All Music Guide

The best CDs, albums & tapes

The experts' guide to
the best releases from thousands
of artists in all types of music

Edited by Michael Erlewine
with Chris Woodstra
and Vladimir Bogdanov

Miller Freeman Books

San Francisco

Published by Miller Freeman Books
600 Harrison Street, San Francisco, CA 94107
Publishers of GPI Books, *Guitar Player*, *Bass Player* and *Keyboard* magazines
A member of the United Newspapers Group

Distributed to the book trade in the U.S. and Canada by
Publishers Group West, P.O. Box 8843, Emeryville, CA 94662

Distributed to the music trade in the U.S. and Canada by
Hal Leonard Publishing, P.O. Box 13819, Milwaukee, WI 53213

Library of Congress Cataloging-in-Publication Data:
All music guide : the best CDs, albums & tapes : the experts' guide to the best releases from thousands
    of artists in all types of music / edited by Michael Erlewine with Chris Woodstra and Vladimir
    Bogdanov.
           p.   cm.
          Includes bibliographical references (p.) and index.
          ISBN 0-87930-331-X
          1. Sound recordings–Reviews. 2. Music–Discography.
          I. Erlewine, Michael. II. Woodstra, Chris. III. Bogdanov, Vladimir, 1965-.
ML156.9.A38 1994
016.78026\6–dc20   94-33583
                                      MN

Cover Design: Tom Erlewine
Copyeditors: Loralee Windsor, Beverly Zegarski, Leslie Tilley, Fran Haselsteiner, Michael Welch, Colleen
Wilder, Michael Katz, Christine de Chutkowski, and Adrienne Armstrong
Page Layout: Brad Greene, Greene Design
Production: Matt Kelsey, Dorothy Cox, Jim Hicks, and Wendy Davis

Printed in the United States of America by Publishers Press, Salt Lake City, UT
   95 96 97 98   5 4 3 2

DEDICATION & FOREWORD

I'd like to dedicate this book to...

> ...*the spirit of the 60s and the music scene in*
> *Ann Arbor, Michigan, at that time.*
> ...*my wife Margaret – I was lucky enough*
> *to find her back there and then.*
> ... *our four children – Iotis, Anne,*
> *May, and Michael Andrew.*

Music, whatever else it may or may not be, is a great healing force. It is the best medicine for the soul that I have ever found, and it comes in all flavors. In my case, the more upset I am by life, the more music I listen to. And it takes some special music to cure those stubborn heartaches, which is how the *All-Music Guide* came into being.

A simple examination of my checkbook dates makes it clear that I buy more music when my life is in turmoil than otherwise. During the period when my aging parents died, I bought and listened to a whole lot of music. If it's true that music is the best medicine for an aching heart, what I most needed at that time was some *very* good music.

But a lot had changed since the 60s, when I was a full-time musician. For one thing, almost 30 years had passed and the recordings I knew just were not around anymore. What I needed was to hear the music I most remembered and maybe try some new stuff too. I set out to find it.

By trial and error I did find some. But I made a lot of mistakes along the way, wasting my time and hard-earned money on worthless recordings, re-recordings, bad sound–you name it. I needed guidance and searched, with some success, through the many books and magazines available on music for more information. In a last-ditch effort to track down the best recordings for different artists, I called the experts themselves–music writers. This worked. They do know their stuff. I started finding some of the music that I craved.

Sharing this information with those around me, it soon became clear that I am not alone. Many people want to know where the good music is or how to venture into new music categories without fear of wasting both time and money guessing at music. This book is intended as an offering to music listeners everywhere. The driving force behind compiling the *All Music Guide* has always been my own need for the book, and I intend to be a major user.

– Michael Erlewine

ALL MUSIC GUIDE DATABASE

The first edition of this book has been well received and we have continued our work. The *All Music Guide* is more than this book. It is an ongoing database project, the largest collection of substantive album ratings and reviews ever assembled. In fact, the 23,000+ albums listed in this book represent a rather small subset (albeit the most important one) of a very much larger collection of over 300,000 albums and reviews. The *All Music Guide* is also available in the following formats:

Books:
All Music Guide to Jazz (Miller Freeman Books)
All Music Guide to World Music (Miller Freeman Books, available Spring 1996)
All Music Guide to Rock (Miller Freeman Books, available Fall 1995)

Electronic Formats:
All Music Guide CD-ROM
MusicRoms (music and data) for Blues, Jazz, R&B, Latin, etc. (SelectWare/Compton's)
All Music Guide (hard disk version) from Great Bear Technology

In-store Kiosks:
Musicland's SoundSite
Sam Goody's
Phonolog's The Source

BBS Systems:
Compact Disc Connection
Entertainment Connection
CD-NOW

Online:
Compuserve (GO ALLMUSIC)
Internet: http://www.allmusic.com/

We welcome your feedback. Perhaps we have left out some of your favorite albums, and/or included ones that you don't consider essential. Let us know about it. We welcome criticism, suggestions, additions, and/or deletions. The All Music Guide is a continuing project. Perhaps you are expert on the complete output of a particular artist or group and would like to participate in future editions of this book and/or our larger computer database. We would be glad to hear from you. Call or write

ALL MUSIC GUIDE
315 Marion Avenue
Big Rapids, MI 49307
616/796-3437
FAX 616/796-3060
A division of Matrix Software

CONTENTS

ABOUT THE EDITORS

Michael Erlewine

All Music Guide editor Michael Erlewine helped form the Prime Movers Blues Band in Ann Arbor, Michigan in 1965. He was the lead singer and played amplified harmonica in this pace-setting band (the first of its kind). The original band included a number of now well-known musicians including Iggy Pop (drums); "Blue" Gene Tyranny (piano; now a well-known avant-garde classical composer); Jack Dawson (bass; became bass player for Siefal-Schwall Blues Band); and Michael's brother Dan Erlewine (lead guitar; now monthly columnist for *Guitar Player* magazine). Michael has extensively interviewed blues performers, both in video and audio, and, along with his band, helped to shape the first few Ann Arbor Blues festivals.

Today Michael is a systems programmer and director of Matrix Software. Aside from the company's work in music and film data, Matrix is the largest center for astrological programming and research in North America. Michael has been a practicing astrologer for more than 30 years and has an international reputation in that field.

Michael is also very active in Tibetan Buddhism and serves as the director of the Heart Center Karma Thegsum Choling, one of the main centers in North America for the translation, transcription, and publication of psychological texts and teachings of the Karma Kagyu Lineage of Tibetan Buddhism. Michael has been married for 23 years, and he and his wife Margaret live in Big Rapids, Michigan. They have four children.

Vladimir Bogdanov

Russian mathematician and programmer Vladimir Bogdanov has been involved in the design and development of *All Music Guide* databases since 1991. Having experience in many different fields such as nuclear physics, psychology, social studies and ancient chronology he now applies his knowledge to the construction of unique music reference tools utilizing the latest computer technologies. His personal interest lies in applying artificial intelligence and other mathematical methods to areas with complex semantic structures, like music, film, literature. Vladimir's ultimate goal is to provide people with the means to find what they need, even if they don't know what they are looking for.

Chris Woodstra

Chris Woodstra has had a lifelong obsession with music and is an avid record collector. He has worked many years in music retail, he was a DJ, hosting programs in every genre of music, and has been a contributing editor for several local arts and entertainment magazines. Working as an editor for the *All Music Guide* database has given him the opportunity to combine his technical skills, a B.S. in Physics and Mathematics, and his love of music for the first time in his life. Being a perfectionist by nature, Chris believes that any information that goes into the database has to be carefully researched and verified.

INTRODUCTION

The *All Music Guide* represents the combined efforts of over 150 experienced music writers to point out the most important artists and their best music. Most are well-known reviewers. Aside from producing scores of liner notes, they also write for magazines like Rolling Stone, Goldmine, Detail, Pulse, Request, Billboard, Music Express, Mix, Agent/Manager, Spin, Musician, CD-Review, Rock & Roll Disc, and many others.

Starting with extensive lists of musicians in their area of expertise, each writer picked the artists they felt should be in the book. These lists were then combined to create a master list for each genre of the most frequently selected artists. Master lists were then submitted to genre editors, further refined and commented upon, and then given to at least one other editor for still more criticism, additions, and suggestions. The final result is in your hands, the 23,000+ top albums selected from a database of over 300,000 albums.

ARTIST NAME   (Alternate name in parentheses).

VITAL STATISTICS   Date and place of birth and death, if known.

INSTRUMENT(S) / STYLE   Major instruments for each performer, and other performace-related credits (bandleader, composer, arranger) are listed here, followed by one or more styles of jazz associated with each performer. A description of these styles is provided in a section at the beginning of the book.

BIOGRAPHY   A quick view of the artist's life and musical career. For major performers, proportionately longer biographies are provided.

MAJOR ALBUMS   These are the 23,000 + albums selected by our editors and contributors. An album listed here (even one without a bullet or comment) is considered an important recording. It's worth a listen. Undistinguished albums are not included here.

KEY TO SYMBOLS ○ ● ☆ ★

☆ ESSENTIAL RECORDINGS   Albums marked with a star should be part of any good collection of the genre. Often, these are also a good first purchase (filled star). By hearing these albums, you can get a good overview of the entire genre. These are must-hear and must-have recordings. You can't go wrong with them.

● ★ FIRST PURCHASE   Albums marked with either a filled circle or a filled star should be your first purchase. This is where to begin to find out if you like this particular artist. These albums are representative of the best this artist has to offer. If you don't like these picks, chances are this artist is not for you. In the case of an artist (like Miles Davis) who has a number of distinct periods, you will find an essential pick marked for each period. It might be best to start with an earlier album (the albums are listed chronologically when possible) and work up to the later ones.

○ LANDMARK RECORDINGS   Albums marked with an open circle are singled out as landmark or career turning points for the particular artist. These are classic albums—prime stuff. A land-mark recording is either a pivotal recording that marked a change in their career or a high point in their recording output.

Booker Ervin (Booker Telleferro Ervin II)
b. 1930, Denison, TX, **d.** Jul. 31, 1970
Tenor saxophone / Hard bop, blues & jazz
Flamboyance, excitement, and bluesy fervor were the trademarks of tenor saxophonist Booker Ervin. He was an aggressive, animated soloist whose repertoire of honks, swaggers, smears, and slurs were matched by his thorough harmonic knowledge and his complete command of the sax. He had one of the hardest tones and biggest sounds among '50s and '60s stylists, something that was even more impressive when he played the blues. Ervin's father was a trombonist who had worked with Buddy Tate. Ervin first played the trombone, then taught himself sax while in the air force. He studied music in Boston for two years, then made his earliest recordings with Ernie Fields's R&B band. This association was Ervin's professional debut as well. During the late '50s and early '60s, he was in Charles Mingus's Jazz Workshop, providing energized, powerful solos. Ervin also played in a group with Horace Parlan, George Tucker, and Al Harewood, and with Randy Weston. He recorded with Weston, and began cutting acclaimed albums as a leader in the '60s. Ervin recorded for Bethlehem, Savoy, and Candid. His crowning achievement was nine albums he did for Prestige in the mid and late '60s. These included such memorable dates as his "books." There were also sessions for Blue Note, Fontana, Pacific Jazz, and a partial album for Enja. Ervin spent most of 1964, 1965, and part of 1966 in Europe, and returned in 1968. Ervin died in 1970. Only a handful of Ervin sessions are currently in print, though others, like *Settin' the Pace*, are being reissued steadily. —*Ron Wynn*

○ Soulful Saxes / **i.** Jun. 1960 / Affinity 758
★ Book Cooks, The / Jun. 1960 / Affinity
Robust, earthy Ervin throughout. This tremendous combo date was originally on Bethlehem. —*Ron Wynn*
Down in the Dumps / Nov. 26, 1960-Jan. 5, 1961 / Savoy 1119
An explosive set from Ervin's prime period, reissued on disc with additional material from the following year (1961), with trombonist Dr. Billy Howell. —*Ron Wynn*
○ Cookin' / Nov. 26, 1960 / Savoy Jazz 150
That's It / Jan. 6, 1961 / Candid 79014
☆ Back From the Gig / Feb. 15, 1963+May 24, 1968 / Blue Note 488
Tenor saxophonist Booker Ervin's *Back From the Gig* is a perplexing volume. It is perplexing because it took Blue Note nearly seven years after Ervin's untimely death to release these valuable and infectious recordings. Apparently, both sessions, one recorded under the tutelage of pianist Horace Parlan (whom Michael Cuscuna thoughtfully documents in his liner notes), were scheduled for release years ago but never materialized. The Parlan sextet (1963) was a tough, no-nonsense blues unit. Ervin, trumpeter Johnny Coles, and guitarist Grant Green are the lead voices and are sly, raw, and often dirty. Ervin, in particular, plays with an inciting bounce and masterful range, lean and to the core. His own 1968 recordings, in cahoots with saxophonist Wayne Shorter and pianist Kenny Barron, are more expansive, evincing a knack for melding his blues romanticism to modal foundations and professing some plain big-band-inspired truths. —*Mikal Gilmore*, Down Beat

HOW TO USE THIS BOOK

ALBUM TITLE   The name of the album is listed in bold as it appears on the original when possible. Very long titles have been abbreviated, or repeated in full as part of the comment, where needed.

DATE   The recording date is given as completely as possible. For the jazz section, in some cases only the date of issue or release is known; these are marked with an **i.** preceding the date. We have made every attempt to verify album dates. However, if you have more accurate information, please write us; we are continually updating and refining our listings.

RECORD LABEL & NUMBER   Record labels and numbers indicate the current (or most recent) release of this recording.

REVIEWERS   The name of each review's author (and the magazine where the review originally appeared, if applicable) are given at the end of the review. "AMG" indicates a review written by the *All Music Guide* staff.

○ **Soulful Saxes** / **i. Jun. 1960** / Affinity 758

★ **Book Cooks, The** / Jun. 1960 / Affinity
Robust, earthy Ervin throughout. This tremendous combo date was originally on Bethlehem. —*Ron Wynn*

Down in the Dumps / Nov. 26, 1960-Jan. 5, 1961 / Savoy 1119
An explosive set from Ervin's prime period, reissued on disc with additional material from the following year (1961), with trombonist Dr. Billy Howell. —*Ron Wynn*

○ **Cookin'** / Nov. 26, 1960 / Savoy Jazz 150

That's It / Jan. 6, 1961 / Candid 79014

☆ **Back From the Gig** / Feb. 15, 1963+May 24, 1968 / Blue Note 488
Tenor saxophonist Booker Ervin's *Back From the Gig* is a perplexing volume. It is perplexing because it took Blue Note nearly ten years after Ervin's untimely death to release these valuable and infectious recordings. Apparently, both sessions, one recorded under the tutelage of pianist Horace Parlan (whom Michael Cuscuna thoughtfully documents in his liner notes), were scheduled for release years ago but never materialized. The Parlan sextet (1963) was a tough, no-nonsense blues unit. Ervin, trumpeter Johnny Coles, and guitarist Grant Green are the lead voices and are sly, raw, and often dirty. Ervin, in particular, plays with an inciting bounce and masterful range, lean and to the core. His own 1968 recordings, in cahoots with saxophonist Wayne Shorter and pianist Kenny Barron, are more expansive, envincing a knack for melding his blues romanticism to modal foundations and professing some plain big-band-inspired truths. —*Mikal Gilmore*, Down Beat

ABBREVIATIONS

The following abbreviations are used in some reviews following the musicians' names to indicate instruments played on a particular recording or session.

as	alto saxophone	org	organ
b	bass	p	piano
bcl	bass clarinet	per	percussion
bj	banjo	pkt-t	pocket-trumpet
bs	baritone saxophone	sno	sopranino saxophone
cnt	cornet	ss	soprano saxophone
cl	clarinet	syn	synthesizer
clo	cello	tpt	trumpet
d	drums	tb	trombone
euph	euphonium	tba	tuba
f	flute	ts	tenor saxophone
flhn	flugelhorn	vib	vibraphone
frhn	french horn	vn	violin
g	guitar	vtb	valve trombone
k	keyboards		

ACKNOWLEDGMENTS

This book would not have been possible without the guidance of Andrew Gun McIver and Ven. Khenpo Kathar Rinpoche.

Special thanks to Scott Bultman, Rick Clark, William Ruhlmann, Ron Wynn, and Scott Yanow. Thanks to Paul Attinello, Brad Balfour, Bruce Bastin, Steve Bergman, Carl Bierling, Rob Bowman, Joe Dandy, Dave Datta, John DeBlaiso, John Evans, Charles Garvin, Aris Hampers, Doug Henkle, Holland Compact Disc, Terry Hounsome, Eben Kent, Matt Kelsey, Bob Koester (of Delmark Records), Peter Lee (*Living Blues* magazine), Robin Lensman, Kip Lornell, Ken Lovett, Jim Maki, Jeffrey Mitchell, Opal Louis Nations, John Norton, Harvey Pekar, Zilgia Quafay, Tom Schmidt, Rex Shudde, Thomas C. Terry, Noel Tyl, Neal Umphred, and Panther White.

To our production staff...

Special thanks to Catherine Armstrong, Judy Dallaguarda, Tana Basham-Hobart, Steve Huey, David Jehnzen, Keith Johnson, Ludmila Lobenko, Angie Pullen, Charles Rathbun, Sara Sytsma, and Lynn Vought.

and to all the Matrix Staff...

Kyle Alexander, Irene Baldwin, Richard Batchelder, Walter Crocket, Bob Daves, Pat Dorset, Phillip Erlewine, Margaret Erlewine, Stephen Erlewine, Tom Erlewine, Kevin Fowler, Carol Garlick, Mary King, Madeline Koperski, David McCarthy, Forest Ray, Tom Roberts, Frantz Sturm, Teresa Swift-Eckert, Brenda Tylak, Robert Walker, Jane Wekenman, and Elizabeth Zielske

Thanks to the staffs of the following magazines, for reviews reprinted by permission: *Cadence, DOWN BEAT, Jazz Times, Coda, Jazziz, Rock & Roll Disc, Request, Pulse, Roundup Newsletter.*

All Music Guide

Editors:
Michael Erlewine
Chris Woodstra
Vladimir Bogdanov

Assistant Editor:
Stephen Thomas Erlewine

Rock, Pop & Soul

Editors:
Stephen Thomas Erlewine
Rick Clark
Chris Woodstra

Contributors:
Steve Aldrich
Ashley Battel
George Bedard
Vladimir Bogdanov
Myles Boisen
John Book
Rob Bowman
Rick A. Bueche
Scott Bultman
Bil Carpenter
Kenneth M. Cassidy
Bill Dahl
Hank Davis
Michael P. Dawson
Robert DeFreitas
Donna DiChario
John Dougan
Bruce Eder

Iotis Erlewine
Meredith Erlewine
Michael Erlewine
Michael Anne Erlewine
Colin Escott
John Floyd
Michael Freedberg
Robert Gordon
Tom Graves
Jeff Hannusch
Dan Heilman
Steve Huey
Mark A. Humphrey
David Jehnzen
Julian Katz
Michael Katz
Kit Kiefer
Cub Koda
Linda Kohanov
Paul Kohler
Larry Lapka
Kip Lornell
Decibel Dennis MacDonald
Brian Mansfield
Richard Meyer
Jas Obrecht
Christine Ohlman
Jim O'Neal
Richard Pack
Roch Parisien
Matthew Plichta
Bob Porter
Jim Powers
Chip Renner
William Ruhlman
Richard Skelly

David Szatmary
Jeff Tamarkin
Neal Umphred
Richie Unterberger
Stephen Winnick
Ron Wynn

Vocal

Editor:
Cub Koda

Contributors:
Bil Carpenter
Stephen Thomas Erlewine
John Floyd
William Ruhlmann
Charles Wolfe
Ron Wynn

Easy Listening

Editors:
Kenneth M. Cassidy
Cub Koda

Rap

Editors:
Ron Wynn
John Floyd

Contributors:
Stephen Thomas Erlewine
Dan Heilman

Bluegrass

Editor:
David Vinopal

Contributors:
Hank Davis
Brian Mansfield
Mark Humphrey
Chip Renner

Blues

Editors:
Bill Dahl
Jim O'Neal
Larry Hoffman

Contributors:
George Bedard
Bil Carpenter
Rick Clark
Hank Davis
Bruce Eder
Dan Erlewine
Michael Erlewine
Stephen Thomas Erlewine
John Floyd
Niles J. Frantz
Robert Gordon
Cub Koda
Mark A. Humphrey
Richard Lieberson
Kip Lornell
Brian Mansfield
Michael G. Nastos
Jas Obrecht
Richard Pack
Roch Parisien
Barry Lee Pearson
Bruce Lee Pearson
Bob Porter
Bruce Boyd Raeburn
Richard Skelly
Jeff Tamarkin
Ron Wynn

Cajun

Editor:
Jeff Hannusch

Contributors:
Danny Carnahan
Michael P. Dawson
Bruce Eder
Mark A. Humphrey
David L. Mayers
Michael G. Nastos
Roch Parisien
Chip Renner
John Storm Roberts
William Ruhlmann
Stephen Winick
Steve Winnick
Ron Wynn

Celtic

Editor:
Stephen Winick

Contributors:
Danny Carnahan
Michael P. Dawson
Bruce Eder
Mark A. Humphrey
David L. Mayers
Michael G. Nastos
Chip Renner
John Storm Roberts
William Ruhlmann
Roch Parisien
Ron Wynn

Christmas

Editors:
Decibel Dennis MacDonald
David A. Milberg

Contributors:
Rick Clark
Bruce Eder
Michael Erlewine
Thom Granger
Bob Hinkle
Tavia Hobart
Cub Koda
Larry Lapka
Brian Mansfield
Richard Meyer
Michael G. Nastos
Chip Renner
William Ruhlmann
Janet Schnol
Roger Steffens
Ron Wynn
Scott Yanow

Country

Editors:
Rick Clark
David Vinopal

Contributors:
George Bedard
Myles Boisen
Bil Carpenter
Rick Clark
Dan Cooper
Bill Dahl
Hank Davis
Michael Erlewine
Stephen Thomas Erlewine
John Floyd
Robert Gordon
Jeff Hannusch
Dan Heilman
Mark A. Humphrey
Cub Koda
Richard Lieberson
Brian Mansfield

Michael McCall
Richard Meyer
Roch Parisien
Barry Lee Pearson
Chip Renner
Tom Roland
William Ruhlmann
Jeff Tamarkin
Ritchie Unterberger
David Vinopal
Charles S. Wolfe
Jim Worbois
Ron Wynn

Folk

Editors:
Richard Meyer
Allan Shaw
William Ruhlmann

Contributors:
Kenneth M. Cassidy
Hank Davis
Michael P. Dawson
Bruce Eder
Michael Erlewine
Stephen Thomas Erlewine
Mike Fleischer
Niles J. Frantz
Robert Gordon
Mark A. Humphrey
Alonso Jasso
Brian Mansfield
Bill McCaully
Michael G. Nastos
Richard Pack
Barry Lee Pearson
Chip Renner
Don Stevens
David Szatmary
Richie Unterberger
Stephen Winick
Charles S. Wolfe
Chris Woodstra
Jim Worbois
Ron Wynn

Gospel

Editors:
Thom Granger
Ron Wynn

Contributors:
Rob Bowman
Rick Clark
Bil Carpenter
Hank Davis
Stephen Thomas Erlewine
Mark A. Humphrey
Cub Koda
Paul Kohler
Kip Lornell
Brian Mansfield
Richard Meyer
Opal Louis Nations

ROCK, POP & SOUL

Ask 20 people for a definition of rock & roll and you'll get 20 different answers, for everyone has their own idea of what the music is and what it should do. And that's good, because if rock & roll could be defined with a simple, concise description, it would've died sometime in the mid 60s. Rock & roll defies categorization: you can't trace its origins back to one particular source, you can't define its content with words like "rebellion" or "sexuality," and you can't pinpoint its sensibility with one clever catch phrase.

More than any other genre of 20th century music, rock & roll has stood the test of time on the strength of its diversity – the diversity of the countless producers, engineers, songwriters, vocalists, and musicians who create the stuff. The hierarchy in anyone's personal history of rock & roll is predestined to include dozens of eclectic names and song titles. And the things people think rock & roll should do vary as wildly as the artistic approaches of the Beatles and the Rolling Stones. Some think it should be full of rebellion, anger, and venom, and they point to the early work of the Who, the Rolling Stones, or the Sex Pistols or to the rantings of some contemporary agit-popster. Others may see it as a vehicle for romantic expoundings, positing their arguments with an armful of doo-wop singles and the complete works of Phil Spector. Still others may argue that the music is simply a White bastardization of Black blues and R&B; these people can point to just about any post-50s group and make a convincing argument.

But rock's origins aren't so easily defined. Many critics and historians credit Jackie Brenston's "Rocket 88," recorded in 1951 at Sam Phillips's Sun Studio in Memphis, TN, as the first "rock & roll" record. Its driving beat, over-amped guitar riffs, blaring horns, and automobile-as-sexual-metaphor theme lend weight to this theory. But what about the blues-laced prewar country work of Jimmie Rodgers or the vivid imagery and pathos in the oeuvre of Hank Williams? What about the prewar and postwar gospel that provided much of the foundation for not only rock & roll but for blues, R&B, and soul? What about the swaggering jump-blues that proliferated in the Midwest and on the West Coast during the 40s and early 50s? What about the Delmore Brothers' choogling, revved-up acoustic country? What about the high, mournful wail of Bill Monroe and the Stanley Brothers? What about the raucous assault of blues pioneers such as Howlin' Wolf, Muddy Waters, Little Walter Jacobs, and Sonny Boy Williamson?

The diversity of rock's origins may explain why the Rock, Pop, & Soul chapter of the *All Music Guide* is the most variegated section of the book. With over 20 critics applying their opinions and critical idiosyncrasies to the canon of 20th century popular music, the variety of music highlighted is certain to be eclectic, to say the least. Whatever your personal definition of rock & roll may be, that eclecticism is necessary, if only to give an accurate overview of what's out there. It also means, however, that not every starred or bulletted album is going to fill everyone's needs. Someone may think Michael Bolton is a pockmark on the face of contemporary pop; someone else may think he's inherited the White-soulman traditions of Van Morrison or the Rascals. Whatever your opinion, in the pages of this section there's a bulletted album recorded by Bolton. We realize no one is going to agree with every critical assessment found in this chapter, and no one should; if they do, they probably aren't asserting their own personality quite as strongly as they should. And some may squabble that we've included contemporary and vintage soul, doo-wop, and jump-blues within the rock and pop section. But without the artists who've worked and continue to work in those genres, the rock & roll section of any book (or record store) would be considerably smaller – and far less interesting.

What this chapter should do, however, is act as a guide-post for the curious, a map to guide readers through areas of music they may not find on their own. You may already know about a lot of the music discussed here, but maybe you'll find a record that somehow slipped through the cracks of popularity. Or maybe you're interested in tracking down the finest album by an obscure New York noise band or an overlooked doo-wop quintet. Odds are, you'll find them both somewhere within these pages. Keep in mind, though, that regardless of how painstakingly the *All Music* editors have worked at making this a definitive portrait of what's good in rock, pop, and soul, it is not definitive – there's no way any one book ever could attain that goal. But if it makes one person purchase an album by an artist they've never heard of, if it makes somebody decide once and for all to dig into the roots of American music to find out where the Rolling Stones got all those cool old songs, the *All Music Guide* has accomplished its task. You, the reader, will be the final judge of its success.

– John Floyd

ABBA

Group / Dance-pop, pop
During the '70s, ABBA's slick light Euro-pop sound made them one of the world's most successful acts, particularly outside America. Each of the four members—Benny Andersson, Bjorn Ulvaeus, Anni-Frid (Frida) Lyngstad, and Agnetha Faltskog—had already enjoyed some professional success previous to the band's formation. The spirited single "Waterloo" earned ABBA much recognition when they won the 1974 Eurovision Song Contest. From there, ABBA scored a seemingly endless string of predomi-nantly bouncy pop hits, featuring well-crafted catchy melodies (some quite good) and the band's distinctive (but occasionally shrill) multilayered female vocals. The string ran out when ABBA disbanded in 1982, with Lyngstad and Faltskog going solo and Andersson and Ulvaeus writing for the musical theater. Of the 14 American Top 40 pop hits, "Dancing Queen" was ABBA's biggest, hitting number one in 1976. ABBA hit the Top 40 in Great Britain 25 times between 1974 and 1983, scoring nine number-one hits. ABBA's influence can be heard in such U.K. groups as Erasure (who recorded a tribute EP, *Abba-esque*) as well as in the Swedish

groups Roxette and Ace of Base. See also the musical *Chess* and *The Munich Philharmonic Orchestra Plays ABBA Classic.* — *William Ruhlmann*

○ **More ABBA Gold** / Jun. 1, 1993 /
All of the singles and important album tracks that aren't featured on *Gold* are available on *More ABBA Gold.* —*Stephen Thomas Erlewine*

★ **Gold—Greatest Hits** / Sep. 21, 1993 / Polydor 517007
A 19-track, 77-minute CD collection released in 1993 to cash in on the resurgence of interest in ABBA, this is an excellent single-disc hits package, and, given that the group's catalog was sold to PolyGram in 1989, probably the only one that's readily available. —*William Ruhlmann*

ABC

Group / New wave, dance-pop, rock/pop
ABC was formed in 1980, when singer Martin Fry teamed up with Stephen Singleton and Mark White, who were members of the group Vice Versa. Their stylish debut, featuring Fry's cartoonishly overwrought delivery backed up by a dramatically lush dance/synth-pop sound, scored well with high-profile videos on MTV, producing the hits "The Look of Love (Part One)" and "Poison Arrow." Except for a quick sidestep into a harder rocking middle-period, Roxy Music-influenced effort with *Beauty Stab*, ABC has increasingly streamlined their sophisticated dance-pop. Their biggest hits have been "Be Near Me," "(How to Be A) Millionaire," and "When Smokey Sings," a tribute to Smokey Robinson. —*Rick Clark*

○ **Lexicon of Love** / 1982 / Mercury 810003
ABC's stylish debut successfuly melded the cool detatchment of Bryan Ferry and David Bowie with a more pop-oriented production than either Roxy Music or Bowie. Even though the songs tended to blend together over the course of the album, the record was successful, scoring two hits with "The Look of Love" and "Poison Arrow." —*Stephen Thomas Erlewine*

Beauty Stab / 1983 / Mercury 814661
For their second album, ABC toned down the synths and turned up the guitars, making an inconsistent set of rocking, Roxy-styled pop that does have its impressive moments, particularly the single "That Was Then but This Is Now." —*Stephen Thomas Erlewine*

How to Be a Zillionaire / 1985 / Mercury 824904
Darkly humorous dance grooves incorporate some hip-hop. The album contains the hit "Be Near Me." —*Rick Clark*

● **Absolutely ABC: The Best of ABC** / 1990 / Mercury 842967
Martin Fry's Bowie-Roxy vocal affectations and sweeping productions (aided by Mark White) are showcased to great effect on this fine anthology that contains all of this act's dance-pop hits. —*Rick Clark*

Paula Abdul

b. Jun. 19, 1962, Los Angeles, CA
Vocals / Dance-pop, urban R&B, pop
In the wake of Madonna's success, many dance-pop divas filled the charts, but out of them all, Paula Abdul was the only one that lasted for more than a hit or two. Abdul had two smash-hit albums not because her singing was exceptional—her voice is thin and transparent—but because she worked with savvy producers that had a knack for picking solid pop hooks; the melodies are what carried "Straight Up," "Forever Your Girl," "Cold Hearted," and "Rush Rush" to the top of the charts. Abdul's days as a cheerleader and choreographer helped her make some exciting videos, which played a major role in her rise to stardom. She has not released an album since 1991's *Spellbound.* —*Stephen Thomas Erlewine*

● **Forever Your Girl** / 1989 / Capitol 86067
Choreographer-turned-diva Abdul debuts with this upbeat collection of dance-pop that yielded a string of Top-40 hits, including four number-one smashes: "Straight Up," "Cold Hearted," "Opposites Attract," and "Forever Your Girl." —*Donna DiChario*

Spellbound / 1991 / Captive 91611
This sophomore set produced another string of hits, with the danceable "The Promise of a New Day" and "Rush Rush," both reaching number one. —*Rick Clark*

AC/DC

Group / Hard rock, heavy metal
When Australia's AC/DC blasted onto the music scene during the mid '0s, they were loud, crude, salacious (did I mention LOUD?), and audiences all over the world ate up their scorch-the-earth policy toward rock & roll. The bazooka roar of the Young brothers' twin guitars and Bon Scott's snarling vocals (they were labeled "crotchgrind" by Chuck Eddy) made them one of the most popular hard-rock bands in the world (with the platinum albums to prove it). Even on a bad night they were very nearly the equals of the Stones or the Who on their best.

The band almost fell apart when singer Bon Scott died in 1980, but they rallied around his successor Brian Johnson, who managed to sound like Scott with an even greater vocal boom. In the '90s they show no inclination toward lowering the decibels. —*Tom Graves*

High Voltage / 1976 / Atlantic 36142
AC/DC kicked things off properly by blowing away the girders with their concussion bomb skronk. Raw, raunchy, and fun-o-plenty, with songs like "The Jack" guaranteed to offend every woman in listening radius. —*Tom Graves*

Let There Be Rock / 1977 / Atlantic 36151
A great follow-up that proved these Aussies would be a nasty itch for a long time. Great meltdown boogie on songs like "Let There Be Rock," "Problem Child," and "Whole Lotta Rosie." —*Tom Graves*

If You Want Blood You've Got It / 1978 / Atlantic 19212
Although the sound engineering lacks, rock & roll still ain't much more in your face than this. Fans had known what a great live band AC/DC was, and this was the album that proved it to everyone else. Collects the best tracks from the early years and spits them back louder than bejeezus. —*Tom Graves*

☆ **Highway to Hell** / 1979 / Atlantic 19244
A classic of hard-rock/heavy metal pillage-and-burn. Earlier AC/DC albums had great riffs and killer chords, but *Highway to Hell* proved the boys could write too. Not a clinker on this thudfest, and songs like "Highway to Hell" and "Girls Got Rhythm" have appropriately become rock staples. —*Tom Graves*

★ **Back in Black** / 1980 / Atlantic 16018
Following Bon Scott's death, AC/DC came back with reinforcements and released another truly great hard-rock album. Brian Johnson ups the ante with his own tough-as-tacks vocals. Robert "Mutt" Lange's production on *Back in Black* remains one of the most powerful in all of hard rock. All in all, this is great diamond-hard, full-throttle rock & roll. —*Tom Graves*

Dirty Deeds Done Dirt Cheap / 1981 / Atlantic 16033
An odds-'n'-sods collection of earlier Bon Scott-era tracks, worth it for the unforgettable title track alone. —*Tom Graves*

○ **For Those about to Rock We Salute You** / 1981 / Atlantic 11111
For Those about to Rock We Salute You is another masterwork from the Brian Johnson period. The title song has become the group's signature track and is featured in AC/DC concerts with pyrotechnics galore. —*Tom Graves*

74 Jailbreak / 1984 / Atlantic 80178
Actually an EP of Bon Scott-period material, this is nonetheless some of AC/DC's best and most blistering blues. In particular, the title song and an incendiary "Baby, Please Don't Go" are worth the admission. —*Tom Graves*

Who Made Who / 1986 / Atlantic 81650
On paper, *Who Made Who* is just a cheap soundtrack to a cheap movie (Stephen King's disasterous *Maximum Overdrive*), but it's actually much more than that. It's a ripping AC/DC retrospective, tearing through such classics as "You Shook Me All Night Long" and "For Those about to Rock," adding the pounding title track to their canon and rescuing overlooked songs like "Sink the Pink" from otherwise mediocre albums. It's not a perfect retrospective—there's no "Back in Black," "Highway to Hell," or "Dirty Deeds Done Dirt Cheap"—but what is here is terrific. —*Stephen Thomas Erlewine*

Blow up Your Video / 1988 / Atlantic 81828
Blow Up Your Video shows signs of the band breaking out of their mid-'80s slump. Angus Young's guitar lurches and growls throughout the album, coming to a blistering head on "This Means War" and "Heatseeker"; any record that has moments this

ROCK, POP & SOUL GENRES AND SUBGENRES

These genre/subgenre descriptions are intended to give the reader a feel for the school of music an artist may have worked within. Since many artists have crossed the line from one style to another over the course of their careers, when artists are mentioned within genres, it is merely intended to illuminate an aspect of the artist's sound.

R&B (RHYTHM AND BLUES) – A term that originated during the 40s, was initially a Black pop synthesis of big-band jump-blues, Tin Pan Alley, swing, and early rock & roll. R&B submerged into soul as that genre gained prominence during the 60s. Examples: Johnny Ace, La Vern Baker, Ray Charles, and Fats Domino.

ROCKABILLY – The mating of hillbilly country and Delta blues, Rockabilly, found its first expression at Sun Studios in Memphis, TN, during the mid 50s. The genre was usually built around small ensembles (string bass; lean, economical, rhythm-heavy electric guitar; minimal drum work; acoustic guitar), supporting an addled singing style (sometimes with hiccuping, stuttering vocals) set in a highly reverberant audio mix. Examples: Elvis Presley, Carl Perkins, Jerry Lee Lewis, Gene Vincent, Wanda Jackson, Eddie Cochran.

ROCK & ROLL (ROCK'N'ROLL) – Like the word "jazz," "rock & roll" was basically a euphemism for sexual intercourse. Rock's emphasis on rhythm, gritty (occasionally abrasive) instrumental sounds, and often salacious lyrical themes underscored the genre's roots in sexuality and things impulsive and earthy. Since the beginning, rock's visceral energy has provided an expression for the young at heart, the rebellious, or anyone looking for some kind of release. Musically, rock & roll drew liberally from Black blues and R&B and from White pop, folk, and country. Like R&B, rock & roll's grooves made for great dance-party music. Examples: Chuck Berry, Bob Seger, and Bruce Springsteen. In the mid 60s, a less dance-oriented, more concert-oriented style of rock & roll emerged, which was usually given the title "rock." Rock music that had specialized leanings was usually indicated by hyphenated subgenre titles such as country-rock, folk-rock, blues-rock, and so forth.

ROOTS-ROCK – The term is usually applied to an acoustic/electric style of rock that draws more obviously from various American music traditions like country, blues, R&B, and folk. Examples: Dave Edmunds, John Hiatt, Stray Cats, Spanic Boys, and the Blasters.

POP – Pop (an abbreviation of the word "popular") music exists for mass-market appeal. Ideally, the intention of pop music is to achieve instant memorability. Most pop music is developed from a well-structured combination of repetitive melody and lyrical lines (referred to as "hooks") that convey messages of varying importance. Pop is even more chameleon-like than rock in the way it can exist in a seemingly endless array of styles while maintaining its essential structural qualities. Generally pop's spiritual home is Top 40 and middle-of-the-road adult radio formats.

Although pop is rarely more than a fairly pleasant diversion, at its best it can possess powerful sentiment and melodic invention that transcend mere craftsmanship; consider, for example, a deceptively simple song like the Beatles' "Yesterday." Examples: Bread, the Carpenters, Culture Club, Neil Diamond, Michael Bolton, Art Garfunkel, Lionel Richie, Sade, Simply Red, Dionne Warwick, and Swing Out Sister.

ROCK/POP – Basically, this description is applied to a commercially accessible blend of pop-song craftsmanship and production values, which still incorporates elements of rock's immediacy. Artists who have delved into this approach include Bon Jovi, Peter Frampton, Fleetwood Mac, Billy Joel, the Guess Who, Extreme, and World Party.

DOO-WOP – During the 50s doo-wop evolved from various Black R&B vocal groups; later, it crossed over to White acts as well, particularly in Northeastern cities. The name doo-wop referred to the application of nonsensical words sung in harmony, usually behind a lead vocal line. Many of the best artists from this genre created absolutely poetic moments with their arranged phonetics. Examples: The Moonglows, the Ravens, Dion & the Belmonts, and the Crests.

MOTOWN – The Detroit record label Motown rose to prominence in the 60s, with a clean, stylized Black pop sound that young White America bought by the truckloads. It was perfect radio music that utilized elements of gospel and sophisticated pop-song craftsmanship, delivered with snappy arrangements that lacked some of the rougher musical aspects of Southern soul music. Examples: The Temptations, the Four Tops, Smokey Robinson & the Miracles, the Supremes, and Martha & the Vandellas.

SOUL – In the American South (particularly in Memphis, TN, and Muscle Shoals, AL), the urgency found in Black gospel and rock helped transform R&B into a grittier, more immediate style known as soul. As the name implies, soul comes straight from the heart and articulates secular concerns and desires with gospel intensity, no matter whether in Sam & Dave's joyous statement of purpose, "Soul Man," Otis Redding's reflective "(Sittin' On) The Dock of the Bay," Wilson Pickett's sexy boast, "I'm a Midnight Mover," or Aretha Franklin's feminist anthems "Respect" or "Think."

BRITISH INVASION – While America was embracing light teen-idol pop during the early 60s, British youth were undergoing a pop and rock revolution, inspired by stateside sounds like blues, country, American pop, and garage-rock. Among the scores of emerging bands, the Beatles and the Rolling Stones best exemplified the diversity of these absorbed influences and created a totally fresh, vibrant sound that reawakened pop and rock from their dormancy. The collective effect was empowering to a generation of post-WWII adolescents, who were beginning to question the expectations of their elders in a Cold War climate.

Both the Beatles and the Rolling Stones initially recorded material that reflected their American influences, but eventually they became formidable sources of original work.

Examples – Peter & Gordon, Gerry & the Pacemakers, Herman's Hermits, and Billy J. Kramer & the Dakotas to rougher rock-oriented acts like the Yardbirds, Them, the Kinks, the Animals, and the Who.

FOLK/ROCK – When Bob Dylan infused his provocative imagistic folk music with a rough and tumble blues-influenced rock & roll sound, he laid the groundwork for taking rock beyond mere boy/girl issues into weightier thematic possibilities.

It was the Byrds, however, who defined what is commonly known as the folk-rock sound. Their distinctive, chiming folk-influenced rhythm-guitar sound (dominated by

Rickenbacker 12-string electric guitars) and clean vocal harmony work (coupled with their soaring arrangements of songs by Dylan and Pete Seeger, as well as traditional folk copyrights and originals) have influenced generations of artists. During the mid 60s, many artists (particularly on the West Coast) followed the Byrds's lead, especially the Turtles, the Beau Brummels, and singer/songwriter P. F. Sloan. The Plimsouls and Tom Petty & the Heartbreakers are more recent examples of folk-rock-influenced artists.

BLUES/ROCK – Blues-rock generally stays true to the initial song forms and themes of blues, set in a rock band context. Usually the no-nonsense groove-oriented arrangements feature improvisary work by a lead instrument, developing ideas from blues scales and tonalities. Examples: Stevie Ray Vaughan, Rory Gallagher, Roy Buchanan, Canned Heat, and early ZZ Top.

R&B/ROCK – This rock subgenre displays more of the swing groove sensibilities of R&B. Horns are also not an uncommon element of the sound. Examples: Delbert McClinton, the J. Geils Band, Van Morrison, and Southside Johnny.

TEX-MEX – Also known as Tejano music, this genre originated in Texas. Tex-Mex, which began in the 1700s, draws from Spanish and Mexican folk music traditions. Over the last 30 years, Tex-Mex has brought in elements of country, rock and R&B. Examples: Joe King Carrasco, Ry Cooder, David Lindley, Doug Sahm, and the Texas Tornadoes.

PSYCHEDELIC – During the 60s, various rock artists sought to broaden the parameters of musical expression through mind-expanding drugs. Psychedelic rock attempted to convey the spirit of these altered states. Examples: Pink Floyd, Jimi Hendrix, Blue Cheer, Jefferson Airplane, Quicksilver Messenger Service, and later-period Beatles.

COUNTRY-ROCK – Country informed rock music from its inception, but it wasn't until the late 60s that rock artists aggressively sought to put their sound back into country. Gram Parsons was a primary facilitator in the creation of what was to be known as country-rock. His presence in the Byrds helped generate the first important album of this subgenre, *Sweetheart of the Rodeo*. Examples: Flying Burrito Brothers, Poco, Pure Prairie League, Linda Ronstadt, and the Eagles.

ART-ROCK/CLASSICAL-ROCK/PROG-ROCK – During the late 60s, many artists were inspired by the Beatles' renaissance approach to making rock a more serious art form. Art-rock, or classical-rock, was the result of realizing those intentions. Groups like the Moody Blues, Procol Harum, Genesis, Gryphon, and Emerson, Lake & Palmer incorporated extended classically structured compositions or grand orchestrally influenced arrangements with rock instrumentation. Thematically, many of these groups reached for lofty sentiment as well. Progressive rock came on the heels of art-rock with a more aggressive, occasionally dissonant style that borrowed from the spirit of hard rock. Examples: King Crimson, Yes, and later Rush.

SINGER/SONGWRITER – The singer/songwriter school fused elements of folk music with pop-song-craftsmanship. Artists like Carole King, James Taylor, Cat Stevens, and Joni Mitchell reached millions of listeners with their soft acoustic-based soft-pop introspections during the early 70s.

POWER-POP/ANGLO-POP – As rock attempted to get heavier and more serious toward the top of the 70s, various artists continued to mine the super-melodic pop/rock sensibilities of the British Invasion. Power-pop and Anglo-pop are basically interchangeable terms used to describe this approach. Generally the sound features fine harmonies and a full mid-period Beatles or Byrds-influenced guitar sound. Unlike most rock & roll or R&B, much of the groove takes a back seat to the melodies. Examples: Badfinger, Big Star, Shoes, the Raspberries, Michael Penn, the dB's, Bill Lloyd, and the Posies.

FUNK – Funk took the gritty appeal of soul and stripped it down to its most basic visceral rhythmic form. James Brown was the master of distilling his sound into barebones one-chord grooves that were stretched out over simple riffs. Sly & the Family Stone explored funk's earthiness as well. During the 70s the Ohio Players, Parliament/Funkadelic, the Brothers Johnson, and Bootsy Collins were some of funk's more prominent players.

SOUTHERN ROCK – This regional form emerged in the early 70s with such artists as the Allman Brothers, Lynyrd Skynyrd, Charlie Daniels Band, Wet Willie, Marshall Tucker Band, and Atlanta Rhythm Section. Thematically, Southern rock addresses the feelings and concerns of those in the American South. Musically, Southern rock draws from the music indigenous to that part of the country, such as gospel, soul, R&B, folk, and some jazz. This music was very much geared toward a high level of improvisation, which managed to maintain a strong sense of groove. Twin lead guitar lineups (with slide guitar) were not uncommon.

GARAGE-ROCK – Rock & roll didn't start out as some highbrow musical conceit, and garage-rock's determined anti-virtuosity underscored that its music was something practically anyone could generate. After all, many of rock & roll's greatest songs featured almost idiot-proof riffs and chord changes, no matter whether it was the Kingsmen's "Louie Louie," the Kinks' "You Really Got Me," Them's "Gloria," or the Ramones' "I Wanna Be Sedated." Garage-rock's amateurism and reckless energy helped pave the way for other genres like punk and alternative rock.

HARD ROCK/HEAVY METAL – The introduction of guitar distortion during the mid 60s created a common ground for blues-influenced rock and psychedelia. The result was an aggressive riff-oriented rock sound. The wider tonalities offered by distortion and fuzz tone, coupled with the larger, more aggressive role of drums and bass, helped bring about hard rock. The Yardbirds set the stage perfectly for the development of this sound, with their experimental sounds and increasingly unconventional arrangements. The Who also laid the groundwork with their anarchic approach to rhythm and their thick choral guitar voicings. Led Zeppelin, Cream, Jimi Hendrix, Steppenwolf, and Deep Purple expanded on the form. Over the years, artists like Van Halen, Blue Oyster Cult, Aerosmith, Bad Company, Scorpions, AC/DC, Tesla, and Guns N' Roses have carried on the spirit of hard rock/heavy metal.

As hard rock became denser and more aggressive-sounding, fans began groping for a way to describe the new attitudes. The designation heavy metal emerged, originating from William Burrough's *Naked Lunch* and later used in Steppenwolf's biker anthem "Born to be Wild." Black Sabbath, with their stripped-down half-speed themes of gloom and doom, laid the groundwork for metal as a stage for the exploration of themes concerning evil.

Thrash incorporated the raw energy of punk and the themes and thick tonalities of heavy metal into a high-speed style. Motörhead was one of the standard bearers for thrash. Over the course of the 80s and 90s, the music evolved further into speed-metal and death-metal, essentially upping the ante in the departments of speed, unintelligibility, and dark subject matter.

HARDCORE – This subgenre mixed elements of punk and thrash into an even more aggressive sound. Examples: Hüsker Dü, Suicidal Tendencies, the Misfits, Bad Brains, Dead Kennedys, and Meat Puppets.

FUSION – During the mid 70s, fusion captured the imagination of certain jazz and prog-rock artists who desired a musical platform to showcase their compositional and musical technique. With few exceptions, fusion lacked any vocal augmentation. In many ways, it was a close cousin to prog-rock; the only real difference came with the jazz chops that certain musicians brought to the genre. Examples: Return to Forever, the Mahavishnu Orchestra, Al Dimeola, and the Dixie Dregs.

PUNK – As rock became more diffuse in the 70s, it also lost much of its primal potency. Punk's willfully confrontational amateurism spat in the face of the pretense that rock had begun to embrace. The movement found much of its roots in the raw aggression of 60s and early 70s groups like MC5, New York Dolls, the Stooges, Velvet Underground, and early Who. Gone were the lengthy lead-instrumental breaks, and in their place was a jack-hammer-beat minimalism that made its point and got out of the way. The Ramones, Richard Hell & the Voidoids, the Sex Pistols, the Buzzcocks, and Clash represented the peak of this spirit.

NEW-WAVE – New-wave emerged in the late 70s with its art-pop-meets-fashionably-punk-ish style. Some vital bands emerged from this scene, such as the Cars, Pere Ubu, Split Enz, and Devo. Many of the artists possessed a sound that had affected vocals; clipped, clean arrangements; and rhythm parts. By the beginning of the 80s, the term new-wave had become such a catch-all for anything that looked left of mainstream rock/pop that it lost resonance as a meaningful designation. Even the Knack and Tom Petty & the Heartbreakers were marketed as such at one point.

ALTERNATIVE ROCK/POP – As new-wave mutated into meaninglessness, the designation alternative rock or pop came to represent music that was more attuned to the college radio market than to Top 40 or mainstream FM rock. Examples: R.E.M., Echo & the Bunnymen, Sonic Youth, and Mojo Nixon, the La's, Julian Cope, XTC, Psychedelic Furs, and the Cocteau Twins.

SKA-REVIVAL – Ska originated in Jamaica during the 60s. The Skatalites and Toots & the Maytals were the most successful exponents of that sound. Around 1980 there was a resurgence of artists in Britain who embraced ska's energetic nervous grooves. The Two-Tone record label was the heartbeat of that sound, with groups like English Beat, Specials, Madness, and Selector.

DISCO – While undanceable hard rock and introspective singer/songwriters seemed to reign during the first half of the 70s, the predominately gay Manhattan discotheque (French for "record library") scene increasingly gained prominence as the purveyors of the type of music eventually called disco, which set out to celebrate one thing: dancing. One of disco's signature qualities was its steady kick-drum-heavy beat. By the late 70s, the genre had become essentially a producer's medium, where the singer's personality was secondary to the groove. Gamble & Huff's glossy production style helped score a considerable number of hits

for artist like the O'Jays, Harold Melvin & the Blue Notes, the Intruders, and the Three Degrees. Giorgio Moroder's clinical synth-heavy approach launched Donna Summer's career. (Summer eventually went beyond disco into major pop success.) In 1977 disco reached its commercial zenith with the 24-million-selling soundtrack to the movie *Saturday Night Fever*, which featured the Bee Gees, Tramps, Tavares, KC & the Sunshine Band, Kool & the Gang, MFSB, and others. Other significant disco artists included Shalamar, George McCrae, Chic, Village People, Sister Sledge, Sylvester, and Barry White. Disco's dominance of the late-70s popular-music landscape was so pervasive that even the sound of such artists as Herbie Hancock and the Rolling Stones incorporated its thumping grooves.

DANCE/DANCE-POP – At the top of the 80s, disco had more than worn out its welcome with many people, so disco's rigid 4/4 groove was replaced by more elastic rhythms and varied synth and other instrumental arrangements. Like disco, much dance-pop is a producer's medium. In a sense, disco never died; it just changed clothes. Over the course of the 80s and 90s, this form of music has remained extremely popular. Examples: Michael Jackson, Janet Jackson, Prince, Madonna, Paula Abdul, and Whitney Houston.

URBAN R&B – Urban R&B blended jumpy grooves like hip-hop and new-jack-swing into classic R&B song structures. Many of these artists are quite adept at covering smooth dance-oriented music as well as romantic ballads. Examples: Luther Vandross, Gregory Abbott, Johnny Gill, and Vanessa Williams.

TECHNO-POP/DANCE – Techno's roots can be traced to the 70s synthesizer experiments of Tangerine Dream, Kraftwerk, and Brian Eno. David Bowie and Roxy Music aided in the cool, arty pop sensibilities that have informed this subgenre. Examples: Ultravox, Depeche Mode, Blue Nile, Human League, Yello, New Order, and Marc Almond.

Radio format terms.

AOR – The emergence of progressive free-form FM rock radio in the renaissance period of the late 60s provided an outlet for many developing artists like Cream, the Doors, Jefferson Airplane, the Who, Janis Joplin, Jimi Hendrix, Crosby, Stills & Nash, and many more. These artists didn't cater to the standard 3-minute hit-single song format but opted instead for extended improvisations and unconventional song structures and arrangements. It was these characteristics of the artists that were played on FM rock stations that helped coin the AOR, or album-oriented rock.

MOR – MOR stands for middle-of-the-road. Most MOR stations feature a style of music that is usually heavy on ballads and light upbeat pop.

CHR – CHR (contemporary hits radio) came into prominence in the early 80s. Essentially a very tightly formatted equivalent to AM's Top 40s sound, CHR came at a time when MTV was beginning to affect the musical tastes of the youth market. Consequently, CHR helped the careers of artists like Thomas Dolby, Simple Minds, and Naked Eyes, while featuring a considerable amount of dance-pop.

–Rick Clark

smashingly visceral deserves at least one listen. —*Stephen Thomas Erlewine*

Razor's Edge / 1990 / Atlantic 91413
The band unarguably slipped a few notches in the late '80s, but *The Razor's Edge* brought them back in the '90s with a vengeance. Great hooks, great sound, and a great single, "Money Talks." Whoever said they sold out? —*Tom Graves*

Ace of Base

Group/Dance-pop
With their 1993 debut album, *The Sign,* Ace of Base became one of the most popular pop bands in the world. Their simple, melodic Euro-disco was equally popular on radio and in the clubs, earning the quartet three hit singles: "All That She Wants," "Don't Turn Around," and "The Sign." —*Stephen Thomas Erlewine*

● **Sign** / 1993 / Arista
Ace of Base's strong point is not versatility—all of their hit singles have exactly the same beat. But that doesn't matter. On their debut album, *The Sign,* they managed to create a piece of melodic Euro-disco that was a huge hit all over the world, appealing to both dance clubs and pop radio. And with singles like "All That She Wants," "The Sign," and "Don't Turn Around," it's easy to see why they were hits—the beat is relentless and the hooks are incessantly catchy. —*Stephen Thomas Erlewine*

Johnny Ace (John Alexander)

b. Jun. 9, 1929, Memphis, TN, **d.** Dec. 25, 1954
Vocals / R&B
One of the more tragic '50s R&B heroes, Johnny Ace (born John Alexander) was a fixture on the Memphis Beale Street blues scene, playing with Bobby Bland and Roscoe Gordon in the fabled Beale Streeters. He struck out solo in the early '50s, recording the gorgeous, stark ballad "Pledging My Love" in 1954, and died playing Russian roulette on Christmas Eve 1954. —*John Floyd*

● **Johnny Ace Memorial Album** / 1974 / MCA 31183
The greatest hits from this ill-fated Memphis blues pianist. Includes the posthumous smash "Pledging My Love." —*Bill Dahl*

Barbara Acklin

b. Feb. 28, 1944, Chicago, IL
Vocals, composer / Soul, R&B
Acklin began singing background vocals at Chess in the mid '60s. Signing with Chicago's Brunswick label (where she was a receptionist), Acklin debuted on the R&B charts in 1968 as Gene Chandler's duet partner before stepping out on her own later that year with the brassy "Love Makes a Woman," her biggest R&B and pop hit. Acklin was also a prolific composer at Brunswick, writing or cowriting hits for Jackie Wilson and the Chi-Lites. —*Bill Dahl*

● **Love Makes a Woman** / 1968 / Brunswick 754137
Unrepresented on CD as yet, this is '60s Chicago soul songstress Acklin's debut album, with her irresistible title-track smash. —*Bill Dahl*

Seven Days of Night / 1969 / Brunswick 754148
More excellent late-'60s soul from Brunswick's top female artist. Includes "Just Ain't No Love" and "Am I the Same Girl," both R&B hits. —*Bill Dahl*

Bryan Adams

b. Nov. 5, 1959, Kingston, Ontario, Canada
Vocals, guitar / Rock/pop
Canadian artist Bryan Adams is one of mainstream rock's biggest hitmakers with his style of Heartland rock—a rhythm guitar-heavy sound that implies roots in the Byrds and the Stones. With his raspy lower tenor, he has a classic rock & roll voice. His grasp of creating memorable melodic and simple lyrical hooks has earned him an enormous string of hits including "Cuts Like a Knife," "Run to You," "Summer of 69," "Heat of the Night," "Heaven," and "(Everything I Do) I Do It for You," the number-one hit from the movie *Robin Hood: Prince of Thieves.* —*Rick Clark*

Cuts Like a Knife / 1983 / A&M 3288

A Top-Ten breakthrough album in America for this Canadian rocker, carried by the strength of "Straight from the Heart" (his first U.S. single) and the title track. —*Donna DiChario*

○ **Reckless** / 1984 / A&M 5013
Radio-friendly pop/rock driven by Adams's trademark gravelly vocals, this album spawned three Top-Ten hits—"Heaven," "Run to You," and "Summer of '69"—as well as a duet with Tina Turner on "It's Only Love." —*Donna DiChario*

○ **Waking Up the Neighbours** / 1991 / A&M 5367
After the disappointing *Into the Fire,* Adams returned to the top of the charts with *Waking Up the Neighbours,* thanks to the massive success of "(Everything I Do) I Do It for You." —*Stephen Thomas Erlewine*

● **So Far So Good** / Nov. 2, 1993 / A&M 540157
Eliminating the filler that tends to clutter his albums and gathering only the hits (including a new one, "Please Forgive Me"), *So Far, So Good* is the only consistently enjoyable album Bryan Adams has released. —*Stephen Thomas Erlewine*

Oleta Adams

b. , Seattle, WA
Vocals, piano / Soul, urban R&B
The youngest daughter of a minister, Oleta Adams's first musical experience was in the choir of her father's church. Discovered by Tears for Fears while performing solo in a Hyatt Regency lounge in Kansas City, she was featured prominently on their *Seeds of Love* album. Tears for Fears member Roland Orzabal went on to produce her 1990 debut album, *Circle of One,* featuring the hit "Get Here." The album earned her a Grammy nomination in 1991. —*Scott Bultman*

○ **Circle of One** / 1990 / Fontana 846346
The former backing vocalist for Tears for Fears performs very well on her debut. Featuring soothing and deep vocals with a heavy gospel influence, the album includes the hits "Get Here" and the relaxing "Rhythm of Life." —*John Book*

Evolution / 1993 / Mercury
After the success of her debut, Adams doesn't change the formula for her second album. Which is not a bad thing—the stylish love ballads that she sings are some of the best adult contemporary pop of the early '90s. —*Stephen Thomas Erlewine*

Hasil Adkins

b. 1936, Madison, WV
Vocals, guitar / Rockabilly
A crazed one-man rockabilly band, Adkins has been recording in a tarpaper shack in the hills of West Virginia since the mid '50s. The absolutely crudest and wildest of all rock & rollers, Hasil's lyrics stray as far from the standard '50s clichés as you can get. Songs about eating peanut butter on the moon, chopping girls' heads off and mounting them on his wall, and doing something called the "hunch" are typical lyrical fare for Adkins. With his combination of a three-octave voice ranging from subglottal Elvis moans to blood-curdling screams that can freeze the blood, with an overamplified guitar that sounds like a gigantic rubber band, there is nothing in pop music that sounds anything like Hasil Adkins, a true rock & roll primitive. —*Cub Koda*

● **Out to Hunch** / 1986 / Norton 201
All the lunatic classics: "She Said," "Chicken Walk," "No More Hot Dogs," "The Hunch," "We Got a Date," and the mind-boggling arrangements of "Memphis" and "High School Confidential." Not for the faint of heart. —*Cub Koda*

○ **Chicken Walk** / 1986 / Dee-Jay Jamboree 2043
More crazed '50s to early-'60s sides. —*Cub Koda*

Wild Man / 1987 / Norton 203
His '80s recordings. Just as crazy. —*Cub Koda*

Aerosmith

Group / Hard rock, heavy metal
Boston's Aerosmith is a riff-heavy American synthesis of Led Zepplin, the Yardbirds, and the Rolling Stones. During their rise to prominence as album rock kings in the mid '70s, Aerosmith managed to produce an impressive collection of hard-rock classics like "Dream On," "Walk This Way," "Back in the Saddle," and "Sweet Emotion."

By the end of the '70s, FM album-rock had become a cynical stale format, and arena rock groups like Aerosmith became the subject of derision among arbiters of the ascending punk and new-wave movements. By then, ensuing personal conflicts and drug problems had weakened Aerosmith's creative power anyway.

Nevertheless, Aerosmith had the good fortune to make the most of a second chance at success. This comeback was fueled by two very different sources: Rap artists Run-DMC scored a huge-hit version of Aerosmith's "Walk This Way" in 1986, and the rise of FM classic-rock radio fed a market nostalgic for something more edgy and organic than synth-pop acts like Tears for Fears, Wham!, and Duran Duran.

The newly sober Aerosmith seized the moment and produced two highly successful albums with *Permanent Vacation* and *Pump*, which ranks with *Rocks* as their best work. —*Rick Clark*

Aerosmith / 1973 / Columbia 32005
The debut from this Boston band shows a sensitive side with their best-known ballad, "Dream On," but the focus remains on its raw, aggressive garage-rock style—amply displayed on "Mama Kin," "One Way Street," and "Make It." —*Donna DiChario*

○ **Get Your Wings** / 1974 / Columbia 32847
Aerosmith took the Yardbird's classic "Train Kept a Rollin'" and made it their own with Steven Tyler's blistering vocals and Joe Perry's ace guitar work. —*Donna DiChario*

☆ **Toys in the Attic** / 1975 / Columbia 33479
A solid slice of classic '70s raunch-and-roll. Aerosmith defined grunge-rock with their best and now-classic "Sweet Emotion" and "Walk This Way." —*Donna DiChario*

☆ **Rocks** / 1976 / Columbia 34165
Although the hits ("Back in the Saddle" and "Last Child") weren't as big as "Sweet Emotion" and "Walk This Way," *Rocks* remains Aerosmith's finest moment, full of relentlessly sleazy rock powered by some of the dirtiest guitar riffs ever committed to tape. —*Stephen Thomas Erlewine*

Draw the Line / 1977 / Columbia 34856
Where the decadent celebration of *Rocks* was glorious, *Draw the Line* collapses in its own hedonism, mainly because the band haven't written enough songs that match even the worst of *Rocks* and *Toys in the Attic*. Only the title track and the pseudo-pomp rock of "Kings and Queens" stand out amid the murk. —*Stephen Thomas Erlewine*

★ **Greatest Hits** / 1980 / Columbia 36865
A solid collection of hits, including their stellar Beatles remake "Come Together." All hits, no misses. —*Donna DiChario*

○ **Done with Mirrors** / 1985 / Geffen 24091
Joe Perry returned to the fold in 1985, and the band turned out their finest record since *Rocks*. Unlike the records that preceded it, *Done with Mirrors* was powered by the same smart-assed lyrics and filthy guitars that formed the core of Aerosmith's best songs. It didn't receive the commerical or critical attention that *Permanent Vacation* did two years later, yet *Done with Mirrors* is the better album; it marks the beginning of their remarkable comeback. —*Stephen Thomas Erlewine*

Classics Live 2 / 1987 / Columbia 40855
A rare case where the sequel surpasses the original release, *Classics Live 2* is the leanest, toughest, and best live album Aerosmith has released. —*Stephen Thomas Erlewine*

Permanent Vacation / 1987 / Geffen 24162
Apart from the strong singles—"Dude (Looks like a Lady)," "Angel," and "Rag Doll"—*Permanent Vacation* isn't as consistent or rocking a record as *Done with Mirrors*. Too often it relies on slick, horn-spiked production instead of genuine grit, making the moments when Joe Perry's guitar does kick into overdrive all the more splendid. —*Stephen Thomas Erlewine*

○ **Gems** / 1988 / Columbia 44487
Gems is not a greatest-hits album. Instead, it's a collection of album tracks and AOR staples ("Mama Kin," "Lord of the Thighs," "Chip Away the Stone," "Rats in the Cellar") that may not make sense as a retrospective, yet rocks harder, stronger and longer than most albums they released during the '70s. —*Stephen Thomas Erlewine*

● **Pump** / 1989 / Geffen 24254
Where *Permanent Vacation* seemed a little overwhelmed by its pop concessions, *Pump* revels in them without ever losing sight

50s R&B Through Soul and Funk to 90s Dance Pop

50s R&B
James Brown – Ray Charles
Sam Cook – Charles Brown

60s Soul
James Brown – Otis Redding
Sam & Dave – Wilson Pickett
Aretha Franklin

Late 60s Funk
James Brown – Sly & The Family Stone

Funk 70's
Funkadelic – Parliament
George Clinton – Bootsy Collins

70s Soul
Curtis Mayfield – Issac Hayes
The Chi-Lites – The Stylistics
Harold Melvin & the Blue Notes – The O' Jays
The Spinners – Rufus

Disco (mid to late 70s)
Chic – Donna Summer
Bee Gees – Sisters Sledge

80s Dance
Michael Jackson – Madonna – The Gap Band
Cameo – Prince – The Time

90s Dance
Michael Jackson – Madonna – Janet Jackson – Keith Sweat
Guy – Bell Biv Devoe – Bobby Brown – Another Bad Creation
Boyz II Men – Paula Abdul

of Aerosmith's dirty hard-rock core. Which doesn't mean the record is a sellout—"What It Takes" has more emotion and grit than any of their power ballads; "Janie's Got a Gun" tackles more complex territory than their previous songs; and "The Other Side" and "Love in an Elevator" rock relentlessly, no matter how many horns and synths fight with the guitars. Such ambition and successful musical eclecticism make *Pump* rank with *Rocks* and *Toys in the Attic*. —*Stephen Thomas Erlewine*

Pandora's Box / 1991 / Columbia 46209
A bare-bones three-CD boxed set concentrating on Aerosmith's glory days at Columbia during the '70s, *Pandora's Box* has plenty of fine music but ultimately fails as a retrospective. All the hits are available in better singles collections (or more consistent original albums), and the rarities are nothing special, nor is the packaging. Because of licensing restrictions, the set isn't able to cover their startling '80s comeback, so it's not comprehensive, either. This one's for die-hard fan only. —*Stephen Thomas Erlewine*

Get a Grip / 1993 / Geffen 24455
Coming on the heels of the commercially and artistically successful *Pump*, the fitfully entertaining *Get a Grip* pales against its predecessors' musical diversity, but not for lack of trying. In fact, Aerosmith tries too hard, making a stab at social commentary ("Living on the Edge"), while keeping adolescent fans in their corner with their trademark raunch-rock ("Get a Grip" and "Eat the Rich"), as well as having radio-ready hit ballads ("Cryin'," "Amazing," and "Crazy"). The problem is, it's a studied performance—it sounds like what an Aerosmith album *should* sound like. Most of the album does sound good; it's just that there's not much beneath the surface. —*Stephen Thomas Erlewine*

Afghan Whigs

Group / Alternative rock

With their 1988 debut, *Big Top Halloween*, the Cleveland-based Afghan Whigs sounded like a more ambitious (and pretentious) Replacements underneath the roar of their guitars. Switching record labels to Sub Pop in 1990 (becoming one of the first non-Seattle bands on that roster in the process), the band increased their volume while lead singer/songwriter Greg Dulli deepened his lyrical word play. With their second Sub Pop album, *Congregation*, and their final independent release, *Uptown Avondale*, the Whigs developed a soul music fixation that added a new dimension to their punky guitar roar. This infatuation came to fruition on their major-label debut, 1993's *Gentlemen*, their strongest, most consistent record to date. It confirmed their status as critics' darlings while substantially increasing their cult following. —*Stephen Thomas Erlewine*

Up in It / 1990 / Sub Pop 60
More pop than you'd expect from a sub-pop release, this is still loud and hard riff-raunch with a thick, unyielding sound. —*John Dougan*

○ **Congregation** / Aug. 1991 / Sub Pop 130
Dulli's songwriting continues to improve on their last full-length independent album, while the band itself sounds tougher and able to keep up with the twists in the songwriting. —*Stephen Thomas Erlewine*

○ **Uptown Avondale** / 1992 / Sub Pop 175
The Whigs' final independent release was a scorching EP of soul and R&B covers that is arguably their finest moment. —*Stephen Thomas Erlewine*

● **Gentlemen** / 1993 / Elektra
On their major label debut, *Gentlemen*, the Afghan Whigs finally come into their own. Throughout *Gentlemen*, the Whigs act as if they were Minneapolis punks ripping through the Stax songbook as written by a young Elvis Costello. It's a riveting, original album, uncompromising in its honesty and punk/soul roots. With this album, the Afghan Whigs have fulfilled the promise of their earlier, independent records. —*Stephen Thomas Erlewine*

Air Supply

Group / Pop

With their heavily orchestrated, sweet ballads, Air Supply became a staple of early '80s radio. The duo of Russell Hitchcock and Graham Russell were able to score eight Top Ten singles before MTV came along, sending their easy-listening pop off the charts. Landing only one hit after 1983, Air Supply disbanded in 1988. Three years later they reunited. —*Stephen Thomas Erlewine*

● **Greatest Hits** / 1988 / Arista 8024
This self-explanatory collection includes "Lost in Love," "The One That You Love," "Every Woman in the World," "All Out of Love," "Sweet Dreams," "Making Love Out of Nothing at All," "Even the Nights Are Better," and many more soft-pop hits. —*Rick Clark*

The Alarm

Group / Alternative pop/rock

An English foursome, the Alarm (inspired by U2's lofty dispatches) initially generated a rock-heavy acoustic guitar-based rock, loaded with anthemic melodies and issue-oriented lyrics. Later the band switched to electric guitars and developed a more mainstream alternative sound that earned them an audience among the MTV set. Even though the Alarm has been quite popular in England, they've only had one pop chart hit stateside, "Presence of Love." —*Rick Clark*

○ **Strength** / 1985 / IRS 5666
In addition to an improved sense of musicality and dynamics, *Strength* featured the Alarm's finest group of songs, making it their single best studio album. —*Stephen Thomas Erlewine*

● **Standards** / 1990 / IRS 13056
Solid anthology covers everything from early aggressive topical folk-rock anthems ("Matching On," "The Stand") to more mainstream rock hits like "Strength" and "Sold Me Down the River." —*Rick Clark*

Arthur Alexander

b. 1942, Florence, AL, d. Jun. 9, 1993

Vocals / R&B, soul

Alexander was one of the first true singing/songwriting stars of country-soul, a genre that wed Southern Black R&B singers to songs written in a country format and played basically by White musicians. Alexander's "You Better Move On" was the first hit to come out of Rick Hall's fledgling Muscle Shoals studio. Alexander's work was immediately appreciated by his peers in the business. Those who have covered his tunes (self-penned or otherwise) read like a Who's Who from both sides of the Atlantic: "Anna" (Beatles), "Soldiers of Love" (Marshall Crenshaw), "Burning Love" (Elvis Presley), "Set Me Free" (Joe Tex, Esther Phillips, Percy Sledge). The Rolling Stones' cover of "You Better Move On" led to valuable contacts for Rick Hall, and the resulting business enabled him to build the new Fame studio. It was the start of the whole Muscle Shoals sound, and Alexander's career was one of its cornerstones. He went on, after a brief retirement, to record for both Warner Brothers and Buddah.

"Anna (Go to Him)," one of Alexander's best-known tunes, epitomizes the anguished, haunting tone of his music. From the onset, the heavily echoed piano and tortured vocal set a mood that is soulful, mysterious, a little spooky, and totally mesmerizing. His work is essential to any country-soul collection.

As Alexander began a comeback in 1993, he died of a heart attack. However, the album he completed before his death, *Lonely Like Me*, is a gentle record that is a fine way to end his career. —*Christine Ohlman*

○ **Lonely Just Like Me** / 1993 / Elektra 61475
The final album from Arthur Alexander was like all his work: simple, unsophisticated and sung with an earthy, direct intensity. This was part of the American Explorers series on Elektra/Nonesuch, and Alexander got some critical attention with his probing, often searing vocals. Unfortunately, he died just as this album was gaining some attention. —*Ron Wynn*

★ **Ultimate Arthur Alexander** / 1993 / Razor & Tie
Alexander's songs are better known in versions by the Beatles, Elvis Presley, and the Rolling Stones, but no one recorded better versions than Alexander himself. *The Ultimate Arthur Alexander* truly lives up to its title, gathering together the best songs (including "Anna (Go to Him)," "You Better Move On," and "Soldiers of Love") from Alexander's remarkably influential and underrated career. I it's essential for any R&B and soul collection. —*Stephen Thomas Erlewine*

○ **Rainbow Road** / 1993 / Warner Archives 45581
Alexander was a natural country-soul artist, whose style easily blended the best of both genres. He had a gospel-tinged, earthy, rural tone in his compositions and performances but never scored a breakout hit. This disc features 15 fantastic singles, most from the great 1972 Warner Brothers album recorded in Memphis that Alexander thought would finally earn him that elusive smash. There are also some singles cut in Nashville as companion records to the Memphis session. The tracks range from the hypnotic title song and "In the Middle of It All" to the up-tempo burners "You Got Me Knockin'" and "Burning Love." There's also a moving gospel number, "Thank God He Came." Alexander repeatedly sang with a power and authority that comes only from someone whose life mirrors their lyrics. This disc is a wonderful tribute to an unjustly ignored artist. —*Ron Wynn*

Alice in Chains

Group / Alternative rock, heavy metal

Although they have been accused of being a metal band in alternative-rock clothing, Alice in Chains is not a traditional metal bands by any means. Eschewing the standard good times of late '80s and early '90s metal, their music wallows in death, despair, and drugs. With guitarist Jerry Cantrell's lean, lethal riffs and Layne Staley's flat, emotionless vocals, the band is relentlessly heavy. What keeps Alice in Chains from being a standard-issue metal band is Cantrell's subtly crafted songs, which rely on shifting textures and dynamics for their impact. Staley's lyrics never celebrate the darkness that he writes about; instead, they intensify the already oppressive atmosphere, making their music frighteningly claustrophobic.

Although their debut,, *Facelift*, was popular in metal circles—particularly "We Die Young" and "Man in the Box"—Alice in Chains' fan base began to build in early 1992 with their acoustic

Sap EP. Their second full-length album, *Dirt*, expanded their audience dramatically, selling over two million copies and earning them a headline slot on Lollapalooza 93. At the beginning of 1994, Alice in Chains released their second EP, *Jar of Flies*, which became the first EP to debut at number one on the *Billboard* album charts. —*Stephen Thomas Erlewine*

Facelift / 1990 / Columbia 46075
Alice in Chains' first album earned them a strong following with crunching, forboding rock like "Man in the Box" and "We Die Young." *Facelift* might not have the grand thematic sweep of *Dirt*, but it makes up for it with its sheer energy and muscular riffs. —*Stephen Thomas Erlewine*

○ **Sap** / Jan. 1992 / Columbia 74182
Before Alice in Chains delivered their second album, they released *Sap*, a five-song EP featuring acoustic-oriented songs. For anyone who pigeonholed them as mere gloom mongers after their debut, *Sap* was a shock—it showed that they were capable of playing quieter, more intricate music without losing any intensity. —*Stephen Thomas Erlewine*

● **Dirt** / Feb. 1992 / Columbia 52475
To say that *Dirt* is a dark album is something of an understatement. But what makes this such a fascinating journey is the lack of wallowing in the muck, of glorifying the negative, of oppressive moroseness. Instead, Alice in Chains convey a stark, stoic beauty to the pain of their protagonists. The violence and disturbing elements (both musical and lyrical) are offset by a mantra-like feel of inner strength and acceptance. Musically, Alice in Chain's rhythm section lays down a heavy, doom-struck base over which twin guitars and double-tracked vocals slash appealingly. —*Roch Parisien*

Jar of Flies / 1994 / Columbia
Like *Sap* before it, *Jar of Flies* is a quieter, acoustic-oriented experimental EP released between full-length albums, but it is also works well as a coda to the epochal *Dirt*. Although the songs are calmer, they are by no means gentle, treading the same harrowing territory as *Dirt*. Thankfully, musical stretches like the instrumental "Whale & Wasp" and the blues of "Swing on This" are successful and the best material here ("I Stay Away" and "No Excuses") rivals the best on *Dirt*. —*Stephen Thomas Erlewine*

Lee Allen

b. Jul. 2, 1926
Sax / R&B
The blasting tenor saxophone of Lee Allen was every bit as integral a factor in the sizzling sound of '50s New Orleans R&B as were the well-documented contributions of Fats Domino, Lloyd Price, and Little Richard. As a key member of the studio band at Cosimo's, Allen played the searing solos that sparked hundreds of Crescent City classics. Allen's wallpaper-peeling sax solos are instantly identifiable—check out Richard's "Slippin' and Slidin'" and "Tutti Frutti" for irrefutably exciting evidence.

But despite his sax mastery, Allen failed to sustain a brief solo career. Signing with Al Silver's New York-based Ember label, he managed one decent-sized hit in 1958, the rocking instrumental "Walkin' with Mr. Lee," while the second-line scorcher "Boppin' at the Hop" inexplicably never received any national airplay.

When the New Orleans sound shifted to a funkier beat, Allen's muscular sound fell out of favor on the local recording scene. But he hasn't been idle—Allen has toured extensively with Domino over the years, as well as working with a variety of young rockers (including the Blasters) who revere his blistering sound. —*Bill Dahl*

● **Walkin' with Mr. Lee** / 1958 / Collectables 5083
New Orleans's leading tenor sax man during the '50s, on his only solo album. Hot rockin' instrumentals. —*Bill Dahl*

The Allman Brothers Band

Group / Southern rock, blues-rock
The Allman Brothers Band was the major instigator of the Southern-rock genre of the'70s and one of the major rock acts of the first half of that decade, and it continues to be popular today. In its original configuration, the group consisted of Duane Allman on guitar, Gregg Allman on organ and vocals, Dickey Betts on guitar and vocals, Berry Oakley on bass; and Butch Trucks and Jaimo (John Lee Johnson) on drums. This sextet was a showcase for the twin-guitar work of Duane Allman and Dickey

Betts and for the bluesy singing of Gregg Allman. It cut three albums between 1969 and 1971. *Live at the Fillmore East*, the Allmans' breakthrough third album, went gold four days before bandleader Duane Allman was killed in a motorcycle accident. The group continued as a quintet, finishing its fourth album, *Eat a Peach* (1972), which was a major success. After bassist Oakley was also killed in a motorcycle accident, the group was augmented with bassist Lamar Williams (1947-1983) and pianist Chuck Leavell to complete its fifth album, *Brothers and Sisters*, which topped the charts and spawned the number-two single "Ramblin' Man." But the group split up in acrimony after the release of *Win, Lose, or Draw* in 1975.

The Allmans re-formed in 1978, this time returning to the sextet format, with Allman, Betts, Trucks, and Jaimo being joined by guitarist Dan Toler and bassist David Goldflies for the gold-selling *Enlightened Rogues* (1979). Two more albums, *Reach for the Sky* and *Brothers of the Road* (for which David Toler replaced Jaimo and Mike Lawler was added on piano), were released before the band split again.

Following the release of a boxed-set retrospective, *Dreams*, in 1989, the Allmans again re-formed, and to date they have released two more albums and toured extensively. —*William Ruhlmann*

○ **Allman Brothers Band** / 1969 / Polydor 823653
The Allmans' aggressive synthesis of blues, rock, jazz, and gospel made an impressive entrance on this 1969 debut, with soon-to-be-standards like "Whipping Post" and the dynamic moody "Dreams." Highlights like "Don't Want You No More," "It's Not My Cross to Bear," "Black Hearted Woman," and "Trouble No More" are further reasons why this was one of the greatest bands to ever emerge from the American South. —*Rick Clark*

○ **Idlewild South** / 1970 / Polydor 833334
The Allmans' second effort may not have been quite as strong as their powerful debut, but *Idlewild South* had more than a handful of gems—songs like the celebratory "Revival," the earthy "Midnight Rider," and the instrumental "In Memory of Elizabeth Reed," with its soaring twin-guitar contrapuntal melodies. —*Rick Clark*

☆ **At Fillmore East** / 1971 / Polydor 823273
The double-disc *Allman Brothers Band at Fillmore East* is one of rock's greatest live albums, featuring amazing interplay within highly dynamic arrangements. Most of the tracks exceed ten minutes, yet the Allmans never stumble. "Hot 'Lanta," "In Memory of Elizabeth Reed," and "Statesboro Blues" are highlights. Contrary to claims that these are untouched performances, *Fillmore East* actually was a skillfully edited document (courtesy of producer Tom Dowd) taken from a run of shows at Bill Graham's Fillmore. —*Rick Clark*

★ **Eat a Peach** / 1972 / Polydor 823654
Half of *Eat a Peach* consists of more fiery improvisations from the *Live at the Fillmore* dates, in the form of the "Mountain Jam." Even though this was released after Duane Allman's fatal motorcycle accident, the studio sides include some tracks showcasing his soaring lead work. Creatively, the band was in peak form with great tracks like "Ain't Wastin' Time No More," "Melissa," "One Way Out," "Stand Back," "Blue Sky," and the delicate acoustic guitar instrumental "Little Martha." —*Rick Clark*

○ **Brothers and Sisters** / 1973 / Polydor 825092
In spite of the inclusion of Dickey Betts's "Ramblin' Man" and "Jessica," *Brothers and Sisters* is a noticeable comedown from the previous four albums. Muddy production doesn't help matters either. —*Rick Clark*

○ **Beginnings** / 1973 / Polydor 827588
Beginnings is nothing more than the Allman Brothers' first two albums on a single disc. Since its release, Polygram has done a markedly improved remastering job, releasing each album separately. —*Rick Clark*

Wipe the Windows, Check the Oil, Dollar Gas / 1976 / Polydor 831595
By the time this, the Allmans' second live album, was released in the fall of 1976, the band had suffered what appeared to be an irrevocable split, which cast a pall over the record and made it their lowest charting since their debut. In retrospect, it's an appealing effort, chronicling the version of the band that existed from the death of Berry Oakley to the first breakup (a one-guitar, two-keyboards lineup) and featuring concert versions of some of the bet-

ter material from *Eat a Peach* and *Brothers and Sisters*. — *William Ruhlmann*

Enlightened Rogues / 1979 / Polydor 831589
After six years of spotty albums, the Allmans made a strong comeback with this Tom Dowd-produced effort. Gregg Allman is in fine voice, and the band kicks up some sparks throughout. Some of the material is a little weak, but "Crazy Love," a duet by Bonnie Bramlett and Dickey Betts, is a highlight. — *Rick Clark*

○ **Dreams** / 1989 / Polydor 839417
This is a thoughtfully compiled boxed set, containing highlights from throughout the Allman Brothers' entire career, as well as solo projects and early pre-Allman recordings. A booklet with generous annotation and photos is included. The remastering is a noticeable improvement over initial CD releases of the Allman catalog. If you've got the bucks for a boxed set, this is a worthwhile acquisition for completists and those looking for a comprehensive introduction. — *Rick Clark*

○ **Seven Turns** / Oct. 1990 / Epic 46144
After a nine-year absence, the Allmans return with a vengeance on *Seven Turns*, with tracks like the hard-swinging opener "Good Clean Fun" and the powerful blues-rock workout "Gambler's Roll." The Dickey Betts-penned title track, a mystical take on life, is the album's spiritual highlight, while "True Gravity" is the musical peak, ranking with "In Memory of Elizabeth Reed" as one of the band's best instrumentals. Overall, *Seven Turns* is their strongest album since 1972's *Eat a Peach*. — *Rick Clark*

○ **Live at Ludlow Garage—1970** / 1991 / Polydor 843260
It's no *Fillmore East*, of course, but this archival release does present the classic lineup of the Allmans at their near peak, and fans especially will be pleased to have more Duane on disc. — *William Ruhlmann*

Shades of Two Worlds / 1991 / Epic 47877
Weaker than *Seven Turns*, *Shades of Two Worlds* still has its moments, particularly the extended rave-up "Kind of Bird." "Bad Rain" and "Nobody Knows" are two other highlights. — *Rick Clark*

○ **Fillmore Concerts** / 1992 / PolyGram 517294
Fillmore Concerts is an expanded version of the classic *At Fillmore East*, featuring several songs that didn't make the original album, re-edited tracks that now run at their original length, and sterling remastered sound. For hardcore fans, it's the ultimate version of this landmark set. — *Stephen Thomas Erlewine*

Where It All Begins / 1994 / Epic
Twenty-five years after their debut album, the Allman Brothers continue to make records in the same basic style, alternating Gregg Allman's bluesy (and increasingly craggy) vocals with Dickey Betts's more country-tinged ones and relying on extended song structures that leave plenty of room for high-pitched, melodic guitar runs by Betts and his current partner, Warren Haynes. There are no classics here, but this is a respectable recreation of the Allmans' standard fare (much of it sounds familiar the first time you listen), which is why it is selling to their fan base and no one else. — *William Ruhlmann*

Duane Allman

b. Nov. 20, 1946, d. Oct. 29, 1971
Guitar / Southern rock, blues-rock
During his brief career, the late Duane Allman managed to become one of rock's greatest guitarists, with his liquid, yet visceral electric lead and slide guitar playing. Allman's consistently high caliber of recorded work as a session sideman (particularly at Rick Hall's Fame Studio in Muscle Shoals) for artists like Wilson Pickett, King Curtis, and Clarence Carter, and in his role in the groundbreaking Allman Brothers Band and Derek & the Dominos, has understandably inspired thousands of guitarists.

Allman's star was still rising when his life was tragically cut short by a motorcycle accident in October of 1971. He was just 24 years old. — *Rick Clark*

● **Anthology** / 1972 / Polydor 831444
A superb collection of Duane's work with the Allmans, as well as many great session gigs. — *Dan Heilman*

○ **Anthology, Vol. 2** / 1974 / Polydor 831445
More great guitar work in tandem with Aretha Franklin, Wilson Pickett, and others. — *Dan Heilman*

Gregg Allman

b. Dec. 8, 1947
Vocals, piano / Southern rock, blues-rock
Gregg Allman is the lead vocalist and keyboardist of the Allman Brothers Band. Fans of the Allman Brothers should find his solo work generally satisfying. — *Rick Clark*

● **Laid Back** / 1973 / Polydor 831941
Debut solo album showcases Allman's soulful, earthy keyboard work and leathery drawl to good effect. "These Days" and the reworked Allman Brothers Band standard "Midnight Rider" are exceptional. — *Rick Clark*

○ **Playin' Up a Storm** / 1977 / Polydor 831942
Weaker material, but the playing and singing more than compensate. — *Rick Clark*

I'm No Angel / 1986 / Epic 40531
The title track was a comeback hit. Allman's voice is distanced in the mix by a little too much reverb, but the band tracks are particularly hot. — *Rick Clark*

Marc Almond

b. Jul. 9, 1959, Southport, Lancashire, England
Vocals / New wave, dance-pop
Marc Almond, the rather unsteady-sounding lead singer of the early '80s techno-cabaret/pop unit Soft Cell, generated a fairly popular solo career in England with his somewhat bleak, decadent Euro-pop. — *Rick Clark*

● **Singles: 1984-1987** / 1987 / Some Bizarre 3
A compilation of Almond's solo work. — *Steve Aldrich*

○ **Stars We Are** / 1988 / Capitol 91042
Accessible "big-pop"; a fine introduction to Almond. — *Steve Aldrich*

Memorabilia / 1991 / Mercury 314510178
A compilation of solo material and Soft Cell sides. — *Steve Aldrich*

Herb Alpert

b. 1935, Los Angeles, CA
Trumpet, vocals / Pop
Trumpeter Herb Alpert started in rock & roll, working with Jan & Dean and others. He took a $200 demo of the instrumental "Twinkle Star," overdubbed bullfight crowd noises, and retitled it "The Lonely Bull." It became his first gold record. Shortly thereafter Alpert formed A&M Records with Jerry Moss, as well as a studio group named the Tijuana Brass. The TJB scored consistently on both the single and album charts over the next ten years, with five albums going to number one. Alpert's laidback vocal style later found mega-success with the smash "This Guy's in Love with You," trading original Latin-flavored style for straight MOR. — *Cub Koda*

Lonely Bull / 1962 / A&M 3101
The early breakthrough sound of the TJB featuring the title track and the cream of Los Angeles session players. — *Cub Koda*

○ **Whipped Cream & Other Delights** / Jan. 1965 / A&M 3157
Whipped Cream & Other Delights is usually celebrated for its cover, but the music here shouldn't be ignored. It's the first time that Alpert recorded an album that was full of tunes with crossover potential. It makes perfect sense that it topped the album charts for eight weeks. — *Stephen Thomas Erlewine*

○ **Rise** / 1979 / A&M 3274
On *Rise*, Alpert experimented with a jazz-funk fusion, which resulted in one of his finest albums. On the strength of the hit title track, the album sold over a million copies, making it his most popular record. — *Stephen Thomas Erlewine*

● **Classics, Vol. 1** / Jan. 1987 / A&M 2501
All the high points from the ten-year dominance of Alpert and the Tijuana Brass. Includes "A Taste of Honey," "Spanish Flea," and others. — *Cub Koda*

● **Classics, Vol. 20** / Feb. 1987 / A&M 2518
This set features Alpert's solo hits from "This Guy's in Love with You" to "Rise." — *Cub Koda*

Gerald Alston

Vocals / Urban R&B

Gerald Alston inherited some big soul shoes and filled them admirably for 17 years. The nephew of gospel great Johnny Fields and Shirley Alston of the Shirelles, the North Carolina-born singer learned his trade in church. As a teen he formed the New Imperials, a group that did both secular and religious music, calling themselves Gospel Jubilee when they appeared in churches. During a local appearance, the Manhattans borrowed some audio equipment from Alston's band. When they came to pick it up they heard him rehearsing with his band. They asked the 17-year-old to join them, and Alston took over as their lead singer in 1971. Alston remained until 1988, and the group enjoyed enormous success in the '70s and '80s. Alston signed with Motown in 1988. He hasn't had much commercial luck as a solo act, though the releases *Gerald Alston* and *Open Invitation* were well produced and wonderfully sung. —*Ron Wynn*

● **Gerald Alston** / 1988 / Motown 6265
Top-flight R&B ballads and excellent singing. —*Ron Wynn*

Open Invitation / 1990 / Motown 6298
The follow-up album that made him a star in sentimental circles. —*Ron Wynn*

○ **Always in the Mood** / 1992 / Motown 6353
Gerald Alston has emerged as one of the '90s best soul and love singers. His passionate, intense leads never lose their steam or conviction, and he wisely avoids doing songs with rappers and doesn't let production gimmicks and studio trappings overwhelm his vocals. —*Ron Wynn*

Altered Images

Group / New wave, power pop
Altered Images was a British power-pop group formed in 1979 and led by film actress Claire Grogan. The group lasted until 1984, their biggest success coming with the U.K. Top-Three hit "Happy Birthday" in 1981. —*William Ruhlmann*

● **Happy Birthday** / 1981 / Portrait 37738
Their debut album contains their first British hit, the title track, produced by Martin Rushent of Joy Division fame. —*William Ruhlmann*

Collected Images / 1984 / Epic 25973
A greatest-hits collection, containing tracks from all three of their albums, that summarizes their career succinctly. —*Stephen Thomas Erlewine*

Dave Alvin

Vocals, guitar / Roots-rock
Most neo-rockabilly artists merely mimic the music without expanding its vocabulary or its creative horizons. Dave Alvin is the exception that proves the rule. From his teeth-cutting days with the now-defunct Blasters (which featured Dave's brother Phil on vocals) up to his current solo career, Alvin has used rockabilly and country as a springboard (as opposed to sole inspiration) for his sympathetic and precise songwriting, which tackles some of the same issues as John Mellencamp's. He's also one hell of an axe slinger. —*John Floyd*

● **Romeo's Escape** / Dec. 1987 / Epic 40921
The former guitarist/songwriter of the Blasters has his solo debut, singing his own songs. As with the Blasters, it's the songs that impress most, notably here "Fourth of July" and "Border Radio." —*William Ruhlmann*

Blue Blvd / 1991 / Hightone 8029
Highlighted by an appearance by the legendary R&B saxophonist, Lee Allen, Alvin's second solo album offers more of his revved-up mix of rockabilly, blues, and rock & roll. —*Stephen Thomas Erlewine*

Ambrosia

Group / Art-rock, pop/rock
Ambrosia, a '70s Los Angeles group, synthesized art-rock with a relatively slick West Coast pop sound, especially toward the end of their career. They produced a few multiformat hits, including "Biggest Part of Me," "How Much I Feel," "Holding on to Yesterday," and "You're the Only Woman." —*Rick Clark*

● **Ambrosia** / 1975 / 20th Century 434
A wonderful debut album, engineered by Alan Parsons. Topnotch mid-'70s art rock, with great musicianship. Features "Holdin' on to Yesterdays" and "Nice, Nice, Very Nice." —*Scott Bultman*

Somewhere I've Never Travelled / 1976 / Warner Brothers 3182
Their second album is more in the symphonic realm, but is just as good as their debut. —*Scott Bultman*

One Eighty / 1980 / Warner Brothers 3368
Contains their biggest pop hits, "Biggest Part of Me" and "You're the Only Woman." —*Scott Bultman*

America

Group / Pop/rock
This light singer/songwriter pop trio scored big with their Neil Young-like number-one hit "Horse with No Name." America generated several more harmony-laden acoustic hits before enlisting Beatles producer George Martin, who gave the band a fuller sound, while maintaining their soft pop approach. —*Rick Clark*

● **History: Greatest Hits** / 1975 / Warner Brothers 3110
A nice roundup of their peak years (1971-1975), including tracks like "A Horse with No Name," "I Need You," "Ventura Highway," "Tin Man," "Lonely People," "Sister Golden Hair," and more. —*Dan Heilman*

○ **Encore: More Greatest Hits** / 1991 / Rhino 70529
This followup to their *Greatest Hits* contains "The Border," "Right Before Your Eyes," "Today's the Day," and "You Can Do Magic." The rest of the tracks are album sides or previously unreleased material. —*AMG*

American Music Club

Group / Alternative pop/rock
A traditional-sounding rock band in these postmodern times? Well, American Music Club, led by Mark Eitzel, may be an anomaly, but it's a pretty engaging proposition on record. Eitzel's songwriting is very straightforward—good people living through hard times—and he's very much the agreeable populist. His bandmates add to this mix by playing no-nonsense, bare bones rock & roll that, if slightly derivative of blues-rock structures, is also loaded with enough panache. Smart and direct, a fine American band. —*John Dougan*

California / 1988 / Frontier 4619
Stark-sounding, highly personal songs that cemented the reputation of band leader Mark Eitzel. —*Steve Aldrich*

United Kingdom / 1990 / Demon 151
Studio and live tracks. This import CD also includes the entire *California* album. —*Steve Aldrich*

○ **Everclear** / 1991 / Alias 15
More expansive production and arrangements without watering down the quality of Eitzel's material. Brilliant album. —*Steve Aldrich*

● **Mercury** / 1993 / Warner Brothers 45226
On their major label debut, American Music Club continues to mine despair from Mark Eitsel's heart, and the results are captivating. Mitchell Froom's production polishes some of their rougher edges, but *Mercury* is by no means a sellout. Eitzel's songs are beautifully sad, etched with grace and elegant suffering, as well as an often overlooked self-deprecating humor. —*Stephen Thomas Erlewine*

Tori Amos

b. , North Carolina
Vocals, piano, singer/songwriter / Alternative pop
Tori Amos gained a considerable cult following with her accomplished "debut" album, *Little Earthquakes*. Actually, that album was released after her false start as a heavy metal seductress in the guise of Y Kant Tori Read, whose record was truly awful and deservedly stiffed. But on *Little Earthquakes* Amos's ambitions and accomplishments were remarkable. She crafted a rich, diverse album of starkly honest songs that feel confessional yet are cryptic at the same time. Amos's music is either spare—just her singing and playing piano—or orchestrated like Kate Bush's grandest moments.

After *Little Earthquakes'* surprise success, Amos released the *Crucify* EP, which featured several covers, including understated versions of Nirvana's "Smells Like Teen Spirit" and Led Zeppelin's "Thank You"—songs which revealed the breadth of her tastes. Her second album, 1994's *Under the Pink*, showcased her more ornate side. —*Stephen Thomas Erlewine*

● **Little Earthquakes** / 1991 / Atlantic 82358

The album just screams Kate Bush, from the cover shot on in. But once past that, we discover plenty of rewards. Amos engages us as few ever attempt. Her lyrical directness and the sparse production draw us almost uncomfortably close to the artist. An album as challenging as it is beautiful, *Little Earthquakes* stands as a major work. —*Steve Aldrich*

Crucify / 1992 / Atlantic 82399
Crucify is a five-song EP that builds upon the success of Amos's *Little Earthquake*. Most notable among the songs is her voice and piano reading of Nirvana's "Smells Like Teen Spirit," which proves what a fine songwriter Kurt Cobain was. The title song (the sole original Amos number) and her versions of the Rolling Stones' "Angie" and Led Zeppelin's "Thank You" are equally noteworthy. —*Stephen Thomas Erlewine*

Under the Pink / 1994 / Atlantic
After the impressive *Little Earthquakes*, *Under the Pink* is bound to be slightly disappointing, and it is. Some of the songs are too labored or suggest Joni Mitchell and Kate Bush too strongly, yet the best material here shows that Amos is just working out the kinks in her style. —*Stephen Thomas Erlewine*

Laurie Anderson (Laura Phillips Anderson)
b. 1950, Chicago, IL
Vocals, violin / Experimental rock
A member of the New York "loft artists" scene in the early '70s, Anderson first started as a sculptor, enhancing her performance-art exhibits by writing and performing music to go along with them. Quirky and unconventional, Anderson has remained a cult figure with strong ties to pop music's alternative scene. —*Cub Koda*

● **Big Science** / 1982 / Warner Brothers 3674
Anderson employs a variety of musical and sound effects (including voice alteration) on this condensation of her mammoth performance-art piece *United States I-IV*, but it is her stories and unusual observations (many of them seriocomic) that really catch the ear. When the album appeared, nothing like it had ever been heard before, and little has been since. —*William Ruhlmann*

Mister Heartbreak / 1984 / Warner Brothers 25077
Anderson becomes more musically involved, using a broad range of backup musicians, including Adrian Belew, Nile Rodgers, and Peter Gabriel. But it's still her spoken observations that carry the record. —*William Ruhlmann*

United States Live / 1985 / Warner Brothers 25192
The complete performance piece that first gained Anderson attention is a grab bag, but it's still full of funny and fascinating individual moments spread across five records. —*William Ruhlmann*

Strange Angels / 1989 / Warner Brothers 25900
On her first new studio album in five years, Anderson ups the musical ante by actually singing on many tracks. It has the effect of reducing her impact, though this remains an unusually inventive and interesting record. —*William Ruhlmann*

Lee Andrews & the Hearts
Group / R&B
Specializing in smooth ballads, this Philadelphia R&B vocal quintet notched three hits in 1957-1958. Andrews formed the Hearts in 1953, and they debuted the next year on the Rainbow label. Chess picked up their first big seller, "Long Lonely Nights," from the tiny Mainline label in 1957. Mainline also originally issued their biggest hit for Chess, "Teardrops." Moving to United Artists, the group charted for the last time in 1958 with the typically polished "Try the Impossible." Andrews and a shifting lineup of Hearts continued to record through the '60s. —*Bill Dahl*

● **Biggest Hits** / 1981 / Collectables 5028
Classy '50s doo-wop, heavy on dreamy ballads. —*Bill Dahl*

Gotham Recording Sessions / Collectables 5003
More attractive '50s doo-wop harmonies. —*Bill Dahl*

The Angels
Group / R&B
One of the leading girl groups of the early '60s, thanks to the number-one hit "My Boyfriend's Back." With Linda Jansen as lead and sisters Jiggs and Barbara Allbut providing harmony, the Orange, NJ, trio signed with Caprice Records in 1961 and hit with

"'Til." Jansen was replaced by Peggy Santiglia, and the trio signed with Mercury's Smash subsidiary in 1963, cutting the bouncy "My Boyfriend's Back" at the height of the girl-group craze. "I Adore Him" proved mildly successful later that year. —*Bill Dahl*

And the Angels Sing / 1962 / Caprice 1001
Nice compilation of their earlier, prehit material. —*Cub Koda*

● **My Boyfriend's Back** / 1963 / Collectables 5085
Their major hit and 11 other solid girl-group performances, including the quirky "Love Me Now." —*Cub Koda*

The Animals
Group / British invasion, rock & roll, psychedelic
As one of the bands originating from England's active R&B scene during the first half of the '60s, the Animals' gritty sound and appearance was a definite contrast to much of the British Invasion's well-scrubbed pop. Like the Rolling Stones, the Animals drew much of their early material from the catalogs of American Black R&B and blues artists.

Under the guidance of producer Mickie Most—whose credits also included Jeff Beck, Herman's Hermits, and Donovan—the Animals scored with a number of great songs, including "We Gotta Get Out of This Place," "Don't Let Me Be Misunderstood," and the number-one "House of the Rising Sun."

Ego problems (particularly between lead singer Eric Burdon and keyboardist Alan Price) and drug abuse resulted in a number of personnel changes, ultimately making the band essentially the backup for Burdon's increasingly psychedelic vision. At one point, future Police guitarist Andy Summers was in the lineup.

The group became Eric Burdon and the Animals in 1966 and produced several wonderfully trippy hits with "Sky Pilot," "Monterey," and "San Franciscan Nights."

In 1969 Burdon closed shop and hooked up with harmonica player Lee Oskar and Los Angeles nightclub band Night Shift, retitling the band War. During his brief time with them, Burdon hit big with "Spill the Wine." Since then, the Animals have knocked off a couple of fairly respectable reunions. —*Rick Clark*

○ **Animalization** / 1966 / PolyGram 829091
A dazzling collection of the group's more ambitious album tracks, mostly sophisticated blues-based rock. —*Bruce Eder*

★ **Best of the Animals** / 1988 / ABKCO 4324
All of the Animals' biggest hits—"House of the Rising Sun," "Don't Let Me Be Misunderstood," "We Gotta Get out of This Place," "It's My Life"—are included on this rather skimpy compilation that nevertheless remains the best domestic hits collection available. —*Stephen Thomas Erlewine*

☆ **Complete Animals** / Jul. 1990 / EMI 1367
Although the title is a bit of a misnomer, this double CD does include the complete sessions that the Animals recorded with producer Mickie Most in 1964 and 1965. The 40 songs capture the band at their peak, including most of their best and biggest hits: "House of the Rising Sun," "Don't Let Me Be Misunderstood," "Bring It on Home to Me," We Gotta Get out of This Place," "I'm Crying," "It's My Life," and "Boom Boom." Most of the rest of the tunes don't match the excellence of these smashes, though they're solid. When they hit the mark, though, the Animals produced some great album tracks that have been mostly forgotten by time, such as "I'm Mad Again," "Worried Life Blues," and "Bury My Body." —*Richie Unterberger*

○ **The Best of Eric Burdon & The Animals, Vol. II** / 1991 / Polydor 827916
The Best of Eric Burdon & the Animals, Vol. 2 is a surprisingly hard-rocking collection from this group's psychedelic period. Excellent songs. —*Bruce Eder*

In the Beginning / 1994 / Sundazed
Recorded in December of 1963 at a live concert, this CD captures the Animals at their rawest and most animated on record, ripping ferociously through a bunch of standards (by Chuck Berry, James B. Odom, et al.), playing the crowd and making snide comments about their London rivals the Rolling Stones, all with Sonny Boy Williamson II hanging somewhere around the stage. Sundazed has actually found the original master to this oft-bootlegged piece of rock/blues history. —*Bruce Eder*

Paul Anka
b. Jul. 30, 1941, Ottawa, Ontario, Canada

Vocals / Pop

Paul Anka was a hugely successful vocalist from 1957 into the '80s, as well as writer of several venerable pop music standards. The young native of Ottawa, Canada, took the United States by storm in 1957 with his rock-slanted ballad "Diana," a number-one smash on ABC-Paramount Records. Dramatic renditions of "You Are My Destiny," "Lonely Boy," "Put Your Head on My Shoulder," and "Puppy Love" elevated the youth to teen-idol status over the next three years. Moving to RCA in 1962, the maturing Anka continued to chart regularly, although some of his most notable '60s copyrights were bequeathed to others—he wrote "My Way" for Frank Sinatra as well as the theme for TV's "Tonight Show." Anka returned to the top pop slot in 1974 with the controversial million-seller "(You're) Having My Baby," cut in Muscle Shoals and issued on United Artists, and he enjoyed several followup smashes, many featuring vocalist Odia Coates. *—Bill Dahl*

● **30th Anniversary Collection** / 1989 / Rhino 71489
The best package of Anka's early teen-idol hits, featuring "Diana," "Puppy Love," "Put Your Head on My Shoulder," and "You Are My Destiny." *—Cub Koda*

Adam Ant

b. Nov. 3, 1954
Vocals / New wave

One of the seminal figures of new wave, Adam Ant had trouble getting his musical career off the ground. Adam and the Ants' 1979 debut, *Dirk Wears White Socks*, suffered from excessive wordplay, stiffness, and an enveloping sourness. Ditching most of the pretentions that plagued the first record, Adam and the Ants opted for a cheerfully campy brand of new wave bubblegum on the follow-up, *Kings of the Wild Frontier*. Adam performed in an outrageous pirate's outfit while the Ants pounded out an intoxicating primal beat and undeniably catchy riffs.

For their next album, *Prince Charming*, the group continued with the same glossy modern pop, but the seams began to show. After the album failed to make an impact, Adam ditched the Ants for a solo career that began with the gloriously trashy *Friend or Foe*, which contained the hit single "Goody Two Shoes."

Although the next album, *Strip*, had some highlights, it marked the end of the road for Adam's commercial success. The Tony Visconti-produced *Vive le Rock* had some fun moments, but was too studied and didn't gain an audience, so Adam Ant turned to a surprisingly successful career in acting.

In 1990, Ant made a surprise comeback with the catchy single "Room at the Top" from the *Manners & Physique* record, but that was the last time he was in the charts. After that, Ant returned to acting and became a staple on the burgeoning new wave nostalgia concert circuit. *—Stephen Thomas Erlewine*

Dirk Wears White Sox / 1979 / Epic 38698
The debut album finds an young Adam Ant exploring a sometimes awkward fusion of punk and glam. While the somewhat pretentious lyrics and inexperienced playing are a drawback, the raw energy can stand up against later releases. *—Chris Woodstra*

○ **Kings of the Wild Frontier** / 1980 / Epic 37033
Combining pounding tom-toms (from two drummers and drum kits) and a guitar style adapted from Ennio Morricone movie soundtracks with a visual motif borrowed from pirates and Native Americans, Adam & the Ants had a brief run as Britain's top band in the wake of the punk/power-pop days of the late '70s. This second album was their apex, featuring the signature tune "Antmusic." *—William Ruhlmann*

Friend or Foe / 1982 / Epic 38370
As a solo artist, Adam Ant struck gold in the United States with this album, which adopts the same musical style as that of the Ants and features the hit "Goody Two Shoes" and a version of the Doors' "Hello, I Love You." *—William Ruhlmann*

● **Antics in the Forbidden Zone** / 1990 / Epic 46819
The most comprehensive overview of the band. In 22 tracks, all of the hits are represented, as well as key album cuts and a rare B-side, "Beat My Guest." An essential part of any new wave collection. *—Chris Woodstra*

Little Anthony & the Imperials

Group / R&B

Formed in 1957, Little Anthony & the Imperials specialized in dramatic pop ballads. Fronted by tenor Anthony Gourdine, the Imperials charted with "Going Out of My Head," "Hurt So Bad," "Take Me Back," "Tears on My Pillow," and "I'm on the Outside Looking In." *—Rick Clark*

Anthrax

Group / Heavy metal, thrash

Nearly as much as Metallica or Megadeth, Anthrax has been responsible for the emergence of speed and thrash metal. Combining the speed and fury of hardcore punk with the prominent guitars and vocals of heavy metal, Anthrax helped create a new subgenre of heavy metal on their early albums. Guitarists Scott Ian and Dan Spitz are a formidable pair, spitting out lightning fast riffs and solos that never seem mastrubatory. Unlike Metallica or Megadeth, they had the good sense to temper their often serious music with a healthy dose of humor and realism.

After their first album, *Fistful of Metal*, singer Joey Belladonna and bassist Frank Bello joined the band. Belladonna helped take the band further away from conventional metal clichés. And over the next five albums (with the exception of 1988's *State of Euphoria*, where the band sounded like it was wearing a creative straightjacket) Anthrax became the arguably the leaders of speed metal.

As the '80s became the '90s, Anthrax began to increase their experiments with hip-hop, culminating in a tour with Public Enemy in 1991 and a joint re-recording of PE's classic "Don't Believe the Hype."

Anthrax kicked Belladonna out of the band in 1992 and replaced him with ex-Armored Saint vocalist John Bush—a singer who was gruffer and deeper, fitting most metal conventions perfectly. Subsequently, their sound became less unique and their audience shrank slightly as a consequence, but it would be foolish to count Anthrax out—these guys are too clever to fade away. *—Stephen Thomas Erlewine*

Fistful of Metal / 1984 / Megaforce 1383
The band's debut album, featuring bassist Dan Lilker who left and formed Nuclear Assault. Not as fast or hard as their later albums. *—John Book*

○ **Spreading the Disease** / 1986 / Island 826668
Spreading the Disease demonstrates that a speed-metal band can still have a knack to create a song accessible for pop audiences. An essential Anthrax album. *—John Book*

● **Among the Living** / 1987 / Island 842447
The Anthrax album to have, a high point in speed-metal history: harsh, powerful, and strong; flawless from beginning to end. *—John Book*

○ **I'm the Man** / 1987 / Island 842448
An EP consisting of a few nonalbum tracks and some live material. The title track pokes fun at rap, the Beastie Boys, Metallica, the Mentors, and themselves. Anthrax was the first heavy metal band to experiment with rap. *—John Book*

State of Euphoria / 1988 / Island 846212
Free-spirited, a showcase for vocalist Joey Belladonna's talent. *—John Book*

○ **Persistence of Time** / 1990 / Island 846480
Second best to *Among the Living*, the band makes strong political statements without sounding preachy. *—John Book*

○ **Attack of the Killer B's** / 1991 / Island 510318
The band gets loose on this one. A compilation of B-sides, covers, and rejects. Shows a lighter side of Anthrax. *—John Book*

○ **Sound of White Noise** / 1993 / Asylum 61430
On their first album with vocalist John Bush, Anthrax emphasized their rhythm section, creating a ballsy, pulsating groove. Bush's aggressive vocals effortlessly meshed with the lean, snarling guitar riffs, making *Sound of White Noise* one of the group's finest. *—Stephen Thomas Erlewine*

Any Trouble

Group / New wave, rock & roll

Led by Clive Gregson, Any Trouble was an underappreciated bright spot on Stiff Records, which had no shortage of talented artists. Gregson's appearance and hardened love songs might have led to (somewhat accurate) compasions with Elvis Costello, but his songs were not as vicious and his band rocked with enthusiasm, not abandon. Any Trouble's records were overlooked when they were released in the early '80s, yet they hold up and contain their fair share of engaging rock and pop. —*Stephen Thomas Erlewine*

● **Where Are All the Nice Girls** / 1980 / Stiff 6
The first album is a pure pub pop-rock delight. Leading off with the infectious "Second Choice" (one of the great "should have been hits") and ending up with the unlikely ABBA cover "Name of the Game," Gregson and company run though 12 tunes, almost all obsessed with love gone wrong. A cult favorite. —*Chris Woodstra*

○ **Live at the Venue** / 1985 / Teldec 625967
Originally released as a promo for radio, this live show from 1980 finds the band in its natural setting. Playing with higher energy than in the studio, this provides the best picture of the band at its peak. —*Chris Woodstra*

Aphex Twin

Keyboard / Techno
The Aphex Twin—also known as Polygon Window or his given name, Richard James—is arguably the leader of ambient techno in the '90s, creating intricately detailed, textured soundscapes. Frequently, his music doesn't even have a pronounced beat—it has rolling washes of synthesizers, samplers, and homemade electronics. However, the Aphex Twin isn't easy listening—it's difficult, complex music that only seems soothing on its surface. —*Stephen Thomas Erlewine*

● **Selected Ambient Recordings 85-92** / 1993 / R&S
A collection of electronic soundscapes by Richard James (a.k.a. the Aphex Twin), arguably the leader in the ambient techno movement, *Selected Ambient Recordings 85-92* is nothing short of stunning. Musically, much of it brings to mind Brian Eno or Kraftwerk, which James never heard until after he recorded this material. Alternately shimmering and desolate, the album points to the future. —*Stephen Thomas Erlewine*

○ **Selected Ambient Works, Vol. 2** / 1994 / Sire 45482
Selected Ambient Works, Vol. 2 is a more difficult and challenging album than the Aphex Twin's previous collection. The music is all texture; there are only the faintest traces of beat and forward movement. Instead, all of these untitled tracks are long, unsettling electronic soundscapes, alternately quiet and confrontational—although most of the music is rather subdued, it is never easy listening. While some listeners may find this double-disc album dull (both discs run over 70 minutes), many listeners will be intrigued and fascinated by the intricately detailed music of the Aphex Twin. —*Stephen Thomas Erlewine*

Argent

Group / Art rock, pop/rock
Ex-Zombies keyboardist Rod Argent formed Argent in 1969. Like the Zombies, Argent was capable of some excellent melodies even when indulging in more extended art-rock forays. Rod Argent had as many chops as Keith Emerson, able to pull out all the stops when needed, but he seemed to have a greater understanding of the value of economy in note selection. Guitarist Russ Ballard was equally tasty, and Argent's rhythm section, bassist Jim Rodford and drummer Rob Henrit, delivered all the right fire and dynamics. Their self-titled debut and sophomore effort *Ring of Hands* are standouts.

Argent's one huge hit, "Hold Your Head Up," went to number one. After the group's demise, Ballard went on to a moderately successful solo career. Both Ballard and Argent became successful producers. Henrit and Rodford went on to join the Kinks. —*Rick Clark*

● **Anthology: The Best of Argent** / 1976 / Epic 33955
"Hold Your Head Up" and other well-crafted rockers. —*Dan Heilman*

Joan Armatrading

b. Dec. 9, 1950, St. Kitts, West Indies
Vocals, piano, guitar, songwriter / Singer/songwriter
Born on the island of St. Kitts in the West Indies, Joan Armatrading moved to England in 1958. In 1969, she met Pam Nestor, with whom she wrote the songs that appeared on her first album, *Whatever's for Us* in 1972. She broke through to pop success in England in 1976 with her Top-Ten single "Love And Affection" and self-titled third album, which also was her U.S.

chart debut. *Show Some Emotion* (1977) and *To The Limit* (1978) confirmed her status as an important singer-songwriter. In the '80s, Armatrading's music took on more of a rock and newwave edge, resulting in her most popular albums, *Me Myself I* (1980), *Walk Under Ladders* (1981), and *The Key* (1983), all of which made the U.K. Top Ten and the U.S. Top 100. Armatrading continues to record and tour regularly. —*William Ruhlmann*

○ **Joan Armatrading** / 1976 / A&M 3228
Her third album was the one most people fell in love with, attracted by her Caribbean-flavored singing of articulate romantic lyrics and Glyn Johns's tasteful folk-rock production, especially on "Love and Affection." —*William Ruhlmann*

Show Some Emotion / 1977 / A&M 3273
A companion piece to *Joan Armatrading*, this lovely album contains the title track, "Warm Love," and "Willow." —*William Ruhlmann*

To the Limit / 1978 / A&M 4732
She began to up the musical ante with a more rock-oriented approach, and her songs also took on a more argumentative tone, especially in the critical "Barefoot and Pregnant." —*William Ruhlmann*

○ **Me Myself I** / 1980 / A&M 3316
On the trio of albums that made her reputation in 1976-78—*Joan Armatrading, Show Some Emotion*, and *To the Limit*—Armatrading relied on the pristine production of Glyn Johns to underscore the sensitivity of her folk-based confessional songs. Here, on her first full-length album in two years, she turned to rock producer Richard Gottehrer and a session band that included Anton Fig, Chris Spedding, and members of the E Street Band, making her case for being a mainstream rocker. The songs were less serious, too, notably the title track, a U.K. hit. The result was the best selling album Armatrading has ever had in either the United States or the United Kingdom. —*William Ruhlmann*

Walk under Ladders / 1981 / A&M 3317
Dominant keyboard lines and the characteristic fat percussion approach of producer Steve Lillywhite completed Armatrading's transformation from folkie to new wave diva on this album. Still, it was songs like "The Weakness in Me" to which old fans responded, though the British hits were "I'm Lucky" and "No Love." Another British Top Ten, the album was less successful in the States, consolidating Armatrading's expanded following without propelling her to major stardom. —*William Ruhlmann*

Key / Mar. 1983 / A&M 3318
The best of Armatrading's later albums, which took on a much harder rock edge. Steve Lillywhite produced, and Armatrading provided some good up-tempo material, including "Drop the Pilot" and "(I Love It When You) Call Me Names." —*William Ruhlmann*

○ **Track Record** / Nov. 1983 / A&M 3319
A reasonable best-of that samples Armatrading's first decade of recording. —*William Ruhlmann*

● **Classics, Vol. 21** / 1989 / A&M 2519
Featuring some of her best songs and covering a bit more ground than *Track Record, Classics* is a good introduction to the rich and varied career of Joan Armatrading. —*Stephen Thomas Erlewine*

P. P. Arnold (Pat Arnold)

b. 1946, Los Angeles, CA
Vocals / Soul
A soul vocalist who came from a family of gospel singers, P. P. Arnold began singing as a four-year-old. She got her start backing Bobby Day before being invited to join the Ikettes, backing Ike and Tina Turner. Arnold toured with them in the '60s, including one stint with the Rolling Stones. Mick Jagger persuaded her to remain in London, and she later recorded for the Immediate label, run by the Stones' manager Andrew Loog-Oldham. Loog-Oldham, Jagger, and Mike Hurst produced Arnold's debut LP, *The First Lady of Immediate*, which included the single "The First Cut Is the Deepest." Arnold also had moderate success with the singles "The Time Has Come," "(If You Think) You're Groovy," and "Angel in the Morning" in the late '60s, though they were hits in England and Europe rather than America. Arnold re-entered the music world in the mid '80s. She sang lead on a Boy George song for the film "Electric Dreams" in 1984. She worked with Dexter Wansel and Loose Ends on the single "A Little Pain," which she

recorded as Pat Arnold. She then had another English hit with the single "Burn It Up." —*Ron Wynn*

● **P. P. Arnold Collection** / 1991 / Sony 47353
Transplanted American R&B singer hits it big with achingly soulful ballads. A '60s curio and more, especially "The First Cut Is the Deepest." —*Bruce Eder*

Art of Noise

Group / Techno-pop, dance
Anne Dudley, Gary Lanagan, and J. J. Jeczalik were members of producer Trevor Horn's in-house studio band in the early '80s, before they formed Art of Noise, a techno-pop group whose music was an amalgam of studio gimmickry, tape splicing, and synthesized beats. After earning a sizable cult following in the latter half of the '80s (as well as scoring two Top-40 hits) the Art of Noise broke up in 1990. —*Stephen Thomas Erlewine*

● **Best of the Art of Noise** / 1988 / Polydor 837367
All of the Art of Noise's best tracks are here, including "Close (to the Edit)," "Legacy," and a cover of Prince's "Kiss" with Tom Jones on lead vocals. —*Stephen Thomas Erlewine*

Ashford & Simpson

Vocals / Soul, disco, urban R&B
Nikolas Ashford and Valerie Simpson have two careers, as songwriters and as performers, with the former seemingly more important than the latter until the mid '80s. The two met in 1964 and scored their first songwriting hit in 1966 with Ray Charles's recording of their "Let's Go Get Stoned." After a period at Scepter Records, they moved to Motown, where they wrote hits for the duo of Marvin Gaye and Tammi Terrell ("Ain't Nothing Like the Real Thing," "You're All I Need to Get By"). When Diana Ross left the Supremes for a solo career, Ashford and Simpson wrote "Reach Out and Touch Somebody's Hand" for her.

Their performing career was launched in 1973 with *Keep It Comin'* on Motown and *Gimme Something Real* on Warner Bros. Their first success came in 1977 with the gold-selling *Send It*, which contained the Top-Ten R&B hit "Don't Cost You Nothing." *Is It Still Good to Ya*, a second gold album, contained the number-two R&B hit "It Seems to Hang On" in 1978. *Stay Free*, their third straight gold album, contained "Found a Cure," another R&B smash that also made the Top 40 on the pop chart. *A Musical Affair*, 1980, featured the hit "Love Don't Make It Right," but was not as successful as previous efforts.

Meanwhile, A&S continued to work with other artists, scoring successes with Ross, Chaka Khan ("I'm Every Woman"), and Gladys Knight. Their own career saw a resurgence in 1984 with *Solid*, which went gold and produced the R&Bnumber one "Solid" (number 12 on the pop charts), "Outta the World," and "Babies." —*William Ruhlmann*

○ **Come As You Are** / 1976 / Warner Brothers 2858
One of Ashford & Simpson's best Warner albums, especially from a production standpoint. The mix between uptempo and slow love songs and dance tunes was perfect, and their interaction had been honed to the point where each anticipated the other. Simpson's soaring vocals and Ashford's less impressive, but still strong, support, plus their outstanding harmonizing, was at its peak. —*Ron Wynn*

○ **Send It** / 1977 / Warner Brothers 3088
Exuberant lead vocals, great teamwork, and excellent production made this set a top entry in the Ashford & Simpson sweepstakes. They were at the top of their production and performance games in the late '70s, cranking out their own hits and also producing everyone in the R&B/soul world from Gladys Knight to themselves. —*Ron Wynn*

○ **Is It Still Good to Ya** / 1978 / Warner Brothers 3219
The disco arrangements are a little dated, but this is still Ashford & Simpson's best '70s album, as their two similar voices intertwine on a collection of songs about devoted love, among them the title track and "It Seems to Hang On." —*William Ruhlmann*

Stay Free / 1979 / Warner Brothers 3357
The title track was spectacular, and the rest of the album was expertly produced, performed, and arranged. —*Ron Wynn*

● **Solid** / 1984 / Warner Brothers 2402501
Ashford & Simpson have always been the prime representatives in R&B of the joys of wedded bliss, and this extended valentine is

their most consistent set as well as their biggest hit ever. —*William Ruhlmann*

Asia

Group / Progressive rock, pop/rock
When they appeared in the early '80s, Asia seemed to be a holdover from the '70s, when supergroups and self-important progressive rockers reigned supreme. Featuring members of such seminal art rock bands as King Crimson (John Wetton), Emerson, Lake & Palmer (Carl Palmer), and Yes (Steve Howe), as well as Geoff Downes from the Buggles, Asia did feature stretches of indulgent instrumentals on their records. However, they also could be surprisingly poppy and that is what brought them to the top of the charts with their debut album, *Asia*, and its hit single, "Heat of the Moment." *Alpha*, their second album, also had a couple of hits ("Don't Cry" and "The Smile Has Left Your Eyes") but its follow-up, *Astra*, was a flop. The group disbanded in 1985, only to reunite in 1990 without Steve Howe; Pat Thrall took his place. After churning out a couple of new songs for a greatest hits collection, the band hit the road, including two sold-out dates in front of 20,000 fans in Moscow, of all places. Since then, they have toured sporadically. —*Stephen Thomas Erlewine*

○ **Asia** / 1982 / Geffen 2008
Debut release for this supergroup, featuring classy pop/rock and several hits. —*Paul Kohler*

Alpha / 1983 / Geffen 4008
Follow-up album with the same lineup as the first. —*Paul Kohler*

● **Then & Now** / 1990 / Geffen 24298
This compilation includes all of their Top-40 hits—"Heat of the Moment," "Only Time Will Tell," "Don't Cry," and "The Smile Has Left Your Eyes"—as well as some unreleased tracks. —*AMG*

The Association

Group / Pop/rock
Between 1966 and 1969, the Association was one of the most successful practitioners of romantic light pop. The band's smooth Lettermen-like harmonies helped make songs like "Cherish," "Never My Love," and "Everything That Touches You" staples of adult easy-listening formats and elevators throughout the planet. Before the Association, founding member Terry Kirkman had actually performed coffeehouses with Frank Zappa for several years.

Their first hit, the upbeat "Along Comes Mary," met with resistance from radio programmers, afraid that the song was about marijuana. The exuberant "Windy," on the other hand, easily sailed all the way to number one, becoming the band's biggest seller. Interestingly, "Windy" (which knocked Aretha Franklin's "Respect" out of the top slot) was originally written as a waltz. Attempts to infuse a more progressive "rock" sound with "Six Man Band" were met with indifference from the public. That was to be their last hit.

The Association ground on until 1972, when the death of bassist Brian Cole, plus the poor commercial response to their Columbia Records debut, *Waterbeds in Trinidad*, provided impetus for the band's dissolution. The band has managed a few reunions, most notably the 1980 HBO reunion special, and a moderate hit, "Dreamer," on Elektra. —*Rick Clark*

○ **Association's Greatest Hits** / 1968 / Warner Brothers 1767
At only 13 songs, this is concise but not definitive. —*Jeff Tamarkin*

● **Songs That Made Them Famous** / 1986 / Pair 1061
Beyond the hits, all of which are included here ("Windy," "Cherish," "Along Comes Mary"), the Association made stunning orchestral folk-pop that still makes the listener feel good. —*Jeff Tamarkin*

Rick Astley

b. Feb. 6, 1966, Warrington, England
Vocals / Dance-pop
With his rich, deep voice and well-crafted dance-pop, Rick Astley became an overnight sensation in the late '80s. Astley was discovered by the producer Pete Waterman in 1985 singing in the English soul band, FBI. After that, Waterman's production team—Stock, Aitken, and Waterman—took Astley under their wing, writing and producing such impeccably crafted pop singles as "Never Gonna Give You Up" and "Together Forever." After two hugely

successful albums in the United States and Great Britain, Astley grew tired of being labeled Stock, Aitken, and Waterman's "puppet" and severed his connections with the team. He resurfaced in 1991 with the soul-injected *Free*, which contained the Top-Ten hit, "Cry for Help." —*Stephen Thomas Erlewine*

● **Whenever You Need Somebody** / 1987 / RCA 6822
A retro-disco sound on this album, which includes the hits "Together Forever" and "Never Give You Up." —*Kenneth M. Cassidy*

○ **Hold Me in Your Arms** / 1988 / RCA 8589
Apart from "She Wants to Dance with Me," Astley's second album didn't have songs that were as strong those on the debut. Most of the album was pleasant dance-pop filler, showing the weaknesses of the Stock-Aitken-Waterman production team. —*Stephen Thomas Erlewine*

Free / 1991 / RCA 3004
On his third album, Astley takes more control, for a streamlined sound. Includes "Cry for Help." —*Kenneth M. Cassidy*

Atlantic Starr

Group / Dance, soul, disco, urban R & B
New York-based Atlantic Starr began in 1976. Brothers David (guitar and vocals), Jonathan (trombone), and Wayne (keyboards) Lewis started a funk and soul band, adding lead vocalist Sharon Bryant, bassist Clifford Archer, drummer Porter Carroll, saxophonist Koran Daniels, percussionist and flutist Joseph Phillips, and trumpeter William Sudderth. They signed with A&M a couple of years later, staying at the label through 1987 and landing several hits, including "Gimme Your Lovin'," "Circles," "When Love Calls," "Stand Up," "Silver Shadow," "One Love," and the crossover hit "Secret Lovers." Their albums *Brillance* and *As the Band Turns* were also Top-20 pop hits. In 1987, the group switched to Warner Bros. and their first release, *All in the Name of Love*, included another pop smash, "Always," the group's sole number-one pop and R&B hit. They enjoyed more R&B successes with Warner through the '80s. Sharon Bryant left in 1989 for a solo career; she was replaced by Barbara Weathers, who later left for a solo career as well. —*Ron Wynn*

○ **Brilliance** / 1982 / A&M 4883
This was the album that came closest to making them superstars. It had two hit singles in "Circles" and "Love Me Down," and by then they had the cohesive, smooth, urban contemporary group sound down cold. —*Ron Wynn*

○ **As the Band Turns** / 1986 / A&M 5019
Their biggest hit album came in 1986, with new singer Barbara Weathers proving the perfect replacement for Bryant. In fact, her lighter, less assured but more sensual sound proved ideal on the duets "Secret Lovers" and "If Your Heart Isn't in It." The Lewis brothers and Joseph Phillips added just enough musical support, and the group's early funk history was by then merely a memory. They'd made the transition to urban (and urbane) balladeers. —*Ron Wynn*

● **Secret Lovers: The Best of Atlantic Starr** / 1986 / A&M 3320
A nice anthology, though it emphasizes the ballad smashes and doesn't convey much of their earlier, harder flavor. Atlantic Starr moved to Warner Bros. in the late '80s, so their former label cranked out a greatest-hits LP to take advantage of their hit status. These songs were staples of '80s urban contemporary radio, and the ballads are still carried in the '90s on many quiet-storm playlists. —*Ron Wynn*

○ **Classics, Vol. 10** / 1987 / A&M 2508
This collection gathers their A&M hits, which also include "Freak-a-Ristic," "Secret Lovers" and "If Your Heart Isn't in It." But the group scored its biggest smash after moving to Warner Bros.—the R&B and pop chart-topping "Always" in 1987. —*Ron Wynn*

Patti Austin

b. Aug. 10, 1948, California
Vocals / Dance, urban R & B
A professional since the age of five, Patti Austin was a protegee of Dinah Washington and Sammy Davis, Jr. Austin cut her debut LP, *End of a Rainbow*, in 1976, followed by *Havana Candy* in 1977 and *Body Language* in 1980. She sang duets with Michael Jackson on "It's the Falling in Love" (from the *Off the Wall* album) and with George Benson on "Moody's Mood for Love" in 1980.

She sang background vocals for sessions by Noel Pointer, Ralph McDonald, Angela Bofill, and Roberta Flack. Austin sang vocals on Quincy Jones's *The Dude* LP in 1981, and was featured on the hit "Razzamatazz."

She inked a solo deal on Jones' Qwest label, and her 1982 album *Every Home Should Have One* included the number-one pop hit "Baby, Come to Me," which got widespread exposure via the ABC soap opera "General Hospital." The follow-up single, "How Do You Keep the Music Playing," was the theme for the film *Best Friends*. Both songs paired Austin with James Ingram.

She continued recording for Qwest throughout the '80s, but couldn't recapture her pop or R&B success, despite working with several top producers, including Jimmy Jam and Terry Lewis in 1985. Austin switched to GRP in 1990 and recorded *Love Is Gonna Getcha*. —*Ron Wynn*

○ **Every Home Should Have One** / 1981 / Qwest 3591
Quincy Jones-produced pop album featuring "Baby, Come to Me," which became a belated hit when it was featured on "General Hospital," two years after the album came out. —*William Ruhlmann*

Patti Austin / 1984 / Qwest 23974
Patti Austin enjoyed good chart action and radio airplay with this mid-'80s release. A pair of singles, "Hot! In the Flames of Love" and "Star Struck" got both R&B and dance attention, while the album had some other competent uptempo material and a couple of good ballads. It wasn't her best on Qwest, but it was far from her worse. —*Ron Wynn*

● **Real Me** / 1988 / Qwest 25696
And how! Austin tackles standards such as "Smoke Gets in Your Eyes" and "They Can't Take That Away from Me," and succeeds brilliantly. Her version of Comden, Green, and Bernstein's "I Can Cook, Too" is enough by itself to make this a pick. —*William Ruhlmann*

The Auteurs

Group / Alternative pop/rock
When the Auteurs released their debut album in 1993, the British press linked them with the massively popular Suede as part of a "glam revival." While the band can blast out guitar-drenched rockers as Suede can, the Auteurs come to life when they draw from the quiet side of such distinctively English guitar-pop musicians as the Kinks, the Smiths, and George Harrison. Luke Haines, the group's guitarist, vocalist, and songwriter, writes highly melodic pop songs that combine the airy lyricism of Harrison with Davies' cutting social observations. They're sharp, intelligent songs, full of humor and gorgeous melancholy, even when they're loud rockers. With their two albums, *New Wave* and *Now I'm a Cowboy*, the Auteurs have earned a devoted following in Great Britain, without gathering much support in the United States. —*Stephen Thomas Erlewine*

● **New Wave** / 1993 / Plan 9 1735
With their 1993 debut album, *New Wave*, the Auteurs established themselves as one of England's best guitar bands of the early '90s. Driven by the bittersweet, ironic songwriting of Luke Haines, the band's carefully crafted, three-minute pop songs are in the vein of the Kinks, the Smiths, and the Beatles, particularly the songs of George Harrison. Yet the band never sounds like imitators—their music combines their influences into a signature sound, distinguished by Haines's sharp lyrics and sighing melodies. —*Stephen Thomas Erlewine*

○ **Now I'm a Cowboy** / 1994 / Hut USA/Vernon Yard
While the Auteurs' second album is harder than their debut, the band never loses sight of their distinctive, melodic guitar-pop. —*Stephen Thomas Erlewine*

Frankie Avalon (Francis Avallone)

b. Sep. 18, 1939, Philadelphia
Vocals / Pop
At the end of the '50s and beginning of the '60s, Frankie Avalon was one of the biggest teen idols around, hitting the top of the charts consistently from 1958 until the end of 1960. Avalon didn't possess a terrific voice, but he did have material that was tailor-made for a receptive teen audience. At the height of his popularity, in 1959, he had five consecutive Top-Ten hits, including "Dede Dinah," "Ginger Bread," "Why," and "Venus." When the '60s began in earnest, Avalon embarked on an acting career; he starred in a

hugely successful series of beach movies with Annette Funicello. After he began acting, Avalon didn't return to music throughout the decade. In the '70s, he began making occasional film and television appearances while he worked the nostalgia and club circuits. He continues to sing and act in the '90s. —*Stephen Thomas Erlewine*

● **Best of Frankie Avalon** / 1984 / Creole 1613
Avalon's biggest hits are collected on this best-of compilation. —*Stephen Thomas Erlewine*

Average White Band

b. , Scotland
Group / Soul, funk
This Glasgow, Scotland, sextet achieved much success during the '70s with their blue-eyed soulful funk. Bonnie Bramlett (of Delaney & Bonnie) jokingly bestowed the name on the band. During their prime, AWB's solid grooves and overall chemistry were anything but average. Their biggest hits came in 1975 with "Cut the Cake," "School Boy Crush," "If I Ever Lose This Heaven," and "Pick up the Pieces," which hit number-one pop at the top of the year. The band members have worked as session sidemen for artists ranging from Chaka Khan to Paul McCartney and Badfinger. —*Rick Clark*

○ **Average White Band** / 1974 / Atlantic 19116
Average White Band's self-titled third album was also their best. It contained their biggest and best hit, "Pick up the Pieces," as well as "Keepin' It to Myself." —*Dan Heilman*

● **Pickin' up the Pieces: The Best of Average White Band (1974-1980)** / 1992 / Rhino 71054
All of the Average White Band's biggest hits, as well as important album tracks, are featured on this definitive 18-track collection. —*Stephen Thomas Erlewine*

Aztec Camera

Group / Alternative pop/rock
More a creative outlet for Glasgowian Roddy Frame than a proper group, Aztec Camera has specialized in lush, acoustic-based cerebral pop, reaching their apex on *High Land, Hard Rain,* their 1983 debut. —*John Floyd*

● **High Land, Hard Rain** / 1983 / Sire 23899
An intelligent and detailed, if somewhat overambitious, debut, showcasing vocalist/songwriter Roddy Frame's catchy and wordy acoustic-based pop songs. Imagine a folkie version of Elvis Costello, with better guitar chops, and you've got the picture here. None of the Camera's other albums have come close to matching this release. —*John Floyd*

Knife / 1984 / Sire 25183
Aztec Camera's second album cuts back the ethereal atmosphere, revealing a stripped-down, vaguely R&B-influenced pop sense. —*Stephen Thomas Erlewine*

○ **Stray** / 1990 / Sire 26211
After a lukewarm stab at soul (*Love*), Roddy Frame returns to a brilliantly textured guitar pop on *Stray*, covering rock, soul, and jazzy pop in the space of one album. It's all tied together by Frame's intelligent, sometimes-precious lyrics and melodic pop sense. It's one of Aztec Camera's finest albums. —*Stephen Thomas Erlewine*

○ **Dreamland** / May 25, 1993 / Sire 45076
Aztec Camera's first album since 1990's lukewarm *Stray* is a surprising return to form for singer/songwriter Roddy Frame. Highlighted by the gorgeous Motown-Byrds hybrid single "Dream Sweet Dreams" and the lush, warm ballads "Valium Summer" and "Let Your Love Decide," *Dreamland* is Aztec Camera's best effort since their debut, *High Land Hard Rain.* —*Stephen Thomas Erlewine*

B. T. Express

b. , Brooklyn, New York
Group / Funk, disco
From their origins as the King Davis House Rockers, Madison Street Express, and Brooklyn Trucking Express, this New York band finally settled on B.T. Express. Their roster included jazz alto saxophonist Carlos Ward and vocalist Barbara Joyce Lomas. They exploded on the funk-disco scene in the mid '70s with back-to-back Number-One R&B hits "Do It ('Til You're Satisfied)" and

"Express," both of which also cracked the pop Top Ten. They had a rougher, less polished sound than their major competitor Brass Construction. "Give You What You Got/Peace Pipe" was another big hit, but the group had peaked by the late '70s. —*Ron Wynn*

● **Golden Classics** / Collectables 5190
This collection includes these three smashes, plus other numbers that earned respectable numbers. They were never great singers, but were a good funk ensemble. —*Ron Wynn*

The B-52's

b. , Athens, Georgia
Group / Alternative pop/rock, dance-pop
Athens, GA, has been a hotbed of alternative talent for quite a while, but the town's rise to cutting-edge musical prominence was aided in no small part by the 1976 formation of the B-52's, a wildly unorthodox party band that featured a guitarist with a five-string Mosrite electric and two mini-skirted female singers (Kate Pierson and Cindy Wilson) who sported extremely bouffant hairdos and go-go boots.

The recklessly exuberant self-titled Warner debut was a left-field success, selling tons of copies with little radio support. The followup, *Wild Planet*, picks up where *The B-52's* left off, with mixed results; nevertheless, it enjoyed even greater success.

A dance-mix EP and two subsequent albums (*Mesopotamia* and *Whammy!*) provide further variations on the band's sound, but the "fun" sounds increasingly forced.

Guitarist Ricky Wilson passed away in 1985 from AIDS, before the release of the uneven *Bouncing off the Satellites*. With drummer Keith Strickland taking over Wilson's guitar duties, the B-52's returned from an extended break and put out the hugely successful *Cosmic Thing*. Produced by Don Was and Nile Rodgers, *Cosmic Thing* successfully synthesized the band's wacky energy with just the right amount of streamlined mainstream pop production. —*Rick Clark*

● **B-52's** / 1979 / Warner Brothers 3355
It's all here on the debut album: the "Secret Agent Man" drum-and-guitar tracks that compel the feet to dance, topped by shrill female vocals and the brash speak-singing of Fred Schneider giving forth with some of the strangest nonsequiturs—as though he were an overexcited carnival barker. Includes "Planet Claire" and the hit "Rock Lobster." —*William Ruhlmann*

Wild Planet / 1980 / Warner Brothers 3471
Wild Planet is more of the same, as the B-52's celebrate the joys of living in your own private Idaho and the wonders of quiche lorraine. —*William Ruhlmann*

Whammy! / 1983 / Warner Brothers 23819
After the still-born *Mesopotamia, Whammy!* is a pleasing return to the classic fun-loving wackiness of the first album, even if some of the songs sound a little forced and self-conscious. —*Stephen Thomas Erlewine*

Bouncing Off the Satellites / 1986 / Warner Brothers 25504
Released about a year after the death of guitarist Ricky Wilson, *Bouncing Off the Satellites* is a disjointed, uneven record that starts off strong but collapses into a mess of studio slickness by the end of the album. —*Stephen Thomas Erlewine*

○ **Cosmic Thing** / 1989 / Warner Brothers 25854
Belatedly, and despite the death of their musical leader Ricky Wilson, the B-52's found enormous commercial success with this album, which effectively recapitulates their zany virtues, especially on the two Top-Three hits "Love Shack" and "Roam." —*William Ruhlmann*

Good Stuff / Jun. 23, 1992 / Warner Brothers 26943
If *Cosmic Thing* found them returned to most-favored party-band status, this follow-up gamely soldiers on in similiar fashion. Without Cindy Wilson, *Good Stuff* becomes Kate Pierson's showcase, even while Fred Schneider turns in his most purely musical performance to date. If the B-52's hit some dead ends while trying to stretch out a bit, be assured there's enough classic bits to make this one worthwhile. —*Steve Aldrich*

Babes in Toyland

Group / Alternative rock
Babes in Toyland are about as harsh as rock music gets—guitarist Kat Bjelland screams and thrashes her guitar to the gut-pounding, throttling beat of bassist Maureen Herman and drummer

Lorie Barbero. Over their two albums and two EPs, the all-female trio offer no escape from their strongly female-oriented, but not necessarily feminist, rock.

Bjelland formed Babes in Toyland in 1987 in Minneapolis, after playing around San Francisco for several years in various bands that featured, at various times, Jennifer Finch of L7 and Courtney Love of Hole. After releasing a single on Sub Pop's singles club, Babes in Toyland came to the attention of Sonic Youth, who took them on a tour of Europe. Soon, they recorded their abrasive debut, *Spanking Machine*, with producer Jack Endino. One more independent EP followed before they signed to Reprise. In between labels, original bassist Michelle Leon left the group.

Sonic Youth's Lee Ranaldo produced their second album, *Fontanelle*, which showed no signs of concession to a major label. In early 1993, the band broke up for several days before re-forming to record the *Painkillers* EP and hitting the road with Lollapalooza 93. *—Stephen Thomas Erlewine*

○ **Spanking Machine** / 1990 / Twintone 89183
A great one first time out of the blocks. Kat Bjelland's guitar is a rampaging string machine, while her vocals pin you to the wall. Not for the weak or fainthearted. *—John Dougan*

● **Fontanelle** / 1992 / Warner Brothers 26998
Fontanelle, Babes in Toyland's major-label debut, is stronger than their previous *Spanking Machine*. The band has grown tighter and more vicious, making their anger sting even harder. *—Stephen Thomas Erlewine*

○ **Painkiller** / Jun. 22, 1993 / Warner Brothers
Painkiller features four solid new tracks, one rerecording, and a brutal, 35-minute live performance of the entire *Fontanelle* album. It's intense and harrowing, but only necessary for fans. *—Stephen Thomas Erlewine*

Babyface (Kenny Edmonds)

Vocals, keyboard / Urban R&B, soul
With his friend Antonio Reid, Babyface formed a Cincinnati-based band, the Deele, in the early '80s. They were introduced by members of Midnight Star to Solar Records executive Dick Griffey, who put them to work producing music for Carrie Lucas, the Whispers, and Dynasty. Since then, they've produced hits for Sheena Easton, Pebbles, and Paula Abdul, as well as several others.

During the '90s, Babyface's dominance has extended beyond the production arena and into the performing circle. A series of hit releases depicting him simultaneously as a vulnerable romantic and an accomplished lover turned Babyface into arguably the decade's biggest urban-R&B male vocalist. The string actually began in the mid '80s with the underrated *Lovers*, but it picked up steam with *Tender Lover* in 1989. *Tender Lover* crossed him over into pop territory and eventually sold more than two million copies, ending any doubts that Babyface would be a major solo star. The singles "Whip Appeal" and "It's No Crime" were Top-Ten R&B and pop hits, and remain staples on urban radio. He followed that with *A Closer Look* in 1991 and 1993's *For the Cool in You* earned another platinum certification and ranked among the year's biggest urban-R&B albums. *—Bil Carpenter and Ron Wynn*

● **Tender Lover** / 1990 / Solar 45288
Babyface's second solo album yielded the first number-one R&B hit of the '90s, while establishing Edmonds as a major personality and performer. He wrote or co-wrote much of the material, and even played several instruments. It was a combination of slick production and nicely sung sentimental tributes and heartache ballads. *—Ron Wynn*

○ **A Closer Look** / Nov. 19, 1991 / CBS 75329
Babyface has established himself as both a performing and production star in the '90s. His alternately innocent, hurt, and disillusioned vocals are this decade's equivalent of the soul love songs of the '70s and '80s. He can sing sentimental material, tender tunes, or seem angry and confused. His lyrics get overly coy, but they've struck many responsive chords in listeners. *—Ron Wynn*

Bachman-Turner Overdrive

Group / Rock & roll, pop/rock
Bachman-Turner Overdrive, formed by two expatriates of Canada's Guess Who, Randy Bachman and C. F. Turner, special-

ized in no-nonsense blue collar rock & roll. In fact, part of the band's name came from the trucking industry magazine *Overdrive*. This isn't to say that BTO was without musical sophistication, the jazzy "Lookin' Out for No. 1." certainly evidenced otherwise.

The band's initial demos were rejected by over two dozen record labels before Mercury picked them up. Several of BTO's radio tracks became substantial hits, particularly "Takin' Care of Business" and the number-one hit "You Ain't Seen Nothing Yet," which had a stuttering vocal hook inspired by the speech impediment of the band's first manager, Gary Bachman. *—Rick Clark*

● **Greatest Hits** / 1981 / Mercury 830039
All the essential hits are here on this good-sounding set. The lack of liner notes keeps this from being an informative place to start, but if you are looking for just the music, the high points are here. *—Rick Clark*

○ **Anthology** / Jul. 20, 1993 / Polygram
This double-disc set features fine remastering from the original masters, plus extensive liner notes. This is an ideal choice for the *true* fan who is just converting to CD and is looking for more than the basic hits package. Hit seekers will still find *BTO's Greatest Hits* more than adequate. *—Rick Clark*

Bad Brains

Group / Hardcore, alternative rock
Along with Black Flag and Minor Threat, the Bad Brains were the leaders of Washington D.C.'s hardcore punk movement in the early '80s, although they didn't sound like either band. The Bad Brains tempered their ferocious hardcore with a good dose of dub and reggae without deviating from the "hard fast loud" rules that were vital to the scene. Led by vocalist H. R. and the blistering guitarist Dr. Know, the Bad Brains were notorious for their exhilarating live show, which had a raw, vital energy that they rarely captured in the studio. As the years passed, the band's reggae elements became more pronounced and—as with most other punk bands—the punk elements lost some of their edge, turning into an honest, brutal version of heavy metal. Throughout their career, H. R. left and rejoined the group, but by the beginning of the '90s, he had left the group permanently, leaving Israel Joseph-I as the lead vocalist. Fifteen years after they formed, the Bad Brains released their first major-label album, *Rise*, in 1993. Between those years, their eclectic, intelligent approach to punk affected a generation of rockers who enthusiastically embrace these ideas in their music. *—Stephen Thomas Erlewine*

Bad Brains / 1982 / ROIR 106
On their debut album, Bad Brains established their explosive mix of reggae and hardcore. At this stage, the mix was still tentative, with the band able to pull off the punk better than the reggae, yet the band's sheer energy made the album successful. *—Stephen Thomas Erlewine*

Rock for Light / 1983 / Caroline 1613
On their Ric Ocasek-produced second album, Bad Brains were able to balance the hardcore and reggae elements more skillfully than they had on their debut, yet *Rock for Light* suffers from a lack of cohesiveness. Even if it is a little inconsistent, the unique power of their vision makes the album worthwhile. *—Stephen Thomas Erlewine*

● **I Against I** / 1986 / SST 065
Slick production helped the Brains make the most satisfying metal/reggae record of their career. Dr. Know's guitar is pushed way up front in the mix, and the funkier backbeat (replacing the hardcore speed blur) kicks every track (especially "Return to Heaven") into high gear. *—John Dougan*

The Youth Are Getting Restless—Live in Amsterdam / 1990 / Caroline 1617
The Youth Are Getting Restless captures the blistering power of the Bad Brains in concert as well as any recording could. *—Stephen Thomas Erlewine*

Bad Company

Group / Hard rock
Supergroups usually don't enjoy lengthy fruitful careers, but Bad Company was a highly successful exception, producing a string of hit records from 1974 to 1982. Paul Rodgers and Simon Kirke of

Free, Boz Burrell from King Crimson, and Mott the Hoople's Mick Ralphs delivered Bad Company's sparse, crunchy hard rock.

Their self-titled debut album, recorded in ten days, exuded an appealing unpolished sound at a time when a lot of rock seemed to be trading its visceral essence for arty pretention. After their second album (*Straight Shooter*), Bad Company began to lose some of its freshness, opting for a more processed sound.

The group broke up in 1983, but by the late '80s, a new lineup with Kirke and Ralphs emerged. Brian Howe filled Rodgers's slot. Even though this incarnation has produced some substantial rock hits, the band's sound is disappointingly interchangeable with a load of other professional radio rock acts. —*Rick Clark*

○ **Bad Company** / 1974 / Swan Song 8501
A powerhouse debut, including "Can't Get Enough," "Ready for Love," and the title track. —*Dan Heilman*

Straight Shooter / 1975 / Swan Song 8502
Their hot streak continues with "Feel Like Makin' Love." A fine follow-up. —*Dan Heilman*

Desolation Angels / 1979 / Swan Song 8506
After a couple of mediocre efforts, *Desolation Angels* marked a return to form for Bad Company. It was also the band's last consistent album, powered by "Rock N' Roll Fantasy" and "Gone, Gone, Gone." —*Stephen Thomas Erlewine*

● **10 from 6** / 1986 / Swan Song 81625
A concise, if overly brief collection of hits, including "Can't Get Enough," "Feel Like Makin' Love," "Ready for Love," "Movin' On," and "Rock N' Roll Fantasy." —*Dan Heilman*

Bad Manners

Group / Ska revival
The English group Bad Manners, formed in 1980 and featuring lead singer Buster Bloodvessel, arrived as part of the early '80s ska revival, with groups like the English Beat, Madness, and the Specials. —*Rick Clark*

● **Klass** / 1983 / MCA 5415
This is most representative collection of the band's fun version of ska/bluebeat. All of their British hits are covered including the endlessly catchy "Ne-Ne Na-Na Na-Na Nu-Nu Nu-Nu." —*Chris Woodstra*

Bad Religion

Group / Hardcore, alternative rock
Of all of the Southern Californian hardcore punk bands of the early '80s, Bad Religion has stayed around the longest. For over ten years, they have kept their underground credibility without turning out a series of records that all sound the same. It wasn't until 1993 that they released an album through a major label, and during the '90s it was much easier to sign to a major and preserve credibility. Although their major label debut, *Recipe for Hate*, didn't have the furious attack of their 1982 debut, *How Could Hell Be Any Worse?*, it didn't sell out. Between those two records, Bad Religion tightened their musical attack while adding thicker riffs and keeping lyrics righteously angry and complex. As a result, the band has leaned toward hard-rock territory on their later albums, but they remain committed to their indie-rock ethics. That dedication blazes through in their music. —*Stephen Thomas Erlewine*

How Can Hell Be Any Worse (1980-1985) / 1981 / Epitaph 86407
Durable standard Southern California hardcore post-punk with brains. —*John Dougan*

○ **Into the Unknown** / 1983 / Epitaph
Slightly spacey, but more direct and hard-hitting. —*John Dougan*

Suffer / 1988 / Epitaph 86404
Featuring a reunited version of the original band, *Suffer* is a fast, stripped-down, blazing record that tears through its songs relentlessly. In terms of sheer sonic intensity, *Suffer* is their best record yet, even if it is lacking in musical diversity. —*Stephen Thomas Erlewine*

● **No Control** / 1989 / Epitaph 86406
No Control is even more uncompromising than *Suffer*, except this time, Bad Religion has concentrated more on songwriting and melody, making the album their most impressive straight hardcore effort. —*Stephen Thomas Erlewine*

Recipe for Hate / 1993 / Epitaph
Although it doesn't sound all that different from what either Bad Religion or X was doing ten years ago, Bad Religion gained a larger audience with *Recipe for Hate*. Featuring guest spots from Eddie Vedder and Johnette Napolitano from Concrete Blonde, the album is a smoother version of punk. All of the trademark anger and guitars are still present, but some of the melodies and riffs lean towards mainstream rock & roll. Fortunately, this all works in Bad Religion's favor—their music is more accessible, yet it doesn't lack integrity. —*Stephen Thomas Erlewine*

Badfinger

Group / Pop/rock, power pop
Rarely has a recorded group had so much apparent opportunity and so much bad luck as Badfinger. Paul McCartney discovered Badfinger's demo and signed them to the Beatles' Apple label. McCartney penned their first hit, "Come and Get It," which was featured (along with a couple of their other songs) in the movie *The Magic Christian*, as well as on their debut, *Magic Christian Music*. With their follow-up, *No Dice*, Badfinger's image as a poor man's Beatles began to evaporate, due to the new sophistication found in the writing skills of all the band members. George Harrison and Todd Rundgren took turns producing their third album, *Straight Up*, which had two more international hits with "Baby Blue" and "Day After Day." Poised to take advantage of this great success, Badfinger lost momentum as Apple Records began to crumble under mismanagement and confusion.

In December 1973, Badfinger released *Ass*—good album, but a little rough around the edges. Only months later, Badfinger released their self-titled debut on Warners, which was eager to regain the momentum from *Straight Up*. The album was an improvement over *Ass*, but it still suffered from the hasty release. Determined to get it right, Badfinger went into the studio with Chris Thomas and produced some of their very best music on *Wish You Were Here*.

Upon discovering a questionable disappearance from Badfinger's publishing escrow account, Warners pulled the record weeks after its release, in spite of glowing reviews. Undaunted but distraught by the situation, the band cut another album, *Head First,* which Warners also barred from release. Depressed by personal and professional problems, Pete Ham (guitar, vocals, and keyboard) hung himself in his garage on April 23, 1975.

After a five-year break, Tom Evans (bass and vocals) and Joey Molland (guitar and vocals) regrouped and released the spotty *Airwaves* on Elektra. The subsequent *Say No More* was even weaker. In 1983, Evans, upset over not receiving proper royalty compensation and plagued by other endless band business problems, took his life. Molland sporadically continued with Badfinger during the rest of the '80s and '90s, hiring different sidemen for each tour while also pursuing a solo career. —*Rick Clark*

○ **Magic Christian Music** / 1970 / Capitol 97579
Magic Christian Music is Badfinger's uneven debut. The band hadn't found their *sound* yet, nevertheless, tracks like "Come and Get It" and "Maybe Tomorrow" gave power-pop fans a good taste of this band's potential. —*Rick Clark*

○ **No Dice** / 1970 / Capitol 98698
Badfinger's distinctive melodic abilities, great vocals, and solid ensemble work on *No Dice*, made a strong case that this quartet could stand on its own, apart from Apple's shadow. "I Can't Take It," "Midnight Caller," the beautifully romantic "We're for the Dark," and "No Matter What" (one of the greatest pop singles ever), are among *No Dice*'s many highlights. —*Rick Clark*

★ **Straight Up** / 1972 / Capitol 3387
George Harrison and Todd Rundgren took turns producing Badfinger's third album, *Straight Up*, which produced two international hits with the gorgeous "Day after Day" and the wall-of-sound pop/rock masterpiece "Baby Blue." Badfinger forges a unique sound with their sweeping, strained high harmonies, thick, edgy rhythm-guitar parts, and a drumming style that featured an exaggerated hi-hat attack on the backbeat. Check out "Take It All," "Sometimes," and the powerful "It's Over" for examples. —*Rick Clark*

Ass / 1973 / Capitol 3411
A step down from Badfinger's two previous classics. *Ass* was the final kiss-off on the Beatles' rapidly deteriorating Apple label. In

spite of some fairly inconsequential tracks, "Apple of My Eye" (the single), "Icicles," "I Can Love You," and "Timeless," the first half of the "I Want You/She's So Heavy" rip, more than redeem this release. —*Rick Clark*

Badfinger / 1974 / Warner Brothers 4081
Tentatively titled *For Love or Money*, this was an unfortunate rush job that, in spite of it all, generated a handful of fine songs. Joey Molland's darkly meditative "Give It Up," "Andy Norris," and "Island" are fine contributions. "Lonely You," "Shine On," and "Song for a Lost Friend" showcase Pete Ham's emotive lower tenor and his considerable melodic skills. On the down side, "Matted Spam" is a horrible attempt at marrying soul with their sound, and "I Miss You" has enough sugar on it to put Paul McCartney into a coma. —*Rick Clark*

○ **Wish You Were Here** / 1974 / Warner Brothers 4082
After many professional and personal distractions, Badfinger refocused their creative energies and, with producer Chris Thomas, created one of their finest albums. The urgent fanfare of the opening track, "Just a Chance," sets the make-it-or-break-it undercurrent here. This features two impressive medleys, "In the Meantime/Some Other Time" and "Meanwhile Back at the Ranch/Should I Smoke," which features stately horn backing by the Average White Band. —*Rick Clark*

○ **Best of Badfinger, Vol. 2** / 1989 / Rhino 70978
A decent attempt at chronicling the last half of their career, which included one of the great lost pop/rock albums of the '70s, *Wish You Were Here*. With the exception of important tracks like Joey Molland's "Love Time" and Pete Ham's "Dennis," *Wish* is well represented. Key tracks from the self-titled Warner debut are included, as well as several sides from the never-released *Head First*. Also included are the only two tracks worth having from their 1979 album *Airwaves*. Until the Warner albums get released on CD stateside (which may be never), this is the only place you can get these fine tracks. —*Rick Clark*

David Baerwald
Vocals, songwriter, / Pop/rock
After the quick dissolution of David + David in the mid '80s, David Baerwald began a solo career, releasing his solo debut, *Bedtime Stories*, in 1990. As with David + David's solo album, it was an album of deceptively laidback pop; the calm production and subtle, memorable melodies hid the fact that Baerwald's characters were either inflicting or suffering from emotional pain. It was a triumph, winning raves from critics, but it sold very few copies. With his second album, 1993's *Triage*, Baerwald decided to have the music match the message, creating soundscapes that recalled a subdued, more pop-friendly Tom Waits. Again the critical praise was substantial but the record sold even less than the first. —*Stephen Thomas Erlewine*

● **Bedtime Stories** / 1990 / A&M 5289
Sparse arrangements lay the foundation for Baerwald's thought-provoking musings and solid vocals. —*Donna DiChario*

Triage / Oct. 6, 1992 / A&M 5392
Like *Bedtime Stories*, *Triage* focuses on deceit and corruption, only this time the political and social is mixed in with the personal. Baerwald's music fits his themes, with dark guitars and synthesizers covering the clanking percussion. It's a remarkably accomplished record, even if its pretensions sometimes overwhelm its accomplishments. —*Stephen Thomas Erlewine*

Dan Baird
Vocals, guitar / Rock & roll
After the Georgia Satellites disbanded at the end of the '80s, their lead singer/songwriter Dan Baird embarked on his own solo career in 1992. Not surprisingly, it sounded a lot like the Satellites' energetic, straightforward rock & roll. Fortunately, in his solo work Baird remains one of the best songwriters of traditional rock & roll to emerge in the past decade. —*Stephen Thomas Erlewine*

○ **Love Songs for the Hearing Impaired** / Oct. 1991 / Def American 26999
Love Songs for the Hearing Impaired is straight, raw rock & roll that only *seems* shallow. It's hard work to write something as irresistably stupid as "I Love You Period" and something as touching as "Julie." Baird's songwriting maintains that peak throughout

the album, while he and his band never stop rocking for a second. —*Stephen Thomas Erlewine*

Anita Baker
b. Dec. 20, 1957, Detroit, Michigan
Vocals / Urban R&B, soul, pop
Anita Baker's strong, sensual alto helped her break down the doors in the middle of the '80s. More than any other singer, she defined quiet storm—smooth, romantic soul for adults. Baker's music is sophisticated without being cold, romantic without being sacchrine. Besides soul, her singing has roots in jazz and classic pop, bringing a refined romanticism to her music. Although her 1983 debut, *The Songstress*, disappeared upon its release, her 1986 album, *Rapture*, was a modern classic that ushered in a new era of urban comtemporary and modern pop singing. None of her following records was quite as good, but her singing remains impressive on each album. —*Stephen Thomas Erlewine*

Songstress / 1983 / Elektra 61116
Not too many people heard it at the time of its release, but this album contains Baker's characteristically tasteful arrangements and remarkably evocative singing. —*William Ruhlmann*

● **Rapture** / 1986 / Elektra 60444
Baker invented a new musical genre, quiet storm, with this gorgeous album of love ballads sung in her compelling voice. Contains "Caught Up in the Rapture" and the Top-Ten hit "Sweet Love." —*William Ruhlmann*

Giving You the Best That I Got / 1988 / Elektra 60827
Baker topped the charts with this worthy follow-up to *Rapture*, which contains the hit title song and "Just Because." —*William Ruhlmann*

Compositions / 1990 / Elektra 60922
As a singer, Baker has more in common with Sarah Vaughan and Nancy Wilson than with most of her contemporaries. *Compositions*, for which Baker cowrote seven of the tunes, evokes a lush, romantic atmosphere like its predecessors, and Baker recorded her vocals live with the rhythm section. —*Brian Mansfield*

Ginger Baker
b. Aug. 19, 1940, Lewisham, London, England
Drums / Progressive rock
Ginger Baker was the fiery drummer for the late-'60s power trio Cream. As a young drummer, Baker embraced jazz and R&B, playing with some of England's finest traditional big bands. While Baker was fully capable of laying down a straight groove, the most distinctive element of his style was in his melodic arrangement-oriented phrasing. After Cream disbanded, Baker formed Ginger Baker's Air Force, which contained three drummers, and also worked in the ill-fated Blind Faith.
Baker moved to Lagos, Nigeria, and built the country's first 16-track studio. Paul McCartney's *Band on the Run* was recorded there. Even though Baker has kept a low profile since the late '70s, his recent solo works, which predominately explore African rhythms, are among his best recorded performances. —*Rick Clark*

Ginger Baker's Air Force / 1970 / PolyGram 837349
Featuring Baker's early-'70s all-star rock band. —*Michael G. Nastos*

● **Middle Passage** / 1992 / PolyGram 846753
Producer Bill Laswell mixes African drummers (Ayib Dieng, Mou Gueye, Magette Fall) with fusioneers (Bernie Worrell, Jonas Helborg, Nicky Skopelitis) and bassists (Jah Wohble and Laswell) to land in a "middle passage" of worldbeat. Not bad at all. —*Michael G. Nastos*

LaVern Baker
b. Nov. 11, 1929, Chicago, IL
Vocals / R&B
One of the greatest figures in '50s rock & roll, Baker's early hits for Atlantic are among the most influential ever produced. Although her best-known songs were pop-rock trifles along the lines of "Tweedlee Dee," Baker's finest work—"I Cried A Tear," "Soul on Fire," "Jim Dandy," and its sequel, "Jim Dandy Got Married"—are uncompromisingly tough rhythm and blues, pro-

pelled by her powerful, robust vocals and the crack Atlantic studio band. —*John Floyd*

○ **Sings Bessie Smith** / Jan. 27, 1958 / Atlantic 90980
From the sassy punch of "Gimmie a Pigfoot," the album's opener to "Preaching the Blues" at the end, the performances on this CD swing with a vibrant confidence. All in all, this is a great disc for those looking for an intoxicating blend of R&B and jazz. —*Rick Clark*

Blues Ballads / 1959 / Atlantic 8030
Before she became a successful rock and roll vocalist, Lavern Baker did straight jazz and gutbucket blues, and that's what she's singing here. These tunes didn't have any crossover appeal, but they're gritty, unpolished, and sung with the intensity and energy that made Baker's later material so memorable. —*Ron Wynn*

★ **Soul on Fire: The Best of Lavern Baker** / 1991 / Rhino 82311
This well-annotated collection rounds up every important hit Baker had with Atlantic, and a few choice rarities as well. —*John Floyd*

Hank Ballard & the Midnighters

b. 1936, Alabama
Vocals, songwriter, bandleader / R&B
Though born in Alabama, Ballard moved to Detroit at an early age, forming a doo-wop group called the Royals by age 16. He signed to the King label in early 1953. Mid-size chart hits followed, and the group's name was changed to the Midnighters to avoid confusion with labelmates the Five Royales when "Work with Me Annie" became a national hit. Banned because of "explicit" lyrics, the song spawned a flurry of answer records (some by Ballard himself), most of them hitting the R&B charts as well. The hits kept coming throughout the early '60s, but the flipside of one of them became a national hit when Chubby Checker rerecorded "The Twist," spawning a national craze. Ballard's best records are informed by Gospel-style harmonies and gritty guitar work, usually played by Alonzo Tucker. —*Cub Koda*

○ **Singin' & Swingin'** / 1959 / King 618
Vintage red-hot R&B: shouting vocals and frenzied instrumentals. Hank Ballard led one of the finest R&B orchestras on the '50s circuit, and his King albums are masterpieces. His singing was usually steamy, his lyrics laden with innuendo, and he kept up a furious pace throughout each album. —*Ron Wynn*

★ **Sexy Ways: The Best of Hank Ballard & the Midnighters** / 1993 / Rhino 71512
Twenty of Ballard's best songs and biggest hits—including "Work with Me Annie," "The Twist," "Finger Poppin' Time," and "Let's Go, Let's Go, Let's Go"—are collected on this fine compilation. —*Stephen Thomas Erlewine*

Bananarama

Group / Pop/rock, dance-pop
This female dance-pop trio came on the scene just as MTV was becoming an influential force in the early '80s. Bananarama's first recordings were with English artists Fun Boy Three. Their slight, airy vocal sound and strong grooves earned them a number of hits, including "Shy Boy," "Robert De Niro's Waiting," "Cruel Summer," "The Wild Life," "Love in the First Degree," "I Heard a Rumour," and "I Can't Help It." —*Rick Clark*

○ **Deep Sea Skiving** / 1983 / London 810107
Though this was not their American breakthrough, it was their biggest British success, hitting the Top Ten and featuring the hits "Really Saying Something," "Shy Boy," and "Na Na Hey Hey Kiss Him Goodbye." It establishes the formula for the group's success with its untrained unison trio singing and pop exuberance. The amateurishness of the singers was what made them so appealing. —*William Ruhlmann*

Bananarama / 1984 / London 820036
The group adopted a more glamorous fashion style for this album, which finally brought them U.S. success with the Top-Ten "Cruel Summer." Also included "Robert De Niro's Waiting." —*William Ruhlmann*

True Confessions / 1986 / London 828031
Bananarama scored its biggest U.S. hit with this third album, earning gold sales with the number-one single "Venus." —*William Ruhlmann*

● **Greatest Hits Collection** / 1988 / London 828158

All of Bananarama's irresistable hit singles are collected on this infectious disc. —*Stephen Thomas Erlewine*

The Band

Group / Rock & roll
Composed of four Canadians and one American, the Band first came together in Toronto in the early '60s as Ronnie Hawkins's backup group. Hawkins recorded nine 45s for Roulette between 1959 and 1963. Drummer Levon Helm plays on all nine, guitarist Robbie Robertson and bass player Rick Danko can be heard on the last three, pianist Richard Manuel on the last two, and organist Garth Hudson plays on the final outing only. Collectively leaving Hawkins in early 1964, they called themselves the Levon Helm Sextet, Levon and the Hawks, and (for a brief spell) the Canadian Squires, releasing two singles before becoming Bob Dylan's backup ensemble for his crazed electric tour of North America, Australia, and Europe in the fall of 1965 through the spring of 1966. (After a couple of gigs, Levon headed back to Arkansas.)
Playing with Dylan had a profound influence on the Band. Woodshedding for two years in Woodstock, NY, they released their debut album, *Music from Big Pink*, in late summer 1968. Over the succeeding eight years, the Band stood completely apart from everything else happening in rock & roll. There was no precedent for what they did and there have been no antecedents. Ironically, given that they were four-fifths Canadian, their music embodied an essence of Americana that no one else in rock & roll has approached. Chief writer, Torontonian Robbie Robertson, wrote about the South, the land, rural America, tradition, and the value and richness of heritage and blood ties. His songs are set in cornfields, during the Civil War, and at carnivals at the edge of town. He was most concerned with displaced people and the passing of a way of life.
Sonically, the Band was equally unique. Hudson played accordion, sax, and organ. Drummer Helm doubled on mandolin and guitar. Pianist Manuel drummed whenever Helm was out front. Bassist Danko played fiddle when they needed a rural or "old-timey" feel. Guitarist Robertson had a pinched, economical style that kept one teetering on the edge with tension. As a unit, they quite consciously avoided any of the current trends. They didn't want their voices to blend, because that was what everyone else was doing; they wanted their piano to sound like a funky old upright, not like a brand spanking new Yamaha Grand; and so on. In the process they created some of the most ethereal and evocative music imaginable. —*Rob Bowman*

☆ **Music from Big Pink** / 1968 / Capitol 46069
Everything about the Band's debut album, *Music from Big Pink*, flew in the face of the ethos of rock & roll circa 1968. For example, the disc opens in an unusual fashion, with a ballad—the Richard Manuel-Bob Dylan composition "Tears of Rage." There is not a guitar solo on the album, and this was a time when Jeff Beck, Eric Clapton, and Jimi Hendrix ruled the world. There was a lot of harmony singing that was deliberately ragged: together but not together—community, where the people that made up the community could be individuals. And then there were the songs, enigmatic tales such as "The Weight," "Chest Fever," and the first released version of Bob Dylan's "I Shall Be Released." —*Rob Bowman*

★ **Band** / 1969 / Capitol 46493
Big Pink had been a fine, even superior, debut. *The Band* was their masterpiece. Robbie Robertson's songwriting had grown by leaps and bounds, and, as players, all five musicians had reached a completely new level of ensemble cohesion. The sum was very much greater than the parts, and the parts were as good as any that existed. The album's single, "Up on Cripple Creek," became the Band's first and only Top-30 release. It was one of several songs on the album that had an "old-timey" feel. Other highlights on this masterpiece include "Rag Mama Rag," "The Night They Drove Old Dixie Down," and "King Harvest." —*Rob Bowman*

Stage Fright / 1970 / Capitol 93593
Stage Fright was a reaction to a level of adulation that the Band members were unprepared for. It was conceived as a lighter, less serious, more rock & roll album. The final product ended up somewhat darker, as the Band themselves were going through a number of changes. "The Shape I'm In" and "Stage Fright" tell the story well. Some of the original feeling manifests itself in romps

such as "Strawberry Wine" and "W. S. Walcott Medicine Show." — *Rob Bowman*

Cahoots / 1971 / Capitol 48420
Cahoots was the first album recorded at Albert Grossman's Bearsville Studios in Woodstock. The sessions were difficult, as the studio was still having the bugs worked out and the Band was experiencing internal problems. Robertson's songs had become much more difficult: The structures, chord changes, and arrangements were increasingly complex. Despite these factors, the album has a number of gems, including "Life Is a Carnival," with its great Allen Toussaint horn arrangement; Dylan's "When I Paint My Masterpiece"; a duet between Richard Manuel and Van Morrison entitled "4% Pantomime"; "The River Hymn"; and "Where Do We Go from Here." —*Rob Bowman*

○ **Rock of Ages** / Jul. 1972 / Capitol 93595
Recorded on New Year's Eve 1971-72, this was the Band's last gig for a year and a half. Allen Toussaint was brought in again to write horn arrangements for many of the Band's classics. The results were inspired. Highlights are many, but of particular note are a cover of the Four Tops' "Baby Don't Do It" and a live recording of a track that had earlier been relegated to B-side status only, "Get Up Jake." —*Rob Bowman*

○ **Northern Lights—Southern Cross** / 1975 / Capitol 93594
The first studio album of Band originals in four years, in many respects *Northern Lights—Southern Cross* was viewed as a comeback. It also can be seen as a swan song. The album was the Band's finest since their self-titled sophomore effort. Totaling eight songs in all, on this album the Band explores new timbres, utilizing for the first time 24 tracks and (what was then) new synthesizer technology. "Acadian Driftwood" stands out as one of Robertson's finest compositions, the equal of anything else the Band ever recorded. —*Rob Bowman*

○ **Last Waltz** / 1977 / Warner Brothers 3146
The Band's farewell gig was held at Winterland in San Francisco on Thanksgiving, 1976. Guests from all periods of their career were invited to participate. The luminaries included Bob Dylan, Van Morrison, Neil Young, Joni Mitchell, Muddy Waters, Eric Clapton, and Paul Butterfield. The four-hour concert was one of the most spectacular in rock history. Two hours of it were released on this three-LP (now two-CD) set. Utilizing horns one more time, this was the gig of the Band's life—and one of the greatest in rock history. —*Rob Bowman*

● **To Kingdom Come** / 1989 / Capitol 92169
If (and only if) you have it in your budget for just *one* Band set, *To Kingdom Come (The Definitive Collection)* provides a good collection of their best songs, presented in remastered form. Even though the sequencing is chronological, experiencing these songs out of the context of their original albums may be disconcerting for some. In other words, the best way to *hear* this great group is to start with their first two albums, then move on to *Rock of Ages* and so on. Nevertheless, this is an exceptionally solid overview. —*Rick Clark*

Jericho / 1993 / Pyramid
A full 17 years after *The Last Waltz,* the Band re-formed without Robbie Robertson (and the late Richard Manuel) and recorded *Jericho.* Far from being an embarrassment, *Jericho* proves the Band can still juggle rock, folk, blues, and country effortlessly, producing a rootsy sound that is distinctly their own. —*AMG*

Band of Susans

Group / Alternative rock, heavy metal
An often-changing lineup does not interfere with this New York City band's love of guitars. Frequently loud and brash, their triple-guitar attack has a solid rock & roll base, nowhere near as pretentious as Glenn Branca nor as discordant as Sonic Youth. —*Bruce Eder*

● **Love Agenda** / 1989 / Restless 71425
Their cover of the Rolling Stones' "Child of the Moon" is a must-hear. —*Robert Gordon*

Word & the Flesh / 1991 / Restless 72534
Triple-guitar attack—a sea of six-strings. —*Robert Gordon*

The Bangles

Group / Pop/rock

This all-female Los Angeles quartet produced some exhilarating music, utilizing impressive four-part vocal work on their generally buoyant power-pop arrangements. At their harmonic best, the Bangles projected the exuberance of the Mamas & Papas, approaching the rich density of the Byrds.

Their first major label effort, *All over the Place,* is an absolute gem. Even though the Bangles achieved much greater success with subsequent efforts, the band's charm became increasingly sanded out.

After the group disbanded in late 1989, primary lead singer Susanna Hoffs pursued a rather uninspiring solo career. —*Rick Clark*

○ **All over the Place** / 1984 / Columbia 39220
Featuring the Bangles' rich harmonies and slightly ragged folk-pop/rock ensemble work, *All Over the Place* is an absolute gem. Highlights like "Hero Takes a Fall," "Dover Beach," "James," "Tell Me," "Live," and "Going Down to Liverpool" easily make this their best album. —*Rick Clark*

Different Light / 1986 / Columbia 40039
The Bangles' most successful album, *Different Light* presented the band with a more polished sheen and depended on a lot more material from outside, professional songsmiths. Prince penned the slight (but tuneful) "Manic Monday," which became their first big hit. That was followed by the novelty-ish "Walk Like an Egyptian," their first number-one hit. The highlights, however, went to an inspired reading of Jules Shears's "If She Knew What She Wants" and a bouncy version of Big Star's "September Gurls." —*Rick Clark*

Everything / 1988 / Columbia 44056
With two fine albums under their belt, the Bangles stumbled on this inappropriately titled effort. Aside from the inspired pop-psychedelic tease of "In Your Room," much of *Everything* suffers from lightweight songwriting. Nevertheless, one of the album's low points, the treacly ballad "Eternal Flame," soared to number one. —*Rick Clark*

● **Greatest Hits** / 1990 / Columbia 46125
Greatest Hits is just that, including a great version of Simon & Garfunkel's "Hazy Shade of Winter," a hit from the *Less Than Zero* soundtrack that's not found on their other albums. Another previously unreleased track is a workmanlike reading of the Grassroots chestnut "Where Were You When I Needed You." The highlights of their weakest album, *Everything,* are also provided. It would've been nice if Sony had utilized the space available on CD to include more essential album tracks from their first two albums, like "September Gurls," "Live," and "James." As collections go, this is a logical place to start, but *All Over the Place* is their most appealing album. —*Rick Clark*

The Bar-Kays

Group / Soul, funk
Even though four group founders were killed in a 1967 plane crash along with Otis Redding, the Bar-Kays came back to reign as one of the top R&B outfits of the '70s. The original Bar-Kays were a Memphis instrumental combo that scored an R&B hit in 1967 on Volt with the rousing "Soul Finger." Guitarist Jimmy King, organist Ronnie Caldwell, drummer Carl Cunningham, and saxist Phalon Jones perished with Redding, leaving trumpeter Ben Cauley and bassist James Alexander to re-form the group. After honing their chops with session work at Stax, the new Bar-Kays kicked off a long string of R&B smashes in 1976 with "Shake Your Rump to the Funk" on Mercury. —*Bill Dahl*

○ **Soul Finger** / 1967 / Rhino 70298
The Bar-Kays were being trained as a second generation Booker T. and the MG's, largely by MG drummer Al Jackson. *Soul Finger* was their first album coming off the success of their debut single, the group-written title cut. The album is in the classic Memphis soul instrumental vein: sparse arrangements, accentuated low-end, walloping snare drum, and slightly delayed backbeat with horns taking the place of vocals. *Soul Finger* was the only album made by this particular version of the group. —*Rob Bowman*

Gotta Groove / 1969 / Stax 4130
After the plane crash in December 1967, trumpeter Ben Cauley and bass player James Alexander regrouped, forming a second edition of the Bar-Kays. *Gotta Groove* was the new group's first release. Modeled on earlier Bar-Kays work, the album is totally instrumental, including covers of the Mar-Keys' "Grab This

Thing" and the Beatles' "Yesterday" and "Hey Jude." No standout cuts, but plenty of fine, hard-driving slices of Memphis instrumental soul. —*Rob Bowman*

○ **Too Hot to Stop** / 1976 / Mercury 9099
One of their best '70s dates, the Bar-Kays were in overdrive throughout this one. The title track was a huge hit, and the other uptempo tunes were equally fast paced and tightly played. The few slow songs provided enough change of pace to keep things varied. The horn charts, production, and arrangements were funk personified, though the group was starting to add synthesized elements in anticipation of changes on the urban front. —*Ron Wynn*

○ **As One** / 1980 / Mercury 844
This was arguably their best Mercury album. It included "Move Your Boogie Body," plus their finest inspirational tune "Deliver Us." And the title cut was a solid winner as well. They'd found the ideal mix of horns, electronics, funk backbeats, and R&B/gospel vocals, and everything clicked on every selection. —*Ron Wynn*

● **Best Of (Stax)** / 1988 / Stax 8542
A nice overview of this major Stax band in their second incarnation. —*Ron Wynn*

○ **Best Of (Mercury)** / May 18, 1993 / Mercury 514823
A solid overview of the Bar-Kays' years as a trailblazing funk outfit. —*Stephen Thomas Erlewine*

Syd Barrett (Roger Barrett)

b. Jan. 6, 1946, Cambridge, England
Vocals, guitar, songwriter / Psychedelic
Like a supernova, Roger "Syd" Barrett burned briefly and brightly, leaving an indelible mark upon psychedelic and progressive rock as the founder and original singer, songwriter, and lead guitarist of Pink Floyd. Barrett was responsible for most of their brilliant first album, 1967's *Piper at the Gates of Dawn,* but he left and/or was fired from the band in early 1968 after his erratic behavior made him too difficult to deal with (he appears on a couple of tracks on their second album, *A Saucerful of Secrets*).

After a period of hibernation, Barrett re-emerged in 1970 with a pair of albums, *The Madcap Laughs* and *Barrett,* which featured considerable support from his former bandmates (especially his replacement, David Gilmour, who produced most of the sessions). Barrett's eccentric humor, sly wordplay, and infectious melodies range from brilliant to chaotic in his solo work. Lacking the taut power of his recordings with the Floyd in 1967, they nevertheless remain fascinating and moving glimpses into a creative psyche gone awry after (it is theorized) too much fame and too many drugs too early. With increasing psychological problems, Syd withdrew into near-total reclusion after these albums. He never released any more material, and these days rarely appears in public, let alone plays music.

Although they attracted little attention upon their release, his albums did gather a cult audience. Barrett's music and mystique achieved a lasting influence that continues to grow more than two decades later. Latter-day new wave psychedelic acts like Julian Cope, the Television Personalities, and (especially) Robyn Hitchcock acknowledge Barrett's tremendous influence on their work. —*Richie Unterberger*

● **Madcap Laughs** / 1969 / Capitol 46607
While this collection bears similarities to the songs found on *The Piper at the Gates of Dawn,* the only Pink Floyd album Barrett contributed to significantly, it nevertheless comes across more as a session of run-throughs and demos than as a finished record. Its very roughness is its charm, undercutting the whimsy of the songs with Barrett's ultimate strangeness. —*William Ruhlmann*

Barrett / 1970 / Capitol 46606
On his second solo album, Barrett was joined by Humble Pie drummer Jerry Shirley and Pink Floyd members Rick Wright and Dave Gilmour (Gilmour and Wright acted as producers as well). Instrumentally, the result is a bit fuller and smoother than the first album, though it's since been revealed that Gilmour and Wright embellished these songs as best they could without much involvement from Barrett, who was often unable or unwilling to perfect his performance. The songs, however, are just as fractured as on his debut, if not more so. "Baby Lemonade," "Gigolo Aunt," and the nursery-rhyming "Effervescing Elephant" rank among his peppiest and best-loved tunes. Elsewhere the tone is darker and more meandering. —*Richie Unterberger*

Opel / 1988 / Capitol 91206
Opel is a collection of six alternate takes and eight unreleased songs, making it essential for hardcore Barrett fans. —*Stephen Thomas Erlewine*

Octopus: The Best of Syd Barrett / May 29, 1992 / Cleopatra 57712
A well-chosen, 14-track, single-disc compilation of Barrett's solo work, presumably discount-priced and aimed at the casual listener. But Barrett is such a specialized taste and has such a small body of work that one wonders why Cema Special Markets would bother. —*William Ruhlmann*

○ **Crazy Diamond** / 1993 / Capitol 771
A three-CD boxed set that enshrines Barrett's complete recorded legacy as a solo artist. Besides including his two 1970 albums, this collection includes the 1988 compilation of unreleased material, *Opel.* The chief attraction of this set for Barrett fans are the no less than 19 previously unreleased alternate takes from throughout his quite brief solo career. All of those alternate takes, it's important to note, are alternate versions of songs that appear on the three previously available albums—no entirely unheard compositions were unearthed. *Crazy Diamond* is a beautifully produced document (including a meticulously detailed booklet) of a uniquely primitive visionary. It has many moments of charming and chilling power. —*Richie Unterberger*

Barry & the Remains

Group / Rock & roll
The Remains, fronted by Barry Tashian, were a blistering, shake 'em down rock & roll teen combo, probably the finest Boston had to offer in the mid '60s They seemed poised for national stardom after signing to Epic for their debut album. Success eluded them, however, and they fell victim to the label's massive "Bosstown sound" promo campaign, which backfired for all the groups signed to Epic at that time. The Remains became cult favorites with '60s collectors, with varied compilations appearing on foreign labels over the years. —*Cub Koda*

● **Remains** / 1967 / Epic 46926
A topflight garage band in this classic collection, painstakingly remastered. —*Bruce Eder*

Dave Bartholomew

b. Dec. 24, 1940, Edgard, Louisiana
Composer, producer / R&B
A major contributor to New Orleans R&B, Dave Bartholomew was a pivotal figure as a writer, arranger, producer, and A&R man for Imperial Records. It was Bartholomew's productions that helped make Fats Domino a major player in R&B and rock & roll, and he assembled the great house band that backed Domino, Little Richard, Lloyd Price, Smiley Lewis, and several other Crescent City greats. This band included pianist Allen Toussaint; bassist Frank Fields; saxophonists Lee Allen, Alvin "Red" Tyler, and Herb Hardesty; and drummer Earl Palmer. Bartholomew recorded as a solo artist for King and others prior to taking over at Imperial, but his fame came from that stint. Bartholomew greatly reduced his activities after Domino left Imperial in the early '60s, but occasionally resurfaced to conduct his band. —*Ron Wynn*

★ **Spirit of New Orleans** / 1993 / EMI 80184
A two-disc set featuring 50 tracks and several different artists (including Fats Domino, Smily Lewis, T-Bone Walker, Shirley & Lee, and Earl King), *Spirit of New Orleans* effectively conveys Bartholomew's groundbreaking achievements in R&B and rock & roll. —*Stephen Thomas Erlewine*

Basia (Basia Trzetrzelewska)

b. , Poland
Vocals / Pop
Basia Trzetrzelewska spent a couple of years in the pop band Matt Bianco before she launched a solo career in 1987. Basia's subtle jazz-pop sound won an audience ready for the smooth, sophisticated pleasures of her albums and her hits, "Time and Tide" and "Cruising for Bruising." —*Stephen Thomas Erlewine*

Time and Tide / 1987 / Epic 40767
A mix of pop-soul, with Brazilian overtones on "Astrud," a tribute to Astrud Gilberto. —*Bil Carpenter*

● **London Warsaw New York** / 1990 / Epic 45472
Melodic pop-jazz. Includes "Cruising for Bruising" and "Baby
You're Mine." —*Kenneth M. Cassidy*

Fontella Bass

Vocals, keyboards / Soul, R&B

An explosive gospel and soul singer, Fontella Bass is the daughter of the great vocalist Martha Bass and sister of David Peaston,
as well as the ex-wife of Art Ensemble of Chicago trumpeter
Lester Bowie. But none of that family history means as much as
her own skills, which include a tremendous voice, great range,
and distinctive delivery. Bass, who is also a fine pianist and organist, sang in several church choirs (her mother was a member
of Clara Ward's gospel troup).

She later moved into R&B, singing in Oliver Sain's band and
working with Little Milton in the early '60s. Bass teamed with
Bobby McClure for two duets on Checker in 1965. "Don't Mess
Up a Good Thing" reached number five on the R&B charts and
inched into the pop Top 30, while "You'll Miss Me When I'm
Gone" got into the R&B Top 30. Bass's debut single as a solo act
was her greatest; "Rescue Me" topped the R&B charts for a
month, peaked at number four on the pop charts, and was among
the era's finest soul singles.

Bass never again attained soul stardom, but has remained busy
in the ensuing years. She has sung with Bowie's group, the Art
Ensemble of Chicago, and was featured on the album *Les Stances
a Sophie*. She has also been part of the gospel group From the
Root to the Source, and has reunited with Bowie on occasional
projects. —*Ron Wynn*

● **Rescued: The Best of Fontella Bass** / 1992 / Chess 9335
"Rescue Me" might have been her only big hit, but Fontella Bass
was a terrific gospel-influenced soul vocalist who cut several
great sides for Checker/Chess Records in the mid '60s. They
might not have gotten the attention they deserved when they
were released, but they have held up very well over the years.
Rescued: The Best of Fontella Bass collects 16 of her finest tracks,
including "Rescue Me," three duets with Bobby McClure, and a
previously unreleased song. It makes a convincing case that she
should have had more hit singles than she did. —*Stephen
Thomas Erlewine*

Bauhaus

b. , Northamptonshire, England
Group / Alternative rock

One of the originators of gloom-and-doom electronic rock, the
British group included Peter Murphy on vocals, Daniel Ash on
guitar, and the Haskins brothers, David Jay and Kevin, for the
rhythm section. The band formed in 1978 and gained notoriety
the next year with the single, "Bela Lugosi's Dead." After achieving chart success and adopting a brighter sound, the group disbanded in July 1983, as Ash and Kevin Haskins re-formed into
Tones on Tail and later, with David J Haskins, into Love and
Rockets. —*David Szatmary*

In the Flat Field / 1980 / Nesak 13
Captures the brooding bleakness of early Bauhaus. —*David
Szatmary*

Mask / 1981 / Beggars Banquet 29
In this followup to *In the Flat Field*, Bauhaus matures by creating
an album that stands on its own, rather than a collection of scattered hits strung together with not-so-strong fillers. Feedback-dri-
ven looped guitars, fuzz bass, and Peter Murphy's ever-haunting,
commanding vocals help to create their best album. More raw
than their later material, yet nicely refined compared to to their
first. Includes "The Passion of Lovers" and "Kick in the Eye." —
Julian Katz

Sky's Gone Out / 1982 / A&M 3324
An upbeat, commercially successful Bauhaus album (number
four in the United Kingdom) that includes a remake of Bowie's
"Ziggy Stardust" and a three-part mini-opera, "The Three
Shadows." —*David Szatmary*

○ **Burning from the Inside** / 1983 / A&M 3325
During the recording sessions for Bauhaus's final album, *Burning
from the Inside*, Peter Murphy suffered from pneumonia, leaving
David J and Daniel Ash to complete most of the record themselves. The result is the band's most pop-oriented album. It's also

their best, even if it is slightly incohesive. —*Stephen Thomas
Erlewine*

● **Singles: 1979-1983** / 1985 / Beggars Banquet 642
Essentially, Bauhaus was a singles band—all of their best moments were individual songs, not entire albums. And the double-
disc *The Singles 1979-1983* collects them all, including some B-
sides and album tracks, making it the one essential Bauhaus
purchase. —*Stephen Thomas Erlewine*

Swing the Heartache: The BBC Sessions / 1989 / Beggars
Banquet 9804
A posthumous collection of five sessions on English BBC, some
from John Peel, on which Bauhaus abandoned hits such as "Bela
Lugosi" and "Dark Entries" to experiment with different songs
and revamp certain prerebased material. The loose, live-recorded
format suits this group, whose creative and skilled musicianship
is highlighted on this recording. "God in an Alcove" and "Swing
the Heartache" are rendered much better here. —*Julian Katz*

The Beach Boys

Group / Surf rock, pop/rock

The Beach Boys are the most successful and important American
band of the rock music era. They were formed in 1961 in
Hawthorne, CA, around the three Wilson brothers: Brian (b.
1942), Dennis (1944-1983), and Carl (b. 1946). Additional members were Mike Love, the Wilsons' cousin (b. 1941), and Al Jardine
(b. 1942). From the start, the focus of the group's music was Brian,
who combined a fascination with vocal harmony in the Four
Freshmen mold with a love of Chuck Berry-derived rock & roll.
Added to that was the subject matter of middle-class teenage life
in southern California: surfing, cars, and girls.

The result was massive popular success for the group, starting
with their first chart entry, "Surfin'," in 1962. "Surfin' Safari" was
their first Top-20 hit the same year, and "Surfin' USA" reached
number three in 1963, while the album of the same name went
to number two and became the first of eight straight gold albums
for the Beach Boys over the next two years.

Most of the music was written and produced by Brian, who retired from touring in 1964 to concentrate on this aspect of the
band's career. After several replacements, the group settled on
Bruce Johnston (b. 1944). This led to a dichotomy between Brian
and the rest of the Beach Boys that continues to this day. Brian's
music became progressively more sophisticated and less like the
teen anthems of the first hits as the '60s wore on, until, with the
1966 recordings *Pet Sounds* and the number-one single "Good
Vibrations," they had become elaborate studio creations taking
months to perfect.

Brian was unable to finish *Smile*, the follow-up to *Pet Sounds*,
and the other members of the band came to assert more say in
the recorded music from 1967 on, as their commercial fortunes
declined. In 1974 they enjoyed a resurgence in popularity, topping
the charts with *Endless Summer*, a compilation of their '60s hits,
and in 1976 they scored with a new album, *15 Big Ones*, again
produced by Brian. Subsequent recordings have been more uneven, though the Beach Boys scored a number-one hit with
"Kokomo" in 1988, the same year Brian Wilson launched a solo
career. —*William Ruhlmann*

Surfin' Safari / Oct. 29, 1962 / Capitol 1808
The Beach Boys' debut album contains the number-14 title track
and chart entries "Ten Little Indians" and "409," as well as a version of "Summertime Blues." It has a youthful exuberance but is
not as accomplished as the group's albums would become shortly.
—*William Ruhlmann*

Surfin' U.S.A. / Mar. 25, 1963 / Capitol 48422
The title track, which was really the music from Chuck Berry's
"Sweet Little Sixteen" with new lyrics (he now gets the writing
credit), was the Beach Boys' breakthrough hit, and the album, a
gold-selling number two, also featured the Top-40 "Shut Down"
and a lovely Brian Wilson falsetto lead on "Farmer's Daughter."
But the rest was filler. —*William Ruhlmann*

Surfer Girl / Sep. 23, 1963 / Capitol 16014
The Beach Boys' third album features the Top-Ten title song, the
number-15 "Little Deuce Coupe," the number-23 paean to
cocooning, "In My Room," and "Catch a Wave." It is also the first
Beach Boys album to be produced by Brian Wilson. But there's
still a little too much filler to merit a higher grade. —*William
Ruhlmann*

Little Deuce Coupe / Oct. 21, 1963 / Pair 57241
The fourth album was also the Beach Boys' fourth to be released within one year—so let's not blame them for the repetitions. Moving the group from the beach to the race track, it features the second LP appearances of the title track, "Shut Down," and "409," as well as a version of "Be True to Your School" that differs from the concurrently released single (which featured the Honeys on cheerleading backup vocals). — *William Ruhlmann*

All Summer Long / Jul. 13, 1964 / Capitol 1016
The Beach Boys rebounded from the British invasion with their first number-one single, "I Get Around" and this summer '64 release, which also includes such lesser (but still good) tracks as "Little Honda," "Wendy," and "Don't Back Down." — *William Ruhlmann*

○ **Beach Boys Today!** / Mar. 8, 1965 / Capitol 2269
The first album to be released after Brian Wilson's retirement from the stage includes a raft of hits: "When I Grow Up To Be A Man," "Dance, Dance, Dance," "Do You Wanna Dance?," "Please Let Me Wonder," and an alternate version of the Beach Boys' second number one, "Help Me, Rhonda." Even the filler, including "Don't Hurt My Little Sister," was improving. — *William Ruhlmann*

○ **Summer Days (And Summer Nights!!)** / Jul. 5, 1965 / Capitol 2354
The summer album for 1965 contains "California Girls" and the single version of "Help Me, Rhonda." Those are the only hits, but the album also contains several examples of Brian Wilson's increasing musical sophistication and eccentricity, among them "Let Him Run Wild," "You're So Good to Me," "Summer Means New Love," and the bizarre "I'm Bugged at My Old Man." — *William Ruhlmann*

Beach Boys Party! / Nov. 8, 1965 / Capitol 16272
Far more than the throwaway it seemed at the time, this contrived party-in-the-studio album finds the Beach Boys commenting on the folk boom and British invasion and turning in fun versions of rock & roll favorites and their own hits. Contains the number-two hit "Barbara Ann," which is actually sung by Dean Torrence of Jan and Dean. — *William Ruhlmann*

☆ **Pet Sounds** / May 16, 1966 / Capitol 48421
The group's most fully realized, ambitious, and well-produced album. A wistful, bittersweet, achingly beautiful foray into postteenage angst ("God Only Knows," "Wouldn't It Be Nice," "That's Not Me") and uncertainty ("Don't Talk") augmented with one hit rock single ("Sloop John B."). The most serious record this band ever did—teens confronting time and aging. — *Bruce Eder*

○ **Smiley Smile** / Sep. 18, 1967 / Capitol 2891
Smiley Smile has long been underrated because of what it is not—namely Brian Wilson's unfinished masterpiece, *Smile*. What it is is an exploratory album containing Wilson's two magnificent singles, "Good Vibrations" and "Heroes and Villains," plus much of the eccentric material intended for *Smile*, albeit as patched together by the other Beach Boys. It remains a curiosity, but nevertheless, some of the most imaginative music of the '60s is found here. — *William Ruhlmann*

Wild Honey / Dec. 18, 1967 / Capitol 16159
Remembered as the album on which the other Beach Boys really took over, *Wild Honey* actually features a lot of Brian Wilson, who has cowriting credits on 9 of its 11 tracks, including the Top-40 title track and the Top-20 "Darlin'." Also included is the original version of "Here Comes the Night," later redone as a disco tune. — *William Ruhlmann*

Friends / Jun. 24, 1968 / Capitol 16160
Brian Wilson's participation is reduced here, but he still contributes the delightful curiosity "Busy Doin' Nothin'," and the album also contains the Top-50 title track and the Wilson-Jardine collaboration "Wake the World." — *William Ruhlmann*

20/20 / Feb. 3, 1969 / Capitol 80133
This was a contractual-obligation album marking the end of the Beach Boys' tenure at Capitol Records, but it is an interesting set nevertheless, containing the singles "Do It Again," "Bluebirds over the Mountain," and "I Can Hear Music," as well as the *Smile* outtake "Cabinessence" and Dennis Wilson's collaboration with mass murderer Charles Manson, "Never Learn Not to Love." — *William Ruhlmann*

Sunflower / Aug. 31, 1970 / Caribou 46950

The group's first '70s album, and a highpoint for all concerned, from the transcendental doo-wop music of "This Whole World" to the simple pleasantries of "Add Some Music." — *Bruce Eder*

○ **Surf's Up** / Aug. 30, 1971 / Caribou 46951
Its title notwithstanding, this album has less to do with surfing than with the band coming to terms with aging and with changing audiences—environmentalism shares space alongside the title track. A poignant, serious masterpiece of modern pop music. — *Bruce Eder*

Holland / Jan. 8, 1973 / Caribou 46952
The California sun mixed with mysticism and some outrageous sound experiments (all with a great beat). A failed effort to renew the group's sound with a change of venue (to Holland) that is salvaged largely by the presence of one great rock number ("Sail on Sailor") and a conceptual piece ("California Saga") that has a phenomenal middle section. — *Bruce Eder*

○ **Endless Summer** / Jun. 24, 1974 / Capitol 46467
A notable collection, and the record that sparked the commercial revival of the band's fortunes during the '70s, although all of the material on it has been remastered in superior form on other Capitol CDs. — *Bruce Eder*

Love You / 1977 / Caribou 46956
The Beach Boys had hailed the return of Brian Wilson with their 1976 album, *15 Big Ones*, but it was on this follow-up (produced by Wilson, who wrote almost all of it as well), that he was heard in all his demented glory, singing with childlike wonder about Johnny Carson, among other topics. Strange, but fascinating, especially for longtime Wilson watchers. — *William Ruhlmann*

★ **Absolute Best, Vol. 1** / 1991 / Capitol 96795
The early hits and their best-known songs ("Surfin' USA," "Fun, Fun, Fun," etc.), and a good anthology from that standpoint. — *Bruce Eder*

☆ **Absolute Best, Vol. 2** / 1991 / Capitol 96796
The second half of this collection is more interesting than the first, containing as it does some of their most celebrated offbeat tracks. — *Bruce Eder*

☆ **Good Vibrations: Thirty Years of the Beach Boys** / Jun. 21, 1993 / Capitol 81294
The Beach Boys get the boxed-set treatment—and it's done right: five discs full of the hits, the best album tracks, rarities, demos, and outtakes, including a generous selection of material from the legendary *Smile* sessions. The quality can't help dipping in the later years, as Brian Wilson's role diminishes and the group subsides into mere professionalism. But the best of the Beach Boys' music is among the best recorded by any American rock band, and it's all here. — *William Ruhlmann*

Beat Happening

Group / Alternative pop/rock
One of the hardest tricks to pull off in rock & roll is to make minimal, primitive music without seeming pretentious. Beat Happening pulls it off with grace. Based in Olympia, Washington, the group's three members switch instruments constantly, providing a spare base for Heather and Calvin Johnson's lead vocals. Heather's voice is soft, calm and feminine; Calvin sounds like Johnny Cash. Beat Happening's Velvet Underground-and-folk hybrid has gained numerous fans in the underground. At times, their unassuming folk-rock and occasional loud guitar workouts sound sloppy and careless, rahter than simple and pure, but at its best, Beat Happening is entirely original and rewarding pleasure.

Beat Happening leader Johnson has also gained fame in the underground as the leader of K Records, a resolutely independent record label that has been the home to the Kill Rock Stars compilations, various riot grrrl groups, and other bands that reflect the trends of the American underground in the '90s. — *Stephen Thomas Erlewine*

○ **Jamboree** / 1988 / Sub Pop 62
As much fun as the title indicates, just screwier. — *John Dougan*

Black Candy / 1989 / Sub Pop 78
Spirited bashing, slightly more cohesive than earlier efforts. — *John Dougan*

○ **Dreamy** / 1991 / Sub Pop 98
A dark, hypnotic record that ranks among the band's best, *Dreamy* features Beat Happening at both their most succinct and their most memorable. — *Stephen Thomas Erlewine*

● **You Turn Me On** / Oct. 2, 1992 / Sub Pop 167
A lighter album than *Dreamy*, *You Turn Me On* combines both
their raw, melodic pop side and their slow, hazy minimalism to a
breathtaking effect. — *Stephen Thomas Erlewine*

The Beatles

Group / Rock & roll, pop/rock, British invasion, psychedelic
The most successful and significant rock group in history, the
Beatles were formed in Liverpool, England, in the late '50s by
John Lennon (1940-1980), Paul McCartney (b. 1942), and George
Harrison (b. 1943). Ringo Starr (b. 1940) joined the group in 1962
in time for their first formal recordings.

The Beatles ingested every popular music style of their day—
the raucous rock & roll of Jerry Lee Lewis and Little Richard, the
more sophisticated rock/pop of Buddy Holly, the soul of Motown
and the Phil Spector-produced girl groups, the pop/R&B of the
Isley Brothers and Larry Williams, the country-rock style of Carl
Perkins, the pop-schmaltz of Broadway show tunes—and synthesized them into a style of their own, most importantly, a style expressed in the original songwriting of Lennon and McCartney.
And that was only the beginning. A year or so into their recording career, the Beatles had already begun to throw off their influences and forge new directions in popular music.

They were also, at the outset, the teenage heartthrobs of their
day. "Beatlemania" struck Great Britain in 1963 and the rest of
the world in 1964 and, in a sense, never let up throughout the rest
of the '60s. Though the teen-phenomenon aspect of their career
became less intense in 1966 (by which time, inevitably, new teen
dreams had cropped up), the Beatles made a successful transition
to an older audience without sacrificing longtime fans. In part
this was because they were so successful that they redefined the
terms of success in the music business, and in part it was because
they managed to be on top of, if not ahead of, popular trends.

Unlike even the most successful musical artists, who tend to
achieve a number of hits in a given style and then base their reputations and their careers on that, the Beatles changed rapidly
and went from success to success. Their early records were short,
bouncy tunes of love, filled with harmony and exuberance. But
by late 1964, melancholy and doubt had begun to surface, along
with an increased musical sophistication and the use of different
instrumentation. By 1965 their style had expanded to include the
timeless ballad "Yesterday," performed with a string quartet, and
the band that released the single "Penny Lane"/"Strawberry
Fields Forever" in 1967 was almost unidentifiable, in appearance
as well as music, as the lovable moptops of 1964. The only thing
the two had in common was that the music was still amazingly
good.

Though the Beatles defined yet another genre of music—art-
rock—with their work of 1967, they returned to a simpler style in
their final years of existence, albeit one that gave greater space to
the individual talents of the band members. The formula sound
of the Beatles was long gone by 1968, replaced by four different,
imaginative musicians still moving in new directions.
Unfortunately, the evident musical differences were mirrored in
personal and business differences, and the Beatles broke up in
1970.

The music, however, remains, and just as the Beatles absorbed
the styles they heard while growing up, so a generation of musicians has grown up absorbing the Beatles, and their influence is
palpable in virtually every rock record made since. — *William
Ruhlmann*

☆ **Please Please Me** / Mar. 22, 1963 / Capitol 46435
Nearly 30 years after its release, the Beatles' first album still
stands not only as a blueprint for what the group itself would accomplish in the next three years, but for what a large part of popular music would sound like from then on. Listening now, one
revels anew at the songwriting of John Lennon and Paul
McCartney (songs include "I Saw Her Standing There"), their remarkable harmonies and solo singing, and the encyclopedia of
pop and rock they offer from other sources—especially light pop
and hard R&B (like the show-stopping closer, Lennon's take on
the Isley Brother's "Twist and Shout"). The CD reissue is in the
original mono, but Mobile Fidelity has issued the album in stereo
on vinyl. — *William Ruhlmann*

☆ **With the Beatles** / Nov. 22, 1963 / Capitol 46436
In only a few months, and despite a torrid schedule, the Beatles
demonstrated enormous growth on their second album (growth

and change would be constants throughout their remarkable career). From the forceful "It Won't Be Long" to the bouncy "All My
Loving," their original songs have made a leap, especially in ensemble playing, and the covers again offer a broad range, from
Broadway show music ("Till There Was You" from *The Music
Man*) to two great Motown songs ("You Really Got a Hold on Me"
and "Money"). The CD reissue is in mono, while Mobile Fidelity
has issued it in stereo on vinyl. — *William Ruhlmann*

☆ **Hard Day's Night (U.K.)**, A / Jul. 10, 1964 / Capitol 46437
Maybe it was all the success of the previous year, but on their
third (U.K.) album, the Beatles sound positively triumphant, roaring through exciting songs like the title tune, "Can't Buy Me
Love," and "Any Time at All." On their first album to be entirely
self-written, it's the material (produced under incredible pressure)
that continues to impress. "I Should Have Known Better," "And I
Love Her", and "If I Fell" are are songs a generation can leap
word-for-word decades later. At the same time, one can hear
around the edges the beginnings of Lennon's darker side and individual voice, as more than once he refers to something he can't
stand. "I'll Cry Instead" is almost bitter. *A Hard Day's Night*'s
freshness has not dated an hour. — *William Ruhlmann*

☆ **Beatles for Sale** / Dec. 4, 1964 / Capitol 46438
In a sense, this fourth U.K. album is a step back for the Beatles as
they return to the formula of their first two albums: eight originals, six covers . Fatigue is clearly setting in. But some of the originals are gems, especially Lennon's "No Reply" and "I'm a
Loser"—songs confirming his sense of anguish. The covers of
Chuck Berry, Carl Perkins, and Little Richard are, once again, inspired recastings of formative material for the group. — *William
Ruhlmann*

☆ **Help! (U.K.)** / Aug. 6, 1965 / Capitol 46439
Their fifth U.K. album contained seven songs used in the film
plus seven other songs, and marked a move to a softer, more reflective style. The lyrics are more prominent and thoughtful, and
the sound more often features slow tempos, acoustic guitars, and
other instruments. Here Lennon continued to cry for "Help!" and
bitterly declared "You've Got to Hide Your Love Away" over a
strummed acoustic. Here McCartney took a bluegrass/country
turn in "I've Just Seen a Face" and achieved his biggest ballad
with "Yesterday" (singing before a string quartet). Once again, the
Beatles had exhibited remarkable growth and pointed the way
for all of pop music to follow. — *William Ruhlmann*

☆ **Rubber Soul (U.K.)** / Dec. 3, 1965 / Capitol 46440
Although their sixth (U.K.) album is less consistent than some of
their other releases, it has its share of memorable songs, among
them Lennon's "Norwegian Wood," "Nowhere Man," and "In My
Life" and McCartney's "Michelle." Again, the sound is softer and
more sophisticated than any of the group's 1964 material. —
William Ruhlmann

☆ **Revolver (U.K.)** / Aug. 5, 1966 / Capitol 46441
The three songs swiped for the American album *"Yesterday" . . .
and Today* were the least of another astonishing leap in songwriting and production that introduced "Eleanor Rigby," "Yellow
Submarine," "She Said, She Said," "Good Day Sunshine," "For No
One," "Got to Get You into My Life," and "Tomorrow Never
Knows." If McCartney was becoming a consummate pop craftsman with a command of horns and strings, Lennon was delving
into a drugged psyche while experimenting with tape loops and
strange sounds. And George Harrison, whose unprecedented
three songs were led by "Taxman," was finally flowering into a
first-rate songwriter. — *William Ruhlmann*

☆ **Sgt. Pepper's Lonely Hearts Club Band** / Jun. 1, 1967 / Capitol
46442
The Beatles' finest album is a song cycle full of childlike whimsy
and irresistibly catchy songs. Its playfulness belies an amazingly
fluid arrangement of melodies, lyrics, and sounds that flow together into a whole, creating its own magical world. An open-
ended embrace of light pop, hard-rock, Indian music, swing, classical music, and blues, the album makes the case for musical
unity-in-diversity, seemingly gathering all that came before it
into surprising yet perfect combinations. The Beatles only occasionally approached this achievement in isolated moments afterwards, and nobody else even came close, then or since. — *William
Ruhlmann*

☆ **Magical Mystery Tour** / Nov. 27, 1967 / Capitol 48062

Music Map

Rock-British Invasion
To America & Back-'64 to '67

Roots-American Blues Robert Johnson – Sonny Boy Williamson Jimmy Reed – Elmore James Muddy Waters – Howlin' Wolf B. B. King – Willie Dixon	**Roots–50s Rock/R&B** Elvis Presley – Little Richard – Jerry Lee Lewis Buddy Holly – Everly Brothers – Gene Vincent	**Roots-Music Hall Shuffle** Vera Lunn Lonnie Donegan

British Invasion Rock '64-'69
The Rolling Stones
The Who – The Kinks – John Mayall – Fleetwood Mac
The Animals – The Yardbirds

American Garage Bands
Post-Beatles era: 1964-1969
The Shadows of Knight
The Leaves
The Seeds
The 13th Floor Elevators
The Chocolate Watch Band
The Barbarians
The Sonics
The Outsiders
Count Five
Blues Magoos
? & the Mysterians
The MC5
Iggy & the Stooges
The Sir Douglas Quintet

British Invasion Rock/Pop '64-'67
The Beatles
The Hollies – Dave Clark 5 – Gerry & the Pacemakers – Herman's Hermits
The Searchers – Freddie & the Dreamers – Billy J. Kramer & the Dakotas
The Zombies – Manfred Mann – The Troggs – The Spencer Davis Group

American Pop Bands
Post-Beatles era: 1964-1967
Gary Lewis & the Playboys – The Grass Roots
The Five Americans – The Beau Brummels
The Monkees – The Box Tops

Folk Rock
Bob Dylan – The Byrds
Mouse & the Traps – The Lovin' Spoonful
Mamas & the Papas – Simon & Garfunkel
Donovan – Sonny & Cher

Six songs from the group's TV film *Magical Mystery Tour*, plus their three 1967 singles. Especially notable among them is "Penny Lane"/"Strawberry Fields Forever," perhaps the most impressive two-sided hit ever recorded. And with songs like "All You Need Is Love," "Hello Goodbye," "The Fool on the Hill," and the title track, the rest of the album isn't too shabby, either. *— William Ruhlmann*

☆ **Beatles (White Album)** / Nov. 22, 1968 / Capitol 46443

In their later recordings, the Beatles largely eschewed the elaborate arrangements and instrumentation of 1967 in favor of a return to the simpler sound of the four-piece band. They did not, however, return to the ensemble style of 1964. Instead, the group served as backup to whichever one of them had written the song. On this sprawling double album, already-apparent individual styles gain ascendency. Likewise, musical styles are not so much combined as separated out in pastiche form: the Beach Boys pop of "Back in the USSR," the blues of "Yer Blues," the folk of "Rocky Raccoon," the hard rock of "Birthday," the schmaltzy pop of "Good Night." The musical facility is amazing but also seems near-parodic. *— William Ruhlmann*

Yellow Submarine / Jan. 13, 1969 / Capitol 153

There are really only four new songs here, and even they predate the material on *The Beatles*, but this is a pleasant enough soundtrack album, dominated by the musical score written by Beatles producer George Martin. *— William Ruhlmann*

☆ **Abbey Road** / Sep. 26, 1969 / Capitol 46446

The Beatles' last unified statement finds them going out at a peak of musical achievement, from Lennon's "Come Together" to Harrison's "Something," with McCartney dominating the Side-2

medley that finds the group rocking out in fine style. *Abbey Road* is the best-selling Beatles album ever. *—William Ruhlmann*

☆ **Let It Be** / May 8, 1970 / Capitol 46447

Flawed, botched, and overproduced by Phil Spector, the final new Beatles album to be released (most of it was recorded prior to *Abbey Road*) nevertheless included the title song, "The Long and Winding Road," an abbreviated version of "Get Back," and such lovely tunes as "Two of Us," which, for one last time, presented Paul McCartney and John Lennon and their acoustic guitars harmonizing together. *—William Ruhlmann*

● **1962-1966** / Apr. 2, 1973 / Capitol 90435

A 26-track double album of the Beatles' greatest hits up through 1966. Though it is primarily devoted to singles, the collection also includes a few key album tracks. *—William Ruhlmann*

● **1967-1970** / Apr. 2, 1973 / Capitol 90438

Twenty-eight songs from the second half of the Beatles' career, focusing on the hits but also including key album tracks. *— William Ruhlmann*

Live at the Hollywood Bowl / May 4, 1977 / Capitol 11638

Previously unreleased live performances culled from shows at the Hollywood Bowl in 1964 and 1965. The screaming never stops, but the group's musical talent and personal charm shine through. *—William Ruhlmann*

☆ **Past Masters, Vol. 1** / Jan. 1988 / Capitol 90043

When EMI and Capitol released the Beatles' recordings on compact disc, it was decided to issue the albums in their original British formats in both the United Kingdom and the United States. The British albums frequently did not contain singles released by the Beatles at the same time, and there were other odd tracks not included on albums. Thus two discs were necessary to gather the stray material (some of which included their biggest hits). This first volume, for example, running from 1962 to 1965, contains "She Loves You," "I Want to Hold Your Hand," and "I Feel Fine." — *William Ruhlmann*

☆ **Past Masters, Vol. 2** / Feb. 1988 / Capitol 90044
Completing the CD release of the Beatles' complete EMI/Capitol catalog, this disc contains "We Can Work It Out," "Paperback Writer," "Lady Madonna," "Hey Jude," "Get Back," "Let It Be," and other later Beatles songs. — *William Ruhlmann*

The Beau Brummels

Group / Pop/rock, folk-rock
The Beau Brummels, from San Francisco, enjoyed a brief run on the Top-0 pop charts in 1965 with a bracing blend of British invasion pop and West Coast folk-rock.

Sylvester Stone (later of Sly & the Family Stone) produced the band's first two albums, as well as their biggest hits, "Laugh Laugh" and "Just a Little." The fatalistic "You Tell Me Why," the band's last Top-40 hit, and the aggressive Byrds-like rocker "Don't Talk to Strangers" revealed the Beau Brummels to be a group possessing much depth. Unfortunately, the band's label (Autumn) folded at the end of 1965.

Two subsequent albums on Warner, *Triangle* and *Bradley's Barn*, are out of print but worth seeking out. In 1975 the Beau Brummels re-formed for an impressive reunion on Warner, then called it quits. — *Rick Clark*

Triangle / 1967 / Warner Brothers 1692
A beautiful venture by the surviving trio into a more authentic form of folk and country-rock, with a repertoire that recalls the more famous Everly Brothers classic, *Roots*. — *Bruce Eder*

● **Best of the Beau Brummels: Golden Archive Series** / 1987 / Rhino 70171
A good collection of their hits and notable tracks. — *Bruce Eder*

The Beautiful South

Group / Alternative pop/rock
This British quintet was formed by Paul Heaton after the demise of the Housemartins in 1988. Their music is characterized by sweet, jazz-pop arrangements that belie their witty, caustic lyrics. — *William Ruhlmann*

● **Welcome to the Beautiful South** / 1989 / Elektra 60917
The difference between the catchy light pop that constitutes the Beautiful South's music and the bitter, pessimistic lyrics innocently sung by Paul Heaton is so great it constitutes a kind of malevolent seduction. But that's the point. — *William Ruhlmann*

○ **Choke** / 1990 / Elektra 60985
The Beautiful South's second album conceals its bitter, mean cynicism in layers of lush, jazz-tinged pop, making all of the bile go down easily. — *Stephen Thomas Erlewine*

0898 / 1992 / Elektra 61308
There are no big poses or walls of crunchy guitars on *0898*. Instead, the group—which includes three lead vocalists—deals in fragile melodies and harmonies, soulful but low-key instrumentation, and lyrics full of subtle social commentary and humour. Producer John Kelly (Peter Gabriel) has contributed an incisive and full-bodied production to *0898*. — *Roch Parisien*

Beck

Vocals, guitar / Alternative pop/rock
Many critics pegged Beck as a one-hit wonder with "Loser," but his music shows he has more to offer than one catchy single. With his portastudio, keyboard, drum machine, and guitar, Beck created music that celebrated the junk culture of the '70s and '80s. His music drew from hip-hop, folk, psychedelia, pop, and rock. His severely warped, satiric lyrics are blessed with striking imagery as well as clumsy poetry. With all of its rootless eclecticism, Beck's music is distinctly a product of the '90s; all of his influences come through television and records, not from real life experiences. But that trashy, disposable quality is what makes his music special.

Although he released an independent album before his breakthrough 1994 major-label debut, *Mellow Gold*, it didn't have the range or musical depth of *Mellow Gold*. Beck's contract with Geffen allows him to release music on indie labels while he's recording for the record company. Since he's so prolific (he re-

leased three albums plus non-LP B-sides in one year), these independent records aren't as consistent as *Mellow Gold*, but anyone hooked on that album should seek out the stranger pleasures of his more obscure recordings. — *Stephen Thomas Erlewine*

● **Mellow Gold** / 1994 / David Geffen Company 24634
Beck's first major label album became a hit, thanks to the lazy folk/hip-hop fusion of "Loser." But *Mellow Gold* proves that he is no one-hit wonder. From the warped TV-folk of "Pay No Mind" and the pounding rhythms of "Beercan" to the trashy garage-rock of "Mountain Dew Rock" and "Soul Suckin' Jerk," Beck shows that his fascination with junk culture can turn into exciting music that refuses to acknowledge any boundaries. — *Stephen Thomas Erlewine*

Jeff Beck

b. Jun. 24, 1944, Surrey, England
Guitar / Rock & roll, hard rock, fusion
Utterly distinctive and certainly one of the most important electric lead guitarists in rock history, Jeff Beck was the wildcard element that gave the post-Clapton Yardbirds' work its futuristic quality. His pioneering experiments with feedback and various effects, particularly on the classic "Shapes of Things," influenced thousands of musicians.

After leaving the Yardbirds, Beck went on to a highly successful solo career that produced an excellent debut (*Truth*), featuring Rod Stewart (vocals), Ron Wood (bass), Nicky Hopkins (keyboards), and Mickey Waller (drums).

The next few albums contained fine moments with Stewart and replacement vocalist Bobby Tench, but during the mid '70s Beck switched gears and released the instrumental jazz/rock fusion *Blow by Blow*, generating his greatest commercial success. Further efforts to delve into that style have been less notable, but even when the material isn't up to par, Beck's liquid yet impulsive style is generally amazing. — *Rick Clark*

★ **Truth** / 1968 / Epic 47412
Along with Led Zeppelin's self-titled first album, Jeff Beck's *Truth* is considered the primo primer for what came to be known as heavy metal. Fusing the thunderous rhythm section of Ron Wood on bass and Mickey Waller on drums with his paint-blistering lead guitar and Rod Stewart's gravel-and-whiskey vocals, Beck's visionary approach to blues and rock & roll influenced practically every rock band that followed, on both sides of the Atlantic. Although Beck could be unpredictable and eclectic (witness his straightforward, acoustic reading of "Greensleeves"), *Truth* features the smoking "Beck's Bolero," "Rock My Plimsoul," and the wah-wah piece de resistance, "I Ain't Superstitious." — *Tom Graves*

Beck-Ola / 1969 / Epic 47411
A year after Jeff Beck recorded *Truth*, he came back with the even heavier *Beck-Ola*. Although the songwriting seems diluted, and the addition of Nicky Hopkins on piano added spice in all the wrong places, *Beck-Ola* is still a gut-slamming good time. Notable tracks include "Spanish Boots" and "Plynth (Water Down the Drain)." — *Tom Graves*

Rough & Ready / Feb. 1971 / Epic 30973
After Jeff Beck nearly died in a car crash, he came back in 1971 with a new group and a new sound, reflecting his more introspective state of mind. Although the firepower and guitar blasts are still there, he burns cooler. With the help of the jazzy Max Middleton on piano, Beck created one of rock's most haunting set pieces, "Raynes Park Blues." Other highlights include the dynamic ballad "Jody" and the hard-grinding rock groove of "I've Been Used." — *Tom Graves and Rick Clark*

Jeff Beck Group / 1972 / Epic 31331
Continuing with the same group lineup as on *Rough and Ready*, *Jeff Beck Group* was slagged off by critics for Steve Cropper's admittedly lazy production. However, several of the songs hold up masterfully, including "Ice Cream Cakes," the superlative redo of Don Nix's "Going Down," and the beautifully sad and wistful instrumental, "Definitely Maybe." — *Tom Graves*

★ **Blow by Blow** / 1975 / Epic 33409
When Jeff Beck announced that he was working on an all-instrumental album, few but his legion of guitar fans could have predicted the far-reaching impact of this pivotal rock/jazz fusion album. Teamed with the Beatles' ex-producer George Martin, Beck singlehandedly created a new subtext for rock & roll. With his vir-

tuosity and taste at an all-time peak, Beck let loose with unforgettable tracks such as the Roy Buchanan-inspired "Cause We've Ended as Lovers" and the percolating "Freeway Jam." One of rock's great instrumental works. — *Tom Graves*

○ **Wired** / 1976 / Epic 33849
Nearly *Blow by Blow*'s equal. Although Beck doesn't venture any further musically, Charles Mingus's "Goodbye Pork Pie Hat" is worth the price alone. — *Tom Graves*

Flash / 1985 / Epic 39483
Produced by Nile Rodgers and Arthur Baker, *Flash* is Beck's surprisingly successful stab at a pop album, featuring a fine performance with Rod Stewart on "People Get Ready." — *Stephen Thomas Erlewine*

○ **Jeff Beck's Guitar Shop** / 1989 / Epic 44313
A guitar hero in his prime, full of fury and finesse, with topnotch support from Terry Bozzio and Tony Hymas. — *Jas Obrecht*

○ **Beckology** / 1991 / Epic 48661
Covering everything from his earliest (and terrific) tracks with the Tridents through his spot-on interpretation of Santo & Johnny's "Sleep Walk," *Beckology* features great remastering, smart packaging (resembling a vintage Fender tweed guitar case), and the essential Yardbirds and solo years material. The set (55 tracks in all) also collects the best material from weaker albums such as *Flash* and *There and Back*. A definitive overview of Beck's career would have included his work as a sideman with artists like Stevie Wonder, Rod Stewart, and Donovan; nevertheless, *Beckology* is as comprehensive a collection as one will find on this innovative guitarist. — *Tom Graves and Rick Clark*

Crazy Legs / Jun. 29, 1993 / Epic
With the Big Town Playboys offering support, Beck rips through 15 Gene Vincent numbers (not "Be-Bop-a-Lulu," however), paying tribute to Vincent's guitarist, Cliff Gallup. Beck sounds terrific as he reconstructs Gallup's parts, but he doesn't add anything to the originals. Nevertheless, *Crazy Legs* is a fun listen and offers many insights into Beck's playing, if not Gallup's. — *Stephen Thomas Erlewine*

George Bedard

b. Nov. 5, 1952, Mt. Clemens, MI
Guitar / Rock & roll, blues-rock, rockabilly
While other youngsters in the '60s were listening to British invasion bands and wishing they were on the Ed Sullivan show, a young George Bedard was in his basement teaching himself guitar, playing along with records by blues legends Howlin' Wolf, B. B. King, and Muddy Waters. By the early '70s, Bedard was teaming up with blues harpist and guitarist Steve Nardella to form the Silvertones, one of the finest Ann Arbor, MI, blues/rockabilly bands of the '70s.

Combining genres is a path Bedard has pursued relentlessly, working in groups both as soloist and sideman, covering a wide range of styles from country to jazz to rockabilly and back to his first love, the blues. There's not much Bedard can't play extremely well in any of these idioms, his style always informed by taste and economy. Though his solo recordings have been few, George Bedard remains a guitar hero's guitar hero. — *Cub Koda*

○ **Upside** / 1992 / Schoolkids 1503
Bedard's debut album features great originals and a rollicking textbook approach to everything from rockabilly to T-Bone Walker-style blues. Worth it just for the explosive solo on "What a Shame." — *Cub Koda*

The Bee Gees

Group / Pop/rck, disco
The Bee Gees' lengthy career has been one of the most successful in all of popular music. Their history could be broken down into two periods, pre- and post-disco. From 1967 to 1972, the Bee Gees (built around brothers Barry, Maurice, and Robin Gibb) produced 13 Top-40 pop hits, which were ornate, lush, and somewhat sentimental. More than most self-contained writing teams, the Bee Gees were adept at creating memorable melodies.

As if the first phase wasn't more success than most artists could hope to attain, the Bee Gees pulled out of a three-year dormancy, courtesy of the rising disco movement, and cashed in big with the Arif Mardin-produced *Main Course*, which contained the hits "Jive Talking" and "Nights on Broadway." The Bee Gees were

then asked to supply material for Robert Stigwood's film *Saturday Night Fever*. Their dominance on the soundtrack, coupled with the film's phenomenal success, made the band quite wealthy. (Over 30 million copies of the soundtrack album sold.)The follow-up album, the disco-heavy *Spirits Having Flown*, contained three number-one hits: "Love You Inside Out," "Tragedy," and "Too Much Heaven." With the death of disco, the group's fortunes subsided, although they scored a few solid chart successes in the '80s. — *Rick Clark*

○ **Odessa** / Jan. 1969 / PolyGram 825451
Odessa is the Bee-Gees' finest moment of the '60s. — *AMG*

● **Best of the Bee Gees, Vol. 1** / Feb. 1969 / PolyGram 831594
Best of the Bee Gees, Volume 1 collects their greatest pop hits from the '60s. — *AMG*

○ **Best of the Bee Gees, Vol. 2** / Feb. 1973 / PolyGram 831960
Best of the Bee Gees, Volume 2 gathers the group's biggest and best hits from the early '70s. — *AMG*

○ **Main Course** / 1975 / PolyGram 833790
Apart from the soundtrack to *Saturday Night Fever*, *Main Course* is the Bee Gees' finest album, featuring the hits "Jive Talkin'" and "Nights on Broadway." — *AMG*

● **Greatest** / 1979 / PolyGram 800071
The cream of their stunning string of late-'70s hits. — *Dan Heilman*

Tales from the Brothers Gibb / 1990 / PolyGram 843911
An exhaustive four-disc boxed set that contains too much for anyone but hardcore fans. — *Dan Heilman*

Bel Canto

Group / Alternative pop/rock
This chamber-rock trio from Norway offers an authentic medieval sound based almost exclusively on the modern techniques of synthesis, with original music that expresses a stream of loss and sorrow from the past. Almost all of their songs are built on a specific type of energy—female power or the power of the earth—sometimes both destructive and hysterical. Bel Canto has an elaborate orchestration, utilizing a wide range of instruments. — *Vladimir Bogdanov*

White-Out Conditions / 1988 / Nettwerk 30030
Bel Canto's first album is refreshing and intriguing. Although it's uneven, it is definitely more than just a search for a new style. — *Vladimir Bogdanov*

● **Birds of Passage** / 1990 / IRS 13031
Completely professional material, well composed and performed. — *Vladimir Bogdanov*

○ **Shimmering, Warm & Bright** / 1992 /
The famous warm "medieval electronic" sound of Bel Canto reaches the point of elaborate purity on this mature album. — *Vladimir Bogdanov*

Adrian Belew

Guitar / Alternative pop/rock
This avant-garde guitar slinger cut his teeth with Frank Zappa and became a critical darling during his stint in the '80s with the Talking Heads and the re-formed King Crimson. He has released albums both as a solo artist and with the late-'80s band, the Bears. — *John Floyd*

○ **Lone Rhino** / 1982 / PolyGram 842844
Lone Rhino, Belew's finest album of straight playing, features the guitarist stretching out over arty rock and funk backdrops, creating a spellbinding array of textures. — *Stephen Thomas Erlewine*

Mr. Music Head / 1989 / Atlantic 81959
Former King Crimson member Belew shines on his own, with aggressive guitar work framing a set of thoughtful alternative rockers. — *Donna DiChario*

○ **Young Lions** / 1990 / Atlantic 82099
Guitar-propelled modern rock, including a duet with David Bowie on "Pretty Pink Rose." — *Donna DiChario*

● **Inner Revolution** / 1992 / Atlantic 82370
Belew uses his well-developed one-man-band and state-of-the-studio abilities to produce a Beatle pastiche record that ranks with the best of such Fab Four idolaters as Todd Rundgren, the Raspberries, and ELO—and that's no mean feat. He can sing (almost) like John Lennon and play guitar like George Harrison. His

sturdy songwriting makes this much more than just a successful genre exercise. —*William Ruhlmann*

Desire of the Rhino King / 1992 / Island 510518
Desire of the Rhino King, a scatter-shot compilation of his earlier, more experimental records for Island, offers some of his best playing, yet the music sounds uncohesive outside the context of the original recordings. —*Stephen Thomas Erlewine*

Bell Biv Devoe

Group / Urban R&B
Former members of New Edition struck pay dirt with their 1990 debut, *Poison,* which crossed over into the White pop charts in addition to dominating the R&B world. Their outside production efforts resulted in hit debuts by the R&B groups Another Bad Creation and Boyz II Men.

Bell Biv Devoe's follow-up arrived three years later; by that time, their audience had moved on to other artists, leaving the group behind with a solid, but unappreciated, album. —*John Floyd*

● **Poison** / 1990 / MCA 6387
BBD describe their style as "R&B on the smooth tip with a hip-hop feel," and that's just what you'll find on this hugely successful debut. Equally adept at sumptuous ballads and big-beat dance thumpers, BBD have taken Teddy Riley's new-jack innovations to both a wider audience and a new creative plateau. —*John Floyd*

Hootie Mack / 1993 / MCA 10682
Hootie Mack not only keeps the same energetic vibe that made *Poison* a hit, it expands upon that base, adding a more street-oriented production that, at its best, is more sexy and funky than the group's debut. Unfortunately, the high points on this album aren't as numerous as those on *Poison.* Not only that, but the good songs didn't receive much airplay, causing the album to drop off the charts quickly. —*Stephen Thomas Erlewine*

Chris Bell

Vocals, guitar / Power pop
Memphis singer/songwriter Chris Bell cofounded the influential power-pop quartet Big Star in 1971, with Alex Chilton. Bell left the group before the release of their second album, *Radio City,* to pursue a solo career. He died in an automobile accident on Dec. 27, 1978. It wasn't until 1992 that Bell's work was released in an album form. —*Rick Clark*

○ **I Am the Cosmos** / 1992 / Rykodisc 10222
A collection of the late Chris Bell's solo work, mostly demos. The title track is a brilliant downer (Big Star and Badfinger at half speed) that opens the album. "You and Your Sister" is a gorgeous heartbreaker, rendered with delicate acoustic guitars and Mellotron and guest vocalist Alex Chilton. Not everything Bell undertakes is so fragile. "I Don't Know" (and its later, inferior incarnation "Get Away"), "Make a Scene," and "Fight at the Table" are relentless rockers. Bell's voice may be an acquired taste for some, as it occasionally gets a little whiney. When it does connect with the music, the results can be quite affecting, particularly on "You and Your Sister," "Speed of Sound," and the title track. Ryko has done a great job remastering these tapes, and the packaging is a first-rate labor of love. —*Rick Clark*

William Bell

b. Jul. 16, 1937, Memphis
Vocals, piano, songwriter / Soul
William Bell was one of the first artists signed to the Stax label during its fledgling years in Memphis, and he greatly influenced the "Stax sound" as both performer and writer. His self-penned "You Don't Miss Your Water" (1961) almost defined the genre known as country-soul, with the unmistakable gospel feel of Bell's elegant, lilting vocal over a country-church piano figure. It was this perfect marriage of styles that became Bell's trademark at Stax and opened the door for others—most notably Otis Redding, who initially mined the same country-soul vein—to follow. With the ascent of Redding, Bell's star began to fade somewhat. He continued to record (the beautiful, string-laden "I Forgot to Be Your Lover" in 1968) and, most importantly, to write (his own "Tribute to a King," written after Redding's death, and Albert King's "Born under a Bad Sign," both cowritten with Booker T. Jones). After Stax's collapse in 1975, Bell moved to Mercury, where he scored his first-ever million-seller with "Trying to Love

Two." Bell continues to live and work in Memphis. —*Christine Ohlman*

● **Soul of a Bell** / 1967 / Atlantic 82252
The 1967 debut album of Stax's resident balladeer, loaded with Memphis soul ballads and an occasional raver. —*Bill Dahl*

○ **Best of William Bell** / 1988 / Stax 8541
Post-Atlantic work from the late '60s and early '70s. Includes Bell's playful duets with Judy Clay. —*Bill Dahl*

A Little Something Extra / 1992 / Stax 8566
A fine collection of Stax outtakes from the '60s, *A Little Something Extra* features several tracks (including his smoldering version of "Will You Love Me Tomorrow?") that rival his original singles. —*Stephen Thomas Erlewine*

Belly

Group / Alternative pop/rock
After spending several years with Throwing Muses and recording an album and EP with the Breeders, guitarist/vocalist Tanya Donnelly formed her own band, Belly, in 1992. In Throwing Muses, her step-sister Kristin Hersh never allowed her more than two songs on an album; in the Breeders, her side project with Kim Deal of the Pixies, she wasn't able to contribute any songs, due to contractual obligations.

In a short time, Belly had surpassed either group's popularity (although the Breeders would outsell them a year later). Belly's debut album, 1993's *Star,* was a major college hit, as well as gathering a respectable amount of mainstream play. Donnelly's songwriting is more straightforward and pop-oriented than either Hersh or Deal; "Feed the Tree" and "Gepetto" were some of the brightest, most melodic pop songs in the grunge-dominated days of alternative music. But that doesn't mean Belly is shallow and slick. Beneath their lush, pretty guitars are some dark undercurrents, which save them from being too precious. —*Stephen Thomas Erlewine*

● **Star** / 1993 / Warner Brothers 45187
Driven by four superb singles—"Gepetto," "Feed the Tree," "Slow Dog," and "Dusted"—Belly's debut album is a terrific set of effortlessly melodic guitar-pop, alternating between bright pop songs and atmospheric ballads. Even with her sweetest melodies, lead singer/guitarist Tanya Donnely has enough realism or dark fantasies in her songs to keep *Star* from being cloying or saccharine. In fact, her songs are so good, it's a wonder she didn't start her own band sooner. —*Stephen Thomas Erlewine*

Jesse Belvin

b. Dec. 15, 1933, San Antonio, TX, d. Feb. 6, 1960
Vocals / R&B
An influential, silky-voiced R&B crooner and songwriter from the '50s, best known for his 1956 hit "Goodnight My Love" and for writing the Penguins' hit "Earth Angel." —*John Floyd*

. . . But Not Forgotten / 196z / United 7220
Terrible sound quality, but this old LP features the balladeer's best-known mid-'50s work for Modern Records. —*Bill Dahl*

● **Blues Balladeer** / 1990 / Specialty 7003
Loaded with previously unissued gems. Belvin's introspective, subdued vocals are delightful. —*Bill Dahl*

Pat Benatar (Pat Andrzejewski)

b. Jan. 10, 1953, Brooklyn, NY
Vocals / Pop/rock
Originally trained as an opera singer, Pat Benatar decided to apply her considerable lung power to rock. Beginning with her first recording in 1979, Benatar adopted the persona of a tough, nononsense woman, which helped make her one of the most popular female performers of the '80s. Much of the material was written by Benatar and/or her guitarist husband Neil Giraldo. *True Love,* a collection of blues tunes with backing by Roomful of Blues, was a departure for Benatar. When the album was a commercial failure, she returned to her arena-ready rock. —*Kenneth M. Cassidy*

○ **In the Heat of the Night** / 1979 / Chrysalis 21236
This debut album features her trademark power-pop song "Heartbreaker." —*Donna DiChario*

○ **Crimes of Passion** / 1980 / Chrysalis 21275

She won the Best Rock Vocal Performance—Female for her revival of the Young Rascals' 1966 hit "You Better Run." — *Donna DiChario*

● **Best Shots** / 1989 / Chrysalis 21715
Multi-Grammy winner Benatar has vocal range to spare on this hits collection, including her rockers "Heartbreaker," "Fire and Ice," and "Hell Is for Children." —*Donna DiChario*

Brook Benton

b. Sep. 19, 1931, Camden, SC, d. Apr. 9, 1988
Vocals / R&B
Silky smooth: that was Brook Benton's byword from his first record to his very last, as the singer parlayed his rich baritone pipes into seven number-one R&B hits and eight Top-Ten items. Stints on the gospel circuit preceded Benton's first secular session for Okeh in 1953, but his career didn't begin to take off until he teamed with writer/producer Clyde Otis. Benton cowrote and sang hundreds of demos for other artists before frequent collaborator Otis signed his friend to Mercury. Together they pioneered a lush, violin-studded variation on the standard R&B sound, which beautifully showcased Benton's intimate vocals.
Good Way," made those tunes pace the R&B lists in 1960.
The early '60s were a prolific period for Benton, but he left Mercury a few years later and bounced between labels before reemerging with the atmospheric Tony Joe White ballad "Rainy Night in Georgia" on Cotillion in 1970. Benton later made a half-hearted attempt to cash in on the disco craze, but his hitmaking reign was at an end long before his death in 1988. —*Bill Dahl*

○ **40 Greatest Hits** / 1989 / Mercury 836755
Everything you need to know about Benton. Bluesy, sexy pop music. Includes the duets with Dinah Washington. —*Hank Davis*

● **Anthology** / Rhino 71497
A slightly more modest version than the *40 Greatest.* —*Hank Davis*

Berlin

Group / Pop/rock
This Los Angeles-based synth-pop group made up of Terri Nunn, John Crawford, David Diamond, Matt Reid, Ric Olsen, and Rob Brill topped the charts in 1986 with "Take My Breath Away." Nunn left for a solo career in 1987. —*William Ruhlmann*

○ **Pleasure Victim** / 1982 / Geffen 2036
Berlin pulled three dance-pop hits from this album, which successfully combined synth-beats with the sexy vocals of Terri Nunn, especially on the uninhibited "Sex (I'm a . . .). *William Ruhlmann*

Count Three and Pray / 1987 / Geffen 24121
Berlin's third album, their last before the departure of Terri Nunn for a solo career, contains their number-one hit, the ballad "Take My Breath Away," which was featured in the film *Top Gun.* — *William Ruhlmann*

● **Best of Berlin 1979-1988** / 1989 / Geffen 24187
All of Berlin's greatest hits and best material are included on this fine single-disc collection. —*Stephen Thomas Erlewine*

Chuck Berry (Charles Edward Anderson Berry)

b. Oct. 18, 1926, San Jose, CA
Vocals, guitar / Rock & roll
It's impossible to give the reader a suitable description of Chuck Berry's rock & roll, and you really don't need one. The innovations he brought to the music—his dazzling, lucid lyrics, a guitar lick that everyone who's ever picked up a guitar has attempted to duplicate, vocals that place you dead-center into his detailed vignettes—can be heard everywhere. They are ingrained in rock's collective conscience, from the '60s shimmy of the Beatles up to the latest heavy metal raving.
The St. Louis-raised Berry brought his unique stylings to pianist Johnnie Johnson's jump-blues boogie trio in 1953. He quickly became the band's leader and began filtering Johnson's tinkly, omnipresent piano runs into his guitar style. In 1955, Muddy Waters suggested that Berry pass a demo tape to Chess-label head Leonard Chess. Chess jumped on a Berry original called "Ida May" (based on an age-old country tune), changed the name to "Maybellene" and gave Berry his first hit in 1955. The song's choogling guitar sound, flowing lyrics, and tight, driving

rhythm laid the groundwork for an amazing string of hits that have inspired generations. "Johnny B. Goode," "Too Much Monkey Business," "Little Queenie," "Carol," "Sweet Little Sixteen," "Back in the USA," "Roll Over Beethoven," and dozens more just like them dealt with everything from tragicomic social drama and teen love and heartbreak to urban protest, all the while giving rock & roll a good deal of its language and most of its style.
A list of rock & rollers who've used Berry's hits for their own jump pads reads like a Who's Who: the Rolling Stones, the Beatles, the Beach Boys, the Yardbirds, Bob Dylan, Bruce Springsteen—the list is endless. Chuck Berry hasn't made a worthwhile record in decades and slops through concerts with only a paycheck on his mind. But if it weren't for Berry's legacy, books like the one you're reading would be considerably smaller. —*John Floyd*

○ **Is on Top** / 1959 / Chess 31260
Berry's best '50s Chess album (his third) features many of his biggest hits, plus atmospheric instrumentals like "Blues for Hawaiians." —*Cub Koda*

☆ **St. Louis to Liverpool** / 1964 / Chess 31261
This album, recorded and issued after Berry's 1964 prison release, is one of the decade's finest albums—a concise shot of brilliance that includes such career-defining statements as "You Never Can Tell," "No Particular Place to Go," and "Nadine." —*John Floyd*

★ **Great Twenty-Eight** / 1982 / Chess 92500
A single-disc compilation of Berry's original Chess greats, every one a gem: "Maybellene," "Johnny B. Goode," "Roll Over Beethoven," "Sweet Little Sixteen," and "Little Queenie" are the music the Beatles and others cut their teeth on. Beyond essential. —*Cub Koda*

☆ **Chess Box** / 1988 / Chess 80001
A three-CD box of Berry's career at Chess, from '50s classics to mid-'70s chart entries, and all the high spots in between. —*Cub Koda*

Bettie Serveert

Group / Alternative pop/rock
With their critically acclaimed 1992 debut, *Palomine*, the Dutch quartet Bettie Serveert became one of the most promising new bands of the '90s. Bettie Serveert's guitar-pop has jangly hooks and sweet melodies to spare, with a sweet toughness like the Pretenders' early albums. Their ballads are achingly gorgeous, yet they're equally capable of playing explosive rockers. *Palomine* established them as alternative stars, yet they have the effortless pop skills to cross over into the mainstream. —*Stephen Thomas Erlewine*

● **Palomine** / 1993 / Matador 46
What makes *Palomine*, Bettie Serveert's debut album, such a wonderful record is how the band balances the sweet guitar-pop of "Tom Boy" with yearning ballads like "Palomine" and gutsy garage-rockers like "The Kid's Alright" without ever sounding forced or clichéd. Instead, all of the band's music is tied together by their weaving guitars, pulsing rhythms, and especially Carol van Dijk's voice, which conveys more genuine emotion and grit than most vocalists in alternative rock. —*Stephen Thomas Erlewine*

Dickey Betts

b. Dec. 12, 1943, Jacksonvile, FL
Guitar / Southern rock
Best known as the guitarist for the Allman Brothers Band, Dickey Betts has made recordings as a solo artist and bandleader during his tenure with the Allmans and during that band's hiatuses, notably leading Great Southern in the '70s and the Dickey Betts Band in the '80s. —*William Ruhlmann*

● **Highway Call** / Nov. 1974 / PolyGram 835115
Betts has made occasional solo albums, starting with this one, which picks up from the country-rock style of his Allmans hit "Ramblin' Man." There's a lot of tasty guitar set in ensemble arrangements, which also feature steel guitar and the prominent fiddle of Vassar Clements. —*William Ruhlmann*

Pattern Disruptive / 1988 / Epic 44289
After a long layoff, Betts cut this blistering guitar rock album in a style strongly reminiscent of the Allman Brothers Band. In fact,

his band contains pianist Johnny Neel and second guitarist Warren Haynes, both of whom would join the next edition of the Allmans when they re-formed. Allmans drummer Butch Trucks guests. — *William Ruhlmann*

Big Audio Dynamite

Group / Alternative pop/rock, dance
After Mick Jones left the Clash, he formed Big Audio Dynamite with video artists Don Letts. BAD followed the more experimental funk elements of the Clash's *Combat Rock,* adding samplers, dance tracks, and found sounds to Jones's concise pop songwriting. Jones suffered a near-lethal bout of pneumonia in 1988 but bounded back vigorously with 1989's *Megatop Phoenix.* After that record, the band split apart in early 1990, with Letts and the rest of the band forming Screaming Target. Jones found three young musicians and formed Big Audio Dynamite II. Releasing *The Globe,* the first full-length album with the new lineup, in 1991, BAD II experienced their greatest success with the hit single "Rush." — *Stephen Thomas Erlewine*

○ **This Is Big Audio Dynamite** / 1985 / Columbia 40220
Since Mick Jones was the more melodic, pop force in the Clash, it was some surprise that the band he formed after that group's demise was such an unusual mix of synthesized drumming and spoken-word tape inserts—although beneath all the gimmicky sounds (or perhaps accentuated by them) were Jones's often winning songs. — *William Ruhlmann*

● **No. 10 Upping St.** / 1986 / Columbia 40705
Reuniting with his former Clash partner Joe Strummer, Mick Jones's second album with Big Audio Dynamite expands on the formula of the debut. *No. 10, Upping St.* features better songs, which meld samples, found sounds, dance rhythms, and elements of hip-hop more completely and effectively than the first record. — *Stephen Thomas Erlewine*

Tighten up Vol. '88 / 1988 / Columbia 44074
Jones tightens the rather free-form structures of the previous BAD albums on *Tighten Up Vol. '88.* While he was aiming for a greater commercial success, the result was only partially successful; the best tracks didn't work as singles and the singles didn't have the creative spark that marks the best of BAD's music. — *Stephen Thomas Erlewine*

○ **Megatop Phoenix** / 1989 / Columbia 45212
On *Megatop Phoenix,* Jones delves even further into a dance-influenced, cut-and-paste approach to pop music that manages to capture all of the inventiveness of late-'80s dance music without losing sight of the melodies that have always been his strength. — *Stephen Thomas Erlewine*

○ **Globe** / 1991 / Columbia 46147
Although the second incarnation of Big Audio Dynamite doesn't sound all that different from the first, Mick Jones's songwriting and concepts are reinvigorated on *The Globe,* making it rank as one of the best BAD albums. — *Stephen Thomas Erlewine*

Big Black

Group / Alternative rock
Proudly and self-consciously abrasive, Big Black's music is polarizing; either you think that Steve Albini's relentlessly thin, metallic, emotionless guitar grind and distorted vocals are an uncompromising work of art, or you think it's self-indulgent crap. The group's clinical noise and grotesque, often misogynist, lyrics easily made them the most extreme, nihilistic band in the American underground in the mid-'80s. After recording three EPs with an unstable lineup, Big Black recorded its first full album with Albini and Santiago Durango on guitar, Dave Lovering on bass, and a drum machine.
   Their recordings don't show much musical progression; the band just gets harder, noisier, and nastier on each subsequent record. Before the band recorded their final and best album, 1987's *Songs about Fucking,* Durango left the group to study law. Albini pulled the plug on the band shortly afterward.
   Although Big Black's life span was short, Albini's influence on the American independent music scene of the late '80s and '90s has been substantial. After Big Black's breakup he formed the equally uncompromising Rapeman, but Albini's real influence has been through his numerous productions. Over the years he has produced literally hundreds of bands; most of the bands he has produced are justifiably unknown, but some are quite fa-

mous— including the Pixies, the Breeders, Urge Overkill, PJ Harvey, and Nirvana. Albini's simple production functions as a type of photograph, capturing the band in aural black and white; the production shows all of a band's strengths, as well as all of their faults. He frequently cuts the bass levels to a minimum, leaving only a harsh guitar grind, which makes his records a bit wearing to listen to. Many young bands of the '90s have embraced his signature guitar grind, as well as his strident punk-rock ethics, as a reaction to alternative music's move into the mainstream. — *Stephen Thomas Erlewine*

Hammer Party / 1986 / Homestead 044
Combining Big Black's first three EPs (*Lungs, Bulldozer,* and *Racer-X*) on one disc, *Hammer Party* shows the band evolving from Steve Albini's one-man guitar and drum machine aggro-fest to the fleshed-out, but no less insular, attack of the bassless trio. It's the band's sparest work, but also some of its most abrasive. — *Stephen Thomas Erlewine*

● **Songs about Fucking** / 1987 / Touch & Go 24
Easily the best album Big Black ever recorded, the bleak noise of *Songs about Fucking* matches the empty nihlism of Albini's ranting lyrics. For once, the sheer force of their music actually makes the band seem threatening, scary, and dangerous. — *Stephen Thomas Erlewine*

○ **Rich Man's 8-Track** / 1989 / Touch & Go 94
Rich Man's 8-Track combines the *Headache* EP and *Atomizer* album on to one disc. *Atomizer,* the band's first full-length album, is a self-consciously aggressive and noxious onslaught of guitars and drums, wallowing in its own depravity. On it, for the first time Albini and company achieved the sound that they were aiming for. *Headache* isn't as good; it's a retread of *Atomizer* without any of the surprise. — *Stephen Thomas Erlewine*

Big Bopper (Jiles Perry Richardson)

b. Oct. 24, 1930, Texas, d. Feb. 3, 1959
Vocals / Rock & roll
Legendary as one of the three rock greats to die in the tragic 1959 Clear Lake, IA, plane crash that also claimed the lives of Buddy Holly and Ritchie Valens, the Big Bopper (born Jiles Perry Richardson) had just established himself as a rock hitmaker with the rollicking "Chantilly Lace." Born in the heart of Texas, Richardson grew up in Beaumont and changed his first name to Jape. He broke into show biz as a DJ over KTRM radio, where he coined the nickname The Big Bopper. He began recording for Mercury in 1957, his animated baritone scaling pop playlists the next year with "Chantilly Lace"—easily his top seller—and the equally raucous novelty "Big Bopper's Wedding." Richardson wrote "White Lightning," a huge country hit for George Jones, and Johnny Preston's number-one smash "Running Bear." — *Bill Dahl*

● **Hellooo Baby!: The Best of the Big Bopper, 1954-59** / 1989 / Rhino 70164
Hellooo Baby! The Best of the Big Bopper, 1954-1959 is a single-CD compilation of the Bopper's finest, including "Chantilly Lace," "Little Red Riding Hood," and "The Big Bopper's Wedding." It's wild and fun. — *Cub Koda*

Big Brother and the Holding Company

b. , San Francisco, CA
Group / Blues-rock, psychedelic
Big Brother and the Holding Company was a psychedelic blues-rock group formed in San Francisco in September 1965. It consisted of guitarist Sam Andrew, guitarist James Gurly, bassist Peter Albin, and drummer David Getz. The group's formal debut was at the Trips Festival in January 1966. In June, singer Janis Joplin joined.
   Big Brother signed to the independent Mainstream label in 1966 and recorded *Big Brother and the Holding Company.* But after their spectacular appearance at the Monterey Pop Festival in May 1967, they switched to major label Columbia, which released the chart-topping, million-selling *Cheap Thrills* in August 1968. Joplin went solo in November, and Big Brother broke up, but it reformed to make *Be a Brother* (1970) and *How Hard It Is* (1971). Big Brother broke up again in 1972, and re-formed in 1987 with singer Michelle Bastian. — *William Ruhlmann*

Big Brother and the Holding Company / 1967 / Mainstream 6099

Big Brother's debut LP was a low-budget quickie, but it included a Joplin classic in Top-50 hit "Down on Me" and was a good example of San Francisco psychedelia. — *William Ruhlmann*

★ **Cheap Thrills** / 1968 / Columbia 9700

Cheap Thrills is a masterpiece of utterly raw psychedelic blues-based rock from the peak of the '60s San Francisco rock scene. Joplin works up a fever unlike anything she ever did on subsequent albums. Her delivery of "Ball and Chain" is a must-hear. Anyone who thinks Guns N' Roses mastered hard electric blues-grunge hasn't heard Big Brother's James Gurley and Sam Houston Andrews duke it out on tracks like "Ball and Chain," "Summertime," and "Combination of the Two." *Cheap Thrills* also features the hit "Piece of My Heart." — *Rick Clark*

Big Country

Group / Pop/rock

Scottish group Big Country burst onto the 1982 rock scene with a uniquely expansive twin-guitar sound (of ex-Skids Stuart Adamson and Bruce Watson) that at times recalled bagpipes. Bassist Tony Butler (whose credits included the Pretenders and Pete Townshend) and drummer Mark Brzezicji (also Townshend) provided an aggressively supple rhythmic foundation.

The Chris Thomas-produced debut effort *Harvest Home* didn't chart, but *The Crossing*, cinematically produced by the innovative Steve Lillywhite, captured the band's sonic vision perfectly. It contains the band's first (and only significant stateside) hit with "In a Big Country."

Big Country followed *The Crossing* with an EP containing the fine "Wonderland," which basically echoed the spirit of "In a Big Country." In England, meanwhile, Big Country scored a brief string of hits, gaining enough popularity to sell out two nights at London's Wembley Stadium in December of 1984. This was further aided by the release of the album *Steeltown*, which entered British charts as number one. After an 18-month layoff, Big Country released *The Seer*. "Look Away" was a 1986 British hit, but only received moderate attention on U.S. rock radio. The rather generic *Peace in Our Time*, released in 1988 on a new label (Reprise), was a misguided redirection of their sound, ditching most of the qualities that made the band so appealing. — *Rick Clark*

○ **Crossing** / 1983 / Mercury 812870

One of the most unique and exciting debut rock releases of the early '80s. Producer Steve Lillywhite (U2, Simple Minds) aided in the band's larger-than-life sound and grand themes. The album contains expansive hits, including "In a Big Country" and "Fields of Fire." Other highlights are "Chance" and "Harvest Home." — *Rick Clark*

● **Best of Big Country** / Feb. 22, 1994 / Mercury 518716

All the significant radio tracks and hit singles, including the fine U.K. hit "Wonderland," plus a pretty thoughtful selection of album tracks. Includes good liner notes and release info. — *Rick Clark*

Big Head Todd & the Monsters

Group / Rock & roll

During the late '80s and early '90s, Big Head Todd & the Monsters built their audience through constant touring, playing college towns across the country. With these tours, they built a solid fan base before they had even signed to a major label. Although they have released several records, they haven't been able to completely translate the live appeal of their laidback, slightly jazzy, blues-based pop to tape. Nevertheless, each of their records contains many fine moments, and 1993's *Sister Sweetly* shows that they are continuing to improve their songwriting, as well as their playing. — *Stephen Thomas Erlewine*

● **Sister Sweetly** / 1993 / Warner Brothers 24486

There was a reason that *Sister Sweetly* expanded Big Head Todd's cult—it's their most consistent and satisfying album yet, full of acoustic charm, relaxed funk, and breezy blues. — *Stephen Thomas Erlewine*

Big Star

Group / Power pop, pop/rock

Next to the Velvet Underground, Memphis's Big Star are the granddaddy of all cult groups. The crisp, succinct pop found on their first two albums was ignored upon release in the early '70s, but by the '80s, Big Star's sound was everywhere. Everyone from

the dB's, R.E.M., and the Replacements to Tommy Keene, Matthew Sweet, and Teenage Fanclub have integrated Big Star's formula into their own styles, and have turned Big Star co-founder Alex Chilton into a cult icon.

Big Star was formed by Memphian Chris Bell in 1971. Although he was living in the home of the blues and soul, it was the Anglo-pop stylings of the Beatles and the Kinks that rang his bell. Alex Chilton, former vocalist for the Box Tops, shared Bell's affection for Brit-pop and joined the group, christened Big Star after a local supermarket chain.

With producer Terry Manning, the group recorded *#1 Record* in 1972, released on the studio's in-house Ardent label. It was well received in the press and seemed like a radio natural, but poor distribution squelched whatever hit potential it had. Bell, disappointed with the poor reception of his band's debut, struck out on his own in 1972.

Chilton was left to mastermind the blistering *Radio City* (1973). The lush charm of *#1 Record* was replaced by Chilton's slashing, skewered guitar runs and his mangy, stray-cat vocals. The album was loaded with would-be classics ("September Gurls," "Back of a Car," "You Get What You Deserve"), but again, the album was poorly distributed and fell between the cracks.

Disenchanted with the politics of the music business, and suffering from drug and alcohol abuse, Chilton hooked up with producer Jim Dickinson and vented his spleen on *3rd/Sister Lovers*, recorded in 1974 but shelved until 1978. More a Chilton solo project than a group effort, the album was an erratic but sometimes brilliant emotional outcry that balanced the beautiful ("Stroke It Noel," "Blue Moon") with the horrific ("Holocaust," "Kangaroo").

With the demise of Big Star, lead singer Alex Chilton went on to pursue a renegade solo career that has taken him full circle from untamed reckless garage rock to his earthy mid-Southern musical R&B roots. Over the years, the effervescent, near-perfect guitar pop found on *#1 Record* and *Radio City* have maintained their vitality, making them legitimate rock classics that deserve more than their cult status. It is fair to say that, in spite of almost nonexistent commercial success, Big Star has been an important influence on many of the post-punk and power-pop bands since the late '70s. — *Rick Clark*

☆ **Third/Sister Lovers** / 1978 / Rykodisc 10220

Basically an Alex Chilton solo project, aided by remaining bandmate Jody Stephens and a slew of Memphis players. Chilton, frustrated at the music biz and career letdowns, enlisted producer Jim Dickinson to aid in this creative tightrope walk without a net. The result is a listening experience that's as uncompromisingly harrowing as Neil Young's *Tonight's the Night*. Not for the casual listener, but essential in any serious rock listener's collection. — *Rick Clark*

★ **#1 Record/Radio City** / 1986 / Stax 60-025

Their first two albums, loaded with amazing songs and performances. Mid-period Beatles, Kinks, and Byrds turned inside out and regurgitated into an utterly unique sound. A must-own for any lover of Anglo pop/rock. — *Rick Clark*

Big Star Live / Feb. 21, 1992 / Rykodisc 10221

A weak performance from a live radio special. It may be of interest to hardcore fans, but it certainly is no place to start discovering Big Star. — *Rick Clark*

Columbia: Live at Missouri University / Sep. 14, 1993 / Zoo 11060

This "reunion" of sorts features original Big Star members Alex Chilton and Jody Stephens, augmented by Ken Stringfellow and Jonathan Auer, the two frontmen for the Posies. The performances are ragged but, for the most part, right. Once Chilton gets down to business, he delivers strong performances on "September Gurls" and Todd Rundgren's "Slut." Auer and Stringfellow particularly shine on Chris Bell's "I Am the Cosmos" and "Back of a Car." — *Rick Clark*

Birthday Party

Group / Alternative rock

After one album and an EP as the Boys Next Door, the band moved to London and switched their name to the deceivingly benign Birthday Party. With their new name, the band's truly demented, knotty post-punk started to gel. Led by Nick Cave's morbid vocals, the band tore through reams of blues and rockabilly licks, hellacious feedback, noise, and stories of religion, violence, and perversity at an unrelenting pace. As the band's career progressed, Cave's vision got darker and their songs varied from dirges to sonic blisters. After three albums and four EPs, the band called it quits in 1983, with all of the members pursuing equally interesting solo careers. —*Stephen Thomas Erlewine*

○ **Prayers on Fire** / 1981 / Nesak 104
Howling, hellacious mangled art-noise. Sure-fire. —*John Dougan*

Junkyard / 1982 / Nesak 207
Slightly less confrontational, but no less disturbing. —*John Dougan*

Drunk on the Pope's Blood / 1982 / 4AD
An extremely harrowing live EP, with Lydia Lunch. —*John Dougan*

● **Hits** / 1992 / Warner Brothers 45087
As an album title, *Hits* is an intentionally ironic misnomer for one of Australia's most influential rock bands of the late '70s and early '80s. Having hits was the furthest thing from the Birthday Party's collective mind over the course of the five tumultuous years that followed the group's move to England from down under—the members reviled anything that hinted at mainstream acceptance. Not for the squeamish (nor for any mood or frame of mind) *Hits* nevertheless compiles, in highly concentrated form, charged, emotional ingredients essential to the makeup of modern rock. —*Roch Parisien*

Elvin Bishop

b. Oct. 21, 1942, Tulsa, OK
Guitar / Blues rock, Southern rock
This blues guitarist, a member of the Paul Butterfield Blues Band from 1965 to 1968, made a series of Southern-rock albums for Capricorn in the '70s. He now cuts blues records for Alligator. —*William Ruhlmann*

● **Let It Flow** / 1974 / Capricorn 0134
The best of Bishop's Southern-rock records, featuring the seven-minute "Travelin' Shoes" and guests Dickey Betts, Toy Caldwell, Sly Stone, and more. —*William Ruhlmann*

Struttin' My Stuff / 1975 / Capricorn 0165
Features the hit single "Fooled Around and Fell in Love," sung by Mickey Thomas. —*William Ruhlmann*

○ **Don't Let the Bossman Get You Down!** / 1991 / Alligator 4791
On *Don't Let the Bossman Get You Down* Bishop projects a good-natured, humorous persona in the extended spoken-word sections of his songs, but he still finds time to play a lot of tasty blues guitar. —*William Ruhlmann*

○ **Sure Feels Good: The Best of Elvin Bishop** / 1992 / PolyGram 513307
A fine collection of this blues-rock guitarist's best moments that covers more material than the earlier compilation, *Best of Elvin Bishop/Crabshaw Rising*. —*Stephen Thomas Erlewine*

Stephen Bishop

b. 1951, San Diego, CA
Vocals / Pop
Bishop has made a career out of light MOR pop songs that range from romantic to humorously quirky. A number of his songs have ended up on movie soundtracks like *Animal House*, *Summer Lovers, Unfaithfully Yours*, and *Tootsie*. His biggest pop hits include "Save It for a Rainy Day," "On and On," and "Everybody Needs Love." —*Rick Clark*

● **Best of Bish** / 1988 / Rhino 70833
Contains "On and On," "Save It for a Rainy Day," and other lesser hits. —*Dan Heilman*

Bjork

Vocals / Alternative pop, dance
When the Sugarcubes dissolved after a string of unsuccessful albums in the early '90s, Bjork rejected the band's arty college guitar-rock pretentions and recorded a smashing, innovative dance record with producer Nelee Hooper. *Debut* made her an artistic force to be reckoned with, as well as an unlikely yuppie hero. Bjork's sensual, elfin looks and thin, expressive voice, which retains all the inflections of her native Iceland, might not make her a natural pop star, yet she has the charisma, as well as the talent, to pull it off. —*Stephen Thomas Erlewine*

● **Debut** / 1993 / Elektra
Bjork's first album since the breakup of the Sugarcubes outshines any of her old group's records. Covering everything from dance-pop to jazzy torch songs, Bjork shows a suprising amount of versatility. *Debut* is one of the strongest, most musically varied and consistent dance records of the '90s. A remarkable debut album. —*Stephen Thomas Erlewine*

The Black Crowes

Group / Rock & roll
At the time of their 1990 debut, the kind of rock & roll the Black Crowes specialize in was out of style. Only Guns N' Roses came close to approximating a vintage Stones-style raunch, but they were too angry and jagged to pull it off completely. The Black Crowes replicated that Stones swagger and Faces boogie perfectly. Few bands borrow as directly as vocalist Chris Robinson's Rod Stewart homage or guitarist Rich Robinson's fusion of Keith Richards and Ron Wood. However, even fewer steal freely without seeming empty and hollow. The Black Crowes are able to make bluesy, '70s rock their own They make it sound hip and modern again.

Since their breakthrough hit was a competent, if unexciting, cover of Otis Redding's "Hard to Handle," the Black Crowes would have disappeared quickly if they didn't have songwriting skills. At their best, the Black Crowes write fully developed rock songs, driven by strong riffs. "Twice as Hard," "Sometimes Salvation," "She Talks to Angels," "Sting Me," and "Jealous Again" have attitude and emotion to spare, and they are seamlessly written. —*Stephen Thomas Erlewine*

○ **Shake Your Money Maker** / 1990 / Def American 24278
The best ideas on this debut album are all about 20 years old, but when those ideas are replicas of vintage Stones and Faces, timelessness is not an issue. The mix of throttling rockers and acoustic ballads doesn't flow with the grace of *Beggars Banquet*, but the best songs here ("Twice as Hard," "She Talks to Angels," "Could I've Been So Blind") act as anchors for a strikingly confident debut. —*John Floyd*

● **Southern Harmony and Musical Companion** / 1992 / Def American 26916
On *The Southern Harmony and Musical Companion* the Crowes avoid the sophomore slump by taking the best elements of their debut and fleshing them out (and giving the rhythm section and keyboards more room to breathe). The Stones/Faces/Humble Pie comparisons are still relevant, but the band's own identity flourishes on such songs as "Remedy," "Black Moon Creeping," and "Sting Me." —*John Floyd*

Black Flag

b. , Los Angeles, CA
Group / Punk, hardcore
Following the footsteps of California punks like the Germs and the Avengers, Greg Ginn and Black Flag took a look around their sun-drenched hometown and got pissed—pissed about the suntans, pissed about suburban decadence, pissed for the sake of being pissed. They released a few decent singles and an EP on Ginn's SST label, and, in 1981, released an album (*Damaged*) that channeled their aggression and hostility through a molten mix of cranky guitars and Henry Rollins's manic vocals. On "Rise Above" and "Six Pack," Rollins expressed the nihilism, cynicism, and outrage of Cali youths better than any of his hardcore peers (and with more humor, as well). The group made the fatal mistake of sticking around too long, though, and after influencing hundreds of similarly disillusioned minds—and forging a career that evolved into self-parody—the group called it quits in 1987. —*John Floyd*

★ **Damaged I** / 1981 / SST 007
A devastating barrage of piss and noise that is a benchmark of West Coast punk. (CD includes their EP *Jealous Again*.) —*John Floyd*

First Four Years / 1984 / SST 021
Rounds up all their early singles, EPs, and compilation cuts. "Nervous Breakdown" and a rewrite of "Louie Louie" are included. —*John Floyd*

○ **Wasted . . . Again** / 1987 / SST 166
A solid collection of some of their greatest hits, including the best cuts from their lame later albums. —*John Floyd*

Black Sabbath

Group / Heavy metal

No other band has come closer to embodying heavy metal than Black Sabbath. Over the years, their lineup may have changed, but their music hasn't—it has remained the same loud, methodical guitar-based heavy rock that it was in the early '70s. Their slow, sludgy attack was part design and part accident. Because of an accident that cut the tips of his fingers, Tony Iommi tuned his guitar down a half-step because he couldn't play comfortably unless the strings were slightly slack; the lower tuning made his mammoth riffs sound heavier. Bassist Geezer Butler's lyrics reveled in black magic, fantasy, drugs, mental illness, and the occult, but never sex. Ozzy Osbourne sang them in a flat, almost tuneless, banshee wail. Butler and drummer Bill Ward never had any flair for playing around with the rhythm, preferring to let the beat plod on and on. Their songwriting was never strayed from one riff, a chorus, another riff, and a guitar solo, but that is part of their appeal. Taken together, the primative musicianship, bad poetry, obsessive fantasy world, crawling tempos, and overpowering volume simultaneously represents everything good and bad about heavy metal.

Critics detested them when they were at the peak of their powers in the early '70s, and they still do. But critical acclaim was never essential to the band's success. Black Sabbath was, in many ways, an underground band—parents hated them, hippies hated them, self-respecting rockers hated them. Everybody hated them except the teenagers. And those were the teenagers that grew up and formed bands, from Metallica to Soundgarden to Henry Rollins. Everybody from the heaviest of metal bands to the sludgiest of grunge bands listened to Black Sabbath when they were teenagers.

Of course, Black Sabbath stuck around past their peak. Some of their first six albums were great, some of them merely had good tracks, but all of them had something to recommend them. Osbourne hung around for two more records before jumping ship for good. Former Rainbow lead vocalist Ronnie James Dio replaced him in 1979. The new lineup released their first record, *Heaven and Hell*, in 1980. It was a far cry from their best, but it sounded like *Paranoid* compared to what they would later release.

Throughout the '80s, the band members kept shifting, with Iommi being the only member to remain in all of the lineups, and at the end of the decade he was the only original member left in the band. Black Sabbath was not only suffering musically, but their credibility with fans was also in question. In 1991, Iommi persauded Butler to rejoin, and, for a brief time, Dio. Black Sabbath continues to lurch forward in the '90s, oblivious to the criticism and declining record sales, but their early records continue to inspire—as well as infuriate—whole new generations of listeners. —*Stephen Thomas Erlewine*

○ **Black Sabbath** / 1970 / Warner Brothers 1871
Their debut album set the tone with the title cut, "The Wizard," "Wasp," and "Warning." —*Cub Koda*

★ **Paranoid** / Jan. 1971 / Warner Brothers 3104
Their second and perhaps best album, featuring the title track, "Iron Man," "War Pigs," and "Fairies Wear Boots." —*Cub Koda*

☆ **Masters of Reality** / Feb. 1971 / Warner Brothers 2562
Sabbath's third album, no less potent than the first two. It includes "Into the Void," "Children of the Grave," and "Lord of This World." —*Cub Koda*

○ **Black Sabbath, Vol. 4** / 1972 / Warner Brothers 2602
A surprisingly song-oriented set of cynical boogie. —*John Floyd*

○ **Sabbath, Bloody Sabbath** / 1974 / Warner Brothers 2695
Sabbath adds some synths to their sludge and comes up with a surprisingly solid album that manages to expand on their patented slow, gloomy sound. —*Stephen Thomas Erlewine*

○ **Sabotage** / 1975 / Warner Brothers 2822
On Ozzy's last album with Sabbath, the band was at their artiest, playing with synths, found sounds, and tight solos and riffs. It may not be their most influential record or their best, but *Sabotage* is certainly one of their most interesting. In fact, it was the last decent thing they ever recorded. —*Stephen Thomas Erlewine*

☆ **Sold Our Soul for Rock & Roll** / 1976 / Warner Brothers 2923

A solid 16-track sampler (over 70 minutes) from the band's first six albums (what you might call Sabbath's glory days). —*John Floyd and Cub Koda*

Heaven & Hell / 1980 / Warner Brothers 3372
Ronnie James Dio's first album with Sabbath is also the best he recorded with the band. As a matter of a fact, it's the only halfway interesting thing the band has recorded since *Sabotage*. —*Stephen Thomas Erlewine*

Frank Black (Black Francis, Charles Thompson)

Vocals, guitar / Alternative pop/rock

Inverting his stage name from Black Francis to Frank Black, the former Pixies lead singer/songwriter embarked on a solo career after he broke up the band in early 1993 (actually, he began recording his solo album *before* he told the band the news). Working with former Pere Ubu member Eric Drew Feldman, Black occasionally heads into the ferocious post-punk guitar territory that marked such landmark albums as *Surfer Rosa* and *Doolittle*, but more frequently he plays up his considerably underrated melodic side. His self-titled 1993 debut album was an adventurous sketchbook of pop styles ranging from surf rock to heavy metal, from Beatlesque pop to new wave. Black's second album, 1994's *Teenager of the Year*, was a sprawling and diverse offering that amplified all the best points of *Frank Black* It received the best reviews of any Black album since 1989's *Doolittle* and had an alternative radio hit with "Headache." —*Stephen Thomas Erlewine*

○ **Frank Black** / 1993 / Elektra 61467
Frank Black is where Charles Thompson (formerly Black Francis of the Pixies) brings to the forefront the pop undercurrents that have always floated through his music. The sonic onslaught of the Pixies is here in small doses (portions of "Los Angeles" and "Parry the Wind High, Low," "Czar," and the Iggy Pop tribute "Ten Percenter"), but there are more Lennon, Bowie, Brian Wilson, and surf-rock influences than Iggy. Even the Ramones tribute is a lovely pop number, not a copy of "Blitzkrieg Bop." —*Stephen Thomas Erlewine*

● **Teenager of the Year** / 1994 / 4AD/Elektra
Frank Black's second album is a wildly ambitious and eclectic piece of guitar-pop, ranging from the full-throttle roar of "Whatever Happened to Pong?" and "Thalassocracy" to the pure pop of "Headache" and the gorgeous winding melodies of "Speedy Marie." It might be a little long, but *Teenager of the Year* is packed with thrilling, innovative pop. —*Stephen Thomas Erlewine*

Blackfoot

Group / Southern rock, hard rock

This Southern rock band originally consisted of Charlie Hargrett, Jackson Spires, Greg Walker, and Ricky Medlocke, three of whom had Indian bloodlines, hence the group's name. With a sound that owed a large stylistic debt to the more musical Lynyrd Skynyrd, Blackfoot cashed in on the last gasp of Southern rock's brief flourishing. After numerous personnel changes, Medlocke still tours and records with a version of the band. —*Cub Koda*

○ **Strikes** / 1978 / Atco 38112
This features Blackfoot's best-known songs, "Train, Train" and "Highway Song." The last gasp of Southern rock. —*Cub Koda*

● **Rattlesnake Rock 'n' Roll: The Best of Blackfoot** / 1994 / Rhino
This solid best-of collection is the place to go. All the hits and key album tracks are here, plus extensive liner notes. —*Rick Clark*

Blake Babies

Group / Alternative pop/rock

While the Blake Babies made several engaging records the late '80s, they never broke out of the collegiate rock circles where they were adored. It wasn't until 1992 that their leader, Juliana Hatfield, began getting recognition as a songwriter in more mainstream publications, but that was after the group had broken up. Over their four albums, Hatfield's songwriting and thin, girlish singing improved drastically as the band's post-R.E.M. alternative pop grew more muscular, branching out into both punkier and folkier territories on each record. By the time of their last full-length album, 1990's *Sunburn*, guitarist John Strohm was emerging as an impressive songwriter in his own right. After a final EP in 1991, the band split, with Hatfield emerging as an alternative superstar and Strohm and drummer Freda Boner forming the acclaimed guitar-pop band, Antenna. —*Stephen Thomas Erlewine*

○ **Earwig** / 1989 / Mammoth 0016
On their first full-length album, the Blake Babies' knack for melodic, chiming guitar-pop became evident, with songs like "Outta My Head" and "Take Your Head Off My Shoulder" leading a pack of fine original numbers. —*Stephen Thomas Erlewine*

○ **Sunburn** / 1990 / Mammoth 0022
Juliana Hatfield's songwriting began to blossom on the Blake Babies' second full-length album, *Sunburn.* Her melodies and hooks are direct and catchy, while her lyrics are disarming in their casual honesty. Which doesn't mean John Strohm's songs don't amount to anything; in fact, his songs and lyrical contributions help balance Hatfield's tendency to be simplistic and childish. At their best, the duo made a surprisingly effective pop songwriting team. *Sunburn* features the band at their best. —*Stephen Thomas Erlewine*

● **Innocence and Experience** / 1993 / Mammoth
Featuring songs from all of their albums as well as a couple of rare tracks, *Innocence and Experience* is a fine collection of the Blake Babies' best work. It's a fine introduction to the ringing, R.E.M.-styled guitar-pop. —*Stephen Thomas Erlewine*

The Blasters

Group / Roots-rock
Among the rock bands that emerged from the Los Angeles scene in the early '80s, the Blasters were the most roots-conscious, producing a sound akin to '50s rockabilly and other 20-year-old musical styles. The group was led by the Alvin brothers (Phil, who sang and played rhythm guitar, and Dave, who played lead guitar and wrote songs) and included John Bazz (bass), Bill Bateman (drums), and Gene Taylor (piano).

The group issued the album *American Music* on the local Rolling Rock label, then switched to Slash for *The Blasters,* which was included in a distribution deal with Warner Bros. They drew national attention in 1982, when the album reached the Top 40. The Blasters released a live EP of rock & roll covers later that year, then returned in 1983 with *Non Fiction,* which was dominated by Dave Alvin's songs. Those songs, steeped in rock, country, and blues traditions, also commented trenchantly on the current state of the American dream in much the same way Bruce Springsteen was doing at the time. They earned the Blasters greater critical respect, though sales did not expand. When *Hard Line* (1985) was also a sales disappointment, Dave Alvin decamped to join X. Phil Alvin kept the band going by hiring another guitarist, Hollywood Fats (Michael Mann), who died a few months later. Dave Alvin returned for a few gigs, then former X guitarist Billy Zoom took his place, but the Blasters had ceased to become a full-time entity. Phil Alvin released a solo album in 1986, then went back to school. Dave Alvin has so far released two solo albums. —*William Ruhlmann*

○ **Blasters** / 1982 / Slash 3680
You might have thought the Blasters had been in suspended animation for 25 years when their major label debut turned up in late 1981 sounding for all the world like something cut in the Sun studios in Memphis in 1956. Dave Alvin knew all the licks and his brother Phil had the country/R&B wail down. Best of all, you couldn't tell the oldies from Dave's newly written classics. Welcome to the birth of rock & roll, all over again. —*William Ruhlmann*

● **Blasters Collection** / 1991 / Slash 26451
One of the leading American "roots" bands of the '80s, this group's anthemic no-frills rock music sounds purer and more real than ever in the post-Milli Vanilli age. —*Jeff Tamarkin*

Blind Faith

Group / Rock & roll
The calculated grafting of ex-Cream members Eric Clapton (guitar, vocal) and Ginger Baker (percussion) to ex-Traffic member Steve Winwood (keyboards, guitar, vocal) and Rick Grech (bass, violin), of the popular British group Family, brought the term *supergroup* to new levels of hype. The talent involved in this amalgamation was quite impressive, but the cynical marketing minds behind this appropriately named fabrication failed to consider natural group chemistry. The volatile personalities in the lineup helped ensure that Blind Faith would almost certainly be nothing more than an interesting one-off.

In spite of unrealistic pressure to live up to fan expectations, Blind Faith delivered an album that at times almost made good on its perceived potential. The memory of the band's auspicious live U.S. debut, selling out Madison Square Garden soured within a matter of weeks, and Blind Faith became yet another historical footnote in the ongoing marriage of commerce and artistic expression. —*Rick Clark*

○ **Blind Faith** / Aug. 1969 / RSO 825094
The only album released by this supergroup. The formula pays off with "Presence of the Lord," the haunting "Can't Find My Way Home" and the art-rock of "Sea of Joy." —*Donna DiChario*

Blind Melon

Group / Rock & roll
Although they may vehemently disagree, Blind Melon fits neatly into the new-hippie movement of the early '90s. While their music is not psychedelic like the Grateful Dead's, Jefferson Airplane's, or even Phish's, it has the same vibe, the same feeling—a call for love, peace, understanding, and good, rocking times. Blind Melon has a harder, guitar-based edge than most hippies, which explains why Axl Rose championed them and featured their lead singer, Shannon Hoon, in Guns N' Roses' single and video, "Don't Cry." If anything, Blind Melon's 1993 breakthrough single, the breezy "No Rain," is decieving—it may capture their spirit faithfully, but the rest of their music favors louder, more meandering guitar jams like the follow-up single, "Tones of Home." —*Stephen Thomas Erlewine*

● **Blind Melon** / Sep. 14, 1992 / Capitol 96585
With its jaunty guitars and memorable melody, "No Rain" was a surprise hit single. It is also the only song of its kind on *Blind Melon.* Throughout the rest of the album, the band relies on a psuedo-hippie formula, sounding like a heavy metal Allman Brothers playing Grateful Dead songs without melodies. —*Stephen Thomas Erlewine*

Blondie

Group / New wave, pop/rock, dance-pop
Blondie started out in the mid-'70s punk/new-wave scene in New York City, along with bands such as the Ramones and the Talking Heads. They would eventually be the most commercially successful new wave band. Their breakthrough came with their third album, the Mike Chapman-produced *Parallel Lines,* containing the rock-disco smash "Heart of Glass." This, along with Debbie Harry's movie-star good looks, propelled the band to stardom. They would continue to ride high on the charts for the next few years with an eclectic mix of hits, including the reggae-flavored "The Tide Is High" and the rap "Rapture." The group disbanded in 1983, with various members pursuing solo careers. —*Kenneth M. Cassidy*

○ **Blondie** / 1977 / Chrysalis 21165
The great '60s girl groups go surfin' in peroxide and run into a bunch of punks with brains. Rock & roll hadn't been this much fun in years. —*Jeff Tamarkin*

○ **Plastic Letters** / 1978 / Chrysalis 21166
Not as startlingly original as the debut, but the follow-up was proof that Blondie was no one-album wonder. —*Jeff Tamarkin*

☆ **Parallel Lines** / 1978 / Chrysalis 21192
Blondie goes image-busting and proves it knows how to create mini-pop masterpieces. Debbie Harry's finest performance on record. —*Jeff Tamarkin*

○ **Eat to the Beat** / 1979 / Chrysalis 21225
While it's not as consistently engaging as *Parallel Lines, Eat to the Beat* features several songs that rank among the band's best material, including "Dreaming." —*Stephen Thomas Erlewine*

Autoamerican / 1980 / Chrysalis 21290
Despite the presence of two of their biggest hits—"The Tide Is High" and "Rapture"—*Autoamerican* is cluttered with filler that obscures the album's occasional pleasures. —*Stephen Thomas Erlewine*

● **Best of Blondie** / 1981 / Chrysalis 21337
All of the hits, and that's the best way to hear this creative singles band. —*Jeff Tamarkin*

Blonde & Beyond / Nov. 16, 1993 / Chrysalis 21990

Although it is a collection of rarities, outtakes, B-sides, and forgotten singles, *Blonde & Beyond* contains enough great music to make the disc enjoyable even to casual Blondie fans. —*Stephen Thomas Erlewine*

Blood Sweat & Tears

Group / Pop/rock
One of the first rock bands to integrate jazz-influenced horns into their sound, Blood, Sweat & Tears burst onto the pop playlists with three million-sellers in 1969. Keyboardist Al Kooper, once a member of the Royal Teens ("Short Shorts"), formed the group in 1968, but soulfully raspy vocalist David Clayton-Thomas was up front when they scored their first smash for Columbia in 1969, a revival of Brenda Holloway's "You've Made Me So Very Happy." "Spinning Wheel" and Laura Nyro's "And When I Die" made it three giants in a row for the band. Clayton-Thomas went solo in 1972 but returned two years later. —*Bill Dahl*

○ **Child Is the Father to the Man** / 1968 / CBS 9619
Brilliant debut effort, seamlessly conceptualized and directed by Al Kooper. Wonderfully arty dynamic production and performances dignify a great batch of songs written by Kooper, Randy Newman, Harry Nilsson, Tim Buckley, Gerry Goffin, and Carole King. —*Rick Clark*

○ **Blood, Sweat & Tears** / 1969 / Columbia 9720
The follow-up to *Child Is Father to the Man* is the band's most successful release. Kooper is gone, replaced by the histrionic David Clayton-Thomas. Big-band arrangements with some rock pretentions dominate here. Contains the hits "And When I Die," "God Bless the Child," "You've Made Me So Very Happy," and "Spinning Wheel." Of the post-Kooper albums, this is the best. —*Rick Clark*

● **Blood, Sweat and Tears' Greatest Hits** / 1972 / Columbia 31170
Self-explanatory collection. —*Rick Clark*

Luka Bloom (Barry Moore)

b. , Ireland
Vocals, guitar / Singer/songwriter
Before making his American debut, Barry Moore recorded three albums in Ireland. Perhaps because his brother is the revered Irish singer Christy Moore, he changed his name to Luka Bloom—Luka is taken from Suzanne Vega's song, Bloom from James Joyce's *Ulysses*. With his literate, melodic original songs and impassioned live performances, Bloom earned a devoted following in the New York area, which led to his record contract with Reprise. While he can occasionally suffer from overworked lyrics and a cloying cuteness, Bloom is one of the best post-punk folk performers and songwriters. —*Stephen Thomas Erlewine*

● **Riverside** / 1990 / Reprise 26092
This songwriter and guitarist has enough help on this album to make it sound good, without taking anything away from his music. —*Chip Renner*

Acoustic Motorbike / 1991 / Reprise 26670
Bloom is a regular old-fashioned songwriter, an unabashed romantic with a sense of humour. *The Acoustic Motorbike* is a warm, cosy album, one rich in depth of emotion and intelligence. Bloom lures the listener in with a congeniality and sense of commitment that is completely contagious. It allows him to get away with a haunting rendition of the Elvis Presley-imprinted "Can't Help Falling in Love" which in other hands would come out maudlin. It even allows him to get away with a heartfelt rap-ballad version—in thick Irish brogue—of LL Cool J's "I Need Love," without sounding silly. —*Roch Parisien*

Blue Cheer

Group / Hard rock, psychedelic, heavy metal
The late '60s was a big time for hard-rock trios, but one of the first, and certainly the most extreme, was Blue Cheer, a San Francisco band whose moniker was also the name of a desirable type of LSD.
Their brain-numbing version of Eddie Cochran's "Summertime Blues" is a hallmark of heavy metal excess. The band's first two crash-and-burn albums (*Vincebus Eruptum* and *Outsideinside*), amateurishly produced by the group's manager, ex-Hell's Angel Abe "Vovo" Kesh, gave a new meaning to the word *loud*. Their

subsequent efforts increasingly degenerated into fairly undistinguished hippie rock wanderings. —*Rick Clark*

○ **Outsideinside** / 1968 / PolyGram 514683
Outsideinside may not have this Frisco trio's death-blast version of Eddie Cochran's classic "Summertime Blues," but there's more than enough tape-saturated hard psychedelic sludge here ("Just a Little Bit" and "The Hunter"). —*Rick Clark*

○ **Vincebus Eruptum** / 1968 / Philips 7839
Blue Cheer's debut psychedelic sludgefest features their explosive reworking of Eddie Cochran's "Summertime Blues." —*Rick Clark*

Louder Than God—Best of Blue Cheer / 1987 / Rhino 70130
The fact that this collection is only available on vinyl may be a drawback for some folks, but (on one level) Blue Cheer, in all its grungy glory, makes even more sense on eight-track than on CD, so what's the complaint? After all, this one has "Just a Little Bit," and the Polygram disc doesn't. —*Rick Clark*

● **Good Times Are So Hard to Find** / 1990 / Mercury 834030
Good Times Are So Hard to Find (The History of Blue Cheer) is an overview spanning Blue Cheer's entire catalog. If only their first two albums of over-the-top psychedelic distorto-blare had been represented a little more. —*Rick Clark*

Blue Oyster Cult

Group / Hard rock, heavy metal
Perhaps it was because two rock writers were working behind the scenes, or perhaps it was because they had a genuine talent in lead guitarist Donald "Buck Dharma" Roeser, but Blue Oyster Cult made some the best heavy metal of the early and mid '70s. Any metal band that can claim Patti Smith as one of their songwriters can't be cut from the same cloth as Black Sabbath, and Blue Oyster Cult's mysticism and darkness were performed with a self-conscious wink, not like Sabbath's lumbering evil. Yet BOC never slid into a hip parody with their early records because they had the songs and skills to back up their image. For several years they made some first-rate metal, yet their first hit was 1976's "Don't Fear the Reaper," which, unlike the rest of their music, featured scores of jangling guitar and a strong chorus. After that, the band began a long, painful slide into unintentional parody that lacked the wit and power of their earlier records. —*Stephen Thomas Erlewine*

○ **Blue Oyster Cult** / 1972 / Columbia 31063
Their debut bogs down under some stupid lyrics, but mostly this is a complex and powerful set. —*John Floyd*

○ **Tyranny & Mutation** / 1973 / Columbia 32017
Blue Oyster Cult's second album sports better lyrics and sharper hooks, culminating in the thunderous "I'm on the Lamb but I Ain't No Sheep." —*John Floyd*

● **Agents of Fortune** / 1975 / Columbia 34164
This bid for mainstream success trades the murky appeal of their early stuff for more coherent themes, crisper production, and ringing guitars. "True Confessions" and "Don't Fear the Reaper" may be their best moments. —*John Floyd*

Spectres / 1977 / Columbia 35019
The follow-up to *Agents of Fortune* doesn't break any new ground lyrically or musically, but it's a solid, workmanlike effort. Includes the AOR staple "Godzilla." —*John Floyd*

Blue Rodeo

Group / Rock & roll, folk-rock
Canadian artists Blue Rodeo incorporate elements of the Band, mid-period Beatles, Buffalo Springfield, and Bob Dylan, to a fine effect. Worth seeking out for those who share those influences. —*Rick Clark*

Outskirts / 1987 / Atlantic 81832
This highly likeable debut is a collection of mid-tempo country rockers. By adding an organ to the arrangements, they were to distinguish themselves from the hordes of other Gram Parson devotees in the mid '80s. —*Chris Woodstra*

Diamond Mine / 1989 / Atlantic 81971
Diamond Mine is a considerably more quiet affair. Beginning with the very Dylanesque "God and Country," a darker, introverted mood is set by their minimalistic approach and slowed tempo. —*Chris Woodstra*

● **Casino** / 1991 / Atlantic 91601

Casino is a more pop-oriented album. They seem to have finally established their fine blend of harmonies and laidback country-rock á la The Band and Bob Dylan. Produced by Pete Anderson (Dwight Yoakam, Michelle Shocked). —*Chris Woodstra*

○ **Lost Together** / 1992 / Atlantic 82412
Lost Together is easily the best Blue Rodeo album to date. Hit the random button on the disc player, and no matter where the laser touches down, you're assured a worthwhile listening experience. —*Roch Parisien*

The Blues Brothers

Group / Soul, rock/pop
During the late '70s, "Saturday Night Live" twosome Dan Aykroyd and John Belushi, as Elwood and Jake Blues, employed the services of Stax rhythm-section players Steve Cropper and Duck Dunn, as well as future David Letterman band leader Paul Shaffer, for a run-through on some soul classics. —*Rick Clark*

● **Definitive Collection** / 1992 / Atlantic 82428
The Definitive Collection is indeed the definitive Blues Brothers disc, containing all of their hits and signature songs. —*Stephen Thomas Erlewine*

The Blues Project

Group / Blues-rock, folk-rock
The Blues Project was New York's first "underground" group. In 1965 guitarist Danny Kalb, who was well established as a player on various Elektra Records folk and early folk-rock and blues albums, played on an Elektra Records sampler called *The Blues Project.* Soon after, he hooked up with Steve Katz (a guitarist with Elektra's Even Dozen Jug Band), Andy Kulberg (a flutist and bassist), Tommy Flanders (singer and harmonica player). Al Kooper came in on keyboards, guitar, and vocals; Andy Kulberg on drums; and Roy Blumenfeld on drums. This sextet quickly built up a reputation for its mix of rock, jazz, classical, and electric blues on numbers such as "Night Time Is the Right Time," "Flute Thing" (which became popular on progressive FM radio stations), and "Catch the Wind."

Kooper exited the band after the third album and went on to join the more jazz-oriented Blood, Sweat & Tears, and Katz quickly followed. The Blues Project also lost Kalb (to ill health) and continued a name only for another album and another year or two. A late-'70s Central Park reunion album recorded by the original sextet attracted a lot of press attention but generated little musical excitement. The three original Verve albums and Rhino's best-of are the records that count. —*Bruce Eder*

Live at the Cafe au-Go-Go / 1966 / Polydor 833346
Arguably the first artistically successful live rock album of the mid '60s. A fine showcase for the band's many talents. —*Bruce Eder*

○ **Projections** / 1966 / Polydor 827918
A groundbreaking record that mixed blues and light jazz with an electric-rock sensibility as solid as that of any band at the time. —*Bruce Eder*

● **No Time Like the Right Time** / 1969 / Rhino 70165
No Time Like the Right Time—The Best of the Blues Project is the best anthology of the band ever likely to be done. It encompasses their wealth of high points in better sound than ever. —*Bruce Eder*

Blues Traveler

Group / Rock & roll
Part of a small group of popular New York-based jam-oriented rock bands in the early '90s, Blues Traveler is arguably the best of the bunch. Like the Spin Doctors and several other like-minded bands, Blues Traveler built their reputation through impressive live shows and constant touring. What sets them apart from the pack is the skills of harmonica player and vocalist John Popper, who is one of the few truly gifted musicians in this scene. Without him, Blues Traveler might spin off into long, pointless blues-based jams, instead of keeping their music relatively tight and concise. —*Stephen Thomas Erlewine*

● **Blues Traveler** / 1990 / A&M 5308
Blues Traveler's loose jam structures on basic blues riffs mark them as a band in the tradition of such predecessors as the Grateful Dead. Unlike that communal effort, however, this group

has a distinct focal point in virtuoso harmonica player and vocalist John Popper, who keeps things from meandering too much. —*William Ruhlmann*

○ **Travelers & Thieves** / 1991 / A&M 5373
"I have my moments," John Popper declares, and many of them, as harmonica player, singer, and lyricist are here, on an album that finds Blues Traveler stretching out much as they do onstage. Popper is a man with a lot on his mind, but when he reaches "The Best Part," his verbosity approaches a Walt Whitman-like exuberance, and guitarist Chan Kinchla is right with him, contributing sweet fills here, Pete Townshend-style strumming there. And as for the rhythm work of bassist Bobby Sheehan and drummer Brendan Hill, as Popper says, "It's all in the groove." —*William Ruhlmann*

Save His Soul / 1993 / A&M 80
Save His Soul is a savory package that dresses obvious influences in a fresh suit of clothes. Thick slabs of acoustic and electric guitars fire off runs that border on trip material, while always returning to a palpable blues structure—like early Paul Butterfield Blues Band on a buzz. While 6- and 12-strings rule, the true inspiration here is Popper's delivery on harmonica and other wind instruments, which spits in machine-gun rapid fire or carries a piercing, emotive melody line with equal ease. —*Roch Parisien*

Blur

Group / Alternative pop/rock
Blur's 1991 debut, *Leisure,* was a collection of relatively straight-forward, energetic guitar-oriented pop released during the end of the Manchester scene and the height of shoegazing. The album signaled a return to a more traditional style of guitar pop in the U.K., without ever sounding like dated music. While *Leisure* was slightly derivative, it was carried by the band's brash pop skills, particularly those of lead singer/songwriter Damon Albarn. With their second album, 1993's *Modern Life Is Rubbish,* the band took a major step backward, aping the Kinks' *Village Green Preservation Society.* Like that classic, it was defiantly British and received no attention outside of the U.K.; however, it helped the group solidify their fan base, while showing that they were capable of a number of different pop styles, from the Beatles to the Kinks to Bowie to the Smiths.

Modern Life set the stage for Blur's breakthrough album, *Parklife,* delivered a mere six months later. While the album was still very British, it had a modern edge that was missing from *Modern Life,* as well as a stronger, more distinctive pop sense. The album's first single, the synthesized dance-pop number "Girls and Boys," was a hit not only in the U.K., but in the United States, making Blur one of a handful of new British bands to have a hit in America in the '90s. —*Stephen Thomas*

○ **Leisure** / 1991 / Capitol 97880
Leisure's most accessible moments, like the singles "She's So High" and "There's No Other Way," blend captivating, fluid melodies with hypnotic, psyched-up instrumentation. More experimental moments like "Repetition" and "Bad Day" are reminiscent of early, Syd Barrett-led Pink Floyd. Fortunately, the group rarely indulges in excess. For the most part, the dreamy atmospheres are firmly anchored by sparse, chunky guitar riffs. —*Roch Parisien*

Modern Life Is Rubbish / 1993 / SBK/Food 89442
On their second album, Blur explores their influences, particularly the Kinks, David Bowie, the Smiths, and the Who. The result is an album that is filled with enjoyable but derivative guitar-pop singles that never manage to capture the spark of Blur's idols or create their own identity. —*Stephen Thomas Erlewine*

● **Parklife** / 1994 / SBK
An audacious fusion of early '80s techno-pop with the timeless guitar pop of the Kinks and the Smiths, *Parklife* is Blur's most ambitious album to date, as well as their best. For once, their songwriting has enough satisfying original hooks to make the entire record consistently enjoyable. —*Stephen Thomas Erlewine*

Eddie Bo (Edwin J. Bocage)

b. Sep. 20, 1930
Piano / R&B
A New Orleans journeyman pianist remembered for his 1961 hit "Check Mr. Popeye" on the Ric label. —*John Floyd*

○ **Check Mr. Popeye** / 1979 / Rounder 2077
Engaging early-'60s New Orleans R&B from a prolific pianist, with a classic title track that spawned a local "Popeye" dance craze. —*Bill Dahl*

BoDeans

Group / Roots-rock
The BoDeans are led by Sammy Llana and Kurt Neumann, guitarists, singers, and songwriters from Wakesha, WI, who play tight, well-arranged guitar rock on their several albums for Slash/Warner Brothers. —*William Ruhlmann*

● **Love & Hope & Sex & Dreams** / 1986 / Slash 25403
On this debut album, Llanas and Neumann are at their best on songs like "Fadeaway," where their sweet-and-sour harmonizing rules over a bouncing rock arrangement full of twangy guitars. There is just enough fidelity to basic rock & roll, and the right number of individual twists, to mark the group's considerable promise. —*William Ruhlmann*

Black and White / Mar. 26, 1991 / Slash 26487
After moderate sales on their first three albums threatened to forever classify them as an alternative band, the BoDeans started tackling bigger themes on *Black and White*, produced by Prince sideman David Z. The band hardly sounds like the roots-oriented band of their previous efforts, Sam Llanas and Kurt Neumann sound more ambitious as songwriters. So "Black, White and Blood Red" is about more than race, the same way the anthemic "Naked" is about more than sex, the same way the hooky "Good Things" is about more than some guy who can't meet a girl. *Black and White* is about using individual problems as analogies to social ones. It's also about loneliness and hardship. It also didn't sell that much better (if any) than the first albums. —*Brian Mansfield*

Tommy Bolin

b. 1951, Sioux City, IA, **d.** Dec. 4, 1976, Miami
Vocals, guitar, keyboard / Hard rock, heavy metal
Tommy Bolin achieved his greatest notoriety in Deep Purple, filling the position of founding member and lead-guitarist Ritchie Blackmore, who left the band to form Rainbow. Previously, Bolin had worked with Zephyr, Billy Cobham, and the James Gang. After Deep Purple folded in 1976, Bolin went solo, releasing two albums. Of particular note was Bolin's slide work. He passed away in Miami in 1976. —*Rick Clark*

○ **Teaser** / 1975 / Columbia 37534
A scattershot collection, but Bolin's forceful slide work on "The Grind" is worth the hunt. —*Rick Clark*

● **Private Eyes** / 1976 / Columbia 34329
A solid showcase for Bolin's no-nonsense lead work in a focused package. —*Rick Clark*

Ultimate—The Best of Tommy Bolin / May 1990 / David Geffen Co. 24248
An overkill boxed set memorializing this late guitarist. Completists will be disappointed that some of Bolin's *Teaser* best moments are not included. —*Rick Clark*

Michael Bolton (Michael Bolotin)

b. Feb. 26, 1954, New Haven, CT
Vocals / Pop/rock, soul
Michael Bolton has suffered more than his fair share of criticism, no matter how much of it was deserved. After spending the '70s churning out arena-friendly hard rock with Blackjack as well as on his own, he turned to soul-inspired pop/rock in the early '80s. As long as he was a faceless hard rocker, critics and audiences paid him no mind because, frankly, he wasn't very good. He *was* good at pop songwriting: Laura Branigan had a hit in 1983 with his "How Am I Supposed to Live Without You," while he was struggling as an AOR singer called Michael Bolotin.
With 1987's *The Hunger*, his second album as Michael Bolton, he began charting on his own. "That's What Love Is All About" cracked the Top Twenty, but it was his carbon copy of Otis Redding's "(Sittin' On) The Dock of the Bay" that brought him the attention and sales that he craved, as well as the start of the blistering criticism.
To be fair, much of the criticism is unwarranted, but some of it is. When he is singing soul covers, Bolton removes any pretense

of subtlety, straining any emotion from the song with his over-wrought delivery. On his own material, he is drastically better. Not only does he restrain his gruff voice and sing musically, but his songs are well-constructed adult-contemporary pop songs that sound perfect on the radio.
Despite all of the criticism, Bolton continued to sell records well into the '90s, even though his writing was starting to lose some of its sharpness. It might have been a massive hit, but 1994's "Said I Loved You (But I Lied)" was his first true piece of hack work. A couple months after that single, he lost a plagarism suit to the Isley Brothers, who claimed that he had appropriated their 1966 "Love Is a Wonderful Thing" for his 1991 hit of the same name. Bolton appealed the ruling, and the case is still in the courts. It remains to be seen whether the case will hurt his sales, but a surprising number of critics came to his defense, agreeing with him that the songs shared little more than the same title. —*Stephen Thomas Erlewine*

Michael Bolton / 1983 / Columbia 38537
Michael Bolton's first album as a blue-eyed pop-soul singer was a minor success, climbing into the Top 100. While it contained a couple of solid tracks, including the single "Fools Game," it was too spotty to capture the superstardom that would come to him in a couple of years. —*Stephen Thomas Erlewine*

Hunger / 1987 / Columbia 40473
One of his best sets, featuring R&B covers and grooving pop and including the hits "That's What Love Is All About" and "(Sittin' On) The Dock of the Bay." —*Bil Carpenter*

● **Soul Provider** / 1989 / Columbia 45012
Featuring such hits as "How Am I Supposed to Live Without You" and "How Can We Be Lovers," *Soul Provider* established Bolton as an adult contemporary superstar. It was also his best, most accomplished album. —*Stephen Thomas Erlewine*

○ **Time, Love & Tenderness** / 1991 / Columbia 46771
Light rock-styled Top 40, with some R&B. Includes the title track and "Love Is a Wonderful Thing." —*Bil Carpenter*

Timeless (The Classics) / Jul. 1992 / Columbia 52783
Timeless (The Classics) won't win Michael Bolton any new fans, but those who have enjoyed his music in the past will find this album of covers (including "Reach Out, I'll Be There," "Yesterday," and "White Christmas") as absorbing as any of his other records. —*Stephen Thomas Erlewine*

The Artistry of Michael Bolotin / 1993 / RCA 66201
A ten-track compilation of Michael Bolton's early recordings of such classic rock staples as Joe Walsh's "Rocky Mountain Way" and the Guess Who's "These Eyes." Since Bolton was still trying to find his style, most of these songs fall flat, yet it's interesting to hear his emotive vocals develop. —*Stephen Thomas Erlewine*

Bon Jovi

Group / Hard rock, pop/rock
One of the most successful teen-geared groups of the last decade, this Jersey-bred group honed their skills as an opening act on the arena circuit until the mid '80s, when the band added some pop to their lite-metal riffs and frontman Jon Bon Jovi (born Jon Bongiovi) took advantage of the possibilities of MTV and became the sex symbol for prepubescent girls across the globe. —*John Floyd*

● **Slippery When Wet** / 1986 / Jambco 830264
Bon Jovi delivers a hook-laden rock album with several of their biggest hits, including "Livin' on a Prayer" and the rocker-as-cowboy opus "Wanted Dead or Alive." —*Donna DiChario*

○ **New Jersey** / 1988 / Jambco 836345
While less instantly catchy than *Slippery When Wet*, this offers many of Bon Jovi's trademark radio-friendly melodies and lyrics that appeal to their faithful following. —*Donna DiChario*

Keep the Faith / Sep. 1992 / Jambco 514045
After being missing in action for nearly four years, Bon Jovi returns with *Keep the Faith*, an update on their trademark pop-metal sound. Because the rules had changed since *New Jersey*, the band knew they had to shake things up a bit. Bon Jovi *wants* to be taken seriously this time around—hence, epics like the ten-minute "Dry County" and stabs at significance like "Fear" (plus new short haircuts). Most of these grand statements fall flat, but there are songs here (like "Bed of Roses" and "Keep the Faith")

that nearly match the glory days of *Slippery When Wet*. — *Stephen Thomas Erlewine*

Gary "U.S." Bonds (Gary Anderson)

b. Jun. 6, 1939, Jacksonville, FL
Vocals / R&B, rock & roll

After moving to the Norfolk, VA, area as a child, young Gary Anderson began plying his vocal wares, first in church and later with a local group called the Turks. At not yet 21, he was approached by local record producer Frank Guida to join his tiny Legrand label. Guida changed Anderson's name to U.S. Bonds, hoping the first release would get extra airplay by disc jockeys mistaking it for a public service announcement. The result was the classic "New Orleans," combining rock-combo raunch with impassioned, scorched soul-singing that set the stage for all that would follow. Guida double- and triple-tracked Bonds's voice, and the resulting murky production gave all the hits (including "Quarter to Three," "Not Me," "School Is Out," and "Dear Lady Twist") a party-in-outer-space quality all their own. Though he's kept recording, making a couple of excellent solo albums over the last decade, Bonds is best seen today dotting the landscape of oldies shows the world over, singing the songs that made him famous. — *Cub Koda*

Dedication / 1981 / Razor & Tie 1986
Bruce Springsteen, a longtime fan, helped revitalize Bonds's career in the '80s by working with him on two albums. This, the first, is the better one, including Springsteen's songwriting and vocals on "This Little Girl." — *William Ruhlmann*

● **School of Rock 'n' Roll: The Best of Gary U.S. Bonds** / 1990 / Rhino 70971
Gary U.S. Bonds was one of the few people trying to make honest rock & roll in the early '60s, and *School of Rock 'n' Roll: The Best of Gary U.S. Bonds* captures his successes, among them his signature song, "Quarter to Three." — *William Ruhlmann*

Boney M

Group / Disco

Although they never had much success in America, the Euro-disco group Boney M was a European phenomenon during the '70s. After German record producer Frank Farian recorded the single "Baby Do You Wanna Bump?" (which was successful in Holland and Belgium), he created Boney M to support the song, bringing in four West Indian vocalists. During 1976 and 1977, the group had four singles in the British Top Ten. In 1978, Boney M was at the height of their popularity with the "Rivers of Babylon" / "Brown Girl in the Ring" single, which became the third-biggest selling single in British chart history. The hits kept coming during 1979, but the group was disbanded in 1980. Their music continues to sell well in Europe, with a compilation hitting the Top Ten in Britain recently. Farian went on to create the early '90s dance sensation Milli Vanilli. — *Stephen Thomas Erlewine*

● **Magic of Boney M (20 Hits)** / 1980 / Atlantic 1
Boney M's top Euro-disco creations—songs that ruled the continent for a while in the mid-'70s—are compiled on this singularly pleasing singles collection. — *Stephen Thomas Erlewine*

Bongos

Group / Power pop

Hoboken's the Bongos made no pretense of being anything other a pop band. Fortunately, they were a good pop band, covering guitar pop from the Byrds to T. Rex, all of it pulled together by the songs of guitarist/vocalist/songwriter Richard Barone. Although he was the focal point, the other members were by no means peripheral. After their first record, guitarist James Mastro joined the trio and contributed some stellar hooks. During the early '80s they made two full-length albums and two EPs. While they might not have been consistently brilliant, at their best the Bongos made some irresistible guitar-pop. — *Stephen Thomas Erlewine & Rick Clark*

Drums along the Hudson / 1982 / Razor & Tie 1999
The Bongo's first proper album is a driving power-pop masterpiece filled with hooks and infectious melodies. Even the unlikely T-Rex cover, "Mambo Sun," comes off well. — *Chris Woodstra*

● **Beat Hotel/Numbers with Wings** / Jul. 24, 1992 / Razor & Tie 1995

This is a two-fer of the Bongos' last two albums. "Barbarella" and the title cut from the Richard Gottehrer-produced *Numbers with Wings* (1983) are the highlights on that set. *Beat Hotel* (1985) is their best-sounding effort, though the songwriting quality isn't as consistent. — *Rick Clark*

The Bonzo Dog Band

Group / Pop/rock, psychedelic

The Bonzo Dog Band (formed in 1965 as the Bonzo Dog Doo-Dah Band) specialized in a peculiarly British absurdist humor and satire that drew from an odd blend of '20s cabaret music, '50s rock & roll, and '60s psychedelia. — *Rick Clark*

Gorilla / 1967 / Imperial 12370
Gorilla, the 1967 debut album by the Bonzo Dog Doo-Dah Band, may be low key, but that's not to say it doesn't retain a good deal of charm. The humor is extremely dry, subtle, and British, leaning more toward their traditional jazz roots than the churning London pop-rock scene. It nonetheless includes a few great moments: the deadpan jazz vamp "The Intro and the Outro" (wherein a swarmy MC introduces a bevy of historical figures in a show band, including Adolf Hitler on vibes), the film noir satire "Mickey's Son and Daughter," and their vicious send-up of *The Sound of Music*. — *Richie Unterberger*

○ **Doughnuts in Granny's Greenhouse** / 1968 / Liberty 83158
They took the "Doo Dah" out of their name for this 1968 LP (their second), which is probably the Bonzos' best. Although they were hardly a rock or pop group in the traditional sense, the Bonzos couldn't help absorbing some of the vibes of British psychedelia, and the heady ambience of the era is reflected in the recklessly diverse and outrageous material. Almost all of the songs were penned by the two top Dogs, Viv Stanshall and Neil Innes, who deflate British blues, psychedelia, and other pop, jazz, and music-hall styles with priceless wit. Star tracks on this saxophone-heavy album include the doo-wop ode to a spacegirl ("Beautiful Zelda"), "Trouser Press" (which gave the late American underground rock magazine its name), the droll series of poker-faced spoken sketches on "Rhinocratic Oaths" (certainly an influence on Monty Python), and the boozy "My Pink Half of the Drainpipe," which ranks as one of the most ridiculous and hysterical songs released by a pop group of any era. — *Richie Unterberger*

Tadpoles / 1969 / Liberty 12445
The Bonzos' third album is a bit of a retreat from the cosmic anything-goes atmosphere of their second LP (*The Doughnut in Granny's Greenhouse*), slanted much more heavily toward their vaudevillian traditional-jazz roots. Perhaps that's because Viv Stanshall and Neil Innes, who dominated the second album, contribute only three tunes here. Still, it's never less than entertaining, and has some stellar moments, like the psychedelic African safari of "Ali Baba's Camel," the skit "Shirt" (another clear forerunner of Monty Python), and the British hit single "I'm the Urban Spaceman," produced by Paul McCartney. — *Richie Unterberger*

● **Best of the Bonzo Dog Band** / 1974 / Rhino 71006
A well-chosen overview of the playful late-'60s British absurdists' work. The precursor to Monty Python. Fans of Python should check this out. — *Rick Clark*

Boo Radleys

b. , Liverpool, England
Group / Alternative pop/rock

When the Boo Radleys released their first album, *Ichabod and I*, in 1990, England was about to enter the height of the shoegazing craze, and it seemed that the group fit neatly into the scene's overpowering loud guitars and airy melodies. With their second record, 1992's *Everything's Alright Forever*, it became clear that not only were the group's ambitions larger than that simple categorization, they had the skills to fulfill them. Their sound had tightened up, and guitarist Martin Carr's songwriting was developing rapidly, as 1993's *Giant Steps* proves. With that album, the Boo Radleys came into their own, incorporating nearly every form of English pop music since the Beatles into one massive record. It was critically praised and sold in large numbers in the United Kingdom and Europe, but it only slightly expanded their cult in America. — *Stephen Thomas Erlewine*

○ **Everything's Alright Forever** / Oct. 1991 / Columbia 52912

An impressive debut album from the Boo Radleys that sketches out their mix of grinding guitars and sweet melodies. *—Stephen Thomas Erlewine*

● **Giant Steps** / 1993 / Columbia 53794
More than anything, *Giant Steps* is a pastiche of every genre of rock & roll, from the '50s to the '90s, in one album. It's an incredibly ambitious notion, but it works. *Giant Steps* has shoegazing guitars, Beach Boys harmonies, the arrangements of love and Beatlesque melodies, forming a remarkably original record, rich in detail and ultimately very rewarding. *—Stephen Thomas Erlewine*

Booker T. & the MG's

b. , Memphis, TN
Group / Soul, R&B
The percolating bass of Duck Dunn, the razor-sharp leads and ringing chords of Steve Cropper, the thick, oozing organ runs of Booker T. Jones, and the deadlocked drum thwap of Al Jackson—known collectively as Booker T. and the MG's—epitomized the sound of Memphis soul. As the house band for the legendary Stax studio, the MG's played on nearly every song released on the label, influencing both other Memphis musicians (such as Willie Mitchell's Hi musicians) and New Orleans luminaries like the Meters. Cropper's choked guitar style had an impact on everyone from Pete Townshend and Eric Clapton to Robert Cray. There's a sameness in the work of the MG's that makes some of their albums blur together, but you will find no better soundtrack for house parties, romancing, or tooling down the interstate. *—John Floyd*

○ **Hip Hug-Her** / 1967 / Rhino 71013
Great album cover and songs—"Groovin," "Soul Sanction," "Double or Nothing," and the classic title track—are just the beginning of the wealth of terrific Memphis soul available on this album. *—Stephen Thomas Erlewine*

★ **Best of Booker T. & the MG's** / 1968 / Atlantic 81281
The title says it all. Includes "Green Onions," "Hip Hug-Her," "Groovin," and "Jellybread." The only one it's missing is "Time Is Tight," which is on Stax's *Best of Booker T. & the MG's*. *—John Floyd*

○ **Mclemore Avenue** / 1970 / Stax 8552
An instrumental reconstruction of *Abbey Road*. The title is derived from the street where Stax was located, and the cover art is a better Beatles parody that anything on *The Rutles*. *—John Floyd*

● **Best Of** / 1991 / Fantasy 60004
Somewhat confusingly, this disc is identically titled to a CD on Atlantic that concentrates on their earlier material. This 17-cut disc draws from 1967-71, and includes three of their four Top-20 pop hits: "Soul Limbo," "Hang 'Em High," and "Time Is Tight." This perhaps lacks a bit of the edge of their mid-'60s recordings, concentrating on loping, relaxed grooves more than biting, incisive chops. The standard remains pretty high though, with the interplay between Steve Cropper's guitar, Booker T. Jones's organ, and the rhythm section never less than telepathic. Most of the material is original, but even on the covers of period pop hits—including unlikely versions of "Something," "Eleanor Rigby," and "Mrs. Robinson"—the group is soulful and tight. *—Richie Unterberger*

The Boomtown Rats

Group / New wave, pop/rock
An Irish punk quintet led by singer/songwriter Bob Geldof. Their early work had the energy and attitude of punk, but on later records (including several British hits), an increased musical sophistication put them closer to the pop-rock mainstream. Geldof left for a solo career in 1986, ending the band. *—William Ruhlmann*

Boomtown Rats / 1977 / Mercury 1188
The Rats posed as a punk group on their debut, but they were always a little too tight to make the tag stick. Still, "Looking Out for No. 1" and "Mary of the 4th Form," both of which made the U.K. charts, had the right energy and the right attitude. *—William Ruhlmann*

○ **Fine Art of Surfacing** / 1979 / Columbia 36248
Lead singer Bob Geldof hit his peak as a Ray Davies-influenced writer of story-songs on this album, which retained the group's

early force while displaying an increased sophistication, especially on the signature song "I Don't Like Mondays." *—William Ruhlmann*

● **Greatest Hits** / 1987 / Columbia 40615
Most of the Boomtown Rats' albums were inconsistent, which is why *Greatest Hits* remains their best album. *—AMG*

Pat Boone

b. Jun. 1, 1934, Jacksonville, FL
Vocals / Pop
He was clean-cut, polite to his elders, and glorified the nutritional value of milk. To folks who hated everything the new music stood for, Pat Boone was the perfect '50s rock & roller. But no matter how music historians judge the career of Pat Boone, nobody can dispute his enormous sales figures. The well-scrubbed crooner in the white buckskin shoes sold many millions of copies of his sanitized R&B covers during the '50s, helping to facilitate acceptance of rock & roll in the pop marketplace.

Boone's family ties are impressive—he's related to frontier legend Daniel Boone through bloodlines and to country great Red Foley through marriage to his daughter. After debuting on the small Republic imprint in 1954, Boone signed with Dot and took the pop world by storm over the next couple of years with covers of R&B items by Fats Domino, Little Richard, the El Dorados, the Flamingos, Ivory Joe Hunter, and too many others to list here.

With his college-boy good looks and an affinity for smooth ballads, Boone crossed over into TV and films, scoring number-one hits in 1957 with "Love Letters in the Sand," from the movie *Bernardine*, and the theme from the movie *April Love*, both of which he starred in.

"Moody River" marked Boone's last chart-topper in 1961, although he gamely tackled everything from novelty rockers ("Speedy Gonzales") to surf songs ("Beach Girl") to sustain his success. These days, you're most likely to encounter Boone and his family (which includes Debby Boone of "You Light Up My Life" fame) on the contemporary Christian circuit or doing work for charitable organizations, the white bucks and crewcut long since retired. *—Bill Dahl*

○ **Jivin' Pat** / Feb. 1986 / Bear Family 15230
All of Boone's rockers—cover versions of Fats Domino, Little Richard, et al. Includes a revealing set of liner notes. You won't find these elsewhere unless you have an enormous singles collection. *—Hank Davis*

● **Greatest Hits** / 1990 / Curb 77298
Nothing fancy. A minimal collection of Pat's '50s hits. *—Hank Davis*

Boredoms

Group / Experimental, alternative rock
With the support of Sonic Youth and Nirvana behind them, the Boredoms released a major label album in 1993, which may be the most impressive thing about this almost unlistenable band. For several years, the Boredoms have been the leaders of Japan's wave of noise bands, inspired by Sonic Youth's early records and other artists from that scene. What separates the Boredoms from early Sonic Youth is songs—the Boredoms don't have any. And they don't care if they do, either. Instead, they get by on sheer willpower and stacks of effects pedals and amplifiers. Unless you have an extreme amount of patience or enjoy listening to the soothing sounds of heavy machinery, chances are you won't be able to tolerate the Boredoms. Which is exactly what they want, by the way. *—Stephen Thomas Erlewine*

○ **Soul Discharge** / 1990 / Shimmy Disc 35
Creative hardcore that is so brash, so noisy, so insane, and so good. Play it loud to guarantee an eviction notice. *—Myles Boisen*

● **Pop Tatari** / 1993 / Reprise 45416
The Boredoms' first major label release is their most accessible record, even if it isn't close to what's generally considered as listenable. *—Stephen Thomas Erlewine*

Earl Bostic

b. Apr. 25, 1913, Tulsa, OK, **d.** Oct. 28, 1965, Rochester, NY
Alto sax / R&B
Bostic began as a jazz player in the big-band jazz era of the '20s and '30s. In the early '40s he worked with Cab Calloway, Lionel

Hampton, and others. He pioneered the hard-driving R&B sax sound of the early '40s. Bostic's band was a training ground for many great artists, including John Coltrane, Stanley Turrentine, Bill Doggett, Mickey Baker, and others. Jazz great Art Blakey says, "Nobody knew more about the saxophone than Bostic, I mean technically, and that includes Bird." Bostic had a number-one R&B hit with "Flamingo." This is hard-rockin', raunchy R&B saxophone at its best. —*Michael Erlewine*

● **Best of Earl Bostic** / 1956 / Deluxe 500
A nice cross section of this fiery alto saxist's '50s output, including his hits "Sleep" and "Flamingo." —*Bill Dahl*

Let's Dance with Earl Bostic / 1957 / Deluxe 529
Take this alto-sax legend up on the invitation! —*Bill Dahl*

○ **Bostic for You** / 1957 / King 503
Bostic's blistering renditions of old dance numbers transcend R&B and jazz barriers. —*Bill Dahl*

○ **Alto Magic in Hi-Fi** / 1958 / King 597
More swinging standards. —*Bill Dahl*

○ **Dance Music from the Bostic Workshop** / 1988 / King 613
Includes an astonishing display of sax technique over a torrid R&B beat on the breathtaking "Up There in Orbit." —*Bill Dahl*

Boston

Group / Pop/rock, hard rock
During the late '70s, Boston dominated AOR (album-oriented rock) FM with their dense multilayered guitars and vocals. The self-titled debut effort, which was basically constructed from band leader Tom Scholz's basement demos, eventually sold over six and a half million copies. "More Than a Feeling," their first single, is a perfect encapsulation of Boston's sound. After a two-year wait, Boston's follow-up, *Don't Look Back*, basically replicated the debut's formula. By then, Scholz was gaining a reputation as an obsessive perfectionist, further underscored by the seven-year wait for the group's third album, *Third Stage*.

During this time, Scholz applied his previous background as a senior product designer for Polaroid and started Scholz Research & Development, which marketed popular professional-musician outboard gear, like the Rockman.

After another long delay—eight years—Boston returned in 1994 with a new album, *Walk On*. —*Rick Clark*

● **Boston** / 1976 / Epic 34188
The album that virtually defined '70s FM rock, selling over six million copies. Featuring the smash hits "More Than a Feeling," "Peace of Mind," and "Let Me Take You Home Tonight." —*Donna DiChario*

○ **Don't Look Back** / 1978 / Epic 35050
Continued success with their rock formula, highlighted by the hit title track. —*Donna DiChario*

Third Stage / 1986 / MCA 6188
A chart-topping comeback after a seven-year hiatus and a lineup reshuffling that kept only singer Brad Delp and guitarist/producer Tom Scholz from the original band. Hits include "Amanda" and "We're Ready." —*Donna DiChario*

Bow Wow Wow

Group / New wave
Bow Wow Wow was a quartet organized by British manager Malcolm McLaren (best known as the mastermind behind the Sex Pistols) at the start of the '80s. McLaren matched the trio of musicians who had constituted Adam Ant's Ants (Matthew Ashman, guitar; Leigh Gorman, bass; and David Barbarossa, drums) with teenage singer Annabella Lwin, retaining the earlier group's African-derived drum sound. In 1983 Lwin quit the group for a solo career, and the remaining three changed their name to the Chiefs of Relief. Both Lwin and the Chiefs issued their own albums. —*William Ruhlmann*

● **I Want Candy** / 1982 / RCA 54375
This album largely recompiles Bow Wow Wow's first album plus its *Last of the Mohicans* EP. It includes the hits "Go Wild in the Country," "I Want Candy," and "Louis Quatorze" and presents the band's urgent, rhythmic sound at its most consistent. —*William Ruhlmann*

○ **Girl Bites Dog—Your Compact Disc Pet** / 1993 / EMI 72438272232

A CD reissue of their first cassette-only release. Featuring a 15-year-old Annabella Lwin singing songs with sex-obsessed themes backed by a driving tribal beat, *Girl Bites Dog* gives a representative view of a band with limited scope. Though it sounds a bit dated today, new wave fanatics will find this newly expanded version essential, especially for the unreleased rarities, B-sides, and extensive discography. —*Chris Woodstra*

David Bowie (David Robert Jones)

b. Jan. 8, 1947, Brixton, England
Vocals / Pop/rock, hard rock, glam rock, dance-pop
Although successful as a singer, musician, songwriter, and film and stage actor, David Bowie's chief artistic accomplishment may have been his astute manipulation of his own image as a star. When he achieved international fame in the early '70s, Bowie brought a new, highly conscious approach to stardom that involved the frequent creation of new personae. No wonder that when he made his film acting debut in 1976, he seemed so good at it: Acting was what a large part of his career was about. Born in Brixton, South London, as David Jones, the singer was already playing in bands by his late teens. He changed his name to avoid confusion with Davy Jones of the Monkees. His early-'60s work was rock and blues oriented, then he turned to an Anthony Newley-style expressive show-music approach. But his breakthrough British hit "Space Oddity" (1969) was a folkie ballad about an astronaut who doesn't come home. By the time of *Hunky Dory* (1971), Bowie had turned again more toward rock, using the first of many strong collaborators, guitarist Mick Ronson.

It was Bowie's concept album *The Rise and Fall of Ziggy Stardust and the Spiders from Mars* (1972) that made him a giant star in England, where he adopted the image of his fantasy rocker, with bright red hair and futuristic stage suits. In America, "Space Oddity" became a belated hit in 1973, the year Bowie "retired" from stage work, only to return in 1974 with an even more elaborate stage show. More an established star than a real record-seller in the United States, Bowie finally hit number one with "Fame" (cowritten by John Lennon and Luther Vandross) in 1975. The late '70s found him collaborating with electronics whiz Brian Eno. He made a major commercial comeback in 1983 with *Let's Dance*, produced by ex-Chic coleader Nile Rodgers. Bowie's work in the '80s was inconsistent, but as late as 1990 he was still able to tour the United States, playing football stadiums. This was supposedly his farewell tour (again) before he turned full attention to a group project, Tin Machine.

After releasing two unsuccessful albums with Tin Machine, Bowie returned to his solo career in 1993, with his first solo album since 1987, *Black Tie White Noise;* although it received favorable reviews, it fell off the charts quickly. —*William Ruhlmann*

○ **Space Oddity** / 1969 / Rykodisc 10131
Originally titled *Man of Words, Man of Music*, this release was a transitional effort from Bowie's earlier Anthony Newley affectations on Decca. Tracks range from the Bob Dylan-influenced future-shock epic "Cygnet Committee" to lightweight rockers like "Janine." Also includes "Space Oddity," Bowie's first major single and the highlight of this album. —*Rick Clark*

○ **Man Who Sold the World** / 1971 / Rykodisc 10132
After the theatrical, acoustic leanings of *Space Oddity*, Bowie undertook a dark foray into British hard rock that at times attempted Cream-style free-for-alls, particularly "She Shook Me Cold." The strangely dense, bass-heavy production (courtesy of Tony Visconti), coupled with Bowie's disturbing imagery, provided some powerful moments. One of Bowie's better efforts. —*Rick Clark*

☆ **Hunky Dory** / 1972 / Rykodisc 10133
This follow-up to *The Man Who Sold the World* found Bowie lightening his sound considerably. Some of his most memorable songs are found on this classic: the catchy pop classic "Changes" (a theme song, of sorts), the beautifully expansive "Life on Mars," the moody dynamics of "Quicksand," "The Bewlay Brothers," and "Oh, You Pretty Things." —*Rick Clark*

☆ **The Rise & Fall of Ziggy Stardust** / 1972 / Rykodisc 10134
Regarded by many to be Bowie's best album, Bowie took the melodicism developed on *Hunky Dory* and beefed it up with a punchy, rigid, freeze-dried "rock" setting. It's a perfect setting for

Bowie's concept of a plastic rock star, Ziggy Stardust. *The Rise and Fall of Ziggy Stardust and the Spiders from Mars*, without a doubt, was an important defining effort for the glam-rock movement. —*Rick Clark*

○ **Aladdin Sane** / 1973 / Rykodisc 10135
Rocks harder than *Ziggy Stardust* but flirts pretty closely at times with cabaret death (courtesy of pianist Mike Garson). "Watch That Man" is a fine rocker that manages to draw inspiration from the Stones' *Exile on Main Street*, while not totally abandoning the rhythmic stiffness inherent in the glam sound. Other highlights: "Jean Genie," "Cracked Actor," and "Panic in Detroit." —*Rick Clark*

Images 1966-1967 / 1973 / London 9
This double album is becoming hard to find, which is unfortunate, as it's easily the most comprehensive collection of Bowie's 1966-67 work for Deram. The 21 tracks include the entirety of his 1967 debut album, plus seven stray songs from singles and sessions that were unreleased at the time. Possibly because it wasn't heard by many listeners until it was reissued in the early '70s during Bowie's ascent to stardom, this material has been unfairly maligned. Critics and fans of *Ziggy Stardust* were shocked to discover an all-around entertainer seemingly bent upon becoming the new Anthony Newley. Indeed, much of his work from this era was overbearingly cloying and saccharine, both in the West End matinee aspirations of the lyrics and the unabashedly theatrical orchestration, which bore hardly any resemblance to good old rock & roll whatsoever. One of these, "Laughing Gnome" (featuring Alvin Chipmunk-like backup vocals) caused Bowie considerable embarrassment when it was reissued—and became a hit—in Britain in 1973. The less idiotically cheerful efforts though, show definite signs of an idiosyncratic talent: the odd character sketches, the fleeting references to transvestites and mysticism, even the occasional London swinging pop number ("Let Me Sleep Beside You"). The best track, "London Boys" (a 1966 single), is a neglected, classic look at the downer side of the mod experience and is the best of his many obscure pre-"Space Oddity" recordings. —*Richie Unterberger*

Pin Ups / 1973 / Rykodisc 10136
Bowie covers a selection of personal favorite songs from the '60s by the Yardbirds, the Kinks, the Who, Pink Floyd, and more. It's an affectionate tribute that makes more of a case for Bowie's excellent taste than for his ability to transcend the original versions. Contains the hit "Sorrow." —*Rick Clark*

Diamond Dogs / 1974 / Rykodisc 10137
An ambitious smudge of an album, it nevertheless contains some standouts in the lean, riff-heavy hit "Rebel Rebel," the fatalistic futurism of "1984" (an early disco-ish harbinger of his thin white duke era), and the title track. —*Rick Clark*

Young Americans / 1975 / Rykodisc 10140
Bowie affects Philly soul and a hodgepodge of other things. Ace sidemen can't save this spotty album, but the title track and "Fame" (cowritten by John Lennon) became worldwide hits. —*Rick Clark*

○ **Station to Station** / 1976 / Rykodisc 10141
A transitional effort that bridges Bowie's clinical pop/disco persona to the icy psychosis and dissonance of his next phase, working with Brian Eno. Almost as ill formed as *Diamond Dogs* (particularly the title track), but the Top-Ten hit "Golden Years" and "TVC15" are highlights. —*Rick Clark*

☆ **Low** / Jan. 1977 / Rykodisc 10142
The first of several efforts with ex-Roxy Music sound painter Brian Eno, *Low* is a willful departure from Bowie's pop persona. Short songs make their point and get out of the way on the first half, followed by four dense synth-instrumental soundscapes. —*Rick Clark*

☆ **Heroes** / Feb. 1977 / Rykodisc 10143
Heroes echos *Low*'s half-sung, half-instrumental approach, this time with longer songs (given a maniacal musical accompaniment by King Crimson's Robert Fripp) and chillingly desolate soundscapes. The brilliant title track features one of Bowie's most passionate performances. Those who like discordant rock should be in heaven with "Beauty and the Beast," "Joe the Lion," and "Blackout." —*Rick Clark*

Stage / 1978 / Rykodisc 10144-45

A great double-disc live document of Bowie's *Heroes* tour, with disc 1 focusing on *Ziggy Stardust* and *Station to Station* material and disc 2 featuring *Low* and *Heroes*. —*Rick Clark*

○ **Lodger** / 1979 / Rykodisc 10146
The third installment with Eno returns Bowie to a more conventional (but not necessarily more commercial) song structure. Production isn't so sharp sounding as on *Heroes*, but it has many engaging moments, particularly the hopeful "Fantastic Voyage" and the goofy "D.J.," plus "Boys Keep Swinging," and the hyperdrive of "Look Back in Anger." —*Rick Clark*

○ **Scary Monsters (and Super Creeps)** / 1980 / Rykodisk
One of the better post-*Low* efforts. Contains the hits "Fashion" and "Ashes to Ashes," and the dissonant rocker "It's No Game (Part 1)." Robert Fripp provides a wonderfully jarring racket on the latter cut, the Tom Verlaine-penned "Kingdom Come," and several others. Pete Townshend guests on "Because You're Young." CD includes four bonus tracks. —*Rick Clark*

Let's Dance / 1983 / EMI America 46002
Bowie guns for big pop success and gets it on this outing, somehow deftly sidestepping appearances of being a sellout. The title track, "China Girl," and "Modern Love" achieved international chart success. This album also includes a nice reworking of Metro's "Criminal World." —*Rick Clark*

○ **Sound & Vision** / 1989 / Rykodisc 90120-21-22
An extravagantly produced three-CD-plus CDV (video mini-disc) boxed set that digs deeper than *Changesbowie*. It features much previously unavailable stuff, but comes up short on certain primary radio tracks. Good complement to *Changesbowie*, in spite of a little track duplication. —*Rick Clark*

★ **Changesbowie** / 1990 / Rykodisc 20171
Except for the substitution of a "Fame '90" remix over the original number-one hit, this is a great sampling of big cuts from all of Bowie's many phases, from "Space Oddity" to "Ashes to Ashes." While Bowie has had some classic albums, the uninitiated should start here. —*Rick Clark*

Early On (1964-1966) / 1991 / Rhino 70526
Before landing his first commercial success with 1969's "Space Oddity," David Bowie released a number of flop records in a variety of styles. He first emerged in the mid '60s as a mod, following the paths of the Who, the Kinks, and the Rolling Stones. The 17-cut CD "Early On (1964-66)" is by far the most comprehensive anthology of his first works, gathering all six of his first singles and adding five previously unreleased demos from 1965. —*Richie Unterberger*

Black Tie White Noise / 1993 / Savage 50212
A fitfully successful comeback effort by Bowie, *Black Tie White Noise* works best when he subtly tries update his sound. When he duets with Al B Sure! on the title track or does a tepid remake of Cream's "I Feel Free," the modernization of soul and glam sounds forced, which never happens on the house beats of "Jump They Say" or the moving reworking of Morrissey's "I Know It's Gonna Happen Someday." Unfortunately, the good songs—and the best material here is easily his best since *Scary Monsters*—are obscured by the filler and ill-conceived dance experimentations. Had it been trimmed by five or six songs, the album could indeed have brought him back to the top of the charts. —*Stephen Thomas Erlewine*

★ **Singles 1969-1993** / 1993 / Rykodisc
Taking *Changesbowie* one step further, *Singles 1969-1993* collects all of David Bowie's biggest hits while picking up such overlooked gems as "Drive-in Saturday" and "Loving the Alien." The comprehensiveness and quality of the songs make *Singles* the best Bowie compilation available. Fans will be pleased with the inclusion of the complete lyrics to all of the songs on this two-disc set. —*Stephen Thomas Erlewine*

The Box Tops

Group / Pop/rock, soul
If you forget about the Rascals and the Righteous Brothers, the Memphis-based Box Tops are the finest blue-eyed soul group. Lead singer (and former Big Star honcho) Alex Chilton had a tough, swaggering voice that belied his teenage years, sounding at times as if he were in a cutting match with the young Steve Winwood. Producers Chips Moman and Dan Penn surrounded

Chilton with a crack American studio band, giving the music more muscle and deep funk than you'll ever find in "Mary Mary."

Instead of knocking off pimply, lightweight teen fodder, the Box Tops managed to add another link in the Memphis soul chain, mixing blues, Beatlesque pop, and the sound of Stax, Hi, and Goldwax. And unlike the Monkees, the Box Tops benefited from top-notch material: Dan Penn and Spooner Oldham's "Cry Like a Baby," and " I Met Her in Church," Wayne Thompson's "The Letter" and "Soul Deep," and the occasional Chilton-penned nugget, such as "I Must Be the Devil." The group's heyday was brief—two years, tops—but their music remains a staple on oldies stations and has retained its vitality for over two decades. —*John Floyd*

● **Ultimate Box Tops** / 1988 / Warner Brothers 27611
Everything you need by this blue-eyed soul combo. Includes "The Letter," "Cry Like a Baby," and "Soul Deep." —*John Floyd*

Boyz II Men

b. , Philadelphia, PA
Group / Urban R&B
Under the guidance of Michael Bivins of Bell Biv Devoe, the five-man vocal group Boyz II Men became a pop sensation in 1992. Although they call their music hip-hop doo-wop, there's very little doo-wop in their music. Instead, they bring the sound of traditional R&B vocal groups into the '90s, adding a little new jack swing to that timeless sound. Their 1991 debut, *Cooleyhighharmoney,* featured a massive hit single, "Motownphilly," which exemplifies the best of their dance work. Their second single, a ballad called "It's So Hard to Say Goodbye," was an even bigger hit. Its success paved the way for "The End of the Road" (taken from the *Boomerang* soundtrack), the group's follow-up single which broke Elvis Presley's record for the most weeks spent at number one. After releasing a Christmas album in 1993, Boyz II Men went to work on their second album. — *Stephen Thomas Erlewine*

● **Cooleyhighharmony** / 1991 / Motown 6320
Bell Biv Devoe vocalist Michael Bivins entered a new arena in the late '80s when he discovered and then became the manager for Boyz II Men, a quartet of Philadelphia high schoolers. Wanya Morris, Michael McCary, Shawn Stockman, and Nathan Morris's retro sound dominated the 1991 pop and R&B marketplaces, with their singles "It's So Hard to Say Goodbye to Yesterday" and "Motownphilly" hitting the Top Ten on both charts. The album eventually sold over five million copies, and put Boyz II Men at the forefront of a movement returning the emphasis to black popular music to vocal harmonies and a cappella interaction. —*Ron Wynn*

Billy Bragg

b. Dec. 20, 1957, Barking, Essex, England
Vocals, guitar / Singer/songwriter
At home with both socialist-geared political dogma and heartbroken love songs, Bragg has blended the one-man-and-a-guitar attack of early Dylan with the passion and big-rock attitude of the Clash and the Jam. His thick British accent may be the reason his clever Costello-esque work hasn't made it big in the States. — *John Floyd*

○ **Talking with the Taxman about Poetry** / 1986 / Elektra 60502
Bragg's one-man approach is fleshed out on *Talking with the Taxman about Poetry,* his second LP. "Levi Stubb's Tears" and "The Marriage" include subtle percussion and horn flourishes, and "Greetings to the New Brunette" is cushioned in layers of overdubbed acoustic guitars. These make it Bragg's most satisfying album musically, but the witty, plaintive songs listed above—in addition to "Ideology" and "The Warmest Room"—make it a stirring and evocative lyrical statement as well. —*John Floyd*

● **Back to Basics** / 1987 / Elektra 60726
This disc brings together Bragg's first three releases (*Life's a Riot with Spy vs. Spy, Brewing Up with Billy Bragg,* and the *Between the Wars* EP) and offers the best introduction to his confessional songwriting and uncompromising politics. Highlights include "A New England," "The Busy Girl Buys Beauty," and "A Lover Sings." —*John Floyd*

Help Save the Youth of America E.P.—Live & Dubious / 1988 / Elektra 60787
An exceptional album. —*Chip Renner*

Workers Playtime / 1988 / Elektra 60824
Bragg's first attempt at working with a full band could be better; most of the songs are mopey and depressing, and some of his socialist manifestos are tiresome and dogmatic. Still, cuts like "She's Got a New Spell," "Must I Paint You a Picture," and "Little Time Bomb" are excellent, and "Waiting for the Great Leap Forward" is a humble and humorous explanation of Bragg's motives and intentions, both political and emotional. —*John Floyd*

○ **Don't Try This at Home** / 1991 / Elektra 61121
With full-blown production by the likes of Johnny Marr and with musical assistance from R.E.M., this would seem like a blatant stab at the postmodern marketplace. Maybe so, but the thrust of his band turns "Accident Waiting to Happen" and "North Sea Bubble" into throttling rockers and makes "Sexuality" his best single. There are also several gorgeous ballads, "Tank Park Salute" and "Wish You Were Here" among them. —*John Floyd*

Peel Sessions Album / May 1992 / Dutch East India 8120
Because Bragg started his career as a solo act, these live-in-the-studio radio transcriptions don't offer anything you can't find on *Back to Basics.* But fanatics will enjoy the occasional lyric deviations, and "A13 Trunk Road to the Sea" (a rewrite of "Route 66" with British directions) is a keeper. —*John Floyd*

Laura Branigan

b. Jul. 3, 1957, Brewster, NY
Vocals / Pop/rock
Laura Branigan is a singer and, increasingly, an actress from Brewster, NY, who first gained notice when she became a backup singer for Leonard Cohen in 1977. Branigan achieved considerable popular success in the early '80s by applying her big, powerful voice to translated versions of Euro-disco hits. She was less successful with subsequent recordings in the second half of the '80s, though by then she had begun to appear on television and in films. —*William Ruhlmann*

● **Laura Branigan** / 1982 / Atlantic 82086
Branigan's big, expressive voice is the draw here, placed in dramatic musical settings that show it off to best advantage, especially on "Gloria," her breakthrough hit and stirring pop performance. —*William Ruhlmann*

Branigan 2 / 1983 / Atlantic 80052
"Solitaire" is the inevitable "Gloria" follow-up, but the album also shows unusual range, including a version of the Who's "Squeeze Box" and the dramatic ballad "How Am I Supposed to Live Without You," which was a minor hit for Branigan and a much bigger hit a few years later for Michael Bolton. —*William Ruhlmann*

Toni Braxton

Vocals / Urban R&B
Toni Braxton made her vocal debut with the single "Love Shoulda Brought You Home" from the *Boomerang* soundtrack. She issued her full-length debut in 1993, and it soared to the top of both the pop and R&B charts. Braxton eventually earned two Grammies and two Soul Train awards, saw her album go platinum, and also reaped both critical and commercial plaudits for such singles as "Love Shoulda Brought You Home" and "Just Another Sad Love Song." —*Ron Wynn*

● **Toni Braxton** / 1993 / LaFace
Toni Braxton's both an elegant songstress and an earthy one. She nicely balances those seemingly divergent sentiments on her self-titled debut disc. Braxton's husky, enticing voice sounds hypnotic on "Breathe Again," dismayed on "Another Sad Love Song," and disillusioned on "Love Shoulda Brought You Home." But she's never out of control, indignant, or so anguished and hurt she fails to retain her dignity. It's a sign of how great the Babyface/L.A. Reid production team was that they kept Braxton's approach divided without sacrificing focus or style. —*Ron Wynn*

Bread

Group / Pop
Bread produced an impressive string of ultra-light pop hits from 1970 to 1976, ten of which were Top-20 pop. In spite of their rather syrupy constitution, Bread had a knack for highly crafted melodies that possessed memorable hooks. "It Don't Matter to Me," with its multiple key and time-signature changes, is a tour

de force in that genre. David Gates, the writer for all their hits, delivered the goods vocally with a silky tenor that had heart. —*Rick Clark*

● **Anthology** / 1985 / Elektra 60414
"Make It with You," "If," "Baby I'm-a Want You," and many other fine-tuned pop gems. —*Dan Heilman*

The Breeders

Group / Alternative pop/rock
Initially, the Breeders were conceived as a way for Pixies' bassist Kim Deal and Throwing Muses' guitarist Tanya Donnely to let out some surpressed creative energy. Deal and Donnely both played guitar, leaving bass for Josephine Wiggs of Perfect Disaster. Taking their name from the group Deal led with her twin sister, Kelly, in their teens, the Breeders combined the spareness of Throwing Muses with the shifting dynamics and warped pop sensibilities of the Pixies. *Pod*, their critically acclaimed debut album, was released in 1990. Two years later, the group delivered *Safari*, a four-song EP that found the band getting more muscular and melodic. Soon after its recording, Donnely left the Breeders to form her own group, Belly. Kim Deal brought in her sister, Kelly, as Donnely's replacement. By this time, their permanent drummer was Jim MacPherson, who was billed as Mike Hunt on *Safari*.

As the Breeders were working on their new album in the beginning of 1993, the Pixies split, leaving Kim Deal able to pursue the Breeders full-time. Released late in the summer of 1993, *Last Splash* was a hazier, more disjointed continuation of the hard pop of *Safari*. With the sonic collage of "Cannonball," the Breeders had a crossover hit that catapulted the group into stardom; within a year, the album had gone platinum and the band had a prime spot on 1994's Lollapalooza tour. —*Stephen Thomas Erlewine*

○ **Pod** / 1990 / Elektra 61331
At the time *Pod* was released, the Breeders were just a side project for Kim Deal and Tanya Donnely, yet the album was much richer than most one-shot records. Taking a little from both the Pixies and Throwing Muses, the Breeders invent a indie-rock style of their own—a sparse, dreamy, elliptical take on guitar pop. While *Pod* may rely on the sheer uniqueness of the band's spare, raw sound, the album wouldn't be nearly as successful if it wasn't for the band's exceptional songwriting. From the wonderful, slow guitar grind of "Glorious" and "Iris" to the stripped-down pop of "Doe" and "Iris," *Pod* is full of original guitar-pop pleasures. —*Stephen Thomas Erlewine*

○ **Safari** / 1992 / Elektra 66432
Only four songs, but it shows that the Breeders continue to improve, with their sound growing more muscular and melodic. All of the songs on the EP, especially "Do You Love Me Now" and a cover of the Who's "So Sad about Us," equal the best on *Pod*. —*Stephen Thomas Erlewine*

● **Last Splash** / 1993 / Elektra
Falling halfway between the adventurous *Pod* and the magnificent heavy guitar-pop of *Safari*, *Last Splash* is ultimately a disappointing second album from the Breeders. On their first album, the band's simple, stripped-down approach sounded fresh. Nearly half of the Breeders' second album is filled with song fragments and incomplete songs that *sound* unfinished—rather than vital, messy garage rock from inspired amateurs, they sound lazy. However, there is no denying that when *Last Splash* is good, it's splendid. From the thrilling sonic collage of "Cannonball" to the more traditional pop melodies of "Invisible Man," "I Just Wanna Get Along," "Divine Hammer," and "Drivin' on 9," the best moments on the album are truly terrific, making the underdeveloped "No Aloha," "Hag," "Mad Lucas," "Roi," and the inferior re-recording of "Do You Love Me Now?" all the more infuriating. —*Stephen Thomas Erlewine*

Edie Brickell

b. , Oak Cliff, Dallas, TX
Vocals / Pop/rock, folk rock
Edie Brickell was born around 1966 in the Oak Cliff section of Dallas. She attended Southern Methodist University for a year and a half before drinking up enough courage in a bar one night in 1985 to get up onstage with a local band, the New Bohemians. She joined the band and wrote songs over the next year as the band changed and evolved. They finally settled on the personnel

of Brad Houser (bass), Kenny Withrow (guitar), and Matt Chamberlain (drums), before taking off for Rockfield Studios in Wales to record their debut album.

That album, *Shooting Rubberbands at the Stars*, revealed Brickell to be a songwriter with a unique perspective and a singer with an intimate, conversational style. The album was hailed by critics and became a massive hit, selling over a million copies and producing the Top Ten hit "What I Am."

After the disappointing performance of their follow-up album, *Ghost of a Dog*, the New Bohemians disbanded. Brickell married Paul Simon and the couple had a child. After several years of remaining artistically quiet, Brickell released her first solo album in late summer 1994. —*William Ruhlmann*

● **Shooting Rubber Bands at the Stars** / 1989 / David Geffen Co. 24192
Lead singer Brickell is charmingly unique on this album of light pop with thoughtful lyrics. Featuring the hit "What I Am." —*Donna DiChario*

Ghost of a Dog / 1990 / David Geffen Co. 24304
An overlooked follow-up that found Brickell expanding on her offbeat vocals. —*Donna DiChario*

Brinsley Schwarz

Group / Rock & roll
Although they were one of England's best and most important bands of the early '70s, Brinsley Schwarz was forever haunted by a well-intentioned, but disasterous, publicity stunt. To promote their first album, the band flew nearly all of the British press, as well as many other journalists, to New York to witness their bottom-of-the-bill showcase gig at the Fillmore East. The problems began when three members of the band were denied work visas until the day of the show. On their way to New York, the reporters were grounded for four hours. Once the press got to the Fillmore, their seats had been taken. Some journalists stayed; some got kicked out after they complained; some went back to the hotel. In any case, they were more than happy to pan Brinsley Schwarz in print once they got back home. Consequently, the group's first album was a commercial failure.

The band decided to regroup by renting a house outside of London and rehearsing for 18 months straight. It was here that the band developed their Byrds-fixated sound into a distinctive, laid-back rock that derived equally from country, R&B, and rock. Bassist and vocalist Nick Lowe became a first-rate songwriter, capable of gorgeous ballads and witty, melodic pop songs. After finding an American band playing a pub called Tally Ho in the summer of 1972, the band decided that pubs provided the perfect, relaxed atomosphere for their music. Brinsley Schwarz became regulars at Tally Ho and persuaded many other pub owners to open their doors for their band.

Brinsley Schwarz soon gained a devoted following. Within a year they were opening for Wings' first British tour. Numerous other bands, including Dr. Feelgood, began playing the same pub circuit as the Brinsleys—the same venues where punk rock was born several years later. Without Brinsley Schwarz, the punk movement would have been very different. At a time when rock & roll was overwhlemingly pompous, the Brinsleys were modest and unpretentious. They played relaxed, rootsy music, and they proved to English pub owners that it was profitable to book left-of-center acts. Without this precedent, the punks would have had nowhere to play.

After releasing six albums, Brinsley Schwarz split up in 1975. Guitarist Brinsley Schwarz and keyboardist Bob Andrews became members of Graham Parker's backing band, the Rumour; Lowe became a successful solo artist and producer in his own right. Over 20 years later, the band's music still sounds splendid and it is still underappreciated. —*Stephen Thomas Erlewine*

Brinsley Schwarz / 1970 / Capitol 11869
A fine country-rock debut that was unfairly panned upon its release, *Brinsley Schwarz* still sounds fresh today. —*Stephen Thomas Erlewine*

Despite It All / 1970 / Liberty 83427
Brinsley Schwarz's second album shows substantial growth, in both the band's playing and Nick Lowe's songwriting. —*Stephen Thomas Erlewine*

○ **Silver Pistol** / 1972 / Edsel 190

Silver Pistol, the band's first consistently entertaining record, is filled with brilliant reconstructions of American country, folk, and rock & roll, featuring excellent songs by both Nick Lowe and Ian Gomm, as well as two covers of Jim Ford songs—"Niki Hoeke Speedway" and "Ju Ju Man." —*Stephen Thomas Erlewine*

○ **Nervous on the Road** / 1972 / United Artists 5647
An even better collection than *Silver Pistol, Nervous on the Road* is an expertly played and superbly written set of country-rock and laidback rock & roll. On the surface it seems all pleasant and gentle, but dig a little deeper and you'll find Nick Lowe slyly subverting the conventions of the genre with his sharp sense of humor. —*Stephen Thomas Erlewine*

○ **Please Don't Ever Change** / 1973 / Edsel 237
Brinsley Schwarz's fifth album is another fine set of exceptional originals and clever covers, all superbly played by the well-seasoned band. —*Stephen Thomas Erlewine*

○ **New Favourites** / 1974 / United Artists 29641
With their final album, Brinsley Schwarz turn in their most pop-oriented record, filled with infectious gems like "The Ugly Things," "Trying to Live My Life Without You," and "(What's So Funny 'bout) Peace, Love, and Understanding." Lowe's songs are the best he had ever written and show that his ambitions were beginning to conflict with those of the rest of the band. Nevertheless, there's not a weak song or uninspired performance on *New Favourites*, making it an excellent farewell album. —*Stephen Thomas Erlewine*

★ **Surrender to the Rhythm** / 1991 / EMI
A terrific sampler of many of Brinsley Schwarz's finest tracks, *Surrender to the Rhythm* is the perfect introduction to this highly underrated band. —*Stephen Thomas Erlewine*

The Brothers Johnson

b. , Los Angeles, CA
Group / Soul, funk, pop/rock
Guitarist/vocalist George Johnson and bassist/vocalist Louis Johnson formed the band Johnson Three Plus One with older brother Tommy and their cousin Alex Weir while attending school in Los Angeles. When they became professionals, the band backed such touring R&B acts as Bobby Womack and the Supremes. Quincy Jones hired them to play on his *Mellow Madness,* and recorded four of their songs, including "Is It Love That We're Missing" and "Just a Taste of Me." Jones took them on a Japanese tour, then produced their debut LP, *Look Out for No. 1.* They scored a number-one R&B and number-three pop hit with "I'll Be Good to You," and enjoyed R&B chart toppers in 1977 and 1980 respectively with "Strawberry Letter 23" and "Stomp!"

The Brothers earned platinum records for *Look Out for Number 1* and *Right on Time.* Jones produced both of these, along with their third and fourth LPs, *Blam* and *Light Up the Night.* After their 1982 hit "Welcome to the Club," they started solo careers. Louis Johnson played bass on Michael Jackson's *Thriller* and recorded a gospel album, while George Johnson worked with Steve Arrington. Leon Sylvers produced their mid-'80s return LP *Out of Control;* it didn't equal their past success but got them another R&B hit with "You Keep Coming Back" in 1984. They recorded *Kickin* in 1988, and cowrote "Tomorrow" with Siedah Garrett for Jones's *Back on the Block* in 1989. —*Ron Wynn*

● **Classics, Vol. 11** / 1987 / A&M 2509
George and Louis Johnson began playing with Billy Preston's band in the '70s. Their performances on Quincy Jones's LP *Mellow Madness* thrust the duo into the spotlight in 1975, and their 1976 debut *Look Out for #1* launched a string of hit albums and singles that continued through 1980. That's the period covered by this anthology, which includes such hits as "I'll Be Good to You," "Stomp," and "Get the Funk out Ma Face." They were never more than functional singers, but their direct funk and party music made its mark. —*Ron Wynn*

Bobby Brown

b. Feb. 5, 1969
Vocals / Dance-pop, urban R&B
At the end of the '80s, former New Edition member Bobby Brown made the album that made new jack swing a dominant force not only on the urban charts but on the pop charts as well. Brown's first album, *King of the Stage,* wasn't that remarkable, but 1988's

Don't Be Cruel is the definitive new-jack album, thanks to the L.A. Reid and Babyface's massive production and songs, including the hits "Don't Be Cruel," "Every Little Step," and "Roni." In 1992, Brown released *Bobby,* a follow-up record that didn't have the commercial success of *Don't Be Cruel,* mainly because it lacked the focused songs and production that made that album such a huge success. In 1994, it was speculated that Brown was working with a reunited New Edition. —*Stephen Thomas Erlewine*

★ **Don't Be Cruel** / 1988 / MCA 42185
Ex-New Edition vocalist Brown released a dud debut in 1985, but his follow-up *Don't Be Cruel,* produced by new-jack kingpin Teddy Riley, was a monster hit and a brilliant statement of Brown's creative purpose. The title cut brought a level of sensitivity into new jack, and "My Prerogative" is one of the greatest dance-groove anthems produced in the late '80s. And the man can smoke on the ballads. —*John Floyd*

● **Bobby** / 1992 / MCA 10417
Brown's follow-up to the groundbreaking *Don't Be Cruel* isn't as innovative or consistent as his previous album, but that doesn't mean it's without its charms; the singles "Humpin' Around," "Good Enough," and "Get Away" are strong and memorable, which almost makes the abundance of filler forgivable. —*Stephen Thomas Erlewine*

James Brown

b. May 3, 1928, Barnwell, SC
Vocals / R&B, soul, funk
When the smoke clears, James Brown will be seen as probably the most influential African-American singer of recent times. Certainly, he is preeminent in terms of chart placings, and his influence on today's Black music is beyond question—it's literally in the grooves, thanks to the magic of sampling.

Brown's career stretches across 40 years—35 or more as a recording artist—so it makes no sense to talk about his style, because it inevitably evolved. He knew something different from the beginning, though ("Please, Please, Please" was not an ordinary record for 1956). The difference was urgency; he went back beyond the gospel progressions of Ray Charles to primordial rhythms and wordless vocals. It was African-American music in the purest sense.

By the mid '60s, with hits like "Papa's Got a Brand New Bag" and "I Got You," Brown had ceased fooling with conventional R&B and had stopped trying to cross over into the pop market (as he had with "Prisoner of Love," for example). He found his groove and he turned it loose. The creative juices began to get a little watered down as the disco era dawned, but from the mid '60s to the mid '70s, James Brown was a force unto himself. Musically and politically, he was the dominant Black musician of the day, an importance that subsequent developments have only served to heighten. —*Colin Escott*

★ **Live at the Apollo** / 1963 / PolyGram 823001
An astonishing record of James and the Flames tearing the roof off the sucker at the mecca of R&B theatres, New York's Apollo. When King Records owner Syd Nathan refused to fund the recording, thinking it commercial folly, Brown single-mindedly proceeded anyway, paying for it out of his own pocket. He had been out on the road night after night for a while, and he knew that the alchemy that was part and parcel of a James Brown show was something no record had ever caught. Hit follows hit without a pause: "I'll Go Crazy," "Try Me," "Think," "Please Please Please," "I Don't Mind," "Night Train," and more. The affirmative screams and cries of the audience are something you've never experienced unless you've seen the Brown Revue in a Black theater. If you have, I need not say more; if you haven't, suffice it to say that this should be one of the very first records you ever own. —*Rob Bowman*

○ **Payback** / 1974 / PolyGram 517137
A superb funk album by James Brown, one of his '70s masterpieces. With its jutting horn charts, lyric hooks, repeated phrases, and striding bass line, the title cut was extremely influential, while Brown's trademark screams on the breaks—and the breaks themselves—were later sampled ad infinitum by various hip-hop groups. —*Ron Wynn*

○ **Roots of a Revolution** / 1984 / PolyGram 817304
A double-CD retrospective of 1956-1964 recordings that charts Brown's progress from doo-wop and Little Richard-influenced

R&B to the verge of his groundbreaking mid-'60s funk. Doesn't include his biggest hits of the era (which are found on *Star Time*), but these are by and large equally exciting. Many fine overlooked R&B hits and B-sides like "Shout and Shimmy," "I've Got Money," the gospel-influenced "Oh Baby Don't You Weep," and "Maybe the Last Time," which inspired the Rolling Stones' "The Last Time." —*Richie Unterberger*

○ **In the Jungle Groove** / 1986 / PolyGram 829624
An interesting anthology of leftover funk selections and items from the vast James Brown catalog. Several of these packages have been supplanted by recent Brown CD anthologies, but this one includes some good extended instrumental and vocal funk numbers that aren't on any of the boxed sets. —*Ron Wynn*

○ **James Brown's Funky People—Part 1** / Jan. 1988 / PolyGram 829417
James Brown the entrepreneur, writing and producing superlative slices of funk for various members of his revue. These two volumes include hits and great misses by Lyn Collins, Vicki Anderson, Marva Whitney, Maceo & the Macks, Bobby Byrd, Fred Wesley & the JB's, and so on. Part 1 highlights include Collins's powerhouse Top-Ten hit "Think (about It)" and the JB's first two hits, "Gimme Some More" and "Pass the Peas." —*Rob Bowman*

○ **James Brown's Funky People—Part 2** / Feb. 1988 / PolyGram 835857
More of the above, including Bobby Byrd's 1971 hits "I Know You Got Soul" and "Hot Pants—I'm Coming, Coming, I'm Coming." Delves into some more obscure tracks, such as Hank Ballard's "From the Love Side." —*Rob Bowman*

★ **20 All Time Greatest Hits** / 1991 / PolyGram 511326
A first-rate greatest-hits package that covers the essential soul singles and some of the funk-period material as well. —*Ron Wynn*

☆ **Star Time** / 1991 / PolyGram 849108
One of the great boxed sets of all time. Over four CDs, Brown's recorded legacy is traced from "Please Please Please" in 1956 through his 1984 duet with Afrika Bambaataa, "Unity Pt. 1." With 71 tunes in all, the set places the Number-one R&B artist ever in his proper perspective as the prime progenitor of funk, one of the architects of soul, and the godfather of rap. To have done any one of these things would have been a bid for immortality, having done all three makes him a god. Four CDs at once is virtually too rich for one sitting. The well-written liner notes provide three different perspectives on Brown's career. A cornerstone of any great collection. —*Rob Bowman*

○ **Love Power Peace** / 1992 / PolyGram 314513389
Live at the Apollo caught James Brown, the '50s gospel/R&B singer; *Love Power Peace —Live at the Olympia, Paris 1971* captures James the funkster. In the early '70s Brown turned up the funk, recording such litanies for Black America as "Ain't It Funky Now," "Sex Machine," "Give It Up or Turn It Loose," "Super Bad," "Get up, Get into It, Get Involved," and "Soul Power." They are all here, along with revved white-hot versions of the early- and middle-period classics. The ferocity of this band is nearly too much for the heart. —*Rob Bowman*

Greatest Hits of the Fourth Decade / 1992 / Scotti Brothers 7529
Collecting Brown's '80s hits that didn't make it on *Star Time*, *Greatest Hits of the Fourth Decade* shows that the decade was not among his most creatively fertile, even with the monster hit of "Living in America." Still, the disc does pick the best tracks from a dry period, making it a nice supplement to the box set. —*Stephen Thomas Erlewine*

○ **Soul Pride—Instrumental 1960-66** / 1993 / PolyGram 517845
Everyone knows how hot James Brown's bands were, but not everyone's aware that he and his sidemen recorded lots of instrumental sides in the '60s. Originally scattered haphazardly over many now-out-of-print singles and albums, *Soul Pride* brings together the best of this work into one cohesive and chronological package. These cuts are nearly equal in power to J.B.'s vocal performances. Not only does the band cook on most of these insinuating vamps, you can also hear the evolution of the man's sound from gritty R&B to tight-as-a-drum soul to freeform funk. Soul Brother Number One himself plays organ and adds unpredictable shouts and screams on most of these tracks, but the chief stars are sidemen like Maceo Parker, Fred Wesley, and Pee Wee Ellis, who broke new ground with their compulsive counterpoint riffs. This fiery two-disc, 36-track boxed set contains over two hours of music, as well as a few non-LP B-sides and previously unreleased tracks. —*Richie Unterberger*

Maxine Brown

b. , Kingstree, SC
Vocals / R&B, soul
An underrated '60s R&B chanteuse from New York responsible for the original "Oh No Not My Baby." With an early gospel background, Brown waxed her first secular hit, "All in My Mind," for the tiny Nomar label in 1960, and quickly encored with "Funny." Switching to Wand Records, Brown recorded some fine uptown-style R&B, including the charming and often-covered "Oh No Not My Baby" in 1964. Teamed with labelmate Chuck Jackson, Brown scored another hit the following year with a duet revival of Chris Kenner's "Something You Got." Brown later recorded for a variety of firms into the early '70s. —*Bill Dahl*

● **Oh No Not My Baby: The Best of Maxine Brown** / 1990 / Kent (uk)
This 28-song CD is undoubtedly the best compilation of this underrated soul singer's work, featuring many of her '60s singles and several tunes from the era that were unreleased until the '80s. This disc draws from her recordings for the Wand label between 1963 and 1967, when Brown was at her artistic peak. Of course, the hit title track is a highlight, but there are no clunkers in this excellent collection of overlooked '60s pop/soul, featuring the New York "uptown" production that also graced the records of fellow Wand/Scepter artists like Dionne Warwick and Chuck Jackson. —*Richie Unterberger*

○ **Golden Classics** / Collectables 5116
One of the underrated soul queens of the '60s. Smoldering vocals and uptown production. —*Bill Dahl*

Ruth Brown

b. Jan. 30, 1928, Portsmouth, Virginia
Vocals / R&B
Jazz/R&B Vocalist Ruth Brown was one of the early hitmakers for Atlantic, netting a slew of Black chart hits in the early '50s: "Teardrops from My Eyes," "5-10-15 Hours," and "Mama He Treats Your Daughter Mean." She has recorded prolifically over the years and enjoyed a comeback in the late '80s thanks to a successful Broadway show. —*John Floyd*

○ **Sweet Baby of Mine (1949-1956)** / 1987 / Route 66 16
Excellent collection covering blues and R&B songs Brown did prior to becoming huge hit artist for Atlantic in late '50s. These were R&B gems, but such artists as Patti Page and Georgia Gibbs were covering them for the White market and Brown was locked out until 1957. Nonetheless, she enjoyed 11 Top-Ten R&B hits, contained on this anthology. —*Ron Wynn*

★ **Miss Rhythm** / 1989 / Rhino 82061
This two-disc set contains all the highly influential early-'50s smashes by this legendary R&B vocalist. Great support from Atlantic's studio aces, including saxophonists Willis Jackson and King Curtis. —*Bill Dahl*

○ **Blues on Broadway** / Jun. 12, 1989-Jun. 13, 1989 / Fantasy 9662
A classy and at times autobiographical session featuring the great jazz, blues, and R&B vocalist Ruth Brown. Since her "comeback," Brown has mainly stuck to the songs she recorded in the pre-Atlantic R&B years, and this set is no different. —*Ron Wynn*

Jackson Browne

b. Oct. 9, 1948, Heidelberg, Germany
Vocals, guitar / Singer/songwriter
As one of the guiding lights from the sensitive 70s singer/songwriter school of pop, Jackson Browne (along with Joni Mitchell) gave the word "introspection" new meaning with his earnest musical epistles from the inside. Like Mitchell and James Taylor (somewhat), Browne provided a weighty soundtrack for scores of apprehensive 60s kids who were trying to come to grips with growing up and finding their place in the world.

Without a doubt, his first four albums are loaded with gems, even if his melodies tend to have a sameness. Browne has always attracted stellar sidemen for his records, many of whom can also be found on records by Linda Ronstadt and James Taylor.

During his career, Browne has proven himself to be a very capable producer for Warren Zevon and Greg Copeland.

Hardcore Browne fanatics will claim their hero ceased to perform to their expectations after his million-selling 1977 opus *The Pretender*, but, his greatest commercial success took place from that album on. Granted, his highest charting single, the lightweight #4 hit, "Somebody's Baby," was quite a departure from his previous work, but maybe Browne needed a breather.

In 1982 Browne's California rock/pop phase ended and he returned with the more topical *Lawyers in Love*, which produced a hit with the title track. Subsequent albums have increasingly addressed global issues over the self-absorbed ruminations of his earlier work. Browne returned to a more introspective style of songwriting with his 1993 album, *I'm Alive*. —*Rick Clark*

☆ **Jackson Browne** / 1972 / Asylum 5051
Jackson Browne's debut album was the accomplished work of a veteran singer/songwriter who'd been kicking around the music business for years. Its songcraft is extremely well developed, and Browne comes off as the kind of wordsmith who never has to strain for a rhyme or limit his imagination to his verbal facility. "Doctor My Eyes," the album's hit, is full of wordplay from the title on, and it's typical. Browne sings in a warm, conversational voice, and his music suggests rock without really working up a sweat. —*William Ruhlmann*

○ **For Everyman** / 1973 / Asylum 5067
This is a less consistent collection than the debut. Some of its songs are examples of promising juvenilia ("These Days"), were originally written for others ("Take It Easy"), or are somewhat coy ("Ready or Not"). Nevertheless, there is the stunning title track, and Browne's overall songwriting ability remains impressive. —*William Ruhlmann*

☆ **Late for the Sky** / 1974 / Asylum 1017
This album is both a reconfirmation of Browne's ability to make words do whatever he wants and something of a musical dead end—people who think all Browne's songs sound alike are thinking of this record. People who think of him as a profound pessimist are too, what with another death song, "Fountain of Sorrow," and another apocalypse song, "Before the Deluge," to add to the Browne collection. But "The Late Show" is his best-realized love song yet, and even if he is a doom-monger, he's so good at it! —*William Ruhlmann*

○ **Pretender** / 1976 / Asylum 107
Browne turns to Bruce Springsteen's producer, Jon Landau, and is rewarded with his best-recorded album, on which he seeks a way out of the gloom in such songs as "The Fuse"— though there may be no more cynical view of middle-class suburban life than the album's title track. —*William Ruhlmann*

★ **Running on Empty** / 1977 / Asylum 113
On the surface, this is the album for anyone who ever had the urge to say, "Hey, Jackson, lighten up." It's a live album of previously unrecorded songs, several of them covers or co-compositions. Its overriding theme is life on the road, but, as the title track suggests, even that life is no more than a temporary escape—and the equally famous medley "The Load-Out/Stay" tells us that the singer wants to stay onstage rather than face life off of it. —*William Ruhlmann*

Lawyers in Love / 1983 / Asylum 60268
After managing to sound romantically mawkish on 1980's *Hold Out*, Browne returned with this album. It showed he has a weird sense of humor when he puts his mind to it. —*William Ruhlmann*

Lives in the Balance / 1986 / Asylum 60457
Enraged by the right-wing Reagan era, Browne puts his heart where his brain should be and starts singing songs like"For America." Even if you agree with his politics, this is strained. "In the Shape of a Heart" shows he can still write an intelligent love song when he tries, though. —*William Ruhlmann*

I'm Alive / Oct. 1993 / Asylum 61524
After several years of doggedly political releases, Browne moves back to the personal territtory of his earlier records with *I'm Alive*. Reportedly inspired by his breakup with Daryl Hannah, *I'm Alive* is a sorrowful song cycle of heartbreak, easily conjuring up the ghosts of *Late for the Sky* and *Jackson Browne*. Even if it is familiar ground, Browne does this music remarkably well, and at its best the album is quite moving. —*Stephen Thomas Erlewine*

Brownsville Station

Group / Rock & roll
A Detroit-area rock & roll band formed in 1969 by guitarist Cub Koda. Original members also included Mike Lutz (guitar), T. J. Cronley (drums), and Tony Driggins (bass). Initially influenced by Chuck Berry, Bo Diddley, Jerry Lee Lewis, and other '50s rockers, their early albums included inspired covers and genre-faithful originals, all presented in Marshall stack, double-bass-drum bigness. Far more effective as a live act (with Koda's onstage banter influencing everyone from J. Geils's Peter Wolf to Alice Cooper), the group finally hit paydirt in late 1973 with their number-three hit, the Koda-penned "Smokin' in the Boy's Room." After disbanding the group in 1979, Koda went on to a career as a solo recording artist and as a journalist for several music magazines. —*Stephen Thomas Erlewine*

○ **No B. S.** / 1970 / Warner Brothers 1888
Their debut album, featuring pedal-to-the-metal renditions of "Road Runner," "Rumble," and "Be Bop Confidential." —*Stephen Thomas Erlewine*

Brownsville Station / 1977 / Private Stock 2026
Their next-to-last album, featuring the cult favorite "The Martian Boogie." —*Stephen Thomas Erlewine*

● **Smoking in the Boy's Room: The Best of Brownsville Station** / 1993 / Rhino 71456
A roaring romp through Brownsville Station's back pages compiled by Cub Koda himself, *Smokin' in the Boy's Room* makes a convincing case that these Ann Arbor, Michigan garage punks were one of the most underrated rock & rollers of the '70s. —*Stephen Thomas Erlewine*

Jack Bruce (John Symon Asher Bruce)

b. May 14, 1943, Glasgow, Scotland
Vocals, bass / Progressive rock
In the pantheon of great rock bassists, Jack Bruce certainly stands tall. His forceful yet elastic technique and his trademark wide tonality and phrasing are utterly unique. As a rock bassist, Bruce incorporated a jazz sensibility by giving the instrument freedom to voice itself beyond merely holding down the pulse with the drummer.

Along with Eric Clapton (guitar, vocals) and Ginger Baker (percussion), Bruce pioneered the hard-rock trio concept, complete with extended free-for-all jams. Bruce has also done exemplary work with the Tony Williams Lifetime, Alexis Korner, the Graham Bond Organization, John Mayall's Bluesbreakers, Carla Bley, Robin Trower, Frank Zappa, West, Bruce & Laing, and the Golden Palominos.

Bruce, with cowriter Pete Brown, penned most of Cream's biggest numbers. As a solo singer/songwriter, Bruce integrated an eclectic sampling of music, ranging from folk to classical overtones to jazz/rock fusion, all focused through a rather impenetrable arty filter. —*Rick Clark*

○ **Songs for a Tailor** / 1969 / PolyGram 835242
There's not a weak song on this first and most accessible solo album. "Theme for an Imaginary Western" (also made popular by Mountain) is one of the finest songs Bruce has ever recorded. Musically, this is more subdued and keyboard-oriented than Bruce's work with Cream. —*Rick Clark*

Harmony Row / 1971 / Atco 365
Bruce's third effort is a much more challenging listen, possessing more complicated arrangements and impenetrable lyrics than *Songs for a Tailor*. Among the album's many highlights is the aggressive multi-time signature rock of "You Burned the Tables on Me" and the haunting "Victoria Sage." —*Rick Clark*

● **Willpower: A Twenty-Year Retrospective** / 1989 / PolyGram 837806
Willpower is a well-compiled overview of Bruce's entire solo output, with choice unreleased tracks. This is the place to start if you are budgeting one disc of his music for your collection. Otherwise, get *Songs for a Tailor*. —*Rick Clark*

○ **Somethin' Els** / 1993 / CMP 1001
Reunited with long-time collaborator Pete Brown, Jack Bruce turns in one of the finest albums of his solo career, with songs that come close to matching the splendor of his work with Cream. —*Stephen Thomas Erlewine*

Peabo Bryson

b. Apr. 13, 1951, Greenville, South Carolina
Vocals / Urban R&B

Vocalist Peabo Bryson was among the premier silky-voiced soul artists who emerged as the softer, more sophisticated urban contemporary sound became dominant in the '70s and '80s. Bryson, who was born in Greenville, South Carolina, sang with Al Freeman & the Upsetters in 1965, and was in the group Moses Dillard & the Tex-Town Display from 1968 to 1973. He was a producer and composer for Atlanta's Bang Records in the early '70s, and sang in Michael Zager's Moon Band.

Bryson recorded several singles and his self-titled debut album for Bang's subsidiary company Bullet, among them "Do It with Feeling," "Undergroud Music," "It's Just a Matter of Time," "Just Another Day," and "I Can Make It Better." All were moderate R&B hits. Bryson moved to Capitol in 1978 His first album there, *Reaching for the Sky*, went gold, and the title track was a number-six R&B hit. He remained in the Moon Band until 1979, departing after "I'm So into You" spent two weeks as the nation's number-two R&B hit in 1978. Bryson has continued a prolific career as both a lead act and duet partner. He has made hit duets with Natalie Cole, Roberta Flack, Melissa Manchester, and Regina Belle. Bryson recorded for Capitol until 1984, when he switched to Elektra, and enjoyed more success with "If Ever You're in My Arms Again." He moved to Columbia in 1991, releasing *Can You Stop the Rain*. —*Ron Wynn*

● **Collection** / 1984 / Capitol 46071
A best-of-covering Bryson's Capitol years, 1978-1983, much of it given over to his collaboration with Roberta Flack, including the hits "Tonight, I Celebrate My Love" and "You're Lookin' Like Love to Me." —*William Ruhlmann*

All My Love / 1989 / Capitol 90641
Peabo Bryson switched labels in 1989, returning to Capitol, the place he'd enjoyed his greatest success in the late '70s and early '80s. The results were both immediate and satisfying. This album was not only one of his strongest in many years, but such songs as "Show and Tell" and "Palm of Your Hand" got widespread urban contemporary airplay, and D'Atra Hicks got a career boost from doing a duet with Bryson on the album. —*Ron Wynn*

Roy Buchanan

b. Sep. 23, 1939, Ozark, Alabama, **d.** Aug. 14, 1986
Guitar / Blues-rock

Buchanan's reputation as a hot-shot guitarist extends back to the beginnings of rock & roll itself. On the road and recording with Dale Hawkins by his teens, Buchanan became the law of the land around the Washington D.C., area by the mid to late '60s. His use of the Fender Telecaster, using high harmonic squeals in place of feedback and distortion, was part and parcel of rock guitar's vocabulary by the early '70s. A reluctant superstar, Buchanan's later work became more unfocused as his career waned, but his unique stylings remain etched into his best records.

Buchanan was on the verge of a comeback in 1986 when he hung himself in a police cell, after being arrested on a drunk-driving charge. He left behind a number of records that testify to the fact that he was a consummate guitarist, capable of tones and techniques that other guitarists only dream of. —*Cub Koda*

○ **Roy Buchanan** / 1972 / PolyGram 831413
His debut album, with a skunk-hot stage band. Buchanan's guitar sizzles on tracks like "Haunted House," "Sweet Dreams," and "The Messiah Will Come Again." —*Cub Koda*

Second Album / 1973 / PolyGram 831412
More blues-based than his debut, with great stretched-out jams showcasing some of his best playing. —*Cub Koda*

That's What I'm Here For / Apr. 1974 / PolyGram 831837
Excellent blues-rock guitar, including the riveting Hendrix tribute "Hey Joe." —*David Szatmary*

○ **Livestock** / 1975 / PolyGram 831414
Brilliant live blues-rock guitar by the legend who turned down the Rolling Stones. A must for guitar-hero fans. —*David Szatmary*

When a Guitar Plays the Blues / 1986 / Alligator 4741
An excellent example of this blues-rock guitar virtuoso's later work. —*David Szatmary*

● **Sweet Dreams: The Anthology** / 1992 / PolyGram 517086

Over two CDs, *Sweet Dreams* collects the finest moments from Buchanan's '70s albums, including nine unreleased tracks. As a career retrospective, it's the finest collection available. —*Stephen Thomas Erlewine*

Lindsey Buckingham

b. Oct. 3, 1948, Palo Alto, California
Vocals, guitar / Pop/rock

Before he joined Fleetwood Mac, Lindsey Buckingham was sketching out his brand of Brian Wilson-influenced pop with Stevie Nicks in the folkie duo Buckingham/Nicks. Mick Fleetwood invited the duo to join his band in late 1974. After Buckingham joined, the band's pop tendencies flowered under his direction. Not only did he provide the group with some brilliant, surprisingly dark pop songs, he sharpened the other members' songs with his production, arrangements, and breathtaking guitar. Buckingham left the band after their 1987 album, *Tango in the Night*, to concentrate on his solo work.

While Buckingham's solo albums are deceptively simple and calm on the surface, there are a great deal of complex arrangements and emotions beneath the smooth production. None of them have sold anything approaching the level of *Rumours*—or even *Tango in the Night*— yet they are rich, layered pop albums. His first solo record, *Law & Order*, had a hit single with "Trouble." —*Stephen Thomas Erlewine*

○ **Law & Order** / 1981 / Warner Brothers 561
Buckingham's studio mastery is placed in the service of a collection of carefully arranged pop confections not unlike the work he was doing with Fleetwood Mac at the time. A good example is the haunting "Trouble," a Top-Ten hit. —*William Ruhlmann*

Go Insane / 1984 / Warner Brothers 60363
Buckingham's second solo album is as experimental as Fleetwood Mac's *Tusk*, only with more elliptical hooks and melodies. —*Stephen Thomas Erlewine*

● **Out of the Cradle** / Jun. 16, 1992 / Warner Brothers 26182
From the world beat tinges of "Don't Look Down" to an instrumental cover of "This Was Nearly Mine" from the musical *South Pacific*, from the paranoid dance rhythms of "Wrong" to the moody ballad "Street of Dreams," Buckingham has enough successful stops to please most listeners. "Countdown" is classic Buckingham pop fused to a squealing guitar solo that complements the song's building climax. Likewise the disc's most inventive number, "This Is the Time," which alternates sombre, acoustic verses with psychotic, power-chording choruses. —*Roch Parisien*

The Buckinghams

Group / Pop/rock

Popular attractions while still in high school, the Chicago quintet changed its name from the Pulsations to the Buckinghams to reflect the British-invasion craze and signed with Chicago's USA Records in 1966. Backing Dennis Tufano's buoyant lead vocals with prominent harmonies and punchy soul-styled brass, the group came across the wistful "Kind of a Drag," and in short order, the Buckinghams had a million-selling pop chart-topper on their hands. They quickly graduated to recording for Columbia.

As long as songwriter Jim Holvay supplied more material of the same high quality as "Kind of a Drag," the Buckinghams were sitting pretty. Holvay cowrote "Don't You Care," "Hey Baby (They're Playing Our Song)," and the pseudo-psychedelic "Susan," and they all proved to be major hits for the band. The group's R&B roots surfaced on a vocal adaptation of Cannonball Adderley's jazz standard "Mercy, Mercy, Mercy," their second-biggest hit.

But the Buckinghams' fortunes soon changed drastically—one of the top-selling rock groups of 1967, they managed only one hit after early 1968, and by 1970 the group was kaput. Two original members, guitarist Carl Giammarese and bassist Nick Fortuna, have since revived the Buckinghams for oldies tours. —*Bill Dahl*

● **Mercy Mercy Mercy (a Collection)** / 1991 / Columbia 47718
These mid-'60s hitmakers from Chicago hold up well with their neat blend of pop and soul. All of their hits and more can be found on this 18-song anthology. —*Jeff Tamarkin*

Tim Buckley

b. Feb. 14, 1947, Washington, D.C., **d.** Jun. 29, 1975

Vocals / Singer/songwriter

Tim Buckley's mournful wail, his synthesis of folk and jazz, and his haunting melodies seemed decidedly out of step with much of the music that was popular at the end of the '60s. Discovered by Frank Zappa manager Herb Cohen, Buckley was signed to Elektra, where he cut several albums. Two of his best from that period, *Goodbye and Hello* and *Happy Sad*, were produced by ex-Lovin' Spoonful Jerry Yester. In 1970 Buckley moved to Cohen's Straight Records and released *Blue Afternoon*, an album that lived up to its title.

Buckley dropped out after 1971's *Starsailor* and became a taxi driver and chauffeur for a while. He returned with a new direction on *Greetings from L. A.*, which featured a down-and-dirty collection of funk rock. In 1975, Buckley died of an accidental drug overdose, mistaking a mix of heroin and morphine for cocaine. — *Rick Clark*

Tim Buckley / 1966 / Asylum 61338

Buckley's 1966 debut was the most straightforward and folk-rock oriented of his albums. The material has a lyrical and melodic sophistication that was astounding for a 19-year-old. The pretty, almost precious songs are complemented by appropriately baroque, psychedelic-tinged production. Buckley was still firmly in the singer/songwriter camp on this album, showing only brief flashes of the experimental vocal flights, angst-ridden lyrics, and soul influences that would characterize much of his later work. It's not his most adventurous outing, but it's one of his most accessible and retains a fragile beauty. — *Richie Unterberger*

○ **Goodbye & Hello** / 1967 / Asylum 74028

With his second album, Buckley began exploring different sonic territory, adding exotic instruments and a distinct, winding jazz influence to his increasingly complex lyrics. — *Stephen Thomas Erlewine*

○ **Dream Letter—Live in London** / Jul. 1968 / Rhino 70361

A live double-disc set capturing Buckley's jazzy folk and passionate mega-octave vocal in fine form. Lee Underwood (guitar), David Friedman (vibes), and Danny Thompson (bass) provide empathic support. — *Rick Clark*

○ **Blue Afternoon** / 1969 / Rhino 70356

Buckley's atmospheric melancholy folk/jazz shines on the first four tracks: "Happy Time," "Chase the Blues Away," "I Must Have Been Blind," and "The River." Those tracks alone make this worth having. — *Rick Clark*

Happy/Sad / 1969 / Asylum 74045

Buckley began to turn toward softer, more introspective and slightly jazzy tunes on his third record. This album of six lengthy compositions features some of his loveliest songs, including "Strange Feelin'," "Sing a Song for You," and the exuberant 12-minute "Gypsy Woman." — *Richie Unterberger*

Lorca / 1970 / Asylum 61339

Buckley stunned and, to a rare degree, alienated fans with the dissonant, at times wearying avant-garde exercises in vocal gymnastics that took up the entire first side of this LP. Side 2 was far more accessible, though Buckley's fusion of folk instrumentation with jazzy improvisation on extended compositions continued to take him further away from his folk-rock roots. — *Richie Unterberger*

○ **Starsailor** / 1970 / Rhino 70360

After his beginnings as a gentle, melodic, baroque folk-rocker, Buckley gradually evolved into a downright experimental singer/songwriter who explored both jazz and avant-garde territory. *Starsailor* is the culmination of his experimentation, and alienated far more listeners than it exhilarated upon its release in 1970. With former Mother of Invention Bunk Gardner augmenting Buckley's group on sax and alto flute, Buckley applies vocal gymnastics to a set of material that's as avant-garde in its songwriting as in its execution. At his most anguished (which is often on this album), he sounds as if his liver is being torn out—slowly. Surrealistic lyrics, heavy on landscape imagery like rivers, skies, suns, and jungle fires top off a record that isn't for everybody, or even for every Buckley fan, but endures as one of the most uncompromising statements ever made by a singer/songwriter. — *Richie Unterberger*

Greetings from L.A. / 1972 / Bizarre 70359

A grittier rock approach supports Buckley's plunge into eroticism. Buckley's uncaged wailing plus his lyrical urgency convey a great deal of sexual tension and an absence of inner peace. Intense stuff—considered by many to be his best. — *Rick Clark*

Buffalo Springfield

b. , USA

Group / Rock & roll, folk-rock, country-rock

Few American groups have produced a wealth of talent like that of Buffalo Springfield. Over a 19-month period, during 1967 and 1968, Buffalo Springfield released three impressive albums. The second one, *Again*, is their masterpiece. In that brief time, they produced a handful of classics, among them "For What It's Worth" and "Bluebird." Buffalo Springfield possessed three strong songwriters (with distinctly different yet complementary styles) in Richie Furay, Stephen Stills, and Neil Young.

Even more than the Byrds, Buffalo Springfield's sound was undeniably American, drawing from rock, folk, and country. The intense clash of creative energies, however, finally caused the demise of the band in May of 1968. Stephen Stills went on to Crosby, Stills & Nash. Neil Young joined that group briefly for *Deja Vu*, then went on to pursue an erratic solo career with periods of great success and brilliant music. After Springfield, Jim Messina and Richie Furay founded the country-rock group Poco. After Poco, Messina recorded a string of hits during the '0s with Kenny Loggins, as Loggins & Messina. — *Rick Clark*

Buffalo Springfield / 1967 / Atco 33200

Their strong debut contains the Stephen Stills classic "For What It's Worth" and Neil Young's "Nowadays Clancy Can't Even Sing," "Sit Down I Think I Love You" and "Go and Say Goodbye" are also highlights. — *Rick Clark*

○ **Buffalo Springfield Again** / 1967 / Atco 33226

By far their best effort. Stills, Furay, and Young each contribute some great songs: the hits "Bluebird," "Mr. Soul," and "Rock & Roll Woman," plus standouts like "A Child's Claim to Fame," "Hung Upside Down," "Broken Arrow," "Everydays," and "Expecting to Fly." Essential stuff for any good rock & roll collection. — *Rick Clark*

Last Time Around / 1968 / Atco 90393

Their last album showcases a couple of gems in Furay's "Kind Woman" and Young's "On the Way Home." — *Rick Clark*

● **Best of Buffalo Springfield . . . Retrospective** / 1969 / Atco 38105

Best of Buffalo Springfield . . . Retrospective is a decent sampler for the uninitiated. Contains all their hits and some key album tracks, but it isn't comprehensive enough to be essential. — *Rick Clark*

Buffalo Tom

Group / Alternative pop/rock

When they released their first album in 1989, the Boston-based trio Buffalo Tom was written off as Dinosaur Jr. junior. Admittedly, their debut was in debt to J Mascis's thundering guitar and folk-tinged songs—it didn't help that Mascis produced the record, either. Over time, Buffalo Tom developed into one of the best straight-ahead rock groups of the early '90s, capable of throttling rockers and beautiful ballads.

Buffalo Tom began to define their loud folk-rock with their second album, *Birdbrain*. While they could still make a gigantic guitar noise, the songs were sharper, and the band began to rely on songwriting, not sound. In 1992, Buffalo Tom made an artistic breakthrough with *Let Me Come Over*, a gritty set of driving rock and achingly melancholy ballads; several of its tracks became alternative radio staples, including the gorgeous "Taillights Fade." Despite an increased amount of critical praise and some radio airplay, the album didn't sell. The follow-up, 1993's *Big Red Letter Day*, was even more accessible, without sacrificing the band's integrity; in fact, it proved that they deserved to break into the mainstream as much as Soul Asylum. Unfortunately, the album received only a small push from radio and MTV, leaving Buffalo Tom as one of the best and most underrated American rock & roll bands of the '90s. — *Stephen Thomas Erlewine*

○ **Birdbrain** / 1990 / Beggars Banquet 2434

A well-produced eccentric batch of underground rock, featuring "Sunflower Suit." — *Dan Heilman*

● **Let Me Come Over** / 1992 / RCA 61105

With *Let Me Come Over* Buffalo Tom came into their own, producing a remarkably strong album, filled with exceptional songwriting. The Dinosaur Jr. comparisons are no longer as strong—now the sound is mixed with R.E.M. and the Replacements. But that's just a starting point—the band has carved out their own brand of guitar-heavy rock & roll, somewhere between college rock and classic rock & roll. Buffalo Tom prove equally adept at pulling off the driving "Staples" and "Mountains of Your Head," the majestic folk-rock of "Mineral," the ballads "Larry," "Frozen Lake," and the gorgeous masterpiece "Taillights Fade." —*Stephen Thomas Erlewine*

○ **Big Red Letter Day** / 1993 / RCA
Following the excellent *Let Me Come Over*, *Big Red Letter Day* features a slightly more polished production, yet it doesn't diminish the band's increasingly powerful songwriting and forceful rock & roll. Buffalo Tom is America's best mainstream rock band that is still undeservedly stuck on the fringes, as *Big Red Letter Day* proves. —*Stephen Thomas Erlewine*

Jimmy Buffett

b. Dec. 25, 1946, Pascagoula, Mississippi
Vocals, songwriter / Country-rock, pop/rock
Buffett is a country-folk-pop singer/songwriter whose songs strongly reflect his Gulf Coast origins: beach bums, booze, sailing, hedonism, and sly humor. He has built up an enormous regional following of fans, who call themselves "Parrotheads." —*William Ruhlmann*

A White Sport Coat & a Pink Crustacean / 1973 / MCA 31090
Buffett was beginning to put in place his folk/rock/country sound and his laidback, humorous, hedonistic persona with this album, which features later concert favorites like "Why Don't We Get Drunk (and Screw)" and "Grapefruit—Juicy Fruit." —*William Ruhlmann*

A-1-A / 1974 / MCA 1590
A little hard-working for a beachcomber, Buffett released a second album in 1974. It was his most perfect evocation of noncareerist hedonism yet, even if its most telling song, "A Pirate Looks at Forty," was unusually thoughtful for a party animal. —*William Ruhlmann*

Living & Dying in 3/4 Time / 1974 / MCA 31059
Jimmy Buffett was already on the second edition of his Coral Reefer Band by the time his third album rolled around. He had also firmly established his Gulf Coast beach-bum/poet persona, but he hadn't written a classic song until "Come Monday," which put him, and the album, on the map. —*William Ruhlmann*

○ **Havana Daydreamin'** / 1976 / MCA 31093
Buffett's best overall collection of songs yet bears the influence of Steve Goodman, who wrote "This Hotel Room" and cowrote "Woman Goin' Crazy on Caroline Street." But a personal favorite is Buffett's own "My Head Hurts, My Feet Stink, and I Don't Love Jesus." —*William Ruhlmann*

○ **Changes in Latitudes, Changes in Attitudes** / 1977 / MCA 31070
Buffett's biggest all-time seller contains his biggest hit single, "Margaritaville." It's also a peak in terms of songwriting, both for the artist himself and in his covers of the work of Steve Goodman and Jesse Winchester, among others. Funny, wistful, and celebratory, the album is the definitive statement of Buffett's worldview. —*William Ruhlmann*

○ **Son of a Son of a Sailor** / 1978 / MCA 31091
If this album was a slight step down from its predecessor, it was almost equally successful commercially, and it contained its share of terrific material, notably the uptempo hit "Cheeseburger in Paradise" and one of Buffett's older songs, "Livingston Saturday Night." —*William Ruhlmann*

Last Mango in Paris / 1985 / MCA 31157
Buffett's rapid recording schedule tended to outrun his muse in the late '70s and early '80s, resulting in some uneven albums with occasional good songs. This time he came up with a far more consistent collection, including three entries on the country charts: "Gypsies in the Palace," "If the Phone Doesn't Ring, It's Me," and "Please Bypass This Heart." —*William Ruhlmann*

● **Songs You Know by Heart** / 1986 / MCA 5633
If anybody ever needed a compilation, it is Jimmy Buffett, who by this time had put out 14 studio albums in 15 years but only managed to accumulate a handful of memorable songs among them.

And just about all of them are here. Unless you're a Parrothead, this will be all you'll need of Jimmy Buffett. —*William Ruhlmann*

○ **Boats, Beaches, Bars & Ballads** / 1992 / MCA 10613
This four-CD, 72-track anthology is essential for Parrotheads who don't miss his concerts but aren't so hardcore that they have to own every single tiny Buffett ever released. Each disc revolves around a theme (Boats, Beaches, Bars, Ballads). All of his hits and popular album tracks are here, as well as some previously unreleased material. The box includes the *Parrothead Handbook*, a 64-page booklet that provides a well-assembled collection of photos, reflections from Buffett, and explanations of his songs. The sound on this set is first rate. —*Rick Clark*

Fruitcakes / 1994 / MCA
On his first new studio album in five years, Buffett starts out talking about an investment banker, an appropriate concern for this sun-bleached entrepreneur. Soon enough, the sprung Calypso rhythms kick in, and you can imagine the Parrotheads swaying and chuckling along, especially when Buffett indulges in the kind of comic raps common to his stage shows. He also covers the Grateful Dead's "Uncle John's Band," one more appropriation in his careful observation of that band's marketing plan. There's also a cover of the Kinks' "Sunny Afternoon," a wealthy man's lament, which is uncomfortably on target. But even with half a decade to come up with original material, Buffett hasn't gotten much to add to his usual sun-and-sand philosophy, and for all his millions he remains a pleasant, but distinctly minor, singer/songwriter. —*William Ruhlman*

Cindy Bullens

b. 1953
Vocals, songwriter / Pop/rock
A rock singer/songwriter who appeared in *Grease*, Cindy Bullens sang backup with Elton John before cutting three albums of her own. —*William Ruhlmann*

● **Desire Wire** / 1978 / United Artists 933
One of the great lost rock albums of the '70s, Bullen's debut release is full of tough, passionate, incredibly catchy rock & roll played to the hilt and sung with fire. Bullens followed it up with *Steal the Night*, in 1979, and ten years later with *Cindy Bullens*—and they're almost as good, though no one noticed. So life is unfair. Search those used-record stores for any of them. —*William Ruhlmann*

Sonny Burgess

b. 1931
Guitar / Rockabilly
Sonny Burgess is one of the wildest rockers to record for the legendary Sun label in Memphis. He and his band, the Pacers, came out of Newport, AR, with a hard-rocking style that, unlike that of most rockabillies, owed little to nothing in the way of a stylistic debt to country music. With his red-dyed hair, matching stage suit and guitar, and wild stage performances, Burgess and the Pacers made mincemeat of the competition on many of the early–'50s rock & roll package tours. Though his Sun releases never brought him much in the way of commercial success, Sonny's recordings nonetheless remain landmarks of the early rockabilly style. Currently touring and recording with other Memphis alumni in the Sun Rhythm Section, the rockin' flame that is Sonny Burgess refuses to be snuffed out. —*Cub Koda*

● **Classic Recordings 1956-1959** / Jul. 1991 / Bear Family 15525
Sonny's complete output for Sun spread over two CDs. Wild and crazed, featuring Burgess's spitfire guitar and booming vocals and the relentless drive of the Pacers in support. —*Cub Koda*

Solomon Burke

b. 1936, Philadelphia, PA
Vocals / Soul
Musically and corporeally imposing, Burke was almost as important as he says he was. His account of how he invented soul music is entertaining but fanciful, but even when SB's BS count is lowered, there is no doubt he was present at the creation of '60s soul music—and at least partially responsible for it.
Starting as Solomon the Boy Wonder Preacher, in Philadelphia, he had been recording for six years when he finally broke through with "Just out of Reach" in 1961. Burke's best recordings probably date from the early '60s, when he was working with

producer Bert Berns. Songs like "Cry to Me," "I'm Hanging Up My Heart for You," "Goodbye Baby," and "The Price" collectively formed the keynote address for soul music. Some of the arrangements sound unnecessarily ornamented today, but the passion Burke brought to those recordings was that of the Boy Wonder Preacher. Live, he's still impressive, as recent recordings attest. — *Colin Escott*

○ **Let Your Love Flow** / Shanachie 9202
Swamp Dogg produced an excellent late '70s soul session for the legendary Solomon Burke on the tiny Infinity label. Williams didn't aim for a slick or polished urban contemporary sound; instead he mixed upbeat numbers with a pronounced Afro-Latin beat and confessional country-soul tunes emphasizing Burke's trademark song sermons. The music was much too raw and rural for the psuedo-sophisticated big city radio set, but Southern soul loyalists treasured it. Shanachie gets high praises for reissuing the date but low marks for the horrendous misspelling of Burke's name all over the CD. — *Ron Wynn*

○ **Soul Alive!** / 1985 / Rounder 11521
Captures masterfully the intensity of Burke's sweaty and raucous stage show. — *John Floyd*

○ **A Change Is Gonna Come** / 1986 / Rounder 2053
Solomon Burke cut one of the great soul statements of the '80s for Rounder in 1985; it should be a revelation for anyone unaware of Burke's singing and performing zeal. The nine-cut disc included powerful versions of "When a Man Loves a Woman," "Love Buys Love," and the splendid title cut. The onetime boy preacher is unequalled in exploiting a lyric and building a song to a shattering climax. This was no nostalgia trip, but a contemporary soul journey that retains its appeal years after its initial release. — *Ron Wynn*

○ **You Can Run but You Can't Hide** / 1987 / Mr. R&B 108
You Can Run but You Can't Hide collects 20 tracks from Burke's formative years at Apollo, recorded between 1955 and 1959. The material tends to be more pop-oriented than his classic Atlantic sides, yet his singing is nearly as impressive as it is on his hits. — *Stephen Thomas Erlewine*

○ **Bishop Rides South** / 1988 / Charly 1187
When Burke left Atlantic, he signed with New York City's Bell Records. Bell wisely sent Solomon down to Muscle Shoals. Two 1969 hits, covers of "Uptight Good Woman" and "Proud Mary" resulted, along with a slew of classic Southern soul covers. — *Rob Bowman*

● **Home in Your Heart** / 1992 / Rhino 70284
Solomon Burke was the first of the great Atlantic Records soul men to hit it big when the country-tinged "Just out of Reach" charted in 1960. This two-disc set contains all of the monumental soul hits that followed, including the great "Everybody Needs Somebody to Love," "Got to Get You off My Mind," "Hanging up My Heart for You," and "Take Me (Just as I Am)." Gerri Hirshey contributes the liner notes. This is the essential compilation on Burke, one of the greatest soul singers on them all. — *Christine Ohlman*

T-Bone Burnett

b. 1945, Fort Worth, TX
Vocals, songwriter / Roots-rock, folk-rock, country-rock
T-Bone Burnett may not be a household word, but he has managed to attain a kind of creative freedom that many more successful artists never see. A virtual renaissance man, Burnett has produced some great albums for Bruce Cockburn, Los Lobos, Elvis Costello, Counting Crows, and Marshall Crenshaw. As a singer/songwriter, he has released a number of albums that have made him somewhat of a critics' darling.

Burnett first gained notoriety with the Alpha Band (after a stint in Bob Dylan's Rolling Thunder Revue) during the middle and late '70s. Among their three albums, *Spark in the Dark* most successfully sidestepped the band's tendency for heavy-handed Christian moralizing. That preachy quality has surfaced periodically in Burnett's solo work. Nevertheless, it is Burnett's intelligent spiritual grounding that has also informed his artistry's many strengths.

Stylistically, Burnett has primarily drawn from folk, country, and roots rock, but he has infused other elements, creating some provocative combinations of music. — *Rick Clark*

○ **Truth Decay** / 1980 / Takoma 72780
The first album after his stint with the Alpha Band. A great mix of Texas roadhouse R&B/blues-based rock, with hard-folk acoustic instrumental augmentation. Thematically, *Truth Decay* was a refreshing departure from some of the Alpha Band's relentless moralizing. Burnett still took some heavy-handed shots on songs like "Madison Ave" and "House of Mirrors," but the presence of tracks like the gritty rocker "Boomerang," "Talk Talk Talk Talk," and "Love at First Sight" makes this a must-own for lovers of Dylanish rock. — *Rick Clark*

Proof through the Night / 1983 / Demon 14
Truth Decay and *Trap Door* had earned Burnett loads of critical praise, but this follow-up featured strong performances (by an all-star lineup) and impressive production, although tracks like "Hefner and Disney" and "The Sixties" were smug, overreaching concept pieces (recalling the Alpha Band's later work) that undermined the overall strength of this release. — *Rick Clark*

Trap Door (EP) / 1984 / Warner Brothers 23691
From his clever reading of the Marilyn Monroe standard "Diamonds Are a Girl's Best Friend" to stunning folk-rock originals like "Hold on Tight" and "I Wish You Could Have Seen Her Dance" to the thoughtful closer "Trap Door," this EP is Burnett's most consistently satisfying release. Too bad it wasn't a full-length album. Too bad it's not out on CD yet. — *Rick Clark*

T-Bone Burnett / 1986 / Dot 31296
Recorded digitally, straight to 2-track, Burnett's self-titled Dot Records release is a heartfelt, low-key affair, featuring flawless country-folk musicianship and a strong collection of originals and covers. Among the highlights are "River of Love," "Shake Yourself Loose," and a version of Tom Waits's "Time." — *Rick Clark*

● **Criminal Under My Own Hat** / 1992 / Columbia 45213
On his first album in four years, Burnett adopts a spare instrumentation dominated by Marc Ribot's angular guitar work to complement a set of close-to-the-bone lyrics that strip love of sentimentality, castigate politicians and evangelists, and, as the album title (echoed in the song "Criminals") attests, do not spare the songwriter himself. The result is a gripping record in the best tradition of Burnett's mentor, Bob Dylan. — *William Ruhlmann*

Johnny Burnette

b. Mar. 28, 1934, Memphis, TN, d. Aug. 14, 1964, Clear Lake, CA
Vocals, songwriter / Rockabilly, pop/rock
A contemporary of Elvis Presley in the Memphis scene of the mid '50s, Burnette played a similar brand of fiery, spare wild-man rockabilly. With his brother Dorsey (on bass) and guitarist Paul Burlison forming his Rock 'N Roll Trio, he recorded a clutch of singles for Decca in 1956 and 1957 that achieved nothing more than regional success. Featuring the groundbreaking fuzzy tone of Burlison's guitar, Johnny's energetic vocals, and Dorsey's slapping bass, these recordings—highlighted by the first rock & roll version of "Train Kept a-Rollin'"—compare well to the classic Sun rockabilly of the same era. The trio disbanded in 1957, and Johnny found pop success as a teen idol in the early '60s with hits like "You're Sixteen" and "Dreamin'." Burnette died in a boating accident in 1964. His brother Dorsey achieved modest success as a solo act in the early '60s, and Burlison recently resurfaced as a member of the Sun Rhythm Section. — *Richie Unterberger*

○ **Tear It Up** / 1978 / Solid Smoke 3001
Seventeen of their purest rockabilly cuts from their 1956-57 prime. Highlights include "Train Kept a-Rollin'," "Rock Therapy," and "Honey Hush." — *Richie Unterberger*

○ **Best of Johnny Burnette: You're Sixteen** / 1992 / Capitol 99997
Burnette's best pop-oriented recordings are featured on this collection, including the classic "You're Sixteen." — *Stephen Thomas Erlewine*

● **Rockabilly Boogie** / Bear Family 15474
All of the Johnny Burnette trio's primal rockabilly records—including the blazing "Train Kept a-Rollin'"—are collected on this single-disc compilation. The alternate takes might border on overkill, but the original takes remain powerful years after they were recorded. — *Stephen Thomas Erlewine*

Kate Bush

b. Jul. 30, 1958, Plumstead, England

Vocals / Progressive rock, pop/rock
A preeminent singer/songwriter with a unique sound and style since her emergence with "Wuthering Heights" in 1978. Bush's high keening voice has mellowed into a beautifully lyrical instrument, while her music and lyrics define the meaning of sensuousness in subject and feeling, especially in the late '80s. Her music is tasteful, intelligent, and stimulating beyond the libido. Her major inspirations were the Beatles and her mentor, Pink Floyd's David Gilmour. It shows in the exquisite lyricism and timbral qualities of her work. —*Bruce Eder*

○ **Kick Inside** / 1978 / EMI America 46012
An amazing debut album. Strident and surprisingly mature for a 20-year-old. Includes "Wuthering Heights." —*Bruce Eder*

Lionheart / 1978 / EMI America 46065
Diffuse compared with her debut, this second album, suffers from unfocused artistic sensibilities and production and overall weak lyrics, despite some pleasant melodies. "Oh England My Lionheart" is the strongest track, followed by "Wow." —*Bruce Eder*

Never for Ever / 1980 / EMI America 46360
Something of a comeback, *Never for Ever* recast Bush in a fiercer musical persona, exploring facets of the dark side of human nature ("The Wedding List") and of tragic melodrama ("Babooshka"). —*Bruce Eder*

Dreaming / 1982 / EMI America 46361
Bush's fourth album is a personal exploration of mysticism and magic and their effect on the mind of the beholder. It's difficult to absorb and—lacking the poetic qualities of her previous work—it's for serious fans only. Generally regarded as a misstep, a trip through variant states of mind. Not lyrical or easily understood, but potentially rewarding. —*Bruce Eder*

○ **Hounds of Love** / 1985 / EMI America 46164
A sexy, sensual masterpiece, embracing love, sex, guilt, and the quest for psychic wholeness within a framework of rich melodies, stunning timbres, and a perfectly developed sense of the dramatic. An outstanding album of the entire decade. —*Bruce Eder*

● **Whole Story** / 1986 / EMI America 46414
A well-thought-out cross-section of the representative tracks from her first five albums, remixed and remastered in some cases. A great way to start on her music. —*Bruce Eder*

○ **The Sensual World** / 1989 / Columbia 44164
Bush's follow-up to *Hounds of Love* lacks the concise structure of the earlier record, but the individual songs stand out, especially the sensual title track. A startling examination of the world through sensuality, guilt, history, and the division of the sexes. —*Bruce Eder*

Red Shoes / 1993 / Columbia
Less brooding and melancholy than either *Hounds of Love* or *The Sensual World*, *The Red Shoes* is a colorful, loose concept album, based on the Hans Christian Anderson story, in which Kate Bush explores world music more deeply than she ever has before. She also comes closer to straight pop (and dance-pop) songs than ever before in "Rubber Band Girl" and a collaboration with Prince. Unfortunately, this experimentation doesn't pay off as well as past adventures by Bush, leaving *The Red Shoes* an only fitfully successful album. —*Stephen Thomas Erlewine*

Jerry Butler

b. Dec. 8, 1939, Sunflower County, MS
Vocals / Soul, R&B
It would be safer to talk about Jerry Butler's *careers* than about his career. Up from Mississippi, he joined Curtis Mayfield in the Impressions around 1957. They began recording the following year and broke through with *For Your Precious Love*, touted by some as the first soul record. Inevitably, he went solo, and fell—or was pushed—into the pop mainstream. Reunited with Mayfield (the latter as writer), Butler announced his return with *He Will Break Your Heart* in 1960. His subsequent recordings for Vee-Jay trod the turf where pop and R&B meet and are variable; the best are excellent.

After Vee-Jay went broke in 1966, Butler signed with Mercury and was soon placed with the team of Gamble and Huff, who produced him in Philadelphia. Jerry Butler's mellow baritone and the sweet Philly sound were a winning combination, as attested by pop and R&B hits like "Only the Strong Survive" and "Hey, Western Union Man." After the Gamble and Huff deal dissolved in

1970, Butler's career went slowly downhill. Deals with Motown and even Gamble and Huff's Philadelphia International label couldn't deliver the goods. There's something for everyone in Butler's prolificacy, but unfortunately little of it is available to sample. —*Colin Escott*

○ **The Ice Man Cometh** / 1969-1966 / Vee-Jay 700
The Ice Man Cometh is one of his best late-'60s albums, produced by the Gamble-Huff team. —*John Floyd*

○ **Ice on Ice** / 1970 / Mercury
The second of two spectacular albums that were collaborations between Jerry Butler and the Gamble-Huff production combine. It resulted in two more super hits, "Moody Woman" and "What's the Use of Breaking Up," and were a high-water mark for Butler, showing his smooth, lush sound could work on upbeat and midtempo tunes as easily as on ballads. —*Ron Wynn*

● **Best of Jerry Butler (Vee-Jay)** / 1987 / Vee-Jay 1048
An excellent 18-song overview of his solo hits and his first recordings with the Impressions. It could use a few more of his later hits. —*John Floyd*

★ **Iceman: The Mercury Years** / 1992 / PolyGram 510968
A glorious 44-song double-disc set collecting Butler's best Mercury sides, with several previously unreleased songs and alternate mixes. Crummy liner notes, though. —*John Floyd*

○ **The Ice Man** / 1992 / Vee-Jay
Featuring 25 of his Vee-Jay singles, including three hits with the Impressions, *The Ice Man* is the best retrospective available of Butler's early years. —*Stephen Thomas Erlewine*

The Butthole Surfers

Group / Alternative rock
There was a time magazines couldn't print their name and radios couldn't say their name. Then there was a time, about ten years later, that they were in heavy rotation on MTV and starring in Nintendo commercials. Throughout it all, the Butthole Surfers haven't changed all that much—they remain the same gleefully gross noise terrorists that they were when their first record was released on Alternative Tentacles in 1983.

Although some critics may say all of their albums sound the same, the only thing that unites the Butthole Surfers' albums is their bracing vulgarity and offensiveness. Unlike many bands whose disgusting lyrics and abrasive music are calculatingly revolting, the Buttholes revel in the filth—they're not making some social commentary with their music, they simply *enjoy* the grotesque. Beneath all of the squalor, the Buttholes remain artpunks. Their albums are never just hard-core noise, they have touches of psychedelia, country, classic rock, rockabilly, techno—anything that comes their way, really. As they get older, their songs rely more on the underpinning guitar grunge of Paul Leary, yet vocalist Gibby Haynes remains a deranged lunatic, giving the band the fuel for their gleeful nightmares. —*Stephen Thomas Erlewine*

○ **Butthole Surfers** / 1983 / Alternative Tentacles 32
Their best album, randy and wild. Smart, stupid, and outrageous all at the same time. —*John Dougan*

Psychic . . . Powerless . . . Another Man's Sac / 1985 / Touch & Go 5
New-age drug music on *Psychic . . . Powerless . . . Another Man's Sac.* —*John Dougan*

Rembrandt Pussyhorse / 1986 / Touch & Go 8
Chunky, cranky, out-of-control pop. —*John Dougan*

○ **Locust Abortion Technician** / 1987 / Touch & Go 19
Good songs, real ugly execution. —*John Dougan*

○ **Hairway to Steven** / 1988 / Touch & Go 29
Actually getting manic here! —*John Dougan*

Pioughd / 1991 / Capitol 98512
Pioughd was the Butthole's first album of original material in three years, and considering the time it took to make the record, it's a bit of a disappointment. Not that it's bad; in fact, some of it is their best. But it's rather uninspired and restates many of their old ideas, only in a more streamlined, accessible fashion. —*Stephen Thomas Erlewine*

● **Independent Worm Saloon** / 1993 / Capitol 98798
Something has definitely changed in the music industry when the Butthole Surfers are recording for a major label, with none other

than Led Zeppelin's John Paul Jones producing. And they *still* haven't sold out. *Independent Worm Saloon* follows the course the past few albums have led the band—a hard '70s-punk metal bottom with lots of avant-noise noodlings and wacked-out vocals on top. The safest it gets is the heavy riff-rocker "Who Was in My Room Last Night?" but that never stops the Buttholes from gross-outs like the heaves that begin "Clean It Up" or "The Annoying Song," which is exactly what it says it is. *Independent Worm Saloon* may run a bit long, but the times that the Butthole Surfers' shock-rock hit the mark make most of the indulgences excusable. —*Stephen Thomas Erlewine*

The Buzzcocks
Group / Punk

With their crisp melodies, driving guitars, and guitarist Pete Shelley's biting lyrics, the Buzzcocks were one of the best, most influential punk bands. The Buzzcocks were inspired by the Sex Pistols' energy, yet they didn't copy the Pistols' angry political stance. Instead, the Buzzcocks brought that intense, brilliant energy to the three-minute pop song. Shelley's alternately funny and anguished lyrics about adolescence and love were some of the best and smartest of his era. The Buzzcocks' melodies and hooks are likewise always concise and memorable. Over the years, their powerful punk-pop has proven enormously influential, with echoes of their music being apparent in everyone from Hüsker Dü to Nirvana.

The Buzzcocks reunited in 1989, releasing their first new studio album since 1979 in 1993. Although no longer as breathtakingly energetic, they are one of the few re-united bands that haven't embarrassed themselves. —*Stephen Thomas Erlewine*

★ **Singles Going Steady** / 1981 / IRS 0001
A magnificent collection of their first eight British singles, both A- and B-sides. Infectious melodies and buzzsaw guitars carry Shelley's finest set of broken-hearted rockers. —*John Floyd*

○ **Product** / 1989 / Restless 72377
One of the first rock & roll boxed sets, as well as one of the finest, *Product* collects nearly every studio record the Buzzcocks ever released, with the exception of their debut EP, *Spiral Scratch*. —*Stephen Thomas Erlewine*

○ **Operator's Manual: The Buzzcocks Best** / 1991 / IRS 13135
A 25-song set that duplicates 11 songs from the *Singles* album. It also contains the best of their three albums, only one of which was released in the United States, and showcases a different side of the band. —*John Floyd*

○ **Different Kind of Tension/Buzzcocks—Parts One, Two, Three** / 1993 / IRS 70055
Even as the band was falling apart, the Buzzcocks were recording an amazing array of ferocious pop songs. Their last album, *A Different Kind of Tension*, featured some of Pete Shelley's best songs, including some of the most personal material he has ever written. *Parts One, Two, Three* collect the band's last three singles, which are all quite impressive. —*Stephen Thomas Erlewine*

Trade Test Transmission / Jun. 2, 1993 / Caroline
While it doesn't have the tight, repressed energy of their earliest records, *Trade Test Transmissions* is a surprisingly effective comeback album from the Buzzcocks that shows the band can still turn out some terrific punk-pop. —*Stephen Thomas Erlewine*

○ **Love Bites/Another Music in a Different Kitchen** / Feb. 22, 1994 / IRS 28309
While the Buzzcocks' singles captured the band's energetic, tightly wound pop style perfectly, the band experimented a bit more with song structures on their full-length albums. Many of the album tracks are in the vein of their classic singles, yet the band also played some twisted, draining instrumental sections that are almost as impressive as their concise pop songs. Of their first two albums, the debut *Another Music in a Different Kitchen* is the stronger record, but *Love Bites* is only a shade weaker. —*Stephen Thomas Erlewine*

The Byrds
Group / Folk rock, country-rock, psychedelic

Aside from the Beatles and the Rolling Stones, there hasn't been another group from the '60s whose sound has been so widely influential. Their trademark bell-like jangle of 12-string electric guitar and rich harmonies has been internalized by artists like

Tom Petty, R.E.M., Big Star, Fairport Convention, the Church, the Bangles, and the Eagles, as well by as much of today's country music.

Before the advent of the British invasion, Jim (later Roger) McGuinn, Chris Hillman, David Crosby, and Gene Clark were active in the Los Angeles folk scene. Fusing the energy of the Beatles and the weightier lyrical concepts developed by Bob Dylan, the Byrds were conceived and folk-rock was born. Over the course of their existence, the Byrds pioneered many musical frontiers, breaking ground in futuristic space-rock and country-rock. Through all their endeavors, the only constant in their many lineup changes was Roger McGuinn. After the band's demise in 1973, McGuinn released a series of solo efforts.

As with Buffalo Springfield, many of the Byrds members went on to even-greater success. David Crosby helped form Crosby, Stills & Nash. Chris Hillman and Gram Parsons formed the Flying Burrito Brothers. Parsons managed two fine albums on Warner before dying in 1973 of a drug overdose. Hillman has continued to have much success in the country field with the Desert Rose Band. Gene Clark, one of the band's finest songwriters, had a sporadic solo career; *Echoes* is a dignified compilation of his highlights. He died in 1991. —*Rick Clark*

☆ **Mr. Tambourine Man** / 1965 / Columbia 09172
An incredibly focused debut, featuring a smart blend of well-chosen song covers and originals, plus the band's trademark 12-string electric sound and transcendent harmonies. The title track and Gene Clark's "I'll Feel a Whole Lot Better," as well as "All I Really Want to Do," are hits. Two highlights, "I Knew I'd Want You" and "Here without You," reveal Clark as the most mature songwriter in the band at this point. —*Rick Clark*

○ **Turn! Turn! Turn!** / Jan. 1965 / Columbia 09254
Continuing in the vein of their debut, this has lots of electrified folk-song covers (Dylan, Seeger, traditional) and Gene Clark shines on "Set You Free This Time," "If You're Gone," and the expansive "The World Turns All Around Her." —*Rick Clark*

○ **Fifth Dimension** / Feb. 1966 / Columbia 9349
Clark left while they were recording this, but David Crosby and Jim McGuinn more than fill the void. The 12-string sound is much more experimental, with McGuinn and Crosby drawing inspiration from jazz and Indian music. Though this album isn't so strong as *Turn! Turn! Turn!* and *Mr. Tambourine Man*, some of their greatest moments are found here in the powerful, hymnlike "5 D," the breathtakingly beautiful psychedelia of "Eight Miles High," or the playful hit "Mr. Spaceman." Other tracks of note are the psychedelic "I See You," "What's Happening?!?!," and the orchestrated folky "Wild Mountain Thyme." —*Rick Clark*

☆ **Younger Than Yesterday** / 1967 / Columbia 9442
Overall a stronger album than *Fifth Dimension*, even though some of the psychedelia lacks much sustaining impact ("C.T.A.-102," "Mind Gardens"). Chris Hillman makes strong contributions, writing or cowriting 5 of the 11 tracks. Among them are the tongue-in-cheek hit "So You Want to Be a Rock 'n' Roll Star" and the spirited "Have You Seen Her Face." Also includes the hit version of Dylan's "My Back Pages." —*Rick Clark*

★ **Byrds' Greatest Hits** / 1967 / Columbia 9516
Even though this collection only covers the first half of their career, it contains more primo stuff than *20 Essential Tracks*. The mastering here isn't quite as good as that on the boxed set. —*Rick Clark*

○ **Notorious Byrd Brothers** / Jan. 1968 / Columbia 9575
A classic psychedelic opus, drawing from the space-rock of *Younger* and *Fifth* while hinting at the country-rock to come with cuts like "Change Is Now" and "Old John Robertson." The 12-string electrics are downplayed. Production techniques like phasing, vari-speeded vocals, sound effects, and baroque string and horn arrangements play a bigger role, while the melodies and vocal execution is much spacier. Highlights include Carole King's yearning "Goin' Back," "Draft Morning," "Dolphins Smile," and "Wasn't Born to Follow" (featured in the movie *Easy Rider*). —*Rick Clark*

☆ **Sweetheart of the Rodeo** / Feb. 1968 / Columbia 9670
The Byrds made this groundbreaking country-rock classic with the songwriting aid of new member Gram Parsons. "One Hundred Years from Now" features some incredibly fine guitar and pedal steel work from Clarence White and Lloyd Green, respectively. Versions of Dylan's "Nothing Was Delivered" and "You

Ain't Going Nowhere" are pure magic, and renditions of the Louvin Brothers' "The Christian Life" and William Bell's "You Don't Miss Your Water" are standouts too. —*Rick Clark*

Dr Byrd & Mr Hyde / 1969 / Columbia 9755
Not one of their best, but it contains two notable tracks in "This Wheel's on Fire" and "King Apathy III." There is a continued country influence, but rock still predominates. —*Rick Clark*

○ **Ballad of Easy Rider** / Feb. 1969 / Columbia 9942
Another beautiful gem with hardly a weak cut. "Gunga Din," with its delicate arpeggios, is one of the finest moments by a later incarnation of the Byrds. By this time, their characteristic 12-string sound was all but gone. —*Rick Clark*

Untitled / 1970 / Columbia 30127
Originally a double-record set (one live LP, one studio) and now on single CD, this contains their last hit of any substance, "Chestnut Mare." The studio tracks are uneven, but tracks like the reflective "Just a Season," "Truck Stop Girl," "All the Things," and much of the live stuff make this set worth having, if only for Clarence White's remarkable guitar playing. —*Rick Clark*

In the Beginning / 1989 / Rhino 70244
A collection of pre-*Tambourine Man* Byrds. Fans might find interest in early versions of "Mr. Tambourine Man," "I Knew I'd Want You," "You Showed Me" (a Byrds original the Turtles scored with), and Gene Clark's "For Me Again." —*Rick Clark*

Never Before / 1989 / Murray Hill 22808
A compilation of previously unreleased sides and alternative versions. The stereo remix of "Mr. Tambourine Man" contains too much spread on the soundstage. The alternative take of "Eight Miles High" and an extended version of "Psychodrama City" will appeal to hardcore fans. The boxed set, however, has since included most of these tracks. Good liner notes and a great picture in the booklet. —*Rick Clark*

☆ **Byrds** / 1990 / Columbia 46773
A thoughtfully compiled four-CD boxed set that features great sound from remastered and remixed tracks. The remixes generally manage to maintain the essential integrity of the original tracks, but there are some that entirely miss the spirit, like "Just a Season" and a toothless "Why" (which is *not* the sought-after version found on the B-side of "Eight Miles High"). Regardless, a must-own for anyone interested in finding out about one of America's greatest groups. —*Rick Clark*

20 Essential Tracks from the Boxed Set: 1965-90 / 1991 / Columbia 47884
That may have been the case for the first 16 cuts, but why include the four 1990 reunion tracks when there's much better material left on the box? An OK choice for the budget-minded, but that's about it. —*Rick Clark*

David Byrne
b. May 14, 1952, Dumbarton, Scotland
Vocals, guitar / Alternative pop/rock
The former lead singer/songwriter and guitarist of the Talking Heads, David Byrne has written theater and film scores (Academy Award winner for *The Last Emperor*), acted and directed (*True Stories*), compiled a series of samplers of South American music, and launched a solo career with *Rei Momo* in 1989. —*William Ruhlmann*

Catherine Wheel / 1981 / Sire 3645
This is Byrne's score for a Broadway dance production choreographed and directed by Twyla Tharp. Its sound—with herky-jerky rhythms and unusual sounds, along with Byrne's own vocals and odd lyrics on many songs—will be familiar to Talking Heads fans. As originally released, only the cassette version contained the full 73-minute score, though an abridged songs-from LP was also issued. —*William Ruhlmann*

Music for the Knee Plays / 1985 / Regal Zonophone 2403811
This music was composed for use in segments of Robert Wilson's opera *The Civil Wars*. Byrne uses a variety of stately horn charts and recites impressionistic lyrics between and over them. The album concludes with the hilariously absurd "In the Future." —*William Ruhlmann*

● **Rei Momo** / 1989 / Luaka Bop 25990
On his first full-fledged solo album, Byrne indulges his fascination with Latin and South American musical styles, employing a variety of native musicians but mixing up the sounds to suit his own distinctly nonpurist vision and singing over the tracks the same kind of witty, oddball lyrics found on Talking Heads albums. When released, the cassette version contained three more tracks than the LP. —*William Ruhlmann*

Uh-Oh / Apr. 1992 / Luaka Bop 26799
David Byrne's debut solo album *Rei Momo* immersed itself in world-beat explorations. His second solo effort, *Uh-Oh*, takes elements of world beat but incorporates them into pop songs that are reminiscent of old Talking Heads numbers. While Byrne's eclecticism is too self-conscious to make the record truly engaging, there are enough fine songs to make it a worthwhile listen. —*Stephen Thomas Erlewine*

C & C Music Factory (Clivilles & Cole)
Group / Dance-pop
C & C Music Factory isn't really a group—it's the product of Robert Clivilles and David Cole, two pop-savvy dance producers. In 1990, Clivilles and Cole hired all the singers and created all the tracks for *Gonna Make You Sweat,* C & C Music Factory's first album. While it was prepackaged, it wasn't necessarily faceless. In Freedom Williams, the producers had a solid, if not original or distinctive, rapper. What was really important to the success of the album was how Clivilles and Cole assembled the tracks, blending hip-hop and club sensibilities to mindlessly catchy pop songs. The three hit singles—"Gonna Make You Sweat (Everybody Dance Now)," "Here We Go," "Things That Make You Go Hmmmm. . . ,"—were very good pop singles, and all of them were massive hits in early 1991.

After the group's moment in the sun, Williams left for an unsuccessful solo career and Clivilles and Cole released *Greatest Remixes, Vol. 1,* a collection of their work with C & C Music Factory as well as other artists. The album had a hit single with their re-recording of U2's "Pride." —*Stephen Thomas Erlewine*

● **Gonna Make You Sweat** / 1990 / Columbia 47093
Their hit pop hip-hop singles are all here—"Gonna Make You Sweat (Everybody Dance Now)," "Here We Go," and "Things That Make You Go Hmmm . . . ." —*Bil Carpenter*

Cabaret Voltaire
Group / Experimental, electronic, dance
Cabaret Voltaire's story is that of a common cult band: They never sold many records and they were never critics' darlings, yet their influence was great. Their effect on techno, industrial, and electronic music is immense. Taking the electronic experiments of Brian Eno and the avant-garde bent of Can, Cabaret Voltaire added a hyponotic, almost trancelike beat, along with television and record sound bites. All of these techniques became popular during the early '90s, when groups like the techno conglomeration Front 242 and the hard, industrial Ministry expanded on these ideas. What sounded avant-garde in the late '70s and early '80s has become the standard in clubs and raves around the world.

Since 1979, Cabaret Voltaire have recorded a staggering amount of albums. Some are impressive, others are almost inaccessible. As they've grown older, their electronics have become more danceable. In 1991, they fit comfortably into acid house, although their music was darker than most of that style. For much of their music, sound is the primary concern, not songs or compositions. Consequently, their albums can be dense, difficult listening that require patience. Even so, it is impossible to deny the importance of Cabaret Voltaire, no matter how inaccessible their music may be. —*Stephen Thomas Erlewine*

○ **Red Mecca** / 1981 / Mute 71473
Cabaret Voltaire's first consistent record, *Red Mecca,* offers a highly stylized revision of Mancini's score for *Touch of Evil* set to a dark, dense electronic landscape. —*Stephen Thomas Erlewine*

○ **Crackdown** / 1983 / Some Bizarre 1
One of Cabaret Voltaire's strongest albums, *The Crackdown* features the band working a number of menacing electronic textures into a basic dance-funk rhythm. The result is one of their most distinctive, challenging records. —*Stephen Thomas Erlewine*

○ **Golden Moments of Cabaret Voltaire** / 1987 / Rough Trade 6001

A solid collection of Cabaret Voltaire's earliest recordings, which features some of the noisiest and bleakest music they have ever recorded. —*Stephen Thomas Erlewine*

○ **Listen Up with Cabaret Voltaire** / 1990 / Mute 71475
It may be a collection of rarities and outtakes, but *Listen Up with Cabaret Voltaire* is one of their strongest albums, giving listeners a good sense of the band's accomplishments. —*Stephen Thomas Erlewine*

● **Living Legends** / 1990 / Mute 71476
Collecting both sides of a number of singles that the band made for Rough Trade, *The Living Legends* offers the best introduction to Cabaret Voltaire's influential electronic soundscapes. —*Stephen Thomas Erlewine*

The Cadillacs

Group / Doo-wop
Equally adept at polished ballads and torrid rockers, the Cadillacs were one of New York's top doo-wop groups. The Harlem quintet signed with Josie in 1954 and debuted with the beautiful "Gloria," but with Earl Carroll's prominent energetic lead vocals, the Cadillacs became known for humorous jump material and hot choreography after "Speedoo" hit big for them in 1956. Tapping into the novelty R&B market pioneered by the Coasters, the Cadillacs cut a load of great rockers during the late '50s, such as "Peek-a-Boo" and "Please, Mr. Johnson," and performed in the quickie flick *Go, Johnny, Go!* in 1959. Carroll left to join the Coasters in 1958, but the group persevered, eventually signing with Mercury. Carroll has re-formed the Cadillacs in recent years. —*Bill Dahl*

Meet the Orioles & The Cadillacs / 1961 / Collectables 5412
A classic doo-wop album featuring one group well known for novelty tracks and another that was among the earliest creators of the genre. Some wonderful jump tunes, silly songs, and romantic ballads. —*Ron Wynn*

★ **Best of the Cadillacs** / 1990 / Rhino 70955
One of the top novelty R&B groups of the mid '50s. Sizzling rockers and a handful of doo-wop ballads. —*Bill Dahl*

○ **For Collectors Only** / Collectables 8800
A 60-track, three-disc collection that will delight hardcore fans of the seminal doo-wop group. Most fans will be content with the single disc collection. —*Stephen Thomas Erlewine*

J. J. Cale

b. Dec. 5, 1938, Oklahoma City, OK
Vocals, guitar, singer-songwriter / Blues-rock, pop/rock
Oklahoma-born songwriter and guitarist known for his laidback style, J. J. Cale wrote several songs ("After Midnight," "Cocaine") that were recorded by Eric Clapton. —*William Ruhlmann*

Really / 1972 / Mercury 810314
Cale's guitar work manages to be both understated and intense here. The same is true of his seemingly offhand singing, which finds him drawling lines like "You get your gun, I'll get mine" with disarming casualness. But he has trouble coming up with original material as strong as that on his debut, and for some, his approach will be too casual—there are many times, when the band is percolating along and Cale is muttering into the microphone, that the music seems to be all background and no foreground. You may find yourself waiting for a payoff that never comes. —*William Ruhlmann*

Okie / 1974 / Mercury 842102
Cale moves toward country and gospel on some songs here, but since those are two of his primary influences, the movement is slight. Longtime-producer Audie Ashworth attempts to place more emphasis on Cale's vocals on some songs by double-tracking them and pushing them up in the mix, but much of this is still low key and bluesy in what was becoming Cale's patented style. —*William Ruhlmann*

○ **Troubadour** / 1976 / Mercury 810001
Producer Audie Ashworth introduced some different instruments, notably vibes and what sound like horns (though none are credited), for a slightly altered sound here. But Cale's albums are so steeped in his introspective style that they become interchangeable. If you like one of them, chances are you'll want to have them all. This one is notable for introducing "Cocaine," which

Eric Clapton covered on his *Slowhand* album a year later. —*William Ruhlmann*

● **Special Edition** / 1984 / Mercury 818633
Sinuous rhythms, conversational singing, and most of all intricate, bluesy guitar-playing characterize Cale's performances of his own songs. This compilation, covering 11 years of recording, includes the songs Eric Clapton (who borrowed heavily from Cale's style in his 1970s solo work) made famous: "After Midnight" and "Cocaine." —*William Ruhlmann*

○ **Travel Log** / May 1989 / Silvertone 1306
Cale's first album in six years finds him taking a more aggressive stance in terms of tempos and playing, though he remains a man with a profound sense of the groove and, especially as a singer, a minimalist. But as he says, "Shuffle or die." —*William Ruhlmann*

John Cale

b. Dec. 3, 1940, Wales
Vocals, keyboards / Art-rock, rock & roll,
A former member of the Velvet Underground (for whom he played viola), Cale has moved between the worlds of rock and avant-garde classical music since launching a solo career in 1969. He also worked as producer for a variety of punk and new wave artists. —*William Ruhlmann*

Vintage Violence / 1970 / Columbia 1037
Fresh out of the Velvet Underground, Cale makes a melodic pop-rock album—which may have been disappointingly tame to fans of the Velvets' sometimes extreme approach, much of which had seemed due to Cale's influence. In any case, this pop move didn't sell, and Cale left Columbia after the label declined to release his collaboration with Terry Riley, *Church of Anthrax*, in the United States in 1971. —*William Ruhlmann*

Academy in Peril / 1972 / Reprise 2079
Cale moved to Warner Bros.' Reprise label in 1972 for his second solo album, an all-instrumental collection on which he made greater use of his classical and avant-garde training, employing the Royal Philharmonic Orchestra for two cuts and naming tunes after Brahms and John Milton. The result is an imaginative though unfocused album that expanded Cale's musical horizons if not his audience. —*William Ruhlmann*

○ **Paris, 1919** / 1973 / Reprise 2131
John Cale's third solo album possessed a rare beauty, demonstrating that the classically trained avant-garde, rock & roll viola player could, when he wished, make melodic pop music with a lush elegance. —*William Ruhlmann*

○ **Fear** / 1974 / Island 9301
Moving to Island Records for his fourth solo album (and third try at a pop vocal approach), Cale brought in Roxy Music guitarist Phil Manzanera and turned to a harder rocking style on the title track and "Gun." But "You Know More Than I Know" and other songs showed he retained the melodic qualities and talent for thoughtful ballads displayed on *Paris 1919*. —*William Ruhlmann*

Slow Dazzle / 1975 / Island 9317
On the second installment of a trilogy made for Island in the mid '70s, Cale played (as one song title had it) "Dirtyass Rock 'n' Roll," anticipating the coming punk movement. *Slow Dazzle* includes Cale's drastic reconstruction of "Heartbreak Hotel." —*William Ruhlmann*

○ **Helen of Troy** / 1975 / Island 9350
Island Records declined to release this, the third of its John Cale albums, in the United States, which meant fans had to scramble for an import copy. The record features guitarist Chris Spedding and a song selection highlighted by the Cale classic "I Keep a Close Watch" and his version of Jonathan Richman's "Pablo Picasso," which he had produced earlier for the Modern Lovers. —*William Ruhlmann*

○ **Guts** / 1977 / Island 9459
Guts is a compilation album selecting the best from Cale's three Island releases of 1974-1975: *Fear, Slow Dazzle,* and *Helen of Troy*. —*William Ruhlmann*

Honi Soit / 1981 / A&M 64849
Cale's first "new" studio album in six years was an excellent pop-rock collection paced by its lead-off track, "Dead or Alive." —*William Ruhlmann*

○ **Music for a New Society** / 1982 / Island 7019
Cale's calmest collection of music since *Paris, 1919* contains an excellent version of "Close Watch," as well as the haunting "Chinese Envoy." *—William Ruhlmann*

○ **Fragments of a Rainy Season** / 1992 / Hannibal 1372
Alternating between piano and guitar backing, *Fragments of a Rainy Season* marks the first time Cale's moving acoustic performances have been captured on a live recording. The disc also serves as a best-of compilation, chronicling tracks like "A Child's Christmas in Wales" from 1973's *Paris 1919* to "Do Not Go Gentle" from 1989's *Words for the Dying*. *—Roch Parisien*

● **Seducing Down the Door** / 1994 / Rhino
The range of John Cale's work can be shocking: It's hard to believe that the piano duets with minimalist composer Terry Riley on *Church of Anthrax*, the lush orchestral pop of *Paris 1919*, and the raucous, dissonant guitar rock of "Gun" and the rest of *Fear* are all the work of the same man, much less that they were all released within a four-year span. This well-chosen 38-track, 2 1/2-hour double-CD anthology does nothing to reconcile the apparent musical contradictions in Cale's classical-to-punk sensibility, but it does bring coherence and consolidation to a recording career that, spread across a multiplicity of labels and plagued by commercial indifference, has been difficult to grasp as a whole. *—William Ruhlmann*

The Call

Group / Rock & roll
The Call, a California-based quartet featuring the passionate singing and writing of Michael Been, incorporated the fire of the Clash and the organic earthy soul of the Band to deliver their spiritually rooted, socially aware themes. *—Rick Clark*

Reconciled / 1986 / Elektra 60440
Features the hit "Everywhere I Go"—Christian mysticism with a nervy edge. One of their best efforts. *—Rick Clark*

Let the Day Begin / 1989 / MCA 6303
The title cut was a rock hit in spite of poor retail distribution. Other highlights include the rude rough-and-tumble rock of "Same Ol' Story." *—Rick Clark*

○ **Red Moon** / 1990 / MCA 10033
Pressured for new product, Been rose to the occasion, creating some of his most affectingly passionate music—particularly in the stirring title cut and "What's Happened to You," "Like You've Never Been Loved," "This Is Your Life," and "Floating Back." The organic style of production works beautifully with the music. *—Rick Clark*

● **The Walls Came Down: Best of the Mercury Years** / 1991 / Mercury 848741
Walls Came Down—Best of the Mercury Years is a great collection of the band's career. Contains the fiery debut "The Walls Came Down." Compiled by Been. *—Rick Clark*

Camel

Group / Progressive rock
The British art-rock band Camel features reflective melodies within the context of extended instrumental workouts. Guitarist Andrew Latimer has been Camel's creative mainstay throughout their many incarnations, which have included keyboardists Pete Bardens and Kit Watkins. *—AMG*

○ **Rain Dances** / 1977 / Deram 820725
Rain Dances, Camel's fifth release, offers the most consistent and representative package in their saga. This is the band at its best. The addition of Caravan cofounder Richard Sinclair proves profitable, as do a few colorist touches by Brian Eno on "Elke." Mel Collins's woodwinds are among the highlights, especially on "Tell Me" and the title track. From beginning to end, this project flows gracefully. *—Matthew Plichta*

○ **Breathless** / 1978 / Arista 4206
While it might not be as consistent as *Rain Dances*, *Breathless* nevertheless contains several fine tracks and remains one of their better efforts. *—Stephen Thomas Erlewine*

● **I Can See Your House from Here** / 1979 / Deram 820614
Although not an honest representation of the band's character, this is undoubtedly their most popular work. The one-time addition of American Kit Watkins produces some fine keyboard lead work. Rupert Hines's resourceful production and appearances by

Phil Collins and Mel Collins round out this strong release. "Survival" and "Who We Are" feature some fine orchestrations, and guitarist Latimer delivers some exceptional lead work on the album's closer, "Ice." *—Matthew Plichta*

● **Echoes—the Retrospective (Chronicles Series)** / Jul. 20, 1993 / Polygram
There might be a song or two that die-hard fans will miss, but this double-disc set is the place to go for anyone looking for that one essential CD purchase of Camel's music. Solid remastering and great liner notes and track annotation. *—Rick Clark*

○ **Compact Compilation** / Rhino 75900
An excellent selection from four of Camel's best albums: *Mirage*, *The Snow Goose*, *Moonmadness*, and *Rain Dances*. *—Michael P. Dawson*

Cameo

b. , USA
Group / Funk, urban R&B
Over the years, Cameo has reflected the numerous changes in the world of funk. When they started in 1974, they frequently toured with Parliament and Funkadelic, which is a clue to how their sound was styled. Even though they were in the hard funk vein of George Clinton's classic outfits, they were not copycats. As the '70s became the '80s, they started to play around with their sound slightly. In 1984, they found a successful style—the synth-powered title track to their album *She's Strange*. But that only hinted at what was to come. With 1986's *Word Up*, Cameo recorded a funk classic. Bass-driven and synth heavy, the album was the sound of the mid '80s. "Word Up" was also the song that broke them into the mainstream, reaching the Top Ten on the pop charts. The album didn't have just one good song, it had a whole album's worth, but *Word Up* was the pinnacle of Cameo's career. Synthesizers took precedence over melody and lyrics in their later records and the funk became somewhat weaker. *—Stephen Thomas Erlewine*

○ **Secret Omen** / 1979 / Chocolate City 2008
Cameo leaped over their rivals with this 1979 release. "I Just Want to Be" was their finest single to that point, and "Sparkle" made a good album cut. It was the band's biggest hit album as well, starting them on a string of five gold records. *—Ron Wynn*

Cameosis / 1980 / PolyGram 514824
Cameo hadn't yet reduced its group size or changed its direction when they released this 1980 LP. Larry Blackmon was still heading a large band that relied on horn-driven funk reflecting the influence of the second-generation Bar-Kays. There were signs of stagnation throughout *Cameosis*, however. Including the neglected single "Why Have I Lost You" from the *We Know Who We Are* album was a stroke of genius. They landed a Top-10 R&B hit with "Shake Your Pants," but this wasn't among their best funk LPs. *—Ron Wynn*

○ **Feel Me** / 1980 / Chocolate City 2016
One of two solid funk albums Cameo issued in 1980. This one had another tremendous single, "Your Love Takes Me Out" and a good second uptempo tune "Keep It Hot." It was also among the few '70s-style productions still viable at that point. *—Ron Wynn*

○ **Knights of the Sound Table** / 1981 / PolyGram 512595
Things were still rolling for Cameo with this album. It scored more hits for them with "Freaky Dancin'" reaching the number-three spot on the R&B charts. Changes were coming soon, but they still retained the familiar horn-dominated sound. *—Ron Wynn*

○ **She's Strange** / 1984 / Casablanca 814984
This was the final large-group Cameo album. Blackmon smartly realized that horn-driven funk was finished as a commercial entity in R&B production, and he stripped the group down to a core trio the next year. However, the title track was the group's biggest R&B hit ever; it stayed atop the charts four weeks—longer than the superior tunes "Word Up" or "Candy." "Talkin' Out the Side of Your Neck" was a good message track. Blackmon showed his savvy by making the change in direction even as he was still reaping commercial dividends from the old style. *—Ron Wynn*

Single Life / 1985 / Casablanca 824546
This was a transitional album for Cameo, the first with a core trio and refocused production and creative emphasis. Now they were a synth-dominated band with a snaking bass sound, rather than

a horn-oriented group playing elaborate arrangements and using multiple vocalists. Blackmon's through-the-nose Sly Stone imitation and a tighter style yielded immediate results: Both the title track and "Attack Me with Your Love" were Top-10 R&B hits. Cameo was now right in the urban-contemporary flow. —*Ron Wynn*

○ **Word Up** / 1985 / Casablanca 830265
Cameo's definitive album came as a surprise to those who'd classed them a good journeyman band. The title track became a national catch phrase in the African-American community, and "Word" remains a linguistic staple in hip-hop circles. It was also a first-rate song, with a hypnotic rhythm track and arrangement and Blackmon's best lead vocal. The follow-up singles "Candy" and "Back and Forth" were also excellent. Cameo eventually scored its only platinum album, and "Word Up" was their lone Top-10 pop hit. —*Ron Wynn*

● **Best of Cameo** / May 18, 1993 / Polygram 514824
These 14 selections range from formative cuts "Rigor Mortis," "Shake Your Pants," and "It's Over" to the definitive "Word Up," "Candy," and "Back & Forth." Blackmon's alternately sneering, defiant, and aggressive vocals were the constant from Cameo's beginnings in the '70s to their emergence as funk's reigning champions in the '80s. —*Ron Wynn*

Tevin Campbell

Vocals / Urban R&B
There's some dispute over who actually discovered Texas child sensation Tevin Campbell. Some accounts credit flutist Bobbi Humphrey, while much of the publicity material credits Quincy Jones. Campbell was in the 1988 television show "Wally & the Valentines" and appeared in Prince's film *Graffiti Bridge*. He made a splashy impression on Jones's *Back on the Block*, singing lead on "Tomorrow"—he was 14 at the time. Campbell made such an impact that he earned a solo deal with Jones's Qwest label. His 1991 debut, *T.E.V.I.N.*, included two big R&B and pop hits, "Round and Round" (first featured on the soundtrack to *Graffiti Bridge*) and "Tell Me What You Want Me to Do." Campbell's second album, *I'm Ready*, was released in 1993. —*Ron Wynn*

● **T.E.V.I.N.** / Nov. 19, 1991 / Reprise 26291
If *T.E.V.I.N.* had been recorded by an adult instead of a teenager, the album would still be impressive, yet the fact that Tevin Campbell was only 14 years old when this was made makes it all the more amazing. Campbell's voice is remarkably expressive, able to handle both ballads and uptempo dance tracks without losing confidence. When he has the right material—like the hit single, Prince's "Round and Round"—the results are flawless. If the material is weak, he's merely enjoyable. —*Stephen Thomas Erlewine*

I'm Ready / 1993 / Reprise
With a voice as strong, romantic, and fluent as Tevin Campbell's, he deserves better material than the smooth, bland urban R&B that dominates *I'm Ready*. Campbell sings rings around these songs, showing that he's a better vocalist than most contemporary singers, as well as proving that he'll need better songs to gain the respect he deserves. —*Stephen Thomas Erlewine*

Camper Van Beethoven

Group / Alternative pop/rock
Of all of their considerable strengths, perhaps Camper Van Beethoven's strongest was the fact that, given all their ambitions and weirdness, they never were inaccessible or pretentious. Whether they were playing country or Middle Eastern music, a Ringo Starr cover or a Black Flag song, Camper Van Beethoven's humor came out of a love of the music—it wasn't just a bunch of in-jokes from a pack of hipper-than-thou, overeducated college wiseasses.

For such a rough, young band, their first album, 1986's *Telephone Free Landslide Victory*, was amazingly inventive and spirited. Over the next four years, Camper Van Beethoven never lost that garagey edge to their music, no matter how arty it was (collaborations with experimental guitarist Eugene Chadbourne) or how simple (numerous covers, as well as originals like "Take the Skinheads Bowling" or "Eye of Fatima"). In 1990, they parted amicably, with several members taking their side project, the Monks of Doom, full time. Lead singer/guitarist David Lowery

formed Cracker, a more straightforward band that experienced a greater commercial success in the 1990s. Camper Van Beethoven's records haven't lost any of their charm over the years—if anything, the music sounds better a decade later than it did when it was recorded. —*Stephen Thomas Erlewine*

● **Telephone Free Landslide Victory** / 1985 / Independent Project 016
"Quirky", "eccentric", "eclectic"— all those words were used often to describe this marvelous debut by Camper Van Beethoven. The Middle East meets country western, and skinheads go bowling. — *Jeff Tamarkin*

II & III / Jan. 1986 / Capitol 13209
Similar to the debut. Well-played but not so humorous or sharp. —*Jeff Tamarkin*

○ **Camper Van Beethoven** / Feb. 1986 / Capitol 13210
Their third album is the apex of their creativity—stunning musicianship, witty lyrics, and a musical melting pot. Alternative rock at its most alternative. —*Jeff Tamarkin*

○ **Our Beloved Revolutionary Sweetheart** / 1988 / Virgin 90918
Camper Van Beethoven moved to a major label and lost none of their wildly eclectic and tuneful spark. In fact, *Our Beloved Revolutionary* contains some of their finest, most accessible songs. —*Stephen Thomas Erlewine*

Key Lime Pie / 1990 / Virgin 91289
Camper Van Beethoven's final record, *Key Lime Pie*, is the darkest album they ever recorded, yet within its gloomy grooves lurk some terrific, fractured pop songs that rank among their best material. —*Stephen Thomas Erlewine*

○ **Camper Vantiquities** / 1993 / Capitol 13211
All of Camper Van Beethoven's odds and ends (ranging from singles and B-sides, songs from tribute albums, and the entire *Vampire Can Mating Oven* EP) gathered together on one CD. *Camper Vantiquities* contains some of the band's finest work, making it equally appealing for hardcore and casual fans. — *Stephen Thomas Erlewine*

Can

Group / Experimental, electronic
Always at least three steps ahead of contemporary popular music, Can was the leading avant-garde rock group of the '70s. From the very beginning, their music didn't conform to any commonly held notions about rock & roll—not even those of the countercultures. Inspired more by 20th-century classical music than Chuck Berry, their closest contemporaries were Frank Zappa, or possibly the Velvet Underground. Yet their music was more serious and inaccessible than either of those artists. Instead of recording tight pop songs or satire, Can experimented with noise, synthesizers, nontraditional music, cut-and-paste techniques, and, most importantly, electronic music. Each album marked a significant step forward from the previous one, investigating new territories that other rock bands weren't interested in.

Throughout their career, Can's lineup was fluid, featuring several different vocalists over the years. The core band members remained keyboardists Irmin Schmidt and Holger Czukay, drummer Jaki Liebezeit, and guitarist Michael Karoli . During the '70s, they were extremely prolific, recording as many as three albums a year at the height of their career. Apart from a surprise British Top-30 hit in 1976, "I Want More," they were never much more than a cult band, and even critics had a hard time appreciating their music. When the band split in 1978, they left behind a body of work that has proven surprisingly groundbreaking. Echoes of Can's music can be heard in Public Image Limited, the Fall, and Einsturzende Neubauten, among others. As with much aggressive and challenging experimental music, Can's music can be difficult to appreciate, yet their albums offer some of the best experimental rock ever recorded. —*Stephen Thomas Erlewine*

○ **Monster Movie** / 1969 / Spoon 71442
Beat-heavy and guitar-driven drones dominate Can's second album. A taste of the tranced eclecticism to come. —*Myles Boisen*

Soundtracks / 1970 / Restless 71443
Psychedelic jams from five late-'50s movie soundtracks. Some inspired, some dated. —*Myles Boisen*

○ **Tago Mago** / 1971 / Restless 71444

All of their seemingly disparate influences are balanced and blended here, with the addition of vocalist Damo Suzuki. —*Myles Boisen*

○ **Ege Bamyasi** / 1972 / Restless 71444
Funky, urgent, and experimental at their 1972 peak, this documents a band that is still ahead of our time. —*Myles Boisen*

○ **Future Days** / 1973 / Spoon 71446
Long, jazzy excursions with few vocal moments. Uncharacteristic but engaging. —*Myles Boisen*

Soon over Babaluma / 1974 / Enigma 71447
The band at its most stripped-down potency. But without Damo, they have a new sound. —*Myles Boisen*

Unlimited Edition / 1976 / Mute 61072
Studio outtakes from Can's history up to 1975. Fascinating electronic and ethnic musical excursions. —*Myles Boisen*

● **Cannibalism 1** / 1978 / Spoon 71453
A sampler of early tracks up to 1974. Many of their most focused grooves and stylistic extremes are here. —*Myles Boisen*

Canned Heat

Group / Blues-rock
A hard-luck blues band of the '60s, founded by Al Wilson and Bob Hite, Canned Heat seemed to be on the right track and played all the right festivals (including Monterey and Woodstock, making it very prominently into the documentaries about both) but somehow never found a lasting audience. Wilson died under mysterious (probably drug-related causes) circumstances in 1970, and Hite carried on with various reconstituted versions of the band until his death in 1981, from a heart seizure just before a show. —*Bruce Eder*

● **Best of Canned Heat** / 1972 / EMI America 48377
All of Canned Heat's best tracks and biggest hits are included on this single-disc collection. —*Stephen Thomas Erlewine*

Uncanned! The Best of Canned Heat / 1994 / EMI America
Uncanned! The Best of Canned Heat is exactly what it claims to be—the definitive portrait of the blues-soaked hippie boogie band. Spreading forty-one tracks (including numerous rarities, alternate takes, and Levi commercials) over two CDs, the set is perfect for the hardcore Canned Heat collector. For casual fans, the collection contains too much music; they should stick with the single disc collection, *The Best of Canned Heat*—*Stephen Thomas Erlewine*

The Capitols

Group / R&B
The energetic Detroit-based Capitols capitalized on mid-'60s R&B dance fever with one of the most memorable entries of the genre, "Cool Jerk." Successful local producer Ollie McLaughlin signed the trio—lead singer Sam George, Donald Norman (who wrote most of the group's material under his real surname of Storball), and Richard Mitchell—to his Karen logo, and the irresistible "Cool Jerk" made them an overnight sensation. After a couple more chart entries later that year, the trio faded quickly. George was murdered on March 17, 1982. —*Bill Dahl*

● **Golden Classics** / Collectables 5105
Dance-oriented mid-'60s Detroit soul, with the notable classic "Cool Jerk." —*Bill Dahl*

The Capris

Group / Doo-wop
The only major Capris hit, the romantic "There's a Moon Out Tonight," is a New York street corner-harmony classic. Doo-wop was back in fashion by 1961, and it was no longer limited to R&B aggregations. Led by Nick Santo (born Nick Santamaria), the Capris named themselves after the Isle of Capri in Italy. The Queens, NY, natives originally cut "There's a Moon Out Tonight" for the obscure Planet imprint in 1958, but it only became a national smash when it was reissued on Lost Nite (and eventually on Old Town) in early 1961. After many moons out of the spotlight, the Capris came back triumphantly in 1981 with an album on Ambient Sound and an appearance on the PBS-TV series "Soundstage." —*Bill Dahl*

There's a Moon Out Again! / 1982 / Ambient Sound 37714

Recorded in 1982, live to two-track, here's a perfect example of what a great modern-day doo-wop album should be. —*Cub Koda*

● **There's a Moon Out Tonight** / Collectables 5016
Nick Santo's anguished, innocent-sounding lead on "There's a Moon Out Tonight" became a hit some three years after the song was originally issued. By this time they'd disbanded, but they regrouped in a hurry trying to milk the hit. It didn't hurt that DJ Murray the K was the person pushing the revived single. This album collects ten tunes they cut for Planet, most of them superior to "There's a Moon Out Tonight," but none of them able to duplicate that song's success. —*Ron Wynn*

Captain & Tennille

Group / Pop
Vibrant, relentlessly upbeat harmonies made the Captain (Daryl Dragon) & Tennille (Toni Tennille) stars during the latter half of the '70s. Dragon, dubbed "The Captain" for his distinctive headgear, had played keyboards with the Beach Boys prior to teaming with his wife. Their first hit on A&M, the buoyant "Love Will Keep Us Together," was a million-selling chart-topper in 1975, and a reissue of their 1974 single "The Way I Want to Touch You" also went gold. The couple hung three more gold records in their den in 1976—"Lonely Night (Angel Face)," "Shop Around," and Willis Alan Ramsey's "Muskrat Love"—and that was enough for ABC-TV to install them as hosts of their own variety program. "Do That to Me One More Time" was the last number-one item for the pair in 1979. —*Bill Dahl*

● **Captain & Tennille's Greatest Hits** / 1977 / A&M 3105
A solid collection of all of their mid-'70s hits. —*Stephen Thomas Erlewine*

Captain Beefheart

b. 1964, California
Vocals / Experimental, psychedelic, rock & roll
Drawing from gut-bucket Delta blues, free jazz, bare-boned rock, and the dissonance of 20th-century avant-garde chamber music, Captain Beefheart (Don Van Vliet) and the Magic Band never sold many records, but they influenced many alternative artists.

Beefheart, an accomplished multi-instrumentalist, exhibited a vocal range that (some claim) spanned seven and a half octaves, at times sounding like an utterly crazed incarnation of Howlin' Wolf. The first lineup of the Magic Band included Ry Cooder, and some of their first recordings on A&M were actually produced by future Bread founder David Gates.

Longtime friend and occasional musical cohort Frank Zappa signed Beefheart to his Straight label, allowing the group complete artistic freedom. The result was the groundbreaking *Trout Mask Replica*. Since then, he has put out a dozen albums, either with the Magic Band, with Zappa, or solo. Beefheart retired from music after the release of 1982's *Ice Cream for Crow*, choosing to concentrate on painting. —*Rick Clark*

○ **Safe As Milk** / 1967 / Buddah 5001
Captain Beefheart's *Safe As Milk* finds him leading his band through a fractured mess of blues and rock & roll, featuring plenty of fine guitar from Ry Cooder. —*Stephen Thomas Erlewine*

★ **Trout Mask Replica** / 1969 / Reprise 2027
Originally released and produced by Frank Zappa as a double album on his Bizarre/Straight label, *Trout Mask Replica* is the definitive Captain Beefheart album. To some, it is just plain weird, perhaps even anti-music. To others, it is blues with a warp or rock & roll at the absolute cutting edge. Deeply rooted in blues and jazz, the Captain taught each member of the Magic Band their extremely complex individual parts over the course of a year. Playful and challenging at the same time, rhythmically kinetic, poetically beautiful, it is an absolute masterpiece. —*Rob Bowman*

○ **Lick My Decals Off Baby** / 1970 / Bizarre 70364
The bookend release to *Trout Mask Replica*, this time produced by the Captain himself. A sample title, "The Smithsonian Institute Blues (The Big Dig)," should give you a sense that this is not an ordinary rock & roll record. Just a shade less essential than *Trout Mask Replica*. —*Rob Bowman*

The Spotlight Kid/Clear Spot / 1972 / Reprise 26249
The Spotlight Kid (1972) and *Clear Spot* (1973) have been released on one CD. The Captain became slightly more accessible on these two early-'70s releases, accenting the rock & roll ingre-

dients. Slide guitar abounds on some of the most asymmetrical riffs imaginable throughout *The Spotlight Kid*. The lyrics are just as playful. *Clear Spot* is the Captain at his most balanced—accessible without deserting the avant-garde. "Big-Eyed Beans from Venus" became one of his all-time classics. —*Rob Bowman*

Mirror Man / 1973 / One Way 22166
An early version of the Captain's Magic Band, recorded live in Los Angeles probably in 1968 (the cover says 1965, but that is undoubted erroneous). Stunning extended versions of four Beefheart originals, including his Robert Johnson-inspired "Tarotplane." —*Rob Bowman*

○ **Shiney Beast Bat Chain Puller** / Jan. 1978 / Bizarre 70365
The Captain's comeback album, with the second edition of the Magic Band. As good as *Clear Spot* or *The Spotlight Kid*, with a slightly different temperament and a touch of synthesizer. —*Rob Bowman*

○ **Doc at the Radar Station** / 1980 / Blue Plate 1824
The masterpiece of the Captain's late-'70s to early-'80s resurrection. This time, the new Magic Band had coalesced into an ensemble of frightening power. Cross-rhythms abut each other in some of the most hyperkinetic settings imaginable. There's not a weak song or performance to be found. —*Rob Bowman*

○ **Ice Cream for Crow** / 1982 / Blue Plate 1632
The Captain's last album as of this writing, with no sign that he'll ever return. A couple of changes in the Magic Band and the Captain perhaps losing a bit of steam make this album undistinguished. But there's nothing poor here; if you are into the Captain, you'll want to own this. —*Rob Bowman*

Legendary A&M Sessions / 1984 / A&M 12150
Before gaining a cult with his avant-garde excursions in the late 1960s, Captain Beefheart wielded a much more traditional sort of blues-rock. That's not to say that these his two obscure mid-'60s A&M singles (packaged together on this five-song EP, which adds a previously unreleased track from the same era) aren't well worth hearing. The Captain's Howlin' Wolf-like growl led a tough outfit that ranked among the best early American blues-rock groups—and among the few that could reasonably emulate the Rolling Stones' toughness. Produced, unbelievably enough, by future Bread leader David Gates, this reissue includes their regional hit cover of Bo Diddley's "Diddy Wah Diddy." The best track, though, is "Moonchild," their shameless derivation of Howlin' Wolf's "Smokestack Lightning." —*Richie Unterberger*

Caravan
Group / Progressive rock
Of all of the progressive-rock bands that came from England in the late '60s, Caravan was certainly one of the most interesting. Instead of indulging in the classical pomp of most of the other groups of that era, Caravan was gentle where others were overbearing, melodic where others were ponderous. That doesn't mean they weren't spontaneous—some of their best moments came when the band launched into extended, intricate improvisations. Caravan's music was based more in traditional English folk and medieval instrumentation; it was not unusual to hear lush strings and woodwinds on their albums. Although the lineup changed slightly over the '70s, they kept releasing records until 1983. That year's *Back to Front* marked the reunion of the original quartet: guitarist and vocalist Pye Hastings, keyboardist David Sinclair, bassist and vocalist Richard Sinclair, and drummer Richard Coughlan. —*Rick Clark*

● **Canterbury Tales—Best Of** / 1993 / See For Miles 505
This double-disc set is the place to go. It contains Caravan's significant airplay tracks, as well as the most popular album tracks, many of which are quite extended. —*Rick Clark*

Mariah Carey
b. Mar. 22, 1970, New York, NY
Vocals / Pop/rock, urban R&B, dance-pop
Mariah Carey has a remarkable multi-octave voice, an astonishing instrument that can reach heights rivaled only by Whitney Houston. Like Houston, Carey works pop-soul ballad territory, occasionally spiked by some catchy dance-oriented pop. Fortunately, Carey hasn't had a shortage of good material; all of her three albums feature impeccably crafted singles designed for continuous radio play.

While she was an overnight sensation with her first single, 1990's "Vision of Love," it wasn't until 1992 that she won over many skeptical critics with her unadorned "MTV Unplugged" performance. Not that negative criticism has hurt her career any—her three albums and one EP have all sold several million copies, and she has dominated the singles chart since her first album. It's a track record very few artists can match. —*Stephen Thomas Erlewine*

○ **Mariah Carey** / 1990 / Columbia 45202
Carey sold over five million copies of her debut, which featured ballads and R&B hits like the Grammy-winning "Vision of Love." —*Donna DiChario*

Emotions / 1991 / Columbia 47980
Carey continues to crank out the hits with her blend of dance, pop, and R&B. The album includes the smash hits "Emotions" and "Make It Happen." —*Donna DiChario*

○ **MTV Unplugged EP** / Mar. 1992 / Columbia 52758
Although Mariah Carey doesn't come close to following the traditional "unplugged" format of only a voice and a guitar (she brought in strings and backup vocalists), her *MTV Unplugged EP* (which includes her hit version of the Jackson 5's "I'll Be There") is her most subtle record to date, proving that her talents as vocalist are considerable. —*Stephen Thomas Erlewine*

● **Music Box** / 1993 / Columbia 53205
Carey reins in her remarkable voice from the previous heights it once reached, and the result is her finest album yet. Apart from the treacly remake of Badfinger's "Without You," each song is a fine example of adult contemporary pop, deserving of all the airplay it receives. *Music Box* includes the hit singles "Dreamlover" and "Hero." —*Stephen Thomas Erlewine*

Eric Carmen
b. Aug. 11, 1949, Cleveland, OH
Vocals / Pop/rock
Eric Carmen was the lead vocalist and songwriter of the Raspberries, an early-'70s band heavily influenced by mid-'60s pop, especially the Beatles. For his 1975 self-titled debut album, Carmen looked even further into the past, to the early 20th century. His two hit singles, the heavily produced ballads "All by Myself" and "Never Gonna Fall in Love Again," were based on pieces by Russian classical composer Sergey Rachmaninoff. The rest of the album and Carmen's subsequent, less commercially successful albums were a pastiche of classic pop styles. Carmen didn't enjoy a big commercial success again until 1987's "Hungry Eyes," from the *Dirty Dancing* soundtrack. —*Kenneth M. Cassidy*

Eric Carmen / 1975 / Rhino 71141
Carmen achieved far greater success with his debut solo album than he ever had with his old group, the Raspberries. In part this was because, freed from the restrictions of leading a rock band, he could indulge his taste in big, lush ballads. That's what he did here, especially on the album's three Top-40 hits, one of which, "All by Myself," was a gold-selling number-two hit. —*William Ruhlmann*

● **Best of Eric Carmen** / 1988 / Arista 8548
This album lacks Carmen's 1988 hit "Make Me Lose Control," but it does sample six of the eight singles-chart entries he enjoyed from 1975 to 1980, plus interesting album cuts such as "Hey Deanie," the Shaun Cassidy hit written by Carmen, and, of course, his comeback hit, "Hungry Eyes," from the *Dirty Dancing* soundtrack. —*William Ruhlmann*

Kim Carnes
b. Jul. 20, 1945, Los Angeles, CA
Vocals / Pop/rock
The raspy-voiced singer's atmospheric number-one smash, "Bette Davis Eyes," was cowritten by Jackie DeShannon. Carnes was once a member of the New Christy Minstrels with Kenny Rogers, who gave her welcome exposure in 1980 with their duet "Don't Fall in Love with a Dreamer." Later that year, a Carnes cover of the Miracles' "More Love" was a smash. She scored numerous pop hits throughout the decade and experimented with country in 1988. —*Bill Dahl*

● **Gypsy Honeymoon: Best of Kim Carnes** / 1993 / EMI 82232
Don't mistake this set as a definitive collection of hits. While it contains her three biggest Top-Ten numbers ("Bette Davis Eyes,"

"More Love," and "Don't Fall in Love with a Dreamer," a duet with Kenny Rogers, six Top-40 hits are missing. Nevertheless, the material that exists here is a good representation of Carnes's considerable singing and songwriting capabilities. —*Rick Clark*

The Carpenters

Group / Pop
Between 1969 and 1981, the brother-sister duo of Richard (b. 1946) and Karen Carpenter (1950-1983), made 20 trips to the Top-40 singles charts with their ultra-sweet light pop featuring Karen's wholesome, even-tempered alto voice. During the first half of the '70s, the Carpenters were one of pop's most successful acts with 12 Top-Ten hits, including "Top of the World," "(They Long to Be) Close to You," "We've Only Just Begun," "Rainy Days and Mondays," "Superstar," "Hurting Each Other," "Yesterday Once More," "For All We Know," and "Sing." —*Rick Clark*

○ **Close to You** / 1970 / A&M 3184
This was the Carpenters' breakthrough album. Its title track was their first major hit, and it spawned the follow-up, "We've Only Just Begun," which has been used in countless weddings since. The album also contained various pop covers of '60s hits like "Help!" and "Baby It's You," reinforcing the group's implied ties to rock while fostering the birth of a new generation of easy-listening music. This album won the Carpenters a Best New Artist Grammy for 1970. —*William Ruhlmann*

● **Singles (1969-1973)** / 1981 / A&M 3601
Exactly what it claims to be, this compilation contains 10 of the Carpenters' 12 Top-Ten hits, from "Close to You" to "Top of the World." They continued to make the charts until 1982, but the bulk of their memorable pop hits—the songs that reintroduced soft, melodic music to the masses and rolled back the rock revolution—are here. —*William Ruhlmann*

○ **Yesterday Once More** / 1985 / A&M 6601
A two-CD set with 27 songs, *Yesterday Once More* includes their big hits, like "We've Only Just Begun" and "Close to You," but there are a few sleeper cuts too. —*Bil Carpenter*

James Carr

b. Jun. 13, 1942, Memphis, TN
Vocals / Soul, R&B
Considered to be among the very greatest of "deep" Southern male soul singers, James Carr's succession of R&B hits on the Memphis Goldwax label were all gems of country-soul, that wonderful '60s marriage of Southern Black R&B vocalists with songs written in a country format and played mostly by White musicians. Carr's dark, gospel-inflected style, marked by a subtle, rich voice that is almost frightening in its intensity and range, has been compared to that of Otis Redding and Percy Sledge. Many reviewers would class him above even these formidable peers. "At the Dark End of the Street," the first songwriting collaboration between Dan Penn and Chips Moman, is Carr's undisputed masterpiece. Also recorded by Aretha Franklin, Clarence Carter, Linda Ronstadt, and Ry Cooder, it is the quintessential country-soul take on adulterous love.

Carr's career initially was short; Goldwax ceased operation in 1969, and he cut only one other single for Atlantic in 1971. However, he has recently emerged from retirement with a new album on Goldwax. His work stands at the apex of '60s soul—with Aretha, Otis, Percy, and Wilson. Essential stuff! —*Christine Ohlman*

Take Me to the Limit / 1991 / Goldwax 5002
Carr's comeback, on a resurrected Goldwax label. Doesn't quite live up to his '60s stuff (maybe nothing could) but it is good contemporary Southern soul in the classic vein, and it's great to have him back! —*Christine Ohlman*

● **You Got My Mind Messed Up** / Vivid Sound 002
A somewhat pricey Japanese import, with its companion *A Man Needs a Woman*, of all the great Goldwax gems. Includes the classic "At the Dark End of the Street," the achingly beautiful "These Ain't Raindrops," plus 19 more. Until a cheaper reissue comes along, this is absolutely essential. —*Christine Ohlman*

Paul Carrack

b. Apr. 22, 1951, Sheffield, England
Vocals, Keyboards / Pop/rock

Despite a distinctive, soulful singing style, British keyboardist Paul Carrack's most popular work has not been done under his own name. He is the voice on Ace's "How Long," Squeeze's "Tempted," and Mike & the Mechanics' "The Living Years." Carrack finally began to score his own hits in the late '80s. —*William Ruhlmann*

○ **One Good Reason** / 1987 / Chrysalis 21578
The third of Carrack's four solo albums of the '80s is the best-realized showcase for his soulful vocals. It produced four singles-chart entries, the most successful of which was the Top-Ten hit "Don't Shed a Tear," Carrack's first big hit under his own name. —*William Ruhlmann*

● **Twenty-One Good Reasons: The Paul Carrack Collection** / 1994 / Chrysalis 27221
Containing not only his solo hits, but also the ones that he sang for Ace ("How Long"), Squeeze ("Tempted"), and Mike and the Mechanics ("Silent Running" and "The Living Years"), as well as two songs with Carlene Carter, *Twenty-One Good Reasons: The Paul Carrack Collection* is the one Carrack disc to own. —*Stephen Thomas Erlewine*

Jim Carroll

b. 1950, New York, NY
Vocals / New wave
New York poet and rock & roll frontman Carroll published *The Basketball Diaries*, an influential book of poetry, and recorded during the early '80s, bringing his cryptic, junkie-framed lyrics to jagged, Big Apple punk. "People Who Died" was his only hit. —*John Floyd*

○ **Catholic Boy** / 1980 / Atlantic 38132
Inspired by beat poets, basketball, and the New York street hustle, Carroll took his tales from the printed pages to the punk-rock stage. —*Jeff Tamarkin*

○ **I Write Your Name** / 1983 / Atlantic 80123
Disappointing follow-up, although some lyrics are worth investigating. —*Jeff Tamarkin*

● **Best of** / 1993 / Rhino
A fine collection of all of the highlights from Carroll's varied career. —*AMG*

The Cars

b. , USA
Group / New wave, pop/rock
The Cars were one of the most popular rock bands in America between 1978 and 1985. Formed in Boston in 1976, the quintet was Rick Ocasek (guitar and vocals), Ben Orr (bass and vocals), Greg Hawkes (keyboards), Elliot Easton (guitar), and David Robinson (drums). Their 1978 debut album *The Cars*, which typified their sleek sound—new wave energy matched to tight rhythms, disembodied vocals by Ocasek and Orr, and an affection for the sound of '60s bubblegum music—was an immediate success, spawning the singles "Just What I Needed" and "My Best Friend's Girl."

After turning out million-selling albums in 1979 (*Candy-O*), 1980 (*Panorama*), and 1981 (*Shake It Up*), the group members took a breather for solo albums before returning for their biggest album yet, *Heartbreak City* (featuring the hits "You Might Think," "Magic," and "Drive"), in 1984. *Door to Door* (1987) marked a falloff in the band's popularity, and they split soon after, with Ocasek so far the most prominent solo star. —*William Ruhlmann*

○ **Cars** / 1978 / Elektra 135
On the heels of new wave, this debut album for the Cars was a mechanized rock delight—its music spare and precise yet undeniably catchy, with sly references to the Beatles and Tommy James & the Shondells. Ocasek and Orr's vocals sounded oddly dispassionate, as if they were being sung in a foreign language. —*William Ruhlmann*

○ **Candy-O** / 1979 / Elektra 507
The Cars' debut album was still charting when its follow-up, *Candy-O*, appeared in the spring of 1979, sporting a cover drawing by Vargas, noted for his *Playboy* illustrations of voluptuous women. It duplicated its predecessor's success; in fact, it outpaced the first album's chart ranking by going to number three as the number-14 single, "Let's Go" (the Cars' biggest hit thus far) be-

came one of the summer songs of the year. "It's All I Can Do" hit as well. —*William Ruhlmann*

Shake It Up / 1981 / Elektra 567
Making extensive use of video promotion, the Cars rebounded sharply with their fourth album, whose title track was actually their first Top-Five single. The album also featured the underrated "Since You're Gone." —*William Ruhlmann*

○ **Heartbeat City** / 1984 / Elektra 60296
A break of three years gave the Cars plenty of time to write strong material. At the same time, Michael Jackson's *Thriller* had expanded the number of singles that could be pulled from one album, good news for the radio-friendly Cars, who scored five hits off this album, including the Top Tens "You Might Think" and "Drive." As a result, the album became the Cars' all-time bestseller. —*William Ruhlmann*

★ **Greatest Hits** / 1985 / Elektra 60464
Ultimately, the Cars were a singles band. Here are those singles, including the biggest ones, "Drive," "Shake It Up," "You Might Think," and "Tonight She Comes." —*William Ruhlmann*

Carter the Unstoppable Sex Machine

Group / Alternative pop/rock, dance-pop
Equally revered and despised in their native England, Carter the Unstoppable Sex Machine has been on the cutting edge of the British dance-pop scene since their first hit single in 1989. Instead of following the disco-derived pop songs of the Pet Shop Boys, Carter relies more on the underground dance club scene, bringing such techniques as spoken-word samples, drum and riff samples, and a relentless beat to tuneful, hook-oriented pop songwriting. In addition, their attitude is inspired by punk rock's mentality, which manifests itself in their satiric lyrics and slash-and-burn approach to ravaging pop's past and present. Their second single, "Sheriff Fatman," is arguably the finest example of their style and it was the song that established them as a force in the United Kingdom.

Perhaps it was coincidence, but after settling a copyright infringment lawsuit with lawyers representing the Rolling Stones in 1991, Carter began to open up their sound slightly (although they were still heavily dance-oriented, there weren't as many recognizable sound bites) but not at the expense of their pop sensibilities. Unfortunately, the pop audience wasn't as receptive to Carter as it had been a couple of years earlier, and they still couldn't earn anything larger than a cult following in the United States. Ironically, the group hasn't declined creatively and are continuing to record some of the most interesting records in the alternative dance-pop world. —*Stephen Thomas Erlewine*

○ **101 Damnations** / 1990 / Chrysalis 21881
Great crafty pop from England that is danceable as well as thought-provoking, using synthesizers and real instruments. Unpredictable, yet never disappointing. —*John Book*

● **1992 —The Love Album** / 1992 / Capitol 21946
With its seamless mix of samples, beats, melody, and social consciousness, Carter the Unstoppable Sex Machine's third album is their best, most fully realized record to date. —*Stephen Thomas Erlewine*

○ **Post Historic Monsters** / Jan. 25, 1994 / IRS 27090
While it didn't receive much critical or commercial attention, Carter's fourth album ranks as one of their finest, filled with inventive fusions of dance and pop. —*Stephen Thomas Erlewine*

Clarence Carter

b. Jan. 14, 1936, Montgomery, AL
Vocals, guitar, keyboards / Soul, R&B
A blind soul singer whose numerous hits of the late '60s and early '70s epitomized the Muscle Shoals R&B sound, Carter hit the big time with his Atlantic single "Patches" (1970) and won a lasting place in the annals of Southern soul with others, like "Slip Away" and "Too Weak to Fight." In 1981 Carter broke out of a dry spell with the Venture album *Let's Burn*, featuring a track called "Workin' (On a Love Building)," which set the theme for much of what was to follow: robust, lascivious lovemaking boasts. More recent tracks, such as his salacious reworking of Tampa Red's "Love Me with a Feeling" and the jukebox favorite "Strokin'" (too risqué for some radio stations), further solidified the carnal Carter image. Still primarily a soul/R&B singer, Carter has incorporated

more hard-blues elements in his music recently than in the Muscle Shoals days, despite his new and unblues-minded penchant for playing and programming all the instruments on his albums. —*Jim O'Neal*

○ **Dr.'s Greatest Prescriptions—The Best of Clarence Carter** / 1971 / Ichiban 1116
A selection of Carter's lascivious recent output on Ichiban Records. —*Bill Dahl*

● **Snatchin' It Back** / 1992 / Rhino 70286
Snatchin' It Back—The Best of Clarence Carter is a great compilation, spotlighting Carter's stellar guitar work and trademark vocals on classics like "Slip Away," "Too Weak to Fight," and "Lookin' for a Fox." His great "Tell Daddy" (covered by Etta James as "Tell Mama") is included. Dave Marsh contributes the liner notes. Soul music at its funky best, and *the* compilation to own if you're a Carter fan. —*Christine Ohlman*

Peter Case

Vocals, guitar / Folk-rock, country-rock
After the breakup of the early '80s power-pop band the Plimsouls, Peter Case followed a different musical path in his solo career. Instead of the concise, rocking pop songs that were the Plimsouls' speciality, Case turned to the folkie territory of a singer/songwriter, making a string of underappreciated albums since 1986, all of them distinguished by a reliance on sharp, clever lyrics supported by a fluid melodicism and spare, stripped-down rock. —*Stephen Thomas Erlewine*

Peter Case / 1986 / Geffen 24482
Case's debut suffers from diverse stylistic jumps, but its best songs (seven, by my count) are compassionate, intelligent, and intriguing. —*John Floyd*

○ **Man with the Blue Postmodern Fragmented Neo-Traditionalist Guitar** / 1989 / Geffen 24238
On *The Man with the Blue Postmodern Fragmented Neo-traditionalist Guitar*, Case sticks to one style, a Mellencampish rocker oozing with compassion. This beats the debut through the range of Case's lyrical concerns and his intense vocals. —*John Floyd*

● **Six-Pack of Love** / 1992 / Geffen 24466
Peter Case's most folk-oriented album to date is also his most inconsistent, yet there are enough solid songs to make it worthwhile for his fans. —*Stephen Thomas Erlewine*

The Castelles

Group / Doo-wop
Sporting the high tenor lead of George Grant, the Philadelphia-based Castelles cut a series of beautiful doo-wop items during the mid '50s. The group was formed in 1949 and signed with Grand Records in 1953, debuting with "My Girl Awaits Me." Specializing in ballads such as "This Silver Ring" (written by '60s soul producer Jerry Ragovoy) and "Heavenly Father," the Castelles briefly moved to Atco in 1956 before calling it quits. —*Bill Dahl*

● **Sweet Sounds of the Castelles** / 1987 / Collectables 5002
Dreamy mid-'50s Philly doo-wop. —*Bill Dahl*

Jimmy Castor

Vocals, saxophone / Funk
A master of novelty/disco funk, saxophonist Jimmy Castor started as a doo-wop singer in New York. He wrote and recorded "I Promise to Remember" with the Juniors in 1956, a group whose roster included Al Casey, Jr., Orton Graves, and Johnny Williams. Castor replaced Frankie Lymon in the Teenagers in 1957, before switching to sax in 1960. He appeared on several soul-jazz and Afro-Latin sessions and had a solo hit with "Hey Leroy, Your Mama's Callin' You" in 1966. Castor also played sax on Dave "Baby" Cortez's hit "Rinky Dink."

He formed the Jimmy Castor Bunch in 1972 and signed with RCA. Their first album, *It's Just Begun*, launched Castor's next phase with the song "Troglodyte (Cave Man)." It was a Top-Ten R&B and pop smash. Castor continued the trend in 1975 with "The Bertha Butt Boogie" and later recorded "E-Man Boogie," "King Kong," "Bom Bom," and "Amazon." The Castor band included keyboardist and trumpeter Gerry Thomas, bassist Doug Gibson, guitarist Harry Jensen, conga player Lenny Fridle, Jr., and drummer Bobby Manigault. Thomas left the band to join the

Fatback Band. Castor recorded as a solo performer from 1976 until 1988. —*Ron Wynn*

● **Hey Leroy** / 1967 / Smash 27091
Long before Jimmy Castor became a successful humorist and funkmeister, he scored a Latin hit with "Hey Leroy, Your Mama's Callin' You." While the title suggests anything but this, it was a smoothly performed bit of Afro-Latin samba with jazz touches by saxophonist Castor. It was such a hit he issued an entire album of similiar tunes that didn't do anywhere near as well as the single, which cracked the R&B Top 20 (number 16) and pop Top 40 (number 31). It would be another five years before Castor formed the Jimmy Castor Bunch and became a comedy/novelty hit via "Troglodyte," and "Bertha Butt Boogie." —*Ron Wynn*

● **Best of the Jimmy Castor Bunch** / 1976 / RCA 10877
This album collected saxophonist/humorist Jimmy Castor's biggest novelty smashes from his mid-'70s days on Atlantic. Castor's "Bertha Butt Boogie" was an R&B and pop hit, and he mined the novelty field again with "E-Man Boogie" and "E-Man Groovin," plus "King Kong." —*Ron Wynn*

Nick Cave

Vocals / Alternative rock
After the Birthday Party called it quits in 1983, singer/songwriter Nick Cave assembled the Bad Seeds, a post-punk supergroup featuring former Birthday Party guitarist Mick Harvey on drums, ex-Magazine bassist Barry Adamson, and Einsturzende Neubauten's guitarist Blixa Bargeld. With the Bad Seeds, Cave continued to explore his obsessions with religion, death, love, America, and violence with a bizarre hybrid of blues, gospel, rock, and arty post-punk, although in a more subdued fashion than his work with the Birthday Party. On his albums with the Bad Seeds, his literary aspirations come to the forefront; the lyrics are narrative prose, heavy on literary allusions and myth-making. Often, Cave's gloomy lyrics, dark musical arrangements, and deep baritone voice recall the albums of Scott Walker, who also obsessed over death and love with a frightening passion. However, Cave brings a hefty amount of post-punk experimentalism to Walker's epic dark pop. By melding the grandeur of Walker to the spareness of the blues, as well as adding the self-conscious eclecticism of post-punk and his own literate lyrics, Cave has emerged as one of the most distinctive and respected figures of alternative rock. —*Stephen Thomas Erlewine*

○ **From Her to Eternity** / 1984 / Mute 71435
Desperate and ominous, this is a chilling love letter. —*John Dougan*

○ **First Born Is Dead** / 1985 / Positive 26
Recorded with the Bad Seeds, this album contains angst directly influenced by early American folk-blues. —*John Dougan*

Kicking against the Pricks / 1986 / Homestead 065
All covers, all unique, all recorded with the Bad Seeds. More rock of your worst nightmare. —*John Dougan*

○ **Your Funeral My Trial** / 1986 / Homestead 073
A double EP. Less focused but still good. —*John Dougan*

Good Son / 1990 / Elektra 60988
Slightly Brazilian-influenced. Still worthwhile, but his least essential. —*John Dougan*

● **Henry's Dream** / 1992 / Mute 61323
Henry's Dream, Nick Cave's apocalyptic, postmodern reading of gospel and the blues, is one of Cave's strongest albums. —*Stephen Thomas Erlewine*

Let Love In / 1994 / Elektra
Let Love In is a darker, more brooding album than *Henry's Dream*, making it one of Nick Cave's most harrowing records. —*David Jehnzen*

Chad & Jeremy

Group / British invasion, pop/rock
This soft-pop duo from England arrived during the first wave of the British Invasion in 1964. Their image and sound echoed (but was softer than) Peter & Gordon, who already had a couple of big hits under their belts when Chad & Jeremy scored with their debut "Yesterday's Gone."
"A Summer Song," their second single, broke the U.S. Top Ten at number seven. Several other hits followed, and Chad & Jeremy became fixtures on TV shows like "Hullabaloo." In keeping with

the times, they released one of the first "concept" albums, *Of Cabbages and Kings*, in 1967. They broke up shortly thereafter, with Jeremy pursuing an acting career and Chad continuing in music. —*Rick Clark*

● **Painted Dayglow Smile** / Jul. 14, 1992 / Columbia 47719
Since their early hits ("Yesterday's Gone," "A Summer Song," "Willow Weep for Me") are only available on various compilations, *Painted Dayglow Smile: A Collection* is the best Chad & Jeremy collection available, featuring their later hits ("Before and After," "I Don't Wanna Lose You Baby," "Distant Shores") as well as several lesser-known songs. Hardcore fans will find all of the albums absolutely necessary, and this disc doesn't even have all the tracks casual fans want, but it'll have to do until a definitive retrospective is available. —*Stephen Thomas Erlewine*

Eugene Chadbourne

b. Jan. 4, 1954, Mount Vernon, NY
Guitar / Experimental, progressive rock
Not strictly a jazz or a rock musician, Eugene Chadbourne is certainly an improviser. His sprawling, skittering, bursting guitar forays are among modern music's most anthemic delights. He combines the wildness of the freest jazz with the unpredictability of manic rock, and adds his own convoluted lyrics and vocals/comments. Chadbourne began playing guitar at 11. He moved from bottleneck blues to bebop and free jazz, then met England's Derek Bailey. Chadbourne's debut included a nod to Anthony Braxton. He began working with Frank Lowe and Billy Bang in the late '70s, then teamed with John Zorn and Tom Cora. Chadbourne's group Shockabilly mixed country, rock, free, and just plain noise, in an inspired, if at times completely chaotic, manner. He recorded with Camper Van Beethoven in the '80s. Chadbourne's material is considered too noncommercial for rock and too outrageous for even most free jazz fans. —*Ron Wynn*

Country Protest / 1985 / Fundamental 7
The warped guitarist/vocalist/deconstructionist puts original political tunes and covers of several '60s staples through his horror-show wringer. Experimental to the max. —*Jeff Tamarkin*

○ **Vermin of the Blues** / 1987 / Fundamental 18
With backing from frantic Austin rockers Evan Johns & the H-Bombs, and originals like "Fried Chicken for Richard Speck" meeting covers of Count Basie and the Count 5, this is Eugene at his most perverse. —*Jeff Tamarkin*

● **LSD C&W** / 1987 / Fundamental 19
The ultimate Chadbourne, featuring medleys of the Beatles, Roger Miller, and Burl Ives, plus much more insanity filtered through post-avant-garde brilliance. —*Jeff Tamarkin*

○ **Dear Eugene** / 1987 / Placebo 025
Dear Eugene, What You Did Was Not Very Nice, So I Am Going to Kill . . . is live, solo, extremely cool. Who else would construct a Bacharach/Manson tune? —*Jeff Tamarkin*

○ **There'll Be No Tears Tonight** / Jan. 1987 / Fundamental 006
Country fans expecting straight, faithful versions of these covers of Roger Miller, Hank Williams, and Merle Haggard will be in shock. Imagine honky-tonk as free jazz, and that's what you'll get. —*Jeff Tamarkin*

Chairmen of the Board

Group / Soul
The Chairmen of the Board were one of the most dynamic acts to emerge on Holland/Dozier/Holland's Invictus label after the legendary songwriters exited Motown. Lead Norman "General" Johnson had previously fronted the Showmen, who hit in 1961 with "It Will Stand," cut in New Orleans. Johnson's pinched, intense vocal delivery powered the pleading "Give Me Just a Little More Time," the first smash for the Chairmen in late 1969, although Danny Woods handled lead duty on the group's biggest R&B seller, "Pay to the Piper." Johnson, who wrote "Patches" for the group's first album, only to see Clarence Carter score the hit, departed in 1974 to start a solo career. —*Bill Dahl*

● **Greatest Hits** / Jan. 9, 1992 / HDH 3901
Driving Detroit soul of the late '60s to early '70s. General Johnson's pungent lead vocals give this quartet a unique sound. Their notable hit was 1970's "Give Me Just a Little More Time," which is here along with 14 other tracks, including the "Pay the Piper" and "Patches." —*Bill Dahl*

Chameleons

Group / Alternative pop/rock
A Manchester, England, intellectual pop outfit, the Chameleons were slightly ahead of their time. Writing stylish, moody guitar-swirled pop, they set the stage for numerous British bands to come, never really reaping the benefits of their (often much better) music. —*John Dougan*

○ **What Does Anything Mean? Basically?** / 1985 / Statik 22
Their second studio album solidly sustains the *Script* formula. —*Steve Aldrich*

● **Script for the Bridge** / 1985 / Statik 17
With dark, dense, but heavily melodic songs equaling the strength of Echo & the Bunnymen and Joy Division, this is a largely undiscovered '80s classic. —*Steve Aldrich*

Fan & the Bellows / 1986 / Caroline 1332
Collection of singles and predebut album material. —*Steve Aldrich*

Gene Chandler

b. Jul. 6, 1937, Chicago, Illinois
Vocals / Soul, R&B
Chandler, a Chicago soul journeyman, worked under the tutelage of Curtis Mayfield during the mid '60s. His understated, balladesque style is best heard on his 1962 Vee-Jay hit, "Duke of Earl." —*John Floyd*

○ **Gene Chandler Situation** / 1970 / MER 61304
Slick Chicago soul from 1970. Includes the smash "Groovy Situation." —*Bill Dahl*

● **The Duke of Earl** / 1993 / Vee-Jay 712
Gene Chandler exploded on the '60s soul scene with "Duke of Earl," a brillant piece of novelty/love song material. His hit singles could be formulaic, but Chandler's expressive, haunting voice never failed to lift a trite lyric or punctuate a great one. This 23-cut set contains many songs previously available only as singles, and mixes the requisite hits with nicely done obscurities like "London Town," "Day to Day" and "Baby, That's Love." Curtis Mayfield provided several gems for Chandler, including "Rainbow," and "Man's Temptation." This isn't the complete Gene Chandler output, but it's certainly got most of his prime early numbers and lots of smashes. —*Ron Wynn*

The Chantels

Group / R&B, doo-wop
This early female R&B quartet was led by powerhouse vocalist Arlene Smith, whose vocals on their 1957 hit "Maybe" remain some of the most moving ever recorded. —*John Floyd*

● **Best of the Chantels** / 1990 / Rhino 70954
One of the leading girl groups of the late '50s, distinguished by Arlene Smith's impassioned leads. —*Bill Dahl*

Harry Chapin

b. Dec. 7, 1942, New York, NY, d. Jul. 16, 1981, Jericho, NY
Vocals, guitar / Singer/songwriter
Singer/songwriter Harry Chapin made a solid career out of essentially setting short stories to music. His most popular tracks were "Taxi," "W.O.L.D.," "Cat's in the Cradle," and "Sequel," which was a followup to the story in "Taxi." Chapin's music possessed a folksy intimacy, further enhanced by the stirring chamber-style string work. His voice, while limited, conveyed the sincerity of his feelings, despite a tendency toward heavy-handed proselytizing. Chapin put his money where his mouth was, however, devoting much of his time and income to aiding the hungry and socially disenfranchised. During his career, he raised over five million dollars for various causes. Chapin died in an auto accident on July 16, 1981, on the way to do a benefit. —*Rick Clark*

○ **Heads & Tales** / 1972 / Elektra 75023
Chapin's breakthrough album, with "Taxi." —*Dan Heilman*

● **Anthology of Harry Chapin** / 1985 / Elektra 60413
A fine summary, featuring "Cat's in the Cradle," "Taxi," and others. —*Dan Heilman*

Tracy Chapman

b. 1964, Cleveland, OH
Vocals, guitar / Singer/songwriter

Tracy Chapman was the most successful folk-based performer to emerge in the '80s. Born in Cleveland, she won a scholarship to the Wooster School in Connecticut, then attended Tufts University. She began singing on street corners and in coffeehouses in the Boston area, then signed with Elektra Records after graduating from college.

Chapman cut her debut album, prominently featuring her throaty alto and acoustic guitar, with minimal added instrumentation. Her songs were closely observed tales of lower-class life (the hit "Fast Car") and political rhetoric ("Talkin' 'bout a Revolution"), sung compellingly. Released on April 1, 1988, *Tracy Chapman* became a number-one international hit, selling three million copies in the United States and a reported six and a half million more overseas. Chapman toured extensively behind it, including a series of Amnesty International benefits around the world. She won three 1988 Grammy Awards, including Best New Artist. *Crossroads*, her second album, was released in 1989 and was also a million-seller. Her third album, *Matters of the Heart*, was released in 1992. —*William Ruhlmann*

● **Tracy Chapman** / 1988 / Elektra 60774
With her choked voice and acoustic guitar, Tracy Chapman reawakened social awareness and demonstrated the power of folk music on her debut album, singing of homelessness and desperation and "Talkin' 'bout a Revolution." Contains the Top-Ten hit "Fast Car." —*William Ruhlmann*

Crossroads / 1989 / Elektra 60888
Coming after her remarkably accomplished debut, the slightly subdued follow-up *Crossroads* is a mild disappointment, but after a few plays, songs like "Bridges" and "Crossroads" reveal themselves to be among her finer work. —*Stephen Thomas Erlewine*

Matters of the Heart / 1992 / Elektra 61215
Less bold and angry than her previous work, Chapman paces *Matters of the Heart* over an acoustic course that touches equally on personal vignettes and social commentary. With her fluid, rapid-fire delivery, Chapman takes aim at society and lands several direct hits devoid of self-righteousness: songs about the downtrodden ("Bang Bang Bang"), greed at the expense of everyone else ("So"), feminism ("Woman's Work"), and freedom ("I Used to Be a Sailor"). A couple of songs suffer from too much sweetening in the studio, diluting the impact of Chapman's potent lyrics. —*Roch Parisien*

Charlatans UK

b. , Manchester, England
Group / Alternative pop/rock
Along with the Happy Mondays, the Charlatans were one of Manchester, England's two leading bands in the late '80s and early '90s. More pop-oriented than either the Happy Mondays or the Inspiral Carpets, the Charlatans brought '60s melodies and hooks—complete with prominent Hammond organs and swirling guitar lines—together with a pulsating dance beat, creating a new psychedelia for the '90s clubgoer. Although they weren't as inventive as the Stone Roses, when the Charlatans were at the top of their form in the early, pregrunge '90s, they made some irresistible singles that were hits in the United Kingdom ("Then" and "The Only One I Know"). They weren't able to duplicate their success in America, where they were forced to tack "UK" to the end of their name because they shared it with a San Francisco garage rock band from the '60s.

As their career progressed, the Charlatans' sound became more streamlined, losing some of the neo-psychedelic club-oriented rhythm tracks that pigeonholed them as part of the Manchester scene, as the 1994 single "Can't Get out of Bed" demonstrates. All the while, they haven't lost their flair for good pop singles, and each of their albums has a few gems scattered among the tracks. —*Stephen Thomas Erlewine*

● **Some Friendly** / 1990 / Beggars Banquet 2411
This British band combines '60s psychedelia with a '90s mentality, creating a strong retro-groove. —*Donna DiChario*

○ **Between 10th & 11th** / Apr. 14, 1992 / Beggars Banquet 61108
The Charlatans' sophomore effort is surprisingly more successful than the group's debut. While lacking the knockout punch of anything as strong as "The Only One I Know," this set steers clear of the underdeveloped material that marred much of the previous album, without deviating from the basic formula. —*Steve Aldrich*

○ **Up to Our Hips** / 1994 / Beggars Banquet 92352

As the Manchester craze fades further into the past, the Charlatans continue to streamline their vaguely psychedelic pop approach. On *Up to Our Hips*, the band refashions '60s British Invasion pop for the '90s, removing most of the dance tendencies that lay beneath the surface of their previous albums. As "Can't Get Out of Bed" shows, their songwriting skills have continued to improve, making the album rank alongside their earlier, more popular releases. —*Stephen Thomas Erlewine*

Ray Charles (Ray Charles Robinson)

b. Sep. 23, 1930, Albany, GA
Vocals, piano, arranger, songwriter / R&B, soul
The seminal '50s Atlantic recordings of Ray Charles virtually defined the very essence of soul, and his radical early '60s R&B-country synthesis helped immeasurably to bridge the gap between the two idioms. If he isn't a certifiable genius, as is often claimed, Ray Charles is certainly one of the most influential musical figures of the 20th century.

Completely blind by age seven, Charles mastered the piano in his teens and, by 1948, was already recording in a Nat Cole/Charles Brown-derived style. But Charles hit upon the daring concept of combining joyous gospel rhythms with secular lyrics just about the time he signed with Atlantic, turning the musical world on its collective ear in the process.

With his jazzy combo in place, Brother Ray sat down at the 88s and began racking up hits during the mid '50s: "I've Got a Woman," "Hallelujah, I Love Her So," and, in 1959, the wondrous "What'd I Say," which combined the call-and-response structure of the church with the sexually charged message of the blues. The number-one R&B seller also showcased Charles's pioneering use of the electric piano.

When Charles signed with ABC-Paramount in 1960, he shifted gears entirely, delving deep into pop and country in his own inimitable style. Ray Charles epitomizes the soul idiom with his gospel-soaked vocals and keyboards, though his recent recording activities have generally been confined to the country field (with the exception of those ubiquitous Diet Pepsi TV ads). —*Bill Dahl*

Great Ray Charles / 1956 / Atlantic 81731
A superb late-'50s instrumental album showcasing the jazz side of Ray Charles. Quincy Jones provided the arrangements, and the Charles band included Fathead Newman and Hank Crawford. The CD version includes six marvelous bonus cuts, among them a remarkable cover of Fats Waller's "Ain't Misbehavin'." —*Ron Wynn*

○ **Genius of Ray Charles** / 1960 / Atlantic 1312
Another instrumental pop, blues, and jazz masterpiece from Ray Charles. Quincy Jones again did the arrangements, and Charles covered everything from "Alexander's Ragtime Band" to "Come Rain or Come Shine." This was the first Charles album to hit the charts, though it certainly wouldn't be his last. —*Ron Wynn*

Genius Hits the Road / Oct. 1960 / Paramount 335
Great blues, soul, and jazzy pop from Ray Charles, then in the midst of perhaps his most creative streak as a performer. Charles's vocals were animated, urgent, and spectacular, while the arrangements, production, material, and instrumental backing were equally splendid. —*Ron Wynn*

And Betty Carter / 1961 / Dcc 39
One of the more intriguing and controversial albums in Ray Charles's distinguished career. He and Betty Carter toured together in the early '60s, cutting this session for ABC-Paramount in 1961. She has since slammed the album; Charles hasn't commented on it. You can hear the differences in style and approach, and at times Carter's jazzy touches don't mesh with Charles's soulful delivery. But there are also plenty of electric moments, and the album has worn well over the years. —*Ron Wynn*

○ **Genius After Hours** / 1961 / Rhino 90464
A great all-instrumental album, with Charles playing straight jazz, pop tunes, blues, and combinations of all those forms and more. Some equally fine solos from Fathead Newman, Hank Crawford, and Charles on keyboards and alto sax. —*Ron Wynn*

○ **Genius + Soul = Jazz** / 1961 / Dcc 38
A memorable early-'60s big-band session that produced the instrumental hit "One Mint Julep." —*Hank Davis*

☆ **Modern Sounds in Country & Western Music, Vol. 2** / 1962 / Rhino 70099

Charles's second installment of *Modern Sounds in Country and Western Music* is every bit as essential as the first, containing stellar interpretations of "Your Cheatin' Heart" and "You Are My Sunshine." —*Stephen Thomas Erlewine*

☆ **Modern Sounds in Country & Western Music** / 1962 / Rhino 70099
The album that sounded shock waves in both the country and R&B camps when it was issued. Ray Charles showed it was possible to take traditional country tunes, sing them in a soulful manner, and not pervert either style. The album was so successful it eventually spawned a follow-up. —*Ron Wynn*

★ **His Greatest Hits—Vols. 1 & 2** / Feb. 1987 / Dcc 037
These discs contain 40 tracks from Charles's ABC-Paramount tenure, covering the years 1960 through 1972. While under contract with ABC, Charles placed 51singles on the *Billboard* charts. Most of the important ones are included here, alongside a few judiciously chosen album cuts. Styles range from country-soul to jazz to stone R&B. Digitally remixed and remastered by Charles and Steve Hoffman, the sound is a joy. Absolutely recommended. —*Rob Bowman*

☆ **Greatest Country Western Hits** / 1988 / Dcc 040
Collecting the highlights from Charles's two *Modern Sounds in Country and Western Music* albums, *Greatest Country Western Hits* features some of the most essential country-soul material ever recorded. —*Stephen Thomas Erlewine*

○ **Anthology** / 1989 / Rhino 75759
Here is perhaps the best single-CD collection of Ray Charles's '60s and '70s ABC-Paramount material. They've also been issued on two separate anthologies, but for someone who only wants the essential items, this disc has them all over its 20 tracks. —*Ron Wynn*

★ **Birth of Soul** / 1991 / Rhino 82310
On three CDs, *The Birth of Soul* contains every R&B recording Ray Charles waxed while at Atlantic between 1952 and 1959. The early recordings are in the Charles Brown/Nat King Cole "Sepia Sinatra" vein; the later recordings go a long way toward defining the birth of soul. Robert Palmer has contributed a superb set of liner notes, contextualizing both Charles and the recordings. The sound is state of the art. This is essential, seminal American music. —*Rob Bowman*

Blues & Jazz / 1994 / Rhino/Atlantic 71667
There's general agreement that much, if not most, of Ray Charles's greatest music was made during his Atlantic tenure. This catalog has been revisited, repackaged, and reissued so often that there's little of value that's not currently available. But Rhino has released another concept set, a two-disc collection that spotlights blues vocals and jazz instrumentals culled from various sessions. The material ranges from an early swingtime date to seminal Atlantic material featuring Charles as a leader and in collaboration with vibist Milt Jackson, David "Fathead" Newman, and Edgar Blanchard. The first disc offers blues, the second jazz pieces. Such seminal albums as *The Genius of Ray Charles*, *Genius Sings the Blues*, *The Genius After Hours*, and *The Great Ray Charles* were tapped for classics like "Drown in My Own Tears" and "I Believe to My Soul," while the two Ray Charles/Milt Jackson releases and Newman's solo debut were the source for fine covers of Fats Waller and Horace Silver originals, among other material. There's nothing wrong with these tracks—they were spectacularly performed and belong in anyone's collection—it's just hard to believe there are that many Ray Charles fans who don't already own them in either their original form or in one of several previously issued Atlantic packages. —*Ron Wynn*

★ **Best of Atlantic** / 1994 / Rhino
For fans who don't want to invest in the three-disc boxed set, this is a good single-disc collection of Charles's groundbreaking Atlantic singles. —*AMG*

Cheap Trick

Group / Power pop, hard rock, pop/rock
This Rockford, IL, quartet arrived at a time (the mid '70s) when FM rock was skidding toward its nadir and punk was emerging. With their audacious debut, Cheap Trick seemed like the panacea for those who loved melodic Anglo-rock and the crash-and-burn of *Live at Leeds*-period Who. Imagewise, Cheap Trick seemed to have their cake and eat it too, with their loony dicotomy of pretty

boys and geeks. Rick Nielsen's amphetamine-nerd personna, with his formidable chops as a lead guitarist and songwriter, flew in the face of popular poseur guitar heros. For their second album, *In Color*, Cheap Trick did an about-face and delivered a collection of concise power-pop songs. Ever since, they've vacillated between mainstream hard rock and power ballads, with mixed results. —*Rick Clark*

○ **Cheap Trick** / 1977 / Epic 34400
A raucous debut loaded with brain-crunching rude noises and attitude, plundering all the right stuff (the Beatles, the Who, the Move). All this supports some primo rockers like "Hot Love," "He's a Whore," "Taxman, Mr. Thief," and "Oh Candy"—which ranks as one of the great lost rock singles of the '70s. Subsequent albums sound tame next to this one. Without a doubt one of their best. —*Rick Clark*

○ **In Color** / 1977 / Epic 34884
Their second album ditches boisterous performances in favor of super-tight pop-rock with hooks galore. All the same influences are there; it's just more mannered. The lightweight "I Want You to Want Me" became their first hit. Also check out "Big Eyes," "Clock Strikes Ten," and "You're All Talk." —*Rick Clark*

○ **Heaven Tonight** / 1978 / Epic 35312
Since Cheap Trick had dispensed with the straight medicine after an excellent debut, this third album recalibrates the band's pop smarts with an impressive handful of tunes. "Surrender," in particular, is a classic. The band wears its good taste well, with a fine cover of the Move's "California Man." —*Rick Clark*

★ **Live at Budokan** / Feb. 1979 / Epic 35795
While their records were entertaining and full of skillful pop, it wasn't until *Live at Budokan* that Cheap Trick's vision truly gelled. Many of these songs, like "I Want You To Want Me" and "Big Eyes," were pleasant in their original form, yet compared to the roaring versions on this album, they seemed like mere sketches. With their ear-shatteringly loud guitars and sweet melodies, Cheap Trick unwittingly paved the way for much of the hard-rock of the next decade, as well as a surprising amount of alternative rock of the '90s, and it was *Live at Budokan* that captured the band in all its power. —*Stephen Thomas Erlewine*

○ **Dream Police** / Oct. 1979 / Epic 35773
With the big time upon them, Cheap Trick went for bigger production sounds. Fortunately, it worked most of the time. The paranoid title cut is an effective, highly orchestrated rocker. Other notable tracks are the appealingly melodic (albeit wimpy) "Voices" and the no-frills rock of "I Know What I Want," complete with a great chorus you can shout to. In spite of its strengths, *Dream Police* marks the beginning of the band's creative decline. —*Rick Clark*

Next Position Please / 1983 / Epic 38794
This release, produced by Todd Rundgren, is Trick's last decent album, opening with a great Robin Zander original "I Can't Take It." "Borderline," "Next Position Please," and "Younger Girls" are all strong, but the Rundgren-penned "Heaven's Falling" is magnificent. —*Rick Clark*

Lap of Luxury / 1988 / Epic 40922
Despite its formulaic approach, *Lap of Luxury* scored a major hit with "The Flame," which briefly returned Cheap Trick to the top of the charts. The rest of the album either featured similar power ballads or half-hearted hard-rockers like their cover of "Don't Be Cruel." —*Stephen Thomas Erlewine*

○ **Greatest Hits** / 1992 / Epic 48681
Hardly a passable collection, certainly not definitive by any standard. Nevertheless, it'll be good for those who prefer the band's more recent cookie-cutter hits like "The Flame" and "Can't Stop Falling in Love." —*Rick Clark*

○ **Woke Up with a Monster** / Jan. 1994 / Warner Brothers 45425
Cheap Trick's Warner debut, produced by Ted Templeman (Van Halen, Little Feat) is their best album in years, certainly since 1983's *Next Position Please;* it's easily an equal to *Dream Police*. In spite of some uneven spots, there is more fire in their sound here, and when they go for the kind of big rock ballads that became their metier in recent years there is enough attitude to counteract most of the tendency toward sappiness. Highlights are "You're All I Wanna Do," "Let Her Go," "My Gang," and the title cut. —*Rick Clark*

☆ **Budokan II** / Feb. 1994 / Epic 53308

Recorded in Japan over 1978 and 1979, this concert set amply displays everything that made Cheap Trick the great band it was—great songs set to a wall of guitars and bass, great over-the-top singing, and crash and bash drumming. It's hard to pick highlights, but they absolutely make the Move's "California Man" their own. Either this album or *Live at Budokan* make a perfect introduction. —*Rick Clark*

Chubby Checker (Ernest Evans)

b. Oct. 3, 1941, South Carolina
Vocals / R&B, rock & roll
He taught America how to twist. Not just the kids, who always learned the latest steps, but everyone—from society matrons and jetsetters to the proverbial man in the street.

Rock & roll was becoming complacent when Chubby Checker came along in 1960 with his note-for-note remake of Hank Ballard and the Midnighters' "The Twist" and got it moving again. The husky Philadelphia lad, known as Ernest Evans until Dick Clark's wife decided he resembled Fats Domino, had already waxed a few 45s for the local Parkway label, including a novelty called "The Class" that found him imitating Fats, Elvis, and even the Chipmunks. But it was "The Twist," a number-one hit not once but twice (in 1960 and 1961), that made him an international celebrity.

Checker quickly became the nation's leading dance specialist, introducing "The Hucklebuck," "The Fly," "Pony Time," and "Limbo Rock" to the gyrating masses and successfully recycling his initial routine into "Let's Twist Again" and "Slow Twistin'." While racking up monster sales figures for Parkway, Checker starred in a couple of quickie exploitation films, *Twist Around the Clock* and *Don't Knock the Twist*, later trying his hand at folk songs when the twist fad finally began to fade.

The British invasion led to some lean years for Checker, although he got a little revenge by charting with a cover of the Beatles tune "Back in the U.S.S.R." in 1969. But he continued to put on a high-energy show that inevitably built to his classic million-seller—and Chubby Checker proved every time out that he was still the king of the Twist. —*Bill Dahl*

● **Greatest Hits** / 1972 / Onyx Classix 269013
The long out-of-print two-LP set contains all of the early-'60s twist and related dance workouts that made this Philadelphian a star. —*Bill Dahl*

Cher

b. May 20, 1946, El Centro, CA
Vocals / Pop/rock
After untying the knot with Sonny Bono in 1974, Cher developed into a pop icon of a magnitude many times brighter than during her '60s duet days with her husband. Even while married to Sonny, Cher was hitting the charts as a solo act with "Bang Bang (My Baby Shot Me Down)" in 1966 and "You Better Sit Down Kids" in 1967, both on Imperial, and her output on Kapp included the 1971 number-one hit "Gypsys, Tramps & Thieves." The gold records continued with "Half-Breed" in 1973 and "Dark Lady" in 1974, both chart-toppers on MCA. 1979's "Take Me Home" was Cher's last smash for eight years, but she wasn't idle, starring in the acclaimed motion pictures *Silkwood* and *The Witches of Eastwick* and winning the 1987 Best Actress Oscar for her role in *Moonstruck*. Cher roared back in 1989 with "After All," a duet with Peter Cetera, and the anthemic solo outing "If I Could Turn Back Time," both on Geffen. Whether she's hawking memberships for a health-club chain or tearing up a concert stage, Cher endures as one of the nation's premier celebrities. —*Bill Dahl*

● **Greatest Hits** / 1974 / MCA 922
Cher's early '70s hits—including "Gypsies, Tramps, and Thieves," "Half-Breed," and "Dark Lady"—are compiled on this collection. —*Stephen Thomas Erlewine*

○ **Cher (Geffen)** / 1987 / Geffen 24164
Cher's late-'80s musical comeback was fueled by her success as an actress, not her songs, yet her first album of the '80s was a surprisingly consistent set of slick contemporary pop, including the hit "We All Sleep Alone." —*Stephen Thomas Erlewine*

● **Heart of Stone** / 1989 / Geffen 24239
One of the most mature albums of Cher's career, focusing on relationships from a 40-year-old's perspective rather than a teenager's. Cuts include "If I Could Turn Back Time," "Just Like

Jesse James," and a duet with Peter Cetera, "After All." —*Bil Carpenter*

● **Bang Bang, My Baby Shot Me Down: The Best of Cher** / 1991 / EMI America 92773

Bang Bang, My Baby Shot Me Down—The Best of Cher collects more than 20 of Cher's '60s solo cuts on the Imperial label. There is the Motown-styled "Dream Baby," but it's mostly folk-pop including little-known gems like the pensive "She's Not Better Than Me." —*Bil Carpenter*

Love Hurts / 1991 / Geffen 24369

Although it isn't quite as varied as its predecessor, *Love Hurts* features many of the same elements of *Heart of Stone* without winding up as a retread. The approach resulted in the hits "Love and Understanding" and "Save Up All Your Tears." —*Stephen Thomas Erlewine*

The Chi-Lites

Group / Soul

Ultra-smooth ballads were the specialty of the Chi-Lites, and they were one of the Windy City's hottest soul exports throughout most of the '70s. Changing their name from the Hi-Lites, the quartet recorded for a number of local firms before hitting in 1969 on Brunswick with "Give It Away." Lead Eugene Record's floating tenor caressed the R&B chart-toppers "Have You Seen Her" in 1971 and "Oh Girl" the next year, and the group scaled the soul playlists regularly through 1976, when Record went solo. Founding member Marshall Thompson keeps the group active today. —*Bill Dahl*

★ **Greatest Hits** / 1992 / Rhino 270532

Outstanding collection containing everything you need, including the hits "Oh Girl" and "Have You Seen Her." —*John Floyd*

Chic

Group / Disco, funk

Chic was the best and most influential disco band of the latter half of the '70s, earning hits with both their own records and the outside productions of coleaders Nile Rodgers and Bernard Edwards. Beginning their career as the Big Apple Band, the group changed their name to Chic in 1977 after Walter Murphy & the Big Apple Band had a number-one hit with "A Fifth of Beethoven." Along with the change in name came a change in music, from fusion to disco. Edwards (bass), Rodgers (guitar), and Tony Thompson (drums) hired Norma Jean Wright and Alfa Anderson to sing, and they recorded a demo of "Dance Dance Dance." Atlantic picked it up in late 1977 after a series of rejections from other record labels. The single sold a million copies in one month, catapulting Chic into the forefront of the disco scene. After Wright left for a solo career, Luci Martin joined the band.

Chic's biggest hits—"Le Freak," "I Want Your Love," and "Good Times"—came in 1978-1979, and as disco started to fade, so did the group's popularity. Still, Chic's influence was apparent throughout the '80s; "Good Times" alone spawned Queen's hit "Another One Bites the Dust" (a complete rip-off), and Sugarhill Gang used the record as the foundation for "Rapper's Delight," arguably the first rap single. Nile Rodgers was one of the most successful producers of the early '80s, scoring hits with David Bowie's *Let's Dance*, Madonna's *Like a Virgin*, and Mick Jagger's solo debut, *She's the Boss*. Edwards' solo productions weren't as consistent as Rodgers's, but Power Station's album (which featured Tony Thompson on drums) was a hit. Chic re-formed in 1992, but failed to recapture the fire of its glory days. —*Stephen Thomas Erlewine*

★ **Dance Dance Dance: Best of Chic** / 1991 / Atlantic 82333

You think disco was nothing more than assembly-line funk and freeze-dried beats? Then you need to step into the crisp grooves and walloping boogie found on this stunning collection of Chic's '70s recordings. Such hits as "Good Times," "Dance Dance Dance," and "Le Freak" used the stylistic innovations of James Brown and Sly Stone as a blueprint for a new era of funk. Bernard Edwards's bass lines are so provocative they seem to talk, while Nile Rodgers's skeletal guitar runs hark back to Steve Cropper's slashing style. Sure, the songs don't say much. Sure, the dance mixes collected here ramble on after about six minutes. But once you step into these grooves—grooves that influenced an entire generation of artists from David Byrne to Prince—you'll realize that these were indeed good times. —*John Floyd*

○ **Best of Chic, Vol. 2** / 1992 / Rhino 71086

Filling in the gaps left by the first volume, *Best of Chic—Vol. 2* proves with its collection of album tracks and singles that Chic was not merely a great disco band, it was a great band, period. —*Stephen Thomas Erlewine*

Chicago (Chicago Transit Authority)

Group / Pop/rock

A rock band with a prominent horn section, Chicago was one of the most popular American groups of the '70s. By the second half of the decade, they were best known for ballads like "If You Leave Me Now." Their success continued with such material through the late '80s. —*William Ruhlmann*

○ **Chicago Transit Authority** / 1969 / Columbia 8

The first rock & roll band to successfully integrate a horn section into its sound, Chicago (fresh from years on the Midwestern bar circuit) demonstrated a wide versatility on its debut. The band seemed capable of playing everything from lounge music to hard rock, and here it mixed ballad material with gritty funk and psychedelic guitar, often on the same song. This time capsule of late-'60s popular music features the hits "Does Anybody Really Know What Time It Is?," "Beginnings," and "Questions 67 And 68." —*William Ruhlmann*

○ **Chicago II** / 1970 / Columbia 24

With its second double album (now on one CD), Chicago became even more ambitious and even more successful, mounting the extended "Suite for a Girl in Buchannon," from which were excerpted the hit singles "Make Me Smile" and "Colour My World." "25 or 6 to 4" is also featured on this album. —*William Ruhlmann*

Chicago III / 1970 / Columbia 24

With this album, Chicago had released three double record sets within two years, which glutted the market and drained the band members' creativity. The result was a falloff in quality and in sales, though *Chicago III* did manage to hit number two and stay in the charts for over a year, selling a million copies. There were only two Top-40 hits, "Free" and "Lowdown," neither of which is among the group's best. —*William Ruhlmann*

Chicago V / 1972 / Columbia 31102

The group's avant-garde roots are explored on the set-opening "A Hit by Varese," while the album also includes the autobiographical "Alma Mater" and the hits "Saturday in the Park" and "Dialogue." —*William Ruhlmann*

○ **Chicago VI** / 1973 / Columbia 32400

Chicago demonstrates all its strength here, turning in one of its great ballads in "Just You 'n' Me" and one of its great rockers in "Feelin' Stronger Every Day." Elsewhere, the group takes on its negative reviews in "Critics' Choice" and acknowledges the impact of Los Angeles stardom on a bunch of Midwestern kids in "Something in This City Changes People." —*William Ruhlmann*

Chicago VII / 1974 / Columbia 32810

Originally intended as a jazz-oriented record, Chicago's first double studio album since *Chicago III* (now on one CD) is an ambitious but ultimately uneven affair, buttressed by the hit singles "(I've Been) Searchin' So Long," "Call on Me," and "Wishing You Were Here." —*William Ruhlmann*

● **Greatest Hits I** / 1975 / Columbia 33900

The biggest hits of Chicago's first five years of recording, including "Just You 'n' Me," "Feelin' Stronger Every Day," "Wishing You Were Here," "Call on Me," and "(I've Been) Searchin' So Long." —*William Ruhlmann*

Chicago X / 1976 / Columbia 34200

It was here that Chicago began to turn toward "power" ballads, but only because it was scoring only modest hits with such more eclectic material as Lamm's "Another Rainy Day in New York City" and Pankow's "You Are on My Mind," while Cetera's "If You Leave Me Now" topped the charts, went gold, and won Grammy Awards for arrangement and vocal performance. —*William Ruhlmann*

Chicago XI / 1977 / Columbia 36517

On its last album to be produced by James William Guercio and to feature guitarist Terry Kath, Chicago turns in another competent but unremarkable effort. Cetera's "Baby, What a Big Surprise" is his follow-up to "If You Leave Me Now," Lamm continues to wax political on "Policeman" and "Vote for Me," and

"Take Me Back to Chicago" accurately expresses an exhausted band's sentiments at this point. —*William Ruhlmann*

○ **Chicago's Greatest Hits, Vol. 2** / 1981 / Columbia 37682
This album chronicles Chicago's gradual transformation in the second half of the '70s into a group that produced big ballads, usually sung by Peter Cetera. And here they are, starting with "If You Leave Me Now" and continuing with "Baby, What a Big Surprise" and the nostalgic "Old Days." —*William Ruhlmann*

Chicago 16 / 1982 / Full Moon 23689
With its back to the wall, Chicago switched record labels, dropped Dacus in favor of Bill Champlin (of the Sons of Champlin), brought in producer David Foster as their new Svengali, and went back to power ballads. And it all worked, at least commercially. "Hard to Say I'm Sorry" was the summer ballad of 1982, the album went Top 10, and Chicago was back in business, albeit with far more limited musical goals than it had had at the beginning. —*William Ruhlmann*

Chicago 17 / 1984 / Full Moon 25060
With sales of four million, this is the biggest selling regular studio album Chicago has made. That's what happens when you really go for the ballads: "Stay the Night," "Hard Habit to Break," "You're the Inspirstion," and "Along Comes a Woman" all fit into that category, all featured Peter Cetera, and all made the Top 15. Not surprisingly, Cetera decamped soon after. —*William Ruhlmann*

○ **Greatest Hits—1982-1989** / 1989 / Full Moon 26080
Chicago returned from a career dip in 1982 with "Hard to Say I'm Sorry" and continued to hit with power ballads, among them "Hard Habit to Break" and "You're the Inspiration," all sung by Peter Cetera. But the streak continued after Cetera departed in 1985, as Jason Scheff stepped in and Chicago went on to score hits like "Will You Still Love Me?" "I Don't Wanna Live without Your Love," and "Look Away," which are all heard here. —*William Ruhlmann*

○ **Group Portrait** / 1991 / Columbia 47416
If the three *Greatest Hits* collections don't look like adequate places to go, yet you want to have some Chicago in your collection, then *Group Portrait* is an extremely comprehensive boxed set that chronicles all the hits and important album tracks. —*Rick Clark*

The Chiffons

Group / Soul
The Chiffons were one of the few girl groups not produced by Phil Spector, maybe because they didn't need him. These NYC gals talked tough and to the point about the intricacies of the heart—whether filled with love or sliced in half. Their best '60s hits are high points of the genre. —*John Floyd*

○ **Greatest Recordings** / 1990 / ACE 293
A generous collection that features not only their greatest hits but many forgotten songs that are surprisingly good. —*Stephen Thomas Erlewine*

● **Best of the Chiffons** / Laurie 104
Everything you need by this delicious ensemble, including some undeservedly obscure gems. —*John Floyd*

Toni Childs

b. , Orange, California
Vocals / Singer/songwriter
Born in Orange, CA, Toni Childs grew up in a variety of locations around the United States and lived in London for four years, where she had a song-publishing deal with Island Music. She then moved to Los Angeles, where she became involved with David Ricketts (of David + David) and collaborated on the soundtrack for the film *Echo Park* (1986). Her debut album, *Union*, was recorded in London, Paris, Los Angeles, and Africa, and reflected an interest in the music of Zimbabwe as well as more conventional singer/songwriter styles. It earned her an opening spot on a Bob Dylan tour and a Grammy nomination for Best Female Rock Vocal, as well as reaching number 67 in the charts. Childs's follow-up, *House of Hope*, was released in 1991. —*William Ruhlmann*

● **Union** / 1988 / A&M 5175
Making her presence felt in the new wave of female singer/songwriters, Childs contrasts her vulnerable, dreamlike lyrics with a powerhouse booming alto voice. Includes the single "Don't Walk Away." —*Donna DiChario*

○ **House of Hope** / 1991 / A&M 5358
Even those who felt *Union*'s power couldn't have been prepared for Child's second album, which dealt with clinging to hope in the face of death, abuse, and indifference. Childs details these experiences not just in her words but in a pain-ravaged voice that reaches into the darkest recesses of the soul. —*Brian Mansfield*

Alex Chilton

b. Dec. 28, 1950, Memphis, TN
Vocals, guitar / Rock & roll
Over the course of the last 25 years, Alex Chilton's artistic career has run the gamut from singing on classic Top-Ten hit records with the Memphis, TN, group the Box Tops ("The Letter" and "Cry Like a Baby") to creating willfully chaotic solo outings with very limited commercial appeal. During the early '70s, Chilton helped form Big Star (with singer/songwriter Chris Bell). In spite of nonexistent sales, Big Star received much critical acclaim, influencing a generation of the post punk/power-pop movement. Chilton's later solo efforts ranged from ramshackle garage rock to tight Memphis-style R&B. —*Rick Clark*

Bach's Bottom / 1985 / Razor & Tie 2010
Recorded during one of Chilton's more chaotic periods, *Bach's Bottom* is an interesting document of misguided talent. It's not so much the music as it is the sense of what is going on around the music that makes this 1975 outing fascinating. Chilton's dismemberment of "Free Again," "Take Me Home and Make Me Like It," the Beatles' "I'm So Tired," and "Jesus Christ" are pretty funny, while his great self-productions of "Bangkok" and the Seeds' "Can't Seem to Make You Mine" reveal his penchant for making something special happen at times when everything seems to be falling apart. —*Rick Clark*

● **19 Years—A Collection** / 1991 / Rhino 70780
While it draws heavily on Big Star's disturbing third album (five tracks), *19 Years* offers a surprisingly coherent and listenable overview of Chilton's wildly inconsistent solo career, collecting some of the finest songs he has written since Big Star, as well as several exuberant covers ("Can't Seem to Make You Mine," "With a Girl Like You," and "Volare"). —*Stephen Thomas Erlewine*

○ **Feudalist Tarts/No Sex** / 1994 / Razor & Tie
By the mid '80s, Chilton had located to New Orleans and recorded *Feudalist Tarts*, his first album in six years. Unlike its predecessor, *Like Flies on Sherbert*, *Feudalist Tarts* marked a return to a more ordered sound that reflected Chilton's love for R&B and blues. Among the highlights are versions of Slim Harpo's "Tee Ni Nee Ni Noo," Carla Thomas' "B-A-B-Y," and his own "Lost My Job." *Feudalist Tarts* was followed by the *No Sex* EP, which is included on this disc. "Underclass" and the title track are among Chilton's finer compositions—rich in rude rootsy sounds and sarcastic deadpan humor. —*Rick Clark*

High Priest/Black List / 1994 / Razor & Tie
High Priest displays a more playful Chilton with versions of Dean Martin's "Volare," Bill Black's "Raunchy," and Charlie Rich's Sun classic "Lonely Weekends." His originals "Dalai Lama" and "Thing for You" are equally fine. *Black List*, which followed *High Priest*, opens with a great send-up of the hot rod anthem "Little GTO," and Walter Lewis's bluesy "I Will Turn Your Money Green" is the high point. Chilton plays all the instruments on both of those cuts. "Magnetic Field" and "Jailbait" are solid originals. —*Rick Clark*

Cliches / 1994 / Ardent
With just an acoustic guitar and voice, Alex Chilton delivers a low-key not too-perfectly performed collection of standards, like "All of You," "Save Your Love for Me," "Let's Get Lost," and even Mel Torme's "The Christmas Song." It's Chilton's subtlest work yet, and one of his best albums. —*Rick Clark*

The Chocolate Watch Band

Group / Psychedelic, garage rock
A legendary ensemble of the '60s, the Chocolate Watch Band's psychedelic punk/garage sound evoked the Rolling Stones at their bluesiest and mixed it up with sitars, bells, flutes, and an enviable array of hooks. —*Bruce Eder*

No Way Out / 1967 / Tower 5096

Debut effort includes the classic garage psychedelia single "Are You Gonna Be There (at the Love-In)," as well as versions of Chuck Berry's "Come On" and Wilson Pickett's "In the Midnight Hour." Other highlights include "Let's Talk about Girls" and "No Way Out." Interestingly, the trippy psycho-surf instrumental "Dark Side of the Mushroom" and the odd "Gossamer Wings" were concocted and tacked onto the album by engineer Richie Podolor (later Three Dog Night's producer) and Bill Cooper. — *Rick Clark*

Inner Mystique / 1968 / Tower 5106
In reality, only about half the tracks on this album are by the Watch Band, the rest being the work of a group of hastily assembled pick-up musicians and sessionmen. But it's all golden—the meandering psychedelic opening numbers have a certain appeal, the fake Watch Band's "In the Past" is a dazzling, glittering hallucinogenic jewel, and the real group's version of the Kinks' "I'm Not Like Everybody Else" is a are punk masterpiece. —*Bruce Eder*

One Step Beyond / 1969 / Tower 5153
The third album is probably the truest representation of the Watch Band, as more of the band and its material can be found here than anywhere else. The sound is a little less Stones, Standells, and Kinks and more a garage version of Moby Grape. Also included is "Blues Theme," a track the Chocolates recorded under the moniker of the Hogs, for the biker flick *The Wild Angels. —Rick Clark*

● **Best of the Chocolate Watch Band** / 1983 / Rhino 70108
A classic, too-little-known collection built on hooks by Brian Jones and Dave Davies, with punk enthusiasm and dope's most beguiling side effects. —*Bruce Eder*

The Church
Group / Alternative pop/rock, psychedelic
At their best, the Church spins out highly textured guitar psychedelia so atmospheric that the melodies work on a subconscious level, or they make a guitar-pop so melodic and hook-laden that it could be straight out of the Byrds and Beatles songbooks as interpreted by David Bowie. At their worst, they're ponderous and pretentious, with only their sonic textures to reccommend them. Fortunately, for most of their nearly 15-year career, they have been at their best, making some of the finest psychedelic-tinged guitar pop of the '80s.
   Although they were always fairly popular in their native Australia, it wasn't until 1988 that they had their first (and only) hit in America, the gorgeous "Under the Milky Way." Before that hit single, they had recorded several albums of rougher pop and psychedelia indebted to the Beatles and Syd Barrett. 1988's *Starfish* was their most polished record, but it also marked the culmination of the band's pop saviness. Since that record, not only has the lineup dwindled to two members, but the music has become more concerned with texture and atmosphere, not hooks and melody. Nevertheless, they remain one of the leading guitar-driven psychedelic bands of their time. —*Stephen Thomas Erlewine*

Of Skins & Heart / 1981 / Arista 8563
The band's first album (now on CD with several extra tracks) is their most straightfoward rock effort and one of their finest moments for that reason. "The Unguarded Moment" stands out as one of the great singles of the '80s. —*Chris Woodstra*

Blurred Crusade / 1982 / Arista 8564
The band defined their now trademark sound on this sophomore effort. Shimmering 12-string guitar work from Marty Willson-Piper more than hints at a Byrds influence. Steve Kilby adds to the lush backdrop with his dreamy, oblique lyric delivery. —*Chris Woodstra*

○ **Seance** / 1983 / Arista 8565
While it's often seen as one of their more excessive works, this neo-psychedelic masterpiece is actually the cullmination of the band's (especially Kilbey's) mystical obsessions. Although the songs are drawn out to nearly epic length, their pop sensibility is not forgotten. —*Chris Woodstra*

○ **Remote Luxury** / 1985 / Arista 8566
A combination of two fine EPs, *Remote Luxury* continues to build on the sound of *Blurred Crusade*. This one takes on an even more meditative and melancholy mood. —*Chris Woodstra*

○ **Heyday** / 1986 / Arista 8567

The band returns to a harder, more straight-ahead rock album with *Heyday*. The more ambitious arrangements, adding horns for the first time, help to flesh out their now-standard jangly retro-'60s sound. —*Chris Woodstra*

● **Starfish** / 1988 / Arista 8521
Engaging alternative rock, appealing to a wider range of listeners than their previous output. This album crystallizes the intensely atmospheric layers of bassist Steve Kilbey's lead vocals with swirling guitar work from Peter Koppes and Marty Wilson-Piper, yielding a Top 40 US hit with "Under the Milky Way." —*Donna DiChario*

Gold Afternoon Fix / 1990 / Arista 8579
The dreamlike essence prevails again as a hypnotic backdrop for the band's cryptic lyrics. —*Donna DiChario*

Priest = Aura / 1992 / Arista 18683
The Australian quartet returns to their earlier sound with less structured alternative-rock tracks. —*Donna DiChario*

Cinderella
Group / Hard rock, heavy metal
When Cinderella released their debut album, *Night Songs*, in 1986, they were packaged like a second-rate Bon Jovi imitation, which isn't surprising, since Jon Bon Jovi was reponsible for bringing the band to Mercury Records. Although the record isn't bad, it was standard lite-metal without much distinction, apart from lead guitarist and vocalist Tom Keifer's exaggerated Steven Tyler howl. With their second album, 1988's *Long Cold Winter*, they began to open up their sound slightly, bringing more blues and Rolling Stones influences to their hard rock. That approach reached its apex with their third album, 1990's *Heartbreak Station*, which swaggers defiantly, appropriating Stones and Aerosmith licks as if they had thought of the whole thing first. Naturally, it didn't sell as much as *Long Cold Winter* did, and the band has been quiet since its release. —*Stephen Thomas Erlewine*

Night Songs / 1986 / Mercury 830076
Jon Bon Jovi discovered this Pennsylvania band, and it's filled with the kind of catchy pop metal his own band plays. —*Stephen Thomas Erlewine*

○ **Long Cold Winter** / 1988 / Mercury 834612
A commercial breakthrough for Cinderella, producing three Top-40 singles "Don't Know What You Got (till It's Gone)," "The Last Mile," and "Coming Home." Cinderella's sound has grown bluesier, more like Led Zeppelin than Bon Jovi, and the songs are better. —*Stephen Thomas Erlewine*

● **Heartbreak Station** / 1990 / Mercury 848018
After successful albums that effectively followed contemporary hard-rock trends, Cinderella reached back into the Stones and Aerosmith songbooks and created a sneering, raunchy hard-rock album that was artistically their finest moment, even if it didn't reach the same commercial heights as its predecessors. But the number of sales doesn't matter (after all, it "only" sold a million copies)—*Heartbreak Station* is the album that shows Cinderella has more genuine rock & roll grit than most of the metal bands of the late '80s. —*Stephen Thomas Erlewine*

Circle Jerks
Group / Hardcore, heavy metal
The Circle Jerks were one of the first West Coast hardcore bands. Smartass ex-Black Flag vocalist Keith Morris was one of the genre's funnier mouthpieces, when his homophobia didn't get in the way. —*John Floyd*

○ **Group Sex** / 1980 / Frontier 34600
Fast and loud debut by this early California thrash combo, offering the best intro to their pungent social commentary and bad jokes. —*John Floyd*

● **Golden Shower of Hits** / 1983 / Rhino 71088
Another batch of gleeful vulgarity, *Golden Shower of Hits* features the notorious "Jerks on 45," along with their trademark wise-ass punk. Throughout the album, the band tempers their attack just slightly, making it their most listenable album. — *Stephen Thomas Erlewine*

Eric Clapton (Eric Patrick Clapp)
b. Mar. 30, 1945, Ripley, England
Vocals, guitar / Pop/rock, blues rock, rock & roll

When Eric Clapton released his first solo album in 1970, he was already considered the foremost guitarist of his generation. During the previous decade, he rocketed to stardom through his thrilling blues guitar heroics in the Yardbirds, John Mayall's Bluesbreakers, and Cream. With those three bands, Clapton became rock & roll's first true guitar hero, a musician who was known for his technical prowess, not hit singles. By doing so, he paved the way for Jimi Hendrix, Jeff Beck, and Jimmy Page, as well as thousands of other guitarists in the following decades.

Given his considerable talent, it is slightly ironic that on Clapton's solo albums, the guitar plays a supporting role. Apart from an occasional long jam, his solo work concentrates on the songs, not the guitar. 1974's *461 Ocean Boulevard* provides the blueprint—laidback rock, with touches of blues, country, and reggae. For the rest of the '70s, Clapton followed this pattern, although never with the commercial and artistic success of *461 Ocean Boulevard*.

By the mid '80s, Clapton's commercial fortunes were sagging, and he turned to Phil Collins for help. Under Collins's direction, Clapton recorded two slick, yet surprisingly ambitious albums that had little chart success. On the heels of the last Collins-produced album, a four-CD boxed-set retrospective of Clapton's career called *Crossroads* (1988) brought him back into the the spotlight.

With his next album, 1989's *Journeyman*, Clapton showed signs of getting his recording career back on track, but his burgeoning comeback was derailed when his young son died in an accident . Released about a year after the tragedy, Clapton's heartfelt tribute to his son, "Tears in Heaven," became his first number-one single. In the next year, an album of his "MTV Unplugged" performance was released; it became a block-buster success, selling over five million copies in the United States alone and winning an armful of Grammies. Although it was a fitting tribute to a long, accomplished career, the success was bittersweet. *—Stephen Thomas Erlewine*

○ **Eric Clapton** / Aug. 1970 / Polydor 825093
The band of Delaney & Bonnie backed Clapton on his first solo outing. Naturally, the results are much closer to Delaney & Bonnie than to Cream. Though Clapton sings about "Blues Power," the heart of this album is in rock & roll. *—Stephen Thomas Erlewine*

★ **461 Ocean Boulevard** / Aug. 1974 / Polydor 811697
Clapton returned from a break in recording to do the best solo album he ever made. *461 Ocean Boulevard* is laidback yet never boring, because Clapton sings and solos equally well. Clapton kept trying to remake this album, but he never recaptured its charming ambience. *—Stephen Thomas Erlewine*

☆ **Slowhand** / Sep. 1977 / Polydor 823276
After a spell of tepid albums, Clapton made a comeback with a recording that strongly recalls *461 Ocean Boulevard*. Certain influences became more pronounced (a country feel on "Lay Down Sally" and the cover of J. J. Cale's "Cocaine"), the blues sound heartfelt, and the guitar sounds as if it had taken a shot of adrenaline. One of his best efforts. *—Stephen Thomas Erlewine*

○ **Just One Night** / May 1980 / Polydor 800093
For once, Clapton's backing band (including guitarist Albert Lee) pushes him into recording an interesting, listenable live album. *—Stephen Thomas Erlewine*

● **Time Pieces: Best of Eric Clapton** / 1982 / Polydor 800014
A fine single-disc retrospective of some, but not all, of Clapton's best singles from the '70s. *—Stephen Thomas Erlewine*

○ **Money and Cigarettes** / Feb. 1983 / Warner Brothers 23773
Recorded with some old friends—including Ry Cooder, Duck Dunn, and Albert Lee—*Money and Cigarettes* is one of Clapton's finest albums. Instead of being an empty exercise in studio professionalism, the record is an appealing, low-key effort that features some of the smoothest blues Clapton has ever played. *—Stephen Thomas Erlewine*

☆ **Crossroads** / 1988 / Polydor 835261
A four-CD boxed set that follows Clapton from his Yardbird days to peddling Michelob on slick TV commercials. Following every different musical path Clapton has traveled over the years, the box is a musical autobiography, detailing both his strengths and weaknesses and revealing many insights to his scattered career. Plenty of unreleased songs are on *Crossroads*, including tracks

from an aborted second Derek & the Dominos album. *—Stephen Thomas Erlewine*

○ **Journeyman** / 1989 / Reprise 26074
While the songs are not always first-rate, Clapton is playing better than he has since the early '70s. Clapton's best album of the '80s. *—Stephen Thomas Erlewine*

○ **Unplugged** / 1992 / Reprise 45024
Paul McCartney may have been the first to release an album of his "MTV Unplugged" performance, but Eric Clapton's *Unplugged* was responsible for making acoustic-based music, and "unplugged" albums in particular, a hot trend in the early '90s. Clapton's concert was not only one of the finest "Unplugged" episodes, it was also some of the finest music he had recorded in years. Departing from the slick productions that tainted his '80s albums, the music was straightforward and direct, alternating between his pop numbers and traditional blues songs. The result was some of the most genuine, heartfelt music the guitarist has ever committed to tape. And some of his most popular—the album sold over seven million copies in the United States and won several Grammy awards. *—Stephen Thomas Erlewine*

Dave Clark Five

Group / British Invasion, rock & roll
For a very brief time in 1964, it seemed that the biggest challenger to the Beatles phenomenon was the Dave Clark Five. Seventeen times between 1964 and 1967, the Dave Clark Five made the Top 40, with memorable hits like "Glad All Over," "Bits and Pieces," "Because," and a remake of Bobby Day's "Over and Over." They made more appearances on the "Ed Sullivan Show" than any other English act. One of the elements that set the band apart from their British contemporaries was their larger-than-life production and their loud stomping drum sound.

Interestingly, and unusual for that time, bandleader Dave Clark managed and produced the band himself, negotiating a much higher royalty rate than artists of that period usually received.

The Dave Clark Five eventually fell out of step with the changing times and called it quits in 1970. *—Rick Clark*

● **History of the Dave Clark Five** / 1993 / Hollywood
For many years, the Dave Clark Five was one of the few major groups of the 1960s whose work was unavailable on compact disc. This two-disc, 50-track reissue not only rectifies that situation, but arguably includes more than all but devoted fans will want to hear. All of the band's mammoth mid-'60s hits—"Glad All Over," "Bits and Pieces," "Because," "Catch Us If You Can," "Anyway You Want It," and others—are included, and while they don't rival the work of British invasion heavyweights like the Beatles, Stones, and the Kinks, they still burst with exuberant melodies and harmonies and dense production. This compilation also features worthy lesser-known hits like "Try Too Hard" and "Everybody Knows."

as well as obscure but commendable beat ballads and raveups from their B-sides and albums. Nonetheless, there is a fair amount of filler, and their post-1966 work is undistinguished by either artistic growth or the hooks and heavy beat of their early material. But at their peak, the DC5 captured the *joie de vivre* of the British Invasion with a lasting power that cannot be dismissed. *—Richie Unterberger*

Dee Clark (Delecta Clark)

b. Nov. 7, 1938, Blytheville, AR, d. Dec. 7, 1990
Vocals / R&B, soul
Dee Clark was a solid R&B vocalist who had some huge hits in the late '50s and early '60s. The Arkansas-born singer moved to Chicago as a child and was in the Hambone Kids with Sammy McGrier and Ronny Strong. They recorded for OKeh in 1952; the next year Clark sang with the Goldentones. This group later became the Kool Gents, which recorded as the Delegates for Vee-Jay in 1956. Clark went solo in 1957, and in 1958 enjoyed his first smash with "Nobody for You," an Abner release that reached number three on the R&B charts and just missed the Top 20 on the pop charts. He continued a string of R&B winners with "Just Keep It Up," "Hey Little Girl," and "How about That" for Abner in 1959 and 1960. Clark teamed with guitarist Phil Upchurch to write "Raindrops" in 1961, his signature tune. The song peaked at number three R&B and number two pop, and was his last major

hit. Clark continued performing through the '60s, '70s, and '80s, but never again was a factor, though "Raindrops" remains a staple on oldies radio. —*Ron Wynn*

● **Rain Drops** / 1994 / Vee Jay 703
Dee Clark was one of the most adaptable R&B vocalists of the '50s and early '60s, as this 25-track disc shows. He did songs in a Little Richard mode, an Afro-Latin setting, and performed ballads, novelty tunes ("Kangaroo Hop") and covers ("Cupid"). Clark's gem was "Rain Drops," a song with enough drama, hooks, and appeal to nearly top both the pop and R&B charts. It was his biggest hit, but not his only fine number. There are many cuts, such as "Nobody but You," "What Kind of Fool," "Hey Little Girl," and the newly issued "Bring Back My Heart," that equal or even top the tune that made him famous. —*Ron Wynn*

Gene Clark

b. Nov. 17, 1941, Tipton, MO, **d.** May 24, 1991
Vocals, songwriter / Country-rock, folk-rock
As a founding member of the Byrds, Clark was inducted into the Rock & Roll Hall of Fame in 1991, a few months before his death. Born in Tipton, MO, in a musical family, Clark was surrounded by bluegrass and country but joined the clean-cut folk boomers, the New Christy Minstrels, at 18. After hearing the Beatles, Clark quit the Minstrels and went to Los Angeles, where a fortuitous meeting with Roger McGuinn led to the forming of the Byrds. Clark wrote some of the best early Byrds songs, one of which, "Feel a Whole Lot Better," Tom Petty recorded in 1990. Clark was the first Byrd to fly, in 1966, and his subsequent solo career flickered with moments of brilliance. He was one of the seminal figures of folk-rock and country-rock. —*Mark A. Humphrey*

● **Echoes** / 1967 / Columbia 48523
Contains six songs with the Byrds, the entire Gosdin Brothers album, and two unreleased tracks. This is a nice companion piece to the Byrds box. —*Kenneth M. Cassidy*

White Light / 1972 / A&M 4292
Good Dylanesque songs. Nice subtle production by Jesse Ed Davis. Low-key and lyrical. —*Kenneth M. Cassidy*

○ **Roadmaster** / 1972 / Edsel 198
Includes two songs from the original early-'70s Byrds that are much better than anything on the ill-fated Byrds reunion album of 1973. A must for fans of Clark-era Byrds. —*Kenneth M. Cassidy*

So Rebellious a Lover / 1987 / Razor & Tie 1992
Clark's last album, recorded with Carla Olson of the Textones. A good mix of folk and country. —*Kenneth M. Cassidy*

Gene Clark with the Gosdin Brothers / 1991 / Sony 2618
Clark's solo debut, recorded with the Gosdin Brothers. —*Kenneth M. Cassidy*

Petula Clark

b. Nov. 15, 1932, Epsom, Surrey, England
Vocals / Pop
By the time Petula Clark made her debut on American pop charts in 1964, she had already developed quite a career as an actress and singer throughout Europe, appearing in over 20 films and selling several million records. "Downtown" is the song that broke her Stateside and placed her firmly in the number-one spot, displacing the Beatles' "I Feel Fine." Not only was she the first female artist from England to land that chart position, but her second record, "I Know a Place," went to number three. Only Cyndi Lauper has had such an impressive entry on her first two singles. Despite the competition, "Downtown" won the Grammy for Best Rock & Roll Recording in 1965. Over the next three years, Clark scored 15 Top 40 pop hits.

Even though Clark's English origins helped her ride in on the first wave of the British Invasion, her music was definitely geared more toward the adult market. —*Rick Clark*

● **Greatest Hits of Petula Clark** / 1986 / GNP 2170
A good selection of hits, marred by substandard sound. The British and French imports are better collections. —*Bruce Eder*

The Clash

Group / Punk, rock & roll
The Clash, 1976-1986, was the most accomplished band to come out of the British punk rock scene of the '70s. The group was formed by guitarist and singer Joe Strummer, guitarist and singer

Mick Jones, bassist Paul Simonon, and drummer Terry Chimes (replaced in 1977 by Topper Headon). They first gained national recognition opening for the Sex Pistols, the other major punk band. But unlike the Pistols, the Clash had a straightforward earnestness to go with their punk anger. Their music was similarly simple, loud, and abrasive.

In December 1979, the Clash released *London Calling*, a critically acclaimed double album that found them expanding their musical style from punk to a more eclectic approach. The album spawned a single in the title song, which became their biggest U.K.single during their existence, getting to number 11, while the album hit number 9 in Britain and was their first real U.S. success at number 27. "Train in Vain (Stand by Me)" from the album was the Clash's first U.S. chart single, reaching number 23.

Sandinista!, a triple-LP set released in December 1980 took their eclecticism to new lengths. The album got to a disappointing number 19 in Britain but was a surprisingly strong number 24 in the United States. The Clash again grazed the Top 40 in Britain with the album's "The Magnificent Seven" in May 1981.

Their next effort, *Combat Rock* (1982), was a straightforward rock collection that was their last album with the original personnel. It was also their most popular. It hit number 2 in Britain and number seven in the States (where it sold a million copies), and its singles "Should I Stay or Should I Go?" and "Rock the Casbah" were hits on both sides of the Atlantic. Meanwhile, Headon left the band in July 1982, and Jones was fired by Strummer and Simonon in September 1983. He formed Big Audio Dynamite. Strummer and Simonon reorganized and added new members, releasing *Cut the Crap* in the fall of 1985, but by the start of 1986, the Clash was no more. —*William Ruhlmann*

○ **Give 'Em Enough Rope** / 1978 / Epic 35543
In retrospect, Sandy Pearlman's production brings a welcome coherence to the Clash's sound, though they sound as aggressive as ever on such songs as "Safe European Home," "English Civil War," and "Tommy Gun." The most moving song is Mick Jones's "Stay Free," however, which may say more about the punk aesthetic than about any of Joe Strummer's angry rants. —*William Ruhlmann*

☆ **Clash** / 1979 / Epic 36060
The revised U.S. version of the Clash's first album, containing most of the vital punk anthems of that record, plus such later tunes as "White Man in Hammersmith Palais" and "I Fought the Law." This and the sole Sex Pistols album, *Never Mind the Bollocks, Here's the Sex Pistols*, tell the story of English '70s punk rock. —*William Ruhlmann*

★ **London Calling** / 1979 / Epic 36328
"What are we gonna do now?" asks Joe Strummer at the start of "Clampdown," one of this album's songs. But by the time you get to that track, it's already clear that the Clash have solved the problem by taking a giant step toward making craftsmanlike rock without sacrificing the urgency that made them punk leaders. From the title track through the reggae, rock, and pop tracks that follow, this is one of the premier albums of its time. —*William Ruhlmann*

Sandinista! / 1980 / Epic 37037
Believe it or not, amidst this messy triple-record (two-CD) set there are some brilliant songs—the trouble is finding them among the dub experiments, half-finished songs, and overlong jams. Listening to all this filler, it's hard to believe that the Clash made a double album the year before that had absolutely no weak tracks. Patient listeners will be rewarded by "The Magnificent Seven," "Charlie Don't Surf," and "Police on My Back," and a couple of other tracks that are among the band's best work; however, most will be happy to hear the highlights on the Clash compilations. —*Stephen Thomas Erlewine*

Combat Rock / 1982 / Epic 37689
The Clash are still a little too individual to be as straight-ahead a rock group as much of this album implies they are, but you can't fault a collection that contains the rock energy of "Should I Stay or Should I Go?" and the absurdist danceability of "Rock the Casbah." —*William Ruhlmann*

○ **Story of the Clash, Vol. 1** / 1988 / Epic 44035
A two-disc, 28-track compilation that ranges over the Clash catalog somewhat haphazardly. Still, this is some of their essential music. —*William Ruhlmann*

○ **Clash on Broadway** / 1991 / Epic 46991

A three-disc, 63-track compilation that treats the catalog coherently and chronologically, with all the major songs included. It's a pricey boxed set, but if you want one album that covers the Clash's career, this is it. —*William Ruhlmann*

○ **Super Black Market Clash** / 1994 / Epic 53191
An expanded version of the *Black Market Clash* EP, *Super Black Market Clash* adds assorted singles and remixes to the original recording. A couple of tracks aren't that interesting, but the majority of the disc is splendid, featuring some of the band's best, but unfortunately overlooked, tracks, including "The Prisoner," "Gates of the West," and "Jail Guitar Doors." —*Stephen Thomas Erlewine*

Otis Clay

b. Feb. 11, 1942, Waxhaw, MS
Vocals / Soul, R&B

Otis Clay made most of his best-known records in Memphis during the early '70s, but he's still universally hailed as Chicago's deep-soul king. In a city filled to overflowing with legendary blues artists, Clay has become the proud standard-bearer for Chicago's enduring soul tradition.

Like so many of his contemporaries, Clay's intense vocal style reflects a gospel background. He made the secular jump in 1965, signing with Chicago's One-derful Records and issuing a series of gospel-tinged soul records that were a lot grittier than the customary Windy City soul sound. Clay inaugurated Atlantic's Cotillion subsidiary in 1968 with a supercharged cover of the Sir Douglas Quintet's "She's About a Mover," produced by Rick Hall in Muscle Shoals shortly before the singer joined forces with Hi Records boss Willie Mitchell. With the relentlessly driving Hi Rhythm Section in tow, Clay waxed his biggest seller in 1972, "Trying to Live My Life without You," later covered very successfully by Bob Seger.

Although Clay's tenure on Hi may have been his most commercially potent, he's steadily recorded and gigged ever since. He is a genuine hero in Japan, where he's recorded two sizzling live albums filled with the churning grooves, punchy horns, and searing vocals that inevitably characterize the best deep soul—no matter where it's recorded. —*Bill Dahl*

Got to Find a Way / 1979 / P-Vine 2195
A Japanese import featuring 19 early Chicago tracks from 1965-1967. —*Richard Pack*

○ **Soul Man Live in Japan** / 1984 / Bullseye Blues 9513
The greatest live soul performer, backed by the Hi rhythm section. —*Richard Pack*

● **That's How It Is** / Hi 110
Twenty-one of the finest tracks Clay recorded for Hi during the '70s are collected on this outstanding compilation. —*Stephen Thomas Erlewine*

George Clinton

b. Jul. 22, 1940, Kannapolis, NC
Vocals / Funk, soul

George Clinton scored a few solo hits on Capitol in the early '80s, but as the president of Parliament, P. Funk, Funkadelic, Bootsy's Rubber Band, and other outfits, Clinton set a new agenda for Black music during the '70s. He combined theater, sci-fi, and funk glossolalia into something that was uniquely his own. On record he loses some of his impact, but it's still the ultimate boom-box music. That Motown passed on him says much for the stripe of Clinton's music. —*Colin Escott*

● **Computer Games** / 1982 / Capitol 96266
Former Parliament and Funkadelic leader George Clinton made a major comeback under his own name with this album, whose irresistible grooves, vocal choruses, and horn arrangements are essentially identical to the music of Funkadelic's salad days. Were you wondering where that "woof-woof" cheer heard on Arsenio Hall and at Black concerts came from? Check out "Atomic Dog."
—*William Ruhlmann*

Some of My Best Jokes Are Friends / 1985 / Capitol 96356
A wildly uneven, but at times first-rate Clinton session. The title cut was fine, and as usual Clinton's studio sophistication, arrangements, and production were frequently incredible. But much of the humor was forced rather than clever, and Clinton seemed to

strain more than usual to find the right mix of synthesized funk and bizarre quips. —*Ron Wynn*

Mothership Connection (Live from the Summit, Houston, Texas) / 1986 / Capitol 15021
A sprawling, often impressive concert recording featuring the immense Mothership Connection organization under George Clinton's reign. This set was perhaps the only time any album conveyed the sense of spectacle, chaos, wild humor, and musical mayhem that were routinely on display during their live shows. —*Ron Wynn*

○ **R&B Skeletons in the Closet** / 1986 / Capitol 96267
Clinton's second and third solo albums had their moments, but he didn't reach the peak of danceable madness of which he is truly capable again until this record, which contains the strange but wonderful "Do Fries Go with That Shake?" Despite its title, it's not a collection of oldies. —*William Ruhlmann*

Best of George Clinton / 1987 / Capitol 48424
This focuses on the best early-Clinton material outside the Parliament/Funkadelic arena. Most of the tracks aren't as humorously spectacular as "Atomic Dog," but there are a couple of clever ones from other albums included besides that masterpiece, among them "Loopzilla." —*Ron Wynn*

○ **Cinderella Theory** / 1989 / Paisley Park 25994
On his first album for Prince's Paisley Park record label, George Clinton's willingness to experiment with samplers and hip-hop (including guest appearances by such artists as Chuck D and Flavor Flav of Public Enemy) resulted in a slightly inconsistent record, yet it has more than enough truly fine songs to make *The Cinderella Theory* rank with his best solo albums. —*Stephen Thomas Erlewine*

○ **Hey Man, Smell My Finger** / 1993 / Paisley Park 25518
Hey Man, Smell My Finger is everything a great George Clinton should be—conceptually disjointed, overlong, silly, sloppy, and funky as hell. Thankfully, the music here is his best since *Computer Games*, and the album proves just how responsible he is for much of the music of the '90s, as the irresistible single "Paint the White House Black" illustrates with its numerous cameos. —*Stephen Thomas Erlewine*

The Clovers

Group / R&B, doo-wop

One of the earliest doo-wop vocal groups, formed in the late '40s in Washington, D.C. Original members were Buddy Bailey, Matthew McQuater, Hal Lucas, Jr, and Harold Winley. Bobby Mitchell replaced Bailey by the time the group was signed to the fledgling Atlantic label in 1950. The Clovers racked up 13 Top Ten R&B hits between 1951 to 1954, all showcasing their solid harmonies and unerring rhythmic verve. After a few years between hits, they scored again in 1959 with their biggest, "Love Potion No. 9." The Clovers went their separate ways by 1961, but they will always be revered by hardcore doo-wop fans the world over. —*Cub Koda*

○ **Love Potion No. 9/The Best of the Clovers** / 1991 / EMI America 96336
The Best of the Clovers/Love Potion No. 9 features their later sides for United Artists including the classic title track. —*Cub Koda*

★ **Down in the Alley: The Best of the Clovers** / 1991 / Atlantic 82312
Down in the Alley: The Best of the Clovers is an excellent compilation of their best and earliest sides, including "Nip Sip," "Don't You Know I Love You," and "One Mint Julep." —*Cub Koda*

The Coasters

Group / R&B

Possibly the most popular R&B vocal group of the '50s, the Coasters started on the West Coast as the Robins, scoring hits under the writing-and-production helm of Jerry Lieber and Mike Stoller. When Atlantic signed Lieber and Stoller as a production team, the group split into two factions: The core of the group became the Coasters and moved to New York to record, while the Robins continued on the West Coast to diminishing acclaim. The Coasters' hits, some of the most finely crafted, well-written, and hilarious in the genre, continued throughout the rest of the decade. Carl Gardner's sly leads and Bobby Nunn's bass singing defined their sound through numerous personnel changes. When their time on the charts came to an end, a number of "Coasters" groups suddenly proliferated (much like the Drifters), many of them still dotting the landscape of a million oldies shows and still singing those classic songs. —*Cub Koda*

☆ **50 Coastin' Classics—Anthology** / 1992 / Rhino 71090
Although it may well be too much for the casual fan, this two-disc set is easily the best Coasters retrospective ever assembled. Besides featuring every one of their hits, it also contains nine strong tunes cut in the mid-'50s by the Robins, who evolved into the Coasters after some personnel changes. As for the enticing obscurities, "Three Cool Cats" and "Besame Mucho" were cut by the Beatles on unreleased recordings in the early '60s, and "Ain't That Just Like Me" would be a small hit for the Searchers. "Down In Mexico" and "Brazil" are cool R&B/Latin melodramas, and "Shoppin' for Clothes," "What about Us," and "That Is Rock & Roll" are half-forgotten vignettes of youthful independence that stack up against the best songs of Jerry Lieber and Mike Stoller, who wrote most of the group's material. Indeed, there's little difference in quality between the hits and the B-sides on this compilation, either in the group's matchless ensemble R&B/comedy vocals or Lieber and Stoller's witty songwriting. The accompanying booklet features comments on most of the tracks by Lieber and Stoller themselves. —*Richie Unterberger*

★ **Very Best of the Coasters** / 1993 / Rhino 71597
Though Rhino's already given them the deluxe two-disc treatment, consumers who either don't want that much Coasters material or prefer only the hits are nicely served by this 18-track anthology. It contains every major release, plus valuable lesser-known selections such as "Shoppin' for Clothes" and "What about Us." The disc features Rhino's usual state-of-the-art remastering and liner notes with entertaining recollections from Lieber and Stoller. —*Ron Wynn*

Eddie Cochran

b. Oct. 3, 1938, Oklahoma City, OK, **d.** Apr. 17, 1960, Wiltshire, England
Vocals, guitar / Rock & roll, rockabilly
As with his friend and contemporary Buddy Holly, Cochran's star has continued to shine ever more brightly since his untimely death. Partially this is because of his "image"—the brash, flamboyantly dressed, hot-guitar-picking, teenage smart-aleck rebel—but the substance is there too. A fine guitarist (I cite the guitar breaks on "Twenty Flight Rock" and "Jeannie Jeannie Jeannie," just to name a couple) and fine songwriter (especially in collaboration with his friend and producer Jerry Capehart), Cochran's best work captured the spirit of its time (the late '50s) so that perfectly it can never seem dated: cars, girls, teenage rebellion, and angst distilled into 2 1/2-minute gems of ringing guitars, throbbing bass (his were among the first rock & roll records to exploit the electric bass's distinctive character), and growling, drawling vocals. Especially influential in Britain (where he was on tour when he was killed in an automobile accident), echoes of Cochran's work (and sometimes his songs) have surfaced in the records of the Who, Rod Stewart, the Clash, Neil Diamond, the Stray Cats, and many, many others. —*George Bedard*

★ **Legendary Masters** / 1990 / EMI America 92809
The definitive single-disc collection of Cochran's best: "Summertime Blues," "Cut Across Shorty," "Something Else," "Come on Everybody," and "Twenty Flight Rock." All the hits, all the feeling. —*Cub Koda*

○ **Singin' to My Baby/Never to Be Forgotten** / Feb. 23, 1993 / Capitol 80240
Two original albums on one compact disc, with only two hits between the two—"Sittin' in the Balcony" and "Twenty Flight Rock." But for devoted fans of Eddie Cochran, this lovingly packaged CD is worth their time, even if some of the material is slightly weak. *Singin' to My Baby* concentrates on ballad material; the posthumously released *Never to Be Forgotten* has more rockers. —*Stephen Thomas Erlewine*

Bruce Cockburn

b. May 27, 1945, Ottawa, Canada
Vocals / Singer/songwriter
Over the course of his lengthy career, Bruce Cockburn has gone from plaintive singer/songwriter folk to aggressive world beat,

rock, and even some jazz. Thematically, Cockburn has gone from deeply introspective musings to human rights activism, all filtered through a distinctly mystical Christian point of view. Cockburn's poetic lyrics are consistently many cuts above those of most artists who choose to tackle this kind of weighty subject matter.

In his native Canada, Cockburn has won many Juno Awards (the equivalent to the Grammy awards). Overseas, he has quite a following, but stateside Cockburn has only managed two significant forays onto the radio playlists, 1980's "Wondering Where the Lions Are" and "If I Had a Rocket Launcher," his 1984 response to injustices he witnessed while in Central America. Most recently, Cockburn has signed with Sony, releasing the fine T-Bone Burnette-produced "Nothing but a Burning Light," which recalls his earlier folkie style. —*Rick Clark*

○ **In the Falling Dark** / 1976 / Columbia 48745
The follow-up to *Joy Will Find a Way* possesses some Cockburn standards in "Festival of Friends," the propulsive folk-jazz of "Silver Wheels," the meditative "Lord of the Starfields," and the title cut. The lyrics involve increasingly complex mystical Christian metaphors. Cockburn's exceptional guitar technique is showcased on the instrumental "Water into Wine." —*Rick Clark*

○ **Dancing in the Dragon's Jaws** / 1979 / Columbia 48736
Cockburn's first Stateside success produced a number-21 pop hit with "Wondering Where the Lions Are," but there is much better material to be found here on one of his best albums. The lyrics tend to be spacier, and musically Cockburn begins to aggressively synthesize Third World rhythms with his singer/songwriter-style folk. —*Rick Clark*

○ **Humans** / Nov. 1980 / Columbia 48748
This follow-up to isn't as accessible as *Dancing in the Dragon's Jaws*, but it's possibly Cockburn's most brilliant artistic statement, where the struggles of the general human condition and (more personally) a divorce cause this Christian mystic to dig deep and grapple with more down-to-earth issues. In some of his most powerfully poetic lyrics, he maintains a fine balance between lofty intentions and grave disappointments. Musically, it is a heady dose of world-beat folk. —*Rick Clark*

Inner City Front / 1981 / Columbia 48749
Transitional self-produced effort featuring more musical diversity, from the techno-dirge of "The Strong One" to the reggaelike "Justice." "Loner" provides a dramatic highlight. Cockburn's human-rights concerns and his left-of-center politics dominate over more mystical fascinations for the first time. —*Rick Clark*

○ **Trouble with Normal** / 1983 / Columbia 48750
Another consistently strong effort. Cockburn's brainy lyrics occasionally border on the didactic, but the imagery is usually brilliant. "Waiting for the Moon" is one of his most beautiful songs. The title cut is released in two totally different versions; the True North rendition is preferable. —*Rick Clark*

Stealing Fire / 1984 / Columbia 48735
Features a more streamlined, sophisticated rock sound. "If I Had a Rocket Launcher" became a powerful left-field AOR hit in 1984. "Lovers in a Dangerous Time" and "Nicaragua" are highlights. "Maybe the Poet," is a low point—the highbrow artistic equivalent to Barry Mann's hideous, self-congratulatory ode to the value of pop-song craftsmen, "Who Put the Bomp (in the Bomp, Bomp, Bomp)." But it's a fine album overall. —*Rick Clark*

○ **Waiting for a Miracle (Singles 1970-1987)** / Jan. 1987 / Gold Castle 71305
This Canadian double-CD best-of collection is geared around Cockburn's Canadian singles—an odd approach, considering that much of his strongest material never enjoyed radio airplay. Because of that, *Waiting for a Miracle (Singles 1970-1987)* isn't definitive, but it is a very good collection. This is mainly because Cockburn is practically incapable of writing a bad song. Nevertheless, Cockburn has yet to receive the kind of treatment he deserves for a collection. *Waiting for a Miracle* is the best overview of Cockburn's music, by default. (A pared-down single-disc version is available in the United States, but it doesn't offer as complete a picture as the Canadian version) —*Rick Clark*

Big Circumstance / 1989 / Columbia 48737
Cockburn tries to balance the edge-rock approach of recent work with more reflective earlier sounds. He's the most successful at illuminating big issues when he's focusing on his personal back-

yard (on "Understanding Nothing," "Don't Feel Your Touch") rather than the "Tibetan Side of Town." Surprise element: Cockburn displays rare flashes of humor. —*Rick Clark*

Nothing but a Burning Light / 1991 / Columbia 47983
This T-Bone Burnett-produced effort finds Cockburn returning to the more introspective, quiet spirit of his earlier work, including his most open Christian expressions in years, particularly "Cry of a Tiny Babe," a Cockburn-style Christmas story, and "Somebody Touched Me." "One of the Best Ones" is classic reflective Cockburn. Although not one of his best albums, it's a nice breather from the relentless heaviness of his last few efforts. —*Rick Clark*

Dart to the Heart / 1994 / Columbia
With the exception of a few revved-up numbers (some with slide guitar and horns), this is a fairly subdued affair, featuring Cockburn's exquisite guitar work and insightful lyricism that is simultaneously grounded and mystical. A typically fine album for this consummate artist. —*Rick Clark*

Joe Cocker (John Robert Cocker)

b. May 20, 1944, Sheffield, England
Vocals / Pop/rock
After starting out in the late '50s as an unsuccessful British pop singer (working under the name Vance Arnold), English soul/rock singer Cocker found his niche in the pubs of England with his superb backing group, the Grease Band. Worldwide success soon followed with a brace of fine recordings based around Cocker's fine interpretive skills. Cocker's first peak of success came when Leon Russell organized the Mad Dogs & Englishmen tour, featuring Cocker and over 40 others. Problems with alcohol (both on stage and off) reduced Cocker's once-powerful voice to a croaking rasp, but he has survived, still scoring hits into the early '80s. It's unlikely we've heard the last of him, since the man still seems capable of making any song his own. —*Cub Koda*

○ **With a Little Help from My Friends** / Jan. 1969 / A&M 3106
The album that foisted Joe Cocker on an unsuspecting public is full of tasteful, raucous covers, Cocker's trademark hysterical vocals, and outstanding studio backing by pros like Jimmy Page and Steve Winwood. —*Tom Graves*

○ **Joe Cocker** / 1970 / A&M 3326
The rare sophomore effort that was an improvement over the first, with great tracks (and vocals) like "Delta Lady" and "She Came in through the Bathroom Window." Arguably Cocker's most soulful album. —*Tom Graves*

○ **Mad Dogs & Englishmen** / 1970 / A&M 6002
Superb document of Cocker's high-energy 1970 tour, which included about a zillion musicians and hangers-on. All the goods are here, and many consider this Cocker's last great moment. —*Tom Graves*

○ **Joe Cocker's Greatest Hits** / 1977 / A&M 3257
Greatest Hits features most—but not all (no "She Came in through the Bathroom Window" or "It's a Sin When You Love Somebody")—of his biggest hits from the early '70s. Nevertheless, there's plenty of fine music here, making the record a solid compilation. —*Stephen Thomas Erlewine*

● **Classics, Vol. 4** / 1987 / A&M 2503
A solid collection from his 1967-1976 peak. Includes "Feeling Alright," "You Are So Beautiful," and "With a Little Help from My Friends." —*Dan Heilman*

Live! / 1990 / Capitol 93416
A solid, R&B-heavy live concert. —*Dan Heilman*

○ **Best of Joe Cocker** / 1993 / Capitol 81243
Although Cocker's Capitol material wasn't as consistent as his A&M work, this compilation successfully distills the highlights, including the splendid "When the Night Comes," on a single CD. —*Stephen Thomas Erlewine*

Cocteau Twins

b. , Scotland
Group / Alternative pop/rock
One of the most unique, distinctive bands of the '80s was the Cocteau Twins, an ethereal, prolific Scottish trio. Over the course of the decade, they became a major force in alternative music, although there isn't much that is forceful about their music. It is a series of soundscapes created with guitars, studio effects, drum machines, and Elizabeth Fraser's expansive vocals; she sings words according to their sound, not their meaning. With their atmospheric records and lush album covers, the band was the embodiment of England's arty 4AD record label during the '80s. As their career progressed, the Cocteau Twins began to harness their sound into more concrete songs, culminating in 1990's *Heaven or Las Vegas*. After one more album on 4AD, the band switched labels. With the new record company, their music started to veer slightly into new age territory, a genre that was in debt to the Cocteau's previous records.

○ **Head over Heels** / 1983 / Capitol 96416
Where the Cocteau Twins' first album relied more on texture than songs, *Head over Heels* melds their dreamy, hazy soundscapes to actual songs. —*Stephen Thomas Erlewine*

○ **Treasure** / 1984 / Capitol 96418
On *Treasure*, the Cocteau Twins' rich, gauzy, layers of sound are positively entrancing. It doesn't matter what Elizabeth Fraser is singing; her voice is only another element in the endless sonic textures. —*Stephen Thomas Erlewine*

● **Pink Opaque** / 1985 / Combat 8040
A compilation of the Cocteau Twins' first records, *Pink Opaque* offers a good introduction to their music. —*Stephen Thomas Erlewine*

Victorialand / 1986 / Capitol 96417
While nearly all of the instrumental support on *Victorialand* is acoustic guitar, the essential structure of the Cocteau Twins' music hasn't changed at all, making the album a bit of retread, no matter how enjoyable it is. —*Stephen Thomas Erlewine*

● **Blue Bell Knoll** / 1988 / Capitol 90892
This, the first Cocteau Twins regular studio album to be released in the United States, is typical of their earlier U.K. output: Keyboards and guitars swirl together into sonic landscapes, over (or rather, buried within) which Elizabeth Fraser sings in a high, ethereal voice reminiscent of Kate Bush and Jane Siberry—the difference being that the lyrics are utterly unintelligible. The result is classy mood music that might appeal to the new crop of Enya fans. —*William Ruhlmann*

Heaven or Las Vegas / 1990 / Capitol 93669
The song structures are more discernible, as are the lyrics, which perhaps makes this a little less mysterious than most Cocteau Twins albums, and a little more accessible, if also less characteristic. —*William Ruhlmann*

Four-Calendar Cafe / Sep. 27, 1993 / Capitol 99375
The Cocteau Twins' first effort outside of 4AD continues in the vein of *Heaven or Las Vegas*, with more recognizable song structures and clearer phrasing from Elizabeth Fraser. Unfortunately, the songs are not as interesting as the ones on *Heaven or Las Vegas* or as intriguing as the sonic explorations of their earlier releases. —*Stephen Thomas Erlewine*

Leonard Cohen

b. Sep. 21, 1934, Montreal, Canada
Vocals / Singer/songwriter
Although he played music during his college years, Canadian poet, novelist, and singer/songwriter Leonard Cohen didn't turn professional until he was in his thirties. A graduate of McGill University, he published several books of poetry starting in the '50s and two novels, *The Favorite Game* and *Beautiful Losers*, in the '60s. After his songs had been recorded by Judy Collins, Cohen turned to singing and released his debut album, *Songs of Leonard Cohen*, in 1968. It contained such typical material as the highly poetic "Suzanne," which had been a singles hit for Noel Harrison. Cohen continued to write and record albums (though less and less frequently) throughout the '70s and '80s, all of them featuring his deepening voice and lyrics that were by turns depressing, comic, and erotic. His 1977 album, *Death of a Ladies Man*, was a collaborative effort with eccentric producer Phil Spector. By the '80s, Cohen's music was being celebrated by the school of doom-rock performers led by Nick Cave and others (resulting in the tribute album *I'm Your Fan*, 1991), but Jennifer Warnes's all-Cohen album *Famous Blue Raincoat* (1987) was a more accessible sampler. The artist himself made one of the best albums of 1988 in *I'm Your Man*. —*William Ruhlmann*

★ **Songs of Leonard Cohen** / 1968 / CBS 9533

His debut album features such standards as "Suzanne," "Sisters of Mercy," and "So Long Marianne." Many of these were featured in the 1971 Warren Beatty film, *McCabe and Mrs. Miller*. — *William Ruhlmann*

○ **Songs from a Room** / 1969 / CBS 9767
Includes his versions of his classics, "Bird on a Wire" and "Story of Isaac." — *William Ruhlmann*

○ **Songs of Love and Hate** / 1971 / CBS 30103
"Famous Blue Raincoat," "Joan of Arc," and more great Cohen songs. — *William Ruhlmann*

○ **Best of Leonard Cohen** / 1975 / CBS 34077
While it isn't a definitive collection, *Best of Leonard Cohen* is a fine cross-section of some of Cohen's best songs. — *Stephen Thomas Erlewine*

○ **I'm Your Man** / 1988 / CBS 44191
Pessimism, humor, and poetry add up to a profound world-view in *I'm Your Man*. — *William Ruhlmann*

○ **Future** / Nov. 10, 1992 / CBS 53226
The Future offers a wealth of lyrical substance, notably on the more political numbers. Both the title track and "Democracy" make for an interesting read. Instrumental backings focus mostly on unobtrusive textures—synths, strings, female backing vocals, and the occasional flavor of pedal steel guitar, mandolin, fiddle, and horns. The tracks have been well labored over—perhaps too much so in places—with a somewhat stale studio feel to them. Cohen's distinctive, deep-throated rasp has lost a couple of notes in recent years. Yet his voice remains a powerfully compelling if somewhat bleak instrument, especially effective on Euro-sounding ballads like "Waiting for the Miracle." — *Roch Parisien*

Marc Cohn
Vocals, piano / Singer/songwriter, pop/rock
This husky-voiced singer/songwriter and pianist from Cleveland released his self-titled debut album in 1991, including the Top-20 hit "Walking in Memphis," and won the 1991 Grammy for Best New Artist. — *William Ruhlmann*

○ **Marc Cohn** / Jan. 30, 1991 / Atlantic 82178
The singer/songwriter album of 1991, and an auspicious debut for a writer of soulful, keenly observed lyrics, who sings them passionately. — *William Ruhlmann*

Rainy Season / May 25, 1993 / Atlantic 82491
While it's a bit lacking in strong material, Cohn's follow-up to his Grammy-winning debut should please fans of his adult-contemporary songwriting. — *Stephen Thomas Erlewine*

Lloyd Cole & the Commotions
b. Jan. 31, 1956, Buxton, Derbyshire, England
Group / Alternative pop/rock
Scottish singer/songwriter Lloyd Cole formed the Commotions, who served as his backup band, in Glasgow in 1983. The group featured guitarist Nick Clark, bassist Lawrence Donegan, keyboard player Blair Cowan, and drummer Steven Irvine. Heavily influenced by Bob Dylan and the Band, Cole and the Commotions developed a familiar-sounding but distinctive folk-rock sound, highlighted by Cole's literate lyrics. The group signed to Polydor in 1984, and scored a series of British hits, including "Perfect Skin." In 1989, he split the band and moved to New York, where he recorded *Lloyd Cole*, his debut solo album, with New York Session players such as Voidoid and Lou Reed guitarist Robert Quine (releasing it in 1990). Cole has garnered considerable critical acclaim, but so far has failed to make a commercial impact in the United States. — *William Ruhlmann*

○ **Rattlesnakes** / 1984 / Capitol 91182
Cole's debut album reflects his Glasgow surroundings in its observations but also incorporates a Dylanish attitude toward them, while the Commotions prove to be a cohesive backup unit. — *William Ruhlmann*

● **1984-1989** / 1989 / Capitol 92223
The compilation *1984-1989* features nearly all of the best moments from Lloyd Cole and the Commotions' three albums, making it the perfect introduction to his music. — *Stephen Thomas Erlewine*

○ **Don't Get Weird on Me Babe** / Sep. 16, 1991 / Capitol 96077

While it's not exactly sunny, *Don't Get Weird on Me Babe* is Cole's most accessible and pop-oriented album to date, filled with fine understated pop/rockers like "She's a Girl and I'm a Man." — *Stephen Thomas Erlewine*

Natalie Cole
b. Feb. 6, 1950, Los Angeles, CA
Vocals, piano / Soul, urban R&B, pop
The daughter of jazz and pop legend Nat "King" Cole, Natalie Cole has forged a successful career in two phases, doing R&B/urban contemporary and then jazz-based pop. She made her stage debut at 11 and sang in college. Cole met the writing and producing team of Chuck Jackson and Marvin Yancey in 1973. The next year they collaborated on some sessions that were recorded at Curtis Mayfield's Curtom studios in Chicago. These helped her land a deal with Capitol, and she teamed with Jackson and Yancey for a string of hit albums and singles from 1975 until 1983. Such LPs as *Inseparable, Natalie, Thankful, Unpredictable*, and *I Love You So* yielded five number-one R&B hits between 1975 and 1977, including "This Will Be, "Inseparable," "Our Love," and "I've Got Love On My Mind." She stayed on Capitol until 1983, then switched to Epic for her final album with the Jackson-Yancey tandem. Cole made duets with Peabo Bryson in 1979 and 1980, and Ray Parker Jr. in 1987. She scored more hits with "Jump Start," "I Live for Your Love," and "Over You" in 1987, and "Pink Cadillac," a cover of a Bruce Springsteen tune, in 1988, and then made her stylistic shift.

Cole eased into the transition with "When I Fall in Love," a number her father recorded in 1957. It was included on her 1987 record *Everlasting*. She fully embraced the move with the 1991 album *Unforgettable with Love*, earning Grammy awards and landing a number-one pop album that eventually sold over five million copies. The title track featured her doing a duet with her father via computer technology. She continued the jazzy trend with *Take a Look* in 1993, and has toured and done television specials working with a large orchestra conducted by Nelson Riddle. — *Ron Wynn*

Inseparable / 1975 / Capitol 97769
Natalie Cole scored her initial fame as a soul singer with a pronounced Aretha Franklin influence. This was her first hit album, and Cole soared to the top of the R&B charts when both "This Will Be" and "Inseparable" were number-one R&B singles ("This Will Be" also was a Top-Ten pop song). Nineteen years later, this album still stands as arguably her finest. It contains more earnest, aggressive, and honest material than most of her other albums, and Cole had not yet been affected by personal and professional struggles that would eventually take their creative toll. — *Ron Wynn*

Natalie Live! / 1978 / Capitol 18
Natalie Cole's first live date had some pleasant and a few boisterous versions of previous studio hits. It followed two consecutive platinum releases and was during her peak period as a straight soul singer. There was an interesting contrast between the tunes that made her a star, such as "Inseparable" and "This Will Be," and the sophisticated, pre-rock pop that she would later turn to almost in desperation. Such singles as "Mr. Melody," "I've Got Love on My Mind" and "Sophisticated Lady (She's a Different Lady)" were an early clue that Cole was not only capable of cutting jazz-based pop, but that she was quite good at it. — *Ron Wynn*

Everlasting / 1987 / Elektra 61114
Fine '80s Top-40 and light-jazz music. — *Bil Carpenter*

○ **Collection** / 1988 / Capitol 46619
This contains the finest Natalie Cole soul and sophisticated pre-rock pop tracks from her days at Capitol (1975-1981). Cole made some superb singles in her early days, especially "This Will Be" and "Inseparable." At the same time, she laid the foundation for the early '90s change that would surprise those who slept on "Mr. Melody" or "I've Got Love on My Mind." Her voice was actually more suited for these songs than the soul numbers, which were as much production and arranging triumphs as vocal victories. — *Ron Wynn*

Good to Be Back / 1989 / Elektra 61115
Natalie Cole overcame drug and emotional problems during the late '80s. This album marked her return and netted her two hits in "Miss You Like Crazy" and "Gonna Make You Mine." It also was

the start of her turn toward softer sophisticated and jazz-based pop that culminated in the 1991 monster hit "Unforgettable." —*Ron Wynn*

● **Unforgettable** / 1991 / Elektra 61049
After enjoying prior hits as a soul vocalist and recycling rock tunes like Bruce Springsteen's "Pink Cadillac," Natalie Cole found new glory with pre-rock pop in 1991. She earned commercial and critical success with an electronically manipulated duet with her father Nat "King" Cole on "Unforgettable." The subsequent album also contained some fine vocals by Natalie Cole doing decent renditions of such songs as "Avalon" and "Lush Life," but it was the title cut that recreated her as a diva in the Anita Baker mode. The album sold over five million copies. —*Ron Wynn*

○ **Take a Look** / 1993 / Virgin
Those who questioned whether Natalie Cole had either the will or skill to succeed with another session of pre-rock popular music need wonder no more; her follow-up to the hugely successful *Unforgettable* is the superior *Take a Look*. It's another 18 jazz-tinged and early pop numbers, with some unexpected pleasures ("Calypso Blues," "It's Sand Man") and spectacular triumphs ("Cry Me a River," "Fiesta in Blue," "I'm Beginning to See the Light"). Cole is now completely comfortable with the pacing, flow, and sensibility of pre-rock material. —*Ron Wynn*

Collins Kids

Group / Rockabilly
By the time Lawrencine (b. 1942) and Lawrence (b. 1944) Collins were 13 and 11, respectively, they were already tearing it up on country package shows, recording for Columbia Records and performing on national TV almost weekly. Older sister Lorrie held up the cowgirl fringe-rustling-against-nylons teenage-sensuality department; kid brother Larry was a bundle of hyperkinetic energy, bopping all over the place while laying down exciting, twangy guitar breaks learned first hand from the "King of Doublenecked Mosrite," Joe Maphis. The Collinses' recordings as time went on veered from mawkish brother-sister country-style duets to white-hot rockabilly, and they were just reaching their peak when Lorrie eloped, effectively breaking up the act. Revered by rockabilly collectors the world over, their filmed television appearances and recordings are testimony to the fact that the Collins Kids weren't just "good for their age," they were just plain good, period. —*Cub Koda*

● **Hop Skip & Jump** / Aug. 1991 / Bear Family 15537
A two-CD boxed set covering the Kids' entire career. —*Cub Koda*

○ **Rockin' on T.V.** / 1993 / Krazy Kat
Thirty-one performances taken from various Town Hall Party television performances from 1957 to 1961. Sound is suspect in spots, naturally, but the energy level makes such arguments superfluous. Highlights include "Kokomo," "Chantilly Lace," "Lonesome Road," "Way Down Yonder in New Orleans," and decidedly left-field takes on three Buddy Holly songs. Highly recommended. —*Cub Koda*

Bootsy Collins

b. Oct. 26, 1951, Cincinnati, OH
Bass / Funk, disco
One of the all-time great funk and R&B bassists and a consummate character, Detroit-born Bootsy Collins formed the Pacesetters during the '60s. Collins and his comrades became part of the JBs from 1969 to 1971, and his inspired, clever progressions and patterns were a vital part of such records as "Get Up, I Feel Like Being a Sex Machine." After departing the JBs, the group became the House Guests, until Collins joined George Clinton's Parliament/Funkadelic empire in 1971. He cowrote "Tear the Roof off the Sucker" with Clinton and Jerome Brailey and established himself so effectively that Clinton urged him to form his own band. Bootsy's Rubber Band emerged in 1976. Their debut album, *Stretchin' Out in Bootsy's Rubber Band*, and second release *Ahh . . . The Name Is Bootsy, Baby!* equaled anything issued during Clinton's peak period for idiomatic diversity, clever, bizarre humor, and outrageous lyrics.

Collins recorded as both a solo artist and with the Rubber Band in the '80s. He also did some special projects, such as a 1984 collaboration with Jerry Harrison of the Talking Heads using the name Bonzo Goes to Washington; the release "5 Minutes (C-C-C-Club Mix)" featured Ronald Reagan declaring nuclear war on the

Soviet Union over a skittering rhythm track. Collins signed with 4th and Broadway in 1990 and also toured England with a group co-led by Parker and Wesley. —*Ron Wynn*

Stretchin' Out in Bootsy's Rubber Band / 1976 / Warner Brothers 2920
The debut album that launched the solo career of bassist Bootsy Collins, after years of playing with everyone from James Brown to George Clinton (with whom he continued working and recording with for years). The title cut and several others established Collins's viability outside the Parliament/Funkadelic empire and contained some excellent uptempo jams. —*Ron Wynn*

○ **Ahh . . . the Name Is Bootsy, Baby!** / 1977 / Warner Brothers 2972
His second album is a fine introduction to Bootsy's bizarre and throbbing funky fairy-tale world. —*John Floyd*

Bootsy? Player of the Year / 1978 / Warner Brothers 3093
Funny jokes, tight ballads, and loads of elastic funk make this album necessary for enthusiasts. —*John Floyd*

● **What's Bootsy Doin'?** / 1988 / Columbia 44107
This pounding set is Collins's best work, with plenty of grooves for the brain and the booty. —*John Floyd*

Phil Collins

b. Jan. 31, 1951, London, England
Vocals, drums, keyboards / Pop/rock
Phil Collins's ascent to the status of one of the most successful pop and adult-contemporary singers of the '80s and beyond was probably as much of a surprise to him as it was to many others. Balding and dimimutive, Collins was almost 30 years old when his first solo single, "In the Air Tonight," became a number-two hit in his native Britain (the song was a Top 20 hit in the United States). Between 1984 and 1990, Collins had a string of 13 straight U.S. Top-Ten hits.

Long before any of that happened, however, Collins was a child actor/singer who appeared as the Artful Dodger in the London production of *Oliver!* in 1964. (He also has a cameo in *A Hard Day's Night*, among other films.) He got his first break in music at the end of his teens, when he was chosen to be a replacement drummer in the British art-rock band Genesis in 1970. (Collins maintained a separate jazz career with the band Brand X, as well.) Genesis was fronted by singer Peter Gabriel. They had achieved a moderate level of success in the United Kingdom and the States with elaborate concept albums before Gabriel abruptly left in 1974. Genesis auditioned 400 singers without success, then decided to let Collins have a go.

The result was a gradual simplifying of Genesis's sound and an increasing focus on Collins's expressive, throaty voice. *And Then There Were Three . . .* went gold in 1978, and *Duke* was even more successful. Collins made his debut solo album *Face Value* in 1981, which turned out to be a bigger hit than any Genesis album. It concentrated on Collins's voice, often in stark, haunting contexts such as the piano-and-drum dirge "In the Air Tonight," which sounded like something from John Lennon's debut solo album, *John Lennon/Plastic Ono Band*. Collins's continuing solo work has not meant the end of Genesis. In fact, he balances group and solo careers with enormous success. —*William Ruhlmann*

○ **Face Value** / 1981 / Atlantic 16029
Collins proves himself a passionate singer (and distinctive drummer) with a gift for both deeply felt ballads and snarling rockers. His debut album transformed him from the frontman of Genesis to a solo star who happened to be in Genesis too. Contains "In the Air Tonight" and "I Missed Again." —*William Ruhlmann*

Hello, I Must Be Going / 1982 / Atlantic 80035
As his hit cover of "You Can't Hurry Love" demonstrates, Collins began to inject his highly melodic pop songwriting with more soul and R&B influences on his second solo album. While some of the material was successful, much of it showed that he was still coming to grips with how to incorporate R&B techniques into his style. In retrospect, *Hello, I Must Be Going* was the ground work for his breakthrough album, *No Jacket Required*, which blended pop and soul much more successfully. —*Stephen Thomas Erlewine*

● **No Jacket Required** / 1985 / Atlantic 81240
From ballads like the number-one "One More Night" to uptempo funk like the number-one "Sussudio," another tour de force in

what was by now one of the most identifiable styles in pop music. The 1985 Grammy winner for Album of the Year. — *William Ruhlmann*

But Seriously / 1989 / Atlantic 82050
This chart-topping fourth album contains "Another Day in Paradise," "I Wish It Would Rain Down," "Do You Remember?," and "Something Happened on the Way to Heaven," all Top-Five hits. — *William Ruhlmann*

Both Sides / 1993 / Atlantic
Returning to the stark, melancholy sounds of *Face Value*, Phil Collins delivers a personal album with *Both Sides* in more than one sense of the world. Collins played all of the instruments on *Both Sides*, and the songs are troubled, haunting tales of regret, romance, and society. Although Collins hasn't lost his flair for melody, the songs are edgier than most of his recent work. Some fans might not go along with Collins on this dark ride, but *Both Sides* is one of his most artistically satisfying albums. — *Stephen Thomas Erlewine*

Color Me Badd

Group / Urban R&B
The New York-based group Color Me Badd formed as high school students in Oklahoma City. They proved adept at both churning dance tunes and sincere, if sometimes lyrically awkward, ballads. Their 1991 debut *C.M.B.* was a huge hit, selling over three million copies and reaching number three on the Top 200 LP chart. They scored two number-one pop hits with "All 4 Love" and "I Adore (Mi Amor)"; "I Wanna Sex You Up" reached number two; and both "Slow Motion" and "Thinkin' Back" made the Top 20. The album was on the charts for 77 weeks. Despite the fact that it was similar to their debut, Color Me Badd's second full release, 1993's *Time and Chance*, didn't come close to matching the success of their debut. — *Ron Wynn*

● **C.M.B.** / 1991 / Giant 24429
Their debut album includes the hit "I Wanna Sex You Up," which is innovative from an instrumental perspective. — *Bil Carpenter*

Time and Chance / 1993 / Giant
On their second album, Color Me Badd still sound superb, but they could have used a couple of songs half as strong as "I Wanna Sex You Up" to make *Time and Chance* more memorable. — *Stephen Thomas Erlewine*

Shawn Colvin

b. Jan. 10, 1958
Vocals, guitar / Singer/songwriter
Singer and songwriter Shawn Colvin was born in South Dakota and lived in London (Ontario) and Carbondale, Illinois, where she graduated from high school. She dropped out of Southern Illinois University to join a hard-rock group, later playing with the Dixie Diesels, a Western swing band in Austin. After a sojourn in San Francisco, she moved to New York City in 1980 and gradually worked her way up to the folk circuit, also appearing in such off-Broadway shows as *Pump Boys and Dinettes*, *Diamond Studs*, and *Lie of the Mind*. Her work appeared in *The Fast Folk Musical Magazine*, and she got her first real break in 1987, singing backup on a Suzanne Vega tour. Recruited by Vega's management, she signed to Columbia Records in 1988 and released her debut album, *Steady On*, in 1989. — *William Ruhlmann*

○ **Steady On** / 1989 / Columbia 45209
Sharp production, surprising arrangements, and Shawn Colvin's alternately breathy and ringing vocals give the best possible forum for her astute reflections on life and love. The album's roots go into rock and country as well as folk. — *William Ruhlmann*

● **Fat City** / Jul. 1992 / Columbia 47122
Produced by bassist Larry Klein, Colvin's second album is looser than the first, with a great cover of Warren Zevon's "Tenderness on the Block" and her own "Another Round of Blues." — *Richard Meyer*

Commander Cody

Group / Country-rock
This Texas ensemble (formed in Ann Arbor, MI) was a good-time blend of roadhouse country swing, rockabilly, and anything else conducive to guzzling mass quantities of Lone Star beer. You could say they were the perfect band for pot-smoking truckers.

They scored one big hit with "Hot Rod Lincoln" in 1972. — *Rick Clark*

Lost in the Ozone / 1971 / MCA 31185
Their remarkable debut album went from gospel to the Andrews Sisters to Eddie Cochran, and was a hoot from top to bottom. — *Jeff Tamarkin*

Very Best of . . . Plus / 1986 / See for Miles 64
More tracks than their U.S. best-of, and costlier, but this collection provides a grand overview of one of the saving graces of '70s rock. — *Jeff Tamarkin*

● **Too Much Fun: Best of Commander Cody** / 1990 / MCA 10092
Not only could they play the hell out of their instruments, but C. C. and his Lost Planet Airmen were a virtual melting pot of American music—country, R&B, rockabilly, western swing. And always too much fun. — *Jeff Tamarkin*

Deep in the Heart of Texas / 1991 / MCA 659
The Airmen were at their best onstage, and this 1973 set caught them at the peak of their game. — *Jeff Tamarkin*

The Commodores

Group / Soul, funk, pop
The Commodores got their start by being the opening act for the Jackson 5. Largely through the prolific lyrics of Lionel Richie, the band broke out nationally in the mid '70s. Their initial success was mainly with dance tunes, but in the late 70s Richie began turning out love ballads such as "Easy," "Still," and "Three Times a Lady." His departure for solo stardom crippled the band, but not before they had one more huge success with "Nightshift" in 1985. Today the group plays state fairs and oldies venues. Members included Lionel Richie (replaced in 1984 by J. D. Nicholas), Thomas McClary (who left in 1984), Ronald LaPread, William King, Walter Orange, and Milan Williams. — *Rick A. Bueche*

○ **Caught in the Act** / 1975 / Motown 5240
A spectacular second album by the Southern funksters, arguably their best overall. It had both powerhouse uptempo tunes and hit ballads, and the group's energy, spontaneity, and drive were still building. It's also the studio album that comes closest to duplicating the quality of their live performances during that era. — *Ron Wynn*

Commodores / 1977 / Motown 5222
The Commodores' early years were spent on the Southern funk circuit, where their energetic, catchy tunes and keyboard-oriented funk made them both a college and a radio staple. They scored seminal hits with "Brick House" and "Slippery When Wet," although it became apparent quite early that lead vocalist Lionel Richie also had a bright future ahead as a solo balladeer, with such tunes as "Easy" signaling his future on adult-contemporary and quiet-storm/urban-contemporary radio. This collection highlights early uptempo and ballad hits. — *Ron Wynn*

Natural High / 1978 / Motown 5293
Another huge hit album for the Commodores, still riding the crest of both R&B and pop waves in the late '70s. "Three Times a Lady" was the group's and Lionel Richie's first pop number-one hit and their fifth R&B chart topper. It began an unfortunate obsession with sappy themes that eventually would redirect both his and the group's focus away from the great funk and uptempo dance tunes that had initially made them famous. — *Ron Wynn*

○ **Greatest Hits** / 1981 / Motown 0912
A very representative anthology gathering the prime Commodores uptempo and ballad material. It shows that they were quite versatile in their heyday, capable of being humorous or romantic with equal ease. They never topped "Brick House" for explosiveness, while "Easy" was arguably their finest slow song. — *Ron Wynn*

● **All the Great Hits** / 1982 / Motown 6028
While there are many Commodores greatest hits packages available, *All the Great Hits* offers most of their biggest hits, making it ideal for the casual fan. — *Stephen Thomas Erlewine*

Nightshift / 1985 / Motown 5400
The Commodores made one final stab at regaining their R&B glory when Lionel Richie and premier producer/arranger James Anthony Carmichael both left in the mid-'80s. J. D. Nicholas became their lead singer, and Dennis Lambert assumed production duties. The Commodores rebounded temporarily when "Nightshift" leaped out of an otherwise ordinary album to be-

come a Grammy-winning R&B and pop smash. It stayed atop the R&B charts for a month and peaked at number-three on the pop charts. Unfortunately, it was also the end for Thomas McClary, who departed the group once the album had run its course. It was their next-to-last hit, and basically the end for the band, although they continued for a couple more years. —*Ron Wynn*

Con Funk Shun
Group / Funk
This Memphis-based group was among the premier funk and soul ensembles of the '70s and '80s. Con Funk Shun began as an in-house band at Stax, backing various acts while recording their own material; some of this was later issued on Fretone. They signed with Mercury in 1976, and had a long run with them until the mid '80s. "Ffun" topped the R&B charts in 1977, and Con Funk Shun overall had eight Top-Ten R&B hits on Mercury through 1986, although they never scored a single Top-Ten or Top-20 pop hit. Their sound and appeal was completely tailored to funk, soul, and urban contemporary audiences. They did danceable ditties, comic pieces, and competent love songs and ballads, especially "Baby, I'm Hooked (Right into Your Love)." Deodato and Leon Ware were two of their producers at various times. Lead vocalist and guitarist Michael Cooper became a star in his own right after Con Funk Shun disbanded in the late '80s. —*Ron Wynn*

● **Best of Con Funk Shun** / 1992 / PolyGram 510275
A solid compilation of Con Funk Shun's influential late '70s and early '80s funk. —*AMG*

Concrete Blonde
Group / Alternative pop/rock
Built around the throaty lead vocals and spare pulsing bass work of Johnette Napolitano and the crunchy guitar execution of former Sparks member Jim Mankey, Concrete Blonde occasionally displays some of the raw fire of the early Pretenders.

After releasing two records that gained some attention in the press and college radio, Concrete Blonde released 1990's *Bloodletting*, which was significantly more accomplished than their previous work. Although the album received good reviews, it took a couple of months before the record began climbing the charts thanks to the surprise hit single, "Joey." Despite two impressive follow-ups, they were never able to match the success of *Bloodletting*. After the modest commercial success of 1993's *Mexican Moon*, the band quietly pulled the plug. During promotional interviews, the band revealed that the record was planned as their swan song. —*Stephen Thomas Erlewine & Rick Clark*

Free / 1989 / IRS 13001
This sophomore effort is an improvement over their slapdash-sounding debut, with punchier arrangements supporting Johnette Napolitano's throaty dramatics. Highlights include the forceful "God Is a Bullet" and the poppish "Happy Birthday." —*Rick Clark*

● **Bloodletting** / 1990 / IRS 13037
Moodier than *Free*. "Joey" is the band's first hit. —*Rick Clark*

○ **Walking in London** / 1992 / IRS 13137
Continues in a vein similar to that on *Bloodletting*. Contains "Ghost of a Texas Ladies' Man." —*Rick Clark*

○ **Mexican Moon** / Oct. 19, 1993 / Capitol 81129
Reportedly their farewell album, *Mexican Moon* finds Johnette Napolitano exploring her fascination with Mexican and Hispanic culture, resulting in album that can be varied and fascinating and, at times, ponderous and tedious. Even with the slight indulgences, the album is among Concrete Blonde's best and is a fine, elegant way to wrap up their rich career. —*Stephen Thomas Erlewine*

Arthur Conley
b. Jan. 4, 1946, Atlanta, GA
Vocals, horn / Soul
A protege of Otis Redding and, like Redding, a musical disciple of Sam Cooke, Conley cowrote (with Redding) and sang "Sweet Soul Music," one of the true anthems of the '60s. Based on Cooke's "Yeah, Man," the record was sweet and hot at the same time, with a readily identifiable horn intro and lyrics that immortalized the soul stars of the day. Conley, although signed to Atco, toured overseas with the Stax/Volt Revue and later joined the Soul Clan with

Atlantic labelmates Wilson Pickett, Solomon Burke, Don Covay, Ben E. King, and Joe Tex. He has lived in France for a number of years. —*Christine Ohlman*

● **Sweet Soul Music** / 1967 / Atlantic 2384
The title track is a real killer! Conley sounds young but assured, and the Otis Redding production is solid throughout. Includes "Let Nothing Separate Us" and "I Can't Stop." —*Christine Ohlman*

○ **More Sweet Soul** / 1969 / Atlantic 33276
This wasn't an album in the classic sense but a collection of singles, as were many soul LPs in the '60s. But Conley's exuberance and spirit are so infectious it overcomes the fact much of this is second level soul at best and clichéd filler at worst. —*Ron Wynn*

The Connells
Group / Alternative pop/rock
This North Carolina rock quartet, led by brothers Mike and David Connell, has a jangly guitar sound. Their debut album, *Darker Days*, was released on Black Park in 1986. —*William Ruhlmann*

Darker Days / 1986 / Tee Vee Toons 2530
The band's first album suffers from inexperience and lack of direction. They show a great deal of promise but fail to distinguish themselves much from the hordes of other southern folk-pop bands. —*Chris Woodstra*

● **Boylan Heights** / 1987 / Tee Vee Toons 2540
Their second album shows a great improvement over its predecessor. With help from producer Mitch Easter, the band effectively combines jangly Southern guitars with Celtic influences. One of the more distinctive college-rock albums of the '80s. —*Chris Woodstra*

Fun & Games / 1989 / Tee Vee Toons 2550
Fun & Games marks a slight dip in quality. The songwriting is still top notch, but at times it's covered by their new heavier sound. —*Chris Woodstra*

○ **One Simple Word** / 1990 / Tee Vee Toons 2580
In the course of four albums, the Connells have evolved their own style within the jangling guitar-rock sound so prevalent in alternative bands of the '80s. Mainly it's been a matter of writing more distinctive songs and having them sung by guitarist George Huntley so they sink in. This is their first album to cross over from the category of "promising" to the beginnings of a fulfillment of that promise. —*William Ruhlmann*

The Contours
Group / Motown, R&B
One of Berry Gordy's earliest discoveries at Motown, the hard-rocking Contours cultivated a new generation of fans when their "Do You Love Me" was featured in the 1987 hit movie *Dirty Dancing*. Led by gravelly voiced Billy Gordon, the quintet scored an R&B chart-topper in 1962 with the rollicking "Do You Love Me" on Gordy's label, then smoothed out their sound just a bit for the mid-'60s soul classics "First I Look at the Purse" and "Just a Little Misunderstanding." Dennis Edwards, who joined the group well after "Do You Love Me," was recruited to replace David Ruffin as lead of the Temptations in 1968. —*Bill Dahl*

● **Do You Love Me** / 1962 / Motown 5415
A rough-edged, early-'60s Motown group that deserves more than its enduring one-hit status for "Do You Love Me." —*Bill Dahl*

Ry Cooder
b. Mar. 15, 1947, Los Angeles, CA
Vocals, guitar, mandolin / Blues-rock, country-rock, roots-rock
Since his self-titled 1970 debut, Ry Cooder has drawn deeply from rich North American colloquial music and pre-rock genres like Tex-Mex, Hawaiian, gospel, vaudeville, country, ragtime, Caribbean, and blues. His passion for dignifying these sounds, plus his earthy emotive guitar technique and choice of stellar sidemen (particularly drummer Jim Keltner), have made for some great albums, especially 1974's *Paradise and Lunch*. Cooder has a knack for inventive song selections, juxtaposing old material with new in a fashion that sometimes illuminates both. It is his understanding of these earlier musical genres that informs Cooder's rock sensibilities with a unique sound, particularly on slide guitar. Besides his solo efforts, Cooder has worked with the Rolling Stones, Taj Mahal, Gordon Lightfoot, Captain Beefheart, John

Hiatt, Randy Newman, and Little Feat, and produced the solid R&B Rounder debut of his backup singers Bobby King and Terry Evans. Cooder has also done extensive soundtrack work for movies, including *The Long Riders, Goin' South, Southern Comfort, Crossroads,* and *Paris, Texas.* In 1992, Cooder worked with John Hiatt, Jim Keltner, and Nick Lowe under the moniker of Little Village. —*Rick Clark*

Ry Cooder / 1970 / Reprise 6402
His debut serves as a neat prototype, with its Sleepy John Estes and Woody Guthrie covers. It also introduces a most talented musician in its leader. But it's still a prototype; the best was yet to come. —*Jeff Tamarkin*

○ **Into the Purple Valley** / Jan. 1971 / Reprise 2052
Cooder perfects his snaky slide guitar technique and introduces exotic ethnic elements on his second album. An American traditional music celebration. —*Jeff Tamarkin*

○ **Boomer's Story** / Feb. 1972 / Reprise 26398
Largely laidback and bluesy, this album features a number of paeans to an America long lost. —*Jeff Tamarkin*

● **Paradise & Lunch** / 1974 / Reprise 2179
Working with an intriguing collection of veteran musicians, the master musician and archivist turns in a stunning set of timeless remakes and new compositions. —*Jeff Tamarkin*

○ **Chicken Skin Music** / 1976 / Reprise 2254
Hawaiian traditional music meets Leadbelly and Ben E. King on Cooder's gospelization of rock and soul. —*Jeff Tamarkin*

Show Time / 1976 / Reprise 3059
Recorded live in 1976, Cooder cooks and struts his stuff on this grand tour of his abilities. The great Flaco Jimenez is on accordion. —*Jeff Tamarkin*

Jazz / 1978 / Reprise 3197
A tribute to Dixieland, with a stopover at the blues hotel. Joseph Byrd's arrangements on tunes by Bix Beiderbecke, Joseph Spence, et al. are inspired. —*Jeff Tamarkin*

Get Rhythm / 1987 / Reprise 25639
Self-producing this time, Cooder gets the old rock & roll right. Johnny Cash and Chuck Berry are pretty darn funky. Cooder can still play slide guitar like no one else. —*Jeff Tamarkin*

Sam Cooke

b. Jan. 22, 1935, Los Angeles, CA, **d.** Dec. 11, 1964, Los Angeles, CA
Vocals / Soul, R&B
Possessing arguably the most glorious voice in Black music, Cooke was never entirely sure what to do with it. Purists prefer his work with the Soul Stirrers (1950-1956) where the gospel edges were untrammeled by any concession to the pop market. When he began recording pop and R&B for Keen, and subsequently RCA, the results varied widely among supper club music, teen ballads, early-60s pop, and proto-soul. That's why the *Live at the Harlem Square* set is important—it captures the way Cooke performed for a Black audience and shows why virtually every soul singer from the '60s and beyond cited him as a primary influence.

For the majority of his years in secular music, Cooke burdened himself with producers for whom the R&B market was at best a secondary consideration. Even the dippiest material is redeemed to an extent by his voice and phrasing, but his unqualified successes are fewer than we might have hoped for. Cooke's death in 1964 meant that he never lived to see his own prophecy, "A Change Is Gonna Come," become truer than he would ever have believed. —*Colin Escott*

○ **Gospel Soul of Sam Cooke & the Soul Stirrers, Vol. 1** / 1964 / Specialty 2116
His pre-pop/soul days. The style is there, but turned toward God. —*Bruce Eder*

Sam Cooke at the Copa / 1964 / ABKCO 2970
Cooke's classic live album is a mixed bag. He was playing to a White supper-club audience and altered his sound accordingly, favoring ballads and folk songs over most of his celebrated classic soul numbers. The voice is there, and the style, but he never does cut loose completely, and the backing band is too clean. —*Bruce Eder*

○ **Gospel Soul of Sam Cooke & the Soul Stirrers, Vol. 2** / 1965 / Specialty 2128
More devotional music, at times overpowering. —*Bruce Eder*

★ **Man & His Music** / 1986 / RCA 7127
The ultimate Sam Cooke collection, and really the only one worth owning, covering his post-1957 career from his pop music breakthrough ("You Send Me") to his final impassioned soul statement, "A Change Is Gonna Come" (which is included in its seldom-heard uncut version). Few stones are left unturned, the sound is clean and sharp, and the tragedy of Cooke's early death is recalled with each play of this collection. —*Bruce Eder*

☆ **Live at the Harlem Square Club** / 1986 / RCA 5181
Long believed lost, this live album—rejected for release in 1963 by Cooke's managers, who wanted to broaden his appeal to White listeners—captures Cooke playing to a largely Black crowd, and it couldn't be more different from his *At the Copa* live album. A hot, sweaty performance, with Cooke and a proper band luxuriating in his most soulful material in its most wrenching and impassioned form. —*Bruce Eder*

○ **His Earliest Recordings** / 1991 / Specialty 7009
A superb collection of 25 of the earliest recordings made by Sam Cooke, including "Touch the Hem of His Garment." —*Stephen Thomas Erlewine*

Cookies

Group / R&B
The forerunner of Ray Charles's Raelettes, the original Cookies were Margie Hendrix, Ethel "Earl-Jean" McCrea, and Pat Lyles. They recorded for Lamp (Aladdin) in 1954, and Jesse Stone brought them to Atlantic in 1955. They recorded three sessions under the Cookies banner and scored a Top-Ten R&B hit with "In Paradise" in 1956. The group also backed Joe Turner and Chuck Willis on their hit recordings in 1956 before being absorbed into the Charles empire and becoming the Raelettes. Almost six years later, a new trio emerged as the Cookies on Dimension, with only McRea from the first group in its lineup. They did backup vocals for Neil Sedaka, Little Eva, and Carole King, while scoring several hits in 1962 and 1963. "Don't Say Nothin' Bad (About My Baby)" was their biggest, peaking at number three R&B (number seven pop) in 1963. "Girls Grow Up Faster Than Boys" was their final chart outing in November of 1963. —*Ron Wynn*

● **Don't Say Nothin' Bad about the Cookies** / 1991 / Teenager 608
This import compilation includes the hits "Chains" and "Don't Say Nothin' Bad about My Baby," and is jammed with obscure Goffin-King tunes. Problem is, most of them aren't anywhere near as good as the hits that the team penned for the Cookies or other girl groups. It does include the obscure gem "Girls Grow Up Faster Than Boys," a sassy cut that's as good as the two hits. —*Richie Unterberger*

Rita Coolidge

b. May 1, 1944, Nashville, TN
Vocals / Pop
After several years as a successful backup singer—either in the studio or on the road—for Delaney & Bonnie, Stephen Stills, Leon Russell, and Eric Clapton, Rita Coolidge launched her own career in 1971. Coolidge's smooth, R&B and gospel-tinged pop didn't land her a hit until 1977, when "We're All Alone" and her cover of Jackie Wilson's "Higher and Higher" hit the Top Ten. Those two hits marked the peak of her career, although she would continue to chart until 1983. "All Time High," from the James Bond movie *Octopussy* was her last hit. Since 1983, Coolidge has only released two albums, and neither record received much notice. —*Stephen Thomas Erlewine*

Rita Coolidge / 1971 / A&M 3107
Her debut album, with Eric Clapton and Stephen Stills. —*Bil Carpenter*

Anytime, Anywhere / 1977 / A&M 4616
Pop covers of R&B standards and ballads. —*Bil Carpenter*

● **Classics, Vol. 5** / 1987 / A&M 2504
Fine cuts from every style Coolidge has recorded, including the hits "(Your Love Has Lifted Me) Higher and Higher," "We're All Alone," and "You." —*Bil Carpenter*

Love Lessons / 1992 / Critique 15410

A comeback album, of sorts, for Coolidge. After a six-year recording hiatus, this is the kind of pop there isn't enough of anymore, including duets with Bonnie from Delaney & Bonnie and Lee Greenwood. Fine mix of adult pop ("Heart Don't Fail Me Now"), sophisticated soul ("Nobody but You"), juke blues ("Ain't No Reason") and a little house music on her update of "I Want to Know What Love Is." —*Bil Carpenter*

Alice Cooper (Vincent Furnier)

b. Feb. 4, 1948, Detroit, MI
Vocals / Hard rock, heavy metal
During the first half of the '70s, Alice Cooper (born Vincent Furnier, son of a preacher), made a name for himself as the king of gross-out, horror hard-rock, touring with guillotines, boa constrictors, and mutilated baby dolls, among other shock props. Fortunately, Cooper's theatrical hard-rock anthems generally weren't upstaged by his performance antics, thanks to smart choices of song covers and crafty plunderings of show-tune melodies. Songs like "I'm Eighteen" and "School's Out" are among some of rock's finest expressions of teen discontent. Cooper fired his original classic lineup in 1974 to pursue a solo career that, while giving him his biggest chart hits, reduced him to an odd middle-of-the-road balladeer. He returned to his old schtick with blood and guts in the late '80s, enjoying something of a comeback. —*Rick Clark*

Pretties for You / 1969 / Bizarre 70351
Alice Cooper's debut album had none of his legendary grotesque hard-rock; instead, *Pretties for You* is an earnest, but flawed, stab at psychedelia, which occasionally catches fire. —*Stephen Thomas Erlewine*

○ **Love It to Death** / Jan. 1971 / Warner Brothers 1883
Features the classic "Eighteen." Other standouts: "Caught in a Dream," "Long Way to Go," and "Black Juju." The best studio album by Cooper. —*Rick Clark*

○ **Killer** / Feb. 1971 / Warner Brothers 2567
Contains the hits "Under My Wheels" and "Be My Lover." Some of the more theatrical pieces undermine the album's strengths. —*Rick Clark*

○ **School's Out** / 1972 / Warner Brothers 2623
The title cut is a Top-Ten hit. One of Cooper's best albums. —*Rick Clark*

○ **Billion Dollar Babies** / 1973 / Warner Brothers 2685
It's not as mind-bendingly outrageous or as hard-rocking as *School's Out, Killer,* or *Love It to Death,* but with its conscious attempt at pop cross-over ("No More Mr. Nice Guy" and "Elected"), *Billion Dollar Babies* is just as perverse as the earlier records, as well as being more consistent than any of his other proper albums. Sometimes selling out just a little bit might not be such a bad thing. —*Stephen Thomas Erlewine*

★ **Greatest Hits** / 1974 / Warner Brothers 3107
While he made many classic hard-rock singles, Alice Cooper never made a consistently enjoyable album, making *Greatest Hits* a necessity. It might not cover *all* of his best tracks, yet everything you need to know is here. —*Stephen Thomas Erlewine*

Welcome to My Nightmare / 1975 / Atlantic 19157
Cooper's solo artist debut contains "Only Women Bleed." It's the best of his solo efforts. —*Rick Clark*

Julian Cope

b. Oct. 21, 1957, Deri, Mid Glamorgan, Wales
Vocals / Alternative pop/rock
By the time Julian Cope called it quits with the Teardrop Explodes in 1982, he had already acquired something of a legendary status in English alternative pop as a wildly creative oddball who fell somewhere between Syd Barrett and Jim Morrison. His solo albums blended '60s psychedelia, synth-pop, and garage rock into a wonderfully twisted stew, with his dry vocal delivery way up in the mix. Subject matter ranges from acid-tinged ruminations to unique manifestos on the state of the planet. Each of his efforts is worth seeking out, but *Peggy Suicide* is an ambitious project that consolidates Cope's many strengths to great effect. —*Rick Clark*

○ **Saint Julian** / 1987 / Island 842686
Former Teardrop Explodes leader Julian Cope adopted a harder, more direct rock style for his solo work, making it more accessi-

ble and bringing out the qualities of his commanding baritone. —*William Ruhlmann*

○ **Peggy Suicide** / 1991 / Island 848388
Peggy Suicide is Cope's idiosyncratic and complexly layered treatise on the state of the earth. Initially inspired by a vision that involved his own self-created mythological characters (Peggy Suicide as Mother Earth, Pollutio as destructive siren), Cope expands his cosmic tragedy beyond the larger political, social, and ecological issues with a healthy dose of mesmerizing psychedelic state-of-the-mind profiles. The unpolished production quality gives *Peggy Suicide* a more immediately believable delivery. Cope juxtaposes pure garage-rock and marimbas, loopy keyboard sounds, and loose-limbed percussion, creating a spellbinding tapestry. Among the many highlights are the ominous AIDS/death epic "Safesurfer" and "Drive, She Said," which is a trashy synthesis of Bowie's Velvet Underground send-ups. —*Rick Clark*

● **Floored Genius—The Best of Julian Cope & the Teardrop Explodes 1979-1991** / 1992 / Island 512788
A sprawling compilation that gives a good sense of the variety of Cope's career, even if it's a bit too scattered to be thoroughly listenable. —*Stephen Thomas Erlewine*

Jehovahkill / 1992 / Island 514052
On first listen, you get the impression that Cope really has gone off the deep end this time. But patience with this 70-minute epic pays off. There is method to Cope's madness. Divided into three "phases," the disc makes an intriguing argument for looking to pre-Christian spirituality for a signpost out of our modern moral conundrums—even if music and lyrics deal with the theme rather more abstractly than the enclosed liner notes, photographs, and poetry.—*Roch Parisien*

Elvis Costello

b. Aug. 25, 1955, Liverpool, England
Vocals / New wave, pop/rock, rock & roll, singer/songwriter,
When Elvis Costello's first record was released in 1977, his bristling cynicism and anger linked him with the punk and new wave explosion. A cursory listen to *My Aim Is True* proves that the main connection that Costello had with the punks was his unbridled passion. He tore through rock's back pages taking whatever he wanted, as well borrowing from country, Tin Pan Alley pop, reggae, and many other musical genres. Over his career, that musical eclecticism has distinguished Costello's records as much as his fiercely literate lyrics. Because he can seamlessly meld his lyrics with his richly diverse music, Costello is one of the most innovative, influential, and best songwriters since the Beatles.

Although *My Aim Is True* was impressive for a debut, his follow-up record, *This Year's Model,* found Costello equaling his accomplishments with a raw, brutal record full of lust and anger. It was also the first record that featured the support of the Attractions, who would back Costello on most of his finest records over the years. After *This Year's Model,* Costello turned toward the intricate, melodic pop of *Armed Forces.* This rapid change in styles is a pattern that he would follow throughout his career. During the '80s and '90s, his records were wildly eclectic, featuring energetic soul, straight country, lushly orchestrated pop, radio-ready Top-40 singles, folk, and chamber music—sometimes every genre would be covered in one sprawling album.

Costello stopped working with the Attractions after 1986's *Blood and Chocolate;* for his next two albums, he recorded with a variety of studio musicians and superstar guests. During the late '80s, Costello indulged too much in his fondness for clever lyrics and musical exploration, yet each album has a number of superbly written songs. After collaborating with the Brodsky Quartet on *The Juliet Letters,* Costello reunited with the Attractions to record 1994's *Brutal Youth.*

In addition to releasing a large number of albums since 1977, Costello has produced a number of artists (including the Pogues, Specials, and Squeeze), written songs for everyone from George Jones to Wendy James, and collaborated with Paul McCartney and Roger McGuinn, among others. Throughout his career, Costello's work has been distinguished by an overwhelming passion for music, making his best records undeniably exciting and emotional. —*Stephen Thomas Erlewine*

☆ **My Aim Is True** / 1977 / Rykodisc 20271

Elvis Costello's debut album is a pop landmark that indicates the future that may exist for the spirit of punk in the wider genre of rock music. Backed by the American group Clover (featuring then-future Doobie Brother John McFee but not harmonica player Huey Lewis), Costello displays all the characteristics that would serve him throughout his career: a caustic wit he uses to savage himself and others, a broad imagination—"(The Angels Wanna Wear My) Red Shoes" is one of the best pieces of rock whimsy ever written—an unsentimental but compelling sense of romance ("Alison"), and an astonishing verbal facility, all enmeshed with a pop encyclopedist's musical knowledge. One of the greatest first albums in pop history. — *William Ruhlmann*

☆ **This Year's Model** / Jul. 1978 / Rykodisc 10272
Backed by his road band, the Attractions, his music becomes harder on the edges, suiting perfectly the bitterness of Costello's best song-for-song set. — *John Floyd*

★ **Armed Forces** / 1979 / Rykodisc 20273
Lavishly produced by Nick Lowe and masterfully programmed, this is Costello's most political album and his most melodic. His bitterness is somewhat subdued, but his passion informs every song. — *John Floyd*

☆ **Get Happy!!** / 1980 / Rykodisc 20275
Featuring 20 tracks of energetic, amphetamine-driven soul, *Get Happy!!* captures Costello at his most vicious and clever. While his words and puns are pithy, it's the constant barrage of songs that make the album work. Not all of the songs are first rate, but the great majority are. — *Stephen Thomas Erlewine*

Taking Liberties / 1980 / Columbia 36839
An interesting jumble of British B-sides and previously unreleased material. Stylistically diverse and occasionally sublime. — *John Floyd*

Almost Blue / 1981 / Rykodisc 20277
Costello's country record, produced by veteran Nashville producer Billy Sherrill. Not one of Costello's best, but it shows an interesting side of his musical sensibilities even as it makes his shortcomings as a singer more obvious. — *Scott Bultman*

☆ **Trust** / 1981 / Rykodisc 20276
Some of the songs are too obtuse to really stick, but the Attractions turn the best of them into edgy and brittle mini-masterpieces. — *John Floyd*

☆ **Imperial Bedroom** / 1982 / Rykodisc 20278
This ornately orchestrated and lush set is Costello's version of *Blood on the Tracks*. It's a musically sophisticated and emotionally devastating tour through the crumbling heart of an incurable romantic. — *John Floyd*

Punch the Clock / 1983 / Columbia 38897
An upbeat set of fairly clear and concise pop songs, supplemented by some punchy horn charts. — *John Floyd*

○ **King of America** / Jan. 1986 / Columbia 40173
Although this is linked thematically to *Imperial Bedroom*, Costello's newfound clarity and the mostly acoustic accompaniment distinguish it from anything in his canon. Remarkable. — *John Floyd*

○ **Blood & Chocolate** / Feb. 1986 / Columbia 40518
A hard-rocking but inconsistent set made worthwhile by "I Want You," "I Hope You're Happy Now," and "Next Time Round," all emotional stunners. — *John Floyd*

Out of Our Idiot / 1987 / Edsel 67
A wildly diverse collection of B-sides and rarities, *Out of Our Idiot* is a treasure for hardcore Costello fans, since many of his throwaways are as fine as his keepers. — *Stephen Thomas Erlewine*

Girls Girls Girls / 1989 / Columbia 46897
Elvis Costello assembled this compilation himself. It is highly idiosyncratic, not the least of its peculiarities being that the CD and cassette versions differ considerably. Costello describes a vague concept in his notes, but the collection of songs (47 on the CDs, 51 on the cassettes) seems a jumble. At least he demonstrates that songs from different periods work well together. A large part of Costello's oeuvre, including *some* of his best work, is represented. — *William Ruhlmann*

Spike / 1989 / Warner Brothers 25848
Throughout his career Elvis Costello has been prolific; thus it was surprising, even given the change in record labels for the United

States, when he took a whole 20 months between *Blood & Chocolate* and this follow-up. But the musical growth he exhibits makes the wait worthwhile. The musical settings range from the stark folk of "Tramp the Dirt Down" to the pop sprightliness of "Veronica" (a collaboration with Paul McCartney that became Costello's first American Top-20 hit) and the New Orleans jazz sound of "Deep Dark Truthful Mirror," featuring the Dirty Dozen Brass Band. The lyrics are among his best. — *William Ruhlmann*

Mighty Like a Rose / 1991 / Warner Brothers 26575
The lyrical concerns here are cumbersome and pretentious, and the music is ponderous and indulgent. But a few decent songs—especially "The Other Side of Summer"—make this 1991 set worthwhile. — *John Floyd*

The Juliet Letters / 1993 / Warner Brothers 45180
Costello's collaboration with the Brodsky Quartet is an intriguing, if flawed, attempt at crossing pop with chamber music. Some songs rely too much on clever arrangements, but most of the tracks are surprisingly successful and accessible. — *Stephen Thomas Erlewine*

☆ **2 1/2 Years** / Oct. 12, 1993 / Rykodisc 90271/74
Rykodisc launched its Elvis Costello reissue series with *2 1/2 Years*, a boxed set featuring his first three albums along with the previously promotion-only *Live at the El Mocambo*, which is only available in the box. While the studio albums are familiar, the live album offers some insights to these highly productive years. The highly sought-after *Live at the El Mocambo* proves that in addition to being an extremely talented songwriter, Costello could also rock *hard* in concert. — *Stephen Thomas Erlewine*

Brutal Youth / 1994 / Warner Brothers 45535
Costello's first album with the Attractions since *Blood & Chocolate*, *Brutal Youth* suffers from soft, mushy production and the inclusion of too many songs. Apart from these two flaws, the record is highly enjoyable, recalling the stripped-down eclecticism of *Trust* and the force of *This Year's Model*. Costello's songs are strong and lean—it's his least affected and pretentious writing since *Blood & Chocolate*. — *Stephen Thomas Erlewine*

Count Five

Group / Psychedelic, garage rock
This San Jose, CA-quintet scored one of the biggest garage-psychedelic hits of the '60s with "Psychotic Reaction," a derivative but riveting American adaptation of the Yardbirds' guitar rave-ups. The single reached number 5 in late 1966, but the group was unable to come anywhere close to duplicating its success. Their sole album and follow-up flop singles emulate the Yardbirds, the Rolling Stones, and the Who—like "Psychotic Reaction," only with less memorable results. Nevertheless, they have their moments. — *Richie Unterberger*

● **Psychotic Reaction** / 1987 / Edsel
Includes seven cuts from their only album, and a few of their ultra-rare flop follow-ups to "Psychotic Reaction." — *Richie Unterberger*

Counting Crows

Group / Alternative pop/rock
With their angst-filled hybrid of Van Morrison, the Band, and R.E.M., Counting Crows became an overnight sensation in 1994. Only a year earlier, the band was a group of unknown musicians, filling in for the absent Van Morrison at the Rock & Roll Hall of Fame ceremony; they were introduced by an enthusiastic Robbie Robertson. Early in 1993, the band recorded their debut album, *August and Everything After*, with T-Bone Burnett; it was released in the fall. It was a dark, sombre record, driven by the morose lyrics and expressive vocals of Adam Duritz. The only up-tempo song, "Mr. Jones," became their ticket to stardom. What made Counting Crows was how they were able to balance Duritz's tortured lyrics with the sound of the late '60s and early '70s. It made them one of the few alternative bands to appeal to listeners who thought that rock & roll died in 1972. — *Stephen Thomas Erlewine*

○ **August & Everything After** / 1993 / DGC 24528
Counting Crows became the surprise success story of 1994 with *August & Everything After*, a record that skillfully filters the classic rock of Van Morrison and the Band through the post-punk sensibilites of R.E.M. and the Cure. With his verbose lyrics and

twisting melodies, lead singer and songwriter Adam Duritz resembles a cross between Morrison and Rick Danko, and his songs are more weathered than anyone would expect from a debut effort. In fact, apart from the single "Mr. Jones," the album is rather gloomy, with melancholy, jangling guitars and a somber mood. What made Counting Crows cross over was the way they are able to make that gloom not sound like Joy Division or the Cure (or even *Automatic for the People*) but like it was recorded straight out of the "classic rock" years of 1968 through 1972. It's modern music for people who don't like modern music. — *Stephen Thomas Erlewine*

Cowboy Junkies

Group / Alternative pop/rock
This low-key quartet from Toronto comes off like a country group with a lava-lamp rhythm section, but occasionally the songwriting of Michael Timmins and the eerie vocals of his sister Margo produce strangely fascinating moments. — *John Floyd*

Whites Off Earth Now!! / 1986 / RCA 2380
VFeaturing only one original song, the Cowboy Junkies' debut *Whites Off Earth Now* captures the band forming their own sound through covers, including songs by Robert Johnson and Bruce Springsteen. It's not as captivating as their later releases, yet it's fascinating to hear their signature country-on-Valium sound develop. And Margo Timmins sings beautifully. — *Stephen Thomas Erlewine*

● **The Trinity Session** / 1988 / RCA 8568
Recorded with one microphone in an abandoned church, their second album achieves a haunting ambience. — *John Floyd*

The Caution Horses / 1990 / RCA 2058
The country influences are clearer and more energetic here, but most of the original material (with the exception of "Sun Comes Up, It's Tuesday Morning") is boring. — *John Floyd*

○ **Black Eyed Man** / 1992 / RCA 61049
The Cowboy Junkies stick with their style of low-key songs steeped in country blues. Songwriter and guitarist Michael Timmins writes story-songs full of rain and street life and regret, and they are movingly sung by Margo Timmins. Two Townes Van Zandt songs, including his classic "To Live Is to Fly," fit right in. — *William Ruhlmann*

○ **Pale Sun, Crescent Moon** / 1993 / RCA
With *Pale Sun, Crescent Moon* the Cowboy Junkies serve up their finest album since *The Trinity Sessions*. The well-chosen covers (including Dinosaur Jr.'s "The Post") mix well with the originals, serving their muted country-rock style well. — *Stephen Thomas Erlewine*

Cracker

Group / Alternative pop/rock, rock & roll
While he was the frontman for Camper Van Beethoven, it seemed that it would take nothing short of a miracle to make guitarist/singer David Lowery a favorite of mainstream rockers, but that's what he and his second band, Cracker, have become. Led by Lowery and guitarist Johnny Hickman, Cracker is much more straightforward than Camper. Cracker concentrates on rock and country, creating a twisted, rootsy rock & roll that sounds like a post-punk Rolling Stones or Little Feat. While their self-titled 1992 debut had moments of raw brilliance, Cracker's second album, 1993's *Kerosene Hat*, fulfilled their promise. Powered by the hit single "Low," the album was a hard-rocking meeting of traditional rock and post-punk sensibilities. Like Camper Van Beethoven's albums, it deserved to be heard by a wide audience. Fortunately, this time Lowery found it—*Kerosene Hat* eventually went gold. — *Stephen Thomas Erlewine*

○ **Cracker** / 1992 / Virgin 86264
Apart from David Lowery's tendency to slip in some smug, self-serving lyrics, Cracker's debut is a terrific rock & roll record, full of energetic three-chord bashers and surprisingly moving ballads. — *Stephen Thomas Erlewine*

● **Kerosene Hat** / 1993 / Virgin
With their second album, Cracker has lost the smarmy self-righteousness that plagued their otherwise fine debut, replacing it with a surprisingly solid, rocking core. *Kerosene Hat* is David Lowery's least affected album yet—its humor is no stranger than the Stones' "Dead Flowers" or Little Feat's "Fat Man in a Bathtub,"

two groups that Cracker strongly recall throughout the album. *Kerosene Hat* is more blues- and country-based than their debut, but it sounds natural since their songwriting has improved and the band has grown tighter. — *Stephen Thomas Erlewine*

The Cramps

Group / Alternative rock, rockabilly
They made their arrival during the first wave of punk-rock, but this New York (via Cleveland, OH) quartet (two guitars, drums, vocals, no bass) found their inspiration in the bizarre sounds of rockabilly and surf guitar and the seedy side of American junk culture. At their best, the Cramps managed to pay homage to their musical heroes without aping them. — *John Floyd*

○ **Songs the Lord Taught Us** / 1980 / IRS 0007
Their first album is a brillant tribute to their inspirations. Its well-chosen covers mingle with ferocious originals. — *John Floyd*

Smell of Female / 1983 / Capitol 73578
A live EP of new material that is a tad lackluster. "Call of the Wighat" conjures the fire of the old days, and "I Ain't Nothin' but a Gorehound" is a career-defining anthem. — *John Floyd*

● **Bad Music for Bad People** / 1984 / IRS 0042
A solid collection of singles, B-sides, and album cuts. A decent introduction made great by "Drug Train" and "New Kind of Kick." — *John Floyd*

The Cranberries

Group / Alternative pop
On the strength of the achingly lush ballad "Linger," the Cranberries' first album, 1993's *Everybody Else Is Doing It, So Why Can't We*, was a surprise success. With its strummed acoustic guitars, soaring strings, and slight Celtic tint, "Linger" is a good example of the guitar-based, Sundays-style atmospheric pop of the Irish group. Although they were stars in Ireland, they hadn't had much success in the rest of Europe. Thanks to their American success, the band also became popular in Britain. — *Stephen Thomas Erlewine*

● **Everybody Else Is Doing It, So Why Can't We** / 1993 / PolyGram 514156
With its gentle, folk-oriented rhythms recalling the finer moments of the Sundays and 10,000 Maniacs crossed with the precious angst of the Smiths, *Everybody Else Is Doing It, So Why Can't We?* is a promising debut album from the Cranberries, highlighted by the gorgeous melancholy of the hit single, "Linger." — *Stephen Thomas Erlewine*

Crash Test Dummies

Group / Alternative pop
With their clever, smug lyrics and cloying folk-tinged melodies, the Crash Test Dummies are a perfect rock band for affluent '90s college students and yuppies. Their first album was a huge hit in their native Canada, but only gained a small cult following in other parts of the world. Thanks to former-Talking Head Jerry Harrison's clean, radio-friendly production, the follow-up *God Shuffled His Feet* (1993), broke big in the States and in turn Europe. The first single from the album, "MMM MMM MMM MMM," became a worldwide Top-Ten hit, making the group a minor sensation with their self-consciously bizarre lyrics and singer/songwriter Brad Roberts's deep baritone. — *Stephen Thomas Erlewine*

Ghosts That Haunt Me / 1991 / Arista 8677
A fine debut album by these smug collegiate folk-pop humorists, featuring the alternative rock hit, "Superman's Song." — *Stephen Thomas Erlewine*

● **God Shuffled His Feet** / 1993 / Arista 16531
Thanks to Jerry Harrison's remarkably clear and focused production, Crash Test Dummies' second album became a surprise hit. Apart from the relatively concise pop-smarts of the singles "MMM MMM MMM MMM" and "Afternoons and Coffeespoons," *God Shuffled His Feet* isn't all that different from the band's first album. — *Stephen Thomas Erlewine*

Crazy Horse

Group / Hard rock
A hard-rock trio consisting of bassist Billy Talbot, drummer Ralph Molina, and guitarist Danny Whitten, they are known best as the

on-again, off-again backup band for Neil Young, though they have recorded occasional albums themselves. Frank Sampedro replaced Whitten after his death in 1973. The current band is Talbot, Molina, singer Sonny Mone, and guitarist Matt Piucci. —*William Ruhlmann*

● **Crazy Horse** / 1971 / Reprise 6438
An exceptional hard-rock album by one of the finest garage-rock bands ever, *Crazy Horse* proves that the band doesn't need Neil Young to make tough, eclectic, and smart rock & roll. —*Stephen Thomas Erlewine*

Crazy Moon / 1978 / RCA 3054
The trio of Molina, Talbot, and Sampedro is frequently joined by compatriot Neil Young on an album of hard rock with a sound not unlike that produced by them on Young's records. —*William Ruhlmann*

"Papa" John Creach

b. May 8, 1917, USA, d. 1994
Violin / Folk rock
Violinist "Papa" John Creach first came to the notice of rock fans when he joined Jefferson Airplane and its spin-off group, Hot Tuna, in 1970. By that time, he was already in his early fifties, a veteran of jazz and blues associations, while his fellow band members were not yet 30. Nevertheless, using an electrified violin, Creach added a new psychedelic edge to the Airplane in its final days. The band split in 1972, by which time Creach had begun to release solo albums on its custom label, Grunt. The Airplane was reorganized and relaunched as Jefferson Starship, and Creach was with it through its million-selling *Red Octopus* album in 1975. He continued to make solo albums through 1992, when be released *Papa Blues*. Papa John Creach died of heart failure in 1994 at the age of 76. —*William Ruhlmann*

● **Papa John Creach** / 1971 / Grunt 1003
At the time this album was recorded, Jefferson Airplane had expanded from a rock group into something of a San Francisco collective of musicians and launched its own record label, Grunt, necessitating a flow of product. As a result, there was a flurry of releases by the Airplane itself and several offshoots, with each of these records featuring several members of the loose aggregation informally dubbed PERRO (the Planet Earth Rock 'n' Roll Orchestra). Papa John Creach, violinist for the Airplane and its spinoff group, Hot Tuna, was the leader on this set, which featured members of the Airplane (Grace Slick, for example, duets with Creach on the leadoff track, "The Janitor Drives a Cadillac"), Quicksilver Messenger Service, and the Grateful Dead. The result sounds like the Airplane records of the period, with a bit more of Creach's electric violin soaring over the proceedings. —*William Ruhlmann*

Cream

Group / Blues rock, hard rock, progressive rock, psychedelic
Eric Clapton (guitar), Jack Bruce (bass), and Ginger Baker (drums) were all veterans of the British blues scene by the time they formed Cream in late 1966, but their brand of highly amplified, freeform playing took the music directions that a band like the Yardbirds could only dream of. They were one of the first bands to legitimatize jamming on stage, with each member a solid soloist in his own right—Baker's solo on "Toad" being a constant highlight of their live show. Their original material (much of it written by Bruce) strayed far from their blues roots, in a more pop direction, expanding their audience in the bargain. When they called it quits in 1969, rock critics mourned their demise, but their two principal contributions (being rock's first "supergroup" and helping to lay the foundation for heavy metal) live on. —*Cub Koda*

Fresh Cream / Dec. 1966 / Polydor 827576
Cream's debut album was largely rooted in the blues, and included here versions of such standards as Willie Dixon's "Spoonful," Muddy Waters's "Rollin' and Tumblin'," and bassist Jack Bruce's "N.S.U." that took on a whole new life on stage. On this record they sound somewhat flat and uninspired. —*Rob Bowman*

○ **Disraeli Gears** / Nov. 1967 / Polydor 823636
Cream's sophomore effort was a substantial step forward. Interestingly, part of the reason seems to be that they stopped covering American blues musicians and started writing their own

psychedelic blues-based hybrids. "Sunshine of Your Love" was the big AM radio hit and "Tales of Brave Ulysses," "Strange Brew," and "Swlabr" received substantial FM play. —*Rob Bowman*

○ **Wheels of Fire** / Aug. 1968 / Polydor 827578
Wheels of Fire was a two-album set, one disc recorded in the studio, the second disc recorded on stage in San Francisco. Side 3 contains the definitive live version of what became Clapton's signature piece, Robert Johnson's "Crossroads," plus a version of "Spoonful" that clocks in at just under 17 minutes. On such pieces, Cream approached blues-based rock with a jazz aesthetic, using the song as a framework to begin and end a performance. The strength of the performance is in the improvisation. When it worked, as it does on "Spoonful," they were brilliant. When it didn't, as on side 4's "Traintime" and "Toad," the band became excess incarnate. The studio disc contained their second Top-Ten single, Jack Bruce's "White Room," as well as a stunning cover of Albert King's "Born Under a Bad Sign." Other tracks, particularly those written by Ginger Baker, do not hold up. —*Rob Bowman*

Goodbye / Mar. 1969 / Polydor 823660
As the title implies, this is Cream's farewell. By the time it was issued, the band had broken up. Three studio recordings that were left were coupled with extended live versions of "I'm So Glad," "Politician," and "I'm Sitting on Top of the World." The live tracks burn. Clapton, Bruce, and Baker each take credit for one of the studio tracks. Clapton's cut, "Badge," was cowritten by George Harrison and remains what was surely the prettiest melody to ever grace a Cream recording. —*Rob Bowman*

Live Cream, Vol. 1 / Jun. 1970 / Polydor 827577
No doubt Cream was best as a live band, but despite the undeniable quality of the playing, does anybody really need these endless jams? —*Jeff Tamarkin*

Live Cream, Vol. 2 / Jun. 1972 / Polydor 823661
More live Cream, concentrating on material from their *Disraeli Gears* and *Wheels of Fire* albums plus an extended workout on Freddie King's "Hideaway." —*Rob Bowman*

★ **Strange Brew: The Very Best of Cream** / 1986 / Polydor 811639
What the title implies, all the finest tracks from the band's four studio albums. The best was brilliant. —*Rob Bowman*

Creedence Clearwater Revival

Group / Rock & roll
Even though Creedence Clearwater Revival hailed from the San Francisco area, the band's soul, which was steeped in R&B, rockabilly, blues, and stripped-down rock & roll, made it hard to believe they came from anywhere but the Mississippi delta. At that time, Bay Area rock was dominated by bands like the Grateful Dead, Quicksilver Messenger Service, and Jefferson Airplane, whose barely had an idea of economical arrangements and a tight rhythmic pocket.

John Fogerty, the band's lead vocalist and lead guitarist, brought a kind of passion to rock & roll that few recorded artists have ever delivered. Not only that, but his songwriting contributions to rock have unquestionably placed him in the ranks of American music legends like Chuck Berry, Willie Dixon, and Carl Perkins. Creedence's rhythm section, with Stu Cook (bass), Doug Clifford (drums), and Tom Fogerty (rhythm guitar), made every note count, doing for rock what Booker T. & the MG's did for Memphis soul.

Any lover of real, earthy rock should own most of Creedence's catalog, since this is the meat-and-potatoes of any decent rock collection. Then again, it is unimaginable that any lover of rock & roll could be unaware of this band. —*Rick Clark*

Creedence Clearwater Revival / 1968 / Fantasy 4512
The band's unique swampy crunch was already well developed on this fine debut. It opens with a riveting version of Screamin' Jay Hawkins's hit "I Put a Spell on You." A gritty psychedelic version of Dale Hawkins's creation "Suzy Q" was Creedence's first hit. —*Rick Clark*

Bayou Country / 1969 / Fantasy 4513
John Fogerty's songwriting voice gains new focus, particularly in "Proud Mary," the band's most popular song, and "Penthouse Pauper." "Bootleg" features a powerfully spare groove, and "Born on the Bayou," with its rock-solid pulse and economical lead guitar work, is one of the band's better attempts at stretching out.

Nevertheless, the long jams found here cause the album to lose some steam. —*Rick Clark*

○ **Green River** / Jan. 1969 / Fantasy 4514

Fogerty tightens things up with this great collection of songs. Contains the truly great hits "Green River," "Lodi," and "Bad Moon Rising." "Wrote a Song for Everyone," "Cross-tie Walker," and "Tombstone Shadow" are classic Fogerty. There's a super version of "The Night Time Is the Right Time." —*Rick Clark*

○ **Willy & the Poor Boys** / Feb. 1969 / Fantasy 4515

Not a weak cut here, just more hits like "Down on the Corner" and the relentless wrong-side-of-the-tracks railing of "Fortunate Son." By the time of *Willy*, this California band had captured the spirit of the South more believably than most bands from that region. Versions of "The Midnight Special," "Cotton Fields," and instrumentals like the down-home "Poorboy Shuffle" and "Side o' the Road," with its Booker T. groove, helped underscore that perception. —*Rick Clark*

○ **Cosmo's Factory** / 1970 / Fantasy 4516

"Ramble Tamble" and a masterful version of "I Heard It through the Grapevine" may run a little too long, but the remainder of the album is letter perfect. Pointing out highlights here is useless. Most of these tracks were hits as well. —*Rick Clark*

Pendulum / 1970 / Fantasy 4517

Creedence loses some steam here by wasting too much time on lengthy groove numbers like "Pagen Baby," "Born to Move," and "Rude Awakening #2"—a horrible attempt at creating something serious-sounding and an irritating waste of time. In spite of those miscalculations, most bands could only hope for as many good songs as "Have You Ever Seen the Rain?" "Hey Tonight," "It's Just a Thought," "Molina," and "(Wish I Could) Hideaway." —*Rick Clark*

Mardi Gras / 1972 / Fantasy 4518

Maybe Fogerty was running out of steam, but in the name of democratization, each of the other band members got to toss in their creative licks on this album. After so many great albums, this one sounds half-hearted. Only "Sweet Hitch-Hiker," "Someday Never Comes," and a cover of the Ricky Nelson tune "Hello Mary Lou" recall the band's earlier magic. —*Rick Clark*

★ **Chronicle, Vol. 1** / 1976 / Fantasy

Essential disc for any serious lover of rock & roll. Contains almost all the Creedence hits plus a generous helping of key album tracks. —*Rick Clark*

Royal Albert Hall Concert / 1980 / Fantasy 4501

This solid, no-frills live document covers many of the band's hits, plus time for some meat-and-potatoes groove-jammin' with ten minutes of "Keep on Chooglin.'" It beats the dismal *Live in Europe* by a long shot. —*Rick Clark*

☆ **Chronicle, Vol. 2** / 1986 / Fantasy 3

A well-compiled set that fills in most of the gaps left by Vol. 1. Sin of omission: Where's "Bootleg" ?! —*Rick Clark*

Marshall Crenshaw

b. 1954, Detroit, MI
Vocals / Pop/rock, rock & roll

When Marshall Crenshaw burst onto the 1982 music scene, his tight well-crafted songs (part Buddy Holly, part Beatles) and exuberant performances were a fresh breeze at a time when robotic pop by Human League and Tony Basil, as well as soul-numbing ballads like Lionel Richie's "Truly," reigned on the airwaves. He even managed a Top 40 hit with the timeless-sounding "Someday, Someway." Crenshaw's albums have been mostly enjoyable. Only on 1989's *Good Evening* does Crenshaw seem creatively adrift. —*Rick Clark*

● **Marshall Crenshaw** / 1982 / Warner Brothers 3673

His incredible debut revealed Crenshaw to be a fully formed songwriter in the Beatles and Buddy Holly super-melodic pop tradition. Like the work of those influences, the best material here seems timeless. "Someday, Someway" was a moderate hit, even though it (and others like "Cynical Girl," "Girls," "The Usual Thing," and "Mary Anne") seemed written in stone. Crenshaw does include one fine cover of "Soldier of Love," recorded originally by Arthur Alexander and later by the Beatles. Criticism: Why has Warner chosen not to include Crenshaw's fine B-sides as bonus tracks from this period on this or his other CDs? —*Rick Clark*

○ **Field Day** / 1983 / Warner Brothers 23873

For those expecting a repeat of his fine debut effort, Crenshaw made an unexpected left turn and sought out in-demand producer Steve Lillywhite, whose credits (Psychedelic Furs, XTC, U2, Ultravox) read like an alternative-rock *Who's Who*. The heavily treated drum sounds and walls of guitar may have initially put off some fans, but *Field Day* demonstrated that Crenshaw was making impressive strides as a songwriter and musician. "Whenever You're on My Mind" (a great single that should've been a hit), "Our Town," "All I Know Right Now," and "Monday Morning Rock" are highlights. —*Rick Clark*

○ **Downtown** / 1985 / Warner Brothers 25319

With the help of producer T-Bone Burnette and a handful of session sidemen, Crenshaw delivered a strong collection of originals and covers. Highlights include a version of Ben Vaughn's "I'm Sorry (but so Is Brenda Lee)" and Crenshaw's own "The Distance Between." This is one of Crenshaw's best efforts. —*Rick Clark*

○ **Mary Jean & 9 Others** / 1987 / Warner Brothers 25583

Not quite as strong as his first three full-length albums, *Mary Jean* does possess some standout tracks in "Calling Out for Love (at Crying Time)," a version of Peter Case's "Steel Strings," and the title cut. Produced by Don Dixon, whose credits include the Smithereens. —*Rick Clark*

Life's Too Short / 1991 / MCA 10223

Crenshaw changes labels and brings on producer Ed Stasium (Cavedogs, Living Colour, Smithereens). The result is a more vibrant, harder-rocking sound. Highlights include "Better Back Off," "Don't Disappear Now," "Face of Fashion," and "Fantastic Planet of Love." —*Rick Clark*

The Crests

Group / Doo-wop

One of the most successful integrated doo-wop groups, the Crests waxed the classic ballad "16 Candles" in 1959. Formed in 1956, they began recording the next year for Joyce, where they inched onto the pop lists with "Sweetest One." Moving to the brand-new Coed logo, Johnny Maestro's warm tenor made "16 Candles" a national smash, and pop/R&B hybrids like "The Angels Listened In" and "Step by Step" also did well. Maestro went solo in 1960, scoring the next year with "Model Girl" on Coed, while the Crests attempted to survive on their own. Maestro eventually reclaimed stardom as leader of Brooklyn Bridge, an 11-piece aggregation that hit with "Worst That Could Happen" in 1968. —*Bill Dahl*

● **Best of the Crests** / 1990 / CoEd

All of the Crests' hits—including the classic "16 Candles" and "Trouble in Paradise"—are collected on this splendid 18-track disc. —*Stephen Thomas Erlewine*

Jim Croce

b. Jan. 10, 1943, Philadelphia, PA, d. Sep. 20, 1973, Natchitaches, LA
Vocals, guitar / Singer/songwriter

Singer/songwriter Croce's enormous pop success of the early '70s was cut short by his death in a plane crash. A Philadelphia native who had worked the coffeehouse circuit for almost ten years when he was signed to ABC Records in 1971, Croce had a warm singing voice that served him well on his comic uptempo hits ("You Don't Mess Around with Jim," "Bad, Bad Leroy Brown") as well as his sincere ballads ("Operator"). The latter became predominant after his death, with "I Got a Name," "Time in a Bottle," and "I'll Have to Say I Love You in a Song," all of which were posthumous Top Ten hits. —*William Ruhlmann*

● **Photographs & Memories: His Greatest Hits** / 1974 / Atlantic 90467

Photographs & Memories: His Greatest Hits is a compilation containing Croce's best songs and biggest hits, including the number-one hits "Bad, Bad Leroy Brown" and "Time in a Bottle." —*William Ruhlmann*

○ **Time in a Bottle/Greatest Love Songs** / 1977 / Atlantic 90469

Since it contains only his love ballads, fans who prefer sweetly sentimental songs like "Operator" and "Time in a Bottle" to story songs like "Bad, Bad Leroy Brown" and "You Don't Mess Around with Jim," will find *Time in a Bottle* the essential compilation. Despite the amount of good material here, *Photographs and*

Memories remains a better collection, since it presents both sides of the popular singer/songwriter. —*Stephen Thomas Erlewine*

○ **50th Anniversary Collection** / 1992 / Saja 92205
While it has too much material for the casual listener, the two-disc *50th Anniversary Collection* is the definitive package for the hardcore Jim Croce fan, covering all his hits, as well as many forgotten album tracks. —*Stephen Thomas Erlewine*

Crosby Stills & Nash (and Young)

b. , USA

Group / Folk rock, pop/rock, singer/songwriter
The musical partnership of David Crosby, Stephen Stills, and Graham Nash, with and without Neil Young, not only was one of the most successful touring and recording acts of the late '60s, the '70s, and the early '80s—with the colorful, contrasting nature of the members' characters and their connection to the political and cultural upheavals of the time—it was the only American-based band to approach the overall societal impact of the Beatles.

The group was a second marriage for all the participants who came together 1968: Crosby bad been a member of the Byrds, Nash was in the Hollies, and Stills had been part of Buffalo Springfield. The resulting trio, however, sounded like none of its predecessors and was characterized by a unique vocal blend and a musical approach that ranged from acoustic folk to melodic pop to hard rock. CSN's debut album, released in 1969, was perfectly in tune with the times, and the group was an instant hit. By the time of their first tour (which included the Woodstock festival), they had added Young, also a veteran of Buffalo Springfield, who maintained a solo career.

The first CSN&Y album, *Deja-vu*, was a chart-topping hit in 1970, but the group split acrimoniousiy after a summer tour. *4 Way Street*, a live double album issued after the breakup, was anotbernumber-one hit. (When it finally was released on CD in 1992, it was lengthened with more live material.) In 1974, CSN&Y reformed for a summer stadium tour without releasing a new record. Nevertheless, the compilation *So Far* became their third straight number one. Crosby, Stills, and Nash re-formed without Young in 1977 for the album *CSN,* another giant hit. They followed with *Daylight Again* in 1982, but by then Crosby was in the throes of drug addiction and increasing legal problems. He was in jail in 1985-1986, but cleaned up and returned to action, with the result that CSN&Y reunited for only their second studio album, *American Dream,* in 1988. CSN followed with *Live It Up* in 1990, and though that album was a commercial disappointment, the trio remains a popular live act. They embarked on a 25th-anniversary tour in the summer of 1994. —*William Ruhlmann*

○ **Crosby, Stills & Nash** / 1969 / Atlantic 19117
The group's debut album is a scintillating blend of personal poetry, topical politics, and splendid, spare production. "Suite: Judy Blue Eyes" caught everybody's ear, but every track here is worthwhile, and the success of the album can be measured by the fact that every song here could have been a single or a B-side. "Marrakesh Express," "Pre-Road Downs," and "Lady of the Island" stand out. —*Bruce Eder*

★ **Deja Vu** / 1970 / Atlantic 19118
This was the group's triumph, displaying a broader musical scope than that found on the CSN debut record. Each of the four members contributed high-quality material, with Stills turning in the leadoff track, "Carry On," Nash contributing such standards as "Teach Your Children" and "Our House," Crosby presenting the title track, and Young adding the characteristic "Helpless." There was also the hit version of Joni Mitchell's "Woodstock." Flawless harmonies, thoughtful lyrics, accomplished playing: this is state-of-the-art '70s rock music and continues to be the best explanation of CSN&Y's enormous stature and enduring legacy. —*William Ruhlmann*

○ **4 Way Street** / 1971 / Atlantic 82406
This expanded version of the original double live album by CSN&Y is now an indispensable part of any collection, with additional Neil Young and Graham Nash material (and even a version of "King Midas in Reverse," the old Hollies tune) that any serious listener will want. Some of the extended guitar jams between Stills and Young ("Southern Man") go on longer than strict musical sense would dictate, but it seemed right at the time, and they

capture a form that was far more abused in other hands after this group broke up. —*Bruce Eder*

● **So Far** / 1974 / Atlantic 19119
Released to coincide with CSN&Y's 1974 reunion tour, this compilation remains the best representation of the group's early work, featuring such hits as "Teach Your Children" and "Suite: Judy Blue Eyes." It also put the one-off single "Ohio"/"Find the Cost of Freedom" (CSN&Y's response to the shooting of four anti-war student protestors at Kent State University) on an album for the first time. —*William Ruhlmann*

CSN / 1977 / Atlantic 19104
A fair and somewhat slick reprise, highlighted by "Dark Star." A valiant attempt to recreate the good spirits of the first album amid the malaise of the '70s. —*Bruce Eder*

○ **CSN (boxed set)** / 1991 / Atlantic 82319
Seventy-seven tracks make up this four-CD boxed-set retrospective of the various permutations of Crosby, Stills, & Nash (& Young) from 1968 to 1990. The set is dotted with unreleased tracks from abortive album sessions (CSN&Y may have recorded only two studio albums, but they sure tried a lot of other times), and there are also good choices from both solo work and the well-known material. For a neophyte, it may be on the long side, but seasoned fans can welcome this lavish tribute. —*William Ruhlmann*

Sheryl Crow

Vocals, guitar / Singer/songwriter, rock & roll
After many years of paying her dues as a backup singer for Don Henley, Eric Clapton, Rod Stewart, and Michael Jackson, Sheryl Crow finally got a chance to make her own album in 1993. Growing out of a series of informal jam sessions with Los Angeles studio veterans, the relaxed yet gritty blues-rock of *Tuesday Night Music Club* became a hit in the spring of 1994, thanks to the single "Leaving Las Vegas," a slightly surreal travelog which only shows the beginning of her talent. —*Stephen Thomas Erlewine*

○ **Tuesday Night Music Club** / Aug. 3, 1993 / A&M 540126
Sheryl Crow's debut album *Tuesday Night Music Club* is a loose, melodic, gritty, record with subtle country underpinnings. Throughout the album, she shows that she not only has an impressive, bluesy voice but that she also is a considerably talented songwriter, as "Leaving Las Vegas" and "Run Baby Run" prove. —*Stephen Thomas Erlewine*

Crowded House

Group / Pop/rock
In 1985, New Zealand-born Neil Finn was left with the task of continuing with Split Enz after the departure of his brother (and founding member) Tim Finn. He opted instead to dissolve the Enz. Taking drummer Paul Hester with him, he formed a stripped-down trio with bassist Nick Seymour. After years of writing Split Enz's synth-pop hits like "I Got You" and "One Step Ahead," Neil concentrated on well-crafted, melodic songs and transparent production. This new Australian band was dubbed Crowded House for the state of congestion in the Los Angeles bungalow the band shared while recording with producer/keyboardist Mitchell Froom.

Their self-titled 1986 debut album was a sleeper hit that waited until the third single, "Don't Dream It's Over," before jumping into the Top Ten. An excellent live act, Crowded House made quite a splash that year. Although their next two albums didn't match the chart success of the first, consistently high quality has earned them many fans and critics'-darling status. Tim Finn joined the band briefly for the *Woodface* album and tour.

Two years later, Crowded House added guitarist Mark Hart and recorded the acclaimed *Together Alone* with Youth, a former member of Killing Joke; the record was a hit everywhere except the United States. During a U.S. tour in the spring of 1994, drummer Paul Hester left the band permanently to spend more time with his family. —*Scott Bultman*

● **Crowded House** / 1986 / Capitol 46693
Their Top-40 debut is loaded with highly melodic, Anglo-pop gems. Strong, upbeat songwriting and vocal harmonies from this talented trio, featuring the hits "Don't Dream It's Over" and "Something So Strong." —*Scott Bultman*

Temple of Low Men / 1988 / Capitol 48763

Darker and more introspective, this still has fine songwriting and performances, including a guest appearance from Richard Thompson. Highlights include "Into Temptation," "Better Be Home Soon," and "When You Come." —Scott Bultman

○ **Woodface** / 1991 / Capitol 93559

This album has the great melodies of their first, the soul-searching depth of the second, and the great vocal harmonies of the re-united Finn brothers. A close contender for their most essential album. —Scott Bultman

○ **Together Alone** / 1993 / Capitol 827048

More experimental and musically varied than any of their previous releases, Together Alone finds Crowded House branching out into traditional Maori music and heavy guitars, all within the shining pop songcraft that is Neil Finn's trademark. Picking up a new guitarist and adding the production skills of ex-Killing Joke member Youth, Crowded House energizes their sound without losing sight of Neil Finn's classic pop songwriting, as the singles "Locked Out" and "Distant Sun" prove. —Stephen Thomas Erlewine

Crystals

Group / Rock & roll

One of Phil Spector's first success stories, the Crystals were at the mercy of the legendary producer. Although the group—Dee Dee Kennibrew, La La Brooks, Pat Wright, Mary Thomas, and Barbara Alston—formed before they met Spector, he owned the rights to the name and he changed the lineup to suit his recording purposes. On their first hit, "He's a Rebel," Darlene Love sang the lead vocals. After that single became a number-one hit, Brooks returned to lead vocals and she sang their next two big hits: "Da Doo Ron Ron" and "Then He Kissed Me." After those two 1963 hits, Spector spent more time with the Ronettes and less with the Crystals. As a result, the group never had another hit. In the following years, their lineup kept shifting as the group played the oldies circuit. —Stephen Thomas Erlewine

● **Best of the Crystals** / 1992 / ABKCO 7214

All of the Crystals' biggest hits are included on this comprehensive collection, which also features many forgotten singles and album tracks. While some of the lesser-known material might not match the standards of the classic singles, many songs do come close. —Stephen Thomas Erlewine

The Cult

Group / Hard rock, heavy metal

Singer Ian Astbury formed the Southern Death Cult in England in 1982 as a doom-rock band. Reorganized in 1983 with guitarist Billy Duffy as Death Cult, by 1984 the rock quartet, quickly moving toward heavy metal, had become simply the Cult. Their hard-rock set Electric (1987) was a commercial breakthrough. —William Ruhlmann

Love / 1985 / Sire 25359

Apart from the monolithic rock & roll masterpiece "She Sells Sanctuary," Love is devoid of memorable riffs and melodies. —Stephen Thomas Erlewine

● **Electric** / 1987 / Sire 25555

After four years of evolving from a goth-rock band with two longer names (Southern Death Cult, Death Cult), the Cult emerged on this Rick Rubin production as a full-fledged heavy metal band. Billy Duffy pulls out monstrous guitar riffs and lead singer Ian Astbury declaims like a latter-day Jim Morrison. Contains "Love Removal Machine." —William Ruhlmann

Sonic Temple / 1989 / Sire 25871

A change of producer and drummers has no discernible impact on the Cult's driving metal assault. —William Ruhlmann

Culture Club

Group / Pop/rock, soul

Culture Club was a successful pop-rock group of the early '80s, led by singer Boy George O'Dowd. It was as well known for O'Dowd's flamboyant fashion sense as it was for its music, but when it was hot, it was hot: Culture Club racked up six straight Top-Ten hits in 1983-1984.

The group was formed in London in 1981. In addition to O'Dowd, it consisted of bassist Mikey Craig, guitarist Roy Hay,

and drummer Jon Moss. They topped the charts with their debut single, "Do You Really Want to Hurt Me." The band's visual flair helped them in the United States, where music video had recently become an important promotional tool, and the single hit number two stateside by early 1983.

Culture Club's music was light, bouncy pop, topped by O'Dowd's appealing tenor. It was anything but outrageous, although O'Dowd's elaborate costumes made the group seem more daring than it was. Kissing to Be Clever, their debut album, was a million-seller and included "I'll Tumble 4 Ya," another Top-Ten hit. The fall of 1983 brought a second album, Colour by Numbers, and more hits: "Church of the Poison Mind," "Karma Chameleon" (a number one), and "Miss Me Blind."

Unfortunately, the group's very novelty was its undoing. The third album, Waking Up with the House on Fire (1984), went platinum by momentum, but its singles were not big hits, and the fourth album, From Luxury to Heartache, was a relative flop in 1986, the same year O'Dowd's heroin addiction became a matter of public knowledge. In 1987 O'Dowd cleaned up, split up Culture Club, and embarked on a solo career. —William Ruhlmann

○ **Kissing to Be Clever** / 1982 / Virgin 38398

Appealing lightly synthesized '80s pop music, featuring the infectious ballad hit "Do You Really Want to Hurt Me." —William Ruhlmann

○ **Colour by Numbers** / 1983 / Virgin 91391

More melodic bouncy pop led by Boy George's engaging singing on "Karma Chameleon" and other songs. —William Ruhlmann

● **At Worst . . . The Best of Boy George and Culture Club** / 1993 / Virgin 72438390142

Not only does At Worst include all of Culture Club's fine hit singles, it also collects selected songs from Boy George's rather unsuccessful career, including his surprise comeback hit, "The Crying Game." —Stephen Thomas Erlewine

The Cure

Group / Alternative pop/rock

The Cure has become one of the most popular groups to emerge from Great Britain's post-punk gloom-rock trend of the late '70s, though it took a relatively long time to achieve its present prominence. Amid a variety of personnel changes, the constant in the group has been singer, songwriter, and guitarist Robert Smith, whose teased hair and black eyeliner dominate the group's look. He formed the Cure as a trio in 1976 with Laurence Tolhurst (drums) and Michael Dempsey (bass). After some work for an independent label (including the single "Killing an Arab," based on Albert Camus's novel The Stranger), they released their first album, Three Imaginary Boys, in 1979.

In January 1980, Dempsey left and was replaced by Simon Gallup. More albums followed at yearly intervals, with the fourth, Pornography, finally breaking the British Top Ten. The fifth album, The Top, became another British Top Ten in 1984, a year that also produced the album Concert —The Cure Live. In 1985, The Head on the Door became the band's biggest British hit yet, reaching number seven. It also broke the U.S. Top-100 list.

By 1986 the Cure had expanded to a quintet. In addition to Smith, Tolhurst (now on keyboards), and Gallup, the group had Port Thompson on guitar and Boris Williams on drums. That year, a compilation album, Standing on a Beach—The Singles, hit number four in the United Kingdom; in America it went gold in early 1987, finally establishing the Cure in the States.

In 1987 they released the double album Kiss Me, Kiss Me, Kiss Me, another success, and added Roger O'Donnell on keyboards. (Tolhurst subsequently departed.) In 1989 Disintegration produced the Cure's first big U.S. hit single, "Love Song" (it was number two). The album itself hit number 12 and went platinum. Wish, released in the spring of 1992, entered the U.S. charts at number two. —William Ruhlmann

○ **Boys Don't Cry** / 1979 / Elektra 60786

Combining the finer moments from Three Imaginary Boys with early singles, this is the best representation of the band's early pop-oriented days. A post-punk masterpiece. —Chris Woodstra

○ **Three Imaginary Boys** / 1979 / Fiction 001

Bursting with high-energy playing and bare-bones production, the band's first album showcases Robert Smith's most concise songwriting. The now common themes of isolation and despair are present, this time presented in perfect three-minute form.

Three Imaginary Boys ends up sounding like a more tuneful version of Wire's *Pink Flag*. —*Chris Woodstra*

Seventeen Seconds / 1980 / Elektra 60784
Although it's still a pop album in many ways, the Cure's second proper album marks a move toward despair, depression, and epic songwriting. The playing is slowed considerably, with synthesizers barely rising above the minimalist arrangements. Hooks are present, but in smaller numbers. —*Chris Woodstra*

Faith / 1981 / Elektra 60783
Continuing the trend of the previous album, *Faith* is an even darker affair. Smith sings with suicidal resignation through eight somber epics, raising the tempo only for the single, "Primary." Typified by the title track and "Funeral Party," the album is chilling, even if it's not particularly memorable. —*Chris Woodstra*

○ **Pornography** / 1982 / Elektra 60785
Pornography is arguably the quintessential goth album. Layers of distorted guitars, heavily echoed vocals, and tribal drumming provide the "wall of doom" backdrop for lyrics like "It doesn't matter if we all die," taking the listener deep into Smith's disturbed psyche. *Pornography* marked the band's move from relative obscurity to cult status. —*Chris Woodstra*

Japanese Whispers/Singles / 1983 / Sire 25076
This collection of the band's mid-'80s lightweight pop singles provides a refreshing contrast to the somber albums that preceded it. —*Chris Woodstra*

Top / 1984 / Sire 25086
Essentially a Robert Smith solo effort, this album lacks the direction of previous albums. Even experiments in different styles can't make up for a lack of real substance in the songs. Only the single, "The Caterpillar," leaves a lasting impression. —*Chris Woodstra*

○ **Head on the Door** / 1985 / Elektra 60435
Head on the Door represents the band's creative high point and most accessible moment. The songs successfully walk a fine line between gloom and pop, including the danceable hits, "In Between Days" and "Close to Me." This move toward the mainstream made them stars in the United Kingdom and helped them make some inroads into the U.S. market. —*Chris Woodstra*

★ **Standing on a Beach—The Singles** / 1986 / Elektra 60477
The Cure's gloom-and-doom (but danceable) greatest hits, 1979-1985. Though not hits in the United States, these helped set the stage for the group's later Stateside success. —*William Ruhlmann*

Kiss Me, Kiss Me, Kiss Me / 1987 / Elektra 60737
The Cure's breakthrough double album containing "Why Can't I Be You?," "Just Like Heaven," and "Hot Hot Hot!!!" —*William Ruhlmann*

○ **Disintegration** / 1989 / Elektra 60855
The Cure became a top-selling group in the United States with this album, which sold a million copies and contains their number-two hit, "Love Song." —*William Ruhlmann*

Wish / 1992 / Elektra 61309
Early notices for this album suggested that Robert Smith and company were getting more optimistic. To be sure, "Doing the Unstuck" contains the lyric "Kick out the gloom," but the chorus to that song is more ambiguous: "It's a perfect day to throw back your head and kiss it all goodbye." In fact, much of this album, from its dirgelike tempos to Smith's just-off-key vocals, bespeaks the depressed state typical of the Cure. There are oddly bouncy pop songs here and there too ("Friday I'm in Love") but the Cure remains the band its fans love to mope to. —*William Ruhlmann*

King Curtis (Curtis Ousley)

b. Feb. 7, 1934, Ft. Worth, TX, **d.** Aug. 13, 1971, New York, NY
Tenor saxophone / R&B
King Curtis was the last of the great R&B tenor sax giants. He came to prominence in the mid '50s as a session musician in New York, recording, at one time or another, for most East Coast R&B labels. A long association with Atlantic/Atco began in 1958, especially on rock recordings by the Coasters. He recorded singles for many small labels in the '50s—his own Atco sessions (1958-1959), then Prestige/New Jazz and Prestige/TruSound for jazz and R&B albums (1960-1961). Curtis also had a number-one R&B single with "Soul Twist" on Enjoy Records (1962). He was signed by Capitol in 1963-1964, where he cut mostly singles, including

"Soul Serenade." Returning to Atlantic in 1965, he remained there for the rest of his life.
Curtis had solid R&B-single success with "Memphis Soul Stew" and "Ode to Billie Joe" (1967). Beginning in 1967, He started to take a more active studio role at Atlantic—leading and contracting sessions for other artists and producing with Jerry Wexler and later on his own. He also became the leader of Aretha Franklin's backing unit, the Kingpins. He compiled several albums of singles during this period. All aspects of his career were in full swing at the time he was murdered in 1971. —*Bob Porter*

New Scene of King Curtis / 1960 / Original Jazz Classics 198
Tenor and soprano saxophonist King Curtis made several R&B and pop recordings during his career and was also a prolific session artist. What's not quite as well known was that he also made some jazz and blues recordings in the early '60s, among them this 1960 date that matched him with Wynton Kelly, Oliver Jackson, and Paul Chambers, doing mostly hard bop, plus some blues backing Little Brother Montgomery. —*Ron Wynn*

Jazz Groove / Apr. 20, 1960+Sep. 18, 1960 / Prestige 24033
A reissue of two King Curtis albums: *The New Scene of King Curtis* and *Soul Meeting*. —*AMG*

○ **Soul Meeting** / Sep. 18, 1960 / Prestige 7833
Sparkling soul-jazz with hot solos. Nat Adderley on trumpet. —*Ron Wynn*

○ **Best of King Curtis** / 1962-1967 / Prestige 7775
Authoritative soul-jazz date. —*Ron Wynn*

● **Soul Twist & Other Golden Classics** / 196z / Collectables 5119
1960-1964 hits. The title cut was a 1962 smash, and this album is worthwhile for that alone. —*Ron Wynn*

Cyrkle

Group / Pop/rock
Cyrkle's biggest hit in 1966, "Red Rubber Ball," was cowritten by Bruce Woodley, a member of the Seekers, and Paul Simon. With Tom Dawes and Don Dannemann as lead vocalists, the folk-tinged group managed by Beatles manager Brian Epstein came together at a Pennsylvania college and signed with Columbia. After "Red Rubber Ball" bounced up the charts, the group encored with another major seller, "Turn-Down Day." They made their last pop-chart appearance in late 1967. —*Bill Dahl*

○ **Red Rubber Ball (A Collection)** / 1966 / Columbia 47717
Basically a two-hit wonder of the mid '60s ("Red Rubber Ball," "Turn-Down Day"), the Cyrkle had Beatles and Paul Simon connections and were themselves fine examples of lightweight folkie pop. Everything of note they ever did is on this album. —*Jeff Tamarkin*

dada

Group / Alternative pop
With their clean pop sound, catchy melodies, and clever lyrics, some journalists labeled dada the Police of the '90s, although they weren't quite as musically adventerous as that group. However, the band's debut, 1992's *Puzzle*, was a fine college-pop record that earned them a sizable amount of attention and a surprisingly large fan base, setting the stage for a possible mainstream crossover with their second record. —*Stephen Thomas Erlewine*

● **Puzzle** / Aug. 1992 / IRS 13141
The L.A. trio dada offers plenty to keep the ears busy—the orchestral sadness of "Timothy," the insidious melody of "Dog," the strung-out ravings of "Here Today, Gone Tomorrow," and the over-the-edge teen angst of "Dizz Knee Land." The absence of tedious jams, tight and memorable songs, and cover art worthy of L.A.'s best psychologists help make this disc an intriguing puzzle. —*Roch Parisien*

Dick Dale & Del-Tones

Group / Surf rock, rock & roll
Through his staccato guitar attack and his revolutionary use of reverb, Dick Dale invented the surf-guitar genre in the early '60s. Although his singles never broke outside of California, "Miserlou," "Surf Beat," and "Let's Go Trippin'" remain some of the most influential instrumentals in rock history. —*John Floyd*

★ **King of Surf Guitar—Best of Dick Dale** / 1989 / Rhino 75756

From "Miserlou" on down, the best Dale document. —*Dan Heilman*

○ **Tribal Thunder** / May 1993 / Hightone 8046
The king of the surf guitar returns with a vengeance on his first new recording in almost a decade. Every track's a gem, but "Nitro" and the title track certainly do pack a wallop all their own. —*Cub Koda*

Damn Yankees

Group / Hard rock, pop/rock
For a brief time in the early '90s, the supergroup Damn Yankees enjoyed a considerable amount of success on the AOR circuit. Composed of guitarist Ted Nugent, Styx guitarist/vocalist Tommy Shaw, Night Ranger bassist/vocalist Jack Blades, and drummer Michael Cartellone, the group came in on the tail end of the heyday of polished pop-metal, and their music didn't stray from that radio-friendly format at all. With their first album they had some hits, including the Top-Ten power ballad "High Enough" and the radio hit "Coming of Age." Although they were popular concert draws, their second album, released in 1992, wasn't as successful. The following year, the group disbanded. —*Stephen Thomas Erlewine*

● **Damn Yankees** / 1990 / Warner Brothers 26159
Well-produced pop/metal debut. Includes "Coming of Age" and "High Enough." —*Kenneth M. Cassidy*

Don't Tread / 1992 / Warner Brothers 45025
Damn Yankees' second album replicated the sound of their debut, but the songs on *Don't Tread* are missing the hooks that made the first record a hit. —*Stephen Thomas Erlewine*

The Damned

Group / Punk
While the Sex Pistols are often considered to be the first English punk band, a motley group of louts called the Damned managed to steal some of their thunder. Not only were the Damned the first punk band to release a proper album (1977's *Damned Damned Damned*), they released the first punk single in the United Kingdom ("New Rose"), and they were also the first to tour the United States. Not only are the Damned historically important, but much of their music retained its power over the years: - "New Rose" is a classic, breathless rocker, and the album, produced by Nick Lowe and released on the seminal label Stiff Records, followed through on its promise. However, they quickly fell out of favor with their second album, *Music for Pleasure*, which was produced by Nick Mason of Pink Floyd.

With their credibility under attack from fans and the press, the band was dropped from Stiff. They briefly parted ways in 1978 Then three of the original members—bassist Captain Sensible, drummer Rat Scabies, and singer Dave Vanian—assembled a new version of the band at the end of the year. The new lineup's *Machine Gun Etiquette* was surprisingly good, yet it was the last good record the band ever released. During the '80s, the band's lineup changed several times, with Vanian and Scabies remaining as the only original members. Their '80s records are, not surprisingly, directionless, ranging from near-power pop to goth rock and hard rock and back to psychedelia. In 1989, the original Damned reunited for a successful U.S. tour. After the tour, the band called it quits for the last time. —*Stephen Thomas Erlewine*

★ **Damned Damned Damned** / Jan. 1977 / Frontier 4621
With its raw, stripped-down production and primal three-chord bashing, the Damned's debut album was a landmark punk album. It never deviated from the sound of "New Rose," but that didn't matter—with its simplistic approach and relentless energy, *Damned Damned Damned* defined an era. —*Stephen Thomas Erlewine*

○ **Light at the End of the Tunnel** / 1987 / MCA 8024
While it would have been much more effective if it was sequenced chronologically, *The Light at the End of the Tunnel* is a fine compilation of the Damned's long and surprisingly varied career. —*Stephen Thomas Erlewine*

Danzig

Group / Heavy metal, hard rock
Most heavy metal bands that sing about Satan aren't threatening because their lyrics and music are never as menacing as their al-

bum covers. Danzig is the exception that proves the rule. Led by singer/songwriter Glenn Danzig, the band has created a dark, bluesy metal that walks the line between being horrifying and being a parody. As the band churns out a bluesy Sabbath-Zeppelin-AC/DC hybrid, he sings about death and evil, but with a knowing wink. All of the satanism is too exaggerated to be taken seriously, but beneath the cartoonish bluster there are some genuinely disturbing imagery and music. This duality, along with some undeniably powerful riffs, have made Danzig one of the best heavy metal bands since Metallica.

Before forming Danzig in the mid '80s, Glenn Danzig performed with the seminal hardcore punk band the Misfits and a transitional metal/punk group, Samhain. With Danzig, his morbid visions flowered. Throughout the late '80s and early '90s, the band's cult grew steadily without the benefit of a hit. In 1994, a live version of the first album's "Mother" became a hit single, thanks to MTV incessantly showing the video. —*Stephen Thomas Erlewine*

● **Danzig** / 1988 / Def American 24208
Glenn Danzig's debut album with his new band. Some incredibly dark and morbid lyrics, including such songs as "Twist of Cain" and "Mother." —*John Book*

Danzig II—Lucifuge / 1990 / Def American 24281
Possibly Glenn Danzig's most interesting work to date, with incredible drumming from Chuck Biscuits. Features "Blood & Tears," "Devil's Plaything," "Long Way Back from Hell," and "Snakes of Christ." —*John Book*

○ **Danzig III—How the Gods Kill** / 1992 / Def American 45134
How the Gods Kill is Danzig's most accessible album to date. Glenn Danzig's vocals aren't as raw as they used to be; they're more defined and toned down, like a real heavy metal vocalist. John Christ's guitar playing is great throughout, and it shows his progression from the band's debut. The cover artwork is by H. R. Giger. —*John Book*

○ **Thrall—Demonsweatlive** / May 25, 1993 / Def American 45286
A combination of a few new studio tracks and some live recordings, *Thrall—Demonsweatlive* featured Danzig's first hit, a live version of "Mother," from the band's debut. Throughout the EP, the band's energy matches the power of the single. —*Stephen Thomas Erlewine*

Terence Trent D'Arby

b. Mar. 15, 1962, New York, NY
Vocals / Pop/rock, soul, urban R&B
Expatriate American D'Arby was one of the most distinctive newcomers of the late '80s, blending the swagger and attitude of Sly Stone and Prince with a penchant for Rolling Stones crunch and Sam Cooke soul. His pretentions are sometimes hard to bear, but he's helped expand the boundaries of both rock and R&B. —*John Floyd*

○ **Introducing the Hardline According to Terence Trent D'Arby** / 1987 / Columbia 40964
Introducing the Hardline According to Terence Trent D'Arby is a strong debut by this young, cocky Black British singer, who wrote virtually every note on this pop album, played a multitude of instruments, and claimed that it was the most important album since the Beatles' *Sgt. Pepper*. Hits included "If You Let Me Stay," "Dance Little Sister," "Sign Your Name," and the number-one "Wishing Well." His first album is a curious mixture of old and new styles. Although the production is quite modern, D'Arby shows his roots in the work of older artists, borrowing a page or two from Michael Jackson and Stevie Wonder, while James Brown appears to have had the strongest influence on D'Arby's stage presence. —*Rob Bowman*

○ **Neither Fish nor Flesh** / 1989 / Columbia 45351
D'Arby's sophomore effort was considered a disappointment by most. More experimental than the first, it was also less focused. If possible, his ego seemed to have grown even larger, with D'Arby taking up to ten playing credits on any given track. —*Rob Bowman*

● **Terence Trent D'Arby's Symphony or Damn** / May 11, 1993 / Columbia 53616
Falling halfway between the modern R&B of *Introducing the Hardline* and the extravagant *Neither Fish nor Flesh*, *Symphony or Damn* is Terence Trent D'Arby's most ambitious album yet. It's

also his best, because it takes the fine songwriting of his debut and melds it to the sonic experimentalism of *Fish*. Sure, some of it is embarassing (it's hard not to cringe during the "Welcome to My Monasteryo" declaration at the beginning of the album), but more often than not D'Arby's experimentations succeed—and succeed grandly, at that. —*Stephen Thomas Erlewine*

Bobby Darin

b. May 14, 1936, Bronx, NY, **d.** Dec. 20, 1973
Vocals / Pop/rock
Who was the real Bobby Darin? Was it the finger-poppin' crooner, the slick '50s rocker, or the introspective folkie of the late '60s? In the end, it really doesn't matter, for Bobby Darin was all of these things and played each of these roles exceedingly well.

The show-biz legend suffered from a number of hardships, health problems in particular, that in the end make his achievements even more impressive. He was one of the first of that breed of white-bread late '50s pop singers, but Darin's sides do indeed rock. Best known for his ring-a-ding-ding style, Darin came across at the outset as a punk Sinatra: He was damn good, and he wasn't about to let you forget it. There was also the much-underrated side of Darin that first turned to the music of Tim Hardin and then started his own record label to record the kind of music he felt deeply about.

Over the years, Bobby Darin has been bagged as kind of a jive, glossy cat and something of an also-ran. But in the end, quite the opposite was true: He gave everything to all his phases, acted honestly on his instincts, and accomplished what most others would never have attempted. —*Steve Aldrich*

Bobby Darin Story / 1961 / Atco 33131
● **Ultimate Bobby Darin** / Jun. 1988 / Warner Brothers 27606
Offers a thorough look at Darin's rock and pop hits, including "Mack the Knife," "Dream Lover," "Splish Splash," and the breathtaking "Beyond the Sea." —*John Floyd*
○ **Capitol Collectors Series** / 1989 / Capitol 91625
A compilation of Darin's mid-'60s singles, songs that showcase Darin's diversity even if the majority of the set leans heavily toward his pop material. —*Stephen Thomas Erlewine*
○ **Splish Splash: Best of Bobby Darin, Vol. 1** / Jan. 1991 / Atco 91794
The first installment of a definitive two-volume Bobby Darin retrospective, *Splish Splash* concentrates on his earlier hits, including "Dream Love," "Baby Face," "You Must Have Been a Beautiful Baby," "Multiplication," and the title track. —*Stephen Thomas Erlewine*
○ **Mack the Knife: Best of Bobby Darin, Vol. 2** / Feb. 1991 / Atco 91795
Darin's later hits—including "Mack the Knife," "Beyond the Sea," "Guys and Dolls," "Black Coffee," and "Artificial Flowers"—are collected on this second volume of Atco's fine two-part retrospective. —*Stephen Thomas Erlewine*

David & David

Group / Pop/rock
Although they only recorded one album, the California duo of David Baerwald and David Ricketts made some of the finest mainstream pop of the '80s. With its slick surfaces and memorable melodies, 1986's *Boomtown* was deceptively smooth—beneath the production, the songs were tales of despair and broken dreams in the Reagan era. David & David scored a surprise hit in 1986 with "Welcome to the Boomtown." It was their only single that charted. Baerwald began a critically acclaimed solo career in 1990; Ricketts hasn't released anything since *Boomtown*. —*Stephen Thomas Erlewine*

● **Boomtown** / 1986 / A&M 5134
Los Angeles musicians David Baerwald and David Ricketts joined forces to create subtle, moody, and darkly atmospheric rock, culminating in their Top-40 hit "Welcome to the Boomtown." —*Donna DiChario*

Spencer Davis Group

Group / British invasion, pop/rock
His ferocious soul-drenched vocals belying his tender teenage years, Stevie Winwood powered the Spencer Davis Group's three

biggest U.S. hits during their brief life span as one of the British invasion's most convincing R&B-based combos.

Guitarist Davis formed the band with Winwood on organ, his brother Muff Winwood on bass, and drummer Peter York. Signing on with producer Chris Blackwell, the quartet got their first hit (the blistering "Keep on Running") from another of Blackwell's acts, West Indian performer Jackie Edwards. After topping the British charts in 1965, the song struggled on the lower reaches of the U.S. Hot 100.

The group's two hottest sellers were self-penned projects. "Gimme Some Lovin'" and "I'm a Man" were searing showcases for the adolescent Winwood's gritty vocals and blazing keyboards and the band's pounding rhythms. Although they burned up the charts even on this side of the ocean in 1967, the quartet never capitalized on their fame with an American tour. At the height of their power, Winwood left to form Traffic, leaving Davis without his dynamic front man. The bandleader focused on producing other acts, including a Canadian ensemble called the Downchild Blues Band during the early '80s. —*Bill Dahl*

● **Best of the Spencer Davis Group** / 1985 / EMI America 46598
Contains "Gimme Some Lovin'" and many good lesser-known songs. —*Dan Heilman*

Tyrone Davis

b. May 4, 1938, Greenville, MS
Vocals / Soul
Perennially a ladies' choice, Tyrone Davis just seems to naturally appeal to women. That's not to say that gents haven't bought his churning Chicago soul records too—his impressive hit-making career harks back to 1968, and there's no end in sight.

His mentor, noted singer Harold Burrage, coached his charge well, and Davis debuted on wax in 1965 as Tyrone the Wonder Boy on the local Four Brothers logo. Far more wondrous were Davis's classy efforts for Chicago's Dakar label, commencing with the remorseful R&B chart-topper "Can I Change My Mind" in 1968, continuing with "Is It Something You've Got" in 1969, and the million-selling classic "Turn Back the Hands of Time" in 1970. With Willie Henderson producing, the cats at Dakar were forging a fresh, vital new Chicago soul sound, and Tyrone Davis was right there at its forefront.

Davis remained with Dakar into 1976, his warm, assured vocals powering the likes of "I Had It All the Time" and "Turning Point," before moving over to Columbia without missing a beat. These days, Tyrone hops from one label to the next, seemingly with each new release—but he's still no stranger to the urban contemporary charts, and the women still love him. What more could he possibly ask for? —*Bill Dahl*

● **Greatest Hits** / 1992 / Rhino 70533
Tyrone Davis combined influences from hard-edged country-tinged urban blues and more tightly arranged, horn-dominated soul. He sang uptempo, surging tunes, midtempo churning ballads, heartache songs, and tribute numbers, and moved from material dominated by brassy arrangements to numbers reliant on his narratives and persona. This 17-track collection begins with his earliest hits, such as "Can I Change My Mind" and "Is It Something You've Got," and continues into smoother but no less urgent tunes like "Turn Back the Hands of Time," "Turning Point," "There It Is," and "One Way Ticket." Because this collection only covers his Dakar material, it ends at 1976, when he left for Columbia. —*Ron Wynn*

Bobby Day

b. Jul. 1, 1932, Fort Worth, TX, **d.** Jul. 15, 1990
Vocals / Doo-wop
An important cog in the Los Angeles doo-wop community during the '50s, Day wrote three often-covered early rock classics in 1957-58. Day was part of the Hollywood Flames, one of the area's top R&B vocal groups, and briefly part of Bob and Earl, who later on hit without Day on "Harlem Shuffle." Day formed his own group, the Satellites, in 1957, cutting the original "Little Bitty Pretty One" for Class Records. A nearly identical cover by Thurston Harris beat the original out, so Day countered with the driving "Rockin' Robin" in 1958, an R&B chart-topper. Its flip side, "Over and Over," was a hit in its own right, although the Dave Clark Five's 1965 revival is better remembered today. Day waxed a few more hits for Class in 1959, including "That's All I Want"

and a derivative "The Bluebird, the Buzzard & the Oriole," and flit from label to label during the '60s. —*Bill Dahl*

● **Original Rockin' Robin** / 1991 / ACE 200
Bobby Day's "Rockin' Robin" remains a classic. That and 25 other original recordings show up on this solid British import. —*Jeff Tamarkin*

The dB's

Group / Alternative pop, power pop
Among the alternative bands who emerged during the early '80s, the dB's clever songs, quirky vocals, and unique arrangements and production made them arguably the best practitioners of the smart power-pop movement that drew much inspiration from Big Star, the Move, the Byrds, and the Beatles, among others.

Regardless, principal singer/songwriters Chris Stamey (formerly of the North Carolina band Sneakers and Alex Chilton sideman) and Peter Holsapple together forged a sound on their two Scott Litt-produced albums (*Stands for Decibels, Repercussion*) that was truly distinctive. Stamey left to pursue a solo career, releasing several EPs and a couple of albums, of which *Fireworks* (1991) is arguably his best.

After Stamey's departure, Holsapple forged ahead with the dB's, releasing *Like This* and *The Sound of Music*, two solid albums that delved deeper into a more Americanized roots/pop sound.

In early 1991, Holsapple and Stamey got together and released *Mavericks*, a charming collaboration that featured a cover of Gene Clark's "Here without You," as well as some great originals like "Angels," "The Child in You," and "Geometry." —*Rick Clark*

● **Stands for Decibels** / 1981 / IRS 13021
Influences like the Beatles, Big Star, and the Move are detectable, but the dB's creatively synthesized those sounds into something unique and personal, with wonderfully twisted melodies, inside-out harmonies, herky-jerky grooves, and quirky arrangements. Every track is noteworthy. —*Rick Clark*

○ **Repercussion** / 1982 / IRS 13022
Their second effort is more polished, but none of their distinctive charm is missing. Consistently fine material from top to bottom. —*Rick Clark*

Like This / 1985 / Rhino 70891
With Stamey gone, the trio (fronted by Peter Holsapple) dropped some of the band's previous eccentricities and got down to a more rootsy rock & roll approach, even touching on a little country. The melodies are still as catchy as ever. —*Rick Clark*

Sound of Music / 1987 / IRS 42055
Sound of Music continues the rootsy pop direction pursued on *Like This*. Even though it is a little weaker than its predecessor, there are some fine standout tracks like "I Lie," "Working for Somebody Else," and the folk-like Holsapple-Syd Straw duet, "Never Before and Never Again." —*Rick Clark*

Ride the Wild Tom Tom / 1993 / Rhino 71299
A wonderful collection of early demos—mostly pre-*Stands for deciBels*. Even though this isn't the place to start with the dB's, it is a must-own for fans of the band who already have the first two albums. —*Rick Clark*

Deacon Blue

Group / Pop/rock
Deacon Blue took their name from a particularly smooth song from Steely Dan, a group that set the precedent for sophisticated jazz-tinged pop. Not coincidentally, the Scottish group Deacon Blue followed a familiar path in their own career. Where Steely Dan relied on jazz, Deacon Blue's singer/songwriter Ricky Ross relied more on soul, and the group wasn't afraid of being known for their pop singles. Even with their numerous British hit singles, they were more serious than the average pop band, mixing in a fair dose of social criticism with their smooth melodies. Deacon Blue were U.K. favorites ever since their first album in 1988, but never gained a large American audience. After struggling for a breakthrough hit for years, the group disbanded in the summer of 1994. —*Stephen Thomas Erlewine*

● **Raintown** / 1987 / Columbia 40915
Inspiring debut of well-crafted adult pop, heavily under the influence of Prefab Sprout. —*Steve Aldrich*

Ooh Las Vegas / 1990 / Columbia 467242

A collection of B-sides and previously unissued material. —*Steve Aldrich*

Dead Boys

Group / Punk
Forming out of the ashes of Cleveland's semi-legendary Rocket from the Tombs, the Dead Boys were one of the first punk bands to escalate punk rock's level of violence, nihilism, and pure ugliness to extreme new levels. After they relocated to New York, ex-Rocket members guitarist Cheetah Chrome and drummer Johnny Blitz hooked up with guitarist Jimmy Zero, bassist Jeff Magnum, and vocalist Stive Bavors to form the Dead Boys. Their music wasn't very special—even by the relaxed standards of punk, it was loose and incompetent, bordering on the stupidity of heavy metal. "Sonic Reducer" and "Ain't It Fun," the band's two best songs, were holdovers from former Rocket from the Tombs members David Thomas and Peter Laughner, who went on to form Pere Ubu. What distinguished the Dead Boys, and what makes them notorious to this day, is their pure nastiness, much of it coming from Bavors. Their two albums—*Young Loud and Snotty* and *We Have Come for Your Children*—are brutal, wallowing in their own self-serving nihilism. They embodied the punk stereotypes held by the mainstream. After two albums, the band split. Bavors formed Lords of the New Church, and the rest of the members slid into obscurity. In 1990, Bavors died of injuries sustained from being hit by a bus in Paris. —*Stephen Thomas Erlewine*

● **Young Loud & Snotty** / 1977 / Warner Brothers 26981
A truly vulgar and tasteless slab of nihilistic punk rock, the Dead Boys' first album included the classic "Sonic Reducer," which was buried in a mess of relentless, sub-heavy metal pounding. —*Stephen Thomas Erlewine*

We Have Come for Your Children / 1978 / Sire 6054
Highlighted by the snarling "Ain't It Fun," the Dead Boys' second album was as nasty and raw as their first. —*Stephen Thomas Erlewine*

Dead Can Dance

Group / Alternative pop/rock
Originally from Australia, this group has a purely European sound (Gregorian chants, Celtic, neo-gothic). Their songs are of lost beauty, regret and sorrow, inspiration and nobility, and of the everlasting human goal of attaining a meaningful existence. —*Vladimir Bogdanov*

Spleen & Ideal / 1985 / Nesak 512
Well-balanced in terms of both mood and style, this album brings you the whole new world of hopeless hope and aimless urge and search. —*Vladimir Bogdanov*

○ **Within the Realm of a Dying Sun** / 1987 / 4AD 705
Probably their most subtle and intelligent album. Touches the deepest levels of our identity. —*Vladimir Bogdanov*

Serpent's Egg / 1988 / 4AD 808
An interesting combination of Slavonic and European medieval music. —*Vladimir Bogdanov*

○ **Aion** / 1990 / 4AD 0007
True medieval sound combined with all the variety of modern studio techniques. Not an imitation at all, just enriched with an old musical tradition. —*Vladimir Bogdanov*

● **A Passage in Time** / Oct. 1991 / Rykodisc 20215
An anthology and best-of. —*Vladimir Bogdanov*

Into the Labyrinth / 1993 / 4AD
Into the Labyrinth explores world-beat territory more heavily than Dead Can Dance's previous releases, and the results are impressive, if not altogether definitive. *Into the Labyrinth* also marks the inclusion of more vocal tracks, some of which that could even be labeled pop songs, and not bad ones at that. —*Stephen Thomas Erlewine*

Dead Kennedys

Group / Hardcore
Next to Black Flag and X, Jello Biafra's Dead Kennedys were the longest lasting of the West Coast hardcore groups. Their music challenged everything and offended everybody, and Biafra's self-righteous morality made him a post-punk role model for thousands of pissed-off kids. In the late '80s, Biafra became a

spokesperson for the indecency of music censorship. When the group disbanded in 1987, Biafra continued with the band Lard for a brief time, before turning to solo recordings, including a series of spoken-word albums. —*John Floyd*

★ **Fresh Fruit for Rotting Vegetables** / 1980 / Virus 1
The DK's 1980 debut was as important to the West Coast hardcore scene as the Sex Pistols' *Bollocks* was to disenfranchised British punks. Despite a few clunkers, *Fresh Fruit* is an explosive and scalding blast of political and social fury, underpinned by Jello Biafra's wise-ass vocals and Klaus Flouride's pseudo-surf guitar wailing. Most of the band's best songs are here. —*John Floyd*

○ **Plastic Surgery Disasters/In God We Trust, Inc.** / 1982 / Alternative Tentacles 12
The DK's second effort captured their frenetic live set—full of mayhem and confusion but with an underlying feeling of greatness. Their nonconformist, anti-establishment sentiment was eloquently made sensible by talented frontman Jello Biafra. Punk at its best, musically and lyrically, with "Terminal Preppie," "Government Flu," and "Winnebago Warrior." —*Julian Katz*

○ **Frankenchrist** / 1985 / Virus 45
More hyperkinetic political punk rock. —*David Szatmary*

Bedtime for Democracy / 1986 / Virus 50
The final political testimony from the DK. —*David Szatmary*

○ **Give Me Convenience or Give Me Death** / 1987 / Virus 57
A useful compilation, in that it not only collects many essential nonalbum cuts but also rounds up the best material from the otherwise desultory follow-ups to *Fresh Fruit.* —*John Floyd*

Dead Milkmen

Group / Alternative pop/rock
Funny guys from Philadelphia whose satire and good-natured humor too often gets the better of them. Playing a melodic strain of radio-friendly pop, the Milkmen seem more outrageous than they really are. In fact, they come off like an occasionally funny party guest who keeps cracking jokes, hoping you'll laugh at one of them. —*John Dougan*

● **Big Lizard in My Backyard** / 1985 / Enigma 72054
You can hardly refer to any Dead Milkmen album as a classic, but *Big Lizard* comes close. Stupid, sophomoric, and quite tuneful, this is when the jokes were still funny or, at the very least, still worth listening to. Features "Bitchin' Camaro" and the tastelessly funny "Takin' Retards to the Zoo." —*John Dougan*

Eat Your Paisley / 1986 / Restless 72131
After *Big Lizard,* Milkmen albums are mostly inconsistent, hit-or-miss affairs. This one is more of a showcase for the dippy side of their sense of humor; only a couple of tracks reproduce the snottiness of their debut. For real diehards only. —*Steve Huey*

○ **Bucky Fellini** / 1987 / Enigma 73260
Another inconsistent outing, but this one is helped out by the dead-on "Instant Club Hit (You'll Dance to Anything)," a satire of pretentious alternative European dance artists, and a few cover tunes, including a parody of "Watching Scotty Grow, Watching Scotty Die." —*Steve Huey*

○ **Beelzebubba** / 1988 / Fever 73351
Probably their best post-*Big Lizard* album, this contains some of the most memorable Milkmen tracks, including songs about wife-beating and drinking bleach, the anthemic "Life Is Shit," and the MTV semi-hit "Punk Rock Girl." There are still a few clunkers, but those are outweighed (for the most part). Anonymous proves on "Stuart" that he would be funnier if he just forgot about trying to sing and instead delivered ranting monologs. —*Steve Huey*

Bill Deal & the Rhondels

Group / R&B, rock & roll
Combining soul-inflected vocals with brassy, uptempo R&B-inspired grooves, Bill Deal & the Rhondels remain favorites on the Carolina "beach music" circuit to this day. The group was part of the Norfolk, VA, scene during the early '60s, and Deal played organ on Jimmy Soul's 1963 smash "If You Wanna Be Happy" on Legrand Records. The Rhondels apparently preferred reviving R&B obscurities to writing their own material, and it paid off—in 1969 their supercharged remake of the Maurice Williams hit "May I" gave the group their first hit, and they followed it up with a pair of blasting Tams covers, "I've Been Hurt" and "What Kind

of Fool Do You Think I Am," all on the Heritage logo. The Rhondels charted for the final time in early 1970 with "Nothing Succeeds Like Success." —*Bill Dahl*

● **Best of Bill Deal & the Rhondels** / May 1986 / Rhino 70129
Contains their biggest and best hit, a cover of "May I," first released by the Zodiacs. —*Dan Heilman*

DeBarge

Group / Pop, urban R&B
Motown hoped this family act would turn into another Jackson 5. Specializing in soft-pop tunes such as "All This Love" and "Time Will Reveal," family members include Eldra, Mark, Randy, Bunny, and Bobby. After hitting big with Richard Perry's "Rhythm of the Night," El began receiving accolades for his fine tenor vocals and in 1986 was singled out for a solo career. He went on to further success, while the remainder of the family floundered at other record companies. —*Rick A. Bueche*

○ **All This Love/In a Special Way** / 1982 / Motown 8145
Another two-in-one CD featuring the Motown family-artists DeBarge, who were solid hitmakers in the '80s before they disintegrated due to intragroup squabbles and family-member legal troubles. Though the songs on these two albums weren't as big as some later material, they were real group projects. El, Bunny, and James hadn't yet gotten in the headlines for nonmusical reasons, and there's an innocence and spirituality (they'd just left the gospel world) that's missing from the cold and calculating crossover material they issued later in the decade. —*Ron Wynn*

● **Rhythm of the Night** / 1985 / Motown 6123
Their best Motown album; includes the number-one title track. —*Rick A. Bueche*

Joey Dee & Starliters

b. Jun. 11, 1940, Passaic, NY
Group / R&B, rock & roll
Joey Dee led the house band at New York's Peppermint Lounge, immortalizing the joint in his 1961 chart topper "Peppermint Twist." Born Joseph DiNicola in Passaic, NJ, Dee teamed with veteran producer Henry Glover to cut "Peppermint Twist" for Roulette, and the huge hit led to a starring role in the film *Hey, Let's Twist.* Most of Dee's hits, including a supercharged revival of the Isley Brothers hit "Shout" in 1962, were firmly in the Twist mode, although he took a successful stab at a softer sound that year with a Johnny Nash tune, "What Kind of Love Is This." Dee gave several future stars early breaks with the Starliters, notably the Ronettes, three-quarters of the Young Rascals, and Jimi Hendrix. Dee is still active on the oldies circuit. —*Bill Dahl*

● **Best of Joey Dee & Starliters—Hey Let's Twist** / 1990 / Rhino 70965
Best of Joey Dee & Starliters: Hey Let's Twist is a representative early-'60s compilation by the man who made the "Peppermint Twist" a national craze. —*Bill Dahl*

Deee-Lite

Group / Dance
Most dance bands based in the house movement of the early '90s concentrated more on the groove than the song; Deee-Lite did not. While they had a strong groove, they also had a strong sense of melody and song structure, as well as a campy, stylish, retro-'70s look and a social conscience. Their music is a heady rush of beats, samples, and hooks, with pop songs—like the hit "Groove Is in the Heart"—that distinguish them from other dance combos. —*Stephen Thomas Erlewine*

● **World Clique** / 1990 / Elektra 60957
World Clique starts with "Good Beat" and keeps them coming for the rest of the album. There are enough thick beats to satisfy house fans plus enough hooks to cross over to the mainstream pop audience, as the success of "Groove Is in the Heart" proves. At times the retro-'70s shtick wears thin, but for the most part *World Clique* is a sheer delight. —*Stephen Thomas Erlewine*

Infinity Within / 1992 / Elektra 61313
Although there are several good tracks and their political consciousness is commendable, *Infinity Within* falls short of the inventive beats and grooves of *World Clique.* —*Stephen Thomas Erlewine*

○ **Dewdrops in the Garden** / 1994 / Elektra

Although it's more focused than *Infinity Within*, *Dewdrops in the Garden* only sporadically lives up to the promise of *World Clique*. —*Stephen Thomas Erlewine*

Deep Purple

Group / Hard rock, heavy metal

Formed in 1968, Deep Purple's initial success was on Bill Cosby's Tetragrammaton label with remakes of Joe South's "Hush" and Neil Diamond's "Kentucky Woman." When Tetragrammaton went under shortly afterward, Deep Purple switched to Warner, with a change in lineup, including the addition of dramatic lead singer Ian Gillan.

Their first effort on Warner, John Lord's *Concerto for Group and Orchestra*, was a ponderously overblown affair that died a quick death in the marketplace. From there on out, the band pursued a hard-rock direction, generating their greatest successes with *Machine Head*, *Burn*, and the live double record set *Made in Japan*. In 1975 Deep Purple earned the dubious distinction of being named the "world's loudest band" in the *Guinness Book of World Records*.

Much of Deep Purple's appeal during their heyday (from 1970's *In Rock* to 1972's *Made in Japan*) came from the lightning-fast duels between keyboardist Jon Lord and lead guitarist Ritchie Blackmore.

Deep Purple successfully carried on after Blackmore, Gillan, and bassist Roger Glover departed (at different times), with a lineup featuring ex-Trapeze member Glen Hughes (bass, vocals), Tommy Bolin (lead guitar, vocals), and David Coverdale (lead vocals). Coverdale would later front the popular MTV/AOR band Whitesnake. —*Rick Clark*

○ **Deep Purple** / 1969 / Tetragrammaton 119
Worthwhile mainly for their psychezilla cover of Joe South's "Hush," which pits Ritchie Blackmore's flame-throwing guitar bursts against Jon Lord's chugging organ. —*Tom Graves*

○ **Deep Purple in Rock** / 1970 / Warner Brothers 1877
The album on which Deep Purple decided they were rockers after all and turned up the amps to prove it. Ian Gillan on vocals (added at this time) became the archetype for heavy metal screamers thereafter. Check out "Speed King," "Bloodsucker," and "Flight of the Rat" for your daily dose of high voltage. —*Tom Graves*

○ **Fireball** / 1971 / Warner Brothers 2564
Fireball solidified the band's reputation as purveyors of maximum-dosage heavy metal. Ritchie Blackmore steals the show with a wall of grinding chords and greased-lightning lead flourishes. At this juncture the band began to challenge Led Zeppelin's position as hard rock's most successful act. —*Tom Graves*

★ **Machine Head** / 1972 / Warner Brothers 3100
The definitive '70s heavy metal album, with each locomotive song ("Highway Star," "Space Truckin'") blasting off like World War III. The highlight is the AOR staple "Smoke on the Water," which has a mandatory riff for anyone owning a guitar. It still fries ears 20 years after the fact. —*Tom Graves*

○ **Made in Japan** / 1972 / Warner Brothers 2701
Not only could they kick ass in the studio but they could stir up a hornet's nest on stage too. This double album (one-CD) set recorded in Japan includes most of their best material ("Highway Star," "Smoke on the Water") and pushes the metal envelope even further. Ritchie Blackmore is in peak form throughout. —*Tom Graves*

Who Do We Think We Are / 1973 / Warner Brothers 2678
The last gasp for the classic Deep Purple lineup, *Who Do We Think We Are* isn't as rock solid as their previous records, but its best moments, including the deliriously stupid "Woman from Tokyo," are bludgeoning hard rock of the highest order. —*Stephen Thomas Erlewine*

○ **When We Rock, We Rock and When We Roll, We Roll** / 1978 / Warner Brothers 3223
When We Rock, We Rock and When We Roll, We Roll is a solid, if incomplete, collection from their 1968-1974 peak years. —*Dan Heilman*

Def Leppard

Group / Hard rock, heavy metal

Def Leppard's catchy, guitar-driven, pop-oriented hard rock was one of the most imitated styles of the '80s. Leppard's hit albums are polished syntheses of heavy, hummable guitar riffs, memorable pop melodies, and simple teen-oriented lyrics. Originally, the band (Joe Elliot, vocals; Pete Willis, guitar; Steve Clark, guitar; Rick Savage, drums; Rick Allen, drums) was associated with the new wave of British heavy metal bands, releasing two albums (*On through the Night* and *High 'n' Dry*) that made a small impact in the United States. Robert "Mutt" Lange produced *High 'n' Dry*, which contained the seeds of the signature Leppard sound. Before the recording of their next album, Pete Willis left the group and was replaced by Phil Collen.

Their third album, *Pyromania*, released in 1983, was a monster success, selling over six and a half million copies in the United States and featuring three Top-40 hits ("Photograph," "Rock of Ages," and "Foolin'"). The album showcased the refinement of Def Leppard's twin-guitar attack, where both parts worked together to create a huge sound instead of merely repeating the riff. In 1984 the group made two attempts to record a follow-up, one with the exhausted Lange and another with Jim Steinman, both ending with the dismissal of the producer. On New Year's Eve, Allen lost his left arm in an auto accident. Despite this, the band wanted to keep him in the group; he was equipped with a customized electronic drum kit to ease his playing.

In 1987 the long-awaited *Hysteria* (also produced by Lange) was released. Although *Hysteria* was a bigger success than *Pyromania*, it took a considerable amount of time for it to gain its sales—after 49 weeks, the album reached number one. Recording for the follow-up to *Hysteria* was under way when Clark was found dead in his apartment after a drinking binge in January 1991. Def Leppard continued the album, with Collen playing all the guitars. *Adrenalize* shot to the top of the charts upon its release in April 1992. Vivian Campbell, a former guitarist for Whitesnake, was announced as Clark's replacement in spring of 1992. —*Stephen Thomas Erlewine*

☆ **Pyromania** / 1983 / Mercury 810308
Although Def Leppard's first two workmanlike metal albums, *On Through the Night* and *High 'n' Dry*, had already established the band in both England and the United States, it was *Pyromania* that broke the sound (and sales) barrier for them. *Pyromania's* acute emphasis on pop sensibilities, in songs like "Photograph" and "Rock Rock ('til You Drop)," over numbing thonk made the album a huge crossover success with the more conservative AOR market. MTV video saturation with key *Pyromania* songs didn't hurt either. —*Tom Graves*

★ **Hysteria** / 1987 / Mercury 830675
If *Pyromania* was great pop metal, *Hysteria* upped the ante a few more notches. With dense, elaborate instrumental layering and meticulous engineering, the album became known almost as much for its production values as for its terrific music. Drummer Rick Allen, who lost an arm in an automobile accident, adds an even harder core of bottom end with his specially rigged drum kit. As hardhitting as it is slick sounding, *Hysteria* became the standard-bearer for pop metal with anthemic tracks like "Rocket" and "Pour Some Sugar on Me." One of the masterpieces of the '80s that renewed the faith, for many, in sensible hard rock. —*Tom Graves*

Adrenalize / 1992 / Mercury 512185
With the band's misfortunes (guitarist Steve Clark died), they can be forgiven for slipping a bit after the mega-success of *Hysteria*. That's not to dismiss *Adrenalize*, however, which still has a heaping helping of Leppard's patented Brit-pop crash-and-burn fusion. —*Tom Graves*

Retro-Active / Oct. 5, 1993 / Mercury 518305
It may be just a collection of B-sides and lost tracks, but *Retro-Active* rocks harder and more convincingly than *Adrenalize*. It also has twice the hooks, making it of interest to more than just hardcore fans. —*Stephen Thomas Erlewine*

Del Amitri

Group / Folk-rock, pop/rock

This Scottish quartet, releasing its first album in 1985, delivers a Byrds-like country-flavored rock. —*David Szatmary*

Del Amitri / 1985 / Chrysalis 21499
The debut album features a bright countrified rock. —*David Szatmary*

● **Waking Hours** / 1989 / A&M 5287
The sound on this effort has a more mainstream-rock sheen to the production than the debut. —*David Szatmary*

○ **Change Everything** / Jun. 9, 1992 / A&M 5385
Del Amitri serves up a slice of Scottish folk-rock on its latest, *Change Everything*. Gritty vocals often hinting at sadness drape themselves over chiming guitars and tasty harmonies, evoking vague memories of Van Morrison in his rockier days.—*Roch Parisien*

Del Fuegos

Group / Roots-rock
Originally including Dan and Warren Zanes (vocalist and guitarist, respectively), bassist Tom Lloyd, and drummer B. Woody Giessmann, this Boston-based band pounds out Rolling Stones-style rock. After critics panned the 1987 album *Stand Up*, Giessmann left the group. The band added horns for a more Stax-oriented sound on *Smoking in the Fields*. Guest appearances on their albums include James Burton and Tom Petty (*Stand Up*) and Rick Danko (*Smoking*). —*David Szatmary*

○ **Longest Day** / 1984 / Warner Brothers 25174
An explosive garage-meets-roots-rock debut from the Boston rockers. —*David Szatmary*

● **Boston, Mass.** / 1985 / Slash 25339
More guitar-driven crunch. —*David Szatmary*

Stand Up / 1987 / Slash 25540
A toned-down, more bluesy effort. Includes guests James Burton and Tom Petty. —*David Szatmary*

Dell-Vikings (Del Vikings)

Group / R&B, doo-wop
One of the first integrated acts during rock & roll's infancy, the Dell-Vikings recorded a beloved classic in 1956, "Come Go with Me." The quintet was formed at Pittsburgh's Air Force Serviceman's Club in 1955 while the members were stationed there. They recorded their immortal "Come Go with Me," written by bass singer Clarence Quick, in the basement of a local DJ and sold the master to tiny FeeBee Records. When given national distribution on Dot, the upbeat tune proved a monster hit. Upon their discharge, four members split to form the "Del Vikings" on Mercury, hitting in 1957 with "Cool Shake." Kripp Johnson, meanwhile, stayed with Dot, assembling a new lineup of "Dell-Vikings" that included a young Chuck Jackson. and hitting at precisely the same time with "Whispering Bells." All the confusion about the two groups may have ultimately sunk both, since those were the last hits for either lineup. —*Bill Dahl*

● **Del Vikings** / 1988 / Collectables 5010
Solid hits by one of doo-wop's first integrated groups. —*Bill Dahl*

Delaney & Bonnie

Group / Pop/rock, blues-rock
Delaney Bramlett and his wife Bonnie recorded a series of blues- and country-influenced albums in the late '60s and early '70s. A variety of musicians played in Delaney & Bonnie's band, including Eric Clapton, Dave Mason, Duane Allman, Leon Russell, Rita Coolidge, Jim Gordon, Bobby Whitlock, and Carl Radle. Clapton, Gordon, Whitlock, and Radle formed Derek & the Dominoes after performing together on Delaney & Bonnie's 1969-70 tour. Delaney and Bonnie's records were a strong influence on Eric Clapton's style in the '70s. The group broke up after the Bramletts' marriage collapsed in 1972. —*Kenneth M. Cassidy*

● **Delaney & Bonnie & Friends on Tour with Eric Clapton** / Jun. 1970 / Atco 33326
Recorded with Eric Clapton, *On Tour* features Delaney & Bonnie's blend of country, rock, blues, and gospel. Includes "I'm Coming Home." —*Kenneth M. Cassidy*

Best of Delaney & Bonnie / 1972 / Rhino 70777
A good overview of their brief career. —*Kenneth M. Cassidy*

The Delfonics

d. 1974
Group / Soul
A sweet ballad-oriented Philadelphia vocal trio who proved highly popular in the late '60s and early '70s. Lead singer William Hart's high-pitched tenor effortlessly sailed into falsetto range on

their first hit in 1968, "La-La—Means I Love You," a typically smooth ballad filled with swirling strings. Hart and co-producer Thom Bell wrote most of the group's early smashes, including the majestic "Didn't I (Blow Your Mind This Time)" in 1970. The group's hit-making reign ended in 1974. —*Bill Dahl*

● **Best of the Delfonics** / 1990 / Arista 8333
Slick late-'60s Philly soul with lush production and polished harmonies. —*Bill Dahl*

The Dells

Group / Soul, doo-wop
After nearly four decades of recording an incredible legacy of hits, the Dells have made only one personnel change in their entire professional career. Perhaps that's why the venerable R&B vocal group can boast such a remarkably consistent track record.

The quintet from Chicago's south suburbs has weathered stylistic shifts from doo-wop and soul to disco and urban contemporary, and every permutation in between. Their harmony remains as striking as ever, with Marvin Junior's earthshaking lead enduring as the group's focal point.

Signing with Vee-Jay in 1955, their creamy vocal blend on "Oh, What a Night" gave the Dells their first major R&B hit the next year, but it would be nearly a decade before they returned to the winner's circle with another dreamy classic, "Stay in My Corner." By then Chicago's R&B sound had changed drastically—doo-wop was dead and soul was king—but the Dells adapted effortlessly, regularly scaling the charts for the Chess subsidiary Cadet with "There Is," "Always Together," "Give Your Baby a Standing Ovation," and a marathon remake of "Stay in My Corner" that afforded Junior's booming baritone room to roam.

Seemingly an indestructible force (turning up on the R&B charts as recently as 1984), the succinct harmonies of the Dells span entire generations of R&B history. —*Bill Dahl*

○ **There Is** / 1968 / Chess 9288
Rich 1966-1968 Chicago soul with little of the overproduction that marred the powerful R&B quintets of the later Chess output. —*Bill Dahl*

○ **Dells** / 1969 / Chess 9103
Tremendous vocals and production, coupled with superb ballads and good uptempo cuts. The Dells were never better than during the late '60s, when they moved to Cadet and Charles Stepney's vision was fulfilled. Though he was never fully credited, lead singer Marvin Junior stands as one of soul's great vocalists, and he showed it repeatedly on this set. Johnny Carter's floating falsetto was another major weapon expertly utilized in the Dells' soul success. —*Ron Wynn*

★ **On Their Corner** / 1992 / Chess 9333
Excellent compilation of their late-'60s sides, like "Oh What a Night," "Stay in My Corner," "The Love We Had Stays on My Mind," and "Give Your Baby a Standing Ovation." —*Stephen Thomas Erlewine*

○ **Dreams of Contentment** / 1993 / Vee Jay 701
The Dells never made it over the hump while at Vee-Jay, despite making many impressive singles. They were a topflight doo-wop group, but they couldn't find a way to advance beyond the R&B margins. Only when they moved to Chess, changed their style, and made Marvin Junior lead singer did they enjoy the success they deserved. Still, as this 24-track compilation shows, there wasn't anything wrong with their Vee-Jay output. They experimented on such numbers as "Lil Darlin'," "It's Not for Me to Say" and "It's Not Unusual" with jazz, pop harmonies and covers. In addition, songs like "Now I Pray" and "Pain in My Heart" are wonderfully sung and harmonized, even if they weren't huge sellers. —*Ron Wynn*

John Denver (John Henry Deutchendorf)

b. Dec. 31, 1943, Roswell, NM
Vocals, guitar / Singe/songwriter, pop, folk-rock
In the '70s, John Denver's simple, melodic, light folk-pop made him one of the decade's biggest stars. In the '60s, he played with his idols the Chad Mitchell Trio, turning into a talented songwriter while he was with the group. Denver left for a solo career in 1969; later in the year, his "Leaving on a Jet Plane" became a big hit for Peter, Paul & Mary. In no time, Denver established himself as a star in his own right, with songs like "Take Me Home, Country Roads," "Rocky Mountain High," "Sunshine on

My Shoulders," "Annie's Song," and "Thank God I'm a Country Boy" becoming pop standards of the decade. After the '70s were over, Denver's career began to lose its commercial momentum and he turned to social causes, while recording the occasional album. Denver continues to record and perform in the '90s, consistently pleasing his fans. —*Stephen Thomas Erlewine*

● **Greatest Hits** / 1973 / RCA 0374
A good collection of his early (and best) era, 1969-1973. —*Dan Heilman*

○ **Greatest Hits, Vol. 2** / 1977 / RCA 2195
More pop, less folk, and more hits. —*Dan Heilman*

○ **Greatest Hits, Vol. 3** / 1985 / RCA 5313
Not many hits, but notable '80s tracks. —*Dan Heilman*

Depeche Mode

Group / Alternative pop, dance-pop
In 1980, Depeche Mode (the name means "fast fashion") was formed in Basildon, Essex, England, by Andy Fletcher, Martin Gore, Vince Clarke, and Dave Gahan. All four played synthesizers, and Gahan sang. They were signed to tiny Mute Records in England in 1982 (distributed by Sire/Warner Bros. in the United States) and scored two Top-20 hits ("New Life" and "Just Can't Get Enough") and a Top-Ten album (*Speak and Spell*) by the end of the year. At that point, Clarke quit and was replaced by Alan Wilder. The band's style—pop songs with ominous lyrics sung in Gahan's distinct baritone and backed by intricate synthesized dance music—did not change, and its commercial success continued as well.

The group only gradually built a following in the States, finally breaking the Hot 100 with "People Are People," which reached number 13 in 1985. The first album to reach the American Top-100 albums was *Black Celebration* in 1986; then *Music for the Masses* went gold in 1987. By 1989 Depeche Mode was big enough in the United States to play a concert at the Rose Bowl in California, and that show was recorded for the live album *101*. But it wasn't until the 1990 album *Violator* and the single "Enjoy the Silence" that Depeche Mode made the Top Ten in this country. By then, they'd also conquered the rest of the world and become one of the most popular "modern" or "alternative" rock groups of the '80s and early '90s. —*William Ruhlmann*

Speak & Spell / 1981 / Sire 3642
Vince Clarke's only album with Depeche Mode is dominated by him (he wrote 9 of the 11 tracks), and the band was never this imaginative or naive. Especially notable is the U.K. Top-Ten hit, "Just Can't Get Enough," which remains the best single track they ever recorded. —*William Ruhlmann*

○ **Some Great Reward** / 1984 / Sire 25194
Depeche Mode's most consistent post-Clarke album contains some of its most provocative material, notably "Blasphemous Rumours" and "Master and Servant," which concern, respectively, religion and sexual domination. —*William Ruhlmann*

● **Catching Up with Depeche Mode** / 1985 / Sire 25346
A U.S.-only compilation that's a well put together best-of from the band's early singles to its current state. If you want to know what Depeche Mode is about, this is the record that will tell you. —*William Ruhlmann*

○ **Black Celebration** / 1986 / Sire 25429
Depeche Mode are frequently called gloom mongers, and much of that criticism stems from this relentlessly bleak album, which is undoubtly the most desolate record they have ever made. —*Stephen Thomas Erlewine*

Violator / 1990 / Sire 26081
Depeche Mode's commercial breakthrough album is a mixed bag. Unlike their previous album, *Violator* truly *is* music for the masses. Throughout the album, occasional spells of catchy hooks emerge from beneath the thudding machines (most notably on the excellent "Personal Jesus" and the hit single "Enjoy the Silence"). On the strength of these flashes of melody, the album crossed over into the mainstream, but for the most part *Violator* is rather tedious. —*Stephen Thomas Erlewine*

Songs of Faith & Devotion / 1993 / Sire 45243
Depeche Mode attempts to reinvent themselves with *Songs of Faith & Devotion*, much as U2 did with *Achtung Baby*. In addition to their signature synthesizers, the group adds more guitar and strings to the music, frequently with rock and gospel flour-

ishes that would previously have been unthinkable on a Depeche disc. Often these moments of departure are the most exciting on the album—like the terrific one-chord stomp of "I Feel You" or the nearly soulful "Walking in My Shoes," which both feature animated vocals by Dave Gahan. Despite the new musical directions, there's nothing here that will alienate old fans, and it might gain Depeche Mode a few new listeners. —*Stephen Thomas Erlewine*

Derek & the Dominos

Group / Blues rock, rock & roll
After touring with Delaney & Bonnie, Eric Clapton formed Derek & the Dominos with members of their backing band. Although they only lasted for one album and tour, the band was Clapton's finest artistic achievement. The Dominos played R&B, rock & roll, and blues that didn't sound like White boys pretending they were Black—it sounded real. Duane Allman sat in on the *Layla* sessions, contributing some beautiful playing. A second album was attempted but never finished. The remains of these sessions can be found on Clapton's *Crossroads*. —*Stephen Thomas Erlewine*

★ **Layla & Other Assorted Love Songs** / Dec. 1970 / Polydor 847090
Quite simply, this is Eric Clapton's finest moment, full of gutsy, impassioned playing and tortured vocals. None of the love songs are simple, and the band rocks away their blues in a series of long jams that are never boring. —*Stephen Thomas Erlewine*

○ **Derek & the Dominos in Concert** / Mar. 1973 / Polydor 831416
While it isn't nearly as intense as *Layla, Derek & the Dominos in Concert* offers some fine playing by Clapton and his band and easily ranks among his best live albums. —*Stephen Thomas Erlewine*

Layla Sessions / Feb. 1991 / Polydor 847083
Featuring two discs of outtakes and jams, the three-CD boxed set *The Layla Sessions* manages to detract from the original by surrounding it with endless, dull instrumentals. Then again, all the unreleased material prove what a well-constructed album *Layla* is. —*Stephen Thomas Erlewine*

Rick Derringer (Rick Zehringer)

b. Aug. 5, 1947, Celina, OH
Guitar / Rock & roll, pop/rock
As a lead guitarist, Rick Derringer (born Rick Zehringer) was the frontman for the McCoys, a group of mid-'60s pop-rockers who recorded the number-one million seller "Hang on Sloopy." The McCoys linked up with Texas guitarist Johnny Winter, and Derringer began producing and backing up Winter and his brother Edgar. Derringer's solo debut, *All American Boy*, generated his only hit with the 1974 number-23 "Rock and Roll Hootchie Koo." In 1976 he formed Derringer, a hard-rock quartet that enjoyed moderate success. More recently, Derringer has produced Weird Al Yankovic's pop parodies. —*Rick Clark*

● **All American Boy** / 1974 / Blue Sky 32481
Derringer's first solo album, featuring great songwriting and performing, with his own version of his classic "Rock & Roll Hootchie Koo." —*Cub Koda*

○ **Live** / 1977 / CBS 34848
A blistering live set from Derringer, featuring most of his best-known songs. —*Stephen Thomas Erlewine*

Jackie DeShannon

b. Aug. 21, 1944, Hazel, KY
Vocals / Singer/songwriter, pop/rock
Primarily known for writing songs recorded by the Byrds, Bruce Springsteen, the Searchers, Brenda Lee, and Marianne Faithful, plus the Grammy-winning Kim Carnes hit "Betty Davis Eyes," DeShannon also enjoyed a sporadic solo-artist career. She generated two Top-Ten hits with her own "Put a Little Love in Your Heart" and a cover of Burt Bacharach and Hal David's "What the World Needs Now." She was one of the few artists to have the privilege of being a warm-up act on the first U.S. Beatles tour. She has worked with Jimmy Page, Van Morrison, Ry Cooder, and an early incarnation of the Crusaders. Over the course of her artistic career, DeShannon's music has ranged from early folk/rock to gospelish pop. —*Rick Clark*

○ **Jackie DeShannon** / 1963 / Sunset 5322

This album features DeShannon's hit version of Hal David and Burt Bacharach's "What the World Needs Now Is Love," but also included is DeShannon's rendition of her own standard, "When You Walk in the Room," and a co-composition with Randy Newman, "She Don't Understand Him Like I Do." *—William Ruhlmann*

Put a Little Love in Your Heart / 1969 / Imperial 12442
DeShannon cowrote her second Top-Ten hit, the title track, with Jimmy Holiday and Randy Myers, and this album contains more of the fruit of their collaboration, including the follow-up, a Top-40 hit called "Love Will Find a Way." *—William Ruhlmann*

New Arrangement / 1975 / CBS 33500
Excellent updating of DeShannon's sound. Includes her co-composition "Bette Davis Eyes," which Kim Carnes took to the top of the charts six years later. *—William Ruhlmann*

○ **Best of Jackie DeShannon** / 1991 / Rhino 70738
This set contains all of DeShannon's best known singles, as well as other notable original songs like "Bette Davis Eyes." *—Rick Clark*

● **Jackie DeShannon: The Definitive Collection** / 1994 / EMI
DeShannon's work on Columbia, Atlantic, RCA, Amherst, Mar-Vel, and Gone isn't represented here. In other words, this isn't the "definitive collection." However, it is a very good one that covers everything from DeShannon's 1958 single release, "Buddy," to 1970's "Brighton Hill." In between are such '60s gems as "Put a Little Love in Your Heart," "When You Walk in the Room," and "What the World Needs Now Is Love." A complete discography, decent liners, and great sound round out this package. *—Rick Clark*

Devo

Group / New wave
Devo comprised two sets of brothers, Mark and Bob Motherbaugh and Jerry and Bob Casale. One of the first new wave groups to get mass-market attention, this Akron, OH band had its own philosophy, "de-evolution"—a sci-fi/satirical view of postmodern cultural values complete with strange costumes and behavior. Their sound was appropriately nervous and jerky, with a heavy emphasis on synthesizers. Their debut album, *Q: Are We Not Men? A: We Are Devo!*, was produced by Brian Eno and featured a great cover of the Rolling Stones' "Satisfaction." After a less interesting second album, they rebounded with the self-produced album *Freedom of Choice*, containing the hit "Whip It."

As one of new wave's most cartoonish and successful bands, they helped define the genre with a minimalist synth sound. Although each successive album provided a new look and theme, their sound became more glossy and less challenging, heading toward straight-synth/dance-pop grooves. *—Scott Bultman*

○ **Q: Are We Not Men? A: We Are Devo!** / 1978 / Warner Brothers 3239
All the mechanized, herky-jerky rhythms and quirky lyrics that first gained attention for Devo are here, among them "Jocko Homo," "Mongoloid," and their drastic recasting of "(I Can't Get No) Satisfaction." *—William Ruhlmann*

Freedom of Choice / 1980 / Warner Brothers 3435
Devo's dance-floor triumph, "Whip It," plus more electro-pop delights. *—William Ruhlmann*

● **Greatest Hits** / 1990 / Warner Brothers 26449
A generous collection of the highlights from Devo's career, *Greatest Hits* is designed for the casual fan. *—Stephen Thomas Erlewine*

Dexy's Midnight Runners

Group / New wave, pop/rock
When Dexy's Midnight Runners were at their peak in the early '80s, U.K. critics hailed their lead singer/songwriter Kevin Rowland as a genius, capable of fusing soul, pop, Irish folk, new wave, and rock into one seamless, unique mix. Although the band wasn't able to fulfill their promise, the best of their music was remarkable. On their first album, *Searching for the Young Soul Rebels*, the group featured scores of horns along with accomplished songwriting from Rowland. It became a sensation in England, although it didn't dent the charts in America. After the album's release, five members of the band split and formed the Bureau, leaving Rowland to refashion Dexy's Midnight Runners.

What he came up with was a departure from the debut, although it shared the same spirit. Instead of soul, the band was rooted in folk and Celtic music on their second album, *Too-Rye-Ay*, which produced the enormous international hit, "Come on Eileen." Rowland seemed lost in the wake of his success, lacking a new idea for his music. The last Dexy album was bland and directionless, as was his solo album, 1988's *The Wanderer*. Rowland hasn't been making music since the late '80s, but his band's first records remain searing displays of passion and musical inventiveness. *—Stephen Thomas Erlewine*

○ **Searching for the Young Soul Rebels** / 1980 / Parlophone 7213
While it's a fascinating mix of punk and soul, Dexy's Midnight Runners' debut album isn't quite as wonderful as the band's cult claims it is, yet it does offer a number of genuinely impressive and impassioned songs. *—Stephen Thomas Erlewine*

● **Too-Rye-Aye** / 1982 / Mercury 810054
For the second Dexy's Midnight Runners album, Kevin Rowland refashioned the band as country-folk punk-rockers. Much like *Searching for the Young Soul Rebels*, *Too-Rye-Ay* is more interesting in theory than in practice, yet it is the stronger of the two records, thanks to the irresistable hit single "Come On Eileen." *—Stephen Thomas Erlewine*

Diamond Head

Group / Heavy metal
Diamond Head was one of the best bands of the New Wave of British Heavy Metal in the late '70s and early '80s, playing a tight and aggressive Zeppelin-derived style of hard rock. The band's power, unassuming sense of melody, and crunching guitars influenced a small generation of American metal bands, including Metallica. After several years of inactivity in the late '80s, the band re-formed in 1991 for a tour and an EP. *—Stephen Thomas Erlewine*

● **Behold the Beginning** / 1986 / Metal Blade 72200
A NWOBHM band that never got noticed in America until Metallica noted that Diamond Head was a major influence in their sound. Liner notes written by Metallica drummer Lars Ulrich. *—John Book*

Neil Diamond

b. Jan. 24, 1941, Brooklyn, NY
Vocals / Pop, pop/rock
Neil Diamond built a career—first as a pop songwriter, and then as a pop singer—that has withstood the changing fashions of music, especially rock, over more than 25 years. Born in Brooklyn, Diamond was writing and recording in New York in his teens, though he graduated from Erasmus High School and attended New York University for a time. In 1965, he signed to Bang Records as an artist while also working as a songwriter. In 1966, he reached the Top Ten with his "Cherry, Cherry," while the Monkees took his "I'm a Believer" to number one. "Cherry, Cherry" was the first of five straight Top-20 hits, among them "Girl, You'll Be a Woman Soon."

Diamond began to develop into more of an individual writer in the mold of Bob Dylan and Paul Simon in the late '60s, and this led to his movement to Uni Records in 1968, where he continued to score hits like "Sweet Caroline," "Holly Holy," and "Cracklin' Rose" in a pop-rock style laced with gospel and country influences. His albums also began to go gold consistently as of 1969's *Touching You, Touching Me*.

Diamond signed a lucrative contract with Columbia Records in 1973 that began with his soundtrack to the film *Jonathan Livingston Seagull*. His 1976 album, *Beautiful Noise*, was produced by Robbie Robertson of the Band—it was his first album to go platinum. In 1980, Diamond starred in a remake of the film *The Jazz Singer*. Its soundtrack was another million-seller for him.

Diamond had developed into a dynamic live performer over the years, and his concert recordings were among his most successful. In the late '80s and early '90s, while updating his sound, he faded from the singles charts, though his albums continued to sell consistently, and his shows continued to sell out: According to *Amusement Business*, he was the top concert draw in the United States for the first six months of 1992. *—William Ruhlmann*

○ **Hot August Night** / 1972 / MCA 6896

This double-record set is the album that established Diamond's reputation as a live performer. Containing passionately performed versions of his biggest hits up to this time, it sold the best of any album he'd had so far, going gold the month of its release. — *William Ruhlmann*

● **His Twelve Greatest Hits** / 1974 / MCA 37252
Actually, this is 12 songs that were hits for Diamond on Uni between 1969 and 1972. "Cracklin' Rosie" is here, along with Diamond's other chart-topper of the period, "Song Sung Blue," as well as "Sweet Caroline," "Play Me," and "Holly Holy." — *William Ruhlmann*

Beautiful Noise / 1976 / Columbia 33965
A beautifully recorded concept album about Diamond's own emergence from the Brooklyn streets and from the Brill Building's Tin Pan Alley. Produced by Robbie Robertson. — *William Ruhlmann*

● **Classics—The Early Years** / 1983 / Columbia 38792
A terrific collection featuring his earliest and best songs—"Kentucky Woman," "Girl, You'll Be a Woman Soon," "Cherry, Cherry," "Thank the Lord for the Night Time," "Solitary Man," "I'm a Believer," and "Red Red Wine." — *Stephen Thomas Erlewine*

○ **The Greatest Hits (1966-1992)** / 1992 / Columbia 52703
Columbia has been Diamond's label since 1973, and it acquired the rights to his Bang material of 1966-1968. But MCA still controls the recordings from 1968-1973. That's why (although you won't find it out by reading the album cover) this two-disc, 37-track retrospective consists of the original versions of such hits as "Cherry, Cherry" (1966) and "You Don't Bring Me Flowers" (1978) but covers the middle period with re-recordings and live renditions of 13 of Diamond's biggest hits. As such, this collection gets only a qualified recommendation. — *William Ruhlmann*

○ **Glory Road—1968 to 1972** / 1992 / MCA 10502
A fine two-disc retrospective of Diamond's late '60s and early '70s tracks, including some of his biggest hits—"Cracklin' Rosie," "Sweet Caroline," and "Song Sung Blue," among others. If *His Twelve Greatest Hits* doesn't offer enough material, *Glory Road* is the definitive retrospective of his years with Uni/MCA. — *AMG*

Diamonds

Group / R&B, doo-wop
One of the leading cover groups of the mid '50s, the Diamonds adapted current R&B hits into pop gold of their own. Hailing from Toronto, the Canadian quartet signed with Mercury in 1955 and immediately zoomed up pop playlists with covers of the Teenagers' "Why Do Fools Fall in Love," the Willows' "Church Bells May Ring," and their biggest hit of all, a sanitized version of the Gladiolas hit "Little Darlin'." Fronted by David Somerville, the quartet hit with an original, the smooth dance outing "The Stroll." After weathering major personnel changes, the Diamonds notched their last hit in 1961. Somerville remains active as a solo, while various aggregations billed as the Diamonds populate the oldies scene. — *Bill Dahl*

● **Best of the Diamonds** / Rhino 209
"Little Darlin'," "The Stroll," and some of their lesser hits are all here. — *Dan Heilman*

The Dictators

Group / Punk, rock & roll
A punk-rock group that predated punk by a few years and was something of a comedy group as well, the Dictators were formed in the Bronx in 1974 by Handsome Dick Manitoba (born Richard Blum), Ross the Boss, Scott Kempner, Andy Shernoff, Mark Mendoza, and Ritchie Teeter . They recorded three albums before breaking up in 1978. — *William Ruhlmann*

● **Go Girl Crazy** / 1975 / Epic 33348
These punk progenitors and rock & roll comedians made only one great album, but it continues to stand up as both a celebration of the joys of three-chord rock and a send-up of the same. — *William Ruhlmann*

Bo Diddley (Ellas Otha Bates McDaniels)

b. Dec. 30, 1928, McComb, MS
Vocals, guitar, composer / Rock & roll, R&B
Bo Diddley (born Ellas Otha Bates McDaniels) is one of the most influential R&B artists of all time. His music resists classification

to this day. Though some critics dismiss him as a one-riff artist, nothing could be further from the truth. His trademark rhythm (based on equal parts hambone beat and sanctified church shout) has many variations, textures, and subtleties, which reveal themselves to the listener with concentrated listening. Though his chart hits were few, the scope and breadth of his influence, both here and abroad, is wide indeed. A major innovator in guitar sounds and designs and a galvanizing live performer with a powerful singing voice and personality to match, his induction to the Rock & Roll Hall of Fame was no less than his due. The only musician in history to have a specific beat named after him, Bo Diddley stands as a true American music original. — *Cub Koda*

○ **Bo Diddley Is a Gunslinger** / 1963 / Chess 9285
One of Bo Diddley's better studio albums, *Bo Diddley Is a Gunslinger* features the classic "Ride on Josephine" as well as a raw version of "Sixteen Tons" and a rewrite of "Somewhere Over the Rainbow" called "Somewhere" among its many highlights. — *Stephen Thomas Erlewine*

○ **Bo Diddley's Beach Party** / 1963 / Checker 2988
A blistering live album. Currently out of print but well worth any search. — *Cub Koda*

○ **Bo Diddley/Go Bo Diddley** / 1986 / Chess 5904
Bo's first and second albums on one CD. — *Cub Koda*

★ **Chess Box** / 1990 / MCA 19502
A two-CD boxed-set overview of Bo Diddley's music. The perfect place to start. — *Cub Koda*

○ **Rare & Well Done** / Sep. 10, 1991 / Chess 9331
Contains unissued and rare sides. The perfect companion piece to *The Chess Box*. — *Cub Koda*

Dinosaur Jr.

Vocals, guitar / Alternative rock
Led by J Mascis's massive guitar roar and drawling vocals, Dinosaur Jr. were one of the most distinctive and influential alternative bands of the late '80s. Taking hardcore punk and Neil Young's splattered electric folk as their starting points, Dinosaur Jr. created a loud, sprawling rock & roll that frequently spun off into the white noise territory of Sonic Youth but just as frequently stayed in Mascis's lazily melodic, folk-based songs. Mascis is one of the few traditional lead guitarists in alternative rock, and his fluid, feedback-drenched guitar expressed all the emotions that his lyrics alluded to. He is also one of the most respected songwriters in alternative rock—his songs have been covered by several artists, including the Cowboy Junkies.

Since their first release in 1985, Dinosaur Jr. have influenced a generation of young guitar bands. Along with the Pixies and Sonic Youth, they provide the link between the post-punk rock of Hüsker Dü and the Replacements and the grunge rock of the '90s. — *Stephen Thomas Erlewine*

Dinosaur / 1985 / Positive 15
Great angst-ridden songs. Tense, with a Neil Young flavor. — *Robert Gordon*

☆ **You're Living All Over Me** / 1987 / SST 130
A collasal slab of snarling indie-rock guitar noise, Dinosaur Jr.'s second album was one of the land mark underground rock records of the late 80s; with its huge sheets of white noise and sighing melodies, it paved the way for the grunge rock of the early 90s. — *Stephen Thomas Erlewine*

○ **Bug** / 1988 / SST 216
Bug is as noisy as *You're Living All Over Me,* but this time out J Mascis's songwriting has sharpened a bit, as evidenced by the brilliant single, "Freak Scene." — *Stephen Thomas Erlewine*

Fossils / 1991 / SST 275
A good collection of non-LP singles and rarities, *Fossils*'s high-points include strangely appropriate covers of Peter Frampton's "Show Me the Way" and the Cure's "Just Like Heaven." — *Stephen Thomas Erlewine*

● **Green Mind** / 1991 / Sire 26479
Many consider *Green Mind* to be a weak, uninspired effort, but Dinosaur Jr.'s major-label debut is a strong, varied album, featuring some of J Mascis's best songwriting as well as some of his best, most fluid guitar work. Essentially a solo effort by Mascis (bassist Murph only appears on three tracks), *Green Mind* finds him stretching and expanding his traditional sonic assault with more acoustic guitars and tighter melodies. With its gentle mel-

lotron and lovely, sighing melody, "Thumb" stands as one Mascis's finest songs. "Muck" is a surprisingly enjoyable stab at funk. "How'd You Pin That One on Me" is a great guitar workout. "Puke & Cry" and "I Live for That Look" are impressive folk-punk. And "The Wagon" rivals "Freak Scene" in its depiction of the underground scene. —*Stephen Thomas Erlewine*

Whatever's Cool with Me / Oct. 22, 1991 / Sire 26761
"Whatever's Cool with Me" is definitive Dinosaur Jr.—roaring rhythm guitars, legato solos, weary lyrics, and a winding, pene-trating melody. The five B-sides on the EP are solid, if unremark-able, highlighted by a tongue-in-cheek rewrite of David Bowie's "Quicksand." —*Stephen Thomas Erlewine*

○ **Where You Been** / 1993 / Sire 45108
Dinosaur Jr.'s full-throttle punk roar keeps diminishing as time goes by, but that doesn't mean the music is any less powerful—if anything, it is getting stronger. *Where You Been* sounds similiar to most other Dinosaur Jr. albums—there's no mistaking J Mascis's trademark wrenching guitar and vocals—but the album is filled with terrific songs like "Get Me" and "Start Choppin'," even if the guitar meanders a bit too much. —*Stephen Thomas Erlewine*

Dio

Group / Heavy metal
Before he assembled Dio, Ronnie James Dio was a well-known figure in the heavy metal world. With Elf, Rainbow, and Black Sabbath, Dio was a top hard-rock singer with a solid commercial appeal. He was responsible for reviving Sabbath's sagging for-tunes in the early '80s. After three years with Sabbath, he left to form his own band in 1983. It featured guitarist Vivian Campbell (who would later play with Whitesnake and Def Leppard), drum-mer Vinny Appice, ex-Rainbow bassist Jimmy Bain, and key-boardist Claude Schnell. For the rest of the '80s, Dio was one of the top metal bands, with a crunchier, more streamlined version of Sabbath's mystical vision. In 1990, Dio disbanded the group, then returned to Black Sabbath for a brief time in 1991 and 1992. He soon left, however, assembling a revamped version of Dio and beginning to tour again. —*Stephen Thomas Erlewine*

● **Dream Evil** / 1987 / Warner Brothers 25612
On *Dream Evil,* Dio manages to record an album where the song-writing doesn't amount to an endless series of riffs. Instead, the record features actual songs with actual melodies, making it their most accomplished album. —*Stephen Thomas Erlewine*

Dion & the Belmonts

b. Jul. 18, 1939
Group / Doo-wop, rock & roll
Doo-wop was just as seductive a musical force in the Bronx as it was in Harlem, and young Dion DiMucci fell under its spell as a lad. With his pompadoured good looks and clear, powerful pipes, he was a natural for rock & roll stardom. And his vocal group, the Belmonts, joined the fledgling Laurie label in 1958 and immediately hit with the upbeat "I Wonder Why." After scor-ing two major pop smashes with "A Teenager in Love" and the pop standard "Where or When," Dion and the Belmonts went their separate ways.

Vocal group harmonies remained integral to Dion's sound even after he went solo, from his initial 1960 hit, "Lonely Teenager," through his swaggering macho classics "Runaround Sue" and "The Wanderer" (still two of the most requested items on any oldies playlist). Moving to Columbia in 1963, Dion's out-put took on a distinctly bluesier tone with remakes of the Drifters' "Ruby Baby" and "Drip Drop" before a recurring prob-lem with heroin forced him to take an extended hiatus from show biz.

America was rocked to its foundations by a series of tragic po-litical assassinations in 1968, and Dick Holler's moving tribute "Abraham, Martin and John" inspired Dion to mount a comeback with the folk-style song. Since then, he's made several more ac-claimed returns to action as a rocker, between stints as a con-temporary Christian performer. He now fittingly enjoys the status of a revered rock legend. —*Bill Dahl*

☆ **Everything You Always Wanted to Hear by Dion** / 1976 / Laurie 4002

The best overall collection of their classic sides. Includes "Teenager in Love," "Where or When," and "I Wonder Why." White New York doo-wop at its best. —*Cub Koda*

★ **24 Golden Greats** / 1983 / Arista 8206
A sampling of every phase of Dion's career from the late '50s to the early '70s. —*Dan Heilman*

○ **Greatest Hits** / 1987 / CBS 31942
A solid compilation of Dion's solo sides, including "Donna the Prima Donna," "Ruby Baby," and others. —*Cub Koda*

Yo Frankie / 1989 / Arista 8549
A solid streetwise effort. —*Dan Heilman*

○ **Bronx Blues: The Columbia Recordings** / 1991 / Columbia 46972
In the mid '60s, Dion turned away from teen-idol doo-wop mate-rial and cut several sides in a solid R&B/blues/folk vein. The best of those sides are collected here. —*Cub Koda*

Celine Dion

b. Mar. 30, 1968, Charlemagne, Quebec
Vocals / Pop
In her native Canada as well as in France, Celine Dion had been a popular singer since she was a teenager. Dion's polished yet soulful adult contemporary pop didn't break in the United States until 1991 (when she released a record recorded in English), but when it did, there was no stopping the hits. From "Where Does My Heart Beat Now" to the theme to *Beauty and the Beast*, Dion has been a fixture on the American pop charts since 1992. —*Stephen Thomas Erlewine*

○ **Unison** / 1990 / Epic 46893
A fine, sophisticated American debut from this popular Canadian singer, featuring the hit singles "(If There Was) Any Other Way" and "Where Does My Heart Beat Now." —*Stephen Thomas Erlewine*

● **Celine Dion** / Mar. 31, 1992 / Epic 52473
Featuring the hit singles "Beauty and the Beast," "Love Can Move Mountains," and "If You Asked Me To," Celine Dion's follow-up to her successful American debut is an even stronger and more ac-complished record than her previous album. —*Stephen Thomas Erlewine*

Dire Straits

Group / Rock & roll
In 1977 disco reigned, and the new wave/punk movements were heralding the death of tired FM rock. It was then that Dire Straits came along with a unique blend of atmospheric blues-flavored rock and literate Dylanesque story-type lyrics. Singer, songwriter, and lead guitarist Mark Knopfler's dry, low-key vocal delivery and economical, clean guitar playing immediately hit a nerve with the public, and the group's self-titled debut effort went num-ber two, aided by the driving number-four hit "Sultans of Swing."

Aside from *Communique*, the band's sophomore effort, Dire Straits increasingly developed a cinematic approach to songwrit-ing and production. *Love over Gold* is a particular highlight. It was only a natural sidestep for Knopfler to score the highly ac-claimed soundtracks for *Local Hero* (1983) and *The Princess Bride* (1987). *Alchemy,* a double-record live set, was released in 1984.

In 1985 *Brothers in Arms* was released, becoming one of the biggest internationally selling albums of the '80s. The song "Money for Nothing" became free advertising for MTV with the hook "I want my MTV."

Knopfler undertook various side projects, including the Notting Hillbillies and a fine duet album with Chet Atkins (*Neck and Neck*). Six years after the release of *Brothers in Arms, On Every Street* was released. —*Rick Clark*

☆ **Dire Straits** / 1978 / Warner Brothers 3266
Even after all their success, the debut is the best example of the intricate style of Dire Straits, dominated by the electric finger-picking of guitarist Mark Knopfler, his smoky voice, and the po-etic lyrics. Features their first hit, "Sultans of Swing." —*William Ruhlmann*

○ **Making Movies** / 1980 / Warner Brothers 3480
The third album displays Knopfler's expanding ambitions as a songwriter with, as the title suggests, a cinematic sweep on such

songs as "Tunnel of Love" and "Romeo and Juliet." —*William Ruhlmann*

○ **Love over Gold** / 1982 / Warner Brothers 23728
The fourth Dire Straits album is their most atmospheric effort, featuring the spacious title track as well as the epic "Telegraph Road," with the extended guitar workout at its conclusion. —*Rick Clark*

○ **Brothers in Arms** / 1985 / Warner Brothers 25264
Their biggest-selling album, containing the mega-hit "Money for Nothing" as well as "Walk of Life" and "So Far Away." —*William Ruhlmann*

● **Money for Nothing** / 1988 / Warner Brothers 25794
This best-of collection contains Dire Straits' biggest hits as well as some key album tracks. "Sultans of Swing," "Walk of Life," "Money for Nothing," plus a live version of "Telegraph Road" from *Love over Gold*, are among the highlights. Even though this may be a fairly representative sampler, listening to the group's better albums in their entirety is the best way to hear this band. —*Rick Clark*

Divinyls

Group / Rock & roll
This Australian band, built around Christina Amphlett's hiccuping vocals and Mark McEntee's rude grungy guitar work, made an impressive debut with *Desperate*, a record that blends the thick chorusy guitar sound of the Pretenders with a punkish hard-rock recklessness.
On their first album for Virgin Records, *Divinyls* (1991), Amphlett's naughty-girl/sexual-fetish persona is brought to the forefront with the Top-Ten ode to auto-eroticism, "I Touch Myself." —*Rick Clark*

● **Essential** / 1987 / Chrysalis 21846
Good compilation. Contains key radio tracks but some great album sides are omitted. Still, a good place to start. —*Rick Clark*

Divinyls / 1991 / Virgin 91397
Only a couple of tracks of note: the highly song-crafted paen to masturbation, "I Touch Myself" (their biggest hit), and "Make Out Alright." —*Rick Clark*

The Dixie Dregs

Group / Fusion
This Georgia-based instrumental fusion band developed quite a following during the late '70s with their musical chops, band chemistry, and complicated (but solidly melodic) compositions, primarily written by guitarist Steve Morse. —*Rick Clark*

Free Fall / 1977 / Polydor 829661
A potent debut that presents the Dregs' melodic instrumental fusion to fine effect. —*Jas Obrecht*

○ **What If** / 1978 / Polydor 831836
Of all the albums by the Dregs, this is the one to get. Steve Morse's melodies have an otherwordly elegance on songs like "Night Meets Light." The band plays with just the right amount of restraint. Ken Scott's production is, at turns, atmospheric and immediate. "Take It Off the Top" is a fine rocker. —*Rick Clark*

Night of the Living Dregs / 1979 / Polydor 831411
A good half-live, half-studio set. —*Jas Obrecht*

● **Divided We Stand: Best of the Dixie Dregs** / 1989 / Arista 8608
A decent selection of their best work while signed to Capricorn. Includes "Cruise Control," a live version of "Refried Funky Chicken," and a healthy sampling off *What If*. —*Rick Clark*

Don Dixon

Vocals / Pop/rock, rock & roll
While his own records never reached a mass audience, Don Dixon was one of the major figures in the post-punk Southern guitar pop of the '80s. Dixon produced R.E.M., Let's Active, the Smithereens, and Marti Jones during the decade, bringing his sharp pop sensibilities to their already highly melodic songs. But his true talents shine in his solo albums. Dixon is able to successfully recall everything from Beatlesque pop and Southern soul to gritty country in R&B with his lean, muscular pop. He adds an engagingly twisted lyrical view to his effortlessly eclectic music, making him one of the best subversive pop singer/songwriters since Nick Lowe. Unfortunately, his records are even more

obscure than Lowe's. On each album, there are several pure pop gems. —*Stephen Thomas Erlewine*

○ **Most of the Girls Like to Dance but Only Some of the Boys To** / 1985 / Enigma 73239
Dixon put together *Most of the Girls Like to Dance but Only Some of the Boys Like To* out of demos cut from 1981-1984. It's a kind of best-of from a man with a pure pop sensibility and a wicked sense of humor when it comes to matters romantic. (The 1986 CD version adds two songs to make a total of 16.) —*William Ruhlmann*

○ **Romeo at Juilliard** / 1987 / Enigma 73243
Dixon's domestic debut featured more of his skewed songs, and here he was aided and abetted by such compatriots as Mitch Easter and Marti Jones (who is his wife). —*William Ruhlmann*

Chi Town Budget Show / 1988 / Restless 72296
An intimate live album featuring many of the best songs from the two previous albums. —*William Ruhlmann*

● **If I'm a Ham, Well You're a Sausage** / Mar. 3, 1992 / Restless 72584
While he is known mainly through his production work, this extensive best-of collection shows Dixon to be an equally sharp songwriter and performer. —*Chris Woodstra*

Dr. Buzzard's Original Savannah Band

Group / Southern rock
Dr. Buzzard's Original Savannah Band was one of the most original musical ensembles of the disco era. They were formed in the Bronx in 1974 by Stony Browder Jr. (b. 1949), his brother August Darnell (Thomas Browder, b. 1951), singer Cory Daye (b. 1952), Andy Hernandez (b. 1950), and Mickey Sevilla (b. 1953). The concept of the group was the re-creation of a '30s dance band á la Cab Calloway, with witty lyrics and a disco beat. All of this was in evidence on their debut album, *Dr. Buzzard's Original Savannah Band*, released in 1976. It produced the dance-floor hit "Cherchez La Femme" and went gold. A follow-up album, *Dr. Buzzard's Original Savannah Band Meets King Pennett*, was less successful. After the release of a third album, *James Monroe HS Presents Dr. Buzzard's Original Savannah Band Goes to Washington*, the group fragmented, with Darnell and Hernandez going off to form Kid Creole and the Coconuts. Browder reorganized and issued a Dr. Buzzard's Savannah Band (dropping the "Original") album titled *Calling All Beatniks!* in 1984. —*William Ruhlmann*

● **Dr. Buzzard's Original Savannah Band** / 1976 / RCA 1504
Dr. Buzzard introduced a big-band sheen to '70s dance music with the hit "Cherchez la Femme" and the rest of this charmingly neo-retro album. —*William Ruhlmann*

Dr. Feelgood

Group / Rock & roll
Although they never strayed from their gritty R&B-based sound, Dr. Feelgood was a fixture of England's rock & roll scene since the early '70s. While their music wasn't particularly influential, their method of playing was. Dr. Feelgood constantly traveled England, playing to sold-out clubs across the country. With their devoted following, they helped create the pub-rock scene in the United Kingdom—venues where rough rock & roll bands could pound out anything from R&B to pop to simple, three-chord rock. By proving these clubs were profitable, the band helped pave the way for the success of punk rock in England—punk bands played the same bars and clubs that Dr. Feelgood, Brinsley Schwarz, and other pub rockers played in the early '70s. Over the years, the band's lineup changed frequently, with vocalist/harmonica player Lee Brilleaux being the only constant member. Brilleaux's consistantly vibrant live performances were the reason Dr. Feelgood was such a concert draw. Even though he had been performing for over 20 years, Brilleaux remained a force to be reckoned when he was on stage, right up until his untimely death in April of 1994. —*Stephen Thomas Erlewine*

○ **Down by the Jetty** / Jan. 1975 / United Artists 29727
Dr. Feelgood's debut album is on a par with the early Rolling Stones albums as a demonstration of R&B fervor. Every track burns. —*William Ruhlmann*

● **Malpractice** / Feb. 1975 / Columbia 34098

Guitarist Wilko Johnson's songs shine against such inspired covers as "Riot in Cell Block #9." And his Stonesy playing takes no prisoners. —*William Ruhlmann*

Sneakin' Suspicion / 1977 / CBS 34806
Wilko Johnson's last album with Dr. Feelgood continues to be dominated by his tough guitar playing, though fewer of his songs are heard. —*William Ruhlmann*

Dr. Hook

Group / Country rock, pop/rock
This American country-rock band was originally named Dr. Hook and the Medicine Show. Formed in New Jersey in 1968, the original members included Ray Sawyer, Dennis Locorriere, Bill Francis, John David, and George Cummings. First coming to prominence with material written by Shel Silverstein, the looniness of their stage show transferred to records well, reaching its peak with the mega-hit "The Cover of the *Rolling Stone*" in 1972. They mellowed their style on record, hitting the charts with ballads as the decade wore on, but they were still crazy in live performances. Sawyer continues to front versions of the band to this day on various oldies package shows. —*Cub Koda*

● **Greatest Hits** / May 1987 / Capitol 46620
Includes "Sexy Eyes," "Sylvia's Mother," "Only Sixteen," "When You're in Love with a Beautiful Woman," and "Cover of the *Rolling Stone*." —*AMG*

Dr. John (Mac Rebennack)

b. Nov. 21, 1940
Vocals, piano / R&B, rock & roll, pop/rock
Dr. John (born Mac Rebennack) honed his skills playing '50s sessions during the heyday of New Orleans R&B. His solo work has alternately paid homage to his inspirations and incorporated those influences into his own distinct rhythmic roux. —*John Floyd*

○ **Gris Gris** / 1968 / Alligator 3904
A haunting and creepy set infused with voodoo imagery from the bayous and acid-tinged variations on New Orleans R&B structures. —*John Floyd*

Babylon / 1969 / Atco 33270
Dr. John's ambition remained undiminished on his second solo album, *Babylon*, released shortly after the groundbreaking voodoo-psychedelia/New Orleans-R&B fusion of his debut, *Gris-Gris*. The results, however, were not nearly as consistent or impressive. Coolly received by critics, the album nonetheless is deserving of attention, though it pales a bit in comparison with *Gris-Gris*. The production is sparser, and more reliant on female backup vocals, than his debut. Dr. John remains intent on fusing voodoo and R&B, but the mood is oddly bleak and despairing, in comparison with the wild Mardi Gras-gone-amok tone of his first LP. "The Patriotic Flag-Waiver" (sic), in keeping with the mood of the late '60s, damns social ills and hypocrisies of all sorts. An FM underground radio favorite at the time, its ambitious structure remains admirable, though its musical imperfections haven't worn well. To a degree, you could say the same about the album as a whole, but it has enough of an eerie fascination to merit investigation. —*Richie Unterberger*

○ **Dr. John's Gumbo** / 1972 / Atlantic 7006
Dr. John's finest album offered a selection of classic New Orleans R&B—including "Tipitina" and "Junko Partner"—updated with a dirty, funky beat. Two decades later, his interpretations sound as timeless as the original singles. —*Stephen Thomas Erlewine*

Ultimate Dr. John / 1987 / Warner Brothers 27612
An adequate overview of the Doctor's Atlantic recordings, including the 1973 hit "Right Place Wrong Time." —*John Floyd*

● **Anthology** / 1993 / Rhino 71450
Over his 35 years of recording, Mac "Dr. John" Rebennack has worn many hats, from '50s greasy rock 'n' roller to psychedelic '70s weirdo to keeper of the New Orleans music flame. All of these modes, plus more, are excellently served up on this two-disc anthology. From the early New Orleans sides featuring Rebennack's blistering guitar work ("Storm Warning" and "Morgus the Magnificent") to the fabled '70s sides as the Night Tripper to his present day status as repository of the Crescent City's noble musical tradition, this is the one you want to have for the collection. —*Cub Koda*

Bill Doggett

b. Feb. 16, 1916, Philadelphia, PA
Organ / R&B, rock & roll
Organist Bill Doggett cut one of the biggest-selling instrumentals of all time in 1956 with the two-part "Honky Tonk." He formed his first band in 1938 and sold the entire outfit to Lucky Millinder for a soda two years later. Doggett worked extensively with Millinder and Louis Jordan and recorded with Ella Fitzgerald before striking out on his own. He signed with King in Cincinnati around 1953, churning out a slew of sizzling instrumentals with Clifford Scott on tenor sax, Billy Butler on guitar, and Doggett on organ, notably "Ram-Bunk-Shush" in 1957 and, in 1958, "Leaps and Bounds" and the often-covered "Hold It." Doggett continues to tour and record—he was recently featured on a disc by the King All-Stars, a distinguished group of alumni from the famous label. —*Bill Dahl*

● **Everybody Dance to the Honky Tonk** / 1956 / King 531
The hugely influential jazz-laced R&B quartet plays their classic two-part instrumental and several more groovers, with guitarist Billy Butler and saxist Clifford Scott incendiary throughout the album. —*Bill Dahl*

○ **Dance Awhile** / 1958 / Deluxe 585
Sizzling R&B-based instrumentals. —*Bill Dahl*

Doggett Beat for Dancing Feet / 1958 / King 557
Doggett's fatback organ cooks in tandem with Butler's licks and Scott's sax. —*Bill Dahl*

Hold It / 1959 / King 609
The title instrumental is a classic. —*Bill Dahl*

Dokken

Group / Heavy metal
Formed in Sacramento, CA, in the late '70s, Dokken's claim to fame was the harmonious vocals of Don Dokken and the engaging guitar work of George Lynch. Although their strength was heavy metal, they weren't afraid to record ballads, which brought them attention from across the world. They soon toured that world and became an important American metal band in the '80s, gathering a few hits along the way before splitting up in 1989 due to "personal indifferences." Don Dokken went solo and Lynch formed the Lynch Mob. —*John Book*

● **Under Lock & Key** / 1985 / Elektra 60458
Melodic heavy metal played by a band that spawned a lot of copycats, both in sound and image. The album features strong vocals from Don Dokken and not-too-flashy guitar playing from George Lynch. —*John Book*

○ **Beast from the East** / 1988 / Elektra 60823
The band's only live album, recorded in Japan. They do their best material. Unfortunately, it was their last as a band. —*John Book*

Thomas Dolby

b. Oct. 14, 1958, Cairo, Egypt
Keyboard, guitar / Techno-pop, dance-pop
This British musician and producer was one of the first artists to explore the possibilities of synthesizers and digital samplers in a straight pop-music context. Besides his dance hits ("She Blinded Me with Science" and "Hyperactive!") Dolby has played on Foreigner's *4* album, produced albums for Joni Mitchell and Prefab Sprout, collaborated with George Clinton (on their respective solo albums and Dolby's Cube project), and written music for the films *Howard the Duck* and *Gothic*.
    He began his career working with Lene Lovich (he wrote "New Toy" for her) and with Bruce Wooley & the Camera Club, a group that also featured Trevor Horn (Yes, Buggles), Geoff Downes (Yes, Asia), and Matthew Seligman (Soft Boys). —*Scott Bultman*

● **Golden Age of Wireless** / 1982 / Capitol 46009
This contains Dolby's biggest hit, the humorously quirky "She Blinded Me with Science." Highlights include "Radio Silence," "Europa and the Pirate Twins," "Windpower," "One of Our Submarines," and "Airwaves"—a track that should've been a single. All in all, this is a very solid collection of early-'80s synth-pop. —*Rick Clark*

Flat Earth / 1984 / Capitol 46028
A departure from the style of his debut, Dolby adds jazz and Joni Mitchellesque elements on this moody and atmospheric album to

warm his synth textures. Only "White City" and the single, "Hyperactive," feature the hard dance beats of his early hits. — *Scott Bultman*

Fats Domino

b. May 10, 1929, New Orleans, LA
Vocals / R&B, rock & roll
New Orleans has produced many musical legends over the years, but none has created a sound that was more recognizable, more influential, or more profitable than Fats Domino. Beginning with "The Fat Man" in 1949, Domino had an enviable run of chart success, selling more than 65 million records and chalking up 23 gold records. Although he's become a rock & roll deity—he was one of the first Rock & Roll Hall of Fame inductees—Domino made his name playing the same New Orleans R&B he'd always played. His best recordings were made for the Imperial label between 1949 and 1963. Of his scores of hits, "Ain't That a Shame," "Blueberry Hill," "I'm Walking," "Whole Lot of Lovin'," and "I'm Ready" were among the biggest. EMI's *They Call Me the Fat Man*, a 100-track boxed set, concisely chronicles Domino's sound and story. —*Jeff Hannusch*

★ **My Blue Heaven: Best of Fats Domino** / Jul. 30, 1990 / EMI America 92808
A crisp, well-thought-out collection that says it all. —*Bruce Eder*

☆ **They Call Me the Fat Man . . . : The Legendary Imperial Recordings** / 1991 / EMI America 96785
Hardcore lovers of Fats Domino's rolling boogie-style piano playing and easy Cajun-inflected tenor voice (if they're ready to plunk down the change for a boxed set) should find this four-CD, 100-song compilation (which includes all of his Imperial hits) a thorough baptism. Sonically, this set is very impressive. Many times when old tracks are cleaned up during remastering, the life gets processed out, but that's not evident here. The 84-page booklet is a fan's delight, with first-rate annotation and plenty of photos. —*Rick Clark*

Don & Dewey

b. , Pasadena, CA
Group / R&B
Wailing in tandem like twin Little Richards, Don & Dewey cut numerous blistering rockers for Specialty from 1957 to 1959 without registering a single hit, only to see other acts revive their songs to much greater acclaim. Don Harris and Dewey Terry were born and raised in Pasadena, CA, joining a group called the Squires and recording for Vita before branching off on their own.

Their Specialty output included the savage rockers "Jungle Hop," "Koko Joe" (written by Sonny Bono), and "Justine," the latter two later covered by the Righteous Brothers. Don & Dewey's Specialty discography also includes the original "I'm Leavin' It Up to You," a hit for Dale & Grace; "Big Boy Pete," ditto for the Olympics; and "Farmer John," the Premiers' only smash. Don laid down his guitar for a violin during the '60s and, billed as "Sugarcane" Harris, sawed his rocked-out fiddle beside John Mayall and Frank Zappa. —*Bill Dahl*

● **Jungle Hop** / 1991 / Specialty 7008
A solid best-of collection featuring the original versions of "Farmer John," "Koko Joe," and "Justine." —*Cub Koda*

Lonnie Donegan (Anthony James Donegan)

b. Apr. 29, 1931, Glasgow, Scotland
Vocals, guitar, banjo / Pop/rock
In Britain, Lonnie Donegan was the king of skiffle, a joyously amateurish interpretation of American folk, blues, and country songs that predated rock & roll. In 1954, Donegan's version of Leadbelly's "Rock Island Line" was an enormous hit in the United Kingdom (it also was successful in America) and set off a skiffle craze—thousands of teenagers formed their own skiffle combos and tried to emulate his spare sound with washboards, broomsticks, and other household items.

Donegan remained a star until Britain raised its own rock superstars with the Beatles in 1962. Although he stopped having hits, he never stopped performing, and he continued to explore different traditional music, from Cajun and Appalachian styles to old time, vaudeville style pub favorites right through the '80s. In the '90s, Donegan is not in perfect health, yet he continues to perform occasionally. —*Stephen Thomas Erlewine*

● **Collection** / 1989 / Castle 223
Containing all of his hits, this disc is the best compilation of all of the anthologies that clutter the market. —*Stephen Thomas Erlewine*

Donovan (Donovan Leitch)

b. Feb. 10, 1946, Glasgow, Scotland
Vocals / British invasion, folk-rock, psychedelic, singer/songwriter
Donovan (born Donovan Leitch), initially touted as the "British Invasion's Bob Dylan," recorded such topical tracks as "The Universal Soldier" and "Catch the Wind" in 1965. However, a new manager, Allen Klein (later to work with the Rolling Stones and the Beatles), and a new producer, Mickie Most (who also cut hits for the Animals, Herman's Hermits, and Jeff Beck), revealed that Donovan was much better suited to synthesizing folk with mystical hippie-pop. Between 1965 and 1969, Donovan scored a series of memorable hits, including "Sunshine Superman," "Mellow Yellow" (containing a Paul McCartney cameo), "Hurdy Gurdy Man" (with Jeff Beck), and "Atlantis." —*Rick Clark*

○ **Sunshine Superman** / 1966 / Epic 26217
Probably the singer/songwriter's best album, embracing folk, blues, and a druggy psychedelia, and driven by crisp rhythm guitars (especially on the title track). It starts to sound the same after a bit, but at its release, even this was a point of recommendation—it set a hazy, drugged-out mood. The use of the mono master helps, because it's punchier. —*Bruce Eder*

A Gift from a Flower to a Garden / 1967 / Epic 171
A blast from hippie past—a flower-decorated double album made up of precious trippy music spiced with a haunting melody or two ("Wear Your Love Like Heaven"). —*Bruce Eder*

Hurdy Gurdy Man / 1968 / Epic 26420
For this performer, this is a hard-rocking album, driven by some loud electric guitar subbing for sitar, which dresses up the plainer folk melodies and turns the title tune into a near-classic. —*Bruce Eder*

● **Donovan's Greatest Hits** / 1969 / Epic 26439
Entertaining but flawed collection of Donovan's psychedelic-era hits, fleshed out with too-languid rerecordings of his pre-CBS folk successes, including "Colours." It's unfortunate that the producers used the stereo versions, which don't sound nearly as good as the mono. —*Bruce Eder*

● **Troubadour: The Definitive Collection 1964-1976** / Aug. 4, 1992 / Epic 46986
This two-disc, 44-track retrospective album chronicles Donovan's decade-long career at Epic Records, with the few folk hits he recorded before joining the label and a couple of early demos added. All the hippie bits of the '60s are included, plus a judicious selection of the less successful '70s recordings. Good liner notes by Brian Hogg and Derek Taylor. —*William Ruhlmann*

The Doobie Brothers

b. Mar. 1970, San Jose, CA
Group / Pop/rock
The Doobie Brothers (*doobie* being slang for a marijuana joint) straddled FM rock and Top-40 pop better than most bands of the '70s, with their good-time grooves and melodies and solid musicianship. During the first part of their career (1970 to 1975), the Doobie Brothers scored with a batch of radio classics in "Listen to the Music," "Long Train Running," "China Grove," and the number-one hit "Black Water." With the arrival of soulful Steely Dan singer and keyboardist Michael McDonald, the Doobie Brothers took on a mellower, more sophisticated musical direction, giving passing nods to jazz and light funk along the way. "Takin' It to the Streets" showcased McDonald's contribution, to fine effect. Their 1977 album, *Living on the Fault Line*, is an artistic pinnacle of the band's new direction, but the number-one follow-up, *Minute by Minute*, was a much bigger success, containing hits "What a Fool Believes" and the title cut.

By the time *One Step Closer* was released in 1980, the Doobies' brand of slick California pop had reached the saturation point in fern bars across the land. The fact that Michael McDonald's aching vocals seemed to appear on every record from the West Coast ensured overkill. The band called it quits in 1981. The pre-McDonald lineup re-formed in 1987 and enjoyed a successful comeback. —*Rick Clark*

○ **Captain & Me** / 1973 / Warner Brothers 2694
Their best early album, featuring "China Grove." —*Dan Heilman*

● **Best of the Doobies** / 1976 / Warner Brothers 3112
A formidable bunch of hard-rock hits from 1972 to 1976. —*Dan Heilman*

○ **Best of the Doobies, Vol. 2** / 1981 / Warner Brothers 3612
The best of the Michael McDonald era. —*Dan Heilman*

The Doors

Group / Rock & roll
The Doors, one of the most influential and controversial rock bands of the 1960s, were formed in Los Angeles in 1965 by UCLA film students Ray Manzarek, keyboards, and Jim Morrison, vocals, with drummer John Densmore, and guitarist Robby Krieger. The group never added a bass player, and their sound was dominated by Manzarek's electric organ work and Morrison's deep, sonorous voice, with which he sang and intoned his highly poetic lyrics. The group signed to Elektra Records in 1966 and released its first album, *The Doors*, featuring the hit "Light My Fire," in 1967.
From the start, the Doors' focus was the charismatic Morrison, who proved increasingly unstable over the group's brief career. In 1969 Morrison was arrested for indecent exposure during a concert in Miami, an incident that nearly derailed the band. Nevertheless, the Doors managed to turn out a series of successful albums and singles through 1971, when, upon the completion of *L.A. Woman*, Morrison decamped for Paris. He died there, apparently of a drug overdose. The three surviving Doors tried to carry on without him, but ultimately disbanded. Yet the Doors' music and Morrison's legend continued to fascinate succeeding generations of rock fans: In the mid '80s, Morrison was as big a star as he'd been in the mid '60s, and Elektra has sold numerous quantities of the Doors' original albums plus reissues and releases of live material over the years, while publishers have flooded bookstores with Doors and Morrison biographies. In 1991, director Oliver Stone made *The Doors*, a feature film about the group starring Val Kilmer as Morrison. —*William Ruhlmann*

☆ **Doors** / Jan. 1967 / Dunhill 1023
One of the most remarkable debut albums in rock history introduced the powerful singing of Jim Morrison, his provocative lyrics, and the group's spare, direct guitar-and-organ sound. "Light My Fire" became an instant standard, but the album also contained such Doors classics as "Break on Through (to the Other Side)," "Twentieth Century Fox," and, of course, that Oedipal odyssey "The End." —*William Ruhlmann*

Strange Days / Feb. 1967 / Elektra 74014
Taking the next step, album number two is flawed but still moving. —*Jeff Tamarkin*

○ **Waiting for the Sun** / 1968 / Elektra 74024
Singles like "Hello, I Love You" and "The Unknown Soldier" are on *The Best of the Doors*, but many of the standouts on this album are gentle songs like "Summer's Almost Gone," "Yes, the River Knows," and "Wintertime Love," which demonstrate that Morrison and company can be lyrical without losing their power. —*William Ruhlmann*

Soft Parade / 1969 / Elektra 75005
Probably the most underrated Doors collection because the addition of horns and strings ("Wishful Sinful") turns it into a more exploratory album than their basic music usually attempted. But "Tell All the People" is the group at its most revolutionary, and the long title track is among its most ambitious. This included the hit "Touch Me" as well as "Wild Child," one of their best rockers. —*William Ruhlmann*

○ **Morrison Hotel/Hard Rock Cafe** / 1970 / Elektra 75007
A bluesy, hard-rock album that nevertheless contains some of Morrison's most visionary poetry. —*William Ruhlmann*

○ **L.A. Woman** / 1971 / Elektra 75011
Morrison's final testament shows him at the height of his ability to bring striking images to the lyrics of rock music, and the group produces some of its most trancelike music. —*William Ruhlmann*

○ **Weird Scenes inside the Gold Mine** / 1972 / Elektra 6001
A two-LP compilation that fills in the Doors hits not included on *13* and concentrates on some of their longer album tracks. —*William Ruhlmann*

★ **Best of the Doors** / 1974 / Elektra 60345
A well-chosen, 18-track compilation balancing the radio hits with the longer, more complex song poems. It's a good sampler, but this is one group for whom you need to hear the whole story. Reissued on CD in 1985 with one bonus track. —*William Ruhlmann*

In Concert / 1991 / Elektra 61082
The Doors could be erratic live, as this double CD shows. Still, it's a fair example of their in-concert charms. —*Jeff Tamarkin*

Lee Dorsey

b. Dec. 24, 1924, New Orleans, LA, d. Dec. 1, 1986
Vocals / R&B, soul
The effervescent approach of Lee Dorsey perfectly summarizes the infectious charm of early-'60s New Orleans R&B. Dorsey specialized in good-humored music with a touch of second-line funk thrown in to make it all the more irresistible. Although he had already waxed a couple of singles, Dorsey caught the country by total surprise in 1961 with his deceptively simple nursery rhyme-style "Ya Ya" on Bobby Robinson's Fury label. Arranged by prolific New Orleans pianist Allen Toussaint, the track proved an R&B chart-topper and a major pop hit to boot.
Dorsey's laconic vocal charms served him well on "Ya Ya" and the Earl King-penned follow-up "Do Re Mi," and the mid '60s found him working with Toussaint on the funky smashes "Ride Your Pony" and "Working in the Coal Mine," this time for Amy Records. It is little remembered that Dorsey was responsible for the original 1970 version of Toussaint's "Yes We Can," revived to much greater acclaim by the Pointer Sisters (who tacked on an extra "Can"). By all accounts, Dorsey remained an exceedingly humble R&B star who preferred tinkering with cars to extensively touring the country. He died of emphysema in 1986. —*Bill Dahl*

○ **Ya Ya** / 1962 / Relic 7013
Terrific overview of the good-humored New Orleans singer's early-'60s classics for Bobby Robinson's Fury label. Direct-from-masters sound quality. —*Bill Dahl*

● **Holy Cow!: Best of Lee Dorsey** / 1985 / Arista 8387
A nice single-disc anthology featuring the best known cuts and biggest pop hits of New Orleans R&B and soul singer Lee Dorsey, one of the Crescent City's best comic/novelty artists and a fine traditional R&B vocalist as well. The title track, "Working in a Coal Mine" and "Ride Your Pony" are superb songs that use the second line rhythm, plus boast outstanding arrangements, clever lyrics, and great vocals. —*Ron Wynn*

Golden Classics / Collectables 5082
Covers Dorsey's Allen Toussaint-produced mid-'60s soul hits as well as some earlier material on the Relic set. —*Bill Dahl*

Downliners Sect

Group / British invasion, rock & roll
Of all the British R&B bands to follow in the Rolling Stones' footsteps, the Downliners Sect were arguably the rawest. The Sect didn't so much interpret the sound of Chess Records as attack it, with a finesse that made the Pretty Things seem positively suave in comparison. Long on crude energy and hoarse vocals, but short on originality and songwriting talent, the band never had a British hit, although they had some sizable singles in other European countries. Despite their lack of commercial success or appeal, the band managed to record three albums and various EPs and singles between 1963 and 1966, with detours into country rock and an EP of death-rock tunes. Although they recorded afterwards, it is the Sect's early work that continues to attract connoisseurs of '60s garage and punk rock. —*Richie Unterberger*

Sect / 1964 / Columbia 1658
Their rawest and most R&B-oriented, firmly rooted in the same influences as the Stones and Pretty Things. Includes punk covers of Chuck Berry, Bo Diddley, Muddy Waters, Jimmy Reed, et al., and a few originals in the same vein. —*Richie Unterberger*

● **Rock Sects In** / 1966 / Columbia 6028
Their wildly erratic third album includes some tepid material, but also has some of their best tracks, especially the vicious run-through of the early British rock & roll standard "Brand New Cadillac." It's most notable for the appearance— through God knows what channels—of "Why Don't You Smile Now," which

was written by Lou Reed, John Cale, and two unknowns before the Velvet Underground formed. —*Richie Unterberger*

Nick Drake

b. Jun. 19, 1948, Worchestershire, UK, d. Nov. 25, 1972
Vocals / Singer/songwriter
Mention the name Nick Drake and it's likely that Van Morrison or Tim Buckley will be mentioned as well. Fans asked to provide a one-word description of Drake's music would most frequently mention "haunting." While his works were known to only a cultish few in his lifetime, the legacy of Nick Drake looms ever larger as the years pass. In discovering the music, most people gravitate to Drake's second album, *Bryter Layter*, a seemingly cheery and agreeable work that stands in sharp contast to the stark and desperate *Pink Moon*. Not even the lush, baroque orchestrations of his first record, *Five Leaves Left*, can mask the real-life gloom—not a studied pose—that Drake was unable to escape from. All three of Drake's actual albums remain astonishingly valuable, with Joe Boyd's production of *Bryter Layter* being a particularly standout effort. That Drake's music has sold increasingly well in recent years comes as little surprise, since Nick Drake has become a most trendy name among contemporary artists. It is safe to say that the sad but beautiful music of Nick Drake will continue to inspire for years to come. —*Steve Aldrich*

● **Five Leaves Left** / 1969 / Hannibal 4434
Nick Drake's debut album skillfully augments his haunting folk-based songs with tasteful string arrangements that accentuate the gorgeous melancholy of his music. —*Stephen Thomas Erlewine*

○ **Bryter Layter** / 1970 / Hannibal 4435
While the strings on Nick Drake's second album are more prominent, they rarely take away from the impact of his music, which is significantly less sad on this record. However, *Bryter Layter* isn't lighthearted—it's a reflective piece of music that gains power from its own introspection. —*Stephen Thomas Erlewine*

○ **Pink Moon** / 1972 / Hannibal 4436
On his last album, Nick Drake strips away all of the excess instrumentation of his first two albums, as well as keeping his songs to their bare essentials. The result is a stark, brilliant album of despair, loneliness, and alienation that is startling in its emotional power. —*Stephen Thomas Erlewine*

○ **Fruit Tree** / 1986 / Hannibal 5402
This multidisc album contains the complete works of this enigmatic British singer/songwriter. —*William Ruhlmann*

Time of No Reply / 1986 / Hannibal 1318
A collection of ten previously unreleased tracks recorded between 1968 and 1974, the songs on *Time of No Reply* rank with Nick Drake's finest work. —*Stephen Thomas Erlewine*

Dramarama

Group / Alternative rock, rock & roll
Dramarama comes on like a hybird of the Clash and the Replacements, playing a spiky, emotionally charged political rock & roll. Unfortunately, their albums have, for the most part, been ignored by both the mainstream and the alternative audiences, leaving them to unjustly suffer unheard in the small gap between the two genres. —*Stephen Thomas Erlewine*

● **Vinyl** / 1991 / Chameleon 61242
With *Vinyl*, Dramarama have captured everything that was good about '70s rock & roll. Hard driving, distorted, and muddy, this sounds more like a classic Rolling Stones album than the Stones themselves have come up with in over a decade. The sound of a turntable needle on the run-out groove midway through (marking the end of side 1) adds authenticity. A cover of the Stones' "Memo from Turner" is a nice touch too. —*Chris Woodstra*

Dramatics

Group / Soul
This popular Detroit R&B vocal aggregation scored numerous hits for Volt and maintained their momentum through the disco era. The early Dramatics hits for Volt lived up to the group's billing with the emphatic vocals of Ron Banks powering the funky "Whatcha See Is Whatcha Get," their first big-seller in 1971, and the R&B chart-topping ballad "In the Rain" the next year. The quintet was just as successful later in the decade, signing with

ABC in 1975 and scoring repeatedly throughout disco-fever days. —*Bill Dahl*

Whatcha See Is Whatcha Get / 1971 / Stax 4111
Great debut album. A Tony Hestor creation. —*Richard Pack*

○ **Dramatically Yours** / 1973 / Stax 8523
One of their finest albums. The Dramatics had solidified their sound and personnel in the early '70s: L. J. Reynolds was now doing the leads, with Ron Banks's feathery falsetto and Willie Ford's booming baritone perfectly positioned at the top and bottom of the arrangements and Reynolds and Lenny Mayes right in the center. Though they didn't generate much crossover success, they were on the R&B charts regularly with the singles pulled from the album. —*Ron Wynn*

● **Best of the Dramatics** / 1976 / Stax 60-003
A solid compilation that includes the hits "Whatcha See Is Whatcha Get," "In the Rain," "Fell for You," and other equally good but lesser-known tracks. —*AMG*

Dream Syndicate

Group / Alternative rock, psychedelic
Of all the bands of the so-called "paisley underground" Los Angeles bands of the '80s, the Steve Wynn-led Dream Syndicate was the one that gained the largest audience and was arguably the best of the lot. Instead of lifting riffs from old Pink Floyd, Jefferson Airplane, or Byrds albums, Wynn relied on the darker sounds of the Velvet Underground and Neil Young, creating a dense, guitar-based pseudo-psychedelia that either soared on ballads or drilled on mid-tempo rockers. It was tailor-made for college radio success, where they received a fair amount of airplay. Dream Syndicate recorded several impressive records over their career, yet they never became big rock stars. The band called it quits in 1989, with Wynn pursuing a solo career. —*Stephen Thomas Erlewine*

Days of Wine & Roses / 1984 / Slash 23844
Karl Precoda plays the kind of noisy guitar associated with the Velvet Underground, while lead singer Steve Wynn pursues his private demons n this perfectly realized low-budget '80s rock record. —*William Ruhlmann*

Ghost Stories / 1988 / Enigma 73341
Paul B. Cutler plays the kind of noisy guitar associated with Neil Young and Crazy Horse, while lead singer Steve Wynn continues to pursue his private demons on what is nevertheless more of a mainstream rock record, maybe courtesy of Young's producer, Elliot Mazer. —*William Ruhlmann*

● **Tell Me When It's Over: The Best of Dream Syndicate** / 1992 / Rhino 70373
These 15 tracks contain the cream of the crop of this Los Angeles band's independent and major label work. Among the highlights are "When You Smile," "Tell Me When It's Over," and "Halloween" off their 1982 Ruby/Slash EP *Days of Wine and Roses*. The fine remastering captures their dense Velvet Underground-style rock in all its trashy glory. The booklet is loaded with a detailed history, many photos, lyrics, and track and personnel listings. —*Rick Clark*

The Drifters

Group / R&B
The Drifters were the longest-lasting of the '50s doo-wop groups simply because they were the best. What other vocal group from those days produced such 20th-century marvels as Clyde McPhatter and Ben E. King? What other group survived numerous personnel changes and changes in audience tastes, keeping their name in the charts for 12 straight years? Doo-wop is certainly full of mythological groups, celebrated as much for their obscurity as their music. The Drifters are the group that turned the myth into fact.

Clyde McPhatter was already an R&B star when Atlantic's Ahmet Ertegun signed him in 1953, thanks to his work with Billy Ward's Dominoes. After leaving them, McPhatter assembled a group to support his glorious, soaring vocals, and in 1953 the Drifters landed their first hit with Jesse Stone's "Money Honey." A slew of meticulously recorded classics followed: "Let the Boogie Woogie Roll," "Such a Night," "Honey Love," and "White Christmas" are among the best. McPhatter took off for a solo career in 1954 but was amply replaced by Johnny Moore, who was on hand when the group recorded three of their finest songs: "Ruby Baby," "Your Promise to Be Mine," and "Adorable."

Drifters manager George Threadwell disbanded the group in 1958 and found an ensemble called the Crowns, who had a lead singer named Ben E. King. A new Drifters was born. Under the wings of Jerry Lieber and Mike Stoller, this new outfit established their own identity in 1959 with the Latin-tinged "There Goes My Baby," a tour de force for King and the first R&B song to include strings, which ushered in a new era of Black music, known as soul. King departed in 1960, but thanks to a string of songs written by the likes of Doc Pomus and Mort Shuman, the Drifters, with Rudy Lewis and Johnny Moore taking leads, became a veritable hit factory. "Save the Last Dance for Me," "On Broadway," "Up on the Roof," and "This Magic Moment" all helped define the sound of soul music and define an era, with their tugging romanticism, dancing strings, and musical innovation and sophistication. —*John Floyd*

☆ **Let the Boogie Woogie Roll—Greatest Hits (1953-1958)** / 1988 / Atlantic 81927
Let the Boogie Woogie Roll—Greatest Hits is the definitive account of the early group and Clyde McPhatter's greatest sides. —*Bruce Eder*

☆ **All-Time Greatest Hits & More: 1959-1965** / 1988 / Atlantic 81931
All the Greatest Hits & More: 1959-1965 is a towering and magnificent collection of some of the best popular R&B ever done this side of Sam Cooke. —*Bruce Eder*

★ **Very Best of the Drifters** / 1993 / Telstar 2280
Combining all of the greatest hits from both the Clyde McPhatter and Ben E. King eras, the single-disc *The Very Best of the Drifters* serves as the perfect introduction to the seminal R&B vocal group. —*Stephen Thomas Erlewine*

Drivin' n Cryin'

Group / Rock & roll
This Georgia quartet boldly mixes country and bluegrass tunes alongside pedal-to-the-metal hard rock and, more often than not, manages to pull it off. It's an over-amped '90s version of the Buffalo Springfield style of earthy rock eclecticism. —*Rick Clark*

Scarred but Smarter / 1986 / Island 842854
Their debut boldly mixes everything from countryish sendups to death-rock. It almost works. Certainly it's an engaging listen. Highlights: "Stand Up and Fight for It," "Another Scarlet Butterfly," and "Saddle on the Side of the Road." —*Rick Clark*

Whisper Tames the Lion / 1987 / Island 842855
The juxtaposition of diverse genres continues, with greater success. Produced by Anton Fier (Grapes of Wrath, Joe Henry). —*Rick Clark*

○ **Mystery Road** / 1989 / Island 842661
New guitarist Buren Fowler adds more punch to the band's sound. Songwriter Kevn Kinney's mature grasp of various genres is shown to great effect, from reckless rockers like "Toy Never Played With" to more laidback tracks like "Peacemaker." —*Rick Clark*

● **Fly Me Courageous** / 1991 / Island 848000
This Atlanta quartet's most fully realized synthesis of aggressive hard rock, country-rock, and folk-rock. Visceral production by Geoff Workman. Standout tracks include the hyperdrive of "Rush Hour" and "Lost in the Shuffle," as well as "Around the Block Again," "Chain Reaction," "Build a Fire," and the title cut. —*Rick Clark*

The Dukes of Stratosphear

Group / Psychedelic, alternative pop/rock
The Dukes of Stratosphear (conceived in 1987) are the psychedelic alter-personalities of the English alternative pop/rock band XTC. —*Rick Clark*

● **Chips from the Chocolate Fireball** / 1987 / David Geffen Co. 24169
Fans of late-'60s psychedelia will love this affectionate Rutles-esque collaboration between XTC (posing as the Dukes) and producer John Leckie (Posies, Let's Active). *Chips from the Chocolate Fireball* is loaded with playful tips of the hat to artists like the Move, the Electric Prunes, early Pink Floyd, the Yardbirds, Spirit, the Zombies, the Beach Boys, and (of course) the Beatles. By the

way, this is a compilation of the Dukes' *25-O-Clock* EP and the full-length album *Psonic Psunspot.* —*Rick Clark*

The Duprees

Group / Doo-wop
Specializing in updated renditions of '40s and '50s pop fare, the Duprees had a classy sound that harked back to an earlier era. Formed as the Parisians in Jersey City, they were discovered by George Paxton, who ran Coed Records in New York. Paxton convinced the quartet to change their name, and they hit big their first time out in 1962 with a polished revival of Jo Stafford's "You Belong to Me." Most sides cut for Coed were in the same big-band mold, including "My Own True Love" and "Have You Heard." Lead singer Joe Canzano left the group in 1964, and the Duprees moved to Columbia the next year, with minimal success. —*Bill Dahl*

● **You Belong to Me** / 1962 / Collectables 9089
Debut album, featuring the title track hit and 11 other doo-wop classics done in typical early-'60s New York City production style. —*Cub Koda*

○ **Have You Heard** / 1963 / Collectables 9091
Second album, companion piece to *You Belong to Me.* —*Cub Koda*

Duran Duran

Group / New wave, dance-pop, pop/rock
Duran Duran (Nick Rhodes, keyboards; John Taylor, bass; Simon Le Bon, vocals; Andy Taylor, guitar; Roger Taylor, drums) formed in 1978 in Birmingham, England, although the final lineup was not set until Simon Le Bon joined in 1980. Taking their name from a character in the Jane Fonda film *Barbarella,* their style of dance music was quickly drawn into the new romantic movement of the British punk/new wave scene. These so-called haircut bands were inspired to their fashion-centered look and hip-synthesizer, neo-disco style by bands like Roxy Music. Duran Duran's lush arrangements and distinct vocal sound, combined with an aggressive new wave, funk-rhythm section caught the attention of the mass market. But it was their visual appeal and exotic/erotic videos for "Girls on Film," "Hungry Like the Wolf," and "Rio" on the newborn MTV that catapulted them into concert arenas and multi-platinum stardom.

Although they were unabashed teen idols, the members tried to gain more critical respect with sideline efforts like Power Station (for John and Andy Taylor) and Arcadia (for LeBon, Roger Taylor, and Rhodes). After these experiments, the band went through a series of lineup changes and artistic wanderings as their teenage fans began to outgrow them. But none of their later works were as successful as *Rio* or *Seven and the Ragged Tiger.* With the end virtually in sight, Duran Duran released the hits/retrospective package *Decade* and one final studio album. The band dissolved but, defying all expectations, they reunited in 1993 with a new album and two very successful singles, "Ordinary World" and "Come Undone." —*Scott Bultman*

● **Decade—Greatest Hits** / Nov. 15, 1989 / Capitol 93178
All their hits—including "Hungry Like the Wolf," "Rio," "Is There Something I Should Know," "Union of the Snake," "The Wild Boys," "Notorious," "I Don't Want Your Love," "The Reflex," and "A View to a Kill"—in a well-selected package. —*Dan Heilman*

○ **Duran Duran** / 1993 / Capitol 98876
Out of nowhere, Duran Duran came back in early 1993 with a new album and a huge hit, "Ordinary World." Duran Duran, now down to a three-piece, doesn't sound like it did during their glory days, but not all that much has changed. Instead of personifying the days of early '80s dance synth-pop, the music is smooth dance-pop for the '90s. Taken on its own terms, *Duran Duran* works every bit as well as *Rio* or *Seven and the Ragged Tiger.* "Ordinary World" and "Come Undone" are wonderful pop singles that sit between some passable album tracks and the occasional embarrassment—namely the wretched cover of the Velvet Underground's "Femme Fatale." In other words, Duran Duran are back and they are as good as they ever were. —*Stephen Thomas Erlewine*

Ian Dury

Vocals / New wave

When Ian Dury released his first record in 1977, he was 35 years old, yet he fit in perfectly with the U.K. punk scene. Dury had energy to spare with his raucous rock & roll and surprisingly incisive lyrics, possibly fueled by anger over the lasting effects of childhood polio. Yet Dury's music wasn't full of bile—it was joyful noise-making. Dury never became a star in America—perhaps his thick Cockney accent was impenetrable—yet he became a beloved figure in the United Kingdom, releasing records until 1984 and performing throughout the '80s and '90s. —*Stephen Thomas Erlewine*

● **Sex & Drugs & Rock 'n' Roll: Best of Ian Dury and the Blockheads** / 1992 / Rhino 70270
A fine 18-track collection that features nearly every worthwhile track Ian Dury ever recorded. —*AMG*

Bob Dylan (Robert Zimmerman)

b. May 24, 1941, Duluth, MN
Vocals, guitar, piano / Singer/songwriter, folk-rock, rock & roll, country rock
The greatest songwriter of his generation and a figure of incalculable influence on popular music from the '60s on, Bob Dylan is also (with the possible exception of Elvis Presley) the most important individual ever in rock music.

Dylan moved from Minnesota to New York City in 1961, at the age of 19, as an acolyte of folksinger Woody Guthrie, although he had played rock music in the late '50s. He met Guthrie (who was slowly dying in a hospital) and was quickly taken up by the New York folk community. He signed to Columbia Records and, in March 1962, released his first album, *Bob Dylan*, consisting largely of folk/blues covers. By this time, however, he had begun to write original songs, many in the philosophical-political style of his Greenwich Village compatriots (though far superior in quality), the best early example being "Blowin' in the Wind." Many of these songs were on Dylan's second album, *The Freewheelin' Bob Dylan*, released in May 1963. That summer, the popular folk group Peter, Paul & Mary took "Blowin' in the Wind" to number two in the national charts. Thereafter, Bob Dylan songs became favorites among many pop and folk performers. As the result of such exposure, *Freewheelin'* became a chart hit in September 1963.

Dylan followed with two albums in 1964, the heavily protest-oriented *The Times They Are a-Changin'* and the more introspective *Another Side of Bob Dylan*. In 1965, he began recording and playing concerts with rock musicians, which vastly increased his following but also led to controversy within the folk community. His singles "Like a Rolling Stone" and "Positively 4th Street" were Top-Ten hits, as were the albums *Bringing It All Back Home* and *Highway 61 Revisited*, and the "folk-rock" sound of his music could be heard on any number of other artists' records, many of the songs written by Dylan himself. Dylan undertook a world tour in 1966 to promote the double album *Blonde on Blonde*, which featured the number-two single "Rainy Day Women #12 & 35." That summer he was in a motorcycle accident, and he withdrew from public view for a year and a half, meanwhile recording the informal material later released as *The Basement Tapes*.

When Dylan returned to action in early 1968, it was with the quieter *John Wesley Harding* album, followed in 1969 by the country-flavored *Nashville Skyline* and its Top-Ten single "Lay Lady Lay." Critics expecting Dylan's more complex work were disappointed, and they savaged his two-disc *Self-Portrait* in 1970, though most saw *New Morning*, released only a few months later, as a return to form.

Dylan was not much heard from in the early '70s (he played at George Harrison's Bangladesh benefit concert in 1971, and in 1973 he appeared in the film *Pat Garrett and Billy the Kid* and wrote its score), but he returned in 1974 with a national concert tour and the number-one album *Planet Waves*. This was followed in 1975 by *Blood on the Tracks*, regarded by many as his best collection of the decade. The same year, Dylan organized a roving band of musicians as the Rolling Thunder Revue and toured the Northeast, appearing in other parts of the country in 1976.

A film crew was part of the entourage, and Dylan put together a sprawling film, *Renaldo & Clara*, released in 1978. With that done, he went on an international tour and released a new album, *Street-Legal*. In 1979, Dylan converted to Christianity and released the first of three overtly religious albums, *Slow Train Coming*.

The religious fervor had become less apparent by the time of *Infidels*, in 1983, and Dylan has released several excellent albums since, while touring more or less continually. The '80s and early '90s have also seen the welcome legitimate release of much previously unissued vintage Dylan material (some of it previously widely available on bootlegs). —*William Ruhlmann*

○ **Bob Dylan** / Mar. 19, 1962 / Columbia 8579
For the most part, Bob Dylan's debut album positions him as an interpretive singer of rural folk songs—and already influential at that. The Animals found "House of the Rising Sun" on this album, while Led Zeppelin borrowed "In My Time of Dyin'." But the most striking track is the Dylan original "Song to Woody," his tribute to Woody Guthrie, which leaves no doubt he intends to carry on in his mentor's footsteps. —*William Ruhlmann*

☆ **Freewheelin' Bob Dylan** / May 27, 1963 / Columbia 8786
The most important collection of original songs issued in the '60s. "Don't Think Twice, It's All Right," "Girl from the North Country," "A Hard Rain's a-Gonna Fall," "Masters of War," and, especially, "Blowin' in the Wind" have long since become standards, and their sheer range, from bitter protest to wry romantic regret, is astonishing. And this is not to mention the absurd apocalyptic humor of some of the album's other tracks. The songs were so strong that they put across Dylan's limited, rough vocal style at a time when such a voice normally would have been completely unacceptable in a professional singer. This album transformed the notion of what "good" singing was. —*William Ruhlmann*

○ **Times They Are a-Changin'** / Jan. 13, 1964 / Columbia 8905
Dylan devoted most of his third album to hard, uncompromising topical or "protest" songs, starting with the anthemic title track and continuing through "The Lonesome Death of Hattie Carroll," "Ballad of Hollis Brown," "Only a Pawn in Their Game," and "With God on Our Side." —*William Ruhlmann*

☆ **Another Side of Bob Dylan** / Aug. 8, 1964 / Columbia 08993
The first of two transitional albums in which Dylan moved first beyond protest and then beyond folk music. Here, in songs like "Chimes of Freedom" and "My Back Pages," he suggested that social issues were much more complicated than the increasingly polarized times made them seem. His lyrics, meanwhile, also became more complicated and poetic. Other singers would mine this album for hits with "All I Really Want to Do" and "It Ain't Me, Babe." —*William Ruhlmann*

☆ **Bringing It All Back Home** / Mar. 22, 1965 / Columbia 9128
Dylan added a bluesy rock-band backing for the first half of this album, and the lyrics of the new songs are compendiums of allusions and witticisms—"Subterranean Homesick Blues," "Maggie's Farm," "Mr. Tambourine Man," "It's All Right, Ma (I'm Only Bleeding)." Even the love songs achieve a new poetic height: "She Belongs to Me," "Love Minus Zero/No Limit," "It's All Over Now, Baby Blue." —*William Ruhlmann*

☆ **Highway 61 Revisited** / Aug. 30, 1965 / Columbia 9189
Dylan only upped the ante, making more extensive use of a crack backup band including Al Kooper and Michael Bloomfield to play his signature song, "Like a Rolling Stone," and other articulate, poetic, and incredibly bitter songs, notably "Ballad of a Thin Man" and "Desolation Row." The gold-disc version possesses a fuller bottom end, and you can hear instruments in the mix with greater detail than ever before, particularly all of Harvey Brooks's bass parts (including his mistakes) and kick drum. (The gold disc available from DCC Compact Classics offers improved fidelity and the complete original artwork.) —*William Ruhlmann*

☆ **Blonde on Blonde** / May 16, 1966 / Columbia 841
The bitterness was transmuted into humor and absurdity on this remarkable album, in which Dylan's gush of wordplay seems endlessly inventive, his wit razor sharp, and his world-weariness overwhelming. The music, meanwhile, has coalesced into a rock backing that influences every musician who hears it. —*William Ruhlmann*

★ **Bob Dylan's Greatest Hits** / Mar. 27, 1967 / Columbia 9463
A ten-song retrospective of the work of the most impressive—and most protean—singer/songwriter of the period from 1963 to 1966. While this album is listed as the "pick" of this period of Dylan's career, due to its general accessibility, a full understanding of the popular music of the '60s is impossible unless the listener is familiar with its three predecessors. *Greatest Hits* combines folk-protest standards like "Blowin' in the Wind" and "The

Times They Are a-Changin'" with his folk-rock hits "Like a Rolling Stone" and "Rainy Day Women #12 & 35." — *William Ruhlmann*

☆ **John Wesley Harding** / 1968 / Columbia 9604
A quieter, simpler album than those Dylan had made in the mid '60s, this "comeback" record nevertheless contained open-ended, parable-like songs, the most memorable of which has turned out to be "All Along the Watchtower." — *William Ruhlmann*

☆ **Nashville Skyline** / Apr. 9, 1969 / Columbia 9825
Dylan reached a sales peak with this album of simple, country-inflected songs (including "Lay Lady Lay"). — *William Ruhlmann*

Self Portrait / Jun. 8, 1970 / Columbia 30050
That Dylan was suffering a writer's block should have been apparent from the skimpy *Nashville Skyline*, but he shocked his following by turning out this two-record set mostly devoted to covers of songs by the Everly Brothers and Simon and Garfunkel. A few tracks were drawn from Dylan's concert performance on the Isle of Wight on Aug. 31, 1969, and they proved ragged. For an audience accustomed to Dylan's classic '60s albums, this first album of the '70s was a crushing disappointment. — *William Ruhlmann*

○ **New Morning** / Oct. 21, 1970 / Columbia 30290
While retaining some of the bucolic, sunny outlook of his recent work, Dylan partially turned back to a grittier rock sound (Al Kooper again in the mix) and to the more ironic, poetic lyrics of his mid-'60s songs. — *William Ruhlmann*

★ **Bob Dylan's Greatest Hits, Vol. 2** / Nov. 17, 1971 / Columbia 31120
A grab-bag of material dating back to 1963, this sprawling two-disc set is notable for its rarities, especially the 1971 single "Watching the River Flow" and the 1963 live performance of "Tomorrow Is a Long Time." — *William Ruhlmann*

Pat Garrett & Billy the Kid / Jul. 13, 1973 / Columbia 32460
Dylan's soundtrack for this Sam Peckinpah-directed Western, in which he co-starred, consists of some folkish instrumentals, several takes of a ballad called "Billy," and "Knockin' on Heaven's Door," a simple song that has become one of his best-remembered compositions. — *William Ruhlmann*

Planet Waves / Jan. 17, 1974 / Columbia 37637
A companion work to its predecessor, *New Morning,* this first album to be recorded with Dylan's backup group, the Band, mixes pronouncements of marital and familial contentment with severe criticisms of the singer himself and others. Contains "Forever Young." — *William Ruhlmann*

Before the Flood / Jun. 20, 1974 / Columbia 37661
This double album chronicles Bob Dylan and the Band's U.S. tour of January and February 1974. It features souped-up performances of many of Dylan's hits and best songs as well as a good selection of work by the Band. — *William Ruhlmann*

★ **Blood on the Tracks** / Jan. 17, 1975 / Columbia 33235
A stunning, mature statement in which the songwriter faced the conflicting elements of his life, the uncertainties of life in general, and the virtues of kindness and generosity. Incidentally, he also invented new songwriting structures and composed some of the most appealing music of his career. Still perhaps Dylan's most listenable and compelling album, this best represents his post-'60s work. — *William Ruhlmann*

☆ **Basement Tapes** / Jun. 26, 1975 / Columbia 33682
A two-disc set of ad hoc performances from 1967, albeit slightly refurbished for this release, *The Basement Tapes* provides the missing link between Dylan's long, poetic songs of the mid '60s and the shorter, more direct songs of the late '60s. Some of the songs had already become well known: "Too Much of Nothing," "Tears of Rage," "This Wheel's on Fire," and "You Ain't Goin' Nowhere." — *William Ruhlmann*

☆ **Desire** / Jan. 16, 1976 / Columbia 33893
A rough-and-tumble collection cut with a band Dylan was assembling for the Rolling Thunder tour. "Hurricane" recounts the tale of an unjustly imprisoned boxer, "Romance in Durango" and "Black Diamond Bay" are short stories in song, and "Sara" is a last plaintive plea from the singer to his wife. — *William Ruhlmann*

Street Legal / Jun. 15, 1978 / Columbia 35453

Using a big band assembled for a world tour, Dylan presents a group of songs, some of which are as imagistic—and as bitter—as his mid-'60s material. Particularly notable are the tone poem "Changing of the Guards" and the desperate but moving "Senior." — *William Ruhlmann*

Slow Train Coming / Aug. 18, 1979 / Columbia 36120
Among Dylan's best-played (members of Dire Straits participate) and best-produced recordings, this album reflects Dylan's religious conversion. At its best, on "Gotta Serve Somebody" and "When You Gonna Wake Up," the album presents cautionary messages similar to those Dylan had served up throughout his career. — *William Ruhlmann*

Saved / Jun. 20, 1980 / Columbia 36553
Just as fervent as he was on *Slow Train Coming,* Dylan is less inspired (sorry) as a songwriter here, and his preachiness is likely to be a bit much even for believers. — *William Ruhlmann*

Shot of Love / Aug. 12, 1981 / Columbia 37496
Dylan's need to sing only about his faith recedes, and his muse returns, notably on "Every Grain of Sand," one of his finest '80s songs. In 1985, this album was rereleased with the addition of the non-LP B-side "The Groom's Still Waiting at the Altar," another of Dylan's better later songs. — *William Ruhlmann*

○ **Infidels** / Nov. 1, 1983 / Columbia 38819
Dylan emerged from his overt references to Christianity with his sense of moral outrage reawakened. He expressed it in songs defending Israel and unions on this impassioned collection, which also includes "Jokerman"—as impressive a piece of socially conscious poetry as he'd ever produced—and the love songs "Sweetheart Like You" and "Don't Fall Apart on Me Tonight." — *William Ruhlmann*

○ **Empire Burlesque** / Jun. 8, 1985 / Columbia 40110
Dylan's strongest song collection since *Blood on the Tracks,* this album also benefits from excellent backup work by members of Tom Petty's Heartbreakers, among others, and a remix by dance expert Arthur Baker. Dylan himself sounds unusually engaged as well, especially on such songs as "Emotionally Yours" (later an R&B hit for the O'Jays) and the moving autobiographical folk ballad "Dark Eyes." — *William Ruhlmann*

☆ **Biograph** / Oct. 28, 1985 / Columbia 38830
A five-LP, three-CD retrospective of Dylan's first 20 years of recording, with an emphasis on presenting some of the mountain of unreleased songs that began leaking out unofficially in the late '60s. The only reason this massive, brilliantly executed album is not listed as an essential pick is its expense—in fact, it's not a bad place to start in trying to appreciate the whole of Dylan's achievement. — *William Ruhlmann*

Knocked Out Loaded / Aug. 8, 1986 / Columbia 40439
A hodgepodge of tracks recorded between 1984 and 1986, some written by others, some in collaboration. Mostly dispensable, it is saved from a "poor" rating by the rambling "Brownsville Girl," co-written with playwright Sam Shepard. — *William Ruhlmann*

Oh Mercy / Sep. 22, 1989 / Columbia 45281
This stunning album demonstrated that, after more than 25 years, Dylan was perfectly capable of writing songs of topical concern, high poetry, and unflinching self-examination to match any of his best work of the '60s and '70s. — *William Ruhlmann*

○ **Bootleg Series** / Mar. 26, 1991 / Columbia 47382
The floodgates opened with the release of this 58-song collection of outtakes and unreleased songs from throughout Dylan's career—an outpouring that demonstrated what the bootleggers and their customers had known all along: Dylan's throwaways are better than everyone else's keepers. It's amazing to think that, while turning out some of the most impressive albums of his time, Dylan was holding back material often equally good. — *William Ruhlmann*

Good as I Been to You / Oct. 27, 1992 / Columbia 53200
After a scattered decade's worth of albums ranging from terrific to terrible, Bob Dylan's second release of the '90s is a return to the acoustic folk that established his career in the early '60s. Naturally, it's not as breathtaking as *The Freewheelin' Bob Dylan* or his debut album, but it is an expert collection of standards by an expert folksinger. *Good as I Been to You* also proves he's a great guitarist, too. — *Stephen Thomas Erlewine*

World Gone Wrong / 1993 / Columbia

Although it follows the same formula as *Good As I Been to You,* *World Gone Wrong* cuts deeper. Dylan's collection of (mainly) obscure blues and folk songs is genuinely moving, one of his best albums of the past decade. On *World Gone Wrong,* Dylan says more with other people's songs than most do with their own, creating a vicious, worried commentary about modern society with a collection of traditional songs. — *Stephen Thomas Erlewine*

(E)

Vocals / Pop/rock
Virginia singer/songwriter and multi-instrumentalist (E) projects a humorously idiosyncratic loser (Woody Allen meets Brian Wilson in the sandbox) mentality. In fact, (E)'s wistful melancholy and tainted hopefulness, as well as his delicately quirky melodicism and dense production smarts, recall the reclusive Beach Boy's better moments. — *Rick Clark*

● **A Man Called (E)** / 1992 / Polydor 511570
A Man Called (E) is a wonderful collection of pop gems, tapped from the soul of the Beach Boys' *Pet Sounds, Tumbleweed Connection*-era Elton John, *White Album* Beatles, and early Todd Rundgren. (E) performed practically every instrument in this keyboard-rich production. Highlights from this impressive debut are "Hello Cruel World," "Fitting in with the Misfits," and "Are You and Me Gonna Happen." — *Rick Clark*

○ **Broken Toy Shop** / Dec. 7, 1993 / Polydor 519976
On his second album, (E) offers more of the same highly crafted pop-rock that graced his debut. Although the overall quality of songs is just a notch lower than his first album, *Broken Toy Shop* nevertheless features many delightful pop gems. — *Stephen Thomas Erlewine*

The Eagles

Group / Country-rock, pop/rock
The Eagles were among the most successful rock groups of the '70s, and their blend of country, folk, and rock continues to sell well in catalog. The group's four original members were Los Angeles session and group veterans assembled by producer John Boylan in 1970 as backup musicians for Linda Ronstadt on her *Silk Purse* album. They then served as her backup band for two years. The four were Glenn Frey, guitarist; Bernie Leadon, banjo and mandolin; Randy Meisner, bass; and Don Henley, drums. All four sang, though Henley and Frey took most leads. Signed to Ronstadt's label, Asylum, they issued their first album, *Eagles,* in June 1972. It was a moderate hit (going gold a year and a half later) and produced the Top-40 hits "Take It Easy" (written by Frey and Jackson Browne), "Witchy Woman" (number 9), and "Peaceful Easy Feeling."

The second Eagles album, a semi-concept album called *Desperado* (1973) that emphasized an "outlaw" image, was somewhat less successful. For their third album, *On the Border* (1974), the group added guitarist Don Felder. This was a breakthrough record, going gold in three months and producing the number-one hit, "Best of My Love," which didn't top the charts until almost a year after the album's release, just in time to set up their fourth album. *One of These Nights* (1975), the first of four straight albums to top the charts, featured the title track, "Lyin' Eyes" and "Take It to the Limit," both Top-Ten hits.

The Eagles released a greatest-hits album in 1976 (it now stands at 12 million sales, the best-selling hits record of all time) and suffered the loss of Leadon, who was replaced by former James Gang leader Joe Walsh. At the end of the year, they released *Hotel California,* which has now sold nine million copies. Its hits included the ominous title track, "New Kid in Town," and "Life in the Fast Lane."

In 1977 Meisner left the band and was replaced by former Poco member Timothy B. Schmit. It took the Eagles until the fall of 1979 to complete *The Long Run,* another million-seller, featuring the chart-topper "Heartache Tonight" and Top-Ten successes in the title track and "I Can't Tell You Why." The next year saw the release of a live album, but by 1981 the Eagles had split up. All five members have since released solo albums, the most successful of which have been by Henley and Frey.

In 1994, the Eagles reunited for a summer stadium tour and recorded an album as part of an appearance on the TV show "MTV Unplugged" that featured several new songs and was due for release in late 1994. — *William Ruhlmann*

Eagles / 1972 / Asylum 5054
The Eagles' tentative debut album is notable for its single bits, "Take It Easy," "Witchy Woman," and "Peaceful Easy Feeling." (It also contains a rare Jackson Browne composition, "Nightingale.") The album has more of a bluegrass tone (courtesy of Leadon) than the band would later pursue. — *William Ruhlmann*

Desperado / 1973 / Asylum 5068
A concept album equating rock & roll musicians with Old West outlaws, the Eagles' second album contains the hit "Tequila Sunrise," the song "Desperado," which has become a standard, and the recurring "Doolin-Dalton," co-written with J. D. Souther and Jackson Browne. — *William Ruhlmann*

○ **On the Border** / 1974 / Asylum 1004
A transitional Eagles album (and their commercial breakthrough), it contained songs like "Already Gone" and "James Dean" (cowritten by Jackson Browne) that hark back to their earlier uptempo rock style, but also "Best of My Love" and Tom Waits's "Ol' 55," ballads that showed off their harmonies and won them a whole new audience. — *William Ruhlmann*

○ **One of These Nights** / 1975 / Asylum 1039
The Eagles' breakthrough album, a convincing mix of heady rockers and lush ballads, featuring the Top-Ten hits "One of These Nights," "Lyin' Eyes," and "Take It to the Limit." — *William Ruhlmann*

★ **Their Greatest Hits (1971-1975)** / 1976 / Asylum 105
The reason this is such a great greatest-hits album is that it includes almost all the best tracks from the Eagles' first four albums, eight Top-40 hits including thenumber ones "Best of My Love" and "One of These Nights," plus the favorites "Tequila Sunrise" and "Desperado." This is the essential Eagles for the period. — *William Ruhlmann*

☆ **Hotel California** / 1976 / Asylum 103
A concept album about the dissipated life of Southern California rock stars, from being the "New Kid in Town" to living "Life in the Fast Lane" to holing up in the "Hotel California" and fearing it's all been "Wasted Time" and turning to "The Last Resort." This album and Pink Floyd's *The Wall* are aural versions of *A Star Is Born* for the rock generation. — *William Ruhlmann*

Long Run / 1979 / Asylum 508
The Long Run, the long-awaited follow-up to *Hotel California* and the Eagles' last studio album, proved a considerable disappointment, though it sold in the expected multimillions and included the hits "Heartache Tonight," "The Long Run," and "I Can't Tell You Why." — *William Ruhlmann*

Eagles Live / 1980 / Asylum 705
The Eagles were always a yawn in concert, and this profit-taking re-creation of their hits demonstrates the lifelessness they brought to live work. Today's fans should listen before forking over all those bucks to sit in the stadiums and experience it themselves. — *William Ruhlmann*

Eagles Greatest Hits, Vol. 2 / 1982 / Asylum 60205
This will save you from having to buy *The Long Run,* an inconsistent album best remembered for its hit songs, all of which are here, along with the ones from *Hotel California.* — *William Ruhlmann*

Earth Wind & Fire

Group / Funk, disco, urban R&B
Earth, Wind & Fire was the most successful R&B group of the second half of the '70s. EW&F was founded by Maurice White and his brother Verdine in Chicago in 1969, and they released their self-titled debut album on Warner Brothers in 1970. After the 1972 release of the second album, *The Need of Love,* White reorganized the group, bringing in Philip Bailey as co-lead singer for the recording of the third album, *Last Days and Time,* on Columbia.

EW&F encapsulated many strains of Black pop from before their time. Their high-pitched harmony vocals called to mind groups such as the Temptations, while their funkiness was reminiscent of Sly and the Family Stone, and their horn section sometimes evoked the work of James Brown and others. Over this, Maurice White laid his own brand of African-inspired kalimba music for a thorough synthesis that nonetheless bore a particular musical stamp unique to Earth, Wind & Fire.

The band began to break through with its fourth album, *Head to the Sky*, in 1973. EW&F's first R&B Top-Ten hit was "Mighty Mighty," from their first gold album, *Open Our Eyes*, which went to number 15 in the pop charts and also contained the R&B hit "Kalimba Story." EW&F's breakthrough to a mass audience, however, came in 1975, with the release of *That's the Way of the World*, the soundtrack to a film in which the group appeared. Led by its gold-selling number-one single, "Shining Star," the album topped the pop charts.

Equally successful were the partially live *Gratitude* (1975), *Spirit* (1976), *All 'n All* (1977), *The Best of Earth, Wind & Fire—Vol. 1* (1978), and *I Am* (1979). Several albums in the early '80s did almost as well, but after the relative failure of *Electric Universe* in 1983, EW&F disbanded. It re-formed for the 1987 release *Touch the World*. —*William Ruhlmann*

★ **Best of Earth, Wind & Fire, Vol. 1** / 1978 / Columbia 35647
Hits compilation covering 1973-1978. —*William Ruhlmann*

○ **Best of Earth, Wind & Fire, Vol. 2** / 1988 / Columbia 45013
The second collection covering hit singles from the 70s top funk and soul band Earth, Wind and Fire. This anthology has recently been supplanted by a boxed set covering virtually all their big Columbia singles and some Warners early material. If you enjoyed their disco and late 70s cuts more than the early tracks, this anthology is worth getting. —*Ron Wynn*

○ **Eternal Dance** / Sep. 8, 1992 / Columbia 52439
Covering three discs and including all the hits, as well as a healthy selection of rarities, *The Eternal Dance* is not designed for the casual listener—only hard-core fans will remain enthralled through the numerous rarities. Most listeners will be content with the two greatest-hits collections, but this comprehensive box set remains essential for hardcore Earth, Wind & Fire fans. —*Stephen Thomas Erlewine*

Sheena Easton

b. Apr. 27, 1959, Glasgow, Scotland
Vocals / Pop/rock
Easton came onto the pop scene in 1980 as an overnight sensation from England, due to her number-eight U.K. hit "Modern Girl" (it later reached number 18 stateside). Her first American hit, "Morning Train (Nine to Five)," went to number one for two weeks. During the early '80s, Easton released a series of light dance-pop hits, but in 1984 she began to pursue hit material with more erotic implications, as in "Strut" and the Prince-penned "Sugar Walls." She dueted with Prince on "U Got the Look," off his *Sign o' the Times* album, in 1987. Easton has released several more singles and, in 1991, pursued an acting stint on Broadway with *Les Miserables*. —*Rick Clark*

● **World of Sheena Easton—The Singles Collection** / 1993 / EMI America 81491
All of Sheena Easton's biggest and best songs—including "Morning Train (Nine to Five)," "For Your Eyes Only," "Telefone (Long Distance Love Affair)," "Strut," and "Sugar Walls"—are collected on this generous 19-track compilation —*Stephen Thomas Erlewine*

The Easybeats

Group / Pop/rock
Although thought of as Australia's answer to the Beatles, this mid-'60s band also owed a little bit to the Kinks—and their sound anticipated the Pretenders. A tight guitar-driven brand of R&B-based rock was their forte, and few groups anywhere played or wrote it ("Friday on My Mind") better. —*Bruce Eder*

● **Best of the Easybeats** / 1967 / Rhino 124
A well-devised collection that pales in sound and content next to its Australian competitor. —*Bruce Eder*

○ **Absolute Anthology** / 1980 / EMI
A two-CD package from Australia, with ear-stunning sound and two hours of golden classics. The collection of choice. —*Bruce Eder*

Echo & the Bunnymen

Group / Alternative pop/rock
Formed in 1978, Echo & the Bunnymen integrated the drama of the Doors and some psychedelia with the syntho-pop feel favored in the early '80s. Lead singer Ian McCulloch's self-absorbed agita-

tion and the band's forceful delivery earned them a substantial devoted alternative-music following in the United Kingdom and Stateside. —*Rick Clark*

○ **Crocodiles** / 1980 / Sire 6096
Arguments rage about these guys, but I prefer this, their debut, when their pop was spacier, moodier, and less coherent—in other words, before they started reading their press clippings. —*John Dougan*

○ **Ocean Rain** / 1984 / Sire 25084
Lots of strings on this one, but the pop is still delivered with flair. Lacks direction, though. —*John Dougan*

● **Songs to Learn & Sing** / 1985 / Sire 25360
A fine anthology collecting all the singles from their golden period of 1980 to 1985. In the end, Echo and the Bunnymen were a great singles band, so this is the ideal way to either get acquainted with the group or to revisit them. —*Chris Woodstra*

Echo & the Bunnymen / 1987 / Sire 25597
Their "mature" record. Actually the sound hadn't varied all that much since the early '80s, just lost a little wallop. —*John Dougan*

Eddie & the Hot Rods

Group / Rock & roll, new wave
Although their music might sound like conventional rock & roll today, Eddie & the Hot Rods played an important role in the birth of U.K. punk rock. The Hot Rods are the bridge between the pub rock of Dr. Feelgood and the punk rock of the Sex Pistols. Tougher, louder, and wilder than Dr. Feelgood, the band gathered a large following in England's clubs, culminating with the release of their 1976 album *Teenage Depression*. At a time when pompous hard rock was dominating rock & roll, the simple pleasures of the joyous, R&B rockers on the album were a refreshing—and important—change of pace.

Released during the beginning of England's punk revolution, 1977's *Life on the Line* featured an equally inspired set of songs that were more pop oriented than their predecessors. However, it was the last time Eddie & the Hot Rods had any impact in Britain. When *Thriller* was released in 1979, the band no longer was on the cutting edge—they couldn't compete with the bands they inspired. After one more lackluster album, the group called it quits. They reunited briefly in 1985. —*Stephen Thomas Erlewine*

Teenage Depression / 1976 / Island 9457
The band's first studio album is a fine effort in the spirit of Dr. Feelgood, bridging the gap between pub rock and punk rock. Wild, raw, and rebellious—everything a rock & roll album should be. —*Chris Woodstra*

● **Life on the Line** / 1977 / Island 9509
Life on the Line has guitarist Graeme Douglas (ex-Kursaal Flyers) helping to bring out the band's pure pop sensibility. This is their finest moment and also their last really great album. Includes the brilliant "Do Anything You Want to Do," a British hit. —*Chris Woodstra*

Duane Eddy

b. Apr. 26, 1938, Corning, NY
Guitar / Rock & roll
One of the '50s most influential guitarists, and one of the more distinct: Unlike other guitarslingers of the era, Eddy forged a sound based on minimalism (and lots of twangy reverb). His best hits ("Rebel Rouser," "Movin' and Groovin'," "Peter Gunn") feature simple reverb-drenched guitar riffs that usually provide a backdrop for a wailing sax. Eddy's chart run was brief (1958 to 1960), but his style is embedded in rock's fiber and continues to shape many young players. —*John Floyd*

★ **Twang Thang: The Anthology** / May 18, 1993 / Rhino
Duane Eddy was America's first bona-fide rock & roll guitar hero, playing minimalistic riffs that any kid with a pawnshop guitar could aspire to with a little determination and elbow grease. This two-CD anthology offers the finest retrospective of his career available, with all facets of his career well documented, from the early hits to later collaborations with the famous rockers he initially inspired. Featuring just enough rarities to keep it from being merely a greatest-hits package, this truly showcases Duane at his best. —*Cub Koda*

Dave Edmunds

b. Apr. 15, 1944, Cardiff, Wales
Vocals, guitar / Rock & roll, roots-rock
Dave Edmunds may not be a musical innovator, but that doesn't mean he's not an original. Where other roots-rockers sound stiff and respectable, Edmunds sounds alive and passionate, even on the tracks he recorded completely by himself. He's not much of a songwriter—all of his best compositions were written with Nick Lowe—but he has a great ear for material. He's able to not only pick the overlooked oldies, but new material that sounds like classic rock & roll (Elvis Costello's "Girls Talk," Graham Parker's "Back to Schooldays"). Edmunds's skills as a producer are formidable: He can replicate and update everything from the sound of Sun Studios and Phil Spector's wall of sound to the crisp guitars of the Everly Brothers and the driving rhythms of Chuck Berry. Although his records after 1982's *D.E. 7* suffer from lackluster material and sound like he's trying to keep up with trends, all of the albums he recorded in the previous decade are brilliant recreations of the best of '50s and '60s rock & roll, and are played with energy and flair.

After spending some time as the lead guitarist of Love Sculpture, Edmunds built his own recording studio in the late '60s. In 1971, he had his only big hit single with a revamped version of Smiley Lewis's "I Hear You Knocking." As he recorded his own albums, he produced several other artists, including Brinsley Schwarz and the Flamin' Groovies. *Get It*, released in 1977, was the first solo album he released that he recorded with other musicians, including former Brinsley bassist Nick Lowe. Lowe and Edmunds formed Rockpile with guitarist Billy Bremner and drummer Terry Williams. Rockpile backed both Edmunds and Lowe on their solo records; during concerts everyone traded songs. With their support, Edmunds's solo records became both tougher and looser. The two albums he recorded entirely with the group—*Tracks on Wax 4* and *Repeat When Necessary*—are his finest.

Rockpile recorded one album as a group before they split in 1980. During the '80s, Edmunds produced several artists, including the Fabulous Thunderbirds, a Carl Perkins television special, and the Everly Brothers. After a couple of years without hits, he turned to Jeff Lynne for production support in 1983. The teaming resulted in two stiff, synth-dominated records. By 1990's *Closer to the Flame*, Edmunds had shed Lynne and returned to the straightforward rock & roll of his earlier records. *—Stephen Thomas Erlewine*

○ **Get It** / 1977 / Swan Song 8418
Driven by the raucous rockers "Get Out of Denver," "I Knew the Bride," and "JuJu Man," *Get It* is one of Dave Edmunds's strongest albums. *—Stephen Thomas Erlewine*

○ **Tracks on Wax 4** / 1978 / Swan Song 8505
A piledriving set of new written-to-orders and covers, powered by Edmunds's dexterous vocals and the bar-band boogie of Rockpile. *—John Floyd*

○ **Repeat When Necessary** / 1979 / Swan Song 8507
His creative breakthrough mines the usual retro-terrain, only the nuevo-oldies are the best he's ever had. Both Edmunds's and Rockpile's finest moment. *—John Floyd*

Twangin'... / 1981 / Swan Song 16034
Twangin. .., Edmunds's first post-Rockpile album, is an inconsistent but enjoyable record, highlighted by the psuedo-new wave of John Hiatt's "Something Happens," the insistent groove of "You'll Never Get Me Up (in One of Those)," and the gorgeous Everly Brothers-styled ballad "(I'm Gonna Start) Living Again If It Kills Me." *—Stephen Thomas Erlewine*

○ **DE7** / 1982 / Columbia 37930
While it follows the same formula as *Twangin'*, *DE7* is a much stronger album, thanks to strong songs like "From Small Things (Big Things One Day Come)," "Bail You Out," and "Warmed Over Kisses (Left Over Love)." *—Stephen Thomas Erlewine*

● **The Dave Edmunds Anthology (1968-1990)** / 1993 / Rhino 71191
By trying to represent all aspects of his career accurately, this double-disc set overlooks a lot of Edmunds's finest material, but the 41 songs on *The Dave Edmunds Anthology (1968-1990)* do offer a good portrait of his career, from his beginnings with Love Sculpture through Rockpile and his solo hits. *—AMG*

The Edsels

Group / Doo-wop
A brief encounter with fame came for the Edsels (from the tiny mill town of Campbell, OH) when they did the doo-wop masterpiece "Rama Lama Ding Dong." However, its success came some three years after its release—diligent record collectors made it a hit . *—Cub Koda*

● **Rama Lama Ding Dong** / 1992 / Relic 7050
A complete 16-track collection of the group's best sides, including the title track, one of the great nonsense doo-wop sides of all time. *—Cub Koda*

Jonathan Edwards

b. Jul. 28, 1946, Minnesota
Vocals / Singer/songwriter
This Minnesota singer/songwriter's claim to fame was the lightly upbeat ditty "Sunshine." Even though he was unable to match the success of that song, Edwards released a string of albums to a small but devoted following. His more recent efforts reflected a return to his bluegrass roots. *—Rick Clark*

● **Jonathan Edwards** / 1971 / Atco 862
His light acoustic folk-pop debut includes the hits "Sunshine" and "Everybody Knows Her." *—Rick Clark*

808 State

Group / House music, dance
With their sample-driven dance music, the pioneering Manchester-based 808 State is one of the first house groups to release trance/ambient dance records. Instead of being an incessant pounding, the beat in 808 State's music is hypnotic and mesmerizing. Occasionally their records feature a vocalist/rapper (including guest appearances by Bjork and New Order's Bernard Sumner) but the music is mainly instrumental. In the late '80s and early '90s, both 808 State's own records, and their remixes were dance club staples. *—Stephen Thomas Erlewine*

● **808 Utd. State 90** / 1989 / Tommy Boy 1033
One of the best house albums ever recorded, *808 Utd. State 90* is a hypnotic, trance-inducing collection of colorful samples and endlessly inventive rhythm tracks. *—Stephen Thomas Erlewine*

Einsturzende Neubauten

Group / Alternative rock, industrial
The German-based industrial group (their name means "collapsing new buildings") brought new meaning to the genre by creating a roaring wall of noise, using many "found" instruments. Their music hinges on the drama wrenched from banging sheets of metal and oil drums, among other junkyard elements, with hammers, wrenches, and other tools. Guitars squeal in whitenoise abandon, and their vocals sometimes conjure your worst nightmares. *—John Floyd*

● **Strategies Against Architecture** / 1984 / Positive 63
Radical noisy primitivism that is occasionally stunning. *—John Dougan*

○ **Strategies Against Architecture, Vol. 2** / 1991 / Mute 61100
Radical noisy primitivism part two.*—John Dougan*

Electric Flag

Group / Blues-rock
A horn-dominated rock band led by guitarist Michael Bloomfield (1944-1981) and featuring drummer and vocalist Buddy Miles, bassist Harvey Brooks (born Goldstein), and vocalist Nick Gravenites. Whereas later, more successful horn-based groups like Chicago and Blood, Sweat & Tears worked from jazz and pop influences, Electric Flag used the Stax/Volt sound, James Brown, and B. B. King's large groups as role models. Bloomfield left after their first album, with Miles taking over the leadership role for the second album. They re-formed with Bloomfield in 1974 for one quick album, released to scant acclaim, but its influence as a trendsetter far exceeds its record sales. *—Cub Koda*

● **A Long Time Comin'** / 1968 / Columbia 9597
Ex-Butterfield Band guitarist/drummer Miles and others put this soul-rock band together in 1967. This debut is a testament to their ability to catch fire and keep on burnin'. *—Jeff Tamarkin*

Electric Light Orchestra

Group / Pop/rock
Formed in 1971 from the ashes of one of Britain's greatest eccentric rock bands, the Move, the Electric Light Orchestra drew heavily from the ornately lumbering "I Am the Walrus"-period Beatles. This is shown to extreme effect on their oddly engaging debut, *No Answer*. Of particular note is the track "10538 Overture."

Move expatriates Roy Wood, Jeff Lynne, and Bev Bevan formed the initial nucleus of ELO, but multi-instrumentalist Wood split after *No Answer* to form the bizarrely '50s-influenced Wizzard. Their sophomore release, *ELO II*, retained some of the off-key crunch of the debut, but it is clearly a transition to what became a very slick, highly orchestrated pop-hit factory. Between 1975 and 1981, ELO managed 17 Top-40 hits, among which were "Evil Woman," "Telephone Line," "Don't Bring Me Down," "Hold on Tight," "Shine a Little Love," and the wonderful "Can't Get It Out of My Head." ELO also scored a hit with "Do Ya," which was the Move's only Stateside chart hit. ELO increasingly became a side project to leader Jeff Lynne's successful outside artist productions, which included Brian Wilson, Dave Edmunds, Tom Petty, the Traveling Wilburys, Randy Newman, and George Harrison. — *Rick Clark*

○ **No Answer** / 1971 / Jet 35524
Their most lively album, this debut is driven by Roy Wood's manic musical sensibilities. An energetic offshoot of the Move's final album. —*Bruce Eder*

○ **On the Third Day** / 1973 / Jet 35525
ELO's sound came togther here, hooked around rocked-up classics and Jeff Lynne's guitar. —*Bruce Eder*

○ **Eldorado** / 1975 / Jet 35526
Pretentious pseudo-concept rock with some hot old-style rock & roll grace notes. —*Bruce Eder*

○ **Face the Music** / 1975 / Jet 35527
Superb production and a good song lineup featuring "Evil Woman" and "Strange Magic." —*Bruce Eder*

Out of the Blue / 1977 / Jet 35530
An overproduced, overwrought piece of pop fluff masquerading as something important. —*Bruce Eder*

● **ELO's Greatest Hits** / 1979 / Jet 36310
Most of ELO's biggest and best hits—"Evil Woman," "Rockaria," "Telephone Line"—are included on this solid but slightly skimpy collection. —*Stephen Thomas Erlewine*

○ **Afterglow** / 1990 / Epic 46090
Although it contains all the hits and the remastering sounds superb, the three-disc boxed set *Afterglow* is likely to be more ELO than anyone but the most devoted fans would want from an anthology. —*Stephen Thomas Erlewine*

Eleventh Dream Day

Group / Alternative pop/rock
A stunning guitar band that grafts relationship angst onto a swirling, intoxicating cushion of electric string damage. Easily one of the (if not *the*) most underrated bands currently in the alternative/independent-label scene. The strength and sass are derived from the formidable pair of Rick Rizzo and Janet Beveridge Bean, who make this country-flavored punk amalgam work hard. —*John Dougan*

Beet / 1990 / Atlantic 82053
Guitar-heavy rock. —*Robert Gordon*

● **Lived to Tell** / 1991 / Atlantic 82179
The overlooked album of 1991, *Lived to Tell* exhibits all of Eleventh Dream Day's strengths without ever sounding forced or generic. Sad, combative, and rageful, this is a triumphant spiritual record that reveals more on repeated plays. —*John Dougan*

○ **El Moodio** / 1993 / Atlantic 82480
Eleventh Dream Day's *El Moodio* is another solid album of raw rock & roll that never is anything less than fiercely intelligent and impassioned. Of course, it didn't sell anything, and the band was dropped by their label shortly afterward. —*Stephen Thomas Er*

Lorraine Ellison

b. , Philadelphia, PA
Vocals / Soul

Music Map

Early Rock Through Punk To Hardcore

50s American Rock n' Roll
Chuck Berry – Little Richard – Link Wray

60s British Rock
The Beatles – The Rolling Stones
The Kinks – The Who

60s American Garage Rock
The Kingmen – The Standells – Count Five
? and the Mysterians – Chocolate Watch Band

Art Garage (late 60s)
Velvet Underground

Late 60s American Garage Punk
The Stooges – MC5

Folk Garage
Neil Young

Early 70s American Proto-Punk
New York Dolls

Mid-70s American Punk
The Ramones – Richard Hell
Patti Smith – Television

Mid 70s British Punk
The Sex Pistols – The Damned
The Buzzcocks – The Clash

Metal/Thrash
Motorhead

80s American Hardcore
Black Flag – Dead Kennedys
Bad Brains – Circle Jerks
Misfits – Husker Du

Grindcore
Carcass – Napalm Death

Thrashcore
Helmet – Prong

A Philadelphia-born gospel singer (with the Ellison Sisters) turned soul diva, Ellison is best known for the poignant, apocalyptical "Stay with Me" (1966), a virtuoso display of vocal pyrotechnics written and produced by Jerry Ragovoy, which instantly garnered Ellison a cult following among her peers in the business. Ellison's stunning soprano, her phrasing by turns ethereal and triumphant, soars above Ragovoy's equally intense arrangements. Her technical perfection in the higher registers infuses each syllable with a purity that has rarely been equaled in the genre. —*Christine Ohlman*

● **Stay with Me** / 1969 / Line 901011
Produced by Jerry Ragovoy. Includes title track, covered by Terry Reid; "Try (Just a Little Bit Harder)," covered by Janis Joplin; "You Don't Know Nothing about Love," covered by Irma Thomas. Few soul albums have ever matched the intensity of this! —*Christine Ohlman*

Lorraine Ellison / 1974 / Warner Brothers 2780
Gospel-tinged effort includes a fine cover of Jimmy Cliff's "Many Rivers to Cross." Out of print. —*Christine Ohlman*

Joe Ely

b. Feb. 9, 1947, TX
Vocals, guitar / Country-rock

In the '70s, country-western was full of artists referred to as "outlaws"—mavericks who bucked the stodgy Nashville music establishment by writing their own songs, recording with their road bands, and producing their own records. The genre produced a slew of acts, but it was Lubbock, TX-native Joe Ely who best epitomized the form. Unlike most of that era's big names, Ely remains a viable artist. He got his start back in the early '70s, working with Butch Hancock and Jimmie Dale Gilmore in a group called the Flatlanders. Their only album didn't go far, and the group broke up. (The album was reissued in 1990 on Rounder.)

Around the mid '70s, Ely formed an eclectic group that was able to swing from Cajun and western to honky-tonk stomps and rockabilly; they were signed to MCA in 1977. Ely released an eponymous debut that year, using songs written by ex-Flatlanders Butch Hancock and Jimmie Dale Gilmore and throwing in some of his own road-worn, oddly poetic originals. The next year brought *Honky Tonk Masquerade*, the cornerstone of Ely's legacy and one of modern country's most ambitious albums. Further albums (especially *Live Shots*, recorded during his European tour with the Clash) brought Ely to the attention of rock fans and netted ecstatic reviews in country and pop magazines (but, mysteriously, produced no hits). Ely was dropped by MCA in 1983 and woodshedded until 1987, when the independent Hightone label signed him and released *Lord of the Highway*. Another Hightone album followed before Ely (whose influence was being felt in the new breed of country neotraditionalists) re-signed with MCA and released another live set. He's yet to top his late-'70s achievements, but Ely remains an energetic and passionate live performer and an occasionally inspired songwriter. Writing him off could be perilous. —*John Floyd*

○ **Joe Ely** / 1977 / MCA 10219
Ely's first album came out while country's outlaw movement was in full swing, but *Joe Ely* took it one better. This is a roots-rocking country album with tunes by Jimmie Dale Gilmore ("Treat Me Like a Saturday Night") and Butch Hancock ("She Never Spoke Spanish to Me," "If You Were a Bluebird") that deserve the near-classic status their cult of fans has bestowed on them. —*Brian Mansfield*

● **Honky Tonk Masquerade** / 1978 / MCA 10220
Ely's best album, *Honky Tonk Masquerade*, contains everything from Texas weepers ("Because of the Wind") to roadhouse rockers ("Fingernails"). Among the best tunes are Jimmie Dale Gilmore's "Tonight I Think I'm Gonna Go Downtown" and Butch Hancock's "West Texas Waltz." Nobody made country records like this in 1978. Come to think of it, they still don't. —*Brian Mansfield*

○ **Live Shots** / 1980 / MCA 5262
Ely partakes of the musical diversity of his hometown, Lubbock, TX, freely mixing country, rock, Tex-Mex, and hard honky-tonk music in excellent songs he writes himself or borrows from his friend Butch Hancock. This is a live best-of covering his first three albums, recorded on tour in England. —*William Ruhlmann*

Lord of the Highway / 1987 / Hightone 8008
After a long recording layoff, Ely picked up where he'd left off in 1984 with this typical collection, whose best songs—"Me and Billy the Kid" and "Are You Listenin' Lucky?"—were Ely originals. —*William Ruhlmann*

○ **Love & Danger** / 1992 / MCA 10584
Ely is stark and restless. . . . His muse still roams the highways in search of whatever, his romance doomed by a twist of fate. Now, he's a more objective observer, a storyteller who captures the tragic side to the well-defined characters of "The Road Goes on Forever" and "Every Night About This Time." Ely conveys much—if not most—of a song's emotion through his inspired electric guitar playing. The string-bending is at high-pressure intensity for "Love Is the Beating of Hearts," then drops deep, sonorous, and echoed for "Slow You Down." —*Roch Parisien*

Emerson Lake & Palmer

Group / Art-rock

By the end of the '60s, many artists became swept up in the wake of the Beatles and their aggressive exploration of the possibilities of pop and rock. In the minds of many young schooled musicians who found release in rock's energy, expanding the form by incorporating motifs and highly arranged extended compositions seemed an appealing notion. The results of this concept became known as art-rock.

Depending on your point of view, Emerson, Lake & Palmer were either guilty of encouraging such tonal indulgence or they delivered some of the genre's better moments. Pianist Keith Emerson had already met much success in Britain with his theatrical pyrotechnics in the Nice. Greg Lake was the vocalist/bassist for the explosively dark King Crimson, and percussionist Carl Palmer backed up the heavy blues-based Atomic Rooster, a band that also contained eventual Fleetwood Mac member Christine McVie.

Months before the arrival of Emerson, Lake & Palmer's self-titled debut, expectations began running high about what the band would contribute to the expansion of rock. The debut was impressive, ranging from delicate acoustic piano and guitar interplay to explosive free-for-alls, but with the second album (*Tarkus*) it became obvious that the band often placed an enormous amount of finesse on playing to the back of the bleachers, rather than focusing that energy into a consistently satisfying musicality.

Nevertheless, Emerson, Lake & Palmer became a staple of FM rock radio during the '70s, even scoring a couple of hits with "Lucky Man" and "In the Beginning." —*Rick Clark*

○ **Emerson, Lake & Palmer** / 1970 / Atlantic 19120
A lively, ambitious, and largely successful debut album, made up of daring instrumentals ("Three Fates," "The Barbarian") and romantic ballads ("Lucky Man"), showcasing three very daunting talents. "Take a Pebble" is rewarding and pretentious enough to have been a Moody Blues track, except that the Moodies could never solo like Keith Emerson. The trio would never be as concise or precise in their work again. —*Bruce Eder*

Tarkus / 1971 / Atlantic 19121
A dark concept album—really as much an offshoot thematically of King Crimson's *Court of the Crimson King* (on which Lake played and sang) as anything derived by the trio—that reaches too far and takes itself too seriously much of the time. The title suite has some haunting moments, but the whole thing is too gloomy and pretentious for all but serious fans. —*Bruce Eder*

Pictures at an Exhibition / 1971 / Atlantic 19122
A live recording of the Mussorgsky piece which, despite its wildness, holds up well as a psychedelic art-rock showcase. —*Bruce Eder*

Trilogy / 1972 / Atlantic 19123
A major improvement over their second album (the convoluted concept effort *Tarkus*) and the group's first success with adapting the music of Aaron Copland ("Hoedown"), which became something of a signature of theirs. The title track is a romantic, almost torch-song number, while "The Endless Enigma" is a curious mixture of pomp and mysticism. —*Bruce Eder*

○ **Brain Salad Surgery** / 1973 / Atlantic 19124
Science-fiction rock, virtually a soundtrack to a nonexistent film. Well-produced and overpowering, but fully rewarding only on the tracks that fall outside the concept. —*Bruce Eder*

Works, Vol. 1 / Oct. 1977 / Atlantic 7000
The trio's last great album, a double-disc set that essentially allowed each of the members a side of his own to produce; on the fourth side they worked as a team. Emerson's "Piano Concerto" is overextended but probably the best work of its kind by a rock figure (and there are quite a few from this period). Lake's solo material is a little too soft and romantic, while Palmer comes off best, with a percussion/production tour-de-force. The group material (including "Fanfare for the Common Man") isn't a major advance (except in dimension) from the preceding record. —*Bruce Eder*

● **Atlantic Years** / 1992 / Atlantic 82403
This double-disc set is a solid 2 1/2-hour overview of ELP's career highlights, including "The Endless Enigma (Parts 1 & 2)," "Fugue," "Knife-Edge," "Take a Pebble," "Lucky Man," "From the Beginning," "Fanfare for the Common Man," "Still . . . You Turn Me On," Greg Lake's "Father Christmas," and excerpts from *Pictures at an Exhibition*. —*AMG*

Return of the Manticore / Nov. 16, 1993 / Victory Music 484004
Coming from this notorious album-oriented art-rock band, the boxed set *Return of the Manticore* works somewhat against the

very structured nature of their albums. For hardcore fans, the music might be disconcerting out of its proper context (although the first studio version of *Pictures at an Exhibition* will delight them), and there is way too much music for casual fans. All in all, the two-CD *Atlantic Years* compilation distills ELP's career much more concisely and successfully, making that set more worthwhile for most fans. —*Stephen Thomas Erlewine*

The Emotions

Group / Soul
A trio of sisters with a strong gospel base, the Emotions (based in Chicago) were one of the leading female R&B acts of the '70s. Lead singer Sheila Hutchinson and her sisters Wanda and Jeanette were only teenagers when they crashed the soul charts in 1969 with the engaging "So I Can Love You," but they sang gospel as children and enjoyed secular fame locally before signing with Memphis-based Volt and working with producers Isaac Hayes and David Porter. When Stax folded in 1975, the group hooked up with Maurice White of Earth, Wind & Fire, an association that led to the number-one pop/R&B hit "Best of My Love" in 1977. —*Bill Dahl*

● **Chronicle** / 1979 / Stax 4121
A fine collection of the Emotions' greatest hits, *Chronicle* also includes several songs that weren't as popular but were nearly as good. —*Stephen Thomas Erlewine*

En Vogue

Group / Urban R&B
Producers Denzil Foster and Thomas McElroy constructed this San Francisco Bay Area vocal quartet. Members include Dawn Robinson, Cindy Herron, Maxine Jones, and Terry Ellis. En Vogue became an unexpected crossover smash when their debut *Born to Sing* produced several Top-40 hits in 1991. The 1992 follow-up, *Funky Divas*, also became a major hit and led some critics to call the dance-floor divas the "new Supremes."

In 1993, the group issued an EP, *Runaway Love*, and teamed with female rappers Salt-N-Pepa on the pop and urban Top-10 hit "Whatta Man." —*John Floyd & Ron Wynn*

● **Funky Divas** / 1992 / East West 92121
En Vogue are incredible singers, which is what makes *Funky Divas* a delight. Naturally the singles are the highpoints of the album, but the rest of the album is hardly filler—it proves that En Vogue possess a great talent. —*Stephen Thomas Erlewine*

The English Beat

Group / Ska-revival
Next to the Specials, the racially mixed English Beat were the best of the "2-Tone" ska-revival bands that flourished in late-'70s England, mixing bluebeat shimmy with punk sensibilities. —*John Floyd*

☆ **I Just Can't Stop It** / 1980 / IRS 0606
A diverse, energetic, and incessantly danceable debut, marked by percolating rhythms and an admirable loathing of England's right-wing government. —*John Floyd*

Wha'ppen? / 1981 / IRS 5070
The rhythms, although less vigorous, incorporate other aspects of third-world boogie and tackle more global social concerns. —*John Floyd*

○ **Special Beat Service** / 1982 / IRS 5069
More jangly pop here, epitomized by the stunning "Save It for Later" and the slinky "I Confess." —*John Floyd*

● **What Is Beat: The Best of English Beat** / 1983 / IRS 0040
This compilation entices the owners of the albums with some previously unreleased live tracks and a couple of great remixes, but it's not definitive. —*John Floyd*

Enigma

Group / Dance-pop
With their 1991 hit, "Sadeness," Enigma brought the new age fascination with Gregorian chants and old world culture to the clubs. The resulting single was both unique and irresistible. The rest of the album followed that pattern successfully, although without quite matching the stunning success of the hit single. On their second album, some of the old world elements remained,

but the new age angle came to the forefront in a set of slick, radio-friendly dance-pop. —*Stephen Thomas Erlewine*

● **MCMXC A.D.** / 1990 / Charisma 91642
Driven by the Gregorian chants of the hit single "Sadeness," Enigma's debut album is an interesting fusion of new age sensibilities and dance-floor rhythms. —*Stephen Thomas Erlewine*

Cross of Changes / Feb. 8, 1994 / Charisma 39236
On Enigma's second album, their latent new age tendencies come to the forefront and occasionally obscure their usually captivating dance tracks. —*Stephen Thomas Erlewine*

Brian Eno

b. May 15, 1948, Woodbridge, England
Vocals, keyboards / Progressive rock, experimental electronic, ambient
Brian Eno may not be a household name, but his influence has been felt on a number of rock's most unique records, some highly successful. Eno first made his appearance as a founding member of British art-pop rockers Roxy Music in 1971. Eno, who fancied himself a manipulator of "treated" sound rather than a formally titled musician, provided Roxy with sweeping tonal washes, peculiar noises, and bleeps and blips on electronic keyboards and tapes.

After leaving Roxy Music, Eno pursued a fascinating career as a solo artist and producer, which has perhaps been the most rewarding and respectable in the pantheon of rock art. His groundbreaking early work influences a slew of budding art-punk rockers; his experiments with synthesized atmospheria serve as intriguing Muzak for rock fans; and his innovative production skills have been enlisted by rockers as varied as David Bowie, U2, Ultravox, Devo, Talking Heads, and James. He's also collaborated with the likes of John Cale, Robert Fripp, Daniel Lanois, David Byrne, and his brother Robert Eno.

Eno's interest in creating "sound landscapes" with sophisticated manipulations of echo and timbre led to the establishment of his "ambient music" ideal in the late '70s, through a series of influential solo albums and ethereal collaborations with Laraaji, Jon Hassell, and Harold Budd. By creating this new subgenre, he unwittingly became one of the fathers of new age music, a genre he was quick to criticize for not encompassing enough "evil and doubt." The intention and effect of Eno's style, however, is markedly different from the soothing sound-baths associated with many new age and contemporary electronic recordings, which are notoriously one-dimensional in their approach to sound construction. Eno makes soundscapes that challenge the listener—his music may be many things, but it is never easy listening

In recent years, Eno has created increasingly sophisticated ambient soundtracks for his own multimedia installations, which have appeared in galleries in Venice, Milan, and Tokyo. Eno continues to release albums in both pop and contemporary instrumental genres. —*Rick Clark, John Floyd, and Linda Kohanov*

○ **Here Come the Warm Jets** / 1973 / EG 11
Eno's solo debut features complex but tight pop songs with bizarre and often hilarious lyrics, which puncture the treated guitar and keyboard textures. —*John Floyd*

○ **Taking Tiger Mountain (by Strategy)** / 1974 / EG 17
They lack the vibrant and energetic rock-laced enthusiasm of *Here Come the Warm Jets*, but these experimentations within the pop format give art-rock a good name. —*John Floyd*

★ **Another Green World** / Jan. 1975 / EG 21
Eno's masterpiece. Containing a sumptuous aural melange of dense ambient instrumental snippets and rich, often beautiful pop melodies, this is one of those albums that should be enjoyed in one concentrated sitting. —*John Floyd*

○ **Discreet Music** / Feb. 1975 / EG 23
Eno's experimental precursor to his ambient series explores his fascination with the element of "chance" in composition. The title cut was created by setting the parameters for a series of synthesizers, equalizers, echo units, and tape players to interact with each other. He then sat back and let the piece follow its own course. The second work, three variations on Pachelbel's famous "Canon in D," involved giving live players fragments of the original score with instructions that caused them to overlay their parts in unusual and unpredictable ways. Both pieces are intriguing and surprisingly musical. —*Linda Kohanov*

☆ **Before & After Science** / 1977 / EG 32
A thrashing partial return to more basic song structures, punctuated by the exhilarating "King's Lead Hat." —*John Floyd*

★ **Ambient 1—Music for Airports** / 1978 / EG 17
Four subtle, slowly evolving pieces grace Eno's first conscious effort at creating ambient music. The composer was in part striving to create music that approximated the effect of visual art. Like a fine painting, these evolving soundscapes don't require constant involvement on the part of the listener. They can hang in the background and add to the atmosphere of the room, yet the music also rewards close attention with a sonic richness absent in standard types of background or easy-listening music. —*Linda Kohanov*

○ **My Life in the Bush of Ghosts** / 1981 / Sire 6093
Talking Heads singer David Byrne teams with Brian Eno to create this unique techno-tribal music by combining tapes of Third World vocalizations with African-like rhythm tracks. It's dense and hypnotic, highlighted by the downright spooky recording of an exorcism. —*Scott Bultman*

☆ **Ambient 4—On Land** / 1982 / EG 20
Eno's most masterful ambient effort to date was created as a musical antidote to the confusion of life in New York City. An earthy sense of repose underlies intricate sonic essays. —*Linda Kohanov*

○ **Desert Island Selection** / 1989 / EG 65
A CD-only survey of Eno's first four albums, with songs hand picked and annotations written by Eno himself. —*John Floyd*

○ **Wrong Way Up** / 1990 / Opal 26421
Both Eno and Cale have flirted with conventional pop music throughout their careers, while reserving the right to go off on less-accessible experiments, which means they've always held out the promise that they would make something as attractive as this synthesizer-dominated collection, on which Eno comes as close to the mainstream as he has since *Another Green World* and Cale is as catchy as he's been since *Honi Soit*. The result is one of the best albums either one has ever made. —*William Ruhlmann*

○ **Eno Box II** / 1993 / Virgin
The first of two retrospective boxed sets devoted to the groundbreaking work of Brian Eno, *II* concentrates on his pop and vocal material, including some selections from the unreleased *My Squelchy Life*. Although his music still makes the most sense in the context of his albums, *II* is solid crash-course introduction to his work, which remains as revolutionary today as it was when it was released. —*Stephen Thomas Erlewine*

○ **Eno Box I** / Mar. 22, 1994 / Virgin 39110
Box I features a cross-section of Eno's influential ambient music; while this music often works better in its original context, the box offers a good introduction to Eno's innovative instrumental work. —*Stephen Thomas Erlewine*

Enuff Z'nuff

Group / Hard rock, power pop
Because of their big hair and lipstick, Enuff Z'Nuff is frequently tagged as another run-of-the-mill pop-metal band. Although there is some truth to that—their guitars are as layered as Def Leppard's—their hearts lie with the trashy pop of Cheap Trick and the classic power pop of Badfinger. Since very few bands have explored the connection between metal and power pop, Enuff Z'Nuff has received barely any airplay and sales, but loads of critical acclaim. And they have earned that praise—this is hard rock that is smarter than it seems, powered by an overwhelming sense of melody. —*Stephen Thomas Erlewine*

○ **Strength** / 1991 / Atco 91638
While the guitars are loud, crunchy, and powerful, *Strength* succeeds because of Enuff Z'Nuff's innate pop sensibility and their fondness for psychedelic flourishes. —*Stephen Thomas Erlewine*

● **Animals with Human Intelligence** / 1992 / Arista 18587
On Enuff Z'Nuff's third album, the band finally makes their catchy, trashy fusion of Cheap Trick, Badfinger, Sweet, and Def Leppard sound completely original. —*Stephen Thomas Erlewine*

Enya

b. , Donegal, Ireland
Vocals / Alternative pop
Enya (Eithne Ni Bhraonain) is from Gweedore, County Donegal, Ireland, which she left in 1980 to join the Irish band Clannad, the group that already featured her older brothers and sisters. She stayed with Clannad for two years, then left, hooking up with producer Nicky Ryan and lyricist Roma Ryan, with whom she recorded film and television scores. The result was a successful album of TV music for the BBC. Enya then recorded *Watermark* (1988), which featured her distinctive, flowing music and multi-overdubbed trancelike singing. The album sold four million copies worldwide. It was followed by *Shepherd Moons* (1991), which confirmed Enya's status as a new age superstar. —*William Ruhlmann*

● **Watermark** / 1988 / Reprise 26774
The United States was a little slower than the rest of the world to admire Enya's blend of ethereal multitracked vocals and subtly flowing music, but this album's single, "Orinoco Flow (Sail Away)," which topped the charts elsewhere, was a Top-25 hit here, and the album went gold. —*William Ruhlmann*

○ **Shepherd Moons** / 1991 / Reprise 26775
More of Enya's textured music, and with this album, the United States succumbed. *Shepherd Moons* shot to number one on *Billboard* magazine's new age albums chart; by 1994, it had sold over three million copies and was still on the Hot-200 chart. —*William Ruhlmann*

Erasure

Group / Alternative pop, dance-pop
After Vince Clarke left Depeche Mode in the early '80s, he first formed the synth-based dance-pop band Yaz, and then Erasure, in 1985, with singer Andy Bell. Clarke wrote and played the majority of the material; the extravagant Bell provided the duo with a voice and image. Like Depeche Mode or the Pet Shop Boys, Erasure sounds cold and detatched while singing about love and alienation, yet they still have a knack for crafting successful pop singles like "Chains of Love." Over the years, the duo's following has expanded with each release, and they have edged their way into the pop mainstream. —*Stephen Thomas Erlewine*

○ **Wonderland** / 1986 / Sire 25354
No matter who the singer is, Vince Clarke's inventive synthesizer music is immediately identifiable. Here the former Depeche Mode/Yaz leader does his electronic wonders behind emotive singer Andy Bell (who bears a certain vocal resemblance to Yaz's Alison Moyet). Clarke's irresistible music is the best argument there is for synthesizers, and Bell is an appealing front man. —*William Ruhlmann*

○ **Innocents** / 1988 / Sire 25730
Erasure emerged from the dance clubs with this gold-selling U.S.-breakthrough album, which contains the Top-15 hits "A Little Respect" and "Chains of Love." —*William Ruhlmann*

Abba-Esque / Jun. 30, 1992 / Sire 61386
A fun EP of ABBA covers, which is worthwhile for any Erasure fan. —*AMG*

● **Pop!—The First 20 Hits** / Nov. 24, 1992 / Sire 45153
Pop!—The First 20 Hits is exactly what it claims to be—a collection of Erasure's biggest singles, which makes it the best place to get acquainted with this synth-pop band. —*Stephen Thomas Erlewine*

Roky Erickson

Vocals / Rock & roll, psychedelic
Aside from Syd Barrett, the Austin, TX-native Erickson is rock's most notorious loony-toon. After forming the 13th Floor Elevators, the quintessential acid-rattled '60s punk band, Erickson embarked on a solo career that has explored his emotional crumbling (due mostly to his nasty penchant for LSD). He's spent several years in institutions, and his voluminous and scattered solo catalog reflects the peculiarities of his vision. At its best, Erickson's music is truly scarifying. —*John Floyd*

● **You're Gonna Miss Me** / Sep. 27, 1991 / Restless 72532
Erickson's peculiar rock vision has been too schizophrenic to produce one essential album. *You're Gonna Miss Me—The Best of Roky Erickson* rounds up the finest cuts from Erickson's solo career, from a remake of "Bermuda" up to the slashing "Don't Slander Me" and "Don't Shake Me Lucifer." An alternately rocking and frightening compilation, with fine liner notes by John Morthland. —*John Floyd*

Esquerita (Eskew Reeder)

b. , Greenville, South Carolina, d. 1986
Vocals, piano, composer / Rock & roll
With a six-inch pompadour, brocaded shirts, rhinestone shades, and a rhythmic, belligerent style of piano playing, Esquerita was the original Little Richard, years before Mr. Penniman tutti-frutti'd his way to stardom. Working the Dallas-New Orleans circuit in the early '50s, Esquerita's shot at the big time came when Capitol Records decided they needed their own version of Little Richard, after signing their answer to Elvis, Gene Vincent. The resulting recordings, though smartly produced, stand as some of the most untamed and unabashed sides ever issued by a major label. Long revered by rock & roll fans the world over, they make Little Richard's Specialty sides look highly disciplined. Though Esquerita continued to record in a tamer style through the '60s, his Capitol sides stand as a monument to the potential of rock & roll's lunatic power and the off-kilter genius of Esquerita. — *Cub Koda*

● **Capitol Collectors Series** / 1990 / Capitol 91871
One of the great lost rock & roll wildmen, Esquerita was as crazed as Little Richard (to whom he was an inspiration musically and visually). All of his key Capitol tracks can be found on this 28-song CD. — *Jeff Tamarkin*

Gloria Estefan & Miami Sound Machine

b. Jan. 9, 1957, Havana, Cuba
Group / Pop, dance-pop
More than any other pop group, Miami Sound Machine and lead singer Gloria Estefan have brought Latin American (particularly Cuban) music into the mainstream. They originated out of the Miami Cuban community, and many of their early recordings were sung in Spanish. Their hits have included "Conga," "Bad Boy," "Words Get in the Way," "Anything for You," "1-2-3," and "Rhythm Is Gonna Get You." — *Rick Clark*

Primitive Love / 1986 / Epic 40131
Gloria Estefan occasionally gets an above-average song, and her live show sometimes includes an Afro-Latin spot where she returns to her roots. Neither was the case on this mid-'80s set, which is certainly well produced, engineered, and arranged. If you're a fan, you enjoyed it. — *Ron Wynn*

○ **Let It Loose** / 1988 / Epic 40769
The group was still billed as "Gloria Estefan & Miami Sound Machine" on this album, which showed the singer and her bandleader husband, Emilio, retaining the jazzy, Latino flavor of their earlier music while moving determinedly into the pop mainstream—and incidentally positioning Gloria as a superstar. Such goals were reached by a record that sold two million copies, went Top Ten, and produced the hits "Rhythm Is Gonna Get You," "Betcha Say That," "Can't Stay Away from You," "Anything for You," and "1-2-3." — *William Ruhlmann*

Cuts Both Ways / 1989 / Epic 45217
Dispensing with the "Miami Sound Machine" name, Estefan continued to successfully to mix Latin-tinged dance numbers with strong ballads on this million-selling Top-Ten solo album, which included "Don't Wanna Lose You," "Get On Your Feet," and "Here We Are." — *William Ruhlmann*

Into the Light / 1991 / Epic 46988
With this successful album, Estefan demonstrated that she had recovered from her serious accident of 1990. The album contains the telling hit "Coming Out of the Dark" but showed her moving even further toward the middle of the road and sacrificing her younger fans in the process—most of the singles from this album performed better on the adult contemporary charts than on the Hot 100. — *William Ruhlmann*

● **Greatest Hits** / Oct. 6, 1992 / Epic 53046
All of Gloria Estefan's hits, with and without the Miami Sound Machine, are included on *Greatest Hits*. — *Stephen Thomas Erlewine*

○ **Mi Tierra** / Jun. 22, 1993 / Epic
Estefan's all-Spanish album will cut down the amount of Top-40 radio play she receives here, but *Mi Tierra* is one of her more consistent albums. — *AMG*

Melissa Etheridge

Vocals / Singer/songwriter, blues-rock, rock & roll

Melissa Etheridge's gutsy electric blues-rock has earned her favorable comparisons to Rod Stewart and Janis Joplin, as well as a considerable fan base across America. Not only is she an solid live performer, but she has written several songs that have became AOR favorites since the late '80s, including "Bring Me Some Water" and "Similar Features." Although she earned some fans with her debut in 1988, her audience has increased with each new album. When she revealed that she is a lesbian, in 1992, her commercial fortunes were not hurt at all—in fact, her audience continued to grow. Because it is rooted in the heartbreak and turmoils of everyday life, Etheridge's music has a widespread appeal that makes her one of the top concert draws and AOR acts of the '90s. — *Stephen Thomas Erlewine*

● **Melissa Etheridge** / 1988 / Island 842303
A powerful debut with occasionally strident performances. Includes "Bring Me Some Water," a fine acoustic rocker. "Similar Features," a scathing indictment of a former lover, is a standout. — *Rick Clark*

Brave & Crazy / 1989 / Island 842302
A little more laidback offering than her self-titled debut, including reflective numbers like "Testify" and "You Used to Love to Dance." There are a few acoustic rockers like "My Back Door," "Skin Deep," and "Let Me Go." — *Rick Clark*

Never Enough / 1992 / Island 512120
Nothing here matches the raw power of "Bring Me Some Water," but this outing blends the thoughtful virtues of *Brave & Crazy* with the more rocking elements of her debut. Etheridge also synthesizes urban-dub rhythms and rap on tracks like "2001" and "Must Be Crazy for Me." Also includes the single "Ain't It Heavy." — *Rick Clark*

Yes I Am / 1993 / Island
Etheridge's gutsy acoustic guitar-based rock is given a slightly more atmospheric treatment on this outing. Her voice is front and center in the mix and the instrumentation conveys power, but there is an evenness to the dynamics here that keep her natural theatrical delivery from totally getting across. Nevertheless, "All American Girl" is a highlight, as is "I'm the Only One." A good album, but not her best. — *Rick Clark*

Eugenius

Group / Alternative pop/rock
Originally called Captain America, Eugenius is the second band from the talented Scottish guitarist/vocalist/songwriter Eugene Kelly. While Eugenius trades in the spare charm of the Vaselines for a more traditional, guitar-driven power-pop rush, the band is no less enjoyable. Kelly's talent for simple, unassuming pop songs hasn't disappeared, and several of the band's best numbers rank with the best of his previous band. Like the Vaselines, Eugenius was helped by the support of Kurt Cobain, who had the band open for Nirvana on their 1991 tour of Europe in addition to praising Eugene Kelly in many interviews. By the time Eugenius's second record was released in 1994, the band had become alternative pop stars in their own right. — *Stephen Thomas Erlewine*

● **Oomalama** / 1992 / Atlantic 82426
Eugenius's debut album is an infectious collection of fuzzy guitars and sweet pop melodies that slowly work their way into the subconscious. — *Stephen Thomas Erlewine*

Mary Queen of Scots / 1994 / Atlantic 82562
While it isn't as catchy or consistent as *Oomalama*, Eugenius's second album has enough strong songs to make it a worthwhile listen. — *Stephen Thomas Erlewine*

Eurythmics

Group / Pop/rock, dance-pop
Formed in December 1980 out of the ashes of the British band the Tourists, Eurythmics (composed of Dave Stewart and Annie Lennox) initially embraced the cool, clinical, synth-heavy sound of German ensembles like Kraftwerk or Can. The musical element that immediately set Eurythmics apart from other techno artists was Lennox's powerful yet subtle voice, which could be extremely icy or soulful, depending on the requirements of the material. Stewart's production skills and multi-instrumental strengths usually provided all the right support.

Visually, Lennox toyed with androgyny as aggressively as David Bowie. As the '80s wore on, Eurythmics progressively infused soul and garage-rock into their sound, producing an impressive string of hits. "Sweet Dreams (Are Made of This)," "Here Comes the Rain Again," "Would I Lie to You?" and a duet with Aretha Franklin, "Sisters Are Doing It for Themselves," are among the numerous hits by Eurythmics. —*Rick Clark*

○ **Sweet Dreams (Are Made of This)** / 1983 / RCA 4681
Their breakthrough second album. Much commotion was caused by the MTV video clip for the hit title track, which played up vocalist Annie Lennox's androgynous image. —*Donna DiChario*

○ **Touch** / 1983 / RCA 4917
The follow-up to the success of *Sweet Dreams* showed a more confident Lennox and Stewart, ready to expand their stylistic range. Contains the Top-40 hits "Here Comes the Rain Again," "Who's That Girl," and "Right by Your Side." —*Scott Bultman*

○ **Be Yourself Tonight** / 1985 / RCA 5429
Showing sparks of Motown influence with the hit "Would I Lie to You?" and others. Stevie Wonder adds a harmonica solo to "There Must Be an Angel." —*Donna DiChario*

★ **Greatest Hits** / 1991 / Arista 8680
Whether cool and sophisticated or impassioned and soulful, this duo of singer Annie Lennox and guitarist Dave Stewart creates stylish and compelling rock. —*Donna DiChario*

Betty Everett

Vocals, piano / Soul
Betty Everett sang gospel growing up in Greenwood, MS before relocating to Chicago and moving into secular music. She began recording for Cobra in 1958, then joined Vee-Jay in the early '60s and started to land hit records. Her original version of "You're No Good," though sung with fire and verve, didn't make much impact until it was turned into a number-one pop hit by Linda Ronstadt in 1975. Her next single, "The Shoop Shoop Song (It's in His Kiss)," was her first major release, peaking at number six R&B in 1964. Her next success was the duet "Let It Be Me" with Jerry Butler, a soul version of the Everly Brothers tune that reached number five R&B that same year. Everett's finest song as a solo act was 1969's "There Comes a Time," which reached number two on the R&B charts and also cracked the pop Top-30 at 26. Everett was now on Uni, where she remained until 1970. She continued recording for Fantasy until 1974, and made one other record for United Artists in 1978. —*Ron Wynn*

● **Shoop Shoop Song** / 1993 / Vee Jay 707
Though sometimes classified as a "girl group" singer because of the Top-Ten success of "The Shoop Shoop Song," Betty Everett's main thrust was much more in the R&B/soul vein. This excellent 25-track anthology of her 1963-65 material shows her facility with various soul, R&B, and pop styles. She had three other minor hits—the original hit version of "You're No Good," the energetic Goffin-King pop-rocker "I Can't Hear You," and Van McCoy's soulful "Gettin' Mighty Crowded"—all of which are featured here. But most of the other material is equally enjoyable, including other early efforts by McCoy, Valerie Simpson and Nick Ashford, and even P. F. Sloan. This CD doesn't include her hit duets with fellow Chicago soulster Jerry Butler, but it's a consistently enjoyable retrospective of an underrated singer who straddled the soul and pop worlds. —*Richie Unterberger*

The Everly Brothers

Group / Rock & roll, pop/rock, country rock
Don (b. 1937) and Phil (b. 1939) were sons of guitarist Ike Everly, said to be a teacher of finger-picking legend Merle Travis. As children, the brothers starred on an early radio program with their parents, going solo when their folks retired in the '50s. After recording in a country-duo style for Columbia with scant results, they switched to rock & roll on the Cadence label and had an immediate smash with "Bye Bye Love," going on to score over 25 Top-40 pop hits between 1957 and 1964. Their unerring harmonies melded well with crisp arrangements featuring top Nashville session players (among them Chet Atkins) and a bountiful supply of top-notch material, most of it coming from the prolific pens of Felice and Boudleaux Bryant. By the late '60s, the strain of touring, lack of record sales, and drug problems were all leading to their eventual and much-publicized split in 1973. Both recorded solo albums without success and reunited in 1983 to much critical acclaim, recording new material and touring with superb backup from a band led by guitarist Albert Lee. A major

influence on any White rock & roll group singing two-part harmony (from the Beatles on down), they continue to impress and delight fans the world over. —*Cub Koda*

○ **Everly Brothers** / Jan. 1958 / Rhino 70211
The definitive album, with exquisite harmonies, a great beat, and teen-angst sentiment galore. —*Bruce Eder*

○ **Songs Our Daddy Taught Us** / Feb. 1958 / Rhino 70212
Retro-music '50s style, but surprisingly hip. —*Bruce Eder*

○ **Fabulous Style of the Everly Brothers** / 1960 / Rhino 70213
Their best album and one of the most listenable rock records of the '50s. —*Bruce Eder*

○ **It's Everly Time** / 1960 / Warner Brothers 1381
While the Everlys' sound was diluted by more elaborate production in the '60s, that's not at all true on this LP, which is one of their very best. Not a stiff among the 12 tracks, most of which are barely known by anyone other than serious Everly fans. Includes six stellar contributions by Boudleaux and Felice Bryant, one of Don Everly's best compositions ("So Sad"), and incredible harmony singing throughout. —*Richie Unterberger*

○ **A Date with the Everly Brothers** / 1961 / Warner Brothers 1395
Though the material is not on the killer level of *Everly Time*, there are some very fine songs on their second Warner LP. Includes "Cathy's Clown," their raucous cover of Little Richard's "Lucille," "Love Hurts" (which preceded Roy Orbison's hit version), and "So How Come" (covered by the Beatles in 1963 on the BBC). —*Richie Unterberger*

☆ **Roots** / 1969 / Warner Brothers 1752
The best album of their Warner period, and the most well crafted of the numerous breakthrough country-rock albums of the late '60s. —*Bruce Eder*

All They Had to Do Was Dream / 1985 / Rhino 70214
Alternate takes of much of their strongest material from the Cadence era, cut between 1957 and 1960. A bit more tentative than the familiar renditions, these aren't as good as the versions that ended up on official releases, but are enjoyable and fascinating glimpses at works-in-progress, and the singing is excellent throughout. Includes different versions of hits like "Wake Up Little Susie," "All I Have to Do Is Dream," "Till I Kissed You," and "When Will I Be Loved." —*Richie Unterberger*

★ **Cadence Classics—Their 20 Greatest Hits** / 1986 / Rhino 05258
Some of the best rock & roll ever recorded. Tough, melodic, innocent, and inventive. More than a road map for the Beatles' sound. —*Bruce Eder*

Hidden Gems from the Warner Years / 1989 / ACE 272
This collects 14 songs that originally appeared on non-hit singles between 1962 and 1965; many of them had never been on LP. This material strongly counters the view that the Everlys faded artistically after "Cathy's Clown." The writing credits for these strong compositions read a bit like a *Who's Who* of early '60s pop-rock, with contributions from Gerry Goffin, Mann-Weill, Doc Pomus and Mort Shuman, Sonny Curtis, Boudleaux and Felice Bryant, and the Everlys themselves. The singing is fabulous, and the arrangements still strong, rock oriented, and tastefully produced. Tracks like "Nancy's Minuet" (1963), a great Don Everly original that is one of their best paeans to lovelorn melancholia, and "You're the One I Love" (1964), a fine brooding midtempo rocker, stand with their very best work. Only three of these appear on the Everlys '60s anthology *Walk Right Back*, making this a necessary purchase for Everlys fans. —*Richie Unterberger*

○ **Classic Everly Brothers** / 1992 / Bear Family 15618
The three-disc boxed set *Classic Everly Brothers* collects all of their Cadence recordings, including alternate takes, as well as several early radio shows and the four tracks the duo recorded for Columbia in 1955. While this music is the most essential the brothers ever made, the disc of rarities is only of interest to devoted fans. Nevertheless, the sound on the box is stellar, the liner notes are excellent, and the whole package is wonderful. For hardcore fans, the set is worth the money. —*Stephen Thomas Erlewine*

☆ **Walk Right Back: The Everly Brothers on Warner Bros.** / 1993 / Warner Archives
This two-CD, 50-track compilation assembles the Everly Brothers' most memorable recordings of the 1960s. Though their work from this period has sometimes been criticized as inferior to their classic '50s recordings for Cadence, the best of these songs are a

match for anything the duo recorded. As it happens, the strongest of these tunes are drawn from their first two albums for Warners in the 1960s, including the hits "Cathy's Clown" and "So Sad." In the following years, their material suffered from increasing inconsistency and ill-suited production. Yet the Brothers continued to intermittently hit the mark squarely—not only with early '60s hits like "Crying in the Rain" and "Temptation," but neglected flop singles like "Nancy's Minuet" and "You're the One I Love," as well as the hard-rocking minor 1964 hit "Gone Gone Gone" (their last Top-40 single). They also showed a willingness to incorporate the hard-rocking beat of the British invasion into their work that was not shared by any of the other major stars of the '50s. This compilation misses a number of fine B-sides and non-hit singles from the early and mid '60s (check the Ace import collection *Hidden Gems* for those), and perhaps leans too heavily on their tepid late '60s country-rock, but it's a good overview of a body of work that is often unfairly overlooked. —*Richie Unterberger*

○ **Mercury Years** / Jul. 20, 1993 / Mercury
Mercury Years collects all of the finest moments from their two '80s albums. Its best moments, like "On the Wings of a Nightingale," are surprisingly strong. —*Stephen Thomas Erlewine*

Everything but the Girl

Group / Pop
A British pop duo with light jazz overtones, formed by Tracey Thorn and Ben Watt in 1983. —*William Ruhlmann*

● **Idlewild** / 1988 / Sire 25721
Thorn and Watt made a couple of albums with a cocktail-jazz backup and one with strings before trying a small unit for the intimate songs of their most accessible recording. The setting is perfect for such moving compositions as "Love Is Here Where I Live" and "Apron Strings." Start here, then go on to the rest of this remarkable group's catalog. —*William Ruhlmann*

The Exciters

Group / R&B
Despite the presence of lone male Herb Rooney, the Exciters made some of the best girl-group records of the early '60s. Led by vibrant-voiced Brenda Reid, the originally all-female quartet came from Jamaica, NY, as the Masterettes. After signing on with saxist Al Sears as their manager, they switched their name to the Exciters and cut "Tell Him" in 1962 for United Artists. Produced by Jerry Lieber and Mike Stoller, the brilliant uptown soul effort proved a major smash. Reid's roaring pipes were expertly spotlighted on the follow-ups "He's Got the Power," "Get Him," and their original reading of "Do-Wah-Diddy," immortalized later that year by Manfred Mann. The group later appeared on Roulette, Band, Shout, and RCA. Reid and Rooney were married for a time, and Reid now performs with her children backing her. —*Bill Dahl*

● **Tell Him /Emi Legends of Rock 'n' Roll Series** / 1991 / EMI America 95202
Girl-group R&B with full-fledged, violin-laden productions backing Brenda Reid's soul-drenched lead vocals. —*Bill Dahl*

Extreme

Group / Hard rock, heavy metal, pop/rock
Although guitarist and band mastermind Nuno Bettencourt's style is derived from Eddie Van Halen, his heart is with the progressive hard rock of Queen, as well as Beatlesque pop and touches of lounge jazz. Consequently, Extreme's music is never easy to classify. It's not just heavy metal, hard rock, or pop—their albums cover all of that territory, with a sweeping ambition and a social conscious to match. By the time of their second album, *Pornograffiti,* Bettencourt was already well respected in the heavy metal world, but it was the Everly Brothers-style acoustic ballad, "More Than Words," that crossed them over into the mainstream. It hit number one and the follow-up single, the acoustic-based pop rocker "Hole Hearted," hit number four. Extreme's third album, *Extreme III: Three Sides to Every Story,* was an overambitious follow-up that sold well at first, but didn't have the staying power of their previous album. —*Stephen Thomas Erlewine*

Extreme / 1989 / A&M 5238
Extreme's first album shows the band struggling to shed their influences—particularly Van Halen—and develop a style of their own. Consequently, it's wildly uneven, but guitarist Nuno Bettencourt is always worth hearing. —*Stephen Thomas Erlewine*

● **Extreme II: Pornograffitti** / 1990 / A&M 5313
MTV-ready mainstream pretty-boy hard rockers, or sensitive acoustic balladeers singing lounge-lizard schmaltz? Candy mint or breath mint? Exceptional lead-guitar chops by Nuno Bettencourt, who also carries fine vocal work with lead singer Gary Cherone. Contains the left-field acoustic hits "More Than Words" and "Hole Hearted." "Song for Love" should have been an AOR hit. —*Rick Clark*

III Sides to Every Story / 1992 / A&M 540006
Highlighted by the single "Rest in Peace," *III Sides to Every Story* stretches three separate musical movements—entitled "Yours," "Mine," and "Truth"—over 70 minutes of music. The disc packs a powerful anti-war message without being drearily pessimistic or nihilistic about its subject matter. Extreme have broken the mold (established on their previous release) of a standard hard rock band milking the occasional power ballad, to assemble a politically correct tour de force. These guys are intent on making strong political statements with loud guitars and on songs such as "Warheads," "Peacemaker Die," and "Who Cares?" They succeed. —*Roch Parisien*

Fabian

Vocals / Pop
Thanks to a series of performances on Dick Clark's "American Bandstand," Fabian rocketed to stardom in the late '50s. With his stylish good looks and mild rock & roll, he became one of the top teen idols of the era. Luckily, he had the support of the legendary songwriting team of Doc Pomus and Mort Shuman, who provided him with "Turn Me Loose," "Hound Dog Man," and "I'm a Man," among other songs. Fabian's fame peaked in 1959 with the million-selling "Tiger" single. After that, he valiantly tried to become a movie star. When Congress fingered him as one of the performers who benefited from payola, his already ailing career was given a nearly fatal blow. Under questioning, Fabian explained that his records featured a substantial amount of electronic doctoring in order to improve his voice. He starred in some more movies in the '60s, without regaining the audience of his peak years. —*Stephen Thomas Erlewine*

● **This Is Fabian!** (1959-61) / ACE 321
The original versions of all of Fabian's hits are featured on this collection. —*Stephen Thomas Erlewine*

The Fabulous Thunderbirds

Group / Blues-rock
The Fabulous Thunderbirds are one of the finest examples of Texas roadhouse R&B/electric blues. The original lineup featured the taut lead-guitar work of Jimmie Vaughan (Stevie Ray's brother). Kim Wilson, the band's frontman, is a master of rude harmonica playing. After years of fine album releases and endless gigging, this journeyman Austin band hit it big in 1986 with the number-ten title cut off the Dave Edmunds-produced *Tuff Enuff.* Since then they've continued to enjoy a string of hits, including a remake of Sam & Dave's "Wrap It Up," "Stand Back," and "Powerful Stuff," featured in the Tom Cruise film *Cocktail.* In 1990 Vaughan left the group and was replaced by Kid Bangham and Duke Robillard. After one more album, the group called it quits, with Wilson pursuing a solo career. —*Rick Clark*

○ **Fabulous Thunderbirds** / 1979 / Chrysalis 21250
Their debut album, with the original lineup of Wilson, Vaughan, Buck, and Ferguson stompin' through a roadhouse set of covers and genre-worthy originals. One of the few White blues albums that works. —*Cub Koda*

What's the Word / 1980 / Chrysalis 21287
Their second album is equally powerful. Some of their best, including the off-kilter "Los Fabulusos Thunderbirds" and "Running Shoes." —*Cub Koda*

Tuff Enuff / 1986 / Epic 40304
Their breakthrough success. The title track and soul covers point the band in a new, more mainstream direction. —*Cub Koda*

● **Essential** / 1991 / Chrysalis 21851
Nice compilation of the early Chrysalis albums on one CD. —*Cub Koda*

○ **Hot Stuff: The Greatest Hits** / 1992 / Epic 53007

The best tracks from the Fabulous Thunderbirds' more rock-oriented years at CBS Associated Records are collected on this single-disc compilation. —*AMG*

Faces

Group / Rock & roll

When Steve Marriott left the Small Faces in 1969, the three remaining members brought in guitarist Ron Wood and lead singer Rod Stewart to complete the lineup and changed their name to the Faces, which was only appropriate since the group now only slightly resembled the mod pop group of the past. Instead, the Faces were a rough, sloppy rock & roll band, able to pound out a rocker like "Had Me a Real Good Time," a blues ballad like "Tell Everyone," and a folk number like "Richmond" all in one album. Stewart, already becoming a star in his own right, let himself go wild with the Faces, tearing through covers and originals with abandon. While his voice didn't have the power of Stewart's, bassist Ronnie Lane's songs were equally as impressive and eclectic. Wood's rhythm guitar had a warm, fat tone that was as influential and driving as Keith Richards's style.

Notorious for their hard-partying, boozy tours and ragged concerts, the Faces lived the rock & roll lifestyle to the extreme. When Stewart's solo career became more successful than the Faces', the band slowly became subservient to his personality; after their final studio album, *Ooh La La,* in 1973, Lane left the band. After a tour in 1974, they called it quits. Wood joined the Rolling Stones, drummer Kenny Jones eventually became part of the Who, and keyboardist Ian McLagan became a sought-after supporting musician. Stewart became a superstar, although he never matched the simple charms of the Faces.

While they were together, the Faces never sold that many records and were never considered as important as the Stones, yet their music has proven extremely influential over the years. Many punk rockers in the late '70s learned how to play their instruments by listening to Faces records. In the '80s and '90s, guitar-rock bands from the Replacements to the Black Crowes took their cue from the Faces as much as the Stones. Their reckless, loose, and joyous spirit has stayed alive in much of the best rock & roll of the past two decades. —*Stephen Thomas Erlewine*

○ **First Step** / 1970 / Warner

On their first album, the Faces established the pattern they would follow throughout their four albums—a ragged mix of breakneck rockers ("Shake, Shudder"), sensitive yet gritty ballads ("Devotion"), folk songs ("Stone"), revelatory covers (Bob Dylan's "Wicked Messenger"), and relaxed, friendly rockers ("Three Button Hand Me Down"). Although two instrumentals on the second side is one too many (Ron Wood's "Pineapple and the Monkey" is pretty great), the Faces seldom got better than the first half of *First Step.* —*Stephen Thomas Erlewine*

☆ **Long Player** / 1971 / Warner Brothers 4037

With their second effort, the Faces grew more muscular and loose, rocking with loose abandon on "Bad n' Ruin" and "Had Me a Real Good Time," two of their best songs. At the same time, their ballads also improved, with Stewart's "Tell Everyone" and Lane's "Richmond" rivalling each other for the most moving number on the album. Out of the two live tracks, "Balling the Jack" goes on a little too long, but "Maybe I'm Amazed" is tremendous—the Faces tear into the song, transforming it from another McCartney ballad to a heartfelt cry of devotion. *Long Player* is a sloppy, terrific record—although it has a couple of weak moments, it has the heart and soul of the band. —*Stephen Thomas Erlewine*

★ **A Nod Is as Good as a Wink . . . To a Blind Horse** / 1971 / Warner

Boasting "Stay with Me," the only hit the Faces ever had, *A Nod Is as Good as a Wink* is their most consistent record, and arguably their best. "Stay with Me" and "Miss Judy's Farm" showcase the band at their best—they're all over the place, threatening to fall apart altogether, before they snap it all back into place. Nobody rocked better than this, and the album is full of such terrific moments, including a rollicking cover of Chuck Berry's "Memphis." As with all Faces albums, it's a little messy, but it shows a classic rock & roll band at the top of their form. —*Stephen Thomas Erlewine*

Ooh La La / 1973 / Warner Brothers 2665

Although it's routinely lambasted as an uninspired effort or a sellout, *Ooh La La* is a tight rock & roll album, with its best moments—"Cindy Incidentally" and "Borstal Boy"—ranking among the Faces' best songs. —*Stephen Thomas Erlewine*

Snakes & Ladders / 1976 / Pioneer 4040

The best available overview of the Faces. Includes the rare "Pool Hall Richard," "Cindy Incidentally," and "Stay with Me." —*Rick Clark*

Donald Fagen

b. Jan. 10, 1948, Passaic, NJ

Vocals, keyboard / Pop/rock

Donald Fagen was one of the two masterminds behind Steely Dan, the seminal jazz-pop band of the '70s. Fagen's solo work has been a continuation of the band's work of the early '80s—carefully constructed and arranged, intricately detailed pop songs that are more substantial than their stylish surface may indicate. His 1982 solo debut, *The Nightfly,* was the best album he had made in years. It covered the same ground as the last two Steely Dan albums, yet surpassed them in terms of ambition and achievement.

After the success of *The Nightfly,* Fagen suffered a case of writer's block. For the rest of the decade he contributed music to the occasional film and briefly wrote a column for *Premiere* magazine in the mid '80s. In the early '90s, he toured with the New York Rock & Soul Revue as he finished the material for his second album. With former Steely Dan partner Walter Becker producing, 1993's *Kamakiriad* sounded like *Aja* recorded with '90s technology. It had some success on the adult contemporary charts, but it was overshadowed by the duo's decision to re-form Steely Dan and tour for the first time in nearly 20 years. The tour was a massive success. —*Stephen Thomas Erlewine*

★ **Nightfly** / 1982 / Warner Brothers 23696

For his debut solo album after leaving Steely Dan, Fagen turned in a typically sophisticated jazz-pop collection tied to a lyrical theme concerning the late '50s and early '60s. One song takes the Kennedy administration's slogan, "The New Frontier," as a title, while another, "The Goodbye Look," is set in Cuba around the time of Castro's takeover. Steely Dan lovers will feel right at home. —*William Ruhlmann*

○ **Kamakiriad** / May 25, 1993 / Reprise 45230

After 11 years, Donald Fagen delivered his second album, *Kamakiriad,* in the summer of 1993. Where sophisticated eclecticism of *The Nightfly* was warm and welcoming, *Kamakiriad* is insular—it takes several listens before all of the pieces fall into place. While all of the album *sounds* terrific, the melodies are subtler and tend to get buried under the meticulous arrangements. However, the hooks and melodies emerge after a couple of plays, as do Fagen's wry, witty lyrics. —*Stephen Thomas Erlewine*

Fairport Convention

Group / Folk-rock

Fairport Convention emerged at the end of the '60s as something of a British response to the American West Coast sound. A wildly eclectic bunch at the outset, Fairport quickly jettisoned their original vocal front line and abandoned the American singer/songwriter material they had often relied on. With the band's third album, *Unhalfbricking,* guitarist Richard Thompson's songwriting skills took hold, and Sandy Denny emerged as England's premier female vocalist.

The album that was to follow, *Liege and Lief,* proved to be the crown jewel of Fairport's career. Inspired by earlier experiments with traditional British folk music, the band crafted a mixture of heavily reworked folk standards and sympathetic originals, topped by the brilliant singing of Denny. Sadly, it was to be her last (for a time) and after another album, Thompson was gone as well.

Fairport continued through the '70s with ever-changing lineups, and even a short-lived reunion with Denny, but despite making several fine, underrated albums, the group eventually waved goodbye.

The mid '80s would see a re-born Fairport, centering around three members from the band's classic era and continuing the legacy with several more fine albums. The complete Fairport story could occupy a massive volume in itself; just let it be known that the influence and importance of this band is substantial. — *Steve Aldrich*

○ **Fairport Convention (1st)** / 1968 / Polydor 835230
A bracing and riveting debut that embraces folk-rock. With Richard Thompson and Ian Matthews on board. — *Bruce Eder & William Ruhlmann*

○ **What We Did on Our Holidays** / Jan. 1968 / Carthage 4430
Their second album introduces Sandy Denny, singing "I'll Keep It with Mine." Dazzling traditional folk, highlighted by "She Moved Through the Fair." — *William Ruhlmann and Bruce Eder*

★ **Unhalfbricking** / Jan. 1969 / Hannibal 4418
Richard Thompson and Sandy Denny at their Fairport peak; three Dylan tunes, including the hit "Si Tu Dois Partir," and Denny's "Who Knows Where the Time Goes." This is worth owning just for the apocalyptic "A Sailor's Life." — *William Ruhlmann and Bruce Eder*

☆ **Liege and Lief** / Feb. 1969 / A&M 4257
This was Sandy Denny's exit album, highlighted by the scintillating "Tam Lin" and "Matty Groves." Voted the best folk album of all time by the readers of Britain's *Folk Roots* magazine. Features Thompson and Denny along with fiddler Dave Swarbrick. — *Stephen Winick, Bruce Eder, and William Ruhlmann*

Full House / Feb. 1970 / Carthage 4417
Denny and bass-player Ashely Hutchings are gone. Thompson and Swarbrick take over as singers, Dave Pegg (now also of Jethro Tull) plays bass. — *Stephen Winick*

● **Fairport Chronicles** / 1972 / A&M 6016
A well-chosen early best-of collection. — *William Ruhlmann*

House Full / 1986 / Hannibal 1319
A revised version of the 1977 album *Live at the L.A. Troubadour*, which, in turn, is taken from a concert performance by the Richard Thompson-led 1970 lineup of Fairport, one of its strongest units. Long versions of "Sloth" and "Matty Groves" dominate. — *William Ruhlmann*

○ **Heyday** / 1987 / Hannibal 1329
This collection of 14 BBC performances from 1968 and 1969 is just as outstanding as their late-'60s studio albums and shows their mastery of an astonishing range of material. Most of these songs were not recorded on the group's official releases. Includes covers of gems by Joni Mitchell, Eric Anderson, Johnny Cash, Leonard Cohen, Gene Clark, Richard Farina, the Everlys, and Bob Dylan. — *Richie Unterberger*

Faith No More

Group / Alternative rock, heavy metal
With their fusion of heavy metal, funk, hip-hop, and progressive rock, Faith No More has earned a substantial cult following. By the time they recorded their first album in 1985, the band had already had a string of lead vocalists, including Courtney Love. Their debut, *We Care a Lot*, featured Chuck Mosley's abrasive vocals but it was driven by Jim Martin's metallic guitar. Faith No More's next album, 1987's *Introduce Yourself*, was a more cohesive and impressive effort—for the first time, the rap and metal elements didn't sound like they were fighting each other.

In 1988, the rest of the band fired Mosley. He was replaced by San Francisco Bay Area vocalist Mike Patton during the recording of their next album, *The Real Thing*. Patton was a more accomplished vocalist, able to change effortlessly between rapping and singing, as well as adding a considerably more bizarre slant to the lyrics. Besides the new vocalist, the band tightened their attack, and the result was the genre-bending hit single, "Epic," which established them as a major hard rock act.

Following up the hit wasn't as easy, however. Faith No More followed their breakthrough success with 1992's *Angel Dust*, one of the more complex and simply confounding records ever released by a major label. Although it sold respectably, it didn't have the crossover potential of the first album. When the band toured in support of the album, tensions between the band and Martin began to escalate, and rumors that his guitar was stripped from some of the final mixes of *Angel Dust* began to circulate. As the band was recording its fifth album in early 1994, it was confirmed that Martin had been fired from the band. — *Stephen Thomas Erlewine*

● **Real Thing** / 1989 / Slash 25878

An unusual combination of heavy metal, rap, and hard rock. Appealing to head-bangers and popsters alike. — *Donna DiChario*

○ **Angel Dust** / 1992 / Slash 26785
Quite diverse and eclectic, with istyles ranging from lounge jazz to power-pop and all-out industrial grindcore. The songwriting shows a lot of talent, especially from Mike Patton, whose vocal range is used to its full potential on this album, the band's fourth. — *John Book*

Marianne Faithfull

b. 1947, London, England
Vocals / Pop/rock
Faithfull gravitated into the London pop scene with model looks and a sweet singing voice. She was discovered by Rolling Stones manager Andrew "Loog" Oldham and was romantically involved for a period with Mick Jagger. Her early work was influenced by the Stones, while her later work, affected by years of pain and substance abuse, was the rock equivalent of Edith Piaf's music, a sort of pop-cabaret singing with a throaty delivery. — *Larry Lapka*

○ **Marianne Faithfull's Greatest Hits** / 1969 / ABKCO 7547
While missing a few fine album tracks, this is an excellent 16-song distillation of her '60s recordings. Includes all of her British and American hits—"As Tears Go By," "This Little Bird," "Summer Nights," and "Come and Stay with Me." Bonuses include "In My Time of Sorrow," an obscure mid-'60s folk-rocker cowritten by Jackie DeShannon and Jimmy Page, and her 1969 single "Sister Morphine" (co-written with the Rolling Stones)—predating the Sticky Fingers version, it's easily her most powerful performance of the decade. — *Richie Unterberger*

● **Broken English** / 1979 / Island 842355
After a lengthy absence, Faithfull resurfaced on this 1979 album, which took the edgy and brittle sound of punk-rock and gave it a shot of studio-smooth dance rock. Faithfull's whiskey-worn vocals perfectly match the bitter and biting "Why'd Ya Do It" and revitalize John Lennon's "Working Class Hero." — *John Floyd*

○ **Strange Weather** / 1987 / Island 842593
Faithfull's 1987 release recast her as a nicotine-stained chanteuse, approaching such standards as "Boulevard of Broken Dreams" and "Penthouse Serenade" with a ravaged, world-weary demeanor that recalls the latter-day recordings of Billie Holiday. She also tackles some blues and jazz material and turns "As Tears Go By" into the gut-wrenching torch ballad neither the Stones nor Faithfull could ever have done in the '60s. A dark, challenging masterpiece. — *John Floyd*

Blazing Away / 1990 / Island 842794
Live disc recorded at the Brooklyn's St. Anne's Cathedral. With a song list that stretches back to her '60s singles, this is something of a career overview. But the wisdom and maturity she applies to the material—both old and new—make this a document that attests to Faithfull's continued vitality and brave artistic commitment. — *John Floyd*

The Falcons

Group / Soul
The Falcons are often credited as having cut the first true soul record in 1959 with "You're So Fine." A host of '60s soul stars called themselves Falcons at one time or another, including founder Eddie Floyd, Wilson Pickett, Sir Mack Rice, and 100 Proof Aged in Soul's Joe Stubbs. Originally an integrated R&B group headed by Floyd, the Falcons debuted on Mercury in 1955. Under the production aegis of Robert West, the Falcons' sound became more gospel-based as time passed, and with Stubbs as lead, the seminal "You're So Fine" was a major hit in 1959. Pickett screamed the gospel-fired ballad "I Found a Love" to national prominence on West's LuPine label in 1962, backed by guitarist Robert Ward's Ohio Untouchables. When Pickett went solo shortly thereafter, the members went their separate ways. West recruited another group, the Fabulous Playboys, who took over the Falcons name, but with little success. — *Bill Dahl*

○ **You're So Fine** / Jan. 1986 / Relic 7003
Prototypical early Detroit soul from this rough-edged vocal group, which featured Eddie Floyd and Joe Stubbs. — *Bill Dahl*

● **I Found a Love** / Feb. 1986 / Relic 7012

A more incendiary collection, thanks to the addition of Wilson Pickett as the Falcons' frontman. — *Bill Dahl*

The Fall

Group / Punk, alternative rock

While the band's audience has never expanded beyond a rabidly devoted cult following across the world, the Fall has had a significant impact on the post-punk music of the '70s, '80s, and '90s. Many fans of the group have gone on to form their own bands, leaving the rock underground with a wealth of groups replicating and expanding the Fall's harsh, jagged guitar experimentalism.

Under the leadership of guitarist/vocalist Mark E. Smith, the band has released an enormous number of albums since their debut in 1977. Every album is a complex, challenging piece of rock & roll, yet none of them sounds the same. With each album, the Fall explores new territory, from guitar noise to club music. Through every incarnation, Smith has retained his reputation as one of rock's foremost experimental artists. — *Stephen Thomas Erlewine*

○ **This Nation's Saving Grace** / 1985 / Beggars Banquet 67
Driven by an unrelenting, tense performance by the band and filled with fractured melodies and elliptical guitar hooks, *This Nation's Saving Grace* is the Fall's masterpiece. — *Stephen Thomas Erlewine*

★ **458489 A Sides** / 1990 / Beggars Banquet 2430
The Fall's singles collection covers their material between 1984 and 1989 and features some of their finest, most innovative material. — *Stephen Thomas Erlewine*

Mylene Farmer

Vocals / Disco

Since 1985, Mylene Farmer (born in Quebec but raised in France) and her musical collaborator Laurent Boutonnat have expanded the Birkin-Gainsbourg bedroom fantasy song into an entire cosmology of sighing songs and pensive, melancholy, and fitfully melodic dances in which fin-de-siecle libertinism is the motive principle and intoxicated hallucination the saving grace. It's fabulously popular throughout Euro-land and not unknown even in the United States. — *Michael Freedberg*

○ **Ainsi Soit Je . . .** / 1988 /
Ambitiously stylish, this thick mix of powerful dance rhythms and sensual melodies is both accessible and subtle. Sometimes uneven in its overall composition, it offers the superb sound quality of the mature artist. — *Vladimir Bogdanov*

● **L'antre . . .** / 1991 /
Marked with the same stylistic integrity as her previous albums, this is without a doubt Mylene Farmer's masterpiece. Compositions are still elaborate and carefully designed but now have a more refined, transparent feel. Deep, dark reflection of life, so typical for the artist, is enriched by the sparkling energy of her powerful, sometimes hysterical irony and the calm confidence of her velvet-soft voice. — *Vladimir Bogdanov*

Fastbacks

Group / Alternative pop/rock

The Fastbacks are a Seattle quartet that generates a sound alternating between punkish pop and poppish punk. Recording sporadically between 1982 and the present, the band benefits from sometime Young Fresh Fellows guitarist Kurt Bloch and the sneering vocals of Kim Warnick, who also doubles as bassist. An extremely underrated group. — *David Szatmary*

○ **And His Orchestra** / 1987 / Pop Llama 803
Recorded between 1981 and 1985, this album features 20 songs from a driving Seattle band that alternates between poppish punk and punkish pop. Fueled by Kurt Bloch's guitar. — *David Szatmary*

Very Very Powerful Motor / 1990 / Pop Llama 011
Thanks to some tougher guitars and rawer vocals, *Very, Very Powerful Motor* is the most punkish album the Fastbacks have released, yet the songs never lack a strong melody. — *Stephen Thomas Erlewine*

● **Zucker** / Jan. 29, 1993 / Sub Pop 184
With its speedy, energetic riffs and bright melodies, *Zucker* is one of the Fastbacks' best albums. — *Stephen Thomas Erlewine*

Fatback Band

Group / Funk

A seminal funk ensemble, the Fatback Band made many great singles through the '70s and early '80s, ranging from humorous novelty tunes to energetic dance vehicles and even occasional political-message tracks. They began recording for Perception in the early '70s, and had moderate luck with "Street Dance" in 1973. They moved to Event in 1974, and while funk audiences loved such songs as "Wicki-Wacky" and "(Are You Ready) Do the Bus Stop," they didn't generate much sales action. Their first sizable hit was "Spanish Hustle" in 1976, which reached number 12 on the R&B charts.

They shortened their name to Fatback in 1977, and landed their first Top-Ten R&B hit with "I Like Girls" in 1978. Their 1979 single "King Time III (Personality Jock)" is widely considered the first rap single in many circles. But their biggest year was 1980, when they scored two Top-Ten R&B hits with "Gotta Get My Hands on Some (Money)" and "Backstrokin'," their finest tune. Fatback kept going through the mid '80s, landing one more Top-20 hit with "Take It Any Way You Can Want It" in 1981. — *Ron Wynn*

● **Best of the Fatback Band** / 1976 / Spring 2391246
Though they earned their biggest hits under the guise of Fatback, for my money their most enjoyable records were recorded as the Fatback Band. The often-infectious funk arrangements and horn lines helped embellish what were without question forgettable group vocals. But there were few East Coast bands making more humorous and delightful singles than the Fatback Band, even if they never got significant airplay or sales, even within the R&B community. This anthology collects most of the tracks that either charted or were underground hits, including the wonderful "Wicky Wacky." — *Ron Wynn*

Fear

Group / Hardcore

With their blistering, nihilistic punk rock, Fear was one of the leading Los Angeles hardcore bands of the early '80s. More than most hardcore bands, Fear relied on shock techniques, dark humor, and vulgarity—frequently, singer Lee Ving's lyrics were outright offensive, particularly concerning women and homosexuals. After two records, the band imploded and Ving pursued a successful acting career. — *Stephen Thomas Erlewine*

● **Record** / 1982 / Slash 23933
Fierce punk-rock, Los Angeles–'80s variety, distinguished by the raw vocals of lead singer Lee Ving. — *William Ruhlmann*

Charlie Feathers

b. Jun. 12, 1932, Hollow Springs, MS
Vocals, guitar / Rockabilly

Charlie Feathers was one of the first country artists to record for Sam Phillips at the legendary Sun studios. He was there at the birth of rock & roll. Marketed during his tenure at the label strictly as a country artist, Feathers went on to record a superb collection of singles for labels like Meteor, King, Kay, and Philwood, all in a highly charged rockabilly vein. Championed by the European rockabilly collector community in the early '70s, he has continued recording for a variety of labels—not varying, only improving, his original '50s style. Charlie Feathers is a superb stylist. His voice is a consummate instrument, full of nuances uniquely his own, whether he's rocking up a storm or singing the most mournful of country ballads. Though never commercially successful, Charlie Feathers nonetheless remains a shining example of raw American music at its finest. — *Cub Koda*

Live in Memphis / 1979 / Barrelhouse 06
Loose early-'70s recordings. Great, but unfortunately out of print. — *Cub Koda*

● **Jungle Fever** / 1987 / Kay 5045
Boasting a generous 20 tracks, *Jungle Fever* is the best available compilation of Charlie Feathers's original rockabilly recordings. All his best-known songs are collected here, including "Get with It" and "Tongue-Tied Jill." — *Stephen Thomas Erlewine*

Charlie Feathers / 1991 / Nonesuch 61147
Recent recordings with Sun alumni. — *Cub Koda*

○ **Rock-a-Billy** / May 1991 / Zu-Zazz 2011

Superb collection of rare and unissued sides, 1954-1973, show-casing Feathers's mastery of rockabilly and country material. — *Cub Koda*

The Feelies

Group / Alternative pop/rock

A New Jersey band fueled by the twin guitars of Glenn Mercer and Bill Million. Since their debut in 1980, the group has produced a sound that combines elements of the Byrds and Velvet Underground under several names besides the Feelies, including the Trypes and Yung Wu. — *David Szatmary*

● **Crazy Rhythms** / 1980 / A&M 5319

The debut of the New Jerseyites fluctuates between folk-rock and Velvet Underground fuzz. — *David Szatmary*

○ **Good Earth** / 1986 / Coyote 8673

A folkish entry with an occasional stinging guitar by the band that re-formed as the Feelies with this album. Coproduced by Peter Buck. — *David Szatmary*

○ **Only Life** / 1989 / A&M 5214

Only Life moves from the light acoustic strumming of 1986's *The Good Earth* into a slightly harder electric sound, while still retaining much of the textured and atmospheric qualities that made its predecessor so charming. There is more of a return of the driving rhythms of the first album, and the entire album has a feeling of the Velvet Underground revisited. — *Chris Woodstra*

Bryan Ferry

b. Sep. 26, 1945, Washington, Durham, UK
Vocals / Pop/rock

Bryan Ferry has been recording solo albums since Roxy Music's early- to mid-'70s heyday, in a bizarre and confounding hodge-podge of styles. His first few solos incorporated mostly eclectic covers that wander everywhere from early rock and soul hits up to Dylan and Beatles tunes. Musically, they share a lot of common ground with his full-time group. — *John Floyd*

○ **These Foolish Things** / 1973 / Reprise 26082

As a side project during his Roxy Music tenure, Ferry recorded this album of drastic rearrangements of a variety of standards, most of them from the '60s. The Beatles, the Rolling Stones, and especially Bob Dylan never sounded like this before. — *William Ruhlmann*

Another Time, Another Place / 1974 / Reprise 26083

Same concept, different songs, as the suave Ferry recasts "Smoke Gets in Your Eyes," Sam Cooke, and several country standards. — *William Ruhlmann*

○ **Boys and Girls** / 1985 / Warner Brothers 25082

With the second (and presumably final) disbanding of Roxy Music, Ferry turned full time to his solo career, so this album is more of a follow-up to 1982's *Avalon*, the last Roxy album, than to 1978's *The Bride Stripped Bare*, the previous Ferry solo release. It brilliantly continues the ethereal dance-floor charm of *Avalon*. — *William Ruhlmann*

● **Street Life (Greatest Hits)** / 1986 / EG 925857

Covering both Ferry's and Roxy Music's best-known songs, *Street Life* is the best introduction to the stylish art-rocker's career. — *Stephen Thomas Erlewine*

○ **Bête Noire** / 1987 / Reprise 25598

Enlisting Madonna-producer Patrick Leonard to assist, Ferry matches his studiedly languorous vocals to densely percussive dance tracks. — *William Ruhlmann*

Taxi / 1993 / Warner Brothers 45246

For Ferry, cover albums have become both artistic statements and a way to buy time. *Taxi*, delivered some six years after *Bête Noire*, is filled with the kind of contradictions that are inherent with such a dual purpose. Nothing on the album is particularly revelatory. It's his third album entirely composed of covers, so Ferry's slick, stylish approach is familiar. Ferry is such a singular singer that *Taxi* escapes being a worthless exercise, however. Although there are some songs that don't hit the mark, there are several moments (particularly "Will You Love Me Tomorrow" and "Amazing Grace") that make up for such missteps. — *Stephen Thomas Erlewine*

5th Dimension

Group / Pop

They didn't sound anything like an R&B group, and their soaring, lighter-than-air harmonic blend frequently proved more palatable to pop audiences than to Black record buyers. But do not suggest, even for a second, that the 5th Dimension was in any way lacking in soul.

Formed as the Versatiles in 1965, the slick quintet changed its name at the request of Johnny Rivers, who had just signed them to his brand-new label, Soul City. Up-and-coming songwriter Jimmy Webb supplied the group with their first pop smash "Up, Up and Away," in 1967, and the group's monumental rise mirrored the song's high-flying imagery. Another prolific composer, Laura Nyro, handed the 5th Dimension several megahits, notably "Stoned Soul Picnic" and "Wedding Bell Blues," but their biggest seller hailed from the groundbreaking musical *Hair*. The Grammy-winning "Aquarius/Let the Sunshine In" held down the number-one slot on the pop lists for six weeks in 1969.

After several more hits, Marilyn McCoo and Billy Davis Jr., who had married while part of the group, successfully branched off as a duo, while Lamonte McLemore, Ron Townson, and Florence LaRue kept the 5th Dimension on the soul charts, losing a head-to-head battle with Diana Ross for hit status on "Love Hangover" in 1976. — *Bill Dahl*

● **Greatest Hits on Earth** / 1972 / Arista 8335

Until Rhino issued its anthology, this was the best hits package for the 5th Dimension, a group that at its peak was among the best at doing light-hearted pop with a soulful foundation. Certainly they weren't a hardcore R&B or earthy singing group, but they did put some punch into songs that were really kind of silly otherwise, like "Wedding Bell Blues." — *Ron Wynn*

○ **Anthology 1967-1973** / 1986 / Rhino 71104

Complete compilation representing the best of this California soul quintet. — *Rick A. Bueche*

Fine Young Cannibals

Group / Pop/rock, dance-pop

When the English Beat splintered in two, bassist David Steele and guitarist Andy Cox formed the Fine Young Cannibals with Roland Gift. Although the band's fusion of rock, Motown-style R&B, pop, and modern dance is tight and loaded with hooks, the real attraction is Gift's soaring falsetto—he sounds like a classic soul singer. Their 1985 debut album was critically acclaimed, but it was the 1989 follow-up, *The Raw & the Cooked*—with the number-one singles "She Drives Me Crazy" and "Good Thing"—that made the band major hit makers. Apart from a remix album in 1990 and Gift's occasional film role, the group has been quiet since their breakthrough success. — *Stephen Thomas Erlewine*

Fine Young Cannibals / 1985 / IRS 5683

Roland Gift's vocals are the find here, backed by the R&B/pop music provided by Ex-Beat members Andy Cox and David Steele. — *William Ruhlmann*

● **Raw & the Cooked** / 1989 / IRS 6273

FYC rode to massive success on the tender-and-terrified singing of Roland Gift and the neo-Motown sheen of the number-one hits "She Drives Me Crazy" and "Good Thing." — *William Ruhlmann*

Tim Finn

b. Jun. 25, 1952, Te Awamutu, New Zealand
Vocals, keyboard / Pop/rock

Singer/songwriter Tim Finn was born in Te Awamutu, New Zealand. Influenced by his Catholic upbringing and the joyous communal singalongs of the native Maori people, Finn founded the '70s new wave band Split Enz. Leaving the band in 1983 for a solo career, he released three albums before he briefly joined his brother Neil's band, Crowded House, for their *Woodface* album and tour. After leaving Crowded House, he recorded his fourth solo album, *Before & After*. Finn's light melodic songs and soaring vocals, while influenced by classic British pop, reflect his unique homeland at the bottom of the world. — *Scott Bultman*

Escapade / 1983 / A&M 4972

His solo debut. Finn broke from Split Enz to exorcise these charming, light, melodic pop songs that didn't quite fit the band's style. Sweet and sappy, his soaring vocal style and introspective lyrics make this worthwhile. — *Scott Bultman*

○ **Big Canoe** / 1988 / Virgin 90879
Much production glitz here from producer Nick Launay, competing for attention with Finn's voice and songs. A very melodic and musical second solo effort. Highlights include "Don't Bury My Heart" and "Hyacinth." —*Scott Bultman*

● **Tim Finn** / 1989 / Capitol 48735
Tim Finn's eponymous record is his most sparsely produced effort. Supported by Los Angeles session musicians and producer Mitchell Froom (Crowded House), Finn is as accessible here as he's ever been. Great melodies, well-turned phrases, and seamless backing vocals from brother Neil Finn of Crowded House, make this one his best. —*Scott Bultman*

○ **Before & After** / 1993 / Capitol 794904
On his fourth solo album, Finn dabbles in dance-pop, psuedo-reggae, and folky ballads, with a different set of producers on nearly every track. While this leads to a certain lack of consistency, Finn's songwriting has never been stronger. He has the most success on the self-produced, stripped-down tracks where his strong sense of melody and knack for catchy pop hooks are allowed to be in the forefront. "Persuasion," cowritten by Richard Thompson and "In Love with It All," written with his brother Neil Finn (Crowded House) are highlights. —*Chris Woodstra*

Firefall

Group / Pop/rock, country rock
When Firefall was formed in 1974, their pedigree included the Flying Burrito Brothers, the Byrds, and Spirit. Their first album (arguably their best) was a very commercial blend of tight harmonies and acoustic/electric, country-flavored pop/rock. Subsequent albums mined that approach, producing hits like "You Are the Woman," "Just Remember I Love You," and "Strange Way." —*Rick Clark*

○ **Firefall** / 1976 / Atlantic 19125
Firefall's self-titled debut effort—featuring the hits "You Are the Woman" and "Cinderella"—was their best album. —*Rick Clark*

● **Best of Firefall** / 1981 / Atlantic 19316
A greatest-hits collection that includes almost all the essential tracks. —*Rick Clark*

fIREHOSE

Group / Alternative pop/rock
Primarily composed of former Minutemen, fIREHOSE is a technically polished, edgy punk/pop band with funk/folkie influences and political overtones.
fIREHOSE quietly disbanded at the beginning of 1994 with a small concert in their hometown. They left behind some of the finest independent rock of the late '80s. —*John Dougan*

Ragin' Full On / 1987 / SST 079
Solid, if unfocused debut. Good songs. —*John Dougan*

● **If'n** / 1988 / SST 115
Kind of mainstream, but this is still great! —*John Dougan*

○ **Fromohio** / 1989 / SST 235
Overlooked and underappreciated. —*John Dougan*

Flyin' the Flannel / 1991 / Columbia 47839
Major-label debut. —*John Dougan*

Mr. Machinery Operator / Feb. 16, 1993 / Columbia 53208
fIREHOSE's final album was a piledriving slab of post-punk rock, tamed by J Mascis's production. Occasionally, the guitars are too thick for the band's style of music, but overall this was a fine way to close the book on their career. —*Stephen Thomas Erlewine*

The Firm

Group / Hard rock
The Firm (incorporated 1985) looked good on paper, with ex-Led Zeppelin guitarist Jimmy Page and former Free lead singer Paul Rogers. Unfortunately, precious little rose above the glut of mass produced-sounding "rock" that filled AOR radio in the '80s (or any other decade for that matter). Nevertheless, the Firm's self-titled debut album went number 17, producing a hit with "Radioactive." Their second album, *Mean Business,* reached number 22. The group disbanded shortly after its release. —*Rick Clark*

● **Firm** / 1985 / Atlantic 81239

Atmospheric rock that relies more on the vocals of former-Bad Company singer Paul Rodgers than on the guitar of ex-Led Zeppelin Jimmy Page. —*Donna DiChario*

Fishbone

Group / Alternative rock, funk
Fishbone is the late-'80s amphetamine equivalent to Sly & the Family Stone (with a healthy dose of eccentric Frank Zappa-style humor) and the early Bus Boys. Originating in Los Angeles, Fishbone tosses ska, hard funk, and hardcore rock into a socially aware stew that, like Sly Stone, blends equal parts of optimism and despair into their intelligently streetwise delivery. The band's hyperkinetic arrangements are well married to their music. All in all, Fishbone is great for those who like their music to be funky and provocative at the same time. —*Rick Clark*

Fishbone / 1985 / Columbia 40032
What a debut! Fierce, funny, and ferocious. —*John Dougan*

○ **Truth & Soul** / 1988 / Columbia 40891
A perfect mix of their anarchic, chaotic debut with their more recent, thrashier sound, *Truth & Soul* still mixes ska beats and licks with Sly and the Family Stone-style funk and harder, Living Colour-style guitar-driven chops. The only difference is, this time it comes together better than ever. *Truth & Soul* prances all over the musical spectrum but never loses its pace or identity. Highlights include "Ma and Pa," "Freddie's Dead," and the funk-punk anthem "Bonin' in the Boneyard." —*Julian Katz*

● **Reality of My Surroundings** / 1991 / Columbia 46142
Needs editing, but contains some inspiring moments. —*John Dougan*

Give a Monkey a Brain and He'll Swear He's the Center of the Universe / May 25, 1993 / Columbia 52764
Fishbone's traditional, careening eclecticism is refined on *Give a Monkey a Brain and He'll Swear He's the Center of the Universe.* Instead of freely flowing between different styles as they did on *The Reality of My Surroundings,* the band's sound is reined in—presumably in an attempt to make Fishbone palatable for the mainstream—making the album impressively diverse but frustrating. They never cut loose like do in almost all of their concerts. Nevertheless, there's enough good material here to make it worthwhile for dedicated fans. —*Stephen Thomas Erlewine*

The Five Royales

Group / R&B
The North Carolina-based Five Royales practically defined Black vocal group singing in the '50s, with their early sides cut for Apollo as well as their latter-day hits on King. Johnny Tanner's vocals anticipated the sound of Southern soul singing, and Lowman Pauling's stinging guitar licks influenced everyone from Steve Cropper to Eric Clapton. —*John Floyd*

Five Royales Sing for You / 1959 / King 616
An exact reproduction of their best original album. Not many hits, but the obscurities will keep you interested. —*John Floyd*

Monkey Hips and Rice / 1994 / King/Rhino 71546
During the '50s, the Five Royales were a dominant vocal ensemble. Bass vocalist, guitarist, and composer Lowman Pauling churned out memorable anthems featuring lyrics a step ahead of the nonsense/novelty fare that comprised the standard doo-wop number. The Royales certainly did their share of forgettable period-piece tunes, but they also had transcendant songs like "Think," "Just as I Am" and "Dedicated to the One I Love." Johnny Tanner was a good, though not virtuoso lead singer. When given the right material, Tanner turned in marvelous performances, but he couldn't elevate substandard or routine cuts. Yet the Five Royales enjoyed a lengthy run, creating many hits plus a few gems, and they're all available on this sparkling two-disc set. The opening disc sets the stage, showing their gospel origins via the single "Let Nothing Separate Me," and also the rather routine cuts the band did in its formative period ("Laundromat Blues" excepted). But they began to evolve into a more substantial unit in the mid-'50s, and by the end of the decade they were a sterling unit cutting emphatic, appealing numbers. Most of these appear on the second disc. By the early '60s, they'd run their course, yet the group turned in one more fine outing in 1962 with "Help Me Somebody." Still, their legacy and impact was secure, as "Dedicated to the One I Love" and "Think" became R&B/pop

Music Map

Rock-Roots,
The 50s thru Early 60s

| **Gospel**
Sister Rosetta Tharpe
The Soul Stirrers | **Pop**
Les Paul – Louis Prima
The Ink Spots | **Blues**
Muddy Waters – Robert Johnson
Howlin' Wolf – Willie Dixon | **Country**
Hank Williams Sr
The Delmore Brothers
Chet Atkins – Merle Travis |

Doo-Wop
The Ravens – The Dominoes
The Drifters – The Moonglows
Frankie Lymon & the Teenagers

Rock & Roll
Chuck Berry – Bo Diddley – Jackie Wilson
Little Richard – Bill Haley & the Comets
The Everly Brothers – Buddy Holly

R & B
Ray Charles

Second-generation Doo-Wop
Dion & the Belmonts – The Crests
The Marcells – The Rivingtons
The Dominoes

50's Woman Rockers
Wanda Jackson – Brenda Lee – Etta James
LaVern Baker – Esther Phillips

Early 60's Rock/Pop
Dion – Del Shannon

Rockabilly
SUN Records
Producer: Sam Phillips
Elvis Presley – Carl Perkins – Johnny Cash
Jerry Lee Lewis – Roy Orbison

Eddie Cochran – Gene Vincent

Phil Spector
The Wall of Sound – The Ronettes
The Crystals – Darlene Love
The Righteous Bros.

Guitar Heroes/50s-early 60s
Chet Atkins – Merle Travis – James Burton
The Ventures – Scotty Moore – Chuck Berry
Bo Diddley – Duane Eddy – Link Wray
Travis Wammack – Carl Perkins – Buddy Holly
Eddie Cochran – Dick Dale & the Del-tones

Motown
Producer: Berry Gordy
Smokey Robinson & the Miracles
The Contours
Junior Walker & the All-Stars
Marvin Gaye – Stevie Wonder
The Temptations – The Supremes
The Marvellettes – Mary Wells
Martha & the Vandellas

Surf Music
Dick Dale – The Beach Boys – Jan & Dean

Brill Building Pop (ca. early 60s)
The Songwriters
Gerry Goffin & Carole King
Jeff Barry & Ellie Greenwich
Barry Mann & Cynthia Weil
Neil Diamond – Neil Sedaka

The Girl-Group Sound
The Shirelles – The Shangri-Las – Little Eva
The Cookies – Rosie & the Originals
The Pixies Three – The Angels – The Raindrops

landmarks. This offers the most complete picture of the Five Royales and their superb music. —*Ron Wynn*

The Five Satins

Group / Doo-wop
Fred Haven and the Five Satins were New Haven, Connecticut's favorite doo-wop sons. Their 1956 hit "In the Still of the Night"

gave rock & roll one of its first cuddle anthems, and set the tone for several tasty follow-ups. —*John Floyd*

● **In the Still of the Night** / 1990 / Relic 7001

Everything you need from this sumptuous late-night doo-wop quintet. The title cut is a work of art worth listening to over and over. —*John Floyd*

The Five Stairsteps

Group / Soul

The Five Stairsteps were a Windy City family affair initially consisting of four brothers and a sister. Later on, five-year-old Cubie Burke toddled aboard, and even mom and pop got into the act. Curtis Mayfield discovered the group at a talent contest, and they debuted in 1966 on his Windy C logo with the tender "You Waited Too Long," their first hit. Lead singer Clarence Burke Jr. was only 15 years old in 1966, yet his attractive leads on "World of Fantasy" and "Come Back" displayed a wealth of emotion. The group enjoyed its biggest pop hit in 1970 with the classic "O-o-h Child" for Buddah. After a few years apart, the group re-formed and notched a final hit, "From Us to You," on George Harrison's Dark Horse label in 1976. Four of the Burkes recorded as the Invisible Man's Band, scoring a sizable seller in 1980 with "All Night Thing," and bassist Keni Burke has recorded as a solo artist. —*Bill Dahl*

● **Greatest Hits** / Collectables 5023
This hits package examines the pubescent Chicago soul group from their mid-'60s beginning through their 1970 bubblegum/soul hit "O-o-h Child." —*Bill Dahl*

The Fixx

Group / New wave, rock/pop

Originally formed in 1980 as the Portraits, the Fixx was one of many early-'80s techno-pop groups that rode the wave of video exposure on the new MTV channel. Hits included "Are We Ourselves," "One Thing Leads to Another," "The Sign of Fire," "Secret Separation," and "Stand or Fall." —*Rick Clark*

● **One Thing Leads to Another—Greatest Hits** / 1989 / MCA 42316
All their hits, including "One Thing Leads to Another," "Are We Ourselves," "The Sign of Fire," "Secret Separation," "Stand or Fall," and "Saved by Zero." —*Larry Lapka*

Roberta Flack

b. Feb. 10, 1939, Ashville, NC
Vocals / Soul, urban R&B

Flack has made a career out of giving composed readings of ultrasmooth ballads. The urbane restraint of her music has attracted fans of light commercial jazz and romantic urban R&B. Flack's biggest include "The First Time Ever I Saw Your Face," "Killing Me Softly with His Song," "Feel Like Making Love," and "Making Love," as well as duets with Donny Hathaway "Where Is the Love" and "The Closer I Get to You." —*Rick Clark*

○ **First Take** / 1969 / Atlantic 8230
The album that launched Roberta Flack's career. She had been doing background vocals and recording with Les McCann, who helped her land at Atlantic. The single "The First Time Ever I Saw Your Face" zoomed into the pop stratosphere after it was included in Clint Eastwood's film *Play Misty for Me.* —*Ron Wynn*

○ **Chapter Two** / 1970 / Atlantic 1569
A great album and the release that made Roberta Flack a major soul and R&B artist in the early '70s. She had a soft, yet compelling and alluring voice, and was able to convincingly switch gears and convey anger, regret, hurt, or despair. Those who thought Flack was a one-hit wonder, or didn't think she could make the transition from jazz to other styles, were convinced otherwise. —*Ron Wynn*

Quiet Fire / 1971 / Atlantic 1594
Another super Roberta Flack album. She had now become one of the masters of what some described as "middle-class soul," restrained, elegant ballads sung in an exuberant but non-gospel fashion. It continued her string of Top 20 albums on both the R&B and pop side, and remains a staple on urban contemporary and adult contemporary outlets. —*Ron Wynn*

○ **Roberta Flack & Donny Hathaway** / 1972 / Atlantic 7216
A duet classic, and perhaps the most popular album Roberta Flack made. Their single "Where Is the Love" dominated urban contemporary radio almost the entire year, while "You've Got a Friend" was just as influential and later was covered by numerous artists (of course Flack and Hathaway didn't write it, but a lot of folks thought they did). It did so well Flack eventually did other duet material and also became very close to Hathaway. —*Ron Wynn*

○ **Killing Me Softly** / 1973 / Atlantic 19154
The title track was another smash for Roberta Flack, and the album continued in the same tradition as *Chapter Two* and *A Quiet Fire.* She made simmering ballads, declarative message songs, and better-than-average uptempo numbers, and at the time was among the top-selling female vocalists in any style. —*Ron Wynn*

○ **Best of Roberta Flack** / 1980 / Atlantic 19317
Showcases her biggest ballads, including "The First Time Ever I Saw Your Face," "Feel Like Making Love," "Killing Me Softly with His Song," as well as her duets with Donny Hathaway, "Where Is the Love" and "The Closer I Get to You." —*Bil Carpenter*

● **Softly with These Songs—The Best of Roberta Flack** / 1993 / Atlantic
While it includes almost everything on *Best of Roberta Flack,* *Softly with These Songs* covers material after 1980—including the hits "Tonight, I Celebrate My Love" and "Making Love"—which makes it the preferable compilation. —*Stephen Thomas Erlewine*

The Flamin' Groovies

Group / Rock & roll, power pop

The second-longest surviving original San Francisco band doesn't sound like the Dead or the Airplane. The Groovies, under original lead singer Roy Loney or lead guitarist Cyril Jordan, are a hard-rocking outfit into Little Richard, Chuck Berry, the Beatles, the Byrds and—amazingly—the Lovin' Spoonful. They've been at it 25 years and are still plugging away. And most of the music is priceless. —*Bruce Eder*

Supersnazz / 1969 / Sony 26487
Flawed, but a good debut album. Roots-rock played with a vengeance. —*Bruce Eder*

○ **Teenage Head** / 1971 / Big Beat 926
Tough and hard rocking, this early-'70s classic is better than anything the New York Dolls ever delivered. —*Bruce Eder*

○ **Shake Some Action** / 1976 / Sire 7521
This and *The Flamin' Groovies Now!* are the greatest "British invasion" albums ever—done a decade late by a California band. Go figure. —*Bruce Eder*

Flamin' Groovies Now! / 1978 / Sire 6059
See the review of *Shake Some Action.* —*Bruce Eder*

● **Greatest Grooves** / 1989 / Sire 25948
Stylistically, a staggering assembly of covers and retro-originals. Loud and beautiful. —*Bruce Eder*

Flaming Lips

Group / Alternative pop/rock, psychedelic

The Flaming Lips' latter-day psychedelia combines the swirling guitar of '60s psychedelia with the smart-ass humor of '80s post-punk, throwing in everything that comes in between. Even when the Lips come close to traditional rock & roll (like 1989's *Telepathic Surgery*), it still has an endearingly weird, catchy eclecticism, if not infectious experimentalism. When the band jumped to a major label in 1992, their music didn't change—it was still the same druggy, alternative psychedelia that they flaunted on their 1985 debut. —*Stephen Thomas Erlewine*

Flaming Lips / 1985 / Enigma 72188
Good early stuff! —*John Dougan*

○ **Hear It** / 1986 / Restless 72173
Trippy, but rocks! —*John Dougan*

○ **Oh My Gawd, the Flaming Lips** / 1987 / Restless 72207
Convoluted, but with plenty of surprises. —*John Dougan*

Hit to Death in the Future Head / 1992 / Warner Brothers 26838
Filled with blazing guitars and elliptical melodies, the band's first album for a major label shows no signs of a sellout. —*Stephen Thomas Erlewine*

● **Transmissions from the Satellite Heart** / Jan. 1993 / Warner
Not as bracingly weird as their previous records, the Flaming Lips' second album for Warner is still stranger than most music. With a good portion of the band now in Mercury Rev, the Flaming Lips veers closer to the inspired wackiness of They Might Be Giants. *Transmissions from the Satellite Heart* is halfway between the psuedo-psychedelic guitar and flute explorations of Mercury Rev and the smart-ass, do-it-yourself jokiness of Ween,

making it their most accessible, as well as consistent, album yet. —*AMG*

The Flamingos

Group / Doo-wop

Seminal in their influence and impact, the Flamingos may have been the greatest harmonizing vocal ensemble ever, and were certainly among the premier units of the doo-wop/R&B era. They recorded with Chance in 1953, and "If I Can't Have You" attracted some attention and did well in the Midwest and on the East Coast. "That's My Desire" and "Golden Teardrops" were marvelously sung numbers, particularly "Golden Teardrops," with its sweeping harmonies on top and bottom framing Sollie McElroy's wondrous lead. But none of their great Chance recordings generated enough national attention to make the R&B charts.

They enjoyed their first chart success with Checker in the late '50s, scoring a Top-Ten R&B hit with "I'll Be Home" in 1956. They temporarily disbanded in 1956 and regrouped in 1957, then signed with End late the following year. "I Only Have Eyes for You," in 1959, was their biggest hit, peaking at number three R&B and number 11 pop. It was the start of a productive period that saw the Flamingos issue four albums for End and get two more R&B Top-30 singles. Hunt left in 1961, and the group returned briefly to Checker in 1964. They later recorded for Phillips, Julman, and Polydor, but couldn't regain their former standing. They remain among the genre's most beloved groups. —*Ron Wynn*

Sound of the Flamingos / 1962 / Collectables 5426
A good collection of Flamingos '50s and '60s tracks on Collectables, a label that in the past hasn't always provided either quality remastering or comprehensive annotation. They're trying to rebuild their image, and this one will help, even if it's not as complete as most Relic sets. —*Ron Wynn*

● **Doo Bop She Bop: Best of the Flamingos** / 1990 / Rhino 70967
A splendid collection of smooth doo-wop. Includes "I Only Have Eyes for You" and the gorgeous "The Vow." Beautiful stuff. —*John Floyd*

Fleetwood Mac

Group / Blues rock, pop/rock

Fleetwood Mac, formed in 1967, initially began as one of Britain's great blues-influenced rock ensembles. Over the course of many lineup changes and a relocation to Los Angeles in 1974, "Big Mac" evolved into one of the most successful pop/rock units in commercial music history.

During the early years, Fleetwood Mac endured a succession of unstable (but brilliant) lead-guitarists/singers/songwriters in Peter Green, Danny Kirwan, and Jeremy Spencer. Green and Spencer eventually jumped ship for cultish religious pursuits, and Kirwan (who ended up in a psychiatric hospital) was fired in 1972 for refusing to go on stage at a Munich gig. Green, in particular, wrote some classics in "Oh Well," "Black Magic Woman" (later a hit for Santana), and "The Green Manalishi (with the Two-Pronged Crown)." Danny Kirwan contributed many of the standout tracks on albums like *Bare Trees*, including the haunting "Dust," the ethereal "Sunny Side of Heaven," and the propulsive title track.

Bob Welch, a Los Angeles resident, was brought on board in 1971. During his time with Fleetwood Mac, Welch penned some standouts as well, like "Hypnotized" and "Sentimental Lady." During all these changes, drummer Mick Fleetwood, bassist John McVie, and vocalist/keyboardist Christine McVie (also a fine songwriter) provided the glue for the proceedings.

In January of 1975 Welch left, and engineer and producer Keith Olsen turned the band on to a tape of Lindsey Buckingham and Stevie Nicks (who had previously released a much sought-after debut on Polydor called *Buckingham Nicks*). They were hired onto Fleetwood Mac, and the rest is history.

Fleetwood Mac, the first album featuring the new lineup, became a gold mine, eventually hitting number one in November 1976, 15 months after its release. After much inner turmoil, Fleetwood Mac put out *Rumours*, which topped charts around the world and became one of the biggest albums in history. Mac never duplicated the impact of *Rumours*, but subsequent albums (*Tusk, Fleetwood Mac Live, Mirage, Tango in the Night*) have been substantial successes.

Buckingham (who left in 1987) and Nicks have enjoyed solid solo careers, and Christine McVie had a hit in 1984 with "Got a Hold on Me" from her self-titled solo album.

Fleetwood Mac reunited with two new guitarists in 1989, releasing the lackluster *Behind the Mask*. In November 1993, confirming the departure of Stevie Nicks and guitarist Billy Burnette, Fleetwood Mac announced the addition of vocalist Bekka Bramlett and veteran singer, songwriter, and guitarist Dave Mason to the band's lineup, joining Fleetwood and the McVies. —*Rick Clark*

○ **English Rose** / 1969 / Epic 26446
Under the direction of Peter Green, Fleetwood Mac is heard as a British blues group, though its most notable performances are on Green's original tunes "Black Magic Woman" and "Albatross," both British hits. —*William Ruhlmann*

Then Play On / 1969 / Reprise 6368
The most diverse and accomplished album by the Peter Green-led lineup. Features some wrenching, introspective originals that draw from both blues and progressive rock, highlighted by the doomy British hit single "Oh Well." —*Richie Unterberger*

Kiln House / 1970 / Reprise 6408
Fleetwood Mac's first album after the departure of their nominal leader, Peter Green, finds the remaining members, Mick Fleetwood, John McVie, Jeremy Spencer, and Danny Kirwan plus McVie's wife Christine trying to maintain the band's guitar-heavy, blues-rock approach, with the burden falling on Spencer and Kirwan. They don't embarrass themselves, but none of this is of the caliber of Green's work. —*William Ruhlmann*

Future Games / 1971 / Reprise 6465
By the time of this album's release, Jeremy Spencer had been replaced by Bob Welch and Christine McVie had begun to assert herself more as a singer and songwriter. The result is a distinct move toward folk-rock and pop; this album sounds almost nothing like Peter Green's Fleetwood Mac. Welch's eight-minute title track has one of his characteristic haunting melodies, and with pruning and better editing could have been a hit. Christine McVie's "Show Me a Smile" is one of her loveliest ballads. Initial popular reaction was mixed: The album didn't sell as well as *Kiln House*, but it sold better than any of the band's first three albums in the United States. In the United Kingdom, where the original lineup had been more successful, *Future Games* didn't chart at all—the same fate that would befall the rest of its albums until the Lindsey Buckingham-Stevie Nicks era. —*William Ruhlmann*

● **Bare Trees** / 1972 / Reprise 2278
On *Bare Trees*, Fleetwood Mac married the gritty electric blues-rock of their earlier incarnations to the classic pop sensibilities that would later become fully realized in 1975's *Fleetwood Mac*. Bob Welch's "Sentimental Lady" and Christine McVie's soulful "Spare Me a Little of Your Love" are highlights. Danny Kirwin revealed an ability to compose highly melodic material that didn't constrain the band's legendary musical chemistry. —*Rick Clark*

Mystery to Me / 1973 / Reprise 25982
At this point, Fleetwood Mac is a mainstream rock band whose songs alternate between guitarist/singer Robert Welch and keyboard player/singer Christine McVie. —*William Ruhlmann*

Heroes Are Hard to Find / 1974 / Reprise 2196
Welch's peak as a songwriter (with new highs by Christine McVie) is also his swan song with the group. —*William Ruhlmann*

☆ **Fleetwood Mac** / 1975 / Reprise 2281
The addition of Lindsey Buckingham and Stevie Nicks, plus the increasing quality of Christine McVie's songs, results in massive success. This number-one album, one of the finest collections of pop-rock in the decade, contains the hits "Rhiannon," "Over My Head," and "Say You Love Me." —*William Ruhlmann*

★ **Rumours** / 1977 / Reprise 3010
Among the best-selling albums of all time, this brilliant song cycle about the travails of love features "Dreams," "Don't Stop," "Go Your Own Way," and "You Make Loving Fun." —*William Ruhlmann*

○ **Tusk** / 1979 / Reprise 3350
In some ways even more impressive than *Rumours*, this two-record set (compressed onto one CD by editing "Sara," one of its hits!) is an ambitious effort full of unusual arrangements and striking instrumental passages, plus a wealth of top-flight songwriting. —*William Ruhlmann*

Mirage / 1982 / Reprise 23607
A tuneful, tastefully produced album that makes up in songcraft ("Hold Me," "Gypsy") what it lacks in the anguished passion that was once Fleetwood Mac's stock in trade. — *William Ruhlmann*

Tango in the Night / 1988 / Reprise 25471
Buckingham's final effort with the group strongly features his dramatic production techniques and striking guitar playing on his own "Big Love" and on Christine McVie's terrific "Little Lies," among other tracks. — *William Ruhlmann*

● **Greatest Hits** / 1988 / Reprise 25801
A well-chosen best-of. The cassette version has three more tracks than the LP. — *William Ruhlmann*

Behind the Mask / 1989 / Reprise 26111

25 Years—The Chain / Nov. 24, 1992 / Reprise 45129
Overall, Fleetwood Mac's four-CD boxed set, *25 Years—The Chain*, contains a lot of great music, with plenty of the hits that made them one of the biggest bands in the world. As a complete chronicle it fails. Not enough weight is given to the early, blues-based Mac with Peter Green (especially to *Bare Trees* and *Future Games*), and there are too many songs (nearly a whole disc's worth) from the lightweight albums of the '80s. Also, the haphazard song sequencing doesn't help matters—it doesn't make the case for Fleetwood Mac's music as a body of work, nor does it trace their musical evolution. Despite these shortcomings, the set is enjoyable, if not definitive. If nothing else, *25 Years—The Chain* offers evidence that Lindsey Buckingham was a brilliant pop composer and that the band's success in the '70s was well deserved. — *Stephen Thomas Erlewine*

The Fleetwoods

Group / Pop
An ultrasmooth White pop vocal trio who, in the late '50s, recorded some of the most delicate hits of the rock era. — *John Floyd*

● **Best of the Fleetwoods** / 1990 / Rhino 70980
Rhino's *Best of the Fleetwoods* contains all of their hits ("Come Softly to Me," "Mr. Blue," and 16 other songs) on a smartly assembled collection. — *Stephen Thomas Erlewine*

○ **Come Softly to Me—The Very Best of the Fleetwoods** / Aug. 10, 1993 / EMI 98830
While the single-disc collection *Come Softly to Me—The Very Best of the Fleetwoods* is a treasure for devoted fans—featuring alternate takes, radio commercials, a comprehensive discography, fine liner notes, and unreleased tracks—casual listeners will find all this material extraneous. Everything they need is on Rhino's collection. — *Stephen Thomas Erlewine*

A Flock of Seagulls

Group / New wave
A Liverpool new wave group with a name derived from the novel *Jonathan Livingston Seagull*, featuring lead singer/keyboard player Mike Score, his brother Ali (drums), Paul Reynolds (guitar), and Frank Maudsley (drums). They formed in 1979, hit with "I Ran (So Far Away)" in 1982, split up in 1986, and have since reformed. — *William Ruhlmann*

○ **Flock of Seagulls, A** / 1982 / Jive 1007
A Flock of Seagulls scored one big hit, "I Ran," in the driving, quick-tempo dance style that characterized most of their work. It's here, along with several similar tracks. — *William Ruhlmann*

● **Best of a Flock of Seagulls** / 1987 / Jive 1034
Every good song A Flock of Seagulls ever recorded is available on this fine collection, including the new wave classic "I Ran (So Far Away)." — *Stephen Thomas Erlewine*

Eddie Floyd

b. Jun. 25, 1935, Montgomery, AL
Vocals / Soul
Floyd came aboard the good ship Stax at the behest of his friend Al Bell and immediately made himself useful as a composer for labelmates Carla Thomas, William Bell, Otis Redding (originally intended to be the recipient of "Knock on Wood"), and Atlantic's Wilson Pickett.

Floyd's own mid-'60s output included "Raise Your Hand," which utilized the same Booker T. & the MG's-powered thrust as "Knock on Wood," and "Big Bird," written partially in shocked re-

sponse to the tragic death of Redding. Floyd remained loyal to Stax right up to its bitter demise, his engaging vocals resulting in major hits with the gentle "I've Never Found a Girl" and a lively remake of Sam Cooke's "Bring It on Home to Me."

Whenever Floyd re-teams with his old Stax pals—guitarist Steve Cropper, bassist Duck Dunn, and sometimes Booker T. Jones on organ—the long-ago Memphis magic instantly returns. With Floyd happily leading the throngs through "Raise Your Hand" and "Knock on Wood," it's 1966 all over again. — *Bill Dahl*

○ **Knock on Wood** / 1967 / Atlantic 80283
The finest album Eddie Floyd ever made for Stax, this late-'60s gem included both "I've Never Found a Girl" and "Knock on Wood," his two most magnificent hits and two Southern soul anthems. Floyd was never as transcendent or striking a vocalist as Otis Redding or even William Bell, but he was consistent and dependable. He was backed by both Booker T. and the MG's and the Memphis Horns (then called the Mar-Kay Horns). A recent CD reissue of this set adds several tracks, including some smoking duets with Mavis Staples. — *Ron Wynn*

Soul Street / 1974 / Stax 8527
A worthwhile set. Funk's Memphis soul. — *Bill Dahl*

● **Chronicle** / 1979 / Stax 4122
A disc spanning Floyd's early output and his softer post-1968 work for Stax. Pumping Memphis grooves back Floyd's energetic vocals. — *Bill Dahl*

○ **Rare Stamps** / 1993 / Stax 880132
Several of Floyd's finest pieces are compiled on the 25-track CD *Rare Stamps*, including a wonderful testimonial to Otis Redding, "Big Bird," which he recorded following the plane crash that killed the soul star in 1967. There are also two super duets with Mavis Staples, "Never Let You Go," and "Ain't That Good," which rank with anything that the label issued. — *Ron Wynn*

The Flying Burrito Brothers

Group / Country-rock
The Flying Burrito Brothers formed in October, 1968 from Byrd expatriates Chris Hillman, Sneaky Pete Kleinow, Gram Parsons, and (later) Michael Clarke, all fresh from recording what was arguably the most important seminal country-rock album, the Byrds's *Sweetheart of the Rodeo*. The Burritos took that concept and focused it into a brilliantly soulful country-rock sound.

Primary lead singer/songwriter Gram Parsons was capable of displaying heartbreaking vulnerability, as evidenced in tracks like "Hot Burrito #1." Parson's influence and the band's overall concept literally laid the groundwork for many artists like the Eagles, Emmylou Harris, and much of today's cutting-edge country music. Parsons died of heart failure following a drug overdose on Sept. 19, 1973, at the Joshua Tree Inn in Joshua Tree, CA. His solo follow-up, *Grievous Angel*, was posthumously released in January 1974. Burrito Brothers cofounder Chris Hillman later formed the Desert Rose Band, which has scored numerous country hits. — *Rick Clark*

☆ **Gilded Palace of Sin** / 1969 / A&M 3122
The birth of country-rock. Gram Parsons and Chris Hillman, aided by Sneaky Pete Kleinow and Chris Ethridge, create a hybrid by combining rock attitude with country sentiments and change the course of popular music. Really. — *William Ruhlmann*

○ **Burrito Deluxe** / 1970 / Edsel 194
The follow-up to the brilliant *Gilded Palace of Sin* finds the band somewhat directionless, with Gram Parsons losing interest and playing a less active role. While the Parson-Hillman penned "Cody Cody" and a touching rendition of the Rolling Stones' "Wild Horses" capture some of the previous album's magic, *Burrito Deluxe* is somewhat of a letdown. Parsons left for a solo career shortly after. — *Chris Woodstra*

Flying Burrito Brothers / 1971 / Mobile Fidelity 772
On their first post-Parsons album, the Burritos (now led by Hillman and Rick Roberts, and with future-Eagle Bernie Leadon replacing Ethridge) make an honest step forward in country-rock. Includes the Roberts song "Colorado." — *William Ruhlmann*

★ **Farther Along: The Best of the Flying Burrito Brothers** / 1988 / A&M 5216
Farther Along: The Best of the Flying Burrito Brothers is an excellent 21-track, 65-minute compilation of the Burritos. — *William Ruhlmann*

Dan Fogelberg

b. Aug. 13, 1951, Peoria, IL
Vocals / Singer/songwriter
When singer/songwriter and multi-instrumentalist Dan Fogelberg arrived in 1973 with his debut *Home Free,* reflective soft-folk/pop was making big inroads into a baby-boomer mass market that was coming of age.

Fogelberg had the good fortune to be previously acquainted (from his University of Illinois days in 1971) with ascending artist-manager and industry powerbroker Irving Azoff, who was managing R.E.O. Speedwagon at the time. Azoff took on Fogelberg and brought in Joe Walsh (another artist client of Azoff's) to produce the sophomore effort *Souvenirs.* It became Fogelberg's first chart success, generating a hit with "Part of the Plan."

During the '70s and early '80s, Fogelberg became a mainstay on FM rock stations and soft adult-contemporary formats, easily managing to share air space with artists like the Eagles, Linda Ronstadt, Jimmy Buffett, and Jackson Browne. "Longer," "Same Old Lang Syne," and "Leader of the Band" were big hits indicative of Fogelberg's thoughtful mellow sound. His attempts at rock have generally failed to score as successfully, particularly the 1988 release *Exiles.* —*Rick Clark*

○ **Home Free** / 1973 / Columbia 31751
This debut, recorded in Nashville and produced by Norbert Putnam, is a nice blend of haunting acoustic-guitar-based numbers ("Stars," "Be on Your Way"), some supported by tasteful string-section work ("To the Morning," "Wysteria," "Hickory Grove"). There are also a few country/light-rock items in "Anyway I Love You," "Long Way Home (Live in the Country)," and "More Than Ever." —*Rick Clark*

Souvenirs / 1975 / Epic 33137
This Joe Walsh-produced effort includes Fogelberg's first hit, "Part of the Plan." Overall, this isn't as strong as the debut. —*Rick Clark*

○ **Netherlands** / 1977 / Epic 34185
Fogelberg returns to Norbert Putnam for this effort, which ranges from the heavily orchestrated, highly dramatic title cut to light CSN-style folk-rock like "Once Upon a Time." One of Fogelberg's better albums, in spite of his tendency for grandiose statement. —*Rick Clark*

Twin Sons of Different Mothers / 1978 / Epic 35339
This album contains duets with flutist Tim Weisberg. It's a nice diversion, featuring a good remake of the Hollies hit "Tell Me to My Face." There are some pleasant instrumental numbers here. Fogelberg scored a hit with "The Power of Gold." —*Rick Clark*

○ **Phoenix** / 1980 / Full Moon 35634
Fogelberg's highest-charting album (number 3) features his widest stylistic stretches, between the ultra-sentimental acoustic hit "Longer," to extended rockish numbers like "Face the Fire," "Wishing on the Moon," and the title cut. —*Rick Clark*

○ **Innocent Age** / 1981 / Full Moon 37393
An ambitious song cycle, detailing the experience of coming of age. Several of Fogelberg's biggest hits ("Leader of the Band," "Same Old Lang Syne," "Hard to Say," and "Run for the Roses") are on this set. —*Rick Clark*

● **Greatest Hits** / 1985 / Full Moon 38308
Even though this collection fails to address much of his best non-single material, most of his obvious hits are here (heavy on the sentimental), making this a fairly safe starting place for someone wanting to get into Fogelberg. —*Rick Clark*

John Fogerty

b. May 28, 1945, Berkeley, California
Vocals, guitar / Rock & roll
John Cameron Fogerty achieved fame as the lead singer/songwriter and guitarist in Creedence Clearwater Revival and has since gone on to a chart-topping solo career. Born in Berkeley, CA, Fogerty and his brother Tom organized the group that would become Creedence as the Golliwogs in the late '50s. As Creedence, they released nine Top-Ten singles, all written by Fogerty, between 1969 and 1971, starting with the standard "Proud Mary." They also scored eight gold albums between 1968 and 1972, all fueled by Fogerty's simple, driving rock songs and his burly baritone, intoning deceptively poetic ("Bad Moon Rising") and even political ("Fortunate Son") lyrics.

Creedence split up in 1972. Fogerty at first confused his considerable following by releasing in 1973 an album of covers, on which he played all the instruments, under the name the Blue Ridge Rangers. This was followed by a formal solo album, *John Fogerty,* in 1975, and then silence for more than nine years while the artist worked out business problems with Creedence's old label. But Fogerty returned at the end of 1984 with a Top-Ten single, "The Old Man Down the Road," and a number-one album, *Centerfield. Eye of the Zombie* was a less successful follow-up in 1986. —*William Ruhlmann*

Blue Ridge Rangers / 1973 / Fantasy 4502
Fogerty as a one-man country band paying tribute to his honky-tonk roots. —*Jeff Tamarkin*

● **Centerfield** / Apr. 1985 / Warner Brothers 25203
The comeback album that proved the ex-Creedence firebrand still knew how to rock and make it count. Includes "The Old Man Down the Road," "Rock and Roll Girls," and "Centerfield." —*Jeff Tamarkin*

Eye of the Zombie / 1986 / Warner Brothers 25449
A disappointing follow-up to *Centerfield, Eye of the Zombie* is too high-tech and low-profile. —*Jeff Tamarkin*

Foghat

Group / Hard rock, heavy metal
Formed in 1971, Foghat enjoyed a string of successful albums with their brand of hard blues-based boogie rock. Biggest hits included "Slow Ride," "Third Time Lucky (First Time I Was a Fool)," "I Just Want to Make Love to You," "Driving Wheel," and "Stone Blue." —*Rick Clark*

● **Best of Foghat** / 1990 / Rhino 70088
Excellent blue-collar rock featuring "Slow Ride" and "Fool for the City." —*Dan Heilman*

○ **Best of Foghat, Vol. 2** / Jan. 24, 1992 / Rhino 70516
If *Best of Foghat* made you hungry for more, *Best of Foghat, Vol. 2*—with no hit singles, only album tracks, including two live cuts and an outtake—should satiate your desire. —*Stephen Thomas Erlewine*

Steve Forbert

b. 1955, Meridian, MS
Vocals, guitar / Singer/songwriter
Mississippi-born Forbert was one of the better received folk-based singer/songwriters of the late '70s. In recent years, he has written hits for country artists as well as continuing to record albums himself. —*William Ruhlmann*

○ **Alive on Arrival** / 1979 / Nemperor 35538
Forbert takes the folk-rock singer/songwriter format, already 13 years old at this point, and gives it a fresh, exuberant, almost punkish appeal. —*William Ruhlmann*

○ **Jackrabbit Slim** / 1979 / Nemperor 36191
Forbert's more elaborately produced second album continues the songwriting quality of his first and includes his number-11 hit single "Romeo's Tune." —*William Ruhlmann*

Streets of This Town / 1988 / David Geffen Co. 24194
Coming back after a six-year layoff, Forbert displays a previously unheard edge of bitterness that only deepens his thoughtful lyrics. And he rocks harder than ever. —*William Ruhlmann*

American in Me / 1992 / David Geffen Co. 24459
With *The American in Me,* Forbert has found a healthier, more balanced perspective. The pressures and uncertainties of growing up, taking on responsibilities, and looking back on missed opportunity make up the central theme linking the disc's ten songs. Forbert alternates between acoustic folk and bracing electric roots-rock, delivering it all up with his distinctively upper-register, raspy vocals. But unlike Forbert's previous outing, hope glimmers through in the end. —*Roch Parisien*

● **Best Of—What Kinda Guy?** / 1993 / Columbia/Legacy 53170
Featuring a generous 19 tracks, including his hit "Romeo's Tune," *Best of Steve Forbert—What Kinda Guy?* is a great place to get acquainted with this underrated singer/songwriter. —*Stephen Thomas Erlewine*

Foreigner

Group / Hard rock, pop/rock

Foreigner was formed in 1976 by Mick Jones (ex-Spooky Tooth) and Ian McDonald (ex-King Crimson). The band was an instant success with the release of their debut album in 1977, which showcased the talents of guitarist Jones and lead singer Lou Gramm. Jones and Gramm also wrote most of the band's material. The songs, mainly hard rock, boasted strong melodies and memorable guitar riffs. The band never strayed far from this formula but, to keep things fresh, added some interesting touches. For example, Junior Walker's sax on "Urgent" and the gospel vocals of Jennifer Holliday and the New Jersey Mass Choir on "I Want to Know What Love Is" helped elevate these songs above the ordinary. Gramm left the band in the late '80s for a solo career. He returned to the fold in 1992. —*Kenneth M. Cassidy*

Foreigner / 1977 / Atlantic 19109
No-nonsense rock & roll catapulted the band's debut all the way to the top of the charts with the hits "Cold as Ice" and "Feels Like the First Time." —*Donna DiChario*

Double Vision / 1978 / Atlantic 19999
Building on the success of the first album, this follow-up yielded the Top-20 hits "Hot Blooded," "Double Vision," and "Blue Morning, Blue Day." —*Donna DiChario*

○ **4** / 1981 / Atlantic 16999
A number-one album on the strength of Lou Gramm's powerhouse vocals and the band's synth-pop texturing. This album produced several major hits, including "Urgent," which featured a sax solo by Junior Walker, and "Waiting for a Girl Like You." —*Donna DiChario*

○ **Records** / 1982 / Atlantic 80999
All the band's early (including those from *4*) radio-friendly hits are here in this collection of straight-ahead rock & rollers. Includes "Waiting for a Girl Like You," "Hot Blooded," and more. —*Donna DiChario*

● **Very Best . . . and Beyond** / 1992 / Atlantic 89999
Very Best . . . and Beyond not only collects all the major hits from Foreigner's early years ("Feels Like the First Time," "Head Games," "Hot Blooded"), it also features their hits from the late '80s ("I Want to Know What Love Is," "Say You Will"), making the set preferable to *Records*. —*Stephen Thomas Erlewine*

Four Tops

Group / Motown, R&B, soul
After passing through five record labels in almost a decade, the Four Tops finally broke big-time on Motown in 1965 with "I Can't Help Myself." Along with many Motown acts, they provided the soundtrack for an era—they were in that heavy rotation on the radio. Immaculately rehearsed, choreographed, and outfitted, they epitomized Motown's value system. With a lead vocal from Levi Stubbs, a Motown backing track, and a Holland-Dozier-Holland song, you had an almost guaranteed hit. Even after H-D-H quit, the hits kept coming. Even after the Tops quit Motown, the hits still kept coming. But there is no doubt about where the classic recordings reside. At their best, the Four Tops were about as soulful as Motown got. More surprisingly, the original group is still together. Reach out—they're still there. —*Colin Escott*

○ **Four Tops** / 1965 / Motown 5122
You'd be hard pressed to find two better singles on a debut album than "Ask the Lonely" and "Baby I Need Your Loving." These were the cornerstones of the Four Tops' first LP, and besides netting one Top-Ten and Top-20 pop single each, it established Levi Stubbs's resounding voice as another unforgettable one at Motown. Even the tunes that didn't do so well like "Left with a Broken Heart" or "Without the One You Love (Life's Not Worth While)" were marvelously sung. It was a debut to remember. —*Ron Wynn*

○ **Second Album** / 1965 / Motown 5264
The Four Tops followed their fine debut album with an even more magnificent second effort. They landed their first number-one pop and R&B hit with "I Can't Help Myself." There was also "Shake Me, Wake Me," a great uptempo shouter that seemed a disappointment at number 18 (number 9 R&B), but didn't lack vocal authority or production genius. Also, don't forget that the album also contained "It's the Same Old Song," a tidy little number that reached number five (number two R&B) and had one of the greatest lyric hooks and titles ever. —*Ron Wynn*

○ **On Top** / 1966 / Motown 5444

Their third album and a classic. The Four Tops never sounded better, more emphatic, or more compelling on Motown than in the mid '60s, when they were getting great songs, production, arrangements, and musical support. —*Ron Wynn*

○ **Reach Out** / 1967 / Motown 5149
Though they were old hands by now, the Four Tops roared out of the gate in high style with this album, their most successful to date on the pop charts. It didn't hurt that Levi Stubbs showed his flair for the oral narrative on "Bernadette," or that "Reach Out, I'll Be There" was their second single to top both the R&B and pop charts. The album peaked at number 11 on the charts, ending any worries that might have occurred because their prior release *Four Tops on Broadway* didn't excite anyone except their fans. —*Ron Wynn*

● **Greatest Hits** / 1968 / Motown 5209
The first of what would be many greatest-hits and anthology packages featuring the Four Tops. At this point, they'd had enough chart hits for a good single album set, which is what this is. —*Ron Wynn*

★ **Anthology** / 1989 / Motown 0809
Until they get the deluxe boxed-set CD treatment, this three-record/two-CD set qualifies as the ultimate Four Tops Motown statement. It includes all the landmark hits, plus good numbers from their final days at Motown in the '70s (they did return in the mid-'80s), among them "Still Water" and "Just Seven Numbers." —*Ron Wynn*

○ **More of the Best—Until You Love Somebody** / 1993 / Rhino 71183
It contains a couple of weak tracks, but over all this compilation of album tracks, B-sides, and live cuts is a good complement to a Four Tops greatest-hits collection. —*Stephen Thomas Erlewine*

○ **Best of the Four Tops (1972-1976)** / MCA 27019
This collection covers their best Dunhill tracks from the '70s, which included two big hits in "Ain't No Woman (Like the One I Got) and "Are You Man Enough." "Keeper of the Castle" was also a Top-Ten R&B single, and it seemed the Four Tops were in stride again. The Dunhill period yielded two more Top-Ten R&B smashes with "One Chain Don't Make No Prison" and "Midnight Flower"; it's a much better period than some fans consider. —*Ron Wynn*

Peter Frampton

b. Apr. 22, 1950, Beckenham, England
Vocals, guitar / Pop/rock
After years of toiling away as an exceptional journeyman guitarist and singer during the late '60s and early '70s, Peter Frampton struck mega-platinum with a double live album entitled *Frampton Comes Alive*. The huge success of that album, coupled with Frampton's pretty-boy looks, almost overshadowed his elegantly melodic musicianship.

The Herd was Frampton's first successful group, but he gained much visibility with the heavy English boogie band Humble Pie. Frampton left just when Humble Pie was becoming a major concert draw, and he released a great 1972 debut solo effort titled *Wind of Change*, following with the strong *Frampton's Camel, Somethin's Happening*, and *Frampton*.

Frampton Comes Alive was a neat summation of Frampton's first four solo albums; it also became the biggest-selling live rock album in history. Frampton's next studio album, *I'm in You*, was a hit, but a series of poor career moves (such as appearing in the ill-conceived movie *Sgt. Pepper's Lonely Hearts Club Band*) and a tragic auto accident undermined his momentum. Frampton continues to release periodic albums and tours regularly. —*Rick Clark*

○ **Frampton Comes Alive** / 1976 / A&M 6505
Fueled by Frampton's voice-box guitar technique and accessible radio-friendly pop-rock songs like "Show Me the Way" and "Baby I Love Your Way," the double album *Frampton Comes Alive* became the biggest-selling live album in rock history, topping the ten-million mark. It's a sensible place to start, since Frampton seems to be in his element here, and the song selection includes the cream of his first four albums. —*Donna DiChario*

● **Classics, Vol. 12** / 1989 / A&M 2510

This overview of Frampton's work may not be definitive but it is a nice sampler that includes all of his hits, plus some favorite album tracks. —*Rick Clark*

○ **Shine On—A Collection** / Oct. 20, 1992 / A&M 540015
This two-disc set is the essential collection for anyone looking for a great overview of Frampton. The packaging and liners are a little skimpy, but the sound is great. —*Rick Clark*

Connie Francis

b. Dec. 12, 1938, Newark, NJ
Vocals / Pop
Considered the leading pop female singer of her era, Connie Francis usually sang of her latest broken heart with a teardrop in her voice. The Newark, NJ native started performing as a child, signing with MGM Records in 1955, but she suffered two years of bombs before the torch ballad "Who's Sorry Now" shot up the charts in 1958. Although she specialized in sobbing tales of woe, Francis proved she could rock with Neil Sedaka's "Stupid Cupid," in 1958, and "Lipstick on Your Collar" the next year. Francis scored two number-one hits in 1960—the twangy "Everybody's Somebody's Fool" and "My Heart Has a Mind of Its Own," and she branched into acting with a starring role in *Where the Boys Are*, the archetypal spring-break movie. "Don't Break the Heart That Loves You" was Francis's last pop chart-topper in 1962, but she continued to rank high in the pop pantheon throughout the decade, with forays into ethnic and country idioms. —*Bill Dahl*

Italian Favorites / 1960 / MGM
The best of Connie's early "international theme" albums. —*Cub Koda*

● **Very Best of Connie Francis** / 1963 / Polydor 827569
Though many best-ofs exist on the market, this one leans more heavily toward her earlier rock & roll hits. —*Cub Koda*

Live at the Sahara in Las Vegas / 1966 / MGM
A late-'60s live album, with Francis in peak form. —*Cub Koda*

Frankie Goes to Hollywood

Group / Dance-pop
Under the production hand of Trevor Horn, this Liverpool group took the "hi-NRG" dance sound into British and American charts in 1984 with the homoerotic "Relax" and the politically trenchant "Two Tribes." The group, however, was a victim of overhype, and by the time their debut album was released, Frankie's fad had worn thin. —*John Floyd*

○ **Welcome to the Pleasuredome** / 1984 / Island 824052
Upbeat British dance music with melodramatic vocals and lyrics that are sexually and politically provocative. The sound of Frankie Goes to Hollywood swept Britain in the years 1983 to 1985. Here is the wide-screen debut double album, containing the hits "Relax," "Two Tribes," "The Power of Love," and the title track. —*William Ruhlmann*

● **Bang! Greatest Hits** / 1994 / Island
A good collection of all the worthwhile songs Frankie Goes to Hollywood ever recorded. —*AMG*

Aretha Franklin

b. Mar. 25, 1942, Memphis, TN
Vocals / Soul, R&B, gospel
Appropriately dubbed "Lady Soul," Aretha Franklin made several false starts before finding consistent artistic direction. It was only when she began integrating her gospel phrasing and passion (heard in its embryonic form on the Chess album) into secular material that she, like Ray Charles before her, elevated herself from the ranks of the also-rans. There were hints of what was to come in her Columbia recordings, but the flowering of Aretha Franklin coincided with her arrival at Atlantic. From the moment "I Never Loved a Man" broke through in early 1967, Aretha rarely put a foot wrong for five or six glorious years. When she went wrong, it was usually because of a poor choice of other people's songs, but even then, Aretha could sometimes turn dross into gold.

By the late '70s, though, the partnership with Atlantic had become stale, and it took a deal with Arista to recharge her chart career. She still has the vocal chops, but many consider that market considerations alone will ensure she will never surpass the artis-

tic high-water mark of her early Atlantic recordings. —*Colin Escott*

○ **I Never Loved a Man (the Way I Love You)** / Jan. 1967 / Atlantic 8139
I Never Loved a Man (the Way I Love You) is Franklin's first Atlantic album—an electrifying breakthrough from her somewhat stymied Columbia career. The Muscle Shoals sound featured here became legendary. —*George Bedard*

Aretha Arrives / Feb. 1967 / Atlantic 8150
Sometimes the most commercially successful material isn't necessarily the finest artistic effort. *Aretha Arrives*, Franklin's second Atlantic album in 1967, didn't yield as many smash singles as some of its successors, nor did it contain much original material. Yet it was a masterpiece, and now, in reissued mono form, the album is an example of how the soul public missed the boat. Franklin's renditions of "Never Let Me Go," "Night Life" and "Going Down Slow," are amazing, while even covers of shopworn tunes like "Satisfaction" and "That's Life" have a punch and appeal that make them worth rehearing. The lone hit, "Baby, I Love You" was another in a series of scorching gems that established Aretha Franklin as the uncontested Queen of Soul, a title she's never relinquished. —*Ron Wynn*

○ **Lady Soul** / 1968 / Atlantic 8176
Great personnel again—King Curtis, Bobby Womack, Frank Wess, and others, including a guest spot by Eric Clapton. Several classic songs, including the lesser-known "Ain't No Way" by Carolyn Franklin and the hits "Chain of Fools" and "Natural Woman." —*George Bedard*

○ **Aretha Now** / 1968 / Atlantic 8186
Aretha Franklin's remarkable late-'60s Atlantic sessions are contemporary music landmarks. While Ray Charles and James Brown showed the link between gospel and soul, as did Sam Cooke, Aretha Franklin offered the climatic evidence. Her sweeping, declarative voice and fervent delivery were compelling and chilling, and they're just as magnificent in digitally remastered form. While the hits are well known, Franklin's covers, especially "The Night Time Is the Right Time" and "I Take What I Want" are so emphatic and exuberantly performed that they sound like new numbers. —*Ron Wynn*

○ **Spirit in the Dark** / Nov. 1970 / Atlantic 8265
Spirit in the Dark was one of Aretha Franklin's more overlooked albums from her Atlantic prime, despite the inclusion of a couple of hit singles (the title track and "Don't Play That Song"). The disc includes five of her own compositions (the most she ever recorded for a single album) and her usual eclectic choice of cover material. On this record, the covers ranged from B.B. King and Dr. John to Jimmy Reed and Goffin-King's "Oh Not My Baby." The album also benefits from great backup players: Both the Muscle Shoals rhythm section and the Dixie Flyers contributed to the sessions, and Duane Allman lends his guitar to a couple of tracks. Though it doesn't rank with her very best Atlantic LPs, it's an exuberant and remarkably consistent effort. —*Richie Unterberger*

☆ **Amazing Grace** / 1972 / Atlantic 906
Aretha Franklin disproved forever with this one the notion that once you leave the church you can't go back. She returned in triumph on this 1972 double album, making what might be her greatest release ever, in any style. Her voice was chilling, sometimes shaking the heavens, other times making it seem God and the angels were conducting a service alongside Franklin, Rev. James Cleveland, the Southern California Community Choir, and everyone else in attendance. Her versions of "How I Got Over" and "You've Got a Friend" are legendary. —*Ron Wynn*

○ **Sparkle** / 1976 / Rhino 71148
A fabulous album, the best Aretha Franklin LP of the mid '70s. Franklin teamed with Curtis Mayfield to make not only a great soundtrack album but just a fantastic album, period. The title track and "Giving Him Something He Can Feel" were hits in 1976, which was much better than the film deserved. En Vogue did a creditable cover of "Giving Him Something He Can Feel," but they didn't come close to equaling Franklin's passion and fire. —*Ron Wynn*

Aretha's Jazz / 1984 / Atlantic 81230
A good anthology that covers various album cuts, B-sides, and assorted material in a jazz vein that Aretha cut for Columbia. It's great to hear her underrated piano playing given some more

space, and Columbia should really reissue her Dinah Washington tribute album from which they pulled a couple of these songs. Aretha wasn't a jazz vocalist from the standpoint of approach or inspiration, but she really can sing anything, and showed it on these cuts, even if they weren't, for the most part, hits. —*Ron Wynn*

Who's Zoomin' Who? / 1985 / Arista 8286
Franklin continued finding ways to accommodate the urban contemporary production style and retain her soulfulness. The single "Freeway of Love" was a monster hit both in clubs and on radio, while the title track and "Another Night" also did well across the board. —*Ron Wynn*

★ **30 Greatest Hits** / 1986 / Atlantic 81668
Contains all of her essential Atlantic hits. A matchless catalog of soul vocalizing that will never be topped. —*George Bedard*

One Lord, One Faith, One Baptism / 1987 / Arista 8497
Though nowhere as anthemic as *Amazing Grace* (what could be?), this was still much better than most "contemporary" gospel. There were sociopolitical speeches by Jesse Jackson and Carl Franklin, for those who wanted earthly concerns addressed alongside spiritual ones, but the real impact came through Franklin's rousing voice and the contributions of such guest stars as Mavis Staples and Aretha's sisters Erma and Carolyn Franklin. If she hadn't issued *Amazing Grace* or *Aretha Gospel* as a teen, this set might have gotten better notices and more critical respect. Instead, it was virtually dismissed, and it deserves better than that. —*Ron Wynn*

Jazz to Soul / 1992 / Columbia 48515
She's Billie Holiday. No, she's Ella Fitzgerald. No, wait, she's Dinah Washington. The conventional wisdom on Aretha Franklin's tenure at Columbia Records is that the label didn't know what to do with her, and that may be true, but you can't say they didn't try. On these 39 recordings, spread across two discs and cut between 1960 and 1965, Franklin and her producers look for ways to frame her obvious vocal talents, but always in terms of uptown jazz and non-rock/pop formats. Much of the result is appealing, and it's only in light of the transcendent soul music Franklin made from her first day at Atlantic Records in 1967 that this work comes across as merely exploratory. "Show me the way to get to Soulville," she demands in 1964. She finally found the way, and that was that. —*William Ruhlmann*

☆ **Queen of Soul: The Atlantic Recordings** / 1992 / Rhino 71063
This four-CD, 86-track collection is a comprehensive look at Franklin's soul genius. All of her great Atlantic hits are here, as well as many significant album tracks. —*AMG*

★ **Aretha Gospel** / Chess 91521
Aretha sings solo and plays piano on these spectacular recordings made at her father's (C. L. Franklin) church in 1956. —*Kip Lornell*

Free

Group / Hard rock
Free, an English quartet formed in 1968 with Paul Rodgers, Andy Fraser, Paul Kossoff, and Simon Kirke, took the then-popular heavy blues-rock sound and stripped it down to a hard yet open minimalistic sound.

Rodgers quickly earned a reputation as one of the greatest singers of the genre, able to deliver lyrics with gritty dark sensuality as well as playful toss-offs. Drummer Simon Kirke was the hard-rock equivalent of soul music's Al Jackson, speaking volumes with a no-nonsense groove. Paul Kossoff's wide sustained leads and rhythm work filled in the band's sounds, allowing Andy Fraser great freedom to pursue his inventive style of very spare, open but melodic bass playing.

The band's sound coalesced into some great moments, particularly the number-four hit "All Right Now," "Fire and Water," and "The Stealer." After some lineup changes and an uneven final album (*Heartbreaker*) in 1973, Free disbanded. Rodgers and Kirke went on to form Bad Company, and Fraser and Kossoff released spotty solo efforts. Kossoff died of heart failure on March 19, 1976.

In spite of Free's brief existence, they have influenced numerous artists, including Lynyrd Skynyrd, the Raspberries, and Bob Seger. —*Rick Clark*

○ **Fire & Water** / 1970 / A&M 3126

Classic Free album that features their biggest hit "All Right Now," as well as key Free tracks "Heavy Load," "Mr. Big," and the title track. —*Rick Clark*

● **Best of Free** / 1973 / A&M 3663
A solid compilation showcasing "All Right Now" and other semi-hits. A worthwhile sampler for the uninitiated. —*Dan Heilman*

● **Molten Gold: The Anthology** / Oct. 5, 1993 / A&M 518456
If you are a Free fan and you haven't purchased any CDs, go no further than here. Great liner notes and sound. All the key tracks are here. —*Rick Clark*

Glenn Frey

b. Nov. 6, 1948, Detroit, MI
Vocals, guitar / Pop/rock
Frey, previously a singer/songwriter and guitarist in the Eagles, launched a solo career upon the band's demise, starting in 1982. He also worked as a TV actor on "Miami Vice" and "Wiseguy." —*William Ruhlmann*

● **Allnighter** / 1985 / MCA 31158
Frey breaks with the old Eagles sound on his second solo album, much of which has a bluesy, rocking feel. Includes the hits "Smuggler's Blues" and "Sexy Girl." —*William Ruhlmann*

Robert Fripp

b. May 16, 1946, Dorset, England
Guitar / Progressive rock
Once a member of the British band King Crimson, this avant-garde guitar virtuoso began recording solo albums during the latter part of King Crimson's seven-year hiatus. Fripp, in addition to his solo efforts, founded a guitar school in the mid '80s, and in 1991 he released an album with his new rock band Sunday All Over the World. —*AMG*

○ **No Pussyfooting** / 1972 / EG 7001
His collaboration with Brian Eno. A musical landscape made up of sedate guitar feedback echoed, repeated, and otherwise treated by tape recorder. Today this would be classified as new age. The follow-up, *Evening Star*, is similar. —*William Ruhlmann*

● **Exposure** / 1979 / EG 41
Though Fripp uses words like "commercial" and "MOR" to describe this music, and though parts of it contain more-or-less conventional pop/rock music, Fripp introduces a variety of tape loops and edits, vocal fragments and sound experiments, resulting in a unique musical sound collage. Guest artists include Phil Collins, Brian Eno, Daryl Hall, and Peter Gabriel. —*William Ruhlmann*

Let the Power Fall (An Album of Frippertronics) / 1981 / EG 10
"Frippertronics" is the name Robert Fripp gives to his instrumental pieces constructed with an electric guitar and a tape recorder. It is characterized by long-lined instrumental passages with sustained notes that reverberate in interesting repetitions and variations. —*William Ruhlmann*

I Advance Masked / 1982 / A&M 4913
An instrumental collaboration between guitarists Andy Summers (formerly of the Police) and Robert Fripp (formerly of King Crimson). Much of it has the rock drive of Summers's work with the Police, along with Fripp's pattern work, making for a surprisingly diverse collection. —*William Ruhlmann*

Fred Frith

Guitar / Experimental
The only ex-Henry Cow member who has been active in the United States, Frith has attained a global reputation as a composer, improviser, multi-instrumentalist, instrument builder, and eclectic collaborator of the first rank. His myriad activities freely cross over the boundaries of rock, world music, improvisation, and the avant-garde. He is one of the few new pioneers to be the subject of a feature-length film (*Step Across the Border*). His work in Henry Cow and related groups (including those of Brian Eno and Soft Machine founder Robert Wyatt) is based on the folk and blues sonic discoveries of British guitarists Derek Bailey, Keith Rowe, and John McLaughlin (among others), yet his originality and self-critical nature have prevented him from being derivative. —*Myles Boisen*

○ **Cheap at Half the Price** / 1983 / East Side Digital 80572

Cheap at Half the Price is the first solo album that features Frith's vocals, but what makes the album succeed is his rough-edged guitar experimentalism. —*Stephen Thomas Erlewine*

● **Step Across the Border** / 1991 / East Side Digital 80462
Although it's theoretically a film soundtrack, *Step Across the Border* features tracks from all phases of Frith's varied career, making it a good introduction to his music. —*Stephen Thomas Erlewine*

Front 242

Group / Alternative pop/rock, techno, industrial, dance
When the Belgian synth-dance group began recording in 1982, their style followed the cold, clinical work of Kraftwerk and Cabaret Voltaire, yet their music had none of the dark mystery or threat of those early electronic bands. As the decade progressed, they captured that mystery; by the end of the decade, Front 242 were on the cutting edge of the experimental industrial dance groups, combining political sound bites with their dance samples and beats.

Their 1988 club hit, "Headhunter," cemented their reputation and provided a good example of their aggressive style. After their 1988 album, *Front by Front,* the group left the seminal industrial record label Wax Trax for a major label, Epic. Front 242's first major label release, 1991's *Tyranny for You,* showed no concessions and was another strong statement. However, their subsequent albums in the '90s showed that the group was beginning to slip from the cutting edge, although each album had some highlights. —*Stephen Thomas Erlewine*

Backcatalogue / Jan. 1987 / Wax Trax 033
A collection of early 12-inch singles, *Backcatalogue* is the best way to get acquainted with the early days of Front 242, Belgium's leading industrial outfit. —*Stephen Thomas Erlewine*

○ **Official Version (1986-1987)** / Feb. 1987 / Epic 52405
With its dense, claustrophobic mix of samples and relentless, hard beats, *Official Version* was the first from Front 242 that was consistently impressive. —*Stephen Thomas Erlewine*

● **Front by Front** / 1988 / Epic 52406
While it reiterates the music of *Official Version, Front by Front* features a stronger political message, as well as their signature single, "Headhunter." —*Stephen Thomas Erlewine*

○ **Tyranny (for You)** / 1991 / Epic 47077
More aggressive and militant than its predecessors, *Tyranny (for You)* is an impressionistic, angry album that captured the underlying chaos of the early '90s just with its dark, brutal rhythm tracks. —*Stephen Thomas Erlewine*

06:21:03:11 Up Evil / May 25, 1993 / Epic 53433
Although it isn't a bad album by any means, Front 242 seems at a loss for ideas on *06:21:03:11 Up Evil,* which lacks the sonic power and conceptual force of their three previous albums. —*Stephen Thomas Erlewine*

Fugazi

Group / Alternative rock, hardcore
Fugazi is as famous for their strident anti-corporate stance as they are for their music. Fugazi's leader, singer/guitarist Ian MacKaye, refuses to charge over five dollars for a concert and keeps the prices of their recordings low by releasing them through his own record label, Dischord. At times, their vehement political stance can overshadow their musical accomplishments, but they are one of the few bands that prove it's possible for hardcore punk to expand beyond its rigid structures. With the seminal Washington DC hardcore band Minor Threat, MacKaye defined straight-edge hardcore; with Fugazi, he breaks and rewrites the very rules he established.

Since their 1988 debut EP, Fugazi has gained a substantial fan base without the help of mainstream press or MTV airplay—the band would rather talk to fanzines than to mainstream press, so they never talk to *Rolling Stone.* By the time of their 1993 album, they charted on *Billboard's* Top-200 album chart without any commercial push. Through their anti-rock star stance, Fugazi have become rock stars. —*Stephen Thomas Erlewine*

● **13 Songs** / 1990 / Dischord 36
A CD combination of their first two EP's, *Fugazi* and *Margin Walker.* —*Meredith Erlewine*

Repeater + 3 Songs / 1990 / Dischord 45

Not quite as polished as *13 Songs,* but a great album. —*Meredith Erlewine*

○ **In on the Kill Taker** / 1993 / Dischord
Another installment from Ian McKaye's straight-edge punk heroes proves to be no different than their previous releases, yet just as satisfying. Well, one aspect was different—it sold more than any previous Fugazi release, breaking into *Billboard's* Top-200 albums chart, which is very impressive for an independent release. Fortunately, it was a record that deserved its success. —*Stephen Thomas Erlewine*

The Fugs

Group / Experimental
The Fugs were a New York City rock/comedy group formed in the mid '60s by beatnik poets Ed Sanders and Tuli Kupferberg. They got their act together while running a way-off-Broadway rock theater presentation, *NYC,* for over 900 performances, filled with scatological satire and crudely performed music. Barely able to sing or play their instruments, the Fugs nonetheless scored big with college audiences when their first album was reissued by the tiny ESP label in 1966. Successful throughout the end of decade (eventually signed to Frank Sinatra's Reprise label!), the Fugs' brand of humor and music exerted an influence on bands as diverse as the Velvet Underground and Frank Zappa's Mothers of Invention. —*Cub Koda*

● **Fugs First Album** / 1965 / ESP 1018
Their debut effort, which combines leftist politics, William Blake, and beatnik sensibilities. Necessary if you want to understand the hippies and acid rock. —*David Szatmary*

○ **Fugs (Kill for Peace)** / 1966 / ESP 1028
At the time of its release, the Fugs' second (self-titled) album contained the most outrageous lyrics ever heard on a Top-100 rock & roll LP. The group, with roots in New York's underground folk and poetry scenes, flung themselves wholeheartedly into all-out rock & roll on this 1966 record, which addresses concerns like free love, the madness of war, and government repression. The CD reissue of this classic includes two previously unreleased live performances, and three tracks from the unreleased album they recorded mid-'60s for Atlantic in 1967. —*Richie Unterberger*

Tenderness Junction / 1967 / Reprise 6280
Listen especially to the live "Exorcising Evil Spirits from the Pentagon." —*David Szatmary*

It Crawled into My Hand, Honest / 1968 / Reprise 6305
Features the classic "Wide, Wide River." —*David Szatmary*

Bobby Fuller Four

d. Jul. 18, 1966
Vocals / Rock & roll
Fuller was Buddy Holly's greatest disciple. Both were Texans who loved the sound of ringing Stratocasters; both knew good hooks when they heard them; and both died at the apex of their careers. Fuller is best remembered for the charging 1965 hit "I Fought the Law" and the follow-up "Let Her Dance." An undeservedly overlooked mid-'60s highlight. —*John Floyd*

● **Best of Bobby Fuller Four** / 1981 / Rhino 70174
He fought something, and it won, but while he was around there were few bands that could churn out rock & roll this raw and determined. —*Jeff Tamarkin*

I Fought the Law/The KRLA King of the Wheels / Nov. 1990 / ACE 956
The first two albums by the legendary '60s rockers, with bonus tracks. For collectors only. —*Jeff Tamarkin*

Live at PJ's Plus! / Jul. 1991 / ACE 314
Killer live show plus assorted rarities, by the ultimate '60s garage band. —*Jeff Tamarkin*

Funkadelic

Group / Funk, rock & roll, soul, psychedelic
Funkadelic was the freewheeling, electric, and rowdy alter-ego band George Clinton co-led during the '60s and '70s. This group performed the loud, surging, improvisational rock-based jams Clinton became attracted to after touring with rock bands. The band's roster included superb guitarists in Clarence "Fuzzy" Haskins and Eddie Hazel, as well as the swirling, creative keyboards of Bernie Worrell and others who rotated between

Funkadelic and Clinton's other band, Parliament. Clinton's bizarre, satiric, razor-sharp wit provided lyrics ranging from highly political material to novelty tunes, from putdowns of musical competitors to songs laced with sexual innuendo.

Funkadelic was the more politicized of George Clinton's psycho-funk spinoffs. Where Parliament offered the butt-tugging ecstasy of "Tear the Roof Off the Sucker" and "Flashlight," Funkadelic tackled racial conflict ("You and Your Folks, Me and My Folks"), government corruption ("America Eats It's Young"), and the power of the boogie ("One Nation Under a Groove"). They were never the singles act Parliament turned out to be, but they tackled tougher issues and made them wiggle and wobble as surely as anything that ever bore Clinton's stamp.

Funkadelic performed a unique, distinctive blend of comedy, protest, soul, funk, and rock fury, and the band burned bright through the '70s, until commercial pressures and internal dissension ripped apart the Clinton empire. *—Ron Wynn and John Floyd*

Funkadelic / 1970 / Westbound 2000
While the music is serious, George Clinton is as tongue-in-cheek as ever. The album opens up with his voice, proposing "If you will suck my soul, I will lick your funky emotions"—for 40 minutes, he weaves in and out of that vein. *Funkadelic* is raw and pure funk, with twangy guitars and deep, low, yet prominent bass lines. It takes the quirky, basic groove of the Meters and renders it heavy and grungy, while maintaining the straightfaced humor that Clinton has made famous. *—Julian Katz*

Free Your Mind Your Ass Will Follow / 1970 / Westbound 2001
Not quite as promising as its title and classic cover would indicate, *Free Your Mind and Your Ass Will Follow* is full of faux religious rambling and spacey studio overdubs and effects. Clinton still manages to pull it off in his style of blending soul, heavy metal, gospel, and bad sci-fi movies, coming up with gems such as "Friday Night, August the Fourteenth," and "Funky Dollar Bill." *—Julian Katz*

☆ **Maggot Brain** / 1971 / Westbound 2007
The best early Funkadelic record. There's some indulgent stuff here that may conjure some art-rock nightmares, but at its best—"You and Your Folks, Me and My Folks"—this is a brave and pioneering recording. *—John Floyd*

America Eats It's Young / 1972 / Westbound 2020
Some fantastic extended guitar jams and bitter, though prophetic, lyrics made this one of Funkadelic's most ambitious and remarkable albums. Few were ready in the early '70s for a Black band that blended acid-rock riffs and angry rhetoric. It wasn't all political however; they were also some silly, joyous tunes and the band's trademark biting satires on their rivals. *—Ron Wynn*

○ **Cosmic Slop** / 1973 / Westbound 2022
Another classic, with furious guitar riffs, inspired, bizarre lyrics, marvelous production, and loose, chaotic, but brillant arrangements. *—Ron Wynn*

○ **Let's Take It to the Stage** / 1975 / Westbound 215
The title track was one of their funniest funk jams, while the other songs run the gamut from blistering rock to zany R&B. George Clinton was in the midst of his greatest commercial/creative run, and this one ranks right alongside the other magical Funkadelic releases of the '70s. *—Ron Wynn*

Tales of Kidd Funkadelic / Jan. 1976 / Westbound 227
Some leftover jams, songs, and funk pieces from the Funkadelic era. George Clinton was in the midst of moving Funkadelic to another label, and the westbound folk released a bunch of vault material to get another Funkadelic album on the market. There were still some fine cuts, but the random element prevented it from being a great album because it lacked the thematic organization and vision Clinton provided for the concept LPs. *—Ron Wynn*

○ **Hardcore Jollies** / Feb. 1976 / Priority
Their major-label debut from 1976 lacks the manic drive of the early stuff, but tightens the grooves and adds some sharp melodies. *—John Floyd*

★ **One Nation Under a Groove** / 1978 / Priority 3209
The title cut is Clinton's supreme goodfoot manifesto, and for the first time in his career he pulls off a start-to-finish masterstroke. *—John Floyd*

○ **Uncle Jam Wants You** / 1979 / Priority

It doesn't keep moving like its immediate predecessor, but this is where you'll find "Not Just Knee Deep," a wonderful piece of erotic esoterica. *—John Floyd*

★ **Music for Your Mother** / 1993 / Westbound 55
This two-disc set collects all the great early Funkadelic singles and B-sides and presents them in remastered glory. The list includes such gems as "Funky Dollar Bill," "Cosmic Slop," "Let's Take It to the Stage" and "I'll Bet You." Unfortunately, some of Funkadelic's finest efforts were album-length and/or suite pieces, so some brilliant material that wasn't issued as singles was omitted. But it's as comprehensive a collection as possible under the circumstances (lacking the later material owned by Priority), and Rob Bowman's notes are extensive and nicely done (though they're also extremely hard to read). *—Ron Wynn*

Billy Fury

b. Apr. 17, 1941, Liverpool, England, **d.** Jan. 28, 1983
Vocals / British invasion, rock & roll
England's best rock singer of the pre-Beatles era. Born in Liverpool, Fury was the most talented of England's Elvis clones and near-clones of the very early '60s and also wrote some of his own songs. A strong singer with a very suggestive stage presence, Fury had the support of a fine backing band, including rockabilly guitarist Joe Brown. His recordings from 1963 onward, backed by the Tornadoes (of "Telstar" fame) lack this power, but Fury still made the charts through the mid '60s, and, prior to his death in the mid '80s, retained the respect and admiration of the British rock establishment he helped to form. *—Bruce Eder*

● **Sound of Fury Plus 10** / 1988 / PolyGram 820627
The best rock album recorded in England before the rise of the Beatles (Andy White, the guest drummer on "Love Me Do," plays the skins on this too). A hard-rocking gem driven by Fury's powerful voice and Joe Brown's superb guitar. This reissue has ten bonus tracks. *—Bruce Eder*

Peter Gabriel

b. May 13, 1950, England
Vocals, keyboards / Progressive rock, pop/rock
Peter Gabriel was one of the founding members of Genesis when it was formed in 1965. Gabriel left Genesis in 1975 to pursue an idiosyncratic but highly successful solo career. He initially drew from the art-rock sounds of his time with Genesis but increasingly infused world-beat and extremely dissonant rock, and eventually some R&B, into his sound.

Gabriel has always surrounded himself with first-class producers (Bob Ezrin, Robert Fripp, Daniel Lanois, Steve Lillywhite) who could sonically push the envelope into new frontiers. Thematically Gabriel's lyrics progressively abandoned the journey through the dark side of the psyche in favor of reaching out with awareness-elevating sentiment. That transition helped expand Gabriel's audience significantly in 1986 with the multi-platinum hit album *So*, which peaked at number two.

Gabriel's hits include "Solsbury Hill," "Games without Frontiers," "Shock the Monkey," "Sledgehammer," "In Your Eyes," and "Big Time." *—Rick Clark*

● **Peter Gabriel** / 1977 / Atco 36147
His strong debut, produced by Bob Ezrin (Pink Floyd, Alice Cooper), features the hit "Solsbury Hill," which addressed Gabriel's breakup with Genesis. The sound reflects some of Genesis's art-rock sensibilities ("Moribund the Burgermeister"), while charting some more accessible styles (in Gabriel's eccentric fashion) like the fairly straight-ahead rock of "Modern Love." Other highlights include the portentous "Here Comes the Flood" and "Humdrum." *—Rick Clark*

Peter Gabriel / 1978 / Atco 19181
King Crimson's Robert Fripp produced this follow-up. Overall, this effort is more uneven, but there are some real highlights in the form of "D.I.Y." and the aggressively dissonant rocker "On the Air." *—Rick Clark*

★ **Peter Gabriel** / 1980 / David Geffen Co. 2035
On this, the third of three self-titled efforts, Gabriel teams up with producer Steve Lillywhite (XTC, Psychedelic Furs, U2) and produces a masterpiece. From the chilling opener, "Intruder," to "Biko," an impassioned tribute to murdered South African poet and activist Steven Biko, Lillywhite's experimental (and very left of center) approach to sound is a perfect match for Gabriel's con-

voluted tales from the dark side of human nature. Arguably Gabriel's best work thus far. —*Rick Clark*

Security / 1982 / David Geffen Co. 2011
Produced by David Lord and Gabriel, this is really a transitional album, borrowing from the heavily treated approach to sound found on the Lillywhite work while embracing more world-beat rhythms. The music is less dissonant. Thematically, Gabriel picks up the human rights thread he started with "Biko" on "Wallflower." "Kiss of Life" suggests a hopefulness emerging in his work. Includes the hit "Shock the Monkey." —*Rick Clark*

Plays Live / 1983 / David Geffen Co. 4012
Gabriel has always been an excellent performer. This live set is excellent proof, in spite of some slight post-gig doctoring. Nevertheless, most of these songs work best in the arid confines of the studio atmosphere. —*Rick Clark*

Birdy / 1985 / David Geffen Co. 24070
This instrumental work was Gabriel's first major soundtrack undertaking. Fans of Gabriel's richly textured arrangements and melodies (some here are drawn from earlier material) should check out this fine work. —*Rick Clark*

○ **Passion** / 1989 / David Geffen Co. 24206
For the soundtrack for Martin Scorsese's film *The Last Temptation of Christ*, Gabriel drew inspiration from field recordings of musicians in the Middle East, fusing those recordings with his own atmospheric sound tapestries for a powerful collection of music. —*Rick Clark*

Shaking the Tree: Sixteen Golden Greats / 1990 / David Geffen Co. 24326
This is an odd best-of collection. True, it includes his hits, but Gabriel isn't merely a singles artist. As a result, there are many important album tracks that are glaring omissions from a more well-rounded picture of Gabriel's artistry. The title, no doubt, is an indicator of the tossed-off nature of this set. —*Rick Clark*

Us / 1992 / David Geffen Co. 24473
Gabriel's proper pop follow-up to his breakthrough *So* is a brooding, introspective affair. Apart from a couple of obvious attempts at hit singles (the most blatant being the "Sledgehammer" knock-off, "Steam"), *Us* is long on slow, atmospheric synthesizer-based numbers with exotic world-beat rhythms. *Us* seems to float away on the first listen, but after a couple of plays, songs like "Come Talk to Me" and "Blood of Eden" work their way into the subconscious. The best songs from *Us* rank among Gabriel's finest work. —*Stephen Thomas Erlewine*

Galaxie 500
Group / Alternative pop/rock
While many bands picked up on the Velvet Underground's more rocking traits, this Boston-based trio reveled in their slower doings. Sparse and not upbeat, they are not dour either. —*Bruce Eder*

● **Today** / 1988 / Rough Trade 266
Working the slow side of the Velvet Underground. Melodic and intense. —*Robert Gordon*

○ **This Is Our Music** / 1990 / Rough Trade 86
More of the same as on *Today*. They knew their trick and stuck to it. —*Robert Gordon*

Game Theory
Group / Alternative pop/rock, power pop
Led by Scott Miller, an Alex Chilton-influenced singer/songwriter, Game Theory produces smart alternative Anglo power-pop, full of engaging quirky melodies and fairly obscure lyrics.
On the down side, Miller's voice can get a little whiny, and his earnest approximations to pitch may be an acquired taste for some. However, their Mitch Easter-produced albums, *Big Shot Chronicles*, *Real Nighttime*, and *Lolita Nation* are worth seeking out.
Big Star and dB's fans should love this band. Then again, they probably know about Game Theory already. —*Rick Clark*

○ **Real Nighttime** / 1985 / Enigma 72022
The band's first effort with Mitch Easter (R.E.M., Let's Active) producing. Miller's Alex Chilton fixation comes to the fore here, and it generally works nicely. "24" was a breezy alternative college hit. Other highlights include "Curse of the Frontierland," with its

Big Star-influenced guitar figure, and the delicately reflective "If and When It All Falls Apart." —*Rick Clark*

○ **Big Shot Chronicles** / 1986 / Enigma 72647
The band's sound and Miller's songwriting are more aggressive here, delivering an appealingly punchy power-pop sound. A fine album with many tracks to recommend. "I've Tried Subtlety" is a strong, over-amped T-Rex rocker, while "Like a Girl Jesus" shines with Easter's mildly psychedelic production touches. "Erica's World" is a wonderfully quirky rocker, and "Regenisraen" showcases the band's harmonic capabilities. —*Rick Clark*

○ **Lolita Nation** / 1988 / Enigma 73280
Many fans of the band claim that this is a creative peak for Game Theory. *Lolita Nation* is loaded with odd juxtapositions of experimental sounds and spoken passages. The material, while dazzling in places, is rather inconsistent. "The Real Sheila" and "We Love You, Carol and Alison" are highlights, and both of them are found on *Tinker*. . . . —*Rick Clark*

Two Steps from the Middle Ages / 1988 / Enigma 73350
Miller's melodies and the band's overall execution sound largely devoid of any real sparks. —*Rick Clark*

● **Tinker to Evers to Chance (Selected Highlights 1982-1989)** / 1990 / Enigma 75351
For the uninitiated, this collection of highlights from 1982 to 1989 is the best place to start, containing a healthy selection from their later Mitch Easter-produced albums. —*Rick Clark*

Gang of Four
Group / New wave, alternative rock
Militant U.K. punk group formed in Leeds in 1977 and featuring Jon King, Hugo Burnham, Andy Gill, and Dave Allen. They made several critically successful albums before splitting in 1984. They were re-formed by King and Gill in 1991. —*William Ruhlmann*

☆ **Entertainment!** / 1978 / Warner Brothers 3446
With their machine-shop rhythms, harsh guitar attacks, and chanted, unmelodic lyrics, GoF is anything but easy listening. But in songs such as "Damaged Goods" and "At Home He's a Tourist," their caustic messages perfectly match the musical lockstep, and both become nearly irresistible—in other words, pop music. —*William Ruhlmann*

Songs of the Free / 1982 / Warner Brothers 23683
Gang of Four fill out their sound with background vocals and rhythmic variety. Most of all, the anguished singing begins to border on the passionate. —*William Ruhlmann*

● **Brief History of the Twentieth Century** / 1990 / Warner Brothers 26448
A well-chosen 20-song compilation taken from the band's four studio albums and miscellaneous singles from 1979 to1983. —*William Ruhlmann*

Gap Band
Group / Soul, funk
This Southern combo bopped around throughout the '70s, offering a rather pedestrian variety of boogie funk. After scaling down and retooling their sound, the Gap Band netted numerous hits with a big mod-funk sound that recalled everyone from Sly Stone to George Clinton and Rick James. —*John Floyd*

Gap Band 1 / 1977 / PolyGram 824141
Ronnie Wilson recruited his brothers Charles and Robert in the late '70s to cement a group vision and sound he'd begun establishing in 1967 but hadn't honed due to constant personnel changes. The Wilsons' first album was titled *The Gap Band* and it laid the groundwork for the George Clinton/Parliament-inspired sound that would become enormously popular with their second album. The debut lacked the production polish, spirited leads and exchanges, and breakout singles that distinguished their best releases. It did, however, contain teasers that were a tipoff that the Wilsons had a sound and style that would be commercially viable. —*Ron Wynn*

○ **Gap Band 2** / 1979 / PolyGram 824142
The seeds laid with their debut flowered on *Gap Band II*. The Wilson Brothers now had their George Clinton/Parliament-with-a-taste-of-Rick James schtick down perfectly, and the chunky riffs and enthusiastic group vocals began to attract attention. "Get Up and Dance (Oops)" was a party and club hit, and "Steppin' Out" had a good track, though it lacked a lyric hook. But this album

eventually went gold, and it helped make the Gap Band a national attraction. —*Ron Wynn*

○ **Gap Band 3** / 1980 / PolyGram 822788
A masterpiece, one of the great funk albums of the '80s. It had such fabulous singles "Burn Rubber on Me" and "Humpin," and marked the fruition of their George Clinton-tinged vocals and humor/grinding Southwestern funk/blues approach. The Wilsons were just starting to hit their stride. —*Ron Wynn*

○ **Gap Band 4** / 1982 / PolyGram 822794
Another smash album and their third funk masterpiece in a row, the Gap Band was still burning up the R&B charts in the early '80s. They had two singles from this album top the charts and a third make it to number two. Robert Palmer later covered "Early in the Morning," and the Wilson brothers were at the top of their game. —*Ron Wynn*

● **Gap Gold** / 1985 / PolyGram 824343
This brief but thorough best-of contains every major hit netted by the revamped, latter-day Gap Band, including such dance crushers as "You Dropped a Bomb on Me" and "Early in the Morning." —*John Floyd*

Jerry Garcia

b. Aug. 1, 1942, San Francisco, CA
Vocals, guitar / Rock & roll
A singer/songwriter and guitarist in the Grateful Dead, Garcia has also worked extensively as a solo and in other configurations since 1972. —*William Ruhlmann*

● **Garcia** / 1972 / Grateful Dead 4003
In essence, this is a Grateful Dead record, featuring as it does the band's leader/singer/guitarist, its drummer, and its lyricist. Except for the few instrumental/experimental cuts, the material has been incorporated into the Dead's concert repertoire. In fact, this is a perfect follow-up to the folk-rock song albums the Dead produced in 1970, *Workingman's Dead* and *American Beauty*—albums the band itself has never really followed up. —*William Ruhlmann*

Reflections / 1976 / Grateful Dead 40082
Again, a Dead album in everything but name, with several tracks featuring the entire band, perhaps most memorably on "It Must Have Been the Roses." —*William Ruhlmann*

Cats under the Stars / 1978 / Arista 8535
The first real "Garcia Band" album is paced by songs that would not sound out of place at a Dead concert. As a matter of fact, the album has garnered increased interest in the '90s as the Dead added the leadoff track "Rubin and Cherise" to its repertoire. —*William Ruhlmann*

Almost Acoustic / 1989 / Grateful Dead 40052
Garcia got his start in bluegrass, and here he assembles the Jerry Garcia Acoustic Band (some of whom he started playing with) to handle a live set full of Jimmie Rodgers, Mississippi John Hurt, and traditional mountain music. —*William Ruhlmann*

○ **Jerry Garcia & David Grisman** / 1991 / Grateful Dead 39032
A guitar-and-mandolin duet album, exquisitely produced, with this pair trying a variety of styles from Garcia's "Friend of the Devil" to the ambitious instrumental "Arabia." —*William Ruhlmann*

Jerry Garcia Band / 1991 / Arista 18690
A double live album recorded in 1990 and featuring extended versions of songs by Bruce Cockburn, Bob Dylan, Smokey Robinson, the Beatles, the Band, Los Lobos, and others. The Garcia Band serves a kind of songbook function for its listeners (as, indeed, the Dead does), which may mean that its chief virtue is as instruction: If you're familiar with the originals, you don't really need to hear Garcia's covers, but if, like many Deadheads, you don't hear much music outside the band's orbit, this may help lead you to other good music. —*William Ruhlmann*

Art Garfunkel

b. Oct. 13, 1941, Queens, NY
Vocals / Pop
As the airy choirboy half of Simon & Garfunkel, Art Garfunkel reached his greatest solo success between 1973 and 1978 with lushly produced soft-pop hits like "All I Know," "I Shall Sing," "Second Avenue," "I Only Have Eyes for You," "Breakaway," and "(What a) Wonderful World," recorded with James Taylor and Paul

Simon. Garfunkel also reunited with Simon in 1975 for the hit "My Little Town." —*Rick Clark*

● **Garfunkel: Best Of** / 1990 / Columbia 45008
This is a good overview of Garfunkel's solo work. Most of his hit singles are included here. —*Rick Clark*

Marvin Gaye

b. Apr. 2, 1939, Washington, D.C., d. Apr. 1, 1984
Vocals / Motown, R&B, soul
He wanted to do it all, from standards to lubricious make-out music—and by his track record he came close. The most troubled of Tamla-Motown's talented stable, Gaye came to the label from the usual background of gospel groups and R&B quartets. He broke through in 1962 with dance-floor specials, but his gentle tenor voice was better suited elsewhere. His music slowly evolved, although the Motown quality controllers ensured that its commerciality rarely slipped.

Gaye's gloriously paranoid interpretation of "I Heard It through the Grapevine" gave him the clout he needed to reshape his career. He worked up some concept albums (most notable, *What's Going On* and *Let's Get It On*, which swiftly ran the gamut from ecological concerns to soft-core porn) and then watched his career fall apart. Divorces, financial woes, and record-label troubles conspired to send Gaye, never an emotionally strong or stable man anyway, into a tailspin that ended tragically when he was shot by his father in 1984. —*Colin Escott*

That Stubborn Kinda Fellow / 1963 / Motown 5218
Vintage Gaye and Motown, following all the formulas that made the label the '60s' finest record company. The title track was an instant classic, and is still among his finest '60s uptempo tunes. The other cuts are just as fantastic, and any doubts anyone might have had about Gaye were immediately and forever quashed with this album. —*Ron Wynn*

○ **I Heard It through the Grapevine** / 1968 / Motown 5395
Here's another Motown classic, superb ballads, striking uptempo tracks, great production and arrangments, and wonderful songs. —*Ron Wynn*

● **Super Hits** / 1970 / Motown 5301
A fabulous anthology, one of the best Motown ever released. —*Ron Wynn*

☆ **What's Going On** / 1971 / Motown 5339
Shortly after Marvin Gaye turned 30, he became the first Motown artist with a measure of creative control. *What's Going On* was the result, surely Marvin's finest moment and, along with a number of Stevie Wonder's early-'70s releases, one of a handful of *great* Motown albums. A concept album, *What's Going On* chronicled a multitude of societal ills. Ironically, Motown owner Berry Gordy did not want to release it. He was convinced it held no commercial potential. Gordy couldn't have been more wrong: *What's Going On* catapulted Marvin Gaye into superstardom. Three number-one singles were pulled from the album: the title song, "Mercy Mercy Me (the Ecology)," and "Inner City Blues (Make Me Wanna Holler)." This was the first album where Marvin overdubbed his voice multiple times, creating a one-man vocal group. The result was a level of timbral integration in the harmonies that became a Gaye trademark. —*Rob Bowman*

Trouble Man / 1972 / Motown 5241
Marvin Gaye turned to soundtracks in the early '70s and came out with one that ranked right alongside the epic scores done by Curtis Mayfield and Isaac Hayes. The film itself was a typical '70s "blaxploitation" effort, but Gaye's vocals, seamless production, and nice mix of uptempo funk, light ballads, and psuedo-macho camp was brilliant. —*Ron Wynn*

☆ **Let's Get It On** / 1973 / Motown 5192
Let's Get It On is one of the most erotic recordings known to mankind. Inspired by Gaye's obsession with a teenage girl, Janis Hunter, who would later become his second wife, side 1 is a self-contained suite. Side 2, including "You Sure Love to Ball," is nearly pornographic. Over time, five songs would chart from the album, including one of his concert standards, "Distant Lover." —*Rob Bowman*

★ **Anthology** / 1974 / Motown 0791
With *Anthology* you can get an overview of Gaye's Motown work without having to plunk the money down for *The Marvin Gaye Collection* boxed set. This two-CD set contains most of his major

hits (although not his number-one hit "Let's Get It On"), including "Inner City Blues (Make Me Wanna Holler)," "Mercy Mercy Me (the Ecology)," "I Heard It through the Grapevine," "Trouble Man," "I'll Be Doggone," "What's Going On," "Hitch Hike," "Can I Get a Witness," and "Pride and Joy," as well as his numerous duets with Kim Weston and Tammi Terrell, like "Ain't No Mountain High Enough," "Ain't Nothing Like the Real Thing," "It Takes Two," and "Your Precious Love." —AMG

Greatest Hits / 1976 / Motown 5191
A good, if unessential, collection that recycles many songs that are available on many other packages. This is strictly for budget-conscious buyers and casual Gaye listeners, though the CD version is mastered pretty well. —Ron Wynn

○ **Here My Dear** / 1978 / Motown 6008
On one of the stranger releases in popular music, *Here, My Dear,* Gaye stands emotionally naked. Over the course of this two-album set, Marvin chronicles the dissolution of his marriage to company president Berry Gordy's sister Anna). The level of detail is nearly painful as Marvin accuses Anna of keeping him from seeing his son, having a restraining order issued against him, and holding their separation up for ransom. Marvin also tells us of his cocaine habit and his obsession with prostitutes. In a trace of irony not lost on the singer, Anna received all royalties from the album as per their divorce agreement. Upon hearing it, she reportedly contemplated suing for invasion of privacy. —Rob Bowman

In Our Lifetime / 1981 / Motown 474
Another of Gaye's uneven, yet appealing releases. He was searching for the right songs, and didn't always find them. He was also hurting again, suffering personal and professional problems that he ultimately failed to solve. This made his songs both poignant and painful, and that's what makes this album worth hearing despite its problems. —Ron Wynn

○ **Midnight Love** / 1982 / Columbia 38197
Gaye's comeback album contains its share of fluff, but "Sexual Healing" is one of the greatest R&B singles of all time. Black radio felt that way as well: The song stayed number one for ten weeks, remaining on the charts for a total of 27 weeks. —Rob Bowman

Marvin Gaye Collection / 1990 / Motown 6311
Marvin Gaye has more than enough great music to make a superb boxed set, but the haphazard *Marvin Gaye Collection* isn't it. The four discs within the set are arranged thematically—one terrific disc of hits, one good disc of duets, one largely uninteresting disc of rarities, and one wildly uneven disc of ballads. By spreading out the material this way, Motown shortchanges Gaye's musical accomplishment; there is no sense of growth or innovation. Although many of the songs are wonderful, some of the selections are puzzling—they seem to be chosen because they are arcane, not because they're significant. Nevertheless, this very quality makes *The Marvin Gaye Collection* essential for his most devoted fans. However, most fans will find this boxed set disappointing. —Stephen Thomas Erlewine

○ **Seek & You Shall Find: More of the Best (1963-1981)** / 1993 / Rhino 71182
Full of album tracks, B-sides, and live tracks *Seek & You Shall Find: More of the Best* is a great complement to Gaye's greatest-hits collections. —AMG

Gloria Gaynor

b. Sep. 7, 1949, Newark, NJ
Vocals / Disco
Gaynor sang with the Soul Satisfiers band before being discovered at the Wagon Wheel in New York in the early '70s. Probably the first "disco queen," Gaynor helped popularize, through her music, the "segue" or "extended mix" that came to represent disco music. Her 1979 cut, "I Will Survive," became a woman's anthem in the vein of Helen Reddy's "I Am Woman." She continues to thrive as a major star in Europe, although not here. —Bil Carpenter

● **Greatest Hits** / 1982 / Polydor 833433
Her disco hits, from "Never Can Say Goodbye" to "I Will Survive." —Dan Heilman

Paul Gayten

b. Jan. 29, 1920, New Orleans, LA, d. Mar. 26, 1991, Los Angeles, CA
Vocals, piano / R&B
Paul Gayten, a seminal figure in New Orleans R&B, led a varied career in the music business as a bandleader, producer, label owner, and onetime overseer of the West Coast operation of Chess Records. A nephew of blues piano legend Little Brother Montgomery, Gayten once led one of the top bands of New Orleans, but he gave up the performing life in 1956 to turn his attention to production and eventually to his own California-based Pzazz label (which featured Louis Jordan, among others). Gayten wrote Larry Darnell's 1949 classic "For You My Love" and recorded a few Top-Ten hits of his own for Regal and DeLuxe (1947-1950), some of them with vocalist Annie Laurie. —Jim O'Neal

● **Chess King of New Orleans/The Chess Years** / 1989 / Chess 9294
Sizzling mid-'50s New Orleans R&B from this veteran. —Bill Dahl

○ **Regal Records in New Orleans** / 1991 / Specialty 2169
Early-'50s New Orleans jump-blues and ballads by pianist Paul Gayten and vocalist Annie Laurie are featured on this generous (27-track) disc. —Bill Dahl

○ **And Annie Laurie** / Specialty 2169
Stomping New Orleans R&B and barrelhouse blues by pianist/vocalist Paul Gayten and vocalist Annie Laurie. Though he moved to Los Angeles from New Orleans in the early '50s, Gayten never lost the second-line beat. The duo didn't enjoy as much success with this Specialty material as they did on Deluxe and Regal, but it's still wonderful, vibrant R&B in the great swing and bawdy tradition. —Ron Wynn

J. Geils Band

Group / Blues rock, rock & roll, pop/rock
From their late-'60s origins as Boston's finest White blues band up to their commerical breakthrough in the early '80s, the J. Geils Band have been one of America's finest bands, with a demolishing live sound and the vision to contort their influences into something derived from, but not confined to, the realm of blues or R&B. This doesn't make them America's answer to the Rolling Stones, but it has produced a surprising number of unique albums, highlighted by Peter Wolf's tough but humorous vocals, J. Geils's economical guitar work, and the Little Walter-like harp calisthenics of Magic Dick. Sadly, just as the group gained the success they'd been working toward for over a decade, the group fired Wolf and released a flat album. Wolf has since made three excellent albums that have failed to find an audience. —John Floyd

○ **J. Geils Band** / 1970 / Atlantic 8275
Their debut paid homage to the likes of Otis Rush, John Lee Hooker, and Motown through blistering covers, but originals such as "Wait" and "What's Your Hurry" more than hold their own. Magic Dick steals the show on this one. —John Floyd

● **Monkey Island** / 1977 / Atlantic 19103
One of the great lost albums, *Monkey Island* is where the Geils Band make the blues their own. It's an elaborately produced, adventurous set that analyzes their commerical failure and looks for answers to hard-to-ask questions. Unlike their 1972 live album *Full House, Monkey Island* refuses to pander to blues conservatives or boogie-rock hammerheads; the album is steeped in the kind of pathos and bitterness that infuse the Stones' *Sticky Fingers.* The album flopped, but it remains the group's most personal statement. —John Floyd

Sanctuary / 1978 / EMI America 17006
The Geils sound is retooled into a streamlined shuffle that owes much to the production and songwriting floriation of keyboardist Seth Justman. Their soul and blues chops are still apparent, but they've worked them into a sound that manages to elaborate on the experiments of *Monkey Island* while still paying homage to their early days. —John Floyd

● **Best of the J. Geils Band** / 1979 / Atlantic 19234
Pulling the decent material from otherwise unspectacular mid-'70s albums makes this an adequate overview of the band's

achievements. It's the best place to sample such minor hits as "Must Of Got Lost" and "Give It to Me." —*John Floyd*

Love Stinks / 1980 / EMI America 92703
The title cut brought the band an across-the-board hit, and the near new wave production touches don't get in the way of the crack rhythm section or Geils's tasty leads. A new sound for a new decade. —*John Floyd*

○ **Freeze-Frame** / 1981 / EMI America 46014
A stylistic retread that nonetheless cemented the band's new-found popularity, thanks to the naggingly catchy "Centerfold" and the noveau-funky "Flamethrower." "Piss on the Wall" and "Rage in the Cage" are blistering rockers. —*John Floyd*

● **House Party: Anthology** / 1992 / Rhino 71164
The superb two-disc anthology *Houseparty* concentrates on the rousing, full-throttle blues-rock boogie of their heyday, including a full album's worth of live material (ten songs from their three live albums). The pop success of the *Love Stinks* and *Freeze-Frame* albums make sense in the context of the set, but the songs that cut the deepest are the blues-rock numbers on the first disc and the live songs. Thankfully, the compilers (*Trouser Press* editor Ira Robbins and band members Peter Wolf and Seth Justman) choose to end *Houseparty* with three songs from *Sanctuary* instead of the dull *You're Gettin' Even While I'm Gettin' Odd*, preserving the image of the J. Geils Band as one of America's top rock and roll groups of the '70s. —*Stephen Thomas Erlewine*

Bob Geldof

b. Oct. 5, 1954, Dublin, Ireland
Vocals / Pop/rock
Born in Dublin, Geldof formed the punk group Boomtown Rats in 1975. During the band's existence, it moved from the pure energy and aggression of hits like "Looking After No. 1" to the more sophisticated but still provocative, "I Don't Like Mondays" (its title derived from the answer given by a San Diego schoolgirl when asked why she'd killed her classmates). The band became a moderate success in the United Kingdom, though it never really broke through in the United States.

In the fall of 1984, Geldof watched a BBC documentary on Ethiopian poverty and was inspired to put together a charity single, "Do They Know It's Christmas." It featured a large number of British pop stars performing under the name Band Aid and became the best-selling single in U.K. history. Michael Jackson and Lionel Richie repeated the feat the following year in the States with "We Are the World." By then Geldof was involved in plans for a massive charity concert that eventually became Live Aid, two marathon shows held July 13, 1985, at Wembley Stadium in London and at JFK Stadium in Philadelphia, featuring a *Who's Who* of pop/rock talent. Millions were raised and distributed to the African poor. Geldof was nominated for a Nobel Prize and knighted, and his autobiography *Is That All?* became a U.K. bestseller.

In 1986, the Rats split and Geldof launched a solo career, again with greater success in England than in the United States. —*William Ruhlmann*

● **Deep in the Heart of Nowhere** / 1986 / Atlantic 81687
On his first solo album, Geldof sheds the new wave sound of the Boomtown Rats for a more straightforward classic Brit-rock approach, notably on the leadoff single, "This Is the World Calling" and on the "Waterloo Sunset" sequel, "Love like a Rocket," which features Eric Clapton. —*William Ruhlmann*

Vegetarians of Love / 1990 / Atlantic 82041
Geldof investigates his Irish folk roots, reveals himself to be a Dylan acolyte, and sends up his "Saint Bob" image on this varied and ambitious second album. —*William Ruhlmann*

General Public

Group / Ska-revival, pop/rock
This U.K. duo of vocalist Dave Wakeling and "toaster" Ranking Roger was formed from the split of the English Beat in 1983. General Public released two albums before they split. In 1994, General Public reunited and had a surprise hit single with their UB40-style interpretation of the Staple Singers' "I'll Take You There," taken from the *Threesome* soundtrack. —*William Ruhlmann*

● **All the Rage** / 1984 / IRS 5046

The vocal duo from the English Beat turn in an album of passionate pop/rock, little of which bears the ska style of the parent group. Most effective are the uptempo, Motown-style songs, especially the Top-30 hit "Tenderness." —*William Ruhlmann*

Hand to Mouth / 1986 / IRS 5782
Although they still have some of the pop smarts that informed *All the Rage*, General Public have toned down their ska and reggae roots, making *Hand to Mouth* a more professional, but less exciting, album. —*Stephen Thomas Erlewine*

Generation X

b. 1978, **d.** 1981
Group / Punk
An early London punk band (1978-1981) featuring Billy Idol and Tony James (later to form Sigue Sigue Sputnik). Often criticized as being too commercially minded, Gen X was definitely the smoothest and most pop-oriented of their rebellious crowd. Their first album is considered the best, with the U.S. version offering a slightly improved song set. Their third and last, *Kiss Me Deadly*, was more an Idol-James project than a band effort and was produced by Keith Forsey, who shaped Idol's solo sound. This album contained an early version of "Dancing with Myself," which was eventually Idol's first big solo pop success. As to whether they were a band of crass opportunists or true champions of the punk spirit, Billy Idol's career and Sigue Sigue Sputnik's dubious distinction of having the first advertisement on a pop record speak volumes. —*Scott Bultman*

○ **Generation X** / 1979 / Chrysalis 21169
Generation X had punk attitude and subject matter on their debut album, which includes their answer song to the Who, "Your Generation," and the generic "One Hundred Punks." But the group's music already had more of a melodic mainstream rock sound than punk's raw assault, and frontman Billy Idol's snarl was straight out of Elvis Presley. —*William Ruhlmann*

Kiss Me Deadly / 1981 / Chrysalis 21327
Idol and bassist Brian James rehearse for their post-Gen X careers, as solo artist and leader of Sigue Sigue Sputnik, respectively. This album contains the dance hit "Dancing with Myself." —*William Ruhlmann*

● **Best of Generation X** / 1985 / Chrysalis 1521
Collecting the highlights from their three uneven albums and their EP, *Best of Generation X* features nearly everything of value the band recorded. —*Stephen Thomas Erlewine*

Genesis

Group / Progressive rock, pop/rock
In the band's original incarnation, the heart and soul of Genesis was singer Peter Gabriel. Gabriel's unique stage presence, involving costumes and bizarre pantomime antics, illustrated the surrealistic story lines of the band's eerie epics. Spooky support for these remarkable performances came from Tony Bank's churning organ and Mellotron and Steve Hackett's unusual synthesizerlike guitar textures. Gabriel's decision to leave Genesis came when the band was at its artistic peak, following 1974's *The Lamb Lies Down on Broadway*. Surprisingly, the remaining quartet found a world-class singer within its own ranks: drummer Phil Collins. With Collins at the helm, Genesis made two solid studio albums before Steve Hackett also quit. Reduced to a trio, the band turned to a mixture of empty pomp and trivial pop, but an example of the latter ("Follow You Follow Me") gave Genesis their first American hit single. The group's success was consolidated as Collins began to guide their music in a funkier and more commercial direction. By the mid '80s, Genesis (which by now bore little resemblance to the art-rock ensemble of bygone days) was regularly scoring smash hit after smash hit, with Collins enjoying a similarly successful solo career on the side. —*Michael P. Dawson*

Trespass / 1970 / MCA 1653
Genesis had changed considerably by the October 1970 release of their second album (which was their first to be issued in the United States, by the Impulse! division of ABC-Dunhill Records, now part of MCA). For one thing, they'd finished school, turned professional, and started playing out. For another, drummer John Silver had left and been replaced for the album by John Mayhew. (Before the release of *Trespass*, both Mayhew and Anthony Phillips left. The group then recruited guitarist Steve Hackett and

former-child actor Phil Collins as new drummer.) Genesis's individual sound began to appear on *Trespass*, with its complex structures and long songs. The driving rocker "Knife," which at nine minutes is the longest track, remains the highlight. — *William Ruhlmann*

Nursery Cryme / 1971 / Atlantic 80030
On their third album, released in the United Kingdom in November 1971 and in the United States in 1972, Genesis is beginning to find a place in the British art-rock movement of the early '70s, as Peter Gabriel constructs elaborate musical set pieces, the most impressive of which is the 10½-minute leadoff track, "The Musical Box." The dense structures, tempo changes, organ/guitar interplay, and fanciful lyrics are not unlike what Yes was doing at the same time, and fans of that band will find music to their liking here. — *William Ruhlmann*

○ **Foxtrot** / 1972 / Atlantic 81848
On its fourth album, Genesis's ambitious music finally starts to show individual identity and accomplishment, mixing elaborate arrangements with stirring rhythms and highly poetic lyrics. Contains "Watcher of the Skies" and the 22-minute "Supper's Ready." — *William Ruhlmann*

☆ **Selling England by the Pound** / 1973 / Atlantic 19277
One of the best examples of '70s British art-rock, this album incorporates a variety of styles, showcasing the musical dexterity of the players as well as the lyrics to story-songs like "I Know What I Like (In Your Wardrobe)," the first British Genesis hit. — *William Ruhlmann*

★ **Lamb Lies Down on Broadway** / 1974 / Atlantic 401
This, the last Genesis album with Peter Gabriel, is a sprawling two-disc thematic album concerning a character named Rael. Keeping with that theme, it includes pastiches of Broadway show music, plus the group's typical mixture of folk, rock, and classical influences. If this is not the first Gabriel-Genesis album to buy, it ultimately may prove the most satisfying. — *William Ruhlmann*

Trick of the Tail / 1976 / Atlantic 38101
At the time of its release in March 1976, Genesis's seventh studio album was a remarkable document, if only because the group had managed to survive the departure of its frontman, Peter Gabriel, by locating a worthy (and similar-sounding) vocalist in drummer Phil Collins and by writing material that was respectable, even if it lacked Gabriel's vision and imagination. As a result, the album hit number three in the United Kingdom and maintained the band's following in the United States, assuring them a future. In retrospect, it isn't a very impressive effort (with the exception of "Robbery, Assault and Battery," which has some of the old spirit), though it gives hints of the pop assembly line Genesis would develop in the coming years. — *William Ruhlmann*

Wind and Wuthering / 1977 / Atlantic 38100
Less impressive than the first Genesis quartet album, *A Trick of the Tail, Wind and Wuthering* nevertheless marked another step in the band's gradual transformation into more of a pop act, containing its first U.S. (and only its second U.K.) chart single, "Your Own Special Way." — *William Ruhlmann*

And Then There Were Three / 1978 / Atlantic 19173
The birth of the modern Genesis, a pop-rock trio led by singer/drummer Phil Collins, playing tightly constructed, short, catchy songs. The best of the bunch here is "Follow You, Follow Me," a hit on both sides of the Atlantic. (It was the first Genesis gold album in the United States.) — *William Ruhlmann*

○ **Duke** / 1980 / Atlantic 16014
Released in April 1980, *Duke* found Genesis completely geared up as a maker of concise, appealing pop singles, and it was an immediate, across-the-board hit, topping the U.K. chart and almost making the U.S. Top Ten, while the singles "Misunderstanding" and "Turn It on Again" became radio favorites on both sides of the Atlantic. — *William Ruhlmann*

● **Abacab** / 1981 / Atlantic 19313
Genesis had perfected its rhythmic, densely chorded, passionate trio music with this, their first U.S. million-seller and Top-Ten hit, which includes the Top-40 singles "Abacab," "No Reply at All," and "Man on the Corner." — *William Ruhlmann*

Genesis / 1983 / Atlantic 80116
Genesis's third straight number-one studio album in the United Kingdom was also its biggest seller yet in the United States, mak-

ing the Top Ten and selling three million copies. Its big U.S. hit was "That's All," while Britain preferred "Mama." "Illegal Alien" and "Taking It All Too Hard" also charted. — *William Ruhlmann*

Invisible Touch / 1986 / Atlantic 81641
The biggest Genesis hit to date, this multimillion-selling release features five Top-Five hits, including the number-one title track, "Throwing It All Away," "Land of Confusion," "Tonight, Tonight, Tonight," and "In Too Deep." — *William Ruhlmann*

We Can't Dance / 1991 / Atlantic 82344
Genesis's first album in five years was another enormous hit, even if it failed to match the sales of 1986's *Invisible Touch*. In the United Kingdom, it was the group's fifth straight studio album to hit number one; in the United States, it was their fifth straight Top Ten and sold four million copies. "No Son of Mine" (something of an answer to "The Living Years," by Mike Rutherford's splinter group, Mike and the Mechanics) broke the group's string of Top-Five singles by getting only to number 12, but it was followed by the number-seven "I Can't Dance," as well as three more Top-25 hits: "Hold on My Heart," "Jesus He Knows Me" (a satire on evangelist preachers), and "Never a Time." — *William Ruhlmann*

Barbara George

b. Aug. 16, 1942, New Orleans, LA
Vocals / R&B, soul
George's "I Know (You Don't Love Me No More)" topped the R&B charts in 1961 and has proven a popular cover item ever since. The New Orleans native had never been in the studio before she brought her extremely catchy melody to Harold Battiste's fledgling A.F.O. label. Benefiting from her pleasing, unpolished vocals and a melodic cornet solo by Melvin Lastie, the tune caught fire, vaulting high on pop playlists. Amazingly, nothing else George did ever dented the charts, although she waxed some listenable follow-ups for A.F.O. and Sue. — *Bill Dahl*

● **I Know (You Don't Love Me Anymore)** / 1962 / Collectables 5141
Catchy New Orleans R&B from the early '60s with coy and charming vocals by George. — *Bill Dahl*

Lowell George

d. Jun. 29, 1979
V/G/COM / Rock & roll
As Little Feat was disbanding in late 1978, their lead guitarist/songwriter Lowell George recorded a solo album, *Thanks, I'll Eat It Here*, that sounded as loose and funky as the band in their prime. After its release the following year, he set out on tour to support the album. Sadly, George died of a heart attack while on the road. He left behind a body of gritty, eclectic, funky rock & roll. On the first five Little Feat albums, his songwriting and instrumental talents are more apparent than on his solo effort, yet that doesn't attract from the record's pleasures. — *Stephen Thomas Erlewine*

● **Thanks I'll Eat It Here** / 1979 / Warner Brothers 3194
While it's surprisingly short on original songs, Lowell George's solo album *Thanks I'll Eat It Here* is as relaxed and funky as any Little Feat album from the last half of the '70s. — *Stephen Thomas Erlewine*

Georgia Satellites

Group / Rock & roll
At a time when rock & roll didn't care about its roots, the Georgia Satellites came crashing into the charts with a surprise hit single to remind everybody where the music had come from. The hit single, 1986's "Keep Your Hands to Yourself," rocked as hard as an old Chuck Berry song, and was almost as clever. The Satellites weren't a back-to-basic roots band, either—their straightforward sound borrowed equally from Berry, the Rolling Stones, the Faces, Little Feat, and AC/DC, with a Southern backwoods bent. At their best, the Satellites were just a damn good rock & roll band, driven by the classic yet fresh songwriting of lead singer/guitarist Dan Baird.

On the strength of "Keep Your Hands to Yourself," their first major-label album sold well, but the follow-up, *Open All Night*, did not. Radio and MTV had treated the band as a kind of novelty—a bunch of hicks kicking out rock & roll offered a break between the slick pop-metal of Bon Jovi and Peter Gabriel's introspective pop. By the time they released *Open All Night* in 1988, no one was interested, even if the album was only slightly weaker than the debut. After one more album, 1989's *In the Land of Salvation and Sin*, the band called it quits. Guitarist Rick Richards joined Izzy Stradlin's Ju Ju Hounds three years later. Baird pursued a solo career and had a small hit in late 1992 with "I Love You Period." —*Stephen Thomas Erlewine*

○ **Georgia Satellites** / 1986 / Elektra 60496
Dirty Rolling Stones-like guitar grunge played by Rick Richards and topped by the adenoidal singing of Dan Baird. Especially enjoyable on the hits "Keep Your Hands to Yourself" and "Battleship Chains." —*William Ruhlmann*

○ **Open All Night** / 1988 / Elektra 60793
Georgia Satellites' follow-up to their surprise hit is as loose and rocking as their previous album, yet it wasn't as successful. The few that did buy the album were treated to some of the rawest and funniest pure rock & roll of the '80s, highlighted by the sleazy humor of "Mon Cheri" and the title track, as well as the stomping cover of the Beatles' "Don't Pass Me By." —*Stephen Thomas Erlewine*

○ **In the Land of Salvation and Sin** / 1989 / Elektra 60887
On the Georgia Satellites' final album, Dan Baird decides he's a songwriter like Lowell George was a songwriter—a traditionalist who adds a healthy dose of ironic humor without losing respect for the music's roots. While his ambitions are ripe with pretentions, his band keeps him in check, and *In the Land of Salvation and Sin* is a terrific record, full of intelligent songs that are never pompous and never fail to rock hell. —*Stephen Thomas Erlewine*

● **Let It Rock: The Best of the Georgia Satellites** / 1993 / Elektra 61336
Most of the band's best tracks are on this generous compilation, which not only features their hits ("Keep Your Hands to Yourself" and "Battleship Chains) but also includes rarities like their sublime John Fogerty medley "Almost Saturday Night/Rockin' All Over the World" from the out-of-print *Rubiyat* collection. —*Stephen Thomas Erlewine*

Lisa Germano

Vocals, violin / Alternative pop/rock
Violinist Lisa Germano became known for her fluid, gutsy style through her work with John Mellencamp, which is captured on the *Big Daddy* and *Lonesome Jubilee* albums. Germano's solo work is much darker and atmospheric than Mellencamp's albums. Her 1991 solo debut, *On the Way Down from Moon Palace*, displayed some promising songwriting along with her acclaimed instrumental prowess. Germano's second album, 1993's *Happiness*, was even better, but the record didn't sell very well when it was first released on Capitol, prompting her to change labels in 1994. She signed with 4AD, which released a resequenced and remixed *Happiness* in the spring of 1994. The new version of the album emphasized her music's underlying dark melancholy, which the original version had only hinted at. —*Stephen Thomas Erlewine*

○ **On the Way Down from Moon Palace** / 1991 / Major Bill 191
Words that come to mind on Germano's debut album: *haunting, delicate, disturbing, abrasive, sparse, intimate, beautiful*. The instrumentals, like the title track, "Dark Irie," and "Simply Tony," have a marvelous fragile beauty, while "Dig My Own Grave" is a herky jerky, rude acoustic rocker. Other highlights include "The Other One," "Guessing Game (or the Music Business)," and "Hangin' with a Demon." —*Rick Clark*

● **Happiness** / 1993 / 4AD
Germano's sophomore effort is a harrowing descent into black humor, anger, and general miserableness. With her deadpan little girl voice, Germano makes "You Make Me Want to Wear Dresses" sound like that is the last thing she wants to do, while she drives the point home on the transcendent dissonance of "Puppet." —*Rick Clark*

The Germs

Group / Punk
One of the first (but certainly not the best) Los Angeles punk groups. Lead singer Darby Crash was a live-fast/die-young nihilist who bemoaned the stodginess of his sunny suburban sur-

roundings. The group recorded from 1977 until 1979, when Crash died of a heroin overdose, like his idol Sid Vicious. —*John Floyd*

● **M.I.A.** / Aug. 3, 1993 / Slash 45239
Everything the seminal Los Angeles punk band ever recorded is on *M.I.A.*, an exhaustive single-disc collection. At their best, the Germs were remarkably good—powerful, gut-wrenching guitars with surprisingly incisive lyrics. At their worst (as on the live tracks), they were messy and almost unlistenable. The Joan Jett-produced "G.I." holds up the best, but there are many quality tracks. It's too much for a single sitting, but *M.I.A.* has more than its share of great punk rock. —*Stephen Thomas Erlewine*

Gerry & the Pacemakers

Group / British invasion, pop/rock
The second group out of the Liverpool starting gate in the early '60s, Gerry and the Pacemakers shared manager Brian Epstein and producer George Martin with the Beatles—and even got the Beatles' hand-me-down material. Their first (U.K.) hit was "How Do You Do It," a song the Fab Four had declined to release. It was a number one for Gerry.

The group was formed in 1959 by singer and guitarist Gerry Marsden, with his brother Freddie on drums, and Les Chadwick on bass. Pianist Les Maguire completed the lineup in 1961. They followed the same path to success as the Beatles, including making trips to Hamburg and hooking up with Epstein and Martin. And shortly after the Beatles topped the charts with "Please Please Me," Gerry and the Pacemakers did so with "How Do You Do It."

Like the Beatles, the group went over to America in 1964 and debuted on the "Ed Sullivan Show," resulting in a hit with their ballad "Don't Let the Sun Catch You Crying." Like the Beatles, they then made a movie (theirs was called *Ferry Cross the Mersey*). But unlike the Beatles, Gerry and the Pacemakers faltered commercially after 1964 and failed to develop musically. As a result, they split up in 1966, with Gerry going solo. By 1975, he had put together a new Pacemakers group and toured on the oldies circuit, his voice still appealing and the Mersey Beat still bouncing. —*William Ruhlmann*

○ **EP Collection** / 1987 / See For Miles 95
A truly definitive collection, with all the hits and the most interesting non-hits. Includes the ultra-rare live *Gerry in California* concert recording from 1966. —*Bruce Eder*

● **Best of Gerry & the Pacemakers: The Definitive Collection** / 1991 / EMI America 96093
The title promises more than it really delivers in content, if not sound. It'll do for the casual listener. —*Bruce Eder*

Debbie Gibson

b. Aug. 3, 1970, Long Island, NY
Vocals / Pop/rock, dance-pop
Of the rash of early teenage female artists who appeared at the last half of the '80s, Debbie Gibson was the most talented and disciplined. Her well-scrubbed image, bouncy dance-pop, and syrupy ballads made her quite a sensation for a couple of years with hits like "Only in My Dreams," "Shake Your Love," "Foolish Beat," and "Lost in Your Eyes." —*Rick Clark*

● **Out of the Blue** / 1987 / Atlantic 81780
A smart, enthusiastic debut that Gibson has yet to top. —*Dan Heilman*

○ **Electric Youth** / 1989 / Atlantic 81932
While it wasn't as carefree and effortless as her debut, *Electric Youth* contained several good hit singles, including "Lost in Your Eyes," "No More Rhyme," and the title track. —*Stephen Thomas Erlewine*

Johnny Gill

b. 1967, Washington, D.C.
Vocals / Urban R&B
Born in Washington, D.C., Johnny Gill was discovered by singer Stacy Lattisaw after singing in his family's group Wings of Faith from age five. His solo career began in 1983 with the Top-30 R&B single "Super Love." In duo with Lattisaw, he scored an R&B Top-Ten hit in 1984 with "Perfect Combination." In 1988 Gill joined New Edition, replacing Bobby Brown. In 1989 he sang on two R&B hits: "Where Do We Go from Here," a number-one by Stacy

Lattisaw, and "One Love," by George Howard. Gill finally scored as a solo singer in 1990 with the release of his album *Johnny Gill*, which sold a million copies, topped the R&B chart, and made the Top Ten in the pop chart. —*William Ruhlmann*

Chemistry / 1985 / Atlantic 90250
It's worth having merely for the awesome pop ballad "Half Crazy." —*Bil Carpenter*

● **Johnny Gill** / 1990 / Motown 6283
Gill's long-in-coming solo breakthrough, featuring the hits "Rub You the Right Way," "My, My, My," and "Fairweather Friend." —*William Ruhlmann*

Provocative / Jun. 8, 1993 / Motown 636355
Basically, *Provocative* is a retread of *Johnny Gill*, but it's a retread done right, since Gill's voice is in prime form and the dueling production teams of Jimmy Jam & Terry Lewis and LA Reid & Babyface make the music smooth, stylish, and funky. —*Stephen Thomas Erlewine*

David Gilmour

b. Mar. 6, 1944, Cambridge, England
Guitar / Progressive rock
David Gilmour, lead guitarist of Pink Floyd, is one of rock's most distinctive players, with his use of echoes, delays, and distorted sustain. His solo efforts have done well, with his self-titled debut reaching number 29 and the follow-up, *About Face*, hitting number 32 on the charts. —*Rick Clark*

● **About Face** / 1984 / Columbia 39296
More accessible than its predecessor, *About Face* is less about mood and more about well-crafted rock. Many highlights grace this underappreciated effort, including "Blue Light," "Love on the Air," and "All Lovers Are Deranged," which was cowritten with Pete Townshend. —*Donna DiChario*

Gin Blossoms

Group / Rock & roll
After an impressive debut EP, the Gin Blossoms rocketed out of the college pop charts and into the mainstream with their 1993 hit single, "Hey Jealousy." Combining the ringing guitar hooks of the Byrds and R.E.M. with a solid, rootsy drive, the band's breakthrough full-length album, *New Miserable Experience*, was filled with songs equally as strong as "Hey Jealousy," including the second hit single, "Found Out About You." *New Miserable Experience* and its singles dominated radio and MTV for the following year—both "Hey Jealousy" and "Found Out About You" were in heavy radio rotation nearly a year after their initial release, which pushed the sales of their debut album over a million copies. —*Stephen Thomas Erlewine*

● **New Miserable Experience** / 1992 / A&M 5403
With their rootsy, melodic fusion of R.E.M. and the Byrds, the Gin Blossoms carry jangle into the '90s with their breakthrough album, *New Miserable Experience*. Powered by the hit singles "Hey Jealousy" and "Found Out About You," *New Miserable Experience* is a solid album that offers an exciting vision of contemporary heartland rock. —*Stephen Thomas Erlewine*

Gary Glitter (Paul Gadd)

b. May 8, 1940, Banbury, Oxfordshire
Vocals, comedy / Glam rock
After many years of trying to become a star, Paul Gadd finally hit the winning formula in 1972: Gary Glitter, the glam rock king. Complete with extravagant makeup, silver outfits, and high boots, Glitter looked as trashy as his music sounded. Glitter and producer Michael Leander created pop records that weren't intended to be serious music—infectious singles that sounded perfect for the three minutes that they were playing; after they were finished, they seemed slightly embarrassing. With its mammoth drum beat, growling guitar, dumb instrumental hook, and incessant chorus of "Hey!" his debut single, "Rock and Roll, Part Two," was a huge hit in both Britain and the United States.

Although he never had another hit in America, Glitter was a superstar in Britain throughout the mid '70s, scoring three number-one singles. Surprisingly, Glitter's cheerfully idiotic, catchy glam rock became somewhat influential over the next decade; Joan Jett covered several of his songs, as did the Human League,

Generation X, Planet Control, and the Brownsville Station. —*Stephen Thomas Erlewine*

● **Rock 'n' Roll: The Best of Gary Glitter** / 1990 / Rhino 70729
Although he's best known for the knuckleheaded sports anthem "Rock & Roll Part Two," Glitter had plenty of other glam-rock delights that were equally as good, if not better than that hit. *Rock 'n' Roll—The Best of Gary Glitter* lovingly collects his best singles, from "Rock & Roll Part Two" to such unsung riff-rockers as "Do You Wanna Touch Me (Oh Yeah!)" and "I'm the Leader of the Gang (I Am!)." It's dumb, it's catchy, it's loud—it's everything good rock & roll should be. A sheer, guilty pleasure. —*Stephen Thomas Erlewine*

The Go-Go's

Group / New wave, pop/rock
Formed in the late '70s, the Go-Go's were the first successful all-female band of the '80s. Their 1981 debut, *Beauty and the Beat*, was a collection of infectious pop songs written and played by the group. It yielded two hit singles, the classic "Our Lips Are Sealed" and "We Got the Beat." They recorded two more albums before splitting up in 1985 to pursue solo careers. —*Kenneth M. Cassidy*

● **Greatest** / 1991 / IRS 0059
An adequate collection of hits, including "Our Lips Are Sealed," "We Got the Beat," "Vacation," and "Head over Heels." —*Dan Heilman*

The Golden Palominos

Group / Alternative pop/rock
Led by drummer Anton Fier, this progressive project band from New York features an ever-changing lineup of current alternative players. At various times, the Golden Palominos have included Michael Stipe of R.E.M., John Lydon, Richard Thompson, Chris Stamey, Jack Bruce, Arto Lindsay, Carla Bley, Bob Mould, Syd Straw, and others. —*Iotis Erlewine*

Golden Palominos / 1983 / Celluloid 5002
Leader Anton Fier (drums) and Bill Laswell (bass) serve as a rhythm section for a revolving group of rockers exploring avant-garde rock. Including Stipe of R.E.M., John Lydon, Jack Bruce, Richard Thompson, Syd Straw, Chris Stamey, and Arto Lindsay. —*William Ruhlmann*

○ **Visions of Excess** / 1985 / Celluloid 6118
A great eclectic mix of alternative-rock songcraft and great musicianship from Jack Bruce, Richard Thompson, and others. Syd Straw shines on "(Kind of) True" as does Michael Stipe on "Omaha." —*Scott Bultman*

Blast of Silence / 1986 / Celluloid 6127
Anton Fier, Syd Straw, and T-Bone Burnett serve up a fine selection of tracks with a country-rock slant, including a Lowell George cover and Peter Holsapple's "Diamonds." —*Scott Bultman*

○ **Drunk with Passion** / 1991 / Charisma 91745
Fier and Bill Laswell are joined by Stipe, Thompson, Carla Bley, and former Hüsker Dü singer/songwriter and guitarist Bob Mould on this album. —*William Ruhlmann*

● **A History (1982-1985)** / 1992 / Metrotone 72651
A fine sampler of the Golden Palominos' first two records. —*AMG*

● **A History (1986-1989)** / 1992 / Metrotone 72652
A fine sampler of the Golden Palominos' last two records. —*AMG*

Bobby Goldsboro

b. Jan. 18, 1941, Marianna, FL
Vocals, guitar / Pop
Singer/songwriter Bobby Goldsboro began his career in the early '60s as a guitarist in Roy Orbison's band. Since departing for a solo career, Goldsboro's success has been marked by a long string of sentimental ballads, the most famous being "Honey," which held the number-one spot for five weeks. Other hits included "See the Funny Little Clown," "Little Things," "Autumn of My Life," "Watching Scotty Grow," and "The Straight Life." —*Rick Clark*

● **Best of Bobby Goldsboro—Honey** / 1991 / EMI America 96094
A definitive 23-track collection of all the Bobby Goldsboro you'll ever need. —*Stephen Thomas Erlewine*

Goo Goo Dolls

Group / Alternative pop/rock, hard rock

Buffalo's Goo Goo Dolls are like the Replacements' goofier brothers—they have all the garage energy of the 'Ments, only without the depth of Paul Westerberg's songwriting. Still, that doesn't deny the pleasure of the band's sonic rush—they have enough hooks and melodies to please fans of both the Replacements and Cheap Trick. As the Goo Goo Dolls make more albums, their songwriting keeps improving and the band gets tighter. 1993's *Superstar Car Wash* edged them into the mainstream, thanks to the single, "We Are the Normal," which was co-written with their idol Westerberg. —*Stephen Thomas Erlewine*

Hold Me Up / 1990 / Metal Blade 26259
A raucous rock record, full of sloppy riffs and energetic hooks—it sounds like the Replacements playing early Cheap Trick. —*Stephen Thomas Erlewine*

● **Superstar Car Wash** / 1993 / Warner Brothers 45206
A tighter, more polished album that features the radio-ready collaboration with Paul Westerberg, "We Are Normal," as well as several spirited hard rockers. —*Stephen Thomas Erlewine*

Lesley Gore

b. May 2, 1946, New York, NY
Vocals / Pop/rock
The petite but big-voiced, Gore hit paydirt with her first record, "It's My Party," after being discovered by Quincy Jones (who produced her) at the age of 16. She held her own for a while against the mounting tide of the British Invasion with several consecutive smashes, and has since branched out into writing her own material, carving out a niche as a cabaret performer. —*Cub Koda*

● **Anthology** / Rhino 71496
Superlative compilation of Leslie's best sides, including "It's My Party," "Judy's Turn to Cry," and "You Don't Own Me." —*Cub Koda*

Grand Funk Railroad

Group / Hard rock
In spite of the fact that Grand Funk Railroad was almost universally reviled by the critical community, FM rock radio and millions of hard rock fans couldn't get enough. Conceived as a trio in 1968, Grand Funk was signed by Capitol after the label caught them live at the 1969 Atlanta Pop Festival. Unlike Cream or the Jimi Hendrix Experience, Grand Funk dispensed with wild interplay and focused on good-time boogie grooves and no-nonsense workmanlike arrangements. Their first album, *On Time*, featuring Mark Farner's earnestly untrained tenor and buzz-saw guitar, Mel Schacher's buffalo-fart bass, and Don Brewer's bashola drumming, was an immediate hit.

The self-titled follow-up stripped down the band's sound to utter basics, but the third effort, *Closer to Home*, showed the band utilizing strings and sound effects to widen their sound. By 1970 the band had sold more albums than any other American band. They broke the Beatles' record at Shea Stadium in 1971.

The band became a four-piece in 1973, and Todd Rundgren produced the hit albums *We're an American Band* and *Shinin' On*. The Jimmy Jenner-produced *All the Girls in the World Beware!!!* continued their winning streak. Subsequent releases did progressively worse, and the band formally disbanded in 1983. —*Rick Clark*

○ **More of the Best** / 1991 / Rhino 70530
This set does a decent job of picking key tracks not found on the *Capitol Collectors Series* album. Included is the fuzz bass-heavy "Paranoid" and boogie numbers like "Are You Ready" and "Got This Thing on the Move." Fans may wish for a more incisive selection from the band's first three albums. —*Rick Clark*

● **Capitol Collectors Series** / 1991 / Capitol 90608
Of the albums available on CD, this is the place to start. All of Grand Funk's hits are here: the classic "We're an American Band," Todd Rundgren's perverse production of "Loco-Motion," their thudding remake of the Animals' "Inside Looking Out," the epic "Closer to Home/I'm Your Captain," "Heartbreaker," and other big favorites. —*Rick Clark*

Grant Lee Buffalo

Group / Alternative pop/rock
Under the leadership of guitarist/songwriter Grant Lee Phillips, Grant Lee Buffalo became a major buzz band in 1993 with their debut album, *Fuzzy*. The band's searching, often political, folk-

rock has shades of everyone from David Bowie and John Lennon to R.E.M. and Bob Mould. Phillips's songwriting received a large amount of critical praise, as did the band's electrifying live performances. They captured a larger following in Europe than in their native America, earning near-universal critical praise upon the release of *Fuzzy*. During 1993, the band toured constantly, building a solid cult following all over the world. —*Stephen Thomas Erlewine*

● **Fuzzy** / 1993 / Warner Brothers 45217
While Grant Lee Phillips's songwriting is quite impressive, what makes Grant Lee Buffalo's debut album, *Fuzzy*, memorable is the band's muscular folk-rock. Equally adept at propulsive rock & roll and haunting ballads, the band turns Phillips's best songs into rough gems, as "Jupiter and Teardrop" and "Fuzzy" prove. —*Stephen Thomas Erlewine*

Grapes of Wrath

Group / Alternative pop
This Canadian soft-alternative pop quartet specializes in appealing airy melodies and harmonies. Instrumentally, they show the influences of early '70s pop/rock and give a passing nod to groups like the Byrds. —*Rick Clark*

○ **Treehouse** / 1987 / Capitol 48018
Early comparisons to R.E.M. are clearly justified on *Treehouse*, a jangly folk-pop masterpiece. On this, their second album, the band seems considerably more confident and focused. Crisp and bright production courtesy of Tom Cochrane (ex-Red Rider) complement the glorious harmonies and melancholy songs perfectly. A sadly overlooked classic of '80s guitar rock. —*Chris Woodstra*

● **Now & Again** / 1989 / Capitol 92581
The production by Anton Fier, leader/drummer of the Golden Palominos, imbues this Vancouver quartet's third full-length album with a lush early-'70s sound, at times approaching an Elton John/Tumbleweed Connection-style blend of orchestration with occasional pedal steel augmentation (by Sneaky Pete Kleinow). Chuck Leavell plays keys on this outing as well. Melodically, the band tends to sound samey, partly attributable to the band's rather light singing tonalities. Highlights: the reflective "All the Things I Wasn't." —*Rick Clark*

These Days / 1991 / Capitol 96431
John Leckie (the Posies, Let's Active) produces this follow-up to *Now & Again* by giving the band a slightly heavier, more organic sound. In spite of improved performance edginess, the band still lacks the proper dynamics to make their melodies memorable. Leckie's production, while loaded with nice touches, fails to help the band in overcoming their limitations. —*Rick Clark*

Grass Roots

Group / Pop/rock
Grass Roots was a Top-40 band with folk-rock and light soul influences, looked down on as a largely faceless studio-spawned ensemble created by the songwriting/production team of Steve Barri and P. F. Sloane. But their sound was powerful as well as marketable, and their best song, "Let's Live for Today," contains the roots of Bruce Springsteen's sound and image. —*Bruce Eder*

Greatest Hits, Vol. 2 / 1987 / MCA 31133
The complement to the above. —*Bruce Eder*

● **Anthology—1965-1975** / 1991 / Rhino 70746
A two-CD set that contains "Midnight Confessions," "Let's Live for Today," and more. Extraordinary sounding and brilliantly annotated. —*Bruce Eder*

Greatest Hits, Vol. 1 / MCA 31132
A decent ten-song collection with some major gaps. —*Bruce Eder*

The Grateful Dead

Group / Psychedelic, rock & roll, country-rock, folk-rock
The Grateful Dead are the longest-lived of the San Francisco "acid rock" groups of the '60s. In the '90s, after more than 25 years in action, the Dead were still playing to enough satisfied customers on the road (most of them "Deadheads") to make them one of the top-grossing concert acts in the music business.

The group was formed in 1965 by bluegrass enthusiast Jerry Garcia (b. 1942) on guitar and vocals, Ron "Pigpen" McKernan (1945-1973) on vocals and organ, Bob Weir (b. 1947) on guitar and vocals, classical music student Phil Lesh (b. 1945) on bass and vocals, and Bill Kreutzmann (b. 1946) on drums. From the beginning, they brought together a variety of influences, from Garcia's country background to Pigpen's feeling for blues (his father was an R&B radio DJ) and Lesh's education in contemporary "serious" music. Add to that the experimentation encouraged at some of the group's first performances—at novelist Ken Kesey's "acid test" parties, multimedia events intended to replicate (or accompany) the experience of taking the then-legal drug LSD—and you had music that could go off in nearly any direction, often with extended improvisational sections.

The band signed to Warner Brothers in 1967, experiencing some difficulties early on with the restrictions of standard recording practices and the company's interest in producing a conventionally commercial product. As a result, the group's first few albums were somewhat tentative but showed promise for the future, especially with the key additions of Mickey Hart as a second drummer in 1967 and Garcia's old friend Robert Hunter as the band's lyricist.

The Dead finally hit their stride with the release of *Live/Dead*, a double album, in 1969. (They were always more comfortable on stage than in the studio.) Two studio albums in 1970, *Workingman's Dead* and *American Beauty*, found them exploring folk-rock and more tightly constructed song forms, and—along with extensive touring—won them a much larger audience.

The second half of the '70s found the Dead recording a series of commercially oriented albums for Arista, then concentrating on road work for the better part of the '80s. *In the Dark*, released in 1987, was their first studio album in seven years. It sold a million copies and produced the band's first Top-Ten hit in "Touch of Grey." The Dead continued to tour, notably doing shows with Bob Dylan, and at the start of the '90s, they began to release vintage material on their own Grateful Dead Merchandising label. — *William Ruhlmann*

Anthem of the Sun / 1968 / Warner Brothers 1749
The Grateful Dead spent six months recording their second album in studios and at concerts. The result came closer to an accurate portrait, highlighted by the four-part, 12-minute "That's It for the Other One." Still, the extensive mixing and editing made the sound dense and uninviting, especially to those not yet converted to the group's approach. — *William Ruhlmann*

Aoxomoxoa / 1969 / Warner Brothers 1790
The addition of poet Robert Hunter as lyricist marked the beginning of a consistent set of imagery in the Dead's words to match their musical interplay, especially on songs like "St. Stephen" and "China Cat Sunflower." But the aural experiments were still making for trying listening as the Dead continued to search for a way to capture their concert feel on disc. — *William Ruhlmann*

○ **Live/Dead** / 1970 / Warner Brothers 1830
Long, trancelike songs with allusive lyrics (such as the classic "Dark Star") and R&B workouts featuring Pigpen's bluesy voice characterize this album, which is the basic document in the early Dead catalog.It's what most fans would like them to sound like every night. — *William Ruhlmann*

☆ **Workingman's Dead** / 1970 / Warner Brothers 1869
A folk-rock, tightly arranged Dead singing (in harmony!) some of their best songs from "Uncle John's Band" to "Casey Jones." — *William Ruhlmann*

★ **American Beauty** / Jan. 1970 / Warner Brothers 1893
Workingman's Dead, part 2: more of the songs that have served as the band's basic repertoire ever since these albums were released. Includes "Box of Rain," "Friend of the Devil," "Sugar Magnolia," "Ripple," and, of course, "Truckin'." — *William Ruhlmann*

Grateful Dead / 1971 / Warner Brothers 1689
The Dead's second double live album (now on a single CD) introduces a couple of excellent Garcia-Hunter compositions, "Bertha" and "Wharf Rat," and allows Bob Weir to indulge his taste for what Deadheads would come to call "cowboy songs:" Merle Haggard's "Mama Tried" and Kris Kristofferson's "Me & Bobby McGee." The album became the Dead's first gold record, probably on the momentum of *Workingman's Dead* and *American Beauty*, though it must have been a disappointment to those expecting another folk-rock album like those. It also failed to match *Live/Dead* as a concert album, so that, coming off the band's recent peaks, it seemed less effective than it was at the time. Now it seems like one of the Dead's better, more coherent records. (Not

to be confused with *The Grateful Dead*, the band's debut album. They resorted to *Grateful Dead* as a title when Warner Brothers Records wouldn't let them call the album *Skull Fuck*.) — *William Ruhlmann*

○ **Europe '72** / 1972 / Warner Brothers 2668
Released as a three-record set, *Europe '72* is now a double CD. But it's still a long album, notable for introducing more Garcia-Hunter songs, especially "Browne-Eyed Woman" and for incorporating onto one album the variety of musical styles to be heard at a Dead concert as well as the sheer duration necessary to appreciate the experience. Which means that, while this may not be the place a new fan wants to start, it's a Deadhead favorite. — *William Ruhlmann*

History of the Grateful Dead, Vol. 1 (Bear's Choice) / Jan. 1973 / Warner Brothers 2721
This is a contractual-obligation album, a record given to Warner Brothers Records to complete the Dead's commitment to the label. It was recorded in February 1970 and is something of a tribute to the late keyboardist/vocalist Ron "Pigpen" McKernan, who is heard frequently. Pigpen highlights an 18-minute version of Howlin' Wolf's "Smokestack Lightnin'." But this is a nonessential Dead album. "Bear" is the band's friend/soundman/drug manufacturer Owsley Stanley. The album is misnamed: It does not provide a "history" and there was never any volume 2. — *William Ruhlmann*

○ **Wake of the Flood** / Feb. 1973 / Grateful Dead 4002
The Grateful Dead's first studio album in three years was also their first for their own record label. It's a strong collection, featuring such Garcia-Hunter songs as "Mississippi Half-Step Uptown Toodleoo," "Row Jimmy," and "Stella Blue," songs that would become concert staples, as well as Bob Weir's "Weather Report Suite." — *William Ruhlmann*

Skeletons from the Closet: The Best of the Grateful Dead / Jan. 1974 / Warner Brothers 2764
This is an 11-song compilation, five of whose songs come from *Workingman's Dead* or *American Beauty*. It presents a sampling of the Dead's 1967-1972 period, focusing on their more accessible material. In that sense, it is recommended to the uninitiated who want to get a feel for the group. Not surprisingly, it is a perennial seller, turning up week after week on *Billboard* magazine's Top Pop Catalog chart. The initiated, however, despise it: In a survey of Deadheads conducted by *DeadBase*, it was rated above only *Dylan & the Dead* as the worst Grateful Dead album. — *William Ruhlmann*

Grateful Dead from the Mars Hotel / Feb. 1974 / Grateful Dead 40072
The Grateful Dead's second independent album was an uneven one, containing favorites like "Scarlet Begonians," "U.S. Blues," and "China Doll," but also a fair amount of filler. — *William Ruhlmann*

○ **Blues for Allah** / 1975 / Grateful Dead 40012
Opening with the suite that has become a concert favorite, "Help on the Way"/"Slip Knot!"/"Franklin's Tower," and also containing the anthemic "The Music Never Stopped," *Blues for Allah* is another Grateful Dead album containing a few band classics and a lot of filler. Note, however, that some fans seem to like the filler. In its survey of Deadheads, *DeadBase* found *Blues for Allah* to be the band's most popular studio album after *Workingman's Dead* and *American Beauty*. — *William Ruhlmann*

○ **Terrapin Station** / 1977 / Arista 8065
The best of the early Arista albums, containing the extended "Terrapin Station" suite. — *William Ruhlmann*

● **What a Long Strange Trip It's Been** / 1977 / Warner Brothers 3091
This is a two-disc compilation of the Grateful Dead covering its tenure at Warner Brothers Records, 1967-1972, and as such is the most extensive sampler of their work in existence. Well-chosen, it contains many of their best songs from the period and is notable for giving album release to the studio-recorded single version of "Dark Star," the Dead's most requested song. Relative newcomers to the band (those who bought *Skeletons from the Closet* and liked it) can get a stronger dose here, and then perhaps go on to the individual albums. Of course, Deadheads hate this record. — *William Ruhlmann*

Reckoning / Jan. 1981 / Arista 8523

Having given up on studio work after the disaster of *Go to Heaven*, the Dead recorded a series of concerts in New York and San Francisco in October 1980 for two live albums. This is the first, a set of acoustic material that will remind many listeners of the rustic feel of the classic *Workingman's Dead* and *American Beauty* albums, though much of it consists of traditional and bluegrass material favored by Jerry Garcia. (The original two-LP set was fit onto one CD in 1987 by eliminating the Dead's cover of Elizabeth Cotten's "Oh Babe It Ain't No Lie.") *—William Ruhlmann*

○ **Dead Set** / Feb. 1981 / Arista 8522
The second of the Dead's two live albums recorded at shows in October 1980, this presents an electric set featuring some material previously heard on Jerry Garcia's solo albums and some of the group's less successful '70s material. As such, it is far from the Dead's best live album, but it is representative of their work at the time. *—William Ruhlmann*

○ **In the Dark** / 1987 / Arista 8452
The comeback, with "Touch of Grey," "West L.A. Fadeaway," and "Black Muddy River." For anyone who wondered how these old hippies could have such a following 20 years after the hippies disappeared, here's the answer. *—William Ruhlmann*

Built to Last / 1989 / Arista 8575
Supposedly, the Dead had broken their studio jinx with *In the Dark* and finally learned how to make good albums without an audience in front of them. So why was this follow-up such a letdown? Perhaps because they hadn't taken seven years to write and perfect new material as they had with the previous album. The dominant songwriter here was keyboard player Brent Mydland (who died the following year), while the crucial songwriting team of Garcia and Hunter contributed only minor efforts. Chastened, the Dead once again retreated from studio work. *—William Ruhlmann*

Without a Net / Apr. 1990 / Arista 8634
A double-CD live album notable for featuring performances by jazz saxophonist Branford Marsalis and the Dead's version of Traffic's "Dear Mr. Fantasy," a concert favorite. Unintentionally, the album serves as the epitaph to keyboard player Brent Mydland, who died shortly after its completion, triggering another change in the band's direction. *—William Ruhlmann*

One from the Vault / 1991 / Grateful Dead 4013
With this album, issued on the group's own merchandising label, the Grateful Dead began to address the needs of an audience that had long since taken to making their own tapes of every Dead performance. Such an audience, of course, would be interested in record releases containing vintage live shows, and the Dead began by issuing this 16-year-old concert, which occurred shortly after they completed their 1975 album, *Blues for Allah*, and while they were nominally retired from live work. It contains all the material featured on that album, plus such recent Dead songs as "U.S. Blues" and such favorites as "The Other One." It made for a modest beginning to the Dead's archival investigations, and only whetted fans' appetites for what might follow. *—William Ruhlmann*

Two from the Vault / 1992 / Grateful Dead 40162
Two discs worth of the Dead in all their psychedelic glory. This second volume of live material from the archives stems from two shows in August 1968, when their improvisational headiness was balanced by Pigpen bringing the proceedings solidly back down to earth. For those who may have wondered what "Anthem of the Sun" might have sounded like minus the studio collage mix, here's the answer. *—Steve Aldrich*

Dobie Gray (Leonard Victor Ainsworth)

b. Jul. 26, 1943, Brookshire, Texas
Vocals / Soul, pop/rock
Journeyman soul singer, composer, and actor Gray has had a checkered career, scoring hit records in two different decades, acting on Broadway, and appearing in the Los Angeles production of *Hair*.
   After moving to Nashville in 1978, Dobie Gray resurfaced in the late '80s as a country songwriter and performer. He continues performing and making occasional appearances on the Nashville Network. *—Cub Koda and Ron Wynn*

● **Dobie Gray Sings for in Crowders** / 1987 / Collectables 5072

Uptown soul from the mid '60s. Gray's commanding baritone delivery is well showcased. *—Bill Dahl*

Great White

Group / Hard rock, heavy metal
For most intents and purposes, Great White wasn't that different from the glut of mid-'80s hard rock/heavy metal bands. Their songs were derivative of Led Zeppelin, AC/DC, and Mott the Hoople, and lead singer Jack Russell had Robert Plant's wail down cold. Despite all their unoriginality, the band was a tight unit that knew the value of a good song—they covered Hunter twice, including their hit single "Once Bitten, Twice Shy." However, Great White could never write as clever and mean as Hunter, nor could they crank out the riffs like Jimmy Page or Angus Young, which made their time in the spotlight very brief. The band continues to record and tour in the '90s, but they have yet to regain the audience 1989's *Twice Shy* captured. *—Stephen Thomas Erlewine*

● **Best of Great White 1986-1992** / Oct. 25, 1993 / Capitol 27185
All of Great White's finest songs are collected on *The Best of Great White*. *—AMG*

Green Day

Group / Alternative rock
Although these brash, third-generation California punks had made a name for themselves in the independent scene in the early '90s, it wasn't until they signed to a major label that they became alternative stars. And when their major-label debut, 1994's *Dookie*, was released, the infectious punk-pop of "Longview" became more than an alternative hit—it quickly crossed over into the mainstream. Green Day come off as bratty punks, not threatening revolutionaries, but it's actually for the music's benefit. Without their healthy, snotty attitude, the speedy, loud guitars and highly melodic hooks wouldn't be nearly as appealing as they are. *—Stephen Thomas Erlewine*

Kerplunk / 1992 / Lookout 46
Green Day's best independent record is fueled more by their attitude and sonic aggression than their riffs. *—Stephen Thomas Erlewine*

● **Dookie** / 1994 / Reprise 45529
After two albums of indie guitar punk, Green Day made the jump to the majors with *Dookie*. Based on MTV's constant playing of "Longview," the band became a major crossover success; *Time* even hailed the album as the best rock & roll record of 1994. While *Dookie* isn't quite that good, it is quite good. For once, Green Day has genuine songs and hooks to go along with their muscular, roaring guitars, making *Dookie* not only their most accessible album, but also their best. *—Stephen Thomas Erlewine*

Green River

Group / Alternative rock
In the mid '80s, Before the word *grunge* became a specific musical style, before Sub Pop was considered as a training league for major labels, many post-punk rock fans didn't believe Seattle had a worthwhile musical scene. Green River helped change that. With its ugly, loud, sub-Stooges guitar grind, Green River was the first band to make Sub Pop a hip underground label. At their best, the band made a powerful, brutal guitar rock that merged '70s heavy metal and '60s garage punk with '80s post-punk; at their worst, they were a sludgy, depressing mess.
   Green River were together for three years before the band splintered apart. Singer Mark Arm and occasional guitarist Steve Turner formed Mudhoney. Guitarist Stone Gossard and bassist Jeff Ament formed Mother Love Bone after the band's demise, which would eventually turn into Pearl Jam. The roots of Mudhoney's garage grunge and Pearl Jam's revisionist '70s hard rock can be heard on Green River's two EPs and their one album. *—Stephen Thomas Erlewine*

● **Rehab Doll** / 1988 / Sub Pop 15
Green River's only album is a brutal collection of primal Stooges-style guitar grind and punked-up metal riffing. The CD includes the equally powerful *Dry as a Bone* EP. *—Stephen Thomas Erlewine*

Al Green

b. Apr. 13, 1946, Forest City, AR

Vocals / Soul, R&B, gospel

Born in 1946 in Forest City, AR, and growing up in Grand Rapids, MI, Al Green became the premier soul singer of the '70s, in the process being the last great purveyor of a music whose time had come and gone. When he was 13, Green started singing with a family gospel group, the Greene Brothers. By 1967 he was singing secular and solo, scoring a number-five R&B, number-41 pop hit with "Back Up Train" on the Hot Line Music Journal label. Touring the chitlin circuit on the strength of the record, Green found himself playing on the same bill in Midland, TX, as Memphis trumpeter and producer Willie Mitchell. Mitchell signed Green to Memphis's Hi Records, and, as they say, the rest is history.

Between 1970 and 1977, Green placed 23 records on the R&B charts and 18 on the pop charts, including seven Top Tens. The Green/Mitchell/Hi Rhythm-section sound was incredibly consistent, making most of the albums listed below somewhat interchangeable. The records are ultra cool; there is little overt sweat. Green's phrases are disjointed, generally behind the beat, always surprising. At regular intervals he dips into his unreal falsetto. Soft girl backup singing is employed, as is a string orchestra. Drummers Al Jackson and Howard Grimes eschew cymbals, replacing them with a ride pattern on the tom-toms. All of this is executed in the context of such compositions by Mitchell, Green, Jackson, and guitarist Teenie Hodges as "Love and Happiness," "Take Me to the River," "Let's Stay Together," and "Tired of Being Alone." Green became "born again" in 1976, splitting from Mitchell a year later and electing to record only gospel music for most of the next decade and a half. In 1985 he reunited with Mitchell for the album *He Is the Light. —Rob Bowman*

○ **Green Is Blues** / 1970 / Hi 32055
The first album linking the soul-singing greatness of Al Green with the production brilliance and expertise of Willie Mitchell. The results were mutually beneficial: Green got the great production, arrangements, and backing from the Hi Rhythm section that often turned good songs into classics, and he sang with the conviction and talent that provided the final component in an artistically and commercially satisfying union. —*Ron Wynn*

○ **I'm Still in Love with You** / 1972 / Motown 5284
Album three sees Green exploring country-soul with an achingly beautiful take on Kris Kristofferson's "For the Good Times." The hits were the title song and "Look What You Done for Me." —*Rob Bowman*

○ **Let's Stay Together** / 1972 / Motown 5290
Green's second album for Hi and the first of a string of brilliant releases. The title song was the big hit, but an extended version of the Bee Gees' "How Can You Mend a Broken Heart" remained a staple for years. —*Rob Bowman*

☆ **Call Me** / 1973 / Motown 5286
Three R&B Top-Ten hits, the title song, "Here I Am (Come and Take Me)," and "You Ought to Be with Me," dominate what is probably his finest album. Once again he tackles some country-soul, turning in moving versions of Hank Williams's "I'm So Lonesome I Could Cry" and Willie Nelson's "Funny How Time Slips Away." Green also returns to the gospel vein on "Jesus Is Waiting." —*Rob Bowman*

Is Love / 1975 / Motown 5432
Two more Top-Ten hits with "L-O-V-E (Love)" and "Oh Me, Oh My (Dream's in My Arms)." —*Rob Bowman*

☆ **Al Green's Greatest Hits** / 1975 / Hi 32089
An excellent single anthology, perhaps the best Green hits package in the pre-CD era. This release was concise and to the point, with absolutely no filler. —*Ron Wynn*

○ **Full of Fire** / 1976 / Motown 5285
Wonderfully sung, expertly produced and performed '70s soul by a vocal master and a superb support-combine. Al Green and Willie Mitchell were so solidly attuned to each other that Green's albums were truly collaborative affairs, with the superb Hi Rhythm section filling in behind and underneath him effortlessly. This is arguably still his greatest overall album. —*Ron Wynn*

☆ **Greatest Hits, Vol. 2** / 1977 / Motown 5291
As good as *Volume 1*, augmented by nonchart items that might have been hits anyway, like "Love and Happiness," "Take Me to the River," and "For the Good Times." —*Rob Bowman*

☆ **Belle Album** / 1977 / Hi 6004

Al Green severed his ties with longtime producer Willie Mitchell in 1977, establishing his own backup band and seizing the production reins. But he hadn't yet made the final break with soul. This was the last secular work he'd make for many years, and it was brillant, even though it didn't come close to equaling his previous commercial heights. Many people just didn't understand where he was going, while others were turned off by the blurred lyric focus of songs like "Belle." But "I Feel Good" had as much danceable energy and soulful fire as any Green uptempo tune, and "Lovin' You" and "Dream" were sorely underrated compositions. —*Ron Wynn*

○ **Higher Plane** / 1981 / Hi 6006
Another superior sacred recording, most notable for a stellar version of the Impressions' "People Get Ready." —*Rob Bowman*

○ **He Is the Light** / 1985 / A&M 5102
At the time of writing, this was Green's last truly great recording. Back with Willie Mitchell, the Hi Rhythm section, and the Memphis Horns, Green has great material and delivers the goods. —*Rob Bowman*

○ **Love Ritual** / 1989 / MCA 42308
Don't let the title lead you into thinking that these are second-rate leftovers, because this album *Love Ritual: Rare & Previously Unreleased 1968-1976* (originally compiled for the British Demon label) is loaded with gems. Highlights are hard to pin down, but one surprise is a spirited version of the Beatles' "I Want to Hold Your Hand"; it should've been a single. Every track except "Ride Sally Ride" has been digitally remixed from the original multitracks. The sound is great—faithful to the spirit of Willie Mitchell's production and mixing style—and the disc includes detailed liner notes. All in all, Green fans should pick up on this. —*Rick Clark*

★ **One in a Million** / 1990 / Word 77000
A compilation from Green's gospel recordings that reveals the emotional depth of his religious work. —*Brian Mansfield*

○ **Sings Gospel** / Motown 5319
Good anthology covering Green's '80s gospel material. The only problem was that Green earned his Grammy awards for complete projects rather than single hits, and some of these songs taken out of their album environment aren't that impressive. But as an overview of his transition from soul to gospel, it's ideal. —*Ron Wynn*

Vernon Green & the Medallions

Group / Doo-wop

The Medallions, a Los Angeles doo-wop quartet with a predilection for songs about speedy cars, formed in 1953. Their first single, "The Letter"/"Buick '59," on the Dootsie Williams Dootone label, was a regional hit, coupling a dreamy ballad with a joyriding rocker complete with automotive sound effects by the group. (Encores in the same vein included "Speedin'," "Pushbutton Automobile," and "Coupe DeVille Baby;" there was even a "'59 Volvo"!). Williams's renamed Dooto label handed Green an opportunity to sing soul in 1973, and he recently reemerged with some doo-wop offerings on the Classic Artists imprint. —*Bill Dahl*

● **Golden Classics** / Collectables 5047
This Los Angeles doo-wop aggregation specialized in "rocking car songs" during the mid '50s. —*Bill Dahl*

Joe Grushecky & Houserockers

Group / Rock & roll

When Pittsburgh-based Joe Grushecky's band the Iron City Houserockers turned up on MCA Records in 1979, their driving bar-band rock & roll and working-class lyrics earned them critical kudos but also made them Johnny-come-latelies in a crowded field headed by Bruce Springsteen and including Bob Seger, John Cafferty, and John Mellencamp. Nevertheless, they managed to release four albums through 1983. Grushecky reorganized, keeping only the bass player for the new edition launched under his own name in 1989, but the approach and sound are the same. —*William Ruhlmann*

● **Pumping Iron & Sweating Steel: The Best of the Iron City Houserockers** / 1992 / Rhino 70375
A generous compilation of the best of an underrated rock & roll band from the late '70s and early '80s. Some of Joe Grushecky's

songs on *Pumping Iron & Sweating Steel* equal the work of Bruce Springsteen, Tom Petty, and Bob Seger during this period. Fans of those artists will definitely find the Iron City Houserockers worth investigating. —*Stephen Thomas Erlewine*

The Guess Who

Group / Pop/rock
A Winnipeg, Canada, band called Chad Allen & the Reflections (formed in 1962) enjoyed some success with a couple of regional 1963 hits ("Tribute to Buddy Holly," "Shy Guy") but quickly shifted over to the new British Merseybeat style and recorded a version of Johnny Kidd & the Pirates' "Shakin' All Over." The song became a number-one Canadian hit. As a publicity stunt, the record label (Quality) listed the artist as "Guess Who?"—implying that it might be some big English act ghosting on the side. The ploy worked, and the American label Scepter picked them up, taking the record to number 22. At the label's request, the Reflections changed their name to the Guess Who.

The band couldn't generate a follow-up hit, and it wasn't until 1968, when they met producer Jack Richardson, that things began looking up. Richardson mortgaged his house to help them record what became the album *Wheatfield Soul.* One of the tracks, "These Eyes," went to number six Stateside, beginning a long string of excellent pop-rock hits.

In banner years 1970 and 1971, the Guess Who cut a pair of hit albums, *American Woman* and *Share the Land,* that displayed a highly developed level of melodic skills. Burton Cummings had developed a compelling vocal style, and new lead guitarists Kurt Winter and Greg Leskiw forged out a distinctive sound. The band scored a few more hits before breaking up in 1975. Cummings went on to experience an uneven solo career after landing a million-selling hit with his debut single, "Stand Tall." —*Rick Clark*

○ **Best of The Guess Who** / 1971 / RCA 3662
A fine single-disc collection of most of the band's greatest hits— it's perfect for listeners who don't want to invest in the double-disc *Track Record.* —*AMG*

● **Track Record: The Guess Who Collection** / 1988 / RCA 61077
A perfect collection, covering the band's whole history on two CDs. Includes the hits "These Eyes," "Laughing," "Undun," "No Time," "American Woman/No Sugar Tonight," "Share the Land," and the noveltyish "Clap for the Wolfman." —*Bruce Eder*

Gumball

Group / Alternative pop/rock
When indie superstar and renowned record producer Don Fleming (Sonic Youth, the Posies, Alice Cooper) decided to form his own group in the early '90s, he brought in his long-time collaborator drummer Jay Spiegel, along with bassist Eric Vermillion, to form Gumball. In Gumball, Fleming's obsession with pop culture and pop music from the Monkees to the Damned to Sonic Youth reached full fruition. Snatches of '60s guitar riffs sat next to '80s guitar noise, and '70s punk rubbed shoulders with '70s schlock metal. All of it proved his knack for treating the worst pop music as serious rock, while dirtying respectable indie sonic tricks with sweet bubblegum pop. Unfortunately, much of their music sounds like the work of an expert record collector, not an expert musician, but at their best they can deliver some solid three-minute rock & roll thrills. —*Stephen Thomas Erlewine*

Wisconsin Hayride / 1992 / CBS 74754
A fun, thrashing EP of several songs that Gumball leader Don Fleming has found particularly inspirational over the years. —*Stephen Thomas Erlewine*

● **Super Tasty** / 1993 / CBS 53023
Gumball's major label debut will not only please their old fans, it may win them some new ones with its trashy combination of indie guitar-rock and shameless pop melodies. —*Stephen Thomas Erlewine*

Revolution on Ice / 1994 / Epic
Another inconsistent but enjoyable set of trashy, melodic punk-pop from Gumball, *Revolution on Ice* virtually duplicates all the same pleasures of *Super Tasty.* —*Stephen Thomas Erlewine*

Gun Club

Group / Rock & roll

This Los Angeles group, led by Jeffrey Lee Pierce, picked up on the Cramps' rockabilly fetish, added some blues and John Fogarty stylings, and crafted a blistering 1981 debut, *Fire of Love.* —*John Floyd*

● **Fire of Love** / 1981 / Slash 23935
Jeffrey Lee Pierce's fusion of punk energy and blues-based themes is linked to (but also derivative of) the Cramps' punk/rockabilly springboard. Pierce's group never matched that band's manic intensity but *Fire of Love* is worthwhile listening for those interested in how the influence of John Fogerty filtered into punk. And with "Sex Beat" and "Jack on Fire," Pierce came up with two minor classics of early-'80s West Coast rock. —*John Floyd*

Miami / 1982 / IRS 13065
Tremendous power. Modern blues, yet original. —*Robert Gordon*

Guns N' Roses

Group / Hard rock, heavy metal
At a time when pop was dominated by dance music and pop metal, Guns N' Roses brought raw, ugly rock & roll crashing back into the charts. They were not nice boys; nice boys don't play rock & roll. They were ugly, misogynist, violent. They were also funny, vulnerable, and occasionally sensitive, as their breakthrough hit "Sweet Child o' Mine" showed. While Slash and Izzy Stradlin ferociously spit out dueling guitar riffs worthy of Aerosmith or the Stones, Axl Rose screeched out his tales of sex, drugs, and apathy in the big city. Bassist Duff McKagan and drummer Steven Adler were a limber rhythm section that kept the music loose and powerful. Guns N' Roses' music was basic and gritty, with a solid hard, bluesy base. They were dark, sleazy, dirty, and honest— everything that good hard-rock and heavy metal should be.

Guns N' Roses released their first EP in in 1986, which led to a contract with Geffen. The following year, the band released their debut album, *Appetite for Destruction.* They started to build a following with their numerous live shows, but the album didn't start selling until almost a year later, when MTV started playing "Sweet Child o' Mine." Soon, the album shot to number one, and Guns N' Roses became one of the biggest bands in the world. By the end of 1988, they released *G N' R Lies,* which paired four new, acoustic-based songs with their first EP.

Guns N' Roses began to work on the follow-up to *Appetite* at the end of 1990. In October of that year, the band fired Adler, claiming that his drug dependency caused him to play poorly. He was replaced by Matt Sorum from the Cult. During recording, the band added Dizzy Reed on keyboard. By the time the sessions were finished, the new album had become two new albums. After being delayed for nearly a year, the albums, *Use Your Illusion I* and *II,* were released in the fall of 1991. The *Illusions* showcased a more ambitious band—while there were still a fair number of full-throttle guitar rockers, there were also stabs at Elton John-style balladry, acoustic blues, horn sections, female back-up singers, ten-minute songs with several different sections, and a good number of introspective, soul-searching lyrics. In short, they were now making art, and, amazingly, they were successful at it.

While the albums sold very well initially, the band soon fell out of favor. Stradlin left the band by the end of 1991, and with his departure the band lost their best songwriter. Once Nirvana's *Nevermind* hit the top of the charts in early 1992, there was a distinct division between what was cool in hard, rock and what wasn't. Guns N' Roses—with all of their pretentions, impressionistic videos, models, and rock star excesses—were very uncool. The band didn't fully grasp the change until 1993, when they released their album of punk songs, *The Spaghetti Incident?* It received some good reviews, but the band failed to capture the reckless spirit of not only the original versions but of their own *Appetite for Destruction.* By the middle of 1994, there were rumors flying that the band was about to break up, since Rose wanted to pursue a new, more industrial direction and Slash wanted to stick with their blues-inflected hard rock. —*Stephen Thomas Erlewine*

★ **Appetite for Destruction** / 1987 / David Geffen Co. 24148
Aggressive, brash, and well-executed hard rockers and ballads that never stray from their chosen target. This major-label debut is one of the finest examples of late-'80s hard rock. "Welcome to the Jungle," "Sweet Child o' Mine," "Mr. Brownstone," "Rocket Queen," and "Paradise City" were highlights from this classic. —*Donna DiChario and Rick Clark*

G N' R Lies / 1989 / David Geffen Co. 24198

The first side of *Lies* features their primitive independent debut EP, full of raw, vital rock & roll. Despite its disturbing lyrics, the second side is even more impressive musically, containing everything from the stark acoustic balladry of "Patience" to the country-rock boogie of "Used to Love Her." —*Stephen Thomas Erlewine*

○ **Use Your Illusion I** / Jan. 1991 / David Geffen Co. 24415

○ **Use Your Illusion II** / Feb. 1991 / David Geffen Co. 24420

Both volumes of *Use Your Illusion* are full of what made classic rock classic: forceful band chemistry and an uncompromising spirit, with results that approach staples like the Stones' *Exile on Main Street,* Led Zeppelin IV, or Aerosmith's *Rocks.* These two separately (but simultaneously) released volumes were a neat sidestep from the indulgent double-album concept. Musically, the band has never sounded better—or rawer. Lyrically, W. Axl Rose still spews out enough venom to offend half the planet, but you'd have to listen hard to catch it through the band-heavy sound mix. Nevertheless, Rose has seasoned his railings with some insight that the world around him isn't hopeless. In spite of his sloppy target shooting, his raw sentiments and delivery are bracing compared to the bulk of rock bands pounding the circuits. Highlights on volume I are "Right Next Door to Hell," "November Rain," "Perfect Crime," "You Ain't the First," and "Don't Cry." Volume II's standout tracks are "Civil War," "You Could Be Mine," "Locomotive," "Breakdown," and "Pretty Tied Up." Of the two albums, the first one is the better choice, but fans of hard rock should get both. —*Rick Clark*

The Spaghetti Incident? / 1993 / David Geffen Co.

As punk albums go, *The Spaghetti Incident?* lacks righteous anger and rage. As Guns N' Roses album go, it's a solid effort, returning to the ferocious, hard-rocking days of *Appetite for Destruction.* The Gunners play Stooges and New York Dolls songs exactly as they do Nazareth—as straight-ahead, driving riff-rockers. After the epic *Use Your Illusions,* the band sounds like it's having fun, not caring about making "art" like "November Rain" or "Estranged." Unfortunately, the tacked-on Charles Manson song leaves a bad aftertaste; the inclusion of the song seems like a publicity-seeking stunt, a way to increase their sales and regain some street credibility. *The Spaghetti Incident?* proves that they didn't need to stoop so low. —*Stephen Thomas Erlewine*

Guy

Group / Dance, soul, urban

By bringing the minimalist swagger of hip-hop into the arena of '80s-style funk and soul, Guy (led by *wunderkind* Teddy Riley) forged a new R&B sound that continues to dominate the genre. Riley has been one of the most respected and sought-after hit-makers of the last decade, producing records for everyone from Heavy D. to Michael Jackson.

In the battle of dueling egos, Guy was the victim; the group never issued a second album. Vocalist Aaron Hall's debut release *The Truth* was released in 1993. Riley returned to the studio wars. —*John Floyd and Ron Wynn*

★ **Guy** / 1988 / MCA 42176

The hottest trend of the late '80s was new jack swing, in which hip-hop production met vintage R&B/soul singing. The man credited with perfecting this style was Teddy Riley, and he was one-third of the trio Guy, along with brothers Aaron and Damion Hall. The New York City threesome roared out of the chute with this album, which eventually became a platinum success, and the hit "I Like" was extremely influential. "Spend the Night" and "Teddy's Jam" were other strong singles, but the key hit was "Groove Me," one of the year's hottest records and Guy's finest single. It had hypnotic beats, was superbly produced, and featured riveting vocals by the Halls and Riley. —*Ron Wynn*

○ **Future** / Uptown/MCA 10115

The second and final album from the new jack trio Guy matched the platinum credentials of its predecessor but didn't have the same dynamic grooves nor the inspired mix of soulful harmonies and futuristic beats. Once more brothers Aaron and Damion Hall teamed with singer and producer Teddy Riley, but only the singles "I Wannna Get with U" and "Let's Chill" came close to generating the buzz and the heat of earlier hits. —*Ron Wynn*

Music Map

Heavy Metal

Influences
Link Wray
The Who – The Yardbirds
The Kinks– Jimi Hendrix

British Metal - 70s
Judas Priest – Led Zeppelin
Black Sabbath – Deep Purple

European Metal - 70s
Scorpions – U.F.O.

Australian Metal - Mid 70s
AC/DC

American Metal - 70s
Van Halen – Kiss – Aerosmith

British Metal - Late 70s
Iron Maiden – Mötörhead– Def Leppard

American Metal - Early 80s
Mötley Crüe – Dio

British Metal - Early 80s
Ozzy Osbourne – Diamond Head

Classical Metal
Yngwie Malmsteen

Thrash Metal - 90s
Anthrax – Metalllica
Slayer – Megadeth

Heavy Metal - 90s
Skid Row – Guns N' Roses – Pantera
Forced Entry

Grindcore - 90s
Napalm Death – Carcass

Death Metal - 90s
Mercyful Fate – Venom – Death
Possessed – Morbid Angel

Gwar

Group / Heavy metal

Gwar is thrash metal's answer to the more mainstream satire of Spinal Tap. Gory, sexually perverse, and scatological in the extreme, Gwar originally formed in Richmond, VA, as an experiment in marketing strategy. The group claims to consist of all-powerful interplanetary warriors, created from the lowest filth in the universe, who have come to Earth to sexually enslave and/or slaughter the human race. All members perform under aliases and wear bizarre costumes made of latex and papier-mache. The main group consists of Oderus Urungus (vocals), Balzac the Jaws of Death (guitar), Flattus Maximus (guitar), Beefcake the Mighty (bass), and Jizmak the Gusher (drums), along with several other auxiliary characters. —*Steve Huey*

Hell-O / 1988 / Metal Blade 14004

Gwar's debut introduces their trademark cartoonish violence and silly gross-out humor (sex with a dead dog). However, given this album's lack of a lyric sheet, character bios, or liner notes to expand on the joke, there are better places to start. —*Steve Huey*

● **Scumdogs of the Universe** / 1990 / Metal Blade 26243
Their heaviest and probably most disgusting album, this brings in some monsters and villains to complement their standard sex-and-violence fare. Lines like "Maggots are falling like rain" pretty much tell the story. The quintessential Gwar album. —*Steve Huey*

○ **America Must Be Destroyed** / Sep. 1991 / Metal Blade 26807
More tales of perversity, mutilation, and horrible creatures. The subject matter broadens a bit, as they take aim at censorship advocates dumb enough to take them seriously ("The Morality Squad") and include a hilarious take on the power-ballad genre ("The Road Behind"), in which they reveal that they enjoy a good cry after senseless slaughters. —*Steve Huey*

This Toilet Earth / 1994 / Metal Blade
Not as consistently deranged as other Gwar releases, this one is at least the best packaged, with fact sheets on all the characters and some truly hideous cartoons. —*Steve Huey*

Sammy Hagar

b. 1947, Monterey, CA
Vocals, guitar / Hard rock, heavy metal
Born in Monterey, CA, Sammy Hagar moved to Fontana, where he formed a lot of small bands before guitarist Ronnie Montrose asked him to join his band Montrose in 1972. Hagar sang with Montrose for three years before deciding to leave and form his own band. After a long line of bestselling albums and memorable songs, he was asked to join Van Halen after the departure of their vocalist, David Lee Roth. With Hagar, Van Halen has since gained more popularity than ever before, with three best-selling albums. —*John Book*

○ **Best of Sammy Hagar** / Nov. 16, 1992 / Capitol 80262
A servicable, but not definitive, collection of some of Hagar's greatest hard-rock tracks. —*AMG*

● **Unboxed** / 1994 / Geffen 24702
All of the hits that weren't on *Best of Sammy Hagar*—including "I Can't Drive 55," "There's Only One Way to Rock," and "Give to Live"—are featured on *Unboxed*. Neither disc is consistently enjoyable, but *Unboxed* is the stronger of the two collections. —*AMG*

Bill Haley (William John Clifton Haley)

b. Jul. 6, 1925, Highland Park, MI, d. Feb. 9, 1981, Harlingen, TX
Vocals, guitar / Rock & roll
The Bill Haley and the Comets recording of "Rock Around the Clock," which topped the charts for eight weeks in 1955, is remembered as the beginning of the rock era. Though it also represented Haley's peak as a performer, his career had begun some time before and would continue for a long time after. Born in Michigan, Haley began leading Western-swing bands under various names in the late '40s, slowly starting to incorporate elements of R&B. Soon after he began recording for Essex in the early '50s, his backup band was named the Comets.
He hit number 15 in the charts in 1953 with "Crazy Man Crazy," a rock & roll song he'd written. Haley signed to Decca in 1954 and went to number 12 with "Shake, Rattle and Roll." In 1955 Haley hit with "Dim, Dim the Lights," "Mambo Rock," and "Birth of the Boogie," but it was "Rock Around the Clock," previously recorded and released as a B-side in 1954 and reissued as the theme song for the movie *Blackboard Jungle*, that became his biggest hit. At that time the band consisted of Haley on guitar and vocals, Danny Cedrone on lead guitar, Joey D'Ambrose on sax, Billy Williamson on steel guitar, Johnny Grande on piano, Marshall Lytle on bass, and Dick Richards on drums.
Following the success of "Rock Around the Clock," Haley and the Comets placed nine more records in the Top 40 over the next three years, among them the Top Tens "Burn That Candle" and "See You Later, Alligator." Haley was largely eclipsed as the king of rock & roll by Elvis Presley and other more flamboyant performers who followed him from 1956 on. Nevertheless, he continued to perform overseas and in oldies shows in the United States, and "Rock Around the Clock" even got back into the Top 40 in 1974. —*William Ruhlmann*

● **From the Original Master Tapes** / 1985 / MCA 5539
The best-sounding Haley collection, but its 20 songs are probably ten more than anyone but the most hardcore fan needs. —*Bruce Eder*

Half Japanese

Group / Experimental, alternative pop/rock
Depending on your point of view, Half Japanese is either a celebration of the pure, amateurish do-it-yourself rock & roll spirit or a pretentious, highly irritating example of noisy, self-conscious experimental rock at its most extreme. Formed by Jad and David Fair in 1977, the group started bashing out music in their parents' basement in Maryland, recording their debut EP by themselves. By the time the Fairs recorded their first album, the three-record boxed set *1/2 Gentlemen/Not Beasts*, they had a acquired a full-time drummer plus a saxophonist, yet their music was no less noisy and primitive—if anything, it was more atonal and difficult than before.
Since then, the band has proudly displayed nothing approaching instrumental virtuosity. David Fair left the band after their third record, rejoining briefly for 1988's *Charmed Life*. Throughout the years, the lineup has changed frequently—at times it has included Velvet Underground drummer Maureen Tucker and guitarist Don Fleming, as well as occasional contributions from Fred Frith and John Zorn—but Jad Fair has remained. This doesn't necessarily the mean the music has stayed the same. Their later records are slightly more musically varied and accessible, yet no less challenging. Jad Fair has released a few solo albums that are stranger (believe it or not) than the typical Half Japanese release. —*Stephen Thomas Erlewine*

● **1/2 Gentlemen/Not Beasts** / 1980 / Fifty Scedillion Watts
As with any album that is three records long, *1/2 Gentlemen/Not Beasts* unwittingly shows some things about Half Japanese that reveal their true roots. Over the three records, the band "covers" such minimalists as the Velvet Underground, the Stooges, and Jonathan Richman, as well as deconstructing such wordsmiths as Bruce Springsteen and Bob Dylan. Although they would like to have you believe that their untuned, almost unlistenable, instrumental clatter is the result of being so enthusiastic that they didn't bother to learn how to play their instruments, it is just the logical, inevitable intellectual extension of Richman's naivety and the Velvet Underground's stripped-down guitar. Half Japanese is consciously primitive and amateurish. —*Stephen Thomas Erlewine*

● **Charmed Life** / 1988 / Fifty Scedillion Watts 5
While *Charmed Life* is the band's most accessible record, it doesn't even come close to the mainstream's concept of what constitutes pop music. Yet when Jad Fair sings about love and joy on *Charmed Life*, he is as straightforward and direct as he ever gets. —*Stephen Thomas Erlewine*

○ **Band That Would Be King** / 1989 / Fifty Scedillion Watts 8
Featuring contributions from John Zorn and Fred Frith, *The Band That Would Be King* is one of the most diverse and challenging records Half Japanese has recorded. It's also one of their most rewarding. —*Stephen Thomas Erlewine*

Hall & Oates

Group / Pop/rock, soul
Daryl Hall first recorded as a member of Kenny Gamble and the Romeos and later became a session man at Sigma studios in Philadelphia. He also recorded one album with the rock group Gulliver. John Oates played with Gulliver too, and when it disbanded in 1972, Hall and Oates signed with Atlantic as a duo. Their biggest hits have (for the most part) been a blend of blue-eyed soul and dance-pop. They enjoyed their greatest success during the first half of the '80s. —*Rick Clark*

○ **Bigger Than the Both of Us** / 1977 / RCA 1467
Includes "Be What You Are" and "Rich Girl." —*Bil Carpenter*

○ **Voices** / 1980 / RCA 3646
This is the album that took Hall and Oates from being a successful '70s pop duo to being one of the four biggest singles acts of the '80s (the others: Michael Jackson, Prince, and Madonna). The sound is a wonderful pop pastiche, from the Beatlesque "How Does It Feel to Be Back" to the neo-Philadelphia soul of the hits "Kiss on My List" and "You Make My Dreams." —*William Ruhlmann*

○ **Private Eyes** / 1981 / RCA 4028
More bouncy, soulful rock & roll, led by the number-one hits "Private Eyes" and "I Can't Go for That (No Can Do)." —*William Ruhlmann*

○ **H2O** / 1982 / RCA 4383
From the Motown beat of "Maneater" to the lush ballad "One on One," Hall & Oates continue to make the top pop of the early '80s. Also contains "Family Man." —*William Ruhlmann*

★ **Rock 'n' Soul Part 1—Greatest Hits** / 1983 / RCA 4858
The best of Hall and Oates, 1974 to 1983, including their biggest '70s hits, "She's Gone," "Sara Smile," and "Rich Girl," plus the '80s chart-toppers and two new hits: "Say It Isn't So" and "Adult Education." —*William Ruhlmann*

Big Bam Boom / 1984 / RCA 5336
The last of the major Hall & Oates albums of the '80s features more of their patented soul-rock sound on the hits "Out of Touch" and "Method of Modern Love." —*William Ruhlmann*

Hanoi Rocks

Group / Hard rock, glam rock
These Finnish glam-rockers tried in the early '80s to pick up where the New York Dolls left off. They broke up after releasing a slew of albums, but have attained cult status thanks to Guns N' Roses' Uzi Suicide label's reissuing their catalog. Vocalist Michael Monroe released a solo album in 1989. —*John Floyd*

○ **Bangkok Shocks, Saigon Shakes, Hanoi Rocks** / 1981 / David Geffen Co. 24262
The sleazy, hard-rocking *Bangkok Shocks, Saigon Shakes, Hanoi Rocks* is the band's best original album.

● **Best of Hanoi Rocks** / 1985 / Hanoi Rocks 8
A solid collection of the band's finest hard-rock moments. —*AMG*

Happy Mondays

Group / Alternative pop/rock, dance
Along with the Stone Roses, the Happy Mondays were the leaders of the late-'80s/early-'90s club-influenced Manchester scene, experiencing a fast moment in the spotlight before collapsing in 1992. While the Stone Roses were based in '60s pop, adding only a slight hint of dance music, the Happy Mondays immersed themselves in the club and rave culture, eventually becoming the most recognizable band of that drug-fueled scene. The Mondays' music relied heavily on the sound and rhythm of house music, spiked with '70s soul licks and swirling '60s psychedelia. It was bright, colorful music that made stabs at melody, but never could quite pull off a cohesive song—the overall texture was more important.

With their second album, 1988's *Bummed*, the Happy Mondays became British superstars, particularly lead singer Shaun Ryder. *Pills 'n' Thrills & Bellyaches*, released in 1990, marked the height of the band's popularity, creativity, and influence. Although the record made the Top 100 albums chart in America, it didn't establish them as stars here.

After that, the fall was quick. By the time they released their last studio album, *Yes Please*, Manchester had disappeared from public consciousness. The record sold respectably, but the group didn't have the commercial impact that they had just two years before. Besides the lack of public interest, Shaun Ryder had become addicted to heroin, tearing the band apart in the process. At a high-level record contract meeting, Ryder walked out for something to eat and never returned. After that, the band was officially finished. —*Stephen Thomas Erlewine*

○ **Bummed** / 1988 / Elektra 60854
The second album by the band, *Bummed*, established the group as premier dance rockers and helped publicize the Manchester scene internationally. —*David Szatmary*

○ **Pills 'n' Thrills & Bellyaches** / 1990 / Elektra 60986
The Mondays sound more kaleidoscopic and more soulful than ever, with '70s soul emerging as the primary stepping-off point. "Kinky Afro" lifts the groove from LaBelle's "Lady Marmalade" for a chilling effect. The group also covers John Kongos' "Step On." More varied and better produced than their previous efforts—the Manchester scene is likely to run out of ideas before the Mondays do. —*Brian Mansfield*

● **Double Easy: The US Singles** / 1993 / Elektra
When everything was said and done, the Happy Mondays were essentially a singles band, and *Double Easy* collects them all, including many superior 12-inch mixes. —*Stephen Thomas Erlewine*

John Wesley Harding

Guitar / Singer/songwriter, alternative pop/rock
John Wesley Harding takes his name from a Bob Dylan song. He's a modern-day folk singer, but with his biting, cynical, clever songwriting, his true forefather is Elvis Costello. On occasion, he also dips into the political commentary of Billy Bragg. Harding's records never slip into self-absored, singer/songwriter mush, thanks to his sharp melodies. At times, his approach is a little too much like Costello's for comfort, yet his lyrical and musical style is distinctly his own. —*Stephen Thomas Erlewine*

○ **It Happened One Night** / 1988 / Rhino 70764
This solo acoustic outing, recorded live in England in 1988, is seems like an odd choice for a debut, but it comes off very well. Capturing both John Wesley Harding's folk roots and his wonderful sense of humor, *It Happened One Night* gives a very representative picture of the singer/songwriter. Included are early versions of songs appearing on the following two albums as well as unreleased gems such as the his fun account of Live Aid ("July 13th 1985") and a cover of Prince's "Kiss." —*Chris Woodstra*

● **Here Comes the Groom** / 1989 / Sire 26087
His second album has him working in the studio with a band called the Good Liars, including Pete Thomas, and Bruce Thomas of the Attractions. Not suprisingly, *Here Comes the Groom* has a feel similar to classic Elvis Costello. Harding's articulate and biting vocal delivery, also reminiscent of Costello, retains a good dark sense of humor. —*Chris Woodstra*

○ **Name above the Title** / 1991 / Sire 26481
The follow-up to *Here Comes the Groom* continues in the same direction. This time the arrangements are filled out with horn sections and strings, but the overall folkie feel remains. —*Chris Woodstra*

Why We Fight / Mar. 1992 / Sire 45032
This 1992 release is more low key and moody than any of his previous work. The subject matter is darker, though the melodies are still catchy and as instantly memorable as always—this time with smoother production. Even a discussion about Hitler ("Hitler's Tears") is musically irresistible, placing him in the ranks of Nick Lowe and Elvis Costello. —*Chris Woodstra*

Roy Harper

b. Jun. 12, 1941, Manchester, England
Vocals / Blues-rock, folk-rock
Harper came out of the United Kingdom in the mid '60s folk boom, in the wake of Bob Dylan's success with songs filled with poetic insight and anger. Guest appearances on his albums over the years by the cream of British Rock (including Jimmy Page, Ian Anderson, Bill Bruford, and Paul McCartney) should have give Harper a larger following, but he has never translated the admiration of his contemporaries into anything beyond cult status. Led Zeppelin's "Hats Off to Harper" was dedicated to Harper. —*Cub Koda*

○ **Stormcock** / 1971 / Chrysalis 1161
With only four tracks (three of which are quite long), this is Harper's most serious, focused work. Though not as melancholy as Nick Drake, it has a similar moody appeal, and features lots of fine acoustic guitar work. "The Same Old Rock" features a virtuoso acoustic lead from none other than Jimmy Page (playing under the pseudonym S. Flavius Mercurius), and one can detect Harper's influence in the acoustic-oriented Led Zep recordings of the early '70s. —*Richie Unterberger*

Lifemask / 1973 / Chrysalis 1162
Lifemask was recorded with Jimmy Page. Side 2 includes "The Lord's Prayer" suite. —*Michael G. Nastos*

● **Flashes from the Archives of Oblivion** / 1974 / Chrysalis 1164
Flashes from the Archives of Oblivion features 14 tracks recorded at various concerts in England. It's some of his most influential work. —*Michael G. Nastos*

Valentine / 1974 / Chrysalis 1163
Valentine includes "Male Chauvinist Pig Blues" and "Magic Woman (Liberation Reshuffle)," which is dedicated to Harper's mates in Led Zeppelin. —*Michael G. Nastos*

○ **When an Old Cricketer Leaves the Crease** / 1977 / Chrysalis 1105

When an Old Cricketer Leaves the Crease is a premiere American release from Harper, featuring seven self-penned cuts. His bandmates include Bill Bruford and Chris Spedding. The album is arresting folk-rock. —*Michael G. Nastos*

George Harrison

b. Feb. 25, 1943, Liverpool, England
Guitar / Pop/rock

As lead guitarist for the Beatles, George Harrison provided the band with a lyrical style of playing in which every note really mattered. Unlike Clapton or many of his other English guitar peers Harrison's style wasn't steeped in American blues, but it often delivered a very real soulfulness. Harrison also developed a uniquely silky slide-guitar sound during his last Beatles days.

Harrison has always been a rather weak singer, but as a songwriter he wrote some classics, both as a Beatle and as a solo artist. His greatest moment of artistic triumph was the triple album *All Things Must Pass,* which Harrison coproduced with the legendary Phil Spector. Both that album and the single "My Sweet Lord" gave Harrison the distinction of being the first Beatle to top the charts after their breakup. In 1971, Bright Songs, publisher of the Chiffons hit "He's So Fine," sued Harrison for plagiarism and won. More hits followed, but Harrison's albums increasingly sounded like afterthoughts. The 1979 album *George Harrison* and 1987's comeback *Cloud Nine* were worthwhile exceptions.

In 1988 Harrison, Bob Dylan, Tom Petty, Jeff Lynne, and Roy Orbison formed the Traveling Wilburys, who have since released two very successful albums. Harrison has also enjoyed success in financing films such as *Monty Python's Life of Brian,, Time Bandits,* and *Brazil.*

Harrison hits include "My Sweet Lord/Isn't It a Pity," "What Is Life," "Give Me Love (Give Me Peace on Earth)," "All Those Years," "Blow Away," "Crackerbox Palace," "Dark Horse," "Got My Mind Set on You," and an ode to the Beatles, "When We Was Fab." — *Rick Clark*

Wonderwall Music / 1968 / Capitol 98706
The first-ever solo album by a Beatle (though John Lennon's *Two Virgins* preceded it in the United States) is a film soundtrack combining Indian-influenced music (some of it played by Indian musicians) with more conventional pop. It's no more essential than most film scores away from the films themselves, but it demonstrates the range of Harrison's musical taste. —*William Ruhlmann*

★ **All Things Must Pass** / 1970 / Capitol 46688
An exquisitely produced album, encompassing rock, mysticism, blues, and folk music under one cover. Every note is memorable. —*Bruce Eder*

Concert for Bangladesh / 1972 / Capitol 93265
A unique live document showcasing Harrison near his best, with ex-Beatle Ringo Starr, Eric Clapton, and many other superstars. It has less-than-perfect sound but overall fine re-creations of his best work, with work by Bob Dylan as an added bonus. —*Bruce Eder*

○ **Living in a Material World** / 1973 / Capitol 94110
Harrison had a lot of songs stored up for his first major solo work, *All Things Must Pass,* and it launched his post-Beatles career with a bang. Two and a half years later, he released its follow-up, which, though it contained some good playing by his band of superstar friends and some good tunes, notably the number-one hit "Give Me Love (Give Me Peace on Earth)," indicated that the first album had contained his best effort and the most he'd be able to do in the future would be to repeat it. — *William Ruhlmann*

Dark Horse / 1974 / Capitol 98079
Rushed through in the preparation for Harrison's first (and last) North American tour, his third solo album found him with a strained throat and not enough first-rate material. Most embarrassing was a rewrite of "Bye Bye Love," in which he commented on the romantic triangle between himself, his wife, and his best friend, Eric Clapton (who later married her). The title track and "Ding Dong, Ding Dong" were Top-40 hits. —*William Ruhlmann*

Extra Texture / 1975 / Capitol 98080
"You," a Top-20 hit, was a terrific pop song, but much of this album is expendable, including an update of the old Beatles song "While My Guitar Gently Weeps" called "This Guitar (Can't Keep

from Crying)." From the superstar status of *All Things Must Pass,* Harrison had declined rapidly. — *William Ruhlmann*

○ **33 & 1/3** / 1976 / Dark Horse 26612
Having suffered the humiliation of being sued successfully over "My Sweet Lord," Harrison turned the ordeal into music, writing "This Song," a Top-25 hit. Even better was "Crackerbox Palace," which hit number 19 and would have fit in nicely on any Beatles album. The rest was slight, though Harrison covering Cole Porter's "True Love" is an interesting idea. This was Harrison's first album on his Dark Horse custom label, formed after the completion of his contract with EMI/Capitol in June 1976, and was initially distributed by A&M. —*William Ruhlmann*

Best of George Harrison / 1976 / Capitol 46682
The Harrison material is matched with some Beatles numbers in a good but routine collection. —*Bruce Eder*

George Harrison / 1979 / Dark Horse 26613
Harrison's sixth solo studio album (released after a two-year hiatus) was another slight affair, boasting the Top-20 single "Blow Away," but otherwise unremarkable. "Not Guilty" was a Beatles-era song once short-listed for the white album." "Here Comes the Moon" was a tepid sequel to "Here Comes the Sun." —*William Ruhlmann*

Somewhere in England / 1981 / Dark Horse 26614
Harrison had trouble getting Warner Brothers Records, which now distributed his Dark Horse label, to accept this album (an early, rejected version even turned up in collecting circles). It finally appeared, heavily revised, featuring a song originally intended for Ringo Starr with different lyrics, "All Those Years Ago." Now pitched as a tribute to the late John Lennon, the song (featuring Starr and Paul McCartney) became a substantial hit and carried the mediocre album, which also features two Hoagy Carmichael songs. —*William Ruhlmann*

○ **Cloud Nine** / 1987 / Dark Horse 25643
A great collection of bright, hard-rocking numbers, even embracing gospel. —*Bruce Eder*

○ **Best of Dark Horse (1976-1989)** / 1989 / Dark Horse 25726
The best of a less than satisfying era. The only way to take it in. —*Bruce Eder*

Live in Japan / Dec. 1992 / Dark Horse 26964
George Harrison returned to the stage for the first time in years in 1991. That Japanese tour is documented on the fine double-disc set, *Live in Japan.* Backed by a stellar supporting band led by Eric Clapton, Harrison turns in surprisingly strong versions of his best solo material—it easily suprasses Paul McCartney's double disc *Tripping the Live Fantastic* or *Paul is Live.* Not bad for a guy who doesn't like to give concerts. —*Stephen Thomas Erlewine*

Wilbert Harrison

b. Jan. 5, 1929, Charlotte, NC
Vocals / R&B

Harrison cut the classic version of "Kansas City" in 1959. The Charlotte, NC, native's laconic vocal style first turned up on Henry Stone's Rockin' label in 1952, and he progressed to Deluxe, Chart, and Savoy before landing on Bobby Robinson's Fury imprint in 1959. With Jimmy Spruill wildly wringing out slashing bent notes on his guitar, Harrison's rocking revival of the Jerry Lieber/Mike Stoller classic "Kansas City" (first cut by Little Willie Littlefield in 1952) topped both the pop and R&B charts. Subsequent Fury 45s (including the sequel "Goodbye Kansas City") undeservedly bombed, and Harrison plied his trade for a time as a one-man band. But he wasn't through—"Let's Work Together," a slight rewrite of his Fury-era "Let's Stick Together," vaulted up the charts in 1970 after being recut for Sue. Like his other bestseller, "Let's Work Together" was prime cover material—for the likes of Canned Heat and Bob Dylan. And once again, he was unable to follow it up with anything of equal potency. —*Bill Dahl*

● **Kansas City** / 1965 / Relic 7035
Harrison's toughest late-'50s to early-'60s output for Fury Records, many in stereo for the first time. —*Bill Dahl*

○ **Greatest Classic R&B Hits** / 1989 / Grudge 4510
The only CD available of Harrison's late-'60s material, long after his 1959 classic "Kansas City." —*Bill Dahl*

Debbie Harry

b. Jul. 1, 1945, New York, NY
Vocals / Pop/rock
Singer/actress who was the lead vocalist in the new wave group Blondie (1974-1982). Harry launched a solo singing career in 1981, as well as acting on stage and film, but she retired in 1983 to nurse seriously ill companion (and Blondie guitarist) Chris Stein. Stein recovered, and Harry returned to action in 1985. — *William Ruhlmann*

Kookoo / 1981 / Chrysalis 1347
Harry teams up with Chic for bass-heavy dance rock, notably on the hit "Backfired." — *William Ruhlmann*

● **Rockbird** / 1986 / David Geffen Co. 24123
A return to the trashy, bubblegum-rock style of early Blondie, featuring the hit "French Kissin'." — *William Ruhlmann*

○ **Once More into the Bleach** / 1988 / Chrysalis 21658
A compilation disc containing Blondie and Debbie Harry solo hits in remixed, extended dance versions. — *William Ruhlmann*

PJ Harvey

Vocals, songwriter / Alternative rock
In terms of sound as well as subject, Polly Jean Harvey is the most challenging singer/songwriter to emerge in the early '90s. With her band, PJ Harvey, she staked out a distinctly personal territory with her brutally honest, darkly humorous songs about sex, love, and hate. At their core, her songs are structured like the blues, but played with the raw aggression of punk. Harvey's voice is equally uncompromising, squeezing all of the emotion out of a song. The sheer overpowing sonic rush of her music can overshadow the fact that her songs are not bitterly angry and violent—they only sound that way. Her music has a very human core.

PJ Harvey became an indie rock sensation, especially in their native Britain, with the 1992 release of their debut, *Dry*. All of the subsequent media attention helped Harvey build a substantial cult following. Instead of expanding her cult, PJ Harvey's uncompromising second album, 1993's *Rid of Me*, only made those same fans more devoted. In the fall of 1993, *Rid of Me*, was followed by *4-Track Demos*, a collection of Harvey's original recordings for the album, plus several unreleased songs.

During the *Rid of Me* tour, PJ Harvey's drummer and backing vocalist Rob Ellis left the band. For a short time, bassist Steven Vaughan also left, only to return by the end of the year. Although Polly Harvey has earned a dedicated cult following, it's unlikely that she'll ever acheive mainstream success—her music is too raw and demanding for casual listening. — *Stephen Thomas Erlewine*

● **Dry** / 1992 / Indigo 5001
Dry is the impressive, original debut album from singer/songwriter Polly Jean Harvey's trio, PJ Harvey. While Harvey has her share of post-feminist anger, the album doesn't lack humor. Although her lyrics are impressive, where she really makes her mark is through her music, a fierce combination of punk rage, sharp songwriting, and surprisingly melodic hooks. *Dry* is one of the most distinctive albums in years. — *Stephen Thomas Erlewine*

○ **Rid of Me** / May 4, 1993 / Indigo 514696
Thanks to Steve Albini's production, PJ Harvey's second album is a harsher, more abrasive affair than *Dry*. Albini has taken the dynamics of Polly Harvey's songwriting to extremes: Sometimes it is nearly impossible to hear the beginning of a song, until an explosive rush of guitars obliterates the silence a minute later. Still, most of the uneasiness of *Rid of Me* can be mainly attributed to Harvey herself—the lyrics are just as scathing as the music. Although the best songs here ("Rid of Me," "50 ft. Queenie," "Yuri G," "Man-Sized") are better than the best on *Dry*, they are more difficult to listen to. Harvey's songs have become harder and angrier, yet she has not completely stripped away the humor that enlivened *Dry*—it's just hard to hear it through the clatter of the guitars and drums. — *Stephen Thomas Erlewine*

○ **4-Track Demos** / Sep. 1993 / Indigo
With Polly Harvey's voice acting as the focal point of these recordings, *4-Track Demos* is no more accessible than the overwhelming guitar attack of *Rid of Me*. So why is it a better album? Harvey's songs are presented as raw, honest emotions, proving that she was not hiding a lack of talent behind noise. The stripped-down instrumentation shows how detailed and well-

written her songs are. Her often-overlooked sense of humor is also more apparent, especially on the sublime "Reeling." All of these factors taken together make *4-Track Demos* an album that should be heard by not just Harvey's devoted fans, but by anyone with a passing interest in her or modern rock. — *Stephen Thomas Erlewine*

Juliana Hatfield

Vocals, guitar / Alternative pop/rock
After leaving the Blake Babies, singer/guitarist Juliana Hatfield pursued a solo career that easily eclipsed her former band, in both commercial and artistic terms. Hatfield's thin, girlish voice accentuates her unassuming, catchy pop songs, which can either be sweet and happy ("Spin the Bottle") or surprisingly honest and moving ("Ugly"). Her first solo album, 1992's *Hey Babe*, was a small gem, full of well-constructed songs that effortlessly evoked the pain and charm of adolescence; rarely has anyone captured teenagers from a female perspective so accurately. It was a college-radio hit that made a small dent in the mainstream, particularly with teenage girls. Afraid that she wasn't being taken seriously as an artist, Hatfield hooked up with a grungy male rhythm section for her next album, 1993's *Become What You Are*. She kept the effortless melody of her first album, while turning up the volume on the amplifiers in an attempt to become harder. It sold more records than *Hey Babe*, but musically, it was only sporadically successful. During the summer of 1994, she was assembling a new band as she prepared to record her third solo album. — *Stephen Thomas Erlewine*

● **Hey Babe** / 1992 / Mammoth 0035
Hey Babe is a terrific debut from former Blake Babies leader Juliana Hatfield, filled with effortless melodies and catchy guitar riffs. Hatfield's thin, girlish voice can be slightly wearing over the course of an entire album, but her intelligent, hook-laden songs make up for that minor flaw. — *Stephen Thomas Erlewine*

○ **Become What You Are** / 1993 / Atlantic
Although she desperately tries to hide behind a grungier guitar sound, Hatfield is still the talented songwriter of girlish power-pop that made the infectious *Hey Babe*. Because she tries so hard to put the innocent pleasures of her debut behind her, *Become What You Are* isn't as satisfying. Most of the loud rave-ups betray her true gifts with melody, which most definitely has not disappeared; her hooks are so strong that she can make such cringe-inducing lyrics as "For the Birds" and "Mabel" easy to ignore. Hatfield's strongest points are apparent on "Supermodel," "My Sister," and "Spin the Bottle"—catchy, honest, and incisive portraits of adolescence. Fortunately, her talents are strong enough to carry the album over the weak spots. — *Stephen Thomas Erlewine*

Dale Hawkins

Vocals, guitar / Rockabilly
This Louisiana guitarist's 1957 hit "Suzy Q," with its crackling bluesy guitar and insistent cowbell, was one of the most exciting early rockabilly singles. Recording for Chess (as one of its few white artists) between 1956 and 1961, Hawkins never quite duplicated its success, either commercially or artistically, but came close enough on a number of occasions to warrant respect as one of the better rockabilly singers. His drawling delivery, sense of humor, affinity for blues, and sharp guitar work (which was actually provided by such ace players as Roy Buchanan, Scotty Moore, and James Burton) are heard to good effect on his 1958 album and a number of non-hit singles. Hawkins went on to become a producer of some note in the 1960s, working with the Five Americans and Bruce Channel. — *Richie Unterberger*

○ **Susie Q** / 1958 / Chess 1429
A way-above average '50s rock & roll album, including both sides of Dale's first four singles. Highlights are "Suzy-Q," its killer B-side ("Don't Treat Me This Way"), and the goofy "See You Soon Baboon" and "Mrs. Mergitory's Daughter."—*Richie Unterberger*

My Babe / 1987 / Argo 1450
Rare singles and other interesting material that Hawkins cut, mostly for Chess, between 1958 and 1962. Includes his sole Top-40 hit besides "Suzy-Q" ("La-Do-Dada") and some fine rockabilly interpretations of blues hits.—*Richie Unterberger*

Ronnie Hawkins

b. Jan. 10, 1935, Huntsville, Madison County, AK

Vocal, guitar / Rockabilly
A rockabilly singer who formed the original backing band, the Hawks, while attending the University of Arkansas. After auditioning unsuccessfully for Sun in 1957, he started working regularly in Canada the following year, eventually taking up permanent residence there. After one release on the Canadian Quality label, he signed with Roulette in New York in 1959, having hits with "Forty Days" and "Mary Lou." The live fervor of Hawkins (known as "Mr. Dynamo") & the Hawks' show continued in Canada after all the original members except Levon Helm headed back to the United States. Hawkins quickly hired Canadian players Robbie Robertson, Garth Hudson, Rick Danko, and Richard Manuel as the new Hawks. They stayed with him until 1963, but later became Bob Dylan's backing group and went on to a career of their own as the Band. Hawkins has remained a legend in Canada, recording unrepentant rockabilly sides and gigging constantly. He's still the original Mr. Dynamo, capable of shaking the walls down any old time he feels like it. *—Cub Koda*

● **Best of Ronnie Hawkins & His Band** / 1990 / Rhino 70966
A good overview of the Hawks' best sides. *—Cub Koda*

Screamin' Jay Hawkins

b. Jul. 18, 1929, Cleveland, OH
Vocals, piano, sax / R&B
Though capable of more conventional blues, sentimental ballads, and R&B, Screamin' Jay Hawkins will be forever remembered for the wild songs and onstage theatrics of his self-created brand of voodoo jive. His act has often featured him emerging from a casket to sing his best-known hit, "I Put a Spell on You." Other novelties, ranging from "Feast of the Mau Mau" to "Constipation Blues," may have stereotyped his talent, but on the other hand, his idiosyncracies have brought him TV and movie appearances that would have eluded him had he played his music straight. Regardless of style, Hawkins's recordings still display a remarkable voice, which would have been used for opera had Screamin' Jay had his way. *—Jim O'Neal*

● **Voodoo Jive: Best of Screamin' Jay Hawkins** / 1990 / Rhino 70947
Opinions vary on Screamin' Jay Hawkins. Some maintain he was a one-hit fluke whose comedy routine peaked with "I Put a Spell On You"—a one-dimensional performer with a limited singing voice and no other discernible skills. Others insist Hawkins was a decent R&B and blues singer, an excellent entertainer and personality whose real talents were overshadowed by the success of "I Put a Spell On You." This anthology doesn't convincingly answer the argument, but it does collect 17 Hawkins singles from Okeh, Enrica, and Phillips, including all of his major hits. Perhaps the high (or low) point is "Constipation Blues," from 1969. *—Ron Wynn*

Hawkwind

Group / Progressive rock, hard rock, heavy metal
Hawkwind is a British acid rock band led by Dave Brock that is famous for long, spacey, improvisational jams. It gained notoriety playing at the 1970 Isle of Wight Festival headlined by Bob Dylan. Hawkwind wasn't on the bill—they set up outside the fence and played for free. Hawkwind's tendency to play gigs almost anywhere for free, as well as press coverage resulting from drug busts, gained them a cult following.

With a few moderately commercially successful albums under their belt, the group played at the 1972 London Roundhouse Greasy Truckers' Festival along with Gong and the Grateful Dead. They also appeared on one side of the live double album resulting from the festival. "Silver Machine," an outtake from the concert recording, was released as a single and became a huge surprise British hit and their only million seller.

Throughout their history, Hawkwind has had an incredible amount of personnel turnaround. Band members have included former Cream drummer Ginger Baker and sci-fi writer Michael Moorcock, who based his 1976 book *Time of the Hawklords* on the band members. Many former Hawkwinders have also released solo albums or formed offshoot groups. Bassist Lemmy Kilmeister was fired from the band in 1974. He went on to form the thrash metal pioneers Motorhead, who took their name from a Hawkwind B-side. *—Jim Powers*

Hawkwind / 1970 / One Way 57658

Includes their best-known hit, "Silver Machine." *—Michael G. Nastos*

● **In Search in Space** / 1971 / One Way 57474
Psychedelic rangers from England go one up on Pink Floyd and Tangerine Dream—and maybe Sun Ra too. Their best studio date. *—Michael G. Nastos*

○ **Quark Strangeness and Charm** / 1977 / Sire 6047
Still at it, in an irreverent way. In many respects they are the standard for many of today's heavy metal bands. *—Michael G. Nastos*

○ **Live** / Gri 3921
More of the same in concert, where they are most likely at their best. Should be a video, because their stage show pulled out all the visual stops. *—Michael G. Nastos*

Isaac Hayes

b. Aug. 29, 1942, Covington, TN
Vocals, piano, sax / Soul, funk, R&B, disco
From the tough urgency of the Stax studio (for whom he was a prolific writer and arranger), Isaac Hayes went on to develop an overwrought style that utilized the potential of the album. To that point, most R&B and soul albums had been a mixture of 2 1/2-minute singles and filler. Hayes concocted mini-symphonies of extraordinary length, which, allied with his personal style (shaved head, designer African clothes, shades, and bizarre jewelry), made him more than a musician: He became an instantly recognizable cultural icon in early-'70s Black music. One album title, *Black Moses*, was probably Hayes's own succinct self-appraisal. Some might argue that his legacy is better represented by his workaday compositions and his arrangements, which include Sam & Dave's immortal "Soul Man" and "Hold On, I'm Coming." *—Colin Escott*

☆ **Hot Buttered Soul** / 1969 / Stax 4114
Isaac Hayes had already co-written many immortal soul singles in the late '60s when he began forging a solo career. Besides composing some landmark soundtracks for the first wave of African-American films during the '70s, Hayes helped focus attention on the album as a creative source in soul and R&B. This seminal album went against the grain in several ways. There were only four cuts, three of them at least nine minutes long. Two had extensive monologues, and he used symphonic backing and elaborate production. The album went gold, cracked the Top 100, and helped usher soul and R&B into the concept album era. It also featured some superb vocals and fine keyboard work by Hayes. *—Ron Wynn*

○ **Isaac Hayes Movement** / 1970 / Stax 4129
His second huge hit album and a great follow-up to the superb *Hot Buttered Soul*. Those critics who thought there was no way Hayes could repeat that triumph got fooled. He included a brilliant remake of Jerry Butler's "I Stand Accused," and also did a 12-minute version of the Beatles "Something," complete with wailing violin solo from jazz-rocker John Blair. This album showed Hayes was going to be around for a long time and be just as consistent on his own as he was teaming with Porter. *—Ron Wynn*

To Be Continued / 1970 / Stax 4133
The third consecutive smash hit album for Isaac Hayes, with more anthemic raps and elaborate symphonic soul. This time he did his production/rap/movement routines remaking the songs "The Look of Love" and "You've Lost That Loving Feeling." Once more Hayes combined inspired vocals with equally creative production and arrangements, getting his third straight platinum album, something that was then unprecedented in R&B and soul circles. *—Ron Wynn*

Black Moses / 1971 / Stax 88006
Isaac Hayes followed his Oscar-winning soundtrack LP, *Shaft*, with another two-record set blending remakes of soul and pop hits, extended monologues, symphonic orchestrations and backing, and the other production devices that made him one of the most successful producers and performers of the '70s. Though *Black Moses* wasn't nearly as commercially dominant as earlier albums, it did make it into the Top Ten briefly, and was on the charts for over 30 weeks. But it was also an indication he was beginning to run a bit dry in the material department. *—Ron Wynn*

○ **Shaft** / 1971 / Stax 88002
Isaac Hayes surprised many in the film and R&B/soul worlds when he produced, arranged, and composed the music for *Shaft*.

Only three of the 15 tracks featured vocals, and Hayes displayed a finesse and capability with strings and mood pieces that his fans already knew he possessed from earlier albums, but that the general audience might have missed. This was a number-one pop LP and eventually earned Hayes an Oscar. It's also held up much better than the film. —*Ron Wynn*

Double Dynamite / 1974 / Stax 88014
Isaac Hayes not only was an innovative composer, songwriter, producer, and performer in the '60s and '70s, he was also an actor, appearing in several popular films during the early '70s. These films, dubbed "blaxploitation" movies in some circles, featured action heroes fighting one-dimensional villians in situations that were little more than vehicles for audiences to enjoy fights and conflict. Hayes did double duty on these projects, writing and conducting the soundtracks for several, including the two featured on this twin-CD reissue *Double Dynamite*. Neither *Truck Turner* nor *Tough Guys* was a particularly memorable film, but Hayes's effective use of symphony orchestras and strings against a vocal backdrop often made the music the best part of the movie. —*Ron Wynn*

● **Best of Isaac Hayes, Vol. 1** / 1986 / Stax 60001
● **Best of Isaac Hayes, Vol. 2** / 1986 / Stax 002
These two compilations dutifully boil down Isaac Hayes's sometimes long-winded albums to their essential parts—in other words, they're both singles collections, highlighted by '70s landmarks such as the "Theme from Shaft" and "By the Time I Get to Phoenix." —*John Floyd*

Jeff Healey Band

Group / Blues-rock
What makes Jeff Healey different from other contemporary blues-rockers is also what keeps some listeners from accepting him as anything other than a novelty—the fact that the blind guitarist plays his Fender Stratocaster on his lap, not standing up. With the guitar in his lap, Healey can make unique bends and hammer-ons, making his licks different than most of the competition. Unfortunately, his material leans toward standard AOR blues-rock, which rarely lets the guitarist cut loose, but when he does, his instrumental prowess can be stunning. —*Stephen Thomas Erlewine*

● **See the Light** / Dec. 1989 / Arista 8553
An assured first effort that contains the hits "Angel Eyes" and "Confidence Man." —*Dan Heilman*

○ **Hell to Pay** / 1990 / Arista 8632
A solid follow-up to Healey's impressive debut, *Hell to Pay* features some of the guitarist's hottest playing to date. —*Stephen Thomas Erlewine*

Feel This / Aug. 1992 / Arista 18706
By his third effort, Healey and the band turn up the heat, while producer Joe Hardy places the emphasis on a live-session feel. Healey's playing and singing have never been better. —*Stephen Thomas Erlewine*

Heart

Group / Hard rock, pop/rock
This Seattle band, led by sisters Ann and Nancy Wilson, has been a staple on FM rock-radio ever since their first hit in 1976, "Crazy on You." It was lead singer Ann Wilson's powerful voice that gave the band an immediate appeal. Heart synthesized Led Zeppelin-style riff-heavy rock and shades of folk. Over the years, the band has continued to churn out hit after hit. In spite of a recent resurgence in the band's popularity, their hits are sounding increasingly formulaic. "Magic Man," "Barracuda," "Straight On," "What about Love," "Never," "These Dreams," "Alone," "There's the Girl," and a remake of Aaron Neville's "Tell It like It Is" are a few of their hits. —*Rick Clark*

○ **Dreamboat Annie** / 1976 / Capitol 46491
Their striking first album was one of the top-selling debuts ever. —*Dan Heilman*

● **Heart Greatest Hits/Live** / 1980 / Epic 36888
This set includes all of the significant rock radio hits that made Heart such a staple during the '70s and early '80s, such as "Barracuda," "Crazy on You," "Straight On," "Dreamboat Annie," "Even It Up," "Magic Man," "Heartless," and "Dog & Butterfly." Filling out the disc are six live tracks, including versions of Led

Zeppelin's "Rock and Roll" and the Beatles' rave-up "I'm Down." —*Rick Clark*

○ **Heart** / 1985 / Capitol 46157
Just when it seemed that Heart was yesterday's news on the radio, they changed labels and experienced a resurgence of huge success with this, their self-titled Capitol debut. Includes the hits "If Looks Could Kill," "What about Love," "Never," "Nothin' at All," and "These Dreams." —*Rick Clark*

Bad Animals / 1987 / Capitol 46676
The winning streak on the radio continues with hits like "Alone" and "Who Will You Run To." —*Stephen Thomas Erlewine*

The Heartbeats

Group / Doo-wop
Lead singer James "Shep" Sheppard cowrote a series of velvety doo-wop ballads for the Heartbeats during the mid '50s; one entry, "A Thousand Miles Away," was a huge R&B seller in 1956. The Queens, NY, quintet began their string of street-corner classics with "Crazy for You" and "Darling How Long," culminating with "A Thousand Miles Away." The Heartbeats recorded for Hull, Rama, Roulette, Gee, and Guyden before packing it in.

In 1961 the lead singer formed a new trio, Shep & the Limelites, and scored on the charts with a heartwarming sequel to his first hit, "Daddy's Home," for Hull. "Our Anniversary" also sold well for the trio the next year, but they broke up soon thereafter. Sheppard was found dead in his auto on the Long Island Expressway in 1970. —*Bill Dahl*

● **Best of the Heartbeats** / 1990 / Rhino 70952
A silky smooth New York quintet from the mid '50s. This album includes five tracks by lead James Sheppard's early-'60s vocal trio, Shep & the Limelites. —*Bill Dahl*

Reverend Horton Heat

Vocals, guitar / Alternative rock, rockabilly
With his highly stylized, backwoods hick-preacher image, it would be easy to dismiss the Reverend Horton Heat as a poseur. But that would be wrong. Instead of treating rockabilly as a campy joke as the Cramps do, the good Reverend rocks the hell out of his modern-day rockabilly, playing it as if it were the hardest of punk, but without any of the self-concious trappings of either genre. Although his lyrics can be too silly, his music never is—t rocks harder than most of his punk and metal contemporaries. —*Stephen Thomas Erlewine*

○ **Smoke 'Em If You Got 'Em** / 1992 / Sub Pop 96
Reverend Horton Heat's first album is filled with tongue-in-cheek songs and killer riffs, made all the more exciting by the good Reverend's raw, gutsy punk-injected rockabilly licks. —*Stephen Thomas Erlewine*

● **Full Custom Gospel Sounds** / 1993 / Sub Pop
On Reverend Horton Heat's second album, the band sounds like they were having a race with the devil. All of their songs are played with a reckless abandon that makes their neo-rockabilly sound rawer and vital than most punk or metal bands. —*Stephen Thomas Erlewine*

Richard Hell & the Voidoids

Group / Punk
With his torn clothes, spiky hair, and recklessly angular rock primitivism, Richard Hell helped define the sound and look of the late-'70s punk movement. Unlike many artists who embraced that esthetic, Hell had the soul of an intellectual and a poet. His band, the Voidoids, featured the jagged interplay of guitarists Ivan Julian and Robert Quine. Anyone interested in investigating the '70s New York punk movement should definitely check out Hell's work. —*Rick Clark*

● **Blank Generation** / 1977 / Sire 26137
A punk-era classic. Snaky, jagged guitar courtesy of Robert Quine wraps around Hell's epiglottal spasms like barbed wire on flesh. All this and you get great song after great song after great song after . . . —*John Dougan*

Destiny Street / 1982 / Combat 5036
It took five years for Hell to follow his debut, but *Destiny Street* is a moderately successful extension of *Blank Generation*. Some of the energy from the old days had disappeared, but Hell com-

pensates with some fine ballads and another screwball classic, "The Kid with the Replaceable Head." —*John Floyd*

Helmet

Group / Alternative rock, heavy metal
Featuring ex-Band of Susans Page Hamilton, Helmet has a take on what is traditionally called heavy metal that is extreme, grinding, and relentless, sometimes more than one can reasonably handle all at once. But the churning wad of guitars, slower-than-muck backbeat, and harsh shouted vocals make for a pretty intimidating display of contemporary power-rock, even if it is a pose. —*John Dougan*

Strap It On / 1990 / Interscope 92235
Helmet's debut isn't as accomplished or powerful as *Meantime*, but it still provides enough gut-busting crunch to satisfy their fans. —*Stephen Thomas Erlewine*

● **Meantime** / 1992 / Interscope 92162
Crude, loud, simplistic thrash-and-bash that sounds like Black Flag and Black Sabbath. In fact, "Give It" could be the best Sab song they never recorded. With its intensity and directness, this is the best Helmet available. —*John Dougan*

○ **Betty** / 1994 / Interscope
On their second major label album, Helmet doesn't change their style at all, making *Betty* essential for fans. —*David Jehnzen*

Jimi Hendrix

b. Nov. 27, 1942, Seattle, WA, **d.** Sep. 18, 1970
Vocals, guitar / Rock & roll, blues rock, hard rock, psychedelic
Jimi Hendrix was one of rock's greatest pioneers on the electric guitar. He fused funky R&B with hard rock, developing and mastering fresh approaches to using feedback, distortion, and various sound effects. As a result of his early immersion in Muddy Waters, Elmore James, B. B. King, and Chuck Berry, as well as his work with the Isley Brothers and King Curtis, Hendrix's rhythm guitar style utilized soul and blues licks and chord inversions as a starting place for many of his songs.

Much has been said about Hendrix's guitar playing, but he was also a formidable songwriter, using sensually trippy lyrics that sometimes drew inspiration from Dylan. "Purple Haze," "Fire," "Little Wing," "The Wind Cries Mary," and "Angel" are a few of Hendrix's classic titles. Along with Cream, Hendrix's group, the Jimi Hendrix Experience (with Mitch Mitchell on drums and Noel Redding on bass), is the most important trio to come out of the rock era.

After the demise of the Experience in July of 1969, Hendrix pursued a hard, funkier (and slightly less imaginative) sound with Band of Gypsys, featuring Buddy Miles and Billy Cox. They released one self-titled live album in May of 1970. On September 18, 1970, Hendrix passed away due to complications brought on from a drug overdose.

In spite of Hendrix's important place in the history of rock, and his great album sales, pop radio was resistant to much of his sound. As a result, Hendrix only had one Top-40 hit, a fiery version of Dylan's "All along the Watchtower," which peaked at number 20. Other hits were "Crosstown Traffic," "Purple Haze," "Foxy Lady," "Up from the Skies," "Freedom," and "Dolly Dagger." — *Rick Clark*

☆ **Are You Experienced?** / 1967 / Reprise 6261
From the dissonant fanfare of "Purple Haze" to the hypnotic closing cadence of the title track, the Jimi Hendrix Experience's audacious debut built upon the experimental hard rock groundwork of groups like the Yardbirds, focusing it through a ferociously interactive trio format. Hendrix fused spacy Dylan-influenced imagery with R&B-derived song structures and chordal voicings to create a unique style. Tracks like "Fire," "Foxy Lady," "Manic Depression," the haunting "The Wind Cries Mary," and "May This Be Love" make this disc essential for any rock collection. —*Rick Clark*

☆ **Axis: Bold as Love** / 1967 / Reprise 6281
Continuing Hendrix's groundbreaking streak, this time matching his guitar pyrotechnics with a more refined collection of originals. The album features gorgeously unconventional ballads like "Little Wing," "Castles Made of Sand," "One Rainy Wish," and "Bold as Love," which shone alongside hyperspace rockers like "You Got Me Floatin'," "Up from the Skies," and the psychedelic hard jazz-rock free-for-all of "If 6 Was 9." —*Rick Clark*

● **Smash Hits** / Jan. 1968 / Reprise 2276
Smash Hits is a solid collection of his most popular radio tracks, and features as well the bluesy "Red House" and "Stone Free," which were not found on previous albums. —*Rick Clark*

☆ **Electric Ladyland** / Feb. 1968 / Reprise 6307
Hendrix's funky psychedelia reached a zenith on *Electric Ladyland*, one of the greatest albums of the rock era. His aggressively otherworldly production did as much for advancing the possibilities of recorded music as Phil Spector's "wall of sound" did in the early '60s. Hendrix's imaginatively fiery guitar work (and the Experience's brilliant interplay) here became the textbook source of inspiration for generations of musicians. Among *Electric Ladyland*'s many highlights are "Voodoo Child (Slight Return)," with its kamikaze lead guitar work; the transcendentally dense "Burning of the Midnight Lamp"; the searing remake of Dylan's "All along the Watchtower," and the beautifully spacy "1983 . . . (a Merman I Should Turn to Be)." —*Rick Clark*

○ **Band of Gypsys** / 1970 / Capitol 472
Hendrix, sans the Experience, hooked up with bassist Billy Cox and drummer Buddy Miles to record this hard electric funk outing live at the Fillmore East in New York on Dec. 31, 1969. While the rhythm section may have lacked the chops for wild free-form excursions, they provided Hendrix with a no-nonsense groove for his funkier R&B experiments. "Machine Gun," the album's highlight, features some of Hendrix's greatest playing. His dramatically violent soundscapes convey the horror of the war experience, with brilliantly controlled use of feedback and rapid-fire bursts of notes. —*Rick Clark*

Cry of Love / 1971 / Reprise 2034
The posthumously released *Cry of Love* revealed Hendrix turning toward a more subdued, less psychedelic style, with songs like "Night Bird Flying" and "Angel." Hendrix does deliver a few strong rockers with "Freedom," "Ezy Ryder," and "Astro Man." — *Rick Clark*

○ **Live at Winterland** / 1987 / Rykodisc 20038
Live at Winterland is one of the best representations of Hendrix's live prowess. The great playing is further enhanced by a top-notch mastering job. —*Rick Clark*

○ **Radio One** / 1989 / Rykodisc 20078
Just when it seemed that the only way to hear more unreleased Hendrix was to put up with doctored Alan Douglas releases, Ryko pulled this live 1967 BBC gem out of the hat. Includes versions of "Day Tripper," "Killing Floor," "Love or Confusion," "Purple Haze," and "Fire," among other tracks. —*Rick Clark*

Stages / 1991 / Reprise 26732
A four-CD boxed set of four raw, complete concerts: Stockholm 1967, Paris 1968, San Diego 1969, and Atlanta 1970. —*Jas Obrecht*

● **Ultimate Experience** / 1993 / MCA 10829
For an introduction to Hendrix, *The Ultimate Experience* is hard to beat. All of the Jimi Hendrix Experience albums are sampled from, in addition to a couple of live tracks and "Red House." The Experience albums are mandatory listening, but *The Ultimate Experience* is a terrific compilation. —*Stephen Thomas Erlewine*

○ **Jimi Hendrix: Blues** / 1994 / MCA 11060
While Hendrix remains most famous for his hard rock and psychedelic innovations, more than a third of his recordings were blues oriented. This CD contains 11 blues originals and covers, 8 of which were previously unreleased. Recorded between 1966 and 1970, they feature the master guitarist stretching the boundaries of electric blues in both live and studio settings. Besides several Hendrix blues-based originals, it includes covers of Albert King and Muddy Waters classics, as well as a 1967 acoustic version of his composition "Hear My Train a Comin'." —*Richie Unterberger*

Jimi Hendrix: Woodstock / 1994 / MCA
Hendrix's entire legendary set at Woodstock is presented for the first time on this set. High points are his incendiary reading of "The Star Spangled Banner" and moments where the playing really comes together. Though hardcore Hendrix fans may enjoy this good-sounding set, it's a lot of endless jamming and general noodling for even the average fan to ingest. Better live Hendrix sets can be found elsewhere, like *Jimi Hendrix in the West*. —*Rick Clark*

Don Henley

b. Jul. 22, 1947, Gilmer, TX
Vocals / Singer/songwriter, pop/rock

After disbanding the Eagles, Don Henley set out on a solo career that artistically eclipsed his previous group's achievements and at times rivaled their commercial success. Beginning with his first solo album, 1982's *I Can't Stand Still*, Henley's songwriting became leaner, making both his cutting political commentaries and bittersweet love songs sound more sincere. *Building the Perfect Beast*, with its layers of synthesizers, was even better. His command of melody and lyrics never got better than "The Boys of Summer" and "All She Wants to Do Is Dance." Its follow-up, 1989's *The End of the Innocence*, was his most ambitious record yet, with more subdued and longer songs that relied on lyrics more than melody.

After that, Henley sued Geffen in the early '90s, requesting the label to release him from his contract; it was eventually settled out of court and he was free to sign to another label. In 1994, Henley reunited with the Eagles for a summer tour. The band was expected to record after the tour was finished. — *Stephen Thomas Erlewine*

○ **I Can't Stand Still** / 1982 / Asylum 60048
A crisply produced and well-conceived debut, highlighted by "The Unclouded Day," "Johnny Can't Read," and "Dirty Laundry." — *John Floyd*

● **Building the Perfect Beast** / 1984 / David Geffen Co. 24026
His commercial breakthrough, defining his solo formula with songs like "The Boys of Summer" and "All She Wants to Do Is Dance," which respond to political and romantic breakdowns. — *John Floyd*

End of the Innocence / 1989 / David Geffen Co. 24217
A conceptual elaboration on his *Beast* album, this frames some wonderfully sarcastic rockers around "The Heart of the Matter," one of the finest ballads of the '80s. — *John Floyd*

Clarence Henry

Vocals, piano / R&B

A bit more eccentric and unpredictable than Fats Domino, not as contemporary or inventive as, say, Lee Dorsey, New Orleans pianist Clarence "Frogman" Henry's vocals were consistently warm and humorous, his recordings always polished. Scoring an unexpected novelty hit with "Ain't Got No Home" in 1956, Henry disappeared from the charts for four years before roaring back with two smashes in the early '60s: "(I Don't Know Why) But I Do" and "You Always Hurt the One You Love."

On his early-'60s singles, Clarence added beefier horn sections that occasionally reached back to the spirit of Dixieland. Crescent City legends like saxophonist Lee Allen and pianists Allen Toussaint and Paul Gayten cropped up on his sessions. When Henry traveled to Memphis to record, he was backed by the all-star band of Bill Justis (guitar), Boots Randolph (sax), and Floyd Cramer (piano). He went on to record a fair number of singles for Chess's Argo subsidiary in the relaxed New Orleans R&B style of his big hits. — *Richie Unterberger*

● **Ain't Got No Home: Best of Clarence "Frogman" Henry** / 1994 / MCA
Includes 18 of Henry's 1956-64 sides, most of which were previously unavailable on a U.S. album. — *Richie Unterberger*

Herman's Hermits

Group / British invasion, pop

Herman's Hermits was one of the most successful bands from the mid-'60s British Invasion, a product of producer Mickie Most's hit factory. During their four-year run on the charts (1964-1968), they scored 18 Top 40 hits. Nine of their 11 Top-Ten hits were consecutive. A couple of their biggest hits, "Mrs. Brown You've Got a Lovely Daughter" and "I'm Henry the VIII, I Am," were rearranged versions of old English pub songs. Most also maximized the band's older-audience appeal by having them do versions of Sam Cooke's "Wonderful World" and Frankie Ford's "Sea Cruise." Herman (born Peter Noone), the band's cute frontman, delivered the material with a light, likable quality. The Hermits' highly melodic, bouncy sound in many ways embodied the pop side of the British Invasion, as they were practically incapable of delivering rock with any conviction. "Can't You Hear My Heartbeat,"

"Silhouettes," "Just a Little Bit Better," "Listen People," "Dandy," "There's a Kind of Hush," "A Must to Avoid," and "Leaning on a Lamp Post" are just a few of their chart successes. — *Rick Clark*

● **Their Greatest Hits** / 1973 / ABKCO 4227
Basic hits package, but it's too brief and is under par soundwise. — *Jeff Tamarkin*

EP Collection / Jan. 1990 / See For Miles 284
This 22-track CD also features most of the major 'erman 'its, with a handful of obscurities thrown in. — *Jeff Tamarkin*

○ **Collection** / Jun. 1990 / Castle 246
All of the hits by Peter Noone and company, with room to spare for some nice surprises. — *Jeff Tamarkin*

Kristin Hersh

Vocals, guitar, singer-songwriter / Alternative, pop/rock

Kristin Hersh, the lead singer/songwriter of Throwing Muses, released her first solo album, the acoustic *Hips and Makers*, in early 1994. She followed it a couple of months later with the *Strings* EP, which featured versions of selected songs from the album recorded with a string quartet. After releasing the record, Hersh finished the next Throwing Muses record and did a solo tour. — *Stephen Thomas Erlewine*

● **Hips and Makers** / 1994 / Sire/Reprise
Taking a temporary break from Throwing Muses, Hersh turns in a stark, introspective acoustic solo album featuring some the best songs she has written in years. By and large, this is truly a solo album—nothing but Hersh and her guitar—but the occasional strings enhance the beautiful, melancholy music. "Your Ghost," featuring a guest appearance by Michael Stipe, is one of the most haunting tracks either artist has recorded. — *Stephen Thomas Erlewine*

○ **Strings** / 1994 / Sire
A beautiful EP featuring several tracks that didn't make *Hips and Makers*, as well as excellent re-recorded versions of several of the tracks that did. — *Stephen Thomas Erlewine*

John Hiatt

b. 1952, Indianapolis, IN
Vocals / Singer/songwriter, rock & roll, country-rock

One of the longest-gestating singer/songwriters of the last quarter century, and one of the best, John Hiatt left his native Indianapolis in 1970 (after high school) to go to Nashville and write songs. He signed up with Epic Records and made two albums, *Hangin' Around the Observatory* (1974) and *Overcoats* (1975), which demonstrated his powerful songwriting ability but didn't draw customers. He signed to MCA in Los Angeles in the late '70s and released *Slug Line* (1979) and *Two Bit Monsters* (1980), still without gaining a commercial following. Then came a stint on Geffen that produced *All of a Sudden* (1982), *Riding with the King* (1984), and *Warming Up to the Ice Age* (1985). All increased his visibility without really breaking through.

But in 1987, Hiatt went into the studio with old friends Ry Cooder and Nick Lowe, plus drummer Jim Keltner, and came out with his first chart album, *Bring the Family*. That album's two follow-ups, *Slow Turning* (1988) and *Stolen Moments* (1990), have demonstrated Hiatt's maturity as a writer and his flowering as a performer, resulting in some of the best singer/songwriter-rock of the era. In 1992, Hiatt again teamed with Cooder, Lowe, and Keltner, this time in a group called Little Village, which released a well-received debut album. After a short, tension-filled tour, the group disbanded. Hiatt released *Perfectly Good Guitar* the following year.

John Hiatt's songs have been covered by Rick Nelson, Dave Edmunds, the Searchers, Three Dog Night, Conway Twitty, Maria Muldaur, Rodney Crowell, Bob Dylan, the Neville Brothers, and many others. — *William Ruhlmann*

Hangin' Around the Observatory / 1974 / Epic 32688
John Hiatt mixed pop, folk, rock, R&B, country, and gospel on his debut album, immediately becoming an uncategorizable (and thus uncommercial) entity. Although this album was cut in Nashville, it owes more to Van Morrison than it does to Conway Twitty, and like the Belfast bluesman, Indianian Hiatt came to his influences somewhat second hand, however sincerely he evoked them. What he really was, of course, was a singer/songwriter—albeit not in a style easily recognizable in 1974. The title indicates

his position: Hiatt's songs show him an acute observer. But the performances require him to dig in, and though he does so with alacrity, the result is too diffuse. Nevertheless, Hiatt earned critical kudos for this album, and Three Dog Night (who knew good songwriting when they heard it) covered "Sure as I'm Sittin' Here," getting a Top-20 single out of it. — *William Ruhlmann*

○ **Slug Line** / 1979 / MCA 31358
Conventional wisdom at the time was that MCA Records had signed John Hiatt (who had languished without a record contract for four years) with the idea that he would be their Elvis Costello: a singer/songwriter in the fashionable punk/New Wave style. Certainly, Hiatt has stripped down and roughed up from his Epic records here, fronting a straight-ahead guitar rock band (capable, of course, of playing the obligatory reggae number), eschewing the stylistic diversity he reveled in before, and throwing out snappy, aphoristic lyrics in a highly processed voice. None of this quite turns him into Elvis Costello, though the mean streak he reveals would serve him well later. — *William Ruhlmann*

Two Bit Monsters / 1980 / MCA 31359
At the time of its release, *Two Bit Monsters* was perceived by critics who had caught up with John Hiatt on *Slug Line* as a less impressive follow-up to that record. In retrospect, it may be the better of the two albums, boasting an even more simplified musical approach and such notable songs (and future Rosanne Cash covers) as "Pink Bedroom" and "It Hasn't Happened Yet." Hiatt here was starting to emerge from the new-Elvis Costello tag that had been affixed to him with *Slug Line*, but his reviewers, however well-meaning, seemed determined to keep him in that category. (In any case, record buyers were paying little attention—
Slug Line was Hiatt's fourth straight album to miss the charts, and MCA dropped him as Epic had before.) — *William Ruhlmann*

○ **Riding with the King** / 1983 / David Geffen Co. 4017
One half of Hiatt's best Geffen album is played by him and Scott Matthews, while the other half features a band including Paul Carrack and Nick Lowe. But what matters is the songs: Hiatt's trenchant observations on life and love, especially the perceptive and painfully funny "She Loves the Jerk." — *William Ruhlmann*

Warming Up to the Ice Age / 1985 / David Geffen Co. 24055
Hiatt turned to veteran country producer Norbert Putnam here, but the result still rocked hard, with the occasional soul touch (notably those obnoxious thumb-struck bass lines that are so prevalent in '80s music). Highlights here are "The Usual," later covered by Bob Dylan, and "She Said the Same Things to Me." There is also an odd duet with Elvis Costello on the old Spinners hit "Living a Little, Laughing a Little" (try and tell them apart). Critics' darling or not, when this album went into the tank, Hiatt was dropped by Geffen—the third label to do so. — *William Ruhlmann*

★ **Bring the Family** / 1987 / A&M 5158
Not only is the small-band playing impeccable, but this is Hiatt's best collection of songs, which is saying a lot for so talented a writer. "Memphis in the Meantime" is a knowledgeable look at the fame game, "Your Dad Did" perfectly skewers domestic life, and "Have a Little Faith in Me" is a touching evocation of persistent love. And that's just three of them. — *William Ruhlmann*

○ **Slow Turning** / 1988 / A&M 5206
Only a notch below *Bring the Famil*, with such strong songs as "Drive South" and the wild criminals-on-the-loose song "Tennessee Plates." — *William Ruhlmann*

Stolen Moments / 1990 / A&M 5310
John Hiatt's highest charting album yet is a step down from the dizzy heights of *Bring the Family* and *Slow Turning*, as he abandons his more acid commentaries and turns in a self-deprecating set full of promises of reformation and celebrations of marriage and family life. But the observations remain acute, and Hiatt's singing (so much camouflaged in his early days) is becoming his secret weapon. — *William Ruhlmann*

Perfectly Good Guitar / 1993 / A&M
A more raucous, guitar-oriented and consistent album than *Stolen Moments*, *Perfectly Good Guitar* finds Hiatt turning up the amplifiers a touch and rocking out to yet another impressive set of original songs. — *Stephen Thomas Erlewine*

Jessie Hill

b. Dec. 9, 1932, New Orleans, LA

Vocals / R&B
Loose and wild, Jessie Hill cut a New Orleans party classic with his crazed "Ooh Poo Pah Doo." The two-sided single, a 1960 Allen Toussaint production on Minit, has Hill shouting the nearly unintelligible lyrics over a strong Crescent City groove, while the flip is an instrumental featuring saxist David Lastie. Hill cut several more boisterous outings with Toussaint at the helm before heading to the West Coast, where he made a disappointing album for Blue Thumb in 1970. — *Bill Dahl*

● **Golden Classics** / Collectables 5164
Good-time New Orleans R&B from the early '60s, produced by prolific pianist Allen Toussaint. — *Bill Dahl*

Peter Himmelman

Vocals, guitar, keyboard, harmonica, percussion / Singer/songwriter, pop/rock
Minnesota native Peter Himmelman was the leader of a rock/pop quintet called Sussman Lawrence, which made two independent albums in the early '80s and earned him comparisons to such new wave singer/songwriters as Elvis Costello and Joe Jackson. The group became Himmelman's backup band for the release of his debut album, *This Father's Day* (1986), which earned him a contract with Island Records. He followed with *Gematria* (1987), *Synesthesia* (1989), and *Strength to Strength* (1991). By the last release, he had moved to Epic Records. — *William Ruhlmann*

● **Synesthesia** / 1989 / Island 842837
Inventive drum tracks highlight Himmelman's spare arrangements of songs that express a personal, poetic world-view full of struggle and vulnerability. — *William Ruhlmann*

○ **From Strength to Strength** / 1991 / Epic 47073
"Woman with the Strength of 10,000 Men" is Himmelman's song of romantic devotion, but it's only one of the driven performances on an album whose song titles—"Crushed," "Midnight Walk in the Ruins"—express its sense of anguish and desperation. — *William Ruhlmann*

Flown This Acid World / Jun. 1992 / Epic 52588
Peter Himmelman is difficult to pigeonhole—rock, pop, and acoustic/folk influences are all present, although none of these categories tell the whole story. Himmelman writes rich, memorable songs which he performs with conviction and a warm but intense vocal delivery. Himmelman's no poet, but he finds original ways to strike some universal chords; he's especially adept at dissecting decaying relationships. Instrumentally, he's just as comfortable on the acoustic guitar-and-mandolin-driven title track, the jangly, electric "Beneath the Damage and the Dust," and the piano ballad "Things to Say." Himmelman has a talent for zeroing in on some of the more unpleasant things about ourselves and society coupled with an equal ability to rise above, while transporting the listener with him. — *Roch Parisien*

His Name Is Alive

Group / Alternative pop/rock
Based in songwriter/guitarist Warren Defever's basement in the Detroit suburb Livonia, His Name Is Alive is an ethereal, yet noisy, experimental rock band that manages to have a generous amount of melody and pop sense in their music. Defever's sonic collages are complemented by the smooth, classically trained vocals of Karin Oliver. Since the band's 1990 debut, Defever's vision has become clearer and more expansive, culminating in 1993's *Mouth by Mouth*. — *Stephen Thomas Erlewine*

Livonia / 1990 / Rykodisc 10244
Unique, quirky effort that transcends its obvious influences—and not without a fair bit of humor. — *Steve Aldrich*

○ **Home Is in Your Head** / 1991 / Rykodisc 20245
More ethereal female vocals married to Robert Fripp-like guitars in a dream state. — *Steve Aldrich*

● **Mouth by Mouth** / 1993 / Warner Brothers 45214
Although *Mouth by Mouth* is His Name Is Alive's most accessible record so far, the band's guitar and tape experiments remain doggedly antimainstream. "Baby Fish Mouth," the breezily melodic pop song that begins the album, is easily their best chance at expanding their cult, but, as should be expected, it wasn't the first single. "Can't Go Wrong Without You," the most disturbing thing they have ever recorded, with a chillingly eerie melody and scattershot feedback guitar, was the choice. The rest

of *Mouth by Mouth* falls somewhere in between, making it *His Name Is Alive*'s best album and a good showcase of their many possibilities. —*Stephen Thomas Erlewine*

Robyn Hitchcock

b. 1952
Vocals / Alternative pop/rock
British singer/songwriter Robyn Hitchcock built up a large cult following and critical acclaim for his highly poetic, if somewhat obscure, songs—especially after his work began to be more generally available in the United States after 1985. Born in London, Hitchcock formed the Soft Boys with Andy Metcalfe and Morris Windsor in 1976. The band continued until 1981, when Hitchcock released his first solo album, *Black Snake Diamond Role*. This was followed by *Groovy Decay* (1982) and *I Often Dream of Trains* (1984). In 1984 Hitchcock formed a backing band called the Egyptians, consisting of Metcalfe, Windsor, Otis Horns Fletcher, and Roger Jackson, and they began playing concerts for the first time in 2 1/2 years. The first recorded output of this band, and the first U.S. Hitchcock album, was *Fegmania!* (1985). It was followed by the live album *Gotta Let This Hen Out!* (1985), *Element of Light* (1986), and a compilation called *Invisible Hitchcock* (1986), all of which built up Hitchcock's following to the point that he was signed by A&M Records, resulting in his major-label debut *Globe of Frogs* (1988), which reached number 111. *Queen Elvis*, Hitchcock's second A&M album, reached number 159 in 1989. He then made *Eye* (1990), an acoustic solo album released on Twin/Tone Records. The following year, Hitchcock and the Egyptians released *Perspex Island*, which contained the alternative radio hit, "So You Think You're in Love." *Respect* (1993) returned to a more abstract pop sound, which meant that he lost most of the audience he had gained with the previous album. —*William Ruhlmann*

○ **Fegmania!** / Mar. 1985 / Slash 25316
Hitchcock's first record with the Egyptians (the Soft Boys reconstituted), *Fegmania* is a strong pop record that plays down his derivative Syd Barrettisms. Snappy, tuneful, and to the point, it's Hitchcock pursuing his muse succinctly, and succeeding. —*John Dougan*

○ **Gotta Let This Hen Out** / Apr. 1985 / Combat 8056
A fine live album that serves as a career overview. Because the band rocks more than usual, even the grim and pretentious numbers sound less irritating. A great sampling from an inconsistent performer. —*John Dougan*

● **Globe of Frogs** / 1988 / A&M 5182
Hitchcock has a considerable catalog, but neophytes might wish to begin with this relatively recent collection, which finds him playing in a folk-rock style while singing highly imagistic lyrics, the tone of which can be suggested by noting some of the titles: "Tropical Fish Mandala," "Sleeping with Your Devil Mask," and "The Shapes Between Us Turn into Animals." Hitchcock is an original lyricist, well worth hearing, but an acquired taste. —*William Ruhlmann*

○ **Queen Elvis** / 1989 / A&M 5241
Hitchcock earned some radio play for this album's lead-off track, "Madonna of the Wasps," which, like several tracks here, features the distinctive guitar of R.E.M.'s Peter Buck. —*William Ruhlmann*

○ **Perspex Island** / 1991 / A&M 5368
While it's a little uneven, *Perspex Island* contains Robyn Hitchcock's best pure pop single, the minor classic "So You Think You're in Love." —*Stephen Thomas Erlewine*

Respect / Feb. 23, 1993 / A&M 64
Hitchcock uses conventional pop structures as a launching pad for whimsical, sometimes abstract, and often wildly imaginative flights. *Respect* is true to form, although his lyrics are at their most accessible here. There's a dark side to Hitchcock's writing—death is a frequent theme—though usually leavened with keen wit. Instrumentally, Hitchcock's layers of acoustic and electric guitars are accompanied not only by bass, keyboards, and drums, but also—when called upon—by water jug, cheese grater, and frying pans. —*Roch Parisien*

Allan Holdsworth

b. Aug. 6, 1948, Bradford, England
Guitar / Fusion, progressive rock

A British, electric guitar, fusion virtuoso who began playing with the progressive rock bands Gong and Soft Machine in the '70s, and later a sideman with the Tony Williams Lifetime, Bill Bruford, and Chuck Mangione. Holdsworth's precise melodic style draws much inspiration from jazz horn phrasing. His most recent albums feature the Synth-axe, a guitarlike synthesizer controller. —*Scott Bultman*

Velvet Darkness / 1977 / CBS 45482
First solo album from this guitarist from such bands as Gong, Soft Machine, and the Tony Williams Lifetime. Includes several excellent acoustic guitar pieces. —*Paul Kohler*

● **Metal Fatigue** / 1985 / Enigma 73222
A terrific album by a most innovative guitarist and composer. First-class. —*Paul Kohler*

I.O.U. / 1985 / Enigma 73252
Brilliant compositions and musicianship on this independent release. Vocal and instrumental material with outstanding guitar solos, and P. Williams on vocals. Recorded on a barge! —*Paul Kohler*

Atavachron / 1986 / Enigma 73203
Atavachron was a landmark album in the history of modern rock guitar instrumentals, because it marked the first time Holdsworth used a Synth-axe guitar synthesizer. Incredible sounds and textures. —*Paul Kohler*

Sand / 1987 / Restless 72593
Instrumental album featuring more of the synth-guitar and regular guitar. Beautiful compositions and fiery guitar solos, with Chad Wackerman and Jimmy Johnson. —*Paul Kohler*

○ **Secrets** / 1989 / Intima 73328
A masterpiece from start to finish. Nice chord changes and wonderful solos. The album includes a mix of guitar and Synth-axe. —*Paul Kohler*

Hole

Group / Alternative rock
Courtney Love's notorious public persona has overshadowed her band Hole's music, which is a shame because it is some of the finest aggressive punk-inspired rock of the early '90s. When their first album, *Pretty on the Inside*, was released in 1991, the band was completely abrasive, violent, and uncompromising, rocketing through such post-hardcore terrors as "Teenage Whore" and "Garbageman." Underneath their massive roar were Love's well-crafted songs, which combined her brutal lyrics with a concise pop structure. The band was critically acclaimed, especially in England, and Love was established as a promising, talented artist.

Then, in early 1992, she married Kurt Cobain, the lead singer/songwriter of Nirvana. For a couple of months, the couple were the king and queen of the new rock world. Soon that world came crashing in. Cobain became addicted to heroin, and the couple fought to keep custody of their baby after a piece in *Vanity Fair* accused Love of shooting heroin while pregnant, charges which she vehemently denied. By 1993, their private world had settled down somewhat.

Part way through 1993, Love reassembled Hole, which had undergone several line-up changes in the two years since their debut. Love's new songs were much more pop-oriented, without losing any of the hard-edged honesty of her previous material. Hole was set to release their second album, *Live Through This*, in April of 1994. Advance word on the album was overwhelmingly positive: For the first time, many of the journalists who had called Love a gold digger were admitting that she was talented. Four days before the album was released, Kurt Cobain's body was discovered in the couple's Seattle home; he had died of a self-inflicted shotgun wound three days before. Cobain's suicide sent Love into seclusion after she tape-recorded a reading of his suicide note.

Two months after Cobain's death, Hole's bassist Kristin Ejlleund was found dead of a heroin overdose in a Seattle apartment. Love announced that the band would continue. Two months later, Hole began touring again, with Courtney Love making special appearances on certain Lollapalooza dates. They embarked on a full US tour in October. —*Stephen Thomas Erlewine*

○ **Pretty on the Inside** / 1991 / Caroline 1710

Hole's debut album is a brutal, scathing record, filled with primal guitars and gut-wrenching vocals. All of the noise and angst is tied together by the exceptional songwriting of Courtney Love, who always manages to provide a reason for anger, whether it's through her lyrics or her music. —*Stephen Thomas Erlewine*

● **Live Through This** / 1994 / David Geffen Company 24631
On their second album, Hole's sound matures without losing its vital edge. Love's songwriting is more melodic and succinct, which makes the band's raging guitars and naked honesty all the more effective. —*Stephen Thomas Erlewine*

The Hollies
b. 1962, Manchester, England
Group / British invasion, pop/rock
The Hollies' string of hits through much of the '60s is one of the most impressive of that decade. Like countless other British beat groups, they were drawn at the outset to American R&B, but their trademark vocal style from the Clarke, Hicks, and Nash front line, coupled with a unique and distinctive rhythm section, caused the Hollies to pull away from the pack quickly. Drawing on the songs of Graham Gouldman (and ultimately their own), the group would reach its creative peak prior to losing the services of Graham Nash. The Nash-less Hollies continued through the '70s, charting huge international hits and creating worthy albums. Still, the Hollies of the mid '60s contributed some of the most vital pop music of the era. —*Steve Aldrich*

● **All Time Greatest Hits** / 1990 / Curb 77377
A 12-track all-singles compilation that includes the Hollies' biggest U.S. hits on both Imperial ("Bus Stop," "Stop, Stop, Stop") and Epic Records from 1964 to 1975. —*William Ruhlmann*

● **Epic Anthology** / 1990 / Epic 46161
Epic Anthology: From the Original Master Tapes! is a 20-track compilation that picks up when the Hollies signed with Epic in 1967 and presents their biggest hits plus select album tracks and rarities through 1975. Includes "Carrie-Anne," "He Ain't Heavy, He's My Brother," "Long Cool Woman (in a Black Dress)," and "The Air That I Breathe." —*William Ruhlmann*

○ **Thirtieth Anniversary Collection** / 1993 / EMI America 99917
This three-CD, 57-track boxed set does a good, if imperfect, job of encapsulating the legacy of one of the British invasion's better bands. This includes all of the Hollies' singles—A and B sides—from the '60s, as well as five previously unreleased tunes. The hits—"I'm Alive," "Bus Stop," "On a Carousel," and others—contain some of the finest beat harmonizing not done by the Beatles. The B sides—many of them originals, some of them never before available in the United States—are often nearly equal in quality to the classic material. The compilation wisely touches upon only the essentials of their post-1970 singles ("Long Cool Woman" and "The Air That I Breathe"), and unwisely closes with three forgettable tracks from the early '90s. Don't be misled into thinking that this box contains all of their best material—their early albums, though inconsistent, featured a fair number of strong original tunes that remain little known beyond collector circles. It's a good set, with an excellent booklet and thoroughly annotated discography, but it's not definitive. —*Richie Unterberger*

Brenda Holloway
b. Jun. 21, 1946, Atascadero, CA
Vocals / Motown, soul
This sultry '60s addition to the Motown roster waxed several memorable ballads for the firm. One of Motown's first Los Angeles signings, Holloway's Tamla debut, "Every Little Bit Hurts," was a soaring ballad that sailed up the pop charts in 1964, while Smokey Robinson wrote and produced Holloway's 1965 smash "When I'm Gone." The voluptuous vocalist opened several concerts for the Beatles on their 1965 U.S. tour, including their Shea Stadium show. In 1967 Holloway cowrote and recorded the original version of "You've Made Me So Very Happy," later a gigantic hit for Blood, Sweat & Tears. —*Bill Dahl*

Every Little Bit Hurts / 1964 / Motown 5242
The title track was one of Motown's grittiest singles ever, but it didn't put Brenda Holloway into the spotlight she deserved. Her sound and style were so gospel-tinged and powerful that she was out of place on a label that wanted more polished, sophisticated material. This album had some marvelous classics, and stands as Holloway's finest. While Motown had many other superb soul

artists, Holloway may have been one who'd have done better at Stax or any of the Southern outlets who specialized in rawer, "deep" country and gospel-tinged productions. —*Ron Wynn*

● **Greatest Hits & Rare Classics** / 1991 / Motown 5485
Brenda Holloway was Motown's second big solo female star, but she spent even less time at the label than Mary Wells. A hard-edged, gospel-tinged belter, Holloway scored two Top-20 hits in the mid '60s with "Every Little Bit Hurts" and "When I'm Gone," and her single "You've Made Me So Very Happy" was later a huge smash for Blood, Sweat & Tears. Holloway lasted on Motown until 1967, then departed after becoming a born-again Christian. She later returned as a background vocalist for Joe Cocker. This album includes her biggest singles for Tamla, plus some other good, though not necessarily "classic," '60s soul numbers. —*Ron Wynn*

Buddy Holly (Charles Hardin Holley)
b. Sep. 7, 1936, Lubbock, TX, **d.** Feb. 3, 1959, Mason City, IA
Vocals, guitar / Rock & roll
An enormously important and influential performer, Holly started out in his native Texas doing country music with boyhood friend Bob Montgomery, eventually adding R&B numbers to the set list after meeting Elvis Presley. He recorded early rockabilly sides in Nashville, but success didn't come until he formed the Crickets and recorded in Norman Petty's studios, producing the number-one hit "That'll Be the Day" in 1957. Holly and Petty continued to experiment in the studio, utilizing different forms of echo ("Peggy Sue"), double-tracking ("Words of Love"), and close-miking techniques, now commonplace in the industry. After his death, much of Holly's earlier pre-Crickets music was overdubbed by Petty, using the Fireballs to keep up with the fan demand for more product. Though his moment in the spotlight lasted barely 18 months, and the movie version of his life story only got it about half right, Buddy Holly's music still sounds fresh and continues to influence to this day. —*Cub Koda*

☆ **Complete Buddy Holly** / 1979 / MCA 80000
Contains every note Buddy Holly every recorded. This six-LP box is essential for hardcore fans. —*John Floyd*

○ **For the First Time Anywhere** / 1983 / MCA 31048
Powerful, undubbed rockabilly sides. —*Cub Koda*

★ **From the Original Master Tapes** / 1985 / MCA 5540
A 20-track best-of with superlative sound. —*Cub Koda*

○ **Something Special from Buddy Holly** / 1986 / Rollercoaster 2013
An import of more undubbed material from 1956. —*Cub Koda*

☆ **Buddy Holly Collection** / 1993 / MCA
For those seeking a more comprehensive CD collection than *From the Original Master Tapes*, the 50 song, two-disc *Buddy Holly Collection* suits the bill. All of his big hits are included here, along with many forgotten treasures. —*Stephen Thomas Erlewine*

Hollywood Flames
Group / Doo-wop
A long-lasting Los Angeles doo-wop aggregation with a very fluid personnel roster. Bobby Day was one of the group's founders in 1950, and they recorded prolifically for Hollywood, Specialty, Lucky, Swingtime, Money, and other firms before cutting their one major hit, the rocking "Buzz Buzz Buzz," in 1957 for Ebb Records. Earl Nelson, who was later half of Bob and Earl, sang lead on the tune, and some of their subsequent Ebb 45s were rocking novelties. Day went on to solo success with "Rockin' Robin," and the group managed one more chart item, "Gee," for Chess in 1961, with Donald Height as lead. —*Bill Dahl*

● **Hollywood Flames** / 1992 / Specialty 7021
Featuring all 27 tracks the group cut for Specialty and EBB, *Hollywood Flames* is the perfect introduction to the band. —*AMG*

○ **Buzz Buzz Buzz** / Specialty 2166
Rockers and doo-wop from this respected West Coast '50s R&B vocal group, including the Top Ten "Buzz Buzz Buzz." —*Bill Dahl*

Holsapple-Stamey
Group / Power-pop
Peter Holsapple and Chris Stamey were two of the principal singer/songwriters in the alternative power-pop band, the dB's.

Much of the music from this collaboration is thoughtfully upbeat, guitar-driven folk-pop, with a few stylistic tips of the hat to the Byrds, Big Star, and mid-period Beatles. —*Rick Clark*

○ **Mavericks** / 1991 / Rhino 70795
A charming low-key power-pop effort, "Geometry" is a perfect Gary Lewis & the Playboys-style sendup. "Angels" is pure power-pop magic. The softer acoustic numbers, "Close Your Eyes" and "Anymore," recall the duo's work on Repercussions. —*Rick Clark*

Honey Cone

Group / Soul
Signing to Holland-Dozier-Holland's Hot Wax label, Honey Cone came together in Los Angeles in 1969 and immediately rolled out one hit after another in a slickly produced, lighthearted soul style. All three members were veterans of the West Coast studio scene, and their experience paid off when "Want Ads" and "Stick-Up" proved back-to-back R&B chart-toppers in 1970, with "Want Ads" also pacing the pop lists. Both hits, along with the Latin-tinged "One Monkey Don't Stop No Show," were cowritten by coproducer General Johnson, who was taking a breather from his frontman role with Chairmen of the Board. —*Bill Dahl*

● **Greatest Hits** / 1990 / HDH 3902
All their hits. —*Richard Pack*

The Honeydrippers

Group / Rock & roll
The Honeydrippers were an ad hoc group put together by ex-Led Zeppelin lead singer Robert Plant and Atlantic Records executive Ahmet Ertegun to record a mini-album of '50s and '60s oldies in 1984. —*William Ruhlmann*

○ **Honeydrippers, Vol. 1** / 1984 / Es Paranza 90220
This five-song EP features Robert Plant singing such oldies as the hit remake of "Sea of Love," with a backup that includes Nile Rodgers, Jeff Beck, and Jimmy Page. —*William Ruhlmann*

The Hoodoo Gurus

Group / Alternative pop/rock, power-pop
The Australian kings of garage Anglo-pop/rock, the Hoodoo Gurus have provided the '80s alternative music scene with a handful of fine, trashy, tuneful classics in "Bittersweet," "Poison Pen," "Like Wow—Wipeout," "What's My Scene," "Come Anytime," and "Where Nowhere Is," among others. They incorporated the grunge of the Cramps with the '60s melodic pop smarts of groups like the Kinks and the Turtles. —*Rick Clark*

○ **Stoneage Romeos** / 1984 / A&M 5012
Their debut effort is '60s garage-punk heaven. Highlights include the raveups "Let's All Turn On" and "Tojo"; "Dig It Up," a Cramps-style rocker; "My Girl," a slice of '60s girl/boy guitar-pop; and the grunge-ola "I Was a Kamikaze Pilot." Highly recommended. —*Rick Clark*

● **Mars Needs Guitars** / 1985 / Elektra 60485
This is the album that gave this Aussie band their break on the American college radio market, thanks to some classic tracks: "Bittersweet," "Poison Pen," "Death Defying," and "Like Wow—Wipeout." The production is a little unfocused, lacking some of the punch the material demands and the trashy sparks of *Stoneage Romeos*. Nevertheless, the songs reflect considerable growth in the band's vision. —*Rick Clark*

○ **Blow Your Cool!** / 1987 / Elektra 60728
The Gurus alternate between appealingly tuneful updates of Turtles-style guitar-pop ("Good Times," "What's My Scene") and wild workouts like "Where Nowhere Is" and "Hell for Leather." The anthemic "I Was the One" is a standout. The Bangles assist on backup harmonies on this effort. All in all, a solid effort. —*Rick Clark*

Magnum Cum Louder / 1989 / RCA 9781
The Gurus continue their once-every-two-year release schedule with this consistent effort that showcases vocalist Dave Faulkner's solid songwriting. "Come Anytime" is primo Gurus, and the moody "Shadow Me" is also a highlight. Even though *Magnum Cum Louder* doesn't shine as brightly as previous efforts, it's still a stronger album than many efforts by groups mining this genre. —*Rick Clark*

Kinky / 1991 / RCA 3009

Kinky blasts out of the gate with pedal-to-the-metal speed, on the hard rocking putdown of substance abuse, "Head in the Sand." No doubt, the inebriated fraternity crowd that worships this band will appreciate Faulkner's sentiments. All in all, this is one of the band's very best releases. *Kinky* portrays a band straddling their playful '60s garage rock esthetic with issues of adulthood, all the while playing as fiercely as ever. —*Rick Clark*

The Hooters

Group / Pop/rock
This regionally popular Philadelphia band, formed in 1978, incorporated folk, ska, reggae, and Heartland rock into a rather mainstream sound. During the mid '80s, the Hooters enjoyed a streak of hits and MTV exposure with "All You Zombies," "And We Danced," "Day by Day," "Where Do the Children Go," "Johnny B," and "Satellite."

By the end of the decade, their popularity had declined, yet the Hooters continued to tour and record, with faithful support from their fans, even as the band moved away from the slick pop that distinguished their biggest hits. —*Rick Clark*

● **Nervous Night** / 1985 / Columbia 39912
Fairly mainstream pop-rock debut, which produced their four biggest hit singles. —*Rick Clark*

Bruce Hornsby & the Range

b. Nov. 23, 1954, Williamsburg, VA
Group / Pop/rock
Hornsby was born in Williamsburg, VA, and grew up in that combination college town and tourist center, later attending the University of Miami and the Berklee School of Music. He then spent years playing in bars and sending demo tapes to record companies. In 1980 he and his brother (and songwriting partner) John Hornsby moved to Los Angeles, where they spent three years writing for 20th Century Fox. There Bruce Hornsby met Huey Lewis, who would eventually produce him and record his material. Hornsby finally signed his band, the Range, to RCA in 1985.

Their debut album, *The Way It Is*, was released in August 1986. It eventually produced three Top-20 hits, the biggest of which was the socially conscious "The Way It Is," which featured Hornsby's characteristically melodic right-hand piano runs. The album hit number 3, stayed in the charts almost a year and a half, and sold two million copies. Hornsby and the Range won the Best New Artist Grammy Award for 1986.

Hornsby's second album, *Scenes from the Southside*, was not as successful as his debut—though it hit number five, sold a million copies, and produced the number-five single "The Valley Road." Hornsby also began to make his mark as a songwriter for others: Huey Lewis had a hit with his "Jacob's Ladder," as did Don Henley with "The End of the Innocence."

Hornsby's third album, *A Night on the Town* (1990), found him trying to break out of his signature sound into other areas. It was less successful than its predecessors, but, along with the pianist's extensive session work, it signaled his determination to tackle new musical challenges. —*William Ruhlmann*

● **Way It Is** / 1986 / RCA 5904
One of the best collections of new songs released in the 1980s, performed to perfection by a versatile band led by a seasoned (if new to the listener) artist. The songs provide an American panorama, in terms both of landscape and social mores. This is smart, compassionate music for thinking adults . . . and you can dance to it too. Includes "The Way It Is" and "Mandolin Rain." —*William Ruhlmann*

○ **Scenes from the Southside** / 1988 / RCA 6686
The Way It Is, part two, featuring some wonderful story songs, not only on the hits "Jacob's Ladder" and "The Valley Road" but also "Defenders of the Flag" and "The Road Not Taken." Hornsby continues to mine a rich American vein on this album. —*William Ruhlmann*

Night on the Town, A / 1990 / RCA 2041
Hornsby's third album found him trying to break out of his signature sound into other areas. It was less successful than its predecessors, but, along with the pianist's extensive session work, it signaled his determination to tackle new musical challenges. —*William Ruhlmann*

Harbor Lights / 1993 / RCA 66114

Bruce Hornsby has dumped the Range, with barely any public notice. Yet there *is* a difference in the music: More than any other Hornsby record, *Harbor Lights* is about playing. It is short on memorable songs, heavy on jazz improvisations. In short, Hornsby has taken the chops he has always had, honed them during his live shows with the Grateful Dead, and applied what he learned to adult contemporary radio. —*Stephen Thomas Erlewine*

Hot Tuna

Group / Rock & roll, blues-rock, folk-rock
Hot Tuna (formed in October 1970) was an offshoot group led by Jefferson Airplane guitarist Jorma Kaukonen and bassist Jack Casady. The group's self-titled debut was a live recording that covered versions of old blues songs by Rev. Gary Davis and Jelly Roll Morton, as well as some originals that became required listening for those inclined toward the Airplane's or Grateful Dead's more laidback material.

By the third album, *Burgers,* Hot Tuna increasingly drew upon their rock background, performing extended jams built around Casady's wide, lumbering bass sound and Kaukonen's tastefully texturous lead work. Even though the band seemed perpetually stuck in medium tempo, they were quite capable of generating sparks, which made them a popular concert draw for a number of years. —*Rick Clark*

○ **Hot Tuna** / 1970 / RCA 3864
This live set includes some solid originals, in particular the instrumental "Mann's Fate" and versions of tunes by Mississippi John Hurt and Rev. Gary Davis. Exceptionally tasteful acoustic guitar work by Jorma Kaukonen. Highlights are "Hesitation Blues" and "Death Don't Have No Mercy." —*Rick Clark*

● **Burgers** / 1972 / RCA 2591
On this third effort, Hot Tuna electrified its initial acoustic country-blues direction and turned in some blistering jams with "Sea Child" and "Sunny Day Strut." "Water Song" is a gorgeous instrumental, featuring some wonderful acoustic guitar and electric bass interplay. David Crosby guests on background vocals. "Keep on Truckin'" was a moderate underground FM hit. —*Rick Clark*

Hothouse Flowers

Group / Pop/rock
At the end of the '80s, Ireland's Hothouse Flowers was one of the most popular groups on the British Isles, with their larger-than-life blend of U2 and Van Morrison. Liam O'Maonlai fronts the band with a commanding, passionate vocal presence, but sometimes their overwrought mega-production sound tends to reduce them to a variation of *Commitments*-style soul. Their first album, *People,* contains some fine moments with "Don't Go," "Forgiven," "Yes I Was," and the single "I'm Sorry." —*Rick Clark*

● **People** / 1988 / London 828101
Irish sensation shoots for the big mystical picture, not unlike U2, but musically owes more to Van Morrison and various R&B rock influences. This debut is fairly solid from start to finish. Highlights are the prayerful "Forgiven," the affirmative "Yes I Was," and the exuberant hit single "I'm Sorry." —*Rick Clark*

Housemartins

Group / Alternative pop/rock
They signed to the independent Go! Discs label in October 1985. Shortly after, vocalist Norman Cook replaced Key. The group's first substantial success came with its third single, "Happy Hour," which reached number three in the United Kingdom in June 1986. The Housemartins' debut album, *London 0 Hull 4,* reached the same position in the album chart. More success followed with the singles "Think for a Minute" and the chart-topping cover of Isley-Jasper-Isley's "Caravan of Love."

In 1987 the Housemartins continued to hit in Britain, while suffering adverse press and personnel conflicts that eventually convinced them to split in 1988. They released two more albums, *The People Who Grinned Themselves to Death* (1987) and *Now That's What I Call Quite Good* (1988), the latter a double-disc compilation that has not been released in the United States. Heaton went on to form the Beautiful South. —*William Ruhlmann*

● **London 0 Hull 4** / 1986 / Elektra 60501
The Housemartins had a bouncy pop-rock sound that was reminiscent of the British beat groups of the mid '60s. This album is full of catchy tunes, though the lyrics are sometimes more serious than the music might suggest. —*William Ruhlmann*

○ **People Who Grinned Themselves to Death** / 1987 / Elektra 60761
Not quite on par with their debut, their second album nevertheless contains some bright moments of bouncy Brit-pop. The band takes a more abstract lyrical approach, but the song craftsmanship can't be denied. The band broke up shortly after the album's completion. —*Chris Woodstra*

○ **Now That's What I Call Quite Good** / 1988 / Go! Discs
A solid collection of singles, B-sides, and rarities released only in the United Kingdom. This combined with the two proper albums represents nearly all of the band's recorded output. Clocking in at over 70 minutes, this isn't a bad place to start, though the actual albums should be heard as well. —*Chris Woodstra*

Whitney Houston

b. Aug. 9, 1963, Newark, NJ
Vocals / Soul, urban R&B, dance-pop, pop
Coming from a solid musical background, this daughter of soul singer Cissy Houston and cousin of Dionne Warwick debuted in 1985. Her first album, *Whitney Houston,* was the first by a woman in *Billboard* chart history to enter at number one. It went on to sell 14 million copies. She scored heavily on MTV with classy videos, helping to break the "color barrier" originally knocked down by Michael Jackson. Her second album, *Whitney,* was just as popular, scoring seven consecutive number ones in the United States, shattering the previous record held by the Beatles.

After the disappointing performance of her third album, *I'll Be Your Baby Tonight,* Houston rocketed back to the top of the charts in late 1992 with the soundtrack from her first movie, *The Bodyguard.* The love theme from the movie, a version of Dolly Parton's *I Will Always Love You,* broke all previous sales and airplay records, becoming the biggest single in pop music history. It also won her an almost innumerable amount of awards, including several Grammy awards.

With pure pop music melded to stunning beauty, Houston's star shines bright whether she is singing ballads, uptempo dance material, the national anthem, or cola commercials. Almost ten years after her first album, she is one of the biggest stars in pop music. —*Cub Koda and Stephen Thomas Erlewine*

● **Whitney Houston** / 1985 / Arista 8212
The legend of Whitney Houston began with this self-titled album. It marked her shift away from the experimental songs she did with the group Material, and a move into heavily produced, very slick urban contemporary and adult pop. Though Houston had learned her craft working in New York nightclubs and singing in a Baptist church in Newark, she was now steered into radio-friendly ballads that emphasized style over substance. The album did yield her an unprecedented string of number-one hits, but "Saving All My Love for You" and "How Will I Know" create an impression of an incredibly talented vocalist that uses only a minimum of her skills. It also contained one of her few legitimate soul workouts in "The Greatest Love of All." —*Ron Wynn*

○ **Whitney** / 1987 / Arista 8405
Whitney Houston became an international star with this album. It sold more than 13 million copies around the world, yielded a string of number of hit singles across the board, like "How Will I Know," "Saving All My Love for You" and "You Give Good Love," and established Houston as the era's top female star. She's since gone on to more than solidify that status with other hit albums and a budding film career. While this is a far cry from soul, it's the ultimate in polished, super-produced urban contemporary material. —*Ron Wynn*

I'm Your Baby Tonight / 1990 / Arista 8616
While Houston's voice always provides some interesting listening, this is a somewhat disappointing release with very few memorable songs. While she attempts to make a larger foray into dance music, she fails to make the crossover impact of such artists as Mariah Carey and Taylor Dayne. The two high points she does reach on this album come in the form of ballads—the uplifting tale of another's love being enough to provide happiness in "All the Man That I Need" and the powerful verses surrounding a love lost through one's own devices in "Miracle." —*Ashley S. Battel*

Human League

Group / New wave, dance-pop
The Human League scored a number of hits in the '80s that
crossed the line between post-new wave rock and dance-pop,
though that was a very different style from the music the group
played at first. The Human League was formed in Sheffield,
England, in 1977 by synthesizer players Martin Ware and Ian
Marsh, along with Addy Newton and singer Philip Oakey.
Newton was soon replaced by Adrian Wright, and the lineup held
for the first two Human League albums, *Reproduction* (1979) and
Travelogue (1980).

Ware and Marsh left the Human League in October 1980, subsequently forming Heaven 17. Oakey and Wright recruited bassist
Ian Burden and backup singers Joanne Catherall and Susanne
Sulley, resulting in a much more pop-sounding version of the
band. Synth player Jo Callis was also added to the group.

The Human League's third album, *Dare*, was its commercial
and international breakthrough. Released in October 1981 in the
United Kingdom and in February 1982 in the United States, it
went to number one in England and number three in the States
largely on the strength of the single "Don't You Want Me," which
topped the charts in both countries. Subsequent hits in 1982 and
1983 included "(Keep Feeling) Fascination" and "Mirror Man."

Hysteria (1984), was far less successful, and the group ago-
nized over a follow-up. *Crash* appeared in 1986, produced by
Jimmy Jam and Terry Lewis (responsible for Janet Jackson's
Control, among other hits). Largely a studio creation, it was nev-
ertheless successful, producing the number-one hit "Human." The
Human League's sixth album, *Romantic?*, was released in 1990.
— William Ruhlmann

○ **Dare** / 1981 / A&M 4892
Martin Rushent's fresh, clean production keeps the synthesized
music from being too cluttered, while Philip Oakey's voice is used
for its self-consciously melodramatic effect and contrasted with
the untrained singing of Joanne Catherall and Susanne Sulley.
The hits are "Don't You Want Me" and (in England) "The Sound
of the Crowd," "Love Action (I Believe in Love)," and "Open Your
Heart," but the album also works as a coherent unit. *— William
Ruhlmann*

● **Greatest Hits** / 1988 / A&M 5227
This well-chosen best-of contains the Human League's U.K.and
U.S. hits from 1978 ("Being Boiled") to 1986, including the chart-
toppers "Don't You Want Me" and "Human" and such nonalbum
singles as "(Keep Feeling) Fascination" and "Mirror Man." It's a
study in '80s dance-pop. *— William Ruhlmann*

Humble Pie

Group / Hard rock
When Humble Pie was formed in 1969, there was much excite-
ment about the possibilities. After all, its founding members
came from very popular English bands. Humble Pie comprised
vocalist and guitarist Steve Marriott, previously with the Small
Faces; Greg Ridley, former bassist for Spooky Tooth; Peter
Frampton, the Herd's frontman and guitarist; and drummer Jerry
Shirley of Little Women.

The band's initial albums (on Andrew Loog-Oldham's
Immediate Records) were surprisingly laidback and melodic.
1971 turned out to be the band's breakthrough to major success,
due to a hard and loud double live album, *Performance—Live at
the Fillmore*, which went to number 21. Frampton left shortly
thereafter to pursue a successful solo career, and Humble Pie progressively turned toward an overamped boogie style of rock.
During the next two years, Humble Pie made three more forays
onto the album charts with *Smoking, Eat It*, and *Lost and Found*,
an anthology of their earlier Immediate label work.

In spite of substantial album popularity, Humble Pie never had
a major single, with their only chart titles being "I Don't Need No
Doctor" and "Hot 'n' Nasty." The group disbanded in 1981, and
Steve Marriott later passed away. *— Rick Clark*

○ **Safe as Yesterday Is** / 1969 / Columbia 47899
Even though many think of Humble Pie as a boogie-rock band,
their first two efforts, originally released on Immediate Records,
possessed a healthy dose of tasty acoustical instrumentation.
Steve Marriott and Peter Frampton applied themselves, through
months of rehearsals, and came up with a solid collection of
songs. Even though *Safe as Yesterday Is* is a little stronger than

the pastoral *Town and Country*, both albums are worth seeking
out. *— Rick Clark*

Rock On / 1971 / A&M 4301
By 1971 Humble Pie had taken on a much harder electric direction. Of their post-Immediate studio albums, this is probably their
best. *— Rick Clark*

○ **Performance: Rockin' at the Fillmore** / 1971 / A&M 6008
This live, extended-play effort, recorded at the Fillmore, show-
cased the band in its element, with Steve Marriott's stratospheric
wail and Peter Frampton's lyrical lead work in fine form.
Frampton split to pursue a successful solo career after this album.
— Rick Clark

Smokin' / 1972 / A&M 3132
With Marriott firmly in control, *Smokin'* featured grittier blues-
based hard rock, with tracks like "Hot & Nasty," "C'mon
Everybody," and the FM hit "Thirty Days in the Hole." *— Rick
Clark*

● **Classics, Vol. 14** / 1987 / A&M 2512
If you are looking for the one place to go for Humble Pie, this
best-of collection covers the essentials, such as "I Don't Need No
Doctor," "Stone Cold Fever," "30 Days in the Hole," "Hot 'n' Nasty,"
"C'mon Everybody," and "Take Me Back." *— Rick Clark*

Ian Hunter

b. Jun. 3, 1946, Shrewsbury, England
Vocals, guitar / Rock & roll, hard rock
Hunter's post-Mott the Hoople work (most of it done in collaboration with guitarist Mick Ronson) has remained true to the boogie roots of his old group, while expanding his beautifully expressed romantic concerns. *— John Floyd*

○ **Ian Hunter** / 1975 / Columbia 33480
A spotty debut, but "Once Bitten Twice Shy," "Who Do You Love,"
and "I Get So Excited" rank with the best Mott the Hoople material. *— John Floyd*

● **You're Never Alone with a Schizophrenic** / 1979 / Chrysalis
1214
Hunter's post-punk return salutes the genre he helped spawn and
brings that old Mott crunch to a fine set of energetic, if somewhat
dated rock & roll. *— John Floyd*

○ **Yui Orta** / 1990 / Mercury 838973
Overlooked upon its release, this is Hunter's most lyrically ambitious and mature disc, with tight rockers and melancholy ballads
working gloriously off one another. *— John Floyd*

Hunters & Collectors

Group / Alternative pop/rock
This Australian collective has taken its penchant for American
R&B and blended it with the righteousness of Midnight Oil. —
Bruce Eder

○ **Human Frailty** / 1986 / IRS 5801
As the title suggests, the band loses some of the edge of earlier releases on *Human Frailty*, revealing a softer, nearly vulnerable
side. A more mainstream pop album, it includes the great love
song "Throw Your Arms Around Me." *— Chris Woodstra*

○ **Human Frailty/Living Daylight** / 1986 / IRS 42024
Touching the "new sensitivity" before its time, laying it over
rhythmic soul. *— Robert Gordon*

○ **Fate** / 1988 / IRS 42110
The finest moment of their later period, *Fate* is a cohesive and
tightly produced album with an edge. "Back on the Breadline" received some attention through college and "modern rock" radio,
making this the closest thing to an American breakthough the
band has seen yet. *— Chris Woodstra*

● **Collected Works** / 1993 / IRS 13053
A good collection of the band's recordings for IRS records in the
mid-to-late '80s. This poppier side of the band is easily the most
palatable of their work, though not definitive. Their varied career
deserves better. *— Chris Woodstra*

Cut / Mushroom
Australia's Hunter's & Collectors have long been the source of
some of down-under's most stately, dignified rock, while never
forsaking an element of challenge. *Cut* peels away several layers
of gloomy lethargy that tended to overpower the group's previous
Ghost Nation—even making an occasional guest appearance on

the dance floor. The group spices the standard instrumental lineup with trumpet, trombone, and French horn, which are used to create a moody, almost string section-like canvas upon which the other instruments paint. Mark Seymour's strong lyrics tackle several topical subjects, but are most successful when dealing with personal politics—especially the quest for self-purpose. — *Roch Parisien*

Hüsker Dü

Group / Alternative rock, hardcore

Hüsker Dü and R.E.M. were the two American post-punk bands of the '80s that changed the direction of rock & roll. R.E.M. became superstars; Hüsker Dü never was more than a cult favorite. Nevertheless, their albums between between 1981 and 1987 have proven remarkably influential, providing a sonic blueprint for the roaring punk-pop hybrid that crossed over into the mainstream in the early '90s. Not only did they shape the sound of the music, they shaped the way independent bands made the transition to the major labels—t'hey showed other bands that it was possible to record uncompromising music on a major label without losing any integrity or creative control. From the Replacements to Nirvana, the Pixies to Superchunk, nearly every major and minor band that appeared in the alternative underground in the late '80s and the '90s owed a major debt to Hüsker Dü, whether they were aware of it or not.

The band's two songwriters, guitarist Bob Mould and drummer Grant Hart, both had a knack for writing songs that essentially followed conventional pop structures, complete with memorable melodies, but were still punk songs. Hüsker Dü took the Buzzcocks' pioneering punk pop and made it harder, both musically and lyrically. Throughout their career, Hüsker Dü never lost their edge, never turned down their amplifiers, never compromised their music. While Hart and bassist Greg Norton were an unfailingly strong rhythm section, Mould would prove to be one of the most influential guitarists of the decade. With his slashing rhythms, distorted strumming, and blazing leads, he set the stage for the alternative guitar heroes of the later years.

After releasing several good, but unspectacular, hardcore records, Hüsker Dü made *Zen Arcade* in 1984. The double album expanded hardcore in previously unimaginable ways. Instead of copying the strident political and social commentary of most hardcore, the band turned the focus inward, writing personal songs were painfully honest. For the next three years, the band consistently recorded and toured, without a lapse in quality.

The band was at the top of its form in 1985, releasing two landmark albums (*New Day Rising* and *Flip Your Wig*) and one non-album single (a cover of the Byrds' "Eight Miles High"). In 1986, they became one of the first post-punk groups to make the jump to the major label. Once they were there, they released two more albums before bitterly breaking up in 1988. After Hüsker Dü split, Grant Hart recorded a solo album, then formed Nova Mob. Mould recorded two solo albums and went on to form another punk-pop-power trio, Sugar. Greg Norton became a chef in the band's hometown of Minneapolis. —*Stephen Thomas Erlewine*

Metal Circus / 1983 / SST 020

This five-song EP, which followed a furiously paced debut, hinted that the confines of hardcore punk couldn't contain the group's collective vision. —*John Floyd*

☆ **Zen Arcade** / 1984 / SST 027

Its four sides are linked by a muddled travelog concept, but this is a remarkable synthesis of hardcore sensibilities and rock & roll themes. "Turn on the News" may be their finest moment. —*John Floyd*

☆ **New Day Rising** / Jan. 1985 / SST 031

From its thin and distorted production to the rich, tugging melodies, this album one-ups *Zen Arcade* through its front-to-back consistency. —*John Floyd*

★ **Flip Your Wig** / Feb. 1985 / SST 055

They finally got the professional production they've always deserved. While it's not the frontal assault of *New Day Rising*, the songs continue to get better, both lyrically and melodically. — *John Floyd*

○ **Candy Apple Grey** / 1986 / Warner Brothers 25385

The band's major-label debut coincidentally happens to be their most lyrically optimistic. —*John Floyd*

☆ **Warehouse: Songs & Stories** / 1987 / Warner Brothers 25544

Hüsker Dü's final record was their second double album. Much like *Zen Arcade, Warehouse* rarely loses momentum over its four sides. While the music here is the band's most accomplished and pop oriented, it never loses its edge. —*Stephen Thomas Erlewine*

Everything Falls Apart and More / 1993 / Rhino 71163

Rhino's reissue of Hüsker Dü's shattering first studio album includes a couple of rare singles, making it a must-have for the band's fans as well as anyone else interested in hardcore punk rock. Anyone unfamiliar with Hüsker Dü's early work should brace themselves for a breakneck force like no other. —*Stephen Thomas Erlewine*

○ **Living End** / Oct. 1994 / Warner Brothers 45582

Recorded on their final tour, *The Living End* is an invigorating document of Hüsker Dü's blistering live power, highlighted by a couple of unreleased songs and a manic cover of "Sheena Is a Punk Rocker." —*Stephen Thomas Erlewine*

Janis Ian (Janis Eddy Fink)

b. Apr. 7, 1951, New York, NY

Vocals / Singe/songwriter, folk-rock

A folk/pop singer/songwriter who gained fame at 16 for her socially conscious ballad "Society's Child" and scored all over again at 24 with "At Seventeen." Lately she is living and writing songs in Nashville. —*William Ruhlmann*

○ **Janis Ian** / 1967 / Forecast 3017

An amazingly precocious set of songs, including the civil rights anthem "Society's Child" and songs touching on religion, prostitution, politics, and other urban concerns, all from the viewpoint of an intelligent teenager. —*William Ruhlmann*

Stars / 1974 / One Way 21397

From precocity to an accelerated maturity, Ian ruefully comments on the fame business in the title track, then turns deeply romantic on "Jesse," a hit for Roberta Flack. —*William Ruhlmann*

● **Between the Lines** / 1975 / Columbia 33394

"At Seventeen" is only one of a group of beautifully written, tastefully performed, and very moving songs. —*William Ruhlmann*

Breaking Silence / Jun. 8, 1993 / Morgan Creek 20023

Janis Ian is the veteran here, the American author of that 1975 feminist bed-sit anthem "At Seventeen." *Breaking Silence*—her first album since 1982—finds her ditching her past waifishness for a confident, mature, contemporary acoustic approach relying mostly on spare guitar and piano textures. Opening with "All Roads to the River" (also recorded by John Mellencamp on his latest), *Breaking Silence* includes among its highlights the Holocaust survivor tale "Tattoo," and the dramatic half-a cappella, half-syncopated rocker title track. —*Roch Parisien*

Billy Idol (William Broad)

b. Nov. 30, 1955, Middlesex, England

Vocals / Hard rock, pop/rock

Billy Idol represents the bridge between punk-rock and hard-rock/metal, a logical-enough connection that somehow seemed unlikely until he made the transition. Idol left Sussex University in 1976 to join the punk movement, specifically the group of rabid Sex Pistols fans called the Bromley Contingent. Many of the members formed their own bands, and Idol began Generation X with Tony James. Generation X became a moderate success during the punk heyday of the late '70s, especially in England, with Idol on snarling lead vocals.

When the band split in 1981, Idol went to New York and hooked up with manager Bill Aucoin (who had handled Kiss, among others). This resulted in Idol's grooming as a more mainstream rock figure. His debut album, *Billy Idol*, came out in 1982 and spent two years on the charts as the result of such video hits as "White Wedding" and "Hot in the City." But it was Idol's second album, *Rebel Yell*, that was his big breakthrough, selling two million copies and spawning hits in the raucous title track and the ballad "Eyes without a Face." Idol followed it up with *Whiplash Smile* in 1986 and *Charmed Life* in 1990. Idol's first commercial failure came in 1993, with *Cyberpunk*, his stab at techno-influenced rock. —*William Ruhlmann*

○ **Billy Idol** / 1982 / Chrysalis 21377

Billy Idol's self-titled debut album was a snarling take on hard rock, injected with the spite and attitude of punk and new wave.

While the record is spotty, Idol pulls it all together on the classic single "White Wedding." — *Stephen Thomas Erlewine*

● **Rebel Yell** / 1984 / Chrysalis 21450
Tight rock arrangements featuring Steve Stevens's slashing guitar playing and Idol's vocal sneer. The dance-rock of "Rebel Yell" is alternated with power ballads like "Eyes without a Face" for a well-rounded pop package. — *William Ruhlmann*

Whiplash Smile / 1986 / Chrysalis 21514
While its Idol's most ambitious album, *Whiplash Smile* only comes to life on hard rocking pseudo-rockabilly like "I Forgot to Be Your Lover." Unfortunately, there aren't many songs that are as good as that single on this album. — *Stephen Thomas Erlewine*

Vital Idol / 1987 / Chrysalis 21620
Dance remixes of Idol's hits, plus a live cover of "Mony Mony" that topped the charts. — *William Ruhlmann*

○ **Charmed Life** / 1990 / Chrysalis 21735
Like any Billy Idol album, *Charmed Life* is wildly inconsistent, yet it has enough strong songs—like the gloriously tongue-in-cheek hard rock of "Cradle of Love"—to make most of the filler on the record forgivable. — *Stephen Thomas Erlewine*

The Impressions

b. 1957, Chicago
Group / R&B, soul
The first Impressions hit, "For Your Precious Love," was an anachronism when released in 1958. Jerry Butler's robust, yearning vocal was a throwback to deep-South gospel, and Curtis Mayfield's arrangement was decidedly barebones. But this song also precipitated the changes coming in R&B—you can hear the groundwork for soul music being laid, from the melisma of Butler's phrasing to Mayfield's skeletal guitar. The song literally flew in the face of then-popular doo-wop formulas.

Butler left the group in 1960, but the pared-down trio, led by Mayfield, cut a path that altered the R&B map. Mayfield's high falsetto and the trade-off vocals of Fred Cash and Sam Gooden framed a new kind of R&B: smooth and graceful, at times lilting, soaked in the history of gospel, and—thanks to Mayfield's lyrical examinations of racism and urban decay—the catalyst for the wave of socially aware Black hits recorded in the '70s.

The group's hits ranged from supple statements of affirmation ("It's All Right," "People Get Ready") and romantic declarations ("Talking about My Baby," "I'm So Proud") to songs that were sociopolitical ("Choice of Colors," "This Is My Country") or mystical ("Gypsy Woman"). Mayfield's outside production work yielded similar-sounding hits for the likes of Major Lance, Walter Jackson, and Billy Butler (and sound of the Impressions was imitated by the likes of the Viscounts and the Knight Brothers). Their chart run had ended by the late '60s, as did Mayfield's Midas touch; after recording the brilliant *Superfly* in 1972, his talents ran dry. Nonetheless, Mayfield's reputation as one of soul's supreme innovators cannot be exaggerated. — *John Floyd*

● **Greatest Hits** / 1965 / MCA 31338
A skimpy but solid collection of Curtis Mayfield's early-'60s soul landmarks. Includes "It's All Right" and "Gypsy Woman," defining the formula of early-'60s soul. — *John Floyd*

Complete Vee-Jay Recordings / 1993 / Vee-Jay 719
The accomplishments of Chicago's Impressions, one of soul's most famed groups, have been well chronicled in terms of their beginnings and Curtis Mayfield's legacy. But their music in the early years has taken a back seat to what they did after Jerry Butler departed and the trio years began with Mayfield doing the lead vocals, writing, producing, and arranging. This excellent 18-track disc helps put the early years into focus, with Butler showcased on seven cuts, Mayfield on eight, Sam Gooden in the spotlight on two and either Richard or Arthur Brooks on the other. The Impressions were not a bad five-member harmony unit; they just weren't a great one in an era when you had to be fantastic simply to break out of the pack. These are nice, simple love cuts with the exception of "For Your Precious Love," but no different lyrically from thousands of similiar tracks. The Impressions didn't become a transcendant act until Mayfield began penning epic protest songs that made his love ballads seem even more poignant in contrast. But this disc shows they did deserve a better fate than to be dropped from the Vee-Jay label 1959. — *Ron Wynn*

Indigo Girls

Group / Singer/songwriter, folk-rock
The Indigo Girls (Amy Ray and Emily Saliers) have earned a devoted following with their thoughtful, introspective lyrics (rich in religious metaphor), sensitive folkie delivery, and earthy harmonies. The dichotomy between Ray's edgier, rock-influenced delivery and Saliers's soft, reflective style creates enough tension to keep their concept interesting. — *Rick Clark*

Strange Fire / 1987 / Epic 45427
Their first proper album, *Strange Fire* hints at future greatness with the duo's lush harmonies and shining acoustic guitars. Beautiful folk-pop, but a diamond in the rough all the same. — *Chris Woodstra*

● **Indigo Girls** / 1989 / Epic 45044
This major-label debut is a strong showcase for the duo's harmonic skills and songwriting virtues. "Closer to Fine" was a moderate hit. Emily Saliers's "History of Us" is particularly affecting. Other highlights include "Secure Yourself," "Tried to Be True," and "Kid Fears," which featured R.E.M. vocalist Michael Stipe on backups. Hothouse Flowers also provide support. — *Rick Clark*

○ **Nomads*Indians*Saints** / 1990 / Epic 46820
Not as dynamic as *Indigo Girls*, this effort includes a few nice songs with "Welcome Me," "Watershed," and "Southland in the Springtime." The dichotomy between Ray's occasionally abrasive vocal strain and Saliers's delicately earthy alto are more apparent, making their delivery feel less focused. Their overreaching lyrics also undermined the success of this outing. — *Rick Clark*

Live—Back on the Bus Y'all / 1991 / Epic 47508
Spirited live set with Saliers and Ray backed by a full band. Features live and studio versions of their radio hit "1 2 3," and a version of Dylan's "All along the Watchtower." — *Rick Clark*

Rites of Passage / Feb. 1992 / Epic 48865
Not straying too far from their nearly formulaic sound, *Rites of Passage* shows great strides in songwriting maturity. The tension between Amy Ray's harsher rock style and Emily Sailer's sweeter melodic sense make a beautiful combination. Only a ridiculous cover of Dire Straits' "Romeo and Juliet" misses the mark. — *Chris Woodstra*

Swamp Ophelia / 1994 / Epic
The most sophisticated-sounding Indigo Girls production to date, *Swamp Ophelia* features some fine material, like "Touch Me Fall," "Mystery," "Language or the Kiss," "Power of Two," and "Least Complicated." For the most part, Amy Ray's occasional lyover-the-top stridency is fortunately restrained, while Emily Saliers's warm, earthy voice continues to pull the listener into considering her lyrical sentiments. As usual, when the two sing together, it's a wonderful sound. — *Rick Clark*

James Ingram

b. Feb. 16, 1956, Akron, OH
Vocals / Soul, urban R&B
Ingram began performing with the band Revelation Funk in the early '70s, moving from Akron, OH, to Los Angeles in 1973. During the '70s, Ingram supported Ray Charles on the road with backup vocals and piano, played keyboards behind the Coasters on Dick Clark's oldies revues, and was Leon Haywood's musical director. After hearing a demo of him singing "Just Once," Quincy Jones asked Ingram to perform on his new album. Released in 1980 on *The Dude*, the number-17 "Just Once" was Ingram's first success, resulting in three Grammy nominations: Best New Artist, Best Pop Male Vocal, and Best R&B Vocal, winning in the two latter catagories. Throughout the '80s, Ingram had steady popular success singing duets, but all of his solo albums failed to make a dent in the charts. In 1990 he scored his first solo hit, "I Don't Have the Heart." — *Stephen Thomas Erlewine*

● **Power of Great Music: Best of James Ingram** / 1991 / Warner Brothers 26700
Includes his Top-40 duets—"Yah Mo B There" (recorded with Michael McDonald), "Somewhere out There" (recorded with Linda Ronstadt), "Baby, Come to Me" (recorded with Patti Austin), and his first solo hit, "I Don't Have the Heart" (number one)—as well as songs that have scored the urban charts. — *Ron Wynn*

Luther Ingram

b. Nov. 30, 1944, Jackson, TN

Vocals / Soul

This Jackson, TN, Southern-soul singer was one of the top artists at Stax during the early '70s. Hooking up with producer Johnny Baylor's tiny KoKo label, Ingram appeared regularly on the R&B charts after Baylor brought his firm into the Stax fold in 1969. Ingram's intimate vocal approach was well suited to ballads, and his 1970 hit revival of "Ain't That Loving You (for More Reasons Than One)" set the stage for his R&B chart-topping classic "(If Loving You Is Wrong) I Don't Want to Be Right" two years later. Long after Stax had folded, Ingram was still releasing hit singles—clear into 1987. —*Bill Dahl*

● **If Loving You Is Wrong (I Don't Want to Be Right)** / 1972 / Koko 2202

Luther Ingram earned his biggest R&B and pop hit with the title track, one of the last hurrahs for gospel-tinged and country-flavored confessional soul. The song would later become a country hit for Barbara Mandrell. Ingram landed one other Top-Ten R&B single with "I'll Be Your Shelter (in Time of Storm)," and the album contained some other earnest soul ballads that weren't hits in "I'Can't Stop" and "Help Me Love." Ingram never again enjoyed similiar crossover heights, and the tide was turning against deep soul in both pop and R&B camps. —*Ron Wynn*

○ **Luther Ingram** / 1986 / Profile 1226

Luther Ingram made a brief return to the R&B charts with this 1986 LP issued on a predominantly dance-oriented label, mixing his classic soul voice with urban contemporary production. It wasn't an early new jack swing number, as there was no hip-hop or rap elements, but it did contain drum machine tracks and synthesizer-dominated arrangements. Otherwise, it was Ingram still singing heartache ballads, doing confessional country-soul and sounding raw and urgent on "Baby Don't Go Too Far" and "Don't Turn Around." The album also contained an interesting, although flawed, remake of Bob Dylan's "Gotta Serve Somebody." —*Ron Wynn*

I Like the Feeling / Urgent! 4119

An overlooked late-'70s Southern soul gem from Luther Ingram. He didn't make any attempt to soften or dilute his raw, country- and blues-tinged delivery and style, which resulted in the album not getting widespread attention. But it did get Ingram a pair of Top-40 R&B hits, and it did much better than a lot of other Southern soul issued at the same time. —*Ron Wynn*

Inspiral Carpets

Group / Alternative pop/rock

Of all of the Manchester bands of the early '90s, Inspiral Carpets were arguably the least interesting. They didn't explore the deep psychedelia of the rave scene as thoroughly as the Happy Mondays, nor did they have the classic pop skills of the Stone Roses. What the band did have was some massive organ hooks, courtesy of Clint Boon; the organ recalled the classic garage punk of the '60s. When the Inspiral Carpets could write a song that matched the sheer pleasure of their sound—and they managed at least two on each album, in addition to their U.K. hit singles—the group made some wonderful pop gems. Unfortunately, their hit-miss ratio was too low to make their albums consistent. When the Manchester fad passed, the Inspiral Carpets were still around and managed to keep scoring hits in Britain by losing some of the dated club beats and experimenting with their music slightly, including a collaboration with Mark E. Smith of the Fall on their 1994 album. —*Stephen Thomas Erlewine*

Life / 1990 / Elektra 60987

An impressive but inconsistent debut that recalled British pop from the '60s more strongly than the current Manchester dance craze, *Life* nevertheless had some fine dance tracks that were made to be played in clubs. —*Stephen Thomas Erlewine*

● **Beast Inside** / 1991 / Elektra 61089

Inspiral Carpets' second album relies more on their organ-driven garage psychedelia than the previous *Life*, and the result is an engagingly diverse set of dance-oriented modern pop. —*Stephen Thomas Erlewine*

○ **Revenge of the Goldfish** / 1992 / Elektra 61397

Inspiral Carpets continue to get further away from their club-oriented dance roots on their third album. Fortunately, their pop songwriting continues to improve, which is why *Revenge of the Goldfish* never sounds like the work of a bunch of has-beens. —*Stephen Thomas Erlewine*

The Intruders

Group / Soul

One of the earliest hitmaking vehicles for producers Kenny Gamble and Leon Huff, the Intruders were a leading R&B act from the mid '60s to the mid '70s. Fronted by Samuel "Little Sonny" Brown, the Intruders hit in 1966 with "(We'll Be) United" and the next year with "Together" on Gamble Records. Their breezy "Cowboys to Girls" and "Love Is like a Baseball Game" garnered plenty of pop crossover action in 1968, and their slick cover of the Dreamlovers hit "When We Get Married" scored in 1970. The quartet enjoyed their last two important R&B hits in 1973—"I'll Always Love My Mama (Part 1)" and "I Wanna Know Your Name"—before switching to Gamble and Huff's TSOP logo. —*Bill Dahl*

● **Super Hits** / 1973 / Philadelphia International 32131

A fine collection of hits by the '70s Gamble and Huff-produced soul team who brought you "Cowboys to Girls" and "Love Is like a Baseball Game." —*John Floyd*

INXS

Group / Rock & roll, pop/rock

After several years as a moderately successful dance-oriented new wave band, INXS began to accentuate the underlying dance and funk elements of their music, as well as vocalist Michael Hutchence's Jaggeresque sexuality. With the strong, funky single "The Original Sin," 1984's *The Swing* was the first album that featured their change in direction, and for the first time INXS had a hit outside of their native Australia. 1985's *Listen Like Thieves* was even more successful, both commercially and artistically. Its title track was a hit on the charts and on MTV, but it was "What You Need" and its stylish, funky rock & roll that gave them their first Top-Ten hit outside Australia. And that was nothing compared to the worldwide success of 1987's *Kick*, which sold over four million copies in the United States alone. From the slow, simmering sexuality of "Need You Tonight" to the lovely ballad "Never Tear Us Apart," the album had no less than four huge hit singles.

Although its 1990 follow-up, *X*, sold well, the record was a carbon copy of *Kick;* it signaled the beginning of INXS's commercial decline. The band released their most consistent and musically adventurous album, *Welcome to Wherever You Are*, in 1992, but it had almost no impact on the chart. The 1993 album, *Full Moon, Dirty Hearts*, was even more disappointing, falling off the charts only a few weeks after its release. Nevertheless, the band continues to be a top concert draw and the best of their work is timeless rock & roll. —*Stephen Thomas Erlewine*

○ **Shabooh Shoobah** / 1982 / Atlantic 90072

The best of INXS's early work. Slowly, the post-punk synthesizers were being replaced with groove, as "The One Thing" proves. "Don't Change" still smacks of the early '80s, but in a positive way: The synthesizer eerily repeats itself over Michael Hutchence's cold vocals. —*Stephen Thomas Erlewine*

Swing / 1984 / Atlantic 90160

A transitional album. INXS was reaching a wider audience with this album, "The Original Sin" was more catchy and danceable than anything they produced up to this point. The rest of the album is nearly as strong. —*Stephen Thomas Erlewine*

○ **Listen Like Thieves** / 1985 / Atlantic 81277

INXS completes its transition into an excellent rock & roll singles band with this album. Unfortunately, the new configuration works only for three songs: "What You Need," "Listen like Thieves," and "Kiss the Dirt (Falling Down the Mountain)." Yet these three songs are so strong (especially "What You Need") that the album cannot be dismissed completely. The album is worth its price just for "What You Need," a strong Stonesy groove with Michael Hutchence singing better than he ever has. —*Stephen Thomas Erlewine*

● **Kick** / 1987 / Atlantic 81796

Kick, INXS's commercial and artistic breakthrough, is overflowing with hit singles, including "Need You Tonight," "Devil Inside," "New Sensation," and "Never Tear Us Apart." The band's mix of Stonesy rock & roll, melodic pop, and dance-oriented beats has never sounded fresher—even the album tracks are fully developed songs, which never seem like filler. It's easily their best album. —*Stephen Thomas Erlewine*

X / 1990 / Atlantic 82140
The follow-up to the smash *Kick* isn't quite as successful as its predecessor, yet it packs quite a punch. Although "Suicide Blonde," "The Stairs," "Bitter Tears," and "Disappear," are as good as anything on *Kick*, the album suffers from songs that sound too similar. —*Stephen Thomas Erlewine*

○ **Welcome to Wherever You Are** / Aug. 4, 1992 / Atlantic 82394
Although they needed to experiment as badly as U2 did when they recorded *Achtung Baby*, INXS's attempt at self-reinvention, *Welcome to Wherever You Are*, didn't even come close to gaining commercial or critical acceptance. Nevertheless, the band did succeed artistically. From the start of the album, it's clear that INXS is out to confuse the standard perceptions of the band; the first instrument on the album is an Eastern-flavored horn. Special effects and exotic rhythms and sounds are abundant on the album. While *Welcome to Wherever You Are* isn't entirely new (there are a few trademark INXS dance-rock songs, like the single "Not Enough Time"), INXS sounds reinvigorated after the rather formulaic *X*. Evidently, the pop audience didn't care about INXS anymore, since nobody bought the album. That's a shame, since it is one of their strongest. —*Stephen Thomas Erlewine*

Full Moon, Dirty Hearts / 1993 / Atlantic
Following the surprisingly adventerous and artistically successful *Welcome to Wherever You Are*, *Full Moon, Dirty Hearts* is as calculated as *X*, but it lacks the pop smarts that made that album listenable. While most of the exotic trappings of *Welcome* have been pared down, there is still some sense of the band experimentation. INXS sounds energetic throughout the album, but their new ideas are poorly executed and there is a serious lack of strong songs and singles. —*Stephen Thomas Erlewine*

Iron Butterfly

Group / Psychedelic, heavy metal
Formed in 1966, Iron Butterfly performed a heavy, minor-key style of psychedelic rock/pop. Their debut album *Heavy* was a promising start, but the follow-up effort, *In a Gadda Da Vida* (number four) became the biggest-selling album in Atlantic Records history until the advent of Led Zeppelin. This was primarily due to the 17-minute title track, which became a staple on the emerging progressive-FM rock format. An edited version became a number-30 hit. The follow-up album, *Ball*, did one better at number three.
Besides "In-a-Gadda-Da-Vida," Iron Butterfly charted with "Soul Experience," "In the Time of Our Lives," and "Easy Rider (Let the Wind Pay the Way)," from the movie *Easy Rider*. The band attempted a reunion in 1975 with two albums, *Scorching Beauty* and *Sun and Steel*, before breaking up again. —*Rick Clark*

○ **In-a-Gadda-Da-Vida** / 1968 / Atco 33250
The title song, in all its glory, is all you need. —*Dan Heilman*

● **Light and Heavy: The Best of Iron Butterfly** / 1993 / Rhino 71166
Though the size of the compilation is quite large (21 tracks on CD), *Light and Heavy: The Best of Iron Butterfly* isn't all that entertaining. Iron Butterfly's entire reputation was built around one song: the 17-minute "In-a-Gadda-Da-Vida"—present on this collection only in its 3-minute single edit format. Which leaves the rest of the *Light & Heavy* to stand on the merits of the band's other songs—frequently spotty '60s psychedelia, ranging from heavy psychedelic rock to light psychedelic pop. Anyone intrigued by the original version of "In-a-Gadda-Da-Vida" might find some things of interest here, but those who just want the full-length "In-a-Gadda-Da-Vida" have to stick with the original album. —*Stephen Thomas Erlewine*

Iron Maiden

Group / Heavy metal
From their origins as a bar band in the mid '70s to the present, England's Iron Maiden has become one of the most imitated bands in heavy metal. The man who has held the group together through the rough times is bassist Steve Harris. Some of their theatrics were somewhat tacky in the early days, but by the late '70s they were already gaining a respectable following. EMI released their self-titled debut album in 1980, featuring Paul Di'Anno on vocals and Dave Smith on guitar. In the United States, the album was released on Harvest.

The band's second album helped them gain a huge following all over Europe and America, but within the band there were problems. Out went Di'Anno and in came Bruce Dickenson, former vocalist for the band Samson. Another change was the addition of guitarist Adrian Smith (replacing Dennis Stratton), and it was this lineup (along with drummer Clive Burr) that took them over the top. The band's impact has been immense, selling millions, and their sound has easily distinguished them from other bands. —*John Book*

○ **Iron Maiden** / 1980 / Capitol 91415
The debut album that started it all for this band. Many of the songs remain all-time metal classics, including "Sanctuary" and "Running Free." —*John Book*

○ **Killers** / 1981 / Capitol 91416
Album number two by Iron Maiden, not as aggressive or as addicting as their self-titled debut but still an essential part of their career. This was the last studio album to feature vocalist Di'anno. Later on he would form Paul Di'anno's Battlezone. —*John Book*

● **Number of the Beast** / 1982 / Capitol 46364
The first Maiden album to feature ex-Samson vocalist Bruce Dickenson. This is one powerful album, with some great guitar work from Dave Murray and Adrian Smith and fantastic bass playing from Steve Harris. This is the album that brought the band success in the United States, and it features two metal classics: "Run to the Hills" and the title track. —*John Book*

○ **Piece of Mind** / 1983 / Capitol 46363
The first Maiden album to feature drummer Nicko McBrain. *Peace of Mind* is easily one of their best efforts. Lead guitarists Adrian Smith and Dave Murray do their most creative work here, and the whole band is in top form. —*John Book*

Powerslave / 1984 / Capitol 46045
Iron Maiden gets more into lyrical themes this time around, featuring the 13-minute classic "Rime of the Ancient Mariner." —*John Book*

○ **Live After Death (the World Slavery Tour)** / 1985 / Capitol 46186
The band at their peak. A great double live album with a wide range of songs going as far back as their first album. Also available as a home video. —*John Book*

Somewhere in Time / 1986 / Capitol 46341
A somewhat controversial album for Maiden fans, as the band prominently used keyboards and synthesizers in their sound. However, there are lots of great songs, including "Heaven Can Wait." —*John Book*

○ **Seventh Son of a Seventh Son** / 1988 / Capitol 90258
The band's first attempt at a concept album. Keyboard and synthesizer sounds are present, but aren't as annoying as on the *Somewhere in Time* album. A good set of songs, including "Can I Play with Madness?," "The Clairvoyant," and the haunting title track. —*John Book*

Chris Isaak

b. Jun. 26, 1956, Stockton, CA
Vocals / Pop/rock, rock & roll
Unlike most modern singers whose work recalls vintage rock & roll, Chris Isaak manages to capture the subtle energy and tension of that music without parodying its mannerisms or excesses. "Wicked Game"—and indeed the entire *Heart Shaped World* album from which it was drawn—is among the better rock & roll recordings of the past decade.
There is an undeniable similarity between Isaak's vocals and the work of Roy Orbison, but it goes far beyond range or timbre. Although Orbison is remembered largely for his operatic ballads, his music was grounded in the blues and country mix that was prevalent at Sun records, where he began. Similarly, Isaak brings a biting intensity and dramatic tension to his vocals. And despite its modernity, Isaak's instrumental backup is surprisingly restrained and minimalist. —*Hank Davis*

● **Heart Shaped World** / 1989 / Warner Brothers 25837
The album that really broke Isaak through to a mainstream audience, this features the title cut, "I'm Not Waiting," "Wrong to Love You," a driving rendition of "Diddley Daddy," and the surprise number-six hit "Wicked Game." Brooding and intense. —*Cub Koda*

○ **San Francisco Days** / 1993 / Warner Brothers 45116

Chris Isaak's records are eerily out of time. The production is too clean and sterile to sound as if it was recorded at Sun Studios (a sound he clearly admires), yet his music doesn't fit neatly into the sounds of contemporary radio. Accordingly, his sound is original yet familiar, appealing both to fans of early '60s rock & roll and a modern audience. At times Isaak tries too hard to emulate his idols—for instance, his strained Orbisonesque falsetto on "Two Hearts"—but when Isaak doesn't try too hard, the results are often startling, as in the cool breeze of the title song and the warm simmer of "Can't Do a Thing (to Stop Me)." *San Francisco Days* is Isaak's most musically diverse album yet. *—Stephen Thomas Erlewine*

The Isley Brothers

Group / Soul, funk, R&B
They're still at it: recording artists since 1957, and hitmakers for almost as long. Inevitably, their music has changed, but this group's chief claim to fame remains their secularization of gospel call-and-response. They found that particular groove on "Shout" (cut for RCA in 1959), later followed by "Twist and Shout" on Wand in 1962—definitely one of the ballsier twist records. Four years in the commercial wilderness followed before they signed with Tamla and came up with "This Old Heart of Mine."

They didn't work long on the Motown assembly line, though, and in 1969 they revived their own T-Neck Records. Twenty years later they were still grinding out hits on the label, although their first T-Neck smash, "It's Your Thing," remains their biggest. Brothers have come and gone, as have sidemen—including Jimi Hendrix at one point. Still, the family that plays together stays together, although the group trading as the Isley Brothers today includes elements of Isley-Jasper-Isley (two younger brothers and a cousin), who had a hit with "Caravan of Love" in 1985. *—Colin Escott*

○ **Doin' Their Thing** / 1969 / Motown 287
An underrated masterpiece. This album really began the 3 + 3 relationship between the older brothers and the younger generation. The single "It's Your Thing" became a national catchphrase and later turned up in a film the brothers financed. More importantly, they now saw they could expand their stylistic frontiers and start doing funk and rock along with the soul. *—Ron Wynn*

○ **3 + 3** / 1973 / T Neck 32453
A masterpiece, one of the defining albums for '70s black music. The original Isley frontline of Ronald, Rudolph, and O'Kelly merged with the next generation featuring younger brothers Marvin and Ernie plus cousin Chris Jasper. The lead single "That Lady" established their new sound and identity on Epic, and was just one of four monster songs that came from the album. *—Ron Wynn*

○ **Isley Brothers Live It Up** / 1974 / T Neck 33070
The album that cemented the revolution begun by the 3 + 3 LP. The title song was a blazing triumph, landing them on "Soul Train" and getting widespread pop and club attention, though it didn't prove to be their biggest hit in those areas. Ernie Isley made his first significant impact as a guitar soloist, and the group also began attracting fans who hadn't heard their earlier cuts, while alerting the faithful that they were really back on the scene. *—Ron Wynn*

○ **Heat Is On** / 1975 / T Neck 33536
Another spectacular album. The Isley Brothers had refined rock/disco and now had it down to a science. The uptempo tunes had extended vamps, slithering, driving backbeats, and funky rhythms, while the ballads were smooth and sentimental. Ernie Isley would get a track to blaze away on guitar, and the whole thing revolved around the group's nonstop excitement and intensity. *—Ron Wynn*

Go for Your Guns / 1977 / T Neck 34432
The Isley Brothers maintained their '70s roll, getting another chart topper with the single "The Pride" and turning out a first-rate rock/disco effort. They were among the dominant acts in the entire business, and were ruling the R&B and urban contemporary airwaves at this time. *—Ron Wynn*

★ **Isley Brothers Story, Vol. 1** / 1991 / Rhino 70908
Rhino's two Isley Brothers compilations provide the definitive portrait of the group. *Vol. 1: Rockin' Soul (1959-1968)* focuses on the Isleys' R&B beginnings, including both parts of "Shout," "This

Old Heart of Mine (Is Weak for You)," and "Twist and Shout." *—Stephen Thomas Erlewine*

★ **Isley Brothers Story, Vol. 2** / 1991 / Rhino 70909
The Isley Brothers founded their own record label, T-Neck, in 1969, and along with the new label came a new direction and sound for the group. Funkier and harder, the Isleys charted more frequently than ever before in their career, including "That Lady," "Fight the Power," and "It's Your Thing." *Isley Brothers Story, Vol. 2: The T-Neck Years (1969-1985)* completes the picture that *Vol. 1* began and is essential for any collection of '70s soul. *—Stephen Thomas Erlewine*

The Jackson 5 (The Jacksons)

Group / Motown, soul
The Jackson 5 was Motown's last great pop group and among the most successful singles acts of the '70s. The group consisted of five brothers: Jackie (b. 1951), Tito (b. 1953), Jermaine (b. 1954), Marlon (b. 1957), and Michael (b. 1958). They grew up in Gary, IN, and were first organized as a group by their father, Joe Jackson, in 1966. In essence, the group was a vocal ensemble centered on Michael, who, though the youngest, was clearly the most talented. The group came to the attention of Motown and was signed in 1969. Their first four singles, "I Want You Back," "ABC," "The Love You Save," and "I'll Be There," all hit number one in 1970; "Mama's Pearl" and "Never Can Say Goodbye" each got to number two in 1971.

In 1972 Motown launched both Michael Jackson and Jermaine Jackson as solo acts, and the group's efforts were gradually less successful in the following years, though "Dance Machine" was a number two hit in 1974. In 1975 Jackie, Tito, Marlon, and Michael signed to Epic Records, replacing Jermaine with younger brother Randy (b. 1961). They also changed their name to the Jacksons, partly because Motown Records owned the name Jackson 5 and partly because of the personnel change. This version of the group continued until 1983, when Jermaine rejoined his brothers for a tour and an album, *Victory*. By 1989 Michael and Marlon had departed, leaving the Jacksons a quartet consisting of Jermaine, Jackie, Tito, and Randy. *—William Ruhlmann*

Diana Ross Presents the Jackson 5 / Jan. 1970 / Motown 5129
This Gary, Indiana family ensemble exploded onto the national scene with immediate and long-lasting impact in 1970. This album's combination of youthful exuberance and innocence, coupled with Motown production magic, yielded quick results as "I Want You Back" topped both R&B and pop charts. Michael Jackson was a national darling as a nine-year-old lead singer. Once they hit the big time, there was controversy over whether Diana Ross actually discovered them, but there was no question Motown had unveiled another superstar act. *—Ron Wynn*

○ **ABC** / Feb. 1970 / Motown 5152
A fabulous album, arguably their best on Motown. While the debut LP established the group's sound, this one cemented it and also made it clear Michael was going to be a huge star for a long time. His blend of gentility, soul, and innocence sparkled on the title cut and throughout the album, while the songs, production, arrangement, and musical support were superb. *—Ron Wynn*

Third Album / Mar. 1970 / Motown 5157
The Jackson 5 solidified the audience they'd enjoyed with their first two albums by turning in a consistently produced and occasionally exciting third record. It included the fine ballad "I'll Be There," and another hit in "Mama's Pearl". The group hadn't yet become hardened by Motown manipulation nor troubled by internal dissension; Michael Jackson was still widely beloved and seen as the '70s Frankie Lymon. This LP became their third Top-Ten album in a row. *—Ron Wynn*

Maybe Tomorrow / 1971 / Motown 5228
Another fine album, with Michael Jackson displaying surprising conviction and earnestness on the title track. The group was rolling along with a strong mix of novelty/dance hits, ballads and soul covers, scoring massive pop success and appearing all over the airwaves. *—Ron Wynn*

Jacksons / 1976 / Epic 34229
Epic turned the Jacksons over to Philly-soul producers Kenny Gamble and Leon Huff for this smooth, danceable label debut featuring the disco-fied hit "Enjoy Yourself." *—William Ruhlmann*

★ **Anthology** / 1976 / Motown 0868
This three-LP/two-CD set contains all 18 of the Jackson 5's pop-chart hits, plus solo hits by Jermaine and Michael, among its 33 cuts. It's the definitive collection and a good sampler of the sound of pop/R&B, circa 1969-1975. — *William Ruhlmann*

○ **Destiny** / 1978 / Epic 35552
The Jacksons are finally turned loose to write and produce themselves, and the result is their best (non-hits collection) ever. The dance tracks still sound fresh ("Blame It on the Boogie," "Shake Your Body (Down to the Ground)"), and the ballads are heartfelt and smooth. This album is a dry run for Michael Jackson's adult solo career. — *William Ruhlmann*

○ **Triumph** / 1980 / Epic 36424
An excellent follow-up, featuring the hits "Can You Feel It" and "Heartbreak Hotel." — *William Ruhlmann*

Chuck Jackson

b. Jun. 22, 1937, Latta, South Carolina
Vocals / Soul, R&B
Chuck Jackson first hit as a member of the Dell-Vikings (1957-1959) before striking out on his own with a string of soulful pop classics ("I Don't Want to Cry," "Any Day Now") on Wand, a subsidiary of Scepter, during the early '60s. With a delivery by turns sophisticated and hoarsely sexy, he was part of a group of singers, Ben E. King among them, whose gospel-tinged style predated and influenced the singing of '60s soul men like Wilson Pickett. Jackson continues to be very active; in 1992 he received the prestigious Pioneer Award from the Rhythm and Blues Foundation. His work is well documented on Capricorn's boxed set, *The Scepter Records Story.* — *Christine Ohlman*

○ **Good Things** / 1991 / Kent
Twenty-four tracks, hits, and unreleased material, from Wand Records (import). — *Richard Pack*

○ **Chuck Jackson's Greatest Hits** / Wand 683
A wonderful anthology that's a fine showcase for an overlooked, superb soul vocalist. Jackson's booming, declarative voice (which still sounds great) was at its best on such songs as "Any Day Now" and "I Don't Want to Cry." This is must-have material for anyone who didn't get either the singles or any of his British-hits sets. — *Ron Wynn*

● **Golden Classics** / Collectables 5115
All the Wand Records hits, including "Any Day Now" and "I Don't Want to Cry." — *Richard Pack*

○ **Starring Chuck Jackson and His Greatest Hits** / Spinorama 123
Another fine anthology. Unlike other artists, Chuck Jackson has been so undervalued for so long that multiple hits packages can only help him. This one qualifies as arguably the best domestic set. It's got both songs that got little crossover action and others that were strictly on the soul charts. — *Ron Wynn*

Janet Jackson

b. May 16, 1966, Gary, IN
Vocals / Urban R&B, dance-pop, pop/rock
Janet Jackson is the ninth and last child in the musically talented Jackson family that includes the Jackson 5, Michael Jackson, and Jermaine Jackson. Janet Jackson performed on stage with her brothers at the age of seven. At ten, she acted in the TV series "Good Times," and was later seen in "Diff'rent Strokes" and "Fame." She released her first album, *Janet Jackson*, in 1982 and her second, *Dream Street*, in 1984, but neither of these records was notably successful. Then, in 1985, Jackson turned to the production team of Jimmy Jam and Terry Lewis (formerly of the Time) for the album *Control*, which, ironically, emphasized the artist's new maturity and independence, even though most of the songs were co-compositions of the three. *Control* was a massive hit: It topped the charts, selling more than four million copies, and spawned five Top-Ten hits, including the number-one "When I Think of You." The follow-up, *Rhythm Nation 1814*, did even better, spawning seven Top-Ten hits, among them the number ones "Miss You Much," "Escapade," and "Black Cat." In 1991 Jackson signed a new recording contract with Virgin Records for a reported $32 million. 1993's *janet.* proved to be as successful as her previous two releases, featuring a series of Top-Ten singles including "If" and "That's the Way Love Goes." — *William Ruhlmann*

★ **Control** / 1986 / A&M 3905

Jam and Lewis tailor their contemporary dance-pop to the emerging personality of Jackson, who is attempting to take "control" of her life on this record. In the course of that attempt, she comes across as an aggressive, independent woman, notably on "What Have You Done for Me Lately." But the album is primarily a production showcase—it may be tailored to Jackson's persona, but the real artists are Jam and Lewis. — *William Ruhlmann*

○ **Rhythm Nation 1814** / 1989 / A&M 3920
Jam and Lewis have more beats up their sleeves, and the singer's own personality is even more submerged than it was on *Control*, but this is the height of '80s dance-pop. — *William Ruhlmann*

janet. / May 18, 1993 / Virgin 87825
Janet Jackson returns with *janet.*, a long (75-minute), ambitious album declaring her sexual maturity. There are good moments here, but it is marred by the torturously long running time and the intros that clutter the entire album. With a CD player, it is possible to program these excesses out and enjoy *janet.* as a solid successor to *Control* and *Rhythm Nation 1814.* — *Stephen Thomas Erlewine*

Joe Jackson

b. Aug. 11, 1955, Burton-on-Trent, England
Vocals, piano, vibraharp / New wave, singer/songwiter, pop/rock
Although Joe Jackson initially appeared to fit in neatly with such new wave singer/songwriters as Elvis Costello and Graham Parker when he appeared in the late '70s, he has displayed a much broader range on his numerous record releases since. Born in Burton-on-Trent, England, Jackson studied music as a youth and earned a piano scholarship to the Royal College of Music, which he attended from 1971 to 1974.

Look Sharp!, his debut album, released in March 1979, featured a fast-paced, guitar-driven rock style, with Jackson spitting out sometimes bitter, sometimes vulnerable lyrics, notably on the single "Is She Really Going Out with Him?," which hit number 21 in the United States. The album got to number 20 and went gold. *I'm the Man*, an album in the same style released in October, got to number 22.

Jackson then began the first of his many changes of style. *Beat Crazy*, released in the fall of 1980, marked a sharp turn toward reggae and a drop in Jackson's commercial fortunes. *Joe Jackson's Jumpin' Jive* (1981) contained big-band and jump-blues standards from the '40s. In 1982 Jackson moved to New York City, adopting some of the sophisticated style of Cole Porter and some of the small-band jazz music found in the city's clubs for *Night and Day*, released in June of that year. The album was Jackson's biggest hit, going to number four and producing the hit singles "Steppin' Out" and "Breaking Us in Two."

Jackson composed the soundtrack for the film *Mike's Murder* in 1983, then made *Body and Soul* in a style similar to *Night and Day*. It hit number 20 and included the Top-15 hit "You Can't Get What You Want (till You Know What You Want)." In 1985 Jackson composed music for the Japanese film *House of the Poet*. Some of the music was later released on his album *Will Power*. Jackson's 1986 album was the three-sided *Big World*, which reached number 34. *Will Power*, issued in 1987, was an instrumental album combining classical and jazz styles. It was followed in 1988 by the double *Live 1980/1986* and the soundtrack to the film *Tucker*. After his next pop album, *Blaze of Glory* (1989), did not succeed commercially, Jackson jumped to Virgin Records, which issued *Laughter and Lust* in 1991. — *William Ruhlmann*

★ **Look Sharp!** / Jan. 1979 / A&M 3187
Hyperactive new wave rock overlaid with the intelligent, caustic world-view of a man as angry as any punk, but far more perceptive. Includes the hit "Is She Really Going Out with Him?" — *William Ruhlmann*

○ **I'm the Man** / Feb. 1979 / A&M 3221
Nearly a rewrite of *Look Sharp* and capturing all of its brilliance, *I'm the Man* is pure power pop—hook filled, concise, and fun. Includes the wonderful "It's Different for Girls," a marginal hit in both the United States and the United Kingdom. — *Chris Woodstra*

○ **Beat Crazy** / 1980 / A&M 3241
Credited to the Joe Jackson Band, *Beat Crazy* completes Jackson's power-pop period. Jackson begins to stretch a bit stylistically, flirting with reggae and more experimental styles while staying in

the confines of the three-minute form he would later dismiss. Every bit as charming as the first two. —*Chris Woodstra*

○ **Jumpin' Jive** / 1981 / A&M 3271
A delightful trip back to '40s and '50s jump blues and big band swing. With faithful covers of Louis Jordan and Cab Calloway, Jackson appears to be having fun while helping a new generation discover these classics. —*Chris Woodstra*

○ **Night and Day** / 1982 / A&M 3334
Since Jackson has already demonstrated his broad musical tastes by turning from rock to "jumpin' jive" on his last album, that he was able to incorporate Latin, dance, and sophisticated ballad styles into his music wasn't so surprising—but that he could do it all so well was delightful. Includes "Steppin' Out" and "Breaking Us in Two." —*William Ruhlmann*

Body and Soul / 1984 / A&M 3286
Continuing in the move away from pop music he began with *Night & Day*, Jackson shows his love of '50s jazz with detail best represented by the cover photo (nearly identical to the Sonny Rollins album of the same name). Features his last U.S. hit, "You Can't Get What You Want" and the beautiful "Be My Number Two." —*Chris Woodstra*

Big World / 1986 / A&M 5139
A brilliant collection of songs, running over an hour, finds Jackson as biting as ever as he surveys the world, but he's also tenderly reflective on "Home Town." —*William Ruhlmann*

Blaze of Glory / 1989 / A&M 5249

Laughter and Lust / 1991 / Virgin 91628
Jackson's work has sometimes been too didactic for its own good, but on *Laughter and Lust* he managed to balance the agenda with a nice blend of humor and heart. His perpetual disdain for the pop music industry found full flower in "Hit Single," in which Jackson finds himself in "pure pop heaven," where angels only want to hear the hits, but not "the whole damn album." Other highlights are the classic acidic Jackson-style rocker "Obvious Song," the hyperkinetic "Jamie G.," a faithful remake of Fleetwood Mac's "Oh Well," and Jackson's ode to the dynamics of love in "Stranger Than Fiction." —*Rick Clark*

Michael Jackson

b. Aug. 29, 1958, Gary, IN
Vocals / Motown, soul, dance-pop, pop/rock, urban R&B
As part of the Jackson 5, a group made up of him and his brothers, Michael Jackson was among the most popular singing stars of the '70s. On his own, he was the biggest pop star of the '80s. Jackson was always the visual and vocal focus of the Jackson 5, who broke through to national success on the Motown label in 1970, when he was 11, with the first of four straight number-one hits, "I Want You Back." Jackson was also promoted as a solo artist, and he scored his first hit, the number four "Got to Be There," in 1971. Subsequent hits included his remake of "Rockin' Robin" and "Ben" in 1972.

Jackson's and the Jackson 5's fortunes declined somewhat after the early '70s, and the group moved to Epic at mid-decade, with Michael temporarily abandoning his solo career and subsuming his group leadership to other members of what was now called the Jacksons. The group gradually built back its popularity by writing its own material. Jackson returned to solo work in 1979 with *Off the Wall*, a mature combination of driving dance songs ("Don't Stop 'til You Get Enough") and feelingly sung ballads ("She's Out of My Life") that outsold any previous group or solo effort, and spawned four Top-Ten hits.

Jackson again recorded and toured with the Jacksons, but his next album, *Thriller* (1982), became a musical phenomenon. It was the biggest-selling album of all time, moving 20 million copies in the United States alone and including seven Top-Ten hits. Clearly Jackson had grown beyond his brothers, but he stayed with them for one more album and tour in 1984.

His follow-up album, *Bad* (1987), accompanied by a solo world tour, sold six million copies domestically. Only six of its seven singles hit the Top-Ten (one stopped at number 11), but five in a row hit number one.

In late 1991 Jackson returned with *Dangerous*, which, by mid 1992, had sold four million copies and spawned the hits "Black and White," "Remember the Time," "In the Closet," and "Jam." Jackson's second world tour was launched in Europe in June 1992, continuing into 1993.

Although numerous rumors had circled around Jackson throughout his career, his reputation remained clean. It wasn't until 1993 that he suffered serious damage to his image. Jackson was accused of child abuse by a teenage friend, sparking a major media frenzy. Through it all, Jackson vehemently denied the accusations. The civil case was settled out of court in early 1994. Jackson began working on a new album shortly after the settlement; it remains to be seen whether the public charges have hurt his sales or not. —*William Ruhlmann*

☆ **Off the Wall** / 1979 / Epic 35745
If you were listening to the Jacksons' *Destiny* from the previous year, maybe you were less surprised than many that Michael Jackson was capable of making an album this accomplished and assured. From the first moments, he seems bursting with the wide range of music included, from the first side's clutch of irresistible dance tracks ("Don't Stop 'til You Get Enough," "Rock with You," "Working Day and Night") to the light pop and ballads ("She's out of My Life," "Off the Wall") of side 2. Throughout, Jackson's flexible tenor coos and growls by turns, always goosing the songs along. Deservedly a massive hit, this is less dated today than much of the dance music of that era. —*William Ruhlmann*

★ **Thriller** / 1982 / Epic 38112
What impresses after a decade is Jackson's range of musical expression, one that touches the schmaltzy pop of Paul McCartney (his duet partner on "The Girl Is Mine") on one side and the hard rock of Van Halen (whose lead guitarist, Eddie Van Halen, is heard on "Beat It") on the other, with plenty of mainstream pop/rock and dance music in between. It's no accident that the record found a home in so many record collections—there's good music here for everyone. And of course, by summing up the state of pop music, Jackson also redefined it—this was a high-water mark for pop music never equaled since, even in his subsequent music. —*William Ruhlmann*

○ **Anthology** / 1986 / Motown 5402
Michael Jackson's greatest hits (1971-1975) emphasize his waiflike charm and youth (he was 13 when the first of these songs appeared) in ballads such as "Got to Be There," "Ben" (even if it is a love song to a rat), and "I Wanna Be Where You Are." The upbeat cover of "Rockin' Robin" is equally appealing. —*William Ruhlmann*

○ **Bad** / 1987 / Epic 40600
A partially successful attempt to remake *Thriller*. Interestingly, Jackson did not turn to a softer, more broadly commercial approach but instead upped the dance-rock ante. Songs such as "Dirty Diana" and "Smooth Criminal" found him striding forward in terms of rhythm and beat. And with seven hit singles out of ten tracks (five at number one), this, like *Thriller*, is in effect a Michael Jackson greatest-hits record, covering 1987-1989. —*William Ruhlmann*

Dangerous / 1992 / Epic 45400
Wisely, Jackson altered his creative process here, jettisoning producer Quincy Jones in favor of Teddy Riley and bringing in several songwriting collaborators. The result is an updated dance-floor success (the drums are way up in the mix), though the songwriting sometimes seems schematic. When Jackson is left more or less to himself, he is less R&B-oriented, notably on the pop ballad "Heal the World" and the guitar-driven rock/pop song "Black or White" (a Stones riff, though taken at a tempo the Stones never attempted). Rather than resting on his laurels, Jackson continues to work hard to maintain and further the quality of his work. —*William Ruhlmann*

Wanda Jackson

b. Oct. 20, 1937, Maud, OK
Vocals / Rockabilly
Fact: Wanda Jackson was the greatest female rockabilly singer of the late '50s and early '60s. Starting out as a Decca country singer in 1954, Oklahoma-born Wanda began her rock & roll career with Capitol in 1956 at age 18. Her trademark growl on the raveup "Fujiyama Mama" sounds like she gargled with nitroglycerine: explosive stuff. The Rhino compilation is evenly divided into Wanda's rocking sides, nine tracks cut between 1956 and 1960, with the remaining nine songs representing some of her best country output of 1958-1970. (For more of Wanda's rockabilly sides, seek out either the French Capitol *Only Rock & Roll* dou-

ble-album set or the British Charly double album, *Let's Have a Party*.) —*Dennis MacDonald*

○ **Rockin' with Wanda** / 1960 / Capitol
Absolutely the best collection of her rockabilly recordings, including her key 1956-60 singles—"Fujiyama Mama," "Mean Mean Man," "Hot Dog! That Made Him Mad," and others. A leading candidate for the best female rock & roll album of the '50s. The British reissue adds four worthwhile bonus cuts, including the essential "Let's Have a Party." —*Richie Unterberger*

● **Rockin' in the Country: Best of Wanda Jackson** / 1990 / Rhino 70990
Perhaps the greatest of the rockabilly women, Wanda Jackson later turned to pure country. Rhino's *Best of Wanda Jackson: Rockin' in the Country* presents the best of both eras here on this 18-track collection. —*Jeff Tamarkin*

Mick Jagger

b. Jul. 26, 1943, Dartford, England
Vocals / Rock & roll, pop/rock
Lead singer/songwriter for the Rolling Stones. After occasional forays away from the group, especially into solo acting, Jagger finally launched a full-fledged solo career in 1985. —*William Ruhlmann*

○ **She's the Boss** / 1985 / Columbia 39940
Jagger employs a *Who's Who* that includes Herbie Hancock, Pete Townshend, and Jeff Beck, for an album that replaces the familiar sound of the Stones with a more sophisticated but no less hard-rock sound. And the voice *is* familiar. Features the hit "Just Another Night." —*William Ruhlmann*

● **Wandering Spirit** / 1992 / Atlantic 82436
More times than not, *Wandering Spirit* works. A lot of the credit goes to Jagger's backing band and producer Rick Rubin, who keep things lean, mean, and simple. The economy of performance allows Jagger to remain credible on a wide variety of styles—he delivers a groovin', sultry version of Bill Withers's soul classic "Use Me," a passionate country ballad on "Evening Gown," and even pulls off an Irish traditional folk piece with "Handsome Molly." —*Roch Parisien*

The Jam

Group / Punk, rock & roll, pop/rock
First-wave mod punks, led by Paul Weller, who began as energetic Who clones but quickly became one of England's most distinct and proudly British combos. Weller's songwriting—alternately political and romantic—invited comparisons with Pete Townshend and Ray Davies, but the band's unflagging energy (and the deadlocked rhythm section of bassist Bruce Foxton and skin-basher Rick Buckler) made them a hit on the then-burgeoning punk scene. Although they never scored a hit in America, by 1980 the group had become British superstars, topping that country's charts with nearly every single. In the mid '80s, just as the group was branching out into soulful new territory, Paul Weller called a halt to the group and quickly formed the Style Council. Foxton and Buckler also struck out on the solo path, but with tepid results. —*John Floyd*

In the City / 1977 / Polydor 817124
A spunky and abrasive debut that mixes a mod's penchant for soul grooves with some fine piss-and-vinegar originals. —*John Floyd*

This Is the Modern World / 1977 / Polydor 823281
While it essentially repeats the formula of their debut, *This is the Modern World* is an exciting, energetic record. —*Stephen Thomas Erlewine*

☆ **All Mod Cons** / 1978 / Polydor 823282
This, their third album, expands their sound and includes some of Weller's most ambitious songs, like "To Be Someone," "The Place I Love," and "Down in the Tube Station at Midnight." —*John Floyd*

☆ **Setting Sons** / 1979 / Polydor 831314
A rough-edged concept album about lost friendships, set to the war-torn angst of "Private Hell," "Burning Sky," and "The Eton Rifles." —*John Floyd*

☆ **Sound Affects** / 1980 / Polydor 823284
A return to the expansive sound and love-and-politics of *All Mod Cons*, highlighted by the snarling "Pretty Green," "Set the House

Ablaze," and "Start!," a fiery rewrite of the Beatles hit "Taxman." —*John Floyd*

○ **Gift** / Jan. 1982 / Polydor 823285
A blatant stab at expanding their soul roots. Pretty spotty, really, but "Town Called Malice," "Ghosts," and "Just Who Is the 5 o'Clock Hero?" are among the band's best work. —*John Floyd*

Dig the New Breed / Feb. 1982 / Polydor 810041
A live hodgepodge culled from material from 1977 to 1982. A rocking affair that's not bad, as far as live albums go. —*John Floyd*

★ **Snap!** / 1983 / Polydor 821712
A generous overview of the band's best, including many British-only singles that are musts for fans. Start with this one. —*John Floyd*

○ **Extras—A Collection of Rarities** / 1992 / Polydor 513177
The exhaustive 26 tracks on *Extras* may not be the ideal introduction for newcomers, but they make up an essential item for fans. As the title suggests, the disc collects single B-sides, demos of well-known songs, cover versions, and overlooked album tracks. Of special interest are two unreleased numbers, a 1980 demo called "No One in the World," and "Hey Mister," recorded in 1979. —*Roch Parisien*

James

Group / Alternative pop/rock
Since the release of their first EP in 1985, the English alternative folk-pop group James have always been on the verge of mainstream success, yet have never quite made it as the superstars they sometimes seem capable of becoming. For all their virtues, their albums have had their share of flaws, too: Vocalist Tim Booth's tendency to go from baritone to falsetto within seconds was impressive at first, but soon grew tiresome; and their songs were occasionally poorly arranged, making them sound directionless. However, if James sounded off-kilter at times it wasn't because of a lack of talent, but rather the height of their ambitions—the band clearly aimed to be transcendent and important, not disposable. Since their first album, 1986's *Stutter,* each record has been drastically improved, with the band consistently reinventing and expanding their sound.

James' reached the Top Ten in the United Kingdom with a single from their live *One Man Clapping*, "Sit Down." It showcased the band at their most direct and simple, which their next album did not. *Gold Mother* (1990) found the band incorporating elements of the current club scene of Manchester, their home town. James was never truly part of that musical trend, yet it helped them re-sign with a major label in their country. Their next album, 1992's *Seven,* didn't have any of the dance style of their previous record, but it showed a significant step forward in their songwriting. And 1993's *Laid* was even better, not only because of Brian Eno's atmospheric, melancholy production, but because James reined in their most excessive tendencies and recorded an album that fulfilled the promise they have always shown. *Laid* gave them their first hit in America, as well as some success in Britain, although the band was publicly angry about what they believed to be a lack of support in their native country. *Laid* proved that James have just begun to hit their stride. —*Stephen Thomas Erlewine*

Stutter / 1986 / Sire 25437
Intelligent, witty songwriting. Their full-length debut. —*Steve Aldrich*

One Man Clapping / 1989 / Rough Trade 001
Excellent live album with exclusive material. —*Steve Aldrich*

James (Sit Down) / 1990 / Fontana 848658
U.S.-only revised edition of *Gold Mother.* —*Steve Aldrich*

● **Laid** / 1993 / Fontana
With *Laid,* James completely changes its direction with a dark, moody album of stunning emotional resonance. Brian Eno's atmospheric production initially makes *Laid* seem if it has only one tone, but with repeated listens the peaks and valleys emerge as clearly as the details within the songs themself. Even the more upbeat-sounding songs, such as "Low Low Low" and "Laid," have a deep undercurrent of sadness, but it is a melancholy that is real and beautiful, making *Laid* an album worth returning to. —*Stephen Thomas Erlewine*

James Gang

Group / Hard Rock, rock & roll

At the top of the '70s, Joe Walsh (the James Gang's lead guitarist and singer) blasted onto the music scene as the new kid to watch. Walsh's distinctive staggered lead-guitar phrasing, barebones boogie riff-work, and tonal integrity immediately earned him high marks, and stories of Walsh upstaging Jimi Hendrix during their warm-up slots with the Experience spread like wildfire.

Walsh backed up the buzz with the James Gang's second album, *Rides Again,* which was a tour de force of dynamic, hard trio rock. What James Gang drummer Jim Fox and bassist Dale Peters lacked in inventive fire (á la Cream or Jimi Hendrix Experience), they made up for in providing a rock-solid foundation for Walsh's soaring guitar flights and wide chordal sound washes.

After one more studio effort, *Third,* and a live album, Walsh split and went solo, leaving the James Gang to flounder, producing a couple of minor FM rock hits before falling apart. —*Rick Clark*

○ **Rides Again** / 1970 / MCA 31145

● **16 Greatest Hits** / 1973 / MCA 6012
A fine collection of the James Gang's best tracks. —*AMG*

Rick James

b. Feb. 1, 1952, Buffalo, NY
Vocals / Funk, disco, urban R&B

Never quite as musically exciting as his cheerfully sleazy image suggests, Rick James was a major funk figure for a short time in the late '70s and early '80s. He called his music "punk funk," which is a reasonable description of his style. James took the basic sound of George Clinton's P-Funk, sang it like was rock, and added cloying drug and sex references. Too often, his music sounded like a string of hooks without any song, but when the hooks worked, as on "Super Freak," the results were undeniably funky and frequently brought him to the top of the R&B and pop charts.

In the early '80s, he brought a number of groups to Motown, most prominently the Mary Jane Girls. Not only did he produce their records, he controlled the direction of their career. However, there was only so far his music could take these artists, not to mention himself, and by 1983 his career had started to slip. By the end of the decade, his music wasn't funk, it was slick urban contemporary R&B; even a change in style couldn't send James back to the top of the charts. Throughout the '90s, his comeback attempts have been plagued by persistent drug and legal problems. The last time he hit the charts was not even as a solo artist, it was as a featured sample in MC Hammer's smash hit, "U Can't Touch This." —*Stephen Thomas Erlewine*

○ **Street Songs** / 1981 / Motown 5405
Rick James's "punk-funk" peaked on this album. James's vocals were never more aggressive nor better produced than on the singles "Super Freak" and "Give It to Me Baby." James was a crossover sensation; the LP peaked at number three on the pop album chart and eventually went platinum. "Give It to Me Baby" topped the R&B charts for five weeks, while "Super Freak" was also a Top-Ten single. —*Ron Wynn*

● **Reflections: Greatest Hits** / 1984 / Motown 6095
A nice collection featuring the best uptempo and left-field ballad hits by Rick James. The anthology shows that James functioned best when riding the rhythm. He was a moderately talented (at best) vocalist, better at yelling and exhorting than trying to interpret lyrics, pace a slow song, or vary a mood. The only significant ballad hit he had was a duet where the contrast between his voice and Smokey Robinson's generated enough response to sell the song. —*Ron Wynn*

○ **Bustin' Out: The Very Best of** / 1994 / Motown
A definitive double-disc anthology that is essential for devoted fans. —*AMG*

Tommy James & the Shondells

b. Apr. 29, 1947, Dayton, OH
Group / Pop/rock

During the last half of the '60s, Tommy James & the Shondells were one of America's most successful pop acts, generating 14 Top-40 hits between 1966 and 1969. James formed the original

Shondells at the age of 12, in 1960. In 1963, they recorded a Jeff Barry-Ellie Greenwich song called "Hanky Panky" for the Snap label. Two years later, a Pittsburgh DJ picked up on the song and made it into a regional hit. James and the original Shondells parted ways because the band members didn't want to relocate from Indiana, and James formed a new Shondells by taking on a group called the Raconteurs. In 1966 they signed to Morris Levy's Roulette, which reissued "Hanky Panky" (it became a number-one million seller).

For the next two years, they embodied lightweight chewy pop with hits like "I Think We're Alone Now" and "Mirage." The group developed a heavier sound with the percussive 1968 hit "Mony Mony." In keeping with the times, they became more psychedelic, best captured in their number-one "Crimson and Clover." The Shondells continued to chart until James left for a moderately successful solo career in 1970. James's biggest hit was "Draggin' the Line." The Shondells changed their name to Hog Heaven, to no appreciable success. During the '80s, the Shondells' material enjoyed a resurgence of popularity among various pop and rock artists. Joan Jett scored with "Crimson and Clover," while Billy Idol's version of "Mony Mony" and Tiffany's "I Think We're Alone Now" took turns at the number-one position in November of 1987. —*Rick Clark*

● **Anthology** / 1990 / Rhino 70920
James and his band had a remarkable string of hits from the mid '60s to the early '70s, largely because of an uncanny ability to keep current with fast-changing pop trends—from their first garage-band hit, "Hanky Panky," to their psychedelicized songs like "Crimson and Clover." Even more remarkable, the music holds up entertainingly today, and this well-annotated, 27-track compilation contains all the hits and more. —*William Ruhlmann*

Jan & Dean

Group / Surf rock, pop/rock

Besides the Beach Boys, no other vocal group captured the sound of California surf music with as much success—both commercial and artistic—as Jan & Dean. The duo actually began as a doowop-soaked harmony act in the late 1950s, reaching the Top Ten with the goofy "Baby Talk" and scoring minor hits with doo-wop updates of standards like "A Sunday Kind of Love" and "Heart and Soul." When the Beach Boys began their climb to superstardom, Jan & Dean changed gears and followed suit with a series of surf and hot rod hits that featured falsetto harmonies, chugging guitars, and Jan Berry's clean production. Brian Wilson himself sang backup vocals on their biggest hit (which he co-wrote with Jan), "Surf City," in 1963. While they lacked the Beach Boys' depth and capacity for artistic growth, Jan & Dean's hits from 1963 and 1964—which included "The Little Old Lady (from Pasadena)," "Drag City," "Honolulu Lulu," and the mini-soap opera "Dead Man's Curve"—are in the same class as the Beach Boys' early work in its infectious, energetic invocation of good times and California sunshine. They added an irresistibly reckless humor to the genre, and were well cast as the fun-loving hosts of the classic 1964 rock & roll hootenanny film *The T.A.M.I. Show* (for which they performed the rip-roaring theme, "(Here They Come) From All Over the World"). The duo's success, already on the wane a bit, was tragically cut short by Jan Berry's near-fatal auto accident in April 1966, which had been eerily foreshadowed by the lyrics of "Dead Man's Curve." —*Richie Unterberger*

● **Surf City—The Best of Jan & Dean** / 1990 / EMI America 92772
Remembered mostly for their surfing hits, Jan & Dean had a bit more range than they're generally given credit for. Their roots were in doo-wop, and after scoring surf and hot-rod hits, they also cut some decent straight pop-rock songs and zany singles that verged on pop satire. *Surf City* includes just about all the material you'd want from the duo. The 22 songs include the big hits "Surf City," "Dead Man's Curve," and "The Little Old Lady (from Pasadena)," of course, but also feature nifty smaller songs like "Honolulu Lulu," "The New Girl In School," and "Ride the Wild Surf." The pair was second only to the Beach Boys in blending high, soaring harmonies with driving vocal surf and hot rod sounds. Of course they weren't nearly as talented as Brian Wilson's group, but even their minor material has an irrepressible sense of fun and sparkling Los Angeles pop-rock production and melodies. —*Richie Unterberger*

Jane's Addiction

Group / Alternative rock, hard rock

Jane's Addiction were one of the most hotly pursued rock bands when they gained notice in Los Angeles in the mid '80s, with record companies at their feet. Flamboyant frontman Perry Farrell, formerly of the band Psi Com, has an undeniable charisma and an interest in provocative art (he designed the band's album covers), and Jane's Addiction plays a hybrid of rock music—metal with strains of punk, folk, jazz, and you-name-it.

The quartet—comprising Farrell, bassist Eric Avery, drummer Stephen Perkins, and guitarist Dave Navarro—had already released their debut album, in the form of a live recording from the Roxy in Hollywood. Finally, Warner Brothers won the bidding war and released *Nothing Shocking*, in 1988. The band's abrasive sound and aggressive attitude (typified by the nude sculpture on the cover) led to some resistance, but Jane's Addiction began to break through to an audience: The album spent 35 weeks in the charts.

Ritual de lo Habitual followed in 1990 and was the band's commercial breakthrough, reaching the Top 20 and going gold. Farrell designed the traveling rock festival Lollapalooza as a farewell tour for Jane's Addiction. After the tour was completed at the end of the summer of 1991, the group split. Farrell would continue to be involved with the organization of the annual Lollapalooza event for the next several years. He also formed Porno for Pyros with Perkins in 1992, releasing their debut record the following year. After a couple of quiet years—which included forming Deconstruction, a band that didn't release any records until 1994, with Avery—Navarro joined the Red Hot Chili Peppers at the end of 1993. *—William Ruhlmann*

○ **Nothing's Shocking** / 1988 / Warner Brothers 25727

The cover (a sculpture of two naked females joined at the hips with their hair ablaze) screams that this is an artsy album, and it is. Jane's Addiction, thanks to frontman Perry Farrell, brings *art* to hard rock. Instead of provoking, the ambitions mostly irritate. Farrell's voice wears thin after a few songs, and it's not helped much by the post-Zeppelin stumble of the band—Navarro is no Jimmy Page. When the music is acceptable, the lyrics are annoyingly self-conscious, making the whole thing implode. Still, if *Nothing's Shocking* is absorbed in concentrated spurts instead of an hour-long session, there are some high points to be found, particularly "Summertime Rolls" and the Lou Reed rip, "Jane Says." *—Stephen Thomas Erlewine*

● **Ritual de lo Habitual** / 1991 / Warner Brothers 26223

Throughout the first half of *Ritual,* Jane's Addiction manages to groove, creating the best rock & roll of their short career. In particular, the two Bo Diddley knock-offs ("Stop!" and the single "Been Caught Stealing") sound tight, but on the second half the indulgent ten-minute songs are hauled out, beginning with the insufferable ménage à trois magnum opus "Three Days." Still, the band manages to salvage the album with "Classic Girl," one of their best songs. *—Stephen Thomas Erlewine*

Japan

Group / Progressive rock

Japan was part of the short-lived "new romantic" movement in British pop. Members of Japan included brothers David Sylvian (b. 1958) and Steve Jansen (b. 1959), who originally shared the family name Batt; Mick Karn (b. 1958); Richard Barbieri (b. 1957); and Rob Dean (b. 1959). Precursors to new age music, Japan combined Eastern influences with synth-pop overlay, giving them a staunch U.K. following that has never translated into U.S. chart success. *—Cub Koda*

○ **Adolescent Sex** / 1978 / Ariola 50037

The debut album is vastly different from later work. *—Steve Aldrich*

Quiet Life / 1980 / Fame 3037

Transitional album in which the band turns from their original glam-rock style to the later Roxy Music-influenced sound. *—Steve Aldrich*

● **Gentlemen Take Polaroids** / 1980 / Blue Plate 1829

First fully realized album in the group's latter-day phase. *—Steve Aldrich*

○ **Tin Drum** / 1981 / Blue Plate 1830

A highly atmospheric effort strongly influenced by folk music of their namesake country. An early-'80s classic. *—Steve Aldrich*

Oil on Canvas / 1983 / Blue Plate 1832

An outstanding live album focusing on *Tin Drum* and *Polaroids*-era material. *—Steve Aldrich*

Jayhawks

Group / Country-rock

On a series of independent albums in the late '80s, the Jayhawks staked out the same territory as Gram Parsons and Neil Young, recording some of the best, grittiest country-rock of the decade. When the band signed to American Records in the early '90s, they started getting a substantial amount of press. Many critics called their 1992 album, *Hollywood Town Hall,* one of the best of the year. While the Jayhawks do nothing particularly new, they do it well; not only do they sound like the classic country-rock of the '70s, they have the songs to support their sound, which keeps them from being an empty exercise in nostalgia. *—Stephen Thomas Erlewine*

○ **Blue Earth** / 1989 / Twintone 89151

A fine debut highlighted by good honky-tonk songwriting. *—Dan Heilman*

● **Hollywood Town Hall** / 1992 / Def American 26829

Right from the distorted, rootsy, opening chords of the lead track "Waiting for the Sun," you can tell that the Jayhawks Minneapolis combo is well versed in early Crazy Horse, á la "Down By the River" and *Everybody Knows This Is Nowhere.* Gary Louris's electric chording is offset by Mark Olson's full-bodied acoustic guitar and harmonica textures. The two trade off heavenly vocal harmonies on "Crowded in the Wings" and "Take Me with You (When You Go)." The tasty mixture of sweet, yearning country and toothsome pop will invite suggestions that Gram Parsons, the Band, and R.E.M. should also be added to the group's list of influences. *—Roch Parisien*

The JB's (Pee Wee Ellis, Fred Wesley, Maceo Parker)

Group / Soul, funk, R&B

Maceo Parker joined James Brown's fabled band in 1964, Alfred "Pee Wee" Ellis joined the fold two years later, and Fred Wesley came on board in 1968. Ellis cowrote such classics as "Cold Sweat" and "Say It Loud—I'm Black and I'm Proud," and both he and Wesley at various points were musical director of the JB's. Parker was immortalized in Brown's famous incantation "Maceo, come blow your horn." Ellis also served as musical director for Van Morrison, while Wesley and Parker were part of the Parliament/Funkadelic gang at their peak in the mid and late '70s.

The three of them have recorded in various permutations as Maceo and All the King's Men, Maceo and the Macks, the JB's, Fred Wesley and the New JB's, Fred Wesley and the Horny Horns, the JB Horns, and simply under any one of their individual names. In the '80s and early '90s, with the resurgence of interest in James Brown and Parliament/Funkadelic, the three horn men have been involved in a plethora of recordings. (Note: All of the albums made by Parker, Ellis, and Wesley in their various permutations have been included here; the artist credited with the album appears at the end of the review.) *—Rob Bowman*

JB Horns / 1964 / Gramavision 79462

On an album made up of 11 originals, the three horn men turn in a fine, if undistinguished mix of jazz and funk. Worth hearing just for Fred's rapping, the gently swinging "Mother's Kitchen," and the sly "Everywhere Is out of Town." *—Rob Bowman*

Doing Their Own Thing / 1970 / House of the Fox

Recorded and released after a mutiny by most of James Brown's late-'60s band, *Doing Their Own Thing* contains 12 slabs of superb early-'70s style funk. Mostly instrumental, radio play for the album and subsequent singles appear to have been blocked by Brown himself. (Credited to Maceo Parker.) *—Rob Bowman*

● **Doing It to Death** / 1973 / People 5603

Extended live "funkafizing" including a ten-minute version of the number-one R&B hit "Doing It to Death." Written, produced, and arranged by James Brown. *—Rob Bowman*

Damn Right I Am Somebody / 1974 / People 6602

More of the same sparse, cutting-edge funk, including a Top-40 R&B hit in the title cut. (Credited to Fred Wesley & the JB's.) — *Rob Bowman*

Breakin' Bread / 1974 / People 6604
The last of the Fred Wesley and the JB's albums. "Breakin' Bread" and "Makin' Love" charted R&B. The funk is still much in evidence, although some new twists and turns manifest themselves on the "rapped" title cut. (Credited to Fred Wesley & the New JB's.) — *Rob Bowman*

○ **A Blow for Me, a Toot for You** / 1977 / Atlantic 18214
Produced by George Clinton and Bootsy Collins and recorded with the company of much of the P-Funk mob, *A Blow for Me, a Toot for You* showcases a new, slinkier, more produced and less hard-edged edition of the JB Horns. The lead cut, a remake of Parliament's "Up for the Down Stroke," received a little R&B airplay. — *Rob Bowman*

New Friends / 1990 / Antilles 848280
Wesley and Parker in the company of jazz musicians Gerri Allen, Anthony Cox, and Robin Eubanks. This is by far the jazziest of Fred, Maceo, and Pee Wee's recordings, covering the likes of Thelonious Monk, Duke Ellington, and Dizzy Gillespie. Wesley also proves himself to be a fine jazz writer, "For the Elders" being particularly notable. — *Rob Bowman*

● **For All the King's Men** / 1990 / 4th & Broadway 444027
Produced by Bill Laswell and Bootsy Collins, this five-cut CD EP includes Wesley, Parker, Bobby Byrd, Bootsy Collins, and Sly Stone on one cut. "Let 'Em Out" is a paean to free James Brown. That and "Sax Machine" appear in two different versions. Hilarious and serious-as-a-heart-attack funk all at once. (Credited to Maceo Parker.) — *Rob Bowman*

Roots Revisited / 1990 / Verve 843751
Ellis, Wesley, and Parker in the company of jazz keyboardist Don Pullen and Bootsy Collins. The first of a string of new recordings, *Roots Revisited* is half jazz, half soul, with a little funk thrown in for good measure. It's the first time these three have played jazz on record. The album includes wonderfully invigorating versions of Charles Mingus's "Better Get It in Yo' Soul" and the Impressions' "People Get Ready." — *Rob Bowman*

Mo' Roots / 1991 / Verve 511068
The second *Roots* installment, *Mo' Roots* was cut minus Pullen and Collins, leaning a little more toward the instrumental soul side. Three fine originals in conjunction with covers of Ray Charles, Marvin Gaye, Otis Redding, Horace Silver, and Lionel Hampton. — *Rob Bowman*

Jefferson Airplane / Starship

Group / Rock & roll, psychedelia, folk-rock, hard rock
Jefferson Airplane (formed July 1965), along with the Grateful Dead, Quicksilver Messenger Service, and Big Brother & the Holding Company, spearheaded the San Francisco rock sound of the '60s and the idealistic hippie message of free drugs and free sex. Compared to many of the Bay Area statements of flower power and peace, Jefferson Airplane always possessed a darker, more revolutionary image. Frontperson Grace Slick was a more-than-willing, outspoken mouthpiece.

Musically, the band ranged from reflective acoustic gems (revealing their folk origins) to explosive excursions into psychedelia. Their performance of "Volunteers" at the legendary Woodstock festival was a highlight.

At the top of the '70s, Jefferson Airplane formed the RCA-distributed Grunt Records, on which they released their subsequent albums as well as albums by Papa John Creach and Hot Tuna. During this time, their counterculture tirades began to sound as tiring as the nagging, parental "establishment."

In 1974 they become the Jefferson Starship. Their 1975 album *Red Octopus* became their biggest-selling album to date, generating lead singer Marty Balin's number-three hit "Miracles." Shortly thereafter, Grace Slick took a leave of absence until 1981. Singer Mickey Thomas (formerly with Elvin Bishop) joined in 1979 and helped usher the band into further mainstream rock-radio success.

After longtime band leader Paul Kantner left Jefferson Starship in 1984, the band dropped the first word in its name. At that point it consisted of Mickey Thomas, Grace Slick, guitarist Craig Chaquico, bassist Pete Sears, and drummer Donny Baldwin. This unit immediately scored with the number-one hits "We Built This

City" and "Sara" and the million-selling album *Knee Deep in the Hoopla.* Sears had left by the time of the 1987 follow-up, *No Protection,* which featured the number-one "Nothing's Gonna Stop Us Now" and the Top Ten "It's Not Over ('til It's Over)." Slick then departed, and the remaining trio recruited keyboard player Mark Moragan and bassist Brett Bloomfield for the 1989 album *Love among the Cannibals,* which featured the Top-20 hit "It's Not Enough." In 1991, when RCA released a Starship greatest-hits album, the one new track on the album had been recorded by Thomas and studio musicians, leading to doubt that Starship remained a functioning band. — *William Ruhlmann*

Takes Off / Sep. 1966 / RCA 3584
The original group's pre-Grace Slick debut album, really closer in spirit to the Mamas & Papas in some respects, is a kind of folk-pop album. Signe Anderson and Marty Balin handle most of the vocals, the instrumental textures are largely acoustic (Jorma Kaukonen contributes some excellent playing, however), and the political sensibilities are almost nonexistent. — *Bruce Eder*

★ **Surrealistic Pillow** / Feb. 1967 / RCA 3766
Their groundbreaking folk-based psychedelic album hit like a shot heard round the world. From "White Rabbit" and "Somebody to Love" to the sublime "3/5 of a Mile in 10 Seconds," the sensibilities are fierce, the material is melodic, and the performances, sparked by new member Grace Slick on most of the lead vocals, are magnificent and inspired. — *Bruce Eder*

After Bathing at Baxter's / Dec. 1967 / RCA 4545
The group's attempt to re-create the psychedelic drug experience as pure music fails in part—the material is too disjointed and the stretch for the listener (except in certain states of mind) too great for the record to be enjoyable. But as an experiment, *Baxter's* is dazzling in its intensity and the playing is superb. — *Bruce Eder*

Crown of Creation / Sep. 1968 / RCA 4058
An impressive but meandering journey through the drugged-out sensibilities of 1967. The science-fiction content gives it some cohesiveness, but not enough. — *Bruce Eder*

Bless Its Pointed Little Head / Feb. 1969 / RCA 4133
A rough but very representative live album that succeeds where the *Baxter's* album failed in capturing the mood of psychedelic music in performance. The music is intense and driving, and the only unfortunate element of the album is that it dates from a period after Marty Balin's songs had largely been dropped from their set. — *Bruce Eder*

Volunteers / Nov. 1969 / RCA 4238
The band's most political album is a somewhat dated statement but also a very joyous and rewarding one. "We Can Be Together" is still a compelling anthem. — *Bruce Eder*

Worst Of / Nov. 1970 / RCA 4459
Above-average '60s hits and major songs in this well-chosen compilation. — *AMG*

Thirty Seconds over Winterland / Apr. 1973 / RCA 0147
Well-produced document of the final days of the Airplane before it evolved into the Jefferson Starship. The singing and playing are all inspired, and the repertory is surprisingly melodic, considering the direction in which the group had been going. The highlight is a live version of the science-fiction anthem "Have You Seen the Saucers." — *Bruce Eder*

Early Flight / Apr. 1974 / RCA 0437
A beguiling collection of bluesy, druggy, and idealistic leftovers from the group's recorded output, partly supplanted by *2400 Fulton Street* and further devalued by the boxed set, but still a handy little disc to have around. — *Bruce Eder*

★ **Red Octopus** / 1975 / RCA 0999
The masterpiece, and a massive seller, too. Grace Slick sings expressively, especially on "Fast Buck Freddie" and "Play on Love," but the real story is the integration of Marty Balin fully into the band, and again he brings a timeless ballad along in the hit "Miracles." — *William Ruhlmann*

Freedom at Point Zero / 1979 / Grunt 3452
Amazingly enough, the band survives the departure of Grace Slick and Marty Balin, adding Mickey Thomas on vocals and scoring hits with "Jane" and Kantner's "Girl with the Hungry Eyes." — *William Ruhlmann*

○ **Gold** / 1979 / RCA 3247

Well-chosen best-of covering the years 1974-1979, after which the band personnel changed significantly. —*William Ruhlmann*

Modern Times / 1981 / RCA 3848
Slick comes back for one song, and "Find Your Way Back" becomes a hit. Also included is "Stairway to Cleveland," as gutsy a statement of purpose as any in rock. —*William Ruhlmann*

● **2400 Fulton Street—An Anthology** / Mar. 1987 / RCA 5724
A more-than-adequate retrospective on the group, with every major song and a lot of oddball favorites as well, all remastered from sources far superior to those used on the original albums. Some of it will be redundant (virtually the whole *Surrealistic Pillow* album is here) but the quality and the order of the programming is rewarding. —*Bruce Eder*

Jefferson Airplane Loves You / Oct. 1992 / RCA 61110
A three-disc boxed set that is loaded with rarities, *Jefferson Airplane Loves You* is necessary for hardcore fans, but the double-disc *2400 Fulton Street* offers a better portrait of the band and is the essential purchase for casual fans. —*Stephen Thomas Erlewine*

Jellyfish

Group / Power pop
In 1990 Jellyfish became a buzz band in certain circles of the music industry for their power-pop direction—essentially a Squeeze-Beatles-Beach Boys synthesis marketed with silly Alice in Wonderland-style psychedelic outfits. For their second album, Jellyfish toned down their image, yet their music remained just as grandiose and colorful. —*Rick Clark*

● **Bellybutton** / 1991 / Charisma 91400
The beginning of the '90s brought a resurgence in Anglo-pop bands, and Jellyfish's debut, *Bellybutton*, was one of the best releases of that style. Highlights on this fine album are the Squeeze-influenced "Baby's Comin' Back," the hit single "The King Is Half-Undressed," and "I Wanna Stay Home," a beautiful pop ballad that draws its melodic and arrangement smarts from McCartney and Burt Bacharach. —*AMG*

Spilt Milk / 1993 / Capitol 86459
Jellyfish's second album is long on technique, stylistic flash, and hooks in the style of Queen, Badfinger, and the Beatles—unfortunately, very few of them stick. *Spilt Milk* sounds splendid while it's being played, while the hooks pile on top of each other, but the end result is slightly cold. Still, there are some pleasures here (particularly the single "The Ghost at Number One") that will make fans forgive the excesses. —*AMG*

The Jesters

Group / Doo-wop
The archetypal New York street-corner group, with soaring falsetto and stirring harmonies. With Adam Jackson and Lenny McKay sharing lead duties, the Jesters recorded several classics of the doo-wop genre for Winley in 1957 and 1958, including "So Strange" and "The Plea." Jackson recast the group in 1960 for their last Winley releases, including an accurate remake of the Diablos tune "The Wind." —*Bill Dahl*

● **Best of the Jesters** / 1969 / Collectables 5036
Falsetto-drenched late-'50s New York City street-corner doo-wop. —*Bill Dahl*

The Jesus & Mary Chain

Group / Alternative pop/rock
This Scottish combo burst out of East Kilbraid in 1984 with a style that piled thick gobs of squalling guitars over tugging Beach Boy harmonies and the lyrical cynicism of Velvets-era Lou Reed. Brothers Jim and William Reid eventually toned down the feedback just a tad—replacing their rhythm section with a drum machine—and have managed to keep their sound fresh, primarily through clever melodies and the occasional inspired lyric hook. —*John Floyd*

● **Psychocandy** / 1985 / Warner Brothers 25383
The fuzzy, super-loud release that introduced JMC to American audiences. —*John Floyd*

○ **Darklands** / 1987 / Warner Brothers 25656
The subdued, depressing follow-up to *Psychocandy*. —*John Floyd*

Barbed Wire Kisses / 1988 / Warner Brothers 25729

A singles and rarities collection that fills in some gaps of this productive band's catalog. —*John Floyd*

Automatic / 1990 / Warner Brothers 26015
The drum-machine beats are too stiff, but this set contains their best songs, including the sorta-hit "Head On." —*John Floyd*

○ **Honey's Dead** / May 1992 / Def American 26830
If Mary Chain albums share that common thread with, say, the Ramones or Motorhead—that as good as they are they're all pretty much interchangeable—then know that *Honey's Dead* stands out. The Reid brothers deliver their concoction of melodic noise with craftsmanship, and this collection stands above much of their previous output. —*Steve Aldrich*

Jesus Jones

Group / Alternative pop/rock, dance-pop
Jesus Jones's murky mix of samples, pop, dance tracks, and techno has resulted in one huge international hit single, "Right Here, Right Now" (taken from their second album, *Doubt*), that pretty much sums up all of the band's virtues: a strong melody and hook, with a flair for making the dance club overtones mesh with the rock guitar. For their flaws, turn to their first album, which suffers from muddy beats, shapeless melodies, and intrusive samples, all of which plagued sections of *Doubt*. But when *Doubt* worked, as it did on "Right Here, Right Now," "International Bright Young Thing," and "Real, Real, Real," it showed that sample-driven dance club music could comfortably fit into pop music.
 Based on the platinum success of *Doubt*, Jesus Jones's leader/guitarist/vocalist Mike Edwards decided it was his mission to make techno palatable for the pop masses and recorded their follow-up album, 1993's *Perverse*, almost entirely on computer. The result was neither good pop music nor good techno. Jesus Jones' subsequent fall from the top of the U.S. and U.K. charts was as fast as their rise to the top. —*Stephen Thomas Erlewine*

Liquidizer / 1989 / SBK 94480
Sampling, synths, and political lyrics all find a home in this electrifying techno-pop debut album. Many of the cuts are from original demos. Includes "Info Freako" and "Broken Bones." —*Donna DiChario and Bil Carpenter*

● **Doubt** / 1991 / SBK 95715
A step forward from their debut, with swirling Beatlesque melodies surrounding clever, often political lyrics, as on their hit "Right Here, Right Now." —*Donna DiChario*

○ **Perverse** / 1993 / EMI 280647
Perverse attempts to expand on the success Jesus Jones enjoyed with their second album, *Doubt*, not only commercially but artistically as well. Jesus Jones has made some history with their third album: It is the first album to be recorded entirely through a computer. Musically, *Perverse* is a synthesis of techno/rave dance music with traditional pop/rock songs and structures—it's an ambitious album that works sporadically. Somewhere during the composition of the album, band leader Mike Edwards lost sight of most of the pop-song sensibility that made "Right Here, Right Now" an across-the-boards smash. Too often the hooks are submerged beneath layers of computerized noise and aren't strong enough to pull themselves out. When *Perverse* clicks—"Zeroes and Ones," "The Devil You Know," "The Right Decision"—Jesus Jones gives the listener an idea of how enjoyable a successful marriage of techno and rock could be. —*Stephen Thomas Erlewine*

Jesus Lizard

Group / Alternative rock
Willfully abrasive and atonal, Jesus Lizard has emerged as Chicago's leading guitar noise band. Formed by former Scratch Acid members bassist David Wm. Sims and vocalist David Yow with guitarist Duane Denison, their albums are almost indistinguishable from each other, yet the band never sounds like they're repeating themselves. When it comes to scathing, disemboweling guitar-driven psuedo-industrial noise, no one else can touch them. —*Stephen Thomas Erlewine*

● **Liar** / May 1992 / Touch & Go 100
Jesus Lizard's third album, *Liar*, it their most focused set of bleak, grinding guitars and angst-ridden vocals. —*Stephen Thomas Erlewine*

Jethro Tull

Group / Progressive rock, hard rock
Led by wild-man flutist/singer/songwriter Ian Anderson, Jethro
Tull has been churning out an oddball synthesis of British Isles
folk and progressive hard rock since the late '60s. During their
heyday (the '70s), Tull became one of the biggest concert draws,
due to Anderson and the band's clownish stage antics and their
amazingly complex interplay.

Their earlier albums, *This Was, Stand Up,* and *Benefit,* laid the
groundwork for Tull's success, but it was 1971's *Aqualung* that
put them over the top.

Not unlike many bands attempting to take rock to new levels
through extended pieces, Tull released two back-to-back albums
(*Thick as a Brick,* and *Passion Play*) containing one musical piece
on each. Unlike many of those bands, both of these albums went
to number one.

Jethro Tull also managed a couple of hits with "Living in the
Past" and "Bungle in the Jungle." The band continues to release
albums and tour. —*Rick Clark*

This Was / 1968 / Chrysalis 21041
Tull incorporated jazz, folk, and blues-based rock into this im-
pressive debut, which included "Dharma for One," "My Sunday
Feeling," and "Song for Jeffrey." —*Rick Clark*

○ **Stand Up** / 1969 / Chrysalis 21042
Tull's second album was as impressive as *This Was.* Anderson's
flute dominates this outing. The instrumental "Bouree" became a
signature song for the band's early sound. Other highlights included "A New Day Yesterday," "Fat Man," and "Nothing Is Easy."
—*Rick Clark*

Benefit / 1970 / Chrysalis 21043
Benefit was almost as strong as *Stand Up.* Anderson had yet to
take the group into the realm of extended pieces. "Teacher,"
"Nothing to Say," and "A Time for Everything" are particularly
nice. —*Rick Clark*

★ **Aqualung** / 1971 / Chrysalis 21044
It was with *Aqualung* that Tull became a staple on FM rock radio, thanks to dynamic riff-heavy tracks like "My God," "Hymn
43," "Locomotive Breath," "Cross-Eyed Mary," "Wind-Up," and the
title track. Thematically, many of these songs were vehicles for
Anderson's railings about how organized religion had restricted
man's relationship with God. —*Rick Clark*

○ **Living in the Past** / 1972 / Chrysalis 21035
Living in the Past was essentially an anthology of key tracks from
Tull's first five albums. Included are extended live tracks as well
as popular numbers like "Christmas Song," "Song for Jeffery,"
"Hymn 43," and their biggest hit, "Living in the Past." The CD ver-
sion has curiously omitted two of Tull's better early tracks—
"Teacher" and "Bouree." Besides "Hymn 43," *Living in the Past*
doesn't include any key tracks from *Aqualung.* —*Rick Clark*

Minstrel in the Gallery / 1975 / Chrysalis 21082
Minstrel in the Gallery was Tull's most successful exercise in synthesizing Elizabethan folk with prog-rock. —*Rick Clark*

M.U.: The Best of Jethro Tull / 1976 / Chrysalis 21078
M.U. is a decent sampling of hits and album picks, but not definitive. —*Rick Clark*

○ **Songs from the Wood** / 1977 / Chrysalis 21132
On *Songs from the Wood,,* Tull's aggressive rock interplay and Ian
Anderson's fascination with early folk melodies from the British
Isles produced a particularly appealing collection of songs. "Cup
of Wonder," and "The Whistler" are particularly successful. —*Rick
Clark*

○ **A** / 1980 / Chrysalis 21301
With the addition of ex-Roxy Music violinist and keyboardist
Eddie Jobson and ex-Fairport Convention bassist Dave Pegg, Tull
produced their most overt (and fully realized) folk-rock album.
"Batteries Not Included," "Black Sunday," and "Crossfire" are
highlights. —*Rick Clark*

○ **20 Years of Jethro Tull—Highlights** / 1988 / Chrysalis 21655
This is a distilled version of tracks taken from Tull's first boxed
set. Broken down into four parts, it includes a smattering of hits,
live tracks, and some key album sides. It might not be definitive,
but it does give the listener a good idea of the band's musical
range. —*Rick Clark*

25th Anniversary / Apr. 20, 1993 / Capitol 26004

Jethro Tull's four-CD celebration of their quarter of a century in
the music business is only worth the time of hardcore Tull fans.
Two discs are full-length live performances (both discs contain
two of the same songs), one disc is full of alternate versions of
their most famous tracks, and a final disc of new remixes of "classic" tracks (which includes the third appearance of "A Song for
Jeffrey" on the four CDs). Casual fans are much better served by
one of the smaller collections. —*Stephen Thomas Erlewine*

Joan Jett

b. Sep. 22, 1960, Philadelphia, PA
Vocals, guitar / Rock & roll, hard rock
She once led the Runaways, but Jett's solo career has been as distinguished and rewarding as Chrissie Hynde's (and less pretentious). She never goes beyond basic two-guitar, three-chord rock
& roll, but her sometimes masterful songwriting and unbridled
enthusiasm are essential to all but the most pointy-headed intellectuals. —*John Floyd*

○ **Bad Reputation** / 1981 / Blackheart 707
Her debut suffers from a lack of coherent sound, but it's an impassioned homage to her glitter-and-punk roots. —*John Floyd*

○ **I Love Rock & Roll** / 1981 / Blackheart 747
The title track was an inescapable hit in 1981, and Jett's new
band, the Blackhearts, gave her a big, crunching hard rock sound.
Could've used some better songs though. —*John Floyd*

○ **Album** / 1983 / MCA 5437
With her best set of songs and big-time production, this is an astonishing statement of purpose, full of gritty Rolling Stones-like
boogie and a cover of Sly Stone's "Everyday People" that works
better than you'd think. But it's all spectacular. —*John Floyd*

★ **Glorious Results of a Misspent Youth** / 1984 / MCA 5476
Another masterful blast of fury and celebration, which shifts from
a blazing cover of the Runaway's "Cherry Bomb" to her best song,
"I Got No Answers." Along with the Pretenders' early work,
Glorious Results . . . ranks with the best rock of the '80s, focused
through a female point of view. —*John Floyd*

Good Music / 1986 / Epic 40544
The production's a bit heavy, but Jett's formula is still a winner.
"Black Leather" and the title cut are fine rock anthems. —*John
Floyd*

Up Your Alley / 1988 / Epic 44146
I Hate Myself for Loving You is a strikingly complex take on re-
lationships and was a hit, but aside from a whopping cover of
Chuck Berry's "Tulane," this album is pretty thin. —*John Floyd*

Pure and Simple / 1994 / Warner Brothers
A solid record that shows she has lost very little of her power,
Pure and Simple contained contributions by several of Jett's fans,
including members of L7 and Bikini Kill. —*Stephen Thomas
Erlewine*

Jive Five

Group / Doo-wop, R&B, soul
One of the groups that was a major instigator in the move from
'50s R&B to '60s soul, the Jive Five produced several outstanding
hits for the New York Belton label during the early '60s. —*John
Floyd*

● **Jive Five** / 1989 / United Artists 3455
A superb 20-track collection that features the Jive Five's finest
material, recorded in the early '60s for Lescay/Belton: Songs include "Rain," "My True Story," "No Not Again," "What Time Is It,"
and "Hurry Back." —*AMG*

○ **Complete United Artists Recordings . . .** / 1992 / Capitol 99669
A superior, 21-track collection of the Jive Five's material for
United Artists, recorded in the mid-'60s. —*AMG*

My True Story / Relic 7007
These hard-hitting doo-woppers testify on the title cut, "What
Time Is It," and on "Hully Gully Callin' Time." Eugene Pitts is one
of the era's most evocative singers. —*John Floyd*

Jodeci

Group / Urban R&B
A new jack swing ensemble whose debut album was a huge hit,
Jodeci pairs North Carolina brothers Joel and Cedric Halley (also
called Jo-Jo and K-Ci) and Dalvin and Donald Degrate Jr. (the lat-

ter better known as Devante Swing). *Forever My Lady* made them huge stars in 1991, selling over two million copies and securing a Top-20 pop hit with "Come and Talk to Me." "Forever My Lady" and "Stay" were also major R&B successes, as was their cover of Stevie Wonder's "Lately," which was featured on the *Uptown Unplugged* release. Jodeci followed that in 1994 with *Diary of a Mad Band*, which debuted at the top of the R&B charts. —*Ron Wynn*

Forever My Lady / 1991 / Uptown/MCA 10198
A pair of brother acts combined forces to form Jodeci, a singing group with one foot in the future and the other squarely in the past. Dalvin and Devante Swing teamed with Jo-Jo and K-Ci Halley for a debut album that mixed vintage soul singing with new jack production and bravado. But it wasn't the hip-hop flavored songs that earned them popularity; instead, urban contemporary audiences embraced the love tunes "Come and Talk to Me" and the title track, signaling the beginnings of a move away from new jack swing that's become a full-fledged retreat as the '90s continue. —*Ron Wynn*

● **Diary of a Mad Band** / 1993 / Uptown/MCA 10915
Jodeci have enjoyed urban contemporary success with two dissimiliar styles. Their debut album was a new jack swing endeavor, with smart raps interspersed within torrid love songs. Then they scored another hit via a cover of Stevie Wonder's "Lately" done in vintage soul style. The group juggles these approaches on their second album, and wind up with a jarring, mis matched release. The disc's love songs, particularly "Cry for You," "What about Us" and "My Heart Belongs to You" are tender, passionately sung, sincere expressions of romance and love. But they diminish these with a string of innuendo-laden come-on numbers, complete with explicit language, tired raps and samples, and the kind of sentiments and appeals better suited to a *Penthouse Forum* entry than an album. —*Ron Wynn*

Billy Joel

b. May 9, 1949, Long Island, NY
Vocals, piano / Singer/songwriter, pop/rock
When pianist, singer, and songwriter Billy Joel came along in 1973 with his major-label debut *Piano Man,* he was perceived as an American alternative to *Tumbleweed Connection*-period Elton John. Both of them tended toward ornate and grand-sounding melodies and progressions, but Joel's musical attack was more assertive, and lyrically he was a straight shooter with something of a chip on his shoulder. Joel's music embraces classic Brill Building and Broadway schools of song structure while drawing from the Paul McCartney side of the Beatles and genres like street-corner doo-wop and early '60s pop.

Joel's first hit, "Piano Man," portrayed him as a guy who endured the lounge-lizard circuit as an observer passing through. On his follow-up hit, "The Entertainer," the punkish pragmatism of his personality is further defined. It is an attitude, along with his decidedly non-rock melodies, that doesn't sit well with critics, but Joel's dynamic shows and his finely tuned composing skills attracted a hardcore fan base.

Joel's initial success began to diminish until he hooked up with producer Phil Ramone (Paul Simon, Julian Lennon) and recorded the mega-platinum *The Stranger.* That album began a string of huge hit singles and albums that remains unabated.

"Just the Way You Are," "My Life," "You May Be Right," "It's Still Rock and Roll to Me," "Tell Her about It," "Uptown Girl," and "You're Only Human (Second Wind)" are among Joel's numerous chart successes. —*Rick Clark*

Cold Spring Harbor / 1971 / Columbia 38984
Joel's debut solo album finds him sounding like a romantic singer/songwriter with a strong sense of melody. The album's single, "She's Got a Way," later turned up in his concerts. The original 1971 album released by Family Productions was mastered wrong and speeds up the tape; in 1984, Columbia Records released a corrected version. —*William Ruhlmann*

○ **Piano Man** / 1973 / Columbia 32544
Joel presents a personal perspective of middle-class teen life in the suburbs ("Captain Jack," "The Ballad of Billy the Kid") followed by life in a cocktail lounge ("Piano Man"), and concludes, "Worse comes to worst, I'll get along." But his already apparent sense of melody and supple singing voice indicate much more promise than that. —*William Ruhlmann*

Streetlife Serenade / 1975 / Columbia 33146
Extending a mean streak he'd already revealed more than once, Joel looks upon the starmaking machinery that broke him the year before and scorns it. But he has such a gift for the putdown, notably in "Los Angelenos" and "The Entertainer," and the melodies are so good, that you can't help singing along and agreeing with him—if you didn't already, that is. —*William Ruhlmann*

○ **Turnstiles** / 1976 / Columbia 33848
Billy Joel's best, most consistent, most accessible record, even if not his best seller. From "Say Goodbye to Hollywood," which signals his return to the Big Apple with a drumbeat borrowed from the Ronettes, through the Sinatra ballad "New York State of Mind," the reflective "Summer, Highland Falls," and the hilarious "Miami 2017," Joel has never been more imaginative or more tuneful. Of course, "Angry Young Man" shows him to be as mean-spirited as ever, but the music carries even that one home. This record was the prototype to a virtual hit assembly line. —*William Ruhlmann*

○ **Stranger** / 1977 / Columbia 34987
The breakthrough to superstardom, containing the hits "Just the Way You are," "Movin' Out (Anthony's Song)," "Only the Good Die Young," and "She's Always a Woman." All those are on *Greatest Hits—Vols. I & II,* but "Scenes from an Italian Restaurant," one of Joel's most compelling story-songs, is not. —*William Ruhlmann*

○ **52nd Street** / 1978 / Columbia 35609
Joel consolidated his position with this somewhat harder rocking follow-up to *The Stranger.* It contained the hits "My Life," "Big Shot," and "Honesty." —*William Ruhlmann*

Glass Houses / 1980 / Columbia 36384
Billy Joel's response to punk, which, being a snotty kid himself, he felt a certain affinity with, and which allowed his usual belligerence unusually free rein (an aspect of his work that can be tolerated only because it is unflinchingly honest and as often directed at himself as at others). Again, most of the best songs are on the greatest hits, but this is the only place you can get "Sometimes a Fantasy." —*William Ruhlmann*

Songs in the Attic / 1981 / Columbia 37461
Joel used his first live album to refocus attention on his pre-*Stranger* catalog, turning in new versions of worthy songs like "She's Got a Way" and "Say Goodbye to Hollywood," both of which now became Top-25 hits. —*William Ruhlmann*

○ **Nylon Curtain** / 1982 / Columbia 38200
Upon release, Joel's eighth studio album was hailed by critics who had previously scorned him because he had decided to take on social concerns—the stress of modern life in "Pressure," unemployment in "Allentown," and the Vietnam War in "Goodnight Saigon." In retrospect, those songs were the best of an uneven collection. —*William Ruhlmann*

Innocent Man, An / 1983 / Columbia 38837
A brilliant evocation of popular styles of the early '60s, from doo-wop to R&B, that is much more than a period exercise because it obviously is so deeply felt and because it is so well executed. And no one has sounded quite so guilty as the singer of the title track, whether he realized it or not. —*William Ruhlmann*

★ **Greatest Hits—Vols. 1 & 2 (1973-1985)** / 1985 / Columbia 40121
Long overdue and exactly what it says it is. —*William Ruhlmann*

Bridge / 1986 / Columbia 40402
The hits are "Modern Woman," "A Matter of Trust," and "This Is the Time," all melodic rockers in Joel's patented style. There is also "Baby Grand," a duet with Ray Charles. But, three years on, this wasn't a patch on *An Innocent Man* and suggested Joel's best work might be behind him. —*William Ruhlmann*

Storm Front / 1989 / Columbia 44366
Joel caused a stampede for high school social science classes with the patter song "We Didn't Start the Fire," a cross between Gilbert and Sullivan and rock & roll that listed events in the news over the last 40 years, broken up by chants of the title. "I Go to Extremes" was a confession of emotional instability set to a strong melody and a rocking beat. There were also minor entries, such as "The Downeaster 'Alexa,'" which was about Long Island fishermen, and "Shameless," which Garth Brooks turned into a country smash. And, as usual, there was about a side's worth of worthless filler. —*William Ruhlmann*

River of Dreams / Apr. 30, 1993 / Columbia 53003
Joel has reached middle age and he's still restless and angry. Fortunately, this results in some fine, adventurous music, making *River of Dreams* his strongest effort since *The Nylon Curtain*. Joel explores all his favorite musical territory on this album, reaching back to doo-wop, moving through Beatlesque pop, toward his trademark balladry. —*Stephen Thomas Erlewine*

David Johansen

b. Jan. 9, 1950, Staten Island, NY
Vocals / Hard rock, rock & roll
The former lead singer with the New York Dolls, David Johansen went on to a solo career but failed to rise above cult status, despite releasing some fine albums. His live 1982 release, *Live It Up*, contains a great Animals medley that almost broke him into a wider market, but a persona change under the moniker "Buster Poindexter" put Johansen over the top, with a big dance hit, "Hot Hot Hot." Subsequent efforts as Poindexter have lacked the freshness of the original concept, which drew from Caribbean dance grooves and '30s and '40s swing and cabaret styles. —*Rick Clark*

● **David Johansen** / 1978 / Razor & Tie 1990
True, the best songs here ("Frenchette," "Funky but Chic," "Girls") are the ones Johansen brought with him from the Dolls. What's intriguing about his solo debut, though, is how well he pulls off ballads like "Donna" and "Pain in My Heart." And Johnny Rao's guitar work *almost* compensates for the absence of Johnny Thunders, the Dolls' guitarist. —*John Floyd*

○ **Live It Up** / 1982 / Razor & Tie 1994
A scorching live set from 1982 that also works as a career-defining best-of. Johansen drives his roadhouse band through a few old Dolls hits, the best cuts from his solo albums, and a medley of Animals hits that damn near outstrips the originals. And don't miss the two Motown covers. —*John Floyd*

Elton John (Reginald Dwight)

b. Mar. 25, 1947, Pinner, England
Vocals, piano / Pop/rock
Elton John was the single most successful pop artist of the '70s, and he continued to score hits for decades after his initial reign of popularity. Born Reginald Dwight in Pinner, England, he showed an early aptitude for the piano and received classical training, winning a scholarship to the Royal Academy of Music at the age of 11. But after six years he turned to pop music, and struggled as a songwriter, sideman, and member of unsuccessful groups for the rest of the '60s.During this period, he hooked up with lyricist Bernie Taupin through a newspaper advertisement, and the two were signed as songwriters to publisher Dick James, who was to have a tremendous impact on John's early career.

A debut album sponsored by James, *Empty Sky*, flopped in 1969, but in 1970, with the album *Elton John* and the single "Your Song," Elton John took off, scoring especially well in America. For the next five years, his output—and the sales that material racked up—was enormous. John always had an ability to hit with ballads like the wistful "Daniel," then turn around and rock as hard as the Rolling Stones on a song like "Saturday Night's Alright for Fighting." There hardly seemed a day from 1972, when "Rocket Man" began a streak of 16 straight Top-20 hits (15 of which went Top Ten), to 1976, when John took a breather, that his songs weren't dominating the airwaves and the record charts.

The late '70s seem to have been a period of recovery and indecision for the singer, but by 1980 he had settled into making one well-crafted album a year, and many of them tossed off hits, if not with such consistency as before. "Little Jeannie" (1980), "I Guess That's Why They Call It the Blues" and "Sad Songs (Say So Much)" (both 1984), and "Nikita" (1986) all showed John could still hit the upper reaches of the charts, especially with his trademark ballads. The late '80s again saw a slowing in John's record success, but by the start of the '90s he had gone public about drug and alcohol problems he said were behind him, and he looked poised for a new start.

After several more years of adult contemporary hits in the early '90s, John moved into scoring films, writing the music for Walt Disney's 1994 animated feature, *The Lion King*. The soundtrack was an enormous success and "Can You Feel the Love Tonight," John's version of the movie's love theme, was his biggest hit in years. —*William Ruhlmann*

Elton John / 1970 / MCA 31105
Ironically, Elton John's breakthrough album (and U.S. debut) is uncharacteristic of his other work, heavily featuring Paul Buckmaster's dramatic string arrangements. John is never overwhelmed by strings or choirs and turns in some powerful performances. Contains "Your Song." —*William Ruhlmann*

☆ **Tumbleweed Connection** / Jan. 1971 / MCA 31103
Elton John's follow-up was a thematic album about the American Old West (a Taupin fascination) that allowed John to rock out on several numbers. There are no hits here (!) but the album stands up well two decades later on. —*William Ruhlmann*

○ **Madman across the Water** / 1972 / MCA 31190
One of John's best-ever collections of songs, containing "Levon," "Tiny Dancer," and the title track, all of which survive in the memory better than they did on the charts. —*William Ruhlmann*

○ **Honky Chateau** / Jan. 1972 / MCA 31104
Notable not only for the hits "Honky Cat" and "Rocket Man" but also for "I Think I'm Gonna Kill Myself" and "Mona Lisas and Mad Hatters." The first of John's seven U.S. number-one albums. —*William Ruhlmann*

☆ **Goodbye Yellow Brick Road** / Feb. 1973 / MCA 6894
Almost certainly Elton John's biggest seller, save his first greatest hits collection. The hits on this sprawling double-disc set include "Saturday Night's Alright for Fighting," the title track, and "Bennie and the Jets," and the album tracks include "Love Lies Bleeding" and "Candle in the Wind" (which became a hit 15 years later in a live version). —*William Ruhlmann*

★ **Greatest Hits** / Feb. 1974 / MCA 37215
A virtual time capsule of the pop music of the first half of the '70s. —*William Ruhlmann*

○ **Captain Fantastic & The Brown Dirt Cowboy** / Feb. 1975 / MCA 31078
Bernie Taupin's most ambitious lyrical effort, *Captain Fantastic & the Brown Dirt Cowboy* is an autobiographical song cycle that also drew an unusually strong musical effort from John, resulting in perhaps his strongest overall record since *Tumbleweed Connection*. —*William Ruhlmann*

Single Man, A / 1978 / MCA 31181
An unusually well-crafted album, and the beginning of John's comeback. "Part-Time Love" was the hit, but "Madness" and the instrumental "Song for Guy" were musical highlights. —*William Ruhlmann*

21 at 33 / 1980 / MCA 31054
An ambitious songwriting effort featuring Tom Robinson's collaboration on "Sartorial Eloquence" and Gary Osborne's on "Little Jeannie," though the best songs are by the returning Bernie Taupin: "Chasing the Crown" and "Two Rooms at the End of the World." —*William Ruhlmann*

☆ **Greatest Hits Volume II** / 1980 / MCA 37216
More of the hottest hit streak of the decade, including such otherwise non-album singles as "Lucy in the Sky with Diamonds" and "Philadelphia Freedom." —*William Ruhlmann*

○ **Too Low for Zero** / 1983 / David Geffen Co. 4006
With Taupin (and his old band) on board full time, John turned out one of his best '80s albums—one full of remorse ("Cold as Christmas") and fierce reaffirmation ("I'm Still Standing"), not to mention such irresistible tunes as "Kiss the Bride" and "I Guess That's Why They Call It the Blues." —*William Ruhlmann*

○ **Greatest Hits, Vol. 3 (1979-1987)** / 1987 / David Geffen Co. 24153
The best of the Geffen years is very good indeed. —*William Ruhlmann*

○ **To Be Continued . . .** / 1990 / MCA 10110
The inevitable Elton John boxed set is a four-disc, 68-track affair covering 25 years of the biggest pop star since the Beatles. Hit after hit is heard, plus good album tracks and rarities. There's a big booklet with commentary by John and his lyricist, Bernie Taupin. In a pinch, you can get by with the two MCA and one Geffen greatest-hits collections, but for a complete overview of Elton John's career, this is the place to come. —*William Ruhlmann*

Greatest Hits, 1976—1986 / 1992 / MCA 10693
It covers much of the same ground as Geffen's *Greatest Hits—Vol. 3* but there's no denying that the hits on *Greatest Hits, 1976-1986* are worth owning in any format by any Elton John fan. —*AMG*

○ **Rare Masters** / 1992 / PolyGram 514138

A two-CD collection of rarities from the early '70s, including B-sides and the entire *Friends* soundtrack which has previously been unavailable on CD, *Rare Masters* is essential for any hard-core Elton John fan. —*AMG*

Eric Johnson

Guitar / Rock & roll

Very few post-Hendrix guitarists can match Eric Johnson's six-string magic. There's no hint of anger, angst, or sloppiness in any of his playing; instead, each note, each phrase, demonstrates his obsession with tone. Joyous celebrations, his solos seem to grow more magnificent with each listening. For years esteemed players proclaimed Eric Johnson one of rock's most imaginative and tasteful guitarists. Despite the praise, Johnson labored in relative obscurity in Austin, TX, until the 1986 release of *Tones*. His goal was to produce music that entertains and heals, and his playing married deep emotion to mind-boggling finesse. The album's collage of guitar tones ran from purest-of-pure Strat to Hendrix-approved psychedelia and majestic, violinlike textures. Johnson spent nearly two years producing his 1990 followup, *Ah Via Musicom*. Full of fire, light, and swirling thunder, it's an artistic triumph, as powerful a statement for Eric Johnson as *Electric Ladyland* was for Jimi Hendrix. —*Jas Obrecht*

○ **Tones** / 1986 / Reprise 25375

A landmark guitar recording. —*Jas Obrecht*

● **Ah Via Musicom** / 1990 / Capitol 90517

Strong songs and exquisite tones. —*Jas Obrecht*

Marv Johnson

b. Oct. 15, 1938, Detroit, MI, d. May 16, 1993

Vocals / Motown, R&B

Johnson played an important role in the founding of the Motown empire, with his "Come to Me" the first release on Berry Gordy's Tamla label in 1959. The tuneful high-pitched tenor's impressive effort was snapped up by United Artists, who promptly issued his two biggest Gordy-produced hits, "You Got What It Takes" (first waxed by Bobby Parker on Vee-Jay) and "I Love the Way You Love." Johnson stayed with UA into the early '60s before returning home to Gordy in 1965 and staying until 1968. —*Bill Dahl*

● **Marvelous Marv Johnson** / 1960 / Collectables 5236

Though he was one of the early artists that helped Motown become a pop and soul empire during the '60s, Marv Johnson made better records while recording for United Artists in the late '50s and early '60s. This is one of several compilations that have chronicled his cuts prior to the Motown days. Though Berry Gordy produced a number of these, the ones that clicked weren't as clever or elaborate, nor as pop-oriented, as Motown's finest cuts. Johnson had a soulful and flexible voice, and is among the transitional artists who deserve more attention for their role in Motown's emergence. —*Ron Wynn*

I Believe / 1966 / United Artists 3187

A wonderful, sorely overlooked late '50s and '60s soul singer, Marv Johnson had the misfortune to have early hits on Tamla, then a tiny label and not the giant wing of Motown it would become by the mid-'60s. He was a dynamic, aggressive vocalist who excelled at heartache ballads, and as these songs repeatedly show, was among the finest of his era in building and pacing a song, delivering a lyric and wrenching emotion out of whatever he was singing. —*Ron Wynn*

○ **You Got What It Takes** / 1992 / EMI America 98895

EMI issued a single-disc CD anthology of Marv Johnson's material in 1993, *You Got What It Takes*. It included all his R&B chart hits, "Come to Me," "You Got What It Takes," "I Love the Way You Love," and "Happy Days." —*Ron Wynn*

Freedy Johnston

Vocals / Singer/songwriter, folk-rock

A fine lyricist from Kansas who resettled in Hoboken, NJ, Johnston brought his heartland rock to the more brash Northeast, and after a shaky start has become a very exciting artist. Johnston's 1992 album *Can You Fly* received a generous amount of critical praise, and deservedly so—his direct, Midwestern viewpoint made for some of the finest folk-rock of the decade. Two years later, the singer/songwriter had become a hot property and

he followed through on his promise with the Butch Vig-produced *This Perfect World*, which easily matched *Can You Fly* with its spare beauty. —*Bruce Eder*

● **Can You Fly** / Apr. 14, 1992 / Bar/None 24

Freedy Johnston's second album is a supremely engaging set of folk-rock that showcases Johnston's considerable talent for writing melodic, literate songs with a gritty emotional core. —*Stephen Thomas Erlewine*

Unlucky / 1993 / Restless/Bar None 24

This CD features Johnston's touring band and includes a great cover of "Witchita Lineman" as well as the acoustic demo of "The Lucky One." —*Richard Meyer*

○ **This Perfect World** / 1994 / Elektra

The follow-up to the critically acclaimed *Can You Fly* is a collection of highly melodic and intelligent folk-rock that confirms Johnston's status as one of the finest singer/songwriters of the '90s. —*Stephen Thomas Erlewine*

Howard Jones (John Howard Jones)

b. Feb. 23, 1955, Southampton, Hampshire

Vocals, keyboard / Pop/rock

Adept at overdubbing himself into a one-man band through his use of synthesizers and drum machines, Jones scored consistently on the charts in the early '80s with an inoffensive pop style on tunes like "New Song," "No One Is to Blame," and "Things Can Only Get Better." —*Cub Koda*

○ **Human's Lib** / 1984 / Elektra 60346

His debut album is almost entirely performed on synthesizers. The material on *Human's Lib*, like all of the following albums, is very inconsistent—Jones either writes hits or flops, with very little in between. Containing two of Jones's best songs, "New Song" and "What Is Love?" —*Iotis Erlewine*

○ **Dream into Action** / 1985 / Elektra 60390

This album shows the synthesizer pop idol at the height of his creativity—*Dream into Action* is definitely the most interesting of Jones's albums. It contains some of his best songs: "Things Can Only Get Better," "Life in One Day," and "No One Is to Blame." The CD includes two bonus tracks, "Bounce Right Back" and "Like to Get to Know You Well," both of which are worthwhile additions. —*Iotis Erlewine*

One to One / 1986 / Elektra 60499

This is Jones's most musically mature and toned down. The synthesizers are less overbearing than on the previous albums, but the songs are mediocre—neither very good nor very bad. The album reached number ten in the United Kingdom, but did not fare as well in the United States, peaking at number 56. This album features the revamped "No One Is to Blame," which is inferior to the original version. —*Iotis Erlewine*

Cross That Line / 1989 / Elektra 60794

After a three-year wait, this album was a bit of a disappointment. Musically, it is his best yet, but it lacked a certain energy that the others had. The songs seemed to replace vivacity with length. The album didn't do very well on the charts, "Everlasting Love" at number 13 on the U.S. charts, was the biggest hit. Ironically, the best song on this album, "Out of Thin Air," does not use a single synthesizer but instead is a solo piano piece performed by Jones himself. After all those years of electronic music, a song featuring a real instrument is a welcome relief. —*Iotis Erlewine*

● **Best of Howard Jones** / Jun. 29, 1993 / Elektra

The Best of Howard Jones successfully distills all the hits and highlights from his albums onto one disc. It could be all the Howard Jones you'll ever need. —*Stephen Thomas Erlewine*

Linda Jones

b. Jan. 14, 1944, Newark, NJ, d. Mar. 14, 1972

Vocals / Soul

A word in support of an artist who will probably be passed over by 999 listeners out of 1,000. Her biggest hit, the tastefully restrained "Hypnotized," came on the Loma subsidiary of Warner Brothers in 1967, but her later recordings for Turbo were probably the most gloriously histrionic soul records of all time. She started at a climax and worked up from there, transforming a ballad like "Let It Be Me" with her towering fury. It was pure gospel—and then some. Jones was already ill with diabetes when she cut those records, and she died in 1972 after collapsing backstage at the Apollo. —*Colin Escott*

● **Hypnotized** / 1967 / Collectables 5120

Linda Jones was a dynamic, sorely neglected late-'60s and early-'70s soul vocalist. There was no mild reaction to Jones's theatrical style—you were either amazed or appalled. She didn't deliver lyrics, she smashed and screamed them. This collection covers her bombastic cuts, among them the classic title track plus "I'll Be Sweeter Tomorrrow," "For Your Precious Love," and several others. Any vocalist picked by Gladys Knight and Patti Labelle as one of their favorites merits closer examination. Unfortunately her premature death in the early '70s prevented Jones from gaining much exposure, as did the fact that she did her recording for a host of small independents and never enjoyed any crossover success. —*Ron Wynn*

Your Precious Love / 1988 / Turbo 7007

Best of the Turbo-label tracks. Superior sound quality. —*Richard Pack*

Marti Jones

Vocals / Singer/songwriter, pop/rock

This Ohio-based singer and former member of Color Me Gone went solo under the tutelage of producer Don Dixon (now her husband). With Dixon she made four albums (1984-1990) interpreting the best of current songwriters. —*William Ruhlmann*

○ **Unsophisticated Time** / 1985 / A&M 5086

Jones applies her smoky alto to a group of ironic love songs, the best of them written by producer Don Dixon. —*William Ruhlmann*

● **Used Guitars** / 1989 / A&M 5208

Another solid effort from Marti Jones. —*David Jehnzen*

Any Kind of Lie / 1990 / RCA 2040

After proving herself an ideal interpreter for the more literate songwriters of the day (Elvis Costello, Peter Holsapple), Jones writes most of her own material here (with Don Dixon). And it's just as good as, if not better than the covers. —*William Ruhlmann*

Rickie Lee Jones

b. Nov. 8, 1954, Chicago, IL

Vocals / Singer/songwriter

A singer/songwriter who emerged in 1979 with a million-selling album and the Top-Ten hit "Chuck E's in Love." Born in Chicago, Jones grew up in Arizona and Washington state and was taught music by her father. Moving to Los Angeles in 1973, she started as a performer by doing rhythmic "Beat" monologs. She began to gain notice after hooking up with singer/songwriter Tom Waits in 1977, and in 1979 Little Feat leader Lowell George recorded her "Easy Money" on his debut solo album. Signed to Warner Brothers, Jones recorded her own debut, *Rickie Lee Jones* (a combination of folk, jazz, and rock styles), its lyrical songs populated by bohemian characters and sung in Jones's slightly slurred voice. It hit number three, and Jones won the Best New Artist Grammy for 1979.

She returned in 1981 with the even more ambitious *Pirates*, which hit number five and went gold. *Girl at Her Volcano* was a 1983 EP made up mostly of cover songs. Jones's next full-length album was *The Magazine*, which hit the Top 50 in 1984. In the second half of the '80s, Jones married and gave birth to a daughter. She returned to recording with the Top-40 *Flying Cowboys* in 1989, and in 1991 she released another record of covers, *Pop Pop*. —*William Ruhlmann*

★ **Rickie Lee Jones** / 1979 / Warner Brothers 3296

One of the most impressive debuts for a singer/songwriter ever, this infectious mixture of styles not only features a strong collection of original songs (the hits are "Chuck E's in Love" and "Young Blood," but "Danny's All-Star Joint" and "Coolsville" are just as good) but also a singer with a savvy, distinctive voice that can be streetwise, childlike, and sophisticated, sometimes all in the same song. —*William Ruhlmann*

○ **Pirates** / 1981 / Warner Brothers 3432

If the songs are less immediately accessible than on Jones's first album, repeated listenings are likely to lead to even greater rewards. Open-ended song structures allow Jones to explore more

fully her closely observed portraits of lowlife characters, and her singing remains entrancing. —*William Ruhlmann*

Janis Joplin

b. Jan. 19, 1943, Port Arthur, TX, **d.** Oct. 4, 1970

Vocals / Blues-rock, rock & roll

Janis Joplin was one of the greatest White female singers to take on the blues. Hailing from Texas, Joplin journeyed to San Francisco in 1963 to sing, playing infrequent gigs with Jorma Kaukonen or Roger Perkins. She returned to Austin in 1966 to sort out her life, briefly giving up singing and making plans for marriage. Nevertheless, word that the Bay Area band Big Brother & the Holding Company was looking for a singer lured Joplin back. With Big Brother, Joplin wowed audiences with her intensity and aching vulnerability. *Cheap Thrills*, a doctored-up live collection, topped a million sales. It contained incredible performances from Joplin and the band, particularly "Ball and Chain," "Summertime," "Combination of the Two," and the hit "Piece of My Heart."

Joplin left for a solo career and released 1969's *I Got Dem Ol' Kozmic Blues Again Mama!*, which featured the track "Try (Just a Little Harder)." Joplin assembled the Full-Tilt Boogie Band and began recording the follow-up album. Unfortunately, Joplin's crippling drug and alcohol addiction got to her, and she was found dead Oct. 4, 1970, at the Landmark Hotel in Hollywood, of an accidental heroin overdose.

Pearl, which was Joplin's nickname, was assembled out of the sessions that had been recorded, and it went to number one for nine weeks. The album produced a number-one hit as well, with a version of Kris Kristofferson's "Me and Bobby McGee." —*Rick Clark*

I Got Dem Ol' Kozmic Blues Again Mama / 1969 / Columbia 9913

Joplin's only solo album to be released during her lifetime heavily employs horns and an R&B band feel, but the dominant sound remains Joplin's impassioned singing on such songs as "Try." —*William Ruhlmann*

○ **Pearl** / 1971 / Columbia 30322

Backed by a tight rock band, Full Tilt Boogie, Joplin puts her mark on everything from the bluesy "Cry Baby" to her hit version of Kris Kristofferson's "Me & Bobby McGee." —*William Ruhlmann*

● **Janis Joplin's Greatest Hits** / 1973 / Columbia 32168

Well-chosen best-of gathers together tracks from Big Brother & the Holding Company and solo material. —*William Ruhlmann*

○ **Janis Box** / 1993 / Columbia/Legacy

This three-CD box set is the most thorough and valuable retrospective of Janis Joplin's career. Besides including all of her most essential recordings with and without Big Brother & the Holding Company, this 49-song package features quite a few enticing rarities; 18 of the tracks were previously unissued. These include a 1962 home recording of the Joplin original "What Good Can Drinkin' Do," which marked the first time her singing was captured on tape; a pair of acoustic blues tunes from 1965 with backup guitar by future Jefferson Airplane star Jorma Kaukonen; an acoustic demo of "Me and Bobby McGee"; a 1970 birthday song for John Lennon; and live performances from her appearance on "The Ed Sullivan Show" in 1969. The real showstopper is the previously unissued, eight-minute version of "Ball on Chain" from Big Brother's first set at the 1967 Monterey Pop Festival (the cut on the "Monterey Pop" boxed set is from their second set). The more forgettable tracks from her solo albums are wisely excised, as are the Big Brother songs that did not feature her vocals. This is the rare multidisc set of a major artist that manages to cover all the official milestones and present a bounty of worthwhile rarities at the same time. —*Richie Unterberger*

Journey

Group / Pop/rock

During its 14-year existence (1973-1987), Journey altered its musical approach and its personnel extensively while becoming a top touring and recording band. The only constant factor was guitarist Neal Schon (b. 1954), a music prodigy who had been a member of Santana in 1971-1972. The original unit, which was named in a contest on KSAN-FM in San Francisco, featured Schon, bassist Ross Valory, drummer Praire Prince (replaced by

Aynsley Dunbar), and guitarist George Tickner (who left after the first album). Another former Santana member, keyboard player and singer Gregg Rolie, joined shortly afterwards. This lineup recorded *Journey* (1974), the first of three moderate-selling jazz-rock albums given over largely to instrumentals.

By 1977, however, the group decided it needed a strong vocal-ist/frontman and hired Steve Perry (b. 1953). The results were im-mediately felt on the fourth album, *Infinity* (1978), which reached number 21 in the charts and had sold a million copies by the end of the year. (By this time, Dunbar had been replaced by Steve Smith.) *Evolution* (1979) was similarly successful, as was *Departure* (after which Rolie was replaced by Jonathan Cain). After a live album, *Captured* (1981), Journey released *Escape*, which broke them through to the top ranks of pop groups by scoring three Top-Ten hit singles, all ballads featuring Perry's smooth tenor: "Who's Crying Now," "Don't Stop Believin'," and "Open Arms." The album topped the charts and eventually sold over seven million copies.

Frontiers (1983), featuring the hit "Separate Ways," was an-other big success, after which Perry released a successful solo al-bum, *Street Talk* (1984). When the group got back together to make a new album, Valory and Smith were no longer in the lineup, and *Raised on Radio* (1986) was made by Schon, Perry, and Cain, who added other musicians for a tour. This, however, was the end of Journey, as Perry and Cain went off to form Bad English. — *William Ruhlmann*

Infinity / 1978 / Columbia 34912
The first album with vocalist Steve Perry. "Wheel in the Sky" was the band's first U.S. chart single, followed by "Anytime" and "Lights." It was the beginning of their climb up the charts with the trademark tenor of Steve Perry. —*Donna DiChario*

Evolution / 1979 / Columbia 35797
Journey got major U.S. radio airplay with "Just the Same Way," "Lovin', Touchin', Squeezin'," and "City of Angels." —*Donna DiChario*

○ **Captured** / 1981 / Columbia 37016
A live double album featuring many of their late '70s hits. —*Donna DiChario*

○ **Escape** / 1981 / Columbia 37408
Jonathan Cain (ex-Babys keyboardist) replaced Gregg Rolie on the band's most popular album to date. On the strength of the hits "Who's Crying Now" and "Don't Stop Believin'," this album spent more than a year in the Top 20. —*Donna DiChario*

○ **Frontiers** / 1983 / Columbia 38504
The ballads "Faithfully" and "Send Her My Love" reap the bene-fits of Steve Perry's crystal-clear vocals. —*Donna DiChario*

● **Greatest Hits** / 1988 / Columbia 44493
A collection of Journey's '70s and '80s radio staples. The band's best-known rockers and ballads, including "Open Arms," "Who's Crying Now," "Any Way You Want It," and "Separate Ways (Worlds Apart)" are here. —*Donna DiChario*

Time3 / Dec. 1, 1992 / Columbia 48937
A three-CD boxed set of Journey is too much by most standards, although hardcore fans will be happy to know that all of the band's hits and best album tracks are included here, among some filler. *Time 3* is more than comprehensive, but if you buy this you will never need to own another Journey album. —*Stephen Thomas Erlewine*

Joy Division

Group / Alternative pop/rock
The unchallenged Kings of Angst, Joy Division would ultimately be recognized as England's most important band of the immedi-ate post-punk era. Starting out as Warsaw, the band failed to dis-tinguish itself beyond the psychotic-looking on-stage behavior of singer Ian Curtis, and the handful of sides the band issued were largely ignored. All that changed with the release of Joy Division's debut album, *Unknown Pleasures*. The music was built around Peter Hook's dominant bass lines, which wound their way around brooding minor-key melodies, while Curtis established himself as a Jim Morrison-like presence with his rigid delivery and often-disturbing lyrics. The album was hailed as an immediate classic.

As difficult and gloomy as Joy Division's music appeared to be, there was also an oddly warmer and sometimes beautiful side to this group, as evidenced by the non-LP single "Atmospheres."

Their upcoming recorded work was highly anticipated, but just prior to its release came the shocking news that Curtis had taken his own life. The ensuing single, "Love Will Tear Us Apart" came packaged in tombstone style graphics, and housed Joy Division's masterpiece. While the group continued as New Order, only their earliest work was directly connected with Joy Division's music—they soon found a voice of their own, away from the spectre of Curtis. Despite the near-hysteria after Curtis's death and the nu-merous tortured souls who attempted to ape the formula, Joy Division's music stands as an impressive and still-riveting achievement. —*Steve Aldrich*

☆ **Unknown Pleasures** / 1979 / Qwest 25840
Their debut is a stark, almost Gothic masterpiece of emotional destruction and inner pain, expressed both lyrically and musi-cally. —*John Floyd*

☆ **Closer** / 1980 / Qwest 25841
An even gloomier set on their second album, released just after Curtis's death. Guitars take a back seat to swirling layers of syn-thesizer, while Curtis's lyrics expand to examine the decay of not only the heart but society. —*John Floyd*

Still / 1981 / Qwest 26495
A double album that contains nine worthwhile studio outtakes, a live version of the Velvet Underground's "Sister Ray," and ten cuts from a 1980 gig. Of interest only to hardcore fans. —*John Floyd*

★ **Substance** / 1988 / Qwest 25747
Collecting some riveting and rare material previously available only on singles and compilations, this offers a more diverse por-trait of the band and works as both an introduction and a sup-plement to the original release. —*John Floyd*

Judas Priest

Group / Heavy metal
Judas Priest is undoubtedly one of the most influential English heavy metal bands of the '70s. With vocalist Rob Halford, gui-tarists K. K. Downing and Glenn Tipton, bassist Ian Hill, and drummer Alan Moore, they released a debut album in 1974, *Rocka Rolla*. It only did well in their native country, but when they released *Sad Wings of Destiny* in 1976, some U.S. radio sta-tions gave airplay to "The Ripper" and "Victim of Changes"; the latter was a song that showed Halford's full vocal range. They soon signed with CBS Records, and it was there they gained worldwide appeal.

Unleashed in the East, recorded live in Japan in 1978, became one of the group's best-selling albums in the United States. Filled with such great songs as "Don't Go" and "Heading Out to the Highway," 1981's *Point of Entry* was the record that put them over the top. Although the follow-up *Defenders of the Faith* featured a speed-metal number called "Freewheel Burning" at a time when thrash and speed metal were still underground phenomenons, they lost some popularity when they experimented with synthe-sizers on 1986s *Turbo*. Since then, the group hasn't maintained the popularity they enjoyed in the late '70s and early '80s, but Judas Priest's sound—from the vocals of Halford to the double at-tack of Tipton and Downing—influenced a generation of bands who proudly claim the Priest as their favorite band. —*John Book*

○ **Sad Wings of Destiny** / 1976 / RCA 4747
Vintage Judas Priest from the mid '70s, an excellent example of British heavy metal coming into its own and of a band beginning to gain acceptance on both sides of the Atlantic. Includes "The Ripper" and "Victim of Changes," the latter of which demon-strates the full vocal range of Rob Halford. —*John Book*

○ **Unleashed in the East (Live in Japan)** / 1979 / Columbia 36179
Recorded live in Japan, this was the album that helped Judas Priest finally break through in America, with support from critics and radio airplay. The album is an exceptional live performance. The songs chosen are a good example of their material from the '70s. —*John Book*

○ **Point of Entry** / 1981 / Columbia 37052
Point of Entry finally made Judas Priest a major-league success. With well-written songs, solid musicianship from the entire band, and powerful vocals from Rob Halford, Judas Priest helped define heavy metal in the '80s. Includes "Heading Out to the Highway," "Hot Rockin'," and "Don't Go." —*John Book*

● **Metal Works '73–'93** / 1993 / Columbia 53932

Over two discs, *Metal Works '73–'93* winds its way through Judas Priest's 20-year career, hitting most of the high points as well as the low points and somehow managing to overlook 7 of their 11 U.K. hits. Still, there isn't a better place to get acquainted with the band, which really was one of the most important metal units in the late '70s and early '80s. —*Stephen Thomas Erlewine*

Henry Kaiser

b. Sep. 11, 1952
Guitar / Experimental
Guitarist Henry Kaiser is a prolific member of the San Francisco Bay Area music scene, as well as being a globally recognized leader of the "second generation" of free improvisers who came of age in the '70s. His earliest musical inspiration came from the spiky sounds of English improvising guitarist Derek Bailey and the many guitarists in Captain Beefheart's Magic Band. Later on, Kaiser absorbed the subtle string textures of the American blues stylists and traditional music of Asia, particularly India, Korea, and Vietnam.

His initial recordings documented solo projects and spontaneous groupings with other energetic improvisers like Fred Frith, the ROVA Saxophone Quartet, pianist Greg Goodman, and vocalist Diamanda Galas. Kaiser's restless creativity unearthed many new and unconventional electric guitar techniques during these years, and he combined these innovations with a strong sense of logic and concise development, often aided by sophisticated sound-processing devices. Recently Kaiser's projects have tended toward the rock sound of the '60s and '70s, with a special fascination for the music of the Grateful Dead. But he has simultaneously explored American folk along with the folk music of Vietnam and Madagascar. —*Myles Boisen*

○ **Aloha: Studio Solo** / 1980 / Metalanguage 109
His first major statement of purpose as a multi-faceted soloist, leader, and producer. A two-fer. —*Myles Boisen*

● **With Enemies like These, Who Needs Friends?** / 1980 / SST 147
A CD compilation of Henry Kaiser and Fred Frith's guitar duo records. *With Enemies like These, Who Needs Friends?* is a masterpiece of studio improvisation and innovative guitar techniques. —*Myles Boisen*

○ **Devil in the Drain** / Oct. 1987 / SST 118
His most fully realized instrumental solo work. Fantastic structures from various creative directions on guitar and synclavier. —*Myles Boisen*

○ **Those Who Know History Are Doomed to Repeat It** / May 1989 / SST 198
Eclecticism reigns supreme here, on his first full exploration of pop music covers and Grateful Dead-style jamming. —*Myles Boisen*

○ **Hope You Like Our New Direction** / 1991 / Reckless 21
From Buddy Holly to Beefheart, Virginia to Vietnam, this musical tour takes you to every corner of Kaiser's wonderful world. Lots of surprises. —*Myles Boisen*

○ **Lemon Fish Tweezer: A History of Henry Kaiser's Solo Guitar Improvisations (1973-1991)** / Aug. 24, 1992 / Cuneiform 45
A retrospective of Henry's boundary-smashing solo projects from the mid '70s on. —*Myles Boisen*

Kansas

Group / Progressive rock, pop/rock
This progressive rock group from Topeka featured Steve Walsh on keyboards, Phil Ehart on percussion, Rich Williams on guitar, Robby Steinhardt on violins, Dave Hope on bass, and Kerry Livgren on piano. They opened on the last Doors tour and were signed by Don Kirshner in 1974. Their music tended to be influenced by British groups such as the Moody Blues and Yes. —*Bil Carpenter*

○ **Kansas** / 1974 / Kirshner 32817
An encouraging debut reflecting an infatuation with English art-rock. —*Rick Clark*

○ **Song for America** / 1975 / Kirshner 33385
The title cut comprises some beautiful passages. While they never really attained the intensity of art-rock bands like Yes, this album is possibly Kansas's most fully realized artistic effort at testing the possibilities of the genre. —*Rick Clark*

○ **Leftoverture** / 1976 / Kirshner 34224
The rock hit "Carry on Wayward Son" catapulted Kansas (and this album) into the big-arena rock circuit. —*Rick Clark*

● **Best of Kansas** / 1984 / Epic 39283
Contains the essential rock radio hits "Dust in the Wind," "Carry On Wayward Son," and "Point of Know Return," as well as improved remastering from the original tapes. —*Rick Clark*

In the Spirit of Things / 1988 / MCA 6254
Pink Floyd producer Bob Ezrin gives Kansas a sonically impressive sound. Fans of orchestral mainstream rock will like this, particularly "One Man, One Heart," "One Big Sky," "House on Fire," and "The Preacher." Ex-Dixie Dregs guitarist Steve Morse and vocalist Steve Walsh shine. —*Rick Clark*

Katrina & the Waves

Group / Pop/rock
Led by ex-Soft Boy guitarist Kimberly Rew, Katrina and the Waves effortlessly evoked the irresistably catchy guitar-pop of the mid '60s with their first three albums in the early '80s. Not only could Rew write songs that were instantly memorable ("Goin' Down to Liverpool" and "Walking on Sunshine") but the band had a dynamic lead singer with the Kansas-born Katrina Leskanich, who could sound sweet or tough according to the material.

After scoring a hit single with "Walking on Sunshine" in 1985, the band began to add a little bit of soul on their next album, *Waves*. While the experimentation was flawed, what really hurt the record was the fact that Rew contributed only two songs. *Waves* marked a downturn in their commercial fortunes, which was fixed with 1989's *Break of Hearts*, when the band turned into indistinguishable commercial hacks. They were rewarded with a Top-20 hit, "That's the Way." However, it marked the end of the road for the group, not only artistically, but literally, too—they disbanded a few years later, without releasing another album. —*Stephen Thomas Erlewine*

● **Katrina & the Waves** / 1985 / Capitol 46169
Combining the highlights from the group's first two albums, *Katrina & the Waves* is a magnificent slice of pure guitar-pop. —*Stephen Thomas Erlewine*

Jorma Kaukonen

b. Dec. 23, 1940
Vocals, guitar / Folk-rock, rock & roll
Guitarist, singer, and songwriter Jorma Kaukonen was born and grew up in Washington, D.C., where he first turned to the guitar. He lived in the San Francisco Bay Area in the early '60s, playing backup to singer Janis Joplin in local clubs. In 1965 Kaukonen became a founding member of Jefferson Airplane, which soared to fame in 1967. Though Kaukonen's songs and vocals were not prominently featured in the band, his distinctive guitar playing was crucial to its sound.

With bassist Jack Casady, in 1970 Kaukonen formed a spinoff duo from the group, called Hot Tuna, and this became his primary musical vehicle after Jefferson Airplane split in 1973. Hot Tuna recorded a series of albums on which Kaukonen sang and played guitar through 1978. After that, Kaukonen worked as a soloist and with such groups as Vital Parts (1980), and he recorded occasional albums. Kaukonen reunited with Casady in Hot Tuna during the '80s, and both participated in the 1989 reunion of Jefferson Airplane. A Hot Tuna reunion album appeared the following year. —*William Ruhlmann*

● **Quah** / 1974 / Relix 2027
Brilliant acoustic album, with Tom Hobson, of Kaukonen originals and folk/blues standards, the highlights being the beautiful "Genesis" and the Rev. Gary Davis's "I'll Be All Right" and "I Am the Light of This World." —*William Ruhlmann*

Magic / 1985 / Relix 2007
Acoustic live album including such folk/blues favorites as "Walkin' Blues" and Kaukonen's Jefferson Airplane tunes "Embryonic Journey" and "Good Shepherd." —*William Ruhlmann*

KC & the Sunshine Band

Group / Disco

In the early '70s, two White men, Harry "KC" Casey (b. 1951) and Richard Finch (b. 1954), created a racially integrated disco band that based its music on various soul styles. They became one of the most commercially successful groups of the early disco era.

KC & the Sunshine Band's disco was funky enough to be a staple in the clubs, while remaining melodic and sweet enough to be huge pop hits. The group continued to have hits until the early '80s. Their last hit single, "Give It Up," was credited to KC in the United States. —*Bil Carpenter*

● **Best of KC & the Sunshine Band** / 1990 / Rhino 70940
A percussive mix of steel drums, whistle flutes, and funky group harmonies on this most soulful disco. Includes all of their hits: "Get Down Tonight," "Please Don't Go," "That's the Way (I Like It)," "I'm Your Boogie Man," "(Shake, Shake, Shake) Shake Your Booty," and KC's solo hit, "Give It Up." —*Bil Carpenter*

Tommy Keene

Vocals, guitar / Power pop
With its instantly memorable melodies and sly guitar hooks, Tommy Keene's music was made to be played on the radio. Unfortunately, he made his pure pop music in the '80s, an era that didn't embrace '60s-styled guitar pop with open arms. So Keene gained a small cult following on college radio, but the best of his songs transcended nearly all of the standard-issue college guitar pop of the '80s. —*Stephen Thomas Erlewine*

● **Real Underground** / 1993 / Alias
A terrific collection that covers all the highlights from Keene's criminally underappreciated career. —*Stephen Thomas Erlewine*

Paul Kelly & the Messengers

b. Jun. 19, 1940, Miami, FL
Group / Rock & roll, folk-rock
A muscular Australian folk-rock combo led by Kelly, a songwriter whose eye for detail and ability to draw the listener into his world rivals Graham Parker's and (sometimes) Elvis Costello's. Kelly's best songs contain the episodic character of Bob Dylan's but with the rocking thwack of John Mellencamp and the occasional flash of the writer Raymond Carver. (Kelly's *So Much Water, So Close to Home* album takes its title and the inspiration for its title track from a Carver short story.) —*John Floyd and Kit Kiefer*

● **Gossip** / 1986 / A&M 5157
Their U.S. debut offers 17 sublime examples of Kelly's compassionate and witty songwriting as well as the group's flexibility and charm. Highlights include "White Train," the gentle "Renwick Bells," "Darling It Hurts," and "Don't Ever Harm the Messenger." —*John Floyd and Kit Kiefer*

○ **Under the Sun** / 1988 / A&M 5207
This covers a lot of stylistic ground, including rockabilly, country, and punk throwbacks. A beautifully arranged set that runs the gamut from Hoodoo Gurus-style raveups ("Dumb Things") to country-rock shuffles ("To Her Door") and pointed social criticism ("Bicentennial"), not to mention the golden title track. —*John Floyd and Kit Kiefer*

So Much Water, So Close to Home / 1989 / A&M 5266
A somewhat light release, but Kelly's writing continues to dazzle, with a song written from the perspective of an abused wife and a touching interpretation of a Raymond Carver story. —*John Floyd*

○ **Comedy** / 1992 / Dr. Dream 9265
A diverse, startling record full of everything from folkie social protest ("From Little Things Big Things Grow") to gorgeous pop ("Brighter"), with a dazzling out-of-left-field homage to Jimmie Dale Gilmore's "Dallas from a DC-9" ("Sydney from a 727"). —*Kit Kiefer*

Chris Kenner

b. Dec. 25, 1929, **d.** Jan. 25, 1976
Vocals / R&B
Kenner wrote a number of enduring New Orleans R&B classics, although subsequent cover versions eclipsed all but "I Like It Like That," his Grammy-nominated greatest hit in 1961. Kenner cowrote "Sick and Tired" with Fats Domino and charted with it in 1957 on Imperial, but Domino's version blew it out of the water. Signing with Joe Babashak's Instant label, Kenner's "I Like It like That," "Land of 1000 Dances," and "Something You Got" sported

Allen Toussaint's rolling piano behind Kenner's raw vocals. —*Bill Dahl*

○ **Land of a Thousand Dances** / 1966 / Atlantic 8117
Slashing soul by the writer of the title cut. One of the great forgotten albums. —*David Szatmary*

● **I Like It Like That—Golden Classics** / 1987 / Collectables 5166
Vocalist Kenner's early '60s sides for Instant, with Allen Toussaint laying down rolling piano behind him, represent New Orleans R&B at its most infectious. —*Bill Dahl*

Chaka Khan

b. Mar. 23, 1953, Great Lakes, IL
Vocals / Soul, funk, urban R&B
The lead singer of the R&B band Rufus from 1972 to 1978, Khan went solo with *Chaka* and the single "I'm Every Woman." Since 1978 she has released several solo albums. The Grammy-winning Khan has also done vocal work for Prince, Steve Winwood, David Bowie, and Quincy Jones. —*William Ruhlmann*

○ **Chaka Khan** / 1982 / Warner Brothers 23729
An excellent album from Chaka Khan, mixing tingling uptempo tunes with her characteristic soaring, glorious vocals. "Got to Be There" reached number five on the R&B charts, but it actually wasn't the album's high point. That was the marvelous "Be Bop Medley," that later lead hardcore jazz purist Betty Carter to proclaim Khan the one female singer working outside the jazz arena that had legitimate improvising credentials. —*Ron Wynn*

● **I Feel for You** / 1984 / Warner Brothers 25162
Smoothly produced funk outing features the Prince-composed title track, an R&B number one, and two more R&B Top-20 hits, "This Is My Night" and "Through the Fire." —*William Ruhlmann*

Destiny / 1986 / Warner Brothers 25425
Another fine album—though more uneven than usual—from Chaka Khan. "Love of a Lifetime" was the latest in her string of definitive singles, while she also elevated several otherwise mundane ballads and uptempo cuts. No matter what her personal situation, Khan seldom made a misstep on any of her albums during the early and mid '80s, and this one might have been the least distinguished of the batch. —*Ron Wynn*

○ **C.K.** / 1988 / Warner Brothers 25707
A first-class release, despite the fact it didn't pack the normal commercial punch. But it had excellent production, many outstanding selections, and uniformly dazzling, booming, and triumphant vocals from Khan. She currently speaks with disdain about the record business, and it's probably due to the relative failure of great records like this to break out and really enjoy the success they merit that's disillusioned her. —*Ron Wynn*

Life Is a Dance (The Remix Project) / 1989 / Warner Brothers 25946
In lieu of a desperately needed greatest-hits album, we'll have to settle for this reconfiguration of such Khan hits as "I'm Every Woman" and "Clouds." —*William Ruhlmann*

Johnny Kidd & the Pirates

d. Oct. 7, 1966
Group / Rock & roll
Pioneering British hard-rock act in the pre-Beatles era, Kidd (real name Fred Heath) and his backing trio the Pirates had a lean, loud, muscular approach to R&B that strongly influenced the Who and the Small Faces, among other bands. When they weren't recording dross like "The Birds and the Bees" at EMI's behest, they were making history with original numbers like "Shakin' All Over" (Heath wrote it) and a brilliant set of (mostly unreleased at the time) R&B covers. Pirates guitarist Mick Green later became well known in his own right. Kidd was in the process of reviving the group in the mid '60s when his life was ended in a car crash. —*Bruce Eder*

● **Hits & Rarities** / 1983 / See For Miles
This collection is the best of three now available. It contains the strongest of Kidd's singles plus superb vault finds. Considered too rough for release in the '60s, they hold up splendidly. —*Bruce Eder*

○ **Complete Johnny Kidd** / 1994 / EMI
A double CD of everything this underrated band ever recorded, assembled chronologically and beautifully remastered and annotated (with great pictures, too). This is the collection to own, es-

pecially since it has been issued at mid-price. And fans of the Who or the Small Faces can double the priority of owning this collection. —*Bruce Eder*

Greg Kihn

b. , Baltimore, MD
Vocals, guitar / Pop/rock
A record store clerk made good, San Franciscan Greg Kihn plays '60s-soaked pop with a smirk, loading up his tunes with so many British invasion quotes you'll become dizzy keeping up. Although his hit-making days have passed, the earnest and likable Kihn still doggedly plays his squeaky-clean pop-rock with panache. —*John Dougan*

● **Kihnsolidation: The Best of Greg Kihn** / 1989 / Rhino 70900
A fine sampling of Kihn's pop sensibility. Drawing on of each of his albums, it includes the hits "The Breakup Song" and "Jeopardy" as well as his better album cuts. —*Chris Woodstra*

Killing Joke

Group / Alternative rock
Heavy and slow, Killing Joke (at least early in their career) was a quasi-metal band dancing to a tune of doom and gloom. They eventually became less heavy and more arty (the latter seems almost impossible), more danceable even, but early on they made some urgent slabs of molten dynamite that oozed with the power of thick guitars, thudding drums, and over-the-top singing. —*John Dougan*

● **Killing Joke** / 1980 / EG 57
Killing Joke's self-titled debut album is a throttling merger of heavy metal, new wave, and noise. It's a dense, claustrophobic record that basically sketched out the path the band would follow over the next decade. —*Stephen Thomas Erlewine*

King Crimson

Group / Art rock
If the Moody Blues provided a heavenly Mellotron-soaked soundtrack for millions of late-'60s cosmic rockers, King Crimson (formed by Robert Fripp on January 13, 1969) balanced the scales with disturbingly dense and explosive sonic trips into the darkside. Even when the band was playing something relatively peaceful, there was a sense that something wasn't quite settled. Founded by guitarist Robert Fripp and saxophonist Ian MacDonald, the group burst forth with an ornate, majestic, savage sound and an approach that owed a greal deal to modern jazz.

Their debut effort, *In the Court of the Crimson King,* made quite a splash on both sides of the Atlantic. The bizarre face painted on the cover enhanced the band's potential for grandly jarring music. The album went Top Five in England and number 28 in the United States. The title track was the band's only charting single, at number 80. MacDonald left after the first tour. Over the years, Fripp would be the only original member remaining in the group.

The second album, *In the Wake of Poseidon,* generally repeated the formula of the debut, but the following two efforts, *Lizard* and *Islands,* lost some of their initial audience. A new lineup (including ex-Family John Wetton, ex-Yes Bill Bruford) and a darker, colder sound emerged with *Larks' Tongues in Aspic.* The next two studio efforts *Starless and Bible Black* and *Red* progressively intensified the dissonance.

Fripp disbanded Crimson in 1974 and pursued solo and side projects, most notably working with Brian Eno (*No Pussyfooting* and *Evening Star*), Andy Summers (*I Advance Masked* and *Bewitched*), and Fripp's own League of Gentlemen. Crimson reformed in 1981, this time with Adrian Belew on guitar and vocals, Tony Levin on bass, and Bill Bruford on percussion. Between 1981 and 1984, they released a trio of fine efforts, particularly *Beat.* —*Rick Clark and Bruce Eder*

★ **In the Court of the Crimson King** / 1969 / Atlantic 8245
Definitive debut album, which was almost too good (it took years for them to come up with a record as concise and distinctive), an orchestrated vision of apocalyptic doom dominated by Ian McDonald's Mellotron, Greg Lake's dignified voice, and the ferocious guitar playing of Robert Fripp. The latter would be the only survivor onto subsequent albums. —*Bruce Eder*

○ **In the Wake of Poseidon** / 1970 / Atlantic 8266

A more carefully produced, better crafted, but more diffuse second album. Fripp took over the keyboard as well as all the compositional chores, with help from Gustav Holst (*The Planets*). —*Bruce Eder*

Lizard / 1970 / Atlantic 8278
A more ornate and purely psychedelic venture, involving extended suites with more of a jazz feel to them. Guest performance by Yes's Jon Anderson on "Prince Rupert Awakes." —*Bruce Eder*

Islands / 1971 / EG 5
A flawed album by what looked like the most stable Crimson lineup in some time (this band actually got to tour), with too much weak material expanded to mammoth proportions. The one compensation is the return of the sense of humor missing since the first two albums. —*Bruce Eder*

○ **Larks' Tongues in Aspic** / 1973 / EG 7
The new King Crimson makes their debut with a violin (courtesy of David Cross) now sharing center stage with Fripp's guitar, and the Mellotron pushed somewhat into the background. The material itself is the most experimental that Fripp had come up with up to that time, and John Wetton's vocals were the strongest since the departure of Greg Lake in 1970. —*Bruce Eder*

Red / 1974 / EG 15
Some final thoughts before Fripp pulled the plug on Crimson—the material is longer, the playing more ferocious, and the whole album seems rushed toward the breaking point of dissolution for the band. The culmination of five years of doom-rock. —*Bruce Eder*

○ **Starless & Bible Black** / 1974 / EG 12
An intriguing follow-up, and overall the band's most satisfying album. —*Bruce Eder*

○ **Discipline** / 1981 / EG 49
The new King Crimson, harder and heavier. —*Bruce Eder*

○ **Beat** / 1982 / EG 51
A superior mid-'80s follow-up with better material. —*Bruce Eder*

3 of a Perfect Pair / 1984 / Warner Brothers 25071
The final chapter? Don't bet on it, but this would be a good way to end, if so. —*Bruce Eder*

○ **Compact King Crimson** / 1986 / EG 68
An OK collection now supplanted by *Frame by Frame.* —*Bruce Eder*

○ **Frame by Frame** / 1991 / Caroline 1595
Frame by Frame is a four-CD boxed set, compiled by band leader Robert Fripp, that does a good job of providing primo samples of each of Crimson's musical periods. Sonically, the excellent remastering makes this the best the band has ever sounded on disc. Three of the discs cover their studio work, while the fourth is a collection of live work, spanning the band's entire career. Enclosed is a richly detailed diary (written by Fripp) of Crimson's entire history, plus interviews with band members and glowing and hateful reviews from critics. Typical of Crimson, precious little of the music on this set would qualify for casual listening. However, those whose taste run towards the dark side of prog-rock will find this set rewarding. —*Rick Clark*

○ **Great Deceiver (Live 1973-1974)** / 1992 / Plan 9 1597
Four CDs full of live King Crimson from 1973 and 1974, an era that many consider their best. Although some songs are repeated, they are never played the same way twice. If you're a King Crimson fan, that's enough of an incentive for purchase; if you're not, the musical expertise of the band might convert you, providing you have the money for a boxed set. —*Stephen Thomas Erlewine*

King's X

Group / Hard rock
Known as the Edge since 1981, this Houston, TX, trio became King's X in 1986. Featuring Ty Tabor's lyrical guitar work, Jerry Gaskill's forceful drumming, and Doug Pinnick's emotive lead singing and distinctive bass work (sometimes on 12-string bass), King's X is a dense instrumental fusion between hard rock and progressive rock. Vocally, King's X exhibits a knack for rich three-part harmonies that, at times, recalls *Abbey Road*-period Beatles. Thematically, they range from *Wizard of Oz*-style fantasy im-

agery to more complex spiritual (particularly Christian) metaphors. —*Rick Clark*

Out of the Silent Planet / 1982 / Megaforce 81825
Out of the Silent Planet (named after the first book of Christian writer C. S. Lewis's space fantasy trilogy) was a brilliant debut for King's X, featuring memorable melodies and sweeping harmonies. This debut's over-the-top performances and well-defined arrangements earned this band a substantial following from both metal and prog-rock audiences early on. —*Rick Clark*

● **Gretchen Goes to Nebraska** / 1989 / Megaforce 81997
King's X sophomore effort contained their smart blend of heavy and melodic rock to a fine effect. Many fans of the band consider this album their best. With fiery tracks like "Over My Head" and "Fall on Me" and ballads like "Summerland" it's easy to understand why. —*Rick Clark*

○ **Faith Hope Love** / 1990 / Megaforce 82145
Faith Hope Love was King's X's commercial breakthrough effort, containing the hit "It's Love." —*Rick Clark*

King's X / 1992 / Atlantic 82372
Their fourth album features harder sounds than previous efforts, but lack enough dynamic dimensionality to the arrangements to make it a consistently satisfying listen. Contains hit "Black Flag," the album's highlight. —*Rick Clark*

Dogman / 1994 / Atlantic
Produced by Brendan O'Brien (Pearl Jam, Stone Temple Pilots), King's X trashes up their sound with an impressive garagey heaviness. "Dogman" was the single, but overall this album shows a shortage of strong songs. —*Rick Clark*

Ben E. King

b. Sep. 23, 1938, Henderson, NC
Vocals / R&B, soul
Swirling strings, subtly shaded orchestrations, and Ben E. King's assured baritone were a blueprint for uptown soul success during the early '60s. King and his vocal group, the Five Crowns, were in the right place at the right time when, in 1959, the manager of the Drifters decided to sack his entire group and solicit replacements. As new lead singer for the Drifters, King crooned the soulful smashes "There Goes My Baby," "Save the Last Dance for Me," and "I Count the Tears" before heading out on his own in 1960. The vocalist's own Atco singles mirrored the sumptuous production of his Drifter sides, and "Spanish Harlem," "Don't Play That Song (You Lied)," and the R&B chart-topping "Stand by Me" were all huge successes. King remained with Atco through 1969, then triumphantly returned to Atlantic in 1975 with another number-one soul hit, "Supernatural Thing (Part 1)."

With the re-release of "Stand by Me" as the theme to the 1986 film of the same title, King was in demand all over again, the stirring song improbably scaling the charts for a second time, despite being a quarter-century old. —*Bill Dahl*

● **The Ultimate Collection** / 1987 / Atlantic 80213
The rich baritone of this ex-Drifter lead is matched by the majestic, violin-drenched, uptown soul arrangements on these early '60s classics. —*Bill Dahl*

○ **Anthology** / 1993 / Rhino 71215
This two-disc, 50-song boxed set thoroughly documents the recordings that Ben E. King cut for Atlantic. Starting as the lead voice of the Drifters on such hits as "There Goes My Baby" and "Save the Last Dance for Me," King went on to a successful solo career with a string of singles that matched his smooth, sexy baritone with tastefully arranged string sections and Latin rhythms. All of those early hits—"Stand By Me" and "Spanish Harlem" were the biggest—are included here, along with nonhit 45s by the likes of Leiber-Stoller, Doc Pomus, Mort Shuman, Phil Spector, and Goffin-King that were nearly equal in worth. As the '60s progressed, Ben moved toward a more mainstream, heavier soul sound and less distinctive material, culminating in his parting from Atlantic in 1969. He returned to the label in the mid '70s for a string of mainstream R&B successes. This compilation includes 16 non-LP singles from the '60s, which together with the hits constitute the definitive overview of this influential soul singer's work. —*Richie Unterberger*

Carole King

b. Feb. 9, 1942, Brooklyn, NY

Vocals, piano / Singer-Songwriter, Pop/Rock
During the early '70s, the singer/songwriter movement emerged as a reflective, folkie alternative to rock and pop. Among the genre's more notable avatars were James Taylor, Joni Mitchell, Cat Stevens, and Carole King. Unlike many of the other artists, King was well grounded in the pop-songcrafting tradition, primarily from her tenure as a writer during the glory days at the Brill Building in New York. It was while she was at the Brill Building, beginning in 1958, that King met Neil Diamond and Paul Simon and began a very successful string of collaborations with Gerry Goffin, whom she would later marry. To list all of those hits would fill a page, but classics like "Up on the Roof," "(You Make Me Feel Like) A Natural Woman," "Will You Still Love Me Tomorrow," "The Locomotion," "Don't Bring Me Down," "Hey Girl," "One Fine Day," "Pleasant Valley Sunday," "Some Kind-a-Wonderful," and "You've Got a Friend" are just a few.

In 1962 King scored a number-22 hit as a solo artist with "It Might as Well Rain until September." With guitarist Danny Kortchmar and her second husband, bassist Charles Larkey, King formed the City, releasing an album titled *Now That Everything's Been Said* on Lou Adler's Ode label. The project fell apart and King focused on her solo career in 1970 with *Writer: Carole King.* That album went nowhere, but its follow-up, *Tapestry,* became one of the biggest-selling albums of the '70s, holding the number-one position for 15 weeks and remaining on the charts for 302 consecutive weeks. *Tapestry,* which featured a blend of old King standards and new compositions, fused the introspection of the singer/songwriter genre with a warm, homey soulfulness and believable passionate delivery.

Since then, King's intimate delivery and quality work have given her a long, rewarding career. In 1987, King was inducted into the Songwriters Hall of Fame. —*Rick Clark*

★ **Tapestry** / Jan. 1971 / Epic 34946
In the world of popular music, the word "classic" gets bandied about like the word "improved" in ad campaigns, ceasing to mean anything after a while. *Tapestry,* however, is a *classic,* no two ways about it. King (already a very successful songwriter) assembled a collection of her best-known songs, plus some new ones, and gave them intimate heartfelt readings. King's voice had a warm earthy quality, with just the right amount of urgency. Listing highlights is fairly pointless, as the whole album is stunning. —*Rick Clark*

○ **Music** / Feb. 1971 / Epic 34949
Without the reserve of self-penned standards to draw upon, *Music* lacked the powerful resonance of its predecessor, *Tapestry,* Nevertheless, songs like "Sweet Seasons," "Brother Brother," "Some Kind of Wonderful," and "Song of Long Ago" make this one of her better efforts. —*Rick Clark*

Fantasy / 1973 / Epic 34962
By this time, King's work was recalling the detached craftmanship of her days as a professional tunesmith. As a result, many of her post-*Tapestry* efforts lacked a sense of emotional investment in their performances. Regardless, *Fantasy* (an improvement over the previously released *Rhymes and Reasons*) produced three hits with "Believe in Humanity," "Corazon," and "You Light Up My Life." Other highlights included "A Quiet Place to Live" and "Directions." —*Rick Clark*

○ **Her Greatest Hits** / 1973 / Epic 34967
All of King's major hits are here, plus a few key album tracks. It's a decent starting place for the uninitiated, but *Tapestry* is a richer listening experience. —*Rick Clark*

○ **Really Rosie** / 1975 / Caedmon 368
This winning soundtrack collaboration for a children's TV special (with children's author Maurice Sendak) was a return to form for King. *Really Rosie* contains some of King's best solo material. This is an enjoyable listening experience for children and adults alike. —*Rick Clark*

Thoroughbred / 1975 / Epic 34963
After a series of solid but unexceptional albums, King re-collaborated with her first husband Gerry Goffin and produced her best album since *Tapestry.* Like *Tapestry,* much of *Thoroughbred* reflected a rich soulfulness. The only thing lacking was *Tapestry's* amazing collection of standards. The emotive "Only Love Is Real" became a substantial hit. —*Rick Clark*

○ **Pearls—Songs of Goffin and King** / 1980 / Fame 3014

King reprises the early-'60s pop gems she wrote with Gerry Goffin, with fine results. —*Dan Heilman*

The Kingsmen

Group / Rock & roll

The rock & roll band from Portland, OR, whose one big hit "Louie Louie" defined the garage-band style and became one of the all-time classics. The original lineup included Jack Ely (lead singer and guitar), Lynn Easton (drums), Mike Mitchell (lead guitar), Bob Nordby (bass), and Don Galucci (piano). After Ely had "incorrectly" taught the rest of the band the Wailers version of Richard Berry's "Louie Louie" (thus altering the basic rhythm into the now-famous duh-duh-duh, duh-duh, duh-duh-duh, duh-duh riff that has become the only way anyone has played it since), they recorded it for 50 dollars at a primitive local recording studio with only three mikes, Ely hollering the lyrics into an overhead boom mike suspended ten feet in the air.

Released on a local label, the record went nowhere after Paul Revere & the Raiders quickly covered it in the Northwest market, although it had already become a standard for all teen bands in that area. In 1964, the record started to break nationally, causing the breakup of the original lineup when Easton copyrighted the group's name, informing the other members that he was now sole owner of the Kingsmen and its new lead singer. Ely formed his own Kingsmen, touring at the same time as Easton, who was lip-synching the record whenever possible. Only Easton and Mitchell were left from the original lineup, but they kept scoring big with frat-band versions of "Money" and "Little Latin Lupe Lu," reaching their peak with "The Jolly Green Giant." (Ely languished in relative obscurity, and Gallucci had formed Don & the Goodtimes.) By the early '90s, history had redressed the situation somewhat. While replacement members from the Easton version of the band toured as the "original" Kingsmen, Jack Ely finally received some of his due, headlining the 30th Anniversary Louie Louie tour. Though the song itself has been covered repeatedly, the version by Ely and the original lineup remains definitive. — *Cub Koda*

● **Best of the Kingsmen** / 1989 / Rhino 70745
All the hits and great sound. —*Cub Koda*

In Person / 1993 / Sundazed 004
Compact disc reissue of the group's first album, including the rock anthem "Louie Louie," issued here for the first time minus the annoying overdubbed crowd noises. Also nice is the inclusion of three bonus tracks. —*Cub Koda*

Volume 2 / 1993 / Sundazed 005
Supposedly another live album, finally issued here without the audience overdubs. Highlights include "Little Latin Lupe Lu," "Long Green," and "David's Mood," plus two CD bonus tracks. — *Cub Koda*

Volume 3 / Sundazed 6006
The group's third album, again issued here without the overdubbed crowd noises. This features their hit "Jolly Green Giant" plus three CD bonus tracks. —*Cub Koda*

The Kinks

Group / British invasion, rock & roll, pop/rRock, hard rock

Formed in 1963, the Kinks were one of the most influential groups to emerge from the first wave of the British invasion. The band's rather sloppy, but energetic ensemble work, coupled with singer/songwriter Ray Davies's (b. 1944) distinctly British point of view and excellent song sense, plus American producer Shel Talmy, generated a substantial body of classic albums. They were a thoroughly British garage-rock bridge (practically devoid of the overt American blues fascination practiced by the Animals or Rolling Stones) for those who desired an alternative to the bright, clean tunefulness of the Beatles.

The Kinks' first Stateside hit, "You Really Got Me," was built around what must be one of rock's most memorable (and influential) guitar riffs. Davies quickly followed suit with the similar (and equally fine) "All Day and All of the Night." Davies's intelligently barbed take on the British class system increasingly dominated their themes. Eventually, the Kinks gravitated toward conceptual albums. *Arthur, or the Decline and Fall of the British Empire* (1969) was one of the first rock operas.

Lola versus Powerman and the Money-Go-Round (1970) would produce their last hit for many years, with "Lola," a song about a transvestite.

A label change to RCA found the band increasingly doing conceptual albums, with fairly spotty results and diminishing sales. Regardless of some good material, the band sounded stale on record compared to their earlier work. In 1977 the Kinks signed with Arista and gradually enjoyed some substantial hits, including the 1983 hit "Come Dancing," which tied the highest charting record of their career, 1965's "Tired of Waiting for You." Other hits include "A Well-Respected Man," "Set Me Free," "Sunny Afternoon," and "Dedicated Follower of Fashion." The Kinks continue to do well as a live and recording unit. —*Rick Clark*

You Really Got Me / 1964 / Rhino 70315
The highlight of this rather spotty debut (consisting of a sampling of originals and covers Kinks churned out at gigs) was, without a doubt, the title track, which single-handedly pioneered riff-oriented hard rock. "Stop Your Sobbing," a song later recorded by Pretenders, was also a standout track, but producer Shel Talmy's "Bald Headed Woman" was an absolute low point. —*Rick Clark*

Kinda Kinks / 1965 / Rhino 70316
Album number two featured a rewrite of "You Really Got Me," with the equally fine "All Day and All of the Night." Ray Davies, however, delivered a strong set of tunes that went beyond riff-rockers with the exuberant "Come On Now," and "You Shouldn't Be Sad." His penchant for memorable melodies emerged with tracks like "Something Better Beginning" and "Tired of Waiting for You." —*Rick Clark*

☆ **Kink-Size/Kinkdom** / 1965 / Rhino 75769
This Rhino reissue contains the Kinks' third and fourth albums, *Kink-Size* and *Kinkdom*, respectively, plus some non-album sides from the same period. *Kink-Size* featured the hit "Set Me Free," another Kinks classic, as well as "Everybody's Gonna Be Happy." By the release of *Kinkdom*, the Kinks had developed an instantly identifiable sound, built around Davies's wavering lower tenor and the group's airy falsetto background vocals and ragged garage rock-like ensemble work. "Dedicated Follower of Fashion," a noisy dance-hall rocker, was a wonderful poke at a Carnaby Street fop in his "frilly nylon panties." Other hits included "Who'll Be the Next in Line" and "A Well Respected Man." This disc also includes the assertive "I'm Not Like Everybody Else," (originally written as a pitch for the Animals and the B-side to "Sunny Afternoon"). —*Rick Clark*

○ **Kink Kontroversy** / 1965 / PRT 6004
This great album is still only available as a British import. The Kinks sludge out some fine trashy rockers with "Where Have All the Good Times Gone" (later re-recorded by Van Halen) and "Till the End of the Day," a moderate hit. Other highlights included "It's Too Late," "You Can't Win," and "I'm on an Island." —*Rick Clark*

○ **Face to Face** / 1966 / Reprise 6228
Face to Face was another extraordinary Kinks album, this time featuring the hit "Sunny Afternoon" and other gems like "Holiday in Waikiki," "Fancy," "Too Much on My Mind," and "Rainy Day in June." —*Rick Clark*

Live at Kelvin Hall / 1967 / Reprise 6260
Outside of the Rolling Stones' *Got Live If You Want It* and the Beatles' *Live at the Hollywood Bowl*, this is the only readily available concert document of a British invasion-era band, complete with all the screaming fans. The Kinks slog through a version of "The Batman Theme," "I'm on an Island," "Milk Cow Blues," and a smattering of hits. —*Rick Clark*

☆ **Something Else by the Kinks** / 1967 / Reprise 6279
The follow-up to *Face to Face* was equally impressive, featuring the wistful "Waterloo Sunset," one of Davies's finest compositions. Other highlights included "Situation Vacant," "David Watts," "Love Me till the Sun Shines," and Dave Davies's "Death of a Clown." Highly recommended! —*Rick Clark*

☆ **Village Green Preservation Society** / 1968 / Reprise 6327
On *The Kinks Are the Village Green Preservation Society*, Ray Davies's eye for the little lyrical details that speak volumes about everyday people hit a zenith. Initially inspired by Dylan Thomas's portrayal of a complacent Welsh village (*Under Milkwood*), this was the Kinks' finest conceptual album. Their first album produced without Shel Talmy, it projected an unassuming, low-key

quality. It is amazing that this album failed to dent the charts. Fortunately, Warner has released it on CD. Highlights include "Picture Book," "Animal Farm," "Big Sky," "Johnny Thunder," "Wicked Annabella," and the title track. —*Rick Clark*

☆ **Arthur (Or the Decline and Fall of the British Empire)** / 1969 / Reprise 6366
After the commercial disaster of *Village Green Preservation Society*, Ray Davies turned his attentions to collaborating on a TV musical titled *Arthur (or the Decline and Fall of the British Empire)* with writer Julian Mitchell. Even though the show got canned, the album received much acclaim, placing the Kinks back on the charts. "Victoria" became a moderate hit. Other highlights included "Brainwashed," "Australia," "Shangri-la," and the title cut. —*Rick Clark*

○ **Lola vs. the Powerman & the Money-Go-Round, Part One** / 1970 / Reprise 6423
Thanks to the hit single "Lola" (about an encounter with a transvestite), *Lola vs. the Powerman & the Money-Go-Round, Part One* became a comeback of sorts for the Kinks. Overall, this album is a Davies-eye view of life as an artist coping with the road ("This Time Tomorrow") and the music industry, which includes blackly humorous portrayals of the musician's union ("Get Back in Line"), music publishers ("Denmark Street"), making it big ("Top of the Pops"), and greed ("Money-Go-Round"). This might be a whinefest from a successful pop artist, but his observations aren't that far off base. Musically, The Kinks still had their ragged delivery, but they increasingly employed more acoustic instrumentation, giving the arrangements a slightly folkie quality at times. —*Rick Clark*

○ **Muswell Hillbillies** / 1971 / Rhino 70934
For their first outing on the RCA label, the Kinks adopted a more laidback rootsy sound that even sported traces of country ("Holloway Jail") and dancehall/cabaret theater styles ("Skin and Bones," "Holiday," "Alcohol"). "Twentieth Century Man" is a nice medium-tempo rocker but lacks the reckless fire of their earlier efforts. —*Rick Clark*

Everybody's in Show-Biz / 1972 / Rhino 70935
One half of this release is a document of the Kinks' spirited live slopfest, including versions of "Top of the Pops," "Holiday," and the "Banana Boat Song." The other half contains a couple of gems like "Celluloid Heroes," "Sitting in My Hotel," as well as "Motorway," and "Maximum Consumption." —*Rick Clark*

★ **Kink Kronikles** / 1972 / Reprise 6454
Anyone wanting a well-chosen sampler of the best Kinks work, from half of their stay at Reprise, should start here. Many of the essential tracks are here. —*Rick Clark*

Preservation: Acts 1 & 2 / 1973 / Rhino 70523
Initially intended as an extension of *The Village Green Preservation Society*, *Preservation* offered relatively little in the way of great songwriting or spirited performances, something *Village Green* had in spades. "Money Talks" is a nice mid-tempo rocker. The Rhino CD includes the single "Preservation." —*Rick Clark*

○ **Kinks' Greatest—Celluloid Heroes** / 1976 / RCA 3869
This is a good collection comprising the cream of the Kinks' RCA years. It includes "Sitting in My Hotel," Twentieth Century Man," "Alcohol," and "Everybody's a Star." —*Rick Clark*

Sleepwalker / 1977 / Arista 8068
For their first release on Clive Davis's Arista label, the Kinks ditched the concept albums and knuckled down to a workmanlike but unexceptional batch of songs. "Full Moon" and "Juke Box Music" are among the stronger tracks. —*Rick Clark*

Misfits / 1978 / Arista 8069
A slight improvement over *Sleepwalker*, *Misfits* boasted their first Top-40 hit in eight years, with "Rock 'n' Roll Fantasy." —*Rick Clark*

Low Budget / 1979 / Arista 8050
Even though the Kinks enjoyed their most consistently satisfying album chart success during their years at Arista, much of this lacks the vision and execution of their work found on Reprise. Regardless of all that, the disco influenced pop-rocker "(Wish I Could Fly like) Superman" was a hit. —*Rick Clark*

○ **Give the People What They Want** / 1981 / Arista 8224

The Kinks delivered their interpretation of the mainstream FM rock sound on this effort, producing three moderate radio hits with "Destroyer," "Better Things," and the title cut. —*Rick Clark*

○ **Come Dancing with the Kinks** / 1986 / Arista 8428
A sampling of their Arista years (1977-1986). Most of the essential tracks are here, including all of their hits from that period. "Come Dancing," "A Rock 'n' Roll Fantasy," "Juke Box Music," "Destroyer," and "(Wish I Could Fly like) Superman" are among the titles found here. —*Rick Clark*

★ **Greatest Hits, Vol. 1** / 1989 / Rhino 70086
If you are going to budget only for one Kinks disc, this is the one to get. It features all of their biggest '60s chart hits, plus some key B-Sides. Nevertheless, their albums from this period feature many fine album cuts worth having, so consider this an excellent primer but not a definitive package. —*Rick Clark*

Kiss

Group / Heavy metal, hard rock
Paul Stanley (born Stanley Harvey Eisen), Ace Frehley (born Paul Frehley), Gene Simmons (born Chaim Whitz), and Peter Criss (born Peter Crisscuola) formed Kiss in New York City, in mid 1973. Taking their cue from Alice Cooper and the New York Dolls, the boys applied makeup and wreaked havoc with their shared passion for good loud hard rock. Signed to the newly formed Casablanca in 1974, they released their debut album and two others within a year.

With three albums under their belt, they gained a foothold on the arena rock circuit, dazzling audiences with a stage show built as much around smoke bombs, floating drum risers, flashpots, and outrageousness as around the music itself. At the height of their popularity, in 1978, the members of the band released simultaneous solo albums with similar covers showing that member's face. All were good, but Frehley's outsold the others.

In the '80s, with lower-quality albums, a possible breakup was rumored. Criss was replaced by Eric Carr; Frehley left one album later, replaced by Vinnie Vincent. Kiss also ditched the makeup in a marketing about-face. Vincent left shortly thereafter, to be replaced briefly by Mark St. John and later by Bruce Kulick. This lineup brought Kiss to a new generation of fans, but at the peak of this new popularity, Carr died of brain cancer in 1991. Not giving up, Kiss recorded *Revenge*, which some cited as their best work in 15 years. Kiss's major influence in heavy metal is obvious in many of today's young bands. —*John Book*

Kiss / 1974 / Casablanca 824146
Their debut album, featuring future stage staples "Deuce," "Strutter," and "Firehouse." —*John Book*

★ **Alive!** / 1975 / Casablanca 822780
The definitive document of the band's power as a live act. Includes "Rock & Roll All Night," "Hotter Than Hell," and "Let Me Go, Rock & Roll." —*John Book*

○ **Destroyer** / 1976 / Casablanca 824149
Produced by Bob Ezrin and featuring the classic "Detroit Rock City," as well as "Beth" and "Do You Love Me?" —*John Book*

● **Double Platinum (Greatest Hits)** / 1978 / Casablanca 824155
An imperfect collection, but the best of their early peak years. —*Dan Heilman*

○ **Smashes, Thrashes & Hits** / 1988 / Casablanca 836427
Companion volume to the above from their later makeup-less period. Includes "Lick It Up," "Let's Put the X in Sex," and "Love Gun." —*Dan Heilman*

Kix

Group / Heavy metal, hard rock
Kix has been recording for over ten years, but they have had exactly one hit—the power ballad "Don't Close Your Eyes," from their 1988 album *Blow My Fuse*. But to call it a power ballad is to imply that the band was no different from the rest of the hard-rock/heavy metal bands of the '80s, and the truth is they were different. Kix was different simply because they were much better—they had better hooks, they rocked harder, and they could write songs. They were also more clever than the average heavy metal band, yet that never meant they treated their adolescent anthems as jokes; it meant that they loved the music they were making so much that their albums sounded like a constant party.

Naturally, they were critics favorites and never became big stars, even in heavy metal circles. When Metallica was all the rage during the '80s, Kix's good-time metal was seen as wimpy by most metal fans. However, their albums hold up better than any of the pop metal bands that sold millions of records while Kix was struggling in the clubs. — *Stephen Thomas Erlewine*

● **Blow My Fuse** / 1988 / Atlantic 81877
Their third album is an amazingly confident mixture of assured rock scorchers and self-respecting power ballads. — *John Floyd*

The KLF

Group / Alternative pop/rock, dance, house, techno
At the height of their career in the late '80s and early '90s, Bill Drummond and Jimmy Cauty were among the top figures in house music. All of their various permutations—Justified Ancients of Mu Mu, the Timelords, and, their most commercially successful group, the KLF—were very popular in the U.K. underground dance scene. The duo created, with their liberal use of samples, a dense, throbbing house mix that spat in the face of pop and all traditions. The best example of their flippant disregard for tradition is their surprise crossover single, "Justified and Ancient," which featured the standard-issue bass-heavy club beat with the vocals of country legend Tammy Wynette. After the success of the single, KLF announced they had broken up and that they were immediately pulling all their recordings off the market. After a little time off, Drummond and Cauty resumed recording under a variety of different names. — *Stephen Thomas Erlewine*

● **White Room** / 1991 / Arista 8657
Formerly known as Justified Ancients of Mu Mu, aka The Jams and the Timelords, the Kopyright Liberation Front (KLF) created dance music with as many samples as possible without getting busted. *White Room* is their major-label debut and contains "Justified and Ancient," a surprise hit with Tammy Wynette on vocals. — *John Book*

KMFDM

Group / Alternative rock, Industrial
KMFDM was one of Wax Trax's first industrial superstars, combining the corrosive scratching of their guitars with a hard, throbbing hip-hop-derived beat. In the late '80s, the German trio (originally a quartet) became an underground sensation not only in America but in much of Europe—clubs became devoted to playing their style of abrasive, distorted guitar-driven dance music. KMFDM continues to be one of the major industrial bands of the '90s, with their recordings becoming even more aggressive, both musically and politically. — *Stephen Thomas Erlewine*

● **Naive** / 1990 / Wax Trax 7148
KMFDM's fourth full-length album is their strongest release to date. It's a claustrophobic wall of noise, driven by a relentless jackhammer beat. — *Stephen Thomas Erlewine*

The Knack

Group / New wave, power-pop
The Knack made a nod to the '60s power-pop sound, pushing the image of themselves as the American Beatles on their 1979 debut album cover. All of the members were experienced musicians, and they didn't try to hide their attempt to market their way to the top. Cleverly crafted pop songs like their smash hit "My Sharona," which sold over five million copies, were aimed straight at the teen-pop market. "Good Girls Don't," the follow-up single to "My Sharona," was another strong hit. Their subsequent albums tried to repeat this initial success, even using blatant copies of previous songs, but failed. After the third album, the Knack folded, with some members staying together as the Game, while vocalist Doug Fieger started the band Taking Chances. In the '90s, the band re-formed with a new drummer, Billy Ward, but didn't make much of a splash. — *Scott Bultman*

● **Get the Knack** / 1979 / Capitol 91848
New wavish pop with the hit "My Sharona." With "Good Girls Don't" and "Maybe Tonight," one gets the feeling that they may have had the talent to do more than just update early Fab Four and '60s bubblegum rock. — *Scott Bultman*

○ **Retrospective: The Best of the Knack** / Nov. 16, 1992 / Capitol 80537

A fine greatest-hits set that collects the best from their debut and their two weaker follow-ups. — *Stephen Thomas Erlewine*

Gladys Knight & the Pips

b. May 28, 1944, Atlanta, GA
Group / R&B, Motown, soul
Gladys Knight's career began when she won first prize on "Ted Mack's Original Amateur Hour" as a child. At the age of 17 she had her first hit record, along with her brother and two cousins, who were known as the Pips. Their career really took off when they signed with Motown in 1966. Moving over to Buddah Records in 1973, they scored another string of hits. Gladys Knight now performs as a solo artist and records for MCA. The Pips are retired; members included Merald Knight, Edward Patten, and William Guest. — *Rick A. Bueche*

Letter Full of Tears / 1961 / Collectables 5154
A good anthology of early tracks by Gladys Knight & the Pips that were recorded for the Fury label in the early '60s. They were far from a polished act at the time, and didn't get the caliber of material or production they'd receive later at Motown. But the potential was shown on several tracks, notably the title cut, which the group had cut years earlier when Knight was only 12 years old. (They later made another version of the song for Motown.) This has better sound than some earlier Collectables titles. — *Ron Wynn*

○ **Greatest Hits** / 1967 / Curb 77321
A final single-album release of the group's great Motown material. If you haven't gotten their anthology or don't feel you need all those discs, then get this one because it's certainly as comprehensive a Motown selection as was available for many years. — *Ron Wynn*

○ **Imagination** / 1973 / Pair 3304
Gladys Knight & the Pips left Motown for Buddah because they felt they'd get more attention, a bigger push from the label, and better material. They sure made their point in a hurry with this album. Knight never sounded more triumphant or soulful than she did on every one of these songs, particularly the title track. This still stands as their finest overall album. — *Ron Wynn*

Neither One of Us / 1973 / Motown 5193
Though they left Motown (actually Soul) shortly after they cut this album, Gladys Knight & the Pips were at their performing peak during the early '70s. This magnificent title track featured stunning vocals by Knight and equally effective backing vocals from the Pips, and had several other outstanding songs on it. Why Motown never pushed them as much as they could have mystified many at the time, and while Knight & the Pips didn't surpass their Motown material at other labels, they created enough outstanding songs to justify their decision to leave. — *Ron Wynn*

● **Anthology** / 1974 / Motown 0792
Atlanta family group Gladys Knight & the Pips had performed together for 14 years before signing with Motown in 1966. Earlier recordings for Huntom (the master recordings were later sold to Vee-Jay), Fury, and Maxx had generated five chart hits, including the Top-Ten R&B smashes "Every Beat of My Heart" and "Letter Full of Tears," but it was on the Motown subsidiary Soul that Gladys Knight and company hit their stride. This compilation more than adequately covers this period of the Pips' career. Working primarily with producer Norman Whitfield from 1967 through 1969, the group created such Motor City classics as "Everybody Needs Love," "I Heard It through the Grapevine," "The End of Our Road," and "Friendship Train." From 1970 through 1973 the Pips worked with a variety of Motown producers concentrating on ballads. Although they were perhaps a little less consistent, there was no shortage of hits, the most notable being 1970's "If I Were Your Woman" and 1973's "Neither One of Us (Wants to be the First to Say Goodbye)." The downside of this compilation is that both the liner notes and the mastering for CD are substandard. — *Rob Bowman*

● **Soul Survivors: The Best of Gladys Knight & the Pips** / 1990 / Rhino 70756
Soul Survivors: The Best of Gladys Knight & the Pips picks up where the Motown anthology left off, containing the most important singles that Gladys Knight & the Pips recorded for Buddah, Columbia, and MCA from the early '70s until the late '80s. The Buddah tracks, highlighted by the Jim Weatherly-written "Midnight Train in Georgia" and "Best Thing That Ever

Happened to Me," contain some of Gladys's most impassioned vocal performances. —*Rob Bowman*

Buddy Knox (Wayne Knox)

b. Jul. 20, 1933, Happy, TX
Vocals / Rockabilly

The brand of Texas rockabilly that Buddy Knox cooked up around 1957 wasn't quite as raw as that of his Memphis cohorts at Sun, but it was just as commercially potent. Knox sported a light, almost gentle vocal style, and his band, the Rhythm Orchids, obliged with upbeat backing that suited him well. Formed at West Texas State University, the Rhythm Orchids also included Jimmy Bowen on upright bass, and it was Bowen's equally lighthearted vocal on "I'm Stickin' with You" that originally graced the flip side of Knox's first smash, "Party Doll." Roulette Records astutely picked up the master from the tiny Triple-D logo, separated the sides, and the fledgling firm enjoyed two giant hits for the price of one.

"Party Doll" soared to the very top of the pops, and Knox encored with the equally tuneful "Rock Your Little Baby to Sleep" and "Hula Love," which he performed in the 1957 rock flick *Jamboree*. Knox waxed the fine rockabilly-based "Swingin' Daddy," "Devil Woman," and a cover of Ruth Brown's "Somebody Touched Me" for Roulette before moving to Liberty and hitting with a pop-flavored rendition of the Clovers' song "Lovey Dovey" in 1960. Over three decades later, the Texas rocker remains a popular act on the oldies front. —*Bill Dahl*

● **Best of Buddy Knox** / 1990 / Rhino 70964
Gentle, catchy Texas rockabilly with a pop slant. —*Bill Dahl*

Cub Koda

b. Oct. 1, 1948, Detroit, MI
Vocals, guitar / Rock & roll, blues-rock, rockabilly

Founder and leader of the rowdy '70s rock group Brownsville Station ("Smokin' in the Boy's Room," "The Martian Boogie"), Koda has gone on to a solo career as a high-spirited archivist of obscure rock, blues, country, and R&B songs and artists. As a producer, Koda unearthed the "world's worst bar band," King Uszniewicz & the Uszniewicztones. As the frontman for Hound Dog Taylor's resurrected Houserockers, he recorded two raucous albums that are encyclopedic in their array of blues songs and styles. But perhaps Koda's most lasting contribution to music is as a writer of liner notes and the long-running "Vinyl Junkie" column for the record-collecting magazine *Goldmine*. —*Kit Kiefer*

○ **Cub Koda & the Points** / 1980 / Fan Club 94
Koda's first solo album after Brownsville Station. Highlights include "Jail Bait" and "Welcome to My Job." —*Stephen Thomas Erlewine*

It's the Blues / 1981 / Fan Club 93
An intense, eclectic, wonderfully played set with the Houserockers. Lots of fun and 100 percent true to its title. —*Kit Kiefer*

Cub Digs Chuck / 1989 / Garageland 002
Koda's tribute album to Chuck Berry, featuring blistering versions of "Johnny B. Goode," "Maybellene," and others. —*Stephen Thomas Erlewine*

○ **Live at B.L.U.E.S. 1982** / 1991 / Wolf 120.290
Powerful blues with the Houserockers, raw and loud, with Koda shining on slide. Special appearance by Chicago legend Eddie Clearwater. —*Kit Kiefer*

○ **Cub Digs Bo** / 1991 / Garageland 001
Koda's tribute album to Bo Diddley, including powerhouse renditions of "Mumblin' Guitar," "Roadrunner," and "Background to a Music." —*Stephen Thomas Erlewine*

● **Welcome to My Job—The Cub Koda Collection 1963-93** / 1993 / Blue Wave 121
Covering everything from his pre-Brownsville Station days to two brand-new songs, *Welcome to My Job* is the definitive collection of Cub Koda's versatile solo career. —*Stephen Thomas Erlewine*

○ **Abba Dabba Dabba—A Bananza of Hits** / 1994 / Schoolkids
Cub Koda's first album for Schoolkids Records is his wildest, funniest, and simply best album in years. —*Stephen Thomas Erlewine*

Kool & the Gang

Group / Funk, urban R&B, pop/rock

One of the leading funk outfits of the '70s and '80s, with gold and platinum platters galore. Formed by bassist Robert "Kool" Bell (b. 1950) as the Jazziacs in Jersey City, the Gang also featured his brothers Robert and Ronald Bell. The crew signed with De-Lite Records in 1969 and began churning out massively funky grooves, hitting full stride in 1973-1974 with "Jungle Boogie," "Hollywood Swinging," and "Higher Plane." The Gang topped the soul charts in 1979 with the high-stepping disco favorite "Ladies Night"; the same year they hired J. T. Taylor as their new lead singer. "Celebrate!" a staple of every respectable wedding reception of the last dozen years, went platinum for the group in 1980, and their non-stop string of incendiary successes stretched into the mid '80s with "Fresh" and "Cherish." Taylor went solo in 1988. —*Bill Dahl*

Something Special / 1981 / Mercury 822534
The beginning of the change in the group's style could be heard on this album, although they wouldn't make the complete shift until the next release. But the horn lines were already being diminished, the backbeat toned down, and the vocals less rowdy and more polished. They still had some funk influences, but you could hear the changes coming. They didn't have J. T. Taylor on board yet, so they couldn't make the complete musical makeover. —*Ron Wynn*

Forever / 1986 / Mercury 830398
Kool & the Gang had their last fling with crossover success with this 1986 album—he last one with J. T. Taylor as their lead vocalist. They got three more chart hits, and while "Stone Love" or "Victory" didn't reach the number-one spot on either survey, they both cracked the pop and R&B Top Ten. They were like most of the hits the group enjoyed during their pop run: likable, lightweight, feel-good material. They lacked the punch of the past but were still viable. —*Ron Wynn*

○ **Everything Is Kool & the Gang: Greatest Hits** / Jul. 25, 1988 / Mercury 834780
Kool and the Gang's long run as a re-created pop act in the '80s formally ended with the release of this late-'80s anthology. It contained all the smooth pop winners sung by J. T. Taylor, who'd already made his exit., and demonstrated how smooth, slick, yet engaging a lead singer he'd been. It also showed how the efforts of such producers as Deodato had successfully turned Kool and the Gang into superstars by erasing the funk beats, making the arrangements mellow and subdued, and providing them with catchy, hook-filled songs like "Celebration" and "Ladies Night." —*Ron Wynn*

● **Best Of** / 1993 / Mercury 514822
Excellent compilation of Kool & the Gang's pioneering funk from 1969-1976. Essential for anyone with an interest in the evolution of modern R&B and funk. —*Stephen Thomas Erlewine*

Al Kooper

b. Feb. 5, 1944, Brooklyn, NY
Vocals, guitar, keyboard / Rock & roll, blues rock

Over the last 30 years, Al Kooper has managed to involve himself in many creative aspects of popular music. As a songwriter, Kooper cowrote the number-one hit for Gary Lewis & the Playboys, "This Diamond Ring." Bob Dylan's "Like a Rolling Stone" and album *Highway 61 Revisited* benefited from Kooper's rolling Hammond B3 organ work. Kooper also played French horn and keys on the Rolling Stones' "You Can't Always Get What You Want." Kooper founded Blood, Sweat & Tears, producing and performing on their classic debut *The Child Is Father to the Man*. He also did side projects with Stephen Stills and Michael Bloomfield, most notably *Super Session*. As a producer, Kooper discovered Lynyrd Skynyrd and produced their first three albums. Kooper's solo output has always been sporadic, due to the many other projects on his plate. More recently, Kooper has relocated to Nashville, where he produces and can be seen playing with the blues-rock band the Blue Bloods. —*Rick Clark*

● **Live Adventures** / 1969 / CBS 6
More jamming, this time at the Fillmore East, with guest appearances by Elvin Bishop and Carlos Santana. —*Cub Koda*

Kraftwerk

Group / Techno-pop, electronic, dance
In the mid '70s, the German quartet Kraftwerk laid the ground-work for most of the electronic and synth-rock bands that followed them in the next two decades. Each of the members played synthesizers, creating a cold, precise, almost mechanical music that was hypnotic in its repetiveness. For the rest of the '70s, the band was on the cutting edge or rock and dance music, influencing numerous musicians in the process. As the '80s progressed, the group's records became less and less innovative, but they still made a number of albums that were very impressive. The band continues to record in the '90s.

Echoes of Kraftwerk's music can be heard in everyone from David Bowie and Tangerine Dream to Depeche Mode and the Human League. Hip-hop is also unwittingly in debt to much of the band's innovative use of electronics. But the underground techno scene of the '80s and '90s owes the greatest debt to Kraftwerk, as artists like the Aphex Twin, Orbital, Vapourspace, and the Orb bring the band's trancelike electronics to new heights, adding a warm, human dimension that the band didn't have when they recorded *Autobahn* in 1974. — *Stephen Thomas Erlewine*

● **Autobahn** / 1974 / Warner Brothers 25326
A cold, hypnotic album, the title song of which was an unlikely hit. — *Dan Heilman*

Billy J. Kramer & the Dakotas

b. Aug. 19, 1943
Group / British invasion
At the outset of the British Invasion in 1964, Billy J. Kramer & the Dakotas was one of the hottest bands of the movement's initial wave. Beatles manager Brian Epstein paired young Liverpool vocalist Kramer with the Dakotas and gave them a surefire hit—the Lennon/McCartney composition "Do You Want to Know a Secret?," which established the group in England. The group broke in America with the two-sided smash "Little Children"/"Bad to Me," in 1964 on Imperial, the latter another Lennon/McCartney effort. Their next two smashes, "I'll Keep You Satisfied" and "From a Window," were also penned by the prolific duo, although Kramer's last U.S. hit, "Trains and Boats and Planes," was written by Burt Bacharach and Hal David. The group appeared in the popular 1964 movie *The T.A.M.I. Show*, but by 1967 the musicians and Kramer had gone their separate ways, the vocalist recording as a solo in Britain. — *Bill Dahl*

● **Best of Billy J. Kramer** / 1991 / EMI America 96055
A strong collection that presents all of his best—including a number of songs written by John Lennon and Paul McCartney—are here in excellent sound. — *Bruce Eder & Jeff Tamarkin*

Lenny Kravitz

b. , New York
Vocals, guitar, bass, drums / Soul, rock & roll, psychedelic, pop/rock
As a musician and a producer, Lenny Kravitz is one of the best. He can successfully recreate the sound and feeling of countless groups from the past; his music recalls everyone from Lennon, Hendrix, and Bowie to the Velvet Underground, Curtis Mayfield, and Prince. What Kravitz can't do is synthesize these influences into a distinctive style—every song on each of his albums sounds like it was recorded by a different artists. However, that's not entirely a bad thing, because Kravitz *can* reproduce the sound of his favorite artists exactly: "It Ain't Over 'til It's Over" sounds like it was recorded in 1972; "Are You Gonna Go My Way" sounds like a forgotten track from 1968. His music might not be original, but it is quite enjoyable.

Since his 1989 debut, *Let Love Rule*, Kravitz's songwriting and production skills have been consistently improving. His second album, *Mama Said*, gave him a number-two hit with "It Ain't Over 'til It's Over." *Are You Gonna Go My Way*, Kravitz's third album, was released in 1993. It was a stronger album than anything he had released in the past and his most commercially successful record yet. — *Stephen Thomas Erlewine*

○ **Let Love Rule** / 1989 / Virgin 91290
Kravitz played the majority of the instruments on this self-produced debut of catchy retro-pop. Kravitz's talent unfortunately does not extend past music, so the album features some em-

barassingly sophomoric lyrics (many from his ex-wife Lisa Bonet) that weigh down some of his better songs. — *Stephen Thomas Erlewine*

○ **Mama Said** / 1991 / Virgin 91610
Like his debut, Kravitz's second album, *Mama Said* works best on its surface—it's filled with undeniable, guilty pop pleasures. Kravitz steals from nearly every major pop artist and style since 1966, which makes for some enjoyable ear candy, including the number-two hit single "It Ain't Over 'til It's Over." Kravitz again plays the majority of the instruments, with Slash contributing some fine guitar to "Always on the Run" and "Fields of Joy." — *Stephen Thomas Erlewine*

● **Are You Gonna Go My Way?** / 1993 / Capitol 86984

Opening with the pounding Hendrix-styled title track, Lenny Kravitz continues his romp through pop history's back pages. This time, he attacks early-'70s soul, much in the vein of Curtis Mayfield. It's always surprising to hear how close Kravitz can come to approximating his idols. *Are You Gonna Go My Way?* is no exception to that rule, but this time out he has created a thoroughly enjoyable, consistent record that is filled with irresistible, hook-laden songs. — *Stephen Thomas Erlewine*

L7

Group / Alternative rock, heavy metal
L7's heavy, punk-inflected, riff-oriented guitar grind—a mix of the Ramones, Motörhead, and Joan Jett—was what earned them a dedicated following of fans in the early '90s, not the fact that they were female. While the band is strongly feminist, they never let their rhetoric stand in the way of their roaring guitars. L7 always relies on the sheer sonic aggression of rock, not its lyrical power.

When the group was on Sub Pop early in the '90s, the band sounded punkier and more abrasive; signing to a major label didn't cause them to lose that aggression—they just had a better production, courtesy of Butch Vig (Nirvana, Smashing Pumpkins, Sonic Youth). Featuring "Pretend We're Dead," 1992's *Bricks Are Heavy* was a major alternative hit; their second major-label album, the coarse *Hungry for Stink*, was released right before L7 toured with 1994's Lollapalooza. — *Stephen Thomas Erlewine*

○ **Smell the Magic** / Jul. 12, 1991 / Sub Pop 79
A wonderfully abrasive set of thrashing guitars and growling vocals. — *Stephen Thomas Erlewine*

● **Bricks Are Heavy** / 1992 / Slash 26784
While their major-label debut is hampered by Butch Vig's rather tame production, it does show that L7 has some strong pop sensibilities underneath their burning guitars, as "Pretend We're Dead" and "Everglade" prove. — *Stephen Thomas Erlewine*

Hungry for Stink / 1994 / Slash
While L7 sounds tremendous on *Hungry for Stink*, the band has neglected to write any songs. But when you're caught in the middle of a massive guitar grind this good, songs don't matter much. — *Stephen Thomas Erlewine*

The La's

Group / Alternative pop/rock
This unique alternative pop/rock band from Liverpool draws heavily from the folky acoustic/electric side of mid '60s Brit pop—á la Hollies and Searchers. — *Rick Clark*

○ **LA's** / 1990 / London 828202
One of the strongest debuts on the 1990 alternative music scene. "There She Goes" was a hit single with its appealing mid '60s-influenced Brit invasion sound and interweaving hooks. Most of the album should be a joy to hear for fans of alternative Anglo-pop. Highlights include "Son of a Gun," "Way Out," "Freedom Song," and "I.O.U." — *Rick Clark*

Patti Labelle (Patricia Holt)

b. May 24, 1944, Philadelphia, PA
Vocals / Soul, urban R&B
Born Patricia Holt in Philadelphia, Patti LaBelle has enjoyed a 30-year-plus career, having sung early '60s girl-group material, soul, and funk and 80s ballad and dance music. From 1962 to 1976 she was a founding member of both Patti LaBelle & the Blue Belles and LaBelle. She began her solo career in 1977. Over the ensuing six years, she scored a number of lower-rung R&B hits with Epic,

coming into her own on Gamble and Huff's Philadelphia International label in 1984 with the #1 R&B hit "If Only You Knew." She has been a consistent chartmaker ever since, renowned for a gospel-trained voice with stunning power and range, capable of exhilarating aural gymnastics. One of the most gifted, idiosyncratic voices in R&B. —*Rob Bowman*

○ **Nightbirds** / 1974 / Epic 33075
The finest of the three LaBelle albums, *Nightbirds* was recorded in New Orleans with funk meister Allen Toussaint handling the production chores and, one assumes, members of the Meters taking care of the session work. Worth the price of admission for the Bob Crewe-written "Lady Marmalade" alone, the album veers between the strutting New Orleans, horn-laden singles and more mainstream pop material. —*Rob Bowman*

Patti Labelle / 1977 / Epic 34847
Patti Labelle's solo debut for Epic closed the book on a 15-year collaboration with Nona Hendryx and Sarah Dash. She mixed light pop and soul covers on this outing, turning in earnestly sung renditions of "You Are My Friend" and The Skyliners' "Since I Don't Have You," but also doing curious material like "Dan Swift Me" and "You Can't Judge a Book by the Cover." Labelle was still finding her niche and hadn't yet become comfortable or established the tendencies that are now commonplace such as the drawn-out lyric emphasis and the embellishments and lengthy holding of notes. —*Ron Wynn*

● **Best of Patti Labelle** / 1986 / Epic 36997
This anthology includes the biggest pop hit that the trio Labelle scored, the classic "Lady Marmalade," plus other staples from Patti Labelle's solo phase, including "You Are My Friend," "Joy to Have Your Love" and "I Don't Go Shopping." Labelle didn't make her best, or at least her most successful, records while on Epic, so these aren't the tunes that are currently associated with her. They were decently produced and often well performed, but lack the depth of her best MCA cuts. —*Ron Wynn*

Winner in You / 1986 / MCA 5737
Patti Labelle enjoyed the biggest hit of her solo career when she switched labels from Phil International to MCA. Though she'd scored a #1 R&B hit on Phil International with "If Only You Knew," none of her albums had consistently clicked since she'd gone solo in 1977. But Labelle's 1986 MCA debut topped the pop album charts, anchored by her huge hit "On My Own." The duet with Michael McDonald dominated both the pop and R&B scenes, staying atop the R&B charts four weeks and also gave Labelle her first #1 pop single as a solo artist. She even earned a second Top 40 hit with "Oh, People," even though there was another fine single on the LP, "Kiss Away the Pain," that was ignored. Still, this album gave Labelle the elusive solo stardom she'd sought since 1977. —*Ron Wynn*

● **Best of the Bluebelles** / Relic 7043
This anthology collects the early, often charming and sometimes overly cute singles from Patti Labelle and the Bluebelles. Besides the classic "I Sold My Heart to the Junkman" (which was really Labelle backed by the Starlets), there are lesser known numbers like "Down the Aisle (the Wedding Song)" and "I'm Still Waiting." Overall, this is competent period piece material, but it's clear Labelle and company preferred more aggressive and assertive material and were never quite comfortable with most of these songs. —*Ron Wynn*

Major Lance

b. Apr. 4, 1941, Chicago, IL
Vocals / Soul
Few vocalists better epitomize the breezy danceability of '60s Chicago soul than whippet-thin Major Lance. Local deejay Jim Lounsbury discovered the loose-limbed singer and arranged his first contract with Mercury in 1959, but Lance needed expert guidance—and he received plenty from innovative producer Carl Davis after joining the OKeh label in 1962. Armed with exceptional dance material by Curtis Mayfield and the brass-heavy, often Latin-tinged charts of Jonny Pate, Lance blasted off with "The Monkey Time" and "Hey Little Girl" in 1963 and followed with the mysterious "Um Um Um Um Um Um" and "The Matador" the next year. When the influence of Mayfield and Davis dimmed, the hits became lesser in magnitude, and Lance left OKeh in 1968, bouncing from Dakar to Curtom to Volt with moderate success.

Lance did a three-year prison stretch from 1978 to 1981 for drug dealing but has been sighted on stage recently. —*Bill Dahl*

● **Um, Um, Um, Um, Um, Um—the Best of Major Lance** / 1964 / Epic 40432
Major Lance had some great novelty/dance tunes and soul ballads in the mid '60s, most of them either written and/or produced by Curtis Mayfield. This album collected them all and showed very quickly that Lance wasn't an album act. He was ideal for the single; he could deliver a short, inspiring performance around a tight, unambitious central concept, be it a dance step or a love affair. —*Ron Wynn*

○ **Greatest Hits** / 1965 / Okeh 14110
This Chicago-based soul crooner was Curtis Mayfield's finest discovery, cutting many Impressions-like hits that captured that group's effervescent spirit and a good deal of its groove appeal. All of Lance's major hits—"Monkey Time," "Um, Um, Um, Um, Um, Um," and "Gotta Getaway"—are included here. —*John Floyd*

Mark Lanegan

Vocals / Alternative pop/rock
The lead vocalist in the neo-psychedelic Screaming Trees favors a more brooding, quietly intense sound on his own. —*Bruce Eder*

○ **Winding Sheet** / 1990 / Sub Pop 61
A dark side of this Screaming Trees vocalist. —*Robert Gordon*

● **Whiskey for the Holy Ghost** / 1994 / Sub Pop
The second solo album from the Screaming Trees frontman is a gloomy, whiskey-soaked song cycle about losers and slackers, told from a surprisingly poetic view; the stark, folk-tinged accompaniment (featuring ample contributions from Mike Johnson from Dinosaur Jr.) fit the songs perfectly and provide Lanegan with a provocative, exciting new direction that only faintly recalls his full-time gig. —*Stephen Thomas Erlewine*

Daniel Lanois

Vocals, guitar, percussion / Alternative pop/rock
Canadian Daniel Lanois has made a name for himself as a producer of very atmospheric albums. He has worked on successful projects with U2, Bob Dylan, the Neville Brothers, and Chris Whitley. Since his relocation to New Orleans, his thoughtful solo work reflects his fascination with the French Cajun rhythms. —*Rick Clark*

○ **Acadie** / 1989 / Opal 25969
Producer Lanois imbues this solo debut with his trademark otherworldly ambience on classics like "Still Water" and "Amazing Grace." Originals like the mystical "The Maker" and the soft French folk melodicism of "O Marie" are other highlights. —*Rick Clark*

● **For the Beauty of Wynona** / 1993 / Warner Brothers
This remarkable followup to his great debut shows Lanois growing as a singer and songwriter. His production is a weirdly magical as ever. "Brother L.A." and "Lotta Love to Give" are highlights among the many delights this album offers. —*Rick Clark*

Latimore

b. Sep. 7, 1939, Charleston, TN
Vocals, keyboard / Soul, funk, disco, R&B
Deep-voiced Latimore's sultry mid '70s output for Miami's Glades label was a steamy marriage of soul and blues. Initially billed as Benny Latimore, the Tennessean began recording for Miami mogul Henry Stone in 1965, and his late '60s Dade singles are solid deep soul. Dropping his first name on Glades, Latimore finally found stardom in 1973 with a jazzy reading of T-Bone Walker's "Stormy Monday." He topped the soul lists in 1974 with the anguished "Let's Straighten It Out," a simmering soul/blues hybrid, and encored with the incendiary "Keep the Home Fires Burnin'" the next year. Most of Latimore's Glades sides were produced in Miami by Steve "Everyday I Have to Cry" Alaimo, and when he wasn't cutting his own hits, Latimore acted as a house pianist for parent TK Records. Latimore moved to Malaco during the '80s, his appeal undiminished. —*Bill Dahl*

More, More, More / 1974 / Glades 6503
Benny Latimore's tough-talking southern soul began to make some inroads in the mid '70s with this LP that included his only #1 R&B hit, "Let's Straighten It Out." The singer, composer, and keyboardist made no-nonsense, unsophisticated confessional soul

and heartache ballads, plus an occasional uptempo number; at the time, he was making tunes with minimal production that put his coarse leads at the center. They were recorded for the Miami-based Glades label and usually were regional rather than national hits. "Let's Straighten It Out" proved an exception. —*Ron Wynn*

○ **Good Time Man** / 1985 / Malaco 7423
Benny Latimore's Malaco albums have been conservatively produced, geared toward southern tastes and moderately successful on a regional basis. That's the case with this date that didn't land national hits, but was a generally good effort. Latimore's voice isn't as commanding as it was during his '70s run, but he can still sing in a menacing fashion, deliver convincing heartache ballads, sound vulnerable or express tenderness and concern. Unfortunately, the lack of a great single and the decidely non-urban contemporary sound doomed this to the fate of most Malaco LPs—little exposure above the Mason-Dixon line and little radio airplay. —*Ron Wynn*

● **Slow Down** / 1989 / Malaco 7443
This was Latimore's best Malaco release and arguably his finest record in the '80s. It had both moving ballads and fine uptempo tunes, and his usually resourceful, deep soul vocals were stronger, more confident and animated. The song "One Man, One Woman, One Love" was the type of simple, yet engaging number that the Malaco tunesmiths didn't deliver consistently enough for their acts in the late '80s. It was also the kind of song that had a vintage sound but a contemporary outlook. —*Ron Wynn*

Cyndi Lauper

b. Jun. 23, 1950, Queens, NY
Vocals, guitar / Pop/rock
As a guitarist, Lauper gigged with several bands in the '70s before cofounding Blue Angel in 1977, which released a highly acclaimed rock & roll album on Polydor three years later. She went solo in 1983 and became a musical and MTV sensation with her pop-feminist song "Girls Just Want to Have Fun" and her tender ballad "Time after Time." She won the 1984 Grammy for Best New Artist.

Although she has had several hits since her debut, most notably the hit ballad "True Colors," Lauper was never able to recapture the excitement that surrounded her debut, *She's So Unusual*. She is still recording in the '90s, scoring a hit every now and then. —*Bil Carpenter and Donna DiChario*

● **She's So Unusual** / 1984 / Portrait 38930
This quirky diva created a musical and MTV sensation with her pop-feminist "Girls Just Want to Have Fun" and her tender ballad "Time after Time." She won the 1984 Grammy for Best New Artist. —*Donna DiChario*

○ **True Colors** / 1986 / Portrait 40313
Includes the Top 5 title track ballad and her Top 20 faithfully remade cover of Marvin Gaye's "What's Going On." Also includes the harder-edged "Change of Heart." —*Donna DiChario*

Amanda Lear

Vocals / Disco
Amanda Lear first surfaced in the early 1970s as a fetishistically clothed album cover model for Roxy Music. She was said to be a transsexual but, as she told *Interview* magazine, that was just a ruse dreamed up by her sponsor, David Bowie, to draw attention. Her importance to disco fans, however, begins in 1977, when, in Germany with production help from Tony Monn, she recorded *I Am a Photograph*, the first of six sleazy, hard-to-find albums in which she flaunts a voice so heavy with low notes you wonder if she really isn't a man after all. But no, Lear's slow notes are simply an exaggeration of the whisky-voiced sultryness created by Marlene Dietrich. Which isn't to say that Lear's lyrics—or the music's inverted proportions—don't exploit her mythology as a kinky concotion to the bursting point. —*Michael Freedberg*

● **I Am a Photograph** / 1977 / Chrysalis 1173
Lear, previously known as a Roxy Music album cover model and a protegee of Salvador Dali, appears here as a cabaret countess. She enunciates naughty suggestions in a smoke-and-velvet rasp that's half Marianne Faithfull and half ventriloquy. Her best subversions hit a dancer's most salacious fantasies dead on: "Queen of Chinatown" (guess), "Pretty Boys" (just so), "Blood and Honey" (instinctual), "Tomorrow" (the blues). Most of these songs support

their studied lewdness with absurdly different music, creating tangible sexual friction that makes Lear's tape-loop voice feel even naughtier. All of Lear's tempos assault disco norms, either as sleaze or ultra-fast hi-hi-NRG. An album not to be missed! —*Michael Freedberg*

○ **Sweet Revenge** / 1978 / Chrysalis 1184
Producer Anthony Monn parades every effect known to Euro-dream imagery in support of Lear as disco vamp (and she's a great one): whispers from inside a tunnel, rhythms that filter subliminally under your thumb, themes that scale up to soprano range like wisps of sexual smoke, choirs of angels singing, guitar rhythm rock-ons, and, of course, Lear's voice. Lear's singing is perhaps Monn's greatest effect: out of reach and horny at the same time, Lear works hard to pretend at playing the merciless siren. She can't properly sing even one note, but what's that got to do with her world of mystery and rhythm? —*Michael Freedberg*

Led Zeppelin

Group / Blues rock, hard rock, heavy metal
In 1968 the Yardbirds' commercial glory days were well behind them. The groundbreaking band had been the nurturing ground for some of the greatest guitarists of the rock era: Eric Clapton, Jeff Beck, and Jimmy Page. It was Page (the last of the three to come on board) who, along with manager Peter Grant, sensed a change in the times and sought to create a heavier, more aggressive sound for the developing album-oriented market.

Initially called the New Yardbirds, Led Zeppelin got its name from a Keith Moon (the Who's drummer) catchphrase ("going down like a lead zeppelin") concerning encountering bad gigs.

From the outset, Led Zeppelin (Page, guitar; Robert Plant, vocal; John Paul Jones, bass and keys; John Bonham, drums) caused a stir with their incredibly heavy yet dynamic sound, their questionable plundering of old blues standards, and Plant's agitated banshee wail of a voice. Their audacious self-titled debut displayed one of the greatest rock production jobs of all time, with its fine balance of room ambience and powerful immediacy. Throughout much of the '70s, Led Zeppelin reigned as the world's most successful rock band, breaking concert records and releasing ten Top 10 albums, eight of which went #1 or #2. In spite of their huge success, Led Zeppelin only had one Top 10 single, "Whole Lotta Love." "Stairway to Heaven," the most requested song ever on rock radio, was never officially released as a single. Over the years, many bands have tried (and failed) to capture the raw power and sonic qualities of Led Zeppelin, but it was the band's shared vision that achieved their sound. They understood that enough to call it quits when Bonham died on Sept 25, 1980. —*Rick Clark*

○ **Led Zeppelin** / 1969 / Atlantic 19126
Led Zeppelin's debut album provided a blueprint for its overall approach—hard rock with ornate guitar textures and powerful riffs, topped by singer Robert Plant's high-pitched singing on roaring rockers like "Good Times Bad Times" and "Communication Breakdown," plus drawn-out blues performances like "Dazed and Confused." —*William Ruhlmann*

☆ **Led Zeppelin 2** / 1969 / Atlantic 19127
Perhaps the definitive heavy metal album, featuring "Whole Lotta Love." —*William Ruhlmann*

○ **Led Zeppelin 3** / 1970 / Atlantic 19128
After the bone-crunching hard rock of *Led Zeppelin II*, Page, Plant, Bonham, and Jones tracked a collection of more acoustic-flavored numbers. Songs like "Gallows Pole" and "Bron-Y-Aur Stomp" were essentially their trademark rockers played on folk instruments, but the reflective "That's the Way" and "Tangerine" indicated a new maturity. A handful of heavy riff-rockers like "Immigrant Song," "Out on the Tiles," "Celebration Day," and the hard blues raveup "Since I've Been Loving You" more than rounded out this solid (but transitional) effort. —*Rick Clark*

★ **Led Zeppelin 4** / 1971 / Atlantic 19129
The perfect mixture of Zeppelin's trademark heavy rock, plus some old-time rock & roll and the band's folkie influences, all of which culminated in its greatest song, "Stairway to Heaven." —*William Ruhlmann*

☆ **Houses of the Holy** / 1973 / Atlantic 19130
Led Zeppelin's followup to their monumental fourth album isn't quite as accomplished as their previous records, yet it is still a remarkably diverse and wonderful set of hard rock, highlighted by

the classic-rock radio staples "Dancing Days," "Over the Hills and Far Away," "The Ocean," "The Rain Song," and "The Song Remains the Same." —*Stephen Thomas Erlewine*

☆ **Physical Graffiti** / 1975 / Swan Song 200
A lengthy two-disc set whose bluesy workouts (plus such new explorations as the Middle Eastern "Kashmir") mark it as the most "Zeppelinish" of Led Zeppelin albums. —*William Ruhlmann*

☆ **Led Zeppelin Boxed Set** / 1990 / Atlantic 82144
This four-CD, 54-track collection, compiled by Robert Plant, Jimmy Page, and John Paul Jones, contains material from all nine of Led Zeppelin's studio albums as well as some previously unreleased cuts, all sequenced in a loosely chronological order. Most of the essential tracks are here, but the main reason to get this set (if you are a fan of this band) is the stunning remastering job. —*Rick Clark*

Led Zeppelin Remasters / 1992 / Atlantic 82371
A collection of most of Zeppelin's best-known tracks, this double-disc set only gives a slight idea of what the band accomplished in its career; spring for the four-disc box set instead. —*Stephen Thomas Erlewine*

○ **Boxed Set 2** / 1993 / Atlantic
Rounding out all of the studio tracks that didn't appear on the first box (as well as the pleasant but unremarkable, "Baby Come On Home"), *Boxed Set 2* is the perfect way to complete a Led Zeppelin library begun with the first stellar set. Only a few tracks are truly essential for casual fans, but it features the same impressive sound as the first box as well as the same intelligent sequencing that reveals new insights about the band. —*Stephen Thomas Erlewine*

Albert Lee

b. Dec. 21, 1943, Leominster, England
Guitar / Country-rock, rockabilly
Lee is an English guitarist, highly proficient in a multitude of styles but primarily gifted in country and rockabilly picking. The ultimate sideman on countless sessions over the last two decades, his Telecaster twangings have graced the recordings of Eric Clapton, Jerry Lee Lewis, and Emmylou Harris, to name just a few. Also notable as the music director when the Everly Brothers reunited a few years back, Lee has released a few solo albums of his own in the last few years, all of them informed by his clean, articulate picking. —*Cub Koda*

○ **Country Guitar Man** / Nov. 1986 / Magnum 037
This collection of Lee's early '70s work with Head, Hands, & Feet is fairly remarkable, particularly Lee's guitar work. —*Jeff Tamarkin*

○ **Speechless** / Feb. 1987 / MCA 5693
One of the guitar world's best-kept secrets, the former Everly Brothers and Emmylou Harris sideman explores his roots in this instrumental jewel. Albert Lee coproduced this album. Very clean sound, very good cover of "Arkansas Traveler" featuring Lee on guitar, mandolin, and piano. —*Jeff Tamarkin and Chip Renner*

● **Gagged but Not Bound** / Mar. 1988 / MCA 42063
The master musician plays unworldly guitar on this acoustic/electric country, rock, and traditional-oriented masterpiece. Exquisitely recorded. —*Jeff Tamarkin*

○ **Black Claw & Country Fever** / Oct. 1991 / Line 9.01057
This collection of late '60s material is raw yet engaging; the musicianship is stunning. —*Jeff Tamarkin*

Laura Lee

b. Mar. 9, 1945, Detroit, MI
Vocals / Soul
Laura Lee sang with the Meditations Singers gospel group in the '50s, but she's primarily known as a tough '60s soul singer whose salty sense of humor is aimed mostly at the men in her life. Her music laid the groundwork for artists like Millie Jackson and Denise LaSalle to expand this proud, sexy, brash-talking corner of "women's" soul music. Lee had a country/soul romantic side as well, as shown on her splendid version of the Penn-Oldham classic "Uptight Good Man." One of the most gifted and overlooked soul singers of the '60s and '70s. —*Christine Ohlman and Bil Carpenter*

○ **That's How It Is—Chess Years** / 1990 / Chess 93005
Her '60s Chess recordings. Bone-chilling vocals. —*Richard Pack*

● **Greatest Hits** / 1991 / HDH 3903
Hot Wax artist Laura Lee took the spirit of the feminist movement and gave it a hard-hitting R&B setting. Assertive titles like "Wedlock Is a Padlock" and "Rip Off" won her more acceptance on R&B stations. "Women's Love Rights," included here, dented the Top 40 charts at #36. —*Rick Clark*

The Left Banke

Group / Pop/rock
This New York group pioneered "Baroque'n'Roll" in the '60s with their mix of pop-rock and grand, quasi-classical arrangements and melodies. Featuring teenage prodigy Michael Brown as keyboardist and chief songwriter, the group scored two quick hits with "Walk Away Renee" and "Pretty Ballerina." Chamber-like string arrangements, Steve Martin's soaring, near-falsetto lead vocals, and tight harmonies that borrowed from British Invasion bands like the Beatles and the Zombies were also key elements of the Left Banke sound. Though their two hits are their only well-remembered efforts, their debut album (*Walk Away Renee/Pretty Ballerina*) was a strong, near-classic work that matched the quality of their hit singles in songwriting and production.

Unfortunately the group, which showed such tremendous promise, was quickly torn asunder by dissension. Brown left in 1967, and most of the group's second and final album, *The Left Banke Too*, was recorded without him. While it still sported baroque arrangements and contained some fine moments, Brown's presence was sorely missed, and the record pales in comparison to their debut. Brown went on to form a Left Banke-styled group, Montage, which released a fine and underappreciated album in the late '60s. He later teamed up to form Stories with vocalist Ian Lloyd. —*Richie Unterberger*

● **There's Gonna Be a Storm: Complete Recordings 1966-69** / 1992 / Mercury 848095
Though it's missing a few rarities—namely the Steve Martin single for Buddah that reunited him with Michael Brown—this is the most definitive Left Banke compilation. It features the entirety of their two late '60s albums, as well as a couple singles that didn't make it onto LPs at the time and a previously unissued cut, "Men Are Building Sand." —*Richie Unterberger*

Lemonheads

Group / Alternative pop/rock
Evan Dando was a hardcore punk when the Lemonheads released their first album, *Hate Your Friends*, in 1987; five years later, he was a teenage heartthrob, thanks to the memorable, punky power pop of *It's a Shame about Ray*. Between those two albums, the rest of the band quit, leaving guitarist/vocalist Dando as the only Lemonhead. The membership wasn't the only thing that changed. Over the years, Dando began to accentuate his fondness for pure pop, which was apparent even on the band's harder earlier records. The Lemonheads moved to a major label in 1990 and released *Lovey*. Dando recorded most of the album by himself, which makes its mix of loud guitars, bright melodies, and charming, simple lyrics all the more impressive; this was the path he would follow to stardom. On the band's next album—1992's *It's a Shame about Ray*, which was recorded with a full band—Dando's songwriting blossomed. Not only could he write catchy, brash power pop, he was able to seamlessly incorporate touches of folk and country rock. Thanks to a loud, irreverant cover of Simon & Garfunkel's "Mrs. Robinson," the Lemonheads began getting mainstream attention; with their next album, 1993's *Come on Feel the Lemonheads*, the band gained an even bigger audience, even if the album was more inconsistent. Even with its dull spots, the album showed that Dando continued to grow as a songwriter as his country influences became more pronounced and genuine. —*Stephen Thomas Erlewine*

○ **Lick** / 1989 / Taang! 32
On their last independent release, the Lemonheads turn in an engaging but incoherent album that bounces back and forth between inspired melodic punk-pop, hardcore, and the occasional ballad; the whole charming mess is highlighted by a muscular cover of Suzanne Vega's "Luka." —*Stephen Thomas Erlewine*

Create Your Friends / 1989 / Taang! 1523
The Lemonheads' first two albums show that beneath the band's relentless hardcore guitar grind, Evan Dando had written some

very good songs with strong melodies. It just takes some effort to *hear* the melodies. —*Stephen Thomas Erlewine*

○ **Lovey** / 1990 / Atlantic 82137
Alternating between melodic hard rock and gentle country and folk rock, *Lovey* was the band's most varied and accomplished album to date. —*Stephen Thomas Erlewine*

● **It's a Shame about Ray** / 1992 / Atlantic 82397
It's a Shame about Ray is a nearly perfect pop album—short, concise, and overflowing with memorable melodies. Although Evan Dando keeps every song between two and three minutes, he isn't cheating the audience by any measure; the 12-song, under-30-minute blitz of *It's a Shame about Ray* provide more quality music than most of 70-minute epics. Dando's songs (particularly the title song, "Rudderless," "Alison's Starting to Happen," "Bit Part," and "Confetti") prove that his true talents as a pop songwriter are just beginning to emerge. —*Stephen Thomas Erlewine*

Come on Feel the Lemonheads / 1993 / Atlantic
More confused and muddled than *It's a Shame about Ray, Come on Feel the Lemonheads* has a number of pure pop pleasures, but they are buried among several lazy, halfhearted numbers. When Evan Dando does hit his target—as on "The Great Big No," "Down about It," and "Into Your Arms"—the results are irresistible; the introspective, moving "Favorite T" and the country rock of "Being Around" and "Big Gay Heart" are among the best songs he has written. Unfortunately, it takes some time to find these small gems amidst the directionlessness of the rest of the album. —*Stephen Thomas Erlewine*

John Lennon

b. Oct. 9, 1940, Liverpool, England, **d.** Dec. 8, 1980
Vocals, guitar, piano / Singer-songwriter, rock & roll, pop/rock
John Lennon was a singer, songwriter, guitarist, record producer, author, actor, filmmaker, artist, political spokesman, and one of the greatest figures in postwar popular music. Lennon was born in Liverpool, England, and became involved in music in the '50s. The group he founded as the Quarrymen eventually evolved into the Beatles, and from 1963 to 1970 they were the most successful rock group in history. Lennon, the group's leader, played an important part in that success, writing and singing many of its biggest hits and best songs.

Lennon began to record and perform outside the group in 1969, usually in the company of his wife, avant-garde artist Yoko Ono. The early Lennon-Ono records (and films and performance events) were experimental in nature, but as Lennon turned to recording as a solo performer, his work became more accessible to pop audiences, though his lyrical concerns were frequently political or scathingly personal. His first formal solo album was *John Lennon/Plastic Ono Band* in 1970, and he followed this with *Imagine* (1971), *Sometime in New York City* (1972), *Mind Games* (1973), *Walls & Bridges* (1974), and *Rock & Roll* (1974). Most of his recordings sold well, with *Walls & Bridges* topping the charts along with its single, "Whatever Gets You through the Night."

Lennon, who had separated from Ono in 1973, was reconciled with her in 1975 and thereafter retired from music to raise their son Sean. He and Ono reemerged with the album *Double Fantasy* in 1980 and had plans for further recordings and performances at the time he was assassinated. —*William Ruhlmann*

Live Peace in Toronto 1969 / 1970 / Capitol 3362
Impromptu concert appearance, with Lennon singing a few rock & roll oldies plus his then-new single, "Cold Turkey," backed by guitarist Eric Clapton. Also 17+ minutes of Yoko Ono screaming and singing over guitar feedback. —*William Ruhlmann*

☆ **John Lennon/Plastic Ono Band** / 1971 / Capitol 46770
A stark, harrowing set of songs in which Lennon recounts the horrors of his childhood ("Mother," "Working Class Hero"), the disillusionment of his adulthood ("I Found Out"), and his loss of faith in all idols ("God," including "Beatles." This album is one of rock's most personal—and most ambitious—statements. —*William Ruhlmann*

☆ **Imagine** / 1971 / Capitol 46641
In addition to the justly revered title track (a #3 hit), this eclectic pop album also contains "Jealous Guy" (later a hit for Roxy Music) and "Gimme Some Truth" (later adopted by such punk rockers as Generation X). —*William Ruhlmann*

Sometime in New York City / 1972 / Capitol 93850
The first album cobbled to John Lennon and Yoko Ono actually to contain recognizable pop music, *Sometime in New York City* found the Lennons in an explicitly political phase, expounding on such topical subjects as the Attica prison riot and the treatment of activists John Sinclair and Angela Davis. Especially in the case of Lennon's songs, there is an appealing rock style to the material (which features the backing of the band Elephant's Memory), even if the lyrics limit the record's appeal. *Sometime in New York City* was released with a second disc that contained on one side a live medley of Lennon's "Cold Turkey" and Ono's "Don't Worry Kyoko" and on the other an appearance by the Lennons at a concert by Frank Zappa and the Mothers of Invention. This slight material, originally intended as a bonus for listeners at no extra cost, now makes the album a two-CD set, and it is priced accordingly. —*William Ruhlmann*

○ **Mind Games** / Sep. 1973 / Capitol 46769
John Lennon retreated from the political tone of *Sometime in New York City* and returned to solo work here, managing a fitting followup to "Imagine" with the piano-based title track and also turning in one of his better ballads with "One Day (at a Time)." —*William Ruhlmann*

○ **Walls and Bridges** / 1974 / Capitol 46768
Craftsmanlike pop-rock featuring the uptempo #1 hit "Whatever Gets You through the Night," its Top 10 followup, "#9 Dream," and some lovely album tracks. —*William Ruhlmann*

○ **Shaved Fish** / 1975 / Capitol 46642
Though superseded by *The John Lennon Collection* (see below), this greatest-hits album is the only place to find such singles as "Cold Turkey" and "Happy Xmas (War Is Over)." —*William Ruhlmann*

Rock 'n' Roll / 1975 / Capitol 46707
It was a common practice in the early '70s for artists to satisfy record companies' demands for frequent LP releases by recording albums of cover songs (see the Band's *Moondog Matinee* and David Bowie's *Pinups* for other examples). The story of John Lennon's covers album is a little more complicated, but the result is the same, with the artist tackling songs from the '50s by many of his favorites, from Gene Vincent to Lloyd Price. Of course, these are the kinds of songs that turned up on early Beatles albums, and while Lennon doesn't reinvent them as strikingly as his old group did, he gives them an affectionate, knowing treatment. —*William Ruhlmann*

○ **Double Fantasy** / 1980 / Capitol 91425
On an album made shortly before his death, Lennon explores his retirement, his artistic rebirth, and his relationship with his family on such songs as "(Just Like) Starting Over," "Woman," and "Watching the Wheels," all of which were Top 10 hits. Lennon's songs are interspersed with surprisingly accessible contributions from Ono. —*William Ruhlmann*

★ **John Lennon Collection** / 1982 / Capitol 91516
Six of the seven Lennon tracks from *Double Fantasy*, plus nine of his best songs from 1969 to 1974, among them the singles "Give Peace a Chance," in its only LP appearance, and "Instant Karma!" The CD version, released in 1989, adds four tracks, including the B-side single "Move Over Ms. L," making this album all the more necessary. —*William Ruhlmann*

Milk & Honey / 1984 / Polydor 817160
Posthumous followup to *Double Fantasy*, featuring sometimes rough takes of perhaps unfinished songs that nevertheless sparkle with Lennon's wit and exuberance, among them the Top 5 hit "Nobody Told Me." (Again, Ono's songs are interspersed with Lennon's contributions.) —*William Ruhlmann*

Live in New York City / 1986 / Capitol 46196
A rare concert performance from 1972, containing live versions of "Instant Karma," "Come Together," "Imagine," and other favorites. —*William Ruhlmann*

Menlove Ave. / 1986 / Capitol 46576
John Lennon is heard in outtakes from the sessions for the albums *Walls and Bridges* and *Rock 'n' Roll*, including alternate versions of songs that turned up on those albums as well as such original songs as "Rock and Roll People," previously heard only in a version by Johnny Winter. —*William Ruhlmann*

○ **Imagine: John Lennon—Soundtrack** / 1988 / Capitol 90803

A two-record set containing a selection of Lennon's work with the Beatles and as a solo artist. This is the original soundtrack album. —*William Ruhlmann*

☆ **Lennon** / 1990 / Capitol 95220
Lennon is given a solid boxed-set treatment with this four-CD, 73-track collection. The set is so complete that there is essentially no need to go out and obtain any of his albums on disc. *Lennon* runs chronologically, from the Plastic Ono Band's "Give Peace a Chance" to "Grow Old with Me" from 1984's *Milk and Honey*. All the best stuff from *Live Peace in Toronto 1969* is here, as well as his live (with Elton John) versions of "I Saw Her Standing There" and "Lucy in the Sky with Diamonds." The book contains a generous collection of photos and lyrics to all of the songs. The A-to-Z color-coded index is overkill in lieu of any track information detailing where and when the songs were cut and who played on them. —*Rick Clark*

Annie Lennox

Vocal / Pop/rock
In 1992, Annie Lennox took a break from Eurythmics and released *Diva*, which was more successful than any record her band has released since 1985, both commercially and artistically. — *Stephen Thomas Erlewine*

● **Diva** / Apr. 28, 1992 / Arista 18704
Diva's framework offers an effective stage for Lennox's husky voice, showcasing her as much more of a chanteuse than in the past. But the music is strangely muted and understated. In fact, the album almost works best as one integrated mood piece rather than a collection of individual songs. —*Roch Parisien*

Let's Active

Group / Alternative pop/rock
Formed in 1981 by North Carolina musician/producer Mitch Easter, Let's Active was one of the premier bands of the Southern alternative pop movement of the '80s. Easter is primarily known for his production of R.E.M.'s *Murmur* and *Reckoning*, yet that only scratches the surface of his work; at his Drive-In Studio, he produced numerous other bands during the decade. However, Easter's main project was Let's Active. Between 1983 and 1989, the band released only three albums and one EP, yet they showed a remarkable proficiency for ringing, melodic guitar pop as well as tangled neo-psychedelia. After their last album in 1988, the group split; Easter has concentrated on production work since then. —*Rick Clark*

○ **Big Plans for Everybody** / 1986 / IRS 5703
Essentially a Mitch Easter solo project, *Big Plans for Everybody* moves into darker territory than the previous album. Though Easter's trademark bright production and quirky songwriting still stand out, the mood is decidedly melancholy. —*Chris Woodstra*

Every Dog Has His Day / Aug. 22, 1988 / IRS 42151
Every Dog Has His Day features some of Easter's strongest songs in a harder edged setting. Almost completely ignored, this is band's last effort before disbanding indefinitely. —*Chris Woodstra*

● **Cypress/Afoot** / 1989 / IRS 0056
This CD combines their first EP, *Afoot*, and their first album, *Cypress*. Featuring infectious hook-filled songs like "Every Word Means No" and "Waters Part," this perfect southern power-pop is worth seeking out. —*Chris Woodstra*

Level 42

Group / Pop/rock
A Manchester pop-funk band led by bassist Mark King since 1972. The lineup has also featured Phil and Boon Gould, Mike Lindup, and part-time member and producer Wally Badarou. Their first singles were on the Elite label, and their biggest hit was "Something about You" in 1986. In 1987 the Goulds left the band, replaced by Alan Murphy and Gary Husband. —*Bil Carpenter*

○ **Level 42** / 1981 / Polydor 821935
The album was produced by label owner Andy Sojka. Highlights include "Love Meeting Love," "Wings of Love," "Love Games," "Turn It On," and "Starchild." —*Bil Carpenter*

Pursuit of Accidents / 1982 / Polydor 810015
Though they didn't really begin to have dance-pop hits until later in the '80s, the English group Level 42 provided some fine per-

formances on this album. While vocals weren't their strong suit, they did a reasonable job of harmonizing and at least getting through the melodies, while the production and arrangements helped embellish and compensate for their singing inadequacies. —*Ron Wynn*

True Colours / 1983 / Polydor 823542
It's hard to understand why this didn't do as well as later albums like *World Machine*, *Running in the Family*, and *Staring at the Sun*, though the obivious reason would be it never broke any singles to compare with the ones from those releases. But it was just as well produced, the songs were almost as cutely performed, and the arrangements are very similar. —*Ron Wynn*

● **Level Best** / 1989 / Polydor 841399
This hits CD draws heavily from *Running in the Family* (1987) and *World Machine* (1985) but offers a good introduction to this band. —*Scott Bultman*

LeVert

Group / Soul, urban R&B
As the offical offspring of the O'Jays, LeVert was a trio from Philadelphia who combined the sweet harmonies that their fathers provided with the "rope-a-dope" style that kept them in the spotlight in the early '90s. Great music all around, and powerful vocals from Gerald LeVert, who also has his own solo album. — *John Book*

Bloodline / 1986 / Atlantic 81669
When O'Jays' lead singer Eddie Levert's two sons, Gerald and Sean, teamed with Marc Gordon to form their own trio, everyone in the R&B community expected great things. The group didn't get off to a good start when they recorded for the tiny Tempre label, but once they moved to Atlantic, Levert began building their image and reputation. They earned a #1 R&B hit with "(Pop, Pop, Pop, Pop) Goes My Mind" and followed it with a Top 20 single in "Let's Go Out Tonight." Gerald's delivery, tone, and approach mirrored his father's; their harmonies and production were contemporary, yet also reflected the O'Jays' influence. —*Ron Wynn*

● **Big Throwdown** / 1987 / Atlantic 81773
Levert's second album started a run of hits that extended into the '90s. They earned their first pop hit and second #1 R&B single with "Casanova," while "My Forever Love" was a solid followup and excellent ballad. Gerald Levert proved his mettle as a lead singer; though not as explosive as his father, he had a similar gift for communicating a lyric, and he teamed nicely with his brother Sean and Marc Gordon on ballads. Levert's singles weren't as anthemic as the O'Jays', but this album's success showed they were now established hitmakers on the urban contemporary scene. — *Ron Wynn*

○ **Just Coolin'** / Oct. 1988 / Atlantic 81926
Levert scored with both uptempo and ballad cuts on their third Atlantic album. The single "Pull Over" clicked with dance audiences and was aided by a video that neatly played off the lyric hook. The title track also was an urban contemporary radio hit and successful single, though the overall record didn't match the level of its predecessor, despite eventually becoming a gold album. In fact, the first signs of creative stagnation that would really surface on their next release were evident on such songs as "Take Your Time" and "Join in the Fun." —*Ron Wynn*

Barbara Lewis

b. Feb. 9, 1943, South Lyon, MI
Vocals / Soul, R&B
From a Detroit-area musical family (both parents had bands in the '30s and '40s), Barbara Lewis was writing songs at the age of nine. And she could sing! She wrote all the songs on her first album, *Hello Stranger*, and the title cut was a major hit in 1963. Other classic Lewis hits include "Baby, I'm Yours" and "Make Me Your Baby." Even with only a few big hits, Lewis has achieved almost a cult status among her admirers. There is something unique about her songs and singing—an enchantment—that goes right to the heart. —*Michael Erlewine*

★ **Hello Stranger—The Best of Barbara Lewis** / 1994 / Rhino
At last! Twenty great Barbara Lewis songs in glorious remastered digital sound. In fact, the sound is so good it's like hearing these classic sides for the first time. The only significant omission is the

song "On Bended Knee," but then I would have liked a two-disc compilation. Thank you, Rhino! —*Michael Erlewine*

Gary Lewis (Gary Levital)

b. Jun. 31, 1946
Vocals, drums / Pop/rock
An American rock group formed in 1964 by the son of comedian Jerry Lewis. After landing a gig at Disneyland, they were immediately signed to Liberty Records and handed over to pop production genius Snuff Garrett. Utilizing the best songwriters and studio players available, Garrett fashioned five Top 5 hits in a matter of 18 months (15 in the Hot 100 by 1969) around Lewis's meager abilities, sometimes augmenting his voice in the studio with backup singers doubling his part. Lewis pretty well held his own against the British Invasion, but the combination his draft call in late 1966 and the rising tide of psychedelia put his days on the charts to an end. Still active on the oldies circuit, he fronts various backup bands under the name the Playboys. —*Cub Koda*

● **Legendary Masters Series** / 1990 / Capitol 80056
One of the most engaging pop acts of the mid '60s, the Playboys benefited from strong songwriting (Al Kooper cowrote "This Diamond Ring") and studio personnel (courtesy of Leon Russell). It's still light, catchy pop with the enjoyable, unaffected vocals of Gary Lewis on top, and still fun. —*William Ruhlmann*

Huey Lewis & the News

b. Jul. 5, 1950
Group / Pop/rock
Before the formation of the News, Huey Lewis (born Hugh Cregg) had been part of the San Francisco band Clover from 1976 to 1980. During that time Clover (sans Lewis) backed up Elvis Costello on his debut *My Aim Is True*. Lewis also did session sideman work on Nick Lowe's *Labour of Lust* and Dave Edmunds's *Repeat When Necessary*. Clover broke up in 1979 after bandleader John McFee split to join the Doobie Brothers.

Lewis returned to a day gig and started jamming at a local Marin County bar called Uncle Charlie's. It was there that the nucleus of the News was formed out of visiting musicians, many of whom had previously backed up Van Morrison.

The News' self-titled debut failed to sell, but "Do You Believe in Love" from their second album, *Picture This*, went to #7. *Picture This* rose to #13 and produced a couple of hits with "Hope You Love Me Like You Say You Do" and "Workin' for a Livin'." The next album, *Sports*, went multiplatinum and generated a number of hits.

Between albums the News scored a #1 hit, "The Power of Love," from the movie *Back to the Future*. Their followup album, *Fore*, included five Top Ten hits: "Stuck with You," "Jacob's Ladder," "Hip to Be Square," and "Doing It All (For My Baby)." 1988's *Small World* marked the beginning of Lewis's commercial decline, which lasted until 1994, when the News became adult contemporary favorites with their covers of classic soul songs. —*Rick Clark*

○ **Picture This** / 1982 / Chrysalis 21340
Their second album broke through with the hits "Workin' for a Livin'" and "Do You Believe in Love." —*Donna DiChario*

● **Sports** / 1983 / Chrysalis 21412
Their brand of spirited, no-frills rock & roll, featuring the hits "I Want a New Drug," "The Heart of Rock & Roll," and "Walkin' on a Thin Line," helped sell more than seven million copies of this album. —*Donna DiChario*

Fore! / 1986 / Chrysalis 21534
More pop-rock featuring the hits "Stuck with You," "Jacob's Ladder," and "Hip to Be Square." —*Donna DiChario*

Jerry Lee Lewis

b. Sep. 29, 1935, Ferriday, LA
Vocals, piano / Rock & Roll
Jerry Lee Lewis, the self-proclaimed "Killer," is a man of prodigous appetites and talent. Egocentric and self-absorbed, Jerry Lee is the last of the original '50s wildmen. A child prodigy who quickly mastered his instrument, Lewis claims to have no influences, but his stylistic quirks point to boogie-woogie master Cecil Gant and country-piano man Moon Mullican. After being run out of Nashville (where he was told he could be signed if he strummed a guitar instead), he came to Memphis, where his au-

dition tape got him hooked up to Sam Phillips's Sun label. In the space of four singles released in a year's time, the Killer was suddenly running neck and neck with Elvis forking of rock & roll honors. When Lewis married his 13-year-old cousin in 1958, his career promptly ground to a halt, leaving him to eke out a bleak existence in the honky-tonks of America.

It took 12 years of his life to fight his way back, but Lewis is nothing less than American music's consummate survivor, and his reemergence (via the country charts, with a string of smashes) was no less than his due. There are few originals in '50s rock & roll, most taking their cue from Elvis or Little Richard, but Lewis is one of the major stylists in the history of American popular music—period. His distinctive piano style is tightly woven into the fabric of that instrument, while his vocal style is easily recognizable as well, whether tackling a mournful country weeper or storming through his prodigious catalog of rock & roll/R&B favorites, putting his individual stamp on each and every one. As he'll be the first to tell you, there is simply no one quite like the Killer. We shall not see the likes of him again in our lifetime. —*Cub Koda*

○ **Greatest Live Show on Earth** / 1964 / Bear Family 1560
Combining two live albums originally issued in the '60s, Lewis proves that the onslaught of the British invasion hadn't lowered his rocking quotient one single bit. Blazing performances. —*Cub Koda*

★ **18 Original Sun Greatest Hits** / 1984 / Rhino 70255
Solid single-disc collection of the records that got Lewis into the Rock & Roll Hall of Fame on the first ballot; "Whole Lotta Shakin' Goin' On," "Great Balls of Fire," "High School Confidential," and "Breathless" were merely the tip of the iceberg. —*Cub Koda*

○ **Killer: Mercury Years—Vol. 1** / Feb. 1989 / PolyGram 836935
○ **Killer: Mercury Years—Vol. 2** / Mar. 1989 / PolyGram 836938
○ **Killer: Mercury Years—Vol. 3** / Apr. 1989 / PolyGram 836941
This three-volume set takes you through the best of the Mercury years, with country, rock, and gospel styles. —*Hank Davis*

☆ **Classic** / 1992 / Bear Family 15420
Eight-disc boxed set of Lewis's complete output for Sun Records. Along with Muddy Waters's Chess recordings, Louis Armstrong's *Hot Fives & Sevens*, and Hank Williams's undubbed MGM sides, this box comprises one of the finest bodies of American music ever recorded. —*Cub Koda*

☆ **Live at the Star Club** / 1992 / Rhino 70268
The Killer at his storming best, dragging his backup group, the Nashville Teens, by the scruff of the neck through a blazing set that earmarks this recording as one of the finest live albums ever made. —*Cub Koda*

★ **All Killer, No Filler** / May 18, 1993 / Rhino 71216
Excellent two-disc retrospective of Lewis's career, featuring all his rock and country hits. If the Bear Family box sets are too much for you to handle, this makes an indispensable alternative. —*Cub Koda*

Smiley Lewis

d. Oct. 7, 1966
Vocals, guitar / R&B
Although he didn't have a lot of hits, Smiley Lewis was among New Orleans's most powerful, striking lead vocalists. A good guitarist as well as singer, Lewis began recording for Deluxe in 1947 under the name of Smiling Lewis. He attained his fame on Imperial as one of several artists whose songs were spiced by Dave Bartholomew's production, arranging, and bandleading acumen. With a brilliant band featuring many superb musicians roaring behind him, Lewis enjoyed one Top 20 and three Top 10 R&B hits from 1952 to 1956, led by "I Hear You Knocking" in 1955. It was #2 for two weeks, while "Bells Are Ringing" peaked at #10 in 1952 and "Please Listen to Me" reached #9 in 1956. "One Night" just missed the Top Ten at #11 that same year. Though his version of "Shame Shame Shame" didn't make the charts, it was used in the soundtrack for the film *Baby Doll* in 1956. Lewis died of cancer in 1966. —*Ron Wynn*

● **Best Of** / 1992 / Capitol 98824
A strong sampling of some of the finest material the seminal New Orleans R&B artist ever recorded, *The Best of Smiley Lewis* isn't definitive, but it's a great introduction to his music. —*Stephen Thomas Erlewine*

Bob Lind

Vocals, guitar / Singer-songwriter, folk rock, pop
Bob Lind's "Elusive Butterfly" was one of the most successful one-shots of the mid '60s folk-rock boom, reaching the Top 5 in early 1966. He never came close to matching that early triumph, although other acts brought his songs to a wider audience with their covers of Lind compositions like "Cheryl's Going Home" (Blues Project), "Counting" (Marianne Faithfull), and "Mr. Zero" (Yardbirds lead singer Keith Relf). The beauty of Jack Nitzsche's intricate production on Lind's two 1966 LPs, favoring acoustic guitars and pretty string arrangements, is admirable, but Lind himself hasn't worn that well. His songs are wordy and on the didactic side; his voice is nervous and lacks emotional range; his melodies are pretty, but not enormously so. —*Richie Unterberger*

○ **Best of Bob Lind** / Jun. 29, 1993 / EMI
This 25-song compilation includes the entire contents of his two 1966 LPs, as well as a 1967 single and two previously unreleased tracks. This period piece is highlighted by "Elusive Butterfly," the original versions of "Counting" and "Cheryl's Goin' Home," "Mr. Zero" (covered by Yardbird lead singer Keith Relf on a flop single), and the previously unreleased, gorgeous baroque rock song "English Afternoon." —*Richie Unterberger*

David Lindley

b. 1944, San Marino, CA
Guitar / Tex-Mex, rock & roll, blues rock
You may remember listening to these great Jackson Browne albums from the '70s and thinking, "This guy not only writes and sings great songs but is also an incredible guitar player and does great arrangements." Well, he did write and sing great songs, but the guitar playing and arrangements are by David Lindley, Los Angeles studio musician extraordinaire. Starting in 1981, Lindley has put out several albums under his own name with his always-changing band, El Rayo-X. He has wide-ranging musical influences: Tex-Mex, zydeco, reggae, blues, and rock & roll. His specialty seems to be taking a song and playing it in the style of a completely different genre of music, for example, a maniacal surf-music version of "Do Ya' Wanna Dance?" or a version of "I Fought the Law" with musicians from Madagascar. His own compositions are sometimes quite wonderful and always at least peculiar and droll. When he plays guitar (and often instruments of his own design), it's as good as it gets. If you grew up on '50s, '60s, and '70s rock & roll, this guy is the best thing going. —*Michael Katz*

○ **El Rayo-X** / 1981 / Asylum 524
His debut album. Highly recommended. —*Michael Katz*

● **Very Greasy** / 1988 / Asylum 60768
His best. Unconditionally recommended. —*Michael Katz*

A World Out of Time / 1992 / Shanachie 64041
Lindley and Henry Kaiser travel to Madagascar, where they record and play with some of that country's best musicians. Great world music. —*Michael Katz*

Little Feat

Group / Rock & roll, blues rock
Little Feat was formed in 1970 when Frank Zappa encouraged his guitarist Lowell George to start his own band after hearing George's original "Willin'." With Zappa bass player Roy Estrada in tow, George enlisted drummer Richie Hayward (formerly of Fraternity of Man) and keyboardist Billy Payne. The band's name came from Jimmy Carl Black's (of the Mothers of Invention) kidding about George's shoe size. Their first albums blended blues, country, and rock with gritty finesse.

With *Dixie Chicken* Little Feat added Kenny Gradney on bass and Sam Clayton on congas. The result was a New Orleans style of rhythmic gumbo and George's incredible slide guitar work. The title cut sums up many of the band's virtues, possessing a rubbery groove, off-kilter instrumental parts, and a classic, drily humorous Lowell George tale. Subsequent albums increasingly sanded off the rough edges in favor of an eccentric fusionlike equivalent to the late '70s Doobie Brothers.

Little Feat disbanded in April 1979, and Lowell George set out for a solo career, releasing the album *Thanks, I'll Eat It Here*. On June 29, 1979, George was found dead of a heart attack brought on from drug abuse.

In 1988 Little Feat reunited, with former Pure Prairie League singer and guitarist Craig Fuller filling George's slot. Since then, the band has regained its status as a solid concert draw and has released several albums. —*Rick Clark*

○ **Little Feat** / 1971 / Warner Brothers 1890
Debut album finds Lowell George's songwriting, singing, and playing style in place on his signature song, "Willin'," as well as "Truck Stop Girl" and "Crazy Captain Gunboat Willie." —*William Ruhlmann*

☆ **Sailin' Shoes** / 1972 / Warner Brothers 2600
A near-peak of songwriting ("Easy to Slip," "Cold, Cold, Cold," "Sailin' Shoes") distinguishes this second album, on which the band finds a perfect second-line groove and Lowell George sings and plays with blues authority. —*William Ruhlmann*

★ **Dixie Chicken** / 1973 / Warner Brothers 2686
A reconfigured group adds greater depth to the percussion, along with a rhythm guitarist who frees Lowell George to slide his way to heaven, and the songs—especially the title track, "Two Trains," and "Fat Man in the Bathtub"—are among George's best. —*William Ruhlmann*

○ **Feats Don't Fail Me Now** / 1974 / Warner Brothers 2784
Whereas earlier albums were carried by Lowell George, this one finds the band as a whole at a writing and performing peak, with Bill Payne and Paul Barrere especially standing out on such songs as "Rock and Roll Doctor," "Oh Atlanta," and "Skin It Back." —*William Ruhlmann*

○ **Waiting for Columbus** / 1978 / Warner Brothers 3140
Excellent double-disc live album. —*William Ruhlmann*

○ **Hoy-Hoy** / 1981 / Warner Brothers 3538
Compilation of best songs and odds and ends makes a good wrapup to the Lowell George years. —*William Ruhlmann*

Little Richard (Richard Wayne Penniman)

b. 1935
Vocals / R&B, rock & roll
With a six-inch-high pompadour topping a face dripping with eyeliner and pancake makeup, Little Richard (born Richard Wayne Penniman, 1935) came out of his native Macon, GA, to become one of the first African American artists not only to cross over to the national White pop charts but also to do it with an uncompromising set of recordings that virtually defined the inherent danger and wildness of rock & roll. Few records explode off a turntable the way the likes of "Tutti Frutti," "Long Tall Sally," "Rip It Up," "Lucille," or "Good Golly Miss Molly" do, and Richard's banshee shrieks and propulsive beat (usually provided by crack New Orleans session players) were catnip to a young White audience who had never heard before an African American gospel singer sing with the brakes off. The hits kept coming, but by the late '50s Richard had quit show business to become a minister. The lure of success (his and the then-emerging Beatles) brought him back, recording dreadful remakes of his earlier hits for one label after another into the '70s and becoming a staple of the talk show circuit with his flamboyant costumes and chatter. The '90s now find him revitalized, making movie appearances and television commercials and recording new material. Though his claim to be "the architect of rock & roll" may be disputed by some, any list of pioneering rock & rollers that doesn't include Little Richard near the top has just become too sophisticated for its own good. —*Cub Koda*

★ **18 Greatest Hits** / 1985 / Rhino 75899
The one definitive package to own. —*Cub Koda*

☆ **Specialty Box Set** / 1989 / ACE 1
Check out this beautiful three-CD boxed set of all the important Specialty sides. —*Cub Koda*

○ **Formative Years 1951-53** / Jul. 1989 / Bear Family 15448
Early Richard, pre-"Tutti Frutti." —*Cub Koda*

★ **The Georgia Peach** / 1991 / Specialty 70122
Perhaps the greatest of Little Richard's greatest hits compilations, the 25-track *Georgia Peach* features all of his biggest hits in chronological order, as well as terrific singles that never were as big as "Tutti Frutti" and "Good Golly Miss Molly." On top of the sublime song selection and sound, the liner notes by compiler Billy Vera are splendid and insightful. —*Stephen Thomas Erlewine*

Little River Band

Group / Pop/rock

Little River Band (formed 1975) enjoyed an impressive string of hits during the late '70s and early '80s with their rather mellow harmony-laden MOR pop. The original lineup included lead singer Glenn Shurrock; guitarists Rick Furmoru, Beeb Birtles, and Graham Goble; Rugo McLachlan on bass; and Derek Pellicci on drums. Later members included David Briggs (guitar), George McArdle (bass), and lead singer John Faraham. — *Rick Clark and Larry Lapka*

● **Greatest Hits** / 1982 / Capitol 46021

All of their best—"Reminiscing," "Lady," "Lonesome Loser," "Cool Change," "The Night Owls," and "Take It Easy on Me." — *Larry Lapka*

Little Willie John

b. Nov. 15, 1937, Camden, AR, **d.** May 27, 1968

Vocals / R&B

He's never received the accolades given to the likes of Sam Cooke, Clyde McPhatter, and James Brown, but Little Willie John ranks as one of R&B's most influential performers. His muscular high timbre and enormous technical and emotional range belied his early age (his first hit came when he was 18), but his mid '50s work for Syd Nathan's King label would play a great part in the way soul music would sound. Everyone from Cooke, McPhatter, and Brown to Jackie Wilson, B. B. King, and Al Green has acknowledged his debt to this most overlooked of rock and soul pioneers. His debut recording, a smoking version of Titus Turner's "All around the World" from 1955, set the pattern for a remarkable string of hits: "Need Your Love So Bad," "Suffering with the Blues," "Fever," "Let Them Talk," and his last, "Sleep," from 1961. His version of "Fever" was copied note for note by Peggy Lee and Elvis Presley, both of whom had bigger hits with it; John's version, however, remains definitive. His second hit, "Need Your Love So Bad," contains one of the most intimate, tear-jerking vocals ever caught on tape.

John had a volatile temper, fueled by a taste for liquor and an insecurity regarding his slight height (5 feet, 4 inches). He was known to pack a gun and knife; in 1966, he stabbed a man and was sent to the Washington State penitentiary, where he died of pneumonia in 1968. James Brown recorded a tribute album to John that year, and his material has been recorded by scores of artists from the Beatles to Fleetwood Mac to the Blasters. Nevertheless, Little Willie John remains a stranger to most listeners and has never received the respect his talent deserves. — *John Floyd*

○ **Mister Little Willie John** / Dec. 1987 / King 603

His third King long-player is one of the '50s finest albums. "You're a Sweetheart" is an R&B landmark. — *John Floyd*

Talk to Me / Jul. 1988 / Sing 596

Reissue of John's second King album includes the title hit, "Person to Person," and the exquisite "There Is Someone in This World for Me." — *John Floyd*

Sure Things / Mar. 1990 / King 739

Another vintage reissue. It features his gorgeous reading of Billy Eckstine's "A Cottage for Sale" and the original version of "I'm Shakin'," which the Blasters covered on their debut. — *John Floyd*

● **Fever: The Best of Little Willie John** / 1993 / Rhino 71511

Little Willie John was both a masterful balladeer and galvanzing uptempo vocalist; he had a commanding delivery, remarkable projection, and a charismatic sound that was both instantly recognizable and unforgettable. He unfortunately didn't enjoy either a lengthy career or a string of R&B hits, yet he made several magical singles. These are all contained on this superb 20-track anthology. It includes his best known song "Fever" (Peggy Lee's cover version became a huge smash) plus such marvelous numbers such as "Home at Last," "Heartbreak (It's Hurtin' Me)" and "You Hurt Me." While John was a dynamic heartache wailer, he could also do excellent dance/novelty and double entendre tunes such as "Let's Rock while the Rockin's Good" and "Leave My Kitten Alone." John's swooping, slashing, and often poignant tones made him an R&B legend; this anthology demonstrates why he's still held in such high regard throughout the world of R&B and soul. — *Ron Wynn*

Live

Alternative pop/rock

With their muscular R.E.M. and U2 hybrid, Live straddles the line between alternative rock credibility and mainstream radio accessibility. When their first album was released, it was a moderate commercial success, made all the more impressive considering the reluctance of radio to alternative-oriented music. *Throwing Copper,* their second album, shot to the top of college charts when it was released in the spring of 1994, as well as receiving a substantial amount of mainstream sales and play on pop radio. — *Stephen Thomas Erlewine*

○ **Mental Jewelry** / 1991 / Radioactive/MCA 10346

Live's debut album was an impressive set of righteous, hard-driving alternative rock; *Mental Jewelry* was in the vein of such college-radio favorites like U2, only it was more vulnerable and less sanctimonious. — *Stephen Thomas Erlewine*

● **Throwing Copper** / 1994 / Radioactive/MCA 10997

Not only did Live's songwriting improve on their second album, *Throwing Copper,* but their sound was much stronger; their hooks were powerful and memorable, and their melodies were carefully crafted and catchy. The result was an actual crossover hit, thanks to the single "Selling the Drama." — *Stephen Thomas Erlewine*

Living Colour

Group / Hard rock, heavy metal

A New York-based hard-rock group formed by guitarist Vernon Reid as part of the fusion-oriented Black Rock Coalition artists group and supported early on by Mick Jagger. Their in-your-face approach, combining Hendrixian guitar with punk-rock fervor, earned them across-the-board hits and a broad-based audience in the late '80s. — *Cub Koda*

● **Vivid** / 1988 / Epic 44099

Living Colour broke through on this debut album with their mixture of heavy metal, guitar heroics (courtesy of Vernon Reid), and thoughtful, sometimes scathing lyrics, suggesting a new direction for hard rock. This Top 10 million-selling album included the songs "Cult of Personality," "Open Letter (to a Landlord)," and the Top 40 hit "Glamour Boys." — *William Ruhlmann*

Time's Up / 1991 / Epic 46202

A powerful, uncompromising sophomore effort, featuring the radio hits "Type" and "Pride" as well as the provocative "Elvis Is Dead" and "Love Rears Its Ugly Head." — *William Ruhlmann*

Stain / 1993 / CBS 52780

With the addition of new bassist Doug Wimbish, Living Colour turns in a harder-edged effort with *Stain,* a record that is driven more by the shattering metal/jazz fusion riffs of Vernon Reed than any of their other albums. While the sheer sonic force of the album is impressive, the songs don't match the power of the music; nevertheless, the music is so strong that it usually overshadows the inadequate songwriting. — *Stephen Thomas Erlewine*

Bill Lloyd

Vocals, guitar / Power pop

As a solo artist, Bill Lloyd (half of country duo Foster & Lloyd) displays his real passion: finely crafted Anglo-power pop/rock—á la Byrds, Big Star, Badfinger- a must for any lover of this kind of music. — *Rick Clark*

○ **Feeling the Elephant** / 1986 / DB 97

Originally released in 1986 on the Throbbing Lobster label, *Feeling the Elephant* was to be the debut for Lloyd's solo career until he got sidetracked with the successful country duo Foster & Lloyd. Lloyd might do country justice, but on *Feeling the Elephant,* his Anglo-pop/rock roots are everywhere to be found. From the urgent drive of "This Very Second," the album's opener, to the spacey melancholy of "Everything's Closing Down," the album exuberantly draws from the best elements of the Byrds, Big Star, Badfinger, mid-period Beatles, and early Who. Highlights include "It'll Never Get Better Than This" and "Lisa-Anne." — *Rick Clark*

● **Set to Pop** / 1994 / East Side Digital

It's hard to find memorable melodies and smart lyrics as abundantly represented on one artist or band's album these days as they are here. Picking a highlight is hard. For lovers of exceptionally melodic power-pop/rock, *Set to Pop* is a real find. —*Rick Clark*

Nils Lofgren

b. Jun. 21, 1951, Chicago, IL
Vocals, guitar / Rock & roll
In 1969 Nils Lofgren formed Grin, a group with much promise and little financial success. During the '70s and early '80s, Lofgren pursued a spotty solo career while contributing some fine work with Neil Young. Lofgren joined Bruce Springsteen's band in 1986. A new deal with Minnesota label Rykodisc produced the moderate-hit album *Silver Lining* in 1991. —*Rick Clark*

● **Nils Lofgren** / 1975 / Rykodisc 4509
After dismantling Grin in 1974, Lofgren signed a solo deal with A&M, releasing a self-titled debut that neatly showcased his strengths as a singer-songwriter and multiinstrumentalist. His reading of Carole King's wistful chestnut "Goin' Back" is a highlight, as are fiery originals like "Keith Don't Go" (a tribute to the Stones' Keith Richards) and "Rock & Roll Crook," with its wonderfully convoluted twin-guitar interplay. "Back It Up" is another gem. —*Rick Clark*

Cry Tough / 1976 / A&M 4573
A little forced on the songwriting side but delivered with enough panache to make it work. —*John Dougan*

○ **Nils** / 1979 / A&M 4756
Lofgren rebounded, after several spotty albums, with this effort, which featured some of the strongest writing in his career, particularly "Shine Silently," "A Fool like You," "Steal Away," and the powerful ballad "No Mercy." —*Rick Clark*

Wonderland / 1983 / MCA 3182
Unfortunately, this one got totally buried. "Across the Tracks," the single, should have been given the push it deserved. A remake of Bobby Womack's "It's All Over Now" is another highlight. —*Rick Clark*

○ **Classics, Vol. 13** / 1987 / A&M 2511
A solid 15-song compilation that gives a good sense of Lofgren's career, but *Nils Lofgren* is a better introduction. —*Stephen Thomas Erlewine*

Crooked Line / 1992 / Rykodisc 10238
There's a free and loose vibe to the recording, a sense that Nils Lofgren is just making the album he wants regardless of "commercial potential". The guitarist leaves flashy pyrotechnics to others, preferring to cut his material with direct, slashing simplicity. —*Roch Parisien*

Loggins & Messina

Group / Pop/rock
Kenny Loggins and Jim Messina were the most successful poprock duo of the first half of the '70s. Loggins was a staff songwriter who had recently enjoyed success with a group of songs recorded by the Nitty Gritty Dirt Band when he came to the attention of Messina, a record producer and former member of Buffalo Springfield and Poco. Messina agreed to produce Loggins's first album, but somewhere along the way it became a duo effort that was released in 1972 under the title *Kenny Loggins with Jim Messina Sittin' In.* The album was a gold-seller that stayed in the charts more than two years.

In the next four years, Loggins & Messina released a series of gold or platinum albums, most of which hit the Top10. They were all played in a buoyant country-rock style with an accomplished band. *Loggins and Messina* (1972) featured the retro-rock hit "Your Mama Don't Dance," *Full Sail* (1973), *On Stage* (a double live album, 1974), and *Mother Lode* (1974) all hit the Top 10. *So Fine* was an album of '50s cover songs. The pair's last new studio album, *Native Sons*, came out at the start of 1976.

Loggins and Messina split for two solo careers by the end of that year, their catalog completed by a greatest-hits album, *Best of Friends*, and a live record, *Finale.* —*William Ruhlmann*

● **Best of Friends** / 1977 / Columbia 34388
Collects their biggest hits from "Your Mama Don't Dance" onward. —*Dan Heilman*

Kenny Loggins

b. Jan. 7, 1948, Everette, WA

Vocals / Pop/rock
Singer, songwriter, and guitarist Kenny Loggins was born in Everett, WA, and moved to Los Angeles in his teens. He got a job as a staff writer and wrote four songs used on a Nitty Gritty Dirt Band album in 1970, among them the hit "House at Pooh Corner." This brought him to the attention of former Poco member Jim Messina, now a staff producer at CBS, who intended to produce Loggins's debut album. The two ended up in a duo, however, and Loggins & Messina made a series of successful albums during the '70s.

Loggins & Messina broke up in 1976, and Loggins went on to solo stardom with such million-selling albums as *Celebrate Me Home, Nightwatch* (which included the hit "Whenever I Call You Friend"), and *Keep the Fire,* all in the cheerful, sensitive style he had displayed in Loggins & Messina. Loggins also became known as the king of the movie soundtrack song, scoring Top 10 hits with "I'm Alright" (from *Caddyshack*), "Footloose" (from *Footloose*), "Danger Zone" (from *Top Gun*), and "Nobody's Fool" (from *Caddyshack II*). His own albums sold less well (and came less frequently) through the '80s. —*William Ruhlmann*

Celebrate Me Home / 1977 / Columbia 34655
Features hit single "I Believe in Love." "Lady Luck," "Why Do People Lie," and the title cut are highlights on this relatively light MOR debut. —*Rick Clark*

Nightwatch / 1978 / Columbia 35387
This super-slick sophomore effort was Loggins's biggest chart success, aided in no small part by the singles "Whenever I Call You Friend," which featured a duet with Stevie Nicks, and "Easy Driver." "Wait a Little While" and remakes of the Doobies hit "What a Fool Believes" and Billy Joe Royal's "Down in the Boondocks" were further highlights. —*Rick Clark*

Keep the Fire / 1980 / Columbia 36172
Produced by Tom Dowd (Rod Stewart, Aretha Franklin, Allman Brothers), Loggins beefs up his sound a little with "Love Has Come of Age." He also enjoys more hits with "This Is It" and the title cut. —*Rick Clark*

● **Kenny Loggins Alive** / 1980 / Columbia 36738
This extended live effort arrived on the wings of Loggins' hit "I'm Alright," off the movie soundtrack of *Caddyshack.* The concert version included here is much better, stripped of some of the cute studio tricks found on the single. Most of the material comes from previously released studio tracks, which are given faithful (but livelier) readings. —*Rick Clark*

○ **High Adventure** / 1982 / Columbia 38127
Loggins continued his successful string of hit albums with this release. A light mainstream rock duet with Journey lead singer Steve Perry titled "Don't Fight It" reached #17, while Loggins turned in a couple of MOR hits with "Heart to Heart" and "Welcome to Heartlight." As with all of his albums to this point, his sound is pleasant and well crafted. Loggins later enjoyed success with songs featured on soundtracks like *Caddyshack II, Top Gun,* and *Footloose.* —*Rick Clark*

Lone Justice

Group / Roots rock
Lone Justice in its original form, ca. 1983, was a quartet based in Los Angeles and featuring singer Maria McKee (b. 1964), guitarist Ryan Hedgecock (b. ca. 1960), bassist Marvin Etzioni, and drummer Don Heffington. The group played in a country-rock style on its debut album, *Lone Justice* (1985). By the time of the second album, *Shelter* (1986), the group had turned more toward mainstream rock and become a sextet, with only McKee and Hedgecock remaining from the original unit. Then Lone Justice broke up, and McKee went on to a solo career. —*William Ruhlmann*

● **Lone Justice** / 1985 / David Geffen Co. 24060
Maria McKee had one of those aching, little-girl voices (not unlike Stevie Nicks's), and it's heard to great effect on these country-rock tunes, especially Tom Petty and Mike Campbell's "Ways to Be Wicked." —*William Ruhlmann*

Los Lobos

Group / Rock & roll, Tex-Mex
Los Lobos were easily one of America's most distinctive and original bands of the '80s. They may have had a hit with "La Bamba"

in 1987, yet that cover barely scratches the surface of their talents. Los Lobos are eclectic in the best sense of the word. While they draw equally from rock, Tex-Mex, country, folk, R&B, blues, and traditional Spanish and Mexican music, their music never sounds forced or self-conscious. Instead, all of their influences became one graceful, gritty sound. From their very first recordings their rich musicality was apparent; on nearly each subsequent record they have found ways to redefine and expand their sound, without every straying from the musical traditions that form the heart and soul of the band.

After releasing an independent EP in the late '70s and an EP in 1983, Los Lobos delivered their first major-label album, *How Will the Wolf Survive*, in 1984; it received an enormous amount of critical acclaim, as well as a dedicated following of fans. In the next four years, they released a marginally successful attempt to make their wildly eclectic sound palatable for a pop audience (*By the Light of the Moon*), a soundtrack of old Richie Valens songs that was a hit (*La Bamba*), and an album of traditional Mexican music (*La Pistola y El Corazon*). The band took two years off and returned with *The Neighborhood* in 1990; the album was a varied and powerful rock & roll record that was better than anything they had released in six years. *Kiko*, released in 1992, brought the band into more experimental territory, without ever abandoning their lovely songwriting. —*Stephen Thomas Erlewine*

○ **... And a Time to Dance** / 1983 / Slash 23963
Only seven songs, but a perfect summation of what the band does and why it's important. A perfectly seamless fusion of Tex-Mex, R&B, and rock & roll, with powerhouse covers of the Ritchie Valens hit "Come on, Let's Go" and the norteño classic "A Te Dejo en San Antonio" thrown in for good measure. —*Kit Kiefer*

● **How Will the Wolf Survive?** / 1984 / Slash 25177
A broader spectrum of music without a measure of the all-out joy of *... And a Time to Dance*, *How Will the Wolf Survive?* features at least two raveup rockers ("Don't Worry Baby" and "I Got Loaded"), an irresistible shuffle ("Evangeline"), two traditional Mexican numbers ("Seranata Norteña" and "Corrida #1"). and a stirring title tune. Well rounded and fully realized. —*Kit Kiefer*

○ **By the Light of the Moon** / 1987 / Slash 25523
A very gentle, very Catholic album summed up by the trilogy of sad songs ("River of Fools," "The Mess We're In," "Tears of God") that closes out the album. —*Kit Kiefer*

○ **La Pistola Y El Corazon** / 1988 / Slash 25790
Los Lobos's album of traditional Mexican music isn't a history lesson, it's a celebration of their heritage and its joyous music, which means it's just as exciting and entertaining as their rock & roll records. —*Stephen Thomas Erlewine*

○ **Neighborhood** / 1990 / Slash 26131
Recharged by their set of Mexican music, Los Lobos return with arguably their finest straight rock & roll record. *The Neighborhood* effortlessly combines rock, R&B, blues, and country into a singular, powerful sound that manages to be as darkly funky as "I Walk Alone" and "Georgia Slop" and as gently moving as "Emily." —*Stephen Thomas Erlewine*

○ **Kiko** / 1992 / Slash 26786
With its highly textured layers of sound, *Kiko* sounds like nothing else Los Lobos has done. Although their music is still based in roots music of all kinds—rock, folk, Mexican, country—the band has shaped it into a dense, impressionistic wall of sound that intensifies the emotions behind such carefully constructed and moving songs like "Two Janes," "Angels with Dirty Faces," and "Kiko and the Lavender Moon." It's certainly their most ambitious album, and it's arguably their best. —*Stephen Thomas Erlewine*

● **Just Another Band from East LA: A Collection** / 1993 / Slash
Just Another Band from East LA: A Collection is a splendid double-disc collection that draws an accurate picture of Los Lobos, one of the most musically versatile bands of the '80s. Featuring all of the band's hits and best-known songs as well as several rare and previously unreleased tracks, there isn't a weak spot among the compilation's 41 songs. —*Stephen Thomas Erlewine*

Loud Family

Group / Alternative pop/rock, power pop
After dissolving Game Theory, Scott Miller formed Loud Family, releasing their first album in early 1993. While it continued the

slightly experimental tendencies of the last Game Theory albums, it did so in a more concise power pop setting. —*Stephen Thomas Erlewine*

○ **Plants and Birds and Rocks and Things** / 1992 / Alias 33
Former Game Theory frontman Scott Miller returns with a new band and his classic style of power-pop. With a sound similar to the experimental *Lolita Nation*, Miller builds on his former band's strong points while leaving behind much of its excesses. *Plants and Birds and Rocks and Things* will be pleasantly familiar to old fans and will no doubt inspire newcomers to seek out Game Theory albums. —*Chris Woodstra*

Love

Group / Psychedelic, pop/rock
Even revisionist rock criticism has overlooked the accomplishments of Arthur Lee and Love, one of the greatest groups to emerge from the psychedelia-shrouded scene of mid '60s Los Angeles. Their early work fused sharp pop hooks with the wiry crunch of early punk, producing instant classics such as "My Little Red Book" and "Seven and Seven Is"; you can hear Lee laying the groundwork for West Coast groups like the Doors and Moby Grape. By the late '60s, Lee moved the group into druggy psychedelic territory; 1968's *Forever Changes* is their best album, a symphonic explosion of lush, orchestrated textures and surreal lyrics. Surprisingly, the album still sounds fresh and innovative. —*John Floyd*

○ **Love** / 1966 / Integrity 003
A grand debut and a prime piece of '60s folk rock. Love didn't peak for another couple of years, but this proves they were one of Los Angeles's hottest bands in the mid '60s. —*Jeff Tamarkin*

○ **Da Capo** / 1967 / Elektra 74005
A beautiful but at times pretentious record (due to the 19-minute closing song), Love's second album includes a few choice tracks. —*Jeff Tamarkin*

★ **Forever Changes** / 1967 / Elektra 74013
Nothing less than a work of genius, Love's third album still shows up on many all-time-best lists. Arthur Lee's most inspired creation, it's everything that progressive, psychedelic folk rock could have been. —*Jeff Tamarkin*

○ **Best of: Golden Archive Series** / 1980 / Rhino 70175
Well-chosen collection of Love's most celebrated tracks makes a case for Arthur Lee and company as one of the most creative, intense West Coast '60s rock bands. —*Jeff Tamarkin*

Love & Rockets

Group / Alternative pop/rock
Formed from the ashes of the English art-punk posers, Bauhaus, Love & Rockets (named after the comic book) became huge by playing a kind of folky postmodern rock, rife with inscrutably pretentious lyrics. Perfect fodder for the dress-in-black college crowd, who read a lot of French Symbolist poetry. —*John Dougan*

○ **Seventh Dream of Teenage Heaven** / 1986 / Beggars Banquet 8507
An album filled with the dark, acoustic-driven work hinted at in their previous group, Bauhaus. —*Steve Aldrich*

● **Earth, Sun, Moon** / 1987 / Big Time 6058
Another solid LP. —*Steve Aldrich*

Love and Rockets / 1989 / Beggars Banquet 9715
Features their only U.S. hit, "So Alive." —*Steve Aldrich*

Darlene Love

R&B, pop/rock
Amazingly, Darlene Love, a superb vocalist, hasn't had much of a track record as a solo singer, at least not in terms of hits. Love was a founding member of the Blossoms in 1957. They did several sessions and were resident singers on the television show "Shindig." Love sang lead vocals on "He's a Rebel," which was credited to the Crystals, and "Zip-A-Dee-Doo-Dah," which was released as Bob B. Soxx and the Bluejeans. She cut six singles for Spector's Phillies label, with "Wait Till My Baby Gets Back Home" the most successful. Love became busy as an actress but reunited with Spector for the 1977 single "Lord, If You're a Woman." Love appeared in all three *Lethal Weapon* films and was also in the Royal Shakespeare Company's co-production of Stephen King's *Carrie*. Her 1990 LP, *Paint Another Picture*, failed to chart in

America. Love later toured as a background vocalist with Cher. She appeared briefly on the soap opera "Another World" in 1993. —*Ron Wynn*

● **Best of Darlene Love** / 1992 / ABKCO 7213
A terrific compilation of Love's Phil Spector-produced hits, including "(Today I Met) the Boy I'm Gonna Marry," "Wait Til' My Bobby Gets Home," and the hits she sang for the Crystals, "He's a Rebel" and "He's Sure the Boy I Love." —*Stephen Thomas Erlewine*

Loverboy

Group / Hard rock, pop/rock
This Canadian commercial hard-rock quintet was a mainstay on FM rock stations during the early '80s. —*Rick Clark*

Loverboy / 1980 / Columbia 36762
Their debut with guitar-heavy pop-metal, including the Top 40 hit "Turn Me Loose." —*Donna DiChario*

○ **Get Lucky** / 1981 / Columbia 37638
Although occasionally overblown, songs like "Lucky Ones" and "Working for the Weekend" were made for blasting on the radio. —*Donna DiChario*

● **Big Ones** / 1989 / Columbia 45411
Loverboy's biggest and best hits, including "Turn Me Loose," "Lovin' Every Minute of It," "This Could Be the Night," "Hot Girls in Love," "Heaven in Your Eyes," and "Working for the Weekend." —*AMG*

Lyle Lovett

b. Nov. 1, 1957, Houston, TX
Vocals / Singer-songwriter
Lyle Lovett represents the increasing diversity of country music as it recovers from a commercial slump in the '80s. Highly literate (he has degrees in journalism and German from Texas A&M), the Houston-born singer comes from the eclectic tradition of Western swing, as filtered through the work of such wry '70s songwriters as Guy Clark and Townes Van Zandt. Lovett has a dry but absurdly hilarious sense of humor, as expressed on "If I Had a Boat" ("And if I had a pony, I'd ride him on my boat"). But he also writes bitingly of love relations, as in "God Will," in which the singer tells his lover that God will forgive her, but he won't, "and that's the difference between God and me." Despite some success in the country market and a Grammy award in the country category, it has been questionable since at least Lovett's second album, *Pontiac*, that his music could be categorized as country. But it's so multigeneric, with elements of folk, jazz, blues, and, lately, gospel, that it's hard to say exactly where it fits. At bottom, he's a singer/songwriter—and an amazingly imaginative one at that. —*William Ruhlmann*

○ **Lyle Lovett** / 1986 / Curb 31307
Lyle Lovett has an ironic overview of the world, expressed in songs he sings with the dead seriousness of the true comic. But he also has a finely defined sense of romantic troubles that sometimes isn't funny at all. Songs like "God Will" and "If I Were the Man You Wanted" mark him as one of the best new writers of the decade. —*William Ruhlmann*

★ **Pontiac** / 1987 / Curb 42028
Lovett's best overall collection of songs includes the gently absurd "If I Had a Boat," the subtly murderous "L.A. County," and the Henny Youngman-style "She's No Lady," among other gems. —*William Ruhlmann*

○ **Lyle Lovett & His Large Band** / 1989 / Curb 42263
On his third album, Lovett continues to explore a synthesis of country and big band. Includes his version of Tammy Wynette's country classic on "Stand by Your Man" and the bittersweet "I Married Her Just Because She Looks Like You." —*Rick Clark*

○ **Joshua Judges Ruth** / 1992 / Curb 10475
There is a southern-fried gospel feel throughout much of the album, even if it's sometimes irreverent. "Church" best displays Lovett's surreal, dry wit, recounting a hunger-driven church rebellion complete with full gospel backing vocals. "I've Been to Memphis" delivers casual, piano-laden southern boogie reminiscent of vintage Little Feat. "She's Leaving Me Because She Really Wants To," featuring guest vocals from Emmylou Harris, is the one sop offered to traditional country. Overall, though, the mood is sombre, bordering on bleak. Like the album cover and insert

photos, *Joshua Judges Ruth* deals in shades of gray and themes of loneliness and death. What one misses the most on this release is the infrequent surfacing of Lovett's weird, playful sense of humor. —*Roch Parisien*

Lene Lovich

Vocals / New wave
A Detroit area new wave pop singer with a quirky vocal style, she had an early '80s hit with "New Toy" (written by Thomas Dolby). She collaborates with her husband (and guitarist) Les Chappell. —*Scott Bultman*

○ **Flex ... Plus** / 1984 / Rhino 70521
Flex shows a Lovich staying true to her unique sound, though it somewhat watered down with superslick production. Now reissued on CD with six extra tracks as *Flex...Plus*. Includes the classic "New Toy" (written by Thomas Dolby). —*Chris Woodstra*

● **Stateless ... Plus** / 1988 / Rhino 70520
Stateless, her aptly titled 1978 debut, is a new wave cult classic. Featuring her offbeat vocals and quirky synth heavy production, this her finest moment. Includes the great single "Lucky Number." Now reissued on CD as *Stateless...Plus* with five extra tracks and extensive liner notes. —*Chris Woodstra*

The Lovin' Spoonful

Group / Pop/rock
The Lovin' Spoonful, a major '60s folk-influenced quartet led by John Sebastian and Zal Yanovsky, made a fair bid to become New York's answer to the Byrds but never overcame their Top 40 radio image and several internal problems. Their catalog was badly abused (lost tapes, etc.) until 1990, but the best-of collection and the early albums reveal flashes of sophistication, humor, and style of near-Beatlesque proportions. —*Bruce Eder*

Hums / 1966 / Pair 3305
Lots of fun, and eminently hummable. —*Bruce Eder*

Daydream / May 1966 / One Way 22165
Blues, hard rock, and folk pop, topped off by the achingly gorgeous "You Didn't Have to Be So Nice." —*Bruce Eder*

★ **Anthology** / 1990 / Rhino 70944
Unquestionably the finest collection of a major band that did much to launch American folk rock in the mid '60s. *Anthology* jams 26 cuts onto a single CD, including all of their hits and some of their strongest album tracks, drawing mostly from their 1965-66 prime. As for the more interesting nonsmashes, these include the original version of John Sebastian's "Younger Girl," which was a hit in a more commercial version by the Critters; the minor 1967 hit "She Is Still a Mystery," a dreamily psychedelic number that holds its own with their other standards, but has somehow been forgotten by oldies radio; and "Good Time Music," recorded early in 1965 for an obscure Elektra sampler (and a small hit in a cover version by the Beau Brummels). The most overlooked find here is the instrumental "Lonely (Amy's Theme)," from the early Francis Ford Coppola film *You're a Big Boy Now*, a lushly orchestrated, melancholy tune featuring Sebastian's wistful harmonica. There are also little-known Sebastian originals, with vocals, from *You're a Big Boy Now* and Woody Allen's early screen venture *What's Up, Tiger Lily?* The accompanying booklet features comments from Sebastian himself about some of the group's most famous songs. —*Richie Unterberger*

Nick Lowe

b. Mar. 25, 1949, Suffolk, England
Vocals, bass guitar / Pop/rock,rock & roll
After the seminal pub rockers Brinsley Schwarz broke up in 1974, Nick Lowe let his love for pop music in all of its trashy, sleazy glory blossom. At a time most artists were concerned about making art, he concentrated on returning to the days when rock & roll was about nothing except love, sex, good times, and rock & roll. The only thing was, Lowe paid tribute to classic rock and pop by twisting their conventions around; he took standard themes and melodies and turned them inside out with a wicked sense of humor. Lowe never sounded dated because at his heart he was a punk—his early records are ragged and raw, positively overflowing with energy. As his career moved into the '80s, he lost that reckless energy, but he always remained an outsider laughing at the mainstream.

Lowe moved to Stiff Records, Britain's first independent record label, in 1976 after releasing several flop singles on Liberty/UA. The label's first record was his "So It Goes"/"Heart of the City" single; it cost 45 pounds to make. Lowe became the label's in-house producer, and he was behind the boards for nearly every one of the label's singles during their early days. By the end of the decade, he had produced an impressive array of artists, including Elvis Costello, the Damned, Graham Parker, the Pretenders, and Dr. Feelgood. During this time he recorded his first solo album, 1978's *Jesus of Cool*, which was retitled *Pure Pop for Now People* in the United States.

By the time his debut was released, Lowe had formed Rockpile with guitarist Dave Edmunds, drummer Terry Williams, and guitarist Billy Bremner; the band functioned as a touring band for Lowe and Edmunds as well as providing support on their records. Lowe's next album, 1979's *Labour of Lust*, was recorded with Rockpile; it contained his only hit, "Cruel to Be Kind." After recording one album in 1980, Rockpile disbanded. Lowe began to experiment with country and Tex-Mex music on his '80s albums, without ever abandoning pop; the records were more polished, but they sold fewer copies than his earlier albums. However, he produced successful records by Carlene Carter, John Hiatt, the Fabulous Thunderbirds, and Paul Carrack during the decade.

While his days as a genuine musical force may be behind him, Lowe's albums have been consistently strong, and when he's at the top of his form, he's an utterly original and inventive pop songwriter; his best songs make wading through his mediocre material worthwhile. —*Stephen Thomas Erlewine*

★ **Pure Pop for Now People** / 1978 / Columbia 35329
A masterpiece from a year that was full of them. This offers the best glimpse into his sometimes demented and ear-catching world. —*John Floyd*

☆ **Labour of Lust** / 1978 / Columbia 36087
The grooves are tighter here than before, mixing the roots-rock sensibilities of Rockpile with his love of a good pop hook. Contains several minor hits, including "Cruel to Be Kind." —*John Floyd*

○ **Nick the Knife** / 1982 / Columbia 37932
Lowe's first album since the breakup of Rockpile was a casually rocking record that recalled his former band, which isn't surprising, considering both Billy Bremner and Terry Williams provide instrumental support. —*Stephen Thomas Erlewine*

○ **Abominable Showman** / 1983 / Edsel 184
On *The Abominable Showman* Lowe's fascination with country music begins to assert itself on a collection of songs that only *seems* lighthearted. While songs like "We Want Action" and "Tanque Ray" are nothing more than solid pop/rockers, "Time Wounds All Heels," "Raging Eyes," "Saint Beneath the Paint," "Wish You Were Here," and "(For Every Woman Who Ever Made a Fool of a Man There's a Woman Who Made a) Man of a Fool" are exceptionally well-written songs, full of subtle emotional power and irresistible melodies. —*Stephen Thomas Erlewine*

○ **Nick Lowe & His Cowboy Outfit** / 1984 / Edsel 185
Thanks to a strong backing band, *Nick Lowe and His Cowboy Outfit* is the most musically satisfying album he's made since *Labour of Lust*. Throughout the record, Lowe touches on all kinds of roots rock, from Tex-Mex and three-chord garage rock to country and pop. And the great majority of the songs—from originals like the organ-driven rocker "Half a Boy and Half a Man" and the sly pop of "God's Gift to Women" to the excellent covers, "You'll Never Get Me Up in One of Those" and "Breakaway"—are simply irresistible. —*Stephen Thomas Erlewine*

○ **Rose of England** / 1985 / Edsel 73
Lowe's second album with his Cowboy Outfit is an even better record than their previous collection. *The Rose of England* retains the band's low-key charm, but now they have a better set of songs to work with. Lowe's originals rank with his best material, and the covers—including Elvis Costello's "Indoor Fireworks" and John Hiatt's "She Don't Love Nobody"—are perfectly suited to his style. —*Stephen Thomas Erlewine*

Pinker & Prouder Than Previous / 1988 / Edsel 99
Pinker and Prouder Than Previous is Nick Lowe's most relaxed and casual album to date, yet it never sounds tossed-off or careless. Instead, Lowe's subtle mastery of pop, rock, R&B, and country results in an unassuming and thoroughly enjoyable set of

clever, well-written originals and fine covers. —*Stephen Thomas Erlewine*

● **Basher: The Best of Nick Lowe** / 1989 / Columbia 45313
A superb collection spanning Lowe's solo career, with a smattering of Rockpile's sides tossed in. A fine introduction, but start with *Pure Pop for Now People*. —*John Floyd*

Party of One / 1990 / Reprise 26132
While Dave Edmunds's production makes *Party of One* Nick Lowe's sharpest-sounding record in years, his songwriting isn't as strong as it has been in the past. Only "(I Want to Build a) Jumbo Ark," "What's Shakin' on the Hill," and "I Don't Know Why You Keep Me On" rank with his best material. —*Stephen Thomas Erlewine*

○ **Wilderness Years** / 1991 / Edsel 203
A wildly entertaining collection of outtakes, demos, and forgotten singles, *The Wilderness Years* captures Nick Lowe at the top of his form. Even seemingly slight songs like "Let's Go to the Disco" and "Bay City Rollers We Love You" are irresistibly rough, melodic pop gems. However, the disc also contains some Lowe's best performances—including the demo "Fool Too Long," the reckless single "Heart of the City," the "erstwhile Stiff advertising jingle" "I Love My Label," and a sublime version of Sandy Posey's "Born a Woman." The sheer quantity of brilliant material on *The Wilderness Years* means that the disc is worthwhile even for Lowe's most casual fans. —*Stephen Thomas Erlewine*

L.T.D.

Group / Funk, urban R&B
Horn-based R&B/funk band originating in North Carolina, formed in 1968. Jeffrey Osborne was the lead vocalist until his departure in 1980; he was replaced by Andre Ray and Leslie Wilson in 1980. L.T.D. is an acronym for Love, Togetherness, and Devotion. —*Bil Carpenter*

● **Classics, Vol. 27** / 1987 / A&M 2525
'70s hard-funk and orchestrated ballads like "Love Ballad" and "(Every Time I Turn Around) I'm in Love Again." —*Bil Carpenter*

Lulu (Marie MacDonald McLaughlin Lawrie)

b. Nov. 3, 1948, Lennox Castle, Glasgow
Vocals / Pop/rock
Most Americans first heard of Lulu when she soared to the top of the charts with the pop ballad "To Sir with Love," the theme to the film of the same name, in 1967. Actually, the Scottish singer—born Marie McDonald McLaughlin Lawrie—had been a star in Britain since 1964, when she hit the Top 10 with a raucous version of "Shout." Lulu's mid '60s recordings (which included a version of "Here Comes the Night" that preceded Them's hit rendition) were often surprisingly rowdy and R&B-influenced. Although she didn't match Dusty Springfield, her Brenda Lee-like rasp could be quite gutsy and soulful. Her career was headed in a determinedly middle-of-the-road direction by the late '60s, which saw her hosting a British variety show and marrying Bee Gee Maurice Gibb (they have since divorced). Recording intermittently ever since, she raised a few eyebrows by traveling to Muscle Shoals studios to record her 1970 album *New Routes* and releasing a single of David Bowie tunes (on which Bowie also played and which he co-produced) in 1973. —*Richie Unterberger*

● **To Sir with Love** / 1967 / Epic 26339
The original album with the hit that made her a star, *To Sir with Love* remains Lulu's finest record. —*AMG*

Independence / Apr. 5, 1993 / Capitol 19779
Lulu works with a host of producers and writers on *Independence* (among them Simon Climie and the Gibb Brothers) to craft an up-to-date set of songs and arrangements. Lulu herself assists in the production and writing on some selections; she helps things even further by turning in assured, confident, and soulful vocals, particularly on "You Left Me Lonely" and "I'm Back for More," with special guest Bobby Womack and the title track. This is a well-crafted, dance-oriented work, but Lulu is never relegated to the backdrop, and the production doesn't subjugate the music to the surroundings. —*Ron Wynn*

Luna

Group / Alternative pop/rock

After Dean Wareham disbanded Galaxie 500 in the early '90s, he formed Luna, which followed in the same dreamy, slow style of his previous group, except the new band had a tendency to accentuate their melodies more frequently; in short, it was a lot like the Velvet Underground's third album but not in a bad way at all. —*Stephen Thomas Erlewine*

○ **Lunapark** / 1992 / Elektra 61360
Luna's first album doesn't sound that different from Galaxie 500, except with his new band Dean Wareham's pop sensibilies come to the forefront, which makes *Lunapark* more enjoyable than most albums his old band made. —*Stephen Thomas Erlewine*

● **Bewitched** / 1994 / Elektra 61617
While it doesn't sound all that much different than their debut, Luna's second album is a stronger record, featuring improved playing and songwriting. —*Stephen Thomas Erlewine*

Luscious Jackson

Group / Alternative Pop/Rock
With their dark hip-hop-influenced rock, Luscious Jackson recreates the dense, multicultural bohemian world of New York in a collage of sound, where Spanish guitars, jazzy keyboards, funky beats, and breathy vocals combine into one. Like the Beastie Boys, Luscious Jackson's eclecticism doesn't acknowledge boundaries; instead, it takes freely from every kind of music, creating an amalgam that is distinctive and original. With their critically acclaimed 1993 debut EP, *In Search of Manny*, they earned a cult following; their first full-length album, 1994's *Natural Ingredients*, was even more eclectic and received terrific reviews. —*Stephen Thomas Erlewine*

● **In Search of Manny** / Oct. 11, 1993 / Grand Royal 1
A darkly funky, atmospheric EP where the hip-hop is used as a basis for the folk-tinged songs, which cut detailed, textured portraits of the New York bohemian slacker scene. —*Stephen Thomas Erlewine*

Lush

Group / Alternative pop/rock
Few bands live up to their names; Lush, however, does so in spades. Paced by Miki Berenyi's paper-thin voice (so thin you'll think she's on a respirator), Lush literally builds its music on a mountain of strummed guitars that approximates a rush of lava. Strong songwriting removes any tedium. —*John Dougan*

○ **Gala** / 1990 / 4AD 26463
A little of it goes a long way, but this is where Lush shines. By this time, their pop craft was developed enough to warrant repeated listenings. Fans of folkie-style guitar, albeit with a touch more volume, will love this. —*John Dougan*

Mad Love / 1990 / Nesak 3
A four-song EP that captures Lush's sound well. —*Dan Heilman*

● **Spooky** / 1992 / 4AD 26798
On their second full-length album, Lush continue to sharpen their melodies and songwriting while keeping their guitars as majestically drenched in fuzz and feedback as before. *Spooky* is the best example yet of their loud dream-pop. —*Stephen Thomas Erlewine*

○ **Split** / 1994 / Sire/Reprise
Featuring improved songwriting and catchier, more muscular hooks, *Split* rivals *Spooky* as Lush's best album. —*Stephen Thomas Erlewine*

Frankie Lymon & the Teenagers

b. 1942, d. Feb. 28, 1968
Group / Doo-wop
Frankie Lymon (1942-1968) & the Teenagers were a New York doo-wop group consisting of Joe Negroni, Herman Santiago, Jimmy Merchant, and Sherman Garnes but centered around the extraordinary talents of their lead singer, 13-year-old Frankie Lymon. Lymon wrote their first big hit, "Why Do Fools Fall in Love." His wise-beyond-his-years vocal and performing abilities not only made the Teenagers a group several notches above the competition but also made Lymon the first African American teenage pop star. Though together for only 18 months, Lymon & the Teenagers exerted an enormous influence, spawning several "kid" vocal groups and providing initial inspiration to Berry Gordy to model his entire Motown production approach around

Lymon's original vocal style. Inexplicably, the group split into two factions at the height of their success, and neither had a hit again. Lymon died from a drug overdose at age 26. Diana Ross, Smokey Robinson, Len Barry, and his principal protege, Michael Jackson (whose early recordings with the Jackson 5 are virtual recreations of the early Lymon sound, merely updated), all show the influence of the groundbreaking work of Frankie Lymon & the Teenagers. —*Cub Koda*

★ **Best of Frankie Lymon & the Teenagers** / 1990 / Rhino 70918
Frankie Lymon wrote "Why Do Fools Fall in Love" at 13 and led his group, the Teenagers, to a brief stardom. They remain one of the finest examples of New York vocal group singing, and all of the essentials are on this album. —*Jeff Tamarkin*

Barbara Lynn (Barbara Lynn Ozen)

b. Jan. 16, 1942
Vocals, guitar / R&B, soul
A bluesy southpaw guitarist from Beaumont, TX, Barbara Lynn Ozen wrote her own ticket to hitdom with the 1962 smash "You'll Lose a Good Thing," an R&B chart-topper. Texas producer Huey Meaux brought Lynn to Cosimo's studio in New Orleans to cut the atmospheric downbeat tune, her debut single on the Jamie label. Followups included the bouncy "Oh! Baby (We Got a Good Thing Goin')"—better remembered through the Rolling Stones' faithful cover—and her minor 1966 hit on the often-covered "You Left the Water Running." Lynn remains active, currently recording for Antone's. —*Bill Dahl*

● **You'll Lose a Good Thing** / 1962 / Jamie 3023
Barbara Lynn Ozen's smokey voice and fine guitar playing (visually arresting because she played lefthand in a manner similar to Albert King) was one of the better blends of soul vocals and blues embellishment. Huey P. Meaux produced the 12 cuts that formed this early '60s record, notably the classic title track. But other Lynn numbers like "I'll Suffer" were equally outstanding; Lynn was sometimes tough and confrontational, other times tender, inviting, or anguished. Meaux didn't clutter the works with unnecessary firepower; his arrangements and chart values were just enough to augment Lynn's sturdy vocals. —*Ron Wynn*

Here Is / 1968 / Atlantic 8171
Guitarist and vocalist Barbara Lynn's Atlantic recordings have been recyled many times, including this recent import compilation. The mastering is good, and the selection thorough, but my preference is for the original Atlantic LP or any Japanese repo that's available. You can't go wrong with any collection that contains "You'll Lose a Good Thing," "I'll Suffer" and the other Atlantic classics. —*Ron Wynn*

● **Barbara Lynn** / 1989 / Goodthing
Yet another Barbara Lynn anthology, this one's more complete than its counterparts in that it includes her material on Jamie and other labels as well as the Atlantic hits. Lynn actually recorded "You'll Lose a Good Thing" for Jamie, but it was later included on an Atlantic release. This has 17 songs from Jamie, Atlantic, and Tribe sessions, including some that weren't big hits but should have been, like "This Is the Thanks I Get" and "It's Better to Have It." —*Ron Wynn*

Lynyrd Skynyrd

Group / Southern rock
From the time of their initial 1970 Sheffield, AL, demos to their tragic plane crash on Oct 20, 1977, the Jacksonville, FL, band Lynyrd Skynyrd fused the spirit of rock & roll with the truth and lyrical directness of great country music.

Lynyrd Skynyrd possessed a highly arranged approach to organizing their material. They also employed a powerful lead guitar triumvirate in Allen Collins, Gary Rossington, and Ed King (later replaced by Steve Gaines), which augmented lead singer/songwriter Ronnie Van Zant's no-nonsense tales of the common man's exploits.

Skynyrd was discovered playing in an Atlanta club by Blood, Sweat & Tears founder Al Kooper in 1972. Kooper signed them to his new Sounds of the South record label and released *Pronounced Leh-Nerd Skin-Nerd*, which included the classic "Freebird," one of the most requested songs in rock history.

The band, which drew heavily from the hard English blues-rock sound (Free, Cream, Stones), had the good fortune to have a fan in the Who's Pete Townshend, who requested that Skynyrd open for the 1973 *Quadrophenia* tour. As a result, the band developed a strong fan base early in their career.

"Sweet Home Alabama" from *Second Helping* was the band's biggest single. Other singles included "Saturday Night Special," "What's Your Name," "Double Trouble," and "You Got That Right." Survivors of the 1977 plane crash played in various amalgamations (Rossington-Collins Band, Allen Collins Band, etc.). Lynyrd Skynyrd reformed for a Tribute tour in 1987. Since then, they have released several albums for Atlantic. —*Rick Clark*

○ **Pronounced Leh'Nerd Skin-Nerd** / 1973 / MCA 1685
With the release of this debut album, Skynyrd was immediately recognized as one of the south's premier bands. The album's highlight is "Freebird," a song that over time has become one of the most requested rock songs in the history of radio. "Simple Man," "Gimmie Three Steps," and "Tuesday's Gone" are several other standards from this classic album. —*Rick Clark*

☆ **Second Helping** / 1974 / MCA 1686
Their appropriately titled followup to their debut was equally impressive, containing their highest-charting hit, "Sweet Home Alabama" (#8). Unlike many albums, where the hit is the highlight, *Second Helping* is chock full of great tunes like "Working for MCA," "Call Me the Breeze," "Don't Ask Me No Questions," and "Ballad of Curtis Loew." —*Rick Clark*

Nuthin' Fancy / 1975 / MCA 31003
Frazzled by too much endless roadwork and too little songwriting preparation, *Nuthin' Fancy* is a step down from its impressive predecessor, *Second Helping*. Nevertheless, "Saturday Night Special," the album's opener, is a classic rocker. Other standouts include the Free-style "On the Hunt," "Whiskey Rock-a-Roller," and "Am I Losin'." —*Rick Clark*

Gimme Back My Bullets / 1976 / MCA 31004
On their first production with the legendary Tom Dowd (Rod Stewart, Eric Clapton, Allman Brothers), Skynyrd sounds relatively uninspired, even as they indignantly call for a return to platinum status with the Free-influenced title cut. Nevertheless, Van Zant's gift for plain-speaking lyrics and the band's undeniable chemistry help this record hold up better than many late '70s AOR rock acts. —*Rick Clark*

One More from the Road / 1976 / MCA 6897
Recorded at Atlanta's Fox Theater and produced by Tom Dowd, Skynyrd returned to their original three-guitar lineup concept with the addition of Steve Gaines. Some might complain that *One More* failed to capture the energy of the band's shows, but overall it ranks as one of rock's finest live releases. Unfortunately, MCA abridged the CD, cutting out some key tracks and dialog. —*Rick Clark*

○ **Street Survivors** / 1977 / MCA 1687
The addition of lead guitarist and singer Steve Gaines goaded Ronnie Van Zant and the band into a dramatic rebirth. *Street Survivors* featured tighter songs, strong melodies, and an exciting element of vocal interplay between Van Zant and Gaines ("You Got That Right"). The contrast between Gaines' clean lead style, Collins' flash, and Rossington's thick-toned lyrical phrasing is something to behold. Without a doubt, Skynyrd's most cohesive body of work since *Second Helping*. —*Rick Clark*

Skynyrd's First and ... Last / 1978 / MCA 31005
Pre-Al Kooper Skynyrd, recorded in Muscle Shoals, may not be their best work, but it shows without a doubt that this Jacksonville band was already heads and shoulders above many major-label bands, even before they were signed. —*Rick Clark*

★ **Gold & Platinum** / 1980 / MCA 6898
Compiled by Gary Rossington and Allen Collins after their tragic 1977 plane crash, *Gold & Platinum* contains most of the band's essential tracks. It would've been nice if annotations had been included, but this is a good primer. —*Rick Clark*

○ **Lynyrd Skynyrd—Box Set** / 1991 / MCA 10390
This attractively packaged and well-chosen collection of the band's most popular tracks also includes early demos and other unreleased tracks. —*Rick Clark*

The Lyres

Group / Punk, garage rock
Led by garage-rock king Jeff "Monoman" Connolly, the Lyres are the Savoy Brown of the punk era, simply because of the band's ever-changing lineup (something like 30-40 members). Playing

classic Farfisa-driven junk-riffing with manic glee, the Lyres are one of Boston's enduring rock legacies, and rightly so. —*John Dougan*

● **On Fyre** / 1984 / Ace of Hearts
Simply their best. For fans of that trebly '60s shit-rock sound and Stooges-style destructo lurch, this is what it sounds like all revved up and ready to go. —*John Dougan*

Lyres Lyres / 1988 / New Rose 103
Not as immediately engaging as *On Fyre*, but this could well be the world's first *mature* garage-rock record. A bit slowed down and more emotionally complex, it's a departure in a genre known primarily for speed and sweat. —*John Dougan*

Kirsty MacColl

Vocals / Singer-songwriter, pop/rock, folk rock
Daughter of folksinger/writer Ewan MacColl and wife of Steve Lillywhite, Kirsty MacColl started as a first-class pop songwriter (penning "They Don't Know," among others, for Tracey Ullman) before branching out with some fine albums of her own. Her uncharacteristic "Walking Down Madison" was a 1991 hit. —*Dan Heilman*

○ **Kite** / 1989 / Charisma 91232
After nearly a decade's absence as solo performer, MacColl released the low key *Kite*, a decidedly more mature effort. Her literate and sharp vocals are perfectly matched with lush, textured folk-pop arrangements. Johnny Marr contributes his distinctive guitar playing on several tracks. —*Chris Woodstra*

● **Electric Landlady** / 1991 / Charisma 91688
MacColl is in peak form on the more experimental *Electric Landlady*. Playing with a different band on nearly every track, she effortlessly moves from hip-hop of "Walking Down Madison," to the Latin-tinged "My Affair," to the Smiths' sound-alike "Children of the Revolution" (cowritten by Smiths guitarist Johnny Marr). Overall, she builds on the folk pop of her previous effort with much stronger material. Her lyrics have become more personal, mainly dealing with her relationship with and the recent death of her father. —*Chris Woodstra*

○ **Essential Collection** / 1993 / Stiff
A fine collection of Kirsty MacColl's early singles for Stiff Records in the late '70s. She wrote effortlessly melodic three-minute pop singles that managed to recast the classic girl-group sound of the '60s into a style that was contemporary and timeless, much like how Rockpile energetically recast '50s and '60s rock & roll. Not only were these singles some of the best she's ever written, they were among the best pop songs of the era, including the original version of Tracey Ullman's hit "They Don't Know". —*Chris Woodstra*

○ **Titanic Days** / Oct. 5, 1993 / IRS 27214
MacColl delivers another brilliant album with 1993's *Titanic Days*. The arrangements have become more ambitious, as evident in the jazzy "Bad" and the heavily orchestrated "Soho Square." The lyrics are still sharp, with biting commentary this time backed by a more dance-oriented pop. —*Chris Woodstra*

Madder Rose

Group / Alternative Pop/Rock
Madder Rose either plays dreamy, jangly guitar-pop like a hazier, jaded R.E.M. or churns out fuzz-drenched punk rockers. When it sticks to pop, the band is wonderful, with ragged harmonies and airy, catchy melodies; on the punkier numbers, the band neglects to write strong hooks and doesn't have enough aggression to make the music a good exercise in noise. Nevertheless, the band usually relies on its pop skills, making its two albums, 1993's debut *Bring It Down* and the 1994 followup *Panic On*, some of the better guitar pop of the mid '90s. —*Stephen Thomas Erlewine*

● **Bring It Down** / 1993 / Seed 4229
Madder Rose's impressive debut album catches fire when they stick with their airy, melodic guitar pop. When they play fast, punky rockers, their songwriting and playing are slightly uninspired, but for the most part, *Bring It Down* is a fine collection of indie-guitar pop. —*Stephen Thomas Erlewine*

Madness

Group / Ska-revival

Madness were a British septet formed in 1976. They gained fame in the late '70s ska revival along with such bands as the Specials and the Beat. Unlike those contemporaries, however, the group had a comic, pop edge that turned them into a well-loved popular singles group. Members were Graham "Suggs" McPherson (vocals), Chas Smash (backup vocals), Chris Foreman (guitar), Mike Barson (keyboards), Lee Thompson (saxophone), Mark Bedord (bass), and Dan Woodgate (drums). The first of their 13 UK Top 10 hits was "One Step Beyond" in 1979.

Though the group's British subject matter and approach tended to preclude American success, Madness did manage one U.S. Top 10 hit, "Our House," in 1983. The group disbanded in 1986. — *William Ruhlmann*

○ **One Step Beyond** / 1979 / Sire 6085
The band's debut shows the band in peak form. More than just the silly novelty act portrayed on the cover, Madness offers a lighthearted approach to ska with an irresistible dance beat. Includes the favorites "One Step Beyond" and "Night Boat to Cairo." A landmark ska-revival album. — *Chris Woodstra*

○ **Absolutely** / 1980 / Sire 6094
Their early ska-influenced material, featuring such UK hits as "Baggy Trousers," "Embarrassment," and "Return of the Los Palmas 7." — *William Ruhlmann*

Seven / 1981 / Stiff 16
Their "nutty sound" seems to fall to the background somewhat on this move toward more mature songwriting. Expanding beyond the limited scope of ska, this is a fine pop effort at times dabbling in more experimental sounds such as sitars and Arabic rhythms. Includes the splendid single "It Must Be Love." — *Chris Woodstra*

○ **Rise & Fall** / 1982 / Stiff 46
Madness Present the Rise and Fall marks the band's most mature effort and artistic statement. Completely devoid of their early ska influence, they paint a picture of British life in the spirit of the Kinks' *Village Green Preservation Society*. Though it was never released in the United States, several tracks were later placed on the compilation *Madness*, including "Our House," their biggest Stateside hit. — *Chris Woodstra*

● **Complete Madness** / 1982 / Stiff
A smartly assembled collection of their early singles. A good starting point for those interested in their self-described "nutty sound" ska/bluebeat. Pure fun. — *Chris Woodstra*

○ **Utter Madness** / 1986 / Zarjazz
Picking up where *Complete Madness* left off, this collection includes all of the key singles from 1982 to 1986. A good collection, though listeners will be better served by simply listening to *Rise & Fall* for a representation of this period. — *Chris Woodstra*

○ **Madness** / 1988 / Geffen 4003
A U.S. compilation album released to coincide with the success of "Our House." It includes that hit, its followup, "It Must Be Love," and such UK successes as "Tomorrow's Just Another Day," "Shut Up," "House of Fun," and "Grey Day." — *William Ruhlmann*

Madonna

b. Aug. 16, 1958, Rochester, MI
Vocals / Dance-pop, pop/rock
The most controversial female artist of the last 30 years has never received her critical due in spite of massive worldwide success. Her unabashed sexual confidence, her canny marketing sense, her support of gay causes, her interracial relationships, and her consistent exposing of the hypocrisy of our male-dominated society have made her the scorn of critics and social commentators; she's been lambasted everywhere, from *Rolling Stone* to "Entertainment Tonight." But Madonna's music deserves to be heard on its own terms. She's been a trailblazing and innovative force in dance-pop. The formula she set with her first album has been mimicked by some of the hottest acts of '80s and '90s, including Janet Jackson and Paula Abdul. Her celebrity and notoriety, however, would be as vacuous as Cher's if her music weren't so good—if it didn't ring in the ears and stick in the brain like all classic pop should. — *John Floyd*

○ **Madonna** / 1983 / Sire 23867
Her introduction to the dance floors and radios of America is short on great songs, but it's significant and mildly intriguing. — *John Floyd*

Like a Virgin / 1984 / Sire 25157

With monster hits like "Material Girl," "Dress You Up," and the title track, this album exploits the traits that defined her then-budding persona. — *John Floyd*

○ **True Blue** / 1986 / Sire 25442
A staggering album from an artist known for hot singles. The hits include "Papa Don't Preach," "Open Your Heart," and "True Blue." "Live to Tell," her best, is also to be found here. — *John Floyd*

You Can Dance / 1987 / Sire 25535
A decent assortment of extended dance remixes. Ideal for parties. — *John Floyd*

☆ **Like a Prayer** / 1989 / Sire 25844
Not as consistent as her *True Blue* album but a diverse and ambitious set, including "Keep It Together," a wonderful single. — *John Floyd*

Dick Tracy—"I'm Breathless" (Music from & Inspired by the Film) [st] / 1990 / Sire 26209
Songs from or inspired by her film *Dick Tracy*—the live-action recreation of the '40s comic strip. Madonna expands her range into the Broadway show tune realm, but the real gem of the record is the brilliant single "Vogue," which brought a new urban dance style (based on fashion model posturing) to middle America. — *AMG*

★ **Immaculate Collection** / 1991 / Sire 26440
A 70-minute singles package that establishes once and for all Madonna's absolute mastery of the pop single. — *John Floyd*

○ **Erotica** / Oct. 20, 1992 / Maverick 45031
While it didn't set the charts on fire like her previous albums, the ambitious *Erotica* contains some of Madonna's best and most accomplished music (including the hit singles "Deeper and Deeper" and "Rain"), even if it runs a bit long. — *Stephen Thomas Erlewine*

Magazine

Group / Punk
An arty angst-rock combo formed in 1978 by former Buzzcocks vocalist Howard Devoto. Before breaking up in 1981, the group recorded one devastating single, 1978's "Shot by Both Sides." — *John Floyd*

○ **Real Life** / 1978 / Blue Plate 1808
A vital album that fired the first shot in defining the UK post-punk scene. A period classic. — *Steve Aldrich*

○ **Correct Use of Soap** / 1980 / Blue Plate 1810
Only a shade less brilliant than their debut. Outstanding work from guitarist John McCeoch. — *Steve Aldrich*

After the Fact / 1982 / IRS 0030
A U.S. compilation that includes non-LP single sides. — *Steve Aldrich*

● **Rays & Hail** / 1990 / Virgin 90891
A comprehensive compilation that samples from all of the band's albums, as well as including the original single version of "Shot by Both Sides." — *Stephen Thomas Erlewine*

The Main Ingredient

Group / Soul, R&B
Originally formed in 1964 as the Poets, this New York soul group (Donald McPherson; Luther Simmons, Jr.; and Tony Sylvester) recorded for Red Bird before changing their name in 1966. After McPherson's death in 1971, Cuba Gooding became the lead singer, and the band scored three Top 40 hits, including "Everybody Plays the Fool," which went to #3.

The Main Ingredient tried again in 1986, with Cuba Gooding returning to his lead spot. They recorded for Zakia but didn't get much response to "Do Me Right." They kept trying, cutting a song on Polydor in 1989. — *Ron Wynn and Bil Carpenter*

● **All-Time Greatest Hits** / RCA 9591
Though they formed in New York City in the mid '60s and were originally called the Poets, it wasn't until 1971 that the Main Ingredient's fortunes changed. When Cuba Gooding replaced Donald McPherson, who'd died earlier in the year, his engaging voice helped make them part of the "sweet" soul trend. Gooding's leads made "Spinning Around (I Must Be Falling in Love)" and "Everybody Plays the Fool" huge hits, as well as "Just Don't Want to Be Lonely" and "Happiness Is Just around the Bend." All these and several other hits are featured on this anthology covering their prime years on RCA. — *Ron Wynn*

Yngwie Malmsteen

Guitar / Heavy metal

By age 21 Yngwie Malmsteen had become one of the most admired guitarists on the planet. Raised in Sweden, the 19-year-old moved to California in 1983 and within two years had debuted on vinyl with Steeler, cut two albums with Alcatrazz, and self-produced a pair of much-lauded solo releases. Onstage, he was energy incarnate—tossing his Strat high in the air and catching it one-handed, playing with his teeth, and offering his instrument in symbolic sacrifice to the gods of feedback. The young Swede's technique was brillant, with a sheer speed and picking control paralleled by few others. Solos were the heart of his art: Roaring masterpieces, they cast high-drama melodies more closely related to Bach and Paganini than any rock forebears. With Yngwie's imprimatur, Paganini, Bach, and Beethoven suddenly became hot items among big-hairs and metal heads.

Meanwhilem hordes of kids armed with copies of *Rising Force* and *Marching Out* scurried to guitar teachers to learn the mysteries of harmonic minor, phrygian, and diminished scales. There was no easy way around it; to approximate Malmsteen's style took hard work. The endless riffing, booze, and star trappings took quick tolls: Yngwie suffered from tendinitis throughout the *Marching Out* sessions. His prediction that he might someday be a race car driver took a chilling turn in June 1987, when he wrapped his car around a tree. An injured picking hand and what he described as "severe brain damage" slowed his career until 1989, when he recorded *Trial by Fire*. —*Jas Obrecht*

○ **Rising Force** / 1984 / PolyGram 825324
Sheer speed, dazzling execution. Result—the birth of the guitar hero. —*Jas Obrecht*

○ **Trilogy** / 1986 / PolyGram 831073
More commercial, but still spectacular. —*Jas Obrecht*

Odyssey / Jan. 1988 / PolyGram 835451
Important additions to his "solography," but no cigar. —*Jas Obrecht*

● **Collection** / 1992 / PolyGram 849271
A nice sampling of Malmsteen's finest songs and solos. — AMG

The Mamas & the Papas

Group / Pop/rock

The leading California-based vocal group of the '60s, the Mamas & the Papas epitomized the ethos of mid to late '60s pop culture: live free, play free, and love free. Their music, built around radiant harmonies and a solid electric-folk foundation, was gorgeous on its own terms, but a major part of its appeal lay in the easygoing Southern California lifestyle it endorsed.

Founder and leader John Phillips came out of early rock roots and a partly successful folk career, as did Cass Elliott and Denny Doherty, while Phillips's wife Michelle was an ex-model who also sang. They got together out of several failed folk groups just as the music was going electric, pulled up stakes in New York, and headed west, where they signed with Lou Adler and wowed the world with a song called "California Dreamin'."

Phillips was a pop poet with a commercial edge, and a good arranger. The group had enviable chart success, lived well, and indulged themselves lavishly yet retained credibility with the counterculture. But it all came apart in a couple of years, as the quartet's intertwining romantic entanglements, coupled with their chemical excesses (detailed in separate books by John and Michelle Phillips), strangled their ability to work. By 1971 they were a fond memory, although a reconstituted version of the quartet was done well on the oldies circuit in the late '80s and early '90s. —*Bruce Eder*

● **16 Greatest Hits** / 1970 / MCA 5701
A great overview of the music from this group, one of the founders of the California sound in the late '60s. This is a good collection of their unforgettable electric folk/pop songs, including "Monday, Monday" and "California Dreaming." —AMG

○ **Creeque Alley** / 1991 / MCA 10195
They weren't the most important folk-rock group of the mid '60s; the Byrds and others produced more enduring music. Yet the Mamas and the Papas were undoubtedly the most commercially successful folk-rock group of their time, racking up an astonishing nine Top 30 hits in little more than a year and a half. This 43-song double CD is by far the most comprehensive document of

their legacy. It draws most heavily from their two 1966 albums (nine songs originate from their debut album *If You Can Believe Your Eyes and Ears* alone), when John Phillips's songwriting talent had yet to exhaust itself. Beyond the hits, the material is variable. The set includes various late '60s and '70s solo recordings by each of the group's members (including small hit singles by John Phillips and Cass Elliott). —*Richie Unterberger*

Manfred Mann

Group / British invasion, pop/rock, progressive rock

A British rock quintet led by keyboard player Manfred Mann (born Michael Lubowitz, October 21, 1940). They scored 13 British and two American Top 10 hits between 1963 and 1969. The biggest was the #1 "Do Wah Diddy Diddy," before Mann disbanded and reemerged in the '70s with Manfred Mann's Earth Band. —*William Ruhlmann*

○ **Roaring Silence** / 1976 / Warner Brothers 3055
A later edition of Mann's band, which had a '70s hit with Bruce Springsteen's "Blinded by the Light," contained on this album. —*William Ruhlmann*

● **Best of Manfred Mann** / 1992 / EMI America 48397
For a guy who claimed to be a jazz buff and to despise pop, Manfred Mann (the keyboard player) sure knew a pop hit when he heard one. And here they are, including "Do Wah Diddy Diddy" and "Pretty Flamingo." —*William Ruhlmann*

Manhattans

Group / Doo-wop, soul, urban R&B

A venerable soul quintet from New Jersey whose career has spanned the dawn of soul and the death of disco, although they have steadfastly preferred ballads over the years. Led initially by George Smith, who died in 1970, the Manhattans first charted in 1965 with "I Wanna Be (Your Everything)." After a string of solid R&B sellers on Carnival and DeLuxe, Gerald Alston replaced the late Smith, and the group moved to Columbia. In 1976 they struck pay dirt with the elegant platinum-selling ballad "Kiss and Say Goodbye," which topped both the pop and soul lists. Several more huge R&B hits preceded their uplifting 1980 gold record "Shining Star," and still more followed.

The Manhattans' fortunes plummeted after Gerald Alston departed in 1988. Roger Harris was a good vocalist, but Alston's sound had become a core component, and they floundered on their final Columbia date. They switched to Valley Vue in 1989 and introduced another new lead singer, Gary Taylor. —*Bill Dahl and Ron Wynn*

● **Dedicated to You—Golden Carnival Classics, Pt. 1** / Collectables 5135
The first of two superb volumes covering the Manhattans early years on the Carnival label, the period many regard as their greatest. While they didn't come close to equaling the crossover/pop success that they'd enjoy with Columbia in their second incarnation, these were the pure soul works. The group featured both a glorious George "Smitty" Smith and young Blue Lovett, and their songs were produced solely with soul/R&B audiences in mind. There was little of the slick, polished orchestrations or smooth arrangements that were the hallmark of the Columbia hits. Instead, Smith's aching, soaring leads and the group's alternately mellow, frenzied, and emphatic harmonies were the high point. No matter what the sound quality, both this album and its counterpart are essential purchases for soul fans. —*Ron Wynn*

○ **For You & Yours—Golden Carnival Classics, Pt. 2** / Collectables 5136
For many Manhattans fans, their earliest singles for the Carnival were their greatest. These featured the wondrous George "Smitty" Smith, a young Blue Lovett, and some classic heartbreak and anguished soul singles, among them the divine "I Wanna Be (Your Everything)." These haven't been available on anthology very often and haven't been available anywhere since the early days of the Solid Smoke series. While Collectables' reissues sometimes leave a lot to be desired in the sound category, these songs are so good and so rare that any anthology featuring them has to get the highest recommendation regardless of technical merit. This is the second of two volumes covering this era. —*Ron Wynn*

○ **After Midnight** / 1980 / Columbia 36411

The finest Manhattan album in their second incarnation. The original group with George Smith had a slightly rougher, more traditional R&B/doo-wop sound, while the soul unit featuring Gerald Alston was smoother, though no less anthemic, especially on ballads. This album didn't make it as high on the pop charts as their self-titled 1976 work, but had more consistently compelling tracks. "Shining Star" and "Girl of My Dream" are masterpiece ballads. —*Ron Wynn*

● **Greatest Hits** / 1980 / Columbia 36861
This spotlights the biggest records from the Manhattans' second phase. After George "Smitty" Smith died, his eventual replacement Gerald Alston brought them a fine heartache and love ballad stylist. The move to a major label in the early '70s also helped, as Columbia provided them much more publicity muscle and promotional assistance than they ever received at Carnival and Deluxe. During the mid '70s and early '80s they also earned their first crossover exposure with the #1 hit "Kiss and Say Goodbye." It's one of the songs featured on this anthology spotlighting their soul and pop hits for Columbia. —*Ron Wynn*

Barry Manilow
b. Jun. 17, 1946
Vocals / Pop
Barry Manilow just can't get any respect. He's been at the butt end of a million remarks regarding what's wrong with radio. Only recently has another act taken that honor away from him, in the form of fellow Arista labelmates Milli Vanilli. At least Manilow could play and sing. It's Manilow's sugary romantic MOR ballads, fortified with throw-in-the-kitchen-sink productions, that have always rankled detractors. Nevertheless, that never kept him from selling over 50 million records worldwide. The biggest successes, among his many hits, include "Mandy," "Could It Be Magic," "I Write the Songs," "Looks Like We Made It," "Can't Smile without You," "Weekend in New England," "Copacabana (at the Copa)," "Ships," "Somewhere in the Night," and "I Made It through the Rain." —*Rick Clark*

○ **Live** / 1977 / Arista 8049
Live was Manilow's only #1 album. The performances are so seamless that it's practically a faithfully performed greatest-hits album. It includes the hit "Daybreak." —*Rick Clark*

● **Greatest Hits, Vol. 1** / 1978 / Arista 8598
Manilow has had a load of albums, but essentially he is a singles artist. This first *Greatest Hits* collection is the place to start for those desiring an introduction to one of the most successful MOR singers of all time. Among the songs included in this collection are "Mandy," "Looks Like We Made It," "Can't Smile without You," "Tryin' to Get the Feeling Again," and "Daybreak." —*Rick Clark*

● **Greatest Hits, Vol. 2** / 1983 / Arista 8102
Includes "Could It Be Magic," "This One's for You," "Weekend in New England," "Copacabana (at the Copa)," and "I Write the Songs." —*Rick Clark*

○ **Greatest Hits, Vol. 3** / 1989 / Arista 8600
Vol. 3 isn't as consistently strong as the first two, since it consists mainly of his less successful tracks. This set contains "The Old Songs," "Memory," "Let's Hang On," "Somewhere Down the Road," "I Made It through the Rain," and his Top 10 version of Ian Hunter's "Ships." —*Rick Clark*

Greatest Hits Box Set / 1992 / Arista 8611
For Barry Manilow fanatics this lavish, expensive box set (which is filled with rarities) will be hard to live without, but more casual fans should stick with the *Greatest Hits* albums. —*AMG*

Aimee Mann
Vocals, guitar / Singer-songwriter, pop/rock
Because of its big video/radio 1985 hit "Voices Carry," Til Tuesday was pigeonholed as a one-hit wonder, but their three albums all featured some fine pop songwriting by singer/guitarist Aimee Mann. Several years after Til Tuesday's breakup and after some legal wrangling, Mann launched a solo career in 1993 with *Whatever*. Even if the album's sales were modest, she finally received some of the critical acclaim that she has always deserved. —*Stephen Thomas Erlewine*

● **Whatever** / 1993 / Imago 21017
Led by the instantly memorable power-pop of "I Should've Known," Aimee Mann's first solo album, *Whatever*, is a strong

collection of pure pop singles and folk-tinged ballads that proves she is a very talented songwriter with a gift for melody, as well as a fine lyricist. —*Stephen Thomas Erlewine*

The Marcels
Group / Doo-wop
This Pittsburgh ensemble deserved a much better fate than being known primarily for a novelty-tinged cover of "Blue Moon." Baritone vocalist Richard F. Knauss teamed with Fred Johnson, Gene J. Bricker, Ron Mundy, and lead vocalist Cornelius Harp, an integrated ensemble. They named themselves after Harp's hairstyle, the marcel. The group did a string of covers as demo tapes that were sent to Colpix. The label's A&R director had them cut several oldies at RCA's New York studios in 1961, one of them being "Blue Moon." They used the bass intro arrangement from the Cadillacs' "Zoom," and the results were a huge hit. It eventually topped both the pop and R&B charts and also was an international smash. The group eventually appeared in the film *Twist around the Clock* with Dion and Chubby Checker. They also recorded an 18-cut album for Colpix. Alan Johnson and Walt Maddox later replaced Knauss and Gene Bricker, making them an all Afrian American unit. The group did score another Top 10 pop single with "Heartaches," another cover of a prerock single; this peaked at #7 pop and #19 R&B in 1961. The group continued recording with varying lineups but never again equaled their past success. —*Ron Wynn*

● **Best of the Marcels** / 1990 / Rhino 70953
An outstanding vocal ensemble that is exceptional on nonsense/novelty tunes like "Blue Moon." —*Ron Wynn*

○ **Summertime** / 1992 / Relic 7030
One of the finest and purest doo-wop albums available, this features 24 a cappella performances and served as the legendary audition tape that got the group signed to their first recording contract. Great singing, arrangements, and performances. —*Cub Koda*

Marillion
Group / Art rock, hard rock
Marillion was one of the leading art rock bands of the '80s, paying homage to the theatrical thrills of early Genesis before evolving into a more straightforward hard rock. Over the years, the group has been quite popular in the United Kingdom, peaking in 1985 with the *Misplaced Childhood* album, but has never been more than a cult act in the United States. They continue to tour and record in the '90s, with a faithful cult of fans supporting their latest efforts. —*Stephen Thomas Erlewine*

○ **Script for a Jester's Tear** / 1983 / Capitol 46237
Their strong debut, showing the influence of Peter Hammill, Pink Floyd, Rick Wakeman, Jethro Tull, and the much-ballyhooed resemblance to Genesis. —*Michael P. Dawson*

○ **Fugazi** / 1984 / Capitol 46027
Gut-wrenchingly powerful lyrics and dynamic prog-rock performance. A classic! —*Michael P. Dawson*

○ **Misplaced Childhood** / 1985 / Capitol 46160
A masterpiece of articulate and emotional lyrics with exciting and colorful musical settings. The songs form a continuous album-length suite. —*Michael P. Dawson*

Clutching at Straws / Jun. 19, 1987 / Capitol 46866
The followup to *Misplaced Childhood* is even more personal and often disturbing, with its ruminations on alcohol abuse and self-betrayal. —*Michael P. Dawson*

● **Six of One, Half-Dozen of the Other** / 1992 / IRS 13157
A fine collection of Marillion's best and most popular tracks, *Six of One, Half-Dozen of the Other* offers a good introduction to the art-rock group. —*Stephen Thomas Erlewine*

The Mar-Keys
Group / Soul
Before Booker T. & the MG's, there were the Mar-Keys, who literally laid the groundwork for the Memphis sound with their powerfully economic early R&B instrumental sound. They enjoyed only one real hit with the #3 "Last Night," which was released in 1961 on Satellite Records, the predecessor to Stax.
Besides including Steve Cropper and "Duck" Dunn in the lineup, the Mar-Keys also had Wayne Jackson, who later formed

the Memphis Horns, and Don Nix, who had a fairly successful career as a solo artist and producer. —*Rick Clark*

● **Back to Back** / 1967 / Atlantic 90307
A smoldering live set featuring the Mar-Keys (aka the Memphis Horns), recorded in Europe during the 1967 Stax/Volt Revue. (Credited to the Mar-Keys and the MG's.) —*John Floyd*

The Marshall Tucker Band

Group / Southern rock

One of the major Southern rock bands of the '70s, the Marshall Tucker Band was formed in Spartanburg, SC, in 1971 by singer Doug Gray; guitarist Toy Caldwell (b. 1948); his brother, bassist Tommy Caldwell (1950-April 4, 1980); guitarist George McCorkle; drummer Paul Riddle; and reed player Jerry Eubanks. The group's style combined rock, country, and jazz and featured extended instrumental passages on which lead guitarist Toy Caldwell shone. The band was signed to Capricorn Records and released its debut album, *The Marshall Tucker Band*, in March 1973. They gained recognition through a tour with the Allman Brothers Band and found significant success during the course of the '70s, with most of their albums going gold. Their peak came with the million-selling album *Carolina Dreams* and its Top 15 single, "Heard It in a Love Song," in 1977. The band was slowed down by the death of Tommy Caldwell in a car accident in 1980, and it faded from the album charts after 1982. Toy Caldwell left for a solo career, and by the early '90s, Marshall Tucker consisted of Doug Gray, Jerry Eubanks, guitarist Rusty Milner, bassist Tim Lawter, drummer Ace Allen, and pianist Don Cameron. —*William Ruhlmann*

○ **Marshall Tucker Band** / 1973 / AJK 618
The Marshall Tucker Band was never better than on its debut, mixing country picking with R&B rhythms and writing topflight songs like "Take the Highway" and "Can't You See." —*William Ruhlmann*

○ **Searchin' for a Rainbow** / 1974 / AJK 702
For their fourth album, Marshall Tucker's synthesis of country and southern rock found its most fully realized expression, particularly on tracks like "Fire on the Mountain" and the title track. Along with their debut, this is Marshall Tucker's best studio effort. —*Rick Clark*

● **Greatest Hits** / 1978 / AJK 799
If you are looking for a place to start with this band, *Greatest Hits* covers all the main bases. Included are "Can't You See," "Heard It in a Love Song," "Fire on the Mountain," and "This Ol' Cowboy." —*Rick Clark*

The Marvelettes

Group / Motown

This quintet came to Motown in 1961 after placing as finalists in their Inkster, MI, school talent contest. They were 16 years old when their first record, "Please Mr. Postman," zoomed to the #1 spot. Their finest work came in the mid '60s under the production of Smokey Robinson. Although they were overshadowed by the Supremes, their vocal styling was representative of the classic girl-group phenomenon of the '60s. By 1967 they were reduced to a trio, finally disbanding in 1970. Members included Gladys Harton (left in 1967 and was replaced by Ann Bogan), Wanda Young, Juanita Cowart (left in 1962), Georgeanne Gordon (left in 1963), and Katherine Anderson. —*Rick A. Bueche*

● **Marvelettes' Greatest Hits** / 1966 / Motown 5180
A good collection spotlighting one of Motown's least appreciated great female groups. The Marvelettes not only gave the label its first #1 pop hit but also strung together a good series of tunes, especially when Smokey Robinson was writing and producing them. —*Ron Wynn*

Richard Marx

Vocals, piano, guitar / Pop/rock

Before he released his first album, Richard Marx sang on commercials and was a backing vocalist for Lionel Richie. It was here that he learned his commercial pop skills. As soon as his first album was released in 1987, he shot to the top of the charts. Marx's first hit was the California rocker "Don't Mean Nothing," but his real strength lay with ballads; "Right Here Waiting" and "Hold On to the Nights" were adult contemporary and pop radio staples

during the late '80s and early '90s. With his first two albums, he had a streak of three consecutive #1 hits in America. With the release of his third album in 1991, his commercial fortunes started to slip somewhat, as the mainstream shifted away from the slick, well-constructed songs that are his forte. Even if he isn't hitting the Top 10 with each single anymore, however, Marx remains a mainstay on adult contemporary and pop radio. —*Stephen Thomas Erlewine*

● **Richard Marx** / 1987 / Capitol 46760
Richard Marx's self-titled debut album was a finely crafted record of mainstream pop/rock. Marx understood how the melody of up-tempo rockers like "Don't Mean Nothing" is driven by thick power chords and how arrangements are as important as melody in ballads like "Hold On to the Nights." Filled with carefully constructed radio-ready tracks, it was no surprise that the album became a huge hit. —*Stephen Thomas Erlewine*

○ **Repeat Offender** / 1989 / Capitol 90380
Marx's second album was almost as strong as his first, even if it showed that his songwriting has a tendency to slip into sappy, saccharine clichés. Nevertheless, it had contained some major hit singles—"Satisfied," "Right Here Waiting," "Angelia," "Children of the Night," and "Too Late to Say Goodbye." —*Stephen Thomas Erlewine*

Rush Street / Oct. 28, 1991 / Capitol 95874
While there are some strong songs on *Rush Street*, it isn't as consistently engaging as his first two albums. —*Stephen Thomas Erlewine*

Paid Vacation / Feb. 8, 1994 / Capitol 81232
Paid Vacation is Marx's calmest and most sophisticated album to date. —*Stephen Thomas Erlewine*

Dave Mason

b. May 10, 1946, Worcester, England

Vocals, guitar / Pop/rock

Mason was a founding member of the influential late '60s group Traffic. He provided some of that group's best material on their first three albums, particularly "You Can All Join In" and "Feelin' Alright," a song that has been covered by numerous artists, including Joe Cocker and Three Dog Night. Mason left Traffic in 1970 and went solo, enjoying sporadic success during the '70s with his style of light melodic rock/pop. —*Rick Clark*

● **Alone Together** / 1970 / MCA 31170
Mason's debut solo album remains his best effort, due to well-crafted tracks like the hit "Only You Know & I Know" and an appealing easygoing rock sound that presents a nice blend of acoustic and electric instrumentation. —*Rick Clark*

○ **Let It Flow** / 1977 / Columbia 34680
On *Let It Flow* Mason delivered a super-slick bid for radio-friendly pop. He succeeded with three hits, "So High (Rock Me Baby and Roll Me Away)," "Let It Go, Let It Flow," and the richly harmonic "We Just Disagree." —*Rick Clark*

Material Issue

Group / Rock, power pop/Anglo pop

A hard power-pop trio from Illinois who draw much musical inspiration from early Who. Lyrically, they stay focused on adolescent love songs.

Material Issue's 1991 debut, *International Pop Overthrow*, had several radio hits ("Dianne" and "Valerie Loves Me"), but their second album didn't receive much airplay—possibly because they were suffering from a bit of a sophomore slump. With its glitzy, '70s-styled hard-rock production, 1994's *Freak City Soundtrack* put an end to their creative doldrums, even if it failed to gather much commercial attention. —*Stephen Thomas Erlewine and Rick Clark*

● **International Pop Overthrow** / 1991 / Mercury 848155
Produced by Jeff Murphy of Shoes, this major label debut contained some power-pop gems like "Renee Remains the Same," "Dianne," "Valerie Loves Me," and the title cut. Fans of Cheap Trick and early Who should love much of this. Also check out their self-titled EP, which preceded this album. —*Rick Clark*

○ **Freak City Soundtrack** / Mar. 8, 1994 / Mercury 518894
Energetic pop-rock abounds on Material Issue's third album. "Goin' Through Your Purse" kicks things off sounding like a garage punk version of "Ballroom Blitz"-era Sweet. The single

"Kim the Waitress" fuses Byrds-style 12-string guitars and electric sitar with rich vocal harmonies. Other highlights include "Funny Feeling" and "The Fan." —*Rick Clark*

John Mayall

b. Nov. 29, 1933
Vocals, guitar, harmonica, keyboard / Blues rock
John Mayall is a major British blues bandleader who sings and plays harmonica, guitar, and keyboards. His bands, starting in London in 1963, have featured some of the most successful rock musicians of the '60s and '70s. Approaching the age of 60, Mayall continues to play and record frequently. —*William Ruhlmann*

★ **Bluesbreakers with Eric Clapton** / Jul. 1966 / PolyGram 800086
One of the seminal blues albums of the '60s with the Bluesbreakers, capturing Clapton on a series of blues standards, after the pop leanings of the Yardbirds and before the heavy indulgence of Cream. —*William Ruhlmann*

○ **Turning Point** / 1969 / Deram 823305
With the possible exception of *A Hard Road* (which featured future Fleetwood Mac founder Peter Green), this is Mayall's best post-Bluesbreakers album. Mayall took a drummerless, acoustic, and sometimes jazzy approach on this album of strong original material, which also featured Jon Mark on guitar and Johnny Almond on sax and flute. —*Richie Unterberger*

○ **London Blues (1964-1969)** / 1992 / PolyGram 844302
Featuring 40 tracks over two discs, *London Blues* is an excellent collection of most of the best moments from Mayall and the Bluesbreakers' early recordings, a time when Eric Clapton, Peter Green, and Mick Taylor all passed through the band. —*Stephen Thomas Erlewine*

○ **Room to Move (1969-1974)** / 1992 / PolyGram 517291
The majority of Mayall and the Bluesbreakers' best material from the early '70s is collected on this 29-track, double-disc set. Although Clapton appears on a couple of songs, the playing on *Room to Move* isn't as universally breathtaking as it is on *London Blues*, yet the collection is thoroughly listenable, and it *does* feature many fine musicians. —*Stephen Thomas Erlewine*

Wake Up Call / 1993 / Jive/Novus 41518
Mayall rarely does the same album twice, and *Wake Up Call* finds him returning to a basic, physical sound after 1990's more progressive/highly produced *A Sense of Place*. No lesser guitar masters than Buddy Guy and Albert Collins also pay respect with guest turns—the later lending some truth-in-advertising muscle to "Light the Fuse." —*Roch Parisien*

Curtis Mayfield

b. 1942
Vocals, guitar / Soul, R&B
Few have had as much influence on African American music, in as many fields of endeavor, as Curtis Mayfield, starting from his early days with the Impressions back in 1958. His sinewy guitar work has become so woven into the basic fabric of R&B guitar that more people know the style than know the man who invented it. He was the first to exhibit racial pride, singing about it on hit singles with the Impressions in the early '60s through '70s. He scored big with the soundtrack to the blaxploitation film *Superfly* in 1972; by this time he had already been running his own record company for four years. Mayfield wrote hits for everyone from Major Lance to Jerry Butler. He continues to persevere today despite the tragic accident that almost took his life in 1990. Curtis Mayfield's stardom is assured by his massive talent. —*Cub Koda and Colin Escott*

☆ **Curtis** / 1970 / Ichiban 2012
A masterpiece, and still one of the greatest urban soul albums of all time. Curtis Mayfield stepped into the spotlight and immediately showed he'd have no trouble away from the Impressions. While he'd done many transcendant singles with them, he'd never made a song as harsh, searing in its indictments, or immediately compelling as "(Don't Worry) If There's a Hell Below We're All Gonna Go." That was just one of many classic tunes. "Move on Up," "We People Who Are Darker Than Blue," and "The Makings of You" retain their impact more than 23 years later. Those who don't think there were great message songs before the hip-hop era should check this one out and then come up with better songs

done by Public Enemy, Ice-T, Boogie Down Productions, or anyone else. —*Ron Wynn*

○ **Roots** / 1971 / Curtom 8009
A fine followup to his hit debut album as a solo artist. Though he only scored one smash single with "Get Down," there were plenty of superb selections, expertly produced numbers, and fine arrangements. Mayfield, Marvin Gaye, Stevie Wonder, and Isaac Hayes were among the innovative composer/producer/performers that helped usher in the album age on the R&B/soul circuit. Mayfield was now doing concept works, with a thematic unity and sophisticated style rather than stringing together singles in the manner of '50s and '60s LPs. —*Ron Wynn*

☆ **Superfly** / 1972 / Curtom 2002
Superfly was a misunderstood film; it was an antidrug film that purported to show the horrors of drugs through the indulgences and flaws of its lead character. Instead, many misguided types assumed the litany of ills depicted were intended as a reaffirmation of the lifestyle rather than an attack. Nonetheless, there were no questions about the music. Such songs as "Freddie's Dead," "Pusherman," and the title track brought home the impact and scourge of drugs with clarity and power. Mayfield's singing was consistently magnificent, and the production and arrangements were equally superb. —*Ron Wynn*

○ **Back to the World** / 1973 / Curtom 8015
Another stirring album by Curtis Mayfield, now in a groove on his own label. Mayfield's works issued challenges across the board, urging everyone to examine his or her prejudices and then seek a solution. While he always included one or two wonderful love songs for balance, these albums were largely examinations of '70s American issues. He scored three R&B chart hits, with "Future Shock" just missing the Top 10, but that was icing on the cake. Mayfield's music had far more importance beyond simply getting hits. —*Ron Wynn*

Got to Find a Way / 1974 / Curtom 8604
Curtis Mayfield continued his run of excellent albums in the '70s with this followup to the huge hit *Superfly* soundtrack. This album had more love songs than some of his earlier material, though he didn't tone down his searing attacks on American injustice and hyprocisy. His vocals continued to be alternately poignant, urgent, and accusatory, while his lyrics, production, and arrangements were once again magnificent. —*Ron Wynn*

○ **There's No Place Like America Today** / 1975 / Curtom 2003
Curtis Mayfield continued his string of powerful, assertive message albums with this mid '70s release, but as luck would have it, the only hit the album scored came with a love tune, "Only You, Babe." Still, the title tune, "Hard Times," "When Seasons Change," and "Blue Monday People" were unrelenting, unapologetic statements expressing frustration and anger. Mayfield also included "So in Love" and "Love to the People" to balance the menu, but the finest cuts addressed the inequities and injustices he saw being ignored. —*Ron Wynn*

○ **Of All Time—Classic Collection** / 1990 / Curtom 2902
This anthology spotlights Curtis Mayfield's hits biggest as a solo star since 1970. It includes his first hit as a lead artist "(Don't Worry) If There's a Hell Below We're All Going to Go," plus "Superfly," "Freddie's Dead," "So in Love," and many other classics recorded for his Curtom label. —*Ron Wynn*

★ **Anthology 1961-1977** / 1992 / MCA 10664
A wonderful collection of both the Impressions' '60s hits and Curtis Mayfield's early '70s solo recordings on his Curtom label. All of the music on the two CDs (including hits like "It's Alright," "People Get Ready," "Superfly," and "Freddie's Dead") is superb, and the liner notes are excellent, making *Anthology* a definitive collection. —*AMG*

Maze featuring Frankie Beverly

Group / Urban R&B, soul
Frankie Beverly and Maze may be the ultimate urban contemporary group, though they're much more soulful and funky than many of their counterparts. They began in Philadelphia as the Butlers and later became Raw Soul. They moved to San Francisco in the mid '70s and switched identities again to Maze. The lineup was lead singer Frankie Beverly, Wayne Thomas, Sam Porter, Robin Duke, Roame Lowry, McKinley Williams, and Joe Provost. Ahaguna G. Sun later replaced Provost, and Sun was subse-

quently replaced by Billy "Shoes" Johnson. Ron Smith replaced Thomas, and Phillip Woo was added on keyboards in 1980. Though they've had only one #1 R&B hit in their long tenure ("Back in Stride" in 1985), Maze's popularity is unquestioned, especially as a live act. They recorded for Capitol from 1977 until 1989, when they moved to Warner Brothers and released *Silky Soul*. —*Ron Wynn*

● **Live in New Orleans** / 1981 / Capitol 46659
A superb live album, one of the finest soul/funk concert dates ever released. Frankie Beverly and Maze managed to capture on this two-album set the energy, spontaneity, and nonstop excitement of their concerts, which have always been among the finest on the R&B/soul/funk circuit. The set functioned as both a greatest hits work and a wonderful introduction to people who'd never seen their live show. The album version of "Joy and Pain" became an international hit and led to other singles being pulled and rereleased in extended versions. —*Ron Wynn*

Maze / 1982 / Capitol 91244
Maze signed with Capitol in the mid '70s, and their first album under the new pact was a fine set with Beverly's energetic lead vocals and an excellent band that included keyboardist Phillip Woo and Sam Porter, bassist Robin Duhe, and guitarist Ron Smith. They made an immediate impact with their hard-driving sound, not as strictly on the beat as the Dayton bands like the Ohio Players or Slave, but just as soulful. —*Ron Wynn*

Silky Soul / 1989 / Warner Brothers 25802
After being on Capitol through much of the '70s and '80s, Maze moved to Warner Brothers in 1989 and scored immediate dividends with this album, which contained some of the group's finest ballads ever. The title track was a poignant tribute to Marvin Gaye, who'd been a supporter and advocate of the group. Frankie Beverly also paid homage to Nelson Mandela, but didn't overdo the political message material. There were plenty of breezy and superbly crafted romantic numbers, while "Love's on the Run" was a decent uptempo number. The album helped reestablish the group as a major urban contemporary act and got them back on the charts for the first time in three years. —*Ron Wynn*

○ **Lifelines, Vol. 1** / Nov. 8, 1989 / Capitol 92810
This collects formative and favorite hits from their years on Capitol, including "Golden Time of Day" and "Joy and Pain." It shows they were both an enjoyable uptempo and funk band and a convincing ballad and love song ensemble. —*Ron Wynn*

Maze featuring Frankie Beverly / 1993 / Pioneer 24218
This 1993 album wasn't much of a departure from previous releases; its relaxed, steady pace and Beverly's infectious leads were the prime components. These were enjoyable, sentimental tunes, bolstered by restrained production and superb performances. The Maze approach hasn't changed much over the years, and that's something that pleases most soul and urban contemporary fans. —*Ron Wynn*

Mazzy Star

Group / Alternative pop/rock
David Roback, veteran of the California paisley-underground group Rain Parade, and singer Hope Sandoval, from Going Home, undertake a cold, reverberant alternative-folk sound, with occasional forays into electric psychedelia. —*Rick Clark*

○ **She Hangs Brightly** / 1990 / Capitol 96508
Roback and Sandoval slog through a collection of Velvet Underground-style pyschedelia and comatose folk. Sandoval's pleasantly detached vocal delivery complements the cold, highly reverberant production. Good for encouraging numb disconnection from the planet. —*Rick Clark*

● **So Tonight That I Might See** / Sep. 27, 1993 / Capitol 98253
Mazzy Star's second album doesn't stray from the spare, haunting guitar-pop of their first record, yet their songwriting has sharpened somewhat; there are discernible melodies and hooks underneath all the atmosphere. After sinking upon its release in the fall of 1993, the album became a surprise hit in the summer of 1994. —*Stephen Thomas Erlewine*

MC5

Group / Hard rock, rock & roll

Detroit rock & roll band whose musical and political stance helped sow the seeds of the British punk movement of the late '70s. Original members included Wayne Kramer (guitar), Rob Tyner (vocals), Bob Gaspar (drums), Pat Burrows (bass), and Fred "Sonic" Smith (guitar). They played around their native Detroit ca. 1966 as the Motor City Five. Both Gaspar and Burrows, who had shaped much of the band's early rhythmic drive, left before the band ever recorded and were replaced by Dennis Thompson (drums) and Michael Davis (bass). After two local singles went nowhere, manager John Sinclair (of the revolutionary White Panther Party) got them signed to Elektra, who recorded them live at Detroit's Grande Ballroom, where they enjoyed a fanatical local following. Troubles with the album's lyrical content (based in large part around the band's sex, drugs, and rock & roll revolutionary rhetoric) and Sinclair's conviction on drug charges saw the band toning down its image for their second album, released on Atlantic. By the time their third album was released in 1971, the band were plagued by drugs and personal problems, and they broke up shortly thereafter. Though never commercially successful, the MC5 personified the Detroit high-energy sound and approach to rock & roll, and their style lives on in the work of punk and alternative bands around the world. —*Cub Koda*

★ **Kick Out the Jams** / 1969 / Elektra 60894
The band in full cry at the Grande Ballroom, 1968; one of the most exciting live albums ever recorded. Highlights include the title track (uncensored on CD), "Ramblin' Rose," and "Borderline." —*Cub Koda*

○ **Back in the U.S.A.** / 1970 / Rhino 71033
Their second album. Not so wild but still exciting. Great original material, like "Shakin' Street" (featuring vocal by Fred "Sonic" Smith), "The American Ruse," "The Human Being Lawnmower," and "Looking at You," which featured some fiery lead guitar work by Wayne Kramer. —*Rick Clark*

○ **High Time** / 1971 / Rhino 71034
Their last studio album, with "Sister Anne" and "Baby, Won't Ya" as principal highlights. —*Cub Koda*

Babes in Arms / 1983 / ROIR 122
Rare and unreleased sides. This includes their first singles, unavailable on album. —*Cub Koda*

Paul McCartney

b. Jun. 18, 1942
Vocals / Pop/rock
In the decade and a half after the demise of the Beatles in 1970, Paul McCartney became one of the most successful figures in popular music. Though he had more trouble scoring hits after the mid '80s, McCartney embarked on a triumphant world tour in 1989 and premiered his first classical work, *Paul McCartney's Liverpool Oratorio*, in 1991.

Born in Liverpool, McCartney teamed with John Lennon and George Harrison in the '50s to form the nucleus of the Beatles, who scored an unprecedented worldwide success in the '60s, much of it fueled by McCartney's melodic songs. The bass player and singer was a musical chameleon, equally capable of performing the most tender love song, the most schmaltzy show tune, or the most raucous rocker on command. McCartney scored a film (*The Family Way*) in 1966 but otherwise restricted his musical activities to the group until the end of the '60s, when he launched his solo career with *McCartney*. In the early '70s, he formed a new group, Wings, and toured while recording frequently. Every new album hit the Top 10, as did nearly every single, such that McCartney and Wings ranked tenth among the Top 20 album artists of the decade and second among the Top 20 singles artists, according to *Billboard* statistics. McCartney finally began to cool off in sales terms after the #1 album *Tug of War* in 1982, but artistically he continued to challenge himself, writing his own motion picture, *Give My Regards to Broad Street* (1984) and entering into a writing collaboration with Elvis Costello that resulted in hits for both of them. —*William Ruhlmann*

○ **McCartney** / 1970 / Capitol 46611
McCartney's handmade solo debut has a rough-hewn, offhand quality that invites the listener into his highly melodic, sometimes whimsical musical imagination. The best songs include "That Would Be Something" (lately revived by the Grateful Dead!), "Teddy Boy" (a Beatles outtake), and "Maybe I'm Amazed" (later a hit in a live 1977 version). —*William Ruhlmann*

○ **Ram** / Jan. 1971 / Capitol 46612
While lacking the polish of his later efforts, McCartney's second post-Beatles effort is brimming with melodies and intriguing ideas. Ultimately, it seems unfinished, but along the way one is treated to the delights of "Uncle Albert/Admiral Halsey" (a #1 hit), "Heart of the Country," and "Back Seat of My Car." —*William Ruhlmann*

○ **Band on the Run** / 1973 / Capitol 46675
On his best post-Beatles album, McCartney uses his mastery of studio technique and gift for musical juxtaposition—from symphonic touches to hard rock to melodic acoustic music- in a wonderful collection of well-constructed songs, including the Top 10 hits "Helen Wheels," "Band on the Run," and "Jet." —*William Ruhlmann*

○ **Venus & Mars** / 1975 / Capitol 46984
A highly polished band album featuring the #1 hit "Listen to What the Man Said," as well as "Letting Go" and "Venus and Mars/Rock Show," which served to introduce the McCartney & Wings world tour of 1975-1976. —*William Ruhlmann*

● **Wings Greatest** / 1978 / Capitol 46056
Most of McCartney & Wings's biggest hits, 1971-1978, among them the singles "Another Day," "Live and Let Die," "Junior's Farm," "Hi, Hi, Hi," and "Mull of Kintyre," which had not previously appeared on an album. —*William Ruhlmann*

McCartney II / 1980 / Capitol 52024
Returning to an all-solo format, McCartney comes up with his best new studio album since *Band on the Run,* though ironically the album's hit is a live band version of "Coming Up," tossed in as a bonus. —*William Ruhlmann*

○ **Tug of War** / 1982 / Capitol 46057
McCartney turns to Beatles producer George Martin for a carefully constructed blockbuster album that features the #1 duet with Stevie Wonder "Ebony and Ivory" and the Top 10 hit "Take It Away," plus McCartney's tribute to John Lennon, "Here Today." —*William Ruhlmann*

★ **All the Best** / 1987 / Capitol 48287
Unfortunately, this second greatest-hits collection repeats many of the tracks from the first. But it does add the singles "C Moon" and "Goodnight Tonight" (previously unavailable on an album) and some of the bigger '80s hits, such as "Say Say Say" and "No More Lonely Nights." —*William Ruhlmann*

Flowers in the Dirt / 1989 / Capitol 91653
A well-constructed comeback album on which McCartney collaborates with Elvis Costello for the Top 30 hit "My Brave Face," recalls his father on "Put It There," rocks out on "Figure of Eight," and turns in one of those lovely McCartney ballads on "This One." —*William Ruhlmann*

○ **Unplugged (The Official Bootleg)** / 1991 / Capitol 96413
A delightful acoustic performance in which McCartney resurrects some Beatles classics, some oldies, and some of his less well known solo songs in a live setting. —*William Ruhlmann*

Michael McDonald

b. 1952, St. Louis, MO
Vocals / Pop/rock, soul
There was a time during the early '80s when Michael McDonald's earnest soulful upper baritone seemed to appear on half the hits coming out of the West Coast, including ones by Christopher Cross, Nicolette Larson, Kenny Loggins, Toto, Donna Summer, and Steely Dan and in hit duets with James Ingram and Patti LaBelle. McDonald's vocal presence was most felt as lead singer for the Doobie Brothers between 1975 and 1982 on hits like "What a Fool Believes," "Taking It to the Streets," and "Minute by Minute." As a solo artist, McDonald scored with "I Keep Forgettin' (Every Time You're Near)" in 1982, off of his debut *If That's What It Takes.* Other hits include "No Looking Back" and "Sweet Freedom." —*Rick Clark*

○ **If That's What It Takes** / 1982 / Warner Brothers 23703
Sweet, romantic blue-eyed soul, containing "I Gotta Try" and "I Keep Forgettin' (Every Time You're Near)." —*Bil Carpenter*

● **Sweet Freedom: The Best of Michael McDonald** / 1986 / Warner Brothers 67
A solid collection that features all of McDonald's greatest hits from the early '80s. —*Stephen Thomas Erlewine*

Roger McGuinn

b. Jul. 13, 1942
Vocals, guitar / Folk rock, rock & roll, country rock
Before he helped found the influential mid '60s group the Byrds, McGuinn (born Jim McGuinn) had been active as a sideman for Bobby Darin and folk artists like the Limeliters, the Chad Mitchell Trio, and Judy Collins. With the Byrds, McGuinn forged the distinctively bright 12-string Rickenbacker electric sound, which has inspired groups too numerous to name. His solo work hasn't risen to the level of his best work with the Byrds, but highlights include his self-titled debut, *Cardiff Rose,* and his 1991 comeback effort, *Back from Rio.* —*Rick Clark*

○ **Back from Rio** / 1990 / Arista 8648
This comeback effort put McGuinn together with Tom Petty & the Heartbreakers, former Byrds Chris Hillman and David Crosby, and other guest artists eager to pay tribute, like Michael Penn and Timothy B. Schmit. "King of the Hill" was a substantial FM rock hit. Other highlights include Elvis Costello's "You Bowed Down" and a fine version of Jules Shear's "If We Never Meet Again." The mainstream AOR production values make McGuinn sound like he's guesting on a Tom Petty record—which is not a bad thing, just an observation. —*Rick Clark*

● **Born to Rock & Roll** / Mar. 1992 / Columbia 47494
A well-chosen overview of McGuinn's post-Byrds solo work, including "American Girl," "I'm So Restless," "Lover of the Bayou," "My New Woman," and "Peace on You." —*Rick Clark*

Maria McKee

Vocals / Rock & roll, country rock
While she was with Lone Justice, Maria McKee always showed promise; her gritty, soulful mix of R&B, rock, and country helped distinguish the band from the multitude of '80s roots rockers. When she released her first solo album in the late '80s, it suffered from the same problem as Lone Justice—lots of potential but no delivery. However, 1993's *You Gotta Sin to Get Saved* showed McKee making good on her promise, with an album of impassioned rockers and ballads. —*Stephen Thomas Erlewine*

○ **Maria McKee** / 1989 / Geffen 24229
Three years after Lone Justice's last album, Maria McKee released her self-titled debut, which showed that her skills as a songwriter had grown considerably since her first band. Not only were her songs better, but McKee's singing had improved; while it was still a little thin, her voice had grown grittier and more soulful, which made her songs all the more convincing. Unfortunately, most of McKee's musical growth was obscured by Mitchell Froom's mushy overproduction. —*Stephen Thomas Erlewine*

● **You Gotta Sin to Get Saved** / Jun. 22, 1993 / Geffen 24508
A few years after releasing an underappreciated solo debut, Maria McKee released *You Gotta Sin to Get Saved,* her best album yet. With Black Crowes and Jayhawks producer George Drakoulias at the helm, *You Gotta Sin to Get Saved* taps into the country-rock vibe of the early '70s (much like the Jayhawks and, to a lesser extent, the Black Crowes) without sounding like a studied replica. McKee sings a dynamic mix of originals and covers with genuine conviction, making *You Gotta Sin to Get Saved* an album that demands repeated listening. —*Stephen Thomas Erlewine*

Sarah McLachlan

Pop/rock
Since her debut album in 1989, Sarah McLachlan's atmospheric folk-pop has gained a devoted following of fans, both in the United States and United Kingdom. Each record has shown McLachlan growing as both a songwriter and a musician. In 1994, she began to work her way into the mainstream with her album *Fumbling toward Ecstasy* and the single "Possession." —*Stephen Thomas Erlewine*

Touch / 1989 / Arista 8594
On her debut effort, McLachlan sets the stage for future greatness. While only in her early 20s, she shows insights beyond her years with highly personal and introspective lyrics. —*Chris Woodstra*

○ **Solace** / Sep. 10, 1991 / Arista 18631
With her second album, Mclachlan shows a marked improvement in songwriting. Yearning lyrics flow perfectly with her 12-string

guitar, a tight rhythm section, and strong Celtic influences. A fine folk-pop effort. —*Chris Woodstra*

● **Fumbling Towards Ecstasy** / Feb. 1, 1994 / Arista 18725
From the heavy dance beats of the opening single, "Possession," to the more delicate "Good Enough," Mclachlan explores self-awareness and sensuality in ways unrivaled by her previous efforts. Lush arrangements back her powerful vocals to build a highly rewarding album. —*Chris Woodstra*

Don McLean

b. Oct. 2, 1945, New Rochelle, NY
Vocals / Singer-songwriter
A singer/songwriter of a fiercely independent character, McLean dominated radio and record sales for weeks in 1971-1972 with his epic-length Buddy Hollyesque hit "American Pie." He could have gotten years more prominence by following it up and milking the sound; instead he wrote from a personal point of view and achieved a level of respect more often associated with folksingers a good decade older than he is for valuing the past and himself more than chart action. —*Bruce Eder*

○ **American Pie** / 1971 / EMI America 46555
The album that made McLean famous. The title track is the only real rocker, but the rest is intelligently produced and at times quite haunting, if a little angst ridden. —*Bruce Eder*

○ **Very Best of Don McLean, Favorites & Rarities** / 1980 / Capitol 98603
Fans of Don McLean should be thrilled with this comprehensive digitally remastered 42-track, double-disc set covering his hits, like "American Pie," "Castles in the Air," "Vincent," and "Everyday." There are also 18 previously unreleased tracks. Also included are an excellent set of liner notes, track annotations, and numerous photos from McLean's collection. —*Rick Clark*

● **Greatest Hits Then & Now** / 1987 / Capitol 17255
An acceptable collection, with few surprises. —*Bruce Eder*

Clyde McPhatter

b. Nov. 15, 1932, Durham, NC, d. Jun. 13, 1972
Vocals / R&B
Along with Ray Charles and Sam Cooke, Clyde McPhatter was one of the most influential and important vocalists to emerge in the '50s. His unusually high, muscular vocals brought gospel fervor and sexual passion to the early '50s hits of Billy Ward's Dominoes, with whom McPhatter cut the showstopping "Have Mercy Baby" and "The Bells." Ahmet Ertegun signed him to Atlantic in 1953, after McPhatter and Ward parted company, and assembled the Drifters around his gorgeous soprano. His solo career began in 1955, while he was serving in the army; "Treasure of Love," "Without Love," and "A Lover's Question" were his best solo hits. He had some minor success with Mercury in the '60s but died in obscurity in 1972. —*John Floyd*

★ **Deep Sea Ball: The Best of Clyde McPhatter** / 1991 / Atlantic 82314
This 19-track compilation contains all of the top hits that McPhatter scored between 1956 and 1959. He also charted singles on MGM and Mercury, but the bulk of his best-remembered work is here, including "A Lover's Question" and "Treasure of Love." —*William Ruhlmann*

Meat Puppets

Group / Alternative rock, rock & roll
One of the weirdest groups from the '80s, and one of the more challenging, this Tempe, AZ, trio has confounded audiences and alternative standard-bearers by honing a singular style based on a genre (hardcore) that thrives on conformity. Their 1981 debut single was standard loud/fast punk, but by their second album the Pups became confident enough to flaunt their influences and their ambitions; traces of Captain Beefheart, Neil Young, ZZ Top, and Blue Oyster Cult seeped through the din of Curt Kirkwood's whining vocals and inventive guitar figures. Their sound has since become more streamlined, but they remain a unique and often-brilliant group, one of the best the '80s produced. Their breakthrough to the mainstream in 1994 with *Too High to Die* was well deserved. —*John Floyd*

Meat Puppets 2 / 1984 / SST 019
Sounds like country, reads like post-punk. —*Robert Gordon*

○ **Up on the Sun** / 1985 / SST 039
Mellow. If they'd stayed in the heat any longer, they'd have melted. —*Robert Gordon*

Mirage / 1987 / SST 100
A bit forced but generally a mellow aura with driving rhythms. —` *Robert Gordon*

● **Huevos** / 1988 / SST 150
Punk ZZ Top wannabees. —*Robert Gordon*

Forbidden Places / 1991 / London 828254
Less contemplative lyrically. A tighter fusion of their disparate musical sides. —*Robert Gordon*

○ **Too High to Die** / 1994 / London
Boosted by an endless stream of praise from groups like Nirvana and Soul Asylum, the Meat Puppets turned in one of their finest albums with *Too High to Die* in 1994. It's a slamming return to form by the country-punk pioneers, full of roaring, twanging guitars and irresistible songs. It also became their first crossover hit, thanks to MTV's airing of the video for "Backwater." —*Stephen Thomas Erlewine*

Meat Loaf

b. Jan. 22, 1946
Group / Pop/rock
A rock singer (real name Marvin Lee Aday) with a full, dramatic voice; also an actor who shot to fame with the multiplatinum album *Bat Out of Hell* in 1977. After everybody had written him off as a has-been, Meat Loaf rocketed back to the top of the charts in 1993 with *Back into Hell: Bat Out of Hell II*, which became an enormous multiplatinum hit. —*William Ruhlmann*

● **Bat Out of Hell** / 1978 / Epic 34974
Meat Loaf's powerful, passionate voice serves as the messenger for Jim Steinman's over-the-top rock songs, which treat teenage angst in practically Wagnerian terms, while Todd Rundgren provides a clean, well-articulated Wall of Sound production in this kitsch masterpiece, which includes "Two Out of Three Ain't Bad" and "Paradise by the Dashboard Light." —*William Ruhlmann*

Dead Ringer / 1981 / Epic 36007
Meat Loaf collects a couple of Steinman songs, and he, Paul Jacobs, and Mack work at recreating the Rundgren production sound for an album of high-voltage rock. —*William Ruhlmann*

○ **Bat Out of Hell II: Back into Hell** / 1993 / MCA
Although Meat Loaf has made several albums since *Bat Out of Hell* (most of them were never released in the United States), *Bat Out of Hell II: Back into Hell* is an explicit sequel to that milestone of '70s pop culture. Reprising the formula of the original nearly to the letter (without Todd Rundgren producing, although he does make a cameo appearance), *Back into Hell* is bombastic with too much detail, thanks to the psuedo-operatic splendor of Jim Steinman's grandly cinematic songs. From the arrangements to the length of the tracks, everything on the album is overstated; even the album version of the hit single, "I Would Do Anything for Love (But I Won't Do That)," is 12 minutes long. Yet that is precisely the point of this album, and it is also why it works so well. —*Stephen Thomas Erlewine*

Megadeth

Group / Heavy metal, thrash
Megadeth formed in 1983 after Dave Mustaine left Metallica and moved to Los Angeles, where he met bassist Dave Ellefson. With guitarist Chris Poland and Gar Samuelson, they landed a contract with Combat Records, releasing their debut album in 1985. After that album's success, they became the first thrash band signed to Capitol Records. The next two albums on that label did extremely well, putting them among the top thrash bands with Metallica, Slayer, and Anthrax. Their music was very tight, and the lyrics showed depth and intelligence. After a slight slump at the end of the decade, Megadeth returned to form with 1990's brutal *Rust in Peace*.

A decade after their first album, Megadeth stands as one of thrash's best bands, influencing a generation of metal bands while releasing some of the most complex records of their genre. —*John Book*

Killing Is My Business ... and Business Is Good / 1985 / Combat 8015

Killing Is My Business ... and Business Is Good! is the album that started it all for ex-Metallica guitarist Dave Mustaine and his new band. This is a lot rawer than *Peace Sells ... but Who's Buying? — John Book*

● **Peace Sells ... but Who's Buying?** / 1986 / Capitol 46370
From the politics of war to the politics of the environment, Megadeth covered them all on an album that brought them from cult status to the eyes and ears of the mainstream. *Peace Sells ... but Who's Buying?* is considered to be one of the best thrash albums of the '80s. —*John Book*

So Far, So Good ... So What! / 1988 / Capitol 48148
Although it featured a new drummer and guitarist, *So Far, So Good ... So What!* was a disappointment after the violent precision of *Peace Sells ... but Who's Buying?* While there are some fine tracks, like "In My Darkest Hour," the album lacks focus and is marred by such ill-conceived songs like "Hook in Mouth" and a bone-headed cover of "Anarchy in the UK." —*Stephen Thomas Erlewine*

○ **Rust in Peace** / Sep. 24, 1990 / Capitol 91935
After kicking drugs, Dave Mustaine returns with yet another new drummer and guitarist with *Rust in Peace*, a stronger collection than *So Far, So Good*, featuring some of Megadeth's most intricately constructed songs riffs to date. —*Stephen Thomas Erlewine*

○ **Countdown to Extinction** / 1992 / Capitol 98531
Countdown to Extinction is proof that good ol' thrash can still survive in the '90s. Strongly written songs, wonderfully executed playing from the entire band, and believable lyrics ranging from suicide ("Skin O' My Teeth") to the destruction of civilization as we know it ("Ashes in Your Mouth"). Arguably the band's best since their *Peace Sells... but Who's Buying? —John Book*

The Mekons
Group / Punk, alternative pop/rock
This critically acclaimed band, led by Jon Langford and Tom Greenhaigh, was founded in Leeds as a punk outfit in 1977 and metamorphosed into a countryish unit by the mid '80s. Now they're more mainstream but still highly eclectic. —*William Ruhlmann*

○ **New York** / 1988 / Combat 5026
An unusually tight version of the band (courtesy of drummer Steven Goulding, formerly of the Rumour) in live performances recorded in 1986 and 1987. Low fidelity, high energy. —*William Ruhlmann*

○ **Fear & Whiskey** / 1989 / Sin 001
Country and folk played in an irreverent rock style like that later adopted by the Pogues, but even looser. —*William Ruhlmann*

● **Mekons Rock 'n' Roll** / 1989 / A&M 5277
The Mekons make like an alternative rock band. They're not, but they do make a lot of noise and have a lot of fun on this typically shambling impersonation. —*William Ruhlmann*

○ **Retreat from Memphis** / 1994 / Quarterstick 26
Retreat from Memphis is the band's best record since the pivotal *Mekons Rock 'n' Roll.* —AMG

John Cougar Mellencamp
(John Mellencamp, John Cougar)

b. Oct. 7, 1951
Vocals, guitar / Rock & roll
Indiana native John Mellencamp is the American small-town boy who made good, selling millions of records while wresting artistic control from the record label and, all along, never disowning his Heartland roots. Unlike Bruce Springsteen, who has been lionized as a practically flawless all-American rocker for most of his career, Mellencamp seems utterly human, bullheaded, idealistic and preachy, indulgent, and very capable of sticking his foot in his mouth.
In 1971 Mellencamp formed a glam-rock band called Trash. It basically went nowhere, but his admiration for David Bowie's music led him to the artist's manager, Tony DeFries. DeFries landed Mellencamp a deal at MCA. When the album *Chestnut Street Incident* was released, Mellencamp discovered his last name had been changed to Cougar, courtesy of DeFries. That event is the beginning of a series of humiliating record-biz miscalculations that (not unlike Tom Petty) caused Mellencamp to cut an image as a regular guy out to beat the system. In 1982

Mellencamp (as John Cougar) scored the rock equivalent of winning a state lottery by selling five million copies of *American Fool*, which produced two huge hits, "Jack and Diane" and "Hurts So Good."
Like anyone from the underbelly of the American middle class who wins big, Mellencamp underwent a running battle trying to figure out how to stay sane while hanging onto the jackpot and trying to figure out why the gnawing vacuum deep inside him wouldn't go away. Ever since then, Mellencamp's albums have been public airings of the American Dream come true, undergoing an initiation through the Book of Lamentations. (In 1983 he added Mellencamp back to his name. In 1991 he dispensed with the Cougar moniker all together.) Mellencamp's sound, while firmly rooted in rock, became increasingly earthy and acoustic until 1991's *Whenever We Wanted*, which was musically a return to a harder-edged sound.
Despite releasing a series of remarkably consistent records, Mellencamp had been in a bit of a commercial rut since 1989's *Big Daddy*. With its sinewy cover of Van Morrison's "Wild Night," 1994's *Dance Naked* put a halt to that decline; the duet with Me'Shell NdegeOcello was his biggest hit in years, appealing to a multitude of radio formats. —*Rick Clark*

American Fool / 1982 / Mercury 814993
One of the biggest albums in 1982, *American Fool* established Mellencamp (then known as John Cougar) as a major star. His fatalistic ode "Jack and Diane" and the radio rock sleezfest "Hurts So Good" were major hits. Even though Mellencamp was occasionally a clumsy lyricist, his small-town punk image, believable intentions, and rhythm guitar-heavy rock were embraced by millions throughout the American Heartland. —*Rick Clark*

○ **Uh-Huh** / 1983 / Mercury 814450
After the mega-platinum *American Fool*, Mellencamp roughened up his sound and began adopting a more topical stance with hits like "The Authority Song," "Pink Houses," and the Stones-ish-sounding "Crumblin' Down." —*Rick Clark*

○ **Scarecrow** / 1985 / Mercury 824865
Recorded at his home studio in Indiana, *Scarecrow* reflected Mellencamp's concern over the plight of the American farmer. The title track is one of the most fully realized statements of purpose in his artistic career. However, there are times when Mellencamp bludgeons the listener with heavy-handed polemics that lack focus. On the plus side, *Scarecrow* was loaded with great rock-radio singles like "Lonely Ol' Night," "R.O.C.K. in the U.S.A.," "Rumbleseat," and "Small Town." The raw noisy production did a good job of enhancing the sparks in Mellencamp's excellent band. —*Rick Clark*

★ **Lonesome Jubilee** / 1987 / Mercury 832465
Here Mellencamp infused his Heartland rock with a strong dose of acoustic and country instrumentation in the form of fiddle, accordian, hammer dulcimer, dobro, banjo, and pedal steel. Thematically, he attempted to flesh out the big statements that predominated his previous album *Scarecrow*. In spite of the fact that Mellencamp's admonishments (with almost biblical undertones) are delivered with the proselytizing earnestness of the recently converted, *Jubilee's* spirited performances and memorable melodies make this one of his best efforts. Highlights include "Check It Out," "Paper in Fire," "Rooty Toot Toot," and "Cherry Bomb." —*Rick Clark*

Big Daddy / 1989 / Mercury 838220
Mellencamp went deeper into acoustic-dominated rock with *Big Daddy*, an album where his focus was fine-tuned through smaller, personalized settings and stories. As a result, *Big Daddy* contained some of Mellencamp's best material, with tracks like "Jackie Brown," "Mansions in Heaven," "Void in My Heart," and "Sometimes a Great Notion." *Big Daddy* is his most subdued album (except for such tracks as his remake of the Hombres's "Let It Out (Let It All Hang Out)," "Martha Say," and his #15 hit whinefest "Pop Singer"). —*Rick Clark*

○ **Whenever We Wanted** / 1991 / Mercury 510151
Two years after Mellencamp released *Big Daddy*, he returned (sans the name Cougar) with electric guitars blaring away on material that represented the thematic extremes of his career. On "Get a Leg Up" (obviously concocted for radio airplay), Mellencamp resorted to his snotty *American Fool* persona, while on tracks like "Now More Than Ever," "Love and Happiness," and the title track he mined the concerns of his more recent work. "I

Ain't Ever Satisfied" pretty much summed up Mellencamp's mortality-aware desire to have it every way. All in all, this is a very strong album, and a must for fans of Mellencamp's brand of forthright Heartland rock. —*Rick Clark*

○ **Human Wheels** / 1993 / Mercury
Arguably Mellencamp's best album to date, *Human Wheels* is a dark, somber portrait of America. Mellencamp's lyrics have been brooding with melancholy for years now, but on *Human Wheels* the music matches his words—the dark R&B and rock sound as anguished as his voice. At one time, he would have sung "What If I Came Knocking" seductively, but here he sounds as if nothing would change is she answered the door. *Human Wheels* might not have the hit singles of *Scarecrow* and *The Lonesome Jubilee* or the punch of *Whenever We Wanted*, but it is more consistent and moving than any of those albums. —*Stephen Thomas Erlewine*

Dance Naked / 1994 / Mercury
A short, stripped-down collection of basic rock & roll, *Dance Naked* isn't quite as powerful as *Human Wheels*, yet it has more good songs in its 30 minutes than most 70-minute albums. — *Stephen Thomas Erlewine*

Harold Melvin and the Blue Notes

Group / Soul, doo-wop
Starting out in 1954 in Philadelphia as a doo-wop group with Harold Melvin as lead singer, the Blue Notes first recorded for the New York-based Josie label two years later. They debuted on the R&B charts in 1960 on the Val-ue label with "My Hero." A 1965 release, "Get Out," with a lead vocal by John Atkins, also charted R&B Top 40 on Landa. But it was not until 1972, when drummer Teddy Pendergrass took over lead vocal chores and the group came under the wing of Kenny Gamble and Leon Huff and their Philadelphia International label, that Harold Melvin and the Blue Notes became consistent chart-makers.

Pendergrass's vocals smoldered with sensuality. Combined with the smooth group harmonies that had always been a Blue Note trademark, Gamble and Huff's superior writing, and lush productions, the superb TSOP house band records, such as "I Miss You," "If You Don't Know Me by Now," and "The Love I Lost," were staples on both African American and White radio from 1972 to 1975. Pendergrass went solo in 1975, and the Blue Notes' glory days came to an end. Recording subsequently for a number of labels (including ABC, Source, MCA, and Philly World), Harold Melvin and the Blue Notes hit the R&B charts another ten times, often with lead vocals by Sharon Paige. Three of those 45s permeated the Top 20, one of which (1977's "Reaching for the World") reached as high as #6. The latter was the only one of the Blue Notes' post-Pendergrass recordings to break the pop Hot 100. — *Rob Bowman*

○ **To Be True** / 1975 / Philadelphia International 33148
The best of their original albums, containing many hits and no filler. —*John Floyd*

★ **Collector's Item** / 1976 / Philadelphia International 34232
Rounds up such hits as "Wake Up Everybody," "Bad Luck," "If You Don't Know Me by Now," and "The Love I Lost," all benchmarks of an era. —*John Floyd*

Melvins

Group / Alternative rock, heavy metal
The Melvins were the first post-punk band to revel in the slow, sludgy sounds of Black Sabbath. Their music is oppressively slow and heavy, only without any of the silly mystical lyrics or the indulgent guitar solos—it's just one massive, oozing pile of dark slime. The Melvins' first record was released in 1987; they've released several albums since then, but it wasn't until 1993 that they went to a major label, thanks to their protege, Kurt Cobain.

While the Melvins can be dull and repetitious, their place in rock history is interesting, even if it is just a minor footnote. The band formed in Aberdeen, WA, the same town that produced Nirvana's Cobain and Chris Novaselic. For Nirvana and many other Seattle-area bands, the Melvins' sludge was inspirational; the younger bands took the Sabbath-styled heaviness of the Melvins while adding an equally important pop song structure, which the group tended to lack. While all of their deciples became famous after Nirvana broke big in 1991 (including Mudhoney, which featured former Melvin bassist Steve Turner),

the Melvins only expanded their cult slightly. —*Stephen Thomas Erlewine*

○ **Gluey Porch Treatments** / 1987 / Alchemy
The Melvins' debut is mandatory for those into slow, aggressive songs, with power chords stretched out beyond compare. Includes such songs as "h," "Steve Instant Newman," and "Over from Under the Excrement." —*John Book*

○ **Ozma** / 1989 / Boner 16
Ozma, the band's second album, became an underground favorite. Fierce guitar work from Osborne, intense drumming from Crover, and mind-numbing bass work from Lori Black make *Ozma* one of the hardest (and harshest) albums of 1989. CD version includes *Gluey Porch Treatment* in its entirety as a bonus. —*John Book*

Bullhead / 1991 / Boner 25
Bullhead represented a slightly different sound for the group. The material on this album made an attempt at being actual "songs" rather than short examples of guitar execution, and the production is not as overpowering as their first two albums. But playing slightly faster songs did appeal to those who thought the band were stuck in molasses. —*John Book*

Lysol / 1992 / Boner 35
Melvins take the Jethro Tull route by recording one lengthy song and releasing it as a full-length album. *Lysol* is a progressive song in the vein of Tull's *Thick as a Brick* and *A Passion Play*, as the band go through different tempo changes, musical moods, and emotions during its 31 minutes. Returning to the large sound they created on their first two albums, this album takes heaviness to an all new plateau. —*John Book*

● **Houdini** / 1993 / Atlantic
The Melvins changed nothing when they went to a major label. They still grind out the same slow, fuzzy, heavy sludge that remains the final word on "grunge." For those who have been wondering what all of the fuss is about, *Houdini* is a good way to catch up. —*Stephen Thomas Erlewine*

Men at Work

Group / Pop/rock
The Australian band Men at Work might still be a sensation relegated to the down under if it weren't for MTV's constant airing of their humorously oddball videos in America's heartland and FM radio's awareness that it was in dire need of some fresh faces. Men at Work's bar-band, Police-like pop/rock did have its share of hooks, particularly the sax line on their #1 international debut hit "Who Can It Be Now?" Their next single, "Down Under," went #1 as well. Both of those tracks came off of *Business as Usual*, which held the #1 spot for 15 weeks in 1982.

Their followup, *Cargo*, peaked at #3 and produced two more big hits with "Overkill" and the topical "It's a Mistake." A two-year layoff effectively killed the band's momentum, and their third album, *Two Hearts*, reached only #50. —*Rick Clark*

● **Business as Usual** / 1981 / Columbia 37978
Their smash debut contains "Who Can It Be Now" and "Down Under." —*Dan Heilman*

○ **Cargo** / 1983 / Columbia 38660
Men at Work's followup to their smash hit debut is a more varied collection, anchored by the fine ballad "Overkill" and the satire of "It's a Mistake." —*Stephen Thomas Erlewine*

Mercury Rev

Alternative pop/rock, psychedelic
Considering the band's leader, guitarist Jonathan Donahue, spent a short time with the Flaming Lips, it's not surprising that Mercury Rev's music is a splendid, scattershot amaglam of psychedelia, pop, experimental noise, rock, free-form jazz, and movie soundtracks. What is surprising is that Donahue's songs are the band's most pop-oriented material, consolidating all of their colorful sonic rush into a three-minute blast. Vocalist David Baker's songs were more languid and less dependent on structure.

It doesn't matter if it is a three-minute or a 12-minute song—it is always impossible to tell where Mercury Rev is coming from and where they are going. After releasing two acclaimed albums in 1991 and 1993, Baker left the band acrimonously and pursued a solo career. —*Stephen Thomas Erlewine*

○ **Yerself Is Steam** / 1991 / Columbia 53030

Mercury Rev's debut *Yerself Is Steam* could be classified as '70s art rock played with '90s post-modern sensibilities, but the band refuses to stay in one place. Instead of the self-absorbed excesses of Pink Floyd, there are elements of psychedelia, punk, free jazz, and warped pop. *Yerself Is Steam* only hints at the band's potential. Columbia's CD reissue includes the Velvet Underground pop of "Car Wash Hair" as a bonus track. —*Stephen Thomas Erlewine*

● **Boces** / Jun. 1, 1993 / Columbia 53217
Boces, Mercury Rev's second album, is an even stronger affair than their first, showcasing the possibilities of their truly mind-bending neo-psychedelic guitar rock. Alternating between brightly colorful blasts of three-minute pop to flowing, lazy extended workouts, the album is never dull. All of their flights into the netherworld are fascinating; even the 11-minute songs seem too short. —*Stephen Thomas Erlewine*

Metallica

Group / Heavy metal, thrash
Metallica was easily the best, most influential heavy metal band of the '80s, responsible for bringing the music back to earth. Instead of playing the usual rock star games of metal stars of the early '80s, the band looked and talked like they were from the street. Metallica expanded the limits of thrash, using speed and volume not for their own sake but to enhance their intricately structured compositions. The release of 1983's *Kill 'Em All* marked the beginning of the legitimization of heavy metal's underground, bringing new complexity and depth to thrash metal. With each album, the band's playing and writing improved; James Hetfield devolped a signature rhythm playing that matched his growl, while lead guitarist Kirk Hammett became one of the most copied guitarists in metal. Lars Ulrich's thunderous, yet complex, drumming clicked in perfectly with Cliff Burton's innovative bass playing.

After releasing their masterpiece *Master of the Puppets* in 1986, tragedy struck the band when their tour bus crashed while traveling in Sweden, killing Burton. When the band decided to continue, Jason Newsted was chosen to replace Burton; two years later, the band released the conceptually ambitious *...And Justice for All*, which hit the Top 10 without any radio play and very little support from MTV. But Metallica completely crossed over into the mainstream with 1991's *Metallica*, which found the band trading in their long compositions for more concise song structures; it resulted in a #1 album that sold over seven million copies in the United States alone. The band launched a long tour that kept them on the road for nearly two years. By the '90s, Metallica had changed the rules for all heavy metal bands; they were the leaders of the genre, respected not only by headbangers but also by mainstream record buyers and critics. No other heavy metal band has ever been able to pull off such a trick. —*Stephen Thomas Erlewine*

☆ **Kill 'Em All** / 1983 / Elektra 60766
The origins of modern thrash-metal are here. One can hear traces of Judas Priest, the Scorpions, and Motörhead on some of the songs. —*John Book*

○ **Ride the Lightning** / 1984 / Elektra 60396
Concise, direct, and to the point. Originally released by the independent Megaforce label, this led to their being signed by Elektra. —*John Book*

★ **Master of the Puppets** / 1986 / Elektra 60439
The album that put thrash-metal into the spotlight and into the mainstream. Flawless. This is one of the best albums of the '80s—period. Also the last album to feature bassist Cliff Burton. —*John Book*

○ **Garage Days Re-Revisited** / 1987 / Elektra 60757
A blistering EP of covers of Metallica's favorite underground metal bands of the late '70s and early '80s, *Garage Days Re-Revisited* is one of the band's purest blasts of raw, primal heavy metal. —*Stephen Thomas Erlewine*

○ **And Justice for All** / 1988 / Elektra 60812
The most sophisticated album in their career. This is also the first full-length release to feature ex-Flotsam & Jetsam bassist Jason Newsted. The thin sound quality stops this from being a masterpiece. —*John Book*

☆ **Metallica** / 1991 / Elektra 61113

Longtime fans may call this one a sellout, but that's hardly the case. Instead, the group has increased the bottom end of their sound and keeps the riff-per-song limit down to about two. This may keep *Metallica* from alienating staunch metal-haters, but it's the quality of the songs—hits such as "Enter Sandman" and the ballad "Nothing Else Matters," but also "Holier than Thou"—that has made this their most successful (and best) album to date. —*John Floyd*

Live Shit...Binge and Purge / 1993 / Elektra
Weighing in at three CDs and three videos plus a bunch of tour memorabilia, the sheer bulk of *Live Shit ... Binge and Purge* scares off anyone but the most devoted fans, which is too bad. Although it is exhausting, this box provides ample proof of the brutal power of Metallica in concert—the entire program of a Mexico City concert is included, and it is awe-inspiring. For hardcore fans, *Live Shit* is a godsend. —*Stephen Thomas Erlewine*

Meters

Group / R&B, soul, funk
The top instrumental band in New Orleans during the late '60s and much of the '70s, both on their own and as a session crew (formed in 1966). Keyboardist Art Neville; guitarist Leo Nocentelli; bassist George Porter, Jr.; and drummer Zigaboo Modeliste played on numerous sessions for producer Allen Toussaint before they climbed the R&B charts themselves in 1969 with "Sophisticated Cissy" and "Cissy Strut" on the Josie label. They remained with Josie into the early '70s, issuing more funky hit instrumentals such as "Look-Ka Py Py" and "Chicken Strut" before spending the mid '70s with the major labels Reprise and Warner. The quartet went their separate ways in 1977 but sometimes reform for the New Orleans Jazz and Heritage Festival. —*Bill Dahl*

● **Look-Ka Py Py** / 1970 / Rounder 2103
The Meters' great '60s singles anticipated the coming of funk with their splendid blend of Afro-Latin grooves, slithering rhythms, and flickering guitar licks backed by a steady bass line and heavy drum backbeat. They made short, catchy tunes and scored occasional hits, particularly the single "Look-Ka-Py-Py." That's one of 12 outstanding tunes on this CD. These were the ultimate party/dance records, and they also showed the link between traditional African rhythms, New Orleans shuffle, and second line sounds, soul, and funk. Keyboardist Art Neville, guitarist Leo Nocentelli, bassist George Porter, Jr., and drummer Zigaboo Modeliste didn't stop cooking until the final note on the concluding tune "Dry Spell." Here's marvelous rhythm music at its hottest. —*Ron Wynn*

Meters Jam / 1972 / Rounder 2105
Only Booker T. and the MGs and possibly the Tower of Power horns ever challenged New Orleans's Meters for supremacy as R&B's finest studio band; their crisply syncopated, rhythmically invigorating arrangements and beats on numerous Crescent City sessions were magical. But the 10 songs on this album are a mixed bag, mainly because the Meters insisted on singing and simply weren't great vocalists. Their leads and harmonies on "Come Together" and "Bo Diddley" among others were exuberant, but didn't add much to the proceedings. However, there haven't been many groups in any style that clicked any more smoothly and soulfully than the Meters. Their playing's so inspired and funky it almost overshadows the tepid vocals. —*Ron Wynn*

Best of the Meters / 1975 / Virgo 12002
A good collection of this quintessential New Orleans funk group's best '70s singles for the Reprise label. Of course they did their finest cuts for Josie, but turned in some reasonably good work on Reprise, though more in a rock/funk direction. "Hey, Pokey-A-Way" was probably the closest Reprise cut to matching the superb Josie singles. But these are the songs that got them their gigs with the Rolling Stones and work with Paul McCartney and Robert Palmer, so they did have some value. —*Ron Wynn*

Good Old Funky Music / May 1979 / Rounder 2104
Unissued material from the Meters' Josie heyday in the late '60s and early '70s. Some good moments, but there's too much filler. —*Bill Dahl*

○ **Uptown Rulers: The Meters Live on the Queen Mary** / 1992 / Rhino 70376

A wonderful live concert from 1975 that showcases the powers of these New Orleans R&B legends. —AMG

George Michael (Yorgos Kyriatou Panayioutou)

b. Jun. 26, 1963, Watford, England
Vocals, guitar / Pop/rock, dance-pop

Yorgos Kyriatou Panayioutou (George Michael) achieved fame in the duo Wham! in his native United Kingdom in 1982. Through 1986, he and his partner, Andrew Ridgeley, scored hit after hit in a variety of styles from rap to uptempo pop to slow ballads. As songwriter and lead singer, Michael gradually overshadowed the group, and by the time they split, he was ready for a massively successful solo career. This began with the 1987 album *Faith,* which featured a series of chart-topping hit singles and sold more than seven million copies. That Michael had not achieved a similar critical success was evident from the title of his followup album, *Listen without Prejudice, Vol. 1,* which, though it sold a million copies, included two Top 10 hits, and hit #2, must be considered a major commercial disappointment. With *Vol. 2* apparently shelved, Michael contributed several songs to the charity album *Red Hot + Dance* in 1992.

After the failure of *Listen without Prejudice,* Michael engaged in a bitter legal battle with his record company, accusing them of not properly promoting the album and asking them to release him from his contract; he stated that he would refuse to release any records if he lost the lawsuit. He lost. After the decision was delivered in summer of 1994, Michael announced he would appeal; it's unclear what his musical plans are. —*William Ruhlmann*

★ **Faith** / 1987 / Columbia 40867
George Michael certainly looked like the biggest pop star to emerge in the second half of the '80s when he released this debut album after his years in Wham! It wasn't just that the record topped the charts for 12 weeks and sold seven million copies and that six of its nine tracks were Top 10 hits (four #1s, a #2, and a #5); it was that Michael, who wrote, arranged, and produced, seemed to have a broad understanding of all aspects of pop, from the rockabilly of the title track and the heartfelt ballad "Father Figure" to the R&B dance grooves of "I Want Your Sex" (indeed, the album also got to #2 on the African American charts). —*William Ruhlmann*

○ **Listen without Prejudice, Vol. 1** / 1990 / Columbia 46898
Michael's followup to the massive success of *Faith* found him turning inward, trying to gain critical acclaim as well as sales. *Listen without Prejudice* is not an entirely successful effort; Michael has cut back on the effortless hooks and melodies that crammed not only *Faith* but also his singles with Wham! and his socially concious lyrics tend to be heavyhanded. Yet the highlights—the light, Beatlesque harmonies of "Heal the Pain," the plodding #1 "Praying for Time," "Waiting for That Day," and the Top 10 "Freedom 90"—make a case for his talents as a pop craftsman. —*Stephen Thomas Erlewine*

Mickey & Sylvia

Group / R&B, rock & roll
The duo of vocalist Mickey Baker and vocalist Sylvia Vanderpool had a number one R&B hit with "Love Is Strange" in 1956, still among the most endearing duo numbers in rock history. They continued recording together into the early '60s, landing another Top 10 R&B hit on Vik with "There Oughta Be a Law" in 1957. Baker was one of rock and R&B's great session guitarists, performing on songs recorded for Savoy, Atlantic, King, Aladdin, and several others. Sylvia Vanderpool first recorded with Hot Lips Page for Columbia as "Little Sylvia" in 1950. She resurfaced solo in 1973, recording as Sylvia. She was also later owner of Sugar Hill Records, one of the earliest labels to chronicle the rap revolution. As Sylvia, she had a #1 R&B and #3 pop hit in 1973, "Pillow Talk," and recorded duets with Ralfi Pagan and the Moments. She married Joe Robinson, owner of All Platinum/Vibration, and recorded for both companies as well as Sugar Hill into the '80s. Their son Joe was leader of the West Street Mob. —*Ron Wynn*

● **Love Is Strange** / 1965 / Bear Family 15438
Unless you're a major R&B collector, it's likely you've never heard anything by this duo besides "Love Is Strange," their only major hit (and a great one). With 20 cuts from 1956 to 1960, this disc

reissues the bulk of their most interesting work. "Love Is Strange" will remain their most memorable tune after you've heard this, but on the whole this is way-above-average '50s R&B/rock. Playing on countless '50s sessions for various labels, Mickey Baker was one of the greatest guitar players of early rock & roll. With Sylvia Robinson, he got to stretch out a bit from his usual role, with some trailblazing, piercing, lean, and bluesy leads. If you're hungering for more great solos like the ones in "Love Is Strange," you'll find some here, especially in "There Oughta Be a Law" and the instrumental "Shake It Up," although his virtuosity doesn't dominate most of the songs. Vocally, Mickey & Sylvia had an engagingly playful, occasionally sly'n'sassy repartee that makes up in charm what it might lack in smoke and firepower. Some of these tunes are routine doo-wop, but a little over half of the material is pretty strong, ranging from the calypso-rock they're best remembered for to straight-ahead R&B shouters, with King Curtis on sax. —*Richie Unterberger*

Midnight Oil

Group / Rock & roll
An Australian quintet formed in 1978 and led by singer Peter Garrett. Other members: Peter Gifford, bass (replaced by Bones Hillman in 1987); Martin Rotsey, guitar; James Moginie, guitar and keyboards; and Rob Hirst, drums. The group came up playing for the surf crowd in Sydney bars but always had a serious political side. Its first three albums, *Midnight Oil* (1978), *Head Injuries* (1979), and *Place without a Postcard* (1981), were released only in Australia. (They appeared in the United States in 1990.) Midnight Oil's first two U.S. releases, *10,9,8,7,6,5,4,3,2,1* (1983) and *Red Sails in the Sunset* (1985), had only modest sales, but *Diesel and Dust* (1988) was a major hit, selling a million copies and featuring the Top 20 hit "Beds Are Burning." *Blue Sky Mining* went gold in 1990, and Midnight Oil released an album of concert recordings dating from 1982 to 1990, *Scream in Blue Live,* in 1992. —*William Ruhlmann*

○ **10,9,8,7,6,5,4,3,2,1** / 1982 / Columbia 38996
Midnight Oil's first album to have a full-scale production, this album effectively brings out the band's driving rock sound, Peter Garrett's impassioned vocals, and the band's forthright political standpoint. —*William Ruhlmann*

● **Diesel & Dust** / 1987 / Columbia 40967
On a thematic album dealing with the plight of Aborigines in Australia, this is Midnight Oil's most focused and compelling music. Its single most impressive song, "The Dead Heart," works powerfully, both as agit-pop and as moving rock music. Also included is the anthemic hit single "Beds Are Burning." —*William Ruhlmann*

○ **Blue Sky Mining** / 1990 / Columbia 45398
Diesel & Dust, only with less aggression. It's still a solid record. —*John Dougan*

○ **Earth & Sun & Moon** / Apr. 1993 / Columbia 53793
On *Earth & Sun & Moon* Midnight Oil sounds revitalized after the slightly uninspired *Blue Sky Mining.* Their most melodic, nearly Beatlesque effort is arguably their best effort yet. —*Chris Woodstra*

Mighty Mighty Bosstones

Group / Hard rock, ska-revival
With their party-ready mix of heavy metal and ska, the Mighty Mighty Bosstones gained a strong following across America in the early '90s, particularly on college campuses. While their records are usually fun, the band hasn't completely captured their kinetic energy on disc. —*Stephen Thomas Erlewine*

● **Don't Know How to Party** / Mar. 1993 / PolyGram 514836
A raucous mix of metal and ska, *Don't Know How to Party* is one of the fiercest party records ever made. —*David Jehnzen*

Steve Miller

b. Oct. 5, 1943, Milwaukee, WI
Vocal, guitar / Pop/rock, blues rock, psychedelic
For my money, the best of the hippie-era San Francisco bands. Maybe that's because the Steve Miller Band actually hailed from Texas, and Miller and early Miller Band vocalist Boz Scaggs were blues fanatics who dabbled in psychedelic song structures and not vice versa. In the '70s Miller turned his tight blues machine

into one of the decade's greatest and most consistent hit machines. His recent stuff, however has been sloppy and desultory, save one fine return to the blues. —*John Floyd*

○ **Children of the Future** / 1968 / Capitol 91245
Recorded in England with producer Glyn Johns (the Who, the Faces), this debut effort presented Miller as someone who was not only immersed in the blues but also fascinated with sound effects and sequencing, not unlike the Moody Blues or Pink Floyd. As a whole, this album flows nicely. Among the album's many highlights are "Baby's Callin' Me Home" (written by Boz Scaggs), "Stepping Stone," "Roll with It," "Junior Saw It Happen," and the spacey Mellotron-heavy ballad "In My First Mind." —*Rick Clark*

○ **Sailor** / 1968 / Capitol 94449
Less than six months after *Children of the Future*, Miller's solid followup proved that he wasn't a flash in the pan. Like its predecessor, *Sailor* dabbled in neat segues and effects, but to a lesser degree. Miller shines on the gently acoustic "Quicksilver Girl" and haunting "Dear Mary." *Sailor* has a couple of great rockers with "Living in the U.S.A." and "Dime a Dance Romance," penned by soon-to-be-departing member Boz Scaggs. —*Rick Clark*

○ **Brave New World** / Jan. 1969 / Capitol 91246
From the anthemic opening title cut, accelerating through to the crash-and-burn closer, "My Dark Hour" (featuring Paul McCartney ghosting on drums, bass, and vocals under the pseudonym of Paul Ramon), *Brave New World* is a tour de force. Other standout tracks include Miller's atmospheric "Seasons," "Kow Kow," and "Space Cowboy," an FM rock classic. —*Rick Clark*

Your Saving Grace / Feb. 1969 / Capitol 94448
This effort is a little more subdued than *Brave New World*, with cuts like "Baby's House" and "Feel So Glad." However, Miller does lay down an authoritative groove on "Don't Let Nobody Turn You Around," while "Little Girl" features some excellent, tasty lead guitar work. Miller also included a spacey reworking of "Motherless Children." Lonnie Turner's daft "Last Wombat in Mecca" is the album's only low point. Considering this was the fourth album Miller released in two years, the weakness is hardly worth mentioning. —*Rick Clark*

Number Five / 1970 / Capitol 436
For this effort Miller went to Nashville, among other places, and recorded a wide range of material that covered everything from waxing poetic about eating hot chili to railing at the industrial military complex. In spite of this album's uneven material, it possesses many strong tunes, including "Going to Mexico," "Good Morning," and "Going to the Country." It also includes "Steve Miller's Midnight Tango." —*Rick Clark*

● **Anthology** / 1972 / Capitol 94488
This is a smartly assembled best-of collection that provides a good introduction to Miller's work up to this point. Those interested in digging deeper than this should check out *Brave New World*, *Sailor*, *Children of the Future*, and *Your Saving Grace*, in that order. —*Rick Clark*

Recall the Beginning: A Journey from Eden / 1972 / Capitol 11022
After the miserable album *Rock Love*, Miller rebounded somewhat with *Recall the Beginning: A Journey from Eden*. One side is largely throwaway stuff, but the other half features a string of dreamy compositions that culminates with the haunting "Journey from Eden." "Love's Riddle," another track from that grouping, is also fine. —*Rick Clark*

Joker / 1973 / Capitol 94445
While not so strong as some of his earlier work, *The Joker's* title cut (built off of a simple guitar riff) was Miller's first huge #1 single. "Sugar Babe" and "Something to Believe In" were also highlights. Nevertheless, Miller's focus on basic catchy material laid the groundwork for his incredibly successful late '70s albums. —*Rick Clark*

○ **Fly Like an Eagle** / 1976 / Capitol 46475
In his effort to create the ultimate playable album, Miller reincorporated his interest in spacey sound effects and neat segues and synthesized them with a batch of tightly crafted light pop/rock tunes. The result generated a load of seamless hits like "Take the Money and Run," "Rock n' Me," and the title track. —*Rick Clark*

○ **Book of Dreams** / 1977 / Capitol 46476
Recorded at the same time as *Fly Like an Eagle*, this album repeated the same formula, with the same big results. Hits included

"Jet Airliner" (a slight reworking of an old R&B tune by Paul Pena), "Jungle Love," and "Swingtown." —*Rick Clark*

★ **Greatest Hits 1974-1978** / 1978 / Capitol 46101
This collection remains, to this day, Miller's most consistent-selling catalog item. It includes all of the hit singles and important album tracks from his biggest albums. —*Rick Clark*

Born 2B Blue / 1988 / Capitol 48303
After a string of incredibly spotty albums, Miller quits noodling around with synthesizers and gimmicky effects and knuckles down with a smooth collection of jazz standards. Utilizing the formidable talents of vibe player Milt Jackson, Phil Woods (alto sax), and Ben Sidran (keys and coproduction), Miller creates an album that is playful and sophisticated. While his guitar playing is downplayed, Miller shines on "Just a Little Bit," "God Bless the Child," and the swinging "Red Top." —*Rick Clark*

○ **Best of Steve Miller (1968-1973)** / 1990 / Capitol 95271
Some duplication with *Anthology*, but a better initiation to the early days, including some cuts from *The Joker*. —*John Floyd*

○ **Steve Miller Band: Box Set** / 1994 / Capitol
This is one case where the project would have, more than likely, been better served if it was compiled without the help of the artist. This three-disc set is broken down into pre-"Joker" (Vol. 1), post-"Joker" (Vol. 2), and "Blues" (Vol. 3). While Miller aced Vol. 2's song selection, and the third disc is enjoyably playable, it's obvious he holds much of his earlier work in disregard. It's hard to justify why he would perform horrible editing jobs and fadeouts on some of his best early work. Why didn't Miller just include *Anthology*, with a couple of extra cuts, as Disc One? The set does feature great sound, and the liner notes and the pictures in the booklet are first-rate. —*Rick Clark*

Garnet Mimms

Vocals, piano / R&B, soul
With his backing band the Enchanters in the early '60s, Garnet Mimms cut several fine, underrated R&B singles, including the hit "Cry Baby." After the Enchanters fell apart in 1964, Mimms pursued a solo career that merged a sophisticated R&B backing with his gospel-influenced singing. He made many terrific records that never hit the charts; it wasn't until 1977 that he had another hit, "What It Is." But in the '60s, Mimms made many records that should have been hits; they remain criminally unheard, but fans of '60s soul and R&B should seek them out. —*Stephen Thomas Erlewine*

● **Cry Baby: The Best of Garnet Mimms** / 1993 / EMI 80183
A terrific collection of Mimms' best tracks, *Cry Baby* is the definitive retrospective of his career. —*AMG*

Ministry

Group / Alternative rock, industrial, heavy metal
When Ministry released their first EP in 1981, it seemed impossible that the band would become one of the biggest industrial terrorists of the late '80s and '90s. On their first album and EP, the band was a synth-funk duo, more similar to the Human League than Einsturzende Neubauten. Yet lead singer/guitarist Al Jourgensen was smart enough to abandon that sound and begin constructing a terrifying new form of dance music. Using heavy guitar, synthesizers, samples, distorted vocals, massive drums, noise, and tape effects, Ministry created some of the first industrial dance records to cross over to a mass audience, and it wasn't because Jourgensen diluted the power of the music. Although the band sometimes approached conventional song structures that were simply fueled by jackhammer guitars, the real reason Ministry appealed to heavy metal fans as much as the alternative crowd is because of how the band looked. Instead of the faceless, abrasive drone of KMFDM or Skinny Puppy, Ministry acted like rock stars, dressing in leather and sunglasses, playing a relentlessly heavy guitar rock that happened to have a dance beat and synthesizers. After years of slowly building a large fan base, the band completed their crossover into the mainstream with 1992's *Psalm 69;* the album's success confirmed that Ministry was one of the most popular hard rock and industrial bands of the early '90s. —*Stephen Thomas Erlewine*

Twelve Inch Singles (1981-1984) / 1987 / Wax Trax 035

All of their best-known hits and great songs before they got signed by a major label. Early techno-industrial music from the early '80s. —*John Book*

○ **Land of Rape and Honey** / 1988 / Sire 25799
Considered to be one of Ministry's best albums, this is the one that crossed them over from the industrial/alternative scene and into the heavy metal crowds. Very heavy and enjoyable from start to finish. —*John Book*

In Case You Didn't Feel Like Showing Up (Live) / 1990 / Sire 26266
A live album recorded during their most recent tour, *In Case You Didn't Feel Like Showing Up (Live)* demonstrates that a band that used a lot of technological wizardry in the studio is fully capable of playing its music on stage. —*John Book*

● **Psalm 69: The Way to Succeed & the Way to Suck Eggs** / 1992 / Sire 26727
Although this is Ministry's most accessible album, it is not a sellout. Al Jourgeson and company never let the intensity up, with the machine-like grind of the rhythm section constantly driving the same 16th-note rhythms again and again. "Just One Fix" is the best track on a remarkable, intense album that also includes "Jesus Built My Hot Rod." —*Stephen Thomas Erlewine*

Mink DeVille

b. Aug. 27, 1953, New York, NY
Vocals, guitar / Rock & roll, pop/rock
From 1977 to 1985, NYC singer and guitar slinger Willy DeVille recorded six albums with his band, Mink DeVille. Willy wrote street-tough songs but was a romantic at heart, showing his inspiration to be closer to Ben E. King and the Drifters than to Lou Reed. Mink DeVille got lumped in with other bands in the burgeoning NYC punk underground, which perhaps helped the band get gigs but also made them misunderstood. In 1987, Willy DeVille was again recording under his name, this time on his third major label. —*Decibel Dennis MacDonald*

○ **Mink DeVille** / 1977 / Capitol 91852
Energetic, no-holds-barred, smoking rock with R&B roots. Excellent. —*David Szatmary*

Return to Magenta / 1978 / K-Tel 5012
Followup to DeVille's self-titled debut. —*David Szatmary*

● **Savoir Faire (A Compilation)** / 1981 / Capitol 48854
Collecting tracks from Mink Deville's first three albums, *Savoir Faire* is a good introduction to the band's raw, stripped-down R&B-influenced rock. —*Stephen Thomas Erlewine*

Minor Threat

Group / Hardcore
Minor Threat was the definitive Washington, DC, hardcore band, writing the rules for straight-edge, hardcore punk rockers. Led by Ian MacKaye, the band was one of the first to reject drugs and alcohol, leading a call for self-awareness, as well as having a fiercely intelligent political bent to their music. Each of their songs were short, sharp, and lethal, made all the more frightening by MacKaye's raging vocals. Minor Threat wouldn't have been half as invigorating and powerful as they were if they didn't have his literate, intelligent lyrics; they were simple, direct, and vicious, much like the band's music. After two years of recording, the band broke up in 1983; MacKaye went on to form the more successful—but no less uncompromising—Fugazi, yet Minor Threat remains his most influential band. —*Stephen Thomas Erlewine*

★ **Complete Discography** / 1988 / Dischord 40
Everything the seminal hardcore band Minor Threat ever recorded is collected on this single disc; it is the ultimate statement of straight-edged, razor-sharp early '80s hardcore. —*Stephen Thomas Erlewine*

Minutemen

Group / Alternative rock, hardcore
At their best, the Minutemen made eclecticism seem as effortless as breathing: in songs that seldom lasted more than a minute (hence their name), this San Pedro, CA, trio touched on everything from jazz and funk to anarchist punk, bohemian beat poetry, and '70s dinosaur rock. Their songs (mostly written by either vocalist and guitarist D. Boon or bassist and vocalist Mike Watt) seethed with political outrage; their wry sense of humor (often

pointed at themselves) separated them from the dead-serious punk brats on the West Coast, as did the diversity of their music. Their career was cut short in 1985 when Boon died in a car crash. Watt and Minutemen drummer George Hurley formed fIREHOSE in 1986. —*John Floyd*

○ **Buzz or Howl under the Influence of Heat** / 1983 / SST 016
Blurts like the earlier records, but goes further. —*Robert Gordon*

★ **Double Nickels on the Dime** / 1984 / SST 028
A double-disc set that remains their finest moment. It was here that the music, activism, and band chemistry coalesced in a forceful document of rage during the Reagan era. Boon's guitar sputters, clanks, and cajoles, while Watt and Hurley explode in rhythmic splendor. —*John Dougan*

○ **Project: Mersh** / 1985 / SST 34
The title stands for "commercial," meaning cool horns and some Mike Watt vocals. —*Robert Gordon*

○ **3-Way Tie (for Last)** / 1986 / SST 058
Their last album shows maturing political involvement and a refinement of musical skills, melding their punk roots with folk's expressionism. —*Robert Gordon*

○ **Ballot Result** / 1987 / SST 068
Post-band, semi-live album, with listener-sent ballots selecting the tracks. —*Robert Gordon*

The Misfits

Group / Hardcore
This influential early hardcore group took the Damned's infatuation with horrific themes and became one of the genre's legendary groups. Frontman Glenn Danzig formed Samhain (and later the group Danzig) following the 1983 breakup of the Misfits. —*John Floyd*

○ **Walk among Us** / 1982 / Ruby 25756
Steeped in sophomoric gore, with relentless guitars and Danzig's growl. —*John Dougan*

● **Misfits** / 1986 / Plan 9 1
A great compilation, which is lean and mean and thankfully tosses out a lot of Glenn Danzig's goofball schlock-violence drooling. As a band, the Misfits simply rampage through these 20 tracks, outtakes, and assorted stuff. The most Misfits for the dollar. —*John Dougan*

Mission of Burma

Group / Punk
This Boston group pioneered the indie-rock ethic in the early '80s, during their brief stint with the Ace of Hearts label. Their music combined avant-garde experimentation with post-punk dynamics, creating a roaring din of wailing guitars and tribal percussion. A major influence on many mid '80s bands, including R.E.M. —*John Floyd*

● **Mission of Burma** / 1987 / Rykodisc 40072
The essential collection of Burma's artful punk rock on one disc. Revised for greater clarity, this thing burns from start to finish, with Roger Miller wielding his guitar like a lethal weapon. —*John Dougan*

Joni Mitchell

b. Nov. 7, 1943
Vocals / Singer-songwriter
One of the most important artists to emerge from the singer/songwriter era of the early '70s. Mitchell first gained notice as a songwriter when her "Both Sides Now" was recorded in a hit version by Judy Collins in 1968. That same year, Mitchell released her debut album, *Joni Mitchell*. It was followed by *Clouds* in 1969 and *Ladies of the Canyon* in 1970, the latter containing the much-covered songs "Big Yellow Taxi" and "Woodstock." *Blue*, her 1971 album, was her first to hit the Top 20 and has now sold over a million copies. *For the Roses* in 1972 was Mitchell's first gold album and included her first Top 40 hit, "You Turn Me On, I'm a Radio."

Mitchell's 1974 album, *Court and Spark*, was a commercial breakthrough, hitting #2, producing two hit singles, selling a million copies, and being nominated for several Grammys. She followed it with a live album, *Miles of Aisles*, that duplicated its success. From the mid '70s on, Mitchell's work became more complicated and less folk/pop-oriented. *Hejira*, for example, paired her acoustic guitar with the bass improvisations of Jaco Pastorious, and *Don Juan's Reckless Daughter* contained impressionistic sidelong songs. Her most experimental album was *Mingus* (1979), which found her setting lyrics to the last tunes written by jazz composer Charles Mingus, at his request. The live *Shadows and Light* (1980), recorded with jazz guitarist Pat Metheny, also leaned in this direction.

Since 1982, Mitchell has adopted a slightly more accessible approach in a series of albums that take into consideration contemporary pop sounds. They have gained critical respect and sold moderately well. — *William Ruhlmann*

Clouds / May 1969 / Reprise 6341
Contains Mitchell's version of "Both Sides Now," as well as the exuberant "Chelsea Morning" and such vulnerable love songs as "I Don't Know Where I Stand." Grammy Award winner for best folk performance. — *William Ruhlmann*

Joni Mitchell / 1970 / Reprise 6293
David Crosby produced this debut album, on which Mitchell sings in a formal, restrained style and writes in a wordy, poetic style, which is nevertheless touching on such songs as "I Had a King" and "Michael from Mountains." — *William Ruhlmann*

☆ **Blue** / 1970 / Reprise 2038
An extraordinarily revealing study in romance and dependency that begins with the girlish infatuation of "All I Want" and ends with the downcast but determined "The Last Time I Saw Richard." The spare music is dominated by Mitchell's newly expressive singing and her guitar and dulcimer work. — *William Ruhlmann*

○ **Ladies of the Canyon** / Apr. 1970 / Reprise 6376
Contains several Mitchell standards, including "For Free," "Big Yellow Taxi," "Woodstock," and "The Circle Game." — *William Ruhlmann*

○ **For the Roses** / Oct. 1972 / Asylum 5057
Mitchell rails against the music industry and defends the position of the artist in isolation, at the same time moving toward more of a pop sound, notably on the Top 25 hit "You Turn Me on, I'm a Radio." — *William Ruhlmann*

★ **Court & Spark** / 1974 / Asylum 1001
Mitchell's commercial peak came with this polished collection, which features the backup of a clutch of jazz-oriented session aces. "Help Me" was a Top 10 hit, and "Free Man in Paris" reached #22. — *William Ruhlmann*

○ **Hissing of Summer Lawns** / Nov. 1975 / Asylum 1051
Mitchell turned her back on stardom with this admirable, idiosyncratic effort. — *Dan Heilman*

Hejira / Nov. 1976 / Asylum 1087
Spare recordings prominently featuring the bass of Jaco Pastorius. Mitchell sings of life on the road, literally and figuratively. — *William Ruhlmann*

○ **Mingus** / Jun. 1979 / Asylum 505
Mitchell sets lyrics to Charles Mingus's last melodies in collaboration with the composer and a Who's Who of prominent jazz musicians. — *William Ruhlmann*

Moby

Keyboards / Techno, dance
During the late '80s and early '90s, Moby established himself as one of the leading DJs and artists in the American and English techno and rave scenes. Moby was a devout Christian and vegetarian, making him an anomaly in the hedonistic world of raves; his throbbing music, not his message, is what earned him a devoted cult following. By the time he signed to a major label in 1993, his bright, danceable techno was going out of style, being replaced by a new wave of ambient artists, yet he continued to make records that were among the best dance music of the decade. — *Stephen Thomas Erlewine*

● **Moby** / 1992 / Instinct 241
Moby's first solo album is a tour de force of contemporary house and rave styles, which proves what an inventive DJ and musical force he is. — *Stephen Thomas Erlewine*

Moby Grape

Group / Psychedelic, folk rock, country rock, rock & roll
There was no shortage of rock & roll in San Francisco in the late '60s. The Grateful Dead, the Jefferson Airplane, Big Brother and the Holding Company—the names go on and on. Moby Grape was, for a short while, one of the great ones. With a triple-guitar attack, the Grape presented taut, deftly arranged rock tunes, eschewing the jam-all-night approach of their contemporaries. They handled a ballad as well as a blistering rocker, and they weren't afraid to throw a country lick or a sweet harmony into the mix.

A combination of overhype and internal disarray killed the Grape after several years, and they never recaptured the brilliance of that debut. But 25 years later, most of the original members were still working together and their brief discography is regarded highly by a battery of loyal fans. — *Jeff Tamarkin*

● **Vintage: Very Best** / May 11, 1993 / CBS
It's hard to imagine a better-produced package of Moby Grape's work than this two-disc, 48-track condensation of their best late '60s recordings. The first disc of this set centers around their entire 1967 self-titled debut record (included in its entirety), which mixed blues, country, and folk influences with hard-charging psychedelic rock & roll. The result was one of the Summer of Love's more enduring works. The second disc boils their wildly inconsistent 1968-69 material down to a fairly strong and coherent selection. While it doesn't match the peak of the group's initial burst, it features some strong folk and country-rock originals that wear much better in the absence of the bloated jams and half-baked hard rock that could make their albums a chore to sit through. Each disc includes interesting demos, outtakes, and live performances that round out the legacy of this prodigiously talented but ill-fated band, which was overcome by internal strife and label/management difficulties after their promising debut. — *Richie Unterberger*

Modern English

Group / New wave
British New Wave quintet from Colchester formed in 1979 and featuring singer and guitarist Robbie Grey, guitarist Gary McDowell, bassist Mick Conroy, keyboard player Stephen Walker, and drummer Richard Brown. By 1990 personnel changes had left the group a trio of Grey and Conroy, with keyboardist, guitarist, and singer Aaron Davidson. — *William Ruhlmann*

● **After the Snow** / 1982 / 4AD 45088
Modern English had evolved into a synthesizer-driven power-pop band by the release of this second album, which features their signature hit, "I Melt with You." Ignore the 1990 remake on Tee Vee Toons. — *William Ruhlmann*

Molly Hatchet

Group / Southern rock
These Jacksonville, FL, Southern boogie boys had the good fortune to emerge at the time of Lynyrd Skynyrd's untimely demise. The group lacked a songwriter as complex and intelligent as Ronnie Van Zandt, but songs like "Flirtin' with Disaster" made them AOR favorites during the late '70s and early '80s. — *John Floyd*

Double Trouble Live / 1985 / Epic 40137
Hatchett captured live in full roar with blistering guitar work. Hot! — *Cub Koda*

● **Greatest Hits** / 1985 / Epic 46949
Nice collection of their best-known tunes. Some of southern rock's finest moments. — *Cub Koda*

Eddie Money

b. Mar. 2, 1949
Vocals / Pop/rock
Since his 1977 self-titled debut, Eddie Money (born Edward Mahoney) has enjoyed a long career as a purveyor of mainstream guitar heavy pop/rock. His hits include "Baby, Hold On," "Two Tickets to Paradise," "Shakin'," "Take Me Home Tonight," "I Wanna Go Back," "Think I'm in Love," and "Walk on Water." — *Rick Clark*

○ **Eddie Money** / 1977 / Columbia 34909
The debut album of his raspy-voiced, pop-rock tunes, which charted in the Top 40 and went platinum. — *Donna DiChario*

○ **Can't Hold Back** / 1986 / Columbia 40096
Featuring his biggest-selling single "Take Me Home Tonight," an upbeat duet with Ronnie Spector of the Ronettes. — *Donna DiChario*

● **Greatest Hits: Sound of Money** / 1989 / Columbia 45381
Money's albums are often uneven combinations of solid tracks
and filler. This collection has all the hits with none of the misses,
including "Baby Hold On," "Two Tickets to Paradise," and "No
Control." —*Donna DiChario*

The Monkees

Group / Pop/rock
To nonmusical TV executives, aware that the pop market was exploding in 1965, the idea of auditioning cute actors to star in a
show featuring a fabricated group called the Monkees (Davy
Jones, Michael Nesmith, Peter Tork, and Mickey Dolenz) seemed
like marketing genius. The public agreed, and the show was a
huge success for several years.
    The Monkees could sing, and Mike Nesmith actually was a
singer/songwriter and guitarist. They also had access to the best
material the professional songwriting world had to offer, covering songs by Neil Diamond, Goffin & King, Harry Nilsson, David
Gates, Boyce & Hart, Mann & Weil, Leiber & Stoller, Paul
Williams, and many more. As a result, the Monkees were a veri-
table pop-hit machine, charting with "Last Train to Clarksville,"
"I'm a Believer," "A Little Bit Me, a Little Bit You," "Daydream
Believer," "Valerie," "Pleasant Valley Sunday," "I'm Not Your
Stepping Stone," and many others. After the initial success, the
Monkees lobbied for more artistic control and got it. The result,
Headquarters, was #1 on the charts, and the album went gold.
Nevertheless, the high quality of material soon diminished and,
with the demise of the show, the Monkees called it quits in 1971.
    Nesmith went solo and recorded some fine country-rock al-
bums, scoring a hit with "Joanne." He also became very involved
with video production, forming the Pacific Arts Corporation in
1977.
    A well-orchestrated Monkees campaign returned the band and
their show to new popularity in 1986, thanks in part to extensive
MTV coverage. In August of 1986, seven of their albums returned
on the charts. —*Rick Clark*

○ **Monkees** / 1966 / Arista 8524
Their debut album, and every bit a winner. Prefab or not, there's
some classic pop-rock here. —*Jeff Tamarkin*

Pisces, Aquarius, Capricorn & Jones Ltd. / Apr. 1967 / Arista
8603
Much of the charm has worn off by the fourth album, *Pisces,
Aquarius, Capricorn & Jones, Ltd.,* but in its place is some real
experimentation. —*Jeff Tamarkin*

○ **More of the Monkees** / Feb. 1967 / Arista 8525
Album #2 contains some killer garage-rock among the fluffy
novelties. Not the American Beatles, but a Top 40 gem anyway. —
Jeff Tamarkin

Headquarters / Mar. 1967 / Arista 8602
Their third album and the first to feature the band as a band playing their own instruments. Not so striking as the first two but a
good Monkees album. —*Jeff Tamarkin*

● **Then & Now ... the Best of the Monkees** / 1986 / Arista 8432
The best of the single-CD collections, with 25 tracks, most of
them true Monkees classics. —*Jeff Tamarkin*

Live 1967 / 1987 / Rhino 70139
Still believe the Monkees didn't play their own music? This concert recording proves otherwise, and you know what? They
played well! —*Jeff Tamarkin*

Missing Links / 1987 / Rhino 70150
A fine selection of rarities and oddities that every Monkee ma-
niac with more than a passing interest should own. —*Jeff
Tamarkin*

Missing Links 2 / 1990 / Rhino 70903
More outtakes and obscurities. Although it's not so interesting as
the first volume, true fans shouldn't hesitate to pick it up. —*Jeff
Tamarkin*

○ **Listen to the Band** / 1991 / Rhino 70566
A four-CD boxed set that includes every Monkees track a fan
could want, and probably much more. Excessive, but a collector's
dream. —*Jeff Tamarkin*

Chris Montez

b. Jan. 17, 1943
Vocals / Rock & roll

One of the leading rockers in the Los Angeles Hispanic community after the tragic death of Ritchie Valens, Chris Montez later
mellowed out under the tutelage of Herb Alpert and tallied several MOR-style hits. His first smash was on Monogram in 1962,
"Let's Dance." It was a grinding rocker with roller-rink organ.
Montez changed his attitude after signing with A&M. With Alpert
producing, Montez adopted an easygoing approach on "Call Me,"
"The More I See You," and "Time after Time," all solid sellers in
1966. The formula quickly faded, however, and his final chart entry came the following year with "Because of You." —*Bill Dahl*

● **All-Time Greatest Hits** / 1991 / Dcc 56
Montez began as a Ritchie Valens-style rocker and reemerged as
a crooner of pop ballads in the mid '60s. He excelled at both
styles, each of which is amply documented here. —*Jeff Tamarkin*

Montrose

Group / Hard rock
After leaving the Edgar Winter Group in 1972, guitarist Ronnie
Montrose decided to form his own band, so he called a young
singer by the name of Sammy Hagar to join his new project.
Hagar left in 1975 to do his own solo project, but the band continued with other singers and various lineups before splitting up
in the early '80s. Ronnie Montrose now performs as a solo artist
and does session work from time to time. —*John Book*

● **Montrose** / 1974 / Warner Brothers 3106
The first album that still rocks as hard as it did way back in 1973,
featuring the vocals of Sammy Hagar. —*John Book*

Paper Money / 1975 / Warner Brothers 2823
The second album from Montrose with Hagar as vocalist, just as
good as their self-titled debut. Great collection of songs. —*John
Book*

○ **Warner Brothers Presents ... Montrose** / 1975 / Warner Brothers
2892
Some of the best guitar work Ronnie Montrose has ever done,
with Bob James on vocals. Contains such songs as "Matriarch,"
"Black Train," "All I Need," and "Twenty Flight Rock." —*John Book*

Moody Blues

Group / British invasion, progressive rock, pop/rock
Formed in Birmingham, England, as an R&B quintet in 1963, the
Moody Blues originally consisted of Denny Laine (guitar), Mike
Pinder (piano), Ray Thomas (harmonica), Graeme Edge (drums),
and Clint Warwick (bass). The band emerged in 1965 with a soulful cover of an American R&B number called "Go Now," which
topped the charts in both England and America. They toured with
the Beatles and seemed poised for stardom, but none of their subsequent records made any impact. The quintet soon returned to
playing the ballroom circuit, discovering at the same time that
their management had filched much of their prior earnings.
Amid these crises, Laine—who, after a furtive solo career and a
tour with Ginger Baker, became Paul McCartney's lead guitarist
in Wings—and Warwick were voted out of the group. In their
places came Justin Hayward (guitar) and John Lodge (bass).
    The Moody Blues 1966 records were heavily influenced by the
Beatles, very upbeat, and unsuccessful. But in 1967 they were
asked to record a stereo demonstration record with a major production budget, and came up with *Days of Future Passed.* Built
around the concept of a day represented by rock songs, which
were bridged by sweeping orchestral passages, this record yielded
two major hits, "Tuesday Afternoon" and "Nights in White Satin,"
of which the latter became their signature tune. The Moodies established themselves as the pop mystics of the Summer of Love,
their music blossoming on a series of impeccably produced albums in pseudo-classical glory, driven by Pinder's lush Mellotron
orchestrations, Hayward's and Lodge's multilayered guitars,
Thomas's flute, and a great beat from Graeme Edge, when he
wasn't reciting overblown poetry. Although many critics looked
down on them, the band was very popular with college-age listeners and broadened the spectrum of rock sounds, thus paving
the way for such art-rock outfits as King Crimson, Yes, and
Emerson, Lake & Palmer.
    In 1973, after seven albums, the Moodies decided to take a five-
year hiatus devoted to solo projects. Pinder exited permanently
following the 1978 comeback album, *Octave,* and was replaced
by ex-Yes keyboard player Patrick Moraz. At this point, they became less interesting—Hayward could be relied on for passionate

love songs, Lodge for driving but predictable rockers, and Thomas for his mysticism, which sounded woefully out of place in the '80s, but except for an occasional hit like 1986's nostagia-laden "In Your Wildest Dreams" (itself a look back at their own history), little of the new material stood out. The Moodies were reduced to the status of an arena oldies act. —*Bruce Eder*

Magnificent Moodies / 1965 / Polydor 820758
The R&B version of the band. A little somber at times but with some major triumphs, including "Go Now" and the Barry-Greenwich number "I've Got a Dream," which is a pretty fair Four Tops imitation. —*Bruce Eder*

○ **Days of Future Passed**/ 1967 / Polydor 18012
An alternately overblown and superbly crafted piece of psyche-delic mood music that established this band's new sound. —*Bruce Eder*

○ **In Search of the Lost Chord** / 1968 / Polydor 820168
An overtly mystical work, facing the mysterious East and laden with sound effects that seem sillier today than they did 25 years ago. But beneath those excesses are a handful of memorable tunes ("Ride My See Saw," "Legend of a Mind") and gorgeous arrangements ("Visions of Paradise"), which make this one of the most successful records ever issued by the band. —*Bruce Eder*

○ **On the Threshold of a Dream** / 1969 / Polydor 820170
Science-fiction elements dominate the theme of this concept al-bum, all about intellect versus emotion. The material lacks the simple melodic beauty of *Lost Chord*, but makes up for it some-what with a production tour de force called "The Dream" and the surrounding "Have You Heard." —*Bruce Eder*

To Our Children's Children's Children / 1969 / Polydor 820364
A beautifully produced, somewhat languid theme album built around mystical concepts of time and the perception of its pas-sage, *To Our Children's Children's Children* features the song "Gypsy," which became one of the group's most requested concert numbers (interestingly, it is said to have been inspired by the TV character Dr. Who), and the haunting and mysterious "Watching and Waiting." —*Bruce Eder*

Question of Balance / 1970 / Polydor 820211
A return to form, and to mysticism, as the group plunges into a Lewis Carroll-like array of symbolic rock songs, all seemingly in search for some mystical meaning in life. All of it is a little pre-tentious but enjoyable, and "Tortoise and the Hare" became one of their best rock numbers on stage, while "Question" became something of an FM hit. —*Bruce Eder*

○ **Every Good Boy Deserves Favour** / 1971 / Polydor 820160
Probably the strongest single album of the group's history, with the Mellotron sound developed to its richest and most distinct, and guitarist Justin Hayward contributing one classic number ("The Story in Your Eye"). The overall attempt at profound state-ment here is balanced by a beautifully dense production and some very majestic tunes ("My Song," "Emily's Song," and so on). —*Bruce Eder*

○ **Seventh Sojourn** / 1972 / Polydor 820159
The group's hardest-rocking album of their post-R&B period, con-structed around Graeme Edge and John Lodge's driving beat and generally a much leaner sound from Mike Pinder's Mellotron. At the time it was hailed as a breakthrough for the band, although it proved to be their last album for six years, and ultimately the most enduring material proved to be Lodge's "I'm Just a Singer in a Rock 'n' Roll Band" and Hayward's "New Horizons," two num-bers completely opposite in terms of orientation, one a driving rock number and the other a romantic ballad. —*Bruce Eder*

○ **This Is the Moody Blues** / 1974 / Polydor 820007
A double CD containing what purports to be the best of the group's material from 1967 through 1972 but is really more a compendium of tracks that were popular on the radio. There are enough holes to make it worth overlooking for the serious lis-tener. —*Bruce Eder*

Caught Live + 5 / 1977 / Polydor 820161
An interesting if not completely successful live recording from a 1970 Royal Albert Hall concert, which leaves something to be de-sired sonically, and padded out with leftover songs from their un-finished 1970 album. Originally released to reintroduce the group after their five-year layoff ahead of the release of the *Octave* al-bum. —*Bruce Eder*

Octave / 1978 / Polydor 820329

The band's comeback album, well written and well produced, with a strong selection of material and a leaner, more muscular sound than their earlier albums. This was their last completely ef-fective record and marked Mike Pinder's exit from the band as well as the point where Hayward and Lodge pretty much took over the songwriting chores. —*Bruce Eder*

● **Voices in the Sky: Best of the Moody Blues** / 1985 / Decca 5341
A good sampling of the Moody Blues' greatest hits from the '60s and '70s; it's fine for those who only want the hits. —*Stephen Thomas Erlewine*

○ **Greatest Hits** / 1989 / Polydor 840659
All of the Moody Blues' best songs and biggest hits from the '80s are collected on *Greatest Hits;* it's the most mainstream pop-ori-ented material the band has ever recorded. —*Stephen Thomas Erlewine*

Moonglows

R&B, doo-wop
Among the most seminal R&B and doo-wop groups of all time, the Moonglows' lineup featured some of the genre's greatest pure singers. The original lineup from Louisville included Bobby Lester, Harvey Fuqua, Alexander Graves, and Prentiss Barnes, with guitarist Billy Johnson. They were originally called the Crazy Sounds but were renamed by disc jockey Alan Freed as the Moonglows. The group also cut some recordings as the Moonlighters. Their first major hit was the #1 R&B gem "Sincerely" for Chess in 1954, which reached #20 on the pop charts. They enjoyed five more Top 10 hits on Chess from 1955 to 1958, among them "Most of All," "We Go Together," "See Saw," and "Please Send Me Someone to Love," as well as "Ten Commandments of Love." Fuqua, the nephew of Charlie Fuqua of the Ink Spots, left in 1958. He recorded "Ten Commandments of Love" as Harvey & the Moonglows with Marvin Gaye, Reese Palmner, James Knowland, and Chester Simmons before found-ing his own label, Tri-Phi. Fuqua went on to create and produce the Spinners in 1961 and wrote and produced for Motown until the early '70s. The Moonglows disbanded in the '60s, then re-united in 1972 with Fuqua, Lester, Graves, Doc Williams, and Chuck Lewis. They recorded for RCA, and a reworked version of "Sincerely" eventually charted, but wasn't a major hit. —*Ron Wynn*

● **Blue Velvet/The Ultimate Collection** / 1993 / Chess Records 9345
The Moonglows didn't invent doo-wop, but ranked among its greatest ensembles. Few rivaled them in musical sophistication, inventiveness, or flair. They could sing gorgeous heartache bal-lads, rollicking uptempo rhythm tunes, creditable period piece novelty numbers, wonderful pop covers, or shattering originals. The original lineup began doing "vocalese," then moved into doo-wop and gospel-influenced R&B harmony. They hit their stride in the mid '50s, and their greatest songs, like "Sincerely" and "Most of All," remain classics. This two-disc set contains 44 outstanding numbers, with every major Moonglows anthem and several oth-ers that weren't big hits but deserved to be, such as "Penny Arcade" and "Love Is a River." It wisely restricts material to the era when they were at their best, the '50s, and includes an excel-lent booklet with lots of anecdotal fare that doesn't neglect musi-cal analysis. —*Ron Wynn*

Gary Moore

Guitar / Hard rock, blues rock
England's Gary Moore played guitar with Colosseum before join-ing a side band created by Thin Lizzy vocalist Phil Lynott called Greedy Bastards. Moore was then asked to join Thin Lizzy in 1977, which is where he gained attention for his musicianship. After two years with them, Moore was asked to leave; Moore then became a solo artist. Although more popular in Europe and Japan, Moore remains an idol among many American guitarists, and his albums continue to sell well around the world; he also does a lot of session work with artists of all types.

During the late '80s and early '90s, Moore received consider-able acclaim for a series of blues albums. In 1994, he formed a supergroup with bassist Jack Bruce and drummer Ginger Baker called BBM. —*John Book*

● **Still Got the Blues** / 1990 / Charisma 91369

Relieved from the pressures of having to record a hit single, he cuts loose on some blues standards as well as some newer material. Moore plays better than ever, spitting out an endless stream of fiery licks that are both technically impressive and soulful. It's no wonder *Still Got the Blues* was his biggest hit. —*David Jehnzen*

○ **After Hours** / 1992 / Charisma 91825
Not wanting to leave a good thing behind, Moore reprises *Still Got the Blues* on its followup, *After Hours*. While his playing is just as impressive, the album feels a little calculated. Nevertheless, Moore's gutsy, impassioned playing makes the similarity easy to ignore. —*David Jehnzen*

Morphine

Alternative rock, rock & roll
Morphine has managed to create a bluesy, bare bones rock & roll without any guitars. Leaving the amps behind, the band relies on sliding bass lines, a squawking baritone saxophone, and understated, powerful drums. With their second album, 1993's *Cure for Pain*, Morphine began receiving a favorable reviews in mainstream publications, as well as earning a sizable cult following. —*Stephen Thomas Erlewine*

○ **Good** / Sep. 8, 1992 / Rykodisc
While it's somewhat uneven, the stark simplicity of the band's stripped-down approach and the barking exchanges between the sliding bass and baritone sex make Morphine's debut album a worthwhile listen. —*Stephen Thomas Erlewine*

● **Cure for Pain** / Sep. 1993 / Rykodisc 10262
With stronger songwriting and a darker, more menacing atmosphere, Morphine's second album improves on their debut. —*Stephen Thomas Erlewine*

Van Morrison

b. Aug. 31, 1945
Vocals / Singer-songwriter, pop/rock
For years, the works of Leadbelly, Robert Johnson, Hank Williams, Howlin' Wolf, Jimmie Rodgers, and other legends of American folk-music forms have inspired subsequent generations of artists to capture the blues within themselves. Many artists may have had the style or inflections down textbook perfect, but with an end result as insubstantial and hollow as the false-fronted buildings of a Hollywood movie set; no matter how much the outside had been dirtied up, investigation usually reveals that the place had truly never been lived in. Irishman Van Morrison is one of those truly gifted artists who goes way beyond the props. There seems to be an almost mystical connection between the soul of the blues and his voice and vision. As a result, Morrison's blues aren't limited to any one form of music; he takes in all that moves him.

While fronting the group Them in the mid '60s, Morrison's intense passion set him apart from the generally poppy British Invasion sound, with songs like "Mystic Eyes," "Here Comes the Night," and the classic "Gloria."

Morrison went solo in 1967 and scored a #10 hit with "Brown Eyed Girl." In 1968 he signed with Warner Brothers and released the brilliant debut *Astral Weeks*, a synthesis of jazz and folk. Cut in 48 hours, it defied pop-radio airplay with its lengthy open-ended compositions. Morrison followed with a series of R&B-influenced albums, many of which are some of the greatest albums ever released in the rock era.

Much of Morrison's music has aged very gracefully, largely due to his commitment to artistic vision rather than fads or trends. Over the years, his work has mellowed with dignity, getting deeper into Christian mystical spirituality. —*Rick Clark*

☆ **Astral Weeks** / 1968 / Warner Brothers 1768
Recorded in a concentrated burst over a couple of days, *Astral Weeks* is one of the most uncompromising albums ever recorded by a major artist. Containing eight cuts that were more like impressionistic sound renderings than conventional melodic song structures, *Astral Weeks* treated the social outsiders that populated its grooves (the transvestite in "Madame George" or the dealer in "Slim Slow Rider") with dignity and compassion. Morrison's free-associative wail, over a sympathetic rhythm section that predominantly drew from folk and jazz, made *Astral Weeks* an album that defied passive listening. His intonation might vary too much for some ears, but if you really *listen*, his

soulful vocal flights will (as Dylan said concerning the function of art) practically stop time. Bassist Richard Davis's lyrical counterpoint and Modern Jazz Quartet drummer Connie Kay's sensitive rhythmic shadings are among this album's most stunning musical elements. Listing highlights is practically pointless, as *Astral Weeks* should be taken as a whole. —*Rick Clark*

☆ **Moondance** / Jan. 1970 / Warner Brothers 3103
After *Astral Weeks*, Morrison switched gears for *Moondance*, a flawless collection of more accessible R&B-rooted material, which drew from easygoing swing ("These Dreams"), upbeat shuffles ("Come Running"), and gospel-influenced song structures like "Crazy Love" and "Caravan," the latter a celebration of radio that didn't pander to that medium's more self-congratulatory nature. The jazzy title cut is a classic, as is "Into the Mystic," a song that essentially encapsulated Morrison's artistic bent. *Moondance's* tasteful production imbued the music with a timeless quality. —*Rick Clark*

○ **His Band & Street Choir** / Feb. 1970 / Warner Brothers 1884
A noticeable step down from the amazing *Moondance*, primarily in the sense that some of the material and performances lack Morrison's characteristic edge. Nevertheless, Morrison's immersion into R&B helped produce his highest-charting track, "Domino," as well as two lesser hits, "Blue Money" and "Call Me Up in Dreamland." —*Rick Clark*

○ **Tupelo Honey** / 1971 / Warner Brothers 1950
The pastoral *Tupelo Honey* was another fine Morrison album, which ranged from the R&B rock of "Wild Night" to the folky gospel of the title cut, a heavenly love letter. —*Rick Clark*

○ **Saint Dominic's Preview** / 1972 / Warner Brothers 2633
Rarely has there ever been so joyous a rocker as "Jackie Wilson Said (I'm in Heaven When You Smile)," with its brilliantly arranged cascading horn lines. That's just one of many delights found here. From the inspirational title cut's tale of resolve to the primally prayerful "Listen to the Lion," *Saint Dominic's Preview* stands as one of Morrison's finest albums. —*Rick Clark*

○ **It's Too Late to Stop Now** / Jan. 1974 / Warner Brothers 2760
This dynamic double-disc set finds Morrison covering everything from his early work with Them, through *Astral Weeks*, to his early '70s Warner hits and album tracks. Morrison is in great vocal form, and the band, the Caledonia Soul Orchestra, is exceptionally hot. Any fan of Morrison's should own this one. —*Rick Clark*

○ **Veedon Fleece** / Feb. 1974 / Warner Brothers 2805
His most willfully introspective album since *Astral Weeks*, *Veedon Fleece* (written in Ireland) is almost a classic, full of delicately rendered reflections and more open-ended vocal excursions. Morrison runs out of steam slightly during the second half of the proceedings, but not enough to keep this from being a pretty magical album. Highlights are "You Don't Pull No Punches but You Don't Push the River," "Fair Play," "Linden Arden Stole the Highlights," "Streets of Arklow," and "Comfort You." —*Rick Clark*

A Period of Transition / 1977 / Warner Brothers 2987
On paper, the collaboration of Morrison with Dr. John looked awfully good. While *A Period of Transition* failed to live up to its potential, it did have some wonderful songs, like "Heavy Connection" and "It Fills You Up" (a particular favorite). The flat-sounding mixes tend to rob the sparks out of the music, making some of this album's more expressive moments sound forced. —*Rick Clark*

Wavelength / 1978 / Warner Brothers 3212
The self-produced *Wavelength* marked an improvement over *A Period of Transition*, producing a near-hit with the title cut. Other highlights included "Santa Fe," cowritten with Jackie DeShannon. —*Rick Clark*

○ **Into the Music** / 1979 / Warner Brothers 26248
Five years after Van's last great album (*Veedon Fleece*), he returned with one of his finest albums, *Into the Music*, which fused the earthly with the spiritual. Highlights included "Bright Side of the Road," "Full Force Gale," "Angelou," and a version of "It's All in the Game." Not the first place to go to discover Morrison, but a masterful album, nonetheless. —*Rick Clark*

Beautiful Vision / 1982 / Warner Brothers 3652
Beautiful Vision improved upon its meandering predecessor, *Common One*, first by having some stronger melodies, and sec-

ond by having a song as mystically upbeat as "Cleaning Windows." —*Rick Clark*

○ **Live at the Grand Opera House Belfast** / 1984 / PolyGram 818336

Not so fiery as *It's Too Late to Stop Now,* but an enjoyable set, featuring "It's All in the Game," "Cleaning Windows," and other tracks from this period. —*Rick Clark*

○ **Poetic Champions Compose** / 1987 / PolyGram 832585

The hypnotic string arpeggios and rolling rhythms of "The Mystery," the gentle exhortation of "Did Ye Get Healed," and even reverberant cocktail-jazz instrumentals like "Spanish Steps" help make the meditative *Poetic Champions Compose* one of Morrison's better albums during the '80s. —*Rick Clark*

○ **Avalon Sunset** / 1989 / PolyGram 839262

Avalon Sunset's evocative melodies and almost prayful sentiments make this one of Morrison's finest albums during the '80s. Some might find this album's rich orchestration a little too close to easy listening, but repeated listenings reveal it adds a quiet dignified elegance and atmospheric unity to the proceedings not unlike the strings on Marvin Gaye's trancendent *What's Going On.* "I'm Tired Joey Boy," "Orangefield," "Have I Told You Lately," "I'd Love to Write Another Love Song," and the supplicatory "When Will I Learn to Live in God" are among the many highlights. *Avalon Sunset* is the mature, timeless work of an artist beyond fashion. —*Rick Clark*

★ **Best of Van Morrison** / Jan. 1990 / PolyGram 841970

This is a strong collection of many of Van Morrison's best songs. Of particular note is the inclusion of "Wonderful Remark," previously only available on *The King of Comedy* soundtrack. That alone makes this worth having. Many of the key Them tracks are here ("Gloria," "Here Comes the Night"), as is Morrison's classic "Brown Eyed Girl." Even though it's a strong sampler, it fails to draw a complete-enough picture of the depth of his work. Sonically, this CD is quite impressive. —*Rick Clark*

Enlightenment / Feb. 1990 / PolyGram 847100

Morrison dispensed with the super-reflective spirit that dominated many of his albums from the '80s and returned to a more relaxed, almost playful effort with *Enlightenment.* "In the Days before Rock 'n' Roll" is a particular highlight. Not one of his best albums, but a nice change of pace. —*Rick Clark*

○ **Bang Masters** / 1991 / Epic 47041

Excellent sound and packaging of Morrison's work at Bert Bern's Bang label. The tracks range from the morose "T. B. Sheets" to his pop standard "Brown Eyed Girl." This is a must for fans who want to go deeper than just obtaining his obviously classic albums. —*Rick Clark*

○ **Best Of Van Morrison, Vol. 2** / Jan. 1993 / PolyGram 517760

Unlike *Best Of Van Morrison*'s dependence on his early Warner Brothers catalog, this collection exclusively features his later Polygram work and pre-Warners sides with his old band Them. While not as strong, there are some wonderful tracks, such as "When WIll I Ever Learn to Live in God," "Coney Island," "Enlightenment," "Hymns to the Silence," and "The Mystery." —*Rick Clark*

A Night in San Francisco / 1994 / PolyGram

A solid double-CD live album, *A Night in San Francisco* features Morrison in fine form running through a set list that features a generous overview of his work, many which have appeared on other live sets. Morrison also delivers a handful of classic numbers like "Stormy Monday," "Have You Ever Loved a Woman," "Good Morning Little Schoolgirl," "Shakin' All Over," and even Sly Stone's "Thank You Falettinme be Mice Elf Agin." This release might not eclipse his great Warners' live set, *It's Too Late to Stop Now*; nevertheless, this set conveys an appealing warmth and accessibility, as well as excellent sound. —*Rick Clark*

Morrissey

b. May 22, 1959

Vocals / Alternative pop/rock

With the Smiths, singer/songwriter Morrissey established himself as a post-punk hero, becoming the spokesman for millions of disaffected teenagers and young adults with his literate, biting, and sensitive lyrics and dramatic vocals. After the band broke up in 1987, he pursued a solo career, releasing his first album the following year. While he released several excellent singles in the

late '80s, he ultimately began to sink into his persona without producing enough quality songs. After 1991's self-absorbed *Kill Uncle,* many critics considered him as a has-been, with his best work in the past. Thanks to the explosive, Mick Ronson-produced *Your Arsenal,* Morrissey regained his credibility. The album was almost universally acclaimed as one of the best of the year, and many said it was his best work since the Smiths' masterpiece *The Queen Is Dead.* His fan base continued to grow, both in size and devotion. With 1994's *Vauxhall and I,* he even had a hit single ("The More You Ignore Me, the Closer I Get") scrape the Top 50 singles chart in America, which would have been unthinkable when "Hand in Glove" was released a decade earlier. —*Stephen Thomas Erlewine*

○ **Viva Hate** / 1988 / Sire 25699

Morrissey pairs with Stephen Street for an album very much in the mold of his Smiths work, i.e., melodic rock dominated by jangly guitar serving as a musical bed for the singer's idiosyncratic lyrical interests and unconcerned delivery on such songs as "Everyday Is like Sunday" and "Hairdresser on Fire." —*William Ruhlmann*

○ **Bona Drag** / 1990 / Sire 26221

This collection of singles somehow plays nicely in as an album, much like the Smiths' *Hatful of Hollow.* Featuring some of Morrissey's finest songs ("Everday Is Like Sunday," "Piccadilly Palare," "The Last of the Famous International Playboys," "Suedehead"), *Bona Drag* is far preferable to *Kill Uncle,* the proper album that followed. —*Steve Aldrich*

Kill Uncle / 1991 / Sire 26514

Clive Langer and Alan Winstanley provide a pop production dominated by keyboards for this typically catchy collection, with typically off-kilter songs like "(I'm) the End of the Family Line." —*William Ruhlmann*

● **Your Arsenal** / 1992 / Sire 26994

Following the dour *Kill Uncle, Your Arsenal* is a hard-rocking, shocking return to form. From the opening of "You're Gonna Need Someone on Your Side," this is the most overt rock & roll of Morrissey's career. The inspired choice of Mick Ronson as producer solidifies the album's link to '70s glam influences. And Morrissey serves up his best material since *The Queen is Dead.* —*Steve Aldrich*

○ **Vauxhall and I** / 1994 / Sire 45451

While it isn't a gutsy rock & roll record like *Your Arsenal,* *Vauxhall and I* is equally impressive. Filled with carefully constructed guitar-pop gems, the album contains some Morrissey's best material since the Smiths. Out of all of his solo albums, *Vauxhall and I* sounds the most like his former band, yet the textured, ringing guitar on this record is an extension of his past, not a replication of it. In fact, with songs like "Now My Heart Is Full" and "Hold on to Your Friends," Morrissey sounds more comfortable and peaceful than he ever has. And "The More You Ignore Me, the Closer I Get," "Speedway," and "Spring-Heeled Jim" prove that he hasn't lost his vicious wit. —*Stephen Thomas Erlewine*

Steve Morse Band

Group / Fusion

Guitarist and composer Steve Morse was the leader and main composer for his band the Dregs during the late '70s and early '80s. He went on to join the band Kansas for two albums in addition to leading his own group, the Steve Morse Band. —*Paul Kohler*

● **Introduction** / 1984 / Elektra 60369

Solo debut album of instrumental fusion rock from the former guitarist with the Dregs/Dixie Dregs. *Introduction* features an excellent mix of styles and top-notch playing. Guitarist Albert Lee guests on this effort. Highlights include the hyperdrive "Cruise Missile," "General Lee," and the anthemic title track. —*Paul Kohler*

Stand Up / 1985 / Elektra 60448

A rock/jazz/country blend and an excellent mix of instrumental and vocal material, with a cameo by guitarist Eric Johnson and guest vocalists. —*Paul Kohler*

Southern Steel / 1991 / MCA 10112

Uptempo, hard-hitting, instrumental rock virtuosity. Morse always delivers. —*Paul Kohler*

Mother Love Bone

Group / Hard rock, heavy metal

When other Seattle bands were releasing singles and EPs of hard garage grunge, Mother Love Bone had their sights set on the arenas, making a grandiose heavy metal that recalled Zeppelin and Aerosmith with a slight punk fervor; in a sense, the band was a response to Guns N' Roses' sleazy guitar boogie. Considering that guitarist Stone Gossard and bassist Jeff Ament formed the rhythmic core of the Stooges-soaked Green River, it was a little strange that the band played it so safe, but that was mainly due to the lead vocalist, Andrew Wood. Wood was a modern day hippie, preaching love and understanding as well as a healthy dose of sex. Most of the hooks came from Gossard and Ament, but Wood was the focal point. The band was set to make their stab at the big time with 1990's *Apple*, but Wood died of a heroin overdose before it was released; the *Temple of the Dog* album, featuring Gossard, Ament, Soundgarden's Matt Cameron and Chris Cornell, and vocalist Eddie Vedder, was released as tribute to him.

Gossard and Ament went on to form Pearl Jam, which took many of the hard rock elements of Mother Love Bone, except it was rawer and more honest. Also, Pearl Jam had a distinctive lead vocalist and lyricist in Eddie Vedder, who easily eclipsed the macho posturings of Wood. —*Stephen Thomas Erlewine*

● **Mother Love Bone** / 1990 / Stardog 512884
Released after the phenomenal success of their descendants Pearl Jam, *Mother Love Bone* collects everything Mother Love Bone ever released. Ever since their record contract was signed, the band was pegged to be huge, but the death of singer Andrew Wood before their first album's release eliminated any hopes of the big time for the band. Mother Love Bone's resurrection of the epic hard rock of the '70s was quite good, but quite derivative. While Wood was a fine singer, he wasn't a very original vocalist and often sounded very similar to Robert Plant. The remaining members of Mother Love Bone found a much better singer and lyricist in Eddie Vedder, resulting in the vastly more original Pearl Jam. —*Stephen Thomas Erlewine*

Mötley Crüe

Group / Hard rock, heavy metal

As far as commercial appeal goes, Mötley Crüe was one of the top heavy metal bands in the '80s, exploiting every trend in metal and hard rock without seeming crass or opportunistic. *Shout at the Devil* had them embracing a theatrical, Kiss-styled Satanism; *Theater of Pain* saw them ride the line between glam and pop metal; *Girls Girls Girls* had them toughening up their image with leather and harder guitars, reaching for a street credibility; *Dr. Feelgood* had them sharpening the guitars of the previous album while adding a pop sensibility that took them straight to the top of the charts. Throughout their changes, the Crue remained joyously sleazy and stupid, with their Zeppelin/Aerosmith-based hard rock making them high school favorites across the country. After the success of *Dr. Feelgood*, singer Vince Neil was fired from the band. When the band reemerged in 1994, they had changed their image again, falling somewhere between Ministry, Stone Temple Pilots, and Soundgarden in an attempt to recapture the new alternative metal audience, but for the first time the band appeared opportunistic and the album flopped. —*Stephen Thomas Erlewine*

Too Fast for Love / 1981 / Elektra 60174
Sleazy heavy metal before all the hype took over their home of Los Angeles. Their debut album, remixed from the original on their own Leathur label. —*John Book*

○ **Shout at the Devil** / 1983 / Elektra 60289
Possibly the best mainstream heavy metal band of the '80s, with their best album to date. —*John Book*

Theater of Pain / 1985 / Elektra 60418
Powered by a sneering remake of Brownsville Station's "Smokin' in the Boy's Room" and the classic power ballad "Home Sweet Home," *Theater of Pain* was Mötley Crüe's biggest hit to date, even if the rest of the album wasn't as strong as its hit singles. —*Stephen Thomas Erlewine*

○ **Girls, Girls, Girls** / 1987 / Elektra 60725
With *Girls, Girls, Girls*, Mötley Crüe toughens up their music as well as their image, turning in an album of greasy, sleazy hard-

rock boogie that, at its best, rivals Aerosmith. —*Stephen Thomas Erlewine*

○ **Dr. Feelgood** / 1989 / Elektra 60829
Producer Bob Rock gives the Crue a high-gloss, corporate rock sheen, eliminating most of the band's self-indulging tendencies. Thanks to a detox program, the Crue itself sounds tighter, giving *Dr. Feelgood* a strong but mindless catchiness. *Dr. Feelgood's* four Top 40 hits—including the ballad "Without You," the driving "Kickstart My Heart," and caustic "Don't Go Away Mad (Just Go Away)—form the heart of the album, but solid album tracks like "S.O.S. (Same Old Situation)" help make *Dr. Feelgood* the band's best record. — *Stephen Thomas Erlewine*

● **Decade of Decadence** / 1991 / Elektra 61204
A collection of some of their hits and the best of their album material. —*John Book*

Motörhead

Group / Heavy metal, thrash

English metal band formed in 1975. Led by bassist Ian "Lemmy" Kilminster, the band was originally named Bastard but soon changed to Motörhead (American slang for speed freak), a name that suited their style of playing very well. Along with guitarist Larry Wallis and drummer Lucas Fox, Lemmy and the boys brought the concept of the power trio to new heights, using the bass almost as a lead instrument behind a wall of noise emanating from the other two instruments. They attracted a huge following in England during the late '70s punk-rock era with their combination of breakneck speed and deafening volume. Though Lemmy remains as the only original member (having revamped the lineup several times over), their style hasn't progressed much in almost 20 years. Their hardcore fans wouldn't have it any other way. —*Cub Koda*

○ **Ace of Spades** / 1980 / Roadrunner 9227
The forefathers of thrash, with one of their better-known albums. *Ace of Spades* features guitarist "Fast" Eddie Clark, who later left and formed Fastway. Highlights include "(We Are) the Road Crew" and the title track. —*John Book*

○ **Iron Fist** / 1982 / Roadrunner 9355
Also a pretty good early album from the band. —*John Book*

★ **No Remorse** / 1984 / Roadrunner 9354
No Remose is a solid collection (in spite of the omission of the band's Chiswick recordings), consisting of key album, EP, and single tracks. Included are Motörhead standards like "Killed by Death" and "Please Don't Touch." Unfortunately, this Roadracer reissue of the 1984 release omits "Leaving Here" and "Louie Louie." Overall, *No Remose* is a great intro to the band's earlier thrash sound. —*Rick Clark*

○ **Orgasmatron** / 1986 / Sinclair 1007
For *Orgasmatron*, Motörhead enlisted producer Bill Laswell, who assisted the band in achieving a dense wall of sound, which was a little too compressed sounding. Highlights on *Orgasmatron* are "Built for Speed," "Deaf Forever," and the title track, an incredible aural sludgefest that borders on psychedelic. —*Rick Clark*

○ **1916** / 1991 / WTG 46858
Produced by Pete Solley and Ed Stasium, *1916* is Motörhead's most diversified effort, including humorous sendups like "Ramones" (a tribute to the New York speed punkers) and "Angel City" (a love letter to Los Angeles), as well as grim topics, like the dying World War I soldier's perspective in the title track. Motörhead manages to cover all this territory without ever losing their basic sonic integrity. All in all, *1916* is arguably this band's finest release thus far. —*Rick Clark*

March or Die / Jul. 14, 1992 / WTG 48997
The original punk-metal fusion band continues to play it raw as sushi. But Motörhead have come out with their most user-friendly and well-produced work. The toned down fury even allows for an emotive ballad-duet with Ozzie Osbourne on "I Ain't No Nice Guy," with guest guitar courtesy of Slash from Guns N' Roses. The Motörhead of 10—or even five—years ago would have chosen death over recording this, but it works—piano, violin and all. —*Roch Parisien*

Motors

Group / Pop/rock

After several years in England's pub-rock scene, ex-Duck Deluxe members Nick Garvey and Andy McMaster formed the Motors in 1977 with vocalist Bram Tchaikovsky and drummer Ricky Slaughter. Their first album was a splendid piece of guitar-driven pop-rock highlighted by the single "Dancing the Night Away." *Approved By* was the album that earned them the UK hits "Airport" and "Forget about You"; the record saw the band's songwriting improving with forceful melodies and invigorating performances. After that record, the Motors split up; Garvey and McMaster used the band's name for the 1980 album *Tenement Steps*, which didn't equal the spark of their first two records. — *Stephen Thomas Erlewine*

Motors 1 / 1977 / Virgin 1821
Their debut features a reworked version of pub rock with an edgier punk feel. Includes the catchy single "Dancing the Night Away," the highpoint of the album. — *Chris Woodstra*

● **Approved by the Motors** / 1978 / Virgin 1820
Their second album shows a marked improvement over the debut, with a stronger melodic base and catchier songs, including the British hits "Airport" and "Forget about You." The CD version adds three bonus tracks. — *Chris Woodstra*

○ **Tenement Steps** / 1979 / Virgin 13139
The band, now reduced to Nick Garvey and Andy McMaster, is a little too ambitious and overproduced. While not their best album, it does include one of their finest songs, "Love and Loneliness," making it worthwhile for those who liked the first two albums. — *Chris Woodstra*

Mott the Hoople

Group / Rock & roll, glam rock, hard rock
Originally a Herefordshire, England, band named Silence, Mott the Hoople was signed to Island in 1969 by A&R man Guy Stevens, who suggested that they change their name (inspired by a Willard Manus novel) and dump their lead singer, Stan Tippens, in their search for a stronger identity. Tippens was made road manager (he later worked for the Pretenders), and Ian Hunter (an engineering apprentice) was brought in to sing and play piano. Stevens, in turn, became the band's manager and producer. Between 1969 and 1972, Mott cut four albums, two of which contained some great rock & roll. Nevertheless, the band's future looked bleak, due to diminishing sales with each release. A happenstance pairing with ascending glam-rock star David Bowie caused a fortuitous turn of events, which culminated in a new sound and a record deal with Columbia. The result of their collaboration was the Bowie-produced *All the Young Dudes*, a blatant glam sendup. The title cut became Mott's first hit, and in the time one could say the words "image makeover," Mott was camping it up, teetering around the stage in makeup and cartoonish platform shoes. Their followup effort, *Mott*, was the band's finest artistic statement, loosely addressing the travails of rock "stardom." After that, Mott began to lose its focus, and the departure of lead singer/songwriter Ian Hunter hastened the band's demise. They eventually broke up in 1976. Hunter went on to enjoy a moderately successful cult following with his solo career. As a songwriter, he scored some substantial hits with artists like Great White ("Once Bitten Twice Shy") and Barry Manilow ("Ships"). — *Rick Clark*

○ **Mott the Hoople** / 1969 / Atlantic 8258
Mott the Hoople, with its hard-rock variation of Dylan's *Blonde on Blonde* sound, stands as one of the band's better efforts. This debut sported some fine originals, particularly "Backsliding Fearlessly" and "Rock and Roll Queen," as well as some unusual (but hip) song covers, like Sonny Bono's "Laugh at Me" and Doug Sahm's "At the Crossroads." The Kinks' garage-riff standard "You Really Got Me" got a high-octane instrumental treatment. Only on the middle section of the lengthy "Half Moon Bay" does *Mott the Hoople* lose momentum. — *Rick Clark*

☆ **Brain Capers** / 1971 / Atlantic 8304
After a couple of fairly dismal efforts, Mott rebounded with one of the great lost hard-rock albums of the '70s. Released with practically no fanfare whatsoever, *Brain Capers* sank without a trace. Certainly, in the decade that produced Styx and Journey, *Brain Capers* (from the audaciously titled "Death May Be Your Santa Claus," to the closing "The Wheel of the Quivering Meat Conception") convincingly drew a line in the sand, revealing most everything called "rock" to be a fraud. Some of this was due, in

part, to the return of Guy Stevens at the production helm. Among the album's highlights are versions of Dion's "Your Own Backyard," the Youngblood's "Darkness Darkness," and Ian Hunter's powerful "The Journey," "Sweet Angeline," and the previously mentioned "Death ...." — *Rick Clark*

○ **All the Young Dudes** / 1972 / Columbia 31750
Just as Mott was about to pack it in due to their amazing lack of public acceptance, David Bowie entered the picture, and with the recording of a few cannily conceived songs, containing strong gay allusions (Bowie's "All the Young Dudes" and Mott's "Sucker" and "One of the Boys"), Mott went from potential has-beens to avatars of the glam-rock movement. The Bowie-produced album contained a version of Lou Reed's "Sweet Jane" and Mick Ralph's "Ready for Love," one of his finest bits of writing to date. As on many albums of that genre, the production sounds tight-assed, stiff, and dry. Nevertheless, Mott makes the proceedings rock fairly convincingly. — *Rick Clark*

☆ **Mott** / 1973 / Columbia 32425
Regarded by many to be their finest album, this self-produced effort was a loosely conceived concept album about the ups and downs of rock & roll success. *Mott* contained two UK hits with "All the Way from Memphis" and "Honaloochie Boogie." Other highlights were "The Ballad of Mott the Hoople," "Whizz Kid," "Violence," and "Drivin' Sister." — *Rick Clark*

★ **Ballad of Mott** / 1993 / Columbia 46973
Mott the Hoople were punks without realizing it. Combining a heavy-metal roar with the sneering hipster stance of 1965 Bob Dylan, Mott the Hoople made some of the best, most original rock and roll of the early '70s. *The Ballad of Mott: A Retrospective* is a terrific chronicle of their Columbia recordings, with four tracks from their early Atlantic albums thrown in for good measure. Because of David Bowie's production of *All the Young Dudes* and their flamboyant stage costumes, Mott was tossed into the glam-rock scene, although their music was smarter, more cynical, and nastier than other glam-rock bands. Their vicious attitude and ferocious riffs made the band an enormous influence on the punk/new wave movement of the late '70s. While it doesn't feature enough material from the early Atlantic albums, *The Ballad of Mott: A Retrospective* is all the Mott most people will need. Nearly all of the songs from their two classic Columbia albums, *All the Young Dudes* and *Mott*, are included, along with a number of tracks from *The Hoople* and several of B sides and unreleased tracks. While the band didn't receive much attention at the time, their music sounds vital over 20 years later. — *Stephen Thomas Erlewine*

Bob Mould

b. 1961
Vocals, guitar / Alternative pop/rock
After Hüsker Dü fell apart in late 1987, guitarist/singer Bob Mould took a year off before reemerging with his solo debut, *Workbook*, in 1989. Compared with the sonic fireworks of his previous band, the largely acoustic *Workbook* was a shock, but a pleasant one. The following year, Mould released *Black Sheets of Rain*, a devastatingly brutal record overflowing with raging guitars; the only thing that tied the two records together was their merciless introspection and consistently strong songwriting. After *Black Sheets*, Mould formed a new trio, Sugar, which released its first album in 1992. — *Stephen Thomas Erlewine*

● **Workbook** / 1989 / Virgin 91240
Mould takes a less raucous, more coherent approach than on his Hüsker Dü work for this solo debut, which combines somewhat pessimistic lyrics with majestic guitar parts matched to a prominent cello. — *William Ruhlmann*

○ **Black Sheets of Rain** / May 1990 / Virgin 91395
A scalding, monolithic collection of soul-baring lyrics and primal guitars, *Black Sheets of Rain* is extremely powerful musically, yet it's slightly monotonous. Nevertheless, the record features several inspired songs from Mould, including the catchy single "It's Too Late." — *Stephen Thomas Erlewine*

○ **Poison Years** / 1994 / Virgin
Drawing heavily from *Black Sheets of Rain*, this anthology of Mould's time at Virgin doesn't give enough space to the brilliant *Workbook*, but it does have several fiery live tracks, including a harrowing version of Richard Thompson's "Shoot Out the Lights." — *Stephen Thomas Erlewine*

Mountain

Group / Hard rock

Founded in 1969 by Cream producer, bassist, and vocalist Felix Pappalardi and 250-pound vocalist and lead guitarist Leslie West (from the Long Island group the Vagrants), Mountain specialized in bottom-heavy mid-tempo hard rock. The band was rounded out by organist Steve Knight and drummer Corky Laing's George-of-the-jungle-style pounding. West's distinctive sustain-drenched lead sound and economical phrasing made him one of the most emulated guitarists at the turn of the '70s.

During their brief existence, Mountain hit the charts with *Mountain Climbing* (which included "Mississippi Queen"), *Nantucket Sleighride*, and *Flowers of Evil. —Rick Clark*

● **Mountain Climbing!** / 1970 / Columbia/Legacy 47361
This includes the hit "Mississippi Queen." All in all, this is Mountain's strongest studio effort. —*Rick Clark*

○ **Best of Mountain** / 1973 / Columbia 32079
This collection contains most of the band's recorded highlights, except for the curious omissions of "Dreams of Milk and Honey" (off of the debut *Leslie West—Mountain*) and "Silver Paper" (off of *Mountain Climbing*). Included are "Mississippi Queen," "The Animal Trainer and the Toad," "For Yasgur's Farm," and their version of Jack Bruce's "Theme for an Imaginary Western." —*Rick Clark*

The Move

Group / Pop/rock

A quintet (later reduced to four) of mod-poseurs from Birmingham and led by guitarist/oboist/songwriter/singer Roy Wood, the Move wasted a lot of time and energy on image and squandered some great music. Influenced by the Beatles, Eddie Cochran, Duane Eddy, and any number of R&B sources (they even covered "Zing Went the Strings of My Heart," a Coasters number that goes back to Judy Garland in the '30s, in creditable doo-wop style), they were equally comfortable doing merry psychedelic odes ("Flowers in the Rain") or pumping their amperage up to planet-cracking levels ("Hello Susie"). They seemed impervious to personnel shifts, which were many, and even got stronger with the addition of Jeff Lynne, a guitarist/songwriter with an even bigger Beatles fixation, in 1970. At around the same time, Wood devised the notion of an offshoot group called the Electric Light Orchestra, which was supposed to co-exist with the Move but instead replaced it, ironically enough without Wood. — *Bruce Eder*

Looking On / 1970 / Capitol 658
The Move's third album was their spottiest collection. Part of the problem came from milking songs longer than necessary. The sludgy sound of the production didn't help matters. Nevertheless, when it all came together in songs like "Brontosaurus," "When Alice Comes Back to the Farm," "Turkish Tram Conductor Blues," and "What?" it was a gloriously murky noise. —*Rick Clark*

☆ **Shazam** / 1970 / A&M 4259
The single most accomplished album to be recorded by any of the Birmingham rock bands (which includes the Moody Blues), *Shazam* is sort of *Sgt. Pepper* with an attitude, a mixture of expansive progressive rock worthy of the Beatles and high-energy music honed by years of playing loud on stage. The rendition of Tom Paxton's "The Last Thing on My Mind" pushes these guys simultaneously into Byrds and Jimi Hendrix territory, while "Beautiful Daughter" is one of the most unabashedly pretty records of this era, and "Cherry Blossom Clinic Revisited" is defiantly strange. The album only exists as an import from Japan, paired up on one CD with the earlier *Flowers in the Rain* album (all songs in print domestically) or a better German version filled out with five live tracks from London's Marquee Club, off of the super-rare *Something Else* EP. —*Bruce Eder*

○ **Message from the Country** / 1971 / One Way 57476
The group's last good album, weaker than *Shazam* but pleasant enough in its sub-*White Album* way. —*Bruce Eder*

○ **Best of the Move (A&M)** / 1974 / A&M 3625
Really the best of the group's early period, ranging from delightfully trippy ("Here We Go Round the Lemon Tree," "Flowers in the Rain") to the downright weird ("Zing Went the Strings of My Heart," "Night of Fear") singles and album sides that helped establish the group's reputation for eccentricity. —*Bruce Eder*

★ **Great Move! The Best of the Move** / Jun. 15, 1994 / EMI America
Newly remastered editon of the group's *Message from the Country* album, fleshed out with five additional songs, including the single "Do Ya." The Beatles influence is even more pronounced here, amid the crunchy hard rock sound, especially on the bonus tracks. —*Bruce Eder*

Alison Moyet

b. Jun. 18, 1961
Vocals / Pop/rock

A bluesy-voiced British singer who gained recognition in the synth-pop duo Yaz in the early '80s. She's had three solo albums since, all of which were big UK hits. —*William Ruhlmann*

● **Alf** / 1984 / Columbia 39956
Moyet's debut attempted a gradual transition from the electronic-pop backgrounds of her Yaz work. She succeeded to the tune of three UK hits—"Love Resurrection," "All Cried Out," and "Invisible." —*William Ruhlmann*

Mudhoney

Group / Alternative rock, garage rock

With their fuzzed-out guitars and Mark Arm's straining vocals, Mudhoney defined '80s and '90s grunge rock. In fact, their 1988 debut single "Touch Me, I'm Sick" is the definitive grunge song—an obnoxious, dirty song driven by massively distorted guitars and a screaming vocal. It was a terrific, invigorating song that the band rewrote on each album that followed, but that's alright because Mudhoney only has one other song— a slow, sludgy Stooges grind. But their limitations are ultimately endearing; the band is a punk band, not like a '70s or '80s group, but like a '60s garage band, kicking out the same three chords with an unbridled enthusiasm. Leave the serious themes to Nirvana, Pearl Jam, Soundgarden, and Alice in Chains—Mudhoney makes everything sleazy and trashy, like the Russ Myers's film they named themselves after. Their records are inconsistent, but when they are good, they are great. —*Stephen Thomas Erlewine*

● **Superfuzz Bigmuff (& Early Singles)** / 1988 / Sub Pop 21
Combining the band's first EP with a handful of early singles, highlighted by the classic "Touch Me, I'm Sick," this disc showcases Mudhoney at their most furious and fine. *Superfuzz Bigmuff* keeps the overextended riffing and hypervocalizing down to a minimum, focusing on maximum-torque metallic garage raunch. A release that provides as much bite as bark. — *John Dougan and Meredith Erlewine*

Mudhoney / Jul. 1989 / Sub Pop 44
This is a collection of catchy tunes sure to make your mother cringe. —*Meredith Erlewine*

○ **Every Good Boy Deserves Fudge** / 1991 / Sub Pop 105
It's no great stylistic breakthrough, but what Mudhoney record is? Instead, it's another solid album of fuzzed-out three-chord garage rockers. There's nothing as great as "Touch Me, I'm Sick" or "In 'N' Out of Grace," but song-for-song, it's their most consistent album. —*Stephen Thomas Erlewine*

Piece of Cake / Oct. 1992 / Reprise 45090
In 1992, the year after Nirvana broke the doors to the major label down, Mudhoney finally released their first major-label album. While it is not as raw as their earlier singles, Mudhoney has not lost their apathetic, slacker attitude. Full of short jokes between tracks (ranging from a rip on techno music to 28 seconds of flatuence), *Piece of Cake* is a muddled album that shows flashes of brilliance. The thundering opener, "No End in Sight," and the pulverizing single "Suck You Dry" fill the grunge quotient, while on other tracks Mudhoney veers off into slower territory ("Blinding Sun" and "I'm Spun") that is equally successful. And the fuzz guitars never let up throughout the entire album. — *Stephen Thomas Erlewine*

○ **Five Dollar Bob's Mock Cooter Stew** / 1993 / Reprise 45439
A stop-gap EP that sounds like it was recorded in a garage, *Five Dollar Bob's Mock Cooter Stew* has some of Mudhoney's rawest and best rock & roll. —*Stephen Thomas Erlewine*

Elliott Murphy

b. Mar. 16, 1949
Vocals / Singer-songwriter, folk rock

A New York-based folk-rock singer/songwriter who emerged with the acclaimed *Aquashow* in 1973 and has since built a cult following in the United States and Europe. —*William Ruhlmann*

● **Aquashow** / 1973 / PolyGram 835587
Highly literate songs played with an instrumentation (rock band, harmonica, piano, and organ) and in a manner strongly reminiscent of mid '60s Bob Dylan. The lyrics provide a telling portrait of suburban life. —*William Ruhlmann*

Just a Story from America / 1977 / Columbia 34653
Murphy travels to England for a streamlined rock sound featuring session aces such as guitarist Mick Taylor and drummer Phil Collins. But it's the songs, such as "Drive All Night," "Rock Ballad," and the title tune, that make the album a standout. —*William Ruhlmann*

Party Girls/Broken Poets / 1984 / Dejadisc 3201
Backed by a seasoned three-piece band, Murphy again turns in a high-quality rocking collection, spearheaded by "Three Complete American Novels" and "Blues Responsibility." —*William Ruhlmann*

Milwaukee / 1986 / EMIS 101459
Murphy adopts a more contemporary rock sound (with production on two tracks by Talking Head Jerry Harrison) for songs often touching on hard and desperate themes. —*William Ruhlmann*

Peter Murphy

Vocals / Alternative pop/rock
After leaving Bauhaus and a short-lived group with ex-Japan member Mick Karn, Peter Murphy launched a solo career in 1986. Murphy's solo albums are a combination of Bauhaus's goth and the synth-based art-rock of Bowie, Roxy Music, and Japan. As his career progressed, he began writing in the stylistic restrictions of a pop song, as well as adding some dance-rock elements. —*Stephen Thomas Erlewine*

● **Deep** / 1990 / Beggars Banquet 9877
Contains Murphy's dramatic alternative rock hit "Cuts You Up." Forceful grooves and thick (somewhat dissonant) arrangements and production propel material reminiscent of David Bowie's work with Brian Eno. —*Rick Clark*

My Bloody Valentine

Group / Alternative rock
My Bloody Valentine is earsplittingly loud, constructing their records with layers of sound and noise. It may sound unlistenable at first, but the sheer sonics of the band are beautiful and shimmering, with the vocals only adding another texture to the overall sound; underneath the white noise, the band plays simple, melodic pop. Comparisons to the Jesus and Mary Chain or Sonic Youth may be inevitable, but My Bloody Valentine is much more atomspheric than either band. Their distorted noise is not confrontational or aggressive; it is rolling sheets of gorgeous dissonance. After several years of independent label releases, the band released the monolithic *Loveless* in 1991, which increased their cult dramatically. Although they haven't released a record since *Loveless*, their fan base has not diminished. —*Stephen Thomas Erlewine*

○ **Isn't Anything** / 1988 / Sire 1006
Shards of twisted, layered guitars, floating female vocals; at once horrifying and beatiful; launched a school of imitators. —*Steve Aldrich*

● **Loveless** / 1991 / Sire 26759
Grindingly assaultive, the big guitars of this monstrous, larger-than-life hunk of lush pop sink into you from track one. —*John Dougan*

My Life with the Thrill Kill Kult

Group / Alternative pop/rock, dance, house
Most house-based dance music is either completely devoid of content or has a fairly serious political consciousness. Not so with My Life with the Thrill Kill Kult. With its schlocky mix of samples, synths, beats, Satan, and sex, the group is a hyped-up, stylized psychdelic dance troupe that revels in bad taste of all kinds. And the sheer tastelessness of their records gained a large cult following in the early '90s, culminating in their *Sexplosion* album and its single, "Sex on Wheels." —*Stephen Thomas Erlewine*

● **Sexplosion!** / 1991 / Interscope 92163
A trashy kaleidoscope of an album, full of campy samples and pulsating rhythm tracks, highlighted by the single "Sex on Wheels." —*David Jehnzen*

Naked Eyes

Group / New wave
This quintessential early '80s MTV synth-pop duo, made up of Pete Byrne (vocals) and Rob Fisher (keyboards), hit it big with "Promises, Promises" and a remake of Dionne Warwick's "Always Something There to Remind Me." —*Rick Clark*

● **Promises, Promises—The Very Best of Naked Eyes** / Apr. 19, 1994 / EMI 27226
Promises, Promises features every worthwhile song Naked Eyes ever recorded, making it the definitve collection. — *AMG*

Graham Nash

b. Feb. 2, 1942, Blackpool, England
Vocals / Singer-songwriter, country rock, pop/rock
One-third of Crosby, Stills & Nash and cofounder of the Hollies, the Manchester-born Nash has long been famed for his high harmony singing and quirky songwriting. —*Bruce Eder*

● **Songs for Beginners** / 1971 / Atlantic 7204
A moving, personal work, filled with lovely nuances and ideas and even lovelier melodies. —*Bruce Eder*

Johnny Nash

b. Aug. 19, 1940
Vocals / Soul, pop/rock, reggae
Native-Texan Johnny Nash experienced his first chart success in 1958 with the hit "A Very Special Love." By the end of the '60s, Nash had begun recording in Jamaica and formed his own record labels, Joda and Jad. He became one of the first artists to bring reggae into the pop mainstream, with the 1968 hit "Hold Me Tight," 1972's #1 "I Can See Clearly Now," and a version of Bob Marley's "Stir It Up." —*Rick Clark*

● **I Can See Clearly Now** / 1972 / Epic 31607
West Indian music for a pop audience, rhythmic and melodic. Nash helped open the mass-market doors to reggae. The title song and "Stir It Up" are winners. —*Hank Davis*

Nazareth

Group / Hard rock
This Scottish hard rock quartet, fronted by Dan McCafferty, produced a string of successful FM rock hits during the '70s and early '80s. —*Rick Clark*

● **Hair of the Dog** / 1975 / A&M 3225
Hair of the Dog is Nazareth's biggest hit, as well as their best album, containing both the thundering title track and their cover of "Love Hurts," which turned out to be the blueprint for the heavy metal power ballads that dominated the pop charts of the late '80s. —*Stephen Thomas Erlewine*

The Nazz

Group / Power pop, psychedelic
The Nazz (named after a Yardbirds song, "The Nazz Are Blue") was a Philadelphia-based quartet formed in 1967 by guitarist and songwriter Todd Rundgren, bassist Carson Van Osten, drummer Thom Mooney, and vocalist and keyboard player Robert "Stewkey" Antoni. Rejecting the free-form psychedelic rock and hippie fashions of the day, the group harked back a couple of years to the British invasion, performing short, catchy pop songs, mostly written by Rundgren (sometimes with a hard-rock edge) and sporting suits and Beatles haircuts. They released their debut album, *Nazz*, in 1968 and scored a minor hit single with Rundgren's plaintive ballad "Hello, It's Me" in 1969 (it recharted in 1970, and Rundgren had a Top 5 hit with a new version in 1973). Critics and a growing audience were charmed, but the Nazz fell apart in 1969, largely because of Rundgren's ascendancy. Predictably, he went on to the greatest success after the split. —*William Ruhlmann*

● **Best of Nazz** / 1983 / Rhino 70116
Contains good examples of the band's powerful uptempo material ("Open My Eyes"), the kind of Rundgren ballad material that defined the group to its pop audience ("Hello, It's Me"), and some

interesting covers ("Kicks," a previously unreleased "Train Kept A-Rollin'"). —*William Ruhlmann*

Rick Nelson (Eric Hilliard Nelson)

b. May 8, 1940, Teaneck, NJ, **d.** Dec. 31, 1985
Vocals / Rock & roll, country rock

Ricky Nelson made it a little safer for "respectable" American teenagers to rock. When 16-year-old Ricky cut his debut single in 1957—a timid cover of Fats Domino's "I'm Walkin'," allegedly on a dare from his girlfriend—the sneering image of Elvis Presley was still taboo in many households. Nelson, the nonthreatening, cleancut youth, commanded the perfect vehicle for spreading his rocking message—his family's beloved TV sitcom, "The Adventures of Ozzie and Harriet."

With a genuine passion for Sun-style rockabilly and the searing lead-guitar work of Joe Maphis initially and later the brilliantly inventive James Burton (from "Believe What You Say" on), Ricky signed with Imperial later in 1957. He waxed one incendiary rocker after another, including "Stood Up," "Waitin' in School," and "It's Late." He introduced them via those TV airwaves, thus ensuring gold record status well into the '60s.

As the demand for unrelenting rock & roll slowly faded, Ricky's sound softened as well, with smoother material such as "Never Be Anyone Else But You" in 1959 and his 1961 chart-topper "Travelin' Man." A much-publicized name switch to Rick on his 21st birthday reflected that maturity.

But Nelson never forgot his roots, not even during the lean mid '60s on Decca, when he ran dry of fresh material and revived too many old Tin Pan Alley standards that should have stayed buried. Returning triumphantly to the top in 1972 with the introspective *Garden Party,* Rick Nelson proved emphatically that he was more than just another teen-idol hunk, right up to his fatal plane crash on New Year's Eve of 1985.

Like his idols at Sun, this kid was born to rock—and showed America that it was no sin. —*Bill Dahl*

★ **Legendary Masters** / 1971 / EMI America 92771
Nelson at his early (1957-1960) best. His youthful vocals are backed by fiery rockabilly pioneers Joe Maphis and James Burton. —*Bill Dahl*

○ **Garden Party** / 1972 / MCA 31364
This comeback introduced Nelson to a new generation. —*Bill Dahl*

Best of Rick Nelson 1963-75 / 1990 / MCA 10098
No longer Rockin' Ricky, but Responsible Rick, his Decca output was wildly inconsistent. The early efforts like "Fools Rush In" and "String Along" still feature guitarist James Burton prominently. —*Bill Dahl*

☆ **Best of Rick Nelson, Vol. 2** / 1991 / Capitol 95219
This continues the showcase of Nelson's triumphant reign on Imperial through 1962. A fascinating smattering of unissued alternate takes is included amidst all the hits. —*Bill Dahl*

Michael Nesmith

b. Dec. 30, 1943, Houston, TX
Guitar / Country rock

You'll get very little argument that Michael Nesmith's songs are the highlights of the Monkees' catalog. If given a chance on his own, Nesmith might have beat Gram Parsons in a race to invent country rock. When he ceased to be "Monkee Mike," Nesmith created rootsy country music, unaffected by the often cynical approach of numerous contemporaries. Nesmith's stature as an outside producer grew, and he eventually shed much of the country influence of his writing before ultimately shelving his musical career entirely. What remains is a sizable body of solo work that too few have investigated. Now that it is readily available again, it would be well worth the effort to check out. —*Steve Aldrich*

Newer Stuff / 1989 / Rhino 70168
This compilation of later solo material is often glossy and overreaching but still quite impressive. —*Jeff Tamarkin*

● **Older Stuff: Best of Michael Nesmith (1970-1973)** / 1991 / Rhino 70763
Post-Monkees country-oriented material is proof that at least one member of the "pre-fab four" possessed genuine musical talent. —*Jeff Tamarkin*

Tropical Campfire's / 1992 / Pacific Arts 50004

Nesmith plays desert music—quiet, contemplative, dignified—embellished, as the album title suggests, with splashes of lush tropical rhythms. His yearning vocals are ably supported by a cast of crack sessioneers, including the legendary Red Rhodes on pedal steel. Nesmith pens nine of the disc's 12 tracks, the others being covers of the samba chestnut Brazil and two Cole Porter tunes (ok, we could have done without the loungy version of Begin the Beguine). —*Roch Parisien*

● **Complete** / 1993 / Pacific Arts Audio 5006
All of Michael Nesmith & the First National Band's three albums are collected on this superb two-disc set that proves what a surprisingly inventive musician the former Monkee is. —*Stephen Thomas Erlewine*

The Neville Brothers

Group / R&B, soul, funk

After more than two decades of performing together and alone, the Nevilles returned to their home turf, New Orleans, in 1977. The music they began making was grounded in that city's rhythms and folklore. Individually, the first Neville to get on record was Art, who joined the Hawketts and scored with "Mardi Gras Mambo" (1955) and on his own with "Cha Dooky Do" (1958). Then Aaron made his mark with "Over You" (1960) and the anthemic "Tell It Like It Is" (1966). The details of how Art, Aaron, Charles, and Cyril passed through the Meters, the Wild Tchoupitoulas, and other outfits to form their family band would defy a genealogist, and their less-than-successful debut on Capitol suggested that it was hardly worth the trouble. But then came *Fiyo on the Bayou* on A&M in 1981. Since then, the brothers have gone from strength to strength, plundering their New Orleans heritage and combining it with an eclectic mix of material to produce music that is virtually without category. Exposure in the band has finally enabled Aaron Neville to gain recognition as one of the truly great, eccentric voices in African American music. *Rolling Stone* and then Linda Ronstadt offered their seals of approval, with the result that the brothers are now both funky and chic. —*Colin Escott*

○ **Fi Yo on Bayou** / 1980 / A&M 4866
A brilliant updating of New Orleans R&B sound to include strains of Cajun, rock, and reggae on standards ranging from "Hey Pocky Way" to "The Ten Commandments of Love" and "Sitting in Limbo." —*William Ruhlmann*

★ **Treacherous— A History of the Neville Brothers (1955-1985)** / 1986 / Rhino 71494
Treacherous: A History of the Neville Brothers (1955-1985) traces the recorded careers of the four brothers' solo efforts, plus the Wild Tchoupitoulas and their more recent group work. Essential to a complete understanding of the Nevilles and New Orleans music in general. —*William Ruhlmann*

○ **Yellow Moon** / 1989 / A&M 5240
The Neville Brothers made a bid for pop/rock stardom with this well-produced album for A&M, their first under a new pact with the label inked in the late '80s. It was certainly as solid as any they cut for A&M; the vocals were both nicely arranged and expertly performed, the arrangements were basically solid, and the selections were intelligently picked and sequenced. The album charted and remained there for many weeks, while the Nevilles toured and generated lots of interest. It didn't become a hit, but it did respectably and represents perhaps their finest overall pop album. —*Ron Wynn*

Brother's Keeper / 1990 / A&M 5312
All the Neville Brothers' recent albums for A&M have been frustrating, uneven propositions, with great performances followed by disjoined numbers, and the studio productions seldom conveying the excitement and fire this group routinely generates in live concert. The same holds true for this release, even though it got more pop exposure and chart penetration than any previous Neville Brothers album. But despite their energetic vocals and often superb instrumental interaction, this release still didn't come close to presenting the Neville Brothers on a good night, much less a great one. —*Ron Wynn*

○ **Treacherous Too!—History of the Neville Brothers, Vol. 2** / 1991 / Rhino 70776
The second collection of Neville Brothers' tracks covers the same '50s to '80s period as its predecessor, but contains more album cuts and nonhits. It also has plenty of unreleased material and

single cuts from Art, Aaron, and Cyril Neville, plus a Hawketts song and four bonus tracks on CD. —*Ron Wynn*

Aaron Neville

b. Jan. 24, 1941, New Orleans, LA
Vocals / Soul, R&B, pop/rock
Although Neville is often compared to singer Sam Cooke in terms of sheer vocal refinement, he has a voice and style uniquely his own. Today he is well known as part of the New Orleans sound of the Neville Brothers. Yet, aside from the 1967 #1 R&B hit "Tell It Like It Is," few have heard his incredible early solo recordings. Many of the first recordings of Aaron Neville, in the early and mid '60s, were arranged, produced, and often written by the brilliant Allen Toussaint—another talent only now being really appreciated. Most of these sides were cut for the Minit (and later) Parlo labels. Songs like "She Took You for a Ride" and "You Think You're So Smart" on Parlo are masterpieces. While his more recent work, including that with Linda Ronstadt, makes for pleasant listening, it lacks the sheer persuasion of his early songs. Aaron has rerecorded his early work often, and it is important to hear the originals. The early sides of Aaron Neville are just waiting to be heard. —*Michael Erlewine*

● **Tell It Like It Is** / 1967 / Curb 77491
Eleven of Neville's best Parlo cuts, including those mentioned above, on one CD. His biggest solo smash from 1966, plus more songs in the same style. Sublime stuff. —*Bill Dahl*

○ **Orchid in the Storm** / Dec. 1986 / Rhino 70956
Aaron Neville's wondrous singing on this poorly distributed record was overlooked by many still unaware of his stunning falsetto. But Neville covered doo-wop, soul, even country on this project, singing with a soaring conviction and poignancy that made it a delightful, though short set. Rhino has thankfully reissued it on CD. It's actually closer to representing Neville's real style than his overproduced, hyped recent pop records. —*Ron Wynn*

Show Me the Way / Aug. 1989 / Charly 162
Here are 22 of his early Minit recordings, many of them incredible. —*Michael Erlewine*

Warm Your Heart / 1991 / A&M 5354
This new set finds Neville's wavering vocals as elegant as ever on a ballad-oriented program. —*Bill Dahl*

New Edition

Group / Urban R&B, pop/rock
When Maurice Starr assembled New Edition in the early '80s, he never could have guessed that the group would produce some of the biggest, most influential urban R&B stars of the following decade. At the time of their first record, Bobby Brown, Ralph Tresvant, Ricky Bell, Mike Bivins, and Ronald Davoe were barely in their teens, yet they had impressive voices and a natural charisma that sent them to the charts with their first single, "Candy Girl." Their second album was even bigger, featuring the #2 single "Cool It Now." New Edition's songs were either light funk or sweet ballads, yet they followed their formula well even if it much of it seems quaint now, especially compared to their groundbreaking solo work.

Brown left the band after their third album, being replaced by Johnny Gill. The band released two more albums before splitting. After the group was finished, they each became successful as solo artists in the early '80s. After their solo careers began to cool down, they decided to reunite; a new record was reportedly in the works during 1994. —*Stephen Thomas Erlewine*

○ **Candy Girl** / 1983 / Warlock 8701
When Maurice Starr uncovered the talents of a Roxbury vocal group in the early '80s, he envisioned a second Jackson 5. That was the direction he took New Edition in its early days, and this album includes such overt Jackson 5 ripoffs as "Candy Girl" and the title track. None of the toughness or street touches that emerged on their later material were evident on this slick pop-oriented session. Ralph Tresvant, Ronald DeVoe, Michael Bivins, Ricky Bell, and Bobby Brown were all aged 13 to 15 when this was released. —*Ron Wynn*

○ **New Edition** / 1984 / MCA 31028
Maurice Starr's vision peaked with this second album by New Edition. They were now thoroughly Jackson 5 clones, and were

reaping similar commercial dividends, thanks to the teen angst cuts "Cool It Now" and "Mr. Telephone Man." They earned their first platinum album, one Top 10 hit, and another Top 20 pop single (both songs topped the R&B charts) and were among the hottest acts in either pop or R&B during this stretch. —*Ron Wynn*

All for Love / 1985 / MCA 5679
New Edition's voices and focus was changing in the late '80s. They'd moved away from the kiddie pop/soul of the early '80s and were singing adult, harder love material and cutting uptempo funk tracks, though there weren't many of those on this session. While sometimes things got a bit sappy lyricwise and other times seemed repetitive, the group compensated with their strongest harmonies and vocal performances to date. —*Ron Wynn*

Under the Blue Moon / 1986 / MCA 5912
Changes were on the horizon for New Edition. They'd become enormously successful by aping the Jackson 5, but were undergoing internal trauma as original member Bobby Brown bolted amid rumors of dissatifaction with the group's direction. This album featured their covers of '50s and '60s standards and was among the early examples of the retro trend that's now so prominent in urban contemporary camps. While they didn't do this type of material nearly as well as the Force MD's, they at least brought fresh attention to such songs as "Earth Angel" and "Tears on My Pillow." —*Ron Wynn*

Heart Break / 1989 / MCA 42207
The arrival of Johnny Gill's lusty baritone and production tactics of Jimmy Jam and Terry Lewis temporarily revived the sagging careers of New Edition. Jam and Lewis gave them current beats, let Gill take the lead on romantic numbers, and put punch and edge into their arrangements. This proved New Edition's biggest album since 1985's *All for Love*, and such songs as "Can You Stand the Rain," "If It Isn't Love," and the autobiographical "Where It All Started" signaled the end of the Jackson 5 ties. —*Ron Wynn*

● **Greatest Hits, Vol. 1** / 1991 / MCA 10434
For anyone who missed New Edition in either its Jackson 5 imitation phase or final days as a funkier, more aggressive urban contemporary vocal group with a slight dance influence, this collection contains examples of both incarnations. Kiddie pop hits such as "Candy Girl," "Cool It Now," and "Mr. Telephone Man" are included, along with their final hits "If It Isn't Love," "Can You Stand the Rain," and appropriately titled "Is This the End." This anthology shows how dominant New Edition was during the '80s and early '90s. —*Ron Wynn*

New Kids on the Block

Group / Urban R&B, pop/rock
After his success with New Edition, producer Maurice Starr decided to replicate the group, subsituting the young African American teenagers for suburban white kids. The result was New Kids on the Block, which quickly eclipsed the popularity of Starr's previous group. Comprising Boston area singers Donnie Wahlberg, Jordan Knight, Jon Knight, Danny Wood, and Joe McIntyre, the New Kids were awkward and enthusiastic on their 1986 debut, which wasn't surprising considering that the oldest members were barely 16. With their next album, 1988's *Hangin' Tough*, the group's image had toughened up, and they had the material to support it. From the saccharine ballad "I'll Be Loving You Forever" to the title track's stab at funk, the band had a seemingly endless streak of hits in 1988 and 1989; their Christmas album even went double platinum. New Kid mania continued with 1990's *Step by Step*; even if it sold five million copies less than *Hangin' Tough*, it still sold three milion copies. But that was the end of the road for their short time in the sun—they were the subject of an endless amount of jokes and were getting no respect. Besides, their audience was growing up. In 1994, they returned with the Starr-less *Face the Music*, which actually showed a remarkable musical maturity—they were a credible urban R&B outfit—but hardly sold anything, even if they were packing theaters on tour. In June of 1994, the band announced that they had acrimoniously parted ways and all of the members were now pursuing solo careers. —*Stephen Thomas Erlewine*

New Kids on the Block / 1986 / Columbia 40475
Debut with "Be My Girl." —*Bil Carpenter*

● **Hangin' Tough** / 1988 / Columbia 40985

Good songs collected by New Kids mastermind Maurice Starr highlight this smash, including "I'll Be Loving You (Forever)," "You Got It (the Right Stuff)," "Please Don't Go Girl," and the title track. Tight, warm, even soulful harmony on the ballads. —*Dan Heilman and Bil Carpenter*

○ **Step by Step** / 1990 / Columbia 45129
In an attempt for some respect, the group wrote some cuts on *Step by Step*, a more serious, harder-sounding album. Although the title track was #1 for three weeks and the followup, "Tonight," went Top 10, they couldn't replicate the success of *Hangin' Tough*. —*Bil Carpenter*

○ **Face the Music** / 1994 / Columbia
Well, the New Kids return after much ridicule and doubt, with the defensive *Face the Music* and, surprise!—it isn't bad at all. Sure, they've changed their style a bit—their new-jack R&B is a bit rougher, the lyrics are a touch nastier, and their hip-hop sounds a little more *real*—but none of it sounds fake, and the best tracks on the album might impress even the most jaded listener. —*Stephen Thomas Erlewine*

New Order

Group / Alternative pop/rock, dance
Of all of the synth-based post-punk bands that emerged in the '80s, New Order is the most important. After Ian Curtis hung himself, the remaining members of Joy Division—Bernard Sumner, Peter Hook, and Stephen Morris—picked up the pieces and formed New Order, adding keyboardist Gillian Gilbert. While the group alleviated some of Curtis's most morbid tendencies, their music still was serious; the band also adhered to pop melodies and structure more frequently than Joy Division. New Order exploited synthesizers and electronics to their fullest, creating a detached yet strangely human soundscape that managed to convey the emotional alienation of the Thatcher and Reagan era. The band was also not afraid to use disco as the basic rhythm in their music, laying the groundwork for the house scene in the United Kingdom at the end of the decade, as well as the cold, detached synth-dance pop that dominated the charts in the United States and United Kingdom for most of the beginning of the decade. In the United Kingdom, New Order were stars, yet they never developed anything larger than a cult following in America.

After 1991's *Technique*, the band members concentrated on solo projects (Sumner in Electronic, Hook in Revenge, Gilbert and Morris in the Other Two), fueling rumors that they had broken up. In 1993, they returned with *Republic*, which earned them their first genuine hit single in America, "Regret." After a tension-filled tour, the members resumed their solo projects, again sparking rumors of the band's split. —*Stephen Thomas Erlewine*

○ **Power Corruption and Lies** / 1983 / Qwest 25308
Synthesized dance music at moderate tempos, plus calmly sung, distanced lyrics, makes for an entrancing effect. —*William Ruhlmann*

○ **Low Life** / 1985 / Qwest 25289
New Order's messages are no less dire here, but the tempos are faster, the singing more engaged, and the melodies more distinct. In fact, "Love Vigilantes" is positively catchy. —*William Ruhlmann*

★ **Substance** / 1987 / Qwest 25621
A collection of New Order singles—some of their best work—little of which had previously turned up on albums or in the United States. —*William Ruhlmann*

Republic / May 11, 1993 / Qwest 45250
New Order's most pop-oriented record actually resulted in a hit single in the United States—the pleasantly catchy "Regret." However, most of the album finds New Order repeating ideas that are now almost a decade old. —*Stephen Thomas Erlewine*

New Riders of the Purple Sage, The

Group / Country rock
A country-rock group that spun off from the Grateful Dead in 1969, originally featuring John Dawson (b. 1945), David Nelson, and Dead members Jerry Garcia (b. August 1, 1942), Mickey Hart (b. September 11, 1943), and Phil Lesh (b. March 3, 1940). The band continues today, with Dawson the only original member left. —*William Ruhlmann*

○ **New Riders of the Purple Sage** / 1971 / Columbia 30888

An album for anyone who liked the sagebrush country-rock of the Grateful Dead's *Workingman's Dead* and *American Beauty* albums, dominated by John Dawson's songs and Jerry Garcia-like voice. —*William Ruhlmann*

● **Best of the New Riders of the Purple Sage** / 1976 / Columbia 34367
A good selection from the group's Columbia catalog, featuring "Glendale Train," "Panama Red," and other favorites. —*William Ruhlmann*

The New York Dolls

Group / Hard rock, glam rock
The New York Dolls were the bridge between the Rolling Stones, the MC5, and the Sex Pistols and the punk-rock movement of the late '70s. Their highly charged, reckless, guitar-heavy sound and lead singer David Johansen's fey stage antics, coupled with the group's inclination toward androgyny, made for a nice diversion in 1973, when their self-titled Todd Rundgren-produced debut came out. Unfortunately, the Dolls were too raw for most of the public, including those who claimed to love rock & roll. As a result, the band became more of a media event and critics' darlings.

The Shadow Morton-produced followup, *Too Much Too Soon*, proved that the Dolls were more than a one-shot wonder. It included a wonderful version of Archie Bell & the Drells's "There's Gonna Be a Showdown." The Dolls lost their deal with Mercury Records and were briefly managed by the outrageous Malcolm McLaren (who later handled the Sex Pistols). They eventually broke up in 1977. Of the five, Johansen has enjoyed the most success as a solo artist, later under the pseudonym Buster Poindexter. Guitarist Johnny Thunders became a punk legend, releasing a series of wildly inconsistent records—both on his own and with his post-Dolls band, the Heartbreakers—before his death in 1990. —*Rick Clark*

★ **New York Dolls** / 1973 / Mercury 832752
Their debut suffers from Todd Rundgren's murky production, but "Personality Crisis," "Pills," and "Frankenstein" manage to break through the clutter. —*John Floyd*

☆ **Too Much, Too Soon** / 1974 / Mercury 834230
Their second (and last) album mixes well-chosen soul/R&B covers with a slew of striking Johnny Thunders-David Johansen originals. Good enough to make their early demise even more regrettable. —*John Floyd*

Randy Newman

b. Nov. 28, 1943
Vocals, piano / Singer-songwriter
Randy Newman, nephew of Lionel and Alfred Newman (Hollywood arrangers and heads of 20th Century Fox Pictures), was already steeped in a rich creative environment when he chose to pursue music as a career. Newman's first attempt as a solo artist was the 1961 Dot single "Golden Gridiron Boy," which was produced by Pat Boone. Even though the record went nowhere, Newman embarked on a successful songwriting career, with songs cut by the Fleetwoods, Jerry Butler, Cilla Black, Judy Collins, Manfred Mann, Nilsson, and Three Dog Night, among others. Since 1968, when he released his self-titled Warner Bros. debut, Newman has employed a seductive blend of ragtime, rolling Fats Domino-style rock & roll, blues, and classic Hollywood cinema-style melodies (with a touch of Stephen Foster), which has been effective in luring the listener into the twisted mindsets of the characters that populate many of his songs. Since Newman often sang from the protagonist's point of view, he rarely wasted time moralizing his position. In 1978 Newman's tongue-in-cheek acerbity produced a hit with "Short People," off of *Little Criminals*, but it also rankled many, who thought the single was mean-spirited. Even Newman's fans began to wonder about the literalness of his sentiment with the 1979 album *Born Again*, which mercilessly skewered each of the protagonists represented.

In 1982 Newman did the soundtrack for the movie *Ragtime*, beginning a successful career in film scoring. Newman has continued to sporadically release solo albums that are many cuts above the average release. —*Rick Clark*

★ **12 Songs** / 1970 / Reprise 6373
Randy Newman's droll humor and ability to render ludicrous settings (through the eyes of protagonists who were obviously not

playing with full decks) made *12 Songs* an instant classic to the handful of people lucky enough to hear it. The bare-bones production, along with assistance from guitarist Ry Cooder, gave the record a homey immediacy. Highlights are hard to single out, but "Mama Told Me Not to Come" (later a hit for Three Dog Night), "Yellow Man," "Lucinda," and "Uncle Bob's Midnight Blues" are great. —*Rick Clark*

Randy Newman Live / 1971 / Reprise 6459
This live set basically reprises much of his first two albums, without adding much to their interpretation. There are a few new tunes, the only standout being a song that Frank Sinatra passed on, called "Lonely at the Top." —*Rick Clark*

☆ **Sail Away** / 1972 / Reprise 2064
Sail Away was Newman's first synthesis of his satirical writing and his impressive orchestral arrangement skills. The result was one of his very best albums. The title cut was a brilliantly twisted take on slaves coming on a ship from Africa, set to a score that owed much to Stephen Foster. "Burn On," Newman's sentimental-sounding ode to the polluted Cuyahoga River (in Cleveland, OH), and his perverse "You Can Leave Your Hat On" (later popularized by Joe Cocker in the movie *9 1/2 Weeks*) are among the many great songs to be found on *Sail Away.* —*Rick Clark*

☆ **Good Old Boys** / 1974 / Reprise 2193
On *Good Old Boys,* Newman increasingly focused his obsessions on the south, but his slant seemed to be rooted more in Steppin' Fetchit and Shirley Temple *Little Rebel* Hollywood films than in reality. As distorted as viewing things through that particular lens may be, the south in *Good Old Boys* is undeniably poignant. "Louisiana 1927" is an affecting account of a spring flood, while "Marie" (a love song from a drunk) is one of the most touching songs written in popular music. The grand, sweeping melodies and arrangements are quite simply beautiful. Newman's sloppy, soulful mumble and understated piano keep this effort from tumbling into drippy sentimentality. A great record. —*Rick Clark*

Little Criminals / 1977 / Reprise 3079
On *Little Criminals,* Newman's penchant for satirically illuminating the quirks in human nature earned him a million-selling #2 hit with "Short People," a song that dealt with the issue of bigotry. It also earned him the loathing of thousands of short people who failed to get the message. Aside from that controversy, *Little Criminals* was relatively tame by Newman standards. "Baltimore," "Sigmund Freud's Impersonation of Albert Einstein in America," and "Rider in the Rain" were among the standout tracks. —*Rick Clark*

○ **Trouble in Paradise** / 1983 / Reprise 23755
After the mean-spirited 1979 release *Born Again,* Newman regrouped and came out with *Trouble in Paradise,* an album that employed more lyrical subtlety and was more successful at skewering its terminally character-disordered targets ("Christmas in Capetown," "Song for the Dead," "My Life Is Good"). "The Blues," a dryly humorous duet with Paul Simon, was a moderate hit at #51. "I Love L.A." failed to chart, in spite of extensive exposure. Musically, Newman downplayed the timeless feel of his best work in favor of a trendier, clean West Coast pop sound. —*Rick Clark*

○ **Land of Dreams** / 1988 / Reprise 25773
After a five-year layoff, Newman returned with the solid *Land of Dreams,* an album that was by turns gentle and reflective ("Something Special," "Falling in Love") or subtly scathing. Among the topics explored in *Land of Dreams* are Newman's childhood memories in New Orleans ("Dixie Flyer," "New Orleans Wins the War"), a beautifully twisted ode to patriotism ("Follow the Flag"), and an explanation from a father to his son ("I Want You to Hurt Like I Do"), concerning the passing down of abusive ways. The cynical "It's Money That Matters" barely dented the charts at #80. Interestingly, Jeff Lynne helped produce this album; only two albums earlier, Newman was skewering Lynne's band ELO for representing some of the worst elements of the music biz. —*Rick Clark*

Olivia Newton-John

b. Sep. 26, 1948, Cambridge, England
Vocals / Pop/rock
Olivia Newton-John ranks at #12 in chart researcher Joel Whitburn's ranking of the most successful singles artists of the '70s. The biggest of her 15 Top 10 hits, "Physical," came in the

'80s, when it spent ten weeks at #1. Born in Cambridge, England, but raised in Australia, she returned to her native country after winning a talent contest at 16 and spent several years struggling before she scored a Top 10 UK hit in 1971 with a cover of Bob Dylan's "If Not for You." But it was not until 1973 that Newton-John made her real American breakthrough with the first of five straight gold-selling Top 10 hits, "Let Me Be There." She scored two #1 albums in 1974 and 1975 with *If You Love Me, Let Me Know* and *Have You Never Been Mellow.* (Newton-John's simultaneous success on the country charts and her winning of Grammy and Country Music Association awards in country categories were controversial in Nashville.)

Newton-John's career cooled in 1976 and 1977, but in 1978 she appeared in the film version of the retro '50s musical *Grease,* which not only added to her hit total but also moved her image from sweetness and innocence to a more aggressive posture. She capitalized on the change and on the disco wave for songs like the sexually provocative "Physical" and enjoyed a new vogue as a dance-pop singer in the early '80s. Her last Top 10 hit, "Twist of Fate," was in 1984, also the year Newton-John married actor Matt Lattanzi. She has since released the gold-selling *Soul Kiss* in 1985, *The Rumour* in 1988, and *Warm and Tender* (1989), an album of children's lullabies. —*William Ruhlmann*

● **Back to Basics: The Essential Collection 1971-1992** / 1992 / David Geffen Co. 24470
An artist well defined by her hit singles, Olivia Newton-John has had a stylistically varied career, as is illustrated on *Back to Basics: The Essential Collection 1971-1992,* a set that ranges from her teary ballad "I Honestly Love You" to that bouncy paean to getting horizontal, "Physical." Fans may quibble that such hits as "Let Me Be There" and "Make a Move on Me" are not included, but Newton-John's two greatest-hits albums are out of print, and this is the only collection to combine both her good-girl and bad-girl personae. —*William Ruhlmann*

Nice

Group / Art rock
Formed in 1967, Nice was keyboardist Keith Emerson's theatrical testing ground before he formed Emerson, Lake & Palmer in 1970. The group never really sold Stateside, but their audacious stage antics and extended trashings of classical pieces made them popular in Europe. —*Rick Clark*

Thoughts of Emerlist Davjack / 1967 / Columbia 52425
An okay, but unambitious first album, heavily influenced by Jimi Hendrix. Lacking discipline, but full of surprises. —*Bruce Eder*

Ars Longa Vita Brevis / 1968 / Columbia 47890
Leonard Bernstein, Bach, and Sibelius interpreted through a musical lens forged by Brubeck, Monk, and a mad keyboard player named Keith Emerson. —*Bruce Eder*

● **Nice** / 1969 / Columbia 47347
Their final statement, with rippling organ passages and a great lineup of songs, plus 20 minutes of a legendary Fillmore live gig. —*Bruce Eder*

Elegy & Five Bridges / 1975 / Mercury 830457
A farewell record of live cuts and outtakes, not showing the band to its best advantage. A good appendix to their superior Immediate recordings on Columbia. —*Bruce Eder*

Stevie Nicks

b. May 6, 1948
Vocals / Pop/rock
A singer/songwriter who gained fame as a member of Fleetwood Mac starting in 1975 and launched a concurrent solo career in 1981, resulting in five gold or platinum albums through 1991. —*William Ruhlmann*

○ **Bella Donna** / 1981 / Modern 38139
Nicks' major attributes—her passionately ragged voice and emotionally vulnerable songwriting- are much in evidence on her debut solo album, given a clean rock production by Jimmy Iovine. Includes "Stop Draggin' My Heart Around" (with Tom Petty & the Heartbreakers), "Edge of Seventeen," and "Leather and Lace" (a duet with Don Henley). —*William Ruhlmann*

● **Timespace: Best of Stevie Nicks** / 1991 / Modern 91711
All the hits, some well-selected album tracks, and two new ones on a generous best-of. —*William Ruhlmann*

Street Angel / 1994 / Modern
Released in 1994, *Street Angel* could've easily been the followup to Nicks's debut 13 years earlier, thanks to production that sounds frozen in her early '80s heyday. Overall, the material isn't that strong; the opening track, "Blue Denim," is the highlight here. — *Rick Clark*

Nico (Christa Paffgen)

d. Jul. 18, 1988
Vocals / Rock & roll, avant-garde, Latin
German-born Christa Paffgen was a model and actress who turned to singing and joined the rock group the Velvet Underground, appearing on their first album, before turning to a solo career in 1968. — *William Ruhlmann*

● **Chelsea Girl** / 1967 / Polydor 835209
Nico's distanced, German-accented voice is presented over austere strings and, in one case, electric guitar on a series of songs reminiscent of her work with the Velvet Underground and written by Velvets John Cale and Lou Reed. Other songs (some unrecorded elsewhere) were written by a young Jackson Browne. — *William Ruhlmann*

○ **Desert Shore** / 1971 / Reprise 6424
John Cale produces, arranges, and plays almost all the instruments on this atmospheric collection of songs well suited to Nico's droning delivery. — *William Ruhlmann*

The End / 1974 / Island 9311
The most remote and Teutonic of Nico's studio albums features Roxy Music guitarist Phil Manzanera, Brian Eno on synthesizer, and John Cale (who also produced) on a dozen instruments. After five Nico originals, it concludes with chilling readings of the Doors' "The End" and "Das Lied Der Deutschen." — *Richie Unterberger*

Peel Sessions / 1988 / Dutch East India 8314
In February 1971, Nico recorded a four-song session for the BBC that included songs from three of her solo albums. "No One Is There" and "Frozen Warnings" had appeared on 1969's *The Marble Index*, and "Janitor of Lunacy" on 1970's *Desert Shore;* "Secret Side" would appear on 1974's *The End*. Frequently bootlegged over the years, this official release presents the performance at the right speed in pristine sound. These renditions are about as bare-boned as they come, with no accompaniment save Nico's own harmonium. In both material and performance, she leans toward the more wistful and gothic of her numbers. It doesn't differ drastically from the LP versions, but it's an interesting addition to fans' collections. — *Richie Unterberger*

Live Heroes / 1989 / Performance 385
A six-track mini-album, four songs recorded live, including David Bowie's title track, which is perfectly suited to the Nico treatment. — *William Ruhlmann*

Harry Nilsson

b. Jun. 13, 1941
Vocals / Pop/rock
Though he is best known as a singer, Harry Nilsson first gained recognition as a songwriter in the mid '60s, when his songs were recorded by the Ronettes, the Modern Folk Quartet, and the Monkees. By the time Three Dog Night took his "One" into the Top 5, Nilsson had released two albums of his own on RCA. Neither of them was a hit, but Nilsson did score with his cover of Fred Neil's "Everybody's Talkin'" when it was used as the theme song of the film *Midnight Cowboy*. Nilsson wrote his own film and television scores and in 1970 made an album of songs written by Randy Newman. His career was not helped by his disinclination to undertake live appearances.

Nevertheless, Nilsson broke commercially with his late-1971 album, *Nilsson Schmilsson*, which contained his version of Badfinger's "Without You," a #1 hit, and his own novelty number, "Coconut," which also hit the Top 10. *Son of Schmilsson*, another appealing collection, was successful the following year. Nilsson's next album was a collection of standards sung against an orchestra conducted by noted '50s arranger Gordon Jenkins, *A Little Touch of Schmilsson in the Night*.

Nilsson had always been a favorite of the Beatles (he was sometimes rumored to be joining the group), and he engaged in projects with Ringo Starr (a film called *Son of Dracula*) and John Lennon (who produced Nilsson's *Pussy Cats*) in the mid '70s.

After Lennon's murder, Nilsson became an outspoken advocate of gun control and devoted much of his time to the cause. In the early '90s, he was holding showings of his art in galleries and starting a comeback in music. Unfortunately, his comeback never materialized—Nilsson died of a heart attack in early 1994. — *William Ruhlmann*

○ **Pandemonium Shadow Show** / 1967 / RCA 3874
It's no wonder that Nilsson was taken up by members of the Beatles after they heard this album, which demonstrated that the singer understood the eclectic whimsy that had given birth to *Sgt. Pepper's Lonely Hearts Club Band* better than most. Contains the bittersweet "1941" and "Cuddly Toy," which was covered by the Monkees. — *William Ruhlmann*

○ **Sings Newman** / 1970 / RCA 4289
Nilsson turns out to be a wonderful interpreter of the work of Randy Newman, his light voice making Newman's satiric humor even drier than when the composer himself sang the songs. — *William Ruhlmann*

○ **Nilsson Schmilsson** / 1971 / RCA 4515
Nilsson's most successful album was a bouncy Richard Perry production, whose catchy songs were deepened by the singer's puckish humor. Contains the hits "Without You," "Jump into the Fire," and "Coconut." — *William Ruhlmann*

○ **Son of Schmilsson** / 1972 / RCA 3812
The humor is starting to take over on this followup, but the songs are still entertaining, and the session players, including "George Harrysong" and "Richie Snare," make for a great backup band. Contains the hits "Spaceman" and "Remember (Christmas)," as well as the ultimate putdown song, "You're Breaking My Heart." — *William Ruhlmann*

A Little Touch of Schmilsson in the Night / 1973 / RCA 3761
Nilsson was nearly a decade ahead of Linda Ronstadt and other nouveau crooners in hiring a conductor/arranger of the pre-rock era (in this case Gordon Jenkins) and recording an album of standards before a full orchestra. And he did it better than most, proving to be a marvelous interpreter of songs like "What'll I Do?" and "Makin' Whoopee!" His version of "As Time Goes By" became a minor hit. — *William Ruhlmann*

○ **Pussy Cats** / 1974 / Edsel 337
A dark, disjointed album of covers (including "Subterranean Homesick Blues," "Rock Around the Clock," and "Many Rivers to Cross"), the John Lennon-produced *Pussy Cats* is the strangest album Nilsson ever recorded; it's an aural document of Lennon and Nilsson's notorious, alcohol-soaked "lost weekend"—the sheer chaos of the album effectively evokes their aimless hedonism. — *Stephen Thomas Erlewine*

● **All-Time Greatest Hits** / 1978 / RCA 9670
Nilsson's albums tended to hang together well, but that didn't keep him from throwing off singles, at least in the late '60s and early '70s. This collection contains all 10 of his chart singles (including "Everybody's Talkin'"), plus his version of his song "One," which was a hit for Three Dog Night. — *William Ruhlmann*

Nine Inch Nails

Group / Alternative pop/rock, industrial
Nine Inch Nails, the one-man band of Trent Reznor, brought industrial music to the masses with 1989's *Pretty Hate Machine*. With its electronic rush, incessant beats, and distorted guitars, the album appeared to be like much industrial music on the surface, yet Reznor wrote pop songs, not the soundtrack to a personal horror movie. NIN's scarred, harsh soundscapes were bleak enough, yet Reznor's lyrics rises the despair and self-loathing to new heights; at times, his relentless darkness can veer dangerously close to self-parody.

Pretty Hate Machine wasn't a hit when it was released; it charted in 1990 and stayed on the charts for years afterward. By the time Reznor assembled a band for the first Lollapalooza tour in 1991, the group had a sizable following that only grew with NIN's ferocious performances on the tour. Legal troubles with his record company delayed the release of a second album; in 1992, he released a stopgap EP, *Broken*, that was harder and more abrasive than the debut, yet still conformed to conventional song structures; it debuted in the *Billboard* Top 10. With their second full-length album, Reznor showed his true roots—'70s progressive rock. *The Downward Spiral* was promoted as a concept album, a cohesive piece of work; it also featured ex-King Crimson guitarist Adrian Belew. Still, NIN is able to straddle two seemingly opposing genres easily, gaining alternative and mainstream hard rock fans alike; whether he likes it or not, Trent Reznor is the man that made industrial palatable for pop fans. *—Stephen Thomas Erlewine*

● **Pretty Hate Machine** / 1989 / Tee Vee Toons 2610

The reason why *Pretty Hate Machine* gained a huge cult following is because Trent Reznor has not made an industrial album, in the strict sense. Reznor's songs are pop songs played in an industrial style. Meanwhile, Reznor constructs a towering monument of angst and hatred in his lyrics, perfect for legions of alienated adolescents. Reznor says, "I'd rather die than to give you control," and he proves it throughout *Pretty Hate Machine*. Full of hooks, beats, and abrasive noise, *Pretty Hate Machine* provided a generation of adolescents a martyr as well as a great way to ventilate anger. *—Stephen Thomas Erlewine*

○ **Broken** / Jan. 1992 / Interscope 92213

After the unexpected success of *Pretty Hate Machine*, Trent Reznor found himself unable to enjoy any of it. Instead, Reznor was embroiled in an ugly lawsuit with his record company, which made him unable to release any new material for three years. Although *Broken* is only an EP, the wait was more than worth it. Those who fell in love with psuedo-industrial *Pretty Hate Machine* will likely be alienated by the raging, angry assault of *Broken*. Instead of blaming everyone else for his troubles, Reznor turns anger inward. "Wish" and "Happiness in Slavery" are busier, angrier, and nosier than anything on *Pretty*, but the songs still have hooks, only that noise is the hook. *Broken* shreds *Pretty Hate Machine* because the anger here is real, not feigned. For those who can stomach undiluted rage, *Broken* is a masterpiece. *—Stephen Thomas Erlewine*

○ **Fixed** / Feb. 1992 / Interscope 96093

Even more than *Broken*, the limited-edition *Fixed* EP sounds like an attempt by Reznor to whittle down the size of his audience. The remixes on *Fixed* totally distort all of the original meanings and intents of the original versions on *Broken;* it's the closest Reznor has come to pure industrial music. *—Stephen Thomas Erlewine*

Downward Spiral / 1994 / Interscope 92346

Although Trent Reznor designed *The Downward Spiral* as a concept album about despair and anger, these are familiar themes for Nine Inch Nails; it's up to the music to carry the album. And it does carry the album, featuring harder guitars and more brutal beats. However, the songwriting has slipped, and the aggression sounds forced. *—Stephen Thomas Erlewine*

Nirvana

Group / Alternative rock

With one album, Nirvana changed rock & roll. Before "Smells Like Teen Spirit" and *Nevermind* were released in 1991, alternative and post-punk rock had never been considered profitable or commercial. Nirvana changed the record industry's, as well as the public's, conception of what was mainstream. *Nevermind* marked a shift in the mainstream, when punk rock finally reclaimed the rock & roll mainstream for themselves. Other post-punk bands that crossed over into the mainstream had done so slowly; by the time U2 and R.E.M. became superstars in 1987, their audiences were large enough to guarantee them a hit album. Besides, neither band had as much raw guitar and naked angst as Nirvana; they were as close to a punk band as possible in the '90s.

Nirvana combined strands of rock from all eras into one explosive burst of rage. Combining the melodic pop of the Beatles, the '70s sludge of Black Sabbath, the spiky song structure of the Pixies, and the fierce indie ethics of the American indie underground of the '80s, the band came up with a signature pop-punk that was distinctly their own.

Bleach, their 1989 debut, made the band underground darlings and led to a major-label contract. In 1990, Dave Grohl became Nirvana's permanent drummer, teaming with bassist Chris Novoselic to form the fiercest rhythm section in rock. Guitarist/vocalist Kurt Cobain's new songs surpassed anything on their debut; his songs were stunning, concise bursts of melody and rage that occasionally spilled over into haunting, folk-styled acoustic ballads.

Nevermind wasn't expected to sell over 100,000 copies; by early 1992, the album was the top-selling record in the country. However, the band's personal fortunes weren't as smooth. During 1992, Cobain developed a debilitating heroin habit, which strained relations with the rest of the band. By the beginning of 1993, Cobain had admitted that he had just detoxed from heroin, which he claimed he used to fight a chronic stomach problem. Nirvana released their third album, *In Utero*, in September of 1993; the album debuted at #1 and soon went double platinum. The band launched a U.S. tour in October; all of the articles about the band portrayed a happier, calmer Cobain.

Those images began to unravel in March of 1994, when Cobain overdosed on champagne and tranquilizers while on vacation in Rome. For all of March, rumors were flying about Nirvana's future. All of the rumors stopped on April 8, when Cobain's body was discovered at his home in Seattle; he had died three days earlier of a self-inflicted gunshot wound.

Since his death, Cobain has been equally revered and reviled; he wasn't universally mourned because he wasn't universally loved. Even after *Nevermind*, Nirvana's music was too raw for many listeners. But that doesn't mean that Cobain was not gifted or that his music was not important. Nirvana proved to both the record companies and the public that post-punk music and culture had a prominent place in mainstream culture. More importantly, the band made some undeniably great music. *—Stephen Thomas Erlewine*

☆ **Bleach** / 1989 / Sub Pop 34

At the time, *Bleach* was a stellar piece of Seattle sludge, state-of-the-art indie-rock from the great northwest. Although it is one of the best albums in the Sub Pop catalog, it pales next to Nirvana's other records. *Bleach* is clearly a debut album; there is a fair amount of filler, and the band sometimes collapses into a sub-Sabbath murk, but "School," "Love Buzz," "Blew," and "Negative Creep" are outstanding, furious rockers, and the gorgeous, Beatlesque ballad "About a Girl" signals the heights the band would reach on their next album. *—Stephen Thomas Erlewine*

★ **Nevermind** / 1991 / Geffen 24425

If "Smells Like Teen Spirit" was the only good song on *Nevermind*, the album wouldn't have inspired the music popular revolution that it did. Although the "Louie Louie"-meets-the-Pixies teen angst of "Teen Spirit" is what made Nirvana cross over into the mainstream, what made the album so remarkable is the quantum leap in Kurt Cobain's songwriting. The throttling punk rockers "Breed" and "Territorial Pissings" demolish anything on *Bleach*, and the haunting "Something in the Way" and "Polly" show Cobain's full range. Even better are "In Bloom," "Drain You," "On a Plain," and "Lithium," which fully combine both the melodicism and the sonic roar that Nirvana does so well. *—Stephen Thomas Erlewine*

○ **Incesticide** / Dec. 1992 / Geffen 24504

More than anyone else, Nirvana was caught surprised by the overwhelming success of *Nevermind*, While they decided what to do next, the released to put out *Incesticide*, a collection of B sides, live performances, outtakes, demos, and indie singles. The majority of the album's second half is of interest only to devoted fans, but the first half—filled with BBC sessions previously only available on the Japanese import *Hormoaning*, the B sides "Been a Son" and "Son of a Gun," and a Sub Pop single—is superb, especially the "Dive"/"Sliver" single, which foreshadow the explosive punk-pop of *Nevermind*. *—Stephen Thomas Erlewine*

☆ **In Utero** / 1993 / Geffen 24607

Despite all of the pre-release rumors predicting a noisy all-out sonic assault, *In Utero* is not an alienating alternative rock monster. Instead, *In Utero* retains all of the melodic splendor of *Nevermind*, injecting it with a raw, primal guitar roar that is louder and harder than anything on *Bleach*. However, Kurt Cobain remains a pop songwriter, and his melodies aren't buried underneath Steve Albini's harsh production, as "Heart-Shaped Box," "All Apologies," and "Penny Royal Tea" prove. *—Stephen Thomas Erlewine*

Nitzer Ebb

Alternative pop/rock, dance, house

With its synth-based songs, supported by throbbing, aggressive beats and half-spoken/half-shouted lyrircs, Nitzer Ebb became a favorite among the British acid house scene in the late '80s. Their albums never show much progression, yet their psuedo-industrial alternative dance music remains an impressive modern vision of angst-filled alienation; it's a nice bonus that you can dance to it. —*Stephen Thomas Erlewine*

● **That Total Age** / 1987 / David Geffen Co. 24155
A towering album of harsh, minimalistic synthesizers, rhythms, and samples, *That Total Age* established Nitzer Ebb as one of the most distinctive alternative dance-rock combos of the late '80s. —*Stephen Thomas Erlewine*

○ **Belief** / 1988 / David Geffen Co. 24213
Belief is essentially the same record as *That Total Age,* but Nitzer Ebb's sonic assault remains just as impressive on their second album. —*Stephen Thomas Erlewine*

Mojo Nixon

Vocals / Alternative rock, rock & roll
Mojo Nixon parlayed an irrepressible personality, a wicked sense of humor, and a taste for high-energy rockabilly into success on a series of novelty albums, and even a place as an MTV VJ. The latter was surprising, since Nixon had first gained notice for a song on his and Skid Roper's second album, *Frenzy* (1986), called "Stuffin' Martha's Muffin," an ode to the joys of intimate contact with MTV VJ Martha Quinn. The song was typical of Nixon's lyrical approach, which he followed with relentless mirth through the course of four albums on which Roper (a mostly silent partner) contributed incidental instrumental backup. *Bo-Day-Shus!!!* (1987), for example, contained "Elvis Is Everywhere," one of the more outrageous tributes to the King. Debunking famous names came more naturally to Nixon, however, and *Root Hog or Die* was introduced by the *National Enquirer*-headline leadoff song "Debbie Gibson Is Pregnant with My Two Headed Love Child." Gibson didn't comment, but when Nixon (now separated from Roper) issued his first solo album, *Otis,* containing the song "Don Henley Must Die," the ex-Eagle was heard to say that the singer needed a laxative. —*William Ruhlmann*

Frenzy / 1986 / IRS 13098
Arguably the duo's best album, highlights include "I'm Living with the Three-Foot Anti-Christ," "The Amazing Bigfoot Diet," and two songs any working musician should understand, "Where the Hell's My Money" and "I Hate Banks." By the way, the *Get Out of My Way* mini-LP, which included some of Mojo's Christmas tunes, is also part of the *Frenzy* CD. —*Rick Clark*

○ **Bo-Day-Shus!!!** / 1987 / Capitol 13099
On *Bo-Day-Shus!!!* Nixon and Roper want you to know that "Elvis Is Everywhere" (but you knew that anyway—right?). They explore the junk-food underbelly of American culture with thoughtful odes like "B.B.Q.U.S.A.," "I'm Gonna Dig Up Howlin' Wolf," and "We Gotta Have More Soul." Declarative odes like "I Ain't Gonna Piss in No Jar" and "Don't Want No Foo-Foo Haircut on My Head" are indications of Mojo and Skid's sensitivity to politically correct issues. —*Rick Clark*

● **Root Hog or Die** / 1989 / IRS 13100
With the help of producer Jim Dickinson and a few sidemen, Skid Roper and Mojo Nixon plow through thoughtful numbers like "Debbie Gibson Is Pregnant with My Two-Headed Love Child," "She's Vibrator Dependent," and "Louisiana Liplock." Nixon indulges his Elvis fixation with "(619) 239-KING," and a version of "This Land Is Your Land" mutates into a pitch for Mojo World. —*Rick Clark*

Otis / 1991 / IRS 13095
After *Root Hog or Die,* Mojo went solo and enlisted a primo group of rude rock sidemen from the Del-Lords, X, Beat Farmers, and Dash Rip Rock. Nixon did a good job making the transition from the bare-bones duo approach to a full band. His putdown of "serious" pop rockers like Don Henley ("Don Henley Must Die") gained quite a bit of publicity. —*Rick Clark*

Nova Mob

Group / Alternative rock
After a solo EP and an album that effectively chronicled his tormented final days with Hüsker Dü, as well as the rehab that followed, Grant Hart formed the punk-pop trio Nova Mob. Abandoning drums for the guitar, Hart's fine songwriting was on display on the group's debut, a rock opera called *The Last Days of Pompeii.* —*Stephen Thomas Erlewine*

● **Last Days of Pompeli** / 1991 / Rough Trade 261
A far-reaching modern-day rock opera. —*Dan Heilman*

NRBQ

Group / Rock & roll
Formed in 1967 in Florida as New Rhythm & Blues Quintet, the original lineup included pianist Terry Adams, guitarist Steve Ferguson, bassist Joey Stampinato, vocalist Frank Gadler, and drummer Tom Staley. After recording two albums for Columbia (including one with Carl Perkins), which went nowhere, guitarist Al Anderson joined in 1971, replacing Ferguson. Gadler left in 1972; Staley was replaced by drummer Tom Ardolino in 1974.

This versatile and witty quartet is at home with everything from atonal jazz to rockabilly to country swing to pop jangle to roadhouse R&B. But they don't always give eclecticism a good name; although there's something worth hearing on each of their albums, the Q's humor is often corny, and their penchant for indulging their every artistic whim means that even their best albums are padded with silly hokum. They've been doing the same stuff for nearly 30 years and have amassed a fanatical cult following. And at times, NRBQ can sound like the greatest rock band in the world.

After two decades without any lineup shakeups, Anderson left the band after the release of their 1994 album, *Message for Our Mess-Age,* to pursue a career writing country songs; he toured as Carlene Carter's guitarist immediately after his departure. NRBQ replaced Anderson with Stampinato's brother, Johnny. —*Cub Koda and John Floyd*

Scraps / 1972 / Polydor 2329018
A spotty album that contains a few necessary gems, like "Magnet" and "It's Not So Hard." —*John Floyd*

All Hopped Up / 1977 / Rounder 3029
A fairly consistent and ballsy offering, containing early classics such as "Ridin' in My Car" and "That's Alright." —*John Floyd*

○ **NRBQ at Yankee Stadium** / 1978 / Mercury 824462
Another winner, sporting three snazzy covers and nine of their best originals. —*John Floyd*

Kick Me Hard / 1979 / Rounder 3030
A decent mix of tough rockers and cheesy pop. —*John Floyd*

○ **Tiddlywinks** / 1980 / Rounder 3048
Stunning. Minimizes the foolishness and ups the ante with at least seven swinging and clever hard-pop nuggets. —*John Floyd*

○ **Grooves in Orbit** / 1983 / Rhino 70945
The same old thing, really, but "When Things Was Cheap" is their only political moment, and "Rain at the Drive-In" is charming in a naive sort of way. —*John Floyd*

RC Cola & a Moon Pie / 1986 / Rounder 3090
An abridged version of *Workshop,* one of their finest early albums. Includes some previously unreleased and rare material. —*John Floyd*

God Bless Us All / 1987 / Rounder 3108
A live album that offers an energetic glimpse at what the "Q" can do on stage. —*John Floyd*

● **Peek-A-Boo: Best of NRBQ (1969-1989)** / 1990 / Rhino 70770
A masterfully executed compilation of nearly every worthwhile song they've done. Could be the only "Q" you'll need. —*John Floyd*

○ **Stay with We: Best Of** / 1993 / Columbia 52432
Featuring 24 songs including eight unreleased tracks, *Stay with We* is the definitive compilation of NRBQ's early years at Columbia. —*Stephen Thomas Erlewine*

○ **Message for the Mess Age** / 1994 / Rhino
After a five-year layoff, NRBQ returned to the studio and made *Message for the Mess Age,* a loose, funny, rocking record that easily ranks among their best albums. —*Stephen Thomas Erlewine*

Ted Nugent

b. 1948
Guitar / Hard rock, heavy metal
Nugent started playing in a local Detroit teen band, the Lourds, and formed the Amboy Dukes in late 1965 or early 1966. He scored his first hit with "Journey to the Center of Your Mind" in 1968. Several albums using the Amboy Dukes tag followed, with the personnel changing with almost every album. Nugent went

solo in 1975, marking his greatest success to date with one album after another in the charts, then put his solo career on hold to become a member of the group Damn Yankees in 1990; the group broke up in 1993. A powerful, high-decibel guitarist, Nugent's energy more than makes up for whatever subtleties he lacks. —*Cub Koda*

○ **Double Live Gonzo** / 1978 / Epic 35069
This is the ultimate document of Nugent's mountain-man persona. —*Dan Heilman*

● **Great Gonzos: The Best of Ted Nugent** / 1981 / Epic 37667
Featuring all of his hard-rock standards from the '70s, *Great Gonzos: The Best of Ted Nugent* is a collection superior to the double-disc *Out of Control*, since there's not a bit of filler. —*Stephen Thomas Erlewine*

○ **Out of Control** / Jun. 22, 1993 / CBS 47039
Out of Control is two CDs of prime Nugent, covering his days with the Amboy Dukes as well as his lengthy solo career. It's the definitive collection of the Motor City Madman. —*AMG*

Laura Nyro
b. 1947, Bronx, NY
Vocals, piano / Singer-songwriter
While Laura Nyro remains best known for providing hit material for a number of late '60s acts, it's a mystery why she never had a smash of her own. Essential college-dorm-room listening for the era, and often bagged as a sort of East Coast answer to Joni Mitchell, in reality Nyro was in a class by herself. Nyro's songs were steeped in classic R&B and framed in stark settings, her vocal gymnastics often accompanied only by her own piano work. Any doubts as to where her music came from were erased by the album *Gonna Take a Miracle*, a brilliant collection of soul covers recorded with the resurrected LaBelle; it was also one of the first albums of all-outside material by a major rock-era songwriter. In the '70s Nyro became more reclusive, releasing only the occasional album. Even now, the promise of new Laura Nyro material is still cause for much hope. —*Steve Aldrich*

○ **First Songs** / 1967 / Columbia 31410
A collection given over to the more conventional, if high-quality early Nyro songs that later became hits (and standards) in the hands of other performers. The album includes "Wedding Bell Blues," "Stoney End," and "And When I Die." —*William Ruhlmann*

● **Eli and the 13th Confession** / 1968 / Columbia 9626
The hits (for others) keep coming—"Sweet Blindness," "Eli's Comin'," and "Stoned Soul Picnic" are all here, sung by their author—but Nyro not only proves herself a powerful singer in her own right, comfortable in styles from jazz to gospel/R&B to stark balladry, she also begins to turn to a more introspective, personal writing and singing that no one will be able to replicate. —*William Ruhlmann*

○ **New York Tendaberry** / 1969 / Columbia 9737
A stunning musical journey through love, loss, religion, and eroticism, by turns passionate, inspired, and suicidal, this is Nyro's most accomplished, most idiosyncratic record, and one of the greatest singer-songwriter works ever made. Using a wide vocal range and her often delicate piano work with deftly added instrumental touches, Nyro creates an aural landscape that spans the extremes of human emotion. It's not listed as her "pick" album only because it's not the place to start; rather, it's the logical conclusion of her musical development. —*William Ruhlmann*

Gonna Take a Miracle / 1971 / Columbia 30987
A joyous change of pace, this album presents inspired readings of pop/R&B hits of the '60s, songs like "Jimmy Mack" and "Nowhere to Run," produced by creamy-smooth soul producers Gamble & Huff and sung rapturously by Nyro, with gorgeous backing by Patti Labelle, Sarah Dash, and Nona Hendryx. —*William Ruhlmann*

○ **Smile** / 1976 / Columbia 33912
This warm comeback album is Laura Nyro's *Double Fantasy*, a return to action by a mature artist, who retains her emotional power but has worked through her problems and beaten back her demons to emerge as a "Sexy Mama." —*William Ruhlmann*

Billy Ocean
b. 1950, Trinidad
Vocals / Soul, pop/rock
Born in Trinidad, Billy Ocean emigrated to the United Kingdom as a child. He worked as a tailor while pursuing music on the side in the '60s, then broke through with the Motown-flavored "Love Really Hurts without You," which hit #3 in the United Kingdom in 1976. Ocean continued to have UK hits through the end of the '70s but didn't achieve mass success in the United States until 1984, when "Caribbean Queen (No More Love on the Run)" became a #1 hit, the first of seven Top 10 hits over the next four years. —*William Ruhlmann*

Nights (Feel Like Getting Down) / 1981 / Epic 37406
Billy Ocean was on his way to superstardom with this album, his first big hit release on Epic. The title song was his first R&B Top 10 record, and he got another couple of chart singles before beginning his run of R&B and pop hits. It also demonstrated his equal ability at doing exuberant uptempo dance tunes and convincing, if at times oversung and vapid, ballads. Epic was later left red-faced when an act they developed moved over to Jive/RCA and became a platinum act. —*Ron Wynn*

○ **Suddenly** / 1984 / Jive 1222
Billy Ocean vaulted into international stardom with this album in 1984. The album peaked at #9, was on the charts over a year and a half, and yielded him three R&B hits that were all also pop smashes. Ocean would sing on the soundtrack for the film *The Jewel of the Nile*, make sold-out appearances around the world, and appear regularly on television and videos. At this point he was also a bigger pop star than R&B artist, as two of his three hits did better as crossover vehicles than R&B tunes. —*Ron Wynn*

○ **Love Zone** / 1986 / Jive 1223
Billy Ocean was riding atop the charts when he released this album in 1986. The title track contained both a fine arrangement and Ocean's emphatic lead vocal and was a huge hit. He topped the R&B charts twice that year with both "Love Zone" and "There'll Be Sad Songs to Make You Cry," each of which was also a huge pop smash ("There'll Be Sad Songs to Make You Cry" also topped the pop charts). This was arguably his finest album and was certainly his most successful. —*Ron Wynn*

Tear Down These Walls / 1988 / Jive 1224
Things were beginning to slip a bit for Billy Ocean in the late '80s. While he was still a successful attraction, this album wouldn't reach the multiplatinum levels of its predecessors. Ocean's voice also lacked the resonance and authority it had on earlier dance tunes and wasn't as convincing or confident on ballads. He'd still land a couple more hits, and one additional chart topper (pop and R&B) with "Getta Outta My Dreams, Get into My Car," but the decline was starting. —*Ron Wynn*

● **Greatest Hits** / 1989 / Jive 1271
Contains his cool '80s disco hits "Caribbean Queen" and "Get Outta My Dreams, Get into My Car" and piano-based ballads like "There'll Be Sad Songs to Make You Cry." —*Bil Carpenter*

Sinéad O'Connor
b. 1967, Dublin, Ireland
Vocals / Alternative pop/rock
From Dublin, Ireland, Sinéad O'Connor came onto the music scene in 1987 with a powerful image of a woman who could express great sensitivity while not losing any qualities of inner strength. In public, O'Connor's seemingly audacious pronouncements about the state of the world around her may have put off those unaccustomed to a woman so forthright with her feelings; nevertheless, it's that courageousness that has endeared her to millions of fans. O'Connor's second album, *I Do Not Want What I Haven't Got*, was a worldwide hit. Musically, O'Connor draws from hard synth-rock, Celtic folk, and funk. Her dramatic alto explores sound in much the same way Peter Gabriel applies varied tonal dynamics.

After the success of *I Do Not Want What I Haven't Got*, O'Connor seemed a bit directionless. Two years later, she released an album of big-band covers, *Am I Not Your Girl?* a strange record that was a commercial disappointment. Even worse, the singer suffered a tidal wave of bad publicity when she tore a photo of the Pope on "Saturday Night Live," saying "Fight the Real Enemy." For the next year, O'Connor laid low, recording a new album that was released in the fall of 1994. —*Rick Clark*

○ **Lion and the Cobra** / 1988 / Ensign 21612

The Lion and the Cobra was an impressive showcase for this Dubliner's vocal and writing skills. On this self-produced effort, O'Connor incorporates bits of hard rock, folk, synth-pop, and light funk onto standout tracks like "I Want Your (Hands on Me)," "Jerusalem," and "Mandinka," a wonderful synth-rocker. —*Rick Clark*

● **I Do Not Want What I Haven't Got** / 1990 / Ensign 21759
O'Connor's debut might have been a strong showing, but her follow-up, *I Do Not Want What I Haven't Got*, was a stunner. Her songwriting skills were much more incisive and, vocally, O'Connor exhibited a greater range of interpretive skills. Highlights include "The Emperor's New Clothes," "I Am Stretched on Your Grave," "Jump in the River," "Black Boys on Mopeds," and the international hit "Nothing Compares 2 U," which was penned by Prince. —*Rick Clark*

Am I Not Your Girl? / 1992 / Ensign 21952
Sinéad O'Connor's version of "You Do Something to Me" (from *Red Hot & Blue*) suggested she may have had the ability to record an album of pop standards with a big band that actually worked. And at times, *Am I Not Your Girl?* a collection of standards and near-standards, *does* work. "Success Has Made a Failure of Our Home" is quite chilling, and O'Connor's sympathetic reading of "Don't Cry for Me Argentina" is better than the song itself. O'Connor runs into trouble with "Bewitched, Bothered and Bewildered" and songs that are heavily identified with other vocalists ("Gloomy Sunday"); O'Connor does not offer a new perspective on the songs, and her airy voice is buried by overwrought string arrangements. —*Stephen Thomas Erlewine*

The Ohio Players

Group / Funk, soul
Originally formed in 1959 as an instrumental R&B group, the Ohio Untouchables (as they were then known) provided backup on the Falcons' records. After the Untouchables broke up, two of the members (Clarence "Satch" Satchell and Marshall "Rock" Jones) formed a new outfit called the Ohio Players and began working as the house band at Compass Records. In the early '70s, the Ohio Players had a steady stream of funky, sexual hit singles, including the #1s "Fire" and "Love Rollercoaster." As the decade progressed, their sound gradually transformed into a throbbing disco pulse, and their sales slowly tapered off. —*Stephen Thomas Erlewine*

Pleasure / 1973 / Westbound 2017
This was the first Ohio Players album to get sizable mileage and attract some attention. "Funky Worm" was their initial #1 R&B hit, got them into the pop Top 20, and alerted the funk and R&B community to the group's mix of sizzling beats, a jazz-rock sensibility, and exuberant collective vocals. They were almost ready to break, and this was an early indication of the band's potential. —*Ron Wynn*

○ **Fire** / 1974 / Mercury 848346
The Ohio Players peaked as a '70s funk band with this record, which became their lone #1 pop hit. The title track was a #1 pop and R&B single, while "I Want to Be Free" was perhaps their best nondance or novelty hit. The horn charts were catchy and energetic, guitarist Leroy "Sugarfoot" Bonner was in his prime, and the vocals were silly but hypnotic. —*Ron Wynn*

○ **Skin Tight** / 1974 / Mercury 848345
The Ohio Players earned their first gold album with this 1974 album, as well as a #2 R&B single with the title cut. The group was honing its punchy funk arrangements and exuberant vocal style, and "Skin Tight" was the first song since "Funky Worm" to earn both R&B and pop attention. It was also their debut album on Mercury, and it did so well their old label Westbound rushed out a compilation of old cuts called *Climax*. But its release didn't hinder the group, who were helping make funk the prime trend in R&B. —*Ron Wynn*

Greatest Hits / 1975 / Westbound 1005
With the Ohio Players established funk superstars on Mercury in the mid '70s, Westbound rushed out a collection of their best early songs, many of which were outstanding. This is actually a worthwhile anthology, particularly many people missed "Pain," "Funky Worm," and other pre-Mercury hits. —*Ron Wynn*

○ **Honey** / 1975 / Mercury 848347

A huge hit album, their second most successful LP ever, peaking at the #2 spot on the R&B charts, though it didn't generate any pop action. The album cover, with its photo of a gorgeous woman having hot honey poured on her, wouldn't even make it to the drawing board in the current environment; it generated a firestorm in the mid '70s when it turned out one of the women they'd used got burned. An interesting aside is that many think the title track was a hit, but it was actually the single "Sweet, Sticky Thing" that cemented the LP's hit status. That and "Love Rollercoaster" were R&B chart toppers. "Honey" didn't even chart. —*Ron Wynn*

★ **Ohio Players Gold** / 1976 / Mercury 824461
A strong overview of their biggest hits and best moments, including "Fire," "Fopp," "Skin Tight," and the shattering "Love Rollercoaster." —*Stephen Thomas Erlewine*

Oingo Boingo

Group / Alternative pop/rock
Led the the wide-ranging musical talent of Danny Elfman (who would go on to score film and TV projects ranging from *Batman* to "The Simpsons"), Los Angeles's Oingo Boingo carved out a respectable reputation among the new wave set with a quirky pop style that owed a heavy debt to bands like XTC. In 1994, Oingo Boingo reemerged as Boingo, releasing a new album that didn't attract much attention. —*Dan Heilman*

● **Best O' Boingo** / 1992 / MCA 10424
Captures their peculiar-yet-catchy style well. —*Dan Heilman*

The O'Jays

Group / Soul, R&B
Perhaps the reigning vocal group of the '70s and '80s, the O'Jays began in Canton as the Triumphs in 1958. The original lineup was Eddie Levert, Walter Williams, William Powell, Bobby Massey, and Bill Isles. They recorded as the Mascots for King in 1961 and were renamed by Cleveland disc jockey Eddie O'Jay. Isles departed in 1965, and Massey left in 1971 to become a producer, making the group a trio. They got their first chart single in 1963 for Imperial, for whom they recorded until 1967. The O'Jays' first major hit was "I'll Be Sweeter Tomorrow (Than I Was Today)" for Bell in 1967, which reached #8 on the R&B charts. They continued on Bell and Neptune until they attained stardom in 1972 on Philadelphia International. "Back Stabbers" was the first of eight #1 R&B hits they would receive on the label from 1972-1987. Others included "Love Train," " "Give the People What They Want," "I Love Music," "Livin' for the Weekend," "Message to Our Music," "Use Ta Be My Girl," "Darlin' Darlin' Baby (Sweet, Tender, Love)," and "Lovin' You." They also had eight other Top 10 R&B hits and four other Top 10 pop smashes, while "Love Train" also topped the pop charts in 1973. They moved to EMI in 1987 and continued recording. —*Ron Wynn*

☆ **Back Stabbers** / 1972 / Philadelphia International 31712
Though you could lean toward *Ship Ahoy,* it would be hard to argue with the general assessment that this is their greatest album. Certainly no other single was as transcendent and definitive in 1970 as "Love Train," without question their greatest song. Yet "Back Stabbers" isn't far behind it; the message, harmonies, Eddie Levert's lead, and the group's refrains are all testimonies to soul's glory. Gamble and Huff were in peak production, writing, and arranging form. It's hard to believe there were some other good songs on the record like "Listen to the Clock on the Wall" and "Shiftless, Shady, Jealous Kind of People"; they were completely blown away and ignored due to "Love Train" and "Back Stabbers." —*Ron Wynn*

○ **Ship Ahoy** / 1973 / Philadelphia International 32408
The "other" O'Jays album masterpiece, *Ship Ahoy,* combined shattering message tracks and stunning love songs in a fashion matched only by Curtis Mayfield's finest material. From the album cover showing a slave ship to the memorable title song and incredible "For the Love of Money," Gamble and Huff addressed every social ill from envy to racism and greed. Eddie Levert's leads were consistently magnificent, as were the harmonies, production, and arrangements. "Put Your Hands Together" and "You Got Your Hooks in Me" would be good album cuts, but on *Ship Ahoy* they were merely icing on the cake. —*Ron Wynn*

○ **Survival** / 1975 / Philadelphia International 33150

The O'Jays followed the spectacular albums *Back Stabbers* and *Ship Ahoy* with the good, though not on the same level, *Survival*. It was unrealistic to expect masterpieces every time out, and the record included many strong ballads and good message tracks. But while it may not have been as epic in its performances and compositions, it was certainly the other albums' equal in its sales strength. The group had two #1 R&B hits in 1975, "Give the People What They Want" and "I Love Music (Part 1)." In addition, the title track made the charts as a B side, the flip to "Let Me Make Love to You," another rousing ballad. —*Ron Wynn*

Family Reunion / 1975 / Philadelphia International 33807
The O'Jays were in one of their most productive periods during the '70s. The Gamble/Huff team was giving them consistently strong material, often classic songs, and their three-member harmonies and shared leads were galvanizing, particulary those by Eddie Levert. The title track did well, but the album tended to be overlooked because it was sandwiched between *Survival* and *Message in Our Music*. Yet it attained more pop attention than the more heralded (and superior) *Ship Ahoy*. Only *So Full of Love* generated more crossover appeal than this album, an interesting achievement. —*Ron Wynn*

★ **Collector's Item** / 1977 / Philadelphia International 35024
After enjoying an impressive string of gold and platinum albums, the O'Jays had this collection of their biggest hits on Philadelphia International released in 1978. There was no way to lose with such songs as "Back Stabbers," "Love Train," "For the Love tf Money," and "I Love Music." Unfortunately, Philadelphia International haphazardly sequenced the collection, ignoring either chronological or stylistic considerations and just sticking tracks on the two sides without any attention to pacing. That gaffe aside, it was (and is) a worthy anthology for the casual listener, though the hardcore fan should look elsewhere. —*Ron Wynn*

So Full of Love / 1978 / Philadelphia International 35355
This was the biggest hit album the O'Jays ever enjoyed, though it wasn't as aesthically transcendant as *Ship Ahoy*. But it came at the right time; there weren't many great group albums being produced in R&B at the time, and that's what this really was, even if Eddie Levert took most of the leads. "Use Ta Be My Girl" was a triumphant success, while "Brandy" was the prototype album cut that became a hit through popular demand. —*Ron Wynn*

● **Greatest Hits** / 1984 / Philadelphia International 39251
When the O'Jays left Columbia for EMI, the company promptly issued this greatest hits package, though they opted to put fewer tracks on it than on the 1978 *Collector's Items*. So, the logical question would be, why would anyone want it? Probably because they've made *Collector's Items* extremely difficult to locate, and also because this mid '80s release had better mastering of such seminal O'Jays' items as "Love Train" and "For the Love of Money." While it has gaping holes, as a single-disc anthology, this release provided an acceptable overview of the group's Epic/Philadelphia International/TSOP material. —*Ron Wynn*

Emotionally Yours / Jan. 21, 1991 / EMI America 93390
A fine early '90s release that demonstrated the trio of Eddie Levert, Walter Williams, and Sammy Strain still packed a solid punch on ballads and uptempo songs and were making the adjustment to New Jack production and hip-hop influences. But while they occasionally used the rapper Jaz, the O'Jays' strengths remained their energized harmonies and the soulful leads of Levert, as well as Williams and Strain at times. Their sound remains timeless and appealing, dependent on material, but superb when they get quality songs. —*Ron Wynn*

Heartbreaker / 1993 / EMI America 89740
The O'Jays have made concessions to changing tastes, adopting drum samples and synthesized backing, and included some new jack swing material on each album. But they wisely haven't tampered with their strength: lush, three-part harmonies anchored by the earnest lead vocals of Eddie Levert. Their newest release contains several intense, urgent ballads, many of them written by group members. Outside of Carlton Hunt's raps on "Trouble" and "Can't Let You Go," many numbers aren't much different from the classic material that made them superstars in the '70s; that's both part of the music's charm and something that might trouble fans hoping the group would experiment with the vocal arrangements as well as the production. —*Ron Wynn*

Olympics

Group / R&B
A sub-Coasters R&B group scored in 1958 with the great novelty hit "Western Movies." In 1965 they recorded the original version of "Good Lovin'," later covered by the Rascals. Despite the rumors, they were not the same group as the Marathons ("Peanut Butter"). —*John Floyd*

● **All-Time Greatest Hits!** / 1991 / Sandstone Music 33078
Somewhat more comprehensive than their Rhino package, this 26-track gem is the definitive homage to this good-time R&B crew. —*Jeff Tamarkin*

Alexander O'Neal

b. Nov. 14, 1953, Minneapolis, MN
Vocals / Urban R&B, soul
This Minneapolis soul man cut his teeth in the Time but was bounced (for looking "too Black") before they signed with Warner Brothers. His tough, ballsy voice has the same grain and range as Otis Redding's. Like that master, O'Neal is comfortable with pumping dance-floor burners and slinky couch-cuddlers. He's certainly the best singer Jimmy Jam and Terry Lewis have ever produced, and the strength of his material and his robust voice make him a candidate for Greatest Soul Singer of the last ten years. —*John Floyd*

Alexander O'Neal / 1985 / Tabu 39331
Former Time member Alexander O'Neal made a smashing debut as a lead artist in the mid '80s. The Jam/Lewis duo found the ideal balance for O'Neal between dance/funk uptempo tunes and urgent urban contemporary ballads. They scored with "If You Were Here Tonight" and "A Broken Heart Can Mend" as well as "Innocent." Suddenly, O'Neal was among the top male urban artists and continued having hits into the '90s. —*Ron Wynn*

○ **Hearsay** / 1986 / Tabu 40320
Alexander O'Neal almost achieved the breakout album he needed for crossover success with his second album. It cracked the Top 30 on the pop album chart, earned a gold record, and included O'Neal's two strongest uptempo tunes, "Fake" and "Criticize." Jam and Lewis linked the material with "party" dialogue and patter and provided their finest and tightest production for any O'Neal record. The beats were catchy, the songs hook laden, and O'Neal's voice alternately explosive, sensitive, and bemused. —*Ron Wynn*

○ **All True Man** / 1991 / Epic 45349
Alexander O'Neal's biggest weakness was timing; he came along during an era when individual soul singers and romantic balladeers had lost their prominence in the urban contemporary equation. While O'Neal had a more rugged sound and natural ebullience than any vocalist except Luther Vandross and Freddie Jackson, his songs could never generate the attention they deserved. Although this album went gold, it couldn't get enough of a breakout single to keep it on the charts long enough. Likewise, O'Neal's voice was never more versatile, convincing, or urgent than on such cuts as "Hang On," "Midnight Run," and "Sentimental." —*Ron Wynn*

● **Greatest Hits: This Thing Called Love** / 1993 / CBS 53833
While it can be argued Alexander O'Neal's track record doesn't merit any greatest hits or best of compilations, that didn't deter Tabu from issuing this compilation. It presented O'Neal's finest uptempo and ballad singles and displayed both his ferocity on such cuts as "Fake" and "Criticize," plus his range and passion on "Never Knew Love Like This." —*Ron Wynn*

The Only Ones

Group / Punk, rock & roll
One of the punk era's most underrated bands. Led by scuzzy romantic Peter Perrett, the Only Ones played not-so-fast guitar rock lifted from numerous listenings to the New York Dolls. Although traditional (actually downright conservative) in their approach to rock craft, their skill with a pop song was, for its time, matched only by the Undertones. —*John Dougan*

○ **Only Ones** / 1978 / CBS 82830
Brilliantly written, sung, and played debut; overlooked in its era, rightfully regarded now as a classic. —*Steve Aldrich*

● **Special View** / 1979 / Epic 36199

237

U.S. collection of tracks from first two LPs and debut single. Easiest access to otherwise rare and classic material. —*Steve Aldrich*

○ **Even Serpents Shine** / 1979 / CBS 83451
Only a shade removed from the standard of debut LP. —*Steve Aldrich*

Baby's Got a Gun / 1980 / Epic 36584
Less consistant than their first two efforts; still rewarding. —*Steve Aldrich*

○ **Peel Sessions** / 1989 / Dutch East India 8109
The essential compilation. Includes the classic "Another Girl, Another Planet" as well as about a dozen more of Perrett's gloomy, sardonic takes on romantic life. Pop so wry it'll make you giddy. —*John Dougan*

Immortal Story / 1992 / CBS 471267
"Official" compilation. Best-ofs including alternate takes and rare tracks. —*Steve Aldrich*

Yoko Ono

Vocals / Experimental, pop/rock
Over the years, Yoko Ono has received an unfair treatment in the press. From being pegged as the reason the Beatles broke up to being called talentless, Ono has been dragged through the press more times than any one person deserves. And she did have talent, although it was primarily as a conceptual and visual artist. As a musician, she is allegedly influential on many post-punk bands, though it is highly unlikely anyone outside of the B-52s actually listened to her records. With her abrasive, frequently atonal pop and rock experimentations, Ono did predict, if not influence, the sound of some experimental post-punk bands, including Public Image Limited. Ono could be even more effective when she conformed to pop songwriting, turning in some surprisingly moving straightforward pop/rock. If you can wade through the pretentions—as well as grow accustomed to her shrill voice—you may find some rewarding music among her many records. — *Stephen Thomas Erlewine*

○ **Onobox** / Jan. 1992 / Rykodisc 10224
Although it inspires countless jokes, the music on the six-disc *Onobox* is, by and large, quite impressive. In terms of experimental rock & roll, Ono was certainly one of the leaders in the '70s, creating intense, almost atonal rock that demanded to be accepted on its own terms. Listening to the music nearly 20 years later, some of it sounds dated, but much of it sounds remarkably contemporary. Nevertheless, the box is rarely dull, and it makes a strong case for her musical talents. —*Stephen Thomas Erlewine*

● **Walking on Thin Ice Compilation** / Feb. 1992 / Rykodisc 20230
A single-disc distillation of the *Onobox* that covers everything the curious listener needs to know. If you still need more after listening to *Walking on Thin Ice*, the *Onobox* is a must-buy. —*Stephen Thomas Erlewine*

Orb

Group / Techno, dance
More than any other techno outfit, the Orb is rooted in the progressive rock tendencies of the '70s, creating a post-post-punk psychedelic dance music for the '90s. While their electronics do occasionally stake out house/rave, the band more frequently explores ambient and trance techno, creating thick, textural sonic landscapes that can last up to 40 minutes a song. While their music is long and repetitive, it is rarely boring; it's hypnotic, much like some of the psychedelic explorations of the late '60s. — *Stephen Thomas Erlewine*

Huge Ever Growing Pulsating Brain That Rules from the Centre of the Ultraworld / 1989 / Island
Pink Floyd-like space music with a variety of water noises. *A Huge Ever Growing Pulsating Brain That Rules from the Centre of the Ultraworld* is suited to those interested in psychedelia and the bizarre. —*David Szatmary*

○ **Adventures Beyond Ultraworld** / 1991 / Island 511034
The Orb's first full-length album expands on the strengths of their debut EP, resulting in one of the most compulsively listenable techno albums ever recorded. —*Stephen Thomas Erlewine*

● **U.f.orb** / Mar. 1992 / Island 513749
So far, the Orb haven't made an album better than *U.F.Orb*, a hypnotic series of trance-inducing rhythms and interweaving synths

that never grows boring, even at its 74-minute length. —*Stephen Thomas Erlewine*

○ **Live 93** / 1993 / Island
Although a live Orb album might sound dull and tedious, the resulting double-disc set is amazing, a complete representation of the group in concert and living proof that techno can be just as captivating in concert as it is on record. Besides, the constant Pink Floyd jokes on the record, including the brilliant cover art, are hilarious. —*Stephen Thomas Erlewine*

Roy Orbison

b. Apr. 23, 1936, Wink, TX, **d.** Dec. 6, 1988
Vocals / Pop/rock, rock & roll, rockabilly
Roy Orbison was the most unlikely of early rock & rollers, the physical and charismatic antithesis of Elvis Presley, Jerry Lee Lewis, and Little Richard. But he forged a style that was as singular as any in rock, assuming the role of pop's master paranoic. He cut some rockabilly for Sun in the late '50s, but it's his string of brilliant '60s hits, produced with Frank Foster for Monument, that established Orbison's formula. His best singles delve into the darkest areas of a soul torn by romantic confusion and terror; "Only the Lonely" and "Running Scared" epitomize Orbison's near-operatic ballad formula. Although he also recorded some convincing and tough rock ("Oh, Pretty Woman," "Candy Man"), his reputation rests on his bleak, uncompromising broken-heart laments, which have influenced rockers from Del Shannon to Bruce Springsteen and Elvis Costello. After spending most of the '70s and '80s on the oldies circuit, Orbison revived his career through an association with a group called the Traveling Wilburys. He died in 1989, just weeks after releasing *Mystery Girl*, the album that put him back on the charts. —*John Floyd*

Crying / 1962 / Sony 21428
Roy Orbison's second album was above average considering the slight standards of the time, but was a fairly slight effort nonetheless. In its favor, the album features nearly all original material by Orbison and some of the writers who frequently tailored songs for him, such as Boudleaux and Felice Bryant and Joe Melson. The trademark early Orbison production flourishes, with swooping strings and full vocal choruses, are also present. What's missing is truly first-rate songwriting. With the exception of "Love Hurts," the title track, and the epic hit "Running Scared," most of the cuts lean toward the Big O's more sentimental side and are pleasantly forgettable. Of the obscure cuts here, the best are the uptempo "Nite Life" and "Let's Make a Memory," with its bouncing string arrangement, but neither could be classified among his best early work. —*Richie Unterberger*

○ **All-Time Greatest Hits** / 1976 / Monument 8600
The All-Time Greatest Hits of Roy Orbison is an essential collection. It rounds up 20 of the Big O's best '60s recordings, with some fine album tracks thrown in. —*John Floyd*

★ **For the Lonely: 18 Greatest Hits** / 1988 / Rhino 71493
For the Lonely: Roy Orbison Anthology (1956-1965) offers the usual Monument hits along with a few Sun tunes—18 in all. Buyers beware: The vinyl version contains more cuts than the CD. —*John Floyd*

○ **Legendary Roy Orbison** / 1988 / Sony 46809
While the Rhino set, *For the Lonely: Roy Orbison Anthology (1956-1965)*, is the most essential single-disc release of Orbison's work, *The Legendary Roy Orbison* tries to flesh out the picture considerably with a four-CD, 75-track boxed set. It may be overkill for some, and certain tracks feel like pointless inclusions, but fans who want more than just a hits collection should like this set. The enclosed booklet contains a wealth of photos, and the annotation is passionate and informative. —*Rick Clark*

○ **Mystery Girl** / 1989 / Virgin 91058
Roy's comeback is remarkable in that every song, from "You Got It" and "She's a Mystery to Me" to "The Only One," proves that the formula of his '60s stuff is still vital 30 years later. An album that really deserved a followup. —*John Floyd*

○ **Sun Years 1956-58** / Apr. 1989 / Bear Family 15461
Contains Orbison's complete Sun output, featuring many undubbed recordings and the pile-driving "Domino." —*John Floyd*

The Originals

Group / R&B, Motown

Led by Freddie Gorman, the Originals took the R&B world by storm in 1969, although they had worked at Motown for years as invaluable background vocalists. Gorman recorded as a solo for Berry Gordy in 1961 and co-wrote "Please Mr. Postman" for the Marvelettes, and the Originals cut a version of Leadbelly's "Goodnight Irene" for Gordy's Soul subsidiary in 1966 with ex-Falcon Joe Stubbs as lead. But Stubbs had split to form 100 Proof Aged in Soul by the time the quartet waxed the beautiful doo-wop throwback "Baby I'm for Real," a R&B chart-topper in 1969 that was co-written and lushly produced by Marvin Gaye. The same combination also produced "The Bells," another major hit in 1970. Former solo act Ty Hunter joined the group in 1971, and the Originals continued to chart into the next decade. —Bill Dahl

○ **Naturally Together** / 1970 / Soul 729
The group's third Motown album didn't fare nearly as well as the previous two, which both made the lower regions of the pop charts. Despite some wonderful production by Clay Murray and fine ballad and uptempo leads from Crathman Spencer and Henry Dixon, they couldn't generate much national action, even though it had one wonderful song in "God Bless Whoever Sent You," which peaked at #14 R&B. —Ron Wynn

● **Motown Superstar Series Vol.10** / Motown 5110
The Detroit-based Originals began singing in 1966, with tenor vocalists Crathman Spencer and Henry Dixon, bassist Freddie Gorman, and baritone Walter Gaines. Marvin Gaye helped bring them to Motown, and later wrote or cowrote three of their singles, including the anthemic "Baby, I'm for Real." That single, their other major hit "The Bells," and the third Gaye single, "We Can Make It Baby," are among the tunes on this anthology. They weren't a great group, but their two hits are as gripping and wonderfully produced and arranged as any Motown material. —Ron Wynn

Jeffrey Osborne

Vocals / Urban R&B

Until 1980, Osborne was the lead vocalist of L.T.D. Throughout the '80s, he had a string of Top 40 hits: "Don't You Get So Mad," "Stay with Me Tonight," "You Should Be Mine (The Woo Woo Song)," and "Love Power," a duet with Dionne Warwick. —*Stephen Thomas Erlewine*

● **Jeffrey Osborne** / 1982 / A&M 3272
A pivotal, career-establishing R&B statement from this love stylist. —*Ron Wynn*

○ **Stay with Me Tonight** / 1983 / A&M 3337
A fine title cut and a good overall session. —*Ron Wynn*

Don't Stop / 1984 / A&M 5017
Good, but no standout cut. —*Ron Wynn*

Only Human / 1991 / Arista 8620
This is the comeback, which returned Osborne to the R&B forefront. —*Ron Wynn*

Ozzy Osbourne (John Osbourne)

b. Dec. 3, 1948, Birmingham, England
Vocals / Heavy metal
The former lead singer of Black Sabbath has carved out a thriving solo career in spite of—or maybe because of—a knack for creating controversy with his lyrics and his behavior. Osbourne's sound is basic and to the point, crafted almost strictly for teenage headbangers, who remain his most loyal followers. While his lyrics rarely hold any relevance for anyone over 17, he is to be admired for his skills as a bandleader who is able regularly to mine talent on the order of his brilliant onetime guitarist, the late Randy Rhoads. —*Dan Heilman*

○ **Blizzard of Oz** / Jan. 1981 / Jet 36812
Ozzy's solo debut not only reestablished him as a viable attraction, it also introduced the ample talents of guitarist Randy Rhoads, whose classically influenced style had a huge impact on rock guitar in the '80s. Say what you will about Ozzy, but the music here is simply great; Osbourne/Rhoads collaborations like "Crazy Train," "Mr. Crowley," and "Revelation (Mother Earth)" still stand today as all-time heavy metal classics. —*Steve Huey*

○ **Diary of a Madman** / Feb. 1981 / Jet 37492
The followup was rushed, and it shows: Rhoads didn't even have time to lay down a real solo on "Little Dolls" (the solo used was intended only as a guide). Even so, Rhoads's classical training

manifests itself even more, and the compositions generally increase in sophistication (especially the epic title track). One wonders how much the Osbourne/Rhoads combination would have accomplished had Rhoads not been killed in a plane crash five months after this recording. —*Steve Huey*

Speak of the Devil / 1982 / Jet 38350
A live album recorded from Osbourne's 1982 tour, featuring powerful new versions of Black Sabbath classics. It caused a minor controversy, since Sabbath (with Ronnie James Dio as vocalist) released their first live album (*Live Evil*) at the same time, also with early Black Sabbath material. Ozzy's band at the time featured drummer Tommy Aldridge, Night Ranger guitarist Brad Gillis, and bassist Rudy Sarzo, later a member of Whitesnake. —*John Book*

● **Tribute** / 1987 / Epic 40714
This live double album, released five years after Randy Rhoads's death, showcases a hard-rock guitarist whose all-around ability was arguably second only to Eddie Van Halen. Osbourne leads his best band lineup through the entire *Blizzard* repertoire, plus a few *Diary* and Sabbath numbers. Of special note are Rhoads's unaccompanied solo, leaving no doubts about his virtuosity, and the studio outtakes of his short solo piece "Dee." Rhoads's entire output is absolutely essential for guitar freaks, but he sounds even better live than in the studio. —*Steve Huey*

○ **No More Tears** / 1991 / Epic 46795
While looking for fresh inspiration, Osbourne started writing songs with Motörhead's Lemmy Kilmister, the kind of collaboration metal fans dream about. As a result, the songs on *No More Tears* are more compact, the sound denser, the musical payoffs more immediate. And not that Ozzy's mellowing in old age or anything, but *No More Tears* contains two of his best ballads—"Mama, I'm Coming Home" and "Time after Time." —*Brian Mansfield*

Live & Loud / 1992 / Epic 48973
Fans will be pleased with this live set from Osbourne, which isn't as consistent as *Tribute* but does feature a hot new band and songs that aren't available on any other live Osbourne album, as well as a one-shot reunion with Black Sabbath on the song "Black Sabbath." —*Stephen Thomas Erlewine*

Jimmy Page (James Patrick Page)

b. Jan. 9, 1944, Heston
Guitar / Rock & roll, hard rock
James Patrick Page is one of the most successful rock guitarists to come out of England in the '60s. Born in Heston, Page was playing recording sessions in London studios while still in his teens, and his guitar can be heard on many of the records made there in the mid '60s. Page turned down an initial offer to join the Yardbirds, then changed his mind and worked with the group until its demise in 1968. He then formed Led Zeppelin, which was the predominant hard-rock/heavy-metal band in popular music until 1980. After the group split, Page was less active, though he formed another hard-rock quartet, the Firm, in the mid '80s. He released his own solo album in 1988. In the '90s, while deflecting Zeppelin reunion rumors, he was working on an album with Whitesnake singer David Coverdale.

In 1993, Page released his collaboration with Coverdale, *Coverdale/Page*. While it featured some fine playing by Page, it was hampered by lackluster songs. Following a tour, the duo broke up. Page and Robert Plant were spotted together several times during 1994—including performing a tribute to Alexis Korner together—and it seemed certain that the two would be recording together in the future. —*William Ruhlmann*

● **Outrider** / 1988 / David Geffen Co. 24188
Page's debut solo album is a heavy guitar treat employing a varying cast of sidemen, including drummer Jason Bonham and Page's old Led Zeppelin partner Robert Plant, who cowrites and sings one song. —*William Ruhlmann*

○ **Session Man, Vol. 1** / 1989 / Bomp! 1041
Prior to his tenure in the Yardbirds and Led Zeppelin, Jimmy Page played numerous recording sessions in England. This is a compilation of his work from 1963 to 1968, including a solo single, some previously unreleased Yardbirds material, and various obscure British artists. —*William Ruhlmann*

○ **Session Man, Vol. 2** / 1991 / Bomp! 1053

With more obscure acts than the previous volume, it also includes such name artists as Brenda Lee and Billy Fury, plus a live Yardbirds cut. —*William Ruhlmann*

Jimmy's Back Pages: The Early Years / 1992 / CBS 52428
Historically, *Jimmy's Back Pages* is interesting because it shows the roots of the overamped blues-rock that Page perfected in Led Zeppelin, but some fans will be disappointed because most of this doesn't sound anything like classic Zeppelin. —AMG

Coverdale/Page / 1993 / Geffen
A fitfully entertaining collaboration with former Whitesnake singer David Coverdale, *Coverdale/Page* shows Jimmy Page can still write the occasional killer riff, but he has trouble pulling together cohesive songs. —*Stephen Thomas Erlewine*

Robert Palmer

b. Jan. 1949
Vocals / Pop/rock
British singer (and occasional songwriter), with a strong taste for R&B, Caribbean, New Orleans, and other rhythmic styles. He made a series of well-received albums in the '70s but finally broke through commercially in the '80s, singing in the Duran Duran project band Power Station and later on his own with his "Addicted to Love" in 1986. —*William Ruhlmann*

○ **Sneakin' Sally through the Alley** / 1974 / Island 842607
On his debut solo album, Palmer employs members of the Meters and Little Feat for a musical gumbo enriched by his husky, percussive voice. —*William Ruhlmann*

○ **Pressure Drop** / 1975 / Island 842594
Palmer's own songs (especially the silky "Give Me an Inch" and "Work to Make It Work") and the backing of Little Feat help make this a worthy followup to *Sally*. —*William Ruhlmann*

○ **Some People Can Do What They Like** / 1976 / Island 842786
Palmer's "Keep in Touch," "Man Smart, Woman Smarter," and "Spanish Moon" (the latter by Little Feat's Lowell George) pace *Some People Can Do What They Like*, another terrific collection. —*William Ruhlmann*

Double Fun / 1978 / Island 842592
Palmer produces and writes more songs than usual, resulting in the hit "Every Kinda People" and a somewhat lighter, more pop approach. —*William Ruhlmann*

○ **Secrets** / 1979 / Island 842354
Palmer scores his biggest hit single of the '70s with the uptempo rocker "Bad Case of Loving You (Doctor, Doctor)" on an album that also includes a wonderful version of Todd Rundgren's ballad "Can We Still Be Friends." —*William Ruhlmann*

Clues / 1980 / Island 842353
A move toward fast-paced electronic dance-rock. It's successful about half the time, especially on Palmer's UK hits "Looking for Clues" and "Johnny and Mary." (Rod Stewart copied "Johnny and Mary" for his hit "Young Turks" the following year.) —*William Ruhlmann*

Maybe It's Live / 1982 / Island 9665
Five oldies recorded in concert and five new songs, among them Palmer's first big UK hit, "Some Guys Have All the Luck." (Rod Stewart had a U.S. hit version two years later.) —*William Ruhlmann*

○ **Riptide** / 1985 / Island 826463
Palmer's commercial breakthrough, much of it in the hard-rock style of his one-shot band Power Station, and featuring the hits "Discipline of Love," "Addicted to Love" (a #1 hit), "Hyperactive," and "I Didn't Mean to Turn You On." —*William Ruhlmann*

● **Addictions, Vol. 1** / 1989 / Island 842301
Thirteen-track compilation containing Palmer's biggest hits, not only the ones on Island but also the Power Station singles and "Simply Irresistible," from Palmer's first EMI album. —*William Ruhlmann*

Addictions, Vol. 2 / 1992 / Island 510345
Apart from "I Didn't Mean to Turn You On," there are no big hits, only album tracks and failed singles, all of which are quite good. Unfortunately, the majority of the material has been remixed, remade, or has new vocal tracks; the album may sound great, but it's not an accurate retrospective. —*Stephen Thomas Erlewine*

Pantera

Group / Heavy metal
Pantera's massively brutal, aggressive, jagged heavy metal earned them a large cult following in the early '90s. During the early '80s, the band explored several different styles of hard rock; sometimes they sounded like Kiss and Aerosmith, at others like Def Leppard. After several years of struggling the band changed their tune in 1988, becoming rougher and harder, much like Metallica. Guitarist Diamond ("Dimebag") Darrell rejected an offer to join Megadeth, concentrating on Pantera's new direction. The change in style proved successful; 1992's *A Vulgar Display of Power* became an underground metal hit, eventually scaling *Billboard's* Top 50. When their new album, *Far Beyond Driven*, was released in 1994, the band debuted at #1. Some chart-watchers were surprised, but anyone that followed their rise from obscurity to *A Vulgar Display of Power* knew that Pantera was one of the most popular metal bands of the early '90s. —*Stephen Thomas Erlewine*

○ **Cowboys from Hell** / 1990 / East West 91372
Technical thrash from Texas. This is the album that put them in the spotlight and opened the door for thrash bands who were a little different. —*John Book*

● **Vulgar Display of Power** / 1992 / East West 91758
A burning, disembowling collection of brutal riffs, pulverizing speed, and hoarse, shouted vocals, *A Vulgar Display of Power* is the record that established Pantera as the most vicious and popular heavy metal band of the early '90s. —*Stephen Thomas Erlewine*

Far Beyond Driven / 1994 / East West 92302
Far Beyond Driven finds Pantera in a bit of a holding pattern. Although the riffs are still lethally fast, the band shows no signs of musical development, and the songs aren't any better than those on *A Vulgar Display of Power*. Nevertheless, there's enough primal metal here to satisfy most of their fans. —*Stephen Thomas Erlewine*

Mica Paris

Vocals / Urban R&B
Though she has yet to attain stardom, English vocalist Mica Paris has a wonderful voice and individualistic delivery and approach. She sang in the Spirit of Watts gospel group before touring and recording in the late '80s with Hollywood Beyond. She signed with 4th & Broadway/Island in the '80s, issuing her debut *So Good*. Her second record, *Contribution*, was released in 1990. Paris moved to Polydor for her third album, *Whisper a Prayer*, in 1993. She also recorded with Will Downing in 1989, doing an updated version of "Where Is the Love." —*Ron Wynn*

So Good / 1988 / Island 842497
British songstress Mica Paris generated some excitement on both sides of the Atlantic with her debut album in 1988. Part of the buzz came from the fact that her tone, huge sound, and approach were much more soul- and R&B-oriented than the ultra-smooth and polished urban contemporary that was commonplace at the time. It also had some dance touches and was looser and more attractive than many of the releases coming from pop and disco divas. —*Ron Wynn*

● **Contribution** / 1990 / Island 846814
Despite improved production, even stronger vocals, and some excellent material, Mica Paris didn't enjoy the same response with her second release that her debut enjoyed. She even ventured into New Jack territory, utilizing rappers Rakim and Danny D, and even recorded some Prince material. But the set's best song, the sizzling "South of the River," was a radio bust, and Paris simply couldn't get enough momentum generated to make the album a success. —*Ron Wynn*

Graham Parker

b. Nov. 15, 1950
Vocals / Rock & roll, pop/rock
Graham Parker is the quintessential angry young man; his early albums are full of righteous passion, vicious sarcasm, and great, powerful rock & roll. Graham Parker is also the quintessential bitter old man; while the occasional good song pops up here and there, his later albums are weighed down by petty anger, disgust, and frustration. But when he was at the top of his form in the late

'70s, Parker was a singer/songwriter like no other. Backed by his superb band the Rumour, he turned out a series of clever, concise songs that bristled with energy; his songs drew heavily from R&B, rock & roll, and rockabilly without ever sounding dated. Parker's music sounded vital because of his unrestrained passion as well as the way his lyrics and song structures redefined and subverted the tradtions of the '50s and '60s.

Howlin' Wind, his 1976 debut album, earned him scores of lavish critical praise, as did its followup, *Heat Treatment*, released the same year. In 1977 he formed the Rumour and released the inconsistent, but occasionaly exceptional *Stick to Me*. Parker left Mercury in 1978, leading to his classic attack on the record label, "Mercury Poisoning"; the company rushed out a live album to fulfill his contract. With 1979's *Squeezing Out Sparks*, Parker had made his finest record; again, he received an overwhelming amount of critical acclaim but no sales.

After *Squeezing Out Sparks*, Parker began to sink into his own cynicism as he tried to refashion his sound for the mainstream marketplace; he had only one hit from the four albums he released between 1980 and 1985—"Wake Up (Next to You)" in 1985. Following that minor chart success, his songs became more direct, as shown by 1988's *The Mona Lisa's Sister*, the best thing he had released in years. It began a string of strong albums that were sometimes undone by his own relentless pessimism. By this time, the anger that fueled his early records had turned into mere bitterness. However, when Parker can keep his sniping to a minimum, he is as good as he has ever been. —*Stephen Thomas Erlewine*

☆ **Howlin' Wind** / 1976 / Mercury 826273
Parker comes across as both tough-minded and optimistic (maybe the word is "determined") on his debut album, on which he sings with conviction against the cohesive backing of the Rumour. —*William Ruhlmann*

○ **Heat Treatment** / 1976 / Mercury 826274
Essentially *Howlin' Wind, Vol. 2*, as Parker and the Rumour demonstrate that their initial burst of high-quality songs can extend to a second album, in the same year as their debut. —*William Ruhlmann*

★ **Squeezing Out Sparks** / 1979 / Arista 8075
Older and more bitter, Parker delves deeper into his demons, and the Rumour just plays harder. Parker's best album, and one of the best albums of the decade. —*William Ruhlmann*

○ **Up Escalator** / 1980 / Arista 8093
On his last album with the Rumour, Parker goes for mainstream rock success, employing the widescreen production style of Jimmy Iovine and such guests as Bruce Springsteen. It didn't sell, but it was a great try. —*William Ruhlmann*

○ **Another Grey Area** / 1982 / Razor & Tie 1982
Parker begins to make his peace with human imperfection (though he can still be sharp-tongued) and starts to look for love ("It's All Worth Nothing Alone"), backed by a smooth session band and a clean Jack Douglas production, which cool his usual fire without putting it out. —*William Ruhlmann*

Real Macaw / 1983 / Razor & Tie 1983
Parker finds love and manages to write about it without losing his usual wit ("Last Couple on the Dance Floor"). He also reemploys Rumour guitarist Brinsley Schwartz and goes back to the uptempo pub rock of his '70s albums. —*William Ruhlmann*

Best of Graham Parker 1988-1991 / Sep. 1992 / RCA 66097
All of the highlights from Graham Parker's brief stint at RCA are here on this single-disc compilation. —*AMG*

○ **Passion Is No Ordinary Word: The Graham Parker Anthology 1976-1991** / 1993 / Rhino 71425
With its smart song selection and entertaining liner notes, *Passion Is No Ordinary Word* is an excellent two-CD anthology covering Parker's entire career, complete with such rarities as "Mercury Poisoning" and "I Want You Back (Alive)" among such signature songs as "White Honey" and "You Can't Be Too Strong." —*Stephen Thomas Erlewine*

Robert Parker

b. Oct. 14, 1930, Crescent City, LA
Vocals, sax / R&B, soul
Parker's dance raver "Barefootin'" was one of the biggest hits to come out of New Orleans during the mid '60s. Parker played ses-

sions as a saxophonist back in 1949 with the legendary pianist Professor Longhair, and his 1959 solo debut for Ron, "All Night Long," was a scorching two-part instrumental. But Parker's underutilized vocal talents suddenly emerged in 1966, when his highly infectious "Barefootin'" became a giant hit on tiny Nola. Only one other Parker single, "Tip Toe," charted the next year, but Parker remains a popular attraction in his hometown. —*Bill Dahl*

● **Barefootin'** / 1966 / Collectables 5163
Originally issued in 1987 on vinyl by England's Charly, this collection includes Parker's main claim to fame, the 1967 R&B and pop dance smash "Barefootin'"; its flip side, "Let's Go Baby (Where the Action Is)"; both sides of a 1969 single Parker cut for Silver Fox; and a number of '70s recordings the erstwhile sax player waxed for Sansu Enterprises. Much of the CD, including the title cut, is infectious New Orleans R&B of a high caliber, but other tracks find Parker attempting to cut mainstream funk and disco, usually with less-than-inspiring results. —*Rob Bowman*

Van Dyke Parks

b. 1941
Composer / Singer-songwriter
Composer, arranger, producer, and musician Van Dyke Parks has had a varied career in popular music without ever getting near the popular mainstream. Parks worked as a songwriter in the early '60s and became a producer, handling such mid '60s acts as Harpers Bizarre. He was enlisted by Beach Boy Brian Wilson to write lyrics for what turned out to be an abortive album project called *Smile* (now one of the legendary lost albums of the '60s), resulting in such songs as the hit "Heroes and Villains." Parks released his own album, the eclectic *Song Cycle*, to critical acclaim and minimal sales in 1968. He then did session work with a variety of artists, not releasing his second album, *Discover America*, which revealed his immersion in Trinidadian music, until 1972. *Clang of the Yankee Reaper*, another eclectic collection, followed in 1975. But Parks maintained his "day job"—film work on scores by Ry Cooder and others, writing and arranging for Shelley Duvall's children's TV series, and other pursuits. Finally, in 1984, came the brilliant *Jump!* a concept album based on the Uncle Remus tales of Joel Chandler Harris. It was followed in 1989 by *Tokyo Rose*, which concerned the state of American-Japanese relations. —*William Ruhlmann*

● **Song Cycle** / 1968 / Warner Brothers 25856
Parks demonstrated an audacious musical imagination on this debut album, which effectively deployed a full orchestra, along with electric instruments, balalaikas, accordions, and an "authentic folk choir," plus nature sounds and God knows what else to produce a unique soundscape. A unique piece of music and a stunning accomplishment. —*William Ruhlmann*

○ **Discover America** / 1972 / Warner Brothers 26145
Parks turns to the music of Trinidad here, especially as it was heard in the '40s, which means tributes to "Bing Crosby" and "The Four Mills Bros.," not to mention "G-Man Hoover" and "FDR in Trinidad," played on steel drums and other indigenous instruments. A charming, idiosyncratic genre exercise. —*William Ruhlmann*

○ **Jump!** / 1984 / Warner Brothers 23829
An exhilarating song cycle based on the Uncle Remus tales. It incorporates the styles of Stephen Foster, ragtime, '30s movie-soundtrack music, you name it, all in the service of playful, touching lyrics that correspond to the source material without actually aping it. A delight from start to finish. —*William Ruhlmann*

Tokyo Rose / 1989 / Warner Brothers 25968
One can hear "America" as played on a Japanese koto on this history of relations between East and West, which covers everything from the "Trade War" to baseball with Parks' typically eclectic and broad musical imagination. A charming album. —*William Ruhlmann*

Parliament

Group / Funk, soul, R&B
Parliament started as a doo-wop group centered around a barber shop owned and operated by George Clinton in New Jersey in the late '50s. One 45 was released on the APT label before Clinton and company headed off to Detroit. Updating their sound to reflect the innovations of Motown, Parliament had a hit with "(I Wanna) Testify" for Revilot in 1967. Leaving Revilot before the

group's contract had legally expired, Clinton lost the right to the name for a few years.

Putting his backup band up front, Clinton signed with Detroit's Westbound label and called the group Funkadelic. By 1971 Clinton regained title to the original name and shortened it to Parliament, while still recording as Funkadelic as well. Parliament's records tended to be more R&B dance-oriented, while Funkadelic leaned toward the psychedelic side of rock & roll.

Parliament was signed first to Invictus and then to Casablanca. In the mid and late '70s, they were at the forefront of funk music, playing crazed shows that included spaceships landing on stage and articulated Clinton's acid-tinged funk cosmology, where the pro-funk and anti-funk forces battled it out. Characters such as Sir Nose D'Void of Funk were routinely forced to give up the funk and dance at the end of Parliament's concerts. Hits included "Up for the Down Stroke," "Chocolate City," "Tear the Roof Off the Sucker (Give Up the Funk)," and "Flash Light." Group members included Fuzzy Haskins, Bernie Worrell, Bootsy Collins, Fred Wesley, Maceo Parker, Eddie Hazel, Gary Shider, and Michael Hampton. Offshoots included the P-Funk All-Stars, Bootsy's Rubber Band, the Brides of Funkenstein, Fred Wesley & the Horny Horns, and Parlet. —*Rob Bowman*

Osmium / 1970 / Invictus 7302
George Clinton was miles away from perfecting his comedic/cosmic lyrics and enhanced funk concept when he began recording his group Parliament. There were many snippets of brilliance on this record, among them the title track, with its clever imagery and some typically chaotic quips and jamming. But Clinton hadn't yet settled on band personnel or musical direction; he moved through bits of R&B, rock, and pop as well as funk. This album has more historical than musical value. —*Ron Wynn*

○ **Up for the Down Stroke** / 1974 / Casablanca 842619
The first album by Clinton's revamped Parliament remains a perfect introduction, although its best songs are on their *Greatest Hits*. —*John Floyd*

○ **Chocolate City** / 1975 / Casablanca 836700
The title track was a masterpiece, one of George Clinton's satirical triumphs. Whether you think it was a political work or not, everything clicked, the production, comic lead vocals, lyrics, and arrangements. The remainder of the album wasn't quite that strong, but was still excellent. It mixed every Clinton element: chaotic jamming, quirky outlook, hilarious vocals, and that sense of the casually absurd that Clinton championed. —*Ron Wynn*

○ **Clones of Dr. Funkenstein** / 1976 / Casablanca 842620
George Clinton had his otherworldly, controlled chaotic vision well in gear for this album. He milked the Frankenstein notion, creating a mad scientist and sonically documenting his warped funk notions. Clinton got instrumental assistance from a crack corps that included keyboardist Bernie Worrell, saxophonist Maceo Parker, and trombonist Fred Wesley, plus numerous vocalists, guitarists, and instrumentalists. The album went gold, though it wasn't as inspired or as successful as *Mothership Connection*. But such songs as "Dr. Funkenstein," "I've Been Watching You (Move Your Sexy Body)," and "Everything Is on the One" were quintessential Parliament jams. —*Ron Wynn*

☆ **Mothership Connection** / 1976 / Casablanca 824502
This *was* the Parliament masterpiece. It mixed creative and clever satirical takeoffs on James Brown, Sly Stone, and classic African American radio with the kind of loose, inventive improvising seldom heard in R&B or soul circles. The narratives were swift and humorous, the music crackling, fast-moving, and progressive. The title cut, "Tear the Roof Off the Sucker (Give Up the Funk)," "Let Me Be," and "If It Don't Fit, Don't Force It" marked the beginning of Clinton and Parliament/Funkadelic's evolution into national celebrities. —*Ron Wynn*

☆ **Funkentelechy vs. the Placebo Syndrome** / 1977 / Casablanca 824501
Funkentelechy vs. the Placebo Syndrome offers an even better introduction to the group than the singles collection, by presenting the most intelligible and rhythmically unstoppable glimpse into Clinton's P-Funk world. —*John Floyd*

Live: P-Funk Earth Tour / 1977 / Casablanca 834941
One of the few live sets that accurately depict the flavor of an epic event. George Clinton's massive P-Funk tour, with all the spinoff groups and support personnel, gave some incredible shows in the

late '70s. Concerts would last three and four hours and would run together in an amazing display of controlled chaos. Songs were open-ended, the pace was nonstop, and it was much more like a ritual than a concert. This album perfectly conveyed the concert's feel and quality. —*Ron Wynn*

Motor Booty Affair / 1978 / Casablanca 842621
Another concept album, only this time the concept is about water and not being able to swim and not wanting to swim. This album is worth hearing, in spite of its occasional Frank Zappa-isms. —*John Floyd*

Gloryhallastoopid / 1979 / Casablanca 842622
Though at the time this album was viewed as a disaster, there's been some critical reassessment in the past years. It was certainly not as inspired, brilliantly executed, or memorable as any one of many '70s Parliament or Funkadelic gems, but it did have its own humorous/bizarre outlook. Clinton was being torn in many directions and plagued by money problems, so he didn't give it the attention it probably needed. Still, it deserves a revisit by Clinton fans who tossed it aside in disgust the first time around. —*Ron Wynn*

● **Greatest Hits (The Bomb)** / 1984 / Casablanca 822637
A solid if scanty assortment of their best singles. —*John Floyd*

★ **Tear the Roof Off** / May 18, 1993 / Casablanca 514417
Two discs of the hardest funk ever recorded, *Tear the Roof Off* is essential for both the casual fan and the hardcore collector. In addition to the presence of the full-length versions of all their hits, several 12-inch mixes make their first appearances on CD here. Without the music on *Tear the Roof Off*, contemporary music would not sound like it does today. —*AMG*

Alan Parsons Project

Group / Progressive rock

Engineer/producer Alan Parsons and his colleague, songwriter and lyricist Eric Woolfson, formed the Alan Parsons Project in 1975. Throughout their career, the Alan Parsons Project have recorded concept albums (including records loosely based on Edgar Allan Poe and Isaac Asimov books), with a revolving cast of session musicians. 1982's *Eye in the Sky* was their greatest success; the title track charted at #3 on the pop charts, and the album went platinum. In recent years, the project has released only a handful of albums, none of which matched the success of *Eye in the Sky*. — *AMG*

○ **Tales of Mystery & Imagination** / 1975 / Mercury 832820
This "project," led by former Beatles engineer Alan Parsons, was recorded at Abbey Road and featured a session group including Terry Sylvester and Arthur Brown (he of the "Crazy World"). It made its first and best album (if not its most popular one) by interpreting the ominous poems and stories of Edgar Allan Poe. Heavy on synthesized keyboards and dramatic choral parts, it's rock soundtrack music minus the film. The group went on to make a series of similar followups, notably including *I Robot* and *Eye in the Sky*, but this is the place to start. —*William Ruhlmann*

● **Best of the Alan Parsons Project** / 1987 / Arista 8193
Although the Alan Parsons Project is a quintessential album rock act, their most effective statements were made on singles and this collection features their best songs, including "Eye in the Sky" and "Games People Play." —*Stephen Thomas Erlewine*

Gram Parsons (Cecil Ingram Connor)

b. Nov. 5, 1946, Winterhaven, FL, **d.** Sep. 19, 1973, Joshua Tree, CA
Vocals, guitar / Country rock

Parsons is considered the founder of country rock. Like Hank Williams, Parsons lived hard and died young, but not before leaving behind a fine recorded legacy. This included stints with the International Submarine Band, the Byrds, the Flying Burrito Brothers, and finally as a solo artist. Parsons strove to break down the barriers between country and rock. He stripped country music down to its basics, while making its concerns more contemporary. For his two solo albums on Reprise, he is backed up by, among others, Elvis Presley's band and Emmylou Harris. The duets with Harris are superb. Harris has since gone on to rerecord most of Parsons's material on her solo albums. His influence has also been acknowledged by the Rolling Stones, Elvis Costello, Dwight Yoakam, and Rodney Crowell. In his field, Parsons is the artist all others must be measured against. His music fits comfortably into any rock or country fan's collection. —*Kenneth M. Cassidy*

Gram Parsons (Safe at Home) International Sub Band / 1967 / Shiloh 4088

Safe at Home represents some of Gram Parsons's earliest recordings as a part of the International Submarine Band. Arguably the first country-rock album, this more than hints at Parsons's greatness to come. This charming document is essential listening. —*Chris Woodstra*

★ G.P./Grievous Angel / 1973 / Reprise 26108

Parson's two best albums on one compact disc. Seeking to synthesize his own ideas with those of classic country and rock, Parsons hired Merle Haggard's recording engineer (he had approached Haggard himself about producing) and members of Elvis Presley's band, including pianist Glen D. Hardin and guitarist James Burton. The result had its roots in everything but sounded like nothing else. Parson's songs were the musings of a wounded soul, and his taste in others' material ran from Harlan Howard to the J. Geils Band. On *Grievous Angel*, Emmylou Harris emerges from the background to provide an angelic foil for Parsons's lost folkie voice. —*Brian Mansfield*

○ Gram Parsons & the Fallen Angels / 1981 / Sierra 1973

A good live document of Parsons's last tour. Recorded at radio station WLIR in New York. —*Kenneth M. Cassidy*

Les Paul (Lester William Poifus)

b. Jun. 9, 1915, Waukseha, WI
Guitar / Pop

The history of recorded music would have been different, much different, if it were not for the pioneering efforts of guitarist and inventor Les Paul. He started as a country musician, working radio spots in the early '30s as Rhubarb Red. Bitten by the jazz bug early on, he formed the Les Paul Trio in 1936, working for bandleader Fred Waring through the end of the decade. By the '40s, he was experimenting with guitars and recording gear. He was among the first to build a solid-body electric and certainly the first to popularize the idea; his Gibson Les Paul models of the '50s are now all highly sought-after collector's items. He was the first to pioneer multitrack recording and overdubbing. The use of tape echo, phase shifting, and so on changed the sound of popular music forever, most notably on the recordings made in the early '50s with his wife, vocalist Mary Ford. Paul is a consummate player, arranger, engineer, and entertainer; his inventions are only part of what makes him one of the giants of American music. —*Cub Koda*

☆ Legend and the Legacy / 1991 / Capitol 97654

Beautiful four-CD boxed set of all of Les and Mary's best Capitol recordings, with the bonus of numerous unissued songs and a track-by-track commentary by Les in the accompanying booklet. A must-have. —*Cub Koda*

★ Best of the Capitol Masters / 1992 / Capitol 99617

A good single-disc distillation of the highlights of Les Paul's epic four-disc box set, *The Legend and the Legacy, Best of the Capitol Years* is all most casual fans will need to own. —*Stephen Thomas Erlewine*

○ Early Les Paul / Capitol 16286

Strictly guitar wizardry here. The best of his '40s and '50s Capitol sides. Stunning. —*Hank Davis*

Pavement

Group / Alternative pop/rock

With their fractured songs, unexpected blasts of feedback, laconic vocals, cryptic lyrics, and defiant low fidelity, Pavement is one of the best bands to emerge from the American underground in the '90s. For several years before their first album, the group had been releasing a series of singles and EPs on small, obscure labels (all of these are now collected on *Westing by Musket and Sextet*); these indie releases were so thin and harsh that they were hard to listen to, even at their average two-minute running time. Pavement's first album, 1992's *Slanted and Enchanted*, took the world of rock criticism by storm; before the album was even available promotionally, critics were lavishly praising it. Initially, the band's following was based more on the press instead of word of mouth, but soon word began to spread on the street as well as in the magazines. Pavement's 1994 album, *Crooked Rain,*

Crooked Rain, saw the band toning down its extreme sonics for a laid-back record that emphasized songs over sound. The album helped the band consolidate its position as alternative stars and critics' darlings, as well as expanding their cult; they even charted in the lower reaches of *Billboard*'s Top 200 Album chart and landed a spot on the "Tonight Show." —*Stephen Thomas Erlewine*

○ Slanted & Enchanted / May 1992 / Matador 038

Listening to *Slanted and Enchanted* is like listening to a college radio station that you can barely get in—melodies are interrupted by shards of white noise, only to have several "sha-la-la's bring the song back into focus. On their first full-length album, Pavement have constructed a cycle of gleeful guitar noise punctuated by fragments of melody floating in and out of the chaos. The first half of the album is the most impressive, where all of the slivers of noise, screams, and melody meld together to form genuine pop hooks, as in "My Summber Babe," "Trigger Cut," and "In the Mouth of the Desert." —*Stephen Thomas Erlewine*

○ Westing (by Musket & Sextant) / 1993 / Drag City 14

A collection of all of Pavement's low-fidelity early singles and EPs that feature considerably less melody than *Slanted and Enchanted*. It's nice to have this rare material on one CD, although the music is defiantly antidigital. Those who boarded the train with the acclaimed *Slanted and Enchanted* should catch up on what they have missed. —*Stephen Thomas Erlewine*

● Crooked Rain, Crooked Rain / 1994 / Matador/Atlantic

Although it's much calmer than the critically acclaimed *Slanted and Enchanted, Crooked Rain, Crooked Rain* shares the same spirit of the band's debut—it's a messy, impossibly catchy catalogue of pop music and culture. On their second full-length album, Pavement have abandoned much of the low-fi squalor of their earlier work, opting for a laid-back, subdued sound that borders on country-rock and jazz-rock at times, and pure pop and rock & roll at others. In other words, it's more accessible than *Slanted and Enchanted* but just as distinctive and original. Ultimately, *Crooked Rain, Crooked Rain* revamps rock history and reinvents it for the slacker generation. —*Stephen Thomas Erlewine*

Freda Payne

b. Sep. 19, 1945, Detroit, MI
Vocals / Soul

Multitalented and beautiful, Payne crashed the soul and pop playlists in 1970 with a series of powerful sides for Holland-Dozier-Holland's Invictus imprint. Payne's early musical experience was quite varied, and she debuted on the jazz-oriented Impulse! label in 1965. Her 1970 blockbuster, "Band of Gold," made Payne a pop star with its strident message and insistent bassline, and she encored with "Deeper & Deeper." The controversial antiwar anthem "Bring the Boys Home" proved her biggest R&B seller the next year. Payne hosted a TV gabfest during the '80s. —*Bill Dahl*

● Greatest Hits / 1991 / HDH 3905

Includes the classic "Band of Gold" and other post-modern Holland-Dozier greats. —*Rick A. Bueche*

Pearl Jam

Group / Alternative rock, hard rock

Pearl Jam rose from the ashes of Mother Love Bone to become the most popular rock & roll band of the '90s. After vocalist Andrew Wood overdosed on heroin, guitarist Stone Gossard and bassist Jeff Ament assembled a new band, bringing in Mike McCready on lead guitar, Dave Krusen on drums, and an unknown vocalist named Eddie Vedder. Calling themselves Pearl Jam, the band recorded their debut album, *Ten,* in the beginning of 1991; when it was released later that year, it didn't begin selling until Nirvana broke down the doors to the mainstream at the end of the year. Once the doors were open, Pearl Jam soon outsold Nirvana—Pearl Jam was always more commercial-sounding than Nirvana. Essentially, the band fused the riff-heavy stadium rock of the '70s with the grit and anger of '80s post-punk, without ever neglecting hooks and choruses; "Jeremy," "Evenflow," and "Alive" fit perfectly into album rock radio stations that were looking for new blood.

No matter how many records they sold or how much AOR embraced them, Pearl Jam remained an underground band at heart. Once they achieved stardom, they used their commercial power to fight rock industry conventions. When the band released their second album, *Vs.*, in 1993, the band refused to release any singles or videos from the album; the record debuted at #1, selling nearly a million copies in its first week; it went on to sell five million records in a short time. On their spring 1994 American tour, the band decided not to play the convential stadiums, choosing to play smaller arenas, including several shows on college campuses.

Pearl Jam planned to tour in the summer of 1994, yet they canceled the tour. The band claimed they could not keep ticket prices below $20 because Ticketmaster was pressuring promoters to charge a higher price; the band took Ticketmaster to the judicial department for unfair business practices. As the band stayed off the road and fought Ticketmaster, they prepared to release a new album, less than year after *Vs.* was released. *—Stephen Thomas Erlewine*

★ **Ten** / 1992 / Epic 47857
With their debut album, *Ten*, and its clearheaded, clean, and politically correct hard rock, Pearl Jam became the most popular band of the early '90s. While Mike McCready and Stone Gossard's dueling guitars are gutsy and muscular and Jeff Ament's bass remarkably rhythmic and fluid, Eddie Vedder's raw, impassioned vocals make already exceptional songs like "Black," "Jeremy," and "Alive" positively transcendent. *—Stephen Thomas Erlewine*

○ **Vs.** / 1993 / Epic
On the first listen, it appears that Pearl Jam's second album has no songs that are as stunning as "Evenflow," "Alive," "Once," "Black," and "Jeremy," but after a couple of plays, *Vs.* reveals its strengths. Instead of copying *Ten*'s signature clear, dark hard rock, *Vs.* is rawer and more open with a number of different textures. From the pulverizing assault of "Go," "Animal," and "Leash" to the folkier, more reflective "Daughter," "Elderly Woman Behind the Counter in a Small Town," and "Indifference," Pearl Jam proves that their initial success was no fluke. Occasionally, the band falls into treacherous politically correct waters (the silly "Glorified G" and the meandering "W.M.A.") but for most of the album, Pearl Jam locks hold, and the best results are riveting. *— Stephen Thomas Erlewine*

Ann Peebles

b. Apr. 27, 1947, St. Louis, MO
Vocals / Soul
Ann Peebles was the queen of Willie Mitchell's Memphis-based Hi Records roster during the '70s, when Al Green was its reigning king. Sung in a voice as bittersweet as it is riveting, her always-dramatic recordings include one undisputed masterpiece, "I Can't Stand the Rain," cited as a favorite by John Lennon and most recently covered by Tina Turner. Other covers abound—Robert Palmer took "I'm Gonna Tear Your Playhouse Down," and Bette Midler claimed "Breakin' Up Somebody's Home." Backed by the brilliant Hi rhythm section and flawlessly produced by Mitchell, Peebles sang and wrote (often in partnership with husband Don Bryant) of the feminine perspective on the darker side of love— sometimes untrusting love, but love, for better or worse. Her work represents, with elegance and grit, some of the best of Memphis soul. *—Christine Ohlman*

○ **Part Time Love** / 1971 / Hi 32059
The title track was a masterpiece, and everything else on this dynamic early '70s soul session is a jewel. Ann Peebles may have been the most overlooked great soul singer, male or female, who emerged in the '70s. HI couldn't strike crossover gold twice, and Al Green was becoming a superstar. But Peebles deserved a better fate than obscurity, as this collection of soul wailers and weepers proves. *—Ron Wynn*

○ **I Can't Stand the Rain** / 1974 / Hi 32079
The title song was an instant classic, and its lyrics are among the most moving and gripping in soul annals. This was Ann Peebles's finest album for Hi Records, and it should have been a massive success. Instead, while it's celebrated in Europe and now considered an anthem, it floundered and barely scraped the pop charts, although the single was her biggest R&B hit. *—Ron Wynn*

○ **If This Is Heaven** / 1978 / Hi 6002
Another exceptional album by Ann Peebles, who was cutting remarkable records for HI in Memphis that no one noticed except deep soul junkies. Her voice was alternately anguished, angry, defiant, and resigned, while Willie Mitchell and the HI Rhythm Section provided minimal, yet spectacular backing. Peebles seldom toured, preferring to stay in Memphis around her family. But

she had a voice surpassed among women soul vocalists only by Aretha Franklin, and equalled by Carla Thomas. *—Ron Wynn*

● **Ann Peebles' Greatest Hits** / MCA 25225
Backed by the vaunted Hi rhythm section and produced by Willie Mitchell. Includes her original "Come to Mama" and "I Can't Stand the Rain." These are classics of the '70s Memphis soul idiom. *—Bill Dahl*

Teddy Pendergrass

b. Mar. 26, 1950
Vocals, drums / Soul, urban R&B
In 1970 Pendergrass joined Harold Melvin and the Blue Notes as their drummer and lead vocalist; he sang on all of the group's Top 40 hits. Pendergrass left the group in 1976 and scored eight Hot 100 hits before he suffered an auto accident that left him partially paralyzed. He made a comeback two years later with *Heaven Only Knows*, which did not fare all that well commercially despite "Hold Me," a Top 50 duet with a young Whitney Houston. Subsequent albums also did not sell particularly well. *—Stephen Thomas Erlewine*

○ **Teddy Pendergrass** / 1977 / Philadelphia International 34390
The skeptics had their suspicions quelled quickly when Teddy Pendergrass's debut album as a solo singer cracked the Top 40. Its lead single, "I Don't Love You Anymore," was among his best uptempo tunes, and the followup ballad, "The Whole Town's Laughing at Me," ended forever any specuation he was returning to Harold Melvin & the Blue Notes. While many thought the album would launch him to consistent R&B success, almost no one thought in a couple of years he'd be R&B's biggest male star. *— Ron Wynn*

○ **Life Is a Song Worth Singing** / 1978 / Philadelphia International 35095
This was the album that convinced anyone who'd had doubts about the wisdom of Pendergrass leaving Harold Melvin and the Blue Notes that he'd made a good decision. Although he only got one R&B hit from the album, there were enough strong ballads and good uptempo cuts to show Pendergrass had the sound, personality, and style to cut it on his own. He'd shortly become R&B's greatest male attraction, but in the interim Philadelphia International was laying the groundwork. *—Ron Wynn*

Teddy / 1979 / Philadelphia International 36003
Teddy Pendergrass scored his greatest hit album with his third solo release, cementing his position at the end of the '70s as the reigning matinee idol and romantic balladeer among R&B male vocalists. This album cracked the pop Top 10, dominated the R&B charts, and ruled the airwaves through much of 1979. While the overt sexual orientation of a song like "Turn Off the Lights" blinded some to the fact Pendergrass's animated vocal was as soulful as you'd ever hear outside the gospel/blues/country axis of the south, this album confirmed Pendergrass had found his niche and would be a dominant singer into the '80s. *—Ron Wynn*

It's Time for Love / 1981 / Philadelphia International 47491
Teddy Pendergrass showed no signs of slowing down in the early '80s. This was another R&B smash and crossover hit, again putting him the Top 20. He got two good R&B singles, remained a popular concert attraction, and demonstrated good rapport with Stephanie Mills on several duets. They teamed so well together Pendergrass eventually appeared on stage with her during a tour of England. *—Ron Wynn*

● **Greatest Hits** / 1987 / Philadelphia International 39252
Teddy Pendergrass's robust baritone, which was greatly influenced by the Dells' Marvin Junior, made its initial impact when he was lead singer for Harold Melvin & the Blue Notes. From there, Pendergrass became the reigning male sex symbol on the R&B circuit in the '70s until a tragic accident crippled him. This collection covers his run of big hits from the Philadelphia International era, including "I Don't Love You Anymore," "Close the Door," and "Turn Off the Lights." *—Ron Wynn*

Joy / 1988 / Elektra 60775
Teddy Pendergrass finally made it back to the top in 1988, when the title track from this album spent two weeks at the head of the R&B list. The song even got mild pop attention, and the album was his first since the accident that really reflected the new Pendergrass sound. Now he sang in a slower, somber, yet appealing way quite different from the swaggering, openly sexual/ma-

cho posturing of the late '70s and early '80s. This was a weary but not beaten Pendergrass, whose manner and delivery underscored the resilent theme in "Joy's" lyrics. —*Ron Wynn*

Truly Blessed / 1991 / Elektra 60891
Teddy Pendergrass's return to recording and performing after the tragic accident that resulted in permanent paralysis was among the greatest stories of the '80s. Pendergrass had been a star dependent as much on sex appeal as his boisterous baritone. He had to learn to sing all over again, with restraint, sensitivity, and control now his keys rather than volume and presence. This 1991 album wasn't quite as moving as 1988's *Joy*, but it still included several poignant numbers, including the title track, which addressed his survival, neither downplaying the problems nor overstating his genuine happiness about still being alive. —*Ron Wynn*

Penguins

Group / Doo-wop
West Coast doo-woppers, led by vocalists Curtis Williams and Cleve Duncan. "Earth Angel," from 1954, was their biggest hit. —*John Floyd*

● **Authentic Golden Hits** / 1993 / Juke Box Treasures 6009
At long last, a well-thought-out compilation that gathers up all of the group's best sides for Dooto Records, including the original versions of the classics "Earth Angel" and "Hey, Senorita" in their original, unedited form. —*Cub Koda*

○ **Golden Classics** / Collectables 5045
Unadorned West Coast doo-wop from the originators of "Earth Angel." —*Hank Davis*

Michael Penn

Vocals, guitar / Singer-songwriter
Michael Penn was one of the best singer-songwriters to emerge in the late '80s, capable of melding Beatlesque pop melodies with word play that rivals Elvis Costello. *March*, in 1989, was critically acclaimed and had a surprise hit single with "No Myth." Although his second album, 1992's *Free-for-All*, didn't have a hit on the size of "No Myth," it displayed his folk roots alongside his pop sensibilities. —*Stephen Thomas Erlewine*

● **March** / 1989 / RCA 9692
A solid debut album, with the hit "No Myth." —*Kenneth M. Cassidy*

○ **Free-for-All** / 1992 / RCA 61113
Free for All, Michael Penn's second album, isn't as immediately accessible as *March*, yet his cryptic lyrics and twisting melodies will work their way into your memory if given some time. —*Stephen Thomas Erlewine*

Pere Ubu

Group / Alternative pop/rock
Named for the French absurdist play by Alfred Jarry, Pere Ubu was one of the most important and long-lived bands of the punk/new-wave era (formed in September 1975 in Cleveland). The current edition of the band features original members David Thomas (vocals) and Scott Krauss (drums). Another current member, Tony Maimone (bass), joined the group in 1976. Pere Ubu was organized by Thomas and fellow rock journalist Peter Laughner (guitar, bass) for the purpose of recording the apocalyptic single "30 Seconds over Tokyo." By spring of 1976, Pere Ubu had recorded a second single, "Final Solution," and traveled to New York, where they gained exposure. The band was then reorganized, minus Laughner, who died the following year. Mercury Records signed Pere Ubu and issued their debut album, *The Modern Dance*, in February 1978. Its combination of uncompromising rock, featuring odd noises and Thomas's high-pitched singing, earned the group critical hosannas and commercial indifference beyond a loyal cult, a situation that would continue for most of their existence. That existence was fitful. Pere Ubu was dropped by Mercury and signed by Chrysalis, which released *Dub Housing* and *New Picnic Time* (both 1979), after which the group split again. But they were back to release *The Art of Walking* in 1980 (on Rough Trade). *360 Degrees of Simulated Stereo* (1981) was an archival live album, and *Song of the Bailing Man* (1981) was the last album before another split. 1985 saw the release of a compilation, *Terminal Tower*, and in 1987 Pere Ubu was reorganized, releasing the slightly more commercially accessible al-

bums *The Tenement Year* (1987), *Cloudland* (1989), and *Worlds in Collision* (1991). —*William Ruhlmann*

○ **New Picnic Time** / 1976 / Rough Trade 20
The last album from the late '70s version of Ubu. Exteme dada, with a beat (sometimes). —*Myles Boisen*

○ **Modern Dance** / 1977 / Blank 001
Aggressive punk rock, punctuated by found sounds and noises and topped by Thomas's remarkably affecting near-falsetto shriek. It's not easy listening, but it's powerful and daring and has lost none of its impact since release. —*William Ruhlmann*

Art of Walking / 1980 / Rough Trade 4
An early '80s recording with guitarist Mayo Thompson. This is a buoyant and groovy accompaniment to Thomas's surrealism. —*Myles Boisen*

390 Degrees of Simulated Stereo (Live) / 1981 / Rough Trade 10
An odds and ends sampler of early band activities, from concerts, singles, and other crazy tidbits. For collectors only. —*Myles Boisen*

Song of the Bailing Man / 1982 / Rough Trade 21
David Thomas becomes more obtuse as the band heads toward breakup again. —*Myles Boisen*

★ **Terminal Tower** / 1985 / Twintone 8561
The songs on *Terminal Tower: An Archival Collection*, many of them taken from Pere Ubu's first singles, demonstrate what helped make them one of the most original and challenging bands of the American new wave of the '70s. Be warned that songs like "30 Seconds over Tokyo" and "Final Solution" will have a polarizing effect on the listener: either this on-the-edge rock is just what you've been looking for, or it isn't. —*William Ruhlmann*

○ **Tenement Year** / 1988 / Enigma 73343
Since the reformed version of Pere Ubu reins in (slightly) the group's more extreme tendencies, this album, which nevertheless presents David Thomas's unique vision and the band's somewhat off-kilter approach to rock more or less intact, may be the place for neophytes to get their feet wet with a highly unusual group. This one should give you the idea—then you're on your own. —*William Ruhlmann*

○ **Cloudland** / 1989 / Fontana 838237
David Thomas returns to his favorite boyhood themes, with his new pop band in tow. —*Myles Boisen*

One Man Drives / 1989 / Rough Trade 61
A second live compilation, *One Man Drives While the Other Man Screams* is more unified than *360 Degrees...*, with lots of their best material. —*Myles Boisen*

○ **Worlds in Collision** / 1991 / Fontana 848564
Worlds in Collision shows a definite commercial aspiration. Still good, but it lacks personality. —*Myles Boisen*

Story of My Life / 1993 / Imago 21024
Although it is the most pop-oriented record Pere Ubu ever cut, *Story of My Life* didn't make much of a dent even in alternative radio. Nevertheless, there are many fine pop tunes here, occasionally spiked with some of their trademark experimentalism, although it's not as challenging as it was years before. —*Stephen Thomas Erlewine*

Carl Perkins (Carl Lee Perkins)

b. Apr. 9, 1932, Lake City, TN, **d.** 1958
Vocals, guitar / Rockabilly, rock & roll
The history of rock & roll guitar would have a gigantic gaping hole without the pioneering efforts of Carl Perkins. He taught Eric Clapton and George Harrison how to play, years before he met either one, and the early Beatles albums were peppered with their versions of Perkins rockabilly classics. Born dirt-poor and ambitious, Perkins started playing the honky-tonks in his native Tennessee with his brothers, fusing elements of hillbilly music with African American blues. He started recording for the Sun label a few months after Elvis, but he was cast as a straight country singer, albeit a fine one, in the Hank Williams mold. Every great singer needs a great lead guitarist, and Carl found one in himself, his combination of fingerpicking chording and rapid spitfire licks becoming instantly recognizable. Turned loose to rock out at his third session, Perkins did just that, producing the ulti-

mate rockabilly anthem, "Blue Suede Shoes." Hitting the #1 slot on the pop, R&B, and country charts, Carl's future seemed assured when he almost perished in a car accident, just as Elvis became a worldwide phenomenon. Minor hits followed (now all acknowledged as classics of the genre), but Carl's star was on the wane. After becoming a member of the Johnny Cash TV show in the '60s (writing hits for Cash and others in the country field), he experienced a comeback when England went rockabilly crazy in the early '70s. Elected to the Rock & Roll Hall of Fame on the second ballot, Carl Perkins keeps on pickin', the ultimate rockabilly survivor. —*Cub Koda*

★ **Up through the Years, 1954-1957** / 1986 / Bear Family 15246
An import collection of Perkins' groundbreaking Sun singles, *Up through the Years* offers eight more tracks than Rhino's *Original Sun Greatest Hits;* both discs are definitive collections. —*Stephen Thomas Erlewine*

★ **Original Sun Greatest Hits** / 1986 / Rhino 75890
Essential, primal rockabilly. Includes "Everybody's Trying to Be My Baby," "Matchbox," "Honey Don't," "Boppin' the Blues," "Glad All Over," and the original "Blue Suede Shoes." —*Hank Davis*

Honky Tonk Gal / Apr. 1989 / Rounder 27
Quirky, obscure, and offbeat. A much deeper look into Perkins's Sun period, with emphasis on hillbilly roots. —*Hank Davis*

○ **Jive after Five: Best of Carl Perkins (1958-1978)** / 1990 / Rhino 70958
His later CBS work, much of it excellent. —*Hank Davis*

○ **Classic** / Feb. 1990 / Bear Family 15494
Simply the most comprehensive collection imaginable. Five CDs, including all of his essential Sun tracks and alternate takes. All the 1958-1962 CBS sides, plus his 1963-1964 Decca sessions. Indispensable for the serious fan and completist. —*Hank Davis*

Restless: The Columbia Recordings / May 12, 1992 / Columbia 48896
A strong collection of Perkins's singles for Columbia, concentrating on the late '50s and early '60s; some of his finest songs, including "Pink Pedal Pushers" and "Jive after Five," are included here. —*Stephen Thomas Erlewine*

The Persuaders

Group / Soul
This group made a pair of marvelous heartache ballads in 1971, but have the unfortunate legacy of having their finest cuts turned into pop hits via covers. Lead singer Douglas Scott—whose nickname appropriately was "Smokey"—Willie Holland, James Barnes, and Charles Stodghill formed in New York in 1969. They signed with Atlantic in the early '70s and had their lone R&B chart topper in 1971, the shattering classic "Thin Line Between Love & Hate"; it was also their only gold single. The followup was nearly as strong; "Love's Gonna Pack Up (and Walk Out)" reached #8 on the R&B charts, but had no crossover appeal. They continued on Win & Lose until 1973, then moved to Atco, where "Some Guys Have All the Luck" was a #7 R&B single in 1973. It was their final hit, though they kept recording until the late '70s, doing their last session for Calla. Besides the Pretenders' remake of "Thin Line Between Love & Hate," Rod Stewart had a Top 10 hit with his version of "Some Guys Have All the Luck" in 1984. —*Ron Wynn*

● **Thin Line between Love & Hate** / 1974 / Collectables 5139
A gritty soul unit, adept at tragic encounter tunes. The title song is a soul anthem. —*Ron Wynn*

The Persuasions

Group / R&B, soul
A cappella singing has been part of the African American musical tradition since the days of slavery. Despite the recent success of the hi-tech a cappella group Take 6, the tradition has suffered a steady decline to the point where it is rare even in gospel circles. The Persuasions, though, are resolutely a cappella. Their chart successes have been minimal (two fleeting R&B entries in 1974-1975), but they carry forward the tradition without appearing ossified. Airplay will probably always elude them—and with it the really big breakthrough—but their music has been a consistently enjoyable sidebar, and never one that has simply reeked of revivalism. —*Colin Escott*

○ **Acappella** / 1970 / Bizarre 70362

The first Persuasions release, recorded live in Los Angeles. The sound is a little two-dimensional, but to my way of thinking, this recording captures the spirit of joy in live harmonizing, which is the very essence of the Persuasions. Includes great takes on the Temptations' "Don't Look Back" and the Drifters' "Up on the Roof," making manifest the intrinsic connection between '50s doo-wop and '60s group singing. —*Rob Bowman*

○ **We Came to Play** / 1971 / Collectables 5234
Better produced than their debut, *We Came to Play* continues what became a formula for the Persuasions—covering '50s and '60s classics (the latter most usually taken from the Motown and Curtis Mayfield portfolios), the occasional Tin Pan Alley standard, and judiciously chosen rock/pop covers. In the '70s, a cappella singing was a lost art that the Persuasions were determined to keep alive. —*Rob Bowman*

○ **Street Corner Symphony** / 1972 / Capitol 872
On this, their highest-charting recording, the Persuasions give more of the same, including gorgeous reworkings of Bob Dylan's "The Man in Me" and the Impressions' "People Get Ready." —*Rob Bowman*

We Still Ain't Got No Band / 1973 / MCA 326
Maintaining their high level of consistency, the Persuasions shy away from Motown here and delve into the blues, tackling Jimmy Hughes's "Steal Away" and a medley of Jimmy Reed's "Baby What You Want Me to Do" and "Bright Lights, Big City." Superb. —*Rob Bowman*

● **Chirpin'** / 1977 / Elektra 1099
After two ill-advised albums for A&M with instruments, the Persuasions returned to their a cappella roots. No longer popular enough to chart, the music was in no way diminished. Highlights include a swinging version of the gospel standard "It's Gonna Rain" and a dramatic reading of Tony Joe White's "Willie and Laura Mae Jones." —*Rob Bowman*

Pet Shop Boys

Group / Dance-pop, techno-pop, disco
Since the Pet Shop Boys work in a genre that isn't considered artistically important, it took most listeners and critics several years before they realized that the duo was one of the finest pop bands of the late '80s. With their detatched, intellectual, and often very funny lyrics and relentlessly hip, melodic, synth-driven disco, Neil Tennant and Chris Lowe were one of the most commercially successful groups in America and England in the late '80s, scoring a consistent string of hit singles through 1991. Through four albums and several singles, the Pet Shop Boys explored every dance trend from disco to house, creating beautifully lush, haunting soundscapes with their synthesizers and drum machines. By the time the sublime *Very* was released in 1993, the popular audience had shifted away from dance-pop, and the group had difficulty receiving mainstream airplay; MTV wouldn't air their videos. However, the duo continued to sell respectably while they continued to expand and redefine their music. —*Stephen Thomas Erlewine*

★ **Discography: The Complete Singles Collection** / 1991 / EMI America 97097
Featuring all of their greatest hits, *Discography* is an excellent overview of their 1985-1990 peak of chart power. —*Dan Heilman*

○ **Very** / 1993 / ERG 89721
Very is one of the Pet Shop Boys' very best records, expertly weaving between the tongue-in-cheek humor of "I Wouldn't Normally Do This Kind of Thing," the quietly shocking "Can You Forgive Her?" and the bizarrely moving cover of the Village People's "Go West." Alternately happy and melancholy, *Very* is the Pet Shop Boys at their finest. —*Stephen Thomas Erlewine*

Peter & Gordon

Group / British invasion, pop/rock
As part of the first wave of the British invasion, Peter Asher (b. June 22, 1944) and Gordon Waller (b. June 4, 1945), as Peter & Gordon, recorded a number of highly successful, lushly orchestrated pop singles that blended Phil Spectorish production sensibilities with Everly Brothers-style harmonies. Their hits included "I Go to Pieces," "World without Love," "Lady Godiva," "Woman," "To Know You Is to Love You," and a version of Buddy Holly's "True Love Ways." —*Rick Clark*

● **Best of Peter & Gordon** / 1991 / Rhino 70748
A duo who synthesized Beatles and Everly Brothers harmonies into a wonderfully seamless string of mid '60s British Invasion lite-pop hits. They are all contained here, with great sound and well-rendered liner notes. —*Rick Clark*

Tom Petty & the Heartbreakers

b. 1953
Group / Rock & roll
Since 1976, Tom Petty & the Heartbreakers have been one of America's finest rock & roll bands, combining the ringing guitars of the Byrds with the gritty rhythmic drive of the Rolling Stones. Petty's tales of American losers and dreamers were simple and direct, but emotionally charged. The Heartbreakers were a lean, tight band that could handle hard rock & roll and melodic pop equally well. The group gained critical attention and solid sales with their first album, but 1979's *Damn the Torpedos* was their commercial breakthrough, selling over two million copies; it couldn't have come at a better time, since Petty filed for bankruptcy before its release.
During the '80s, Petty sold consistently well, as he expanded his sound with the release of each album. In 1989, he released his first solo album, *Full Moon Fever*, which became his biggest hit yet. That momentum carried over into the next Heartbreakers release, 1991's *The Great Wide Open*, which went platinum. As they were preparing their next album, the group released a greatest hits album in 1993 that contained the hit single, "Mary Jane's Last Dance"; it proved that nearly two decades after he began recording, Tom Petty remains a vital artist. —*Stephen Thomas Erlewine*

Tom Petty & the Heartbreakers / 1976 / MCA 10135
Originally released on Denny Cordell's Shelter label, the 1976 self-titled debut was a real sleeper until the single "Breakdown" became Petty's first hit almost a year and a half later. This album's release coincided with the advent of the punk and new-wave movements. The lean, edgy production and arrangements only enhanced that perception, in spite of the fact the songs clearly drew inspiration from the Byrds and '60s Anglo-rock. Among the highlights are the gritty riff-rocker "Strangered in the Night" (which guests Dwight Twilley), "American Girl" (a song so shamelessly influenced by the Byrds that even Roger McGuinn covered it), "Hometown Blues" (later covered by Rosanne Cash), and "The Wild One, Forever." —*Rick Clark*

You're Gonna Get It! / 1978 / MCA 10134
Not quite so strong as the debut, *You're Gonna Get It* exhibited a denser, Rickenbacker-heavy guitar sound. Petty's voice was practically buried in the mix, particularly on the rockers. Nevertheless, this album does have some great songs, particularly "I Need to Know" and "Listen to Her Heart." —*Rick Clark*

☆ **Damn the Torpedoes** / 1979 / MCA 31161
Petty switched producers to Jimmy Iovine, and together they created the masterful *Damn the Torpedoes*. For once, Petty's voice was up front in the mix, giving him much more character. The band never sounded so full or punchy before this. *Torpedoes* opens with a seamless string of great rockers, "Refugee," "Here Comes My Girl," and "Even the Losers." Other highlights include "Century City" and "Don't Do Me Like That." —*Rick Clark*

○ **Hard Promises** / 1981 / MCA 31066
Pre-album publicity made much of the fact that Petty was taking issue with his big bad record label (MCA) over gouging his fans with a list-price increase on this album. Petty won, reinforcing the notion that he was a principled people's artist. The aptly titled *Hard Promises* became platinum hit. Even though *Hard Promises* is a slight step down from its predecessor, there is plenty of strong material. "The Waiting," one of Petty's finest songs, is the stylistic epitome of his Byrds fixation. Other standouts include the rockers "Kings Road," "A Thing about You," and the darkly humorous "Something Big." —*Rick Clark*

Long after Dark / 1982 / MCA 31027
The highlights of this album, "Straight into Darkness," "Change of Heart," "Deliver Me," and "You Got Lucky," may be some of Petty's best, but much of *Long after Dark* suffers from weak melodies and flat-sounding production. —*Rick Clark*

Pack Up the Plantation—Live! / 1985 / MCA 8021
A solid-as-a-brick live set, featuring incredible symbiotic playing from all the Heartbreakers. —*Cub Koda*

Southern Accents / 1985 / MCA 5486
Produced by Dave Stewart, *Southern Accents* is an ambitious album, attempting to incorporate touches of psychedelia, soul, and country into a loose concept about the modern south. Occasionally, the songs work—"Rebels" and "Spike" are fine rockers, and "Don't Come Around Here No More" and "Make It Better (Forget about Me)" expand the Heartbreakers' sound nicely—but too often the record is weighed down by its own ambitions. —*Stephen Thomas Erlewine*

○ **Let Me Up (I've Had Enough)** / 1987 / MCA 5836
After the failed *Southern Accents*, Petty and company return to a fairly straight-ahead collection of rock & roll. Except for a handful of strong tunes like the free-associative rocker (cowritten with Dylan) "Jammin' Me," "Runaway Trains," and "My Life/Your World," much of this album feels like the product of an uninspired band. —*Rick Clark*

☆ **Full Moon Fever** / 1989 / MCA 6253
Recorded as a casual side project, Petty's first solo album possessed more flashes of brilliance than most of his albums put together. It also produced four hits, with "Free Fallin'," "A Face in the Crowd," "Runnin' Down a Dream," and "I Won't Back Down." Another highlight was a great remake of the Byrds' "I'll Feel a Whole Lot Better." Petty ought to moonlight more often. —*Rick Clark*

○ **Into the Great Wide Open** / 1991 / MCA 10317
This is Petty's first Heartbreakers album after his multiplatinum solo effort, *Full Moon Fever*. The band sounds a little more lively than on the previous two efforts, and the material is generally better than much of their previous two studio albums. —*Rick Clark*

★ **Greatest Hits** / 1993 / MCA
All of Petty's biggest hits collected, along with the excellent "Mary Jane's Last Dance" and "Something in the Air," on one essential disc. Everything from "American Girl" to "Free Fallin' is included, with the 16 tracks proving that Petty is one of the best rockers of the past 15 years. —*Stephen Thomas Erlewine*

Liz Phair

Vocals, guitar, piano / Alternative pop/rock
For several years, singer/songwriter Liz Phair recorded homemade tapes under the name Girlysound; one of the cassettes reached Matador Records, which offered her a contract. Phair's first album, the double-length *Exile in Guyville*, was released in the early spring of 1993; by the end of the year, it was topping nearly every critic's poll in America. During the course of the year, Phair became the figurehead for the new movement of female artists, particularly those in alternative rock. Combining elements of both traditional singer/songwriters and alternative rockers, Phair stands as an original; although her roots are identifiable, nothing in her music sounds derivative. She is capable of playing straight pop songs, rock, folk, and atmospheric experimentalism effortlessly and unpretentiously. Her lyrics are simple, yet layered with detail and meaning; her hooks and melodies are memorable and withstand repeated playings. —*Stephen Thomas Erlewine*

★ **Exile in Guyville** / 1993 / Matador
Liz Phair's stunningly accomplished and ambitious debut album *Exile in Guyville* is loosely based on the Rolling Stones' classic *Exile on Main Street*, retelling that album's weary tales of love and sex from a female perspective. While there is some anger here ("Fuck and Run" and "6' 1"), there are also love songs ("Never Said"), lust songs ("Flower"), haunting character sketches ("Canary" and "Explain It to Me"), and exceptional narratives ("Divorce Song," "Stratford-on-Guy," and "Help Me Mary"). While her lyrics are literate without being pretentious, what makes the album so impressive is her musical diversity; from rock & roll to folk, from experimental rock to just a piano and a voice, *Exile in Guyville* is an endlessly inventive album that only gets better with repeated plays. —*Stephen Thomas Erlewine*

Sam Phillips

b. Jan. 5, 1923, Florence, AL
Vocals / Pop/rock
Sam Phillips the singer, not the former head of Sun Records, is a California-based singer/songwriter, whose 1987 debut album, *The Turning* (released under her given name of Leslie Phillips)

was a contemporary Christian recording issued by Myrrh and produced by fellow Christian and then-future husband T-Bone Burnette. He also handled the boards for Phillips's three secular albums, which have garnered considerable critical praise. — *William Ruhlmann*

○ **Indescribable Wow** / 1988 / Virgin 90919
T-Bone Burnette surrounds Phillips's voice, which has both a little-girl bounce and a teenage ache in it, with neo '60s pop arrangements on songs whose lyrics are often more serious than the inevitably cute-sounding production. But that only means that, once the music has seduced you, the words surprise you. — *William Ruhlmann*

Cruel Inventions / 1991 / Virgin 91617
A somewhat less accessible but nevertheless impressive followup. — *William Ruhlmann*

● **Martinis & Bikinis** / Mar. 8, 1994 / Virgin 39438
Sam Phillips's third album is a remarkably rich and varied set of Beatlesque pop, distinguished by her exceptional songwriting. — *Stephen Thomas Erlewine*

Phish

Rock & roll
Phish has gained a devoted cult since the release of their 1988 debut album, *Junta*. Most of their support derives from their concerts; their wildly eclectic music—incorporating rock, folk, country, bluegrass, jazz, and pop—catches fire in an improvised setting. On record, their experimentations can sometimes fall flat, but often the band's rich musical diversity and goofy charm usually carry them over the dull spots. — *Stephen Thomas Erlewine*

● **A Picture of Nectar** / Aug. 1991 / Elektra 61274
A wildly eclectic album in the vein of the Grateful Dead, *A Picture of Nectar* is the best example of their genre-jumping good-time rock & roll. — *David Jehnzen*

Rift / 1993 / Elektra 61433
Rift, Phish's followup to their major-label breakthrough *A Picture of Nectar*, follows the same pattern as its predecessor but doesn't quite live up to the surprising adventurous music as *Nectar*. Phish fans won't be too disappointed, since most of the album is enjoyable. — *Stephen Thomas Erlewine*

Wilson Pickett

b. Mar. 18, 1941, Prattville, AL
Vocals / Soul, R&B
The Wicked Pickett, as he dubbed himself, first achieved a measure of success as the apoplectic lead tenor on the Falcons' "I Found a Love" in 1962. Fleeting success followed (his original of "If You Need Me" was scooped up by Solomon Burke) before he signed with Atlantic Records in 1964. After a couple of false starts, he was shipped down to Memphis and came back with "In the Midnight Hour." It was followed by similarly compelling entries such as "Don't Fight It," "634-5789," "Mustang Sally," and a hysterical revival of Chris Kenner's mid-tempo shuffle "Land of 1000 Dances." Scouring old albums, one will also notice that Pickett never lost his feel for a slow ballad, despite his reputation as the prince of the dance floor. Some have charged that Pickett went on to reduce spontaneous emotion to a cliché, and most of his later records certainly reinforce that notion, but at his considerable best, Pickett was an immensely compelling performer at any tempo. The hit movie *The Commitments* hinted broadly at the esteem in which vintage Pickett is held. Sampled at his best, he was a titan. — *Colin Escott*

In the Midnight Hour / 1965 / Atlantic 8114
Wilson Pickett's first album, from 1965, was a bit of a hodgepodge, including singles from as far back as 1962. Three of these tracks were actually issued as singles by the Falcons (for whom Pickett sang lead) before he started his solo career; others were issued as singles before Pickett broke through as a national star with the title track. This 12-track album doesn't really suffer as a result, however. Besides the all-time classic "In the Midnight Hour," it includes the Mann/Weil-penned single "Come Home Baby," covered by several rock and soul artists; "Don't Fight It," which reached the R&B Top 10 in late 1965; "I'm Gonna Cry," a 1964 single that Pickett wrote with fellow soul legend Don Covay; and "I Found a Love," the Falcons single that made the R&B Top 10 in 1962. Working with several collaborators (includ-

ing Steve Cropper), Pickett himself wrote most of the tunes on this album. The record also featured the first recordings he made with the Stax rhythm section in Memphis—a combination that would yield much fine soul music throughout the rest of the '60s. — *Richie Unterberger*

○ **Wicked Pickett** / 1966 / Atlantic 8138
A fabulous album, done when Pickett was in the midst of his best period at Atlantic. It had everything: great songs, wonderful production and arrangement, and a hungry, galvanizing Wilson Pickett hollering, screaming, shouting, and soaring on anything he covered from ballads to uptempo dance and midtempo wailers. It also has been deleted at present. — *Ron Wynn*

☆ **Exciting Wilson Pickett** / 1966 / Atlantic 8129
This 1966 record included several Pickett anthems, among them "Ninety-Nine and a Half (Won't Do)," "634-5789 (Soulsville U.S.A.)," and "Land of 1,000 Dances." Pickett was at his flaming, screaming, and testifying best, doing short, hot, and torrid uptempo tunes and equally blazing wailers and ballad weepers. Even the nonhits like "Danger Zone" and "It's All Over" were monsters. — *Ron Wynn*

○ **Sound of Wilson Pickett** / 1967 / Atlantic 8145
A masterpiece, perhaps his finest '60s album. This wasn't a hits collection, but a batch of great singles. His version of "Funky Broadway" may still be the best; it was certainly the most swaggering and posturing, punctuated by his screams and jubilant cries. Pickett was all over the R&B charts in 1967, and this was one of three albums Atlantic issued on him that year. Each one was a classic. — *Ron Wynn*

○ **Wilson Pickett in Philadelphia** / 1970 / Atlantic 8270
A landmark album, one of Pickett's all-time best and without question his finest '70s date. "Engine, Engine, Number 9" was a return to the great funky days of the '60s. The edited single was a big radio and crossover hit, while the extended version was a club smash. It revived his career, although he was now feuding with Atlantic and would take almost a year and a half to follow this with any new material. — *Ron Wynn*

○ **Wilson Pickett's Greatest Hits** / 1973 / Atlantic 2501
Atlantic issued this greatest hits anthology on Pickett to go along with two previous best of packages that had been released in the late '60s and early '70s. Pickett's personal problems and feuds with Atlantic studio heads had led him to jump ship and head to RCA in 1973. The company rushed this out and kept them scrambling to fill the void because he was back on top and was coming off a string of R&B hits and a successful album. As with the other packages, the Rhino is now the set to grab. This is the only other hits set that isn't out of print. — *Ron Wynn*

○ **A Man and a Half: The Best of Wilson Pickett** / 1992 / Rhino 70287
A Man and a Half: The Best of Wilson Pickett is a double-disc set that collects the absolute cream of Pickett's early sides with the Falcons and all the highlights of his successful alliance with the Atlantic label. With "Mustang Sally," "In the Midnight Hour," "Ninety Nine and a Half," "Hey Jude," "Land of a 1000 Dances," "You're So Fine," and "634-5789" all included, this excellent compilation should be one of the cornerstones of anybody's soul collection. — *Cub Koda*

★ **Very Best Of** / 1993 / Rhino 71212
A terrific single-disc collection of all of Pickett's biggest hits; it's the place to go for casual fans. — *Stephen Thomas Erlewine*

Pink Floyd

Vocals / Progressive rock, psychedelic
Practically from its inception in 1965, Pink Floyd was on the cutting edge of psychedelic rock experimentalism, utilizing feedback, sound effects, light shows, unorthodox lyrical themes, and spacey productions. It was band member Syd Barrett (b. January 6, 1946) who gave the band its moniker, inspired by the Georgia bluesmen Pink Anderson and Floyd Council. Barrett's trippy songwriting on their debut album, *The Piper at the Gates of Dawn* (which included the English hit "See Emily Play"), set the band even further apart from most bands of the time. Barrett, however, left the band due to psychological deterioration encouraged by drug abuse, leaving bassist Roger Waters (b. September 9, 1944) to take over the primary songwriting duties.

The band's sonic explorations achieved focus with 1973's seamless *The Dark Side of the Moon,* an album that firmly placed them in the big time. Followup albums *Wish You Were Here, Animals, The Wall,* and *The Final Cut* enjoyed phenomenal success.

Waters reveals an increasingly vitriolic spirit in his conceptual themes as he addressed the breakdown of individual dignity in the face of a perceived Orwellian post-WWII social order.

It should be said that guitarist David Gilmour's (b. March 6, 1946) soaring guitar work and songwriting contributions on *The Wall*'s "Comfortably Numb" gave him a high profile in the band. After *The Final Cut,* Waters and the band acrimoniously split up in 1983, leaving them to pursue various solo efforts, with moderate success.

Gilmour reformed Pink Floyd in 1987 with drummer Nick Mason (b. January 27, 1945) and keyboardist Rick Wright (b. July 28, 1945), releasing *A Momentary Lapse of Reason,* which sparked a flurry of lawsuits between Waters and the band over the ownership of the name. While the album lacks the thematic bite of Waters's input, the band's sound is intact, helping the album become a worldwide hit. Seven years after their triumphant comeback, Pink Floyd released *The Division Bell,* which shared had the same flaws and pleasures as *A Momentary Lapse of Reason.* —*Rick Clark*

☆ **The Piper at the Gates of Dawn** / Sep. 1967 / Capitol 46384
The debut album combines long, group-written, largely instrumental compositions with shorter, whimsical, eclectic pop songs written by lead singer and guitarist Syd Barrett (his only full-length album appearance with the group). A wonderful evocation of the distinctly British take on '60s psychedelic music. (Note: Avoid the out-of-print LP version *Pink Floyd,* Tower 5093, which abridges the original UK album.) —*William Ruhlmann*

○ **Ummagumma** / Nov. 1969 / Capitol 46404
A two-disc set, the first disc containing a definitive live set, the second experimental contributions from each of the band members. —*William Ruhlmann*

○ **Relics** / May 1971 / Barclay 701290
A singles collection from the Syd Barrett era, containing the British hits "Arnold Layne" and "See Emily Play," among other psychedelic nuggets. —*William Ruhlmann*

○ **Meddle** / Nov. 1971 / Capitol 46034
With *Meddle,* Pink Floyd instrumentally arrived at an airy ensemble sound, which would eventually find full flower on their 1973 classic *The Dark Side of the Moon.* This approach is particularly evident on "Echoes," a periodically languorous jam that takes up half of the album. Nevertheless, there are enough sonic concepts and pleasant melodies at work on this album to make it worthwhile to the Floyd fan looking to dig deeper than *The Dark Side of the Moon* or *The Wall.* —*Rick Clark*

★ **Dark Side of the Moon** / Mar. 1973 / Capitol 46001
Pink Floyd's instrumental prowess and mastery of sound effects, married for the first time to bassist Roger Waters's lyrics about madness, "Time," "Money," and other concerns, make for the most impressive mood music of the decade (and sales of 25 million copies so far). —*William Ruhlmann*

☆ **Wish You Were Here** / Sep. 1975 / Columbia 33453
A concept album paying tribute to Syd Barrett ("Shine On You Crazy Diamond") and lambasting the music industry ("Have a Cigar"). —*William Ruhlmann*

☆ **The Wall** / Nov. 1979 / Columbia 36183
This is Roger Waters's two-disc meditation on the travails of a rock star, whose unhappy life causes him to build a psychological barrier between himself and the rest of the world. Contains the #1 hit "Another Brick in the Wall (Part 2)" and the concert favorite "Comfortably Numb" (cowritten by David Gilmour). —*William Ruhlmann*

The Final Cut / Apr. 1983 / Columbia 38243
A Roger Waters solo album in all but name, containing the composer's response to Britain's Falklands War in the form of a massive condemnation of war and government. —*William Ruhlmann*

A Momentary Lapse of Reason / 1987 / Columbia 40599
A David Gilmour solo album in all but name, heavily featuring the kind of atmospheric instrumental music and Gilmour guitar sound typical of the Floyd before the now-departed Roger Waters took over but lacking Waters's unifying vision and lyrical ability. —*William Ruhlmann*

The Division Bell / 1994 / Columbia 64200
Another album of Floyd-by-numbers by David Gilmour, *The Division Bell* carefully reconstructs the band's classic '70s sound with the occasional ambient update to keep the band current. —*Stephen Thomas Erlewine*

Gene Pitney

b. Feb. 17, 1941
Vocals / Pop/rock
Between 1961 and 1968, Gene Pitney's seamless pop sound scored 16 Top 40 hits, with songs like "Town without Pity," "Only Love Can Break a Heart," "(The Man Who Shot) Liberty Valance," "It Hurts to Be in Love," and "I'm Gonna Be Strong." Pitney, with his expressive tenor voice, was one of the few artists who successfully bridged the gap from early '60s light pop to the British invasion sound. Much of this came from his extensive music-industry background as a producer, engineer, and songwriter, penning hits for Ricky Nelson, the Crystals, Roy Orbison, and others. He also worked with producer Phil Spector and had a knack for identifying promising upcomers like Al Kooper and Randy Newman. Pitney's shrewd business sense, coupled with the compliance of manager/publisher Aaron Schroeder, positioned him to record with much more favorable artistic control and greater participation in publishing and royalties. —*Rick Clark*

● **Anthology 1961-1968** / 1986 / Rhino 75896
The voice still sounds surreal, like no one else in pop music, and this collection of hits exudes class. Emotional, pained, stunning. Pitney is a master—rock's Caruso. —*Jeff Tamarkin*

Pixies

Group / Alternative pop/rock
With their jagged, roaring guitars and undeniable pop melodies, the Pixies were arguably the best American alternative rock band of the late '80s. Many critics accussed the band of being pretentious, amateurish college students just wanting to make noise, and some of that criticism is rather accurate; their records are filled with squealing guitar noise that could only be made by enthusiastic, inexperienced musicians and rabid rock fans. But the band was able to meld punk and post-punk indie guitar rock, classic pop, surf rock, and stadium-sized riffs with singer/guitarist Black Francis's (born Charles Thompson) bizarre, fragmented lyrics about space, religion, sex, mutilation, and pop culture; while the meaning of his lyrics may have been impenetrable, the music was direct and forceful. The Pixies' busy, brief songs, extreme dynamics, and subversion of conventional song structures were very influential on many bands of the '90s; Nirvana, in particular, cited them as one of their favorite bands, admitting that "Smells Like Teen Spirit" was a Pixies rip-off.

By the time of their last album, 1991's *Trompe Le Monde,* the band was increasingly becoming a solo project for Black Francis; bassist/vocalist Kim Deal barely sang on the record and was reportedly angry that she wasn't allowed any space for her songs on the last two albums. After a tension-filled final tour opening U2's 1992 Zoo TV stadium extravaganza, Black Francis informed the band in early 1993 that they were officially broken up. He inverted his stage name to Frank Black and released his first solo album three months later. Lead guitarist Joey Santiago played with Black; drummer David Lovering joined Cracker. At the time, Deal was already at work on the Breeders' second album, which became a much bigger commercial success than any Pixies record. —*Stephen Thomas Erlewine*

○ **Come on Pilgrim** / 1987 / Elektra 61296
Filled with raw, noisy guitars, the Pixies' debut EP *Come on Pilgrim* is a thrilling collection of eight rough pop gems that are extremely catchy and extremely abrasive.

☆ **Surfer Rosa** / 1988 / Elektra 61295
A stunning full-length debut album loaded with the guitar-driven angst and feral pop that define the Pixies' sonic onslaught. —*John Dougan*

★ **Doolittle** / 1989 / Elektra 60856
Muscular, jarring post-punk pop with brains. As skewed melodies explode into a netherworld of alternately harsh and sweet vocalizing, the Pixies rewrite the book of love in their own singular and compelling way. —*John Dougan*

○ **Bossanova** / 1990 / Elektra 60963

Although it occasionally sounds like an afterthought, *Bossanova* makes up for its shortcomings (which are mostly lyrical) with its alternately assaultive and lush sound. —*John Dougan*

○ **Trompe le Monde** / 1991 / Elektra 61118

While it's noisier than *Bossanova, Trompe Le Monde* is anything but a return to the raw punk-pop of the Pixies' earlier records. Instead, it's a highly textured record, filled with distinctive melodies and subtle production flourishes that embellish their subversive pop songs. —*Stephen Thomas Erlewine*

Robert Plant

b. Aug. 20, 1948

Vocals / Hard rock, pop/rock
British hard-rock/heavy-metal singer Robert Plant had released a couple of singles and worked with a number of bands before he hooked up with Jimmy Page's New Yardbirds, subsequently renamed Led Zeppelin, around the time of his 20th birthday in 1968. For the next 12 years, Plant was one of the biggest rock stars on the planet. He gradually developed as a singer, branching out into other styles within Zeppelin's hard-rock framework, and he blossomed as a songwriter as well.

Plant launched a solo career in 1982 with the album *Pictures at Eleven*, a gold-selling hit. He did even better the following year with *The Principle of Moments*. It sold a million copies, included the Top 20 hit "Big Log," and led to his first post-Zeppelin concert tour. Surprisingly, Plant then organized a one-off mini-album, *The Honeydrippers, Vol. One*, recording some rock oldies with a superstar pickup band. He faced greater consumer resistance with his third solo album, *Shaken 'n' Stirred*, perhaps because joint appearances with Page led an audience to desire for a Zeppelin reunion. To an extent, Plant fed that desire with *Now and Zen*, which sampled Zeppelin tracks and featured Page. It was another million-seller. Plant's 1990 followup, *Manic Nirvana*, went gold. —*William Ruhlmann*

○ **Pictures at Eleven** / 1982 / Swan Song 8512

The directions in which Plant seemed to be heading in the later Zeppelin records- toward lighter, more melodic music, tempered with sometimes odd rhythms—are continued on his first solo album, which finds him singing more and screaming less. It wasn't Led Zeppelin, but then, that was the whole point. —*William Ruhlmann*

● **Principle of Moments** / 1983 / Es Paranza 90101

Plant reinvents rock and pop oldies in much the way Led Zeppelin did old blues songs. "Other Arms" recasts "Lay Down Your Arms," as Plant declares, "I'm not a prisoner of the big parade," while "In the Mood" retools an old pop theme. The playing is propulsive (thanks to guest drummer Phil Collins) and Plant's singing unusually supple. —*William Ruhlmann*

Now & Zen / 1989 / Es Paranza 90863

Robert Plant hires a new band, prominently featuring keyboardist Phil Johnstone, and also adds a backup singer for a fuller sound. At the same time, the appearance of Jimmy Page on "Tall Cool One," a Top 25 hit, casts a glance back at Plant's Led Zeppelin days. —*William Ruhlmann*

Fate of Nations / May 27, 1993 / Atlantic

At first, *Fate of Nations* seems so light and airy that it slips away (quite a remarkable feat for a man who fathered heavy metal) through the layers of acoustic guitars, violins, and keyboards. Upon further listenings, more textures appear, and the album gains a calm sense of tension and reflectiveness. Needless to say, it also is Plant's most personal record ever; he addresses the death of his son in the beautiful "I Believe." Simultaneously, *Fate of Nations* is, as its title suggests, a political album—the booklet is filled with environmental information in addition to the lyrics of "Great Spirit" and "Network News," two of the most socially conscious songs Plant has ever written. Yet the album never is heavyhanded, falling into sermonizing or sentimentality. —*Stephen Thomas Erlewine*

The Platters

Group / R&B, doo-wop
During the '50s and early '60s, this Los Angeles vocal quartet, featuring the soaring tenor of lead singer Tony Williams (b. April 15, 1928), successfully straddled the line between teen and adult audiences with their romantically charged material. The Platters charted 35 Top 100 hits while on Mercury Records.

Their hits, many of which were penned by manager Buck Ram, included "Only You (and You Alone)," "The Great Pretender," "My Prayer," "Twilight Time," "Smoke Gets in Your Eyes," "Harbor Lights," "(You've Got) the Magic Touch," and "Enchanted." —*Rick Clark*

Very Best of the Platters / 1991 / Mercury 510317

The Platters' 12 biggest hits are featured on this brief but solid collection; it's fine for those who don't want to spend the money on the double-disc set. —*Stephen Thomas Erlewine*

★ **Magic Touch: An Anthology** / 1991 / Mercury 510314

Double-disc set of all their best sides, including "The Great Pretender," "Smoke Gets in Your Eyes," "Only You," "Harbor Lights," and the title track. Great annotation and impeccable sound. All compilations should be done this well. —*Cub Koda*

Plimsouls

Group / New wave
With their sharp guitar hooks, memorably sweet melodies, and raggedly beautiful harmonies, the Plimsouls made music that invigorated power pop in the early '80s. Led by Peter Case's strong songwriting, the group released only two albums and an EP before breaking up in 1983, yet their records sound fresh and exciting more than a decade after their split. —*Stephen Thomas Erlewine*

○ **Everywhere at Once** / 1983 / David Geffen Co. 24481

The second album retains all of the fiery spirit of the debut with a smoother production. This album holds up much better than many others of the period. Includes the infectious "A Million Miles Away." —*Chris Woodstra*

● **Plimsouls ... Plus** / 1992 / Rhino 71061

Now reissued as *Plimsouls...Plus* with bonus tracks from the *Zero Hour* EP, the band's first album showcases their blend of power-pop and gritty southern soul. Hook-laden and filled with raw energy, this is a lost masterpiece that shouldn't be missed this time around. —*Chris Woodstra*

Poco

Group / Country rock
Founded by Jim Messina and Richie Furay during the dying days of Buffalo Springfield, with Randy Meisner (who dropped out shortly before the recording of their first album), Rusty Young, and George Grantham, the band built a solid reputation in Los Angeles as an innovative country-rock ensemble. Their first album, *Pickin' Up the Pieces*, was one of the strongest debut records of its era, a blend of country and western influences, Beatlesque harmonies, and mainstream rock, all within one cover. They began developing a major national reputation with the release of their second album, *Poco*, at the same time that the group's membership entered what proved to be a virtually constant state of flux. By the mid '70s, the band had become an established fixture in the middle reaches of the national charts, but Messina and Furay were long gone. The band continued recording well into the late '70s on MCA after leaving Epic, and their following was strong enough to justify a posthumous live album from Epic at the same time. The original quintet, which never did get to record, finally went into the studio under the auspices of RCA in the late '80s. —*Bruce Eder*

○ **Pickin' Up the Pieces** / 1969 / Epic 48514

Their debut album, which is as accomplished as anything by Buffalo Springfield, also recalls the Beatles and the Byrds in its musical orientation. —*Bruce Eder*

Poco / 1970 / Epic 26522

Their still fresh, and very Beatlesque, debut album is a fine continuation from the early Buffalo Springfield. —*Bruce Eder*

Deliverin' / 1970 / Epic 30209

The first of two live albums, and consisting of entirely new material—a major country-rock success, capturing not only the lyricism and upbeat approach of the band but also the infectiously positive attitude of its fans. —*Bruce Eder*

From the Inside / 1971 / Epic 30753
A most unusual record, produced by Memphis guitarist Steve Cropper. Much harder-edged than the rest of the group's output, this album is much more a solid rock album and relies less on the harmony sound than their other records. —*Bruce Eder*

A Good Feelin' to Know / 1972 / Epic 31601
The title track is a failed attempt at a hit single, but the record as a whole is a much more pure rock album than they were known for. —*Bruce Eder*

● **Forgotten Trail (1969-1974)** / 1986 / Epic 46162
This definitive two-CD collection is full of wonderful moments and great songs, so it is the obvious starting point. —*Bruce Eder*

Crazy Loving: Best of Poco 1975-1982 / 1989 / MCA 42323
An anthology of the group's second era, distilling the strongest tracks from those seven years. —*Bruce Eder*

The Pogues
Group / Alternative pop/rock
The Pogues combined traditional folk of all stripes (with an emphasis on Irish folk) with rock muscle, producing some of the most original and remarkable music of the '80s. Originally known as Pogue Mahone (Gaelic for "kiss my ass"), the group (Shane MacGowan, vocalist and songwriter; Philip Chevron, guitar; Spider Stacy, tin whistle; Andrew Ranken, drums; James Fearnley, accordion; Darryl Hunt, bass; Jem Finer, banjo; Terry Woods, mandolin) formed in 1982. The Elvis Costello-produced *Rum Sodomy & the Lash* proved MacGowan was a gifted songwriter and earned the band several UK hits. Original bassist Caitlin O'Riordan left the band in 1985 and married Costello; O'Riordan was replaced by Hunt. The Pogues signed to Island, releasing *If I Should Fall from Grace with God*, arguably their best album, in 1988. MacGowan's health began to deteriorate due to drug use, culminating in a breakdown in the fall of 1990; he left the band after *Hell's Ditch*, dropping out of sight for a couple of years. After his departure, the Pogues toured with ex-Clash leader Joe Strummer for a short time.

MacGowan resurfaced on a one-off Christmas single with Nick Cave; he formed a new band late in 1993. The Pogues continued with Spider Stacy on lead vocals, releasing a new album in 1993; it received a lukewarm critical and commercial reception. By the beginning of 1994, there were rumors that the band had decided to call it quits. —*Stephen Thomas Erlewine*

Red Roses for Me / 1984 / Enigma 73225
A very raw but enjoyable debut. —*Stephen Winick*

○ **Rum Sodomy & the Lash** / 1985 / MCA 5744
A triumph, produced by Elvis Costello. Shane MacGowan has never sounded so intense, nor has the band played with such authority. A classic melding of punk-era-defined sensibilities and the magic of Celtic traditionalism. Features a stirring version of Eric Bogle's classic "And the Band Played Waltzing Matilda" (import). —*John Dougan*

● **If I Should Fall from Grace with God** / 1988 / Island 842878
If I Should Fall from Grace with God, The Pogues' third album, is another fiery, eclectic meld of traditional Celtic music and rock played with punk venom. The band can barely keep up with the breakneck pace of songs like "Bottle of Smoke," which is what makes the album so appealing. Overall, this album has more of a rock spirit than *Rum Sodomy and the Lash,* and MacGowan's songs show significant strides in quality. —*Stephen Thomas Erlewine*

Peace and Love / 1989 / Island 842838
Kind of a letdown—good but not up to their high standards. —*Chip Renner*

Hell's Ditch / 1990 / Island 846999
Less than pristine production makes this provocative CD a bit hard to listen to repeatedly. —*Robert Gordon*

○ **Essential Pogues** / 1991 / Island 510610
Essential Pogues doesn't cover *Red Roses for Me* or *Rum Sodomy and the Lash,* so it isn't the definitive collection. However, it does capture the majority of the highlights from their Island albums and functions as a good introduction to the band. One complaint: the tedious extended remix of "Yeah, Yeah, Yeah, Yeah, Yeah" was included instead of the punchy, energetic original single. —*Stephen Thomas Erlewine*

Waiting for Herb / 1993 /

Without Shane McGowan, the Pogues are a competent Irish folk-rock band with several strong songs, yet they lack the fire of their earlier albums. For the diehard, *Waiting for Herb* will be necessary, even if it is a little disheartening. —*Stephen Thomas Erlewine*

Buster Poindexter (David Johansen)
b. Sep. 1, 1950, New York, NY
Vocals / Pop/rock, R&B
"Buster Poindexter" is the pseudonym rock singer David Johansen adopted in the mid '80s for a semi-comic nightclub-singer act he began to perform. Eschewing his hard-rock solo career (which followed a stint as lead singer of the New York Dolls), Johansen turned up at the New York club Tramps in a tuxedo, with a band he dubbed the Banshees of Blue, and sang pop standards, jump blues, and various novelty material. Eventually, the act won him a record contract, resulting in a few albums on RCA, but it was basically a live attraction. Since then, Johansen has pursued an acting career, though he maintains the Buster persona, appearing, for example, in the Catskills in the summer of 1992. —*William Ruhlmann*

● **Buster Poindexter** / 1987 / RCA 6633
You can't experience Buster Poindexter's campy nightclub act on a studio recording, but you can get a sense of the material by listening to the Caribbean dance strains of "Hot Hot Hot" and the Wynonie Harris hit "Good Morning Judge." There are also a couple of good songs by one David Johansen. —*William Ruhlmann*

○ **Buster's Happy Hour** / 1994 / Rhino/Forward
This collection of jump blues and roadhouse rockers is an excellent party album. Poindexter's smart choice of material and obvious love of the music should cajole even the stodgiest stick-in-the-mud to lighten up and have a good time. —*Rick Clark*

The Pointer Sisters
Group / Soul, pop/rock, urban R&B
Versatile Ruth, Anita, June, and Bonnie Pointer regularly scored pop and soul hits throughout the '70s and '80s in a chameleonic variety of styles. Formed in Oakland, with their first successes for Blue Thumb Records blending funky rhythms with a novel nostalgic attitude (beginning with their 1973 revival of Allen Toussaint's "Yes We Can Can"), leading up to their first #1 R&B item in 1975, "How Long (Betcha' Got a Chick on the Side)."

Bonnie signed with Motown in 1978 and kicked off her own string of R&B hits with "Free Me from My Freedom/Tie Me to a Tree (Handcuff Me)." (June and Anita also tried the solo route during the '80s, without leaving the fold.)

By 1979, when the remaining trio covered Bruce Springsteen's "Fire," the Pointers were headed in a more contemporary direction on the Planet label, and "He's So Shy" (1980), "Slow Hand" (1981), "Automatic," and the anthemic "Jump (for My Love)" (the last two both 1984) were savvy ditties that blazed trails across the R&B and pop charts. —*Bill Dahl*

Pointer Sisters / 1973 / MCA 31377
The Pointer Sisters stepped out of session anonymity and into stardom with their debut. After working with Elvin Bishop, Esther Phillips, and many others, the foursome got into the spotlight in a hurry with "Yes We Can Can." They did a mix of jazzy pop, scat, light R&B, and even some country, and their harmonies and shared leads were reminiscent of both cabaret acts and early '60s female ensembles. The album cracked the pop Top 20 and established them as a viable frontline singing act. —*Ron Wynn*

○ **Steppin'** / 1975 / Blue Thumb 6021
The second Pointer Sisters album didn't do as consistently well as its predecessor, though it earned them their second gold album and also won them a country Grammy for the song "Fairy Tale." They may have been the most unlikely country success story of all time, with their sassy attitudes and irreverent stage show. But they did appear all over the country landscape that year, even at the Grand Ole Opry. Regretably, it was an indication of how wide the splits are musically and demographically that "Fairy Tale" didn't even chart on the R&B side. —*Ron Wynn*

○ **Black & White** / 1981 / Planet 18
The Pointer Sisters were beginning to hit their stride on Planet with this album. They earned their second #2 pop hit with "Slow Hand." "Should I Do It" was a throwback to the camp and novelty tunes that launched their careers, while they also did a cover of

"Someday We'll Be Together" and handled other straight pop pieces such as "Take My Heart, Take My Soul" and "Sweet Lover Man." —*Ron Wynn*

● **Greatest Hits** / 1982 / RCA 9816
The Pointer Sisters had their run of hit albums on Planet briefly interrupted in the early '80s, when their label rushed out this anthology as their second album of 1982. They were just coming off a huge R&B and pop hit in "Slow Hand," had another song on the R&B charts, and were red hot. This album didn't do much saleswise, but served to keep their name alive and clear the way for what would prove their biggest album as a group the next year, *Break Out*. —*Ron Wynn*

○ **So Excited** / 1982 / Planet 6001
The Pointer Sisters put the title track on the charts twice; this was the original version that peaked at #30 and was the cornerstone for this 1982 album. There was also the mild hit "American Music," which spoke to their eclecticism, and the less successful "If You Wanna Get Back Your Lady" and "Heart Beat." They were still carefully building their fan base, mixing soul-oriented cuts with lighter pop ones and not letting any single sister dominate the spotlight. —*Ron Wynn*

○ **Break Out** / 1983 / Planet 4705
The Pointer Sisters landed the biggest album of their careers with this Richard Perry-produced glossy pop package. The album eventually became a double platinum success, while "Automatic," "Jump," and "Neutron Dance" were each pop and R&B hits. There was little surprise to these cuts, but they were excellently produced and arranged, and the Pointer Sisters sang them with class and zest. —*Ron Wynn*

Contact / 1985 / RCA 5487
This was the first album that the Pointer Sisters did directly for RCA. Richard Perry produced once more, and they scored their biggest hit in quite a while with the single "Dare Me," while several other songs from the album charted in subsequent months. They were almost about to move to Motown, and Anita was making noises about a solo career. She finally did issue her own session, but didn't stay out of the fold very long. —*Ron Wynn*

● **Jump: Best of the Pointer Sisters** / 1989 / RCA 90319
Jump covers their hits for the Planet record label. They'd moved beyond their camp/novelty origins and away from their country flirtation and were comfortable making exuberantly sung, conservatively produced soul-tinged pop. During this period, they scored a number of crossover smashes, including "Jump," "He's So Shy," "Automatic," and "Slow Hand;" all of their '80s hits are included on this album. —*Ron Wynn*

Poison

Group / Hard rock, pop/rock, heavy metal
A hard-rock quartet consisting of singer Bret Michaels, guitarist C. C. Deville, bassist Bobby Dall, and drummer Rikki Rockett, Poison was formed in Harrisburg, PA, in 1983, though the band members relocated to Los Angeles early on, where their highly visual approach (drummer Rockett was also a hairdresser who advised them on clothes, hair, and makeup) made them favorites in the city's glam-rock underground. C. C. Deville left the band in early 1992. Deville's replacement, Richie Kotsen, appeared on 1993's *Native Son*, their unsuccessful attempt to become a grittier, serious rock band; he was fired during the subsequent tour. —*William Ruhlmann*

Look What the Cat Dragged In / 1986 / Capitol 46735
Glam-metal gets revived with the Los Angeles group Poison, who turned many heads with their hook-filled songs as well as their looks. Although subsequent albums were more diverse, this one was loose and fun without a care for safety. Includes their first hit, "Talk Dirty to Me." —*John Book*

● **Open Up & Say ... Ahh!** / 1988 / Capitol 48493
This, the group's most popular album, presents its taste for straightforward hard rock ("Nothin' but a Good Time"), for acoustic ballads ("Every Rose Has Its Thorn"), and for its roots in simple pop-rock ("Your Mama Don't Dance"). —*William Ruhlmann*

○ **Flesh & Blood** / 1990 / Capitol 91813
On their third album, vocalist Bret Michaels puts in his best performance. "Unskinny Bop" and the anthemic "Something to Believe In" were both Top 10 hits. —*John Book*

○ **Swallow This Live** / 1991 / Capitol 98046
A two-disc concert release that captures Poison in all its excess (six-and-a-half-minute drum solo, nine-and-a-half-minute guitar solo) and hard-rock glory, with live versions of the hits that are better produced and more impassioned than the original studio cuts. —*William Ruhlmann*

Native Tongue / Feb. 8, 1993 / Capitol 98961
Ditching most of their party anthems as well as guitarist C. C. Deville because he supposedly couldn't play, Poison added guitar whiz Richie Kotzen and made a bid for respect. Leader Bret Michaels decided to accentuate the populist strains of ballads like "Something to Believe In" throughout *Native Tongue*. Often it falls short—Kotzen's playing is too proficient for the lite-metal hooks that the rest of the band have mastered—but Poison gets points for trying, and they do come up with some tracks, like the single "Stand," that could stand with their anthems from *Open Up and Say Ahh* and *Look What the Cat Dragged In*. —*Stephen Thomas Erlewine*

The Police

Group / New wave, pop/rock
In 1977, Sting (a British ex-schoolteacher born Gordon Sumner) and Stewart Copeland (a young drummer from the United States) met up with guitarist Andy Summers (of Soft Machine) and the three formed the final lineup of the Police—the rock group that would later take the early '80s by storm. The band's debut album, *Outlandos d'Amor*, which sported jazz and reggae rhythms in a rock/pop format, was released in 1978. The album, with such classic songs as "Roxanne," was popular with college radio, marking the beginning of the band's ascent to fame. The followup, *Regatta de Blanc*, was released the next year; with its bouncy, lively songs, it hit #1 in the United Kingdom for four weeks. *Zenyatta Mondatta*, released in 1980, achieved the same success on the UK charts and became the band's first album to place into the U.S. Top 10. *Ghost in the Machine* was a success as well, and in 1983 *Synchronicity* was released and went multiplatinum. It was #1 on the U.S. charts for 12 weeks, winning three Grammy Awards, including Song of the Year for the single "Every Breath You Take." In 1985 the three band memebers split to pursue solo careers. Apart from reuniting in 1986 to record a new version of "Don't Stand So Close to Me" for their stellar compilation *Every Breath You Take—The Singles*, the band has remained inactive. —*Iotis Erlewine*

○ **Outlandos d'Amour** / 1978 / A&M 3311
The Police's first album, although fairly rough, is still an impressive first effort. Although "Can't Stand Losing You" was their first hit (it made the Top 50), the best-known track on this album is definitely "Roxanne", still a favorite among college-radio stations. The influence of the punk era on this album is evident, as is bass player Sting's jazz background. A great deal of fun. —*Iotis Erlewine*

○ **Regatta de Blanc** / 1979 / A&M 3312
The very title, *Regatta de Blanc* (rough French for "White reggae"), describes the style of the Police's second album. This speedy mix of reggae and mainstream rock spawned two #1 UK hits with "Message in a Bottle" and "Walking on the Moon." The reggae influence is most noticeable in the rhythms, especially on the tracks "Bring On the Night," "Walking on the Moon," and "The Bed's Too Big without You." —*Iotis Erlewine*

☆ **Zenyatta Mondatta** / 1980 / A&M 3720
This album, although a bit rough around the edges, marks a transitional point in the band's career. "Don't Stand So Close to Me" became a #1 hit on the UK charts, and the band edged further into the mainstream. The sound became more pop oriented on this album, with songs like "De Do Do Do, De Da Da Da" and "Canary in a Coalmine," although they retained their unique sense of rhythm. For a good introduction to early Police, this album is a wise choice. —*Iotis Erlewine*

Ghost in the Machine / 1981 / A&M 3730
One of the Police's best songs, "Every Little Thing She Does Is Magic," is featured on this album, but as a whole, *Ghost in the Machine* is bland. Besides being poorly mixed (the music overpowers the vocals), the songs lack the musical simplicity and direction that are so appealing in the earlier albums. —*Iotis Erlewine*

○ **Synchronicity** / 1983 / A&M 3735

A departure from early Police, this album completed the band's transition into mainstream pop while, at the same time, becoming more musically refined. *Synchronicity* had the complexity of *Ghost in the Machine* without the boredom. The Police get louder and angrier, making this a stronger, more driving album. *Synchronicity* contains some of the band's most well-known work: "Every Breath You Take," which went #1 on both the U.S. and the UK charts; "Wrapped around Your Finger"; and "King of Pain." The pinnacle of the band's career, it went multiplatinum and secured the Police's claim to the title of "rockgods" in the early '80s. With the exception of Andy Summers's "Mother," there is not a bad song on the album. The CD contains the bonus track "Murder by Numbers." —*Iotis Erlewine*

★ **Every Breath You Take: The Singles** / 1986 / A&M 3902
A collection of singles from the five Police albums, this provides a consistent sampling of some of the Police's best work, from "Roxanne" to "Every Breath You Take." It's a good overview of the band's work and an excellent place to get an introduction to their music. This also includes a 1986 remake of "Don't Stand So Close to Me," featuring all three members of the band. —*Iotis Erlewine*

○ **Message in a Box** / 1993 / A&M
All of the studio recordings the trio made during their short career (except for a handful of foreign language recordings, remixes, and live tracks) are collected on the four-disc set *Message in a Box*. There are enough rarities in this attractive, sonically impressive package to justify its purchase for hard-core fans; for anyone who doesn't own any Police, it is an easy way to have the entire collection at once, but casual fans will be more satisfied by *Every Breath You Take: The Singles*. —*Stephen Thomas Erlewine*

Iggy Pop (James Newell Osterberg)

b. 1947
Vocals / Hard rock
Iggy Pop (born James Newell Osterberg, 1947; original stage name was Iggy Stooge, the Iggy appellation coming from his drumming tenure with local teen band the Iguanas) formed the Detroit rock & roll group the Stooges as the Psychedelic Stooges in 1967. The group also comprised Ron Asheton (guitar), Scott Asheton (drums), and Dave Alexander (bass). If local favorites the MC5 were striking fear into the hearts of Motor City parents with their manifesto of sex, drugs, rock & roll, and politics, they looked normal in comparison to the stage antics of Iggy and the Stooges. Violent interaction with members of the audience (both verbal and physical), vomiting, and self-mutilation with beer bottles were some of the more predictable aspects of their live presentation, while the music itself was simplistic and angry one- to three-chord grunge-rock, with lyrics ranging from teenage disorientation to animal lust. Two excellent albums for Elektra followed (they were signed the same night as the MC5), but the drug lifestyle of the band caused its breakup in the early '70s. They reformed with James Williamson on guitar and Asheton moving over to bass for the next album in 1973, but disbanded again a year later. Working with David Bowie, Iggy cut two good solo albums in the mid '70s, when bands like the Sex Pistols defined him as "The Godfather of Punk." He has kept recording and touring to his hardcore cult following up to the present time, with small acting roles in *The Color of Money* and *Cry Baby* as well. —*Cub Koda*

○ **Stooges** / 1969 / Elektra 74051
Debut album; the true birth of punk-rock. —*Cub Koda*

☆ **Fun House** / 1970 / Elektra 74071
Their second album, equally as great. —*Cub Koda*

★ **Raw Power** / 1973 / Columbia 32111
The title says it all. The blueprint for the Sex Pistols and the entire punk-rock movement. —*Cub Koda*

○ **Metallic K O** / Jan. 1977 / Skydog 1015
The last Stooges live show; scary as hell. Bootleg import. Worth the search. —*Cub Koda*

○ **Idiot** / Feb. 1977 / Virgin 91342
Iggy's first solo album. —*Cub Koda*

● **Lust for Life** / Mar. 1977 / Virgin 91343
Iggy Pop's second solo album is a boldly aggressive, upbeat record that is easily one of the best things he has ever recorded. —*Stephen Thomas Erlewine*

Music Map

Power Pop

The Sixties

British Influences
The Beatles – The Kinks – The Move

American Influences
The Byrds – Nazz

The Seventies
Badfinger – Big Star
The Raspberries – Stories
Dwight Twilley – Cheap Trick
Shoes

The Eighties
The dB's
Let's Active – Smithereens
Hoodoo Gurus – The Bangles

The Nineties
The Posies – Material Issue – Matthew Sweet
Cavedogs – Jellyfish – Teenage Fanclub

Porno for Pyros

Alternative rock
Perry Farrell's post-Jane's Addiction band, Porno for Pyros, followed the same path as his previous band, combining art rock, punk, heavy metal, and funk into one shrieking whole. On their self-titled 1993 debut, Farrell's pretentions got out of hand at times, resulting in some ridiculously self-absorbed conceptual pieces sitting next to some straightforward rockers and pop songs; it sold well at first, but soon slipped down the charts. While he prepared new Porno material in 1994, Farrell returned to the organization of Lollapalooza—the traveling rock festival he conceived—for the first time since 1992. —*Stephen Thomas Erlewine*

● **Porno for Pyros** / 1993 / Warner Brothers 45228
Although Porno for Pyros was supposed to sound radically different than Perry Farrell's former band, Jane's Addiction, Porno sounds like Jane's without the Zeppelinesque grandeurs of David Navarro. Their debut album, *Porno for Pyros*, should please Farrell's fans, although it does show the limits of his vision. —*Stephen Thomas Erlewine*

The Posies

Group / Power pop
This Seattle-based power-pop quartet is influenced by the Move, Big Star, Badfinger, and the Beatles. The songwriting and harmonic skills of Jonathon Auer and Kenneth Stringfellow are particularly striking, at times sounding like Graham Nash-period Hollies. —*Rick Clark*

○ **Failure** / 1988 / Pop Llama 2323
Failure is worth looking up, not so much because it represents a mature work but because it's a nice diamond-in-the-rough portrait of a band with a deep creative resource and a strong sense of pop history. —*Rick Clark*

● **Dear 23** / 1990 / David Geffen Co. 24305
From the Move-influenced "My Big Mouth" to the delicate, wistful "Everyone Moves Away," through tracks that would do Badfinger or Big Star proud, like "Apology," "Golden Blunders," and "Suddenly Mary," *Dear 23* is Anglo-rock/pop heaven. John Leckie's larger-than-life production might be a little overwhelming at times, but overall it highlights this band's gorgeous harmonies and arrangements to great effect. —*Rick Clark*

Frosting on the Beater / 1993 / Geffen 24522

The Posies turn up the rockets for their third album with an appealingly huge wall of guitars and bashola drumming. For the most part, the melodies and harmonies are still intact, but song for song, *Frosting on the Beater* doesn't hold up to *Dear 23.* Nevertheless, songs like "Different Door," "Solar Sister," and "Flavor of the Month" are wonderful. —*Rick Clark*

Prefab Sprout

Group / Pop/rock
Prefab Sprout, featuring singer/songwriter Paddy McAloon, are an adult-alternative/smart-pop quartet from England, who integrate their music with a Steely Dan-like sophistication in an airy bed of texturous synthwork and acoustic instrumentation. —*Rick Clark*

○ **Two Wheels Good** / 1985 / Epic 40100
A strong album debut of atmospheric, breathy, and clever pop music, with Thomas Dolby's light production. Earthy and ethereal at the same time. Released overseas as *Steve McQueen,* but with a different name for the U.S. version due to protests from the actor's estate. —*Scott Bultman*

○ **From Langley Park to Memphis** / 1988 / Epic 44208
A good but inconsistent record, with shining tracks like "The Golden Calf," "Cars and Girls," and "I Remember That." Paddy McAloon begins to explore his fixation with pop icons like Elvis and Springsteen. A must for fans. —*Scott Bultman*

○ **Jordan: The Comeback** / 1990 / Epic 46132
A stunning masterwork with 19 tracks (over 70 minutes) tied together by recurrent themes of God and Elvis. This one is stylistically all over the map—gospel, soul, rock, and pop. Pop songwriting with acknowledged influences from Jimmy Webb and Paul McCartney. —*Scott Bultman*

● **A Life of Surprises: The Best of Prefab Sprout** / 1992 / Epic 52847
This hits packaged offers a well chosen set and two previously unreleased tracks, "The Sound of Crying" and "If You Don't Love Me." The 16 tracks draw more selections from the *From Langley Park to Memphis* than the other albums, but this is a good single-disc introduction to Prefab Sprout's music. —*Scott Bultman*

Elvis Presley

b. Jan. 8, 1935, Tupelo, MS, d. Aug. 16, 1977, Memphis, TN
Vocals, guitar, piano / Rock & roll, pop/rock
Elvis Presley astonished the White culture of the American '50s with his overt sexuality and synthesis of hopped-up hillbilly music spot welded to the most African American of blues sources. Preachers railed against it, parents hated it, teenage boys emulated it, and girls went hog-wild in ecstasy over it. It took the world by storm, and while his visual and musical styles had their cultural antecedents in Hollywood and the Mississippi Delta, no one had ever seen anything like him before. At some point in 1953, the 19-year-old Presley entered Sam Phillips's Sun studios and cut a vanity disc under the auspices of its being a gift for his mother. Truth be known, Elvis (too proud to risk rejection at a formal audition) developed the ploy in hopes of being discovered. By July of 1954, Presley was in the studio again, laying down a series of recordings that transformed Western culture, achieving effortlessly what others would spend their careers pursuing in vain. In 1955, after no commercial success of major consequence, virtually every label of standing was bidding for his services, including Atlantic, who (with a predominantly African

American roster) were prepared to hock their entire assets to sign the unproven singer. His contract was eventually sold to RCA Victor under the guidance of Colonel Tom Parker, a former carnival hustler who aided in Presley's meteoric rise to the top and just as easily assured his slide into mediocrity. In 1957, at the height of his success, Elvis was drafted into the army, only to return two years later into a world of grade-Z movies and equally abominable soundtrack albums that exhibited only periodic flashes of his original brilliance. In December of 1968, on his first-ever television special, Elvis (recently married and a father extolling family virtues) took the NBC stage sweating, greasy, and passionate, growling his way nervously through his past, rediscovering his roots, and reinventing his persona as the King of Rock & Roll.

To cap this achievement, he returned to Memphis and recorded there for the first time since 1955. The resulting recordings were the most mature and passionate of his career. This was followed

by a much-ballyhooed conquest of Las Vegas, the town that chased him out in 1956. By the end of 1970, after a two-year run of hits and another wall full of gold records, Elvis Presley was the single most successful entertainer in the world. But with worldwide success came the personal problems that would eventually overwhelm him. During the last few years of his life, Presley stumbled onto stages around the country to croon his former glories, an unreliable entertainer, bloated beyond belief, a parody of his former self.

On June 26, 1977, Elvis was presented with a plaque commemorating his two-billionth record pressed by RCA. Less than two months later, on August 16, he died at Graceland, the victim of the progressively toxic effects of the veritable cornucopia of prescription drugs he had been taking for a decade or more. Whether his death was accidental, planned, or staged has been tabloid-magazine fodder ever since. What *is* certain is that, within days of his death, every record and tape on the planet earth with his name on it had been purchased by someone, somewhere. The real merchandising of Elvis Presley had begun in earnest. —*Neal Umphred, Rick Clark, Cub Koda, and Stephen Thomas Erlewine*

☆ **Elvis Presley** / Mar. 1956 / RCA 5198
While RCA had the material, they opted to play it safe and combine five Sun outtakes with seven new recordings and release the Hillbilly Cat's first album. This is a great way to begin a career! The best material here is on a par with the Sun singles. While "Blue Suede Shoes" is a cultural cornerstone of sorts, hearing Elvis's version of Clyde McPhatter's "Money Honey" is still, after four decades, revelatory. —*Neal Umphred*

☆ **Elvis** / Oct. 1959 / RCA 5199
A solid rock & roll album that almost any rocker of the '50s could claim as their best album. While there are some excellent rhythm numbers ("Rip It Up," "Paralyzed," and the too-country "When My Blue Moon Turns to Gold Again"), the album's standout is the panting "Love Me." —*Neal Umphred*

Elvis Is Back! / Apr. 1960 / RCA 2231
The first album after the army, *Elvis Is Back!* captures him at his secular best, which is nonetheless moved by gospel undertones. The sheer intensity of the performances from both Elvis on vocals and rhythm guitar and the all-star band (which, aside from the regulars, includes Floyd Cramer, Hank Garland, and Boots Randolph) overcomes any shortcomings the material might offer. "Make Me Know It," "Fever," and "The Girl of My Best Friend" (a hit for sound-alike Ral Donner here and for Elvis abroad) could have been chart-toppers. "Dirty, Dirty Feeling," "Reconsider Baby," and "Such a Night" are among the very best—and "dirtiest"—numbers Elvis had ever cut. —*Neal Umphred*

☆ **His Hand in Mine** / Dec. 1961 / RCA 1319
Presley cut several gospel albums over the course of his career, most of them overblown affairs. This one's easily his best: stripped-down arrangements with Elvis passionately involved every note of the way. —*Cub Koda*

○ **How Great Thou Art** / Mar. 1967 / RCA 3758
Between 1966 and 1968, Elvis recorded just enough studio material to fill one complete secular album and *How Great Thou Art,* a far more polite (and slightly surreal) reading of traditional religious material than the previous outing a half-dozen years earlier. The performances throughout are superb, the sound impeccable; this actually beat *Sgt. Pepper* as the Best Engineered Album of 1967 in the Grammys! This album is also much closer to mainstream gospel and may not be so immediately accessible to the unconverted; don't let that steer you away from an otherwise great record. —*Neal Umphred*

☆ **NBC TV Special** / Dec. 1968 / RCA 61021
After years of making abysmal movies, Presley appeared before a live audience, scared to death. That he more than rose to the challenge is evidenced here, a masterly performance highlighted by the jam-session segment with DJ Fontana and Scotty Moore, where Presley plays electric guitar and knocks out drop-dead versions of "Baby, What You Want Me to Do" and "Tiger Man." —*Cub Koda*

○ **From Elvis in Memphis** / May 1969 / RCA 51456
Presley returned to Memphis, recording 30 odd songs in Chips Moman's America Sound Studios in 1969, leading to his artistic and commercial resurgence ("In the Ghetto" and "Suspicious Minds") and what may be his single greatest album, *From Elvis in Memphis.* The first track opens with Elvis hoarsely shouting "I

had to leave town for a little while" and then announcing—in no uncertain terms—that he's back. Brilliant selection of material with Elvis singing like his life depended on it. (It didn't; his career did.) The musicians (all regulars from Chips Moman's American Sound Studios) cook, and the overdubbed horns and background vocals are among the most appropriate ever used on a white singer's record. —*Neal Umphred*

○ **Worldwide 50 Gold Award Hits, Volume 1** / Aug. 1970 / RCA 6401
A combination of the two four-LP *Worldwide* boxes, this two-CD set contains each of the 50 sides that RCA credits with accumulated worldwide sales in excess of one million copies! And in chronological order of release in mono! One can either trace the obvious decline of the artist into entertainer or marvel at how good the bad stuff sounds in context. Million-selling B sides and EPs that most assuredly had topped the seven-digit figure but were routinely ignored by most compilations are also included. If all you want in your collection from Elvis is the most obvious hits, this is the one to go with. —*Neal Umphred*

○ **In Person at the International Hotel, Las Vegas, NV** / Nov. 1970 / RCA 53892
When Elvis and the Colonel decided it was time to start appearing live again, they assembled a crackerjack band (featuring guitarist James Burton) and took on Vegas full bore. Easily the King's best live album, the highlights on *In Person (at the International Hotel, Las Vegas, NV)* include "Johnny B. Goode," the "My Babe/Mystery Train/Tiger Man" medley, and "Suspicious Minds." —*Cub Koda*

○ **That's the Way It Is** / Dec. 1970 / RCA 4114
Returning to the more familiar haunts of Nashville in 1970, Elvis & Co. recorded three dozen tracks, the best of which are on a par with the Memphis recordings from the preceding year. From these two albums emerged, both flawed, both excellent. *That's the Way It Is*, purporting to be the soundtrack from the documentary of the same name, contains eight of those sides, with Elvis at his most delicious ease. The live recordings are negligible and sink the album's basic level *except* for Elvis's magnificent "I Just Can't Help Believin'." —*Neal Umphred*

Collector's Gold / 1971 / RCA 3114
Here's a veritable treasure trove for Elvis fans. All of its 48 tracks on three CDs are previously unreleased. Hence, my fear of having to wade through a lot of dreck to get two or three good cuts. Instead, it came as a pleasant surprise to find a remarkable number of top-notch performances as well as consistently high-quality recorded sound throughout. Disc one covers numerous Hollywood outtakes and alternates highlighted by "You're the Boss," a red-hot duet with Ann-Margaret, originally recorded for "Viva Las Vegas," but which appeared neither in the film nor on the soundtrack album. Disc two is from Nashville sessions and contains a rocking version of Chuck Berry's "Memphis." Disc three comprises unreleased live material from Las Vegas, with a cover of Del Shannon's "Runaway" and the infamous "laughing" version of "Are You Lonesome Tonight." This set is well worth having and will add immeasurably to your Elvis collection. —*Randy Richardson*, Roundup Newsletter

○ **Elvis Country** / Jan. 1971 / RCA 6330
Elvis Country was the second album from the June 1970 sessions. It is Elvis's best single album from the '70s and one of his very best ever. Every performance has something to offer; one can argue about the outstanding selection, although I tend away from the pleading of "I Really Don't Want to Know" to the raving "(I Washed My Hands in) Muddy Water." Even "Snowbird" is sung with passion! —*Neal Umphred*

○ **Sun Sessions** / Mar. 1976 / RCA 6414
The place where rock & roll begins. "That's All Right," "Baby, Let's Play House," "Mystery Train," "Milkcow Blues Boogie," and "Good Rockin' Tonight," plus fascinating outtakes like "When It Rains, It Really Pours." The cornerstone of any rock & roll collection, and great notes by Peter Guralnick too. —*Cub Koda*

☆ **Reconsider Baby** / 1985 / RCA 5418
Since Elvis's death in 1977, the market has been inundated with an array of repackages, most of them artless, pointless, and, a fan might wish, profitless. Part of the 50th Anniversary celebration, *Reconsider Baby* offered little that was new, but the concept—Elvis as an R&B singer—was overdue. The selection is impossible

to argue with, the programming perfect, and the album makes its argument aptly. —*Neal Umphred*

○ **Number One Hits** / 1987 / RCA 6382
Number One Hits contains 18 #1 records from the charts of *Billboard*, who somehow didn't rank "Crying in the Chapel," "In the Ghetto," "Burning Love," and "Way Down" as chart-toppers, although other national surveys did. In fact, according to RCA, every copy of "Way Down" was sold out within days after Presley's death, not just here but all over the planet, and somehow, amazingly, it didn't even make the magazine's Top 10! —*Neal Umphred*

★ **Top Ten Hits** / 1987 / RCA 6383
The one definitive collection to own, 38 essential tracks spread over two CDs. Think of any of Elvis's biggest chartbusters: they're all here. —*Hank Davis and Cub Koda*

☆ **Memphis Record** / 1987 / RCA 6221
Coming hot off the heels of his breakthrough NBC special in 1968, Presley returned to Memphis to record for the first time in 12 years and laid down 20 tracks in the space of four days. He was hot, he was inspired, and it's all here. —*Cub Koda*

☆ **Million Dollar Quartet** / 1990 / RCA 2023
For years available only as a poor-fidelity bootleg, this is Elvis jamming in the Sun studios with Carl Perkins, Jerry Lee Lewis, and others on a set of primarily gospel and hillbilly material. Loose as a goose, with a true jam-session spirit to it, it offers a fascinating glimpse of one of the few times Presley let his true musical soul come up for air with somebody (Sam Phillips) there to record it. —*Cub Koda*

☆ **King of Rock 'n' Roll: Complete 50s' Masters** / 1992 / RCA 66050
Boxed five-CD set that contains every studio recording Elvis made from 1954 to 1958 in chronological order on the first four discs; the fifth is a collection of outtakes and alternates. The sound is the best we have heard on CD by Elvis with virtually every track taken from an original tape of a first-generation safety copy. Great booklet with more note from Peter Guralnick. *Absolutely* the single finest package RCA of America has ever released on Elvis Aaron Presley and indispensable to any collection that pretends to deal with American music. —*Neal Umphred*

☆ **From Nashville to Memphis: The Essential 60's Masters** / 1993 / RCA 66160

Billy Preston

b. Sep. 9, 1946
Vocals, piano, keyboard / Soul, R&B
It's advantageous to get an early start on your chosen career, but Billy Preston took the concept to extremes. By age ten, he was playing keyboards with gospel diva Mahalia Jackson, and two years later, in 1958, he was featured in Hollywood's film bio of W. C. Handy, *St. Louis Blues*, as young Handy himself. Preston was a prodigy on organ and piano, recording during the early '60s for Vee-Jay and touring with Little Richard. He was a loose-limbed regular on the mid '60s ABC-TV "Shindig" series, proving his talent as both vocalist and pianist, and he built an enviable reputation as a session musician, even backing the Beatles on their *Get Back* and *Let It Be* albums. That impressive Beatles connection led to Preston's big break as a solo artist with his own Apple album, but it was his early '70s soul smashes "Outa-Space" and the high-flying vocal "Will It Go Round in Circles" for A&M that put Preston on the permanent musical map. Sporting a humongous Afro and an omnipresent gap-toothed grin, Preston showed that his enduring gospel roots were never far removed from his joyous approach, less so now than ever. —*Bill Dahl*

○ **Most Exciting Organ Ever** / 1965 / Vee Jay 1123
The hyperbole of the title aside, Preston did produce some flamboyant organ solos and keyboard work throughout this album. His use of bass pedals, dazzling intervals, octave jumps, phrases, and chordal maneuvers were impressive. This hasn't been reissued by Vee Jay and certainly should be if the label hasn't lost the masters. It's another side of Preston, one that became lost as he gained more and more popularity in the '70s as a singer. —*Ron Wynn*

Wildest Organ in Town! / 1966 / Capitol 2532
A late '60s Capitol set with Preston displaying his jazz/blues side as an organist. Unfortunately, nothing on this album caught fire,

even in the R&B community, and Preston would soon go on to work for Ray Charles and subsequently the Beatles. His early prowess as a flashy organ equivalent of Jimi Hendrix has been largely forgotten or overlooked, and the fact this album hasn't been in print for many years hasn't helped. —*Ron Wynn*

○ **That's the Way God Planned It** / 1969 / Apple 97580
A great bit of gospel/soul in the title cut, and otherwise a fine record that didn't make Billy Preston a huge star but alerted everyone he was more than just a talented keyboard player backing the Beatles. This was one of two albums Preston did on the Beatles' Apple label, and while nothing made the charts, it was a good introduction for those unaware of Preston's multiple skills. —*Ron Wynn*

○ **Music Is My Life** / 1972 / A&M 3516
Though this was an erratic album, keyboardist and vocalist Billy Preston landed his lone #1 pop hit with "Will It Go Round in Circles." Preston tried everything from gospel and message tracks to rock and pop, but outside of "Circles," nothing else generated even a listen. But among Preston album cuts, "God Loves You" and "Ain't That Nothin'" are quite interesting. —*Ron Wynn*

● **Best of Billy Preston** / 1988 / A&M 3205
Contains several fun pop hits, including "Will It Go Round in Circles" and "Outa-Space." —*Dan Heilman*

The Pretenders

Group / Rock & roll, New Wave, rock/pop
The Pretenders, fronted by singer/songwriter Chrissie Hynde, released their 1980 self-titled debut at the height of the punk/New-Wave movement. Hynde's bracing, tough-as-nails female take on rock & roll and permutations of love, coupled with the band's inspired musical aggression, stood out in a market flooded with alienated, torn-shirt posturing. Sonically, the Pretenders were a tuneful fusion of mid '60s Anglo rock and late '70s punk energy.

After their sophomore effort, *Pretenders II*, the band's distinctive guitarist, James Honeyman Scott, died as a result of drug addiction, as did bassist Pete Farndon, who had been previously fired for incompatibility. Reeling from the losses, the Pretenders released the fine *Learning to Crawl*, which possessed a less aggressive, more melodic sound.

Over the course of their career, the Pretenders have softened their sound, but Hynde's honest (occasionally awkward and outspoken) search for personal growth has provided many provocative songs. —*Rick Clark*

☆ **Pretenders** / 1980 / Sire 3563
Chrissie Hynde's tough-girl persona, allied with the aggressive onslaught of Pete Farndon, James Honeyman Scott, and Martin Chambers, makes this the top debut album of its year and prime evidence of the enlivening influence punk had on mainstream rock. —*William Ruhlmann*

○ **Pretenders II** / 1981 / Sire 3572
A well-named followup, since this album successfully repeats the formula of the debut, from its punky leadoff track, "The Adultress," to its catchy pop-rock single, "Talk of the Town," and even to its Kinks cover, "I Go to Sleep." But if you liked the first one ... —*William Ruhlmann*

☆ **Learning to Crawl** / 1984 / Sire 23980
Half the band is dead, Chrissie Hynde has taken time off to have a baby, and the world has changed. The Pretenders are now a front for Hynde, solo artist, an adult rock singer-songwriter, and, on such songs as "Middle of the Road," "Back on the Chain Gang," and "My City Was Gone," a damn good one too. —*William Ruhlmann*

Get Close / 1986 / Sire 25488
By now, Hynde is writing songs to her child and taking on social issues. But the chiming guitars are gorgeous, and Hynde's caught-in-the-throat voice has never been more expressive. —*William Ruhlmann*

★ **Singles** / 1987 / Sire 25664
Though the singles-only format makes the Pretenders sound more pop-oriented than they were, especially in the beginning, this album essentially addresses the legacy of punk in the 10 years after its peak, tracing a heritage back to mid '60s Merseybeat and forward to a more rock-based pop music. It also makes the case for Chrissie Hynde as a major artist. —*William Ruhlmann*

Pretty Things

Of all the original British invasion groups, perhaps none is as underappreciated in the United States as the Pretty Things. Featuring the hoarse vocals of Mick Jagger lookalike Phil May and the stinging leads of guitarist Dick Taylor (who actually played in early versions of the Rolling Stones with Jagger and Keith Richards), the Pretties recorded a clutch of raunchy R&B rockers in the mid '60s that offer a punkier, rawer version of the early Stones' sound. Their first two albums, as well as a brace of fine major and minor British hits (of which "Don't Bring Me Down" and "Honey I Need" were the biggest), feature first-rate original material and covers and remain the group's most exciting and influential recordings. Unfortunately, the band remained virtually unknown to American audiences, most of whom would first hear "Don't Bring Me Down" on David Bowie's *Pinups* album (which also included a version of the Pretties' "Rosalyn").

After their initial run of success, the group took a sharp left turn into psychedelia with the orchestrated album *Emotions* (1967), impressive singles that owed more to Pink Floyd than Bo Diddley, and, most significantly, *S.F. Sorrow* (1968). The first rock opera, *S.F. Sorrow* was a major influence upon Pete Townshend, who released his much more successful opera, *Tommy*, with the Who the following year. Founding member Taylor left shortly after *S.F. Sorrow*, and the group continued to record progressive rock and hard rock with less impressive results through the mid '70s, although *Parachute* (1970) was named by *Rolling Stone* as album of the year. The group reunites sporadically for occasional gigs and recordings in their early R&B vein. —*Richie Unterberger*

Singles A's & B's / 1977 / Harvest 2022
Thirteen tracks from their progressive/psychedelic era, 1967-1971. Of special interest is the non-LP 1967 single "Defecting Grey," a brilliant cop of the Syd Barrett-era Pink Floyd. Its B side ("Mr. Evasion") and the followup single "Talkin' about the Good Times"/"Walking through My Dreams" were also non-LP and also rank among the more coveted rarities of the early British psychedelic era. —*Richie Unterberger*

● **Get a Buzz: The Best of the Fontana Years** / 1992 / Fontana 512446
It's missing a few good tracks, but this is a good retrospective of their British invasion-era work, running through the 1967 *Emotions* LP. Includes all their major singles—"Rosalyn," "Don't Bring Me Down," "Honey I Need," "Midnight to Six Man," "Come See Me." —*Richie Unterberger*

Lloyd Price

b. Mar. 9, 1933, Kenner, LA
Vocals / R&B, rock & roll
Having taken New Orleans by storm in 1952 with his often-covered #1 R&B hit "Lawdy Miss Clawdy" and a raft of sizzling encores, Lloyd Price yearned for new horizons in 1958, when he signed with ABC-Paramount Records. Price wanted to be a pop star, and it didn't take him long to achieve his goal. Price's pleading style worked brilliantly on his initial New Orleans sides for Specialty Records, resulting in a string of 1952-1953 R&B hits, but his later ABC output left the second-line rhythms behind in favor of prominent female choruses and giant supper-club-style horn sections. His socko reading of the old Crescent City chant "Stagger Lee" deservedly topped the R&B and pop lists in 1958, and he followed it with the utterly pop-styled "Personality" and "I'm Gonna Get Married," another pair of R&B #1s that sported no hint of Price's New Orleans roots. As the '60s dawned, Price insisted on interpreting a variety of Tin Pan Alley standards on his albums, although "Come into My Heart" and "Lady Luck," both hits, swung with a brassy, R&B-based drive. Price formed his own Double-L logo in 1963, issuing hits by Wilson Pickett and one for himself—a Vegas-oriented treatment of "Misty." Price seemed to prefer the business end of show biz after that rather than focusing on his singing career. —*Bill Dahl*

● **Greatest Hits** / 1990 / Curb 77305
Price's biggest hits, vintage 1957-1959, like "Personality" and "Stagger Lee." Catchy, brassy, and overarranged. —*Hank Davis*

○ **Lawdy!** / 1991 / Specialty 7010
Only five years earlier than the pop hits, but what a difference! Wonderful New Orleans R&B, including the memorable "Lawdy Miss Clawdy"; it's an excellent first installment in Specialty's two-volume Price series. —*Hank Davis*

○ **Vol. 2: Heavy Dreams** / 1993 / Specialty 7047

Lloyd Price hit the bigtime with a pair of R&B/novelty gems, "Personality" and "Lawdy Miss Claudy." But he was also a fine "straight" singer, something that's evident on this second volume covering his '50s Specialty material. The list includes hard-rocking covers of "Aint' It a Shame" and "Oooh-Oooh" in which Price scores with soaring vocals rather than humorous lyrics or asides. That's also true on "Restless Heart" and "Night and Day." There's also more playful material such as "Chee Koo Baby" and "Woe Ho Ho," but this collection spotlights Lloyd Price's singing approach and shows he was much more than merely a successful comic. With musical support from an all-star New Orleans lineup that includes Dave Bartholomew, Herb Hardesty, Lee Allen, Earl Palmer, and even Fats Domino on "Chee Koo Baby" and "Oo-EE Baby," the arrangements and rhythms add plenty of kick behind Price's voice. —*Ron Wynn*

Primal Scream

Group / Alternative pop/rock, dance, rock & roll
Primal Scream might be the greatest charlatans of the '90s. With their third album, *Screamadelica*, the band was hailed as great musical innovators, dragging rock & roll kicking and screaming into the drug-soaked dance club scene of the early '90s. As it turns out, the record was merely a means to an end—Primal Scream just want to be rock stars, and they don't care what they actually sound like, as long as they get there.

On their first two albums, the band recycled '60s and early '70s guitar pop and hard rock to some acclaim in the United Kingdom, but it was 1991's *Screamadelica* that established Primal Scream as major stars in England and earned them a cult in America. *Screamadelica* took the classic early '70s rock of the Stones and the Faces and submerged it in techno and house dance music, creating a blissed-out, colorful pseudo-psychedelic extravaganza. It was a distinctive, innovative album, but Primal Scream's actual contribution to the sound of the record is questionable. What carried the album was its admittedly amazing production, mainly provided by Andrew Weatherall; there were few songs that could actually be attributed to the group, and those that could were blatantly derivative.

Primal Scream's true roots appeared on their followup album, 1994's *Give Out But Don't Give Up*, which saw the band accentuating the classic rock currents that ran beneath their music and refashioning themselves as retro-rockers like the Black Crowes. Of course, that may again be the work of their producers—R&B veteran Tom Dowd, George Clinton, and Black Crowes mastermind George Drakoulias—but either way, the band lost many of its fans in the dance world while gaining a new audience of rockers. —*Stephen Thomas Erlewine*

● **Screamadelica** / Oct. 8, 1991 / Sire 26714

Screamadelica is an impressive, innovative album that seamlessly combines classic rock with the throbbing beat of the dance club. While it doesn't contain any concise pop songs besides "Movin' On Up," the album is remarkably consistent and proved that it was possible to inject some true grit into the highly stylized world of techno, house, and rave. —*Stephen Thomas Erlewine*

Give Out But Don't Give Up / Apr. 1994 / Sire 45538

The rock undercurrents that ran throughout dance extravaganza *Screamadelica* come to the forefront on the tired *Give Out But Don't Give Up*. While Primal Scream turn out a couple of good songs—"Jailbird" and "(I'm Gonna) Cry Myself Blind"—the band sounds too mannered to be a truly successful ripoff of the Stones and Faces. And the colorful, wreckless experimentation of their previous album is sorely missed. —*Stephen Thomas Erlewine*

Primus

Group / Alternative rock
Primus is all about Les Claypool; there isn't a moment on any of their other records where his bass isn't the main focal point of the music, with his vocals acting as a bizarre side show. Which isn't to deny guitarist Larry LaLonde or drummer Tim "Herb" Alexander any credit—no drummer could weave in and around Claypool's convoluted patterns as effortlessly as Alexander, and few guitarists would as willingly push the spotlight away like LaLonde, so he can produce a never-ending spiral of avant-noise. All of this means that they are miles away from being another

punk-funk combo like the Red Hot Chili Peppers; Claypool may slap and pop his bass, but there is little funk in the rhythm he and Alexander lay down. Instead, they're a post-punk Rush spiked with the sensibility and humor of Frank Zappa. Primus doesn't want to make you dance, they want to play music; songs are secondary to showcasing their instrumental prowess.

Primus's music is willfully weird and experimental, yet it's not alienating; the band was able to turn its goofy weirdness into pop stardom. At first, the band was strictly an underground phenomenon, but in the years between their third and fourth albums, their cult grew rapidly. 1991's *Sailing the Seas of Cheese* went gold shortly before the release of *Pork Soda*. By the time of the album's 1993 release, Primus had enough devoted fans to make *Pork Soda* debut in the Top 10. After touring for a year—including a headlining spot on 1993's Lollapalooza—Claypool revived his Prawn Song record label in 1994 and released a reunion record by Primus's original lineup under the name Sausage. —*Stephen Thomas Erlewine*

Suck on This / Jan. 1990 / Caroline 1620

Originally recorded on their own Prawn Song label (a parody of Led Zeppelin's Swan Song Records), this is their debut, recorded live in a small club and featuring all of the greatness this trio has. Hard, thrashy funk and punk with a sense of humor. The reissue on Caroline sounds a little muddy. Find the original vinyl pressing on Prawn, which sounds more like a CD than the CD. —*John Book*

Frizzle Fry / Feb. 1990 / Caroline 1619

Their first studio album, although some of the songs seem rushed. —*John Book*

○ **Sailing the Seas of Cheese** / 1991 / Interscope 91659

The band's major-label debut, featuring an appearance by Tom Waits on "Tommy the Cat" (originally found on *Suck on This*). Guitarist Larry Lalonde, formerly with Possessed and Blind Illusion, shows his death-metal roots on some of the songs on this album. —*John Book*

○ **Miscellaneous Debris** / 1992 / Interscope 96208

What makes this five-song EP of covers Primus's best release is the material. For once, Les Claypool's crew plays actual songs instead of sketching out a few ideas as an excuse for jamming. As a result, *Miscellaneous Debris* isn't as weird and alienating as previous albums, and often their reinterpretations—from the clever ribbing of XTC's "Making Plans for Nigel" and Pink Floyd's "Have a Cigar" to the relatively respectful readings of the Meters, the Residents, and Peter Gabriel's "Intruder"—show flashes of brilliance, largely due to the loose yet focused musicianship. —*Stephen Thomas Erlewine*

● **Pork Soda** / 1993 / Interscope 92257

Apart from the bizarre murder tale "My Name Is Mud," there are few tracks on *Pork Soda* that rival "Tommy the Cat" or "Jerry Was a Race Car Driver" as individual tracks; another troubling sign of a lack of songwriting ideas is that one track, "The Pressman," was originally released on their live debut album, *Suck on This*. Yet the overall quality of the playing is so good that it almost doesn't matter that the songs are frequently simplistic and occasionally awful. *Pork Soda* is hardly a terrible album—in fact, it's their best, most consistent full-length effort to date, even though it would benefit from some editing. —*Stephen Thomas Erlewine*

Prince (Prince Rogers Nelson)

b. Jun. 7, 1958
Vocals, guitar, keyboard / Pop/rock, soul, funk, dance, urban R&B
Few artists have created a body of work as rich and varied as Prince. During the '80s, he emerged as one of the most singular talents of the rock & roll era, capable of seamlessly tying together pop, funk, folk, and rock. Not only did he release a series of groundbreaking albums, he toured frequently, produced albums, wrote songs for many other artists, and recorded hundreds of songs that still lie unreleased in his vaults. With each album he has released, Prince has shown remarkable stylistic growth and musical diversity, constantly experimenting with different sounds, textures, and genres. Occasionally, his music can be maddeningly inconsistent because of this eclecticism, but his experiments frequently succeed; no other contemporary artist can blend so many diverse styles into a cohesive whole.

Prince's first two albums were solid, if unremarkable, late '70s funk-pop. With 1980's *Dirty Mind*, he recorded his first masterpiece, a one-man *tour de force* of sex and music; it was hard funk, catchy Beatlesque melodies, sweet soul ballads, and rocking guitar-pop, all at once. The follow-up, *Controversy*, was more of the same, but *1999* was brilliant. The album was a monster hit, selling over three million copies, but it was nothing compared to 1984's *Purple Rain.*

Purple Rain made Prince a superstar; it eventually sold over ten million copies in the United States and spent 24 weeks at #1. Partially recorded with his touring band the Revolution, the record featured the most pop-oriented music he has ever made. Instead of continuing in this accessible direction, he veered off into the bizzare psycho-psychedelia of *Around the World in a Day* (1985), which nevertheless sold over two million copies. In 1986, he released the even-stranger *Parade*, which in its own way was as ambitious and intricate as any art-rock of the '60s; however, no art-rock was ever grounded with a hit as brilliant as the spare funk of "Kiss."

By 1987, Prince's ambitions were growing by leaps and bounds, resulting in the sprawling masterpiece *Sign O' the Times*. Prince was set to release the hard funk of *The Black Album* by the end of the year, yet he withdrew it just before its release, deciding it was too dark and immoral. Instead, he released the confused *Lovesexy* in 1988, which was a commercial disaster. With the soundtrack to 1989's *Batman* he returned to the top of the charts, even if the album was essentially a recap of everything he had done before. The following year he released *Graffiti Bridge*, the sequel to *Purple Rain*, which turned out to be a considerable commercial disappointment.

In 1991, Prince formed the New Power Generation, the most versatile and talented band he has ever assembled. With their first album, *Diamonds and Pearls*, Prince reasserted his mastery of contemporary R&B; it was his biggest hit since 1985. The following year, he released his 12th album, which was titled with a cryptic symbol; in 1993, Prince legally changed his name to the symbol. In 1994, he independently released "The Most Beautiful Girl in the World" single, which became his biggest hit in years. Later in the year, he released *Come* under the name of Prince; he was expected to continue to release recordings under both the symbol and the name of Prince until his record contract with Warner Brothers expired.

Although he's no longer topping the charts with each album, Prince is currently making some of the wildest, most fully realized music of his career. His eclecticism encompasses more styles of music, yet he's able to meld the different sounds together subtly and seamlessly. After a decade and a half of spectacular music, Prince might just be beginning to hit his artistic peak. — *Stephen Thomas Erlewine*

For You / 1978 / Warner Brothers 3150
Prince's debut is a fairly conventional blend of erotic funk, highlighted by the horny "Soft and Wet" and subverted by too much mediocre material. —*John Floyd*

Prince / 1979 / Warner Brothers 3366
The followup makes his rock leanings more apparent, culminating in the Hendrix guitar-driven single "I Wanna Be Your Lover." —*John Floyd*

☆ **Dirty Mind** / 1980 / Warner Brothers 3478
A delirious, hard-on masterpiece, dedicated to the joy of sex. The guitars are revved up a few notches, the funk has more muscle, and the songs make explicit just how unique (and sometimes twisted) Prince's vision can be. —*John Floyd*

Controversy / 1981 / Warner Brothers 3601
Synthesizers move to the forefront, but though the sound is riveting, and while "Do Me, Baby" and the title cut are among his best, this is a tad short on decent songs. —*John Floyd*

☆ **1999** / 1982 / Warner Brothers 23720
Double-album mingling of politics and sex features Prince's sturdiest dance grooves and his first crossover hits ("Little Red Corvette," "Delirious," and the title track). This album is a near-masterpiece. —*John Floyd*

☆ **Purple Rain** / 1984 / Warner Brothers 25110
Upon its release, the soundtrack from Prince's big-screen debut sounded as if his artistry had blossomed fully. Today it remains essential for the singles, like "When Doves Cry" and "Let's Go Crazy." —*John Floyd*

○ **Around the World in a Day** / 1985 / Paisley Park 25286

Prince got his first negative reviews when this album was originally issued in the mid '80s. Cries of ripoff and imitator were leveled his way while defenders rushed into the fray. The album was hardly the flop it's been perceived. While it did reflect Prince's love of the Beatles' psychedelic period, it topped the charts for three weeks and ultimately yielded the hits "Pop Life" and "Raspberry Beret." Prince would return to a funkier sound the next time out, and the album seems a logical end to a direction he began with *Purple Rain. —Ron Wynn*

○ **Parade (Music from the Motion Picture "Under the Cherry Moon")** / 1986 / Paisley Park 25395
Another soundtrack (from Prince's second film, *Under the Cherry Moon*) that boasts some strong singles ("Kiss," "Mountains," and "Anotherloverholenyohead") and some dreary, neo-psychedelic filler. —*John Floyd*

☆ **Sign o' the Times** / 1987 / Warner Brothers 25577
A two-disc, one-man-band romp through everything he does best, from galvanizing grooves (one of which was recorded with the Revolution) to some slinky smoochers, which show for the first time sympathy and genuine affection for his romantic objects. This is Prince's greatest album. —*John Floyd*

The Black Album / 1987 / Bootleg
Recorded in 1987 but shelved in favor of *Lovesexy*, the *Black Album* is a sinister funk-fest, long on the boogie but short on anything really remarkable. —*John Floyd*

Lovesexy / Feb. 1988 / Paisley Park 25720
Lovesexy was a better album, anyway. It's not perfect, but it does find Prince attempting to make clear his philosophy, which likens sex to godliness and vice versa. It doesn't fully convince, but "Anna Stasia" and "I Wish U Heaven" should keep you interested. —*John Floyd*

Batman / 1989 / Warner Brothers 25936
Soundtrack for the hugely successful film is a mildly amusing set of competent funk, but nothing he hasn't done better elsewhere. —*John Floyd*

Graffiti Bridge / Aug. 21, 1990 / Warner Brothers 27493
Prince was shooting for the top of the charts with *Graffiti Bridge*, and he missed. The movie was a disaster, causing the soundtrack to sell very poorly. Despite its poor showing, *Graffiti Bridge* is not a bad album; in fact, it's often very good. Prince wrote all of the songs, but performed a little over half the tracks, leaving the rest for the Time, Mavis Staples, and Tevin Campbell. With the exception of the Time's slamming "Release It" and Campbell's "Round and Round," the best songs are the ones Prince performed himself. The George Clinton collaboration "We Can Funk," the psycho-blues of "The Question of U," the sinewy single "Thieves in the Temple," and the pop/rock of "Can't Stop This Feeling I Got," "Tick, Tick, Bang," and "Elephants & Flowers" make *Graffiti Bridge* a thoroughly enjoyable listen. — *Stephen Thomas Erlewine*

○ **Diamonds and Pearls** / 1991 / Paisley Park 25379
Out of nowhere, Prince suddenly regathers his strengths, assembles the New Power Generation, the best band of his career, and shimmies and strolls through his best album since *Times*. An eclectic yet seamless attestation of Prince's vitality in the '90s. — *John Floyd*

○ **Love Symbol Album** / Oct. 13, 1992 / Paisley Park 45037(
The New Power Generation is the most talented and versatile band Prince has ever fronted, and they fulfill their potential on *Symbol*. Although the NPG played a big part on *Diamonds and Pearls*, it still sounded like a solo Prince album. *Symbol* sounds like a band performing together, working off of each other's strengths and weaknesses. Opening with the dance smash "My Name Is Prince" and the deep funk "Sexy M.F.," *Symbol* has Prince's best dance tracks since the unreleased *Black Album*. But Prince isn't interested in producing an album full of nothing but funk. Instead, he decides to run the entire gamut of modern pop/R&B/dance, and the music is uniformly accomplished and excellent. Disregard his ridiculous attempt at a "rock soap opera" and Kirstie Alley's annoying sound bridges, because *Symbol* has some of the finest, most inventive music of Prince's career. — *Stephen Thomas Erlewine*

★ **Hits/B-Sides** / 1993 / Paisley Park 45440
While it isn't a truly comprehensive set, Prince's singles collection does contain most of his biggest hits. The two volumes are avail-

able separately or in a box set with a third disc of B sides; apart from the glorious "Erotic City," the flip sides are only of interest to devoted fans. —*Stephen Thomas Erlewine*

John Prine

b. 1946, Maywood, IL
Vocals, guitar / Singer-songwriter
Prine is from the Bob Dylan school of talented folkies who like to play with words. But unlike most Dylanites, Prine also evokes the sly, dry humor of Woody Guthrie, and his brokenhearted laments are never chauvinistic and only seldom wallow in self-pity. If he's never made one album as great as prime Dylan, that's because he isn't Dylan; he makes great albums that flaunt his own personality, not the personality of his inspirations. —*John Floyd*

☆ **John Prine** / 1971 / Atlantic 19156
A revelation upon its release, this album is now a collection of standards: "Illegal Smile," "Hello in There," "Sam Stone," "Donald and Lydia," and, of course, "Angel from Montgomery." Prine's music, a mixture of folk, rock, and country, is deceptively simple, like his pointed lyrics, and his easy vocal style adds a humorous edge that makes otherwise funny jokes downright hilarious. —*William Ruhlmann*

○ **Sweet Revenge** / 1973 / Atlantic 7274
A bold and brilliant stab at (almost) straight country that tempers Prine's cynical streak with the tone of a jaded humorist and social commentator. —*John Floyd*

Common Sense / 1975 / Atlantic 18127
A brash album, full of aggressive rock rhythms and morose tunes. Even the Chuck Berry cover, "You Never Can Tell," is shot full of melancholy. —*John Floyd*

○ **Bruised Orange** / 1978 / Asylum 139
Despite some brilliant songs, Prine's followup albums to his stunning debut were uneven until this, his fifth, produced by his friend Steve Goodman. Here, Prine's always finely tuned sense of absurdity once again collides with his ability to depict pain sympathetically for a whole album, typified by "That's the Way That the World Goes 'Round," a neat statement of his philosophy, and "Sabu Visits the Twin Cities Alone," perhaps the best depiction ever written of life on the road in the entertainment business. —*William Ruhlmann*

Storm Windows / 1980 / Oh Boy 008
A relaxed effort, defined by straightforward love songs and subdued vocals. Modest but quite nice. —*John Floyd*

German Afternoons / 1986 / Oh Boy 3
Another straight country set, but unlike *Sweet Revenge*, this is a sleepy-town stroll, highlighted by some beautiful ballads and snappy accompaniment by the New Grass Revival. —*John Floyd*

● **The Missing Years** / 1991 / Oh Boy 009
Prine took five years between his ninth studio album and this, his 10th—enough time to gather his strongest body of material in more than a decade. From the caustic "All the Best" to the cliché compilation "It's a Big Old Goofy World," Prine's gifts for emotional revelation and off-the-wall humor are on display in abundance, and he's aided by excellent production (courtesy of Heartbreaker Howie Epstein) and strong backup musicians. *The Missing Years* won the 1991 Grammy Award for Best Contemporary Folk Album. —*William Ruhlmann*

★ **Great Days: The John Prine Anthology** / 1993 / Rhino 271400
Prine's career has been rich but scattered, and *Great Days* gathers together almost all of his finest moments, providing a comprehensive introduction to one of the best songwriters of the past 20 years. —*Stephen Thomas Erlewine*

Proclaimers

Group / Pop/rock
When the Scottish duo of Craig and Charlie Reid emerged in 1987, they were immediately compared to the Everly Brothers. Considering their energetic, melodic folk-rock, the comparison made some sense, even though the Proclaimers didn't really sound like the Everlys. Instead, the band were a post-punk pop band, aggressively displaying their thick accents on sweet, infectiously melodic songs about love. After two albums in the late '80s, the band disappeared for several years, suffering from personal problems and severe writer's block. When their 1988 song "I'm Gonna Be (500 Miles)" was used in the 1993 film *Benny &*

Joon, the duo began to receive massive radio airplay in America, sending them into the Top 10 in the United States, as well as the rest of the world; it was their first taste of real success. Luckily, the band was close to completing their third album at the time, leaving them in a position to capitalize on its success. When the album was released the following year, it received strong reviews but little airplay. —*Stephen Thomas Erlewine*

● **Sunshine on Leith** / 1988 / Chrysalis 21668
The Proclaimers' second album is a delightful set of folk-pop, highlighted by the belated hit single, "I'm Gonna Be (500 Miles)." —*David Jehnzen*

Hit the Highway / Mar. 22, 1994 / Chrysalis 28602
After six years, the Proclaimers delivered their third album. While it was a strong record with many fine songs, it lacked a knockout single. Consequently, the duo wasn't able to follow through on the success of "I'm Gonna Be (500 Miles)." —*David Jehnzen*

Procol Harum

Group / Progressive rock, psychedelic, rock & roll
Formed in 1967, Procol Harum incorporated a weighty classicism into their sound, with occasional traces of R&B and rock & roll. This British group was originally formed around the core of lyricist Keith Reid and singer-songwriter Gary Brooker, who hailed from the R&B club band the Paramounts. Their first collaboration, the stately "A Whiter Shade of Pale," was loosely built off of Bach's "Air on a G String." A band was formed (named after Reid's cat), and in short order, Procol Harum had a record deal and an international hit on their hands. Part of the success of the band's sound was due to Matthew Fisher's stately organ work and Robin Trower's lyrical blues-based lead-guitar playing, which appeared on Procol's second and third albums—*Shine on Brightly* and *A Salty Dog.*

In spite of further lineup changes (eventually incorporating most of the Paramounts), Procol Harum went on to enjoy even greater chart success during the early '70s, particularly *Live in Concert with the Edmonton Symphony Orchestra.* By this time, the band seemed to be trading on its past glories, with flashes of their earlier brilliance briefly resurfacing on their 1974 release *Exotic Birds and Fruit.* Procol Harum eventually broke up in 1977, after the spotty *Something Magic.* —*Rick Clark*

○ **Procol Harum** / 1967 / Deram 18008
Their spectacular debut showed remarkable songwriting and became a late '60s classic, due to the immense popularity of "A Whiter Shade of Pale," which made their reputation. —*Cub Koda*

○ **Shine on Brightly** / 1968 / A&M 4151
Procol's ambitious sophomore effort expanded upon their symphonic-style rock, particularly the 18-plus-minute conceptual opus "In Held 'Twas in I." The title track was another highlight. —*Rick Clark*

○ **A Salty Dog** / 1969 / A&M 3123
Procol's synthesis of blues and grand classically inspired melodies reached an apex on their third album. The tasteful production featured sweeping orchestrations, subtle sound effects, and dynamic arrangements. *A Salty Dog* became one of Procol's signature numbers. —*Rick Clark*

Home / 1970 / A&M 4261
With Matthew Fisher gone, Procol embraced a harder, more rock-oriented approach best displayed on the herky-jerky riff-rocker "Whiskey Train," a Robin Trower showcase. —*Rick Clark*

Procol Harum Live: In Concert with the Edmonton Symphony Orchestra & the Da Camera Sin / 1972 / A&M 4335
With the help of the Edmonton Symphony Orchestra (Canada), Procol Harum does an impressive job recreating their more stately numbers, complete with sound effects and a full choir. "Conquistador" became a #16 hit. —*Rick Clark*

○ **Best of Procol Harum** / 1973 / A&M 3259
A fine wrapup of the band's 1967-1973 output. Their most creative era. —*Dan Heilman*

● **Classics, Vol. 17** / 1987 / A&M 2515
This best-of collection covers the hits, plus a decent collection of album tracks. —*Rick Clark*

Prong

Group / Heavy metal

Prong could be the perfectly named heavy metal band. From the ashes of New York speed-thrash, Prong plays slower, stripped-down metal without the egregious marketing flourishes (for example, sexism, satanism). Perhaps a tad derivative, Prong makes up for its lapse in stylistic originality with speed and power. — *John Dougan*

Force Fed / 1988 / In-Effect 3004
Brutal and bloody, Prong achieves maximum riff thrust here as Tommy Victor's guitar penetrates the wall-of-steel sonic boom. A dense and forceful album, which is worth many headbangs. — *John Dougan*

○ **Beg to Differ** / 1990 / Epic 46011
Technical thrash with a band who continues to stretch the boundaries of their genre. —*John Book*

○ **Prove Your Wrong** / 1991 / Epic 47460
Tighter riffs and stronger songwriting on *Prove Your Wrong* helped Prong expand their cult substantially. —AMG

● **Cleansing** / 1994 / Epic
Cleansing offers a cleansing of Prong's sound, tightening up their trademark drilling guitars while adding some slight techno and industrial touches, which only hightens the tension. Thankfully, none of this comprimises the band; it only strengthens their already muscular metallic roar and, in fact, helps makes *Cleansing* their most varied and best record yet. —*Stephen Thomas Erlewine*

The Psychedelic Furs

Group / Alternative pop/rock
The Psychedelic Furs, whose name belies their punk-influenced music, were formed in England in 1977 by brothers Richard Butler (vocals) and Tim Butler (bass), along with saxophone player Duncan Kilburn and guitarist Roger Morris. By the time they released their self-titled debut album in 1980, the group had become a sextet, adding guitarist John Ashton and drummer Vince Ely. That album, featuring Butler's hoarse voice (the tone of which suggested John Lydon without the sneer) was a bigger hit in England, where it reached the Top 20, than in the United States.

Talk Talk Talk (1981) did better, reaching the U.S. Top 100 and producing two British singles-chart entries, one of which was "Pretty in Pink," later also a hit in the United States when a new version was used as the title song of a film. *Forever Now* (1982) saw the band reduced to a quartet with the departure of Kilburn and Morris. The rest moved to the United States, turned to producer Todd Rundgren, and scored a U.S. Top 50 hit with "Love My Way." Ely then left, and the remaining trio of the two Butlers and Ashton made *Mirror Moves* (1984), the biggest Psychedlic Furs hit yet.

The film *Pretty in Pink* helped spread their name further before the release of their next album, *Midnight to Midnight* (1986), which consequently got to #12 in the United Kingdom and the Top 30 in the United States and included the Top 30 U.S. hit "Heartbreak Beat." *Book of Days* (1989) marked the return of Vince Ely but was a considerable commercial disappointment. *World Outside* (1991) also failed to find an audience. The band broke up shortly afterward. — *William Ruhlmann*

○ **Psychedelic Furs** / 1980 / Columbia 36791
This auspicious debut finds the sextet turning out thick, noisy rock (especially in the saxophone-guitar combination) through which Richard Butler's voice cuts like a buzzsaw. Best track: "Imitation of Christ." — *William Ruhlmann*

○ **Talk Talk Talk** / 1981 / Columbia 37339
An even better followup makes explicit the Furs's connection to the Velvet Underground (their name comes from the Velvets' song "Venus in Furs"). Their strongest overall collection, this includes the original (superior) version of "Pretty in Pink," "Dumb Waiters," and the definitive Psychedelic Furs song, "Into You like a Train." — *William Ruhlmann*

Forever Now / 1982 / Columbia 38261
Actually, Todd Rundgren's much-vaunted clean, sharp production style has very little effect on the Furs' sound, which is still pretty noisy and still dominated by Butler's hoarse, slightly scornful voice on such songs as "Love My Way," "President Gas," and the title track. — *William Ruhlmann*

● **All of This and Nothing** / 1988 / Columbia 44377

Not a perfect Furs compilation, but this 12-track look back does contain the notable tracks from the albums *Mirror Moves* and *Midnight to Midnight*, plus some of the necessary ones from the albums listed above and a good new song, "All That Money Wants." — *William Ruhlmann*

Public Image Limited (PiL)

Group / Alternative pop/rock
Public Image Ltd. (PiL) originally was a quartet led by singer John Lydon (formerly Johnny Rotten, b. January 31, 1956) and guitarist Keith Levene, who had been a member of the Clash in one of its early lineups. The band was filled out by bassist Jah Wobble (John Wordle) and drummer Jim Walker. It was formed in the wake of the 1978 breakup of Lydon's former group, the Sex Pistols. For the most part, it devoted itself to droning, slow-tempo, bass-heavy noise rock, overlaid by Lydon's distinctive, vituperative rant.

The group's debut single, "Public Image," was more of an up-tempo pop-rock song, however, and it hit the UK Top 10 upon its release in October 1978. The group itself debuted on Christmas Day, shortly after the release of its first album, *Public Image*. Neither the single nor the album was released in the United States.

Metal Box, the band's second UK album, came in the form of three 12-inch, 45 RPM discs in a film cannister. It was released in the United States in 1980 as the double album *Second Edition*. (By this time, PiL was a trio consisting of Lydon, Levene, and Wobble.) The third album, not released in the United States, was the live *Paris in the Spring* (1980). Lydon and Levene, plus hired musicians, made up the group by the time of *The Flowers of Romance* (1981), the much-acclaimed fourth album, which reached #11 in the United Kingdom.

In 1983, PiL scored its biggest UK hit, when "This Is Not a Love Song" reached #5. By this time, however, Levene had left, and the name from here on would simply be a vehicle for John Lydon. A second live album, *Live in Tokyo*, appeared in England in 1983.

1984 saw the release of *This Is What You Want ... This Is What You Get*, only PiL's third album to be released in the United States, though the group now had six albums out. It marked the start of Lydon's move toward a more accessible dance-rock style, a direction that would be pursued further in *Album* (1986) (also called *Cassette* or *Compact Disc*, depending on the format), notably on the hit "Rise," as well as on *Happy?* (1987) and *9* (1989). In 1990, PiL released the compilation album *The Greatest Hits, So Far*, and in 1991 came the new album, *That What Is Not*. After completing his memoirs in late 1993, Lydon decided to put an end to PiL and pursue a solo career. — *William Ruhlmann*

○ **Second Edition** / Jul. 1980 / Warner Brothers 3288
A two-disc deconstruction of traditional rock music, its tempos steady but slow, its bass track mixed high as in a reggae dub album, and Lydon's droning voice, with its scornful lyrics, wafting in the back. It is what PiL called it at the time, "anti-rock & roll," and it's fascinating. — *William Ruhlmann*

Flowers of Romance / 1981 / Warner Brothers 3536
The drums are loud and sharp, and Lydon wails like some sort of Middle Eastern street singer on this forbidding but rewarding album. — *William Ruhlmann*

○ **This Is What You Want ... This Is What You Get** / 1984 / Virgin 2309
Lydon adds keyboards, horns, and even a violin, double-tracks his vocals, and writes shorter songs with faster tempos. *This Is What You Want ... This Is What You Get* doesn't quite add up to a pop album, but you can dance to it. Contains the UK hit "This Is Not a Love Song." — *William Ruhlmann*

○ **Album/Compact Disc/Cassette** / 1986 / Elektra 60438
Hot guitars and 4/4 time signatures make this sound more like a hard-rock album than anything Lydon's done since the Sex Pistols. And the hit single "Rise" is actually a catchy number, believe it or not. — *William Ruhlmann*

● **Greatest Hits So Far** / 1990 / Virgin 91581
Fourteen tracks, recorded between 1978 and 1990, that trace PiL from the punk energy of the first single, "Public Image" (not previously released in the United Staes), through the antirock of "Death Disco" and "Flowers of Romance" to the almost pop of "This Is Not a Love Song" and "Rise" and the best of the late '80s material. — *William Ruhlmann*

Gary Puckett & Union Gap

b. Oct. 17, 1942
Group / Pop/rock

Very popular during the late '60s, this San Diego-based band rode Gary Puckett's soaring vocal cords to pop gold. Formed in 1967 and signed to Columbia, the band's smooth accessibility and full-bodied pop arrangements quickly led to four 1967-1968 million sellers: "Woman, Woman," "Young Girl," "Lady Willpower," and "Over You." Puckett notched his last couple of chart entries as a solo act, including a Paul Simon tune, "Keep the Customer Satisfied." —*Bill Dahl*

● **Greatest Hits** / 1970 / Columbia 1042
All you would ever need from the "Lady Willpower" man, and more. —*Dan Heilman*

Pure Prairie League

Group / Country rock

Pure Prairie League fused singer-songwriter pop with mellow country rock. They scored several hits from the mid '70s to early '80s, with "Let Me Love You Tonight," "I'm Almost Ready," "Still Right Here in My Heart," and their most popular track, "Amie." — *Rick Clark*

○ **Bustin' Out** / 1972 / RCA 4656
Bustin' Out was this band's most distinctive album, featuring very bright, thin-sounding acoustic guitars and dramatic string arrangements, courtesy of David Bowie's lead player Mick Ronson. "Amie" became a standard of sorts for the college coffee-house crowd. Other highlights include "Jazzman," "Early Morning Riser," "Boulder Skies," "Call Me Tell Me," and "Angel," a song originally recorded on J. D. Blackfoot's *The Ultimate Prophecy.* — *Rick Clark*

● **Amie & Other Hits** / 1981 / RCA 52163
This best-of collection contains all the hits and most of the essential album cuts, including a healthy sampling from *Bustin' Out.* —*Rick Clark*

James and Bobby Purify

Group / Soul, R&B

James (b. May 12, 1944) and Bobby (b. September 2, 1939) of this Southern soul duo were not actually brothers but cousins. James Purify and Robert Lee Dickey joined forces for some classic Southern soul duets during the mid '60s. Producer Papa Don Schroeder brought the soulful Floridians to Muscle Shoals in 1966 to record at Rick Hall's Fame studios, and the result was the gorgeous mid-tempo "I'm Your Puppet." The Dan Penn/Spooner Oldham ballad proved their biggest hit for the Bell label, although "Let Love Come Between Us" and their revival of the Five Dutones's "Shake a Tail Feather" also made some major noise in 1967. When Bobby mutinied, James went it alone for a while before recruiting a new Bobby (Ben Moore), and they picked up right where the old duo left off. —*Bill Dahl*

● **100% Purified Soul** / 1988 / Charly 1182
A fine album collection (not issued on CD at the time of writing), containing the Purifys' chart hits for Bell. Light and understated, with less fire and brimstone when compared with Sam & Dave, but worthy nonetheless. —*Rob Bowman*

Do It Right (Best of James & Bobby Purify) / Arista 8392
This collection covers the few hits James & Bobby Purify enjoyed, including "I'm Your Puppet" and "Shake a Tail Feather." —*Ron Wynn*

Pylon

Group / Alternative pop/rock

The group that put Athens, GA, on the musical map in the early '80s, thanks to their arty, angular dance-rock. Vanessa Briscoe's clipped melodies figured into the early sound of the B-52's, and her chopped lyrics and the band's minimalist punch influenced R.E.M. (who later covered Pylon's "Crazy"). The group broke up in 1983, but reformed in 1989 for an album and a tour. —*John Floyd*

● **Hits** / 1988 / DB 91
Since they had no hits, the title is more than a little ironic, but this collection is the best of Pylon's a quirky college-educated dance pop. With a blistering rhythm section and quirky singer in Vanessa Briscoe, this gets better with age. —*John Dougan*

Chain / 1990 / Dog Gone 2020
In 1990, the band regrouped for this fine album that, while breaking no new ground, loses none of the energy of the band in its heyday. —*Chris Woodstra*

Queen

Group / Hard rock, progressive rock, pop/rock

Queen was a quartet that combined elements of hard rock, heavy metal, and art rock, adding other styles along the way for an often-majestic sound that also contained a distinct element of campy humor. The group was formed in England in 1971 by singer Freddie Mercury (born as Frederick Bulsara; September 5, 1946-November 24, 1991), guitarist Brian May (b. July 19, 1947), bassist John Deacon (b. August 19, 1951), and drummer Roger Taylor (b. July 26, 1949). They released their first album, *Queen,* in 1973, and it first reached the charts in the United States (going gold in 1977). It wasn't until the following year that Queen broke through in its native country, getting a Top 10 hit with "The Seven Seas of Rhye" and reaching the album chart with *Queen II. Sheer Heart Attack,* later the same year, was a substantial hit on both sides of the Atlantic (a #2 UK hit with "Killer Queen," #12 in the United States).

The biggest of Queen's early albums, however, was *A Night at the Opera* (1975), which topped the UK chart, made the Top 5 in the United States, and included the gold-selling single "Bohemian Rhapsody," the longest-running UK #1 in 18 years and voted the best song of all time in radio polls (in 1992, bolstered by its appearance in the film *Wayne's World,* it would be a hit all over again in the United States). *A Day at the Races* (1976) was also a substantial hit, though it couldn't match its predecessor.

Queen turned to a harder rock approach for 1977's *News of the World,* which included the Top 5 hit "We Are the Champions," still a sporting-event favorite. *Jazz* (1978) and *Live Killers* (1979) were successful, if less substantial albums, but Queen took a sharp stylistic turn for *The Game* in 1980 and was rewarded with two uncharacteristic #1 hits, the rockabilly-tinged "Crazy Little Thing Called Love" and the disco-rock "Another One Bites the Dust."

Though Queen scored gold in the United States with the subsequent releases *Hot Space* (1982) and *The Works* (1984), the group was in a gradual commercial decline throughout the '80s. It returned to gold-selling status with *Innuendo* in 1991, but singer Freddie Mercury died of AIDS in November of that year. That set off a sales bonanza in Europe and, belatedly, in the United States, with a giant benefit concert held in Mercury's honor at Wembley Stadium in England in April 1992. Posthumous releases began to appear, with a boxed set promised. —*William Ruhlmann*

○ **Sheer Heart Attack** / 1974 / Hollywood 61036
An effective demonstration of the range of Queen's musical tastes, from the guitar pyrotechnics of "Brighton Rock" to the vocal histrionics of "Killer Queen" and the on-the-road diary "Now I'm Here." —*William Ruhlmann*

○ **A Night at the Opera** / 1975 / Hollywood 61065
In case there was any doubt that Queen was devoted to over-the-top effects, this massively overdubbed combination of hard rock and opera, paced by May's monster guitar riffs and Mercury's million-voiced choir and emotive solo singing, should have erased it. Contains "Death on Two Legs," "You're My Best Friend," and, of course, "Bohemian Rhapsody." —*William Ruhlmann*

News of the World / 1977 / Hollywood 61037
In the balance between Queen's operatic tendencies and its desire to rock out, the rock side once again gained an upper hand on this release. Not that the bombast lessened, but songs like "We Will Rock You" were actually dry runs for the stripped-down approach of *The Game,* and even "We Are the Champions" was a ballad. Well, almost. —*William Ruhlmann*

○ **Game** / 1980 / Hollywood 61063
The basic elements of Queen's approach, from May's heavy guitar to Mercury's vocal army, were in attendance here, but the album owes its success to its novelties, especially "Another One Bites the Dust" and "Crazy Little Thing Called Love." —*William Ruhlmann*

★ **Greatest Hits** / 1981 / Elektra 564
They may not have started out that way, but by 1981 Queen definitely was perceived as a singles act. This record gathers their biggest U.S. and UK hits from 1973 through 1981, including the

collaboration with David Bowie, "Under Pressure." — *William Ruhlmann*

Queensryche

Group / Heavy metal, progressive rock, hard rock

During the early '80s, Queensryche was a standard heavy metal band, sounding like a cross between Iron Maiden and Judas Priest. In the middle of the decade, the band shifted to a more progressive sound, adding elements of '70s art rock, particularly Pink Floyd, to their music. Queensryche came into their own in 1988's *Operation Mindcrime*, a concept album about a media-dominated future. With *Empire* two years later, the band crossed over into the mainstream with the hit "Silent Lucidity." Although they haven't released any new material since that album, they continue to be a one of the more respected heavy metal bands of the early '90s. — *Stephen Thomas Erlewine*

○ **Operation Mindcrime** / 1988 / EMI America 48640
Seattle's best kept secret is let out of the box with a concept album that brought comparisons of Pink Floyd and the Who. Fantastic lyrics with a great story line and powerful playing by the band and powerful vocals by Geoff Tate, finally noticed by fans a year after its release. — *John Book*

● **Empire** / 1990 / EMI America 92806
An album by a band who know what they want and how to get it. Masterfully produced (recorded digitally), this is the one that made the band international superstars. — *John Book*

? & the Mysterians

Group / Rock & roll, garage rock

Originally formed in Flint, MI, in 1962, this group took its name from the obscure science-fiction movie, "The Mysterians." They recorded the anthemic "96 Tears" for the local Spanish music label Pa-Go-Go in 1966. It was immediately picked up for national consumption by Cameo-Parkway, going on to be one of the most covered garage band classics of the '60s. Lead singer Question Mark (real name listed as both Rudy Martinez and Reeto Rodriguez) continues to front a version of the band on oldies package shows across the United States. — *Cub Koda*

● **96 Tears** / 1966 / Cameo 2004
A true garage-band classic, featuring the title track and 11 others straight from the band's set list. (Out of print.) — *Cub Koda*

Quicksilver Messenger Service

Group / Psychedelic

The band that became Quicksilver Messenger Service originally was conceived as a rock vehicle for folk singer-songwriter Dino Valenti (b. November 7, 1943), author of "Get Together." Living in San Francisco, Valenti had found guitarist John Cipollina (August 24, 1943-May 29, 1989) and singer Jim Murray. Valenti's friend David Freiberg (b. August 24, 1938) joined on bass, and the group was completed by the addition of drummer Greg Elmore (b. September 4, 1946) and guitarist Gary Duncan (b. September 4, 1946).

They debuted at the end of 1965 and played around the Bay Area and then the West Coast for the next two years, building up a large following but resisting offers to record that had been taken up by such San Francisco acid-rock colleagues as Jefferson Airplane and the Grateful Dead. Quicksilver finally signed to Capitol toward the end of 1967 and recorded their self-titled debut album, which appeared in 1968 (by this time, Murray had left). *Happy Trails*, its 1969 followup, was recorded live. After its release, Duncan left the band and was replaced for *Shady Grove* (1970) by British session pianist Nicky Hopkins. By the time of its release, however, Duncan had returned, along with Valenti, making the group a sextet.

This version of Quicksilver, prominently featuring Valenti's songs and lead vocals, lasted only a year, during which two albums, *Just for Love* and *What about Me*, were recorded. Cipollina, Freiberg, and Hopkins then left, and the remaining trio of Valenti, Duncan, and Elmore hired replacements and cut another couple of albums before disbanding. There was a reunion in 1975, resulting in a new album and a tour, and in 1986, Duncan revived the Quicksilver name for an album that also featured Freiberg on background vocals. — *William Ruhlmann*

○ **Shady Grove** / 1969 / One Way 57339

Even though the opening title track featured all the elements that made Quicksilver one of the great Bay Area bands (particularly John Cipollina's vibrato-laden lead guitar), *Shady Grove* was a transitional album. The addition of pianist Nicky Hopkins (Rolling Stones, Steve Miller) gave the band more colors to work with. One of Quicksilver's better albums, *Shady Grove* shines brightest on tracks like "Joseph's Coat," the dazzling Hopkins keyboard instrumental showcase "Edward (the Mad Shirt Grinder)," and the title cut. The sound on this disc isn't particularly good. — *Rick Clark*

○ **Happy Trails** / 1969 / Capitol 91215
Quicksilver was heard at its best on this partially live album, which contained a 25-minute version of Bo Diddley's "Who Do You Love." — *William Ruhlmann*

● **Sons of Mercury (1968-75)** / 1991 / Rhino 70747

The thorough two-disc best-of contains Quicksilver's most familiar material from its various lineups, plus some rarities. The only thing keeping this from being essential is the exclusion of the complete live version of "Who Do You Love" over a single edited version. — *William Ruhlmann*

Quiet Riot

Group / Heavy metal

In the early '80s, Quiet Riot became one of the first metal bands to hit the top of the pop charts with their remake of Slade's "Cum On Feel the Noize." By that time, Quiet Riot had been recording for a number of years, experiencing several changes. During the late '70s, the band was a straight-ahead metal group, distinguished only by the talented young guitarist Randy Rhoads; he left in 1979 to join Ozzy Osbourne's band, causing Quiet Riot to change their sound slightly, adding more pop elements to their hard rock. It paid off with 1983's *Metal Health*, which hit #1. However, their following albums didn't have the same crossover appeal and started to slip down the charts. Throughout the '80s, the band was a solid concert attraction even if their albums didn't sell particularly well. In 1988 the band broke up; vocalist Kevin DuBrow assembled a new version of Quiet Riot in 1993 for a tour and album. — *Stephen Thomas Erlewine*

● **Metal Health** / 1983 / Pasha 38443
On the strength of their gloriously stupid cover of Slade's "Cum on Feel the Noize," Quiet Riot shot to the top of the charts with *Metal Health*. While it was easily the best thing the band ever recorded, it is very inconsistent, but the album does contain some of the best dumb heavy metal of the early '80s. — *Stephen Thomas Erlewine*

○ **Randy Rhoads Years** / 1993 / Rhino 71445
A fine collection of Quiet Riot's earliest records, *Randy Rhoads Years* captures the influential guitarist in his formative years. That alone would have made the disc essential for his fans, but it also includes some prime unreleased material, making it all the more desirable. — *Stephen Thomas Erlewine*

Rage Against the Machine

Group / Alternative rock

On the strength of their fiercely political debut album, Rage Against the Machine became an alternative rock sensation in 1993. Combining a technically advanced post-punk guitar roar with an amateurish stab at hip-hop, the band's sound is polarizing: you believe either they're the most uncompromising rockers on earth or they're whining, simplistic hypocrites (after all, how many revolutionaries sign to Sony Records). Either way, with their fiery, militant rock, the band managed to gain more fans than most stridently political bands, as well as earning a considerable amount of critical acclaim for their abrasive sound. — *Stephen Thomas Erlewine*

● **Rage Against the Machine** / Nov. 3, 1992 / Epic 52959
Rage Against the Machine's debut album is overflowing with barely contained anger that comes across better in the scalding music than the half-baked, clichéd lyrics. — *Stephen Thomas Erlewine*

Raincoats

Group / Alternative pop/rock

The Raincoats were one of the most experimental bands that immediately followed the initial burst of punk rock in the late '70s. With their minimalistic approach to guitar-driven folk rock, the band developed a distinctive, jagged sound, punctuated by a shrill violin. The Raincoats were also one of the first all-female post-punk bands, which wasn't common in the late '70s and early '80s. When they were recording, the band gained a small cult following in their native England and an even smaller audience in America; they broke up in 1984. Nearly ten years later, the band became a hip name in alternative rock, thanks to Kurt Cobain's mention of the group in the liner notes to a Nirvana album. Geffen picked up the rights to the Raincoats' catalog and reissued their albums in late 1993 and 1994. The band reunited and toured with Nirvana in Europe before heading out on their own tour of the United States in 1994. —*Stephen Thomas Erlewine*

● **Raincoats** / 1979 / Geffen
Their ebullient debut is vibrant and enthralling. It is truly wonderful. —*John Dougan*

○ **Odyshape** / 1981 / Geffen
A bit funkier and still great! —*John Dougan*

Kitchen Tapes / 1983 / Geffen 120
Live tracks; thoroughly entertaining. —*John Dougan*

Moving / 1984 / Rough Trade
More insistent, driving beats. More joy. —*John Dougan*

Bonnie Raitt

b. Nov. 8, 1949, Cleveland, OH
Vocals, guitar / Blues rock, singer-songwriter, pop/rock
In 1989, Bonnie Raitt, singer-songwriter and guitarist, finally hit major success, after almost 20 years of performing, with the aptly titled *Nick of Time*. The album came at a time when the market was ready for something earthy, and fortunately Capitol Records, who had just signed Raitt, had the foresight to encourage her love of sexy folk-blues, R&B, and intelligently thoughtful sentiment. Raitt, who has always championed quality songwriters like John Prine, John Hiatt, Terry Adams, Jackson Browne, and Jerry Williams, is quite an accomplished songwriter herself, penning songs for *Nick of Time* that equal anything she has covered.

Before Raitt's late '80s success, she had enjoyed a few moderate successes and a respectable cult following. By 1986, with the release of *Nine Lives*, Raitt's career seemed to be stagnating, and Warner Bros. (her label of 15 years) cut her loose.

Raitt's soulful guitar playing, particularly slide, has sadly been overlooked. Lesser male guitar players have graced the covers of major music magazines. Hopefully, her time of recognition in that area will arrive as well. —*Rick Clark*

Bonnie Raitt / 1971 / Warner Brothers 1953
By the time Raitt had recorded this impressive self-titled debut, she had developed quite a set of blues chops playing with artists like Mississippi Fred McDowell, Howlin' Wolf, and other blues greats. In fact, she enlisted Chicago bluesmen Junior Wells and A. C. Reed to aid in the proceedings, which are relaxed and earthy. A fine record. —*Rick Clark*

★ **Give It Up** / 1972 / Warner Brothers 2643
Raitt's sophomore release is a classic. Of all the albums from her days with Warner, this is the one that put together her folky singer-songwriter sensitivities with her love for country blues. *Give It Up*, which took 13 years to go gold, showcased an intelligent song selection, with tracks by Jackson Browne ("Under the Falling Sky"), Eric Kaz ("Love Has No Pride"), and Joel Zoss (Been Too Long at the Fair"). Her self-penned "Love Me like a Man" highlighted her impressive guitar technique. —*Rick Clark*

○ **Takin' My Time** / 1973 / Warner Brothers 2729
Raitt continued her streak of quality albums with *Takin' My Time*. Like her previous efforts, Raitt drew from the cream of the songwriting crop. Randy Newman's "Guilty" and Jackson Browne's "I Thought I Was a Child" are highlights. —*Rick Clark*

Streetlights / 1974 / Warner Brothers 2818
This album was undermined by slick production and unnecessary orchestration. At the time, Raitt seemed to be fighting the production by Jerry Ragovoy. Versions of Joni Mitchell's "That Song about the Midway" and Allen Toussaint's "What Is Success" are the main highlights of the album. —*Rick Clark*

Homeplate / 1975 / Warner Brothers 2864

A return to form. Raitt shines with some great songs, particularly "Good Enough," "Your Sweet and Shiny Eyes," and "Run Like a Thief." —*Rick Clark*

Sweet Forgiveness / 1977 / Warner Brothers 2990
One of Raitt's lesser efforts. Her version of Del Shannon's "Runaway" was a moderate hit, in spite of the fact that it's pretty lifeless-sounding. Even though the production isn't quite as slick as *Streetlights*, the relatively weak selection of material is this album's failing. —*Rick Clark*

Glow / 1979 / Warner Brothers 3369
With the success of "Runaway," Warner felt it was time to take Raitt all the way by pairing her up with hit producer Peter Ascher (Linda Ronstadt, James Taylor). Gone is the natural earthiness Raitt possessed on her first albums. In its place was an airbrushed slickness—from the cover photo all the way down to the grooves. A rendition of Isaac Hayes and David Porter's "Your Good Thing" and an original, "Standing by the Same Old Love," are among *The Glow*'s few highlights. The single off this album was a Robert Palmer song, "You're Gonna Get What's Coming." —*Rick Clark*

○ **Green Light** / 1982 / Warner Brothers 3630
Raitt dumps the slick stuff and goes for the grit with this energetic set, featuring her band, which included keyboardist Ian MacLagan, whose credits included the Stones and Faces. Raitt's sensitive electric slide-guitar work was finally up front in the mix. It's one of her very best albums. Raitt does spirited versions of NRBQ's "Green Light" and "Me and the Boys." Other standouts include the reckless rockers "Willya Wontcha" and "I Can't Help Myself." "River of Tears" is a powerful track that Raitt has dedicated to the memory of Little Feat's Lowell George in shows over the years. —*Rick Clark*

★ **Nick of Time** / 1989 / Capitol 91268
Few comebacks have been as celebrated as Raitt's multiplatinum hit *Nick of Time*, an album that included some of her strongest performances as a musician and singer. The determined "I Will Not Be Denied" seemed to say it all. Her poignant self-penned title cut revealed Raitt as a mature songwriter, on the level of the best writers whose work she had covered. She dug deep with some solid roadhouse R&B in "Love Letter," "Road's My Middle Name," and "Real Man." Her playful version of John Hiatt's "Thing Called Love" was another highlight. All in all, this is a very seamless album. Highly recommended. —*Rick Clark*

○ **Bonnie Raitt Collection (Double)** / 1990 / Warner Brothers 26242
A good (not great) sampler of Raitt's years at Warner, and a good starting place. —*Rick Clark*

○ **Luck of the Draw** / 1991 / Capitol 96111
Raitt followed *Nick of Time* with *Luck of the Draw*, another great album. Among the album's many highlights are "I Can't Make You Love Me" and a duet with Delbert McClinton on "Good Man, Good Woman." —*Rick Clark*

Longing in Their Hearts / Mar. 14, 1994 / Capitol 81427
Raitt continues her winning streak with this fine stew of Don Was-produced R&B and blues-influenced pop/rock. Like her two previous albums, Raitt touches on issues of the preciousness of life and love, but she doesn't dwell there so long that it spoils the celbration of good times found in these grooves. Contains the single "Love Sneakin' Up on You," as well as Teenie Hodges great Memphis-style stomper "I Sho Do." —*Rick Clark*

The Ramones

Group / Punk
With a crisp, militaristic shout of "1-2-3-4" introducing a sonic barrage the likes of which had never been heard, the Ramones declared that rock & roll had become fatuous and ostentatious, embarrassingly prissy, and way too serious. They cranked up the volume, took out the stuffing, and let it be known that henceforth endless solos, pseudo-poetry, and concept albums were being relegated to the dustbin, to be mocked and scorned as digressions.

Perhaps all this quartet from Queens, NY, was really doing was reminding those who had strayed that simple is often best, that the first rockers had the right idea (just get a guitar and make some noise with it), that one should not have to study in a conservatory to play rock. The Ramones stripped it back to the basics, a few chords and some d-u-m-b words, and before they knew it they'd been congratulated—and blamed—for inventing something called punk-rock.

Two decades later they were still at it, the Kings of Doofus, true to their original vision. Maybe they weren't able to rid the world of the scholarly approach to rock after all, but they sure "shook it up good." —*Jeff Tamarkin*

○ **Ramones** / 1976 / Sire 6020
Punk-rock begins here. The cartoon kings of Queens at their most primitive and threatening. Rock's mainstream didn't know what hit it. —*Jeff Tamarkin*

○ **Ramones Leave Home** / 1977 / Sire 7528
The disappointing second album was still hipper than, well, Peter Frampton or something. —*Jeff Tamarkin*

○ **Rocket to Russia** / 1977 / Sire 6042
The epitome of "stoopidity"—the Ramones at their peak. Includes "Rockaway Beach," "Teenage Lobotomy," and other fine examples of Ramonedom. —*Jeff Tamarkin*

○ **Road to Ruin** / 1978 / Sire 6063
Power ballads, even a (gasp!) "country" tune, but also "I Wanna Be Sedated." In other words, the Ramones get versatile but remain on target. —*Jeff Tamarkin*

End of the Century / 1980 / Sire 6077
The Ramones as produced by Phil Spector. Not a disaster but not all it should've been. —*Jeff Tamarkin*

Pleasant Dreams / 1981 / Sire 3571
The group reportedly wasn't happy with this Graham Gouldman-produced album, but it holds up well—one of their more solid '80s releases. —*Jeff Tamarkin*

Animal Boy / 1986 / Sire 25433
The Ramones get d-u-m-b again and score with a back-to-basics roaring set. —*Jeff Tamarkin*

○ **Ramones Mania** / 1988 / Sire 25709
The best of the Ramones, or, how to pack 30 songs onto one CD—not all of their "hits" but a crash course in stripped-down genius. —*Jeff Tamarkin*

★ **All the Stuff & More, Vol. 1** / 1990 / Warner Brothers 26220
The first two albums, *Ramones* and *Leave Home*, condensed onto one CD, plus bonus tracks. —*Jeff Tamarkin*

☆ **All the Stuff & More, Vol. 2** / 1990 / Sire 26220
The third and fourth albums, *Rocket to Russia* and *Road to Ruin*, combined the present Ramones at their peak on one CD plus bonus tracks. —*Jeff Tamarkin*

Acid Eaters / 1994 / Radioactive/MCA
Tearing through a bunch of psychedelic and garage-rock classics from the '60s, the Ramones regain much of the fun and abandon of the earlier records, making *Acid Eaters* easily their best record in a decade; the guest appearances of Pete Townshend ("Substitute") and ex-porn star Traci Lords ("Somebody to Love") help make the record a blast. —*Stephen Thomas Erlewine*

Willis Alan Ramsey

Vocals, guitar / Singer-songwriter
Few artists have sustained a devout cult following from only one album as Willis Alan Ramsey has. In a way, it's understandable. Ramsey's 1972 self-titled debut, on Denny Cordell's Shelter label, contained some real gems: "Satin Sheets," "Ballad of Spider John," "Painted Lady," and "Muskrat Love," a song that became a huge hit for Captain & Tennille. —*Rick Clark*

○ **Willis Alan Ramsey** / 1972 / Dcc 8008
One of the great (and sadly overlooked) albums of the '70s, Willis Alan Ramsey's self-titled debut had great impact among Austin's progressive country-folk songwriters. Although best known as the writer of "Muskrat Love," which Captain & Tennille took to the Top 10, Ramsey's muse was rooted much deeper in American lore and folk music. Influences from Robert Johnson to Jimmie Rodgers to Woody Guthrie can be felt if not actually heard on these 11 highly original tracks. Unfortunately, Ramsey, a unique talent with a clear and idiosyncratic artistic vision, hasn't been heard from since. —*Tom Graves*

The Rascals

Group / Pop/rock, soul
The Young Rascals from New York (formed 1965) successfully integrated soul and rock into a sound that earned the band considerable success on pop and R&B radio formats with songs like "Good Lovin'" (remake of the Olympics 1965 R&B hit), "Groovin'," "People Got to Be Free," "A Beautiful Morning," and "How Can I Be Sure," as well as other hits, many of which were penned by keyboardist Felix Cavaliere (b. November 29, 1944) and vocalist and percussionist Eddie Brigati. The Young Rascals possessed an explosive rhythm section with jazz drummer Dino Danelli (b. July 23, 1945) and guitarist Gene Cornish (b. May 14, 1945). "Young" was dropped from the band name, as they wanted to portray a more serious image. As the Rascals progressively immersed themselves in indulgent album projects like *Freedom Suite*, their audience shrank. The band called it quits in 1972, after dismal success with their last three albums, *Search and Nearness*, *Peaceful World*, and *The Island of Real*, which were actually pretty good, but their audience had left them. —*Rick Clark*

Young Rascals / 1966 / Warner Brothers 27617
A vital, driving debut album, with a nice, grungy garage-band feel to it. The old mono LPs of this album are a real treat. —*Bruce Eder*

○ **Groovin'** / 1967 / Warner Brothers 27619
A smooth, soulful collection. Carefully and subtly crafted production wrapped around superb songs. —*Bruce Eder*

○ **Time Peace: The Rascals' Greatest Hits** / 1968 / Atlantic 8190
Arguably the greatest greatest-hits album of the '60s. A Whitesoul classic. —*Bruce Eder*

● **Anthology (1965-1972)** / 1992 / Rhino 71031
Anthology is the most comprehensive overview of one of the greatest bands of the '60s. All 18 of their hits as well as important album cuts (including tracks from their Columbia releases) are here on this two-CD, 44-track set. —*Rick Clark*

● **Very Best of the Rascals** / 1994 / Rhino/Atlantic 271277
Although Rhino issued a deluxe two-CD set covering the Rascals a couple of years ago, this single disc set contains enough essential songs for you to get the point. The Rascals, along with the Righteous Brothers, defined blue-eyed soul singing, making records that were as churchy, earthy, and convincing as anything that came out of the south or Motown in the '60s, and it was backed by tight, anthemic arrangements and excellent combo playing. The 16 cuts include their first hit, "I Ain't Gonna Eat Out My Heart Anymore," and continues on into their flirtation with psychedlica in 1970. —*Ron Wynn*

The Raspberries

Group / Power pop
Led by Eric Carmen (b. August 11, 1949), the Raspberries (from Cleveland, OH) brought out their exuberant Beatles-style Anglopop and matching outfits at a time in the early '70s when art rock, concept albums, and serious "statements" were being heralded. It was a time when pop for pop's sake was decidedly uncool. Capitol Records accentuated the band's teenybopper appeal by marketing their self-titled debut with a raspberry-scented scratch-and-sniff sticker on the cover. The band's dynamic first single, "Go All the Way," was a huge hit.

Carmen's tenor had the range of Paul McCartney, and he had the goods to write a handful of truly great guitar pop hits. Lead guitarist Wally Bryson, who filled out their sound with a Beatles-meets-Free crunch, also contributed some solid material. Unfortunately, the public increasingly cooled off on the band, unwilling to buy into harder-rocking single releases like "I'm a Rocker," "Ecstasy," and the truly amazing "Tonight."

Drummer Jim Bonfanti (b. December 17, 1948) and bassist Dave Smalley (b. July 10, 1949) left in 1973, frustrated over the group's image problems. They were replaced by drummer Michael McBride and bassist Scott McCarl.

The 1973 followup effort, *Starting Over*, documented the dreams and frustrations of wanting to be pop stars. The track "Overnight Sensation (Hit Record)" went to #18, but the album ended up being one of the great lost pop albums of the '70s. The group disbanded shortly afterward, and Eric Carmen went on to pursue a sporadically successful solo career that resembled Barry Manilow more than rock & roll. —*Rick Clark*

★ **Capitol Collectors Series** / 1991 / Capitol 92126
Delightful and exciting old-style Top 40 rock, played like it mattered (which it did). Weighty enough to stand the test of time. —*Bruce Eder*

Ratt

Group / Hard rock, heavy metal
The Los Angeles quintet Ratt gained a lot of acceptance in the early to mid '80s with the MTV-friendly style of their glam-influenced mainstream hard rock. —*John Book*

○ **Out of the Cellar** / 1984 / Atlantic 80143
The first album by Los Angeles's Ratt, it brought them instant success and a number of memorable hits. The cover featured actress Tawny Kitaen. —*John Book*

○ **Invasion of Your Privacy** / 1985 / Atlantic 81257
They may have been influenced by Aerosmith, but at this stage Ratt were recording songs that were powerful as well as masterful hits. This album also showed they were a lot more than a hitmaking machine. —*John Book*

○ **Dancin' Undercover** / 1986 / Atlantic 81683
The band's last album before falling into a slump when their imitators got more attention. —*John Book*

● **Ratt & Roll 8191** / 1991 / Atlantic 82260
A greatest-hits package with the best of Ratt's impressive 10-year (and still counting) career. —*John Book*

Lou Rawls

b. Dec. 11, 1935
Vocals / Soul, R&B, pop/rock
When Chicago-born Lou Rawls croons a soulful love song, his deep-hued pipes rumble with simmering passion. Rawls did the usual gospel apprenticeship before breaking out on a landmark jazz album with pianist Les McCann's trio for Capitol that launched his secular career. But it took Rawls a while to establish himself as a soul artist—perhaps he was perceived as a little too sophisticated and jazzy (although his uncredited responses on Sam Cooke's "Bring It on Home to Me" certainly proved he could wail). "Love Is a Hurtin' Thing" instantly changed that notion when it topped the R&B charts in 1966, and the unyielding "Dead End Street" and "Your Good Thing (Is About to End)" perpetuated his success.

After memorably delivering Bobby Hebb's powerful "A Natural Man" in 1971, Rawls joined forces with Philadelphia producers Kenny Gamble and Leon Huff in 1976, emerging with the silky "You'll Never Find Another Love like Mine," another gigantic R&B and pop smash tailor-made for nattily sweeping across the classiest disco dance floors. The disco era's long gone now, but Rawls maintains elegantly. He's still as cool as cool can be. —*Bill Dahl*

○ **Lou Rawls Sings/Les Mccann Plays Stormy Monday** / 1962 / Capitol 1714
A highly popular soul-jazz duo in the '60s, this reissue spotlights the Lou Rawls/Les McCann team in peak form. Rawls sang gritty blues and R&B, McCann added funky keyboard solos and accompaniment. The album was early indicator that McCann would be steady, consistent seller working same territory as Ramsey Lewis. The reissue included three bonus cuts. —*Ron Wynn*

Live! / 1965 / Capitol 91207
Riding high on the success of his mid '70s soul and R&B dates, Philadelphia International issued this live recording featuring Rawls doing the straight blues, jazzy ballads and pre-rock standards he normally reserved for clubs and concerts. There were none of the big radio hits on this date; instead Rawls covered such songs as "Six Cold Feet of Ground," "Blues for a Four String Guitar," and "Everyday I Have the Blues." It also didn't stay on the charts very long, and Gamble and Huff got back to commercial basics the next time out. Still, it's one of his finest and most representative albums. —*Ron Wynn*

○ **All Things in Time** / Oct. 1976 / Philadelphia International 33957
Fine Philly-sound disco and warm romantic ballads. —*Bil Carpenter*

○ **Unmistakably Lou** / 1977 / Philadelphia International 34488
Lou Rawls was riding another hot streak in the late '70s, his career rejuvinated by a string of fine albums and singles on the Philly sound Philadelphia label. This was the followup to his huge hit *All Things in Time*. He only had one R&B chart song from the album, yet in ways his vocals are superior to those on the prior album. Where the Gamble/Huff production team's efforts on the preceding project rivaled Rawls's vocals, this time he took the

spotlight, while their arrangements and productions were more on the subdued side. —*Ron Wynn*

Let Lou Be Good to You / 1979 / Philadelphia International 36006
An above average album that did much better than anyone thought it would be at the time. The title track just missed the R&B Top 10, and the album almost made the pop Top 40, though it wasn't on the charts for a long time. Rawls was still singing in a confident, relaxed, yet earnest and convincing fashion, and the Gamble/Huff production team continued to let his voice be at the forefront and just give him miminal arranging support. —*Ron Wynn*

○ **Stormy Monday** / 1985 / Blue Note 91441
Lou Rawls has enjoyed success in almost every musical arena, from traditional gospel to R&B, soul, pop, and blues. This was his strictest jazz material, as he received excellent backing from the Les McCann trio. McCann, himself a pretty fair singer, played funky keyboards and fronted the trio, while Rawls did both shouting stompers and blues like the title cut, plus mellow ballads, standards and pre-rock pop. But the bulk of this material was blues and ballads. —*Ron Wynn*

○ **At Last** / 1989 / Blue Note 91937
He's never deserted either blues or jazz, but Lou Rawls hasn't always found a receptive audience for these styles at notoriously conservative major labels. That wasn't the case on this 1989 album, in which Rawls performed either straight-ahead jazz and pre-rock pop or blues and was backed by an all-star lineup that included Ray Charles, Cornell Dupree, Steve Khan, Richard Tee, and Dianne Reeves. His voice had an exuberance and fervor that spoke volumes about how happy he was in the setting. —*Ron Wynn*

● **Best of Lou Rawls** / Capitol 91147
A nice collection of Rawls's Capitol singles, which include his number one hit "Love Is a Hurting Thing" and many other fine chart singles, all produced by David Axelrod. Rawls got in a groove during his Capitol years, singing songs that had a soul feel but a jazz and blues base. In some ways, he's never made better songs than his late '60s and early '70s stint at Capitol. —*Ron Wynn*

James Ray

b. 1941
Vocals / Soul, R&B
The Washington, DC, native's 1962 hit, "If You Gotta Make a Fool of Somebody," inspired a raft of covers, while one of his lesser-known efforts, "I've Got My Mind Set on You," provided George Harrison with a recent big-seller. Ray's pop-slanted R&B output for Caprice Records, including his less successful followup "Itty Bitty Pieces," was arranged by pianist Hutch Davie. All three of the songs cited above were written by prolific New York tunesmith Rudy Clark. —*Bill Dahl*

● **Golden Classics** / 1976 / Caprice 1002
An overlooked R&B stylist whose best songs were triumphs of form over thin lyrics. —*Ron Wynn*

Chris Rea

b. Mar. 4, 1951
Vocals / Rock & roll, singer-songwriter
After a string of dull albums in the '70s, Rea released a pair of late '80s and early '90s albums that were astonishing in many ways, revealing the passion of the best kind of singer-songwriter and a rocker's heart that conjures images of everyone from Springsteen to Mark Knopfler. And he's one hell of an evocative vocalist. —*John Floyd*

○ **New Light through Old Windows** / 1988 / Atco 91732
A decent assortment of cuts from his early albums. —*John Floyd*

● **Road to Hell** / 1989 / Atco 91733
The title only hints at the horror that lurks in this album's message. "Texas," "Looking for a Rainbow," and "You Must Be Evil" pick apart the atrocities of our society, while "Let's Dance" offers some much-needed tension release. A modern masterpiece. —*John Floyd*

○ **Auberge** / 1991 / Atco 91662

This one can't help but stand in the shadow of *Road to Hell;* it lacks that set's thematic cohesion. But it's still a hefty testament to the singularity of Rea's world vision. —*John Floyd*

The Records

Group / Power pop
A UK quartet, active from 1979 to 1982, employing a jangly guitar, '60s-pop approach. The band was led by songwriter and guitarist Will Birch and also featured John Wicks, Phil Brown, and guitarist Huw Gower. Their first album, *Shades in Bed,* was released in the United States as *The Records* and featured the minor hit single "Starry Eyes." Gower left, replaced by American Jude Cole for *Crashes* (1980). Their last album, *Music on Both Sides* (1982), featured a quintet of Birch, Wicks, Brown, Dave Whelan, and Chris Gent. — *William Ruhlmann*

○ **Records** / 1979 / Virgin 13130
Virtually every song here is a catchy guitar-driven pop song with sweet harmonies, from the single "Starry Eyes" through "Teenarama" and "Another Star." The album includes a bonus record containing the Records' versions of such oldies as the Kinks' "See My Friends" and Spirit's "1984." — *William Ruhlmann*

● **Smashes Crashes and Near Misses** / 1988 / Virgin 13
Beginning with the nearly perfect single, "Starry Eyes," this 20 track import-only collection gives a good sampling of the band's first three albums. Pure power-pop that shouldn't be missed. — *Chris Woodstra*

The Red Hot Chili Peppers

Group / Alternative pop/rock, funk
A quartet with varying personnel, anchored by lead singer Anthony Kiedis and bassist Flea (born Michael Balzary), the Red Hot Chili Peppers play a hybrid rock incorporating punk, funk, rap, and metal. Though the mixture was ahead of its time when the group was first organized in the early '80s in Los Angeles, the music industry has since caught up to it, which earns the group the right to call itself the forerunner of an approach now adopted by such acts as Living Colour and Faith No More, and also means the Peppers themselves have finally hit the big time. In 1988 guitarist Hillel Slovak died of an overdose and the band reorganized, with John Frusciante on guitar and Chad Smith on drums. This lineup scored a commercial breakthrough with *Mother's Milk,* which went gold after its release in 1989. They ascended to real star status with the release of *Blood Sugar Sex Magik,* which sold two million copies and included the Top 10 hit "Under the Bridge." In mid 1992, Frusciante left the group and was replaced by Arik Marshall. Marshall was replaced by Jesse Tobias in 1993. Tobias's tenure with the group was extremely brief; after a couple of months, he was replaced by ex-Jane's Addiction guitarist Dave Navarro. — *William Ruhlmann*

○ **Freaky Styley** / 1985 / EMI America 90617
Funk-rock explosion on this George Clinton production. Standouts include "Blackeyed Blonde," the Dr. Seuss satire "Yertle the Turtle," and a cover of Sly Stone's "If You Want Me to Stay." — *Bil Carpenter*

Uplift Mofo Party Plan / 1987 / EMI America 48036
The Peppers' best album before they crossed over into the mainstream and their last album with the original band members. Includes "No Chump Love Sucker" and "Fight like a Brave." — *Meredith Erlewine and Bil Carpenter*

Mother's Milk / 1989 / EMI America 92152
While *Mother's Milk* is not their most adventurous or best release, it's a good album that expanded the Red Hot's cult. Mainstream listeners were attracted to the band in large part because of their cover of Stevie Wonder's "Higher Ground," the best song on *Mother's Milk.* Other highlights include "Knock Me Down," "Taste the Pain," "Nobody Weird like Me," and "Sexy Mexican Maid." — *Meredith Erlewine and Stephen Thomas Erlewine*

○ **Blood Sugar Sex Magik** / 1991 / Warner Brothers 26681
It isn't just that the world has finally come around to the Peppers' funk-rock mixture, it's that, with the help of producer Rick Rubin, they've found a focus and that, as musicians, they've reached a sufficient level of competence to execute their ideas. The result is their best album, containing the hit "Under the Bridge." — *William Ruhlmann*

● **What Hits!?** / 1992 / EMI America 94762
A sampling of tracks from the band's 10-year career, including the hit "Under the Bridge," plus "Higher Ground" and "Fight like a Brave." —AMG

Red House Painters

Group / Alternative pop/rock
With their slow, atmospheric, weaving alternative folk-rock, Red House Painters have earned considerable critical acclaim and a cult following. Prolific to a fault, the band released their first EP late in 1992, following it with two full-length albums the next year. On each record, leader Mark Kostelich's introspective melancholia is detailed over a spare, moody soundscape that is occasionally interrupted with bursts of distorted guitar. At their best, Red House Painters are absorbing and hypnotic; at their worst, they are long-winded and boring. Since they are still developing their style, it's understandable that they occasionally fall into their own mire; fortunately, they are often more mesmerizing than dull. — *Stephen Thomas Erlewine*

● **Red House Painters** / May 25, 1993 / 4AD 45256
A slow, stark mood piece, with its folk-pop roots in the somber meditations of Nick Drake, Love's *Forever Changes,* and fellow San Franciscans' American Music Club, *Red House Painters* will either mesmerize or act as a cure for insomnia, depending on your mood. — *Stephen Thomas Erlewine*

Leon Redbone

Vocals, guitar / Pop
Leon Redbone got his start in Toronto at the start of the '70s, then (as now) performing songs primarily of the 'teens, '20s, and '30s and accompanying his affectionate crooning baritone (which some found funny, either intentionally or unintentionally) with simple, syncopated guitar playing. Folk stars such as Maria Muldaur and Bob Dylan spread the word, and Redbone eventually signed to Warner Bros., for whom he recorded three albums (*On the Tracks* [1976], *Double Time* [1977], and *Champagne Charlie* [1978]) whose sales were increased by his appearances on the TV show "Saturday Night Live." His recordings from 1981 on were infrequent and on small labels, but he made a good living as the voice (on and off screen) in many TV commercials. — *William Ruhlmann*

● **On the Track** / 1976 / Warner Brothers 2888
Debut album contains a typical collection of campy oldies ("Ain't Misbehavin'," "Lulu's Back in Town"), accompanied by a varied cast including folkie Don McLean and jazz stars Milt Hinton and Ralph McDonald. — *William Ruhlmann*

○ **Leon Redbone Live** / 1985 / Pair 1309
A live setting is just about ideal for a performer like Redbone, and he does not disappoint on this two-record set, which features "Diddy Wah Diddy," "Champagne Charlie," and other favorites. — *William Ruhlmann*

○ **Red to Blue** / 1985 / August 8888
Redbone's best overall album veers from country to jazz to folk to blues. Backup includes members of Vince Giordano's old-time jazz band, Dr. John, David Bromberg, and the Roches on songs ranging from "Lovesick Blues" to Bob Dylan's "Living the Blues," and with two Redbone originals, as well. — *William Ruhlmann*

Otis Redding

d. Dec. 10, 1967
Vocals / Soul
We are left to guess the direction Otis Redding's music would have taken had he lived. His last hit, the gently affecting "Dock of the Bay," pointed away from the impassioned soul ballads with which he'd made his name and strayed further yet from the Little Richard imitations with which he'd begun his career. Like many others during the mid '60s, Redding discovered what was special about his music in Memphis. He had been recording sporadically and unsuccessfully for three or four years when he arrived at Stax and cut "These Arms of Mine." It gave us everything we could expect from him for the next few years: the almost exaggeratedly impassioned vocals couched in the sparse elegance of the Stax/Volt rhythm and horn sections. Wrenching ballads such as "I've Been Loving You" and "That's How Strong My Love Is" were judiciously mixed with uptempo stomps like "Mr. Pitiful" and "Respect." The individual albums inevitably contain some

duds, but Otis rarely fired blanks on his singles. Redding's appearance at the Monterey Pop Festival and on the West Coast club circuit was beginning to spread word of his music beyond the traditional confines of the R&B market when he was tragically killed in a plane crash in December 1967. —*Colin Escott*

○ **Pain in My Heart** / 1964 / Atco 80253
Redding's first release. Includes the title track, a deep-soul gem, plus "These Arms of Mine" and "Security." —*Christine Ohlman*

○ **Great Otis Redding Sings Soul Ballads** / 1965 / Atco 91706
Redding's second album includes "Mr. Pitiful," "That's How Strong My Love Is," and "Chained and Bound." He moves out of the country-soul genre into his own stompin' thing. —*Christine Ohlman*

☆ **Otis Blue** / 1966 / Atco 80318
Pretty essential if you can only afford individual albums. Three Sam Cooke covers, including "Shake" and "A Change Is Gonna Come," are included, as well as "I've Been Loving You Too Long," "Satisfaction," and the original version of "Respect." —*Christine Ohlman*

○ **Live in Europe** / 1966 / Atco 90395
Ten of Redding's biggest hits, live before an ecstatic audience. Includes "Respect," "I Can't Turn You Loose," "Try a Little Tenderness," and so on. Soul rave-up! —*Christine Ohlman*

☆ **Dictionary of Soul** / 1966 / Atco 91707
If you can only afford one Redding album, start here. Includes "Try a Little Tenderness," "My Lover's Prayer," and "Fa-Fa-Fa-Fa (Sad Song)." One of the best album covers ever! —*Christine Ohlman*

Soul Album / 1966 / Atco 91705
Includes "Chain Gang," "Good to Me," and "Cigarettes and Coffee." —*Christine Ohlman*

○ **King and Queen** / 1967 / Atco 82256
Eleven duets by the undisputed ruler and his consort, Carla Thomas. Includes "Tramp" and "Lovey Dovey." Sweet and soulful! —*Christine Ohlman*

○ **In Person at the Whisky a Go Go** / 1968 / Rhino 70380
Redding captured live in 1966, at the peak of his form! —*Christine Ohlman*

○ **Dock of the Bay** / 1968 / Atco 80254
Includes the posthumously released classic title track plus the great "Ole Man Trouble." —*Christine Ohlman*

Immortal Otis Redding / 1968 / Atco 80270
His later sides, including the wonderful "I've Got Dreams to Remember" and the super-funky "Hard to Handle." Produced by Steve Cropper. Redding on the border of a new soul frontier as a writer and performer, before his untimely death. —*Christine Ohlman*

Remember Me / 1992 / Stax 8572
Twenty-two previously unreleased tracks, finished and unfinished, from the Stax vaults. Includes outtakes, remakes, cover tunes, and some very tasty never-before-heard originals. A historically important release covering all of Otis's remaining studio material. —*Christine Ohlman*

★ **Very Best of Otis Redding** / 1993 / Rhino 71147
For a single-disc collection, *The Very Best of Otis Redding* is unbeatable. All of his biggest hits are here—it's a dynamite album, essential for any lover of soul. —*AMG*

☆ **Otis! the Definitive Otis Redding** / 1993 / Rhino 71439
Although it includes the same studio tracks, *Otis!* supplants the previous, excellent *Otis Redding Story* by adding improved liner notes and sound, as well as a fourth disc of prime live material, gathered from various performances. —*Stephen Thomas Erlewine*

Lou Reed

b. Mar. 2, 1942, Freeport, Long Island, NY
Vocals, guitar / Rock & roll
Lou Reed would be important even if his career had ended with the passing of the Velvet Underground. It didn't, though, and Reed has forged a rich and varied solo career spanning some 20 albums. Not everything he has released has been great, but the best is formidable, and most is worth investigating. Equally interested in poetry and guitar/bass/drums rock & roll, Reed has always felt

that rock & roll can be made interesting and valid for those over 40.

Born in Brooklyn, Reed guided the Velvet Underground from 1965 to 1970. His first, eponymously titled solo album came out in 1972. From his second album, *Transformer*, came his only chart hit in "Walk on the Wild Side." Peaking in popularity in the mid '70s with the *Rock 'n' Roll Animal* and *Sally Can't Dance* albums, Reed became increasingly hostile, frustrated, and erratic. Cleaning himself up in the '80s, from 1982's *The Blue Mask* through 1992's *Magic and Loss*, he has made some of the finest, most engaging nonformulaic rock music ever conceived. —*Rob Bowman*

Lou Reed / 1972 / RCA 4701
Reed's first solo album, with "Walk It & Talk It," "Wild Child," and "Lisa Says" being particular standouts. —*Cub Koda*

● **Transformer** / 1972 / RCA 4807
Produced by David Bowie and Mick Ronson, *Transformer* has a lushness and beauty to its production and arrangements that Reed's material had never before received. The hit single "Walk on the Wild Side" was a fluke brought about by the actions of one fill-in disc jockey at the BBC. The song chronicles several personages from Andy Warhol's Factory retinue, including speed-freaks and transvestites giving head; it is boggling to this day that it got by AM radio programmers. Other Reed classics such as "Vicious" and "Satellite of Love" get similar treatment. —*Rob Bowman*

Berlin / 1973 / RCA 0207
Canadian studio whiz Bob Ezrin and Reed concocted a brilliant album-length concept loosely constructed around the song "Berlin" from Reed's first solo album. Reed, of course, wrote the basic songs (several stemming back to demos recorded but not released by the Velvet Underground), and Ezrin and Allan MacMillan wrote orchestral arrangements for each track. Recording in London, Ezrin assembled a dream band including Jack Bruce, Steve Winwood, Aynsley Dunbar, and, from Detroit, two relatively unknown guitar heroes, Steve Hunter and Steve Wagner. —*Rob Bowman*

Rock & Roll Animal / 1974 / RCA 3664
Retaining guitarists Hunter and Wagner from the *Berlin* sessions, Reed hired a rhythm section consisting of Prakash John on bass, Pentti Glan on drums, and Ray Colcord on keyboards. Two shows were recorded at New York's Academy of Music in 1973. Behind Reed the band produced fierce near-heavy-metal twin-guitar apotheosis for 90 minutes. Just under half of the concert made it onto this album. An FM radio staple at the time, *Rock 'n' Roll Animal* includes searing versions of the Velvet Underground classics "Sweet Jane," "Heroin," "White Light/White Heat," and "Rock 'n' Roll," plus "Lady Day" from *Berlin*. —*Rob Bowman*

Lou Reed Live / 1975 / RCA 3752
Most of the rest of the above-mentioned concert. Three songs from *Transformer*, two songs from *Berlin*, and the Velvet Underground's "I'm Waiting for the Man." Just a shade less visceral than *Rock 'n' Roll Animal*. —*Rob Bowman*

○ **Coney Island Baby** / 1976 / RCA 0915
Coney Island Baby was an album of renewal for Reed. The year 1974 had witnessed one of his worst albums ever in *Sally Can't Dance*, and, early in 1975, in reaction to a career spinning out of control, he had released the lyric-less sonic feedback assault of *Metal Machine Music. Coney Island Baby* was a return to peak songwriting form. The title track reflected Reed's early love of doo-wop. It is probably the grandest love song of his career. "Kicks" is a rather frightening internal study of a diseased mind that eventually turns to murder. As with most of Reed's writing in the '60s and '70s, he draws no conclusion; he simply paints a picture. —*Rob Bowman*

Street Hassle / 1978 / Arista 18499
Reed's second album for Arista has a few weak spots but most of it, including the 11-minute title song, is unmitigated brilliance. The sound is rather odd as Reed began experimenting with Manfred Schunke's binaural recording process. Some tracks on the album are part live and part studio while others are near totally live or totally studio. *Street Hassle* includes Reed's tongue-in-cheek take on racial stereotypes, "I Wanna Be Black," and a quite strange reinterpretation of the Velvet Underground's "Real Good Time Together." —*Rob Bowman*

○ **Blue Mask** / 1982 / RCA 14221

Reed took nearly two years off at the end of the '70s to dry out and clean up. When he did return to recording it was with a vengeance. In an odd quirk of fate Reed had resigned with RCA, and he had also gone back to a lineup of two guitars, a bass, and drums. *The Blue Mask* sounds immaculate. The guts of Reed's sound are still present in no uncertain terms, but there is also a richness to the finished mix that is striking. The bass player, Fernando Saunders, became Reed's right-hand man for the next several years, and guitarist Robert Quine was Reed's ideal foil for this and the subsequent *Legendary Hearts*. The result was Reed's best album since *Berlin*. His songwriting had taken a quantum leap since cleaning up. The maturity was inspiring, as was the breadth of the material. —*Rob Bowman*

Legendary Hearts / 1983 / RCA 4568
Continuing with Quine and Saunders, coupled with a different drummer in Fred Maher, Reed delivered his second superb album in a row. This was a more subdued affair than *The Blue Mask*, but the writing was no less impressive. —*Rob Bowman*

● **New Sensations** / 1984 / RCA 4998
After a few challenging and critically acclaimed albums, Reed dispensed with densely literate and dissonant excursions into the dark side of the human psyche and delivered a solid, upbeat, and at times humorous collection of accessible rock & roll. Reed celebrated love ("I Love You Suzanne"), poked fun at power plays between the genders ("My Red Joystick"), and, as the title track suggested, generally looked forward with optimism. Reed's dirty-electric rhythm, Fernando Saunders's elastic bass work, and Fred Maher's forceful drumming provide a solid bed of ragged but tight ensemble work behind Reed's dry narratives. —*Rick Clark*

○ **New York** / 1989 / Sire 25829
Reed's first album in three years hailed another peak in his recording career. In the past he had always painted pictures of any given social situation. Positive or negative, he had never stated a point of view. On *New York* he rails. Sporting a new band, including bass virtuoso Rob Wasserman and Reed's brother-in-law guitarist Mike Rathke, Reed indicts everyone from slum lords to polluters. *New York* contains, perhaps, his finest writing. —*Rob Bowman*

○ **Songs for Drella** / Jul. 1990 / Sire 26140
Reed and former Velvet Underground partner John Cale reunite to create a song cycle based around the life of Velvet's mentor Andy Warhol. Recorded with just the two of them, the range of sound and mood is masterful. Reed's ballads give way to angst-ridden feedback-charged guitar freakouts. This is an astonishingly moving album. —*Rob Bowman*

○ **Magic and Loss** / 1992 / Sire 26662
The third installment in what feels loosely like a trilogy. This time out Reed tackles death itself as his theme, having recently experienced the loss of two friends. A number of reviewers and fans have attacked the recording, claiming it is too depressing. Reed's irrefutable response is that if books and films are able to deal with death, why not popular songs and rock & roll? As an addendum, the man deserves respect for giving Little Jimmy Scott a cameo vocal on "Power and Glory." —*Rob Bowman*

Between Thought and Expression: The Lou Reed Anthology / 1992 / RCA 62356
For those whose pocketbook can handle a boxed set as an introduction to an artist's work, this three-CD, 45-track set, compiled by Reed himself, is intelligently conceived and executed, spanning his 17-album career with the Arista and RCA labels. *Between Thought and Expression: The Lou Reed Anthology* is a generous selection of his best solo material, outtakes, and other rarities. The box contains extensive liner notes, providing many fine quotes from Reed, who clarifies numerous factual "corrections" made by others concerning his mythology. Sonically, *Between Thought and Expression* is a great improvement over previous reissues of Reed's solo material from this period. —*Rick Clark*

Martha Reeves & the Vandellas

b. Jul. 18, 1941, Detroit, MI
Group / Motown
Perhaps the perfect product of the Motown machine, Martha Reeves was working as a secretary at the label, occasionally doubling as a demo singer, when she was called upon to do some

background vocals for Marvin Gaye. That chance was parlayed into a recording deal for Motown's Gordy subsidiary, and her breakthrough came with her second record, "Come and Get These Memories." There were the inevitable comparisons with the Supremes, but Martha was an incomparably earthier singer than the slinky Ms. Ross, as witnessed by her storming leads on "Heatwave" and, especially, "Dancing in the Street." It was, as the Motown brass well knew, perfect party music, and it was a vein they mined successfully for several more years. The Vandellas came and went, and chart success grew increasingly elusive as the '60s closed, with the result that Martha left the label in 1972 to sign with MCA. Despite the fact that her Martha Reeves set was the most expensive album released to that point (1974), it failed to recharge her career, which has been largely confined to reprising her old hits—where the magic transcends mere nostalgia. —*Colin Escott*

Heat Wave / 1963 / Motown 5145
Martha & the Vandellas began making their first noise on the pop and soul charts with this 1963 album. The title song was a classic, while there were also decent remakes of such vintage tunes as "Mocking Bird" and "My Boyfriend's Back." These proved that the group was a singles rather than an album act and that a little more effort needed to be extended toward finding more material (they even put "Danke Schoen" on this album). But no one really cared, since "Heat Wave" was such a triumph. —*Ron Wynn*

○ **Dance Party** / 1965 / Motown 5433
Another collection of singles rather than a unified album, but who cared when the songs included "Dancing in the Street" and "Nowhere to Run," as well as "Wild One." Martha Reeves was singing with as much energy, sensuality, and joy as any Motown performer during the mid '60s, at least the killer for this record was "Hitch Hike" and "Jerk" instead of "Danke Schoen." —*Ron Wynn*

○ **Anthology** / 1974 / Motown 0778
Until the label issued the definitive two-disc set *Live Wire: The Singles 1962-1972* in 1993, this two-record set was the ultimate Martha Reeves & the Vandellas set. It's still worth hearing, as it contains all the essential hits from their early '60s run. But the two-CD set has better sound than the original vinyl and more extensive notes, discographical information, and photos. —*Ron Wynn*

★ **Martha & the Vandellas Greatest Hits** / 1987 / Motown 5204
The one definitive package to own, with all their biggest and best, including "Come and Get These Memories," "Heat Wave," and "Dancing in the Streets." —*Cub Koda*

○ **Live Wire! The Singles 1962-1972** / 1993 / Motown
This two-CD box set includes all the top, and many of the flip, sides of the singles that Martha Reeves and the Vandellas cut for Motown. All the hits are here, of course; the collector will be especially interested in the B sides and nonhit singles, many of which employed the songwriting talents of Motown regulars like Holland-Dozier-Holland and Mickey Stevenson. There's also the rare single (featuring Gloria Williamson on lead vocals) cut by the Vells in 1962, before Reeves took top billing and the group changed their name. Eight of these cuts have never been released on album before. Among the nonhits, there isn't anything to match "Heat Wave" or "Dancing in the Street," but Reeves's astonishingly powerful voice never falters. —*Richie Unterberger*

R.E.M.

Group / Alternative pop/rock
R.E.M., along with their English counterparts the Smiths, mark the point when post-punk turned into alternative rock. When their first single, "Radio Free Europe," was released in 1981 it created a massive buzz in the American underground that continued to grow through the release of their first full-length album, 1983's *Murmur*. What made R.E.M. so different from other guitar-driven pop bands of their time was the subtlety of their influences; although they were clearly influenced by punk, they didn't sound like any punk group. Instead, Peter Buck's arpeggiated rhythm guitar recalled the Byrds and the Velvet Underground, while Mike Mills was reminiscent of the melodic bass lines of the Beach Boys and the Beatles. But the band was never a retro group or pop revivalist—Bill Berry's strong drumming place and Michael Stipe's mumbled vocals and abstract lyrics place them squarely into the

post-punk era. While their influences are discernible, the clean, atmospheric folk rock of their early records are clearly their own.

Murmur was adored by critics, as well as earning legions of listeners in the college rock underground. Even with Stipe's inaudible, cryptic lyrics, the band's guitar pop was highly melodic and accessible, yet it didn't fit into the strict confines of AOR or Top 40 radio; consequently, it stayed in the American underground, gaining an enormous following over the years, as well as countless imitators. Yet, R.E.M. continued to improve with each record, continually expanding their fan base through constant touring and uniformly excellent albums. By the time they had their first hit single in 1987—the Top 10 "The One I Love"—their underground fans were devoted enough not to be scared off by the success; besides, R.E.M. had not compromised their music in order to sell records.

During the late '80s, the band became genuine rock stars, selling out arenas across the world. Stipe was becoming the focal point for many of the new fans, as well as the press, but R.E.M. has always functioned as a band, not as a backing group and a singer. Their albums were always the result of a collaborative effort between their members, which is the reason they continued to be musically inventive in the '90s.

Although the band hasn't toured since 1989, they are arguably at the height of their popularity in the early '90s. Countless bands have cited R.E.M. not only as a musical influence but also as an ideological model. By the time they sold millions of records, R.E.M. had already developed a solid fan base, so they could afford to play the music they wanted to, whether it was the lush pop of *Out of Time* or the haunting melancholia of *Automatic for the People*. Throughout their career, they have never lost their desire to explore new music, nor have they lost their integrity. —*Stephen Thomas Erlewine*

☆ **Murmur** / 1983 / IRS 0014
All of R.E.M.'s imitators base their homages on this strange, eerie album. Out of all of R.E.M.'s albums, none have the mood this one has- it is the aural equivalent of the creeping kudzu on the cover. The music belongs to no time—the guitars and rhythms may have their roots in '60s pop and folk, but the vocals couldn't have been produced before 1977 and punk-rock. —*Stephen Thomas Erlewine*

☆ **Reckoning** / 1984 / IRS 0044
The guitar still rings and chimes, the vocals still mumble, but the rhythm section is brought toward the front of the mix—the sound is brighter. While the mood has changed (it isn't out of time like *Murmur*), the songs are better—nothing on *Murmur* had the power of "(Don't Go Back to) Rockville" and "So. Central Rain." —*Stephen Thomas Erlewine*

○ **Fables of the Reconstruction** / 1985 / IRS 5592
Fables of the Reconstruction is R.E.M.'s most folk-oriented record, yet it never strays from the band's highly developed pop sensibilities, as "Can't Get There from Here," "Green Grow the Rushes," and "Driver 8" prove. —*Stephen Thomas Erlewine*

☆ **Lifes Rich Pageant** / 1986 / IRS 5783
This is not R.E.M.'s most successful album, but it captures the band at an important crossroads. The ringing guitars of *Murmur* and *Reckoning* remain ("Fall on Me," "Flowers of Guatemala," "What If We Give It Away?"), but the bombastic directness of their next two albums, *Document* and *Green*, is anticipated with tracks like "Just a Touch," "Begin the Begin," and their cover of "Superman." —*Stephen Thomas Erlewine*

○ **Dead Letter Office** / 1987 / IRS 0054
A collection of B sides and outtakes—including a drunken cover of Roger Miller's "King of the Road" and three Lou Reed songs—which confirms the fact that R.E.M. have not only a better sense of melody than most bands but also a better sense of humor. The CD version includes their fine 1982 debut EP, *Chronic Town.* —*Stephen Thomas Erlewine*

☆ **Document** / 1987 / IRS 42059
R.E.M.'s first Top 10 (hell, their first Top 40) single, "The One I Love," is featured on *Document*, as is the anthem "It's the End of the World As We Know It (and I Feel Fine)." Those two songs illustrate the difference in the band—loud guitars, driving rhythms, and clear (well, at least clearer) vocals. "It's the End of the World ..." may be unintelligible, but Stipe's vocals are audible throughout the album, even though the lyrics are murky. —*Stephen Thomas Erlewine*

● **Eponymous** / 1988 / IRS 6262
Basically a singles collection from R.E.M.'s first five albums, *Eponymous* gives the listener a sense of R.E.M.'s change from a folk-rock band to a rock band. The songs are intelligently selected, distilling many of the highlights from their five albums for IRS. The original single version of "Radio Free Europe," different mixes of "Gardening at Night" (where it is actually possible to hear the vocal) and "Finest Worksong," and the previously unreleased (and unspectacular) "Romance" are included for the hardcore fans. —*Stephen Thomas Erlewine*

Green / 1988 / Warner Brothers 25795
Green is R.E.M.'s most disjointed and strange recording. Alternating between eerie acoustic numbers and all-out guitar rave-ups, there is no cohesion here. Nevertheless, there is some good material: the goofy "Stand," the veiled confessions of "Hairshirt" and "World Leader Pretend," the guitar workout of "Turn You Inside Out," the mocking "Pop Song 89," and the charming untitled 11th track. —*Stephen Thomas Erlewine*

○ **Out of Time** / 1991 / Warner Brothers 26496
Highlighted by the hit single "Losing My Religion," *Out of Time* is a mature, balanced, and graceful collection of pop songs quite different from *Murmur* and *Reckoning*. Buck, Berry, and Mills switch instruments frequently, keeping the music fresh and exciting. —*Stephen Thomas Erlewine*

☆ **Automatic for the People** / 1992 / Warner Brothers 45055
After electing not to support the success of *Out of Time* with a tour, R.E.M. promised a hard, driving guitar rock album by the end of the next year. Fortunately, R.E.M. delivered *Automatic for the People*, a beautifully sad album that is the anything but hard rock & roll. A dark, brooding meditation on loss of all sorts, *Automatic for the People* is arguably R.E.M.'s finest moment. Largely acoustic with lush string arrangements by John Paul Jones, *Automatic for the People* is sorrowful and nostalgic without being crass, shallow, or pandering. Whether it is the adolescent memories of "Nightswimming" and "Find the River," the celebrity deaths of "Monty Got a Raw Deal" and "Man on the Moon," or the consolations of "Everybody Hurts" and "Sweetness Follows," R.E.M. never falls into false sentiment. —*Stephen Thomas Erlewine*

REO Speedwagon

Group / Pop/rock

REO Speedwagon may not have been the most talented arena rock band of the '70s, but they were almost certainly worked harder than any other group on the same circuit. In 1971 they released their first album of competent hard rock, but they didn't chart until 1974 with *Ridin' the Storm Out.* That album was recorded with temporary vocalist Michael Murphey, who would later have some solo success of his own; regular vocalist/rhythm guitarist Kevin Cronin rejoined the band in 1975. The first album released after Cronin rejoined REO was only moderately successful, but 1977's *REO Speedwagon Live/You Get What You Play For* began a string of gold and platinum albums, culminating with the 1980 album *Hi Infidelity*, which sold over seven million copies in the United States. Although their style had shifted to a slick, mainstream AOR rock and they were known for the power ballads, the hits didn't stop coming until 1990, when the band's support dropped off sharply; their 1991 album didn't even chart. However, the band remains a solid touring attraction, and they continue to release albums into the '90s. —*Stephen Thomas Erlewine*

○ **R.E.O. 2** / 1972 / Epic 31745
An early album defining what was best about them in their opening act days of the early '70s. —*Cub Koda*

○ **Decade of Rock and Roll '70-80** / 1980 / Epic 36444
A well-chosen recap of REO's dues-paying years. —*Dan Heilman*

○ **Hi-Infidelity** / 1982 / Epic 36844
The band's breakthrough album with the masses. Heavy on the syrupy ballad formula that brought them success. —*Cub Koda*

● **Hits** / 1988 / Epic 44202
This collects their chart hits and some old favorites. —*Dan Heilman*

The Replacements

Group / Alternative pop/rock, rock & roll

Minneapolis band the Replacements blasted onto the scene with a perfectly inspired blend of irreverence, sloppiness, and heart, the stuff from which great rock & roll is created.

Paul Westerberg, the band's primary singer-songwriter, has produced an impressive body of work that ranges from moronically inspired rock to reflective numbers possessing heartbreaking vulnerability. No other band from the post-punk age has worn such an interesting and complex heart on their torn-up sleeve or used an imperfect voice to such great advantage. On their initial releases (*Sorry Ma, Forgot to Take Out the Trash, Stink,* and *Hootenanny*), the band puked out frantic song-bites (many less than two minutes long) with clown punk titles like "I Hate Music," "Shiftless When Idle," "White and Lazy," "F*** School," and "God Damn Job."

Let It Be, their fourth release, reflected a new maturity while not sacrificing their spirit of reckless fun. The next two efforts, *Tim* and *Pleased to Meet Me,* maintained the magic.

After that, the Replacements addd guitarist Slim Dunlap and softened their ragged-but-right sound with *Don't Tell a Soul* (which produced a #1 college-rock hit in "I'll Be You"). Original drummer Chris Mars left the band before they recorded their final album, the more acoustic-oriented *All Shook Down,* which was essentially a solo project for Westerberg.

They were called "the last great band of the '80s" by *Musician.* You'd better believe it. *—Rick Clark & John Floyd*

Sorry Ma, Forgot to Take out the Trash / 1981 / Twintone 8123
Sorry Ma, Forgot to Take Out the Trash is a thrashy, Ramones-like debut. "Johnny's Gonna Die," "I'm in Trouble," and "Takin' a Ride" hint at things to come. *—John Floyd*

○ **Hootenanny** / 1983 / Sire 74804
A hodgepodge of hard rock, country, punk—everything. It's patchy, but "Color Me Impressed," "Willpower," and "Within Your Reach" are among their best. *—John Floyd*

☆ **Let It Be** / 1984 / Sire 74805
This is where they realized their potential and consolidated their diversity into a masterpiece that screams, cries, comforts, and antagonizes. Highlights include "Unsatisfied," one of Westerberg's finest songs and vocal performances, as well as the reckless swinging "I Will Dare" and the playful "Androgynous." *—John Floyd*

☆ **Tim** / 1985 / Sire 25330
Their major-label debut isn't a great leap forward, but their raggedness is retained, and Westerberg contributes anthems of rebellion and insecurity, like "Bastards of Young" and "Hold My Life." Also included is a hard-rockin' nod to alternative radio (with Alex Chilton), "Left of the Dial." *—John Floyd*

★ **Pleased to Meet Me** / 1987 / Sire 25557
Pared down to a trio, the band offers a complex set of ballads and guitar blazers and continues its examination of the effects of rock stardom. Producer Jim Dickinson (Ry Cooder, Big Star) gives the group a piledriver sound, like a boombox with the loudness up to 10. "Alex Chilton," a hard-rocking ode to Big Star's founder; "Can't Hardly Wait," with its great Memphis groove and Box Tops-style horn and string parts; and the haunting "Skyway" are among this album's highlights. *—John Floyd*

Don't Tell a Soul / 1989 / Sire 25831
The full-blown production made some cry sell out, but *Don't Tell a Soul* contained a heightened level of melodicism that produced some wonderful moments, particularly the expansive "Darlin' One," "Talent Show," "Achin' to Be," and their first #1 AOR hit, "I'll Be You." With that song, Westerberg practically achieved the magic he so much admired on Big Star's records. If *Don't Tell a Soul* hadn't been a Replacements album, its appealingly sloppy melodic power-pop would have, more than likely, earned rave reviews. This contains their most desolate work, highlighted by "I'll Be You" (their first #1 AOR hit), "Talent Show," the expansive psychedelia of "Darlin' One," and the creepy "Rock & Roll Ghost." *—John Floyd*

○ **All Shook Down** / 1990 / Sire 26298
More a Westerberg solo album than a band effort, this is a weary acoustic-based set, which finds him finally facing the perils of adulthood. *—John Floyd*

Paul Revere & the Raiders

Group / Rock & roll

In 1959, two natives of Caldwell, ID, met and decided to form a band. Paul Revere (b. January 7, 1942) and Mark Lindsey (b. March 9, 1942) called their group the Downbeats, after the jazz magazine. At first the group was largely instrumental, featuring Revere's pounding roadhouse piano (in the style of Jerry Lee Lewis) and Lindsey's sax playing. The band was renamed Paul Revere & the Raiders in 1960, after a pressing plant owner suggested Revere ought to capitalize on his memorable name.

Their first single was an instrumental called "Beatnick Sticks," a takeoff on "Chopsticks." Their third single, an instrumental called "Like Long Hair," was their first national hit, getting them played on Dick Clark's "American Bandstand." Eventually Clark became one of the most important people in furthering the band's career.

Columbia signed the band, and Terry Melcher was given the job of producing them and toughening up their sound. Beginning with "Steppin' Out," the band had a long stretch of substantial hits, aided by their residency on Dick Clark's "Where the Action Is" TV show.

Melcher managed to get songwriters Barry Mann and Cynthia Weil to give the Raiders an antidrug song, "Kicks" (originally written for the Animals), and it became one of their biggest hits. Mann and Weil supplied the followup hit, "Hungry."

Other hits included "Good Thing," "Him or Me—What's It Gonna Be?" "Indian Reservation," "Just Like Me," and "The Great Airplane Strike." Mark Lindsey concurrently pursued a solo career, scoring a hit with "Arizona" during the latter part of the Raiders' existence. Paul Revere continued to perform with a modified lineup of Paul Revere & the Raiders. *—Rick Clark*

● **Greatest Hits** / 1967 / Columbia 9462
A good single-disc collection, containing most of their biggest hits; for those who don't want the comprehensive *Legend of Paul Revere,* it's a good buy. *—Stephen Thomas Erlewine*

○ **Legend of Paul Revere** / 1990 / Columbia 45311
This two-CD anthology, with 55 songs, may be a lot more Raiders than the average fan would want. But go for it and be amazed at how consistently strong this rocking band from the Great Northwest was. Includes all the hits. *—Jeff Tamarkin*

Revolting Cocks

Alternative rock, industrial
Revolting Cocks have been the sleaziest and ugliest industrial band in the land since their debut album in 1986. Over the years, their records have featured many musicians, but the core members of the band are Ministry's Al Jourgensen, ex-Fini Tribe member Chris Connely, and Belgian producer Luc Van Acker. Combining samples, guitars, synths, and pounding dance rhythms, their records are a trashy synthesis of the most extreme industrial noise, the silliest pop culture, and classic art rock. Because of their irreverence, they are the industrial band that is the most fun to listen to, if not the best or most influential. *—Stephen Thomas Erlewine*

● **Beers, Steers & Queers** / 1990 / Wax Trax 7063
A sleazy set of campy, vulgar samples and rhythms, *Beers, Steers & Queers* is the Revolting Cocks' most entertaining record. *—David Jehnzen*

Linger Fickin' Good / 1993 /
Revolting Cocks' major-label debut treads no new ground but it contains a giddy, demented reworking of Rod Stewart's "Do Ya Think I'm Sexy" that has to be heard to be believed. *—Stephen Thomas Erlewine*

Rezillos

Group / Punk new wave
One of Scotland's great punk bands, the Rezillos came on like gangbusters with a hip attitude, a revved-up band (featuring soon-to-be Human Leaguer Jo Callis), and the remarkable pipes of Ms. Fay Fife. With a flair for garish '60s pop-art artifacts (something I'm positive influenced the B-52s), the Rezillos were decidedly less serious than their punk contemporaries, but their debut album *Can't Stand the Rezillos* is a cheesy classic. *—John Dougan*

● **Can't Stand the Rezillos: The Almost Complete Rezillos** / 1993 / Sire 26942

Nearly everything this energetic new-wave band ever recorded is on this splendid one disc compilation. —*Stephen Thomas Erlewine*

Cliff Richard (Harry Webb)

b. Oct. 14, 1940, Lucknow, India
Vocal / Pop/Rock

Britain's answer to Elvis Presley, Richard (born Harry Webb) dominated the pre-Beatles British pop scene in the late '50s and early '60s. An accomplished singer with a genuine feel for the music, Richard's artistic legacy is nonetheless meager, as he was quickly steered toward a middle-of-the-road pop direction. Several of his late '50s recordings, however, were genuinely exciting Presleyesque rockers—especially his first hit, "Move It" (1958)—and gave British teenagers their first taste of genuine homegrown rock & roll talent. Backed by the Shadows—clean-cut instrumental virtuosos who became legends of their own—Richard embarked on a truly awesome string of hit singles in Britain, scoring no less than 43 Top 20 hits between 1958 and 1969. One of these, although it was by no means one of the more successful, was an actual Mick Jagger-Keith Richards composition (the ballad "Blue Turns to Grey").

In his homeland, Cliff's popularity was diminished only slightly by the rise of the Beatles, but in his prime, he had a much rougher time in the United States, hitting the Top 40 only twice (with "Living Doll" in 1959 and "It's All in the Game" in 1963). Richard belatedly cracked the U.S. Top 10 in 1976 with "Devil Woman," and racked up a few other hits ("We Don't Talk Anymore," "Dreaming," "A Little in Love") in a mainstream pop-rock style. He remains an institution in Britain, where he is one of the nation's most popular all-around entertainers of all time. —*Richie Unterberger*

● **20 Rock'n'Roll Hits** / 1979 / EMI 07145
Concentrating mostly on his 1958-1959 material, this has Cliff's most untamed recordings (bearing in mind that they're still pretty polished compared to most U.S. rockabilly). Includes his first brace of hits—"Move It," "High Class Baby," "Mean Streak," and "Never Mind"—along with the megasmash "Livin' Doll," which pointed the way toward the pop ballad path he would follow in the '60s. —*Richie Unterberger*

○ **Cliff Richard & the Shadows** / 1984 / EMI
Cliff Richard & the Shadows rock out like nobody's business on this classic live album (arguably rock's first authorized and professionally recorded concert album). Recorded in February 1959 at EMI in front of 500 screaming fans, the sound is raw and raunchy by British standards of the time. —*Bruce Eder*

Keith Richards

b. Dec. 18, 1943, Dartford, Kent, England
Vocals, guitar / Rock & roll

One of the few White guitarists with strong blues roots who has been able to take the form to new places, Richards's contribution to the vocabulary of rock guitar cannot be overestimated. His heavy reliance on Delta blues open tunings (mostly played on guitars with only five strings) has provided licks that are part and parcel for any player who wants to get the joint rocking and the dance floor packed. Though much has been made of his lifestyle, and time has reduced his voice to a sore-throated husk, it is as a guitarist and songwriter that Richards will ultimately establish his reputation. —*Cub Koda*

● **Talk Is Cheap** / 1988 / Virgin 86079
Richards's first solo album includes "Take It So Hard," "Struggle," "I Could Have Stood You Up," and "Make No Mistake," with a classic Hi Rhythm Section groove and featuring great guest vocals by Sarah Dash. —*Cub Koda*

○ **Live at the Hollywood Palladium (Dec 15, 1988)** / 1991 / Virgin 91808
A nicely ragged live album that captures Richards and the Winos at the top of their form. —*Stephen Thomas Erlewine*

Main Offender / 1992 / Virgin 86499
Richards's second solo album is even more delightfully focused than his first. Highlights include "Wicked As It Seems," "Eileen," and the searing "999." New Rolling Stones albums should rock this hard. —*Cub Koda*

Lionel Richie

b. Jun. 20, 1949, Tuskegee, AL
Vocals / Soul, urban R&B, pop

After he left the Commodores in 1981, Lionel Richie became one of the most successful solo artists of the early '80s, earning a string of 13 Top10 hits between 1981 and 1987, including five #1 singles ("Endless Love," "Truly," "All Night Long (All Night)," "Hello," "Say You, Say Me"). Between 1986 and 1992 he didn't release any new material, but in 1993 he reemerged with a new album that sold well, but not up to the standards he set a decade earlier. —*Stephen Thomas Erlewine*

○ **Lionel Richie** / 1982 / Motown 6007
Lionel Richie was perhaps the dominant songwriter and performer of the early '80s. His almost overwhelmingly sentimental love tunes were massive crossover hits, and he turned awkwardness into an art form. This was his first big album, and it peaked at #3 on the pop albums chart, eventually selling over four million copies and staying on the charts 140 weeks. —*Ron Wynn*

● **Can't Slow Down** / 1983 / Motown 6059
The Lionel Richie gravy train was in full throttle on this second big hit album, which eventually sold over eight million copies. Richie earned the 1984 Grammy for Album of the Year, and such tunes as "Hello," "Running with the Night," "Stuck on You," and "Love Will Find a Way" were all over the R&B, pop, even country airwaves. —*Ron Wynn*

Dancing on the Ceiling / 1986 / Motown 6158
Lionel Richie had a slump of sorts after the incredible success of *Can't Slow Down*. This record, which came some three years later, only sold four million instead of eight million copies, stayed atop the pop album charts only a month instead of two, and only had a few pop hits in "Love Will Conquer All," "Say You, Say Me," "Se La," and "Deep River Woman." —*Ron Wynn*

Back to Front / 1992 / Motown 6338
After six silent years, *Back to Front* is a respectable comeback from Lionel Richie, although it rarely catches fire or is as memorably melodic as his records from the early '80s. —*Stephen Thomas Erlewine*

Jonathan Richman & the Modern Lovers

b. 1951, Boston, MA
Vocals / Rock & roll, pop/rock

Jonathan Richman (b. 1951) is a certifiable rock weirdo. In 1971 he and the Modern Lovers cut some demos for Warner Bros. (produced by John Cale) that funneled the influence of the Velvet Underground into the twisted vision of a high-school geek. Those demos were finally released in 1976. On everything he's done since then Richman has pushed the parameters of cuteness into theme albums (*Jonathan Goes Country* and so on), amplifying his lighthearted approach. —*John Floyd and Cub Koda*

☆ **Modern Lovers** / 1977 / Rhino 70091
This is a reissue of the 1971 John Cale-produced demos that unknowingly precipitated what would eventually become punk-rock. As he states on "Roadrunner," he's in love with the modern world but also with girls. His odes to a lack of love make for a cogent debut. —*John Floyd*

○ **Jonathan Richman & the Modern Lovers** / Jan. 1977 / Beserkeley 0048
Richman's second collection of Modern Lovers, over which he was billed (eventually, the group name would be dropped), had a lighter rock & roll sound than the first. In fact, as often as not, Richman played acoustic guitar. And his lyrical concerns had similarly lightened up, to the point of childlike whimsy on such songs as "Hey There Little Insect" and "Here Come the Martian Martians." But the focus was still Richman's unabashed vocalizing (the word "sings" is put in quotes on the back cover), giving the whole album an amateurish charm. —*William Ruhlmann*

○ **Rock 'N' Roll with the Modern Lovers** / Feb. 1977 / Rhino 70093
Richman branches out to Japanese music, a "South American Folk Song," and even "Egyptian Reggae" (the last earning him a UK Top 5 hit), but the real highlight on *Rock 'N' Roll with the Modern Lovers* is that ode to a totaled car, "Dodge Veg-O-Matic." —*William Ruhlmann*

● **Beserkley Years** / 1987 / Rhino 75889
After the first Modern Lovers album, Richman's records were enjoyable but fairly spotty. Thankfully, *The Beserkley Years* collects

the best moments from his '70s records, when his cuteness was endearing, not irritating. With "Roadrunner," "Pablo Picasso," "Here Come the Martian Martians," "Important in Your Life," "Ice Cream Man," and "Dodge Veg-O-Matic" forming its core, this collection definitive portrait of his goofy, catchy minimalist pop/rock. —*Stephen Thomas Erlewine*

Ride

Group / Alternative pop/rock

Trancelike vocals and dance grooves, coupled with walls of ambient distorted guitar, are this Manchester, England, quartet's stock in trade. In the style of Echo & the Bunnymen, psychedelic dance-pop filtered through early Pink Floyd psycho-drone. —*Rick Clark*

○ **Smile** / Jan. 1990 / Sire 26390
The first two EPs from Britain's Creation label on one American collection. Sonically muddier than *Nowhere* (if that can be possible), but the tuneful crash-and-burn of "Like a Daydream" is one of their best. —*Rick Clark*

● **Nowhere** / Feb. 1990 / Sire 26462
Rackety, reverberant, psychedelic drone-rock from Manchester, England. Fans of hypnotic detached singing against numbing waves of dissonance should find this somewhat interesting, particularly the throbbing "Polar Bear," the lumbering yet airy "Vapour Trail," the fairly accessible "Taste," and the reckless "Here and Now." The title cut is an effective fusing of early Pink Floyd sonic freakout and industrial noise sludge. —*Rick Clark*

Going Blank Again / Oct. 1991 / Sire 26836
Ride's second full-length album finds the band in a holding pattern. While the loud, atmospheric guitars and gorgeous melodies *sound* good, it isn't a big departure from their *Nowhere*, and it doesn't point the band in a new direction. Fortunately, they experienced a creative rebirth on their next album. —*Stephen Thomas Erlewine*

○ **Carnival of Light** / 1994 / Sire
A thoroughly impressive, assured set of swirling guitar psychedelia that recalls classics British pop without ever sounding dated. —*Stephen Thomas Erlewine*

The Righteous Brothers

Group / Soul, pop/rock

The Righteous Brothers vocal duo consists of Bill Medley and Bobby Hatfield (both b. 1941). Generally regarded as the popular originators of "blue-eyed soul," they originally formed as the Paramours in a stronger doo-wop style, eventually tackling harder R&B material in a more gospel-oriented fashion, prompting the name change. Early recordings featured the hit "Little Latin Lupe Lu," written by Medley. It quickly became a garageband staple of the '60s, successfully covered by both the Kingsmen and Mitch Ryder. With producer Phil Spector, they went on to score Top 10 hits consistently with classic ballad material like "You've Lost That Lovin' Feelin'" and "Unchained Melody," the latter featured prominently in the movie *Ghost*. Even with label and production changes, the hits kept coming through the end of the '60s, when they went their separate ways. They reunited in 1974-1975, had another Top 10 smash with "Rock and Roll Heaven," and are still performing today to appreciative audiences. —*Cub Koda*

★ **Anthology 1962-74** / 1989 / Rhino 71488
Excellent two-CD retrospective covering the hits from the early Moonglow R&B sides up to "Rock and Roll Heaven." The definitive overview. —*Cub Koda*

Live 1967 / Live Gold 30003
Great live performance from Anaheim Stadium, running the gamut from familiar hits to doo-wop and gospel favorites. With dynamic singing and energetic backing, this one catches them pretty much at the top of their form. —*Cub Koda*

Billy Lee Riley

b. 1933
Vocals, harmonica, bass, guitar, drums / Rockabilly

An alumni of Sun Records, Riley was one of the most crazed, unabashed rockers that label had to offer—and in the company of Jerry Lee Lewis, Carl Perkins, and Sonny Burgess, that's saying a lot. Proficient at harmonica, guitar, bass, and drums, Riley con-

tributed as a sideman to many a classic Sun session, and his combo the Little Green Men (most notably guitarist Roland Janes and drummer J. M. Van Eaton) in time became the Sun house band. Riley went on to record for a number of labels in a variety of styles, especially effective with blues. Though never commercially successful, Riley's Sun recordings of "Flying Saucer Rock 'n' Roll" and "Red Hot" (both covered in wooden renditions by Robert Gordon) remain landmarks of the genre. —*Cub Koda*

● **Classic Recordings, 1956-1960** / Jul. 1990 / Bear Family 15444
All the classic Sun sides, plus later Memphis recordings in a brilliant two-CD set. Raw rockin' at its finest. —*Cub Koda*

Johnny Rivers (John Ramistella)

b. Nov. 7, 1942
Vocals / Pop/rock

Johnny Rivers, intent on getting a break in the music business, left his Baton Rouge home for New York and Nashville. It is DJ Alan Freed who suggested the name change to Rivers, since he originated from the Delta South. After a series of moves and song cuts and a stint with Louie Prima, Rivers gained attention on the Los Angeles club scene, particularly the Whiskey a Go-Go, where he recorded his debut, *Johnny Rivers at the Whiskey a Go-Go*, for Imperial Records. Versions of Chuck Berry's "Memphis" and "Maybellene" hit #2 and #12, respectively, launching a series of live hit singles that reflect his tendency to draw from the blues and old rock & roll. Rivers scored with "Secret Agent Man," capitalizing on the then-current fascination with foreign espionage. After that he increasingly turned his attentions to a lusher MOR formula with "Poor Side of Town," "Baby I Need Your Lovin'," "The Tracks of My Tears," and the haunting "Summer Rain." During the '70s, Rivers had a comeback with several remakes of old rock hits, as well as a hit with the romantic "Swayin' to the Music (Slow Dancin')." Besides his artistry, Rivers displayed good commercial instincts by discovering and signing the 5th Dimension and assisting the career of songwriter Jimmy Webb. Rivers continues to perform, sounding like he hasn't aged a day since his biggest hits. —*Rick Clark*

● **Best of Johnny Rivers** / 1987 / EMI America 46594
A fine single-disc collection, *Best of Johnny Rivers* features most of his biggest hits, making it a good purchase for those who don't want the definitive double-disc set. —*Stephen Thomas Erlewine*

○ **Anthology** / 1991 / Rhino 70793
One of the great interpretive singers in rock & roll. Rivers made every song his own, and this two-CD package is proof that he rarely faltered. —*Jeff Tamarkin*

The Rivieras

Group / Doo-wop

Moonlight Cocktails / Relic 7025
A nice anthology covering the Rivieras singles on Coed, among them the title track and "Count Every Star." Never a huge hit group, they were among the many journeyman doo-wop ensembles that plugged away in the '50s, always one step away from scoring a hit but never quite able to take the next step. —*Ron Wynn*

The Rivieras

Group / Rock & roll

A South Bend, IN, rock & roll band whose one big hit was one of the last great gasps of pure American rock & roll before the British invasion took over the charts. Original members Otto Nuss (organ), Doug Gean (bass), Marty "Bo" Fortson (vocals and guitar), Joe Pennell (guitar), and Paul Dennert (drums) were local teen ballroom heroes. They recorded a supercharged version of the Joe Jones R&B semihit "California Sun" featuring a powerful drum intro and the now-famous signature guitar and organ riff. The song became a hit in the midst of the first flush of Beatlemania, only nudged out of the #1 spot on the national charts by "I Want to Hold Your Hand." Although several equally fine 45s and two albums followed, the band's relatively young ages, coupled with numerous personnel changes caused by the draft and the changing musical climate, caused the band to break up by 1966. Nuss, Gean, and Fortson reunited the Rivieras in mid '80s, recording and doing local shows, sounding as great as ever. Though their time in the spotlight was brief, their one big hit continues to define for future generations everything that's pulsatingly great about American teen-band rock & roll. —*Cub Koda*

○ **Campus Party** / 1965 / Riviera 701
Second album; classic frat-band sound. Out of print and impossibly rare but worth the search at any cost. —*Cub Koda*

● **California Sun** / Sonet 9922
Import reissue of their first album. —*Cub Koda*

The Rivingtons

Group / Doo-wop
The Rivingtons were a West Coast vocal group featuring Al Frazier, Carl White, John "Sonny" Harris, and Turner "Rocky" Wilson, Jr. Though they are best known for their string of early '60s novelties, the Rivingtons in reality had a rich tradition of doo-wop in their background, going back to their original recordings for Federal as the Lamplighters in 1953. They did extensive backup group work throughout the '50s between their own stray releases under a number of different names: the Sharps (singing on the original "Little Bitty Pretty One" and "Over and Over" by Thurston Harris), the Tenderfoots, the Rebels (they do all the backups on the Duane Eddy hits), the Four after Fives, the Crenshaws. They even sang backup on Paul Anka's first record, credited as the Jacks! In 1962 they became the Rivingtons and hit pay dirt with their first record, the self-penned "Pa Pa Ooh Mow Mow," one of the truly great rock & roll songs to make a virtue of sheer gibberish. They hit the charts again a year later with "The Bird's the Word," capitalizing on a current West Coast dance fad that teenagers were doing to "Pa Pa Ooh Mow Mow." A landlocked surf-teen combo from Minnesota called the Trashmen combined the two songs, revved up the beat to warp factor nine, and scored a massive hit with "Surfin' Bird." No further chart success, their place in rock & roll history (both for the classic performances they recorded and for being the inspiration behind one of the great noise-rock anthems of all time) is assured. —*Cub Koda*

● **Liberty Years** / 1991 / EMI America 95204
An excellent 23-track CD with detailed notes and great sound, featuring both sides of all their original-issue 45s (including the insane followup "Mama Ooh Mow Mow") plus all the tracks from their lone Liberty album, *Doin' the Bird*. —*Cub Koda*

Robbie Robertson

b. Jul. 5, 1943
Guitar / Singer-songwriter, pop/rock
After dissolving the Band in late 1976, guitarist/songwriter Robbie Robertson acted in and produced *Carny*, wrote and/or chose the music for the soundtracks of Martin Scorsese's *Raging Bull, King of Comedy,* and *The Color of Money* and in 1987 released his first solo album. Relatively inactive in the late '80s, Robertson's second solo album, *Storyville,* was not released until 1991. —*Rob Bowman*

● **Robbie Robertson** / 1987 / David Geffen Co. 24160
Robbie Robertson's first solo album, released 11 years after the Band called it quits at *The Last Waltz,* found the singer-guitarist mining radically new territory. Hiring Daniel Lanois as coproducer, Robertson crafted an album that owed very little to the Band's roots-Americana sound. Instead Robertson opted for a quirky, enigmatic modern approach, using drum programs, the stick, and guest musicians such as U2, Peter Gabriel, and Bill Dillon. If the album had a weakness, it was in the vocal department. Robertson had only sung lead on a couple of songs with the Band. His reedy ghost of a voice can be quite effective but wears a bit thin over the course of a whole album. Ultimately that is a minor complaint, as the songwriting, arrangements, playing, and sound-painting are superb. —*Rob Bowman*

Storyville / 1991 / David Geffen Co. 24303
Robertson's second album was four years in the making. Once again he set out to explore an approach and sound markedly different from any of his previous work. The album is conceptual, roughing out a story over 10 songs set in New Orleans's legendary turn-of-the-century Storyville red-light district. Coproduced by Robertson, Stephen Hague, and Gary Gersh, the record was recorded in New Orleans with members of the Neville Brothers, Mardi Gras Indians, the Meters, and the Zion Harmonizers. Legendary New Orleans arranger Wardell Quezergue contributed stunning horn charts. More aggressive

than Robertson's first solo release, *Storyville* is perhaps a little less mysterious and enigmatic. —*Rob Bowman*

Smokey Robinson & the Miracles (William Robinson)

b. Feb. 19, 1940, Detroit, MI
Group / Motown, R&B, soul, urban R&B
Bob Dylan called him "America's greatest living poet." Certainly, he was—and is—one of America's greatest living voices; he has brought his thrilling high tenor to a wide variety of material, most of it marked by his innate good taste. Smokey Robinson's association with Motown founder Berry Gordy goes back to the late '50s, when Gordy produced and cowrote the singles that the Miracles recorded for Chess and Roulette. Subsequently, the Miracles were one of the first acts to record for Tamla—and one of the first to break; "Shop Around" was a hit in 1960 and was followed by 38 more before Robinson quit the group in 1972. He also wrote for other acts (including "The Way You Do the Things You Do" and "My Girl" for the Temptations and "My Guy" and "Two Lovers" for Mary Wells).

Perhaps Robinson's masterpiece was "Tracks of My Tears," which he recorded with the Miracles. Its success was all the more surprising because the group had largely confined themselves to dance-oriented novelties before then. Robinson's contributions to Motown as an artist, writer, and producer were rewarded with a vice presidency, although the group's momentum was sagging. Their career was temporarily bolstered in 1970 when "Tears of a Clown" (cut three years earlier) became their first #1 pop hit. Robinson went solo two years later, and his solo albums trace the journey of a man who peaked early in life but has never lost the creative spark. —*Colin Escott*

○ **Going to a Go-Go** / 1965 / Motown 5269
This was the first truly great Miracles album, and their first to crack the Top 10 on the LP chart. The title song was arguably Robinson's finest uptempo composition (along with "Get Ready"), and the album also contained the majestic ballads "Ooh Baby Baby" and "My Girl Has Gone," plus Robinson's signature tune "Tracks of My Tears." After those heavyweights, it didn't matter what else was there, but "In Case You Need Love" and "My Baby Changes Like the Weather" were the kind of afterthought gems Motown churned out with regularity during their prime. —*Ron Wynn*

Tears of a Clown / 1967 / Motown 5156
The title track revisited the arena of heartache and confessional soul that few have ever exploited more skillfully and memorably than Smokey Robinson. This album was actually an example of corporate greed at work; it was only grafting a new title onto an old album. Motown merely reissued *Greatest Hits, Vol. 2* with a fresh title to fill the gap as internal problems were preventing the completion of a new Miracles record. Of course, most of the songs were great, since "More Love" and "Love I Saw in You Was Just a Mirage" were among the many fine tunes on the album. But it was just an early example of the label's constant recyling of their hits that's now standard operating procedure. —*Ron Wynn*

Hi, We're the Miracle / 1969 / Motown 5160
A wonderful late '60s album from the period when Smokey Robinson was still producing, writing for, and singing with the Miracles. They scored five R&B chart hits in 1969, among them the transcendent ballad "Baby, Baby, Don't Cry" and equally fine "Doggone Right" as well as his version of "Abraham, Martin and John." It's one of the few Miracles' releases that's close to being a genuine album rather than a collection of singles. —*Ron Wynn*

Time out For ... / 1969 / Motown 5437
Smokey Robinson was in peak form on this 1969 album, even though he would end his involvement with the group three years later. His voice was still splendid, his delivery and soaring falsetto magical, and his writing and production skills keen. The album boasted "Doggone Right" and "Here I Go Again" as its prime hit material and was done with the soulful charm and elegance that marked every Miracles record from the mid '60s until Robinson went solo in 1972. —*Ron Wynn*

★ **Anthology** / 1973 / Motown 0793
Detroit vocal group the Miracles were a fixture at Motown from day one. Driven by Robinson's superior writing and smooth, silky falsetto, the Miracles placed a stunning 48 singles on the *Billboard* charts, 39 of those with Smokey in tow. All but six are

included on this collection. Songs such as "Ooh Baby Baby," "The Tracks of My Tears," and "The Tears of a Clown" define much that was good about the '60s. As usual with Motown's reissues, the sound is substandard, and there is no decent set of liner notes. — *Rob Bowman*

☆ **Quiet Storm** / 1975 / Motown 5197
The landmark artistic release of Smokey Robinson's solo career. This album didn't equal the sales of his '80s LPs, but was extremely influential. Robinson linked the songs conceptually and produced the album with almost no breaks between selections. *A Quiet Storm* was as influential as Marvin Gaye's "What's Going On" or Isaac Hayes' "Hot Buttered Soul." It also spawned the rise of a new sound: adult soul aimed at a nonteen audience. Many radio stations aired various cuts unedited from this LP late at night or after dark. Soon an entire format was developed that emphasized adult ballads and played album cuts as much as, if not more than, edited singles. This format was called "The Quiet Storm." — *Ron Wynn*

Being with You / 1981 / Motown 12151
Smokey Robinson landed his first big album of the '80s with this release. The title track soared to the top on the R&B charts and stayed there, while it just missed topping the pop charts. Robinson's wonderful lead vocals, timing, dramatic delivery, and overall technique were as impressive as ever, and he got two more chart hits from the album. It eventually became his most successful LP ever from a commercial standpoint, although his artistic landmark as a solo artist remains *A Quiet Storm.* — *Ron Wynn*

○ **Blame It on Love and Other** / 1984 / Motown 5401
A fine compilation covering recent Smokey Robinson love songs and hits. While some of these lack the staying power and integrity of the Motown hits, they were certainly superior to much of what was being marketed as romantic fare. Robinson's ageless falsetto, masterful lyrics, and professionalism have enabled him to survive numerous trends and changes in both the business and among the audience. The success of these tracks reaffirmed his special qualities as one of the greatest performers in the history of American music. — *Ron Wynn*

One Heartbeat / 1987 / Motown 6226
Another superb Robinson album. He continued scoring hit singles throughout the '80s, and this time out the song "Just to See Her" was another huge pop and R&B smash, and the title track did almost as well. Robinson was thriving despite the fact hip-hop was steadily gaining strength, and New Jack Swing would soon force its way into the urban contemporary spotlight. — *Ron Wynn*

○ **Whatever Makes You Happy: More of the Best** / 1993 / Rhino 71181
Solid compilation of 18 of the most interesting nonhits from Smokey's (and Motown's) golden era. Culled from 11 albums, this is an intelligent and consistent overview of Robinson's relatively unknown tunes. These cuts show the stylistic evolution of Motown as surely as any greatest hits collection, moving from bluesy, raucous R&B to assembly-line soul to songs reflecting the lyrical and instrumental innovations of the psychedelic era. Robinson's peerless soul songwriting and the Miracles' smooth harmonies remained constant no matter what the era and make this a much more fluid set than you might expect. Ultimately, the songs don't boast hooks quite as memorable as their classic hit singles, despite their similarities in structure and production. The early '60s tracks are perhaps the record's most interesting, displaying a gritty, almost salacious approach that had yet to be toned down by slicker production values. — *Richie Unterberger*

☆ **Thirty-Fifth Anniversary Box** / 1994 / Motown
A splendid four-disc box set covering all the essential tracks Smokey Robinson and the Miracles ever recorded. — *AMG*

Tom Robinson

Vocals / New wave
Robinson emerged amid the British punk explosion with overtly political lyrics and a punkish pop sound. A former London folkster, he released his most successful album, *Power in the Darkness*, in 1978, which included the minor hit "2-4-6-8 Motorway." After a tamer followup inappropriately produced by Todd Rundgren, Robinson formed the short-lived, more electronic sounding Sector 27 in 1980. The singer subsequently abandoned

his political messages for more commercial rock in a series of albums during the '80s. — *David Szatmary*

● **Power in the Darkness** / 1978 / Razor + Tie 11778
Angry British political punk at its best. — *David Szatmary*

TRB Two / 1979 / Razor + Tie 11930
A good followup to a brilliant debut. — *David Szatmary*

Rockpile

Group / Rock & roll, pop/rock
During the late '70s, Rockpile was the touring band for both Dave Edmunds and Nick Lowe. Like Edmunds, the band was passionate about traditional rock & roll. Like Lowe, the band played with a reckless, trashy abandon. Driven by the powerful rhythm section of drummer Terry Williams and Lowe's bass, guitarists Billy Bremner and Edmunds were left free to spit out crushing rock, blues, rockabilly, and country licks. With their fierce live energy and unpretentious rock & roll, the band fit easily into the post-punk new wave at the end of the decade.

Although they only released one album as a group—1980's *Seconds of Pleasure*—the band provided support for most of the albums Lowe and Edmunds recorded in the late '70s. After the rushed release of *Seconds of Pleasure,* the band toured one last time before splitting apart, largely due to mismanagement. All of the members continued to occasionally collaborate with each other throughout the '80s. — *Stephen Thomas Erlewine*

○ **Seconds of Pleasure** / 1980 / Columbia 36886
Rockpile's only proper album is an inspired collection of old-fashioned rock & roll, which sounds vital because of the band's unrelenting energy and Nick Lowe's consistently inventive songwriting. The CD includes the bonus EP of Everly Brothers covers that was included in the album's original pressing. — *Stephen Thomas Erlewine*

Tommy Roe

b. May 9, 1942
Vocals / Pop
Widely perceived as one of the archetypal bubblegum artists of the late '60s, Tommy Roe cut some pretty decent rockers along the way, especially early in his career—many displaying some pretty prominent Buddy Holly roots. In fact, Roe's initial pop smash, 1962's chart-topping "Sheila," was quite reminiscent of Holly's "Peggy Sue," utilizing a very similar throbbing drumbeat and Roe's hiccuping vocal. The singer had previously cut the song for the smaller Judd label before remaking it in superior form for ABC-Paramount. The infectious "Everybody"—another hot item the next year—was waxed in Muscle Shoals at Rick Hall's Fame studios, normally an R&B-oriented facility (it's not widely known that Roe wrote songs for the Tams, a raw-edged soul group from his Atlanta hometown).

Once Roe veered off on his squeaky-clean bubblegum tangent, he stuck with it for the rest of the decade. His lighthearted "Sweet Pea" and "Hooray for Hazel" burned up the charts in 1966, and he was still at it three years later when he waxed his biggest hit, "Dizzy," and "Jam Up Jelly Tight." — *Bill Dahl*

○ **Greatest Hits** / 1993 / Onyx Classix 266112
With "Sheila," "Dizzy," and the rest, this is the place to start and finish. — *Dan Heilman*

The Rolling Stones

Group / Rock & roll
The Rolling Stones are the definitive rock & roll band and, by now, the longest-lived rock & roll band to remain consistently popular throughout their (30-year) career. The group came together in London, where singer Mick Jagger (b. July 26, 1943) and guitarist Keith Richards (b. December 18, 1943), who had been grade school classmates, joined with guitarist Brian Jones (February 28, 1942-July 3, 1969) and a rhythm section then consisting of pianist Ian Stewart, bassist Dick Taylor, and drummer Mick Avory (later of the Kinks) at a debut show at the Marquee on July 12, 1962. Taylor was replaced soon after by Bill Wyman (b. October 24, 1936), and Avory eventually by jazz drummer Charlie Watts (b. June 2, 1941).

The Rolling Stones played an eight-month residency at the Crawdaddy Club in 1963, during which they signed a management contract with Andrew "Loog" Oldham (who demoted Ian Steward to road manager) and a recording contract with Decca.

The group was devoted to playing Chicago blues and its off-shoots, notably the rock & roll of Chuck Berry, and its early records were either covers of such music or extremely derivative originals. The Stones' first single, for example, was a cover of Berry's "Come On." It was followed by "I Wanna Be Your Man," a song written for the Stones by John Lennon and Paul McCartney.

The Stones' first really successful single, however, was a version of Buddy Holly's "Not Fade Away," which reached #3 in England and became their first American chart entry. Their next five UK singles all hit #1, and by 1965 they had established themselves as second only to the Beatles as the most popular British rock group, a position they held until the Beatles broke up.

The important factor setting the Stones apart from their lesser competition was that they successfully moved from being a blues-rock cover band to being a band that performed primarily original pop-rock material with a blues base. Jagger and Richards turned into a songwriting team as early as 1964, and by 1965 such Stones hits as "The Last Time" and "(I Can't Get No) Satisfaction" were scoring on both sides of the Atlantic.

The Stones toured extensively in the mid '60s, with their success partially attributable to frontman Mick Jagger, who became the most prominent lead singer in rock. They followed many of the trends of the '60s as the decade wore on, and their involvement with drugs curtailed their ability to play in the United States after 1966. By that time, like the Beatles and others, their musical horizons had expanded to include a variety of eclectic styles. Unlike the Beatles, however, the Stones were never really comfortable with psychedelia, and after their 1967 *Sgt. Pepper* knock-off, *Their Satanic Majesties Request*, they returned to a more basic hard-rock style on the single "Jumpin' Jack Flash" and the album *Beggars Banquet*.

In 1969 the Stones reemerged as a concert attraction after firing Brian Jones (who died shortly after) and hiring guitarist Mick Taylor (b. January 17, 1948), who in turn was replaced by Ron Wood (b. June 1, 1947) in 1976. They released the single "Honky Tonk Women" and the album *Let It Bleed* and embarked on an American concert tour that culminated in the disastrous Altamont Festival. Despite that debacle, after the Beatles' split the following year, the Stones were undisputed in their claim to being "the greatest rock & roll band in the world."

In the '70s, the Stones toured every three years and released a series of million-selling, chart-topping albums, despite guitarist Keith Richards's descent into heroin addiction. The drug problem came to a head when Richards was arrested in Toronto in 1977. He subsequently cleaned up, however, and took a more active role in the Stones' creative efforts, resulting in improved albums in the late '70s and early '80s.

The band played a world tour 1981-1982 and continued actively into the mid '80s, but when Jagger made a solo album in 1985 and then refused to tour behind the Stones' 1986 *Dirty Work* album, their long career together seemed to be over. Richards reluctantly began work on a solo album and publicly voiced his anger. Jagger released a second solo album in 1987 and toured Japan in 1988, but by the time of the release of Richards's solo album, *Talk Is Cheap*, the Stones were in discussions about a reunion. A new album, *Steel Wheels*, was recorded and released in 1989, accompanied by another world tour lasting into 1990.

Bill Wyman left the group for good after the *Steel Wheels* tour. For a couple of years, the Stones had no bassist; they signed a multimillion-dollar deal with Virgin Records in 1992 as a four-piece. After all four members released solo records in 1992 and 1993, the band began auditioning bassists during rehearsals for their new album. Released in the summer of 1994, *Voodoo Lounge* was recorded with former Miles Davis and Sting bassist Darryl Jones; after the album's release, he was named as Wyman's permanent replacement. *—William Ruhlmann*

○ **Rolling Stones (England's Newest Hitmakers)** / May 30, 1964 / ABKCO 7375
The group's debut album, a bit bluesier and more acoustically textured than the sound they later became famous for, with the influence of Slim Harpo and Muddy Waters getting equal time with Chuck Berry and Bo Diddley. "Carol," "King Bee," and "Route 66" are just a few of the indispensable highlights. *—Bruce Eder*

☆ **12 X 5** / Oct. 17, 1964 / ABKCO 7402

A much more rock-oriented album than their debut, *12 X 5* is the album that solidified the group's Chuck Berry- and Bo Diddley-based sound, and on which guitarists Keith Richards and Brian Jones first flexed their muscles. *—Bruce Eder*

○ **Out of Our Heads** / Jul. 1965 / ABKCO 7429
The first of the American patchwork albums, assembled from sessions on two continents and some London concerts, and it all works—"Satisfaction" was the hit, but "I'm Alright" was a concert favorite for years. *—Bruce Eder*

○ **December's Children** / Jul. 1965 / ABKCO 7451
A much more artful release, compiled from various singles and album sessions. The blues material is subservient to rock numbers like "Get Off of My Cloud" and elegant R&B such as "You Better Move On." *—Bruce Eder*

○ **Rolling Stones Now!** / Jul. 1965 / ABKCO 7420
The group's second album is a louder blues record, moving toward rock, with Mick Jagger beginning to stretch out as a vocalist and the band hardening its sound. "Everybody Needs Somebody to Love" and "Mona" are among the best parts of a near-perfect record. *—Bruce Eder*

○ **Big Hits, Vol. 1** / Mar. 1966 / ABKCO 8001
Big Hits, Vol. 1 (High Tide & Green Grass) is a concise collection of the group's early hits, without any surprises. *—Bruce Eder*

☆ **Aftermath** / Jun. 1966 / ABKCO 7476
The group's most accomplished studio record of the '60s and the first to feature all Jagger-Richards originals. The sound also expands here to embrace the mild psychedelic/Eastern sound of "Paint It Black," and the barrier-bursting 10-minute-plus "Goin' Home," highlighted by Brian's workout on blues harp. *—Bruce Eder*

☆ **Between the Buttons** / Jan. 1967 / ABKCO 7499
A spaced-out, trippy mix of psychedelia, vaudeville, and Dylan homages that has worn well despite the inclusion of two hits ("Let's Spend the Night Together" and "Ruby Tuesday") that had nothing to do with the rest of it. A self-conscious album, and very theatrical. *—Bruce Eder*

Flowers / Jun. 1967 / ABKCO 7509
Somewhat repetitive collection of odd B sides and unanthologized singles that is worth owning just for the Bo Diddley-styled "Please Go Home." *—Bruce Eder*

Their Satanic Majesties Request / Nov. 1967 / ABKCO 8002
Underrated psychedelic venture by the Stones, who seem to lack confidence in their abilities and material (and lacked a producer at the time as well). The dross is balanced out by a couple of minor hits ("2000 Light Years from Home," "She's a Rainbow") and a couple of brilliant album tracks ("2000 Man" and "Citadel"). *—Bruce Eder*

☆ **Beggars Banquet** / Nov. 1968 / ABKCO 7539
The group's newly matured sound came together on this album, a mixture of blues and politics that proved almost too controversial to release at the time. "Salt of the Earth," "Parachute Woman," "Street Fighting Man," and "Jigsaw Puzzle" make it worthwhile. *—Bruce Eder*

☆ **Let It Bleed** / Nov. 28, 1969 / ABKCO 8004
A coda to the Brian Jones era, and the start of the Mick Taylor era, with a dazzling collection of numbers ("Gimme Shelter," "Midnight Rambler," "Love in Vain," "You Can't Always Get What You Want," "Let It Bleed," and so on), most of which figured prominently in the group's subsequent tour. *—Bruce Eder*

☆ **Get Yer Ya-Ya's Out** / Sep. 4, 1970 / ABKCO 8005
This live album, released largely to counteract the effect of the bootleg *Liver Than You'll Ever Be*, captured the new-era Stones in their top form, doing all of the key material from their preceding pair of albums. *—Bruce Eder*

☆ **Sticky Fingers** / Apr. 23, 1971 / Virgin 39255
A ballsy, bluesy masterpiece made up of leftovers and works in progress from the preceding two years, including "Wild Horses," "Brown Sugar," and "Sister Morphine." *—Bruce Eder*

● **Hot Rocks 1964-1971** / Jan. 1972 / ABKCO 6667
A straightforward hits package (1964-1971) and a radio programmer's dream. Includes "Satisfaction," "Gimme Shelter," "Brown Sugar," and many more of their greatest hits and album tracks. *—Bruce Eder*

☆ **Exile on Main Street** / May 12, 1972 / Virgin 39524

Originally rock's most musically successful double album, this epic collection has aged magnificently. Includes the hit "Tumbling Dice," as well as "Rocks Off," "Happy," "Rip This Joint," and "Sweet Virginia." —*Bruce Eder*

● **More Hot Rocks (Big Hits and Fazed Cookies)** / Nov. 1972 / ABKCO 6267
Highlighted by a unique stereo edition of "It's All Over Now." Often thought of as secondary, this anthology is really a lot more interesting than *Hot Rocks*. —*Bruce Eder*

Goats Head Soup / Aug. 31, 1973 / Virgin 39519
Compared to the monumental *Exile on Main St.*, *Goats Head Soup* is bound to sound inferior, and it does. Nevertheless, the album doesn't deserve its bad reputation. It might be careless and decadent, but that excess is quite intoxicating, as the nasty rocker "Star Star" and the finely crafted ballad "Angie" prove. —*Stephen Thomas Erlewine*

○ **It's Only Rock and Roll** / Oct. 18, 1974 / Virgin 39522
It's uneven, but at times *It's Only Rock and Roll* catches fire. The songs and performances are stronger than those on *Goats Head Soup;* the tossed-off numbers sound effortless, not careless. Throughout the Stones wear their title as the "World's Greatest Rock & Roll Band" with a defiant smirk, which makes the bitter cynicism of "If You Can't Rock Me" and the title track all the more striking and the reggae experimentation of "Luxury," the aching beauty of "Time Waits for No One," and the agreeable filler of "Dance Little Sister" and "Short and Curlies" all the more enjoyable. —*Stephen Thomas Erlewine*

Black & Blue / Apr. 20, 1976 / Virgin 39520
Ron Wood's first album with the Stones finds the band work through a number of reggae and funk-tinged numbers, trying to expand their sound. Consequently, songs are sacrificed for grooves; only the ballads "Memory Motel" and "Fool to Cry" are fully developed, but the grooves that dominate the album are strong enough to make the record successful. —*Stephen Thomas Erlewine*

☆ **Some Girls** / Jun. 9, 1978 / Virgin 39526
A nasty hard-rocking album, *Some Girls* finds the Stones turning out a set effortlessly brilliant and eclectic set of material, encompassing the disco pulse of "Miss You," the sleazy snarl of "When the Whip Comes Down," the campy country of "Far Away Eyes," the moving ballad "Beast of Burden," and Keith's best outlaw song, "Before They Make Me Run." —*Stephen Thomas Erlewine*

Emotional Rescue / Jun. 23, 1980 / Virgin 39523
While it isn't a great album, *Emotional Rescue* is a good album. The Stones have made a set of skillfully crafted pop/rock numbers that embrace disco and new wave to a greater extent than *Some Girls*, and when *Emotional Rescue* is on- as on "She's So Cold," "Where the Boys Go," "Send It to Me," and the hypnotic, pulsing title track—it is damn good. —*Stephen Thomas Erlewine*

○ **Tattoo You** / Aug. 30, 1981 / Virgin 39521
Tattoo You remains the Stones' last great album. While the rockers on side one provide some sparks, the heart of the album lies in the second side with the gorgeous ballads "Worried about You" and "Waiting on a Friend." —*Stephen Thomas Erlewine*

Undercover / Nov. 7, 1983 / Virgin 39649
A glorious return to form, with topical politics, sex, and decadence all colliding to create some memorable sparks. In addition to the title track, "She Was Hot" was also a hit and managed to create a fair amount of controversy with its subject matter and the accompanying video clip. —*Bruce Eder*

Rewind (1971-1984) / 1984 / Rolling Stones 40505
A collection of material from 1971 through 1984. —*Bruce Eder*

Dirty Work / 1986 / Virgin 39648
At its best, *Dirty Work* captures the sparks that were flying between Mick and Keith during the album's recording; at its worst, it's simply a competent collection of hard rock, spiked with some unnecessary synthesizers. —*Stephen Thomas Erlewine*

☆ **Singles Collection: The London Years** / 1989 / ABKCO 1218
The best individual collection of their classic hits ever assembled, for sound and content. —*Bruce Eder*

Steel Wheels / 1989 / Virgin
The band's best album of the '80s, embracing blues, classic rock, and even psychedelia ("Continental Drift"). —*Bruce Eder*

Voodoo Lounge / 1994 / Virgin

While *Voodoo Lounge* sounds amazingly like the Stones' classic records from the early '70s, it's rather inconsistent and too long to make it one of their major works. Instead, it's simply another solid Stones record with some fine tracks and typically strong playing. —*Stephen Thomas Erlewine*

Henry Rollins

Vocals / Alternative rock
In the '90s, Henry Rollins emerged as a post-punk renaissance man, without the self-conscious trappings that plagued such '80s self-conscious artists as David Byrne. Since Black Flag's break-up in 1986, Rollins has been relentlessly busy, recording albums with the Rollins Band, writing books and poetry, performing spoken word tours, written a magazine column in *Details*, acting in several movies, and, most surprisingly, appearing on MTV as an occasional VJ. All the while, he has kept his artistic integrity, becoming a kind of father figure for many alternative bands of the '90s.

The Rollins Band's records are uncompromising, intense, cathartic fusions of hard-rock, funk, post-punk noise, and jazz experimentalism, with Rollins shouting angry, biting self-examinations and accusations over the grind. On his spoken word albums, he is remarkably more relaxed, showcasing a hilariously self-deprecating sense of humor that is often absent in his music. —*Stephen Thomas Erlewine*

○ **Hot Animal Machine** / 1987 / Texas Hotel 23
A good solo effort, raw and powerful. This CD includes the EP *Drive by Shootings*. —*John Dougan*

Turned On / 1990 / Quarterstick 02
A perfect example of the Rollins Band at work, recorded live in Vienna, Austria, in 1989 with some of his best songs from that era. Recorded digitally, but the CD treats the entire recording as one track. —*John Book*

● **The End of Silence** / Jan. 1992 / Imago 21006
Intense is the only word that can describe Henry Rollins, and his band is the most intense unit recording today. *The End of Silence* is arguably the Rollins Band's best effort to date, full of angry, abrasive hardcore/jazz fusion, highlight by the crushing "Low Self Opinion." —*Stephen Thomas Erlewine*

○ **Deep Throat** / Feb. 1992 / Quarterstick 13
All of Rollins's early spoken-words releases are gathered in the reasonably priced six-disc box set *Deep Throat*. As with each of his spoken albums, Rollins is incisive, moving, self-effacing, and very funny; it's worth the price of the discs. —*Stephen Thomas Erlewine*

● **Rollins: The Boxed Life** / 1993 / Imago 21009
Rollins's spoken word records are comedy records, more like Lenny Bruce or Richard Pryor than Andrew Dice Clay or Eddie Murphy. Underneath all the laughter there are some serious themes; the humor is drawn from pain. But the main reason to hear *The Boxed Life* (or any of Rollins's spoken-word records) is that he's a superb storyteller with a wicked sense of humor. Some of the topics are squeamish (animal testing, safe sex, depression), and there is a generous helping of profanity, but it is genuinely funny and moving. —*Stephen Thomas Erlewine*

○ **Weight** / Apr. 12, 1994 / Imago 21034
The latest effort from the Rollins Band is able to mix the musicians' love for jazz with a blindingly direct hard-rock assault, making a twisted form of metal-jazz. Rollins' lyrics have also begun to move away from his relentless self-examination, adding a touch of the self-effacing humor that distinguishes his spoken records. The new lyrical dimension adds depth to the band's music, making *Weight* the most impressive album they have released to date. —*Stephen Thomas Erlewine*

Romantics

Group / Power pop, pop/rock
In the early '80s, the Romantics were a terrific rock band, joyously tearing through loose, infectious power pop gems like the classic "What I Like about You." After two albums of energetic pop/rock, the band shifted its direction to a slicker, more radio-friendly pop; the change of style worked, resulting in the hit singles "Talking in Your Sleep" and "One in a Million" in 1983. Surprisingly, their drummer Jimmy Marinos left after their success; the band recorded one more album in 1985 before breaking up.

In the early '90s, "What I Like about You" began appearing in television commercials, leading the band to reunite; they have recorded one EP and have toured several times since reforming. —*Stephen Thomas Erlewine*

● **What I Like about You (& Other Romantic Hits)** / 1991 / Nemperor 47043
The title track was their finest hour, but there are a couple of other hits here too. —*Dan Heilman*

The Ronettes
R&B, rock & roll
Before Phil Spector took them under his wing in the early '60s, the Ronettes had already recorded several singles and were regionally successful. But the Spector-produced records are what everyone remembers, and for a good reason—they featured some of his biggest, best productions along with equally impressive songs. Beneath his monumental wall of sound, lead vocalist Ronnie Bennett, who would later marry Spector, sang songs of teenage love in a plain, girlish voice; "Be My Baby," the group's first and biggest hit, was the pinnacle of the group's talent, as well as the producer's. None of their following singles were quite as successful commercially, although they were nearly as strong artistically. While Spector was inactive in the mid '60s, the Ronettes were also inactive; together they reemerged in 1969 to a small commerical reception. After Ronnie divorced Spector in 1973, she formed a new version of the Ronettes that lasted for three years; after the group disbanded, she launched a solo career. —*Stephen Thomas Erlewine*

○ **Ronettes: The Early Years** / 1965 / Rhino 70524
The early Ronettes' songs weren't as immaculately produced or as evocative as Phil Spector's productions. Their sound was more generic and resembled other girl groups like the Shirelles or Chiffons. They recorded for Colpix and Dimension during 1961 and 1962, with Veronica (Ronnie) Bennett (later Ronnie Spector) doing most of the leads, while her sister Estelle and cousin Nedra added soothing harmonies and backgrounds. At times, as on "My Guiding Angel" or "You Bet I Would," they came close to the appealing mix of innocence and earnestness that characterized their later (and greatest) tracks. But despite getting material from such songwriters as Jackie DeShannon and Carole King, many of these cuts were more serviceable than classic. Still, here's the foundation for the sound that exploded in the mid '60s, when Spector's production gave the Ronettes the final ingredient they needed for superstardom. —*Ron Wynn*

★ **Best of the Ronettes** / 1992 / ABKCO 7212
For a couple of years, the Ronettes made music that was as moving and unforgettable as any made during the rock era. Their voices merged sensuality, longing, innocence, and sentimentality, with Ronnie (Bennett) Spector's angelic leads framed by Phil Spector's sweeping production, the lyrics of Ellie Greenwich, Jeff Barry, Barry Mann, Cynthia Weil, Spector, and others, plus the backing and sighs of her sister Estelle and cousin Nedra. While such songs as "Walking in the Rain," "Be My Baby," "Baby, I Love You," and "(The Best Part) of Breakin' Up" may seem hopelessly naive and possibly sexist in today's cynical world, they're still classic love poems. Ronnie Spector's voice retains its allure and appeal, and the 18 tracks on this CD will never become dated. —*Ron Wynn*

Linda Ronstadt
b. Jul. 15, 1946, Tucson, AZ
Vocals / Pop/rock, country rock, pop
Coming out of the Los Angeles folk music coffeehouse circuit in the mid '60s with her original group, the Stone Poneys, Ronstadt was an early proponent of the country-rock movement spearheaded by groups like Poco and the Eagles, who were originally her backup band. With wide-ranging tastes and spot-on intonation, the sweet-voiced Ronstadt has dealt with many different styles in the intervening years with great popular success. —*Dan Heilman*

☆ **Heart Like a Wheel** / 1974 / Capitol 46073
Ronstadt's breakthrough album, and her most perfectly realized. Solid from top to bottom, featuring the title track, "When Will I Be Loved?" "Desperado," and "You're No Good." Essential. —*Cub Koda*

● **Greatest Hits, Vol. 1** / 1976 / Asylum 106
A concise collection of her chart successes. —*Dan Heilman*

○ **Retrospective** / 1977 / Capitol 11629
A nice compilation of primarily country-influenced, prehit material. —*Cub Koda*

Greatest Hits, Vol. 2 / 1980 / Asylum 516
Her next dozen hits, more formulaic in content, but bigger on the charts. —*Cub Koda*

○ **What's New** / 1983 / Asylum 60260
Some of Ronstadt's best work to date—her first collaboration with bandleader Nelson Riddle ('40s and '50s standards). —*Cub Koda*

Canciones De Mi Padre / 1987 / Asylum 60765
Rondstadt's first all-Spanish album is a heartfelt tribute to her heritage. It also contains some of her finest performances of the '80s. —*AMG*

Diana Ross
b. Mar. 26, 1944, Detroit, MI
Vocals / Pop/rock, soul, disco
Diana Ross, protege of Motown president Berry Gordy, stepped out of the Supremes in 1970 for a solo career that has included successes on record, stage, and film. As lead singer of the Supremes and as a soloist, she has had more #1 records than any other female artist in history. She left Motown for RCA in 1981, a move that diminished her record-selling power. Today she is back at Motown searching for a new musical identity. —*Rick A. Bueche*

○ **Diana's Duets** / 1970 / Motown 5214
An excellent collection featuring Diana Ross singing with the Temptations, Stevie Wonder, Smokey Robinson, the Supremes, and Marvin Gaye. These songs, all brilliantly produced and arranged with wonderful lyrics, show how great a vocalist Ross was before she became weighed down with being a star and celebrity. Her delivery, vocal range, lyric interpretations, and performances are so much better than what she turned in during the late '70s and '80s that it's amazing. While her album with Marvin Gaye might be her best single duet work, this anthology will more than fit the bill. —*Ron Wynn*

○ **Diana Ross** / May 1970 / Motown 5294
This remains arguably her finest solo work at Motown, and perhaps her best ever; it was certainly among her most stunning. Everyone who doubted whether Diana Ross could sustain a career outside the Supremes found out immediately that she would be a star. The single "Reach Out and Touch (Somebody's Hand)" remains a staple in her shows and is still her finest message track. —*Ron Wynn*

Lady Sings the Blues / Dec. 1972 / Motown 0758
Diana Ross forever ended any association with the Supremes after this film. She not only got an Oscar nomination and more roles but also really captured the spirit and flavor, if not the sound and timbre, of Billie Holiday's music. The film was woefully inaccurate and more of a soap opera than a portrait of a great but troubled vocalist. Ross's performance was the only saving grace. —*Ron Wynn*

Diana Ross / 1977 / Motown 5135
Diana Ross landed one of the decade's definitive singles with "Love Hangover," instantly making this a major hit album. While it surprisingly didn't sell as well as some '80s LPs, the single was a double chart topper and also a huge club hit for much of the next two years. It vaulted the album into the pop Top 10 and even managed to break the followup single onto the charts. —*Ron Wynn*

● **All the Great Hits** / Oct. 1981 / Motown 0960
Yet another Motown anthology/greatest hits package. The songs are fine, and the mastering is good. It's really a question of choice and need. If you want everything, get either the new Ross boxed set or the original anthology. If you only want a few hits, then either this or any other package will suffice. —*Ron Wynn*

★ **Anthology** / May 1983 / Motown 6049
A complete collection of nonstop Motown hits. A must-have. —*Rick A. Bueche*

Forever Diana: Musical Memoirs / Oct. 5, 1993 / Motown 6357
Plagued by inferior sound and poor track selection, *Forever Diana* is a major disappointment for fans. Only one disc is devoted to the Supremes, with Ross's spotty solo career occupying the other three discs, featuring markedly worse sound than pre-

vious Motown releases. Besides poor audio, the liner notes are skimpy and incomplete. Ultimately, *Forever Diana* is a wasted opportunity. —*Stephen Thomas Erlewine*

David Lee Roth

b. Oct. 10, 1955, Bloomington, IN
Vocals / Hard rock, pop/rock, heavy metal
With Van Halen, vocalist David Lee Roth raised the role of a heavy metal frontman to a performance art. Once he left the band in 1985, he released an EP that displayed his blatant pop roots, covering everything from the Beach Boys to Louis Prima. For his first full-length album, 1986's *Eat 'Em and Smile*, Roth hired instrumental big-guns guitarist Steve Vai and bassist Billy Sheehan for a grossly exaggerated take on heavy arena rock. With this album, Roth's showmanship and tongue-in-cheek humor were enormously inflated. It was a mammoth hit, as was the more pop-oriented follow-up, *Skyscaper*. After *Skyscraper*, Vai and Sheehan left to form their own bands. Roth put together a new band for 1991's *A Little Ain't Enough*, which marked his first commercial decline. Sensing that it was time for a change, he tried to refashion himself as a hard-rock singer-songwriter with 1994's *Your Filthy Little Mouth*, but it resulted in his least successful album yet. —*Stephen Thomas Erlewine*

○ **Crazy from the Heat** / 1985 / Warner Brothers 25222
For his first solo effort, Roth stripped away the gonzo guitars that are Van Halen's trademark and accentuated his lounge lizard as rock star persona, resulting in an EP that succeeds *because* of his persona, not because the music is anything special. Certainly, he doesn't add anything to "California Girls" and "Just a Gigolo/I Ain't Got Nobody" other than his joking, over-the-top vocals. Then again, that's all he needs to do. —*Stephen Thomas Erlewine*

● **Eat 'Em & Smile** / 1986 / Warner Brothers 25470
This flamboyant frontman is flanked by bassist Billy Sheehan and guitar-shredder Steve Vai, blazing the solo trail with these big and bawdy rockers, like "Goin' Crazy!" —*Donna DiChario*

Skyscraper / 1988 / Warner Brothers 25671
On his second full-length solo album, Roth turns down the guitars, adds more melody, and makes a more polished, but less interesting record, highlighted by the soaring pop of "Just Like Paradise." —*Stephen Thomas Erlewine*

Roxette

Group / Pop/rock
It's tempting to write Roxette off as nothing more than a shallow pop/rock band, but their shameless hooks are precisely what makes them so enjoyable. Roxette has a knack for writing extremely catchy and simple hooks and melodies that are sweet but not saccharine; it's radio-friendly pop, but the hooks don't wear thin with repeated plays. The duo of guitarist Per Gessle and vocalist Marie Fredriksson released an album in 1986 that didn't display much of their talents, but the infectious follow-up, 1988's *Look Sharp*, brought them to the top of the charts in America and England; 1991's *Joyride* was almost equally successful. After a couple of years off, Roxette returned with a new album in 1994. —*Stephen Thomas Erlewine*

● **Look Sharp** / 1988 / EMI America 91098
A fun, dynamic debut, featuring the hit singles "The Look," "Dressed for Success," "Listen to Your Heart," and "Dangerous." —*Dan Heilman*

○ **Joyride** / 1991 / EMI America 94435
Their second album, featuring infectious, solid song construction from Gessle and dynamite singing from Fredriksson. "Knock on Every Door," "Watercolours in the Rain," and the title track are among the highlights. —*Cub Koda*

Tourism (Songs from Studios, Stages, Hotelrooms & Other Strange Places) / 1992 / EMI America 99929
A completely live hits package from Roxette's first world tour (1991-1992). This features both concert and in-studio performances of some of their biggest hits, including "Joyride," "The Look," and "It Must Have Been Love." Recorded in their native Stockholm as well as in Zurich, Buenos Aires, and Sydney, Australia. —*Stephen Thomas Erlewine*

Roxy Music

Group / Progressive rock

Roxy Music scored enormous success in its native England in the '70s, first as a leader of the glam-rock movement and later for its sophisticated sound. The group was formed in London in 1971 around lead singer Bryan Ferry (b. September 26, 1945). Personnel came and went until the group solidified by the time of its 1972 debut album with a lineup of Ferry, reed player Andy Mackay (b. July 23, 1946), guitarist Phil Manzanera (b. January 31, 1951), keyboardist Brian Eno (b. May 15, 1948), and drummer Paul Thompson (b. May 13, 1951). The band's original bassist, Graham Simpson, left during the album sessions and was replaced initially by Rik Kenton, though the group employed a series of bassists throughout its career.

Roxy Music was a Top 10 UK hit in the summer of 1972, spinning off the Top 10 single "Virginia Plain." *For Your Pleasure* (1973) did even better, getting to #4. Eno had left the band by the time it made its third album, *Stranded* (going on to an extensive career as a solo artist and record producer), and was replaced by Eddie Jobson (b. April 28, 1955), who played violin and keyboards. *Stranded* was another UK hit, going to #1, and it was followed by *Country Life*, Roxy Music's first album to sell in even modest numbers in the United States. *Siren* (1975) contained the American Top 30 hit "Love Is the Drug" (#2 in the United Kingdom).

At the point of American commercial breakthrough, however, Roxy Music disbanded, with Ferry, Mackay, Manzanera, and Jobson going off to solo careers. The group reformed in 1978, minus Jobson, and recorded *Manifesto* (1979), after which Thompson left. The remaining trio released *Flesh and Blood* and *Avalon* (the latter was Roxy's only U.S. gold album), albums made in a smooth, melodic art-rock style before the group folded again in 1983. — *William Ruhlmann*

For Your Pleasure / 1973 / Reprise 26040
For Your Pleasure, Roxy's schizophrenic second album, vacillates between campy rockers like "Do the Strand" and "Editions of You" (both UK hits) and creepy mood pieces like "In Every Dream Home a Heartache" (an ode to an inflatable sex doll) and the title cut, which showcases lead singer Bryan Ferry's goulish croon over an instrumental track that would work well on "Twin Peaks." —*Rick Clark*

○ **Stranded** / 1973 / Reprise 26041
On *Stranded*, their first album without sound manipulator Brian Eno, Roxy affected a more sophisticated, self-absorbed stance with elegant numbers like "A Song for Europe" and "Psalm." Roxy's penchant for fine oddball pop-rockers continued with "Street Life," "Amazona," and the soaring "Serenade." —*Rick Clark*

☆ **Country Life** / 1974 / Reprise 26042
Arguably their best album, *Country Life's* everything-and-the-kitchen-sink art-rock production and steely dissonance reached a pinnacle with tracks like the "The Thrill of It All," "All I Want Is You," and "Casanova." "Out of the Blue," one of their finest songs, showcased Eddie Jobson on a powerfully phase-shifted violin solo. The beautifully unsettling "Bitter-Sweet" reflected Bryan Ferry's flirtation with Germanic melodicism and fascist imagery. —*Rick Clark*

☆ **Siren** / 1975 / Reprise 26043
Siren provided Roxy Music with their first international hit, the coolly funky "Love Is the Drug." Except for "Sentimental Fool," "Both Ends Burning," and "Whirlwind," most of this album fails to deliver the power or memorable melodies of either *Country Life* or *Stranded*. —*Rick Clark*

Viva! / 1976 / Reprise 26044
While their studio work is the place to start with this group, this is a good live set. —*Rick Clark*

○ **Manifesto** / 1979 / Reprise 26046
After a four-year layoff, Roxy shed their aggressively dense rock sound and returned with a more streamlined (but still weird) danceable pop. Detractors claimed that the band had lost their edge, but *Manifesto* introduced Roxy Music to a new audience looking for a sophisticated alternative to generic late '70s disco. Highlights include "Angel Eyes," "Dance Away," and the title cut. —*Rick Clark*

Flesh & Blood / 1980 / Reprise 26075
Flesh & Blood finds Roxy making a further transition away from dissonant arrangements. The sleepwalking delivery of "In the Midnight Hour" is oddly fascinating, as is the discoish streamlin-

ing of the Byrds's classic "Eight Miles High." Nevertheless, many of the originals lack any memorable qualities. —*Rick Clark*

☆ **Avalon** / 1981 / Reprise 23686
From the beautifully longing romanticism of Bryan Ferry's melodies to the dreamy soundscapes rendered by Rhett Davies, Roxy Music, and Bob Clearmountain, *Avalon* is fashion-plate cool, yet somehow exudes a weird, intoxicating kind of detached soulfulness that makes this one of the most elegant-sounding releases ever committed to disc. —*Rick Clark*

○ **Atlantic Years (1973-1980)** / 1983 / Atco 90122
Atlantic Years (1973-1980) provides the cream of *Flesh & Blood* and *Manifesto* (as well as a couple of key tracks from Roxy's earlier work on Reprise). Overall it lacks the substance of the original 1977 Atco *Greatest Hits* package, which was an essential showcase for their earlier work. —*Rick Clark*

● **Street Life: 20 Greatest Hits** / 1986 / Reprise 25857
This compilation is a more general (not entirely satisfactory) overview of Roxy tracks and Bryan Ferry's urbane dance-pop hits. —*Rick Clark*

Rufus & Chaka Khan

Group / Funk, soul
Rufus was one of the most commercially successsful funk bands of the mid '70s, primarily because lead vocalist Chaka Khan was a dynamic singer, capable of making even the band's pedestrian material seem interesting. Their self-titled debut album suffered from a lack of strong single material, but the follow-up featured Stevie Wonder's "Tell Me Something Good," which he wrote specifically for the band after hearing Khan sing; it became a #3 hit single. After that song, the hits kept coming until the end of the '70s. Chaka Khan began a solo career that eventually eclipsed Rufus's success in 1978, continuing to record with the band until 1983; the group fell apart shortly after her departure. —*Stephen Thomas Erlewine*

○ **Rufusized** / 1974 / MCA 10236
With the addition of guitarist-songwriter Tony Maiden, Rufus delivers one of their best albums. It features the hits "Once You Get Started" and "Please Pardon Me (You Remind Me of a Friend)." —*Rick Clark*

● **Rags to Rufus** / 1974 / MCA 31365
From the hard-funk opener of "You Got the Love" to the Stevie Wonder-penned "Tell Me Something Good," *Rags to Rufus* is a fine showcase for Chaka Khan's amazing vocals. Even though it's not one of their best albums, fans will definitely enjoy this effort. —*Rick Clark*

Rufus Featuring Chaka Khan / 1975 / MCA 31373
Rufus continued their string of successful albums with this 1975 release, featuring the mellow soul of "Sweet Thing," a million-seller, as well as jolting funk tunes like "Dance wit Me." —*Bil Carpenter*

Ask Rufus / 1977 / MCA 10449
This solid album includes "Hollywood" and "At Midnight (My Love Will Lift You Up)." —*Rick Clark*

The Runaways

b. 1975, d. 1980
Group / Hard rock, heavy metal
Rock & roll band featuring vocalist Cherie Currie and guitarists Joan Jett and Lita Ford. Organized by producer Kim Fowley in 1976, their raw, punkish style became a cult item in Japan and Europe, but unfortunately never connected with any kind of mainstream success stateside until Jett and Ford each went solo. —*Cub Koda*

○ **Runaways** / 1976 / Mercury 3079
Their debut album, produced by mentor Kim Fowley, loaded with excitement and featuring the classic "Cherry Bomb." —*Cub Koda*

○ **Queens of Noise** / 1977 / Mercury 3080
Their definitive statement, with Joan Jett taking over lead-singing chores on six of the 10 tracks. The title cut says it all. —*Cub Koda*

● **Best of the Runaways** / 1987 / Mercury 826279
A good collection of the Runaways' finest moments, *Best of the Runaways* is the only consistently enjoyable disc from these trashy hard-rockers. —*Stephen Thomas Erlewine*

Todd Rundgren
....
b. Jun. 22, 1948, Upper Darby, PA
Vocals / Pop/rock
Over the course of his lengthy career, Todd Rundgren (b. June 22, 1948) has created some of popular music's finer moments, as well as some of its most frustrating. He has proven to be a master of great pop melodies (with influences from the Beatles to Philly Soul) and heartfelt lyrical sentiment, while also releasing albums of tedious prog-rock that only a diehard fan could care about. At times Rundgren's productions seemed to have existed independently of the music, rather than enhancing it; nevertheless, Rundgren is an influential Renaissance man in the history of rock. Rundgren's first taste of success came with the psychedelic pop-rock group Nazz, in 1967. "Hello, It's Me" charted twice, while the heavily phased riff-rocker "Open My Eyes" became a signature tune of sorts. Rundgren left Nazz (future Cheap Trick guitarist Rick Nielson was his replacement) and pursued a solo career with his 1971 debut *Runt*.

Something/Anything, Rundgren's third album, was his finest showcase as a songwriter. It was during this time that Rundgren began making a name for himself as an innovative producer. Over the years he has worked on projects for Badfinger, New York Dolls, Foghat, Patti Smith, Cheap Trick, XTC, Meat Loaf, and others. In 1974 Rundgren formed Utopia, a quartet that helped fulfill his prog-rock tendencies. By the late '70s, Rundgren was actively exploring the medium of rock video, opening his own computer video studio in Woodstock, NY. He continues to produce various artists and to release solo albums that enjoy a solid cult success. —*Rick Clark*

○ **Runt** / 1970 / Rhino 70862
Runt, Todd Rundgren's debut, might have been a little uneven, but its homemade production, spirited arrangements, and great tunes like "We Gotta Get You a Woman" and "I'm in the Clique," made this one of the most appealing albums of his career. —*Rick Clark*

Runt: Ballad of Todd Rundgren / 1971 / Rhino 70863
Rundgren's sophomore release didn't contain the flashes of brilliance found on *Runt*, but "Be Nice to Me," "Parole," and "Remember Me" are standouts on this relatively low-key effort. —*Rick Clark*

★ **Something/Anything?** / 1972 / Rhino 71107
From beginning to end, *Something/Anything?* is Rundgren's best album, featuring the hit singles "I Saw the Light" and "Hello, It's Me." There are also a load of gems like "It Wouldn't Have Made Any Difference," "Wolfman Jack," and "Couldn't I Just Tell You," one of the finest power-pop tracks ever cut. Rundgren plays every instrument and sings all the parts on three-fourths of this self-produced release. Even though Rundgren had flashes of brilliance after *Something/Anything?* he never came up with an album with performances and material as consistently satisfying. —*Rick Clark*

○ **A Wizard a True Star** / 1973 / Rhino 70864
Rundgren's keen sense for writing tight pop songs is almost nowhere to be found on this over-the-top production job. That's not to say that *A Wizard a True Star* doesn't have its virtues. Rundgren's take on *Peter Pan*'s "Never Never Land" is otherworldly, and his Philly-soul medley is quite fine. "International Feel" and "Just One Victory" are other standout tracks. —*Rick Clark*

Faithful / 1976 / Rhino 70868
One half of this outing features Rundgren delivering almost letter-perfect versions of '60s classics like "Good Vibrations" and "Rain," which are impressive in their attention to detail but sound strangely lifeless. On the other half of the album, he delivers some of his best work since *Something/Anything?* particularly on "Black & White" and "When I Pray." —*Rick Clark*

○ **Hermit of Mink Hollow** / 1978 / Rhino 70871
By the release of this album, Rundgren had ditched the homemade charm of *Something/Anything?* for a warbly hard-rock/pop sound. Tracks like "Determination," "Out of Control," "You Cried Wolf," and "Fade Away" best exemplify that approach. "Can We Still Be Friends" became a hit. —*Rick Clark*

○ **Ever Popular Tortured Artist** / 1983 / Rhino 70896

This album, one of Rundgren's best do-it-yourself efforts of the '80s, contains his hit "Bang the Drum All Day" and a swell remake of Small Faces's "Tin Soldier." —*Rick Clark*

● **Anthology (1968-1985)** / 1986 / Rhino 71491
Anthology is a fairly comprehensive overview of Rundgren's entire career, starting with "Open My Eyes" by Nazz and including "Something to Fall Back On," from Rundgren's 1985 solo album *A Cappella*. All of his radio hits are included, as well as many important album tracks. Nevertheless, there are several key tracks missing, like "Wolfman Jack," "International Feel/Never Never Land," and Nazz's "Forget All about It" and "Hang On Paul." Like all of Rundgren's reissues on Rhino, *Anthology* has been given a first-class remastering job. —*Rick Clark*

Rush

Group / Hard rock, progressive rock
Inspired by Cream, Led Zeppelin, and Jimi Hendrix, the Toronto, Canada, power trio Rush formed in 1969, comprising guitarist Alex Lifeson, bassist Geddy Lee, and original drummer John Rutsey—later replaced by Neil Peart. Their first few albums were rather pedestrian hard rock, but the addition of Peart in 1974 prodded the group into a more complicated, heavy art-rock mode: King Crimson and Yes meet Led Zeppelin.

"The Trees," metaphorically addressing the Quebec secessionist movement (off of 1978's #47 *Hemispheres*) became a controversial rock-radio hit. The 1980 album *Permanent Waves*, containing two substantial AOR hits with "Freewill" and "Spirit of the Radio", marked the beginning of a golden period for the band, which peaked with the #3 followup *Moving Pictures*.

Rush briefly flirted with a more synthesized sound, sublimating the band's natural interplay. Fortunately, recent albums indicate Rush is back in top form with *Presto* and *Roll the Bones*. — *Rick Clark*

○ **2112** / 1976 / Mercury 822545
Rush's first successful stab at a concept album. Like many of Rush's albums during the '70s, this one deals with a futuristic scenario where an individual triumphs over an impersonalized high-tech society. —*Rick Clark*

A Farewell to Kings / 1977 / Mercury 822546
Rush continues to explore their sci-fi fantasy themes and lofty concepts with this effort, which featured "Closer to the Heart," a substantial FM rock hit that also went #76 pop. —*Rick Clark*

Hemispheres / 1978 / Mercury 822547
Includes the FM hit "The Trees," which can be found on *Chronicles*. Their extended pieces here aren't among their best, but the playing and dynamics of the arrangements keep things fairly interesting. —*Rick Clark*

○ **Permanent Waves** / 1980 / Mercury 822548
The cumulative effect of endless tours and obvious growth with each studio effort, Rush hit it big with this effort, delivering with their best material to date. "Spirit of the Radio," "Freewill," and "Entre Nous" were big FM rock hits. "Jacob's Ladder" was another highlight. —*Rick Clark*

★ **Moving Pictures** / 1981 / Mercury 800048
On *Moving Pictures*, Rush's aggressive prog-rock hit a zenith, with challenging playing that never became formless or devoid of good melodic integrity. The trio's active ensemble work reached new levels of interplay. "Tom Sawyer," "Limelight," "Red Barchetta," and the instrumental "YYZ" are standouts. —*Rick Clark*

○ **Exit Stage Left** / 1981 / Mercury 822551
A good live collection, possibly the best of their three such releases. —*Rick Clark*

○ **Signals** / 1982 / Mercury 810002
The third in a trio of great albums. "Digital Man" and "Analog Kid" are powerful riff-rockers. "New World Man" was a #21 hit, and "Subdivisions" was an FM rock favorite. The soundstage lacks some of the ambience found on *Moving Pictures*, but the performances still pack quite a punch. —*Rick Clark*

Power Windows / 1985 / Mercury 826098
An improvement over the sterile techno-crap of the 1984 release *Grace under Pressure*. "Big Money" recalls the highlights of *Moving Pictures*, while "Manhattan Project" and "Territories" also shine. —*Rick Clark*

Hold Your Fire / 1987 / Mercury 832464

Even though the playing is typically exceptional, the clinical production keeps this album from really catching fire. "Time Stand Still," "Force Ten" and "Turn the Page" are among the highlights. —*Rick Clark*

○ **Presto** / 1989 / Atlantic 82040
Presto, Rush's 13th album of new studio material and their first for Atlantic, showed this Canadian trio coming out from under a succession of bloodless-sounding techno-excursions (*Grace under Pressure, Hold Your Fire*) and going for a much more open, accessible sound. From beginning to end, the arrangements reflect more straightahead rock playing than on any of their other albums. *Presto* contains some of Neil Peart's best lyrics, and along with *Moving Pictures*, smartly presents many of Rush's virtues in their best light. —*Rick Clark*

● **Chronicles** / 1991 / Mercury 838936
Anyone wanting an essential overview of this Canadian band's prog-rock work should start here. All of their FM rock hits and most of the important album tracks are here. —*Rick Clark*

○ **Roll the Bones** / 1991 / Atlantic 82293
Roll the Bones continues with the organic-sounding hard prog-rock spirit of *Presto*, and it's equally fine. After many years of albums and touring, it's obvious that Rush has maintained its edge as a musical unit. The playing and material are primo throughout. Highlights include "Neurotica," "Big Wheel," "Ghost of a Chance," and the title cut. —*Rick Clark*

Counterparts / 1993 / Atlantic
A solid collection of songs, including the AOR rock radio tracks "Stick It Out," "Animate," and "Nobody's Hero," the band's statement on the AIDS situation. The playing is typically top-notch, but the type of reverbs and equalization setting on this Peter Collins production make the band sound colder and more distant than usual. —*Rick Clark*

Leon Russell

b. Apr. 2, 1941
Vocals, piano / Singer-songwriter, pop/rock
Leon Russell has had a widely varied career as an artist, a songwriter, a record label owner, a producer, and an in-demand session sideman. As part of Phil Spector's "Wall of Sound" wrecking crew, Russell played on hits by the Crystals. He also played on Herb Alpert's *Taste of Honey* and the Byrds' *Mr. Tambourine Man* and played and arranged tracks for Gary Lewis & the Playboys. Russell also toured with Delaney & Bonnie and briefly with Paul Revere & the Raiders when Revere was drafted. Russell organized Joe Cocker's Mad Dogs & Englishmen tour, which led him to tours with Bob Dylan, Eric Clapton, and the Rolling Stones, and a performance at George Harrison's Concert for Bangladesh.

In 1970 Russell formed Shelter Records with English producer Denny Cordell. The label eventually released albums by Willis Alan Ramsey, Dwight Twilley, and Phoebe Snow, among others. In October 1971, the Carpenters had a huge hit with Russell's "Superstar." (Years later, another Russell composition, "This Masquerade," became a career-making hit for George Benson.)

All of this visibility set the stage for Russell's lucrative solo career, which fused gospel, blues, country, rock, and light jazz behind his quirky warble of a voice. Russell had seven Top 40 albums, with 1972's *Carney* peaking at #2 for four weeks. "Tightrope," "Lady Blue," and a double-sided single remake of Hank Williams's "Roll in My Sweet Baby's Arms"/"I'm So Lonesome I Could Cry" are a few of Russell's hits. In 1992, he released a comeback effort, *Anything Can Happen. —Rick Clark*

○ **Leon Russell** / 1970 / Dcc 8001
Russell's self-titled debut features his strongest set of songs and performances, with tracks like "A Song for You," "Dixie Lullaby," "Shoot Out at the Plantation," and "Delta Lady," which became one of Joe Cocker's early signature songs. The CD includes a brief version of Dylan's "Masters of War." —*Rick Clark*

○ **And the Shelter People** / 1971 / Dcc 8005
Released hot on the heels of his Mad Dogs & Englishmen tour with Joe Cocker, Russell released this spirited outing, which included covers of tunes by George Harrison ("Beware of Darkness") and Dylan ("It's a Hard Rain Gonna Fall," "It Takes a Lot to Laugh, It Takes a Train to Cry") and some fine originals: "Alcatraz," "Home Sweet Oklahoma," "Stranger in a Strange Land" (an FM hit), and the title cut. The CD includes three bonus versions of Dylan tunes. —*Rick Clark*

Carney / 1972 / Dcc 8006
Carney became Russell's highest charting album with the aid of the oddball #11 hit "Tightrope." Also included is "This Masquerade," a song that later became an international hit for George Benson. "If the Shoe Fits" is a great putdown of pop-star sycophants. Other highlights include "Manhattan Island Serenade" and "Cajun Love Song." —*Rick Clark*

Hank Wilson's Back / 1973 / Dcc 8009
A skewed but interesting Hank Williams tribute album, with capable country backing. —*Cub Koda*

● **Best of Leon Russell** / 1976 / Dcc 8017
This is a straightforward hits and key-album-tracks collection, including "Lady Blue," "Tightrope," "A Song for You," "This Masquerade," and "Stranger in a Strange Land," among others. —*Rick Clark*

Rutles

Originally broadcast on network television in 1978, ex-Monty Python member Eric Idle's satire of the Beatles legend was one of the very few successful rock parodies; only Spinal Tap, perhaps, has outdone it. One of the key elements of this mock "rockumentary" was the brilliantly executed "soundtrack" by Python associate and ex-Bonzo Dog Band member Neil Innes (he also played the character loosely based upon John Lennon in the film itself). As an actual peer of the group in the '60s (the Bonzos even appeared in the *Magical Mystery Tour* film), Innes was well qualified to satirize the Fab Four phenomenon in song. With the exception of Idle, each of the four "Rutles" played their own instruments on the recording in addition to acting in the film. — *Richie Unterberger*

○ **Rutles** / 1978 / Rhino 75760
Ex-Bonzo Dog Band member Neil Innes was well qualified to satirize the Fab Four phenomenon in song. And he delivered, with catchy, harmony-laden tunes that deftly and lovingly parodied every phase of the moptops' career, from their Hamburg/Cavern Club days through "Get Back" (here retitled "Get Up and Go"). In between are fully realized send-ups of "If I Fell," "I Want to Hold Your Hand," "Penny Lane," "Lucy in the Sky," "I Am the Walrus," "All You Need Is Love," and more. "Ouch!" their hilarious mockery of "Help!" is perhaps the album's highlight. The 1990 CD reissue adds six very worthwhile "bonus tracks" that were used in the special, but were unavailable on the original 1978 Warner album, making for 20 cuts in all. —*Richie Unterberger*

Mitch Ryder (William Levise)

b. Feb. 26, 1945
Group / Rock & roll
Mitch Ryder & the Detroit Wheels blended the Motown soul sound with over-revved Midwestern rock & roll. Mitch Ryder's (born William Levise) gutsy soul shouting and superhuman screams were some of the most electrifying sounds to charge AM radio in the mid '60s, landing somewhere between the Rascals' Felix Cavaliere and Wilson Pickett. The Wheels sported two strong lead guitarists in Joe Cubert and Jim McCarty (later in Cactus and Detroit), and they were pushed along by one of the great unsung rock drummers of all time, John "Johnny Bee" Badanjek.

It was producer Bob Crewe who signed the band to his New Voice label, releasing a string of high-octane raveups in "Jenny Take a Ride," "Little Latin Lupe Lu," "Devil with a Blue Dress On/ Good Golly Miss Molly," "Sock It to Me-Baby!" and "Too Many Fish in the Sea." In spite of all the hits and visibility, Mitch Ryder & the Detroit Wheels were victims of the era, making loads of money for Crewe and New Voice, but ending up broke. —*Rick Clark*

★ **Rev-Up: The Best of Mitch Ryder & the Detroit Wheels** / 1990 / Rhino 70941
Perhaps the most raucous White soul band of the '60s, Ryder and the Detroit Wheels scored a series of hits from 196 through 1968 by souping up rock and R&B ravers to fever pitch. This is hard party music. —*William Ruhlmann*

Sade (Helen Folsade Adu)

b. Jan. 16, 1959, Ibadan, Nigeria
Group / Urban R&B, pop

Sade's smooth, silky jazz-tinged pop-oriented R&B earned several hits and a large following in the mid '80s. Borrowing the spirit, if not the sophisticated sound, of her idols Billie Holiday and Nina Simone, her music was lush and stylish, helped considerably by her talented supporting band. After her 1988 album, *Stronger Than Pride*, Sade disappeared for several years, returning in 1992 with *Love Deluxe*, which returned her to the spotlight, selling over a million copies in the first few months after it was released. —*Stephen Thomas Erlewine*

● **Diamond Life** / 1984 / Portrait 39581
Former model Sade made an immediate and huge impact with her 1985 debut album. Her sound and approach were deliberately icy, her delivery and voice aloof, deadpan, and cold, yet she became an instant sensation through such songs as "Smooth Operator" and "Your Love Is King," where the slick production and quasi-jazz backing seemed to register with audiences thinking they were hearing a jazz vocalist. Sade won the Best New Grammy Award for 1985, and *Diamond Life* sold more than two million copies. —*Ron Wynn*

Promise / 1985 / Portrait 40263
Sade's second LP improved on the performance of her debut, as the single "Sweetest Taboo" was a huge hit, and "Never as Good as the First Time" landed in both the R&B and pop Top 20. She was once again the personification of cool, laid-back singing, seldom extending or embellishing lyrics, registering emotion, or projecting her voice. This demeanor made her more desirable in the minds of many fans and was perhaps the ultimate misapplication of the notion of sophistication. But this album topped the pop album charts and eventually went triple platinum. —*Ron Wynn*

Stronger Than Pride / 1988 / Epic 44210
After two LPs with little or no energy, Sade demonstrated some intensity and fire on her third release. Whether that was just an attempt to change the pace a bit or a genuine new direction, she had more animation in her delivery on such songs as "Haunt Me," "Give It Up," and the hit "Paradise." Not that she was suddenly singing in a soulful or bluesy manner; rather, Sade's dry and introspective tone now had a little more edge, and the lyrics were ironic as well as reflective. This was her third consecutive multiplatinum album, and it matched the two-million-plus sales level of her debut. —*Ron Wynn*

○ **Love Deluxe** / Oct. 20, 1992 / Epic 53178
Sade's fourth album included the hit "No Ordinary Love" and marked a return to the detached, cool jazz backing and even more icy vocals that made her debut album a sensation. Though Sade's style is more suggestive than hynotic, and her production and arrangements are in an urbane mode rather than a jazz one, she's maintained her popularity among the fusion and urban contemporary audiences. This release also included "Mermaid," "Pearls," and "Feel No Pain." —*Ron Wynn*

Doug Sahm

b. Nov. 6, 1942, San Antonio, TX
Vocals, guitar, piano / Rock & roll, Tex-Mex, R&B
Since his days with the Sir Douglas Quintet in the '60s, Doug Sahm has been preaching the gospel of Texas music traditions. He's mastered everything from barrio Latin rock to Western swing to shuffle blues to doo-wop to Cajun, yet his work always bears his distinctive stamp. He's recorded a ton of albums with a wide array of sidemen and, regardless of the style, his laconic, reefer-headed vision comes through. Everything he's recorded is worth hearing, but most of it has been out of print for decades. But the stuff that's in print offers an adequate estimation of the beautiful music he's made for the last 30 or so years. —*John Floyd*

● **Juke Box Music** / 1989 / Antone's 0008
Sahm shimmies and strolls through this set of doo-wop and R&B covers. A gorgeous slow-dancing gem. —*John Floyd*

○ **Best of Doug Sahm: Atlantic Sessions** / 1992 / Rhino 71032
In 1972 Atlantic bought out Sahm's contract with Mercury, giving him the freedom to create an all-star ensemble of musicians. Throughout the year Sahm recorded with the likes of Bob Dylan, Dr. John, and David Bromberg, producing a typically rich body of work that was released on two albums in late 1973. Rhino has collected various cuts from the albums, adding five previously unreleased tracks (on CD only), giving an excellent portrait of Sahm's music. —*Stephen Thomas Erlewine*

Saint Etienne

Group / Alternative pop, dance
Formed by UK rock journalist Bob Stanley and Pete Wiggs in late
1988, St. Etienne became one of the leading British dance-pop
bands of the early '90s, combining elements of house, techno, pop,
disco, and hip-hop in a melodic, hypnotically rhythmic music that
not only was popular in dance clubs but also had crossover appeal. Considering their detatched, intellectual approach to pop, it's
not surprising that the group has experienced its greatest success
in Europe—particularly in England—and has only been a cult
band in America. After a series of female singers, Sarah
Cracknell became their permanent lead vocalist during the
recording of their debut album, 1991's *Fox Base Alpha*. —*Stephen
Thomas Erlewine*

● **So Tough** / 1993 / Warner Brothers 45166
British duo Bob Stanley and Pete Wiggs deserve recognition as
the genius pop svengalis of their generation that they are. Eerie,
dreamy, moody, hypnotic, and all those cliché terms don't disguise the fact that under the group name Sainte Etienne, they
craft superb, digital aural candy on *So Tough*. While delicately-ap-
plied Prophet, Roland, Moog, and Emax sampler synths comprise
the duo's main stock in trade, their key weapon is Sarah
Cracknell's waifish vocals. Bottom line: "Avenue," "Mario's Cafe,"
and "Hobart Paving" are simply some of the most achingly pretty
songs imaginable. —*Roch Parisien*

○ **Tiger Bay** / 1994 / Sire
While its not as consistently engaging as *So Tough, Tiger Bay* has
a number of excellent, innovative dance-pop tracks. —*Stephen
Thomas Erlewine*

Sam & Dave

Group / Soul
Perhaps no act epitomized soul music as the secularization of
gospel more than Sam & Dave. The original pairing of Sam
Moore and Dave Prater met in Florida in 1961, and they recorded
unsuccessfully for several years before being signed to Atlantic
Records in 1965. Atlantic persuaded their Memphis affiliate Stax
Records to produce them, and in December that year the writing
and production team of Isaac Hayes and David Porter delivered
the crisply soulful "You Don't Know Like I Know." Hayes and
Porter became the "eminences grises" behind Sam & Dave, much
as Holland-Dozier-Holland pulled the strings behind the
Supremes. They wrote, they produced—and the result was a
string of hits, including "Soul Man," "Hold on I'm Coming," and "I
Thank You," songs that survive as the very epitome of southern
soul. Certainly, Sam & Dave's hits are among the most soulful
ever to crack the Hot 100. Their albums often bore the hallmarks
of hasty execution, though. The dissolution of the partnership between Stax and Atlantic virtually sealed the fate of Sam & Dave;
there were a few more hits (and, later, a revival of interest thanks
to the Blues Brothers), but the glory days were over. —*Colin
Escott*

○ **Hold On, I'm Comin'** / 1966 / Atlantic 80255
The finest single Sam & Dave album, featuring the superb title
track and several other brilliant works. They were the greatest
soul duo ever, with Sam Moore's crackling leads and Dave
Prater's less intense but equally effective contrast and their perfect harmonizing supported by wonderful compositions, production, and arrangements by David Porter and Isaac Hayes. —*Ron
Wynn*

○ **Double Dynamite** / 1967 / Atlantic 80305
This was the second Sam & Dave album to enjoy significant
crossover appeal. The 1967 record included such hits as "Said I
Wasn't Gonna Tell Nobody," "Soothe Me," and "When Something
Is Wrong with My Baby." Isaac Hayes and David Porter were now
rolling as songwriters, and even though the record didn't attain
big pop numbers, the singles clicked with both soul and pop audiences. More importantly, Sam & Dave's teamwork and vocal interaction were establishing them as major stars. —*Ron Wynn*

I Thank You / 1968 / Rhino 71012
Straight reissue of an original Atlantic album, one of Sam &
Dave's better efforts. Highlights include "Wrap It Up," "These
Arms of Mine," "Don't Turn Your Heater On," "If I Didn't Have a
Girl Like You," and the title track. —*Stephen Thomas Erlewine*

● **Best of Sam & Dave** / 1969 / Atlantic 81279

For many years this late '60s Atlantic collection was the finest
value available to soul fans who hadn't purchased the original albums. But Rhino's extensive two-volume set that was issued in
1993 supplanted this collection, though it's still a nice set and is
ideal for anyone who doesn't want the B sides and extra tracks
from Rhino. —*Ron Wynn*

★ **Sweat 'N' Soul** / 1993 / Rhino/Atlantic 271253
Sam Moore and Dave Prather were the ultimate soul duo: one a
high-voiced wailer, the other a low-toned blaster. They came together in the mid '60s to form a superb duo, singing tunes
penned by soul's finest writing tandem, Isaac Hayes and David
Porter. They made a host of great singles before ego battles broke
them apart. This 50-cut, two-disc anthology not only has every
song of significance, but plenty of obscure worthwhile items, like
a "Stay in School," promo, some overlooked material done with
the Dixie Flyers, and a couple of numbers cut by Moore as a single act in the early '70s. The sound quality, annotation, and song
sequencing are as outstanding as the songs themselves. —*Ron
Wynn*

Sam the Sham & the Pharaohs

Group / Rock & roll, garage rock
This mid '60s Dallas party band blended Tex-Mex and Memphis-
rooted rock & roll for hits like "Wooly Bully," "Li'l Red Riding
Hood," "Ju Ju Hand," "Ring Dang Doo," and "The Hair on My
Chinny Chin Chin." —*Rick Clark*

● **Pharaohization! (The Best of Sam the Sham & the Pharaohs)**
/ Rhino 122
This one gets the nod for a great selection of songs. —*Dan
Heilman*

Samples

Pop/rock
With their relaxed, slightly jazzy pop, the Samples have become
one of the most popular touring bands of the early '90s. After a
bad experience with a major label, the band began releasing their
own records independently, building supporting through a grassroots network of fans. Through constant touring, the Samples
were able to keep building their network of fans. They were also
busy in the studio, recording three albums between 1992 and
1993. With none of their albums deviating from their folky, Sting-
meets-the Grateful Dead pop, their albums are virtually indistinguishable from each other. However, none of them are bad—each
record has a couple of first-rate songs, showing why the group are
concert favorites across the country. —*Stephen Thomas Erlewine*

● **Underwater People** / Feb. 1992 / WHAT ARE 70020
All of the Samples' records feature a pleasant mix of pop, jazz,
and blues, but *Underwater People* is the only album that features
consistently strong songwriting throughout the entire record. —
Stephen Thomas Erlewine

Carlos Santana (Devadip Carlos Santana)

b. Jul. 20, 1947, Tijuana, Mexico
Guitar / Rock & roll, blues rock, fusion
Santana is the name of a band that has successfully married elements of blues, rock, and Latin music and enjoyed international
acclaim for more than two decades. It is also the name of the guitarist, Carlos Santana, who has led that band and made other
recordings over the same period of time. In its original manifes-
tation, the Santana Blues Band was a group of equals, with Carlos
named as leader only because of a musicians union requirement
that such a designation be made. The group was formed in San
Francisco in the mid '60s and first gained recognition in the same
dance halls that hosted the psychedelic rock groups of the era, although, with its Latin and African roots, Santana never quite fit
in with the psychedelic sound. The group came under the direction of promoter Bill Graham and had already scored a contract
with Columbia when it appeared at the Woodstock Festival in
August 1969. Personnel at that time, in addition to Carlos, included Gregg Rolie (vocals and keyboards), Dave Brown (bass),
Mike Shrieve (drums), Armando Peraza (percussion and vocals),
and Mike Carabello and Jose Areas (percussion).
    Santana, the debut album, was a massive success, including
the #4 hit "Evil Ways." *Abraxas* (1970) did even better, topping the
charts for six weeks and featuring the hits "Black Magic Woman"
and "Oye Como Va." For *Santana III* (1971), the group expanded

to a septet with the addition of guitarist Neal Schon, though an additional six sidemen were listed in the album credits. This album was #1 for five weeks.

Guitarist Santana released a live duet album with drummer and vocalist Buddy Miles (later a member of Santana) in 1972; then came the fourth Santana Band album, *Caravanserai*, on which different musician credits were listed for each track, none of them including bassist Dave Brown or percussionist Mike Carabello. The album was a Top 10 hit. Carlos released another duet album in 1973 with guitarist John McLaughlin (the two shared a guru), followed by *Welcome*, credited to "The New Santana Band," its only remaining original members being Santana, Mike Shrieve, Armando Peraza, and Jose Areas (Rolie and Schon had decamped to found Journey).

In subsequent years, "Santana" for the most part referred to Carlos and a band of hired musicians playing in the established Santana style, while the leader also made occasional solo albums that varied the style somewhat. In 1992, Santana ended his long association with Columbia and signed to Polydor, which set up a custom label for him, calling for him to sign his own new acts. — *William Ruhlmann*

○ **Santana** / 1969 / Columbia 9781
A brilliant combination of rock with Latin and African influences, prominently featuring the organ playing and husky vocals of Gregg Rolie; the energetic, precise drumming of Mike Shrieve; and, especially, the soaring, immediately identifiable guitar sound of Carlos Santana. Justifiably a massive hit and the prototype for an assembly line of similar records. Contains "Evil Ways" and "Soul Sacrifice." — *William Ruhlmann*

○ **Abraxas** / 1970 / Columbia 30130
Excellent continuation of the first album, with songwriting credits to four of the six band members, plus a terrific version of Tito Puentes's "Oye Como Va." The hit was a cover of the Fleetwood Mac song "Black Magic Woman." — *William Ruhlmann*

○ **Santana III** / 1971 / Columbia 30595
Completes a trilogy of tightly constructed, exciting band albums filled with percolating, multirhythmic percussion and fiery guitar work. The last album that is the work of the Woodstock-era Santana band. — *William Ruhlmann*

★ **Greatest Hits** / 1974 / Columbia 33050
Carlos Santana was an album artist, yet this *Greatest Hits* set collects his best tracks from his band's first five albums and offers a fine introduction to his work. — *Stephen Thomas Erlewine*

○ **Viva Santana!** / 1988 / Columbia 44344
A lovingly assembled three-disc retrospective set that collects the best of the Santana band, along with many interesting rarities. — *William Ruhlmann*

Joe Satriani

b. 1956
Guitar, vocals / Hard rock, pop/rock, fusion
Joe Satriani was one of the best, most influential rock guitarists of the late '80s, equally capable of fast flights of blinding technique as well as sweet, lyrical passages. What also separates Satriani from most technically gifted guitar virtuosos is that he treats a song as a song, not as an excuse to shred. For these reasons, he appeals not only to guitarists but also to many rock fans who have never touched the instrument—his breakthrough 1987 album, *Surfing with the Alien*, was the first rock instrumental album in years to chart in the Top 30 on *Billboard's* Top 200 Albums. Since then, he has added vocals to his records; while his voice can't compare to his guitar, it added another dimension to an artist that was already more versatile than the majority of contemporary musicians.

Before Satriani became a recording star, he taught guitar in San Francisco; several of his students became famous, influential guitarists in their own right before he even recorded his first album in 1988. Metallica's Kirk Hammett was the first of his students to hit the big time, followed by Steve Vai and Larry LaLonde of Primus. — *Stephen Thomas Erlewine*

Not of This Earth / 1986 / Combat 8110
Major debut from this San Francisco guitarist. An eclectic mixture of sounds and styles. — *Paul Kohler*

● **Surfing with the Alien** / 1987 / Combat 8193

Hard-hitting, intense, and foot-to-the-floor guitar playing. All instrumental. — *Paul Kohler*

Flying in a Blue Dream / Feb. 1990 / Combat 1015
His first album to feature Satriani's vocals, with a total playing time of over 66 minutes. — *Paul Kohler*

○ **Extremist** / Jul. 1992 / Combat 1053
Satriani returned to the all-instrumental format for *The Extremist*. It's a smart move, and not just because he's a better guitar player than he is a singer. Whether it's guitar-god rock like "Friends" and the neo-folk "Rubina's Blue Sky Happiness," Satriani always shows that he's got a real knack for melody—his voice may hide that, but his guitar only emphasizes it. — *Brian Mansfield*

○ **Time Machine** / 1993 / Combat
Satriani has proven to be one of the most technically gifted and influential guitarists of the '80s, and the two-CD *Time Machine* compiles his long out-of-print first EP with several live tracks, making it a good showcase for his considerable talents. —*AMG*

Savoy Brown

Group / Blues rock
Along with John Mayall's Bluesbreakers and the Byrds, English blues-influenced rock band Savoy Brown should win some kind of distinction for having the most line-up changes—almost a different one for each of their 14 albums on Deram between 1967 and 1978. Lead guitarist Kim Simmonds was the constant element throughout. Among the band's expatriates were members of Foghat. — *Rick Clark*

○ **Blue Matter** / 1969 / Deram 820923
A great album, a classic that includes "Louisiana Blues" and "Train to Nowhere." — *Michael G. Nastos*

○ **Raw Sienna** / 1970 / Deram 844016
A blues-rock standard. Classic. — *Michael G. Nastos*

● **Savoy Brown Collection** / Jul. 20, 1993 / Polygram/Deram
This double CD set is all you may ever need of Savoy Brown. Includes their biggest hit, "Tell Mama." Like all Polygram *Chronicles* sets, this features great sound, smart track selections, thoughtful liner notes, and good photos. — *Rick Clark*

Boz Scaggs (William Royce Scaggs)

b. Jun. 8, 1944, Ohio
Vocals, guitar / Pop/rock, soft rock
Boz Scaggs got his start in 1959, playing with Steve Miller in the Dallas, TX, band, the Marksmen. It was Miller who taught Scaggs guitar. Scaggs and Miller eventually formed the Steve Miller Band, with Scaggs leaving after their classic second album, *Sailor*. Rolling Stone editor Jann Wenner helped Scaggs secure a solo deal with Atlantic. Scaggs's self-titled debut (produced by Wenner) failed to sell in spite of critical praise and the presence of sidemen like Duane Allman on the album. A deal with Columbia in 1970 was more fruitful, with each of Scaggs's albums selling in increasing numbers. In 1976 Scaggs achieved major stardom, thanks to the elegant urban pop of *Silk Degrees*. Over the next five years, he released a string of sophisticated R&B-influenced pop hits. In recent years, Scaggs's output has been very sporadic, as he became a restaurant owner in San Francisco. — *Rick Clark*

○ **Boz Scaggs** / 1969 / Atlantic 19166
Produced by Jann Wenner and featuring crack accompaniment by the Muscle Shoals house band, Scaggs's solo debut is a near-masterwork, mingling the pathos and heartbreak of vintage honky-tonk with the celebration and release of southern soul. The highlights of the album also flaunt its diversity: "Loan Me a Dime," an extended blues dirge, which features some of Duane Allman's finest work, and "Waiting on a Train," Scaggs' marvelous revamping of Jimmie Rodgers's classic hobo song. — *John Floyd*

Moments / 1971 / Columbia 30454
Scaggs' first album for Columbia is so low-key you barely notice the magic conjured on this set of introspective ballads. That is, until you really *listen*. — *John Floyd*

○ **My Time** / 1972 / Columbia 31384
Scaggs' last rock & roll gasp. The ballads that would become his trademark are already surfacing, but you need this one for "Full-Lock Power Slide" and "Dinah Flo," two scorching rockers that give this album the muscle it needs. — *John Floyd*

○ **Silk Degrees** / 1976 / Columbia 33920
Scaggs reached his commercial peak with this elegant collection of soulful urban pop, thanks to hits like the ultra-smooth disco of "Lowdown," the revved-up "Lido Shuffle," and "We're All Alone," Scaggs's finest ballad. —*Rick Clark*

● **Hits** / 1980 / Columbia 36841
In spite of the inclusion of "Dinah Flo," *Hits!* primarily focuses on Scaggs's '80s pop hits like "Lowdown," "Jojo," "Break Down Dead Ahead," and "Look What You've Done to Me." —*Bil Carpenter*

○ **Some Change** / Apr. 5, 1994 / Virgin 39489
This album has a nice organic feel to it that many of Scaggs's more commercially successful albums lacked. Scaggs plays a lot more guitar here, and his singing has a nice, relaxed soulfulness. One of his very best albums. —*Rick Clark*

Scorpions

Group / Heavy metal
A German metal band formed in 1970 by guitarists Rudolf and Michael Schenker; also included vocalist Klaus Meine, bassist Lothar Heimberg, and drummer Wolfgang Dziony. The original lineup stayed intact for three years, until Michael quit in 1973 to join UFO. The band broke up briefly and was reformed at the end of the same year by Rudy Schenker with Meine, guitarist Uli Roth, bassist Francis Buchholz, and drummer Jorgen Rosenthal, who was replaced in 1975 by Rudy Lenners. Lenners was replaced in 1977 by Herman Rarebell. Roth left to form Electric Sun in 1978, replaced by Matthias Jabs, the two of them in and out of band during the '80s. Undoubtedly the biggest group to come out of Germany, the Scorpions have survived in a genre not noted for longevity, cutting several classic sides along the way. —*Cub Koda*

Fly to the Rainbow / 1974 / RCA 5057
First U.S. release features the title track, "Speedy's Coming," "Drifting Sun," and "They Need a Million." Early meisterwerk from these German hard rockers. —*Cub Koda*

○ **Virgin Killers** / 1976 / RCA 3659
Features the title track, "Hell Cat," "Backstage Queen," "Polar Nights," and "Yellow Raven." —*Cub Koda*

Tokyo Tapes / 1978 / RCA 28331
Tokyo Tapes pulled this German band out of obscurity and into the spotlight. A quality sampling of their early material and a performance that is considered one of the band's best. Includes "All Night Long," "Back Stage Queen," and "Flight to the Rainbow." — *John Book*

○ **Lovedrive** / 1979 / Mercury 822555
Well-written songs and powerful singing from Klaus Meine are some of the reasons given for calling *Lovedrive* one of the best Scorpions ever. Rudolf Schenker and Matthais Jabs provide many of this album's highlights, with lots of great guitar. —*John Book*

○ **Blackout** / 1982 / Mercury 818885
The band experiments with pop smarts in a few of the songs, while retaining the solid hard-rock sound they have molded over the years. *Blackout* provided this German band with their first major hit, "No One Like You." —*John Book*

● **Best of Rockers 'n' Ballads** / 1989 / Mercury 842002
A good collection spotlighting the band's best tracks from the '80s, including "Rock You Like a Hurricane," "Rhythm of Love," Non One Like You," and "Still Loving You." —AMG

○ **Crazy World** / 1990 / Mercury 846908
Crazy World featured the Scorpions' biggest (and best) hit single, the reflective ballad "Wind of Change," which was the highlight on one the band's most consistent, accomplished albums. — *Stephen Thomas Erlewine*

Gil Scott-Heron

b. Apr. 1, 1949, Chicago, IL
Piano, vocals / Fusion
Pianist, composer, and poet Gil Scott-Heron has had a prime influence on contemporary African American popular music. He attended Lincoln and Johns Hopkins University, and wrote two novels that are highly popular among African American college students, *The Vulture* and *The Nigger Factory*. He began working with musician Brian Jackson on putting music to his oral narratives and monologs. His 1972 release *Small Talk at 125th and Lenox* attracted underground attention, while the followup *Pieces of a Man* was a major hit. Throughout the '70s and early '80s,

Heron's commentaries on racism, injustice, and inequality, with side trips on jazz, romance, and family life, were very popular among jazz fans with left-wing views as well as rock, R&B, and pop audiences. Although disputes with Arista over artistic direction and production control have resulted in very few Scott-Heron recordings in recent years, he continues to tour and give interviews. —*Ron Wynn*

○ **Revolution Will Not Be Televised** / 1975 / Bluebird 6994
The poem "The Revolution Will Not Be Televised" was perhaps Gil Scott-Heron's first major hit. It wasn't on any charts, but its searing message resounded on college campuses across the nation. This was the centerpiece for the album that also included several crackling protest pieces such as "Pieces of a Man," "Home Is Where the Hatred Is," and "Save the Children," plus the poignant "Lady Day and John Coltrane." The guest list of jazz participants included Ron Carter and Hubert Laws. —*Ron Wynn*

From South Africa to South Carolina / 1975 / Arista 4044
The Gil Scott-Heron/Brian Jackson collaboration was now a formal one, as they were issuing albums as a team. This was their second duo project to make the pop charts, and it included antinuclear and antiapartheid themes, plus less political, more autobiographical/reflective material like "Summer of '42," "Beginnings (The First Minute of a New Day)," and "Fell Together." Scott-Heron was now a campus and movement hero, and Brian Jackson's production and arranging savvy helped make his albums as arresting musically as they were lyrically. —*Ron Wynn*

Winter in America / Sep. 4, 1975+Oct. 15, 1973 / Strata East 19742
Gil Scott-Heron was at his most righteous and provocative on this album. The title cut was a moving, angry summation of social injustices that Scott-Heron felt had led the nation to a particularly dangerous period, while "The Bottle" was a great treatise on the dangers of alcohol abuse. He also offered his thoughts on Nixon's legacy with "The H2O Gate Blues," a classic oral narrative. Brian Jackson's capable keyboard, acoustic piano, and arranging talents helped make this a first-rate release, one of several the duo issued during the '70s. —*Ron Wynn*

● **Best of Gil Scott-Heron** / 1984 / Arista 18306
An exemplary firebrand poet whose raps and lyrics influenced the entire hip-hop generation, yet who has said his own influence was jazz. —*Ron Wynn*

Screaming Trees

Group / Alternative rock, hard rock, psychedelic
Putting their post-punk guitar noise within traditional hard-rock song structure, the Screaming Trees crafted a new form of psychedelia. Instead of the long, spacy trips of the late '60s, the band took the sonic explorations of indie guitar bands and used it for a mind-altering journey instead of expressions of aggression. Their late '80s releases on SST are raw, on the level of the label's other groups but trading angst for a drug-inspired mysticism that is too realistic and gritty for the Screaming Trees to be called hippies. When the band signed to a major label in the early '90s, some of the rough edges in their sound were smoothed out, yet they continued to produce some fine hard rock, incorporating more traditional rock styles (like the country-tinged "Dollar Bill") that kept the band's sound from growing stale. —*Stephen Thomas Erlewine*

Invisible Lantern / 1988 / SST 188
Solid neo-psychedelic pop. —*Robert Gordon*

● **Anthology: SST Years** / 1991 / SST 260
A scalding collection of their finest moments from the late '80s. —*Stephen Thomas Erlewine*

○ **Uncle Anesthesia** / 1991 / Epic 46800
Major-label bucks don't detract from their punch. —*Robert Gordon*

● **Sweet Oblivion** / Mar. 1992 / Epic 48996
While it's the band's most accessible record yet, the Screaming Trees' second album for Epic isn't as consistently captivating as the previous *Uncle Anesthesia*. However, when the band kicks their update of psychedelic hard-rock in gear on "Dollar Bill" and the spectacular "Nearly Lost You," the shortcomings of the rest of the album are easy to ignore. —*Stephen Thomas Erlewine*

Seal

Vocals / Pop/rock, dance-pop, soul
Seal's mix of classic soul melodies and contemporary dance
rhythms and instrumentation made him a pop star after the release of his debut album in 1991. "Crazy," his Top 10 hit single,
and the dance hit "Killer" are the best examples of his fusion of
soulful pop and '90s club culture and sound. — *Stephen Thomas
Erlewine*

○ **Seal** / 1991 / Sire 26627
This debut album features great dance music, some acoustic
tunes, and moody ballads, highlighted by the hit singles "Crazy"
and "Killer." — *John Book*

● **Seal** / 1994 / Sire
This self-titled second album continues Seal's richly produced
style of dance-influenced pop with a soul. Themes of uncondi-
tional love, compassion, and spirituality prevail throughout.
Includes the hit "Prayer for the Dying." A fine album. — *Rick
Clark*

Seals & Crofts

Group / Singer-songwriter, pop
The '70s were big years for this soft acoustic-pop duo, who had
previously enjoyed success with the late '50s/early '60s group the
Champs (remember "Tequila"?). From 1971 to 1978, Jim Seals (b.
October 17, 1941) and Dash Crofts (b. August 14, 1940) charted 14
times with hits like "Summer Breeze," "Diamond Girl,"
"Hummingbird," "We May Never Pass This Way Again," "I'll Play
for You," "You're the Love," and "Get Closer."
    Besides their pleasant tenor harmonies, both of them were
multiinstrumentalists, showcasing instruments like mandolin
and fiddle on some of their material. — *Rick Clark*

● **Greatest Hits** / 1975 / Warner Brothers 3109
This album has all their hits, including "Summer Breeze,"
"Hummingbird," "We May Never Pass This Way (Again),"
"Diamond Girl," and "When I Meet Them." — *Dan Heilman*

The Searchers

Group / British invasion, pop/rock
The Searchers (formed in 1961) came on the first wave of the
British invasion in 1964, with a million-selling hit, "Needles and
Pins," written by Jack Nitzsche and Sonny Bono (of Sonny &
Cher). The "Needles and Pins" jangling guitar arrangement was a
Merseybeat forerunner to the 12-string Rickenbacker sound of
the Byrds.
    Subsequent hits capitalized on that sound, as well as on the
band's slightly husky vocals. Other hits included a hit remake of
the Clovers's "Love Potion #9" (another million-seller), a version
of Jackie DeShannon's "When You Walk in the Room," "Don't
Throw Your Love Away," "Some Day We're Gonna Love Again,"
"Bumble Bee," and "What Have They Done to the Rain."
    They enjoyed a brief comeback in 1980 with their self-titled
Sire debut. To this day, the Searchers continue as an active touring unit. — *Rick Clark*

○ **It's the Searchers** / 1964 / Castle 167
Their best and most representative album. Major hits surrounded
by their unique renditions of folk and rock standards, including
some surprising Phil Spector covers. A seminal British invasion
album. — *Bruce Eder*

● **Greatest Hits** / 1985 / Rhino 75773
An okay way to whet the appetite, but not the definitive collection. — *Bruce Eder*

○ **30th Anniversary Collection** / 1992 / Sequel 170
An 84-song anthology, containing *not* every important track (*It's
the Searchers* and the other early albums are still worth owning)
but a good overview of their history, with two dozen rarities
(German-language versions of their early hits, outtakes, solo
numbers, live performances) included for good measure. If the
Rhino hits package whets your appetite, this triple CD is the next
step up. — *Bruce Eder*

Live at the Star Club / 1994 / PolyGram
Of all the British bands that recorded at the Star Club in 1962
and 1963, the Searchers gave the best performance—polished, exciting, and utterly professional, lacking the finely honed 12-string
guitar sound that their subsequent hits would display but still a
fine testament to their early work and history. — *Bruce Eder*

Sebadoh

Group / Alternative rock
After leaving Dinosaur Jr., Lou Barlow formed Sebadoh. Instead
of working like a traditional rock band and collaborating on each
song, Sebadoh acts as a backing band for the material of each individual band member. Consequently, their albums can be a little
schizophrenic, covering all kinds of indie guitar-rock from R.E.M.-
style pop to Dinosaur-style melancholy and Sonic Youth sonic explosions, all recorded in ragged lo-fidelity. Fortunately, each
member is a talented songwriter, managing to wear their influences without sounding exactly like any of them; they are one of
the most unique bands of the early '90s. Sebadoh's artistic
breadth makes them critical and cult favorites; their jagged playing and oblique songwriting guarantee that they will never cross
over into the mainstream, but that has never seemed a concern of
the band. — *Stephen Thomas Erlewine*

● **Smash Your Head on the Punk Rock** / 1992 / Sub Pop 176
Smash Your Head on the Punk Rock is a lo-fi masterpiece, full
of noise and subverse pop songs. — *Stephen Thomas Erlewine*

○ **Bubble & Scrape** / 1993 / Sub Pop 192
Nearly as impressive as *Smash Your Head*, *Bubble & Scrape*
shows that Sebadoh is continuing to grow as songwriters, turning
out a number of rough, fracture pop gems. — *Stephen Thomas
Erlewine*

John Sebastian

b. Mar. 17, 1944, New York City, NY
Vocals, guitar, harmonica / Singer-songwriter, folk rock, pop/rock
Born in New York City, the son of a classical harmonica player,
John Sebastian grew up in the Greenwich Village coffeehouses
and was a popular sideman to various folk artists prior to forming the folk-rock band, the Lovin' Spoonful, for which he served
as lead singer and songwriter in the mid '60s. When the Spoonful
broke up, Sebastian went solo, appearing at the Woodstock
Festival in 1969 and releasing the Top 20 *John B. Sebastian* album in 1970. Subsequent efforts were less successful, but in 1976
Sebastian scored a #1 hit with "Welcome Back," the theme song
from the TV series "Welcome Back, Kotter." Sebastian has continued to tour and play on occasional sessions; he released his first
album since the '70s in 1993. — *William Ruhlmann*

○ **John B. Sebastian** / 1970 / MGM 4654
A strong debut solo album spotlighting Sebastian's warm voice
and optimistic, melodic folk-pop songwriting. — *William
Ruhlmann*

○ **Cheapo Cheapo Production Presents Real Live** / 1971 / Reprise
2036
Cheapo-Cheapo Productions Presents Real Live is an exuberant
solo appearance at which Sebastian's humor and wit are at their
apex. A wide variety of songs, from old folk-blues standards to
Spoonful favorites. Makes you wish you'd been there. — *William
Ruhlmann*

● **Best of John Sebastian** / 1989 / Rhino 70170
A 16-track selection from Sebastian's solo albums from 1970 to
1976, including the hit "Welcome Back." — *William Ruhlmann*

Tar Beach / 1993 / Shanachie 8006
A low-key comeback album from Sebastian that shows that his
melodic folk-pop hasn't lost its charm in the 17 years since he
recorded his last record. — *Stephen Thomas Erlewine*

Jon Secada

Urban R&B, pop
With only one album, Jon Secada became one of the biggest adult
contemporary artist of the '90s, selling over six million albums
worldwide. Secada's smooth mix of R&B, pop, and Latin music
appealed to a number of different audiences. What separates him
from the overly slick sound of most adult contemporary artists
are his considerable songwriting skills; he's able to write sweet,
affecting ballads that never seem contrived or saccharine. As well
as becoming a huge pop star, Secada is one of the hottest Latin
artists recording in the '90s; his Spanish language album *Otro
Dia Mas Sin Verte* was *Billboard*'s #1 Latin album in 1992 and
won a Grammy for best Latin pop album. — *Stephen Thomas
Erlewine*

● **Jon Secada** / 1992 / SBK 98845

Secada has a beautifully versatile voice, which would mean nothing if his material didn't equal his talents. Fortunately, this collection of smooth adult contemporary R&B does serve his talents well, making *Jon Secada* a satisfying and promising debut. — *Stephen Thomas Erlewine*

Heart, Soul & a Voice / May 24, 1994 / SBK 29272
While there aren't as many obvious singles on Jon Secada's second album, his voice sounds better than ever, making it a worthwhile sophomore effort. — *Stephen Thomas Erlewine*

Neil Sedaka

b. 1939
Vocals, piano / Pop
An excellent songwriter, Sedaka came from a doo-wop background (working with an early version of the Tokens). He sharpened his skills with Juilliard training and enjoyed much success with a number of pre-Beatles-era hits. Though the British invasion stopped the flow of hits, he reentered the charts in the mid '70s with a string of chart-toppers that extended into the following decade. A major influence on Elton John, Sedaka continues performing today. — *Cub Koda*

● **All-Time Greatest Hits** / 1975 / RCA 6876
Includes "Calendar Girl," "Happy Birthday, Sweet Sixteen," "Breaking Up Is Hard to Do," and other sprightly pop numbers. — *Dan Heilman*

○ **Oh! Carol & Other Hits** / 1990 / RCA 2088
Early '60s album with the title track and other pop material one step removed from white doo-wop. — *Dan Heilman*

○ **All-Time Greatest Hits, Vol. 2** / Aug. 1991 / RCA 2406
Companion volume to the above, equally fine. — *Dan Heilman*

The Seeds

Group / Rock & roll, psychedelic, garage rock
The Seeds (formed in 1965 in Southern California) produced five albums of magically limited garage-psychedelia extolling the virtues of sex and drugs and drugs and sex. Sky Saxon, the band's self-absorbed singer-songwriter, evidently understood arrested development quite well, making the Seeds records a pretty enjoyable '60s punk sleazefest.

The urgent trashola snarl (and corny "Rawhide"-style backup vocals) of "Pushin' Too Hard" helped give them their only hit. "Can't Seem to Make You Mine," probably their best song, was later affectionately covered by Alex Chilton. Both of those songs can be found on their self-titled debut. Even though subsequent albums recycled the basic formula of the Seeds, their second album, *A Web of Sound*, is worth checking out. — *Rick Clark*

Web of Sound / 1966 / GNP 2033
A more ambitious, but less successful venture into teenage rages and lusts. — *Bruce Eder*

● **Seeds** / 1966 / GNP 2023
Punk sneers, cheesy organ, and an attitude. A garage-band classic. — *Bruce Eder*

The Seekers

Group / Folk rock, pop
During the '60s, this quartet from Australia deftly bridged folk vocal-ensemble work with shades of British invasion pop. Their stirring harmonies and memorable melodies earned them a series of big hits, as first the Seekers (on Capitol) and, with a totally different lineup, as the New Seekers on Elektra. Their biggest hits were "Georgy Girl," "I'll Never Find Another You," and "I'd Like to Teach the World to Sing (in Perfect Harmony)," a song that also became a theme song for a Coca-Cola ad campaign. Their work on Capitol is their best. — *Rick Clark*

○ **Seekers** / Aug. 1965 / EMI 107
A compilation featuring over one hour of hits and key album tracks on this British import. Completely comprehensive, with the best sound ever. — *Bruce Eder*

○ **Come the Day** / 1966 / Columbia 6093
Their best album, with their biggest hit and the Simon-Woodley songs. Also includes a killer rendition of Tom Paxton's "The Last Thing on My Mind." U.S. title is *Georgy Girl*. — *Bruce Eder*

● **Capitol Collectors Series** / 1992 / Capitol 91846

The Seekers' rich folky harmonies, fronted by the clear alto of Judith Durham, are given an excellent presentation on this 23-song anthology. All of their Capitol hits are here, including "Georgy Girl," "A World of Our Own," "Come the Day," and "I'll Never Find Another You." Typical of *Capitol Collectors Series* reissues, this set contains ample annotation, track info, and photos. — *Rick Clark*

Bob Seger

b. May 6, 1945
Vocals / Rock & roll, pop/rock
At his best, Detroit rocker Bob Seger has produced some incredibly clearheaded music speaking to and about the working class's fleeting joys, shortchanged dreams, and grinding existence. Many of the people who populate Seger's material possess some kind of resolve and dignity. Seger grew up as one of these people, and he's never really forgotten it. Musically, Seger's influences range from Chuck Berry to Creedence Clearwater Revival, the Rolling Stones, and Bob Dylan to Bruce Springsteen and the Eagles, all merged together in a Heartland rock stew.

Seger's first hit was the 1969 heavy soulful stomper "Ramblin' Gamblin' Man." For years after that, he consistently landed regional Top 10 hits that never saw the light of day anywhere else in the country. That was until the release of 1976's *Live Bullet*, a great concert album that encapsulated Seger's career to that point with an impassioned delivery. It became his first million-seller, charting at #34. His next two studio efforts, *Night Moves* and *Stranger in Town*, were artistic highlights. By this time, Seger had become a major arena attraction. He stumbled on the mediocre *Against the Wind*, reducing once-effective sentiment to hack wordplay, but he regained his focus on *The Distance*. His latest effort, *The Fire Inside*, is solid but fails to mine any new territory.

Blessed with a voice that could sing the phone book and sound great, Seger has even scored hits with his most pedestrian work. Nevertheless, he has created a body of work that, at its best, celebrates the spirit of rock in the face of mortality with a hard-won wisdom. — *Rick Clark*

○ **Ramblin' Gamblin' Man** / 1968 / Capitol 96261
The title track on Seger's Capitol debut is one of the all-time great rock & roll stompers with its bone-crunching two- and four-drum groove and gospel-choir backup. Other highlights include the incredibly hard-rocking antiwar track "2 + 2 =?" and "Down Home," a rude harmonica-driven rocker that sports an absolutely addled rhythm section. In spite of some cornball psychedelic-period mixes, *Ramblin' Gamblin' Man*, with its reckless over-the-top delivery, is Seger's hardest-rocking album. Throughout many of these tracks, Seger wails like a banshee. Seger's later rock hits sound absolutely tame next to this stuff. — *Rick Clark*

Smokin' O.P.'s / 1973 / Capitol 99077
Smokin' O.P.'s was a fine showcase for Seger's workmanlike rock & roll approach. "Heavy Music," an original, became a huge Detroit hit. Other highlights included Seger's versions of such standards as "Bo Diddley," "Let It Rock," and "Turn on Your Lovelight." — *Rick Clark*

○ **Beautiful Loser** / 1975 / Capitol 91424
After several years of relative obscurity, Seger emerged with this rather reflective effort. The hard-rocking "Katmandu," however, was a substantial hit in the Midwest. — *Rick Clark*

○ **Live Bullet** / 1976 / Capitol 46085
A blistering live show from Cobo Hall, containing raucous versions of early material like "Nutbush City Limits" and "Get Out of Denver" as highlights. — *Cub Koda*

★ **Night Moves** / 1976 / Capitol 46075
Seger's breakthrough album, a classic of blue-collar rock, featuring such standouts as the wistful "Mainstreet," the no-frills rock of "Rock and Roll Never Forgets," and the title track, a reflective coming-of-age masterpiece. Throughout, Seger believably details the characters in his songs with compassion. — *Rick Clark*

○ **Stranger in Town** / 1978 / Capitol 46074
It's not quite as strong as *Night Moves*, but *Stranger in Town* continues Seger's streak of great songwriting and performance. Highlights include the relentless rockers "Hollywood Nights" and "Feel like a Number." Seger's facility with the ballads "Still the Same" and "We've Got Tonight" produced substantial hits. — *Rick Clark*

Against the Wind / 1980 / Capitol 46060
Against the Wind became Seger's first #1 album, producing the hits and key album-rock-radio tracks "Fire Lake," "You'll Accomp'ny Me," "The Horizontal Bop," and the title cut. However, after two fine albums, Seger's lyrical abilities and melodic skills began to reveal a cookie-cutter sameness. His singing still had plenty of passion. —*Rick Clark*

Nine Tonight / 1981 / Capitol 46086
Features the title-track contribution to the *Urban Cowboy* movie soundtrack and an affective cover of "Trying to Live My Life without You." —*Cub Koda*

○ **Distance** / 1982 / Capitol 46005
The Distance was a strong rebound after the spotty *Against the Wind*, featuring his rocking Chuck Berry-like auto worker's tribute, "Makin' Thunderbirds," the resolute rock anthem "Even Now," and a fine version of Rodney Crowell's "Shame on the Moon." —*Rick Clark*

Selecter

Group / Ska-revival
An interracial ska group that emerged during the late '70s two-tone era, spearheaded by the Specials. —*John Floyd*

● **Too Much Pressure** / 1980 / Chrysalis 1274
Extremely danceable propulsive fusion of '70s British punk and Jamaican ska music. —*David Szatmary*

○ **Selected Selecter Selections** / 1989 / Chrysalis 21723
Greatest hits from their two studio albums. —*David Szatmary*

The Sex Pistols

Group / Punk
The Sex Pistols may have only been together for two years in the late '70s, but they changed the face of popular music. Through their raw, nihlistic singles and violent performances, the band revolutionized the idea of what rock & roll could be. In England, the group was considered dangerous to the very fabric of society and were banned across the country; in America, they didn't have the same impact, but countless bands in both countries were inspired by the sheer sonic force of their music, while countless others were inspired by their independent, do-it-yourself ethics. Even if they didn't release any singles by themselves, their was an implicit independence in the way they played their music and handled their career. The band gave birth to the massive independent music underground in England and America that would soon include bands that didn't have a direct musical connection to the Sex Pistols' initial three-minute blasts of rage, but couldn't have existed without those singles.

Guitarist Steve Jones and drummer Paul Cook were regulars were regulars at a boutique owned by their manager, Malcolm McLaren, bassist Glen Matlock worked at the store. Vocalist John Lydon, who would later perform under Johnny Rotten, met the rest of the group at the shop and was asked to join the band. While the band played simple rock & roll loudly and abrasively, Rotten arrogantly sang of anarchy, abortion, violence, facism, and apathy; without Rotten, the band wouldn't have been threatening to England's government—he provided the band's conceptual direction, calculated to be as confrontational and threatening as possible. The publicity caused by their caustic first single, "Anarchy in the UK," caused the band to be dropped by their record label, EMI. Matlock was fired before their next single, "God Save the Queen," which was released on Virgin; it was banned by the BBC. Matlock's replacement was Sid Vicious, a street tough who, unlike the rest of the band, couldn't play his instrument.

After releasing one album in 1977, the band headed over to the United States for a tour in January of 1978; it lasted 14 days. Rotten left the band after their show at San Francisco's Winterland Ballroom on January 14, heading back to New York; he would form Public Image Limited later that year. McLaren tried to continue the band, but Cook and Jones soon turned against him. In the following years, an endless stream of outtakes, repackages, and live shows have appeared, but their one proper album, *Never Mind the Bollocks—Here's the Sex Pistols*, remains their most concise and effective record; without it, popular music would have been much different. —*Stephen Thomas Erlewine*

★ **Never Mind the Bollocks** / 1977 / Warner Brothers 3147

Never Mind the Bollocks (Here's the Sex Pistols) is a delightfully vulgar and viscerally pulverizing debut. Everything you need is here, including "God Save the Queen," "Pretty Vacant," "Holidays in the Sun," and "Anarchy in the U.K." —*John Floyd*

○ **Great Rock & Roll Swindle** / 1979 / Warner Brothers 45083
The soundtrack to a muddled film from 1979. Loaded with rubbish, but there are some live and studio cuts that should be heard. —*John Floyd*

○ **Flogging a Dead Horse** / 1980 / Virgin 2142
This collects the band's seven British singles. Some duplicates with *Never Mind the Bullocks*, but the B sides can't be found elsewhere. —*John Floyd*

The Shaggs

Group / Alternative pop
In 1969 the Shaggs, comprising three sisters, Dorothy, Betty, and Helen Wiggin, entered a Revere, MA, recording studio under the encouragement and financial support of their father, Austin Wiggin. The recording engineer, upon hearing the band, tactfully suggested that they weren't ready to be a recording unit, but their father insisted on catching the band on tape "while they were hot." The result of this session, their first album, was called *Philosophy of the World.* Their followup effort, the appropriately titled *Shaggs' Own Thing,* actually reflects some growth in the area of technical facility.

Depending on your point of view, either this is the most hilarious-sounding mish-mash of ineptitude ever committed to CD, or it's an unconscious musical realization of everything great naive American art desires to be, believably innocent. Either way, you'll either love them or hate them. —*Rick Clark*

● **Philosophy of the World** / 1972 / Rounder 11547
This release compiles the Wiggins sisters' (otherwise known as the Shaggs) two releases *Philosophy of the World* and *Shaggs' Own Thing.* Anyone with unconventional tastes interested in taking a harrowing trip into the twilight zone of naive Americana pop should check this out. —*Rick Clark*

Shai

Group / Urban R&B
At the end of 1992, the four-man urban contemporary vocal group Shai shot to the top of the R&B and pop charts with their debut album, *...If I Ever Fall in Love,* and its #1 title track. Although they sometimes lack quality material, the smooth silkiness of their voices usually makes such weaknesses easy to ignore; the group has remained hot on the R&B charts, even if they haven't duplicated the pop success of their first single. —*Stephen Thomas Erlewine*

○ **... If I Ever Fall in Love** / 1992 / Gasoline Alley Music 10762
Apart from the gorgeous title tracks, most of the material on *If I Ever Fall in Love* is underdeveloped; although Shai sounds terrific, their material doesn't match their vocal talents. There are occasional signs of promise, but the single is the only flat-out impressive track here. —*Stephen Thomas Erlewine*

The Shangri-Las

Group / Rock & roll
Street-tough and smart, the Shangri-Las were like nothing that had come before in the history of rock & roll female groups. Hailing from Queens, NY, the group comprised two sets of sisters (one set identical twins, at that). They cranked out 11 hits in the space of two years, all of them enduring classics of the girl-group genre. Masterminded by oddball writer and producer George "Shadow" Morton, these narratives have a disturbing edge—tales of girls who run away from home, doomed girls who go all the way with bad boys; the spectre of death hangs over most of their songs. Eerie and creative production makes fatalistic melodramas such as "I Can Never Go Home Anymore" (1965) truly haunting—and the girls' voices, ranging from New York snotty to wistful and breathy, are ideally utilized.

The epitome of "biker girls in heat," their live presentation devastated audiences on package shows, while their offstage antics left a string of trashed hotel rooms, tour buses, and male groupies in their wake. The formula of teen-biker melodramas with a tough-as-nails image worked like a charm until they were eclipsed by the progressive rock movement of the late '60s. —*Cub Koda and George Bedard*

● **Golden Hits of the Shangri-Las** / 1984 / PolyGram 24807
Includes all the eerie three-minute melodramas from one of the
all-time great girl groups: "Leader of the Pack," "Remember," "I
Can Never Go Home Anymore," "Past, Present, and Future," and
more. —*George Bedard*

Del Shannon (Charles Westover)

b. Dec. 30, 1934, Coopersville, MI, **d.** Feb. 8, 1990
Vocals, guitar / Rock & roll
Del Shannon (born Charles Westover) came out of Grand Rapids,
MI, in 1961 with a sound that no one had ever heard before. A
rocker by inclination in a time when rock was supposedly dead,
his first single, "Runaway," became a monster hit and a half with
its catchy guitar hooks, great beat, and Shannon's strong yet vulnerable vocal (which leaped to falsetto range without compromising his manliness).
   Shannon had several followup hits, none quite as memorable
or driving, and in 1963 also became the first American artist to
cover a Beatles song ("From Me to You"). By 1964, however, he
began concentrating equally on songwriting and production and
wrote "I Go to Pieces," a romantic rocker that became a hit for
Peter and Gordon. He made numerous attempts at finding a new
and successful sound, signing with Liberty, which was able to sell
his records in England and other parts of Europe but not
Stateside. An attempt at updating his sound, first with Andrew
"Loog" Oldham and later with Dave Edmunds and Tom Petty as
producers, met with very limited success. In the mid '80s, however, Shannon seemed poised for a comeback when "Runaway"
emerged as a hit in an updated version by Todd Rundgren from
the TV show "Crime Story." Unfortunately, just as he was completing a comeback album on MCA, Shannon took his own life.
—*Bruce Eder*

○ **I Go to Pieces** / 1990 / Edsel 174
A British import and an indispensable complement to the Rhino
hits package. Sixteen important tracks, capturing Shannon's
sound at its most achingly beautiful. —*Bruce Eder*

★ **Greatest Hits** / 1990 / Rhino 70977
An almost-perfect collection of his best tracks from the U.S. cata-
log. The gaps can (and should) be filled by his album *I Go to
Pieces. —Bruce Eder*

Jules Shear

b. Mar. 7, 1952, Pittsburgh, PA
Vocals / Pop/rock
Singer-songwriter Shear (born in Pittsburgh) is best known for
hits he's written for others, notably "All through the Night" for
Cyndi Lauper and "If She Knew What She Wants" for the Bangles.
He has been a member of the groups the Funky Kings, Jules and
the Polar Bears, and the Reckless Sleepers in addition to making
solo albums. He was also an early host of the successful MTV series "Unplugged." —*William Ruhlmann*

○ **Got No Breeding** / 1978 / Columbia 35601
A cult favorite, reissued on CD. —*Dan Heilman*

Third Party / 1989 / IRS 13008
Shear sings his songs with no more accompaniment than the
acoustic guitar of Marty Willson-Piper of the Church. The results
are stark but impressive. —*William Ruhlmann*

○ **Great Puzzle** / 1992 / Polydor 511200
Full-band production gives a pop sheen to Shear's excellent
songs, notably the ballad "We Were Only Making Love." —
William Ruhlmann

● **Horse of a Different Color (1976-1989)** / 1994 / Razor & Tie
This retrospective covers everything from Shears's work with
Funky Kings, Jules & the Polar Bears, and Reckless Sleepers to
his solo work. Of particular note is the beautiful Byrds-like "If We
Never Meet Again" and "If She Knew What She Wants," later
recorded by the Bangles. —*Rick Clark*

The Shirelles

Group / Rock & roll
The premier female vocal group of the late '50s/early '60s, the
Shirelles was one of the very few groups who wrote their own
material. Led by Shirley Alston, the girls started singing as the
Poquellos in high school at parties and so on. A friend hooked
them up with her mother, who had music business connections.

The result was their first record and first hit, "I Met Him on a
Sunday." The hits flowed steadily from then on, all becoming en-
during classics and staples of oldies station formats to this day.
The Shirelles are still active on the revival circuit. —*Cub Koda*

★ **Anthology (1959-1967)** / 1988 / Rhino 75897
One of the most consistently creative and diverse of the 60s girl
groups, the Shirelles were a hit-making machine. "Soldier Boy,"
"Dedicated to the One I Love," "Will You Still Love Me
Tomorrow," and 13 others can be found here. —*Jeff Tamarkin*

Shirley & Lee

Group / R&B
Shirley Goodman's (b. June 19, 1936) screechy vocals and
Leonard Lee's (June 29, 1936-October 23, 1976) bluesy retorts
added up to R&B gold during the '50s for the young Crescent City
duo. The teenagers' debut on Aladdin, the Dave Bartholomew-
produced "I'm Gone," was a major R&B hit in 1952. Shirley and
Lee caught fire in 1955-1956 with three rocking smashes: "Feel
So Good," the R&B chart-topping "Let the Good Times Roll," and
"I Feel Good," all written by Lee. The pair stayed on Aladdin into
1959 before moving to Warwick and re-doing "Let the Good
Times Roll." The "Sweethearts of the Blues" broke up after a few
1962-1963 singles for Imperial. In 1974 Goodman returned under
the sobriquet of Shirley and Company with a #1 R&B smash, the
disco-fied "Shame, Shame, Shame," for producer Sylvia Robinson
on the Vibration logo. —*Bill Dahl*

● **Legendary Masters** / 1974 / EMI America 92775
The "Sweethearts of the Blues" in all their glory, with "Let the
Good Times Roll" and more. —*Dan Heilman*

Michelle Shocked

b. 1962, Texas
Vocals, guitar / Alternative pop/rock, singer-songwriter
A postmodern feminist folkie whose career has incorporated
blitzspeed-punk and '40s swing, Michelle Shocked's eclectic folk
is in the grand neo-tradition of acoustic performers in the post-
post-punk era. —*John Dougan*

Texas Campfire Tapes / 1987 / Mercury 834581
Her debut, recorded live around a campfire on a Walkman, is a
wildly overrated but interesting introduction to her talents. —
John Dougan

● **Short Sharp Shocked** / 1988 / Mercury 834924
With the great miss-you song "Anchorage," this is Shocked's
strongest record from start to finish. Rich and evocative, there's
hardly a clinker in the bunch. Special credit to Pete Anderson for
a sympathetic production job. —*John Dougan*

Captain Swing / 1989 / Mercury 838878
Whoa, stop right there. Read the title. This is swing music like
your parents listened to. That's right, Goodman, Herman, the lot.
Includes "On the Greener Side." —*John Dougan*

○ **Arkansas Traveler** / Oct. 1991 / Mercury 512101
Part three of the trilogy that began with *Short Sharp Shocked,
Arkansas Traveller* focuses this time on American roots music of
the south, mainly rural blues and country; according to her theory in the album's liner notes, all of these songs are based on
blackface minstrels. Recorded with a mobile studio at various
nonconventional locations around the country, it features an
amazing array of guest musicians, including Pops Staples, Doc
Watson, and Gatemouth Brown. Those who were put off by the
unexpected direction of *Capain Swing* will certainly welcome
this return to form—her best since *Short Sharp Shocked. —Chris
Woodstra*

Shoes

Group / Power pop
If there was a band that typified all that was good about that post-
punk permutation known as power pop, it was the Shoes. This
Zion, IL, quartet burst from their studio home with a string of terrific records that took Beatles-inspired pop and sprinkled it liberally with their own airy melodies and steady, sturdy playing. —
John Dougan

Black Vinyl Shoes / 1977 / Black Vinyl 10092
A homemade demo that became their first national release, this
is a dazzling collection of pop songs driven by thick sheets of guitar and warm, emotive singing. —*John Dougan*

○ **Present Tense** / 1979 / Elektra 244

Their major-label debut suffers from a bit of overwhelming post-production, but there's not enough interference to ruin this great collection of tunes. —*John Dougan*

● **Shoes Best** / 1987 / Black Vinyl 9787

A 22-song compilation, this is a wonderfully comprehensive overview of this wonderful band. Good liner notes by former *Trouser Press* head honcho Ira Robbins. —*John Dougan*

Shonen Knife

Group / Alternative rock

At their best, the Japanese punk-pop band Shonen Knife is an irresistable delight, combining sweet Beatlesque pop with buzzing Ramones power chords, singing about the schlockiest things pop culture has churned out. At their worst, the band's cuteness seems contrived, as if they were using their fractured English and obsession about Barbie Dolls, ice cream, and Hello Kitty as a deliberately cloying, cutesy marketing ploy. Even worse, at times it seems that their fans are not laughing with the band, they're laughing *at* their fascination with American kitsch culture and their bad English. Nevertheless, when taken on a strictly musical level, Shonen Knife's best records are truly intoxicating, rocking hard with a melody you can hum for days. —*Stephen Thomas Erlewine*

Shonen Knife / 1990 / Positive 6047

Early sides, sung mostly in Japanese. Super! —*John Dougan*

○ **712** / 1991 / Rockville 6065

A little sleeker but still terrific. —*John Dougan*

● **Let's Knife** / 1993 / Capitol 86638

Not everyone is going to "get" Shonen Knife, but there is lots of fun to had on *Let's Knife* for those who do. Picture three female Japanese 20-somethings who filter an obsession with junky American pop culture through equally cheesy domestic Godzilla movies. No? How about three propulsive chords that draw equally from punk and bubblegum (plus occasional forays into surf, folk rock, and Spector-ish girl group), with earnest lyrics that refreshingly never quite capture all the nuances of the language? Songs titles "Twist Barbie," "Flying Jelly Attack," and "I Am a Cat" offer an accurate snapshot. —*Roch Parisien*

Showmen

Group / R&B

Norman "General" Johnson's first group was based in New Orleans, but their best hit—"It Will Stand," from 1961—became a rock & roll anthem with global appeal. In the '70s, Johnson led the Chairmen of the Board ("Give Me Just a Little More Time"). —*John Floyd*

○ **It Will Stand** / Collectables 5162

A nice collection featuring the stuttering, sputtering vocals of General Norman Johnson and company, otherwise known as the Showmen. The title track was one of the great pieces of rock and R&B testimony. They never quite equaled it, though they produced some fine ballads and good uptempo tunes. "It Will Stand," incidentally, wasn't a hit the first time out of the box; it didn't make it onto the R&B charts until 1964, three years after it had peaked at #61 on the pop charts, and then it only reached #80. That just shows once again songs often become classics in hindsight. —*Ron Wynn*

Shriekback

Group / Alternative pop/rock, dance

A UK dance-rock band, 1982-1989, with varying personnel. The only constant member was keyboard player Barry Andrews, a former member of XTC. The original lineup was a trio also featuring former Gang of Four bassist Dave Allen and guitarist and vocalist Carl Marsh. They reached the U.S. charts with their first album, *Care*, in 1983, and the UK charts with their second, *Jam Science*, in 1984. *Oil & Gold* (1985), *Big Night Music* (1987), and *Go Bang!* (1988) also made the lower reaches of the U.S. charts, but the group's real home was in discos devoted to the kind of electronic, industrial-noise dance music of such peers as Ministry. Hits include "Nemesis" and "My Spine (Is the Bassline)." —*William Ruhlmann*

● **Dancing Years** / 1990 / Island 846356

An idiosyncratic compilation devoted to remixes and extended dance versions and lacking some of the group's best-known songs, though it *is* very danceable and gives a good sense of what Shriekback sounded like. If possible, find the UK import *The Infinite*, a good best-of, covering the early years. —*William Ruhlmann*

Jane Siberry

b. 1956, Canada

Vocals / Singer-songwriter

This Canadian singer-songwriter has been compared to both Joni Mitchell and Laurie Anderson, perhaps because she mixes traditional folk styles with various electronic effects and because of quirky lyrics that border on humor. —*William Ruhlmann*

Jane Siberry / 1980 / East Side Digital 80512

Siberry's first (low-budget) recording is her most conventional and folk-oriented, but already she is warning us that "Writers Are a Funny Breed" and is showing the offbeat perspective that will charm listeners later on. —*William Ruhlmann*

○ **No Borders Here** / 1984 / Open Air 0302

The sound has a new-wave rock energy. The songs poke fun at "Extra Executives" as well as the artist, who muses that she'd probably be famous by now if she weren't such a good waitress. —*William Ruhlmann*

Bound by the Beauty / 1991 / Reprise 25942

Siberry has by now mastered an ability to make her unorthodox song forms (changing time signatures, surprising alterations of melody) work for her, and she's struck a balance between revealing too much and too little in her lyrics, so that such songs as "The Life Is the Red Wagon" really do reveal all the levels she's given it. And "Everything Reminds Me of My Dog" is one of the funniest and best songs of the year. —*William Ruhlmann*

● **When I Was a Boy** / Aug. 3, 1993 /

This is a very personal, introspective album, its intimate textures consistent with the ambient work that production collaborators Brian Eno and Michael Brook are well known for. There are good songs and good performances here. In particular, her vocal interplay with guest k. d. lang on "Calling All Angels" is a treat. Still, *When I Was a Boy* is not the album that will cross Siberry over to the mainstream. At the same time, longstanding fans may be puzzled by the muting of her trademark verve and eccentricity. —*Roch Parisien*

Simon & Garfunkel

Group / Folk rock

Between Paul Simon's (b. October 13, 1941) warm lower tenor and Art Garfunkel's (b. November 5, 1941) sweet, airy choirboy upper tenor, Simon & Garfunkel's delicate harmonic interplay (coupled with Simon's brilliant songcraftsmanship) earned them the distinction of being the most successful folk/pop duo of the '60s and early '70s. As early as 1955, the twosome were seriously working on music together and registering their originals at the Library of Congress. Under the moniker Tom & Jerry, they landed a deal (while in high school) on the Big label in 1957. Their first single, "Hey Schoolgirl," reached #49 nationally, landing them a spot on "American Bandstand."

They went to separate colleges in 1959 but continued to release singles as solo artists under various pseudonyms. In 1964 Simon traveled to England and became active in the folk scene. While there, he met up with the vacationing Garfunkel, and they became Simon & Garfunkel. Shortly thereafter, Tom Wilson signed them to Columbia.

Their first album, *Wednesday Morning, 3 AM,* was a pretty straightforward folk effort, blending originals with song covers. It failed to make an impression on the marketplace. Without informing the duo, Wilson took a track called "Sounds of Silence" off the album, added electric guitars, drums, and bass, and remixed it as a single. It soared to the #1 position for two weeks and boosted their debut up to #30. The album *Sounds of Silence,* featuring the electrified title track, hit #21. It included three other hit singles, "I Am a Rock," "Homeward Bound," and "The Dangling Conversation." By this time, Paul Simon's writing was being mentioned in the same breath as Dylan and Lennon/McCartney, but much of his best writing was yet to come.

Their next three albums—*Parsley, Sage, Rosemary and Thyme, Bookends, Bridge over Troubled Water*—and the soundtrack album from the movie *The Graduate* were huge artistic and commercial successes. The duo broke up during the recording of *Bridge over Troubled Water*. Simon had become increasingly frustrated with Garfunkel's absence while Art pursued a career in movie acting.

Bridge over Troubled Water, its #1 hit title track, and Simon & Garfunkel cleaned up at the 1971 Grammy Awards. Other hits include "Mrs. Robinson," "The Boxer," "Cecilia," "Fakin' It," "Scarborough Fair/Canticle," "At the Zoo," "A Hazy Shade of Winter," "El Condor Pasa," and "My Little Town," recorded as a reunion single in 1975 and released on Simon's solo *Still Crazy after All These Years*. —*Rick Clark*

● **Greatest Hits** / 1972 / Columbia 31350
Nothing much more than what it says, although the live tracks are interesting. —*Bruce Eder*

☆ **Collected Works** / 1981 / Columbia 45322
This three-CD set is the only way to get the original albums with the best sound that's ever likely to turn up. —*Bruce Eder*

Carly Simon

b. Jun. 25, 1945
Vocals / Singer-songwriter, pop
Simon, who possesses an airy, somewhat unsteady alto, was one of the more popular female artists of the '70s, presenting a blend of singer-songwriter introspection and slick pop-smarts. After working with her sisters in a music group (The Simon Sisters) and experiencing a false solo-artist start in 1966, Simon's career took a turn for the better with her self-titled debut. It produced hits in "That's the Way I've Always Heard It Should Be." *Anticipation*, her second album, went gold and produced another hit with its title track. With her third effort, *No Secrets*, Simon linked up with producer Richard Perry, resulting in a #1 album that included her politely snotty putdown hit, "You're So Vain." The followup, *Hotcakes*, was practically a duet album with then-husband James Taylor (they split in 1982).

Simon has continued to enjoy periodic chart success in recent years. Her hits include "Nobody Does It Better," "The Right Thing to Do," "Haven't Got Time for the Pain," "You Belong to Me," "Jesse," and "Coming Around Again." —*Rick Clark*

● **Best of Carly Simon** / 1975 / Elektra 109
Good collection from Simon's most popular period, including "Anticipation," "That's the Way I've Always Heard It Should Be," and "You're So Vain." —*Cub Koda*

Joe Simon

b. Sep. 2, 1943
Vocals / Soul
His plaintive baritone equally conversant with R&B and country phrasing, Joe Simon married the two genres with startling success during the late '60s, adapting Nashville material to the soul sound and repeatedly coming up a winner. Simon began recording in the Bay Area, but a switch in recording sites (first to Muscle Shoals for Vee-Jay and then to Nashville, upon signing with deejay John Richbourg's Sound Stage 7 label in 1966) heightened his national appeal. With easy access to prime country-oriented material, Simon soon found his true calling, scoring major hits with "Nine Pound Steel," "(You Keep Me) Hangin' On," and the #1 R&B smash "The Chokin' Kind," penned by Music Row tunesmith Harlan Howard. Still dabbling in country covers after switching to the Spring imprint in 1970, Simon was even more successful when assigned to Philadelphia wizards Kenny Gamble and Leon Huff, who produced the moody "Drowning in the Sea of Love" the next year. Simon tried his hand at disco in 1975 with the sizzling "Get Down, Get Down (Get on the Floor)" and "Music in My Bones," two of the most palatable artifacts of the era. Simon eventually retired from active performing to devote his life to the church. —*Bill Dahl*

● **Greatest Hits** / 1962 / Monument 231916
Probably the best single album collection covering Simon's '60s hits, among them "The Chokin' Kind" and "Drowning in the Sea of Love." He sung these almost effortlessy, yet never lost either his soulful underpinning or his folksy narrative tack. Simon later had an album produced by Porter Wagoner and should have made as big a splash doing country as Ray Charles. —*Ron Wynn*

○ **Simon Sings** / 1969 / Sound Stage 7 15005

Joe Simon was just a step away from being a star when he issued his third album in 1969. His voice was becoming deeper, his style and delivery were more confident, and he was getting stronger material. The country/soul blend came together on this album, and he was now mixing sassy uptempo tunes with smokin' ballads and starting to break beyond Dixie. —*Ron Wynn*

Paul Simon

b. Oct. 13, 1942
Vocals, guitar / Singer-songwriter, pop/rock
After disbanding Simon & Garfunkel after *Bridge Over Troubled Water*, Paul Simon embarked on a solo career that has been even more diverse and complex than his work with Art Garfunkel. Simon can occasionally slip into precious poetry or pretentious wordplay, yet his albums have been consistently rich, drawing from reggae, gospel, jazz, rock, folk, African and Brazilian rhythms, and traditional pop. On each of his solo albums, Simon has experimented with distinctly different musical territory without abandoning his distinctive, literate, and melodic songwriting. During the '70s, his albums were consistent best-sellers; all three of his solo albums reached the Top 5, and even his live album went gold. After releasing the brilliantly understated *Hearts and Bones* in 1983, Simon suffered a dry spell, which was conquered by the African explorations of the acclaimed 1986 album, *Graceland*. Since then, he has released only one album—the Brazilian- and South American-influenced *The Rhythm of the Saints* (1990)—but Simon has never been one to work quickly; since 1972, he has only released seven albums of original material. —*Stephen Thomas Erlewine*

☆ **Paul Simon** / 1972 / Warner Brothers 25588
Backing away from the heavy production of the last Simon & Garfunkel album, Paul Simon's first solo outing is a quiet affair based around acoustic guitar. "Mother and Child Reunion," a successful experiment with reggae, is included as is "Me and Julio Down by the Schoolyard;" the great Stephane Grappelli guests on "Hobo's Blues." Many of Simon's finest songs are found here. — *Stephen Thomas Erlewine*

☆ **There Goes Rhymin' Simon** / 1973 / Warner Brothers 25589
Simon listened to R&B when he was growing up, and on *Rhymin' Simon* he returns to those roots. At times the results are some true R&B, and even gospel ("Loves Me like a Rock" recorded with the Dixie Hummingbirds), but mainly there is a lot of beautiful, sophisticated pop, shaded with blues ("St. Judy's Comet" and "Something So Right.") Not as fully realized as *Paul Simon*, but there is much rewarding listening to be found. —*Stephen Thomas Erlewine*

☆ **Still Crazy after All These Years** / 1975 / Warner Brothers 25591
Replacing the guitar with the piano as the primary instrument, Simon produced a quiet, introspective Grammy-winning album centering around love lost. Simon reunites with Garfunkel on "My Little Town," a track that sounds nothing like old S&G songs. *Still Crazy* doesn't much resemble Simon's two previous albums; it is a serious, somber album with none of the light touches present on *Paul Simon* and *Rhymin' Simon*. —*Stephen Thomas Erlewine*

One Trick Pony: Soundtrack / 1980 / Warner Brothers 3472
This is usually categorized as a regular Paul Simon album, although its songs were featured in the Simon-written-and-starring film of the same name. Featuring New York session aces like Steve Gadd, Richard Tee, Tony Levin, and Eric Gale, the music has a contemporary jazz feel, and typical of a Simon album there are some extraordinary lyrics. "Late in the Evening" was the hit, but that's only the beginning. —*William Ruhlmann*

○ **Hearts & Bones** / 1983 / Warner Brothers 23942
An understated set of introspective folk-rock that contains some of Simon's finest, most literate songs. —*Stephen Thomas Erlewine*

☆ **Graceland** / 1986 / Warner Brothers 25447
Graceland is immediately accessible because the music is exotic yet familiar. As Simon says in the liner notes, he was drawn to South African music because it sounded "like 50s rock & roll out of the Atlantic Records school of simple three-chord pop." Simon put his own melodies and lyrics to South African rhythms and chords, producing a remarkable hybrid. Simon's songs are some of his best, recovering from a 10-year dry spell. Los Lobos guests on "All Around the World." *Graceland* is not only Simon's best al-

bum but one of the classic rock & roll albums. —*Stephen Thomas Erlewine*

★ **Negotiations & Love Songs 1971-1986** / 1988 / Warner Brothers 25789
A good sampler of Paul Simon's personal favorites and hits. Many of his frequent changes in style are captured here, as are the highlights of the *One Trick Pony* and *Hearts and Bones* albums. —*Stephen Thomas Erlewine*

○ **Rhythm of the Saints** / 1990 / Warner Brothers 26098
Simon moved from Africa to Brazil and produced an album that resembles *Graceland*, yet is harder to grasp. The songs are more oblique than *Graceland*'s and the music is harder to absorb in one listen. After a couple of repeat listenings, the album begins to take shape, and melodies emerge under the heavy percussion. It's necessary to put some time into this album, but the results are well worth it. —*Stephen Thomas Erlewine*

○ **Paul Simon's Concert in the Park, August 15, 1991** / 1992 / Warner Brothers 26737
Simon plays all the favorites from his African and Brazilian albums and recasts some old favorites in these settings. Sometimes the results are thought-provoking (Bridge over Troubled Water" and "Sound of Silence"), other times severely faulted ("Kodachrome" and "Cecilia"), yet the album is immensely entertaining and listenable. —*Stephen Thomas Erlewine*

1964/1993 / 1993 / Warner Brothers
Simon's box set contains a great deal of fine music, including all of his hits as well as a smattering of rare and unreleased material. However, he has already released two other fine compilations and *1964-1990* treads the same ground as those. It also draws too heavily on *Graceland* and *The Rhythm of the Saints*, devoting an entire disc to these two albums, while shortchanging his work with Simon & Garfunkel. Collectors will also be frustrated by the small amount of rarities as well as the poorly executed packaging. There is no denying the music here is great but this box could have been much more than what it is. —*Stephen Thomas Erlewine*

Simple Minds

b. 1978, Glasgow
Group / Alternative pop/rock
Simple Minds was conceived in 1977 out of the remains of the Glasgow, Scotland, band Johnny & the Self-Abusers. Their initial albums were rather dissonant, moody, synth-heavy dance-music excursions that enjoyed increasing popularity in the British Isles, due to the band's incessant touring. The 1982 album *New Gold Dream (81, 82, 83, 84)* spent a year on the British charts and produced three hit singles; the followup, *Sparkle in the Rain*, was a #1 hit in England. In 1984, lead singer Jim Kerr's marriage to Chrissie Hynde of the Pretenders became a pop-media event.

Nevertheless, it wasn't until the band recorded a nonoriginal track, "Don't You Forget about Me," for the 1985 brat-pack film *The Breakfast Club* that the group began making a big impression Stateside. During that time, Simple Minds played at the historic Live Aid benefit in Philadelphia. Their next album, *Once Upon a Time*, featured a clean, radio-friendly production by Bob Clearmountain and Jimmy Iovine and generated a few Top 40 hits.

Subsequent efforts have included a fine live album and a couple of dramatically produced studio releases that continue the band's hopeful humanitarian themes. —*Rick Clark*

○ **New Gold Dream** / 1982 / A&M 4928
New Gold Dream (81-82-83-84) was the first effort (after many spotty earlier releases) to exhibit a focused collection of strong songs. The material, overall, is a coolly elegant style of synth-rich dance-pop. Among the album's highlights are "Promised You a Miracle," "Glittering Prize," and the title song. —*Rick Clark*

○ **Sparkle in the Rain** / 1984 / A&M 4981
On *Sparkle in the Rain*, Simple Minds assembled the best songs of their career and brought in producer Steve Lillywhite (XTC, Psychedelic Furs, U2) to help articulate their vision. The result was the best album of their career thus far. Lillywhite's sweeping cinematic soundscapes perfectly suited grand songs like "WaterFront," "Book of Brilliant Things," "Up on the Catwalk," "East of Easter," and a version of Lou Reed's "Street Hassle." "Kick inside of Me" rocks harder than anything the band has ever done. —*Rick Clark*

○ **Once upon a Time** / 1985 / A&M 5092
On the wings of the popular 1985 *Breakfast Club* soundtrack hit, Simple Minds enlisted in-demand producers Jimmy Iovine and Bob Clearmountain and released the ready-made-for-American-FM-radio *Once upon a Time*. In spite of the fact that this album generated three hits with "Alive & Kicking," "Sanctify Yourself," and "All the Things She Said," Simple Minds had lost the inspirational edge they had attained on *Sparkle in the Rain*. —*Rick Clark*

Live in the City of Light / 1987 / A&M 6850
Simple Minds has a reputation as an excellent live unit, and this well-recorded 1986 set done in Paris is a testament to that fact. With the help of extra sidemen (background vocalists, computer programmer, and violinist), Simple Minds runs through a wide sampling of their best material. —*Rick Clark*

● **Glittering Prize** / 1993 / A&M 52
Glittering Prize falls short of being a definitive anthology of Simple Minds by eliminating many key tracks (not even the "Glittering Prize," the song the album is named after, is included) and giving too much weight to the band's later years (an inexplicable three tracks from 1991's *Real Life* are included). Still, all the mid '80s hits are here, including "(Don't You) Forget about Me," making its first appearance on a Simple Minds album, which will be enough for most casual fans. —*AMG*

Simply Red

Group / Soul, pop/rock
Led by the vocalist Mick Hucknall, the English blue-eyed soul band Simply Red became international stars with their debut album, *Picture Book*. With the hit ballad "Holding Back the Years," Hucknall proved that he could sing soulfully without affectation, and their cover of the Valentine Brothers' "Money's Too Tight to Mention" proved that they could do light funk capably. With each album, their fan base has expanded, especially in the United Kingdom; their latest album, 1991's *Stars*, outsold the latest albums from U2, Guns N' Roses, and Michael Jackson in Britain. —*Stephen Thomas Erlewine*

● **Picture Book** / 1985 / Elektra 60452
The band finds a steady R&B groove reminiscent of '60s Stax house band the MG's, and, as with the MG's, it's all in the service of a big-voiced soul singer, in this case a British redhead. Features the U.S. #1 "Holding Back the Years" and the UK Top 20 "Money's Too Tight (to Mention)." —*William Ruhlmann*

Men & Women / 1987 / Elektra 60727
After a monster debut, Simply Red's followup album simply didn't get the job done. It wasn't a halfhearted effort; Mick Hucknall's crackling vocals were just as exuberant, and the band's Stax/Volt-influenced lines were effectively played. The songs were tightly produced and nicely arranged, but were an uneven batch and lacked the kind of standout single Hucknall had enjoyed on the previous album with "Holding Back the Years." They did turn in an interesting version of "Ev'ry Time We Say Goodbye." —*Ron Wynn*

○ **A New Flame** / 1989 / Elektra 60828
Although Hucknall tries to resurrect soul in his own original songs, he's most successful at evoking the past, notably on Simply Red's second #1, a remake of the Harold Melvin & the Blue Notes classic "If You Don't Know Me by Now." —*William Ruhlmann*

○ **Stars** / 1991 / East West 91773
Although it didn't have a single as strong as "Holding Back the Years" or "If You Don't Know Me by Know," *Stars* was Simply Red's best album since their debut. It was smoother and more polished than their previous work, yet Mick Hucknall was singing better than ever, and his songwriting was improving. —*Stephen Thomas Erlewine*

Siouxsie & the Banshees

Group / Punk, alternative pop/rock
One of the first UK punk bands inspired directly by the Sex Pistols, Siouxsie & the Banshees fashioned their own dark, confrontational brand of rock, becoming one of the first goth bands. Led by the cold, detatched vocals of singer Siouxsie Sioux, the band's music was abrasive but not fast; it was a wall of terror and darkness. On stage she frequently flirted with Nazi symbols, causing quite a controversy in Britain; despite the onstage imagery,

the band's music was gathering quite a following in the United Kingdom.

After their first few albums, the band began softening its harsh sound, wandering into pop territory; in 1983, the group had a UK hit with its sublime version of the Beatles' "Dear Prudence." Siouxie's voice had become warmer and more accessible, which helped the band become more commercially successful. All the while, the band has never lost their creative edge, exploring new territory with each new album. —*Stephen Thomas Erlewine*

○ **Scream** / 1978 / Geffen 24046
By waiting until punk essentially had blown over to sign a contract, the Banshees had a clear field for their harsh rock attack and plenty of time to prepare it. The result is this fierce debut, which fulfills the promise of punk and suggests (unlike most of its progenitors) that it has a future. —*William Ruhlmann*

Juju / 1981 / Geffen 24050
They're shifting gradually toward a more straightforward rock sound, but the Banshees also add Middle Eastern touches here. Contains the British hits "Spellbound" and "Arabian Knights." —*William Ruhlmann*

● **Once upon a Time: The Singles** / 1981 / Geffen 24051
This compilation of UK singles (some appearing on an album for the first time) emphasizes the more pop sound of Siouxsie & the Banshees. Still not easy listening, though. —*William Ruhlmann*

Hyaena / 1984 / Geffen 24030
Siouxsie & the Banshees's first album to benefit from a major-label push in the United States (and make the charts) finds them taking a more melodic, expressive approach and even covering the Beatles' "Dear Prudence." Old fans howled, but there were a lot of new fans. —*William Ruhlmann*

Through the Looking Glass / 1987 / Geffen 24134
Well-selected album of rock and pop cover songs, including everything from Sparks's "This Town Ain't Big Enough for Both of Us" to "Strange Fruit." —*William Ruhlmann*

● **Twice upon a Time: The Singles** / Oct. 13, 1992 / Geffen 24492
A good collection of singles, *Twice upon a Time* picks up where *Once upon a Time* left off—1981 to 1993, their more mainstream period. The albums from this time span may be too ambitious for some, but the singles shouldn't be missed. This is probably the best introduction to the band. —*Chris Woodstra*

The Sir Douglas Quintet

Group / Rock & roll, Tex-Mex
Texas had always had its own brand of rock & roll—a little bit o' country, a little bit o' blues, with a heapin' helpin' o' hot sauce poured over the top. Doug Sahm was no stranger to the studio when he formed the Sir Douglas Quintet in 1964; he'd been at it since the age of six and already possessed an encyclopedic knowledge and innate understanding of those local flavors when the band cut its first big hit, "She's about a Mover."

The ingredient that set the Quintet apart was Tex-Mex, that curious, joyous, irresistible, danceable, festive feast that married the jumpy Mexican *conjunto* to good ol' rock & roll. With Augie Meyers on the organ and a rhythm section that couldn't stop cookin', Sir Doug Sahm let it be known that good-time music was alive and kickin' in San Antone.

After the Quintet itself dissolved, Sahm went on to cut numerous solo albums and collaborations, spreading the Tex-Mex influence. In the late '80s he and Meyers teamed up with two of their mentors, Freddy Fender and Flaco Jimenez, to form the Texas Tornados, keeping that high and happy sound alive. —*Jeff Tamarkin*

○ **Sir Doug's Recording Trip: The Mercury Years** / 1988 / Edsel 255
An incredible 30-song sampling of his Quintet and solo years, featuring most of the hits, some rare delicacies, and an educational set of notes by Ed Ward. —*John Floyd*

● **Best of Doug Sahm & Sir Douglas Quintet** / 1990 / Polygram 846586
This is not as thorough as *Sir Doug's Recording Trip*, but it's easier to find and gives you 22 essential tracks in sterling digital fidelity. —*John Floyd*

Sister Sledge

Group / Disco, soul

Sisters Debra, Joan, Kim, and Kathie began recording as Sisters Sledge in 1971. Dropping the "s" from Sisters, the group collaborated with Chic for some seminal dance/soul hits in the late '70s and early '80s. Sister Sledge enjoyed two #1 R&B hits and two other Top 10 singles from 1979 to 1981, as well as Top 10 pop hits. Both "He's the Greatest Dancer" and "We Are Family" were international smashes, with the Pittsburgh Pirates adopting "We Are Family" as their theme song during their world championship season in 1979. "Got to Love Somebody" and "All American Girls" were also major hits. The group began producing its own singles in 1981, but ran into tough sledding in the wake of the anti-disco backlash. They began recording for Atco in 1974 and remained on Cotillion from 1976 to 1983. They moved to Atlantic in 1985, but were unable to regain their former glory. Kathy Sledge issued her own album, *Heart*, in 1992. —*Ron Wynn*

● **Sister Sledge Collection** / 1992 / Atlantic
This collection covers both formative tracks and well-known Sister Sledge hits for Atco and Atlantic from the days when they tried everything from light R&B to teen pop on through the disco classics "We Are Family" and "He's the Greatest Dancer." It ends at the early '80s, about the time they began producing their own material and started struggling once more, though they were also undone by the antidisco backlash. This anthology also contains photos and some competent, though not exhaustive, liner notes. —*Ron Wynn*

Sisters of Mercy

Group / Alternative rock
A Leeds outfit, headed by lyricist Andrew Eldritch, that started with pounding heavy metal in its 1982 debut EP and since then has moved steadily toward danceable pop-funk. —*David Szatmary*

○ **Vision Thing** / 1990 / Elektra 61017
Guitar-based pop fueled by the bright-sounding sensibilities of ex-Generation X axeman Tony James. —*David Szatmary*

● **Singles Compilation** / 1993 / Mute 61399
Collecting a number of their better singles of the past decade, *Singles Compilation* offers a good introduction to the Sisters of Mercy. —*AMG*

Skid Row

Group / Hard rock, heavy metal
Before alternative music crossed over into the mainstream, Skid Row was one of the top heavy metal bands of the '90s, pounding out a radio-friendly mix of Bon Jovi, Aerosmith, and Led Zeppelin. On the strength of the "18 and Life" and "I Remember You" singles, their 1989 debut album sold over three million copies. The 1991 followup, *Slave to the Grind*, sold a million copies and hit #1. Later that year, the band began a quick fall from the limelight, as Nirvana's success (who, ironically, were called Skid Row in an earlier incarnation) changed the rules of hard rock, making Skid Row seem irrelevant. They haven't recorded an album since *Slave to the Grind*. —*Stephen Thomas Erlewine*

Skid Row / 1990 / Atlantic 81936
With enough exposure, Skid Row became impossible to ignore. The beginning of a good band. —*John Book*

● **Slave to the Grind** / 1991 / Atlantic 82278
Skid Row's impressive second album, with some great rockers, a nice ballad or two, and even a heavy venture into thrash. One of the best metal albums of 1991. —*John Book*

Skinny Puppy

Group / Alternative rock, industrial
Skinny Puppy was one of the pioneers of industrial music, cultivating a scalding mix of electronics, samples, found sounds, and beats. All of their albums are thunderously menacing experimentations with dance and synthesizers, creating a consistent body of dense, dark music that owes a debt to the nightmarish vision of Cabaret Voltaire and Throbbing Gristle. Skinny Puppy were primarily responsible for popularizing the cut-and-paste techniques of those '70s electronic forefathers during the late '80s; Ministry and Nine Inch Nails picked up much of their sonic terrorism from Skinny Puppy's early records. After industrial music had worked its way into the mainstream in the early '90s, Skinny Puppy

landed their first major-label contract with American Records. — *Stephen Thomas Erlewine*

Bites / 1985 / Nettwerk 30002
Skinny Puppy's first album recalls the gloomy throb of Cabaret Voltaire, only with a more pronounced beat; their debut EP, *Remission*, is included on the CD version of *Bites*. — *Stephen Thomas Erlewine*

Mind: The Perpetual Intercourse / 1986 / Capitol 90467
Skinny Puppy doesn't deviate from their dark vision on their second album; in fact, the record doesn't sound all that much different than the first. — *Stephen Thomas Erlewine*

○ **Cleanse Fold & Manipulate** / 1987 / Capitol 46922
While it doesn't deviate from their previous lyrical territory, the music is more intense and scary; for the first time, Skinny Puppy has made an album that actually *sounds* frightening. — *Stephen Thomas Erlewine*

○ **VIVIsectVI** / Jul. 1988 / Capitol 91040
VIVIsectVI is the first Skinny Puppy album that is explicitly political, which adds some depth to their standard throbbing, gloomy industrial dance rock. — *Stephen Thomas Erlewine*

Rabies / 1989 / Capitol 93007
Despite the presence of Ministry's Al Jourgensen and his brutal guitar riffs, Skinny Puppy sounds at a loss for ideas on their fifth album. — *Stephen Thomas Erlewine*

● **12-Inch Anthology** / 1990 / Nettwerk 30041
Featuring both sides of four 12-inch singles from 1985 through 1989, *12-Inch Anthology* offers a good introduction to Skinny Puppy's psycho-terrorist dance music. — *Stephen Thomas Erlewine*

○ **Too Dark Park** / 1990 / Capitol 94683
Skinny Puppy's first album of the '90s is a thicker, more layered and bass-heavy record than their previous work, which makes it one of the most interesting albums they have ever released. — *Stephen Thomas Erlewine*

Skyliners

Group / Doo-wop
This Pittsburgh vocal group made a magnificent heartache ballad in 1959, "Since I Don't Have You"; it remains among R&B's ultimate agonizing triumphs. Jimmy Beaumont was the lead vocalist, with Janet Vogel, Wally Lester, Joe VerScharen, and Jackie Taylor. Beaumont, Taylor, and Lester had been in the Crescents, while Vogel and VerScharen were alumni of the El Rios. Their followup, "This I Swear," was a creditable effort that peaked at #20 on the R&B charts, but few remember it. Oddly, "Since I Don't Have You" only reached #3 on the R&B side and #12 on the pop charts. But it's certainly one song for whom the numbers really don't come close to telling the story. The Skyliners had two chart singles on Callico and then had one other song reach the R&B Top 40 in 1965, "The Loser." — *Ron Wynn*

● **Since I Don't Have You** / 1963 / ACE 78
The Skyliners were among the more dramatic, theatric white doo-wop groups. Their hit "Since I Don't Have You" has been covered by numerous performers, and it's among the 21 singles featured on this Ace anthology covering numbers recorded for Calico and Laurie. Jimmy Beaumont's tremendous leads distinguished "I Swear," "It Happened Today," and the title track among others. It's no surprise such flamboyant performers as Patti Labelle and Chuck Jackson are big Skyliners fans. — *Ron Wynn*

Slade

Group / Hard rock, glam rock
One of the most successful British bands of the early '70s, Slade made it to the top of the charts after several years on the road. The band formed in 1966 in Wolverhapton as the N'Betweens. After taking on former Animals bassist Chas Chandler as their manager, they changed their name to Ambrose Slade, then shortened it to Slade.

Many of their records were a variations of upfront lead vocals, fat, loud, distorted guitar chords, a basic foot-stomping beat, and anthemic choruses. The simplicity of it all was played up even further by the deliberate misspelling of words in the song titles. At the turn of the '70s, "Get Down and Get with It" cracked the UK Top 20, and there was no turning back. Their next dozen singles were UK Top 5 hits, six of them reaching #1. The group's success wasn't limited to the singles charts, either; three of their albums also topped the charts during the same period. Their holiday song "Merry Xmas Everybody" has entered the UK charts seven times as well.

Despite their British success Slade barely cracked the U.S. Hot 100. Even in England, the big hits stopped coming during the punk revolution in the late '70s. They enjoyed a brief revival in the early '80s when Quiet Riot covered "Cum on Feel the Noize" and took it to the top of the charts around the world. This revival even enabled Slade to chart in the American Top 40 with "Run Runaway" and "My Oh My." Slade recently celebrated its 25th anniversary and shows no sign of stopping. — *Jim Powers*

● **Sladest** / 1973 / Reprise 2173
All the British hits that bombed in America. — *Larry Lapka*

○ **Keep Your Hands off My Power Supply** / 1984 / Epic 39336
An early '80s album that managed to climb into the American Top 40, thanks to the success of Quiet Riot's versions of "Cum on Feel the Noize" and "Mama Weer All Crazee Now." On *Keep Your Hands off My Power Supply*, Slade shows that they are still the masters of loud, trashy hard rock. — *Stephen Thomas Erlewine*

Slave

Group / Funk, soul, disco
Arguably the hottest of the '70s Ohio funk bands, Slave had a great run in the late '70s and early '80s. Trumpeter Steve Washington formed the group in Dayton in 1975. Vocalist Floyd Miller teamed with Tom Lockett, Jr.; Charles Bradley; Mark Adams; Mark Hicks; Danny Webster; Orion Wilhoite; and Tim Dozier. Vocalists Steve Arrington and Starleana Young came aboard in 1978, with Arrington ultimately becoming lead vocalist. Their first big hit was the thumping single "Slide" in 1977 for Cotillion, where they remained until 1984. Their best tracks were lyrically simple and at times silly, but the arrangements and rhythms were intense and hypnotic. Other Top 10 R&B hits were "Just a Touch of Love" in 1979, "Watching You" in 1980, and "Snap Shot" in 1981. Young, Washington, and Lockett departed to form Aurra in 1979; Arrington himself left in the early '80s. They added Charles C. Carter, Delburt Taylor, Sam Carter, Kevin Johnson, and Roger Parker as replacements and continued on, though much less successfully, into the late '80s. They moved to Atlantic for one record in 1984, then switched to Ichiban in 1986 for singles and albums that were just a shade of the former vibrant Slave sound. — *Ron Wynn*

● **Stellar Funk: Best of** / 1994 / Rhino/Atlantic 71592
This excellent 15-track anthology contains Slave's finest hits, each with a captivating, thudding bass riff: "Slide," "Just a Touch of Love," and "Watching You," among others. There are also five Arrington numbers, among them his best dance cut ("Weak at the Knees") and topical tune ("Feel So Real"). Though not as acclaimed as Parliament/Funkadelic or Earth, Wind and Fire, this CD shows that Slave deserves recognition for its ability to keep the funk with style and verve. — *Ron Wynn*

Slayer

Group / Heavy metal, thrash
The thrash/speed-metal world would be a very cold place and metal would be very different without Slayer. Tom Araya (vocals/bass), Jeff Hanneman (guitar), Kerry King (guitar), and Dave Lombardo (drums) formed the band in their hometown of Los Angeles in 1982. In their early days they wore heavy eye makeup like Alice Cooper and sang songs about doom, darkness, and the devil, topics many Los Angeles bands of the time wouldn't touch. They played heavy metal, but their lyrics and stage presence (often including crosses worn upside-down by one or more of them) earned their music the name death-metal.

In 1984 Slayer was signed to Metal Blade Records, who released their debut album. On 1985's *Hell Awaits*, the band played a little bit faster, the lyrics were more brutal, and Araya's vocals were getting better. They caught the attention of producer Rick Rubin, cofounder of Def Jam Records, a hip-hop label, who signed them to the label. When their third album was recorded in 1986, CBS refused to distribute it because of so-called demonic overtones. After a few months, Geffen Records came to the rescue and took over distribution. The controversy caused well-deserved publicity, and when critics reviewed the album, they almost unanimously called it a masterpiece in speed-metal. Not wanting to repeat themselves, the band slowed the speed down slightly, and Araya did more singing than all-out screaming on their next album, *South of Heaven;* it was released in 1988 to a lukewarm reception.

They have had many imitators in the following years. Still, there's only one Slayer, a unique and talented band. —*John Book*

Show No Mercy / 1984 / Enigma 71034
Slayer's debut, when the band wore makeup and were considered a joke in some circles. A big difference and a far cry from what they sound like now. —*John Book*

○ **Hell Awaits** / 1985 / Restless 72297
The fear of being in hell is explored on this classic album, right up there with *Reign in Blood.* —*John Book*

● **Reign in Blood** / 1986 / Def American 24131
One of the best albums in thrash/speed-metal, if not the best. Proof that playing fast doesn't result in monotonous boredom. Slayer's major-label debut. —*John Book*

South of Heaven / 1988 / Def American 24203
Slayer's first major-label effort is a devilish delight. —*Dan Heilman*

○ **Seasons in the Abyss** / 1990 / Def American 24307
Their best since *Reign in Blood.* —*John Book*

Decade of Aggression: Live / 1991 / Def American 26748
A double-length set with all of Slayer's great songs done in the only way the band should be experienced: in concert. The best-sounding live speed-metal album so far. —*John Book*

Percy Sledge

b. Nov. 25, 1941, Leighton, AL
Vocals / Soul
"When a Man Loves a Woman" existed long before Michael Bolton ever came on the scene—it's hard to believe that anyone could be unaware of Percy Sledge's original version of the song. As the first southern soul recording to top both the R&B and pop charts in 1966, the emotionally supercharged ballad was a groundbreaker, and Sledge's remarkably anguished performance ranks as an unrivaled masterpiece of the soul genre. Sledge often seems to teeter on the verge of tears on his best Atlantic label releases of the late '60s. A product of the musically fertile area around Muscle Shoals, AL, Sledge recorded "When a Man Loves a Woman" and the equally moving followups "It Tears Me Up," "Out of Left Field," and "Take Time to Know Her" with the same session aces that played on most Muscle Shoals classics of the period. By the turn of the decade, Sledge's well had run dry, although he's recorded off and on ever since. —*Bill Dahl*

★ **It Tears Me Up** / 1992 / Rhino 70285
This stunning compilation from the vaults of Atlantic Records spotlights the voice that gave us the original version of "When a Man Loves a Woman." Lesser-known hits like "It Tears Me Up," "Take Time to Know Her," and "Warm and Tender Love" are equally wonderful, and all are included in this must-have package. Great liner notes by Dave Marsh. Soul music just doesn't get any more heart-wrenching than this. Absolutely essential! —*Christine Ohlman*

P. F. Sloan

Vocals / Singer-songwriter, folk
He was there at the dawn of surf music, he was crowned king of the West Coast protest folkies, and he created some of the great American pop records of the '60s, yet today, the name P. F. Sloan is scarcely remembered outside of a circle of collectors and other '60s enthusiasts. Teamed early with Steve Barrik, Sloan found a lasting partner. The duo cashed in on the surf craze as the Fantastic Baggies, and Sloan has claimed to be involved with countless more surf productions. Sloan and Barri wrote and produced hits for the likes of the Turtles ("Let Me Be"), Herman's Hermits ("Must to Avoid"), and Johnny Rivers ("Secret Agent Man") and may best be remembered for Barry McGuire's "Eve of Destruction." Sloan's own albums for Dunhill were based on the kind of material he had given McGuire, and despite being dismissed by the "serious" protest-folk community of the day, they stand as excellent on their own merits today.

Sloan's attempt to shift away from the West Coast folk-rock he largely created was reflected with the R&B-tinged album "Measure for Pleasure," and following another album in the early

'70s, he was gone. In spite of the occasional live gig and rumors of a comeback, it appears that P. F. Sloan will remain forever connected with his '60s work, with his behind-the-scenes efforts overshadowing the fine music under his own name. —*Steve Aldrich*

● **Anthology** / 1993 / One Way 22097
A well compiled 18-track anthology featuring Sloan's overlooked recording career. This is essential folk-rock in the singer-songwriter tradition. Included is his wonderful version of "Eve of Destruction," which was written by Sloan and popularized by Barry McGuire. —*Chris Woodstra*

Sly & the Family Stone

b. Mar. 15, 1944, Dallas, TX
Group / Soul, funk, R&B, pop/rock
Sylvester Stewart came charging out of the psychedelic environs of San Francisco in 1967 with a band—and a sound—that made good on the communal spirit most acid-scorched bands only talked about. The Family Stone was rock's first fully integrated group: men and women, African American and White, they refused to play the music-business game of racial and sexual segregation, mixing rock and R&B until, as critic Dave Marsh pointed out, "you couldn't find where one began and the other left off."

Songs such as "Everyday People" explained Stone's desire to mix everything up, while "I Want to Take You Higher" and "Dance to the Music" made explicit the community of the Family Stone. But Stone's optimism began to sour in the wake of Dr. Martin Luther King's assassination and the return of segregation, and his music took on a chilling tone. The dizzy glee of "Hot Fun in the Summertime" gave way to the scathing "Thank You (Falettinme Be Mice Elf Agin)" and *There's a Riot Goin' On.* Eventually, his career bogged down under a shroud of drug problems. But Sly Stone's stamp is as indelibly placed on pop music as James Brown's, and his influence can be heard and felt in the work of Kool and the Gang, Prince, George Clinton, and dozens of others. —*John Floyd*

Dance to the Music / 1968 / Epic 26371
Sly's second album reached the lower echelons of *Billboard*'s album charts due to the quintessential psychedelic soul single "Dance to the Music." The rest of the album is uneven, early, and tentative, with the full funk being a little further around the bend. —*Rob Bowman*

Life / 1968 / Epic 26397
The Family Stone's third album was a step forward with a harder drum sound, sharper horn lines, and more focused writing. Despite these developments, *Life* failed to yield a hit single ("Plastic Jim," "Life," and "M'Lady" were all fine candidates). —*Rob Bowman*

☆ **Stand!** / 1969 / Epic 26456
The album on which Sly's integrationalist vision paid big dividends. Four of the record's seven songs, including "I Want to Take You Higher" and "Everyday People," charted as singles. The group contained African Americans and Whites, men and women; voices and instruments careened off one another in one apocalyptic vision of community. At the time, such an album seemed to be the clarion call of a new day. Brilliant. —*Rob Bowman*

★ **Greatest Hits** / 1970 / Epic 30325
This greatest-hits package was released as a stopgap while Sly was taking two years to record *There's a Riot Goin' On.* It's what you would expect from a greatest-hits package, with the addition of two newly recorded monster-hit singles, "Hot Fun in the Summertime" and "Thank You (Falettinme Be Mice Elf Agin)." —*Rob Bowman*

☆ **There's a Riot Goin' On** / 1971 / Epic 30986
Sly gets darker and funkier. By *Riot,* Sly was a bona fide superstar. His personal behavior became more erratic, and his songwriting became more eclectic and adventurous. There is no precedent for such a record; songs were conceived from the rhythm up and often left in sparse, naked, seemingly semifinished form. Sly's earlier hit, "Thank You (Falettinme Be Mice Elf Agin)" is slowed down, turned inside out, and retitled "Thank You for Talkin' to Me Africa." The result is an extremely personal stab at exorcism that takes the listener through the new reality of African American and White America in the early '70s. Mesmerizing. The album's most accessible songs, "Family Affair"

and "Runnin' Away," were R&B and pop hit singles, the former reaching the #1 spot on both charts. —*Rob Bowman*

○ **Fresh** / 1973 / Epic 32134
Stripped down and funky, minus thumb-popping bass whiz Larry Graham (who had left to found Graham Central Station), Sly turned in a fine album. One Top 10 R&B hit resulted with "If You Want Me to Stay," while two other songs, "Frisky" and "If It Were Left Up to Me," also received substantial airplay on African American radio. In the wake of Sly's politics on *Riot* and his increasingly erratic personal and concert behavior, most pop-radio programmers seemed to grow leery of the Family Stone. The first single, "If You Want Me to Stay," reached #12 pop, but it was to be the last Sly Stone record to receive any significant pop success. —*Rob Bowman*

Small Talk / 1974 / Epic 32930
A new bass player and drummer signaled a toned-down Family Stone sound. Partially in keeping with changes in much of popular music in the early '70s, and maybe the result of marriage and a child, Sly became more introspective, quieter, calmer, even employing a string section on various cuts. Less exhilarating album than earlier efforts, there is still much of merit here, including the Top 10 R&B hit "Time for Livin'." —*Rob Bowman*

★ **Anthology** / 1981 / Epic 37071
Repeats cuts from *Greatest Hits* but also includes highlights from *Riot* and *Fresh*. But you should hear those albums in their entirety. —*John Floyd*

The Small Faces

Group / British invasion, pop/rock
America remembers them only for their hit "Itchycoo Park," but the Small Faces were one of England's most wonderful bands of the mid '60s, and their music remains some of the most valuable of the era. The diminutive mods came out roaring in 1965, basing their sounds around American R&B, but unlike countless of their contemporaries, the Small Faces were not about to merely mimic American soul sounds. The group was a powerhouse instrumental unit capped off by the incredible vocals of Steve Marriott. They stayed largely within the R&B-based formula through their stay at Decca. As thrilling as these sides often were, recording time was often rushed between live dates, and, as a result, the band never really had a chance to discover its studio potential during its stay at that label.

That situation changed when the Small Faces hooked up with Andrew "Loog" Oldham's Immediate in 1967. From the outset, the band created some of the most brilliant pop records of the day, far outdistancing their early work. They worked with expanded instrumentation, both live and in the studio, and also began to feature the voice of bassist Ronnie Lane, whose flat, cockney delivery was used brilliantly to contrast with Marriott's. The album *Ogden's Nut Gone Flake* was the pinnacle of their work; unfortunately, it was also their last album. A brief reunion, sans Lane, in the mid '70s added nothing to the band's legacy, but the Small Faces' work of the previous decade would have been hard to equal. —*Steve Aldrich*

Small Faces / 1966 / PolyGram 820572
A testament to greatness. The declaration of true Cockney rebel Steve Marriott singing out against the world. —*Bruce Eder*

From the Beginning / 1967 / PolyGram 820766
The early history of the band, at this time a quartet of earnest White soul shouters. —*Bruce Eder*

○ **There Are But Four Small Faces** / Jan. 1968 / Sony 47895
The Steve Marriott-Ronnie Lane songwriting team spreads its wings, and the band grinds and crunches its way through a collection of excellent (but not outstanding) songs, including the psychedelic anthem "Itchycoo Park." —*Bruce Eder*

● **Ogden's Nut Gone Flake** / Feb. 1968 / Sony 46964
A concept album with soul. A lot of great songs, and an off-center Cockney personality. A classic. —*Bruce Eder*

○ **All or Nothing** / CBS 52427
Extraordinary collection of the band's outtakes, forgotten B sides, odd album tracks that only showed up in certain specific countries, and four live tracks recorded at Newcastle in 1968, all gathered together for the first time and with improved sound. the outtakes and unmixed instrumental backing tracks are all worthwhile, and the live cuts—especially the classics "All or

Nothing" and "Tin Soldier"—are so powerful they're scary, showing Steve Marriott as a vocalist of almost superhuman power and the entire band in high-decibel glory. —*Bruce Eder*

Smashing Pumpkins

Group / Alternative rock
Smashing Pumpkins played the indie rock game, although they didn't quite fit in with the rest of the crowd. Out of his affection for '70s stadium and progressive rock, guitarist/vocalist Billy Corgan fashioned a distinctive, layered sound for the band, dripping with distortion, thick hooks, and airy melodies. Unlike most alternative bands, Smashing Pumpkins don't try to disguise their pretentions or their roots; they are an album rock band, in the tradition of Queen and Black Sabbath. Where most alternative bands use guitar for sonic texture, they use it as a lead instrument in intricate compositions. Smashing Pumpkins rose to success through the alternative scene instead of AOR for two reasons. First, their music was too detailed, creative, and different to fit easily into the conservative hard-rock radio formats of the pre-Nirvana '90s. Secondly, Corgan's lyrics are definitely post-punk, celebrating self-proclaimed geeks and detailing depression and angst. Their mammoth guitars and fragility made them alternative superstars with their 1991 debut *Gish*. When they honed their riffs and Corgan tightened his songwriting for the followup, 1993's major-label debut *Siamese Dream*, the band crossed over into the mainstream. After all, most of their new fans didn't pay attention to the lyrics of "Cherub Rock" or "Today"—they just liked the way those guitars sounded. —*Stephen Thomas Erlewine*

○ **Gish** / 1991 / Caroline 1705
A fine, fine debut album that follows a simple structural philosophy: fast songs good, slow songs not-so-good. Snazzy sound courtesy of hip independent producer Butch Vig. —*John Dougan*

● **Siamese Dream** / 1993 / Virgin
Dense with detail and texture, Smashing Pumpkins' breakthrough second album is a highly personal, ambitious record that unfolds after a few plays. *Siamese Dream* expands on all of the promises of *Gish*, offering more pop melodies, heavy metal riffs, bombastic progressive instrumental sections, and punk angst. Apart from the succinct "Today," the music is so dense and insular that it requires some patience for it to make sense, but given some time *Siamese Dream* becomes addictive. —*Stephen Thomas Erlewine*

Huey Piano Smith

b. Jan. 26, 1934, New Orleans, LA
Piano / R&B
Both a madcap vocalist and underrated pianist, Huey "Piano" Smith was a star in New Orleans during the '50s. He sang with Earl King in the early '50s, then recorded with Guitar Slim from 1951 to 1954. He did several sessions and also led the Clowns, whose roster at one point included Bobby Marchan. Smith's biggest hit wasn't the song he's best known for, "Rocking Pneumonia and the Boogie Woogie Flu," but "Don't You Just Know It," which was his only Top 10 pop and R&B hit. It reached #4 R&B and #9 pop in 1958, a year after "Rocking Pneumonia" peaked at #5 R&B. Smith kept performing until he became a Jehovah's Witness and left the music business. —*Ron Wynn*

● **Rock & Roll Revival** / Jan. 1991 / ACE 2021
A terrific 16-track collection of Huey "Piano" Smith & the Clowns' biggest hits and best material, including "Rocking Puneumonia" and "Don't You Just Know It," plus a couple of fine previously unreleased tracks. —*Stephen Thomas Erlewine*

Patti Smith

b. Dec. 30, 1946
Vocals / Rock & roll
Patti Smith is a poet and rock singer who first gained notice when reading her poetry at gatherings in New York City in the early '70s. By 1974 Smith had edged toward music by reading with the backup of electric guitarist and rock critic Lenny Kaye, notably on her independent-label single "Piss Factory." By 1975 Smith had organized a band that was playing in such clubs as the punk birthplace in New York, CBGB's, and she earned a contract with Arista Records. This resulted in the release of *Horses*, a critically acclaimed album that featured her songs, sometimes melded to dramatic readings, and such rock oldies as "Land of

1,000 Dances." *Radio Ethiopia* was both mainstream-rock-oriented and more experimental, depending on which track you played. With 1978's *Easter*, Smith was definitely moving in a more commercial direction, especially by pairing with Bruce Springsteen for the hit single "Because the Night." That marked the high point of Smith's rock career. *Wave* (1979) found her waving goodbye; she married ex-MC5 guitarist Fred "Sonic" Smith and retired from the music business. Her return came with the promising 1988 album *Dream of Life*, but she was not back to full-time duty. —*William Ruhlmann*

★ **Horses** / 1975 / Arista 8362
One of the more successful matings of poetry and rock, this landmark changed the role of women in rock and paved the way for rock without excess. —*Jeff Tamarkin*

○ **Radio Ethiopia** / 1976 / Arista 8161
Her disjointed second album takes the focus off of Smith's words and shifts it to her excellent band. Intelligent rock & roll, minus a bit of the edge. —*Jeff Tamarkin*

○ **Easter** / 1978 / Arista 8166
Although it contained the hit cover of Springsteen's "Because the Night," Smith's writing was weaker on this third album. The group burns though. —*Jeff Tamarkin*

Wave / 1979 / Arista 8546
The Todd Rundgren-produced final album by the PSG in unfocused and overproduced. Smith was smart to quit while she was ahead. —*Jeff Tamarkin*

Dream of Life / 1988 / Arista 8453
The long-awaited comeback of 1988 was certainly the work of an older, more settled artist. If Smith was still viable, there were few signs here. —*Jeff Tamarkin*

Warren Smith

b. Feb. 7, 1933, d. Jan. 31, 1980
Vocals, guitar / Rockabilly
For sheer, heartfelt vocalizing abilities, Warren Smith may have been the most talented of all the folks who stood in front of the microphone at Sun studio. Equally adept at storming rockabilly and the most gut-wrenching of country ballads, Smith always sang it from the heart, without giving in to phony rasping or histrionics. Though typecast as strictly a rocker, Smith left Sun and achieved minor success in the '60s as a country singer, his first love. —*Cub Koda*

● **Classic Recordings 1956-59** / 1992 / Bear Family 15514
Smith's entire output (31 tracks in all) for Sun Records. Includes the rockabilly classics "Rock & Roll Ruby," "Ubangi Stomp," and "Miss Froggie," as well as heartfelt country performances on "The Darkest Cloud," "I'd Rather Be Safe Than Sorry," and "Goodbye Mr. Love." No Sun collection can really be considered complete without this one . —*Cub Koda*

The Smithereens

Group / Rock & roll
Pat DiNizio (vocals, guitar), Jim Babjak (guitar), Mike Mesaros (bass), and Dennis Diken (drums) make up the Smithereens, formed in New Jersey in 1980 when DiNizio answered an ad placed by the three others. The band plays in a '60s British invasion rock & roll style, DiNizio's songs overtly evoking that era. The Smithereens gigged around the New York area and recorded a couple of EPs on small labels in the early '80s, then scored a record contract with the independent Enigma, which issued *Especially for You* in 1986. It stayed on the charts nearly a year. Its followup, *Green Thoughts* (1988), also showed staying power in the charts, producing the AOR radio hit "Only a Memory." The Smithereens reached the pop Top 40 with "A Girl like You" from their third album, *11*, in 1989. A fourth album, *Blow Up*, stirred college and AOR radio interest for the track "Top of the Pops" in 1991, but it was less of a sales success. —*William Ruhlmann*

Beauty & Sadness / 1983 / Capitol 96841
The Smithereens' second EP is an impressive collection of melodic guitar-driven power-pop, particularly the title cut. Fans of the band should seek this out, but the uninitiated will get a better picture of the band with *Especially for You* and *Green Thoughts*. —*Rick Clark*

● **Especially for You** / 1986 / Capitol 97499

On *Especially for You*, Smithereens achieved a near-perfect blend of exuberant rockers and moody excursions. Don Dixon's production captured the band's exciting chemistry, while keeping lead singer Pat DiNizio up front in the mix, on this, their best album. "Behind the Wall of Sleep" and "Blood and Roses" were big college-music favorites, helping pave the way for greater success. Other highlights included "Strangers When We Meet," "Time and Time Again," "Groovy Tuesday," and "Alone at Midnight." —*Rick Clark*

○ **Green Thoughts** / 1988 / Capitol 48375
The followup to *Especially for You* was another impressive batch of power-pop rockers. "Only a Memory" and "House We Used to Live In" were FM rock hits. Again, Dixon's production demonstrated his empathy for the band's sound. Other highlights included "Something New," "Drown in My Own Tears," and the title track. —*Rick Clark*

11 / 1990 / Capitol 91194
On *11*, Smithereens employed alternative hard-rock producer Ed Stasium (Living Colour) to beef up their sound. The result was a thick guitar-riff-heavy sound. The approach helped "A Girl like You" become a big rock and MTV hit, but, as a whole, *11* lacked the dynamics and natural soundstage that made their earlier work so fresh-sounding. "Yesterday Girl," "Baby Be Good," and "A Girl like You" are highlights, though. —*Rick Clark*

Blow Up / 1991 / Capitol 94963
An improvement over *11*, *Blow Up* displays Stasium's state-of-the-art power-rock production and a greater range of material. The soulful "Too Much Passion" was a hit, as was "Top of the Pops." —*Rick Clark*

A Date with the Smithereens / 1994 / RCA
Producer Don Dixon returns to the helm, creating an album that synthesizes the jangly melodic appeal of *Green Thoughts* with the finesse of *11*. Includes the single "Miles from Nowhere." —*Rick Clark*

The Smiths

Group / Alternative pop/rock
At the beginning of the '80s, both the British pop and independent charts were filled with synth-pop, goth-rock, and lightweight new wave. In this climate, the Smiths' first single, "Hand in Glove," caused a quiet revolution. With their first album and early singles, the Smiths led rock & roll into a new era, where songs were again of the utmost importance, guitars replaced synthesizers as the prominent instrument on the pop and indie charts, and lyrics were unabashedly personal and poetic; in short, they helped post-punk become alternative rock. In their native England, the band were superstars; each of their albums hit the Top 10. America never warmed to their distinctly British sensibility, yet they did earn a sizable cult following across the United States. Ten years after the release of their first album, their influence is still substantial; from the Stone Roses to Suede, the Smiths were the root of nearly every significant development in British music since 1984.

At its core, the Smiths' music was pure guitar-based pop/rock, recalling hooks and textures from the '60s. While their music was rooted in British pop, it also borrowed significantly from the energy and independence of punk; it never sounded dated or derivative. Morrissey's yearning voice and literate lyrics complimented Johnny Marr's understated, textured guitar to the point where the two were inseparable. Marr had a skill for writing melodic hooks that sounded simple and direct, yet were an incredibly complex web of interweaving guitar lines. But Morrissey was the focal point of the band. Some critics accused him of being tuneless, yet he was a great vocalist, effortlessly conveying the exaggerated angst and self-deprecating humor of his words with unusual, unexpected pitches and phrasing. Morrissey's introspective lyrics strongly connected with disaffected youth around the world, yet they aren't adolescent; beneath his grandly dramatic vocals, there are genuine emotion, humor, melancholy, and compassion in Morrissey's writing.

The songwriting team of Morrissey and Marr was remarkably inventive and prolific; during their brief four-year career, the Smiths released four proper albums, several non-LP singles and B-sides, and two singles compilations. All of their material was remarkably consistent, proving the band's mastery of pop songwriting.

The Smiths broke up in early fall of 1987, just before the release of their fourth and final album, *Strangeways Here We Come.*
Bassist Andy Rourke and drummer Mike Joyce supported Sinéad
O'Connor for a time; Joyce eventually joined the reunited
Buzzcocks. Marr went on to work with the Pretenders, the The,
and Electronic. Morrissey began a solo career that proved just as
popular as the Smiths'. —*Stephen Thomas Erlewine*

☆ **Smiths** / 1984 / Sire 25065
The Smiths make ear-pleasing, catchy pop-rock, and it seduces
the listener into paying attention to Morrissey's deadpan lyrics,
which are deliberately self-pitying, sometimes caustic, and usually funny. "Reel around the Fountain" is a classic, and the album
also contains the UK singles "Hand in Glove" and "What
Difference is it Make?" —*William Ruhlmann*

☆ **Hatful of Hollow** / 1984 / Sire 45205
A collection of singles, B sides, and BBC radio sessions, *Hatful of
Hollow* shows how rapidly the Smiths were evolving. Containing
some of the best songs—"William, It Was Really Nothing," "How
Soon Is Now?" "This Charming Man," "Hand in Glove," "Reel
around the Fountain," "Please, Please, Please, Let Me Get What I
Want"—the album is a more exciting and effective record than
their debut album. —*Stephen Thomas Erlewine*

Meat Is Murder / 1985 / Sire 25269
The Smiths' second album isn't a great leap forward, but it does
contain some fine guitar pop, including "The Headmaster Ritual,"
"Rusholme Ruffians," and "That Joke Isn't Funny Anymore." The
American version included the pulsating "How Soon Is Now?"
which doesn't fit the mood of the rest of the album. —*Stephen
Thomas Erlewine*

★ **The Queen Is Dead** / 1986 / Sire 25426
The Queen Is Dead is the Smiths' masterpiece, boasting an amazingly accomplished set of songs, including the surrealistic humor
of the title track, the lilting "The Boy with the Thorn in His Side,"
the deceptively sunny pop of "Cemetery Gates," the nasty
"Bigmouth Strikes Again," and the gorgeous "There Is a Light
That Never Goes Out." Morrissey's lyrics have never been better,
and Marr's hooks are among his best. —*Stephen Thomas
Erlewine*

☆ **Louder Than Bombs** / 1987 / Sire 25569
The Smiths' second singles and B-sides collection is every bit as
essential as the first, containing such brilliant songs as "Panic,"
"London," "You Just Haven't Earned It Yet, Baby," and "Is It Really
So Strange." There's a bit of duplication with *Hatful of Hollow*,
but the music on *Louder Than Bombs* was some of the most vi-
tal and timeless pop music of the '80s. —*Stephen Thomas
Erlewine*

○ **Strangeways Here We Come** / 1987 / Sire 25649
While there are some fine songs here, *Strangeways Here We
Come* is ultimately a disappointing final effort from the Smiths.
Nevertheless, the album's best songs—"Stop Me If You've Heard
This One Before," "I Won't Share You," "Last Night I Dreamt That
Somebody Loved Me," "Girlfriend in a Coma"—are among the
best the band recorded. —*Stephen Thomas Erlewine*

Rank / 1988 / Sire 25786
A solid but unexceptional live album recorded on the *Queen Is
Dead* tour. —*Stephen Thomas Erlewine*

Best of the Smiths, Vol. 1 / 1992 / Sire 45042
With or without its companion volume, this remains a less than
excellent compilation. Even when viewed with *Volume 2*, these
collections include odd selections at the expense of more obvious
ones. The faithful will already have everything here. And neophyte fans would do better with *Louder than Bombs* along with
Queen and the debut. —*Steve Aldrich*

Best of the Smiths, Vol. 2 / Dec. 8, 1992 / Sire 45097
Best of, Vol. 2 fills in the gaps from the first volume, but like its
predecessor, it lacks cohesion or a sense of what made the Smiths
important. Many great songs but, ultimately, it cheats the legacy
of Britain's most important band of the 80s. —*AMG*

Sneakers

Power pop
While the Sneakers never made much of an impact when they
were together, the band marks the first appearance of several
seminal figures of the alternative pop scene of the early '80s.
Chris Stamey, Mitch Easter, and Will Rigby formed the core of the

Sneakers, writing well-crafted, guitar-driven pop rockers; their
self-titled debut EP was engineered by Don Dixon, who went on
to be a successful producer as well as a solo artist. After one excellent full-length album, the Sneakers broke up. Stamey and
Rigby went on to form the dB's, one of the '80s best American
guitar-pop bands; Easter led Let's Active as well as becoming a
record producer (including R.E.M.'s first two albums). However,
the Sneakers are more than a historical curiosity; although they
didn't record very much, their album and EP contain some of the
finest power pop of the late '70s. —*Stephen Thomas Erlewine*

● **Racket** / 1993 / East Side Digital 80672
This disc contains selections from the Sneakers' unfinished third
record, *Wig Cleaner*, as well as all the original compositions from
In the Red and the band's first release, *Carnivorous #1*. While all
of the songs were written in the late '70s, some of the recordings
were done as recently as 1992. Songs like "Some Kinda Fool" and
"Story of a Girl" exude an effortless sophistication of chord structure and melody. Lovers of quirky guitar pop/rock (read: early
dB's fans) should have this one. —*Rick Clark*

Phoebe Snow (Phoebe Laub)

b. Jul. 17, 1952, New York City, NY
Vocals / Singer-songwriter, pop
This pop-jazz singer-songwriter with a broad, melismatic contralto voice broke through in 1975 with her debut album on
Shelter, then made several albums for Columbia and Atlantic despite legal and personal difficulties that distracted her from her
career. She returned to recording on Elektra in 1989 after an
eight-year layoff and was also part of Donald Fagen's New York
Rock and Soul Revue. —*William Ruhlmann*

● **Phoebe Snow** / 1974 / Dcc 8004
A wondrous folk, pop, and jazz album of Snow's original songs
and some well-chosen covers, all showcasing her one-of-a-kind
voice. Includes the Top 5 hit "Poetry Man." —*William Ruhlmann*

○ **It Looks like Snow** / Feb. 1976 / Columbia 34387
The cover songs start to overwhelm the originals, but when Snow
is able to bring such powerful interpretations to "Don't Let Me
Down," "Shakey Ground," and "Teach Me Tonight," who could
complain? —*William Ruhlmann*

Social Distortion

Group / Rock & roll, punk
An early high mark in California punk. Actually, with their 1977-
era power chords and an artistic scope that was comfortable
enough to include Johnny Cash covers, this Fullerton, CA, band
came on like a throwback to British punk groups like Stiff Little
Fingers and the Vibrators. They were also able to move their
chunky punk rock into the mainstream without cutting back on
the energy, the power chords, or the nihilism. And that's something few West Coast hardcore bands can claim. —*John Floyd*

○ **Mommy's Little Monster** / 1983 / Triple X 51019
Their debut is full of wailing guitars, sharp lyrics, tugging
melodies, and snarling vocals. —*John Floyd*

Prison Bound / 1988 / Restless 72251
The release of lthis album brought acoustic guitars, ballads, and
a cautious step toward the rock mainstream that makes their music of use for more than just hardcore nihilists. —*John Floyd*

○ **Social Distortion** / 1990 / Epic 46055
Their major-label debut repeated the winning formula of *Prison
Bound*—Ramones meet the Blasters meet Johnny Thunders—but
with better production. —*John Floyd*

● **Somewhere between Heaven and Hell** / 1991 / Epic 47978
Social Distortion wallows in rock & roll rebellion and fatalism.
The combination of urgent lyrics and unbeatable riffs make this
their best album. —*John Floyd*

The Soft Boys

Group / Punk, alternative pop/rock
While they were together, the Soft Boys recorded three discs of
blissful post-punk weirdness, fueled by the winding guitar of
Kimberly Rew and the warped vision of Robyn Hitchcock. Rew
joined the band after an independent EP in time for the recording of their full-length debut, *A Can of Bees*. But the focal point
of the band was singer-guitarist Hitchcock, a bizarrely gifted pop
songwriter with an affection for Syd Barrett and John Lennon.

Hitchcock melded the psychedelic guitars of *Revolver*-era Beatles with the sheer dementia of Barrett, creating a stripped-down guitar rock unlike anything else in the post-punk world. And the Soft Boys were assuredly inspired by punk—both their raw sound and lyrical obsessions were outgrowths of the punk era. Their time together was brief—about three years—yet their music has inspired a cult of devoted fans. Hitchcock went on to a successful cult career as a singer-songwriter; Rew formed Katrina & the Waves, where he earned a surprising amount of pop success. —*Stephen Thomas Erlewine*

● **Underwater Moonlight** / 1980 / Rykodisc 20232
Wry, savage humor permeates this near-virtuoso album. Extraordinarily well played, especially the guitars. —*Bruce Eder*

Soft Cell

Group / New wave, dance-pop
Like the traditional synthesizer-driven dance-pop of the early '80s, Soft Cell was detatched from their material, yet they were not cold. Instead, the duo of vocalist Marc Almond and keyboardist David Ball were warm and human; they were joyfully sleazy, celebrating kinky sex and trashing pop standards. Their finest moment came with a single from their first album, *Non-Stop Erotic Cabaret*, in 1981. "Tainted Love" represents everything Soft Cell wanted to achieve, and it was an enormous success, spending nearly a year on the *Billboard* singles charts. After that, the duo occasionally recaptured some of the spark of that single (their cover of "Where Did Our Love Go?" in particular) but more frequently slipped into self-parody; they broke up in 1984. —*Stephen Thomas Erlewine*

● **Memorabilia: Singles** / 1991 / PolyGram 510178
Although it doesn't contain a couple of key tracks—including the 12-inch version of "Tainted Love/Where Did Our Love Go"—*Memorabilia* is the best Soft Cell collection available. —*Stephen Thomas Erlewine*

Soft Machine

Group / Progressive rock, psychedelic
Named after a William Burroughs novel, Soft Machine (formed 1966) was one of the most exciting prog-rock bands to emerge from England during the late '60s. Their first two albums were brilliantly whimsical fusions of jazz and hard psychedelia. Robert Wyatt's inventive drumming and appealingly unstable tenor rasp of a voice enhanced the band's oddball musical attack, as did Michael Ratledge's off-center keyboard parts, Hugh Hopper's distorto-splat bass work and Kevin Ayers's manic lead guitar work. After their second album, the Soft Machine adopted a more pronounced instrumental space-jazz approach. After their appropriately titled *Third*, the group's lineup began to change dramatically. Subsequent albums became less interesting. —*Rick Clark*

○ **Third** / 1970 / Columbia 30339
This album marks the beginning of their penchant for long, jazz-influenced pieces and the end of the youthful, madcap era. —*Myles Boisen*

Live at the Proms 1970 / 1988 / Reckless 5
A masterful exposition of their more serious jazz side. —*Myles Boisen*

● **Volumes 1 & 2** / Sep. 1989 / Big Beat 920
Their influential early recordings, combining Bonzo Dog Band's zaniness with a strong progressive vision in concise song structures. —*Myles Boisen*

Sonic Youth

Group / Alternative rock
When Sonic Youth began as a downtown New York band in the early '80s, they rejected most traditional rock & roll formalities such as Western tuning and song structure. With screwdrivers randomly stuck into their guitar necks, the quartet created discordant, droning, mantralike songs, which were quietly forceful. As they matured, their material became more accessible and the songs more conventional, even as they retained their discordance. By the early '90s, Sonic Youth was approaching mainstream acceptance.

The band (Kim Gordon, bass and vocal; Thurston Moore, guitar and vocal; Lee Ranaldo, guitar; Steve Shelley, drums) had several releases before their sound crystallized. *Sonic Youth,*

Confusion Is Sex, Kill Yr Idols, and *Sonic Death* document a band learning to express their complex ideas. These releases are often coarse and brash, sometimes unlistenable, and frequently startling in their power.

The band's cult following continued to grow throughout the late '80s, culminating in a major-label contract with Geffen Records. The corporate machine helped them develop a still-larger following. After their Geffen debut, 1990's *Goo*, Sonic Youth rested for two years.

The band reemerged with *Dirty*, their most direct stab at traditional pop/rock songwriting. The album was more successful than any of their past efforts, making the band popular with MTV-weaned adolescents. Naturally, Sonic Youth responded with a change in direction. *Experimental Jet Set, Trash and No Star* (1994) was their calmest record, yet it was more abstract than either of their major-label releases; it had an instant alternative radio/MTV hit with "Bull in the Heather." —*Robert Gordon*

Bad Moon Rising / 1985 / Blast First 1
On *Bad Moon Rising,* the songs gained a focus so that moods and styles that formerly had spread scross several releases could be accomplished in one album. —*Robert Gordon*

○ **EVOL** / 1986 / SST 059
Leaving their most experimental stage, *EVOL* retains that sense of adventure and packages it in concise, deliberate bites. *EVOL* ("love" spelled backward) is composed of catchy rhythms and melodies, even some hooks; however, a menacing darkness remains, even dominates. Vocals are split pretty evenly between Gordon and Moore. *EVOL* remains a high point for the band, with provocative songs that force us, even after punk, to question what was commonplace in pop. Features "Green Light" and "Expressway to Yr Skull." —*Robert Gordon*

☆ **Sister** / 1987 / SST 134
Sister found them largely embracing the rock aesthetic, though with little sacrifice to their own code. The album retains its menace and punkish attitude while totally rocking out. It's sort of the other side of the *EVOL* coin. They achieve a similar end, but instead of using spacious and brooding songs, they play hard, succinct, and tight. The CD features the bonus track "Master Dik." —*Robert Gordon*

★ **Daydream Nation** / 1988 / Geffen 75403
Daydream Nation is a double album that warrants its indulgences; if the songs run long, they're worth it. When "Total Trash" devolves into a furious jam, its cacophony is beautiful, surpassed only by the surprise return to structure. The appeal of the "Teenage Riot" single brought the band a greater audience, and, if it seems to compromise their stance, in the context of the album it makes perfect sense. —*Robert Gordon*

Goo / 1990 / David Geffen Co. 24297
Though *Goo* is not a sellout, it didn't advance the band in the leaps their previous few albums had. Mostly it sounds like *Daydream Nation* rehashed. Includes "Tunic," "Dirty Boots," and "Kool Thing." —*Robert Gordon*

○ **Dirty** / 1992 / David Geffen Co. 24485
Sonic Youth could never sell out, no matter how hard they tried. Their sound—a jarring barrage of distorted guitars and feedback—is entirely too singular and avant garde to ever completely cross over into the mainstream. However, *Dirty* is the closest Sonic Youth has ever come to the mainstream, and it is their most accessible album to date. "100%" is nearly a pop single, complete with hooks and an identifiable song structure. But Sonic Youth hasn't lost their edge, as Kim Gordon's tracks (like "Swimsuit Issue") in particular prove. —*Stephen Thomas Erlewine*

Experimental Jet Set, Trash and No Star / 1994 / David Geffen Company 24632
Opening with their first acoustic number ever, *Experimental Jet Set, Trash and No Star* is Sonic Youth's calmest record to date. While the band's sound is different, they're ideas aren't—they're essentially repeating *Sister*. There's a couple of interesting tracks, but most of the album is surprisingly boring. —*Stephen Thomas Erlewine*

The Sonics

Group / Rock & roll, garage rock

Forming in the wake of the early '60s success of local favorites the Kingsmen and the Wailers (whose Etiquette label they recorded for), the Sonics combined the classic Northwest-area teen-band raunch with early English band grit (particularly influenced by the Kinks), relentless rhythmic drive, and unabashed '50s-style blues shouting for a combination that still makes their brand of rock & roll perhaps the raunchiest ever captured on wax. Lead singer Gerry Roslie was no less than a White Little Richard, whose harrowing soul screams were startling even to the Northwest teen audience, who liked their music powerful and driving with little regard to commercial subtleties. With hit after hit on the local charts (and influencing every local band that ever took the stage), the band inexplicably was never able to break out nationally, leaving their sound largely undiluted for mass consumption. Breaking up in the late '60s (after one ill-fated album attempt to water down their style for national attention), the Sonics continue today to be revered by '60s collectors the world over for their unique brand of rock & roll raunch. —*Cub Koda*

● **Here Are the Ultimate Sonics** / 1991 / Etiquette 024027
Combining all the tracks from their first two Etiquette albums, three tracks from the label's Christmas album, live tracks, and an alternate take of "The Witch," this compilation more than lives up to its title. The definitive overview. —*Cub Koda*

Sonny & Cher

Group / Pop/rock
Sonny & Cher proved one of the magical musical combinations of the '60s, with their wisecracking repartee providing counterpoint to a series of adoring hit duets. Sonny Bono (b. February 16, 1935) started out at Los Angeles-based Specialty Records as a songwriter in the late '50s. While working sessions with legendary producer Phil Spector, Bono met and married background singer Cher (born Cherilyn Lapierre, May 20, 1946) and formed a duet with his new wife. Neither was blessed with an outstanding vocal range, but no matter—they went gold in 1965 with the pop chart-topper "I Got You Babe" on Atco and did well with "Baby Don't Go" on Reprise. At the same time, both enjoyed success separately—Sonny with "Laugh at Me" for Atco, Cher with "All I Really Want to Do" and "Bang Bang (My Baby Shot Me Down)" on Imperial. "The Beat Goes On" in 1967 and "All I Ever Need Is You" four years later presaged the pair's anointment as popular TV variety-hour hosts from 1971 to 1974 (the year they were divorced). Since then, Cher has gone on to mega-stardom on record and on the silver screen. Sonny, meanwhile, was elected mayor of Palm Springs, CA. —*Bill Dahl*

● **Beat Goes On: The Best of Sonny & Cher** / 1975 / Atco 91796
They were the ultimate "hip luv" couple of the '60s, and their many hits are still fun to listen to. "I Got You Babe," "Laugh at Me," and the title track are three of the 21 original recordings included in this definitive collection. —*Jeff Tamarkin*

Soul Asylum

Group / Alternative rock, rock & roll
Initially, Soul Asylum didn't sound that much different from their Minneapolis peers Hüsker Dü and the Replacements, churning out fast, spirited punk rockers. Even at that stage, there were hints of musical diversity, from folk and country to straight-ahead pop, beneath the roar. As the band's career progressed, the songwriting of lead vocalist/guitarist Dave Pirner became sharper, relying on conventional, melodic song structure instead of aimless, raging sound; guitarist Dan Murphy's writing was equally as good. After they signed to A&M in 1988, Soul Asylum hit their artistic stride, releasing two excellent albums that suffered from poor promotion on the label's part; the label dropped the band after their *And the Horse They Rode On* album.

Soul Asylum's last chance for success was 1992's *Grave Dancer's Union*, an album that was more accessible than their previous albums without compromising their artistic integrity. Amazingly, the band *did* hit the big time, thanks to the folkie ballad "Runaway Train." The band became superstars, touring the world for nearly two years and going platinum several times over; they even performed at the White House. For a band that seemed destined to the same fate as their long-gone Minneapolis contemporaries, their success was nothing short of a miracle. —*Stephen Thomas Erlewine*

Made to Be Broken / 1986 / Twintone 8666

Early Soul Asylum blitzkreig-raunch at its best. Sure, it sounds a little like Hüsker Dü. But only a little. —*John Dougan*

Clam Dip and Other Delights / Jan. 1988 / Twintone 88144
A great EP with a very funny cover. Loud, fun, and funky. —*John Dougan*

● **Hang Time** / Feb. 1988 / A&M 5197
More of a riff record than usual, this is the strongest collection of Dave Pirner songs in one place. Lenny Kaye's production does a good job of translating the roar of Pirner and lead guitarist Dan Murphy to tape. A great place to start. —*John Dougan*

○ **And the Horse They Rode On** / 1990 / A&M 5318
Thanks to Steve Jordan's live production approach and some great material, *And the Horse They Rode On* is this Minneapolis quartet's best effort. Among this album's many highlights are "Veil of Tears" (a nice Stones riff), the spastic hyperdrive of "Spinnin'," the ugly funk of "Something Out of Nothing," and the dynamic rocker "Nice Guys (Don't Get Paid)." —*Rick Clark*

○ **Grave Dancers Union** / May 1992 / Columbia 48898
Although Soul Asylum's first Columbia release, *Grave Dancer's Union,* is a bit of a step down from the excellent *And the Horse They Rode On,* it was their first hit album, due to Dave Pirner's more streamlined songwriting. Instead of relying on a spiky, riff-oriented punk roar, Soul Asylum covers everything from the straightforward rock of "Somebody to Shove" and "99%" to the folky "Runaway Train" and "Black Gold." While these songs are among the best the band has ever recorded, much of the rest of the record doesn't compare to the previous album. Nevertheless, *Grave Dancer's Union* is the band's most accomplished, accessible album; it deserved to be a hit. —*Stephen Thomas Erlewine*

Soul II Soul

Group / Dance, urban, soul, pop
The best of the pack of late '80s/early '90s British retro-soul groups, Soul II Soul (led by DJ, producer, and vocalist Jazzie B) blends elements of '70s Motown and Philly soul with the easy-groove approach favored by Loose Ends and the incessant thump of Chicago house music. —*John Floyd*

● **Keep on Movin'** / 1988 / Virgin 91267
The group's debut (originally titled *Club Classics Vol. One* in Europe) contains their finest single, "Keep On Movin'," and "Back to Life" but is padded by stilted raps and plodding beat fodder. —*John Floyd*

○ **Vol. II: 1990: A New Decade** / 1990 / Virgin 91367
A better album but a deceptive one: even the best songs here don't intoxicate as thoroughly as "Keep On Movin'," but within the context of the album, each plays a vital part. In other words, this is a genuine *album,* and not a pastiche of singles. —*John Floyd*

Soundgarden

Group / Alternative rock, heavy metal
Never one for true musical diversity—and that includes their breakthrough album, *Superunknown*—Soundgarden was responsible for making true, gutsy heavy metal hip in the American underground of the late '80s. Fueled by the primal, sub-Sabbath riffing of guitarist Kim Thayil and the shrieking wail of vocalist Chris Cornell, Soundgarden offers a revamped, post-punk take on heavy metal. While they never dispense with the traditions of metal—pummeling riffs, long solos, machismo—they add a significant amount of angst and irony. Their songs are always more intricate than the average Black Sabbath number, yet never as detailed as Led Zeppelin.

Soundgarden worked its way into the mainstream through a series of late '80s independent releases, culminating in a major-label deal with A&M; their first major label album, *Louder Than Love,* was released in 1989. Before Nirvana exploded down the doors for alternative rockers in general and Seattle bands in particular in 1991, Soundgarden had earned a following that was larger than any other Seattle band; with songs like "Big Dumb Sex" and "Hands All Over" they were appealed both to the riff-hungry heavy metal fans as well as the cool, detatched alternative rock fans. But their real mainstream breakthrough didn't come until 1994, when the band released the critically acclaimed *Superunknown.* On that album Soundgarden expanded their primal metal into a variety of new musical territory without ever losing sight of the core of their music—their overpowering riffs. It established the band as one of the most popular rock bands of the early '90s. —*Stephen Thomas Erlewine*

○ **Ultramega OK** / 1989 / SST 201

A noticeable improvement from their EPs, Soundgarden's first full-length release is an impressive mixture of slow Zeppelin/Sabbath-style riffs updated for a new generation with even more murkiness. Cornell's vocals can be irritatingly overblown, and the band can be unfocused (hear their cover of Howlin' Wolf's "Smokestack Lightning"), but the whole thing sounds fresh. —*Stephen Thomas Erlewine*

Louder than Love / 1990 / A&M 5252

The first major-label release from Soundgarden is a step down from the independent *Ultramega OK*, as Thayil's guitar drowns in the murkiness of the production that Cornell tries to bellow through. It's uneven, but there are some staple Soundgarden songs that are among their best, including "Full on Kevin's Mom," "Hands All Over," "Ugly Truth," and the extraordinarily stupid "Big Dumb Sex." —*Stephen Thomas Erlewine*

Screaming Life / Fopp / 1990 / Sub Pop 12

A reissue of two early (1987 and 1988) EPs, which capture the band in its formative stages. Worth any true fan's time. —*Stephen Thomas Erlewine*

○ **Badmotorfinger** / 1991 / A&M 5374

Soundgarden's most accessible and accomplished album to date captures the band stretching out and successfully experimenting. Unlike those on the previous *Louder than Love*, the songs have varied tempos and textures, along with memorable riffs. With Cornell singing better than he ever has on a Soundgarden album, the band has delivered a set of songs that now stands as their signature statement. —*Stephen Thomas Erlewine*

● **Superunknown** / Mar. 8, 1994 / A&M 540198

Superunknown expands on the bottomless heavy metal of *Badmotorfinger* by adding touches of psychedelia and pop to Soundgarden's signature sludge. The result is the band's best album, full of powerful, expertly crafted hard rock that improves with repeated listens. —*Stephen Thomas Erlewine*

Joe South

b. Feb. 28, 1940

Vocals, guitar / Singer-songwriter, pop/rock

By the time Joe South hit as a solo artist, he had become a veritable jack-of-all trades, being a country DJ and an in-demand session guitar player, providing electric guitar for Simon & Garfunkel's hit "Sounds of Silence." As a producer, he produced Billy Joe Royal, who scored with two South compositions, "Down in the Boondocks" and "I Knew You When." South also penned "Hush," a hit for Royal and for the British band Deep Purple.

South signed to Capitol Records in 1968 and released his debut, *Introspect*, with the single "Birds of a Feather." The song didn't chart but became a hit for the Raiders. The second single off of that album, "Games People Play," was his first big solo hit, and it established South as a rather preachy straight-talking southern artist. His followup singles were "Walk a Mile in My Shoes," "Don't It Make You Want to Go Home," and "Fool Me."

In 1971 South had his greatest songwriting success when country singer Lynn Anderson landed a worldwide million-selling hit with "Rose Garden," which Elvis Presley and many other artists recorded as well. Except for a few relatively obscure mid '70s solo albums, South dropped out and hasn't been heard from since. —*Rick Clark*

● **Best Of** / 1990 / Rhino 70994

This is an essential collection featuring South's brand of southern-style pop idealism. Classic hits like "Games People Play," "Walk a Mile in My Shoes," "Don't It Make You Want to Go Home," and "Birds of a Feather" as well as notable South originals like "Down in the Boondocks," "Rose Garden," "I Knew You When," and "Hush" are here, too. Good liner notes and sound round out this package. —*Rick Clark*

John David Souther

b. 1946

Vocals, guitar / Singer-songwriter

This Detroit-born songwriter, singer, and guitarist is best known for the cover versions of his songs found on Linda Ronstadt albums and his hit cocompositions with members of the Eagles ("Best of My Love," "New Kid in Town," "Heartache Tonight"). Also a member of the Souther, Hillman, Furay Band in the mid '70s. —*William Ruhlmann*

John David Souther / 1971 / Asylum 5055

It may be that the only thing that kept Souther from becoming a major star in the '70s was that his friends the Eagles beat him to the country-rock style demonstrated on this album, which features "The Fast One" and "Run like a Thief," both recorded by Linda Ronstadt. —*William Ruhlmann*

○ **Black Rose** / 1976 / Asylum 1059

Excellent album steeped in the Southern California country-rock sound of the '70s, with all the usual suspects (Danny Kortchmar, Waddy Wachtel, Kenny Edwards, and Russ Kunkel and producer Peter Asher—all Ronstadt veterans—plus Glenn Frey and Don Henley from the Eagles) in place on such songs as "Faithless Love," "Simple Man, Simple Dream," and "Silver Blue." —*William Ruhlmann*

● **You're Only Lonely** / 1979 / Columbia 36093

Souther finally scored a hit single with the '50s-ish title track, and the album also includes such lovely ballads as "White Rhythm and Blues," as well as the solo version of the Souther, Hillman, Furay song "Trouble in Paradise." —*William Ruhlmann*

Southside Johnny & the Asbury Jukes

Group / Rock & roll

A ragtag collection of Jersey-shore bar-band vets led by harmonica-playing, late-night-voiced "Southside" Johnny Lyon. The Jukes coalesced under the direction, production, and songwriting assistance of Miami Steve Van Zandt and Bruce Springsteen, churning out a string of superb albums that merged horn-driven R&B raveups with strong original material. Some seldom-heard Springsteen-written chestnuts show up on the Jukes' albums, including "The Fever," "Love on the Wrong Side of Town," "When You Dance," and the ravishing "Hearts of Stone." The group fell apart when guitarist Billy Rush left, but then reformed for a stunning comeback album, *Better Days*. —*Kit Kiefer*

○ **I Don't Want to Go Home** / 1976 / Epic 34180

The Jukes's debut and an R&B revivalist's delight, capped by splendid duets with Lee Dorsey ("How Come You Treat Me So Bad?") and Ronnie Spector ("You Mean So Much to Me"). —*Kit Kiefer*

○ **This Time It's for Real** / 1977 / Epic 34668

Southside Johnny's sophomore release was another strong collection of early '60s R&B- and doo-wop-influenced rock/pop. To underscore those elements, *This Time It's for Real* features guest appearances by the Drifters, the Coasters, and the Five Satins. Highlights include "Without Love," "Love on the Wrong Side of Town," and the title track. —*Rick Clark*

○ **Hearts of Stone** / 1978 / Epic 35488

The most successful merger of old R&B with modern songwriting and sensibilities in the Jukes' catalog. "Hearts of Stone" features more great Van Zandt originals ("Got to Be a Better Way Home," "This Time Baby's Gone for Good") and Springsteen's knockout title tune. —*Kit Kiefer*

○ **Havin' a Party with Southside Johnny** / 1979 / Epic 36246

The highlights of this New Jersey band's first few albums, plus a fine remake of Sam Cooke's "Having a Party." It's a great starting place for the uninitiated. —*Rick Clark*

○ **Better Days** / 1991 / Impact 10445

A comeback album that by all rights shouldn't be this good, *Better Days* reunites Southside Johnny with his old cohorts Springsteen and Van Zandt and some special guests (Jon Bon Jovi, Flo and Eddie) for 11 bittersweet originals capped by the gorgeous soul ballad "It's Been a Long Time." —*Kit Kiefer*

● **Best of Southside Johnny & the Asbury Jukes** / Aug. 11, 1992 / Epic 52733

Concentrating on the highlights from the late '70s albums of Southside Johnny & the Asbury Jukes, *Best of Southside Johnny* offers a good introduction to the hard R&B-influenced rock of the New Jersey band. —*Stephen Thomas Erlewine*

Spacemen 3

Group / Alternative rock

Spacemen 3 were psychedelic in the loosest sense of the word; their guitar explorations were colorfully mind-alterating, but not in the sense of the acid rock of the '60s. Instead, the band developed its own minimalistic psychedelia, relying on heavily distorted guitars to clash and produce their own harmonic overtones; frequently, they would lead up to walls of distortion with overamplified acoustic guitars and synths. Often the band would jam on one chord or play a series of songs all in the same tempo and key. After several albums in the late '80s, the band fell apart after in 1991; guitarist Jason Pierce made his side-project Spirtualized his full-time band. —*Stephen Thomas Erlewine*

○ **Perfect Prescription** / 1987 / Genmark 1
Spacey, with lots of guitar noise and simplistic drum thumping. —*John Dougan*

Performance / 1988 / Genius 6
Ugly and noisy, in front of a tiny audience. —*John Dougan*

● **Recurring** / 1991 / Dedicated 3047
Kinda danceable in an odd way. —*John Dougan*

Spandau Ballet

Group / New wave, dance-pop, pop
After recording two albums in the early '80s of new romantic synth-pop that resulted in only one great single ("To Cut a Long Story Short"), Spandau Ballet abruptly changed their style to a smooth, soul-influenced pop sound. The change in direction resulted in their biggest success, with the international hit "True" and its accompanying album. After another album in the same vein didn't sell, the changed their direction again, becoming an arena rock outfit; the new records failed miserably. By 1989, the band combined *all* of their previous incarnations into one faceless album. At that time, the acting careers of guitarist Gary Kemp and bassist Martin Kemp took off, earning a substantial amount of critical acclaim for their roles in the English gangster film *The Krays*. —*Stephen Thomas Erlewine*

● **Singles Collection** / 1985 / Chrysalis 21498
Traces the group's development from the melodramatic, "new-romantic" dance-pop style of "To Cut a Long Story Short" to the lush ballad "True." Spandau Ballet always went in for big effects, but they became more subtle as they went along. —*William Ruhlmann*

Spanic Boys

Group / Roots-rock
Spanic Boys are a father-son duo from Milwaukee who specialize in driving roots-rock, with an alien Everly Brothers-influenced vocal harmony sound. —*Rick Clark*

○ **Spanic Boys** / 1990 / Rounder 9022
Good collection of rockabilly-based, '50s-style rock. —*David Szatmary*

● **Strange World** / 1991 / Rounder 9027
Rockin' rawness from Milwaukee's finest. —*David Szatmary*

Sparkletones

Group / Rockabilly
Five 16-year-olds from Spartanburg, SC, the Sparkletones were one of the finest rockabilly acts ever to record. Mostly their style was fast and spirited, with a frenetic energy that made most of the competition (even Elvis) seem geriatric by comparison. Singer and guitarist Joe Bennett's "Black Slacks" remains their defining song, but everything they did was worthwhile. —*Bruce Eder*

○ **Black Slacks** / MCA 1553
This topflight collection does not contain everything, but the 10 best songs this rockabilly quintet left behind are here. As fine as any Elvis collection of 1956. —*Bruce Eder*

Sparks

Group / Pop/rock
An American pop/rock group led by two brothers Ron (keyboards) and Russell Mael (vocals), with varying backup. They were especially popular in the mid '70s in England, where the singles "This Town Ain't Big Enough for Both of Us," "Amateur Hour," and "Beat the Clock" and the albums *Kimono My House* and *Propaganda* all hit the Top 10. —*William Ruhlmann*

○ **Kimono My House** / 1974 / Island 9272

Sparks specializes in keyboard-based pop songs with clever, ironic lyrics (by Ron Mael) sung in a near-falsetto by Russell Mael. Examples include "Here in Heaven" (in which a disappointed, dead Romeo sings to a still-living Juliet, who "broke our little pact"), "Thank God It's Not Christmas," and the UK hits "This Town Ain't Big Enough for Both of Us" and "Amateur Hour." —*William Ruhlmann*

○ **Propaganda** / 1974 / Island 9312
More of Ron's wit ("Don't Leave Me Alone with Her," "Who Don't Like Kids") and Russell's operatic singing with catchy rock backings, though it's hard to get the jokes without the lyric sheet. —*William Ruhlmann*

Number One in Heaven / 1979 / Elektra 186
After flirting with hard rock, Sparks turned to disco producer Giorgio Moroder and scored three UK hits, "Tryouts for the Human Race," "Beat the Clock," and "The No. 1 Song in Heaven," all in an aggressive electro-dance rock style. —*William Ruhlmann*

Angst in My Pants / 1982 / Atlantic 19347
Sparks turns to power-pop and scores their first U.S. singles chart entry with the hilarious "I Predict" on an album that also includes such novelties as "Eaten by the Monster of Love." —*William Ruhlmann*

Sparks in Outer Space / 1983 / Teldec 25520
"Cool Places," an uptempo duet with ex-Go-Go Jane Wiedlin (and #49 hit) paces this collection, perhaps Sparks' biggest U.S. seller. —*William Ruhlmann*

● **Profile: Ultimate Collection** / 1991 / Rhino 70731
A double-disc collection of Sparks' finest moments, *Profile* is the definitive anthology of the quirky '70s pop/rockers. —*AMG*

The Specials

Group / Ska-revival
Jerry Dammers and the Specials kicked off the 2-Tone fad in late '70s England, where the hyperactive bounce of blueboat met the energy and concise punch of punk. Their influence was widespread and culturally significant, in that most of the bands on Dammer's 2-Tone label (including the Specials) were racially mixed. —*John Floyd*

☆ **Specials** / 1979 / Chrysalis 21265
The Specials' self-titled debut sparked the Two-Tone movement in the late '70s. With well chosen ska classics and Prince Buster-inspired originals, the band mixed political and social activism and blended punk's intensity with an infectious dance beat. This is essential listening. Produced by Elvis Costello. —*Chris Woodstra*

○ **More Specials** / 1980 / Chrysalis 21303
Losing some of their ska roots, the band moves directionlessly into a neo-lounge act. Still in full force is the biting social commentary, only in a slightly skewed environment. While somewhat of a disappointment after the brilliant debut, with time *More Specials* can be nearly as rewarding. —*Chris Woodstra*

In the Studio / 1984 / Chrysalis 21447
When Hall, Staples, and Golding left to become Fun Boy Three, Jerry Dammers decided to continue with the addition of vocalist Stan Campbell. Nearly three years in the making, *In the Studio* lacks any hint of ska, and Campbell's vocals, while good, lack the tension needed for the overtly political direction of the band. The highpoints, "Racist Friend" and the anthem "Free Nelson Mandela," can be found on the *Singles Collection*, so only completists need to bother. —*Chris Woodstra*

★ **Singles Collection** / 1991 / Chrysalis 21823
All of the essential singles from their three albums are present on this 15-track collection. Not only the perfect starting point for the curious, the inclusion of B sides and rarities like an inspired cover of Dylan's "Maggies Farm" makes this essential for fans. —*Chris Woodstra*

Benny Spellman

b. 1938
Vocals / R&B
His deep bass voice booms through loud and clear on many early '60s Allen Toussaint productions, but Benny Spellman enjoyed a major hit of his own in 1962, "Lipstick Traces (on a Cigarette)." Spellman spent some time with Huey "Piano" Smith and the Clowns before signing with Minit, where Toussaint utilized his

deep pipes to full advantage as a backing vocalist behind Ernie K-Doe on "Mother-in-Law" and countless others. The Rolling Stones covered "Fortune Teller," the flip side of this hit. Spellman recorded through much of the '60s, his "Word Game" turning up on Atlantic in 1965, before he took a day gig as a beer salesman. —*Bill Dahl*

○ **Fortune Teller** / 1988 / Collectables 5165
Infectious and influential early '60s New Orleans R&B. Spellman's low-pitched vocals, perfectly produced by pianist Allen Toussaint. —*Bill Dahl*

Spiders

R&B
A fine New Orleans vocal ensemble who started as a gospel group, the Spiders scored five Top 10 R&B hits for Imperial in 1954 and 1955. They were originally the Zion City Harmonizers in the '40s and also did radio work as the Delta Southernaires in 1952 and 1952. Lead singer Hayward "Chuck" Carbo, Joe Maxon, Matthew West, Oliver Howard, and Leonard "Chick" Carbo got their first hit with "I Didn't Want to Do It" in 1954. It was also their biggest, peaking at #3. They continued the string until the end of 1955. The Carbo brothers departed in 1956, moving on to solo careers. —*Ron Wynn*

● **Complete Imperial Recordings** / 1993 / Bear Family 15673
All of the Spiders' best songs are collected on this extensive double-disc set. — *AMG*

Spin Doctors

Group / Rock & roll, pop/rock
There were many psuedo-hippie, jam-oriented blues rockers in New York during the early '90s, but only the Spin Doctors made it big. And they made it big because they not only could immerse themselves in a groove but also had concise pop skills. "Little Miss Can't Be Wrong" and "Two Princes" were cleverly written singles, full of clean, blues-inflected licks and ingratiating pop melodies. *Pocket Full of Kryptonite* had been around for nearly a year when MTV and radio began playing "Little Miss Can't Be Wrong," but once they started playing it, they couldn't stop. The Spin Doctors became an overnight sensation, selling millions ofablums around the world.

Their second album, 1994's *Turn It Upside Down*, didn't sell very well when it was released, largely because the first single, "Cleopatra's Cat," was a failed experiment in funk. But the second single, "You Let Your Heart Go Too Fast," was nearly as good as "Two Princes," and the album began to sell after the song was released. —*Stephen Thomas Erlewine*

● **Pocket Full of Kryptonite** / 1992 / Epic 47461
This sleeper album took a while to catch on, but when it did, the Spin Doctors' slightly jazzy style of funky groove rock went multiplatinum. The first single, "Little Miss Can't Be Wrong," is a likable, lightweight bit of pop that sounds like something Steve Miller could've done. "Two Princes" was another huge hit. Other highlights include "Jimmy Olsen's Blues," "What Time Is It?" and "Forty or Fifty." —*Rick Clark*

Homebelly Groove: Live / Nov. 24, 1992 / Epic 53309
While the band was undergoing the endless tour in support of *Kryptonite*, Epic rereleased a remixed version of their first EP, a live recording called *Up for Grabs*, and added several more tracks. The result is this disc. A good example of the band's concert chops. —*Rick Clark*

Turn It Upside Down / 1994 / Epic
A weaker album than *Kryptonite*, *Turn it Upside Down* suffers from weaker material and lifeless production. Nevertheless, the first single, "Cleopatra's Cat," is an appealing slice of bop funk/rock. A few steps down there's "Big Fat Funky Booty," "Biscuit Head," and "You Let Your Heart Go Too Fast." —*Rick Clark*

The Spinners

Group / Soul, disco
There were plenty of Philly-soul groups that were as good as the Spinners, but none of them were better. They never cut anything as searing as the O'Jays' "For the Love of Money"; Teddy Pendergrass brought more eroticism to the hits of the Blue Notes; and they never matched the breathy, helium croon of the

Stylistics' Russell Tompkins. What the Spinners and producer Thom Bell did was consolidate the best elements of Philly soul into a hit-making machine that could be as topical ("Ghetto Child"), romantic ("Could It Be I'm Falling in Love"), and blistering ("I'm Coming Home") as anything Gamble and Huff ever whipped up for Eddie LeVert and Teddy Pendergrass. And Spinners lead vocalist Philippe Wynne had a voice that damn near outflanked anyone for versatility and sheer gospel slow burn; think of him as soul's answer to Claude Jeter, with the mental imbalance of James Carr.

The group didn't last as long as their slick-soul contemporaries: Wynne left the fold in 1977, and they never found a suitable replacement. (Wynne died of a heart attack in 1984 while performing in San Francisco.) Most of their work is still in print, and urban stations regularly program the hits from the Spinners's glory years. If you think pure soul singing died in the '60s (and some people do), a session with the Spinners should change your mind. —*John Floyd*

Second Time Around / 1970 / VIP 405
The Spinners began making some soul noise in 1970, when Stevie Wonder produced a pair of hit singles for them. "It's a Shame" was their first Top 10 R&B song since 1965 and was the swan song for G. C. Cameron as lead vocalist. Phillipe Wynne stepped in and shortly after made everyone forget (who remembered) that Cameron was ever in the band. The followup tune "We'll Have It Made" wasn't bad either. —*Ron Wynn*

○ **Mighty Love** / Jan. 1974 / Atlantic 7296
Phillippe Wynne's twisting, soulful, and frequently captivating voice was at its finest on this 1974 album. The title track was a smash in edited single form, and the extended album version contains marvelous Wynne ad-libs and exchanges nicely contrasted by the group's harmonizing. The album contains many other fine songs like "Ain't No Price on Happiness" and "I'm Coming Home" and was their second Atlantic release. It equaled the gold-selling pace of its predecessor and cemented the Spinners' status as R&B stars. —*Ron Wynn*

○ **Pick of the Litter** / 1975 / Atlantic 50155
The Spinners were rolling in the '70s, and this proved their biggest album ever. It peaked in the pop Top 10 at #8, and they racked up four consecutive R&B Top 10 singles, including the chart topper "They Just Can't Stop It (the Games People Play)." Phillippe Wynne, for a stretch in the '70s, sang with an amazing mix of class and fire, sophistication, and earthiness that hadn't been heard in soul circles for years. Of course, this is now out of print. —*Ron Wynn*

○ **Spinners** / 1977 / Atlantic 7256
A superb album, arguably their finest, though it wasn't their biggest crossover work. But the Spinners teamed with Thom Bell and made Motown look stupid with this album of glorious anthems. "I'll Be Around" and "Could It Be I'm Falling in Love" forever ended any discussions, mentions, or even thoughts of their former lead singer G. C. Cameron, as Phillippe Wynne was emerging as the '70s king of immaculate sophisticated soul. They had three R&B chart toppers from this album and were now dominating the Motown acts they'd once idolized. —*Ron Wynn*

Dancin' and Lovin' / 1979 / Rhino 71115
While soul purists recoiled in horror, the Spinners climbed off the ropes and soared back into the spotlight by recasting themselves as a modified dance/crossover band with soul/R&B influences. It worked in the short run, as their remake of the Four Seasons' "Working My Way Back to You" mixed with their own wailer "Forgive Me Girl" made a nice sandwich at #2 pop and #6 R&B. It took nearly a year, but they were revived. While they wore the formula out with a similiar followup, it gave them a fresh start and necessary credibility to eventually return to their customary sophisticated soul. —*Ron Wynn*

☆ **One of a Kind Love Affair—The Anthology** / 1991 / Atlantic 82332
Spanning from their first single, "That's What Girls Are Made For" in 1961, to their last charting single more than 20 years later, *One of a Kind Love Affair: The Anthology* is the definitive collection of the Spinners. The bulk of the two-CD compilation is the Spinners' work with Thom Bell during the mid '70s, easily the best work they ever recorded and arguably the finest Philly-soul singles. All of the Spinners' major hits are here, as are excellent,

informative liner notes (including complete personnel, discography). —*Stephen Thomas Erlewine*

★ **Very Best Of** / 1993 / Rhino 71213
Featuring all of their big hits, *Very Best of the Spinners* is a nice, condensed version of Atlantic's excellent double-CD collection that is perfect for those who don't want such a comprehensive Spinners compilation. —AMG

Spirit

Group / Progressive rock, psychedelic
Of all the unusual musical groups that graced the West Coast in the late '60s, Spirit was certainly one of the most peculiar, both visually and musically. At a time when psychedelic music was in its most dissonant and disorganized state, the band performed elegantly quirky music with a kind of disciplined restraint. Except for the band's biggest hit, "I Got a Line on You," from *The Family That Plays Together*, Spirit never really was a rock band in the usual sense; rather they were an ensemble of musical iconoclasts who sometimes embraced rock's abandon. The unique sustain-drenched lead work of Randy California (born Randy Wolfe) and the forcefully melodic percussion playing of his stepfather, Ed Cassidy, were readily identifiable signatures for Spirit's ambient fusion of jazz, rock, and folk.

After the band's third album, *Clear Spirit*, it became apparent that their sales were slipping. They released "1984," which linked police brutality to a developing Orwellian nightmare in America.

In 1971, Neil Young producer David Briggs worked with Spirit on their next and last album with the original lineup. *The 12 Dreams of Dr. Sardonicus* ultimately earned the band their greatest commercial success, with the FM hits "Nature's Way," "Mr. Skin," and "Animal Zoo." That year, bassist Mark Andes and vocalist Jay Ferguson left to form the marginally successful Jo Jo Gunne. Cassidy and California continue to tour and release periodic albums as Spirit. —*Rick Clark*

○ **Spirit** / 1968 / Epic 31457
This is a strong debut by this quartet, featuring "Fresh Garbage," "Elijah," "Mechanical World," and "Uncle Jack." —*Rick Clark*

○ **Clear** / 1969 / Edsel 268
Previous to the recording of this album, Spirit had been working on music for a soundtrack for the movie *The Model Shop. Clear* reflected that effort with an odd blend of off-the-wall (occasionally goofy-sounding) rock-influenced songs and strangely sparse instrumentals (with titles like "Ice" and "Clear"). Highlights include "Dark Eyed Woman" (#118), "Policeman's Ball," "Give a Life, Take a Life," and "New Dope in Town." —*Rick Clark*

○ **Family That Plays Together** / 1969 / Edsel 162
Lou Adler's unusual production, coupled with Marty Paich's ethereal orchestrations, on songs like "Aren't You Glad," "It Shall Be," "Poor Richard," and "Silky Sam" gave Spirit's music a quality of icy distance. The only other band that comes to mind who employed such otherworldly arrangements was Love, with their masterful *Forever Changes*. This is a wonderful album worth getting. —*Rick Clark*

○ **12 Dreams of Dr. Sardonicus** / 1970 / Epic 30267
One of Spirit's most successful albums. Contains "Nature's Way," "Mr. Skin," "Animal Zoo," and "Nothin' to Hide." —*Rick Clark*

● **Time Circle** / 1991 / Epic 47363
A generous helping of practically everything Spirit accomplished in their years on Lou Adler's Ode Records and Epic Records. The collection is sonically satisfactory (although the Mobile Fidelity version of *Dr. Sardonicus* sound stronger), and there are generous, informative liner notes. —*Rick Clark*

Split Enz

Group / New wave
This New Zealand band was formed in 1972 by art student and guitarist Phil Judd and singer/keyboardist Tim Finn. Drawing from Roxy Music, Genesis, the Move, and post-*Sgt. Pepper* Beatles, the band's music covered everything from art rock to catchy new wave pop/rock. They were known for their wild costumes and haircuts as much as for their eccentric blend of British dancehall and rock music. After Phil Judd left the band in 1977, he was replaced by Tim's younger brother Neil, and the Finn brothers took the band in a more commercial direction. Pleasing melodic pop with some still-lingering offbeat impulses made

their middle-period albums enjoyable. Neil's budding songwriting talent garnered attention with the pop hit "I Got You" from the 1979 *True Colours* album (also the world's first laser-etched LP, whose surface was covered with prismatic designs). He went on to write several of the band's better-known hits like "One Step Ahead" and "History Never Repeats," but the band never received much chart success. Tim left for a solo career in 1983, and Neil carried on for one more album before disbanding the Enz and forming the trio Crowded House. —*Scott Bultman*

○ **Mental Notes (Mushroom)** / 1975 / Mushroom 19217
The first proper Enz album features the band at its eccentric best. *Mental Notes* is completely noncommercial art rock filled with ambitious arrangements and slightly disturbing themes courtesy of the Phil Judd and Tim Finn songwriting partnership. Finn's bittersweet crooning perfectly complements Judd's madman persona on tracks like "Stranger than Fiction." Although the album would be repackaged, renamed, and rerecorded in years to come, the band would never again produce anything like it. —*Chris Woodstra*

Dizrhythmia / 1977 / Mushroom 19219
With Tim Finn's leadership and brother Neil replacing founding member Phil Judd, the band makes a move into the mainstream. While the eccentricity is still evident, the album shines with a melodic pop sensibility. Contains the classics "Bold as Brass," "Charlie," and "Crosswords." —*Chris Woodstra*

○ **Frenzy** / 1978 / A&M 3153
Although often thought of as a trasitional album, *Frenzy* shows the band in top form. Produced in England on a diminished budget, the album showcases pure pop with a hungry edge. "I See Red," added after the initial pressing, became a huge hit in Australia and New Zealand, allowing the band the financial freedom to follow up with the blockbuster *True Colours* in 1980. The album was reissued in the United States in 1981, dropping half of the tracks and adding songs from the legendary "Rootin' Tootin' Luton Tapes" recorded in 1978. —*Chris Woodstra*

○ **True Colours** / 1979 / A&M 3235
This is the New Zealand band's most cohesive pop statement and their most successful American release. Clever pop songs with synthesizer textures. Neil Finn comes into his own as a writer in his brother's band. —*Scott Bultman*

○ **Beginning of the Ends** / 1979 / Mushroom 19220
A compilation of demos from 1972 through 1975. This Australian-only release shows the band in its eccentric formative years before a recording contract. Light acoustic arrangements of songs appearing on later albums coupled with long-forgotten gems make this a favorite among diehard fans. Not the most representative picture of the band, but an interesting one. —*Chris Woodstra*

Waiata / 1981 / A&M 64848
Also titled *Corroboree* (in Australia and New Zealand), this followup to the successful *True Colours* album offers more Neil Finn-penned gems like "One Step Ahead" and "History Never Repeats," although the music is less edgy, with more emphasis on pleasant synth pop. Includes three instrumentals: "Iris," "Ships," and "Albert of India." —*Scott Bultman*

○ **Time & Tide** / 1982 / A&M 64894
Time and Tide is the band's creative high point and most fully realized effort. Combining beautiful melodies with introverted, soul-searching lyrics, the album gives listeners new insights into the band. Both Tim and Neil Finn reach new peaks in their songwriting. Includes the hits "Dirty Creature" and "Six Months in a Leaky Boat." —*Chris Woodstra*

Conflicting Emotions / 1983 / A&M 4963
Less focused than *Time and Tide, Conflicting Emotions* is still a high point for the band. With Tim Finn stepping back and Neil Finn playing a more dominant role in the songwriting, the album is both dark and beautiful. Neil Finn's strong sense of melody builds on heavy rhythms and direct playing to produce a solid if not exceptional album. Highlights include "Message to My Girl" and "Bullet Brain and Catus Head." —*Chris Woodstra*

● **History Never Repeats: The Best of Split Enz** / 1987 / A&M 3289
All the best songs from their American albums are here, although many other great songs can be found on their import

CDs. A good place to get acquainted with the band. —*Scott Bultman*

Spongetones

Group / Power-pop

One of the most underrated pop bands of the '80s, the Spongetones released several albums of effortlessly melodic, catchy guitar pop that captured the feel of '60s British invasion pop with remarkable accuracy and feeling. While they never received much critical or commercial attention, their music has aged much better than most power pop from the era; the band continues to record and perform in the '90s. —*Chris Woodstra*

● **Oh Yeah!** / 1991 / Black Vinyl 12064

The Spongetones return after a long absence with 1991's *Oh Yeah*. They effectively pick up where they left off in the '80s with their infectious Beatlesque power-pop. Easily their best songwriting and a good place to get acquainted with the band. —*Chris Woodstra*

○ **Beat & Torn** / 1994 / Black Vinyl

Now combined on one CD, *Beat Music* and *Torn Apart* represent the band's earliest recordings and some of their finest. —*Chris Woodstra*

Spooky Tooth

Group / Hard rock, blues rock

Few bands in the late '60s rivaled England's Spooky Tooth for delivering bone-breaking heavy-metal blues. Fronted by two fine blues-influenced lead singers, Gary Wright and Mike Harrison, and sparked by the lyrical crunch of lead guitarist Luther Grosvenor, Spooky Tooth produced a couple of great albums in *Spooky Two* and *The Last Puff*. Wright split in 1970 after the horrible experimental-music effort *Ceremony* and went on to a briefly successful solo career with *Dream Weaver*. —*Rick Clark*

● **Spooky Two** / 1969 / A&M 3124

A late '60s and early '70s English rock band featuring Mike Harrison, Gary Wright, and Luther Grosvenor. Rivals to Procul Harum, with a harder edge. Excellent group vocals. Includes classic "Evil Woman." —*Michael G. Nastos*

Dusty Springfield (Mary O'Brien)

b. Apr. 16, 1939, London, England

Vocals / Soul, rock/pop

Born Mary O'Brien before changing her name professionally, Dusty Springfield first emerged during the early '60s as one-third of the British folk-pop trio the Springfields, which also included her brother Tom. They had several hits, including "Island of Dreams" and "Silver Thread and Golden Needles," and the latter topped the U.S. charts a year before the Beatles' first records.

In 1964, the Springfields split up, with Tom going off to produce the Seekers. Dusty made herself over vocally, evolving from a folk alto into a powerful white soul singer, capable of credibly covering Motown material (she dueted with Martha Reeves on television's "Ready, Steady, Go" without embarrassing herself at all) and belting out British pop numbers with seismic intensity. "I Only Want to Be with You," "Stay Awhile," "Wishin' and Hopin'," and "24 Hours from Tulsa" were just a few of her successes, and all were heavily played in either England or America. In 1969, Springfield recorded *Dusty in Memphis*, a landmark white soul album done at Stax studios, which received critical raves and is something of a legendary record.

Since the early '70s, Springfield has recorded and made infrequent appearances, but none of her work since the Memphis album has been embraced by the public. In 1987, she experienced something of a revival when she was recorded a duet with the Pet Shop Boys, "What Have I Done to Deserve This?" Springfield remains a respected and much-loved figure from British rock's heyday, even 30 years on. —*Bruce Eder*

○ **Golden Hits** / 1966 / PolyGram 824467

A fair representation of her mid '60s hits, with major gaps. The imported CDs are preferable. —*Bruce Eder*

★ **Dusty in Memphis** / 1969 / Rhino 71035

A sultry, subtle, soulful classic, key in any collection. —*Bruce Eder*

○ **A Brand New Me** / 1970 / Rhino 71036

While it's not quite as uniformly excellent as *Dusty in Memphis*, *A Brand New Me* comes close to recapturing its predecessor's

magic and is easily one of Springfield's best albums. —*Stephen Thomas Erlewine*

● **Silver Collection** / Jan. 1988 / Philips 834128

Twenty-four songs, encompassing her British and American chart history for the '60s. Superb sound. —*Bruce Eder*

Rick Springfield

b. Aug. 23, 1949, Sydney, Australia

Vocals, guitar / Pop/rock, power pop

Before he became a soap star, Rick Springfield was a rock star in his native Australia. After scoring several hits with his band Zoot in the early '70s, he went solo and tried to make the big time in America. Springfield released several power pop albums to no success; he then decided to become a television actor, landing a role on "General Hospital." While he was acting on the soap opera, he gained a strong following, which led him to revive his singing career in the early '80s. This time his records were more successful—"Jessie's Girl," his first single since returning to music, hit #1. Several other Top 10 hits followed, before his career started to slip in the mid '80s; despite his diminished sales, he continued recording and acting through the rest of the decade. —*Stephen Thomas Erlewine*

● **Working Class Dog** / 1981 / RCA 3697

Forget that Rick Springfield was a soap star for a moment and listen to his music, because he made some of the finest guitar-driven mainstream pop-rock of the early '80s. *Working Class Dog* is his finest moment, filled with expertly crafted pop songs, highlighted by the massive hit "Jesse's Girl." —*Stephen Thomas Erlewine*

○ **Greatest Hits** / 1989 / RCA 9817

A good collection of Springfield's greatest hits. —*David Jehnzen*

Bruce Springsteen

b. Sep. 23, 1949, Freehold, NJ

Vocals, guitar / Rock & roll

It could be argued that Bruce Springsteen has never made a wrong artistic move. His spirit is embedded in rock traditions that are as varied as singles on a jukebox: Woody Guthrie, Chuck Berry, Elvis, Buddy Holly, Phil Spector, Bob Dylan, the Rolling Stones—the bedrock of rock history. From his first album in 1973 up to 1987's *Tunnel of Love*, Springsteen has continually improved, tightening his strengths, growing with his vision, and proudly proclaiming a sense of purpose that's nearly unrivaled in rock.

Springsteen established a set of characters on his first two albums who grappled with the pain of adolescence, the reluctance to embrace adulthood, and the conflicting emotions of heartache and romance. But instead of succumbing to eternal adolescence, he let those characters grow and become adults who faced the grime and ecstasy of their lives in admirably uncompromising terms, all of which are realistic and fascinating, all of them outgrowths of the complexities of his own personality, and all of them unique in the pantheon of rock drama. Springsteen treats his women with compassion and charity; his men try to maintain honor in a society bereft of that concept; and the settings in which they are placed reflect Springsteen's awareness of and contempt for an America that chews up and spits out its working class without care or concern. That he's managed to do this consistently without any lapse in quality or sureness of vision is remarkable. That he's done it without becoming a chest-thumping agit-pop irritant, but rather a performer whose concerts and albums are cathartic celebrations of ecstasy and release, is reason enough to call him the greatest American rocker of the last two decades. —*John Floyd*

Greetings from Asbury Park NJ / Jan. 1973 / Columbia 31903

The songs, laced with Dylanistic wordplay, are gorgeous street vignettes fused with romance, idealism, and a true sense of wonder. —*John Floyd*

☆ **Wild, the Innocent and the E Street Shuffle** / Feb. 1973 / Columbia 32432

The Wild, the Innocent & the E Street Shuffle is a subtle masterpiece. The grooves are tougher, revealing the R&B heart that *Greeting from Asbury Park* stifled, and the songs are long enough to let him develop his characters and their situations. —*John Floyd*

☆ **Born to Run** / 1975 / Columbia 33795
A bombastic masterpiece. His breakthrough is a testament not only to the sound of Phil Spector's '60s hits but also to the romanticism, the longing, and the determination of those hits. The title cut and "Thunder Road" are anthems that deserve that status. —*John Floyd*

○ **Darkness on the Edge of Town** / 1978 / Columbia 35318
The flip side of *Born to Run*. The idealism of those characters turns into stark terror once they hit adulthood. This is where Springsteen's reputation as a working-class mouthpiece is based, but there's much more here than that. —*John Floyd*

☆ **River** / 1980 / Columbia 36854
In many ways his best album, balancing the dashed dreams of *Darkness on the Edge of Town* with the hope of *Born to Run*, but it trades the Spectorian wallop for a taut, frat-rock sound that is alternately wiry, delicate, and full-blown. —*John Floyd*

☆ **Nebraska** / 1982 / Columbia 38358
A set of acoustic demos offering ravaged tales of despair, defeat, and defiance. —*John Floyd*

★ **Born in the U.S.A.** / 1984 / Columbia 38653
The album that pushed him into superstar status ironically examines the dirty underbelly of America in both political and domestic terms. The big, catchy, hard-slamming rock & roll that carries the lyrics only adds to the irony. —*John Floyd*

○ **Live 1975-1985** / 1986 / Columbia 40558
A career-defining three-disc live collection. Among the three or four greatest boxed sets ever issued. —*John Floyd*

☆ **Tunnel of Love** / 1987 / Columbia 40999
A moody and dark inquiry, which asks why people fall in love, why they get married, why they lose faith in the people closest to them, and why they even bother. Required listening for anyone contemplating the altar. —*John Floyd*

Chimes of Freedom / 1988 / Columbia 44445
A four-song live EP from his 1988 tour, which includes a riveting version of Dylan's "Chimes of Freedom" and an acoustic rendering of "Born to Run." —*John Floyd*

Human Touch / Jan. 1992 / Columbia 53000
His first proper recording without the E Street Band continues the conversation started on *Tunnel of Love* through the pleading urgency of "Soul Driver" and the forthright admissions on "Real World." Musically, the set balances E Street retreads ("Roll of the Dice," "All or Nothin' at All") with taut soul grooves and slashing hard rock, emphasizing Springsteen's astonishing guitar playing. —*John Floyd*

Lucky Town / Feb. 1992 / Columbia 53001
Lucky Town, recorded chiefly by Springsteen, with occasional assistance from E Street keyboardist Roy Bittan, is the thematic antithesis of Dylan's *Blood on the Tracks*, an album devoted to the requisiteness of love and romance and how empty lives are without that love and romance. *Lucky Town* offers living proof that Bruce Springsteen's grappling with domestic bliss and superstardom is just as enlightening as his struggle to attain them. —*John Floyd*

Squeeze

Group / New wave, pop/rock
Squeeze is a British pop/rock quintet that serves as a forum for the songs of its lead singer Glenn Tilbrook (b. August 31, 1957) and his partner, guitarist Chris Difford. The duo formed Squeeze in 1974 with keyboardist Jools Holland (b. January 24, 1958), whose bubbly personality made him a natural frontman, bassist Harry Kakouli (replaced by John Bentley after the first album), and drummer Gilson Lavis (b. June 27, 1951). They reached the UK Top 20 in 1978 with the single "Take Me I'm Yours," but really broke through the following year, when their second album, *Cool for Cats*, produced two UK Top 10 hits in the title track and the Difford-sung "Up the Junction." *Argybargy*, their third album, was a moderate success in 1980 (and their first U.S. chart entry), but their next milestone came in 1981 with *East Side Story*, an album for which Holland was replaced by former Ace lead singer Paul Carrack (b. April 22, 1951), who sang lead on "Tempted," Squeeze's first U.S. chart single. The album, which hit the UK Top 20, also featured a #4 British hit, "Labelled with Love." As it turned out, Carrack left after the one album, replaced by Don Snow (b. January 13, 1957) for *Sweets for a Stranger*, after which

Squeeze disbanded. They reformed in 1985 with Tilbrook, Difford, Holland, and Lavis, plus Keith Wilkinson on bass, to release *Cosi Fan Tutti Frutti* and then, in 1987, *Babylon and On*, which featured "Hourglass," a Top 20 hit on both sides of the Atlantic. *Frank* came out in 1989, followed in 1990 with the live album *A Round and a Bout*, which finished Squeeze's contract with A&M. They then signed to Warner Bros. and released *Play* in 1991. After the sluggish sales of *Play*, Warner dropped the band; they resigned with A&M soon afterward. Gilson Lavis left the band before they recorded 1993's *Some Fantastic Place*, leaving Difford and Tilbrook as the band's only original members. — *William Ruhlmann*

U.K. Squeeze / 1978 / A&M 3185
Their debut of rough-edged British pub-rock during the peak of the punk years. —*Scott Bultman*

○ **Cool for Cats** / 1979 / A&M 3231
The band's second album shows a great leap in songwriting skills. While an emphasis on English themes can leave most Americans bewildered, the catchy pop melodies crossed with a pub-rock sensibility are simply irresistible. Highlights include "Cool for Cats" and "Up the Junction," a pure pop masterpiece. —*Chris Woodstra*

○ **Argybargy** / 1980 / A&M 3232
Upbeat, cleverly crafted pop-rock with decidedly British themes. Tilbrook's guitar work and Jools Holland's keyboards shine as Squeeze move from being pub-rockers to critics' darlings. —*Scott Bultman*

○ **East Side Story** / 1981 / A&M 3253
Their U.S. breakthrough album featured the hit "Tempted," sung and written by Paul Carrack (of the '70s band Ace), who was Squeeze's keyboardist for this one album. This is the album that sparked the comparisons of Difford/Tilbrook to Lennon/McCartney. A broader pop style with classical overtones and a country influence courtesy of producers Elvis Costello and Dave Edmunds. Great songs. —*Scott Bultman*

Sweets from a Stranger / 1982 / A&M 3254
Still riding high on the success of *East Side Story*, Squeeze continues to write perky, upbeat tunes, but with the blue-eyed soul influence of the quickly departed Paul Carrack, they begin their move away from their classic sound. The hit "Black Coffee in Bed" sounds amazingly like a Paul Carrack song, perhaps an attempt to duplicate the success of Carrack's "Tempted." —*Scott Bultman*

● **Singles 45's & Under** / 1982 / A&M 3338
Twelve early Squeeze singles and one nonalbum track ("Annie Get Your Gun"). This is classic Squeeze, the songs that made them. Includes "Tempted," "Black Coffee in Bed," and "Another Nail for My Heart." —*Scott Bultman*

○ **Cosi Fan Tutti Frutti** / 1985 / A&M 3339
After *Sweets from a Stranger* and the Difford/Tilbrook solo effort, this reformed Squeeze (with Jools Holland returning on keyboards) make a move in another direction, with a less overt soul influence. High pop-craft and experimentation. Laurie Latham's technicolor/cinerama production makes this their most glossy album. Keith Wilkinson takes over on bass. —*Scott Bultman*

○ **Classics, Vol. 25** / 1987 / A&M 2523
A 19-cut sampler of their 1978-1987 work and the 25th CD in A&M's 25th-anniversary reissue of the best material on the label. Six cuts overlap with the *Singles 45 & Under* package, but the other 13 tracks make this a worthwhile companion for those not up to buying the original albums. At 72+ minutes, this is a bargain. —*Scott Bultman*

Babylon and On / 1987 / A&M 5161
Yet another step back to their classic sound, this time rewarded with minor chart success. Squeeze regains their drive and perkiness, firing on all cylinders. —*Scott Bultman*

Frank / 1989 / A&M 5278
Along with the return of keyboardist Jools Holland comes a return to the classic Squeeze sound. "If It's Love" and "She Doesn't Have to Shave" more than make up for the blandness of the previous album with their memorable hooks and irresistible melodies. —*Chris Woodstra*

○ **Play** / 1991 / Reprise 26644
This unfortunately overlooked album finds the songwriting team of Difford and Tilbrook still in strong form through a 12-track song cycle. Now a four-piece band, they have less dependence on

keyboards and a focus on more acoustic arrangements. A considerably more subdued mood but no less rewarding on repeated listening. —*Chris Woodstra*

Some Fantastic Place / Sep. 14, 1993 / A&M 540140
The band's 10th proper album reunites the core of Glen Tilbrook and Chris Difford with former member Paul Carrack and adds drummer Pete Thomas (Elvis Costello & the Attractions). Their classic sound is still there through the melodic power-pop of "Third Rail" to the blue-eyed soul of "Loving You Tonight" (nearly a rewrite of "Tempted"). Another in a series of commercial sleepers, but it's sure to delight those who give it a try. —*Chris Woodstra*

Billy Squier

b. May 12, 1950, Wellesley, MA
Vocals, guitar / Hard rock
Billy Squier was making pop metal years before Bon Jovi came along. With his sharp, hard-rocking riffs and sweet, slick melodies, Squier became one of the biggest hard rock stars of the early '80s, earning two multiplatinum albums. But his fall from commercial prominence was just as quick as his rise; 1984's *Signs of Life* was his last album to sell over a million copies, and even then he seemed slightly behind the times. Squier wasn't able to translate his AOR hits over to MTV, causing him to fall down the charts. However, he never lost his hard-core fans; he continued to tour and record successfully right into the '90s. —*Stephen Thomas Erlewine*

● **Don't Say No** / 1981 / Capitol 46479
Far and away the most consistent and solid work from this hard-rock singer-songwriter and guitarist. This studio-polished debut plays like a greatest-hits album. Includes "In the Dark," "The Stroke," and "Lonely Is the Night." —*Donna DiChario*

Rock Me Tonight / 1984 / Capitol
His guitar heavy rock. —*Bil Carpenter*

Chris Stamey

Vocals, Guitar / Power pop
Chris Stamey might not be a household name, but among the cult of melodic guitar pop/rock fans, he's a major player. Stamey played in the seminal North Carolina '70s pop band the Sneakers and was a founding member of the dB's. After the dB's fell apart, Chris Stamey recorded an album with his fellow dB Peter Hollsapple; after that album, Stamey released his first solo record in 1991. —*Rick Clark*

○ **It's Alright** / 1987 / A&M 5180
With the help of Alex Chilton, Richard Lloyd, Mitch Easter, Marshall Crenshaw, and others, Stamey presented a cohesive body of fine pop/rock songs, most notably "Cara Lee," "Incredible Happiness," "27 Years in a Single Day," and "The Seduction." —*Rick Clark*

● **Fireworks** / 1991 / Rhino 70766
Fireworks, the album that A&M allegedly rejected, surfaced on Rhino's new artist imprint RNA. While it is arguably his best solo album, the overly reverberant production and thin sounds steals the thunder from this album. Another problem comes in the lyric department. Stamey's earnest lyrics are often too arty, while failing to communicate any real enhancing art. Nevertheless, Stamey delivers some beautiful melodies and songs like "The Company of Light," "Something Came over Me," "Glorious Delusion," and "On the Radio (for Ray Davies)" are wonderful listens. —*Rick Clark*

It's a Wonderful Life / 1992 / East Side Digital 80682
This playful disc includes Stamey's 1982 solo effort, *It's a Wonderful Life* and 1984's *Instant Excitement*. Stamey experiments with percussion triggering other types of instrumental sounds—something he calls the Groovegate System. All in all this disc feels more like an idea scrapbook than a polished release. —*Rick Clark*

The Standells

Group / Garage rock
The Standells had the greasy garage-band sound down to perfection, and their pounding ode to Boston's "Dirty Water" was a huge hit in 1966. Prior to hitting national playlists, the band had recorded for MGM and Liberty and appeared in the 1964 movie

Get Yourself a College Girl. Signed to Capitol's Tower subsidiary, drummer (former Mouseketeer) Dick Dodd's snarling vocal and pounding backbeat made "Dirty Water" (produced by Ed Cobb of the Four Preps, who were about as far opposed to the Standells' approach as could possibly be) their top-seller. Three subsequent 1966-1967 Standells singles also charted, but the quartet fell apart before the end of the decade. —*Bill Dahl*

● **Best of the Standells** / 1984 / Rhino 70176
Most '60s punk bands could barely fill an album side with decent material. This 18-song compilation is a tribute to the vitality of the Standells' raunch-and-roll attack, including not only their one hit ("Dirty Water") but salacious essentials ranging from the swaggering "Sometimes Good Guys Don't Wear White" to the horny wail of "Barracuda." —*John Floyd*

Lisa Stansfield

b. 1965
Vocals / Urban soul, disco
English vocalist Lisa Stansfield was the lead singer of the group the Blue Zone and featured on Coldcut's "People Hold On" in 1989. She zoomed into the spotlight with *Affection* in 1990. The album went platinum and earned her a #3 pop and #1 R&B single with "All Around the World." *Affection* and its followup CD *Real Love* were deeply influenced by the '70s disco sound of Barry White, from arrangements to mood and even Stansfield's own technique. —*Ron Wynn*

● **Affection** / 1989 / Arista 8554
Stansfield's voice serves this retro-disco material extremely well, best exemplified by the hits "All around the World" and "You Can't Deny It." An impressive debut. —*Stephen Thomas Erlewine*

○ **Real Love** / 1991 / Arista 18679
Another strong effort from Stansfield. —*Stephen Thomas Erlewine*

Mavis Staples

b. 1940, Chicago, IL
Vocals / Soul
Most of Mavis Staples's (b. 1940 in Chicago) career has been as lead singer for the Staple Singers. She first recorded solo for Stax subsidiary Volt in 1969. Subsequent efforts included a Curtis Mayfield-produced soundtrack on Curtom, a disappointing nod to disco for Warner in 1979, a misguided stab at electro-pop with Holland-Dozier-Holland in 1984, and, most recently, two uneven albums for Paisley Park. Staples has a rich contralto voice that has neither the range of Aretha Franklin nor the power of Patti LaBelle. Her otherworldly power comes instead from a masterful command of phrasing and a deep-seated sensuality expressed through timbre manipulation. —*Rob Bowman*

Mavis Staples / 1969 / Stax 4118
A powerhouse soul belter and wailer, Mavis Staples doesn't have to take second fiddle to anyone, including Aretha Franklin, when it comes to just pure, house-rocking, testifying authority. She's seldom gotten a complete album of quality material, but on this 1969 debut she took half-baked material and made it memorable. "I Have Learned to Do without You" wasn't a classic, but her vocal came mighty close. —*Ron Wynn*

○ **Only for the Lonely** / 1970 / Stax 880122
Mavis Staples never attained national stardom during her Stax years, yet she made many brilliant soul recordings, displaying the vocal power, authority, and intensity that reflected her extensive gospel background. This 21-track anthology collects songs recorded in 1969 and issued on three albums. The roster includes a strong duet with Johnny Taylor called "That's the Way Love Is" and her signature tune "A House Is Not a Home." Steve Cropper produced and arranged 11 cuts, with Don Davis producing another eight; Al Bell produced the duet with Taylor. Staples's energy, delivery, timing, and technique were consistently awesome. Unfortunately, only a few of these songs got much attention outside R&B circles but their quality shows Staples's greatness as a soul vocalist. —*Ron Wynn*

Time Waits for No One / 1989 / Paisley Park 25798
Prince took a great interest in Mavis Staples after she provided him some rousing background vocals and appeared in the film *Graffiti Bridge* in 1990. He signed her to his label and wrote and produced some of the tracks on this disc. Unfortunately, it en-

joyed little impact sales wise, though Staples soared, shouted, and roared with splendor. But her sound and approach were so soulful it seemed out of place in the detached, urbane setting of urban radio. There were both fiery message tracks and blistering love songs, with Staples's alternately assertive, tender, and intense vocals. However not even Prince's name could break the embargo on acts considered too old school for modern audiences. —*Ron Wynn*

● **Don't Change Me Now** / 1990 / ACE 014
Mavis Staples' solo career has been largely undistinguished. *Don't Change Me Now* pulls together most of her better efforts, being a composite of Staples's two Volt solo albums, *Mavis Staples* and *Only for the Lonely*, recorded for Stax subsidiary Volt in 1969 and 1970, respectively. Ace has added a number of originally unreleased tracks to this collection. The liner notes are well written and the sound is fine. —*Rob Bowman*

Edwin Starr

b. Jan. 21, 1942, Nashville, TN
Vocals / Soul
One of the best soul shouters to come from the Motown stable, Starr's style was closer to James Brown than to any of the other male Motown artists. Best known for his 1970 hit "War," he made a brief comeback during the disco craze, but he now tours Europe and plays the oldies circuit. —*Rick A. Bueche*

● **Motown Superstar Series, Vol. 3** / Motown 5103
Not every vocalist enjoyed consistent success on Motown. Edwin Starr, despite having a bombastic style and striking voice, only enjoyed a few hits during his Motown tenure. But they were definitive ones, notably "25 Miles" and the landmark "War." Though the Temptations also cut the single, it was Starr's shattering, angular version that made it unforgettable. Those and other less well known Starr tracks are included on this anthology. It's an interesting release that shows sometimes Starr didn't get first-rate material, and other times his own performances weren't that grabbing. —*Ron Wynn*

Ringo Starr (Richard Starkey)

b. Jul. 7, 1940, Dingle, Liverpool
Vocals, drums / Pop/rock
Ringo Starr, born Richard Starkey, was the drummer in the Beatles from 1962 to 1970 and thus one of the most famous musicians of the '60s. Though the least prominent member of the quartet, he distinguished himself as an occasional singer of good-natured material and as an actor. Upon the group's split, Starr went solo with two novelty projects: the first, an album called *Sentimental Journey*, found him covering prerock standards, and the second, *Beaucoups of Blues*, was a country music collection.

Starr then scored Top 10 hits with two nonalbum singles, "It Don't Come Easy" in 1971 and "Back off Boogaloo" in 1972. In 1973 he paired with producer Richard Perry and, with assistance from the three other ex-Beatles, made *Ringo*, which featured two #1 hits, "Photograph" and "You're Sixteen." "Oh My My," a Top 10 hit, was also included. Almost as successful was the 1974 followup, *Goodnight Vienna*, which featured the hits "Only You" and "No No Song."

Starr continued to release albums through 1981, though with diminishing success. His 1983 album *Old Wave* did not find a U.S. distributor. Starr was also suffering from the excesses of his lifestyle, but by the late '80s he had cleaned up, and in 1989 he toured with his "All-Starr Band." In 1992, he signed to Private Music and released a new studio album, *Time Takes Time*. —*William Ruhlmann*

Sentimental Journey / 1969 / Apple 3365
A trip down memory lane—Ringo does the '40s. —*Jeff Tamarkin*

○ **Beacoups of Blues** / 1970 / Apple 3368
More sentimental nostalgia while Ringo decided whetherthere was life after Beatles. —*Jeff Tamarkin*

● **Ringo** / 1973 / Capitol 95637
One of the great Beatle solo albums, and the only one to feature a little help from all three ex-friends in the band. Starr's apex. —*Jeff Tamarkin*

Goodnight Vienna / 1974 / Capitol 80378
Even with Johns Lennon and Elton and a couple of bona fide hits, little here holds up. —*Jeff Tamarkin*

● **Blast from Your Past** / 1975 / Capitol 46663
A formidable collection, including a couple of the more venerable hits. —*Jeff Tamarkin*

○ **Starr Struck: Best of, Vol. 2** / 1989 / Rhino 70135
For Beatle loyalists only. —*Jeff Tamarkin*

All-Starr Band / 1990 / Rykodisc 10190
Soundtrack from the 1989 tour, with contributions from not only Starr, but Joe Walsh, Billy Preston, and others. —*Jeff Tamarkin*

○ **Time Takes Time** / 1992 / Private Music 82097
A sober, reflective Ringo Starr returns, after a near decade's absence, with a solid set of songs that could have been the work of, well, a Beatle. —*Jeff Tamarkin*

Starship

Group / Pop/rock
After longtime band leader Paul Kantner left Jefferson Starship in 1984, the band dropped the first word in its name. At that point it consisted of singers Mickey Thomas and Grace Slick (b. October 30, 1939), guitarist Craig Chaquico (b. 1955), bassist Pete Sears, and drummer Donny Baldwin. This unit immediately scored with the #1 hits "We Built This City" and "Sara" and the million-selling album *Knee Deep in the Hoopla*. Sears had left by the time of the 1987 followup, *No Protection*, which featured the #1 "Nothing's Gonna Stop Us Now" and the Top 10 "It's Not Over ('Til It's Over)." Slick then departed, and the remaining trio recruited keyboard player Mark Moragan and bassist Brett Bloomfield for the 1989 album *Love among the Cannibals*, which featured the Top 20 hit "It's Not Enough." In 1991, when RCA released a Starship greatest-hits album, the one new track on the album had been recorded by Thomas and studio musicians, leading to doubt that Starship remained a functioning band. —*William Ruhlmann*

○ **Knee Deep in the Hoopla** / 1985 / Grunt 5488
Keyboard arrangements dominate here, along with Thomas's soaring vocals, with Grace Slick along mostly for counterpoint (though her showcase is the stirring "Rock Myself to Sleep") on the hits "We Built This City" and "Sara." —*William Ruhlmann*

● **Starship's Greatest Hits: Ten Years of Change** / 1991 / RCA 2423
The Mickey Thomas era, half of it is also the Paul Kantner era, the choices reflecting taste ("Stranger" and "Layin' It on the Line" are included) rather than strict chart rankings (hits like "Be My Lady" and "Tomorrow Doesn't Matter Tonight" are missing). —*William Ruhlmann*

Status Quo

Group / Psychedelic, hard rock
During the late '60s, Status Quo was one of England's best psychedelic bands, creating an indisputable classic with their 1967 debut single "Pictures of Matchstick Men." After a couple more psychedelic albums that weren't successful, the group was pegged as a has-been. However, Status Quo refashioned themselves as a heavy, hard-rocking boogie band in 1970. The change in direction proved to be a massive success; since the release of *Ma Kelly's Greasy Spoon* in 1970, they have been stars in England. In America, they've managed only one album in the lower reaches of *Billboard's* Top 200 chart in 1976. Status Quo continues to tour and record into the '90s, and in England they are considered almost legendary. —*Stephen Thomas Erlewine*

● **Collection: Status Quo** / 1985 / Pickwick 046
Featuring everything from their early psychedelic days to the years when they were the kings of simply heavy guitar boogie, *Collection: Status Quo* is the definitive single disc collection of one of England's most popular bands. —*Stephen Thomas Erlewine*

Steely Dan

Group / Rock/pop
If most art-rock bands borrowed from the European folk and classical-music traditions for their attempts at heightened hybrids of rock, Steely Dan (formed in 1972) drew inspiration from American jazz, big band, and R&B artists like Charlie Parker, Stan Kenton, and Ray Charles, as well as Brill Building pop, to arrive at their sophisticated rock mutations. Steely Dan was not a rock band in the convential sense. True, they employed rock in-

strumentation and various production values, but rock & roll was clearly not the bottom line in their artistic vision. Built around Donald Fagen (b. January 10, 1948) and Walter Becker (b. February 20, 1950), Steely Dan was more a studio vehicle for their songwriting and arrangement concepts than a real live touring unit. In fact, as Steely Dan shed members, Becker and Fagen merely plugged the holes by incorporating more session sidemen, as opposed to maintaining a band.

Thematically, Becker and Fagen relished exploring the fetishes, twisted logic, and misadventures of society's losers and misfits, with a blackly humorous, cryptic lyric style. Sonically, Steely Dan's albums have earned them raves from practically ever corner of the audiophile world. Their 1973 debut, *Can't Buy a Thrill,* presented a six-piece band (with a handful of sidemen), sounding like a sophisticated alternative to fellow ABC labelmates Three Dog Night on tracks like "Midnight Cruiser," "Kings," and "Dirty Work." That album produced Steely Dan's first two hits, "Do It Again" and "Reeling in the Years."

By the time of their fifth album, the 1977 platinum *Aja,* Becker and Fagen had fine-tuned their spare grooves, quirky melodies, and mildly dissonant jazz chordal clusters into a peculiarly seamless pop sound that was embraced by practically every radio format outside of country music. Sophisticated hits like "FM (No Static at All)," "Deacon Blues," "Peg," and "Josie" were among the many songs that became required soundtracks for every fern bar in the country. Becker and Fagen disengaged Steely Dan indefinitely after the 1981 release *Gaucho,* which included the classy title cut and hits "Hey Nineteen" and "Time Out of Mind."

Since then Becker has produced other artists, like China Crisis, and Fagen released a successful solo album, *The Nightfly,* which produced a hit with "I.G.Y. (What a Beautiful World)." Fagen has also recorded "Century's End" for the movie *Bright Lights, Big City.* Becker produced Fagen's second solo album, 1993's *Kamakiriad;* the collaboration led to a Steely Dan reunion, which has resulted in two successful tours but no recordings to date. —*Rick Clark*

Can't Buy a Thrill / 1972 / MCA 31192
The Steely Dan that appeared on this debut was basically a sophisticated perversion of the sound forged by fellow ABC labelmates Three Dog Night. Check out "Dirty Work," "Kings," and "Midnight Cruiser" and say that it isn't true. It's certainly one of the best debuts by any group to emerge out of the '70s. *Can't Buy a Thrill* also produced two classic hits with the dirty Latin-influenced groove of "Do It Again" and the edgy shuffle "Reelin' in the Years." —*Rick Clark*

☆ **Countdown to Ecstasy** / 1973 / MCA 31156
Compared to their debut, *Countdown to Ecstasy* was a commercial failure (rocketing up and down the charts in three weeks) once it became apparent that this wasn't *Reelin' in the Years: Part II.* The melodies and arrangements were more subtle and the lyrics a little more inpenetrable. Nevertheless, this is the album that initially hooked many hardcore Dan fans. "Show Biz Kids" and "My Old School" became moderate hits. Other standouts include the jazzy rocker "Bodhisattva" and "King of the World." —*Rick Clark*

☆ **Pretzel Logic** / 1974 / MCA 31165
On *Pretzel Logic* Steely Dan most successfully synthesized their love for jazz into their dense pop-rock sound. The grooves were funky ("Night by Night," "Monkey in Your Soul") and the arrangements sophisticated ("Parker's Band," "Through with Buzz"). "Rikki Don't Lose That Number," featuring an incredibly lyrical guitar solo by Jeff Baxter, became Dan's biggest hit at #4. The title track and "Any Major Dude Will Tell You" are more highlights. —*Rick Clark*

☆ **Katy Lied** / 1975 / MCA 31194
With its appealing melodies and oddball themes, this was a strong successor to *Pretzel Logic.* By this time, Steely Dan was Becker and Fagen, aided by an army of Los Angeles's A-list session stars—Hugh McCracken, Larry Carlton, Jeff Porcaro, Hal Blaine, Michael McDonald, and more. Sonically, *Katy Lied's* superclean mix pointed the way to the elegantly shrinkwrapped sound of their later work. Among the standout tracks are "Black Friday," "Daddy Don't Live in That New York City No More," "Chain Lightning," and "Throw Back the Little Ones," featuring an expressive closing piano improvization by Michael Omartian. —*Rick Clark*

Royal Scam / 1976 / MCA 31193
With *The Royal Scam,* Steely Dan delivered a rather cluttered, abrasive-sounding collection of tracks, which were further undermined by weaker melodies. If fusion ever found a home in disco, "Kid Charlemagne" was it. Smugly humorous tracks like "Haitian Divorce," "Green Earrings," and the fetish sendup "The Fez" are some of *Scam's* highlights. —*Rick Clark*

○ **Aja** / 1977 / MCA 37214
During the late '70s, *Aja* became required soundtrack music for fern bars throughout the country whose owners desired an upscale ambience. This was due to precision-crafted jazz-fusion pop/rock tracks like "Deacon Blues," "Josie," "Peg," and the title track, which featured a wonderfully musical drum solo by Steve Gadd. —*Rick Clark*

Gaucho / 1980 / MCA 37220
Three years after *Aja,* Becker and Fagen returned with the obsessively streamlined *Gaucho.* This impeccably recorded set contained two fine hits, "Hey Nineteen" and "Time Out of Mind." "Babylon Sisters" was another memorable highlight, while the title track sported one of the most entrancingly convoluted melodies of their career. However, "Glamour Profession," with its sophisticated disco feel, seemed tailor-made for the perpetual happy hour. —*Rick Clark*

○ **Gold** / 1982 / MCA 10387
Now expanded past its original length, this companion to *Decade* features newly remastered versions of tracks like "FM (No Static at All)," Donald Fagen's "Century's End," and previously unreleased live work. —*Rick Clark*

★ **A Decade of Steely Dan** / 1985 / MCA 5570
This collection features many of Dan's high spots, but it's hardly definitive. Nevertheless, this is the place to go if you are only budgeting for a single disc. —*Cub Koda*

Citizen Steely Dan / 1993 / MCA
Collecting all of Steely Dan's albums in chronological order, plus all of their two or three B sides and one demo in a four-CD box, *Citizen Steely Dan* is only worthwhile for the fan replacing their old records. The remastering on the box is exactly the same as the newly upgraded CDs, and everything but the demo is available on other discs. —*Stephen Thomas Erlewine*

Steppenwolf

b. Apr. 12, 1944
Group / Hard rock, psychedelic
Led by John Kay (b. Joachim Krauledat, April 12, 1944), Steppenwolf's blazing biker anthem "Born to Be Wild" roared out of speakers everywhere in the fiery summer of 1968, John Kay's threatening rasp sounding a mesmerizing call to arms to the counterculture movement rapidly sprouting up nationwide. German immigrant Kay got his professional start in a bluesy Toronto band called Sparrow, recording for Columbia in 1966. After Sparrow disbanded, Kay relocated to the West Coast and formed Steppenwolf, named after the Herman Hesse novel. "Born to Be Wild," their third single on ABC-Dunhill, was immortalized on the soundtrack of Dennis Hopper's underground film classic *Easy Rider.* The song's reference to "heavy metal thunder" finally gave an assignable name to an emerging genre. Steppenwolf's second monster hit that year, the psychedelic "Magic Carpet Ride," and the followups "Rock Me," "Move Over," and "Hey Lawdy Mama" further established the band's credibility on the hard-rock circuit. By the early '70s, Steppenwolf ran out of steam and disbanded. Kay continued to record solo, as other members put together ersatz versions of the band for touring purposes. During the mid '80s Kay reformed his own version of Steppenwolf, grinding out his hits (and some new songs) at oldies shows. Nevertheless, they'll be remembered for generations to come for creating one of the ultimate gas'n'go rock anthems of all time. —*Bill Dahl and Cub Koda*

Early Steppenwolf / 1969 / MCA 31356
Early live recordings made when the band was still called "Sparrow," working more out of a blues-band mold; features a surprisingly great version of Junior Wells' "Messin' with the Kid." —*Cub Koda*

● **16 Greatest Hits** / 1973 / MCA 37049
Just what the name implies; "Born to Be Wild," "Magic Carpet Ride," "The Pusher," and "Rock Me" are just some of the high-

lights. Everything you're going to want to hear in one neat little package. —*Cub Koda*

○ **Born to Be Wild: A Retrospective** / 1991 / MCA 10389
A double-disc collection of Steppenwolf's lengthy career, *Born to Be Wild: A Retrospective* includes more music than anyone but hardcore fans need, but the song selection and packaging are superb, making it essential for those devoted fans. —*Stephen Thomas Erlewine*

Stereolab

Group / Alternative pop/rock
Stereolab's music is not about songs, it's about textures. The band's one-chord, guitar- and organ-driven songs can last up to 20 minutes, repeating the same patterns over and over. Fortunately, their music is never cold and boring—it is positively hypnotic, full of warmth and depth. The band became alternative stars in Europe, particularly England, in the early '90s before releasing their first major-label effort in America in 1993 to considerable critical acclaim. —*Stephen Thomas Erlewine*

○ **Switched On** / 1992 / Slumberland 22
A fine example of Stereolab's hypnotic, trance-inducing guitar and organ pop. —*AMG*

Cat Stevens (Steve Georgiou)

b. 1947, London
Vocals, guitar / Singer-songwriter
Cat Stevens (born Steve Georgiou in London) was the son of a Greek father and a Swedish mother. Stevens became interested in folk and rock & roll in his teens and scored his first UK hit, "I Love My Dog," before he turned 20. Stevens reached the singles charts four more times, getting to #2 with "Matthew and Son" and releasing the similarly titled Top 10 album before he contracted tuberculosis in 1968 and was forced to retire from music.

He reemerged with a new, mature style in 1970 with the album *Mona Bone Jakon* and hit the UK Top 10 with "Lady D'Arbanville." But it was his late 1970 followup, *Tea for the Tillerman*, that made him an international success. The album hit the Top 10 and went gold in the United States, producing the #11 hit "Wild World." *Teaser and the Firecat*, released in 1971, did even better, getting to #2 and including the hits "Peace Train" and "Morning Has Broken." Stevens became so successful as an albums artist that, even though his next couple of albums did not generate big hit singles, they were still big sellers: *Catch Bull at Four* (1972) went to #1, and *Foreigner* (1973) reached #3. Stevens's 1974 album *Buddha and the Chocolate Box*, which included the #10 hit "Oh Very Young," reached #2.

Stevens's records were gradually less successful during the second half of the '70s. In 1979 he became a Muslim, adopted the name Yusef Islam, and retired from music. He was not heard from for another 10 years, until he shocked admirers at the end of the '80s by supporting the death sentence ordered by the Ayatollah Khomeini against novelist Salman Rushdie for writing the book *The Satanic Verses*. Some "classic rock" radio stations discontinued playing him as a result, though his music remains popular. —*William Ruhlmann*

Mona Bone Jakon / 1970 / A&M 3160
Mona Bone Jakon was Stevens's first effort for A&M records, unveiling him as a sensitive singer-songwriter, with gentle tracks like "Trouble," "Katmandu," "Lady D'Arbanville," "Lily White," and "I Wish I Wish." Fans of *Teaser and the Firecat* or *Tea for the Tillerman* should check this one out. —*Rick Clark*

☆ **Tea for the Tillerman** / 1970 / A&M 4280
Tea for the Tillerman is like a musical collection of children's tales by Stevens. The delicacy of the arrangements, Paul Samwell-Smith's brilliant otherworldly production, and Stevens's entrancing melodies and images easily make this his best work. "Wild World" was a huge hit, but emotive tracks like "Father and Son," "Where Do the Children Play," and the haunting "Into White" and "Sad Lisa" make this a must-own for fans of singer-songwriter pop. This is Stevens's best album. —*Rick Clark*

○ **Teaser & the Firecat** / 1971 / A&M 4313
The followup to *Tea for the Tillerman* was almost as impressive. Sonically, less energy was put into creating empty real soundscapes, with more emphasis on tighter song constructions and immediacy. The result paid off with three international hits, "Peace Train," "Moonshadow," and "Morning Has Broken." Other

highlights included "Tuesday's Dead," "The Wind," "Bitter Blue," and "Ruby Love." After *Tea for the Tillerman*, this is the one to get. —*Rick Clark*

○ **Catch Bull at Four** / 1972 / A&M 4365
Catch Bull at Four was Stevens's commercial peak, holding the #1 spot for three weeks. Much of the reason for this was probably public anticipation that this would be as smoothly appealing as his previous two outings. With this album, Stevens's melodies became more ornate, and his delivery became a little gruffer. Overall, it is one of his better albums, with "18th Avenue," "Sitting," and "Can't Keep It In" as highlights. —*Rick Clark*

Buddha & the Chocolate Box / 1974 / A&M 3623
At the time of its release, this was heralded as Stevens's best effort since *Tea...*. It wasn't. It did have a few good tunes, particularly "Oh Very Young" and "Ready," both hits. —*Rick Clark*

● **Greatest Hits** / 1975 / A&M 4519
This is the most popular best-of collection. It has his biggest hits and a couple of important album tracks. The CD version is just a straight reissue of the original LP release, therefore utilizing only about half of the time available on disc. —*Rick Clark*

○ **Footsteps in the Dark** / 1984 / A&M 3285
This is a spotty attempt to fill the holes left open from the first *Greatest Hits* collection. Key tracks from *Mona Bone Jakon* and *Harold & Maude* are here. Unfortunately, the remastering on this disc is less than desirable. —*Rick Clark*

○ **Classics, Vol. 24** / 1987 / A&M 2522
After several collections, there has yet to be a definitive representation of Stevens's work. Half of his Top 40 hits (like "Wild World," "Another Saturday Night," "Two Fine People," "The Hurt," and "Ready") are missing. On the plus side, some nice album cuts like "The Wind" and "18th Avenue" and highlights from the movie *Harold & Maude* are here. —*Rick Clark*

Al Stewart

b. Sep. 5, 1945
Vocals, guitar / Singer-songwriter, folk rock, pop
Al Stewart has made a career out of wistful pop odes obsessed with time and historical events, all delivered with a slightly cosmic twist. During the early and mid '60s, Stewart embraced the English folk scene and released the albums *Bedsitter Images* and *Love Chronicles*, which featured the guitar work of then-future Led Zeppelinite Jimmy Page.

Stewart made his first dent on the U.S. charts with *Past, Present & Future*, an album inspired by the works of the ancient soothsayer Nostradamus. His followup, *Modern Times*, did even better, reaching #30, but it was the Alan Parsons-produced *Year of the Cat* that catapulted Stewart into brief stardom. The title track went #8, and "On the Border" rode to #42.

Stewart changed labels to Clive Davis's Arista in 1978, releasing *Time Passages*, also produced by Parsons. At #7, the title cut became the highest charting hit of Stewart's career. By this time, Stewart's sound possessed a sweeping airy quality brought on in part by his light voice and Parsons's cinematic production style. "Song on the Radio" and "Midnight Rocks" were Stewart's remaining hits. Stewart continues to play live and record. —*Rick Clark*

Love Chronicles / 1969 / Epic 48535
Notable for the 18-minute coming-of-age title cut, which caused a stir at the time for its use of the word "f**cking." Jimmy Page is featured on guitar. —*Rick Clark*

○ **Modern Times** / 1975 / Rhino 71046
Stewart's airy (sometimes sentimental) obsessions with the passage of time take on a special resonance on this outing. Highlights include "Carol," "Apple Cider Re-Constitution," "Dark and Rolling Sea," and "The Modern Times." —*Rick Clark*

○ **Year of the Cat** / 1976 / Arista 8229
Stewart's calm delivery gives his songs a reserved, tasteful sense of understatement, especially on the title track, one of those "mysterious woman" songs, which captivated listeners and turned the album into a million-seller. —*William Ruhlmann*

○ **Time Passages** / 1978 / Arista 8342
A return to Stewart's historical themes lyrically, though it's still the overall smoothness of his music that connected with another million listeners. —*William Ruhlmann*

● **Best of Al Stewart** / 1988 / Arista 8433

All of Al Stewart's Stateside hits are available here, as well as most of the best cuts from the hit albums *Year of the Cat* and *Time Passages*. Not a comprehensive overview of his career, but the best sampler available. —*Rick Clark*

Billy Stewart

b. Mar. 24, 1937, Washington, DC, d. Jan. 17, 1970
Vocals, piano / Soul
Billy Stewart was one of the most distinctive vocal stylists of the '60s. His stuttering, word-doubling attack owed more to jazz scat singing than to the gospel influences of many of his peers. A jovial, rotund piano player who toured with Bo Diddley and, through him, gained entry to Chess Records, Stewart scored biggest in 1966 with a smash Top 10 version of George Gershwin and Dubose Heyward's "Summertime," an atypically (for Chess) big-band arrangement (featuring Earth, Wind & Fire's Maurice White on drums) with Stewart in a vocal tour de force, masterfully scatting around, stuttering through, and generally turning the melody inside out. It was not your typical '60s soul music, but Stewart's success opened the door for other jazz-influenced singers like Georgie Fame to gain a place on radio playlists of the day. Stewart died tragically at age 33 in a 1970 auto accident. —*Christine Ohlman*

● **One More Time: The Chess Years** / 1990 / Chess 6027
Although a minor soul star of the '60s, Stewart possessed one of the most unique and sweetest styles. His hits "Summertime," "I Do Love You," and "Sitting in the Park" are classics of the era. —*Jeff Tamarkin*

Dave Stewart

Vocals, guitar, keyboards / Pop/rock
Dave Stewart was the musical mastermind of the Eurythmics, but on his solo recordings with the Spiritual Cowboys, he made more atmospheric, guitar-based albums that became minor hits in the United Kingdom in the early '90s. Stewart also has written several soundtracks and produced many artists, including Bob Dylan and Mick Jagger. —*Stephen Thomas Erlewine*

● **Dave Stewart & Spiritual Cowboys** / 1990 / Arista 8626
Dave Stewart's first album with the Spiritual Cowboys is a fine collection of atmospheric pop/rock. —*AMG*

Rod Stewart

b. Jan. 10, 1945, London, England
Vocals / Rock & roll, rock/pop
Before he married models, before he cared if you thought he was sexy, before he crooned pablum like "Forever Young," Rod Stewart was a rock & roll singer/songwriter with a sharp eye for detail and the ability to suck you into his world and make you feel welcome, as if you were among friends. Stewart's boozy, good-timey spirit allowed him to find humor in even the darkest corners of life, and he had the heart of a born rocker. On his early to mid '70s work, he wrote songs that overflowed with self-deprecating humor and commitment, anchored by a rambunctious sound that remains one of the most communal in all of rock.

Once he became a rock star, that joyous spirit went out the window, as he concentrated on being simply a pop singer. At times he recorded some fine Top 40 pop, but nothing he's released since 1973 has had the same creative energy and spark as his early records. —*John Floyd*

○ **Rod Stewart Album** / 1969 / Mercury 830572
An interesting if spotty hodgepodge of delicate folk ballads and blazing raveups, highlighted by "An Old Overcoat Won't Ever Let You Down." —*John Floyd*

☆ **Gasoline Alley** / 1970 / Mercury 824881
A full-blown folk outing, conjuring the despair and humor of Woody Guthrie and, on occasion, the wildcat appeal of rockabilly. —*John Floyd*

★ **Every Picture Tells a Story** / 1971 / Mercury 822385
Achieving the same variety as the debut, Stewart's title cut and "Maggie May," plus his covers of vintage Temptations, Arthur Crudup, and Tim Hardin material flaunt the versatility and savvy of his vision. A grand statement by a major player. —*John Floyd*

☆ **Never a Dull Moment** / 1972 / Mercury 826263

This repeats the formula of *Every Picture Tells a Story*, but the originals, with the exception of the beautiful "Italian Girls," are just slightly below par. Still worthwhile, though. —*John Floyd*

○ **Tonight I'm Yours** / 1981 / Warner Brothers 3602
This lacks the muscle of the early stuff but remains Stewart's last burst of creativity. This is the last time he sounds like he cares. —*John Floyd*

○ **Storyteller: Complete Anthology** / 1989 / Warner Brothers 25987
A four-disc set containing most of the essentials (but not enough material from the Faces) and all the late '70s and '80s hits for those who care. Should've been better. —*John Floyd*

Downtown Train (Selections from the Storyteller Anthology) / Mar. 6, 1990 / Warner Brothers 26158
Downtown Train: Selections from the Storyteller Anthology is a single-disc collection of some of the highlights from the *Storyteller* boxed set. —*AMG*

● **Mercury Anthology** / 1992 / Mercury 512805
A two-disc anthology of Rod Stewart's early Mercury recordings, which, along with the albums he recorded with the Faces, are inarguably his finest (however, nothing from the Faces' records is included). Most of the highlights of his terrific first four albums are here—"Maggie May," "You Wear It Well," "Handbags and Gladrags," "Gasoline Alley"—as well as selections from the lukewarm *Smiler,* a live album recorded with the Faces, and a couple of rare B sides. Although most of his biggest hits aren't here, this is the finest Stewart anthology available. —*Stephen Thomas Erlewine*

○ **Unplugged ... and Seated** / May 25, 1993 / Warner Brothers 45289
With *Unplugged ... and Seated* Stewart returns to the acoustic rock & roll and folk that marked his greatest recordings. Ron Wood's supporting guitar is a nice bonus that recalls the glory days. Naturally, *Unplugged* can't hope to match *Gasoline Alley* or *Every Picture Tells a Story,* but the amazing thing is how close it comes at times, even with the knowledge that it is a supremely calculated move on Stewart's part. He sounds fine, if a little bit ragged at first, but as the album progresses his performances become more genuine and heartfelt, culminating in yet another sublime Tom Waits cover with "Tom Traubert's Blues (Waltzing Matilda)" as well as a hit single with Van Morrison's "Have I Told You Lately?" —*Stephen Thomas Erlewine*

Stiff Little Fingers

Group / Punk
A brash, inflammatory Irish combo who released one of punk's finest debuts, then made the mistake of sticking around too long. —*John Floyd*

● **Inflammable Materials** / 1979 / Restless 72363
Despite the title, this is a scalding set that funnels the influence of the Sex Pistols into a unique and riveting debut. Includes "Alternative Ulster" and "Suspect Device." —*John Floyd*

Stephen Stills

b. Jan. 3, 1945
Vocals, guitar / Singer-songwriter, pop/rock
Singer-songwriter and multiinstrumentalist Stephen Stills first gained prominence with the legendary late '60s group Buffalo Springfield. Their first hit was the Stills-penned "For What It's Worth," inspired by Los Angeles police oppression of the youth community. Another Springfield classic written by Stills was "Bluebird," which featured his distinctive gutsy acoustic lead guitar style and his mildly husky lower tenor voice. Stills left Buffalo Springfield in 1968 to form the distinctively harmonic Crosby, Stills & Nash.

As a solo artist, Stills has produced several successful albums that mine a blend of acoustic/electric folk-rock with occasional gospelish undertones. He recorded two albums with his own group Manassas in 1972 and 1973. His biggest hits were "Love the One You're With," "Sit Yourself Down," "Change Partners," "Marianne," and "It Doesn't Matter." —*Rick Clark*

● **Stephen Stills** / 1970 / Atlantic 7206
Stephen Stills's self-titled debut started out his solo career with much promise. The opening cut, "Love the One You're With," was a huge hit. His warm, husky voice is used to great effect on most

of these tracks, and the album features a cast of 1970 all-stars like Jimi Hendrix, Eric Clapton, David Crosby, Graham Nash, John Sebastian, and Rita Coolidge. Hendrix's lead contribution is occasionally buried by Stills's overbearing organ work, and Clapton's guitar tone is too thin and brittle, but the hit "Sit Yourself Down," with its powerful piano introduction, is flawless in production and performance. —*Rick Clark*

○ **Manassas** / 1972 / Atlantic 903

After the uneven 1971 release *Stephen Stills 2*, Stills formed a band around him of some solid players (Chris Hillman, Joe Lala, Al Perkins, Fuzzy Samuels, Dallas Taylor, and others) and called it Manassas. Their first of two albums was a self-titled double-record set. Many consider *Manassas* to be Stills's finest effort; it would have made a grand single album. Atlantic has managed to fit the whole thing on a single CD. —*Rick Clark*

○ **Best of Stephen Stills** / 1977 / Atlantic 18201

This is a decent sampling of his solo work up to this point. It includes "Change Partners" from *Stephen Stills 2* as well as main tracks from the debut. —*Rick Clark*

Sting (Gordon Sumner)

b. Oct. 2, 1951
Vocals / Pop/rock

Sting launched his musical career as the lead singer of the successful rock band the Police. After the Police split in 1984, the English singer-songwriter and bassist embarked upon a successful solo career. Sting's solo works focus less on achieving pop success, instead voicing his political views and concerns. His 1985 debut album, *Dream of the Blue Turtles*, is heavily jazz-influenced and boasts a number of jazz musicians, including Branford Marsalis. This album, while it contained lyrical references to turbulent Soviet-American relations and the British coal-miners' strike, still managed to sell two million copies. The *Dream* tour resulted in a two-disc live album, *Bring on the Night*, which featured some new live renditions of Police songs. In 1987 Sting released a second solo album, *Nothing like the Sun ...*, which was very politically based as well. One of the most powerful songs on the album is "They Dance Alone," an outright criticism of the regime of Chilean General Augusto Pinochet. *The Soul Cages*, released in 1991, deals with the deaths of Sting's mother and father and veers away from political issues. It was a more introspective work, although rather gloomy, dealing with the ideas of death and loss.

In addition to his music, Sting has also appeared in a number of movies and plays, including *The Bride* and *The Threepenny Opera*. Sting has used his status as a well-known performer to lend assistance to many worthy organizations, including Band Aid, Live Aid, Special Olympics, Greenpeace, Amnesty International, and the Rainforest Foundation. —*Iotis Erlewine*

○ **Dream of the Blue Turtles** / 1985 / A&M 3750

Sting's early jazz experience was very evident on his solo debut album. Kenny Kirkland (piano), Omar Hakim (drums), Darryl Jones (bass), and Branford Marsalis (sax) contributed greatly to the jazz "feel" of the songs. This captures some of the energy and exuberance of the early Police, like *Regatta de Blanc*, but also maintains some of the somber, serious tone of *Synchronicity*. Sting's first album is his most impressive, boasting such songs as "Love Is the Seventh Wave," "Fortress around Your Heart," "Children's Crusade," and "Moon over Bourbon Steet." —*Iotis Erlewine*

○ **Bring on the Night** / 1986 / A&M 6705

A terrific live-concert album, this contains songs dating back to Sting's years with the Police, as well as works from his first solo album, *Dream of the Blue Turtles*. In addition to performances of well-known songs, Sting performs the haunting "I Burn for You," a song written for the film *Brimstone and Treacle* (in which Sting had a role) but not included on any of Sting's own albums. This two-CD set features Branford Marsalis (sax), Omar Hakim (drums), Darryl Jones (bass), Kenny Kirkland (keyboards), and Janie Pendarvis and Dolette McDonald (vocals). —*Iotis Erlewine*

○ **Nothing like the Sun** / 1987 / A&M 6402

This album is more somber than *Dream of the Blue Turtles* and light on the jazz influences, focusing more on Brazilian and Hispanic rhythms. Not as lively and concise as *Dream ...* due to the heavy, political lyrics (on such songs as "They Dance Alone" and "Fragile"), this is a good album, nevertheless. Along with

Sting's own songs, the album includes a cover of Hendrix's "Little Wing." This album includes guests Mark Knopfler, Eric Clapton, the Gil Evans Band, former Police bandmember Andy Summers (who plays on "Lazarus Heart"), and, once again, Branford Marsalis featured on sax. —*Iotis Erlewine*

Soul Cages / 1991 / A&M 6405

This long-awaited album followed the death of Sting's father, which may explain the melancholy, pained tone of these songs. The focus here is very much on death and dying, making the album a bit of a downer and hard to listen to at a single sitting. Although the material may not be as good overall as Sting's previous work, the song "All This Time" is definitely one of his best. —*Iotis Erlewine*

● **Ten Summoner's Tales** / Mar. 9, 1993 / A&M 70

Ten Summoner's Tales is the most song-oriented, lighthearted collection Sting has delivered since his debut, *The Dream of the Blue Turtles*. Sting's songs remain densely literate, although the melodies aren't; they are devoid of the jazz pretensions of *Nothing like the Sun* and the oppressive seriousness of *The Soul Cages*. When he doesn't get carried away by his own cleverness—as he does in "Love Is Stronger than Justice (the Munificent Seven)," the spoken word section of "Saint Augustine in Hell," and the schmaltzy lounge-jazz bridge of the jumping "She's Too Good for Me"—Sting can deliver the goods with some terrific pop songs ("If I Ever Lose My Faith in You," "It's Probably Me," "Epilogue [Nothin' 'Bout Me]," and "Seven Days"). Those songs help make *Ten Summoner's Tales* one of his strongest solo releases. —*Stephen Thomas Erlewine*

Stone Poneys

Pop/rock

Before becoming a solo act, Linda Ronstadt was the lead singer of the Stone Poneys, an L.A.-based trio with an acoustic, folkish sound and strong original material. Ronstadt's clear, powerful vocals were the band's focal point and greatest asset. Originally recording in a coffeehouse folk style not far removed from Peter, Paul & Mary, the group rocked up their sound slightly and scored a top 20 hit with "Different Drum," written by Mike Nesmith of the Monkees, in 1967. —*Richie Unterberger*

● **Stone Poneys Featuring Linda Ronstadt** / 1976 / Capitol 11383

It doesn't have "Different Drum," but the first Stone Poneys album is their folkiest and best, dominated by close harmonies and strong original material by the group's guitarists, Bob Kimmel and Ken Edwards. —*Richie Unterberger*

The Stone Roses

Group / Alternative pop/rock

Meshing '60s-styled guitar pop with an understated '80s dance beat, the Stone Roses defined the Manchester scene of the late '80s and early '90s. With their self-titled 1989 debut, the group mastered the subtle art of catchy guitar hooks and sighing melodies, mainly supplied by guitarist John Squire; even when they stretch out into a jangly funk jam (as on "Fool's Gold" or "I Am the Resurrection"), their music never loses its direction. After the album became an English sensation, countless other groups in the same vein became popular, including the Charlatans (UK), Inspiral Carpets, and Happy Mondays. However, none of them had the strong songwriting of the Stone Roses; "I Wanna Be Adored," "She Bangs the Drums," and "Made of Stone" are smart, melodic pop songs that rank among the best of the '80s.

After their remarkable first album, the group became embroiled in several severe lawsuits with their record companies; after a few years, the suits were settled and the band wound up on Geffen. With the exception of one single, the band has released no new material since 1989. The followup album, *Second Coming*, was expected in 1993, but it was pushed back to spring of 1994; when that didn't pan out, it was announced that the album would be out sometime in the fall. After all this time, the Stone Roses' reputation hasn't diminished. In 1993, the British newspaper *New Musical Express* voted *The Stone Roses* as the best album of the '80s and placed it in the Top 10 albums of all time. —*Stephen Thomas Erlewine*

★ **Stone Roses** / 1989 / Silvertone 1184

A vital debut that defined late '80s UK rock, maintaining a strong link with psychedelic-tinged '60s guitar-pop sounds and current dance-club beats. —*Steve Aldrich*

Turns into Stone / Oct. 27, 1992 / Silvertone 41507
Not a new Stone Roses album, but a collection of European B
sides and singles. If they don't already own the singles, hardcore
fans will want to purchase this despite the inclusion of several
tracks from the debut. —AMG

Stone Temple Pilots

Group / Alternative rock, hard rock
Stone Temple Pilots were able to make alternative rock into stadium rock; naturally, they became the most critically despised
band of their era. Accused by many critics of being nothing more
than ripoff artists, pilfering from Pearl Jam, Soundgarden, and
Alice in Chains, the band nevertheless became major stars in
1993. And the influences of those bands *are* apparent in their music, but Stone Temple Pilots do manage to change things around
a bit. STP are more concerned with tight song structure and riffs
than punk rage. Their closest antecedents are not the Sex Pistols
or Hüsker Dü; instead the band resembles arena rock acts from
the '70s—it's popular hard rock that sounds good on the radio and
in concert. No matter what the critics might say, Stone Temple
Pilots have undeniably catchy riffs and production; there's a reason why over three million people bought their debut album,
Core, and why their second album, *Purple,* shot to #1 when it was
released. —*Stephen Thomas Erlewine*

● **Core** / 1992 / Atlantic 82418
While the Stone Temple Pilots may not be sincere alternative
rockers, they do know how to write a killer riff, which is why
their debut album sold nearly as many copies as Pearl Jam.
Admittedly, STP can sound like either Pearl Jam ("Plush"), Alice
in Chains ("Sex Type Thing" and "Wicked Garden"), Soundgarden
("Dead & Bloated"), or even R.E.M. ("Creep"), depending on their
mood, but their hooks are undeniably catchy, making the songs
much better than they have any right to be. —*Stephen Thomas
Erlewine*

The Stories

Group / Pop/rock
After the demise of the Left Banke, classically trained keyboardist
and songwriter Michael Brown formed Stories in 1972 with
singer Ian Lloyd. Their first two albums, *Stories* and (particularly)
About Us, featured a brilliant collection of ultramelodic pop-rock
songs that were less baroque than those of Left Banke and (at
times) harder hitting than those of fellow pop-rockers like
Badfinger.
 Neither of these albums achieved any real success, and Stories
would have (more than likely) sadly sunk without a trace had fate
not intervened with the totally left-field hit (about an interracial
encounter) titled "Brother Louie," written by Errol Brown of the
British group Hot Chocolate. Their label, Kama Sutra, jammed
the tune on *About Us,* and the album ended up charting at #29.
 Brown left the group, and they released the spotty *Travelling
Underground,* which produced the "Brother Louie" carbon-copy
"Mammy Blue" and "If It Feels Good, Do It." Stories broke up
shortly thereafter. —*Rick Clark*

● **About Us** / 1973 / Pair 3303
The second Stories album melded ornate Anglo-pop with ever-so-
slight art-pop tendencies. Loaded with great melodies and smart
arrangements. Fans of Badfinger and Beatles-style rock/pop
should love this outing. A commercial sleeper until the band
stuck their version of Hot Chocolate's "Brother Louie," which became a #1 hit. Unfortunately, the song didn't resemble anything
else on the album. Highlights include "Darling," "Hey France,"
Please Please," "What Comes After," and "Top of the City." This
disc may be hard to find, since their reissue label has historically
done little to promote reissue product. —*Rick Clark*

Izzy Stradlin

Group / Rock & roll
After leaving Guns N' Roses, guitarist Izzy Stradlin formed a
band, the JuJu Hounds, that accentuated the Stones and Faces undertones that were always in his music. His 1992 debut is an underrated record, full of great songwriting and effortless rocking.
—*Stephen Thomas Erlewine*

○ **Izzy Stradlin & the Ju Ju Hounds** / Oct. 13, 1992 / David Geffen
Co. 24490

Izzy Stradlin was always the most gifted member of Guns N'
Roses, able to put a modern spin on the classic rock of Chuck
Berry, the Stones, the Faces, as well as the New York Dolls and
Sex Pistols. Axl may have had the angst, and Slash may have had
the chops, but Izzy had the smarts and the heart. On his debut album, the traditional elements that had always formed the backbone of Stradlin's music with Guns N' Roses comes to the forefront—it's Stones and Faces, all the way, folks, but it is done well.
Izzy Stradlin & the Ju Ju Hounds is terrific only half of the time,
which is good enough for a debut album. —*Stephen Thomas
Erlewine*

Straitjacket Fits

Group / Alternative pop/rock
New Zealand's Straitjacket Fits were a moody, ethereal pop band
that recorded several albums from 1987 to 1994. —AMG

● **Hail** / 1990 / Rough Trade 73
Dissonant, dreamy, and hypnotic garage-rock with an aggressive
edge from this New Zealand band. Highlights include "She
Speeds" and "All That That Brings." The import CD contains additional tracks. —*Scott Bultman*

Melt / 1991 / Arista 8645
Not as soaring as their first U.S. album, but their musicianship
and dark hypnotic energy make it worthwhile. —*Scott Bultman*

The Stranglers

Group / Punk, rock & roll
The Stranglers—Hugh Cornwell (b. August 28, 1949),
guitarist/vocalist; Jean Jacques Burnel, bassist/vocalist; Dave
Greenfield, keyboard player; and Jet Black, drummer- are one of
the longest-lived bands associated with the British punk explosion of the '70s, but they were never really a punk group. Formed
in Guildford in 1975, the group adopted a spare sound reminiscent of the Doors. They were categorized as punk because they
came up at the same time as the punk originators and because
their demeanor was angry and threatening.
 The Stranglers broke through in 1977, scoring three Top 10
hits, "Peaches," "Something Better Change," and "No More
Heroes," and two Top10 albums, *IV Rattus Norvegicus* and *No
More Heroes.* The group never achieved commercial success in
the United States but did well consistently in the United
Kingdom. They gradually evolved from the hard-edged style of
their early hits to a more mainstream rock sound. —*William
Ruhlmann*

● **Greatest Hits 1977-1990** / 1990 / Epic 47081
This 15-track compilation takes the Strangers from the overtly
sexist, tough-talking "Peaches" through more textured pop songs
like "Always the Sun" to recent rock remakes like "96 Tears." —
William Ruhlmann

The Strawbs

Group / Folk rock, progressive rock
Originally a folk and bluegrass trio formed by Dave Cousins,
with Sandy Denny as lead singer, the Strawbs evolved into an
acoustic folk quartet and later into a progressive rock quintet,
complete with electric keyboards and an epic/classical orientation. The exits of bassist John Ford and drummer Richard Hudson
in the early '70s led to a toughening of the group's sound but also
a weaker songwriting contingent. Their return, and Cousins's
hookup with guitarist Brian Willoughby, made them musically if
not commercially viable again in the '80s and '90s. —*Bruce Eder*

○ **Sandy Denny & the Strawbs** / 1968 / Hannibal 1361
Acoustic folk and bluegrass. Mostly a showcase for Denny, plus a
few clues to the group's future evolution. —*Bruce Eder*

Strawbs / 1969 / A&M
Still an acoustic sound, but with a much more expansive song
structure and growing seriousness. —*Bruce Eder*

● **Grave New World** / 1972 / A&M 4118
Fulfillment! Singer-songwriter Dave Cousins finds a space somewhere between Bob Dylan and John Bunyan, Hudson and Ford
come up with some superb hooks, and the electric sound is powerful and majestic. Powerful and sincere, if a little too serious and
downbeat. —*Bruce Eder*

○ **Bursting at the Seams** / 1973 / A&M 394383

A magnum opus: romantic, mystical, electrifying, and it rocks with a defiant smile. "Down by the Sea" is as fine a piece of progressive rock as was ever produced. *—Bruce Eder*

Strawbs by Choice / 1974 / A&M
A concise retrospective of some of the better moments from the first four A&M albums. *—Bruce Eder*

Hero & Heroine / 1974 / A&M 3607
The group's last great album, filled with mysticism and sexuality but lacking melodic subtlety. Loud, but with less richness of expression. *—Bruce Eder*

● **A Choice Selection of Strawbs** / 1993 / A&M
Very few of the UK group's albums are easily available, and this comprehensive 74-minute collection goes a long way to sating the resultant thirst. While there are elements of the Strawbs Mellotron-based sound that make *A Choice Selection* sound dated at times, the material survives better than many of the group's "progressive-minded" contemporaries. The Strawbs' roots went back to folk and bluegrass, and leader David Cousins never let instrumental virtuosity get in the way of a good song and well-turned lyric. The fervent folk-rock of "Lay Down and Benedictus," chilly atmosphere of "Autumn," wry wit of "Part of the Union," and enticing riffs of "Hero and Heroine" and "Down by the Sea" all hold up nicely. *—Roch Parisien*

The Stray Cats

Group / Rockabilly
A neo-rockabilly trio consisting of Brian Setzer, guitar and vocals; Slim Jim Phantom, drums; and Lee Rocker, string bass. They formed in 1979 in Massapequa, Long Island, after the demise of Setzer's punk band, the Bloodless Pharaohs. The group moved to England in 1980 and broke through there, scoring Top 10 hits with "Rock This Town" and "Runaway Boys," as well as their debut album, *Stray Cats*.

That album was not released in the United States, nor was its followup, *Gonna Ball*, but EMI America combined tracks from the two albums to create their U.S .debut, *Built for Speed*. It sold a milllion copies in 1982 and produced the U.S. Top 10 hits "Rock This Town" and "Stray Cat Strut." *Rant N' Rave with the Stray Cats* (1983), featuring "(She's) Sexy + 17," was also successful. Setzer then split from Phantom and Rocker and went solo. (The rhythm section formed Phantom, Rocker, and Slick.) There was a contractual-obligation album, *Rock Therapy*, in 1986; they reformed in 1988 and released *Blast Off* in 1989. They split again shortly afterward. *—William Ruhlmann*

○ **Built for Speed** / 1982 / EMI America 46103
The best tracks from the Stray Cats's two UK albums, the best produced by Dave Edmunds, as the group updates rockabilly and Brian Setzer comes on like a rock star. Infectious. *—William Ruhlmann*

● **Best of the Stray Cats: Rock This Town** / 1990 / EMI America 94975
Best of the Stray Cats: Rock This Town is a nice, solid compilation, featuring the title track, "Stray Cat Strut," and others. *—Cub Koda*

Nolan Strong & the Diablos

b. 1934, d. 1977
Group / R&B
Early Detroit R&B vocal group formed in 1950, which originally featured Nolan Strong, Juan Guiterriec, Willie Hunter, Quentin Eubanks, and Bob "Chico" Edwards on guitar. Strong was blessed with a beautiful high tenor voice (and even higher falsetto) and writing and arranging skills far surpassing those of most doo-wop groups of the era. What surpasses his recordings (with and without the Diablos) so special is that we're hearing the Motown sound in its embryonic form. Nolan was the original Smokey Robinson, the original Michael Jackson, years before either of them stood before a microphone at Motown. Recording his entire career for the tiny independent Fortune (Detroit's first Black R&B label), Strong's influence on Smokey and the early Motown stable of talent was unmistakable. As late as the early '60s, Berry Gordy tried to buy Nolan's contract from Fortune and install him as head arranger and producer, but to no avail. (The job went instead to Robinson.) Incredibly handsome, with a strong stage presence, Strong came close to the big time on several occasions (when his "Mind over Matter" started to break nationally, Gordy recruited the Temptations to cover it under the name the Pirates,

the only time in the history of Motown that this was done), but his erratic temperament and lifestyle ensured that it was not to be. The genius of one of the greatest and yet most underappreciated artists in the history of pop music lives on in the 20-odd years of recordings Strong did in a tiny, crudely equipped studio situated in the back of a record shop. The original sound of the Motor City, indeed. *—Cub Koda*

● **Fortune of Hits, Vol. 1** / 1961 / Fortune 8010
All the early hits, and the perfect place to start. *—Cub Koda*

○ **Fortune of Hits, Vol. 2** / 1962 / Fortune 8012
The companion piece to *Fortune of Hits, Vol. 1.* *—Cub Koda*

Mind over Matter / 1963 / Fortune 8015
Early '60s. Very soulful. *—Cub Koda*

Daddy Rock / 1963 / Fortune 8020
A great batch of rare and unreleased sides. *—Cub Koda*

The Style Council

Group / Pop/rock
After Paul Weller broke up the Jam in 1982, he formed the Style Council with pianist Mick Talbot. Together they elaborated on the slick soul music the Jam were perfecting, and, at their best, they maintained Weller's fierce liberal political agenda. Although they never hit it big in the United States, the group was successful in Europe. *—John Floyd*

○ **Introducing the Style Council** / 1983 / Mercury 815277
A solid EP collection of the band's initial British singles, including the ersatz soul of "Long Hot Summer," the bubbling pop of "Speak like a Child," and "Money-Go-Round," a fine British-funk manifesto. *—John Floyd*

● **Singular Adventures of the Style Council** / 1989 / Mercury 837896
An adequate hits collection, which skims the cream from their otherwise disappointing albums. Includes "You're the Best Thing," the closest they've ever come to a U.S. hit. *—John Floyd*

The Stylistics

Group / Soul
One of the sweetest soul groups hailing from Philly, with an incredible run of soul smashes from 1971 to 1975. The fragile falsetto of Russell Thompkins, Jr. (b. March 21, 1951), and sumptuous production of Thom Bell added up to serious long-term success for the Stylistics. The quintet debuted on the charts in 1971 with "You're a Big Girl Now" and proceeded to set the soul and pop markets ablaze with "You Are Everything," "Betcha by Golly Wow," "I'm Stone in Love with You," "Break Up to Make Up"—all ballads—and the untypical rocker "Rockin' Roll Baby" on Abco. Although they left the label in 1976, the hits rolled on for another decade, albeit not on so lofty a scale. *—Bill Dahl*

○ **Love Hits** / 1974 / Amherst 9746
Another anthology, this one covering the beautiful love songs and romantic ballads that were the Stylistics' specialty. These are all magnificent, some of the finest sentimental soul that's ever been recorded. But it's also been issued before, and Amherst's mastering isn't anything to write home about, especially the way they tend to wash out the high notes of Russell Tompkins, Jr. *—Ron Wynn*

● **Best of the Stylistics** / 1975 / Amherst 9743
Any of their collections are good, but this one features their biggest and best hits, including "I'm Stone in Love with You," "Rockin' Roll Baby," "Betcha by Golly Wow," and "You Make Me Feel Brand New." *—Cub Koda*

○ **All-Time Classics** / 1976 / Amherst 9744
When the Stylistics switched labels to Amherst in the '80s, their glorious "sweet" soul hits were repackaged on a couple of collections. This was a singular set covering their finest '70s numbers; another package split them into a two-part release. It's slightly improved in sound quality over the 1975 *The Best of the Stylistics*, and hearing Russell Tompkins, Jr., quavering falsetto at any time is a treat. *—Ron Wynn*

● **Best of the Stylistics, Vol. 2** / 1976 / Amherst 9745
This was the second volume in a two-part collection that resulted in Amherst Records issuing the same music three times. The songs are wonderful, the tactic ethically dubious at best. *—Ron Wynn*

Styx

Group / Progressive rock, hard rock
Styx were one of the biggest art rock bands of the late '70s, capable of producing monster hits with their stadium rock, power ballads, and concept albums. More than any other art-rock band, Styx was able to cross over into the pop charts, scoring hits with "Babe," "Lady," "Come Sail Away," "Too Much Time on My Hands," and "Don't Let It End." Never one for subtlety, their ballads featured sweeping, overarranged guitars and keyboards while their rockers were long and detailed, with several different sections and gargantuan guitar solos. When MTV rolled around in the early '80s, the hits stopped coming; the group broke up in 1984. Six years later, they reunited and released *Edge of the Century;* the record featured "Show Me the Way," which became popular as a Gulf War anthem. The band went on hiatus a couple of years after the album's release. —*Stephen Thomas Erlewine*

○ **Cornerstone** / 1979 / A&M 3239
DeYoung once said this album was about American thinking before the Vietnam War and wasn't autobiographical as many people thought. Includes "Babe." —*Bil Carpenter*

○ **Paradise Theater** / 1980 / A&M 3240
The height of their musical maturity, "The Best of Times." —*Bil Carpenter*

○ **Kilroy Was Here** / 1983 / A&M 3734
Includes "Mr. Roboto" and "Don't Let It End." —*Bil Carpenter*

● **Classics, Vol. 15** / 1987 / A&M 2513
This best-of collection amply covers this group's primary radio hits and key album cuts. Included are "Babe," "Best of Times," "Too Much Time on My Hands," "Mr. Roboto," "Don't Let It End," "Blue Collar Man (Long Nights)," "Come Sail Away," "Crystal Ball," and "Grand Illusion." —*Rick Clark*

Edge of the Century / 1990 / A&M 5327
Melodic hard pop and power ballads, obviously cut from the same cloth as Journey, but with a nod to modern metal. "I've Got a Lot to Learn about Love," the song that sounds the most like classic Journey, was an AOR hit. —*Brian Mansfield*

The Subdudes

Group / Rock & roll
The Subdudes embrace New Orleans and Memphis soul and filter it through an earthy acoustic/electric style, with rich, heartfelt harmonies. The fact that the Subdudes lack a drummer makes them unique in an idiom that traditionally is built on a foundation of solid drumming. They compensate with a percussionist who manages to make a tambourine sound like a trap set. —*Rick Clark*

● **Subdudes** / 1990 / East West 82015
Lovers of earthy soulful music, heavy in New Orleans spirit, should check out this impressive debut, produced by Don Gehman (John Mellencamp, Treat Her Right). "Need Somebody," "Any Cure," "Got You on His Mind," and a version of the Crescent City standard "Big Chief" are among the highlights. —*Rick Clark*

Lucky / 1991 / East West 91671
This sophomore outing contains a nice version of Al Green's "Tired of Being Alone." Overall it's almost as consistent-sounding as their debut. —*Rick Clark*

Suede

Group / Alternative rock
Like many English bands that receive massive praise from the British press, Suede were dismissed as mere hype by most listeners before they had even released a record. However, this was one time that the press were right. Suede might not be entirely original, yet their sweaty, sensual mix of the decadent elegance of '70s glam rock and the tortured angst of the post-punk British rock of the '80s makes them one of the most exciting English guitar bands of the '90s. Bernard Butler's guitar combines the crunch of Mick Ronson with the innovative, intricate rhythms and textures of Johnny Marr; Bret Anderson's exaggerated accent can be grating to some ears, yet it fits the grandly theatrical ballads "So Young" and "Stay Together," as well as throttling rockers like "Metal Mickey" and "Animal Nitrate." Anderson's impressionistic lyrics can be a little precious, but the band's musical ability saves him from his pretentions. Suede's self-titled 1993 debut was a huge hit in England, but they only gained a small cult in

America. As the band was recording their followup in 1994, an obscure American jazz-pop singer that called herself Suede forced the band to change their name to the London Suede in the United States; in the rest of the world, they've been able to retain their name. —*Stephen Thomas Erlewine*

● **Suede** / 1993 / CBS 53792
It's not often that an album can live up to its prerelease hype, but Suede's debut album is one of those rare occasions. A unique amalgam of glam-rock and post-punk pop, *Suede* takes the snarling guitars of early '70s rock and sets them to the angst of the Smiths. Although he is a fine singer, there is no doubt that Brett Anderson's grandly theatrical vocals are an acquired taste, but the strength of their material warrants such indulgences. No other band of the '90s has captured adolescent sexual yearnings and fears quite so well. —*Stephen Thomas Erlewine*

Sugar

Group / Alternative rock
After two solo albums, ex-Hüsker Dü guitarist/vocalist Bob Mould formed Sugar, another punk-pop trio, with bassist David Barbe and drummer Malcom Travis. Sugar recalls Mould's days with the seminal Hüsker Dü more than his solo albums, yet the band is not a carbon copy of *Flip Your Wig* or *New Day Rising.* Instead, Sugar's music is more streamlined and pop-oriented than Husker, without sacrificing Mould's trademark intensity—*Beaster* is one the most uncompromising recordings he has ever released. Although their first two releases were dominated by Mould, he has insisted that Sugar is a group in all senses of the word and from the sound of the band, he's right—they interact brilliantly with each other, producing a cohesive sound that was missing from Mould's last solo album, *Black Sheets of Rain.* —*Stephen Thomas Erlewine*

● **Copper Blue** / 1992 / Rykodisc 10239
Featuring some of Mould's best songwriting, Sugar's debut album is a stunning piece of hook-laden punk-pop, highlighted by the '60s-styled "If I Can't Change Your Mind," the loud, beautiful guitars of "Man on the Moon" and "Helpless," and the tongue-in-cheek Pixies tribute, "A Good Idea." —*Stephen Thomas Erlewine*

Beaster / 1993 / Rykodisc 50260
Recorded at the same time as *Copper Blue, Beaster* is a darker, more intense record than Sugar's debut, yet it never is as black as Bob Mould's *Black Sheets of Rain.* All of the qualities that made *Copper Blue* so magnificent are here, but the guitars are harsher, and the loose crucifixion concept provides a downbeat atmosphere—providing you can hear the lyrics. Mould's vocals are mixed beneath all the other instruments, contributing to the claustrophobic, oppressive atmosphere. Yet *Beaster* is not nihilistic. In fact, Mould has chosen to end the EP optimistically, albeit cautiously, with the gorgeously circular organ-based "Walking Away." —*Stephen Thomas Erlewine*

Sugarcubes

Group / Alternative pop/rock
To call them the greatest rock band from Iceland is like saying you know the greatest hockey player from Chile—it just doesn't mean much. Arty and pretentious, the Sugarcubes took the British pop press by storm with their artifice-laden pop. After releasing several flawed follow-up albums, the Sugarcubes disbanded in 1992; lead singer Bjork began a more successful solo career the following year. —*John Dougan*

● **Life's Too Good** / 1988 / Elektra 60801
With strong songs built around Bjork Gudmusdottir's piercing, striking voice, this record lived up to all the advance hype. With songs like "Birthday" and "Motorcrash," this is the perfect introduction to the 'Cubes. —*John Dougan*

Here Today Tomorrow Next Week / 1989 / Elektra 60860
A slip from the first album, but not so much that it's without merit. —*John Dougan*

○ **Stick Around for Joy** / 1992 / Elektra 61123
While it's a bit better than their second record, the Sugarcubes' final album isn't as exciting as their debut, even if it shows more musical range. Too often, it slips into a self-conscious goofiness, and even Bjork's fine vocals can't save the music from its smirking, self-involved in-jokes. —*Stephen Thomas Erlewine*

Suicidal Tendencies

Group / Hardcore, heavy metal
This Los Angeles hardcore metal quintet (originally formed as a quartet in 1981) has earned a reputation for addressing unpleasant social topics. —*John Book*

● **Suicidal Tendencies** / 1983 / Frontier 4604
The album that started it for this band. Not heavy metal but hardcore punk. A lot of aggression, with some fun. Includes the classic song "Institutionalized." —*John Book*

Join the Army / 1987 / Caroline 1336
The band incorporates a little more metal influences on this one. Includes "Possessed to Skate." —*John Book*

○ **How Will I Laugh Tomorrow When I Can't Even Smile Today** / 1988 / Epic 44288
The band is a bit more metal-oriented but still as aggressive as in their punk days. *How Will I Laugh Tomorrow When I Can't Even Smile Today* has lots of great songs, including "Trip to the Brain" and the title track. —*John Book*

○ **Lights ... Camera ... Revolution!** / 1990 / Epic 45389
Their strongest album since the debut, with great songs like "Send Me Your Money" and "You Can't Bring Me Down." —*John Book*

Suicide

Group / Alternative pop/rock, electronic
This early punk duo featuring Alan Vega and Martin Rev brought punk dynamics to their minimalist synthesized art rock. —*John Floyd*

● **Suicide** / 1977 / Restless 72519
Harsh, demanding, relentless—the best place to start. —*John Dougan*

○ **Half Alive** / 1981 / ROIR 103
Nasty live stuff. Singer Alan Vega is especially obnoxious. —*John Dougan*

Ghost Riders / 1986 / ROIR 145
Tenth anniversary gig, less confrontational. —*John Dougan*

Donna Summer

b. Dec. 31, 1948, Boston, MA
Vocals / Disco, pop
Born Donna Gaines, to a churchgoing family in the Mission Hill section of Boston, Summer took her name from Helmut Sommer, whom she married while living in Munich, Germany, as a member of a travelling cast of *Hair.* Italian electro-pop arranger Giorgio Moroder met her, and in 1975 they recorded "Love to Love You Baby," a 16-minute, riff-driven update of Jane Birkin and Serge Gainsbourg's version of "Je t'aime...moi non plus." But Summer, as it turned out, had a sturdiness quite different from Birkin's short bursts of this and that, and a flair for kitschy show tunes and overproduced slickness, both of which ideally complemented the transparent impersonality of Moroder's electronic rhythms. She and Moroder created entire subgenres of disco, and there was no stopping them until Summer stopped herself.

Beginning with 1980's *The Wanderer* she began to sing exactly the kind of pop/rock material her daring impressionism had fought against. She tried to become a pop singer; and when, as in *She Works Hard for the Money,* she drew upon gospel styles, she was listened to. But during the '70s, she wasn't merely listened to, she was a leader. Today Summer tries to catch up, sadly, with a generation whose greatest esthetic achievement was to catch up with her. —*Michael Freedberg*

○ **Love to Love You Baby** / 1975 / Casablanca 822792
"Love to Love You Baby"'s 16:50 of arousal and refill—ticklishly sensitive rhythm and fusion—threw disco into a tizzy overnight, but the tonally starved blues-of-isolation on the B side isn't to be missed, either: the broken promises Summer bemoans in "Full of Emptiness"; "Need-a-Man Blues," with its unrequitedly sexy guitar rhythm as out of range of Summer's voice as she of satisfaction; the imaginary seaside hold-me in "Whispering Waves"; and "Pandora's Box," where Summer and guitar scream icily at one another as they turn their backs on each other's body music. —*Michael Freedberg*

Love Trilogy / Jan. 1976 / Casablanca 822793

Summer's quizzical "Try Me," "I Know," and "We Can Make It" wing her nervous little falsetto from risk to dare and from dare to mad hope, and her rhythm section gropes from testy touch beats to tightrope-walkers' guitar figures and safety net harmonies. The second side substitutes dance with imaginary lovers for the debut album's love starvation blues. Don't dismiss its subtle mood poems the way fans of "Love to Love You" sped right past the B side of Summer's debut; the flightier Summer plays a rhythm, the dicier her resolution. —*Michael Freedberg*

I Remember Yesterday / Jan. 1977 / Casablanca 826237
Donna Summer continued her climb to superstardom with this late '70s album, her first since the attention-grabbing *Love to Love You Baby* album in 1975 to crack the pop Top 10. The single "I Feel Love" was her second Top 10 R&B and pop hit and paved the way for Summer to emerge shortly after as disco's reigning queen. —*Ron Wynn*

Once upon a Time / Feb. 1977 / Casablanca 826238
Summer and her liberators have created one audience and redefined another, and this record's four sides of dreamworlds without end sometimes manipulate each audience. The candy girl music of "Fairy Tale High," "Queen for a Day," and "If You Got It, Flaunt It" explicitly recognizes her newly created gay audience, a daring acknowledgment coming from a mainstream pop star. As for her redefined audience of naive young things who live in the suburbs and dream of romance, adventure, and sex while they search for identity, Summer works her music into a true-to-life Cinderella story staged as four acts of impatient pulse, delirious space noise, wish-upon-a-star voice monologues, and motion. —*Michael Freedberg*

○ **Bad Girls** / 1979 / Casablanca 822557
Summer defined feminine for an age in love with femininity and made the disco experience an adventure/vacation even for those who had trouble learning how to fantasize. Now, in her third two-record set in two years, she has altered her outlook on femininity and changed her mind about the adventure. The disco queen becomes a streetwalker ready to sell her voice to any guy (read: producer) for a dime ("Bad Girls," "Hot Stuff") or anyone at all blindly searching for a lover they'll never find ("Sunset People"). Once a Cinderella, she now sees through a (looking) glass darkly—and is not afraid. It's chilling to hear Miss Love-to-Love-You describe bad girls as sad girls who, like you and me, just want to be a star; when she says that bad girls and she are the same though each use different names, it's clear that disco innocence has gone. —*Michael Freedberg*

★ **On the Radio (Greatest Hits)** / 1979 / Casablanca 822558
If you want to be unadventurous and just go for the '70s hits, stop here; however, you will still be missing some of Summer's finest work. Besides, in order to cram all the hits into a two-record set, many of them were abridged, including the stunning guitar solo on "Hot Stuff." —*Bil Carpenter*

○ **Wanderer** / 1980 / David Geffen Co. 99124
First post-Casablanca set with hard rock edge shining best on title, "Cold Love," and "Night Life." —*Bil Carpenter*

○ **She Works Hard for the Money** / 1983 / Casablanca 812265
Summer's brassy, matter-of-fact mezzo does not play the sexy sanctified diva, and her musicians' crisp loud beats don't evoke rapture or delirium. Instead, she and her rhythm men live up to the title of "She Works Hard for the Money." Here's praise for a waitress's 12-hour workday that sums up Summer's own post-dance queen job status as well as disco fans' own spotlighted lives and maintains the pressure from the steel-and-synth riffs of "Stop, Look & Listen" to the impatient tenderness of "People, People." No one writes about love with as mesmeric a sense of wonder as Summer confesses in "Love Has a Mind of Its Own," "Unconditional Love," and "I Do Believe (I Fell in Love)." —*Michael Freedberg*

● **Donna Summer Anthology (Chronicles Series)** / Sep. 21, 1993 / Casablanca 518144
A double-disc set that collects all of Summer's biggest hits and finest moments; it's the definitive anthology. —*AMG*

The Sundays

Group / Alternative pop
A British alternative-pop band, the Sundays feature the airy vocal phrasing of Harriet Wheeler and the R.E.M.-meets-Smiths ambi-

ent guitar jangle of David Gavurin. Their sound is simultaneously atmospheric and driving. —*Rick Clark*

● **Reading Writing & Arithmetic** / 1990 / David Geffen Co. 24277
The delicate vocals of lead singer Harriet Wheeler propel this top-notch collection of modern rock tracks. —*Donna DiChario*

○ **Blind** / 1992 / David Geffen Co. 24479
Featuring gentle, folk-based guitars and pop melodies, the Sundays' second album isn't much of a sonic departure from their first album. While it does have several fine numbers, it doesn't have as many outstanding songs as *Reading Writing & Arithmetic;* nevertheless, *Blind* will please most fans of the group. —*Stephen Thomas Erlewine*

Superchunk

Group / Alternative rock
In the big-business world of '90s alternative rock, Superchunk remains a staunchly independent guitar rock band. When their record label, Matador, signed a major-label distribution deal, the band refused to be a part of the deal; with their next record, they switched labels to their privately owned Merge label. All the while, the band continues to gain more fans. Superchunk's stripped-down, speedy punk rock is proudly low-fidelity, yet their songs are well written, packed with hooks and raw, energetic rocking. Although their singles and albums show little stylistic variation, they rock so hard the similarity hardly matters. —*Stephen Thomas Erlewine*

● **Tossing Seeds (Singles 89-91)** / 1992 / Merge 20
A superb collection of early singles by one of the best indie-guitar bands of the early '90s. —*Stephen Thomas Erlewine*

○ **No Pocky for Kitty** / 1992 / Matador 35
No Pocky for Kitty is the band's finest record to date, filled with blistering punk rockers. —*Stephen Thomas Erlewine*

○ **On the Mouth** / 1993 / Matador 49
On the Mouth is one of Superchunk's best albums not because it offers anything different from their previous work but because the band's songwriting is at a peak, which make songs like "The Question Is How Fast" sound fresh and exciting, not empty exercises in punk nostalgia. —*Stephen Thomas Erlewine*

Supertramp

Group / Progressive rock, pop/rock
In 1969, a young Dutch millionaire by the name of Stanley August Miesegaes gave his acquaintance vocalist and keyboardist Roger Davies a "genuine opportunity" to form his own band; he could form the band of his dreams, and Miesegaes would pay for it. After placing an ad in *Melody Maker,* Davies assembled Supertramp. Supertramp released two longwinded progressive rock albums before Miesegaes withdrew his support. With no money or fan base to speak of, the band was forced to redesign their sound. Coming up with a more pop-oriented form of progressive rock, the band had a hit with their third album, *Crime of the Century.* Throughout the decade, Supertramp had a number of best-selling albums, culminating in their 1979 masterpiece, *Breakfast in America. Breakfast in America* marked their first album that tipped the scale in completely in the favor of pop songs; on the strength of the hit singles "Goodbye Stranger," "Logical Song," and "Take the Long Way Home" it sold over 18 million copies worldwide. After that album, Supertramp continued to develop a more R&B-flavored style; the change in direction was successful on 1982's *Famous Last Words,* but they soon ran out hits. The band continued to record and tour into the '90s. —*Stephen Thomas Erlewine*

○ **Crime of the Century** / 1974 / A&M 3647
This Ken Scott-produced concept album made it into the U.S. Top 40. It includes the hits "Bloody Well Right," "Hide in Your Shell," and "Dreamer." —*Bil Carpenter*

○ **Even in the Quietest Moments** / 1977 / A&M 3297
The group produced this one without Ken Scott. The title track and "Give a Little Bit" are standouts. —AMG

○ **Breakfast in America** / 1979 / A&M 3708
Not only was *Breakfast in America* their biggest hit, it was their best album, thanks to singles like "Goodbye Stranger," "Take the Long Way Home," and "The Logical Song." —AMG

● **Classics, Vol. 9** / 1987 / A&M 2507

This is a fairly good sampler of this band's bigger radio tracks as well as key album numbers. Included are "Bloody Well Right," "Ain't Nobody but Me," "The Logical Song," "Give a Little Bit," "It's Raining Again," "Goodbye Stranger," "Take the Long Way Home," and "Dreamer." Unfortunately, "Even in the Quietest Moments" is curiously omitted. —AMG

The Supremes

Group / Motown
The Supremes evolved from the Primettes to become the preeminent female group of their day, and Diana Ross emerged from the Supremes to become one of the all-time great pop divas. The Primettes were a local Detroit group that had recorded unsuccessfully for Lupine before they signed with Motown and changed their name to the Supremes- a name that seemed to create a self-fulfilling prophecy. After a few false starts, they broke through in 1964 with "Where Did Our Love Go?" From there, the roll call of hits is as familiar as Diana Ross's false eyelashes; they are part of the collective unconscious of anyone who lived through the '60s. The hits were the work of the production team of Holland-Dozier-Holland, which had been seconded from Martha & the Vandellas, a move that was later the font of considerable acrimony. Whether the hits were R&B or pop is a moot point. Certainly Diana Ross had pop aspirations aplenty, as her solo recordings showed, but it was a trend already evident on forlorn albums of standards that the Supremes cut at Motown. There is every indication that Motown founder Berry Gordy saw Diana Ross (with whom he had a close personal relationship) and the Supremes as his ticket into legitimate show business.

Ross left in 1970, immediately after "Someday We'll Be Together," and although the Supremes soldiered on (even scoring another #1 R&B hit with "Stoned Love"), there is no doubt that to most people the Supremes will be forever associated with their former lead singer. —*Colin Escott*

○ **Where Did Our Love Go** / Jan. 1965 / Motown 5270
The group's second album and the first to explode onto the charts. The suggestion that Diana Ross replace Florence Ballard as lead singer forever altered the course of Motown and popular music and is still being felt to this day. The decision to put them in the hands of Holland-Dozier-Holland was equally pivotal; they crafted the title track and started the group on its way to superstardom. This album has a charm and innocence sorely missing from their later LPs, when Ross was aware that she was a star. Now, it was just three young women expressing what was in their hearts with no affectation, primness, or fluff. —*Ron Wynn*

○ **I Hear a Symphony** / Feb. 1966 / Motown 5147
The Supremes ruled the roost in 1966, topping the pop charts, dominating the R&B/soul surveys, and establishing themselves as the greatest women's vocal group of all time. They'd had a brief slump with the single "Nothing but Heartaches," but were back on top with the title track and during the year destroyed any competition with four R&B and pop hits, half of them #1 on both sides, plus two Top 10 albums, with this one also a chart topper. Diana Ross had become the group star, but her vocals indicated she deserved that position. —*Ron Wynn*

○ **Supremes A-Go-Go** / Aug. 1966 / Motown 5138
A #1 album and the greatest dance-based release Motown ever issued. The Supremes were lapping the field at this point, getting superb material, production, and arrangements, plus musical backing from pop's finest instrumentalists. "Love Is Like an Itching in My Heart" set the stage for another run of smash #1 hits, and this was one of only two Supremes' LPs that stayed on top more than one week (the other was their first greatest hits album). —*Ron Wynn*

Magnificent 7 / Sep. 1970 / Motown 5123
Motown tried to recapture the success of their previous Temptations/Supremes pairing by putting the post-Diana Ross Supremes alongside the Four Tops. It proved an inspired idea; the album not only was one of the best that this Supremes lineup ever made but also revitalized the Four Tops. Their version of "River Deep, Mountain High" shocked everyone by cracking the R&B Top 10 and pop Top 20 almost a year after it had been issued and certainly helped make the ordinary followup tune "Nathan Jones" a hit. —*Ron Wynn*

★ **Anthology** / May 1974 / Motown 794

A complete collection of their nonstop Motown hits. A must-have. —*Rick A. Bueche*

70's Greatest Hits & Rare Classics / Motown 5487
An interesting anthology, one of the few that don't merely recycle shopworn hits. This collection covers the Supremes in the post-Diana Ross era, with tracks that featured both the group and solo tracks from Jean Terrell and Scherrie Payne, plus the few hits they had when Mary Wilson shared the leads with Terrell. It also contains some rare Supremes album tracks. —*Ron Wynn*

Keith Sweat

Vocals / Urban R&B
Keith Sweat is a Harlem-born R&B singer-songwriter who released his debut album, *Make It Last Forever*, at the end of 1987. The album sold over three million copies, spawning the hits "I Want Her," "Something Just Ain't Right," "Make It Last Forever," and "Don't Stop Your Love." It was followed in June 1990 by *I'll Give All My Love to You*, another million-seller, that featured the hits "Make You Sweat," "Merry Go Round," "I'll Give All My Love to You," and "Your Love, Part 2." Sweat's third album was *Keep It Comin',* an R&B chart-topper at the end of 1991, whose title track was another #1 R&B hit. —*William Ruhlmann*

○ **Make It Last Forever** / 1988 / Elektra 60763
Featuring "I Want Her" and several other equally danceable tracks. —*Bil Carpenter*

● **I'll Give All My Love to You** / 1990 / Vintertainment 60861
Keith Sweat represents a new generation of R&B love men who combine the ballad strength of singers like Luther Vandross with percussion-heavy dance music, called new jack swing, that answers the needs of the current dance floor. His second album, with its four hit singles, is typical of his approach. —*William Ruhlmann*

Sweet

Group / Glam rock, rock & roll
Mid '70s English glam-rock pioneers, the Sweet churned out Who-like Chapman- and Chinn-composed teen raunch that, by the '90s, approached neoclassic status. With their chirpy harmonies and fuzzy (but never too dangerous) guitars, the Sweet's commercial grunge became far more influential than anyone had predicted. —*John Dougan*

○ **Desolation Boulevard** / 1974 / Capitol 48452
A surprisingly solid hard-rock record; features "Ballroom Blitz." —*Dan Heilman*

● **Best of Sweet** / Mar. 1, 1993 / Capitol 80324
Nobody played rock & roll trashier or dumber than Sweet, and their best moments shine on this terrific 16-track compilation. Every one of their hits was powered by an irresistibly stupid melody, big dumb guitars, and, on occasion, a whining synthesizer. It was glitter rock for teens at its best, without the dark sensuality of T. Rex. Even today, Sweet's best songs—"Ballroom Blitz," "Little Willy," "Blockbuster," "Teenage Rampage," and the nearly perfect "Fox on the Run"—still sound gloriously trashy. —*Stephen Thomas Erlewine*

Matthew Sweet

Vocals, guitar / Alternative pop/rock
For the most of the '80s, Matthew Sweet played guitar with Oh-OK and Lloyd Cole; he released his first solo album, *Inside*, in 1986. Both *Inside* and 1989's *Earth* showed promise, drawing equally from the jangly guitar pop of the Byrds and Big Star and the southern pop of R.E.M. and the dB's. But it wasn't until 1992's *Girlfriend* that Sweet made came into his own artistically. Where his other albums were good, *Girlfriend* was exceptional, full of raging guitars (courtesy of Richard Lloyd and Robert Quine) and aching melodies; it expertly fused the Beatles, Big Star, and Neil Young into one distinctive, melodic style. The album was critically acclaimed as well as relatively commercially successful; Sweet had a minor hit with the title track and he earned many fans. *Altered Beast*, released the following year, was sloppier, yet it expanded his cult and helped him inch his way into the mainstream. —*Stephen Thomas Erlewine*

● **Girlfriend** / 1991 / Zoo 11015
Matthew Sweet's third album is a remarkable artistic breakthrough. Grounded in the guitar pop of the Beatles, Big Star,

Byrds, R.E.M., and Neil Young, *Girlfriend* melds all of Sweet's influences into one majestic, wrenching sound that encompasses both the gentle country rock of "Wynonna" and the winding guitars of the title track and "Divine Intervention." Sweet's music might have recognizable roots, but *Girlfriend* never sounds derivative; thanks to his exceptional songwriting, the album is a fresh, original interpretation of a classic sound. —*Stephen Thomas Erlewine*

○ **Altered Beast** / Feb. 1993 / Zoo 11050
Compared to the concise songwriting of *Girlfriend*, *Altered Beast* is all over the place, both emotionally and musically. Ranging from piercing guitar raveups ("Dinosaur Act") to gorgeous country rock ("Time Capsule"), the album not only covers all sides of Sweet's musical personality but also pastes them together haphazardly. Consequently, it takes a bit of time for it all to make sense, but after a few listens, it falls together, and its best moments equal *Girlfriend*. —*Stephen Thomas Erlewine*

Son of Altered Beast / Mar. 15, 1994 / Zoo 11078
Collecting several B sides and outtakes, *Son of Altered Beast* is actually more consistent and enjoyable than the full-length *Altered Beast*. —*Stephen Thomas Erlewine*

Rachel Sweet

b. 1963, Akron, OH
Vocals / New wave, pop/rock
After a couple of failed singles as a teenage country singer, the diminutive Sweet plugged her big voice into the burgeoning punk movement after being signed to Stiff Records. Along with Lene Lovich, she was one of the early women recording for the label, with a succession of great records that garnered much critical acclaim but failed to catch on in the marketplace. She dropped out of sight for a few years, then came back working for director John Waters both on and off the screen (*Hairspray*, *Cry Baby*), and has recently turned up working on cable's Comedy Channel. —*Cub Koda*

● **Fool Around** / 1978 / Rhino 70313
A solid best-of collection showcasing Sweet's dazzling vocal capabilities. —*Cub Koda*

○ **Protect the Innocent** / 1980 / Rhino 70313
Sweet's second and most perfectly realized album features "Take Good Care of Me" and a slam-bang version of "Baby, Let's Play House." Out of print, but it's worth the search. —*Cub Koda*

SWV

Urban R&B
SWV scored several hits in the early '90s with their smooth, silky harmonies and lush urban contemporary material. —*Stephen Thomas Erlewine*

It's about Time / 1992 / RCA 66074
SWV's debut album is a good example of the best of contemporary urban R&B, mixed with a hint of new jack swing style and hip-hop. Naturally, the singles are the strongest songs on the album, but the rest of the material reveals that this talented trio has quite a bit of promise. —*Stephen Thomas Erlewine*

David Sylvian

Vocals / Art rock
After Japan broke up in 1982, vocalist David Sylvian embarked on a solo career. His solo efforts include work with progressive sidemen such as Robert Fripp (King Crimson), Bill Nelson (Be Bop Deluxe), and Holger Czukay (Can). He draws his style from '70s art-rock fixtures like Roxy Music and David Bowie, with a spark from the experimental electronic movement of the '80s. —AMG

Gone to Earth / 1986 / Virgin 90577
Sylvian is joined by guitarists Robert Fripp and Bill Nelson on this 68-minute CD, which features tracks of Sylvian's trademark vocals and instrumentals. Dreamy, atmospheric works, with nice musical support from Steve Nye, Kenny Wheeler, and Mel Collins. —*Scott Bultman*

● **Secrets of the Beehive** / 1987 / Virgin 90677
A consistent mood is sustained throughout this one. Sylvian is joined by Ryuichi Sakamoto, David Torn, Mark Isham, ex-Japan drummer Steve Jansen, and others. Includes a vocal version of

the Sylvian/Sakamoto cut "Forbidden Colours" from the *Merry Christmas, Mr. Lawrence* soundtrack. —*Scott Bultman*

○ **Plight & Premonition** / 1988 / Venture 90904
A collaboration between David Sylvian, frontman for Japan, and Holger Czukay, the bassist for Can. —*Michael P. Dawson*

Flux and Mutability / 1989 / Venture 1602
A followup to *Plight and Premonition,* with Holger Czukay. Two lengthy, dreamlike pieces. —*Michael P. Dawson*

Tad

Group / Alternative rock, heavy metal
More than any other Seattle, Tad fits the stereotypical image of heavy, grizzled Northwestern lumberjacks. Fittingly, the band sounds like it looks—loud, heavy, slow, grimy, sweaty, spitting out recycled '70s metal licks with a slow-burning fervor. Led by guitarist/vocalist Tad Doyle, the band has gained a solid fan base since their first Sub Pop release in 1989; the band released its first major-label album in 1993. They were the last Seattle band from Sub Pop's late '80s/early '90s roster to sign to a major label. They were also the first to be dropped, when their record company objected to Tad's 1994 promotional posters for their *Inhaler* album, which featured President Bill Clinton smoking a joint, saying "This Is Heavy Shit." —*Stephen Thomas Erlewine*

○ **Salt Lick** / Jan. 1990 / Sub Pop 49
Notable Seattle grunge for Soundgarden fans. The CD contains most of the group's previous effort, *God's Balls.* —*David Szatmary*

○ **8-Way Santa** / Feb. 1991 / Sub Pop 89
More noise from this grunge outfit. —*David Szatmary*

● **Inhaler** / 1993 / Giant
Thanks to producer J. Mascis, Tad gets a more focused and driven sound on their major label debut, *Inhaler,* easily their best and most consistent album to date. Fortunately, the group has lost none of the grit that marked them as the grungiest of the Seattle scene, while keeping their songs full of sledgehammer hooks. —*Stephen Thomas Erlewine*

Talk Talk

Group / New wave
Synthesizer rock by Londoners Mark Hollis, Paul Webb, and Lee Harris. Formed in 1981 and signed amid the synth-pop craze, Talk Talk released its debut and toured with Duran Duran in 1982. —*David Szatmary*

○ **It's My Life** / 1984 / EMI America 46063
The followup is more polished. Less like Duran Duran, more like Roxy Music. Features the hit title track. —*Scott Bultman*

○ **Colour of Spring** / 1986 / EMI America 46228
Talk Talk begins their move away from light pop into more adventurous ground. The results are hit and miss, but several good tracks like "Life's What You Make It" are worthwhile. —*Scott Bultman*

● **Natural History: The Very Best of Talk Talk** / 1990 / EMI America 93976
Natural History: The Very Best of Talk Talk is a collection of the best material from their first four albums, plus two live tracks. All their hits and highlights are here, like "It's My Life," "Such a Shame," and "Life's What You Make It." —*Scott Bultman*

○ **Laughing Stock** / 1991 / Polydor 847717
Hauntingly beautiful dissonance, almost like free-form jazz. Not pop music, to be sure, but interesting atmospheric instrumentals. This is the culmination of the direction they were taking on their previous two albums. —*Scott Bultman*

Talking Heads

Group / New wave, pop/rock
At the start of their career, Talking Heads were all nervous energy, detached emotion, and subdued minimalism. When they released their last album about 12 years later, the band had recorded everything from art funk to polyrhythmic worldbeat explorations and simple, melodic guitar pop. Between their first album in 1977 and their last in 1988, Talking Heads became one of the most critically acclaimed bands of the '80s, while managing to earn several pop hits. While some of their music can seem too self-consciously experimental, clever, and intellectual for its own good, at their best Talking Heads represents everything good about art-school punks.

And they were literaly art-school punks. Guitarist/vocalist David Byrne, drummer Chris Franz, and bassist Tina Weymouth met at the Rhode Island School of Design in the early '70s; they decided to move to New York in 1974 to concentrate on making music. The next year, the band won a spot opening for the Ramones at the seminal New York punk club CBGB's. In 1976, keyboardist Jerry Harrison, a former member of Jonathan Richman's Modern Lovers, was added to the lineup. By 1977, the band had signed to Sire Records and released their first album, *Talking Heads '77.* It received a considerable amount of acclaim for its stripped-down rock & roll, particularly Byrne's geeky, overly intellectual lyrics and uncomfortable, jerky vocals.

For their next album, 1978's *More Songs about Buildings and Food,* the band worked with producer Brian Eno, recording a set of carefully constructed, arty pop songs, distinguished by extensive experimenting with combined acoustic and electronic instruments, as well as touches of surprisingly credible funk. On their next album, the Eno-produced *Fear of Music,* Talking Heads began to rely heavily on their rhythm section, adding flourishes of African-styled polyrhythms. This approach came to a full fruition with 1980's *Remain in Light,* which was again produced by Eno. Talking Heads added several sidemen, including a horn section, leaving them free to explore their dense amalglam of African percussion, funk bass and keyboards, pop songs, and electronics.

After a long tour, the band concentrated on solo projects for a couple of years. By the time of 1983's *Speaking in Tongues,* the band had severed their ties with Brian Eno; the result was an album that still relied on the rhythmic innovations of *Remain in Light,* except within a more rigid pop-song structure. After its release, Talking Heads embarked on another extensive tour, which would turn out to be their last; it's captured on the Jonathan Demme-directed concert film, *Stop Making Sense.* After releasing the straightforward pop album *Little Creatures* in 1985, Byrne directed his first movie, *True Stories,* the following year; the band's next album featured songs from the film. Two years later, Talking Heads released *Naked,* which marked a return to their worldbeat explorations, although it sometimes suffered from Byrne's lyrical pretensions.

After its release, Talking Heads were put on "hiatus"; Byrne pursued some solo projects, as did Harrison; Franz and Weymouth continued with their side project, the Tom Tom Club. In 1991, the band issued an announcement that they had broken up. —*Stephen Thomas Erlewine*

☆ **Talking Heads '77** / 1977 / Sire 6036
An edgy set of weird, funk-like rockers, which introduced David Byrne's skewed world outlook. "Pull Me Up" and "New Feeling" are the standouts. —*John Floyd*

☆ **More Songs about Buildings & Food** / 1978 / Sire 6058
Producer Brian Eno added muscle and flair to the group's arty funk rock, making this a dense and beautiful set. —*John Floyd*

Fear of Music / 1979 / Sire 6076
A weird, dance-worthy album, made creepy by Byrne's paranoid vision and Eno's dense production. But "Life during Wartime" is one hell of a single. —*John Floyd*

☆ **Remain in Light** / 1980 / Sire 6095
Song structure shimmies out the window as Eno and the band flex their Afro-funk muscles. Works as both brain music and dance music. —*John Floyd*

○ **The Name of This Band Is Talking Heads** / 1982 / Sire 3590
A live double album that traces the band's progression, culminating in two sides of scalding material from *Remain in Light.* —*John Floyd*

○ **Speaking in Tongues** / 1983 / Sire 23883
A pulsating mix of the heavy funk of *Remain in Light* and song structures that hark back to *More Songs about Buildings & Food.* Contains the hit "Burning Down the House" and the hypnotic "This Must Be the Place." —*John Floyd*

Stop Making Sense / 1984 / Sire 25186
Like *The Name of This Band Is Talking Heads,* the soundtrack to their concert film *Stop Making Sense* captures the group at the peak of their live powers. Even though it duplicates three numbers from the previous live album, the performances on *Stop Making Sense* are so energetic that the album never sounds like a retread. —*Stephen Thomas Erlewine*

○ **Little Creatures** / 1985 / Sire 25305
Musically, this is a return to spare production and simple melodies, but this is also Byrne's most coherent and mature set of songs. —*John Floyd*

True Stories / 1986 / Sire 25512
Featuring songs written for David Byrne's film of the same name, *True Stories* is even more pop-oriented than *Little Creatures*, full of simple, catchy melodies and guitar hooks. Unfortunately, Byrne thinks pop should be not only simple but also simplistic; too often, his genuinely engaging songs are weighed down by his trite lyrics and condescending attitude. Fortunately, with their exceptional musical versatility, the rest of the band keeps the album from being a complete failure. —*Stephen Thomas Erlewine*

Naked / 1988 / Fly 25654
Another dense set of Third World funk, this time with some help from genuine African musicians and lyrics that talk loudly but mostly say nothing. —*John Floyd*

● **Popular Favorites, 1984-1992: Sand in the Vaseline** / Oct. 13, 1992 / Sire 26760
Featuring material from every Talking Heads album except the live *The Name of This Band Is Talking Heads*, *Sand in the Vaseline* is a terrific double-disc retrospective of the band's long and varied career. Featuring all of their hit singles and tradmark songs ("Psycho Killer," "Take Me to the River," "Burning Down the House," "And She Was," "Once in a Lifetime," "Swamp," "Memories Can't Wait," "Crosseyed and Painless," "Road to Nowhere," "(Nothing but) Flowers," "Life During Wartime"), the set also includes five previously unreleased tracks. —*Stephen Thomas Erlewine*

James Taylor

b. Mar. 12, 1948
Vocals / Singer-songwriter
When people use the term "singer-songwriter" (often with the word "sensitive"), in praise or in criticism, it's James Taylor that they're thinking of. Yet in a career now extending over a quarter-century, Taylor's biggest hits have come with his cover versions of other people's songs. Go figure. Taylor grew up in Massachusetts and North Carolina, forming the band the Flying Machine with guitarist Danny Kortchmar in 1967. He was signed as a solo artist by Apple in 1968 and released his debut album, *James Taylor*, in 1969. But it was his 1970 album, *Sweet Baby James*, with its understated autobiographical hit, "Fire and Rain," that was his commercial breakthrough. *Mud Slide Slim and the Blue Horizon* went to #2 in 1971 and contained the #1 single "You've Got a Friend," written by Carole King. Taylor scored his next big hit with a remake of Marvin Gaye's "How Sweet It Is (to Be Loved by You)" in 1975, and hit again in 1977 with Jimmy Jones's "Handy Man." He has recorded with Simon & Garfunkel, his ex-wife Carly Simon, and J. D. Souther, and he continues to release gold-selling albums every few years. —*William Ruhlmann*

○ **James Taylor** / 1969 / Capitol 97577
A lovely debut album, beautifully produced by Peter Asher. It features Taylor's sometimes dour sentiments sung in his compelling but quiet voice. Includes "Something in the Way She Moves," "Carolina in My Mind," and "Rainy Day Man." —*William Ruhlmann*

☆ **Sweet Baby James** / 1970 / Warner Brothers 1843
The heart of James Taylor's appeal is that you can take him two ways. On the one hand, his music, including that warm voice, is soothing; its minor key melodies and restrained playing draw in the listener. On the other hand, his world view, especially on such songs as "Fire and Rain," reflects the pessimism and desperation of the '60s hangover that was the early '70s. Either way, this is impressive stuff. —*William Ruhlmann*

○ **Mud Slide Slim and the Blue Horizon** / 1971 / Warner Brothers 2561
The changeover here—and it's the big changeover in Taylor's work—is that he is trying to jettison the past ("Don't come to me with your sorrows anymore" is the album's opening line) and look to a hopeful future. That he doesn't quite succeed makes the album itself a success. You need a little darkness to make the light stand out. —*William Ruhlmann*

Gorilla / 1975 / Warner Brothers 2866

After a three-year slump, Taylor made *Gorilla*, a comeback album of sorts. Its slick blend of light reflective originals and *Big Chill*-style song covers set the tone for many of his subsequent releases. Highlights included a remake of Marvin Gaye's "How Sweet It Is (to Be Loved by You)," "Mexico," the steamy "You Make It Easy," and "Sarah Maria," an ode to his daughter. All in all, *Gorilla* is one of Taylor's more enjoyable post-*Sweet Baby James* efforts. —*Rick Clark*

● **Greatest Hits** / 1976 / Warner Brothers 3113
Pretty great. Be warned, however, that the versions of "Something in the Way She Moves" and "Carolina in My Mind" are rerecordings. —*William Ruhlmann*

○ **JT** / 1977 / Columbia 34811
The bad news is that by the time he switched to Columbia, Taylor had made the transition to craftsmanlike pop music, abandoning the shadows of his earlier work. The good news is that the Columbia work *is* so well crafted, forcing you to acknowledge what a good singer Taylor is. If the songs are less thoughtful, they are no less appealing as music. This is the best of six Columbia albums so far, but they're all of a piece. Good, easy listening. —*William Ruhlmann*

Live / 1993 / Warner Brothers
Since there is there is no comprehensive domestic greatest hits album available, the pleasant *Live* will suit the needs of those who want a collection of Taylor's best-known songs, although his performance is unremarkable. —AMG

Johnnie Taylor

b. May 5, 1938
Vocals / Soul
Aptly dubbed the "Philosopher of Soul" by the Stax publicity department, Johnnie Taylor set the ladies' hearts aflutter during the early '70s with his tender brand of Memphis soul.
    Taylor wasn't always the sincere crooner he developed into. A Sam Cooke protege who took over with the Soul Stirrers when Cooke went secular, and who retained a hint of his mentor's mellifluous delivery, Taylor took the same pop route via Cooke's SAR label in 1961. Once he got on the Stax label in 1966, the vocalist forged a sublime blues/soul synthesis with a series of absolutely gorgeous efforts. But there was nothing subtle about Taylor's first #1 R&B hit in 1968: "Who's Making Love" was an uncompromising treatise on cheating lovers, with storming brass and slashing guitar. The followups "Take Care of Your Homework" and "Jody's Got Your Girl and Gone" pounded the same message home from different angles.
    As the decade turned, though, Taylor perceptibly mellowed, turning increasingly to ballads for inspiration—"I Believe in You (You Believe in Me)" and "We're Getting Careless with Our Love." By the time he went platinum with the horribly repetitive "Disco Lady" in 1976, the rough edges that made his early work so absorbing were smoothed away, although his recent Malaco output sometimes manages to suggest Taylor's glory years. —*Bill Dahl*

○ **Wanted: One Soul Singer** / 1967 / Atlantic 82253
Johnnie Taylor was just emerging as a credible soul vocalist in 1967, and this album didn't enjoy the widespread acclaim or exposure later albums would garner. But it didn't lack good material; Taylor got a mild hit with "Somebody's Been Sleeping in My Bed," and this album's concentration on romantic tactics and love tales helped earn Taylor his nickname as "The Soul Philosopher." —*Ron Wynn*

Philosophy Continues / 1970 / Stax 8563
Johnnie Taylor had a string of fabulous soul albums in the early '70s, works that both defined and transcended the genre. They were the essence of gritty, gospel-tinged soul, while the themes and the lyrics had an appeal to pop, blues, and country fans as well as soul mavens. The singles "Love Bones" and "I Could Never Be President" had everything; hooks, great production and arrangements, and Taylor's smashing leads. Unfortunately, it's yet to be reissued. —*Ron Wynn*

○ **One Step Beyond** / 1971 / Stax 2030
A great soul album, one of Taylor's finest. It included the opening installation of the Jody story, plus the outstanding "I Am Somebody, Part II." Stax let Taylor wail, strut, holler, and preen and turned him loose at the right moments so he could also show those who'd forgotten that the Soul Stirrers didn't fall far when

he'd replaced Sam Cooke as lead singer in his gospel days. —*Ron Wynn*

○ **Taylored in Silk** / 1973 / Stax 8537
Perhaps Taylor's best pure soul release. It contained the shattering "We're Getting Careless with Our Love," and the equally bittersweet/humorous "Cheaper to Keep Her." Taylor was in peak form as a vocalist, while he was getting superb productions, arrangements, compositions, and musical backing from the Stax braintrust. —*Ron Wynn*

Eargasm / 1976 / Columbia 33951
Johnnie Taylor's biggest hit album also proved his undoing. Stax had collapsed in the wake of questionable financial dealings, and he ended up on Columbia's roster. The disco boom was beginning, and Taylor had the perfect single. "Disco Lady" was vocally quite similar to his earlier material, but its lyrics embraced the hedonism and dance-your-troubles-away ethic of the era. It was not only a #1 hit, but *the* song of the year for 1976, and Taylor was shoved into territory where he wasn't comfortable. Indeed, the rest of the album was standard soul tunes like "You're the Best in the World" and "Don't Touch Her Body (If You Can't Touch Her Mind)," but those were overlooked in the rush. Taylor eventually left the label after subsequent attempts to pigeonhole him as a dance singer bombed. —*Ron Wynn*

★ **Chronicle** / 1977 / Stax 88001
The definitive Johnny Taylor retrospective/anthology package. It contains every major Stax hit, some album cuts, and an extensive set of liner notes from Robert Palmer. While the soul hardcore have already purchased it in vinyl, anyone who missed it that time around should immediately rush and get the CD. If you love soul, you can't be without it. —*Ron Wynn*

Tears for Fears

Group / Pop/rock
Childhood friends Curt Smith (b. June 24, 1961) and Roland Orzabal (b. August 22, 1961) first worked together in 1980 with the ska/pop quintet Graduate, which produced an oddball British single "Elvis Should Play Ska." After the demise of Graduate, the twosome began recording demos of some of Orzabal's morose synth-pop tunes "Suffer the Children" and "Pale Shelter," which eventually become part of *The Hurting,* their debut release as Tears for Fears (the name was inspired by primal scream therapy psychologist Arthur Janov).

Their 1985 sophomore release, *Songs from the Big Chair,* became a worldwide success, containing several huge hits in "Shout," "Everybody Wants to Rule the World," "Head over Heels," and "Mother's Talk."

Perfectionism delayed their overreaching third album, *The Seeds of Love,* by four years. One of the album's highlights was the addition of soulful American singer Oleta Adams, whom Orzabal and Smith discovered singing in a Kansas City hotel lounge. That album's hits included "Sowing the Seeds of Love," "Woman in Chains," and "Advice for the Young at Heart."

Before the recording of their fourth album, Smith and Orzabal had a falling out, leaving Orzabal as the only member of Tears for Fears; he released *Elemental* in 1993 to respectable sales. —*Rick Clark*

○ **Hurting** / 1983 / PolyGram 811039
Roland Orzabal and Curt Smith's debut, featured the morose synth-pop hits "Pale Shelter" and "Mad World." —*Scott Bultman*

○ **Songs from the Big Chair** / 1985 / PolyGram 824300
Their best album. A good mix of synthesizers and traditional instruments. Includes the hits "Shout," "Head over Heels," and "Everybody Wants to Rule the World." —*Kenneth M. Cassidy*

Seeds of Love / 1989 / PolyGram 838730
Their third album was an overreaching effort that produced a couple of gems in spite of itself, particularly "Sowing the Seeds of Love" and "Woman in Chains." Oleta Adams's soulful voice added life to the proceedings. —*Rick Clark*

● **Tears Fall Down (The Hits 1982-1992)** / 1992 / PolyGram 510939
All of this duo's hits, plus some other key tracks, from throughout their career. It's a perfect overview and (essentially) the only disc to have. This anthology includes "Pale Shelter," "Shout," "Everybody Wants to Rule the World," "Head over Heels", and "Sowing the Seeds of Love," among others. —*Rick Clark*

Elemental / Jun. 22, 1993 / PolyGram 514875
On *Elemental,* Tears for Fears *is* Roland Orzabal and he backs away from the cinematic production of *The Seeds of Love,* preferring a more direct and soulful style of pop music that appealed to both adult contemporary and adult alternative radio audiences. While some of the material was a little weak, the record was easily as good as its immediate predecessor. —*Stephen Thomas Erlewine*

Teenage Fanclub

Group / Alternative pop/rock
Although their music may not be particularly innovative, Teenage Fanclub are great synthesizers of pop music, tying together everything from the Beach Boys and Big Star to Sonic Youth, Neil Young, and Madonna. On their earlier records, they leaned toward loud guitar pop, drenched in dissonance. Starting with 1991's *Bandwagonesque,* the band toned down the noise and reached deeper into their melodic gifts; the result was a brilliant homage to Big Star's chiming guitars and Neil Young's lazy melodies. The record earned them substantial critical praise—*Spin* named it the record of the year—as well as some critical scorn. While the album helped the band gain a cult following in America, it made them stars in England. Two years later, they delivered *Thirteen,* which showed the band incorporating their influences into their own signature sound instead of just paying homage to them. While it wasn't a big as a success as *Bandwagonesque,* it showed that Teenage Fanclub hadn't lost their gift for loud, lush guitar pop. —*Stephen Thomas Erlewine*

Catholic Education / 1990 / Matador 12
A grimy pop record that never loses its charm, even when it becomes nearly impenetrable. Filled to the brim with charm and ebullience (as well as a snotty attitude), this is a dazzling record. —*John Dougan*

○ **Bandwagonesque** / 1991 / David Geffen Co. 24461
Much cleaner than the debut, this is a slice of Big Star worship that never fails to deliver the goods. Although it gets bogged down in obviousness from time to time, Teenage Fanclub proves they are a fine pop band, loaded with ringing guitars and breathtaking choruses. —*John Dougan*

● **Thirteen** / 1993 / David Geffen Co. 24533
Opening with the snarling T. Rex meets Nirvana guitar of "Hang On," which soon melts away into a sea of gorgeous Beatlesque harmonies, *Thirteen* marks a shedding of the Big Star devotions that made *Bandwagonesque* so delicious but that doesn't make it any less enjoyable. Instead of concentrating on one band, Teenage Fanclub pillages through all of the pages of pop history, producing a layered, infectious slice of guitar pop that only gets better with repeated listenings. —*Stephen Thomas Erlewine*

Television

Group / Punk
This four-piece vehicle for the expoundings of guitarist/vocalist Tom Verlaine was an enigma on the '70s CBGB scene: Verlaine's songs reflect the influence of punk in structure and content, but the guitar duels between Verlaine and Richard Lloyd harken back to the dense jams of old-school rockers. Despite their influence on '80s indie-rockers, their reputation is somewhat inflated. Their three releases, however, are more than worthwhile for both historians and guitar fiends. —*John Floyd*

★ **Marquee Moon** / 1978 / Elektra 1098
It's hard to overrate this one, which features whiplash guitars, thrusting rhythms, and Verlaine's piercing vocals on his best set of songs. —*John Floyd*

Adventure / 1979 / Elektra 133
This is a subdued set in both sound and content, but the songs sport stronger melodies, and "Glory" anticipates R.E.M.'s sound. —*John Floyd*

Blow Up / 1990 / ROIR 114
Crappy fidelity mars this live set, but Verlaine and Lloyd conjure some scarifying and beautiful six-string magic. —*John Floyd*

Television / Sep. 28, 1992 / Capitol 98396
Once again, guitarist and nerve centre Tom Verlaine's dry, '50s-instrumental, murder-mystery style entwines masterfully with Richard Lloyd's more emotive, pealing riffs. The performances range from hypnotically atonal to ragingly cascading; the mood

from paranoid to blissful. *Television*'s highlights include the blistering ecstasy of "Call Mr. Lee" and the trance and dance of "Shane, She Wrote This." —*Roch Parisien*

Temple of the Dog

Group / Alternative rock, hard rock
Soundgarden's singer Chris Cornell and drummer Matt Cameron teamed with guitarist Stone Gossard and bassist Jeff Ament from Mother Love Bone to record this 1990 tribute to the deceased Mother Love Bone lead vocalist, Andrew Wood. Several tracks feature vocalist Eddie Vedder, who would had recently joined Gossard and Ament to form Pearl Jam. —*Stephen Thomas Erlewine*

○ Temple of the Dog / Dec. 1990 / A&M 5350
While it doesn't sound all that different than either Soundgarden or Pearl Jam, *Temple of the Dog* does feature some of the finest music members of either band have ever made. Chris Cornell displays a better grasp of melody and song structure than he ever has on any previous Soundgarden album, and Eddie Vedder shows signs of developing into a distinctive, original vocalist. But the real power of the album is in the guitars of Stone Gossard and the rhythm section of Jeff Ament and Matt Cameron; together, they make the occasionally clichéd tributes to the late Andrew Wood into a genuinely moving, heartfelt elegy for their departed friend. —*Stephen Thomas Erlewine*

The Temptations

Group / Motown, R&B, soul
The early history of the Temptations parallels that of the Supremes. The Tempts started as the Primes, the Supremes as the Primettes. They joined Motown at roughly the same time and broke through at the same time. The Temptations had a more thorough grounding in the R&B tradition, though, a fact evident in their work. They employed the classic gospel-group formula: a light tenor against a gutbucket rasp, with flashes of falsetto for emphasis. The Temptations had the benefit of the writing and production skills of Norman Whitfield and Smokey Robinson, who crafted songs for them such as "The Way You Do the Things You Do" and "My Girl."

With a classic lineup that included David Ruffin and Eddie Kendricks, the Temptations were the hottest R&B group during the 10-year period between 1965 and 1975. Ruffin left in 1968, the year the group experimented with psychedelia ("Cloud Nine" and later "Psychedelic Shack"); Kendricks quit in 1971. Increasingly, they fell under the spell of Norman Whitfield's preoccupations and grandiose productions, although Whitfield rose to the occasion magnificently in 1972 with "Papa Was a Rolling Stone." It was the group's last #1 pop hit, and in 1976 the group left Motown for a brief stint with Atlantic before returning to the fold. They continue to record and score R&B hits, but most people associate them with their golden period. —*Colin Escott*

Meet the Temptations / Mar. 1964 / Motown 5140
The album that effectively introduced soul's greatest vocal group. It was quite tentative in retrospect, containing only one hit, "The Way You Do the Things You Do." But that glittering single, with Eddie Kendrick's feathery tenor floating out of the arrangement and smashing harmonies nicely punching home the theme, were an indication lightning would soon strike. —*Ron Wynn*

○ Sing Smokey / Feb. 1965 / Motown 5205
A fabulous album, the Temptations' first masterpiece, and the LP that established them as soul's finest vocal group. Smokey Robinson's spectacular productions, lyrics, and arrangements were sung in majestic fashion by the David Ruffin/Eddie Kendricks vocal frontline, and what more need be said about immortal songs like "My Girl," "It's Growing," and "The Way You Do the Things You Do," a carryover from the first album—but who's complaining? —*Ron Wynn*

○ Gettin' Ready / Jun. 1966 / Motown 5373
The marvelous title track alone, with Eddie Kendricks's gliding into the stratosphere, made this an instant winner. But there were several fine songs that weren't hits such as "Not Now, I'll Tell You Later" and "I've Been Good to You." There sure wasn't anything wrong, though, with powerhouse cuts like "Ain't Too Proud to Beg." The Temptations would score four straight #1 hits in the mid '60s, each one an unforgettable classic. —*Ron Wynn*

Greatest Hits, Vol. 1 / Nov. 1966 / Motown 5411

The original Temptations greatest hits album, which came awfully early in their reign, but contained nothing but nuggets. It's long since lost its value with about a million Temptations collections, compilations, and anthologies issued since, but it had a certain charm back in the '60s. —*Ron Wynn*

○ With a Lot o' Soul / Jul. 1967 / Motown 5299
A fabulous album, and one that's thankfully available on CD. It contained scorching uptempo hits with David Ruffin in blazing, anthemic form on "(I Know) I'm Losing You" and "(Loneliness Made Me Realize) It's You That I Need." He and Kendricks alternated the leads brilliantly on "You're My Everything." Sadly, Ruffin's push to get his name placed in front of the other Temptations would eventually result in him being booted from the band. But that doesn't detract from this album's brilliance. —*Ron Wynn*

○ Temptations Wish It Would Rain / 1968 / Gordy 927
Another in their impressive string of remarkable albums that began with their second in 1965, *The Temptations Sing Smokey*, and continued until *Hear to Tempt You* in 1977. The title cut was a David Ruffin triumph, among his best anguished/heartache numbers. Kendricks equaled his emotional brilliance without registering identical pain on "Please Return Your Love to Me." —*Ron Wynn*

Puzzle People / Sep. 1969 / Motown 5172
A sorely overlooked album, this late '60s release included a pair of great commentary pieces, "Message from a Black Man" and "Don't Let the Joneses Get You Down." But the song that made the album was "I Can't Get Next to You," the greatest Dennis Edwards lead vocal in his Temptations tenure. Though Edwards always sang with passion and exuberance, on this track he came close to surpassing David Ruffin's zeal and shattering brilliance; he only equalled this performance one other time, and it wasn't with the Temptations. Rather, it was on the classic single "Don't Look Any Further." —*Ron Wynn*

Greatest Hits, Vol. 2 / Sep. 1970 / Motown 5412
This second hits collection, which was issued in 1970, a time when things were going nicely commercially, but not so nicely behind the scenes. Paul Williams was being replaced on concerts by Richard Street and would tragically commit suicide in three years. Eddie Kendricks would shortly be leaving. But none of that mattered as Motown recycled hits from the late '60s and did quite nicely. —*Ron Wynn*

Sky's the Limit / Apr. 1971 / Motown 5474
Eddie Kendricks said so long to the Temptations on this early '70s album, with his swan song being the glorious "Just My Imagination." The song that everyone missed was their lengthy, imaginative version of "Smiling Faces Sometimes," which wasn't a huge hit for them, but became a smash for the Undisputed Truth. Though their success continued after Damon Harris replaced Kendricks, things would never be the same. —*Ron Wynn*

○ All Directions / Jul. 1972 / Motown 5417
A monster album, the one that put them back in the spotlight and signaled that Norman Whitfield had saved the day. Damon Harris had replaced Eddie Kendricks, and there were many doubters that were convinced the band was finished. Instead Whitfield revitalized them via the majestic single "Papa Was a Rolling Stone." Despite its length, Whitfield's decision to open with an extensive, multilayered musical suite and tease listeners was a master stroke. By the time Dennis Edwards's voice came rushing in, no one would dare turn it off. The single as well as "Law of the Land" and others ended the funeral arrangements that had been prepared for the Temptations. —*Ron Wynn*

★ Anthology / Feb. 1973 / Motown 0782
The best hit collection available. Exhausting! —*Rick A. Bueche*

● All the Million-Sellers / 1982 / Motown 5212
An excellent anthology even though the Temptations had many great tunes that weren't big sellers. But it does contain almost every major hit, and they're well-mastered versions. —*Ron Wynn*

○ More of the Best-Hum Along & Dance / 1993 / Rhino 71180
A good collection of lesser-known tracks and rarities from the Temptations that fills in some of the gaps left by the numerous other Motown collections. —*AMG*

10cc

Group / Pop/rock

Formed in 1972, 10CC mixed pop craftsmanship with art-rock affectations. The band members already had quite a professional pedigree: Graham Gouldman had already penned hits for the Yardbirds ("For Your Love") and the Hollies ("Bus Stop"), among others. While working in the Mindbenders, Gouldman met Eric Stewart, as well as Kevin Godley and Lol Creme, both graphic arts students who had signed with ex-Yardbirds manager Giorgio Gomelsky's Marmalade label under the moniker of Frabjoy and Runcible. While they were recording their first single, "I'm Beside Myself," they met Gouldman and Stewart, sidemen for the session.

The foursome produced a number of records under a variety of fake band names, scoring a worldwide two-million-selling hit, "Neanderthal Man," using the name Hotlegs. Brit pop impresario Jonathon King heard the foursome's satirical '50s-style demos, "Donna" and "Waterfall," and signed them to his UK Records label, giving them the name 10CC along the way. "Donna" quickly became a huge English hit at #2. The bouncy "Rubber Bullets" went #1 in the United Kingdom. Subsequent albums became increasingly ambitious until the departure of Godley and Creme, who went on to pursue an idiosyncratic duo career and a very successful venture into video direction. Stewart and Gouldman continued with 10CC until 1983. —*Rick Clark*

● **10CC/Sheet Music** / 1973 / Dcc 53
This includes both of 10CC's first two albums on a single disc. The self-titled debut featured material that spoofed lightweight late '50s/early '60s pop, with songs like "Donna" and "Johnny Don't Do It." "Rubber Bullets," off that album, became a #1 UK hit, reaching #73 Stateside. On *Sheet Music*, 10CC took a more sophisticated arty direction. With that album, they became favorites of college-radio programmers, who liked the band's clever pretensions. Highlights on *Sheet Music* include "Wall Street Shuffle" and "The Worst Band in the World." Even though none of the band's major hits are here, this is probably the best starting place for the uninitiated. —*Rick Clark*

Original Soundtrack / 1975 / Mercury 830776
There are some very nice *sounding* songs here. The atmospheric "I'm Not in Love" was a worldwide hit. "Brand New Day" and "Second Sitting for the Last Supper" are highlights, but extended pieces like "Une Nuit a Paris" come off like art pop for the terminally cute. —*Rick Clark*

How Dare You? / 1976 / Mercury 836949
"Lazy Days" and the title cut are nice, and fans of the band champion tracks like "I'm Mandy, Fly Me," "Art for Art's Sake," and "I Want to Rule the World" as evidence of 10CC's smarts, but the end result is a little too smug at times. In terms of production, 10CC's ultraclean production sound is impressive. —*Rick Clark*

Deceptive Bends / 1977 / Mercury 836498
After *How Dare You*, Lol Creme and Kevin Godley left Eric Stewart and Graham Gouldman to their own devices. The result was *Deceptive Bends*, a poppier, at times McCartneyish album, which produced three hits: "People in Love," "Good Morning Judge," and the internationally successful "The Things We Do for Love." —*Rick Clark*

10,000 Maniacs

Group / Alternative pop, folk rock
10,000 Maniacs (named after the low-budget horror movie *2,000 Maniacs*) was formed in Jamestown, NY, in 1981 by singer Natalie Merchant and guitarist John Lombardo. Other members of the sextet were Robert Buck (guitar), Steven Gustafson (bass), Dennis Drew (keyboards), and Jerry Ausugstyniak (drums). The group gigged extensively and recorded independently before signing with Elektra and making *The Wishing Chair* in 1985. Cofounder Lombardo left the band in 1986, and they continued as a quintet, releasing the second album, *In My Tribe*, in 1987. This album broke into the charts, where it stayed 77 weeks, peaking at #37. *Blind Man's Zoo*, the 1989 followup, hit #13 and went gold.

After 1992's *Our Time in Eden* had finished its run on the charts, Natalie Merchant announced that she was leaving for a solo career, bringing an end to 10,000 Maniacs. *MTV Unplugged* was released a few months after their breakup. —*William Ruhlmann*

Wishing Chair / 1985 / Elektra 60428

Put simply, 10,000 Maniacs sound a lot like Fairport Convention with Sandy Denny, so it's appropriate that Fairport's original producer, Joe Boyd, was brought in to handle their major-label debut. The result is a gentle folk-rock record that highlights the haunting voice of Natalie Merchant. —*William Ruhlmann*

● **In My Tribe** / 1987 / Elektra 60738
Guest vocal by Michael Stipe of R.E.M. Includes "Like the Weather" and their remake of "Peace Train." The album was produced by Peter Asher. —*Kenneth M. Cassidy*

Blind Man's Zoo / 1989 / Elektra 60815
Natalie Merchant's lyrics have a subtle urgency on such tracks as "Eat for Two" and "Trouble Me," while the band contrives textured folk-rock backing, and producer Peter Asher creates a well-articulated rock sound. —*William Ruhlmann*

Hope Chest: The Fredonia Recordings 1982-1983 / 1990 / Elektra 60962
A reissue of the band's first recordings. —*Kenneth M. Cassidy*

○ **Our Time in Eden** / Sep. 29, 1992 / Elektra 61385
On their last album *Our Time in Eden*, 10,000 Maniacs experiment with their trademark sound without ever losing sight of their gentle, melodic folk rock that has gained them legions of fans. They wind up with their best album since *In My Tribe*, highlighted by the rolling "These Are Days" and the horn-spiked "Candy Everybody Wants." —*Stephen Thomas Erlewine*

○ **MTV Unplugged** / 1993 / Elektra 61569
When it was recorded, nobody knew that *MTV Unplugged* would be 10,000 Maniacs' last album. As it stands, it's a quiet, gentle way to say goodbye. While the album offers no new revelations, it includes solid versions of many of the group's signature songs (although it features too many tracks from the recent *Our Time in Eden*) and a strong cover of Patti Smith's "Because the Night." —*Stephen Thomas Erlewine*

Ten Years After

Group / Blues rock
Ten Years After is a British blues-rock quartet consisting of Alvin Lee (b. December 19, 1944), guitar and vocals; Chick Churchill (b. January 2, 1949), keyboards; Leo Lyons (b. November 30, 1944), bass; and Ric Lee (b. October 20, 1945), drums. The group was formed in 1967 and signed to Decca in England. Its first album was not a success, but its second, the live *Undead* (1968) containing "I'm Going Home," a six-minute blues workout by the fleet-fingered Alvin, hit the charts on both sides of the Atlantic. *Stonedhenge* (1969) hit the UK Top 10 in early 1969. Ten Years After's U.S. breakthrough came as a result of its appearance at Woodstock, at which it played a nine-minute version of "I'm Going Home." Its next album, *Ssssh*, reached the U.S. Top 20, and *Cricklewood Green*, containing the hit single "Love Like a Man," reached #14. *Watt* completed the group's Decca contract, after which it signed with Columbia and moved in a more mainstream pop direction, typified by the gold-selling 1971 album *A Space in Time* and its Top 40 single "I'd Love to Change the World." Subsequent efforts in that direction were less successful, however, and Ten Years After split up after the release of *Positive Vibrations* in 1974. They reunited in 1988 for concerts in Europe and recorded their first new album in 15 years, *About Time*, in 1989. —*William Ruhlmann*

○ **Undead** / 1968 / Deram 820533
A live album from a group best experienced live, including some amazing guitar playing at phenomenal speeds from Alvin Lee. —*William Ruhlmann*

○ **Greatest Hits** / 1977 / Deram 820324
The group's 1968-1970 best, including the hit "Love like a Man" and the Woodstock version of "I'm Going Home." —*William Ruhlmann*

● **Essential** / 1991 / Chrysalis 21857
While it doesn't include all of their prime material, *Essential* features enough of their best songs to make it a fine introduction. —AMG

Tammi Terrell

b. 1946, Philadelphia, PA, d. Mar. 16, 1970
Vocals / Motown
Although she signed to Motown in the mid '60s as a solo artist, Tammi Terrell's greatest successes were duets with Marvin Gaye,

including the original "Ain't No Mountain High Enough." Her solo successes were limited, and her potential was never fully realized, due to her illness and subsequent death from a brain tumor in 1970. —*Rick A. Bueche*

○ **Irresistible** / 1968 / Motown 5231
Tammi Terrell had a sexy, hypnotic voice and alluring sensibility that not only made her an ideal partner for Marvin Gaye, but could have resulted in substantial impact as a solo singer. This album includes her finest solo single, "I Can't Believe You Love Me," and some other interesting numbers, though Terrell never received any songs for herself that matched what she did with Gaye. —*Ron Wynn*

● **Greatest Hits** / 1970 / Motown 5225
This is actually a greatest hits LP for Marvin Gaye and Tammi Terrell, and there's little more that needs to be said about these numbers—the writing of Ashford and Simpson and the vocals of Gaye and Terrell were an epic collaboration. "Ain't No Mountain High Enough," "Ain't Nothing Like the Real Thing," "If This World Were Mine," and the list continues, classics each and every one. —*Ron Wynn*

Tesla

Group / Hard rock, heavy metal
With their first album, *Mechanical Resonance*, Tesla quickly established themselves as one of the better hard rock/heavy metal bands of the late '80s. Although they weren't utterly original, the band was tight and showed an ability for crafting melodic, driving riffs. What made Tesla different from other metal bands with pop inclinations was the fact that their music was grounded in gritty, bluesy hard rock instead of slick, arena rock.

Although their debut climbed all the way to #32 on the *Billboard* charts, their second album, 1989's *The Great Radio Controversy*, was an even greater success, scoring a Top 10 hit with the ballad "Love Song." Their followup album, *Five Man Acoustical Jam*, showed that the band didn't need overdriven amplifiers in order to play; it also showed that they had a fondness for sentimental hippie oldies, as their hit version of "Signs" proved. The record also turned out to be their biggest hit, reaching #12 on the charts. While its followup, *Psychotic Supper*, wasn't as commercially successful, it captured Tesla branching into new musical territories; it proved that the band hadn't lost its creative spark. —*Stephen Thomas Erlewine*

○ **Mechanical Resonance** / 1986 / David Geffen Co. 24120
Tesla's debut and one of their stronger albums. —*John Book*

● **Great Radio Controversy** / 1989 / David Geffen Co. 24224
More use of acoustic instruments make this a treat. Features the Top 10 hit "Love Song," as well as "The Way It Is" and "Heaven's Trail (No Way Out)." —*John Book*

Five Man Acoustical Jam / 1990 / David Geffen Co. 24311
With the advent of "MTV Unplugged," it became popular for all types of groups to prove that they didn't have to rely on walls of amps and outboard gear to get their music across. *Five Man Acoustical Jam* was one of the most successful outings of that type, featuring versions of the Five Man Electrical Band's "Signs," Creedence's "Lodi," and a smattering of originals. —*Rick Clark*

Psychotic Supper / 1991 / David Geffen Co. 24424
One of the few heavy metal bands who can release albums with more than 10 songs and still end up with a consistent, high-quality record. —*John Book*

Joe Tex (Joe Arrington, Jr.)

b. Aug. 8, 1933, Rogers, TX, d. Aug. 13, 1982
Vocals / Soul, funk
An oddball figure, Tex came to soul music via Nashville after a decade covering all the bases from sappy pop to ersatz Little Richard. His mentor, country music publisher Buddy Killen, founded Dial Records specifically to record him. Tex had a preachy, didactic style that was a virtual parody of black ministers. His records were sermonettes on various subjects that generally got back to sex and relationships at some point. When his homespun homilies worked, they worked marvelously ("Hold What You Got," "I Want to Do Everything for You," "Buying a Book," and so on). Unfortunately, it was a style that eventually tended toward self-parody, and his work cannot be indiscrimately recommended. At his best, though, Tex was a true eccentric with

Techno/House/Rave

As long as man has been around, so has dance music. From early caveman dances, to African tribal dances, to the Shamanic ceremonies of Eskimos and Indians, dance music has played a major role in every culture.

Today, dance music is bigger than ever. The recent popularity of techno and house closely mimics the 1970s disco explosion. Dance music dominates today's pop charts. Techno, house, and other "rave" styles have changed the face of music today and continue to break new musical ground. The origins of techno are hard to pin down. Many styles have been blended together to create today's distinctive sound. The great funk and soul bands of the '70s have played a large part. Parliament, James Brown, The Gap Band, and many others have made an indelible mark on the genre. Seminal electronic bands such as Kraftwerk, Cabaret Voltaire, and Tangerine Dream were major influences as well. While the term "techno" is relatively new, the roots of the music lie firmly here.

House music's pedigree is more clear-cut. The basic elements of disco (a driving beat and a great vocal), updated with modern instrumentation, form the essence of house. Many house tracks have a strong, uplifting theme. This may help to account for its wide appeal. The positive, anthemic nature of house songs has propelled many of them into the pop charts.

Electronic music has been popular since the late 60s, but the techno heard today is unlike anything that has come before. Today, hard electronic sounds from synthesizers and drum machines are often combined with short sampled vocals and drum loops from old rap or funk records. The resulting songs are fast and hard; the unrelenting beat is the focus. As with most styles of music, splinter genres exist. Techno and house have spawned many. "Acid-house," "tribal," "hardcore," "trance," and "progressive" are just some of these sub-genres. There are huge differences amongst these. Artists like The Orb cover the lighter, more ambient side of techno, while at the other extreme Acen and The Prodigy offer a harder sound. Snap, Rozalla, and Technotronic are some of the more popular house artists, but the far reaching influences of house can be heard in many pop songs today. Madonna's "Vogue" is a good example.

An essay on techno and house wouldn't be complete without mentioning the concept of "raves". A rave is essentially a large dance party, often advertised solely by word of mouth. It may take place in a warehouse or at a secluded park or beach. A great location can contribute a lot to the overall feeling, but a rave can occur anywhere. What separates a rave from a regular dance club is "the vibe." There is an absence of the "singles bar" mentality often found at a dance club. Raves are places where people go to dance—pure and simple.

A large part of the rave experience is based on sensory overload—a barrage of sounds and visuals are brought together to elevate people into an altered state. Rave lighting may range from a single strobe light to a full blown laser show with computer generated visuals. The DJs play an endless onslaught of music, often manipulating a crowd through the extremes of emotion. The recent explosion of techno and house can be directly attributed to the popularity of raves. This is the music of choice at a rave. Techno and house are young styles. There is much exploration still to be done. New sounds are appearing every day, and new artists are constantly pushing the limits of the genre.

—*Dennis Barton*

a completely different slant on the music and concerns of the day. —Colin Escott

● **I Believe I'm Gonna Make It** / 1988 / Rhino 70191

First-rate country/soul, sung with the just the right blend of whimsy, worry, and relief. Joe Tex was routinely turning out excellent cuts throughout the mid '60s, but it wasn't until his novelty/disco tunes of the mid '70s that he finally attained any widespread recognition. Sadly, none of his great Dial albums are currently in print, a travesty. —Ron Wynn

The Texas Tornados

Group / Tex-Mex, rock & roll

A Tex-Mex supergroup—Doug Sahm, Augie Meyers, Flaco Jimenez, and Freddy Fender—whose sound is a well-done rollicking version of country music in the Mexican style, accordion and all. The Tornados are good enough to have been twice nominated for a Grammy; they won with "Soy de San Luis." Play it at any party and forget about things being dull the rest of the night. — David Vinopal and Jeff Tamarkin

○ **Zone of Our Own** / 1991 / Reprise 26683

Not quite as jubilant as the first album, but these guys are incapable of not being fun. —Jeff Tamarkin

● **Best of Texas Tornados** / 1994 / Reprise 45511

Featuring material from all of their albums, *The Best of Texas Tornados* is a terrific compilation of one of the best Tex-Mex bands of the last two decades. —AMG

That Petrol Emotion

Group / Alternative pop/rock

After the Undertones broke up, brother Sean (formerly known as John) and Damian O'Neill formed That Petrol Emotion. While they were more politically oriented and noisier than the Undertones, they managed to keep their former band's energetic, melodic kick. With their first album, *Manic Pop Thrill*, That Petrol Emotion became critics' favorites, as well as earning a respectable following in the United Kingdom. Over the years, their music remained endlessly diverse, incorporating elements of every style of independent guitar rock. Occasionally, their albums would be wildly uncohesive because of this, yet they managed to turn in several excellent songs on each record. Sean left the band after their third album, *End of the Millennium Psychosis Blues*. The album showed signs that That Petrol Emotion's exuberant diversity was beginning to wear thin; their next albums proved that they were running out of things to say. After eight years, That Petrol Emotion broke up in 1994. —Stephen Thomas Erlewine

● **Babble** / 1987 / Polydor 833132

On their second album, That Petrol Emotion's electrifying mix of spiky guitar hooks, direct melodies, and righteous, socially conscious lyrics solidifies into a distinctive sound that's a little messy but completely invigorating. Although they released several records in the next seven years, the band were never able to replicate the sheer power and solid hooks of *Babble*. —Stephen Thomas Erlewine

The The

Group / Alternative pop/rock

The The is essentially the solo project of Londoner Matt Johnson. Johnson released a solo album, *Burning Blue Soul*, in the early '80s that sketched out the The's sound—atmospheric, experimental songs that rely more on sound than song. With the first official the The album, 1983's *Soul Mining*, Johnson expanded his sound somewhat, concentrating more on songwriting while retaining the hollow, haunting ambience of his sound. With 1986's *Infected*, he began recording with studio musicians; this allowed him to embellish his music with several different styles, particularly dance. On the The's next album, 1989's *Mind Bomb*, former Smiths guitarist Johnny Marr joined the band, which helped Johnson to present his music more clearly. With each release, the The became more direct, and 1993's *Dusk* was their most straightforward album yet. Even though Johnson has strayed slightly from his spare, experimental roots, he remains an ambitious artist that has always satisfied and challenged his cult. — Stephen Thomas Erlewine

Soul Mining / 1983 / Epic 39266

On the The's first album, Matt Johnson crafted a pleasant but unengaging set of dance-pop that just barely hinted at the experimentalism he would develop on later records like *Infected* or *Mind Bomb*. —Stephen Thomas Erlewine

○ **Infected** / 1986 / Epic 40471

Infected is such a leap forward from *Soul Mining* that the album hardly seems like the work of the same band. Instead of the light, agreeable dance-pop of the previous album, *Infected* draws a dense, dark sonic landscape that accurately conveys the alienation and despair Matt Johnson sings about. —Stephen Thomas Erlewine

● **Mind Bomb** / 1989 / Epic 45241

With the addition of former Smiths guitarist Johnny Marr, the The attempted their most ambitious album yet with *Mind Bomb*. Instead of the darky, polished dance-pop stylings of *Infected*, *Mind Bomb* opens up the music to reveal a slow, winding, textured world of sound that celebrates its rough edges instead hiding them. It's serious, dance-influenced rock of the highest order. —Stephen Thomas Erlewine

○ **Dusk** / Jan. 5, 1993 / Epic 53164

If nothing else, Matt Johnson is consistent. *Dusk* is another dark, lush album, both musically and lyrically, fitting neatly into the The's catalog. The only difference this time is the quality of the songs—they're stronger and more melodic than the bulk of his past work. —Stephen Thomas Erlewine

Them

Group / British invasion, rock & roll

Unlike many of the squeaky-clean acts that were part of the British invasion, the rough-and-tumble Them (formed 1963), fronted by the scruffy Van Morrison, delivered fiery blues-informed rock & roll. During their brief career, Them produced a handful of classics in songs like "Gloria," "Mystic Eyes," "Baby Please Don't Go," and "Here Comes the Night." In 1966 Them parted ways, with Morrison going on to a successful solo career and keyboardist Peter Bardens forming British art-rock band Camel. —Rick Clark

● **Them Featuring Van Morrison** / 1973 / Deram 810165

Remembered today as the starting point for Van Morrison, Them was a tough, bluesy Irish rock group that made two of the most compelling singles of the mid '60s: "Gloria" and "Here Comes the Night." Both are here, along with the best of the rest of their small catalog. —William Ruhlmann

Therapy?

Group / Alternative rock, heavy metal

With their buzzing guitars, tortured lyrics, and undeniable melodic gifts, Therapy? is one of the best postmodern heavy metal bands. Hailing from Belfast, Ireland, Therapy? combines the sonic rush of Hüsker Dü and the Buzzcocks with the straightforward riffing and sensibility of Black Sabbath. Guitarist Andy Cairns's soul baring can be embarrassingly clichéd at times, yet the melodrama of the lyrics can be easily ignored when the band locks into their intense, tuneful grind. —Stephen Thomas Erlewine

○ **Nurse** / 1993 / A&M 44

Therapy?'s debut album is a brutal fusion of heavy metal and hardcore punk with a surprising dose of straight melody. Their ability to write songs that are simultaneously abrasive and melodic separates them from such one-dimensional riff-mongers like Helmet. —Stephen Thomas Erlewine

Hats off to the Insane / Sep. 7, 1993 / A&M 540139

A stopgap EP that finds Therapy? honing their melodic skills while keeping the aggressive guitar assault. Although its best moments are repeated on the full-length *Trouble Gum*, the rest of the EP is strong enough to satisfy fans. —Stephen Thomas Erlewine

● **Trouble Gum** / 1994 / A&M

On their second album, Therapy? hit their stride, strengthing their considerable melodic gifts while sharpening their razor-sharp guitars. At times, Therapy's assault resembles a more straightforward Bob Mould or a more melodic Helmet. Unfortunately, the trite, angst-ridden lyrics sometimes undercut the power of their music, but when faced with the drilling guitars and irresistible hooks of "Screamager" and "Nowhere" such minor complaints are forgotten. —*Stephen Thomas Erlewine*

They Might Be Giants

Group / Alternative pop/rock
This Brooklyn-based duo, made up of John Flansburgh and John Linell, gives a new twist to pop music. Their lyrics (which are frequently funny and always offbeat) are often accompanied by Flansburgh's guitar and Linnell's accordion, giving their songs a unique sound. Only in 1994 did they begin recording with a full band. Full of puns, wisecracks, and thesaurus-dependent lyrics, TMBG's music is always entertaining. —*Iotis Erlewine*

○ **They Might Be Giants** / 1987 / Restless 72603
TMBG's debut album. The album includes a few good songs, such as "Don't Let's Start," "Put Your Hand inside the Puppet Head," and "I Hope That I Get Old before I Die." Overall, the album is too rough and tedious, featuring TMBG's trademark "under three-minute" songs. —*Iotis Erlewine*

● **Lincoln** / 1989 / Restless 72600
TMBG's most entertaining album lets you have fun with the songs without trying to ferret out any deeper meaning in the bizarre lyrics. Here, TMBG reaches a good balance between goofy lyrics and listenable music. The songs won't spark any deep intellectual conversations, but you might just enjoy yourself. —*Iotis Erlewine*

Flood / 1990 / Elektra 60907
Musically, this is their best album, but in their attempt to put meaning into their lyrics, they have lost sight of TMBG's most appealing quality—the fun. *Flood* features a cover of "Istanbul (Not Constantinople)," written by J. Kennedy and N. Simon. There are a few outstanding songs, such as "Birdhouse in Your Soul" and "Particle Man." —*Iotis Erlewine*

Miscellaneous T / 1991 / Bar/None 72646
This album is a collection of TMBG's B sides that includes several previously unreleased songs. For diehard fans only. —*Iotis Erlewine*

Apollo 18 / 1992 / Elektra 61257
Apollo 18 offers a dizzying array, opening with the one-minute punkish rave "Dig My Grave" and concluding, 18 tracks later, with "Space Suit," an instrumental merging East Euro cafe accordion with outer-space sound effects. Turning over other stones on the way reveals snippets of jazz, folk, samba, progressive electronic, and worldbeat. Beach Boys melody meets heavy-rap rhythm and a psychedelic finale on "See the Constellation." "The Guitar" is actually a surrealist version of the Tokens' hit "The Lion Sleeps Tonight." TMBG are possibly the first group to take full advantage of the "random" feature of most CD players. The song "Fingertips" is composed of 21 separate sound bites which, in random mode, pop up unexpectedly between the 17 other tracks. —*Roch Parisien*

Thin Lizzy

Group / Hard rock, heavy metal
An Irish rock quartet led by Hendrix lookalike Phil Lynott (1951-1986). Band members came and went over the years, but Lynott's rebel stance and intelligent, working-class lyrics won them a huge worldwide following. —*Cub Koda*

○ **Jailbreak** / 1976 / Mercury 822785
Their most perfectly realized album, featuring the title track and "The Boys Are Back in Town," a staple of classic-rock radio to this day. —*Cub Koda*

○ **Life** / 1983 / Vertigo 6
As a live album, *Life* holds up as an excellent example of what Thin Lizzy were like on stage. All of the 19 songs were true Thin Lizzy classics (including "Jailbreak" and the arena standard "Boys Are Back in Town") and are a better introduction to the band than the *Dedication* compilation on PolyGram. —*John Book*

● **Dedication: The Very Best of Thin Lizzy** / 1991 / Mercury 848530
A good, if somewhat brief look at all the high spots, featuring great guitar from fretmeisters Gary Moore, Eric Bell, John Sykes, and others. —*Cub Koda*

Thirteenth Floor Elevators

Group / Psychedelic, garage rock

Featuring the yelping vocals and visionary, occasionally demented lyrics of Roky Erickson, the Thirteenth Floor Elevators were one of the original acid-rock bands. Formed in Texas in the mid '60s, the Elevators started as a garage rock outfit, scoring their one and only modest national hit with "You're Gonna Miss Me." While Erickson's loopy persona, along with Tommy Hall's odd "jug" percussion, was the band's most distinguishing feature, several members of the group's original lineup contributed strong material to their albums. Although these inconsistent efforts sometimes wander off into a cloudy haze, they also include sturdy folk-rock tunes and driving psychedelic rockers. Trips to San Francisco established the group as up-and-coming underground favorites, but Erickson's drug problems led to the singer's commission to a state mental hospital in the late '60s, an ordeal from which he has never fully recovered. The band was really at full power for only a couple of albums, although all of their releases for the legendary International Artists label—produced by, of all people, Kenny Rogers's brother Leland—are revered among psychedelic collectors. Live recordings and outtakes from the Elevators continue to surface, though a cogent compilation of the best of these erratic pioneers' work remains overdue. —*Richie Unterberger*

● **Thirteenth Floor Elevators** / 1966 / International Artists
Their first album is their best, although their second (*Easter Everywhere*) also had some good material. Besides "You're Gonna Miss Me," it includes "Fire Engine," "Tried to Hide," "Roller Coaster," and Erickson's best composition, the gentle folk-rocker "Splash 1." —*Richie Unterberger*

.38 Special

Group / Rock, southern rock
This hard-touring Jacksonville-based band (formed 1975) featured lead singer Donnie Van Zant, brother of Lynyrd Skynyrd's lead singer Ronnie Van Zant. .38 Special delivered a brand of Southern pop-rock that wasn't quite so hard-hitting as Skynyrd's, while showcasing an Allman Brothers-like lineup, with two lead guitarists and two drummers. They also charted more hits than either of those bands. Their most popular hits included "Caught Up in You," "Hold on Loosely," "Back Where You Belong," "Like No Other Night," "Second Chance," "If I'd Been the One," and "Rockin' into the Night." —*Rick Clark*

Wild Eyed & Live / 1978 / A&M 61702
A live album featuring an even balance of hits and smokin' crowd pleasers. —*Cub Koda*

● **Flashback: Best of .38 Special** / 1987 / A&M 3910
An excellent retrospective, featuring all the hits from the early '80s. The last commercial flowering of southern rock. —*Cub Koda*

This Mortal Coil

Group / Alternative pop/rock
This Mortal Coil is the brainchild of 4AD's president, Ivo Watts. It's not really a band, it's a way for Watts to explore different musical territory and cover his favorite artists, including Syd Barrett, Alex Chilton, Talking Heads, Tim Buckley, and Gene Clark. Over the years, the lineup has featured various stars from the record label's roster, including Kim Deal, Tanya Donnelly, Heidi Berry, and Robin Guthrie and Elizabeth Fraser from the Cocteau Twins. Like most 4AD bands, This Mortal Coil is atmospheric, sometimes dreamy, other times haunting. Watts has said that 1991's *Blood* is the last album the outfit will release. —*Stephen Thomas Erlewine*

○ **It'll End in Tears** / 1984 / 4AD 90269
A studio project by various artists from the 4AD stable. —*Michael P. Dawson*

● **Filigree & Shadow** / 1986 / 4AD
Ethereal, nostalgic, and wonderful. —*Michael P. Dawson*

Blood / 1991 / 4AD 1005
Notable for a cover of Syd Barrett's "Late Night." —*Michael P. Dawson*

1983-1991 / 1993 / Warner Brothers 45135
All three of This Mortal Coil's albums packaged in an expensive slipcase, along with a disc of the original version of the songs they covered. Fans of 4AD bands like Throwing Muses, the Cocteau Twins, and Dead Can Dance will thoroughly enjoy This Mortal Coil's lush, haunting music; some members of these bands

play on various tracks on the box, including a standout duet between Kim Deal and Tanya Donnely on Chris Bell's "You and Your Sister." Although the packaging is beautiful, there is a lack of liner notes. *—Stephen Thomas Erlewine*

Carla Thomas

b. Dec. 21, 1942, Memphis, TN
Vocals / Soul
In the glorious decade and a half of sound that was Stax in the '60s and early '70s, Carla Thomas was the Queen of Memphis Soul. She was born in Memphis in 1942, and 18 years later she recorded a duet with her father, Rufus Thomas, giving the fledgling Satellite label its first taste of success with the regional hit "Cause I Love You." As her 18th birthday drew nigh, she cut her first solo single, the teen ballad "Gee Whiz (Look at His Eyes)." Written a few years earlier and rejected by Vee-Jay in Chicago, it gave Satellite its first national hit, breaking the Top 10 mark on both the R&B and pop charts. Shortly thereafter Satellite became Stax, and Carla proceeded to claw her way onto the national charts another 22 times with such immortal slices of soul as her answer song to Sam Cooke, "I'll Bring It on Home to You," as well as "Let Me Be Good to You," "B-A-B-Y," "Tramp" (with Otis Redding), and "I Like What You're Doing to Me." Carla released six solo albums and, with Otis Redding, one duet album on Stax between 1961 and 1971. *—Rob Bowman*

Gee Whiz / 1961 / Atlantic 8057
Carla Thomas's first album was typical fare for the R&B market of the time, combining two chart entries (the title song and "A Love of My Own") with covers of recent chart hits (the Drifters' "Fools Fall in Love" and "Dance with Me," the Five Satins' "To the Aisle"), standards ("The Masquerade Is Over"), and a handful of originals. This was the first album produced by the then-fledgling Stax label, and the unique Stax sound was not yet manifest. *—Rob Bowman*

○ **Carla** / 1966 / Atlantic 82340
Paired with Stax writing whiz-kids Isaac Hayes and David Porter, Thomas had her greatest chart run, beginning with the hit "B-A-B-Y" and continuing with "Let Me Be Good to You." Both of those appear here, alongside evocative slabs of country-soul in covers of Hank Williams's "I'm So Lonesome I Could Cry" and Patsy Cline's "I Fall to Pieces." For good measure, Thomas also tries her hand at the blues with covers of Howlin' Wolf's "Little Red Rooster" and Jimmy Reed's "Baby What You Want Me to Do." *—Rob Bowman*

○ **Comfort Me** / 1966 / Atlantic 80329
A collection of 12 tracks recorded over a year and a half, *Comfort Me* showcases Thomas in the midst of the developed Stax sound. Backed by Booker T. and the MG's and the Mar-Key horns, Thomas turns in fine covers of Baby Washington's "Move on Drifter," the Marvelettes's "Forever," the Shirelles' "Will You Love Me Tomorrow," the Everly Brothers' "Let It Be Me," Jackie DeShannon's "What the World Needs Now," the Toys' "Lover's Concerto," and Barbara Mason's "Yes I'm Ready," coupled with a number of efforts by Thomas herself, Steve Cropper, and Eddie Floyd. The highlight is the Cropper-Floyd title cut, with utterly gorgeous backing by Gladys Knight and the Pips. *—Rob Bowman*

○ **Queen Alone** / 1969 / Rhino 71015
The queen of Stax shines on tracks like "When Tomorrow Comes," "Unchanging Love," "Lie to Keep Me from Crying," and "Any Day Now" (the Chuck Jackson classic). This album was recorded in 1967, a year after her hit "B-A-B-Y"; the mood is funky, the singing self-assured. Fine Memphis soul music. *—Christine Ohlman*

Memphis Queen / 1975 / Stax 8538
Half recorded in Memphis with the usual stellar Stax crew and half recorded in New York with local session musicians (all overdubbed in Detroit), *Memphis Queen* finds Thomas and the Stax label in transition. Motown alumnus Don Davis handled production, draping many cuts in large, lush orchestral settings. "I Like What You're Doing (to Me)" was a Top 10 R&B hit, and three other tracks had brief chart runs. *—Rob Bowman*

● **Chronicle: Their Greatest Stax Hits** / 1979 / Stax 4124
Rufus and Carla Thomas helped launch the Stax era, both individually and as a team. Thomas bought his daughter to Stax in the hopes they'd find suitable material, and she soon had "Gee Whiz" soaring to the top. Had Carla Thomas chosen to tour ex-

tensively, she might have been a great star in Aretha Franklin's class: she sang with equal ferocity and power during this period. Rufus Thomas parlayed his dance/novelty tracks into international superstardom, but he was also a fine straight soul vocalist. This album splits its bill between the two, offering each a side to showcase their hits. *—Ron Wynn*

○ **Hidden Gems** / 1992 / Stax 8568
Twenty outtakes recorded for Stax between 1960 and 1968, a number of which are gems. In fact, it is really surprising just how good the unreleased Stax stuff was in the '60s. "Loneliness," "Sweet Sensation," and "It Ain't No Easy Thing" all could have been superb singles. *—Rob Bowman*

● **Gee Whiz: The Best of Carla Thomas** / 1994 / Rhino
A sterling collection of all of Carla Thomas's biggest hits and best material *—AMG*

Irma Thomas

b. Feb. 18, 1941
Vocals / Soul, R&B
Radiating an outgoing joy that's inevitably at the heart of her infectious vocal delivery, Irma Thomas has no rival as the Soul Queen of New Orleans. Working at a Crescent City nightery as a waitress in 1959, Thomas sat in one night with Tommy Ridgely's band and made such a favorable impression that the veteran bandleader hustled her into the studio shortly thereafter to wax her first hit for the Ron label, the driving "Don't Mess with My Man." She joined forces with producer Allen Toussaint to make some of her most moving outings for Minit Records during the early '60s, notably "It's Raining," "Ruler of My Heart," and "Cry On," before venturing to the West Coast, where she cut both her biggest seller, the lushly produced "Wish Someone Would Care," and her best-known song, the original "Time Is on My Side"—and she's still bitter enough about the Rolling Stones' cover stealing her thunder to discourage requests for the tune.

The highly adaptable chanteuse also made some sizzling soul at Rich Hall's Muscle Shoals studio for Chess in the summer of 1967 before cooling off for a while during the '70s. But she's back now, as radiant as ever—and for convincing proof, listen to her buoyant 1990 concert performance on Rounder, *Live! Simply the Best.* Now that's truth in packaging! *—Bill Dahl*

○ **Wish Someone Would Care** / 1964 / Imperial 9266
Irma Thomas has been New Orleans's reigning soul queen since the early '60s, and this landmark album was her most stunning and complete session. It didn't make her a national star, but it showed vulnerability that was as captivating as lust, anger, or pain. Thomas's voice seemed at times deliberately frail, but she made "Time Is on My Side" and "I Wish Someone Would Care" remarkable triumphs. There were many other fine songs, among them "I Need Your Love So Bad," "Please Send Me Someone to Love," and "Break-A-Way." It remains one of the greatest soul albums ever recorded. *—Ron Wynn*

New Rules / 1986 / Rounder 2046
Irma Thomas balanced classic and contemporary sensibilities on this album. She did such songs as "Gonna Cry 'til My Tears Run Dry" and "I Gave You Everything" that were arranged, performed, and felt like her triumphant heartache songs from the '60s. She also did more recent tunes such as the title track and a good remake of "The Wind Beneath My Wings (Hero)" that showed she wasn't locked into the past. *—Ron Wynn*

○ **Way I Feel** / 1988 / Rounder 2058
Wonderful, contemporary soul from the great Irma Thomas, intelligently produced and sung with warmth, depth, and conviction by a vocalist who truly sounds better today than she did when she was a hit act. Her voice may not have its former range or innocence, but in its place are an emotional fiber, convincing edge, and passion that give her songs even more urgency and appeal. *—Ron Wynn*

Ruler of Hearts / 1989 / Charly 195
Sides from her early '60s Minit sessions. The most New Orleans R&B-influenced of Thomas's early work, it includes "Cry On," "It's Raining," and "Ruler of My Heart," as well as lesser known but equally moving cuts like "Two Winters Long" and "It's Too Soon to Know." *—Richie Unterberger*

○ **Live: Simply the Best** / 1991 / Rounder 2110

Though she hasn't had a hit artist since the '60s, Irma Thomas has retained the luster, emotional authority, and vocal majesty that highlighted her big singles. There are a credibility and integrity underscoring any song she does, quite evident throughout the 14 numbers on this album. Thomas hasn't tried to be something she's not; she remains a soul singer and great storyteller, and while "It's Raining," "Time Is on My Side," and "Wish Someone Would Care" are certainly from another era, Thomas's treatments made them relevant to the '90s. Irma Thomas can still belt out unforgettable songs whether she ever lands another hit. —*Ron Wynn*

★ **Time is on My Side (The Best of Irma Thomas), Vol. 1** / 1992 / EMI America 97988
Twenty-three sides representing the cream of Irma Thomas's brilliant Minit/Liberty years (1961-1966), when her reputation as "The Soul Queen of New Orleans" was built. Virtually all her best-known tunes are here—"Wish Someone Would Care," "Ruler of My Heart," "It's Raining," and "Time Is on My Side" (covered note for note by the Stones). Beautiful singing from one of the first ladies of soul music. Essential. —*Christine Ohlman*

Rufus Thomas

b. Mar. 26, 1917
Vocals / Soul, R&B
The self-proclaimed "world's oldest teenager" has been a staple on the Memphis music scene since the '20s. He recorded the first hit for Sun Records ("Bear Cat," from 1953); was a celebrity DJ on Memphis's WDIA; and, with his daughter Carla, he gave Stax their first hit (1960's "Cause I Love You"). He recorded an album for Alligator in 1988, but his best work was done for Sun and Stax. His Sun material is available on several various-artist collections. —*John Floyd*

○ **Walking the Dog** / 1964 / Rhino 82254
Thomas's first album on Stax contains many of his best early hits, including the title track and several other dance- and novelty-oriented gems. —*John Floyd*

● **Chronicle** / 1986 / Stax 4124
Half of *Chronicle* features the greatest hits of Rufus Thomas's daughter, Carla, while the other half features the best of the man himself; it's a good introduction to the music of both artists. —AMG

The Thompson Twins

Group / Pop/rock, dance-pop
This British trio, comprising Tom Bailey (b. January 18, 1956), Alannah Currie (b. September 28, 1957), and Joe Leeway (b. November 15, 1957), specialized in accessible early-MTV-style synth/dance-pop. Among their hits were "Hold Me Now," "Lay Your Hands on Me," "King for a Day," "Doctor! Doctor!" and "Lies." —*Rick Clark*

● **Into the Gap** / 1984 / Arista 8200
Their American breakthrough album, with the hits "Doctor, Doctor" and "Hold Me Now." The best single album. —*Kenneth M. Cassidy*

Greatest Mixes: Best of the Thompson Twins / 1988 / Arista 8542
A collection of their best on Arista. It was downhill once they switched record labels. —*Kenneth M. Cassidy*

Richard Thompson

b. Apr. 3, 1949, London, England
Vocals, guitar / Singer-songwriter, folk rock, rock & roll
From his days in the Fairport Convention, through his albums recorded with his wife, Linda, to his solo records of the past decade, Richard Thompson has remained a brilliantly gifted songwriter and guitarist. Since the beginning of his career, Thompson has been melding traditional British folk and Celtic music with rock & roll, creating a unique, innovative body of work. He mas made a remarkably consistent body of work; every album features songs that are complexly detailed, full of forboding and regret. Even when he was in his early 20s, Thompson sounded like an old man scarred by lost love and hope. This consistency can make some of his lesser songs sound repetitious, but the overwhelming majority of his music is excellent; both his writing and his playing are distinctive and greatly rewarding.

Thompson's greatest work came during the '70s, when he recorded with his wife, Linda. Linda's clear, warm alto added another dimension to the fear and melancholy of Richard's lyrics. His own deep baritone voice was naturally filled with sadness, which only made his music more serious and sombre. Together, the duo provided a beautiful balance of light and darkness, recording six albums that were critically praised, but were commercial failures.

After performing together for 10 years, the Thompsons' marriage fell apart in 1982, around the time their masterpiece *Shoot Out the Lights* was released. The following year, both Richard and Linda pursued their own solo careers. Linda released her only solo album in 1985, but Richard's *Hand of Kindness* came out in 1983. Since that record, Thompson's stature as a songwriter has only grown, as fellow artists and critics alike rush to praise his talents. However, his albums have been slightly similar in sound, although each has featured several exceptional songs. Nevertheless, Thompson remains one of the finest songwriters of his generation, as well as one of the best guitarists in rock & roll. —*Stephen Thomas Erlewine*

☆ **I Want to See the Bright Lights Tonight** / 1974 / Hannibal 4407
I Want to See the Bright Lights Tonight contains some of Richard Thompson's darkest songs and several beautiful vocal performances by Linda Thompson. "When I Get to the Border," "Calvary Cross," and "Withered and Died" define their early direction. —*John Floyd*

★ **Shoot Out the Lights** / 1982 / Hannibal 1303
One of the most mesmerizing recordings ever committed to tape by a husband/wife team, *Shoot Out the Lights* is the sound of a marriage falling apart—particularly Richard and Linda Thompson's. Linda's beautifully world-weary alto and Richard's indignant quaver deliver some monumental performances on tracks like "Wall of Death," "Don't Renege on Our Love," "Did She Jump or Was She Pushed," "Walking on a Wire," and "Just the Motion." The title track features some incredible lead guitar playing by Richard. Indispensible for any comprehensive rock collection, particularly fans of folk rock. —*Rick Clark*

○ **Hand of Kindness** / 1984 / Hannibal 1313
His first post-divorce release is an uncharacteristically bouncy set, shifting from 12-bar stompers to lilting folk ditties. —*John Floyd*

Across a Crowded Room / 1985 / Polydor 825421
A somewhat predictable set of bitter love songs, accompanied by radio-ready production and, unfortunately, not enough guitar. —*John Floyd*

○ **Daring Adventures** / Mar. 1986 / Polydor 829728
Produced by Mitchell Froom, this album has some great rockers on it; "A Bone through Her Nose," "Valeriem," and the "Wall of Death" sound like "Dead Man's Handle."However, it's also got "Al Bowley's in Heaven." —*Richard Meyer*

○ **Amnesia** / 1988 / Capitol 48845
This dynamic and diverse set is his best, with loads of droll, biting rockers and broken-heart manifestos. —*John Floyd*

● **Rumor and Sigh** / 1990 / Capitol 95713
Another creative triumph. Not quite as lashing as *Amnesia*, but here's the source of many future Thompson classics. —*John Floyd*

○ **Watching the Dark** / May 11, 1993 / Hannibal 5303
A sprawling three-CD compilation tracing Richard Thompson's career from his beginnings with Fairport Convention, through his days with his ex-wife Linda, to his recent solo recordings, *Watching the Dark* is a treasure for longtime fans as well as those who want an introduction to his distinctive English folk-rock. Instead of being assembled chronologically, each disc contains three separate eras, which helps illustrate how consistently rich his music has been through the years. Nearly half of the tracks are rare or unreleased; instead of betraying Thompson's gifts, the song selection helps convey the breadth and scope of his talents. Although the material might be skewed towards hardcore fans, anyone unfamiliar with Thompson will realize why he is one of the most revered (and, unfortunately, unknown) songwriters and guitarists of his era by listening to *Watching the Dark*. —AMG

Mirror Blue / 1994 / Capitol
In many ways, *Mirror Blue* is Thompson's pop radio record, with shorter songs and a crisp, slick production. While that may put some fans off, the songs prove to another set of rich, detailed stories; even the supposed tossoffs are bright, catchy, and memo-

rable. In fact, the best moments of *Mirror Blue* equal the best of *Rumor and Sigh*—it's hard to equal the subtle power of "Mingus Eyes" or "Mascara Tears," and the closing song, "Taking My Business Elsewhere," is one of the best things he has ever written. —*Stephen Thomas Erlewine*

George Thorogood & the Destroyers

b. , Wilmington, DE
Group / Blues rock
A Delaware-based blues band formed in 1973 and led by guitarist/singer George Thorogood, who brings a rough-voiced enthusiasm to the music of John Lee Hooker, Elmore James, and others. The group scored five gold albums in 1980-1988. — *William Ruhlmann*

○ **George Thorogood & the Destroyers** / 1978 / Rounder 3013
Contains Thorogood's crowd-pleasing rendition of John Lee Hooker's "One Bourbon, One Scotch, One Beer." Its basic approach—heavy on Thorogood's bluesy guitar playing—serves as the prototype for every Destroyers record that followed. — *William Ruhlmann*

Move It on over / Jan. 1979 / Rounder 3024
This was Thorogood's second album, and what's now almost a cliché then sounded fresh and vital. Thorogood's energy, rousing vocals and driving guitar playing, plus the catchy three-member support offered by drummer Jeff Simon, bassist Billy Blough, and percussionist Uncle Meat Pennington, came roaring through on inspired covers of Elmore James' "The Sky Is Crying," Bo Diddley's "Who Do You Love," and Chuck Berry's "It Wasn't Me." He even did a credible Piedmont blues on Brownie McGhee's "So Much Trouble." While Thorogood went on to make more commercially succesful albums, the spirit and innocence in his early releases have seldom been duplicated. —*Ron Wynn*

More George Thorogood / 1980 / Rounder 3045
George Thorogood was honing his focus and getting the Destroyers concept down pat on this record. Thorogood's playing and singing on such tracks as "House of Blue Lights," "Night Time," and "I'm Wanted" were earnest enough to make the treatments convincing and retain interest while saxophonist Hank Carter, bassist Billy Blough, and drummer Jeff Simon added driving backgrounds and assistance underneath and behind him. While this wasn't quite as memorable as his earlier dates, George Thorogood still had the hunger that fueled his breakout sessions. —*Ron Wynn*

○ **Bad to the Bone** / 1982 / EMI America 46083
Though songs such as "Back to Wentzville" are credited to G. Thorogood, he'd be the first to admit that they are proudly derivative of Chuck Berry and his other mentors. The title track, another Thorogood copyright, has become ubiquitous in *Terminator 2* and the *Problem Child* movies and elsewhere, but it's still terrific. —*William Ruhlmann*

● **Baddest of George Thorogood and the Destroyers** / 1992 / EMI America 97718
The aptly titled *The Baddest of George Thorogood and the Destroyers* offers a dozen tracks that cleanse the church of rock & roll of all but its most basic elements: guitar, bass, drums, and a pile of Chuck Berry, Bo Diddley, and Rolling Stones licks. Thorogood has never quite captured his wildman live presence in the studio, but having all his best material gathered on one disc—including "Bad to the Bone," "Move It on Over," and "One Bourbon, One Scotch, One Beer"—makes for a great party. Fans will be pleased with two previously unreleased inclusions—a cover of Robert Johnson's "I'm a Steady Rollin' Man" and a decade-old version of Berry's "Louie to Frisco" with Stones' pianist Ian Stewart tinkling the keys. —*Roch Parisien*

Three Dog Night

Group / Pop/rock
At a time when rock elitists deemed Top 40 radio decidedly uncool, the slick multivocal blend of soulful pop-rock of Three Dog Night (formed 1968) made 21 trips to the charts from 1969 to 1975.

The centerpiece of Three Dog Night's sound was the band's trio of lead singers: Danny Hutton (b. September 10, 1946), Chuck Negron (b. June 8, 1942), and Cory Wells (b. February 5, 1944). Composed of seasoned players, the band displayed quite a bit of

proficiency musically, even though their lurching, soulful dance rhythms occasionally sounded awkward.

Since the band lacked any real songwriting resource from within, they were smart enough to look outside for material and had the good taste to plug into some of the era's best songwriters. While Three Dog Night's versions of the material may not have been definitive, they opened the door to the mass market's awareness of talented writers like Steve Winwood, Harry Nilsson, Robbie Robertson, Randy Newman, Hoyt Axton, Neil Young, Laura Nyro, and many others. Elton John and Bernie Taupin had their first Stateside success with Three Dog Night's cover of "Lady Samantha." —*Rick Clark*

● **Best of Three Dog Night** / 1983 / MCA 6018
This collection contains all of Three Dog Night's hits, plus a few key album tracks. Among the tracks included are "One," "Easy to Be Hard," "Eli's Coming," "Mama Told Me Not to Come," "Joy to the World," "Black & White," "Shambala," "An Old-Fashioned Love Song," "Never Been to Spain," and "Celebrate." —*Rick Clark*

Celebrate: The Three Dog Night Story, 1965-1975 / 1993 / MCA 10956
A comprehensive double-disc anthology, *Celebrate* is necessary for devoted fans of Three Dog Night, but most listeners will be content with *Best of Three Dog Night*, which features all of the hits on a single disc. —*AMG*

Throbbing Gristle

Group / Alternative rock, industrial
This is the group that defined the industrial sound, forging their distinctively dark outlook with sonic experimentation and dance beats at the dawn of the punk age. Although Throbbing Gristle followed no formulas—producing many unpredictable albums and hundreds of live tapes in just a few years—the pop aspects of industrial dance music became an identifiable mainstream genre. Consequently, Throbbing Gristle split up into two entities, with members Chris and Cosey following the dance trend, while Genesis P. Orridge took the underground route in Psychic TV. — *Myles Boisen*

2nd Annual Report / 1977 / Mute 61093
Actually their first album, with singles and different live versions of two early pieces. —*Myles Boisen*

D.O.A. / 1978 / Mute 61094
A dark lyrical content dominates these 15 tracks. —*Myles Boisen*

○ **20 Jazz Funk Greats** / 1979 / Mute 61095
As close as they got to the industrial-dance style of their many imitators. Fairly accessible. —*Myles Boisen*

Heathen Earth / 1980 / Mute 61096
Live in the studio, combining the best of both harrowing worlds. —*Myles Boisen*

Mission of Dead Souls / 1981 / Mute 61097
Their final and perhaps most extreme musical assault, live in San Francisco. —*Myles Boisen*

● **Greatest Hits** / 1984 / Mute 61001
Like the title says (with irony). An industrial primer with song sensibility. —*Myles Boisen*

CD 1 / 1986 / Resonance 71457
A very raw studio session. —*Myles Boisen*

Throwing Muses

Group / Alternative pop/rock
Led by Kristin Hersh, Throwing Muses produced some of the most exciting, distinctive music of the late '80s. When they began recording in 1986, Throwing Muses didn't sound like any other band; after several albums and lineup changes, they still sound utterly original. Combining elements of folk, pop, and punk, the band's music is a swirling, guitar-based rush of sound. Hersh's cryptic, metaphoric lyrics and highly emotive singing were equally as original and challenging. Although their music might have sounded strange, it never was alienating; Hersh's songwriting is emotional, not intellectual. Throwing Muses gained a substantial cult following on the basis of their first album; they were never able to break into the mainstream because, no matter how close they came to direct guitar pop on their later albums, their music is always too emotional and abstract to qualify as easy listening.

After releasing three albums and two EPs, Hersh's stepsister, guitarist Tanya Donnelly, decided to leave the band while they were recording 1991's *The Real Ramona;* she formed Belly the following year. After releasing *Red Heaven* in 1992, Hersh recorded a solo acoustic album in late 1993; the record, *Hips and Makers,* was released in early 1994, just as Throwing Muses headed back into the studio to record their next album. —*Stephen Thomas Erlewine*

○ **Throwing Muses** / 1986 / 4AD
A challenging set of fractured pop-rock, *Throwing Muses* sounds as original today as it did when it was originally released. — *Stephen Thomas Erlewine*

House Tornado / 1988 / Sire 25710
Throwing Muses' second album continues in the vein of their first album. —*Stephen Thomas Erlewine*

Hunkpapa / 1989 / Sire 25855
A more pop-oriented album than their previous records, *Hunkpapa* finds Kristin Hersh attempting to open up her rather insular songwriting with intriguing results. —*Stephen Thomas Erlewine*

● **Real Ramona** / 1991 / Sire 26489
With some strong pop melodies from both Hersh and Tanya Donnelly, *The Real Ramona* is the band's lightest, most accessible record. —*Stephen Thomas Erlewine*

○ **Red Heaven** / 1992 / Sire 26897
Throwing Muses' first release since Donnelly's departure manages to retain the more straightforward songwriting of their recent albums while recapturing the raw energy of their earlier records. — *Stephen Thomas Erlewine*

Johnny Thunders

b. 1941, **d.** Apr. 23, 1991
Vocals, guitar / Rock & roll, punk
This ex-New York Doll guitarist recorded a slew of albums before a fatal 1990 heroin overdose. Unfortunately, most of them are garbage, consisting mostly of live shows that, more than anything, document the perils of heroin addiction and its effects on someone who should've remained a rock & roll contender well into the '90s. —*John Floyd*

New Too Much Junkie Business / 1978 / Combat 5029
The best of Thunders's live and outtake documents. For diehards only. —*John Floyd*

● **So Alone** / 1978 / Sire 26982
Thunders' first solo shot enlisted members of the Sex Pistols, the Hot Rods, and the Only Ones, featuring a variety of material that showcased both his mangy vocals and his strangling guitar attack. —*John Floyd*

'Til Tuesday

Group / Pop/rock
Aimee Mann was the lead singer and bass player in the Boston-based 'Til Tuesday, which scored a Top 10 hit with "Voices Carry" and a gold-selling album of the same name in 1985. The rest of the group was Michael Hausmann, drums; Robert Holmes, guitar; and Joey Pesce, keyboards. The group recorded two more albums but broke up after *Everything's Different Now* in 1988. —*William Ruhlmann*

○ **Voices Carry** / 1985 / Epic 39458
'Til Tuesday showed a lot of promise with this debut album, which focused on Aimee Mann's emotive singing, notably on the title track. —*William Ruhlmann*

● **Everything's Different Now** / 1988 / Epic 44041
Til Tuesday's final album is their best record, showcasing Aimee Mann's emergence as a songwriter capable of impeccably crafted guitar-pop gems. —*Stephen Thomas Erlewine*

Sonny Til & the Orioles

d. Dec. 9, 1957
Group / R&B, doo-wop
A smooth, early '50s group best known for the 1953 hit "Crying in the Chapel," the Orioles were arguably the most important R&B vocal group of the late '40s and early '50s; as much as anyone, they were responsible for the shift from the straight pop harmonies to doo-wop. —*John Floyd*

☆ **Jubilee Sides (Boxed Set)** / 1993 / Bear Family 15682
This exhaustive five-CD box set shows you all the reasons why the Orioles, led by smooth-as-silk vocalist Sonny Til, were one of the most pivotal, if not the most important, of all the early African American vocal groups. The group's honey-smooth harmonies perfectly framing Til's soaring, sexy vocals against the simplest of backgrounds on their earliest sides, while later sessions with full orchestras surprisingly do little to intrude, with interesting results. With typical Bear Family completeness, this rounds up everything the group cut for Natural-Jubilee from two different tenures with the label. —*Cub Koda*

● **Greatest Hits** / Collectables 5014
A good overview of this historic '50s and '60s harmony group. One of the pioneering R&B vocal groups. A decent collection of their hits, marred by putrid sound. —*Ron Wynn*

Time

Group / Funk, soul, pop/rock
From their origins as Prince's first pet project, to their self-produced funk-rock oeuvre, the Time has been a fascinating and outrageous congregation. Vocalist Morris Day infused his cocky, swaggering personality into dance hits that would make Rufus Thomas envious, and, unlike most of the competition, the band managed to do something unique with Prince's genre-busting innovations. Time broke up in the late '80s, with Day going on to a somewhat disastrous solo career, Jesse Johnson crafting two dazzling solo albums, and Jimmy Jam and Terry Lewis becoming one of the most successful production teams this side of Gamble-Huff, working with everyone from Full Force and Janet Jackson to the S.O.S. Band and Human League. The group reformed in 1990 and released the excellent *Pandemonium.* —*John Floyd*

Time / 1981 / Warner Brothers 3598
The former backing band for Prince became stars in their own right in the early '80s. Their debut album had a smart combination of funk, rock, pop, and punk, with Morris Day the erstwhile lead singer, and the cast also including Terry Lewis, Jimmy "Jam" Harris, Jesse Johnson, and Jellybean Johnson. Their early singles "Get It Up" and "Cool" were surly, suggestive, and just as energetic and electric as Prince's. —*Ron Wynn*

● **What Time Is It?** / 1982 / Warner Brothers 23701
After a tentative debut, the Time bounced back with one of 1982's best dance albums, full of hilarious stompers and braggadocio ballads. —*John Floyd*

○ **Ice Cream Castle** / 1984 / Warner Brothers 25109
Ice Cream Castle finds the band stepping out of Prince's purple shadow and discovering their own persona. The relentless "Jungle Love" is their best song. —*John Floyd*

○ **Pandemonium** / 1990 / Paisley Park 27490
Jam and Lewis bring their groundbreaking production techniques to a set that alternately demonstrates just how timeless the Time's boogie can be and just what the band members picked up during their sabbatical. —*John Floyd*

Tin Machine

Group / Hard rock
To some ears, Tin Machine's sheets of guitar feedback and bash-ola drums may be overkill, but this quartet, fronted by pop chameleon David Bowie, takes aggressive, dissonant hard rock to bracing extremes, particularly on their exciting self-titled debut. —*Rick Clark*

● **Tin Machine** / 1989 / EMI America 91990
For fans of wildly dissonant hard rock, Tin Machine's debut effort (uneven as it is) is a gem. The band's chemistry, on tracks like "Heaven Is Here" (check the lead ride at the end), "I Can't Read," "Crack City," and "Baby Can Dance," is great. "Amazing" sports a nice descending guitar pattern and one of the album's more memorable melodies, but their version of Lennon's "Working Class Hero" rings hollow. Lyrically, most of this is Bowie at his most half-baked. —*Rick Clark*

Toad the Wet Sprocket

Group / Folk rock, pop/rock
Toad the Wet Sprocket's second-generation, R.E.M.-derived guitar pop made them stars in 1992, with the gentle, highly melodic *Fear.* Although they released two albums before their commercial

breakthrough, they hadn't yet developed a signature style; with *Fear* the band's songwriting improved and their sound developed into a graceful, folk rock that incorporated the band's influences instead of mimicking them. Both radio and MTV played the singles "All I Want" and "Walk on the Ocean" constantly, making the album a hit. In 1994, the band released *Dulcinea,* which was a hit upon its release, thanks to the single "Fall Down." —*David Jehnzen*

● **Fear** / 1991 / Columbia 47309
Since their first release, *Bread and Circus,* Toad have grown dramatically as players and songcrafters. *Fear* is the pleasant result of these developments. Contains the Top 40/alternative hit single "All I Want"; the opening track, "Walk on the Ocean," is another highlight. —*Rick Clark*

Dulcinea / 1994 / Columbia
Over two years in the making, *Dulcinea* builds upon the sound laid down in *Fear.* "Fall Down" was the first hit, while "Fly from Heaven" and "Inside" have the same potential for both alternative and mainstream pop/rock appeal. —*Rick Clark*

Tom Tom Club

Group / Alternative pop/rock, dance-pop
Tom Tom Club began life as a side project for Talking Heads members Chris Frantz and Tina Weymouth, who adopted a light, tropical dance style that won them a gold album in *Tom Tom Club* in 1981 and a Top 40 single in "Genius of Love." They continued to make albums under this moniker between Heads production projects: *Close to the Bone* (1983) and *Boom Boom Chi Boom Boom* (1989). They even toured as Tom Tom Club in the summer of 1989. When the Heads broke up in late 1991, Tom Tom Club became Frantz and Weymouth's main outlet. They released *Dark Sneak Love Action* in 1992. —*William Ruhlmann*

● **Tom Tom Club** / 1981 / Sire 3628
Frantz and Weymouth pulled off a surprising mixture of rap and dance music with light humor, expecially on "Genius of Love." Maybe it was a fluke: they never equaled the effervescence of this album, though they tried. —*William Ruhlmann*

Tony! Toni! Tone!

Group / Urban R&B, soul, funk
Brothers Dwayne and Raphael Wiggins and cousin Timothy Christian have proven themselves durable guardians of the soul and funk tradition, while also infusing their music with enough contemporary devices to remain popular. This Oakland trio scored a #1 R&B hit right out of the box in 1988 with "Little Walter," a song that generated some criticism from gospel audiences for its use of the melody from "Wade in the Water." But they've since been able to keep things going on their own, as their LPs *The Revival* in 1990 and *Sons of Soul* in 1993 have also been enormously successful. —*Ron Wynn*

Who? / Jan. 1988 / Wing 835549
Dwayne and Raphael Wiggins, along with cousin Timothy Christian, made a quick and lasting impact with their 1988 debut album. The lead single, "Little Walter," used the melody from "Wade in the Water" and laid out in vivid detail the rise and fall of a comrade who lacked control and direction. It proved a huge R&B hit and got moderate pop attention, but it helped establish the trio and their creative mix of vintage soul and contemporary hip-hop and new jack production. "Baby Doll" and "For the Love of You" also got sizable pop attention, and Tony! Toni! Tone! were on their way. —*Ron Wynn*

○ **Revival** / 1990 / Wing 841902
This Oakland trio followed their fine debut album with an even more polished and better produced second effort. "Feels Good" was an uptempo, hook-laden hit, while "It Never Rains in Southern California" was a nicely sung, elegantly arranged, and tightly performed ballad and a sign they were real craftsmen rather than trendy followers. "The Blues" expressed their love for vintage music, while "Whatever You Want" was another love tune that displayed genuine style and compositional depth, rather than dumb luck. —*Ron Wynn*

● **Sons of Soul** / 1993 / Wing
With their third album, Tony! Toni! Tone! received their greatest chart success, without compromising their music; it was still the finely crafted, highly eclectic, and highly funky pop-soul that dis-

tinguished their first two albums, but the band's songwriting and playing had improved. The result was the band's most successful album yet, both commercially and artistically. —*Stephen Thomas Erlewine*

Tool

Group / Heavy metal, alternative rock
When their first full-length album was released in 1993 (they released an EP a year earlier), Tool won lots of fans with their grinding, post-Jane's Addiction heavy metal. With their dark, angry lyrics and numbing guitar drilling, they appealed both to metalheads and alternative rock fans. When they landed an opening spot on Lollapalooza, their audience grew by leaps and bounds; the increased exposure helped their debut album, *Undertow,* go gold. —*Stephen Thomas Erlewine*

○ **Opiate** / 1992 / Zoo 11027
Tool's debut EP, *Opiate,* is as tough and brutal as *Undertow* and will more than satisfy fans of that album. —*Stephen Thomas Erlewine*

● **Undertow** / 1993 / Zoo 11052
With their angst-ridden heavy metal, Tool appear to be something new; the band fall right into metal's grand tradition of white male adolescent aggression. It's the angry, politically aware lyrics that qualify this as "alternative rock," because their grinding, assaultive attack is not that different from Helmet, or Iron Maiden and Black Sabbath, for that matter. Anyone who found "Sober" both rocking and disturbing will undoubtedly be thrilled with *Undertow*'s pulverizing consistency. —*Stephen Thomas Erlewine*

Tornados

Group / Rock & roll
Britain's premier instrumental group of the early '60s, the Tornadoes' fame rests principally on "Telstar," a haunting instrumental written by their producer, Joe Meek, which rocketed to the top of the charts in both England and the United States in early 1962. Although none of their subsequent work went so far (or deserved to), they achieved additional recognition after becoming Billy Fury's backup band—they played on his live album, *We Want Billy*—and their bass player, blond, German-born Heinz Burt (who went by the moniker "Heinz") later became a low-level chart success as a vocalist ("Just Like Eddie" and others). —*Bruce Eder*

○ **Roots of British Rock** / Sire 3711
"Telstar" is one of the good reasons (among many) for owning this out-of-print collection. —*Bruce Eder*

Toto

Group / Pop/rock
Formed in 1978, Toto immediately became favorites on FM rock and pop formats with their million-selling mainstream rocker "Hold the Line," followed by the mildly funky "Georgy Porgy." Their sound, honed from years of session work, had a steely precision that, while sounding impressive, seemed bloodless. Nevertheless, their fourth album, *Toto IV* (1983), became the biggest album of their career, earning six Grammy awards. During this time, Toto continued doing session work for many artists, in a sense defining much of the sound of radio during the mid '80s. —*Rick Clark*

○ **Toto IV** / 1982 / Columbia 37728
This is the album that cleaned up at the 1982 Grammys. Most of *Toto IV* is a seamless collection of precision-crafted hard-rockers and power ballads. The album contains five hits, the biggest being "Africa," "Rosanna," and "I Won't Hold You Back." —*Rick Clark*

● **Past to Present 1977-1990** / 1990 / Columbia 45368
Past to Present 1977-1990 is a complete set of the biggest songs from this group of Los Angeles session pros, including "Africa," "Hold the Line," "Rosanna," "I Won't Hold You Back," "Stranger in Town," "99," "Make Believe," and "Georgy Porgy." —*Rick Clark*

Tourists

Group / New wave, pop/rock
In a brief career lasting from 1979 to 1980, the Tourists recorded three albums, *The Tourists, Reality Effect,* and *Luminous Basement,* all of which made the UK charts. They also scored five

chart singles, two of which, "I Only Want to Be with You" and "So Good to Be Back Home Again," made the Top 10. The band included singer Annie Lennox (b. December 25, 1954), keyboardist/guitarist Dave Stewart (b September 9, 1952), vocalist/guitarist Pete Coombes (who wrote most of the songs), bassist Eddie Chin, and drummer Jim Toomey. After the split, Stewart and Lennox formed the Eurythmics. —*William Ruhlmann*

● **Should Have Been Greatest Hits** / 1984 / Epic 39318
A best-of released in the wake of Eurythmics' success and therefore emphasizing Stewart and Lennox's contributions over Coombes's. Nevertheless, it's a well-chosen selection and includes four of their five UK hits, among them their sole U.S. chart entry, a terrific remake of Dusty Springfield's "I Only Want to Be with You." —*William Ruhlmann*

Allen Toussaint

b. 1938
Vocals, piano / R&B

His inherently funky piano work heavily influenced by his Crescent City forefathers—Professor Longhair, Huey "Piano" Smith, and Fats Domino—and with a heavy dose of Ray Charles, a young visionary named Allen Toussaint almost singlehandedly fashioned a fresh, vital New Orleans R&B sound for the early '60s.

Earning a vaunted reputation as a session pianist, Toussaint debuted on vinyl in 1958 with an obscure RCA album whimsically billed as "A. Tousan." When Joe Banashak inaugurated his Minit label in 1960, Toussaint joined the firm as A&R man and quickly proved himself the ultimate behind-the-scenes wizard on the New Orleans scene. During the early to mid '60s, Toussaint tirelessly wrote, arranged, produced, and played on hits by Ernie K-Doe, Irma Thomas, Jessie Hill, Chris Kenner, Barbara George, Lee Dorsey, Benny Spellman, the Showmen, and many more, his rolling keyboards vital to the charm of virtually all of them.

After unleashing the Meters on the world, Toussaint finally began to step out as a front man in 1970, although his low-key vocals have never achieved quite the same level of success as his previous productions for others. His brilliant compositions have been covered by everyone from Herb Alpert & the Tijuana Brass to Robert Palmer and Bonnie Raitt. Allen Toussaint's stature as a New Orleans musical giant endures. —*Bill Dahl*

○ **Wild Sound of New Orleans** / 1958 / RCA Victor 1767
His debut album, featuring a killer band, storming second-line instrumentals, and Toussaint's rolling 88s. —*Bill Dahl*

● **Allen Toussaint Collection** / 1991 / Warner Brothers 26549
A representative cross-section of the legendary New Orleans piano man's solo output—uneven but interesting. —*Bill Dahl*

○ **Complete "Tousan" Sessions** / 1992 / Bear Family 15641
A compilation of instrumentals from 1958 and 1959 that feature Toussaint at the top of his form, *The Complete "Tousan" Sessions* is a wonderful portrait of the seminal New Orleans pianist; it's also the first time this material has ever been available on CD. —*Stephen Thomas Erlewine*

Tower of Power

Group / Soul

Studio session work has never lent itself to wide recognition except among other musicians, yet when not on the road as Tower of Power, the individuals who make up the critically acclaimed West Coast horn section might as well go by another name: "Backup for the World." Individually and in various incarnations, members of Tower of Power (fronted by Emilio Castillo) have recorded as sidemen for Elton John, Santana, Bonnie Raitt, Huey Lewis, Little Feat, David Sanborn, Michelle Shocked, Paula Abdul, Aaron Neville, and Riot.

Tower of Power has had their share of personnel changes over the years, but the core group members (including Castillo on saxes and vocals, Stephen "Doc" Kupka on baritone sax, Greg Adams on trumpet and vocals, and Rocco Prestia on bass) have remained, giving the band a percussive horn-based sound that is not rooted in any one genre. —*Richard Skelly*

○ **Tower of Power** / 1973 / Warner Brothers 2681
The Tower of Power finally found their ideal lead singer on this album. Lenny Williams came aboard and gave them both the up-tempo belter and convincing balladeer they'd been previously lacking. They landed their biggest single hit "So Very Hard to Go"

and also had two other top tunes in "What Is Hip" and "This Time It's Real." The arrangements and production were also excellent, and the horn section was at its explosive best. —*Ron Wynn*

○ **Urban Renewal** / 1974 / Warner Brothers 2834
A fine workout album, with surging horn funk and charts, punchy songs, excellent lead vocals from Lenny Williams, and only an occasional out-of-place tune. The Tower of Power were the finest West Coast funk/soul band of the early and mid '70s, and organist/keyboardist Chester Thompson provided them with another strong instrumentalist in the rhythm section. —*Ron Wynn*

● **Back to Oakland** / May 1974 / Warner Brothers 2749
The Tower of Power followed their self-titled gold album with an even better album that didn't enjoy similar sales success. Yet *Back to Oakland* had tougher, funkier, and better produced cuts, stronger vocals from Lenny Williams, who was now more comfortable as their lead singer, and included an excellent ballad "Time Will Tell," plus the rousing "Don't Change Horses (in the Middle of a Stream)." The Tower of Power horn section reaffirmed its reputation as the hottest in both soul and pop circles, and the album included a powerhouse instrumental. —*Ron Wynn*

Pete Townshend

b. May 19, 1945
Vocals, guitar / Rock & roll

Pete Townshend was the guitarist and songwriter for the Who from 1964 to 1982. Best known for his conceptual works, he wrote *Tommy* and *Quadrophenia* for the group. Townshend made his first tentative solo album, *Who Came First*, in 1972. Dedicated to his guru, Meher Baba, the album continued themes pursued in the previous Who album, *Who's Next*, and contained material from an abortive conceptual work, *Lifehouse*. The album sold modestly. In 1976, Townshend made a duo album, *Rough Mix*, with Ronnie Lane, formerly the bassist in the Small Faces.

Townshend's first full-fledged solo effort, however, was *Empty Glass* (1980), which sold half a million copies, reached the Top 5, and featured the Top 10 hit "Let My Love Open the Door," as well as the minor hits "A Little Is Enough" and "Rough Boys." Townshend followed this in 1982 with *All the Best Cowboys Have Chinese Eyes*.

Following the demise of the Who, Townshend released *Scoop*, a two-disc collection of demos, in 1983 (a second volume appeared in 1987). In 1985 he returned to thematic efforts with the album *White City—A Novel*, which included the Top 30 single "Face the Face." In the same year, Townshend published a book of short stories, *Horse's Neck*. As part of the *White City* project, Townshend appeared in an accompanying film, for which he organized a band called Pete Townshend's Deep End. The unit played only a few gigs, but one was videotaped and recorded, resulting in the 1986 album *Pete Townshend's Deep End Live!* In 1989 Townshend released an album based on Ted Hughes's children's story, *The Iron Man*. The record featured guest vocals by John Lee Hooker and Nina Simone, as well as two tracks featuring the three surviving members of the Who. Simultaneous with the album's release, Townshend embarked on a reunion tour with the Who.

Although the reunion tour was successful, it didn't help *The Iron Man* at all. Four years later, Townshend delivered *Psychoderelict* to mixed reviews and lukewarm sales. By that time, he had successfully reinvented himself as a Broadway tunesmith—the Broadway production of *The Who's Tommy* had become a runaway hit, earning Townshend a Tony and prompting him to pursue more stage musicals. —*William Ruhlmann*

Who Came First / 1972 / Rykodisc 10246
Pete Townshend's first solo album was a homespun, charming forum for low-key, personal songs that weren't deemed suitable for the Who, as well as spiritual paeans (both direct and indirect) to his spiritual guru Meher Baba. Who fans will be immediately attracted by the presence of a couple songs from the aborted Who concept album *Lifehouse* (much of which ended up on *Who's Next*), "Pure & Easy" and "Let's See Action." But Townshend's own versions aren't the highlights of this record, which shows a folkier and gentler side to the Who's chief muse than his albums with the group. —*Richie Unterberger*

○ **Rough Mix** / 1977 / Atco 90097

Pete Townshend and Ronnie Lane rock it up, with some good melodies thrown in. Tops among Townshend's non-Who projects. —*Bruce Eder*

★ **Empty Glass** / 1980 / Atco 32100
A bright, energetic rock album, tightly played and sung in a manner equaling the best Who albums. —*Bruce Eder*

○ **Scoop** / 1983 / Atco 90063
Townshend's first batch of Who demos. Not viscerally exciting, but musically intriguing. —*Bruce Eder*

○ **Another Scoop** / 1987 / Atco 90539
The second batch of Who demos, with better songs than the first. Some surprises for the serious fan. —*Bruce Eder*

Traffic

Group / Rock/pop, progressive rock, psychedelic
Among all the bands to emerge from England in the '60s, Traffic is one of the few who have aged gracefully.

At the time of Traffic's inception in 1967, former Spencer Davis bandmate Stevie Winwood (b. May 12, 1948) was its most noted member, but with the release of their debut, *Mr. Fantasy*, it became clear that this was truly a band of four equally creative multiinstrumentalists. Their initial efforts fused an ecumenical range of musical genres through a fairly psychedelic sensibility, most of it among the best examples of that approach to late '60s pop-rock. Guitarist and vocalist Dave Mason (b. May 10, 1947) penned some particularly strong material on those first Traffic albums, especially "Feelin' Alright," a song that was later popularized by Joe Cocker, Three Dog Night, and many others.

After many instances of quitting the band over creative differences (the remaining three were resistant to his obvious pop tendencies), Mason left for good after 1971's *Welcome to the Canteen*, a live album. By then, he had already earned a gold album for his 1970 debut, *Alone Together*.

After their second self-titled album, Traffic parted ways when Winwood joined the short-lived supergroup Blind Faith. After Blind Faith's demise, Winwood began a solo effort, tentatively titled *Mad Shadows*. As the project developed, Winwood increasingly sought the input of Chris Wood and Jim Capaldi. The result was the funkier, earthier *John Barleycorn Must Die*.

Traffic's studio followup, *The Low Spark of High Heeled Boys*, incorporated a spacier improvisational sound. The title cut became an FM rock-radio standard. Several more albums followed, and the band parted ways in 1974.

Wood died on July 12, 1983, of liver failure. Capaldi and Dave Mason have experienced sporadically successful solo careers. Winwood, in contrast, had a profitable string of releases.

When Winwood's solo career began to sag in 1994, he reformed with Capaldi; Mason didn't participate, choosing to stay in Fleetwood Mac. While the album proved a commercial disappointment, the reunited Traffic tour was successful, although neither proved to be as stimulating as their earlier work. —*Rick Clark*

○ **Mr. Fantasy** / Jan. 1967 / Island 842783
Produced by Jimmy Miller (Rolling Stones, Blind Faith), *Mr. Fantasy* is sonically decked out in *Sgt. Pepper*-period psychedelic splendor. Although much music of the period sounds quite dated, *Mr. Fantasy* and the self-titled followup have aged gracefully. This is in no small part due to Dave Mason's refined pop sensibilities. Even though he occasionally gets lost in a sea of sitars ("Utterly Simple"), Mason gives the material much of the form and restraint that the latter-period Traffic, at times, desperately needed. Even Winwood turns in some of the tightest pop-song constructions in his career, thanks to Jim Capaldi and Chris Wood's cowriting input. The band's almost whimsical approach to integrating its eclectic influences keeps the material sounding fresh too. Traffic's hodgepodge of psychedelia always sounds like the product of a band that really plays together rather than existing as a studio concoction. —*Rick Clark*

● **Traffic** / Feb. 1968 / Island 842590
It's songs like "Feelin' Alright," "Pearly Queen," "You Can All Join In," "Vagabond Virgin," and "40,000 Headmen" that make Traffic's self-titled second effort a classic. Although not quite as trippy as their debut, most of the sonic observations mentioned for *Mr. Fantasy* apply here. —*Rick Clark*

Last Exit / Jan. 1969 / Island 842787

This collection of leftover studio tracks and live recordings from their 1968 tour was thrown together after Winwood jumped ship to go play with Blind Faith. It's a little spotty, but "Shanghai Noodle Factory" and the funky "Medicated Goo" are among their best early recorded work. —*Rick Clark*

○ **John Barleycorn Must Die** / Jan. 1970 / Island 842780
Upon the demise of the short-lived supergroup project Blind Faith, Stevie Winwood began work on a solo album entitled *Mad Shadows*. As the project developed, it evolved into a Traffic reunion of sorts, as Winwood brought in Wood and Capaldi. The result, *John Barleycorn Must Die*, became an instant success, with its lengthy funky, R&B, jazz, and folk explorations. The playing is top-notch throughout, with Wood blowing some inspired sax, Capaldi laying down his trademark fluid percussion grooves, and Winwood's Hammond B3 and piano work in peak form. "Glad," "Freedom Rider," "Empty Pages," and the title cut are the highlights. —*Rick Clark*

○ **Low Spark of High Heeled Boys** / Jan. 1971 / Island 842779
Opening with the pastoral "Hidden Treasure," *Low Spark* flows effortlessly, almost lazily, to the last song, "Rainmaker." The band does shake things up a little with "Rock & Roll Stew" and "Light Up or Leave Me Alone." The title cut, at over 12 minutes of spacey jamming, is one of Traffic's most well known FM hits. —*Rick Clark*

Welcome to the Canteen / Feb. 1971 / Island 842417
This fine live effort revealed Traffic as a seven-man touring unit, a precursor to their upcoming studio directions. On board for this outing were percussionist Reebop Kwaku Baah, drummer Jim Gordon, bassist Rick Grech, and Dave Mason, who briefly rejoined Winwood, Capaldi, and Wood for the tour. A revamped version of the Spencer Davis classic "Gimmie Some Lovin' (Part One)" became a moderate hit. —*Rick Clark*

Shoot out at the Fantasy Factory / 1973 / Island 842781
The title cut has its moments, but the augmentation of Muscle Shoals studio heavies Barry Beckett, Roger Hawkins, and David Hood ultimately turned down most of the remaining sparks in search of the eternal groove. —*Rick Clark*

★ **Smiling Phases** / 1991 / Island 510553
Island remastered the tracks included in this double-CD anthology, and the difference is remarkable. Except for a few curious omissions, this is absolutely essential. —*Rick Clark*

Far from Home / 1994 / Virgin
In terms of capturing the spirit of playful creativity found on Traffic's best early work, this polished 1994 reunion album is indeed *Far from Home*. Traffic lovers may be disappointed, but fans of Winwood's later solo work will probably like this. Essentially, it is an extension of the sound he's created for the last 10 years, with more instrumental stretching out—a nod to the band esthetic of '70s-era Traffic. —*Rick Clark*

Trammps

Group / Disco, soul
Disco's most soulful vocal group began in the '60s as the Volcanos and were also called the Moods for a time. Gene Faith was the original lead vocalist, with Earl Young, Jimmy Ellis, guitarist Dennis Harris, keyboardist Ron Kersey, organist John Hart, bassist Stanley Wade, and drummer Michael Thomas rounding out the lineup. But by the time they'd gone through various identities and emerged as the Trammps in the mid '70s, the lineup featured lead vocalist Ellis, Harold and Stanley Wade, Robert Upchurch, and Young. A snappy revival of Judy Garland's '40s tune "Zing Went the Strings of My Heart" was their first chart single, reaching #17 on the R&B charts in 1972. Despite their well-deserved reputation and boisterous, jubilant harmonies and sound, the Trammps were never huge commercial successes even during disco's heyday. Indeed, they had only three R&B Top 10 hits from 1972 through 1978, and such wonderful records as "Soul Bones," "Ninety-Nine and a Half," and "I Feel Like I've Been Livin' (on the Dark Side of the Moon)" stiffed on the charts, though they were beloved by club audiences and R&B fans alike. Their only huge hit was "Disco Inferno" in 1977, which was a #9 R&B single in 1977 and was also featured in *Saturday Night Fever*; it missed the pop Top 10, peaking at #11. But the Trammps' prowess can't be measured by chart popularity; Jimmy Ellis's booming, joyous vocals brilliantly championed the celebra-

tory fervor and atmosphere that made disco both beloved and hated among music fans. —*Ron Wynn*

● **Best of the Trammps** / 1978 / Atlantic 19194
A good collection of the band's best tracks, including the monolithic "Disco Inferno" and "Disco Party." —*Stephen Thomas Erlewine*

The Trashmen

Group / Rock & roll, garage rock
A Minneapolis rock & roll band that evolved from a local group, Jim Thaxter & the Travelers, recording one single under that name ("Sally Jo"/"Cyclone"). The group comprised Tony Andreason (lead guitar), Dan Winslow (guitar/ vocals), Bob Reed (bass), and Steve Wahrer (drums/vocals). Unfairly depicted as a novelty act, the Trashmen were in actuality a top-notch rock & roll combo, enormously popular on the teen-club circuit, playing primarily surf music to a landlocked Minnesota audience. Drummer Steve Wahrer combined two songs by the Rivingtons ("The Bird's the Word" and "Pa Pa Ooh Mow Mow"), added freakish vocal effects and a pounding rhythm to the mix, and, by early 1964, the group was in the Top 10 nationwide with "Surfin' Bird." Though the group continued to release great followup singles and an excellent album, their moment in the sun had come and gone, the group disbanding by late 1967/early 1968. They reformed in the mid '80s and continued to play locally until Wahrer's death. The Trashmen are revered by '60s collectors as one of the great American teen-band combos of all time, their lone hit exemplifying wild, unabashed rock & roll at its most demented, bare-bones-basic, lone-E-chord finest. —*Cub Koda*

Live Bird '65-'67 / Sundazed 11006
Storming unreleased live recordings. —*Cub Koda*

○ **Great Lost Trashmen Album!** / Sundazed 11007
Fine unreleased studio recordings. —*Cub Koda*

● **Best of the Trashmen** / Sundazed 11011
The original "Surfin' Bird" album, plus all the original Garrett singles from that period. The perfect primer set. —*Cub Koda*

The Traveling Wilburys

Group / Pop/rock
Reversing the usual process by which groups break up and give way to solo careers, the Traveling Wilburys are a group made up of solo stars. The group was organized by former Beatle George Harrison, former Electric Light Orchestra leader Jeff Lynne, Bob Dylan, Tom Petty, and Roy Orbison, thus representing three generations of rock stars. In 1988 the five (who had known each other for years) came together to record a Harrison B-side single and ended up writing and recording an album on which they shared lead vocals. It turned out to be a way to transcend the high expectations made of any of them as individuals, and a delighted public sent the album to #3, with two singles, "Handle with Care" and "End of the Line," hitting the charts. Unfortunately, Orbison died of a heart attack only a few weeks after the album's release.

Two years later, the remaining quartet released a second album, inexplicably titled *Vol. 3*. It was another million-selling hit. —*William Ruhlmann*

● **Traveling Wilburys** / 1988 / Wilbury 25796
The idea of Dylan, Orbison, Harrison, Lynne, Petty, and session drummer Jim Keltner getting together on a single album was pretty bizarre, inspiring curiosity and a little dread. Instead of trying to create something on a grand scale, these guys achieved much more by tossing together a refreshingly playful and unpretentious collection of homey pop-rock tunes. "Handle with Care" and "End of the Line" were the hits from this release. —*Rick Clark*

Traveling Wilburys, Vol. 3 / 1990 / Wilbury 26324
Skipping over *Volume 2*, the Wilburys managed a more unified and harder-rocking sound. Party raveups like "Wilbury Twist" and "She's My Baby" indicate that these guys seem to enjoy how their fabricated identities have allowed them to ditch their living legends status and possibly become more themselves in the process. —*Rick Clark*

The Tremeloes

Group / British invasion, rock/pop

After splitting from Brian Poole, this quartet went off on their own in 1965. Their music altered from a relatively taut, R&B-inspired base to a softer, more upbeat and relaxed sound, which was subsequently replaced by a disastrous attempt to become a serious, progressive band. —*Bruce Eder*

● **Best of the Tremeloes** / 1992 / Rhino 70528
A generous 20-track collection of the band's finest moments, including all of their U.S. hits. —AMG

Ralph Tresvant

Vocals / Urban R&B
A charter member of New Edition, vocalist Ralph Tresvant went out on his own in 1990 and came close to duplicating the success of fellow New Edition vocalists Bell Biv Devoe and Johnny Gill. The album *Ralph Tresvant*, featuring his light, at times whiny leads and pleading lyrics, got him a Top 10 R&B and pop hit with "Sensitivity," while the album went platinum. —*Ron Wynn*

● **Ralph Tresvant** / 1990 / MCA 10116
This one-time New Edition member scores with his wispy, almost weepy falsetto. —*Ron Wynn*

T. Rex

Group / Glam rock, rock & roll
Britain has a long history of championing style-over-substance flavor-of-the-week artists. Former fashion model Marc Bolan (b. Marc Feld, September 30, 1947) was a particularly fascinating self-promoter. Between 1970 and 1973, Bolan (operating under his group moniker, T. Rex) took England by storm with his lightly funky, fantasy-heavy, glam-rock songs, producing 11 Top 10 hits.

Stateside, T. Rex didn't quite catch on, generating a single hit with the #10 "Bang a Gong (Get It On)," which came off of the #32 album *Electric Warrior*. His followup album, *The Slider*, went to #17 on the wings of enormous hype. Nevertheless, Bolan's quavering tenor, mutated Chuck Berry rhythm parts, and plodding grooves generated some fine moments, thanks in no small part to Tony Visconti's creative production input. By late 1973, though, their success had waned. Bolan died from injuries sustained in an automobile accident on September 16, 1977. —*Rick Clark*

★ **Electric Warrior** / 1971 / Reprise 6466
Kicking off with the fat guitars of "Mambo Sun," *Electric Warrior* winds through all of Marc Bolan's obsessions, from sleazy teenage rock & roll to spacey mysticism. "Bang a Gong (Get It On)" was the well-deserved hit, full of lust and flamboyance, but it's by no means the only good thing here. With the trashy blues stomps of "Jeepster" and "Lean Woman Blues" sitting next to the space-age rock of "Monolith" and "Planet Queen," *Electric Warrior* has nothing but teenage kicks; it's glam rock at its absolute best. —*Stephen Thomas Erlewine*

☆ **Slider** / Jan. 1972 / Combat 8253
Surprisingly, *The Slider* was T. Rex's highest charting record, without the benefit of a hit single. Even without a hit, the record was a gas, powered by killer riffs like "Baby Strange," "Buick Mackane," "Telegram Sam," "Boomerang," and "Chariot Choogle." *The Slider* offers nothing new—it's still the same trashy glam rock that made *Electric Warrior* sublime—but that's why it's special. No one else could get away with "Metal Guru," "Baby Boomerang," and "Chariot Choogle" without seeming like a fool. Bolan does it with style and grace, and with a wink. It's tremendous fun and the last great record he would ever make. —*Stephen Thomas Erlewine*

○ **Tanx** / Feb. 1973 / Combat 8254
Although the songs are not quite as well constructed as those on *Electric Warrior*, *Tanx* still finds Bolan and T. Rex in top form, storming through a set of songs that kick as hard like "Country Honey," swing like "Mad Donna," and sigh like "Brokenhearted Blues." It's prime T. Rex—a terrific record. —*Stephen Thomas Erlewine*

Essential Collection / 1991 / Combat 1063
T. Rex is worthy of a great box set, but *The Essential Collection* isn't it. Bypassing all of Bolan's earlier folk work, the set has no cohesion—it's just a bunch of tracks, piled together haphazardly. "Jeepster," not "Bang a Gong (Get It On)," is the only track from *Electric Warrior* to make the box, leaving their best record woefully underrepresented; instead, the box concentrates on the spot-

tier records from the mid '70s. Ultimately, *The Essential Collection* does a disservice to T. Rex. —*Stephen Thomas Erlewine*

The Troggs

Group / British invasion, rock & roll
Remembered chiefly as proto-punkers who reached the top of the charts with the "caveman rock" of "Wild Thing" (1966), the Troggs were also adept at crafting power pop and ballads. Hearkening back to a somewhat simpler, more basic British invasion approach as psychedelia began to explode in the late '60s, the group also reached the Top 5 with their flower-power ballad "Love Is All Around" in 1968.

While more popular in their native England than the United States, the band also fashioned memorable, insistently riffing hit singles like "With a Girl Like You," "Night of the Long Grass," and the notoriously salacious "I Can't Control Myself" between 1966 and 1968. Paced by Reg Presley's lusting vocals, the group—which composed most of its own material—could crunch with the best of them, but were also capable of quite a bit more range and melodic invention than they've been given credit for. The hits dried up after 1968, but the group continued to work, record, and produce the odd memorable track well into the '70s. —*Richie Unterberger*

● **Best of the Troggs** / 1988 / PolyGram 512936
"Wild Thing" is the hit, but there's lots of good, raunchy rock here. —*Dan Heilman*

○ **Archeology (1967-1977)** / 1992 / Polydor 512936
A double-CD, 52-track box set that proves there was a lot more to the Troggs than "Wild Thing" and "Love Is All Around." This archetypally primitive British invasion quartet scored many hits in the United Kingdom that barely dented the charts in the United States, like "With a Girl Like You," "Night of the Long Grass," and the notoriously racy "I Can't Control Myself." They're all here, along with notable album cuts, B sides, and worldwide post-1968 flops. Primitive they may have been, but the Troggs—who wrote most of their own material—did not lack a flair for hard pop hooks and could display a surprising delicacy in their ballads. Several of their obscure singles and album tracks are equal in worth to their hits, like the gothic but pretty "Cousin Jane" and the witty light psychedelia of "Maybe The Madman" and "Purple Shades." Some of the '70s hard rockers and glammish novelties are unimpressive, and 52 songs are arguably excessive, but there's a fair number of obscure gems to be found on this well-annotated package. —*Richie Unterberger*

Athens Andover / 1992 / Rhino 71064
Most comebacks albums never work; *Athens Andover* is the rare exception that does. Backed by members of R.E.M. and the dB's, the Troggs make some of their best pop ever, full of ringing guitars and chiming melodies. —*Stephen Thomas Erlewine*

Trouble Funk

Group / Funk, disco
A pioneering early '80s go-go band from the Washington, DC, area, Trouble Funk plays deep, grooving funk; they broke up in the late '80s, after the go-go fad had passed. —*AMG*

● **Drop the Bomb** / 1982 / Sugar Hill
Trouble Funk ushered in the go-go sound, a throbbing mix of heavy funk, rap, and hip-hop. This is their best album, but it's almost impossible to find. —*John Floyd*

Trouble over Here, Trouble over There / 1987 / Island 842711
This Boosty Collins-produced set could use some better songs, but fans will dig it. *Trouble over Here, Trouble over There* includes some vocals by Kurtis Blow. —*John Floyd*

Robin Trower

b. Mar. 9, 1945
Guitar / Blues rock, hard rock
Robin Trower's expressive lead guitar style possessed some of Clapton's lean blues sensibilities while embracing Hendrix's fascination with altered tonalities, sustain, and feedback. His lead work with the late '60s British band Procol Harum distinguished Trower as one of the finest players of that period. He left them in 1973 to pursue a highly successful solo career. During the '70s, Trower's albums were a staple of FM rock playlists. —*Rick Clark*

○ **Twice Removed from Yesterday** / 1973 / Chrysalis 21039
The solo debut by this former Procol Harum guitarist. Moody Hendrix-inspired guitar, plus James Dewar's magnificent whiskey-throated vocals. A classic. —*Michael P. Dawson*

○ **Bridge of Sighs** / 1974 / Chrysalis 21057
Trower's second album is another solid effort. —*Michael P. Dawson*

○ **Live** / 1976 / Chrysalis 21089
A truly fine live set, recorded in Sweden. —*Michael P. Dawson*

Long Misty Days / 1976 / Chrysalis 21107
A good mix of down-and-dirty blues with Trower's ethereal ballads. —*Michael P. Dawson*

○ **No Stopping Anytime** / 1989 / Chrysalis 21704
A compilation from Trower's two collaborations with Cream bassist Jack Bruce. —*Michael P. Dawson*

● **Essential** / 1991 / Chrysalis 21853
A well-chosen compilation. —*Michael P. Dawson*

The Tubes

Group / Pop/rock
A rock group fronted by vocalist Fee Waybill. Taking their cue from Frank Zappa's Mothers of Invention, the Tubes were one of the first to bring performance art (albeit with a satirical edge) to arena rock & roll. By the early '80s they had toned their image down to a more commercial, MTV-acceptable format. —*Cub Koda*

Tubes / 1975 / A&M 3161
The debut album for the Tubes, featuring the anthem "White Punks on Dope." —*Cub Koda*

○ **Young & Rich** / 1976 / A&M 3222
Their breakthrough album and the best representation of the band's early days. —*Cub Koda*

What Do You Want from Life / 1978 / A&M 6003
A great live album, featuring a good sampling from their mind-boggling '70s stage act. —*Cub Koda*

● **Best of the Tubes** / Nov. 9, 1992 / Capitol 98359
The Best of the Tubes is the best Tubes disc available, containing all of their hits and trademark songs. —*AMG*

Maureen Tucker

Vocals, drums / Alternative pop/rock
In the mid '80s, the ex-Velvet Underground drummer turned into a wonderful primitive-pop performer. —*John Dougan*

● **Life in Exile after Abdication** / 1989 / Fifty Scedillion Watts 7
Fantastic! Straightforward, wonderfully succinct songs about life's assorted problems. —*John Dougan*

Ike and Tina Turner

Group / R&B, soul
There was a time when the Ike and Tina Turner Revue was one of the hottest, most durable, and potentially most explosive of all R&B ensembles. Fronted by Tina, with one of the rawest, most sensual, and impossibly dynamic voices in African American music, the Ike and Tina Revue was an ensemble that dripped musical discipline while manifesting nearly unbearable tension, eventually giving way to wave upon wave of catharsis.

Their story is a long and convoluted one. Ike was born in 1931 in Clarksdale, MS; Tina was born Anna Mae Bullock in 1938 in Nutbush, TN. They met in 1959 in East St. Louis, where Ike's Kings of Rhythm were the reigning patriarchs of the local R&B scene. Up to that point, Ike had been a DJ on WROX in Clarksdale, a talent scout and producer for Modern Records (waxing sides for the likes of B. B. King, Rosco Gordon, Elmore James, and Junior Parker), and a recording artist, his Kings of Rhythm appearing in one guise or another on Chess, Modern, King, Cobra, Artistic, and Stevens. Their most famous record, "Rocket 88," appeared under the moniker "Jackie Brenston with his Delta Cats" in 1951. It played an integral part in jump-starting the rock & roll revolution.

Once Tina joined the Kings of Rhythm, life changed for all concerned. They recording a demo of "A Fool in Love" in late 1959; by the autumn of 1960 the record was a #2 R&B hit on Sue Records. "I Idolize You," "It's Gonna Work Out Fine," "Poor Fool," and "Tra La La La La" all quickly followed, giving the Revue five Top 10 R&B hits in two and a half years. All told, from 1960 to

1975 Ike and Tina Turner placed 25 records on the R&B charts for nine separate record companies. Their most successful pop recording was a reworking of Creedence Clearwater Revival's "Proud Mary" in 1971. —*Rob Bowman*

○ **River Deep & Mountain High** / 1966 / A&M 3179
These sessions, recorded in 1966, were produced by Phil Spector. Spector's production chops and Tina's voice were a match made in heaven. Tina possesses one of the strongest voices ever committed to wax; Spector envelops it in the grandest version of his Wall of Sound that he ever conceived. Besides the title track, Spector cut the Turners redoing their first three chart hits, "A Fool in Love," "I Idolize You," and "It's Gonna Work Out Fine." —*Rob Bowman*

Workin' Together / 1970 / Liberty 83455
The most successful album ever issued by Ike and Tina Turner, this contains their best message song in the title selection, plus arguably their best known song in their version of "Proud Mary" and a good cover of "Ooh Poo Pah Doo." Things went plunging downhill from here, as Tina Turner's autobiography vividly detailed years later. —*Ron Wynn*

○ **Nutbush City Limits** / 1973 / United Artists 180
The album that marked the end of the Ike and Tina Turner alliance, though it wasn't their last album. But the turmoil that they were undergoing off stage would soon shatter their personal and professional union. They scored a major hit with the title cut nationally and internationally and also told their life story, though it turned out this tale was a fantasy. Here's one of the few Ike and Tina Turner albums that deserves to be back in print. —*Ron Wynn*

★ **Proud Mary: The Best of Ike & Tina Turner** / Mar. 18, 1991 / EMI America 95846
Proud Mary: The Best of Ike & Tina Turner is a fine 23-track collection that looks at the Turners' career at the beginning and the end. Their early '60s hits on Juggy Murray's Sue label are included, as are their early and mid '70s successes on Liberty and United Artists. The mid and late '60s recordings for Kent, Loma, Modern, Innis, Blue Thumb, and Minit are not here, unfortunately. Superior liner notes round out a fine package. —*Rob Bowman*

Tina Turner (Annie Mae Bullock)

b. Nov. 26, 1938, Nutbush, TN
Vocals / Soul, R&B, pop/rock
The woman who taught the world how to dance in high heels, Tina Turner has never been less than electrifying. Her full-throated rasp, full of low-note rumblings and soulful shrieks, is one of the most distinctive in any field of music, and her overtly sexual stage presence is nothing short of mesmerizing. The early part of her career, with then-husband Ike Turner, has been well documented (see entry for Ike and Tina Turner), but she really hit her stride and found a whole new audience with the coming of the MTV generation, her solo career bringing her the acclaim that had been long overdue. —*Cub Koda*

● **Private Dancer** / 1984 / Capitol 46041
The one that won her a pile of awards, and rightly so, because it's simply her finest solo album. Using a multitude of producers and cut in a variety of locations, *Private Dancer* still sounds amazingly unified. Includes the title cut, "What's Love Got to Do with It," "Let's Stay Together," "Better Be Good to Me," and a blistering Jeff Beck solo on "Steel Claw." —*Cub Koda*

Break Every Rule / 1986 / Capitol 46323
A moderately succesful Tina Turner album, but far from the levels she'd reached with *Private Dancer*. Turner sounded more a comfortable, posturing singer than the dynamic, take-no-stuff vocalist who roared, testified, and strutted through such hits as "What's Love Got to Do With It." "Typical Male" was a good put-down tune, and "Two People" and "What You Get Is What You See" came close to recapturing *Private Dancer's* haughty/sassy mood, but the album was more a restatement than another step foward. —*Ron Wynn*

○ **Simply the Best** / 1991 / Capitol 97152
A solid greatest-hits collection culled from her solo Capitol albums. Includes "Typical Male," "Steamy Windows" (written and produced by Tony Joe White), "I Can't Stand the Rain," and a duet with Rod Stewart on "It Takes Two." —*Cub Koda*

What's Love Got to Do with It / Jun. 15, 1993 / Capitol
This is the soundtrack for the Tina Turner film that got Oscar nominations for Angela Bassett and Laurence Fishburne. There's little here that you couldn't get elsewhere in better versions, but if you only want a hint of the music Tina Turner's made in various contexts with and without Ike, this would be a serviceable purchase. Otherwise, get the film and hear the music in the correct setting. —*Ron Wynn*

The Turtles

Group / Folk rock, pop/rock
The Turtles were a pop-rock quintet from 1963 to 1969, with varying personnel, though always featuring lead singer Howard Kaylan (b. June 22, 1945) and backup/harmony singer Mark Volman (b. April 19, 1944). Other original members were guitarists Al Nichol (b. March 31, 1945) and Jim Tucker and bassist Chuck Portz (b. November 8, 1945). They began life as a surf band called the Crossfires, but by the time of their debut album on White Whale Records, they'd become a folk-rock group singing Bob Dylan songs, including their first hit, "It Ain't Me Babe." More characteristic of their style, however, was the sweet pop hit "You Baby" of 1966. The Turtles topped the charts with "Happy Together" in 1967 and scored several more romantic pop hits before they split up at the end of the '60s, after which Kaylan and Volman hooked up with Frank Zappa in the Mothers, then performed on their own as Flo and Eddie. Today, they continue to perform under that name and as the Turtles. —*William Ruhlmann*

○ **It Ain't Me Babe** / 1965 / White Whale 111
The Turtles' first album presents them as a folk-rock group covering a lot of Dylan and P. F. Sloan material. They also found "It Was a Very Good Year" on a Kingston Trio album and cut it. Frank Sinatra heard their version and had one of his bigger hits with it, but their version is good too. —*William Ruhlmann*

○ **Happy Together** / 1967 / White Whale 114
The Turtles' best studio album includes the title hit, "She'd Rather Be with Me," "Guide for the Married Man," and then-unknown Warren Zevon's "Like the Seasons," among other songs. —*William Ruhlmann*

○ **Turtles' Greatest Hits** / 1982 / Rhino 05160
Fourteen tracks tracing the Turtles' evolution from folk to pop, with some oddities thrown in for fun. —*William Ruhlmann*

● **20 Greatest Hits** / 1983 / Rhino 5160
A witty and underrated band, the Turtles compiled this fine set themselves. —*Dan Heilman*

Dwight Twilley

b. Jun. 6, 1951
Vocals, keyboard / Power pop
Dwight Twilley fused rockabilly, mid '60s Anglo-pop, and Byrdsy jangle into a distinctly reverberant sound. In 1976 Twilley and his partner, Phil Seymour, released the exceptional Anglo-rockabilly hit "I'm on Fire" on Denny Cordell's Shelter label. Unfortunately, Shelter's lack of organization delayed the release of Twilley's debut album, *Sincerely*, by over a year. In spite of glowing reviews concerning the album's rich melodicism and sparkling production, *Sincerely* sank without a trace.
After the followup, *Twilley Don't Mind*, Twilley jumped ship for Arista, releasing a self-titled album. In spite of some brilliant power pop ("Alone in My Room," "It Takes a Lotta Love"), problems arose at the label, and Twilley jumped again to EMI, releasing *Scuba Divers*. It was on his next album that he scored his next hit, "Girls." —*Rick Clark*

● **Sincerely** / 1976 / DCC
From the opening Anglo-pop/rock-meets-rockabilly blast of Top 20 hit single "I'm on Fire," through breezy jangle-rock numbers like "You're So Warm," "Just Like the Sun," and "England," to the dirge-like psychedelia of the title song, *Sincerely* is Twilley's finest album. It's a must-own for fans of guitar pop/rock. The CD includes four bonus tracks. —*Rick Clark*

Twilley Don't Mind / 1977 / Dcc 8002
Twilley drops the ball slightly on this second album, in spite of good tracks like "Looking for the Magic," "Here She Come," "Sleeping," and the title cut. —*Rick Clark*

○ **Twilley** / 1979 / Arista 4214

This self-titled third album rivals Twilley's debut as best album with super tracks like "Alone in My Room," "It Takes a Lot of Love," "Darlin'," and "I Want to Make Love to You." As of this printing, this fine pop/rock album has yet to see a CD release. If you like Twilley's other albums, then this is worth the search. — *Rick Clark*

Great Lost Twilley Album / Apr. 1993 / Shelter 8020
This collection of unreleased tracks from 1974 to 1980 will please fans. Good songs, but the uninitiated should go to the first or third albums. —*Rick Clark*

Bonnie Tyler (Gaynor Hopkins)

b. Jun. 8, 1953, Swansea, Wales
Vocals / Pop/rock

Welsh female singer Bonnie Tyler (born Gaynor Hopkins) was touted as the female Rod Stewart when she arrived on the charts with her 1978 international hit "It's a Heartache." Her raspy delivery was brought about by a 1976 operation to remove throat nodules. In 1983, Tyler scored a #1 hit with the overwrought Jim Steinman-penned hit "Total Eclipse of the Heart." Since then, little has been heard from Tyler, save a few moderate hits between 1984 and 1986. —*Rick Clark*

● **Faster than the Speed of Night** / 1983 / Columbia 38710
Gutsy rock and Top 40 cuts in her rasp of a voice. —*Bil Carpenter*

U2

Group / Alternative pop/rock

In 1976, four Dublin schoolboys started the band that, under the name U2, would dominate rock music in the late '80s. Consisting of lead singer Bono (born Paul Hewson, May 10, 1960), guitarist the Edge (born David Evans, August 8, 1961), bassist Adam Clayton (b. March 13, 1960), and percussionist Larry Mullen, Jr. (b. October 31, 1961), U2 has helped to open up the doors for many other Irish bands.

U2 started out as a Dublin pub band and began earning recognition after the band won a talent contest sponsored by Guinness in 1979. This led to the Irish release of a three-track EP, *U2-3*, that topped the charts in Ireland and won them quite a following. They were signed by the Island label in 1980 and released their debut album, *Boy*, later that year. Unfortunately, *Boy* and the band's 1981 followup, *October*, did not gain much recognition outside of Ireland (where the band was playing soldout concerts). It was not until the 1983 release of the critically acclaimed album *War* that U2 began to get a taste of success. *War* was the band's major breakthrough in the United States, going platinum, although the first two albums had never made it into the Top 40. *Under a Blood Red Sky*, a live concert album from the *War* tour, was released in 1983, followed by *The Unforgettable Fire* in 1984; both went platinum in the States as well.

With the release of *The Joshua Tree* (1987), U2 became one of the world's leading rock bands. Entering at #1 on the UK charts, *The Joshua Tree* went platinum within 48 hours. The album also spent nine weeks at #1 on the U.S. charts, and "With or Without You" became the band's first #1 single in America, followed by "I Still Haven't Found What I'm Looking For." As the new rock sensation, U2 appeared on the covers of *Time, Musician,* and *Rolling Stone* and won two awards at the 1988 Grammy Awards, including Album of the Year. In 1988 the band went on to release a full-length concert film, *Rattle and Hum*, and an album of the same name.

Achtung Baby, released in late 1991, proved to be quite a departure from their previous work. Darker and more atmospheric than their other albums, it not only proved to be only successful commercially and artistically but also preserved their image of being on the cutting edge. After the release of *Achtung Baby*, U2 embarked on a major world tour, called *Zoo TV*, that featured state-of-the-art video images. During the tour, they recorded *Zooropa*, which was released in 1993; it was even more experimental and darker than their previous album. Naturally, it was a worldwide hit, even if it didn't have any hit singles as big as "One" or "Mysterious Ways."

U2 could arguably be called the greatest rock band of the '80s. Out of sheer determination (or cockiness), they have avoided the musical ruts that stardom can produce and have gone out of their way to experiment with new sounds and musical ideas. It is this musical growth and exploration that make U2 a great band. — *Iotis Erlewine*

○ **Boy** / 1980 / Island 842296
The inexperience of the band, not yet at its musical peak, is compensated for by its raw power. The songs on *Boy* are full of teen angst and rebellion, a result of the influence of punk bands like the Virgin Prunes. In spite of the roughness of this album, its simplicity and directness are very appealing. Including "I Will Follow" and "Out of Control," this album is a good example of U2's early work; so far, the band has been unable to match the sheer energy of *Boy*. —*Iotis Erlewine*

October / 1981 / Island 842297
U2's second album lost a lot of the fire and momentum that was in *Boy*. The band is better musically on this album, but it lacks spontaneity and seems a little too rehearsed. *October* incorporates Christian religious symbolism, apparent in songs like "Gloria" and "Rejoice." The album has some great songs (such as the minor UK hit "Gloria" and the melancholy "Tomorrow") but as a whole is a rather weak followup. —*Iotis Erlewine*

☆ **War** / 1983 / Island 811148
This album was a major turning point for U2- the band went from being a minor Irish band to being a world-renowned rock group. *War* retains some of the anger that is found on *Boy*, but it is more subtle and mature. This album features some of U2's best-known songs—"New Year's Day," "Sunday Bloody Sunday," "Seconds," and "Two Hearts Beat as One." In spite of all the protest, aggression, and outrage in these songs, the album ends with the optimistic "40," a song that sets the uplifting words of Psalm 40 to music. With such spectacular songs and emotion, *War* is a must for any fan of rock music. —*Iotis Erlewine*

○ **Under a Blood Red Sky** / 1983 / Island 818008
This is a great concert album from U2's *War* tour, most of which was recorded during their concert at the Red Rocks Festival in Colorado. The album includes "11 O'Clock Tick Tock" and "Party Girl" (which previously were available only as singles) and intense performances of "New Year's Day" and "Sunday Bloody Sunday." *Under a Blood Red Sky* captures some of the power and charisma that make U2 such a great live band. —*Iotis Erlewine*

Unforgettable Fire / 1984 / Island 822898
After *War*, this was U2's second #1 album in the United Kingdom (#12 in the United States), and it features two of the band's better-known songs, "Pride" and "Bad." Ironically, even in spite of its relative success, this remains one of U2's "forgotten" albums. The quality of the songs may play a part in this—either the songs are outstanding, or they are not even worth mentioning. It is this kind of inconsistency that causes this album to be so frequently overlooked. —*Iotis Erlewine*

Wide Awake in America / 1985 / Island 842479
This is a four-song EP that includes excellent live versions of "A Sort of a Homecoming" and "Bad," plus two largely forgettable songs, "Three Sunrises" and "Love Come Tumbling," that had previously only been released on singles. Unless you have to own the complete U2 collection, this album is not a necessity. —*Iotis Erlewine*

★ **Joshua Tree** / 1987 / Island 842298
Joshua Tree is the album that won the United States (and the rest of the world) over. Before this release, the band had met with considerable success, but nothing like what was to follow *Joshua Tree*. This album moved away from the loud anger of *War* and focused on a more subtle, refined sound. The wistful, searching quality of this album captures U2 at a transition, as the band attempt to rediscover themselves. Including such songs as "With or without You," "I Still Haven't Found What I'm Looking For," "Where the Streets Have No Name," "In God's Country," and "Running to Stand Still," this album is among U2's best works. — *Iotis Erlewine*

Rattle & Hum / 1988 / Island 842299
U2's ego manifests itself. Billed as U2's "exploration of America," this album was a grave disappointment. There are, however, some excellent tracks, such as "When Love Comes to Town" (featuring B. B. King), "All I Want Is You," "Desire," and "Angel of Harlem." —*Iotis Erlewine*

☆ **Achtung Baby** / 1991 / Island 510347
This album was a big change in style for U2. On this album, the group drops some of the pretentiousness of the last few albums

and stops taking itself so seriously, and the result is very impressive. Although some of the lyrics are downright laughable, *Achtung Baby* is more direct and honest than some of the previous, preachier albums. Promoted as U2's "dark, trashy" album, this is, as far as I'm concerned, the most sophisticated work the band has yet created. The songs on this album (like the powerful "One" and "Love Is Blindness") revolve around human emotion instead of politics. *Achtung Baby* may be a shock the first time you hear it, but the more you listen, the better it gets. —*Iotis Erlewine*

○ **Zooropa** / May 1993 / Island 518047
After their successful artistic renewal with 1991's *Achtung Baby*, U2 mounted a staggering world tour filled with glitz, empty slogans, mammoth TV screens, and stunning music. Originally intended as an EP, *Zooropa* was recorded in a short break in their European Zoo TV tour. Instead of being a pure piece of product, *Zooropa* is a complex album that takes the sonic experimentations of *Achtung Baby* even further—listen to the grinding "Numb" or "Lemon" for proof. Some of the songwriting isn't as fully developed as it could have been, but the album creates a terrific claustrophobic atmosphere that comes to an incredible close with "The Wanderer," where Johnny Cash's lead vocal sounds completely natural among the ominous synthesizers. —*Stephen Thomas Erlewine*

UB40

Group / Reggae, pop/rock
Along with the 2-Tone groups that emerged during the late '70s ska revival that dominated the British charts, UB40 managed to insinuate their own personality into the conservative genre of reggae. Mixing leftist politics with pop-based melodies, the band scored many hits in England, but it was "Red Red Wine," a song recorded by the band in 1984 but rereleased in 1988, that broke them in America.

After "Red Red Wine," the band began to hit the charts frequently with their smooth, reggae-tinged versions of classic oldies like "Way You Do the Things You Do" and "I Can't Help Falling in Love." In the process, the band became less politicized and lost the spark that had distinguished their early albums. —*John Floyd*

Best of UB40 (1980-1983) / 1983 / A&M 4955
This U.S. compilation gathers the best of the early days of the United Kingdom's top White reggae band, displaying their love of dub and some of their best songs of the period, such as the caustic "One in Ten." —*William Ruhlmann*

● **Labour of Love** / 1983 / A&M 4980
Long stars in England, UB40 finally found Stateside success (and that belatedly) by recording an album of their favorite Jamaican cover tunes. One of these, "Red Red Wine," finally took off in the United States in 1988 and went to #1. —*William Ruhlmann*

Little Baggaridim / 1985 / A&M 5090
UB40 actually got their first U.S. hit with a cover of Sonny and Cher's "I Got You Babe," set to a reggae beat and sung with the Pretenders's Chrissie Hynde, heard on this min-album. —*William Ruhlmann*

Labour of Love II / 1989 / Virgin 91324
UB40 repeats their formula for even more success, with reggae versions of "Here I Am (Come and Take Me)" and "The Way You Do the Things You Do." —*William Ruhlmann*

Promises and Lies / 1993 / Virgin
Carried by the hit "I Can't Help Falling in Love with You," *Promises and Lies* finishes UB40's transition from a reggae band to an adult-contemporary band that plays reggae-pop. Fans of the single will be satisfied by *Promises and Lies*, but older fans will find the whole affair rather disenheartening—there's not much reggae here. —*Stephen Thomas Erlewine*

UFO

Group / Heavy metal, hard rock
During the '70s, UFO was one of the most popular heavy metal bands in the world, thanks in no small part to the blistering guitar work of Michael Schenker. After recording several best-selling albums, Schenker quit in 1978 to join the Scorpions. With his departure, UFO lost their personality; working through several lineup changes, they continued to record right into the '90s, churning out faceless arena rock. It was a far cry from when their metallic riffs were a sure thing for teenagers across the world. —*Stephen Thomas Erlewine*

● **Essential UFO** / 1992 / Chrysalis 21888
UFO's best tracks, compiled on one smartly assembled single-disc collection. —*Stephen Thomas Erlewine*

U.K.

Group / Progressive rock
A progressive rock band featuring John Wetton, Allan Holdsworth, Bill Bruford, and Eddie Jobson. Bill Bruford was later replaced by drummer Terry Bozzio. —*Paul Kohler*

● **U K** / 1978 / EG 35
An impressive debut album featuring Allan Holdsworth, John Wetton, Bill Bruford, and Eddie Jobson. —*Paul Kohler*

Danger Money / 1979 / EG 39
Followup album, with Terry Bozzio taking over the drumming. Exceptional synth work by Eddie Jobson and bass and vocals from John Wetton. —*Paul Kohler*

Night after Night / 1979 / EG 42
A live album with the *Danger Money* lineup and songs from both studio recordings. A great show! —*Paul Kohler*

Tracey Ullman

Vocals / Pop/rock
Before she became a famous TV comedian, Tracy Ullman recorded two albums in the early '80s that effortlessly recalled the classic girl group sound of the '60s. Ullman covered everything from Doris Day ("Move Over Darling") to Blondie ("[I'm Always Touched by Your] Presence, Dear"), finding the underlying conncections between classic pop songs of all eras. *You Broke My Heart in 17 Places*, her debut album, was a hit in the United Kingdom, and she even managed to have a Top 10 hit in America with a version of Kirsty MacColl's "They Don't Know." Although it had some fine numbers, the followup, *You Caught Me Out*, wasn't as successful, prompting Ullman to return to television. By the end of the '80s, her comedy show, "The Tracy Ullman Show," was one of the most critically acclaimed television shows in America; she hasn't recorded any music since. —*Stephen Thomas Erlewine*

○ **You Broke My Heart in 17 Places** / 1983 / Stiff 51
Ullman's first album, recorded in the middle of the new wave and synth-pop movements, provided a refreshing break with its retro girl-group sound. Includes her only U.S. hit, "They Don't Know" (written by Kirsty MacColl), as well as carefully chosen obscure oldies. One of the great lost classics. —*Chris Woodstra*

● **Best of Tracey Ullman** / 1991 / Rhino 70292
This 20-track compilation provides an extensive look at the nearly forgotten singing career of this now famous actress. Combining the entire first LP, *You Broke My Heart in 17 Places*, the highlights from her second effort *You Caught Me Out*, and well chosen B sides, it more than lives up to its name. Although this material was recorded in the early '80s, lovers of the classic '60s-girl-group sound will find these retro-gems a familiar delight. —*Chris Woodstra*

Ultra Vivid Scene

Alternative pop/rock
Ultra Vivid Scene is a one-man project for Kurt Ralske, a Berklee School of Music dropout. With UVS, he creates lush, detailed soundscapes that have a dark undercurrent buried deep beneath the layers of sound and melody. Since 1988, he has recorded a series of critically acclaimed albums that manage to be highly artistic and experimental, without ever losing their accessibility. —*Stephen Thomas Erlewine*

● **Joy 1967-90** / 1990 / 4AD 46227
Joy 1967-90 is Ultra Vivid Scene's most accomplished, pop-oriented record. —*David Jehnzen*

Ultravox

Group / New wave, pop/rock
Ultravox (or Ultravox!—as it was called at first) had two separate identities and styles of music during its existence. Formed in London in 1974, it was originally intended as a platform for singer John Foxx (born Dennis Leigh) and included guitarist Stevie Shears, keyboardist and violinist Billy Currie, bassist Chris Cross, and drummer Warren Cann. With this lineup, the group

recorded its debut album, *Ultravox!* (1977), produced by Brian Eno and Steve Lillywhite during the height of the punk/new wave movement. A second album, *Ha! Ha! Ha!* (1977), was released only in the United Kingdom. A third, *Systems of Romance* (1978), marked the last appearance of Foxx, who went solo, and of guitarist Robin Simon, who had replaced Shears. The remaining trio enlisted singer/guitarist Midge Ure, formerly of the teenybop band ilk, and recorded *Vienna* (1980), which marked a sharp turn toward synthesizer pop and helped give birth to the British "new romantic" movement of the early '80s. The album was Ultravox's first to chart; the title track went to #2, and "All Stood Still" reached the Top 10. There followed a series of successful albums in the United Kingdom: *Rage in Eden* (1981), *Quartet* (1982), *Monument: The Soundtrack* (1983), *Lament* (1984), and *U-Vox* (1986). *The Collection* (1984) was a hits album. Of these, only *Quartet* made any significant inroads in the United States. Ultravox split in mid 1987, when Ure decided to turn his full attention to his solo career. —*William Ruhlmann*

○ **Ultravox** / 1976 / Island 9449
John Foxx proves to have an odd, Bowie-influenced vision, here aided and abetted by Brian Eno (then a Bowie crony) and Steve Lillywhite. "My Sex" and "I Want to Be a Machine" are standouts. —*William Ruhlmann*

Vienna / 1980 / Chrysalis 21296
The new Ultravox, under Midge Ure, has a dreamy, ethereal sound heard at its best on its debut album, which features the title song, "All Stood Still," "Passing Strangers," and "Sleepwalk," all UK hits. —*William Ruhlmann*

Three into One / 1980 / Antilles 7079
A compilation of Ultravox's three albums with John Foxx. —*William Ruhlmann*

● **Collection** / 1984 / Chrysalis 21490
Ultravox's UK hit singles during the Midge Ure era. —*William Ruhlmann*

Uncle Tupelo

Group / Alternative rock, country rock
Uncle Tupelo's skillful updating of country and folk for the post-punk era made the band one of the best of the early '90s. Beginning with their first independent record in 1990, the band played direct, hardcore country, injecting it with the loud fervor of punk. Over the course of four albums, the overt punk elements of their music became less dominant, as the group's fascination with country came to the forefront. By the time of their major-label debut in 1993, Uncle Tupelo had developed a familiar, yet distinct, sound that had traces of the Flying Burrito Brothers, Neil Young, and Hank Williams; their music was based in tradition, yet it didn't sound nostalgic—their conviction and passion made it sound vital and contemporary. Unfortunately, the band broke up the following year; the group's two songwriters—Jar Farrar and Jeff Tweedy—each had formed new bands by the end of the year. —*Stephen Thomas Erlewine*

○ **March 16-20, 1992** / 1992 / Gasatanka 6090
A remarkably accomplished set of contemporary country rock. —*Stephen Thomas Erlewine*

● **Anodyne** / May 1993 / Sire 45424
Uncle Tupelo's other albums are impressive, but their final record, *Anodyne,* is a brilliant reinterpretation of traditional country, folk, and country rock. Filled with excellent songs, it sounds both contemporary and timeless. —*Stephen Thomas Erlewine*

Undertones

Group / Punk, new wave
With their 1978 debut, "Teenage Kicks," this Irish quintet blended the wail of the Sex Pistols with the pop sensibilities of the Ramones. Although the group, led by vocalist Feargal Sharkey and John O'neill, released four fine albums between 1978 and 1983, they were at their best on singles. —*John Floyd*

● **Teenage Kicks** / 1978 / Rykodisc 4
The Undertones' first album remains their best, filled with rough, melodic punk-pop gems. —*Stephen Thomas Erlewine*

Unrest

Group / Alternative pop/rock

Although they formed during the prime days of the Washington, DC, hardcore scene in the early '80s, Unrest was never quite part of that movement. Their early records were filled with aching pop and jagged rock, covered with shards of noisy guitar. During the late '80s they gained a small but devoted cult following by releasing several acclaimed independent albums. By 1992's *Imperial f.f.r.r.,* the guitars weren't as jarring; Unrest had created a shimmering, stripped-down melodic pop that shined with joyful experimenation. Unrest seemed primed for alternative pop superstar status when they released their major-label debut, *Perfect Teeth,* in 1993. It was one of their finest records and received favorable reviews, but the band decided to break up several months after its release; their leader, Mark Robinson, immediately went to work on several projects, including his second band, Grenadine. —*Stephen Thomas Erlewine*

● **Imperial F.f.r.r.** / Jul. 14, 1992 / Number Six 018
Alternating between minimalistic pop and noisy guitar explorations, *Imperial F.f.r.r.* is a wonderfully inventive and surprisingly accessible record. —*Stephen Thomas Erlewine*

○ **Isabel Bishop** / 1993 / Warner Brothers 45271
Featuring the wonderful, charming pure pop of the title track, *Isabel Bishop* is a fine EP that showcases Unrest's pop sensibilities as well as their experimental tendencies. —*Stephen Thomas Erlewine*

● **Perfect Teeth** / 1993 / 4AD
Perfect Teeth, Unrest's major-label debut, is their finest album yet, full of shimmering left-of-center pop songs. All of the instruments function as one, providing a distinctive, instantly recognizable sound that serves their full yet spare melodic tales of love and alienation exceedingly well. Not many bands could deliver "Make-Out Club," "Six-Layer Cake," and "West Coast Love Affair" so directly, with humility, humor, and affection. With each play, the hooks on *Perfect Teeth* become more memorable. —*Stephen Thomas Erlewine*

Urge Overkill

Group / Alternative rock, rock & roll
Unlike most alternative rock bands, Urge Overkill set out to be rock stars. They found an image—stylish, hip swingers with impeccable taste in fashion, music, and women—and made music that suited that persona. Picking up their Les Pauls and turning up their Marshall stacks, Urge Overkill made rock & roll that was full of instantly memorable choruses, guitar solos, loud and catchy guitars, and a powerful backbeat; in short, music that *rocked.* Of course, it took them a couple of albums before they got that good. Initially, they were another Steve Albini-produced, buzzing guitar band from Chicago. With their second album, *Americruiser,* they began to write actual songs. By 1991's *Supersonic Storybook* album, the band's lineup was set in stone—Nash Kato on guitar and vocals; "Eddie" King Roeser on bass, guitar, and vocals; and drummer Blackie Onassis—and Urge released their first consistent album; it had stadium-sized riffs played with punkish aggression. Before they made the jump to the major labels, they released their most varied and diverse recording, the *Stull* EP. And with 1993's *Saturation,* Urge finally perfected the glamorous, powerful rock & roll that they always wanted to record. While it didn't make them the superstars they wanted to be, it sold well and had a minor hit with "Sister Havana." —*Stephen Thomas Erlewine*

Americruiser/Jesus Urge Superstar / 1990 / Touch & Go 52
Urge's first two albums were recorded at a time when their vision eclipsed their talent; while there's a lot of good indie-guitar bluster here, there's not that many memorable songs. With its flat, Steve Albini-production, *Jesus Urge Superstar* is the weaker of the records. *Americruiser,* with production courtesy of Butch Vig, not only has a fuller sound, it also has some real songs. "Ticket to L.A." is a classic rocker, with a locomotive riff and great lyrics. It was a sign of things to come. (The CD also includes their gonzo cover of Jimmy Webb's "Wichitaw Lineman.") —*Stephen Thomas Erlewine*

○ **Supersonic Storybook** / 1991 / Touch & Go 70
With the addition of drummer Blackie Onassis, Urge Overkill shapes up into a killer rock & roll combo. It also doesn't hurt that the songs are the finest they have written to date. Although the production is a little flat, there's no denying the force of the best tracks. "The Candidate" boasts a huge, stadium-size riff, "The Kids

Are Insane" is a frenzied, frenetic rocker, "Today Is Blackie's Birthday" is gleefully stupid, and the band is surprisingly sexy on the old Hot Chocolate song "Emmaline." Things bog down a bit on the second side, but Urge are starting to sound like the rock stars they always knew they were. —*Stephen Thomas Erlewine*

○ **Stull Ep** / 1992 / Touch & Go 86
It's not the full-throttle rock masterpiece that *Supersonic Storybook* suggested, but the *Stull EP* is quite remarkable. Opening with a straight cover of Neil Diamond's "Girl, You'll Be a Woman Soon" (which fits Urge Overkill's image perfectly), the EP is an atomospheric guitar workout. While "Stitches" is a salute to their punk roots, the most impressive moments come during the stylish kiss-off to indie-rock, "Goodbye to Guyville" and "Stull," with its sly, laid-back groove. As the richness of *Stull* proves, Urge's vision was too large for the band to remain on an independent record label. —*Stephen Thomas Erlewine*

● **Saturation** / Jun. 8, 1993 / Geffen 24529
When they hit the major labels, Urge Overkill followed through on their promise with the blistering *Saturation.* It's stadium rock by clever post-punkers who are smart enough to not let their carefully crafted image interfere with the music. Every one of the 12 songs is a killer, from the outlandish menace of "Stalker" to the moving ballad "Back on Me," as well as the tongue-in-cheek "Woman 2 Woman" and the radio hit "Sister Havana." —*Stephen Thomas Erlewine*

King Uszniewicz & His Uszniewicztones

Group / Rock & roll
A hilariously inept Detroit bowling-alley/lounge band fronted by Ernie "King" Uszniewicz (b. 1945) from 1969 to 1979. The crudest tenor saxophonist in the history of rock & roll, King Uszneiewicz (pronounced "you-snev-vitch") & the U-Tones had only one single, issued on a local label during the '70s. Dubbed by one critic as "the worst oldies band I ever heard in my life," they played with a bludgeoning energy, oblivious to the fact that they were woefully shy in the talent department. However, when the group's first album showed up on several college-radio playlists in 1989, they earned a minor cult following among both record collectors and collegiate alternative-music fans. —*Stephen Thomas Erlewine*

Teenage Dance Party / Norton 208
Their first album, featuring both sides of their original and lone 45 ("Surfin' School"/"Cry on My Shoulder") and insane versions of "Papa Ooh Mow Mow," "Little Latin Lupe Lu," and "This Should Go on Forever." Raw, crude, tuneless, and wonderful. —*Stephen Thomas Erlewine*

● **Twistin' and Bowlin'** / Norton 221
Subtitled "just when you thought it was safe to go back into the bowling alley" and more than living up to all that implies. Drunken, out-of-control versions of "Way Down Yonder in New Orleans," "Peppermint Twist," and Johnny Mathis's "Chances Are" are among the numerous highlights. Scary. —*Stephen Thomas Erlewine*

○ **Doin' the Woo-Hoo** / Norton 239
More oldies-band mayhem. "At the Hop," "G.T.O.," "Love Letters in the Sand," the title cut, and King Uszniewicz's wife, Arlene, belting out "It's My Party" are just a few of the standout tracks. Extremely potent stuff. —*Stephen Thomas Erlewine*

Utopia

Group / Progressive rock, pop/rock
Utopia is a rock quartet that theoretically features equal participation by its members, although singer and guitarist Todd Rundgren (b. June 22, 1948), who formed the band, is a recognized solo star and frequently dominates the group. The first two albums found them billed as Todd Rundgren's Utopia, a six-piece unit. But as of the third album, *Ra,* Utopia was a four-piece unit, including Rundgren, Roger Powell, John Wilcox, and Kasim Sulton, and that lineup was still in place as of 1986, which is the last time they released new material. —*William Ruhlmann*

Deface the Music / 1980 / Rhino 70873
This album ranks up there with the Rutles as a pastiche/parody of the Beatles, presenting a series of original songs in the evolving '60s styles of the Fab Four, from Merseybeat to *Sgt. Pepper* psychedelia. —*William Ruhlmann*

● **Anthology (1974-1985)** / 1989 / Rhino 70892
Some of Todd Rundgren's best pop-rock material is found among the 16 tracks of this well-chosen compilation, including the Top 30 hit "Set Me Free." —*William Ruhlmann*

Steve Vai

Guitar / Hard rock, fusion
A former "stunt guitarist" for Frank Zappa and student of Joe Satriani, Steve Vai has gained exposure with the bands he has played with in the past (Alcatrazz, David Lee Roth, Whitesnake), as well as for his flashy, technically advanced guitar style. —*John Book*

○ **Flex-able** / 1984 / Akashic 777
Self-released solo album from this former Zappa guitarist, featuring Zappa-influenced vocals. Recorded by Vai at home on an eight-track machine. The CD offers extra material from the *Flex-able* sessions originally released as a 10-inch EP. —*Paul Kohler*

● **Passion & Warfare** / Sep. 1990 / Combat 1037
One of the most creative, musical, and mystical guitar albums ever made. Truly a musical genius. A must-have. —*Paul Kohler*

Ritchie Valens

b. May 13, 1941, **d.** Feb. 3, 1959
Vocals, guitar / Rock & roll
A singer/guitarist of mixed Mexican-American and Native American descent, Valens was the first Hispanic rocker of any consequence. During an effective career of barely a year (until to his death in the same plane crash that killed Buddy Holly in 1959), Valens emerged with a basic high-energy rock sound that, at its most raucous, became an influence on performers up through the Kinks and Jonathan Richman. He delivered two classic songs, "Donna" and "La Bamba." —*Bruce Eder*

In Concert at Pacioma Jr. High / 1960 / Rhino 70233
A bizarre piece of work: a homemade tape of a high school concert. Possibly rock's earliest "official" live album, padded with narration and unfinished studio tracks. In shaky sound, but unique. —*Bruce Eder*

● **Best of Ritchie Valens** / 1986 / Rhino 70178
The virtually complete recording legacy of an all-too-brief career. —*Bruce Eder*

Ritchie Valens Story / Jun. 15, 1993 / Rhino 71414
While this compilation features the official versions of Ritchie's three biggest songs ("La Bamba," "Donna," and "Come On, Let's Go"), the bulk of it is turned over to recently unearthed rehearsal takes and demos of his better known sides. Not the place to start your Valens collection, but a real good place to go after you've absorbed the hits. —*Cub Koda*

Frankie Valli & the Four Seasons

b. May 3, 1937, Newark, NJ
Group / Pop/rock
The Four Seasons were the most successful male vocal group of the rock era. Although the personnel have changed through the years (especially after the '60s), the group has nearly always been a platform for the singing of Frankie Valli (b. May 3, 1937). It was formed in Newark, NJ, in 1956, first as the Variatones and then as the Four Lovers, and featured Valli, brothers Tommy and Nick DeVito, and Hank Majewski. Under that name and with that lineup, they scored their first, minor hit, "You're the Apple of My Eye."

Over the next five years, the Four Lovers became the Four Seasons, songwriter Bob Gaudio replaced Nick DeVito, Nick Massi replaced Hank Majewski, and the group began working with producer Bob Crewe. With this team—Valli singing lead, Gaudio and Crewe writing songs, and Crewe producing, plus Charlie Callelo arranging—the Four Seasons launched a series of teen-oriented hits in 1962 with the chart-topper "Sherry." The hits continued long into the Beatles era, totaling 13 Top 10s among 34 chart entries by the end of 1967. Valli also launched a solo career and had his own hits.

After more personnel changes, the group's career seemed to take a backseat to Valli's in the early '70s, though they came back in a multiple-lead-singer format for another series of hits in the mid '70s. —*William Ruhlmann*

○ **25th Anniversary** / 1987 / Rhino 72998

Frankie Valli and the Four Seasons scored hits from 1962 to 1978 under a variety of guises. Lead singer Valli started making solo records in 1965, and he had his own hits. They are all included in this long-overdue four-disc set, which runs from the Seasons's "Sherry" to Valli's "Grease." — *William Ruhlmann*

Four Seasons Sing Big Hits by Burt Bacharach...Hal David...Bob Dylan / Jul. 20, 1988 / Rhino 70248
How Bacharach/David and Bob Dylan ended up the subject of the same album is anyone's guess, but Valli and the boys pull it off with panache. — *Jeff Tamarkin*

★ **Anthology** / 1989 / Rhino 71490
Over the course of 20 tracks, *Anthology* covers all of the Four Seasons' essential hits, as well as Valli's solo "Can't Take My Eyes Off You"; it's the definitive collection. — *Stephen Thomas Erlewine*

Van Der Graaf Generator

Group / Art rock
An art-rock group principally centered around keyboardist, composer, and vocalist Peter Joseph Andrew Hammill (b. 1948). With floating personnel, which changed from record to record, and "sound paintings" that varied from heavyhanded to somber, Van Der Graaf Generator was cited by British punk bands as a seminal influence. Hammill continued to release solo albums in a similar vein throughout the '80s. — *Cub Koda*

Least We Can Do Is Wave / Feb. 1969 / Blue Plate 1826
Their ambitious second album. Bandleader Peter Hammill was already writing enduring songs. — *Michael P. Dawson*

● **H to He, Who Am the Only One** / Jan. 1970 / Blue Plate 1638
A superb album, which includes the heavy metalish "Killer" and a guest appearance by guitarist Robert Fripp. — *Michael P. Dawson*

○ **Pawn Hearts** / 1971 / Blue Plate 1639
Lengthy prog-rock epics with Peter Hammill's intensely emotional lyrics. Robert Fripp guests on guitar. — *Michael P. Dawson*

○ **Still Life** / 1976 / Blue Plate 1641
The second and best of the mid '70s comeback albums, highlighted by the incredible title track. Brilliant. — *Michael P. Dawson*

Van Halen

Group / Heavy metal, hard rock
Van Halen was one of the most popular American hard-rock/heavy metal bands to emerge in the '70s, primarily distinguished by the fleet fingers of guitarist Eddie Van Halen. Actually, Eddie and his brother Alex, who played the drums, were born in the Netherlands, though they moved to California as children, as did bassist Michael Anthony and singer David Lee Roth. They formed the group in Pasadena in 1974 and worked their way up the Southern California club circuit, signing with Warner Brothers in 1977. Their debut album, *Van Halen*, released in 1978, went gold in three months, platinum in eight. Every album since has sold at least a million copies.

The group hit a popular peak in 1984 with *1984*, which sold four million copies in its first year of release, and its #1 single, "Jump," after which Roth left the band for a solo career. He was replaced by Sammy Hagar, and the success has continued, with three successive chart-topping albums to date. — *William Ruhlmann*

★ **Van Halen** / 1978 / Warner Brothers 3075
The prototype: Eddie Van Halen proves the hand is quicker than the ear, while David Lee Roth plays the role of outrageous frontman to perfection. Includes "You Really Got Me" and "Runnin' with the Devil." — *William Ruhlmann*

☆ **1984** / 1984 / Warner Brothers 23985
Adding synthesizers to the mix, Van Halen turned pop while retaining much of its hard-rock propulsion, resulting in a quantum leap in sales. Includes "Jump," "I'll Wait," "Panama," and "Hot for Teacher." — *William Ruhlmann*

5150 / 1986 / Warner Brothers 25394
Van Halen proves it can survive in the post-Roth era, as Eddie continues to burn up the fretboard, and Sammy Hagar turns out to fit into the group's style just fine. Includes "Why Can't This Be Love," "Dreams," and "Love Walks In." — *William Ruhlmann*

Luther Vandross

b. 1951
Vocals / Soul, urban R&B
In R&B music, Luther Vandross ranked with Prince, Stevie Wonder, and Michael Jackson as one of the most successful singer-songwriters and producers of the '80s. Amazingly, unlike those peers, Vandross for the most part did not cross over to widespread pop appeal, a situation that finally began to change at the end of the '80s and the start of the '90s. Born in New York City, Vandross has an elastic tenor that made him a natural for backup singing and commercial work in the '70s, when he became a top session vocalist. In 1975 Vandross worked with David Bowie on the latter's *Young Americans* album, even cowriting (with Bowie and John Lennon) the #1 hit "Fame." In the second half of the '70s, he recorded under a variety of guises, cutting two albums for Cotillion under the name "Luther," recording with the session groups Roundtree and Change, and singing on hits by Chic.

In 1981 Vandross signed with Epic and released his debut album *Never Too Much*, which topped the R&B chart and sold a million copies. The title track was also an R&B #1 single and reached the pop Top 40. Vandross went on to produce albums for Aretha Franklin and other female singers, while maintaining his own career through the '80s. His albums *Forever, for Always, for Love* (1982), *Busy Body* (1983), *The Night I Fell in Love* (1985), *Give Me the Reason* (1986), and *Any Love* (1988) were all million-sellers that spawned major R&B hits, but Vandross's pop success was spotty until 1989, when Epic released *The Best of Luther Vandross ... The Best of Love*, a double-pocket greatest-hits album containing the new track "Here and Now," which became Vandross's first Top 10 pop hit. That proved his breakthrough, and Vandross's next album, *Power of Love* (1991), another million-seller, featured two pop hits, "Power of Love/Love Power" and "Don't Want to Be a Fool." Vandross released *Never Let Me Go* in 1993, and while it did well, it wasn't quite the commercial powerhouse of his past releases. — *William Ruhlmann*

○ **Never Too Much** / 1981 / Epic 37451
The auspicious debut, demonstrating Vandross's gorgeous vocal arrangements and his lush, romantic singing on the #1 R&B smash "Never Too Much" and the Top 10 "Don't You Know That?" plus the tour de force version of "A House Is Not a Home." — *William Ruhlmann*

Forever for Always for Love / 1982 / Epic 38235
Luther Vandross scored his first platinum album and cemented his status as the new heartthrob king of the '80s with this fine second release. Strangely, his sublime version of "Since I Lost My Baby" wasn't issued as a single, but the combination hit "Bad Boy/Having a Party" was an R&B sensation and helped secure the album's crossover success. — *Ron Wynn*

Busy Body / 1983 / Epic 39196
An accurate title for a man who seemed to be producing all the divas in the business at this time, including Dionne Warwick, who turns up for a duet on "How Many More Times Can We Say Goodbye." It's one of three R&B Top 10 hits here, the others being "I'll Let You Slide" and the brilliant medley "Superstar/Until You Come Back to Me (That's What I'm Gonna Do)." — *William Ruhlmann*

○ **Night I Fell in Love** / 1985 / Epic 39882
A wonderful version of Stevie Wonder's "Creepin'" almost gets lost on another hit-filled collection, which includes the Top 5 R&B smashes "'Til My Baby Comes Home" and "It's Over Now." — *William Ruhlmann*

Give Me the Reason / 1986 / Epic 40415
Luther Vandross was riding high in the '80s, dominating the R&B charts and slowly but steadily increasing his pop exposure. This was his fourth consecutive platinum smash, second straight double platinum winner, but beyond that was a superbly sung, soulful, and expressive triumph. "Stop to Love" and "Give Me the Reason" were beautifully produced, arranged, and performed numbers, huge R&B hits (the latter a chart topper), and deserved a better pop fate. — *Ron Wynn*

○ **Any Love** / 1988 / Epic 44308
There were some who felt Vandross suffered a slight slump, as this album only reached the platinum level after two consecutive double platinum winners. But "Here and Now" was a huge

smash, and by now the pop crowd was fully aware of Vandross's vocal charms and allure. "She Won't Talk to Me" was a bit to the posturing side, but still managed to do decently, while there were also fine album cuts like "I Wonder" and "Are You Gonna Love Me." —*Ron Wynn*

★ **Best of Luther Vandross...The Best of Love** / 1989 / Epic 45320
By the time this way-overdue double-record hits collection came out, Vandross had done many more R&B singles than could fit on it, so *The Best of Luther Vandross ... The Best of Love* is inadequate to encompass him. It does, however, contain "Here and Now," which broke Vandross through to the pop Top 10 long after most people had given up hope that he'd ever cross over. — *William Ruhlmann*

Vanilla Fudge

Group / Hard rock, psychedelic
Specializing in thundering psychedelia, Vanilla Fudge gave the Supremes hit "You Keep Me Hangin' On" an ultraserious, somewhat indulgent arrangement and hit big in 1968. The quartet was introduced to Atco by veteran producer Shadow Morton and fronted by keyboardist Mark Stein. "You Keep Me Hangin' On" was only a minor seller in 1967. Reissued a year later, it proved far more potent its second time around. Bassist Tim Bogert and drummer Carmine Appice later played with Jeff Beck and Rod Stewart. —*Bill Dahl*

● **Psychedelic Sundae: The Best of Vanilla Fudge** / 1993 / Rhino 71154
A generous compilation of the best of this heavy, progressive, psychedelic band from the late '60s. —AMG

Vaselines

Group / Alternative pop/rock
Eugene Kelly and Frances McKee were bored with their town, so they decided to form a band; they were called the Vaselines. Adding Charles Kelly on drums and bassist James Seenan, the Scottish quartet began rehearsing in their basements; soon they began recording their rough, simple, and highly melodic pop songs in studios in Glasgow and Edinburgh. They recorded about 20 pure pop gems that were barely heard by anyone. The Vaselines would likely have faded away into obscurity if it weren't for Nirvana, who recorded two of their songs (both appear on the *Incesticide* compilation); Kurt Cobain was very vocal about his admiration for the band, and Eugene Kelly in particular. By this time, the Vaselines had broken up, and Kelly had formed Captain America, which later became Eugenius; soon, Eugenius became a hip band in alternative circles and the Vaselines' music was reissued. —*Stephen Thomas Erlewine*

● **Way of the Vaselines** / Jul. 31, 1992 / Sub Pop 145
The Way of the Vaselines collects everything the Vaselines ever recorded; it's a rough gem of raw pop. —*Stephen Thomas Erlewine*

Stevie Ray Vaughan

b. Oct. 3, 1954, d. Aug. 27, 1990
Vocals, guitar / Blues rock
Stevie Ray Vaughan was the most impressive blues guitarist to appear in the '80s, which made his death in a helicopter crash at the start of the '90s all the more tragic. Vaughan grew up in Dallas, the younger brother of Jimmie Vaughan (cofounder of the Fabulous Thunderbirds). Stevie began playing in clubs at 12, and by 17 had dropped out of high school and moved to Austin. There followed years of struggling until April 23, 1982, when Vaughan and his group, Double Trouble, played a private audition for the Rolling Stones in New York. The gig led to an invitation to appear at the Montreux Jazz Festival, at which Vaughan was seen by David Bowie, who hired him to play guitar on his *Let's Dance* album, and Jackson Browne, who offered the free use of his recording studio. Vaughan took up that offer after being signed by legendary talent scout John Hammond to Epic, recording his debut album, *Texas Flood*, in the fall of 1982.

The release of the album led to a wave of recognition that included gold albums, Grammy awards, and other accolades over the next seven years. In 1987, Vaughan took time out to go through a rehabilitation program to overcome alcohol and drug addiction, and he wrote about the experience on his final studio album, *In Step* (1989). In the last year of his life, he embarked on

a coheadlining tour with Jeff Beck and recorded a duo album with his brother. He had just finished a jam with Eric Clapton and Robert Cray at a show at Alpine Valley in East Troy, WI, when he was killed. In 1991 Epic released the posthumous *The Sky Is Crying*, assembled by Jimmie Vaughan. —*William Ruhlmann*

Texas Flood / 1983 / Epic 38734
A late-arriving star, Vaughan did not make his first album until the age of 28. By that time he had become a seasoned player, so this doesn't really sound like a debut album; rather, it sounds like a blues guitar master at the top of his form. Highlights include "Pride & Joy," "Love Struck Baby," "Lenny," and the hard blues title cut. —*William Ruhlmann*

○ **Couldn't Stand the Weather** / 1984 / Epic 39304
Vaughan does not ease up on this second set, even taking on Jimi Hendrix in a rendition of "Voodoo Chile (Slight Return)" and handling it beautifully. —*William Ruhlmann*

○ **Soul to Soul** / 1985 / Epic 40036
Soul to Soul shows that Vaughan is a great guitarist—but everybody already knew that. What makes this album different from his two previous efforts are the inspired backing of Double Trouble—who finally sound like they're not intimdated by their leader—and Vaughan's considerably more soulful and assertive vocals. —*Stephen Thomas Erlewine*

Live Alive / 1986 / Epic 40511
Live not only covers many of Vaughan's most popular album tracks but also showcases a version of Stevie Wonder's "Superstition." Other standout tracks include "Look at Little Sister," "Willie the Wimp," and "Cold Shot." —*Rick Clark*

★ **In Step** / 1989 / Epic 45024
Vaughan sounds just as fierce sober as he did before, and he is beginning to bloom as a songwriter, a fact most notable on the driving "The House Is Rockin'" and the confessional "Wall of Denial." —*William Ruhlmann*

Family Style / Jan. 1990 / Epic 46225
Jimmie and Stevie Ray Vaughan team up for this relaxed one-off, produced by Nile Rodgers. In spite of a couple of throwaway songs, "Hard to Be," and "Good Texan" showcase their lean Austin-style electric blues/roadhouse R&B to good effect. "Tick Tock" became a poignant hit, released just after Stevie Ray died in a helicopter crash. —*Rick Clark*

○ **Sky Is Crying** / 1991 / Epic 47390
The posthumously released *The Sky Is Crying*, assembled out of tracks recorded between 1984 and 1989, is a lovingly assembled tribute to Vaughan's brilliance as a guitarist. Arguably this is Vaughan's finest album. The first-rate playing is unforced and natural in execution. On the songs, from his impeccable version of Hendrix's "Little Wing" to the hard blues shuffle of "Empty Arms," Vaughan's execution is unforced and his phrasing is relaxed. The release contains great liner notes and track information. Fans of hard blues-rock should check this one out. —*Rick Clark*

In the Beginning / Oct. 6, 1992 / Epic 53168
Although it is a very rough early concert from 1980, this album captures an energetic Stevie Ray Vaughan developing still developing his signature style, which makes it essential for fans. —*Stephen Thomas Erlewine*

Bobby Vee

Vocals / Pop/rock
Bobby Vee enjoyed his greatest success in the early '60s, with five Top 10 singles, including the classic "Take Good Care of My Baby." Vee's vocal style was similar to that of his hero, Buddy Holly. Ironically, Vee's break came when he filled in for Holly the day after his death in a plane crash. Like those of many of his contemporaries, his career went into a tailspin with the arrival of the British invasion in 1964. He did score one more Top 10 single in 1967 with "Come Back When You Grow Up." —*Kenneth M. Cassidy*

● **Legendary Masters** / 1990 / EMI America 92774
The most complete collection of Vee's recordings, including "Take Good Care of My Baby," "Rubber Ball," and "The Night Has a Thousand Eyes." —*Kenneth M. Cassidy*

Suzanne Vega

b. Aug. 12, 1959, Santa Monica, CA

Vocals / Singer-songwriter
Vega was born in Santa Monica, CA, and moved to New York City at age two. She attended the High School of Performing Arts, then Barnard College. Vega was still at Barnard when she began attracting attention at Greenwich Village folk clubs and was featured on several issues of the songwriters' magazine/record album *The CooP* (later *The Fast Folk Musical Magazine*) in 1982. She was signed to A&M Records in 1984 and released her first album, *Suzanne Vega,* in 1985. It was a critical success and a moderate seller. Vega's second album, *Solitude Standing,* featured "Luka," a song about child abuse that became a surprise hit single, reaching #3 in 1987. The album itself went gold. Vega took three years to release the followup, *Days of Open Hand* (1990), which was a commercial disappointment, though a few months later a couple of British DJs, under the name D.N.A., put out a dance version of her a cappella song "Tom's Diner" from the album *Solitude Standing,* and it became a #5 hit. On her next album, 1992's *99.9 Degrees F.,* Vega experimented with the dance rhythms that made "Tom's Diner" a hit; although the result was interesting, it didn't give her any hits. — *William Ruhlmann*

○ **Suzanne Vega** / 1985 / A&M 5072
Vega's most consistent collection of songs spotlights her hushed, restrained singing style and the spare, precise backup produced by Lenny Kaye. But it's those songs—"Small Blue Thing," "Undertow," "Marlene on the Wall"—with their brittle imagery (things are always frozen, flat, or cracking) and restraint—that let you know there's a big new talent here. — *William Ruhlmann*

● **Solitude Standing** / 1987 / A&M 5136
A more uneven but still striking album, featuring "Tom's Diner" (in its pre-disco version) and the hit "Luka." — *William Ruhlmann*

○ **99.9 Degrees F.** / Sep. 8, 1992 / A&M 540005
While this is not the techno album that Suzanne Vega was rumored to be making, *99.9 Degrees F.* does offer a significant departure from her previous contemporary folk albums. Vega uses more synthesizers and drum machines, often evoking a bizarre carnivalesque atmosphere on the album. Still, at its heart *99.9 Degrees F.* is a folk album; every song is steeped in traditional song form, not those of techno or synth-pop. Vega's writing is strong, hitting highpoints on the title track, "Blood Makes Noise," "In Liverpool," and "As Girls Go," which features a typically tasteful solo by Richard Thompson. Fans of Vega's previous work might be taken aback by the turn she has taken on *99.9 Degrees F.,* but those willing to listen will find that Vega has produced one of her strongest records yet. — *Stephen Thomas Erlewine*

Velocity Girl

Group / Alternative pop
After all their grunge bands left for the majors, Sub Pop's most popular band was, surprisingly, Velocity Girl. Velocity Girl is the exact opposite of grunge; their guitars may be a little dirty, but their music is pure pop, with shiny melodies and Beach Boys harmonies. Their hooks are sharp enough to make the band one of the few college-radio favorites that don't wear thin with repeated listens. — *Stephen Thomas Erlewine*

○ **Copacetic** / 1993 / Sub Pop 196
A consistent, enjoyable collection of alternative guitar-pop in the vein of R.E.M. and the Velvet Underground, Velocity Girl's debut album is distinguished by Sarah Shannon's thin, girlish voice, which is showcased to its best effect on "Audrey's Eyes." — *Stephen Thomas Erlewine*

The Velvet Underground

Group / Rock & roll
The Velvet Underground was one of the few bands of consequence to emerge from New York City in the '60s. They played their first gig near the end of 1965, and shortly thereafter they hooked up with pop artist Andy Warhol. Warhol in effect "sponsored" the band, allowing them to rehearse at his studio, known as the "Factory," and putting together a multimedia extravaganza featuring the Velvets, entitled *The Exploding Plastic Inevitable.* Warhol also grafted German chanteuse, model, actress, and would-be singer Nico onto the group's core: Lou Reed (vocals, guitar), John Cale (vocals, bass, viola), Sterling Morrison (guitar), and Maureen Tucker (drums).

Reed was the group's main songwriter. With material such as "Heroin," "Sister Ray," "Candy Says," and "I'm Waiting for My Man," he chronicled a number of aspects of his community, as all folksingers have done. In Reed's case, the community was that of lower Manhattan: a mix of artists, junkies, homosexuals, and transvestites. Such being the case, the Velvets had problems even having radio ads for their first album. Their deliberate aesthetic of amateurish primitivism; raw, distorted production; drones; and feedback did not help win them radio play. On top of all this, their stage presence (wearing wraparound shades and black clothes, making deadpan stage announcements, and at all times projecting ennui) appeared to be closed and hostile, flying directly in the face of the then-prevailing ethos of "love, peace, happiness, and the dawning of a new age." It is one of the great ironies of rock that they sold very few albums while together (1967-1970), yet in the '80s and early '90s their influence was pervasive, manifesting itself in the work of groups as disparate as R.E.M. and the Jesus & Mary Chain. The joke has always been that they didn't sell a lot of albums, but everyone who bought one started a band. One of the results of this is that everything they issued is still in print.

After years of denying reunion rumors, the original Velvet Underground (Reed, Cale, Morrison, Tucker) reunited for a European concert tour in 1993. Although they planned to tour the United States and record an "MTV Unplugged" album, tensions between John Cale and Lou Reed escalated quickly, and the band split again, only a few months after their European tour. Cale and Reed vowed never to work with each other again because, as Reed said, they "can't stand each other." — *Rob Bowman*

☆ **Velvet Underground & Nico** / Jan. 1967 / Verve 823290
Many of the songs are melodic pop tunes, and the lyrics can be charming, but they also take on the experience of shooting heroin and other hard-edged subjects, and some of the music reflects Cale's taste for avant garde music. All together, a remarkable document for 1967, and far more provocative than any debut album released since. — *William Ruhlmann*

☆ **White Light/White Heat** / Feb. 1967 / Verve 825119
By the time of *White Light/White Heat,* Nico had departed to embark upon a solo career. The Velvets, now also minus Warhol, concocted an extraordinarily abrasive, tension-filled album, full of mind-numbing feedback and incessant drones. The playing and production on this album herald a punk aesthetic eight years ahead of the fact. Standout tracks include the sidelong improvisatory "Sister Ray" and the John Cale-narrated, Lou Reed-written "The Gift." — *Rob Bowman*

☆ **Velvet Underground** / 1969 / Verve 815454
A complete turnabout, as Reed and company (minus Cale) make a quiet, cautiously optimistic album typified by "I'm Set Free" and "Beginning to See the Light." — *William Ruhlmann*

☆ **Loaded** / 1970 / Warner Brothers 27613
Recorded in the summer of 1970 while the band was playing a summer-long residency at Max's Kansas City in New York. Feeling increasingly disaffected, Reed walked out after the last gig at Max's, never to return. The album was remixed and edited without him, much to his later chagrin. Whatever imperfections may have consequently occurred, *Loaded* remains an absolute must. The Velvets were now playing stripped-down rock & roll, and Reed was writing such enduring classics as "Sweet Jane" and "Rock & Roll," as well as the underrated "New Age," "Train round the Bend," and "Oh! Sweet Nuthin'." — *Rob Bowman*

Live at Max's Kansas City / 1972 / Cotillion 9500
Low-fidelity recording of the final Velvets' appearance with Lou Reed at a small New York club in the summer of 1970. Essential for Reed's stage remarks alone. — *William Ruhlmann*

☆ **1969: Velvet Underground Live** / 1974 / Mercury 2-7504
Originally a double album and released in two volumes with added songs on CD, *1969: Velvet Underground Live* is a stunning document of the Reed, Yule, Morrison, Tucker edition of the Velvets at their pinnacle. Recorded privately in Texas and San Francisco, the Velvets play extended, intensely driven, out-and-out versions of songs from their first three albums as well as then-unreleased material such as "Ocean," "Real Good Time Together," and "Sweet Bonnie Brown." — *Rob Bowman*

☆ **Vu** / 1985 / Verve 823721
This is a lost Velvets album, recorded in 1969 as their fourth album, but rejected by MGM at the time. Some of its songs turned up in other versions on Lou Reed's solo albums. — *William Ruhlmann*

Another View / 1986 / Verve 829405
More outtakes and unreleased tracks, recorded from 1967
through 1969, including an early version of "Rock and Roll." —
William Ruhlmann

● **Best of the Velvet Underground: Words and Music of Lou
Reed** / 1989 / Verve 841164
*The Best of the Velvet Underground: Words and Music of Lou
Reed* is a 15-track summary of the Velvets' career, borrowing
heavily from the debut (six tracks) and featuring "Sweet Jane"
and "Rock & Roll," licensed from Atlantic. — *William Ruhlmann*

The Ventures

Group / Rock & roll, surf rock
Instrumental rock & roll group from Tacoma, WA, formed in 1959
originally named the Versatones. The early lineup consisted of
Don Wilson (b. 1937), rhythm guitar; Bob Bogle (b. 1937), lead
guitar; Nokie Edwards (b. 1939), bass; and Howie Johnson, drums.
They pressed a twangy, rocked-up version of Johnny Smith's
"Walk Don't Run" on their own Blue Horizon label, which was
later picked up by Dolton Records. It became a #2 hit in 1960.
Bogle and Edwards switched instruments, and Mel Taylor replaced Johnson on drums in 1963. More hit singles featuring
their cleanly played but rockin' style followed, but the band
wisely entered the album market early on, and it was there they
found their true format, placing 37 chart entries and more than
50 albums between 1960 and the mid '70s.
     The Ventures are the biggest-selling instrumental group of all
time, but their influence extends far beyond mere record sales.
With their solid-body Fender guitars (later switching to Mosrite
Ventures models) and matching suits, their album covers defined
what a rock & roll combo should look like. Likewise, their sound
was so popular that they released several successful instructional
albums in the *Play with the Ventures* series that many later rock
stars cut their teeth on. Because they played instrumentals, they
were among the first American bands to break big in Japan (no
language barrier), eventually honored as the first foreign members of that country's Conservatory of Music for selling over 40
million records. Edwards left and was replaced for a while by
Jerry McGee, but he returned in 1972, restoring the early '60s
lineup, which has endured to the present day. They continued to
tour and record, sounding better than ever, their place in rock &
roll guitar history assured. — *Cub Koda*

○ **Ventures on Stage Around the World** / 1965 / Dolton 8035
Explosive live recordings from Japan, England, and the United
States, with a hot greatest-hits medley and a wild "Driving
Guitars" being among the highlights. *The Ventures on Stage
around the World* is out of print but worth any search. — *Cub
Koda*

★ **Walk, Don't Run: The Best of the Ventures** / 1990 / EMI
America 93451
A perfect 29-track CD compilation, with great notes and superla-
tive sound. All the hits, from "Walk Don't Run" to "Hawaii Five-
O." Important album sides, plus interviews and radio spots. A per-
fect introduction. — *Cub Koda*

Tom Verlaine

b. 1949, Wilmington, DE
Vocals, guitar / Alternative pop/rock
Guitarist Tom Verlaine recorded numerous albums following the
breakup of his groundbreaking band Television. The best of his
solo albums hint at what that group could've done, had they stuck
it out for a few more albums. — *John Floyd*

○ **Tom Verlaine** / 1979 / Elektra 216
This, his solo debut, expands the musical vocabulary of
Television, while elaborating on Verlaine's sometimes sketchy
lyricisms. — *John Floyd*

● **Dreamtime** / 1981 / Warner Brothers 56919
The closest he's come to crafting a solo masterpiece. Dense guitar
structures and his best set of songs since Television's *Marquee
Moon* hit the racks. — *John Floyd*

Words from the Front / 1983 / Warner Brothers 3685
The material is patchy enough to make this one worthwhile only
for devotees, who will no doubt scarf up the angst-ridden title cut.
Others will groove on the picture-pop-perfect "Postcards from
Waterloo." — *John Floyd*

○ **Cover** / 1985 / Warner Brothers 25144
Dense, synth-heavy production notwithstanding, this 1984 set is a
sharp and poignant set of desperate romantic gems. — *John Floyd*

Warm and Cool / 1992 / Rykodisc 10216
Warm and Cool serves as a primer of instrumental electric guitar
stylings, from the '50s rumble of Link Wray, twang of Duanne
Eddy, and surf of the Ventures right up to contemporary, white-
light experimental feedback. These influences are filtered
through Verlaine's moody grasp of urban paranoia. The overall
feel of the 14 tracks is hypnotic, mysterious, and somewhat foreboding, like the soundtrack to a good film noir. — *Roch Parisien*

Verve

Group / Alternative pop/rock
In the early '90s, Verve gained a strong following in the native
England with their crushingly loud, guitar-soaked neo-psyche-
delic pop. In America, the band had to change their name to the
Verve in order to avoid a lawsuit with Verve Records. — *Stephen
Thomas Erlewine*

● **A Storm in Heaven** / Jun. 1993 /
The Verve's debut album is a collection of cascading guitars and
meandering melodies that are made memorable by the band's elliptical sense of songwriting. — *Stephen Thomas Erlewine*

No Come Down / May 17, 1994 / Vernon Yard 39583
No Come Down collects various singles, B sides, and rarities; it's
for devoted fans only. — *Stephen Thomas Erlewine*

Vibrators

Group / Punk
In 1977 British pub-rock veterans Knox and John Ellis made one
punk rock classic, 1977's *Pure Mania*, then became a relic of an
era full of forgotten one-shotters. — *John Floyd*

○ **Pure Mania** / 1977 / Columbia 35038
These early punks rock & roll with the energy of the new school,
but the grooves are tighter, and they have a genuinely creepy
sense of humor. Not just for punk enthusiasts. — *John Floyd*

● **Power of Money: The Best of the Vibrators** / Dec. 1991 /
Continuum 10002
By taking the best moments from the Vibrators' debut *Pure
Mania*, as well as their inconsistent followups, *Power of Money*
winds up as a fine collection of their energetically melodic punk
rock. — *Stephen Thomas Erlewine*

Village People

Group / Disco
Part clever concept, part exaggerated camp act, the Village People
were worldwide sensations during disco's heyday and keep reviving like the phoenix. Producer Jacques Morali in 1977 assembled
a group designed to attract gay audiences while parodying (some
claimed exploiting) that same constituency's stereotypes. He
landed a deal with Casablanca, then carefully recruited an appropriate cast of characters. Songwriters Phil Hurtt and Peter
Whitehead were tabbed to compose songs with gay underpinnings, and other roles and costumes were carefully selected;
among them were a cowboy, biker, soldier, policeman, and construction worker complete with hard hat. The group clicked first
in England with the single "San Francisco (You Got Me)" in 1977,
then reaped stateside honors with "Macho Man" in 1978.
"Y.M.C.A." and "In the Navy" were worldwide smashes, both peaking at #2 on the pop charts.
     Although they were a disco band rather than an R&B, soul, or
funk unit, the Village People's ranks included at one time or another three solid singers in original lead vocalist Victor Willis, his
replacement Ray Simpson, and later Miles Jaye, who took
Simpson's place. After two more successful singles, "Go West"
and "Can't Stop the Music," the group's fortunes plummeted, in
large part due to their participation in the ill-fated film also titled
Can't Stop the Music. They tried a comeback with updated dance-
rock material, but flopped. They've resurfaced in the '90s with
more new cuts, though they haven't rekindled past success. Jaye
became a major figure in urban contemporary circles in 1987 and
continues recording and performing as a solo vocalist. — *Ron
Wynn*

● **Greatest Hits** / 1988 / Rhino 70167

The best collection of their campy disco hits available. —*Stephen Thomas Erlewine*

○ **Best of the Village People** / Mar. 22, 1994 / Casablanca 522039
Although it isn't as listenable as Rhino's collection, this disc does contain all of their hits, making it a good purchase. —*Stephen Thomas Erlewine*

Gene Vincent (Vincent Eugene Craddock)

b. 1935, d. Oct. 12, 1971
Vocals / Rock & roll
Though his chart hits were few, no one defined the initial greasy-haired, leather-jacketed, hot-rods 'n' babes spark of rock & roll more than Gene Vincent. Far more influential as a live performer, Vincent, with his backing group the Blue Caps, defined the lifestyle and visual prowess of the music, as well as touring with a wild-ass stage show that usually left a sea of destroyed equipment and hotel rooms, deflowered schoolgirls, and musical converts in its wake. Dogged by tax problems and the emerging teen-idol trend in pop music, by the early '60s he emigrated to the United Kingdom, where he found himself revered as a founding father of the music. Several bids for a chart comeback failed, and by the late '60s, alcoholism had reduced his once-energetic stage prowess to a bloated self-parody. But a quick spin of his '50s Capitol sides dispels all that: the rebellious spirit of rock & roll's first flowering lives on in the supercharged recordings of Gene Vincent & the Blue Caps. Be-Bop-A-Lula, indeed. —*Cub Koda*

○ **Capitol Years 1956-63** / 1987 / Charly
While Vincent recorded a fair number of overlooked gems during his prime, he also cut a greater number of uninspired tracks. This lavishly packaged and exhaustively annotated 10-album set inadvertently charts the rapidly plummeting quality of his recordings, even as it unearths worthy obscurities. It does manage to gather all of his classic 1956 sessions with guitarist Cliff Gallup in the same place, but Gene's subsequent efforts could have easily been boiled down to a supplementary disc or two. —*Richie Unterberger*

★ **Capitol Collectors Series** / 1990 / Capitol 94074
Breathless, unintelligible, and spirited rockabilly at its non-Sun best, this 21-track compilation covers Vincent's Capitol recordings (including "Be-Bop-A-Lula," "Race with the Devil," and "Lotta Lovin'") in admirable form. —*Hank Davis and Stephen Thomas Erlewine*

○ **Gene Vincent Box Set** / 1994 / EMI
Six CDs containing the complete Capitol and EMI-Columbia recordings by Vincent, from 1956 through 1964. The 151 tracks may seem excessive, but the sound glitters, and since most of the post-1962 material was never issued in the United States, this stuff could be revelatory to serious fans. And the booklet is filled with detailed notes, sessionographies, and great photos. —*Bruce Eder*

Violent Femmes

Group / Alternative pop/rock
With their geeky, nervous folk pop, the Violent Femmes became one of the '80s biggest cult bands. The new-wave group features Gordon Gano (vocals, guitar, songwriter), Brian Ritchie (bass), and Victor DeLorenzo (drums). The Femmes formed in the early '80s in Milwaukee, WI. In 1982, they released their self-titled debut, which has approached neo-classic status in some circles. Their following albums weren't as popular or consistent, yet each one has a few good songs. —*Anne Erlewine*

★ **Violent Femmes** / 1984 / Slash 23845
One of the seminal albums in alternative rock. On their first album (by far their best) the Violent Femmes began their professional career with a style that proves both entertaining and distinctive. Includes "Blister in the Sun," "Add It Up," and "Gone Daddy Gone." —*Michael Anne Erlewine*

○ **Hallowed Ground** / 1985 / Slash 25094
Though mistaken for a parody when it was released, *Hallowed Ground* features Gordon Gano's serious Christian convictions. The teenage angst is pushed aside on this more mature effort based, for the most part, in traditional American folk—of course, it's slightly skewed. —*Chris Woodstra*

○ **Blind Leading the Naked** / 1986 / Slash 25340

A more mainstream effort courtesy of producer Jerry Harrison (Talking Heads). Gano returns to his troubled teen persona, and the band rocks harder than on the previous two releases. A nice cover of the T. Rex classic "Children of the Revolution" and the yearning "I Held Her in My Arms" complete with a horn section. —*Chris Woodstra*

3 / 1989 / Slash 25819
The fourth album finds the band in somewhat of a rut creatively. Fans of the band's early days will appreciate the slightly stripped back acoustic production but will find not much energy; the album falls flat in most places. Only the single "Nightmares" and the confessional "See My Ships" leave any lasting impression. —*Chris Woodstra*

Why Do Birds Sing? / 1991 / Reprise 26476
After a several-year absence, the Femmes make a comeback of sorts with the charming *Why Do Birds Sing?* Returning to their street busking roots, the band plays stripped-back acoustic songs as a three piece. Though they can't fight the fact that they have grown up, the songs show that they can still have fun. —*Chris Woodstra*

○ **Add It Up** / 1993 / Reprise
Although it isn't as comprehensive as it seems, *Add It Up* is a good collection of most of the Violent Femmes' best tracks. —AMG

The Waitresses

Group / New wave
The Waitresses existed for the purpose of performing the witty, often female-oriented songs of guitarist Chris Butler, who had previously led a series of new wave bands in Cleveland. The personnel of the band as of its 1982 debut album, *Wasn't Tomorrow Wonderful*, was, in addition to Butler, singer Patty Donahue, backup singer Ariel Warner, reed player Mars Williams, bassist David Horstra, drummer Billy Ficca (a once and future member of Television), and keyboardist Dan Klayman. The group recorded two albums and a mini-LP in the early '80s, stirring critical acclaim and international interest before both Donahue and Butler left. Ficca fronted the band for a while, then they broke up. —*William Ruhlmann*

○ **Wasn't Tomorrow Wonderful?** / 1982 / Polydor 6346
"No Guilt," in which Donahue's matter-of-fact voice details what a spurned lover has found out since the breakup ("I learned the reason for a three-pronged outlet"), and "I Know What Boys Like" are the standouts among these clever songs, but the whole album has an attitude that won't quit. —*William Ruhlmann*

● **Best of the Waitresses** / 1990 / Polydor 847249
A fine collection of the Waitresses' best tracks and biggest hits. —AMG

Tom Waits

b. Dec. 7, 1949, Pomona, CA
Vocals / Singer-songwriter, rock & roll, alternative pop/rock
Singer-songwriter and actor Tom Waits has garnered considerable critical acclaim and a cult following during a 20-year singing career (he has also built up quite a resumé as a film actor since the late '70s), and his songs have been successfully covered by such mainstream artists as the Eagles and Rod Stewart, though he himself has never scored a notable commercial hit.

Born in Pomona, CA, Waits was heavily influenced by the Beat writers of the '50s and, by the early '70s, had developed a performing persona as a heavy-drinking, heavy-smoking street poet. He signed to Elektra/Asylum and released his debut album, *Closing Time*, a relatively conventional singer-songwriter album of the day, in 1973. One of its songs, "Ol' 55," turned up on an Eagles album. Waits followed it with *Heart of a Saturday Night*, which found him celebrating the same street life found in Bruce Springsteen's early albums. (Springsteen later recorded Waits' song "Jersey Girl.") *Nighthawks at the Diner*, a double live album, represented a peak in his material.

On his albums after the mid '70s, Waits's voice, already a raspy one, seemed to drop an octave, and his songs became less melodic. In the early '80s he switched to the Island label, and on albums such as *Swordfishtrombones*, his music became more experimental. He wrote and starred in a stage presentation called *Frank's Wild Years* in the mid '80s, and it was transferred to film under the title *Big Time*. —*William Ruhlmann*

● **Closing Time** / 1973 / Asylum 5061
The bluesy cocktail-jazz accompaniment underscores Waits's boozy, sentimental tales of life after hours. But songs like "Ol' 55" and "Martha" transcend the somewhat hackneyed form to be genuinely touching. — *William Ruhlmann*

○ **Small Change** / 1973 / Asylum 1078
On *Small Change*, Waits alternates between playing the sleazoid barker with "Step Right Up" and the sentimental bum on tracks like "Tom Traubert's Blues" and "I Wish I Was in New Orleans." This might not be one of Waits's best efforts, but fans of his drunken croak of a voice will find this enjoyable. Like many of his recordings from his Asylum period, *Small Change* was recorded live to two-track and produced by Bones Howe. Sonically, these albums are quite impressive. — *Rick Clark*

Heart of Saturday Night / 1974 / Asylum 1015
The touchstone here isn't so much Charles Bukowski as it is Hoagy Carmichael, even if, in Waits' interpretation, it's a "bloodshot moon in that burgundy sky." — *William Ruhlmann*

○ **Nighthawks at the Diner** / 1975 / Asylum 2008
There are those who consider this two-record live set the culmination of Waits's nightlife persona, and others who worry that it's a comedy act in which the singer veers into self-parody. It's one of those tough questions, like, how drunk is *too* drunk? — *William Ruhlmann*

Foreign Affairs / 1977 / Asylum 1117
Foreign Affairs continues Waits's immersion into orchestrated street short stories with tracks like "Burma-Shave," "A Sight for Sore Eyes," and "Muriel." Bette Midler duets with Waits on "I Never Talk to Strangers." — *Rick Clark*

Blue Valentine / 1978 / Asylum 162
With this effort, Waits continues the bum-fronting-an-orchestra approach he started on *Small Change*. Particularly striking is his interpretation of *West Side Story*'s "Somewhere." Other highlights include the bittersweet sentimentality of "Christmas Card from a Hooker in Minneapolis," the bluesy "$29.00," and "Romeo Is Bleeding." — *Rick Clark*

☆ **Swordfishtrombones** / 1983 / Island 842469
On *Swordfishtrombones*, Waits (by now with a voice even deeper and more gravelly than ever) dropped Hoagy Carmichael as his chief influence and adopted Kurt Weill and Bertolt Brecht. Employing odd percussive instruments and horns, he turned to this imaginative, impressionistic approach, which is also followed on subsequent albums. — *William Ruhlmann*

○ **Anthology of Tom Waits** / 1985 / Asylum 60416
Anthology collects most of the key tracks from Waits's Asylum years, except for *Nighthawks at the Diner*. — *Rick Clark*

★ **Rain Dogs** / 1985 / Island 826382
From the New York streets to the Orient ("Singapore") and back, Waits continues his colorful survey, alternately challenging the listener (especially in Marc Ribot's guitar playing) and returning to the melodic style of the past ("Downtown Train"). Keith Richards guests on gritty "Big Black Mariah," while "Time" is one of his best ballads. — *William Ruhlmann*

○ **Frank's Wild Years** / 1987 / Island 842357
Frank's Wild Years continued Waits's weird blend of theatrical melodies and unusual production, which he began on *Swordfishtrombones*. "Rainville" and "Hang on St. Christopher" are highlights. Not as strong as *Rain Dogs*, this is still one of his better albums from this period. — *Rick Clark*

Big Time / 1988 / Island 842470
This is the soundtrack to Waits' in-concert film *Big Time*. It covers tracks from *Frank's Wild Years* and *Rain Dogs*, plus two new tracks, "Falling Down" and "Strange Weather." His careening version of "Big Black Mariah," with its dissonant guitar and roller rink organ, is even ruder than the original version. — *Rick Clark*

○ **Early Years** / 1991 / Bizarre 70557
A collection of early demos and recordings that is fascinating for devoted fans. — *Stephen Thomas Erlewine*

☆ **Bone Machine** / Feb. 1992 / Island 512580
A set of dark, stripped-down songs, *Bone Machine* is a bleak, melancholy song cycle of decay and despair. It's also his best album, full of wonderfully evocative songs and haunting, primitive sounds. — *Stephen Thomas Erlewine*

○ **Early Years, Vol. 2** / Jan. 1993 / Rhino 71089

A second collection of early demos, recorded before Waits received a record contract, *Early Years, Vol. 2* is just as fascinating as the first volume. — *Stephen Thomas Erlewine*

Black Rider / Feb. 1993 / Island 314
Written with William S. Burroughs and Robert Wilson, Tom Waits's version of their operetta is an intriguing mess that tends to be too scattered to be truly effective. — *Stephen Thomas Erlewine*

Junior Walker & the All-Stars

b. 1942, Blytheville, AR
Vocals, sax / Motown
Of all the great musicians who played on scores of Motown records, none of them got label credit, much less a chance to bask in the spotlight. The lone exception was Junior Walker (born Audrey Dewalt), whose tenor sax wailings were made up of equal parts Illinois Jacquet high-note shrieks, Coleman Hawkins growls, and pure Midwest soul. Never much of a vocalist, Walker nonetheless scored hits with his rough-grained chops, though the sax solos remained the definite focal point. He was highly influential on the Tom Scott/David Sanborn crowd. Walker should be close to the top of any list of rock & roll's great tenor saxophonists. — *Cub Koda*

○ **Shotgun** / 1965 / Motown 5141
All the early hits, including "Cleo's Mood," "Shake & Fingerpop," and "Road Runner"—along with King Curtis and Maceo Parker, the soul sax man—and probably the most influential. — *George Bedard*

● **Greatest Hits** / 1982 / Motown 5208
All the hits, including "Shotgun," "What Does It Take to Win Your Love," and "Roadrunner." The definitive package. — *Cub Koda*

Scott Walker (Noel Scott Engel)

b. Jan. 9, 1944, Hamilton, OH
Vocals / Pop/rock
One of the most enigmatic figures in rock history, Scott Walker was known as Scotty Engel when he cut obscure, flop records in the late '50s and early '60s in the teen idol vein. He then hooked up with John Maus and Gary Leeds to form the Walker Brothers. They weren't named Walker, they weren't brothers, and they weren't English, but they nevertheless became a part of the British invasion after moving to the United Kingdom in 1965. They enjoyed a couple years of massive success there (and a couple hits in the United States) in a Righteous Brothers vein. As their full-throated lead singer and principal songwriter, Scott was the dominant artistic force in the group, which split in 1967.

While remaining virtually unknown in his homeland, Scott launched a hugely successful solo career in Britain with a unique blend of orchestrated, almost MOR arrangements with idosyncratic and morose lyrics. At the height of psychedelia, Walker openly looked to crooners like Sinatra, Jack Jones, and Tony Bennett for inspiration, and to Jacques Brel for much of his material. None of those balladeers, however, would have sung about the oddball subjects—prostitutes, transvestites, suicidal brooders, plagues, and Joseph Stalin—that populated Walker's songs. His first four albums hit the Top 10 in the United Kingdom—his second, in fact, reached #1 in 1968, in the midst of the hippie era. By the time of 1969's *Scott 4*, the singer was writing all of his material. Although this was perhaps his finest album, it was a commercial disappointment and unfortunately discouraged him from relying entirely upon his own material on subsequent releases.

The 1970s were a frustrating period for Walker, pocked with increasingly sporadic releases and a largely unsuccessful reunion with his "brothers" in the middle of the decade. His work on the Walkers' final album in 1978 prompted admiration from David Bowie and Brian Eno. After a long period of hibernation, he emerged with an album in 1984, *Climate of Hunter*, which drew critical raves for a minimalistic, trance-like ambience that showed him keeping abreast of cutting-edge '80s rock trends. As of mid 1994, that was his last appearance on records, although a new album has been said to be in the offing for years from this notoriously reclusive figure, who has rarely been interviewed or even seen in public since his days of stardom. He was a substantial, if largely overlooked, influence upon the vocal style of David Bowie and Bryan Ferry. A biography, *Scott Walker: A Deep Shade* of Blue, was published by Virgin in the United Kingdom in 1994. —Richie Unterberger

○ **Scott** / 1967 / Fontana

Scott Walker's success as a teen idol singer of Spectorish ballads with the Walker Brothers in no way prepared listeners for the mordant, despairing lyrics of his solo debut. To compound the surprise, he does his best to imitate the vocal girth of Tony Bennett and Frank Sinatra on this mix of original tunes and covers, which also features sweeping, bloated orchestral arrangements. It was hardly rock, and pop of a most oddball sort, but it found a surprisingly large audience—in Britain, anyway, where it reached the Top 3 in 1967. Poke behind the velvet curtain of the languid MOR arrangements, and one finds a surprisingly literate existentialist at the helm of these proceedings. His lyrical nuances were probably lost on his audience of predominately teenage girls, though they've earned him a small cult audience that endures to this day. Besides presenting three of his own compositions, Walker covers tunes by Weill/Mann, Tim Hardin, and Andre and Dory Previn on this album, as well as three songs by his favorite writer, Jacquel Brel. Highlights include his exquisitely anguished rendition of Brel's classic "Amsterdam," and his dramatic cover of the early '60s Timi Yuro pop ballad "The Big Hurt." —Richie Unterberger

○ **Scott 2** / 1968 / Philips 7840

Although Walker's second album was his biggest commercial success, actually reaching #1 in Britain, it was not his greatest artistic triumph. His taste remains eclectic, encompassing Bacharach/David, Tim Hardin, and of course his main man Jacques Brel (who is covered three times on this album). And his own songwriting efforts hold their own in this esteemed company. "The Girls from Streets" and "Plastic Palace People" show an uncommonly ambitious lyricist cloaked behind the over-the-top, schmaltzy orchestral arrangements, one who is more interested in examining the seamy underside of glamor and romance than celebrating its glitter. The Brel tune "Next" must have lifted a few teenage mums' eyebrows with its not-so-hidden hints of homosexuality and abuse. Another Brel tune, "The Girl and the Dogs," is less controversial, but hardly less nasty in its jaded view of romance. Some of the material is not nearly as memorable, however, and the over-the-top show ballad production can get overbearing. The album included his first solo Top 20 UK hit, "Jackie." —Richie Unterberger

Scott 3 / 1969 / Philips 7882

Scott Walker's final British Top 10 album was the first to be dominated by his own songwriting. Ten of the 13 tunes on this 1969 LP are originals; the remaining three, naturally, were written by one of his chief inspirations, Jacques Brel. There are some interesting moments here. "Big Louise" talks about a hefty prostitute with shocking explicitness for a pop star album of the era. "Copenhagen" (like much of Walker's '60s work) foreshadows David Bowie. "No Last Tango" is a particularly vicious Brel song. "30 Century Man" is uncommonly folkish and focused tune for Walker. "We Came Through" is an oddball cavalry charge featuring one of his occasional forays into Ennio Morricone spaghetti western-like production. The tension between Walker's dense, foreboding lyrics and orchestral production is unusual, to say the least. But too often, it's too difficult to penetrate Walker's insights through Wally Scott's string-drenched production. It shrouds the lyrics in a fog that's often too syrupy to justify the effort needed to fight through it. —Richie Unterberger

○ **Scott 4** / 1969 / Philips 7913

Walker dropped out of the British Top 10 with his fourth album, but the result was probably his finest '60s LP. While the tension between the bloated production and his introspective, ambitious lyrics remains, much of the over-the-top bombast of the orchestral arrangements has been reined in, leaving a relatively stripped-down approach that complements his songs rather than smothering them. This is the first Walker album to feature entirely original material, and his songwriting is more lucid and cutting. Several of the tracks stand among his finest. "The Seventh Seal," based upon classic film by Ingmar Bergman, features remarkably ambitious (and relatively successful) lyrics set against a haunting Ennio Morricone-styled arrangement. "The Old Man's Back Again" also echoes Morricone and tackles no less ambitious a lyrical palette; "dedicated to the neo-Stalinist regime," the "old man" of this song was supposedly Joseph Stalin.

"Hero of the War" is also one of Walker's better vignettes, serenading his war hero with a cryptic mix of tribute and irony. Other songs show engaging folk, country, and soul influences that were largely buried on his previous solo albums. —Richie Unterberger

● **Boy Child: Best of 1967-1970** / 1990 / Fontana 842832

This collection of "Scott's best self-composed songs" features 20 Walker originals from his 1967-1970 heyday. While he covered some interesting material on his albums during this period, paying tribute to Jacques Brel with special devotion and frequency, his original compositions are his most enduring achievements. Besides such highlights as "Big Louise," "We Came Through," "The Seventh Seal," "Plastic Palace People," and "The Old Man's Back Again," it includes half a dozen songs that were not included on the four other solo albums that Fontana UK has reissued on CD. Some of those cuts are very strong, especially "The Rope and the Colt," a dramatic western ballad with an arrangement that would do Ennio Morricone proud; the positively eloquent despair of the ennui-ridden "Time Operator"; and "The Plague," a representative sampling of Walker's taste for the disquieting and bizarre. This is a recommended starting point for those interested in checking out this singularly strange '60s phenomenon, who was a relatively unacknowledged and undetected, but nonetheless substantial, influence on David Bowie and other fashionably decadent British singers. —Richie Unterberger

● **No Regrets: Best of Scott Walker & Walker Brothers** / 1992 / Fontana

Including both the Walker Brothers' hits ("The Sun Ain't Gonna Shine Any More," "Make It Easy on Yourself") and material from Scott Walker's solo albums, No Regrets: Best of the Walker Brothers is the best introduction to Walker's music. —Stephen Thomas Erlewine

Joe Walsh

b. 1947

Guitar / Rock & roll

After coming to national fame as the leader of the James Gang, Walsh's skewed humor and bluesy guitar chops have forged a nice solo career for him. Walsh's solo debut Barnstorm displayed him as not only an innovative guitarist but a competent keyboardist and a songwriter with much scope. Walsh's second solo effort, The Smoker You Drink, the Player You Get, perfectly suited the tastes of FM rock programmers and firmly established his career. "Rocky Mountain Way" and "Meadows" are hits off that album. Walsh also produced some outside projects, including Dan Fogelberg's first hit album, Souvenirs.

The Eagles enlisted Walsh as a replacement for Bernie Leadon in December of 1975. Their next studio album, Hotel California, heavily featured Walsh's playing, particularly on "Life in the Fast Lane" and "Hotel California." Walsh played on their live album and The Long Run, the band's swan song.

All along, Walsh has continued his solo efforts, scoring big in 1978 with But Seriously Folks ..., an album that brings his goofy humor to the forefront with the hit "Life's Been Good." "All Night Long," a track off The Urban Cowboy soundtrack, continued Walsh's string of success. During the '80s, Walsh has had sporadic success.

In addition to Dan Fogelberg, Walsh has produced other atists, including Spirit's Jay Ferguson and Ringo Starr (working as bandleader on Starr's late '80s/early '90s tours). In 1994, Walsh joined the reunited Eagles for their Hell Freezes Over tour. —Cub Koda and Rick Clark

○ **Barnstorm** / 1972 / Dunhill 50130

Even though he had developed quite a rep as the lead guitarist for the James Gang, Joe Walsh's debut (under the band moniker Barnstorm) was an impressive showcase for his songwriting and arranging. Produced by Bill Szymczyk, Barnstorm exudes a thick, textured sound. Some of Walsh's most distinctive guitar sounds are found here. Sonically, Barnstorm is shown to fine effect on this Mobile Fidelity reissue. Highlights include "Here We Go," "Mother Says," and "Turn to Stone." —Rick Clark

○ **The Smoker You Drink, the Player You Get** / 1973 / MCA 31121

On Walsh's second outing, he fused the dynamics and textures of Barnstorm, mixed in a few well-crafted tunes, perfect for FM radio, and scored his highest charting album. Smoker's centerpiece was the plodding "Rocky Mountain Way," a perfect vehicle for his soaring slidework and squirrelly tenor strangle. "Meadows" was also a substantial FM hit. Other highlights are "Days Gone By" and "Happy Ways." —*Rick Clark*

○ **But Seriously Folks** / Jan. 1978 / Asylum 141
This is his biggest solo success, featuring the hit "Life's Been Good." —*Cub Koda*

● **Best of Joe Walsh** / Feb. 1978 / MCA 1601
Featuring the biggest James Gang hits and early solo hits. —*Cub Koda*

Travis Wammack

b. 1946
Vocals, guitar / Rock & roll
A guitarist, singer, and young instrumental genius from Memphis who cut his first record at the tender age of 12, Travis Wammack is one of the great unheralded guitarists of rock & roll. A contemporary of Lonnie Mack, Wammack was simply the fastest guitar player in a town bursting at the seams with great guitarists. By the time he was 17, he appeared on the national charts with "Scratchy," a speed-burner instrumental featuring incredible distortion and dazzling technique. Several incredible singles followed, but none charted. By the late '60s, Wammack had moved into session work at the FAME Studios in Muscle Shoals, AL, playing on countless hits. He continues recording and touring to the present day (recently working as musical director for Little Richard), his hot and speedy guitar chops intact. —*Cub Koda*

○ **That Scratchy Guitar from Memphis** / 1987 / Bear Family 15415
Wammack's best instrumental and vocal sides from 1964 to 1967. Simply incredible. —*Cub Koda*

War

Group / Soul, funk, pop/rock
Freewheeling War mixed rock, jazz, and soul influences into a spicy stew throughout the '70s, resulting in a series of R&B and pop hits sporting funky melodies and politically aware messages. Born in Long Beach in 1969, the large combo initially served as rocker Eric Burdon's group, backing the ex-Animal on his 70-million-seller "Spill the Wine." Bidding Burdon adieu, the band signed with United Artists in 1971 and enjoyed its first smash the next year with "Slippin' into Darkness." Tapping into a sizzling, horn-fueled rock/soul synthesis, "The World Is a Ghetto," "The Cisco Kid," and "Why Can't We Be Friends?" all went gold during the mid '70s. Despite numerous personnel and label changes, War remained eminent throughout the '80s.

In the early '90s, War experienced a revival, partially due to the fact that all of their albums were reissued. But the group was also acknowledged as a primary influence on contemporary R&B and hip-hop. War released a new album in 1994 to capitalize on their newfound popularity. —*Bill Dahl*

○ **All Day Music** / Feb. 1971 / Rhino 71042
A great War album, the first where all their influences meshed. They blended gospel-tinged soul, funk, Afro-Latin and light jazz with enthusiastic group vocals and interplay, plus just the right amount of instrumental support and occasional solos by Lee Oskar on harmonica, Lonnie Jordan on keyboards, and Charles Miller on saxophones and flute. It also contained the fantastic "Slippin' into Darkness," one of their best arranged and performed numbers ever. —*Ron Wynn*

○ **World Is a Ghetto** / 1972 / Rhino 71043
War hit its peak with this 1972 album, the only one they ever released that topped the pop charts. The title track was a triumphant blend of great exchanges and unison vocals, plus concise and spirited musical contributions all around. It also contained the delightful "Cisco Kid" and elaborate "City, Country, City," plus the curious "Beetles in the Bog." Harmonica player Lee Oskar and percussionist Papa Dee Allen were at their best, as were keyboardist Lonnie Jordan and saxophonist/flutist Charles Miller, who would sadly be murdered eight years later. —*Ron Wynn*

○ **Deliver the Word** / 1973 / Rhino 71044
War began to slide a bit from their early '70s peak with this release. The best selection, "Gypsy Man," had to be edited, and thus Lee Oskar's roaring harmonica solo wasn't heard by anyone who didn't purchase the album. "Me and Baby Brother" was another of their mock-humorous hits, but overall, this wasn't nearly as sharp

or effective an album as they'd normally been making. —*Ron Wynn*

Why Can't We Be Friends / 1975 / Rhino 71051
War returned with a vengeance and new material in the mid '70s, as the title hit was both a pop and R&B Top 10 smash, and "Low Rider" did even better, topping the soul surveys and peaking at #7 pop. More importantly, they were once more a carefree, loose, and jamming band, mixing and matching soul, Afro-Latin, funk, and jazz. Unfortunately, it was the last definitive War album, as ego and production battles would soon undermine their success. —*Ron Wynn*

★ **Greatest Hits** / 1976 / United Artists 648
If you can find this collection (only available on vinyl), get it. *Greatest Hits* truly lives up to the title, with tracks like "Summer," "All Day Music," "Cisco Kid," "Slippin' into Darkness," "The World Is a Ghetto," and more. —*Rick Clark*

★ **Best of War & More** / 1991 / Rhino 70072
It's not a perfect compilation by any means—there's no "The World Is a Ghetto" and a bad remix of "Low Rider," for starters—but *Best of War & More* is the only compilation available from this influential band, so it's the pick by default. But search for that original vinyl, because it was definitive. —*Stephen Thomas Erlewine*

Billy Ward

Piano / R&B
Though they were often billed on records as Billy Ward & the Dominoes, Ward was, in fact, not their lead singer. But as group leader and musical director, he sure knew how to pick them, as evidenced by the back-to-back tenures of frontmen Clyde McPhatter and Jackie Wilson. Originally formed in 1950, the Dominoes were one of the first groups to infuse their music with a strong gospel flavor, changing the sound of R&B vocal-group stylings forever and influencing everyone from Nolan Strong to Smokey Robinson in the process. —*Cub Koda*

★ **Sixty Minute Men: The Best of Billy Ward & His Dominoes** / 1993 / Rhino 71509
Billy Ward and the Dominoes were not R&B's first great group, but they were among its earliest flamboyant, openly sexy aggregations. "Sixty Minute Man" might have been played for laughs on one level, but there was no mistaking its theme or its intended audience. The Dominoes included Clyde McPhatter and later Jackie Wilson, a pair of dynamos. McPhatter and Wilson possessed thunderbolt voices, shimmering, radiant, and rangy vocal weapons that generated immediate impact and reaction. Ward was far too much of a disciplinarian and taskmaster to accomodate these free spirits, and once Wilson departed, the Dominoes were never again an R&B factor. But during their golden years, they ruled the R&B roost. McPhatter's eubilent tenor is featured on 16 cuts. There was once an entire Wilson album of King/Federal material, but unless the old Gusto albums reappear on CD, you will have to be content with these three selections. Since one is the riveting "Rags to Riches," that is acceptable. The other tunes include their signature song, "Sixty Minute Man," the one classic that did not feature either McPhatter or Wilson on lead but instead highlighted Bill Brown. The final number is the past-their-prime "Star Dust." The bonus is two Little Esther tunes, "The Deacon Moves In" and "Heart to Heart." —*Ron Wynn*

Jennifer Warnes

b. , Seattle, WA
Vocals / Pop, country rock
Over the last 25 years, Jennifer Warnes has enjoyed a widely varied career, including performing the lead female role in the Los Angeles production of *Hair*, appearing as a regular on the '60s hit show "The Smothers Brothers Comedy Hour," scoring hits as a country-rock/pop singer ("Right Time of the Night," "I Know a Heartache When I See One"), winning a Grammy for her duet with Joe Cocker on their version of "Up Where We Belong" from the movie *An Officer and a Gentleman*, and garnering critical acclaim for her solo interpretations of Leonard Cohen's songs on the album *Famous Blue Raincoat*. In 1987 Warnes was featured on Roy Orbison's TV special, and she also landed a #1 hit duet with former Righteous Brother Bill Medley on "(I've Had) the Time of My Life" from the film *Dirty Dancing*. —*Rick Clark*

○ **Best of Jennifer Warnes** / 1982 / Arista 8348

This collection covers Warnes' earlier hits, like "Right Time of the Night," "I Know a Heartache When I See One," "When the Feeling Comes Around," and "Could It Be Love." The omission of her chart-topping duets with Bill Medley ("The Time of My Life") and Joe Cocker ("Up Where We Belong") as well as key *Famous Blue Raincoat* tracks keeps this from being definitive. —*Rick Clark*

● **Famous Blue Raincoat** / 1987 / Private Music 82092
Leonard Cohen's material never received a more elegant treatment than the one Jennifer Warnes gave him on *Famous Blue Raincoat*. Warnes is supported by an impressive cast of sidemen, including Stevie Ray Vaughan. The quality of this recording is first-rate. Among the many great songs found here is a powerful version of "Joan of Arc." "Song of Bernadette," "Coming Back to You," and "Came So Far for Beauty" are other highlights. —*Rick Clark*

Dionne Warwick

b. Dec. 12, 1940
Vocals / Pop
The magically melodic voice of Dionne Warwick and the sophisticated pop compositions of Burt Bacharach and Hal David were the proverbial match made in heaven. Warwick proved the prolific songwriting team's favorite interpreter, scaling the pop and soul charts time and again with her soaring renditions of their memorable songs.

Warwick hailed from a musical brood with a strong gospel heritage, and her sister Dee Dee scored a few hits of her own. Dionne's sultry pipes stood out, even on the highly competitive background vocal scene in New York, and she got a chance to step out front in 1963, hitting big on Scepter with the uptown soul classic "Don't Make Me Over."

Under the expert tutelage of Bacharach and David, who doubled as her producers, Warwick's sound soon became smoother and more accessible to pop programming—a formula that resulted in the massive acceptance of her "Walk on By," "I Say a Little Prayer," "This Girl's in Love with You," and a slew of others.

Strangely, Warwick never made it to the top of the pop charts until she broke away from her mentors, traveling to Philadelphia to record the R&B-oriented "Then Came You" with the Spinners in 1974. As elegant and tasteful as ever, Dionne Warwick's breathy vocals still haven't gone out of style—she's managed to remain contemporary while never jeopardizing her appeal. —*Bill Dahl*

★ **Dionne Warwick Collection: Her All-Time Greatest Hits** / Jan. 1989 / Rhino 71100
The finest collection of Warwick material compiled by anyone, this excellent set gathered every Warwick gem and smartly remastered them. It's a definitive CD, containing several landmark releases featuring the collaborative compositions of Burt Bacharach and Hal David. These songs underscored Warwick's ability to embody her pop tunes with a soulful, but also light and innocent, quality. "Don't Make Me Over," "Message to Michael" and "You'll Never Get to Heaven" are among the triumphs. It also has excellent liner notes and intelligent sequencing. This is by far the set to get if you want a comprehensive presentation of Warwick's pop/soul greatness. —*Ron Wynn*

Greatest Hits 79-90 / Feb. 1989 / Arista 8540
This collection gathered the great hits from Dionne Warwick's rebirth on Arista. Barry Manilow wisely recast her doing sophisticated pop and moved her into adult contemporary love ballads and away from straight soul and R&B. It was an inspired move and returned her to the top charts frequently in the late '70s and '80s. But while the songs were good, the collection didn't fare so well. —*Ron Wynn*

○ **Hidden Gems: Best of Dionne Warwick, Vol. 2** / 1992 / Rhino 70329
A fine collection of rarities and forgotten singles from Warwick's heyday with Bacharach/David; it's a good supplement to Rhino's *Dionne Warwick Collection.* —*Stephen Thomas Erlewine*

Was (Not Was)

Group / Pop/rock, soul
Was (Not Was) plays contemporary R&B dance music, with lyrics that range from the satiric to the bizarre. The group is led by Detroit natives David Weiss (David Was), who plays flute and writes those lyrics, and Don Fagenson (Don Was), who plays bass

and writes music, but the group is fronted by singers Harry Bowens and Sweet Pea Atkinson. Was (Not Was) first gained notice for a dance single called "Wheel Me Out" in 1980. Their first album, *Was (Not Was)* (1981), did not reach the charts, but its followup, *Born to Laugh at Tornados* (1983), did. Then little was heard from the group for five years. They returned in 1988 with *What Up, Dog?* which featured the #16 hit "Spy in the House of Love" and the #7 hit "Walk the Dinosaur." (During this period, Don Was had become a prominent record producer, handling the board for Bonnie Raitt's Grammy-winning *Nick of Time,* among many other mainstream pop records.) The fourth Was (Not Was) album, *Are You Okay?* appeared in 1990.

Are You Okay? wasn't as commercially successful as the previous *What Up, Dog?* After the album's release, Don Was continued to pursue his production career, which began to increase tensions between him and David. In 1993, Was (Not Was) officially parted ways. —*William Ruhlmann*

Born to Laugh at Tornados / 1983 / David Geffen Co. 24251
The Was brothers provide a strange bunch of songs with irresistible dance beats, plus an array of guest singers that is, well, unusual to say the least: Mitch Ryder, Dough Fieger (of the Knack), Ozzy Osbourne, and, on the ballad "Zaz Turned Blue," Mel Tormé. —*William Ruhlmann*

● **What Up, Dog?** / 1988 / Chrysalis 21664
The guests are fewer (though Frank Sinatra, Jr., sings one song), but the oddities go on, with "11 MPH," a review of the JFK assassination, and "Dad I'm in Jail," a proud rant by David Was. Also included: the hits "Spy in the House of Love" and "Walk the Dinosaur." —*William Ruhlmann*

Are You Okay? / 1990 / Chrysalis 21778
The "hit" is a remake of "Papa Was a Rollin' Stone," but the album is more memorable for typically oddball tunes like "I Blew Up the United States" and "Elvis' Rolls Royce," which features a droll vocal by Leonard Cohen. —*William Ruhlmann*

Baby Washington

b. Nov. 13, 1940, SC
Vocals / R&B, soul
Her sultry delivery earned Justine "Baby" Washington R&B chart bows in four different decades, most notably on the delectable uptown soul classic "That's How Heartaches Are Made" for Sue Records in 1963. Born in South Carolina but raised in Harlem, Washington was a member of the Hearts in 1956 before tallying her first R&B hit in 1959 with "The Time" for Neptune. Billed occasionally as Jeanette or Justine Washington, she scaled the soul charts into the mid '70s with hits still hot from the '60s, such as her nugget "Only Those in Love." —*Bill Dahl*

That's How Heartaches Are Made / 1963 / Collectables 5124
Jeanette "Baby" Washington cut her finest songs for Sue in the early '60s. Though few made the charts, all were delivered with conviction, sung in an earnest and riveting manner, and produced with minimal gimmicks. While the title track's perhaps her best cut, this album thankfully covers many lesser known tracks and avoids the singles that have frequently popped up on numerous anthologies. "Careless Hands" and "Standing on the Pier" are superior to material that did get airplay; even the always troublesome Collectables sound quality can't override the importance of this release. —*Ron Wynn*

● **Best of Baby Washington** / 1987 / Collectables 5040
Jeanne "Baby" Washington could one moment sound like a hard-edged, no-nonsense wailer and the next a wounded sparrow. She never enjoyed any pop attention, but equaled Dionne Warwick and Maxine Brown among female light soul singers. This collection covers her late '50s and early '60s songs for Neptune and Sue, including "The Bells," "The Time," and "That's How Heartaches Are Made." —*Ron Wynn*

The Waterboys

Group / Alternative pop/rock, folk rock
A critically acclaimed folk-rock band led by Scottish singer-songwriter and guitarist Mike Scott. The group's first recording was a five-track mini-album, *The Waterboys,* released in 1984, at which time the only other regular band member was sax player Anthony Thistlewaite. By the time their second album, *A Pagan Place,* was released, they had added keyboard player Karl Wallinger. They first gained extensive recognition for their third

album, *This Is the Sea* (1985), which got to #37 in the UK charts and included the #26 single "The Whole of the Moon." Wallinger then left to form World Party, and Scott spent more than three years preparing *Fisherman's Blues*, which, when it appeared in late 1988, showed a distinct turn toward Irish folk music. It was followed two years later by *Room to Roam*. Scott backed away from Irish folk on 1993's *Dream Harder*, which featured a more straightforward, epic rock that recalled their earlier albums. — *William Ruhlmann*

○ **This Is the Sea** / 1985 / Chrysalis 21543
Mike Scott combines the forcefulness of rock with the earnestness of folk and adds a mystical poetic soul to this brilliant album, which also features notable musical contributions from saxophonist Anthony Thistlewaite and keyboardist Karl Wallinger. — *William Ruhlmann*

○ **Fisherman's Blues** / 1988 / Ensign 21589
The Waterboys turn into a neo-traditional Irish folk band, complete with mandolins and fiddles, and Mike Scott's poetic muse just gets better. — *William Ruhlmann*

● **Best of the Waterboys (1981-1990)** / 1991 / Ensign 21845
Sums up the story so far, tracing the band's evolution from rock to folk, the constant sensibility of Mike Scott remaining intact. — *William Ruhlmann*

Roger Waters

b. Sep. 6, 1944
Vocals, bass / Progressive rock
Roger Waters was the bassist for Pink Floyd from 1965 to 1983. Waters assumed an increasingly dominant position in the band, writing all lyrics in addition to some of the music as of *The Dark Side of the Moon* (1973) and singing most of the lead vocals on *The Wall* (1979). Waters issued his debut solo album, *The Pros and Cons of Hitch Hiking*, in 1984. In the mid '80s, he engaged in a protracted legal battle, arguing that the other members of Pink Floyd could not continue using the name without him in the band; he lost. In 1987 Waters released his second album, *Radio K.A.O.S.*, and in 1990 he staged a concert version of *The Wall* in Berlin. In 1992 he finished his third album, *Amused to Death*. — *William Ruhlmann*

○ **Radio K.A.O.S.** / 1987 / Columbia 40795
There's more story than can be effectively told on this concept album dealing with radio, computers, and the threat of nuclear war, but many of the songs are up to Waters's Pink Floyd standard, and some rock out more than his former band ever did. — *William Ruhlmann*

Wall in Berlin 1990 / 1990 / Mercury 846611
This is a gala two-disc live rendition of the Pink Floyd concept album, employing a raft of guest stars including Van Morrison, Sinéad O'Connor, Joni Mitchell, the Scorpions, and others. — *William Ruhlmann*

● **Amused to Death** / Sep. 1, 1992 / Columbia 47127
Yet another installment in Waters's lectures about the horrors of war and man's inhumanity to man, *Amused to Death* is helped considerably by the presence of Jeff Beck, who contributes some brilliant, free-form guitar to the meandering songs. Waters himself is in fine form, spitting out bitter, sarcastic lyrics over his slow, grandiose instrumental backdrops. While he could have fleshed out the melodies a little bit more, his execution is what matters, and his performance on *Amused to Death* is the liveliest of any of his solo records. — *Stephen Thomas Erlewine*

Jody Watley

b. Jan. 30, 1959, Chicago, IL
Vocals / Urban soul, dance-pop
Jody Watley got her start as a dancer on the TV show "Soul Train." From 1977 to 1984, she was a singer in the group Shalamar. Her debut solo album, *Jody Watley* (1987), sold a million copies and produced three Top 10 hits—"Looking for a New Love," "Don't You Want Me," and "Some Kind of Lover." As a result of its success, Watley won the Grammy Award for Best New Artist of 1987. Her second album, *Larger Than Life* (1989), went gold and contained the #2 pop hit "Real Love" as well as the Top 10s "Friends" and "Everything." *You Wanna Dance With Me?* released at the end of that year, contained dance remixes of her hits. Watley's

third album, *Affairs of the Heart*, was released at the end of 1991. — *William Ruhlmann*

● **Jody Watley** / 1987 / MCA 5898
State-of-the-art R&B/dance pop by a singer who was a veteran of the genre long before cutting her debut album. — *William Ruhlmann*

○ **Larger Than Life** / 1989 / MCA 6276
The former Shalamar member and goddaughter of Jackie Wilson followed her hit debut album with a solid second entry, though it was much more uptempo and dance-dominated. Watley secured a huge pop and R&B hit with "Real Love," and "Friends" was a new jack swing number with rap contributions from Whodini. "Everything" was another Top 10 pop and R&B success. While the thinness of Watley's vocals and the preponderance of predictable beats seemed to indicate trouble lay ahead, she happily took the gold record certification for the album. — *Ron Wynn*

Jimmy Webb

Vocals / Singer-songwriter, pop/rock
Even if you never have heard a Jimmy Webb album, you have at least heard his songs. During the late '60s and early '70s, Webb was writing a series of hits for the Fifth Dimension, Glen Campbell, Richard Harris, and Cher, including "Wichita Lineman" and "By the Time I Get to Phoenix"; both songs have become pop standards. His first hit was the Fifth Dimension's "Up, Up and Away," which was eventually used in TWA television commercials.

After having many different artists record his songs successfully, Webb officially launched a solo career in 1970; a collection of his demos had been released against his will in 1968. Although his debut album, *Words and Music*, earned mixed reviews, it helped him gain a sizable cult following. While he recorded a series of overlooked albums in the '70s, other artists continued to record his songs, including Art Garfunkel, Judy Collins, Joe Cocker, and Lowell George. During the '80s, he concentrated on scoring films and television shows, releasing only one album. In 1993, he returned to the studio to record his first album since 1982; produced by Linda Rondstadt, *Suspending Disbelief* earned good reviews, but poor sales, which seems to be Webb's curse. Even though he has never has had success with his own recordings, Jimmy Webb remains one of the best-loved and most-recorded songwriters of his generation. — *Stephen Thomas Erlewine*

○ **El Mirage** / 1977 / Atlantic 18218
Produced by George Martin, *El Mirage* is one of Webb's strongest albums. As always, the songs are perfectly constructed but this time sung with more confidence than ever before. Highlights include "If You See Me Getting Smaller" and "Christian No." — *Chris Woodstra*

○ **Suspending Disbelief** / 1993 / Elektra 61506
After a several-year absence, Webb returns with one of his most polished efforts to date. His hook-filled melodies are instantly endearing while he sings a love song to his sports car and remembers a meeting with Elvis. His voice, never one of his strong points in the past, has aged particularly well. — *Chris Woodstra*

● **Archive** / 1993 /
This 20-track anthology takes an exhaustive look at Webb's overlooked career as a recording artist from 1970 to 1977. Though he recorded some of his finest songs during this period to much critical acclaim, the four albums represented here were almost completely ignored commercially. Includes his own versions of the hits "Galveston" and "The Highwayman" as well as lost classics like "P. F. Sloan," "Christian No," and the hauntingly beautiful "Met Her on a Plane." — *Chris Woodstra*

Wedding Present

Group / Alternative pop/rock
Sometimes jangly and sometimes brash, the Wedding Present, from Leeds, takes Joy Division and puts it on motorcycles. — *Bruce Eder*

○ **Bizarro** / 1990 / RCA 2173
Suprisingly listenable frenetic rock. — *Robert Gordon*

● **Hit Parade, Part 1** / 1992 / First Warning 75711
Britain's Wedding Present has hit on an interesting marketing ploy in its home country: the group has been releasing one lim-

ited edition single for each month of 1992. Hit Parade 1 (First Warning/BMG), a 12-track compilation of the first six, presents a rather unrelenting onslaught of fuzzy guitars and dour, aggressive vocals. The effect can be riveting or disconcerting, depending on your mood. Definitely a love 'em or hate 'em band. *—Roch Parisien*

Ween

Group / Alternative pop/rock
Since 1990, Ween have been making records that consume pop culture whole and smirkingly spit it back out. The duo of Dean and Gene Ween (born Mickey Melchiondo and Aaron Freeman) make records that read like parodies but sound like pop albums. Essentially, they are two spoiled, overeducted suburban college kids, screwing around with a four-track cassette recorder in their parents' basement; they sing in funny voices, speed up the tape, make noises with their instruments, slow down the tape, and write some incredibly enjoyable, subversive pop songs. It's like what They Might Be Giants would sound like if they relied on smartass humor instead of hooks and melodies. *—Stephen Thomas Erlewine*

● **Pure Guava** / 1992 / Elektra 61428
Ween's third album is their most accessible yet, but it remains true to their gleefully demented, fractured pop visions. *—Stephen Thomas Erlewine*

Bob Weir

b. 1947
Vocals, guitar / Rock & roll
Bob Weir is a guitarist and vocalist in the Grateful Dead. He was a founding member of the group in 1965 and has been with it throughout its history. Weir began making records under his own name and in other configurations in 1972 and has released solo albums as well as leading Kingfish and Bobby and the Midnites. Most recently Weir has toured in a duo with bassist Rob Wasserman. *—William Ruhlmann*

● **Ace** / 1972 / Grateful Dead 40042
Weir's debut solo album is really a Grateful Dead album in disguise and, at that, not a bad followup to the group's *American Beauty* album. While Weir handles lead vocals, the rest of the band is on the album, and the selections, including "Greatest Story Ever Told," "Playing in the Band," "One More Saturday Night," and "Cassidy," have entered the Dead's concert repertoire and the list of Dead Head favorites. *—William Ruhlmann*

Heaven Help the Fool / 1978 / Arista 8165
A slickly produced pop-rock album, but one that demonstrates the range of Weir's abilities. *—William Ruhlmann*

○ **Bobby & the Midnights** / 1981 / Arista 8558
Weir gets jazzy with drummer Billy Cobham and others. *—Jeff Tamarkin*

Paul Weller

Vocals, guitar / Soul, pop/rock
After disbanding the Style Council, former Jam leader Paul Weller went solo, making a series of soul-inspired pop/rock records. While his self-titled 1992 debut a return to form, it was the following year's *Wild Wood* (not released in the United States until 1994) that showed he was still a vital songwriter and artist. Like the rest of Weller's work, the album was a hit in nearly every country except the United States. *—Stephen Thomas Erlewine*

○ **Paul Weller** / 1992 / London 828343
The lyrics from Weller's debut solo album suggest that much of late '80s retreat was spent wrestling with past demons and self-doubt. Take "Uh Huh Oh Yeh": "I took a trip down boundary lane/Try an' find myself again/At least a part I left somewhere/Buried under a hedgerow near." Musically, the better moments have neither the hard edge of the Jam or the mellow vibe of the Style Council, but mine some funky ground in between. Jacko Peake's sax and flute contributions give several tracks a summery, mid-period John Mayall blues-jazz feel. Weller's voice has matured into a deep, soulful, resonant instrument, in keeping with his new inward-looking material. He's obviously come to terms with being an effective chronicler of his own feelings rather than being the spokesperson of a generation. *—Roch Parisien*

● **Wildwood** / 1993 / London

Mary Wells

b. May 13, 1943, Detroit, MI, **d.** Jul. 26, 1990
Vocals / Motown
Motown's first female star, Wells received international acclaim under the wing of Smokey Robinson. Her original recording of "My Guy" in 1964 is one of the most recorded songs from the Motown label. She was ill advised to leave the company in 1964, and future productions planned for her made Diana Ross a superstar. Wells never again scored a hit. Her voice was silenced by throat cancer in 1990. *—Rick A. Bueche*

○ **My Guy** / 1964 / Motown 5167
The Temptations weren't the only Motown act that benefited from Smokey Robinson's production genius. He demonstrated on this album his ability to craft and then hone great material for female acts, something he'd later repeat with the Marvelettes. Besides the title track, which became Motown's first Top 10 and #1 pop hit, there were other strong tunes such as "He's the One I Love" and "At Last" that weren't hits but certainly should have been. *—Ron Wynn*

● **Compact Command Performances** / 1985 / Motown 9058
The recent two-disc Mary Wells collection eclipses the value of this set, which previously was perhaps the definitive Wells anthology. It contains just what you'd expect: "My Guy" and "You Beat Me to the Punch," plus hits with Marvin Gaye and other representative cuts. It was decently remastered as well. *—Ron Wynn*

○ **Looking Back 1961-1964** / 1993 / Motown
This two-CD, 43-track box set is the most comprehensive retrospective of Motown's biggest female star before Diana Ross. Although her first hit, "Bye Bye Baby," presented Wells as a blues belter, she quickly settled into a sly and sassy groove. Subsequent hits like "You Beat Me to the Punch," "Two Lovers," and "My Guy" (all included here) made the most of her shy, seductive voice by teaming her with some great songs and production by Smokey Robinson. Though many of these tunes were relegated to B sides, album tracks, or even the can (11 were previously unreleased), the material—written by Motown stalwarts like Berry Gordy, Holland-Dozier, Holland, and Mickey Stevenson when Smokey was unavailable—is not far below the hits in quality. *—Richie Unterberger*

Paul Westerberg

Vocals, guitar / Rock & roll
After disbanding the Replacements in 1991, singer-songwriter Paul Westerberg resurfaced the following year with two songs on the *Singles* soundtrack. A year later, he began his solo career in earnest with *14 Songs*, a loose effort that recalled a cross between the driving pop-rock of *Pleased to Meet Me* and the weary, acoustic ballads of *All Shook Down*. *—Stephen Thomas Erlewine*

● **14 Songs** / Jun. 15, 1993 / Sire/Reprise 45255
Falling somewhere between the sound of *All Shook Down* and the songwriting of *Tim*, Paul Westerberg's first solo album since the breakup of the Replacements is a strong yet incoherent set of songs from one of the best songwriters of the '80s. Sounding like the optimistic version of the last Replacements album, *14 Songs* is not as raw as *Let It Be* or *Tim* or as consistent as *Pleased to Meet Me*, but it is a solid collection of expertly crafted rock and pop songs. *—Stephen Thomas Erlewine*

Wham!

Group / Dance-pop, pop/rock
Wham! was a UK pop/dance duo formed in 1981 by George Michael (born Yorgos Panayiotou, June 26, 1963) and Andrew Ridgeley (b. June 25, 1963). Combining light soul music with slow, romantic ballads, they first hit the UK charts in the fall of 1982 with "Young Guns (Go for It)." It hit #3, the first of 10 UK Top 10 hits for the duo. The first Wham! album, *Fantastic*, topped the UK charts in 1983. The group broke through in the United States the following year with "Wake Me Up before You Go-Go," the first of three straight #1 hits. The second of those chart-toppers was "Careless Whisper," billed as "featuring George Michael," the first sign that Michael, who sang lead and wrote the songs, was emerging as a solo entity. Nevertheless, Wham! continued through 1986, finishing their career at Wembley Stadium

in England, after which Michael went on to a successful solo career. —*William Ruhlmann*

● **Make It Big** / 1984 / Columbia 39595
George Michael demonstrates a thorough knowledge of danceable pop, from the '60s-ish "Wake Me up Before You Go-Go" to the tear-jerking ballad "Careless Whisper." Also includes "Everything She Wants" and "Freedom." —*William Ruhlmann*

Music from the Edge of Heaven / 1986 / Columbia 40285
More of a hodgepodge of tracks than a coherent album, this still includes the Top 10 hits "I'm Your Man," "A Different Corner," and "The Edge of Heaven." —*William Ruhlmann*

The Whispers

Group / R&B, soul, urban
The Whispers are a veteran R&B quintet with an impressive 23-year legacy of R&B hits. Formed in Los Angeles by twins Walter and Wallace Scott, Nicholas Caldwell, Marcus Hutson, and Gordy Harmon (who left in 1973), the Whispers turned up on the Dore label in 1964 with "I Was Born when You Kissed Me." In 1969 the quintet climbed the soul charts for the first time with "The Time Has Come" on Soul Clock, and they cracked the R&B Top 10 the next year with "Seems Like I Gotta Do Wrong." They've remained hitmakers ever since for the labels Janus, Soul Train, and Solar, with smashes like the solid gold chart-topper "And the Beat Goes On" in 1980 and another #1 urban-contemporary hit, "Rock Steady," in 1987. After being their backbone and selling point since the group's inception, twin lead vocalists Walter and Wallace Scott departed for solo careers in 1993. —*Bill Dahl and Ron Wynn*

● **Best of the Whispers** / 1982 / Solar 4242
This isn't a completely accurate title, as the collection doesn't contain their Dore or Janus material. Instead, it focuses on their best known cuts from the Solar years, when they became an R&B power. The twin leads of Walter and Wallace Scott plus their polished productions and smoother sound made them quite popular in the '70s, and such singles as "It's a Love Thing," "Lady," and "Make It with You" were included. —*Ron Wynn*

Just Gets Better with Time / 1987 / Solar 75303
A reissue of their landmark release. —*Ron Wynn*

○ **More of the Night** / Jul. 23, 1990 / Capitol 92957
A highly representative session. —*Ron Wynn*

Dr. Love / Quicksilver 5075
Cool, smooth soul from this California vocal group. —*Ron Wynn*

○ **In the Mood** / Solar 75321
Marvelous ballads and great contemporary dance hits. —*Ron Wynn*

● **Vintage Whispers** / Solar 75306
A reissue of their prime hits. —*Ron Wynn*

White Zombie

Group / Heavy metal
All garish colors and trashy noise, White Zombie brought some sleazy fun back to heavy metal, celbrating the sheer schlock of cheap sex and bad horror movies. Although they gathered a cult following with a series of independent albums in the late '80s, it wasn't until their video for "Thunder Kiss '65" was aired on MTV's "Beavis & Butt-head" in 1993 that the band crossed over to a large audience. And they were the rare metal band that could appeal to jaded, post-modern hipsters; with their campy lyrics and theatrics, it was clear that the band didn't take themselves seriously. —*Stephen Thomas Erlewine*

● **La Sexorcisto: Devil Music Vol. 1** / 1992 / David Geffen Co. 24460
White Zombie carves out a unique identity for itself in the grunge/thrash genre with this one. The prerequisite loud guitars and shouting vocalist are here, but this album shows an obsession with '60s trash culture, particularly fast cars and grade-B horror movies. The subject matter of Rob Zombie's lyrics, along with frequent movie samples, help this group stand out from their more generic, disaffected brethren. —*Steve Huey*

Barry White

b. Sep. 12, 1944
Vocals / Disco, soul, urban R&B

Barry White has been involved in the popular music industry since age 11, when he played piano on Jesse Belvin's hit single "Goodnight My Love." He recorded with the Upfronts for Lumntone in 1960, then as a lead vocalist for Atlantic in 1964 and for Downey and Veep in 1965 under the name of Barry Lee. He was an A&R man for Mustang/Bronco Records in 1966 and 1967. White formed the female trio Love Unlimited in 1969, and also became leader of the 40-piece Love Unlimited orchestra. His solo career was revitalized in the early '70s as his formidable, deep, captivating bass, coupled with psuedo-sophisticated strings and elaborate productions, helped him rack up five #1 hits and seven other Top 10 R&B hits from 1973 until 1978 for 20th Century Records. He also scored five Top 10 pop singles and one #1 in that same stretch. "I'm Gonna Love You a Little More Baby" started the string in 1973, and his final Top 10 R&B single was "Your Sweetness Is My Weakness," which peaked at #2 in 1978. Throughout the '80s, White had a hard time keeping his audience, although he recorded consistently through the decade. He scored a mild comeback by being one of the featured vocalists on Quincy Jones's single "The Garden" in 1989 and continues recording in the '90s. —*Ron Wynn*

○ **Greatest Hits, Vol. 1** / 1975 / Casablanca 822782
Before a definitive multidisc boxed set was issued in the '90s, there were two single-album volumes of Barry White hits released by Casablanca in the '70s. The first edition was the best, with sweeping versions of such disco classics as "Can't Get Enough of Your Love Babe" and "You're the First, the Last, My Everything." White's productions and arrangements were never as intricate as they seemed, but his booming baritone and romantic dialogue sounded convincing when underscored by the lush backgrounds. —*Ron Wynn*

○ **Greatest Hits, Vol. 2** / 1981 / Casablanca 822783
This second set of Barry White hits isn't quite as impressive or essential as its predecessor. White's arrangements and compositions grew stale as the '70s wore on, and he recycled the romantic dialogue and exploited the robust baritone until he became a caricature of himself. —*Ron Wynn*

○ **Just for You** / 1992 / Casablanca 514143
A three-disc box set that contains more music than anyone but the most devoted fan could want. —*Stephen Thomas Erlewine*

● **Best of Barry White** / 1994 / Casablanca
Condensing the best moments from the two *Greatest Hits* collections onto one disc, *The Best of Barry White* is the deep-voiced disco crooner's one essential album. —*Stephen Thomas Erlewine*

Maurice White

b. Dec. 19, 1941
Vocals / Soul, funk
Best known as the brains behind Earth, Wind & Fire, one of the most innovative and wildly successful funk aggregations of the '70s and '80s, White's solo history is also fascinating. Born in Memphis, he moved to Chicago in his teens and became house drummer at Chess Records during the '60s, playing on countless Windy City soul sides. In 1967, he replaced drummer Red Holt with the Ramsey Lewis Trio and remained with the popular jazz group into 1969. White then formed the Salty Peppers with his brother Verdine, regrouping as Earth, Wind & fire two years later. In 1985, White stepped out briefly as a solo, updating Ben E. King's ever-popular "Stand by Me" on Columbia, but two followups failed to match the impressive sales figures of his initial solo project. —*Bill Dahl*

● **Maurice White** / Columbia 39883
Not a high point for this talented Earth, Wind & Fire leader gone solo. —*Ron Wynn*

Whitesnake

Group / Hard rock, heavy metal
After recording two solo albums, former Deep Purple vocalist David Coverdale formed Whitesnake around 1977. In the glut of hard rock and heavy metal bands of the late '70s, their first albums got somewhat lost in the shuffle, although they were fairly popular in Europe in Japan. During 1982, Coverdale took some time off, so he could take care of his sick daughter. When he re-merged with a new version of Whitesnake in 1984, the band sounded revitalized and energetic. *Slide It In* may have relied on Led Zeppelin and Deep Purple's old tricks, but the band had a

knack for writing hooks; the record became their first platinum album. Three years later, Whitesnake released an eponymous album that was even better. Portions of the album were blatantly derivative—"Still of the Night" was a dead ringer for early Zeppelin—but the group could write powerul, heavy rockers like "Here I Go Again" that were driven as much by melody as riffs, as well as hit power ballads like "Is This Love." *Whitesnake* was an enormous international success, selling over six million copies in the United States alone.

Before they recorded their followup, 1989's *Slip of the Tongue*, Coverdale again assembled a completely version of the band, featuring guitar virtuoso Steve Vai. Although the record went platinum, it was a considerable disappointment after the across-the-boards success of *Whitesnake*. Coverdale put Whitesnake on hiatus after that album. In 1993, he released a collaboration with former Led Zeppelin guitarist Jimmy Page that was surprisingly lackluster. The following year, Whitesnake released a greatest hits album, and it seemed likely that Coverdale was going to form a new version of the band. —*Stephen Thomas Erlewine*

○ **Slide It In** / 1984 / David Geffen Co. 4018
With its combination of stadium-sized hard-rock riffing and solid commercial melodies, *Slide It In* laid the groundwork for the blockbuster followup *Whitesnake*. Nevertheless, the album is rawer and cruder than their subsequent pop hit and is more representative of the band's metal roots. —*Stephen Thomas Erlewine*

○ **Whitesnake** / 1987 / David Geffen Co. 24099
After slugging it out in the British hard-rock market for almost 10 years, Whitesnake achieved multiplatinum success with this highly crafted mainstream AOR. Includes the #1 "Here I Go Again," "Is This Love," and the Led Zeppelin rip "Still of the Night." —*AMG*

Slip of the Tongue / Feb. 1989 / David Geffen Co. 24249
A replica of the mega-hit *Whitesnake*, *Slip of the Tongue* wasn't as successful because the band's songs weren't as catchy and the riffs weren't as powerful. Not even the presence of guitar superhero Steve Vai could add excitement to the band's bland, futile attempt at keeping its pop audience. —*Stephen Thomas Erlewine*

● **Whitesnake's Greatest Hits** / 1994 / David Geffen Co.
All of the best moments from Whitesnake's late '80s glory days collected on one disc. —*Stephen Thomas Erlewine*

Chris Whitley

Vocals / Singer-songwriter, blues rock
Chris Whitley writes and sings provocatively dark folk/blues/pop. His debut featured an appropriately haunting production job by Daniel Lanois (U2, Bob Dylan). —*Rick Clark*

○ **Living with the Law** / Dec. 5, 1991 / Columbia 46966
A stirring and classy debut of well-crafted blues, which was released to a flurry of critical praise. Whitley combines dreamy storytelling with commanding electric guitar work—all with the touch of a journeyman's blues. —*Donna DiChario*

The Who

Group / British invasion, hard rock
Founded in the early '60s by Pete Townshend, John Entwistle, and Roger Daltrey (with Keith Moon coming along slightly later), the Who were originally a fairly conventional R&B-based outfit, with Townshend and Daltrey sharing guitar chores, Enwistle on bass, and Doug Sanden (later replaced by Keith Moon) on drums. Early on, however, they fell under the influence of Johnny Kidd & the Pirates, a British band that pioneered a lean, muscular sound built around a single guitar and a rhythm section of bass and drums (most British bands of the period also featured a rhythm guitar very prominently) behind a lone singer. Kidd had hit originally with "Shakin' All Over," a number that the Who would adopt into their repertoire. Daltrey gave up the guitar to concentrate on singing, Townshend turned his rhythm guitar into a lead instrument, and the band emerged with a powerful, sweaty brand of R&B, all very Memphis-influenced ("Green Onions" was long part of their stage act) and louder than anything that London audiences were used to. They quickly became favorites of the R&B-loving mods, and by 1964 were ready to cut their first single, a quickie rewrite of "Got Love If You Want It" entitled "I'm the Face" ("face" being a key part of mod slang) under the temporary name the High Numbers.

It was around this time that Pete Townshend discovered two key talents. As a songwriter, Townshend showed a remarkable capacity for writing anthem-like songs, which, if not exactly Top 40 material, were certainly memorable to their core audience and just different enough to get airplay. "My Generation" was the first and most important of these, and while his songwriting would broaden in coming years to embrace longer thematic canvases (including the so-called rock opera), it was songs like "My Generation," "The Magic Bus," and the epic-length "Won't Get Fooled Again" that would make the most lasting impact on rock & roll. Townshend's other major talent was in the area of destruction—by accident one night, he shattered the neck of his guitar during a performance, and the crowd seemed to appreciate it. Gradually guitar smashing became a trademark of the band's sets, an effective but extremely expensive publicity vehicle.

Meanwhile, Roger Daltrey emerged as one of the most powerful singers of his generation, a soul shouter whose voice could be heard even above Townshend's ringing power chords and Keith Moon's flamboyant drumming. They built their reputations gradually in the United States during the mid '60s, emerging as one of the better acts at the Monterey Pop Festival (alongside Jimi Hendrix), but it was their rock opera, *Tommy*, that finally transformed the group into a major international rock act.

Tommy's pretensions aside, the passions and seemingly allegorical search for truth behind the story of the deaf, dumb, and blind boy seemed to strike a chord with an entire generation of teenagers and college students who were searching for something different and more genuine in their own lives—the opera's clear rejection of drugs (which echoed Townshend's own philosophy) was conveniently ignored, and the sky seemed to be the limit for the band for the 10 years after *Tommy*'s release.

A live album followed, reminding audiences of the group's R&B roots, and after a false start on a film project, in 1971 the Who released *Who's Next*, which was probably their strongest individual album. Very little that they did afterward was quite as successful artistically as this brilliant compendium of religious musings, idealism at high volume, and revolutionary anthems, but it didn't matter. *Quadrophenia* was too vague a subject for Americans who were unfamiliar with its mod-culture roots; *Who by Numbers* seemed slight after the records that had preceded it; *Who Are You* showed a certain softening of the edges, but the audiences kept buying albums and, even more important, kept going to concerts. Then in 1978, shortly after the release of *Who Are You*, Keith Moon died, and that was pretty much it for the Who. Their work became softer and less urgent (a process that might have been hastened also by Pete Townshend's progressive hearing loss), and while the audiences still bought tickets, their music no longer seemed very important. What little musical capital the group still possessed in the late '80s was squandered on one-too-many farewell tours. —*Bruce Eder*

○ **Sings My Generation** / 1966 / MCA 31330
The group's debut album is more R&B-oriented than their subsequent records, but it's honest and direct. Includes covers of James Brown material amid the Beatlesque originals such as "The Kids Are Alright." —*Bruce Eder*

○ **A Quick One (Happy Jack)** / 1966 / MCA 31331
The group's second album is a transitional work, containing a rudimentary rock opera ("A Quick One") and a bizarre collection of originals by Roger Daltrey and Keith Moon as well as the expected Pete Townshend and John Entwistle. The flashes of brilliance make up for the defects in the writing, and Entwistle's "Boris the Spider" and "Whiskey Man" are among the best songs he has ever written. —*Bruce Eder*

☆ **Who Sell Out** / 1967 / MCA 31332
Arguably rock's first important concept album and infinitely more effective and humorous than *Tommy* or *Quadrophenia*, this is a full-length tribute to Britain's pirate radio stations, complete with commercials by the band. "I Can See for Miles" was the hit off of the record, but the material ranges from the ethereal "Sunrise" to the proto-*Tommy* mini-opera "Rael." Funny as well as scintillating. —*Bruce Eder*

Magic Bus / 1967 / MCA 31333
A second-rate collection of leftover tracks surrounding the Bo Diddley-based title song, better than much of what else was coming out of England at the time, but difficult to accept. —*Bruce Eder*

○ **Tommy** / 1969 / MCA 10005
The original rock opera. The material hasn't worn well as a conceptual creation, but the individual songs still have an energy that is refreshing. Keith Moon's nasty sense of humor stands out. —*Bruce Eder*

☆ **Live at Leeds** / 1970 / MCA 31196
A loud, raunchy concert showcase for the group, with surprisingly little material from *Tommy*. The group's R&B roots are showcased here far better than on their post-*My Generation* studio albums, and the only problem for some listeners is the lack of the sophisticated studio sound they'd developed on previous releases. —*Bruce Eder*

★ **Meaty, Beaty, Big & Bouncy** / 1971 / MCA 37001
The first halfway decent retrospective on the group, covering their American singles as of 1972, including "I Can See for Miles," "My Generation," "The Magic Bus," "The Seeker," and a lot of other material that subsequently became staples of FM radio. —*Bruce Eder*

★ **Who's Next** / 1971 / MCA 37217
The group's magnum opus, a rich, expressive, loud piece of hard rock that summed up the first six years of the band's history. "Won't Get Fooled Again" became a major radio anthem, and "Behind Blue Eyes" unexpectedly became a favorite Pete Townshend number as well. Roger Daltrey never sang better, and John Entwistle's bass achieved new heights of prominence, while Keith Moon turned in an explosive performance on drums. —*Bruce Eder*

○ **Quadrophenia** / 1973 / MCA 6895
The group's second rock opera wasn't nearly the success that *Tommy* had been, but it proved more fertile in other media—"Love Reign o'er Me" was a moderate success as a single, but precious little else seemed to register with the public. Ironically, this is a finely produced album, with a sound that is both hard and lush, and Roger Daltrey seemed to achieve a larger-than-life performance as the embattled mod Jimmy. —*Bruce Eder*

Odds & Sods / 1974 / MCA 1659
Odds is right—a collection of outtakes and mistakes from the first eight years of the group's history, all of it listenable and half of it indispensable. "Long Live Rock" (which later turned up on the *Quadrophenia* soundtrack album) was the best song, but most of the rest is worth a listen. —*Bruce Eder*

Who Are You / 1978 / MCA 37003
The final worthwhile album by the band, a somewhat arch collection of pretentious rock anthems and failed concepts surrounding a powerful title track whose video clip marked Keith Moon's final public appearance with the band. —*Bruce Eder*

○ **Kids Are Alright** / 1979 / MCA 6899
Soundtrack to a dazzling video portrait of the band, better in many ways than any of the hits collections out of the group for the surprises and odd takes that it contains. —*Bruce Eder*

Hooligans / 1982 / MCA 12001
Surprisingly unimpressive collection of hits and major songs, because of its redundancy—there were too many hits collections out previously, and the sound is amazingly flat. —*Bruce Eder*

Greatest Hits / 1983 / MCA 1496
One of too many similar packages. Okay, but nothing more. —*Bruce Eder*

Who's Missing / 1985 / MCA 31221
A collection of loose ends from the group's early years, mostly B sides and some R&B covers. —*Bruce Eder*

Two's Missing / 1987 / MCA 31222
A followup to *Who's Missing*, with more obscure B sides, little-known R&B covers, and other relics of the band's early history, of which the best part is their soulful rendition of "Anytime You Want Me." —*Bruce Eder*

○ **Thirty Years of Maximum R&B** / 1994 / MCA
It's amazing that, after years of box sets glutting the marketplace, it took until 1994 for the Who to get their treatment. Was it worth the wait? Absolutely! With the unfortunate omission of the single version of "Substitute," all the hits and key album tracks are represented, as well as other curiosities that help round out the band's picture. Excellent liner notes, track info, and photos complete this great-sounding package. One unfortunate note: Roger Daltrey might have disdained Kenny Jones's drumming, but to

give Jones hardly a cursory representation in this package is bad form. —*Rick Clark*

Widespread Panic
Group / Rock & roll
Widespread Panic has developed a devoted cult of fans who appeal to the band's blend of Allman Brothers chops and occasional Grateful Dead looseness. Their albums highlight the band's well-developed musical interplay. —*Rick Clark*

● **Space Wrangler** / Feb. 4, 1988 / Capricorn 42001
Widespread's debut album, *Space Wrangler*, is regarded by many of their fans as their finest work. It's understandable, thanks to strong material like "Travelin' Light," "Coconut," "Driving Song," "Chilly Water," and the title cut—the album's musical centerpiece. —*Rick Clark*

○ **Widespread Panic** / Mar. 1991 / Capricorn 10001
The band's Capricorn debut is another strong collection of songs and extended instrumental workouts. Includes "Walkin' (for Your Love)," "Mercy," "Send Your Mind," "Makes Sense to Me," and "Barstools and Dreamers." —*Rick Clark*

Everyday / 1993 / Warner Brothers 42013
Not as strong or fresh sounding as the previous two albums. However, there are enough good tunes here to hold the interest of anyone checking out this band. —*Rick Clark*

Andre Williams
b. 1936
Vocals / R&B
A singer, songwriter, arranger, producer, and one of the mightiest talents to emerge from Detroit's pre-Motown era, Andre Williams started recording in 1957 for the tiny Fortune label, with his group, the Five Dollars (aka the Don Juans), and as a solo artist. Employing his stop-time "wavy gravy" beat and hitting the charts with oddball spoken-word numbers like "Bacon Fat," "The Greasy Chicken," and "Jail Bait," Williams was the original rapper before there was ever a name for it. Moving to Chicago in the early '60s, he wrote "Shake a Tail Feather" for the 5 Du-Tones and "Twine Time" for Alvin Cash, produced albums for Bobby Blue Bland, and scored national hits of his own for Chess with "Cadillac Jack," "Girdle Up," and "Humpin', Bumpin' & Thumpin'." He continues to record and produce other artists sporadically, still keeping abreast of the times, still "Mr. Rhythm," the original rappin' man. —*Cub Koda*

● **Jail Bait** / Fortune 8019
Good (though not complete) overview of Andre's Fortune period. —*Cub Koda*

Deniece Williams
b. Jun. 3, 1950, Gary, IN
Vocals / Soul, pop, gospel
Born in Gary, IN, Deniece Williams sang with Wonderlove before signing with Columbia in 1976 and cutting sweet soul sides in a high soprano. She has had, from 1975 to the present, solo hits with "Let's Hear It for the Boy" and the duet "Too Much, Too Little, Too Late." After 1988, Williams returned to her roots in gospel music. —*Bil Carpenter*

● **This Is Niecy** / 1976 / Columbia 34242
After singing in Stevie Wonder's backup band Wonderlove from 1972 to 1975, Deniece Williams made her solo debut and enjoyed an immediate impact. Her lilting, rising voice and upper-register range, which she nicely exploited on "Free," sounded daring and refreshing in 1976, coming on the heels of Minnie Riperton's hits. Williams also had several other solid secondary tunes like "Because You Love Me Baby" and "If You Don't Believe." She smartly blended inspirational fervor and quasi-sophistication, including a couple of pop gospel tunes. This record holds up much better than most of her other albums. —*Ron Wynn*

○ **Let's Hear It for the Boy** / 1984 / Columbia 39366
Williams's pop breakthrough, featuring the title song and several other good pop/rockers. —*All-Music-Guide*

○ **So Glad I Know** / 1988 / Sparrow 1121
Deniece Williams raised some eyebrows when she decided to begin splitting her focus between urban contemporary and contemporary gospel. The results have thus been quite mixed, and this first gospel venture not only wasn't a major success, it didn't even

get widespread exposure in the gospel ranks. It was likewise ignored by pop and R&B audiences. The vocals were competent, the production dull, and the material surprisingly timid. —*Ron Wynn*

Larry Williams

b. May 10, 1935, New Orleans, LA, **d.** Jan. 7, 1980
Vocals, piano / R&B, rock & roll
Specialty groomed Williams to reinforce their rock & roll credentials after they lost Little Richard to religion in the late '50s. Williams recorded a few standards ("Bad Boy," "Dizzy, Miss Lizzy," "She Said Yeah"), which were covered by the Beatles and the Rolling Stones during their formative years. —*John Floyd*

Unreleased Larry Williams / 1986 / Specialty 2158
A deeper look into the obscure and alternate takes of Williams's work. For collectors. —*Hank Davis*

★ **Bad Boy** / 1989 / Specialty 7002
Vintage (1957-1958) rock from this Little Richard soundalike, with backing from hot New Orleans and Los Angeles sidemen. Excellent 23-track collection with informative notes. —*Hank Davis*

Maurice Williams & the Zodiacs

Group / Doo-wop
After recording one single for Excello as the Marigolds ("Little Darlin,'" later covered by the Diamonds), Maurice Williams rechristened his group and scored a huge hit in 1960 with "Stay," which contains one of the greatest falsettos in the pantheon of soul. Later hits included "May I" and "Come Along." —*John Floyd*

● **Best of Maurice & the Zodiacs** / 1989 / Relic 7004
Not much thought went into this set, but it'll do. —*Dan Heilman*

Vanessa Williams

b. Mar. 18, 1963
Vocals / Urban soul, dance-pop
When Vanessa Williams lost her Miss America crown in 1984, it seemed like her career was over. Actually, the truth was quite different. Four years later, she remerged as an urban R&B vocalist with *The Right Stuff*, which featured the Top 10 hit "Dreamin'." Her next album was an even bigger success, thanks to the smash hit "Saving the Best for Last" ;it confirmed her status as one of urban R&B's most popular vocalists. —*Stephen Thomas Erlewine*

○ **The Right Stuff** / Feb. 1988 / Wing 835694
Club dance music and soulful ballads. —*Bil Carpenter*

● **Comfort Zone** / 1991 / Wing 843522
Former Miss America Vanessa Williams retained the momentum from her hit debut release, *The Right Stuff*, with this prototype urban contemporary album. She utilized different producers, arrangers, and songwriters on almost every track, nicely balancing the menu between dance-oriented uptempo numbers like the title track and "Running Back to You" with syrupy but extremely popular ballads like "Save the Best for Last" and "Just for Tonight." While far from being soulful, Williams's voice had enough earnesty and conviction to make the love songs seem sincere and not be buried in the mix on the rhythm cuts. —*Ron Wynn*

Victoria Williams

Vocals, guitar / Singer-songwriter, folk rock
During the late '80s and early '90s, singer-songwriter Victoria Williams recorded two critically acclaimed albums, featuring her distinctive, lyrical songwriting. Occasionally, her thin voice can be a little shrill, yet her music is consistently complex, drawing from folk, pop, gospel, and country. At times, Williams's lyrics can be slightly cloying, but more often, she writes rich, detailed narratives.

After the release of 1990's *Swing the Statue!* Williams was diagnosed as being ill with multiple sclerosis. She had no money or insurance to pay for her expensive hospital bills. Her dire situation led to a bunch of her musician friends assembling a relief fund for her; the fund led to the 1993 tribute album *Sweet Relief,* which featured 14 artists covering her songs. The proceeds were donated to Williams, as well as the Sweet Relief Musicians Trust Fund, designed to help musicians who, like Victoria Williams, have no money for health insurance. After the album was a suc-

cess, her two records were reissued by Geffen. During this time, Williams went into remission; it is likely she will release a new album in the future. —*Stephen Thomas Erlewine*

● **Swing the Statue** / 1990 / Rough Trade 50
Victoria Williams's second album was her most accomplished set of folk rock, featuring the remarkable "Summer of Drugs." —*Stephen Thomas Erlewine*

Chuck Willis

b. Jan. 31, 1928, Atlanta, GA, **d.** Apr. 10, 1958
Vocals / R&B
Chuck Willis was one of the greatest R&B songwriters and vocalists, from his early '50s stint with Okeh up to his work with Atlantic. His best songs, "It's Too Late," "I Feel So Bad," and "What Am I Livin' For," focused on romantic pain and suffering, but he also produced one of rock's finest statements of longevity: "Hang Up My Rock and Roll Shoes." Willis died of peritonitis in 1958. —*John Floyd*

○ **King of the Stroll** / 1958 / Pioneer 4587
Chuck Willis had a short but eventful career. He'd just begun riding the wave of his hit "The Stroll" when he died of peritonitis in 1958. Willis had begun recording at Okeh, then moved to Atlantic, where his singles "C .C. Rider," "Betty & Dupree," and "It's Too Late" were among early crossover hits. These are the numbers that preceded them, Willis's rousing Okeh hits that displayed his dynamic sound and energetic style. They've been reissued on some other compilations, so this may no longer be around. —*Ron Wynn*

★ **My Story** / 1980 / Sony 36389
The best Okeh recordings by this brilliant R&B songwriter and vocalist, best known for his later work in the '50s on Atlantic. Great liner notes by Peter Guralnick. —*John Floyd*

Wilson Phillips

Group / Pop
A female vocal trio consisting of Carnie and Wendy Wilson (daughters of Beach Boy Brian Wilson) and Chynna Phillips (daughter of John and Michelle Phillips of the Mamas & the Papas). They broke through to enormous pop success with their debut album, which sold four million copies. The followup, *Shadows and Light*, got off to a fast start in the spring of 1992. However, it slipped down the charts quickly; Wilson Phillips broke up soon after. —*William Ruhlmann*

Wilson Phillips / 1990 / Capitol 93745
A pleasant, harmony-filled pop-rock album, featuring hits such as "Hold On," "Release Me," and "You're in Love." —*William Ruhlmann*

Shadows & Light / Jun. 2, 1992 / SBK 98924
While it contains a couple of strong tracks—most notably the single "Give it Up"—none of the songs on Wilson Phillips's second album are as appealing as "Hold On" or "Dream Is Still Alive," and the entire record sounds like a forced attempt to replicate the multiplatinum success of their debut. —*Stephen Thomas Erlewine*

Brian Wilson

b. Jun. 20, 1942
Vocals, keyboards, bass / Pop/rock
Brian Wilson is arguably the greatest American composer of popular music in the rock era. Born and raised in Hawthorne, CA, Wilson formed the Beach Boys, with his two younger brothers, cousin Mike Love, and school friend Al Jardine, and they became the most successful American rock band in history by performing his songs, which initially combined the rock urgency of Chuck Berry with the harmonies of the Four Freshmen. Wilson's musical imagination expanded during the '60s to the point of such remarkable works as "Good Vibrations," a chart-topping Beach Boys single of 1966. Wilson retreated from his dominance of the Beach Boys after 1967, as their popularity declined. He made sporadic contributions to their records, returning briefly as a songwriter and producer in the mid '70s. Wilson issued a debut solo album in 1988, but his second one, *Sweet Insanity,* was rejected by Sire Records. Wilson is said to be preparing his next album. —*William Ruhlmann*

● **Brian Wilson** / 1988 / Sire 25669

Any suggestion that Wilson's talents had waned was erased by this solo masterpiece, which found his sense of composition and arrangement—especially the gorgeous harmonies- intact, and even growing. —*William Ruhlmann*

Jackie Wilson

b. Jun. 9, 1934, Detroit, MI, **d.** Jan. 21, 1984
Vocals / R&B, soul
In terms of range, vocal gymnastics, and showmanship—not to mention the ability to simply belt out a song—nobody could match Jackie Wilson. Graduating from Billy Ward's Dominoes, he signed with the Brunswick label and began his career performing songs cowritten by fellow Detroiter Berry Gordy, later the founder of Motown. These included "To Be Loved," "Lonely Teardrops," and "Reet Petite." Wilson trod the line between R&B and pop, often favoring the latter, where he could use his astonishing range to good effect. His records were frequently characterized by a surfeit of brass and "Tonight Show" arrangements. Fans contend that Jackie Wilson was incapable of making a bad record, but his output remains a mixed bag to most ears. The best is among the most thrilling music to emerge from the late '50s and early '60s. —*Colin Escott*

○ **Mr. Excitement** / 1992 / Rhino 70775
A three-CD box from the experts of reissue at Rhino, *Mr. Excitement* takes Wilson's career from his first sides with Billy Ward and the Dominoes in 1956 through his final recordings in the early '70s. The former Detroit boxer hit either the R&B or pop chart over 50 times, making him the 26th most successful R&B artist, in chart terms at least. Every one of those recordings is contained in this set, including such classics as "Reet Petite," "Lonely Teardrops," and "(Your Love Keeps Lifting Me) Higher and Higher." Wilson had an explosive falsetto and a downright weird sense of phrasing that made him utterly unique. Some of his productions were a little overwrought, but even in the most extreme cases, that voice was a gift from God. Seminal. —*Rob Bowman*

★ **Very Best of Jackie Wilson** / 1993 / ACE 913
A terrific single-disc collection of Jackie Wilson's biggest hits and finest moments. —*Stephen Thomas Erlewine*

Jesse Winchester

b. May 17, 1944, Shreveport, LA
Vocals / Singer-songwriter
The country-folk singer-songwriter Jesse Winchester first gained notice for his debut album, *Jesse Winchester* (1970), produced by the Band's Robbie Robertson. It featured such songs as "The Brand New Tennessee Waltz" and "Yankee Lady," which were covered by a wide range of performers. The subtext of his appeal, however (and of songs like "Yankee Lady"), was that Winchester was an American living in Canada to avoid the draft. Born in Shreveport, LA, he had grown up in Memphis and attended Williams College, from which he graduated in 1966. While studying in Germany in 1967, he received his draft notice and moved to Montreal.

Winchester's second album, *Third Down 110 to Go*, was released in 1972 and got into the charts briefly, but he was hindered by his inability to play in the United States. In 1973 Winchester became a Canadian citizen. He released more records, but it wasn't until 1977, when President Jimmy Carter instituted an amnesty for draft resisters, that Winchester was able to appear in the United States. His appearances made his next album, *Nothing but a Breeze*, his biggest-seller yet. *A Touch on the Rainy Side* (1978) was a more moderate success, while *Talk Memphis* (1981) featured the Top 40 hit "Say What." This was his last album for seven years, until the independent Sugar Hill label issued *Humour Me* (1988). Winchester continues to tour. —*William Ruhlmann*

○ **Jesse Winchester** / 1970 / Rhino 70885
Robbie Robertson and Levon Helm lend a Bandlike sound to these tracks, which, while not typical of Winchester's later work, nevertheless have a pleasing rock feel. Some of Winchester's best songs are here, and the album made him a legend. —*William Ruhlmann*

○ **Third Down, 110 to Go** / 1972 / Rhino 70886
Winchester's best album is full of songs about following your desires and taking risks against high odds, though they're sung and

played buoyantly: "If we're treading on thin ice," Winchester sings, "then we might as well dance." —*William Ruhlmann*

Let the Rough Side Drag / 1976 / Bearsville 6964
A well-produced country-rock album with more songs offering sage advice, from the title track to "Damned If You Do" and "Blow On, Chilly Wind." —*William Ruhlmann*

● **Best of Jesse Winchester** / 1988 / Rhino 70085
Not a perfect selection, but good enough to give a reasonable representation of Winchester's Bearsville years, 1970 to 1981. Includes this transplanted southerner's haunting "Mississippi You're on My Mind," as well as "The Brand New Tennessee Waltz," "Bowling Green," "Biloxi," and "Talk Memphis." —*William Ruhlmann*

Edgar Winter

b. Dec. 28, 1946, Beaumont, TX
Vocals, guitar / Rock & roll
Johnny's younger brother. Multiinstrumentalist and possessor of a vocal range of about a zillion octaves, Edgar has zipped through so many styles he's simply not worth pinning down. If you like unhinged blues-rock and R&B, you'll like the early part of his career. If you like commercial hard rock, there are songs like the mega-hit "Frankenstein." Whatever you fancy, chances are Edgar's recorded it. —*John Dougan*

○ **White Trash** / 1971 / Epic 30512
A full R&B outfit with horns. Texas raunch. Only the ballad sounds dated. —*Robert Gordon*

● **They Only Come out at Night** / 1972 / Epic 31584
Commercial hits, with "Free Ride" and "Frankenstein." —*Robert Gordon*

Johnny Winter

b. Feb. 23, 1944
Vocals, guitar / Blues rock
Blues guitarist Winter became a major star in the late '60s and early '70s. Since that time he's confirmed his reputation in the blues by working with Muddy Waters and continuing to play in the style, despite musical fashion. Born in Leland, MS, Winter formed his first band at 14 with his brother Edgar in Beaumont, TX, and spent his youth in recording studios cutting regional singles and in bars playing the blues. His discovery on a national level came via an article in *Rolling Stone* in 1968, which led to a management contract with New York club owner Steve Paul and a record deal with Columbia. His debut album (there are numerous albums of juvenilia), *Johnny Winter*, reached #24 in 1969. Starting out with a trio, Winter later formed a band with former members of the McCoys, including second guitarist Rick Derringer. It was called Johnny Winter And. He achieved a sales peak in 1971 with the gold-selling *Live/Johnny Winter And*. He returned in 1973 with *Still Alive and Well*, his highest-charting album. His albums became more overtly blues-oriented in the late '70s, and he also produced several albums for Muddy Waters. In the '80s he switched to the blues label Alligator for three albums and has since recorded for the labels MCA and Virgin. In 1992 he released *Scorchin' Blues* on Columbia. —*William Ruhlmann*

○ **Johnny Winter** / 1969 / Columbia 9826
Winter's stunning debut features his fiery blues playing in both electric and acoustic settings, with backup that includes Willie Dixon. —*William Ruhlmann*

● **Second Winter** / 1969 / Columbia 9947
Winter leans more toward mainstream rock & roll, though the guitar playing remains fierce. Originally a *three*-sided LP, this now makes a long CD. —*William Ruhlmann*

○ **Johnny Winter and ...** / 1970 / Columbia 30221
Winter puts together a new band and takes on the assistance of Rick Derringer, who coproduces and provides such great songs as "Rock and Roll, Hoochie Koo." —*William Ruhlmann*

Johnny Winter and ... Live / 1971 / Columbia 30475
Winter and his new band turn out hard-rock versions of "Jumpin' Jack Flash," "Johnny B. Goode," and other rock & roll favorites. —*William Ruhlmann*

○ **Nothin' but the Blues** / 1977 / Blue Sky 34813

After a long period making rock records, Winter fronts the Muddy Waters Band (with Waters singing) on this Chicago blues workout. He sounds happier than ever before. — *William Ruhlmann*

○ **Guitar Slinger** / 1984 / Alligator 4735

The first of three blues albums recorded after a four-year studio hiatus finds Winter as fleet-fingered as before and sounding more vocally involved than in some of the later Columbia material. — *William Ruhlmann*

○ **Birds Can't Row Boats** / 1988 / Relix 2034

Aside from "Ice Cube" (a 1959 instrumental), these tracks date from 1965 through 1968. Many are previously unissued or only available on rare 45s. Those accustomed to his more famous recordings are in for a jolt, as this shows Johnny in several unexpected settings: grinding Texas psych-punk, the British invasion-cum-folk-rock garage single "Gone for Bad," blue-eyed R&B/soul, an Everly Brothers cover, a *Highway 61*-era Dylan imitation, and even a shit-kickin' C&W tune. There are also some straight, predominantly acoustic blues numbers. — *Richie Unterberger*

Steve Winwood

b. May 12, 1948

Vocals, keyboard, guitar / Pop/rock

Singer-songwriter, keyboardist, and guitarist Steve Winwood was a well-known musician long before he finally embarked on a solo career in the second half of the '70s. Born in Birmingham, England, Winwood joined the Spencer Davis Group with his older brother Muff when he was only 15. His was the soulful, Ray Charles-like voice on such hits as "Gimme Some Lovin'" and "I'm a Man," songs he also cowrote. In 1967 he formed Traffic, which he led, with time off for the supergroup Blind Faith in 1969, until 1974. Winwood finally released his first solo album in 1977, and in 1981 had his first million-seller with his second album, *Arc of a Diver*. *Talking Back to the Night* (1982) was not as much of a success, and Winwood spent four years preparing *Back in the High Life* (1986), which sold three million copies. *Roll with It* (1988) went to #1, but *Refugees of the Heart* (1990) was not up to his usual standard. After the relative failure of *Refugees of the Heart*, Winwood and Jim Capaldi reformed Traffic in 1994; although their record and tour were well received, the reunion wasn't as successful as expected. — *William Ruhlmann*

○ **Arc of a Diver** / 1980 / Island 842365

Utterly unencumbered by the baggage of his long years in the music business, Winwood reinvents himself as a completely contemporary artist on this outstanding album, leading off with his best solo song, "While You See a Chance." Winwood also plays all the instruments. — *William Ruhlmann*

● **Back in the High Life** / 1986 / Island 830148

Turning to involved percussion tracks and horns, Winwood turns another musical corner on this sophisticated album, which contains echoes of everything from gospel to Caribbean music. Contains the #1 hit "Higher Love." — *William Ruhlmann*

○ **Chronicles** / 1987 / Island 842364

This isn't an adequate compilation of the years 1977 to 1986, but it does manage to gather some of the better songs of the period. — *William Ruhlmann*

Roll with It / 1988 / Virgin 90946

Winwood manages to reintroduce some of the R&B elements of the Spencer Davis Group and some of the psychedelic effects of early Traffic here, though this is also an effective followup to the directions indicated on *Back in the High Life*. Contains the #1 title track and "Don't You Know What the Night Can Do?" — *William Ruhlmann*

Wire

Group / Punk, alternative pop/rock

Wire's brief, fractured songs and minimalistic sound made the band the artiest of all punk bands, as well as one of the most influential. Unlike most other punk bands, their stripped-down approach was not an attempt to get back to rock's roots; it was cutting the music to its raw nerve, so nothing extraneous was left. On their 1977 debut, *Pink Flag*, Wire managed to tear through 21 in under 40 minutes. Although they never managed to match that album's accomplishment, they recorded two other excellent albums before breaking up in late 1979.

Wire was quiet for several years. They returned to recording in 1986 with the *Snakedrill* EP, quickly following it with 1987's full-length *The Ideal Copy*. Amazingly, Wire's capabilities were still intact; the only concession the group made was adding synthesizers to their music, which they managed to work in quite well. However, after *The Ideal Copy*, the band began to slip, as they were attempting to incorporate synths and samplers to a greater degree; their experimental tendencies began to overshadow their musical sense. Eventually, the band shortened their name to Wir; their first release in this new incarnation was 1991's *The First Letter*. — *Stephen Thomas Erlewine*

☆ **Pink Flag** / 1977 / Restless 72360

Wire's debut effort, *Pink Flag*, was one of the strongest releases during the late '70s British punk scene, mixing the aggressive punch of the Sex Pistols with the humor and brevity of the Ramones. *Pink Flag* packed 22 tracks into the space of 37 minutes; 12 of the tracks were under a minute and a half. ("Field Day for the Sundays" clocked in at just 28 seconds.) Somehow none of these tracks felt short; Wire merely made their point and moved on to the next idea. — *Rick Clark*

○ **Chairs Missing** / 1978 / Restless 72361

In *Chair's Missing*, Wire stretched out into longer pieces and artier production. Not as impressive as *Pink Flag*, *Chair's Missing* does contain some standout tracks with "Outdoor Miner," "French Film Blurred," "I Am the Fly," and "Question of Degree." — *Rick Clark*

○ **154** / 1979 / Restless 72362

154 integrated more keyboards and slowed the pace down a bit, but Wire didn't lose any of the eccentric edge. They just kept getting stranger. If *Ummagumma*-period Pink Floyd, early King Crimson, and the Moody Blues at their musically most cosmic were filtered through the punk movement, you'd get an idea what a peculiar album *154* is. Call it psychedelic punk. Among the highlights are "Two People in a Room," "The 15th," "Map Ref. 41 N 93 W," "The Other Window," "Single K.O.," and "40 Versions." — *Rick Clark*

● **On Returning (1977-1979)** / 1989 / Restless 72358

A magnificent 31-song overview that collects highlights from *Pink Flag* and many of the best songs from the two followups, plus some interesting rarities. — *John Floyd*

Bill Withers

b. Jul. 4, 1938, Slab Fork, WV

Vocals / Soul, urban R&B

It was a chance 1970 meeting with the legendary Booker T. Jones (of Stax's Booker T. & the MG's) that opened the door for Bill Withers into the world of pop success. At the time of their meeting, Withers was working in a factory that built toilet seats for jet airplanes. Jones, impressed with Withers's demos, helped secure a deal with Sussex Records. Withers's Jones-produced debut, *Just As I Am*, was a classic of folky acoustic-guitar-driven soul, complemented by Withers's earthy vocal delivery and largely autobiographical tales. His next few albums capitalized on that sound, but as the late '70s came around, Withers gravitated toward a sophisticated urban R&B sound, sometimes collaborating with groups like the Crusaders. — *Rick Clark*

● **Greatest Hits** / 1981 / Columbia 37199

A good sampler of Withers's hits, plus a few key album tracks, covering his transition from funky acoustic-rooted soul to smooth urban pop. Included are "Use Me," "Lean on Me," "Just the Two of Us," "Ain't No Sunshine," and "Who Is He and What Is He to You." Now if only Withers's early albums, like *Still Bill*, would see the light of day on CD. — *Rick Clark*

Peter Wolf

b. Mar. 7, 1946

Vocals / Rock & roll, pop/rock

Peter Wolf was the lead singer of the J. Geils Band from 1967 to 1983. After splitting from the band, he released three solo albums from 1984 to1990, with varying success. — *William Ruhlmann*

● **Lights Out** / 1984 / EMI America 17121

On his own, Wolf achieves a more contemporary pop sound than that of the bluesy J. Geils Band and scores three chart hits: "Lights Out," "I Need You Tonight," and "Oo-Ee-Diddley-Bop!" — *William Ruhlmann*

○ **Come As You Are** / 1987 / EMI America 46563
Wolf gets back in the Top 15 with the title track, but the best song
is the leadoff, an R&B raveup ironically called "Can't Get Started."
—*William Ruhlmann*

Womack & Womack

Group / R&B, soul
Cecil Womack (b. 1947) and his wife, Linda (b. 1952), had a long
history before the release of their first duo album in 1983. Cecil
was one of the gospel-singing Womack brothers who became the
Valentinos and toured with Sam Cooke in the early '60s; Linda
was Cooke's daughter. Both Womacks were successful songwrit-
ers for such performers as Teddy Pendergrass, Wilson Pickett, and
Aretha Franklin prior to hooking up as a performing team. The
focus is on songwriting in their collaboration; they began with
Love Wars, which featured the Top 40 R&B hit "Baby I'm Scared
of You." *Radio M.U.S.I.C. Man* (1985) contains unfinished Sam
Cooke songs completed by the duo. It was followed by
Conscience in 1988 and *Family Spirit* in 1991. —*William
Ruhlmann*

● **Love Wars** / 1983 / Elektra 60293
Womack and Womack are steeped in the early '60s style of Cecil's
Valentinos and Linda's father, Sam Cooke, but they have updated
the style. Nevertheless, this is contemporary soul likely to be em-
braced by fans of Cooke, Otis Redding, and others of the genre. —
William Ruhlmann

Radio M.U.S.I.C. Man / 1985 / Elektra 60406
Nice interaction and captivating lyrics. —*Ron Wynn*

Family Spirit / 1991 / RCA 3072
A good, although not great, session. —*Ron Wynn*

Bobby Womack

b. Mar. 4, 1944
Vocals, guitar / Soul, R&B
Few careers in American popular music have been as consistently productive and influential as that of singer-songwriter and
guitarist Bobby Womack. Sam Cooke, for whom Womack was
playing guitar, financed his first recordings in the early '60s. With
his brothers as the Valentinos, he cut two R&B classics, "It's All
Over Now" (later a hit for the Stones) and "Lookin' for a Love" (a
mega-hit for J. Geils). The Valentinos' combination of shouting
lead vocals and blues/gospel harmonies predated late '60s soul
music.
 Womack knew and championed Jimi Hendrix early on, befriending him during a 1962 soul package tour. Womack's lean,
groundbreaking guitar work, so similar in flavor to that of his
contemporary Curtis Mayfield, influenced Hendrix. Later,
Hendrix would return the favor by popularizing the wah-wah- an
effect Womack would use it to chilling effect on Sly Stone's
There's a Riot Goin' On album and its smash single, "Family
Affair" (he doubled here on bass). That's also Womack's guitar on
Wilson Pickett's "Funky Broadway" and on Aretha Franklin's
Lady Soul album.
 In fact, Womack himself was one of the legendary "wild" soul
men, friend and partying companion of Wilson Pickett, for whom
he wrote "Midnight Mover" and "I'm in Love." He even scored a
movie, *Across 110th Street,* which came out at the same time as
the landmark blaxploitation film *Shaft.*
 Womack's singing career resumed in the '70s; James Taylor
covered his #1 R&B hit, "Woman's Got to Have It." He made a
stunning 1981 comeback with the #1 R&B album *The Poet* and
reunited with old Memphis studio friends and producer Chips
Moman on 1986's *Womagic.*
 Bobby Womack's career is far from over. Look for more greatness from this soulful, innovative musician and singer. P.S.: He
belongs in the Rock & Roll Hall of Fame! —*Christine Ohlman*

○ **Lookin' for a Love** / Jan. 1993 / Razor & Tie 2009
A strong collection of Bobby Womack's influential early R&B
songs. —AMG

● **Midnight Mover** / Feb. 1993 / EMI Records 72438276732
Spanning the length of his influential career, *Midnight Mover* features two discs of one of the major figures of contemporary soul
and R&B, covering all of his hits and best moments. —AMG

The Wonder Stuff

Group / Alternative pop/rock
When the Wonder Stuff released their first album, *The Eight
Legged Groove Machine,* in 1988, the British press wrote scores of
articles about the band, mainly because of the arrogant self-confidence of their leader, vocalist/guitarist Miles Hunt. Hunt's brash
public image was the Wonder Stuff personified—mean, self-satis-
fied, self-serving, and scathingly witty. Accordingly, their colorful
mixture of pop melodies, loud guitars, sneering lyrics, and
touches of dance music was sometimes brilliant and sometimes
banal. Between 1988 and 1993, the band kept incorporating more
stylistic flourishes to their basic punk- and new wave-inspired
pop/rock. The band were instant stars in England; America never
warmed to their music. After trying to gain a worldwide audience
for five years, the band broke up in 1994. —*Stephen Thomas
Erlewine*

● **Eight Legged Groove Machine** / 1988 / Polydor 837802
A brash, scattershot debut that is driven by the band's sheer ar-
rogance as their catchy, but erratic, guitar hooks. —*Stephen
Thomas Erlewine*

Hup! / 1989 / Polydor 841187
The Wonder Stuff's second album isn't as snotty as their first, but
it's more ambitious, adding bits of folk, psychedelia, and art-rock
to their self-involved punk-pop. Unfortunately, they didn't bring
as many hooks and melodies this time around, leaving *Hup!* an
admirable but failed experimentation. —*Stephen Thomas
Erlewine*

○ **Never Loved Elvis** / 1991 / Polydor 847252
The Wonder Stuff's carefully constructed melodies, endless ambition, spiky guitars, and self-confidence combined into a consistently engaging sound on their third album. —*Stephen Thomas
Erlewine*

Construction for the Modern Idiot / Oct. 5, 1993 / Polydor
 519894
With *Construction for the Modern Idiot,* the Wonder Stuff re-
bounds from a somewhat lackluster streak of records with an album of brash guitar pop that rivals its earlier releases. —*Stephen
Thomas Erlewine*

Stevie Wonder (Steveland Morris)

b. May 13, 1950, Saginaw, MI
Vocals, piano / Motown, soul, pop/rock
When Stevie Wonder began recording in 1963, he was only 11
years old. Even then, his talent was evident, although there was
no sign of how deep it was. After all, the music was the work of
a startlingly gifted child; it was all exuberant flash, with little
complexities. Soon, Wonder would go far beyond the infectious
energy of "Fingertips (Part 2)." In two years, he became one of
Motown's finest artists, recording a series of brilliant singles for a
solid nine years, the overwhelming majority of which he wrote
himself. During this time, his albums were like other Motown albums—a combination of killer singles and pleasant filler, only
Wonder was allowed to record the occasional number that reflected his increasing social consciousness, like his hit version of
Bob Dylan's "Blowin' in the Wind." By the end of the '60s, he was
not only hitting the charts with his own records, but writing material for many other Motown artists, including the Spinners' "It's
a Shame" and cowriting "The Tears of Clown" with Smokey
Robinson.
 With his creativity growing by leaps and bounds, Wonder soon
felt limited by Motown's strict production and publishing contracts. When his record contract expired in 1971, Wonder recorded
two full albums by himself and used them as a bargaining tool
during contract negotiations with Motown. The record label gave
him total artistic control of his albums, as well as the rights to his
own songs. Soon afterwards, the two albums—*Where I'm Coming
From* and *Music of My Mind*—were released.
 Music of My Mind, especially, helped usher in a new era of
soul/R&B. Along with Sly Stone and Marvin Gaye, Wonder was
responsible for making soul and R&B albums not just collections
of singles, but cohesive artistic statments, where artists could extend their music beyond the confines of a three-minute hit single.
With his next two albums, *Talking Book* and *Innervisions,*
Wonder's music became richly complex and inventive; in addition
to his musical innovations, Wonder's lyrics addressed social and
racial issues as eloquently and incisively as any other pop song-

writer. Wonder sustained his creative peak through 1974's *Fulfillingness' First Finale* and 1976's *Songs in the Key of Life*.

Three years later, he released the ambitious and bewildering *Journey through the Secret Life of Plants*, which received terrible reviews upon its release. Wonder released the more straightforward *Hotter than July* in 1980; the album received substantially better reviews and became his first platinum album. However, he wasn't able to sustain that momentum for the rest of the decade. Although his records sold well and he scored the occasional hit—including the smash hit ballad "I Just Called to Say I Love You"—his albums weren't as focused as they were a decade earlier. By the '90s, he was still an immensely respected musician, but his music was no longer on the cutting edge. —*Stephen Thomas Erlewine*

○ **Up-Tight (Everything's Alright)** / May 1966 / Motown 5183
Stevie Wonder began demonstrating his production skills and compositional acumen on his first of two albums in 1966. Though still just a teen, Wonder was already anxious to do more than simply grind out love tunes. He covered Bob Dylan's "Blowing in the Wind" and also contributed "Pretty Little Angel" alongside the monster hits "Nothin's Too Good for My Baby" and the title song. It was also a signal Wonder had moved beyond simply paying homage to his idol Ray Charles and now wanted to establish his own musical identity. —*Ron Wynn*

Signed, Sealed & Delivered / Aug. 1970 / Motown 5176
Stevie Wonder was beginning to rebel at the Motown hit factory mentality in the early '70s. While he certainly hadn't lost his commercial touch, Wonder was anxious to address social concerns, experiment with electronics, and not be restricted by radio and marketplace considerations. Still, he gave the label another definitive smash with the title track, while sneaking in a cover of the Beatles' "We Can Work It Out" and penning more intriguing tunes like "I Can't Let My Heaven Walk Away" and "Never Had a Dream Come True." —*Ron Wynn*

○ **Music of My Mind** / Mar. 1972 / Motown 0314
When Wonder turned 21 he renegotiated his Motown contract; the key issue was control. Stevie Wonder had a vision that veered far away from that of the Motown hit-making machine. Influenced by the work of Isaac Hayes in 1969 and 1970 and labelmate Marvin Gaye in 1971, Wonder no longer was content with putting out albums that were a collection of two or three hit singles plus filler; he wanted to record full-length albums that had an integrity unto themselves. *Music of My Mind* was the first such effort. Wonder produced, wrote the songs, and played the majority of the instruments. At the time it was a revelation. Compared with Wonder's subsequent efforts, it pales just slightly. —*Rob Bowman*

☆ **Talking Book** / Nov. 1972 / Motown 0319
Talking Book is the album that crystallized Wonder as the self-contained singer-songwriter. "Superstition" and "You Are the Sunshine of My Life" were both #1 singles. The rest of the album maintains an equally torrid level. —*Rob Bowman*

☆ **Innervisions** / Aug. 1973 / Motown 0326
For my money, Stevie Wonder's finest moment. Three massive hits, "Higher Ground," "Living for the City," and "Don't You Worry 'bout a Thing," were drawn from the album. "Golden Lady" and "He's Misstra Know-It-All" could have been equally successful. From the titles alone, one can see that Wonder had developed a social concience and, as were many other singer-songwriters of the time, he was politicizing his music. Intelligent lyrics that one can boogie to—what more could one want from popular music? —*Rob Bowman*

○ **Fulfillingness' First Finale** / Jul. 1974 / Motown 0332
Two funky, clarinet-dominated singles, "Boogie On, Reggae Woman" and "You Haven't Done Nothin'," are the high points of this record. Much of the rest of the album is centered around the electric piano, a sound ubiquitous in African American music in the early '70s. Wonder occasionally gets a little syrupy on the non-hit material, although his phrasing is so fine that one tends to be forgiving. —*Rob Bowman*

○ **Songs in the Key of Life** / Sep. 1976 / Motown 0340
Wonder the auteur, began to get out of hand with this sprawling double album plus four-song-EP set. Much is maudlin, cloying, and pretentious; yet great songs, such as "Sir Duke," rear their heads at various junctures throughout the set. —*Rob Bowman*

Journey through the Secret Life of Plants / Oct. 1977 / Motown 6127
Perhaps the most curious album in Stevie Wonder's career, this was ostensibly a soundtrack for a film few people saw (if indeed it was ever released). These were mostly instrumentals plus a few oddball vocals, but most observers didn't know what to make of it at the time. Wonder was so hot (he'd earned three consecutive Grammy Awards for Album of the Year in 1973, 1974, and 1976) that the record peaked at #4 on the pop albums chart despite the lack of any real singles and confounding almost everyone who heard it. "Outside My Window" was the lone tune to scrape the middle regions of the pop charts, while the R&B community ignored the entire album. —*Ron Wynn*

★ **Looking Back** / Dec. 1977 / Motown 804LP3
Between 1963 and the end of 1971, Little Stevie Wonder placed 25 songs on *Billboard*'s charts. Twenty-four of those, including such radio staples as "Fingertips, Pt. 2," "Uptight (Everything's Alright)," "I Was Made to Love Her," "For Once in My Life," "My Cherie Amour," and "Signed, Sealed, Delivered, I'm Yours" appear on *Looking Back*. Wonder's recordings in the '60s stand apart from most Motown acts partially because he was paired with producers and writers who very rarely worked with the Temptations, Supremes, and so on. In the beginning Wonder was often produced by Clarence Paul and/or William Stevenson; during the golden years Henry Cosby was usually manning the controls. Then in 1970 Wonder started producing himself, beginning with "Signed, Sealed, Delivered." Most of Wonder's singles were written by Wonder himself in tandem with a variety of others, or by Ron Miller. The hits alternated between stomping barnburners and midtempo, understated ballads. —*Rob Bowman*

★ **Original Musiquarium I** / May 1982 / Motown 6002
Most of Wonder's chart hits from 1972 through 1982 (although why "You Haven't Done Nothin'" is not here I will never know) are included on *Stevie Wonder's Original Musiquarium I*, plus three newly written and recorded tunes. Simply put, some of the finest African American music made in the '70s. Essential. —*Rob Bowman*

In Square Circle / 1985 / Motown 6134
Though it went platinum, nothing stands as better evidence of how cylical the pop experience is than the response to *In Square Circle*. Wonder actually wrote some superb songs, and several—like "Overjoyed" and "I Love You Too Much"—were superior to the hit single "Part-Time Lover." But that one zoomed to the top spot and became the album's definitive tune in the minds of many. —*Ron Wynn*

Jungle Fever / May 28, 1991 / Motown 6291
Despite all of the hype surrounding it, the soundtrack to *Jungle Fever* is Stevie Wonder's best work in years. Although it can't compare to Wonder's glory days of the early '70s, *Jungle Fever* is a considerable improvement from his bland late '80s albums. Wonder still borders on saccharine on his ballads, although even the sappiest of them ("These Three Words") isn't as sickingly sugary as his 1984 hit "I Just Called to Say I Love You." While the keyboard funk of "Chemical Love," "Gotta Have You," and "Queen in the Black" doesn't sound new, it does sound alive, which is better than Wonder has sounded in years. *Jungle Fever* pales in comparison to *Innervisions* and *Talking Book, but stands head and shoulders above* In Square Circle *and* Characters. — *Stephen Thomas Erlewine*

Brenton Wood

b. Jun. 26, 1941, Shreveport, LA
Vocals / Soul
Wood's quirky rhythmic sense and happy-go-lucky vocal delivery clicked with R&B and pop audiences in 1967, when "The Oogum Boogum Song" and "Gimme Little Sign" both proved potent hits. Born in Shreveport, LA, Wood moved west to San Pedro and found inspiration in the mellifluous styles of Sam Cooke and Jesse Belvin. He formed a vocal group called the Quotations while attending college, before signing with Double Shot Records and hooking up with producers Joe Hooven and Hal Winn. After making it three hits in a row with "Baby You Got It," Wood only notched a couple more minor chart items for the label in 1968. — *Bill Dahl*

● **Best of Brenton Wood** / Rhino 70223
The best, and much of the rest. —*Dan Heilman*

Ron Wood

b. Jun. 1, 1947
Vocals, guitar / Rock & roll
UK guitarist Ron Wood has spent most of his career in groups—
the Jeff Beck Group, Faces, and, since 1976, the Rolling Stones—
but he's found time to make a variety of nongroup albums, including duet albums with Ronnie Lane and with Bo Diddley, and
even a few solo albums that serve as assemblages of his friends.
— *William Ruhlmann*

● **Gimme Some Neck** / 1979 / Columbia 35702
Wood leads a pickup band that includes, on various cuts, fellow
Rolling Stones Charlie Watts, Mick Jagger, and Keith Richards,
plus Mick Fleetwood, Dave Mason, and other notables. The highlight is a then-unreleased Bob Dylan song called "Seven Days,"
where the rough-voiced Wood sounds uncannily like Mr. D himself. — *William Ruhlmann*

○ **Slide on This** / Sep. 1992 / Continuum 19210
Ron Wood's first solo album in over 10 years is a relaxed, rocking,
star-studded affair, including appearances by Charlie Watts,
Hothouse Flowers, Joe Elliott from Def Leppard, and the Edge.
Nothing here is earth-shaking, but the quality of "Knock Yer Teeth
Out," "Show Me," and a cover of the Parliaments' "Testify" makes
Slide on This Wood's best solo album. — *Stephen Thomas
Erlewine*

World Party

Group / Pop/rock
Basically, World Party *is* singer-songwriter and multiinstrumentalist Karl Wallinger. Formerly of the popular British band the
Waterboys, Wallinger's albums are fascinating, unapologetic exercises in pop self-referentialism. At times Wallinger's retro '60s obsessions and his vocal blend of Dylan and Jagger (less distinctive
than either), coupled with his occasional forays into funk, make
him sound like Prince fixated on classic rock. All in all, Wallinger
manages to make the effect flow seamlessly. — *Rick Clark*

○ **Private Revolution** / 1986 / Ensign 21552
This debut album from World Party is a solid release, even if it is
a bit heavy on the synthesized sounds (what can you expect from
a one-man band?). Wallinger's insightful songs deal primarily
with the responsibility of the individual to recognize and cope
with the problems of the world. Features mainly original songs
like "Private Revolution," "World Party," and "It's All Mine," as
well as a cover of Dylan's "All I Really Want to Do," which remains surprisingly true to the original version. — *Iotis Erlewine*

● **Goodbye Jumbo** / 1990 / Ensign 21654
This excellent followup album from World Party is much tighter
than the debut. Dealing with issues from the environment ("Take
It Up," "Put the Message in the Box") to relationship woes ("And I
Fell Back Alone"), these tracks manage to maintain a hopeful,
positive mood without becoming trivial. In these songs, Wallinger
has developed his own distinct style. A great album, worth checking out just for the uptempo groove of "Way Down Now." — *Iotis
Erlewine*

Bang! / 1993 / Capitol 21991
In his previous releases Wallinger has displayed a social conscience, but never has it taken prominence like it does on *Bang!*
World Party's third album. *Bang!* does contain some glorious music that is the equal of his masterpiece *Goodbye Jumbo*, but the
album slows down when he tries to say too much (as in the quasi-
operatic "And God Said"). Even then, Wallinger's preaching does-
n't obliterate the considerable pleasures of the music. Wallinger
has often been accused of recycling the Beatles, but the truth is he
can combine the Beatles, Beach Boys, Sly Stone, Dylan, and
Prince into a musical style that is distinctive and unique yet familiar. *Bang!* for all of its shortcomings, is as strong an album as
any Wallinger has released. — *Stephen Thomas Erlewine*

Link Wray

b. 1930
Guitar / Rock & roll
Up until Link Wray's groundbreaking instrumental "Rumble"
(1958), White guitarists in the main either took the jazz route or
tried their best to emulate some form of the Chet Atkins/Merle
Travis style. Link changed all that. With the pioneering use of distortion, tremolo, and feedback, plus an unabashed attack that

owed much to soul-blues, Wray created a style that was years
ahead of its time. Creating one great instrumental after another
on primarily chordal themes (making him the godfather of the
now-common power chord), his music contained the groundbreaking roots of heavy metal, 10 years before it came into being.
A seminal influence on Pete Townshend, Jeff Beck, and others,
Wray continues to record sporadically, sounding wilder and cra-
zier than ever, giving the lie to the cliché of being "too old to rock
& roll." — *Cub Koda*

Link Wray & the Wraymen / 1960 / Edsel 149
Sides from the '50s and early '60s; some of his best. — *Cub Koda*

○ **Walkin' with Link** / Apr. 1992 / Epic 47904
An excellent 20-track compendium of Wray's tenure with
Columbia-Epic back in the late '50s and early '60s. Nasty, searing,
guitar instrumentals like the title cut, "Ramble," "Rawhide,"
"Comanche," and "Radar" make this an indispensable part of any
Link collection. — *Cub Koda*

★ **Rumble! The Best of Link Wray** / 1993 / Rhino 71222
Finally, a multilabel Link Wray collection spanning his lengthy
career is available. Starting, appropriately enough, with
"Rumble," *Rumble! The Best of Link Wray* illustrates through its
20 tracks (15 on cassette) that Wray was indeed one of the pioneering guitarists of rock & roll, expanding the sonic possibilities
of the instrument with a variety of effects. All of the tracks feature
some truly warped genius fretboard work from Wray, and a few
also feature his equally demented vocals. *Rumble! The Best of
Link Wray* is the definitive Wray collection. — *Stephen Thomas
Erlewine*

○ **Missing Links, Vols. 1, 2, & 3** / ACE 931
A brilliant three-volume set of rare recordings. — *Cub Koda*

Wreckless Eric

Vocals / New wave
Wreckless Eric's music wasn't much more than simple, basic rock
& roll played with an energetic abandon, but at his best, he made
pop singles that were immediately gripping and surprisingly
timeless. During the late '70s, he recorded several minor
punk/new wave classics on Stiff Records, including "Whole Wide
World" and "Semaphore Signals," which sound fresh and exciting
a decade and a half after they were recorded. Those two songs,
benefited from the brilliant pop sense of Nick Lowe, who produced the single and provided instrumental support for Eric's
snarling vocals. After Lowe left Stiff, Wreckless Eric was left without a strong producer and bandleader, making his music much
more inconsistent, yet still highly enjoyable. During the '80s, his
sound was polished up slightly, which removed much of the
crackling energy of his early records. Now, he lives in France and
continues to tour and record, playing for a small cult of fans over
in Europe. — *Stephen Thomas Erlewine*

○ **Wreckless Eric** / 1978 / Stiff 6
A wonderful collection of sloppy, snarling rock & roll that nearly
makes good on the promise of "Whole Wide World." — *Stephen
Thomas Erlewine*

○ **Wonderful World of Wreckless Eric** / 1979 / Stiff 9
Wreckless Eric's second album is a tighter, more pop-oriented col-
lection that still has a vital, ragged edge. — *Stephen Thomas
Erlewine*

● **Big Smash** / 1980 / Stiff 36463
Taking the best moments from Wreckless Eric's first two exciting
but spotty albums, *Big Smash* contains everything you need to
know about this forgotten but charming punk/new wave rocker.
— *Stephen Thomas Erlewine*

Betty Wright

b. Dec. 21, 1953, Miami, FL
Vocals / Soul
A consistently strong presence on the Miami music scene
throughout the '70s and '80s, Betty Wright was just 15 when she
cut the Top 40 "Girls Can't Do What the Guys Do." A child gospel
star who switched to R&B at age 13, she put the Miami scene on
the map in 1971 with the #6 hit "Clean Up Woman," notable for
its prominent guitar riff and Wright's swaggering lead vocal. She
went on to win a Grammy in 1974 for "Where Is the Love?" (not
to be confused with the Roberta Flack/Donny Hathaway tune of
the same name). She collaborated with Stevie Wonder in 1981 on

the Epic hit "What Are You Gonna Do with It?" Betty continues to live and work in the Miami area. —*Christine Ohlman*

Live / 1978 / Rhino 70796
This may not be live, but it is an accurate record of Wright's energetic R&B approach in concert during the mid '70s. —*Bill Dahl*

● **Best of Betty Wright** / 1992 / Rhino 71085
An excellent collection, covering the years between 1968 and 1978; it's 20 tracks of Betty Wright at her best. —*Stephen Thomas Erlewine*

○ **Clean Up Woman** / Collectables 5118
Her earliest Miami soul sides are also her most charming. —*Bill Dahl*

Charles Wright

Vocals, guitar, piano / Soul, funk
Charles Wright headed one of the late '60s and early '70s great funk groups, the Watts 103rd Street Band. Wright, who was born in Clarksdale, MS, was a singer, pianist, guitarist, and leader of the eight-member band, recruited from Watts in Los Angeles. They were originally known as the Soul Runners. Bill Cosby helped get the band off the ground by giving them appearances at his gigs. They began recording for Keyman in 1967, then moved to Warner Bros. in 1969. While "Do Your Thing" and "Till You Get Enough" were Top 20 R&B hits, their finest selection was "Express Yourself," a song that expressed the urge for freedom as adroitly as the Isley Brothers' "It's Your Thing" had in the '60s. It has also been among the most sampled funk tracks for hip-hop and rap groups. "Your Love (Means Everything to Me)" was their final R&B hit in 1971, peaking at #9 R&B and #12 pop. The group's best ballad, "Love Land," did better pop-wise than among R&B fans, many of whom saw it as a bit soft. They continued recording for Dunhill in 1973 before disbanding. Drummer James Gadson and guitarist Al McKay, who later joined Earth, Wind and Fire, were among the instrumental corps of the Watts 103rd Street Rhythm Band. —*Ron Wynn*

● **Express Yourself: The Best of** / 1993 / Warner Brothers
A definitive, 16-track collection of Charles Wright's best material. —*Stephen Thomas Erlewine*

Gary Wright

b. Apr. 26, 1943, Creskill, NJ
Vocals, keyboard / Pop/rock
Gary Wright initially found success with the British hard blues/rock band Spooky Tooth, from 1967 to 1970. He then pursued a solo career that peaked in 1975 with the atmospheric synth-pop hits "Dream Weaver" and "My Love Is Alive," both reaching #2. —*Rick Clark*

● **Dream Weaver** / 1975 / Warner Brothers 2868
During the fall of 1975, the title cut off of this album became an enormous hit, with its atmospheric synthesizer washes and spacey sentiments. The followup, "My Love Is Alive," did just as well. Most of the album trades on the same themes but with less success. —*Rick Clark*

O. V. Wright

b. Oct. 9, 1939, d. Nov. 16, 1980
Vocals / Soul
A truly incendiary deep-soul performer. O. V. Wright's melismatic vocals and Willie Mitchell's vaunted Hi Rhythm Section combined to make classic Memphis soul during the early '70s. Overton Vertis Wright learned his trade on the gospel circuit with the Sunset Travelers before going secular in 1964 with the passionate ballad "That's How Strong My Love Is" for Goldwax in Memphis. Otis Redding liked the song so much that he covered it, killing any chance of Wright's version hitting.

Since Wright was already under contract to Houston-based Peacock as a gospel act, owner Don Robey demanded his return, and from then on, Wright appeared on Robey's Backbeat subsidiary. Wright's sanctified sound oozes sweet soul on the spine-chilling "You're Gonna Make Me Cry," a 1965 smash, but it took Memphis producer Willie Mitchell to wring the best consistently from Wright. Utilizing Mitchell's surging house rhythm section, Wright's early '70s Backbeat singles "Ace of Spades," "A Nickel and a Nail," and "I Can't Take It" rank among the very best southern soul of their era.

No disco bandwagon for O. V. Wright—he kept right on pouring out his emotions through the '70s, convincing his faithful that "I'd Rather Be (Blind, Crippled & Crazy)," that he was "Into Something (Can't Shake Loose)." Unfortunately, he apparently was—drugs have often been cited as causing Wright's downfall; the soul great died at only 41 years of age in 1980. —*Bill Dahl*

● **Soul of O. V. Wright** / 1992 / MCA 10670
This collection of '60s and '70s material for Don Robey's Back Beat label includes evocative ballads like "You're Gonna Make Me Cry," "Gonna Forget about You," and "I've Been Searching," plus lightweight but enjoyable numbers like "Monkey Dog," "I Don't Want to Sit Down," "Motherless Child," and "I'm Going Home (to Live with God)," which returned him to his gospel days. While several foreign anthologies spotlighting Wright have been issued, this 18-track CD stands as the most complete domestic reissue package currently available. —*Ron Wynn*

Robert Wyatt

Vocals, drums / Art rock
The former Soft Machine drummer and vocalist has recorded a slew of albums in the British art-rock vein. —*John Floyd*

● **Rock Bottom** / 1974 / Blue Plate 1634
A progressive rock-era masterpiece. Brilliantly simple songs, poems, and textures, with all-star support. —*Myles Boisen*

○ **Ruth Is Stranger than Richard** / 1975 / Blue Plate 1635
Another enduring collaboration with Brian Eno, Fred Frith, and other '70s luminaries. On a par with *Rock Bottom*. —*Myles Boisen*

○ **Compilation** / Nov. 1, 1991 / Gramavision 79459
A reissue of his two strongest '80s albums, *Nothing Can Stop Us* and *Old Rottenhat*. Both are political and lyrical triumphs. —*Myles Boisen*

X

Group / Punk, rock & roll
X was a Los Angeles-based punk-rock band of the '80s. It was an outstanding critical success, especially in its first years of record making, but it never broke through to the kind of record sales necessary to sustain a band on a national level. X was formed in the winter of 1977-1978 by singer and bassist John Doe (b. February 24, 1954), guitarist Billy Zoom (b. February 20, late 1940s), singer Exene Cervenka (b. February 1, 1956), and D. J. Bonebrake (b. December 8, 1955).

Over the next couple of years, they rose to the top of a punk-rock scene that had begun to emerge just as the ones in New York and London were fading away. The group signed to the local Slash label and released their debut album, *Los Angeles* (produced by Ray Manzarek of the Doors), in 1980. The album, with its driving rock, led by Zoom's Chuck Berry-influenced guitar, and the colead vocals of Cervenka and Doe on a series of poetic, socially conscious lyrics, was a critical success and sold well for an album on a small label. *Wild Gift* (1981) did even better, even reaching the national charts.

Inevitably, X then signed to a major label, Elektra, and went from being a big fish in a small pond to the opposite. Their third album, *Under the Big Black Sun* (1982), was well received, but *More Fun in the New World* (1983) and *Ain't Love Grand* (1985) failed to expand their audience or to excite critics the way earlier records had done. Billy Zoom left X in late 1985 and was replaced by former Blasters guitarist Dave Alvin, who had played with Cervenka and Doe in a country-rock spinoff band, the Knitters. Tony Gilkyson, formerly of Lone Justice, was added as a second guitarist in March 1986. This quintet recorded *See How We Are* (1987) (though Alvin had quit for a solo career before it was released); it was considered a critical comeback, but its sales were unimpressive. X released a double live album in 1988, then announced a hiatus; during the next five years, Cervenka and Doe both made solo albums. X reunited in 1993, releasing the *Hey Zeus!* album and touring the country; although the album received respectable reviews, it didn't sell very many copies. —*William Ruhlmann*

○ **Los Angeles** / 1980 / Slash 23930
Although classified as punk because of their simple hard-rock sound and caustic lyrics ("The World's a Mess; It's in My Kiss"), X always had more of a rockabilly edge, courtesy of former Gene Vincent guitarist Billy Zoom, and were always funnier than the

punk label implies, which may be why they were a cut above their competition. —*William Ruhlmann*

○ **Wild Gift** / 1981 / Warner Brothers 23931
As with many groups, X had more good songs in their repertoire than could fit on their debut, and their second album presents the rest. Appropriately, the two albums have been packaged together on a single CD. —*William Ruhlmann*

○ **Under the Big Black Sun** / 1982 / Elektra 60150
Unlike many groups, X responded to the pressure to write a new body of material after their initial burst of songs by coming up with the goods, especially "The Hungry Wolf" and "Riding with Mary." —*William Ruhlmann*

○ **See How We Are** / 1987 / Elektra 60492
X had moved toward becoming more of a mainstream hard-rock act by the time of their last studio album and, given how good the song "4th of July" is, it's a shame its writer, Dave Alvin, didn't stay with the band long enough to contribute more. —*William Ruhlmann*

★ **Los Angeles/Wild Gift** / Sep. 20, 1988 / Slash 25771
X's two classic early albums combined on one essential CD. —*AMG*

XTC

Group / New wave, alternative pop/rock
England's XTC emerged during the late '70s, when new wave and punk were informing rock with a renewed urgency. Their early recordings drew heavily from those movements, with arrangements that were edgy and dissonant. Early on, though, it became evident that XTC had a spiritual affinity for post-*Revolver* Beatles and *Pet Sounds*-era Beach Boys. Their clever (often humorous) off-centered pop increasingly addressed adult topics (from whimsical takes on parenting to religion and class-structure divisions) that, by turns, exuded heady idealism, childlike wonder, or sober skepticism. All in all, XTC has produced some of the finest pop-rock of the '80s and early '90s. —*Rick Clark*

White Music / Jan. 1978 / David Geffen Co. 24373
XTC's first full album shows the band going full throttle in true punk spirit. More dissonant than their latter period, the young band shines with directionless energy and a good sense of humor. Highlights include the catchy singles "This Is Pop" and "Radios in Motion" as well as a jumpy version of "All Along the Watchtower." The *3D* EP has been added to the CD version. –*Chris Woodstra*

Go 2 / Feb. 1978 / David Geffen Co. 24375
The band's second album, *Go 2* continues in the same high energy vein as *White Music* with slightly less memorable results. —*Chris Woodstra*

○ **Drums & Wires** / 1979 / David Geffen Co. 4034
By the release of the Steve Lillywhite-produced *Drums and Wires*, XTC had developed a unique sound that integrated (and plundered) late '70s new wave, '60s-style pop, and psychedelia. The album produced XTC's first big British hit with "Making Plans for Nigel" (#17 UK). —*Rick Clark*

○ **Black Sea** / 1980 / David Geffen Co. 24376
On *Black Sea*, again produced by Steve Lillywhite, XTC turned influences (like the Beatles and Beach Boys) inside out with agitated rhythms and mildly dissonant instrumental voicings. *Black Sea* generated four moderate British hit singles. One of them, "Towers of London," features a marvelously twisted Badfinger-style guitar hook set against a wonderfully galumphing bass line. "Respectable Street" is another standout on this, one of their best albums. —*Rick Clark*

○ **Waxworks: Some Singles 1977-1982** / 1982 / David Geffen Co. 4037
A smartly assembled collection of the band's better early tracks. —*Rick Clark*

○ **English Settlement** / 1982 / David Geffen Co. 4036
English Settlement, a double-album set, heightened XTC's stateside visibility with the track "Senses Working Overtime." Unfortunately, the album lacked the consistency of *Black Sea*, primarily because of the flat-sounding production, which seemed to steal the impact of the music. —*Rick Clark*

○ **Mummer** / 1983 / David Geffen Co. 24374

With a couple of exceptions, *Mummer* is a relaxed, somewhat flat-sounding affair. Andy Partridge still manages to get a little venom out with the acidic "Funk Pop a Roll." Other highlights are Colin Moulding's "Love on a Farmboy's Wages" (#50 UK), "Wonderland," and "Great Fire." —*Rick Clark*

Big Express / 1984 / David Geffen Co. 24054
Following up the relatively somnolent *Mummer*, *The Big Express* was a return to the playful upbeat pop/rock of some of XTC's previous works. "The Everyday Story of a Small Town" is a highlight, as well as "All You Pretty Girls." —*Rick Clark*

● **Compact XTC, the Singles 1978-85** / 1986 / Virgin
Taking the *Waxworks* collection one step further, this 18-track disc collects all of the pre-*Skylarking* singles. A nice place for beginners to start. —*Chris Woodstra*

★ **Skylarking** / 1986 / David Geffen Co. 24117
With *Skylarking*, XTC addressed coming-of-age issues like marriage ("Big Day"), supporting a family ("Earn Enough for Us"), and the existence of a loving God ("Dear God"), while clothing them with performances that suggested XTC hadn't lost the capacity for childlike wonder. Todd Rundgren's production of *Skylarking* is one of his best, bathing the album in a pleasantly trippy soundstage. Other highlights include "The Meeting Place" and "Grass." —*Rick Clark*

○ **Oranges & Lemons** / 1989 / David Geffen Co. 24218
Compared to their best work, *Oranges & Lemons* is a little uneven—a case of a double album that would have made a great single release if XTC had pared it down. *Oranges & Lemons* did produce two big alternative pop-rock hits with "The Mayor of Simpleton" and "King for a Day." Other highlights include the optimistic "The Loving" and "Pink Thing." —*Rick Clark*

Rag 'n' Bone Buffet / 1991 / David Geffen Co. 24417
This is a collection of B sides, live performances, and alternative versions culled from throughout their career. Among the oddities contained here is a cleaned-up-for-radio version of "Respectable Street" off of *Black Sea*. Among the live recordings is "Another Satellite," taken from a BBC broadcast, and a great version of "Scissor Man," originally on *Drums and Wires*. Also included are various solo recordings by bandmates Andy Partridge and Colin Moulding. All in all, *Rag 'n' Bone Buffet* is a desirable item for any XTC fans looking to round out their collection of this band's work. —*Rick Clark*

○ **Nonsuch** / 1992 / David Geffen Co. 24472
Nonsuch, produced by Gus Dudgeon (Elton John, Bowie), trims the excesses found on *Oranges and Lemons* and recalls the pastoral refinement of *Skylarking* and the rocky edge found on *The Big Express*. Andy Partridge's "The Ballad of Peter Pumkinhead," "The Disappointed," and "Crocodile" are highlights, as are Colin Moulding's "Books Are Burning" and "Bungalow." One of their better albums. —*Rick Clark*

The Yardbirds

Group / British invasion, rock & roll, blues rock, psychedelic
Formed in 1963, the Yardbirds are one the most influential groups in the history of rock & roll. (The term "Yardbird" came from the designation given to hobos in a Jack Kerouac novel.) During the course of their career, the Yardbirds featured three of rock's greatest guitarists in Eric Clapton, Jeff Beck, and Jimmy Page. During their early period with Clapton, they pursued a highly charged style of electric blues, highlighted best on *Five Live Yardbirds*. Clapton split when he sensed the band was getting too pop with the release of their first single, "For Your Love."

Jeff Beck brought on phase two of the band's development with a highly experimental style that pioneered the application of feedback, fuzz, and unusual melodic scales. It was here that the Yardbirds achieved their creative peak, with songs like "I'm a Man," "Heart Full of Soul," "Evil Hearted You," "Lost Woman," and the masterly "Shapes of Things."

Around the time Beck began unraveling at the seams, Jimmy Page came on board. For a very brief time, the Yardbirds had a dream twin-lead guitar lineup, best chronicled on the hits "Happenings Ten Years Time Ago" and "Stroll On," from the movie *Blow Up*.

After Beck left, Page hung on for a little over a year, recording the rather lightweight album *Little Games*. Shortly afterward, the band feel apart, with Page going on to form Led Zeppelin. Lead singer Keith Relf helped form the art-rock group Renaissance, and bassist Paul Samwell-Smith went on to a successful production career for artists like Cat Stevens and Carly Simon. Even though the Yardbirds weren't among the most commercially successful bands of the '60s British invasion, their profound impact on rock laid the groundwork for hard blues-based rock and heavy metal.

Of particular note to those seeking out the best-sounding Yardbirds discs: none of their CD reissues utilize the original first-generation masters. EMI England has them but won't license them out, due to an unpaid studio bill dating back from the mid '60s. However, the Edsel import of *Roger the Engineer* sounds impeccable. The reason: The band owns the original masters. —*Rick Clark*

○ **Five Live Yardbirds** / Dec. 1964 / Rhino 70189
Recorded live at London's Marquee Club, *Five Live Yardbirds* is the best document of Eric Clapton's work with the band. Tracks like "Too Much Monkey Business," "Got Love If You Want It," and "Smokestack Lightning" were good representations of the Yardbirds's "raveups," which were open-ended improvisations that helped lay the groundwork for groups like Cream and the Jimi Hendrix Experience. —*Rick Clark*

○ **Roger the Engineer** / 1966 / Edsel 116
Roger the Engineer is a classic Yardbirds studio album, thanks to tracks like "Lost Woman," "Over Under Sideways Down," "What Do You Want," "Psycho Daisies," and "Ever Since the World Began." Not available in the States, this British import (on Edsel) is the best-sounding Yardbirds CD by a long shot. A must-own for fans of this band. —*Rick Clark*

★ **Greatest Hits, Vol. 1: 1964-1966** / 1986 / Rhino 75895
Sonically, these tracks fail to match the brilliance and warmth of the original vinyl pressings, but *Greatest Hits* has more punch. "For Your Love" is an exception, with the record version sounding extremely compressed. Of the various Yardbird collections that exist, this is still the most intelligently chosen, even though it lacks key tracks from *Roger the Engineer*. —*Rick Clark*

○ **Vol. 1: Smokestack Lightning** / 1991 / Sony 48655
This double-disc set focuses on tracks from *For Your Love* and *Having a Rave-Up with the Yardbirds*. Included are live tracks recorded at the Crawdaddy Club while touring with Sonny Boy Williamson. Most of these tracks on *Smokestack Lightning* (as well as *Blues, Backtracks*) were mastered off of safety tapes, as opposed to the original masters, since EMI England has possession of them. Considering that EMI won't release the masters to anyone, this is a respectable sound—though not as good as the first vinyl pressings. —*Rick Clark*

○ **Vol. 2, Blues, Backtracks & Shapes of Things** / 1991 / Sony 48658
Vol. 2, Blues, Backtracks & Shapes of Things, another double-disc set, covers some later hits (including the classic future-rock of "Shapes of Things"), *Roger the Engineer* outtakes, and various other oddities. The sound on some of the outtakes is pretty respectable, considering some of them were taken from the original acetates. —*Rick Clark*

Yardbirds Little Games Sessions & More / 1992 / EMI America 98213
This digitally remastered 39-track double-disc set covers Jimmy Page's tenure with the Yardbirds. This period didn't contain the band's best work, mainly because Mickie Most's poppish production reined in the band's experimental strengths. Nevertheless, tracks like "Little Games," "Puzzles," "Smile on Me," "Drinking Muddy Water," and a wonderful acoustic version of Jimmy Page's "White Summer" make this a good overview of the Yardbirds' final stretch as a band. This set includes extensive liner notes and discography—a real treat for fans. —*Rick Clark*

Yaz

Group / New wave, dance, dance-pop
Yaz was the American name taken by Yazoo, a British duo made up of former Depeche Mode synthesizer player Vince Clarke and singer Alison Moyet (b. June 18, 1961). The two stayed together only about a year and a half (1982-1983), but that was long enough to score four British hit singles and two top-selling albums. Moyet then went solo, and Clarke eventually formed another successful duo, Erasure. —*William Ruhlmann*

○ **Upstairs at Eric's** / 1982 / Sire 23737

Yaz's music is spare, striking electronic backup contrasted with full-throated, emotional singing, but one shouldn't discount some remarkable songwriting, especially the hits "Don't Go," "Only You," and "Situation." —*William Ruhlmann*

● **You & Me Both** / 1983 / Sire 23903
Perhaps a more consistent collection overall than the first album, this one demonstrates that the duo was anything but played out. While both have gone on to successful careers, you can't help regretting that this is the end of Yaz. —*William Ruhlmann*

Yello

Group / Progressive rock, dance
This group from Switzerland is a picture of professionalism, although none of the members are trained musicians. Boris Blank, Dieter Meier, and Carlos Peron do not go overboard trying to be innovative and original, but that is certainly the outcome. They have created a distinctive and bright listening style, unusual and very simplistic, not based on traditional harmony or pretensions. Their rich, unique sound and strong emphasis on modern synthesizer technology make this group one of the most interesting in contemporary music history. —*Vladimir Bogdanov*

○ **Stella** / 1985 / Mercury 822820
This is one of their disco-oriented albums. Includes "Desire" and "Sometimes." —*Vladimir Bogdanov*

One Second / 1987 / Mercury 832675
This album offers a great variety of styles, effects, textures, and rhythms. Includes the songs "The Rhythm Divine" and "The Secret Fazida." —*Vladimir Bogdanov*

○ **Flag** / 1988 / Mercury 836426
This is Yello's most dynamic album, with excellent compositions. Picking highlights would be difficult, since the songs segue, and the album just begs to be listened to as a whole. —*Vladimir Bogdanov*

● **Essential** / Smash 8002
A good compilation that will satisfy fans of their infamous "Oh Yeah." —*AMG*

Yes

Group / Progressive rock, pop/rock
Yes is, without a doubt, the definitive English progressive-rock band, purveyors of cosmic lyrics, virtuoso playing, and vast musical tapestries topped off with heart-stoppingly gorgeous melodies and sealed with a rock & roll kick. Yes was formed in London in 1968 by singer Jon Anderson and bassist Chris Squire, both owners of high, clear tenor voices that blend seamlessly in the band's trademark harmonies. The history of Yes is one of constant changes in personnel, but the group's most celebrated lineup came about when founding members Anderson, Squire, and drummer Bill Bruford, plus guitarist Steve Howe (who had enlisted in 1970), were joined in 1971 by keyboard whiz Rick Wakeman. Thus constituted, the band cut its signature tune, "Roundabout" (from the fourth Yes album, *Fragile*), not to mention the sumptuously symphonic magnum opus *Close to the Edge*. A further series of comings and goings led to a disastrous 1980 lineup (documented on "Drama") in which Squire was the only remaining original member. After a three-year hiatus, a revamped Yes (Anderson, Squire, original keyboardist Tony Kaye, longtime drummer Alan White, and South African guitarist Trevor Rabin) emerged in 1983 with a streamlined, commercialized sound, topping the charts with the danceable "Owner of a Lonely Heart." Anderson split in 1988, teaming up with some old cohorts as Anderson Bruford Wakeman Howe—essentially a rival version of Yes! The two bands joined forces in 1991 as an eight-man "mega-Yes," combining their separately recorded efforts on *Union*. —*Michael P. Dawson*

Yes / 1969 / Atlantic 8243
Early pop/folk rock. Their first, and it should be taken as such. —*Bruce Eder*

Time and a Word / 1970 / Atlantic 8273
A more ambitious second album, in search of a style. —*Bruce Eder*

○ **Yes Album** / 1971 / Atlantic 19131
This is the album that first gave shape to the established Yes sound, built around science-fiction concepts, folk melodies, and soaring organ, guitar, and vocal showpieces. "Your Move" actually

got some airplay as a single, and "Starship Troopers" became a much-loved part of the band's set. —*Bruce Eder*

★ **Fragile** / Jan. 1971 / Atlantic 19132
The breakthrough album for the band, in which the science-fiction and fantasy elements of the songs became dominant and the addition of Rick Wakeman on organ added a larger-than-life element to the group's sound. Ironically, the album was a patchwork job, hastily assembled to help cover the cost of Wakeman's expanded array of instruments, but the short form of "Roundabout" clicked on AM radio, album buyers liked the long version, plus the rest of the material they found, and the band was made. —*Bruce Eder*

☆ **Close to the Edge** / Feb. 1972 / Atlantic 19133
The group's sound broke more boundaries here, as side-long suites allowed Jon Anderson even more opportunity for vocal acrobatics and Wakeman an even bigger canvas on which to paint his electronic-synthesizer swirls and organ arpeggios. The poetry also had a peculiarly hypnotic quality, which overcame its relatively obscure passages. —*Bruce Eder*

Yessongs / 1973 / Atlantic 100
The best live album to emerge from the entire art-rock scene, a compendium of blazing performances covering the previous three studio albums by the group and the accompanying solo career of Rick Wakeman. Some of the performances are superior to their studio originals, although "And You and I" is something of a disappointment next to the version on *Close to the Edge.* —*Bruce Eder*

Yesterdays / 1975 / Atlantic 19134
A slightly disappointing compendium of odd early tracks. For true fanatics. Supplanted, in part, by *Yesyears.* —*Bruce Eder*

Yesshows / 1980 / Arista 32P228901
A double album chronicling the late '70s repertoire of the group, less interesting than *Yessongs* but probably the best compendium of this material that is likely to emerge. —*Bruce Eder*

○ **90125** / 1983 / Atlantic 90125
A ridiculously successful "comeback" album with a slightly different membership. —*Bruce Eder*

○ **Yesyears** / 1991 / Atlantic 91644
This four-CD set is sonically so far superior to the individual CDs by the group that on this basis alone it is worth owning. Unfortunately, there are important songs that didn't get the remastering treatment, and they are missed. —*Bruce Eder*

● **Very Best of Yes** / 1993 / Atlantic 82517
The very best of Yes is hard to stick on merely one disc; the set includes tracks from each era of the band. Not essential, but a decent sampler. —*Rick Clark*

Talk / 1994 / Victory
The opening song, "The Calling," is solid later-era Yes. Overall, an album hardcore fans will accept, but not one of their best. —*Rick Clark*

Yo La Tengo

Group / Alternative pop/rock
Formed by music critic Ira Kaplan, Hoboken-based Yo La Tengo (Spanish for "I got it") mixes a little acoustic folk rock with their noise. Their music alternates and blends folky melodicism with postpunk aggression. Mostly, they sound as though they're enjoying what they're playing. —*Bruce Eder*

○ **Ride the Tiger** / 1986 / Coyote 8676
Basking in guitars. —*Robert Gordon*

○ **President Yo La Tengo/New Wave Hot Dogs** / 1989 / Twintone 89153
President Yo La Tengo was the first album where the band was able to tie their eclectic mix of folk and noisy rock into a cohesive whole. —*Stephen Thomas Erlewine*

○ **Fakebook** / 1990 / Bar/None 20
A collection of mostly covers, Tengo-ized. —*Robert Gordon*

● **Painful** / 1993 / Matador/Atlantic
Yo La Tengo have released several fine albums before, but only *Painful* encapsulates their folky guitar experimentalism perfectly. Alternating between dreamy Velvet Underground-style ballads and raving, Sonic Youth guitar squalls, *Painful* also finds the group improving their songwriting skills immeasurably. Before, they relied on their soundscapes—now the sound fleshes out their

songs, from the trance-like "Nowhere Near" to the dense "From a Motel 6" and the two versions of "Big Day Coming," which cover both ends of the spectrum. —*Stephen Thomas Erlewine*

Neil Young

b. Nov. 12, 1945, Toronto, Canada
Vocals, guitar, piano / Singer-songwriter, rock & roll, country rock, hard rock, folk rock
With the exception only of Bob Dylan, Neil Young is the most acclaimed and accomplished singer-songwriter of his generation. Born in Toronto, Young learned to play ukelele and then guitar in his teens and played in a variety of groups. He moved to Los Angeles with his friend bassist Bruce Palmer and hooked up with Stephen Stills, Richie Furay, and Dewey Martin to form Buffalo Springfield in 1966. After the Springfield split in 1968, Young went solo, releasing his first album, *Neil Young,* an acoustic effort with strings, in January 1969. Characteristically, Young followed it only four months later with the hard-rock *Everybody Knows This Is Nowhere,* backed by the electric three-piece band Crazy Horse; it became his first gold-selling album. Young joined Crosby, Stills & Nash in June 1969 and combined solo and group careers until the band split the following summer. His third solo album, *After the Gold Rush* (August 1970), reached the Top 10 and included his first Top 40 hit, "Only Love Can Break Your Heart." But Young's commercial peak came early in 1972, when he released the #1, three-million-selling album *Harvest,* which contained the chart-topping gold single "Heart of Gold."

Instead of following up such success, Young worked on the documentary film *Journey through the Past* (and its accompanying soundtrack album) for the rest of the year, then launched a concert tour in early 1973, by which time Crazy Horse's guitarist Danny Whitten had died of a heroin overdose. The tour was a ragged affair chronicled on the live album *Time Fades Away.* After it, Young recorded (but did not release) *Tonight's the Night,* which memorialized Whitten and Bruce Berry, a Young roadie who had also overdosed.

Young's first new studio album in 18 months, *On the Beach,* was released in the fall of 1974. Much of it was acoustic, and it expressed dire sentiments. He finally put out *Tonight's the Night* in the summer of 1975, and the hard-rocking *Zuma* the following autumn. In the spring of 1976, Young toured with Stephen Stills, and the two recorded the duo album *Long May You Run.* Young's next solo album was 1977's *American Stars 'n' Bars,* made up of studio tracks dating back three years. In the fall of 1977, he released *Decade,* a three-album (later two-CD) career retrospective. 1978 saw the release of *Comes a Time,* Young's most country-folk-oriented album since *Harvest,* and his first since *Harvest* to reach the Top 10. In 1979 Young launched a tour with Crazy Horse under the banner *Rust Never Sleeps,* including a critically acclaimed album of the same name and, eventually, a tour film and a live album called *Live Rust.*

Young spent the better part of the '80s veering from one musical style to another, as his commercial fortunes declined. He turned to electronic music on *Trans,* to rockabilly on *Everybody's Rockin',* to country on *Old Ways,* and to horn-backed R&B on *This Note's for You.* In 1989, however, Young returned to his more familiar folk and rock styles for *Freedom* and was rewarded with critical hosannas and his first gold album in a decade. The hard-rocking *Ragged Glory* was even more rapturously received, topping the *Village Voice* critic's poll for Best Album of 1990. In late 1991 Young issued a double live album, *Weld,* as well as *Arc Weld,* an album of instrumental guitar feedback.

In 1992, Young was being hailed as "the Godfather of Grunge," as dozens of new rock & roll bands from Pearl Jam to the Jayhawks were claiming him as an influence. Naturally, Young backed away from the hard, overdriven rock of *Weld* and *Ragged Glory,* releasing the quiet *Harvest Moon,* the sequel to his country-rock landmark, *Harvest.* In 1993, he released a rarities collection (*Lucky Thirteen*) and a live album (*Unplugged*) while he worked on his long-awaited box set; he released another album recorded with Crazy Horse, *Sleeps with Angels,* in late summer of 1994. —*William Ruhlmann*

☆ **Everybody Knows This Is Nowhere** / 1969 / Reprise 2282
Young's breakthrough album is also the first one to feature the backup of Crazy Horse for a seminal rock session that produced the Young favorites "Cinnamon Girl," "Down by the River," and "Cowgirl in the Sand." —*William Ruhlmann*

☆ **After the Gold Rush** / 1970 / Reprise 2283
The years have only been kind to what sounded like Young's best album when it was released. It's a mixture of his folkie ("Tell Me Why"), country ("Oh, Lonesome Me"), and hard-rocking ("Southern Man") selves, and there's also that mystical title track, which remains Neil Young's definitive statement of purpose. — *William Ruhlmann*

○ **Harvest** / 1972 / Reprise 2277
Uneven, yes, perhaps due to the overambitiousness of the orchestral pieces, but this album, Young's biggest seller, still contains "Heart of Gold," the rocker "Alabama," and such telling ballads as "Old Man." — *William Ruhlmann*

Time Fades Away / 1973 / Reprise 2151
The beginning of Young's mid '70s descent into decadence, this is part of a trilogy including *Tonight's the Night* and *On the Beach* that explores drug addiction, desperation, and determination, and the subject matter isn't only expressed in the lyrics, it's in the roughly played music and the strained vocals. The most gripping music of Young's career. — *William Ruhlmann*

○ **On the Beach** / 1974 / Reprise 2180
Part three of the doom trilogy was actually the second to be released, as Young began to dig himself out of the depression of the previous year, noting that "Sooner or later, it all gets real" but also fearing that he's "just pissing in the wind." — *William Ruhlmann*

☆ **Tonight's the Night** / 1975 / Reprise 2221
This belatedly released masterpiece (part two of the trilogy) is one of the scariest records ever released. It names names and spares no one in its depiction of the ravages of the druggy life of rock & roll. Least of all spared is the author, who often sounds like he's about to nod out himself. Probably the best album Neil Young will ever make, and not listed as his pick only because it's not the place to start. — *William Ruhlmann*

○ **Zuma** / 1975 / Reprise 2242
"Don't cry no tears around me," Young declares, trying for the second album in a row (after *On the Beach*) to put the past behind him and take on new topics and directions. And so he does, though by calling on other aspects of his past. Crazy Horse is back, with Frank Sampedro replacing Danny Whitten, and Young even includes "Through My Sails," a track from an abortive Crosby, Stills, Nash, and Young session. But the highlight is "Cortez the Killer," Young's best guitar workout since *Everybody Knows This Is Nowhere*. — *William Ruhlmann*

★ **Decade** / 1977 / Reprise 2257
A three-LP/two-CD retrospective with material dating back to Buffalo Springfield (some of it unreleased) and including such previously non-LP gems as "Sugar Mountain." As a best-of, it's idiosyncratic, but as a rarities album, it's invaluable. — *William Ruhlmann*

○ **Comes a Time** / 1978 / Reprise 2266
From the reflective opener "Goin' Back" to the airy remake of Ian & Sylvia's "Four Strong Winds," *Comes a Time* is Young's most delicately (and oddly) atmospheric album. The album's dreamy country/folk music frames Young's homey discourses on "Peace of Mind," the "Field of Opportunity," and the "Human Highway." The collective effect is a lulling optimism, even when his mind at times seems to be bangin' on one cylinder—merely dishing out alien-sounding toss-offs clothed in plainspeak. Overall, *Comes a Time* is a strangely entrancing high point in Young's willfully erratic career. — *Rick Clark*

☆ **Rust Never Sleeps** / Jan. 1979 / Reprise 2295
Like the album that followed it, *Live Rust*, this is a live album. The difference is that this is a single disc containing all-new material. The songs are among Young's best ever, "My My, Hey Hey (Out of the Blue)," "Thrasher," and "Powderfinger," among them. — *William Ruhlmann*

○ **Freedom** / 1989 / Reprise 25899
"Rockin' in the Free World" represents a renewal of Young's commitment to his artistic vision and to his audience, and, as with all his best work, it recognizes the worst while it hopes for the best. A stunning return to form for an artist who seemed to have wandered too far from his original promise ever to find his way back. — *William Ruhlmann*

☆ **Ragged Glory** / 1990 / Reprise 26315
Young is reunited with Crazy Horse for an album of noisy guitar rock that sounds perfect when played right after *Everybody Knows This Is Nowhere*, and that's a high recommendation. — *William Ruhlmann*

○ **Weld** / 1991 / Reprise 26671
With the double-disc *Weld*, Neil Young closes the door on his return to overamplified guitar grunge. Recorded at various tour stops during the Gulf War in 1990, *Weld* is full of anger, patriotism, optimism, and confusion—it perfectly captures the atmosphere of the time. Although there is a heavy political undertow on *Weld*, the main reason to listen to it is that it rocks like a demon. Neil Young has never released such a towering monument of noise before, and the sheer rage and volume of *Weld* are overpowering. Live albums rarely are this good or this relevant. (Note: The first editions of *Weld* featured *Arc*, a 35-minute aural collage of feedback recorded throughout the tour. Although the premise sounds frightening, *Arc* is a surprisingly accessible, enjoyable listen. It was later issued separately as an EP.) — *Stephen Thomas Erlewine*

○ **Harvest Moon** / Nov. 3, 1992 / Reprise 45057
After he took feedback as far as it could go with *Weld/Arc*, Neil Young finally decided to release the sequel to *Harvest*, his most commercially successful album. Twenty years have passed between the two albums, and Young's talents have grown over time. *Harvest Moon* is a better album than *Harvest*, lacking the orchestral bombast that stifled some of the songs on *Harvest* and boasting a stronger overall selection of songs. *Harvest Moon* manages to be sentimental without being sappy, wistful without being nostalgic. Featuring the lovely "Unknown Legend," "From Hank to Hendrix" and the gorgeous title track, *Harvest Moon* is a beautiful album that proudly displays its scars, heartaches, and love. — *Stephen Thomas Erlewine*

○ **Lucky Thirteen** / 1993 / Geffen 24452
It would be difficult to argue with the fact that 1982 to 1988 was not Young's most consistent period. Even many diehard fans were able to find something to dislike among the pseudo-synth pop of *Trans*, straight rockabilly of *Everybody's Rockin',* pure country of *Old Ways*, or MOR rock of *Landing on Water* and *Life*. Apart from compiling the best material from most of these releases (nothing from *Rockin'*), what makes *Lucky Thirteen* valuable is that Young himself scoured the vaults for interesting outtakes and live tracks from the period. There's some real gold mined here, especially the heartfelt, previously unreleased ballad "Depression Blues" (a shelved outtake from *Old Ways* that would have been right at home on *Harvest Moon*) and heavy riff-rocker "Don't Take Your Love Away from Me," recorded live in 1983 with the Shocking Pinks. Another find never available before is the 1988 live recording "Ain't It the Truth," with its horn-driven R&B feel. Also essential is the tough, original full-length version of "This Note's for You," recorded live in 1988 at the Palace in Hollywood. — *Roch Parisien*

○ **Unplugged** / Jun. 15, 1993 / Reprise
Like Paul McCartney's *Unplugged*, Neil Young's *Unplugged* seems to be an attempt to thwart bootleggers by releasing the material before they get their chance. Unlike McCartney's album, which was special because it showed that he could still perform with vigor when the occasion called for it, Young's album doesn't offer any revelations—it is just a solid, thoroughly enjoyable concert. Acoustic performances of "Mr. Soul," "World on a String," "Like a Hurricane," and especially the synthesized "Transformer Man" are essential for the serious Young collector. Fans of *Harvest*, *After the Gold Rush*, *Comes a Time*, and *Harvest Moon* will find that this, not *Live Rust* or *Weld*, is the live Neil Young they need in their collection; hardcore fans will realize this is the acoustic equivalent of the stunning *Weld*. — *Stephen Thomas Erlewine*

Paul Young

b. Jan. 17, 1956
Vocals / Pop/rock, soul
A soulful UK interpretive singer who gained fame in his native country in 1983 with a cover of Marvin Gaye's "Wherever I Lay My Hat (That's My Home)" and in the United States with Daryl Hall's "Everytime You Go Away" in 1985. Young found less success writing his own songs, then returned to the U.S. Top 10 with a cover of the Chi-Lites's "Oh Girl" in 1990. In 1992 he left Columbia and moved to MCA. — *William Ruhlmann*

● **From Time to Time: The Singles Collection** / 1991 / Columbia 48829

All Young's UK and U.S. hits, among them "Everytime You Go Away," "Come Back and Stay," "I'm Gonna Tear Your Playhouse Down," "Love of the Common People," "Wherever I Lay My Hat (That's My Home)," and "Oh Girl." —*William Ruhlmann*

The Youngbloods

Group / Folk rock
The Youngbloods, formed in 1965, were led by singer-songwriter Jesse Colin Young (born Perry Miller, November 11, 1944). They incorporated bluegrass, folk, country, rock, and bits of psychedelia into their music. Their biggest hit was an up-with-people-style folk-rock anthem called "Get Together," which charted twice (at #62 in 1967, #5 in 1969). Other hits included the jug band-influenced "Grizzly Bear," the dramatic rocker "Darkness, Darkness," and the gentle, acoustic "Sunlight." —*Rick Clark*

Earth Music / 1967 / Edsel 274
In a mood similar to their first, this followup presents an eclectic blend of pop-folk-jazz-blues. —*Jeff Tamarkin*

Youngbloods / 1967 / Edsel 271
The debut from this folk-rocking, blues-loving quartet is a smile-inducing pleasure in a Lovin' Spoonful vein. —*Jeff Tamarkin*

○ **Elephant Mountain** / 1969 / Mobile Fidelity 792
The majestic beauty of the Northern California landscape and the idyllic lifestyle it inspires have never been as perfectly portrayed as on this free-flowing, easygoing 1969 album. —*Jeff Tamarkin*

● **Best of the Youngbloods** / 1970 / RCA 3280
It's a bit short at 10 songs, but this collection offers a nice overview of this '60s band's growth from good-time ragtimers to laidback jammers. —*Jeff Tamarkin*

Frank Zappa (Francis Vincent Zappa)

b. Dec. 21, 1940, Baltimore, MD, **d.** Dec. 4, 1993
Vocals, guitar, keyboards / Experimental, fusion, hard rock, progressive rock
Frank Zappa is one of the most accomplished composers of the rock era; his music combines an understanding of and appreciation for such contemporary classical figures as Stravinsky, Stockhausen, and Varese with an affection for late '50s doo-wop rock & roll and a facility for the guitar-heavy rock that dominated pop in the '70s. But Zappa is also a satirist whose reserves of scorn seem bottomless and whose wicked sense of humor and absurdity have delighted his numerous fans, even when his lyrics crossed over the broadest bounds of taste. Finally, Zappa is perhaps the most prolific record-maker of his time, turning out massive amounts of music on his own Barking Pumpkin label and through distribution deals with Rykodisc and Rhino after a long, unhappy association with industry giants like Warner Brothers and the now-defunct MGM.

Zappa became interested in music early and pursued his studies in school, up through a six-month stint at Chaffey College in Alta Loma, CA. He scored a couple of low-budget films and used the money to buy a low-budget recording studio. In 1964 he joined a local band called the Soul Giants, which, over the course of the next two years, evolved into the Mothers, who played songs written by Zappa. The band was signed to the Verve division of MGM by producer Tom Wilson in 1966 and recorded its first album, a two-LP set called *Freak Out!* which introduced Zappa's interests in both serious music and pop as well as his scathing wit. (Verve insisted on adding "of Invention" to the band's name.)

Subsequent albums extended the musical and lyrical themes of the debut, and they came frequently. Three albums, for example, hit the charts in 1968: *We're Only in It for the Money*, a Mothers album that made fun of hippies and *Sgt. Pepper*; *Lumpy Gravy*, a Zappa solo album recorded with an orchestra; and *Cruising with Ruben & the Jets*, on which the Mothers played neo-doo-wop. Toward the end of the '60s, Zappa expanded the Mothers lineup, turning more toward instrumental jazz/rock, much of which displayed his technically accomplished guitar playing. But by the end of the decade, he had broken up the band.

In 1971, however, Zappa reassembled a new edition of the Mothers, featuring former Turtles lead singers Mark Volman and Howard Kaylan as frontmen. The lineup moved the group more in the direction of X-rated comedy, notably on the album *Fillmore East June 1971*, but it was short-lived: during a performance at the Royal Albert Hall, Zappa was pushed from the stage by a demented fan and was seriously injured.

While he recovered, Zappa released several albums, then he reformed the Mothers with himself as lead singer and made pop-rock albums, such as *Over-nite Sensation*, which were among his best-selling records ever. By the end of the '70s, Zappa was recording on his own labels, distributed in some cases by the majors, and he had attracted a consistent cult following for both his humor and his complex music. (Zappa's band, in fact, became a training ground for high-quality rock musicians, much as Miles Davis's was for jazz players.)

In the '80s Zappa gained the rights to his old albums and began to reissue them, at first on his own and then through the pioneering Rykodisc CD label. He published his autobiography and embarked on a world tour in 1988. That was the end of his live performing, except for such isolated appearances as one in Czechoslovakia at the invitation of its post-Communist president, Zappa fan Vaclav Havel.

In late 1991, it was confirmed that Zappa was seriously ill with cancer of the colon. Nevertheless, his schedule of album releases continued to be rapid.

Sadly, Zappa succumbed to the illness in December of 1993. He left behind a remarkably diverse body of work that never once conformed to traditional musical conventions. That spirit lives on in a countless number of contemporary musicians, no matter if they're rockers or if they're classically trained. —*William Ruhlmann*

○ **Freak Out** / 1966 / Rykodisc 40062
Once an LP, now an hour-long CD, but still featuring the Mothers' opening salvo to the world, playing what is often melodic '60s pop-rock with doo-wop influences. But the lyrics in songs like "Who Are the Brain Police?" and "Trouble Every Day" mark composer Frank Zappa as having a social conscience and a wickedly satiric sense of humor. —*William Ruhlmann*

○ **Absolutely Free** / 1967 / Rykodisc 10093
The satire gets even sharper on such songs as "Plastic People" and "Status Back Baby," while the references are often only local to the band's Los Angeles environs (and, increasingly, part of a private, absurdist language), and the music gets increasingly complicated. —*William Ruhlmann*

★ **We're Only in It for the Money** / 1967 / Verve 5045
A simultaneous condemnation of the straights and the hippies, its songs segue as on *Sgt. Pepper* and, with verbal asides included, a sound collage that was the original Mothers' highest-charting album. (Note: Recommendation is for the original LP release, not the CD reissue—which, available on one disc with *Lumpy Gravy*, has rerecorded rhythm tracks.) —*William Ruhlmann*

○ **Hot Rats** / 1969 / Rykodisc 10066
Zappa disbanded the original Mothers group in 1969 and cut this solo album, most of which consists of well-organized jazz-rock instrumentals such as "Peaches En Regalia," one of his most appealing compositions. Captain Beefheart provides a guest vocal on "Willie the Pimp," which also features violin by Jean-Luc Ponty. —*William Ruhlmann*

○ **Uncle Meat** / 1969 / Rykodisc 10064
A sprawling, largely instrumental soundtrack to a movie that was never finished, including everything from the pop tune "The Air" to the extended "King Kong," complete with variations. —*William Ruhlmann*

○ **Weasels Ripped My Flesh** / 1970 / Rykodisc 10163
An album of live material recorded from 1967 to 1969 and featuring an expanded lineup with horn section. Highlights include Sugar Cane Harris's violin work on Little Richard's "Directly from My Heart to You" and Zappa's vocal on "My Guitar Wants to Kill Your Mama." —*William Ruhlmann*

★ **Apostrophe/Over-Nite Sensation** / 1973 / Rykodisc 40025
Over-Nite Sensation was Zappa's first new studio album of vocal music in three years, and it finds him with another edition of Mothers (from this point, Mothers group albums and Zappa solo albums become indistinguishable). This time Zappa took the lead vocals himself and wrote a new set of catchy, satiric rock-pop songs like "Camarillo Brillo" and "Montana." *Apostrophe* is Zappa's only gold-selling Top 10 album, featuring the satiric "Don't Eat the Yellow Snow," along with other parodic songs in the same style as *Over-Nite Sensation*. Rykodisc has combined the two 1973 albums onto one CD. —*William Ruhlmann*

Bongo Fury / 1975 / Rykodisc 10097

A live album recorded with Captain Beefheart on lead vocals, it combines Zappa's provocative songs with Beefheart's peculiar perspective. Contains the should-have-been-a-hit "Carolina Hard-Core Ecstasy." —*William Ruhlmann*

○ **Shut Up 'n Play Yer Guitar** / 1981 / Rykodisc 10028-29
A compilation of crazed solo Zappa with the spotlight on his guitar work. —*Cub Koda*

Tinsel Town Rebellion / 1981 / Rykodisc 40166
From the mid '70s on, Frank Zappa's music divided ever more extremely into complex instrumental passages and broadly satiric songs, which stopped sounding clever and started seeming smutty and sophomoric. There are elements of these excesses on this live double album, but for the most part the appeal of the music and the fine performances overcome objections. There are also remakes of such old favorites as "Brown Shoes Don't Make It." —*William Ruhlmann*

Ship Arriving Too Late to Save a Drowning Witch / 1982 / Barking Pumpkin 74235
Ship Arriving Too Late to Save a Drowning Witch features the novelty hit "Valley Girl," with vocals by Zappa's daughter, Moon. (Steve Vai is featured on the appropriately credited "impossible guitar.") —*William Ruhlmann*

○ **Broadway the Hardway** / 1988 / Rykodisc 40096
A live album culled from Zappa's final world tour of 1988. It features his comments on Elvis Presley ("Elvis Has Just Left the Building"), televangelists ("Jesus Thinks You're a Jerk"), and other objects of political scorn. —*William Ruhlmann*

● **You Can't Do That on Stage Anymore, Vol. 1** / 1988 / Rykodisc 10081-82
In the late '80s, Frank Zappa, already the most prolific artist in rock history, began releasing large amounts of archival material. The *You Can't Do That on Stage Anymore* series was to consist of six two-CD sets (the final two of which were scheduled for release in 1992), on which Zappa mixed and matched live recordings from throughout his career, editing different versions of songs together (sometimes by different bands). For an artist as inconsistent as Zappa, the results were bound to be uneven, but for those willing to wade through the hours of recordings, there are hidden gems. The first release is typical of the series. —*William Ruhlmann*

Fillmore East: June 1971 / 1990 / Rykodisc 10167
A new Mothers lineup led by ex-Turtles singers Mark Volman and Howard Kaylan makes for a virtual comedy act based on the theme of life on the road. Very funny, and some of the playing is amazing too. —*William Ruhlmann*

Beat the Boots! Box / 1991 / Rhino 70372
Frank Zappa frequently has been the victim of bootleggers, and with this release he turns the tables on his tormentors. This boxed eight-cassette set (also available as separate CDs) presents a series of bootlegs as they appeared, without any improvement. Nevertheless, the sound is often surprisingly good, and especially the recordings by the original Mothers (for instance, *The Ark*, RHI 70538) will be of interest to Zappaphiles. (A second version of *Beat the Boots!* available only as a boxed set, appeared in 1992.) —*William Ruhlmann*

Warren Zevon

b. Jan. 24, 1947, Chicago, IL
Vocals, piano, guitar / Singer-songwriter, rock & roll
How did a guy with such a wickedly black sense of humor and a love for tough rock & roll get to be a '70s Los Angeles songwriting pro? By tempering that dark streak with some evocative and personal ballads, which surveyed the trappings of the Los Angeles lifestyle. Even at his worst, Zevon was always better than the Eagles, and with less sexism to boot. —*John Floyd*

○ **Warren Zevon** / 1976 / Asylum 1060
A beautiful and ambitious debut that paints a gloomy and cryptic portrait of Hollywood's casualties through gripping songs like "Carmelita," "I'll Sleep When I'm Dead," and "Mohammed's Radio." —*John Floyd*

○ **Excitable Boy** / 1978 / Asylum 118
A disappointing followup in that Zevon's sensitivity is sacrificed for mere weirdness. Nevertheless, there's some fine music here. —*John Floyd*

Stand in the Fire / 1981 / Asylum 519

This live set rocks harder than his studio discs and also works as a career overview. —*John Floyd*

● **A Quiet Normal Life: The Best of Warren Zevon** / 1986 / Asylum 60503
An adequate but skimpy best-of. —*John Floyd*

Transverse City / 1989 / Virgin 91068
Zevon's attempt to integrate the influence of Stravinsky makes this album is a complex, dense, but still absorbing blast of jagged rock. —*John Floyd*

Mr. Bad Example / 1991 / Giant 24431
First release in some time from Zevon, featuring guitarist Waddy Wachtel and an all-star cast of studio assistance from Bob Glaub, Jeff Porcaro, Jim Keltner, Jorge Calderon, and David Lindley. Dwight Yoakam guests on "Heartache Spoken Here." Other tunes include "Model Citizen," "Renegade," "Quite Ugly One Morning," and "Things to Do in Denver When You're Dead." —Roundup Newsletter

Learning to Flinch / 1993 / Warner Brothers 24493
Warren Zevon recorded the acoustic *Learning to Flinch* at various venues all over the world. All of his best-known songs are here, in riveting rough acoustic forms. Longtime Zevon fans will find this essential, and it may win him a few new ones too. —AMG

Zombies

Group / British invasion, pop/rock
A British invasion band with a soulful but sophisticated sound, whose hard-luck history ended with their biggest hit topping the U.S. charts and racking up two million sales after they'd split up. Member Rod Argent later formed the early '70s band Argent. —*Bruce Eder*

○ **Odessey & Oracle** / 1968 / Rhino 70186
A psychedelic effort whose best song, "Time of the Season," became a monster hit with a sultry, soulful sound not replicated elsewhere on the album. —*Bruce Eder*

● **Greatest Hits** / Dcc 52
The early sides. All well-chosen Brit-beat with a strong R&B influence. —*Bruce Eder*

ZZ Top

Group / Blues rock, rock & roll
An American blues-rock trio from Texas consisting of Billy Gibbons (guitar), Dusty Hill (bass), and Frank Beard (drums), ZZ Top formed in 1970 in and around Houston from rival bands—the Moving Sidewalks (Gibbons) and the American Blues (Hill and Beard). Their first two albums reflected the strong blues roots and Texas humor of the band. The third album (*Tres Hombres*) gained them national attention with hit "La Grange," a signature riff tune to this day. Their success continued unabated throughout the '70s, culminating with the year-and-a-half-long Worldwide Texas Tour. Exhausted from the overwhelming workload, they took a three-year break, then switched labels and returned to form with *Deguello* and *El Loco*, both harbingers of what was to come. By their next album, *Eliminator*, and its worldwide smash followup, *Afterburner*, they had successfully harnessed the potential of synthesizers to their patented grunge-groove, giving their material a more contemporary edge while retaining their patented Texas style. Now sporting long beards, golf hats, and boiler suits, they met the emerging video age head on, reducing their "message" to simple iconography. Becoming even more popular in the long run, they moved with the times while simultaneously bucking every trend that crossed their path. As genuine roots musicians, they have few peers; Gibbons is one of America's finest blues guitarists working in the arena of rock idiom, while Hill and Beard provide the ultimate rhythm section support. The only rock & roll group that's out there with its original members still aboard after 20-plus years, ZZ Top's music is always instantly recognizable, eminently powerful, profoundly soulful, and 100% American in derivation. —*Cub Koda*

ZZ Top's First Album / 1970 / Warner Brothers 3268
This Texas trio's debut was a gritty exercise in bare-boned blues boogie. Tracks like "Brown Sugar," "Neighbor Neighbor," and "Shakin' Your Tree" helped establish them as a regionally successful act in the south. —*Rick Clark*

Rio Grande Mud / 1972 / Warner Brothers 3269

Rio Grande Mud possessed a beefier sound than its predecessor. The "Brown Sugar"-style "Francene" became their first hit at #69. Other highlights included "Chevrolet" and "Just Got Paid." *—Rick Clark*

○ **Tres Hombres** / 1973 / Warner Brothers 3270
Constant touring and favorable radio exposure made *Tres Hombres* ZZ's first hit album, thanks in no small part to "La Grange," an ode to a whorehouse. By this album, Billy Gibbons had practically perfected his distinctively dirty electric guitar sound. His riffs and chordal voicings were also more memorable. Highlights included "Beer Drinkers & Hell Raisers," "Precious & Grace," and the twosome "Waitin' for the Bus," and "Jesus Just Left Chicago." *—Rick Clark*

Fandango / 1975 / Warner Brothers 3271
Fandango is a half-studio/half-live effort. The concert side is a fairly straightahead, no-nonsense affair that includes a version of "Jailhouse Rock." The studio side featured their first Top 40 hit, "Tush." The hyper-boogie of "Heard It on the X" was another popular track off this release. *—Rick Clark*

★ **Best of ZZ Top** / 1977 / Warner Brothers 3273
The sound may be a little muddy, but this anthology is still the best representation of ZZ's early work. Contains classic rude, riff-heavy blues rockers like "Just Got Paid," "Jesus Just Left Chicago," "Heard It on the X," "Tush," and "La Grange." *—Rick Clark*

○ **Deguello** / 1979 / Warner Brothers 3361
Deguello was ZZ's best album from their pre-robotic blues-rock period—the last reminder of what a tough ensemble this trio could be. It was the first time they infused their lunkhead approach to fast cars, kinky girls, and partying with some bizarre humor. Their version of Sam & Dave's "I Thank You" became their first Top 40 hit in five years. Other highlights included the oddball "Manic Mechanic," a rip-roaring version of Elmore James's "Dust My Broom," the funky boogie of "Cheap Sunglasses," and "Fool for Your Stockings," a down-and-dirty fetish blues. *—Rick Clark*

El Loco / 1981 / Warner Brothers 3593
Not as strong as *Deguello*, *El Loco* vacillates between half-baked ballads ("Leila") and novelty rockers ("Party on the Patio," "Groovy Little Hippie Pad," "Heaven, Hell or Houston"). "Pearl Necklace," with its not-too-subtle sexual double entendre and Police-inspired groove, was a big AOR hit. *—Rick Clark*

● **Eliminator** / 1983 / Warner Brothers 23774
Hardcore fans might have cried "sellout," but ZZ's introduction of a streamlined synth-heavy sound (and three slickly produced T&A videos) turned this trio from potential blues-rock has-beens to multiplatinum purveyors of space boogie. Most of this album became a staple on album rock radio, with "Gimmie All Your Lovin'," "Sharp Dressed Man," and "Legs" becoming the primary hits. *—Rick Clark*

Afterburner / 1985 / Warner Brothers 25342
Basically a carbon copy of *Eliminator*, *Afterburner* continued ZZ's winning streak, which includes four hit singles: "Sleeping Bag," "Stages," "Rough Boy," and "Velcro Fly." *—Rick Clark*

Six Pack / 1987 / Warner Brothers 25661
The idea of compiling albums one through five, plus their seventh effort, onto a three-CD set seemed like a good one. After all, there's a load of great playing on these discs. Unfortunately, the first five albums were hastily remixed from the original multitracks. The sound might have more definition and punch, but the effort to update the drum sounds with triggered samples, reamped guitars, and cold digital reverbs gave some of the music a stiff, clinical quality. Seeing a band that touts the power of an organic game like the blues so insensitively plunder the recordings they made when they really were a real live band makes one wonder if the sequencers had finally gone to their brains. That ZZ's management and Warner allowed such a half-baked job on the market seems to support that assertion. *—Rick Clark*

Recycler / 1990 / Warner Brothers 26265
ZZ seemed to be running low on good material as they cranked up the Fairlights for a third go-round. "My Head's in Mississippi," however, is a fine rocker that synthesized the gritty virtues of their earlier sound with the hi-tech gloss of their later work. *Recycler* also includes "Doubleback," their hit from the movie *Back to the Future, Part III. —Rick Clark*

Greatest Hits / 1992 / Warner Brothers 26846

An 18-song compilation that features the greatest hits of ZZ Top's MTV era, including "Gimme All Your Lovin'," "Sharp Dressed Man," "Tush," "Pearl Necklace," "Cheap Sunglasses," "Sleeping Bag," "Rough Boy," and a remixed version of "Legs." It's a good, fun collection that should have been sequenced better and, unfortunately, omits a few good songs. —AMG

Antenna / 1994 / RCA
Like precious few bands from the '70s whose best work is mummified daily thanks to classic rock radio, ZZ Top just keeps rolling on into the next decade. There's much to love here, from the downright nasty stomp of "Fuzzbox Voodoo," the powerhouse slow blues of "Cover Your Rig," the bass pumping looniness of "Girl in a T-Shirt," to the slow grind of "Breakaway." While Billy Gibbons's guitar tones on this album are highly reminiscent of *Tres Hombres* (an early high-water mark for the band), the high production sheen from their '80s albums remains intact. But Gibbons hasn't played with this much over-the-top abandon since their pre-beard'n'babes days, and that's what separates this album from the three that came before it. *—Cub Koda*

Rock, Pop & Soul Collections

○ **Ace Story, Vol. 1** / ACE 2031
With five separate volumes, *The Ace Story* is the most comprehensive portrait of the seminal New Orleans R&B record label. Over the course of the series, each of the label's hits are featured—including "Sea Cruise," "Rockin' Pneumonia," and "Pop Eye," among others—as well as many lesser-known gems. During the late '50s and early '60s, Ace's roster featured such R&B giants as Huey "Piano" Smith, Eddie Bo, Jo Tex, Lightnin' Hopkins, Charles Brown, Amos Milburn, and Earl King. Each artist is featured on at least one disc of *The Ace Story*, along with several acts that didn't have hits but recorded some outstanding tracks. Start with the first volume, then proceed to the other discs. Every one is filled with timeless R&B. *—Stephen Thomas Erlewine*

● **Ace Records, Best of, Vol. 2: R&B Hits** / 1993 / SCB
Scotti Brothers' two volumes of highlights from the Ace Records roster are the best available sampler of the label's late '50s to early '60s R&B and pop hits, featuring such stars as Huey "Piano" Smith, Frankie Ford, Joe Tex, and Jimmy Clanton. Both volumes have detailed liner notes and great songs. And both are essential for comprehensive rock and R&B collections. *—Stephen Thomas Erlewine*

Acid Jazz: Collection 1 / Scotti Brothers 5218
Scotti Brothers has issued three separate volumes of acid jazz, a popular dance genre of the late '80s and early '90s that combines elements of jazz, hip-hop, funk, and R&B. Like most dance music, it is primarily a singles medium, so compilations serve the music well. None of the featured songs was a pop hit, yet almost every track has something to recommend it, whether it's the beat, vocals, or instrumentals. While some major names of the genre are missing from the three discs, any volume of *Acid Jazz: Collection* is a good place to get introduced to the music. *—Stephen Thomas Erlewine*

○ **All Star Funk** / Priority 8658
Good collection of '70s funk hits, including definitive cuts by Parliament, Funkadelic, and Bootsy Collins. *—John Floyd*

○ **At Death's Door: Brutal Death Metal** / Oct. 30, 1990 / Roadrunner 9362
A diverse selection of death-metal bands on the Roadrunner label. *—John Book*

★ **Atlantic R&B: 1947-1974, Vols. 1-7** / 1991 / Atlantic 82305
Along with Specialty, Aladdin, Chess, Sun, and a few other labels, Atlantic paved the way for rock & roll. Started by Ahmet Ertegun and Herb Abramson in 1947, Atlantic brought meticulous recording techniques—usually reserved only for jazz sessions—to R&B. They assembled a revolving cast of crack studio musicians. This seven-disc set (eight CDs in the boxed set) is a perfect collection of all the best singles from Atlantic Records. *—John Floyd*

○ **Atlantic Sisters of Soul** / 1992 / Rhino 71037
A fine collection of lesser-known female soul artists on Atlantic, including such artists that aren't normally associated with the la-

bel like Mary Wells and the Pointer Sisters. All of the songs were recorded in the late '60s and early '70s and only three of the disc's 23 tracks scratched the R&B Top 20, although most of the tracks were good enough to be hits. While the songs may not be familiar, their sweet sound is, making the disc a worthwhile purchase for fans of early '70s soul. —*Stephen Thomas Erlewine*

○ **Atlantic Soul Classics** / Warner Brothers 27601
This was the first CD collection of Atlantic's greatest '60s soul burners. You can now find most of these on better collections, but this still isn't a bad place to start your education. —*John Floyd*

○ **Back Seat Jams** / 1987 / Dunhill 31
A good oldies collection remastered by Steve Hoffman, featuring such hits as Ritchie Valens's "Donna," the Shirelles' "Dedicated to the One I Love," the Skyliners' "Since I Don't Have You," and the Capris' "There's a Moon Out Tonight." —*Dan Heilman*

Battle of the D.J.'s / Jive 1112
A good hip-hop anthology covering material from Eric B. & Rakim, DJ Jazzy Jeff & the Fresh Prince, Run-D.M.C., Steady B, Cash Money & Marvelous Marv, Whodini, Grandmaster Flash, Kurtis Blow, Schoolly D, and Too Short. —*Ron Wynn*

☆ **Beach Classics: All Original Recordings** / 1987 / Dcc 30
A terrific 20-song collection of surf hits from the early '60s, including the classics "Miserlou," "California Sun," and "Surfin' Bird," as well as many forgotten gems. Not only is the song selection first rate, but the sound is as good as it could be, considering the original master tapes probably were not well preserved. —*Stephen Thomas Erlewine*

○ **Beachbeat Shaggin'** / Dcc 33
A good overview of the light '60s soul nuggets known on the Atlantic coast as beach music, including "Maurice Williams & the Zodiacs" "Stay," Freda Payne's "Band of Gold," and "Give Me Just a Little More Time" by the Chairmen of the Board. —*John Floyd*

○ **Beat Generation** / 1992 / Rhino 70281
This three-CD boxed set is an ambitious musical and spoken portrayal of the late '50s and early to mid '60s Beat Generation, as well as later practitioners of that aesthetic. Among those represented are Jack Kerouac, Langston Hughes, Ken Nordine, William S. Burroughs, Dizzy Gillespie, John Drew Barrymore, Lenny Bruce, Allen Ginsberg, Tom Waits, and Lambert, Hendricks & Ross. —*Rick Clark*

Beavis & Butt-Head Experience / 1993 /
Based on the popular and controversial MTV show, *The Beavis & Butt-Head Experience* is a collection of hard-rock bands that . . . well . . . that don't suck. Although the humor sketches wear thin after only one play, the music doesn't. Some of the songs—especially Jackyl's—are sub-par, but Nirvana, Primus, White Zombie, and Beavis & Butt-Head's "Come to Butt-Head" make the disc worthwhile. —*Stephen Thomas Erlewine*

☆ **Best of Chess R&B, Vol. 1** / MCA 31317
This Chess R&B anthology came out initially in a pair of double album sets. Then it was reissued on two CDs, though they left some tracks off each volume due to programming restrictions. This CD covers the first double album and includes cuts from the Moonglows, some early Miracles, Etta James, Sugar Pie Desanto, Jan Bradley, Billy Stewart, and Little Milton. —*Ron Wynn*

☆ **Best of Chess R&B, Vol. 2** / MCA 31318
The second Chess CD covers the second double album and features later R&B cuts from Billy Stewart, Mitty Collier, the Dells, Jackie Ross, Etta James, the Ramsey Lewis Trio, and the Radiants. The stylistic lines are blurred a bit here, since some of these artists were also featured on the Best of Chess soul anthology that had been previously issued. —*Ron Wynn*

☆ **Best of Chess Rock & Roll** / Chess 6024
Over two separate volumes, *Best of Chess Rock & Roll* gives a good portrait of the seminal record label's massive contributions to rock & roll. Not only are landmarks like Chuck Berry's "Johnny B. Goode" and Bo Diddley's "Bo Diddley" covered, cult favorites like the Moonglows and the Students are also featured. With "Johnny B. Goode," "Maybellene," "Who Do You Love," "Ain't Got No Home," "Rocket 88," and "Susie Q" all on the first volume, it is one of the most essential single-disc rock collections ever assembled. The second volume is nearly as important, with "Book of Love," "High Heel Sneakers," "No Particular Place to Go," "Ten

Commandments of Love," and "Road Runner" among the featured tracks. —*Stephen Thomas Erlewine*

○ **Best of Chess Vocal Groups** / Chess 6029
Rounding out the trilogy of Chess sampler albums, this series features "Long Lonely Nights" by Lee Andrews & the Hearts, the Marathons' "Peanut Butter," "See Saw" by the Moonglows, the highly influential "Every Day of the Week" by the Students, and the Southern soul of the Knight Brothers' "Temptation 'bout to Get Me." The first disc is the place to start, with the second giving with a nod toward rare material. —*Cub Koda*

☆ **Best of Doo Wop Ballads** / 1989 / Rhino 75763
☆ **Best of Doo Wop Uptempo** / 1989 / Rhino 75764
Rhino's *Best of Doo Wop* compilations are a glorious pair of discs that salute the finest doo-wop hits. Most collectors already have this stuff, but novices would do well to start right here. —*John Floyd*

☆ **Best of Excello Records, Vol. 1** / 1991 / Rhino 270896
The Nashville-based Excello label specialized in obscure blues, R&B, and rock & roll from the '50s and early '60s. This first volume of *Sound of the Swamp: The Best of Excello Records* covers the best from Crowley, Louisiana-producer Jay Miller's blues, rockabilly, and swamp-pop sides. —*John Floyd*

☆ **Best of Excello Records, Vol. 2** / 1991 / Rhino 270897
The second volume of *The Best of Excello Records* isn't as consistent as the first, but there is nevertheless some fine material here. —*AMG*

○ **Best of Metal Blade, Vol. 1** / 1988 / Metal Blade 72117
The first best-of package from Metal Blade. Contains very early tracks from Bitch, Celtic Frost, Fates Warning, Hallow's Eve, Hirax, Lizzy Borden, Metal Church, Slayer, Trouble, and Voivod. —*John Book*

○ **Best of Mountain Stage** / Blue Plate 1
An ongoing series of discs culled from one of the finest radio programs in America, each disc of *The Best of Mountain Stage* features terrific, rare performances from artists like Richard Thompson, R.E.M., and Dr. John. Each volume is worthwhile. —*AMG*

☆ **Best of Nuggets** / Rhino 75892
Punk and garage-rock from the '60s, raw and essential. Probably the best compilation ever done on the genre, featuring classics by the Seeds, Syndicate of Sound, Count Five, Chocolate Watchband, and others. Part of a continuing series. —*Cub Koda*

○ **Best of Sue Records** / Collectables 5123
Find out why Sue Records was one of New Orleans's greatest and most revered R&B/soul labels and the early home to such artists as Aaron Neville and Ike & Tina Turner. —*John Floyd*

○ **Best of Techno, Vol. 1** / 1991 / Profile 1420
Techno is a rapidly expanding and changing genre, so no collection can possibly capture the full diversity of the music. Still, Priority's three discs of *Best of Techno* does a fair job of conveying part of the music's excitement and stylistic variety. It's strictly for novices, and any volume serves as an adequate introduction to techno. —*Stephen Thomas Erlewine*

○ **Big Itch** / Mr. Mannicotti 328
Insane compilation of extremely raw, crude, and obscure rock & roll tracks. Side 1 is all "Pa Pa Ooh Mow Mow" and "Surfin' Bird"-related tunes, while side 2 charts the territory of the awesomely arcane, featuring the title track and offerings by King Uszniewicz and Trez Trezo. Not for the faint of heart. —*Cub Koda*

Big Itch, Volume 2 / Mr. Mannicotti 340
More nutzo offerings on this memorial album for Joe E. Ross, which features Ross (of "Car 54 Where Are You?" fame) doing "Ooh-Ooh," Archie Pier's "Tamales & Rock 'n' Roll," and the best/worst version of "Heartbreak Hotel" you'll ever hear. —*Cub Koda*

Big Itch, Volume 3 / Mr. Mannicotti 341
The third offering in an ongoing series, this time featuring the cast of "McHale's Navy" doing "Pa Pa Ooh Mow Mow," Terry Tene's "Curse of the Hearse," Jerry Coulston's "Cave Man Hop," and T. Valentine's "Hello Lucille, Are You a Lesbian?" as some of the crazed highlights. As insane as the first two volumes and then some. —*Cub Koda*

○ **Billboard Top Dance Hits** / 1992 / Rhino 70490

Covering the disco years in detail, Rhino's five-volume *Billboard Top Dance Hits* series is a worthwhile budget retrospective. It is not as complete or definitive as the label's *Disco Years* series, yet it features several tracks that did not make that series, as well as songs that aren't easily available on other compilations, making it necessary for disco fans. Ten of the top dance hits for each year from 1976 to 1980 are featured on each disc, including such hits as "You Should Be Dancing," "Love Hangover," "Ring My Bell," "You Make Me Feel (Mighty Real)," "Funkytown," "Got to Give It Up," and "Call Me" in their original single form. Unlike the other *Billboard* series, *Top Dance Hits* actually has liner notes about the songs, not trivia about a particular year. —*Stephen Thomas Erlewine*

☆ **Billboard Top Hits** / 1991 / Rhino 70670
Rhino ended its *Billboard Top Rock & Roll Hits* series with the 1974 volume, replacing it with the *Billboard Top Hits* series beginning with the year 1975. It has the same faults and attributes as the *Rock & Roll* series. The only difference is the fact that it merges R&B hits with the pop singles. Since the late '70s were filled with cheerfully disposable pop singles, each volume differs greatly in quality. The 1978 and 1979 discs are the most consistent, with several soft rock and disco hits on each album. Rhino's *Have a Nice Day* and *Disco Years* series cover this era in greater detail, with more hits and novelty items on both series; however, these are concise, fun snapshots of a particularly embarrassing and enjoyable moment in pop history. —*Stephen Thomas Erlewine*

☆ **Billboard Top Hits** / 1992 / Rhino 70675
When Rhino's *Billboard Top Hits* series hit the '80s, the collection began to lose a little steam. For the first few years—1980 through 1985—the discs are enjoyable and representative of the pop mainstream, although there were the usual major artists missing. Still, the discs contained plenty of one-hit wonders and classic singles like "Bette Davis Eyes," "Jessie's Girl," "Down Under," "Maneater," and "Centerfold," with the highest concentration of good singles on the 1983 volume. As the series approached the end of the decade, the problem of licensing reared its ugly head. Not only were major artists like Madonna, Prince, Phil Collins, and Guns N' Roses unavailable (although U2 was available), smaller artists like Rick Astley, Roxette, Poison, and Michael Damien also don't appear. Although there are a couple of enjoyable period pieces like Donny Osmond's "Soldier of Love," the bulk of the tracks can't cover the abscence of "Never Gonna Give You Up," "Every Rose Has Its Thorn," and "The Look." Perhaps they should have waited a couple of years. Oh well. Otherwise, the '80s installments are every bit as good as the previous volumes. —*Stephen Thomas Erlewine*

☆ **Billboard Top R&B Hits** / 1989 / Rhino 70641
Despite its faults, Rhino's *Billboard Top R&B Hits* was one of the finest retrospectives of R&B from 1955 to 1974 ever assembled. Its excellence wasn't based on impeccable song selection, informative liner notes, nor a generous amount of tracks on each disc—in fact, the song selection was frequently puzzling, the liner notes nonexistent, and each disc only had ten tracks, frequently clocking in at under a half hour. However, the series featured most of the major artists and singles for each year, giving a good sense of that year, as well as a rough sketch of the evolution from R&B to soul to disco. For beginners, such an affordable introduction was invaluable; for collectors, the brevity of the discs may have been frustrating, but they couldn't argue with the fidelity or the fact that many of these songs were appearing on disc for the first time. Over 20 discs, the series featured legends like Johnny Ace, Clyde McPhatter, Little Richard, Jackie Wilson, James Brown, Ben E. King, Lee Dorsey, Brook Benton, Marvin Gaye, the Temptations, the Supremes, Aretha Franklin, Smokey Robinson, the Isley Brothers, Sly Stone, and Curtis Mayfield. The 1955, 1956, 1963, 1964, 1965, and 1972 installments are arguably the most consistent discs, but any volume is worthwhile. Unfortunately, the R&B series didn't sell as well as its rock & roll counterpart and is currently out of print. Fortunately, they can still be found in cut-out bins. —*Stephen Thomas Erlewine*

☆ **Billboard Top Rock & Roll Hits** / 1988 / Rhino 70598
Despite its many faults, Rhino's *Billboard Top Rock & Roll Hits* is as good an introduction to this consistently diverse music as possible. Like the *Top R&B Hits* series, it's marred by a confusing song selection, poor liner notes, and brevity, as well as the omis-

sion of several important artists like the Beatles, the Rolling Stones, the Kinks, the Who, and most album rock acts like Cream, Jefferson Airplane, and Jimi Hendrix. However, the series is not attempting to be that comprehensive. Instead, it offers a view of the popular mainstream for each year from 1955 to 1974 at an affordable price—the great sonics are an additional bonus. With Elvis, Chuck Berry, Fats Domino, Jerry Lee Lewis, the Everly Brothers, Buddy Holly, and Carl Perkins on the initial '50s volumes, the discs are essential. As the series moves into the '60s, the discs remain remarkably consistent, featuring several Phil Spector hits, the Beach Boys, Dion, and the Kingsmen. It is only in the mid-'60s that the series begins to represent only radio hits, instead of portraying what was really happening during the era. Nevertheless, the discs remain enjoyable listening right up until the 1974 volume, as well as sketching a fairly representive picture of the popular mainstream for each year. Sure, the early '70s installments can't compete with the late '60s editions in terms of creativity, innovation, or artistic quality, yet they evoke their time just as well as the earlier discs. Out of the series' exhaustive 20 discs, the 1955, 1957, 1958, 1959, 1963, 1965, and 1966 installments are the most consistent, yet each disc is enjoyable and gives a taste of popular music history. —*Stephen Thomas Erlewine*

○ **Black Rock Coalition: History of Our Future** / 1990 / Rykodisc 10211
Black Rock Coalition: History of Our Future is a fantastic collection of Black rock & roll from the organization formed by Living Colour's Vernon Reid. Diversity is the game here, with cuts by Blackasaurus Mex, Michael Hill's Bluesland, and Shock Council, mixing up funk, metal, and hip-hop as though they'd never heard of segregated radio playlists. —*John Floyd*

Black on White: R&B Covers of Rock / May 18, 1993 / Rhino 71227
Black on White collects a bunch of R&B covers of pop hits, including Run DMC's "Walk This Way," Wilson Pickett's "Hey Jude," and Aretha Franklin's "Satisfaction." Although it sounds like a cheap gimmick, the results are surprisingly good and thoroughly listenable, with no embarrassing tracks. In fact, the best material is positively transcendent. —*Stephen Thomas Erlewine*

○ **Blues Dimension** / 1969 / Decca 254
A very good collection of in-concert recordings from Stevie Ray Vaughan, Sugar Blue, and more. —*Niles J. Frantz*

● **Blues Masters, Vol. 14: More Jump Blues** / 1993 / Rhino 71133
The second volume saluting the booming vocals-booting tenor sax sound of the late '40s to early '50s yields several gems from Louis Prima, Joe Liggins & His Honeydrippers, Ruth Brown, Big Maybelle, and LaVern Baker. Every bit as potent as its companion volume, number five in the series. —*Cub Koda*

Born Bad Volume 1 / Born Bad 1
A five-disc series of supermely rare and trashy rockabilly and '60s garage punk, *Born Bad* showcases some of the wildest and most bizarre records ever recorded. A couple of artists and songs are familiar—most notably Little Willie John, Dale Hawkins, Wanda Jackson, Tommy James & the Shondells, and Charlie Feathers—but the bulk of the series is devoted to "Chop Suey Rock," "Bop Pills," and "Hot Lips Baby," which is what great rock & roll is made of. The first volume is the best starting place, but don't miss volume 4, which includes the *Mad Magazine* flexi-disc "It's a Gas." —*Stephen Thomas Erlewine*

Born to Choose / 1993 / Rykodisc 10256
A benefit album for abortion rights, *Born to Choose* features an almost standard cast of alternative musicians (including R.E.M., Natalie Merchant, Matthew Sweet, Bob Mould, and Soundgarden) supporting the most overtly political of all recent tribute collections. *Born to Choose* would be meaningless if the music was weak. Even though it is the standard mix of outtakes, B-sides, and live tracks, the music is worth the price, with R.E.M. & Natalie Merchant's "Photograph" and Sweet's "She Said, She Said" being particular highlights. —*Stephen Thomas Erlewine*

○ **Brace Yourself!: A Tribute to Otis Blackwell** / 1994 / Shanachie Records C 5702
Most tribute albums fail because the interpretations are too diverse to make the album consistent. *Brace Yourself!: A Tribute to Otis Blackwell* sidesteps that problem by having the artists record with a house band that is well-versed in the legendary rock & roll/R&B songwriter. Thankfully, the approach works—

none of the artists turns in a bad performance and the disc rocks (albeit rather gently) from start to finish. But then again, it wasn't that hard to make a good album when the artists included Dave Edmunds, Graham Parker, Chrissie Hynde, Frank Black, the Smithereens, and Kris Kristofferson. *—Stephen Thomas Erlewine*

○ **Bridge: A Tribute to Neil Young** / 1989 / Caroline 1374
In theory, *The Bridge: A Tribute to Neil Young* was a perfect concept, since most alternative bands of the late '80s owed the singer/songwriter a heavy debt. In practice, it wasn't entirely satisfying. Some groups, made their interpretations self-consciously distinctively, as in Bongwater's collage of "Mr. Soul," while others, like Soul Asylum and Loop, played it close to the original. But the best moments came when a band played the song like it was their own. Listen to Sonic Youth's rampaging "Computer Age," Dinosaur Jr's faithful "Lotta Love," or the Pixies' gorgeous take on "Winterlong" for proof. *—Stephen Thomas Erlewine*

☆ **Brief History of Ambient, Vol. 1** / Feb. 22, 1994 / Virgin Records Amer 39434
Although it seemed to arrive out of nowhere in the early '90s, ambient music actually has a long and varied history, from Brian Eno's and Kraftwerk's electronic experiments in the '70s right up to Aphex Twin's textural techno soundscapes. As an introduction and history lesson, the two-disc *Brief History of Ambient Music* can't be beat. It shows that the latest techno trend has roots that most fans wouldn't even realize existed. *—Stephen Thomas Erlewine*

☆ **British Invasion: History of British Rock, Vols. 1-9** / Jan. 21, 1992 / Rhino 72022
Imagine nine CDs (available separately or in a box) of those classic AM radio hits of the '60s, all of them from England, most of them as fresh-sounding and exciting as they were more than two decades ago. Now imagine that these nine CDs are devoid of Beatles (except for one early track), Stones, Who, early Animals, Dave Clark Five, and Herman's Hermits (all due to licensing problems)—but you won't miss them—and you'll get an idea of just how much quality pop/rock & roll came out of Britain in those several years. Included are the Kinks, Zombies, Hollies, Small Faces, Yardbirds, Manfred Mann, Them, Donovan, Peter and Gordon, Bee Gees, Cream, and much more. *—Jeff Tamarkin*

○ **Carnival Time: The Best of Ric Records, Vol. 1** / Rounder 2075
Stomping, romping good-time numbers are the menu on this 14-track anthology issued in 1988. Such artists as Joe Jones, Al Johnson, Johnny Adams, and Edgar Blanchard were hit acts in New Orleans at the time, but made music that was raw and intended for only for the R&B faithful. While an occasional number like Adams' "I Won't Cry" or Jones' "You Talk Too Much," got a little pop attention, most, like Blanchard's hot "Let's Get It" and Tommy Ridgley's "She's Got What It Takes," didn't move anyone who didn't already have the soul spirit, and that's what made them great. *—Ron Wynn*

○ **Chartbusters: The Best of Beserkley, 1975-1978** / Rhino 70096
Beserkley never scored any chart hits, but they were one of the best American independent record labels of the late '70s and early '80s, featuring such cult favorites as Jonathan Richman and Greg Kihn. *Best of the Beserkley Years* gathers up some the label's best stripped-down rock & roll, offering a good picture of their music. *—Stephen Thomas Erlewine*

Classic Rock Box: WNEW-FM 25th Anniversary Box / 1992 / PolyGram 515913
One of the more confusing boxed sets, *Classic Rock Box* collects a slew of FM album rock standards in one hulking black box. No rarities are included—it would defeat the intent of the box. Listening to this box is exactly like listening to the radio for four hours straight. In that regard, the *Classic Rock Box* fills its purpose perfectly. *—Stephen Thomas Erlewine*

Classic Soul / 1991 / MCA 10288
A good blend of Stax, Chess, and even a bit of blues and Afro-pop from Hugh Masekela. *—Ron Wynn*

○ **Cobra Records Story: Chicago Rock & Blues 1956-58** / Apr. 26, 1993 / Warner Brothers 42012
A fine two-CD retrospective of the Chicago Blue label, including all of its 39 singles by such seminal figures as Magic Sam, Otis Rush, Buddy Guy, Ike Turner, Sunnyland Slim, and Walter Horton. *—AMG*

★ **Complete Stax-Volt Singles 1959-1968** / 1991 / Atlantic 82218

This 244-track, nine-CD boxed set includes *all* of the 45 RPM A-sides ever released (as well as a few choice B-sides) on these legendary Memphis labels, during and preceding their association with Atlantic Records. Even though Stax/Volt continued to release more strong sides after 1968, with Isaac Hayes ("Shaft") and the Staple Singers, many consider that their classic sound is the one represented here. The consistently great songs and performances found on this collection, by artists like Otis Redding, Carla Thomas, Sam & Dave, Booker T. & the MG's, Eddie Floyd, and many more, are a testament to Stax/Volt's vision. The tracks (remastered from the original mono masters on specially modified equipment) sound amazingly warm and full. Included is a booklet with extensively detailed liner notes and a generous selection of photos. For anyone who has the change to part with for a boxed set of this size, this is absolutely essential, provided you are a serious lover of gritty soul music. *—Rick Clark*

○ **Complete Stax-Volt Soul Singles, Vol. 2, 1968-1971** / 1993 / Stax 4411
A massive nine-CD deluxe boxed set containing all 216 singles released by the seminal soul label from 1968-1971. During their first four years after leaving Atlantic's distribution wing, Stax had some of the biggest soul hits (and stars) of the day, and they're all here, with deluxe packaging and superb sound. This is a perfect companion to the first Stax-Volt box set. *—Cub Koda*

Concussion! / Mr. Mannicotti 342
A rock-solid compilation of 18 stompin' instrumentals from the golden age of guitar combos, 1958-1965. No hits, no big names (unless you count Punk Carson & the Chucklers), just great, raw rockin'. *—Cub Koda*

○ **Conmemoritivo: A Tribute to Gram Parsons** / 1993 / Rhino 71269
Conmemoritivo is a scattered, yet enjoyable, tribute to Gram Parsons, the legendary father of country-rock. As with most tribute records, the results are a mixed bag—some bands play the songs as straight rock without any trace of country—yet the best moments capture the spirit, if not the exact sound, of Parsons's originals. Bob Mould and Vic Chestnutt's mournful rendition of "Hickory Wind" is a particular highlight. *—Stephen Thomas Erlewine*

☆ **Creole Kings of New Orleans** / 1992 / Specialty 2168
Creole Kings of New Orleans is a splendid 26-track sampler of Specialty Records' numerous R&B legends, including Professor Longhair, Percy Mayfield, Lloyd Price, Joe Liggins, and Guitar Slim. Although only a couple of big hits are included, the material is consistently strong, making the disc an excellent purchase. *—Stephen Thomas Erlewine*

★ **D.I.Y.: Anarchy in the UK—UK Punk I (1976-77)** / Jan. 19, 1993 / Rhino 71171
Rhino Records has masterfully chronicled with its *D.I.Y.* series the explosive early years of punk and its better-behaved kid brother new wave. It comprises an essential body of work in the history of rock. The first installment in the series, *Anarchy in the UK*, compiles such early punk luminaries as the Sex Pistols, the Jam, the Buzzcocks, the Stranglers, the Adverts (the brilliantly bizarre "Gary Gilmore's Eyes"), Australia's Saints, and the first female entrants with X-Ray Spex and Penetration. *—Roch Parisien*

★ **D.I.Y.: Blank Generation—The New York Scene (1975-78)** / 1993 / Rhino 71175
Featuring essential singles from the Ramones, Richard Hell & the Voidoids, Blondie, Television, Patti Smith, the Dictators, the Heartbreakers, and the Dead Boys, *Blank Generation* is where the story chronicled on *D.I.Y.* begins. It was the mid-'70s rumblings of Patti Smith and the Ramones emanating from New York City's famed C.B.G.B. club that served as the catalyst for what followed. The Ramones' debut album, released in May 1976, lit a match to the dry tinder of England's alienated youth and set the pace for the Sex Pistols and the Damned, who—in turn—are captured in all their primitive glory on *Anarchy in the UK.* *—Roch Parisien*

★ **D.I.Y.: Come out and Play—American Power Pop Part I** / 1993 / Rhino 71177
Come Out and Play, the first of two discs of American power-pop in the *D.I.Y.* series, is a terrific 19-track collection of heavyweights such as Cheap Trick, Flamin' Groovies, Chris Stamey, and Chris Bell, as well as more obscure bands like Fotomaker, Pezband, and

the Diodes. It's essential for fans of power-pop or anyone who loves a good melody. —*Stephen Thomas Erlewine*

○ **D.I.Y.: Mass. Ave.—The Boston Scene (1979-83)** / 1993 / Rhino 71179
Out of all of the volumes in the *D.I.Y.* series *Mass. Ave—The Boston Scene (1975-1983)* is probably the weakest—but that doesn't mean it's worthless. *Mass. Ave* chronicles its scene very well; it's just that Boston's punk/new wave scene wasn't as strong as New York's or Los Angeles's. Yet the CD is full of wonderful moments, including Mission of Burma, the Lyres, a demo from the Cars, Willie Alexander, and Human Sexual Response among its 19 tracks. It is definitely worth purchasing for punk and new wave aficionados. —*Stephen Thomas Erlewine*

○ **D.I.Y.: Shake It Up—American Power Pop Part II** / 1993 / Rhino 71178
Shake It Up! D.I.Y.'s second volume of American power-pop, is slightly less consistent than the first, but it is still full of wonderful music, making it just as essential as the first volume. Includes the Shoes, Chris Stamey & the dB's, Pearl Harbor & the Explosions, the Plimsouls, and the Romantics' infectious "What I Like about You." —*Stephen Thomas Erlewine*

☆ **D.I.Y.: Starry Eyes—UK Pop, Vol. 2** / 1993 / Rhino 71174

★ **D.I.Y.: Teenage Kicks: UK Pop (1976-79)** / Jan. 19, 1993 / Rhino 71173
Concurrently with the new punk sounds (and in a symbiotic relationship), British pub-rock was evolving into tight, frenetic, and witty pop that would soon be called new wave. *Teenage Kicks* and its companion volume *Starry Eyes* capture this evolution from the early Stiff Records sound of Nick Lowe and Wreckless Eric, to hard, crystalline gems from Ireland's the Undertones and the comic-book hyberbole of Scotland's the Rezillos. The list of performers contained on these two volumes who produced magical singles which (in some cases) charted in England but went virtually ignored in North America, is impressive: the Boys, the Motors, the Distractions, the Jags, the Records, and the criminally underrated Yachts from Liverpool. Early tracks from longer-lived names like XTC, Squeeze, and Joe Jackson are also included. —*Roch Parisien*

★ **D.I.Y.: The Modern World: UK Punk II (1977-78)** / 1993 / Rhino 71172
The Modern World chronicles the splintering of the initial punk wave into different factions and styles: mod-inspired workouts from the Jam, working-class anthems by 999 and Sham 69, the progressive tendencies of Magazine and the Fall, emerging psychedelia from the Soft Boys, and powerful politics from Ireland's Stiff Little Fingers. —*Roch Parisien*

○ **D.I.Y.: We're Desperate—The L.A. Scene (1976-79)** / 1993 / Rhino 71176
Twenty-one tracks of raw Los Angeles punk form *We're Desperate—The L.A. Scene (1976-79)*, another solid installment in Rhino's punk/new wave series, *D.I.Y.* Although it isn't a front-to-back blowout like the New York volume, *We're Desperate* is a disc all punk and new wave fans will want to add to their collection, considering that the original versions of all the singles have been included. The CDs feature such bands as the Germs, the Dickies, the Weirdos, the Plugz, the Zippers, the Motels, and X, Los Angeles's quintessential punk band. —*Stephen Thomas Erlewine*

○ **Dance Craze** / 1983 / Two Tone 21783
Finally available on CD, a classic collection of live tracks from the English Beat, the Specials, Bad Manners, and other '80s ska-revival bands. — *Scott Bultman*

○ **Deadicated—A Tribute to the Grateful Dead** / 1991 / Arista 8669
This tribute record features everyone from Elvis Costello to Midnight Oil to Dr. John doin' the Dead. An attempt to showcase the Dead's songwriting. The rigid arrangements could have used more imagination, but the interpretations are mostly agreeable. —*Jeff Tamarkin*

Desperate Rock 'n' Roll, Vol. 2 / Flame 2
Storming compilation of extremely rare early rock & roll sides. The master tapes are history, but the music and the energy contained here more than make up for the lack of fidelity. —*Cub Koda*

☆ **Disco Years, Vol. 1: Turn the Beat Around** / 1990 / Rhino 70984

A comprehensive series featuring many of the greatest disco songs ever recorded, Rhino's five-volume *Disco Years* set accurately chronicles the pop music sensation of the mid-'70s. The first two volumes are the places to start; the other three are necessary for devoted disco fans and pop music historians. —*Stephen Thomas Erlewine*

☆ **Doo Wop Box** / 1994 / Rhino
Rhino's four-disc collection, *The Doo Wop Box*, may not contain every classic doo-wop single ever recorded, but it comes damn close. Featuring a hundred tracks, superb sound, and amazingly detailed liner notes, the set is one of the best various-artist boxed sets ever assembled. Although these four discs will be all the doo-wop some listeners will ever need, hopefully the set will make most listeners want to investigate the genre further. —*Stephen Thomas Erlewine*

○ **Doo-Wop from Dolphin's of Hollywood, Vol. 1** / 1992 / Specialty 2173
Mid-'50s Los Angeles doo wop, produced by John Dolphin. Groups include the Turbans, the Voices, the Gassers, Bobby Relf, the Turks, Gaynell Hodge and the Blue-Aires, Bobby Byrd, and the Jaguars. —*AMG*

○ **Doo-Wop from Dolphin's of Hollywood, Vol. 2** / Specialty 2174
More mid-'50s Los Angeles doo wop. Groups include the Hollywood Arist-O-Kats, the Turks, the Hollywood Flames, Grady Chapman and the Suedes, the Sunrisers, and others. —*AMG*

○ **Dope Guns & F***ing in the Streets, Vols. 1-3** / 1989 / Amphetamine Reptile 89172
Released in 1989, this is alienated, second-generation, post-hardcore guitar rant. —*John Dougan*

Down & Dirty: Immediate Blues Story, Vol. 3 / CBS 47897
Eric Clapton and Jimmy Page are the big names on this anthology, but the real value lies in songs by the late Jo Ann Kelly, who sounds utterly authentic. —*Bruce Eder*

☆ **Duke-Peacock's Greatest Hits** / 1992 / MCA 10666
Don Robey, something of an infamous figure even in the rough-and-tumble world of 1950s R&B labels, owned one of the first successful Black-owned labels in the country, and his output was rich and varied. *Duke-Peacock's Greatest Hits* offers a revealing overview of his operation, beginning with major hits by two of the company's humongous female belters: Big Mama Thornton's "Hound Dog" and Marie Adams's "I'm Gonna Play the Honky Tonks." Johnny Ace, Bobby Bland, and Junior Parker are represented by a few of their biggest hits, but it's the relatively unknown "Pack Fair and Square" by San Antonio pianist Big Walter Price that wields a knockout punch. Vocal groups aren't forgotten, with sides by Norman Fox, the Rob Roys, and the El Torros, and a foray into "rockabilly" is recalled by the Original Casuals' "So Tough." —*Bill Dahl, Goldmine*

80's Greatest Rock Hits, Vol. 1: Passion & Power / Priority 7073
Like Priority's corresponding *70's Greatest Rock Hits* series, *80's Greatest Rock Hits* arranges several hit singles according to loose themes like *Arena Rock* and *The Agony & the Ecstasy*. Each disc contains the original hit version in good fidelity, but like other Priority releases, this lacks liner notes. However, the discs are enjoyable and several discs feature songs that are hard to find on other releases. Priority later began their *Rock of the 80's* series, which covered the same ground in a more haphazard, yet more enjoyable, manner. —*Stephen Thomas Erlewine*

Fillmore: The Last Days / 1972 / CBS 31390
In the summer of 1971, Bill Graham closed the two halls that had redefined the way live rock music was heard. In San Francisco, the Fillmore Auditorium (later Fillmore West), had been home to virtually every major performing band of the era—a neighborhood meeting place and dance palace rolled into one. It was the place to see the Dead, the Airplane, Santana, and any visiting musical act with any hipness quotient at all. This two-CD package features some of the recordings from the final week of shows at the fabled Fillmore West. Not all of the bands are remembered today (Lamb, anyone?) but with hot entries from Quicksilver Messenger Service, Tower of Power, Hot Tuna, Boz Scaggs, the Dead, Santana, and more, it's a tribute both to a time and place and to the inestimable contributions of the late Graham. The sound quality is lacking by today's standards, but the free 'n' easy Fillmore atmosphere comes through. —*Jeff Tamarkin*

○ **Fire/Fury Records Story** / 1993 / Capricorn 42009

A fine two-CD compilation of the seminal blues label and its many groundbreaking artists. —*AMG*

☆ **Frat Rock** / 1991 / Rhino 75778
Rhino's *Frat Rock* series is an excellent overview of '60s rock & roll and R&B party anthems like the Kingsmen's "Louie Louie," "Double Shot of My Baby's Love" (Swinging Medallions), "La La La La La" (Blendells), "Shout" (Isley Brothers), "Do You Love Me" (the Contours), and "Mony Mony" (Tommy James & the Shondells). —*John Floyd*

○ **Funky Stuff: The Best of Funk Essentials** / May 18, 1993 / Polygram 514821
A terrific compilation of the highlights of Mercury's *Funk Essentials* series (which features individual titles by Parliament, the Bar-Kays, Cameo, and Con Funk Shun) plus songs from artists who don't have their own individual CDs. Essential for anyone curious about the funk. —*AMG*

○ **Get Down Tonight: Best of T.K. Records** / 1990 / Rhino 71003
A fine collection of the best tracks from the seminal disco label from the '70s, including tracks by KC & the Sunshine Band, George McCrae, Gwen McCrae, Betty Wright, Latimore, and Little Beaver. —*Stephen Thomas Erlewine*

○ **Get Hot or Go Home: Vintage RCA Rockabilly '56-'59, Vols. I & II** / Country Music Found 14
This two-fer contains an extensive set of recordings from some of the top legends in rockabilly, artists like Milton Allen, Roy Orbison, Janis Martin, Homer & Jethro, Joe Clay, Martha Carson, Pee Wee King, and many more. The informative booklet includes photos and a discography. —*AMG*

● **Golden Groups** / 1993 / Specialty 2155
Doo-wop in its heyday had ten worthy groups for every hit attraction. There was so much material that many outstanding songs, vocalists, and ensembles got lost in the shuffle. This 15-song, hour-long CD spotlights superb numbers that didn't generate much impact but were still outstanding examples of the style. The contributors' list includes the Chimes, Tropicals, Arthur Lee Maye and the Crowns, the Twilighters, and the Monitors. The focus is on love, of course, every type from unrequited to tragic to joyous. Sometimes harmonies aren't totally on pitch; other times the lyrics seem incredibly innocent or a song's message reflects a sensibility honed in another era. But the passion, earnestness, and honesty of the vocals overcomes any and all of these problems, conveying to '90s audiences the magic that made (and makes) doo-wop so compelling. —*Ron Wynn*

● **Golden Throats: The Great Celebrity Sing Off** / May 18, 1988 / Rhino 70187
A hilarious compilation of famous personalities killing well-known songs. So bad it's funny! —*Larry Lapka*

○ **Golden Throats 2: More Celebrity Rock Oddities** / 1991 / Rhino 71007
The second volume of *Golden Throats* isn't quite as consistent, but there are wonderful moments here, including Sammy Davis Jr.'s take on "Shaft" and Mae West's "Light My Fire." And *anything* William Shatner ever recorded is hysterical. —*Stephen Thomas Erlewine*

○ **Groove 'n' Grind: 50's & 60's Dance Hits** / Rhino 70992
An 18-cut assemblage of '50s and '60s rock, soul, and R&B/dance tunes. Essential for strollers, peppermint twisters, hully-gulliers, monkey-timers, and cool-jerks. —*John Floyd*

★ **Hardcore Doo-Wop: In the Hallway—Under The Street Lamp** / 1993 / Specialty 7049
The Specialty vaults are bulging with solid tracks that for various reasons didn't see the light of day when they were recorded. There's little filler on this 25-song CD featuring cuts from many acts issued not only on Specialty but other independents like Ebb and Antone. Jesse Belvin's creamy lead on "Where's My Girl," Arthur Lee Maye and the Crows' version of "Gloria," The Chimes' "Pretty Little Girl," and the Jaguars' "Hold Me Tight" are merely a few of the disc's great cuts. There's also Eugene Church's brilliant vocal on "How Long" and Belvin's pairing with Marvin Phillips on "Dream Girl." This 60-minute disc will trigger wonderful memories for those whose musical preferences were built during the era. Others who've only heard about the music's charms can now understand why so many revere it. —*Ron Wynn*

○ **Harlem Shuffle: 60s Soul Classics** / Charly 85

A perfect selection (and disc order) of lesser-known but essential soul hits, including the Barbara Lewis hits "Hello Stranger," "Make Me Your Baby," and "Baby I'm Yours," plus "Oogum Boogum Song" and "Gimme Little a Sign" by Brenton Wood, and "Get On Up and Get Away" by the Esquires. Twenty-one classic sides in all, every one a delight. An import, but worth the trouble to find. —*Michael Erlewine*

☆ **Hi Records Story** / Hi 101
Marvelous tribute to Willie Mitchell's Hi label, which, like Stax, revolutionized Memphis soul. A 24-song disc featuring the best of the two American volumes and a few different cuts. —*John Floyd*

○ **History of Hi Records R&B, Vol. 1: Beginnings** / 1988 / MCA 25226
A terrific two-volume tribute to Willie Mitchell's Hi label, featuring a hodgepodge of rockabilly and soul from such artists as Mitchell and Ace Cannon. —*John Floyd*

○ **History of Hi Records R&B, Vol. 2: Glory Years** / 1988 / MCA 25227
Great '70s soul from Al Green, Ann Peebles, and associates. —*Ron Wynn*

☆ **Hits from the Legendary Vee Jay Records** / Motown 9067
A comprehensive survey of this seminal blues and soul label, including hits by the Dells, John Lee Hooker, and Jerry Butler. Plus Little Richard's obscure soul masterpiece, "I Don't Know What You Got." —*John Floyd*

☆ **Hitsville USA: The Motown Singles Collection 1959-1971** / 1992 / Motown 6312
A terrific four-disc boxed set that features many of Motown's greatest hits in superb sound. While nearly every song is a gem, this is one of the few boxed sets that isn't comprehensive enough. If anything, it could have used another disc to fit in some more material, particularly more songs by the Supremes. Nevertheless, what is here is transcendent. —*Stephen Thomas Erlewine*

Hitsville Usa, Vol. 2: The Motown Singles Collection (1972-1992) / Oct. 19, 1993 / Motown 6358
Where the first *Hitsville* box suffered from not featuring enough material, the sequel suffers from having too many tracks. During the '70s, the label lost its distinctive sound, although the hits continued to come for a number of years. Unfortunately, as the years progress, the hits become fewer and less distinctive—they follow the trends, instead of setting them. Perhaps this could have been a successful two-CD set, but at four discs there aren't enough gems to justify the hefty price ticket. —*Stephen Thomas Erlewine*

☆ **Best of House Music** / 1988 / Profile 1248
Use this as an introduction to the frenetic world of house music. —*Ron Wynn*

○ **I'm Your Fan (Tribute to Leonard Cohen)** / 1991 / Atlantic 82349
An incoherent tribute to Leonard Cohen, *I'm Your Fan* contains some fine versions of some of his best songs, but too often these renditions are half-hearted. Of particular interest are R.E.M.'s "First We'll Take Manhattan" and the Pixies' "I Can't Forget." —*Stephen Thomas Erlewine*

○ **Immediate Singles Collection, Vol. 1** / 1991 / Sony 47351
Interesting 20-song compilation of veddy British tunes by Small Faces, the Nice, and others, with an American or two thrown in. —*Jeff Tamarkin*

Immediate Singles Collection, Vol. 2 / 1991 / Sony 46994
For collectors of obscure '60s British rock only. Includes Humble Pie, P. P. Arnold, Amen Corner, and more. —*Jeff Tamarkin*

○ **In Yo' Face! (The History of Funk), Vol. 1** / Rhino 71431
Funk fans eagerly anticipated Rhino's four-part series, thinking that they would get something equivalent to the label's wonderful '70s soul line. Well, while the final results are good, things are not quite as rosy as earlier reports indicated. The most disappointing thing in my view was the apparent decision to settle for single versions of tracks rather than extended ones. I'm sure the reason was that this was how the songs sounded on radio, but the results are truncated versions of *Sex Machine* and *Keep On Truckin'* rather than glorious full cuts with complete musical interludes. Otherwise, most song choices are great, especially the JB's, Funkadelic, and Lyn Collins. —*Ron Wynn*

○ **In Yo' Face! (The History of Funk), Vol. 2** / Rhino 71432

Volume 2 of Rhino's Funk series offers 15 more mostly strong cuts, although again it is disappointing to hear edited versions of great anthems. The marvelous trumpet solo and additional chorus from the O'Jays *For the Love of Money* has been trimmed, and though they don't tell you, only part of B.T. Express's "Do It ('til You're Satisfied)" is included. There is still plenty of wonderful funk, including classics by Sly & the Family Stone, James Brown, Kool & the Gang, Rufus, Parliament, and the Temptations. *—Ron Wynn*

○ **In Yo' Face! (The History of Funk), Vol. 3** / Rhino 71433
By the third volume of Rhino's generally solid funk series it has become apparent who did and did not permit their songs to be licensed. Once more there are songs from James Brown, Sly & the Family Stone, Parliament, Funkadelic, the O'Jays and AWB, and it's great that George McRae's delightful "I Get Lifted" made the cut as well as Graham Central Station's "The Jam." Cameo's "Funk Funk" reveals how close to Parliament they were early in their career, while the Brothers Johnson, Kool and the Gang in their great pre-J. T. Taylor phase, and one-hit wonders Wild Cherry complete the disc. *—Ron Wynn*

○ **In Yo' Face! (The History of Funk), Vol. 4** / Rhino 71434
Familiar names comprise the bulk of the fourth volume in Rhino's funk series. There are more tracks by James Brown, Sly & the Family Stone and AWB, plus entries from the Isley Brothers, Kool & the Gang, Graham Central Station, and Earth, Wind & Fire. But new acts offer prototype funk on some smoking numbers such as Slave's "Slide," the Bar-Kays' "Shake Your Rump to the Funk," Brick's "Dazz," and George Duke's "Reach for It," with a snaky electric bass line by Stanley Clarke, dense arrangements, and heavy backbeats. Bootsy's "The Pinocchio Theory" was a classic, and the same is true of Marvin Gaye's "Got to Give It Up, Part 1." Only Brass Construction's "L-O-V-E-U" falls below the standard. *—Ron Wynn*

○ **In Yo' Face! (The History of Funk), Vol. 5** / Rhino 71435
Another solid installment in the *In Yo' Face* series, the fifth volume contains essential tracks from Parliament, Con Funk Shun, Rick James, Zapp, and Cameo. *—AMG*

○ **Island Story 1962-87** / 1987 / Island 842901
A fine, if too brief, look at the influential reggae and rock label. *—Dan Heilman*

○ **Juke Box: R&B** / 1993 / Virgin 86302
A fine collection of '50s R&B featuring solid but frequently uncelebrated tracks by classic artists like B. B. King, Elmore James, Ike & Tina Turner, Etta James, and Lowell Fulsom. *—AMG*

☆ **Just Can't Get Enough: New Wave Hits of the 80s, Vols. 1-5** / 1994 / Rhino
Rhino's first 5 volumes of their 15-disc new wave retrospective are filled with classic tracks from the early '80s, from "Love Will Tear Us Apart" to "867-5309/Jenny." Each disc is loosely chronological and contains a number of obscurities and novelites along with the hits. For sound and content, this is likely to be the best series of new wave hits ever to be released. Start with the fifth volume, which contains "I Want Candy," "Someday, Someway," "The Kids in America," "Love Plus One," "Valley Girl," and other gems. Then work your way through the rest of the discs. *— Stephen Thomas Erlewine*

○ **Kill Rock Stars** / 1991 / KK 201
Excellent modern-day punk rock collection of various cutting-edge artists, including Nirvana and riot grrrls Bikini Kill. Alternative-rock fans will find much to savor here. (The Courtney Love band's acoustic "Don't Mix the Colors" is particularly noteworthy). *—Stephen Thomas Erlewine*

○ **King Biscuit Live: Best of, Vol. 1** / 1991 / San Francisco Sound 33005
Getting down with Tull, Rod Stewart, Skynyrd, and others, in concert. *—Jeff Tamarkin*

○ **King Biscuit Live: Best of, Vol. 2** / 1991 / San Francisco Sound 33006
An odd assortment, including the Stray Cats, Elton John, Foghat, and Iggy Pop, all recorded live for vintage radio broadcasts. *—Jeff Tamarkin*

○ **King Biscuit Live: Best of, Vol. 3** / 1991 / San Francisco Sound 33007
More '70s and '80s live radio, this time with Lou Reed, Linda Ronstadt, the Allmans, and more. *—Jeff Tamarkin*

○ **King Biscuit Live: Best of, Vol. 4** / 1991 / San Francisco Sound 33008
Queen, Nugent, Thin Lizzy, and others, captured on this too-brief collection of radio tapes. *—Jeff Tamarkin*

○ **Legends of Guitar—Guitar Player Presents Rock: The 50s, Vol. 1** / 1991 / Rhino 270719
Nice collection of tracks featuring dazzling guitar work and classic sides from Chuck Berry, Bo Diddley, Les Paul, James Burton, Carl Perkins, and 12 others. *—Cub Koda*

○ **Legends of Guitar—Guitar Player Presents Rock: The 50s, Vol. 2** / 1991 / Rhino 270561
Companion volume to the above, with dynamite tracks from Ike Turner, Joe Maphis, Ritchie Valens, Scotty Moore, Duane Eddy, Larry Collins, and 12 more. *—Cub Koda*

○ **Legends of Guitar—Guitar Player Presents Rock: The 60s, Vol. 1** / 1991 / Rhino 270720
Excellent 18-track CD featuring dazzling guitar work by the Ventures, Steve Cropper, Dave Edmunds, the Byrds, Chet Atkins, Lonnie Mack, and others, showing the breadth of '60s guitar work. *—Cub Koda*

○ **Legends of Guitar—Guitar Player Presents Rock: The 60s, Vol. 2** / 1991 / Rhino 270562
Companion volume to the above, featuring tracks by Jeff Beck, the Fendermen, Travis Wammack, Roy Buchanan, Eric Clapton, and other guitar giants of the '60s. *—Cub Koda*

○ **Legends of Guitar—Guitar Player Presents Rock: The 70s, Vol. 1** / 1991 / Rhino 270721
Showcasing a selected sampling of the lesser-heralded guitarists of the era, this 18-track CD features selections by Rick Derringer, Brownsville Station's Cub Koda, the Outlaws, Ted Nugent, James Gang, and others. A nice selection with excellent sound. *—Dan Heilman*

○ **Legends of Guitar—Guitar Player Presents: Surf Guitar, Vol. 1** / 1991 / Rhino 270724
Guitar was always the driving force in surf rock, which means this edition of the *Legends of Guitar* series serves as a good introduction to the sub-genre in general. *—AMG*

○ **Legends of Guitar—Guitar Player Presents: Electric Blues, Vol. 2** / Rhino 70564
Eighteen tracks from blues guitarists Buddy Guy, Albert Collins, Mike Bloomfield, Magic Sam, and more. Includes Rufus Thomas's great Sun-era cut, "Bear Cat," featuring Joe Hill Louis on guitar, and the steamy "Okie Dokie Stomp" by Clarence "Gatemouth" Brown. *—Roundup Newsletter*

○ **Live Stiffs** / Edsel 621
Recorded on the first "Live Stiffs" tour in the late '70s, this record contains some fine performances by Elvis Costello, Nick Lowe, and Graham Parker. *—AMG*

○ **Living in Oblivion: The 80s Greatest Hits** / 1993 / EMI 81417
A somewhat haphazardly assembled retrospective of '80s pop, *Living in Oblivion* contains not only classic new wave cuts, it also features several MTV hits from the mid '80s and radio hits from the end of the decade. While there are some great songs on every volume, each disc is wildly inconsistent; only the first disc is somewhat coherent. Nevertheless, *Living in Oblivion* captures the fractured mainstream of the decade quite well and manages to include some classic pop songs along the way. *—Stephen Thomas Erlewine*

Lonely as an Eyesore / 4AD 703
Rare tracks from the 4AD label, including the Cocteau Twins, Throwing Muses, Dead Can Dance, and This Mortal Coil. *— Michael P. Dawson*

○ **Lost in the Stars: The Music of Kurt Weill** / A&M 5104
Eclectic updates of Kurt Weill's distinctive German theater music, with Sting, Marianne Faithfull, John Zorn, Lou Reed, Carla Bley, Tom Waits, Charlie Haden, and more. *—Myles Boisen*

Louisiana Scrapbook / Rykodisc 20058
Contemporary Louisiana sounds were presented on this 18-track compilation culled from various albums. While veteran stylists like Irma Thomas, Tuts Washington and Johnny Adams were included, the disc contained cuts by other acts not so readily identified with the state (Marcia Ball), plus sorely neglected artists (Phillip Walker, James Booker, Lonesome Sundown), as well as then-emerging stars (The Dirty Dozen Brass Band, Beausoleil)

and both Zydeco (Buckwheat Zydeco) and Cajun performers (D. L. Menard, Jo-El Sonnier). —*Ron Wynn*

○ **Max Weinberg Presents Let There Be Drums, Vol. 1: The '50s** / 1994 / Rhino
Although it is the foundation of rock & roll, it seems a little silly to build an entire anthology around drums. Amazingly, *Let There Be Drums* works incredibly well, not only as a history of the role of drums in rock, but also as a splendid history of rock itself. On the first volume, nearly all of the major players of the '50s are featured, as well as several obscure treasures, making the disc a great deal of fun. —*Stephen Thomas Erlewine*

○ **Max Weinberg Presents: Let There Be Drums, Vol. 2: The '60s** / 1994 / Rhino
The second volume of *Let There Be Drums* is nearly as successful as the first, even if it doesn't feature Ringo Starr, Charlie Watts, or Keith Moon. However, it does cover a good portion of the broad spectrum of pop music made during the decade, making it a fun and revealing listen. —*Stephen Thomas Erlewine*

Max Weinberg Presents: Let There Be Drums, Vol. 3: The '70s / 1994 / Rhino
Like the decade itself, the '70s volume of *Let There Be Drums* is a bit all over the place. Although Ringo Starr and Charlie Watts are both featured, John Bonham is missing along with entire other sub-genres of the decade, including disco and punk. Still, the disc contains enough variety and good music to make it a worthy conclusion to the series. —*Stephen Thomas Erlewine*

Mega Hits Dance Classics, Volumes 1-14 / Priority
A spotty but exhaustive series of '70s and '80s disco hits. The packaging is awful, with horrid graphics and no liner notes, but there are some rarities to be found on some of the sets. Every volume contains at least one treasure. —*John Floyd*

○ **Mercury Rhythm & Blues: 1946-1962** / 1990 / PolyGram 838243
Though it leaned more toward pop-flavored R&B like the Platters, Mercury had some fertile years. This set catches them well. —*Dan Heilman*

Metal Age: The Roots of Metal / 1992 / Rhino 70272
Actually, *Roots of Metal* comes closer to representing the heyday of heavy metal. From Status Quo to Motorhead, all kinds of '70s arena hard rock and metal are covered. Over the course of the disc, it becomes clear that metal does *not* all sound the same—there's quite a difference between thuggish Wishbone Ash, melodic Cheap Trick, snarling Runaways, and the bloated blues of Beck, Bogert, and Appice. Some of it holds up surprisingly well, and some of it is embarrassing, but there's no question that it captures its era particularly well. —*Stephen Thomas Erlewine*

○ **Monster Rock 'n Roll Show** / Dunhill 050
Hilarious and well-programmed collection of Halloween-geared blues, rock, and R&B cuts. Collectors will like the tunes by the Revels, the Hollywood Flames, and Johnny Fuller, while everyone will like the movie-trailer voiceovers that separate the songs. —*John Floyd*

★ **Monster Summer Hits: Wild Surf** / Jul. 22, 1991 / Capitol 96861
The two-volume *Monster Summer Hits* (the above album, *Drag City*, and this one, *Wild Surf*) *is surf and hot rod material culled from the Capitol archives. Lots of obvious cuts by the Beach Boys, Jan and Dean, and the Ventures, but there's plenty of rare stuff to keep you interested. Great sound quality too.* —John Floyd

○ **Monterey International Pop Festival Box Set** / Jun. 1967 / Rhino 70596
The Monterey Pop Festival was one of the greatest of the late-'60s music festivals. This 4-CD boxed set generously documents performances by artists as varied as the Byrds, the Association, Jimi Hendrix, Jefferson Airplane, Lou Rawls, Ravi Shankar, Booker T. & the MG's, the Who, Otis Redding, the Mamas & Papas, Eric Burdon & the Animals, Big Brother & the Holding Company, and more. —*Rick Clark*

○ **Muscle Shoals Sound** / Rhino 71517
Everything on *Muscle Shoals Sound* has been featured on countless compilations before, but in terms of song selection, sound quality, and liner notes, this is one of the best of its genre. —*Stephen Thomas Erlewine*

New Orleans Jazz & Heritage Festival 1976 / 1976 / Rhino 71111

Lightnin' Hopkins on three tracks, playing a Stratocaster, raw and distorted, dragging the rhythm section by the scruff of the neck. Worth it for these three tracks alone. —*Cub Koda*

○ **New Orleans Ladies: Rhythm & Blues from the Vaults of Ric and Ron** / 1988 / Rounder 2078
With the exception of Irma Thomas, this 1988 anthology covered good female vocalists whose contributions to New Orleans R&B were overlooked or devalued. Both Martha Nelson (Carter) and Leona Buckles were excellent uptempo, dance-oriented vocalists who had no trouble maintaining their vocal authority and clout over driving arrangements and could shift gears and handle low-key, steamy ballads or confessional material. Carter's entertaining answer cut to Joe Jones's hit "You Talk Too Much" was "I Don't Talk Too Much." It's included along with "I'm Through Crying," "Bless You" and "One Man's Woman." Buckles's songs "I'm Waiting (to Give You My Love)" and "Baby We're Through" were exuberantly sung and nicely produced and arranged. The Thomas tracks include her outstanding "Don't Mess with My Man" and three other lesser-known early 1960 numbers that weren't smashes but displayed the majestic voice and dramatic delivery that ultimately became a dominant part of New Orleans soul. These aren't throwaway numbers, despite their obscurity. All three vocalists were vital parts of the Crescent City legacy, and Martha Carter (Nelson) and Leona Buckles hopefully will eventually get the wider recognition they deserve. —*Ron Wynn*

★ **Best of New Orleans Rhythm & Blues, Vol. 1** / 1988 / Rhino 75765
Some of the greatest music ever, period: the Meters, Clarence Henry, Lloyd Price, and so on. Endless groovin'. —*Jeff Tamarkin*

☆ **Best of New Orleans Rhythm & Blues, Vol. 2** / 1988 / Rhino 75766
More funky gumbo, from Smiley Lewis, Irma Thomas, Earl King, and others who know how to have a good time. —*Jeff Tamarkin*

○ **New Wave of British Heavy Metal** / 1990 / Metal Blade 2200
Many of today's thrash bands, like Metallica and Anthrax, were heavily influenced by British '80s bands, including Samson, Iron Maiden, Def Leppard, and Diamond Head. In the '70s these bands offered something different from metal/hard rock, appealing to kids looking for a change. —*John Book*

○ **Nipper's Greatest Hits: The 50's, Vol. 2** / RCA 8467
The label was on a roll: Elvis, Jim Reeves, Belafonte, even the Isley Brothers. A fascinating collection. —*Jeff Tamarkin*

Nipper's Greatest Hits: The 60's, Vol. 1 / RCA 8474
Country and easy listening marked the early part of RCA's '60s, but by the end of the decade, the hippies had arrived. This is a fun study. —*Jeff Tamarkin*

○ **Nipper's Greatest Hits: The 60's, Vol. 2** / 1988 / RCA 8475
A nice collection running from the Tokens to Jefferson Airplane. Great songs. —*Jeff Tamarkin*

Nipper's Greatest Hits: The 70's / 1988 / RCA 9684
The Guess Who to Hall & Oates—and the King was still holding on. Not the greatest period, but some fine records. —*Jeff Tamarkin*

○ **Nipper's #1 Hits: 1956-1986** / RCA 9902
A good cross section of RCA's pop hits, featuring everyone from Perry Como to Elvis and beyond. An interesting chronicle of pop music in general. —*Cub Koda*

○ **No Alternative** / 1993 / Arista 18737
A mixture of B-sides, outtakes, live tracks, and newly recorded songs, *No Alternative* was the most successful benefit album of 1993, both commercially and artistically. Exceptional songs from Nirvana, Bob Mould, Urge Overkill, Smashing Pumpkins, American Music Club, and Pavement enhance fine outtakes from Buffalo Tom and Matthew Sweet, strengthen Uncle Tupelo and Soul Asylum's strong covers, and make the weak live tracks from the Beastie Boys, Sonic Youth, and the Breeders tolerable. However, nothing can save the Goo Goo Dolls atrocious pop-metal take on the Rolling Stones' "Bitch." Still, that is only one song out of 19, making *No Alternative* a worthy purchase. —*Stephen Thomas Erlewine*

○ **Oh Yeah! the Best of Dunwich Records** / 1992 / Sundazed 11010
Dunwich Records was to '60s garage bands what Sun was to rockabilly. This CD features a generous sampling of the best of Chicago's teen scene of that period. Great sound and liner info too. —*Cub Koda*

○ **Okeh Rhythm & Blues** / Apr. 1, 1993 / Columbia 37649
A fine three-disc box that features most of the greatest hits from the seminal R&B label. —*AMG*

○ **Okeh Soul** / 1982 / Columbia Special Pr 37321
Here's Chicago soul from Major Lance, the Vibrations, and other artists. —*Dan Heilman*

Oldies but Goodies, Vol. 1 / Original Sound 8850
Oldies but Goodies was the first rock & roll anthology, setting the standards for various artists anthologies when it was originally issued in the early '60s. Over the years, the series has held up well in many respects, although there isn't a unifying theme to any of their albums—not by genre, year, or label—the music is first-rate, full of popular singles that form the basis of oldies radio stations. However, when the series made its transition to compact disc in 1987, it wasn't nearly as successful. Taken on their own terms, the fidelity of these 14 discs is quite bad, with muffled, distorted sound on almost every song. Compared with CD reissues by other labels, the discs sound positively atrocious. So it's a mixed bag. If bad sound doesn't stand in your way, there's plenty of good music to be found on these CDs; the original records remain fine items. —*Stephen Thomas Erlewine*

○ **One Hit Wonders: The 60s, Vol. 1** / Rhino 70995
So what if Barry & the Tamerlanes and Jimmy Soul never had another hit? The dozen tracks here by them and others like them will hold up long after a bigger star's music has faded. —*Jeff Tamarkin*

● **One Hit Wonders: The 60s, Vol. 2** / Rhino 70996
This stuff is too much fun! The Hombres, Soul Survivors, and more are a sure thing every time. —*Jeff Tamarkin*

Original Blues Classics / Original Blues Clas 1202
This 15-track compilation serves as a fine sampler of the OBC label. Included are "Trouble in Mind" (King Curtis), "I've Got Mine" (Pink Anderson), "The Dyin' Crapshooter's Blues" (Blind Willie McTell), and "Say No to the Devil" (Rev. Gary Davis). —*Roundup Newsletter*

☆ **Phil Spector: Back to MONO (1958-1969)** / 1991 / ABKCO 7118
If you look hard enough, you can find decent one-album samplers of Phil Spector's greatest recordings, but this four-disc boxed set (three sets of singles and the entire *A Christmas Gift for You* on the fourth) is the jewel of Spector's legacy. Aside from his sporadic '70s productions, *Back to Mono* contains everything you'd ever want by rock's supreme romantic: early productions with Curtis Lee, Ben E. King, and Gene Pitney; the girl-group effervescence of the Ronettes, the Crystals, and Darlene Love; the soul innovations of the Righteous Brothers and the Checkmates; and his notorious sessions with Ike and Tina Turner. Throughout the set, Spector's artistic vision (which has influenced dozens of producers and hundreds of performers) shines like the smile on a lover's lips. One of the greatest and most fully realized boxed sets ever issued. —*John Floyd*

Philly Classics (1973-1977) / 1988 / Philadelphia Intern 34940
A decent sampler of '70s soul hits from the Philadelphia International label. Could've been better. —*John Floyd*

○ **Pimps, Players & Private Eyes** / Jan. 14, 1992 / Sire 26624
An entertaining collection of early '70s funk and soul, featuring classic cuts by Isaac Hayes and Curtis Mayfield. —*AMG*

Rare Soul: Beach Music Classics, Vol. 1 / 1992 / Warner 70277
A fine collection of '60s soul, including excellent tracks from Barbara Lewis and Archie Bell & the Drells. —*AMG*

Rare Soul: Beach Music Classics, Vol. 2 / 1992 / Warner 70278
The second volume of *Rare Soul* is just as enjoyable as the first, featuring tracks by the Clovers, Mary Wells, and Sam & Dave. —*AMG*

Rare Soul: Beach Music Classics, Vol. 3 / 1992 / Warner 70279
The final volume of *Rare Soul* is arguably the best, featuring dynamite songs by Ruth Brown and Willie Tee. —*AMG*

○ **Rarest Rockabilly & Hillbilly Boogie** / ACE 311
This is actually two earlier vinyl compilations on one compact disc, 28 tracks in all, hence the overlong title. The first compilation features artists incredibly obscure, playing music with a delightful, homespun crudity that makes it homegrown rock & roll in its most embryonic stage. The second features more name-brand artists, the majority of them from the Starday catalog, and

offers classic '50s sides from Sonny Fisher, Sleepy LaBeef, and a very young George Jones. —*Cub Koda*

○ **Rebel Rousers: Southern Rock Classics** / Jan. 24, 1992 / Rhino 70586
A solid 12-track collection of some of the finest moments in Southern rock, *Rebel Rousers* features such seminal bands as the Allman Brothers and Lynyrd Skynyrd, as well as Black Oak Arkansas, Elvin Bishop, Marshall Tucker Band, 38 Special, and the Rossington Collins Band. —*AMG*

○ **Red Hot & Blue** / 1991 / Chrysalis 21799
A fitfully entertaining collection of contemporary pop stars interpreting classic Cole Porter songs, *Red Hot & Blue* highlights include U2, Sinead O'Connor, Kirsty MacColl & the Pogues, Neneh Cherry, and David Byrne, but the best part of the disc is the wonderfully campy duet between Deborah Harry and Iggy Pop on "Well Did You Evah." —*AMG*

Red Hot & Dance / Jun. 30, 1992 / Columbia 52826
A compilation to raise money for AIDS research featuring George Michael, Madonna, Seal, PM Dawn, Lisa Stansfield, Young Disciples, Sabrina Johnston, Crystal Waters, Sly & the Family Stone, EMF, and Tomandandy. —*AMG*

Rhythm Country & Blues / 1994 / MCA 10965
An interesting collection of duets between country and soul artists, *Rhythm Country & Blues* works better in theory than in practice, despite a couple of fine tracks. —*AMG*

Rig Rock Jukebox / 1992 / First Warning 75710
Diesel Only is a New York-based label that releases amazing country-rock vinyl singles that it markets via jukeboxes in truck-stops and diners across the United States—hence "Rig Rock." *Rig Rock Juke Box* compiles (on CD) a delicious blend of male and female performers, hard-edged country-rockers, and more traditional twangers. Basically, all 16 tracks are truck-drivin', footstompin', greasy-spoon great. —*Roch Parisien*

○ **Risque Rhythm: Nasty 50s R&B** / 1991 / Rhino 70570
A superb collection of racy R&B, featuring such classics as "Big Ten-Inch Record" and "It Ain't the Meat." —*AMG*

Rock & Roll: Early Days / RCA 5463
Paltry but powerful collection of a dozen classics by Elvis, Haley, Waters, Berry, and more. —*Jeff Tamarkin*

○ **Rock Goes to the Movies #1** / CBS 46808
A wide-ranging, four-album collection of rock tracks, covering various styles and periods. It is all movie-related and most of it hard to find. —*Bruce Eder*

☆ **Rock Instrumentals** / 1994 / Rhino 70137
Rhino's five-volume series of *Rock Instrumentals* is an ambitious and successful collection of the most overlooked subgenre of pop music. Since the '50s and '60s were the high-water mark for pop instrumentals, the first two discs are the best, although the volume dedicated to surf music is equally excellent. The '70s and soul discs aren't quite as consistent, yet they both contain some fine tracks. All in all, the five-disc *Rock Instrumentals* series is the best available collection of a frequently neglected style of rock & roll. —*AMG*

☆ **Rock This Town: Rockabilly Hits, Vol. 1** / 1991 / Rhino 70741
This devastating '50s rockabilly anthology expertly cuts across label and stylistic restraints. —*Bill Dahl*

☆ **Rock This Town: Rockabilly Hits, Vol. 2** / 1991 / Rhino 70742
The second volume of this anthology is just as satisfying through the first ten tracks, when it suddenly veers toward contemporary interpreters. —*Bill Dahl*

○ **Rock of the 80s** / Priority 7994
Like Priority's *70s Greatest Rock Hits* series, the 15 volume *Rock of the 80s* offers a haphazard, yet enjoyable, presentation of hit singles and one-hit wonders from each year of the decade. While the '70s discs are loosely arranged according to theme, the '80s discs just feature ten songs, regardless of when they were released or what they are about. Nevertheless, the series features several songs that can't be easily found anywhere else—Dexy Midnight Runner's "Come on Eileen" on *Vol. 14*, for example—and the sound is good, even if there are no liner notes. Despite its flaws, the series remains a good sampler of '80s pop hits, arguably one of the best on the market today. —*Stephen Thomas Erlewine*

○ **Rockabilly in Memphis; 1954-1968** / 1954-1968 / Smithsonian 051
The rockabilly story has been romanticized and mythologized to the point it seems everyone has heard it a zillion times. But many superb rockabilly acts never got their day in the sun, and the genre hasn't received the documentation it merits. This 18-cut anthology goes a long way toward correcting the problem. It includes cuts from such neglected performers as Ray Harris, Sonny Burgess, Carl Mann, Malcolm Yelvington, and Ray Smith. Robert Gordon's notes detail exactly how the intersection of Southern Black and White cultures resulted in rockabilly. A genuine hybrid that shared characteristics of both, it had the rural vocal inflections of the hillbilly and earthiness of the delta Black. The music was so spontaneous and unsophisticated that it couldn't last. It was the product of an era bound to change, and once the environment changed, so did the sound. While such selections as Johnny Cash's *I Walk the Line* and Roy Orbison's *Ooby Dooby* have been reissued to death, hearing them one more time isn't much to ask for the chance to get Carl McVoy's version of *You Are My Sunshine*. —*Ron Wynn*

○ **Rockin' in the Farmhouse: Original Rockabilly and Chicken Bop, Vol. 2** / 1992 / Sundazed 12002
Rockin' in the Farmhouse: Original Rockabilly and Chicken Bop, Vol. 2 is an excellent 20-track compilation featuring the best of the Roulette label's rarest rockabilly tracks. Highlights include Don "Red" Roberts's "Only One," Jimmy Isle's "Goin' Wild," Jimmy Lloyd's "Rocket in My Pocket," and five chaotic unissued tracks by the Rock-a-Teens. —*Cub Koda*

○ **Rumble** / Relic 7005
An excellent New York doo-wop anthology featuring mid-'50s work by the Channels, the Bop Chords, the Love Notes, and the Continentals. Great sound quality from the original master tapes. —*Bill Dahl*

○ **Todd Rundgren: An Elpee's Worth of Productions** / 1992 / Rhino 70519
Essentially a scrapbook of Rundgren's productions with artists like Patti Smith, Meatloaf, New York Dolls, Grand Funk Railroad, Pursuit of Happiness, XTC, and more. The diversity of artists makes a nice case for Rundgren's wide range of taste, but many of the selections seem odd choices, considering that better material existed on those albums. —*Rick Clark*

○ **San Francisco Nights** / 1991 / Rhino 70536
Probably the most interesting and accessible collection of its kind ever to come from America, more substantial than many European collections. Featuring the obvious and the weird, including the Beau Brummels, the Charlatans, the Vegetables, and the Mystery Trend. —*Bruce Eder*

☆ **Scepter Records Story** / May 26, 1992 / Capricorn 42003
During the '50s and early '60s, NYC-based Scepter Records and its subsidiary, Wand, were part of a group of independents whose artists churned out hit after hit, defining the sound of the day and shaping the sound of the future. The Shirelles, Dionne Warwick, and the Isley Brothers all got their start there. If you love tough, pre-soul era records like "Will You Still Love Me Tomorrow," "Twist and Shout," and "Walk On By," then this is for you. The label's roster also included singers Chuck Jackson, Maxine Brown, and Tommy Hunt; instrumentalist King Curtis; proto-pop/country artists B. J. Thomas and Ronnie Milsap; and punksters the Kingsmen. That's right—"Louie Louie" is here, along with lots of other truly great music. I would have condensed the three discs down to a killer two, but on the whole this box gets high marks. —*Christine Ohlman*

70's Greatest Rock Hits, Vol. 1: Hard n' Heavy / 1991 / Priority 8662
Priority has released 15 volumes of '70s hits, loosely arranged around such themes as *Southern Comfort, High Times,* and *Kickin' Back.* While the discs aren't definitive, they nevertheless offer a good portrait of their particular theme. Each disc features the original hit version. The remastering is fine, but the liner notes are nonexistent. Despite its flaws, *70's Greatest Rock Hits* is one of the best budget-line series available—each disc presents the original version of popular singles in one hit-filled, ten-track disc. —*Stephen Thomas Erlewine*

Shut Down '66 / Ernie Douglas 66
Subtitled *The World's Only 60s Punk Record,* this compilation features 18 garage-band rockers from the wimpier, "My Baby

Shot Me Down" side of the equation. Plenty of 12-string guitars, Farfisa organ, and teenage angst—great fun all. —*Cub Koda*

Slash Early Sessions / Warner Brothers 23937
Decent overview of '80s cuts from the West Coast label that brought you Los Lobos, the Blasters, X, and the Gun Club. —*John Floyd*

○ **Son of Super Bad** / 1991 / K-Tel 60122
As long as K-Tel keeps issuing collections like the *Super Bad* series, they should have no trouble upgrading their public reputation. *Son of Super Bad* doesn't have the outstanding track listing of the first disc, yet there is nothing but prime funk and soul here, presented in their original versions in fine fidelity. While it's not as definitive as Rhino's *Didn't It Blow Your Mind* series, *Super Bad* is mighty fine on its own terms. —*Stephen Thomas Erlewine*

Songs of Protest / Rhino 70734
A wide variety of topical songs from the '60s, ranging from the Kingston Trio's "Where Have All the Flowers Gone?" to Edwin Starr's "War." —*Kenneth M. Cassidy*

☆ **Soul Hits of the 70s: Didn't It Blow Your Mind** / 1991 / Rhino 70781-70790
This 15-volume set was released in 1991 and is a veritable Comstock Lode of overlooked hits from an era most rock fans have yet to discover. By offering the best recordings by the likes of the O'Jays, the Blue Notes, the Chi-Lites, and many others, *Soul Hits* gives the listener a feel for just how vital Black pop and disco was in an era when rock was starting to sag. But the inclusion of dozens of forgotten one-shot hits makes each volume a history lesson in the continued innovation and sheer joy of R&B, proving that Blacks didn't stop making great music after Muddy Waters and Sly Stone bit the dust. —*John Floyd*

○ **Soul Shots, Vol. 1: 60s Soul Classics** / 1988 / Rhino 75774
Soul Shots, Vols. 1-4 are CD compilations of *Soul Shots* collection albums. Devoted to the greatest soul sounds of the '60s, these CDs feature major players such as James Brown and the Impressions, as well as one-shots like the Show-Stoppers and Billy Stewart. This volume features Johnnie Taylor and J. J. Jackson. —*Larry Lapka*

Soul Survey / Black Top 1078
This 18-song blues compilation is a tasty sampling from the solid roster of the New Orleans-based Black Top label. It features songs by seasoned musicians like Earl King and Snooks Eaglin, as well as younger players like Bobby Radcliff and Anson Funderburgh. Highlights include Ronnie Earl and the Broadcasters' "Blind Love," Robert Ward's "Your Love Is Amazing," and Carol Fran and Clarence Holliman's feisty "Golden Girl." If you like blues rhythms, vocals, guitars, horns, harmonicas, and keyboards, you'll find plenty to enjoy here. —*Roundup Newsletter*

○ **Soul Train: Hall of Fame, 20th Anniversary** / 1994 / Rhino Records, Inc. 71618
A lavishly produced three-disc boxed set, *Soul Train: Hall of Fame, 20th Anniversary* follows soul's metamorphosis into disco, hip-hop, new jack swing, and urban contemporary. Over its three discs, it manages to include many of the greatest R&B hits of the '70s, '80s, and '90s. —*AMG*

○ **Specialty Story** / 1994 / Specialty Records, 4412
A definitive five-disc boxed set of the seminal R&B record label, featuring all the essential tracks from such major artists as Little Richard, Larry Williams, and Percy Mayfield, as well as overlooked acts like Don & Dewey. —*AMG*

○ **Stax Blues Brothers** / 1970 / Stax 8547
Twelve tracks by various artists make up this 1988 LP. Artists include John Lee Hooker ("Slow and Easy"), Jimmy McCracklin ("Think"), and Albert King ("Drownin' on Dry Land"). —*Roundup Newsletter*

Stax Blues Masters: Blue Monday / Stax 8528
A decent overview of Stax blues artists, but inferior to individual records by Albert King and Little Milton. —*Ron Wynn*

○ **Stay Awake: Interpretations of Vintage Disney Films** / 1989 / A&M 3918
Cinematic, star-studded, highly inventive interpretations of the music of Disney, lovingly assembled by Hal Wilner. —*Steve Aldrich*

○ **Stiff Records Box Set** / 1992 / Rhino 71062
Stiff Records was the first independent record label in England and partially responsible for starting the fires of the punk and

new wave revolution of the late '70s. Under the guidance of house producer Nick Lowe, Stiff turned out an enormous number of seminal punk and new wave singles in their first years, including classic tracks by the Damned, Elvis Costello, Graham Parker, the Adverts, Ian Dury, and Lowe himself. But what really gave the label its wild, original flavor were minor artists like Ian Dury, Wreckless Eric, Tenpole Tudor, the Yachts, Lene Lovich, Rachel Sweet, and Mickey Jupp, who turned out a series of raw pop gems that were everything good rock & roll singles should be: catchy, energetic, memorable songs that sounded immediate and timeless. While their most talented artists (most prominently Lowe and Costello) left the label immediately, Stiff was able to develop Madness into a major artist in the early '80s. However, they were the only band on Stiff's roster that could turn out consistent albums for a number of years—by the time the Pogues signed to the label, Stiff was pretty much finished. Over the years, the label's early singles have aged remarkably well; they sound as immediate and vital as they did when they were originally released. All of Stiff's finest tracks are collected on this wonderful four-disc boxed set, which contains over a hundred tracks. While most of these songs weren't hits—in fact, many of them were barely noticed in the United States—they are classic rock & roll. The first three discs are excellent; the fourth disc contains some bright moments, but by that time, their artists were pretty much spent. However, the box remains one of the most compulsively listenable sets ever assembled, and it provides the definitive retrospective of arguably the most important and influential British record label of the late '70s. —*Stephen Thomas Erlewine*

Stone Free: A Tribute to Jimi Hendrix / 1993 /
A confused tribute album that is more worthwhile as a curiosity than as an album, *Stone Free* gathers several artists that have nothing in common other than the fact that they have recorded a Hendrix tune. Some of the results are surprisingly good, but most of it is cringe-inducing (Spin Doctors and Body Count) or predictably rote (Eric Clapton and the Pretenders). —*AMG*

☆ **Street Jams: Electric Funk** / 1992 / Rhino 70575
An excellent multi-disc series of 12-inch mixes of influential dance records from the early '80s. Essential for any funk, rap, and dance collection. —*AMG*

○ **Sub-Pop-2000** / 1988 / Sub Pop 25
A fine overview of the hottest new scene today, Seattle grunge rock. —*John Dougan*

Summer & Sun / 1989 / Rhino 70087
An entertaining roundup of summer-oriented hits from the '50s, '60s, and '70s. —*Dan Heilman*

Summer of Love / 1987 / Rhino 71065
Although there is good music on both volumes of *Summer of Love*, the concept is too loose to tie the collections together cohesively. Still, this is the only place to find some of these songs and the sound is terrific. —*AMG*

Sun City / 1985 / Razor & Tie 2007
Sun City was certainly the most political of all of the charity rock albums of the '80s—while everybody agrees hunger is a bad thing, there were still many rock acts that were playing clubs and theaters in South Africa, a country ruled by apartheid. Little Steven organized a number of artists for this protest against apartheid, including such heavyweights as Miles Davis, Bob Dylan, Peter Gabriel, Jimmy Cliff, Bruce Springsteen, Jackson Browne, Run-D.M.C., and Lou Reed. Thankfully, the result was extremely listenable as well as fiercely political; it is one of the few charity or protest albums that stands up to repeated listenings, thanks to the extended instrumental workouts. Arguably the finest moment on the record is one that was added at the last minute—a stripped-down version of U2's "Silver and Gold" by Bono, Keith Richards, and Ron Wood. —*Stephen Thomas Erlewine*

☆ **Sun Records: The Rockability Years** / Charly 106
Gigantic 12-record import with a 52-page book anthology of Sun's landmark contribution to the genre it virtually founded. Many classic sides by the better-known artists and even more great unissued sides by unknown rockers like Jimmy Wages and Tommy Blake, among others. Beyond classic. —*Cub Koda*

☆ **Sun Rockabilly: Classic Recordings** / Rounder 37
As the title suggests, Memphis rockabilly at its best. Featuring Carl Perkins, Warren Smith, Billy Riley, and a stellar cast of musical pioneers. —*Hank Davis*

☆ **Sun Story** / Rhino 75884
This collection contains the work of the country and the rock artists discovered by Sun Records in Memphis during the '50s. Elvis Presley, Jerry Lee Lewis, Johnny Cash, Roy Orbison, Carl Perkins, Sonny Burgess, and others are featured. —*AMG*

○ **Super Bad** / 1991 / K-Tel 60112
An excellent collection of early-'70s funk that features Sly & the Family Stone, Parliament, the Isley Brothers, Kool & the Gang, War, Curtis Mayfield, Ohio Players, and James Brown on one disc. "Thank You (Falettinme Be Mice Elf Agin)," "Up for the Down Stroke," "Fight the Power," "Superfly," "Super Bad"—it doesn't get better than this. —*Stephen Thomas Erlewine*

☆ **Super Hits of the '70s: Have a Nice Day, Vol. 1** / Jan. 1990 / Rhino 70921
Rhino's ridiculously large (over 20 discs) series of the schlockiest pop hits of the '70s provides the definitive portrait of that decade's musical mainstream. Each of the volume contains at least two pop classics, but the most consistent volumes are 2, 5, and 14. —*Stephen Thomas Erlewine*

○ **Surf & Drag, Vol. 1** / 1989 / Sundazed 11003
All the great surf and hot-rod sides from the Challenge label. Features Gary Usher, the Four Speeds, the Knickerbockers, Jan & Dean, the Royal Coachmen, Donna Loren, and the Rhythm Rockers. Powerful genre material—this is as good as it gets. —*Cub Koda*

○ **Sweet Relief: Benefit for Victoria Williams** / Jul. 6, 1993 / CBS
Sweet Relief: A Benefit for Victoria Williams works better than most tribute albums because the quality of the performances match the quality of the songs. There's not a weak track to be found among the 15 songs, including stellar performances by Soul Asylum, Matthew Sweet, Buffalo Tom, Lou Reed, Lucinda Williams, the Jayhawks, Maria McKee, and a stunning version of "Crazy Mary" by Pearl Jam. —*AMG*

○ **A Taste of Doo-Wop, Vol. 1** / 1993 / Vee-Jay 709
No R&B label had more prolific doo-wop talent than Vee-Jay, which turned the fertile Chicago area into a goldmine in the '50s and early '60s. This 25-cut anthology contains a healthy sample and, thankfully, focuses on acts like the 5 Echoes, Orchids, Magnificents, and Rhythm Aces—fine ensembles that didn't score the huge hits of their contemporaries but made several solid records nonetheless. There are also acts that became bigger on other labels, like Sonny Till (spelled Til here) and his Orioles, the Pips (later Gladys Knight and the Pips), and a funky unreleased version of "The Twist" with the Midnighters (Hank Ballard and company). —*Ron Wynn*

○ **A Taste of Doo-Wop, Vol. 2** / 1993 / Vee-Jay 715
The second Vee-Jay various-artists anthology showcasing diverse doo-wop hits takes the same formula as its predecessor, featuring strong songs by more obscure acts rather than huge hits from established greats. The Kool Gents (a group that once included Dee Clark), Prodigals, Hi-Liters, and El Dorados, plus holdovers from volume 1 the Magnificents, 5 Echoes, and Impressions are on hand—providing 25 more examples of marvelous harmony singing, jump cuts, and swooning romantic ballads.—*Ron Wynn*

○ **Teenage Riot!** / Atomic Passion 1957
Insanely great rock & roll compilation centered around juvenile-delinquent themes and featuring promo drop-ins from teen-gang movies and anti-rock & roll sermons. Gene Maltais's "Gang War" is not to be missed. —*Cub Koda*

○ **Ten Years of Collectors Records** / White Label 8816
Highlights culled from a decade of issuing great rockabilly comps, this one features the Lonesome Drifters hit "Eager Boy" and Charles Dean's "Train Whistle Boogie" and "Parking in the Dark" as just some of the highlights. —*Cub Koda*

○ **Texas Kat Music** / Gulf Coast 102
A 15-track collection of rockabilly and rock & roll from the Texas-based Felco label. Cuts by Billy Taylor ("Wombie Zombie"), Irwin Russ ("Crazy Alligator"), and the Twisters (the awesome "Bandstand Rocket") are featured. —*Cub Koda*

☆ **That'll Flat Git It!, Vol. 2: Rockabilly From . . .** / 1992 / Bear Family 15623
A sterling collection of obscure rockabilly from the vaults of Decca Records. Both hardcore and casual rockabilly fans will find much to treasure in this wonderful package. —*AMG*

☆ **That'll Flat Git It!, Vol. 3: Rockabilly From . . .** / 1992 / Bear Family 15624

More raw rockabilly and country bop, this time from the vaults of Capitol Records. While the label had Gene Vincent and Esquerita, a quick listen to these will reveal rockabilly sounds—with the accent on the 'billy. Skeets McDonald's "You Ought a See Grandma Rock" goes a long way toward defining the compilation's strengths, and Tommy Sands, long thought of as a teen idol singing pop mush, stokes the fires here with "The Worryin' Kind" and "Playin' the Field." While Ferlin Husky masquerading as Simon Crum on "Bop Cat Bop," the Rio Rockers' "Mexicali Baby," and Bobby Lee Trammell's "You Mostest Girl" show the length and breadth of the genre, perhaps the most fascinating earful of all is the Louvin Brothers testing the waters of rockabilly with "Red Hen Hop" and "Cash on the Barrelhead." —*Cub Koda*

☆ **There's a Riot Goin' On!: Tthe Rock 'n' Roll Classics of Leiber & Stoller** / Rhino 70593

An amazing collection of 18 of Jerry Leiber and Mike Stoller's greatest hits, *There's a Riot Goin' On* contains classic tracks like Wilbert Harrison's "Kansas City," "Stand By Me," "Hound Dog," and "Jailhouse Rock." —*AMG*

These People Are Nuts / 1989 / IRS 13010

A fine overview of the greatest hits of I.R.S. Records. —*Dan Heilman*

○ **This Are Two Tone** / 1983 / Chrysalis 21745

The best of the neo-ska label of the early '80s, featuring the Specials, English Beat, and others. —*Dan Heilman*

☆ **Top of the Stax: Twenty Greatest Hits** / Stax 88005

Memphis Soul 101. *Top of the Stax* is the history of Stax in two concise volumes, tracing the music from the early hits of the Mar-Keys, Otis Redding, and Sam & Dave up to the major hits of the '70s. —*John Floyd*

○ **Treasure Chest of Musty Dusties, Vol. 1** / 196? / Fortune 8011

Twelve-song compilation (originally issued in the early '60s) featuring the best-known sides of the lesser-known Fortune Records vocal groups. Some of the best of Detroit's pre-Motown R&B era is presented here, the Swans' "Wedding Bells" being a particular highlight. —*Cub Koda*

○ **20 Hard to Find Motown Classics, Vol. 2** / Motown 9062

This second volume contains some not-so-rare tracks that remain ageless. —*Rick A. Bueche*

○ **20 Hard to Find Motown Classics, Vol. 1** / Motown 9061

A good set of superb but overlooked Motown singles. —*AMG*

★ **25 Hard to Find Motown Classics, Vol. 3** / 1986 / Motown 9069

The best of the *Hard to Find* series. —*Rick A. Bueche*

☆ **Two Tone Compilation: Checkered Past** / Nov. 16, 1993 / Chrysalis Records 27677

An essential double-disc set that provides all the greatest tracks from the seminal ska-revival record label, including classic singles by the Specials and the English Beat. —*AMG*

○ **The Unavailable 16 & the Original Nitty Gritty** / 1962 / Vee-Jay 708

This pair of early '60s albums from the Vee-Jay vaults has some interesting history. The first 16 numbers are old doo-wop tunes by such groups as the Quintones and El Dorados and single vocalists Harold Dorman and Tony Bellis. There's a good ratio of hits to flops, notably the Moonglows' "Secret Love" and "Angel Baby" by Rosie & the Originals, plus fine performances from the Dells, Spaniels, Impressions, and Magnificents. The other album has a mixed bag of pop, doo-wop, R&B and even blues, with a diverse artist list ranging from Roscoe Gordon and Harold Burrage

to Pee Wee Crayton, Eddie Taylor, Jerry Butler, and Joe Buckner. —*Ron Wynn*

Uptown MTV Unplugged / 1993 / MCA/Uptown 10858

New jack vocals are the main course on this latest entry in the unplugged sweepstakes, a collection featuring artists from MCA's Uptown label. Jodeci, Mary J. Blige, Father M. C., Christopher Williams, and Heavy D and the Boyz are the participants, with Jodeci and Williams in particular sounding energetic and animated, if at times a bit overwrought. Blige, who one might expect to dominate the proceedings, comes across more understated than expected, while Heavy D. turns in his customary mix of humor and hip-hop insolence, and Father M. C. does something that's in between balladry, rapping, and comedy. —*Ron Wynn*

○ **Vee-Jay Story, 1953-1993** / 1993 / Vee-Jay Limited Par 400

A definitive three-disc retrospective of the seminal R&B and blues record label. —*AMG*

WCBS FM-101 History of Rock: The Doo-wop Era, Part 2 / Collectables 2508

WCBS FM 101 History of Rock: Doo-Wop Era is a two-part anthology built around the old End, Gone, and Roulette catalogs, featuring Frankie Lymon and the Teenagers, the Chantels, and so on. The songs are good, but the sound quality is at times very rough—audiophiles beware. —*Bruce Eder*

○ **We Got a Party: Best of Ron Records, Vol. 1** / 1988 / Rounder 2076

There's something for R&B, blues, and soul fans of all persuasions on this anthology spotlighting various New Orleans artists that recorded for the Ron label in the late '50s and early '60s. There were celebrities like rollicking pianist Professor Longhair and the sultry soul queen Irma Thomas, country/rockabilly singers like Warren Lee, novelty specialist Chris Kenner, and shouters such as Bobby Mitchell. The 14 tracks on the CD are all good and most are wonderful—even if most of the singers never attained any recognition outside Crescent City R&B circles. —*Ron Wynn*

○ **West Coast Doo-Wop** / ACE 87

Nice collection of vocal group sides from the vaults of Modern Records. Arthur Lee Maye & the Crowns' "Loop-De-Loop-De-Loop" and "Oochie Pachie" are among the numerous highlights. —*Cub Koda*

○ **Wild Men Ride Wild Guitars** / 1991 / Sundazed 12001

Great rockabilly/hillbilly-boogie compilation of tracks from the vaults of Challenge Records. Highlights include Big Al Downing's "Down on the Farm" and Charlie Ryan's "Hot Rod Rocket." —*Cub Koda*

○ **Yellow Pills, Vol. 1** / 1994 / Big Deal

A dynamic power-pop collection featuring new and old tracks by some of the leading groups of the last ten years, including Dwight Twilley, the Shoes, the Rubinoos, and Tommy Keene. The music on *Yellow Pills* is strong enough to convert casual fans into hardcore power-pop fanatics. —*Stephen Thomas Erlewine*

○ **Yesterday's Heroes: '70s Teen Idols** / Rhino 71228

A collection of the lightweight pin-up stars of the '70s, *Yesterday's Heroes: '70s Teen Idols* is the perfect complement to Rhino's *Have a Nice Day Series*. It's some serious fun. —*AMG*

Zoo Rave 1 / 1992 / Zoo 11030

Zoo's two volumes of rave music are cursory introductions to the early '90s dance phenomenon, giving a good impression of the hard, relentless drive of the underground style. While *Zoo Rave* isn't definitive nor respected by hardcore rave fans, it's a worthwhile introduction for listeners unfamiliar with the subgenre. —*Stephen Thomas Erlewine*

REGGAE

"Reggae music is boring; it all sounds the same."

Those are fighting words in the torpid back alleys of Kingston, because nowhere on the face of the earth is there more recorded output per capita than on this Isle of Springs, where literally hundreds of 7-inch singles are released each week, in a staggering variety of styles. It started as the 60s dawned, when steamy-hot and ripe-for-revolution JA was about to oust its British master, and the music (ska) drove the engine of change – double-time, frenetic, and as un-yielding as a fully loaded cane truck on a hairpin turn. Ska turned to the half-time lope of rock-steady for a couple of years, producing some of the most lyrical and lasting musical mementos of the century, songs of freedom that will be chanted by sufferers I-ternally. Then reggae burst on the scene in 1968, and the world has never stopped listening.

Reggae is as close to a universal music as this receding century has – with superstars like Bob Marley, Peter Tosh, Jimmy Cliff, Toots and the Maytals, and other touring pioneers; with the cult classic movie "The Harder They Come" and a soundtrack that has never stopped selling; with the success of the annual Sunsplash extravaganzas in Montego Bay and their touring counterparts from Japan, Europe, and North America; and with major American labels turning gold and platinum with artists such as Ziggy Marley and Shabba Ranks.

Check it! Maori, Tongan, and Fiji Islanders put aside age-old battles to form a reggae band called Herbs; a Japanese boy toasts (raps) in the rattle-blasted patter of a Kingston speed-rapper; Havasupai Indians at the foot of the Grand Canyon regard Marley as a prophet and display his picture in their homes; Poland's top ethnic fiddler joins a Twinkle Brother for a Polski hoedown/dub showdown, while at the shipyards in Gdansk, 10,000 people (most in red, gold, and green clothing) cheer an eight-hour reggae festival; and Aboriginals form a protest group whose chosen rhythm of resistance is reggae, calling themselves No Fixed Address. Reggae is triumphant, the irresistible heartbeat call to consciousness, the call of the LA rioters – "No Justice, No Peace!"

It is a call that can be as deep and spooky as a bad dream; as lopey and leering as Red Foxx after hours; ethereal and eternal – the true new Psalms; as understated as a pause and as robust as a rocket. This is the music of the Movement of Jah People, future folk who know God is a living man and paradise is right here right now. It is Jah love made manifest, not fe de weakheart, and definitely not boring.

– Roger M. Steffens

Abyssinians

Group / Reggae
Dreadly serious purveyors of praise-filled Rastafarian religious music, this superb trio began by writing and recording "Satta Massagana" in 1969. The song became a heavily covered standard. Although their output has been spotty, the group is still active. —*Roger Steffens*

● **Forward** / 1982 / Alligator 8305
"Satta" and other hymns for the hearticle. —*Roger Steffens*

Laurel Aitken

Ska, ska-revival
Though born in Cuba, Laurel Aitken played a pivotal role in bringing Jamaican music to international attention. He moved to Jamaica from Cuba in the '50s, then went to England in the '60s. Aitken's recording "Boogie in My Bones" was the first Jamaican single issued in England in 1958. Aitken's debut Bluebeat label release, "Boogey Rock," was released two years later. More important, his evolution from an imitative R&B vocalist to a premier ska and reggae singer influenced many ska, bluebeat, and reggae vocalists. Aitken recorded hundreds of singles, ranging from incendiary protest to sentimental romance and crass sexual innuendo. He continued performing with his band The Full Circle well into the '80s. —*Ron Wynn*

● **Rasta Man Power** / ROIR 205
Laurel Aitken was one of the pioneers of the bluebeat sound, as ska was called in '60s England. His vocals blend soulfulness with a touch of grit while his backing musicians kick out thumping, horn-powered ska. The bulk of this collection was originally recorded between 1960 and 1971, but even the two tracks from 1990 boast a rootsy feel. Because many of the original master tapes have vanished, vinyl copies were used for this cassette. Aitken himself selected the songs to be included here. – *Mark J. Cadigan, Roundup newsletter*

Dennis Alcapone (Dennis Smith)

b. Aug. 6, 1947, Clarendon, Jamaica
Ska
Dennis Alcapone became a dominant toaster-DJ during the early '70s, using a style similar to U-Roy's, though it was neither as fast nor as clever. Alcapone worked with such top producers as Prince Tony and Keith Hudson. Alcapone also recorded for many labels including Studio One and Treasure Isle. Alcapone's popularity began to dip when toasters praising Jah and decrying political, social, and moral injustices began winning the audience's hearts and minds and those doing comedic and novelty tunes were losing favor. Alcapone moved to England but also found the going there tough. Despite teaming with Bunny Lee on such records as *Investigator Rock* and *Six Million Dollar Man*, Alcapone was a non-factor by the end of the '70s. —*Ron Wynn*

● **Universal Rockers** / RAS 3221
Toaster-DJ Dennis Alcapone was at his humorous, barbed, and bizarre best on this collection of '70s material. His style was often near mirror imitation of Big Youth's, but he was also at his performing peak during this period. —*Ron Wynn*

Roland Alphonso

b. 1936, Jamaica
Tenor sax, flute / Reggae
A fine saxophonist with a rubbery tone and catchy sound, Roland Alphonso was a prolific studio musician during the '60s and a founding member of the Skatalites. During the group's existence, Alphonso's solos were prominently featured on several Studio One and Treasure Isle hits, including "Phoenix City," "Blackberry Brandy," "The President," and "Crime Wave." The Skatalites worked extensively through the ska and rock-steady eras before disbanding. Alphonso has recorded as a leader for Studio One and Wackies. In the mid '80s he assembled a revamped Skatalites that appeared at the 1984 Sunsplash. —*Ron Wynn*

Reggae Sax / Rohit 7781
Tasty jazz-tinged sax solos and smart, aggressive playing highlight this collection featuring one of Jamaica's premier studio musicians. —*Ron Wynn*

Bob Andy

Vocals / Reggae
An early member of the mid '60s Paragons (famed for "Tide Is High"), Bob Andy has written some of Jamaica's most lasting songs, such as "Desperate Lover" and "Feeling Soul." With Marcia Griffiths, he hit the UK Top Ten in the early '70s. Andy is a strong, lyrical singer of powerful love songs and incisive social statements. His "Fire Burning" became one of 1992's most-used rhythms. —*Roger Steffens*

● **Retrospective** / 1986 / Heartbeat 32
A fine overview of a sorely overlooked reggae vocalist, composer, arranger, and session singer. —*Ron Wynn*

○ **Song Book** / 1988 / Studio One 1121
Among Coxsone Dodd's most important albums ever, virtually every cut a classic. —*Roger Steffens*

Horace Andy

b. Jamaica
Reggae
An animated, often compelling tenor vocalist, Horace Andy was featured on many '70s reggae hits. These included "Love of a Woman" and "You Are My Angel." He made his recording debut in the mid '60s, then left the music scene to sharpen his skills. Upon his return in 1970, Andy's popularity rose as he recorded for Studio One, Crystal, Santic, Randy's, Ja-Man, Channel One, and Jackpot. Andy later moved to America and established his own label. A prolific composer as well as a singer, Andy scored an international hit in 1980 when Tapper Zukie produced "Natty Dread A Weh She Want," recorded during a brief return trip to Jamaica. Andy issued several albums and LPs during the '80s and '90s, the most recent being *Rude Boy* for Shanachie in 1993. —*Ron Wynn*

Best of Horace Andy / Liberty 51159

Aswad

Group / Reggae
These three longtime UK singers and musicians started hard in the '70s but failed to break through commercially. By the end of the '80s, their sweet-soul/pop/reggae soared in the UK charts, but they lost their roots authenticity in the process. Their earliest work, however, reverberates still. —*Roger Steffens*

Aswad / 1976 / Mango 539399
Their leadoff album that established the group's sound. —*Ron Wynn*

Live & Direct / 1983 / Mango 539723
This compiles several group favorites. A solid live outing. —*Ron Wynn*

○ **Rebel Souls** / 1984 / Mango 539780
Good covers of Marvin Gaye and Toots Hibbert classics. —*Ron Wynn*

○ **New Chapter** / 1984 / CBS 32473
Aswad made its debut on Columbia (British division) with this 1981 release. It marked a musical shift as keyboardist Tony Gad (aka Tony Robinson) moved to bass, replacing the departed George Oban. The songs were well produced and exuberantly performed, and there was a good mix between fiery uptempo tunes and passionate love songs. —*Ron Wynn*

○ **To the Top** / 1986 / Mango 539866
Contains the wonderful single "Bubbling" and good vocal harmonies. —*Ron Wynn*

● **Crucial Tracks—The Best of Aswad** / 1989 / Mango 539833
The best collection for both fans and novices. —*Ron Wynn*

Buju Banton

Reggae
The style of this contemporary dancehall star accents the lewd, sex-dominated approach favored by '90s acts. Banton also mines the hip-hop/reggae field, incorporating production elements and influences from rap into his material. He triggered a firestorm of protests with widely quoted homophobic remarks in 1993. His CD *Voice of Jamaica* was among the most popular major label reggae releases of '93. —*Ron Wynn*

Voice of Jamaica / 1993 / Mercury
Growling, gravelly-voiced toaster Buju Banton has gained notoriety for some foolish homophobic statements. His recent Mercury release contains entertaining "slack" material such as *Good Body* and *Willy (Don't Be Silly)* and respectable social commentary with *Deportees (Things Change)* and *No Respect*. But Banton is not that creative or imaginative a wordsmith, and once the delivery wears thin, the lightness of his sentiments becomes acute. The single *A Little More Time* features a great soulful vocal from the criminally underrated Beres Hammond. For the most part, this is a competently produced and performed major label dancehall. —*Ron Wynn*

Big Youth

b. 1952, Jamaica
Vocals / Reggae
In the early '70s, no toaster (the Jamaican word for rapper) was bigger than Big Youth. His choice of cuts over which to chat was always impeccable, and he had multiple entries in the Jamaican Top Ten. From a whisper to a scream, hearing him even once explains why he was Bob Marley's favorite DJ. —*Roger Steffens*

★ **Natty Cultural Dread** / 1976 / Trojan 123
A definitive early-period album from this reggae toaster. A must for every reggae lover. —*Michael G. Nastos*

○ **Dreadlocks Dread** / 1976 / Frontline 1682
An outstanding set of early material, with the spotlight on their compositional prowess. —*Ron Wynn*

○ **Hit the Road Jack** / 1983 / Trojan 137
One to own. —*Michael G. Nastos*

● **Excellent Skank—The Best of Big Youth** / 1983 / Trojan 189
A tremendous anthology containing early, out-of-print singles and album cuts. —*Ron Wynn*

A Luta Continua / 1984 / Heartbeat 28
Songs of the '80s' worldwide struggle—sung, not toasted. —*Roger Steffens*

○ **Chanting Dread Inna Fine Style, The** / 1985 / Heartbeat 08
Originally released in 1982 and now available on CD, this captures Big Youth's unique chanting style in conjunction with the smoother backing vocals of Gregory Isaacs, Dennis Brown, and the Heptones. Big Youth addresses poverty, healing, and salvation in his original tunes and a reworked version of War's "The World Is a Ghetto" entitled "Streets in Africa." Providing roots reggae atmospheres and occasional dub effects are solid musicians such as bassist George Fullwood, drummers Carlton "Santa" Davis and the late Carlton Barrett, guitarist Earl "Chinna" Smith, and keyboardists Earl "Wire" Lindo and Augustus Pablo. —*Mark J. Cadigan, Roundup newsletter*

Black Uhuru

b. Jamaica
Group / Reggae
By 1992, Black Uhuru (Black Sounds of Freedom) had gone through six distinct incarnations, the only common factor being Duckie Simpson, their dreadly serious harmonist and sometime composer. Founded in the mid '70s, the group hit their key period in the early '80s with a charismatically scowling lead singer named Michael Rose, who remade his classic "Dreadlocks Coming . . . " as "Guess Who's Coming to Dinner." A fearsome prowler onstage with a Far East style of roots warbling, Rose was often touted as the "next Bob Marley," an observation that has ruined the career of many a lesser performer.

The militancy of the group was enhanced by an African-American woman with a Masters degree from Columbia University, Puma Jones, whose wavy-armed dancing and high, chromatic harmonies echoed the communal gatherings she had witnessed while working in Mama Africa. Add to this the essential underpinnings of rhythm twins Sly & Robbie, who were considered equal members of the group while Rose was aboard, and you have the quintessential reggae lineup of the post-Marley era and reggae's first-ever Grammy winners. However, internal problems and dissatisfaction with their record label broke up that lineup.

Music Map

Reggae

SKA

Jamaica's first indigenous music,
a double-horn-driven amalgam
of R&B shuffle, Nyabinghi, calypso,
Afro-Cuban, pocomania, jazz, and rock & roll.
Skatalites, Byron Lee, Prince Buster,
Toots & the Maytals,
Desmond Dekker, Laurel Aitken

SKA REVIVAL

UK Skinheads in late 60s
(Judge Dread) UK
Two-Tone movement 1980
(Specials, Selector, Madness)
US, Japan, Europe currently

ROCK-STEADY 1966-1968

Half-speed ska: trombone replaced by piano
and prominent bass. More conscious lyrics.
Concern with harmonies, particularly in trios
like Heptones, Gaylads, Dominoes,
Aces, Wailers. Also Alton Ellis and Ken Boothe

REGGAE 1968 – present

Off-beat, sensuously slowed rhythm.
Lyrics marked by religious and
political concerns, often with a
Rastafarian religious underpinning.
Wailers, Lee Perry, Jimmy Cliff,
Gregory Isaacs, Black Uhuru,
Burning Spear, Sly & Robbie

DUB ca. 1969 – present

Instrumental reggae.
Pure dub is a rhythm track
with a bit of special effects.
A dub version interpolates bits of
the vocal. From the early
70s, nearly all JA 7-inch records
had a vocal on the A side and
a dub instrumental version
of the same song on the B side.
King Tubby, Lee Perry,
Augustus Pablo, Adrian Sherwood,
Mad Professor, Scientist

DJ late 60s – present

Over a dub track, rappers
(called "toasters" in JA)
would chat lyrics of topical timely concern.
The form began live at sound-system
dances, eventually leading to the
recording of toasts on disc.
U-Roy, Big Youth, I Roy,
Dennis Alcapone

LOVERS ROCK early 70s – present

Primarily a UK-fostered style;
secular, mostly romantic concerns sung
over a reggae rhythm,
but divorced from reggae's
lyrical emphasis on social justice
and Rasta.
John Holt, Maxi Priest

DUB POETRY

Mutabaruka, Linton Kwesi Johnson

RAGGAMUFFIN (DANCEHALL)

DJ or "sing-jay" material, half sung, half rap,
often dealing with bawdy ("slack") themes.
Primarily heard in the dancehalls.
Yellowman, Shabba Ranks

A surprisingly strong resolve to continue the group was apparent in 1986's *Brutal*, featuring new lead singer Junior Reid. Eventually, visa problems sidelined Reid and Jones died of cancer. But coming full circle, the three original members joined together to take the group to a new level.

The current lineup is composed of solo star Don Carlos (whose style is hauntingly similar to Reid's and Rose's), Duckie Simpson, and former Wailing Soul Garth Dennis, demonstrating that the Black Uhuru concept could be successfully molded to fit almost anyone willing to give voice to these Black sounds of freedom and righteous indignation. —*Roger Steffens*

★ **Sinsemilla** / 1980 / Mango 539593
An outstanding set that helped break them in the States. —*Ron Wynn*

Black Sounds of Freedom / 1981 / Shanachie 48005
A reissued remix of the early *Love Crisis* album. —*Ron Wynn*

☆ **Red** / 1981 / Mango 539625
This album is a landmark release, one of the great reggae sessions of the '80s. —*Ron Wynn*

○ **Chill Out** / 1982 / Mango 539752
Superb Sly & Robbie backing—dark, haunting, and bare. —*Roger Steffens*

Tear It Up / 1982 / Mango 9696
A strong live date, though an overly familiar selection. —*Ron Wynn*

Dub Factor, The / 1983 / Mango 539756
A great dub date. —*Ron Wynn*

Reggae Greats / 1985 / Mango 539791
An adequate collection of past hits. —*Ron Wynn*

Brutal / 1986 / RAS 3015
Black Uhuru's late '80s trio didn't garner that much crossover attention or the publicity of earlier editions but was equally outstanding from the standpoint of content and performance. While Sly Dunbar and Robbie Shakespeare's production embraced the computerized mode, Junior Reid's lead vocals were as dynamic and explosive as those of former lead singer Michael Rose, and the occasional leads and sparkling harmonies of Puma Jones and Duckie Simpson were expertly incorporated into the mix. *Brutal* included strong message tracks in the title tune; "Conviction or a Fine" and "Vision," good love/romantic fare; and a fine spiritual number, "Dread In the Mountain." In addition, "Great Train Robbery" was as frenetic as any Black Uhuru single and should have been a bigger international hit. —*Ron Wynn*

Brutal Dub / 1986 / RAS 3020
This dub version of Black Uhuru's 1986 *Brutal* benefited from a great mixing job by Scientist, whose snaking patterns and boosting of Robbie Shakespeare's bass illuminated the appeal of the original production and songs. Even those who find dub unappealing or distracting should be hooked by this fine release. —*Ron Wynn*

Now / 1990 / Mesa Blue Moon 79021
A more recent session. —*Ron Wynn*

Now Dub / 1990 / Mesa Blue Moon 79022
Dub one more time. —*Ron Wynn*

○ **Iron Storm** / 1991 / Mesa Blue Moon 79035
The latest from this anthemic ensemble. —*Ron Wynn*

● **Liberation—The Island Anthology** / Sep. 21, 1993 / Mango
With remastering and carefully chosen tracks, this two-disc anthology is essential for fans and newcomers alike. A perfect starting point. —*Chris Woodstra*

Alpha Blondy

b. 1953, Dimbokora, Cote d'Ivoire
Vocals / Reggae

An Ivory Coast native whose name means "First Bandit," Blondy was one of Africa's biggest stars in the '80s. His initial album, *Jah Glory*, sold a million copies in Africa. He dresses as a Rasta, wears a Star of David, carries a Bible and Koran. He sings in Arabic in Israel and in Hebrew in the Arab world. Wailers-like music with African accents. —*Roger Steffens*

Jerusalem / Shanachie 43054
Blondy sings in Arabic, Hebrew, French, English, and many African languages in an effort to reach as many people as possible. On this disc, one of his most popular titles, he's backed by the Wailers (sans Bob Marley) for a simmering, roots-heavy session. —*J. Poet*

○ **Jah Glory** / 1983 / Moya 387101
Alpha Blondy's smash-hit first album with an all-local band, the Natty Rebels, had all the accessibility and directness that made him an international star. Two cuts are agreeable reggae in English; the rest is Afro reggae and a lot more interesting for that. In some ways Blondy's music is typical of the Ivory Coast: light, accomplished, and geared to a regional rather than local audience. —*John Storm Roberts*

○ **Cocody Rock!!!** / 1984 / Shanachie 64011
Though the notes don't tell you so, *Cocody Rock* is a rerelease of Blondy's 1984 second album, recorded in Paris and Kingston with a mix of African and Jamaican musicians (plus Kassav's Jocelyne Beroard on backup vocals!) Presuperstar Blondy, with the freshness you'd expect from somebody pretty much just starting out. He sure believes in touching all bases!
Blondy's best-selling African album. —*J. Poet*

○ **Apartheid Is Nazism** / 1985 / Shanachie 43042
This is Blondy's most militant statement, and a continent-wide hit. —*J. Poet*

○ **Prophets, The** / 1989 / Capitol 91793
Blondy's first international release under a new worldwide contract with EMI. It's as soulful and militant as past efforts, with an added gloss to the production that may win new listeners. —*J. Poet*

● **Best of Alpha Blondy, The** / 1990 / Shanachie 43075
This disc lives up to its title with hits like "Jerusalem," "Cocody Rock," and "Apartheid Is Nazism." —*J. Poet*

Yami Bolo (Rolando McLean)

Dance

Yami Bolo emerged as a popular reggae and dancehall artist in the '80s. He began working for the Youth Promotion sound system, then performed with Stur-Mas and Third World. Winston Riley tabbed him for the Techniques label, and Bolo cut three singles for Techniques in the mid '80s. Although he recorded extensively with Sugar Minott, none of the tracks they did were ever issued. Bolo made an LP with Junior Delgado and another with Augustus Pablo before his debut Heartbeat CD *He Who Feels It Knows It* in 1989. Unlike many of his contemporaries, Bolo hasn't disdained political or protest music; both his debut and second release *Up Life Street* contain fiery message tracks alongside softer love tunes and dance cuts. —*Ron Wynn*

● **Ransom** / Shanachie 47003

Cedella Marley Booker

Vocals / Reggae

Bob Marley's mother. Hear this big-voiced one-of-a-kind gospel-reggae singer, and you'll know instantly where Bob got his power. —*Roger Steffens*

● **Awake Zion** / 1990 / Rykodisc 10204
As was her son Bob Marley, the "Grandmother of Reggae" is a strong Rastafarian. In the fullness of her years she speaks to her sorrow as a mother separated from her child—for instance, in "Mother Don't Cry"—and of consolation, resolution, strength, and faith. Here she fulfills Bob Marley's request that she should sing, in an impressive album complete with many original songs combining reggae and gospel styles, with backup by many members of the Wailers. Originally released under the title *Redemption Songs*. —*Ladyslipper*

Ken Boothe

b. 1948, Kingston, Jamaica
Vocals / Rock steady, reggae

Dubbed "Mr. Rock-steady" in the mid '60s by legendary producer Coxsone Dodd, this hard-belting crooner had some of that genre's biggest hits. His career has spanned the past 30 years, and his style is rooted in the Jamaican fundamentalism called "pocomania" but mixed with a touch of Otis Redding. His cover of Bread's "Everything I Own" hit number 1 on the UK pop charts. —*Roger Steffens*

● **Live Good** / 1978 / United Artists 801
Coxsone sessions including the hits "Moving Away," "Live Good," and "Thinking." —*Roger Steffens*

Call Me / Rohit 7763
One of reggae and Jamaican music's finest pure singers. —*Ron Wynn*

Brigadier Jerry

Vocals / Dance, reggae, DJ

A speed-rapping pioneer, "Briggy" was the featured toaster of the Jah Love sound system run by an uptown Rasta organization called the Twelve Tribes that counted Bob Marley among its membership. His raps are invariably cultural, not slack (bawdy), and he ruled the mid '80s DJ clashes in Jamaica. —*Roger Steffens*

● **Jamaica Jamaica** / 1985 / RAS 3012
His first album, featuring some of his best-known toasts. —*Roger Steffens*

Peter Broggs

Vocals / Reggae

An '80s rootsman, better known in the US than home in Jamaica, Broggs has become a convincing singer thanks to strong support from his US label, RAS. —*Roger Steffens*

○ **Rastafari Liveth!** / 1982 / RAS 3001

● **Reasoning** / 1990 / RAS 3051
A fine, aware collection. Broggs is backed by the Wailers and Roots Radics. —*Roger Steffens*

Dennis Brown

b. 1957, Kingston, Jamaica
Vocals / Reggae

Often referred to as "Emmanuel, the Crown Prince of Reggae," Dennis Brown was Bob Marley's favorite singer. He was 13 when his career began, recording initially (and typically) for Coxsone Dodd, scoring big with a 1968 cover of the Impressions' "No Man Is an Island." In the '70s he made a series of exciting albums for Joe Gibbs and had a UK hit with his classic "Money in My Pocket." From 1977 to 1982 he recorded for Joe Gibbs, in his peak period producing such classics as "Revolution," "Have You Ever Been Lonely (Have You Ever Been Blue)," "The Promised Land," and "Sitting and Watching." A live album was cut in Montreux in 1979, a year after he was featured in the film *Heartland Reggae*. With a no-nonsense, straight-ahead style, Brown is capable of wrapping a love song in a crooning caress or inciting a crowd (as he did memorably at the 1983 Sunsplash in Montego Bay) to heights of uncontrolled hysteria. He continues to be one of Jamaica's classiest and most riveting performers. —*Roger Steffens*

○ **Super Hits** / 1972 / Trojan 57
Although only a complete reggae novice would need any convincing, here's a set that displays the lyric mastery and soulful-

ness that have made Dennis Brown a legend since his days as a youthful star. —*Ron Wynn*

○ **Visions** / 1977 / Shanachie 44002
Wonderful work from Brown. —*Ron Wynn*

○ **Words of Wisdom** / 1979 / Shanachie 44004
Outstanding. —*Ron Wynn*

● **20 Classic Reggae Tracks** / 1985 / Meteor 002
Another special collection intended for the casual or novice buyer rather than the hardcore fan, but it's an opportunity to get some seminal Dennis Brown material on one CD. Otherwise, grab the entire albums from which these songs were culled to get their full and accurate context. —*Ron Wynn*

History / 1986 / Live & Love 009
Despite some pro forma nods to Jah, Brown was one of the first of the post-Rasta wave. In this album he used a mellow late-reggae style to put over the new word of dancehall music—"We Should Make Love," "Dance All Night"—and the rest of the party-time ethos. —*John Storm Roberts, Original Music*

Slow Down / 1987 / Shanachie 48017
Good-to-great leads. —*Ron Wynn*

Greatest Hits / 1988 / Rohit 7709
An arguable title, but no problems otherwise. —*Ron Wynn*

○ **Inseparable** / 1988 / VP 7
Simply stunning. —*Ron Wynn*

My Time / Jan. 1989 / Rohit 7713
Keeps things at a generally high level. —*Ron Wynn*

Good Vibrations / May 1989 / Rohit 77500
A harder edge and tone. —*Ron Wynn*

○ **Unchallenged** / 1990 / VP 1115
The songs, production, and arrangements on this album are all first-rate. —*Ron Wynn*

Over Proof / 1991 / Shanachie 43086
Uniformly excellent. Exuberant, passionate vocals. —*Ron Wynn*

Go Now / Jun. 1991 / Rohit 77960
Another fine session. —*Ron Wynn*

Hold Tight / Live & Learn 021
Since he was a child star in Jamaica, Dennis Brown's golden voice has been among the island's most evocative and striking, regardless of lyric content or musical setting. This mid '80s date featured him doing gorgeous love ballads and probing message tracks with sensitive, laidback production that had instrumental backing underlining Brown's svelte vocals without intruding on his frequently brilliant leads. Al Campbell joined him on "I've Got Your Number," a fine performance that saw both vocalists soaring and uniting on a tune that was convincing, neither trite nor overly sentimental. Brown, like Gregory Isaacs and a few others, seems to cut an album a day, but most are decent, some above average, and a few exceptional. By Brown's standards this fell in the above-average category, which meant that it was excellent by almost all other singers' criteria despite its brevity (35 minutes). —*Ron Wynn*

Victory Is Mine / RAS 3072
This session released in 1991 includes a skillful remake of "Sea of Love" and has stirring romantic material ("Call Me," "We Are in Love," and "Sunday Morning"), plus competent, though not great, roots and message tunes ("Jah Can Do It," "Victory Is Mine"). With Brown you'll never get anything less than solid vocals; the trick is whether he sings up or down to the material. On this one, the ratio of stirring to detached performances makes it well worth hearing. —*Ron Wynn*

Burning Spear (Winston Rodney)

Group / Reggae
Winston Rodney took his stage name from Jomo Kenyatta, hero of Kenyan independence. "The Spear," as he is called, first recorded in 1969 for Coxsone Dodd. Those productions, collected six years later on a pair of Studio One albums, were lean, mysterious, and way ahead of their time: a similar sound would sweep Jamaica in the late '70s and be dubbed the "rockers" style. Not meeting much initial success, Spear retreated to his rural home in St. Ann's, in the northern coastal hills of Jamaica. Eventually he returned in 1975 as part of a self-named trio for producer Jack Ruby. This time the world woke up, and Spear was recognized as a major figure. After two albums Spear dismissed his backing

trio, journeyed to London, and cut one of the most astonishing live reggae sets ever for Island, with whom he recorded until 1980. That same year he was featured unforgettably in an a cappella performance of "Jah No Dead" in the reggae movie *Rockers.* Since then he has skipped through several major and minor labels, returning in 1990 to Island.

Spear is one of those artists whose style is so immediately recognizable that those who liked him from the start seem to have followed his every move with joy. He is similar to a trance singer, especially in his horn-lofted live performances, whirling around the stage with arms outstretched, a dreadlocked dervish chanting of dark carnal nights of captivity and imminent deliverance. By the end of his best shows he is often repeating phrases in delicious delirium, reaching the higher heights ("irie ites") that is reggae and Rasta's promised land. Without question, Spear is one of reggae's greats. —*Roger Steffens*

★ **Marcus Garvey** / 1975 / Mango 539377
A reggae cornerstone. The most focused and musically exhilarating tribute to Marcus Garvey, a recurring theme in his music. —*John Floyd*

Garvey's Ghost / 1976 / Mango 9382
A pulsating dub version of his album *Marcus Garvey.* —*John Floyd*

○ **Man in the Hills** / 1976 / Mango 539412
Nearly repeating the success of his debut, through a wide-ranging array of topics and a sturdy groove. —*John Floyd*

☆ **Live** / 1977 / Mango 539513
Aswad backs Spear's solo debut, one of reggae's greatest ever live sets. —*Roger Steffens*

○ **Dry & Heavy** / 1977 / Mango 539431
Originally released in 1977, *Dry and Heavy* finds Burning Spear in fine form—vocally, lyrically, and musically. Winston Rodney's incantatory vocals mesmerize on cuts like "Throw Down Your Arms" and "Any River." He's backed up by some of the best reggae musicians in the business, including bassists Robbie Shakespeare and Aston "Family Man" Barrett, drummer Leroy "Horsemouth" Wallace, guitarist Earl "Chinna" Smith, keyboardist Earl "Wire" Lindo, and tenor saxophonist "Dirty Harry" Hall. This is compelling, message-laden roots reggae full of potent but seductive grooves. —*Mark J. Cadigan, Roundup newsletter*

★ **Harder Than the Best** / 1979 / Mango 539567
A magnificent career overview that includes every highlight from Spear's canon. The best songs from otherwise turgid albums. —*John Floyd*

Hail H.I.M. / 1980 / Radic 2003
This '80 date had no American distribution and was only briefly available as an import. It contains the kind of undiluted, furious leads only Rodney could provide on such cuts as "Columbus," "Follow Marcus Garvey," and "Cry Blood Africans." Heartbeat deserves the highest possible praise for unearthing it. —*Ron Wynn*

○ **Farover** / 1982 / Heartbeat 22
Some superb compositions and searing vocals. —*Ron Wynn*

○ **Fittest of the Fittest, The** / 1983 / Heartbeat 22
Taut production, memorable leads from Winston Rodney. —*Ron Wynn*

○ **Resistance** / 1985 / Heartbeat 33
A great pairing of Rodney vocals and horn section. A Grammy nominee, this boasts the added bonus of a wonderful nonpolitical piece, "Love to You." —*Ron Wynn*

People of the World / 1987 / Slash 25524
A nice debut on a major label not known for reggae. This release also includes eclectic material and a female horn section. —*Ron Wynn*

○ **100th Anniversary: Marcus Garvey + Garvey's Ghost** / 1987 / 539377

○ **Mek We Dweet** / 1990 / Mango 539863
Spear makes a triumphant return to the label where he started his international career. —*Ron Wynn*

○ **Jah Kingdom** / 1992 / Mango 539915
Burning Spear remains one of reggae's most rooted bands, planted firmly in the traditional Rastafarian spiritualism from which reggae music was born. While other reggae artists encroach upon the topical mainstream, Winston Rodney and the Burning Band continue to sing praises to Jah Rastafari, Jamaica,

and freedom on their newest, *Jah Kingdom*. Complete with horns, politics, religion, and Rodney's classic vocals, the disc also includes "Estimated Prophet," Burning Spear's seven-minute Grateful Dead cover originally released on the Dead tribute album *Deadicated. —Erin Ryan, Roundup newsletter*

Don Carlos & Gold

Vocals / Reggae

A founding member of Black Uhuru and an outstanding "sweet" vocalist, Don Carlos has been an international reggae star since the '70s. He's recorded for Roots, Greensleeves, Negus Roots, Ras, Empire, and several other labels as a solo performer as well as with the group Gold. Carlos, Rudolph Dennis, and Derrick Simpson were the original Black Uhuru, but this trio made only one single for Top Cat, "Folk Song," before disbanding. Carlos rejoined Black Uhuru along with Dennis for the CD *Now* in 1990. Their most recent release was *Iron Storm* for Mesa in 1994. — *Ron Wynn*

● **Just a Passing Glance** / 1972 / RAS 3008
One of reggae's finest "sweet" vocalists, Don Carlos's earnestness and sincerity overcome sometimes overwrought and sentimental material. He was more forceful on the message cuts. —*Ron Wynn*

Charlie Chaplin

Reggae

● **Two Sides of Charlie Chaplin** / RAS 3043
If there's such a thing as the Rasta equivalent to a rowdy Knights of Columbus lodge meeting, Chaplin, the Roots Radics, and the crowd assembled to witness and cheer on this live-in-the-studio project have succeeded at capturing it. For those living too far away to catch live reggae anytime soon, this may be as good a surrogate as you'll find. —*Jamie Lee Rake, Option*

○ **20 Super Hits** / SONICSOU 003
Toaster/DJ Charlie Chaplin dispenses wit and wisdom on a variety of subjects on this anthology covering his most popular singles. Most were done for small Jamaican labels, with sound and production quality varying appropriately. —*Ron Wynn*

Johnny Clarke

b. Jan. 1955, Jamaica
Vocals / Reggae
A crucial '70s vocalist, Clarke made some of his biggest marks for producer Bunny Lee, especially "Enter into His Gates with Praise." His numerous cover versions often outstripped the originals, and he is acknowledged as one of the great unknown masters of Jamaican singing. —*Roger Steffens*

○ **Enter into His Gates** / 1975 / Attack 1015
Mid '70s tracks, mixed by virtuoso King Tubby. Gripping. —*Roger Steffens*

● **20 Massive Hits** / 1985 / Striker Lee 110
A superb and soulful vocalist, Johnny Clarke never sounds less than inspired on this anthology. The cuts range from evocative to commonplace, the lyrics from enlightening to clichéd, humorous to vulgar. —*Ron Wynn*

Reggae Archives / 1991 / Gong Sounds 70025
An up-to-the-second production that brings well-deserved exposure to the mellifluous Mr. C. A real winner with 16 cuts. —*Roger Steffens*

○ **Authorised Rockers** / Jul. 26, 1991 / Frontline 1866
Another great pure singer, adept at soul, reggae, or lovers-rock styles. —*Ron Wynn*

Jimmy Cliff (James Chambers)

b. 1948, St. Catherine, Jamaica
Vocals / Reggae, soul
The first artist in Leslie Kong's groundbreaking Beverly's label stable in 1962, Jimmy Cliff has been a figure of major influence in the internationalization of Jamaican music for 30 years. Bob Dylan called Cliff's late '60s hit "Vietnam" the best protest song he ever heard. Hearing that same tune led Paul Simon to travel to Kingston; book the same rhythm section, engineer, and studio; and record "Mother and Child Reunion," the first Yankee reggae song ever. Despite a number of ska hits and an Island Records contract in 1967, it wasn't until he was recruited to act in Perry Henzell's rollickingly hypnotic film *The Harder They Come* that

Cliff achieved true stardom. He sang a number of his own compositions in the movie, including "Many Rivers to Cross," "Sitting in Limbo," and the title track, three standards that helped make the soundtrack album one of the biggest sellers in reggae history. The follow-up albums, however, were generally unfocused, their spotty material spoiling Cliff's bid to become reggae's main exponent, a gap rushed into and filled brilliantly by Bob Marley. By 1976, Cliff had regrouped and enlisted Wailers tutor Joe Higgs to be his bandleader. A yearly stream of albums followed, with songs as good as anything he had ever recorded ("Beyond the Boundaries," "Bongo Man"); and Cliff became a mainstay on the international festival and touring circuit, achieving huge fame in places like Nigeria, where he keeps a second home. Cliff's style is a high, almost gospel plaint, with a keen rhythmic sense that echoes Africa as well as R&B. A concert film, *Bongo Man*, was released around 1980 as Cliff looked unsuccessfully for the proper vehicle to follow up on the worldwide penetration of *The Harder They Come*. Cliff, a father figure to several generations of young musicians, can still be counted on to deliver thoroughly professional shows and recordings. —*Roger Steffens*

○ **Wonderful World, Beautiful People** / 1970 / A&M 3189
Contains the Cliff anthem "Vietnam." —*William Ruhlmann*

★ **Harder They Come, The** / 1972 / Mango 9202
Jimmy Cliff starred in this gritty film about street life in Kingston, Jamaica. The album is a brilliant compilation of early reggae music, and Cliff's own songs. "You Can Get It If You Really Want It," "Many Rivers to Cross," "The Harder They Come," and "Sitting in Limbo," are among the best of a very good lot. —*William Ruhlmann*

○ **Struggling Man** / 1973 / Mango 539235
Though not as well regarded nor as vocally spectacular as *The Harder They Come*, this was nevertheless some outstanding early Jimmy Cliff material. The title cut was especially strong, and there were also some good ballads. —*Ron Wynn*

Hanging Fire / 1987 / CBS 40845
Cliff has long since been eclipsed by other reggae stars, but this later release shows him effectively mixing his own quick-step version of the music with general pop trends. —*William Ruhlmann*

Reggae Greats / 1991 / Mango 539794
This is a good overview of his hits, including "Vietnam," "The Harder They Come," "Many Rivers to Cross," and "Struggling Man." —*Scott Bultman*

Culture

Group / Reggae
The gritty vocal textures and poetic invocations that characterize lead singer Joseph "Culture" Hill's genius are evident in all his work. Like Burning Spear, he mixes prophecy with his personal experiences. He managed to close down the entire country of Jamaica when the "Two Sevens Clashed" on 7-7-77. "Fussing and Fighting" became an anthem for the ghetto peace movement in Kingston the following year. It's as if Elijah, the Old Testament prophet, came back with a trio. —*Roger Steffens*

★ **Two Sevens Clash** / 1977 / Shanachie 44001
The landmark debut, with gorgeous vocals, concise rhythms, and tough and properly impassioned heart makes this a cornerstone of any reggae collection. —*John Floyd*

○ **Cumbolo** / 1979 / Shanachie 44005
A classic, almost on par with *Two Sevens*, utilizing similar themes and sung with like amounts of passion. —*John Floyd*

○ **International Herb** / 1979 / Shanachie 44006
The politics have subsided just a notch, but this is still a beauty. —*John Floyd*

○ **Too Long in Slavery** / 1980 / Frontline 1687
Here is a decently compiled collection of their output up to *Cumbolo*. —John Floyd

Lion Rock / 1985 / Heartbeat 12
An exemplary '80s session with Hill in top form. —*Ron Wynn*

○ **Culture in Culture** / 1988 / Heartbeat 67

○ **Nuff Crisis** / 1988 / Shanachie 43064
Topical, passionate, and, as always, beautifully sung. —*Ron Wynn*

Desmond Dekker (Desmond Dacres)

b. 1943, Kingston, Jamaica
Vocals / Rock-steady, ska
Born Desmond Dacres in Kingston, Desmond Dekker scored a stunning international hit with an unlikely ode to a small Christian/Rastafarian cult in 1969. Propelled by obscure lyrics and a quirky, galloping beat, Dekker's "Israelites" brought Jamaican rock-steady music to the Top Ten in America and Europe largely on the strength of an incredible, soaring tenor rarely heard in pop. But back home Dekker was already a mainstay with a succession of drop-dead beautiful singles beginning with "Honor Your Mother and Your Father" in 1963 and including 1967's rude-boy anthem "007 (Shanty Town)" featured in the film "The Harder They Come." As rock-steady made way for reggae, Dekker faded from the scene. Despite a pair of solid albums for Stiff Records in 1980 and 1981 (both out of print but worth seeking) and the use of "Israelites" in two recent movie soundtracks, he hasn't made the comeback other rock-steady-era pioneers like Lee Perry, Johnny Clarke, or Toots Hibbert have achieved. The purity of his voice and his witty approach to songwriting are sorely missed. Gift us again, Desmond. *—Bob Tarte*

○ **Black and Dekker** / 1980 / Stiff 26
A fierce ska version of "Israelites" sets the tone and tempo for this release, which came at the crest of the UK twin-tone revival, initiated by such bands as the English Beat and the Specials. Not meant to take the place of the originals, the punk-intense versions of a half-dozen of Dekker's biggest hits are cleverly arranged, meticulously albeit loosely performed. Shed not a single nostalgic tear, not when the music remains this fresh. *—Bob Tarte*

★ **Rockin' Steady: The Best of Desmond Dekker** / 1992 / Rhino 70271
His unmistakable voice is irrevocably tied to the rock-steady era—not because of limitation but because of the versatility that the times demanded. Dekker could be as light as a sigh in the strangely portentous "Fu Manchu," wax comic in "Licking Stick," or summon enough raucousness to blow down a picket fence in "Warlock." At his most righteous he never succumbed to preachy, shifting instead into an other-worldly eccentricity that shaped an outstandingly memorable body of work, including one of the most transcendent records in anybody's canon, the still-jarring "Israelites." *—Bob Tarte*

Chaka Demus

Reggae
One-half of an extremely popular reggae duo, Chaka Demus and Pliers had a monster hit with "Murder She Wrote" in 1993. *—Ron Wynn*

● **Reggae Dance Hall Sensation** / 1970 / Rohit 7764
A contemporary dancehall star, Chaka Demus's music is neither compelling nor very original. But it is extremely popular, and you can hear the hip-hop and rock influences within this conventional pop-reggae material. *—Ron Wynn*

Dillinger (Lester Bullocks)

Reggae, DJ
Dillinger was a seminal stylist in DJ/toaster circles during the '70s. His blazing, witty, and irreverent style, sometimes comedic, sometimes tragic or poignant, was featured on many singles as he moved from simply recyling Big Youth and U-Roy's style to developing his own gripping approach. Dillinger began as a DJ on Prince Jackie and El Brasso's sound systems during the early '70s. He enjoyed his first hit with "Freshly" in 1974, cutting it for Yabby U. Later came singles for Augustus Pablo, Joe Joe Hookim, and Coxsone Dodd. Dodd issued the LP *Ready Natty Dreadie* in '75 establishing Dillinger as a star, while Kim issued the second album containing the classics "Cocaine in My Brain" and "Crank Face," a superb duet with Trinity. Dillinger tried to repeat the cocaine magic later with "Marijuana in My Brand," which did reasonably well. But as audience interests shifted during the '80s, Dillinger's fortunes plummeted. He eventually left music but returned with "Say No to Drugs" in 1990. *—Ron Wynn*

● **Cocaine** / 1983 / Charly 12
Dillinger's "Cocaine" remains an all-time anthem. It's without question the high point on an otherwise erratic album, one whose rambling qualities accurately reflect Dillinger's entire career. The songs are great one moment, utterly forgettable the next. *—Ron Wynn*

Mikey Dread (Michael Campbell)

Vocals / Dance, reggae
Mikey Dread changed the face of JA radio (albeit briefly) in the late '70s with a post-midnight weekend program of weird sound effects, dub-wise mixing techniques, and almost no talk for hours. Of course he was fired. His cave-deep voice has a narrow range, but on record it penetrates to the core of heartfelt and conscious concerns. A tour with the Clash exposed him to US audiences a decade ago, and constant reissues and new material have kept him in the public eye. *—Roger Steffens*

○ **Beyond WW3** / 1972 / Heartbeat 02
Mikey Dread was at his toasting best on this '81 session, peppering his commentary with fiery topical references and quips. Producer Scientist provided swirling electronic backing and multitracked sonic support. This was among the most influential reggae-meets-punk/new wave LPs of its day. *—Ron Wynn*

● **Dread at the Controls** / 1979 / Trojan 178
Mikey Dread made his recording debut at this '79 session, and it was a good but tentative one. His toasting was functional, his compositions occasionally arresting. *—Ron Wynn*

Don Drummond

d. 1969
Trombone / Ska
A magnificent trombonist, Don Drummond ranks with Roland Alphonso, Jackie Mittoo, Tommy McCook, Rico, and Dean Fraser in the upper tier of Jamaica's finest instrumentalists. Drummond's meaty, fluid trombone solos graced numerous singles in the '60s, and prior to that he'd been a first-rate jazz player. Drummond was educated at the Alpha Catholic Boys Home and School, where he later served as an instructor. Like Alphonso, Drummond was in the original Skatalites. He was among the first major musicians to publicly embrace Rastafarianism, and such singles as "Far East" and "Addis Ababa" reflected that faith. Sadly, Drummond became mentally unstable following the mid '60s murder of his common-law wife. He was committed to Kingston's Belle Vue asylum, where he died in 1969. *—Ron Wynn*

● **Best of Don Drummond** / 1989 / Studio One 9008
Here's a collection highlighting some of the most popular material Don Drummond and the Skatalites performed during the ska era. There's little thematic variety, but it's a good anthology of early Jamaican music. *—Ron Wynn*

Lucky Dube

Vocals / African, reggae
Of the many reggae artists at one time or another dubbed "the next Bob Marley," South Africa's Lucky Dube seems a likely candidate for the crown. Not only is he the biggest-selling recording artist in his country, but his first release (*Prisoner*, 1989) was also the top-selling South African album of all time. His success is partly due to charismatic live performances featuring Zulu-inspired choreography and revealing unmatched energy and vocal verve. For the international fans who know him simply through his recordings, Dube's combination of a strong melodic gift and his straightforward approach to social-issue songwriting recalls many of Jamaica's greatest at top form. Even when the message of his music is the most serious, a buoyancy and spirit of unity make the heavy reasonings go down easy. *—Bob Tarte*

Slave / 1990 / Shanachie 43060
Another strong statement of militant "sufferation," liberation, and love. *—J. Poet*

● **Prisoner** / 1991 / Shanachie 43073
One of the best efforts from a South African reggae superstar whose vocal style owes much to Peter Tosh. Dube is one of the finest post-Marley singers/songwriters in the reggae field. *—J. Poet*

○ **House of Exile** / 1992 / Shanachie 43094
The latest refinement of Dube's sound features his toughest songwriting yet and several numbers with the expanded version of his band, the Slaves. *—Bob Tarte*

Captured Live / Shanachie 43090

This intense live recording captures Lucky Dube's charismatic force as none of his studio discs do—plus he's backed by a hot horn section. —*Bob Tarte*

Eek-A-Mouse (Ripton Hylton)

Group / Reggae

Born Ripton Hylton, this "six-foot-six above sea level" toaster was named after a race horse. The Mouse's Far Eastern "bong-gong-giddy-mem-giddy-hoy" style set the pace for many early '80s imitators. His sing-jay lyrics run the gamut from wildly funny to terrifying and touching. A master of stagecraft, he performs in witty costumes ranging from Mexican caballero to samurai warrior that help keep him touring successfully into the '90s. —*Roger Steffens*

○ **Wa-Do-Dem** / 1982 / Shanachie 48006
Classic innovative title track and autobiographical material make this a major debut. —*Roger Steffens*

● **Mouseketeer** / 1984 / Shanachie 48014
Definitive toasting from Ripton Joseph Hylton aka Eek-A-Mouse. This LP included the definitive "Star, Daily News or Gleaner," in which he examined the bitter rivalry between Jamaica's newspapers, and the entertaining "How I Got Me Name" for all those interested in his origins. —*Ron Wynn*

● **Best of Eek-A-Mouse, The** / Shanachie 48001
A strong anthology collecting Eek-A-Mouse's most clever and popular cuts from the early '80s. —*Ron Wynn*

Alton Ellis

Vocals / Reggae, ska

One of Jamaica's first singers, the silken-smooth Alton Ellis made his first hit "Muriel" in 1959 as part of a duo with Eddie Perkins. Producer Coxsone Dodd oversaw a string of subsequent successes. Eventually Ellis, seeing little financial remuneration, left for Coxsone's archrival Duke Reid and his Treasure Isle label. Tunes like "Dance Crasher," "Cry Tough," and "Girl, I've Got a Date" gave Reid his first chance to pass Dodd in the popular mind as Jamaica's heaviest producer.

By 1966 the red-hot double-time ska beat had given birth virtually overnight to a much slower, hiccuping rhythm dubbed "rock-steady," and it was Ellis who was to be its midwife. "One evening in the studio," Ellis recalls, "the bass man didn't show up. So Jackie Mittoo, the keyboardist, had to play the bass pattern on the piano with his left hand, but he couldn't hold it steady, and we all thought the line was so fresh and nice. When the bass player turned up next time, Jackie insisted that he play what Jackie was playing with his left hand. That's how rock-steady was born; we called it so that night."

Coxsone lured Ellis back, and by 1968 Ellis was the undisputed king of rock-steady with shots like "Willow Tree," "I'm Just a Guy," and "Sitting in the Park," often highlighted with his trademark yelp of "Looka here now!" Again, the money failed to follow the hits, and somewhat disillusioned, Ellis spent several years in the US and Canada before pulling up stakes and moving permanently to England in 1973. Scores of songs were issued steadily, cementing his reputation as one of the most consistent reggae artists around. By 1984 he was celebrated internationally for his 25 years in show business, making a pair of critically acclaimed appearances at Jamaica's Sunsplash festival in 1983 and 1985. From 1989 on, he has been releasing compilations of his early masterpieces on his own Alltone label, and he even recorded *Man from Studio One*, a new 12-inch, for Coxsone in 1991. One of the real gentlemen of reggae, Ellis is a satisfying and scintillating singer, one of Jamaica's extraordinary gifts to the world, right up there with Bob Marley. —*Roger Steffens*

○ **Best of Alton Ellis** / 1988 / Coxsone 8019
A great cross-section of mid '60s covers that sound far better than the originals, along with self-penned classics. —*Roger Steffens*

○ **Legendary Alton Ellis** / 1990 / Alltone 012
Ska, rock-steady, and early reggae singles, including the essential "Cry Tough" and "Dance Crasher." —*Roger Steffens*

Alton and Hortense / 1990 / Heartbeat 64
This outstanding 1990 CD collected several rare singles by each singer and included only one duet number, their marvelous rendition of "Breaking Up Is Hard to Do." Roger Steffens's authorita-

tive and insightful notes complete an extremely attractive set of classic rockers and lovers rock reggae. —*Ron Wynn*

★ **Cry Tough** / 1993 / Heartbeat 106
This 20-track collection features the finest moments from one of Jamaica's great vocalists. Concentrating mainly on his strong mid 60's rock-steady material, this serves as the best introduction for newcomers. Longtime fans will also be pleased with the inclusion of rare takes from the long-lost Treasure Isle sessions. Essential for any lover of reggae or rock-steady. —*Chris Woodstra*

Ethiopians

Group / Reggae, ska

A duo founded in 1966, the Ethiopians featured Leonard "Jack Sparrow" Dillon leading songs like "Owe Me No Pay Me," "Train to Skaville," and "The Whip." Their biggest hit, "Everything Crash" in 1968, spoke of the quotidian realities of life in the ghetto, a common concern in their literally hundreds of singles. This is classic roots music by one of the most critically acclaimed Jamaican groups ever. —*Roger Steffens*

○ **Slave Call** / 1977 / Heartbeat 56
A potent, hypnotic rhythmic foundation pulsates through this new release by the Ethiopians, simultaneously grounding the music and paying homage to reggae's African roots. Singer Leonard Dillon addresses the troubles and struggles of culturally and financially disenfranchised people everywhere on tracks like "Slave Call," "Guilty Conscience," and "Nuh Follow Babylon." A moving cover of the Beatles' "Let It Be" offers hope and redemption amid the turmoil. Contributing musicians include bassist George Fulwood, guitarist Earl Smith, and a horn section of trumpeter Bobby Ellis, trombonist Vin Gordon, and tenor saxophonist Lennox Brown. —*Mark J. Cadigan, Roundup newsletter*

★ **Ethiopians** / 1986 / Trojan 228
These 21 songs from 1966 to 1972 give the best available overview of a major Jamaican duo. —*Roger Steffens*

○ **Owner Fe De Yard** / 1994 / Heartbeat
Contemporary dancehall reggae may be enjoying a popularity boom, but for lovers of the classic sound nothing will ever match the music that came out of Coxsone Dodd's Studio One in the '60s, '70s, and '80s. The 15 tracks on this superb anthology spotlight the Ethiopians, one of Jamaica's most consistent vocal groups thanks largely to the tremendous leads of Leonard Dillon. Whether singing love tunes, protest songs, soul covers or in patois, Dillon turned each number into a shimmering, confident, and radiant masterpiece. Dodd's production lacked the multitrack sophistication, computerized synth-backing, and other colorations that are now routine. Instead, he relied on the brilliance of individual musicians and provided either rocking backgrounds or lush, swaying ones. The Studio One sound was special in reggae annals, and this collection reaffirms that fact. —*Ron Wynn*

Majek Fashek (Majekodunmi Fasheke)

Vocals, guitar / Reggae, African

Nigerian Majekodunmi Fasheke, otherwise known as Majek Fashek, is (along with South Africa's Lucky Dube) Africa's prime proponent of reggae. But while Dube keeps the music close to its Jamaican source, Fashek lights a polyrhythmic fire under the familiar reggae beat, with ferocious talking-drum volleys and multilayered percussion. Though Fashek was influenced by Jimmy Cliff and Bob Marley, his initial love (and the music he first sang) was Indian film music. He began playing guitar while in secondary school in Benin, forming a band called Jah Stix, which made the club circuit in Lagos. In 1988 he struck out on his own. The African release of his first reggae album, *Prisoner of Conscience*, sold 200,000 copies and spawned two singles that rode high on the Nigerian charts for over a year. —*Bob Tarte*

Prisoner of Conscience / 1989 / Mango 9870
Heavily influenced by Marley—Fashek sounds more like the reggae avatar than Ziggy—this batch of Nigerian-flavored "skanking" is startlingly redeemed by the brilliant "Send Down the Rain," which took on near-incantatory intensity on Fashek's tours across the drought-stricken continent. —*Bob Tarte*

● **Spirit of Love** / 1991 / Interscope 91742
Seamlessly blending elements of juju with reggae, Fashek turns from imitator to innovator on a disc with so much clear-eyed enthusiasm and vision you'd think reggae was his personal inven-

tion. "Majek Beware" is the most powerful reggae song in years, awash in talking drums, jungle chants, and shamanistic lead vocals. —*Bob Tarte*

Dean Fraser

Sax / Reggae

Whether Roland Alphonso, Tommy McCook or Dean Fraser is Jamaica's premier saxophonist really depends on personal taste. Fraser's certainly no less accomplished than the other two; his tone and range are extensive, and he's appeared on mellow ballads, instrumentals, fiery uptempo tunes, and message tracks. He gained international prominence while backing Dennis Brown during his late '70s tour and has done numerous sessions in Jamaica. He's also issued a handful of LPs as a leader, the most recent being *Dean Plays Bob,* a Bob Marley tribute CD in 1994. —*Ron Wynn*

● **Sings and Blows** / 1989 / Shanachie 47001
Saxophonist Dean Fraser's most exciting and spirited instrumental release. His solos were nicely played, the production wasn't too elaborate, and there was a good balance between improvisational and popular concerns. —*Ron Wynn*

Albert Griffiths & the Gladiators

Group / Reggae

A harmony group fronted by Griffiths, whose high-pitched, slightly nasal voice gave them an instantly identifiable sound influenced by the Wailers and the Techniques in the '60s. Still active after 25 years. —*Roger Steffens*

● **Trenchtown Mixup** / 1976 / Virgin 2062
Captured at their peak, with some of their most representative compositions, such as "Hello Carol" and "Thief in the Night." —*Roger Steffens*

On the Right Track / 1989 / Heartbeat 52
Their best '80s effort, with assistance from members of the I-Tones. —*Ron Wynn*

Marcia Griffiths

Vocals / Dance, reggae

Jamaica's longest-running and perhaps biggest female vocalist ever. Griffiths began as a teenager in Coxsone's Studio One, racking up hit after hit, then joined with paramour Bob Andy as Bob & Marcia for the Top Five UK pop hit "Young, Gifted and Black." She formed the I Threes to back Bob Marley's international tours and recordings from 1974 to 1980 and scored a massive international hit with "Electric Boogie" in the '80s. Although she did a few Rasta tunes like "Stepping Out of Babylon" in the '70s, she is known primarily for her strong, smooth-as-mousse love songs and captivating live performances. —*Roger Steffens*

● **Naturally** / 1978 / Shanachie 44014
Ten of her greatest early hits, seven written by Bob Andy. —*Roger Steffens*

○ **Steppin'** / 1979 / Shanachie 44007
Stirring leads from a wonderful singer. —*Ron Wynn*

Marcia / 1988 / RAS 3047
This wasn't a strict reggae effort; she did a straight soul version of "Don't Let Me Down" and a quasi-jazz/pop turn on "Blue Skies." But when Griffiths turned to reggae, she was as captivating as usual. Her duet with Bunny Clark, "It's Not Funny," was beautifully performed on both sides, while "Trenchtown Rock" and "I'm Leaving" were the type of unadorned, from-the-heart singing that's sorely lacking in contemporary reggae and a lot of urban music. —*Ron Wynn*

Carousel / 1990 / Island 842334
A wonderful example of the West meeting the Islands and both being the better for it. —*Danny McCue, Rock & Roll Disc.*

Half Pint

Vocals / Reggae

Important roots rocker whose 1985 release "Cost of Living" ("there are more sellers than buyers") was a career-making single. Mick Jagger has covered him, and Sunsplashes have starred him. Impassioned delivery, great voice, conscious poetry mark him as a long-termer. —*Roger Steffens*

● **Victory** / 1986 / RAS 3031

Beres Hammond

Vocals / Soul, reggae

Arguably the most soulful vocalist among '90s reggae stars, Beres Hammond has issued many recordings on various Jamaican labels. —*Ron Wynn*

● **Live & Learn Presents: Beres Hammond & Barrington Levy** / 1991 / Live & Learn 31
Beres Hammond and Barrington Levy rank among reggae's greatest pure vocalists, and this eight-track CD presents five Levy numbers. Hammond is more soulful, Levy more vocally flexible and spirited. Levy does playful fare such as "Some Girls Are Trouble" and political/topical material like "Juggling Soldier," though the emphasis is clearly on entertainment rather than relevance. "Sho-Be-Do-Sho" showcases Levy's verbal facility, and "Strictly Rocker" features his classic reggae sound. Hammond's "Never Let Go" and "I Will Follow You" are gloriously sung, powerful performances; "When the Grass Is Green" falters lyrically, but Hammond's evocative singing elevates it. —*Ron Wynn*

The Heptones

Group / Reggae

Bigger in the mid '60s than the Wailers, the Heptones were led by Studio One bassist and singer Leroy Sibbles, one of Jamaica's most compelling vocalists. The belting Sibbles lead, with the harmonies of Earl Morgan and Barry Llewellyn, made the Heptones a model for trios through the late '70s, when Sibbles left. Now fronted by Naggo Morris, the Heptones '80s material has never recaptured the majesty of the earlier era. Sibbles continues as a highly popular international touring artist. —*Roger Steffens*

Night Food / 1973 / Mango 539381
Wonderful harmonies. —*Ron Wynn*

○ **Party Time** / 1973 / Mango 539456
Sizzling. One of the first reggae vocal groups to hook Americans. —*Ron Wynn*

★ **Book of Rules** / 1976 / Island 9381
The title track is transcendent poetry. This album includes brilliant updates of classics such as "Fatty Fatty," "I've Got the Handle," and "Mama Say." —*Roger Steffens*

Better Days / 1981 / Rohit 7715
Top-flight singing. —*Ron Wynn*

On the Run / 1982 / Shanachie 43008
A reggae institution. —*Ron Wynn*

Toots Hibbert & the Maytals

Group / Reggae

Toots Hibbert sings as if he's determined to summon the ghost of Otis Redding. Since his arrival on the ska scene in the early '60s, Hibbert and the Maytals have provided the clearest evidence of the link between American soul and the hometown bop of Jamaica. Some of his albums have been spotty, but his enthusiastic vocals make everything he's cut worth hearing (and not just for reggae aficionados). —*John Floyd*

★ **Funky Kingston** / 1973 / Mango 539330
This is the album that brought Toots's soul-infused testifying to American audiences. Forget about this being a great reggae album; this set transcends categorization. —*John Floyd*

○ **Reggae Got Soul** / 1976 / Mango 539374
Among his landmark releases, this album wasn't quite as magnificent as *Funky Kingston* but still contained plenty of explosive numbers and Otis Redding-influenced leads. —*Ron Wynn*

Reggae Greats / 1984 / Mango 539781
It's skimpy, but this one offers an adequate smattering of essentials, including their first hit, "54-46 Was My Number," "Funky Kingston," and "Sweet and Dandy." —*John Floyd*

○ **Toots in Memphis** / 1988 / Mango 539818
Recorded with a slew of Memphis studio pros, Toots pays homage to the power of southern soul with sterling covers of "I Can't Stand the Rain," "Knock on Wood," "Love and Happiness," "Hard to Handle," and six others. An amazing return to form. —*John Floyd*

○ **Do the Reggae** / Attack 103
Sixteen cuts from their early days, when the Maytals were perfecting their sound. Includes some seminal and rare early material. —*John Floyd*

Joe Higgs

Vocals / Reggae

The "Godfather of Reggae Music" and teacher of Bob Marley and the Wailers, the Wailing Souls, and dozens of other Trenchtown youths, Higgs is also known as the "Jazz Connection" to Jamaican music. He became one of Jamaica's first indigenous stars in the late '50s, helping turn R&B covers into a new kind of music called ska. In the mid '70s he was Jimmy Cliff's bandleader on worldwide tours. His career continues into its fourth decade with regularly released albums showcasing his sharp-shock style and vocal daring. *—Roger Steffens*

● **Life of Contradiction** / 1975 / Vulcan 508
Remakes of big '60s hits including "There's a Reward" and "Song My Enemy Sings." Passion personified. *—Roger Steffens*

Triumph / 1985 / Alligator 8313
Smashing, defiant vocals from a legendary figure, done during the brief time Alligator was involved in reggae. *—Ron Wynn*

○ **Blackman Know Yourself** / 1990 / Shanachie 43077
Wonderful in every aspect. *—Ron Wynn*

Justin Hinds & Dominoes

Group / Reggae

This sugarcane-sweet country/gospel trio (begun in 1964) spotlighted the inimitable round warmth of leader Justin Hinds. Their music is marked by themes of righteousness often cloaked in hoary folk sayings. The 1980 ska revival in the UK renewed interest in the group, although Hinds remains a recluse in the North Coast bush and rarely leaves Jamaica. *—Roger Steffens*

Jezebel / 1976 / Mango 9416
Well sung and well produced. *—Ron Wynn*

● **Just in Time** / 1979 / Mango 9532
Hot leads, piercing harmonies. *—Ron Wynn*

Travel with Love / 1984 / Nighthawk 309
Eight perfectly beautiful midtempo country croonings. *—Roger Steffens*

John Holt

Vocals / Lovers rock

The father of lovers rock (non-Rasta, nonpolitical reggae rhythm in service of the ultimate emotion), Holt is a founder of the Paragons and the songwriter of some of the biggest hits of '60s Jamaica, such as "On the Beach" and "Wear You to the Ball," as well as a consistently interesting, smooth-voiced coverer of US and UK pop hits. Still active, he finally got his payday when Blondie covered his "Tide Is High." *—Roger Steffens*

● **Love I Can Feel, A** / 1970 / Bamboo 210
Fine Coxsone productions from the early '70s. *—Roger Steffens*

Sweetie Come Brush Me / 1980 / Volcano 001
This mid '80s career reviver includes "Ghetto Queen," backed by the Radics. *—Roger Steffens*

I Roy

Vocals / Reggae

A reggae toaster and original rapper, I Roy uses quick wit and sharp rhythms to make modern poetry in a stylish roots-skank mode. *—Michael G. Nastos*

● **Truth & Rights** / 1975 / Grounation 504
Horns, organ, and a rhythm section by Sly & Robbie. Top-drawer toasting. *—Michael G. Nastos*

○ **Musical Shark Attack** / 1976 / Virgin 2075
This album features "Semi-classical Natty Dread" and "Tribute to Marcus Garvey." *—Michael G. Nastos*

Ijahman (Trevor Sutherland)

Vocals / Reggae

Folk poet Trevor Sutherland, under the nom de chanteur Ijahman Levi, has since the late '70s issued yearly compilations of (generally) acoustic, lengthy meditations on Jah, repatriation, and the healing power of love, occasionally abetted by his wife, Madge. Soft, subtle, sensuous—he's a one-of-a-kind balladeer in an otherwise electrified music. *—Roger Steffens*

○ **Haile I Hymn (Chapter 1)** / 1978 / Mango 539521

Four extended tracks that epitomize spiritual longing; includes "Jah Heavy Load" and "I'm a Levi." *—Roger Steffens*

● **Are We a Warrior** / 1979 / Mango 539557
The title track and "Moulding" are two of reggae's most haunting meditations ever. *—Roger Steffens*

Inner Circle

Group / Rock/pop, reggae

Jacob Miller's backup band struggled on after their lead singer's untimely death in 1980, finally topping the reggae charts with the "Cops" TV theme "Bad Boys" a decade later. They continue to tour with new vocalist Carlton Coffie, mixing rock-oriented messages for the masses. *—Roger Steffens*

○ **One Way** / 1987 / RAS 3030
"Bad Boys" highlights a return to form. *—Roger Steffens*

● **Best of Inner Circle—The Capitol Years 1976-1977, The** / Aug. 24, 1993 / The Right Stuff
Before they were fluke pop stars, Inner Circle recorded a series of solid reggae singles in the '70s; the best of these are compiled here on this 14-track collection that draws from their two Capitol albums. Anyone who was turned on to the group through "Bad Boys" should continue exploring here. *—Stephen Thomas Erlewine*

Gregory Isaacs

Vocals / Soul, reggae

Nobody sings a love song quite like Gregory Isaacs, reggae music's "Cool Ruler." His voice is languidness personified, insinuating itself around snatches of rhythm like a duppy through a canefield. There's no insistence here, more an intimation. His is the voice of lullabies and laments and loneliness, of indignation and sufferation, of soothing and seething. Few singers in Jamaica have had as many hits as he, few his impressive durability. A recent issue of *Reggae Directory* was devoted entirely to a discography of Isaacs, listing more than 400 releases in the past 20 years. Recording initially in the late '60s as part of the Concordes, he cut his first solo disc, "Another Heartache," for WIRL, the label founded by onetime Jamaican prime minister Edward Seaga. Almost immediately, Isaacs decided to establish his own labels, Cash and Carry and African Museum, and produce himself. On his third album, *Extra Classics*, he found his own voice on such laidback laments as "Mr. Cop" and "Rasta Business," and most especially on "Loving Pauper." The follow-up, *Mr. Isaacs*, joined him with Sly & Robbie and the Heptones and gave the world the four *S*s: "Sacrifice," "Slavemaster," "Smile," and "Storm." As an example of the respect other artists accord Isaacs, on the *Soon Forward* album he is backed by the voices of Junior Delgado, Dennis Brown, and Leroy Sibbles. The *Cool Ruler* collection continued the streak of classics, which culminated in 1983's *Night Nurse*, one of his all-time best-sellers. Throughout the '80s, Gregory released more music than any other artist of the time, sometimes offering six singles in the space of a week. Many of them were critically and commercially successful, such as "Rumours" and "Private Beach Party." Isaacs has had frequent and well-publicized run-ins with the law throughout his career, contributing to his image as the ultimate rude-boy artist, with his head in the clouds and his feet in the street. Ultimately, though, as Gregory says, "Only love can win the war!" *—Roger Steffens*

○ **Best of Gregory Isaacs, The** / 1977 / Tassa 7004
Misleading, since his output can't be compiled on a single (or even double) album. *—Ron Wynn*

○ **Extra Classic** / 1981 / Rohit 77930
Outstanding. *—Ron Wynn*

○ **Early Years, The** / 1981 / Trojan 196

Mr. Isaacs / 1982 / Shanachie 43006
Heartfelt, exuberant. *—Ron Wynn*

● **Night Nurse** / 1982 / Mango 539721
Isaacs's strongest vocal performance and most memorable album. Essential lovers rock. *—Chris Woodstra*

Out Deh / 1983 / Mango 539748
Almost as brilliant vocally as *Night Nurse*, despite its erratic songs. *—Ron Wynn*

All I Have Is Love / Feb. 1983 / Trojan 121

First-rate vocals, and great coproduction by Isaacs and Alvin Ranglin. —*Ron Wynn*

Private Beach Party / 1985 / RAS 3007
Enchanting, if sometimes off-center, vocals. —*Ron Wynn*

Victim / 1987 / VP 1033
Excellent, with a harder edge. —*Ron Wynn*

Watchman of the City / 1987 / Rohit 93100
Fine song selection. —*Ron Wynn*

○ **Sly & Robbie Present Gregory Isaacs** / 1988 / RAS 3206
This early '70s session for Sly & Robbie's Taxi label certainly ranks among his finest full LPs. There were no flimsy soul or pop covers, and Isaacs sang with clarity, depth, verve, and confidence, no matter if he were covering "Slave Driver," ripping through "Soon Foward" and "Going Downtown," or embellishing "Motherless Children." The CD includes both vocals and versions and also has a bonus track in the 1987 single "I'm Coming Home." —*Ron Wynn*

Heartbreaker / 1990 / Rohit 7788
A superb title track. —*Ron Wynn*

Call Me Collect / 1990 / RAS 3067
The songs on this '90 session are excellently produced by Fatis and include first-rate bass/drums interaction and support from Sly Dunbar and Robbie Shakespeare, plus synthesized assistance from Clive Hunt that's neither rigid nor obtrusive. Isaacs wrote nine of the 10 numbers, and though nothing is along the lines of "Night Nurse" or "Private Beach Party," there's a good blend of urgent love songs and one or two spirited protest numbers. Isaacs can still croon, moan, and sigh with the best of Jamaica's wailers. —*Ron Wynn*

● **Cool Ruler; Soon Forward Select** / 1990 / Frontline 1688
A good twin set, pairing past releases. —*Ron Wynn*

Dancing Floor / 1990 / Heartbeat 79
The excellent digital production fully captures his vocal quality. —*Ron Wynn*

My Number One / 1990 / Heartbeat 61
A thorough compilation of past hits, plus rare cuts and remixes. —*Ron Wynn*

Once Ago / 1990 / Frontline 1680
As good as it gets, though after a while Isaacs falters. —*Ron Wynn*

Come Again Dub / 1991 / ROIR 193
A good dub version of *Come Again.* —*Ron Wynn*

Love Is Overdue / 1991 / Heartbeat 98
Soulful and vibrant. —*Ron Wynn*

○ **Best of Gregory Isaacs, Vols. 1 & 2, The** / 1992 / Heartbeat 97
Gregory Isaacs, the "Cool Ruler," bears an apt nickname. His vocals drip with a laidback sexuality that mirrors the romantic yearnings of his lyrics. Songs like his big hit, "My Number One," function both as direct come-ons and catchy tunes. But he also reveals a more socially conscious side on songs like "Border." Both songs are included in this 20-track collection, which features drummer Sly Dunbar, bassist Robbie Shakespeare, saxophonist Dean Fraser, and other stellar reggae musicians. — *Roundup newsletter*

Feature Attraction / VP 1066
Any of his albums on VP are worth hearing. —*Ron Wynn*

Past & Future / VP 1116
Hot, anguished leads. —*Ron Wynn*

Israel Vibration

Group / Reggae
Israel Vibration consists of three young men who met in a polio rehab center. Their voices are among the holiest of Jamaican trinities. Dr. Dread of RAS Records arranged their reunion following a mid '80s period of breakup, and reggae fans have been thanking him ever since. Ever soulful, ever sure, their voices are so close to the roots you can hear the earth itself in their blending. Roots *exemplaire.* —*Roger Steffens*

● **Forever** / 1991 / RAS 3080
The flowing "Reggae on the River" celebrates some of America's most famous reggae locales; a satisfying and sultry collection. — *Roger Steffens*

Why You So Craven / RAS 3210

Contains "Highway Robbery" and a great title track. A formative album produced by Junjo and engineered by Scientist. —*Roger Steffens*

The Itals

Group / Reggae
Keith Porter and Ronnie Davis, joined by either Lloyd Ricketts or David Isaacs, are lead singers with big voices capable of filling a club without a mike. The result is often stunning as this powerful trio takes on songs with consciousness at their core, delivered with meltdown intensity. —*Roger Steffens*

● **Brutal Out Deh** / 1982 / Nighthawk 303
A powerhouse reggae trio. —*Ron Wynn*

Give Me Power! / 1983 / Nighthawk 307
Intense and energized. —*Ron Wynn*

○ **Cool & Dread** / Nighthawk 311
Nicely sung. A fine set of compositions. —*Ron Wynn*

○ **Early Recordings 1971-1979** / Nighthawk 310
Groundbreaking records that brought this trio initial recognition. —*Ron Wynn*

Winston Jarrett

Vocals / Reggae
He came to Kingston to sing with his idol, Alton Ellis, whose voice is very similar to Jarrett's. Joining the Flames in the mid '60s to back Ellis, he soon branched out on his own to record a series of albums that often featured Marley and Ellis covers, and self-penned ghetto plaints as evocative as Bosch paintings. — *Roger Steffens*

● **Kingston Vibrations** / 1991 / RAS 3079
Strong, forceful, and rootical. —*Roger Steffens*

Linton Kwesi Johnson

Vocals / Dub poetry
"I coined the phrase *dub poetry* because I was trying to argue that what the DJs in Jamaica were actually doing is poetry—improvised, spontaneous, oral poetry." Johnson's initial recorded work, *Dread Beat an' Blood* (recorded in the UK in 1978), provided an entirely different way to look at Caribbean rhythms and life, and had a major impact on Jamaican poet-performers like Mutabaruka, Michael Smith, and Oku Onuora. Johnson had emigrated with his family to England in 1963, eventually receiving an honors degree in sociology from the University of London. He joined the British arm of the Black Panthers in 1970 and began writing poetry and reciting it publicly. His writings, which used Jamaican patois to reflect the realities of immigrant life in the ghettos of Britain, were revolutionary in both content and style. *Forces of Victory,* his second album, was a musical novel about oppression and confrontation, backed by the machine-gun force of Dennis Bovell's Dub Band. The follow-up *Bass Culture* expanded Johnson's themes to include meditations on the relationship of art to its audience, and was followed by *LKJ in Dub,* an instrumental version of his most powerful sessions. *Making History,* released in the Orwellian year of 1984, broadened his rhythmic horizons and added a pan-Caribbean flavor to his sound. A live album, summing up his career to date, came out the following year, after which Johnson claimed he had retired. But in 1991 he made a well-received return to the scene with *Tings and Times,* another multirhythmic outing of indignant rhymes. Taking stage in a porkpie hat and modest demeanor, Johnson gives understated performances that belie the power of his carefully observed imagery and uncompromising calls for change. He is one of the true internationalizers of the form, a musical Marxist with upheaval on his mind. —*Roger Steffens*

○ **Dread Beat an' Blood** / 1977 / Frontline 1685
Debut album with political statements about racism and inequality. A powerful forum. —*Michael G. Nastos*

★ **Forces of Victory** / 1979 / Mango 539566
Johnson's best studio date. Many of his finest numbers, recorded for the first time. —*Michael G. Nastos*

Bass Culture / 1980 / Mango 539605
A studio date, with this rapper at his best. —*Michael G. Nastos*

○ **LKJ in Dub** / 1980 / Mango 539650

Desert-island dub. Johnson's better early material, with vocals deleted. All instrumental, all outstanding. —*Michael G. Nastos*

In Concert with the Dub Band / 1986 / Shanachie
A fine live show and a good introduction. —*Michael G. Nastos*

Tings An' Times / 1990 / Shanachie 43084
A wonderful reunion of Johnson and Bovell, plus several brilliant compositions. —*Ron Wynn*

Ini Kamoze

Vocals / Reggae
Ini Kamoze burst full-grown on the scene in 1983 with one of the touchstone albums of the '80s, the self-titled *Ini Kamoze*. Produced by Sly & Robbie at their creative peak, all of its half-dozen tracks are essential. In 1985 *Settle with Me* included the jarring "Call the Police" and "Taxi for Me." His output has been erratic lately, but it's always compelling. —*Roger Steffens*

★ **Ini Kamoze** / 1984 / Island 7
Essential to the understanding of early '80s roots. Simply brilliant. —*Roger Steffens*

Byron Lee

Vocals / Soca, party soca
Lee is a Jamaican artist who, with his band the Dragonnaires, is always a part of T&T carnival, both as a live performer and through his annual release of cover versions of the year's most popular tunes. In the '90s he began to release his own tune each year and has been one of the strongest proponents of Jamaican dancehall-influenced soca. —*Gene Scaramuzzo*

○ **Tiney Winey** / 1985 / Dynamic Sounds
The first recording of "Tiney Winey," a song written by Arrow but set aside as second-rate, was later recorded by Lee to become one of the huge hits of the Caribbean in 1985. Arrow went on to record the song in 1988. —*Gene Scaramuzzo*

● **Soca Bacchanal** / Dynamic Sounds 3461
Hot tunes and fine leads. —*Ron Wynn*

○ **Wine Miss Tiny** / Dynamic Sounds 3449
The Dragonnaires' biggest contemporary hit was the title track. —*Ron Wynn*

Barrington Levy

b. Apr. 30, 1964
Vocals / Reggae
A sweet midrange lovers rocker, Levy goes from strength to strength as he matures and internationalizes. From the late '70s *Bounty Hunter* to the recent US release *Here I Come*, Barrington is as satisfying as dancehall reggae gets. —*Roger Steffens*

● **Broader Than Broadway: The Best of . . .** / 1990 / Profile 1294
A fine collection of his best hits of the '80s. —*Roger Steffens*

Teach Me Culture / Profile 1294
Barrington Levy's earlier material doesn't have the sophisticated production of his recent MCA release but was more lyrically varied and intense. This nine-track set presents Levy doing the rich, powerful, traditional reggae that made him a legend in the '70s and early '80s. The menu includes the anguished "To Love Someone" and "Lonely Man," the prophetic title cut, and poignant "Jah Is with Me." While these songs often invoke a melancholy note or bittersweet mood, there's nothing dispirited or solemn about Levy's soaring vocals and vigorous delivery. —*Ron Wynn*

J. C. Lodge

Vocals / Reggae
With her classic girlish pop voice, J. C. Lodge helped bankrupt producer Joe Gibbs when he failed to pay songwriter's royalties to Charley Pride for her million-selling cover of "Someone Loves You, Honey." In the late '80s, J. C.'s "Telephone Love" became a massive, long-lasting international hit penetrating the dancehalls as well as radio stations. She seems poised for a genuine breakthrough in the '90s by piecing rock, reggae, and soul into a highly seductive mosaic. —*Roger Steffens*

● **Revealed** / 1985 / RAS 3010
A remade "Can't Hurry Love" and other dancehall faves. —*Roger Steffens*

Tropic of Love / 1992 / Tommy Boy 1032

Her debut for a major label has both high and low points. Contains the smash "Telephone Love." —*Ron Wynn*

Bob Marley (Robert Nesta Marley)

b. Feb. 6, 1945, St. Ann, Jamaica, d. May 11, 1981, Miami, FL
Vocals / Reggae
Born of a middle-age White father and a teenage Black mother, Robert Nesta Marley transcended the humility of his rural beginnings to become not only a million-selling artist and stadium-filling entertainer but also—and more important—a nearly religious figure whose pleas for brotherhood and justice achieved universal anthemic status.

He began singing professionally at 16 with his self-penned "Judge Not!" It and its follow-up were not successful, and he returned to his ghetto neighborhood of Trenchtown to be tutored by Joe Higgs, a recording artist who coached promising youngsters like Marley, Bunny Livingstone, and Peter Tosh (who would become the Wailers). Signed in 1963 to Coxsone Dodd's influential, pacesetting Studio One, the Wailers saw their first release, "Simmer Down," become an instant number-one hit. During the next two and a half years, the group recorded over a hundred songs, and at one point in 1965 held five of the top ten slots on the Jamaican charts.

Forming their own label, Wail 'n Soul 'm, in 1966, the Wailers continued a series of local hits, with little financial remuneration. Following an album with Leslie Kong *(Best of the Wailers)*, they hooked up with the seminal oddball producer Lee Perry and produced an amazing series of singles that are collected under a variety of names and remain their finest hour.

In 1972, Island Records prez Chris Blackwell signed the Wailers, but after two albums the group broke up, leaving Marley at the head of the band, to which he added a female backing trio, the I Threes. By 1975 Marley had become a revolutionary standard-bearer, the inheritor of the activist energy and hippie ganja enlightenment of the '60s. Almost assassinated in 1976 in Kingston, Marley was given the UN Peace Medal on behalf of 500 million Africans in 1978 for his humanitarian achievements. He headlined a Peace Concert that same year in Jamaica, uniting the warring factions in the Kingston slums. But his greatest honor came when he was invited to headline the Zimbabwe Independence Celebrations in 1980. He outdrew the pope in Milan, fathered 11 children by seven women, sold tens of millions of records worldwide, left a $30 million estate, wrote "the new Psalms," and died at 36 of melanoma (cancer). —*Roger Steffens*

Best of the Wailers, The / 1970 / Beverly's 011
Pressed under dozens of subsequent names, this is the Leslie Kong collection, reggae's first real album project. Includes "Soul Shakedown Party," "Soon Come," and "Stop the Train." The Wailers' moving pep talk to themselves. —*Roger Steffens*

○ **Soul Rebels** / 1970 / Trojan 126
Bare, haunting Lee Perry productions with the Wailers, echoing into eternity. —*Roger Steffens*

☆ **African Herbsman** / 1973 / Trojan 62
Sixteen Perry tracks, brilliant late '60s classics that may be the best-ever work of the Wailers. "Put It On," "Sun Is Shining," "Small Axe," and "Brain Washing" are standouts. —*Roger Steffens*

☆ **Catch a Fire** / Jan. 1973 / Tuff Gong 846201
This was the Wailers' first album on Island, their first with a real budget, their first international success. It is very nearly the birth of international reggae music. Songs include Peter Tosh's "Stop That Train" and Marley's "Concrete Jungle," "Kinky Reggae," and "Stir It Up." —*William Ruhlmann*

☆ **Burnin'** / Feb. 1973 / Tuff Gong 846200
Another extraordinary collection, strongly featuring the vocal blend of Marley, Peter Tosh, and Bunny Livingstone on such songs as "Get Up, Stand Up," "I Shot the Sheriff," and "Burnin' and Lootin'." The last album to feature the original group. —*William Ruhlmann*

☆ **Natty Dread** / 1975 / Tuff Gong 846204
Adding a female vocal trio, Marley proved himself up to the task of carrying on without Tosh and Livingstone, delivering the memorable songs "Lively Up Yourself," "No Woman, No Cry," and "Them Belly Full (But We Hungry)." —*William Ruhlmann*

○ **Live** / 1975 / Tuff Gong 846203

One of the great live albums of all time, this collection demonstrated not only Marley's charismatic presence as a leader, but also the power and subtlety of the Wailers as a band. It's one live recording that captures the feel of the concert perfectly. — *William Ruhlmann*

○ **Rastaman Vibration** / 1976 / Tuff Gong 846205
Marley's breakthrough American album finds him discovering new polyrhythms while continuing to turn out powerful new songs, among them the title tune, "Who the Cap Fit," and "War." — *William Ruhlmann*

Exodus / 1977 / Tuff Gong 846208

Kaya / Jan. 1978 / Tuff Gong 842362
Laidback ganja meditations, love songs, and "Running Away," which tells the critics he hasn't gone soft. — *Roger Steffens*

☆ **Babylon by Bus** / Feb. 1978 / Tuff Gong 846197
Double album. Arguably the most powerful live album in reggae's history, recorded with the Wailers at various international stops over a three-year period. Demonstrates how Marley remade his music constantly, especially in performance. — *Roger Steffens*

Survival / 1979 / Tuff Gong 842460
Perhaps Marley's most militant statement, its bare-bones production put many off at first, but it returned him to the political realm in powerful fashion. "One Drop," "So Much Trouble," and "Babylon System" are among his best. — *Roger Steffens*

○ **Uprising** / 1980 / Tuff Gong 846211
The last album Marley released in his lifetime, this collection is one of his most impassioned, especially the acoustic folk song that closes it, "Redemption Song." — *William Ruhlmann*

★ **Legend** / 1984 / Tuff Gong 818994
This well-chosen 14-track collection of greatest hits serves as an excellent introduction to the definitive reggae musician. Songs like "No Woman, No Cry" and "I Shot the Sheriff" remain among Marley's most powerful efforts. Start here. — *William Ruhlmann*

○ **Soul Revolution 1 & 2** / 1988 / Trojan 406
Thoughtful repackaging of 14 of the best Perry vocal sessions plus the only "legitimate" Wailers dub album ever, with four bonus tracks. — *Roger Steffens*

Reggae Greats / 1989 / Mango 539795
A good, although not formidable, compilation. — *Ron Wynn*

All the Hits / 1990 / Rohit 77570
A great but disgracefully packaged, 20-cut collection of works from 1969 to 1972, mostly Lee Perry productions. Includes the only available copies of rarities like "Satisfy My Soul Jah Jah," abetted by ten dub tracks, eight of which have never appeared before. — *Roger Steffens*

☆ **One Love at Studio One** / 1991 / Heartbeat 111-112
The only Studio One collection pressed from the unaltered master tapes. There are 40 tracks, many never before available, including a 1965 rehearsal and several alternates. Essential 1963-1966 Bunny, Bob, and Peter. — *Roger Steffens*

Talkin' Blues / 1991 / Tuff Gong 848243
This live broadcast recorded during the band's first US tour in 1973, is an amazing testament to Marley's power. It's a soul-tingling treat to hear Marley, Peter Tosh, and Joe Higgs . . . harmonizing on these early Wailers' classics as the Barret brothers and the rest of the Wailers lay down an earthshaking reggae rhythm. — *J. Poet, Rock & Roll Disc*

☆ **Songs of Freedom** / Oct. 6, 1992 / Island 314-512280
A limited-edition four-CD box set, *Songs of Freedom* concentrates on rarities instead of hits. This approach paints a full picture of Bob Marley as an artist, so it is perfectly suited to listeners who are willing to spend the money on a box set as an introduction to an artist (even though they will still need to own the greatest-hits collection *Legend*, because most of the famous versions of his hits are not included here). For Marley's devoted fans, *Songs of Freedom* is absolutely essential for the abundant rarities, including a stunning 12-minute acoustic medley. — *Stephen Thomas Erlewine*

○ **Early Years—3 CD Box** / 1993 / Pickwick 32

Rita Marley (Rita Anderson)

Vocals / Reggae
Rita Anderson was the leader of the Soulettes, a Studio One trio in 1964, when she met her husband-to-be Bob Marley. She recorded with two separate lineups of her group in the '60s, backed several early Wailers recordings, and then became a solo artist. In 1974 she helped form the I Threes (along with Marcia Griffiths and Judy Mowatt), who backed Bob on his world-spanning tours through 1980. Following her husband's passing in 1981, she had the biggest hit of her career, a frothy pro-ganja delight called "One Draw." She devoted the '80s to guiding her children's careers in the Melody Makers. Now that the Marley estate's legal battles have been mostly settled, she continues to showcase her teenage-high voice again. — *Roger Steffens*

● **Who Feels It Knows It** / 1981 / Shanachie 43003
Too long defined as "Bob Marley's wife," Rita Marley has emerged from his shadow to express her beliefs, mostly spiritual, to the world. Her first album, which she coproduced, is *pure* reggae, very smooth and tightly arranged. Includes "One Draw," a humorous anthem to the Amazon of Marijuana, sinsemilla, plus "Thank You," "Jah," "Play Play," and "Easy Sailing." — *Ladyslipper*

Ziggy Marley & the Melody Makers

Group / Reggae
Raised in the studio, these four children of Bob and Rita Marley (Ziggy, Stephen, Sharon, and Cedella) are third-generation professionals. Their debut album was named after a song Bob wrote for them years earlier ("Children Playing in the Streets"), and now all four have become composers. "We are here to complete Bob's mission," says Ziggy. They have had stupendous early success, becoming the first reggae group to top the US R&B singles chart with "Tumbling Down" and already winning two Grammies. Their material is revivifying modern roots music, with an occasional nod to dancehall in Stephen's attitude-rich speed-rapping. — *Roger Steffens*

Play the Game Right / 1985 / Capitol 92705
An interesting concept, but underdeveloped potential. — *Ron Wynn*

Hey World / 1986 / EMI America 92706
Establishing a style, sound, concept, and direction. — *Ron Wynn*

Time Has Come—The Best of . . . / 1988 / EMI America 90952
A compilation of Ziggy's formative material. — *Ron Wynn*

One Bright Day / 1989 / Virgin 91256
An excellent follow-up album that helped cement Ziggy's popularity. — *Ron Wynn*

● **Conscious Party** / Aug. 1989 / Virgin 90878
A pivotal release, with special guest Keith Richards. — *Ron Wynn*

Jahmekya / 1991 / Virgin 91626
Possibly Ziggy's best-overall release, it didn't enjoy the same impact as other material. — *Ron Wynn*

Larry Marshall

Disco, reggae
Despite being an energetic, convincing, and soulful vocalist, Larry Marshall's not well known except among the reggae faithful. He's both a superb romantic balladeer and an excellent message and roots vocalist. Marshall's single "Nanny Goat" was among the early transitional tunes signaling the music's evolution from rocksteady to reggae. He cut his first single at Studio One in the mid '60s; it was later remade by Clancy Eccles. Sessions for the Prince Buster and Top Deck labels followed; then a return to Studio One, where he attained stardom. He eventually became an engineer as well as a vocalist at the label. He's since recorded for various companies, among them Heartbeat and King's Music. — *Ron Wynn*

● **Presenting Larry Marshall** / Jan. 15, 1992 / Heartbeat 3508
A fine ballad stylist and effective uptempo singer, Larry Marshall's an obscurity to all except the reggae faithful. Here's a nice album featuring more recent material. — *Ron Wynn*

Freddie McGregor

Vocals / Reggae
"Little Freddie" joined the Clarendonians at the age of seven in 1963 and hasn't stopped singing since. He was with Coxsone Dodd's Studio One first, the Soul Syndicate in the late '70s, then became his own producer in the '80s. *Bobby Bobylon* is one of the finest productions in Dodd's history, compiling a decade's worth of unreleased tracks into McGregor's masterpiece. Equally at home in lovers rock or Rasta roots, composer-singer McGregor is consistently satisfying. — *Roger Steffens*

Across the Border / 1984 / RAS 3009
This wasn't one of his most consistent releases, but it reaffirmed that Freddie McGregor, unlike some of reggae's other great voices, never coasts or plods on a session, even on tepid tunes. — *Ron Wynn*

Come On Over / 1984 / RAS 3002
The soulful, jubilant voice of Freddie McGregor was equally outstanding on every track from this mid '80s session. The gem of the set was the soothing "Go Away Pretty Woman," but McGregor also ventured into topical material with "Stand Up and Fight" and "Brotherman" and spicy romantic ballads like "Rhythm So Nice" and "Shirley Come On Over." It was short, sweet, and to the point, and performed minus the slack lyrics and gun imagery that are now almost mandatory on dancehall material. — *Ron Wynn*

○ **Big Ship** / 1988 / Shanachie 48008
A fine reissue of a classic session. — *Ron Wynn*

Reggae Rockers / 1989 / Rohit 7714
More exciting, enthused vocals. — *Ron Wynn*

★ **Sings Jamaican Classic** / 1991 / VP 1200
Excellent vintage tracks brilliantly sung by one of reggae's all-time greats. — *Ron Wynn*

☆ **Bobby Bobylon** / Heartbeat 3502
Freddie's overall best, the product of a decade's work, sung over nothing but classic Coxsone rhythms. — *Roger Steffens*

Live at the Town & Country Club / VP 1150
A good choice for live settings. — *Ron Wynn*

Meditations

Group / Reggae, meditation
An early reggae trio whose smooth vocal stylings were tuned mainly to Rasta consciousness. "Tricked," "Woman Is Like a Shadow," and "Running from Jamaica" are examples of harmony at its most effective. — *Roger Steffens*

● **Greatest Hits** / 1984 / Shanachie 43015
Just as it says; two sides of pleasing meditations. — *Roger Steffens*

The Melodians

Group / Rock-steady
This rock-steady vocal trio is led by soulful Brent Dowe. "Rivers of Babylon," featured on the crucial soundtrack of the film *The Harder They Come*, is a world-class standard, often covered but never duplicated. — *Roger Steffens*

● **Sweet Sensation** / 1976 / Mango 539635
Sweet Sensation is the finest collection of the trio's soulful rock-steady. This showcases the period 1969-1971, when the Melodians found their greatest success, thanks in part to Leslie Kong's brilliant production. Includes the anthem "Rivers of Babylon," their international hit. — *Chris Woodstra*

○ **Pre-Meditation** / 1986 / Sky Note 18
"Swing and Dine" and "Don't Get Weary" make this an exemplary collection of the rock-steady style. — *Roger Steffens*

○ **Swing & Dine** / 1992 / Heartbeat 129
This outstanding 16-track collection, produced by Duke Reid and Sonia Pottinger, includes the Melodians' biggest hits for Treasure Isle . The threesome glided atop skipping, light rhythms provided by such bands as the Gaytones, Lyn Taitt and the Jets, the Soul Syndicate, and Tommy McCook and the Supersonics. They adjusted to rhythmic changes as reggae put more emphasis on heavy bass lines and aggressive horn charts. The Melodians primarily did poignant love tunes, though they could also handle evangelical or political material. The set features classics like "Little Nut Tree," "Hey Girl," "You Don't Need Me," and "Love Is a Doggone Good Thing." It's also thoroughly annonated and superbly mastered. — *Ron Wynn*

Michigan & Smiley

Reggae
Papa Michigan and General Smiley were among the first toaster duos on the Jamaican scene. Beginning in the late '70s while still in school, the humorous duo (Smiley was so named because he never smiles) scored immediately with "Rub-a-Dub Style" and "Nice Up the Dance," two ubiquitous songs on the dancehall circuit. "One Love Jam Down" became a popular anthem, and 1982's "Diseases" established them as major stars, especially at the annual Sunsplash festivals. They broke up in the late '80s, although occasional attempts at reunions have been made recently. — *Roger Steffens*

● **Rub-a-Dub Style** / 1992 / Heartbeat 3512
General Smiley and Papa Michigan helped pioneer the DJ duo format in reggae. Trading rhymes over versions of crucial roots reggae songs, they've created ripples of excitement in Jamaican dancehalls. Their talent for word play energizes tracks like "Rub-a-Dub Style" and "Nice Up the Dance," both of which were massive hits on the island. Find out why with this welcome reissue, produced by Clement "Coxsone" Dodd. — *Roundup newsletter*

The Mighty Diamonds

Group / Reggae
The most consistent and longest-running vocal trio in Jamaican musical history, consisting of the judge (Judge), the jester (Bunny), and the prophet (Tabby, the lead singer). Possessing one of the most achingly pure voices on earth, Tabby croons mini morality plays, limning life on the island of suffering with the precision of a microscope. — *Roger Steffens*

★ **Right Time** / 1976 / Shanachie 43014
The right album at the right time, with the right musicians, the right mix, and the right things to say. Eternal. — *Roger Steffens*

○ **Ice on Fire** / 1977 / Virgin 34235

Indestructible / 1982 / Alligator 8303
The only release that was issued and licensed on Alligator Records. — *Ron Wynn*

Roots Is There, The / 1982 / Shanachie 43009
Well done. — *Ron Wynn*

Struggling / 1985 / RAS 15
Though it says 1985 on the back of this CD, it might as well be the early '70s, for the Mighty Diamonds remain steadfastly committed to the principles that guided vintage reggae. They're still singing devout praise songs, defiant protest tunes, and infrequent but moving love ballads. Lead vocalist Tabby's alternately reverent, anguished, angry, and sentimental delivery turns even plodding numbers into triumphs, while Judge and Bunny's harmonies are among reggae's most attractive. The Diamonds wrote seven of the 10 tracks and also cover three fine Al Campbell originals, including the dynamic "Reggae-Lution." The production blends contemporary and classic touches, from Mallory Williams's teasing keyboards and synthesizer colors to David Madden and Chico's trumpet/sax interplay and contributions. If you've had problems in determining where the hip-hop and pop ends and the reggae begins in current material, you'll have no such problems with the Mighty Diamonds. — *Ron Wynn*

Reggae Street / 1987 / Shanachie 43004
A fine, funky knockout. — *Ron Wynn*

Real Enemy, The / Jul. 1987 / Rohit 77110
The title track is another memorable message piece. — *Ron Wynn*

Get Ready / 1988 / Rohit 77100
Nice harmonies, but the leads vary in energy and quality. — *Ron Wynn*

Go Seek Your Rights / Jul. 1990 / Frontline 1678
The title cut is among the best message tracks. — *Ron Wynn*

Jacob Miller

d. Mar. 23, 1980
Vocals / Reggae
One of reggae's brightest lights was abruptly snuffed out in a car crash in 1980. Miller's death occurred at a time when he had become more popular than Marley among the in-crowd. Huge, bubbling, and boyish, Miller blew spliff smoke in the face of authority (literally) and demanded that "we jam all night until daylight." His songs are timeless testaments to Jah and the healing power of herb. His loss is immense. — *Roger Steffens*

Natty Christmas / 1978 / RAS 3103
Along with DJ Ray I, Miller sends up Xmas; "Deck the Halls with Boughs of Collie" sets the pace. — *Roger Steffens*

● **Reggae Greats** / 1984 / Mango 539793
The true greatest hits. — *Roger Steffens*

○ **Collector's Classics** / 1988 / RAS 32045
Though they've enjoyed pop success in the post-Jacob Miller era, Inner Circle's never been the same since his death. Here's a com-

prehensive anthology featuring Miller's powerful, captivating voice at its finest. —*Ron Wynn*

Lincoln Sugar Minott (Sugar Minott)

Ragamuffin
Penning hit after hit for two decades, Minott is not only one of dancehall reggae's all-timers, but also a mentor to two generations of young stars developed by his Youth Promotions organization. Timely and touching, Minott at his best is utterly irresistible, as enticing as his nickname. —*Roger Steffens*

● Slice of the Cake / 1984 / Heartbeat 24
"Buy Out the Bar," "Level Vibes," "No Vacancy." All killer, no filler. —*Roger Steffens*

Extra Hot / 1986 / RAS 3018
"Herbman Hustling" and other '80s standouts. —*Roger Steffens*

○ Showcase / 1992 / Heartbeat 3510
Singer-songwriter Sugar Minott has carved out an impressive niche for himself in the reggae world, gaining more and more fans all over the world with each release and tour. This reissue of an earlier Studio One album, produced by Clement "Coxsone" Dodd, features extended mixes of popular Minott songs like "Oh Mr. D. C." and "Vanity." Backing musicians include drummer Leroy "Horsemouth" Wallace, bassist Earl "Bagga" Walker, and keyboardist Jackie Mittoo. — *Roundup newsletter*

Pablo Moses

Vocals / Reggae
Moses possesses a nasal, untutored voice that seems perfectly matched to his ghetto-aware lyrical concerns. His masterpiece, *A Song*, juxtaposed that voice against avant-Euro-disco arrangements for a one-of-a-kind triumph. —*Roger Steffens*

★ Song, A / 1980 / Mango 539541
A masterpiece of forward-looking sophistication from a roots perspective. —*Roger Steffens*

In the Future / 1983 / Alligator 8308
Always reliable and dependable—frequently electrifying. —*Ron Wynn*

Reggae Greats / 1984 / Mango 539790
A decent collection. —*Ron Wynn*

Tension / 1985 / Alligator 8311
This second album on Alligator Records tops the first. —*Ron Wynn*

Live to Love / 1988 / Rohit 9301
A capable production, first-rate vocals. —*Ron Wynn*

We Refuse / Nov. 1990 / Profile 1295
Updated, forthright, and to the point. —*Ron Wynn*

Judy Mowatt

Vocals / Reggae
Starting as lead singer for the Gaylettes in the mid '60s, Judy Mowatt has been one of reggae's leading female vocalists for a quarter-century with no signs of diminishment. Originally planning to become a preacher, Mowatt posesses one of the most sweetly powerful voices in Jamaica, an instrument she places at the service of Rastafarian and feminist causes above all else. After a series of local hits for her group or under the temporary pseudonym of Juliann, Mowatt became an international celebrity by helping form the I Threes, Bob Marley's backup singers, in 1974. When Marley built Tuff Gong, his own studio in Kingston, in 1977, Mowatt's seminal album *Black Woman*, considered by many critics to be the finest female album ever made in Jamaica, was the first to be recorded there. Mowatt wrote nearly all its tracks (Freddie McGregor and Bob Marley wrote the others). The title track and "Sisters Chant" are two ethereally beautiful cuts that encapsulate women's concerns everywhere and have achieved the status of anthems. Following Bob Marley's death, Mowatt has carved out a successful solo career, releasing a series of carefully crafted albums of canny originals and clever covers ("Grooving" and "Sing Our Own Song") that have solidified her forefront position in reggae's pantheon. —*Roger Steffens*

★ Black Woman / 1979 / Shanachie 43011
The debut by this former Bob Marley backup vocalist blends touching romanticism with impassioned feminism and religious Rastafarian fervor. —*John Floyd*

Only a Woman / 1982 / Shanachie 43007
Wonderful vocals, fine production, and a quiet but discernible edge. —*Ron Wynn*

○ Mellow Mood / Tuff Gong 70
This 1975 recording, probably her first LP, is a must for serious Judy Mowatt collectors. The arrangement and lyrics are simpler than those on her later LPs, but two songs make this album worth the price: "Mr. Big Man," a warning to the men in power that "your time is over," and "Rasta Woman Chant," a stark account of slavery. —*Ladyslipper*

Hugh Mundell

Reggae, protest
Vocalist Hugh Mundell made some stirring records during the late '70s and early '80s, particularly the landmark *Africa Must Be Free by 1983*. Unfortunately, Mundell didn't live to see South Africa eliminate apartheid. He was killed in a shooting incident in the early '80s. —*Ron Wynn*

● Africa Must Be Free by 1983 / RAS 3201
Hugh Mundell's protest masterpiece proves to be the highlight of this conservatively produced but otherwise good LP. —*Ron Wynn*

Junior Murvin

Vocals / Reggae
A high-pitched alto verging on falsetto distinguishes this languid singer from his peers. "Police and Thieves," produced by the wacky genius Lee Perry, is a prophetic standard that Murvin himself has rewritten several times in various versions. —*Roger Steffens*

● Police and Thieves / 1977 / Mango 539499
A mid '70s golden age of reggae masterwork. —*Roger Steffens*

Mutabaruka

Vocals / Dub poetry
Just above his forehead, poet Mutabaruka has a strip of white hair that bisects his jet black locks. That is the only white thing about this revolutionary writer whose "Every Time I 'Ear Dis Sound" burst through the mellow reggae of the early '80s like a bullet from an AK-47. Muta's deep voiced, uncompromising rants and his performances sans shoes and shirt make him a unique, almost fearsome figure. Listening to his melding of poetry and dub music, one can imagine an Old Testament prophet bellowing "Listen—or else!" —*Roger Steffens*

● Check It! / 1983 / Alligator 8306
Brilliant debut for Jamaica's hardest dub poet. Essential. —*Roger Steffens*

Outcry / 1984 / Shanachie 43023
More militant poetry with a rock-hard beat. —*Roger Steffens*

Mystery Unfolds, The / 1986 / Shanachie 43037
Poems with more highly orchestrated backing. —*Roger Steffens*

Any Which Way . . . Freedom / 1989 / Shanachie 43061
His first release in three years was as potent, abrasive, and defiant as any of the prior dates. —*Ron Wynn*

Blakk Wi Blak . . . Kkk / 1991 / Shanachie 43083
Strong, assertive, but nothing new. —*Ron Wynn*

Sonny Okosuns

b. 1947, Benin City, Nigeria
Vocals, guitar / African, reggae
With 16 African album releases to his credit—many of them gold—Nigeria's Sonny Okosuns is one of the continent's most enduringly popular performers. Okosuns initially caught the pop music bug via Elvis and the Beatles, forming his first band, the Postmen, in 1964. In the early '70s he helped usher in a back-to-African-roots trend with a stylistic mix of Western pop and local highlife he called "ozzidi." He later broadened it to include the rapidly spreading gospel of reggae. His diversity has kept him from being pigeonholed. He was featured in *Black Star Liner*, a 1983 anthology of African reggae, and more recently appeared on the antiapartheid *Sun City* LP produced by Steve Van Zandt. His albums typically feature vocals in English as well as in the Nigerian Ishan language. —*Bob Tarte*

● 3rd World / 1981 / OTI 0500
This is one of his best African records. —*J. Poet*

African Soldiers / 1991 / Profile 1414
Okosuns expands his music, moving away from a predominantly reggae-based music by adding highlife, funk, soca, and some punchy horn chants. —*J. Poet*

Johnny Osbourne

Vocals / Reggae
A 25-year career—ranging from soulful reggae to a massive dancehall catalog—that shows no sign of letting up. With his warm voice filled with conviction and yearning, he's one of the island's best, especially on standards like "Ice Cream Love," "Water Pumping," and countless rub-a-dub singles. —*Roger Steffens*

★ **Truth and Rights** / 1980 / Heartbeat 3513
Johnny Osbourne's heartfelt, soulful vocals have the capacity to captivate with sweet melodicism alone. The fact that he sings enlightened lyrics—about love, unity, honesty, respect, and bringing up children with warmth and guidance—increases the potency of these songs. And they're all wrapped up in a roots reggae package that's adorned with organ swirls, buoyant harmonies, and occasional horn blasts. Songs like the steadfast "Jah Promise" and gospel-influenced "Eternal Peace" are among the gems from Osbourne's Studio One days. —*Mark J. Cadigan, Roundup newsletter*

○ **Water Pumping** / 1983 / Greensleeves 61
The title track remains a reggae dancehall classic. Otherwise the material ranges from soulful to tepid, though Osbourne's seldom less than first-rate vocally. —*Ron Wynn*

Rougher Than Them / 1989 / VP 1048
A standout, whether singing fast or slow. —*Ron Wynn*

Cool Down / 1989 / VP 1051
An expert with reggae, soul, or even quasi-pop. —*Ron Wynn*

Augustus Pablo (Horace Swaby)

Vocals / Reggae, dub poetry
The name hasn't gained the international recognition of Bob Marley's, but Augustus Pablo is one of reggae's legitimate legends, a pioneer who flipped the genre completely upside down. Along with producer King Tubby, Pablo almost singlehandedly invented dub, wherein reggae's fat bass and popping drums are twisted and contorted until they crack like bullwhips and rumble like syncopated earthquakes. This is instrumental music: voices will emerge from the supple rhythms only to trickle into an echo-shrouded void, forsaking their contribution to the bedrock grooves. And Pablo's haunting splashes of melodica (which at times conjure images of Ennio Morricone's Sergio Leone soundtracks) give his music a sound that is immediately identifiable and as singular as anything Marley managed. As a youngster, Swaby hung around Kingston's jostling recording studios, watching the masters. There he met the original Augustus Pablo—the Upsetters' keyboardist Glen Adams—who invented the name and played the melodica, the odd instrument that gave reggae its "Far East" sound. Adams moved to the States in 1971 and left the concept to Swaby, who began recording in 1972. Under his new name, he released a string of brilliant singles over the next five or so years on his Rockers label. The best of those singles are collected on *Original Rockers;* his best early album is *King Tubby Meets Rockers Uptown* (1976). His more recent work has only occasionally matched the breathtaking innovation of the old stuff. Only the 1981 *East of the River Nile* has equaled his early triumphs. But he's still at it, occasionally striking a balance between the technical wizardry of his Tubby years and the slick production style of modern reggae. The results aren't always great, but they're always interesting. —*John Floyd & Roger Steffens*

Rebel Rock Reggae—This Is Augustus Pablo / 1972 / Heartbeat 34
Augustus Pablo formed his mysterious dub style on these early sessions, with Lee Perry producing and the best reggae session players backing. —*Myles Boisen*

○ **King Tubby Meets Rockers Uptown** / 1975 / Shanachie 1007
A personal favorite, with Robbie Shakespeare and members of Bob Marley's band. —*Myles Boisen*

★ **East of the River Nile** / 1977 / Shanachie 1003
Many regard this as Pablo's masterpiece, a superlative blending of earthy dub techniques with floating melodic lines in an exotic, oriental mode. —*Myles Boisen*

Original Rockers / 1979 / Shanachie 44008
Yet another heavy early work. —*Myles Boisen*

East of the River Nile / 1979 / Message ?

Meet King Tubby Inna Fire House / 1981 / Shanachie 43001
Another early gem, *Rockers Meet King Tubby Inna Fire House* shows the influence of dub pioneer King Tubby. —*Myles Boisen*

○ **Earth's Rightful Ruler** / 1982 / Shanachie 44011
Top session players and some vocal assistance from Hugh Mundell, Delroy Williams, and others makes this an early classic. —*Myles Boisen*

Rising Sun / 1985 / Shanachie 44009
This 1985 effort is a little slicker than others but still worthwhile. —*Myles Boisen*

Eastman Dub / 1988 / RAS 3038
Pablo extends his musical arsenal to include xylophone and various keyboards in addition to his trademark melodica. —*Myles Boisen*

Rockers International Showcase / 1991 / Rykodisc 10177
This compilation of Pablo tracks gives a nice cross-section of his work. —*Myles Boisen*

Blowing with the Wind / Jun. 1991 / Shanachie 43076
One of his newest recordings, with a Far Eastern sound reminiscent of *East of the River Nile.* —*Myles Boisen*

Frankie Paul

Vocals / Dance, soul, reggae
Nearly blind from birth, young Frankie Paul is one of the most dependable dancehall singers of the '80s. With a pleasant midrange voice, he eschews slackness in his well-regarded live performances. Consistent and exemplary. —*Roger Steffens*

● **Pass the Tu-Sheng-Peng** / 1985 / Greensleeves 75
Frankie goes to the dance and lives to sing about it. Lots of fun. —*Roger Steffens*

● **Get Closer** / 1990 / Profile 1296
Stalwart dancehall numbers. Good leads and production. —*Ron Wynn*

Lee "Scratch" Perry

Vocals / Reggae
The "bumpity riddim" of Lee "Scratch" Perry, Jamaica's most outrageous producer, percolates like an aural gallop through a minefield in a hailstorm. Why is he named "Scratch"? "Because," he cackles, "all things start from scratch. So check it out—who am I?" Whenever a dub track is shattered by an earthshaking shriek from the ninth dimension, whenever a glossolalia-quick burst of word salad blurts over an acid-tinged assault of bass and drums, whenever a "Croaking Lizard" grunts toward some "Roast Fish and Cornbread"—chances are great that the diminutive Mr. Perry has had his flexible fingers in it. Starting as an assistant to Coxsone Dodd as he struggled to begin his seminal Studio One in the mid '50s, Perry soon was mixing, arranging, and engineering sessions. Shortly thereafter he was producing and singing as well. By the late '60s he had established a series of labels under the Upsetter umbrella and forged one of the most critical links in the chain of reggae's worldwide successes by joining his studio band with Bob Marley, Peter Tosh, and Bunny Livingstone (the Wailers). The result was a pair of crucial albums that have never stopped selling since 1970—*Soul Rebels* and *African Herbsman*—rereleased all over the world under dozens of different titles, most notably Trojan's recent vocal-and-dub triumph called *Soul Revolution Vols. I and II,* an absolutely essential Wailers compilation and a triumph of early reggae minimalism.

Perry suffers from a combination of glossolalia (he speaks in tongues—, for example, he says "wizzy wizzy" instead of *wisdom*) and "graphalalia" (he fills every available surface with writing). He's a beat poet times ten, the original speed-rapper whose Black Ark studio became home to myriad noteworthy '70s artists who were discovered by him or whose careers were revivified by his take-no-prisoners production techniques. These singers included the Heptones (the essential *Party Time* album), Big Youth, the Mighty Diamonds, Max Romeo (*War Ina Babylon*), Gregory Isaacs, Delroy Wilson, U-Roy, I Roy, Junior Murvin (*Police and Thieves*), and Dillinger, to name a tiny fraction. As the '80s dawned, artists from Paul McCartney to the Clash beat a path to the graffiti-scrawled door of Perry's Black Ark in Kingston.

During periods of controlled madness in the past decade, Perry toured Europe with a stage lineup similar to Marley's, right down to the three female backup singers. Recently, he married an allegedly titled Swiss woman and began spending half of each year in the Alps. His music is unmistakable still: wacky, wondrously histrionic, and as persistent as a jackhammer to the brain. Long may he rave! —*Roger Steffens*

○ **Roast Fish Collie Weed & Corn** / 1978 / VP 1000
A fairly typical all-Jamaican effort done at Perry's Black Ark studio (before he burned it down). —*Myles Boisen*

Lord God Muzick / 1981 / Heartbeat 65
Recent dementia, recorded with the Upsetters after a European tour and dedicated to his new European and American fans . . . hmm! —*Myles Boisen*

History, Mystery & Prophesy / 1984 / Mango 539774
More contemporary rantings. —*Myles Boisen*

● **Reggae Greats** / 1984 / Mango 539792
Perry productions featuring the Heptones, Junior Murvin, Max Romeo, Prince Jazzbo, and the upsetter himself—fairly straightforward but brilliant song settings. —*Myles Boisen*

Scratch Attack / 1988 / Clock Tower 1415
Two albums on one CD—the imaginative *Chapter 1* and the dubbed-out *Blackboard Jungle Dub* session, from Perry's own Black Ark studio. —*Myles Boisen*

○ **Upsetter Compact Set, The** / 1988 / Trojan 1
Returning to the days when music of sheer genius was being made by one of the most influential men, this set collects three albums issued under the name of Perry's studio band, the Upsetters. — *Ed Ward, Rock & Roll Disc*

Chicken Scratch / 1989 / Heartbeat 53
Mid '60s material with the Upsetter from Studio One. Perry is the featured vocalist on singles with the Wailers, Rita Marley, the Skatalites, and more. —*Myles Boisen*

Open the Gate / 1989 / Trojan 2
Here we are presented with full-length songs and their "versions," of dubs. This is tape manipulation to the same extent as Pierre Henry's early *musique concrète* experiments. What these pieces have is a deep groove that sucks in the listener and, usually, makes invisible the incredible art of the mixer. At least a few of the earlier numbers have been dubbed off of records. — *Ed Ward, Rock & Roll Disc*

From the Secret Laboratory / 1990 / Mango 539869
Produced by modern dub master Adrian Sherwood, with Perry presiding regally over a crew of Jamaican, English, and American players. —*Myles Boisen*

○ **Some of the Best** / 1991 / Heartbeat 37
Odds and ends from the reggae/rockers era (1968-1972), with Bob Marley and the Wailers, Junior Byles, Linval Thompson, and the ever-creative Upsetters. —*Myles Boisen*

Pinchers (Delroy Thompson)

Vocals / Reggae
Delroy Thompson may be named after a pair of pliers, but there's nothing mechanical about his soothing, melodic dancehall singing style. Going against the genre's grain, Pinchers does not chant slackness but seeks to elevate, educate, and entertain, although "Agony," his trademark, walks a fine line between the profane and the profound. —*Roger Steffens*

● **Pinchers Meets Sanchez** / VP 1100

Prince Buster (Cecil Bustamanate Campbell)

Ska
Prince Buster was among Jamaica's first international stars. His singles were outrageous, sexist, hilarious, widely influential, and inspirational. A onetime boxer, Prince Buster began working as a combination sound engineer and bouncer for Coxsone Dodd. His claims to be ska's inventor make him a Jamaican equivalent of Jelly Roll Morton for exaggerated importance, but Buster certainly helped popularize it. After parting company with Dodd, Buster established his own sound system, label, and record store. His first recording session yielded the anthemic original "Oh Carolina" by the Folks Brothers. Buster soon had multiple labels operating: Wild Bells, Voice of the People, and Buster's Record Shack. His singles were distributed on the Blue Beat label in

England, and his fame rose while such hits as "Al Capone" and "Madness" exploded. His talking/toasting records, filled with lewd imagery and vivid language, proved enormously popular. Buster doubled as a prolific performer and busy recording executive in the '70s, cutting sessions with Dennis Brown, Big Youth, John Holt, and Alton Ellis, among others. He reissued his old records, churned out compilations, bought record stores, and built a huge empire. Buster stopped performing in the late '70s, then returned to the stage in the late '80s. He was still cutting fresh tracks as recently as 1992. —*Ron Wynn*

● **Fabulous Greatest Hits** / 1980 / Melodisc 1
This is arguably the set to get if you're unaware of Prince Buster's charms. There are several outlandish, outrageous numbers spiced by Prince Buster's madcap toasting and energetic presence. —*Ron Wynn*

Prince Far I

Vocals / Reggae
With a voice deeper and more darkly shaded than a mid-ocean trench, Prince Far I rapped tales of eccentrics like Bedward, the "Flying Preacher," and prophesied the holocausts of these "last days," before being murdered in his bed at the close of the '80s. —*Roger Steffens*

★ **Black Man Land** / 1990 / Frontline 1681
A reissue of his penetrating vocal raps on the Virgin/Caroline label. —*Myles Boisen*

Ras Michael & the Sons of Negus

Group / Reggae, Nyahbinghi
Negus is a title of Ethiopian Emperor Haile Selassie, the Almighty God of the Rastafarian movement, and no one pays him more eloquent homage than Ras Michael and his group. This is the beat of the heart, based on the original "instrument of ten strings," the hand-beaten drum. On *Dadawah* in 1975, Michael took a religious ceremonial gathering as the basis for an album of elegant poetry and raw, visceral power. Later, eschewing minimalism, such works as *Promised Land Sounds* added electronics and produced a primeval psychedelia without compare in Jamaican history. This is the sound of the Roots Church in the 21st century, highly charged hymns for humanity's future survival. —*Roger Steffens*

○ **Rastafari** / 1975 / Top Ranking
More Rasta gospel music, including the essential "None a Jah Jah Children No Cry" and "Mr. Brown." —*Roger Steffens*

Promised Land Sounds / 1980 / Lions Gate 1202
Four extended Nyabinghi jams; the Grateful Dread meets 2001. —*Roger Steffens*

Rally Round / 1985 / Shanachie 43027
More Rasta standards from their primary musical spokesperson. —*Roger Steffens*

★ **Dadawah** / Trojan
The best Rasta testament from the '70s. Spin it and become a "Man in the Hills." —*Roger Steffens*

Junior Reid

Reggae
Junior Reid found himself in a difficult spot when he joined Black Uhuru in 1986. He replaced Michael Rose, who'd become quite popular as a longtime Uhuru contributor. Though essentially a good vocalist, Reid had a style so close to Rose's he didn't establish his own identity. The group also suffered compositional difficulties and personal crisis during Reid's tenure. Puma Jones left and was replaced by Olafunke. They also didn't always get quality material or support from Sly & Robbie during this period. Reid departed in 1990 and has since been struggling as a solo artist to fulfill his considerable potential. —*Ron Wynn*

● **Long Road** / 1991 / Cohiba 221100
Junior Reid's been unable to attain consistent stardom despite being among reggae's better vocalists. This was his finest LP, marked by tremendous singing and both strong romantic and effective roots/message material. —*Ron Wynn*

Max Romeo & the Upsetters

Group / Disco, Reggae

His leering '60s UK smash "Wet Dream" was really (said Max) about "a leaky roof." In the '70s he made several roots reggae standards, most notably for producer Lee Perry. Although still active, he's had no material in the '80s that equals his talent and sweet intensity. —*Roger Steffens*

● **War Ina Babylon** / 1976 / Mango 539392
One of Lee Perry's most perfect '70s productions, especially on the chilling title track and "One Step Forward." —*Roger Steffens*

○ **Reconstruction** / 1978 / Mango 9503
Several stirring vocal performances, even on otherwise shaky numbers, made this an above-average vehicle for Max Romeo. —*Ron Wynn*

Roots Radics

Group / Reggae
The key studio band of the '80s in Jamaica, they've recorded with everyone from Gregory Isaacs (*Night Nurse* is his greatest) to Bunny Wailer (*Rock 'n' Groove*). With Dwight Pinkney on finger-picked guitar, Flabba Hold on wicked punchy bass, Style Scott on hard metronomic drums, and Bingy Bunny on precise rhythm guitar, along with Steely on scintillating keyboards, they set the standard for a decade of increasing, unceasing, international penetration of Jamaican music. —*Roger Steffens*

● **World Peace III** / 1992 / Heartbeat 110
Lots of singing, with a great Garvey song, "International Hero." The culmination of two decades' work in the studios. —*Roger Steffens*

Leroy Sibbles

Reggae
Both a wonderful vocalist and fine bassist, Leroy Sibbles initially gained fame as the lead singer for the Heptones. The trio began at Caltone, then became stars when they moved to Studio One in 1966. They were accomplished at both rock-steady and reggae, and Sibbles's wondrously soulful leads and excellent compositions were augmented by his smooth, hypnotic bass lines, which were reproduced on numerous Heptones' knockoffs and versions. Unfortunately a once musically profitable relationship soured, and the Heptones left Studio One under bitter circumstances in 1971. Sibbles has since enjoyed a successful solo career but retains his bitterness toward Dodd and Studio One. He remained with the Heptones a couple more years, and their 1973 LP *Party Time* was an international reggae favorite. —*Ron Wynn*

Mean While / Attic 1226

Sister Carol

Vocals / Reggae
Toaster Sister Carol, a Jamaican immigrant who lives in Brooklyn, is one of the most forceful exponents of women's rights in reggae today. A decade in the business, she has recorded duets with Judy Mowatt (Bob Marley's "Screwface") and appeared in several movies, including Johnathan Demme's riotous *Something Wild* in which she sang "Wild Thing" over the closing titles. A Sunsplash headliner, Carol has become an example for many younger people coming up in the music, someone who shows that slackness is not the only way to gain a contemporary audience. —*Roger Steffens*

● **Jah Disciple** / RAS 3053
Sister Carol emphasized truth and rights over sex and love on this session issued by Ras in 1989. She had harsh words for outer space exploration, internal African problems, and rude boys who disrupt social affairs, while recalling an earlier, more enjoyable time on "Remember When" and calling for respect and dignity from an ignorant male on "A No Me Name Peggy." Her toasts were slower and paced differently than the rapid-fire dancehall mode; the arrangements and backing combined electronic and acoustic instrumentation, and there was more than a trace of vintage reggae in her style and sound. —*Ron Wynn*

Skatalites

Group / Reggae, ska
Ska was Jamaica's first indigenous creation, a compelling mix of fast R&B, Rastafarian African rhythms, and Afro-Cuban percussion highlight. This double-time delight ruled Jamaica from 1962 to 1966, and no one played it more convincingly than its creators,

the Skatalites. Led by a mentally disturbed world-class trombonist named Don Drummond, the Skatalites were an amalgam of the top instrumentalists on the island at the time: Tommy McCook, Roland Alphonso, and "Ska" Campbell on tenor sax; Lester Stering on alto; Karl Bryan on baritone; "Dizzy Johnny" Moore and Baba Brooks on trumpet; Lloyd Brevett on bass; Lloyd Knibbs on drums; Jackie Mittoo on piano; and Lyn Tait and Jah Jerry on guitar. Viewed from today's perspective, this is a roster of Jamaica's musical gods, the originators of all that would come out of this tiny land of two million people to influence the entire world of music for the next 30 years. Rock-steady, reggae, rockers, dub—all are merely tempo reworkings of their skipping ska beat. It is remarkable, then, to note that the Skatalites existed for a mere 14 months. As 1965 dawned, Drummond murdered his wife and was put away in "de Bellevue" mental hospital, where he died a couple years later. The band then broke up into several different lineups, most notably Tommy McCook and the Supersonics, and the Soul Brothers. Their rhythm slowed in 1966 to the rock-steady, a twin result of Drummond's loss and a torpid steamy summer during which people didn't want to dance as frenetically as they had before. But ska underwent periodic revivals, particularly among British skinheads in the late '60s; Northern British two-tone skanksters in 1980; and massive movements in the '80s in places as far afield as Brussels, Tokyo, and California. Today, ska has achieved a permanent place in the world's beats, as alive, fresh, and exciting as rock & roll. Yet even now, no interpretation sounds more compelling than the original Studio One recordings made by its masters, the Skatalites. —*Roger Steffens*

○ **Ska Authentic** / 1967 / Studio One
Early '60s ravers, including "Lee Oswald" and "Bridge View" (any Studio One Skatalites collection is worth owning). —*Roger Steffens*

● **Scattered Lights** / 1984 / Alligator 8309
Recorded from 1962 to 1965 for Justin Yap's Top Deck, and featuring some of the final shots of Don Drummond. Admirable. —*Roger Steffens*

Sly & Robbie

Dance, reggae
Drummer Sly Dunbar and bassist Robbie Shakespeare have arguably been reggae's preeminent production team since the early '70s. Besides appearing on countless sessions, they patented the "Taxi" sound; a clean, less choppy style with Shakespeare's bass lines augmented by Dunbar's use of syndrums, which added a different sound to the reggae mix. This helped bring more electronic and production effects into reggae (detractors viewed them as gimmicks) and created changes in style, tone, and emphasis that have continued nonstop ever since. Sly & Robbie have produced sessions by Gregory Isaacs, Black Uhuru, Grace Jones, Joan Armatrading, Bob Dylan, Ian Drury, the Mighty Diamonds, and many, many others. They've also issued many compilations and sessions featuring their productions as well as Dunbar's cut solo dates for Front Line and Mango. —*Ron Wynn*

● **A Dub Experience—Reggae Greats** / 1984 / Mango 539787
A good sampling of dub from this in-demand rhythm duo on this installment of Island/Mango's *Reggae Greats* series. —*Scott Bultman*

○ **Rhythm Killers** / 1987 / Island 842785
Another session with Bill Laswell. The all-star guest lineup includes Bootsy Collins, Bernie Worrell, Bernard Fowler, Henry Threadgill, Nicky Skopelitis, Shinehead, and Pat Thrall. Features a killer version of the Ohio Players hit "Fire," with funky Bootsy Collins grooves throughout the album. —*Scott Bultman*

○ **Tribute to King Tubby, A** / 1990 / Rohit 7791

Leroy Smart

Reggae
A master of love songs and roots material, Leroy Smart's been on the reggae scene since the early '70s. He was raised in Kingston's Alpha Catholic Boys Home and began recording in the early '70s. Smart worked with such producers as Gussie Clarke, Joe Joe Hookin, and Bunny Lee while gaining fame for a flamboyant performance style, exceptionally anguished delivery, and penetrating vocal manner. Smart's smashing voice often seemed about to collapse from anxiety and earnestness in mid-song. He's maintained

his popularity through the '70s, '80s, and '90s, never scoring any crossover or international hits, but retaining his pull with the notoriously fickle Jamaican audience. —*Ron Wynn*

● **Dread Hot in Africa** / 1988 / Burning Sounds 1004
Piercing, poignant, and topical fare from a legitimate reggae great. Leroy Smart's cutting delivery and wailing leads are as moving and hypnotic as those of Dennis Brown, Gregory Isaacs, Freddie McGregor, or any other better-known superstar. —*Ron Wynn*

Slim Smith

Vocals / Reggae
In the '60s, Slim Smith was one of the lead singers of the seminal Techniques, then went on to form (with Jimmy Riley) the Uniques. Often compared to Curtis Mayfield (his major influence), Smith never achieved the financial rewards his extensive, big-selling output deserved. He died tragically in the early '70s when he punched his fist through a glass door in frustration and bled to death before he could summon help. He remains one of Jamaica's most venerated and gifted interpreters. Virtually everything he cut is worth owning, particularly if your tastes run to Impressions-style harmonies. —*Roger Steffens*

○ **Born to Love** / 1979 / Heartbeat 3501
Includes the eternal "You Don't Care" and the oft-versioned "Rougher Yet." —*Roger Steffens*

Steel Pulse

Group / Soul, R&B, reggae
Formed in the early '70s in industrially depressed Birmingham, England, Pulse created a new kind of reggae, adapting such disparate influences as flamenco and Euro-pop to give voice to an alienation as hard as the times. Such tracks as "Ku Klux Klan" and "Handsworth Revolution" led Bob Marley to declare Pulse among his favorite groups. In the '80s they created a super successful album with "True Democracy," their highpoint, but then, like contemporaries Aswad, they seemed to lose direction and militancy in a search for mainstream commercial success, largely at the urging of their record labels. —*Roger Steffens*

● **True Democracy** / 1970 / Elektra 60113

Handsworth Revolution / 1978 / Mango 539502
The title track is another among several unforgettable numbers penned and performed by Steel Pulse during their tenure on Island. The LP as a whole was just a shade below *Babylon the Bandit*. —*Ron Wynn*

○ **Babylon the Bandit** / 1985 / Elektra 60437
Biting, frequently riveting protest material from Steel Pulse. The title track's one of several anthemic numbers punctuated by the remarkable David Hinds. Only Aswad compares to them among British reggae bands, and they've never produced any roots or political tracks superior to routine Steel Pulse material. —*Ron Wynn*

Steely & Clevie

Group / Reggae
The Sly & Robbie of contemporary '90s dancehall, Wycliffe "Steely" Johnson and Cleveland Browne are the in-house rhythm programmers from studios like Jammy's, Techniques, Powerhouse, Redman, and Gussie Clarke's Music Works. Those they have backed include Gregory Isaacs, Frankie Paul, Maxi Priest, Freddie McGregor, and Grammy winner Shabba Ranks. Highly digital. —*Roger Steffens*

● **Twenty-First Century Sound Clash** / 1988 / VP 1059

The Tamlins

Group / Disco, reggae
The Tamlins—Carlton Smith, Junior Moore, and Derrick Lara—are among the most widely respected backup singers in reggae, especially for their years of international touring in support of Peter Tosh. They have backed John Holt, Delroy Wilson, Pat Kelly, Marcia Griffiths, and a host of others, as well as recording on their own. Lara's ethereally high lead vocals bring to mind the best of '70s Philly soul music, a style they have often covered. —*Roger Steffens*

Love Devine / Heartbeat 44
Soothing, often enjoyable, but not substantive. —*Ron Wynn*

Third World

Group / Reggae
Third World's cover of "Now That We Found Love" is an R&B radio staple, along with the reggae classic "96 Degrees in the Shade." Composed of well-educated and -connected uptown Jamaicans, Third World blends a sophistication in instrumentation (note guitarist Cat Coore's live cello excursions) with a pop consciousness that seems ironically unable to penetrate the mainstream market despite years of major label attempts. —*Roger Steffens*

● **96 Degrees in the Shade** / 1977 / Mango 539830
The album that cemented their stateside popularity. —*Ron Wynn*

Rock the World / 1981 / CBS 37402
Well meaning, this juggles R&B, pop, and reggae. —*Ron Wynn*

All the Way Strong / 1983 / CBS 38687
Teetering on the pop tightrope. —*Ron Wynn*

Reggae Greats / Mar. 1985 / Mango 539789
A decent place to start with reggae's longest-lasting pop ensemble. —*Ron Wynn*

○ **Sense of Purpose** / Apr. 1985 / CBS 39877
A-1 production and arrangements. —*Ron Wynn*

You've Got the Power / 1989 / CBS 37744
Some above-average ballads and social cuts. —*Ron Wynn*

● **Reggae Ambassadors: 20th Anniversary Collection** / Oct. 5, 1993 / Mercury
While they didn't make groundbreaking albums, this pop-reggae outfit found a great deal of success with their singles. This two-disc anthology may be too much for the casual listener but the more ambitious will want to start here. All of the essential tracks are here, as well as some fine live performances. —*Chris Woodstra*

Tiger

Vocals / Dancehall
Gruff-voiced '80s DJ Tiger leaped to prominence in the Jamaican dancehalls with an anti-fat rap called "No Wanga Gut." A scintillating live performer, Tiger overcame an extended period of substance abuse to return in the early '90s and regain his growly crown. —*Roger Steffens*

● **Me Name Tiger** / 1987 / RAS 3021
"No Wanga Gut" and "Puppy Love" anchor his US debut. —*Roger Steffens*

Andrew Tosh

Vocals / Reggae
Eldest son of the late Wailer Peter Tosh, Andrew made his debut at his father's funeral in 1987, wowing the mourners with his physical and vocal similarities to Peter. Two promising albums later, Andrew is looked upon as one of conscious reggae's greatest hopes. A tour with the Wailers in 1991 solidified his live reputation. With strong material he could fill his famous father's shoes in a manner similar to that of Ziggy Marley. —*Roger Steffens*

● **Make Place for the Youth** / 1989 / Tomato 79752
Self-penned mini-dramas showcase Andrew's promising growth. —*Roger Steffens*

Peter Tosh (Winston Hubert McIntosh)

b. Oct. 9, 1944, Jamaica, d. Sep. 11, 1987, Kingston, Jamaica
Vocals, guitar, melodica, organ / Reggae
In the early Wailers lineup, Peter Tosh stood apart from the other members not only because of his six-foot-plus height but also because of his boasty-boy attitude. He was known as the "stepping razor" after a song Joe Higgs had written, and his knife-sharp temper could whittle many a bad man down to size. But he had a soft, extremely humorous side as well, as evidenced by his frequent word play: he complained about the "crime ministers who shit in the House of Represent-a-Thief" and called America "A-*sada*-ca, because there is nothing merry about it." Tosh joined up with Bunny Wailer and Bob Marley in 1962, and they rehearsed nearly two years before they made their Studio One debut with "Simmer Down." Tosh played guitar, melodica, piano, and organ on many of their early tracks; he even played behind American pop star Johnny Nash's Columbia Records ses-

sions in the late '60s, when Nash had hired the Wailers as song-writers. By 1973 Tosh felt the need to pursue a solo career because of the mass of material he had written and his dissatisfaction with Island Records' boss Chris Blackwell. *Legalize It* was his debut in 1976, remaking many of his earlier Jamaican recordings and giving the marijuana movement its most potent anthem in the title track, which Tosh would perform not once but twice in his '70s live concerts.

A firm opponent of the hypocritical "shitstem," Tosh was a favorite target of Babylon's legal forces. Police in Jamaica beat him nearly to death on at least three occasions, and he bore the scars till his death. *Equal Rights*, 1977's follow-up, provided a key line that echoed 15 years later in the mouths of LA rioters: "I don't want no peace, I want equal rights and justice!" The Rolling Stones, impressed by Tosh's ferocious and unflinching posture, signed him to their fledgling label and released *Bush Doctor* in 1978, another series of hymns and harangues. *Mystic Man* (1979) and *Wanted: Dread & Alive* (1981) kept a militant attitude while trying to cross over to the mainstream that Marley had conquered, without achieving anything near Marley's success. Following 1983's *Mama Africa* and a live album from that tour, Tosh disappeared for four years, seeking advice from traditional medicine men in Africa and trying to extricate himself from various recording agreements when he found his records released in South Africa against provisions in his contracts. In 1987, shortly after the release of *No Nuclear War*, Tosh was assassinated at his home in Kingston. Only one of the three gunmen responsible was arrested; he was sentenced to hang after a brief trial. Like Marley, Tosh left at least ten children and no will. A brilliant documentary, *Peter Tosh: Red X-Stepping Razor*, was released in 1992, and there is hope that at least one more album will come out of the vaults. —*Roger Steffens*

○ **Legalize It** / 1976 / CBS 34253
Tosh cut this album after leaving the Wailers but used virtually the entire Wailers band (minus Bob Marley) to do it. His "Legalize It," a plea about marijuana with a twist ("I'll advertise it"), is still winning. —*William Ruhlmann*

★ **Equal Rights** / 1977 / CBS 34670
Tosh's most political album includes his own version of "Get Up, Stand Up," as well as the chilling "Stepping Razor." The music, anchored by Sly & Robbie, is as tough as the lyrics. —*William Ruhlmann*

Bush Doctor / 1978 / Trojan 2100
"Creation" is Genesis set to music; "Moses" continues the story; "Don't Look Back" teams Tosh with Jagger. An appealing collection. —*Roger Steffens*

Wanted Dread & Alive / 1981 / EMI America 91670
Great Binghi roots-rave on "Rastafari Is," plus the gorgeous ballad "Fools Die" and other mixed pleasures. —*Roger Steffens*

○ **Mama Africa** / 1983 / EMI America 91671
A strong collection with the hit "Johnny B. Goode" and remakes of "Maga Dog" and "Stop That Train." —*Roger Steffens*

No Nuclear War / 1987 / EMI America 46700
His valedictory album, with "Lesson in My Life," strangely foreshadowed his murder by a "friend." —*Roger Steffens*

Twinkle Brothers

Group / Reggae, dub poetry
Norman Grant is the unifying factor in the various lineups of the Twinkles over the past 20 years. Possessing a rootical North Coast sensibility, as opposed to the harder-edged Kingston vibe, the Twinkle Brothers' music is Rastafarian belting at its best. Grant is even a big star in reggae-loving Poland, where he has cut five albums for that market. —*Roger Steffens*

○ **Live at Reggae Sunsplash—Since I Throw** / 1984 / Sunsplash 8907
Superb vocals and a representative live set. —*Ron Wynn*

★ **Free Africa** / 1990 / Frontline 1684
Grab anything you can find by this tremendous outfit. —*Ron Wynn*

U-Roy (Ewart Beckford)

Vocals / Reggae
In the late '60s, U-Roy almost single-handedly invented the modern DJ rap style in Jamaica by toasting on the sound system of pi-oneer King Tubby, who was the first engineer to mix reverb and echo effects on deconstructed rhythm tracks. This led directly to the Jamaican peculiarity of having only one song per seven-inch single (the A-side being the vocal, the B-side being the "dub version" or rhythm bed that any local toaster could "skank" over with the events of the day). But U-Roy remains the most trickily tasteful exemplar of the style, largely owing to his uncanny choice of tracks over which to toast, and on which he created ad hoc dialogs with the singer, commenting on and responding to the lyrics. His toasts, classics of the form, include "On the Beach," "Wear You to the Ball," and "Tide Is High" In his royalty-ridiculing '70s scat "Chalice in the Palace," he invites the Queen herself to suck on the ganja pipe (chalice). Still active, living in Los Angeles, he is now referred to respectfully as Daddy U-Roy. —*Roger Steffens*

● **Dread in a Babylon** / 1976 / Frontline 1683
This is the veteran rapper's best album, comparable to any in this idiom. —*Michael G. Nastos*

Bunny Wailer (Neville O'Reilly Livingstone)

Vocals / Reggae
This crucial Jamaican singer and songwriter was raised as Bob Marley's brother from the age of nine. As cofounder of the Wailers (along with Peter Tosh), Bunny gave high chromatic shadings to some of the most exhilarating harmonies ever pressed on wax, the equal of the finest work done by their contemporaries, the Impressions. Bunny's "Pass It On" was one of the standout tracks on the final album the Wailers did together as a trio, 1973's *Burning*. Three years later, Bunny released his first solo project, one of reggae's most majestic achievements, the roots classic *Blackheart Man*, which included hymnlike chants with titles like "Dreamland," "Bide Up," and "Rastaman." Bunny's baritone has been showcased in as many as three albums a year, most notably *Struggle* (1980); *Bunny Wailer Sings the Wailers* (1980's collection of covers); *Rock & Groove* (1981 dancehall classics); *Live* (recorded at his first solo concert in Kingston in December 1982); and *Liberation* (1988's consciousness-raiser that is the acknowledged peer of his spectacular debut album *Blackheart Man*). He won a Grammy in 1991 for *Time Will Tell*, a tribute collection of covers of Bob Marley songs. He has toured abroad twice, trying to overcome his reputation as reggae's most reclusive artist, backed by members of the original Skatalites, Sly & Robbie, and the Roots Radics. A spectacular show at New York's Madison Square Garden (1986) has been released on video. Today Bunny is obsessed with reaching the teenage dancehall crowd, attempting to wean them away from the predominant slackness of the form and back to a recognition of the truth and rights that were reggae's original concerns. He also feels the need to continue the work of his late partners, Tosh and Marley, bringing to oppressed people everywhere the twin messages of hope and the faith to carry on. —*Roger Steffens*

★ **Black Heart Man** / 1976 / Mango 539415
Maybe his best, certainly a classic. —*Ron Wynn*

Struggle / 1980 / Solomonic 3
The title cut is anthemic; everything else is superb. —*Ron Wynn*

Bunny Wailer Sings the Wailers / 1980 / Mango 539629
As poignant a tribute as you'll ever hear. —*Ron Wynn*

○ **Rock'n'Groove** / 1981 / Solomonic

○ **Live** / 1983 / Solomonic 9
Tough to find, but worth the effort. —*Ron Wynn*

Roots Radics Rockers Reggae / 1983 / Shanachie 43013
A reggae original runs the genre's gamut. —*Ron Wynn*

Marketplace / 1985 / Shanachie 43071
Entertaining and enriching. —*Ron Wynn*

Rootsman Skanking / 1987 / Shanachie 43043
Emphatic vocals. —*Ron Wynn*

Rule Dance Hall / 1987 / Shanachie 43050
Controversial content, but outstanding. —*Ron Wynn*

○ **Liberation** / 1989 / Shanachie 43059
A textbook Wailer outing. —*Ron Wynn*

Time Will Tell / 1991 / Shanachie 43072
Heartwarming, Grammy-winning remakes of Marley compositions. —*Roger Steffens*

Wailing Souls

Group / Soul, reggae

If lead singer Winston "Pipe" Matthews sounds like a slightly higher-pitched version of Bob Marley, that may be because he was tutored by the same teacher (Joe Higgs) in the same yard that produced the Wailers. The Souls have gone through many different lineups, but Pipe and his partner Lloyd "Bread" McDonald have survived as a duo and currently record for Columbia Records. Through most of the Souls' history, they were one of reggae's only quartets that gave voice to Jamaican folk sayings and righteous religious rumblings through shimmering harmonies. — *Roger Steffens*

★ **Wild Suspense** / 1979 / Island 9523
Brilliant quartet triumphs, echoing the harmonic heights of the early Wailers. Virtually their greatest hits, backed by Sly & Robbie. —*Roger Steffens*

Firehouse Rock / 1980 / Shanachie 48004
Junjo-produced, with the Radics mixed by Scientist at King Tubby's. What's not to like? —*Roger Steffens*

○ **Best of the Wailing Soul, The** / 1984 / Empire
Channel One classics produced by Jo Jo Hookim and backed by the Revolutionaries. —*Roger Steffens*

○ **All Over The World** / 1992 / Chaos 48653
A genre-busting all-star duo debut; guest shots from L. Shankar to U-Roy. —*Roger Steffens*

Delroy Wilson

Dance, soul, reggae

A great veteran of the Jamaican vocal scene, Delroy Wilson's been performing and recording since he was 11 years old. His song "Better Must Come" became the theme song for Michael Manley during Jamaica's 1972 prime ministerial election. Wilson's recorded for Studio One, CCAS, Empire, BP, Pioneer, Top Rank, and Vista, among others. He has a vibrant, extremely soulful sound and can also easily handle roots material. —*Ron Wynn*

● **Best of Delroy Wilson, The** / 1991 / Heartbeat 3507
Superb soul-tinged reggae from a veteran of the Jamaican music wars. —*Ron Wynn*

Yabby You (Vivian Jackson)

Vocals / Reggae

Yabby You is the odd-man-out in roots reggae, professing deep conviction in traditional Christian beliefs while sporting a mane of dreadlocks. His 17 albums are spare, dark, and meditative, a turgid view of the "downpression" of ghetto living, chanted in ominous fugues. —*Roger Steffens*

Conquering Lion / 1975 / Prophet
Debut beauties, deliciously menacing and admonitory. —*Roger Steffens*

○ **Deliver Me from My Enemies** / 1977 / Prophet
Timeless social commentary and Rasta prophecy. —*Roger Steffens*

● **One Love, One Heart** / 1983 / Shanachie 43016
An anthology of some of his greatest hits: what to bring when you summer in the Cave of the Dead Sea Scrolls. —*Roger Steffens*

Yellowman (Winston Foster)

Popular, reggae

DJ Winston "Yellowman" Foster, a tall, lanky Jamaican albino, became the biggest star in the wake of Bob Marley's death in 1981. He released over four dozen records in 1982 alone and was the undisputed star of that year's Sunsplash in Montego Bay. Yellowman knows how to work a crowd to a frenzy, although he is highly controversial because of his homophobic, sexist lyrics and his extremely "slack" style of toasting, which have made him as many detractors as fans. He continues to perform internationally, but his recorded output has diminished to a trickle in the '90s. —*Roger Steffens*

○ **Mister Yellowman** / 1982 / Shanachie 48007

● **One in a Million** / 1989 / Shanachie 44003
One of the few nonslack albums in his career, this boasts Yellowman's signature rap "Mad over Me" and serious scenarios of guns and fire. —*Roger Steffens*

Reggae Collections

○ **Best of Reggae Dance Hall, Vol. 1** / Rohit 7705

Best of Reggae Dance Hall, Vol. 2 / Rohit 7719
An outstanding retrospective, with many unknown or obscure artists. — *Ron Wynn*

★ **Best of Studio One, Vol. 1, The** / Heartbeat 07

○ **Best of Studio One, Vol. 2, The** / 1983 / Heartbeat 14

○ **Best of Studio One, Vol. 3: Downbeat the Ruler** / Heartbeat 38
A stunning series devoted to the voluminous output of Coxsone Dodd's Jamaican studio. The first two volumes cover the best stuff from the '60s and '70s, from shimmying ska to the rock-steady period. The third installment features a scalding set of instrumentals, full of crashing cymbals, twisting bass lines, and razor-sharp guitars. — *John Floyd*

○ **Black Star Liner: Reggae from Africa** / Heartbeat 16
Subtitled *Reggae from Africa*, this makes a welcome antidote to most of the computerized dancehall beats that are making Jamaican reggae so bland. Includes the smash hit "Fire in Soweto" by Sonny Okosuns as well as work by Victor Uwaifo, Cloud 7, and Bongos Ikwue. — *J. Poet*

● **Calling Rastafari** / Nighthawk 304
An excellent anthology, with gems from Culture, Itals, and others. — *Ron Wynn*

● **Celebration— 25 Years of Trojan Records** / 1992 / Trojan 413

○ **Club Ska '67** / 1980 / Mango 9598
This decent assortment of latter-day ska tracks serves as a nice complement to the label's *Intensified!* series. — *John Floyd*

Country Man (Soundtrack) / 1983 / Mango 9001
A double album of fab remakes of Toots Hibbert and Bob Marley and a dozen other early '80s performers. — *Roger Steffens*

○ **Dance Hall Ensemble, Vol. 1** / Cosmic Force 4022
Good variety. A nice cross-section of modern reggae. — *Ron Wynn*

○ **Dance Hall Session** / RAS 9001
This is an excellent retrospective featuring red-hot dancehall tunes. — *Ron Wynn*

Dance Hall Sizzling, Vol. 1 / VP 2011

Dance Hall Sizzling, Vol. 2 / VP 2012

Dance Hall Sizzling, Vol. 3 / VP 2013
A trio of burners, many unheard in America except in dancehalls. — *Ron Wynn*

○ **Dance Hall Stylee— Best of Reggae Dancehall** / Profile 1271
A comprehensive collection geared toward American audiences. — *Ron Wynn*

○ **Duke Reid's Treasure Chest** / 1992 / Heartbeat 95/96
Duke Reid's Treasure Isle label achieved massive popularity in Jamaica during the rock-steady years between ska and reggae. It's easy to understand why when listening to this thoroughly enjoyable double set of material from Reid's vaults. With ska's often hyper rhythms slowed down a bit and American soul growing in influence, rock-steady retained ska's danceability and added an undeniable feeling of emotional warmth. The vocals here— whether they're sung by individuals (Alton Ellis, Phyllis Dillon, the Ethiopians) or by groups (the Melodians, the Paragons, the Techniques)—are a joy to hear. Likewise, instrumentals such as Duke Reid Group's gliding "Soul Style" and Ernest and Tommy's cool, jazz-inflected "Ranglin on Bond St." have the power to soothe frayed nerves. This compilation, which contains 40 tracks by a variety of talented performers, is indeed a musical treasure chest. — *Mark J. Cadigan, Roundup newsletter*

● **Explosive Rock Steady: Joe Gibbs' Amalgamated Label** / 1992 / Heartbeat 72
If ska reflected the clamor for Jamaican independence in the early '60s, rock-steady signified the hopeful innocence of a new beginning, partly through the stuttered bass line and pre-reggae skank but especially through its fragile lead vocals and yearning choruses perpetually on the verge of a swoon. The exception, of course, is Lee "Scratch" Perry, whose "Upsetter" signature song bristles with understated menace—and whose pointy producer's ears honed classic performances by Roy Shirley, Errol Dunkley, and the lost-in-the-mists-of-history Overtakers. — *Bob Tarte*

○ **Fresh Reggae Hits** / Pow Wow 7406
Everything from sultry soul to funky and funny contemporary
material. – Ron Wynn

○ **From Kongo to Zion** / Heartbeat 17
Vocal and percussion music from Jamaica's four major local religious traditions: Central African-based Kumina, Afro-Christian,
Revival Zion, and Rastafari. Splendid music in its own right, these
selections dramatically illustrate the diversity of neo-African
adaptations in the Caribbean and the importance of this music in
reggae's evolution. The notes are unusually good. — *John Storm
Roberts*

○ **Greensleeves Sampler** / Shanachie 48002

Greensleeves Sampler 2 / Shanachie 48003
Both contain superb and seminal cuts. This is rare, hard-to-get
reggae. — *Ron Wynn*

★ **Groove Yard** / Mango 9849
If you're looking for a crash course in reggae, this is the place. The
biggest names from Island Records with their biggest hits are included on this generous 70-minute set. There are key songs from
Jimmy Cliff, the Melodians, Augustus Pablo, Junior Murvin, and
15 others. — *John Floyd*

○ **Heartbeat Reggae** / Heartbeat 50
A tremendous collection, culled from labels on the Heartbeat roster. — *Ron Wynn*

○ **Intensified! Original Ska 1962-66** / 1979 / Mango 9524

○ **Intensified! Original Ska, Vol. 2 1963-67** / 1979 / Mango 539 597
The first volume is a 16-track disc offering a fine introduction to
reggae's roots and featuring innovators such as Don Drummond,
the Skatalites, and the Maytals. Volume 2 contains some of the
better-known ska songs from the Ethiopians ("Train to Skaville")
and Don Drummond ("Man in the Street"), but its strength lies in
its coverage of often-overlooked artists like Marguerita and Sir
Lord Comic. Both volumes offer a good overview of ska. – *Chris
Woodstra*

● **Jammin'** / Mango 162-539924
Offering the best-known artists and songs, this 23-track sampler
is one of the best single-disc introductions to reggae. — *Chris
Woodstra*

○ **Joe Gibbs & Errol Thompson: The Mighty Two** / Heartbeat 73
Roots reggae, dub, and DJ styles mesh on this compilation produced by Joe Gibbs and Errol Thompson (Thompson also engineered the bulk of them). Amazingly, most of the songs were
recorded and mixed live in the studio during the '70s, prior to the
advent of multitrack recording in Jamaica. But the sound is righteous, and the lineup of talent is prodigious: Peter Tosh, Culture,
Dennis Brown, Prince Far-I, the Mighty Diamonds, Black Uhuru,
and high-caliber musicians such as drummers Sly Dunbar and
Carlton Barrett, bassist Robbie Shakespeare, guitarist Earl
"Chinna" Smith, keyboardist Franklyn "Bubbler" Waul, saxophonist Dean Fraser, and others. — *Mark J. Cadigan, Roundup
newsletter*

★ **"King" Kong Compilation— The Historic Reggae Recordings,
The** / 1981 / Mango 9632
As a producer, Leslie "King" Kong was as important to reggae's
early years as Sam Phillips was to rock & roll and Jerry Wexler
was to soul. Kong was an entrepreneur of Asian descent raised in
Jamaica; his status as an outsider made him the ideal choice to
shepherd the outlaws turning ska into reggae in the late '60s.
Kong died in 1971, only 38, from heart problems, and this 16-song
collection is a straight CD reissue of Mango's posthumous 1981
salute to Kong's ability to construct forceful yet friendly productions out of the most unassuming rhythms and harmonies. The
50-minute set features nearly all of Kong's most prominent
clients, among them Desmond Dekker, the Maytals, the
Melodians, and the Pioneers, as well as sideman-turned-star
Ansel Collins. Only Lee Perry approached Kong's range and insight as a reggae producer. This CD is highly recommended. —
Jimmy Guterman, Roundup newsletter

○ **Legends of Reggae Music** / Rohit 7718
An authoritative collection of top reggae stars and cuts. — *Ron
Wynn*

○ **Lloyd Daley's Matador Productions, 1968-1972** / Heartbeat 92
Producer Lloyd Daley, aka the Matador and the Originator, sought
out musicians who wanted to create their own sound rather than

mimick American soul records, and thereby spearheaded a movement within the Jamaican music industry that found inspiration
in a purely homegrown sensibility. This fine roots reggae compilation, which includes Little Roy's hit "Bongo Nyah," as well as
songs by Dennis Brown, U-Roy, the Ethiopians, and others, chronicles Daley's successes. It also displays his nice touch with the dub
style on "Y Mas Gan Version." – *Roundup newsletter*

○ **MUP: Reggae from Around the World** / 1989 / RAS 3050
A solid international compilation. . . . All 13 tracks are danceable,
the production and sound quality are superb, and the music flows
smoothly from cut to cut. — *J. Poet, Rock & Roll Disc*

○ **Musical Feast: Mrs. Pottinger's High Note and Gayfeet Label** /
1991 / Heartbeat 84
In contrast to the brittle edges of digital production, these recordings from the back of the Tip-Top Record Shop at 37 Orange Street,
Kingston, bask in the kitchen-table warmth of vacuum tube equipment technology. Sweet and fragile harmonies, bouncing bass
lines, and taffy-pull organ phrases contribute to the atmosphere of
intimacy, but most of all, label owner Sonia Pottinger's auteur's
touch provides the sense of an unwavering attention to quality. All
the hallmarks of a great pop collection are here: a novelty number
worthy of an idiot savant (the Gaylads "ABC Rocky Steady"), uncredited cover versions (appropriating both the Beatles and Nat
King Cole), an early duff ditty by a future star (Judy Mowatt's "I
Shall Sing"), verses to inspire (from Strange Cole's "Let the Power
Fall"), and flat-out scorchers like the Conqueror's "Look Pon You"
and Ken Boothe's "Say You." – *Bob Tarte*

○ **ROIR Reggae: 10 Years of Crucial Roots Music** / ROIR 206
A wide variety of reggae is featured on this 90-minute cassette,
from the seminal ska of the Skatalites to the eerie dub of Black
Uhuru (complete with backwards vocals) to the dub poetry of
Oku Onuora and Sister Breeze to the hypnotic, African-style percussion of Ras Michael and the Sons of Negus. The breadth and
depth of material is impressive, and the emphasis on dub styles,
including some experimental adventures, gives the compilation a
definite edge. A worthy addition to any reggae collection. — *Mark
J. Cadigan, Roundup newsletter*

○ **Raggadubbin' U.K.** / ROIR 190
A good overview of the British scene, with obscure sounds and
names. — *Ron Wynn*

○ **Ram Dancehall** / 1990 / Mango 9853
Focuses on current dancehall hits. — *Ron Wynn*

Ras Tapes, The / 1990 / Ryko 20151
There are 25 certified reggae hits on this CD anthology culled
from Ras's vaults. It's heavy on dancehall selections but also has
several rockers and traditional reggae songs by Dennis Brown,
Hugh Mundell, Freddie McGregor, Ijahman, and Israel Vibration.
The other numbers feature artists considered to be among the
hottest dancehall performers: Sugar Minott, Pinchers, Charlie
Chaplin, Frankie Paul, Half Pint, and Admiral Tibet. Unlike the
more sexually oriented material that now dominates dancehall
releases, this anthology had a hefty amount of sociopolitical
protest material alongside the requisite tunes like Minott's "Rub-
a-Dub Sound." — *Ron Wynn*

Ras Tapes 2: Nice Up Dance / 1991 / Ryko 20202
This second set of reggae hits from the Ras vaults issued on CD
included two classics— *Tiger's "Bam Bam" and Paul Blake and
Bloodfire Posse's "Get Flat"* – plus some other super numbers,
notably Foxy Brown's reggae remake of Tracy Chapman's "Fast
Car" and Little Kirk's variations on Michael Jackson's "Man in the
Mirror." The dancehall slant was heavy, with other songs featuring Little Lenny, Johnny P., Sanchez, Tippa Lee & Rappa Robert,
and Super Glen, among others. — *Ron Wynn*

R.A.S. Tapes—Reggae Jamdown / 1990 / Rykodisc 20151

R.A.S. Tapes, Vol. 2 (Nice up Dancee) / May 24, 1991 / Rykodisc
20202
Both are essential sets that compile authentic and hard-to-find
reggae. — *Ron Wynn*

○ **Reggae Classics** / 1990 / Dcc 46
A good collection, but most of the selections are available elsewhere. — *Ron Wynn*

○ **Reggae Dance Party** / RAS 3018
Reggae's link to dance was explored on this 11-cut anthology that
featured single vocalists, groups, and an occasional toaster doing
cuts celebrating or extolling dance. It included an interesting re-

working of "Let the Good Times Roll" by Michigan & Smiley retitled "Reggae Ska," plus the complete ten-minute-plus hit "Get Flat" by Paul Blake & Bloodfire Posse, as well as Gregory Isaacs's superb "Private Beach Party" and Sugar Minott's swaying "Rub-a-Dub Sound." Also included were Wayne Smith's "Teach Me to Dance" and Barrington Levy's "Do the Dance," both novelty numbers made into effective vocal and musical workouts. Black Uhuru's "Great Train Robbery" and Horace Andy's "Elementary" were sociopolitical tracks with a dance beat, and J. C. Lodge's "You Can Dance" explored the steamier side of meeting on the dancefloor, as did Don Carlos's "Springheel Skanking." — *Ron Wynn*

● **Reggae Greats—Strictly for Lovers** / Mango 9788

★ **Reggae Greats—Strictly for Rockers** / Mango 9796
The first is a high-caliber review of artists who popularized the "lovers" style; the second is a well-done overview of "rockers" artists. — *Ron Wynn*

Reggae Legends / Rohit 7753
More from the prolific vaults of Rohit. — *Ron Wynn*

○ **Reggae Roll Call 1989—Reggae DJ's & Singers** / IRS 13029
Part of a series that highlights songs and "toasts" of top reggae Brits from Papa Levi to Dee Sharpe. — *Ron Wynn*

○ **Reggae Sunsplash '81** / Elektra 60035
Tribute to Bob Marley. A heartfelt tribute to a departed genius, although the performances don't always match the passion of the occasion. — *Ron Wynn*

○ **Reggae Superstars, Vol. 2** / Rohit 77320
A good addition to Rohit's anthology line. — *Ron Wynn*

○ **Rockers (Soundtrack)** / 1980 / Mango 162-539587
A super soundtrack of the 1980 film. — *Roger Steffens*

★ **Ska Bonanza: The Studio One Ska Years** / Heartbeat 86/87
In the '60s ska was a major musical force in Jamaica, and in the late '70s it resurfaced in England as the two-tone movement. This outstanding collection focuses on producer Coxsone Dodd's work at Jamaica's Studio One during the music's heyday, when the lively, horn-pumped sound became massively popular on the island. Among the many highlights are Bob Marley and the Wailers' infectious "Simmer Down," Toots Hibbert and the Maytals' "Shining Light," and one of the all-time great ska instrumentals, Don Drummond's "Man in the Street." Other artists featured on *Ska Bonanza* include the Skatalites, Ken Boothe with Stranger Cole, Derrick Harriott, Rita Marley (with the Wailers), Lee Perry, Aubrey Adams with Rico Rodriguez, Roland Alphonso, the Gaylads. Burning. — *Mark J. Cadigan, Roundup newsletter*

Solid Gold—Coxsone Style / 1992 / Heartbeat 80
Harder edged than any of the smooth Studio One reissues, this anthology confirms my growing suspicion that—until something new skanks along—reggae hit its artistic peak some 20 years ago. The songs are tougher than usual too, including versions of "Rivers of Babylon" and the one-stanza-short-of-perfecton "Declaration of Rights," plus flinty instruments by Jackie Mitoo and Ernest Ranglin that led me back to PiL's "metal box." Only quibble: where are the women? With the addition of four new tracks on this reissue, the compilers could have easily included the sistren and righted past oversights. — *Bob Tarte*

★ **Story of Jamaican Music—Tougher Than Tough, The** / Mango 162-539935
Island's importance as the American reggae source has just been reaffirmed with a marvelous four-disc anthology. *The Story of Jamaican Music* rivals great jazz and classic popular lines normally the province of foreign import companies. The discs are chronologically arranged, with the first covering the amalgam of American genres that were absorbed into Jamaican culture: bebop and swing, New Orleans R&B, Chicago and Memphis soul, country, and film soundtracks. It shows the industry evolving from imitation into its own idioms: the hectic syncopation of ska; the slower, more soulful singing of rock-steady; and the coming of reggae. Prince Buster, Don Drummond, the Skatalites, and Laurel Aitken were among this era's pioneers.
The second volume cements reggae's emergence as an evocative love music and a voice of the new, nationalist/militant Rasta generation. The toasting DJs like U-Roy, Jimmy Cliff's *The Harder They Come*, and Bob Andy and Marcia Griffith's soaring cover of Nina Simone's *Young, Gifted and Black* are only a few highpoints.

The third and fourth volumes chronicle reggae's final maturation into a hit form and showcase the inevitable production uniformities and assembly-line tendencies that arise when any style must reproduce hits en masse for a large audience. But there are superb songs galore on both discs: the emphatic lead vocals of Jacob Miller, Joseph Hill of Culture, Dennis Brown, and, of course, Bob Marley, as well as evocative, compelling harmonies by the Heptones, Mighty Diamonds, Wailing Souls, and Black Uhuru. The purists became steadily more appalled by the rise of dancehall, and the vulgarity of Admiral Bailey's *Punanny* or Supercat's *Boops* does seem somewhat shocking when contrasted with the Rasta/spirituality of earlier eras. But these songs are also often hilarious, and while Wayne Smith's *sleng teng* did generate a cottage industry with umpteen songs cut on the same "riddem" (melody), there are plenty of hypnotic rhythms and final songs on the fourth volume as well.

This does not claim to be the definitive reggae anthology; it could not be anyway, since there were lots of tiny, seminal labels like Studio One that were not distributed by Island and that were making equally vital music. So take it for what it is: Island's portrait of reggae's beginnings, growth, and flowering into a prime international style. On that basis, here is arguably the finest boxed set you will hear this year on the world music circuit. — *Ron Wynn*

● **Street Reggae** / K-Tel 529-2
A decent place for the novice to get an introduction to the music of present-day reggae stars like Shelley Thunder as well as veterans. — *Ron Wynn*

Strictly the Best / VP 1147
A possibly deceptive title, but great music throughout. — *Ron Wynn*

○ **Studio 1 Presents Rare Reggae—Collector's Edition** / Heartbeat 47
Culled from the fruitful Coxsone Dodd laboratory. — *Ron Wynn*

○ **This Is Lovers Reggae** / 1991 / RAS 61

This Is Lovers Reggae, Vol. 2 / Ariwa 069
Lovers rock was reggae's sentimental, sometimes sappy, but often hypnotic end. These were frequently soul or R&B covers, done either by male crooners or innocent-sounding female balladeers. The 12 tracks on the first of two volumes culled from Ariwa's catalog include Sandra Cross's wonderful cover of "So in Love," Brown Sugar's coy version of Barbara Lewis's "Hello Stranger," and a great remake of Curtis Mayfield's "I'm So Proud" by Kofi. These aren't some of reggae's biggest names, but they acquit themselves well. Another gem is Slim Linton's "Two's Company," a brilliant number that nicely balances jealousy and anticipation.
The second volume has two fewer tunes than its predecessor and includes repeat appearances from Sandra Cross, Kofi, Slim Linton, John McLean, and Robotiks, although this time Just Dale is their featured vocalist. Cross again sounds sublime, as does Kofi on a marvelous reworking of The Emotions' "Don't Ask My Neighbors." Tomorrow's People makes the original Royalettes version of "Gonna Take a Miracle" seem like a cynical, bitter effort by comparison, while Sister Audrey's "My Thing" matches any contemporary dancehall tune in its lyrical boldness and suggestiveness. — *Ron Wynn*

☆ **This Is Reggae Music, Vol. 3** / 1976 / Island 9391
A compilation with Junior Murvin, Prince Jazzbo, and Bunny Wailer. — *Michael G. Nastos*

○ **Towering Dub Inferno—Roir Tapes** / Rykodisc 20152
A powerhouse compilation, with Lee Remy, Scientist, and others. — *Ron Wynn*

Towering Dub Inferno / 1990 / Ryko 20152
Dub, the stripped down instrumental covers of prior vocal hits, has long been a favored style in Jamaica. Ryko issued on CD in 1990 a 14-song anthology using great songs that had been previously released on cassette by ROIR. The selections include numbers by the idiom's finest producers— *Scientist, Niney the Observer, and the Mad Professor*— taking classics originally done by Lee Perry, Prince Far I, and many others. — *Ron Wynn*

○ **Wiser Dread** / Nighthawk 301
A marvelously annotated collection of vintage '70s tributes to Rastafarianism. Not many big names here, but everything from the Bunny Wailer cuts to "Cut Them Down" by the Morwells comes on like a classic. — *John Floyd*

BLUES

To paraphrase the incomparable Delta blues performer Robert Johnson, "The blues is a low-down aching chill; if you ain't never had 'em, I hope you never will."

Blues is the most emotional, gut-wrenching style of 20th-century American secular music. It evolved in the deep South shortly before the turn of the century from the spirituals, work songs, and country-dance instrumentals sung or performed by African-Americans. This music has long exhibited strong regional as well as racial characteristics. Consider, for example, the light, easily understood ragtime-influenced music of Blind Boy Fuller in contrast to Texas Alexander's moaning, which sounds close to an old field holler. But not all blues are sorrowful and low-down – witness the "hokum" blues of Tampa Red and Georgia Tom, Frankie Jaxon, and others. They are laced with clever double-entendre as well as such salacious food metaphors as "hot nuts" and "jelly roll."

The blues have always kept up-to-date. The classic Chicago blues sound of Muddy Waters, Howlin' Wolf, and Little Walter is the perfect example of this. It is basically the Mississippi Delta blues sound, amplified and adapted for a Northern audience of southside Chicago immigrants who themselves had moved up from the mid South. When Charlie Christian, T-Bone Walker, and a handful of others began experimenting with electric guitars in the mid to late 30s, many of the popular blues singers like Big Bill Broonzy were right with them. Ultimately, this resulted in the commercial success of B. B. King and other similar urban blues legends, beginning in the early 50s.

In the 90s it is perfectly clear that this music and its 12-bar musical form have influenced not only most of our contemporary popular music but many musicians from outside the United States. This is particularly true in Europe and Great Britain, where rock stars ranging from Eric Clapton to U2 have long acknowledged their debt to the blues. In the middle of this latest blues boom, which has been partially fueled by the new wave of CDs, we are fortunate to have an immense range of blues. In 1968 I never thought I'd live to see a convenient way to have all of Sleepy John Estes's Victor and Decca 78s or a comprehensive retrospective of the Trumpet and Chess selections of Sonny Boy Williamson #2. With so much wonderful blues material around, the Hokum Boys summed it up well: "You can't get enough of that."

– Kip Lornell

Johnny Adams

b. Jan. 5, 1932, New Orleans, LA
Vocals / Soul, R&B, Soul blues

Though a lifelong New Orleans resident and a renowned R&B singer for more than 30 years, Johnny Adams is not a New Orleans R&B stylist in the traditional sense but more a modern soul singer—"perhaps America's greatest soul singer," in fact, according to Crescent City music historian Jeff Hannusch. In New Orleans, "Johnny is known as "The Tan Canary," ... esteemed by musicians for his unerring ear, taste, and imagination, loved by club and concert audiences for his always engaging performances." Adams sang in gospel quartets before cutting his first R&B record in 1959 (produced by Dr. John) and had a national Top Ten hit with "Reconsider Me" in 1969. His recent albums for Rounder have won him new acclaim among contemporary blues audiences. *—Jim O'Neal*

From the Heart / 1983 / Rounder 2044

New Orleans's most versatile blues and R&B vocalist, Johnny Adams was captured in peak form during this mid-'80s set recorded in Louisiana. Adams's soaring vocals and excellent, sensitive production made this a first-rate outing focusing on both vintage blues tunes and more recent soul and R&B wailers. *—Ron Wynn*

○ **After Dark** / 1986 / Rounder 2049

After Dark included amazing covers of Doc Pomus's "I Don't Know You" and "Give A Broken Heart A Break," John Hiatt's "Lovers Will" and the Dan Penn/Chips Moman soul classic "Do Right Woman—Do Right Man." There's also Adams' own composition "Fortune Teller" and versions of Hiatt's "She Said The Same Thing to Me" and Paul Kelly's "Missing You." This was one of the first records on which Adams' wondrous voice, with its extensive range at the top and bottom, as well as his distinctive delivery, great tone, and understated swinging abilities were both well produced and effectively mastered and recorded. *—Ron Wynn*

○ **Reconsider Me** / 1987 / Charly 89

New Orleans's giant Johnny Adams does his biggest soul hits, among them the title track and his first smash single "I Won't Cry." This was recorded in the early '60s for small local and regional labels like SS, Sansu, and Maison De Soul. They've previously been available only as singles or scattered on import anthologies. *—Ron Wynn*

Room with a View of the Blues / 1988 / Rounder 2059

Adams demonstrated his blues proficiency on this 1988 date. The ten numbers covered every emotional base, from the social protest themes of "A World I Never Made" to the setting-the-record straight sentiments of "How Wrong Can a Good Man Be?" (CD bonus track). With great support from an instrumental corps that included guitarists Walter "Wolfman" Washington and Duke Robillard, keyboardist Dr. John, and saxophonists Red Tyler and Foots Samuel, plus Ernie Gautreau on valve trombone, Adams didn't just cut a blues album, he made unforgettable blues statements. *—Ron Wynn*

● **I Won't Cry** / 1992 / Rounder 2083

Johnny Adams's marvelous, assertive, and triumphant voice made its earliest mark on the New Orleans scene in the late '50s and early '60s. He made several singles for the Ric and Ron labels, songs that marked his departure (lyrically) from the gospel world and gave him a foothold in R&B. This '91 collection featured 14 early Adams songs, many of them immediate classics like the remarkable "I Won't Cry." While he retained the vocal maneuvers, emotional intensity, and fervor of his gospel days, Adams showed his ability to sing everything from straight love tunes to bluesy denunciations, songs of regret and woe to celebratory pieces. This CD's a great starting point for those unfamiliar with Adams's formative material, while others who don't have all the Ric and Ron singles can now add these to their collections. *—Ron Wynn*

Johnny Adams Sings Doc Pomus: The Real Me / Rounder 2109

The brilliant compositions of Doc Pomus are covered in a marvelous fashion by Johnny Adams, New Orleans's finest living vocalist. Adams covers "Still in Love," "Prisoner of Life," and the title track plus several other Pomus classics with his customary power and authority. He's supported by a great session band that includes Dr. John, Alvin Tyler, and guitarist Duke Robillard. — *Ron Wynn*

○ **Walking on a Tightrope** / Rounder 2095
As with his Doc Pomus session, whenever Johnny Adams does a repertory date it's as much his own showcase as a forum for the spotlighted composer. Even Percy Mayfield's lyrically brilliant works didn't hamper Adams from displaying his special magic; his treatments on the session's 10 tunes ranged from excellent to magnificent. —*Ron Wynn*

Luther Allison

b. Aug. 17, 1939, Mayflower, AR
Vocals, guitar, sometimes harmonica / R&B, Modern electric blues, Chicago Blues
Allison emerged as the fresh new face on the Chicago blues scene with his debut album in 1969 (Delmark) and soon put other notches on his guitar when he became the only outright blues artist on the Motown (Gordy) roster. A talented and expressive singer and guitarist from what has become known as the post-B. B. King school, Allison has veered between straight West Side blues, soul, and high-intensity blues/rock. His recordings range from raw live albums of blues standards to crossover-oriented European studio productions. —*Jim O'Neal*

○ **Luther's Blues** / 1973 / Gordy 967
The most representative album showcasing his modern Chicago blues approach. —*Bill Dahl*

● **Love Me Papa** / Dec. 13, 1977 / Evidence 26015
Allison was on throughout most of the nine tracks (three bonus cuts) on this 1977 date, playing with the ferocity, direction, and inventiveness that is often missing from his more uneven efforts. His covers of Little Walter Jacobs's "Last Night" and "Blues with a Feeling" are not reverential or respectful but are launching pads for high-octane, barreling riffs; snappy phrases; and exciting solos. His vocals are not always that keen, but Allison at least stretches them out and adds verbal embellishments, yells, and shouts of encouragement. —*Ron Wynn*

○ **Serious** / 1987 / Blind Pig 2287
This album highlights Allison's contemporary rock-tinged approach. —*Bill Dahl*

Billy Boy Arnold

b. Sep. 16, 1935, Chicago, IL
Vocals, harmonica / Electric Chicago blues
Arnold is one of the last surviving original postwar Chicago bluesmen, and a great one at that. A major disciple of John Lee "Sonny Boy" Williamson, Arnold honed his craft on the streets of the Windy City, most often working with a young Bo Diddley. His best works are enlivened with witty, urbane lyrics and powerful harmonica playing, several of them going on to become certified classics of the idiom. —*Cub Koda*

● **More Blues on the South Side** / 1964 / Bellaphon 40108
Billy Boy Arnold initially surfaced during the mid-'50s with several excellent hard-driving singles that mixed a funky beat, blistering harmonica, jagged vocals, and searing lyrics. His debut full-length album paired him with guitarist Mighty Joe Young, pianist Lafayette Leake, bassist Jerome Arnold, and drummer Junior Blackmon for 12 short, biting heartache and lament numbers, plus an occasional drinking song. Arnold's vocals on "You Don't Love Me No More," "I Love Only You" and "You Better Cut That Out" were gripping and anguished, while his harmonica playing was torrid. —*Ron Wynn*

○ **Crying and Pleading** / 1980 / Charly 1016
Collection of Billy Boy's complete Vee Jay output. Chicago blues at its best. Includes "I Wish You Would," "I Was Fooled," and the original "I Ain't Got You," later covered by the Yardbirds. (Import) —*Cub Koda*

○ **Back Where I Belong** / 1993 / Alligator Records 4815
Arnold's first new album in years finds the veteran harpman in top form, contributing powerhouse material and recasting his older Vee-Jay hits while interpreting some classic songs by others. With powerful support from the West Coast band the Taildraggers, the sound of this album is that of a mature blues-

man at the peak of his powers. All modern-day blues albums should sound this good. —*Cub Koda*

Kokomo Arnold (James "Kokomo" Arnold)

b. Feb. 15, 1901, Lovejoys Station, GA, d. Nov. 8, 1968, Chicago, IL
Vocals, guitar / Blues, Acoustic blues
A popular recording artist of the '30s, James "Kokomo" Arnold was a left-handed bottleneck guitarist who usually recorded solo, occasionally with piano accompaniment. His first Chicago session (Decca, 1934) produced the widely covered "Milk Cow Blues" and "Old Original Kokomo Blues" (the model for Robert Johnson's "Sweet Home Chicago"), as well as the first appearance on record of the classic "I believe I'll dust my broom" line (in "Sagefield Woman Blues"). Critic Hugues Panassi wrote, "Arnold is one of the greatest blues singers ever recorded." Arnold continued to play for a few years in Chicago after his last session (1938) but later took a job in a steel mill, disillusioned with the music business. Interviewed by two Frenchmen in 1959, Arnold said, "I'm finished with music and that mad way of life." —*Jim O'Neal*

Complete Recorded Works, Vol. 1 (1930–35) / Docun.ent 5037
A four-volume series covering every recording Kokomo Arnold made between 1930 and 1938. —*Stephen Thomas Erlewine*

● **Kokomo Arnold/Peetie Wheatstraw** / Blues Classics 4
Eight tracks each by Kokomo Arnold and Peetie Wheatstraw. Includes "Milk Cow Blues." —*Michael Erlewine*

Marcia Ball

Vocals, piano / R&B, Country, Modern electric blues, Piano blues
Long, tall Marcia Ball is the reigning crawfish circuit queen, a piano-pumping Louisiana gal transplanted to Austin, TX. Her vocal influences include Irma Thomas, Etta James and Sugar Pie DeSanto. On "Hot Tamale Baby," Marcia's original "That's Enough of That Stuff" pays tribute to one of her piano-playing heroes, Professor Longhair. Marcia Ball is capable of writing strong material for herself but also shows great taste in her selection of soul (and more) covers by Laura Lee, O. V. Wright, and others. — *Dennis MacDonald*

○ **Hot Tamale Baby** / 1986 / Rounder 3095
Marcia Ball solidified the favorable impression she'd made on her debut Rounder effort with this rousing second outing. Ball ripped through Booker T. Jones's soul gem "Never Like This Before" and Clifton Chenier's title composition, while also demonstrating her own facility with struttin' R&B on "That's Enough of That Stuff" and "Love's Spell." Marcia Ball proved that her good debut was no fluke, and that she'd be on the contemporary blues/R&B scene for quite a while. —*Ron Wynn*

● **Gator Rhythms** / 1989 / Rounder 3101
Marcia Ball explored R&B and honky-tonk country on this album, keeping her blues chops in order while expanding her repertoire. She included a pair of tunes by country vocalist Lee Roy Parnell, "What's a Girl to Do" and "Red Hot," doing both in a feisty, attacking fashion. Her third Rounder album was her most entertaining and dynamic, as Ball became less of an interpreter and more of an individualist. —*Ron Wynn*

Soulful Dress / 1989 / Rounder
Marcia Ball got things started in a celebratory fashion on her debut Rounder release *Soulful Dress*, doing the title track in a taunting, challenging manner aided by flashy guitar riffs from the late Stevie Ray Vaughan. From there, she artfully displayed other sides of her personality, from dismayed on the cover of "I'd Rather Go Blind" to defiant on "Jailbird" and assured on "My Mind's Made Up." —*Ron Wynn*

Barbecue Bob (Robert Hicks)

b. Sep. 11, 1902, Walnut Grove, GA, d. Oct. 21, 1931, Lithonia, GA
Vocals, guitar / Acoustic country blues
Barbecue Bob may be a familiar name to some blues fans today because at least two young White musicians have adopted the name, but back in the '20s the original Barbecue Bob (born Robert Hicks) was a big name on the Black "race records" scene. Recording for Columbia from 1927 to 1930, Hicks was the most popular of the Atlanta blues guitarists of his time, and Columbia's best-selling bluesman. But Barbecue Bob died of pneumonia at the age of 29, and some of his contemporaries like Blind Willie

McTell are much better known to modern-day audiences. Most of Bob's recordings were solo outings featuring rhythmic 12-string bottleneck-guitar work and original lyrical themes. In historian Stephen Calt's opinion, "For sheer musical verve and punch, Hicks easily rivals Charley Patton." —*Jim O'Neal*

● **Chocolate to the Bone** / Yazoo 2005
Fourteen selections from popular '20s Atlanta 12-string slide artist Barbecue Bob. A fine American collection, with good sound quality. —*Barry Lee Pearson*

Complete Recorded Works, Vol. 1 (1927–28) / Document 5046
A three-disc series covering everything Barbecue Bob recorded between 1927–30. —*AMG*

Roosevelt "Booba" Barnes

b. Sep. 25, 1936, Longwood, MS
Vocals, guitar, harmonica / Blues
Barnes and his Playboys band rocked the hardest of all the juke-joint combos in the Mississippi delta during the '80s, and after the release of his debut album (*The Heartbroken Man*, 1990), "Booba" took his act and his band north to Chicago, following the trail of his idols Howlin' Wolf and Little Milton. In a *Guitar Player* review, Jas Obrecht called Barnes "a wonderfully idiosyncratic guitar player and an extraordinary vocalist by any standard." —*Jim O'Neal*

● **Heartbroken Man, The** / 1990 / Flying Fish 2623
No-frills recording of hair-raising modern Delta blues. —*Jas Obrecht*

Lou Ann Barton

Vocals / Rock, Blues, Blues rock
Barton is arguably the queen of the Austin, TX, roadhouse R&B/blues scene. Her recordings on Antone are well worth seeking out. —*Rick Clark*

○ **Old Enough** / 1982 / Antone's 21

● **Read My Lips** / 1989 / Antone's 0009
Barton's lascivious delivery of roadhouse R&B chestnuts by Hank Ballard, Slim Harpo, and others is hotter than four-alarm chili on a Texas summer night. Members from the Fabulous Thunderbirds, Stevie Ray Vaughan's band, and other Austin heavy-hitters ensure that songs like "Sexy Ways," "Shake Your Hips," "You Can Have My Husband," and "Rocket in My Pocket" have the right amount of grease. —*Rick Clark*

Carey Bell

b. Nov. 14, 1936, Macon, GA
Vocals, harmonica, sometimes bass and guitar / Electric Chicago blues
One of the reigning blues harp virtuosos, Bell was a protégé of Big Walter Horton and a former sideman with Muddy Waters and Willie Dixon. Head of one of the most talented blues families, Carey has often worked with his sons, including Lurrie (guitar) and Steve (harmonica), his adopted stepfather Lovie Lee (piano), and occasionally with famous cousins such as guitarist Eddy Clearwater. Bell first recorded as a bassist on a live Robert Nighthawk album in 1964. He cut his first album as a singer/harmonica player for Delmark in 1969. —*Jim O'Neal*

○ **Heartaches and pain** / 1977 / Delmark
These 1977 dates were recorded by legendary producer Ralph Bass but were withheld from domestic circulation until this recent reissue. Despite their brevity, Bell shows his harmonica mastery with swirling phrases, dipping lines, and vigorous solos even on the most basic cuts. He wasn't (and isn't) a compelling singer, but he effectively states the theme, then starts blowing fiercely. —*Ron Wynn*

Son of a Gun / 1984 / Rooster Blues 2617
The raucous pairing of this harpist and his guitarist son Lurrie creates some sparks. —*Bill Dahl*

● **Mellow Down Easy** / 1991 / Blind Pig 74291
Bell's full-toned harp is showcased in a marvelous update of the original '50s Chicago sound. —*Bill Dahl*

Buster Benton

b. Jul. 19, 1932, Texarkana, AR
Guitar / Dance

An underrated, entertaining guitarist and vocalist whose style hugs the line between blues, R&B, and soul, Buster Benton sang in a gospel choir while growing up in Texarkana, AR. He started playing guitar after moving to Toledo, OH, in 1952, and then relocated to Chicago in the late '50s. There Benton formed a band and began recording for Melloway, Twinight, and Alteen. He played with Willie Dixon for several years and also owned the Stardust Lounge. Ralph Bass produced many good Benton recordings for Jewel in the '70s, and he scored a regional hit with "Spider in My Stew." He's remained active into the '90s, recording for Blue Phoenix and Ichiban. —*Ron Wynn*

● **Spider in My Stew** / 1978 / Ronn 8002
Intruigingly soul influenced debut LP by Chicago blues guitarist. Great grooves! —*Bill Dahl*

○ **Blues Buster** / 1979 / Red Lightnin' 26

○ **Blues at the Top** / Nov. 22, 1983–May 2, 1985 / Evidence 26030
Buster Benton's brand of soul and funk blues is not pretty, fancy, or artful; it is raw, nonstop attacking, powerful material, sung without subtlety or flair. Benton is not just a wailer; he is an unsophisticated yet compelling one, and the 15 cuts are not for fans interested in intricate guitar solos, clever lyrics, or flamboyant singing. But those who enjoy rough-edged, soulful vocals and taut, tight phrases, riffs, and licks will find Benton's music quite enticing. —*Ron Wynn*

Big Maybelle (Maybelle Smith)

b. May 1, 1924, Jackson, TN, d. Jan. 23, 1972, Cleveland, OH
Vocals, sometimes piano / R&B, Electric jump blues
Big Maybelle lived up to her billing in more ways than one. Her thundering voice was every bit as large as her physique, and she was one of R&B's leading belters during the mid-'50s. After gaining early professional experience with the Sweethearts of Rhythm and Tiny Bradshaw's outfit, Maybelle Smith hooked up with producer Fred Mendelsohn, who negotiated her a contract with Columbia's R&B subsidiary Okeh. In 1953, she notched a trio of Top Ten R&B hits: "Gabbin' Blues," "Way Back Home," and "My Country Man." But her best-known Okeh release never made the charts, at least for her. Two full years before "Killer" Jerry Lee Lewis set the world on fire with his seismic rendition, Big Maybelle cut the first waxing of "Whole Lotta Shakin' Goin' On" with Leroy Kirkland's band in New York. Her version was much closer to rockabilly pianist and co-writer Roy Hall's original vision of the tune than the subsequent megahit reading by the Killer. Maybelle's jumping appearance in *Jazz on a Summer's Day*, the acclaimed documentary of the 1958 Newport Jazz Festival, affords us rare film footage of Maybelle's commanding stage presence. Heroin was allegedly a recurring problem for Maybelle. Although she later mounted a mini-comeback with a cover of Question Mark & the Mysterians' "96 Tears," she died much too soon in 1972. —*Bill Dahl*

Blues, Candy and Big Maybelle / 1958 / Savoy 1168
Sixteen tracks of late-'50s R&B from the Savoy label. Mickey Baker on guitar. —*Bill Dahl*

Saga of the Good Life and Hard Times / 1969 / Rojac 123
A mix of soul and blues from her last sessions, sung with despair. —*Richard Pack*

● **Okeh Sessions, The** / 1983 / Charly 108
A mix of R&B and blues on 22 tracks, 1952–55. —*Richard Pack*

Big Twist & the Mellow Fellows

b. 1937, Terre Haute, IN, d. Mar. 14, 1990, Broadview, IL
Group / Blues
Larry "Big Twist" Nolan and the Mellow Fellows developed their brassy, soul-influenced act in Southern Illinois and transported it to Chicago, where North Side and suburban White audiences of the '80s embraced their style of R&B, a genre generally more popular with the Black audiences who support the music's originators like Little Milton and Bobby Bland. Big Twist was one of the first Chicago acts to do a blues video (*300 Pounds of Joy*, Alligator). The Mellow Fellows, now billed as the Chicago Rhythm & Blues Kings, have continued to tour and record since Nolan's death in 1990. —*Jim O'Neal*

Big Twist & The Mellow Fellows / Jun. 1981 / Flying Fish 70229
This debut set proved accessible to even casual blues fans. —*Bill Dahl*

Blues Styles

CLASSIC FEMALE BLUES – The earliest recorded form of the blues. This genre features female vocalists singing material with close connections to pop music of the period (mid 20s to early 30s) and primarily jazz backings. Main proponents: Mamie Smith, Bessie Smith, Ma Rainey, Lucille Bogan, and Victoria Spivey.

DELTA BLUES – Also known as Mississippi blues, this is the earliest guitar-dominated music to make it onto record. Consisting of performers working primarily in a solo, self-accompanied context, it also embraces the now-familiar string-band/small-combo format, both precursors to the modern-day blues band. Main proponents: Charlie Patton, Robert Johnson, and Son House.

COUNTRY-BLUES – A term that delineates the depth and breadth of the first flowering of guitar-driven blues, embracing all regional styles and variations (Piedmont, Atlanta, early Chicago, ragtime, folk, songster, etc.). Primarily acoustic guitarists, some country-blues performers later switched to electric guitars without changing their style. Major proponents: Henry Thomas, Skip James, Barbecue Bob, Leadbelly, Mississippi John Hurt, Lonnie Johnson, Blind Blake, and Tommy Johnson.

MEMPHIS BLUES – A strain of country-blues all its own, the Memphis style gives us the rise of two distinct forms, the jug band (humorous, jazz-style blues played on homemade instruments) and the beginnings of assigning parts to guitarists for solo (lead) and rhythm, a tradition that is now part-and-parcel of all modern-day blues bands. The later, post-WWII electric version of this genre featured explosive guitar work, thunderous drumming, and declamatory vocals. Main proponents: Cannon's Jug Stompers, Furry Lewis, Memphis Minnie, and the early recordings of B. B. King and Howlin' Wolf.

TEXAS BLUES – A subgenre earmarked by a more relaxed, swinging feel than other styles of blues. The earlier, acoustic version embraced both songster and country-blues traditions, while the post-war electric style featured jazzy, single-string soloing over predominately horn-driven backing. Main proponents: Blind Lemon Jefferson, Lightnin' Hopkins, Clarence "Gatemouth" Brown, and T-Bone Walker.

CHICAGO BLUES – Delta blues fully amplified and put into a small-band context. Later permutations of the style took their cue from the lead guitar work of B. B. King and T-Bone Walker. Main proponents: Muddy Waters, Howlin' Wolf, Little Walter, Big Walter Horton, Jimmy Rogers, Elmore James, Jimmy Reed, Otis Rush, Magic Sam, and Buddy Guy.

JUMP BLUES – Uptempo, jazz-tinged blues, usually featuring a vocalist in front of a large, horn-driven orchestra with less reliance on guitar work than other styles. Main proponents: Amos Milburn, Johnny Otis, Roy Brown, Wynonie Harris, and Big Joe Turner.

NEW ORLEANS BLUES – Primarily (but not exclusively) piano- and horn-driven, this genre strain is enlivened by Caribbean rhythms, party atmosphere, and the "second-line" strut of the Dixieland music so indigenous to the area. Main proponents: Professor Longhair, Guitar Slim, and Snooks Eaglin.

WEST COAST BLUES – More piano-based and jazz-influenced than anything else, the West Coast style (California in particular) also embraces post-war Texas guitar expatriates and jump-blues practitioners. Main proponents: Charles Brown, Pee Wee Crayton, Lowell Fulson, and Percy Mayfield.

PIANO BLUES – A genre that runs through the entire history of the music itself, this embraces everything from ragtime, barrelhouse, boogie-woogie, and smooth West Coast jazz stylings to the hard-rocking rhythms of Chicago blues. Main proponents: Big Maceo Merriweather, Leroy Carr, Sunnyland Slim, Roosevelt Sykes, Albert Ammons, and Otis Spann.

LOUISIANA BLUES – A looser, more laidback and percussive version of the Jimmy Reed side of the Chicago style. Production techniques on most of the recordings utilize massive amounts of echo, giving the performances a "doomy" sound and feel. Main proponents: Slim Harpo, Lightnin' Slim, and Lazy Lester.

R&B/SOUL BLUES – A more modern form, this fuses elements of Black popular music (the rhythm and blues strain of the 50s and the Southern soul style of the mid 60s) to a wholly urban blues amalgam of its own.

MODERN ACOUSTIC BLUES – Newer artists reviving the older, more country-derived styles of blues. Main proponents: John Hammond, Rory Block, John Cephas, Taj Mahal, and the earlier recordings of Bonnie Raitt.

MODERN ELECTRIC BLUES – An eclectic mixture, this genre replicates older styles of urban blues while simultaneously recasting them in contemporary fashion. Main proponents: Stevie Ray Vaugahn, the Fabulous Thunderbirds, Robert Cray, and Roomful of Blues.

BRITISH BLUES – More than a mere geographical distinction, the British style pays strict adherence to replicating American blues genres, with an admiration for its originators bordering on reverence. Main proponents: Alexis Korner, John Mayall, and the early recordings of Fleetwood Mac and the Rolling Stones.

– Cub Koda

● **Playing for Keeps** / 1983 / Alligator 4732
Slickly produced soul-blues from this Chicago outfit. —*Bill Dahl*

Scrapper Blackwell (Francis Blackwell)

b. Feb. 21, 1903, Syracuse, NC, **d.** Oct. 7, 1962, Indianapolis
Vocals, guitar, sometimes piano / Acoustic Chicago blues
Best known for his duets with blues kingpin Leroy Carr, Blackwell was an exceptional instrumentalist who recorded several sessions on his own (usually unaccompanied) in 1928–35 and again in 1958–61. Blackwell's melodic single-note guitar work presaged much of the blues that was to follow. He had begun to record again, his talent reportedly undiminished, when he was shot to death in early 1962 in an Indianapolis alley. —*Jim O'Neal*

● **Virtuoso Guitar 1925–34** / Yazoo 1019

This early and influential guitarist is known for his work with his partner, pianist/singer Leroy Carr, two examples of which are found here among a collection of solo performances. His high-note, "string-snapping" solo style, developed to be heard over Carr's rolling piano, is echoed in the work of Johnny "Guitar" Watson, among others. —*George Bedard*

Bobby "Blue" Bland

b. Jan. 27, 1930, Rosemont, TN
Vocals, guitar, Tenor sax / Soul, Soul, R&B, R&B, Soul blues
Bland's early years around Memphis were closely associated with Junior Parker, Johnny Ace, and B. B. King. His earliest recordings (Chess, Modern) are very rough, but beginning in the mid-'50s on Duke Records, he became a distinctive blues/R&B voice. The Duke period produced a continuous stream of hit R&B singles. His work mellowed and became more album-oriented in the '70s.

Music Map ## Blues History

African Roots

Work Songs, Field Hollers

Church & Gospel Music
Standard Quartette (rec. 1894)
Dinwiddie Colored Quartet (rec. 1902)
Apollo Male Quartette (rec. 1912)

Black Entertainment
Minstrel, Ragtime, String Bands

Medicine Shows
Papa Charlie Jackson – Pink Anderson
Daddy Stovepipe

Early Blues Recorders (ca. 1920)
● W. C. Handy (1873-1958) – Perry Bradford (1893-1970)
Clarence Williams (1898-1965)

Songsters
● Henry Thomas (1874-1950) – Frank Stokes (1888-1955)
Peg Leg Howell (1888-1966) – ● Leadbelly (1889-1949)
● Mance Lipscomb (1895-1976) – ● Mississippi John Hurt (1893-1966)

Classic Female Blues Singers
Mamie Smith (1883-1946) – ● Ma Rainey (1886-1939)
●Bessie Smith (1894-1937) – Lucille Bogan (1897-1948)
Sara Martin (1884-1955) – Clara Smith (1894-1935)
Ida Cox (1896-1967) – Sippie Wallace (1898-1986)
Victoria Spivey (1906-1976) – Chippie Hill (1905-1950)

Postwar Female Blues
Big Maybelle (1924-1972) – Big Mama Thornton (1926-1984)
Little Esther Phillips (1935)

Religious Music That Influenced Blues
● Blind Willie Johnson (1900-1947)

Piano Blues
Origins – 1890s – Barrelhouses, Railroad & Lumber Camps
● Clarence "Pine Top" Smith (1904-1929)
Cow Cow Davenport (1894-1955) – George Thomas
Henry Townsend (1929-1971) – ● Roosevelt Sykes (1906-1983)
Albert Ammons (1907-1949) – Meade "Lux" Lewis (1905-1964)
●Big Maceo (1905-1953) – ● Sunnyland Slim (1907)
Peetie Wheatstraw (1902-1941) – Leroy Carr (1905-1935)
Johnnie Jones (1949-1964) – ● Otis Spann (1930-1970)
● Pinetop Perkins (1913)

Major Influences
● Lonnie Johnson (1889-1970)
● Blind Lemon Jefferson (1897-1929)

Mississippi Blues

Delta-Style Blues
● Charley Patton (1887-1934) – Willie Brown (1900-1952)
● Son House (1902-1971) – ●Robert Johnson (1911-1938)
● Fred McDowell (1904-1972) – Bukka White (1906-1977)
Big Joe Williams (1903-1982) – Arthur Crudup (1905-1974)
Tommy McClennan (1908-ca. 1962)
John Lee Hooker (1917)

Jackson-Style Blues
Rubin Lacy (1901-1972) – Ishmon Bracey (1901-1970)
Charles McCoy (1909-1950) – Tommy Johnson (1896-1956)

Bentonia-Blues
Henry Stuckey (1897-1966) – ● Skip James (1902-1969)
Jack Owens (1904)

Regional Down-Home Blues

Atlanta
●Barbecue Bob (Robert Hicks) (1902-1931)
Blind Willie McTell (1901-1959) – ● Curley Weaver (1906-1962)
Buddy Moss (1906)

Piedmont School
● Blind Blake (1890-1933) – ● Blind Boy Fuller (1908-1941)
● Sonny Terry (1911-1984) – ●Brownie McGhee (1915)
● Rev. Gary Davis (1896-1972)

Tennessee

Memphis Jug Bands
●Gus Cannon's (1885-1979) Jug Stompers – ● Memphis Jug Band
Will Shade (1898-1966) – ● Noah Lewis (1895-1961)

Memphis
Furry Lewis (1893-1981) – Frank Stokes (1888-1955)
Robert Wilkins (1896-1987) – ●Memphis Minnie (1897-1973)

Brownsville, Tennessee
Sleepy John Estes (1899-1977)
Yank Rachell (1910) – Sonny Boy Williamson (1914-1948)

The End of World War II – The Rise of Live Blues Radio – "King Biscuit Time" – KFFA – Helena, Arkansas 1941

● Sonny Boy Williamson II (Rice Miller) (1899-1965) – ● Robert Lockwood Jr (1915) – Willie Love (1906-1953)
Joe Willie Wilkins (1923-1979) – Houston Stackhouse (1910-1981) – Peck Curtis (1912-1970)
Doctor Isaiah Ross (1925) – ● Elmore James (1918-1963) – ● Hound Dog Taylor (1917-1975)

Music Map **Blues History**

Chicago
The Bluebird Sound (mid 30s - late 40s)
Producer: Lester Melrose
Recorded:
● Big Bill Broonzy – Washboard Sam (1935-1964) – Jazz Gillum
● Tampa Red – Memphis Minnie – Walter Davis
● Sonny Boy Williamson – Big Joe Williams – Arthur Crudup
Tommy McClennan – Henry Townsend (1909)

Chicago – Early Artists
● Big Bill Broonzy (1893-1958) – ●Tampa Red (1900-1981)
Jazz Gillum (1904-1966) – Leroy Carr (1905-1935)
Big Maceo (1905-1953) – ● Robert Nighthawk (1909-1967)
Scrapper Blackwell (1903-1962) – Kokomo Arnold (1901-1968)
● Sonny Boy Williamson (1914-1948)

Chess Records
Producer: Leonard Chess
Recorded
● Muddy Waters – Little Walter – Elmore James
Howlin' Wolf – Buddy Guy – Sonny Boy Williamson II
Jimmy Rogers

The Muddy Waters Band
● Muddy Waters (1915-1983) – ●Little Walter (1930-1968)
● Jimmy Rogers (1924) – ●Otis Spann (1930-1970)

The Howlin' Wolf Band
Memphis ca. 1952
● Howlin' Wolf – Willie Johnson – Willie Steele

Chicago ca. 1954-1975
● Hubert Sumlin – Henry Gray – Eddie Shaw
Sam Lay – Detroit Jr. – Jody Williams

2nd Generation Chicago Bands
● Buddy Guy (1936) – ●Otis Rush (1934) – ●Junior Wells (1934)
● James Cotton (1935) – ●Magic Sam (1937-1969)
● Hound Dog Taylor (1917-1975) & the Houserockers

Postwar Chicago Harmonica
● Little Walter – ●Big Walter Horton – Snooky Pryor
● Jimmy Reed – James Cotton – Billy Boy Arnold
Junior Wells – George "Harmonica" Smith
Sonny Boy Williamson II

● Jimmy Reed – ● Eddie Taylor

Modern Postwar Blues Guitar
● T-Bone Walker (1910-1975)
● B. B. King – ●Albert King – ●Freddy King

Texas Guitar
● Clarence Gatemouth Brown (1924) – ●Lowell Fulson (1921)
Albert Collins (1932) – Johnny Copeland (1937)

Chicago Guitar
Mississippi - influenced:
● Elmore James – ● Eddie Taylor – Johnny Young
Johnny Shines – Homesick James – ●Hound Dog Taylor
● Earl Hooker – Joe Carter – J. B. Hutto – Louis Myers
B. B. King - influenced (West Side School):
● Otis Rush – ●Magic Sam – ● Buddy Guy – ●Hubert Sumlin
Magic Slim (1937) – Son Seals (1942) – Lonnie Brooks (1933)

Jump Blues
● Big Joe Turner (1911-1985) – ●Amos Milburn (1927-1980)
Roy Brown (1920-1981) – Wynonie Harris (1915-1969)

Texas Bluesmen
Smokey Hogg (1908) – ●Lightnin' Hopkins (1912-1982)
Lil Son Jackson (1915-1976) – Frankie Lee Sims (1917-1970)

West Coast
Jimmy McCracklin (1921) – Lowell Fulson (1921)
● Percy Mayfield (1920-1984) – ● Jesse Fuller (1896-1976)
K. C. Douglas (1913-1975) – Floyd Dixon (1929)
Charles Brown (1920) – Johnny Otis (1921)
Jimmy Witherspoon (1923) – Pee Wee Crayton (1914)

Detroit
● John Lee Hooker (1917) – ● Baby Boy Warren (1919-1977)
Bobo Jenkins (1916) – Eddie Burns (1928)
Eddie Kirkland (1928)

The Memphis Sound
Producer: Sam Phillips/Sun Records
Originally Recorded:
● B. B. King – ●Howlin' Wolf – ● Bobby Bland – ● Junior Parker
● Big Walter Horton – Joe Hill Louis – Willie Nix – Dr. Ross
Ike Turner – Roscoe Gordon

New Orleans
● Professor Longhair (1918-1980) – ● Fuitar Slim (1907-1975)

Zydeco
● Clifton Chenier (1925-1987) – Boozoo Chavis
Rockin' Dopsie – Fernest Arceneaux

Louisiana (Excello Records)
● Lightnin' Slim (1913-1974) – ● Slim Harpo (1924-1970)
Lonesome Sundown (1928) – Lazy Lester (1933)
Silas Hogan (1911)

● Robert Pete Williams (1914-1980)

More Modern Blues - Mid 60s to present:
Country Blues (White Interpreters)
John Hammond (1942) – Dave Van Ronk (1936)
John Koerner (1938) – Rory Block
Some Electric Blues
● Paul Butterfield (1942-1987) – ●Michael Bloomfield (1944-1981)
Taj Mahal (1940) – Johnny Winter (1944)
Elvin Bishop (1942) – Roy Buchanan (1939-1988)
Lil' Ed and the Blues Imperials – Roomful of Blues
● Fabulous Thunderbirds – ● Stevie Ray Vaughan (1956-1990)
Robert Cray (1953) – ●William Clarke

Soul Blues
● Junior Parker – Bobby Blue Bland (1930)
Little Milton (1934) – Little Johnny Taylor (1943) – Otis Clay
Z.Z. Hill (1940-1984)

Two joint meetings with B. B. King are highlights of those ABC/MCA years. His work for Malaco (mid-'80s to present) is formula blues and soul but quite satisfying in general. —*Bob Porter*

○ **Two Steps from the Blues** / 1962 / MCA 27036
One of his classic early albums. —*Michael Erlewine*

○ **Call On Me** / 1963 / MCA 27042
A near-perfect collection of early '60s sides. The man at his best. —*Hank Davis*

Ain't Nothing You Can Do / 1964 / MCA 27040
Fine soulful mid-'60s sides, including the title track, "Loneliness Hurts," and a cathartic reading of the soul classic "Blind Man." —*Cub Koda & Hank Davis*

○ **Touch of the Blues** / 1968 / Duke 88
During his Duke tenure, Bobby "Blue" Bland's rich, creamy voice was at its stark and dramatic peak. Like his other label releases, even when he got overly sentimental or sang just plain corny material, or the songs were over-arranged, Bland's smashing leads made everything work. —*Ron Wynn*

★ **Best of Bobby Blue Bland, The** / 196z / MCA 31219
Excellent compilation of the sides that made the legend. Includes "Call On Me," "Farther Up the Road," "I Pity the Fool," and "Turn On Your Love Light." —*Cub Koda*

His California Album / 1973 / MCA 10349
One of the gems of Bobby "Blue" Bland's post-Duke Records discography, originally released on ABC-Dunhill. Includes "Goin' Down Slow," "(If Lovin' You Is Wrong) I Don't Want to Be Right," and covers of songs by Van Morrison and Leon Russell. —*Roundup Newsletter*

Dreamer / 1974 / MCA 10415
Reissue of Bobby Bland's second album for ABC/Dunhill. Features all-star sidemen including Larry Carlton, Wilton Felder, Michael Omartian, Ernie Watts, and Pete Christlieb. Songs include "Ain't No Love in the Heart of the City" and "I Wouldn't Treat a Dog (The Way You Treated Me)," both Top Ten R&B hits. —*Roundup Newsletter*

Members Only / 1985 / Malaco 7429
A move to Malaco reenegized Bland's recorded output. —*Bill Dahl*

☆ **Best of Bobby Blue Bland, Vol. 2, The** / 198z / MCA 27045
Features the classics "It's My Life Baby," "Queen for a Day," and "Two Steps from the Blues." —*Cub Koda*

★ **I Pity the Fool: The Duke...** / 1992 / MCA 10665
A well-thought-out two-disc retrospective, this compiles Bland's first 44 recordings and perfectly chronicles his early development as an artist. Highlights are many, but the inclusion of the highly impassioned "Little Boy Blue" on disc two is worth the purchase price alone. — *Cub Koda*

○ **Turn On Your Love Light** / 1994 / MCA
The second two-CD installment in MCA's comprehensive Bobby "Blue" Bland reissue series is as impressive as the first, *I Pity the Fool*, and—with such highlights as the title song—nearly as essential. —*Stephen Thomas Erlewine*

Touch of the Blues/Spotlighting the Man / Mobile Fidelity 770
Two of Bland's best 1960s Duke LP's on one great-sounding CD. —*Bill Dahl*

Blind Blake (Arthur Phelps)

b. Jacksonville, FL, **d.** CA.
Vocals, guitar / Acoustic country blues
The high sales of Blind Lemon Jefferson 78s sent Paramount scouts scrambling to sign blues artists. In the fall of 1926, they recorded Arthur Blake, a swinging, sophisticated ragtime guitarist whose warm, relaxed voice was a far cry from harsh country blues. Paramount's newspaper ads boasted of Blind Blake's "famous piano-sounding guitar." Not much is known of Blind Blake, and the single surviving photograph only seems to deepen the mystery. He was a traveling man whose sponsors claimed he hailed from Jacksonville, FL. He worked in South Georgia and on the East Coast and spent at least part of the '20s living in a Chicago tenement. He made most of his 78s as a solo artist, although he sometimes featured sidemen and did some of his finest work as a sideman for women singers. "When he started to drink too much—you can hear it toward the end—it just doesn't work anymore," observes Ry Cooder. "He's physically past it, be-

cause you've got to be sharp to sound that good." After his final 1932 Paramount session, Blind Blake dropped out of sight and died in obscurity. For a while, though, his records sold almost as well as Blind Lemon's, and he had a tremendous impact, setting the standard for ragtime-influenced blues fingerpicking. —*Jas Obrecht*

★ **Ragtime Guitar's Foremost Fingerpicker** / 1984 / Yazoo 1068
Brilliantly facile guitar playing, with great arrangements. —*Jas Obrecht*

Complete Recorded Works, Vol. 1 (1926–27) / Document 5024
Complete Recorded Works in Chronological Order—Vols. 1–4.
Can't get enough of that stuff! —*Jas Obrecht*

Rory Block

Vocals, guitar / Modern acoustic blues
Rory Block is one of the brightest stars among a galaxy of modern-day country blues interpreters. Rory's superb renderings of classic songs by Robert Johnson, Tommy Johnson, Charley Patton, and others display her deep passion and instinct for historic preservation, but seldom are her covers mere mimics. With its body-pounds, potent bass-string snaps, and precision rhythms, her fierce acoustic guitar attack recalls the great Willie Brown. Rory's originals are often as strong as her covers, a standout being the title track from *Mama's Blues*. Her urgent, soulful voice is in a class of its own. As Taj Mahal says, "She's very simply the best there is." —*Jas Obrecht*

● **High Heeled Blues** / 1982 / Rounder 3061
A breathtaking, breakthrough CD of country-blues covers. —*Jas Obrecht*

Rhinestones & Steel Strings / 1984 / Rounder 3085
Delta blues meets sweet, sweet soul. —*Jas Obrecht*

Best Blues & Originals / 1988 / Rounder 11525
Sweet and tender, or down and dirty, but always uplifting. —*Jas Obrecht*

Mama's Blues / 1991 / Rounder 3117
Though she competently covers many musical areas, Rory Block's best genre has always been traditional blues. She emphasized that idiom on this album, doing strong, declarative versions of Robert Johnson's "Terraplane Blues," Tommy Johnson's "Bye Bye Blues," and "Big Road Blues" and her own originals "Ain't No Shame," "Got to Shine," and the title track. —*Ron Wynn*

○ **Ain't I a Woman** / 1992 / Rounder 3120
Rory Block's 11th album marked both a personal and professional milestone. Now a thoroughly experienced singer, Block sounded much more confident and assured doing traditional blues tunes. Block's vocals and guitar work have blossomed, toughened, and greatly improved over her career, and on this album were in prime form. —*Ron Wynn*

Michael Bloomfield

b. Jul. 28, 1944, **d.** Feb. 15, 1981
Electric guitar / Rock, Electric Blues, Blues rock
Bloomfield was one of the first White players who got right into the Chicago blues scene and could actually play the music. As lead guitar for the Butterfield Blues Band, he exerted a powerful influence with far-reaching effect on young rock guitarists. He almost single-handedly pioneered the extended guitar solo, introducing many Western ears to the sounds of the Far East with his sitar-inspired solos. The Butterfield Blues Band album *East-West* (and the lovely title cut) broke new ground in the progressive rock scene—psychedelic rock was born. Bloomfield also backed Bob Dylan in his move into electric-land on *Highway 61 Revisited,* one of the landmarks of modern rock music. He went on to record albums with his own band, the Electric Flag, and with others (*Super Session* with Al Kooper). These later efforts saw only limited success. He was best at blues, and those first two Butterfield albums mark a high point. Part of Bloomfield's enormous influence on younger rock guitar players was due to his very outgoing and generous spirit. Bloomfield was one of those rare performers who cared as much for sharing his vision with others as he did for the music he loved. —*Michael Erlewine*

● **Super Session** / 1968 / Columbia 9701
Al Kooper was the mastermind behind this appropriately named album, one side of which features his "spontaneous" studio collaboration with Mike Bloomfield and the other a session with

Stephen Stills. The recordings have an off-the-cuff energy that displays the inventiveness of the two guitarists to best advantage. The best-selling recording of Bloomfield's career, it inspired the followup *The Live Adventures of Mike Bloomfield and Al Kooper.* —*Jeff Tamarkin*

○ **It's Not Killing Me** / 1969 / CBS 9883

Triumverate / 1973 / CBS

The late guitarist Mike Bloomfield, blues master John Hammond, and timeless New Orleans funk of Dr. John blend well on this one-time-only outing. —*Jeff Tamarkin*

Living in the Fast Lane / 1980 / AJK 5006

Michael Bloomfield was a pioneer in blues-rock, one of the performers who found a way to maintain his own sound while paying tribute to the blues greats that created the music he idolized. The ten tracks presented on *Living in the Fast Lane,* weren't as vital as his earlier material, but they were done with the same intensity and passion that marked all his numbers. —*Ron Wynn*

Lucille Bogan (Lucille Armstrong)

b. Apr. 1, 1897, Amory, MS, **d.** Aug. 10, 1948, Los Angeles, CA
Vocals / Classic female blues
The big-voiced Bogan made some important sides in the classic female blues tradition throughout the the mid-'20s and early '30s. Unlike other women singers from the genre, she seldom strayed into pop-style music, remaining essentially a straightahead blues stylist. —*Cub Koda*

○ **1923–35** / 1923–35 / Story Of Blues 3535

A solid 18-track compilation of Lucille's best sides from her peak period. —*Cub Koda*

Son Bonds

b. Mar. 16, 1909, Brownsville, TN, **d.** Aug. 31, 1947, Dyersburg, TN
Vocals, guitar, sometimes kazoo / Acoustic country blues
An associate of Sleepy John Estes and Hammie Nixon, Bonds played very much in the same rural Brownsville style that the Estes-Nixon team popularized in the '20s and '30s. Curiously, either Estes or Nixon (but never both together) played on all of Bonds's recordings. The music to one of Bonds's songs, "Back and Side Blues" (1934), became a standard blues melody when John Lee "Sonny Boy" Williamson from nearby Jackson, TN, used it in his classic "Good Morning, (Little) School Girl" (1937). According to Nixon, Bonds was shot to death, while sitting on his front porch, by a nearsighted neighbor who mistook him for another man. —*Jim O'Neal*

○ **Complete Recorded Works in Chron. Order** / Wolf 003

Blues from Brownsville, 1934–41, with Hammie Nixon and Sleepy John Estes. —*Jas Obrecht*

Juke Boy Bonner

b. Mar. 22, 1932, Bellville, TX, **d.** Jun. 29, 1978, Houston, TX
Vocals, guitar, harmonica / Electric Texas blues
A modern-day Texas blues poet with an insightful sense of lyricism, Bonner usually performed as a one-man band, playing basic rhythm on guitar accented by soulful bursts from the harp he wore in a rack around his neck. While his music was down-home and countrified, some of his most notable songs dealt with the urban ghetto life of Houston. Bonner's blues are of the caliber destined to bring him greater fame as a posthumous legend than he was ever able to enjoy during his alcohol-shortened life, when he was known mostly to local blues-bar patrons in Houston and to European fanatics. —*Jim O'Neal*

○ **Life Gave Me a Dirty Deal** / 1969 / Arhoolie 375

Essential for Bonner fans; his best work. —*Bill Dahl*

★ **Struggle, The** / 1981 / Arhoolie 1045

Recorded in extreme stereo, with drums on one channel and Bonner's guitar on the other, this is Juke Boy Bonner's most cohesive album. Great songwriting and performances throughout. —*Cub Koda*

Juke Boy Bonner, 1960—1967 / 1991 / Flyright 38

A Lightnin' Hopkins–meets–Jimmy Reed sound on these delightfully funky guitar/harp-accompanied blues by this Houstonian, whose ironic lyrics are half the fun. —*Jas Obrecht*

Roy Book Binder

An often stirring folk/blues guitarist and vocalist, Roy Bookbinder's been playing country blues since the mid-'60s, when he began recording for Blue Goose. Greatly influenced by Rev. Gary Davis and Pink Anderson, Bookbinder played in East Coast coffeehouses in the early '60s, then began accompanying Rev. Davis on tours in the mid-'60s. He also played with Larry Johnson, Arthur "Big Boy" Crudup, and Homesick James. Besides constant concerts and tours, Bookbinder's made additional recordings for Blue Goose, as well as Adelphi and Rounder. —*Ron Wynn*

● **Hillbilly Blues Cats, The** / 1992 / Rounder 3121

Roy Bookbinder and his Hillbilly Cats band expertly convey the urgency of vintage blues by performing them with a brash rockabilly attitude. They cover classic songs in a manner that's neither reverential nor disrespectful, putting their own spin on such numbers as Blind Willie McTell's "Statesboro Blues" or Happy Traum's "Mississippi John." —*Ron Wynn*

Live Book... Don't Start Me Talkin'... / May 2, 1994 / Rounder Records

James Booker (James Carroll Booker III)

b. Dec. 17, 1939, **d.** Nov. 8, 1983
Piano / R&B, Blues, Piano blues, Boogie-woogie
Certainly one of the most flamboyant New Orleans pianists in recent memory, James Carroll Booker III was a major influence on the local rhythm and blues scene in the '50s and '60s. Booker's training included classical instruction until age 12, by which time he had already begun to gain recognition as a blues and gospel organist on radio station WMRY every Sunday. By the time he was out of high school he had recorded on several occasions, including his own first release, "Doing the Hambone," in 1953. In 1960 he made the national charts with "Gonzo," an organ instrumental. In 1967 he was convicted of possession of heroin and served a one-year sentence at Angola Penitentiary, which took the momentum out of an otherwise promising career. The rediscovery of "roots" music by college students during the '70s provided the opportunity for a comeback by 1974, with numerous engagements at local clubs like Tipitina's, the Maple Leaf, and Snug Harbor.

Booker's left hand was simply phenomenal, often a problem for bass players who found themselves running for cover in an attempt to stay out of the way; with it he successfully amalgamated the jazz and rhythm & blues idioms of New Orleans, adding more than a touch of gospel thrown in for good measure. His playing was also highly improvisational, reinventing a progression (usually his own) so that a single piece would evolve into a medley of itself. In addition, he had a plaintive and seering vocal style which was equally comfortable with gospel, jazz standards, blues, and popular songs. Despite his personal eccentricities, Booker had the respect of New Orleans's best musicians, and elements of his influence are still very much apparent in the playing of pianists like Henry Butler and Harry Connick Jr. —*Bruce Boyd Raeburn*

○ **Junco Partners** / 1976 / Hannibal 1359

A superb effort from a premier New Orleans piano master who made far too few recordings. The rumbling licks, often astonishing technique, and variety of rhythms and styles that Booker fused were always matched by his energy and exuberance. These sessions have since been reissued on CD. —*Ron Wynn*

● **New Orleans Piano Wizard: Live!** / Nov. 27, 1977 / Rounder 2027

Why so much of what pianist/vocalist James Booker recorded in the '70s didn't surface until the '90s is a mystery. But that's secondary compared to the greatness routinely presented on this CD. It contains nine Booker selections, which he performed at the 1977 Boogie Woogie and Ragtime Piano Contest held in Zurich. I don't know who won, but if they surpassed Booker the results ought to be on record somewhere. His relentless, driving style, ability to switch from a hard-hitting tune to a light, soft one without skipping a beat, and wild mix of sizzling keyboard licks and bemused, maniac vocals is uniformly impressive. It's a bit short for a CD at 37 minutes, but it has so much flamboyant music and singing it shouldn't be missed. —*Ron Wynn*

○ **Resurrection of the Bayou Maharajah** / 1977–82 / Rounder

This collection of late '70s and early '80s tracks feature amazing chordal forays, splintering riffs, barrelhouse, boogie-woogie, second-line tinged R&B solos and state-of-consciousness vocals. Booker rambles, cajoles, exaggerates, mocks, and soars while punctuating his wry singing with astonishing keyboard maneuvers. Singling out tracks is useless because there is nothing here that is not first-rate. —*Ron Wynn*

Spiders on the Keys / 1993 / Rounder Records 2119
Eclectic New Orleans piano master captured live in a local bar; plenty of surprises. —*Bill Dahl*

○ **King of the New Orleans Keyboard** / Junco Partner 1
Spectacular date by a great New Orleans pianist whose personal difficulties prevented him from both long life and sustained career achievement. He seamlessly fused blues base, jazz touches, and R&B/gospel feeling, and this was among his best (and few) recordings. —*Ron Wynn*

Eddie Boyd (Edward Riley Boyd)

b. Nov. 25, 1914, Stovall, MS
Vocals, piano / Chicago Blues, Piano blues
One of the most popular piano-playing bluesmen around Chicago in the early '50s, Eddie Boyd contributed one certified classic to the idiom in the much-covered "Five Long Years." —*Cub Koda*

● **Five Long Years** / Fontana 905
Mid-'60s session with superb backing reprising most of Boyd's '50s hits. —*Cub Koda*

Ishmon Bracey

b. Jan. 9, 1901, Byram, MS, d. Feb. 12, 1970, Jackson, MS
Vocals / Acoustic Delta blues
One of the early giants of the Delta blues, Bracey's best work is marked by a tremulous vibrato to his largely nasal voice and simple but effective guitar work. —*Cub Koda*

○ **Complete Recorded Works (1928–29)** / Document 5049
Bracey's complete recorded works (1928–29) in chronological order, with the bonus of four tracks by the elusive Charley Taylor. —*Cub Koda*

Tiny Bradshaw

b. Sep. 23, 1905, Youngstown, OH, d. Nov. 26, 1958, Cincinnati, OH
Vocals, drums, piano / Electric jump blues
Tiny Bradshaw was one of the most prominent bandleaders of the '30s and '40s who led groups of essentially jazz-trained musicians into the developing (and more commercial) field that came to be known as rhythm & blues. A vocalist with other bands early in his career, Bradshaw formed his own band in 1934 and kept it going through the early '50s, enjoying five *Billboard* hits (and also recording the original "Train Kept A-Rollin'") with King Records (where he was a labelmate to many of the other leading jump-blues performers of the era). Bradshaw's band produced such saxophone stars as Sonny Stitt, Red Prysock, and Sil Austin; among the vocalists to record with the group were Roy Brown, Arthur Prysock, Lonnie Johnson, and Tiny Kennedy. —*Jim O'Neal*

○ **Great Composer** / 1959 / King 653
Jump-blues bandleader of the '40s and '50s rocks the house. — *George Bedard*

● **Breakin' Up the House** / Charly 43
Best available CD of jump blues bandleader's swinging early '50s King Material. —*Bill Dahl*

Lonnie Brooks

b. Dec. 18, 1933, Dubuisson, LA
Vocals, guitar / Modern electric blues
Lonnie Brooks has emerged as a standard-bearer of "genuine houserocking music" for Alligator Records over the past decade and a half, with a bright, energetic style that draws from blues, rock & roll, and Louisiana R&B. Brooks (born Lee Baker Jr.) began his recording career in Lake Charles, LA, releasing "Family Rules," "The Crawl," and other '50s rhythm & blues sides under the name Guitar Jr. A move to Chicago put him in closer touch with hardcore blues (one of his first jobs in the city was with Jimmy Reed) and soon brought him a new stage name. Most of his singles continued to be in an R&B or soul vein, until he

adopted a bluesier approach when he began waxing albums for the blues market. —*Jim O'Neal*

● **Bayou Lightning** / 1979 / Alligator 4714
One of the hottest good-time blues albums of the late '70s. —*Bill Dahl*

Turn On the Night / 1981 / Alligator 4721
The second Alligator album is enjoyable in its own right, though inconsistent. —*Bill Dahl*

Hot Shot / 1983 / Alligator 4731
A sizzler, with an impressive Brooks on guitar. —*Bill Dahl*

Wound Up Tight / 1986 / Alligator 4751
Johnny Winter pays homage to Brooks (an early influence) by guesting on two tracks of this rocked-up set. —*Bill Dahl*

Live from Chicago / 1988 / Alligator 4759
On *Live from Chicago—Bayou Lightning Strikes*, Brooks shows he knows how to incite a packed nightclub. —*Bill Dahl*

Satisfaction Guaranteed / 1991 / Alligator 4799
The most rock-oriented album of this high-energy guitarist's career. Koko Taylor duets on one cut, and Lonnie's son on another. —*Bill Dahl*

Big Bill Broonzy (William Lee Conley Broonzy)

b. 1893, Scott, MS, d. Aug. 14, 1958, Chicago, IL
Vocals, guitar / Acoustic country blues
Big Bill Broonzy's performing career spanned five decades, taking him from Mississippi to Chicago, and on to Europe—where he served as one of the first and finest spokespersons and role models for the blues. Over the course of his life he played multiple roles equally well: down-home country fiddler, "race records" recording star, Chicago studio sideman, and blues revival folksinger.

A songwriter, vocalist, and guitar hero, Broonzy recorded some 250 sides prior to WWII, and hundreds more after, for a dozen labels; wrote innumerable songs; and played on countless sessions other than his own. A terrifically influential artist, he played in several styles, including down-home finger-picking, ragtime, and single-string electric. Later on he effortlessly produced rich acoustic finger work targeted to the guitar-conscious folk-revival audience. During his later years he sang protest pieces and other "folk" material to a coffeehouse and cabaret crowd.

But most of his musical life, his repertoire of blues, ragtime, hokum, and pop was specifically directed to the "race market." Beyond his extensive recordings, he left an autobiography, *Big Bill Blues*, which shows him to be an engaging storyteller and a master of the spoken word as well as song. One of the first to become a star after moving from Mississippi to Chicago, Broonzy earned the love and respect of his fellow musicians. As the central character in the first generation of Chicago blues, his work bridged tradition and popular categories. He was known as a musician not just in the technical sense, but in the sense of a supportive co-worker and a friend who could be counted on to help others in need. Aside from his towering skills as a musician and his self-promoted predilection for whiskey, Broonzy was a venerated member of the blues community.

Slick enough to deal with shifts in musical taste, Broonzy changed styles in his younger days and changed audiences in his later days. One of the first artists to successfully work to Northern and European audiences, he shaped the way a generation thought about the blues. —*Barry Lee Pearson*

Big Bill Broonzy & Washboard Sam / 1962 / MCA 9251
This chronicles the last commercial hurrah (1953) for this pair of prewar blues greats. —*Bill Dahl*

☆ **Young Big Bill Broonzy (1928–35), The** / 1968 / Yazoo 1011
Traditional as well as commercial material from a major bluesman. A must for those who only know Broonzy's later blues revival work. —*Barry Lee Pearson*

☆ **Do That Guitar Rag (1928–35)** / 1973 / Yazoo 1035
Great blues ragtime and hokum from a major singer, composer, guitarist, and sideman, whose recording career spanned four decades. —*Barry Lee Pearson*

☆ **Big Bill's Blues** / 198z / Portrait 44089
Big Bill at his most representative. Includes "When I've Been Drinkin'," in which he supposedly takes several drinks on microphone as part of the cut. —*Barry Lee Pearson*

★ **Good Time Tonight** / 1990 / CBS 46219
Twenty cuts from the '30s Columbia, ARC, and Vocalion sessions with various sidemen, including Blind John Davis and Joshua Altheimer. —*Barry Lee Pearson*

☆ **Blues in the Mississippi Night** / 1990 / Rykodisc 90155
Writer, producer, and historian Alan Lomax managed something truly unique in 1946: He not only brought together pianist Memphis Slim, guitarist Big Bill Broonzy, and harmonica player Sonny Boy Williamson for a concert, he managed to get them to talk frankly and specifically about their experiences in the segregated Deep South. At this time, few people outside the region really knew what was happening there, and even fewer that lived under the system ever discussed it openly. The anecdotes and incidents described, even from the vantage point of hearing them on this 1990 CD, are shocking and disgusting; they were even more shocking when aired in 1946. So much so that they were issued in semifictious form and in excerpts for years. The complete version appears here in all its hard-hitting glory. —*Ron Wynn*

In Chronological Order / 1991 / Document 5052
Three CDs of Broonzy's earliest and best sides, 1932–35. Includes "C-C Rider," "Milkcow Blues," and his finest instrumental, "House Rent Stomp." —*Cub Koda*

○ **Sings Folk Songs** / Smithsonian/Folkways 40023
Big Bill Broonzy was a narrative genius; someone who could take lyrics, situations, and themes and make them resonate with pain, sadness, anger, or joy. This 11-song set takes a slightly different tack. It's a compilation with Broonzy doing his renditions of well-known (and some obscure) folk songs. From the woeful laments of "Backwater Blues" and "Tell Me Who" to the assertive strains of "This Train" and "I Don't Want No Woman (To Try to Be My Boss)," Broonzy puts his own stamp on every number, even shopworn items like "John Henry" and "Bill Bailey." —*Ron Wynn*

Buster Brown

b. Aug. 15, 1911, Georgia, **d.** Jan. 31, 1976, Brooklyn, NY
Vocals, harmonica / R&B, Electric Blues
Brown was an obscure NY/NJ-based singer/harmonica player who came out of nowhere in late 1959 with the Fire Records issue of "Fannie Mae," which was a #1 R&B hit. Apart from one minor hit some years later and one album, *The New King of the Blues,* very little is known about this performer. The Fire album has been reissued on a variety of different labels. —*Bob Porter*

● **New King of the Blues, The** / 1959 / Collectables 5110
Best of the Fire sessions, including #1 hit "Fannie Mae" and "Is You Is or Is You Ain't My Baby?" —*Barry Lee Pearson*

Charles Brown

b. Sep. 13, 1922, Texas City, TX
Vocals, piano / R&B, Electric West Coast blues
The West Coast club-blues genre can be traced back directly to pianist Charles Brown, whose groundbreaking mid-'40s work as part of guitarist Johnny Moore's Three Blazers deeply influenced a legion of younger wizards of the ivories—notably Floyd Dixon, Amos Milburn, and Ray Charles. Theirs was a quieter, more introspective brand of blues, with obvious pop and jazz overtones.

Influenced himself by the ultra-smooth stylings of Nat "King" Cole, Brown's cool vocals communicated a proper mood of isolation and heartbreak on the classic Blazers tune "Driftin' Blues" and the Yuletide perennial "Merry Christmas Baby." Brown broke out as a solo artist in 1948, signing with Aladdin and continuing his string of hits with the doomy "Trouble Blues" and "Black Night."

Best classified as a blues balladeer, the pianist saw his suave style fall out of favor as rock & roll swept the country, and he recorded only intermittently from the '60s on. But Brown never gave up hope, and he recently made the sort of miraculous comeback normally reserved for contrived Hollywood melodramas. His 1990 Bullseye Blues disc *All My Life* brilliantly spotlights Brown's timeless approach, and a three-month stint opening for Bonnie Raitt in stadiums nationwide exposed this venerated R&B pioneer to a fresh mob of potential fans. —*Bill Dahl*

○ **Sunny Land** / 1979 / Route 66 5
Nice cross-section of the pianist's smooth early work for a variety of labels. —*Bill Dahl*

○ **All My Life** / 1990 / Bullseye Blues 9501

Fresh and triumphant performances from the year of Brown's celebrated "second coming." In the company of old pal Ruth Brown, incomparable saxman Clifford Solomon, Dr. John, and other top-drawer players, Brown sparkles. —*Mark A. Humphrey*

★ **Driftin' Blues: The Best of** / 1992 / EMI America 97989
This is a nice 20-track compilation of 1992 Grammy Award Winner Charles Brown's Aladdin label recordings. The keyboardist/singer works through tunes such as "Driftin' Blues," "Black Night," "Trouble Blues," and "Merry Christmas, Baby." Smooth vocals and tasteful accompaniment provide positive proof of Brown's musical prowess. No wonder why Bonnie Raitt is such a big fan of his. —*Roundup Newsletter*

Just a Lucky So and So / 1993 / Bullseye/Rounder
Brown's casual yet stunning phrasing, inventive voicings, and piano accompaniment are wonderfully presented on this ten song set. —*Ron Wynn*

Clarence "Gatemouth" Brown

b. Apr. 18, 1924, Vinton, LA
Vocals, guitar, violin, mandolin, drums / Texas Blues, Violin blues, Country & Western
Labeling Clarence "Gatemouth" Brown a blues artist is an injustice. While it's an undeniable fact that he's one of the pioneers of the blistering Texas blues guitar style, he's as likely to whip out his fiddle and play country, jazz, or calypso as he is to lay down a smoldering Texas shuffle.

Brown fell under the spell of Lone Star blues legend T-Bone Walker early on, adopting his crisp single-string picking and turning up the heat. While Brown was playing at a Houston nightclub, owner Don Robey took an interest in his career, inaugurating Peacock Records to issue Brown's work. Although he only enjoyed two R&B chart items, Brown's 1949–60 Peacock output was immensely influential on younger Texans such as Albert Collins and Johnny Copeland. With a torrid jazz-laced combo sizzling behind him, Brown dug in on the searing "Dirty Work at the Crossroads" and "Rock My Blues Away," setting nearly impossible standards for his proteges to duplicate on the incendiary instrumentals "Boogie Uproar" and "Okie Dokie Stomp." Brown left Peacock after a session showcasing his violin talent, later serving as house bandleader for the R&B TV variety program "The Beat." With the resurgence of interest in Texas blues, Gatemouth was ready to answer the call. Three acclaimed Rounder albums (including the 1981 Grammy-winning *Alright Again!*) and three more Alligator discs proclaim that Gatemouth Brown is much more than a bluesman, although the genre will always be his inspiration. —*Bill Dahl*

○ **Makin' Music (Roy Clark)** / 1979 / MCA 3009
Sparks fly when Brown teams with brilliant country icon Clark. —*Bill Dahl*

○ **San Antonio Ballbuster** / 1982 / Red Lightnin' 0010
Fine collection of Brown's late '40s and early '50s Peacock sides. Dubbed from old 78s. —*Bill Dahl*

○ **Alright Again!** / 1982 / Rounder 2028
Clarence Gatemouth Brown earned both notoriety and a reputation he later tried to shed at every opportunity with this 1981 session. The ten songs were superb examples of contemporary blues, plus a brilliant reworking of Lou Donaldson's soul-jazz tune "Alligator Boogaloo." It contained superior horn arrangements and brilliant guitar and violin playing by Brown. It earned him a 1982 Grammy and unanimous plaudits, but it also led many to typecast him as a blues musician. This ranks among the handful of truly great Gatemouth Brown albums, and was his finest release of the '80s. —*Ron Wynn*

★ **Original Peacock Recordings, The** / 1984 / Rounder 2039
Brown's earliest recordings feature tons of smoldering guitar with brassy, high-powered arrangements. Those only familiar with his mellow later work will be startled by the gutsy wallop these tracks have to offer. Milestones in Texas blues. —*Cub Koda*

J. T. Brown

b. Apr. 2, 1918, **d.** Nov. 24, 1969
Chicago Blues, Electric Blues, Sax blues
Saxophonist J.T. Brown was a honking, stomping soloist whose licks embellished recordings by numerous blues musicians from Little Brother Montgomery to Roosevelt Sykes, Elmore James,

Muddy Waters, Howlin' Wolf, and Willie Dixon among others. His braying, bleating sound was also featured on his own recordings for Harlem and United. Brown's early years were spent touring and playing with various medicine and ministrel shows. He moved to Chicago from Mississippi in the mid-'40s, and played on RCA sessions for Washboard Sam, Eddie Boyd, and Memphis Jimmy Clarke. He also frequently worked with Jump Jackson, whom he introduced to producer Lester Melrose. Brown began cutting his own dates in 1950 and continued through the mid-'50s. —Ron Wynn

● **Rockin' with J T** / 1984 / Krazy Kat 7240
Chicago jump blues, wailing stuff from late 1940s and early '50s. —Bill Dahl

○ **With Wille Dixon** / Delmark 9

Nappy Brown

b. Oct. 12, 1929, Charlotte, NC
Vocals / R&B, Electric jump blues
Nappy Brown has, alternately and often simultaneously, devoted his considerable vocal talents to both blues and gospel music for most of his life. It was as a member of a gospel group that he went to record for Savoy Records, but the company fancied him as a blues singer. With Savoy he hit the national charts four times from 1955–59, singing blues and novelty material that made use of his improvisational vocal phrasing. His modernized R&B version of "Night Time Is the Right Time," by Roosevelt Sykes, was not one of the big hits, but it did provide the model for Ray Charles's 1959 classic, and critics such as Peter Guralnick still cite Brown's rendition as the best. In the '60s Brown gave up the touring life and returned home to a renewed career in gospel, yet he would still heed the call of the blues on occasion, more and more so since 1984. He has since recorded several blues albums and enlivened many a blues stage with his energetic and humorous presence. —Jim O'Neal

○ **Right Time, The** / 1958 / Savoy 14025
Scorching N.Y. R&B from 1950's. —Bill Dahl

○ **That Man** / 1985 / Swift 100
This release features 1954–61 soul music recordings by this influential Savoy recording artist. It includes cuts with Budd Johnson, Sam "The Man" Taylor, and others. —Roundup Newsletter

● **Don't Be Angry!** / 1985 / Savoy 1149
An album containing several examples of the great singer's work for Savoy. Besides the title tune, it also contains "It Is True," "Open Up That Door," "Little By Little," "Two Faced Woman," etc. —Roots & Rhythm Newsletter

○ **Tore Up** / 1989 / Alligator 4792
A joyful noise: bright and brassy production with Brown in full belt. No mothballs here. The Heartfixers teaming up with the legendary singer Nappy Brown works very well. —Mark A. Humphrey & Michael G. Nastos

Roy Brown

b. Sep. 10, 1925, New Orleans, LA, d. May 25, 1981, San Fernando, CA
Vocals, sometimes piano / R&B, Rock & Roll, Electric jump blues
One of the premier shouters of the jump-blues era, Brown has been called "the first singer of soul" (in John Broven's *Walking to New Orleans*), "one of the great blues lyricists of all time" (in Jeff Hannusch's *I Hear You Knockin'*), and the artist responsible for the breakthrough of New Orleans rhythm & blues. An acknowledged and obvious influence on Bobby Bland, B. B. King, Junior Parker, Little Milton, James Brown, and Jackie Wilson in the blues and R&B fields, Brown also had followers on the rock & roll side by the names of Elvis Presley and Buddy Holly. He was a trendsetter both in his use of fervent gospel-style singing in Black secular music and in the infectious rhythms that helped pave the way for rock & roll in songs such as "Good Rockin' Tonight" and "Rockin' at Midnight." Though never again as commercially successful as he was in 1948–51, when he had 15 records on the charts, Brown continued to perform and record now and again in later years, still boasting the magnificent voice that enthralled and inspired listeners when he was "the mighty, mighty man" of rhythm & blues. —Jim O'Neal

★ **Good Rocking Tonight: The Best of Roy Brown** / Rhino Records, Inc.
Roy Brown's groundbreaking King sides, including "Rocking at Midnight" and "Good Rocking Tonight," are collected on this essential CD. —AMG

George "Mojo" Buford

b. Nov. 10, 1929, Hernando, MS
Harmonica / Electric Chicago blues
An alumni of the Muddy Waters band, Buford moved to Minneapolis in the early '60s, where he recorded and worked as a solo artist, eventually heading back to Chicago to work again with Muddy and on his own. A good, solid harp player in the Chicago tradition. —Cub Koda

Exciting Harmonica Sound of Mojo Buford / 1964 / BluesRecordSoc 324116
One of his best and earliest LPs. —Bill Dahl

● **Mojo Buford's Blues Summit** / 1981 / Rooster Blues 7603
Buford in the company of guitarists Little Smokey Smothers, Pee Wee Madison, Sammy Lawhorn, and Sonny Rogers, with a rhythm section pounding it out like crazy. —Cub Koda

Bumble Bee Slim (Amos Easton)

b. May 7, 1905, Brunswick, GA, d. 1968, Los Angeles, CA
Guitar, piano / Acoustic country blues
Popular and prolific, Bumble Bee Slim parlayed a familiar but rudimentary style into one of the earliest flowerings of the Chicago style. —Cub Koda

● **1931–37** / Document 506
A solid 18-track compilation of all his best sides. —Cub Koda

George "Wild Child" Butler

b. Oct. 1, 1936, Hernando, MS
Vocals, guitar, harmonica
An alumni of the Muddy Waters band, with a strong style that owes a heavy debt to both Little Walter and Sonny Boy Williamson II. —Cub Koda

● **Open up Baby** / 1984 / Charly 1104
Solid collection of Butler's best sides for the Jewel label. —Cub Koda

○ **These Mean Old Blues** / 1992 / Bullseye Blues 9518
His best offering in many moons. —Bill Dahl

Paul Butterfield

b. Dec. 17, 1942, Chicago, IL, d. May 4, 1987
Amplified harmonica, Vocals / Modern electric blues, Blues rock
Chicago-born Paul Butterfield started out on classical flute before switching to amplified harmonica. He hung out and jammed with Chicago South Side blues players, starting his own band in 1963. The first Butterfield album (1965) had an enormous impact on young rock players who were used to getting their blues via groups like the Rolling Stones. This album was no deferential imitation of Black music by shy Whites, but a hard-driving blues album that rocked. It was a signal to White players to stop making respectful tributes to Black music and just play it. In a flash, the image of blues as old-time music was gone, and modern Chicago-style urban blues was out of the closet and introduced to mainstream White audiences.
The first two Butterfield Blues albums are essential from a historical perspective. While *East-West*, the second album, set the tone for psychedelic rockers with its Eastern influence and extended solos, it was that incredible first album (*The Paul Butterfield Blues Band*) that put the music scene on alert to what was coming. Later Butterfield material somehow misses the mark. Butterfield was one of the only White harmonica players to develop his own style—one respected by Black players (another is the brilliant William Clarke). Butterfield has no credible imitators. His harp playing was always understated, concise, and serious—only Big Walter Horton has a better sense of note selection. —Michael Erlewine

☆ **East-West** / 1966 / Elektra 7315
These Chicago-based musicians took blues to a whole new level on this, their second album, paving the way for the experimentations that are still being explored today. —Jeff Tamarkin

○ **Resurrection of Pigboy Crabshaw, The** / 1968 / Elektra 74015

A new direction was tried on this third album, stressing horn arrangements over guitar-fueled improvisations. —*Jeff Tamarkin*

★ **Blues Band** / 1971 / Elektra 7294
Butterfield's unique amplified harmonica style is already present on his classic first album—a wakeup call for a generation of young White players wondering if they, too, could play the blues. Great guitar from Michael Bloomfield and Elvin Bishop. With Mark Naftalin (organ), Jerome Arnold (bass), and Sam Lay (drums). —*Michael Erlewine*

Better Days / 1973 / Rhino 70877
Paul Butterfield with Geoff Muldaur, Howard Johnson, Ronnie Barron, Bobby Charles, and others. —*AMG*

Chris Cain Band

Vocals, guitar / Modern electric blues
The San Jose, CA, native's crisp lead guitar and gravelly vocals have brought him national recognition, with a solid 1990 album on Blind Pig to his credit. Influenced by B. B. and Albert King as well as various jazz players, Cain has cooked up a jumping sound on the Bay Area circuit. —*Bill Dahl*

Late Night City Blues / 1987 / Blue Rock-It 105
This debut album was rewarded with four Handy Award nominations. —*Bill Dahl*

● **Cuttin' Loose** / 1990 / Blind Pig 74090
A wonderful, big-voiced, contemporary West Coast bluesman and superb guitar player. There are several horns in the band, giving it a great, huge sound. —*Niles J. Frantz*

○ **Can't Buy a Break** / Blind Pig 75000
The latest release from the Chris Cain Band emphasizes originals that swing hard. The West Coast guitarist/vocalist, who also plays piano on two cuts here, is backed by bass, drums, keyboards, and two saxophones. This is blues with a twist, as on the gospel-laced "My Life Is Getting Sweeter" and jazzy instrumental "Gin 'n' Soda." —*Roundup newsletter*

Eddie C. Campbell

b. May 6, 1939, Duncan, MS
Vocals, guitar / Modern electric blues
The self-styled "King of the Jungle" from Chicago's West Side, Campbell has employed a clever and often whimsical sense of humor in his songs to go along with a solid blues foundation built on the music of Magic Sam, Muddy Waters, and James Brown, among others. Campbell was a member of Willie Dixon's Chicago Blues All Stars when he cut his first album in 1977, backed by Dixon sidemen Carey Bell, Lafayette Leake, and Clifton James. Campbell. A man of many interests, he maintained blues as only a part-time occupation and did little to further his musical career until he moved to Europe in 1984. The receptive European blues climate has afforded him renewed opportunities to perform and record, and although he remains a refreshing entertainer, he also remains little known in his home country. —*Jim O'Neal*

● **King of the Jungle** / Jan. 1977 / Rooster Blues 7602
Tough contemporary blues from Chicago's West Side. —*Bill Dahl*

○ **Let's Pick It** / Oct. 1984 / Evidence 26037
Campbell keeps it down to earth on this collection, vacillating between solid original material and great versions of Magic Sam's best. Highly recommended. —*Cub Koda*

John "Blues" Campbell

Guitar / Cool
Contemporary Texas bluesman whose 1991 domestic debut on Elektra, *One Believer*, is a gloomy, intense collection with lots of fiery guitar. Born in Shreveport, LA, and reared in Texas, Campbell cites Lightnin' Hopkins as a principal influence. He cut his first album, *A Man and His Blues*, for the German Crosscut imprint, and it earned a 1989 Handy Award nomination. Tragically, he died a short time after his third album, the critically acclaimed *Howlin' Mercy*, was released, cutting short a promising career.—*Bill Dahl*

○ **One Believer** / 1991 / Elektra 61086
A ten-tune program of mostly original compositions co-written with Dennis Walker, who coproduced it. The Robert Cray Band rhythm section is on hand for half the album. A very impressive artist and album. —*Bob Porter*

● **Howlin' Mercy** / 1993 / Elektra 61440
On the whole, *Howlin' Mercy* is anchored by a thundering rhythm section and Campbell's grinding, cement-mixer voice—a riveting instrument that expresses the torment of a life experience you really only want to know about second hand. *Howlin' Mercy* is contemporary blues at its most powerful. —*Roch Parisien*

Cannon's Jug Stompers (Gus Cannon)

b. Sep. 12, 1885, Red Banks, MS, d. Oct. 15, 1979, Memphis, TN
Vocals, banjo, guitar, sometimes jug, kazoo, piano / Acoustic Memphis blues
Gus Cannon was the best known of all the jug band musicians and a seminal figure on the Memphis blues scene. His recollections have also provided us with much of our knowledge of the earliest days of the blues in the Mississippi Delta. Cannon led his Jug Stompers on banjo and jug in a historic series of dates for the Victor label in 1928–30. The ensemble usually included a second banjoist or guitarist, one of whom often doubled on kazoo, and the legendary Noah Lewis on harmonica. The jug-band style enjoyed a revival during the folk boom of the '50s and '60s, resulting in an ultra-rare Gus Cannon album on Stax, of all labels, after his "Walk Right In" became the nation's best-selling record for the Rooftop Singers in 1963. Cannon's Victor output was also a favorite source of early blues material for the Grateful Dead. —*Jim O'Neal*

○ **Complete Recordings, The** / Yazoo 1082
This innocent and exuberant Memphis good-time blues was the inspiration for '50s British skiffle and Greenwich Village folkies alike. —*Mark A. Humphrey*

Leroy Carr

b. Mar. 27, 1905, Nashville, TN, d. Apr. 29, 1935, Indianapolis, IN
Vocals, piano / Piano blues
The term "urban blues" is usually applied to post-WWII blues band music, but one of the forefathers of the genre in its preelectric format was Leroy Carr. Teamed with the exemplary guitarist Scrapper Blackwell in Indianapolis, Carr became one of the top blues stars of his day, composing and recording almost 200 sides during his short lifetime, including such classics as "How Long, How Long," "Prison Bound Blues," "When the Sun Goes Down," and "Blues before Sunrise." His blues were expressive and evocative, recorded only with piano and guitar, yet as author Sam Charters has noted, Carr was "a city man" whose singing was never as rough or intense as the country bluesmen's; and as reissue producer Francis Smith put it, "He, perhaps more than any other single artist, was responsible for transforming the rural blues patterns of the '20s into the more city-oriented blues of the '30s." —*Jim O'Neal*

★ **Blues Before Sunrise** / 1962 / Portrait 44122
Despite minimal sound quality, this reissue contains some prime Leroy Carr/Scrapper Blackwell material. They were arguably the greatest piano and guitar duo to emerge in the late '20s and early '30s. You can find these tracks on other import collections, but this was among the first reissues available on a domestic label. —*Ron Wynn*

○ **Singin' the Blues** / 1973 / Biograph 9
This is late period Carr, superb material done in 1934. It's hard to believe, considering the depth of his piano playing and the vocal quality, that by the end of the next year, Carr's career would be finished. The sound quality is good enough to convey the range and might in Carr's piano fills and his delivery. —*Ron Wynn*

☆ **Naptown Blues (1929–34)** / 1988 / Yazoo 1036
A seminal piano/guitar duo. Leroy Carr was among the most influential early blues singer/pianists, and Scrapper Blackwell was a remarkably fluid guitarist. —*Mark A. Humphrey*

Bo Carter (Armenter Chatmon)

b. Mar. 21, 1893, Bolton, MS, d. Sep. 21, 1964, Memphis, TN
Vocals, guitar, sometimes banjo, bass, clarinet / Acoustic Delta blues
Bo Carter (born Armenter "Bo" Chatmon) had an unequaled capacity for creating sexual metaphors in his songs, specializing in such ribald imagery as "Banana in Your Fruit Basket," "Pin in Your Cushion," and "Your Biscuits Are Big Enough for Me." One of the most popular bluesmen of the '30s, he recorded enough

material for several reissue albums, and he was quite an original guitar picker, or else three of those albums wouldn't have been released by Yazoo. (Carter employed a number of different keys and tunings on his records, most of which were solo vocal and guitar performances.) Carter's facility extended beyond the risqué business to more serious blues themes, and he was also the first to record the standard "Corrine Corrina" (1928). Bo and his brothers Lonnie and Sam Chatmon also recorded as members of the Mississippi Sheiks with singer-guitarist Walter Vinson. —*Jim O'Neal*

● **Greatest Hits, 1930–40** / Feb. 1970 / Yazoo 1014
Mostly solo selections by Bo, with a couple of Mississippi Sheiks songs included. Features very fine and distinctive country-blues guitar playing and singing. Most of the songs are of the double-entendre variety—a possible reason why he's not as well known as he deserves to be, since some blues researchers did not deem his material worthy. As with most Yazoo releases, the liner notes include various guitar tunings and chord progressions for each song—fascinating for guitarists. —*George Bedard*

Banana in Your Fruit Basket / 1978 / Yazoo 1064
Some of Carter's best double-entendre material, including the salacious "I Got Ants in My Pants." —*Cub Koda*

John Cephas with/ Phil Wiggins

b. 1988
Guitar, harmonica / Blues, Modern acoustic blues
Products of the Washington, D.C., area, Cephas and Wiggins have been working as an acoustic guitar and harmonica duet for over 15 years. Their music has its roots in the rural African-American dance music of Virginia and North Carolina and shows the influence of Blind Boy Fuller, Gary Davis, and Sonny Terry.

Their broad repertoire consists of Piedmont blues standards as well as an eclectic sampling of Delta stylings, R&B, ballads, ragtime, gospel, and country & western. Two of their best albums, *Dog Days of August* and *Guitar Man,* were voted the Best Traditional Blues Albums of the Year by the Handy Awards. In 1989 Cephas received a National Heritage Award in recognition of his efforts as a teacher and spokesperson for the traditional arts.

Cephas and Wiggins have literally toured the world, playing every major festival and winning new friends for their regional blues style. Their sound combines sophisticated traditional instrumentation and modern gospel-edged vocals, applied to traditional standards and their own hard-hitting compositions, offering a soulful acoustic option to electric blues. Today Cephas and Wiggins are the most visible exponents of Piedmont blues, gracefully carrying their tradition into the '90s. —*Barry Lee Pearson*

● **Dog Days of August** / 1986 / Flying Fish 90394
Handy Award–winning acoustic guitar and harmonica Piedmont blues. Includes ballads "John Henry," "Staggerlee," and ten original compositions. —*Barry Lee Pearson*

Guitar Man / 1987 / Flying Fish 470
Their second Handy Award winner includes slide guitar, Piedmont finger-picking, and wonderful harmonica. —*Barry Lee Pearson*

○ **Walking Blues** / 1988 / Marimac 8004
A fine assortment of Piedmont blues, ragtime, and country. Includes "Walking Blues." —*Barry Lee Pearson*

Sam Chatmon

b. Jan. 10, 1897, Boltmon, MS, **d.** Feb. 2, 1983, Hollandale, MS
Vocals, guitar, strings / Acoustic country blues
A product of the prodigious Chatmon family that included not only Lonnie of the famous Mississippi Sheiks but also the prolific Bo Carter and several other blues-playing brothers, Sam Chatmon survived to be hailed as a modern-day blues guru when he began performing and recording again in the '60s. Sam continued brother Bo's tradition of sly double-entendre blues to entertain a new generation of aficionados, but he also showed a more serious side on songs like the title track of the early Arhoolie anthology *I Have to Paint My Face.* —*Jim O'Neal*

○ **Mississippi Sheik** / 1970 / Blue Goose 2006

● **Sam Chatmon's Advice** / 1979 / Rounder 2018
Outstanding blues and double-entendre delights. —*Ron Wynn*

Sam Chatmon & His Barbecue Boys / 1987 / Flying Fish 202

An excellent set of trio recordings by this underrated performer. —*Ron Wynn*

William Clarke

b. Mar. 29, 1951, Inglewood, CA
Amplified harmonica / Modern electric blues
I had given up hope of ever seeing a new voice on amplified blues harp (harmonica) again in my life. It seemed that the best players out there couldn't even live up to classic harp players like Big Walter Horton or Little Walter, much less carry blues harmonica the next step. Then came William Clarke. Technically, Clarke is a master of both the cross and chromatic harps. He takes blues on the chromatic up to and beyond where Little Walter left it years ago. But far more important than the technique is the music. Clarke plays music to my ears, and it has been a long time since I have heard any really new sounds on a blues harp. Raised in the West Coast blues scene, Clarke studied with many players, in particular George "Harmonica" Smith—a veteran of the Muddy Waters band. Clarke (along with Big Walter Horton and Paul Butterfield) has an almost impeccable sense of which notes to play. Give him a listen. Harmonica recording artist Charlie Musselwhite says that Clarke is his "favorite living harp player—no doubt about it." I am in total agreement with Musselwhite. —*Michael Erlewine*

Can't You Hear Me Calling / 1983 / Rivera 502
Clarke's debut album only gives a glimmer of what's to come from this new genius of the blues, but it is enjoyable nonetheless. —*Cub Koda*

Rockin' the Boat / 1988 / Rivera 503
Recorded live in 1987, this features Clarke and his regular working band on a wide variety of material showcasing his formidable talents as a vocalist and harmonica man extraordinaire. —*Cub Koda*

★ **Blowin' Like Hell** / 1990 / Alligator 4788
The title says it all. William Clarke cooks on this one. These are new sounds. —*Michael Erlewine*

○ **Serious Intentions** / 1992 / Alligator 4806
Clarke's second album for the label burns with a ferocious intensity, particularly for his groundbreaking work on chromatic harp and his ability to cover all styles with remarkable elan. —*Cub Koda*

Gary B. B. Coleman

b. 1947, Paris, TX
Vocals, guitar, sometimes keyboards, bass / Modern electric blues
After a career as a local bluesman and blues promoter in Texas and Oklahoma, Gary Coleman found his niche when he signed over his first album, a self-produced outing originally issued on his own label, to the fledgling Ichiban company out of Atlanta in 1986. Since that time, both Coleman and Ichiban have made their marks in the blues field—not only has Coleman released half a dozen of his own albums, he has also overseen production of the bulk of Ichiban's hefty blues catalog, bringing to the studio a number of artists he's booked or toured with in his previous career (Chick Willis, Buster Benton, and Blues Boy Willie, among others). A singer/guitarist onstage, Coleman has often taken on a multiinstrumentalist's role in the studio. His music remains true to the blues and to the King legacy saluted in his "B. B." moniker and in his acknowledged debt to fellow Texan Freddie King. —*Jim O'Neal*

○ **Nothin' But the Blues** / 1987 / Ichiban 1005
Darker overall tone; sadder and more introspective. One of his more consistent records. Includes two very good slow blues, "Let Me Love You Baby" and "Shame on You." —*Niles J. Frantz*

○ **If You Can Beat Me Rockin'...** / 1988 / Ichiban 1018
Highlights here are the title track and the Coleman-penned "Watch Where You Stoke." —*Niles J. Frantz*

● **Best of Gary B. B. Coleman, The** / 1991 / Ichiban 1065
Good career overview. Exposes a certain lack of originality and diversity. —*Niles J. Frantz*

Romance without Finance ... / 1991 / Ichiban 1107
Romance without Finance Is a Nuisance is a little funkier and a little more naughty. —*Niles J. Frantz*

Albert "Jazzbeaux" Collins

b. Oct. 3, 1932, Leona, TX
Vocals, guitar / R&B, Electric Texas blues
One of the most influential guitarists in the post-WWII period, Collins was a prominent performer in the Houston area who began recording in the '50s but lingered in obscurity until discovered by members of the rock group Canned Heat in 1966. His early recordings for the Hall label were collected in *The Cool Sound of Albert Collins*, which featured primarily instrumentals with similar titles ("Frosty," "Sno-Cone," "Frost Bite"). Collins has kept this identity since. Three albums on Imperial are a mixed lot—gems mixed in with commercial dross. The '70s were largely uneventful for the guitarist until a 1978 relationship with Alligator Records. Here Collins began to blossom, and the Alligator albums, which continued to be released until 1986, are uniformly excellent and reveal a previously obscured ability as a blues singer. Collins was a popular live performer and was actively recording until his death in 1993; he will always be remembered as the "Master of the Telecaster." —*Bob Porter*

○ **Truckin' with Albert Collins** / 1969 / MCA 10423
Classic early-'60s ice-laden instrumentals that established Collins as "the Master of the Telecaster." —*Bill Dahl*

★ **Ice Pickin'** / 1978 / Alligator 4713
A killer album, with loads of icy guitar and Collins's understated vocals. Classic contemporary blues! —*Bill Dahl*

Frostbite / 1980 / Alligator 4719
More searing Texas guitar. "Brick" just may be his hottest shuffle to date! —*Bill Dahl*

Frozen Alive! / 1981 / Alligator 4725
This first legitimate live album is typically spellbinding. —*Bill Dahl*

Don't Lose Your Cool / 1983 / Alligator 4730
This fourth Alligator Records effort is consistently satisfying. —*Bill Dahl*

Showdown / 1987 / Alligator 4743
A summit meeting between Texas guitar veterans Collins and Johnny Copeland and newcomer Robert Cray. Scorching all the way. —*Bill Dahl*

★ **Complete Imperial Recordings, The** / 1991 / EMI America 96741
A complete, two-disc set of Collins's 1968–70 work on Imperial Records. Mostly instrumental. —*Bill Dahl*

Sam Collins

b. Aug. 11, 1887, Louisiana, d. Oct. 20, 1949, Chicago, IL
Vocals, guitar / Acoustic country blues
One of the earliest generation of blues performers, Collins developed his style in South Mississippi (as opposed to the Delta). His recording debut single ("The Jail House Blues," 1927) predated those of legendary Mississippians such as Charley Patton and Tommy Johnson and was advertised as "Crying Sam Collins and his Git-Fiddle." Collins did not become a major name in blues—in fact, his later records appeared under several different pseudonyms—but his rural bottleneck guitar pieces were among the first to be compiled on LP when the country blues reissue era was just beginning. Sam Charters wrote in *The Bluesmen*: "Although Collins was not one of the stylistic innovators within the Mississippi blues idiom, he was enough part of it that, in blues like "Signifying Blues" and "Slow Mama Slow," he had some of the intensity of the Mississippi music at its most creative level." —*Jim O'Neal*

● **Jailhouse Blues** / 1990 / Yazoo 1079
One of the '20s' most fascinating, eccentric obscurities, although a little Collins goes a long way. —*Mark A. Humphrey*

Complete Recorded Works (1927–31) / Document 5034

Johnny Copeland

b. 1938, Homer, LA
Vocals, guitar / R&B, Electric Texas blues
Copeland is associated with the Texas blues and has been headquartered both in Houston and New York for many years. A fine blues composer as well as guitarist and vocalist, he is one of the most well rounded performers of the genre. Early recordings on Home Cooking and Crazy Cajun and two volumes on Mr. R&B are collections of singles originally recorded for many labels from the early '60s to the late '70s. Copeland's albums for Rounder Records begin in 1981, and it is here that the mature Copeland is to be found. A total of six albums were issued (and two collections from the earliest albums), and Copeland appears on the Grammy-winning *Showdown* with Robert Cray and Albert Collins. Of the Rounder albums, all the U.S.-recorded studio sessions are fine, leaving one live album (*Ain't Nothin' but a Party*) with a session recorded in Africa (*Bringin' It All Back Home*) for specialists only. —*Bob Porter*

● **Copeland Special** / 1977 / Rounder 2025
This immaculate collection put the veteran Houston axeman among the blues elite. Features searing guitar and soulful vocals. —*Bill Dahl*

○ **Texas Twister** / 1983 / Rounder 11504
The 15 numbers on this anthology cover four Rounder sessions and include competent renditions of familiar numbers "Claim Jumper," "Copeland Special," and "Houston." But what makes things special are the final three selections; these were part of Copeland's superb and unjustly underrated *Bringing It Back Home* album, a date recorded in Africa that matched Texas shuffle licks with swaying, riveting African rhythms. The eight-minute "Ngote" in particular was a delight, and the other two numbers—"Kasavubu" and "Abidjan"—were so great they'll make you want to immediately grab the entire African CD and play it at maximum volume. —*Ron Wynn*

○ **I'll Be Around** / 1984 / Mr. R&B 1001
Exceptional collection of Copeland's primordial work. —*Bill Dahl*

○ **Down on Bending Knee** / 1985 / Mr. R&B 1002
A second volume of his early sides, equally impressive. —*Bill Dahl*

○ **Bringin' It All Back Home** / 1986 / Rounder 2050
Imaginative hybrid of blues and African idioms. —*Bill Dahl*

Ain't Nothing But a Party (Live) / 1988 / Rounder 2055
Copeland didn't turn in a formula job on these six tunes recorded live at the 1987 Juneteenth festival. Indeed, the concert setting seems to put some juice in Copeland's singing: His voice isn't raspy or detached, and he actually seems exuberant about doing the umpteenth version of "Big Time" and "Baby, Please Don't Go." Even Copeland's shuffle licks and patterns, which can become awfully predictable, were executed with some sharp twists and surprising turns. —*Ron Wynn*

Collection, Vol. 1 / 1988 / Collectables 5221
Early 1960–68 Houston sides. Obscure but satisfying. —*Bill Dahl*

James Cotton

b. Jul. 1, 1935, Tunica, MS
Vocals, harmonica, sometimes drums, guitar / Rock & Roll, Electric Chicago blues
James Cotton learned blues harmonica from Sonny Boy Williamson. He was playing in Howlin' Wolf's Arkansas Band at the age of 13 and even recorded with Wolf on his early Chess sessions. After Little Walter left, Cotton went on to become Muddy Waters's main harp player and worked with him for more than ten years before leaving to form his own band in 1965. Along with Junior Wells, Cotton is one of the two greatest Chicago harmonica players alive today. Branching out from straight blues, Cotton's recent albums show the influences of jazz, gospel, and pop music. His singing is often in the style of Bobby Bland, and his harp playing combines elements of amplified down-home harp with the high-compression Chicago style. —*Michael Erlewine*

○ **Chicago/ the Blues/ Today!, Vol. 2** / 1964 / Vanguard 9217
Classic compilation, also starring Otis Rush and Homesick James. —*Bill Dahl*

James Cotton Blues Band, The / 1967 / Verve 3023
Upbeat, soul-influenced mid-'60s work by Cotton's initial solo aggregation. —*Bill Dahl*

Cut You Loose! / 1967 / Vanguard 79283
One of Cotton's earlier solo efforts. —*Bill Dahl*

○ **100% Cotton** / 1974 / One Way 27670
Boogie burners from this searing harp master at his absolute hottest. —*Bill Dahl*

● **High Compression** / 1984 / Alligator 4737

Half low-down Chicago blues, half brassy, R&B-influenced fare, this spotlights his high-energy harp and vocals. —*Bill Dahl*

Take Me Back / 1988 / Blind Pig 72587
The harpist pays tribute to his roots with a tasty album of covers done Chicago-style. —*Bill Dahl*

Live at Antone's / 1988 / Antone's 0007
A relaxed club setting of Cotton picking some old favorites, with Matt Murphy contributing blistering guitar. —*Bill Dahl*

Mighty Long Time / 1991 / Antone's 0015
A classy contemporary collection of standards with crisp all-star backing. —*Bill Dahl*

Ida Cox (Ida [née Prather] Cox)

b. Feb. 25, 1896, Toccoa, GA, d. Nov. 10, 1967, Knoxville, TN
Vocals / Classic female blues, Blues jazz, Ballads, Swing
A stalwart performer whose career began in minstrel shows, Ida Cox was a bawdy, free-wheeling performer with a love for "blue" jokes and double-entendre vocals. During the '20s she made memorable cuts with first-rate jazz musicians and was a tent-show star in the '30s. She was one of the earliest, biggest stars on the Black circuit. Cox made a final triumphant recording for Riverside, backed by the Coleman Hawkins group in 1961. —*Ron Wynn*

★ **Blues for Rampart Street** / 1961 / Riverside 1758
This is latter-period Cox, with jazz all-stars, including Coleman Hawkins. Some of her best tunes. —*Michael G. Nastos*

○ **Wild Women Don't Have the Blues** / 1961 / Rosetta 1304

Robert Cray

b. 1953, Columbus, GA
Vocals, guitar / Rock, Modern electric blues, Blues
Cray is the man responsible for bringing the blues into the pop charts at a time when synthesized dance pop was the rage. He did it through songs that defined blues themes but added modern and personal twists. He's also a fine bandleader and a masterfully subtle guitarist. —*John Floyd*

○ **Who's Been Talkin'** / 1979 / Atlantic 81730
Cray's debut LP, one of his bluesiest and best. Reissue of Tomato album. —*Bill Dahl*

Bad Influence / 1983 / Hightone 8001
Classic harbinger of what would soon follow; very consistent LP. —*Bill Dahl*

○ **False Accusations** / 1985 / Hightone 8005
Cray's most developed and consistent Hightone release, cut a year before he signed with Polygram. —*John Floyd*

★ **Strong Persuader** / 1986 / Mercury 830568
Cray's commercial breakthrough is a set of songs that work off one another and sound great as singles. It is evocative enough to have made him the most innovative bluesman of the last 20 years. —*John Floyd*

Don't Be Afraid of the Dark / 1988 / Mercury 834923
A followup to *Strong Persuader*, this suffers from weak songs but is worthwhile for fans. —*John Floyd*

○ **Midnight Stroll** / Jun. 1990 / Mercury 846652
Cray adds the Memphis Horns to the permanent lineup, resulting in an album that recalls the dark, driving soul of Stax/Volt's heyday even more than previous efforts. —*Brian Mansfield*

I Was Warned / Apr. 1992 / Mercury 512721
Heavy on Southern soul influence and Cray has the voice to pull it off. —*Bill Dahl*

○ **Shame + a Sin** / Oct. 5, 1993 / Mercury
Back to the blues set—impressive. —*Bill Dahl*

Pee Wee Crayton

b. Dec. 18, 1914, Rockdale, TX, d. Jun. 25, 1985, Los Angeles, CA
Vocals, guitar / R&B, Electric West Coast blues
One of the preeminent West Coast bluesmen of the postwar era, Crayton was one of the first blues artists to scorch the charts with an electric guitar instrumental ("Blues after Hours," a #1 hit on Modern Records in 1948). A student of T-Bone Walker (and later his rival), Crayton did his most successful and influential work for Modern, but he maintained his stature as a blues guitar master throughout a career that found him still going strong until a

heart attack felled him at the age of 70. In *Living Blues* magazine, Dick Shurman described Crayton's style as a mix of "jazzy single-note lines, wide bends, fancy picking, and some of the biggest, prettiest chords ever waxed by a blues player." —*Jim O'Neal*

★ **Pee Wee Crayton** / 1959 / Crown 5175
An ancient but indispensable collection of his Modern label output. It includes the instrumentals "Texas Hop" and "Blues after Hours." —*Bill Dahl*

○ **Things I Used to Do, The** / 1970 / Vanguard 6566
A later work by this influential Texas guitarist. The only domestic CD available. —*Bill Dahl*

○ **Peace of Mind** / 1982 / Charly 601
Mid-'50s Vee-Jay rockers. —*Bill Dahl*

○ **Rocking Down on Central Avenue** / 1982 / ACE 61
Classic late-'40s/early-'50s sides on Modern that showcase Crayton's smooth, T-Bone Walker-influenced guitar work. —*Bill Dahl*

Arthur "Big Boy" Crudup

b. Aug. 24, 1905, Forest, MS, d. Mar. 28, 1974, Nassawadox, VA
Vocals, guitar / R&B, Electric Blues
Although a major contributor to American music history, Arthur "Big Boy" Crudup remains in relative obscurity, known more as a name associated with Elvis Presley than as a blues recording artist whose voice and songs are familiar. Presley, early in his career, credited Crudup with being a model. Asserting the juke-joint roots of his own style, Elvis claimed that if he could "feel" what Crudup felt, he'd have it made.

Crudup saw several of his songs transcend blues tradition and have an impact on pop music. These include "That's All Right Mama" and "Rock Me Mama," the first a hit for Elvis, the second a standard associated with B. B. King.

Crudup's recorded legacy shows an unusual consistency and dependence on tradition. A limited guitarist who learned to play late in life, he stuck with the key of *E*, reworking the same basic guitar figures time and again. His voice was high-pitched, keening, and strong enough to cut through to his juke-joint listeners. Above all, he was a songwriter with a gift for reworking traditional poetry into memorable songs. His best works have become staples for blues players past and present. —*Barry Lee Pearson*

○ **That's Allright Mama (Relic)** / 1961 / Relic 7036
Fine fine sides from '61. —*Bill Dahl*

○ **Mean Ol' Frisco** / 1962 / Collectables 5130
These are his '60s Fire sessions. It fits into the second stage of his recording career, with *Look on Yonder's Wall* and *Coal Black Mare*. —*Barry Lee Pearson*

Look on Yonder's Wall / 1969 / Delmark 614
This late-'60s Delmark session represents the third stage of his career history. —*Barry Lee Pearson*

★ **That's Allright Mama** / 1991 / RCA 61043
Superior 22-track compilation of Arthur Big Boy Crudup material. Elvis Presley recorded "That's All Right Mama" and it soon became a signature tune for him. This includes title track plus "If I Get Lucky," "My Baby Left Me," "Cool Disposition," and "That's Your Red Wagon." — *Roundup Newsletter*

Charles "Cow Cow" Davenport (Charles Edwards Davenport)

b. Apr. 23, 1894, Anniston, AL, d. Dec. 3, 1955, Cleveland, OH
Organ, piano / Piano blues
One of the great early exponents of boogie-woogie piano playing, Davenport is principally noted as the composer of his signature tune, "The Cow Cow Boogie." —*Cub Koda*

● **Alabama Strut** / 1979 / Magpie 1814
Mostly solo instrumental, this is Davenport at his best. —*Cub Koda*

○ **Charles "Cow Cow" Davenport 1926–38** / Best of Blues 5
Material ranges from magnificent Cow Cow Davenport solo tunes to good and not-so-good duets with a host of performers. Ivy Smith and Dora Carr are the artists with whom Davenport works best. Since these were dubbed from 78s, don't expect pristine sound. —*Ron Wynn*

Cyril Davies

b. 1932, England, **d.** Jan. 7, 1964, England
Vocals, harmonica / Electric British blues
Balding, gnome-like Cyril Davies was, with Alexis Korner, the co-founder of the entire British blues scene, whence sprang the Rolling Stones, the Yardbirds, et al. A virtuoso on harmonica, he split with Korner in 1963 over the latter's insistence on adding horns to their band, Blues Incorporated. Davies died of leukemia in early 1964. —*Bruce Eder*

Legendary Cyril Davies, The / 1970 / Folklore
Acoustic blues, rougher and somewhat more persuasive than his Decca album. Recorded with Alexis Korner. —*Bruce Eder*

● **R&B from the Marquee** / 1971 / Decca
The first British blues album ever to make the U.K. charts. The playing is more than competent, although not as flashy as anything by the Rolling Stones. —*Bruce Eder*

Blind John Davis

b. Dec. 7, 1913, Hattiesburg, MS, **d.** Oct. 12, 1985, Chicago, IL
Vocals, piano / Piano blues
The piano work of John Davis was featured on blues records by the score during the '30s and '40s. His accompaniments to Tampa Red, Sonny Boy Williamson, Big Bill Broonzy, and others brought him fame as a blues musician, but like his piano compatriot Little Brother Montgomery, Davis did not care to be typecast as such and often expressed a preference for the sweet, sentimental favorites he played in countless piano lounges. But as with Montgomery, most of Davis's own recording opportunities came from blues companies, and he never failed to acquit himself well when it came to blues and boogie-woogie. He was the first pianist to do a European blues tour (with Broonzy in 1952), returning to the continent frequently as a solo act during the '70s and '80s. With blues piano appreciation in Europe being what it is and has been, it's not surprising that most of the albums of Blind John Davis were recorded there and not in Chicago, his home from the age of two until his death. —*Jim O'Neal*

● **Stompin' on a Saturday Night** / 1978 / Alligator 4709
Solid blues piano. Excellent phrasing and rhythms. —*Ron Wynn*

You Better Cut That Out / 1985 / Red Beans 008
His final session, with hot piano licks and failing vocals. —*Ron Wynn*

James "Thunderbird" Davis

b. Nov. 10, 1938, Prichard, AL, **d.** Jan. 24, 1992, St. Paul, MN
Vocals / Modern electric blues
James "Thunderbird" Davis was an inspiring vocalist whose records were far better known than he himself was until he reappeared on the blues scene in 1988. The handful of Davis recordings in 1963–64 for Houston's Duke Records produced such gems as "Bad Dream," "Your Turn to Cry," and the oft-covered "Blue Monday." He was presumed dead by many blues fans and fellow musicians until Black Top Records turned him up in Gray, LA, and brought him back to blues life via new recording sessions and personal appearances. Davis was on tour at the Blues Saloon in St. Paul when he collapsed and died as he ended the song "What Else Is There to Do?" —*Jim O'Neal*

○ **Check out Time** / 1989 / Black Top 1043
After years of musical inactivity, Davis returns with a roaring set that expertly spotlights his melismatic vocal delivery. —*Bill Dahl*

Larry Davis

b. Dec. 4, 1936, Kansas City, MO
Vocals, guitar / Soul blues, Contemporary Delta blues
A fine guitarist and singer, Davis is principally noted for composing the classic "Texas Flood," covered in fine fashion by Stevie Ray Vaughan on his first album. —*Cub Koda*

○ **Funny Stuff** / Jun. 1983 / Rooster Blues 2616
One of his best efforts to date. —*Bill Dahl*

○ **I Ain't Beggin' Nobody** / 1985 / Evidence 26016
Davis recorded the nine tracks on this '85 date with longtime blues and soul producer and instrumentalist Oliver Sain at the controls. Davis demonstrated his convincing appeal on Sain's title track as well as the defiant "I'm a Rolling Stone" (another Sain

original), Davis' own anguished "Giving Up on Love," and "Please Don't Go," a Chuck Willis composition. —*Ron Wynn*

● **Sooner or Later** / 1992 / Bullseye Blues 9511
Larry Davis mixes brisk soul ravers like "I'm Workin' on It" with after-hours blues excursions like "Goin' Out West (Part 1 and Part 2)" on his latest release. The Arkansas native, who won four W.C. Handy Awards in 1982 and composed the late Stevie Ray Vaughan's hit, "Texas Flood," should earn a lot of new fans with this one. He sings with aching passion, particularly on "Letter from My Darling," and lets his guitar slice through tracks like the instrumental "102nd St. Blues." —*Mark J. Cadigan, Blues Access*

Rev. Gary Davis

b. Apr. 30, 1896, Laurens, SC, **d.** May 5, 1972, Hammonton, NJ
Vocals, guitar / Acoustic country blues, Gospel
This blind South Carolina–born country-blues/gospel singer and guitarist was, after Blind Blake, the foremost exponent of the East Coast ragtime school of country-blues guitar. Davis recorded mostly gospel material, with an occasional ragtime or pop instrumental. His impassioned, gravelly vocals drew on his church and preaching experience. He recorded only a handful of sides in the '30s, but after a number of years spent singing on the streets of New York City, he became a fixture of the '50s and '60s folk revival, recording and performing extensively. Using finger-picks, Davis drew a tremendous sound from the jumbo Gibson guitars he favored. His guitar style (simplified and copied by his much-recorded protege Blind Boy Fuller) enjoyed complex rhythms and countermelodies far more involved than the garden-variety alternating-bass style of finger-picking. To hear Davis perform his spectacular reworking of Blind Willie Johnson's "Samson and Delilah" is an electrifying experience, and humbling for aspiring guitar pickers. —*Richard Lieberson*

○ **Pure Religion & Bad Company** / 1957 / Smithsonian/Folkways 40035
A solid sampling of Davis's influential finger-picking and singing on this one. —*Kip Lornell*

Say No to the Devil / 1958 / Bluesville 519
A strong early-'60s session. —*Richard Lieberson*

At Newport / 1959 / Vanguard 73008
This live set includes instrumentals and novelty tunes, as well as gospel, and gives one a feel for the man. —*Richard Lieberson*

★ **1935–49** / 1960 / Yazoo 1023
Powerful stuff. Some of the finest East Coast country-blues guitar ever waxed. —*Richard Lieberson*

Gospel, Blues & Street Songs / Jul. 1961 / Riverside 524
Seven tracks by Pink Anderson, including "John Henry" and "He's in the Jailhouse Now," and eight by Rev. Gary Davis, including "Samson and Delilah" and "Keep Your Lamp Trimmed and Burning." These two singer/guitarists were adept at a wide variety of material, including blues, folk, minstrel, popular, and gospel. —*Roundup newsletter*

From Blues to Gospel / Mar. 1971 / Biograph 123
This particular set was recorded one year before Davis's death, when he was 76 years old. Producer Arnold Caplin has combined two LPs to create this package and believes these to be the artist's very last recordings. Although the master-picker pulls off some prodigious playing here—on both the 6- and 12-string guitars—he is no match for his own earlier work recorded between 1935 and 1960. Listeners already familiar with the younger Davis's playing will feel great affection and gratitude for these last recordings. —*Larry Hoffman*

When I Die I'll Live Again / 1972 / Fantasy 24704
This twofer offers Davis's best work of the '60s. —*Richard Lieberson*

Jimmy Dawkins

b. Oct. 24, 1936
Modern electric blues, Chicago Blues
Jimmy Dawkins has been successful as a rhythm guitarist, vocalist, and bandleader. He moved from Mississippi to Chicago in 1955, and later worked briefly with Lester Hinton before forming his own band. Dawkins' career began to take off after he won France's Grand Prix of the Hot Club award as the Best Jazz/Blues guitarist in 1971, and also captured Record of the Year for *Fast Fingers*. The blistering Dawkins style has been featured on re-

leases for Delmark, JSP, and Earwig, most recently his acclaimed *Kant Sheck Dees Bluze* for Earwig in '92. —*Ron Wynn*

● **Fast Fingers** / 1969 / Delmark 623
Still his toughest and most worthwhile LP. —*Bill Dahl*

Tribute to Orange / Nov. 30, 1971-Nov. 2, 1974 / Black & Blue 33538
This disc features eight numbers pairing Dawkins and the great Gatemouth Brown and another four matching him with equally sensational Otis Rush. The Brown/Dawkins tandem duel, match, and challenge each other as Dawkins's sometimes enigmatic, sometimes bemused and often compelling vocals set the stage for their instrumental encounters. The same holds true on the Rush/Dawkins cuts, especially Dawkins's "Serves You Right to Suffer" and "Mean Atlantic Ocean." —*Ron Wynn*

All for Business / 1973 / Delmark 634
Well worth seeking out, Dawkins is solid, Otis Rush handles second guitar, and Andrew "Big Voice" Odom sings. —*Bill Dahl*

○ **Kant Sheck Dees Bluze** / Jun. 1991 / Earwig 4920
Every song cuts to the bone. Dawkins's "Rockin' D. Blues" is a fine twist on the classic "Rock Me Baby." The title track finds Jimmy talking blues truth, as he has always done, about the realities of living. Longtime sideman "Professor" Eddie Lusk shines with crisp clear piano counter to Dawkins's fevered intensity. —*Jeff Story, Roundup Newsletter*

Floyd Dixon

b. Feb. 8, 1929, Marshall, TX
Vocals, piano / R&B, Electric West Coast blues
Though his name is not as recognizable as Charles Brown's or T-Bone Walker's, Dixon was also a major contributor to the West Coast blues sound that came to life in the '40s, and his contributions have continued over the years. In many ways an upbeat counterpart to the mellow Charles Brown style, Dixon's music incorporated jump, boogie, and humor. He sang the original versions of "Saturday Night Fish Fry" (known as a Louis Jordan standard) as well as the more recently revived "Hey Bartender." As with most of the leading jump-blues artists, Dixon had some hits in the late '40s and early '50s but none since, despite the quality of many of his later efforts. —*Jim O'Neal*

○ **Opportunity Blues** / 1976 / Route 66 1
Jump blues from late '40s and the '50s. Classic stuff. —*Bill Dahl*

○ **Houston Jump** / 1979 / Route 66 11
More vintage Dixon, swings like crazy! —*Bill Dahl*

● **Marshall Texas Is My Home** / Specialty 7011
A swinging 22-song collection of this influential jump-blues pianist's finest '50s sides, including the original "Hey Bartender." —*John Floyd*

Willie Dixon

b. Jul. 1, 1915, Vickburg, MS, **d.** Jan. 29, 1992, Burbank, CA
Vocals, upright bass, sometimes guitar / Acoustic and electric Chicago blues
The premier blues composer of the post-WWII era, Willie Dixon was also probably the single most influential figure in shaping the Chicago-blues sound of the Chess Records heyday in his role as writer, arranger, producer, and bassist. The recordings of Muddy Waters, Howlin' Wolf, Koko Taylor, Otis Rush, and innumerable others bore the Dixon stamp. He frankly admitted that such artists could perform his songs better than he himself could; hence he did little recording on his own (apart from some early work with blues harmony groups like the Big Three Trio) until fairly late in the game. His growing renown for songs like "Little Red Rooster," "Seventh Son," and "Hoochie Coochie Man" enabled him to start touring and recording with his Chicago Blues All Stars from the late '60s through the '80s. Much of his important later writing was in a socially conscious vein, dedicated to world peace and to improving the human condition. Dixon founded the Blues Heaven Foundation to secure the blues its rightful respect, protection, and recognition and to educate present and future generations about what he liked to call "the facts of life"—the blues. —*Jim O'Neal*

I Am the Blues / 1970 / Mobile Fidelity 872
Dixon's vocals can't match previous versions of these classic songs, but the album's still worth owning. —*Bill Dahl*

○ **Catalyst** / 1973 / Ovation 1433

One of his better latter-day efforts. —*Bill Dahl*

I Feel Like Steppin' Out / 1986 / Dr. Horse 804
Formed right after World War II (and taking its name from the tag given to the Allied leaders), the Big Three Trio was a unique group. Its emphasis on unison singing, hokum, and sweet pop tunes separated it from other blues groups, while mainly straight blues material set it apart from the vocal groups of the day. What keeps it from being more than a historical footnote is the charm of its vocalizing and the fact that Willie Dixon was the largest of the B3T. Coupling this release with its CBS release would give you almost all of the group's recordings, with only "Signifying Monkey" being duplicated. The Dr. Horse disc has a much fuller sound than the CBS set, although it has more pop tunes as well. —*Rick Swenson, Roundup Newsletter*

★ **Chess Box, The** / 1989 / Chess 16500
A two-CD box of Dixon's best-known vintage compositions, performed by his Chess Records labelmates with a few by Dixon himself. —*Bill Dahl*

○ **Big Three Trio, The** / 1990 / CBS 46216
Smooth three-part harmonies and sizzling instrumentals from the late '40s and early '50s. —*Bill Dahl*

Georgia Tom Dorsey (Thomas Andrew Dorsey)

b. Jul. 1, 1899, Villa Rica, GA, **d.** Jan. 23, 1993
Guitar, piano / Acoustic country blues
Though he started out firmly entrenched in the vaudeville and hokum blues traditions of the '20s and '30s, Dorsey found his true calling as the composer of several enduring gospel classics. —*Cub Koda*

○ **Come on Mama Do That Dance 1931-40** / Yazoo 1041
Hard to believe that America's greatest writer of gospel songs could come up with this solid a collection of risqué blues tunes in his earlier, "sinful" days. Believe it. —*Cub Koda*

K. C. Douglas

b. Nov. 21, 1913, Sharon, MS, **d.** Oct. 18, 1975, Berkeley, CA
Vocals, guitar / Electric country blues
K. C. Douglas was a Mississippi bluesman who transplanted himself and his music not to Chicago but to the San Francisco Bay Area in 1945. He became one of the rare Californians with such a down-home rural style, as many of his recordings were remakes of old blues he knew from Mississippi. (His first album, an obscure item on the Cook label, was entitled *K. C. Douglas, a Dead Beat Guitar and the Mississippi Blues*.) His re-creations of Tommy Johnson's blues were of particular interest to fans of prewar blues, but his own compositions attracted attention as well. —*Jim O'Neal*

● **K. C.'s Blues** / Jan. 1961 / Bluesville 533
Traditional Mississippi Delta blues. A 1990 CD reissue of 1961 recordings. —*Niles J. Frantz*

Champion Jack Dupree

b. Jul. 4, 1910, New Orleans, LA, **d.** Jan. 21, 1992, Hanover, Germany
Vocals, piano, sometimes drums, guitar / Piano blues
One of the blues world's most colorful characters, Dupree was both a first-rate entertainer and a top-quality artist, whether he took the role of merry mirthmaker or down-and-out denizen of the gutters of life. The first of the American blues greats to emigrate to Europe, Dupree managed, perhaps better than any of the other expatriate bluesmen, to infuse his work on the continent (both live and on record) with a continuing sense of freshness and vitality. His recording career spanned 51 years, beginning with the 1940-41 sessions for Okeh that produced, among other classics, "Junker Blues" (later rewritten by Fats Domino as "The Fat Man"). After having recorded in Europe since 1959, Dupree returned for triumphant U.S. tours in 1990-91, waxing his final sessions for Bullseye Blues. —*Jim O'Neal*

★ **Blues from the Gutter** / 1958 / Atlantic 82434
Dupree's masterpiece. His pounding piano contrasts with some very downbeat subject matter. —*Bill Dahl*

○ **Sings the Blues** / 1961 / King 735
Some of his best '50s work. —*Bill Dahl*

○ **Cabbage Greens** / 1963 / Okeh 12103
First sides. —*Bill Dahl*

○ **Blues for Everyone** / 1969 / King 1084
1950s gems. —*Bill Dahl*

Blues at Montreux / 1973 / Atlantic 1637
Sloppy but swinging. —*Bill Dahl*

Blues for Everybody / 1990 / Charly 243
Two records of mid-'50s Dupree on King, cut in N.Y.C. and Cincinnati with top-flight support. —*Bill Dahl*

○ **New Orleans Barrelhouse Boogie (The Complete Champion Jack Dupree)** / 1993 / Columbia/Legacy 52834
Dupree's early '40s work for Okeh rocks with a vengeance; makes his influence on other New Orleans pianists to follow all the more obvious. —*Bill Dahl*

One Last Time / 1993 / Bullseye Blues 9522
His last, posthumously issued, disc is quite satisfying. —*Bill Dahl*

Snooks Eaglin

b. Jan. 21, 1936, New Orleans, LA
Vocals, guitar, sometimes percussion / Acoustic and electric New Orleans blues
The blind Crescent City guitar virtuoso was hailed in some circles as the hot new talent of the blues world during the folk-music boom of the early '60s, but the versatile Eaglin's eclecticism reportedly soon put him in disfavor with the tastemakers. Though absent from the studio for some time thereafter, Snooks continued to perform in New Orleans, evincing a talent for whatever funky, folky, or farfetched styles he chose. Since the '70s he has recorded several times, with and without backup bands, his wide-ranging repertoire often still in evidence. In recent years Eaglin has won a new following among fans of hot contemporary blues guitar for his electric axework. —*Jim O'Neal*

○ **Country Boy Down in New Orleans** / 1958 / Arhoolie 348
An album of early works, including ancient blues ("Jack O'Diamond") and Crescent City R&B in an easygoing, understated mix. —*Mark A. Humphrey*

● **Baby, You Can Get Your Gun** / 1987 / Black Top 1037
A funky album showing Eaglin in a contemporary New Orleans R&B setting. —*Mark A. Humphrey*

○ **New Orleans 1960-61** / 1988 / Sundown 70904
Great R&B sides for Imperial with full band. —*Bill Dahl*

○ **Teasin' You** / 1992 / Black Top 1072
Backed by a top-shelf band—George Porter, Sammy Berfect, Herman Ernest III, and some of the Black Top brass regulars—Snooks tears through a mixed bag of blues, gospel, soul, rock & roll, and swing. —*Tom Smith, Roundup Newsletter*

Ronnie Earl & the Broadcasters

Guitar / R&B
A New England–based blues band fronted by guitarist Ronnie Earl (born Ronald Horvath, 1953). Earl did a stint in the early '70s with Boston's Guitar Jonny & the Rhythm Rockers, a group featuring John Nicholas (Asleep at the Wheel), Fran Christina (The Fabulous Thunderbirds), plus Mark Kazanoff and Sarah Brown, now both mainstays of the Austin, TX, blues circuit. Earl then replaced Duke Robillard in the nine-piece Roomful of Blues in the early '80s, forming the Broadcasters in the late '80s as a side project. Capable of playing most any style of blues there is, Earl is a consummate guitarist and is well represented on record. —*Cub Koda*

○ **Peace of Mind** / Nov. 1990 / Black Top 1060
Nice, swinging stuff. —*Bill Dahl*

Surrounded by Love / May 1991 / Black Top 1069
Ronnie Earl's fifth Black Top album features a new edition of the Broadcasters: He's reunited with the fantastic Sugar Ray Norcia on vocals and harmonica; bassist Michael "Mudcat" Ward has returned to the fold after some years; drummer Per Hanson kicks things along righteously; and keyboard chores are shared by organist Tony Zamagni and pianist Dave Maxwell. But the icing on the cake is the appearance on three tracks by blues legend Robert Jr. Lockwood, who plays guitar on "One of These Mornings" and sings and plays on "Mr. Downchild" and "Jelly Jelly." —*Roundup Newsletter*

● **Test of Time** / Black Top 1082
This 18-track collection gathers material from six releases, including instrumentals as well as tunes sung by Kim Wilson,

"Sugar Ray" Norcia, Darrell Nulisch, and Mighty Sam McClain. Earl's taste, tone, and sense of dynamics qualify him as one of the best guitarists playing today, in the blues genre or in general. His songwriting talents are also in evidence on the nine songs he wrote or co-wrote, including "Soul Searchin'," "Narcolepsy," and "I Want to Shout About It." —*Mark J. Cadigan, Roundup Newsletter*

Tinsley Ellis & the Heartfixers

Vocals, guitar / Modern electric blues
A blues-based guitarist from the Atlanta, GA, area, notable for his stage work and his recordings both with the Heartfixers and as a solo artist. —*Cub Koda*

Live at the Moon Shadow / 1983 / Landslide 1007
Atlanta blues/rockers Tinsley Ellis and the Heartfixers hit in concert with vocalist Chicago Bob Nelson. —*Michael G. Nastos*

Cool on It / Jan. 1986 / Alligator 3905
High-energy roadhouse-rock and blues/rock with the Heartfixers. —*Niles J. Frantz*

● **Fanning of the Flames** / 1989 / Alligator 4778
Blues/rock in the Stevie Ray Vaughan tradition. —*Cub Koda*

Sleepy John Estes (John Adams Estes)

b. Jan. 25, 1899, Ripley, TN, d. Jun. 5, 1977, Brownville, TN
Vocals, guitar / Acoustic country blues
Big Bill Broonzy called John Estes's style of singing "crying" the blues because of its overt emotional quality. Actually his vocal style harks back to his tenure as a work-gang leader for a railroad maintenance crew, where his vocal improvisations and keen, cutting voice set the pace for work activities. Nicknamed "Sleepy" John Estes, supposedly because of his ability to sleep standing up, he teamed with mandolinist Yank Rachell and harmonica player Hammie Nixon to play the house-party circuit in and around Brownsville in the early '20s. Forty years later, the same team reunited to record for Delmark and play the festival circuit. Never an outstanding guitarist, Estes relied on his expressive voice to carry his music, and the recordings he made from 1929 on have enormous appeal and remain remarkably accessible today.
Despite the fact that he worked to mixed Black and White audiences in string band, jug band, or medicine show format, his music retains a distinct ethnicity and has a particularly plaintive sound. Astonishingly, he recorded during six decades for Victor, Decca, Bluebird, Ora Nelle, Sun, Delmark, and others. Over the course of his career, his music remained simple yet powerful, and despite his sojourns to Memphis or Chicago he retained a traditional down-home sound. Some of his songs are deeply personal statements about his community and life, such as "Lawyer Clark" or "Floating Bridge." Other compositions have universal appeal ("Drop Down Mama" or "Someday Baby") and went on to become mainstays in the repertoires of countless musicians. One of the true masters of his idiom, he lived in poverty, yet was somehow capable of turning his experiences and the conditions of his life into compelling art. —*Barry Lee Pearson*

Legend of Sleepy John Estes, The / 1962 / Delmark 603
The best of his Delmark rediscovery recordings. —*Barry Lee Pearson*

Jazz Heritage—Down South Blues (1935–40) / 1970 / MCA 1339
Part of an '80s MCA budget blues series, this album includes "Drop Down Mama" and "Someday Baby." With Hammie Nixon on harmonica. —*Barry Lee Pearson*

★ **Sleepy John Estes 1929–40: I Ain't Gonna Be Worried No More** / 1992 / Yazoo 2004
This set is vintage Estes, 22 cuts that serve as an ideal showcase for this fine singer and writer from western Tennessee. Estes was influenced by sundry fellow Memphis-area blues masters (particularly Ashley Thompson of Cannon's Jug Stompers), but what truly set him apart was his slippery lyrical approach, direct yet unpredictable. —*Jimmy Guterman, Roundup Newsletter*

Frank Frost (Frank Otis Frost)

b. Apr. 15, 1936, Augusta, AR
Vocals, guitar, harmonica / R&B, Electric Delta blues
A fine singer, guitarist, and harmonica player, Frost upholds the rich tradition of Delta blues. Responsible for some of the finest down-home blues records of the '60s, he holds the distinction of

being the last bluesman to record for the Sun label in Memphis. —*Cub Koda*

○ **Hey Boss Man** / 196z / Philips 1975
The last great blues record Sam Phillips ever produced. —*Bill Dahl*

Frank Frost / 1973 / Jewel 5013
More down-home eclectic blues from the harpist/keyboardist. —*Bill Dahl*

● **Ride with Your Daddy Tonight** / 1985 / Charly 1103
Frost's best sides for the Jewel label. Some of the most down-home '60s blues ever recorded. —*Cub Koda*

Jelly Roll Blues / PR 20
This is a likable, very solid collection of mellow, small-band blues. Frank, though a multiinstrumentalist, only sings here—leaving the well-sculpted harp lines to be delivered by Oscar Williams, beautifully supported by a tightly knit band. —*Larry Hoffman*

Blind Boy Fuller

b. 1908, Wadesboro, NC, **d.** Feb. 13, 1941, Durham, NC
Vocals, guitar / Acoustic country blues
Unlike blues artists like Big Bill or Memphis Minnie who recorded extensively over three or four decades, Blind Boy Fuller recorded his substantial body of work over a short, six-year span. Nevertheless, he was one of the most recorded artists of his time and by far the most popular and influential Piedmont blues player of all time. Fuller could play in multiple styles: slide, ragtime, pop, and blues were all enhanced by his National steel guitar. Fuller worked with some fine sidemen, including Davis, Sonny Terry, and washboard player Bull City Red. Initially discovered and promoted by Carolina entrepreneur H. B. Long, Fuller recorded for ARC and Decca. He also served as a conduit to recording sessions, steering fellow blues musicians to the studio.

In spite of Fuller's recorded output, most of his musical life was spent as a street musician and house-party favorite, and he possessed the skills to reinterpret and cover the hits of other artists as well. In this sense, he was a synthesizer of styles, parallel in many ways to Robert Johnson, his contemporary who died three years earlier. Like Johnson, Fuller lived fast and died young in 1942, only 33 years old. Fuller was a fine, expressive vocalist and a masterful guitar player best remembered for his uptempo ragtime hits "Rag Mama Rag," "Trucking My Blues Away," and "Step It Up and Go." At the same time he was capable of deeper material, and his versions of "Lost Lover Blues" or "Mamie" are as deep as most Delta blues. Because of his popularity, he may have been overexposed on records, yet most of his songs remained close to tradition and much of his repertoire and style is kept alive by North Carolina and Virginia artists today. —*Barry Lee Pearson*

★ **Blind Boy Fuller** / 196z / Document 5091
The finest collection ever of blues and ragtime. Fuller is here both solo and with Gary Davis, Sonny Terry, and Bull City Red. This is Piedmont blues at its best (1935-40), a must for anyone interested in down-home blues. —*Barry Lee Pearson*

○ **Truckin' My Blues Away** / 1978 / Yazoo 1060
Piedmont blues at its best, with fine guitar work from this popular and influential bluesman. —*Barry Lee Pearson*

○ **East Coast Piedmont Style** / Aug. 1991 / CBS 46777
A very good 20-cut roots and blues collection with Sonny Terry, Gary Davis, and Bull City Red. —*Barry Lee Pearson*

Jesse Fuller

b. Mar. 12, 1896, Jonesboro, GA, **d.** Jan. 29, 1976, Oakland, CA
Vocals, guitar, harmonica, kazoo, footdella / Acoustic country blues
Equipped with a bandful of instruments operated by various parts of his anatomy, Bay Area legend Jesse Fuller was a folk music favorite in the '50s and '60s. His infectious rhythm and gentle charm graced old folk tunes, spirituals, and blues alike. One of his inventions was a homemade, foot-operated instrument called the "footdella" or "fotdella." Naturally, Fuller never needed other accompanists to back his one-man show. His best-known songs include "San Francisco Bay Blues" and "Beat It on Down the Line" (the first one covered by Janis Joplin, the second by the Grateful Dead). —*Jim O'Neal*

○ **Jazz, Folk Songs, Spirituals & Blues** / Apr. 1958 / Good Time Jazz
The title of this recently reissued 1958 date adequately described the session's musical width and depth; Fuller handled everything from old spirituals such as as "I'm Going to Meet My Loving Mother" to the rollicking "Memphis Boogie" and "Fingerbuster" and the concluding "Hesitation Blues." As sole performer and melodic, rhythmic, and performing focus, Fuller's energy never wanes through the CD's 11 numbers. —*Ron Wynn*

Favorites / 1965 / Prestige 528
Skiffle roots in full cry. —*Mark A. Humphrey*

○ **Frisco Bound** / 1968 / Arhoolie 360
A one-man band with guitar, harmonica, kazoo, and "footdella" bass. Some of his first recordings, ca. 1955. Innocent echoes of turn-of-the-century rural America. —*Mark A. Humphrey*

● **San Francisco Bay Blues** / 1988 / Good Time Jazz 537
Fuller's hit and more. No misses. —*Mark A. Humphrey*

Lowell Fulson

b. Mar. 31, 1921, Tulsa, OK
Vocals, guitar / R&B, Acoustic and electric West Coast blues
One of the great blues guitarists, singers, and composers of all time, Fulson began recording after WWII in California in a country-blues context but soon made a transition to a more urban sound. His recordings for Swingtime (1949-52) have been collected on a variety of labels and are notable for Fulson's Texas guitar, slick piano (usually Lloyd Glenn), and subtle horns. Notable hits from the period include "Every Day I Have the Blues," "Blue Shadows," and "Low Society."

Fulson joined Chess Records in 1954 and had an immediate smash hit with "Reconsider Baby" on the Checker label. Though he had no other commercial successes for Checker, he continued to record for them until late 1963. By 1965, he began recording for Kent Records in Los Angeles (owned by the Bihari family of Modern/RPM/Flair fame). Once again he scored an enormous hit with "Tramp" and had other strong items with "Black Nights" and "Make a Little Love." Moving to Jewel in 1969, he began recording albums with some rock background. Since that time his recordings have been album projects with varying degrees of success. He has also recorded in France and Japan. Invariably Fulson's performances are fine—if the results are less than satisfactory as a whole, it is usually a failed concept or an inappropriate accompaniment that is at fault. —*Bob Porter*

○ **Hung Down Head** / 1954 / Chess 9325
A reissue of his '50s Chess recordings. —*Barry Lee Pearson*

Lowell Fulson / 1959 / Chess 92504
The rest of Fulson's 1955-62 Chess output, classic stuff. —*Bill Dahl*

Back Home Blues / 1959 / Night Train 7001
This disc focuses on Lowell Fulson's early uptempo jump blues sides. Material is taken from direct-to-disc sessions in Oakland, 1947-48, and from 1949-52 sessions for the Swing Time label, featuring the Lloyd Glenn combo. Two alternate takes and one unissued instrumental. — *Roundup Newsletter*

Now / 1969 / United 7752
More funky blues with lots of covers. —*Bill Dahl*

○ **Lowell Fulson (Early Recordings)** / 1975 / Arhoolie 2003
Fulson's roots are on full display on this varied collection of '40s/'50s cuts. —*Bill Dahl*

○ **San Francisco Blues** / 1988 / Black Lion 760176
Fulson helped establish his reputation with a string of fine songs for the Swingtime label in the late '40s and early '50s. Fulson showed he could belt out hard-hitting blues, do sentimental ballads, double-entendre novelty pieces, or irony-filled laments, and also play riveting solos. —*Ron Wynn*

● **Tramp/Soul** / 199z / Capitol 86300
Fulson's two best mid-'60s albums for Kent on one CD; includes his hits "Black Night" and "Tramp". —*Bill Dahl*

River Blues / Arhoolie 2003
Reissues of his '40s Swingtime material. —*Barry Lee Pearson*

Anson Funderburgh & the Rockets

Vocals, guitar / Modern electric Texas blues

This Texas-based blues guitarist is a mainstay of the Austin, TX, circuit. A master of Stratocaster-tinged, single-string-style blues, Funderburgh fronts his band, the Rockets, sometimes working with harmonica legend Sammy Myers as well. —Cub Koda

My Love Is Here to Stay / 1986 / Black Top 1032
The first record where Sam Myers (who had been performing with Robert Jr. Lockwood, Myers's latest gig in a professional career that began in the mid-'50s) joined Funderburgh's band. This successful coupling has made some truly wonderful music. —Niles J. Frantz

○ **Sins** / 1987 / Black Top 1038
The best of old and new: straightforward, no-nonsense blues. A successful combination of Texas and Delta sounds. —Niles J. Frantz

○ **Tell Me What I Want to Hear** / 1991 / Black Top 1068
First-rate, contemporary Texas shuffle and blues with tasteful, biting guitar from Funderburgh and great vocals and harp from Mississippian Sam Myers. This is their most varied and ambitious release to date (the band seems to get better with each album). —Niles J. Frantz

● **Thru the Years—a Retrospective (1981–92)** / 1992 / Black Top 1077
Anson Funderburgh has distinguished himself as a tasteful guitarist who's capable of unleashing concise musical punches. This retrospective features songs from several releases and performances by different versions of his Rockets band, including those fronted by singer/harmonica players Darrell Nulisch and Sam Myers. Songs like "My Heart Cries Out for You," "Changing Neighborhoods," and "Meanstreak" exemplify Funderburgh's modern Texas blues sound. — Roundup Newsletter

Clifford "Grandpappy" Gibson

b. Apr. 17, 1901, **d.** Dec. 21, 1963
Guitar / Prewar acoustic blues
Though not a particularly great singer, Clifford "Grandpappy" Gibson was an excellent guitarist, among the finest pure players in country blues. Gibson moved from Kentucky to St. Louis in the '20s, where he lived the remainder of his life. He frequently played St. Louis clubs during the '20s and '30s, and began recording for QRS and Victor in 1929. Greatly influenced by Lonnie Johnson, Gibson also accompanied Jimmie Rodgers on a Victor single in 1931, then spent parts of the next three decades playing in the streets around St. Louis. Gibson resurfaced on recordings in 1960 with a Bobbin date, and worked another three years in St. Louis's Gaslight Square before his death in 1963. —Ron Wynn

● **Beat You Doing It** / 1972 / Yazoo 1027
Important prewar country blues. —Bill Dahl

Jazz Gillum (William McKinley Gillum)

b. Sep. 11, 1904, Indianola, MS, **d.** Mar. 29, 1966, Chicago, IL
Harmonica / Blues, Urban
Next to John Lee "Sonny Boy" Williamson, no harmonica player was as popular or as much in demand on recording sessions during the '30s as Jazz Gillum. His high, reedy sound meshed perfectly on dozens of hokum sides on the Bluebird label, both as a sideman and as a leader. —Cub Koda

● **Roll Dem Bones 1938-49** / Wolf 002
Best selection of Gillum sides available. Not a bad one in this bunch. —Cub Koda

Lloyd Glenn

b. Nov. 21, 1909, San Antonio, TX, **d.** May 23, 1985, Los Angeles, CA
Piano / Piano blues
An instrumental giant and pioneer figure in postwar California blues, Glenn was a prime contributor to recordings by Lowell Fulson, T-Bone Walker, B. B. King, and many more, as a pianist and sometime arranger or songwriter. In 1950–51, when mellow blues instrumentals were in vogue, Glenn's own combo had two national R&B hits, "Old Time Shuffle" and "Chica Boo" (which displaced "Rocket 88" as *Billboard*'s #1 record). At the time, Glenn also teamed with Lowell Fulson on "Everyday I Have the Blues" and "Blue Shadows." Glenn's renown was such that when a young Ray Charles went on the road as Fulson's pianist, he reportedly had to pass himself off as Lloyd Glenn. A boogie-woogie

devotee since his early years, Glenn continued to display his piano mastery throughout a long and distinguished career. —Jim O'Neal

● **After Hours** / 1957 / Oldie Blues 8002
After Hours: Piano Blues & Boogie Woogie is a solid collection of instrumentals recorded in the mid-'40s and '50s. —Cub Koda

Piano Styling / 1957 / Score 4006
Smooth West Coast '50s piano. —Bill Dahl

○ **Honky Tonk Train** / 1983 / Night Train 7002
Fifteen tracks from pianist Glenn, who worked with T-Bone Walker and Lowell Fulson. Includes one alternate and three unissued tracks. — Roundup newsletter

Old Time Shuffle / Black & Blue 33077
European sessions from the late '70s. Swinging piano throughout, showing off Glenn's patented Texas-cum-West-Coast lope to good advantage. —Cub Koda

Henry Gray

b. Jan. 19, 1925, Kenner, LA
Vocals, piano, sometimes organ / Electric Chicago blues
Though a Louisiana native and current resident (since returning home in 1969), Gray is still known to many enthusiasts as a Chicago bluesman. His 20-plus years on the Chicago scene included an extensive stint as Howlin' Wolf's piano man, along with a few recordings on his own and countless club dates with various blues bands. He has come to prominence in his own right during his more recent years in the Baton Rouge area, playing in the company of swamp blues musicians who complement Gray's robust blues work in fine down-home style. Gray has also toured and recorded in Europe as a solo act. —Jim O'Neal

● **Lucky Man** / 1988 / Blind Pig 2788
Gray's first solo album features the pounding piano work that earmarked his best work with Howlin' Wolf and others. —Cub Koda

Clarence Green & the Rhythmaires

b. 1937, Houston, TX
Vocals, guitar / Blues
Though not one of the best known of the modern Texas blues guitarists, Clarence Green is regarded by his peers as one of the best. Green (not to be confused with the late Clarence "Candy" Green, a Texas blues pianist) did session work for Duke Records in the '60s with Junior Parker, Bobby Bland, and others, and performed with stars from Fats Domino to Johnny Nash. His own recordings have mostly been for small Houston labels. As Marcel Vos from Double Trouble Records wrote, "The Clarence Green of today plays a brand of Texas blues that is mixed with soul, jazz, and funk, not unlike the music of fellow Texans such as Roy Gaines, Cornell Dupree, and of course, his brother Cal Green." —Jim O'Neal

○ **Green's Blues** / 1991 / Collectables 5229
A CD reissue of Texas blues, R&B, and pop. All very danceable and very enjoyable. Recordings from 1958 to 1965. —Niles J. Frantz

Guitar Slim (Eddie Jones)

b. Dec. 10, 1926, Greenwood, MS, **d.** Feb. 7, 1959, New York, NY
Vocals, guitar / Electric New Orleans blues
A torrid guitarist, impassioned vocalist, and legendary showman who took electric blues guitar playing to savage new levels of intensity, Eddie "Guitar Slim" Jones inspired a whole generation of musicians from Buddy Guy to Earl King to Jimi Hendrix. He spent most of his professional career in New Orleans, yet his music owed little to the syncopated '50s R&B so popular in the area. Neither is he typically regarded as a Delta bluesman, although he was raised in the Mississippi Delta and performed in Hollandale, MS, and Lake Village, AR, in his early years. His slashing guitar work, though rooted in the Texas jump style of Gatemouth Brown, burst forth from his recordings as something uniquely and identifiably his. Slim's #1 hit of 1954, "Things That I Used to Do" (featuring Ray Charles on piano), has become a standard in the modern blues band repertoire. His son Guitar Slim Jr., who was just a boy when Guitar Slim died of pneumonia on a trip to New York, carries on his legacy in New Orleans today. —Jim O'Neal

○ **Atco Sessions** / Jul. 1988 / Atlantic 81760
These later (1956–58) sides seem slightly subdued, but still include highly rewarding material. *—Bill Dahl*

★ **Sufferin' Mind** / 1991 / Specialty 7007
Monumentally influential 1953–55 tracks by this wild, charismatic axeman, including the R&B chart-topper "The Things That I Used to Do." *—Bill Dahl*

Guitar Slim Jr. (Rodney Armstrong)

b. 1951, New Orleans, LA
Vocals, guitar / Electric New Orleans blues
Despite the fact that his first and only album to date earned a Grammy nomination, Guitar Slim Jr. remains a somewhat shadowy figure to the blues public. The son of Eddie "Guitar Slim" Jones, his real name is Rodney Armstrong. According to New Orleans historian Jeff Hannusch's notes on Slim's 1988 album, he "has been a fixture on the Black New Orleans club circuit for the better part of 20 years ... [but] doesn't get to play the posher uptown clubs." His Orleans album featured mostly covers of his father's inspirational blues, which he was loath to play earlier in life, but Slim is also known for his extensive soul repertoire. *—Jim O'Neal*

○ **Story of My Life** / 1988 / Orleans 4188
Contemporary blues, blues/rock, and soul from the son of the late blues/R&B legend. Mostly credible covers of his father's tunes. Grammy nominee. *—Niles J. Frantz*

Buddy Guy

b. Jul. 30, 1936, Lettsworth, LA
Vocals, guitar / Electric Chicago blues
The idol of many a blues and rock guitarist from the '60s on through the present, Buddy Guy has been called the world's best, although his performances in person and on record have been inconsistent. The moments of awe-inspiring guitar continue to set a blistering pace for the axemen who follow in his path. Some of Guy's tastiest work has come not as a pyrotechnician but as a sideman par excellence, particularly with Junior Wells. Buddy cut his teeth on the Baton Rouge blues scene, influenced by the guitar heroes of his youth, Guitar Slim and B. B. King, before moving to Chicago in 1957. Today Guy owns his own blues club in the city, appropriately named Legends. *—Jim O'Neal*

○ **I Left My Blues in San Francisco** / 1967 / Chess 31265
Some of Buddy's best from Chess. *—Mark A. Humphrey*

○ **Buddy Guy & Junior Wells Play the Blues** / 1972 / Rhino 70299
The Guy and Wells team were nearly perfect. Whether in the studio or on stage, theirs was a challenging partnership, an ongoing cutting contest. The results were, for the most part, amazing. Outside the well-intentioned addition of the J. Geils Band on "This Old Fool," a song that never gets off the ground, this is about as good as they got. *—Mark E. Gallo, Blues Access*

○ **I Was Walkin' through the Woods** / 1974 / Chess 9315
Searing guitar, tortured vocals—the best of Guy's early-'60s Chess recordings. *—Mark A. Humphrey*

○ **Pleading the Blues** / Oct. 1979 / Evidence
Recorded on Halloween night in 1979, this pairs up Wells and Guy in a fashion that hasn't been heard since *Hoodoo Man Blues*, their first, and best collaboration. Solid backing by the Philip Guy band (Buddy's brother) makes this album a rare treat. *—Cub Koda*

Drinkin' Tnt 'n' Smokin' Dynamite / 1982 / Blind Pig 71182
Recorded live at Montreux 1974. Accurately represents the long-standing partnership of Guy and Junior Wells. *—Bill Dahl*

☆ **Damn Right, I've Got the Blues** / 1991 / Silvertone 1462
This is the album that Buddy Guy fans have always hoped for. His last studio album was released a decade ago and was a rather lackluster affair. This time Buddy has a proper producer in John Porter (who's worked with Eric Clapton) and a brilliant supporting cast of rhythm section players in Greg Rzab, Pete Wingfield, Mick Weaver, and Neil Hubbard; Little Feat drummer Richie Hayward; the Memphis Horns; and guitarists Eric Clapton, Mark Knopfler, and Jeff Beck. *—Roundup newsletter*

○ **Complete Chess Studio Sessions, The** / 1992 / Chess 9337
A two-CD compilation of Guy's seminal work for the legendary Chicago label. Full of explosive guitar and impassioned vocals, these are some of Buddy's finest recordings. *—Cub Koda*

★ **Very Best of Buddy Guy, The** / 1992 / Rhino 70280
While plowing through the immense catalog of Guy's recorded work can sometimes be an uneven experience at best, this 18 track collection hits all the high spots. Buddy's brutal solo on "Blues at My Baby's House" is worth the price of admission alone. *—Cub Koda*

○ **My Time After Awhile** / 1992 / Vanguard 141-42
Best of selection from Guy's Vanguard catalog. *—Bill Dahl*

○ **Feels Like Rain** / 1993 / Jive/Novus 41498
The followup to the Grammy winner *Damn Right I've Got the Blues!*, this mines similar turf with similar results. Buddy turns in powerhouse renditions of James Brown's "I Go Crazy," Guitar Slim's "Sufferin' Mind," and Ray Charles's "Mary Ann," while the obligatory guest duets reach their high point with Bonnie Raitt's turn on John Hiatt's title cut. The synthesizer lushness of Marvin Gaye's "Trouble Man" may enrage true believers, but Guy pours his heart into it, making it a surprise highlight. *—Cub Koda*

Travis "Moonchild" Haddix

Vocals, guitar / Modern electric blues
A native of Walnut, MS, "Moonchild" Haddix was inspired in his early years by B.B. King's broadcasts on WDIA out of Memphis. In Cleveland, OH, where he has lived since 1959, Haddix developed into a fine modern bluesman and songwriter with an original and soulful touch. His albums for Ichiban contain some of the best blues material that label has released. *—Jim O'Neal*

Wrong Side Out / 1988 / Ichiban 1033
Impressive debut for this Cleveland-based vocalist. *—Bill Dahl*

● **Winners Never Quit** / 1991 / Ichiban 1101
An interesting contemporary-blues/soul synthesis. *—Bill Dahl*

John Hammond Jr. (John Paul Hammond)

b. Nov. 13, 1942, New York, NY
Vocals, guitar, harmonica / R&B, Modern acoustic blues
Now enjoying over 30 years of recording, Hammond remains one of the greatest White performers of traditional acoustic blues. Although he's also an excellent electric guitarist and knows how to work with a band, most of Hammond's shows these days are solo presentations, complete with harmonica, voice, slightly amplified guitar, and foot stomps. During the course of one of his performances, Hammond carefully arranges his song list to bring the listener to several peaks, during which he sings, plays guitar, stomps, and wails away on harmonica, all with an enthusiasm and energy that belies his age. Thirty years after he began performing professionally, John Hammond is one of the most intense and energy-filled performers on the scene. *—Richard Skelly*

○ **So Many Roads** / 1965 / Vanguard 79178
One of young Hammond's better early albums. *—Bill Dahl*

○ **I Can Tell** / 1967 / Atlantic 82369
On this 1967 LP, Hammond digs into the songbags of Willie Dixon, Howlin' Wolf, Elmore James, John Lee Hooker, and others, emerging with a batch of sturdy songs to which he applies his considerable vocal, guitar, and harmonica skills. Four bonus tracks—taken from Hammond's 1970 LP, *Southern Fried*—feature the Muscle Shoals rhythm section, bolstered by some Duane Allman slide. Great stuff. *— Mark J. Cadigan, Blues Access*

○ **Live** / 1983 / Rounder
This 18-song album, recorded live in 1983, may have been his definitive session. It was certainly a masterpiece date, with Hammond doing confident, thoroughly distinctive versions of signature Delta and Chicago blues classics by Robert Johnson, Muddy Waters, Willie Dixon, Son House, and others. While "Dust My Broom," "Drop Down Mama," "Wang Dang Doodle," and all the rest have certainly been done to death, Hammond's spirited vocals, riveting guitar work on acoustic or bottleneck, and overall charismatic performances made them seem like fresh discoveries. *—Ron Wynn*

Nobody But You / 1988 / Flying Fish 70502
Hammond usually performs solo, but here he is backed by a five-piece band, including pianist Gene Taylor. It's good to hear him in this context. All the numbers are blues classics or standards written by John Lee Hooker, Muddy Waters, Arthur Crudup, Little Walter, and B. B. Fuller. *—Michael G. Nastos*

● **Best of John Hammond, The** / 1989 / Vanguard 11-12

The best early works of this folk-blues artist. Acoustic and essential. —*Michael G. Nastos*

Got Love If You Want It / 1992 / Charisma 92146
It's doubtful that John Hammond will ever be known as a musical innovator, since he leans so heavily on the repertoires of blues and R&B masters. But he sings and plays guitar and harmonica with such conviction that it doesn't even matter. It's obvious that this man is thoroughly immersed in the blues—he growls, blows frenetic harp outbursts, and snaps off slide guitar slashes on a National Steel with the best of them. This new release, produced by J. J. Cale (who adds guitar to one cut), features Hammond solo, in a duet with John Lee Hooker, and backed by Little Charlie and the Nightcats. — *Mark J. Cadigan, Blues Access*

○ **John Hammond Live** / Jan. 15, 1992 / Rounder 3074
A definitive live set featuring Hammond on guitar and harmonica. —*Michael G. Nastos*

Slim Harpo (James Moore)

b. Jan. 11, 1924, Lobdell, LA, **d.** Jan. 31, 1970, Baton Rouge, LA
Vocals, guitar, harmonica / Electric Louisiana blues
Born James Moore, this popular Louisiana blues singer played both guitar and neck-rack harmonica in a more down-home approximation of Jimmy Reed, who plowed similar turf with a more pronounced Chicago edge to it. Slim's music was more laid back than Reed's (if such a notion is possible) but the rhythm was insistent, and Harpo's material not only made the national charts from time to time but also was quite adaptable for White blues-rock bands, including the Rolling Stones, the Yardbirds, the Kinks, and the Fabulous Thunderbirds. —*Cub Koda*

○ **Rainin' in My Heart** / 1961 / Excello 8001
The original Excello album. —*Cub Koda*

★ **Best of Slim Harpo, The** / 1989 / Rhino 70169
All the hits, including the original "I'm a King Bee," "Baby, Scratch My Back," "I Got Love If You Want It," "Shake Your Hips," "Rainin' in My Heart," "Tip On In," and "Strange Love." A best-of that really is, with top-flight sound as a bonus. —*Cub Koda*

○ **I'm a King Bee** / 1989 / Flyright 05
Unissued sides and alternate takes, the perfect companion volume to *The Best of Slim Harpo*. —*Cub Koda*

Peppermint Harris (Harrison Nelson)

b. Jul. 17, 1925, Texarkana, TX
Vocals, guitar / Electric jump blues
Harrison "Peppermint" Nelson's story is one of many hidden or mistaken identities. He acquired the name Harris when a producer couldn't remember the singer's name when his first hit single, "Raining in My Heart," was released in 1950. The following year Peppermint (retaining the Harris billing) recorded his biggest seller, "I Got Loaded"—one of a number of drinking songs waxed by a man who maintained that he wasn't even a drinker at the time. As a songwriter, he said he often sold his compositions outright, relinquishing both royalties and writer's credits on songs recorded by B. B. King, Bobby Bland, and others. As a youth he looked to Lightnin' Hopkins as his main inspiration, yet his own style was nothing like that of Hopkins. A smooth city stylist, the college-educated Harris had an urbane approach to the blues, singing with a deep, often mellow tone while employing the guitar sparingly. He has continued to compose and record blues over the years, and rates as one of the more interesting Texas blues tunesmiths, even based solely on the songs that do list his name. —*Jim O'Neal*

Peppermint Harris / 1962 / Time 5
Nice early '50s Texas R&B. —*Bill Dahl*

○ **Sittin' in with** / 1979 / Mainstream 907
Fifteen tracks recorded for the Sittin' In With label, 1950-53, including "Come on Let's Ride," "Got a Big Fine Baby," "Gimme Gimme," "Mabel, Mabel," and "Rainin' in My Heart." —*Roundup Newsletter*

● **I Got Loaded** / 1987 / Route 66 23
An import collection of classic R&B sides by this deep-voiced Texas bluesman. Booze-related songs derived mostly from '50s Aladdin singles. —*Hank Davis*

Being Black Twice / Collectables 5230
These are '60s and '70s sides from the Jewel label. A good vocalist with some unusual material. —*Hank Davis*

Wynonie Harris

b. Aug. 24, 1915, Omaha, NE, **d.** Jun. 14, 1969, Los Angeles, CA
Vocals, sometimes drums / Electric jump blues
One of the most popular and powerful singers to contribute to the birth of '40s rhythm & blues, Wynonie Harris achieved his greatest hits by rocking long and hard or by making his listeners laugh the same way. His two #1 hits were the Roy Brown–penned "Good Rockin' Tonight" and "All She Wants to Do Is Rock," while other chart records were often in a comic novelty vein. But his nickname was "Mr. Blues" and a blues powerhouse he was, as well as a humorist, showman, and "a profane and raucous individual," in the words of his lifelong friend Preston Love. Many of his 1946–52 hits were recorded with top-flight jazz accompanists. Harris recorded sporadically afterwards but never again enjoyed the glory or success he'd known as one of the kings of jump-blues. —*Jim O'Neal*

★ **Bloodshot Eyes: The Best of** / King/Rhino
There are many hilarious cuts on this 18-track anthology, among them "I Like My Baby's Pudding," "Grandma Plays The Numbers," and "Good Morning Judge." Harris roars, struts, and wails over equally feverish arrangements, and earns a draw with Joe Turner on "Battle of the Blues." Both the raw quality and overt tone of his lyrics and his sound limited Harris to the R&B market, but within that sphere he was a dominant figure through much of the '40s and '50s. These songs give a good portrait of a delightful, often spectacular vocalist who could be both provocative and compelling. —*Ron Wynn*

Buddy B Hawkins

Walter "Buddy Boy" Hawkins' background and origins are uncertain. He's been cited being born in four different states and at least three different times. What's truly clear is that he was a marvelous vocalist and relaxed, distinctive guitarist in the vintage country-blues mode. He recorded for Paramount in the late '20s; these are his finest tracks. Hawkins also did some dates with William Harris. —*Ron Wynn*

○ **Buddy B Hawkins and His Buddies** / Yazoo 1010
This is somewhat deceptive packaging, as Hawkins only has half the selections and the "buddies" have the second half. But since the buddies include Texas Alexander, their contributions are worth close scrutiny. Hawkins's fine vocals and distinctive guitar are still dominant, though. —*Ron Wynn*

Ted Hawkins

b. 1936, Biloxi, MS
Vocals, guitar / Soul, Modern acoustic blues
Hawkins is one of the greatest blues/soul finds of the last three decades, a smoky-voiced singer from the streets of Venice, CA, who evokes the spirit of Sam Cooke and writes songs packed with subtle, heartbreaking details. —*John Floyd*

● **Watch Your Step** / 1972 / Rounder 2024
His acoustic-based debut, recorded in 1971, was released while Hawkins was serving a prison sentence. This album runs the gamut from moody, tormented ballads to celebratory moments of release. —*John Floyd*

○ **Happy Hour** / 1987 / Rounder 2033
Happy Hour features Hawkins's memorable compositions plus an occasional cover, this one a wonderful version of Curtis Mayfield's "Gypsy Woman." Hawkins' vocals were even more gritty and striking, as was his acoustic guitar backing and chording. He teamed with his wife Elizabeth on "Don't Make Me Explain It," "My Last Goodbye," and "California Song," and with guitarist Night Train Clemons on "Gypsy Woman" and "You Pushed My Head Away." Hawkins blended soul and urban blues stylings with country and rural blues inflections and rhythms, making another first-rate release that deserved wide recognition beyond acoustic music and blues circles. —*Ron Wynn*

○ **Next Hundred Years, The** / 1994 / Dgc (David Geffen Company)
Hawkins's first album for DGC Records is a beautiful, understated record that easily ranks with his finest works. —*Stephen Thomas Erlewine*

Clifford Hayes

Violin / Big band, Swing

Violinist Clifford Hayes provided some rich, joyous solos for various jug bands in the '20s and '30s. He was best known for his work with Sara Martin's Jug Band. —*Ron Wynn*

○ **Dixieland Jug Blowers** / Jun. 7, 1927-Jun. 1, 1928 / Yazoo 1054
My own personal taste prefers jazzier jug band material to the hokum and country blues variety. This one goes about as far to the margin as any jug band ever journeyed, thanks to Clifford Hayes's violin and Earl McDonald's jug. —*Ron Wynn*

Johnny Heartsman

b. Feb. 9, 1937, San Fernando, CA
Vocals, guitar, keyboards, flute, sometimes bass / Modern electric blues
Another extremely talented and severely underrecorded blues performer, Johnny Heartsman's name belongs in any short list of pivotal West Coast performers. A dazzling guitarist and powerful, convincing vocalist, Heartsman has sadly made only a handful of recordings as a leader. He's absorbed ideas from such guitarists T-Bone Walker, Lowell Fulson, and Charlie Christian, and began making his mark on the West Coast scene in the '50s. He became a studio musician for Bob Geddins at 16, appearing on recordings by Johnny Fuller, King Solomon, Jimmy McCracklin, and Jimmy Wilson. A gifted multiinstrumentalist and arranger who also plays bass, piano, organ, flute, and trombone, Heartsman backed Lou Rawls, Lavern Baker, and several others during the '60s, but dropped off the scene for several years in 1967. He returned in the mid-'70s, and has remained active ever since, with recent recordings on the Crosscut and Alligator labels. —*Ron Wynn*

● **Touch, The** / 1991 / Alligator 4800
Finally, a worthy showcase for this Bay Area multiinstrumentalist. Heartsman's prodigious talents are shown on guitar, organ, and flute. —*Bill Dahl*

Z. Z. Hill (Arzell Hill)

b. Sep. 30, 1935, Naples, TX, d. Apr. 27, 1984, Dallas, TX
Vocals / Soul, R&B, Soul blues
Arzell "Z. Z." Hill toiled for years as a second-line act on the chitlin circuit, recording soul, blues, and R&B in whatever vein was contemporary for various labels both big and small, until he signed with Malaco Records in 1980. His early Malaco singles did fairly well, but neither Hill, Malaco, nor anyone else was prepared for the astonishing success of his second album for the label, *Down Home*, featuring the now-standard "Down Home Blues," which was quickly adapted into every blues or R&B band's repertoire. *Down Home* became one of the best-selling blues albums of all time and has been credited as a major force in reviving the blues in the '80s. The journeyman soul singer became the #1 blues man in Black America; there was little crossover to the White blues market. Hill's approach was designed to appeal both to the mature blues audience and to younger R&B listeners, and in trying to promote a youthful image he usually subtracted several years from his age (hence there are a number of different published birthdates). The fruits of his success were tragically short-lived, as Z. Z. Hill died suddenly in 1984, just two years after *Down Home* had turned his career around. —*Jim O'Neal*

Brand New Z.Z. Hill / 1971 / Mankind 201
A '70s Swamp Dogg–produced concept album. —*Richard Pack*

Z. Z. Hill / 1981 / Malaco 7402
Beginning of his great comeback. —*Bill Dahl*

○ **Rhythm & The Blues, The** / 1982 / Malaco 7411
More fine modern blues. —*Bill Dahl*

☆ **Down Home** / 1982 / Malaco 7406
Straight blues, not trendy but timeless. —*Richard Pack*

● **In Memorium (1935–84)** / 1985 / Malaco 7426
A nice anthology covering the career of blues and soul vocalist Z.Z. Hill, who shocked everyone during the '80s by scoring huge hits with traditional, acoustic country and bluesy soul. His albums *Down Home Blues* and *The Rhythm and the Blues* busted the East Coast radio embargo on nonurban material. Sadly, Hill had a heart attack and died en route to what would have been his Brooklyn debut. These songs are a worthy tribute to what he accomplished at Malaco. —*Ron Wynn*

Willie "Smokey" Hogg (Willie Anderson Hogg)

b. Jan. 27, 1914, Westconnie, TX, d. May 1, 1960, McKinney, TX

Vocals, guitar, sometimes piano / Blues
The most prolific of the postwar down-home Texas bluesmen next to Lightnin' Hopkins, Hogg recorded steadily in the late '40s and early '50s for a number of different labels and hit the *Billboard* R&B charts twice with "Long Tall Mama" and "Little School Girl" (both on Modern Records). His recorded repertoire and vocal approach owed more to various popular blues recordings of the '30s and '40s than to the Texas tradition, though he also apparently made up a number of his own songs in the studio. While producers usually teamed him with three- or four-piece combos, often including sax, his blues remained countrified and unadorned in keeping with his roots as a solo street musician. —*Jim O'Neal*

○ **Sings** / 1961 / Crown 5226
Smokey Hogg was a fine guitarist and good vocalist, better at mid-tempo and slower material than uptempo numbers. These are some of his best early '60s cuts; the sound quality is good but not exceptional. —*Ron Wynn*

Smokey Hogg / 1962 / Time 6
Early '50s Texas blues. —*Bill Dahl*

○ **Original Folk Blues** / 1965 / United 7745
Some of Hogg's best early '50s sides for Modern here. —*Bill Dahl*

● **Angels in Harlem** / 1992 / Specialty 7020
Generous compilation of the Texas guitarist's early '50s Specialty sides. —*Bill Dahl*

○ **Sittin' in with** / Mainstream 906
Fourteen tracks recorded for the Sittin' In With label, 1949-50. Tunes include "You Won't Stay Home," "Why Should I Worry," "I'm So Lonely," "Shake a Leg," and others. —*Roundup Newsletter*

Holmes Brothers, The

Group / Soul, R&B, Modern electric blues
The Holmes Brothers Band (guitarists Sherman and Wendell, Gib Wharton, and drummer Willie "Popsy" Dixon) has emerged as the most appealing "new" blues band of the '90s. What they do is actually far from new, and they have been doing it in New York for many years. They have created their own version of soul through the ultimate blending of the church and the juke, merging gospel, blues, rock, and hillbilly. Their vocalizing effectively erases the boundaries between sacred and secular songs. With the freshest, most welcome blues sound today, they remind us that good music is not confined to any single genre. —*Barry Lee Pearson*

● **Soul Street** / 1993 / Rounder Records 2124
This album continued their tradition of doing tremendous covers ("You're Gonna Make Me Cry," "Down In Virginia," and "Fannie Mae"), authentic originals ("I Won't Hurt You Anymore," "Dashboard Bar") and adding gospel ("Walk in the Light") and honky-tonk ("There Goes My Everything") into their blend. —*Ron Wynn*

○ **Where It's at** / Rounder 2111
If there were any thoughts that the Holmes Brothers may have been one-disc wonders or a curiousity that would fade from view, their second release in 1991 ended that speculation. It contained another 11 wonderful tunes that easily moved from surging R&B to rousing blues with an occasional venture into gospel or country. They covered "Drown in My Own Tears" and "High Heel Sneakers" and got the requisite qualities for each one down pat, as well as "Never Let Me Go," "The Love You Save" and "I Saw the Light." But their own numbers, like "I've Been a Loser" and the title track were even better, displaying a contemporary sensibility and classic style and sound. —*Ron Wynn*

○ **In the Spirit** / Rounder 2056
This 1990 set included some riveting gospel tunes like "None But the Righteous" and "Up above My Head," plus a credible (if a little lengthy) version of "When Something Is Wrong with My Baby" and tighter, hard-hitting tunes "Please Don't Hurt Me," "Ask Me No Questions," and "The Final Round." If straight-ahead, rousing shared leads and booming harmonies interest you, the Holmes Brothers do it the way they used to throughout the South in the '60s and '70s. —*Ron Wynn*

Honeyboy Edwards (David Edwards)

Though he's recorded fitfully over the years, Edwards was a staple of the Delta blues circuit, working with Robert Johnson, Rice

Miller and Elmore James, among others. His powerful voice is complimented by his dazzling guitar work that has Mississippi stamped all over it. —*Cub Koda*

○ **White Windows** / Sep. 1988 / Evidence 26039
Edwards does not rely on slickness, inventiveness, or niceties; his riffs, lines, phrases, and licks are as aggressive and fiery as his vocals. He showed what real traditional blues singing was all about when he recorded for Blue Suit in 1988. Edwards's triumphant, resounding voice rings through such classics as Bukka White's "Shake 'Em On Down," Muddy Waters's "Don't Say I Don't Love You," and his own "The War Is Over" and "Build Myself a Cave." It is certainly a vintage approach, but Honeyboy Edwards's music will never be dated. —*Ron Wynn*

● **Delta Bluesman** / 1992 / Earwig 4922
In the shadow of Robert Johnson, Johnny Shines, and Son House, there's been a lot less attention placed on David "Honeyboy" Edwards. *Delta Bluesman* should go a long way toward righting that wrong. The CD includes Edwards's 1942 Library of Congress recordings for Alan Lomax, even a humorous—and revealing—retelling of the two men's first encounter. —*Bryan Powell, Blues Access*

Earl Hooker (Earl Zebedee Hooker)

b. Jan. 15, 1930, Clarksdale, MS, **d.** Apr. 21, 1970, Chicago, IL
Vocals, guitar / Electric Chicago blues
The blues artist and singer generally acknowledged by his peers as the finest all-around guitarist in Chicago blues circles, Earl Hooker brought much of a modern flavor to his music while never straying far from his Clarksdale, MS, roots. A cousin of John Lee Hooker and a major disciple of Robert Nighthawk, Hooker's slide guitar work was the most technically advanced of all bluesmen. Adept at a multitude of styles ranging from hillbilly to jazz, Hooker worked as a sideman and leader in more configurations than any other modern bluesman. While his lead guitar work graced the recordings of Muddy Waters ("You Shook Me"), Junior Wells, G. L. Crockett, and others, Hooker's solo career didn't really blossom until the late '60s, by which time the tuberculosis that dogged him throughout his life cut his career short. Perhaps the only traditional bluesman to successfully utilize electronic gimmicks like wah-wah pedals and distortion units without sounding ridiculous in the process, Earl Hooker remains one of the great listening surprises of the blues. —*Cub Koda*

● **Two Bugs and a Roach** / 1966 / Arhoolie 324
A nice representative sample from Chicago's unsung master of the electric guitar. Includes the title track, "Anna Lee," and the atmospheric instrumental "Off the Hook" —*Bruce Lee Pearson*

Sweet Black Angel / 1970 / Blue Thumb 8812
With Ike Turner credited as one of the set's producers, Hooker offers a mostly instrumental program with a wide stylistic range; blues to soul to country. —*Bill Dahl*

○ **Leading Brand** / 1978 / Red Lightnin' 0018
Hooker's best early '60s instrumentals for Mel London, along with a few sides that feature his guitar by Ricky Allen, Lillian Offett, etc. Also featured are several equally memorable workouts by guitarist Jody Williams. —*Bill Dahl*

○ **Blue Guitar** / 1981 / PR 18
Twenty-one–track collection of Earl's early '60s output for Mel London's Chief-Profile-Age labels, both as a sideman and as a featured soloist. His wide variety of styles, encompassing rockabilly to the creamiest of slide work, shows why Muddy Waters dubbed him "the best guitarist in Chicago." —*Cub Koda*

○ **Play Your Guitar Mr. Hooker** / 1985 / Black Magic 9006
A perfect companion piece to Blue Guitar, this features Earl's recordings for the tiny Cuca label, along with privately recorded live recordings from 1968. Great guitar playing by one of the most unheralded of the genre. —*Cub Koda*

John Lee Hooker

b. Aug. 22, 1917, Clarksdale, MS
Vocals, guitar / Indie, R&B, Acoustic & electric Delta blues
By the time blues singer and guitarist John Lee Hooker made his recording debut in 1948 and had a national hit with "Boogie Chillen," he was already an anachronism. Except for his thunderous electric guitar, Hooker's one- and two-chord modal stylings sounded much like those of a Delta blues artist from the '20s.

This was not surprising, since Delta legend Charley Patton was Hooker's childhood inspiration. But Hooker's music was altogether more fierce and rhythmic, solo for the most part, coupled with his dark, hypnotic voice on one end and his relentless footstomping on the other. Over the years he recorded with full-band support, though he never really found one to keep up with his odd approach to meter and his violent bursts of solo guitar. Recording right up to the present time for seemingly every large and small blues label that's ever existed (and with little to no variation in his approach), Hooker's music is raw, riveting, doom-laden Mississippi blues that demands much from the listener. One of the great emotional listening experiences in the blues, John Lee Hooker stands alone as a true creative original, often imitated but never equaled. —*Cub Koda*

○ **House of the Blues** / 1960 / Chess 9258
Seminal early Hooker. —*Bill Dahl*

☆ **John Lee Hooker Plays and Sings the Blues** / 1961 / Chess 1454
Recorded in 1951 and 1952, *Plays and Sings the Blues* features 12 songs of John Lee Hooker at his best, including "Baby Please Don't Go," "Bluebird," "Hey Baby," and "Worried Life Blues." —*Stephen Thomas Erlewine*

Dont Turn Me from Your Door / 1963 / Atlantic 82365
Recorded mostly in 1953, this is a stunning example of Hooker's intense, primitive blues stylings. Guttural moans and clanging, psychotic guitar compete for space in the mix as Hooker wails ominous messages, many directed at assorted, treacherous women. Eddie Kirkland assists on vocals and guitar on 3 of the 16 tracks and an unknown bassist sits in on 4 others. But Hooker and his notoriously loud footstomp have no trouble filling out the sound. Tunes include "Stuttering Blues," "Goin' South," "My Baby Put Me Down," and a cover of Charles Brown's "Drifting Blues." —*Roundup Newsletter*

○ **John Lee Hooker at Newport** / 1964 / Vee Jay 1078
Arguably his finest live date, this was John Lee Hooker minus the self-congratulatory mugging that's a now almost mandatory part of his sets. Instead, there's just lean, straight, and defiant Hooker vocals and minimal but effective backing. —*Ron Wynn*

○ **Real Folk Blues, The** / 1966 / Chess 9271
Some good mid-'60s material, featuring second guitarist and vocalist Eddie Burns. Hooker wasn't quite as strong or combative as he was during his first Chess period or with Vee-Jay, but there are plenty of prime vocal moments. —*Ron Wynn*

★ **Ultimate Collection (1948–90), The** / 1991 / Rhino 70572
A two-CD boxed set overview of Hooker's best sides, more than living up to its title. Indispensable. —*Cub Koda*

More Real Folk Blues—the Missing Album / Sep. 10, 1991 / Chess 9329
Nine songs previously unavailable, culled from the same sessions as *The Real Folk Blues*, recorded in 1966. Includes "This Land Is Nobody's Land," "Catfish," "Want Ad Blues," "House Rent Blues," and a cover of Willie Dixon's "I Can't Quit You, Baby." —*Roundup Newsletter*

Best of John Lee Hooker 1965—1974, The / 1992 / MCA 10539
The decade covered in this 16-cut compilation did not yield many of Hooker's most lasting recordings, and it saw many of his producers making all sorts of concessions to open up new commercial markets (lots of wah-wah pedals, if you get the idea). Still, Hooker wasn't totally down and out in the sixties and seventies. Compiler Dave Booth has done a fine job of plucking good tracks from otherwise mediocre records (like "Bluebird" from *Free Beer and Chicken*, and "Bang, Bang, Bang, Bang" from *If You Miss 'Im ... I Got 'Im*), and Colin Escott's notes are up to his usual high standard. These are far from Hooker's greatest recordings, but *The Best of John Lee Hooker*, 72 minutes long, is the first collection that presents this period of the Hook's career with care and sense. —*Jimmy Guterman, Roundup Newsletter*

☆ **Graveyard Blues** / 1992 / Specialty 7018
Searing early sides. —*Bill Dahl*

★ **On Vee-Jay 1955–58** / 1993 / Vee-Jay 713
John Lee Hooker made some of his hardest hitting, finest recordings for Vee-Jay in the '50s, working with such greats as Jimmy Reed and Eddie Taylor. He had not yet worn out the "boogie" idiom, and his lyrics and playing were intense, inspired, and creative, while his voice was in peak shape. The set includes some hot numbers never before available, among them "Wheel and

Deal," "Everybody's Rockin'," and "Little Fine Woman." —*Ron Wynn*

Lightnin' Hopkins (Sam Hopkins)

b. Mar. 15, 1912, Centerville, TX, **d.** Jan. 30, 1982, Houston, TX
Vocals, guitar, sometimes piano, organ / Acoustic and electric Texas blues

A true giant in blues history, Lightnin' Hopkins cut an imposing figure on the Texas blues scene and set a standard for postwar down-home blues. His work influenced not only countless country bluesmen all across the land but also many of the younger urban blues stylists. His songs might hark back to Blind Lemon Jefferson or they might deal with the latest-breaking news. Whether traditional or topical, acoustic or electric, whether recording solo or with a small combo, Hopkins was a natural: a master musician, singer, and blues poet/storyteller. He recorded electric country blues and boogies for the Black R&B market as well as acoustic guitar albums for the folk market. Throughout a lengthy and prolific recording career that began in 1946, he was a consistent, engaging, and immediately identifiable artist who made many outstanding records and very few bad ones. —*Jim O'Neal*

○ **Lightnin' Hopkins** / 1959 / Smithsonian/Rounder 40019
Sam "Lightnin" Hopkins was a master storyteller, underrated guitarist and marvelous performer whose albums could be irritating, inspirational, or uneven, but were seldom predictable or tepid. This 1959 session, reissued without bonus cuts or alternate takes, has mostly short, crisply narrated anecdotes or songs with ironic resolutions sung in Hopkins's usual declarative, wry tone. His "Reminiscenses of Blind Lemon" spins one of his wonderful yarns, while "See That My Grave Is Clean" and "Bad Luck and Trouble" pivot around his sparse guitar and emphatic, dry vocals. —*Ron Wynn*

How Many More Years I Got / 1962 / Fantasy 24725
A repackaging of three earlier albums: *Walkin' This Road by Myself, Lightnin' & Co.,* and *Smokes Like Lightnin'.* Lightnin' plays electric with small-band support on these sides, which probably come the closest to what he sounded like in the juke joints around Houston in the early '60s. —*Cub Koda*

○ **In New York** / 1970 / Candid 79010
Recorded in one day in 1960 for jazz critic Nat Hentoff's small Candid label, its combination of superb sound quality and exceptional performances by Hopkins makes it the definitive Lightnin' Hopkins set, if not the definitive recorded example of the Texas songster tradition. — *Ralph Stewart Jr., Rock & Roll Disc.*

☆ **Herald Material 1954, The** / 1988 / Collectables 5121
Killer electric sides by the prolific Texas troubadour from Herald vaults. —*Bill Dahl*

○ **Herald Recordings, Vol. 2, The** / 1989 / Collectables 5181
More savage Texas guitar licks from the blues master. —*Bill Dahl*

☆ **Gold Star Sessions** / 1991 / Arhoolie 330
The two separate discs of the *Gold Star Sessions* are some of the earliest and most uncompromising work in the Hopkins pantheon, late '40s vintage. —*Bill Dahl*

☆ **Complete Prestige/Bluesville Recordings** / 1991 / Bluesville 4406
A seven-disc boxed set of Hopkins's complete Prestige/Bluesville recordings. Includes Sam Charter's brilliant liner notes. —*Jas Obrecht*

○ **Sittin' in with** / 1992 / Mainstream 905
Compilation of 17 tracks recorded for Bob Shad's Sittin' In With label between 1951and 1953. Touring the south with then-partner Joe Bihari, Shad recorded Lightnin' Hopkins on a portable tape recorder at locations including clubs, hotel rooms, churches, and brothels. Songs on this disc include "Back Home Boogie," "New York Boogie," "Long Way from Texas," and "Cemetery Blues." —*Roundup Newsletter*

☆ **Complete Aladdin Recordings, The** / 1992 / EMI America 96844
A double-CD boxed set of Hopkins's first recordings, primarily solo and acoustic. Powerful and riveting. —*Cub Koda*

★ **Mojo Hand: The Anthology** / May 18, 1993 / Rhino
A two-disc set, drawing from a variety of different labels, that is a definitive introduction to the Texas bluesman's lengthy career. Anyone who wants to learn about Lightnin' Hopkins should start

here. Many tracks have been out of print for years, making the *Mojo Hand: The Lightnin' Hopkins Anthology* tempting for collectors as well. —*AMG*

Big Walter "Shakey" Horton

b. Apr. 6, 1917, Horn Lake, MS, **d.** Dec. 8, 1981, Chicago, IL
Harmonica, Vocals / Electric Chicago blues

Raised in the South, Horton recorded with a Memphis jug band in 1927 before migrating to Chicago. He is without a doubt one of the all-time great blues harmonica players. Along with Little Walter (whom he claims to have taught), Horton defined modern amplified harp (harmonica). There is no harp player (and that includes Little Walter) with Horton's big tone and spacious sense of time. Although his early acoustic recordings in Memphis (1951) are excellent, it is his amplified harp work that will be most remembered. He plays just incredible backup harp (and solos) with both Muddy Waters and Jimmy Rogers; and his instumental "Easy" with guitarist Jimmy DeBerry is a classic. Horton recordings from the late '50s and mid-'60s are unrivaled. In particular, the album *Chicago/The Blues/Today! Vol. 3* on Vanguard is a landmark recording—his contrapuntal backup harp seems to float behind the singer, loping along, always stretching and opening up the time. And Horton's taste in notes is unparalleled. Big Walter Horton is one of the high-water marks of modern Chicago-style blues. —*Michael Erlewine*

● **Soul of Blues Harmonica, The** / Jan. 13, 1964 / Chess 9268
A classic album with Horton in great form—sort of a musical tour of the wide variety of musical styles that Horton has mastered. Includes a fine verion of "Hard Hearted Woman." The all-star band includes Buddy Guy (guitar), Jack Myers (bass), Willie Dixon (vocals), and Willie Smith (drums). —*Michael Erlewine*

★ **Chicago/The Blues/Today!, Vol. 3** / 1967 / Vanguard 79218
Here is one of the all-time great blues albums. A classic! —*Michael Erlewine*

Big Walter Horton with Carey Bell / Jan. 1973 / Alligator 4702
Enjoyable meeting of two blues harp giants in an informal setting. —*Bill Dahl*

○ **Fine Cuts** / Apr. 1979 / Blind Pig 70678
Perhaps the best of later Horton. Contains rerecordings of some of his better early material. —*Michael Erlewine*

Little Boy Blue / 1980 / JSP 208
A 1980 live recording in Boston. Working with a pickup band consisting of Ronnie Earl on guitar, Mudcat Ward on bass, and Ola Dixon on drums, Horton catches fire and quite simply blows his heart out. The album features some of Big Walter's best late-period playing. —*Cub Koda*

Mouth Harp Maestro / 1988 / ACE 252
Sixteen cuts from the early '50s. Classic acoustic harp! —*Michael Erlewine*

○ **Memphis Recordings 1951** / 1991 / Kent
Some of Horton's best early efforts for Sam Phillip's prior to Sun's advent. —*Bill Dahl*

Eddie James "Son" House Jr.

b. Mar. 21, 1902, **d.** Mar. 21, 1988, Detroit, MI
Vocals, guitar / Acoustic Delta blues

His blues were intense, anguished, and powerful. Unlike his '30s playing partner Charley Patton—a "clowning man" with a guitar—Son House took his music mighty seriously. Sitting on a straight-back chair, he'd suddenly whip his head back, roll his eyes inside his skull, and slide a bottleneck up his guitar's neck. Veins bulging in his forehead, he'd moan, thump a bass note, and sing with the deep conviction of a sinner on judgment day. Seeing him in 1930 caused a teenage Robert Johnson to abandon harmonica for guitar. House cast a lifelong spell over Muddy Waters too.

Eddie James "Son" House remained true to his Mississippi roots. His 1930 Paramount 78s captured unsurpassed Delta blues singing but brought him little money or recognition. He made superb field recordings—solo and with a band—in 1941 and 1942, and then followed a girlfriend to Rochester, NY, where he took a job on the New York Central Railroad. Blues researchers located House in 1964 and prompted him into playing again. The hard-drinking guitarist recorded passionately primitive albums for Columbia, Verve/Folkways, Vanguard, and other labels, giving concerts until deteriorating health forced his retirement in 1974. He lived with his family in Detroit until March 21, 1988, when the last great voice of first-generation Delta blues was finally stilled. —*Jas Obrecht*

☆ **Son House & The Great Delta Blues Singers** / 1990 / Document 5002
The complete 1930 session, with Willie Brown, Rube Lacy, and others. Stunning vocals. (Import) —*Jas Obrecht*

○ **Delta Blues** / 1991 / Biograph 118
Digital transfers from the Library of Congress acetates, 1941–42. —*Jas Obrecht*

★ **Delta Blues—the Original Library of Congress Sessions from Field Recordings 1941–42** / 1991 / Biograph Records, Inc.
All of the recordings Alan Lomax made of Son House in 1941 and 1942 are collected on this essential CD. —*Stephen Thomas Erlewine*

○ **Father of the Delta Blues: The Complete 1965 Sessions** / 1992 / CBS 48867
After being rediscovered by the folk-blues community in the early '60s, Son House rose to the occasion and recorded this magnificent set of performances. Allowed to stretch out past the shorter running time of the original 78s, House turns in wonderful, steaming performances of some of his best-known material. —*Cub Koda*

Howlin' Wolf (Chester Arthur Burnett)

b. Jun. 10, 1910, West Point, MS, **d.** Jan. 10, 1978, Hines, IL
Vocals, harmonica, guitar / R&B, Electric Chicago blues
The Wolf was six-foot-six, weighed close to 300 pounds in his prime, and possessed a voice that could shake the city down to the last radio. There is no sound in the blues more primal and ferocious than the recordings of the Howlin' Wolf. A pupil of Charley Patton and a contemporary of Robert Johnson, Wolf didn't start recording until the early '50s (first in Memphis for Sam Phillips, then in Chicago for Leonard Chess), quickly racking up one classic after another, all of them precisely focused on Wolf's dominating personality. "How Many More Years," "Riding in the Moonlight," "Back Door Man," "Spoonful," and "I Ain't Superstitious" (all featuring the stinging guitar work of Willie Johnson or Hubert Sumlin, Wolf's two main musical partners throughout his career) are just a few of his tunes that have been covered again and again by rock groups and bluesmen alike. Though his sandpaper growl of a voice has been widely imitated from Wolfman Jack on down, and his disciples are many, there exists no real "school" of Wolf, since the man and his music were uniquely of one piece. Capable of simultaneously rocking the house while scaring its patrons out of their wits, the Howlin' Wolf stands alone in the annals of American music. —*Cub Koda*

○ **Real Folk Blues, The** / 1963 / Chess 9273
An absolutely majestic collection with the Wolf at his snarling, threatening, defiant best. When it came to making great ornery blues, no one in the Chess kingdom could beat Howlin' Wolf. —*Ron Wynn*

★ **Howlin' Wolf/Moanin' in the Moonlight** / 1964 / MCA 5908
Wolf's first and second Chess albums on one CD. With all the early hits, it's the perfect introduction to his music. —*Cub Koda*

○ **More Real Folk Blues** / 1967 / Chess 9279
Early Chicago classics. —*Bill Dahl*

○ **Ridin' in the Moonlight** / 1982 / ACE 52
A great collection of the Memphis/RPM sides issued in the early '50s. A great companion piece to *Memphis Days.* —*Cub Koda*

☆ **Cadillac Daddy** / 1989 / Rounder 28
Great compendium of pre-Chess tracks produced by Sam Phillips. The sheer power of Wolf's voice and Willie Johnson's guitar work never cease to amaze. —*Bill Dahl*

○ **Memphis Days: The Definitive Edition** / 1989 / Bear Family 15460
Memphis Days: The Definitive Edition comprises two volumes of Wolf's earliest and rarest sides at the Sun studios, featuring previously unissued material culled from long-lost acetates. Raw and explosive, this is Wolf at his most primitive. Highly recommended. —*Cub Koda*

☆ **Chess Box, The** / 1991 / Chess 9332

A three-CD boxed set. The definitive overview of Wolf's career. Great booklet and mastering, with Wolf interview snippets interspersed throughout. —*Cub Koda*

○ **Howlin' Wolf Rides Again** / 1993 / Capitol 86295
If you've heard the legendary Wolf material found on Chess, you may wonder how there could be room in this world for any more. Well, these sides are even more rough, raw, and ready. Cut for Sam Phillips's Sun Studios, these first, ferocious sides commemorate Bigfoot's Memphis tenure, when he was fresh out of the Delta. The masters were farmed out to the Biharis Brothers for release on labels such as RPM and Crown. This is the Howlin' Wolf band that featured sidemen such as Willie Johnson, Ike Turner, and Willie Steel. Essential for any real Wolf fan. —*Larry Hoffman*

○ **Ain't Gonna Be Your Dog** / 1994 / Chess Records
A terrific two-CD set of rare and unreleased Chess tracks, none of which are on the Wolf's box set; for hardcore fans, *Ain't Gonna Be Your Dog* is essential. —*AMG*

Alberta Hunter

b. Apr. 1, 1895, Memphis, TN, **d.** Oct. 17, 1984, Roosevelt Is, NY
Vocals / Classic female blues
The influence of the late legendary vocalist can be heard today in the singing styles of many of the current crop of women blues singers, including Carrie Smith and Ruth Brown. Hunter was the perfect example of how changing public tastes were able to make singers of her ilk fashionable again. In the early '80s, Hunter, then over 80 years old, began a series of weekly engagements at New York's Cookery, simultaneously rekindling the public's interest in blues as well as in the fire in her voice. Her most exceptional recordings were made in the early '80s for Columbia, with legendary impresario John Hammond at the helm. —*Richard Skelly*

Chicago: The Living Legends / 1988 / Riverside 510
Alberta Hunter, one of the classic blues women, was coaxed out of retirement to record this heartfelt reunion with veteran Chicago pianist Lovie Austin for Riverside in 1961. Songs include "Moanin' Low" and "St. Louis Blues." —*Roundup Newsletter*

● **Young Alberta Hunter** / Vintage Jazz 6
1921–40. Twenty-three classic tracks, both small and large backup bands (Fletcher Henderson). Good sound. —*Michael Erlewine*

Ivory Joe Hunter

b. Oct. 10, 1914, Kirbyville, TX, **d.** Nov. 8, 1974, Memphis, TN
Vocals, piano / R&B, Electric jump blues, Prewar acoustic blues
Best known for his classic ballads "I Almost Lost My Mind" and "Since I Met You Baby" (both #1 hits), Ivory Joe Hunter was one of the major '50s R&B stars to cross over into the pop market. Prior to that, he'd been a popular blues singer/pianist in the urbane West Coast style of the '40s. In the beginning he was a Texas barrelhouse blues pianist who recorded for the Library of Congress in 1933, and in later years he did sessions as both a soul singer and a country & western artist. As a songwriter, Hunter claimed over 7,000 compositions. His recorded output was so varied as to defy any overall categorization, but for the blues enthusiast the reissues of his '40s sides are of greatest interest. —*Jim O'Neal*

○ **Ivory Joe Hunter** / 1957 / Atlantic 8008
His hit making peak. —*Bill Dahl*

● **16 of His Greatest Hits** / 1958 / King 605
Late-'40s ballads and blues. —*Bill Dahl*

Sings the Old and The New (Black Label) / 1958 / Atlantic 8015
More fine '50s sides. —*Bill Dahl*

Return of Ivory Joe Hunter, The / 1971 / Epic 30348
Funky Memphis comeback LP. —*Bill Dahl*

○ **Seventh Avenue Boogie** / 1980 / Route 66 66Kix4
These are wonderful mid-'40s and early '50s sides from an extremely versatile vocalist and sorely neglected composer and pianist. Ivory Joe Hunter could and did sing everything from blues to soul to gospel to country magnificently; this is predominantly blues and R&B fare. —*Ron Wynn*

○ **I'm Coming Down with the Blues** / Collectables 5226
Obscure later sides by this piano-playing balladeer. —*Bill Dahl*

Mississippi John Hurt

b. Jul. 1, 1893, Teoc, MS, **d.** Nov. 2, 1966, Grenada, MS
Vocals, harmonica, sometimes guitar / Blues
An exquisite country blues singer/guitarist with a subtle voice and refined fingerpicking guitar style, Hurt recorded in the '20s and again in the '60s. Both periods are well worth hearing: acoustic country blues with real technical clarity that is also comforting and easy to listen to. He never made a recording not worth hearing. With a gospel flavor in his blues, Mississippi John Hurt projects a sense of dignity and kindliness through all of his recordings. If you have trouble with the frequent heaviness of many blues players, you may find Hurt refreshing. He is one of a kind, and a kind one at that. —*Michael Erlewine*

○ **Avalon Blues** / Apr. 1963 / Rounder 1081
The 12 tunes on this '91 CD are sung without frills and played in elegant, evocative fashion. Whether doing brief pieces like "Salty Dog" and "Spanish Fandango" or more elaborate ones such as "Cow Hooking Blues," Hurt's style was the same. He just told stories in a lean and piercing manner, never failing to make the lyrics register merely through his vocals and instrumental support. —*Ron Wynn*

○ **Worried Blues** / Apr. 1963 / Rounder 1082
This second of two sessions devoted to Mississippi John Hurt's first recordings, following his "rediscovery," followed the identical pattern of its predecessor. Hurt did mostly blues, with an occasional spiritual number like "Oh Mary Don't You Weep." He sang in a fragile yet powerful manner, backing his vocals on acoustic guitar in an equally simple, gentle manner with lines and riffs that weren't complicated, but often surpassed passages with far more intricate voicings. These two CDs restored into public circulation very valuable recordings, and the sympathetic remastering gave Hurt the sonic forum his music always deserved. —*Ron Wynn*

Last Sessions / 1966 / Vanguard 79327
Still fine on his last recordings. —*Mark A. Humphrey*

Today / 1966 / Vanguard 79220
A fine '60s album. —*Michael Erlewine*

○ **Immortal, The** / 1967 / Vanguard 79248
The best of Hurt's '60s "rediscovery-era" recordings. —*Mark A. Humphrey*

Mississippi John Hurt, The / 1968 / Vanguard 19-20
A great double-album collection of '60s Hurt. —*Michael Erlewine*

★ **1928 Sessions** / 1988 / Yazoo 1065
Justifiably legendary, with gentle grace and power on these understated masterpieces of fingerpicked guitar and vocals. This is the one to get. These are the early (1928) recordings, which are very fine. —*Michael Erlewine & Mark A. Humphrey*

○ **Greatest Songsters—Complete Works (1927–29), The** / 1990 / Document 5003
You can get a lot of arguments started declaring which "Mississippi" blues musician is the best, so let's just say here's first-rate "Mississippi" John Hurt material and leave it at that. —*Ron Wynn*

J. B. Hutto (Joseph Benjamin Hutto)

b. Apr. 26, 1926, Blackville, SC, **d.** Jun. 12, 1983, Harvey, IL
Vocals, guitar / Electric Chicago blues
A contemporary Chicago blues singer and slide guitarist in an Elmore James mold, Hutto also developed a fierce, raw style of his own. Recording from the early '50s to the mid-'80s, Hutto was also a dynamic live performer. His good-time approach to the music held sway on his recordings, giving a loose, barroom feel to almost all of them, regardless of who was backing him. —*Cub Koda*

★ **Chicago/The Blues/Today!, Vol. 1** / 1967 / Vanguard 79216
Hutto only has five tracks on this album, sharing it with solo turns by Junior Wells and Otis Spann, but it's truly the place to start, because it doesn't get much better than this: "Too Much Alcohol," "Please Help," "Going Ahead," and "That's the Truth" are all classics. —*Cub Koda*

○ **Hawk Squat!** / 1968 / Delmark 617
Good Delmark sides from a major Chicago artist who later relocated to Boston. Not as good as his '50s material. —*Barry Lee Pearson*

Slideslinger / Apr. 1, 1982 / Evidence 26009
While he was not in top shape during the early '80s, J.B. Hutto could still bend strings, churn out whiplash chords, and offer exuberant shouts, which he did on this '82 set, reissued on CD with two bonus cuts. Hutto originally recorded these tracks for Black and Blue. He did not always hit every note on the fretboard or maintain his vocal depth, but his spirit never flagged. —*Ron Wynn*

Slippin' & Slidin' / 1983 / Varrick 006
A well-produced, modern-sounding set by the Chicago style guitarist. —*Bill Dahl*

Jim Jackson

b. 1890, Hernando, MS, **d.** 1937, Hernando, MS
Guitar / Acoustic Memphis blues
Coming from the rich medicine-show tradition of the Memphis area, Jackson's "Kansas City Blues" is one of the great classics of the idiom. —*Cub Koda*

● **Kansas City Blues** / 1980 / Agram 2004
Sixteen tracks from Jackson's peak creative period. Includes many variations of the title track. —*Cub Koda*

John Jackson (John H. Jackson)

b. Feb. 25, 1924, Woodville, VA
Vocals, guitar, banjo / Acoustic country blues
For much of his life, John Jackson played for country house parties in Virginia, or around the house for his own amusement. Then in the '60s he encountered the folk revival, and since that time he has been the Washington, D.C., area's best-loved blues artist. Undoubtedly the finest traditional Piedmont guitarist active today, Jackson exemplifies the songster tradition at its best. His eclectic repertoire embraces the music of his guitar heroes Willie Walker (who once visited his father's house), Blind Boy Fuller, and—most notably—Blind Blake. Besides the blues, rags, and dance tunes associated with these masters, Jackson plays ballads, country songs, and what he terms "old folk songs," such as "The Midnight Special." His confident finger-picking, down-home Virginia accent, and contagious good humor mark his performances, live or on record, as something special. A world-class storyteller and party-thrower as well as a National Heritage Award–winning musician, Jackson has recorded a half-dozen albums and toured the world as often as he has wanted to. Today he often performs with his son James. —*Barry Lee Pearson*

○ **Blues and Country Dance Tunes from Virginia** / 1965 / Arhoolie 1025
John Jackson was an excellent country blues musician whose repetoire also included reels, mountain music, and folk tunes. This was an outstanding collection of vintage material done in what was about as contemporary a fashion as you could get in that genre in the mid-'60s. —*Ron Wynn*

● **Don't Let Your Deal Go Down** / 1970 / Arhoolie 378
Fine compilation of Arhoolie sides. —*Bill Dahl*

○ **Step It up & Go** / 1979 / Rounder 2019
Virginia ragtime, blues, and hillbilly from this amiable singer/guitarist. —*Mark A. Humphrey*

Melvin "Lil' Son Jackson (Melvin Jackson)

b. Aug. 16, 1915, Barry, TX, **d.** May 30, 1976, Dallas, TX
Vocals, guitar / Electric Texas blues
A Texas country-blues guitarist/singer who adapted his laconic rhythms to electric guitar, Jackson enjoyed brief fame in the late '40s and early '50s, resurfacing again in the early '60s. —*Cub Koda*

● **Lil' Son Jackson** / Mar. 1962 / Arhoolie 1004
One of the few '60s "rediscovery" recordings that really works. Highly recommended. —*Cub Koda*

Papa Charlie Jackson (Charlie Carter)

b. , New Orleans, LA, **d.** 1938, Chicago, IL
Vocals, banjo, guitar, ukelele / Acoustic country blues
Jackson was the earliest of the bluesmen to record. His rich vein of material drew from vaudeville, minstrel show, and folk-song material. —*Cub Koda*

○ **Papa Charlie Jackson** / 1972 / Biograph 12042

Jackson's mid-'20s material blended topical fare with hokum hilarity and blues laments, and Jackson's four- and six-string banjo accompaniment was among country blues' most striking. His guitar work wasn't bad either. —*Ron Wynn*

Elmore James

b. Jan. 27, 1918, Richland, Mississippi, d. May 24, 1963, Chicago, IL

Vocals, guitar / Electric Chicago blues

A major link between the traditional Mississippi Delta blues and the modern electric Chicago blues sound of today, Elmore James played throughout the Delta—often with his friend Sonny Boy Williamson II (Rice Miller). Elmore's brilliant singing and slide guitar playing helped define Chicago blues, along with Muddy Waters, Howlin' Wolf, and the other Southern bluesmen who had migrated from the Delta to Chicago. Heavily influenced by Robert Johnson, Elmore became well known after recording his own version of Robert's "Dust My Broom" in 1951. Elmore always played, and recorded, with the finest musicians—usually featuring harmonica, piano, or tenor sax as a complement to his passionate singing and slide playing.

Elmore and his band, the Broom Dusters, played an intense, emotional blues that drove the audience wild. Stories are told of patrons becoming so spellbound by Elmore's plaintive singing and sensual slide guitar work that they'd throw money at his feet as he played. The passion of Elmore's music comes through on any of his recordings—listen to "Something Inside of Me," "Look over Yonder Wall," "The Sky Is Crying," or "Standing at the Crossroads" for starters.

As a slide guitarist, Elmore was more accurately in tune than most others, and his full, rich tone—bordering on feedback with the amplifier—had a sound much like the human voice. This tone may well have inspired B. B. King to develop the voicelike string-bending technique for which he has become famous. Elmore's playing has certainly influenced all the modern blues guitarists—from J. B. Hutto and Earl Hooker to Jimi Hendrix, Duane Allman, Eric Clapton, and Johnny Winter. Elmore died of a heart attack in 1963 and was buried near Durant, MS. —*Daniel Erlewine*

○ **Whose Muddy Shoes** / 1969 / Chess 9114
These Chess sides from the mid-'50s to the early '60s are chock-full of classics, including "Madison Blues," "I Can't Hold Out (Talk to Me Baby)," and Elmore's version of "Stormy Monday." Also features definitive tracks by Chicago bluesman John Brim. —*Cub Koda*

☆ **Original Meteor & Flair Sides, The** / 1984 / ACE 112
The best of Elmore's early '50s sides with stunning slide and driving band support. Elmore at the top of his form. —*Cub Koda*

○ **Rollin' & Tumblin'—the Best of Elmore James** / 1992 / Relic 7026
A great single-disc compilation containing the best of the Fire & Enjoy sessions, with Bobby Robinson producing. —*Cub Koda*

☆ **King of the Slide Guitar** / 1992 / Warner Brothers 42006
King of the Slide Guitar, a two-CD box set collecting all of Elmore James's final recordings for the Fire/Fury/Enjoy labels, is full of wonderful material, making it an essential purchase, despite the tacky cover art. —*Stephen Thomas Erlewine*

★ **Sky Is Crying: The History of, The** / 1993 / Rhino 71190
With the confusing plethora of Elmore James discs out on the market, this is truly the place to start, featuring the best of his work culled from several labels. Highlights include Elmore's original recording of "Dust My Broom," "It Hurts Me Too," "T.V. Mama" with Big Joe Turner, and the title track. Slide guitar doesn't get much better than this. Essential piece for any blues collection. —*Cub Koda*

○ **Let's Cut It: Very Best of Elmore James** / Flair 91800
The jolting sound of Elmore James' electric slide guitar represents powerhouse blues at its best. Right from the start, with the blistering opening notes of "Dust My Blues," this 18-song collection shows the intensity of one of the most fiery blues guitarists ever. Also includes "Blues Before Sunrise" and "Mean and Evil." (The sessions date from between 1953 and 1956.)— *Roundup newsletter*

Etta James (Etta James Hawkins)

b. Jan. 25, 1938, Los Angeles, CA

Vocals / Soul, Soul, R&B, R&B, Soul blues

R&B/Soul singer. A growling and purring stylist who is at the top of her genre, Etta was discovered at the tender age of 16 by bandleader Johnny Otis, fronting an all-girl vocal trio called the Peaches. They quickly hit paydirt with her waxing of an answer record to Hank Ballard's "Work with Me Annie" entitled "The Wallflower." This tune, also known as "Roll with Me Henry," was cleaned up for White cover record chart consumption by Georgia Gibbs as "Dance with Me Henry," its national success prompting a flurry of lawsuits over composer royalties. Though Etta continued to record classic sides for Modern (some with Little Richard's band backing her), nothing clicked until she signed with Chess Records in 1960. It was here that she really hit her stride, charting 24 crossover pop/R&B hits between 1960 and 1970. Her reading of ballads ("All I Could Do Was Cry" and "At Last" being notable examples) and uptempo material (the definitive reading of "Something's Got a Hold of Me") presaged the Soul music movement to come. After several bouts with drugs and drinking, she is recording and touring again, her incredibly soulful voice delivering the goods every time, making her new recordings every bit as satisfying as her old classics. —*Cub Koda*

○ **Second Time Around** / 1961 / Chess 9287
This was the followup to Etta James's debut Chess album *At Last*, and was very much in the same mold: big orchestra productions, arranged and conducted by Riley Hampton, over which she crooned mostly '40s standards with a couple of R&B/rockin' cuts. James dropped that formula after this LP, but it was a great side of her singing talents. It includes "Don't Cry Baby" and "Fool That I Am." —*Roundup Newsletter*

○ **At Last** / 1961 / Chess 9266
Most of these are also on *Greatest Sides*. Those that are not, are well worth hearing. —*George Bedard*

○ **Rocks the House** / 1964 / MCA 9184
James tears it up on this live 1964 recording. Highlights include incredible versions of Jimmy Reed's "Baby What You Want Me to Do" and B. B. King's "Sweet Little Angel." James at her scorching best. —*Cub Koda*

○ **Tell Mama** / 1968 / Chess 9269
More fine '60s Chess sides. —*George Bedard*

○ **Sweetest Peaches/Chess Years, The** / 197z / Chess 6028
The third compilation in the outstanding *The Chess Years* series chronicles Etta James's sides cut for Chess from 1960 to 1975, all the years this tough R&B/soul queen recorded for the label. Even if you have the out-of-print *Peaches* collection or her *Greatest Sides* LP, there is much here not on those. The album and cassette each have 20 tracks, and the CDs have 12 apiece, 2 extra cuts on each, with her biggest hits, "Something's Got a Hold on Me," "Stop the Wedding," and her signature soul-belter "Tell Mama," alongside three singles never before on LP, "Miss Pitiful" (an adaption of Otis Redding's "Mr. Pitiful"), "Lovin' Arms," and her Chess recording of "W.O.M.A.N." The liner notes are by Roberta Penn, who has been writing James's authorized biography, and James is not holding back some of the sordid details. —*Roundup Newsletter*

○ **Her Greatest Sides** / 1987 / Chess 9110
This album contains most of James's greatest '60s Chess and Cadet singles. Soul with a vengeance. —*George Bedard*

○ **R&B Dynamite** / 1987 / Virgin 91695
A young, sultry Etta James is in fine voice here. Stellar backing from the bands of Johnny Otis and Maxwell Davis in Los Angeles and Cosimo Matassa in New Orleans. The New Orleans sessions feature Lee Allen, Harold Battiste, Dave Bartholomew, and Earl Palmer—all veterans of recordings with Fats Domino and Little Richard. Includes "W-O-M-A-N," "Good Rockin' Daddy," "The Pick Up," "Market Place," "Tough Lover," and more. —*Roundup Newsletter*

★ **Essential Etta James, The** / 1993 / Chess Records
Etta James's best Chess sides are collected on this terrific two-CD collection that lives up to its title. —*AMG*

Skip James (Nehemiah Curtis James)

b. 1902, d. 1969

Vocals, guitar / Acoustic Delta blues

Among the earliest and most influential Delta bluesmen to record, Skip James was the best-known proponent of the so-called Bentonia school of blues players, a genre strain invested with as much fanciful scholarly "research" as any. Setting an odd-ball guitar tuning against eerie, falsetto vocals, James's early recordings could make the hair stand up on the back of your neck. It was even more surprising when blues scholars rediscovered him in the '60s and found his singing and playing skills intact. He influenced everyone from a young Robert Johnson (James's "Devil Got My Woman" became the basis of Johnson's "Hellhound on My Trail") to Eric Clapton (who recorded James's "I'm So Glad" on the first Cream album). Although James's music is from a commonly shared regional tradition, it remains infused with his own unique personal spirit. —Cub Koda

○ **She Lyin'** / 1964 / Genes
This mid-'60s album features songs James recorded for the Adelphi label in 1964 that were never issued. They range from his signature song "Devil Got My Woman" to the poignant "Broke and Hungry," the engimatic title tune, the interesting "Black Gal" and "Crow Jane," and the exciting "Goin' Away to Stay," "Cypress Grove Blues," and "Look Down the Road." Once again, it's hard to understand why this wasn't issued at the time it was recorded. It's just as solid as the albums James recorded for Columbia during the same period. —Ron Wynn

☆ **Skip James Today!** / 1965 / Vanguard 19001
As quiet as it was kept then, Skip James might have made the best music of anyone who resurfaced during the mid-'60s "discovery" era for Mississippi country blues types. Certainly, there weren't many albums made during that time as good as this one; wonderful vocals, superb guitar and a couple of tunes with tasty piano make this an essential date. —Ron Wynn

Devil Got My Woman / 1968 / Vanguard 79273
Fine blues-revival sides from a very influential artist. —Barry Lee Pearson

★ **Complete 1931 Session** / 1986 / Yazoo 1072
A magnificent sampler of the '30s repertoire of a major Mississippi artist. Blues, ballads, and religious songs are included among the major songs from this idiosyncratic musical genius who has influenced current artists such as John Cephas. —Barry Lee Pearson

Blind Lemon Jefferson

b. Jul. 11, 1897, Couchman, TX, d. Dec. 1929
Vocals, guitar / Blues, Texas acoustic blues
One of the first blues guitar stars, Blind Lemon Jefferson went on to become the most famous bluesman of the Roaring Twenties. His 78s shattered racial barriers, becoming popular from coast to coast and influencing a generation of musicians. His best songs forged original, imagistic themes with inventive arrangements and brilliantly improvised solos. He was a serious showman, balancing a driving, unpredictable guitar style with a booming, two-octave voice. His guitar became a second voice that complemented rather than repeated his lyrics. He often halted rhythm at the end of vocal lines to launch into elaborate solo flourishes, and he could play in unusual meters with a greal deal of drive and flash. A man well acquainted with booze, gambling, and heavy-hipped mamas, Blind Lemon lived the rough-and-tumble themes that dominate his songs. Portraits of Afro-American life during the early 1900s, his lyrics create a unique body of poetry—humorous and harrowing, jivey and risqué, a stunning view of society from the perspective of someone at the bottom. To this day, he ranks among the most gifted and individualistic artists in blues history. —Jas Obrecht

○ **Complete Recorded Works, Vol. 1** / 1901 / Document 5020
A four-volume set of Jefferson's complete recordings, sequenced in chronological order. —Jas Obrecht

○ **Blind Lemon Jefferson** / Mar. 1961 / Milestone 47022
The legendary Blind Lemon Jefferson was the embodiment and symbol of the early country blues, influencing great bluesmen for nearly half a century. The 25 tracks here were originally issued as 78 RPM singles on the Paramount label and reissued on LP by Milestone in 1974. Titles include "Jack o' Diamonds Blues," "That Black Snake Moan," "Broke and Hungry," "Matchbox Blues," and "Long Distance Moan." Due to space limitations, several tracks from the double LP reissue have been deleted from this disc. —Roundup Newsletter

★ **King of the Country Blues** / 1985 / Yazoo 1069

Jefferson was the most popular male blues artist of the '20s, and here's why! Superior sound. —Jas Obrecht

One Dime Blues / Aldabra 1006
Blind Lemon Jefferson was the first artist to introduce country blues to a national audience. His contribution to the lyric tradition of blues cannot be overstated. Beginning in 1925 for Paramount, he recorded a hundred tracks before his death four years later. Collected here are 16 of his best, including "Black Snake Moan" and "Corrina Blues," later recorded by Bob Dylan. —Roundup Newsletter

Big Jack Johnson

Vocals, guitar / Modern electric blues
A member of Frank Frost's Jelly Roll Kings. Johnson's powerful voice and biting guitar evokes comparisons with Magic Slim, but Johnson has a rougher flavor to his blues. —Cub Koda

● **Oil Man, The** / 1987 / Earwig 4910
A solid album from a fine, down-home artist, with "I'm Gonna Give Up Disco and Go Back to the Blues." —Cub Koda

Jimmy Johnson

b. Nov. 25, 1928, Holly Springs, MS
Vocals, guitar, sometimes keyboards, harmonica / Modern electric blues, Chicago Blues
Jimmy Johnson grew up in a blues family, sang gospel in his early years, established himself in Chicago (playing soul and R&B), and then switched back to the blues in the mid-'70s. Now recognized as one of Chicago's finest blues singers and guitarists, Johnson performs with an emotion and commitment that belie his claim that he only turned to the blues because he couldn't get jobs playing more "commercial" music. Johnson's blues are distinguished by high gospel-rooted vocals (not unlike his brother Syl Johnson) and string-bending guitar from the Otis Rush/Albert King school. —Jim O'Neal

Johnson's Whacks / 1979 / Delmark 644
His ambitious domestic debut exhibits a witty, irreverent, lyrical approach. —Bill Dahl

North/South / 1982 / Delmark 647
Funkier than his Delmark debut. Johnson's soaring vocals stand out. —Bill Dahl

● **Bar Room Preacher** / 1983 / Alligator 4744
This record contains mostly covers, but it's still the best representation of Johnson's slashing style. —Bill Dahl

Johnnie Johnson

R&B, Rock & Roll, Blues piano
A great boogie-woogie pianist, Johnnie Johnson's a self-taught player who's integrated the influence of Meade "Lux" Lewis, Earl Hines, and Clarence "Pinetop" Smith into his own highly delightful style. Johnson's professional career began after he ended a stint in the Army in 1946. His association with Chuck Berry began in 1952, when he hired Berry as the guitarist for his Sir John Trio. Berry shortly graduated to head songwriter and then group leader. Berry was signed to a Chess solo deal after Muddy Waters suggested the group audition. Berry recruited Johnson for the sessions, and his flaming piano riffs and licks were a vital ingredient on all of Berry's fabulous singles. Berry's been quoted as saying "Johnny B. Goode" was written for Johnson. After leaving Berry in the '60s, Johnson played for a time with Albert King. He began heading his own band in the '70s. Johnson was featured in the Berry concert/retrospective film *Hail! Hail! Rock and Roll* and played on Keith Richards's debut solo release. He's recorded as a leader for Pulsar and Elektra, and also recorded with the Kentucky Headhunters. —Ron Wynn

Blue Hand Johnnie / 1988–90 / Evidence 26017
Johnson's rolling, barrelling licks are as enticing as ever on this CD, but there are some other things that are not so grand. These include barely tolerable vocalists Barbara Carr and Stacy Johnson, whose enthusiasm is commendable, but their vocals often get in the way. Johnson's covers of Fats Washington's "O.J. Blues" and "Black Nights" are great, as are his versions of "Honky Tonk" and "See See Rider." It's a decent effort that might have been a superior one with a couple of added touches. —Ron Wynn

○ **Rockin' Eighty-Eight** / Apr. 1990 / Modern Blues 1201

Three underrated pianists, Clayton Love, Johnnie Johnson, and Jimmy Vaughn, typify the St. Louis Blues piano tradition on this solid sender. —*Bill Dahl*

● **Johnnie B. Bad** / 1991 / Nonesuch 61149
Keith Richards, Eric Clapton, and various NRBQ members guest on this pianist's inconsistent major-label debut. —*Bill Dahl*

Lonnie Johnson (Alonzo Johnson)

b. Feb. 8, 1889, New Orleans, LA, **d.** Jun. 16, 1970, Toronto, Canada
Vocals, guitar, sometimes piano, violin, harmonium / Acoustic and electric Chicago blues, Blues and jazz
A guitarist and vocalist with a career spanning over 40 years (born Alonzo Johnson). Working with everyone from Louis Armstrong to Duke Ellington, Lonnie Johnson may have been the most durable of all the bluesmen. Certainly, few could even come close to his versatility. With jazz orchestras, small groups, piano-guitar duos, and solo, he recorded everything from low-down blues and the then-popular hokum style to duets with jazz guitarist Eddie Lang. Johnson's backup work behind vocalists or as part of a larger group (he soloed on one of the earliest versions of "Stardust") is as interesting as any of his better-known solo sides. His execution and knowledge of his instrument was a major influence on a young Robert Johnson (some of whose more obscure numbers are virtual homages to his namesake) and other Delta bluesmen, and he was lauded as a well-known recording star.
Lonnie Johnson was primarily noted for the cleanly picked, highly intricate patterns used on his turnarounds. Though his recording career goes as far back as 1925, Johnson had an R&B hit with the self-penned ballad "Tomorrow Night" in 1948. He recorded for folk labels in the '60s, mostly using an electric guitar, as durable and versatile as ever. —*Cub Koda*

○ **Losing Game** / 1960 / Bluesville 543
This 1960 solo session finds blues crooner/guitar master Lonnie Johnson digging into tunes like "What a Difference a Day Makes" and "Summertime." Also includes a rare instance of Johnson accompanying himself on piano ("Evil Woman") and a sublime guitar instrumental ("Slow and Easy"). —*Roundup Newsletter*

★ **Blues & Ballads** / 1960 / Bluesville 531
Later Johnson, doing blues and ballads with jazz guitarist Elmer Snowden. Johnson's vocals are refined and sensitive. It is hard to hear him sing his own composition "I Found a Dream" and remain unmoved. Such a lovely album. —*Michael Erlewine*

Idle Hours / Jul. 1961 / Bluesville 518
Singer/guitarist Lonnie Johnson and singer Victoria Spivey had recorded a number of best-selling sides together between 1925 and 1929. After 32 years had elapsed, the two were reunited for this 1961 Bluesville session, but they hit it off in the studio as if no time had passed at all. Songs include "End It All" and the title track. —*Roundup Newsletter*

Complete Folkways Recordings, The / 1967 / Smithsonian/Folkways
Later sides that vary stylistically from bitter blues to sweet ballads. —*Bill Dahl*

Blues By / 1979 / Bluesville 502
This 1960 release marked the comeback of one of the giants of blues and jazz guitar. Lonnie Johnson had given up on the music business by the late 1950s, but was enticed from his position as a janitor in a Philadelphia hotel to record this, the first of five albums for the Prestige subsidiary, Bluesville. Twelve tracks, including "No Love for Sale," "She Devil," "She's Drunk Again," and "Blues 'Round My Door." —*Roundup Newsletter*

○ **Originator of Modern Guitar Blues, The** / 1980 / Blues Boy
Here's later Lonnie Johnson, demonstrating his proficiency on everything from pop to blues and R&B. It's excellently remastered, sequenced, and presented, covering '40s and '50s cuts. —*Ron Wynn*

★ **Steppin' on the Blues** / 1991 / CBS 46221
A fine collection of 19 blues, ragtime, and pop songs from one of the best guitarists, vocalists, and composers around. —*Barry Lee Pearson*

○ **Complete Recorded Works, Vol. 1 (1925–32)** / 1991 / Document 5069
A fantastic seven-CD collection of Johnson's earliest works. Includes "Bed of Sand," "Treat 'Em Right," "Woke Up with the

Blues in My Fingers," "When a Man Is Treated like a Dog," "Have to Change Keys to Play These Blues," "Blues Is Only a Ghost," "Not the Chump I Used to Be," and the romantic "She's Making Whoopee in Hell Tonight." —*Cub Koda*

Complete Recorded Works, Vol. 1 (1937–40) / 1992 / Document 5
Two CDs from a full decade of Lonnie's best, featuring "Man Killing Broad," "I'm Nuts over You," and "Laplegged Drunk Again." —*Cub Koda*

Luther Johnson

b. Aug. 30, 1934, **d.** Mar. 18, 1976
Guitar / Electric Blues
One among many Luther Johnson's, this one's vocal quality and guitar style are closest to Muddy Waters's. But he was no mere imitator; Johnson's playing and singing had sufficient power and authority to stand on its own. He began playing guitar as a child, and honed his skills while serving a reform school stretch for running away from home. Johnson sang in gospel groups around Milwaukee in the early '50s, before forming a blues trio in the late '50s. He worked with Elmore James in the early '60s, then joined Muddy Waters's band in the mid-'60s. He stayed with the band until 1970, recording with it and with Otis Spann for Spivey, Bluesway, and Douglas. He appeared at several festivals in the '70s, and toured almost up until his death in '75. —*Ron Wynn*

○ **Come on Home** / 1969 / Douglas 789

● **Lonesome in My Bedroom** / Dec. 18, 1975 / Evidence 26005
This was Johnson's final album before his death in 1976, and it was originally cut for Black and Blue (now reissued with three bonus tracks). While various tracks, among them "Long Distance Call," "Hush, Hush," and "Please Don't Take My Baby Nowhere" reflect the influence of Waters, Jimmy Reed, and John Lee Hooker, respectively, Johnson's own inimitable vocals, raspy lines, and tart guitar eventually create his own aura. He is nicely backed by the great drummer Fred Below, plus bassist Dave Myers, guitar burner Lonnie Brooks, and the solid rhythm work of Hubert Sumlin. This was a fine final session for a good, occasionally outstanding blues artist. —*Ron Wynn*

Luther "Guitar Jr." Johnson

b. Apr. 11, 1939, Itta Bena, MS
Vocals, guitar / Modern electric blues, Blues
A solid Chicago bluesman in the West Side tradition of Magic Sam, Johnson toured the world with the Muddy Waters band from 1973 to 1980. He parlayed his Chicago credentials into a new career as a bandleader and a popular act on the East Coast blues-bar circuit after moving to Boston. (Johnson should not be, but often has been, confused with another ex-Muddy Waters sideman named Luther Johnson (1934–76) who also moved from Chicago to Boston; Luther "Houserocker" Johnson, from Atlanta, GA, is yet a different artist.) —*Jim O'Neal*

Luther's Blues / Nov. 1, 1976 / Evidence 26010
Though not in either Buddy Guy or Otis Rush's class as a pure soloist, Johnson could match them in dramatic personna, pacing a song and weaving a narrative. This good natured set was recorded for Black and Blue in 1976 and was recently reissued by Evidence with three bonus cuts, one of them a nice nod to Chuck Berry via a cover of "Little Queenie." —*Ron Wynn*

Doin' the Sugar Too / 1984 / Rooster Blues 7607
The group Roomful of Blues provides swinging support. —*Bill Dahl*

● **I Want to Groove with You** / 1990 / Bullseye Blues 9506
An excellent outing by this former Chicago guitarist. Full of blazing integrity. —*Bill Dahl*

It's Good to Me / 1992 / Bullseye Blues 9516
Johnson and his band, the Magic Rockers, tear into Chicago blues, country blues, and soulful testifying on this new release. The dozen tracks include covers of Waters's "Deep Down in Florida" and Howlin' Wolf's "I'm Leaving You" as well as originals like "Raise Your Window," "Come on Back to Me," and the funkified title cut. — *Roundup Newsletter*

Luther "Houserocker" Johnson

Vocals, guitar / Modern electric blues

The latest Luther Johnson to add his name to the blues directory is an adept singer/guitarist who is a current favorite on the Atlanta blues scene. Proficient in various shadings of the electric blues idiom, Johnson has recently extended his repertoire from covers of blues standards to his own material, performed with the same '50s/'60s flavor. —*Jim O'Neal*

● **Houserockin' Daddy** / Ichiban 9010
Johnson is a traditional electric bluesman (now living and working in the Atlanta, GA, area) who was heavily influenced by Jimmy Reed. The album includes covers of Jimmy Reed, Lightnin' Slim, Howlin' Wolf, and Guitar Slim tunes. Simple, driving, to the point, streamlined, no-frills blues. —*Niles J. Frantz*

Robert Johnson

b. May 8, 1911, Hazlehurst, MS, d. Aug. 16, 1938, Greenwood, MS
Vocals, guitar / Indie, Acoustic Delta blues
Robert Johnson lived his blues, spending most of his life wandering the Depression-era South. An inveterate womanizer and drinker, he performed mostly at juke joints, levee camps, and street corners. While his slide- and finger-style playing drew from the work of Son House, Charley Patton, Willie Brown, Lonnie Johnson, Kokomo Arnold, and others, his amazing finesse made him the most sophisticated of the Delta bluesmen. (His former traveling partner Johnny Shines remembers him as something of a human jukebox, able to play almost anything after a single listening.) Robert could blend his guitar and lyrics into one inseparable voice, and the 29 songs he recorded form a uniquely passionate and poetic body of work. His playing had an immediate impact on his contemporaries and inspired generations of players ranging from Muddy Waters in the '40s to Eric Clapton in the '60s and Steve Vai in the '90s. A half-century after Johnson's murder, the emotion-charged voice, troubled lyrics, and superb guitarmanship of "Cross Road Blues," "Rambling on My Mind," "Kindhearted Woman Blues," "Sweet Home Chicago," and "I'll Believe I'll Dust My Broom" remain as fresh and potent as any blues ever recorded. —*Jas Obrecht*

○ **King of the Delta Blues Singers** / 1966 / CBS 1654
Until *The Complete Recordings* was issued, *King of the Delta Blues Singers* was the definitive Robert Johnson; it was the record that influenced many blues and rock players of the '60s. Even with the release of the two-CD set, it has lost none of its value, since it offers many of his greatest songs—including "Stones in My Passway," "Come On in My Kitchen," "Terraplain Blues," "Crossroads Blues," and "Hellhound on My Trail." —*Stephen Thomas Erlewine*

○ **King of the Delta Blues Singers, Vol. 2** / 1970 / CBS 30034
A truly excellent collection of Johnson's other material, almost as good as the first volume of this pair. A must for any collector. —*Barry Lee Pearson*

★ **Complete Recordings, The** / 1990 / CBS 46222
Among the most impressive blues ever recorded. Absolutely essential! —*Jas Obrecht*

Tommy Johnson

b. 1896, Terry, MS, d. Nov. 1, 1956, Crystal Springs, MS
Vocals, guitar, kazoo / Acoustic Delta blues
One of the great Delta musicians of the late '20s and early '30s, Johnson was influenced by Charley Patton and Dick Bankston. But he soon developed his own style and became highly influential in his own right, with Howlin' Wolf, Floyd Jones, and Boogie Bill Webb among his many disciples. —*Cub Koda*

○ **Complete Recorded Works** / 1929 / Document 5001
The complete Victor and Paramount sides from 1928-29, sequenced in chronological order. —*Jas Obrecht*

Curtis Jones

b. Aug. 18, 1906, Naples, TX, d. Sep. 11, 1971, Munich, Germany
Vocals, piano / Electric Chicago blues, Piano blues
A fine piano player and singer, best known for his songs "Lonesome Bedroom Blues" and "Tin Pan Alley." —*Cub Koda*

○ **Lonesome Bedroom Blues** / 1962 / Delmark 605
Introspective solo piano blues, cut shortly before Jones relocated to Europe. —*Bill Dahl*

● **1937-40** / Document 592
A solid collection of Jones's earliest sides. —*Cub Koda*

Floyd Jones

b. Jul. 21, 1917, Marianna, AR, d. Dec. 19, 1989, Chicago, IL
Vocals, guitar / Electric Chicago blues
One of the earliest of the Chicago Maxwell Street gang to record, Jones's mournful voice and rudimentary guitar work in perfect tandem with harmonica man Snooky Pryor and guitarist cousin Moody Jones. —*Cub Koda*

○ **Masters of Modern Blues, Vol. 3** / Testament 22154
Don't be put off by the murky sound on this one, because it features Jones, guitarist Eddie Taylor, harmonica wizard Walter Horton, pianist Otis Spann, and drummer Fred Below playing their hearts out. —*Cub Koda*

Little Johnny Jones

b. Nov. 1, 1924, Jackson, MS, d. Nov. 19, 1964, Chicago, IL
Vocals, harmonica, piano / Piano blues
One of the great blues piano men of all time, Jones is well known for his striking work on a number of seminal sides by slide guitar legend Elmore James. He recorded very little as a solo artist, but what few recordings exist are all classics of the Chicago style. —*Cub Koda*

○ **Johnny Jones W/ Billy Boy Arnold** / 1979 / Alligator 4717
Beautiful but tough Chicago piano blues. Real good. —*Niles J. Frantz*

Charley Jordan

b. 1890, d. Nov. 15, 1954
Acoustic blues
A fine St. Louis guitarist and vocalist, Charley Jordan teamed with many blues luminaries for some fine recordings in the '20s, '30s, and '40s. After traveling throughout the Southeast as a hobo in the '30s, Jordan settled in St. Louis. He played with Memphis Minnie, Roosevelt Sykes, Casey Bill Weldon, Peetie Wheatstraw, and many others. Jordan overcame a permanent spine injury he suffered during a shooting incident in 1928. He recorded for Vocalion and Decca in the '30s, and also doubled as a talent scout for both labels. Jordan worked often with Big Joe Williams in the late '30s and the '40s. —*Ron Wynn*

● **Charley Jordan V.1, 1930-31** / Document 5097
A fine St. Louis singer and guitarist, this was the first volume of songs Charley Jordan did in the early '30s. He could be very humorous or cuttingly poignant, and there are examples in both veins on this anthology. The sound quality ranges from good to awful. —*Ron Wynn*

Willie Kent

Modern electric blues
Among the rare blues bassists who double as bandleaders, Willie Kent's made a couple of good Delmark recordings. Kent moved from Iverness, MS, to Chicago in the '50s, and began playing bass when one of his band members missed a gig. Kent played with Little Walter, Muddy Waters, and Junior Parker in addition to heading his own band. He doubled as a truck driver until a 1987 heart bypass operation, opting since then to be a full-time musician. —*Ron Wynn*

● **Ain't It Nice** / 1991 / Delmark 653
Kent sings and plays bass in front of a seven-piece group that features two guitars, harp (by no less than Lester Davenport), keyboards, and rhythm. Davenport is the only "name" in the group and even he is hardly a star. Maybe that's the secret of this album's success, because it offers some of the best ensemble playing since Muddy's band in the '50s. Band members don't just play together, they play with and off each other, creating a full and powerful sound. The uptempo cuts show off Davenport's exemplary harp style and include "Memory of You," Check It Out," the soul-tinged "Ain't It Nice," and "What You're Doing to Me." Slower cuts, framed by Kent's heartfelt vocals, are "Worry, Worry," "One More Mile," and "Come Home." The latter pair are gut-wrenching emotional experiences, not easily forgotten. On all of these, Kent's vocals and Davenport's harp are never far from each other, one filling in the under-pinning where the other leaves off. —*Kerry Kudlacek, Blues Access*

○ **Too Hurt to Cry** / 1994 / Delmark
If his compositions aren't lyrically transcendent, Kent's rendering of the words elevates them. You never tire of hearing him sing,

and he makes you feel and believe his messages, even as his backing band plugs in familiar progressions and lines behind him. Indeed, it's only when Kent covers someone else's music, notably "The Night Time Is the Right Time," that things become less interesting. Kent's own blues view is more than enough to hold the attention of blues audiences. —*Ron Wynn*

Albert King

b. Apr. 25, 1923, Indianola, MS, **d.** Dec. 21, 1992
Vocals, guitar / Soul, R&B, Modern electric blues
Albert King first played the guitar in his early teens—at times in a gospel quartet. Albert was in and out of music until the early '50s when, after playing drums for Jimmy Reed, he again took up the guitar and decided to go it on his own. His first single, "Bad Luck Blues"/"Be on Your Merry Way," was recorded for the Parrot label in the early '50s. In the years to follow—and into the '60s—King sang and played his way onto the blues charts with songs such as "Laundromat Blues" and "Don't Throw Your Love on Me So Strong." Then, during the so-called blues revival (the discovery of blues music by a White audience in the '60s), King's recordings of "Born under a Bad Sign" and "Personal Manager" caught the fancy of British blues guitarist Eric Clapton. In fact, Eric Clapton copied King's "Personal Manager" guitar solo note-for-note on the Cream's song "Strange Brew" (*Disraeli Gears* album)—thereby introducing King's style to a new audience. From that point on, King was more famous than ever and began getting more lucrative bookings, including many of the rock clubs of the day, such as the Fillmore Auditorium in San Francisco.

Albert King is truly a "King of the Blues," although he doesn't hold that title (B. B. does). Along with B. B. and Freddie King, Albert King is one of the major influences on blues and rock guitar players. Without him, modern guitar music would not sound as it does, and his style has influenced both Black and White blues players from Otis Rush and Robert Cray to Eric Clapton and Stevie Ray Vaughan (Stevie Ray was especially influenced by King). It's important to note that while almost all modern blues guitarists seldom play for long without falling into a B. B. King guitar cliche, Albert King never does—he's had his own style and unique tone from the beginning.

Albert King plays guitar left-handed, without restringing the guitar from the right-handed setup; this "upside-down" playing accounts for his difference in tone, since he pulls down on the same strings that most players push up on when bending the blues notes. King's massive tone and totally unique way of squeezing bends out of a guitar string has had a major impact. Many young White guitarists—especially rock & rollers—have been influenced by King's playing without even knowing it. Many players who emulate his style may never have heard of Albert King, let alone heard his music. His style is immediately distinguishable from all other blues guitarists, and he's one of the most important blues guitarists to ever pick up the electric guitar. Albert King is a tough act to follow. —*Daniel Erlewine*

☆ **Born under a Bad Sign** / 1967 / Mobile Fidelity 577
King's original album for Stax features many of his classics, now part and parcel of the language of the blues. Includes the title cut and "Crosscut Saw." —*Cub Koda*

○ **Live Wire/Blues Power** / 1968 / Stax 4128
Powerful 1968 live set at the Fillmore West. —*Bill Dahl*

○ **Years Gone By** / 1969 / Stax 8522
Typically inspired Stax work from the King of the Flying V. —*Bill Dahl*

○ **Albert King: King of the Blues Guitar** / 1969 / Atlantic 42183
No blues guitarist who emerged during the '60s wielded more influence. This incendiary collection contains his best '60s workouts for Stax. —*Bill Dahl*

○ **I'll Play the Blues for You** / 1972 / Stax 8513
A moody, R&B-influenced set with plenty of intensity. —*Bill Dahl*

I Wanna Get Funky / 1974 / Stax 8536
Another very solid, early-'70s outing. —*Bill Dahl*

Tomato Years / 197z / Rhino/Tomato
This anthology culls 14 cuts from his Tomato releases, among them slashing numbers "Blues at Sunrise" and "I'm Gonna Call You Soon As the Sun Goes Down," that vividly illustrated King's guitar prowess. Others like "Truckload of Lovin'," and "We All

Wanna Boogie" show how he skillfully crammed moments of inspiration into formulaic outings. —*Ron Wynn*

I'm in a Phone Booth, Baby / 1984 / Stax 8560
King's last studio album. Still tough. —*Bill Dahl*

Blues at Sunrise: Live at Montreux / 1988 / Stax 8546
A searing live set from the 1973 Montreux Jazz Festival. —*Bill Dahl*

○ **Let's Have a Natural Ball** / 1989 / Modern Blues 723
Great compilation of King's Bobben sides of the late '50s and early '60s. —*Bill Dahl*

Wednesday Night in San Francisco: Recorded Live at the Fillmore Auditorium / 1990 / Stax 8556
Recorded live at San Francisco's Fillmore in June, 1968, this album finds blues maven Albert King applying his vocal and guitar skills to tracks like "I Get Evil," "Born under a Bad Sign," and the sly "Personal Manager." —*Roundup Newsletter*

Thursday Night in San Francisco: Recorded Live at the Fillmore Auditorium / 1990 / Stax 8557
This album features material from Albert King's second night at the Fillmore in June, 1968, including "You Upset Me Baby," "Drifting Blues," and the sharp-edged "Crosscut Saw." It's no wonder he was one of the late Stevie Ray Vaughan's favorite guitarists. —*Roundup Newsletter*

★ **Ultimate Collection** / 1993 / Rhino
A solid, two-CD anthology of most of this highly influential artist's best sides. Although his seminal sides for the King label are not included due to licensing restrictions, this truly is the best place to start as it features all the hits and much great guitar playing from Albert. —*Cub Koda*

B. B. King (Riley B. King)

b. Sep. 16, 1925, Indianola, MS
Vocals, guitar / R&B, Modern electric blues
Born Riley B. King, B. B. King is perhaps the most important and influential electric guitarist ever. Inspired by Lonnie Johnson, Django Reinhardt, T-Bone Walker, Elmore James, and Blind Lemon Jefferson, B. B. studied their music and then took the electric guitar to new heights by developing a blues guitar "vibrato"—used primarily for soloing—that hadn't previously existed. B. B.'s vibrato (his method of trilling, slurring, or bending the string) has become the major lead guitar "tool" of every blues and rock guitarist since—White or Black.

Now known as "The King of the Blues," B. B.'s roots are in the music of the Mississippi Delta and Southern church choirs. Within the Black community B. B. has been a famous recording artist and entertainer from the late '40s until the present, so when White audiences "discovered" the blues in the '60s, B. B. was already on top and was finally greeted by a worldwide audience. Since then, Mr. King has received more awards and honors in recognition of his music than could ever be listed here (Grammy, Best R&B Vocal by a Male in 1970 for "The Thrill Is Gone"; Honorary Doctor of Music, Yale University) and has toured the world many times over, playing for presidents, kings, and world leaders.

B. B. is as great a singer as he is a guitarist, his vocal artistry influencing the styles of the younger Texas bluesmen—from Freddie King and Magic Sam to Luther Allison and Mighty Joe Young. Fame has never changed B. B. King, either. He's a humble entertainer who names his audience as the reason for his greatness. B. B. lives for his music, and he still plays some 150+ engagements a year! —*Daniel Erlewine*

★ **Live at the Regal** / 1965 / MCA 31106
Full of some amazingly inspired moments, King's *Live at the Regal* (arguably his finest album) outdistances his usual rock-solid studio efforts. Recorded in November 1964, the album is nothing short of magical, one of the greatest live performances ever committed to tape, ranking with James Brown's classic *Live at the Apollo 1962*. King's rendering of "How Blue Can You Get" is sure to convert anyone resistant to the power of the blues. —*Rick Clark*

○ **Blues on Top of Blues** / 1967 / Bluesway 6011
One of his best ABC albums. —*Bill Dahl*

His Best—The Electric B.B. King / 1968 / Bluesway 6022
Very solid effort. —*Bill Dahl*

Lucille / 1968 / MCA 10518

This 1968 release is notable for the ten-minute title track, in which B.B. King proclaims his devotion to his guitar. The song has since become a staple in King's live shows. The other eight songs on this disc also feature his deeply emotional vocals and jolting guitar lines of pure blues. A band that includes organist Maxwell Davis and pianist Lloyd Glenn backs him up on tunes like the rollicking "Watch Yourself." —*Roundup Newsletter*

Live & Well / 1969 / MCA 31191
Another enjoyable collection. —*Bill Dahl*

○ **Completely Well** / 1969 / MCA 31039
Contains "The Thrill Is Gone"; his big crossover album. —*Bill Dahl*

Indianola Mississippi Seeds / 1970 / MCA 31343
B.B. King hasn't made many better pop-flavored albums than this '70 date. Besides making Leon Russell's "Hummingbird" sound like his own composition, King showed you can put the blues into any situation and make it work. Carole King was one of several pop luminaries who did more than just hang on for the ride. —*Ron Wynn*

○ **Live at Cook County Jail** / 1971 / MCA 31080
A burning, intense performance from the master of modern blues, in front of a captive audience. The best live version King ever recorded of "The Thrill Is Gone." —*Cub Koda*

○ **Memphis Masters** / 1982 / ACE 50
Only the absence of substantial or even minimal recording information keeps this from being a showcase release. The songs, culled from early '50s sessions, are formative King material and should be closely studied by the hordes who only know King from overarranged major label LPs and "Tonight Show" appearances. —*Ron Wynn*

Blues 'n' Jazz / Aug. 1983 / MCA 27119
Swinging session that plays to King's strengths. —*Bill Dahl*

○ **Do the Boogie** / 1989 / ACE 916
Great early sides from Modern vaults. —*Bill Dahl*

★ **Best of B. B. King, Vol. 1, The** / 1991 / Flair 91691
Transferred off the original master tapes, this compilation of King's earlier work with the Kent, RPM, and Modern labels sounds surprisingly full, with fairly clean highs and a respectable bottom end. The performances shine through, with "Everyday I Have the Blues," "Sweet Little Angel," and "You Don't Know" being some of the highlights. —*Rick Clark*

○ **Spotlight on Lucille** / 1991 / Flair 91693
Fans of King's jazzy big-band synthesis with electric blues should be in heaven with this smartly compiled release. A collection of instrumentals from King's work with the Kent, Modern, and RPM labels that feature plenty of his heartfelt guitar style. —*Rick Clark*

☆ **King of the Blues** / 1992 / MFP 50259
A four-CD box spanning King's entire career, *King of the Blues* is worth its hefty price tag for most fans. Although some listeners might want more early material (which is not easily available on CD) and the original versions of some of his signature songs, *King of the Blues* offers a balanced, complete portrait of this seminal guitarist. —*AMG*

☆ **Singin' the Blues/The Blues** / 1992 / Capitol 86296
Two great original Crown albums from the '50s on one CD, including most of King's Top Ten R&B hits from the period: "3 O'Clock Blues," "Please Love Me," "You Upset Me Baby," "You Know I Love You," "Woke Up This Morning," and "Sweet Little Angel," plus one of his best, "Crying Won't Help You." This is the stuff that was so hugely influential to other blues guitarists and singers in its original recorded version. Here is lots of the real early, gritty stuff: "That Ain't the Way to Do It," "When My Heart Beats Like a Hammer," "Don't You Want a Man Like Me." The guitar intro to "Early in the Morning" is one of the finest examples of King in a jazzy mode. Great guitar! —*George Bedard*

○ **My Sweet Little Angel** / Oct. 5, 1993 / Flair
Fine collection of mid- to late-1950s sides. Particularly stirring is the torrid instrumental "String Bean," a true jaw dropper. Plenty of rarities and alternate takes make this one a collector's dream. —*Bill Dahl*

Earl King

b. Feb. 7, 1934, New Orleans, LA
Vocals, guitar / Soul, R&B, Electric New Orleans blues

One of the key figures in New Orleans blues and R&B, Earl King has been a constant presence either on or behind the scenes for more than 40 years. From powerful blues à la Guitar Slim (a huge influence on King's early work for Specialty) and South Louisiana–style ballads to classic New Orleans "second line" rhythms and contemporary R&B, King has proven his mastery time and again. He has produced or written songs for most of the major New Orleans artists, including Fats Domino and Professor Longhair, as well as recording hits of his own such as "Those Lonely, Lonely Nights" (Ace, 1955) and "Trick Bag" (Imperial, 1962). King also did the original version of "Come On," later repopularized by Jimi Hendrix. —*Jim O'Neal*

Street Parade / 1981 / Charly 2021
Funky second-line beats predominate on this joyous collection. —*Bill Dahl*

○ **Let the Good Times Roll** / 1983 / ACE 2029
This collection originally came out on the British Ace label in the early '80s. It includes "Darling Honey Angel Child," which evolved into "Come On" (a/k/a "Let the Good Times Roll"); "Everybody's Carried Away," one of his catchiest rock & roll numbers; the hit "Those Lonely Lonely Nights;" and more. —*Roundup Newsletter*

● **Trick Bag** / 1983 / EMI America 17238
Funky, irresistible early-'60s R&B, with King's guitar brought to the fore. —*Bill Dahl*

Glazed / 1988 / Black Top 1035
Less of an overt New Orleans second-line feel, and plenty of well-written originals. —*Bill Dahl*

○ **Sexual Telepathy** / 1990 / Black Top 1052
King's piercing guitar and charming vocals are prominent on this exceptional modern New Orleans blues set. —*Bill Dahl*

Freddie King (Freddy King)

b. Sep. 3, 1934, Gilmer, TX, d. Dec. 28, 1976, Dallas, TX
Vocals, guitar / Modern electric blues

An influential blues guitarist and singer who rode to early-'60s fame with a spate of catchy instrumentals that became instant bandstand fodder for fellow bluesmen and White rock bands alike. Employing a more down-home (thumb- and finger-picks) approach to the B. B. King single-string style of playing, Freddie went on to late-'60s/early-'70s success. He recorded for a variety of labels and was one of the first bluesmen to employ a racially integrated group onstage behind him. Influenced by Eddie Taylor, Jimmy Rogers, and Robert Jr. Lockwood, King influenced the likes of Eric Clapton, Mick Taylor, Stevie Ray Vaughan, and Lonnie Mack, among others. —*Cub Koda*

○ **Freddy King Sings** / Jan. 1961 / Modern Blues 722
Great stuff from this influential Texas bluesman—the haunting "Lonesome Whistle Blues," "I'm Tore Down," and other classics. From the B. B. school, but with his own searing style of singing and playing. A must for fans of modern blues. —*George Bedard*

○ **Hide Away** / 1969 / Starday 5033
Fine retrospective of early work. —*Bill Dahl*

Texas Cannonball / 1972 / Dcc 8018
King's sound began to change into a more rock slanted mode with his Shelter LPs. —*Bill Dahl*

Burglar / 1974 / BGO 137
An even more rock oriented album, but still quite powerful. —*Bill Dahl*

17 Hits / 1977 / King 5012
Good retrospective of his Federal sides. —*Bill Dahl*

○ **Just Pickin'** / 1986 / Modern Blues 721
Both of Freddie's all-instrumental albums for the King label (*Let's Hide Away and Dance Away with Freddy King* and *Freddy King Gives You a Bonanza of Instrumentals*) on one CD. "Hide Away," "The Stumble," and "San-Ho-Zay" influenced guitarists on both sides of the Atlantic. —*Cub Koda*

★ **Hide Away: The Best of Freddie King** / Rhino
Though not always placed in the upper echelon of blues performers alongside the other Kings (B.B. and Albert), Freddie King was a dynamo. He was both a powerhouse, fiery, imaginative guitarist and a glorious, soulful vocalist who could belt out come-ons, shout with gusto, or wail in anguish. His instrumentals were also catchy, usually simply structured but vigorous and vividly ar-

ticulated. This tremendous 20-cut compilation from his time on King Records includes familiar hits like "Going Down" and the title cut plus the shattering "Have You Ever Loved a Woman" and the poignant "Lonesome Whistle Blues" as well as the entertaining "Remington Ride" and "The Stumble." The tracks are exquisitely remastered, intelligently sequenced, and the notes informative and thorough, without being academic or fawning. —Ron Wynn

Kinsey Report

Group / Rock, Modern electric blues, Chicago Blues
Donald Kinsey (b. May 12, 1953, in Gary, IN), (vocal, guitar); Ralph "Woody" Kinsey, (drums); Kenneth Kinsey, (bass); Ronald Prince, (guitar). Solidly based in the blues as a result of lifelong training in the Big Daddy Kinsey household, the Kinsey scions are also versed in a broad range of music. The older brothers Donald and Ralph had an early blues-rock trio (White Lightnin') in the mid-'70s, long before they regrouped as the Kinsey Report in 1984 and began to launch new excursions into rock. Donald also recorded and toured with Albert King and with Bob Marley, and the influence of those giants (as well as that of Big Daddy Kinsey, naturally) show through in the music of the Kinsey Report. The band expertly covers all the bases from Chicago blues through reggae, rock, funk, and soul, and their recordings are also distinguished by the songwriting talents and self-contained production approach of the Kinseys. —Jim O'Neal

● **Edge of the City** / 1987 / Alligator 4758
An engaging, original blues/rock album from this family band. —Niles J. Frantz

Big Daddy Kinsey (Lester Kinsey)

b. Mar. 18, 1927, Pleasant Grove, MS
Vocals, guitar, harmonica / Modern electric blues, Chicago Blues
Long before Lester "Big Daddy" Kinsey and his clan hit the international blues circuit, he established himself as the modern-day blues patriarch of Gary, IN, and as the Steeltown's answer to Muddy Waters. A slide guitarist and harp blower with roots in both the Mississippi Delta and postwar Chicago styles, Kinsey worked with local bands only long enough for his sons to mature into topflight musicians, and since 1984 (when Big Daddy recorded his debut album, *Bad Situation*) the family act has become one of the hottest attractions in contemporary blues. Big Daddy's material ranges from deep blues in the Muddy Waters vein to hard-rocking blues with touches of funk and even reggae, courtesy of sons Donald and Ralph (who venture even further afield in their own outings as the Kinsey Report). —Jim O'Neal

● **Can't Let Go** / 1990 / Blind Pig 73489
Fine patriarchal blues from this little-known Chicago artist, backed by his sons (Kinsey Report). —Cub Koda

○ **Can't Let Go** / Blind Pig 93489
Decent encore LP, with an emphasis on Kinsey's enduring delta roots. —Bill Dahl

Eddie Kirkland

b. Aug. 16, 1928, Jamaica
Vocals, guitar, harmonica / Modern electric blues
A multitalented artist who was performing essentially in a high-energy blues style years before the genre (or even the term) came into vogue, Kirkland has traversed the many byways of the blues, sometimes to acclaim but often in obscurity. Jamaica-born but Alabama-raised, Kirkland played a seminal role in the Detroit blues scene, recording his first sides there (1952, RPM) in the company of John Lee Hooker. Over the next decade, his style evolved into one of burning intensity, and during the '60s and '70s he fused his blues with raw, hard-edged soul funk. Onstage with a band he was (and is) a pulsating, somersaulting live wire, yet he can also be convincing as an acoustic rural blues act. His recordings find him in or between all these moods and settings, while Kirkland himself might be found living in Georgia, Florida, or the Hudson Valley. He and his music may be off the beaten blues path, but they're well worth the search. —Jim O'Neal

○ **It's the Blues Man!** / 1961 / Original Blues Classics 511
Exuberant and eclectic album featuring King Curtis on sax and Kirkland on guitar and harp. —Bill Dahl

Devil and Other Blues Demons, The / Apr. 1975 / Trix 3308

Eddie Kirkland has long straddled the fence between bluesy soul and soulful blues. His repertoire mixes novelty tunes and pop fare with straight blues and wailing soul. He was at a low point when he recorded for Trix in 1973, but this session recharged him musically, if not saleswise. It is great to have it available again; whether Kirkland is doing such silly numbers as "Spank the Butterfly," offering taut blues licks on "Mink Hollow Slide," or giving examples of his philosophy on "Hard to Raise a Family Today" and "Tell Me, Baby," he finds creative ways to utilize the standard 12-bar scheme. —Ron Wynn

● **Three Shades of the Blues** / 198z / Original Blues Classics 513
Kirkland's eight sides on this compilation are as hard-driving and intense as you could possibly ask for. It also includes four sides each from B. B. King disciple Mr. Bo and the Ohio Untouchables, with dazzling guitar work from Robert Ward on the latter. —Cub Koda

Alexis Korner (Alexis Koerner)

b. Apr. 19, 1928, Paris, France, d. Jan. 1, 1984, London, England
Vocals, guitar / R&B, Electric British blues
The cofounder of British blues (with Cyril Davies), guitarist Alexis Korner never achieved anything like the fame of the younger players who learned from him (among them Charlie Watts, who played in Blues Incorporated). Gifted though he was, Korner lacked the vocal skills or the commercial edge needed for mass success. After splitting up the last of his various incarnations of Blues Incorporated, he began popularizing the blues as the host of a children's TV show. He toured with the Rolling Stones in the mid '70s, and then formed his last (and best) band, Rocket 88, late in the decade, prior to his sudden death in the early '80s. —Bruce Eder

○ **R&B from the Marquee** / 1962 / Ace Of Clubs 1130
Britain's first home-grown blues album to make the U.K. charts is a landmark with good playing, even if none of the flash associated with Korner alumni like the Rolling Stones or Yardbirds is present. —Bruce Eder

○ **Rocket 88** / 1981 / Atlantic 50776
Arguably the best record ever for an offshoot of the Rolling Stones, with Korner on guitar, Ian Stewart on piano, Charlie Watts on drums, and Jack Bruce on upright bass. This has tight, rippling, rollicking interpretations of blues and jazz standards and is a seminal part of any collection. —Bruce Eder

● **Alexis Korner Collection, The** / 1988 / Castle
A strong import anthology featuring Korner's various bands over the years. Probably the best extant collection. —Bruce Eder

The Smokin' Joe Kubek Band

Vocals, guitar / Modern electric Texas blues
Another young Texas axeman from the old school, Smokin' Joe Kubek issued his band's debut disc in 1991 on Bullseye Blues, *Steppin' Out Texas Style*. Kubek was already playing his smokin' guitar on the Lone State chitlin circuit at age 14. The vocalist in his current crew, B'nois King, hails from Monroe, LA, and plays rhythm guitar as well. —Bill Dahl

● **Steppin' out Texas Style** / 1991 / Bullseye Blues 9510
Just like the title says. —Niles J. Frantz

Chain Smokin' Texas Style / 1992 / Bullseye Blues 9524
Listeners who favor hard blues done Texas style should check out this new release by the Smokin' Joe Kubek Band. Kubek lights the torch to his lead, slide, and tremolo guitar arsenal on tracks such as the original "Chain Smokin'" and covers of T-Bone Walker's "Little Girl" and Willie Dixon's "Love to Live the Life." He gets able support from lead vocalist/second guitarist B'nois King, bassist Greg Wright, drummer Phil Campbell, and guests such as saxophonist Jim Spake and organist/producer Ron Levy. —Roundup Newsletter

○ **Texas Cadillac** / 1993 / Bullseye/Rounder
Smokin' Joe Kubek's third Rounder album juggles blues-rock originals with faithful, exuberant covers of Jimmy Reed, Willie Dixon, Muddy Waters, and Little Walter Jacobs (among others) tunes. Kubek's a good, sometimes captivating guitarist and entertaining singer, if not the greatest pure vocalist, and the band rips through the CD's 11 cuts in a relaxed yet passionate fashion. —Ron Wynn

Lazy Lester

b. Jun. 20, 1933, Torras, LA
*Vocals, harmonica, guitar, washboard, percussion / Electric
Louisiana blues*
The definitive swamp-blues harmonica player since the '50s, Lazy
Lester has also become the most active member of the original
down-home Louisiana blues circle on the national performing
circuit today. Lester's harp was once a trademark on Excello labelmate Lightnin' Slim's records, often introduced by Slim's exhortations to "Blow your harmonica, son." Lester's session discography encompassed appearances on a number of recordings by
other Louisiana artists, playing harp, washboard, or impromptu
rhythm accompaniment on cardboard boxes or rolled-up newspapers. He also recorded regularly on his own, and both sides of
his best-known single ("I'm a Lover, Not a Fighter/Sugar Coated
Love," 1959) inspired rock cover versions. Long after Lester left
Louisiana for Pontiac, MI, he recorded a new album on a 1987
tour of England, home to many an Excellophile. With that album,
he bounced back into the spotlight and has continued to delight
blues devotees with his harp, homespun humor, and high spirits.
—*Jim O'Neal*

★ **True Blues** / 196z / Excello 8006
Lester's original album, collecting the best of his early Excello
sides. Includes "Sugar Coated Love," "I Hear You Knockin'," and
"I'm a Lover, Not a Fighter." —*Cub Koda*

○ **Lester's Stomp** / 1987 / Flyright 07
Primitive and rocking '50s sides by an overlooked harmonica ge-
nius who epitomized the ragged-but-right ethic of producer Jay
Miller. —*John Floyd*

○ **Rides Again** / 1988 / Sunjay 377
Lester's original rediscovery album pairs him with English blues
musicians, with surprisingly great results. —*Cub Koda*

Leadbelly (Huddie William Ledbetter)

b. Jan. 20, 1888, Mooringsport, LA, **d.** Dec. 6, 1949, New York, NY
Vocals, guitar, piano, accordion / Acoustic country blues
Huddie Ledbetter is one of the best-known 20th-century folk and
blues singers. Leadbelly had begun putting together his wide
repertoire of blues, gospel, dance tunes, pop songs, and ballads by
about 1900. Leadbelly was primarily known as a 12-string guitar
player, though he also played the piano and accordion. One-and-
a-half years after being "discovered" by John and Alan Lomax at
the Louisiana State Penitentiary in 1933, Ledbetter moved to New
York City. Leadbelly's fame was spread through his personal appearances, radio work, recordings, and the legends that circulated
about this "Sweet Singer of the Swamplands." "Goodnight, Irene"
and "Midnight Special" are the two songs most closely associated
with Leadbelly. His influence upon folk revival musicians like
Woody Guthrie and Pete Seeger was immense. New York City remained Huddie's base of operation until his death in 1949. —*Kip
Lornell*

○ **Good Mornin' Blues (1936–40)** / 1969 / Biograph 12013
Wonderful mid-'30s and early-'40s material from Leadbelly, some
of his finest and most colorful blues tunes and/or good folk numbers as well. —*Ron Wynn*

○ **Leadbelly Sings Folk Songs** / 1990 / Smithsonian/Folkways
3106
Leadbelly was a consummate song stylist; not necessarily a blues
artist, though he certainly could deliver the blues with earnestly
and authority. His forte was taking all types of songs, whether
they be simple, filled with chilling metaphors, funny stories, or
tragic events, and making them unforgettable personal anthems.
That what he does on all 15 cuts on *Leadbelly Sings Folk Songs*,
teaming with such fellow greats as Woody Guthrie, Cisco
Houston, and Sonny Terry. Leadbelly made many great albums
with Folkways; this was certainly among them. —*Ron Wynn*

○ **Alabama Bound** / 1990 / RCA 9600
Wonderful performances from the late '30s, some with the
Golden Gate Quartet. —*Mark A. Humphrey*

☆ **Gwine Dig Hole to Put the Devil In** / 1991 / Rounder 1045
Rounder's second installment of Leadbelly's Library of Congress
Recordings is just as essential as the first edition. —*AMG*

○ **Let It Shine on Me** / 1991 / Rounder 1046
The third volume of Leadbelly's incredible Library of Congress
sessions includes several searing spiritual numbers, among them

"Down in the Valley to Pray," "Must I Be Carried to the Sky," "Run
Sinners," and "You Must Have That Religion, Hallaloo." The CD
begins with a highly informative interview/performance segment
that features Leadbelly answering questions about his life and
stylistic influences, then demonstrating techniques and recounting the origins of particular songs. The disc also contains an interesting rendition of the number "When I Was a Cowboy" and
superb topical tunes "Mr. Hitler," "The Scottsboro Boys," and "The
Roosevelt Song." Leadbelly's mournful, moving, and authoritative
vocals, plus his sometimes surging, sometimes reflective guitar
playing, were never more moving or appealing than during the
Library of Congress sessions. No one should pass on them, regardless of their musical preferences. —*Ron Wynn*

☆ **Midnight Special** / 1991 / Rounder 1044
Leadbelly made the most exciting music of his legendary career
between 1937 and 1942, when he was regularly recording for the
Library of Congress. The original three-record set was unavailable for many years, but in the early '90s Rounder reissued it on
CD. This first volume includes early and brilliant versions of such
Leadbelly classics as "Irene," "Ella Speed," "Midnight Special,"
and "Roberta." There's also the wonderful lament "I'm Sorry
Mama" and the intriguing "You Don't Know My Mind." Leadbelly
was a true vocal and instrumental giant; his guitar playing had a
ragged rhythmic vitality that only underscored the rampaging
quality of his singing. Rounder deserves unqualified praise ·for
putting the series on CD, and anyone who misses it deserves only
jeers. —*Ron Wynn*

○ **Nobody Knows the Trouble I've Seen, Vol. 5** / Mar. 30, 1994 /
Rounder Records
Another excellent installment in Rounder's reissue of Leadbelly's
Library of Congress recordings. —*AMG*

○ **Pickup on This** / Mar. 30, 1994 / Rounder Records
Like the other volumes that came before it, *Pickup on This* is full
of wonderful music and interviews from Leadbelly's Library of
Congress recordings. —*AMG*

○ **Titanic, The** / Mar. 30, 1994 / Rounder Records
This fourth volume of Leadbelly's Library of Congress Recordings
includes several works that he'd previously done and others that
were vigorous reworkings of classic numbers. Unlike some other
sessions, this one wasn't punctuated by interview inserts or remembrances. Instead, except for the last cut, Leadbelly concentrated on his vocals, storytelling, and guitar playing, and offered
some shattering, frequently spectacular singing and instrumental
accompaniment. His energetic, booming pace and swaggering vocals on "Blind Lemon Blues," "Tight Like That" and "I Ain't
Bothered a Bit" demands and gets the listener's full attention. He
bowls through many songs so fiercely, yet manages to make
every word seem important and relay the story in an unforgettable manner. The 19-track CD, which runs over an hour, seems
short when it's completed. That was the power of Leadbelly: You
couldn't get enough of his music. —*Ron Wynn*

★ **King of the 12-String Guitar** / 199z / CBS 46776
From 1935, his first and bluesiest commercial recordings. —*Mark
A. Humphrey*

○ **Convict Blues** / Aldabra 1004
Historic Leadbelly material quite apart from his known discogra-
phy. Leadbelly was discovered by the folklorists John and Alan
Lomax in Louisiana's Angola Prison. He recorded over 130 songs
for them in 1933 and 1934 for the Library of Congress Archives.
However, these titles were recorded by New York's American
Record Corporation in 1935 and were largely unreleased. Among
the 16 titles are "Pig Meat Papa," "Mr. Tom Hughes Town," "Death
Letter Blues," and "New Black Snake Moan." — *Roundup
Newsletter*

○ **Congress Blues** / Aldabra 1007
More historic Leadbelly. However, this collection focuses not on
the blues recordings for labels like A.R.C. and Banner, but on his
masterful, wide-ranging repertoire of every type of American
song. Titles include "Rock Island Line," "Easy Rider," "New York
City," and "Stew-ball." — *Roundup Newsletter*

Frankie Lee

b. 1942, Mart, TX
Vocals / Soul, R&B, Soul blues

Lee, whose early records billed him as Little Frankie Lee, gained some degree of erroneous notoriety among blues collectors who assumed (and stated in print) that he was the son of Texas bluesman Frankie Lee Sims; however, the two were not related, nor is their music similar. Frankie Lee started as a gospel singer, and the flavor and fervor of the church has remained a part of his secular performing style. Influenced by such singers as Little Willie John and Bobby Bland, Lee has recorded sporadically since the early '60s, mostly in a soul or soul/blues style. A long-time fixture on the Oakland blues scene, Lee has recently taken his act East in hopes of hitting the big time that has eluded him despite his renown as a live performer. —Jim O'Neal

○ **Ladies & the Babies** / Apr. 1986 / Hightone 8004
On these soul-styled contemporary blues, Lee's vocals exhibit a strong gospel influence. —Bill Dahl

Legendary Blues Band

Group / Electric Chicago blues
Calvin Jones (b. 1926, Greenwood, MS; bass, violin); Willie Smith (b. 1935, Helena, AR; drum); various others on vocals, guitar, harmonica, piano. When the Muddy Waters band quit the master en masse in 1980, most of the sidemen stuck together and formed their own group. The Legendary Blues Band, as they were named, included Pinetop Perkins, Jerry Portnoy, Willie Smith, and Calvin Jones throughout its early years. Short-term member Louis Myers, another Muddy Waters alumnus, appeared as guitarist on the band's first album. The band has since changed personnel with some regularity, and while its lineup has become progressively less "legendary" in name or historic associations, its music has remained solid and true to the mainstream Chicago style. In a later configuration, they even made the *Billboard* Black Music charts. Recent albums have featured guitarist Billy Flynn and harmonicist Madison Slim. The rhythm section of Jones and Smith has anchored the unit throughout the changes, never failing to deliver the Chicago blues with aplomb. —Jim O'Neal

● **Red Hot 'n' Blue** / 1983 / Rounder 2035
Very solid vocals by Pinetop Perkins and Clavin Jones. Above average LBB set. —Bill Dahl

○ **Keepin' the Blues Alive** / 1990 / Ichiban 1052
Only bassist Calvin Jones and drummer Willie Smith remain from Muddy Waters's old crew, but guitarist John Duich helps keep the traditional Chicago sound in place. —Bill Dahl

Money Talks / Wild Dog
All of a sudden, drummer Willie Smith has become a very credible singer. —Bill Dahl

J. B. Lenoir

b. May 5, 1929, Monticello, MS, **d.** Apr. 29, 1967, Urbana, IL
Vocals, guitar, harmonica / Electric Chicago blues
Combining high-pitched vocals, driving boogie guitar, an unusual off-time drumbeat, and a riff-oriented sax section, Lenoir was one of the few Chicago bluesmen to constantly turn to topical themes in his music. A wild and popular stage performer, Lenoir was starting to inject African percussion and rhythms into his music at the time of his death. His best songs are still staples of the Chicago blues circuit. —Cub Koda

○ **Natural Man** / 1968 / Chess 9323
Equally fine mid-'50s recordings for Chess. —Cub Koda

○ **Mojo Boogie** / 1980 / Flyright 564
J.B. Lenoir made some marvelous recordings for the J.O.B. label in the early '50s, often working with pianist Sunnyland Slim and saxophonist J.T. Brown. They're avaiable on this reissue. —Ron Wynn

★ **Parrot Sessions, 1954-55: Vintage Chicago Blues, The** / 1989 / Relic 7020
J. B. at his creative and performing best, including "Mama Talk to Your Daughter," "Eisenhower Blues," and "Give Me One More Shot." The lyrics are as metaphorically powerful as any in blues and are sung against grooves alternating between low-down blues and Lenoir's patented boogie. —Cub Koda

○ **His J. O. B. Recordings 1951-54** / Jewel 4
Lenoir's earliest sides, including "Let's Roll" and the classic "Mojo Boogie." —Cub Koda

Furry Lewis (Walter Lewis)

b. Mar. 6, 1893, Greenwood, MS, **d.** Sep. 14, 1981, Memphis, TN
Vocals, guitar, sometimes harmonica / Acoustic Memphis blues
Furry Lewis became Memphis's favorite blues character late in life, famed for a bottle in one hand and a bottleneck in the other. His clowning nature sometimes overshadowed his considerable blues talents, but his best work (especially the early 1927-28 sides) was moving and memorable. Furry's music was not only the Memphis blues, it was the music of early 20th-century medicine shows, country suppers, and riverboats. His lyrics were often colorful and sly, and few bluesmen have ever seemed to enjoy themselves as much as Furry, who became something of a TV/movie celebrity after his return to action in the '60s. —Jim O'Neal

★ **In His Prime (1927-28)** / 1988 / Yazoo 1050
Lewis is the Memphis-based "songster" singer and guitarist whose gently rollicking early work flows from the same country font as John Hurt's. —Mark A. Humphrey

○ **Furry Lewis—Complete Works (1927-29)** / Document 5004
A full plate (25 tracks in all) of early, great sides. Includes "Sweet Papa Moan," "Black Gypsy Blues," and two takes of the best version of "John Henry" you may ever hear. —Cub Koda

Jimmy Liggins

b. Oct. 14, 1922
Guitar / R&B, Jump blues
Important West Coast jump-blues guitarist and vocalist (and younger brother of Joe Liggins) who became one of Specialty's first success stories in the late '40s and early '50s, thanks to such hits as "Cadillac Boogie," "Teardrop Blues," and "I Can't Stop It." —John Floyd

○ **Rough Weather Blues, Vol. 2** / 1992 / Specialty 7026
More house-rocking, horn-leavened jump blues. —Bill Dahl

● **And His Drops of Joy** / Specialty 7026
Swinging West Coast jump-blues of the late '40s, with a slightly harder edge than his older brother Joe's sound. —Bill Dahl

Joe Liggins

b. 1915, **d.** Aug. 1, 1987
Piano / R&B, Electric jump blues
Jimmy Liggins's older brother was also a Specialty hitmaker, but his first hits (including "The Honeydripper") came on Exclusive during the mid-'40s. The pianist signed with Specialty in 1950 and placed several songs in *Billboard*'s Black charts. "Pink Champagne," "Frankie Lee," and "Little Joe's Boogie" were his biggest hits with the label. —John Floyd

★ **And His Honeydrippers** / 1985 / Specialty 7025
Bouncy, danceable early-'50s jump-blues by this pianist's brassy combo. CD version has nine bonus cuts. —Bill Dahl

○ **Dripper's Boogie, Vol. 2** / 1992 / Specialty 7025
Vintage jump blues. —Bill Dahl

Lightnin' Slim (Otis Hicks)

b. Mar. 13, 1913, St. Louis, MO, **d.** Jul. 24, 1974, Detroit, MI
Vocals, guitar / Electric Louisiana blues
The acknowledged kingpin of the Louisiana school of blues, Lightnin' Slim had a style built on his grainy but expressive voice and rudimentary guitar work, with generally nothing more than Lazy Lester's harmonica and drums (usually a cardboard box!) in support. This formula worked successfully, scoring him regional hits for the Excello label for over a decade. Combining the country ambience of a Lightnin' Hopkins with the plodding insistency of a Muddy Waters, Slim's music remained uniquely his own, even when reshaping others' material to his dark, somber style. Lazy, rolling and insistent, Lightnin' Slim (born Otis Hicks) is Louisiana blues at its finest. —Cub Koda

○ **Early Years, The** / 1976 / Flyright 524
There's duplication here with *Bell Ringer*, though there's also some numbers done even earlier than those. —Ron Wynn

○ **Bell Ringer** / 1987 / Excello 8004
Superb early Slim Excello material. He never sang with more clarity or conviction, nor did his harmonica or guitar playing ever sound more electrifying than on these songs, many of which were popular singles. Other than Rice Miller's (Sonny Boy Williamson

II) definitive anthem, Slim's rendition of "Don't Start Me tTo Talking" was the finest. —*Ron Wynn*

○ **Rooster Blues** / 1987 / Excello 8000
The original Excello album. Excellent from start to finish. —*Cub Koda*

★ **Rollin' Stone** / 1991 / Flyright 08
With all six sides from Lightnin's earliest singles for the Feature label, plus excellent alternate takes of his best-known Excello numbers, this album is the perfect place to start. —*Cub Koda*

☆ **King of the Swamp Blues 1954-61** / 1992 / Flyright 47
A perfect companion volume to the other Flyright CD, this collects more rare tracks from Lightnin' Slim. —*Cub Koda*

Lil' Ed & the Blues Imperials (Lil' Ed Williams)

b. Apr. 8, 1955, Chicago, IL
Vocals, guitar / Modern electric blues
Lil' Ed Williams (vocal, guitar); "Pookie" Young (bass); various others (guitar, drums). Lil' Ed Williams learned his trade as a teenager from his uncle, Chicago slide guitarist J. B. Hutto, and the resemblance to Hutto, vocally and instrumentally, continues to be no less amazing some 20 years later. If Ed, half-brother Pookie Young, and the latest members of the revamped Blues Imperials never do much to modernize their blues or develop a new sound, that will be just fine with the band's growing legion of followers ("Ed Heads," no less), to whom the raucous, rocking slide guitar heritage of Hutto, Hound Dog Taylor, and Elmore James is blues nirvana. —*Jim O'Neal*

Roughhousin' / 1986 / Alligator 4749
Wild and greasy blues at its best. A two-song session for an anthology turned into an all-night, live-in-the-studio jam. Sounds like it was great fun. —*Niles J. Frantz*

● **Chicken Gravy & Biscuits** / 1989 / Alligator 4772
Wild, raw, rough-edged Chicago slide guitar blues, this is jumpin', partyin' music in the tradition of Hound Dog Taylor and J. B. Hutto (Lil' Ed's uncle). Recorded live in the studio with no overdubs. Includes nine original compositions plus covers of Hutto and Albert Collins tunes. —*Niles J. Frantz*

Mance Lipscomb

b. Apr. 9, 1895, Navasota, TX, **d.** Jan. 30, 1976, Navasota, TX
Vocals, guitar, violin / Acoustic Texas blues
As with Leadbelly and Mississippi John Hurt, the designation as a strictly blues singer dwarfs the musical breadth of Mance Lipscomb. A sharecropper/tenant farmer all his life, Mance didn't record until 1960 and the term "songster" fits what he did best. A proud yet not boastful man, Lipscomb would point out that he was an educated musician. His ability to play everything (classic blues, ballads, pop songs, spirituals) in a multitude of styles and keys was his particular mark of originality. With a wide-ranging repertoire of over 90 songs, Lipscomb may have gotten a belated start in recording but left a remarkable legacy (eight albums in 15 years) to be enjoyed. —*Cub Koda*

★ **Texas Sharecropper & Songster** / 1960 / Arhoolie 306
Includes '60s Texas blues, traditional songs, and jackknife slide by a country master. —*Jas Obrecht*

○ **You Got to Reap What You Sow** / 1964 / Arhoolie 398
Mance Lipscomb was a great "songster," someone who knew hundreds of songs and could deliver any and all of them in different yet effective ways. He sang blues, spirituals, and old folk numbers, and he composed his own tunes. Lipscomb had few rivals when it came to telling stories, setting up situations, and creating characters and depicting incidents. This 24-song reissued disc from 1964 puts Lipscomb in a perfect context; ripping through various songs, talking about everything from drugs to domestic conflict, police worries to spiritual concerns. —*Ron Wynn*

Little Charlie & the Nightcats

Group / Modern electric blues
This West Coast–based blues band features the jazz-tinged guitar work of Little Charlie Baty, plus off-kilter original material from vocalist and harmonica player Rick Estrin. —*Cub Koda*

All the Way Crazy / 1987 / Alligator 4753
A very happening debut album—funny and danceable. —*Niles J. Frantz*

● **Disturbing the Peace** / 1988 / Alligator 4761
Jumpin' blues. Wild antics, a good sense of humor, tons of fun, often outrageous. Very, very good guitar from Charlie Baty and interesting harp from lead vocalist Rick Estrin. —*Niles J. Frantz*

Captured Live / 1991 / Alligator 4794
This enjoyable live set captures the group's manic energy. —*Niles J. Frantz*

Little Milton (Milton Campbell)

b. Sep. 7, 1934, Inverness, MS
Vocals, guitar / Soul, R&B, Soul blues, Boogie-woogie
One of the great blues guitarists, singers, and composers of all time, Milton began his recording career in Memphis with Sun Records in 1953. Small-label singles followed for Meteor and Bobbin before he landed at Chess records in Chicago in 1961. He became one of the best-selling blues artists of the '60s, with many hit singles, including a #1 R&B hit "We're Gonna Make It" and items such as "Feel So Bad," "If Walls Could Talk," and "Baby I Love You." There may be soap opera elements in much of Milton's work, but it is always done with flair and good humor. While the mold was pretty much established during his Checker period, it also worked with his later affiliations at Stax and Glades. His Malaco recordings (dating from 1984) bring the formula of strings, horns, and background vocals up to date, but the blues artistry of Milton still shines through. —*Bob Porter*

○ **If Walls Could Talk** / 1970 / Chess 9289
Chess sides. —*Mark A. Humphrey*

Grits Ain't Groceries / Jan. 1970 / Checker 3011
Another splendid soul set. —*Bill Dahl*

Blues 'N Soul / 1974 / Stax 8518
One of his best Stax sets. —*Bill Dahl*

☆ **Chess Blues Master Series** / 1976 / Chess 2ACMB204
Little Milton hit his creative and playing stride at Chess, at least in terms of blues. "Grits Ain't Groceries," "We're Gonna Make It," and many other gems were available on this LP anthology. It's no longer available except in used record stores, but is still worth pursuing. —*Ron Wynn*

○ **Chronicle** / 1979 / Stax 4123
A fine single LP/CD collection spotlighting Little Milton's best Stax tracks. Whether you accept the premise he did better songs on Sun and Chess, there's still lots of good soul-oriented blues cuts here. —*Ron Wynn*

○ **Walkin' the Back Streets** / 1981 / Stax 8514
Excellent blues/soul set. —*Bill Dahl*

○ **Greatest Sides** / 1984 / Chess 9112
Milton's '60s Chess performances are hot and bothered. —*Mark A. Humphrey*

Annie Mae's Cafe / 1987 / Malaco 7435
The best of his Malaco recordings are on this '80s album. —*Mark A. Humphrey*

★ **Sun Masters** / 1990 / Rounder 35
Early-'50s Sun label material with searing guitar and pleading vocals. This is Milton's moment. —*Mark A. Humphrey*

○ **We're Gonna Make It/Little Milton Sings Big Blues** / 199z / Chess 5906
Two of Milton's classic mid-'60s Chess albums on one CD; a great value. —*Bill Dahl*

Little Walter (Marion Walter Jacobs)

b. May 1, 1930, Marksville, LA, **d.** Feb. 15, 1968, Chicago, IL
Amplified harmonica, Vocals, sometimes guitar / R&B, Electric Chicago blues
Little Walter was one of the two greatest Chicago-style amplified blues harp players, the other being Big Walter Horton. No one else can touch Little Walter. He pretty much defined modern amplified blues harp by virtue of his sheer genius, his extended recording career with Muddy Waters, and his own solo recordings. Perhaps the first to play amplified harmonica in the now classic Chicago style, Walter is the undisputed master of the blues shuffle. His jazz-influenced harmonica style did much to shape the direction of the Muddy Waters band, lending it a more modern sound. Walter was a fine songwriter, with 14 Top Ten R&B hits between 1952 and 1958. He also had great recording groups

that included such players as Robert Jr. Lockwood, Louis Myers, Fred Below, and Luther Tucker. —*Michael Erlewine*

★ **Best of Little Walter** / 1958 / Chess 1428
A quarter century after his death, Little Walter is still the standard that most harmonica players aspire to. This 12-track compilation of sides recorded in 1952-55 shows exactly why. A cornerstone for any blues collection, this album features the classics "My Babe," "Sad Hours," "Blues with a Feeling," "You Better Watch Yourself," "Off the Wall," and "Juke," the national anthem of harp players. —*Cub Koda*

○ **Hate to See You Go** / 1969 / Chess 9321
Another solid collection of tracks recorded between 1952 and 1960. Standout cuts abound anywhere the laser beam falls, but the set closer, "Blue and Lonesome," just may be the most emotionally terrifying masterpiece of Walter's illustrious career. —*Cub Koda*

Blues World of Little Walter, The / 1988 / Delmark 648
The title is a bit of a misnomer, because Walter is featured more as a sideman to Baby Face Leroy, Muddy Waters, and others on early Parkway, Regal, and Savoy sides. The explosive slide work from Waters on this pre-Chess version of "Rollin' and Tumblin'" is not to be missed. Many of these sides have appeared on previous compilations, but this one features superior sound, taken from the original lacquer masters. —*Cub Koda*

☆ **Best of Little Walter, Vol. 2, The** / 1989 / Chess 9292
Vol. 2 continues the overview of Walter's enormous output for the Chess label, with more definitive tracks, including "It Ain't Right," the blistering instrumental "Boogie," and "Boom Boom (Out Go the Lights)." —*Cub Koda*

☆ **Essential, The** / Jun. 8, 1993 / MCA
A two-CD, 46-track career retrospective of what many believe to be the most influential harmonica player who ever lived. A cornerstone of any blues collection, making all previous compilations obsolete. —*Cub Koda*

"Little" Willie Littlefield

b. Sep. 16, 1931, Houston, TX
Vocals, piano / R&B, Electric jump blues, Boogie-woogie
Piano player/vocalist probably best known for recording the original version of the classic "Kansas City." —*Cub Koda*

● **It's Midnight** / 1979 / Route 66 10
Nice compilation of Litlefield's best sides, 1949-57. —*Cub Koda*

Johnny Littlejohn (John Funchess)

b. Apr. 16, 1931, Lake, MS
Vocals, guitar / Electric Chicago blues
Recording only sporadically, Littlejohn remains one of Chicago's best slide guitarists. —*Cub Koda*

● **Johnny Littlejohn & the Chicago Blues All Stars** / 1968 / Arhoolie 1043
Tight and intense, this is Littlejohn's finest record to date. Great slide guitar work. —*Cub Koda*

Robert Jr. Lockwood

b. Mar. 27, 1915, Marvell, AR
Vocals, guitar, harmonica / Chicago Blues, Acoustic and electric Delta blues
Lockwood was actually christened after his father, but the junior part of his name has stuck with him to the present day because of his association with his "stepfather," Delta legend Robert Johnson. When he first started recording in 1941, it was with a heavy debt to Johnson (few play that style better than Lockwood, and for good reason), but playing with harmonica wizard Sonny Boy Williamson on the original "King Biscuit Time" radio show broadened his tastes. The resulting jazz-influenced tinges remain hallmarks of his later work and, in the process, influenced a young B. B. King. One of the main house musicians used by Chess Records in the '50s, Lockwood played behind Sonny Boy, Little Walter, and Chuck Berry, to name a few, but never appeared as a solo artist. Moving to Cleveland, OH, in the early '60s, Lockwood formed his own bands, exploring every strain of music that appealed to him in his typically stubborn and adventuresome manner. Not merely slavishly recycling or exploiting his connection to the Robert Johnson legend, Robert Jr. Lockwood has remained his

own man, with a fine brace of solo recordings from his later years to prove it. —*Cub Koda*

● **Steady Rollin' Man** / 1967 / Delmark 630
A fine, low-key set from a major contributor to the Chicago blues sound, recorded with the Aces, Louis Myers, Davey Myers, and Freddy Below. —*Barry Lee Pearson*

○ **Contrasts** / 1974 / Trix 3307
Robert Jr. Lockwood made a pair of spectacular albums for Trix in the '70s; the newly reissued *Contrasts* offered probing originals, while *Does 12* spotlighted his instrumental magic as well as penetrating vocals. Johnson's version of "Driving Wheel" maintains the spirit of Roosevelt Sykes's familiar rendition but has his own compelling twists. Otherwise, the session featured Lockwood songs, and he demonstrated the probing, animated qualities that made him a legend and a survivor. —*Ron Wynn*

○ **Does 12** / 1977 / Trix 3317
Robert Jr. Lockwood made two excellent albums for the Trix label that didn't get the publicity or distribution they merited, then quickly disappeared. Muse has recently begun reissuing Trix material, but thus far hasn't gotten to this Lockwood date or its companion. Grab it whenever and wherever you can. —*Ron Wynn*

Plays Robert and Robert / Nov. 28, 1982 / Black & Blue 33740
Robert Jr. Lockwood played with and knew the great blues musicians of the '30s, particularly his stepfather Robert Johnson. No living artist was or is better suited to interpret Johnson's songs, which was part of Lockwood's agenda when he cut this lovely 13-track (one bonus cut) session in 1982. Additional motivation was a chance for him to showcase his own originals, which comprise 5 of the cuts. —*Ron Wynn*

Cripple Clarence Lofton (Albert Clemens)

b. Mar. 28, 1887, Kingsport, TN, d. Jan. 9, 1957, Chicago, IL
Vocals, piano / Piano blues
A consummate entertainer, Lofton helped to spearhead the boogie-woogie movement in the Windy City, influencing everyone from Meade "Lux" Lewis to John Mayall in the bargain. —*Cub Koda*

○ **Cripple Lofton & Walter Davis** / Yazoo 1025
Marvelous blues piano and singing from Cripple Clarence Lofton, and nearly as fine an effort from Walter Davis. —*Ron Wynn*

● **Cripple Clarence Lofton, Vol. 1** / RST 6006
Some of Lofton's best, with the selections "Strut That Thing," "Monkey Man Blues," and "Pitchin' Boogie" being particular standouts. —*Cub Koda*

Lonesome Sundown (Cornelius Green)

b. Dec. 12, 1928, Donaldsville, LA
Vocals, guitar, piano / Electric Louisiana blues
Cornelius Green was renamed Lonesome Sundown when he made his first records for the Excello label in 1956, and it was Sundown and his similarly renamed counterparts Slim Harpo, Lightnin' Slim, and Lazy Lester who helped define the Louisiana blues sound. Sundown has been called the most versatile and urbane of the group, as his material extended beyond the down-home guitar and harmonica stylings most often associated with swamp blues. Though he made a number of fine singles, none of them hit it big, and a disillusioned Lonesome Sundown went back to being Cornelius Green again after his last Excello sessions in 1965. Producer Bruce Bromberg brought him out of retirement to record some solid new material in the '70s, some of it featuring Sundown's protege Phillip Walker. Though he gave the blues life a brief shot again, Cornelius Green has since settled into the sunset back in Baton Rouge. —*Jim O'Neal*

Been Gone to Long / 1977 / Hightone 8031
A comeback effort for this veteran swamp-blues guitarist. —*Bill Dahl*

● **Lonesome Sundown** / 1990 / Flyright 16
Classic Southern Louisiana swamp blues from the studios of producer J. D. Miller. —*Bill Dahl*

Louisiana Red (Iverson Minter)

b. Mar. 23, 1936
Louisiana Red (born Iverson Minter) is a flamboyant guitarist, harmonica player, and vocalist. He lost his parents early in life through multiple tragedies; his mother died of pneumonia a

week after his birth, and his father was lynched by the Ku Klux Klan when he was five. Red began recording for Chess in 1949, then joined the Army. After his discharge, he played with John Lee Hooker in Detroit for almost two years in the late '50s. Since then he's maintained a busy recording and performing schedule, having done sessions for Chess, Checker, Atlas, Glover, Roulette, L&R, and Tomato among others. —*Ron Wynn*

● **Lowdown Back Porch Blues** / 1963 / Collectables 5419
Still his best album; early '60s sides that provide an attractive showcase for the guitarist's eclectic talent. —*Bill Dahl*

Midnight Rambler / 1982 / Tomato 70664
At times harrowing, this is one of Red's more intense efforts. —*Bill Dahl*

Willie Love

b. Nov. 4, 1906, Duncan, MS, d. Aug. 19, 1953, Jackson, MS
Vocals, piano / Electric delta-piano blues
A playing and drinking buddy of Rice Miller (Sonny Boy Williamson II), the spats wearing Love had a hammering, two-fisted style of piano playing that's been preserved on many fine recordings. —*Cub Koda*

● **Trumpet Masters, Vol. 1** —**Lonesome World Blues** / Collectables 5240
Willie Love played exciting, if sometimes unorganized piano and sang in an equally unpredictable and galvanizing fashion. This is how Mississippi juke joints sounded during the early '50s (they're not that different now). —*Ron Wynn*

Willie Mabon

b. Oct. 24, 1925, Hollywood, TN, d. Apr. 19, 1985, Paris, France
Vocals, harmonica, piano / R&B, Blues, Piano blues
The piano playing and singing Mabon struck it big in the early '50s with a swinging set of novelty-style numbers, including the often-covered "I Don't Know" and "Poison Ivy." —*Cub Koda*

○ **Chicago 63** / 1974 / America 6136
Stylish piano and vocals that range from clever to cranky to anguished. Willie Mabon's an artist who's seldom powerful but can convey more shadings and nuances than many blues vocalists or singers in several other genres. —*Ron Wynn*

● **Blue Roots, Vol. 16** / 1982 / Chess 1439
Nice cross-section of Mabon's best Chess sides. —*Cub Koda*

Lonnie Mack

b. Jul. 18, 1941
Guitar / R&B, Rock & Roll, Modern electric blues
Guitarist Lonnie Mack took the organ-like tone of guitarist Robert Ward's Magnatone amp, added blinding speed and devastating-for-their-time whammy-bar techniques, and spot-welded them to the most bluesy and soulful of sources. He influenced numerous guitarists in the process, his most devoted disciple being the late Stevie Ray Vaughan. Not content to merely grind out his old hits and rest on his laurels, Mack continues to write, record, and tour to this day, sounding better than ever. —*Cub Koda*

★ **Wham of That Memphis Man, The** / 1963 / Alligator 3903
A reissue of Lonnie's first album—the one thousands of guitarists cut their teeth on. —*Cub Koda*

○ **Memphis Sounds of Lonnie Mack** / 1974 / Trip 9522
Fine Fraternity rarities. —*Bill Dahl*

Strike Like Lightning / 1985 / Alligator 4739
On this album, coproduced by Stevie Ray Vaughan, the highlight is an inspired duet with Vaughan and Mack on "Wham (Double Whammy)." —*Cub Koda*

Second Sight / 1987 / Alligator 4750
New recordings, with Lonnie in excellent form. —*Cub Koda*

Magic Sam (Samuel Maghett)

b. Feb. 14, 1937, Grenada, MS, d. Dec. 1, 1969, Chicago, IL
Vocals, guitar / R&B, Modern electric blues, Electric Chicago blues
From his collected Cobra sides to his Delmark masterpieces *West Side Soul* and *Black Magic*, Magic Sam's recordings prove that (with the possible exception of Otis Rush at his best) nobody captured the spirit and soul of the '60s Chicago blues like the late Sam Maghett. When Sam died, Chicago lost its brightest star, yet

because of his deserved reputation for guitar techniques and vocal passion, most of his recorded sides are available in some format. Along with several other artists, Luther Allison and Jimmy Dawkins for example, Magic Sam was associated with the so-called West Side sound, a '60s shift away from the Chess Studio sound associated with Howlin' Wolf and Muddy Waters. According to West Side musicians, the innovations were economically motivated because the tough West Side clubs paid so little. In the stripped-down guitar/bass/drums format, the guitarist worked overtime filling lead and rhythm roles simultaneously. Moreover, the demanding West Side audiences, many of them recently up from the South, took their blues seriously, and musicians had to play full-tilt to win their approval. During the '60s, blues musicians also needed to cover the soul hits on the charts. Put it all together, and you have three-piece bands alternating between innovative hard treatments of blues classics and contemporary soul material reduced to bare-bones readings. It made for some of the very best high-energy blues ever created.

Vocally, Magic Sam drew on the church-based soul styling favored by B. B. King and Otis Rush. Instrumentally, he preferred the haunting minor-key phrases and upbeat rhythmic treatment of John Lee Hooker or J. B. Lenoir riffs. Add in Sam's songwriting skills and a heavy dose of charisma, and you come up with the embodiment of '60s Chicago blues at its best. There will never be another like him. —*Barry Lee Pearson*

★ **West Side Soul** / 1968 / Delmark 615
The best '60s West Side sound album, the best Magic Sam album, and probably the best blues album ever made. —*Barry Lee Pearson*

○ **Black Magic** / 1969 / Delmark 620
More West Side soul. —*Barry Lee Pearson*

○ **Otis Rush & Magic Sam** / 1980 / Flyright 562
A pair of blues giants, each given ample room. While you can find better Rush and Sam, that's no slam on what's here. What you're getting is excellent songs that didn't make it onto the first reissue of Magic Sam/Shakey Jake material, plus powerhouse Rush that didn't make *Groaning The Blues*. In other words, this isn't exactly fodder. —*Ron Wynn*

Live at Ann Arbor & in Chicago / Jul. 1982 / Delmark 645-646
Don't let the homemade recording quality put you off for a second, because this is Magic Sam at his whiplash best. —*Cub Koda*

☆ **1957–66** / 1991 / Paula 2
Excellent collection of Sam's earliest sides for the Cobra and Crash labels. —*Cub Koda*

Give Me Time / 1991 / Delmark 654
Relaxed, loose, informal home recordings of Sam playing solo, interpreting a variety of soul and blues classics. —*Cub Koda*

○ **Magic Touch** / 1992 / Black Top 1085
Great live-in-a-club set. —*Bill Dahl*

Magic Slim (Morris Holt)

b. Aug. 7, 1937, Grenada, MS
Vocals, guitar / Modern electric blues
Principally influenced by Magic Sam (whom he claims gave him his stage name), Slim's jagged guitar style and powerful voice are mainstays of today's Chicago blues sound. —*Cub Koda*

Highway Is My Home / Nov. 19, 1978 / Evidence 26012
Magic Slim is not trying to soft pedal or entice anyone. His style is a full-speed ahead, hard-edged and ragged one, with a deep, sometimes sloppy vocal approach and an equally cutting guitar approach. It is not pretty, flashy, pop-oriented, or even particularly appealing, but it is genuine. The stripped-down Slim sound was mostly on target throughout the ten tracks (one bonus cut) on this late-'70s date. —*Ron Wynn*

● **Raw Magic** / 1982 / Alligator 4728
One of the best contemporary Chicago bands, unadorned and to the point. —*Barry Lee Pearson*

Grand Slam / 1982 / Rooster Blues 2618
An interesting tribute to Florence's, one of Chicago's most famous blues bars and an old Magic Slim venue. —*Barry Lee Pearson*

Taj Mahal (Henry Saint Clair Fredericks)

b. May 17, 1942, New York, NY

JERRY McCAIN

Vocals, guitar, piano, sometimes banjo, bass / Modern acoustic blues

Guitar/piano playing rural blues revivalist Taj Mahal was quite a rarity in the late '60s—a young black who accurately revived classic country blues for a new generation of listeners. Mahal took an archival interest in folk blues while matriculating during the early '60s. He began playing his blues and rags in various Boston folk joints, then formed a short-lived band with Ry Cooder in Los Angeles called the Rising Sons. He debuted on vinyl in 1968 with a self-titled album for Columbia, and continually placed on the album charts throughout the '70s with his electric blend of blues, folk, reggae, and ragtime influences. Mahal has done several movie soundtracks, notably *Sounder* in 1972. —*Bill Dahl*

○ **Natch'l Blues** / 1968 / CBS 9698
For some reason, Taj Mahal gets the back of the hand treatment from a lot of blues "purists." Sure, his records can get very self-indulgent, but when he turns to blues you can hear a lot worse than Mahal. This was among his best LPs, with both strong originals and good remakes. —*Ron Wynn*

● **Taj Mahal** / 1968 / CBS 2779
His debut, with Ry Cooder and Jesse Ed Davis. First and foremost. —*Mark A. Humphrey*

Mule Bone / Nov. 1, 1991 / Gramavision 79432
Taj Mahal won a Grammy nomination with this music from the Broadway production of the Hurston/Hughes play. —*Mark A. Humphrey*

○ **Taj's Blues** / Jun. 16, 1992 / CBS 52465
Taj Mahal was multicultural before the phrase "world music" came into vogue, but his forte was—and still is—the blues. He's no traditionalist, but his unique and innovative style borrows heavily from all the early legends. This enjoyable 12-track collection takes the listener through a series of "varied bluesscapes"—half solo acoustic, half electric band—and includes the previously unreleased "East Bay Woman." —*Roundup Newsletter*

Dancing The Blues / 1993 / Private 82112
Taj Mahal has always been a more inclusive, eclectic musician than even some admirers understand; his work was never simply or totally blues, even though that strain was at the center and seldom far from anything he performed either. That's the case with this newest collection: a 12-song set that includes splendid covers of Muddy Waters and Howlin' Wolf tunes, but also equally respectful, striking renditions of soul standards such as "Mockingbird" with special guest Etta James and "That's How Strong My Love Is." —*Ron Wynn*

Martin Bogan & Armstrong

Group / Blues

Only violinist, storyteller, and philosopher Howard Armstrong remains to tell of the exploits of this remarkable African-American string band. Virginia-born guitar and mandolin blues artist Carl Martin died in 1979, and guitarist Ted Bogan passed away a few years ago. But in their prime, Martin, Bogan, and Armstrong enjoyed multiple incarnations, first (in the '30s) as "The Four Keys," "The Tennessee Chocolate Drops," and the "Wandering Troubadours." They played individually and collectively throughout the mid-South on radio, with medicine shows, and at country jukes before eventually making it to Chicago in the late '30s and '40s, where they made records but mostly supported themselves by what Armstrong calls "pulling doors." This meant going into different cafes and taverns and playing for tips if they weren't thrown out. Playing various ethnic neighborhoods, the group took advantage of Armstrong's gift with languages and learned to sing in a variety of tongues. Best described as an acoustic string band (violin, guitar, mandolin, bass), the group played blues, jazz, pop, country, and various non-English favorites. As skilled musicians eager to earn tips by playing whatever their audiences wanted, they built a necessarily large repertoire.

After years of separation the group reunited as Martin, Bogan, & Armstrong in the early '70s and enjoyed substantial blues revival acclaim. After Carl Martin died, Bogan and Armstrong continued. When I worked with them in 1986, Bogan and Armstrong were still the greatest living exponents of the African-American string-band style, equally at home playing blues, swing, jazz, ragtime, or older Black string-band material. Armstrong, who speaks seven languages and is a painter and a sculptor, was a National Heritage Award winner in 1990. What made their music so won-

derful, besides its energy and flawless presentation and their personable good humor, was their ability to remind us that good music transcends classifications and a skilled artist can draw from many streams. —*Barry Lee Pearson*

● **Martin Bogan & Armstrong** / Flying Fish 003
A fine Black string band. —*Barry Lee Pearson*

That Old Gang of Mine / Flying Fish 3
A mixed repertoire for all ethnic audiences. —*Barry Lee Pearson*

Sara Martin

b. May 18, 1884, Louisville, KY, **d.** May 24, 1955, Louisville, KY
Vocals / Classic female blues

Known in her heyday as "the blues sensation of the West", the big-voiced Martin was one of the best of the classic female blues singers of the '20s. —*Cub Koda*

○ **1922–28** / Best of Blues 19
All of Martin's best, featuring fine support from Fats Waller and Clarence Williams. —*Cub Koda*

Percy Mayfield

b. Aug. 12, 1920, **d.** Aug. 11, 1984
Vocals, piano / Soul, R&B, Nostalgic, West Coast blues

After his #1 R&B lament "Please Send Me Someone to Love" established him as a subtly moving singer in 1950, a disfiguring auto accident forced Percy Mayfield to accentuate his songwriting skills instead. It was lucky for Ray Charles that he did, since the introspective composer penned some of Brother Ray's best material (notably "Hit the Road, Jack"). Based in Los Angeles, Mayfield proved to be one of his own best musical interpreters during the early '50s when he racked up seven Top Ten R&B sellers for Specialty Records. The despairing "Strange Things Happening," "The River's Invitation," and "Please Send Me Someone to Love" tabbed Mayfield as the poet laureate of R&B, a writer whose material has grown in stature with time. Although his own sound was based in sax and piano, Mayfield's recordings were apparently too gentle and troubling to weather the onslaught of early rock & roll. While under contract to Charles as a writer during the '60s, Mayfield cut a couple of nice albums for the Genius's own Tangerine logo, and he remained semi-active on the West Coast until his 1984 death. —*Bill Dahl*

○ **My Jug and I** / 1962 / Tangerine 1505
Known as the "poet laureate of the blues," Percy Mayfield remains arguably the genre's greatest singer/songwriter. This classic, long-out-of-print recording places him in front of the Gerald Wilson band featuring Ray Charles as producer/keyboardist. It first appeared on Charles' own label, Tangerine, and is perhaps Mayfield's finest outing. The songs, vocals, ensemble performances, arrangements, and instrumental solos are simply superb and combine to make this one of the greatest recordings of its kind. —*Larry Hoffman*

Bought Blues / 1969 / Tangerine 1510
Mayfield's Tangerine sides are eminently tasty. —*Bill Dahl*

★ **Poet of the Blues** / 1990 / Specialty 7001
The original 1950–54 recordings by this influential songwriter and vocal stylist. The superb combo backing was led by Maxwell Davis. —*Hank Davis*

○ **Memory Pain** / Specialty 7027
More Specialty gems from the '50s, including many rarities. Gentle and plaintive. —*Bill Dahl*

For Collectors Only / Specialty 7000
As the title suggests, this gives a deeper look at Mayfield's early career. Alternate takes and unissued material. —*Hank Davis*

Jerry McCain

b. Jun. 18, 1930, Gadsden, AL
Vocals, harmonica, guitar / R&B, Modern electric blues

McCain blows harp with a heavy debt to idol Little Walter, while bringing a raucous, almost rock & roll slant to his music. He has recorded prolifically from 1954 to the present day for Trumpet, Excello (arguably his best sides, available only as singles or stray tracks on compilation albums as of press time), Rex, Okeh, Jewel, and Ichiban, among others. —*Cub Koda*

○ **Choo Choo Rock** / 1981 / White Label 9966

These demo recordings for Excello (ca. 1956) are wild and raucous, featuring overamplified guitars, crashing drums, and bizarre lyrics. What a rock & roll album by Little Walter might have sounded like. —*Cub Koda*

Tommy McClennan

b. Apr. 8, 1908, Yazoo City, MS, **d.** CA. , Chicago, IL
Vocals, guitar / Soul blues, Acoustic R&B
A gravel-throated back-country blues growler from the Mississippi Delta, McClennan was part of the last wave of downhome blues guitarists to record for the major labels in Chicago. His rawboned 1939–42 Bluebird recordings were no-frills excursions into the blues bottoms. He left a powerful legacy that included "Bottle It Up and Go," "Cross Cut Saw Blues," "Deep Blue Sea Blues" (aka "Catfish Blues"), and others whose lasting power has been evidenced through the repertoires and re-recordings of other artists. Admirers of McClennan's blues would do well to check out the 1941–42 Bluebird sessions of Robert Petway, a McClennan associate who performed in a similar but somewhat more lyrical vein. McClennan never recorded again and reportedly died destitute in Chicago; blues researchers have yet to even trace the date or circumstances of his death. —*Jim O'Neal*

★ Travelin' Highway Man / 1990 / Travelin' Man 06
Paint-peelin' Delta blues, 1939–42. —*Jas Obrecht*

Delbert McClinton

b. 1940
Vocals, guitar, harmonica / R&B, Modern electric blues, Blues rock, Country-Rock
A Texas music institution, McClinton honed his musical chops to razor sharpness as a teenage harmonica man, learning firsthand from blues legends traveling through the area. He got on the bigtime circuit via his harp work on Bruce Channel's hit, "Hey Baby," making it over to tour England and eventually giving harmonica lessons to a young John Lennon. Much behind-the-scenes work throughout the '60s ensued, with McClinton fronting the Rondells, who hit the Hot 100 with "If You Really Want Me to, I'll Go." He hit the charts again in the '70s with Glen Clark as Delbert and Glen. Around this period, McClinton's songs started getting covered by country acts, Waylon Jennings and Emmylou Harris both having hits with his material. The Blues Brothers used his "B-Movie Box Car Blues" on their first album and in their hit movie. He has released idiosyncratic solo efforts and has guested on albums with everyone from Roy Buchanan to Bonnie Raitt. We've not heard the last of Delbert McClinton, a Texas music treasure. —*Cub Koda*

Victim of Life's Circumstances / 1975 / ABC 907

Genuine Cowhide / 1976 / ABC 959
Both *Victim of Life's Circumstances* and *Genuine Cowhide* contain a few strong originals and successfully capture Clinton's aggressive blend of country and R&B. —*Rick Clark*

Second Wind / 1978 / Capricorn 0201
McClinton lays on the grease with two great originals, "'B' Movie" and "Maybe Someday Baby" (featuring a wailing support vocal by Clydie King). Also includes a decent collection of covers ("Spoonful" and "Big River"). —*Rick Clark*

● Best of Delbert McClinton, The / 1989 / Curb 77415
This adequate overview contains mostly familiar material but lacks the cohesiveness of his best early albums. —*Rick Clark*

Live from Austin / 1989 / Alligator 4773
Rock-solid, gritty roadhouse R&B, performed with a no-nonsense spirit. —*Rick Clark*

Never Been Rocked Enough / 1992 / Curb 77521
Never Rocked Been Rocked Enough covers the whole checkerboard while remaining vintage McClinton: his harp wails on "Everytime I Roll the Dice;" "Can I Change My Mind" flirts with Motown soul; "Blues As Blues Can Get" defines the confessional blues ballad; "I Used to Worry "and the title track chug into Band/Little Feat territory. The disc also includes the performer's Grammy winning duet with Bonnie Raitt, "Good Man, Good Woman." —*Roch Parisien*

Jimmy McCracklin

b. Aug. 13, 1921, St. Louis, MO

Vocals, piano, sometimes harmonica / R&B, Electric West Coast blues
Along with Lowell Fulson and Johnny Otis, the most durable of the West Coast rhythm and blues pioneers, McCracklin is still going at it, keeping up with the times after making records for almost 50 years. McCracklin has enjoyed relatively few hits but has managed to record again and again, though now with less regularity than in earlier days. As tastes in blues have moved on since he first recorded with only piano accompaniment, McCracklin has also moved his music onward through small combos, bigger bands, and more current styles, yet he has never strayed far from the blues. A distinctive singer and a gifted songwriter, McCracklin lists among his hits "The Walk" (1958), "Just Got to Know" (1961), "Every Night, Every Day" (1965), and "Think" (1965), as well as Lowell Fulson's "Tramp" (1967), a McCracklin-Fulson composition. —*Jim O'Neal*

○ Twist With / 1961 / Crown 5244
Blistering 1950s sides; originally on Modern. —*Bill Dahl*

○ I Just Gotta Know / 1961 / Imperial 12219
Some of his very best early '60s sides. —*Bill Dahl*

○ Jimmy McCracklin Sings / 1961 / Chess 1464
Great late-'50s rocking R&B. —*Bill Dahl*

○ Everynight Everyday / 1965 / Imperial 12285
Another standout early-'60s LP. —*Bill Dahl*

○ My Story / 1991 / Bullseye Blues 9508
A recent album by this great '50s and '60s R&B singer. —*Mark A. Humphrey*

● Everybody Rock: Let's Do It! The Best of / Domino 1008
Sixteen rockin' blues tracks by the phenomenal Jimmy McCracklin. This album contains the original versions of "Georgia Slop" and "The Walk," plus many more fine numbers, including "The Wobble" (two versions), "Let's Do It," "Club Savoy," "Get Tough," "I'm Through," and a cover of Chuck Berry's "Reeling and Rocking." —*Roundup Newsletter*

Larry McCray

b. Apr. 5, 1960, Magnolia, AR
Vocals, guitar / R&B, Modern electric blues
Raised in Arkansas where his grandmother, father, and older sister all played the blues, McCray formed a band with his brothers Carl and Steve after the family moved to Saginaw, MI. While still in his 20s, McCray chalked up a wide range of experience on the Saginaw music scene, encompassing blues, jazz, country, R&B, and rock. From the combination of a deep blues background and fluency in a variety of styles, McCray has forged a hot blues sound for the '90s. —*Jim O'Neal*

Ambition / 1990 / Charisma 91388
Along with Joe Louis Walker, McCray is the best of the contemporary bluesmen. He's a superb, rock-influenced guitar player. This album includes good songs with blues, R&B, and Motown influences. —*Niles J. Frantz*

Mississippi Fred McDowell

b. Jan. 12, 1904, Rossville, TN, **d.** Jul. 3, 1972, Memphis, TN
Vocals, guitar / Blues
A driving, propulsive bottleneck guitarist, McDowell hoboed around the South throughout the '20s and '30s, working as an itinerant musician. Eventually settling down to become a farmer in 1940, he was discovered and subsequently recorded by folklorist Alan Lomax in 1959. These recordings coincided with renewed interest in Delta blues during the folk-music boom of the '60s, and soon McDowell was recording for a variety of labels and touring the world to deserved acclaim. A major influence on Bonnie Raitt (whose slide work shows a major stylistic affinity to his), McDowell's "You Got to Move" brought him a small fortune in belated royalties when covered by the Rolling Stones. —*Cub Koda*

★ Mississippi Delta Blues / Aug. 1964 / Arhoolie 304
Nineteen great tracks (1964–65) of bottleneck slide guitar. Excellent liner notes. —*Jas Obrecht*

○ My Home Is in the Delta / Sep. 1964 / Testament 2208
Mississippi Fred McDowell's home may have been in the Delta, but his music belonged to the world. This is heartfelt, raw, and glorious country blues, delivered without an ounce of pretension or nostalgia. —*Ron Wynn*

Fred McDowell / 1966 / Flyright 14
Another well-rounded collection. —*Jas Obrecht*

Mississippi Fred McDowell and Johnny Woods / 1977 /
Rounder 2007
A nice, laid-back set from guitar legend McDowell and his old
harmonica sidekick, Johnny Woods. —*Barry Lee Pearson*

Brownie McGhee (Walter McGhee)

b. Nov. 30, 1915, Knoxville, TN
*Vocals, guitar, sometimes kazoo or piano / Acoustic country
blues*
Probably the most underrated, or at least underappreciated,
bluesman on the planet, Brownie McGhee is a master musician
whose most familiar recordings have for some time been out of
vogue with current tastes in blues. The same music that made
Brownie and his partner Sonny Terry a hot item during the boom
years of folk music now tends to be dismissed as too smooth and
folksy for contemporary fans, not raw enough for country blues
aficionados, and not hard-hitting enough for the more electric-
oriented crowd. While perhaps the folk-blues routine was overdone, it is still a disservice to dismiss Brownie McGhee and his
music, for he has written and recorded many fine blues in a variety of styles since his recording career began in 1940. For ears not
attuned to the folk idiom, McGhee's '40s output as the Piedmont
successor to Blind Boy Fuller, the early postwar electric guitar
combo sides from New York, and various post–Sonny Terry albums with different bands will all provide different and sometimes surprising perspectives; for the folk/blues fan, the Terry-
McGhee collaborations still set the standard. —*Jim O'Neal*

○ **Back Country Blues** / Nov. 1958 / Savoy 14019
Brownie McGhee's solo material had a certain charm and compelling quality missing from his collaborations with Terry. For
whatever reason, he tended to try more things alone, and vary his
approach, sound, and delivery. This is first-rate country and topical material, delivered without the forced humor that eventually
made his dates with Terry more camp than substance. —*Ron
Wynn*

Brownie's Blues / 1971 / Bluesville 505
Outstanding 1962 Bluesville album featuring Brownie McGhee
and Sonny Terry. It was McGhee's date, with Terry taking the role
of harmonica accompanist and soloist to McGhee's sophisticated
vocals and jazzy guitar. Tunes include "Trouble in Mind" and
"Everyday I Have the Blues." —*Roundup Newsletter*

● **The Folkways Years, 1945–59** / 1991 / Smithsonian/Rounder
40034
Brownie McGhee was among the last generation of blues musicians with deep country and traditional ties that maintained
some level of popularity into the '50s. The onslaught of electrified, urban blues would change the music's direction and result in
many Delta and country artists losing stature among the genre's
core constituency. But McGhee managed to continue working,
both with longtime musical companion Sonny Terry and as a
solo act. The 17 cuts presented on this CD were taken from six
McGhee albums, and include ballads, folk tunes, originals, and
comedic numbers. They depict the versatility and idiomatic range
that was commonplace in the music of Brownie McGhee. —*Ron
Wynn*

○ **Complete Brownie McGhee** / 1994 / Columbia/Legacy
A terrific two-CD set of all of the recordings McGhee made in the
early '40s for OKeh and Columbia; these 47 tracks are the very
first recordings he ever made. —*Stephen Thomas Erlewine*

"Blind" Willie McTell (William Samuel McTell)

b. May 5, 1901, Thomson, GA, d. Aug. 19, 1959, Milledgeville, GA
Vocals, guitar, accordion, harmonica / Acoustic country blues
A Depression-era recording star, Blind Willie McTell worked until just before his death in 1959. His repertoire was phenomenal,
covering mellow blues, hillbilly music, spirituals, quick-fingered
rags, minstrel show tunes, and even semipornographic ditties. He
played with a light touch on a big-bodied Stella 12-string, specializing in shifting rhythms and resonant melodies that were as
distinctive as his clear, somewhat nasal voice. His best-known
song is "Statesboro Blues," a 1928 fingerpicking showpiece
named after his Georgia hometown. (Four decades later, the
Allman Brothers turned it into their signature song.) A shrewd,
intelligent man, McTell is remembered as having extraordinary
powers of perception and memory, as well as an uncanny sense
of direction. A great improviser, he sometimes composed with
great deliberation, while other tunes reflect a stream-of-con-
sciousness approach bordering on poetry. He kept a large 78 collection and occasionally learned songs from Braille sheet music.
During the Depression, he recorded as Georgia Bill for Okeh,
Blind Willie for Vocalion, and Hot Shot Willie for Bluebird. He
was often accompanied by a second guitarist, and his wife Kate
McTell sometimes joined in on vocals. Folklorist John Lomax
recorded McTell in 1940 for the Library of Congress's Archive of
Folk Song, capturing a remarkable array of blues, ballads, rags,
spirituals, and insightful monologs. McTell reactivated his recording career in 1949, cutting for Regal and Atlantic Records. By
then, however, his solitary blues seemed a thing of the past. —*Jas
Obrecht*

○ **Atlanta Twelve String** / 1949 / Atlantic 82366
McTell's greatest performances are undoubtedly his twenties and
thirties material. Although *Atlanta Twelve String* presents McTell
toward the end of his career (recorded in 1949, though not released on LP until 1972), he's not coasting here. By 1949, the
sound of a bluesman alone on his acoustic guitar was already
something of an anachronism, and McTell knows it: He wields his
12-string like two dueling guitars, constantly putting one rhythm
or theme in contrast with another. He's traditional and modern,
making no concessions to either market. This is remarkably complex stuff, often breathtaking work from an aging master
nowhere near ready to give up his crown. Recommended. —
Jimmy Guterman, Roundup Newsletter

Last Session / 1960 / Bluesville 517
Blind Willie McTell had an instantly recognizable style of his own,
yet he spent over 25 years jumping from one label to another and
recording under a variety of pseudonyms. Bitter about record
companies in general, McTell had by 1956 returned to playing for
tips on Atlanta street corners. Fortunately, an Atlanta record store
owner nudged him back in front of a tape recorder shortly before
his death. Songs include "Kill It Kid" and "The Dyin'
Crapshooter's Blues." — *Roundup Newsletter*

○ **Complete Library of Congress Recordings (1940)** / 1969 /
Document 6001
Songs and autobiographical monologs. —*Jas Obrecht*

Complete Recorded Works, Vol. 1 (1927–31) / 1990 /
Document 5006
A three-volume set of McTell's complete recordings from 1927 to
1935. Some of the most imaginative 12-string guitar work ever
recorded. —*Jas Obrecht*

★ **Early Years 1927-33, The** / 1990 / Yazoo 1005
A good sampler, emphasizing 12-string guitar. —*Jas Obrecht*

☆ **Definitive Blind Willie McTell, The** / 1994 / Columbia Records
All of the recordings Blind Willie McTell made for Columbia,
OKeh, and Vocalion between 1929 and 1933 are collected on this
essential two-disc set. —*Stephen Thomas Erlewine*

Memphis Jug Band

Group / Acoustic Memphis blues
One of the definitive jug bands of the '20s and early '30s, this
seminal group was comprised of Will Shade, Will Weldon, Hattie
Hart, Charlie Polk, Walter Horton, and others, in various configurations. —*Cub Koda*

○ **Complete Recorded Works—Vols. 1-3** / Document 5023
A definitive three-CD set with all the issued material from this
groundbreaking jug band. Includes "Cocaine Habit Blues," "Cave
Man Blues," the original "He's in the Jailhouse Now," and the al-
ways wonderful "I Whipped My Woman with a Single Tree." —
Cub Koda

★ **Memphis Jug Band** / Yazoo 1067
Definitive 28-song collection by the city's finest jug band, spanning their output from 1927 to 1934. —*John Floyd*

Memphis Minnie (Lizzie Douglas)

b. Jun. 3, 1897, Algiers, LA, d. Aug. 6, 1973, Memphis, TN
Vocals, guitar, banjo / Acoustic Memphis blues
Tracking down the ultimate woman blues guitar hero is prob-
lematic because woman blues singers seldom recorded as guitar
players and woman guitar players (such as Rosetta Tharpe and
Sister O. M. Terrell) were seldom recorded playing blues.

Excluding contemporary artists, the most notable exception to this pattern was Memphis Minnie. The most popular and prolific blueswoman outside the vaudeville tradition, she earned the respect of critics, the support of record-buying fans, and the unqualified praise of the blues artists she worked with throughout her long career. Despite her Southern roots and popularity, she was as much a Chicago blues artist as anyone in her day. Big Bill Broonzy recalls her beating both him and Tampa Red in a guitar contest and claims she was the best woman guitarist he had ever heard. Tough enough to endure in a hard business, she earned the respect of her peers with her solid musicianship and recorded good blues over four decades for Columbia, Vocalion, Bluebird, Okeh, Regal, Checker, and JOB. She also proved to have as good taste in musical husbands as music and sustained working marriages with guitarists Casey Bill Weldon, Joe McCoy, and Ernest Lawlers. Their guitar duets span the spectrum of African-American folk and popular music, including spirituals, comic dialogs, and old-time dance pieces, but Memphis Minnie's best work consisted of deep blues like "Moaning the Blues." More than a good woman blues guitarist and singer, Memphis Minnie holds her own against the best blues artists of her time, and her work has special resonance for today's aspiring guitarists. —*Barry Lee Pearson*

★ **Hoodoo Lady (1933–37)** / 1933-37 / CBS 46775
Great early stuff. —*Mark A. Humphrey*

○ **Blues Classics by Memphis Minnie** / Oct. 1965 / Blues Classics 1
Shaking, rockin', volcanic material from the great Memphis Minnie. There weren't many stylists, male or female, who could match Lizzie Douglas when it came to conveying a lyric. She was in peak form on every selection here . —*Ron Wynn*

○ **Complete Recorded Works, Vol. 1 (1935–41)** / 1991 / Document 12
A five-volume CD set of Memphis Minnie's entire output from 1935 to 1941. Highlights include "Me and My Chauffeur Blues," "Good Biscuits," "You Can't Rule Me," "If You See My Rooster," and "Selling My Porkchops." An essential collection by the greatest female blues guitarist ever. —*Cub Koda*

☆ **And Kansas Joe—1929–34** / 1991 / Document 31
Minnie's earliest recordings with first husband Kansas Joe McCoy. Includes "I Want That," "Bumble Bee," "Squat It," "I Don't Want That Junk outta You," and the original version of "When the Levee Breaks," later covered by (and recredited to) Led Zeppelin. —*Cub Koda*

○ **1934–42** / Biograph 124
You can't go wrong with Memphis Minnie at almost any point in her estimable career. During the '30s and early '40s, she made the adjustment to changing styles, but in the early '30s she *made the style*. The sound quality's pretty good throughout the set, though it's better on the later tunes. —*Ron Wynn*

○ **With Kansas Joe** / Blues Classics 13
When she was married to Kansas Joe McCoy, Memphis Minnie was making wailing blues, memorable laments, and brillant double-entendre tunes. He in turn supplied her with excellent accompaniment and nice complimentary vocals. These are simply marvelous songs. —*Ron Wynn*

Memphis Slim (Peter Chatman)

b. Sep. 3, 1915, Memphis, TN, **d.** Feb. 24, 1988, Paris, France
Vocals, piano, keyboards / R&B, Piano blues
One of the most prolific of all blues recording artists, Memphis Slim was never away from the studio for too long after he cut his first records in 1940 (OKeh). Although a sophisticated vocalist with a suave approach, Slim seldom strayed from his deep blues roots when it came to piano playing. He recorded in various solo, band, and small combo settings, primarily in Chicago until he began touring abroad in 1960. In 1962 he moved to Paris and became the most successful of the transplanted American bluesmen in Europe. Recording album after album on the continent, he wore his licks and repertoire thin, but among the plethora of Memphis Slim releases are a number of prize blues items. —*Jim O'Neal*

○ **At The Gate of Horn** / 1959 / Vee-Jay 800
Only this disc's short length (34 minutes) qualifies as something worthy of complaint; otherwise this is seminal blues piano, performed by a great rocking player and singer, Memphis Slim. This 1959 session had everything: super piano solos; a strong lineup of horn players; clever, well-written and sung lyrics; and a seamless pace that kept things briskly moving from beginning to end. —*Ron Wynn*

○ **Memphis Slim** / 1961 / Chess 9250
Pounding Chicago piano blues and boogies from Slim's early '50s Chess Records stint. —*Bill Dahl*

○ **Memphis Slim—U.S.A.** / 1962 / Candid 79024
Exceptional 1954 material from the United Records vaults, with Matt Murphy's blistering guitar. —*Bill Dahl*

All Kinds Of Blues / 1963 / Bluesville 507
As Leroi Jones writes in the liner notes, "Slim's blues serves as a natural link between earlier blues tradition and the more recent rhythm and blues styles." On this 1960 session, Slim dished out plenty of rough-and-tumble boogie piano, remarkable homespun monologues, and some great songs, including a haunting remake of "Mother Earth." — *Roundup Newsletter*

○ **Real Folk Blues, The** / 1966 / Chess 9270
More classics from the Chess Records vault. —*Bill Dahl*

Mother Earth / 1969 / Buddah 7505
Excellent singing and rousing, sparkling barrelhouse, boogie-woogie, and straight blues piano playing from a certified legend. Memphis Slim wasn't shy about making records, and they were seldom not worth hearing. This one didn't break the string of quality efforts. —*Ron Wynn*

○ **Messin' Around with the Blues** / 1970 / King 1082
He wasn't messing around with either his singing or playing on this date. Memphis Slim made dozens of albums; most were good, some were very good, and a handful were great. This was among the handful. —*Ron Wynn*

★ **Rockin' the Blues** / 1981 / Charly 210
The immaculate late-'50s Vee Jay sessions are collected on this one album. Thundering piano and authoritative vocals are by the prolific Slim. Matt Murphy is astonishing on guitar. This is *the* Memphis Slim album, with roaring saxes adding more power. — *Bill Dahl*

I Just Keep on Singing the Blues / 1981 / Muse 5219
He kept singing and playing the blues with gusto and distinction his entire career. This came a bit later in the Memphis Slim legacy, when he was more established artist than maverick performer, but it's still almost as essential as his landmark recordings from the '50s. —*Ron Wynn*

Big Maceo Merriweather (Major Merriweather)

b. Mar. 31, 1905, Atlanta, GA, **d.** Feb. 26, 1953, Chicago, IL
Vocals, piano / Piano blues
With his smoky husk of a voice and absolute command of the 88 keys, Merriweather influenced every blues piano from Willie Mabon to Otis Spann and most everybody in between. There never has been a blues piano man quite as omnipresent or as influential as Big Maceo, and we'll certainly never see the likes of him again. —*Cub Koda*

○ **Chicago Breakdown** / Oct. 1975 / Bluebird 5506
Simply fabulous piano playing and nearly as wonderful vocals from the estimable "Big" Maceo Merriweather. Whether working alone or with Tampa Red, his was a sound to behold. —*Ron Wynn*

○ **Best of Big Maceo, The** / 1992 / Arhoolie 7009
Thundering Chicago boogie and blues piano; essential. —*Bill Dahl*

● **King of Chicago Blues Piano, Vol. 1 & 2** / Arhoolie 210
The first of two essential compilations gathering vintage Big Maceo Merriweather singles from the early '40s. This is about as close to perfection as prewar blues singing and piano playing came from any level. —*Ron Wynn*

Amos Milburn

b. Apr. 1, 1927, Houston, TX, **d.** Jan. 3, 1980, Houston, TX
Vocals, piano / Piano blues, Electric jump blues
Important jump-blues pianist who scored numerous hits with Aladdin from the mid-'40s to the '60s. A hard-drinking Texan, Milburn fashioned a slew of stomping, house-party classics, in-

cluding "Chicken Shack Boogie," "Let's Have a Party," "Good Good Whiskey," and its sequel, "Bad Bad Whiskey." —*John Floyd*

★ **Down the Road Apiece—The Best of Amos Milburn** / Jan. 11, 1994 / Emi Records Group North Ameri
Pianist Amos Milburn mixed boogie-woogie brilliance with vocal energy and intensity to forge a style that was among early R&B's most exciting and appealing. Milburn's '40s and '50s singles were sometimes fiery, sometimes silly, and ranged from drinking songs and celebratory uptempo numbers to stomping instrumentals and an occasional blues or love tune. This excellent 26-track anthology contains such classic Milburn anthems as "Chickenshack Boogie," "One Scotch, One Bourbon, One Beer," "Let's Have A Party," and "Bad, Bad Whiskey," as well as lesser known but just as spirited romps "Let's Rock a While," "House Party (Tonight)," and "Real Pretty Mama Blues." —*Ron Wynn*

Roy Milton

b. Jul. 31, 1907, Wynnewood, OK, **d.** Sep. 1983, Canoga Park, CA
Vocals, drums / R&B, Electric jump blues, Blues & jazz
West Coast jump pioneer who recorded for Specialty during the mid '40s to early '50s. His group, the Solid Senders, was a tight rocking machine able to swing from slow grinding blues ("R. M.'s Blues") to barrelhouse stomps ("What Can I Do," "Waiting on Baby"). A neglected R&B genius. —*John Floyd*

★ **Roy Milton and His Solid Senders** / 1990 / Specialty 7004
Seminal cuts, part of the R&B revolution.

○ **Groovy Blues, Vol. 2** / 1992 / Specialty 7024
More polished jump blues from a master of the genre. —*Bill Dahl*

Mississippi Sheiks

Group / Acoustic country blues
One of the classic string bands of the late '20s and early '30s, this group featured the talents of Walter Vinson, Bo Carter, and Lonnie Chatmon in various configurations. —*Cub Koda*

☆ **Mississippi Sheiks—Vols. 1-4** / Document 5084
There's absolutely no way you can go wrong with this superlative four-CD import set of this seminal blues band. Covers everything they ever recorded from 1930 to 1936. —*Cub Koda*

★ **Stop and Listen** / Yazoo 2006
The Mississippi Sheiks were one of the most popular blues acts of the 1930s. Guitarist Walter Vinson and fiddler Lonnie Chatmon blended elements of hard-edged blues, popular music, hokum, country, and traditional material. This 20-track collection includes "Sitting on Top of the World," "Stop and Listen Blues," and the previously unissued "Livin' in a Strain." — *Roundup newsletter*

Little Brother Montgomery (Eurreal Montgomery)

b. Apr. 18, 1906, Kentwood, LA, **d.** Sep. 6, 1985, Champaign, IL
Vocals, piano / Piano blues
A virtual encyclopedia of blues piano styles, Eurreal "Little Brother" Montgomery was a consummate musician who often parlayed his sparkling memory of countless obscure piano men from Mississippi and Louisiana into recordings of his own, many decades later. Of course, Montgomery created plenty on his own, most notably the classic "Vicksburg Blues" (Paramount, 1930), which he claimed was a collaborative effort with two of those forgotten piano greats. His 1936 recording of "The First Time I Met You" was transformed into a modern-day Chicago masterpiece when reworked by Buddy Guy as "First Time I Met the Blues." Montgomery was a perfectionist who could work solo, with a Dixieland group, or with a Chicago blues band. One of his biggest complaints was that record companies only wanted him to record blues and not the old popular songs and sentimental ballads he also loved; fortunately for the blues fan, the record companies persevered. —*Jim O'Neal*

○ **Tasty Blues** / 1960 / Original Blues Classics 554
One of the Chicago blues piano great's most swinging LPs. —*Bill Dahl*

● **Chicago: the Living Legends** / 1961 / Original Blues Classics 525
Little Brother Montgomery was a singer/pianist who was at ease with both blues and traditional jazz styles. This 1961 Riverside date features Montgomery originals plus classics from the pens of

Jelly Roll Morton, Duke Ellington, and Irving Berlin. —*Roundup Newsletter*

Goodbye Mister Blues / 1973–76 / Delmark
While Little Brother Montgomery was among the blues' greatest barrelhouse and boogie pianists, he was also well versed in traditional jazz. This disc's 13 cuts feature him working with the State Street Swingers, an early jazz unit, doing faithful recreations of such chestnuts as "South Rampart St. Parade," "Riverside Blues," and "Panama Rag." —*Ron Wynn*

At Home / 1990 / Earwig 4918
Very informal performances. —*Bill Dahl*

○ **Complete Recorded Works (1930–36)** / Document 5109

Alex Moore

b. Nov. 22, 1899, Dallas, TX, **d.** Jan. 20, 1989, Dallas, TX
Vocals, piano / Piano blues
One of the last of the old-time Texas barrelhouse pianists, Alex Moore was an institution in Dallas, his lifelong home. A colorful entertainer with a poetic gift for rambling improvisations, Moore had one of the longest recording careers in blues history (his first sides for Columbia were made in 1929; his final session was in 1988). Yet it was hardly one of the most prolific, as there were usually lengthy gaps between sessions. The spontaneous, autobiographical nature of his latter-day recordings imbue his albums with a special charm. —*Jim O'Neal*

○ **Wiggle Tail** / 1988 / Rounder 11559
Late recordings by this venerable Texas blues pianist. —*Mark A. Humphrey*

Buddy Moss (Eugene Moss)

b. Jan. 26, 1906, Jewel, GA, **d.** Oct. 19, 1984, Atlanta, GA
Vocals, guitar, sometimes harmonica / Acoustic country blues
Called "probably the finest of the North Carolina school of Piedmont blues artists" by blues author and reissue producer Bruce Bastin, Eugene "Buddy" Moss enjoyed only a brief period of real popularity on the blues scene (1933–35), when he was recording regularly for the American Record Company label group. In his later years, he was still an excellent musician by most accounts, yet for reasons of his own he did little to revive his career in the way of public performances or new recordings. (Bastin also described Moss as "moody" and "temperamental" in his 1971 book *Crying for the Carolines*.) However, Moss left a substantial recorded legacy that included two-guitar sessions with such illustrious accompanists as Josh White, Curley Weaver, and Brownie McGhee. —*Jim O'Neal*

Rediscovery / Biograph 12019
Piedmont blues master Buddy Moss featured in a good blues revival session. —*Barry Lee Pearson*

● **Buddy Moss 1933-35** / Document 528
A fine collection of blues from one of the major Piedmont guitarists and composers. —*Barry Lee Pearson*

Matt "Guitar" Murphy

b. Dec. 29, 1927, Sunflower, MS
Guitar, sometimes Vocals / Electric Chicago blues, Guitar-pop
Matt "Guitar" Murphy, once called the best guitar player in the blues by Willie Dixon, built a new, although not particularly illustrious career in the '80s based on his association with the Blues Brothers. (Not only was he a band member, he also had a memorable scene with Aretha Franklin in the movie.) Murphy, formerly a sideman extraordinaire with Memphis Slim, Bobby Bland, and others, subsequently put together a touring band of his own. He found ample nightclub work, but one noted blues club owner ostensibly hired the band, then told all of them except Murphy to stay in their hotel rooms, because it was only Murphy's legendary guitarmanship that the diehard blues fans wanted to hear, not another pseudo-blues revue. And it has only been in the role of blues guitar hero, not Blues Brothers bandsman, that Murphy has been able to record on his own in recent years, including his first full album (for the Austin-based Antone's label). His incendiary '50s work, most of which was with Memphis Slim, was revelatory for its time and sounds no less remarkable today. —*Jim O'Neal*

○ **Way Down South** / 1990 / Antone's 0013

Primarily an instrumental release, spotlighting Matt's fluid guitar playing. Matt's brother Floyd Murphy (who did session work for Sun Records in the early '50s) joins in on guitar. —*Niles J. Frantz*

Charlie Musselwhite

b. Jan. 31, 1944, Kosciusko, MS
Vocals, harmonica, sometimes guitar / Electric Chicago blues
One of the most heralded new harp players to emerge from the Chicago scene of the '60s, Musselwhite differed from the other White musicians on the circuit in that, like many Black bluesmen, he came from a working-class Mississippi family via Memphis to the Windy City. His early Chicago experience came at various South and West Side clubs with the city's blues veterans. In the late '60s he followed the westward movement to California, where he has lived since, but unlike some of the other transplanted Chicagoans, "Memphis Charlie" never attempted to become a pop-rock "star" and, over the years, has mellowed into a powerful, mature stylist with a continuing dedication to the roots of the blues. —*Jim O'Neal*

Stand Back Here Comes Charlie Musselwhite's Southside Band / 1967 / Vanguard 79232
Musselwhite's debut album is ambitious and self-consciously authentic. —*Mark A. Humphrey*

Memphis Charlie / 1969 / Arhoolie 303
The 14 performances on *Memphis Charlie* include some loose live sides and even a taste of slide guitar from Musselwhite. They're the work of a more mature artist than the brash kid on *Stand Back!* —*AMG*

● **Ace of Harps** / 1990 / Alligator 4781
Musselwhite's spurred on by a harder, more contemporary-sounding band than he's had before, a tough bass/drums/guitar trio. —*AMG*

Signature / Oct. 1991 / Alligator 4801
If you liked his *Ace of Harps* release, you won't be disappointed with *Signature*. The vocalist/harmonica ace has the same solid backing, with ripping guitar leads from Andrew Jones Jr., funk riffs and jazzy blues from bassist Artis Joyce, and Tommy Hill hitting the skins. The band is very urban and tight, and Musselwhite has horns backing him on two cuts. — *Jeff Story, Roundup Newsletter*

○ **In My Time** / 1993 / Alligator
Musselwhite takes four different approaches on *In My Time*. On two tracks he turns to guitar and proves a competent instrumentalist and convincing singer in vintage Delta style. He also does two gospel numbers backed by the legendary Blind Boys of Alabama that are heartfelt, but not exactly triumphs. Musselwhite reveals his jazz influence on "Revelation," "Movin' and Groovin'," and "When It Rains It Pours," making them entertaining harmonica workouts backed by guitarist Andrew Jones, bassist Felton Crews, and drummer Tommy Hill. But for blues fans, Musselwhite's biting licks and spiraling riffs are best featured on such numbers as "If I Should Have Bad Luck" and "Leaving Blues." —*Ron Wynn*

Louis Myers

b. Sep. 18, 1929, Byhalia, MS
Vocals, guitar, harmonica / Electric Chicago blues
A member of Little Walter's Jukes, Myers is one of the idiom's finest guitarists and an excellent harmonica player as well. —*Cub Koda*

● **I'm a Southern Man** / 1978 / Advent 2809
Myers's debut album, with fine playing and singing throughout. —*Cub Koda*

Tell My Story Movin' / 1992 / Earwig 4919
Of the 12 tracks here, 7 are originals. Louis plays harp throughout—"Bottom of the Harp" and "Tribute to the Aces" feature especially strong harp solos. Myers plays guitar on "Blue and Lonesome" and leaves the rest of the guitar work to the agile hands of Steve Freund and John Primer, whose slide work is exceptional as always. —*Jeff Story, Roundup newsletter*

Kenny Neal

b. 1957, Los Angeles
Vocals, guitar, harmonica, sometimes bass and piano / Modern electric blues

A versatile and dynamic new-generation bluesman, Kenny Neal grew up with the blues in Baton Rouge. He made his performing debut at the age of 6 with his father, harmonica player Raful Neal, and joined the family band when he was 13. After a late-'70s apprenticeship as the bass man in Buddy Guy's Chicago band, Kenny struck out on his own with his brothers Larry, Raful Jr., and Ronnie in Toronto. Adept at playing soulful down-home blues as well as high-energy contemporary styles, Kenny Neal has recently taken his blues to the theatrical stages of New York City. —*Jim O'Neal*

Big News from Baton Rouge!! / 1987 / Alligator 4764
A debut from this hot young Louisiana blues guitarist. —*Mark A. Humphrey*

Devil Child / 1988 / Alligator 4774
Hot chops and a mite slicker production than needed. —*Mark A. Humphrey*

○ **Walking on Fire** / 1991 / Alligator 4795
This album includes a couple of neat acoustic blues numbers from the musical *Mule Bone*. —*Mark A. Humphrey*

● **Bayou Blood** / 1992 / Alligator 4809
Kenny Neal straddles the line between traditional and contemporary demands with his compositions and playing. He sounds like a modernist, incorporating soul and funk influences and elements into his singing, playing, instrumentation, and writing. But there's also a strain of the old-time wailing and moaning that runs through his music, as would be expected of the son of Louisiana legend Raful Neal. —*Ron Wynn*

Raful Neal

b. Jun. 1936, Baton Rouge, LA
Vocals, harmonica / Modern electric blues
The patriarch of the most prolific of Louisiana's blues families, Raful Neal performed for some 30 years around Baton Rouge before recording his first album. His first band included Buddy Guy and, at one point, bayou blues legend Lazy Lester, but Neal waxed only a handful of singles during the heyday of Louisiana blues recording. As his sons Kenny Neal and the Neal Brothers came to prominence on the international blues scene during the '80s, so did Dad, who has finally assumed a hard-earned position in the annals of swamp blues, carrying on the tradition of his old friend Slim Harpo. —*Jim O'Neal*

● **Louisiana Legend** / 1990 / Alligator 4783
An album that is grittier and nearer the swamp than his son Kenny's music. —*Mark A. Humphrey*

I Been Mistreated / 1991 / Ichiban 9004
More fine Baton Rouge blues. —*Mark A. Humphrey*

Robert Nighthawk (Robert McCollum)

b. Nov. 30, 1909, Helena, AR, d. Nov. 5, 1967, Helena, AR
Vocals, guitar, harmonica / Acoustic and electric Chicago blues
Though he recorded from the '30s right up to his death, Nighthawk never achieved the success of his more celebrated pupil, Muddy Waters. Instead, he found himself being relegated to one-nighters in taverns and the Maxwell Street open market on Sundays. But his resonant voice and creamy-smooth slide guitar playing (played in standard tuning, unusual for a bluesman) would influence players for generations to come, and many of his songs would later become blues standards. —*Cub Koda*

Bricks in My Pillow / 1977 / Pearl Flapper 11
Superb Robert Nighthawk slide guitar, originally recorded in Chicago for the United label in the early '50s. —*Barry Lee Pearson*

○ **Complete Recorded Works (1937–40)** / 1985 / Wolf 002
Perhaps the finest bottleneck player outside Elmore James, Robert Nighthawk sang with a brooding, piercing quality that could make your hair stand and your ears ring. These are early Nighthawk performances, some rudimentary and others masterful. None of them are throwaways, nor delivered with anything except spirit and passion. —*Ron Wynn*

★ **Live on Maxwell Street** / 1988 / Rounder 2022
Recorded live on the street (one can actually hear cars driving by!) in 1964 with minimal duo support. Nighthawk's slide playing (and single-string soloing, for that matter) are nothing short of elegant and explosive. One of the top three live blues albums of all time. —*Cub Koda*

The Nighthawks

Group / R&B, Rock, Rock & Roll, Blues, Hard Rock, Heavy Metal
A hard-driving D.C.-based bar band with strong Chicago blues roots. Formed in 1972 by harpist and vocalist Mark Wenner and guitarist Jimmy Thackery, the band earned a reputation as a solid outfit through more than a decade of touring and recording projects with John Hammond and former members of Muddy Waters's band. Thackery left in 1986, but Wenner regrouped around longtime members Jan Zukowski on bass and Pete Ragusa on drums. *Trouble*, their recent release on Powerhouse, is a blend of blues, R&B, and rock influences, with a typically energetic sound born in thousands of one-night stands across the country. —*Bill Dahl*

● **Open All Nite** / 1976 / Mobile Fidelity 754
This longtime Washington, D.C., blues-rock aggregation made one of its more complete and satisfying albums with this date. Everything from the vocals to the good mix of bar-band arrangements and explosive solos, clicked. —*Ron Wynn*

○ **Jacks & Kings** / 1977 / Genes 4120-4125
Classic material and stirring playing. A must-find. —*Michael G. Nastos*

Side Pocket Shot / 1977 / Adelphi 4115
A studio album with the Rhythm King's Horns. Another solid album. —*Michael G. Nastos*

10 Years Live / 1982 / Varrick 1
A highly recommended two-fer that celebrates their decade together. —*Michael G. Nastos*

Jimmy Oden (James Burke Oden)

b. Jun. 26, 1903, Nashville, TN, d. Dec. 30, 1977, Chicago, IL
Vocals, piano / Electric Chicago blues, Piano blues
The piano-playing Oden contributed one certifiable classic, the much-recorded "Goin' Down Slow." —*Cub Koda*

○ **1932–48** / Story of Blues 3508
A solid 16-track import collection of Oden's earliest and best sides. —*Cub Koda*

Johnny Otis

b. Dec. 28, 1921, Vallejo, CA
Vocals, drums, vibes, piano / R&B, Electric West Coast blues
There was probably no one who played a greater role—or as many roles—in catalyzing rhythm and blues on the West Coast than Johnny Otis. Bandleader, club owner, producer, writer, DJ, and musician, Otis was responsible for recording such artists as Charles Brown, Little Esther, and Big Mama Thornton. Off and on since the '40s, he has led a revue that features both big names and new discoveries. Otis has sung on record, with "Willie and the Hand Jive" being his best-known vocal (Capitol, 1958), but he has usually preferred to put other singers out front, and the majority of his hits featured Little Esther and/or Mel Walker during the Otis aggregation's peak of popularity in 1950–52. The Johnny Otis Show made a resurgence in the early '70s, with vocalists such as Big Joe Turner and Cleanhead Vinson heading an all-star cast that included Otis's son Shuggie on guitar. In varying configurations, the Otis crew has periodically regrouped to tour and record when the leader was not occupied with preaching or other new pursuits. —*Jim O'Neal*

○ **Johnny Otis Show, The** / 1958 / Savoy 2221
Some of the R&B bandleader's earliest and best work (1945-51) for Savoy. Cast includes singers Little Esther and Mel Walker, The Robins, and guitarist Pete Lewis. —*Bill Dahl*

○ **Live at Monterey** / 1971 / Epic 30473
An R&B oldies show with a difference, the artists represented the cream of the crop of jump blues, and in 1970, they were still in fine fettle. The disc stars Otis, Esther Phillips, Eddie Vinson, Joe Turner, Ivory Joe Hunter, Roy Milton, Roy Brown, Pee Wee Crayton, and Johnny's guitar weilding son, Shuggie. —*Bill Dahl*

● **Capitol Years, The** / 1988 / Capitol 92858
Big-band R&B, scaled down and jived up, from the early rock era. Includes his 1958 hit "Willie and the Hand Jive." —*Mark A. Humphrey*

Be Bop Baby Blues / 1989 / Night Train 7003
In the late forties and early fifties, great bandleaders such as Joe and Jimmy Liggins, Roy Milton, and Maxwell Davis were busy hammering out a rocking rhythm and blues style that would soon sweep the country. Preeminent among these was Johnny Otis, functioning as a sort of all-around blues godfather. Collected on this disc are 14 early direct-to-disc recordings, including acetates and three unissued tracks. —*Roundup Newsletter*

● **Complete Savoy Recordings, The** / Savoy

Lets Live It Up / Charly 269
Nice early '60s R&B twist rhythms and Johnny "Guitar" Watson on several cuts. —*Bill Dahl*

Creepin' with the Cats: The Legendary Dig Masters / ACE 325
Rarities from the vaults of Otis's own Dig label, mid-'50s vintage. —*Bill Dahl*

Junior Parker (Herman Parker)

b. Mar. 27, 1932, Clarksdale(?), MS, d. Nov. 18, 1971
Vocals, harmonica / Soul, R&B, Soul blues
Though his creamy-smooth, Roy Brown–influenced voice stood him in good stead in later years in translating more soul-oriented material, Junior Parker contributed some of the best down-home blues recordings ever committed to wax. While Parker worked with Howlin' Wolf and B. B. King around Memphis, his initial recordings for the Sun label produced two enduring classics, "Feelin' Good" and "Mystery Train," later a hit for a young Elvis Presley. Moving to the Duke label, his sound became more urbane and polished, while still interpreting down-home material like Robert Johnson's "Sweet Home Chicago," Howlin' Wolf's "Riding in the Moonlight (Pretty Baby Blues)," and Roosevelt Sykes's "Driving Wheel," the latter a Top Ten R&B hit for him. Later recordings drifted further away from hard blues (no doubt influenced as much by constant touring with R&B stylist Bobby "Blue" Bland as by prevailing market trends), but Parker continued to work and record, having R&B chart hits up until his death from a brain tumor in 1971. —*Cub Koda*

○ **Blues Consolidated (Barefoot Rock and You Got Me)** / May 1958 / Duke 72
Half Parker, half Bland, all great '50s Texas blues and R&B. —*Bill Dahl*

○ **Driving Wheel** / 1962 / MCA 27039
One of the best historical recordings, featuring Memphis blues vocalists and harmonica players from the Duke recordings of the '60s. —*Barry Lee Pearson*

Sometime Tomorrow / 1973 / Bluesway 6066
Some fine lesser known Duke sides. —*Bill Dahl*

○ **Mystery Train** / 1990 / Rounder 38
A fine set of Parker's Sun recordings, including the cool original version of the title cut. It's great to compare with the hot Presley version. These classic uptown presentations also feature tracks by James Cotton and Pat Hare. —*Barry Lee Pearson*

★ **Junior's Blues/the Duke Recordings, Vol. 1** / 1992 / MCA 10669
Junior Parker combined rugged Sonny Boy Williamson II–styled harmonica with a velvet-smooth urban-derived vocal delivery and developed a blues style all his own during the 1950s. Although he debuted on Sun fronting the rip-roaring Blue Flames, he moved to Houston-based Duke Records in 1954 and soon became an R&B star. This great-sounding 18-track disc makes a profound case for the late bluesman's consistent brilliance. Dating from 1954-64, the contents show that Little Junior Parker, as he was initially billed, seldom stopped experimenting. Great urban blues from a vastly underrated harpist and singer. —*Bill Dahl, Goldmine*

Charley Patton

b. 1887, d. 1934
Vocals, guitar / Acoustic Delta blues
If the Delta country blues had a convenient source point, it would probably be Charley Patton, its first great star. His hoarse, impassioned singing style, fluid guitar playing, and unrelenting beat made him the original "King of the Delta Blues." A major influence on Howlin' Wolf, Robert Johnson, and John Lee Hooker, Patton truly excelled as a live performer, making him tremendously popular throughout the Delta. The first blues guitarist to introduce the kind of flashy performing gymnastics modern audiences normally associate with artists like Jimi Hendrix, his music embraced everything from blues, ballads, and ragtime to gospel. Recorded in the late '20s to early '30s on primitive equip-

ment (no masters of any kind exist), Patton's music gives us the first flowering of the Delta blues form, before it became homogenized with turnarounds and 12-bar restrictions. —*Cub Koda*

★ **Founder of the Delta Blues** / 1969 / Yazoo 1020
A 24-track best-of compilation featuring all of Patton's best titles, this is a cornerstone of any blues collection. —*Cub Koda*

☆ **King of the Delta Blues** / 1991 / Yazoo 2001
An excellent companion to *Founder of the Delta Blues.* —*Cub Koda*

Complete Recorded Works—Vols. 1-3 / Document 5009
A three-CD set of Patton's complete recorded works, sequenced in chronological order. Superior sound. —*Cub Koda*

Peg Leg Sam (Arthur Jackson)

b. Dec. 18, 1911, Jonesville, SC, **d.** Nov. 27, 1977, Jonesville, SC
Vocals, harmonica / Acoustic country blues
Peg Leg Sam was a performer to be treasured, a member of what may have been the last authentic traveling medicine show, a harmonica virtuoso, and an extraordinary entertainer. Born Arthur Jackson, he acquired his nickname after a hoboing accident in 1930. His medicine show career began in 1938, and his repertoire—finally recorded only in the early '70s—reflected the rustic nature of the traveling show. "Peg" delivered comedy routines, bawdy toasts, and monologs; performed tricks with his harps (often playing two at once); and served up some juicy Piedmont blues (sometimes with a guitar accompanist, but most often by himself). Peg Leg Sam gave his last medicine-show performance in 1972 in North Carolina and was still in fine fettle when he started making the rounds of folk and blues festivals in his last years. —*Jim O'Neal*

○ **Joshua** / Sep. 1990 / Tomato 269665
Rootsy '70s performances by this Southeastern country-blues harmonica player and singer. —*Mark A. Humphrey*

Pinetop Perkins

b. Jul. 13, 1913, Belzoni, MS
Vocals, piano, sometimes guitar / Piano blues
Pinetop Perkins has been recognized by blues audiences as one of the world's top blues pianists ever since he replaced Otis Spann in the Muddy Waters Band in 1969. His talent had already been proven in his earlier years in the South with the King Biscuit Boys, Robert Nighthawk, Earl Hooker, and others, but his name never appeared on record until he settled in Chicago. (He had recorded "Pinetop's Boogie Woogie" for Sam Phillips in Memphis in 1953, but a British reissue label finally released the track more than 20 years later.) Perkins recorded one album and a few scattered tracks of his own during his 11-year stint with Muddy and has waxed several albums since his departure from the band, including two with the Legendary Blues Band. —*Jim O'Neal*

Boogie Woogie King / Nov. 1, 1976 / Evidence 26011
Though he did not have an album issued under his name as a leader until 1988, pianist Pine Top Perkins actually should have had one released in 1976. That is when he cut the eight tracks on this recently reissued Evidence CD for the Black and Blue label. They did not appear until 1992, which is a shame. Perkins trademark boogie-woogie riffs, rumbling rhythms, left-hand lines and spinning phrases were in fine form on such songs as his signature piece "Pinetop's Boogie Woogie," Memphis Slim's "Lend Me Your Love," and Robert Jr. Lockwood's "Take a Little Walk with Me." —*Ron Wynn*

● **After Hours** / 1986 / Blind Pig 73088
Easy-grooving blues and boogie, backed by the competent New York City–based blues band Little Mike and the Tornadoes. Though Perkins followed Otis Spann as the piano player in the Muddy Waters band, these are the first domestically available recordings under his own name. —*Niles J. Frantz*

Lucky Peterson

b. Dec. 13, 1964, Buffalo, NY
Vocals, guitar, organ, piano, sometimes drums, bass / Modern electric blues
A former child prodigy who recorded his first album and appeared on the "Tonight Show" at the age of five, Lucky Peterson has continued to burn as one of the bright lights on the contemporary blues scene. As a teenager, Lucky toured with Little Milton, followed by a stint with Bobby Bland, and he now performs with his own unit in addition to doing session work with many of the top names in blues. A superb organist who has also become an excellent guitarist, Lucky was raised with the blues, and his musical instincts allow him to play down-home blues, funk, R&B, jazz, and up-to-the-minute original blues with equal ease. —*Jim O'Neal*

● **Ridin'** / Mar. 1984 / Evidence 26033
The spiraling solos, excellent bridges, turnbacks, pedal maneuvers, and soulful accompaniment are executed with a relaxed edge and confident precision. Guitarist Melvin Taylor is another gem, offering a loose, funky, and dead-on-the-case blues solo, while bassists Titus Williams and Ray Allison do not let the groove waver. If you have wondered whether Lucky Peterson deserves the hype and major label bonanza, these songs are the real deal. —*Ron Wynn*

Lucky Strikes / 1989 / Alligator 4770
His first LP as an adult; crisp and contemporary blues. —*Bill Dahl*

○ **Triple Play** / 1990 / Alligator 4789
Very good, contemporary high-energy blues. Lucky sings and plays guitar and keyboards. —*Niles J. Frantz*

Piano Red (William Lee Perryman)

b. Oct. 19, 1911, Hampton, GA, **d.** Jul. 25, 1985, Decatur, GA
Vocals, piano / Piano blues
An albino Black, this "Piano Red" was the cousin to another piano man, "Speckled Red." —*Cub Koda*

○ **Jump Man, Jump** / 1956 / Groove 1001
Raucous barrelhouse blues and boogies with a hot R&B combo on these swinging sides. —*Bill Dahl*

Atlanta Bounce / 1992 / Arhoolie 379
Combination of later solo Arhoolie material and a handful of great live items from '56 Magnolia Ballroom set on Groove. —*Bill Dahl*

● **Wildfire** / Matchbox 902
A dozen tracks of Red at his poundin' best. —*Cub Koda*

Rod Piazza and the Mighty Flyers

Vocals, harmonica / Modern electric blues
A California-based blues bandleader, harmonica, and singer, Piazza's stratospheric harmonica wailings owe a heavy debt to both Little Walter and George "Harmonica" Smith. —*Cub Koda*

○ **Blues in the Dark** / 1991 / Black Top 1062
Blues in the Dark is a contender for the title of Black Top's best, head and shoulders above many of the label's better known efforts. —*Roundup Newsletter*

○ **Alphabet Blues** / 1992 / Black Top 1076
Rod Piazza and the Mighty Flyers follow up their acclaimed *Blues in the Dark* with this smokin' new release. Piazza's harp playing paints both bold splashes of color and subtle shadings, while his sturdy vocals are supported by a tight combo of piano, guitar, bass, and drums. Of the 12 tunes here, 10 are originals, with 7 penned by Piazza and 3 by pianist Miss Honey. This West Coast band knows how to cruise in the pocket on the slow-burning blues numbers and turn up the heat on the uptempo shuffles. —*Roundup newsletter*

● **Essential Collection, The** / 1992 / Hightone 8041
Compilation of fairly recent sides by the powerhouse West Coast harpist; like most of his work, it smokes! —*Bill Dahl*

Dan Pickett

Vocals, guitar / Acoustic country blues
Reissuers have unearthed little information about Dan Pickett: He may have come from Alabama, he played a nice slide guitar in a Southeastern blues style, and he did one recording session for the Philadelphia-based Gotham label in 1949. That session produced five singles, all of which have now been compiled along with four previously unreleased sides on a reissue album that purports to contain Pickett's entire recorded output—unless, of course, as some reviewers have speculated, Dan Pickett happens also to be Charlie Pickett, the Tennessee guitarist who recorded for Decca in 1937. As Tony Russell observed in *Juke Blues*, both Picketts recorded blues about lemon-squeezing, and Dan uses the

name Charlie twice in the lyrics to "Decoration Day." 'Tis from such mystery and speculation that the minds of blues collectors do dissolve. —*Jim O'Neal*

○ **1949 Country Blues** / 1990 / Collectables 5311
A CD reissue of beautiful, ragtime-esque acoustic blues. Generally very lighthearted. —*Niles J. Frantz*

Sammy Price (Samuel Blythe Price)

b. Oct. 6, 1908, Honey Grove, Texas, **d.** Apr. 14, 1992
piano, leader / Blues, Piano blues, Boogie-woogie, Traditional bluegrass, Swing, Stride
Among the last of the vintage stomping barrelhouse, blues, and boogie pianists, Sammy Price actually got his start professionally as a singer and dancer with Alphonso Trent's band in the late '20s. He arrived in Kansas City in 1930 and spent three years immersing himself in the swing sound of Count Basie and Pete Johnson before he moved to Chicago and later Detroit. Price moved to New York in 1938, becoming house pianist for American Decca and providing the pianistic foundation for great sessions featuring such vocalists as Trixie Smith and Sister Rosetta Tharpe. He subsequently worked on 52nd Street, appearing at such clubs as the Famous Door and Cafe Society. Price organized the first Black-supervised and -administered jazz festival in Philadelphia in 1946, and he later appeared at the Nice Festival with Mezz Mezzrow. Price worked a decade with Allen, until the latter's death in 1967. —*Ron Wynn*

○ **In Paris** / 1956 / Brunswick 54037
With Sidney Bechet, Price's "Bluesicians" hit on old-time and good-time standards—Bechet, as always, in good tune. —*Michael G. Nastos*

★ **Fire** / May 1, 1975 / Black & Blue 233079
The Texas blues and jazz pianist plays in good time and old time format with the basic trio of J. C. Heard, Carl Pruitt, and guests Ted Buckner, The Mighty Flea (Gene Connors), and Doc Cheatham. Includes ten Price originals. —*Michael G. Nastos*

○ **And the Blues Singers** / Wolf 007
Unbelievably huge four-disc set examines Price primarily as accompanist to a variety of 1940s vocalists. —*Bill Dahl*

○ **Rib Joint/Roots of Rock & Roll** / Savoy 4417
Great mid-'50s instrumental R&B with Price's 88s abetted by King Curtis on sax and guitarist Mickey Baker. —*Bill Dahl*

Professor Longhair (Henry Roeland Byrd)

b. Dec. 19, 1918, Bogalusa, LA, **d.** Jun. 30, 1980, New Orleans, LA
Vocals, piano, drums, guitar / R&B, Rock & Roll, Acoustic New Orleans blues
Born Henry Roeland Byrd and known affectionately as "Fess" to most New Orleans residents, Professor Longhair began his musical career as a street entertainer in the early '30s. By the late '40s he was playing piano, leading small combos with arcane names such as the Four Hairs Combo and Professor Longhair and His Shuffling Hungarians. He worked as part of Dave Bartholomew's big band in 1949, then began a series of recordings for various labels, including Star Talent, Mercury, and Atlantic. For the next 20 years Professor Longhair continued to record for obscure labels but remained on the fringes of the New Orleans scene, forced to supplement his meager earnings from music with odd day jobs.

In 1971 he re-created the Four Hairs Combo for an appearance at the New Orleans Jazz and Heritage Festival. This inaugurated the comeback phase of his musical career and attracted the interest of a small but dedicated cadre of college students who undertook his rehabilitation as part of a burgeoning roots revival.

As he stated, "I'm a little rowdy with my playing," and the synthesis he developed of calypso and rhumba rhythms, boogie-woogie, and street-parade music became the basis for young groups like the Neville Brothers and the Radiators as they sought to translate their own respective musical visions of the New Orleans "good-time" heritage. Despite his often unorthodox approach, Fess remained true to the essence of New Orleans music in never straying too far from the basic maxims of "feeling, freedom, and fun."

At the time of his death in 1980, he was the most popular and revered musician in New Orleans. His passing left a vacuum in the city's long-standing piano traditions, seemingly closing the book on an illustrious musical heritage. —*Bruce Boyd Raeburn*

Piedmont Blues

"Piedmont blues" refers to a regional substyle characteristic of African-American musicians of the southeastern United States. Geographically, the Piedmont means the foothills of the Appalachians west of the tidewater region and Atlantic coastal plain stretching roughly from Richmond, VA, to Atlanta, GA. Musically, Piedmont blues describes the shared style of musicians from Georgia, the Carolinas, and Virginia as well as others from as far afield as Florida, West Virginia, Maryland, and Delaware. It refers to a wide assortment of aesthetic values, performance techniques, and shared repertoire rooted in common geographical, historical, and sociological circumstances; to put it more simply, Piedmont blues means a constellation of musical preferences typical of the Piedmont region.

Piedmont artists include guitarists Blind Blake, Gary Davis, Josh White, Pink Anderson, Blind Boy Fuller, Buddy Moss, John Cephas, and John Jackson as well as harmonica players Sonny Terry and Phil Wiggins. The Piedmont guitar style employs a complex fingerpicking style in which a regular, alternating-thumb bass pattern supports a melody on treble strings. The guitar style is highly syncopated and connects closely with an earlier string-band tradition integrating ragtime, blues, and country dance songs. It's excellent party music with a full, rock-solid sound.

– Barry Lee Pearson

○ **New Orleans Piano** / 1972 / Atlantic 7225
The ultimate Professor Longhair album (Volume 2 of the *Blues Originals* series), featuring New Orleans legends Lee Allen and Earl Palmer. —*Bruce Boyd Raeburn*

○ **Rock 'n Roll Gumbo** / 1977 / Dancing Cat 3006
Featuring great renditions of New Orleans standards such as "Junco Partner" and "Rockin' Pneumonia" with an all-star band that features Clarence "Gatemouth" Brown on guitar and violin. —*Bruce Boyd Raeburn*

Crawfish Fiesta / 1980 / Alligator 4718
Fess's revival-period band burns through a mixed bag of vintage favorites, complete with a horn section. The presence of Dr. John on guitar is a special treat. —*Bruce Boyd Raeburn*

○ **Mardi Gras in New Orleans** / 1982 / Nighthawk 108
A compendium of early Longhair classics (1949–57) via the Shuffling Hungarians, the Blues Jumpers, and the Blues Scholars. —*Bruce Boyd Raeburn*

House Party / 1987 / Rounder 2057
A classic pairing of Professor Longhair with New Orleans guitar legend Snooks Eaglin and drummer "Zig" Modeliste of the Meters. —*Bruce Boyd Raeburn*

★ **Fess: Professor Longhair Anthology** / 1993 / Rhino
An essential two-CD set that covers the highlights of Professor Longhair's career, including all of his best-known songs and performances. —*Stephen Thomas Erlewine*

○ **Houseparty New Orleans Style** / 1994 / Rounder
Boiling blues and his trademark Afro-Latin and boogie-woogie riffs were the menu when Professor Longhair brought his Crescent City music show to Baton Rouge, LA, and Memphis in 1971 and 1972. The 15 numbers on this set matched the great pianist with an esteemed array of musicians that included outstanding guitarist Snooks Eaglin on both sessions, and fine rhythm sections as well. —*Ron Wynn*

Snooky Pryor (James Edward Pryor)

b. Sep. 15, 1921, Lambert, MS
Vocals, harmonica, drums / Electric Chicago blues
A staple of the Chicago scene from the mid-'40s onward, Pryor contributed solid harp work to numerous early Chicago classics, as both a leader and a sideman. His signature instrumental,

"Boogie," became the basis for Little Walter's hit "Juke," while his "Someone to Love" was later adapted by the Yardbirds. A true journeyman, Pryor worked with just about every major (and minor) bluesman at one time or another, and continues to record and perform today, his workmanlike skills intact. —*Cub Koda*

★ **Snooky Pryor** / 1969 / Jewel 11
These tracks from the JOB label, recorded from the early '50s to early '60s, include the classics "Boogie" and "Stockyard Blues" and the raucous, echo-laden stomp of "Boogie Twist." These are Pryor's finest moments on wax. —*Cub Koda*

○ **Snooky & Moody** / 1980 / Flyright 565
The team of Snooky Pryor and Moody Jones don't have the same reputation as other tandems like Leroy Carr and Scrapper Blackwell or Tampa Red and Big Maceo Meriweather, but they certainly created several fine numbers themselves. This collection highlights several of them, and shows each musician was a capable performer and interpreter. —*Ron Wynn*

Snooky / Blind Pig 72387
Fine recent effort. —*Bill Dahl*

○ **Snooky Pryor** / Paula 11
Pryor's pioneering late-'40s/early-50s sides for various small Chicago firms. —*Bill Dahl*

Yank Rachell

b. Mar. 16, 1910, Brownsville, TN
Vocals, guitar, harmonica, mandolin / Acoustic country blues
Best known for his down-home mandolin playing, guitarist, vocalist, and songwriter Yank Rachell played a central role in several of the most exciting chapters in blues history. Born in either Mississippi or Tennessee, he took up mandolin as a youngster and was soon making the rounds with the Brownsville, TN, blues crowd: John Estes, John Lee "Sonny Boy" Williamson, Jab Jones, and Homesick James Williamson. During the '30s he was part of the vibrant St. Louis blues community, working with Henry Townsend and Big Joe Williams before moving on to Chicago. For the past 30 years he has resided in Indianapolis, presiding over still another blues community, which once included Shirley Griffith, J. T. Adams, and guitarist Pete Franklin. When I met Rachell in the early '70s, he had put an electric band together with his son-in-law and some local R&B players. Although much of his recording career with Victor, ARC, Bluebird, and Delmark was spent accompanying others, he composed and sang powerful songs such as "Lake Michigan Blues" and "Gravel Road Woman." When he visited my classroom in 1976, he told the students he coauthored the classic "Schoolgirl" with his onetime partner Sonny Boy Williamson. Explaining his music, he said: "I learned it the hard way, out in the country all by myself—so far back in the woods my breath smelled like cord wood." Throughout his lengthy career, his music changed little, holding a country dance flavor. At the same time, he demonstrated a remarkable ability to play with other musicians—the mark of a seasoned string-band veteran. For 60 years Rachell worked in various ensemble formats, but his heart remained with his string-band roots. —*Barry Lee Pearson*

Blues Mandolin Man / 1902 / Blind Pig 1986
This contains fine material by one of the few great mandolin bluesmen. —*Barry Lee Pearson*

● **Chicago Style** / 1987 / Delmark 649
While Yank Rachell was past his prime when he began recording for Delmark in the '60s, he was still an effective, often exciting vocalist and mandolin player. He seldom sounded more striking and enjoyable than on the nine cuts that comprised *Chicago Style*. Rachell sang with a spirited mix of irony, anguish, dismay, and bemusement on such numbers as "Depression Blues," "Diving Duck," and "Going to St. Louis." —*Ron Wynn*

Bobby Radcliff

Vocals, guitar / R&B, Modern electric blues
Although blues guitarist and singer Bobby Radcliff has been honing his craft for the last 20 years around his native Washington, D.C., the 40-year-old veteran only recently entered the national blues spotlight with a couple of stellar recordings for the Louisiana-based Black Top Records label.
   Radcliff's fiery playing and strong, energetic vocals are sure to make him one of the guiding lights of blues music throughout

the '90s. His two Black Top releases, "Dresses Too Short" and "Universal Blues," were received well by the critics but were not big sellers. Perhaps the most exciting thing about Radcliff is knowing that he's only just begun. The best is yet to come. —*Richard Skelly*

● **Dresses Too Short** / Oct. 1989 / Black Top 1048
A Magic Sam devotee who tastefully updates the Chicago sound. —*Robert Gordon*

Universal Blues / 1991 / Black Top 1067
Again, tasteful. Searing but not showy. —*Robert Gordon*

Ma Rainey (Gertrude Rainey)

b. Apr. 26, 1886, Columbus, GA, d. Dec. 22, 1939, Columbus, GA
Vocals / Classic female blues
Ma Rainey wasn't the first blues singer to make records, but by all rights she probably should have been. In an era when women were the marquee names in blues, Ma Rainey was once the most celebrated of all—the "Mother of the Blues" had been singing the music for more than 20 years before she made her recording debut (Paramount, 1923). With the advent of blues records, she became even more influential, immortalizing such songs as "See See Rider," "Bo-Weavil Blues," and "Ma Rainey's Black Bottom." Like the other classic blues divas, she had a repertoire of pop and minstrel songs as well as blues, but she maintained a heavier, tougher vocal delivery than the cabaret blues singers who followed. Ma Rainey's records featured her with jug bands, guitar duos, and bluesmen such as Tampa Red and Blind Blake, in addition to the more customary horns-and-piano jazz-band accompaniment (occasionally including such luminaries as Louis Armstrong, Kid Ory, and Fletcher Henderson). —*Jim O'Neal*

★ **Ma Rainey's Black Bottom** / Jun. 1975 / Milestone 47021
The archetypical "classic" blues femme belter on 1924–28 recordings, with Fletcher Henderson on piano and Coleman Hawkins bass sax on two tracks. —*Mark A. Humphrey*

A. C. Reed

b. May 9, 1926, Wardell, MO
Vocals, Sax / Electric Chicago blues
One of a handful of sax players to ever assume a featured role as singer/bandleader in Chicago blues, Aaron Corthen once based his act on a reputed relationship to Jimmy Reed, going so far as to assume the last name in addition to the musical posture. After years of sideman duty with Buddy Guy, Albert Collins, and others, recording occasional singles along the way, A. C. thrust his songwriting wit to the fore and came up with a successful new persona—that of the anti-blues bluesman. Coproducing his own albums with sidekick Casey Jones, Reed has become noted for titles such as "Take These Blues and Shove 'Em," "I Am Fed Up with This Music," and "I'm in the Wrong Business." Despite the comic-yet-sincere sentiments expressed, Reed has remained a bluesman through and through. —*Jim O'Neal*

Take These Blues and Shove 'Em / 1982 / Rooster Blues 7606
Take These Blues and Shove 'Em is a very nice record of seven of Reed's originals, plus a cover of Willie Dixon and Howlin' Wolf's "Howlin' for My Darling." —*Niles J. Frantz*

● **I'm in the Wrong Business** / 1987 / Alligator 4757
Solid, soulful blues, often with humorous, self-deprecating lyrics, from the well-respected vocalist, tenor player, composer, and veteran of the bands of Albert Collins, Buddy Guy, Magic Sam, and Son Seals. Reed has been called "the definitive Chicago blues sax player." This album features Reed's band, with guests Bonnie Raitt and Stevie Ray Vaughan. —*Niles J. Frantz*

Jimmy Reed (Mathis James Reed)

b. Sep. 6, 1925, Dunleith, MS, d. Aug. 29, 1976, Oakland, CA
Vocals, guitar, harmonica / R&B, Electric Chicago blues
Lazy, loping, and insistent, Reed's music revolved around his mush-mouthed vocals and countryish harmonica solos against the driving boogie guitar of long-time partner Eddie Taylor. The formula proved to be enormously successful, as Reed crossed over to the pop charts on many occasions, a rare feat for an unreconstructed bluesman. Songs like "Baby, What You Want Me to Do," "Bright Lights, Big City," "Going to New York," and "Big Boss Man" have become such an integral part of the standard blues repertoire, it's almost as if they had existed forever. Because

Reed's style was simple and easily imitated, his songs were accessible to everyone from high school garage bands to Elvis Presley and the Rolling Stones, making him, in the long run, perhaps the most influential bluesman of all. —*Cub Koda*

★ **Live at Carnegie Hall/Best of Jimmy Reed** / 1961 / Suitebeat 3001
Not a live album at all; two LPs of Reed's finest studio efforts for Vee-Jay. —*Bill Dahl*

○ **High & Lonesome** / 1981 / Charly 1013
A great collection of Reed's earliest and rarest sides. —*Cub Koda*

○ **Big Boss Blues** / 1986 / Charly 389
Although many "best of Jimmy Reed" compilations exist on the market (most with variable sound quality and maddening duplication), this import features all the influential hits and is a perfect place to start. —*Cub Koda*

○ **Ride 'Em on Down** / 1989 / Charly 171
A compilation shared with Eddie Taylor (with Reed in support on four tracks), this features a dozen tracks from Reed's early days. It's the perfect companion piece to *Big Boss Blues.* —*Cub Koda*

★ **Speak the Lyrics to Me, Mama Reed** / Vee Jay 705
Jimmy Reed's singles for Vee-Jay were the ultimate in simplicity; he recycled his loping, shuffle beat continually, sang in laconic, steady fashion, and played his guitar and harmonica in a relaxed, easy manner. He didn't dazzle anyone with technique, and each song was almost a replay of its predecessor. Yet they were enormously popular, and had their own charm and appeal, mainly Reed's joyous enunciations, wailing harp, and flickering riffs. This 25-track disc includes most of his best-known hits—"You Don't Have to Go," "Honest I Do," "Take Out Some Insurance," "Baby What You Want Me to Do," "Bright Lights, Big City"—plus four cuts in stereo and is a good introduction to his sound. —*Ron Wynn*

Sonny Rhodes

b. Nov. 3, 1940, Smithville, TX
Vocals, guitar, lap steel guitar, sometimes bass / Modern electric blues
Sonny Rhodes is a bluesman who has found ways to set himself apart from the rest of the pack—visually with his trademark turban, musically with his tantalizing lap steel guitar playing, and philosophically with his "Disciple of the Blues" tag. The steel has been part of his act only since 1977, when he decided to carry on the Bay Area tradition of L. C. "Good Rockin'" Robinson; Rhodes is also a fine instrumentalist on the conventional electric guitar. As a songwriter of some note, Rhodes was a disciple of the legendary Percy Mayfield. With several European and American albums now to his credit, Rhodes is best known for his work in California during the '70s and '80s. He felt it was time for a change a few years ago and, always wanting to be different, now lives in New Jersey. —*Jim O'Neal*

○ **Disciple of the Blues** / 1991 / Ichiban 9002
This be-turbaned bluesman plays lap steel guitar. This is a good one, but I know he's got an even better one in him. —*Niles J. Frantz*

● **Livin' Too Close to the Edge** / 1992 / Ichiban 9016
Sizzling contemporary blues. —*Bill Dahl*

Tommy Ridgley

b. Oct. 30, 1925, New Orleans, LA
Vocals, piano / R&B, Electric New Orleans blues, Dixieland
Tommy Ridgley has been right with the New Orleans rhythm and blues movement ever since the early Imperial recording era, achieving his share of local renown and regional success despite a lack of national hits. Influenced in his younger days by the blues shouting style of Roy Brown and Big Joe Turner, Ridgley eventually became known for his ballad singing; a similarity to Chuck Willis also earned him the title "The New King of the Stroll." After recording for Imperial, Atlantic, and Herald, Ridgley turned to local New Orleans labels in the '60s. After an ensuing lull, he has been recording again in recent years and is still a talent to be reckoned with. —*Jim O'Neal*

● **New Orleans King of the Stroll, The** / 1988 / Rounder 2079
This 15-track collection mostly covers Ridgley material from 1960 to 1964 for the Ric label, and ranges from laments like "Please Hurry Home" and "I Love You Yes I Do" to such comic

material and dance-based numbers as "Double-Eyed Whammy," "The Girl from Kooka Monga." There's also two numbers produced by Wardell Quezergue for Watch Records, "All My Love Belongs to You" and "I Want Some Money Baby." Ridgely wasn't as booming nor as dynamic as some other Crescent City vocalists, but made several nice period pieces and soul tunes, several of which are included on this set. —*Ron Wynn*

She Turns Me on / 1992 / Modern Blues 1203
Credible comeback set for the Crescent City veteran vocalist. —*Bill Dahl*

○ **Herald Recordings, The** / Collectables 5182
Rocking New Orleans R&B; Ridgley's strong vocals match the roaring rhythms of the vaunted Casimo's studio crew. —*Bill Dahl*

Fenton Robinson

b. Sep. 23, 1935, Minter City, MS
Vocals, guitar / Modern electric blues, Chicago Blues
"The Mellow Blues Genius," as his Japanese fans have dubbed him, is a widely praised and honored artist, yet Robinson has had to struggle financially throughout a career that has most often found him an undeniably distinctive and original stylist in search of a market. After recording in a Memphis-based blues style early in his career (Meteor, 1957, and Duke, 1959), Robinson moved from Arkansas to Chicago in 1961 and began staking out his own stylistic territory, one that made use of his extensive and growing knowledge of musical structures and progressions. His well-known "Somebody Loan Me a Dime" (Palos, 1967, later re-recorded for Alligator) was an early culmination of his blues vision. A thinking man of the blues, Robinson seems forever ready to explore something new, moving to a new city every few years and continually experimenting with his fluid, jazz-flavored blues, perhaps just too far ahead or too far removed for the rest of the blues world to catch up. —*Jim O'Neal*

○ **Somebody Loan Me a Dime** / 1974 / Alligator 4705
As good as modern blues gets. —*Bill Dahl*

● **I Hear Some Blues Downstairs** / 1977 / Alligator 4710
Mellow blues, featuring Robinson's jazz-inflected guitar work and smooth, soaring vocals. Very, very nice. —*Niles J. Frantz*

Blues in Progress / 1984 / Black Magic 9005
Smooth and jazzy. —*Bill Dahl*

Nightflight / 1984 / Alligator 4736
Solid, innovative guitar and mellow vocals. —*Bill Dahl*

Jimmy Rogers (James A. Lane)

b. Jun. 3, 1924, Ruleville, MS
Vocals, guitar, harmonica, piano / R&B, Electric Chicago blues
Rogers was an original founding member of Chicago's first electric blues band with Muddy Waters and Little Walter, in a trio originally known as the Headhunters. He worked as a guitarist in Waters's band throughout the '50s, cutting solo sides for Chess at the tail end of Muddy's sessions, using the same lineup. The first record issued in his name, "That's All Right," became a huge hit and a blues standard to this day. Further sessions throughout the '50s utilized the cream of Chicago blues players, making every side a gem of that genre. The most notable was Big Walter Horton's earth-shattering solo on Jimmy's "Walking by Myself." With his Mississippi roots fully intact, Jimmy Rogers stands as one of the last great Chicago blues artists actively performing and recording today. —*Cub Koda*

Gold Tailed Bird / 1971 / Shelter ?
Roger's attempt to break through to a new younger audience was less exciting than his Chess years but plausible none the less. —*Bill Dahl*

○ **Bluemasters** / 1976 / Chess 207
Fine two-LP compilation of his early Chess sides that deserves CD reissue soon. —*Bill Dahl*

★ **Chicago Bound** / 1976 / Chess 93000
Classic '50s Chess sessions with Little Walter and Muddy Waters, including the 1956 hit "Walking by Myself." —*Barry Lee Pearson*

Ludella / 1990 / Antone's 0012
Representative of one of Chicago's most important artists. —*Barry Lee Pearson*

Jimmy Rogers / Chess 92505

The ultimate in El Cheapo packaging, and with barely acceptable sound quality to boot, nevertheless this set contains absolutely essential music. There's several Rogers gems from the early and mid-'50s, and also some other cuts culled from various reissues. —*Ron Wynn*

Roomful of Blues

b. , Providence, RI
Group / Modern jump blues
This nine-piece blues/jump band from Providence, RI, formed in 1967. They have recorded and toured tirelessly for over two decades while eschewing the standard Chicago blues band/Muddy Waters approach for a horn dominated style that owes more to jazz learnings and late-'40s blues masters like Wynonie Harris, Roy Brown, and Big Joe Turner. More than capable of backing artists like Turner and Eddie "Cleanhead" Vinson (both had Roomful back them for complete albums) as well as delivering the goods on their own, major players who have come through the ranks over the years have included guitarists Duke Robillard and Ronnie Earl, bassist Preston Hubbard, and drummer Fran Christina (Fabulous Thunderbirds). —*Cub Koda*

● **Let Have a Party** / Nov. 1979 / Antilles 7071
Decent-to-good R&B-influenced jump and party blues. This group live has always been great. Their albums have always been mixed affairs, and this was no different. —*Ron Wynn*

○ **Hot Little Mama** / 1981 / Varrick 21

Dr. Isiah Ross

b. Oct. 21, 1925, Tunica, MS
Vocals, guitar, harmonica / Acoustic country blues
A triple-threat guitarist, harp blower, and vocalist, Dr. Ross decided to fire his sidemen over 30 years ago and carry on as a one-man band, a tradition that also includes Joe Hill Louis, Daddy Stovepipe, and Jesse Fuller. Ross's music does not depend on novelty effect, yet it has a distinctly recognizable sound, in part because he learned to play his own way and essentially plays everything backwards. His guitar is tuned to open *G* (like John Lee Hooker and other Delta artists), but Ross plays it left-handed and upside-down. He also plays harmonica in a rack, but it is turned around with the low notes to the right. As an instrumentalist, Ross has perfected the interplay between guitar and harmonica. Unlike other Delta artists who tune in *G*, Ross doesn't use slide, preferring a series of banjolike strummed riffs, a percussive approach reminiscent of Atlanta 12-string guitarist Barbecue Bob. A strong vocalist and excellent songwriter, Ross gained early experience playing Delta jukes and eventually landed radio shows in Clarksdale and Memphis, where he also recorded for Sam Phillips's Sun label.

At the peak of Ross's career, he quit Sun, concerned that his royalties were being used to promote Elvis Presley's recordings. Relocating to Michigan, he recorded for his own label and for several Detroit labels while working for General Motors. Returning to music as a recording artist, he recently worked the festival circuit. To the present day, Ross's music retains the spirit of his live radio and juke-joint work. I feel the sides he recorded with a band for Sun produced his best material, including classics like "Chicago Breakdown" and "Boogie Disease." As Dr. Ross put it in an interview ten years ago, "I'm kind of like the little boy from the West; I'm different from the rest." Different, yes, but very good. —*Barry Lee Pearson*

● **Boogie Disease** / Arhoolie 371
This one will make your teeth rattle. Veteran of the early '50s Sun Studio in Memphis, Ross became known as the "one-man band," a routine gleaned from his mentor Joe Hill Louis. He plays both fine harp (out of the Sonny Boy I mold) and exciting rhythm guitar characterized by churning, mesmerizing rhythms spiced by treble fills. These 22 infectious tracks are the good doctor's very first recordings, and they present him with a rhythm section—a style that predates his "one-man" days. —*Larry Hoffman*

Otis Rush

b. Apr. 29, 1934, Philadelphia, MS
Vocals, guitar / Soul, R&B, Electric Chicago blues
Part of the celebrated West Side school of guitarists (the other two notables being Buddy Guy and Magic Sam), Rush quickly distanced himself from the pack by coming up with a style that was more broodingly intense and introspective than either of them. His early recordings combined Robert Johnson–like anguished vocals with sweet, stinging guitar solos in a B. B. King mode, both with a unique voice. Influencing countless young guitarists on both sides of the Atlantic (Jimmy Page, Eric Clapton, and Stevie Ray Vaughan being just the tip of the iceberg), Rush continues to record and tour to this day, still occasionally connecting with the private demons that make his brand of blues so compelling. —*Cub Koda*

Mourning in the Morning / Aug. 1969 / Atlantic 82367
Mourning in the Morning has aged pretty well. On this Mike Bloomfield–produced set, guitarist and singer Rush is surrounded by some extremely sympathetic players (especially the horns) and the presence of Duane Allman on second guitar frequently inspires Rush to sing and play harder. But the material is inconsistent and Rush's lead lines sometimes seem in opposition to the song he's supposedly trying to put over. There's much here worth hearing, but those unfamiliar with Rush have many better places to start. — *Jimmy Guterman, Roundup Newsletter*

○ **Door to Door (With Albert King)** / Jun. 1970 / Chess 9322
Rush's performance of "So Many Roads" here should not be missed at any cost. Also includes tracks by Albert King. —*Cub Koda*

Screamin' & Cryin' / Nov. 26, 1974 / Evidence 26014
Otis Rush's crunching guitar and vocals were never more emphatic than during the '70s, when it seemed that he would actually find the pop attention and mass stardom he deserved. These mid-'70s tracks were originally cut for the Black and Blue label, with Rush playing grinding, relentless riffs and creating waves of sonic brilliance through creatively repeated motifs, jagged notes, and sustained lines and licks. —*Ron Wynn*

○ **Cold Day in Hell** / 1976 / Delmark 638
The blues legend's maddening inconsistency surfaces from time to time on *Cold Day In Hell*, a 1975 album that catches fire just enough to make it essential to Otis Rush's ardent followers. When he's in the mood, as on a slashing reprise of Ricky Allen's wicked "Cut You A Loose" and the indulgent but intriguing title cut, Rush unleashes his vibrato-laden axe and wailing vocals with frightening intensity, his solid combo lending tough support. —*Bill Dahl, Goldmine*

☆ **Right Place, Wrong Time** / Feb. 1976 / Hightone 8007
The material is excellent, the sound fine, and this album is deservedly a minor legend, albeit nowhere so raw as Rush's '50s Cobra sides. — *Mark A. Humphrey, Rock & Roll Disc*

★ **Cobra Recordings, 1956–58** / 1989 / Flyright 01
The songs that made the legend—"All Your Love," "Double Trouble," "I Can't Quit You, Baby." All 16 Cobra sides plus the bonus of 4 alternate takes. These are milestone recordings in the history of blues. —*Cub Koda*

○ **This Way** / 1994 / Mercury
On *This Way*, Rush gets first-rate production, engineering, and material. There's only one original out of 12 cuts, but when he's putting his stamp on classics by Albert and B.B. King, Sam Cooke, Ray Charles, and Percy Mayfield, it's hard to complain. Rush emphasizes uptempo, surging numbers rather than slow, teeming tunes, and there aren't many examples of his jagged, cutting solos, but his vocals are among his most dynamic and arresting in many years. It's certainly his finest work since the '70s Bullfrog sessions. —*Ron Wynn*

Saffire

Group / Modern acoustic blues
Saffire, a trio of women from Fredericksburg, VA, have been making fine acoustic blues together since 1984. They began pursuing blues as professionals in the mid-'80s and have been delighting audiences around the country with their interpretations of the sassy blues tunes of Ma Rainey, Bessie Smith, and other blues divas from the '20s and '30s ever since. But the three are also talented lyricists and arrangers, and their original tunes are firmly rooted in the blues tradition. —*Richard Skelly*

● **Hot Flash** / 1991 / Alligator 4796
A great place for blues beginners, but not for purists. Good variety. —*Robert Gordon*

Satan & Adam

Vocals, guitar, harmonica / Modern acoustic blues
Sterling "Satan" Magee (b. May 20, 1936, Mount Olive, MS; vocals, guitar, hi-hats); Adam Gussow (harmonica). Dubbed "a PR man's dream" by *Chicago Reader* critic David Whiteis, "this pairing of a grizzled veteran Harlem street singer and a young refugee from the Broadway theater" created something of a sensation after the release of their first album in 1991, following up on the buzz started by the inclusion of a Satan & Adam track in U2's *Rattle & Hum* (both on film and on record). Their material, while rarely falling within the typical guidelines of blues, is nonetheless spirited and moving, with enough of a blues base that the duo has now appeared at a number of major blues festivals. Adam, the Broadway refugee, never lets up on his harp, while Satan (who was an R&B session man before embarking on his New York street musician's career) stomps a hi-hat rig with both feet, as streams of rhythm flow from his guitar. Satan, who also recorded under his real name for the Ray Charles Tangerine label back in the '60s, is a Mississippi native who is as consumed by his music as the blues greats from his home state have been by theirs. *—Jim O'Neal*

● **Harlem Blues** / 1991 / Flying Fish 70567
Satan (an outrageous and unique street musician/bluesman) meets Adam (a young harp player) with magic results! A wonderful album. *—Niles J. Frantz*

Mother Mojo / Jan. 1993 / Flying Fish
More magical root music. *—Bill Dahl*

Son Seals

b. Aug. 13, 1942, Osceola, AR
Vocals, guitar, sometimes drums / Electric Chicago blues
When Son Seals recorded his debut album in 1973, he quickly earned a reputation as the hottest new talent in blues. Not long up from Arkansas, he brought with him a searing, relentless guitar attack and a gruff vocal manner. His style was based mostly on Albert King but came across quite a bit more rough and urgent. (Seals had once been King's drummer.) Over the years, Seals acquired more of his mentor's musical polish, and although the fiery rawness has mellowed some, Seals remains one of Chicago's most highly regarded bluesmen. *—Jim O'Neal*

● **Son Seals Blues Band, The** / 1973 / Alligator 4703
The debut album from this fiery Chicago stringbender. *—Mark A. Humphrey*

Midnight Son / Jun. 1977 / Alligator 4708
More hot stuff. *—Mark A. Humphrey*

○ **Live & Burning** / 1978 / Alligator 4712
This lives up to its title! *—Mark A. Humphrey*

Bad Axe / 1984 / Alligator 4738
Truth in advertising. *—Mark A. Humphrey*

Johnny Shines (John Ned Shines)

b. Apr. 26, 1915, Frayser, TN, d. Apr. 20, 1992
Vocals, guitar / Acoustic & electric Delta blues
Johnny Shines's best material crackles with energy. In his prime, his slashing slide guitar carried more of the spirit of his onetime running mate Robert Johnson than any other traditional blues artist. Shines, however, was never a Johnson imitator. He had his own sound, his own guitar style, and a voice that can still take you on a roller coaster ride. (However, he did learn from Johnson and his classic recordings. "Ramblin'" and "Dynaflow Blues" feel like Johnson's best work.) Shines has too much personal magnetism to be confused with anyone else. Like many artists of his generation, he is also master of the spoken word, a gifted storyteller, a social critic, and a historian dedicated to telling the truth. On stage or off, he pulls no punches, and his independent spirit and readiness to fight for what he perceives as fair have no doubt ruffled the feathers of the movers and shakers in Chicago's blues business.

Shine's distinctive style and songwriting skills should have brought him fame and fortune in music, but such was not the case. During the '40s and '50s, when he was at his peak, he only issued a handful of records. Although critically acclaimed today, these were not sufficient to keep him in the business at the time. Working outside of music in the '50s and over much of his career, he returned to the studio with Pete Welding in the '60s. These

Chicago sessions showed his musical power had not diminished. Subsequent recordings, including his collaboration with Robert Jr. Lockwood, have generally maintained a high quality. His later guitar work was hampered by a stroke, but he remained a powerful artist sustained by one of the all-time great blues voices. *—Barry Lee Pearson*

○ **Last Night Dream** / 1968 / Blue Horizon 63212
Recorded in '68 with all-star backing—harpist Walter Horton, bassist Willie Dixon, drummer Clifton James—this is one of Shines's best band backed sets, cut not too long after he mounted his successful comeback. *—Bill Dahl*

○ **Johnny Shines with Big Walter Horton** / Nov. 1969 / Testament 2217
Here's outstanding late '60s Shines material matching him with a sterling lineup. Big Walter Horton's awesome on harmonica, a young Luther Allison doesn't dissipate his brilliance on haphazard soul and funk, and pianist Otis Spann and drummer Fred Below are super on their cuts. The date combines a '66 and a '69 session; there's another LP with a full collection culled from 1966. *—Ron Wynn*

○ **Hey Ba-Ba-Re-Bop** / 1978 / Rounder 2020
Shines hadn't yet encountered the physical difficulties that made his final years so troubling when he recorded the 13 selections on this CD. Instead, Shines could still sing and moan with intensity and passion, hold a crowd hypnotized with his rembrances and asides, and play with a mix of fury and charm. While the menu includes oft-performed chestnuts "Sweet Home Chicago," "Terraplane Blues," and "Milk Cow Blues," there wasn't anything staid or predictable about the way Shines ripped through the lyrics and presented the music. If you missed it the first time around, grab this one immediately. *—Ron Wynn*

★ **Johnny Shines & Robert Lockwood** / 1979 / Flyright 10
Essential JOB sides, 1952–53. *—Jas Obrecht*

○ **Traditional Delta Blues** / 1991 / Biograph 121
Robert Johnson's pal pays homage on acoustic recordings from 1972–74. *—Jas Obrecht*

J. D. Short

b. Feb. 26, 1902, d. Oct. 21, 1962
Acoustic blues
Gifted with a striking and almost immediately identifiable vocal style characterized by an amazing vibrato, J. D. Short was also a very versatile musician. He played piano, saxophone, guitar, harmonica, clarinet, and drums. Growing up in the Mississippi Delta, Short learned guitar and piano. He was a frequent performer at house parties before he moved to St. Louis in the '20s. Short played with the Neckbones, Henry Spaulding, Honeyboy Edwards, Douglas Williams, and Big Joe Williams from the '30s until the early '60s. He recorded for Vocalion, Delmark, Folkways, and Sonet. Short was in the 1963 documentary "The Blues," but he died before it was released. *—Ron Wynn*

○ **Stavin' Chain Blues** / Jul. 1965 / Delmark 609
He could sing, wail, holler, or moan traditional Delta blues with a lot of names that were much bigger. J. D. Short didn't make a lot of records, but the few he cut during the '30s should be heard over and over to truly enjoy their quality. *—Ron Wynn*

Frankie Lee Sims

b. Apr. 30, 1917, New Orleans, LA, d. May 10, 1970, Dallas, TX
Vocals, guitar / Electric Texas blues
A Texas blues singer and guitarist who recorded in the late '40s and early '50s in a style similar to fellow Texas bluesman Lightnin' Hopkins, only much more percussive and electric. Sims had a better ability to work with full bands than did Hopkins. Sims's lyrics borrow from traditional sources, with inventive twists of their own, while the music at times sounds like a strong precursor to rock & roll. *—Cub Koda*

○ **Lucy Mae Blues** / 1970 / Specialty 7022
Sims's only album, primarily in a drums-and-electric-guitar format. *—Cub Koda*

Bessie Smith

b. Apr. 15, 1894, Chattanooga, TN, d. Sep. 26, 1937, Clarksdale, MS
Vocals / R&B, Classic female blues

Generally regarded as the greatest female blues vocalist ever, Bessie Smith—a protégé of Ma Rainey—surpassed her mentor to become the #1 blues act of the '20s. Smith's life and death were the stuff of legend, and no other blues singer has been so frequently memorialized in books and stage productions. Her music has been constantly revived over the years by leading jazz and blues vocalists. Among her most recognizable classics were "Tain't Nobody's Business If I Do," "The St. Louis Blues," "Nobody Knows You When You're Down and Out," "Careless Love Blues," and "Empty Bed Blues." Altogether Smith recorded more than 200 sides in 1923–33, many of them featuring her powerful, dramatic singing backed only by piano (Clarence Williams, Fletcher Henderson, James P. Johnson et al.), on others adding horns (Coleman Hawkins, Louis Armstrong, and Don Redman, to name just a few). —*Jim O'Neal*

★ **Collection, The** / Dec. 1989 / CBS 44441
Featuring her classics, from "Downhearted Blues" to "Gimme a Pigfoot." —*Jas Obrecht*

☆ **Complete Recordings, Vol. 1, The** / Apr. 9, 1991 / CBS 47091
Her earliest work on two discs. Nice packaging and notes. —*Bill Dahl*

○ **Complete Recordings, Vol. 2 (1924–25), The** / Sep. 10, 1991 / CBS 47471
Excellent liner notes and state-of-the-art remastering of acetates on these companion boxed sets. —*Jas Obrecht*

○ **Complete Recordings, Vol. 3, The** / Sep. 22, 1992 / CBS 47474
The third installment of Bessie Smith's complete recordings is as excellent as the first two volumes, including terrific sound and liner notes. —*AMG*

○ **Vol. 4-Complete Recordings** / CBS 52838
The fourth installment of Bessie Smith's complete recordings is as excellent as the first three volumes, including terrific sound and liner notes. —*AMG*

Byther Smith

b. Apr. 17, 1932, Monticello, MS
Vocals, guitar, sometimes bass / Modern electric blues, Chicago Blues
Byther Smith's cousin J. B. Lenoir was once Chicago's most intriguing lyricist, but these days Smith himself rates as a prime candidate for the honor. While Lenoir often wrote of political and social ills, Smith's most striking songs are disturbingly dark and deadly excursions into his own psyche. A former sideman with Junior Wells and others, Smith worked hard over the years at his musicianship, inspired especially by the guitar sound of Otis Rush. Although musically quite derivative (and usually quite a bit less dramatic) on past recordings, Smith arrived at a stylistic and emotional plane of his own, described by Chicago critic David Whiteis as one of "ominous, almost primal intensity." Though this kind of music seems not destined to win him a broad audience given current tastes in blues, Smitty's handful of releases have spawned a growing corps of true believers. —*Jim O'Neal*

○ **Tell Me How Do You Like It** / Oct. 1985 / Grits 100
Fine guitar from this longtime Chicago bluesman, including four originals. —*Barry Lee Pearson*

● **Housefire** / 1991 / Bullseye Blues 9503
A great vocalist and Chicago stalwart and former bandleader for Theresa's Lounge. —*Barry Lee Pearson*

Funny Papa Smith (John T. Smith)

b. 1890, Texas?
Vocals, guitar / Acoustic Texas blues
J. T. "Funny Papa" Smith acquired the name Howling Wolf from the title of his first record in 1930. Any influence on the more famous Chester "Howlin' Wolf" Burnett from Mississippi was probably in name only, but Smith was an influential musician within the Texas blues idiom. In fact, the liner notes of his Yazoo reissue album refer to his recordings as "practically definitive of what is known as Texas blues-playing." The notes also tout Smith's originality as a composer and his skill as an instrumentalist, "despite the fact that his guitar was chronically out of tune." Little biographical information has been published on Smith; blues guitarist Tom Shaw remembered him as the overseer of an Oklahoma plantation who was sent to prison for murder. He made his last recordings in 1935, presumably after his release.

According to *Blues Who's Who,* Smith toured with Texas Alexander in 1939; "whereabouts unknown thereafter." —*Jim O'Neal*

○ **Howling Wolf (1930–31), The** / 1971 / Yazoo 1031
Fine guitar-based Texas country blues by an artist completely unlike the later Howlin' Wolf. —*Mark A. Humphrey*

Little George Smith (George Allen Smith)

R&B
George Allen Smith was a master harmonica soloist and fine singer. He learned harmonica from his mother as a child in Helena, AR, and left home in 1934 to travel through the South. Smith played in streets and lived as a hobo, often using the name "Hip-Cat." After working in various government programs in the early '40s, Smith settled in Rhode Island. Later came gigs with the Jackson Jubilee Singers of Mississippi, and a stint as a projectionist and promoter in Mississippi. He resettled in Chicago during the early '50s, and played with Otis Rush, Muddy Waters, Champion Jack Dupree and Big Mama Thornton in the '50s and '60s. Smith made numerous festival appearances and club dates during those decades, while recording for Checker, Lapel, Sotoplay, World Pacific/Liberty, Blue Horizon, BlueTime, Advent, and Vanguard among others. Waters, Thornton, T-Bone Walker, Dupree, and Eddie Taylor were some of the musicians he recorded with and/or accompanied. Smith also recorded under various names, among them "Little Walter Jr.," "Harmonica King" and "George Allen." —*Ron Wynn*

● **Harmonica Ace** / 1993 / Capitol 86298
Some red-hot harmonica solos and often delightful vocals by a chromatic master. Known alternately as "Little" and George "Harmonica" Smith, what never changed about him was his blistering licks and amazing skills. Anything you can find by Smith you should grab, especially if you enjoy blues harmonica. —*Ron Wynn*

Mamie Smith

b. May 26, 1883, Cincinnati, OH, d. Aug. 16, 1946, New York, NY
Vocals, piano / Classic female blues
A pillar in the classic female blues tradition, Mamie Smith is generally recognized as the first to record in the genre. Her version of "Crazy Blues" was the first major hit of the blues. —*Cub Koda*

☆ **In Chronological Order, Vol. 1** / Document 551
This first volume of a five-volume import set of her complete recordings features her earliest and best sides, including the classic "Crazy Blues." —*Cub Koda*

Chris Smither

b. , New Orleans
Vocals, guitar / Modern acoustic blues
Chris Smither has forged a blues/folk synthesis from his adopted hometown of Boston. Leaving the Crescent City in 1966, Smither wrote "Love You Like a Man" for Bonnie Raitt and recorded for Poppy during the '70s and Adelphi in 1984. Smither's 1991 set for Flying Fish, *Another Way to Find You,* showcases his rough-hewn vocals and slide-guitar work. —*Bill Dahl*

● **Another Way to Find You** / 1991 / Flying Fish 70568
Recorded live in the studio in Boston in 1989 with an audience of friends and guests. Smither is a very talented folk/blues singer/songwriter and a very good guitarist. He has an attractive, low-key, introspective way about the blues. —*Niles J. Frantz*

○ **Happier Blue** / 1993 / Flying Fish

Otis Spann

b. Mar. 21, 1930, Jackson, MS, d. Apr. 24, 1970, Chicago, IL
Vocals, piano, organ, harmonica / R&B, Electric Chicago blues
Otis Spann did more than anyone else to define the pianist's role in postwar Chicago blues. His rhythmic support of Muddy Waters throughout the '50s and '60s was superb, and during his last decade Spann recorded an impressive number of his own albums, convincingly showcasing the depth of his blues. Many of Spann's recordings were made with various configurations of the Muddy Waters band, but among his most memorable sessions were those pairing him with only a guitarist or a drummer. Spann's rumbling piano and ruminant vocals were sometimes reminiscent of the previous Chicago blues piano king, Big Maceo

Merriweather. Ironically, Spann's only minor hit single, "Hungry Country Girl," was released after his death. —*Jim O'Neal*

○ **Otis Spann Is the Blues** / Aug. 1960 / Candid 79001
He may not have been *the* blues, but he was sure close to being *the blues pianist.* Spann provided wonderful, imaginative, and tasty piano solos and better than average vocals, and he was arguably the best player whose style was more restrained than animated. Not that he couldn't rock the house, but Spann's forte was making you think as well as making you dance. —*Ron Wynn*

○ **Complete Candid Recordings** / Aug. 23, 1960 / Mosaic 139
With Robert Lockwood Jr. Two classic Spann albums: *Otis Spann Is the Blues* and *Walkin' the Blues.* Early, potent Spann with flawless liner notes and a complete discography. Also included are the Candid sessions of Lightnin' Hopkins. —*Michael Erlewine*

○ **Blues Never Die, The** / Oct. 1969 / Prestige 530
Muddy Waters had the prototypical Chicago blues band of the '50s and '60s and, in Otis Spann, the most formidable down-home blues piano stylist of the modern era. This 1964 Prestige date, although issued under Spann's name, featured the entire Muddy Waters band of the period—including Waters himself, who's listed on guitar as "Dirty Rivers" for contractual reasons. Tunes include "One More Mile to Go" and the title track. —*Roundup Newsletter*

★ **Walking the Blues** / 1987 / Candid 79025
With guitarist Lockwood on many cuts. Haunting! A must-have for blues fans. —*George Bedard*

Victoria Spivey (Victoria Regina Spivey)

b. Oct. 15, 1906, Houston, TX, d. Oct. 3, 1976, New York, NY
Vocals, organ, piano, Ukelele / Classic female blues
A classic female blues singer who outlasted her competition by several decades, Spivey formed her own label in the early '70s, giving both young talent and forgotten artists a chance to reach a wider audience. —*Cub Koda*

● **1926–31** / Document 590
Spivey is in marvelous form throughout. This album features the classics "Steady Grind," "Black Snake Blues," and "Blood Thirsty Blues." —*Cub Koda*

Frank Stokes

b. Jan. 1, 1888, Whitehaven, TN, d. Sep. 12, 1955, Memphis, TN
Vocals, guitar / Acoustic Memphis blues
Frank Stokes and partner Dan Sain recorded as the Beale Street Shieks, a Memphis answer to the musical Chatmon family string band, the Mississippi Shieks. According to local tradition, Stokes was already playing the streets of Memphis by the turn of the century, about the same time the blues began to flourish. As a street artist, he needed a broad repertoire of songs and patter palatable to Blacks and Whites. A medicine show and house-party favorite, Stokes was remembered as a consummate entertainer who drew on songs from the 19th and 20th centuries with equal facility. Solo or with Sain and sometimes fiddler Will Batts, Stokes recorded 38 sides for Paramount and Victor. These treasures include blues as well as older pieces: "Chicken You Can't Roost Too High for Me," "Mr. Crump Don't Like It," an outstanding version of "You Shall" (commonly known as "You Shall Be Free"), and "Hey Mourner," a traditional comic anticlerical piece. Stokes possessed a remarkable declamatory voice and was an adroit guitarist. His duets with Sain merit special attention because of their subtle interplay and propulsive rhythm. —*Barry Lee Pearson*

★ **Victor Recordings, The** / 1902 / Document 5013
Declamatory deep blues, Memphis style, recorded in 1928–29. —*Jas Obrecht*

Beale Street Sheiks, The / 1990 / Document 5012
Contains his Paramount 1927–29 sides with Dan Sain. —*Jas Obrecht*

○ **Memphis Blues, The** / Yazoo 1008
No one in the Memphis ministrel/traveling show or early blues tradition had a more distinguished career than Frank Stokes. This is marvelous, inspiring guitar, done in such a spry and captivating manner you forget Stokes got his start working alongside a blackface comedian in the early '20s, or that much of this material by even '50s standards was borderline offensive at best. —*Ron Wynn*

Sugar Ray & the Bluetones

Vocals, harmonica / Modern electric blues
This East Coast-based blues band is fronted by singer/harmonica player Ray Norcia. Over the years, they have featured guitar work by Ronnie Earl (Roomful of Blues, Ronnie Earl & the Broadcasters) and Kid Bangham (the Fabulous Thunderbirds). —*Cub Koda*

○ **Knockout** / 1989 / Varrick 37
A surprisingly tasteful and solidly swinging album. Sugar Ray is a powerhouse vocalist and a more-than-respectable harp player. There are some good songs, too, especially the slow blues "I'm Tortured." —*Niles J. Frantz*

Don't Stand in My Way / 1990 / Bullseye Blues 9507
More swagger, less swing, and still quite good. —*Niles J. Frantz*

Hubert Sumlin

b. Nov. 16, 1931, Greenwood, MS
Vocals, guitar / Electric Chicago blues
Hubert Sumlin's lasting fame will likely remain with the slicing guitar work that emblazoned Howlin' Wolf's Chess singles of the late '50s and early '60s. The trademark sound of the longtime Wolf sideman earned him such renown that, even with virtually no experience as a bandleader or vocalist, he was seldom without an invitation to perform as a featured act or special guest on the blues club circuit after Wolf's death (1976). An early European release of Sumlin's recordings bore this quote from Jimi Hendrix on the jacket: "My favorite guitar player is Hubert Sumlin." His albums have been a varied and not always dynamic lot, but when Sumlin pulls out the stops, it's easy to understand why he's a guitar hero's hero. —*Jim O'Neal*

● **Blues Party** / 1987 / Black Top 1036
A solo recording from the '80s by the former lead guitarist for Howlin' Wolf. —*Mark A. Humphrey*

○ **Healing Feeling** / Black Top 1053
Better than the previous Black Top CD. —*Bill Dahl*

Heart & Soul / Blind Pig 73389
The vocals are more confident here. —*Bill Dahl*

Sunnyland Slim (Albert Luandrew)

b. Sep. 5, 1907, Vance, MS
Vocals, piano / Piano blues
A two-fisted barrelhouse piano man armed with a voice that in his prime was rumored to be capable of frying microphones, Sunnyland Slim has probably graced more recordings, both as sideman and leader, than any other blues piano player in history. —*Cub Koda*

○ **House Rent Party** / 1949 / Delmark 655
This is the blues as interpreted by the legendary Sunnyland Slim and some of his contemporaries, including Oden, Willie Mabon, and Jimmy Rogers. Recorded for the most part in 1950 and modeled after his popular basement jams that were happening around the same time, these classic sides present the King of the Southside Piano Players in his rollicking and blues prime. —*Mark E. Gallo, Blues Access*

○ **Slim's Shout** / 1969 / Prestige 7723
One of his best LPs, with King Curtis on roaring tenor sax and Slim swinging his best material. CD reissue boasts two bonus tracks. —*Bill Dahl*

Live at the D.C. Blues Society / Mapleshade 512630
Sunnyland Slim's brand of weary blues punctuated by rolling piano accents and boogie riffs predates both the rise and fall of Delta blues and the emergence of its urban successor. Slim toured the South in the '20s, '30s, and early '40s, then left for Chicago and has been there ever since. This blend of Delta and urban sensibilities has been infused in his songs since he began recording, and it permeates the 14 selections on the 1987 CD *Live at the D.C. Blues Society.* Though long since passed his vocal peak, Slim still spins a nifty yarn and mournful lament, while the piano keeps pounding away in the background. —*Ron Wynn*

★ **Sunnyland Slim** / Flyright 566
Here is Slim at his indefatigable best, with great support from J. B. Lenoir and Snooky Pryor. (Import) —*Cub Koda*

Roosevelt Sykes

b. Jan. 31, 1906, Elmar, AR, **d.** Jul. 17, 1983, New Orleans, LA
Vocals, piano, sometimes organ, guitar / Piano blues
Sykes was a major contributor to the blues idiom, one of the most influential figures both as an artist and a composer from the time he made his first record, the classic "44 Blues," in 1929 (Okeh). Sykes did the original versions of such timeless staples of the blues as "Driving Wheel Blues" and "Night Time Is the Right Time," and as a pianist he exerted an impact in his day on younger men such as Memphis Slim and Otis Spann in much the way that B. B. King set the standard for upcoming guitarists in later years. Sykes recorded nearly every year from 1929 through the early '50s, retaining his popularity through all the changes in music. He moved from solo piano to small combo to jump-blues band to electric postwar blues, and when the blues revival hit, Sykes was on his way again, recording robust and ribald albums for the new young audiences of the '60s and '70s. *—Jim O'Neal*

○ **Honeydripper, The** / 1961 / Prestige 7722
Roosevelt Sykes expertly fit his classic down-home piano riffs and style into a fabric that also contained elements of soul, funk, and R&B on the '60 session *The Honeydripper*. The nine-cut date included such laments as "I Hate to Be Alone," "Lonely Day" and "She Ain't for Nobody," as well as the poignant "Yes Lawd" and less weighty "Satellite Baby" and "Jailbait." Besides Sykes alternately bemused, ironic, and inviting vocals, there's superb tenor sax support from King Curtis; Robert Banks' tasty organ; and steady, nimble bass and drum assistance by Leonard Gaskins and drummer Belton Evans. *—Ron Wynn*

Roosevelt Sykes Sings the Blues / 1962 / Crown 287
Sturdy, satisfying set, no nonsense band-backed effort. *—Bill Dahl*

○ **Country Blues Piano (1929–32), The** / 1972 / Yazoo 1033
Featuring this Arkansas-born pianist/songster in some of his best early outings. *—Mark A. Humphrey*

☆ **Raining in My Heart** / 1987 / Delmark 642
United recordings from the '50s by this enduring blues belter and pianist. *—Mark A. Humphrey*

Complete Recorded Works, Vol. 1 (1929–30) / Document 5116
All of Roosevelt Sykes's recordings between 1929 and 1942 are collected on this seven-volume series; essential for hardcore fans of blues piano. *—AMG*

★ **Roosevelt Sykes (1929–41)** / Story Of Blues
A good sampling of some of Sykes's best tracks, offering a perfect introduction to this seminal pianist. *—AMG*

Tampa Red (Hudson Whittaker)

b. Jan. 8, 1904, Smithville, GA, **d.** Mar. 19, 1981, Chicago, IL
Vocals, guitar, piano, kazoo / Acoustic & electric Chicago blues
Out of the dozens of fine slide guitarists who recorded blues, only a handful—Elmore James, Muddy Waters, and Robert Johnson, for example—left a clear imprint on tradition by creating a recognizable and widely imitated instrumental style. Tampa Red was another influential musical model. During his heyday in the '20s and '30s, he was billed as "The Guitar Wizard," and his stunning slide work on steel National or electric guitar shows why he earned the title. His 30-year recording career produced hundreds of sides: hokum, pop, and jive, but mostly blues (including classic compositions "Anna Lou Blues," "Black Angel Blues," "Crying Won't Help You," "It Hurts Me Too," and "Love Her with a Feeling"). Early in Red's career, he teamed up with pianist, songwriter, and latter-day gospel composer Georgia Tom Dorsey, collaborating on double-entendre classics like "Tight Like That."

Listeners who only know Tampa Red's hokum material are missing the deeper side of one of the mainstays of Chicago blues. His peers included Big Bill Broonzy, with whom he shared a special friendship. Members of Lester Melrose's musical mafia and drinking buddies, they once managed to sleep through both games of a Chicago White Sox doubleheader. Eventually alcohol caught up with Red, and he blamed his latter-day health problems on an inability to refuse a drink.

During Red's prime, his musical venues ran the gamut of blues institutions: down-home jukes, the streets, the vaudeville theater circuit, and the Chicago club scene. Due to his polish and theater experience, he is often described as a city musician or urban artist in contrast to many of his more limited musical contempo-

raries. Furthermore, his house served as the blues community's rehearsal hall and an informal booking agency. According to the testimony of Broonzy and Big Joe Williams, Red cared for other musicians by offering them a meal and a place to stay and generally easing their transition from country to city life.

Today's listener will enjoy Tampa Red's expressive vocals and perhaps be taken aback by his kazoo solos. His songwriting has stood the test of time, and any serious slide guitar student had better be familiar with Red's guitar wizardry. *—Barry Lee Pearson*

★ **Bottleneck Guitar (1928–37)** / 1974 / Yazoo 1039
Prime cuts from one of the greatest guitarists ever to strap on a slide. *—Cub Koda*

☆ **Tampa Red: Guitar Wizard** / Oct. 1975 / RCA 25501
A 32-song collection of great slide guitar from 1934–53, featuring sidemen Carl Martin, Black Bob, Blind John Davis, Johnnie Jones, and Walter Horton. Produced by Frank Driggs, this captures the full range of blues, hokum, and pop from a most popular and influential blues player. *—Barry Lee Pearson*

○ **It's Tight Like That** / 1976 / Blues Document 2001
Superb slide and suggestive hokum from 1928–42. *—Jas Obrecht*

Bawdy Blues / 1977 / Bluesville 544
Latter-day Tampa, from the late '50s to the early '60s, with Memphis Slim and Lonnie Johnson. *—Jas Obrecht*

Don't Tampa with the Blues / 1982 / Bluesville 516
Lured out of retirement in 1960, guitarist/vocalist Tampa Red had, by that time, traded his acoustic guitar for an electric, but his trademark style was still intact. Songs include "Goodbye Baby" and "Kansas City Blues." *—Roundup Newsletter*

Complete Recorded Works, Vol. 1 (1928–29) / Document 5073
Tampa Red's complete recordings from 1928 to 1934 are collected on this five-disc series. *—AMG*

○ **Tampa Red (1928–42)** / Story Of Blues 3501
Tampa Red sang and played the guitar and kazoo with a joy and flair that made almost every tune he did instantly unforgettable. His early work's been reissued and repackaged so often, it's easy to get caught in the mire. These are marvelous cuts, matching him with various accompanists, among them Georgia Tom (later Dr. Thomas A. Dorsey), and offering the best in double-entendre, rags, topical, and novelty material. *—Ron Wynn*

Eddie Taylor

b. Jan. 29, 1923, Benoit, MS, **d.** Dec. 25, 1985, Chicago, IL
Vocals, guitar / R&B, Electric Chicago blues
One of the cruel ironies of blues history is that the boogie lines on all the great Jimmy Reed records, always referred to as the "Jimmy Reed rhythm," were in fact played by Reed's long-time partner Eddie Taylor. But Taylor was no mere sideman, having started as a juke-joint performer in Mississippi back in the late '30s. When he finally got a chance to record in the mid-'50s, his approach, though completely electric, drew its inspiration from his down-home roots, making every song a true gem of early Chicago blues. His playing on the Jimmy Reed sides may make him one of the most influential (if unheralded) guitarists in the history of the music. *—Cub Koda*

○ **I Feel So Bad** / 1972 / Hightone 8027
Fine 1972 album by underrecorded Chicago guitarist; cut in L.A. *—Bill Dahl*

● **Big Town Playboy** / 1981 / Charly 1015
Nice cuts from the sorely underrated Eddie Taylor, who found in death the respect and widespread praise he'd earned while alive. This contains some of his best songs and hottest playing. *—Ron Wynn*

Still Not Ready for Eddie / Jul. 1988 / Antone's 0005
Live set cut at Antone's Bar in Austin; some nice moments. *—Bill Dahl*

★ **Ride 'Em on Down** / Charly 171
All the classic Vee Jay sides: "Bad Boy," "Big Town Playboy," "Find My Baby," the title track, and eight others, plus a dozen more early Jimmy Reed sides with Taylor in support. *—Cub Koda*

Hound Dog Taylor (Theodore Roosevelt Taylor)

b. Apr. 12, 1917, Natchez, MS, **d.** Dec. 17, 1975, Chicago, IL
Vocals, guitar, piano / Electric Chicago blues

A truly great and influential slide guitarist, Taylor worked in a two-guitars-drums-no-bass format with guitarist Brewer Phillips and drummer Ted Harvey for well over a decade, putting his own raucous slant on the popular Elmore James style. His music was loud, raw, and totally infectious, with Phillips and Harvey driving the beat home like no one else. After seeing only two 45s issued locally in the '60s, Hound Dog became the first artist to record for Alligator Records in 1971, enjoying international success. One of his pupils, a young George Thorogood, would later co-opt Hound Dog's stage act and music with great success in the White teen market. —*Cub Koda*

★ **Hound Dog Taylor & the Houserockers** / 1971 / Alligator 4701
Hound Dog's primitive, slashing bottleneck style gave Alligator Records its start, providing them with their first star and the model for their slogan of "houserocking music." Wild, raucous, crazy music straight out of the South Side clubs, this is the perfect place to start. Features "Give Me Back My Wig," "55th Street Boogie," "She's Gone," and "Taylor's Rock," the tune that became the basis for Freddie King's signature piece, "Hideaway." —*Cub Koda*

○ **Natural Boogie** / 1973 / Alligator 4704
A second album, just as wild as his debut. Features the high-octane kick of "Take Five" and "Hawaiian Boogie" and the throbbing boogie of "See Me in the Evening." —*Cub Koda*

○ **Beware of the Dog** / 1975 / Alligator 4707
His first live album, perhaps even steamier than the first two studio efforts. Features driving versions of "Dust My Broom," "Kitchen Sink Boogie," and "Comin' 'Round the Mountain." His unique take on soul music in "Let's Get Funky" is simmering in 100-proof lunacy. —*Cub Koda*

Genuine Houserocking Music / 1982 / Alligator 4727
Previously unissued tracks from the first two studio albums. "Crossroads," Brewer Phillips's version of "Kansas City," and a wild "What'd I Say" are the standouts on this one. —*Cub Koda*

○ **Live at Joe's Place** / 1992 / New Rose 5100
Live recordings with the Houserockers from 1972 in Boston. They're drunk, they're out of tune, but the whole shebang rocks like crazy, and the crowd goes nuts. I wouldn't be without it for a second, and neither should you. —*Cub Koda*

Have Some Fun / 1992 / Wolf 120.300
More 1972 live recordings from Boston, done with the Houserockers. Better fidelity, different song selection, and a much tighter performance make this one a nice addition to Taylor's meager discography. —*Cub Koda*

Freddie's Blues / 1993 / Wolf
Third volume of live recordings from Joe's Place in Cambridge, MA, in 1972. Of the 11 tunes here, 6 are instrumentals (4 of them featuring the lead guitar of Brewer Phillips), and while Taylor and the Houserockers are generally in rare form here, some chaotic moments ("Let's Get Funky") do abound, but that's half the fun and charm of it all. —*Cub Koda*

Koko Taylor

b. Sep. 28, 1935, Memphis, TN
Vocals / R&B, Electric Chicago blues
The reigning queen of the blues has been greatly influenced by Chicago blues artists like Howlin' Wolf. She's been recording professionally since the '60s and is renowned for her gospel-style ashy contralto and her contemporary blues repertoire. —*Bil Carpenter*

○ **Koko Taylor** / 1968 / Chess 1532
Taylor's first album with top-notch band-backing including Buddy Guy and Willie Dixon (who produced). —*Bill Dahl*

○ **Koko Taylor** / 1972 / Chess 9263
A funky blues set. —*Bil Carpenter*

South Side Lady / Dec. 1, 1973 / Evidence 26007
Vocalist Koko Taylor was not a star, known commodity, or even under contract when these 15 songs were initially recorded in 1973. Instead, she had recently left Chess and was scuffling on the juke joint/honky-tonk trail, developing the voice, mannerisms, and approach that became an institution on the blues circuit thanks to her '70s and '80s Alligator albums. While many of the songs featured on this CD are now established set pieces, Taylor's voice then was still growing. Her trademark octave-leaping screams, urgent delivery, and spirited mix of innuendo, assertive-

ness, and vulnerability solidify during such numbers as "What Kind of Man Is This," "I Got What It Takes," and "I'm Gonna Get Lucky." The disc includes "Wang Dang Doodle" and energetic but not so great covers of "Big Boss Man" and "I Got My Mojo Working." —*Ron Wynn*

Southside Baby / 1975 / Black & Blue 33505
Taylor's first Alligator album; as tough and uncompromising as any she's done for the firm. —*Bill Dahl*

○ **I Got What It Takes** / 1975 / Alligator 4706
This is '60s barrelhouse blues, featuring "Wang Dang Doodle." Produced by Willie Dixon. —*Bil Carpenter*

● **What It Takes—The Chess Years** / 1977 / Chess 9328
A good overview of Koko Taylor's Chess career from 1964 to 1972, highlighting her successful collaboration with producer and mentor Willie Dixon. Includes "Wang Dang Doodle," "The Egg or the Hen," and several tracks either previously unreleased or unavailable on a U.S. album. —*Roundup Newsletter*

○ **Earthshaker, The** / 1978 / Alligator 4711
One of her best, with "I'm a Woman" and "Hey Bartender". —*Bill Dahl*

Little Johnny Taylor (Johnny Lamar Taylor)

b. Feb. 11, 1943, Memphis, TN
Vocals, sometimes harmonica / Soul, R&B, Soul blues
A former member of the Mighty Clouds of Joy best known for his modern-day blues classic "Part Time Love" (Galaxy, 1963), Taylor has long been one of America's top gospel-based blues vocalists, though not always one of the most visible. As the story goes, his failure to tour behind Part Time Love allowed a like-named rival, Johnnie Taylor, to step in and reap the benefits; Johnnie later recorded the song himself for Stax. LJT has been a chitlin circuit favorite but has remained within that sphere, recording consistently enough to keep his name going. His early '70s work for Ronn (including "Everybody Knows About My Good Thing," "It's My Fault Darling," and "Open House at My House") clearly presaged the popular Malaco soul/blues sound of the '80s and '90s. The confusing Taylor rivalry has continued: With Johnnie now at Malaco, Little Johnny signed with the label's main competitor, Ichiban, in 1988. —*Jim O'Neal*

○ **Little Johnny Taylor** / 1963 / Galaxy 203
Terrific brass, heavy charts by Roy Shanklin push Taylor's soulful pipes heavenward on this great LP that includes hit "Part Time Love". —*Bill Dahl*

● **Greatest Hits** / 1964 / Fantasy 4510
This singer's best '60s output, originally on Galaxy Records. Full of gospel-fired fervor. —*Bill Dahl*

○ **I Shoulda Been a Preacher** / 1981 / Red Lightnin' 0030
Only his pastor knows that for sure, but this is one wailing collection. It contains the hottest gospel-tinged singles "Little" Johnny Taylor cut for Galaxy, and anyone turned off by the tepid material coming out for Ichiban should consult these before hopping off the bandwagon. —*Ron Wynn*

Johnnie "Geechie" Temple

b. Oct. 18, 1906, Canton, MS, **d.** Nov. 22, 1968, Jackson, MS
Vocals, guitar, mandolin, piano / Urban blues
Johnnie Temple is one of the great unsung heroes of the blues. A contemporary of Skip James, Son House, and other Delta legends, Temple was one of the very first to develop the now-standard bottom-string boogie bass figure, generally credited to Robert Johnson. —*Cub Koda*

○ **1935-39** / Document 511
A solid collection of Temple's earliest sides, including the killer "Lead Pencil Blues." —*Cub Koda*

Sonny Terry

b. Oct. 24, 1911, Greensboro, GA, **d.** Mar. 11, 1986, Mineola, NY
Vocals, harmonica / Acoustic country blues
Often cited as the greatest and certainly most famous of the acoustic blues harmonica players, Terry was also famed for the exuberant whoops and hollers he worked into his blues numbers, fox-chase imitations, and folk songs. Although much of his best work came with long-time partner Brownie McGhee, whom he met in 1939, Terry recorded with other accompanists, including Woody Guthrie, Lightnin' Hopkins, and Johnny Winter, in settings

ranging from pure folk to rocking electric blues. Like Brownie, he went through an early-'50s blues-band period in the New York studios, followed by extensive albums in the folk-blues vein before the pair stopped speaking to one another and finally went their separate ways a few years before Terry's death. —*Jim O'Neal*

★ **The Folkways Years, 1944–63** / 1944–63 / Smithsonian/Rounder 4003
The 17 songs on this anthology include Terry playing with Brownie McGhee's brother Sticks, Pete Seeger, and others, as well as several featuring Terry's biting harmonica and wry leads relating stories of failure, triumph, and resiliency, backed by McGhee's flickering, but always audible, guitar alongside. The title's a bit misleading since the earliest date for any session is 1946 (one number) and most are done between 1955 and 1959. —*Ron Wynn*

Sonny's Story / 1960 / Bluesville 503
Throughout the prolific career of Sonny Terry and Brownie McGhee, many fans felt that singer/harmonica player Terry too often took a back seat to his singer/guitarist partner. On this Prestige/Bluesville album, Terry got a chance to really strut his delightful whooping and hollering stuff. Tunes include "I Ain't Gonna Be Your Dog No More" and "Worried Blues." —*Roundup Newsletter*

Sonny Is King / 1963 / Bluesville 521
Though they'd never performed together previously, vocalist/harp player Sonny Terry and guitarist Lightnin' Hopkins hit it off famously when paired at Rudy Van Gelder's studio in October 1960. Their collaboration, which yielded "She's So Sweet" and "One Monkey Don't Stop the Show," among others, fills the A side of this LP. The B side was recorded a year later with Terry's longtime partner, guitarist Brownie McGhee. — *Roundup Newsletter*

○ **Whoopin'** / 1984 / Alligator 4734
The textbook charge usually levelled against Alligator sessions are that they're sanitized. You couldn't lodge that one against this set with a straight face; if anything, somebody turned Sonny Terry loose. It didn't hurt that Johnny Winter was around on guitar and piano, playing gritty blues with a passion. It didn't help that Terry didn't put some amplified muscle behind his harmonica, however. Otherwise, this is a strong session. —*Ron Wynn*

○ **Sonny Terry** / 1987 / Collectables 5307
Harmonica player and vocalist Sonny Terry cut some stunning material for Gotham in the early '50s. Some of it got issued, much of it didn't. Here's a healthy chunk of things that were and weren't released, with good remastering helping embellish Terry's cutting vocals and splintering harmonica. —*Ron Wynn*

Sonny Terry & Brownie McGhee

Harmonica, guitar / Blues
Although they also recorded separately over the years, harpist Sonny Terry and guitarist Brownie McGhee will always be indelibly connected as one sturdy unit, and their lengthy and often stormy tenure together marks them as the most prolific duo in blues history.

Terry and McGhee became musical partners in 1941, when the guitarist was drafted to accompany the blind harpist to a Library of Congress recording session. Although they were products of the Southeastern blues tradition—McGhee hailed from Tennessee, Terry from North Carolina, where he had played with Blind Boy Fuller—the pair found their way into New York City's folk music "hootenanny" scene during the '40s. Contrary to popular belief, the two didn't do everything together—Terry's solo activities included a 1946 stint on Broadway in *Finian's Rainbow*, while McGhee recorded in an urban jump blues setting through the late '40s and early '50s.

When they did share a stage, the pair sang and played up a rollicking storm, Terry's trademark whooping style of harmonica contrasting with McGhee's full-bodied chording, and they cashed in on the budding folk boom by recording numerous acoustic albums along with various solo projects. Terry died in 1986, although the partnership had perished sometime earlier. —*Bill Dahl*

★ **Brownie McGhee & Sonny Terry Sing** / 1958 / Smithsonian/Folkways 40011
A great album by this influential folk/blues guitar-and-harmonica duo. —*Mark A. Humphrey*

Just a Closer Walk with Thee / Nov. 1960 / Fantasy 541
A live recording from 1957 by Sonny Terry (harmonica, vocals) and Brownie McGhee (guitar, vocals), but with a twist: It consists of all religious material like "Just a Closer Walk with Thee," "Get Right, Church," and "If You See My Saviour." — *Roundup Newsletter*

○ **At the 2nd Fret** / Mar. 1963 / Bluesville 1058
Brownie McGhee and Sonny Terry were the ultimate blues duo until long simmering personality conflicts finally dissolved their union. But until that happened, they were an ideal team: McGhee's stylized singing and light, flickering guitar was wonderfully contrasted by Terry's sweeping, whirling harmonica solos and intense, country-tinged singing. They were in great form during the ten tunes featured on this '62 live date, recently reissued on CD. Sometimes as on "Custard Pie" or "Barking Bull Dog," they're funny; other times they were prophetic, chilling, or moving. —*Ron Wynn*

○ **Brownie McGhee & Sonny Terry (at the 2nd Fret)** / Prestige 7803
Prototype Piedmont-styled blues from that genre's finest guitar/harmonica duo. They were so tight and interconnected it's no wonder when things soured they got so vicious. There's plenty of familiar material, but they were in a groove at this point and sounded fantastic. —*Ron Wynn*

Henry Thomas

b. 1874, Big Sandy, TX?
Vocals, harmonica / Acoustic country blues
Texas songster Henry Thomas remains a relative stranger who made some great recordings, then returned to obscurity. Evidence suggests he was an itinerant street musician, a musical hobo who rode the rails across Texas and possibly to the World Fairs in St. Louis and Chicago just before and after the turn of the century. Most agree he was the oldest African-American folk artist to produce a significant body of recordings. His projected 1874 birthdate would predate Charley Patton by a good 17 years. Like Patton and a handful of other musicians generally termed songsters (including John Hurt, Jim Jackson, Mance Lipscomb, Furry Lewis, and Leadbelly), Thomas's repertoire bridged the 19th and 20th centuries, providing a compelling glimpse into a wide range of African-American musical genres. The 23 songs he cut for Vocalion between 1927 and 1929 include a spiritual, ballads, reels, dance songs, and 8 selections titled blues. Obviously dance music, his songs were geared to older dance styles shared by Black and White audiences.

Thomas's sound, like his repertoire, is unique. He capoed his guitar high up the neck and strummed it in the manner of a banjo, favoring dance rhythm over complex fingerwork. On many of his pieces, he simultaneously played the quills or panpipes, a common but seldom-recorded African-American folk instrument indigenous to Mississippi, Louisiana, and Texas. Combining the quills, a limited-range melody instrument, with his banjo-like strummed guitar produced one of the most memorable sounds in American folk music. For example, his lead-in on "Bull Doze Blues" still worked as a hook when recycled 40 years later by blues/rockers Canned Heat in their version of "Going Up the Country." "Ragtime Texas," as Thomas was known, provides a welcome in-road to 19th-century dance music, but his music is neither obscure nor merely educational: It has a timeless quality—and while it may be an acquired taste, once you catch on to it, you're hooked. —*Barry Lee Pearson*

★ **Texas Worried Blues** / Yazoo 1080
Songster Thomas plays a cross-section of blues and pre-blues with a unique guitar-and-panpipes instrumentation. Although it may sound archaic to the beginner, given time it will get your toes tapping and quickly become a favorite. —*Barry Lee Pearson*

Rockin' Tabby Thomas

Electric Louisiana blues
A solid Louisiana vocalist who plays both guitar and piano, "Rockin'" Tabby Thomas has been cutting stirring recordings since the mid-'50s. He's teamed often with harmonica players Whispering Smith and Lazy Lester, and done several sessions for Maison De Soul and various labels owned by Jay Miller. —*Ron Wynn*

● **King of Swamp Blues** / Maison de Soul 1026

Good, hard-rocking Louisiana blues with just a tinge of swamp from "Rockin'" Tabby Thomas. What he lacks in vocal range, he compensates for with his exuberance. The backing band's no all-star unit, but they provide some solid grooves behind Thomas's surging leads. —*Ron Wynn*

"Big Mama" Thornton (Willie Mae Thornton)

b. Dec. 11, 1926, Montgomery, AL, **d.** Jul. 25, 1984, Los Angeles, CA

Vocals, harmonica, drums / Electric West Coast blues
Despite her religious home environment, Willie Mae Thornton was working the Southern club circuit by the time she was 14. While appearing at Houston's Bronze Peacock, she caught the attention of Don Robey, the club's owner and a major African-American record producer, who signed her to his Peacock label, named in honor of his club. Thornton's hard-edged blues voice contrasted with the sweeter, smoother style currently in vogue; nevertheless, her energy and showmanship allowed her to work with the best Southwestern and West Coast R&B bands, fronted by Johnny Otis, Roy Milton, Joe Liggins, and Gatemouth Brown. Along with fellow Duke/Peacock artists under contract to Robey (including Junior Parker, Johnny Ace, and Bobby Bland), she toured the Southern club and theater circuit. In 1953 she scored a #1 R&B hit with her grits-and-gravy version of "Hound Dog," later a hit for Elvis Presley. Continuous West Coast club work kept her active until the blues revival expanded her audience. In 1969, at the Ann Arbor Blues Festival, she proved to be the reigning woman artist, interacting as an equal with her peers Big Joe Williams, Howlin' Wolf, and Muddy Waters. Although she played several instruments, her voice was her strength, and she served as a model for female rock vocalists. Despite her bluff exterior, she was a warm, considerate person and a respected member of the blues community. During the '70s she was by far the premier down-home blueswoman in America. —*Barry Lee Pearson*

● **Hound Dog: The Peacock Recordings** / 1992 / MCA 10668
Too often recalled as either the artist who inadvertently supplied Elvis Presley with one of his biggest early hits or a major influence on Janis Joplin, Willie Mae "Big Mama" Thornton left much more behind than the original "Hound Dog." Thornton's 1952-57 output for Don Robey's Peacock imprint will always be overshadowed by the R&B chart-topping success of her original 1952 reading of the title track, enlivened further by the snarling guitar of Pete Lewis. But the other 17 crisp-sounding gems on this disc are no less enchanting. With so much solid jump blues distinguishing her Peacock discography, Big Mama Thornton doesn't need the recommendation of Elvis or Janis to deserve your purchase. —*Bill Dahl, Goldmine*

Henry Townsend (Too Tight Henry)

b. Oct. 27, 1909, Shelby, MS
Vocals, guitar, piano / Acoustic country blues
Influenced by Roosevelt Sykes and Lonnie Johnson, Townsend was a commanding musician, adept on both piano and guitar. —*Cub Koda*

○ **Mule** / 1980 / Nighthawk 201
Venerable St. Louis guitarist and pianist Henry Thomas mostly stuck to the keyboard on this outstanding '79 session. It was forceful, wonderfully sung and alternately moving, impressive and inspiring. —*Ron Wynn*

● **Henry Townsend & Henry Spaulding** / 1986 / Wolf 117
Topflight country-blues from Townsend, with the bonus of two cuts from the seldom-heard Henry Spaulding. —*Cub Koda*

Big Joe Turner (Joseph Vernon Turner)

b. May 18, 1911, Kansas City, MO, **d.** Nov. 24, 1985, Inglewood, CA

Vocals / R&B, Electric jump blues, Swing, Blues & jazz
Big Joe Turner enjoyed stardom in two related, but quite different eras. The Big Chill generation appreciates Turner for his contribution to rock & roll; those who know pre-rock history cherish his vocal contributions to the boogie-woogie and Kansas City jazz eras. He was among the greatest, most vociferous shouters ever, able to holler and roar above a striding big band, yet also fit his huge sound into situations with boogie-woogie players relying on timing and pace. Turner was tending bar and singing at 14 in Kansas City. Known as the "singing bandleader," the youth at-

tracted the attention of such bandleaders as Bennie Moten, Andy Kirk, and Count Basie. He and pianist Pete Johnson became great friends and a popular touring act in the late '30s and the '40s. After his appearance with Johnson at the "Spirituals to Swing" Carneigie Hall concert in 1938, Turner made his first recordings, notably the spectacular "Roll 'Em Pete." Turner's huge voice half shouts, half sings, with the piece's tension superbly developed via his use of repeated phrases and Johnson's rumbling, churning riffs, and accompaniment. Turner was an equally gifted slow blues and ballad stylist, and his work with pianists and bands reflected his fluidity, knowledge of inflections, and ability to develop themes and embellish lyrics. He recorded with Joe Sullivan, Benny Carter, and Art Tatum, among others. But his early '50s R&B hits "Still in the Dark," "Chains of Love" and "Sweet Sixteen" were forerunners of a new era. "Honey Hush" and "Shake, Rattle and Roll" marked Joe Turner's move to the pop arena, even though cover versions of both songs did better saleswise than his originals. But after his rock success ebbed, Turner returned to the jazzy blues he'd always done; he made fine dates in the '70s with Count Basie, the Trumpet Kings, Cleanhead Eddie Vinson, and Jimmy Witherspoon. In 1983, two years before his death, Turner recorded with Roomful of Blues. —*Ron Wynn and John Floyd*

○ **Joe Turner Sings Kansas City Jazz** / 1953 / Decca 8044
Long before he became the darling of the first rock & roll generation, Big Joe Turner was singing surging, swinging jazz and boogie tunes. That was the menu on this date, and Jimmy Rushing had nothing on Turner when it came to stretching out notes, hollering, cavorting and shouting. —*Ron Wynn*

○ **Boss of the Blues** / Sep. 19, 1956 / Atlantic 8812
A smoldering, jazz-based set from 1956 features pianist Pete Johnson and some of Turner's most confident vocals. —*John Floyd*

Big Joe Rides Again / 1959 / Atlantic 90668
More '50s sides in the vein of *Boss of the Blues*. —*John Floyd*

I Don't Dig It / 1986 / Juke Box Lil 618
Sixteen '40s performances from the incomparable Boss of the Blues, 5 from his Decca years and 11 others waxed in the late '40s for such labels as MGM and Coast. Decca sides excepted, these are Turner rarities which display the first 'n foremost blues shouter's big heart and timeless taste for the slowly sensuous as well as the rockin' rollers. — *Mark Humphrey, Roundup Newsletter*

★ **Greatest Hits** / 1987 / Atlantic 81752
These are Turner's finest early-rock-era recordings, including his best (and best-known) hits and some tasty obscurities. A must-have. —*John Floyd*

○ **Memorial Album—Rhythm & Blues** / 1987 / Atlantic 81663
More Atlantic-era rock & roll sides, including many obscurities. —*John Floyd*

○ **I've Been to Kansas City** / 1991 / MCA 42351
A superb assortment of his finest '40s sides with bands led by Pete Johnson and Art Tatum. —*John Floyd*

○ **Big, Bad & Blue: The Big Joe Turner Anthology** / 1994 / Rhino
This three-disc anthology shows how Turner, without really ever changing his style, moved from strict Kansas City swing to pioneering rock & roll and back to basic jazzy blues. It contains 62 songs, everything from treasured hits to slow, sweltering ballads, strident uptempo wailers, moaning blues, novelty tunes, and some fiery pieces with lyrics and sentiments that wouldn't make it in today's environment. His collaborations with pianist Pete Johnson, songwriter Jesse Stone, and dates heading various combos and bands, are presented in digitally remastered glory. A comprehensive, well-written and lavishly prepared and illustrated booklet with numerous anecdotes and remembrances are the icing on a superb cake. —*Ron Wynn*

○ **Jumpin' with Joe—The Complete Aladdin & Imperial Recordings** / Jan. 11, 1994 / Emi Records Group North Ameri
Big Joe Turner's remarkable recordings for Atlantic and Decca have been frequently reissued and evaluated. But his singles for other labels haven't gotten similar treatment, which makes this 18-cut single disc anthology of Aladdin and Imperial material so welcome. These were recorded in the late '40s and early '50s, before his robust, swaggering Atlantic singles earned R&B and rock & roll immortality. They were closer to the Kansas City swing

Turner had done earlier in his career; there was more emphasis on lyric interpretation, swing, and timing than sheer volume and volcanic, nonstop hollering. But they also show Turner was more versatile than sometimes thought; he made a great duet partner for Wynonie Harris on the opening four cuts and final selection. —*Ron Wynn*

○ **Early Big Joe (1940-44)** / MCA 1325
Vital early-'40s Joe Turner when he was ripping and shouting the blues, doing Kansas City Swing numbers, and working with long-time friend and musical companion Pete Johnson. These are tracks cut for Decca, among them prehit version of "Corrine, Corrina" and tremendous composition "Wee Baby Blues." —*Ron Wynn*

Maurice John Vaughn

b. Nov. 6, 1952, Chicago, IL
Vocals, guitar, Sax / Modern electric blues
One of the sharp young guitarists to make his mark in '80s Chicago blues, Vaughn produced an impressive debut album and released it on his own Reecy label in 1984. The cleverly packaged *Generic Blues Album* and up-to-the minute songs such as "Computer Took My Job" attracted a reissue deal with Alligator. Vaughn, whose previous experience included R&B, funk, and blues guitar work for A. C. Reed and Casey Jones, has done little to follow up this auspicious blues recording debut, but new releases are eagerly awaited by contemporary blues enthusiasts. —*Jim O'Neal*

● **Generic Blues Album** / Apr. 1986 / Alligator 4763
Anything but generic, actually this is powerful, contemporary, funky Chicago blues. With excellent musicianship, Vaughn performs interesting songs focusing on the trials of modern urban life and work. Vaughn, a top session player, sings and plays guitar and sax. —*Niles J. Frantz*

In The Shadow of The City / 1993 / Alligator 4813
On *In the Shadow of the City* Maurice John Vaughn plays single-note leads and chords that express jocularity or apprehension, pushed along by bassist Freddie Dixon and three different sets of pianists and drummers (and sometimes a trombone and his saxophone). Vaughn's voice, neither large nor supple, carries an air of confident nonchalance as his crisply appealing songs (only "Eager Beaver" sputters) preserve the tradition in a modern context with galvanizing strains of R&B. —*Frank-John Hadley, Downbeat*

Joe Louis Walker

b. Dec. 25, 1949, San Francisco, CA
Vocals, guitar / R&B, Modern electric blues
By majority ruling of the music critics, the blues in its modern-day form has reached a peak in the work of San Francisco's Joe Louis Walker, whose individual creative vision has forged progressive musicianship and contemporary urban sensibilities with a blues/roots ethic. Gospel, funk, and soul flavor Walker's music, yet it remains identifiable and emotionally the blues (with strong Delta and Chicago elements). Perhaps for that very reason, Walker has not crossed over into the commercial market the way some of his more pop- or rock-oriented blues contemporaries have. Still, Walker has a strong following, especially in England, and regularly scores at or near the top in blues polls and awards—all this since he recorded his first album as a virtual unknown in 1986, having only recently returned to the blues life after turning to gospel in the '70s. —*Jim O'Neal*

Cold Is the Night / 1986 / Hightone 8006
A head-turning debut album of mostly original compositions. Walker's potential for greatness is in evidence. —*Niles J. Frantz*

● **Gift, The** / 1988 / Hightone 8012
The Gift is the bluesiest of Walker's four releases to date. Walker plays blues, R&B, and funk, with a distinct and overriding gospel influence on his singing and songwriting. Still, he has been known to play a set of slide guitar pieces in concert and to rearrange band songs for solo guitar and voice. He is a bluesman in the best and broadest sense of the word, incorporating almost every aspect of 20th century African-American popular music into his unique and expressive style. —*Niles J. Frantz*

Blue Soul / 1989 / Hightone 8019

An appropriately titled and excellent showcase of Walker's soul- and gospel-influenced songwriting and singing. Highlights include the chilling slow blues of "City of Angels" and the solo "I'll Get to Heaven on My Own." —*Niles J. Frantz*

○ **Live at Slim's, Vol. 1** / 1991 / Hightone 8025
A great live show, with guest appearances by Angela Strehli and Huey Lewis. A beautiful solo reworking of "Don't Play Games" from *Cold Is the Night. —Niles J. Frantz*

○ **Live at Slim's, Vol. 2** / Nov. 1992 / Hightone 8036
More gems from same memorable shows. —*Bill Dahl*

Phillip Walker

b. Feb. 11, 1937, Welsh, LA
Vocals, guitar / Modern electric blues
When *Playboy* magazine launched a record company in the early '70s, Phillip Walker was chosen to be the label's contemporary bluesman, and his first album (*Bottom of the Top*) was exemplary. Both the expectations and accolades for Walker have remained high, although he has never enjoyed a breakthrough beyond blues cult status. Raised in Port Arthur, TX, Walker was influenced by Lonesome Sundown (with whom he later recorded a reunion album), Lonnie Brooks, and Long John Hunter, and he spent three years as Clifton Chenier's guitarist before relocating to Los Angeles in 1959. Walker's smoky vocals and crackling guitar work are flavored by both his Louisiana/Texas background and his associations with such West Coast figures as Lowell Fulson and Percy Mayfield. —*Jim O'Neal*

● **Blues** / 1973 / Hightone 8013
A very talented, and very underrated bluesman, Walker was originally a member of Zydeco legend Clifton Chenier's band. He has also worked with Little Richard, Etta James, Lowell Fulson, and Percy Mayfield, among others. Striking, upper-register vocals cut right to the bone. Powerful, stately guitar. —*Niles J. Frantz*

Someday You'll Have These Blues / 1977 / Hightone 8032
An exciting and eminently listenable second album. —*Niles J. Frantz*

From L.A. to L.A. / 1982 / Rounder 2037
Walker's tunes from 1969, 1970, and 1976 sessions, produced by Bruce Bromberg and recorded with Lonesome Sundown. Very nice. —*Niles J. Frantz*

○ **Tough As I Want to Be** / 1984 / Rounder 2038
Hotter and fiercer than other recordings. Originals and covers from Lowell Fulson and Jimmy McCracklin. —*Niles J. Frantz*

○ **Bottom of the Top** / 1990 / Hightone 8020
Walker's first album. Los Angeles recordings done 1969-72. Confident, tuneful, and resonant. —*Niles J. Frantz*

Big Blues from Texas / JSP 248
Good entry; cut with Otis Grand's combo. —*Bill Dahl*

T-Bone Walker (Aaron Thibeaux Walker)

b. May 28, 1910, Linden, TX, **d.** Mar. 16, 1975, Los Angeles, CA
Vocals, guitar / Electric Texas blues
One of the great guitarists, vocalists, and composers of all time, Walker was the inventor of the Texas shuffle and a major influence on guitarists since the '40s. His recordings for Black & White (1945–47), including his best-known hit "Call It Stormy Monday," were purchased by Capitol Records, which also won his Imperial recordings. These recordings were combined in a boxed set of six LPs/CDs by Mosaic Records, giving the best possible overview of Walker's distinguished career. The Imperial recordings (1950–54) are available in a double CD on EMI. Also worth seeking is *T-Bone Blues* (1955–57) on Atlantic. Walker's album projects in Europe (where he became a major star) included *Feeling the Blues*, among his finest. Also worth finding is *Stormy Monday Blues*, although Walker's later work does not generally compare with his magnificent work from the '40s and '50s. —*Bob Porter*

☆ **T Bone Blues** / 1959 / Atlantic 8020
Walker's finest mid-period album. Classics abound any place you look, and T-Bone's guitar work is nothing short of extraordinary. —*Cub Koda*

○ **Sings the Blues** / 1959 / Imperial 9098
Early '50s Imperial sides that find the Texas guitar pioneer in top form. —*Bill Dahl*

○ **Singing the Blues** / 1960 / Imperial 9116

More early '50s gems. —*Bill Dahl*

○ **Original 1945-50 Performances** / 1976 / EMI 2C06886523
A deep look into T-Bone's roots: 12 classic performances, including the original "Stormy Monday Blues." —*Hank Davis*

○ **Jumps Again** / 1981 / Charly 1019
1942-47 sides, early and terrific. —*Bill Dahl*

○ **Natural Blues** / 1983 / Charly 1057
More 40's Walker classics. —*Bill Dahl*

○ **Inventor of the Electric Guitar Blues** / 1983 / Blues Boy 304
Some formative and masterful recordings by Aaron T-Bone Walker, among the greatest pure vocalists in modern blues history. The find is a side with Walker playing 1929 country blues and sounding just as comfortable and exciting as he does on the 16 other '40s and '50s numbers. —*Ron Wynn*

○ **Hustle Is on, The** / 1990 / Sequel 124
Nice CD compilation of Imperial material. —*Bill Dahl*

☆ **Complete T-Bone Walker Recordings, The** / Oct. 1990 / Mosaic 130
1940–54. A six-CD boxed set—an education in the lineage of urban blues. It appears that T-Bone Walker had a greater influence on urban blues players than any other single talent. His guitar, vocals, song selection, and sheer style live on today in nearly every blues performer. He is the master. —*Michael Erlewine*

★ **Complete Imperial Recordings, The** / 1991 / EMI America 96738
The 1950–53 recordings by the man who virtually invented electric guitar blues. Performances range from soulful and mellow to jump blues. A double CD. —*Hank Davis*

Rare T-Bone / Off-Beat 22053
T-Bone Walker was the master and driving force behind the electric blues guitar. While several fine T-Bone compilations and album reissues exist, this is the only currently available CD to feature his work on ABC/Bluesway Records, for whom Walker recorded three albums, believed by many to be some of his best. There are a total of ten tracks here, including "Cold Hearted Woman," "Confusion Blues," "Stormy Monday Blues," "Treat Me So Low Down," and "Goin' to Funky Town." —*Roundup Newsletter*

Sippie Wallace (Beulah Wallace)

b. Nov. 1, 1898, Houston, TX, d. Nov. 1, 1986, Detroit, MI
Vocals, organ, piano / Classic female blues
A classic female blues singer from the '20s, who kept performing and recording until her death. She was a major influence on a young Bonnie Raitt, who recorded several of Wallace's songs and performed live with her. —*Cub Koda*

● **1923–29** / Alligator 4810
Sippie's earliest and best sides, including "I'm a Mighty Tight Woman." —*Cub Koda*

Robert Ward

Vocals, guitar / Soul, R&B, Soul blues
Robert Ward created a classic guitar sound on the 1962 hit "I Found a Love" by the Falcons (featuring lead vocalist Wilson Pickett). That same vibrato-drenched Magnatone amp sound has propelled Ward to guitar-hero status since his much-touted return to public performing and recording in 1990. This time around, Ward (who worked with the Ohio Untouchables, later known as the Ohio Players, and made the rounds backing various R&B singers before retreating to Dry Branch, GA, some years ago) is in the spotlight for his soulful vocals as well as his trademark guitar work (which retains more of a gospel-based R&B approach than a blues soloist's attack). —*Jim O'Neal*

★ **Fear No Evil** / 1991 / Black Top 1063
Though recently recorded, this sounds like vintage soul. Ward is an exceptional individualist on the guitar. —*Robert Gordon*

Rhythm of the People / 1993 / Black Top 1088
OK encore to classic *Fear No Evil.* —*Bill Dahl*

Washboard Sam (Robert Brown)

b. Jul. 15, 1910, Walnut Ridge, AR, d. Nov. 13, 1966, Chicago, IL
Vocals, washboard / Acoustic Chicago blues
A popular hokum blues artist, usually found in the company of singer/guitarist Big Bill Broonzy. —*Cub Koda*

Washboard Sam (1935–47) / Jan. 1991 / Story Of Blues 3502
Forget the washboard, which was almost more a prop than an instrument. Robert Brown was a captivating vocalist, expert at working off his sidemen, and he coaxed creditable riffs out of that washboard, even if they all sounded the same. This is peak material, done when he was in excellent voice and hadn't yet gotten stagnant in his material or approach. —*Ron Wynn*

○ **Rockin' My Blues Away** / Feb. 1992 / RCA 61042
These 1940s recordings feature Washboard Sam in the superb company of Big Bill Broonzy, Memphis Slim, Roosevelt Sykes, and Willie Dixon, among others. Interesting mix of country blues, evolving into full-tilt, post-war urban blues. Tunes include "My Feet Jumped Salty," "Do That Shake Dance," and the title track. —*Roundup newsletter*

● **Blues Classics by Washboard Sam 1935–41** / Blues Classics 10
This still ranks as the best collection of Washboard Sam's finest, or at least popularly known, pieces. —*Ron Wynn*

○ **Washboard Sam, Vol. 1** / Document 507
Eighteen sides from the classic Bluebird period, with solid support from Big Bill Broonzy, Black Bob, and Blind John Davis. Includes "Who Pumped the Wind in My Doughnut" and "He's a Creepin' Man." —*Cub Koda*

Tuts Washington

b. 1907, d. 1984
Piano / Boogie-woogie, Traditional bluegrass
Isidore "Tuts" Washington (also widely known as "Papa Yellow") was 76 years old at the time of the release of his first solo recording. He began playing piano at age ten and worked with a number of famed New Orleans bandsmen—Kid Rena, Papa Celestin, Kid Punch Miller—over the course of his long career. In the late '30s he made trips to California and in 1950 joined the Tab Smith Orchestra in St. Louis for a time. During the better part of the '40s he worked in a trio backing up blues singer Smiley Lewis, which took him to various locations from Oklahoma to Florida. In 1958 he was with the Clyde Kerr Orchestra in New Orleans, and a decade later made several excursions up the Mississippi River on the Delta Queen. From 1968 to 1973 Tuts held forth at the Court of Two Sisters Restaurant in the French Quarter, then moving on to the piano bar at the Caribbean Room of the Pontchartrain Hotel in the early '80s. He died while performing on stage at the 1984 New Orleans World's Fair.

Tuts Washington identified Joseph Louis "Red" Cayou, an itinerant New Orleans pianist, as a prime influence on his early playing. He developed his repertoire by following the brass bands on the streets of New Orleans, memorizing the tunes and working out his own versions at home. He was self-taught at first but eventually took lessons at age 18; apparently his "professor" felt that Tuts was already too advanced to benefit from basic instruction, and at that point he turned to "Red" Caillou, whose hands he described as "like lightning." Washington specialized in instrumental pieces, but he also maintained a number of bawdy blues songs which he delivered with an impish relish. As the recognized "dean" of New Orleans piano players by the mid-century, he is credited frequently as a major influence on Fats Domino, Professor Longhair, James Booker, Dr. John, and Allen Toussaint. —*Bruce Boyd Raeburn*

● **New Orleans Piano Professor** / Apr. 1984 / Rounder 11501
The venerable New Orleans pianist Tuts Washington didn't get many chances to record during his lifetime. This 1983 session was his most extensive project with 23 songs covering everything from spirituals to traditional jazz numbers, pop pieces, novelty tunes, rippling blues and country. Washington played them all in a seamless manner, displaying the mix of boogie-woogie and barrelhouse riffs, R&B, blues and gospel elements, Afro-Latin and Caribbean rhythmic accents, plus jazz phrasing and licks that he'd mastered through many decades of playing in bars and clubs on Bourbon Street and elsewhere. This was his chance in the spotlight, and Washington didn't waste it. —*Ron Wynn*

Walter Washington

Vocals, guitar / Soul, R&B, R&B, Soul blues
Walter Washington became a local legend in the Black clubs of New Orleans in the '70s and '80s and worked his way up to national status with a series of well-received albums and appearances. His recording affiliations have likewise moved from local

to national independent to major label. An innovative guitarist and fine singer who has also done some excellent work with vocalist Johnny Adams, Washington does not perform in the classic New Orleans R&B mold but incorporates soul, funk, jazz, and blues with fluency and power. —*Jim O'Neal*

Wolf Tracks / May 1987 / Rounder 2048
Washington's first nationally distributed album contains contemporary R&B filtered heavily through gospel and traditional New Orleans influences. —*Niles J. Frantz*

Out of the Dark / 1988 / Rounder 2068
Truly soulful blues and R&B. Funky and inspired. —*Niles J. Frantz*

○ **Out of the House** / 1988 / Rounder
Washington's second Rounder session in 1988 mixed Crescent City R&B and jazz licks with contemporary and vintage songs and production. Washington's cover of "Ain't That Loving You," while not quite as dramatic as Bobby "Blue" Bland's, was still outstanding, while he was appropriately ironic and bemused on "You Can Stay But the Noise Must Go" and vividly soulful on "Save Your Love for Me" and "Steal Away." It wasn't the kind of glossy, trendy work that garners the pop spotlight, but Walter "Wolfman" Washington showed good progress and skills with a nice followup to a solid debut. —*Ron Wynn*

Sada / 1991 / Point Blank 91743
Moving and tuneful, this album is more reflective and more inward. —*Niles J. Frantz*

● **Wolf at the Door** / 1991 / Rounder 2098
Inventive, passionate, and irresistibly groovin', with very tasty guitar and snarly vocals. Walter writes great songs, along with creating unique versions of other people's compositions. This guy is undeservedly obscure, for he is a major talent. Highlights here are a slow blues called "At Night in the City," the rocking shuffle of "Tailspin," and Walter's eerie reading "Hello Stranger," penned by Doc Pomus and Dr. John. —*Niles J. Frantz*

Muddy Waters (McKinley Morganfield)

b. Apr. 4, 1915, Rolling Fork, MS, d. Apr. 30, 1983, Westmont, IL
Vocals, guitar, harmonica / R&B, Electric Chicago blues
Rolling his eyes toward heaven and shaking his head like a man possessed, Muddy Waters cast a powerful spell. He could easily work audiences into a frenzy, marrying the unmistakable sexual urgency of his lyrics to the vocal slide statements that for 40 years were as much a part of his signature as his voice, which many claim was the best in electric blues. A native Mississippi Delta bluesman, Muddy instinctively understood the unpretentious beauty and power in simplicity. Time and again, he transformed basic patterns into blues masterpieces. Like the superstitions and voodoo images prominent in Waters's best-known lyrics, the primal earthiness of his rhythms contains a deep, almost subconscious appeal.

As a vocalist, Muddy Waters had few parallels. As a blues bandleader, he had none. More than any other performer, he was responsible for forging Delta acoustic music into the electrified, band-oriented urban blues of today. And some of his own bands were the stuff legends are made of. British groups copied his songs in the early '60s, one naming themselves after his "Rollin' Stone." Guitarists such as Buddy Guy, Mike Bloomfield, Eric Clapton, and Johnny Winter came to share his stage. By the end of his life, Muddy Waters was hailed as "Father of Electric Blues." Through the years and various sidemen, Muddy's music remained intensely his own. His vocals and playing patterns have often been imitated, but no one has ever quite captured his touch. —*Jas Obrecht*

○ **Muddy Waters Sings Big Bill Broonzy** / 1964 / Chess 9197
Muddy's tribute album to the man who gave him his start on the Chicago circuit. Features "When I Get to Drinkin'," "The Mopper's Blues," and great harp from James Cotton as an added bonus. —*Cub Koda*

Folk Singer / 1964 / Chess 9261
Unadorned, down-home acoustic blues, with Buddy Guy on second guitar. —*Jas Obrecht*

○ **Real Folk Blues, The** / 1965 / Chess 9274
A mixed bag of early Chess sides from 1949–54. Highlights include "Walkin' through the Park" and the "I'm a Man"-derived strut of "Mannish Boy." —*Jas Obrecht & Cub Koda*

○ **More Real Folk Blues** / 1967 / Chess 9278

More early Chess sides from 1948–52. Features essential tracks not found on *The Chess Box*, with the bludgeoning stomp of "She's Alright" and the moody introspection of "My Life Is Ruined" among the numerous highlights. —*Jas Obrecht & Cub Koda*

○ **They Call Me Muddy Waters** / 1971 / Chess 1553
Sizzling leftovers. —*Bill Dahl*

○ **Hard Again** / 1977 / Blue Sky 34449
Recorded in two days, this is absolutely brilliant. —*Jas Obrecht*

○ **Muddy "Mississippi" Waters—Live** / 1979 / Blue Sky 35712
Fierce, declamatory vocals and an other worldly slide. A bluesman at the height of his powers. —*Jas Obrecht*

King Bee / 1981 / Blue Sky 37064
Muddy's 1981 swan song, recorded with Johnny Winter. —*Jas Obrecht*

Rare & Unissued / 1984 / Chess 9180
Great but relatively obscure Chess sides from 1947–54. —*Jas Obrecht*

★ **Best of Muddy Waters, The** / 1987 / Chess 31268
Twelve tightly compacted gems of seminal Chicago blues. Features the original versions of "I'm Your Hoochie-Coochie Man," "Long Distance Call," "I'm Ready," "Honey Bee," "I Just Wanna Make Love to You," "Still a Fool," and a song called "Rollin' Stone," which provided the name inspiration for a hippie rock magazine and a group of British musicians. The perfect primer for those on a budget. —*Jas Obrecht & Cub Koda*

☆ **At Newport** / 1987 / Chess 31269
A sensational 1960 performance with crackerjack support from James Cotton, Otis Spann, and Pat Hare. This features Muddy delivering first-rate live renditions of "I Got My Mojo Workin'," "Baby Please Don't Go," "Tiger in Your Tank," and the brutally macho "I Got My Brand on You." —*Jas Obrecht & Cub Koda*

☆ **Chess Box, The** / 1989 / Chess 80002
The best of the best-ofs, the three-CD box collects 72 classics from 1947 through the '70s. —*Jas Obrecht*

○ **Trouble No More/Singles (1955–59)** / 1989 / Chess 9291
Slim but solid hits package. —*Bill Dahl*

○ **Blues Sky** / Jun. 16, 1992 / Epic 46172
Muddy Waters's genius is showcased on these recordings for Blue Sky Records from 1976-80, inspired by admirer and guest guitarist/producer Johnny Winter. The Blue Sky albums were widely praised and garnered three consecutive Grammy Awards (for Best Ethnic or Traditional Recording) for Waters. This 12-track collection features "I Can't Be Satisfied," "(My Eyes) Keep Me in Trouble," and a live version of "Deep Down in Florida." —*Roundup Newsletter*

☆ **Complete Plantation Recordings, The** / Jun. 8, 1993 / MCA
At long last, Muddy's historic 1941-42 Library of Congress field recordings are all collected in one place, with the best fidelity that's been heard thus far. Of particular note is the inclusion of several interview segments with Muddy from that embryonic period. Beyond essential. —*Cub Koda*

○ **One More Mile** / 1994 / Chess Records
A fine two-CD collection of unreleased and rare Chess tracks, none of which are featured on Waters's box set. —*AMG*

Johnny "Guitar" Watson

b. Feb. 3, 1935
Guitar, piano / Soul, R&B, Blues, Guitar-pop
Besides being a wonderful entertainer and showman, Johnny "Guitar" Watson's a marvelous guitarist, fine vocalist, and competent pianist. His flashy, shuttering guitar style is one of the most complete and accomplished among Texas blues musicians. His approach was greatly influenced by Aaron "T-Bone" Walker, and he in turn had a strong impact on the style of Jimi Hendrix. Watson's father was a pianist and taught the instrument to his son as a child. Watson moved from Houston to California at 15, and he appeared in many local talent shows during the '50s. Watson worked in the bands of Chuck Higgins, Amos Milburn, and Big Jay McNeely in '50s. He recorded as a leader for RPM, Federal, Keen, King, Decca, and his own DJM label among others. He also toured and recorded domestically and internationally with Larry Williams in the '60s. Watson made numerous club and festival appearances in the '50s, '60s, and '70s. He's best known to contem-

porary audiences for his novelty and humorous recordings of the late '70s and early '80s, earning a number five R&B single in 1977 for "A Real Mother for Ya," his biggest hit. —*Ron Wynn*

Gangster of Love / 1958 / Charly 267
Watson's terrific blues/R&B output from King vaults; 1950s/'60s vintage. —*Bill Dahl*

Gangster Is Back / 1975 / Red Lightnin' 0013
Boot-quality compilation of his searing early work. —*Bill Dahl*

○ **Ain't That a Bitch** / 1976 / DJM 3
Reborn as a funkmeister, Watson gets down on the ironic title track. —*Bill Dahl*

A Real Mother for Ya / 1977 / DJM 7
More seriously funky Watson. —*Bill Dahl*

○ **I Heard That** / 1985 / Charly 48
King-Federal sides from '50s/'60s includes amazing "Space Guitar". —*Bill Dahl*

● **Three Hours Past Midnight** / 1991 / Flair 91696
Sixteen tracks from the great Johnny "Guitar" Watson: a domestic issue of a fine compilation previously available only as a British import from Ace. Includes "Hot Little Mama" (covered by Roomful of Blues), "Too Tired," "Motor Head Baby," and a fine cover of Earl King's "Those Lonely, Lonely Nights." Also included are both sides of a very rare single, "The Bear" and "One More Kiss." — *Roundup Newsletter*

Greatest Hits / Fantasy 4503
Later funk-oriented sides. —*Bill Dahl*

Curley Weaver

b. Mar. 25, 1906, **d.** Sep. 20, 1962
Acoustic country blues
A wonderful vocalist and guitarist, Curley James Weaver didn't get as much attention as other Atlanta blues musicians like Blind Willie McTell and Barbecue Bob, but was a fine performer. He was a link between early and later styles, influenced by Kokomo Arnold and Blind Boy Fuller, and was able to adapt and work effectively from the '20s until the '50s. After learning guitar in his teens, Weaver recorded for Columbia and QRS in the late '20s. He frequently worked with Buddy Moss, Eddie Anthony, and Slim Kirpatrick in Atlanta clubs, and later recorded with Clarence Moore, Georgia Brown, and McTell. Weaver did sessions for Okeh, Banner, ARC, Decca/Champion, and Regal/Sittin' In during the '30s and '40s. —*Ron Wynn*

● **Georgia Guitar Wizard (1928–35)** / Story Of Blues 3530
Why Atlanta blues guitarist and vocalist Curley Weaver would be so obscure when his cohorts Blind Willie McTell and Buddy Moss are so well known is one of those why ask why deals. Weaver was an outstanding player and convincing singer, and this collection nicely outlines his attributes. By the way, McTell and Moss appear here in accompanying roles. —*Ron Wynn*

Sylvester Weaver

Guitar / Acoustic country blues
The pioneering guitarist from the early days of the blues who created the enduring classic "Guitar Rag," later popularized as "Steel Guitar Rag." Weaver was adept at everything from ragtime to slide-guitar stylings, all performed with great technical skill and a marvelous sense of time. —*Cub Koda*

● **Smoketown Strut** / Agram 2010
Weaver's earliest and best sides, including "Guitar Rag." The sound is horrible in spots, but every note of the music is great. —*Cub Koda*

Katie Webster

b. Jan. 9, 1939, Houston, TX
Vocals, piano, sometimes organ / R&B, Electric New Orleans blues
Katie Webster, a music major in college, grew up playing gospel, classical, blues, boogie-woogie, and jazz. She was such an accomplished and in-demand pianist that discographers will probably never be able to count the number of recording sessions she played on, especially those from the '50s and '60s in Louisiana, where she accompanied everyone from Clifton Chenier to Slim Harpo. Although Webster recorded a number of early R&B singles of her own, it was not until the '80s that she really started

hitting the touring circuit (especially in Europe) as a featured act. The momentum has carried over into a renewed career in the U.S., where Webster's saucy, energetic performances both on stage and on record have made her not only a favorite among contemporary blues fans but also a spokesperson for the female point of view in a typically male-dominated field. —*Jim O'Neal*

I Know That's Right / 1987 / Arhoolie 393
Decent swamp blues CD. —*Bill Dahl*

○ **Swamp Boogie Queen** / 1988 / Alligator 4766
Jay Miller's swamp-blues pianist of the '50s is unmuzzled in the '80s. A joyful noise. —*Mark A. Humphrey*

Two-Fisted Mama! / 1990 / Alligator 4777
More powerhouse piano and vocals. —*Mark A. Humphrey*

● **Katie Webster** / 1991 / Paula 13
The swamp-boogie queen's rockingest sides from late '50s and early '60s; she plays rippling 88s and sings bayou blues. —*Bill Dahl*

Casey Bill Weldon (Will Weldon)

b. Jul. 10, 1909
Acoustic blues, Prewar country blues
Among the premier "Hawaiian" guitarists, Will "Casey Bill" Weldon's voicings, fluidity and tunings were creative and imaginative, as were his arrangements. He was married to Memphis Minnie in the '20s, and they made some superb recordings together in the late '20s. Weldon played in medicine shows before beginning his recording career in 1927 for Victor. There were later dates for Champion, Vocalion, and Bluebird. Weldon recorded and played with the Memphis Jug Band, Charlie Burse and the Picaninny Jug Band, and the Brown Bombers of Swing. He moved to the West Coast in the '40s and purportedly recorded for several soundtracks. Weldon moved to Detroit and left the music world in the '60s. —*Ron Wynn*

○ **Bottleneck Guitar Trendsetters of the 1930's** / Yazoo 1049
Outstanding bottleneck guitar and above average singing from Casey Bill Weldon, one of the lesser publicized but tremendous prewar stylists. —*Ron Wynn*

Valerie Wellington

b. Nov. 14, 1959, Chicago, IL, **d.** Jan. 3, 1991
Vocals, piano / Modern electric blues
Valerie Wellington took the Chicago blues scene by surprise in 1982, perhaps not forgoing her classical training as an opera singer as much as using it to enhance her work in the blues. As a blueswoman she fit right in, not only becoming a regular in the blues clubs but also compiling an impressive theatrical résumé for her portrayals of Ma Rainey and Bessie Smith—women who, like opera singers, learned to project their voices without microphones. The influence of Koko Taylor has also been evident in Wellington's blues approach, which combines classic vaudeville-era blues with hard-driving Chicago sounds. Her power-packed voice has been heard on only a few record releases but has been featured frequently in TV and radio commercials. —*Jim O'Neal*

● **Million Dollar $ecret** / Oct. 1984 / Flying Fish 2619
Wellington is a powerful yet subtle vocalist, backed by some of the best Chicago blues players, including Sunnyland Slim, Billy Branch, Casey Jones, and Magic Slim and the Teardrops. The CD reissue contains two bonus tracks. —*Niles J. Frantz*

Junior Wells (Amos Blackmore)

b. 1934
Vocals, harmonica / R&B, Electric Chicago blues
Wells started on the streets of Chicago, playing for tips as a teenager, and graduated to house parties with the Aces, who became Little Walter's Jukes when Wells replaced him in Muddy Waters's band. Wells recorded on his own throughout the '50s and into the early '60s for a spate of smaller, Chicago-based labels, then came to national attention by teaming up with guitarist Buddy Guy in the mid-'60s and recording a brilliant set of landmark recordings for collector-oriented labels like Delmark and Vanguard. Generally acknowledged as the last of the great Chicago harmonica players, Wells continues to record and perform to the present day, his skills honed to a fine edge, a perfect ambassador to the music he's represented for so long. —*Cub Koda*

☆ **Hoodoo Man Blues** / 1965 / Delmark 612
This is the album that started the collector blues label trend of
the late '60s—a simple, unadorned recording of a working
Chicago blues band captured in all their unbridled glory.
Features smoldering guitar from Buddy Guy and a crack rhythm
section in support. —*Cub Koda*

On Tap / 1966 / Delmark 635
A loose set of jams, including a powerful version of "Mystery
Train." Phil Guy replaces Buddy Guy, while A. C. Reed and
Charles Miles add saxes. —*Barry Lee Pearson*

South Side Blues Jam / 1967 / Delmark 628
Five Delmark cuts that capture the Theresa's Lounge feel.
Includes Buddy Guy, Otis Spann, Louis Myers, and Freddy Below
of the Aces. —*Barry Lee Pearson*

South Side Jam / 1969 / Delmark 612
You can't go wrong with any Wells mid-'60s release. This had
hard-driving, powerful, uptempo tunes and equally impressive
slow wailers. Wells was joined by the likes of Buddy Guy and
Fred Below among others, and there were absolutely no stylistic
excesses or LP padding. —*Ron Wynn*

★ **Blues Hit Big Town** / 1977 / Delmark 640
A fine reissue set of Wells's early '50s States recordings. —*Barry
Lee Pearson*

Drinkin' Tnt 'n' Smokin' Dynamite / Jun. 1982 / Blind Pig 1182
Live at Montreux; Jr. and Buddy. —*Bill Dahl*

○ **1957–66** / 1991 / Paula 3
The best of Wells's output for Mel London's Chief and Profile labels, including the original "Messin' with the Kid." —*Cub Koda*

The Devil's Son-In-Law

b. Dec. 21, 1902, Ripley, TN, **d.** Dec. 21, 1941, East Saint Louis, IL
Vocals, guitar, piano / Piano blues
A very popular bluesman in the '30s and early '40s, Wheatstraw's
signature phrase, "Oh well well," was adapted by several bluesmen, Muddy Waters among them. —*Cub Koda*

● **Devil's Son-in-Law, The** / Blues Document 2011
A 20-track import compilation of Wheatstraw's best. Includes "I
Want Some Seafood" and "Fairasee Woman." —*Cub Koda*

Artie White

b. Apr. 16, 1937, Vicksburg, MS
Vocals / Soul, R&B, Soul blues
As Artie White tells it, he was walking down the street one day
during his Chicago gospel-singing days when "a guy drove up in
a Cadillac and offered me ten grand to record some blues." It took
years of dues-paying on Chicago's South Side club scene and the
Southern and Midwestern chitlin circuit, but Artie White has
proved his worth in the blues. A solid, hearty vocalist who has
surrounded himself with a talented crew of musicians, White (at
one time billed as Artie "Blues Boy" White) has most often performed squarely within the soul/blues territory staked out by
Little Milton and Bobby Bland. If White's style is too close for
comfort, Little Milton doesn't show it—he's even played guitar on
some of Artie's recent tracks. —*Jim O'Neal*

Nothing Takes the Place of You / 1987 / Ichiban 1008
Warm vocals, hot band. —*Bill Dahl*

○ **Thangs Got to Change** / 1989 / Ichiban 1044
An excellent, varied mixture of tempos and tunes. —*Niles J.
Frantz*

○ **Tired of Sneaking Around** / 1990 / Ichiban 1061
White is a B. B. King–sounding singer, with an original overall
sound, who makes great records with big band feel. Lots of horns
and stuff. —*Niles J. Frantz*

● **Best of Artie White, The** / Ichiban 1131
The one to get. —*Bill Dahl*

Bukka White (Booket T. Washington White)

b. Nov. 12, 1906, Houston, TX, **d.** Feb. 26, 1977, Memphis, TN
Vocals, guitar, harmonica, piano / Acoustic Delta blues
Achieving a distinctive musical voice is a highly prized blues
value, yet few artists develop an easily recognizable vocal and instrumental style that is uniquely theirs. Bukka White was one of
those remarkable artists with an overall approach and composition style that were unusual, yet he was a popular house-party

musician and a successful recording artist. Although he had a second career during the blues revival and remained a powerful performer, his best work was on his 1937 and 1940 Vocalion sides,
reissued by Columbia. They feature down-home country-blues at
its best, personal, moving, and instrumentally compelling. White's
percussive approach to his open *G*-tuned steel National can be
imitated but not duplicated. Like other Delta artists, White's
sound was melodically simple but rhythmically complex.
Sporting an attack vaguely reminiscent of Big Joe Williams,
White worked his guitar like a drum, adding rhythmic nuances
with his chording hand on the guitar neck. On his '40s session, he
added further percussive rhythm. Many of White's pieces employ
spoken or chanted passages, especially his train songs, which
combined talking blues and train effects. His compositions generally either fall outside mainstream blues or bridge sacred and
secular traditions, as in his classic "Fixing to Die." Moody and introspective, his songs let you into his life, detailing his experiences as a prisoner at Mississippi's notorious Parchman Farm or
as a hobo riding the rails. His dance songs, such as "Bukka's
Jitterbug Swing," aptly demonstrate his skills as a house-party
performer and bear out his reputation as a breakdown artist,
which means people danced so hard to his beat that they literally
broke the floors down at the jukes and plantation balls over
which he reigned. —*Barry Lee Pearson*

☆ **Complete Sessions 1930–40, The** / 1976 / Travelin' Man 03
Delta blues as propulsive as a runaway freight train. Not for the
weakhearted! —*Jas Obrecht*

★ **Complete Bukka White, The** / 1994 / Columbia Records
All of Bukka White's landmark recordings for Vocalion and Okeh
Records are collected on this brilliant single disc. —*AMG*

Robert Wilkins (Rev. Robert Timothy Wilkins)

b. Jan. 16, 1896, Hernando, MS, **d.** May 26, 1987, Memphis, TN
Vocals, guitar / Acoustic country blues
A superior guitarist, Robert Wilkins projected a relaxed ease on
his exquisite country blues 78s. He was working as a Pullman
porter in Memphis when he was hired by Victor to record in 1928.
He was soon back in the studio for Brunswick and Vocalion. The
1929 "That's No Way to Get Along," the most famous of his prewar 78s, was covered by the Rolling Stones as "Prodigal Son."
Wilkins's great Mississippi vibrato was similar to that of Frank
Stokes and Joe Callicott, and his records show considerable finesse with rag and blues guitar. Ungoverned by standard 12-bar
conventions, Wilkins created his own structures and was especially strong in open *E*, as heard in "That's No Way to Get Along"
and the spooky one-chord "Rollin' Stone." He crafted lyrics into
coherent narratives, carefully avoiding any hint of the risqué. He
showed up at the Chicago World's Fair but did most of his playing in Memphis and Hernando. Unnerving violence at a house
party prompted him to quit the blues in 1936 and find Jesus. In
1964 a rediscovered Rev. Robert Wilkins, spiritual singer and
minister of the Church of God in Christ, hit the folk circuit and
made some deeply moving records. He refused to play blues but
did recycle some old riffs. Near the end of his life, Rev. Wilkins
was seen working as a root doctor on a Memphis side street. He
lived to be 91. —*Jas Obrecht*

Memphis Blues 1928–35 / 1901 / Document 5014
Wilkins's complete works, plus sides by Tom Dickinson and Allen
Shaw. —*Jas Obrecht*

● **Original Rolling Stone, The** / 1980 / Yazoo 1077
Fourteen prewar tracks, with adequate liner notes. —*Jas Obrecht*

Big Joe Williams

b. Oct. 16, 1903, Crawford, MS, **d.** Dec. 17, 1982, Macon, MS
*Vocals, guitar, harmonica, accordion, kazoo / Acoustic and elec-
tric Delta blues*
Big Joe Williams may have been the most cantankerous human
being who ever walked the earth with guitar in hand. At the same
time, he was an incredible blues musician: a gifted songwriter, a
powerhouse vocalist, and an exceptional idiosyncratic guitarist.
Despite his deserved reputation as a fighter (documented in
Michael Bloomfield's bizarre booklet *Me and Big Joe*), artists who
knew him well treated him as a respected elder statesman. Even
so, they may not have chosen to play with him, because—as with
other older Delta artists—if you played with him you played by
his rules.

As protégé David "Honeyboy" Edwards described him, Williams in his early Delta days was a walking musician who played work camps, jukes, store porches, streets, and alleys from New Orleans to Chicago. He recorded through five decades for Vocalion, Okeh, Paramount, Bluebird, Prestige, Delmark, and many others. As a youngster, I met him in Delmark owner Bob Koester's store, the Jazz Record Mart. At the time, Big Joe was living there when not on his constant travels. According to Charlie Musselwhite, he and Big Joe kicked off the blues revival in Chicago in the '60s.

When I saw him playing at Mike Bloomfield's "blues night" at the Fickle Pickle, Williams was playing an electric nine-string guitar through a small ramshackle amp with a pie plate nailed to it and a beer can dangling against that. When he played, everything rattled but Big Joe himself. The total effect of this incredible apparatus produced the most buzzing, sizzling, African-sounding music I have ever heard. —Barry Lee Pearson

Piney Woods Blues / 1958 / Delmark 602
Fine Delmark cuts from the late-'50s rediscovery phase of Big Joe's career. —Barry Lee Pearson

○ **Nine-String Guitar Blues** / 1961 / Delmark 627
One of his finest albums (of many). —Bill Dahl

○ **Back to the Country** / 1964 / Testament 2205
Fellow Mississippians Jimmy Brown on fiddle and Willie Lee Harris on harmonica augment Big Joe's down-home Delta blues from the blues revival of the '70s. —Barry Lee Pearson

● **Early Recordings 1935-41** / 1965 / Mamlish 2047
This blues legend and guitar wizard's best initial Bluebird recordings, including the best versions of "49 Highway" and "Baby Please Don't Go" from 1935. —Barry Lee Pearson

○ **Stavin' Chain Blues** / 1966 / Delmark 609
A CD reissue of 1958 recordings, including four previously unreleased tracks. Raw but beautiful country-blues, featuring the otherworldly sound of Big Joe's nine-string guitar. —Niles J. Frantz

● **Shake Your Boogie** / 1990 / Arhoolie 315
Arhoolie reissued two of Big Joe Williams's seminal rediscovery albums on one disc in 1990. The first, 1960's Tough Times, ranks among his best; the second, 1969's Thinking of What They Did, isn't as strong, yet the two albums provide an excellent introduction to this Delta bluesman. —Stephen Thomas Erlewine

○ **Delta Blues—1951** / 1991 / Trumpet 702
Though the early '50s were not a great time for delta blues musicians, there remained some proficient players performing in this vein throughout the South. The three presented on this new collection of classic Trumpet recordings include Big Joe Williams, known for his nine-string guitar and robust singing, Luther Huff, a good, if derivative vocalist/guitarist and the spry pianist and vocalist Willie Love, an exuberant performer whose Three Aces band at various times contained Elmore James and Little Milton. This anthology includes 18 selections that show the link between older, traditional blues and the urban, electric sounds that emerged as the idiom's dominant form later in the decade. —Ron Wynn

Robert Pete Williams

b. Mar. 14, 1914, Zachary, LA, **d.** Dec. 31, 1980, Rosedale, LA
Vocals, guitar, kazoo / Acoustic Louisiana blues
Discovered at the Louisiana State Penitentiary, Williams became one of the great blues discoveries during the folk boom of the early '60s. His disregard for conventional patterns, tunings, and structures kept him from a wider audience, but his music remains one of the great, intense treats of the blues. —Cub Koda

Robert Pete Williams, Vol. 2 / 1959 / Arhoolie
This second volume of newly released Robert Pete Williams material was mostly recorded in Louisiana in 1959, shortly after Williams was paroled from Angola by Governor Earl Long. For five years Williams was not allowed to travel, and instead worked for a farmer in Denham Springs, LA, before receiving a full pardon in 1964. The cuts recorded during this time reflect both his appreciation for being out of jail and his understanding that he was still not completely free. —Ron Wynn

★ **Angola Prisoner's Blues** / Mar. 1961 / Arhoolie 2011
Not enough great things to say about this one, one of the finest field recordings ever done anywhere. If Robert Pete's "Prisoner's

Talking Blues" doesn't move you, check your heart into your refrigerator's freezer section. —Cub Koda

○ **Rural Blues (With Snooks Eaglin)** / 197z / Storyville 8001
Not only does Snooks Eaglin prove a fine partner for Robert Pete Williams, but his vocals and playing have seldom been more disciplined and exciting. —Ron Wynn

Robert Pete Williams, Vol. 1 / 1994 / Arhoolie
These songs were mostly recorded at the Angola State Penitentiary and such numbers as "Pardon Denied Again," "Angola Special," and "Please Lord, Help Me On My Way" (a superb previously unissued cut) take on a deeper meaning in this context. While Williams sings mournful, anguished blues with spectacular impact, he also can turn around and do more joyous fare such as "Louise" or "Come Here Baby" effectively. His vigorous accompaniment, especially on six-string guitar, is just as creative and stunning as his vocals. This 15-cut disc, which has 5 bonus cuts, is most welcome and makes the listener eager to hear the second volume. —Ron Wynn

○ **When a Man Takes the Blues** / 1994 / Arhoolie
Important collection of Williams' best early work. —Bill Dahl

○ **I'm as Blue as a Man Can be** / 1994 / Arhoolie
More classic early sides. —Bill Dahl

Sonny Boy Williamson I (John Lee Williamson)

b. Mar. 30, 1914, Jackson, TN, **d.** Jun. 1, 1948, Chicago, IL
Vocals, harmonica / Blues
John Lee Williamson, known to bluesologists as "the first Sonny Boy" or "Sonny Boy I" because he preceded another famed bluesman (Aleck "Rice" Miller) who also used the SBW moniker, can rightly be considered the forefather of the postwar Chicago blues style. It was he who brought the harmonica to prominence in the blues, and he who pioneered the harmonica-led small-combo format that defined the Chicago idiom in its '40s development. Williamson's records exuded charm and swing. His vocals and harp playing were widely imitated, and many of his songs survived in the repertoires of artists like Junior Wells, Snooky Pryor, and Little Walter. Before he died on a Chicago street, the victim of murder by icepick, Sonny Boy had contributed a wealth of memorable works to the discography of the blues, including "Good Morning (Little) School Girl," "Blue Bird Blues," and "Hoodoo Hoodoo" (the "Hoodoo Man Blues" of Junior Wells fame). —Jim O'Neal

★ **Throw a Boogie Woogie (With Big Joe Williams)** / Apr. 1990 / RCA 9599
The 1930s Bluebird recordings from the influential harp-playing "Sonny Boy I" and the archetypical bluesman drifter Big Joe Williams, whose powerful vocals and percussive nine-string guitar epitomized the Delta. —Mark A. Humphrey

○ **Complete Recorded Works—Vols. 1-5** / Document
His complete works 1937-47 in chronological order. Sonny Boy was a major influence (both harmonica and vocals) on many of the younger Chicago bluesmen, in particular: Junior Wells. —Michael Erlewine

Sonny Boy Williamson II (Aleck Ford "Rice" Miller)

b. Dec. 5, 1899, Glendora, MS, **d.** May 25, 1965, Helena, AR
Vocals, harmonica / R&B, Blues
One of the three greatest blues harmonica men who ever lived (Little Walter Jacobs and Big Walter Horton being the other two), Sonny Boy's style was 100 percent his own. A contemporary of Robert Johnson and other early Delta blues legends, Williamson worked under the name "Little Boy Blue." He began using the "Sonny Boy" tag when he started broadcasting over KFFA on the "King Biscuit Time" radio show in the early '40s. Williamson, however, didn't start recording until the early '50s. Early recorded success for the Mississippi-based Trumpet label brought him to Chicago's Chess label, where he remained for the rest of his career, having R&B chart hits into the early '60s. His appearance on European blues tours made him a direct influence on the then-burgeoning English R&B scene as well, and he recorded with the Yardbirds, the Animals, and Jimmy Page. Whether he worked solo or with a full band, Sonny Boy could keep any audience spellbound with his rhythmic bursts of harmonica, his sly singing of some of the best blues lyrics ever constructed, and a gift for entertaining that went back to his days of hoboing around the

South. One of the true originals in the blues, Sonny Boy Williamson's recordings are classics of the genre. —*Cub Koda*

☆ **Down & out Blues** / 1959 / Chess 31272
The long overdue first CD reissue from the extensive recorded output of harp wizard Sonny Boy Williamson to be included in MCA's Chess Masters series. It was Williamson's first Chess LP, originally released in 1959 and contains tracks culled from sessions dating from 1955 through 1958. — *Ralph Stewart Jr., Rock & Roll Disc.*

○ **Real Folk Blues, The** / 1965 / Chess 9272
Contains some of his most memorable sides, "One Way Out," "Checkin' Up on My Baby," and "Bring it on Home." — *Ralph Stewart, Rock & Roll Disc.*

○ **More Real Folk Blues** / Sep. 1967 / Chess 9277
Fine Chess tracks. —*Bill Dahl*

○ **One Way Out** / 1968 / Chess 9116
Wide ranging classic compilation. —*Bill Dahl*

★ **King Biscuit Time** / 1989 / Arhoolie 310
Sonny Boy's early Trumpet sides from 1951. The original "Eyesight to the Blind," "Nine Below Zero," and "Mighty Long Time" are Sonny Boy at his very best. Added bonuses include Williamson backing Elmore James on his original recording of "Dust My Broom" and a live broadcast from 1965. —*Cub Koda*

○ **Clownin' with the World** / 1989 / Trumpet 700
This batch of mostly unreleased Trumpet blues cuts from the early '50s offers some sizzling, if sometimes uneven, material by Sonny Boy Williamson II and Willie Love. Each gets eight numbers, with Williamson's being recorded both in Houston and Jackson, MS, while Love did all his dates in Jackson. This is undiluted, frequently chaotic, and always enjoyable music. —*Ron Wynn*

○ **Chess Years, The** / 1991 / Ch 1303
This import multidisc boxed set of Sonny Boy's Chess sides (1955–64) is a definitive overview. —*Cub Koda*

Keep It to Ourselves / 1992 / Alligator 4787
Acoustic solo sides, recorded in Europe in 1963. Intimate and wonderful. —*Cub Koda*

★ **Essential Sonny Boy Williamson** / 1993 / MCA-Chess 9343
This magnificent two-CD anthology with its sumptuous booklet makes all previous compilations of Williamson's Chess recordings (excepting the complete Japanese box set) by and large obsolete. This is one time when the "essential" in the title is no mere hyperbole; indispensable is more like it. —*Cub Koda*

○ **Goin' in Your Direction** / Trumpet 801
This is a great compilation of pre-Chess Rice Miller, only a step below Arhoolie's *King Biscuit Time,* with which it shares one song: "She Brought Life Back to the Dead." This is essential stuff for anyone interested in the transition of country blues to the full-blown Chicago style. —*Jimmy Guterman, Roundup Newsletter*

○ **Trumpet Masters, Vol. 5 —From the Bottom** / Collectables 5244
As you would expect, Sonny Boy Williamson II's Trumpet sides were rough, raspy, and combative, punctuated by biting harmonica and accented by his piercing vocals. This CD cleans up the sound a bit, but not enough to rob it of its energy or grit. —*Ron Wynn*

Hop Wilson (Harding Wilson)

b. Apr. 27, 1927, Grapeland, TX, d. Aug. 27, 1975, Houston, TX
Vocals, guitar / Electric Texas blues
Slide guitar blues with an Elmore James flavor, played on an eight-string table (nonpedal) steel guitar, was the trademark sound of Houston blues legend Hop Wilson. Strictly a local phenomenon, Wilson recorded fitfully and hated touring. Though he played fine down-home blues on conventional electric guitar and was a powerful singer as well, it is Wilson's unique slide stylings that remain a signature influence on Johnny Winter and Jimmie Vaughan, to name a few. —*Cub Koda*

○ **Rockin' Blues Party** / 1989 / Charly 115
Featuring a full side of Hop Wilson, with alternate (and superior) takes of all the classic Goldband sides on this album. —*Cub Koda*

● **Houston Ghetto Blues** / Nov. 1993 / Bullseye Blues
Hop Wilson was a legitimate trail blazer in a genre where innovation was almost nonexistent after the '50s. He played blues on steel guitar and did not simply spotlight its unusual sound as a

gimmick but played flaming chords, fiery phrases, sparkling riffs, and unforgettable solos. Whether it is the hoodoo/voodoo intimations on both takes of "My Woman Has a Black Cat Bone," the novelty themes of "Dance to It (the Chicken Stuff)" and "Toot Toot Tootsie," the cautionary tones of "Be Careful with the Blues" and the crushed yet relieved "My Woman Done Quit Me," Wilson brings a vitality and edge to these songs that more than justify his long-held reputation. —*Ron Wynn*

Jimmy Witherspoon (James Witherspoon)

b. Aug. 18, 1923, Gurdon, AR
Vocals, bass / R&B, Electric jump blues
One of the great blues singers of the post-WWII period, Witherspoon began recording with Jay McShann for Philo and Mercury in 1945 and 1946. His own first recordings, using McShann's band, resulted in a #1 R&B hit in 1949 with "Ain't Nobody's Business Parts 1 & 2" on Supreme Records. Live performances of "No Rollin' Blues" and "Big Fine Girl" provided Spoon with two more hits in 1950. Later singles were tried for Federal, Chess, Atco, Vee Jay, and others with little success. His album *Live at the Monterey Jazz Festival* from 1959 lifted him back into the limelight. Partnerships with Ben Webster (tenor sax) or Groove Holmes (organ) were recorded, and some memorable music resulted, but Jimmy's best '60s album is *Evening Blues* (Prestige), which features T-Bone Walker on guitar and Clifford Scott on saxophone.

Inactive for a time in the '70s due to throat cancer, Witherspoon has made a complete recovery and made one of his most memorable albums for Muse Records (*Midnight Lady Called the Blues*). Muse also released an album recorded in France, featuring Witherspoon with the Savoy Sultans. His newer records lack the spark of some of his earlier work, but given the proper circumstances Jimmy Witherspoon always delivers. —*Bob Porter*

○ **Jimmy Witherspoon & Jay McShann** / 1947–49 / DA 760173
Here's vintage blues shouting, jump blues and boogie piano performed by two giants at their performance peaks. Vocalist Jimmy Witherspoon hollered, roared and strutted with authority, while pianist Jay McShann not only headed a superb combo and backed Weatherspoon stylishly, but when given the spotlight he supplied connecting riffs, offered emphatic solos, and helped keep things roaring. There are 24 numbers on this 1992 CD reissue, and they illustrate the potency and appeal of Weatherspoon and Mcshann, while also revealing the links between swing, blues, and early R&B. —*Ron Wynn*

○ **Baby Baby Baby** / 1963 / Prestige 527
Originally released on Prestige in 1963, this is one of the finest albums the singer recorded during his tenure there. Eight of the 12 cuts feature jazz guitar giant Kenny Burrell playing some smoky blues. Songs include "Mean Old Frisco" and "One Scotch, One Bourbon, One Beer." —*Roundup Newsletter*

○ **Evenin' Blues** / 1964 / Original Blues Classics 511
This informal 1963 session for Prestige is one of singer Jimmy Witherspoon's rarest. It was the only time he ever recorded with T-Bone Walker, who contributed his trademark electric blues guitar to a set of tunes including "Money's Getting Cheaper" and "Good Rockin' Tonight." —*Roundup Newsletter*

● **Hey Mr. Landlord** / 1965 / Route 66 31
A thorough import survey of Witherspoon's earlier (1945–56) blues-shoutin' days. —*Hank Davis*

○ **Spoon Concerts, The** / 1972 / Fantasy 24701
A classic Monterey Jazz Festival date with Ben Webster, Roy Eldridge, and Coleman Hawkins. —*Hank Davis*

Spoon So Easy—the Chess Years / 1990 / Chess 93003
Chicago sides from 1945–55 that are closer to R&B than jazz. —*Hank Davis*

○ **Call Me Baby** / 1991 / Night Train 7004
Features a young Jimmy Witherspoon in his prime, backed by great bands led by Jay McShann and Count Basie veteran Buddy Tate. Fifteen tracks including three alternates. Direct-to-disc recordings. —*Roundup Newsletter*

★ **Blowin' in from Kansas City** / 1993 / Capitol 86299
These 20 tunes pair the great Mr. Witherspoon with the finest jazz, jump, and blues talent around. Jay McShann, Maxwell Davis, Tiny Webb, and Chuck Norris are only a few of the first-

rate session men and arrangers who grace the tracks of this essential CD. —*Larry Hoffman*

○ **Jays Blues** / Charly 270
Fine early-'50s jump blues for Federal. —*Bill Dahl*

Billy Wright

b. May 21, 1932
R&B
A first-rate talent scout who was among Little Richard's and James Brown's earliest boosters, Billy Wright was also a fine vocalist. He recorded for Savoy and Duke/Peacock in the '40s and '50s, and was a dominant emcee in Atlanta clubs during the '70s. —*Ron Wynn*

○ **Goin' Down Slow (blues, Soul & Early R 'n' R, Vol. 1)** / 1984 / Savoy 1146
Crying and pleading the blues, Wright's early 50's Savoy output was very influential. —*Bill Dahl*

Jimmy Yancey (James Edward Yancey)

b. Feb. 20, 1898, Chicago, IL, **d.** Sep. 17, 1951, Chicago, IL
Vocals, piano, harmonium / Piano blues, Boogie-woogie, Traditional jazz
Yancey was a truly great stride and boogie-woogie piano man who influenced numerous players during his heyday in the '30s and '40s. —*Cub Koda*

○ **Chicago Piano, Vol. 1** / 1972 / Atlantic 82368
This reissue of a 1951 Yancey session that briefly surfaced in 1959 and 1972 is fine hard-yet-delicate piano soul. Jimmy cut this after his stints with Bluebird, Victor, and Vocalion, but these duets are prime boogie woogie, a spirited middle ground between Meade Lux Lewis and Jerry Lee Lewis. —*Jimmy Guterman, Roundup Newsletter*

★ **Vol. 1 (1939–40)** / Document 5041
Yancey's earliest and best sides for the Solo Art label. Beautiful and sensitive performances. —*Cub Koda*

Johnny Young (John O. Young)

b. Jan. 1, 1918, **d.** Apr. 18, 1974, Chicago, IL
Vocals, mandolin, guitar / Acoustic and electric Chicago blues
Although the mandolin is not an instrument commonly associated with Chicago blues, it has been used by Chicago-based string bands or on Chicago-made recordings by artists such as Carl Martin, Charles and Joe McCoy, and Yank Rachell. However, the only artist to use it successfully in the later electric blues format was Mississippi-born bluesman Johnny Young. An important figure in blues history, Young loved the rough-and-tumble string-band tradition of the Delta, a style that readily coexisted with blues.

Young's initial 1947 Chicago classic, "Money Taking Women," exhibits the same exuberant down-home sound, fusing blues with the older country breakdown traditions. The string-band ensemble sound suited street performance as well, whether in Memphis or in Chicago's open-air Maxwell Street Market, where Young and his cronies were brought in off the streets to record. Over the years, Young's mandolin activity declined as Chicago's African-American blues audience demanded a more modern and urban sound. Since Young was also a skilled guitarist and a fine vocalist, he easily weathered the transition.

During the late '60s, an emerging White blues-revival audience proved eager for Young's mandolin styling. Unlike Yank Rachell, whose mandolin playing retained an older string-band feel, Young's style was firmly grounded in a more contemporary postwar blues idiom, and he interacted well with other electric blues artists. Through his life, he had worked with the major figures of blues history, including Sonny Boy Williamson, Muddy Waters, Walter Horton, and Otis Spann. He was, he insisted, born to be a musician. When I interviewed him shortly before he died, he told me how he had struggled all his life trying to make it in the music business. An emotional man, he hoped he would live long enough to make enough money to buy a house. He never made it. —*Barry Lee Pearson*

○ **Chicago Blues Band** / 1966 / Arhoolie 1029
James Cotton nearly blew the roof off on harmonica, and Otis Spann added some wonderful rumbling piano. Johnny Young's

spirited guitar, vocals, and occasional mandolin provided the final element for a superb mid-'60s date. —*Ron Wynn*

○ **Chicago/ the Blues/ Today!, Vol. 3** / 1967 / Vanguard 79218

● **Chicago Blues** / 1968 / Arhoolie 325
Excellent '60s recordings by this down-home urban singer, guitarist, and mandolinist, accompanied by Otis Spann on piano and James Cotton and Big Walter Horton on harmonicas. —*Mark A. Humphrey*

Mighty Joe Young

b. Sep. 23, 1927, Shreveport, LA
Vocals, Guitar / Electric Chicago blues
Although massively popular in the sweaty blues clubs of Chicago and surrounding environs during the 1970 and '80s, energetic guitarist Mighty Joe Young's recording career never really equaled his live popularity, despite a handful of solid offerings.

After stints in the combos of Billy Boy Arnold, Jimmy Rogers, and Otis Rush, Young waxed a series of solid, brassy blues during the '60s for small local logos such as Webcor, Celtex, and USA that never progressed past local status. Young's debut album for Delmark, *Blues with a Touch of Soul*, was quite inconsistent, but a pair of mid-'60s sets for Ovation spotlight his tough lead guitar work and vocals in a slick contemporary setting that perhaps best reflects his high-energy approach. —*Bill Dahl*

● **Chicken Heads** / 1974 / Ovation 1437
Funky and contemporary. —*Bill Dahl*

○ **Mighty Joe Young** / 1976 / Ovation 1706
Another laudably modern set. —*Bill Dahl*

Bluesy Josephine / Nov. 28, 1976 / Evidence 26023
Energetic 1976 French recordings. Young treats the whole project as just another club set in Chicago, so tracks do have a tendency to wander a bit. But this stands as some of the better recordings capturing what this highly derivative artist does best. —*Cub Koda*

Blues Collections

○ **Alabama Blues, 1927-1931** / Yazoo 1006
This 14-track compilation includes Barefoot Bill ("Snigglin' Blues"), Jay Bird Coleman ("Coffee Grinder Blues"), Ed Bell ("Mean Conductor Blues"), Clifford Gibson ("Whiskey Moan Blues"), and others. —*Roundup Newsletter*

○ **All Night Long They Play the Blues** / 1992 / Specialty 7029
Excellent '60s soul/blues anthology from the Galaxy label's vaults. —*Bill Dahl*

○ **Alley Special** / 1990 / Collectables 5320
Blues of various styles and consistently high quality, released on the Gotham and 20th Century labels, with three previously unreleased cuts. Raw, early electric blues from the late '40s and early '50s. Includes Muddy Waters's first commercial recording. —*Niles J. Frantz*

Alligator 20th Anniversary / 1991 / Alligator 105/6
A brilliant, inexpensive two-CD or two-cassette collection that emphasizes the high points of the planet's greatest new-recordings blues label. —*Roundup newsletter*

○ **Angels in Houston** / Rounder 2031
Great Duke recordings of Bobby Bland, James Davis, Larry Davis, and Fenton Robinson from the late '50s and the '60s. Includes Bland's classic "Yield Not to Temptation." —*Barry Lee Pearson*

○ **Antone's—Bringing You the Best in Blues** / 1989 / Antone's 9901
A sampler of artists on this Austin, TX, label. A variety of Texas blues and R&B, originally released from 1987 to 1990. Includes Otis Rush, Angela Strehli, Doug Sahm, Matt "Guitar" Murphy, and several others. —*Niles J. Frantz*

○ **Antone's 10th Anniversary Anthology, Vol. 1** / 1986 / Antone's 0004

○ **Antone's Anniversary Anthology, Vol. 2** / 1991 / Antone's 0016
Both volumes consist of live recordings at a popular Austin, TX, club in July 1985. Volume 1 includes Chicago blues living legends Buddy Guy, Jimmy Rogers, Eddie Taylor, James Cotton, Snooky Pryor, Otis Rush, Albert Collins, and more. The CD has three bonus cuts. Volume 2 includes incendiary tracks by Buddy Guy

and Matt "Guitar" Murphy. Good sound and very good performances.
—Niles J. Frantz & Bill Dahl

● **Atlanta Blues** / Sep. 1967 / RBF 15

☆ **Atlantic Blues Box** / 1986 / Atlantic 82309
Atlantic takes one step forward with a revamped *Atlantic Rhythm and Blues* boxed set and two steps back with this *Atlantic Blues Box*, which was originally issued in 1986 as four double LPs (now out of print). To completely reproduce the collection on CD would have required a fifth CD, which Atlantic opted not to produce. Maybe they limited the set to four CDs to keep the four genres of Atlantic blues separated, as each CD features one genre—guitar, piano, Chicago, and vocalists. If so, that's a lousy reason to keep the additional material out of print. Still, there is some great stuff here, and the accompanying book does give us generous-sized photos: Mississippi Fred McDowell, John Lee Hooker, T-Bone Walker, Albert King, and B. B. King in the guitar section; Little Brother Montgomery, Meade Lux Lewis, Jay McShann, and a dashing Willie Mabon in the piano section; Sippie Wallace and Wynonie Harris in the vocalists section; and Chicago greats Freddie King (he's from Texas but recorded in Chicago, too), Otis Rush, Buddy Guy, Muddy Waters, and Koko Taylor in the final section. A sessionography is provided along with the original liner notes. Other artists on the CDs include Guitar Slim, Cornell Dupree, Mikey Baker, Jimmy Yancey, Champion Jack Dupree, Percy Mayfield, Ted Taylor, Big Joe Turner, Johnny Copeland, Johnny Shines, J. B. Hutto, and others. Although this 83-track set has 20 fewer tracks than the LP original, what you do get is a sample of fine Atlantic blues, little of it available elsewhere. —*Decibel Dennis MacDonald, Roundup newsletter*

○ **Beauty of the Blues** / 1991 / CBS 47465
A beautiful 18-track collection from a sampling of Columbia/Legacy's *Roots 'n' Blues* series. The recordings, from 1929 to 1947, include a wide variety of traditional blues and blues-related styles. Excellent sound, with music from Robert Johnson, Big Bill Broonzy, and others. —*Niles J. Frantz*

Best of Chess Blues / MCA 6025
A continuing series, containing six volumes to date, of rare and obscure '50s tracks by Chess blues stalwarts, including Howlin' Wolf, Little Walter, Sonny Boy Williamson, and many more. —*Hank Davis*

○ **Best of Chicago Blues** / 1973 / Vanguard 1
Mostly '60s recordings of tough Chicago blues, produced by Samuel Charters. Features James Cotton, Junior Wells, Otis Spann, Buddy Guy, J. B. Hutto, Homesick James, Big Walter Horton, and Johnny Young. Very successful snapshots of what was happening in the Chicago blues bars at that time. Beautiful, powerful music. —*Niles J. Frantz*

Best of Duke-Peacock Blues / 1992 / MCA 10667
Sizzling sampler of '50s and '60s blues from Don Robey's Houston base firm. —*Bill Dahl*

○ **Black Top Blues Cocktail Party** / 1991 / Black Top 1066
This features nonalbum tracks from the label's roster. —*Robert Gordon*

Black Top Blues Pajama Party / May 15, 1992 / Black Top 1075
Following in the tradition of *Black Top Blues Cocktail Party* (Black Top 1066) comes *Blues Pajama Party*, a mixture of sizzling blues and unreleased tracks. —*Roundup newsletter*

Black Top Blues-A-Rama, Vol. 1 / Black Top 1044
Volume 1 includes 1988 live sides by Anson Funderburgh, Sam Myers, organist Ron Levy, and sax wailer Grady Gaines—all of it typically hot and sweaty. —*Bill Dahl*

Black Top Blues-A-Rama, Vol. 2 / 1988 / Black Top 1045
Three R&B vets; Nappy Brown, Earl King, James Davis and relative newcomer Ronnie Earl live in '88.—Bill Dahl

Black Top Blues-A-Rama, Vol. 7—Live at Tipitinas / Black Top 1089
Robert Ward makes his live recording debut on Volume 7's simmering '92 set. Also aboard: bluesy zydeco expert Lynn August and Carol Fran and Clarence Holliman with three numbers. —*Bill Dahl*

○ **Black Top Blues-A-Rama: A Budget Sampler** / 1990 / Black Top 2

A 21-track sampler of Black Top Records' music. A very good example of contemporary blues, with a focus on Texas and Louisiana. —*Niles J. Frantz*

○ **Blind Pig Sampler** / Blp 78001
Representative collection of prolific label's bluesy catalog. —*Bill Dahl*

○ **Blow It 'Til You Like It** / Charly 27
More blues and R&B harmonica on this generous 24-track import sampler. —*Hank Davis*

☆ **Blue Flames—Sun Blues Collection** / 1990 / Rhino 70962
A skimpy (18 songs) but tremendous set of Sam Phillips's gutbucket blues recordings, all of early '50s vintage and exquisitely remastered. Most of the big names are here. —*John Floyd*

Blues Around Midnight / 1991 / Flair 91801
This 20-song compilation focuses on the slower, softer side of the blues, making it ideal for late-night listening. It contains over an hour's worth of music, including B. B. King's "You're Breaking My Heart," Ray Charles's "I'm Wondering and Wondering," Larry Davis's "Three O'Clock in the Morning," T-Bone Walker's "Love Will Lead You Right," Jimmy Witherspoon's "I Need Somebody," and Lowell Fulson's title track. —*Roundup newsletter*

○ **Blues As Big as Texas, Vol. 1** / 1991 / Collectables 5220
Previously unreleased Texas blues, digitally remastered from the original tapes. Various artists recorded between 1958 and 1971 in Houston (one cut in Beaumont, TX). Features Johnny Copeland, Clarence "Gatemouth" Brown, Percy Mayfield, and more. A good and varied set. —*Niles J. Frantz*

○ **Blues Came Down from Memphis** / Charly 67
A nice overview of Sun's early '50s blues recordings on a single-disc CD, primarily sticking to an issued-singles format. This is a perfect place to start. —*Cub Koda*

○ **Blues Deluxe** / 1989 / Alligator 9301
A 1989 CD reissue. Recorded live at the 1980 Chicagofest. A budget CD with only 38 minutes of playing time. Muddy Waters, Koko Taylor, Willie Dixon, and three others. —*Niles J. Frantz*

○ **Blues Is Killin' Me** / 1991 / Jewel 19
A 20-track, rock-solid collection of classic blues sides from Chicago's JOB label, primarily focusing on both sides of original-issue 78s by Floyd Jones, Memphis Minnie, Baby Face Leroy, and Little Hudson's Red Devil Trio, with a few unissued surprises rounding out the already excellent package. —*Cub Koda*

☆ **Blues Masters, Vol. 1: Urban Blues** / 1992 / Rhino 71121
Covering over a quarter-century in its scope, this volume features the big band sound of Erskine Hawkins's "After Hours" and Count Basie's "Every Day (I Have the Blues)" with Joe Williams on vocals. Guitar fanatics will prize Pee Wee Crayton's "Blues After Hours," Guitar Slim's "The Things That I Used to Do," T-Bone Walker's "T-Bone Blues," Albert King's "Laundromat Blues," and Otis Rush's original Cobra recording of "I Can't Quit You, Baby." A great overview. —*Cub Koda*

☆ **Blues Masters, Vol. 2: Post-War Chicago Blues** / 1992 / Rhino 71122
Expertly compiled by Dick Shurman, this is about as solid a compilation as you could ask for, and one of the best volumes in the series. Highlights include Big Walter Horton and Johnny Shines's shattering "Evening Sun"; Baby Face Leroy, Muddy Waters, and Little Walter teaming up on "Rollin' & Tumblin'"; Jody Williams's obscure but wonderful "You May"; and classic tracks from Buddy Guy, Otis Rush, and Magic Sam. Highly recommended. —*Cub Koda*

☆ **Blues Masters, Vol. 3: Texas Blues** / 1992 / Rhino 71123
This volume recounts the history of Texas blues from Blind Lemon Jefferson's "Matchbox Blues" and early sides by Lightnin' Hopkins to the modern sounds of Stevie Ray Vaughan and the Fabulous Thunderbirds. Also included are seminal sides by Pee Wee Crayton, Albert Collins, Frankie Lee Sims, and Clarence "Gatemouth" Brown. —*Cub Koda*

★ **Blues Masters, Vol. 4: Harmonica Classics** / 1992 / Rhino 71124
Postwar electric blues harmonica at its best—Little Walter, Jimmy Reed, Lazy Lester, Paul Butterfield, Sonny Boy Williamson, Slim Harpo, Junior Wells, and Charlie Musselwhite. There's no better one-stop introduction on the blues harp. —*AMG*

☆ **Blues Masters, Vol. 5: Jump Blues Classics** / 1992 / Rhino 71125

Part one of two volumes devoted to the horn-dominated strain of the genre, this features hard-driving sides by tenor saxophonists Red Prysock and Big Jay McNeely as well as the best sides by blues shouters Wynonie Harris, Tiny Bradshaw, and Big Joe Turner. —*Cub Koda*

Blues Masters, Vol. 10: Blues Roots / 1993 / Rhino 71135

Expertly compiled, annotated, and, in most cases, recorded by pioneering blues researcher Samuel Charters, this volume explores all areas of the blues' origins. Featuring devastating recordings of prison work hands, from native African music to Texas prison songs, this is as hardcore a collection as you're likely to find, yet it's still very accessible to the average fan. —*Cub Koda*

★ **Blues Masters, Vol. 6: Blues Originals** / 1993 / Rhino 71127

Out of all the volumes of the *Blues Masters* series, *Vol. 6: Blues Originals* is the rock & roll fan's best introduction to the blues. *Blues Originals* has 18 originals of songs that famous rock bands later covered or appropriated for their own purposes. Most rock fans will be familiar with the majority of this material ("That's All Right," "I'm a Man," "I Can't Quit You Baby," "Love in Vain," "You Need Love," "Back Door Man") in one form or another. What makes this such a splendid introduction to the blues is the number of styles (from electric Chicago blues to acoustic Delta blues) featured and the number of major performers represented. (Muddy Waters, Howlin' Wolf, Robert Johnson, Jimmy Reed, Little Walter, Arthur "Big Boy" Crudup, Elmore James)—all of whom had a major part in shaping rock & roll. Listeners familiar with the major artists will also find some treasures here, like Henry Thomas's "Bulldoze Blues" (Canned Heat reworked this for "Goin' Up the Country), Big Walter & His Thunderbirds' "Pack Fair and Square" (which the J. Geils Band covered), and Larry Davis's "Texas Flood," which is remarkable not only for the way Stevie Ray Vaughan borrowed the guitar licks for his version, but also its vocal phrasing. —*AMG*

○ **Blues Masters, Vol. 7: Blues Revival** / 1993 / Rhino 71128

With the blues revival of the '60s, Whites entered the music's history both as performers and rediscoverers-promoters of the original artists, who were brought back to record again. Blues was being accepted by the White audience in a big way, and this 17-track compilation touches on all the important moments and artists from that time. For anyone who was there, this volume will bring back a flood of memories. —*Cub Koda*

Blues Masters, Vol. 8: Mississippi Delta Blues / 1993 / Rhino 71130

The title for this volume is a bit of a misnomer. While there is easily half a compilation's worth of authentic acoustic material here (including classics by Tommy Johnson, Charley Patton, Willie Brown, and Robert Johnson), the inclusion of tracks by B. B. King and Albert King and sides by Howlin' Wolf, Elmore James, and Robert Nighthawk recorded in Chicago do much to blur the distinctiveness of this package. —*Cub Koda*

○ **Blues Masters, Vol. 9: Postmodern Blues** / 1993 / Rhino 71132

A wonderful compendium of artists and styles illustrating the coming of blues into the mainstream. This volume features representative tracks by B. B. King, Albert Collins, Albert King, George Thorogood, Stevie Ray Vaughan, Johnny Winter, and the Fabulous Thunderbirds. The modern sound at its best and most diverse. —*Cub Koda*

☆ **Blues Masters, Vol. 11: Classic Blues Women** / 1993 / Rhino 71134

Although blues is now male dominated, the earliest to record and have success in the field were women. This volume not only collects many of the great recordings by these women (Mamie, Trixie and Bessie Smith, Billie Holiday, Sippie Wallace, Ma Rainey), but it is also one of the few volumes in the series that offer multiple selections by some of these artists. Highly recommended. —*Cub Koda*

☆ **Blues Masters, Vol. 12: Memphis Blues** / 1993 / Rhino 71129

Recounting the blues history of America's craziest city, from early offerings by Cannon's Jug Stompers and the Memphis Jug Band to early Sun recordings from the '50s by Junior Parker, Rufus Thomas, and Joe Hill Louis, this is undoubtedly one of the best compiled volumes in the series. —*Cub Koda*

○ **Blues Masters, Vol. 13: New York City Blues** / 1993 / Rhino 71131

While other volumes in the series focus on the down-home aspects of the music, this one highlights the big band sound. Great sides by Lionel Hampton ("Hamp's Boogie Woogie"), Duke Ellington, Buddy Johnson, Count Basie, Sam "The Man" Taylor ("Oo-Wee"), and Lucky Millinder showcase a side of the music that is seldom heard. —*Cub Koda*

○ **Blues Masters, Vol. 15: Slide Guitar Classics** / 1993 / Rhino 71126

The final volume in the series (at least for now) features seminal and classic tracks from Elmore James ("Dust My Broom"), Muddy Waters ("Honey Bee"), and Hound Dog Taylor as well as from modern-day disciples like Johnny Winter and Ry Cooder. Blind Willie Johnson's "Dark Was the Night, Cold Was the Ground" alone is worth the price of admission. —*Cub Koda*

○ **Blues Piano Orgy** / 1972 / Delmark 626

A sensational keyboard anthology with great cuts by Speckled Red, Roosevelt Sykes, and Little Brother Montgomery. —*Ron Wynn*

Blues at Newport - Newport Folk Festival / 1959 / Vanguard 115

Blues at Newport—Newport Folk Festival 1959-64 offers fine performances by Mississippi John Hurt, Skip James, Rev. Gary Davis, Robert Wilkins, and others. —*Mark A. Humphrey*

○ **Blues in the Mississippi Night** / Jul. 13, 1991 / Rykodisc 90155

Pioneering documentary-style recording produced by Alan Lomax, which laid unissued for decades after it's 1946 recording because it includes a frank discussion of racism by Big Bill Broonzy, Sonny Boy Williamson, and Memphis Slim. —*Bill Dahl*

○ **Bottleneck Guitar Masterpieces** / Yazoo 1046

Here are 14 tracks highlighting various bottleneck guitar styles. Artists include Barbecue Bob ("Goin' Up the Country"), Rambling Thomas ("Ground Hog Blues"), the Too Bad Boys ("Corrine Corrina Blues"), Roy Smeck ("Laughing Rag"), and others. —*Roundup newsletter*

○ **Canned Heat Blues: Masters of the Delta Blues** / Aug. 1928 / Bluebird 61047

This disc features 21 tracks divided nearly evenly among three Delta blues greats: Furry Lewis, Tommy Johnson, and the lesser-known Ishmon Bracey. Tunes include "Mistreatin' Mama," "Big Fat Mama Blues," and "Saturday Blues." —*Roundup newsletter*

☆ **Chess Blues** / 1992 / MCA 9340

MCA's new *Chess Blues* set is worth acquiring, even for veteran aficionados who have the earlier releases. Sure, icons like Muddy Waters, Howlin' Wolf, Sonny Boy Williamson, and Willie Dixon are represented here, but it's the cuts by a slew of lesser knowns that distinguish this new four-disc anthology, which covers the years 1947-1967.

Among the talented but largely forgotten performers represented here are Baby Face Leroy ("My Head Can't Rest Anymore"), Andrew Tibbs ("Bilbo Is Dead," a landmark racial/political statement), pianist Henry Gray & Morris Pejoe (untitled instrumental); Rocky Fuller ("Funeral Hearse at My Door"), the witty Detroit Jr. ("Too Poor"), Forest City Joe ("Memory of Sonny Boy"), and Arbee Stidham ("Mr. Commissioner").—*Dan Emerson, Request*

○ **Chicago—The Blues Today!, Vol. 1** / Oct. 1966 / Vanguard 79216

Junior Wells, J. B. Hutto, and Otis Spann are all superlative on this groundbreaking anthology. —*Bill Dahl*

○ **Chicago—The Blues Today!, Vol. 2** / 1966 / Vanguard 79217

This series (vols. 1-3) is one of the enduring gems from producer Sam Charters' tenure with Vanguard Records in the '60s. James Cotton's vocals and harp playing are both in top form on his 5 tracks; among them Ike Turner's "Rocket 88" and a make-over of Charles Brown's "Black Night". Slide guitarist Homesick James and his Dusters are fierce in Elmore James' "Dust My Broom" and "Set a Date", and Otis Rush is simply magnificent on his 5 tracks which include "It's a Mean Old World" and "I Can't Quit You Baby" which Led Zeppelin would later copy note for note on their first album. This disc is certain to climb to the top 10 of any blues fan's collection. —*Larry Hoffman*

☆ **Chicago—The Blues Today!, Vol. 3** / 1966 / Vanguard 79218

Aside from the classic Chess albums (Muddy Waters, Little Walter, Howlin' Wolf, etc.), there is no better introduction to Chicago-style blues than this three-volume set. Each one is incredible. This third album contains the Johnny Shines Blues Band, Johnny Young's South Side Blues Band, and Big Walter Horton's Blues Harp Band with Memphis Charlie Musselwhite. Here are the original Chicago artists who have grown up and played together for most of their lives, so the musical time is spacious—wide open. This is South Side Chicago blues with a trace of country at its best. Big Walter Horton plays some of the best harmonica of his career on this album. Listening to Horton on backup and solo harp is an education. This album is definitive. —*Michael Erlewine*

○ **Chicago Ain't Nothin' but a Blues Band** / 1972 / Delmark 624
Chicago Ain't Nothin' but a Blues Band is a solid collection of sides from Chicago's Atomic H label, with JoJo Williams, J. T. Brown, and Eddy Clearwater's earliest recordings among the highlights. —*Cub Koda*

☆ **Chicago Blues—Early 50's** / Blues Classics 8
At the time of its release this was an important examination of pioneering postwar Chicago blues. Now the LP's worth has been superseded by better-sounding CD reissues. —*Bill Dahl*

○ **Chicago Blues Anthology** / 1984 / Chess
A wonderful 24-cut set of raw, early Chicago blues from the Chess label. Delta blues influences are evident in the work of Johnny Shines, Robert Nighthawk, and Floyd Jones. A more modern, urban style is shown by Buddy Guy and Otis Rush. A worthwhile collection. —*Niles J. Frantz*

○ **Chicago Boogie—1947** / 1983 / St. George 1001
All the earliest Maxwell Street acetate recordings from the short-lived Ora Nelle label, including debut sides of Little Walter, Jimmy Rogers, Johnny Young, and Othum Brown. A particular standout: Delta bluesman Johnnie Temple's "Olds 98 Blues," done Robert Johnson-style on an electric guitar. —*Cub Koda*

○ **Chicago Boss Guitars** / 1991 / Paula 9
Chicago's West Side blues guitar school, as recorded for Cobra/Artistic Records, with a rash of Otis Rush and Magic Sam alternate takes and Buddy Guy's very first recordings. Featuring impassioned vocals and bright, stinging lead work, this anthology succeeds on every level. —*Cub Koda*

○ **Cincinnati Blues (1928-1936)** / Story of Blues 3519
Good vibes fill much of *Cincinnati Blues*, billed as the "Complete Recordings of Bob Coleman's Cincinnati Jug Band and Associates." The band's instrumental "Newport Blues" was once a favorite for old-time music anthologies, and it's nice to hear there was more good stuff where it came from. Susan Swain's liner notes assume that Kid Cole, Bob Coleman, and Walter Coleman were all the same person, so the 15 tracks here are from the three sources. Included are two takes of Walter Coleman's "Mama, Let Me Lay It on You," an early "Baby, Let Me Follow You Down." Like the music of the Georgia musicians, the Cincinnati Ohio River style wanders in and out of "blues" terrain. But then the boundary lines that we now pretend exist, didn't exist. —*Blues Access*

○ **Clownin' with the World** / 1989 / Acoustic Archives 700
This wonderful CD from the vaults of Trumpet Records features unissued Sonny Boy Williamson sides and great tracks by his piano-playing buddy, Willie Love. —*Cub Koda*

○ **Cobra Records Story** / 1993 / Capricorn 42012
Two-disc examination of Chicago's mid to late '50s label; west side blues classics by Otis Rush, Buddy Guy, and Magic Sam. —*Bill Dahl*

☆ **Copulatin' Blues Compact Disc** / Vintage Jazz 1
The first release that vindicated the value of Stash's special Jass line was a 1987 anthology featuring 27 overtly sexual blues tunes. *Copulatin' Blues* covers numbers by artists as diverse as Sidney Bechet, Clara Smith, Tampa Red, and Lil Johnson, and has a good balance between singers and instrumentalists, males and females, jazz and classic blues types. Sometimes the tunes are suggestive, other times explicit, but they're all prime examples of just how much sex was in the minds of many early jazz and blues performers and songwriters and of their willingness to admit it. —*Ron Wynn*

☆ **Country Blues Bottleneck Guitar Classics** / 1972 / Yazoo 1026
The first and possibly best anthology of prewar bottleneck guitar (1926-1937), this includes the singing slides of Robert Johnson, Bukka White, and Memphis Minnie, and—although scarcely country blues—a stunning "St. Louis Blues" by Jim and Bob, the Genial Hawaiians! —*Mark A. Humphrey*

Dapper Cats, Groovy Tunes & Hot Guitars / 1992 / ACE 351

Sizzling blues and R&B from the mid '50s vaults of Johnny Otis's Dig Records. —*Bill Dahl*

○ **Dark Muddy Bottom Blues** / 197? / Specialty 2149
Most of the 12 tracks on this 1972 blues compilation were previously unissued. Artists include John Lee Hooker, Lightnin' Hopkins, Mercy Dee, Big Joe Williams, and others. —*AMG*

Dealing with the Devil: Immediate Blues Story, Vol. 2 / 1980 / CBS 47894
This is a collection of early British blues featuring Eric Clapton, Jeff Beck, Jon Lord, Ron Wood, and other not-yet superstars in some rough, raw performances. —*Bruce Eder*

○ **Deep in the Soul of Texas** / 1991 / Collectables 5224

○ **Deep in the Soul of Texas, Vol. 2** / Collectables 5255
Texas soul from the '60s and '70s. Some previously unissued material. —*Niles J. Frantz*

○ **Delta Blues—1951** / 1990 / Acoustic Archives 702
A great compilation from Trumpet Records (Jackson, MS) featuring early '50s sides by Big Joe Williams, wonderful acoustic duets by the Huff Brothers, and the first recordings by the original King Biscuit Boy, Willie Love. A wonderful document. —*Cub Koda*

○ **Detroit Blues—Early 1950's** / Blues Classics 12
Tough, raw-edged, and primitive urban blues from Motor City. —*Bill Dahl*

○ **Dig These Blues: The Legendary Dig Masters** / ACE 334
Johnny Otis produced these hot R&B sides for his Dig label during the mid '50s. —*Bill Dahl*

○ **Don't Leave Me Here** / Yazoo 1004
A collection of rare country blues featuring Blind Lemon Jefferson, Henry Thomas, Buddy Boy Hawkins, Little Hat Jones, Texas Alexander, Willie Reed, King Solomon Hill, and others. —*Roundup newsletter*

○ **Drop Down Mama** / 1970 / Chess 93002
A fine early '50s Chess blues anthology, with classic tracks by slide guitarists Robert Nighthawk and Johnny Shines, brooding Floyd Jones, Arthur Spires, and fleet-fingered Blue Smitty. —*Bill Dahl*

○ **Drove from Home Blues** / Flyright 48
This is an interesting collection of tunes recorded by virtually unknown artists. The music is excellent, finding its niche in the stylish, pre-rockabilly/R&B world—a reflection of the work being done in the late '40s and early '50s by artists such as Arthur Crudup, Lightnin' Hopkins, Tommy McClennan, and Blind Boy Fuller. The music of Wright Holmes, for example, is cast in a Lightnin' Hopkins' mold, but his imaginative guitar style is very wild and unconventional. In addition, harpist Sonny Boy Johnson emerges from the John Lee "Sonny Boy" Williamson school. Also present is Muddy Waters' very first commercial recording. —*Larry Hoffman*

○ **East Coast Blues—1926-1935** / Yazoo 1013
A fine assortment from Carl Martin, Willie Walker, William Moore, Blind Blake, Bayless Rose, and other East Coast guitarists. There are several very traditional blues like "Black Dog Blues" and "Crow Jane," plus lots of good ragtime blues. For serious guitar players and Piedmont blues fans. —*Barry Lee Pearson*

Evidence Blues Sampler / Evidence 26000
Evidence's blues reissue campaign has been exhaustive and diverse in its artistic and stylistic range, qualities reflected in this 15-cut sampler culled from various sessions. There is vintage material from John Lee Hooker, J. B. Hutto, and the tandem of Junior Wells and Buddy Guy, plus classic R&B by Louis Jordan and Big Joe Turner and contemporary blues by Magic Slim, Lonnie Brooks, and Luther Johnson, Jr. You can also hear Otis Rush and Luther Allison at their string-bending, note-swaying best and Pinetop Perkins offering prototypical boogie-woogie and rumbling piano licks. —*Ron Wynn*

○ **Fifties: Juke Joint Blues** / Virgin 86304
A valuable look at some of the toughest Delta and West Coast blue sides issued by Modern Records in the '50s. —*Bill Dahl*

○ **Frank Stokes' Dream: The Memphis Blues** / Yazoo 1008
Early Memphis gems; prewar acoustic. —*Bill Dahl*

○ **Genuine Houserockin' Music, Vol. 1** / 1986 / Alligator 101
Good-time, high-energy, modern R&B produced by Chicago's Alligator label. Lonnie Brooks, Lonnie Mack, Koko Taylor, Fenton

Robinson, Albert Collins, and others. Slick and well produced. — *Hank Davis*

Genuine Mississippi Blues / ACE 2028
Fifteen tracks from eight artists. In the tradition of the recent domestic Ace releases, it's kind of a hodgepodge—most of these tracks were recently recorded in Jackson, with several different artists sharing the same rhythm section. There's a Mississippi Fred McDowell track (accompanied by electric bass), no date given. The Frankie Lee Sims tracks include his original Ace recording of "Hey Little Girl" from about 30 years ago. — *Roundup newsletter*

○ **Georgia String Bands (1928-1930)** / Story of Blues 3516
Black/White musical lines are really blurred by Lonnie Coleman on *Georgia String Bands*. The singer-banjoist's "Old Rock Island Blues" is a wonderful, rocking performance, with terrific lyrics like "I got the raging arthritis and my baby's got the Mobile blues." Coleman's "Wild about My Loving" sounds like Uncle Dave Macon doing the Louis Armstrong Hot 5's "I'm Not Rough." Pink Anderson and Simmie Dooley provide four 1928 tunes on *Georgia String Bands*, including their classic "C. C. and O. Blues." Anderson, a South Carolina native, was a humorous vaudeville songster who gave off the same vibrations as Mississippi John Hurt. Most of the disc contains the music of Macon Ed and Tampa Joe, who did spirited "beedle-um-bum" fiddle-guitar material with titles like "Wringing That Thing" and, believe it or not, "Warm Wipe Stomp." —*Blues Access*

○ **Going Away Blues** / 1969 / Yazoo 1018
Magnificent tracks here, circa 1926-1935, featuring Robert Wilkins, Frank Stokes, Henry Thomas, Charley Jordan, Lottie Beaman, Jelly Jaw Short, and others. —*Roundup newsletter*

○ **Gonna Head for Home** / Flyright 517
A nice compendium of rare and unissued Excello sides by lesser-known names (Boogie Jake, Mr. Calhoun, Silas Hogan, and Jimmy Anderson) who recorded for the label. Excellent Louisiana swamp blues, crude and low-down. —*Cub Koda*

○ **Good Time Blues: Harmonicas, Kazoos, Washboards &** / 1991 / CBS 46780
Twenty-one performances waxed between 1930 and 1941 of hokum blues accompanied by rhythmic kitchenware. Ragtime romps (with many clanks) abound: typical of the material are two covers of Blind Boy Fuller's "Step It Up and Go" (Charlie Burse and His Memphis Mudcats' "Oil It Up and Go," and Sonny Terry and Jordan Webb's "Touch It Up and Go"). Other movers 'n shakers are performed by the Georgia Cotton Pickers, featuring Barbecue Bob and the deft bottleneck of Curley Weaver. The Pentecostal ragtime of the Mississippi Jook Band is great fun. Big Joe (Joe McCoy) and his Washboard Band (with Robert Nighthawk on harmonica) bring a smooth professionalism to their four performances. The nearest thing to a star this funky blues subgenre produced, Washboard Sam is heard doing "Diggin' My Potatoes No. 2." Irresistible spastic cartoon blues, remastered to sound great and thoroughly annotated by David Evans. — *Mark Humphrey, Roundup newsletter*

○ **Got Harp If You Want It** / Blue Rock-It 111
A decent overview of postwar blues harmonica, but hardly comprehensive. —*Ron Wynn*

○ **Got My Mojo Workin'** / 1991 / Flyright 41
A collection of blues sides recorded for New York's Baton label in the mid to late '50s, featuring Chris Kenner's first recording and Ann Cole's original, pre-Muddy Waters performance of the title track. —*Cub Koda*

Great Blues Guitarists: String Dazzlers / Aug. 1991 / CBS 47060
A high-quality survey of some of the finest blues guitar players, recorded from 1924 to 1940. Includes, among others, Tampa Red, Blind Willie Johnson, and Big Bill Broonzy. Highlights include three instrumental duets featuring Lonnie Johnson and Eddie Lang. They take your breath away. —*Niles J. Frantz*

☆ **Great Bluesmen at Newport** / 1976 / Vanguard 78
Performances from 1959 to 1965 by rediscovery legends Son House, Mississippi John Hurt, Skip James, Sleepy John Estes, and other compelling singers and guitarists such as Robert Pete Williams, John Lee Hooker, and Mississippi Fred McDowell. — *Mark A. Humphrey*

○ **Great Harp Players (1927-1936)** / 1992 / Document 5100

● **Greatest in Country Blues (1927-1930), The, Vol. 1** / Story of Blues 3521/3522

● **Greatest in Country Blues (1927-1936), Vol. 2** / Story of Blues 3522

● **Greatest in Country Blues (1929-1956), Vol. 3** / Story of Blues 3523
Congratulations to Story of Blues for snaring these gems from the vaults of Johnny Parth, the Austrian King of the Blues Reissue! Anyone interested in a survey of early blues will be thrilled with any of these three historical volumes, suited to both novice and connoisseur alike. Each provides a dazzling, panoramic survey of artists both famous and obscure and covers every region known to have nurtured this music.
Volume 1 leads with Charley Patton's "High Water Everywhere" and follows with Blind Lemon Jefferson's "See That My Grave Is Kept Clean." It delivers other such master spirits as Blind Willie McTell, Tommy Johnson, Gus Cannon's Jug Stompers, Son House, Blind Willie Johnson, and Mississippi John Hurt—each represented by perhaps their greatest recorded performance.
Volume 2 features Skip James's "Devil Got My Woman," Robert Johnson's "Preaching' Blues," and Kokomo Arnold's "Paddlin' Madeline Blues." From Texas Alexander there is a version of "Levee Camp Moan Blues" that is made timeless by the incomparable guitar of Lonnie Johnson. Great instrumentals like Palmer McAbee's "Railroad Piece" and the Dallas String Band's "Dallas Rag" add spice, and there are also first-rate entries by more obscure giants like King Solomon Hill, George "Bullet" Williams, "Hi" Henry Brown, and Blind Joe Taggart. —*Lawrence Hoffman, Blues Access*

○ **Guitar Wizards—1926-1935** / Yazoo 1016
An excellent collection of great prewar blues guitarists. —*Mark A. Humphrey*

○ **Gulf Coast Blues, Vol. 1** / 1990 / Black Top 1055
Contemporary Texas and Louisiana blues from four artists deserving wider attention. Two cuts each from Carol Fran, Joe "Guitar" Hughes, and Grady Gaines, with four from Teddy Reynolds. Fran and Reynolds are the highlights, and each deserve their own full releases. —*Niles J. Frantz*

○ **Hand Me Down Blues Chicago Style** / 1990 / Relic 7015
This is one of the finest '50s Chicago blues compilations in existence, taken from the vaults of Parrot-Blue Lake Records. Unissued sides and rare singles create an incredible ambiance here. Essential listening. —*Cub Koda*

○ **Harmonica Blues** / 1991 / Yazoo 1053
A fine collection of prewar harp performances. —*Mark A. Humphrey*

○ **Harmonica Blues Kings** / 1986 / Delmark 12
Featuring a side each of Big Walter Horton and Alfred "Blues King" Harris in primarily supporting roles behind various vocalists from the vaults of United/States Records. Featuring raw, lively harmonica, it's another missing piece of the early Chicago blues puzzle. —*Cub Koda*

○ **Harp Attack!** / 1991 / Alligator 4790
An 11-track CD spotlighting four Chicago harmonica players—Carey Bell, Billy Branch, James Cotton, and Junior Wells—in new recordings. All have played with Muddy Waters or Willie Dixon's Chicago Blues All-Stars (or both). Solid electric-band-style Chicago blues. —*Niles J. Frantz*

★ **How Blue Can You Get?—Great Blues Vocals in the Jazz Tradition** / Bluebird 6758
Excellent reissue shows the links between jazz and blues. —*Ron Wynn*

○ **If It Ain't a Hit . . .** / Zu-Zazz 2009
X-rated blues is the theme here, with selections ranging from totally raunchy to mildly titillating. Great listening and a full dollop of humor throughout. Features under-the-counter performances by Jackie Wilson, LaVern Baker, Chick Willis, the Clovers, and the Fred Wolff Combo. Blues with a nudge and wink to it. —*Cub Koda*

Jewel/Paula Records Story / 1993 / Capricorn 42014
Uneven but worthwhile two-disc treatment of Stan Lewis's Shreveport, LA, family of labels (Jewel, Paula, Ronn). The soul/R&B sides are generally more satisfying than that of the marquee blues names. —*Bill Dahl*

Jump 'n Shout! (New Orleans Blues) / Pearl Flapper 15
Solid New Orleans anthology. —*Bill Dahl*

Keys to the Crescent City / Rounder 2087
The revelation on this 1991 CD anthology spotlighting three New Orleans greats and one West Coast blues legend (Charles Brown) is the late Willie Tee. Tee, who died in 1993, was known for his soulful vocals and skillful writing but was undervalued as a pianist. He demonstrated with his voicings and solos on "Can It Be Done" and "In the Beginning" that he also merited attention as a keyboard stylist. Charles Brown turned in his customary polished, first-rate vocal and instrumental job on his three tunes, while Eddie Bo's singing exceeded his piano playing and Art Neville again demonstrated why he should do more recording outside the arenas of the Neville Brothers and the Meters. —*Ron Wynn*

○ **Legends of Electric Blues Guitar, Vol. 1** / Rhino 70716

Legends of the Guitar—Electric Blues, Vol. 2 / 1991 / Rhino 70564
Volume 1 is a very consistent postwar blues guitar collection; Muddy, T-Bone, B. B., Guitar Slim, Earl Hooker, and Otis Rush contribute their vintage classics. Volume 2 is slightly less consistent than its predecessor but is still loaded with gems from "Gatemouth" Brown, Albert Collins, Lowell Fulson, Magic Sam, and others —*Bill Dahl*

○ **Legends of the Blues, Vol. 1** / Feb. 1991 / CBS 46215
Though this set begs comparison with Columbia's double LP anthology of 20 years ago, *The Story of the Blues*, *Legends* isn't nearly as expansive as *Story*. A top flight collection of guitar oriented blues, with Blind Lemon Jefferson, Leadbelly, Bukka White, Big Joe Williams, and Memphis Minnie, among others, playing and singing at the top of their game. Includes a Charley Patton performance, "Revenue Man Blues," not found elsewhere on CD —*Mark Humphrey, Rock & Roll Disc.*

○ **Legends of the Blues, Vol. 2** / CBS 47467
Volume 2 is just as diverse and entertaining as Volume 1, though the artists included are, in general, somewhat less well known. This collection (featuring recordings from 1929 to 1941, presented in chronological order) includes piano blues from Roosevelt Sykes, Charlie Spand, and Champion Jack Dupree; guitar greats Tampa Red, Buddy Boss, and Casey Bill Weldon; and "classic" blues from Lil' Johnson, Victoria Spivey, and Bessie Jackson. Also here is one of T-Bone Walker's first-ever recordings (as "Oak Cliff T-Bone," from 1929) as well as 13 sides that were previously unissued by Columbia or are alternate takes of issued recordings. —*Niles J. Frantz*

○ **Living Chicago Blues, Vol. 1** / 1978 / Alligator 7701
Review:Arguably the best entry in this pioneering anthology series, with excellent sides by guitarist Jimmy Johnson and saxophonist Eddie Shaw. —*Bill Dahl*

Living Chicago Blues, Vol. 2 / 1978 / Alligator 7702
Almost as incendiary as the first, thanks to four sides each from Magic Slim, Lonnie Brooks, and Pinetop Perkins. —*Bill Dahl*

Living Chicago Blues, Vol. 3 / 1980 / Alligator 7703
Laconic saxman A. C. Reed and crisp guitarist Lacy Gibson are standouts on Volume 3. —*Bill Dahl*

Living Chicago Blues, Vol. 4 / 1980 / Alligator 7704
The fourth volume is not quite as strong, although witty pianist Detroit Jr. and guitarist Andrew Brown contribute strong tracks. —*Bill Dahl*

○ **Lonesome Road Blues: 15 Years in the Mississippi Delta, 1926-1941** / Yazoo 1038
Tommy Johnson's influence once again appears on *Lonesome Road Blues—15 Years in the Mississippi Delta*, which includes fine prewar Delta blues by him and other artists. —*Mark A. Humphrey*

○ **Long Man Blues** / Pearl Flapper 17
Chicago blues obscurities from the '50s United/States vaults; Dennis Binder, Harold Burrage, Arbee Stidham, Jack Cooley, and Cliff Butler are solid. —*Bill Dahl*

○ **Louisiana Blues** / 1970 / Arhoolie 1054
Distinctive swamp blues by Henry Gray, Silas Hogan, Whispering Smith, and Guitar Kelley. —*Hank Davis*

○ **Low Blows—Anthology of Chicago Blues** / Rooster Blues 7610

Low Blows is a scatter-gun compilation of great early '70s recordings by Chicago's better-known (Big Walter Horton, Carey Bell) and lesser-known (Big John Wrencher, Good Rockin' Charles Edwards) harmonica men. A missing chapter in blues history. —*Cub Koda*

☆ **Mama Let Me Lay It on You (1926-1936)** / Yazoo 1040
A fine collection of East Coast blues, including vintage Josh White, Pink Anderson, and guitarists Blind Blake and Willie Walker. —*Barry Lee Pearson*

○ **Masters of the Delta Blues: The Friends of Charley Patton** / 1991 / Yazoo 2002
Subtitled *The Friends of Charley Patton*, this CD perfectly anthologizes some of the best and rarest tracks by early Delta blues legends like Son House, Tommy Johnson, and Bukka White. Sounds rough in spots, but it's indispensable nonetheless. —*Cub Koda*

○ **Mississippi Blues—1927-1941** / Yazoo 1001
Another well-programmed anthology. —*Mark A. Humphrey*

Mississippi Delta Blues Jam in Memphis, Vol. 1 / 1993 / Arhoolie 385

Mississippi Delta Blues Jam in Memphis, Vol. 2 / 1993 / Arhoolie 386
Volume 1 is a field recording from 1967 and 1968. Best-known artist on it is Robert Nighthawk. Volume 2 is the more satisfying of the pair, cut in 1967 and 1968. It includes one of R. L. Burnside's best solo works, impressive country blues by Joe Callicott (along with sides of his 1930 78), and four items by guitarist Houston Stockhouse and his combo. —*Bill Dahl*

☆ **Mississippi Girls** / Sep. 1991 / Story of Blues 3515
This is an important collection because it helps fill the gap in the recorded history of blueswomen who played and sang outside of the well-known sphere of the "classic singers" such as Ma Rainey and Bessie Smith. The highlights here are the two recordings of Mattie Delaney, a wonderful singer-guitarist about whom almost nothing is known. Fine also are the more rough-hewn offerings of Rosie Mae Moore, who is accompanied by talented veterans Charlie McCoy and Ishmon Bracey. Although a scratchy background mars the Geechie Wiley/Elvie Thomas duets, they also are well worth hearing. —*Larry Hoffman*

○ **Mississippi Moaners—1927-42** / Yazoo 1009
Lots of Mississippi vocals and blues guitar by the best of the genre—Charley Patton, Skip James, Son House, Rube Lacy, Mississippi John Hurt, and others. — *Roundup newsletter*

○ **Mister Charlie's Blues—1926-1938** / Yazoo 1024
A fascinating exploration of blues-drenched, prewar hillbilly recordings, including the great fingerpicked guitar of Sam McGee. —*Mark A. Humphrey*

○ **New Bluebloods** / 1987 / Alligator 7707
An attempt to document "the next generation of Chicago blues." Generally a very exciting and successful collection, it includes the Kinsey Report, Lil' Ed & the Blues Imperials, Valerie Wellington, and several more. —*Niles J. Frantz*

○ **New Orleans Blues—Troubles Troubles** / Rounder 2080
A sampler of late '50s and early '60s Ric and Ron label music by Edgar Blanchard, Mercy Baby, and Eddie Lang. —*Hank Davis*

○ **News & Blues: Telling It Like It Is** / Feb. 1991 / CBS 46217
Along with juicy thematic meat there's a variety of music settings here, making this one of the brightest gems in the R&B series.— Mark A. Humphrey, Rock & Roll Disc

○ **Original American Folk Blues Festival** / 1962 / PolyGram 25502
Recorded live in a studio in Hamburg, Germany, in October 1962, it includes artists involved with that year's American Folk Blues Festival tour. Performances are generally relaxed and reflective. The artists include T-Bone Walker, Sonny Terry, and John Lee Hooker. —*Cub Koda*

○ **Original Blues Classics, Vol. 1** / 1990 / Fantasy 53306
Budget-priced, seven-cut, cassette-only release for non-record-store retail outlets (such as drug stores). Features blues and soul by Albert King, Etta James, and Lightnin' Hopkins plus four more. Not for real blues fans. —*Niles J. Frantz*

○ **Out of the Blue (Rykodisc)** / 1985 / Rykodisc 20003
A 17-cut sampler of some of Rounder's blues and blues-related releases of the modern period. Features "straight" blues from J. B. Hutto, Phillip Walker, and Johnny Copeland; blues/rock from the

Nighthawks and George Thorogood; soulful blues from Johnny Adams and Ted Hawkins; plus cuts from Buckwheat Zydeco, piano great James Booker, John Hammond, Solomon Burke, and several more. The Adams, Walker, and Copeland cuts are particularly nice, as is one entry from Marcia Ball and the Legendary Blues Band. —*Niles J. Frantz*

○ **Piano Blues, Vol. 2 1927-32** / Magpie 05
Twenty stunning barrelhouse piano blues from the legendary Paramount label—need more be said? Okay, there are three performances by the brilliant and chaotic Jabo Williams; two from the irrepressible and salacious Louise Johnson, whose upfront vocals are as much a treat as her piano pounding; the 1927 original of "Lux" Lewis's influential "Honky Tonk Train Blues"; Skip James's explosive and inimitable "22-20 Blues"; a fine 1929 boogie, "Walking Blues," from the obscure Raymond Barrow; and at least a dozen other treats from Charley Taylor, Will Ezell, and Barrel House Welch, among others. The dismal sound of Paramount 78s is almost as legendary as the blues the label recorded, but these transfers are remarkably clean, and the set is nicely annotated. — *Mark Humphrey, Roundup newsletter*

☆ **Play My Juke Box—East Coast Blues (1943-1954)** / Flyright 45
Bruce Bastin's English Flyright label—only one of the magnificent tributaries of his Interstate Music Company—has consistently demonstrated a union of fine scholarship and great music. This collection of mostly little-known East Coast blues artists is no exception. There are seven tracks of singer-guitarists, four harp/guitar duets, four piano/guitar pairings, two guitar duos, and one arresting cut featuring three harps plus vocal. Artists such as Skoodle-dum-Doo & Sheffield, Boy Green, Robert Lee Westmoreland, Marilyn Scott, and Sonny Jones serve up a startling reminder of all the amazing talent that has gone unrecognized over the years. —*Larry Hoffman*

○ **Prime Chops—Blind Pig Sampler** / 1990 / Blind Pig 78001
A 14-track sampler, with a variety of contemporary blues sounds. —*Niles J. Frantz*

○ **Raunchy Business—Hot Nuts & Lollypops** / Aug. 1991 / Columbia 46783
A sampler of risqué blues. —*Mark A. Humphrey*

○ **RCA Victor Blues & Rhythm Revue** / Dec. 1987 / RCA 8423
Great 25-cut cross-section of Nipper's R&B activities from 1940 to 1959. Everyone from Count Basie to Little Richard to the Dew Droppers to the Isley Brothers. —*Bill Dahl*

○ **Real Blues Brothers** / 1987 / Dcc 26
Ignore the meaningless, opportunistic title of this collection, and instead just listen to the music, an enjoyable collection of sides recorded between 1956 and 1962 by mostly well-known and successful artists. Included here are four performances by Jimmy Reed and five from John Lee Hooker, plus Pee Wee Crayton, Lightnin' Hopkins, Brownie McGee, Sonny Terry, Billy Boy Arnold, and others. These were mostly recorded for, and eventually released by, Vee Jay Records. Just over 60 minutes of playing time. —*Niles J. Frantz*

Reefer Songs: Original Jazz & Blues Vocals / Vintage Jazz 7
Entertaining if somewhat controversial anthology that presents early jazz and blues songs celebrating the joys of marijuana. These tunes aren't so much pro-drug as they are pro-party, but changed attitudes would result in far more criticism coming in this set's direction if it were issued today, rather than in the '70s. —*Ron Wynn, AMG*

Regal Records in New Orleans / Specialty 2169
Regal Records enjoyed a rather stormy two-year history as an offshoot of Linden, NJ's Deluxe Records. After a talent-scouting trip to New Orleans, Regal Records was born. Quickly signing and recording great talent, they cut numerous top-notch sides with artists like Paul Gayten, Annie Laurie, Dave Bartholomew, and Roy Brown. The 27-track collection includes several alternates and six demos. —*Roundup newsletter*

☆ **Riot in Blues** / Mobile Fidelity 874
Excellent Lightnin' Hopkins, Sonny Terry, Brownie McGhee, James Wayne, and early Ray Charles scat singing. Partially field recorded by Bob Shad in the early '50s. The best cuts include "Wayne's Junco Partner" and "Hopkins' Buck Dance Boogie." — *Barry Lee Pearson*

Rockin' Eighty-Eights / Modern Blues 1201

A gem that only shines brighter as the days go passing by; a swinging, jumping, gutsy masterpiece. Johnnie Johnson, Clayton Love, and the late Jimmy Vaughn take turns leading Johnson's band through a live-to-DAT journey that covers a variety of St. Louis blues and R&B. — *Roundup newsletter*

○ **Roots 'n' Blues/The Retrospective 1925-1950** / Jun. 30, 1992 / CBS 47911
This collection is composed of 107 tracks, 47 of which are previously unissued, with a total of over five hours of music. Among the genres covered are boogie-woogie, White and Black string bands, Cajun music, blues, spiritual and gospel music, jugband, country, and some very early indications of R&B. Artists range from the celebrated and well known (Lonnie Johnson, Mississippi John Hurt, Blind Willie McTell, Charley Patton, Bill Monroe) to the talented but obscure (Papa Too Sweet, Blues Birdhead, Pelican Wildcats, George Curry). The overall concept of the set is to showcase both the Black and White traditions as recorded by Columbia Records and various allied labels (Vocalion, Okeh, Arc) over a 25-year period predating rock music. The producers of this compilation, Lawrence Cohn and Gary Pacheco, deserve credit for this mesmerizing tribute to traditional song. —*Roundup newsletter*

○ **Roots of Rhythm & Blues: A Tribute to the Robert Johnson Era** / Sep. 1, 1992 / CBS 48584
Live program featuring some of the late legend's old partners: Honeyboy Edwards, Johnny Shines, Robert Jr Lockwood, and some of his contemporary successors; Lionel Pitchford, John Cephas, and Phil Wiggins pay heartfelt tribute. —*Bill Dahl*

☆ **Roots of Robert Johnson** / 1990 / Yazoo 1073
Robert Johnson's small body of recordings have made him almost larger than life. Many novice listeners probably think the Delta blues began and ended with Johnson. This 14-song collection traces the origins of Johnson's music, uncovering the roots of his tormented, anguished lyrics, and the origins of his wildly influential guitar style. Some of the finest songs by luminaries like Skip James, Charley Patton, Son House, Kokomo Arnold, and Lonnie Johnson are included. Not only of use to Johnson archivists but also to anyone interested in the greatest prewar Delta blues. —*Bruce Boyd Raeburn*

St. Louis Blues (1929-1935) / Yazoo 1030
More fine prewar blues. —*Mark A. Humphrey*

○ **St. Louis Town—1929-1933** / Yazoo 1003
Guitar and piano blues from this Mississippi River city. —*Mark A. Humphrey*

○ **Saturday Night Blues** / 1991 / Stony Plain
A compilation album of Canadian blues artists who have been featured on "Saturday Night Blues" on the AM network of CBC Radio. It includes Colin James, Dutch Mason, Amos Garrett, Rita Chiarelli & the Road Rockets, Paul James, and others. The 20 songs on the album are a great way to check out the great blues scene in Canada. —*Chip Renner*

Sissy Man Blues: Str't & Gay Blues / Vintage Jazz 13
Twenty-five straight and gay blues, from 1924 to 1941, by various artists. —*Jas Obrecht*

☆ **Slide Guitar—Bottles Knives & Steel** / CBS 46218
A super collection of slide guitar pieces in such styles as blues, hokum, gospel, and dance, from Blind Willie Johnson, Tampa Red, Bukka White, and other bottleneck masters. The Leadbelly cut, "Packing Trunk Blues," shows off his masterful slide style. For every blues guitarist. —*Barry Lee Pearson*

Vol. II-Bottles Knives & Steel / CBS 52725
Another excellent volume of various styles of blues slide guitar from Columbia's *Roots 'n' Blues* series. —*AMG*

○ **Smackin' That Wax—The Kangaroo Records Story** / Collectables 5266
Obscure but solid '50s and '60s Texas blues and R&B; includes a very early Albert Collins single. —*Bill Dahl*

☆ **Story of the Blues** / CBS 30008
An excellent blues sampler, ranging from prewar years to the '60s, offering a broader palette of "shades of blue" than most. — *Mark A. Humphrey*

○ **Sun Records—The Blues Years** / Charly 105
Gigantic nine-record box with a 44-page booklet. This comes the closest to documenting the wide breadth of blues recordings

done by Sam Phillips at the Sun studios in Memphis during the early '50s. A landmark achievement. —*Cub Koda*

○ **Sun Records Harmonica Classics** / 1990 / Rounder 29
A brilliant compilation of blues sides, cut at the Sun studios in the early '50s, featuring indispensable tracks by Big Walter Horton ("Easy" being one of the greatest harmonica instrumentals of all time), Joe Hill Louis, and Dr. Ross. —*Cub Koda*

Superblues: All-Time Classic Blues Hits / 1991 / Stax 8559
Fine companion volume to *Superblues Volume 1*, featuring 18 great artists and about the same number of signature tunes. Check out Guitar Slim's "The Things That I Used to Do," Big Joe Turner's "Chains of Love," Percy Mayfield's "Please Send Me Someone to Love," Lowell Fulson's "Reconsider Baby," Roscoe Gordon's "No More Doggin'," Sonny Boy Williamson's "Don't Start Me to Talkin'," Albert King's "Breaking Up Somebody's Home," and 11 more. — *Roundup Newsletter*

○ **Sweet Home Chicago** / Nov. 1988 / Delmark 618
Solid '60s sides by Magic Sam, Eddie Shaw, Luther Allison, Louis Myers. —*Bill Dahl*

Taste of the Blues, Vol. 1 / 1993 / Vee Jay
Terrific compilation of '50s Vee Jay blues; artists include Jimmy Reed, Billy Boy Arnold, Pee Wee Crayton, and Harold Burrage. —*Bill Dahl*

○ **Texas Blues** / Arhoolie 352
This excellent collection features eight little-known blues artists who recorded for Bill Quinn's Gold Star label in Houston. There are 27 tracks in all—split unequally between acoustic guitar/vocal (16) and piano/vocal (11). Lil Son Jackson is perhaps the best known, and his ten tracks are all good, rocking acoustic blues. There are also tunes by L. C. Williams, a polished and imaginative guitarist, and one magnificent track by the obscure Buddy Chiles. —*Larry Hoffman*

Texas Blues Guitar (1929-1935) / Story of Blues 3532
The number of blues and folk reissues is absolutely mind numbing, so let's hope there's a market out there for historic recordings. There certainly should be. Some of the best music you'll find is the older stuff, and you don't need a musicology degree to appreciate it, either. Just don't expect high-tech, hip-hop, Top 30 danceability. Look on these as antiques, every bit as valuable as those overpriced pieces of Americana that fill antique stores crosscountry. One company that's really pumping out discs is Story of Blues, which is releasing American versions of the catalog of Johnny Parth's Document Records in Vienna. Parth and his associates amassed a huge collection of old 78s and have been arranging them into comprehensive packages—possibly too comprehensive, because no one really needs the complete recorded works of, say, Little Hat Jones, who shares the *Texas Blues Guitar* disc with J. T. "Funny Paper" Smith. Still, if you're into Texas or into roots, maybe you'll like Jones, just as some people like carnival glass. The better half of the disc belongs to J. T. Smith, aka The Howling Wolf because he had a series called *Howling Wolf Blues* #1, #2, and so on. A couple of his *Howling Wolf* numbers, as well as the portion of Smith's output not on *Texas Blues Guitar,* have been reissued on Yazoo 1031. —*Blues Access*

Texas Guitar Greats / 1991 / Collectables 5223
Texas blues, boogie, and blues/rock recorded from 1962 to 1988. Includes several previously unreleased cuts, with Johnny Winter,

Freddie King, Clarence "Gatemouth" Brown, and Johnny Copeland, among others. —*Niles J. Frantz*

★ **Texas Piano Blues 1929-48** / Story of Blues 3509
This is a good collection of piano-accompanied vocals by bluesmen who worked the lumber camps and oil fields of rural Texas, as well as the red-light districts of cities like Galveston and Houston. Big Boy Knox shows a strong city influence in his decorative right-hand work, as does Robert Cooper, whose playing points to the influence of Fats Waller. Joe Pullem is on board with his hit "Black Gal," which is perhaps overstated by three takes and a variation. The vocals are good, however, and the piano playing is uniformly excellent. Stylistically, this music falls somewhere between ragtime, blues, and vaudeville. —*Larry Hoffman*

○ **Texas Sax Greats** / Collectables 5261
Slightly inconsistent but rewarding R&B sax compilation; Big Sambo, Link Davis, and Henry Hayes provide the best moments. —*Bill Dahl*

Them Dirty Blues / Jass 11
A two-CD set of 50 songs by various artists that shocked your grandparents. —*Jas Obrecht*

Tuesday's Just As Bad / K-Tel 60082
Companion volume to K-Tel's *Best of the Blues*, this one features ten more indispensable cuts from Muddy Waters, Howlin' Wolf, Elmore James, B. B. King, and others. Great listening even if you already have the songs on other compilations. —*Cub Koda*

○ **Voice of the Blues—Bottleneck Guitar Masterpieces** / Dec. 1976 / Yazoo 1046
Voice of the Blues contains an eclectic hodgepodge of prewar slide guitar styles, encompassing everything from blues and Hawaiian to ragtime and country. —*John Floyd*

We Love You Bobby: A Tribute to Bobby Bland / 1992 / Collectables 5270
Not much Bland influence on many of these Texas R&B sides, but soulful nonetheless. Mostly '60s sides. —*Bill Dahl*

○ **White Country Blues 1926-38** / Apr. 27, 1993 / CBS
Country artists sing prewar blues-influenced songs. —*Bill Dahl*

○ **Wizards from the Southside** / Chess 9102
This is a great sampler of the finest in classic Chicago blues—perfect for those listeners who are looking for a taste of the genre's best. The album contains two Howlin' Wolf tracks, including"Evil"; five Muddy Waters tracks, including "Rollin' and Tumblin'"; John Lee Hooker's "Walkin' the Boogie"; Sonny Boy Williamson's "Bring It on Home"; two tracks by Bo Diddley, including "I'm a Man"; and two tracks by Little Walter, including "Mellow Down Easy." All of these fabulous sides were cut between 1950 and 1961—-the Golden Era of Southside Chicago blues. —*Larry Hoffman*

○ **Wrapped in My Baby** / 1989 / Pearl Flapper 16
Basement rehearsal recordings from the early '50s for the United/States labels, featuring Morris Pejoe's raw and rockin' "Let's Get High" from a full unissued session, plus four amazing sides from Arthur "Big Boy" Spires. Another missing chapter of Chicago blues history brought to light—simply incredible. —*Cub Koda*

CAJUN/ZYDECO

Zydeco and Cajun are the premier cultural expressions of the spirited and hardy people of southwest Louisiana. While the two styles have some similarities, they are also quite different.

Cajun music as we know it today can be traced back to early Acadian, French, Creole, and Anglo-Saxon folk songs. These early ballads and lullabies – typically concerned with troubles and hard times – were often sung a cappella. For the most part, they were performed at home and passed down orally from generation to generation; however, the singers of these traditional songs were eventually accompanied by simple instrumentation.

Cajun music is of course meant for dancing – one-step, two-step, and waltzes. Traditionally, the Cajun dance ("Fais-do-do" in Cajun) was the major social function in Cajun society. The principal instrument in Cajun music is the diatonic accordion, preferably in the key of C. Although it is a German instrument, the Cajun people adopted it in the 1870s. To a lesser degree, the fiddle is also a favorite instrument in Cajun music. Early Cajun bands featured both of these instruments as well as a triangle to keep the rhythm. Acoustic guitars were added to the lineup by 1920, then, three decades later, steel, electric guitars, and sometimes drums. Although Cajun music has changed somewhat over the years and has been influenced by other styles of music – notably country and blues – it has remained a distinctive style.

The first Cajun record was Joe Falcon's "Allons à Lafayette" from 1928. Although the style was recorded only sporadically for several decades, Iry Le Jeune, Harry Choates,

Nathan Abshire, Lawrence Walker, Leo Soileau, and Vin Bruce had become influential Cajun artists by the middle of the 20th century. While the music's popularity continued to grow within Louisiana, it didn't enter the spotlight nationally until the mid 80s, riding on the coattails of the Cajun food explosion. Today several traditional and contemporary Cajun artists – including Dewey Balfa, Zachary Richard, and Beausoleil – tour nationally and internationally.

Compared to Cajun music, zydeco music has a much shorter history. Like Cajun music, the dominant instrument is the accordion, but unlike Cajun music, zydeco adds electric bass, horns, and sometimes keyboards. In a nutshell, zydeco is creole (Black) dance music of southwest Louisiana that blends Cajun music with rhythm & blues and soul. The word "zydeco" is actually a bastardization of an early zydeco song, "L'Haricots Sont Pas Salés" (The Snap Beans Aren't Salted). The first Black-French recordings were made in 1928 by Amadé Ardoin, an accordion player who played in the Cajun style. However, the music we know as zydeco today didn't begin to evolve – at least on record – until the mid 50s, when Clifton Chenier and Boozoo Chavis made their initial recordings.

Like Cajun music, zydeco didn't achieve national popularity until 1980, buoyed somewhat by Rockin' Sidney's surprise hit "My Toot Toot." By the 90s, several zydeco artists were signed to major labels, including Terrance Simien, Boozoo Chavis, Buckwheat Zydeco, and Rockin' Dopsie.

– Jeff Hannusch

Nathan Abshire

b. 1915, d. 1981
Vocals, accordion / Cajun

Abshire, the best-known accordionist of the modern era, played more of a honky-tonk style of Cajun music, one often heard in the barrooms and dancehalls of Louisiana. Abshire's playing and singing were strongly rooted in the blues.

Along with the legendary Iry LeJeune, Abshire is credited with restoring the accordion to its former prominence in Cajun Music following WWII. His 1949 O.T. label hit "Pine Grove Blues" became his signature song, and its bluesy barroom bark epitomizes the best rough-edged Cajun honky-tonk. Abshire recorded extensively and often appeared at folk festivals with the Balfa Brothers. *—Jeff Hannusch & Mark A. Humphrey*

○ **Cajun Social Music** / 1990 / Smithsonian/Folkways 40006
A summit meeting of Cajun stars yields outstanding renditions covering classics and originals. *—Ron Wynn*

● **Cajun Legend: Best of Nathan Abshire** / 1991 / Swallow 6061
With "The Good Times Are Killing Me" emblazoned on his accordion case, Abshire embodied the Cajun musician's ethos. There are 20 two-steps and waltzes here, some with the Balfa Brothers—includes a remake of the great "Pine Grove Blues" and a heartfelt "Tramp Sur La Rue" with wailing vocals from Nathan. *—Mark A. Humphrey*

Johnnie Allan

b. Mar. 10, 1938, Rayne, LA
Guitar

Johnnie Allan's been a prominent Cajun performer since his teens, when he joined accordionist Lawrence Walker's band as a steel guitarist. When the band split, Allan teamed with pianist/fiddler U.J. Meaux, producer Huey Meaux's cousin, in the Krazy Kats, a rock band. Allan continued singing rock and roll and R&B in the late '50s and early '60s. He alternated between music and education for a while, at one point even becoming principal of an elementary school. But his popularity soared when his Cajun-flavored cover of Chuck Berry's "Promised Land" became a hit. Allan's style mixes rock flamboyance with Cajun authenticity, and he has been featured on many regional labels.— *Ron Wynn*

● **South to Louisiana** / 1985 / ACE 145
A compilation featuring Allan doing both prime rocking and traditional Cajun material. *—Ron Wynn*

○ **Johnnie Allan & Krazy Kats 1959—1960** / 1985 / Krazy Kat 792
Here's a collection highlighting Johnnie Allan's straight rock and R&B singles recorded in 1959 and '60. The high point is the cover of Chuck Berry's "Lonely Days and Lonely Nights." *—Ron Wynn*

Ardoin & Fontenot

Accordion, fiddle / Cajun, Creole

Accordionist Alphonse "Bois Sec" ("dry wood") Ardoin (b. 1914) grew up idolizing his legendary uncle, Amadé Ardoin, as did fiddler Canray Fontenot (b. 1922). Ardoin and Fontenot began playing together in their youth, though they were unrecorded until the '70s. Their music is a still-strong reflection of the early Cajun/Creole traditions, with an added burst of bluesiness in Canray's fiddling. *—Mark A. Humphrey*

○ **Musique Creole** / Arhoolie 1070
Haunting. The music on this album shaped modern Cajun/zydeco music. —*Jeff Hannusch*

Amadé Ardoin

b. 1896, d. 1941
Vocals, accordion / Blues, Cajun
Although he recorded some of the purest early Cajun records, Amadé Ardoin (his name has also been spelled Amadie or Amedee) was a French-speaking Black singer/accordionist who was popular with both Cajun and Creole audiences. His crying, high-pitched vocals were the model for much that came later in Cajun music, as was his empathetic squeezebox playing. Ardoin's recordings with fiddler Dennis McGee are noteworthy not only because they are among the first racially integrated folk recordings, but also for an emotional/artistic integrity to which traditionalists like the Savoy-Doucet band continue to aspire. —*Mark A. Humphrey*

● **Louisiana Cajun Music, Vol. 6** / Old Timey 124
A stunning collection of 14 of his 30 recordings. (Ardoin also appears on several Cajun compilations, such as *J'Etais Au Bal—Vol. 1.*) —*Mark A. Humphrey*

First Black Cajun Recording Artist / Arhoolie 9056
Violinist Dennis McGhee is featured on this 14-track album, which contains recordings from 1929, 1930, and 1934. —*AMG*

Lynn August

Blind accordionist/vocalist Lynn August's brand of zydeco sometimes annoys purists with its high concentration of R&B and pop. August's CDs for Maison de Soul and Black Top have been erratic but generally entertaining.—*Ron Wynn*

Creole Cruiser / Jan. 1992 / Black Top 1074
A blind keyboardist, accordionist, singer, and drummer, Lynn August has had a long and varied career, including playing drums for Esquerita while still in his early teens, working the crawfish circuit in various soul and lounge acts, even directing a church choir for a while. He arrived at the accordion relatively late (1988), but he plays zydeco like he was born to it and shows a special flair for the ultra-traditional "jures"—vocal chants and song accompanied by nothing but percussion. *Creole Cruiser* was recorded early this year in New Orleans, with a band including keyboardist Sammy Berfect and bassist George Porter, Jr., of the Meters. "I like old cars and I like old music," says Lynn August. "I really think they made the best music and the best cars a long time ago." He means it, too—he owns a pink 1958 Fleetwood Cadillac and plays strong, blues-based zydeco in the tradition of Clifton Chenier. —*Roundup newsletter*

The Balfa Brothers

Group / Cajun
The Balfas helped keep alive the traditional Cajun sound when it was disappearing in the '60s. Their style can be traced to the beginning of the century and is dominated by the fiddle. Unfortunately, Rodney and Will were killed in a car wreck in 1979, but Dewey continued to keep their sound alive until his death in 1992. —*Jeff Hannusch*

● **Play Trad. Cajun Music—Vols. 1 & 2** / 1987 / Swallow 6011
From the '60s recordings that helped launch the Cajun revival. Stirring performances still. —*Mark A. Humphrey*

○ **J'ai Vu Le Loup, Le Renard Et La Belette** / 1988 / Rounder 6007
The Balfa Brothers' long heritage in traditional Cajun music has never been better represented than on this 13-cut CD recorded in 1975. The songs are mostly short (only one longer than four minutes) and predominantly uptempo dance numbers, with some two-steps, waltzes, and romantic pieces mixed in, as well as an interesting version of "Casey Jones." The lineup includes Dewey and Will Balfa on violins, Tony and Rodney Balfa on guitar and triangle, with Dewey also on accordion; Dewey, Rodney, and Will divide the vocal leads and harmonies. The session was produced and recorded by Gerard Dole, was originally issued on the Cezame label in France, and is thoroughly traditional. True believers and purists couldn't find a better example of the vintage sound anywhere. —*Ron Wynn*

○ **Let's Get Cajun** / Flying Fish 539

Modern Cajun sounds played by young musicians. —*Jeff Hannusch*

Dewey Balfa

b. 1927, d. 1992
Fiddle / Cajun, Zydeco
The son and grandson of Cajun fiddlers, Dewey Balfa played fiddle in a relaxed yet spirited style and inspired much of the best of the Cajun revival. A gentle and gracious man, he was passionate about his culture and was a father figure and guiding light for Cajun music. With his brothers, he helped introduce this music to the world at the Newport Folk Festivals of the '60s and won renewed attention and support for Cajun music in Louisiana. He died in 1992 and is sorely missed. —*Mark A. Humphrey*

○ **Souvenirs** / 1987 / Swallow
A low-key but excellent effort from the late king of Cajun fiddle. —*Jeff Hannusch*

Cajun Legend / Swallow
Features such artists as Tracy Schwartz, Robert Jardell, and others of Balfa's friends on this album's 21 tracks. —*AMG*

● **Fait à La Main** / Swallow
Twenty-one tracks compiled from two 1980s Swallow albums offer a fine introduction to the fiddling of one of the architects of the Cajun music revival. Homespun and heartfelt, this set exudes the generosity of spirit of a rare man who has inspired many younger musicians to follow his example. — *Mark Humphrey, Roundup newsletter*

Beausoleil

Group / Cajun, Zydeco, New Orleans
Responsible for much of the cajun craze in the late 80's, thanks to the film *The Big Easy*, in which their music was featured. Formed in 1975 by fiddler and folklorist Michael Doucet, Beausoleil has worked with Mary Chapin Carpenter (#1 country hit *Down at the Twist and Shout*), Richard Thompson (*Cajun Conja* and other projects), Keith Richards, and the Grateful Dead. Beausoleil has also appeared on National Public Radio's *A Prairie Home Companion* starring Garrison Keillor. —*Liz Opoka*

Bayou Boogie / 1987 / Rounder 6015
A fine modern Cajun collection, including "Cajun Dead" at full tilt. —*Jeff Hannusch & Mark A. Humphrey*

Allons à Lafayette / 1988 / Arhoolie 308
A more traditional sound as compared with the group's other albums. —*Jeff Hannusch*

● **Hot Chili Mama** / 1988 / Arhoolie 5040
The perfect blend of Cajun, zydeco, and rock & roll. —*Jeff Hannusch*

Bayou Cadillac / 1989 / Rounder 6025
While they sometimes ventured a bit far afield, as with the concluding "Island Zydeco," much of Beausoleil's fare did artfully cross genres and successfully combine divergent influences and material. Besides the enthusiastic vocals of fiddler Michael Doucet and his brother David (guitar), accordion player Jimmy Breaux also deserved plenty of credit for his instrumental underpinnings, and bassist Tommy Comeaux, banjo/fiddler Al Tharp and drummer Tommy Alesi were integral group members. Here's a disc that should satisfy audiences regardless of idiomatic preference. —*Ron Wynn*

Live from the Left Coast / 1990 / Rounder 6035
An excellent example of this popular group's live sound. —*Jeff Hannusch*

Déjà Vu / 1991 / Swallow 6080
Leader Michael Doucet's musical concoctions. —*Jeff Hannusch*

Cajun Conja / Sep. 1991 / Rhino 70525
A 1991 Grammy nominee. —*Mark A. Humphrey*

Parlez-Nous à Boir & More / Oct. 1991 / Arhoolie 322
Traditional Cajun, with a taste of the modern sound. The best of their Arhoolie albums. Cajun/zydeco zip with rock and ethno-synergistic overtones. —*Jeff Hannusch & Mark A. Humphrey*

☆ **Cajun & Creole Music** / Music of the World 110
This recording combines the great masters of the Creole music tradition with the internationally acclaimed Cajun group, Beausoleil. This Library of Congress Award-winner belongs in every Cajun lover's collection. —*Music of the World*

Vin Bruce (Ervin Bruce)

Vocals, guitar / Cajun
Known as the "King of Cajun Singers," this native of Cut Off, LA, born Ervin Bruce, first recorded for Columbia in 1951, where he found some success with the ballad "Dans La Louisianne." A decade later this singer/guitarist was recording for Floyd Soileau's Swallow label, where he scored a hit with "Jole Blon" (at least the third go-round for "the Cajun national anthem"). Bruce currently resides in Galliano, LA, and is widely respected in Louisiana for his country-tinged Cajun traditionalism. —*Jeff Hannusch & Mark A. Humphrey*

○ **Greatest Hits** / 1979 / Swallow 6002
Recorded by one of the pioneers of Cajun music, these early '60s sides are a mix of traditional songs and French interpretations of country hits. —*Jeff Hannusch*

Cajun Country / 1979 / Swallow
A good country-tinged album featuring "Dog" Guidry on fiddle, Harry Anselm on guitar, and Eldridge "Johnny" Comeaux on steel guitar. —*Chip Renner*

Buckwheat Zydeco (Stanley Dural)

b. 1947, Lafayette, LA
Accordion, keyboard / Cajun, Zydeco
Currently one of the best-known zydeco artists, thanks to his work with Rounder and Island Records, Buckwheat Zydeco (Stanley Dural) got his first taste of zydeco working as a keyboardist with Clifton Chenier, and it was Chenier who inspired him to pick up the accordion. His style has a very modern edge. —*Jeff Hannusch*

★ **100% Fortified Zydeco** / 1985 / Black Top 1024
Currently the most visible zydeco artist nationally. This mid '80s effort is his best, as the material recorded is more inventive. The sound is great, and the song selection is superior. —*Jeff Hannusch*

On a Night Like This / 1987 / Island 422-842739
Not bad, but not as good as his Black Top or Rounder label work. —*Jeff Hannusch*

Turning Point / 1988 / Rounder 2045
A good sampling of modern zydeco. —*Jeff Hannusch*

Menagerie: The Essential Zydeco Collection / Mango 9929
A good compilation of some of the best tracks of one of today's top zydeco artists. —*AMG*

Chubby Carrier (Roy Carrier)

Accordion, vocals / Cajun, Zydeco
Louisiana-born Carrier got his training with Terrance Simien and the Mallet Playboys, going on to form his first band in 1990. Although his music is steeped in the tradition of the area, Carrier adds an original twist with a heavy reliance on rock & roll rhythms and electric guitar solos. —*Cub Koda*

☆ **Boogie Woogie Zydeco** / 1991 / Flying Fish 575
One of the best new albums in the genre today, this is loaded to the brim with great songs and performances. Highlights include the title track, "Bernadette," "Good for the Goose," and "Young Creole Man." It's infectious beyond belief! —*Cub Koda*

Hadley J. Castille

Vocalist, composer, and fiddler Hadley J. Castille has been a prolific performer since learning music from his uncle as a boy in the Opelousas, LA area. Castille's song "200 Lines: I Must Not Speak French" won the '92 Cajun Music Association Heritage Award and he's made several fine releases for Cajun labels. —*Ron Wynn*

200 Lines: I Must Not Speak French / 1991 / Swallow 6088
Here's Hadley J. Castille's award-winning composition, plus several other instrumentals, originals and covers, including a strong rendition of Nathan Abshire's "Nathan's Blues." —*Ron Wynn*

● **Cajun Swamp Fiddler** / 1993 / Swallow 6112
Fiddler and vocalist Hadley J. Castille plays and sings vintage French and Cajun material featuring his sometimes comical, sometimes autobiographical originals like his award-winning "200 Lines: I Must Not Speak French." That song is one of 16 on his most recent CD, which is a treat for fans of entertaining, often evocative Cajun material. Castille and the Louisiana Cajun Band perform both his own traditional tunes "Panique Et Lodie" and

"Cyprien Et Marie" and covers of Austin Pitre's, "Chere Joue Rouge" and Nathan Bashire's, "Nathan's Blues." There's the good-time flavor of "Lake Arthur Stomp" and "Fifi Poncho" and the haunting "Blue Acadin Sky" penned by his son J. Blake Castille. Here's excellent and undiluted Cajun material. —*Ron Wynn*

Boozoo Chavis

b. Oct. 23, 1930, Lake Charles
Vocals / Zydeco
Chavis supplied the first-ever zydeco hit in 1954 with "Paper in My Shoe." Unfortunately, he was in musical semi retirement for three decades, but he returned in the mid '80s with a bang. His many great albums underline his traditional but rocking zydeco style. —*Jeff Hannusch*

○ **Louisiana Zydeco Music** / 1986 / Maison de Soul 1017
A zydeco masterpiece and a down-home foot-stomper. —*Jeff Hannusch*

● **Paper in My Shoe** / 1987 / ACE 214
Fifty-seven-year-old Chavis has been playing zydeco accordion since he was 9 and releasing singles since he was 24 (when he had the 1954 minor hit "Paper in My Shoe"), yet this is his first album. On this recording Boozoo and his band (which includes three of his sons) perform various tunes he's previously released on hard-to-find singles ("Dog Hill," the raunchy "Deacon Jones"), as well as various zydeco standards and other Boozoo Chavis originals. Boozoo's cajun drawl can be tough to understand, but the irresistibly catchy dance beat he and his band create musically manage to draw one in regardless. The washboard, guitar, bass, and drums mesh tightly with the dominant accordion to create this rocking sound. —*Steve Kiviat, Option*

Zydeco Homebrew / 1988 / Maison de Soul 1028
Chavis had an early zydeco hit (1954) with "Paper in My Shoe," a song that helped define the style. Then he took to raising horses and betting on his crop, and he and vinyl did not meet again for some 30 years. With his third release of his second recording career, Boozoo makes dancing easy, playing his accordion to the two-step rhythm. Listening to this, it's easy to forget that other types of music exist, not because this is so singular, but because it sounds so natural. It is absorbing and all-encompassing, and the fact that many of the words are in cajun patois makes it that much better, that much more romantic. This is the kind of record you could play loud in an apartment with thin walls, and the neighbors wouldn't mind. —*Robert Gordon, Option*

★ **Zydeco Trail Ride** / 1989 / Maison de Soul 1034
This collects his best sides from the Maison de Soul label. Whoopti-yo cover and bootin' sounds to match. —*Jeff Hannusch & Mark A. Humphrey*

Lake Charles Atomic Bomb / 1990 / Rounder 2097
Boozoo Chavis vaulted to fame in Zydeco circles during the mid-'50s, when his gritty, anthemic "Paper in My Shoe" helped get the fledgling Zydeco industry off the ground. The song was equally popular on radio, at dances and in clubs. But shortly after that success, Chavis bolted the music business, disgruntled at the corruption he'd sampled first-hand. He stayed away until the '80s, when he returned to deserved acclaim and fresh stardom. But the 14 tracks on this 1990 anthology showcase a younger, more vocally spry and dynamic Chavis, singing short, simple two-step tunes and Zydeco/blues hybrids. There wasn't anything intricate or complicated about pieces like "Hamburgers and Popcorn," "Oh Ho She's Gone" and "Telephone Won't Ring." They were either anguished heartache songs, novelty tunes, or wailing, uptempo pieces, and Chavis didn't vary his approach, attack or treatment. But they were direct, honest, and often memorable. It's good to have them available on one anthology. —*Ron Wynn*

Boozoo, That's Who! / 1993 / Rounder 2126
The 14 cuts on his most recent release are primarily vintage Zydeco numbers, though they also do an occasional novelty song like "Billy Goat Number Three." There's one tune, "Oh Black Gal," that might ruffle the feathers of those who don't bother to hear a song before objecting to a title. But otherwise, these are sizzling two-step pieces, waltzes, and driving Zydeco numbers, with Chavis' aging but still effective vocals leading the way. —*Ron Wynn*

C. J. Chenier

b. Sep. 28, 1957, Port Arthur, TX
Accordion / Zydeco
The son of Clifton Chenier, accordionist C. J. Chenier carries on in his father's tradition, updating it with a blend of R&B and zydeco. *—Mark A. Humphrey*

● **Hot Rod** / Oct. 30, 1990 / Slash 26263
This 12-song effort, C.J.'s second, is produced by Arhoolie's Chris Strachwitz, who helps bring out the best in accordionist Chenier and his band. C.J. does a fine job of carrying on his father Clifton's name. In fact, one of C.J.'s best original compositions here is a tribute to his dad called "You're Still the King to Me." C.J. and company's blues-drenched zydeco is never staid or overly respectful of tradition; this stuff moves. Guitarist Harry Hypolite, sex and harmonica man Wilbert Miller, and drummer Joseph Edwards also deserve credit for this well-done release. *—Steve Kiviat, Option*

I Ain't No Playboy / Mar. 1992 / Slash 26788
○ **My Baby Don't Wear No Shoes** / Arhoolie 1098
Let Me in Your Heart / Arhoolie 1098

Clifton Chenier

b. Jun. 25, 1925, Opelousas, LA, **d.** Dec. 12, 1987
Vocals, accordion / R&B, Cajun, Zydeco
There is no way to overstate the importance of this great artist. Known as the "King of Zydeco," Chenier was responsible for nearly every stylistic innovation that zydeco has displayed since the mid '50s. Although Chenier died in 1987, his son C. J. and several other artists keep his style alive. *—Jeff Hannusch*

○ **Zodico Blues & Boogie** / 1955 / Specialty 7039
Clifton Chenier's mid-'50s singles for Specialty were among his rawest and simplest; they were short ditties with rippling accordion and gritty vocals on top, driving rhythms and surging instrumental accompaniment underneath. This formula is displayed on *Zodico Blues & Boogie*, a 20-cut presentation of Chenier's early work, where he was often backed by guitarists Phillip Walker or Cornelius Green (Lonesome Sundown) with his brother Cleveland handling rubboard duties. Here's Chenier in his stylistic infancy, building and nurturing what ultimately became a signature sound. *—Ron Wynn*

Louisiana Blues & Zydeco / 1965 / Arhoolie 329
Excellent small-combo zydeco. *—Jeff Hannusch*

○ **Bayou Blues** / 1970 / Specialty 2139
Compilation of 12 tracks by the legendary accordion master. Original mono recordings. Includes "Boppin' the Rock," "All Night Long," "I'm on My Way (Parts 1 & 2)," and "Zodico Stomp." *—Roundup Newsletter*

○ **Out West** / 1974 / Arhoolie 350
Special guests Elvin Bishop and Steve Miller joined Chenier for an excellent outing blending blues and rock influences with zydeco. Chenier's vocals were tough and convincing, while Bishop and Miller along with saxophonist Jon Hart were outstanding. *—Ron Wynn*

○ **In New Orleans** / 1979 / GNP 2119
The folks at Crescendo have transferred [this 1978 session] to CD and now we have a second chance to appreciate Clifton and his fine band of the 1970s featuring his brother Cleveland on rubboard, Paul Senegal on guitar, and the hot sax of John Hart. "Boogie Louisiane," "Boogiein' in New Orleans," and "Mardi Gras Boogie" all live up to their names, but "Rumblin' on the Bayou" is the most exciting of the fast cuts. Other jump tunes are "I Love Corn Bread" (in French), "Hello Rosalee", and "I'm Gonna Take You Home Tonight." Standout slow blues include "Cotton-Picker" and "Crying My Heart Out to You." Throw in a waltz here and a ballad there and you've got another batch of classic zydeco by the man who virtually invented it. *—Chicago Kerry, Blues Access*

○ **Bon Ton Roulet** / May 1981 / Arhoolie 345
Great rock'em-sock'em zydeco. *—Jeff Hannusch*

I'm Here! / May 1982 / Alligator 4729
Although not as good as his Arhoolie albums, this one won Chenier a Grammy. *—Jeff Hannusch*

King of Zydeco Live at Montreux / 1984 / Arhoolie 355
A nice concert set. *—Mark A. Humphrey*

Live! / 1985 / Arhoolie 404
The 19 selections on this disc were done in the early '80s, when Chenier was past his romping prime but still keeping the zydeco engine running. He has done them all before on other releases but keeps them entertaining and enjoyable through sheer will and personality. There are not many people whose entire output is worth hearing; if you have not added Clifton Chenier to the list, do so immediately. *—Ron Wynn*

Sings the Blues / 1987 / Arhoolie 351
Lots of great accordion and unique vocals from the blues side of the bayou. *—Jeff Hannusch & Mark A. Humphrey*

Bogalusa Boogie / Jul. 1987 / Arhoolie 347
Backed by a fuller band on this release, Clifton sounds great. Here's the hottest of the red-hot Louisiana bands, and they're feelin' frisky. *—Jeff Hannusch & Mark A. Humphrey*

Live at St. Mark's / 1988 / Arhoolie 313
... a live recording Chenier made in front of an audience of transplanted Creoles who'd moved to the Bay Area. The rumbling bass lines, barreling vocals, and seamless blend of blues, traditional tunes, his own works, and comedic elements expertly convey Chenier's special qualities. *— Ron Wynn, Rock & Roll Disc*

☆ **60 Minutes with the King of Zydeco** / 1988 / Arhoolie 301
Zydeco at its best. Clifton's greatest hits from the Arhoolie label. *—Jeff Hannusch*

★ **Zydeco Dynamite: The Clifton Chenier Anthology** / 1993 / Rhino 71194
Clifton Chenier was to zydeco what Elvis Presley was to rockabilly, only more so—he was also the genre's founding father and tireless ambassador. Rhino has done an admirable job of collecting the accordionist's important work for this two-disc, 40-track set, harking back to a wonderfully chaotic "Louisiana Stomp" that he waxed in Lake Charles, LA in 1954 for J.R. Fullbright's tiny Elko label. Whether you're in the market for one zydeco collection to summarize the entire genre or ready to delve deeply into the legacy of the idiom's pioneer, this is precisely where to begin. *—Bill Dahl, Goldmine.*

Harry Choates

b. 1922, **d.** 1951
Fiddle / Cajun
Choates's 1946 recording of "Jole Blon" (My Pretty Brunette) presented a simple traditional waltz, sung in Cajun French, and played with few frills. Yet it became a national hit, was covered (in English) by Roy Acuff and others, and became as essential to any Cajun music performance as "The Star-Spangled Banner" is to a baseball game. "Jole Blon" was actually atypical of the frenetic Choates, whose Western-swing-tinged fiddling was jazzier than that of any Cajun before or since. Choates was also a passable singer who punctuated his songs with an energetic "Eh, hah hah!" in the manner of Bob Wills. Hard drink and fast living got the better of Choates, who died in an Austin jail in 1951. Disparaged by Cajun purists, he is the Acadian that Western swing enthusiasts find most approachable. *—Mark A. Humphrey*

● **Jole Blon** / 1979 / 'D' 7000
The title cut "Jole Blon" has become the "Cajun national anthem," plus many other great fiddle-led Cajun tunes. *—Jeff Hannusch*

Five-Time Lobster / 1990 / Krazy Kat
A followup to "Jole Blon" and 13 other performances, including the Hank Williams-inspired "Cat 'n Around." Rough sound but great music, blending Cajun, swing, and honky-tonk. *—Mark A. Humphrey*

His Original 1946-1949 Recordings / Arhoolie
Sixteen performances by the man dubbed "The Godfather of Cajun Music," including his swingin' takes on such standards as "Allons à Lafayette" and "Grand Mamou." *—Mark A. Humphrey*

Clark & Duhon

Group / Cajun
Accordionist OctClark and fiddler Hector Duhon formed their group, the Dixie Ramblers, in 1930, performing in contests alongside Nathan Abshire and Amedé Breaux. Years later, in the '80s, they hooked up with fiddler Michael Doucet and his brother, guitarist David Doucet. *—Liz Opoka*

○ **Old-Time Cajun Music** / Arhoolie 5026
Old-time Cajun music played right. *—Jeff Hannusch*

Bruce Daigrepont

b. 1959
Vocals, accordion / Cajun
An admitted child of the Cajun revival, Daigrepont only began regarding Cajun music as something other than the music of his
grandparents' generation when he heard such young Turks as
Michael Doucet and Zachary Richard in the '70s. Ironically, this
singer and accordionist developed a style somewhat more traditional than that of his mentors. Writing his own material and
fronting a tight band, Daigrepont has earned both the approval of
his elders and the respect of his peers. *—Mark A. Humphrey*

● **Stir Up the Roux** / 1988 / Rounder 6016
Bruce Daigrepont's music and approach are emblematic of recent
Cajun performers. While he's aware of other sounds like rock and
country, he integrates their edge and sensibility into his work
without losing or deserting the basic Cajun mode. The 10 tunes
on his '87 release are predominantly driving, uptempo, and energetic pieces, with his frenetic accordion and infectious vocals setting the pace, backed by a sharp band that includes tremendous
fiddler Waylon Thibodeaux and right-in-the-groove drumming
from Kenny Blevens, plus Sharon Leger harmonizing. Daigrepont
makes no lyric concessions, but the color and flair of his singing
should overcome any hesitancy non-French speakers might have
about the material. It's certainly up-to-date, but it's also thoroughly steeped in the old ethic. *—Ron Wynn*

Coeur Des Cajuns / 1989 / Rounder 6026
Bruce Daigrepont's second album for Rounder in 1989 was even
more traditional Cajun than his award-winning first effort. The title track and other works such as "Les Mains du Bon Dieu,"
"Acadie a la Louisiane", and "Laissez Moi Tranquille" presented
tales of Cajun life and times ranging from struggles to triumphs,
and sung with power, earnestness, and verve. His accordion playing was equally assertive, and his band was once more keyed by
fiddler Waylon Thibodeaux and drummer Kenny Blevins, as well
as bassist Scott Goudeau, harmony and lead fiddler Gina
Forsythe and such special guests as guitarist David Doucet, pianists Roscoe Horton and Sue Daigrepont, and saxophonist Ray
Moore. It's artists such as Bruce Daigrepont that indicate the future is bright for Cajun music. *—Ron Wynn*

John Delafose

b. 1939
Vocals, accordion / Zydeco
Delafose's driving but down-home zydeco is indebted to Clifton
Chenier but reaches back to African-tinged Creole roots. He
played sporadically while farming, before committing to music
with a family-based band that included sons Tony on drums (now
bass) and John Jr.on washboard. A fine singer and fiery accordionist, Delafose's unique traditionalism is a refreshing counter-
weight to the more R&B and funk-tinged zydeco bands. *—Mark
A. Humphrey*

○ **Heartaches and Hot Steps** / 1984 / Maison de Soul 1035
Explosive arrangements, powerhouse vocals and accordion playing and good band support make this a first-rate contemporary
zydeco date.*—Ron Wynn*

● **Joe Pete Got Two Women** / 1988 / Arhoolie 335
Delafose's best, containing his popular saga of Joe Pete. Zydeco
fundamentalism from this singer/accordionist, who's so down-
home, his music clearly echoes African hypnotic grooves. *—Jeff
Hannusch & Mark A. Humphrey*

Pere et Garcon Zydeco / 1992 / Rounder 2116
While zydeco and Cajun-influenced hybrids have been the norm
in many circles during the '80s and '90s, John Delafose & the
Eunice Playboys have remained true to the classic style. This '92
session featured predominantly hardcore material, emphasizing
the two-steps, waltzes, and French language lyrics that are at the
heart of zydeco/Cajun rather than the blues and R&B tunes that
have won it wider exposure. Delafose and his son Geno alternated lead vocals and accordion support, each singing and playing with vigor, conviction, and authenticity. Meanwhile the band
backed them with equal electricity, and while such tunes as
"Watch That Dog," "Morning Train," and "Go Back Where You
Been," were lyric departures, they were as fully in the zydeco
framework as "Mon Coeur Fait Mal" and "Grand Mamou."

Delafose presents the best of both worlds here; old and new
school zydeco, each done in brilliant style. *—Ron Wynn*

David Doucet

Guitar / Cajun
The guitarist in the group Beausoleil, Doucet is adept mixing tra-
ditional Cajun sound with more modern stylings. *—Jeff
Hannusch*

○ **Quand J'ai Parti** / Jan. 1990 / Rounder 6040
David Doucet both expanded and narrowed his scope on this '91
release. He decided to concentrate on guitar and incorporate it
into a traditional Cajun setting; at the same time he used the
wide-ranging band Beausoleil and recruited special guests bluegrass great Josh Graves on dobro and bassist Josh Stewart. The
results were gratifying; Doucet's guitar playing was unpredictable, edgy, and crisp, while Beausoleil, Graves, and Stewart
made fine partners on 13 tracks that were thoroughly Cajun,
right down to the French lyrics, waltz, and two-step arrangements, and accordion/fiddle backing fortified by mandolin/do-
bro/bass. Here was music with a familiar style and base, but a
fresh, vital feel and energy. *—Ron Wynn*

Michael Doucet

Vocals, fiddle / Cajun
Since the mid '70s, Doucet has been one of the dominant figures
of the Cajun music revival, respected for his scholarship and admired for his showmanship. On the one hand Doucet dredges up
ancient Cajun tunes with medieval French roots, and on the other
plays flamboyant fiddle with Beausoleil. Aside from Beausoleil,
singer and fiddler Doucet has performed and recorded with the
more purely traditional Savoy-Doucet Cajun Band. He is as passionate about Cajun tradition as he is eager to drop-kick it into
the 21st century, and for that reason Doucet has earned the applause of both purists and plebians who just wanna boogie. *—
Mark A. Humphrey*

○ **And Cajun Brew** / 1988 / Rounder 6017
Sometime Beausoleil member Michael Doucet heads a different
type of ensemble in Cajun Brew. This band's a fusion/rock/pop
group, and their '87 release began with a reworking of Sam the
Sham's "Wooly Bully" and included covers of "Hey, Good
Looking" and "Louie Louie." The roster included flamboyant, stirring guitarist Sonny Landreth, whose blues-rock leanings were
quite evident in his solos and riffs. At the same time, the band
also featured Doucet holding court on fiddle, mandolin, and guitar as well as vocals, Pat Breaux on sax and accordion, Niles
Hokkanen on fiddle and mandolins, and veteran drummer Kenny
Breaux. As if aware that there might be questions about alle-
giances, the group's song roster contained such numbers as "Un
Autre Soir Ennuyant" and "Like A Real Cajun" alongside the covers. While they sometimes blurred or hedged their focus, there
was enough Cajun flavor in the arrangements, performances, and
instrumentation to keep purists from grumbling, while they
aimed for a wider audience with their joyful rock/pop remakes.
—Ron Wynn

Beau Solo / 1989 / Arhoolie 321
... a 22-song feast of old-time Cajun music. *— Ron Wynn, Rock &
Roll Disc*

Le Hoogie Boogie: Louisiana French Music for Children /
1992 / Rounder 8022
Vocalist and multi instrumentalist Michael Doucet, along with
some of his friends, family members, and musical allies in the
group, Beausoleil, got together to record something special for
children. As Doucet says, "You'll find songs full of colors, numbers, animals, and clothing, along with lots of different musical
sounds and rhythms for dancing." *— Roundup Newsletter*

● **Bayou Deluxe: The Best of Michael Doucet** / 1993 / Rhino
71169
An excellent collection of some of the best tracks from this leader
in the Cajun music revival. *—AMG*

Joseph Falcon

b. 1900, **d.** 1965
Accordion / Cajun
One of the pioneers of Cajun music, Falcon made the first com-
mercial Cajun recording, "Lafayette ("Allons à Lafayette")" with

his wife Cleoma in 1928. Cleoma's simple guitar and emotive singing, driven by Joe's crying accordion, was an instant hit in Cajun country, foisting a regional stardom on the team, who recorded for Columbia, Decca, Bluebird, and Okeh in the '30s. Cleoma's death in 1941 and changes in listeners' taste (the accordion was out, the fiddle in) led Falcon away from performing, though he and his second wife, Theresa, were fronting a band in the years before his death. Falcon's early recordings are among the enduring classics of the Cajun genre. —*Mark A. Humphrey*

File

A fun, contemporary Cajun/zydeco dance band, File's influences include Zachary Richard and Beausoleil. They have recorded Cajun zydeco standards, but also delve into other genres for variety (namely their brilliant version of Richard Thompson's "Two Left Feet"). —*Liz Opoka*

● **Cajun Dance Band** / Oct. 1987 / Flying Fish 418
The debut album by one of the more popular contemporary Cajun bands. —*Jeff Hannusch*

○ **Two Left Feet** / 1990 / Flying Fish 507
Excellent dancehall music. —*Jeff Hannusch*

Allen Fontenot

Vocals, fiddle
An enjoyable vocalist/fiddle player based in New Orleans. —*Jeff Hannusch*

○ **Jole Blon & Other Cajun Honky Tonk Songs** / Jan. 1980 / Great Southern 11012

Wade Fruge

b. 1916
Accordion, fiddle / Cajun
Fruge, a Cajun fiddler, has performed with *Mark Savoy* and singer *Vorance Borgas*. Fruge is best known for his renditions of Cajun standards, but he has also been influenced by blues fiddler Douglas Bellard. —*Liz Opoka*

○ **Old-Style Cajun Music** / Arhoolie 5044
The title says it all. —*Jeff Hannusch*

Hackberry Ramblers

Group / Cajun
Started by a group of teenagers in 1930, the Hackberry Ramblers went on to become the most popular and influential Cajun band of the '30s. Fiddler Luderin Darbone (b. 1913) led this accordionless Cajun band with as many as three supporting guitarists. Their recordings featured songs in both French and English, and their music was deeply influenced by the jazzy Western swing string bands of Texas. In a sense, the Hackberry Ramblers were the first "hybrid" Cajun musicians, reflecting the impact of records and radio on an isolated regional culture. Despite long periods of inactivity, Darbone and a revived Hackberry Ramblers continue to appear at folk festivals across America. —*Mark A. Humphrey*

○ **Early Recordings—1935-1948** / 1988 / Old Timey 127
No accordions here: This strain of Cajun music includes fiddles and guitars. —*Jeff Hannusch*

Jambalaya

Group / Cajun
Primarily a local *cajun* outfit, they've won numerous local and regional awards. Bassist Kenneth David has performed with the Church Point Players and has worked with accordion player Ambrose Thibodeaux. —*Liz Opoka*

○ **C'est Fun** / Swallow 6085
An enjoyable mix of two-steps and waltzes from this four-piece group. —*Jeff Hannusch*

Doug Kershaw (Douglas James Kershaw)

b. Jan. 24, 1936, Tiel Ridge, LA
Fiddle / Country, Cajun
Cajun country fiddler Kershaw emerged from the steamy South Louisiana swampland with his own wildly energetic approach on the violin. He is widely recognized as a Cajun music pioneer. Paired with his brother as Rusty & Doug, he first hit the country charts in 1955 for Hickory with "So Lovely Baby." In 1961 the pair

issued the original "Louisiana Man" and "Diggy Liggy Lo," both solid country sellers and now the songs perhaps most vividly associated with the manic violinist. While Kershaw sawed his fiddle like a man possessed, his solo career took off during the '70s, although his popularity was never properly reflected by the charts. —*Bill Dahl*

Cajun Way / 1969 / Warner Brothers 1820
Kershaw's first calling card. Very good. —*Jeff Hannusch*

Louisiana Man / 1971 / Warner Brothers 3166
Contains the infamous title-track hit and several other goodies. —*Jeff Hannusch*

★ **Best of Doug Kershaw** / Aug. 8, 1989 / Warner Brothers 25964
A compilation of Kershaw's '60s/'70s Warner Bros. sides. The "Everly Brothers-on-the-Bayou" vocal harmonies, Doug Kershaw's fiddle, and crisp Nashville production make these a joy. —*Mark A. Humphrey*

Rusty Kershaw

The younger brother of Doug Kershaw, Russell "Rusty" Kershaw hasn't enjoyed as much success operating on his own as he has performing with brothers Doug and Sammy Kershaw. His most recent LP was issued on Domino in '92. —*Ron Wynn*

Cajun in Blues Country / 1970 / Cotillion 9030
Rusty's best Cajun LP as a leader includes both solid vocals and first-rate playing. —*Ron Wynn*

Shorty LeBlanc (Vorris LeBlanc)

Accordion / Cajun
LeBlanc is best remembered as the accordionist on the bluesy "Sugar Bee" by Cleveland Crochet and his Hillbilly Ramblers, which climbed to #80 in the *Billboard* Hot 100 in early 1961. LeBlanc's performance was Cajun accordion played to sounds such as amplified blues harmonica. Sidney Brown was an accordion maker and repairer who scored a regional hit with "Pestauche Ah Tante Nana" ("The Peanut Song"). —*Mark A. Humphrey*

Great Shorty Leblanc / 1979 / Goldband 7742

● **Best of Two Cajun Greats** / 1987 / Swallow 6067
Shorty Le Blanc and Sidney Brown are two lesser-known but great Cajun artists. These are their best sides waxed for Swallow. —*Jeff Hannusch*

Eddie LeJeune

Accordion / Cajun
Son of the legendary accordionist Iry LeJeune. Eddie's band is the Morse Players. LeJeune also performs with fiddler Lionel LeLeux, singer/guitarist D. L. Menard, and fiddle virtuoso Ken Smith. —*Liz Opoka*

● **Cajun Soul** / 1988 / Rounder 6013
Though he'd been singing traditional, anguished, and evocative Cajun music for many years, Eddie LeJeune didn't record an album for a general label until this 1988 date. He made the most of his opportunity, singing with abandon, fervor, and intensity on 15 tunes. Some such as "Jolie Blon" (a CD only cut) were familiar efforts; others like "Don't Cry My Children," "The Mistake I Made," and "Little Broken Heart" had some country flavor, but were Cajun through and through. The backing, which included assistance from the great D.L. Menard on guitar and LeJeune's own spicy accordion, never veered from its straight Cajun path yet was quite invigorating. The lack of thematic and musical variety might have been a detriment to the session having appeal outside Cajun circles, but within them it was a winner. —*Ron Wynn*

○ **Le Trio Cadien** / Jul. 15, 1992 / Rounder 6049
Fans of Cajun music should definitely pick up this collaboration between singer/acoustic guitarist D.L. Menard, singer/accordionist Eddie LeJeune, and fiddler Ken Smith. The music dances with a spry liveliness that's thoroughly infectious. Throughout, the members of the trio justify their reputations as masters of their respective instruments, particularly on Menard's "Elle Savit Pas J'Etais Marie (She Didn't Know I Was Married)" and traditional tunes like "Blues de Port Arthur," "Bayou Pon Pon," and "Mamou Two-Step." A warm, rich, and fun musical experience. —*Roundup newsletter*

Mamou Playboys

A contemporary Cajun group whose recordings expertly mix traditional French songs with originals merging pop and rock elements.—*Ron Wynn*

Mamou Playboys / Rounder 6036

D. L. Menard (Doris Menard)

Vocals, accordion / Cajun

One of the purest examples of Cajun music around today, the sound of D. L. Menard & the Louisiana Aces harks back to the genre's ground-floor days and has changed very little in style over the years. Menard's impassioned vocals (largely sung in French) have invited comparisons to country legend Hank Williams. — *Cub Koda*

● **Cajun Saturday Night** / 1985 / Rounder 198
"The Cajun Hank Williams" in Nashville with Ricky Skaggs, Jerry Douglas, and others. No one can imitate Menard or the great sounds on this album. —*Jeff Hannusch & Mark A. Humphrey*

No Matter Where You At ... / 1988 / Rounder 6021
D.L. Menard's among the most successful Cajun musicians ever, and a master at working the common ground between that idiom and classic country. Though most of the songs on his '88 release were two-steps and/or waltzes, Menard also sang such country-flavored numbers as "The Little Black Eyes," "I Went to the Dance Last Night" and "The Heart of the City." His voice rang with clarity, conviction and intensity whether doing heartache tunes, bittersweet narratives, or exuberant dance numbers. Menard's vocals got an additional boost on several tunes by the hot accordion of Eddie LeJeune, giving the songs a backing that was just slightly superior to what they received without him, though accordion player and harmony vocalist Blackie Forestier and fiddler Ken Smith were also accomplished musicians. Though he's not even an obscurity outside Cajun circles, to his fandom D.L. Menard remains their king. —*Ron Wynn*

Nathan & the Zydeco Cha-Chas

Accordionist and bandleader Nathan Williams symbolizes the new breed among zydeco and Cajun artists. He speaks and plays French songs wonderfully, but can also handle R&B, blues, and pop.—*Ron Wynn*

Steady Rock / 1989 / Rounder 2092
Nathan Williams has emerged near the head of the class among contemporary zydeco artists, and this '89 release helped cement his status. It featured mostly zydeco-tinged versions of blues and R&B tracks, though the cuts "Zydeco Joe" and "Everything on the Floor" were closer in structure and arrangements to straight zydeco. But Williams' voice, flair, and energy, coupled with his band's ability to keep the beat moving, helped him retain a sizable following among Louisiana music purists, yet also branch out and do material that could gain attention from less knowledgeable fans. It was fiery, non stop, and enjoyable music, produced with a modern sensibility yet performed in vintage fashion. —*Ron Wynn*

Your Mama Don't Know / Oct. 1990 / Rounder 2107
Nathan Williams continued his string of solid releases with this 1991 date. It included good pop and R&B tracks like "Outside People" and "Don't Burn No Bridges," plus vibrant traditional material such as "El Sid O's Zydeco Boogaloo" and "Mardi Gras Zydeco." Williams again sung with zest, drive, and non stop intensity, while the band showed once more they're considered the tightest unit working in the genre. There weren't any surprises nor low points, just a consistently fine set spotlighting the best group in '90s zydeco. —*Ron Wynn*

● **Follow Me Chicken** / 1993 / Rounder Records 2122
While Nathan Williams has generally been more contemporary in his song selection, approach, and performance style on the zydeco circuit, he's also proficient doing traditional French tunes and two-steps. He shows on this '93 date that he can handle the demands of older material with fine performances on "Tout Partout Mon Passe" and "Elle Est Jolie," a French cover of Stevie Wonder's "Isn't She Lovely." But Williams remains the champion of churning blues and R&B-flavored numbers, and the band rips through "Zydeco Road," "Follow Me Chicken," and "One Track Mind," as well as the more low-key "I Need Someone to Love Me" and "I'm in Love." With Allen Broussard providing burning alto

sax and James Benoit stoking the guitar fires, Williams's vocals and whirling accordion lines punctuate the music of modern zydeco's finest group. —*Ron Wynn*

Queen Ida

Accordion / Cajun, Zydeco

Ida Guillory is an inspiration to all latebloomers: she was over 40 when she left her job as a San Francisco school bus driver and moved to the button accordion and stardom as the first woman to front a zydeco band. Though a native of Lake Charles, LA, Ida has spent much of her adulthood on the West Coast, which may account for her music's being more breezy than swampy. An ebullient performer, Ida won a 1982 Grammy (ethnic-folk category) for *Queen Ida and the Bon Temps Zydeco Band on Tour*. A festival favorite, Queen Ida maintains a busy road schedule. —*Mark A. Humphrey*

Caught in the Act / 1985 / GNP 2181
Live from San Francisco. Includes classics "Jole Blon," "Don't Mess with My Tu Tu," and Nick Lowe's "Half a Boy, Half a Man." Rollicking zydeco from the Queen. —*Michael G. Nastos*

○ **In San Francisco** / 1988 / GNP 2158
A Grammy Award-winning, live, and potent album, with Al Rapone on accordion. —*Michael G. Nastos*

★ **Cookin' with Queen Ida** / 1989 / GNP 2197
She cooks up a hearty menu of traditional zydeco and Cajun harmony, blending in blues, reggae, and more, on this 1989 release. Includes "Hard Headed Woman" and "C'est Moi," her personal lament to life on the road. —*Ladyslipper*

○ **Band on Tour** / GNP 2147
Winner of the 1982 Grammy Award for Best Ethnic/Traditional Folk Album! —*Ladyslipper*

Belton Richard

○ **At His Best** / Swallow 6043
Cajun honky-tonk music at its best. This is what Cajun barroom music is supposed to sound like. —*Jeff Hannusch*

Zachary Richard

Rock, Cajun, Zydeco

Like others of his generation, this native of Scott, LA, discovered his Cajun roots circuitously. Richard started out playing rock and country-rock in the '70s but found his way to Cajun music partly through his experiences in Quebec and France. The music he wound up creating was an aggressive, eclectic blend of rock, zydeco, and R&B, causing one scribe to dub the flamboyant Richard "the Mick Jagger of zydeco."—*Mark A. Humphrey*

That this contemporary Cajun accordionist/songwriter has performed with *Michael Doucet*, slide guitarist *Sonny Landreth*, saxophonist *Steve Berlin*(of Los Lobos) and *Parrothead* Jimmy Buffett. Of late, Richard has become more commercially accessible, incorporating a pop/rock sensibility into his Louisiana roots, as illustrated on his A & M recordings "Women in the Room" and "Snake Bite Love". —*Liz Opoka*

Live / 1970 / Arzed 1003
An exciting live performer, Richard is at his best here. —*Jeff Hannusch*

★ **Looking Back** / 1985 / Arzed 1011
The greatest hits from this important artist. —*Jeff Hannusch*

Zack's Bon Ton / 1990 / Rounder 6027
The 12 tracks included hot versions of "Jolie Blonde," "La Valse de Grande Riviere" and "Ma Petite Fille Est Gone." Richard also demonstrated his country proficiency with a heady cover of Johnny Horton's "The Battle of New Orleans," as well as "Big River" and "Take Me Deep (Song for C)." The Bon Ton Playboys also include outstanding musicians in fiddler Rufus Thibodeaux, saxophonist Pat Breaux, keyboardist Craig Lege, with Richard doubling on Acadian accordion, harmonica, and acoustic guitar in addition to doing leads. This was alternately spicy and reflective material, providing a good look at Cajun music's past, present, and future. —*Ron Wynn*

☆ **Women in the Room** / 1990 / A&M 75021-5302
Zach's writing comes together on this release with his most powerful songs to date. "No French, No More" is a sad tale about how teachers denied the Cajun people the use of their language. "Who

Stole My Monkey" is a knock-you-out fun song. A very diverse release. Highly recommended. —*Chip Renner*

Bayou des Mysteres / 1991 / Arzed 1017
Richard's traditional album. —*Jeff Hannusch*

Steve Riley & the Mamou Playboys

Group
Riley is a talented fiddler and accordionist whose mentor was the great Dewey Balfa. —*Mark A. Humphrey*

○ **Steve Riley and the Mamou Playboys** / 1990 / Rounder 6038
An exceptional debut from what is currently one of Louisiana's most popular contemporary Cajun groups. —*Jeff Hannusch*

Mamou Playboys / Rounder 6036
Two-steps and waltzes. —*Jeff Hannusch*

Rockin' Dopsie

Vocals, accordion / Cajun, Zydeco
Rockin' Dopsie enjoys an international reputation as one of zydeco's top exponents, thanks to a number of fine albums and numerous overseas tours. As you'd expect, Dopsie's early recordings are very bluesy, while his recent material tends to sound more contemporary. —*Jeff Hannusch*

○ **Big Bad Zydeco** / 1988 / GNP 2154
Hot Louisiana R&B/zydeco from one of its most popular modern practitioners. —*Hank Davis*

Good Rockin' / 1988 / GNP 2167
Upbeat and spirited zydeco. —*Hank Davis*

● **Louisiana Music** / 1991 / Atlantic 82307
Jumping Atlantic debut by Rockin' Dopsie and the Zydeco Twisters. Killer dance blend of rootsy zydeco full of grit, funk, and soul with pedal-to-the-metal rhythms. Tunes include "I'm in the Mood," "Keep a Knockin'," "The Things I Used to Do," "Zydeco Two-Step," and six others. — *Roundup Newsletter*

Rockin' Sidney

b. 1938
Guitar, organ, harmonica, accordion / Soul, Cajun, Zydeco
Sidney Simien began playing guitar and harmonica before discovering accordion (he also played organ in Lake Charles lounges). He cut his first demo in 1958 and worked the zydeco circuit in Louisiana and Texas before the unlikely 1985 success of "My Toot Toot" (a term of endearment, "my special one") made Rockin' Sidney a star and "Toot Toot" a Grammy winner and the first zydeco record to get extensive pop, rock, and country air play. —*Mark A. Humphrey*

● **My Toot Toot** / 1986 / Maison De Soul 1009
Rockin' Sidney had the biggest zydeco release of all time—"My Toot Toot"—and it has enjoyed many subsequent covers. Some of this release is unfortunately unacceptable, as it includes updated covers, but Sidney rises above it most of the time. —*Jeff Hannusch*

Roddie Romero

Cajun
Zydecajun accordionist whose first effort, The New Kid in Town, was produced by Rick Lagneaux, the keyboardist with the Wayne Toups Band. Romero was nominated as the Berst New and Upcoming Act by the Cajun French Music Association. —*Liz Opoka*

○ **New Kid in Town** / Swallow 6086
Much of this music sounds alike, but Romero's definitely one to watch. —*Jeff Hannusch*

Sam Brothers

A good, young zydeco ensemble that gained fame for its recordings on Arhoolie and appearances at the New Orleans Jazz and Heritage Festival.—*Ron Wynn*

Zydeco Brotherhood / Maison de Soul 1029
Not the most original of zydeco groups, the Sam Brothers still manage to jam a lot of energy into the covers they interpret. —*Jeff Hannusch*

Marc Savoy

b. 1940

Accordion / Cajun
Savoy labels himself a "crusader" for Cajun culture and, as such, is ranked at the top of the revivalists who followed the Balfa Brothers' example and championed pure Cajun music. Savoy's dedication to the music includes building Cajun accordions at his workship in Eunice, LA, as well as playing the music and discussing its background at festivals around the world. He and his wife Ann (singer and guitarist with the Savoy-Doucet Cajun Band and author of the excellent *Cajun Music: A Reflection of a People*) were the subject of Les Blank's PBS documentary, "Marc and Ann." In September 1992, Savoy received the prestigious Heritage Award from the National Endowment for the Arts. — *Mark A.*

○ **Oh What a Night** / 1988 / Arhoolie 5023
Some excellent dance music. This album proves that not only is Savoy an accomplished accordion maker, but he can play one too. —*Jeff Hannusch*

Savoy-Doucet Cajun Band

Group / Cajun
The Savoy-Doucet Cajun Band, comprised of Marc Savoy on accordion, Michael Doucet on fiddle and Ann Allen Savoy on guitar, perform traditional cajun music. —*Liz Opoka*

○ **Two Step D'Amade** / Arhoolie 316
This is the kind of acoustic music you used to hear only at Cajun houseparties. Very spirited and a timepiece. A glorious tribute to Cajun pioneer Amadé Ardoin. —*Jeff Hannusch*

Terrance Simien

Cajun, Zydeco
Terrance Simien and his band, the Mallet Playboys, have built upon the legacy of the late Clifton Chenier. Simien has worked with Paul Simon and has cowritten and performed a song with actor Dennis Quaid for the film, *The Big Easy*. *Billboard* Magazine rated Simien and Mallet Playboys as one of the top 10 performance acts of 1987. —*Liz Opoka*

○ **Zydeco on the Bayou** / 1992 / Restless 72368
A modern zydeco artist whose songs aren't yet in an essential category. More rock than zydeco, but lots of energy nonetheless. — *Ron Wynn &Jeff Hannusch*

Rufus Thibodeaux

b. 1934
Fiddle / Cajun
Thibodeaux is the consummate Cajun-fiddle session player and sideman. He worked at Jay Miller's Crowley studios in the '50s, playing various stringed instruments on everything from blues to rockabilly, and toured with Bob Wills and George Jones. But he is best known for a long association as sideman to Jimmy C. Newman: Thibodeaux's fiddle added Cajun spice to Newman's sometimes bland country fare. —*Mark A. Humphrey*

● **Cajun Country Fiddle of ...** / 1987 / La Louisianne 129
This album demonstrates the emotive style of one of the premier Cajun fiddlers. —*Jeff Hannusch*

Wayne Toups

Accordion / Cajun
A native of Crowley, LA, Toups began playing accordion at age 14. Like Zachary Richard, Toups is noted for his flamboyance and rock-derived rhythms. Not high on any purist's list of faves, Toups is nonetheless a great crowd pleaser. —*Mark A. Humphrey*

★ **Zydecajun** / 1985 / Mercury 846584
When rock meets Cajun, it must be Zydecajun. —*Jeff Hannusch*

○ **Johnnie Can't Dance** / 1990 / Mercury 846585
Uptown zydeco. Slick, with strong rock and Western-swing elements, and a touch of swamp-pop as well. —*Hank Davis*

Fish out of Water / 1991 / Mercury 848289
... this crisp, rocking Lousiana quintet impresses me. Toups mixes ballads with the boogie to good effect and pins it all down with some tasty accordian licks. The band's last release made minor inroads into the pop market; this one could make the full cross-over leap. — *Richard Riis, Rock & Roll Disc*

Justin Wilson

The best known Cajun comedian in Louisiana; the rest of the country probably knows him best as a chef, via his syndicated cooking show. —*Jeff Hannusch*

● **Ol' Favorites** / 1987 / Great Southern 11013
From the top-rated Cajun comedian; this is Wilson's only CD, and it is very funny. —*Jeff Hannusch*

Cajun Collections

○ **101-Proof Zydeco** / Maison de Soul 1030
A good collection of contemporary zydeco from the Maison de Soul label. —*Jeff Hannusch*

○ **14 Cajun Hits** / 1987 / Swallow 6066
An exceptional sampling of modern Cajun music from the Swallow label. —*Jeff Hannusch*

☆ **Alligator Stomp, Vol. 1** / 1991 / Rhino 70946
☆ **Alligator Stomp, Vol. 2** / 1991 / Rhino 70740
☆ **Alligator Stomp, Vol. 3** / 1992 / Rhino 70312
Third volume of this series, which is incredibly popular with music fans and critics alike. Most of the tracks are making their CD debut and many were previously available only in zydeco specialty shops and regional markets. Many popular artists, including Clifton Chenier, C. J. Chenier, Buckwheat Zydeco, Rockin' Dopsie, File', and many more. Titles include "Mamou Two-Step," "Hot Tamale Baby," "Parlez-Nous A Boire," and 15 more. —*Roundup Newsletter*

Best of La Louisianne Records / 1001

Features 23 cuts from such Cajun artists as Zachary Richard, Ambrose Thibodeaux, Michael Doucet, Eddy Raven, and many others. —*AMG*

Best of Louisiana Cajun, Vol. 2 / Mardi Gras 1010
Some top artists in the Cajun and zydeco fields. —*AMG*

○ **Cajun, Vol. 1: Abbeville Breakdown 1929-1939** / Feb. 1991 / Columbia 46220

○ **Cajun Home Music** / Smithsonian/Folkways 2620

Cajun Music / Arhoolie 5008
Features Nathan Abshire, Shuk Richards, and other Cajun artists from the 50s. —*AMG*

○ **Cajun Music & Zydeco** / Rounder 1572
This 17-track compilation chronicles some of the best recorded moments in the renaissance of south Louisiana's French-based music styles, Cajun and zydeco. Culled from the catalogues of several labels—including Rounder, Swallow, Arhoolie, Maison de Soul, and La Louisianne—the songs highlight some of the best fiddle, frottoir (rub board), and accordion players of the genres. Contributors include: Clifton Chenier, Boozoo Chavis, Dewey Balfa, Buckwheat Zydeco, Beausoleil, Dennis McGee, Zachary Richard, Steve Riley and the Mamou Playboys, and Bruce Daigrepont. An exemplary gathering of talent. —*Roundup Newsletter*

○ **Cajun Social Music** / 1987 / Smithsonian/Folkways 40006
Field recordings from various Cajun groups, recorded in the '60s. —*Jeff Hannusch*

Cajun Songs from Louisiana / Smithsonian/Folkways 4438
Field recordings from various Cajun groups, recorded in the '60s. —*Jeff Hannusch*

FOLK

In its widest possible application, "folk music" refers to music composed and performed by amateurs and passed down in an oral tradition devoid of formal training. In this sense, folk music is not only the ballads that derive from the Scots and the Irish and have descended from the Appalachian Mountains, it is also the rural blues of the Mississippi Delta and the drum-heavy music of northwestern Africa, not to mention any other tribal or traditional genres.

In the 20th century in the US, however, the definition of folk music has tended to narrow over time, as other musical styles have encroached on it. Thus, though the Carter Family was an obvious influence on Woody Guthrie, and though they played their traditional music on acoustic instruments and sang it with untrained voices, we think of them as country musicians, not folk ones. Woody Guthrie, however, is resolutely categorized as folk, even though he introduced two main innovations to the form: first, he moved to the city, and second, he wrote his own songs.

It is probably the second factor that's the most important. By the early post-WWII era, Guthrie's songs were getting pop treatments in the hands of the Weavers, and by the mid 50s, two distinct camps had grown up, both of whom benefited from the boomlet of popular interest in folk music that lasted roughly from the 1955 Weavers comeback concert at Carnegie Hall (after years of blacklisting) to the summer day in 1965 when Bob Dylan turned up on stage at the Newport Folk Festival with an electric guitar in his hands.

The first camp followed in Guthrie's footsteps, writing their own songs and singing them in some approximation of Guthrie's Oklahoma accent. This camp tended to be more political and artistic, and most of them were individuals. Dylan was the most prominent of them, though Phil Ochs, Tom Paxton, Dave Van Ronk, and many others were included.

The second camp followed in the footsteps of the Weavers, singing the songs of others (including many of the Child ballads, but also songs written by those in the first camp) in sweet harmonies and clearly enunciated phrases. This camp tended to be apolitical and entertainment-oriented, and most of them were singing groups. Peter, Paul, and Mary were preeminent in this camp, along with the Kingston Trio, the Limeliters, and others. Joan Baez started in the second camp and gradually moved to the first.

After 1965, the first camp merged with pop and rock & roll, especially the "sensitive singer/songwriter" school of the early 70s, and the second camp retreated into a nostalgic past. By the end of the 70s the folk boom was over, but folk music remained healthy, continuing to flourish in the places it always had – in hundreds of small clubs spread across the US and Europe and at dozens of summer festivals. A new crop of singer/songwriters was emerging, and if they didn't have the clear road to national recognition enjoyed by their 60s forebears, they were nevertheless gradually able to build up reputations on a viable circuit, record their own tapes, and even eventually move up to independent labels like Flying Fish and Rounder.

You will find in the listings that follow, therefore, records by the old hands (many of them reissued on CD in recent years) and a healthy sampling of those younger artists operating in what is now, as perhaps it always should have been, a highly decentralized field. It's likely that many of those names will be unfamiliar, but the reader is encouraged to try out a recording or two by the new folk acts and to keep an eye out for their appearances in local venues. That's where folk music lives today.

– William Ruhlmann

Pat Alger

Vocals, guitar

Pat Alger, who is among the most successful country songwriters of the late '80s and early '90s, comes from a folk background, and that colors the unusually thoughtful, articulated songs he writes. He first turned up on record himself playing guitar and singing with the loosely constructed Woodstock Mountains Revue on the album *More Music from Mud Acres* in 1977. He was a coauthor of the song "Ocracoke Time"— which appeared on the Revue's third album, *Pretty Lucky,* in 1978—and "Old Time Music" on its fourth album, *Back to Mud Acres,* in 1981; he was the sole author of "Southern Crescent Line" on the same album.

But Alger really began to gain recognition as a songwriter with the release of Nanci Griffith's third album, *Once in a Very Blue Moon* in 1985. Alger cowrote the title song, which reached the country charts in 1986. He was also heard from on Griffith's fourth album, *The Last of the True Believers,* in 1986, for which he cowrote the song "Goin' Gone." (He also played guitar on the album and did its graphics.) Alger was coauthor of the title song on Griffith's 1987 album, *Lone Star State of Mind,* and that song became a Top 40 country hit. In 1988 Kathy Mattea's version of "Goin' Gone" hit the top of the country charts. In 1990 Mattea took Alger and Fred Koller's "She Came from Fort Worth" to number two.

It's no surprise, then, that when Alger came to record his debut album, *True Love & Other Short Stories,* in 1991, he was able to call on the help of the cream of the young Nashville writers and performers. Trisha Yearwood, Nanci Griffith, Mary Black, Ashley Cleveland, Kathy Mattea, and Lyle Lovett all turn up, though Alger himself is the focus, singing his best-known songs. "No one sings or plays Pat Alger like Pat Alger himself," Griffith writes. — *William Ruhlmann*

○ **True Love & Other Short Stories** / 1991 / Sugar Hill 1029

This country-folk songwriter sings his own versions of such hits as "Lone Star State of Mind" and "Goin' Gone." Guests include Nanci Griffith and Kathy Mattea. — *William Ruhlmann*

Amy & Leslie

Vocals

Amy Fradon and Leslie Ritter are Woodstock-based composers and vocalists. — *Chip Renner*

○ **Amy & Leslie** / 1990 / Alcazar 110

Vocals are strong—these women were meant to sing together. Artie Traum plays and coproduced; Rory Block plays some sweet slide guitar. —*Chip Renner*

Take Me Home / 1994 / Shanachie/Cachet
Their second album frames the duo's clear harmonies in warm spacious arrangements. The Lennon-McCartney song "Rain" is given a dreamy and effective treatment. This album has a slightly new age feel to it, due to the production, but the playing is dynamic. "Your Move" and "From Time to Time" are standout tracks. —*Richard Meyer*

Eric Andersen

b. Feb. 14, 1943, Pittsburgh, PA
Vocals
Eric Andersen has maintained a career as a folk-based singer-songwriter for 30 years. In contrast to such peers as Tom Paxton and Phil Ochs, Andersen's writing has had a romantic, philosophical, poetic bent for the most part, rather than a socially conscious one, though one of his best-known songs, "Thirsty Boots," has as its background the Freedom Rides of the early '60s. (The song has been recorded by Judy Collins and others.)

After emerging from the Northeast folk-club circuit, Andersen began to record in 1965 with *Today Is the Highway*. His second album, *'Bout Changes & Things*, contained some of his most accomplished writing, including the highly poetic "Violets of Dawn," "Thirsty Boots," and "I Shall Go Unbounded." All were sung in Andersen's flexible tenor (he shaded toward a baritone later), backed by rapid, intricate fingerpicking. In the late '60s and early '70s, Andersen experimented with country, pop, and rock music, settling on an amalgamation by the time of his masterpiece *Blue River* in 1972. This was also his most commercially successful album, but Andersen, like friends Leonard Cohen and Townes Van Zandt, was always too serious minded for the mainstream. In the '70s and '80s, he recorded sporadically while playing folk-clubs around the United States and especially Europe, where he took up residence. His newest recording is the remarkable *Ghosts upon the Road*, in which he reflects ruefully on the '60s. —*William Ruhlmann*

○ **'bout Changes & Things** / 1966 / Vanguard 79206
The best early Andersen. Includes "Violets of Dawn" and "Thirsty Boots." —*William Ruhlmann*

○ **Tin Can Alley** / 1968 / Vanguard
This record, which contains "Hello Sun" and "Rollin' Home," is one of his solidest early albums. It begins and ends with the title cut played by a great junkyard band. —*Richard Meyer*

★ **Blue River** / 1973 / CBS 31062
One of the best folk-rock singer-songwriter albums of the early '70s. —*William Ruhlmann*

Be True to You / 1975 / Arista 4033
Includes the tender title track and the epic "Time Runs Like a Freight Train." —*William Ruhlmann*

Ghosts upon the Road / 1989 / Gold Castle 71327
Evocative songs that reflect on Andersen's past and current concerns. —*William Ruhlmann*

○ **Stages: Lost Album** / Mar. 1991 / CBS 47120

Añel, Lili

Once the winner of the best unsigned artist in the New York Music Awards, Añel has been a fixture on the New York City songwriter's scene since 1979, performing at most of the major venues there. She combines blues, Caribbean, and jazz influences in original material that is powerful and honest. —*Richard Meyer*

○ **Laughed Last** / 1994 / Palmetto Records
This album is marked by beautiful production and arrangements that never call undue attention to themselves. Lili Añel's singing is relaxed and expressive. In a style reminicent of Phoebe Snow, Añel stakes out a personal territory. The title song and "Let Her Go" are particularly strong cuts. Recommended. —*Richard Meyer*

Jenny Avila and Amy Torchia

Change Is / 1993 / Jenamy Music
This Pennsylvanian duo's CD showcases their lovely vocal style, which can be quite forceful at times. The songs find them search-

ing for comfort in a complicated world. "Defy Gravity" and "Hiding Place" are two of the best. —*Richard Meyer*

Joan Baez

b. Jan. 9, 1941, Staten Island NY
Vocals
The most accomplished interpretive folksinger of the '60s, Joan Baez has influenced nearly every aspect of popular music in a career still going strong after more than 30 years. Baez is possessed of a once-in-a-lifetime soprano, which, since the late '50s, she has put in the service of folk and pop music as well as a variety of political causes. Starting out in Boston, Baez first gained recognition at the 1959 Newport Folk Festival, then cut her debut album, *Joan Baez*, released in December 1960. The record was made up of 13 traditional songs, some of them Child ballads, given near-definitive treatment. A moderate success on release, the album took off after the breakthrough of *Joan Baez—Vol. 2*, released a year later, and both albums became huge hits, as did Baez's third album, *Joan Baez in Concert*. Each album went gold and stayed on the bestseller charts more than two years.

From 1962 to 1964, Baez was the popular face of folk music, headlining festivals and concert tours and singing at a variety of political rallies, including the August 1963 March on Washington led by Dr. Martin Luther King Jr. During this period, she began to champion the work of folk songwriter Bob Dylan, and gradually her repertoire moved from traditional material toward the socially conscious work of the emerging generation of '60s artists like him.

In the late '60s and early '70s, Baez moved toward country and rock music and also began to write her own songs, culminating in the gold-selling *Diamonds & Rust* in 1975. Since then, while her recording career has gradually declined, she has maintained her status on the concert circuit and her commitment to social issues. —*William Ruhlmann*

☆ **Joan Baez** / 1960 / Vanguard 2077
Revelatory first album features Baez singing traditional folk songs. —*William Ruhlmann*

Joan Baez in Concert, Part 2 / 1963 / Vanguard 2123
A superb followup to *Part 1*, with some more interesting material. —*Bruce Eder*

5 / 1964 / Vanguard 79160
A good folk set, from a variety of sources. —*Bruce Eder*

Joan / 1967 / Vanguard 79240
Ornate, heavily orchestrated versions of other people's songs. Overproduced, but quite beautiful. —*Bruce Eder*

Any Day Now / 1968 / Vanguard 79306-7
All-Dylan album includes definitive performance of "Love Is Just a Four-Letter Word." —*William Ruhlmann*

○ **Best of Joan C. Baez** / 1968 / A&M 3234
Emotionally charged songs from her '70s albums on A&M. Not early Baez, this album of touching songs is probably too commercial for diehard folk fans. Excellent. —*Michael Erlewine*

● **First Ten Years** / 1970 / Vanguard 6560-61
A nearly perfect cross-section of her most enduring work, both traditional and contemporary. —*Bruce Eder*

Joan Baez 2 / 1970 / Vanguard 79094

● **Blessed Are** / 1971 / Vanguard 6570

Come from the Shadows / 1972 / A&M 3103
After recording for the folk label Vanguard for more than a decade, Baez moved to A&M. On this label debut, she maintained her interest in country music, recording in Nashville with some of the city's session aces. She also continued to dedicate herself to radical politics, from her set opener "Prison Trilogy," which pledged, "We're gonna raze the prisons to the ground," to the closer, John Lennon's "Imagine." In between were her call on Bob Dylan to return to protest music ("To Bobby") and her sister Mimi Farina's touching tribute to Janis Joplin, "In the Quiet Morning." —*William Ruhlmann*

Hits/Greatest & Others / 1973 / Vanguard 79332
An alternate cross-section of Baez's Vanguard music, including her monster hit "The Night They Drove Old Dixie Down." —*Bruce Eder*

Where Are You Now, My Son? / 1973 / A&M 4390

This isn't only *not* the place to start listening to Joan Baez, it's the album that separates the true fans from the, um, fellow travelers. Side 2 is taken up by the title song, a musical account of Baez's trip to Hanoi over Christmas of 1972, complete with the sound of U.S. bombs falling on the city. Side 1, on the other hand, contains one of Baez's best original songs, "A Young Gypsy," and two by her sister, "Mary Call" and "Best of Friends." —*William Ruhlmann*

Joan Baez in Concert / 1976 / Vanguard 2122
A vibrant concert recording with a radiant sound, humor, and topicality. —*Bruce Eder*

Honest Lullaby / 1979 / Portrait 35766
On her second album for CBS's Portrait label (and her last new album issued in the United States for eight years), Baez was given a full-scale pop-rock production by veteran Barry Beckett and the studio band in Muscle Shoals, AL. The result, on songs that range from "Let Your Love Flow" to "Before the Deluge," is accessible but not particularly memorable '70s-style pop. If you always wanted to know what the words to "No Woman, No Cry" are, however, this is the place to find out. —*William Ruhlmann*

○ **Live Europe 83—Children of the Eighties** / 1983 / Ariola
While Baez declined to record again in the United States unless she could get on a major label, she did make several live albums in Europe in the interim. This is the best of them, mixing old favorites like "Farewell, Angelina" with new originals like her heartfelt "For the Children of the Eighties." (Import) —*William Ruhlmann*

Very Early Joan Baez / 1983 / Vanguard 79446
A masterful raid on the vault, recapturing the purity and simplicity of her debut recording. —*Bruce Eder*

○ **Recently** / 1988 / Gold Castle 71304
Baez returned to U.S. record shops with a vengeance here, delivering her interpretations of songs by Dire Straits, Johnny Clegg, U2, and Peter Gabriel, performers whose political consciousness had been formed by listening to old Joan Baez albums. And on the title track, a stunning original, she boldly answered ex-husband David Harris's downbeat memoir of the '60s, *Dreams Die Hard*, as well as other '80s revisionists. —*William Ruhlmann*

★ **Diamonds and Rust in the Bullring** / 1989 / A&M 3233
Baez's peak as a songwriter (title track) and folk-rock interpreter, singing songs of Jackson Browne, John Prine, and Bob Dylan. —*William Ruhlmann*

○ **Play Me Backwards** / 1992 / Virgin 86458
This 1992 release, reflecting Joan's fourth decade of performance, shows her musically as strong and vibrant as ever. Includes several originals plus outstanding songs by Janis Ian ("Amsterdam"), Mary-Chapin Carpenter ("Stones in the Road"), and other contemporary songwriters. —*Ladyslipper*

○ **Rare, Live & Classic** / Sep. 1993 / Vanguard 705
Spanning three discs, the boxed set *Rare, Live & Classic* is an odd mix of Baez's best-known songs and rarities. For the hardcore collector, there are plenty of interesting items here—including previously unreleased duets with Bob Dylan, Donovan, Bill Wood, and Jeffrey Shurtleff—but for the casual fan there's too much material; they would be better off with her original albums or single-disc compilations. —*Stephen Thomas Erlewine*

Bill Baker

Wolves of Winter, The / 1994 /
His voice and story-song style call David Mallet to mind. These are introspective songs arranged for guitar with dashes of piano, viola, and bass. —*Richard Meyer*

Geoff Bartley

Guitar

○ **Blues Beneath the Surface** / 1986 / Magic Crow
The title track here is an extraordinary example of Bartley's guitar work. His lyric songs are also quite fine. —*Richard Meyer*

Interstates /
This album is more produced than his first release and well done with lots of rage. "Death is the Robber" is a cool edgy blues, and "The Sanderlings" is a very moving extended spoken piece. —*Richard Meyer*

Cathy Barton and Dave Para

Cathy is a protege of Roy Acuff, Jimmy Driftwood, and Grandpa Jones. A master of the frailing banjo style, she has twice won the Tennessee old-time banjo championship. She introduced the hammered dulcimer to the Walnut Valley festival at Winfield. She holds a Masters degree in folklore. Playing with old-time performers, Dave has developed a great repertoire of traditional songs and stories, and a fantastic stage presence that carries over into their recordings. They have befriended many old-time musicians, encouraging them to join in both performing and recording. Many of their recordings include other folk-legacy artists, Missouri old-time fiddlers and Bob Dyer (the Bard of Boonville). Cathy, Dave, and Bob are currently working on a project of collecting and recording Civil War songs from the midwest. Dave's great 6- and 12-string guitar work, coupled with Cathy's banjo, dulcimer, and autoharp, and their fine harmony singing make these recordings a listening treasure. —*Don Stevens*

February March / Cornbelt

● **For All The Good People—A Golden Ring Reunion** / Folk-legacy

In The Days I Went A Courtin... / Acoustic Revival

Movin' On Down The River / Srg

New Harmony / Folk Legacy

Old Time Gospel Hymns / Cumberland

Reflections On The Carter Family / Take Two

Treasure In The River / Big Canoe

Wendy Beckerman

New Jersey native Wendy Beckerman came to the Greenwich Village songwriters community in 1989 and has gone on to become a regular performer on the Northeast coffeehouse circuit. —*Richard Meyer*

○ **By Your Eyes** / 1992 / Great Divide Records
On her debut release, Wendy Beckerman offers a well-paced collection of 14 of her direct and poetic songs. Her clear voice is well served by the all acoustic band with background harmonies. Standout tracks include "Lion's Mane," "If I Ask for Love," and "Now Is the Dream." —*Richard Meyer*

Jennifer Berezan

Borderlines / Flying Fish 70615
Canadian Jennifer Berezon's album of originals and voice have the feel of Karla Bonoff's albums. There is a soft rock gloss over her straightforward songs of love and longing for home. —*Richard Meyer*

Cindy Lee Berryhill

Vocals

A savvy, witty singer-songwriter in what has been called the "antifolk" style of the mid '80s, she has released two albums on Rhino Records. —*William Ruhlmann*

○ **Naked Movie Star** / 1989 / Rhino 70845
This quirky, Los Angeles-based folkie, aided by a folk-rock production courtesy of Lenny Kaye, comments on life in Hollywood, Donald Trump, and other subjects with a sometimes flip, sometimes self-deprecating attitude. —*William Ruhlmann*

Peter and Lou Berryman

Vocals

Lou and Peter write and perform great "feel good" music. They are excellent at cerebral satire. When listening to the words, you sometimes forget the great musical accompaniment provided by them (accordian and guitar). Their great stage presence carries over into their recordings. —*Don Stevens*

Forward Hey—Wisconsin Songs / Cornbelt

Your State's Name Here / Cornbelt

● **So Comfortable** / Cornbelt 300

Peter & Lou Berryman

○ **We Don't Talk about That!** / 1993 / Cornbelt Records
Here is the eighth collection of the Wisconsin-based duos gentle and humorous songs. "We Don't Talk about That" is about skele-

tons in the family closet, "Spray Them Gold" recommends decorating ideas for old LPs. "Hard Work and Perseverence" is a moral tale that brings free will into play along with Darwinian rules of survival. —*Richard Meyer*

Sohipa Bilides

A Massachussetts artist who performs traditional Greek music. —*Richard Meyer*

○ **Greek Legacy** / 1991 / E. Thomas 101
This Greek-Italian second-generation American presents traditional songs from the mainland, island, and Asia Minor populations of Greece for both listening and dancing. Comfortable with a wide variety of regional vocal styles, from island syrto to urban zeibekiko, her voice is deep, rich, and expressive. She accompanies herself on the traditional santouri (hammered dulcimer), while being supported on laouto (lute), violi (violin), clarino (clarinet), and dumbeleki (drum). These aren't updated, westernized versions of traditional songs with dance beats or synthesized instrumentation; it's the pure stuff, well researched, with an "old world" sound of ageless beauty. —*Ladyslipper*

Milo Binder

Vocals
This Los Angeles-based singer-songwriter is sly, romantic, and childlike. He is a contributor to *The Fast Folk Musical Magazine* and Windham Hill's *Legacy*. —*Richard Meyer*

☆ **Milo Binder** / 1991 / Alias 10
"Effigy," "New Toys," and "Donald Thorn" are gems. —*Richard Meyer*

Tony Bird

b. , Malawi
Vocals
Malawi-born Tony Bird was effecting a mixture of modern Western musical styles with traditional African ones ten years before Paul Simon was ever heard on mbaqanga. Though his excellent '70s recordings went ignored, the surge of interest in African pop in the late '80s got him back in the studio for "Sorry Africa" (Philo 1135) in 1990. —*William Ruhlmann*

○ **Bird of Paradise** / 1978 / CBS 34988
Malawi-born Tony Bird's first album anticipated Paul Simon's fusion of African music and Western folk-pop by ten years. On this, his second album, he combines thoughtful lyrics about such African concerns as apartheid with celebrations of the continent's flora and fauna, using music that evokes both African and U.S.-U.K. folk styles. —*William Ruhlmann*

○ **Sorry Africa** / 1990 / Philo 1135
Twelve years after his last album, Bird's social commentary is more anguished ("Athlone Incident"), his political statements more plaintive ("Sorry Africa"), and his celebratory songs more fervid ("Mango Time"). He remains the only songwriter honestly taking on the issue of what it means to be White and African. —*William Ruhlmann*

David Blue (S. David Cohen)

b. 1941, Providence, RI, **d.** Dec. 2, 1982
Vocals
Born in Providence, RI, as S. David Cohen (a name he returned to for one of his albums), David Blue was a member of the folk singer-songwriter community of Greenwich Village in the '60s and a close friend of Bob Dylan's (he recounts this period of his life in Dylan's movie *Renaldo & Clara*). Blue made several albums for Elektra, Reprise, and Asylum in the '60s and '70s and is best remembered for his songs "I Like to Sleep Late in the Morning" and "Wanted Man" (recorded by the Eagles). —*William Ruhlmann*

○ **David Blue** / 1966 / Elektra 74003
Blue's debut album features the first recording of his remarkable "Grand Hotel" and other well-written folk-rock songs. —*William Ruhlmann*

Nice Baby and the Angel / 1973 / Asylum 9009
Blue is joined by an all-star California cast (Dave Mason, Graham Nash, David Lindley, and Glenn Frey) for this excellent '70s singer-songwriter collection, which includes his "Outlaw Man." —*William Ruhlmann*

Com'n Back for More / 1975 / Asylum 1043
Blue takes a more jazz-rock approach here, using members of the crony group the Los Angeles Express, whose employer, Joni Mitchell, makes an appearance, as does Blue's old crony, Bob Dylan. —*William Ruhlmann*

Hugh Blumenfeld

b. 1958
Songwriter
Brooklyn-born but now residing in Connecticut, Hugh Blumenfeld was a mainstay in the late '80s Greenwich Village scene, an associate editor and contributor of songs to the *Fast Folk Musical Magazine*, winner of the Kerrville New Folk Competition, is featured on Christine Lavin's *On a Winter's Night* compilation, and was the first artist signed to the new 1 800 Prime CD label. He is a Ph.D. in poetry but doesn't let that get in the way of honest songwriting. —*Richard Meyer*

○ **Strong in Spirit** / 1987 / Grace Avenue 001
Hugh's first collection contains some of his signature tunes, including "Brothers," "Sailing to the New World," and "Rising Moon." Its simple production showcases his intimate vocal style very well. —*Richard Meyer*

Barehanded / 1991 / Grace Avenue
Originally released independently in cassette, *Barehanded* was remixed with some additional parts and crisper sound on this 1 800 Prime CD release. Blumenfeld's songwriting continues to mature as evidenced by "Bring Stones," "Watertowers," and "Jerusalem." —*Richard Meyer*

Eric Bogle

b. 1944, Peebles, Scotland
Vocals
An Australian singer-songwriter best known for ". . . And the Band Played 'Waltzing Matilda,'" —*Richard Meyer*

Scraps of Paper / 1981 / Flying Fish 70311

When the Wind Blows / 1985 / Flying Fish 354
Eric Bogle with John Munro & Brent Miller. —*AMG*

Singing in the Spirit Home / 1987 / Flying Fish 447
An emotional collection of songs composed by one of Earth's finest political songwriters. These are songs that cut deep into the emotions of the listener, much as Phil Ochs did 20 years earlier. —*Steve Romanoski, Option*

● **Something of Value** / 1988 / Philo 1125

Bob Bouvee & Gail Heil

No one handles old-time cowboy and humorous songs better than Bob. His vocals are hauntingly rough. His guitar and harmonica are as good as you will ever hear. Gail is one of the top fiddlers in the country, and her vocals are worth the price of admission. Whether performing in concert, playing for a barn dance, or recording, Bob and Gail leave you wanting more. —*Don Stevens*

Behind The Times / Marimac

● **For Old Time's Sake** / Train On The Island

From The Heart / Bob Bovee

Minnesota Minstrel / Train On The Island

Roundup, The / Train On The Island

Tunes From Home / Bob Bovee

Oscar Brand

b. Feb. 7, 1920, Winnipeg, Manitoba, Canada
Vocals
Oscar Brand traveled with Woody Guthrie and has hosted the FolkSong Festival on New York's WNYC for 45 years. He has recorded over 80 albums of folk songs of all kinds—political, romantic, children's, and ribald. His performances are often clean and academic, but his scope as a disseminator of songs cannot be denied. Probably the best known is the series entitled Bawdy Backroom Ballads. —*Richard Meyer*

○ **Wild Blue Yonder** / 1956 / Specialty 168

● **Best of Oscar Brand** / 1975 / Tradition 2053

Brandywine Singers

Group

From 1962 through 1965 The Brandywine Singers were one of the hottest acts on the college folk circuit. Then life, the Vietnam War, and other careers intervened. The Brandywines re-formed in 1992 with original members Rick and Ron Shaw and Les Clark joined by multiinstrumentalist, multitalented Taylor Whiteside. The result is pure magic, folk music as we remember it in its popularity heyday and still able to send chills up and down one's spine. Folk favorites, beautifully sung, played, and arranged, spiced with a couple of originals. —*Allan Shaw*

○ **World-Class Folk** / 1993 / Folk Era 1402
The group you've never forgotten and never can forget. —*Mike Fleischer*

Andy Breckman

Guitar

A New York singer-songwriter, guitarist, and writer for both "Saturday Night Live" and David Letterman, Breckman has written many sly, comedic "folk" songs. —*Chip Renner & Richard Meyer*

● **Don't Get Killed** / 1990 / Gadfly 121089
A collection of 14 live songs that are guaranteed to make you laugh. The audience is into Breckman's songs. It makes for an enjoyable experience! This contains the surrealist revisionist folksong "Railroad Bill." —*Chip Renner & Richard Meyer*

○ **Proud Dad** / 1994 / Gadfly
Another set of Far Side-style songs from screenwriter Breckman. It begins with a cheery tune about Russian Roulette and gets stranger from there. It's all live taken from recordings as far back as 1981 to the present. It's all really funny. A good follow-up to his first distinguished collection. —*Richard Meyer*

David Bromberg

b. Sep. 19, 1945, Philadelphia, PA
Guitar, mandolin, dobro, fiddle

Often referred to as a musician's musician, throughout his career Bromberg has spent almost as much time being a sideman to people like Bob Dylan and Jerry Jeff Walker as he has fronting his own band. Session credits for albums by Tom Paxton and Jerry Jeff Walker started getting Bromberg attention in the mid-'60s, and he began making the transition from sideman to frontman in the early '70s, when he got signed to record for Columbia records.

The key to appreciating Bromberg is to realize he has an equal passion for blues, folk, country and western, bluegrass, and rock & roll. This diverse range of influences is reflected on all his recordings for Columbia, Fantasy, and Rounder, and in his performances as well. His musical eclecticism over the years may have cost him some fans, but a typical Bromberg concert can be a musical education. —*Richard Skelly*

● **David Bromberg** / 1971 / CBS 31104
David Bromberg was already a well-known folk instrumentalist before this album proved he was also a top-notch songwriter and an appealing vocalist as well. The styles mix folk, blues, rock, and jug-band music, and the songs alternate from the painfully sensitive ("Sammy's Song") to the rib-tickling "The Holdup," which was cowritten by George Harrison. —*William Ruhlmann*

Wanted Dead or Alive / 1974 / CBS 32717
Reissue of Bromberg's 1974 album. Backing musicians include several members of the Grateful Dead, as well as Andy Statman on mandolin and tenor sax. Some of Bromberg's strongest and best-loved material can be found here, including "The Holdup," "Danger Man," "Send Me to the 'Lectric Chair," "The New Lee Highway Blues," and Bob Dylan's "Wallflower." —*Roundup Newsletter*

Midnight on the Water / 1975 / CBS 33397
A big-band blowout album with guest appearances by Bonnie Raitt, Linda Rondstadt, Emmy Lou Harris. Key tracks are "The Joke's on Me" and "Don't Put That Thing on Me." —*Richard Meyer*

How Late'll Ya Play 'til? / 1976 / Fantasy 79007
Bromberg's band, with two horns and a fiddle player, is capable of playing just about any style of popular music, and most of them are here on a double album, half recorded in the studio and half live. (Fantasy has also issued the two discs separately.) The standout inclusion is Bromberg's "Will Not Be Your Fool," which

became his onstage showstopper from here on out. —*William Ruhlmann*

Out of the Blues—Best of David Bromberg / 1977 / CBS 34467

Bandit in a Bathing Suit / 1978 / Fantasy 9555
A lot of hot playing, including Pink Anderson's "Travelin' Man" and "If You Don't Want Me Baby." —*Richard Meyer*

Brothers Four

b. 1958, USA
Group

Formed in 1958 by four University of Washington students (Bob Flick, Michael Kirkland, John Paine, and Richard Foley) who met in a fraternity. The group signed with Columbia in 1959 and immediately hit the charts with "Greenfields." Between 1961 and 1963, they toured over 300 college campuses, and in 1961 they performed on the Academy Awards Show. The Brothers also made TV appearances on "The Ed Sullivan Show," "The Pat Boone Chevy Showroom," and "Mitch Miller's Singalong." They recorded their last Columbia album in 1967. —*David Szatmary*

★ **Greatest Hits** / CBS 8603

Saul Broudy

Vocals

This New Jersey-based folksinger primarily interprets others' songs. —*Richard Meyer*

○ **Travels with Broudy** / 1977 / Arista 2011

Greg Brown

Vocals

Greg Brown is from southwestern Iowa, and he brings a rural Midwestern sensibility to his songs that is alternately homey, tender, and witty. Gaining recognition on the "Prairie Home Companion" radio show, Brown has made a series of albums for Minnesota-based Red House Records. —*William Ruhlmann*

In the Dark with You / 1985 / Red House 8
Humorous and sardonic reflections on domestic life and aging, from a journeyman folksinger. —*William Ruhlmann*

● **One More Goodnight Kiss** / 1986 / Red House 23
Brown's best collection of touching, funny, small-town songwriting. —*William Ruhlmann*

One Big Town / 1989 / Red House 28
Brown turns his eye outward and views the world cynically on "America Will Eat You." —*William Ruhlmann*

Sandy Bull

b. 1941, New York, NY
Guitar

Long before Ry Cooder, Leo Kottke, Richard Thompson, and others were impressing us with their ability to hop from genre to genre, Sandy Bull glided from classical and jazz to ethnic music and rock & roll with grace and verve on his first two albums. Accompanied on his first two albums by renowned jazz drummer Billy Higgins, Bull produced some of the first extended instrumental compositions for guitar that incorporated elements of folk, jazz, and Indian and Arabic-influenced dronish modes. Not "rock" by any stretch of the imagination, it's nevertheless easy to see that it could have had an influence on the rock musicians who began incorporating eclectic and Middle Eastern sensibilities into their music a few years later. After his debut, Bull expanded his arsenal from the acoustic guitar and banjo to include oud, bass, and electric guitar. After his second album, however, his recordings were less focused and less impressive. In the '70s, he dropped out of music altogether due to drug problems, although he began recording again in the late '80s. —*Richie Unterberger*

Fantasias for Guitar and Banjo / Aug. 1963 / Vanguard 79119
Bull's debut is most notable for the side-long cut "Blend," a 22-minute track on a folk (more or less) album in the days when that just wasn't done outside of classical and jazz records. Accompanied by renowned jazz drummer Billy Higgins, Bull produced one of the first extended instrumental compositions for guitar that incorporated elements of folk, jazz, and Indian and Arabic-influenced dronish modes. The second side features imaginative interpretations of traditional gospel and southern moun-

tain tunes, as well as a work by German composer Carl Orff. — *Richie Unterberger*

● **Inventions for Guitar & Banjo** / 1965 / Vanguard 79191
On his second and best album, Bull expanded his arsenal from the acoustic guitar and banjo to include oud, bass, and electric guitar. The centerpiece of the record is "Blend II"; like "Blend" from his first album, it is a melange (somewhat more electric in tone) of folk, jazz, and the Middle East, this time 24 minutes worth. Also included on this 54-minute LP are two versions (electric and acoustic) of a Bach passage, a composition from the 14th century (Guillaume de Machaut's "Triple Ballade"), and Luiz Bonfa's "Manha de Carnival." A heavily reverbed (with drums), extended version of Chuck Berry's "Memphis, Tennessee" closes the set with an unexpected blast of rock & roll. —*Richie Unterberger*

○ **Sandy Bull** / Vanguard
Good solid album. —*Chip Renner*

Jane Byaela
Vocals
New York-based singer-songwriter of the '80s and '90s, with a sound that crosses the purity and perfection of Judy Collins with the quirkiness and drama of Suzanne Vega, without ever imitating either. Byaela is a classically trained guitarist, and her songs are all characterized by a virtuoso's command of her instrument and rich tonal colorations amid their intimacy. —*Bruce Eder*

Burning Silver / 1994 / 1-800 Prime
Jane Byaela's second album continues the deeply revealing confessional songwriting that marked her first fine album. Producer David Seitz has recorded her with exceptional clarity. Jane plays the intricate classically inspired guitar and viola parts. The title song is one of the strongest, though many others will be deeply affecting to the listener if they are willing to take some time with this record. —*Richard Meyer*

● **On the Edge** / Spark 903
An especially pleasing all-acoustic record, soaring artfully and plunging bluesily along on a beguiling and stylized roller coaster ride that is twice as interesting and three times more honest than Suzanne Vega's best work. —*Bruce Eder*

Andrew Calhoun
Vocals
Andrew Calhoun is a Chicago-based singer-songwriter with a sly but deeply reverent view of life. He released two albums on the Flying Fish and recently founded his own Waterbug Records for his recordings, as well as compilations and individual artist releases. —*Richard Meyer*

○ **Hope** / Waterbug Records
This album finds Calhoun in fine form. He is humorous in the face of domestic disaster; "Better Get a Lawyer," and passionate in "I Love You All the Time." His rich voice lend a traditional sound to all he does, but his songs are rooted in a modern poetic sensibility that is uncluttered and powerful. —*Richard Meyer*

Walk Me to the War / 1980 / Flying Fish 398

● **Gates of Love** / 1989 / Flying Fish 341

Hamilton Camp
Vocals
An early '60s city folksinger, Camp was an early interpreter of otherwise-unrecorded Bob Dylan songs. Best known for his song "Pride of Man," popularized by Quicksilver Messenger Service. —*Richard Meyer*

● **At the Gate of Horn** / 1963 / Elektra 207
Bob Gibson and Hamilton Camp both play on this album. —*AMG*

Sarah Elizabeth Campbell
Vocals
Sarah Elizabeth Campbell is a Texas singer-songwriter who also resides in California. She was part of the popular California bluegrass band Fiddlestix. Her songs have been covered by Jim Messina, Rick Danko, and Levon Helm (of the Band); Blue Rose; and others. —*Chip Renner*

○ **Little Tenderness** / 1986 / Kaleidoscope 42

This CD is a collection of slow-paced, bluesy folk ballads that almost remind you of songs that could have been written 50 years ago. Her songs are from the heart. She is backed by Nina Gerber on guitar (producer of the CD), and three members of the Good Ol' Persons: John Reischman, mandolin; Sally Van Meter, lap steel and dobro; and Kathy Kallick, harmony vocals; along with Barbra Higbie, Sam Page, Jake Lampert, Joe Craven, Ed Johnson, Joe Goldmark, Sharon O'Connor, and Joe Weed. —*Chip Renner*

Fred Campeau & Michelle (mitch) Thomas
Fred is best know as a performer of old-time music with groups like the Volo Bogtrotters. Performing alone or with Mitch, and as a part of More the Merrier, Fred is even more outstanding. He plays a variety of instruments, including banjo, fiddle, harmonica, and guitar. Michelle plays piano and recorder and has one of the most beautiful voices around. Some of their best work in ragtime and blues has never been recorded. That leaves us with a lot to look forward to on their future recordings. —*Don Stevens*

Backside Of Buncombe / Marimac

In The Dead Of Night / Porcupine

More The Merrier, The / Porcupine

Prarie Dog & Other Fiddle Tunes From The Midwest / Marimac

Tough Luck / Marimac

● **Volo Bogtrotters, The** / Marimac

Guy Carawan
b. Jul. 28, 1927, Los Angeles, CA
Hammer dulcimer, guitar, banjo
Guy Carawan is a hammer dulcimer, guitar, and banjo player from Tennessee. He plays traditional Appalachian music. —*Chip Renner*

★ **Been in the Storm So Long** / 1967 / Smithsonian/Folkways 3842

Green Rocky Road / 1977 / June Appal 21
Songs from Appalachia and the British Isles. Features "Soldiers Joy," "Green Rocky Road," and "St. Anne's Reel." —*Chip Renner*

Jubilee / 1979 / June Appal
Covers of David Mallet's "Inch by Inch" and "Road to Lisdoonvarna," plus 14 more. —*Chip Renner*

Songs of Struggle & Celebration / 1982 / Flying Fish 272
Fifteen songs recorded at workshops. Good backup. —*Chip Renner*

○ **Hammer Dulcimer Music** / 1985 / Flying Fish 329
Guy Carawan and his son Evan play great traditional music on this release. —*Chip Renner*

Cliff Carlisle
○ **Volume 1 & 2** / Old Timey
Born in 1904 in Mt. Eden Kentucky, Cliff Carlisle was raised in tobacco country. He drew on songs he heard growing up, and wrote a number of his own incorporating themes of the old West. His style is uptempo with a lot of yodeling and Hawiian guitar licks. He performed on the radio in the '30s and with his brother. These LPs collect his rare original recordings. —*Richard Meyer*

Doyle Carver
Vocals
A Houston-based singer-songwriter who writes mostly about local issues and conditions. —*Richard Meyer*

○ **Live at the Circle K** / 1970 / Carver Music 101
Carver's first album is a fine collection and includes the beautifully balanced "Deer Hunter," which is about hunting, coming of age, and love of family tradition, all in three minutes without one extra syllable. —*Richard Meyer*

High Ground / 1971 / Carver Music 201
"Red Iron Rain" and the title song are particularly fine songs on this album. —*Richard Meyer*

Patti Casey with Bob Gagnon
○ **Around Again** / 1993 / Long Shot Music
Patti Casey has vocal style similar to Karla Bonoff, mixed with Mary Chapin Carpenters. The story songs are her own and she

sings of love and longing with her heart. "Highway Blues" and "Centrifugal Force" are highlights. —*Richard Meyer*

Central Park Shieks

Group
An important mid-'70s New York band that gave an urban slant to country swing. —*Richard Meyer*

○ **Honeysuckle Rose** / Flying Fish 27026
Great playing and arrangements throughout. —*Richard Meyer*

The Chenille Sisters

Group
The Chenille Sisters feature Cheryl Dawdy, Connie Huber, and Grace Morand. They sing songs on the humorous side, with tight harmonies. —*Chip Renner*

Chenille Sisters / 1970 / Red House 29
First album. Good, humorous songs. —*Chip Renner*

● **At Home with the Chenille Sisters** / 1988 / Red House 26
A good record, featuring "Girl Shoes," "Crazy People," and "Bad Habits." —*Chip Renner*

Mama, I Wanna Make Rhythm / 1989 / Red House 39
The Chenilles lift their artistry to new heights on this 1991 release. —*Ladyslipper*

Whatcha Gonna Swing Tonight? / 1992 / Red House 50
Joined on this 1992 release by James Dapogny's Chicago Jazz Band, this talented vocal trio takes us back to the Swingland era . . . . Their fabulous harmonies and ability to be equally expressive whether punching out a lickety-split bop or slinking along in a langorous croon make these gals a must! —*Ladyslipper*

Kathy Chiavola

○ **Labor of Love** / 1990 / MY Label
Her voice is like Katy Moffat's and Mary Chapin Carpenter. She's got the usual spread of uptempo and ballads. She covers songs by Buddy Holly and Jimmy Rushing in addition to a tune of her own. They are all honestly sung and well produced. This is a good solid album. It includes some odd moments such as "Twinkle Twinkle Little Star" recorded in 1954 at the artist's childhood home and another cut live in Lisbon. —*Richard Meyer*

Frank Christian

Guitar
An exceptional guitarist and songwriter, Christian released one album in addition to his participation on the Italian Song Project record and various cuts on the *The Fast Folk Musical Magazine*. —*Richard Meyer*

○ **Somebody's Got to Do It** / 1982 / Great Divide
Includes his signature song, "Where Were You Last Night." —*Richard Meyer*

Chrysalis

Group
A folk-rock band based in Ithaca, NY, in the late '60s. Their leader, Spider Barbour, went on with solo work and with the Mothers of Invention. —*Richard Meyer*

○ **Definition** / 1967 / MGM 4547
Key songs are "Cynthia Jerome," "Lacewing," "30 Poplar," and "Lake Hope." The writing has a particularly sophisticated sense of psychology for this style in this era. —*Richard Meyer*

Sheila Clark

Guitar, banjo
Sheila Clark collects murder ballads and performs them with guitar and banjo. —*Richard Meyer*

○ **Legend of Tom Dula** / 1986 / Smithsonian/Folkways 31110
The Legend of Tom Dula and Other Tragic Love Ballads is a group of her finds. —*AMG*

Paul Clayton

Vocals, dulcimer
A '60s folk song collector and writer. —*Richard Meyer*

● **Folk Ballads ...** / Smithsonian/Folkways 2310

Folk Ballads of the English Speaking World is a good example of Clayton's work. —*AMG*

Slaid Cleaves

Cleaves is an Austin based singer-songwriter by way of Maine and is a winner of the 1992 Kerrville Folk Festival's New Folk competition. His rootsy songs have a folk and honkey-tonk feel to them that—combined with his honest delivery, reminicent of Peter Case—make them easily accesible. —*Richard Meyer*

Promise / 1990 / Rock bottom Records
The Promise contains 13 straighforward solo performances. These are melodic songs of romantic longing. —*Richard Meyer*

★ **Life's Other Side** / 1992 / Play Hard Records
This simply produced CD contains songs of wandering and wanderers. Many of the lyrics have an underlying theme of mystery. "Willie of the Wind" is one of the highlights. —*Richard Meyer*

○ **For The Brave & Free** / 1993 / Slaid Cleaves
The songwriting here is darker than the previous two releases. Like Springsteen's *Nebraska*, this album is comprised of sparse, sketched out stories. The band is simple and tight. —*Richard Meyer*

Judy Collins

b. May 1, 1939, Seattle, WA
Vocals
Judy Collins was one of the major interpretive folksingers of the '60s. A child prodigy at classical piano, she turned to folk music at the age of 15 and released her first album, *A Maid of Constant Sorrow*. in 1961 when she was 22. That album and its follow-up, *The Golden Apples of the Sun*, consisted of traditional folk material, with Collins's pure, sweet soprano accompanied by her acoustic guitar playing. By the time of *Judy Collins #3*, she had begun to turn to contemporary material and to add other musicians. (Jim, later Roger, McGuinn tried out his first arrangements of "The Bells of Rhymney" and "Turn, Turn, Turn" on this album, before using them with the Byrds.)

Collins's musical horizons were expanded further by 1966 and the release of *In My Life*, which added theater music to her repertoire and introduced her audience to the writing of Leonard Cohen; it was one of her six albums to go gold. Her first goldseller, however, was 1967's *Wildflowers*, which contained her hit version of "Both Sides Now" by the then-little-known songwriter Joni Mitchell.

By the '70s, Collins had come to be identified as much as an art song singer as a folksinger and had also begun to make a mark with her original compositions. Her best-known performances cover a wide stylistic range: the traditional gospel song "Amazing Grace," the Stephen Sondheim Broadway ballad "Send in the Clowns," and such songs of her own as "My Father" and "Born to the Breed."

Collins recorded less frequently after the end of her 23-year association with Elektra Records in 1984, though she made two albums for Gold Castle. In 1990, she signed with Columbia Records and released *Fires of Eden*, her 23d album. —*William Ruhlmann*

Maid of Constant Sorrow / 1961 / Elektra 7209
Prettily sung traditional songs. Collins talent is to sing these chestnuts, even at the time, without the prissiness of so many female folk singers. Her phrasing has enough strength to stand up to the "Prickile Bush" and give in to "Wild Mountain Thyme." —*Richard Meyer*

Golden Apples of the Sun / 1962 / Elektra 7222
Judy takes on such diverse repertoire as Gary Davis's "Twelve Gates to the City," "Crow on the Cradle," and her setting of "Golden Apples of the Sun." —*Richard Meyer*

#3 / 1963 / Elektra 7243
Having established herself as one of the foremost interpreters of traditional material, Collins did the same for contemporary folk songwriters on this album, which mixed standards with pristine covers of compositions by Dylan, Bob Gibson, Pete Seeger, Ewan MacColl, and Shel Silverstein. With Jim McGuinn arranging and playing second guitar and banjo, this album, which included a fine version of Seeger's "Turn! Turn! Turn!," had a clear (if overlooked) influence on the folk-rock he pioneered with the Byrds a couple years later. —*Richie Unterberger*

Judy Collins' Concert / 1964 / Elektra 7280

On this live set recorded at Town Hall in New York in 1964, Judy stirs up the audience with a rich mixture of traditional and contemporary covers; Billy Ed Wheeler's "Coal Tattoo" and Paxton's "Ramblin' Boy." —*Richard Meyer*

○ **In My Life** / 1966 / Elektra 74027
Collins, who by this point has moved from the acoustic renderings of traditional folk ballads to more extensive instrumentation and the work of contemporary folk writers, takes another step here, turning to tasteful string arrangements by Joshua Rifkin and adding theater music from *Threepenny Opera* and *Marat/Sade* to the Bob Dylan covers. She also starts covering Leonard Cohen ("Suzanne," "Dress Rehearsal Rag"). —*William Ruhlmann*

Wildflowers / 1967 / Elektra 74012
Passionate and filled with memorable passages. Includes her hit "Both Sides Now" and her first major original composition "Since You Asked." Leonard Cohen's "Priests" has not appeared elsewhere. —*Bruce Eder and William Ruhlmann*

Who Knows Where the Time Goes / 1968 / Elektra 74033
Rock and country leanings are found on this album featuring guitarists James Burton and Stephen Stills. Includes the hit "Someday Soon" and Collins's own brilliant "My Father." —*William Ruhlmann*

○ **Recollections** / 1969 / Elektra 61350
Judy sings "Tomorrow Is a Long Time," "Early Mornin' Rain," and "Winter Sky." This is a best of compilation. —*Richard Meyer*

● **Colors of the Day—Best of Judy Collins** / 1972 / Elektra 75030
The biggest hits of her early career, well chosen. —*Bruce Eder*

True Stories and Other Dreams / 1973 / Elektra 75053
Collins at her most political, saluting Che Guevara, among others. Elaborately produced and well sung. —*Bruce Eder*

Judith / 1975 / Elektra 111
A soaring collection of songs from the Depression, '70s Broadway ("Send in the Clowns"), and modern C&W. —*Bruce Eder & William Ruhlmann*

★ **So Early in the Spring ...** / 1977 / Elektra 6002
So Early in the Spring, the First 15 Years. Double-album best-of covering the years 1961 to 1976; the place to start and also some of the best singing in contemporary folk music. —*William Ruhlmann*

○ **Fires of Eden** / 1990 / CBS 46102
A graceful, personal, and finely crafted work that crosses between art song and folk music. —*Bruce Eder*

Lui Collins

Vocals
A Connecticut singer-songwriter and interpreter of songs by Jack Hardy and Julie Snow. —*Richard Meyer*

● **Baptism of Fire** / 1980 / Green Linnet 1060
The title song is lush. Jack Hardy's "Tinker's Coin" is another highlight. —*Richard Meyer*

Bob Coltman

Bob Coltman is one of the best-kept secrets in traditional music. He has written hundreds of songs, and many have entered folk music credited to "traditional." Even when you hear Bob's songs for the first time, you feel as though you have heard them before. Very few musicians have had Bob's ability to write a song and have it accepted, immediately, as traditional. An excellent instrumentalist on banjo, fiddle, guitar, mandolin, and harmonica, Bob is admired by all of his contemporaries, and it is a rare performance by traditional musicians that does not include at least one of his songs. His recordings are rare but well worth the time and effort searching for them. —*Don Stevens*

Before They Close The Minstrel Show / Minstrel

Lonesome Robin / Minstrel

Original & Traditional Country Music / Biograph

People Like You / Folk-legacy

Telling Takes Me Home, The / Folk-legacy

Phil Cooper & Margaret Nelson W/paul Goelz

Hits of the '90's! (1690-1790-1890) Death! Murder! Seduction! More death! This is the agenda of Phil and Margaret—and no one

ever did it better. Phil is one of the best instrumentalists performing today. He plays guitar, cittern, and bowed psaltery. Margaret has the perfect voice for these old ballads from the British Isles. Margaret's voice is so beautiful that she holds your attention on the 40th verse as well as she does on the first. With Paul Goelz, a master on hammered dulcimer playing on most of their recordings, and joined by many other talented musicians, it seems that these songs were written years earlier, and just sat there waiting for Phil and Margaret to perform them. —*Don Stevens*

Across The Water / Porcupine

Full Moon / Ippel

In The Dead Of Night / Porcupine

Notes From Home / Holly Williams

Pretty Susan / Porcupine

Cornerstone

Group
A group of five musicians with musical roots in Florida, Virginia, Texas, and upstate New York can add up to only one thing: a bluegrass band with a solid folk base that does stunning original material. That's what Cornerstone, based near Ithaca, NY, is all about. Led by banjo player-songwriter Chris Stuart (FL), Cornerstone is made up of vocalist-fiddler Dee Specker (NY), mandolinist-fiddler Rick Manning (TX), bassist Dana Paul (VA), and virtuoso guitarist Tim Wallbridge (NY). This fusion of musicians from old-timey and bluegrass traditions makes for a special sound, one that features twin fiddles on some cuts, cajun accordion on others, Irish harp, and even the traditional five-piece bluegrass band lineup. The vocals are stunning, the feelings real, the instrumental backup exactly right for each tune. —*Allan Shaw*

○ **Out Of The Valley** / Folk Era
A bluegrass sensation. —*Mike Fleischer*

Elizabeth Cotten

b. 1893, Syracuse, NY, d. Jun. 29, 1987 , Syracuse, NY
Guitar
Elizabeth Cotten has influenced the fingerpicking style of every guitarist who has tried it since she began performing publicly in the '50s. Cotten worked as a domestic for the Charles Seeger family (whose children included Pete, Peggy, and Mike) in Washington, DC, and was persuaded by Mike Seeger to take up performing at the age of 60. The song "Freight Train," which she wrote when she was 12, became a Top Five hit in the United Kingdom and is now a standard. She recorded several albums for Folkways in the '50s and '60s, displaying her remarkably dexterous style, which (like stride piano playing) mixed a strong rhythmic backing with precisely yet delicately picked melody work. She continued to perform until shortly before her death in her mid '90s. —*William Ruhlmann*

★ **Folksongs & Instrumentals ...** / 1958 / Smithsonian/Folkways 3526
Folksongs & Instrumentals with Guitar. This first LP collection by a widely influential guitarist includes her classic "Freight Train." —*William Ruhlmann*

○ **Freight Train & Other Nc Folk Songs** / Smithsonian/Folkways 40009
Reissue of initial recordings of this National Heritage Award-winning Piedmont guitarist. A major model for fingerpickers. —*Barry Lee Pearson*

Mike Cross

Guitar, fiddle
Mike Cross is a gifted musician (guitar and fiddle), who started playing late in his life. He is known for his high-energy live shows. His songwriting styles lean toward folk, country, and Gaelic. —*Chip Renner*

Best of the Funny Stuff /
The title says it; "The Great Strip Poker Massacre," "The Scotsman," and "Dear Boss" are high points. —*Richard Meyer*

Carolina Sky / 1975 / Sugar Hill 1006
Another well-done studio album of Cross's energetic songs, played with a crack band. —*Richard Meyer*

Irregular Guy / Sugar Hill 1009
A solid collection of intrumental rave-up and fun songs from this multiinstrumentalist. Includes "Carolina Calling" and the tongue twisting "Directions." — *Richard Meyer*

○ **Live & Kickin'** / Sugar Hill 1005
Cross mixes country, folk, bluegrass, and Scots-Irish music, playing fiddle and guitar and singing on material ranging from spirited dance tunes to off-the-wall novelties. He is thus best heard in a live setting, especially one that includes the infectious "Whiskey 'Fore Breakfast." — *William Ruhlmann*

★ **Prodigal Son** / Sugar Hill 1008

Culley & Elliott

○ **Culley & Elliott** / 1993 / Culley and Elliott Pr
This duo was a winner at the 1993 Kerrville Folk festival New Folk Competition. Their first release contains strong melodic acoustic guitar-based songs. They are primarily story-songs in a style similar to David Mallett's. — *Richard Meyer*

Catie Curtis

Vocals
A Boston-area singer-songwriter whose politics are at once humanist, feminist, and gentle. — *Richard Meyer*

○ **Dandelion** / 1989 / Mongoose
Curtis's debut cassette, featuring 12 songs, is not as polished as her *From Years to Hours* CD. Her acoustic guitar work is good, and she uses just enough backup to add to her music without overpowering it. Good effort. — *Chip Renner*

● **From Years to Hours** / 1991 / Mongoose 102
Curtis shines on her second release, really maturing as a songwriter. Her music is well produced (Darleen Wilson), and her songwriting is intelligent and thought-provoking. "Hole in the Bucket" is the key song on this collection. — *Chip Renner & Richard Meyer*

Erik Darling & Border Town

b. Sep. 25, 1922, Baltimore, MD
Vocals, banjo
Erik Darling was an important influence on the folk scene in the late '50s and early '60s. Inspired by the Weavers, in the '50s he formed the Tunetellers, later called the Tarriers. Darling left that group to replace Pete Seeger in the Weavers, staying with them from 1958 through 1962. He then formed the Rooftop Singers (*see* separate entry in this section). His solo album *True Religion* for Vanguard was influential on younger folksingers in the '60s. — *Michael Erlewine*

Border Town at Midnight / Folk Era
This group is setting new trends. — *Mike Fleischer*

● **True Religion** / 1961 / Vanguard 9099
Darling performs on banjo and 6- and 12-string guitar. He is good command of the idiom, more than many other contemporaries, on such tunes as "Moanin' Dove" and "Blackeyed Susan." — *Richard Meyer*

○ **Train Time** / 1962 / Vanguard 9131

Possible Dream / 1975 / Elektra
Featuring guest Patricia Street. — *Michael Erlewine*

The Deighton Family

Group
A six-piece band that plays a combination of bluegrass, blues, Celtic folk, and Cajun music. — *Chip Renner*

○ **Mama Was Right** / 1980 / Philo 1130
More fun performances with squeezebox, tin whistles, and mandolin. Includes a wiggy take on George Harrison's "Tax Man." — *Mark A. Humphrey*

★ **Acoustic Music to Suit Most Occasions** / 1988 / Philo 1120
A delightful British folkabilly band that defies easy pigeonholing. National Public Radio named this its Album of the Year. — *Mark A. Humphrey*

Rolling Home / 1991 / Green Linnet 1116
For those who may have missed their first two albums, the Deightons are a seven-member family band from England. Befitting the Anglo-Moluccan marriage of Dave and Josie

Deighton, their music is a delightful, slightly off-kilter hybrid of Anglo-Celtic folk with sundry American folk, country, and rock elements delivered via wheezy melodeon, electric guitar, flute, mandolin, and so on. The Deightons find the unexpected in the familiar, slipping an old-time Creole-Cajun lilt into "Save the Last Dance for Me" and unleashing a snarling fuzz guitar on "Reuben's Train," which is as startling as it is somehow right. This 13-track collection is the Deightons' most winning yet, featuring more of the Deighton daughters' vocals this time, though Dave's imploring busker's rant is still prominent. The Carter Family of the "global village" is among the most inventive traditionalist groups you'll ever hear. — *Mark Humphrey, Roundup Newsletter*

Jackson Delta

A Canadian trio based in Peterborough, Ontario, Canada. — *Richard Meyer*

○ **Lookin' Back** / 1993 / Jackson Delta
This independently produced CD is just great. It was recorded live and sounds more immediate and present than 98 percent of live records. The performances are loose, fun, and honest, with great playing all around. There is nothing precious or falsly authentic about this R&B flavored record. Best cuts are "My Mistake" and "My Ears Keep Hearing Voices" (available c/o PO Box 2384 -Peterbrough, Ontario K9J 7Y8) — *Richard Meyer*

Iris Dement

Vocals
A very lyrical singer-songwriter from Arkansas who plays country-edged folk music, and whose view of the world is relaxed and filled with lovely irony. — *Richard Meyer & Chip Renner*

● **Infamous Angel** / 1992 / Philo 1138
Iris DeMent's strong family roots are reflected in this stunning collection of country-folk tunes dealing with the simplicity of innocence and the heartache of growth. DeMent has a tender but strong voice that evokes such pure emotion that at times it's breathtaking. A wide range of approaches work nicely: the bluesy gospel feel of "Sweet Forgiveness," an acknowledgement of frailties and strengths; the growing pains of "When Love Was Young"; and the aptly titled "Hotter Than Mojave in My Heart," which hurries with the exuberance of love. It's tough to listen to DeMent without getting choked up—but the funny thing is, you're smiling the whole time. That's talent. — *J.J. Rassler, Roundup Newsletter*

○ **My Life** / 1993 / Warner Bros. Records, Inc.
Since her beautiful debut record on Philo, Iris DeMent has graduated to the majors with her style intact. She has a confessional spirit and maintains her perspective as a free thinker all the while. The album is dedicated to her father, and it is lovely through it out. These are songs that sound like they've always been around. — *Richard Meyer*

Sandy Denny

b. Jan. 6, 1941, London, England, **d.** Apr. 21, 1978
Vocals
From her debut with Fairport Convention in 1968, Sandy Denny was one of England's most important folk stylists and a major influence in rock as well, with a striking alto voice and daunting compositional style. Prior to her accidental death a decade later, Denny recorded a brace of superb solo albums with her former Fairport stablemate, guitarist Richard Thompson, and her husband Trevor Lucas (d 1990). She left behind one classic song ("Who Knows Where the Time Goes"). Major influence: Isla Cameron. — *Bruce Eder*

North Star Grassman and the Ravens / 1971 / Carthage 4429
Some second thoughts and reapproaches to older work. — *Bruce Eder*

Sandy / 1972 / A&M 4371
Those seeking initiation into the ranks of Denny fans may consult listings for Fairport Convention and Fotheringay. Also try this solo album, which features many of the same players (Richard Thompson, Dave Swarbrick, etc.) and contains a good collection of Denny originals along with her rendition of Dylan's "Tomorrow Is a Long Time." — *William Ruhlmann*

Rendezvous / 1977 / Hannibal 4423
Stylistically varied, if not so fresh as her album *Sandy*. — *Bruce Eder*

Original Sandy Denny / 1984 / Trojan 2
Denny's first recording, originally released in 1967, is her most traditional effort. Backed only by her own acoustic guitar, Denny's 20-year-old voice is assured, pure, and powerful on her debut. The album features traditional folk staples like "This Train," "Make Me a Pallet on Your Floor," and "Pretty Polly," as well as covers of Tom Paxton's "Ramblin' Boy" and "Milk and Honey." There are also a couple of songs by the obscure American songwriter Jackson Frank, one of which she would soon perform with Fairport Convention ("You Never Wanted Me"). Although this has little of the folk-rock cross-pollination that Denny would soon master with Fairport and others, it is still an impressive LP that shows her voice in as haunting and commanding form as her more renowned recordings. —*Richie Unterberger*

Sandy Denny & The Strawbs / 1985 / Hannibal 1361
Denny with a British bluegrass band that later moved into progressive rock (without her). Her voice and a moody rendition of her classic "Who Knows Where the Time Goes" make it worthwhile. —*Bruce Eder*

○ **Who Knows Where the Time Goes** / 1986 / Hannibal 5301
This magnificently produced multidisc boxed set presents a complete portrait of Sandy Denny, the haunting singer; melodic, mournful songwriter; and mesmerizing bandleader of Fairport Convention and Fotheringay. Much of the material is previously unheard, but it's all of a piece with Denny's accomplished work on her solo albums and in her groups. The album makes the case for Denny as a major folk artist. —*William Ruhlmann*

● **Best of Sandy Denny (Best of Box)** / 1989 / Hannibal 1328
Selections from the three-CD boxed set *Who Knows Where the Time Goes*. . . sort of the best of the best, from one of the most formidable folk talents who ever lived. Includes, of course, "Who Knows Where the Time Goes," plus "Listen, Listen," "The Lady," "Late November," "The Pond and the Stream." —*Ladyslipper*

Devonsquare

Group
Devonsquare is a New England-based folk trio featuring Alana MacDonald (vocals, violin), Herb Ludwig (vocals), and Tom Dean (vocals, guitar, and percussion). They were voted "Act of the Year" by WNEW-FM of New York City. Tight harmonies and solid songwriting are their trademark. —*Chip Renner*

Walking on Ice / 1987 / Atlantic 81843
A very rich album. Folk with a pop flavor. "Black Africa" and "Walking on Ice" are very strong songs. —*Chip Renner*

● **Bye Bye Route 66** / 1991 / Atlantic 82343
It's hard to believe this is the same band. It has a Fleetwood Mac sound: more rock. Highly recommended. —*Chip Renner*

Brian Dewan

○ **Tells the Story** / 1993 / Bar/None
Artist songwriter Brian Dewan plays the electric zither. These songs are truer to the old ballad tradition than many contemporary folk songs. He deals with dark material; disrespect for chain letters, 100-year-old cowboys put on display, and the influence of a single copy of a record. It might not sound like folk music, but it is. —*Richard Meyer*

Hazel Dickens

b. , West Virginia
Vocals
One of 11 children of a West Virginia preacher, Hazel Dickens has recorded self-penned songs of deep conviction delivered with rough-edged passion. A country singer too raw for Nashville, Dickens is generally pegged a folksinger, albeit one without a dulcet warble. She's more akin to Sara Carter than to Joan Baez. Dickens also has been placed in the bluegrass camp, though one suspects her labor activism and feminism make much of her company there uneasy. Twenty years ago, her album with Alice Gerrard, *Hazel & Alice* (Rounder), was a cult classic that inspired, among others, Emmylou Harris. Her anthemic "They'll Never Keep Us Down" appeared in the award-winning documentary *Harlan County, USA*. Dickens's solo albums for Rounder are uniformly excellent, the title of one (borrowed from Woody Guthrie) neatly summarizing her work: *Hard Hitting Songs for Hard Hit*

People. This is a woman Guthrie would've loved as a kindred spirit. —*Mark A. Humphrey*

Hard Hitting Songs / 1980 / Rounder 0126
Hard Hitting Songs for Hard Hit People is a very good record that deals with the out-of-work, down-on-his-luck, average American. It features Nancy and Norman Blake, Tony Trischka, Ross Barenberg, James Bryan, Matt Glaser, Barry Mitterhoff, and Buddy Spicher. —*Chip Renner*

★ **By the Sweat of My Brow** / 1983 / Rounder 0200
A great record, which features "By the Sweat of My Brow," "Old and in the Way," "The Ballad of Ira Hayes," and "Your Greedy Heart." —*Chip Renner*

○ **Hard to Tell the Singer from The Song** / 1987 / Rounder 0226
Dickens covers Dylan's "Only a Hobo" and Dallas Frazier's "California Cottonfields." Jerry Douglas, Pat Enright, Roy Husky, Ross Barenberg, and Mike Compton back her up. —*Chip Renner*

Few Old Memories / Rounder 11529
Good songs. —*Mark A. Humphrey*

○ **Hazel & Alice** / Rounder 0027

Domestic Science Club

○ **Domestic Science Club** / 1994 / Discovery
A trio featuring Sarah Hickamn and the Dixie Chicks. Good energy and fun all around. —*Richard Meyer*

Kitty Donohoe

Vocals
A Michigan singer and songwriter. —*Richard Meyer*

As Sparks Fly Upward / 1990 / Roheen Records
Her lovely singing and precise playing are heard to best effect on the originals "Steady as a River" and "Emma Sutter." —*Richard Meyer*

● **Farmer in Florida** / Roheen 001

Connie Dover

Vocals, keyboard
Connie Dover is a Kansas City-based singer-songwriter. She is also the lead singer and keyboard player in the Celtic band Scartaglen. —*AMG*

● **Somebody** / Taylor Park Music 101
Vocalist with the American Celtic group Scartaglen, Connie's soaring, crystal-clear voice and sensitive interpretation of traditional songs make this 1991 release noteworthy. She is joined by instrumentalists from the Scots-Irish bands Silly Wizard, Capercaillie, and Boys of the Lough to create a collection of songs that spans the music of 1000 years. From the monasteries of eighth century Ireland to the Shenandoah River Valley, the album is a powerful testament to the elusive beauty of traditional Celtic music. —*Ladyslipper*

Barry Dow

Vocals
Barry Dow is a California singer and songwriter, a winner at the 1991 Kerrville Folk Festival (Emerging Songwriting Award). Dow's music combines contemporary folk with occasional ventures around the edges of ragtime and blues, all fingerpicked in an easy, rolling style. —*Chip Renner*

○ **Barry Dow's Urban Folk Tales** / Barry Dow Music
Dow's album is full of imagery dealing with love—love of whiskey, love of the West Coast and Pacific Ocean, and love of memories. His vocals are a cross between Jim Croce and Phil Ochs. Dow is an artist to watch for. —*Chip Renner*

Judy Dunaway

From rural Missisipi, Dunaway uses balloons, bottle brushes, and standard instruments for songs about monsters, nudity, death, and immigration. Her songs range in style from rock to salsa to country to blues to noise, suspended over irregular rhythms and forms that often incorporate free improvisation. This is experimental but not at all self-indulgent. —*Richard Meyer*

○ **Judy Dunaway** / 1990 / Lost 90141
Remarkable variety, "Missionary Kid" and "El Norte." —*Richard Meyer*

Richard Dyer-Bennett

Vocals

Dyer-Bennet began his performing career in 1934 and became one of the preeminent "concert folksingers" of his generation. His genteel interpretations did much to popularize old English and American ballads. —*Richard Meyer*

Ballads / 1970 / Stinson 35
The key song is "Spanish Is the Loving Tongue." —*Richard Meyer*

Twentieth Century Minstrel / 1980 / Decca 5045
Includes "The Devil and the Farmer's Wife," "Swapping Song," and "Eggs and Marrowbone." —*Richard Meyer*

● **Richard Dyer-Bennett—Vols. 1–7** / DYB 7000
These comprehensive collections of Dyer-Bennett form the most complete collection of his work. Recorded in the mid-to late '50s. —*Richard Meyer*

Cliff Eberhardt

Vocals, guitar

New York-based singer-songwriter Cliff Eberhardt combines a hoarse, expressive voice with a dynamic guitar style for some of the most moving music to be heard in the "new folk" music of the '80s and '90s. Though his debut album released in 1990, *The Long Road*, shows how stirring he can be, *The Songwriters Exchange*, a compilation made ten years earlier, shows he's been that good for a long time. —*William Ruhlmann*

● **Long Road** / 1990 / Windham Hill 1092
The debut from one of the best of the new crop of folksinger-songwriters. —*William Ruhlmann*

○ **Now You Are My Home** / 1993 / Sanachie/Cachet 8008
On his second release, Pennsylvania-born Eberhardt gets closer to the energy of his live sound with this well-produced album. He is joined by Patty Larkin, John Gorka, and Nanci Griffith. The collection is engaging all the way through to the driving "Make Me Believe." —*Richard Meyer*

Ed's Redeeming Qualities

Group

Quirky contemporary folk trio. Singing of distributor caps, lawn darts, and guys named Bob, Ed's Redeeming Qualities is responsible for two cleverly amusing albums that transcend genre limitations. Sharing vocals are violinist-guitarist Carrie Bradley, ukelele ace Dan Leone, and bongos-clarinet man Neno Perrotta (who also shakes a mean jar of rice). The San Francisco-based ERQ debuted on Flying Fish Records with "More Bad Times" in 1990 (the set is dedicated to Dom Leone, writer of "Buck Tempo," who died before its release), and encored with "It's All Good News," another delightfully off-the-wall 1991 collection. —*Bill Dahl*

○ **More Bad Times** / 1990 / Flying Fish 70549
Creative, low-fi folk with a silliness that is almost, but not quite, cloying. Humorous lyrics, with instruments like xylophones, ukeleles, and a coffee can. —*Robert Gordon*

Kat Eggleston

○ **Second Nature** / 1993 / Waterbug
Eggleston has a beautiful voice with a great deal of tenderness and strength, which she makes good use of on her song "Fury." "Home" and "Banks of Sweet Dundee" are excellent also. —*Richard Meyer*

Ramblin' Jack Elliott

b. Aug. 1, 1931, Brooklyn, NY
Vocals, guitar

Ramblin' Jack Elliott, who has been playing folk music since the '40s, is an important link between Woody Guthrie (Elliot's dominant influence) and the folk artists of the '60s and after. A repository of folk-blues, cowboy songs, and early country; an archivist; and an excellent performer. —*William Ruhlmann*

Ramblin' /
Ramblin' contains some of the songs he still performs with vitality '30 years later ("San Francisco Bay Blues," " Railroad Bill"). He was beginning to find his distinct voice as a performer on this disc. —*Richard Meyer*

★ **Essential Ramblin' Jack Elliott** / 1970 / Vanguard 89

Elliott was the complete folksinger of the '60s, singing and yodeling traditional material derived from folk, country, and blues sources and (especially) carrying on the tradition of Woody Guthrie. This two-pocket set, some of which is taken from a 1965 concert, provides a representative sampling of his repertoire and style. —*William Ruhlmann*

Sings Woody Guthrie & Jimmie Rodgers / 1976 / Monitor 380
Elliott devotes one side each to his two chief influences, re-creating Guthrie standards such as "Grand Coulee Dam" and "I Ain't Got No Home" as well as Rodgers favorites like "T for Texas" and "Waitin' for a Train." Not coincidentally, he brings out the similarities between them. —*William Ruhlmann*

○ **Hard Travelin'** / 1990 / Fantasy 24720

Country Style / Prestige 7804
Elliott knows how to tell a story as we hear on this album, which has him interpreting "Wabash Cannonball," "Wreck of the Old 97," and "Lovesick Blues." —*Richard Meyer*

Peter Elman

b. , Washington, DC
Piano, guitar

Elman was born in Washington, DC, and moved to California. He is a talented piano and guitar player. He has played with Roy Buchanan, Mike Marshall, Darol Anger, Lacy J. Dalton, and others. His music falls between folk and new age. —*Chip Renner*

○ **Durango Saloon** / 1990 / Acorn 004
There is a nice balance between Elman's piano and guitar playing and his brother Tony's hammer dulcimer. Flaco Jimenez's accordion and Pete Grant's pedal steel add nicely to the recording. Todd Phillips (bass), John Blakeley (guitar and dobro), Darol Anger (violin), and Jon Eriksen (harmonica and percussion) are all skilled musicians. This release has a real Western feel to it. —*Chip Renner*

Tony Elman

Hammer dulcimer

Elman is one of the better hammer dulcimer players around. He has sold over 400,000 copies of his recordings. His music is a combination of folk and new age. —*Chip Renner*

● **Winter Creek** / 1991 / Acorn 005
This is a beautiful album featuring traditional Christmas carols and winter tunes; however, it's one to enjoy all year round. Elman is a skilled hammer dulcimer player and is backed by his brother Peter (piano, guitar, and synthesizer), along with Mike Marshall (guitar, mandolin, and violin), Todd Phillips (string bass), Pete Grant (pedal steel, dobro, autoharp), Jon Eriksen (percussion, harmonica), Barry Phillips (cello), and the Arlekin String Quartet. All solid and well-crafted, it's a good buy. —*Chip Renner*

Shakin' Down the Acorns, Vol. 1 / Acorn Music

Shakin' Down the Acorns, Vol. 2 / Acorn Music

Michael Elwood

Vocals

Michael Elwood is a Texas-based singer-songwriter and a fine lyricist. —*Richard Meyer*

○ **Scarecrow's Prayer** / Agua Azul 22
Texas singer-songwriter Michael Elwood's debut showcases his thought-provoking lyrics and gentle vocals. His material ranges from "Who Am I to Say," a simple song to a child, to "One Too Many Questions," which addresses some of the dilemmas adults face. The folk ambiance expands on the title track, which moves to a rhythmic world beat. Cellist John Hagen, guitarist John Inmon, and violinist Susan Voelz add to the disc's rich sound. —*Roundup Newsletter*

Alejandro Escovedo

Formerly a member of the bands True Believers and Rank and File, Escovedo has released two fine solo albums. —*Richard Meyer*

● **Gravity** / 1992 / Watermelon 1007
He's got a sandpaper quality to his voice that gives credibility to these songs, many of which have an edge of danger or desperation. This is guitar-based music enhanced by dramatic arrangements making use of orchestral touches and a rockin' band.

"Broken Bottle" is like a beautiful chamber work. —*Richard Meyer*

○ **Thirteen Years** / 1993 /
Austin musician, Escovedo continues his development as a solo artist. After winning the 1993 Musician of the Year he has released another haunting great record. There are more string-oriented tunes. —*Richard Meyer*

Nancy Eversole

Nancy performs as the "Kentucky Woman" playing harp, mountain dulcimer, and guitar. She plays and sings in a hauntingly beautiful voice the old songs she learned from her family in the mountains of Kentucky. For many years Nancy has been a favorite at festivals throughout the Midwest. In recent years she has performed at Dollywood. Her songs are mostly old ballads, handed down for generations by members of her family. Beautiful. —*Don Stevens*

At Home W/Kentucky Woman / Kentucky Woman

Ballad Weaver / Kentucky Woman

Come By The Hills / Lemco

● **Kentucky Woman** / Kentucky Woman

John Fahey

b. Feb. 28, 1939, Cecil County, MD
Guitar
One of the greatest and certainly among the most influential acoustic guitarists in folk and popular music, Fahey started his own record label, Takoma, in 1959, to release his debut album, *The Transfiguration of Blind Joe Death*. He has since recorded 40 or more albums. A student of rural blues music, Fahey did a Ph.D. thesis on Charley Patton and incorporated the Delta blues into his increasingly eclectic style. Also important as a record company executive, Fahey recorded what he liked, resurrecting the career of Bukka White and taking on young protAgA Leo Kottke, who has never really escaped his influence. Nor have the army of new age guitarists of the '70s and beyond, many of whom sound like Fahey in isolated moments, though none can keep up with his musical ability and imagination. By now there are elements of almost all genres in his music, yet his playing remains his own. —*William Ruhlmann*

★ **Transfiguration of Blind Joe Death** / 1959 / Takoma 72715
This is the definitive work by this influential acoustic guitar master. —*William Ruhlmann*

○ **Great San Bernadino Birthday Party** / 1966 / Takoma 1008

Requia / 1967 / Vanguard 79259
Originally released on Vanguard in 1967, *Requia* is a very contemplative album of Fahey guitar instrumentals. Titles include "Requiem for John Hurt," "Requiem for Russell Blaine Cooper," "When the Catfish Is in Bloom," "Requiem for Molly (Parts 1-4)," and the hymn, "Fight on Christians, Fight." Produced by Samuel Charters. —*Roundup Newsletter*

Fare Forward Voyagers (Soldier's Choice) / 1974 / Shanachie 99005
This 1973 release features three compositions by guitarist John Fahey. In addition to the title track, the tunes are: "When the Fire and the Rose Are One" and "Thus Krishna on the Battlefield." —*Roundup Newsletter*

○ **Fahey, Leo Kottke, Peter Lang** / 197z / Takoma 1040

Railroad / 1983 / Shanachie 99003
Ten solo acoustic pieces from the unique perspective of guitarist John Fahey. Titles include "Enigmas and Perplexities of the Norfolk and Western," "Delta Dog through the Book of Revelation," and "Summer Cat By My Door." —*Roundup Newsletter*

Old Girlfriends & Other / 1992 / Varrick 031
John Fahey, whose seminal solo guitar albums led the way for a zillion other guitar players, has made another fine one himself. All his trademark elements are here, eclectic song choices, dark and precise playing, and a sense of fun. "Twilight Time" and "Sea of Love" are particularly memorable. —*Richard Meyer*

Mimi Farina

b. Apr. 30, 1945, CA
Vocals

Mimi Farina, Joan Baez's younger sister, first got into performing professionally in partnership with her husband, novelist and songwriter Richard Farina, whom she married in 1963. Singing harmony, the couple released two remarkable albums on Vanguard, *Celebrations for a Grey Day* in 1965 and *Reflections in a Crystal Wind* (1966), before Richard was killed in a motorcycle accident. Mimi Farina was 21.

She subsequently released an album of the duo's outtakes, *Memories.* (The two albums made during Richard's lifetime were reissued as a best-of twofer.) In the late '60s, Farina, based in California, worked with the couple and began to write her own songs. She reemerged on record in 1971 on *Take Heart*, a duo album with Tom Jans that included her tribute song to Janis Joplin, "In the Quiet Morning." (This and other songs of hers were also recorded by her sister.)

In the '70s, Farina founded Bread & Roses, a charity organization devoted to putting on musical performances in hospitals and prisons. Several of the organization's annual benefit concerts, featuring some of the biggest names in folk and popular music, have been recorded and released. In 1985, Farina finally released a solo album, appropriately entitled *Solo*, and undertook a national tour. —*William Ruhlmann*

★ **Best of Mimi and Richard Farina** / 1970 / Vanguard 21-22
The brilliant novelist, singer, and songwriter Richard Farina died young, but not before recording two great albums with his wife, Mimi, that are combined here. —*William Ruhlmann*

Solo / 1985 / Philo 1102

Fiction Brothers

Group
Alan Senauke (guitar) and Howie Tarnower (guitar, banjo, and mandolin) play a blend of bluegrass to blues. —*Chip Renner*

Country Cooking with the Fiction Brothers / 1984 / Flying Fish 27019
A fine recording from this new bluegrass group. —*AMG*

● **Things Are Coming My Way** / 1984 / Flying Fish 204
Very good old-time music with a new-time freshness. Featuring Tony Trischka, Kenny Kasek, and Matt Glaser. —*Chip Renner*

Sally Fingerette

Vocal
Ohio resident Sally Fingerette has a polished style for her personal songs. She tours on her own and with the Four Bitchin' Babes. She consistently well-produced solo albums have many lovely songs, most notably "Home Is Where the Heart Is." —*Richard Meyer*

● **Unraveled** / 1990 / Ams 798
A woman of many identities, Sally's also known as one of the "Four Bitchin' Babes," and should be considered Shawn Colvin's stylistic soul sister. . . . Her ten original songs explore the landscape of the myriad of relationships, whether it's enjoying the nostalgia of an old flame ("Smilin' Boy"), realizing the nature of her love for her child ("The Return"), or what sounds like the lament of anyone's parents ("He Loved Her So," "The Ballad of Harry and Esther"). . . . All in all, the treatment is tender and feeling, the music beautiful, and her voice warm and inviting. —*Ladyslipper*

Five Chinese Brothers

Group
The Five Chinese Brothers are not Chinese or brothers. What they are is a five-piece band that plays a combination of folk, rock, and country. The New York-based band is made up of Tom Meltzer (lead vocals, acoustic guitar), Paul Foglino (bass), Charlie Shaw (drums), Neil Thomas (accordion, piano, vocals), and Kevin Trainor (lead guitar, vocals). —*Chip Renner*

○ **Singer, Songwriter, Beggarman, Thief** / 1992 / (Independent)
After some remixing of their indie cassette and the addition of a few tracks, Five Chinese Brothers have released their first album after ten years of the New York scene. Tom Meltzer and Paul Foglino handle the writing, separately, though their styles complement each other so well you'd think they were a team. These songs have open-hearted humor, and the performances are tight but animated with a very live feeling. This is a great record that captures the fun of the band live but with the precision of a stu-

dio. Not a bad cut on this record; it's a must have. —*Richard Meyer*

Folk Like Us

Group

A traditional band featuring Debra Bagwell (flute, piccolo, pennywhistle, recorder, piano), Johnny Carlisle (guitar, five-string banjo), Doug Reid (fiddle), David Shaw (string bass, tenor banjo), Mark Shelton (hammer dulcimer, bodhran bones, snare drum, spoons), Dave Yonley (fiddle), and special guest Beth Shelton on oboe. —*Chip Renner*

○ **Spring Dance** / 1992 / North Star 29
A fine collection of reels, polkas, jigs, and traditional standards. If you enjoy traditional instruments played to perfection, pick up this CD. —*Chip Renner*

Kim Forehand

○ **Kim Forehand** / 1992 / Heartland
This Kansas artist has a lighthearted, agreeable style and writes songs that take hard issues and treat them with generosity and openness, as in "Cinderella's Song," "Greenhouse Effect," and "The Drifter." —*Richard Meyer*

Stephen Foster

b. Jul. 4, 1826, **d.** Jan. 13, 1864
An American songwriter of hundreds of popular songs like "Jeannie with the Light Brown Hair" (1854), "My Old Kentucky Home" (1853), "Oh! Susanna" (1848), and "Camptown Races" (1850). —*AMG*

○ **Songs of** / Columbia/Legacy 332

Fotheringay

Group

A short-lived offshoot of Fairport Convention, featuring key member and leader Sandy Denny. A second album was planned but never completed; tracks from it turn up on the triple-CD Denny anthology *Who Knows Where the Time Goes*. This is far more interesting and beguiling than their work with Fairport Convention, especially the Bob Dylan songs, but it lacks Fairport's precision and focus. —*Bruce Eder & William Ruhlmann*

○ **Fotheringay** / 1970 / Carthage 4426
Also featured are Trevor Lucas and Jerry Donahue, both of whom eventually joined Fairport when Denny rejoined. The album is a close relative of Denny's other solo and group work and features several of her flowing ballads, showcasing her lovely voice. A footnote, but a pleasing one. —*Bruce Eder & William Ruhlmann*

Kinky Friedman (Richard Friedman)

b. Oct. 31, 1944, Palatine, TX
Vocal
Texas-born Richard "Kinky" Friedman operated on the outer fringe of the "outlaw" country movement of the '70s, forming a band called the Texas Jewboys and performing highly satiric country-rock material. He has since written successful detective novels. —*William Ruhlmann*

○ **Sold American** / 1973 / Vanguard 79333
A renegade figure who often stresses the outrageous. The title song is a gem. Part of the '70s country-folk-rock wave. —*Hank Davis*

● **Lasso from El Paso** / 1976 / Epic 34304
Of the many albums that grew out of Bob Dylan's *Rolling Thunder Revue*, this must be the strangest. Friedman has a husky voice and an off-kilter sense of humor best captured on the live-from-the-revue track, "Sold American." Also notable for a version of the Bob Dylan outtake, "Catfish." —*William Ruhlmann*

Annie Gallup

○ **Cause and Effect** / 1994 / Flying Hair
This Seattle singer-songwriter has made an album of very personal songs that are filled with a woman's reveries in a voice reminiscent of Jane Gillman. There are some tasteful instrumental embellishments on this release. The album as a whole has a smokey, late-night quality. This album was produced by the late Bruce Paskow of the Washington Squares. —*Richard Meyer*

Jim Gaudet

Albany-based singer-songwriter Jim Gaudet began writing in his 30's after a long hiatus building a family life and playing in the local Lost Country Ramblers before that. Now he tours the Northeast performing his own witty and heartfelt material. Before the release of *Its a Colorful Life* Jim released three independent cassettes. —*Richard Meyer*

○ **Its A Colorful Life** / 1994 / 1-800 Prime
This 15-cut CD offers a combination of studio and live cuts that offer a strong selection of his material. He has songs of social awareness like "In Real Life" and the lighthearted title track, "Phone in My Car." This is essentially a solo direct to two-track record with occasional fiddle and harmonies. —*Richard Meyer*

Paul Geremia

Guitar
A bluesy acoustic guitarist with a new age sound. —*Chip Renner*

● **I Really Don't Mind Livin'** / 1982 / Flying Fish 270
A good selection of blues songs, all written by Geremia. Highly recommended. —*Chip Renner*

My Kinda Place / 1986 / Flying Fish 70395
Geremia covers Leadbelly, Blind Willie McTell, Lonnie Johnson, and Blind Lemon Jefferson. Some fine playing. —*Chip Renner*

Bob Gibson

b. Nov. 16, 1931, New York, NY
Guitar, banjo
Gibson and Hamilton Camp were one of the most popular folk duets in the '60s, touring the world with unique song stylings accompanied by Gibbon's near virtuoso 12-string guitar and banjo playing. Thirty years after the folk boom, the duo got together for a reunion concert celebrating Chicago's Gate of Horn nightclub. The songs include all the tunes from the original 1961 release "Gibson and Camp at the Gate of Horn," plus their "must" songs "Well, Well, Well," "You Can Tell the World about This," and "For Lovin' Me." —*Allan Shaw*

● **Revisited** / Folk Era
A must for every serious fan of the popular folk era. —*Mike Fleischer*

○ **Carnegie Concert** / 1957 / Riverside 12-816

○ **I Come for to Sing** / 1957 / Riverside 12-806

○ **There's a Meetin' Here Tonight** / 1959 / Riverside 1111

○ **Homemade Music** / 1978 / Mountain Railroad 52781
Bob and Hamilton Camp—featuring several Shel Silverstein songs and a Steve Goodman cover "Lookin' for Trouble." —*Chip Renner*

Perfect High / 1980 / Mountain Railroad 52794
Bob cowrites with Shel Silverstein and Tom Paxton. —*Chip Renner*

Uptown Saturday Night / 1984 / Hogeye 005
A good record, featuring "Tequila Sheila" and the title track, "Uptown Saturday Night." —*Chip Renner*

Eliza Gilkyson

Vocals
Daughter of singer and songwriter Terry Gilkyson (who hit with "Marianne" in 1957), Eliza Gilkyson has made three albums; the first, *Love from the Heart*, was under the name Lisa Gilkyson. —*William Ruhlmann*

● **Pilgrims** / 1987 / Gold Castle 71307
Said to be concerned with "Jungian archetypes," this album can be enjoyed for the impassioned singing, song structures that sometimes recall Joni Mitchell at her most accessible, and the ethereal instrumental backgrounds that got the album tagged "new age" upon release. —*William Ruhlmann*

Legends of Rainmaker / 1989 / Gold Castle 71323
More directly autobiographical and issue-oriented material (including Gilkyson's version of her song "Rosie Strike Back," done earlier by Rosanne Cash) played with more of a backbeat characterizes this striking follow-up to *Pilgrims*. —*William Ruhlmann*

Jane Gillman

Vocals, guitar, harmonica, dulcimer

Gillman is a DC-based singer-songwriter who performs nationally in a play about Woody Guthrie. She plays guitar, harmonica, and dulcimer and is known for her well-crafted songwriting. —*Richard Meyer & Chip Renner*

Pick It Up / 1970 / Green Linnet 1068
A great debut album. Gilman plays some good cross-picking guitar and is backed by Lyle Lovett and Mark O'Connor. —*Chip Renner*

● **Jane Gillman** / 1980 / Green Linnet 2101
A beautifully produced album. Mary Chapin Carpenter, Marcy Marxer, Lucy Kaplansky, John Gorka, Nina Gerber, and Seamus Egan back Gillman up. There is something about her vocals that catches you. Gillman's songwriting is top-notch, especially on songs such as "Listen to the Thunder," "Three Quarters," and the '90s folk view of romance in the pop '60s, "Song on the Radio." —*Chip Renner*

Neal Gladstone

Vocals
Gladstone is a singer-songwriter from Oregon who uses humor in his brand of folk-rock. —*Chip Renner*

○ **Sleep Neat** / 1988 / Kaleidoscope 28
Gladstone likes to use humor in his songs to get you thinking. "Get Cloned" is about the uses of personal clones, "Country ClichA" hits the old country music industry for its songwriting clichAs, and "Dodge Dart" is about that old indestructible car—all great songs. The music style is more rock-pop. —*Chip Renner*

Jeff Gold

○ **Streets Cracked** / 1993 / Miracle Baby Producti
A New Yorker, part of the fast folk community in the '80s transplanted to LA, Jeff Gold has released an independant album of his songs, including the beautiful "Three Strangers." Production is simple, and the songs are relaxed and inviting. —*Richard Meyer*

Good Ol' Persons

Group
The Good Ol' Persons are a California-based bluegrass band. The band is currently made up of Kathy Kallick (guitar), Sally VanMeter (dobro), John Reischman (mandolin), Kevin Wimmer (fiddle), and Bethany Raine (bass). They play a more contemporary bluegrass style with good rich vocals. Laurie Lewis was a member of the band in the mid-'70s. —*Chip Renner*

● **Anywhere the Wind Blows** / 1986 / Kaleidoscope 38
○ **I Can't Stand to Ramble** / 1986 / Kaleidoscope 17
○ **Part of a Story** / Kaleidoscope 26

Cynthia Gooding

A major interpreter of folk songs from around the world in their original language and translation. —*Richard Meyer*

● **Best of Cynthia Gooding** / Prestige 13010
Early English Folk Songs / Elektra 131

Steve Goodman

b. Jul. 25, 1948, Chicago, IL, d. Sep. 20, 1984
Vocals
Chicago-based singer-songwriter Steve Goodman made a number of excellent albums on Buddah, Asylum, and his own Red Pajamas Records before his premature death from leukemia. His best-known song was "The City of New Orleans," which was a hit for Arlo Guthrie and was recorded by many others. —*William Ruhlmann*

○ **Steve Goodman** / 1972 / Buddah 5096
The debut of a great new songwriter. —*William Ruhlmann*

Somebody Else's Troubles / 1973 / Buddah 5121
Another great mixture of ballads ("The Dutchman") and fun songs ("Somebody Else's Troubles"). —*Richard Meyer*

Jessie's Jig & Other Favorites / 1975 / Asylum 1037
Has Michael Smith's "Spoon River," "Door Number Three," and the rave-up "Mama Don't Allow." —*Richard Meyer*

Unfinished Business / 1975 / Red Pajamas 5
Released posthumously after Goodman's death from leukemia, it contains "A Fool Such as I," "My Funny Valentine," and "The Whispering Man." A sweet, more subdued collection. —*Richard Meyer*

Words We Can Dance To / 1976 / Asylum 1061
A good collection of mostly Goodman originals, along with rockers like "Tossin' and Turnin'." —*Richard Meyer*

○ **Say It in Private** / 1977 / Asylum 1118
A full-blown studio affair with chestnuts like "Is It True What They Say about Dixie" and wonderful originals like "The Twentieth Century Is Almost Over." —*Richard Meyer*

Hot Spot / 1980 / Asylum 297
He may have been trying to be more mainstream with this LP, but the great "Sdrawkcab klat (Talk Backwards)" shows that his sense of fun can rise to new heights. —*Richard Meyer*

○ **Artistic Hair** / 1983 / Red Pajamas 1
Goodman achieved artistic control with this album, featuring his "City of New Orleans" and other classics. —*William Ruhlmann*

○ **Tribute to Steve Goodman** / 1985 / Mobile Fidelity 854
Affordable Art / 198z / Red Pajamas 2
This one features "A Dying Cub Fan's Last Request" and "Watchin' Joey Glow." —*William Ruhlmann*

Best of Asylum Years, Vol. 2 / Red Pajamas 7
● **Best of the Asylum Years, Vol. 1** / Red Pajamas 006

John Gorka

Vocals
This perceptive, husky-voiced singer-songwriter spent the early '80s hustling around the Northeast folk circuit and then won the Kerrville Folk Festival's New Folk award in 1984. He has since recorded four albums. —*William Ruhlmann*

○ **I Know** / 1987 / Red House 18
Still some of his best work, including "Blues Palace," "Downtown Tonight," and "Down in the Milltown." —*Richard Meyer*

○ **Land of the Bottom Line** / Jun. 8, 1992 / Windham Hill 1089
Keen observations and an earnest performance style mark Gorka as a major new folk talent. —*William Ruhlmann*

Jack's Crows / Dec. 8, 1992 / High Street 10309
The songwriting is particularly strong on this album. His ballad of the Marines and his father demonstrates how he can handle the most sentimental subjects well. "Silence," the first cut, is a crystalline beauty, and "Where the Bottles Break" is a rockin' song about personal convictions and the real estate business. —*Richard Meyer*

Out of the Valley / May 10, 1994 / High Street Records
On this, Gorka's fifth album, he continues the steady stream of bluesy and lyrical songs. Produced by John Jennings, this CD has a larger more filled out sound than any release since his debut. His songwriting has remained consistent in quality and style. —*Richard Meyer*

Green Grass Cloggers

Group
A mountain dance troup. —*Charles S. Wolfe*

○ **Through the Ears** / 1988 / Rounder 0228
A splendid collection of never-before-released tracks by many of the old-time country groups who toured with or performed with the Cloggers. —*Charles S. Wolfe*

Robin Greenstein

Vocals
A New York singer-songwriter and interpreter with a light jazz sensibility. —*Richard Meyer*

○ **Slow Burn** / Windy 216
Her beautiful song "When You Leave Amsterdam" is here. —*Richard Meyer*

Clive Gregson & Christine Collister

Group
Clive Gregson and Christine Collister were the most moving U.K. folk-rock duo to emerge since Richard and Linda Thompson. Gregson (b. 1955) was the founder of Any Trouble, a rock quartet, in Manchester in 1975. The band's sound, and Gregson's songwriting and singing, reminded some of Elvis Costello, and Any Trouble was signed by Stiff, Costello's label. The band made sev-

eral well-remembered but poor-selling albums and then split up. Gregson made a solo album, *Strange Persuasions*, in 1985 and then hooked up with Collister. Gregson first introduced Collister into Richard Thompson's band (Gregson was backup guitarist at the time) and then they began performing as a duo. The duo's first release was a homemade tape sold at gigs and later released as *Home and Away*. It was followed by their first formal album, *Mischief*, in 1988 and by a *Change in the Weather* in 1990. *Love is a Strange Hotel*, released later the same year, was an album of cover versions of Gregson and Collister's favorite songs. Their songs, all written by Gregson, are wry tales of the ins and outs of love, sung in Collister's heartbreaking voice. *—William Ruhlmann*

○ **Home & Away** / 1986 / Flying Fish 0473
A collection of songs recorded during an early acoustic tour in 1986. The duo run through new originals, some songs from Gregson's Any Trouble days, and a few well-chosen covers in a warm, intimate setting. *—Chris Woodstra*

○ **Mischief** / 1987 / Rhino 70842
Clive Gregson's songs treat romance with ironic charm: "We're Not Over Yet" is a compendium of reasons why they ought to be over, and "Everybody Cheats on You" is about more than just romantic infidelity. Christine Collister gives the songs a depth that often keeps them from being a bit too glib and clever, as do the folk-pop arrangements. *—William Ruhlmann*

Love Is a Strange Hotel / 1990 / Rhino 70961
A departure from the expansive arrangements of the previous two albums, *Love Is A Strange Hotel*, is a low key acoustic collection of covers. Even unlikely choices, like Aztec Camera's "How Men Are," and 10cc's "Things We Do for Love" are pulled off in their own charming way. *—Chris Woodstra*

● **Change in the Weather** / 1990 / Rhino 70914
The self-insight continues in Gregson's lyrics, but the concerns are expanded. Collister does a fine job covering "Tryin' to Get to You." *—William Ruhlmann*

○ **Last Word** / 1992 / Rhino 70282
Gregson and Collister have perfected their now classic sound on their final effort. Their extraordinary harmonies have never sounded better on Gregson's moody songs mixing folk, jazz, country, and blues. *—Chris Woodstra*

Stefan Grossman

b. Apr. 16, 1945
Guitar
Stefan Grossman is a student of the folk, blues, and ragtime styles of the Reverend Gary Davis (with whom he studied) and a variety of other performers. He has become a virtuoso guitarist, as is demonstrated by numerous recordings and concert appearances. *—William Ruhlmann*

● **Shining Shadows** / 1988 / Shanachie 97020
Stirring guitar instrumentals. *—William Ruhlmann*

Arlo Guthrie

b. Jul. 10, 1947
Vocals, guitar
Like his father Woody Guthrie, Arlo Guthrie has carved out a career as a folksinger and songwriter with a social conscience who leavens political messages with humor. Though Woody Guthrie was hospitalized for much of Arlo's youth, the youngster nevertheless grew up in a musical community that included Pete Seeger, Leadbelly, and Cisco Houston. He learned to play the guitar at age six and was performing in coffeehouses by his late teens.

Guthrie's early fame was based on his anti-Establishment shaggy-dog story in song, "Alice's Restaurant," actually a comic monolog about the singer's troubles with the police and the draft board that was extremely timely when it appeared on record in 1967. The *Alice's Restaurant* album became Guthrie's only gold record, but he made a series of folk-rock records through the '70s, filling them with his own songs and those of his contemporaries, notably Steve Goodman's "The City of New Orleans," which became Guthrie's sole hit single in 1972.

Guthrie's commercial fortunes, like those of most folkies, declined by the end of the '70s, and he made his last album for Warner Bros. in 1981. Since then, he has launched his own label,

Rising Son, which has reissued his Warner's albums and released his new recordings. He continues to tour extensively and to work for such causes as environmentalism. *—William Ruhlmann*

★ **Alice's Restaurant** / 1967 / Warner Brothers 6267
In 1967 when this LP came out it was totally radical, directly political, and so deliciously funny that it deflated a great deal of the seriousness of the growing antiwar movement. In this one stroke Arlo established himself as more than the son of the famous man and major star. Aside from the title cut people often forget about the "Motorcycle Song" and "Chillin' of the Evening," which were on side two. *—Richard Meyer*

Arlo / 1968 / Rising Son 6299
On this LP Arlo continued his monologue with and extended "Motorcycle Song" and other originals. *—Richard Meyer*

Washington County / 1970 / Reprise 6411
This album is more homey and roots flavored, with cuts like "Valley to Pray" with Doc Watson, and "Lay Down Little Doggies." A good relaxed effort. *—Richard Meyer*

○ **Hobo's Lullaby** / 1972 / Rising Son 2060
Contains his hit version of "City of New Orleans" and "1913 Massacre." *—Richard Meyer*

Last of the Brooklyn Cowboys / 1973 / Rising Son 2124
A strong collection with good versions of "Ramblin' Round," "Gypsy Davey," "Love Sick Blues" and "Gates of Eden." *—Richard Meyer*

○ **Together in Concert** / 1975 / Reprise 2214
Separately and together, Arlo Guthrie and Pete Seeger delight in a live setting. *—William Ruhlmann*

○ **Amigo** / 1976 / Rising Son 2239
An excellent, rocking collection, including Guthrie's adaptation of "Guabi, Guabi," a song about Victor Jara, and a knockabout cover of the Rolling Stones song "Connection." *—William Ruhlmann*

○ **Best of Arlo Guthrie** / 1977 / Warner Brothers 3117
This includes "Alice's Restaurant," the equally comic "Motorcycle Song," "Coming into Los Angeles," and "City of New Orleans." *—William Ruhlmann*

● **Precious Friend** / 1982 / Warner Brothers 3644
A second excellent collection by Pete Seeger and Arlo Guthrie, veterans of two generations. *—William Ruhlmann*

Woody Guthrie

b. Jul. 14, 1912, **d.** Oct. 3, 1967
Vocals, harmonica
Woody Guthrie was the most important American folk music artist of the first half of the 20th century. Coming out of Oklahoma, Guthrie had firsthand knowledge of the dustbowl diaspora chronicled in John Steinbeck's novel, *The Grapes of Wrath*. In fact, Guthrie wrote his own version of the story in the song "Tom Joad." By the time he gained recognition in the '40s, Guthrie had written hundreds of songs, many of which remain folk standards to this day. When he was interviewed by Alan Lomax for the Library of Congress in March 1940, Guthrie punctuated his reminiscences by singing "So Long, It's Been Good to Know You," "Dust Bowl Blues," "Do-Re-Mi," "Pretty Boy Floyd," "I Ain't Got No Home," and others. He later wrote "Pastures of Plenty," "The Grand Coulee Dam," and his masterpiece, "This Land Is Your Land." He was also an author (*Bound for Glory*) and a newspaper columnist.

Guthrie made some recordings for RCA in 1940, but much of his work was issued on the small Folkways label. Meanwhile, in the late '40s and early '50s, versions of his songs became hits for such artists as the Weavers. By then, Guthrie himself was in physical decline, suffering from a hereditary paralytic disease. But during his long illness, Guthrie's influence spread to the next generation, fostering the folk boom of the late '50s and early '60s. Not only is Bob Dylan unimaginable without him, but also large segments of popular music are permanently affected by his concerns as a songwriter and his approach to the form. Guthrie also composed a body of children's music toward the end of his performing career in the early '50s, when he was raising a family with his wife Marjorie. The songs, many sung from a child's point of view, have been covered and performed extensively since. *—William Ruhlmann*

○ **Sings Folk Songs** / 1962 / Smithsonian/Folkways 40007

Guthrie sings traditional material here, with Leadbelly and others. —*William Ruhlmann*

☆ **Dust Bowl Ballads** / 1964 / Rounder 1040
His classic Okie songs, "Talking Dust Bowl Blues," "Do-Re-Mi," and more. —*William Ruhlmann*

☆ **Library of Congress Recordings—Vols. 1-3** / 1964 / Rounder 1041
A multidisc set of songs and conversations from 1940. —*William Ruhlmann*

☆ **This Land Is Your Land** / 1967 / Smithsonian/Folkways 31001
The title track and some of the Columbia River songs. —*William Ruhlmann*

Struggle / 1976 / Smithsonian/Folkways 40025
This album features Woody Guthrie, Cisco Houston, and Pete Seeger playing political songs, including "The Dying Miner," "Ludlow Massacre," and "Union Burying Ground." It's an energetic album. —*Richard Meyer*

Columbia River Collection / 1988 / Rounder 1036
An intelligent reconstruction of Guthrie's Columbia River songs, including "Grand Coulee Dam" and "Pastures of Plenty." —*William Ruhlmann*

Chuck Hall
Songwriter
A Boston-area writer of quite graceful, direct songs about day-to-day life. —*Richard Meyer*

○ **One Night in a Cheap Hotel** / Cheap Hotel Music 101
"Dollmaker's Secret" is a key cut. —*Richard Meyer*

Kristen Hall
Atlanta-based singer-songwriter, Kristen Hall has built a strong reputation in folk circles with her infectious Indigo Girls style of acoustic folk-rock. Her raspy-voiced delivery of highly personal lyrics are the center of attention, often accompanied only by acoustic guitar. While her first album, released independently, consisted of minimalistic arrangements of nearly demo quality, subsequent releases have been bigger productions featuring high-profile guests such as Emily Saliers of Indigo Girls, Cindy Wilson of the B-52s, and Jules Shear. —*Chris Woodstra*

● **Fact and Fiction** / 1991 / Daemon 5053
This mainly acoustic album ranges from introspective ballads to catchy upbeat folk-rock anthems. Hall's world-weary voice, both rough and delicate, tells reflective tales of yearning and love lost while retaining an uplifting spirit. Guests include Emily Sailers (Indigo Girls) and Cindy Wilson (B-52s). —*Chris Woodstra*

○ **Be Careful What You Wish For** / 1994 / High Street Records
Kristen Hall has a gutsy voice that never sounds forced. The rocking guitar-based arrangements have a sound not unlike some of John Hiatt's recent records. These are very personal songs, some with political centers, such as "Proud Man," sung with commitment and deep emotion. The opening cut, "Cry Tomorrow" sets the tone of the album and she maintains the drive and quality through to the end. —*Richard Meyer*

Real Life Stuff / Dog Gone 5055
An outstanding independent release from this Atlanta-based singer-songwriter. Her debut, a self-produced low-key folk album centered around Hall's raspy voice and guitar, gives the blueprint for her later releases. Well worth seeking out. —*Chris Woodstra*

Butch Hancock
b. Jul. 12, 1945, Lubbock, TX
Vocals, guitar
An obscure, legendary Texas songwriter whose work has been covered by Jerry Jeff Walker and Joe Ely, Hancock has a gift for wordplay and nuance. The songs become gradually more accessible, as the tentative voice-and-guitar approach is replaced by surprisingly full folk-rock settings and assured singing. —*William Ruhlmann*

Firewater / 1981 / Rainlight 100
Off-the-cuff versions of Butch's classics are here, including "The Wind's Dominion," and "If You Were a Bluebird." The band includes Jimmy Dale Gilmore. —*Richard Meyer*

Yella Rose with Marce Lacoutre / 1985 / Rainlight 13711

This album has a rather big band with occasional horns, congas, and accordion, Marce Lacouture songs on the title cut. A good one. —*Richard Meyer*

● **Own & Own** / 1989 / Sugar Hill 1036
This compilation is culled from Hancock's many albums on his own Rainlight label from 1978 to 1987 (plus four tracks from 1989). —*William Ruhlmann*

Live in Australia / 1990 / Virgin
An energetic live album of duets by Hancock and Gilmore recorded in Sydney in 1990. The Flatlander hit "Dallas" is here and other ragged but right cuts from these musical pals. —*Richard Meyer*

○ **No Two Alike** / Rainlight
This 14-tape series (available by subscription only) is a document of six nights at the Cactus Cafe, where Butch performed with a host of great guests and never repeated a single one of his songs. —*Richard Meyer*

Tim Hardin
b. Dec. 23, 1941, Eugene, OR, d. Dec. 29, 1980
Vocals, guitar
Tim Hardin brought a trancelike personal touch to the songs he wrote, though in the hands of others they became more accessible pop hits, notably "If I Were a Carpenter" and "Reason to Believe." Hardin's own music spanned folk and jazz, and his talent belied his uneven career. —*William Ruhlmann*

○ **Tim Hardin I** / 1966 / MGM

○ **Tim Hardin Ii** / 1967 / MGM

○ **3-Live in Concert** / Jan. 1969 / Verve 3049
A great live recording that captures Hardin at his peak as a performer. —*Kenneth M. Cassidy*

● **Reason to Believe** / 1970 / PolyGram 833954
The early work of a top-flight '60s singer-songwriter includes the title track, "If I Were a Carpenter," and "Misty Roses." Great stuff. —*Kenneth M. Cassidy & William Ruhlmann*

Bird on a Wire / 1971 / Columbia 30551
His last new American release, and a good one. —*Kenneth M. Cassidy*

○ **Shock of Grace** / 1981 / CBS 37164
His best from the '70s, including "Bird on a Wire" and "First Love Song." —*William Ruhlmann*

○ **Tim Hardin Memorial Album** / 1981 / Polygram

● **Hang on to a Dream—the Verve Recordings** / Feb. 22, 1994 / Polydor Records
Double-CD set of 47 tracks that Hardin recorded for Verve between 1964 and 1966. His expressive, blues-inflected vocals and confessional songwriting are heard on covers and famous compositions like "If I Were a Carpenter," "Lady Came from Baltimore," and "Reason to Believe." The compilation includes every studio recording that Hardin released on the Verve label, as well as two alternate takes and 15 previously unreleased tracks. —*Richie Unterberger*

Jack Hardy
b. 1948
Songwriter
Jack Hardy has been a central figure in folk music since his arrival in Greenwich Village in 1978. Instrumental in founding The Songwriter's Exchange, The SpeakEasy Musician's co-op, and *The Fast Folk Musical Magazine*, Hardy has released nine albums domestically on his Great Divide label. Considered a writer's writer, he is known for politics in his songs, Americanized Irish influences, and a preoccupation with mythological imagery, mixed up with standard New York folk & roll. —*Richard Meyer*

○ **Mirror of My Madness** / 1976 / Great Divide 1760
New York urban folk-rock period. Includes "The Tailor" and "Go Tell the Savior." —*Richard Meyer*

Landmark / 1980 / Great Divide 1762
These two albums (*The Nameless One, Landmark*) show Hardy's Irish influence and some of his best work, including "The Tinker's Coin," "Orphan from Madrid," and "The Inner Man." —*Richard Meyer*

● **White Shoes** / 1982 / Great Divide 1763

A brilliant collection of songs by this husky-voiced founder of New York's "Fast Folk" movement. —*William Ruhlmann*

Cauldron / 1984 / Great Divide 1767
Politically charged and neo-traditional originals, adeptly performed. —*William Ruhlmann*

Hunter / 1986 / Great Divide 1769
An excellent example of Hardy's various lyric preoccupations. Includes "Dublin Farewell" and "The Changing Wind." —*Richard Meyer*

Civil Wars / 1994 / Great Divide
These songs describe civil wars of all sorts, political, domestic, and artistic. Highlights are "The 111th Pennsylvane" and "Double-Edged Sword." Recorded direct to DAT, the album has an intimate, immediate mood that is perfectly suited to these often very personal songs. —*Richard Meyer*

Kim & Reggie Harris

From school programs to major folk festivals and huge concert halls, from Chicago Stadium to church social halls, Kim & Reggie Harris have been delighting audiences for years. Their songs come to us in the spirit of Phil Ochs, Richie Havens, Bob Dylan, and David Roth. The central message is one of hope, love, and unity done with a musicality and vocal power that compels attention. This husband-wife team sparkles on everything from traditional spirituals and "Underground Railroad" songs to stunning originals and interpretations of well-known material. —*Allan Shaw*

○ **In The Heat of the Summer** / Folk Era
A musical message that everyone can join. —*Mike Fleischer*

Richie Havens (Richard Pierce Havens)

b. Jan. 21, 1941, Brooklyn, NY
Vocals, guitar
Born in the Bedford-Stuyvesant section of Brooklyn, Richie Havens moved to Greenwich Village in 1961 in time to get in on the folk boom then taking place. Havens had a distinctive style as a folksinger, appearing in such clubs as the Cafe Wha? His guitar set to an opening tuning, he would strum it while barring chords with his thumb, using it essentially as percussion while singing rhythmically in a gruff voice for a mesmerizing effect. Havens was signed to Douglas Records in 1965 and recorded two albums that gained him a local following. In 1967 the Verve division of MGM Records formed a folk section (Verve Forecast) and signed Havens and other folk-based performers. The result was Havens's third album, *Mixed Bag*. It wasn't until 1968 and the *Something Else Again* album, however, that Havens began to hit the charts—actually, Havens's fourth, third, and second albums charted that year, in that order. In 1969 came the double album *Richard P. Havens 1983*.

Havens's career benefited enormously from his appearance at the Woodstock festival in 1969 and his subsequent featured role in the movie and album made from the concert in 1970. His first album after that exposure, *Alarm Clock*, made the Top 30 and produced a Top 20 single in "Here Comes the Sun." These recordings were Havens's commercial high-water mark, but by this time he had become an international touring success. By the end of the '70s, he had abandoned recording and turned entirely to live work.

Havens came back to records with a flurry of releases in 1987: a new album, *Simple Things;* an album of Bob Dylan and Beatles covers; and a compilation. In 1991, Havens signed his first major label deal in 15 years, when he moved to Sony Music and released *Now*. —*William Ruhlmann*

○ **Mixed Bag** / 1967 / PolyGram 835210
Havens's first major label album, and his best, featuring his distinctive interpretations of such songs as Dylan's "Just Like a Woman" and the scathing antiwar anthem "Handsome Johnny." (It should be noted that, while it is his best overall collection, *Mixed Bag* is also a characteristic album: If you like it, you'll probably like other Havens records, which adopt much the same style.) —*William Ruhlmann*

Collection / 1987 / Rykodisc 20036
A compilation of Havens's '60s and early '70s material. It leaves out some of his signature material, but it's the only means of get-

ting hold of this music at present. It does include his version of "Here Comes the Sun." —*William Ruhlmann*

● **Resume: Best of** / 1993 / Rhino 71187
Resume: The Best of Richie Havens is the best Havens available, covering material from throughout his career and including most of his trademark songs. —*Chris Woodstra*

Cuts to the Chase / 1994 / Forward
Richie Havens has been a consistent performers of his own songs and others for 30 years. On *Cuts to the Chase,* his new release, he maintains the unique driving guitar style and impassioned vocals that are his tradmark. He takes a modern studio sound and uses it to support these new performances. The album is divided into two sections; The Declaration and The Independence. Exceptional cuts are Cliff Eberhardt's "My Father's Shoes," "How the Nights Can Fly," and a knowing, world-weary version of "The Times They Are a-Changin'." —*Richard Meyer*

Ginny Hawker & Kay Justice

Ginny and Kay find old songs from the mountains and perform them so beautifully, it seems that their voices are a part of the mountain mist. Their rendition of "Going to the West" is one of the most beautiful songs ever recorded. Many traditional performers now include this song in their performances, always crediting Ginny and Kay. Ginny and Kay are instructors in vocal harmony at Augusta. Their recordings are proof positive of their qualifications. —*Don Stevens*

Signs & Wonders / June Appal

● **Come All You Tenderhearted** / June Appal

Pathway To West Virginia / Pathway

Mark Heard

Vocals
Performer-producer Mark Heard released 14 albums of Christian-oriented rock. His later albums are more acoustically oriented and more spiritual than religious with increasingly sophisticated lyrics. He died of a heart attack in 1993. —*Richard Meyer*

Stop the Dominoes / 1981 / Home Sweet Home Recor
More straight rock and roll than his later efforts and more obviously Christian-oriented songs. —*Richard Meyer*

○ **Dry Bones Dance** / 1990 / Fingerprint 9001
Includes the great "House of Broken Dreams," the rockin' "Rise from the Ruins," and "Lonely Road." This acoustic album is very forceful but never forced. Each song has a real drive and committed vocals. A great record. —*Richard Meyer*

○ **Second Hand** / 1991 / Fingerprint 9102
On this album Heard has adopted a more contemporary electric sound. His songs keep getting stronger. Some key tracks are "Nod Over Coffee," " Love Is Not the Only Thing," and "Look Over Your Shoulder." Highly recommended. —*Richard Meyer*

Satellite Sky / 1992 / Fingerprint
Mark Heard has gone into overdrive on this, his third Fingerprint CD. Most songs are arranged around his electrified metal-bodied mandolin. The personal spiritual message is still here in full force, but the songs stand up well. The desparate "Tip of My Tongue," "Love Is So Blind," and "Satellite Sky" are key tracks. —*Richard Meyer*

● **High Noon** / Myrrh
This 18-song posthumous collection includes selections from his three previous Fingerprint CDs plus four additional tracks. —*Richard Meyer*

Heartbeats Rhythm Quartet, The

☆ **Spinning World** / 1993 / Green Linnet
This is a joyous album by the Heartbeats Rhythm Quartet. It combines elements of jazz, swing, and old-timey. The sound of this CD is warm and present, and the vocals are so tight that they sound like one big voice. The title cut is terrific, as is "Hollywood Dream," and Jean Richie's "Blue Diamond Mines." —*Richard Meyer*

Margo Hennnebach

Margo Hennebach served as a backup musician for many of Greenwich Village's established singer-songwriters in the 1980s. She also performed as a member of the group Idle Rumors. Now she is on her own touring nationally and has released an album of her own. —*Richard Meyer*

○ **Margo Hennebach** / 1994 / 1-800 Prime

On her eponymous release, Margo effectively performs the songs that have made her a favorite of fans of the traditionally oriented contemporary song. A trained musician, Hennebach arranged the vocals and instruments with a classical feel that never weighs down the essence of her songs. Her very clear voice floats over the music in a way that is similar to many Celtic singers. — *Richard Meyer*

Jane Henshaw

Jane Henshaw / 1992 / CPG Records

Indiana resident Henshaw sings in an agreeable light quiver. Her country-flavored album inclues a pair of her own tunes, along with covers such as T-Bone Burnett's "The Bird That I Once Held in My Hand," and Bill Staines's "Street of Old Quebec." —*Richard Meyer*

Judy Henske

b. , Chippewa Falls, WI

Vocals

A West Coast folksinger, Judy Henske started out working with ex-Kingston Trio member Dave Guard in 1962 as part of the Whiskeyhill singers. A fine folksinger who was very popular in the early '60s, Henske has never achieved real commercial success. —*Michael Erlewine*

○ **Judy Henske** / 1963 / Elektra 7231

High Flying Bird / 1964 / Elektra 7241

Henske sings with a full-throated, bluesy style reminiscent of Mama Cass on her best album, which was one of the first contemporary folk records to use a rhythm section (including Earl Palmer on drums). Highlighted by the title track, a moody, soaring ballad that was covered by Jefferson Airplane. —*Richie Unterberger*

● **Death Defying Judy Henske** / 1965 / Reprise 6203

Priscilla Herdman

Vocals, guitar

A folksinger and guitarist from New York, she has released five albums since 1976, including *Stardreamer, Nightsongs,* and *Lullabies,* which is a collection of songs for children. —*Mark A. Humphrey*

○ **Seasons of Change** / 1983 / Flying Fish 309

Herdman presents a compelling rural landscape, singing in a clear, reassuring voice of struggling farmers, family ties, and feminist consciousness. She continues the interpretive folksinging tradition of Joan Baez and Judy Collins, updating it for the '80s and '90s. —*William Ruhlmann*

● **Water Lily** / 1987 / Philo 1014

Herdman presents a more traditional set of songs on this collection, which was recorded in 1976. Accompanied by fiddle, mandolin, and cello, along with her own guitar, she is remarkably affecting on such emotional selections as "The Drover's Sweetheart" and, especially, "The Band Played Waltzing Matilda," which is all but guaranteed to provoke tears. —*William Ruhlmann*

Forgotten Dreams /

Haunting, lyrical music for guitar and voice. —*AMG*

Carolyn Hester

b. 1937, Waco, Texas

Vocals

Singing songs from her Southwestern roots, as well as standard folk items, Carolyn Hestor was a mainstay of the folk scene in the '60s. Her first album for Columbia, *Carolyn Hester,* received rave reviews. She graduated to a more contemporary folk music and in the early '80s was still providing rare appearances on the folk circuit. —*Michael Erlewine*

○ **That's My Song** / 1964 / Dot 25604

● **At Town Hall** / 1965 / Bear Family 15520

. . . a compilation of two live albums recorded for Dot Records in 1965 by this seminal and gifted folk performer. With all of her other material out of print, this disc is the sole document of Hester's rich contralto voice and engaging performing style.

Fortunately, both are well-served by the excellent sound of the recording and song selection, including a couple of self-penned numbers and a version of Bob Dylan's sing-a-long "Playboys and Playgirls." — *Richard Riis, Rock & Roll Disc.*

Chris Hickey

Vocals

A Los Angeles-based singer-songwriter, Hickey is a member of the band Show of Hands (with one album on IRS). —*Richard Meyer*

● **Frames of Mind, Boundaries of Time** / 1970 / CNC 1001

○ **Looking for Anything** / 198z / CNC 1374

Looking for Anything is packed with good compositions, and one that is an absolute masterpiece. Hickey is a quality songwriter who has a real grip on his lyrics. When you read through the words, they hold up as poetry, a quality that is lost with most songwriters. Though the backup work is limited, one cut simply jumps out and demands additional play. "Another War" is as good a picture of how innocents must endure the wars of others as you're gonna get. It cuts deep like Prine, Paxton, and Dylan did during their prime. Most of the other songs are well worth listening to, though the absolute quality of "Another War" simply overshadows the rest. —*Steve Romanoski, Option*

Anne Hills

Vocals, guitar, banjo, autoharp

A mainstay on the folk circuit for years now, Anne Hills has recorded with Priscilla Herdman and Cindy Mangsen and on her own. Originally from Chicago, Hills is known for her clear, expressive singing. —*Richard Meyer*

○ **Don't Explain** / Hogeye 006

● **October Child** / Flying Fish

October Child is a collection of fellow Chicagoan Michael Smith's songs. Peter Erskine's arrangements are respectful of the song's carefully crafted lyrics. One of the great benefits of this CD is the chance to hear some of Smith's less well known songs, "Disappearing Heart," for example. —*Richard Meyer*

Tish Hinojosa

Vocals

In the liner notes to her album *Homeland,* Tish Hinojosa writes of a dilemma she faced as she began to emerge as a singer-songwriter. She writes of ". . . wondering how my love for my parents' humble Mexican heritage and language would mix with idealistic images of a musical future." With four albums and one EP now behind her, Hinojosa has fashioned her blend of cultures into a compelling voice in American music. Typically a Tish Hinojosa album or concert moves effortlessly from songs of loves forgotten and family struggles remembered to eloquent cries against injustice, evocations of sawdust dance floors, the rolling endless highways of the Southwest, and the lonely struggles of the disenfranchised.

Hinojosa was born in San Antonio to a large blended family, went to parochial school, listened to the songs of her parents as well as the Beatles and Woodstock, began her musical career doing jingles and recording for a small Tejano label before leaving Texas for Taos. In the spectacular beauty of northern New Mexico, she further honed her art and recorded an EP featuring three original songs. Nashville was her next stop.

Although she worked steadily—touring, doing demo work, even recording a successful single, "I'll Pull You Through" for Curb Records—she never felt that she could find her niche in Music City. She says, "Nashville requires a delicate balance. I began to see that incorporating aspects of my ethnic heritage into my music was a problem, at least at that time (early '80s)."

In 1985 Hinojosa returned to New Mexico where she recorded an independent cassette, *Taos to Tennessee.* The recording features some of her compositions that would later appear on *Homeland,* her 1989 A&M/Americana major label debut. Finding the opportunity for work limited as a Taos-based artist, she moved to Austin in the summer of 1988. She rapidly became an integral part of the vibrant Austin musical scene not only making many club appearances but also standing tall for her social concerns by being a willing participant in benefits for migrant farmworkers. Her concern for the dangers of picking pesticide-laced crops was also evident in her song "Something in the Rain," a moving account of the tragedy of unsafe crop spraying practices told through the eyes of a small boy. Hinojosa also has a loyal following overseas, and her touring itinerary often includes stops in Amsterdam and Scandinavia, as well as the more familiar confines of clubs in Houston, Cambridge, and Taos.

The highpoint of her recording career so far is the 1992 album *Culture Swing* on Rounder Records. This is an essential album in the classic folk tradition of Baez and Dylan. With all of the songs written by Hinojosa, *Culture Swing* is a singer-songwriter tour-de-force that bridges the folk and country idioms. The 1994 album *Destiny's Gate* carries on the Hinojosa tradition in the vein of *Culture Swing*. —*Alonso Jasso & Michael Erlewine*

○ **Homeland** / 1989 / A&M 5263
Her first mainstream LP containing the beautiful "Border Trilogy," "Voice of the Big Guitar," and "Who Showed You the Way to My Heart." —*Richard Meyer*

★ **Culture Swing** / Aug. 27, 1990 / A&M 5328
With a voice that rivals Joan Baez in quality and a sense of humor all her own, Tish Hinojosa is proof that really great singer-songwriters still appear from time to time. Each generation has but a few perfect folk albums and *Culture Swing* (all songs are written by Hinojosa) is one of these—an instant classic. —*Michael Erlewine*

Aquella Noche / 1991 / Watermelon 1005
A live recording of original and classic Spanish songs. —*Richard Meyer*

○ **Taos to Tennessee** / 1992 / Watermelon 1008
Recorded in 1987, *Taos to Tennessee* predates the more successful *Culture Swing* and shows the same kind of style and clarity in presenting folk-country songs. Six of the songs are written by Hinojosa. —*Michael Erlewine*

Destiny's Gate / 1994 / Warner Brothers
Hinojosa continues to move into the mainstream with *Destiny's Gate*, a decidedly more pop-oriented effort, without losing the magic of *Culture Swing*. With a beautiful voice blending elements of both Joan Baez and Emmylou Harris, she seems to have perfected her unique style of Mexican folk and country music. "I Want to See You Again" stands out as one of her finest songs. —*Chris Woodstra*

Hobo Jim

Vocals
Hobo Jim is a Nashville-based singer-songwriter whose songs depict life in the Northwest. —*Chip Renner*

○ **Thunderfoot** / 1971 / Flying Fish 344
Debut album. Hard to find, easy to listen to. —*Chip Renner*

Lost & Dyin' Breed / 1972 / Flying Fish 345
A good folk-bluegrass album. Not so mature as his follow-up record, but worth checking out. —*Chip Renner*

● **Where Legends Are** / 1973 / Flying Fish 520
Solid songs. Hobo Jim stacks the deck with some fine musicians, including Sam Bush, Bela Fleck, Pat Flynn, and Kenny Malone. Short in length, but long on quality. —*Chip Renner*

Robin Holcomb

b. 1954, Georgia
Vocals, piano
This Georgia-born singer-songwriter, composer, pianist, and poet incorporates elements of gospel, blues, R&B, and rock into her music. Holcomb has had a varied background in chamber music, ethnomusicology (including performing in a Javanese gamelan ensemble), musical theater, and work with her husband, Wayne Horvitz of the New York downtown avant-garde experimental scene. After attending the University of California at Santa Cruz, she and Horvitz moved to New York before settling in Seattle in 1988. —*AMG*

● **Robin Holcomb** / Nov. 19, 1990 / Elektra 60983
The songs are arty, piano-based, spooky, and very sensual. "Deliver Me" is particularly fine. —*Richard Meyer*

○ **Rockabye** / Sep. 8, 1992 / Elektra 61289

David Holt

Banjo, Vocals

Holt is a banjo player and storyteller based in Nashville. He has hosted *The American Music Shop* and other specials on TNN. —*Chip Renner*

○ **Reel & Rock** / 1986 / Flying Fish 372
Holt plays some great banjo. This album is all music, featuring Doc and Merle Watson and Jerry Douglas. —*Chip Renner*

The Holy Modal Rounders

Group
Peter Stampfel (b. 1939) and Steve Weber (b. 1944) formed one of the strangest groups to come out of Greenwich Village in the '60s, mixing traditional music with novelties and off-kilter originals. They had added more instruments by the end of the '60s, by which time their recordings had become infrequent. They have reunited occasionally since. —*William Ruhlmann*

● **Indian War Whoop** / 1967 / ESP 1068
Comic, absurdist folk with Peter Stampfel as ringleader. —*William Ruhlmann*

○ **Moray Eels Eat the Holy Modal Rounders** / 1968 / Elektra 74026
Like a psychedelic folkie fusion of the Fugs and the Mothers of Invention, this ranks as one of the best "acid folk" albums. This sprawling, demented LP includes "Bird Song," which was featured on the *Easy Rider* soundtrack. —*Richie Unterberger*

Last Round / 1978 / Adelphi 1030
More madness, with "Pink Underwear" and "Romping through the Swamp." —*William Ruhlmann*

Caroline Horn

○ **Caroline Horn** / 1993 / Koho
This Brooklyn, NY, singer-songwriter has produced a strong album of her slightly gospely pop songs. Her arrangements have left a lot of room for her soulful vocals to come through. These tunes have a little bit of the early Laura Nyro feel to them. This is a folk album in its most elastic definition. These love songs have a good strong pop construction. —*Richard Meyer*

Bobby Horton

We are currently going through a revival of the Civil War. There are dozens of good recordings of songs from the Civil War era available today. There are none better than the tapes recorded and performed by Bobby Horton. Bobby, who has recorded with Three on a String and the Front Porch String Band, has put together the most songs ever recorded by a single artist covering the Civil War. It is almost a misnomer to call Bobby a "single" artist. On these tapes (available on his own label—Homespun) he produced and sang songs as a single, duet, trio, quartette, and chorus! He plays over a dozen instruments. The research that he has done to put together this set of tapes is unequaled. Anyone remotely interested in this phase of our American heritage must have these tapes. —*Don Stevens*

Homespun Songs Of The C.S.A., Vol.1 / Homespun

Homespun Songs Of The C.S.A., Vol.2 / Homespun

Homespun Songs Of The C.S.A., Vol.3 / Homespun

Homespun Songs Of Faith: 1861-1865 / Homespun

Cisco Houston

b. Aug. 18, 1918, Wilmington, DE, d. Apr. 29, 1961
Vocals
An associate of Woody Guthrie, with whom he made many recordings, Houston scored a hit single with "Rose, Rose, I Love You" in 1951. He was a popular folk interpreter until his death from cancer. —*William Ruhlmann*

● **900 Miles and Other Railroad Ballads** / 195z / Smithsonian/Folkways 2013

○ **Sings Songs of the Open Road** / 1968 / Smithsonian/Folkways 2480
This Woody Guthrie sidekick sings Guthrie's songs and traditional tunes. —*William Ruhlmann*

Randy Howard

○ **Survival of the Fiddlist** / 1993 /
This album proves you don't have to be Mark O'Conner to make a scorching hot fiddle record. The title tune drives along like

"Orange Blossom Special" as do many of the others, with great support playing by Kathy Chiavola and Roy Husky Jr. —*Richard Meyer*

Reverend Jim (James Dale) Howie

Reverend Howie is one of our national treasures, in the mode of Bradley Kincaid. Reverend Howie is a pastor in the United Presbyterian Church. His mother's family were members of the Scottish Covenanters, whose music was a part of the earliest music in America. His father was a Southern Baptist. Everyone in his family sang the old religious songs and secular ballads. Reverend Howie learned these songs from his parents, grandparents, and other family members. It is estimated that Reverend Howie knows over a thousand of these songs. To hear him sing them while strumming his autoharp is a blessing and an inspiration. — *Don Stevens*

Gooseberry Pie & Other Old-Time Delights / Prarie Schooner
● **Psalm Singing Of The Covenanters** / Prarie Schooner

Reeva Hunter

☆ **Lucky Penny** / 1994 / Hunter's Moon music
This Los Angeles-based singer-songwriter has completed her first album. She is a great new country-influenced songwriter. This woman's songs have a great big heart and lots of brains. Her stylistic versatility is evident with tunes like the ballad "Somebody Loves You for You" and the dark and mystical "Walking Map of Fate." She's a serious writer who has fun. Contact PO Box 912 Malibu, CA 90265 —*Richard Meyer*

Sonya Hunter

Vocals
This San Francisco-based singer-songwriter has a sound like vintage English folk-rock combined with a hip urban-American sensibility. —*Richard Meyer*
○ **Favorite Short Stories** / 1992 / Heyday 10
It's easy to be fooled by a glance at Sonya Hunter's album: It starts with the traditional "Once I Had a Sweetheart," which is followed by a group of originals. "Aha, just another woman singer-songwriter," you think. Wrong. A singer-songwriter she may be, but her work is unusual and the instrumentation diverse, ranging from solo with acoustic guitar, to spare arrangements with cello and bass, to full band arrangements with other guitars and drums. Hunter has an uncanny ability to write and sing about those little subtle moments in life that so often go unnoticed. Her writing is understandable and thought-provoking without being annoying or mawkish. The only fault of the album is its length: Just as it really begins to satisfy, it's over! —*Mike Fleischer, Roundup Newsletter*

Ian & Sylvia

Group
The '60s duo of Canadians Ian Tyson (b. 1933) and Sylvia Fricker (b. 1940) was notable for its combination of contemporary folk with the countryish music of rural Canada, once described as "country and Northwestern." Both singers wrote original songs that became standards (Tyson's "Four Strong Winds" and "Someday Soon," Fricker's "You Were on My Mind"), and they championed the work of little-known writers like fellow-Canadians Gordon Lightfoot and Joni Mitchell. —*William Ruhlmann*

Ian & Sylvia / 1962 / Vanguard 79215
Ian & Sylvia's debut album is their most standard affair, and indeed a fairly typical folk recording for the era, with such traditional warhorses as "Rocks and Gravel" (also recorded, but not released, by Dylan during this time), "C.C. Rider," and "Handsome Molly." What made the pair immediately distinctive was their superb vocal dueting, which was definitely a case of the sum being greater than its parts. Blended together, they canceled each other's weaknesses and gave the material great freshness and vigor. Ian's guitar and Sylvia's autoharp are backed by stellar playing from guitarist John Herald and string bassists Bill Lee (director Spike Lee's father) and Art Davis. —*Richie Unterberger*

● **Four Strong Winds** / 1964 / Vanguard 2149
Ian & Sylvia hit their stride on their second LP, which features the first in a line of talented second guitarists (John Herald) that they

used to augment their original guitar-autoharp-bass lineup. The album featured an assortment of largely traditional material that was unsurpassed in its time, encompassing bluegrass, spirituals, gospel, hillbilly, the French-Canadian standard "V'La L'bon Vent," a British prison song, and two tunes from the Cecil Sharp collection of Southern Mountain folksongs of British origin. Two of the most impressive cuts, however, were contemporary compositions. One was their version of Bob Dylan's "Tomorrow Is a Long Time," one of the first obscure Dylan tunes to be committed to vinyl. The title cut, an Ian Tyson original, would prove to be the duo's first song to influence rock musicians, as the Searchers covered it shortly afterwards with a reverent version that was quite close to the original; Neil Young revived it in the late '70s. —*Richie Unterberger*

Early Morning Rain / 1965 / Vanguard 79175
Side one of their fourth LP continues in the eclectic folkie style of their earlier albums, containing only one original (Tyson's "Marlborough Street Blues"). The other cuts include the fine Gordon Lightfoot title track, a Johnny Cash cover ("Come In Stranger") that heralded their increasing interest in country and western music, one of their finest interpretations of a bona fide traditional warhorse ("Nancy Whiskey"), and "Darcy Farrow," a fine obscure composition that could pass for a traditional standard (written for the duo by an unknown Californian singer-songwriter pair). Side two, however, with the exception of one traditional tune and another Lightfoot cover, is composed entirely of originals. The most notable of these is Tyson's "Song for Canada" (written with Pete Gzowski). A bittersweet plea for greater communication between French- and English-speaking Canadians, it could just as well be heard as a comment on any sort of deteriorating relationship. —*Richie Unterberger*

● **Greatest Hits** / 1987 / Vanguard 5
This compilation (CVSD 5/6) captures much of their best work. Do not confuse it with the identically titled Vanguard album 73114, which includes only half the material found on this set. —*William Ruhlmann*

Incredible String Band

Group
Scotland-born Mike Heron (b. 1941) and Robin Williamson (b. 1943) led one of the most eclectic folk groups of the 1960s, starting as a duo and later expanding and electrifying into a folk-rock group. —*William Ruhlmann*

Wee Tam / 1968 / Elektra 74036
Mixing English and American folk with what we now call "world music," the multiinstrumental Scottish duo of Robin Williamson and Mike Heron achieves a whimsical, delicate style that has never been duplicated. It reaches a peak here with such songs as "You Get Brighter." (*Wee Tam* is sometimes packaged with the simultaneously released *The Big Huge*, which is also recommended.) —*William Ruhlmann*

● **Relics of the Incredible String Band** / 1970 / Elektra 2004
The ISB's prolific output makes a compilation a virtual necessity, and this two-record set selects wisely from the seven albums the group released in the United States between 1967 and 1970. From Robin Williamson's "First Girl I Loved" (covered by Judy Collins) and "Way Back in the 1960s" (recorded in 1967), to Mike Heron's "Air," and "This Moment," the ISB's eclectic, fanciful acoustic style is well portrayed. —*William Ruhlmann*

No Ruinous Feud / 1973 / Edsel 367
The ISB began to change its approach in 1971, cutting back on its sometimes open-ended song structures and adding a rock rhythm section to selected tracks. But it wasn't until this album that everything came together, resulting in a delightful collection of songs that range from reggae to light pop, along with the traditional folk styles that had always been the group's strong suit. —*William Ruhlmann*

Jim Infantino

○ **Strawman** / 1993 / Melville Park Records
Bostonian, Jim Infantino is a high-energy performer who mixes his politics and humor well; it's heard on his instant urban classic "Stress." —*Richard Meyer*

Tom Intondi

Originally based in Greenwich Village and now residing in the Northwest, Intondi has toured throughout the United States and internationally, alone and as a member of the Song Project. He has three albums on his own and various cuts on *The Fast Folk Musical Magazine*. —*Richard Meyer*

● **House of Water** / 1983 / City Dancer 2001
Exuberant folk-pop with jazzy overtones makes up the musical base for this earnest New York singer, whose songs carry a warmth and depth of feeling rare even in the singer-songwriter genre and a melodic sense welcome in any musical style. The title song and "High Times" are highlights on this self-produced album. —*William Ruhlmann & Richard Meyer*

Bringin' up the Sun / 1992 / City Dancer 003
Includes a guest appearance by Nanci Griffith. —*Richard Meyer*

Burl Ives

b. Jun. 14, 1909, Jaspar County, IL
Vocals

Ives traveled as an itinerant handyman throughout the United States after a brief stay at New York University. He became a working actor and performed concerts of folk ballads. He has published several songbooks and an autobiography, *Wayfaring Stranger*. —*David Szatmary*

★ **Wayfaring Stranger** / 1959 / CBS 628
This is traditional folk from the smooth-sounding Ives. Includes "On Top of Old Smokey," "Roving Gambler," and "Green Broom." —*David Szatmary*

Kate Jacobs

○ **Calm Comes After** / 1993 / Bar None Records
Originally an independent artist, *The Calm Comes After* was picked up by Bar None records and amended with three new cuts. The charm of this album is in Jacobs's friendly, almost naive delivery. Her lyrics have a deeply knowing womanly innocence that really says she sees more than she says and acts on it. Think of this artist as a less religious, urban Iris Dement. Kate is supported by a sparse country-sounding band. —*Richard Meyer*

Bert Jansch

b. Nov. 3, 1943, Scotland
Vocals, guitar

Born in Scotland, Jansch moved to England and popularized the "folk baroque" movement. His style is a combination of jazz-flavored folk, traditional, and blues. —*Chip Renner*

○ **Early Bert, Vol. 2** / 1966 / Xtra 1164
This was originally titled *Jack Orion*. More folk than his other releases. —*Chip Renner*

Nicola / 1967 / Transatlantic 157
Jansch's third solo album is perhaps too lightly dismissed by both folk critics and the artist himself. Bowing slightly to commercial pressures, he allowed orchestration to be used on 5 of the 12 tracks. Actually, the orchestrated cuts aren't bad at all, and the remainder are pretty much in keeping with the character and high standard of his other '60s work. Of the 12 cuts, 9 are Jansch originals, and ably display his nimble guitar work, incorporation of blues and traditional British Isles folk influences into a contemporary style, and his Donovanesque vocals. For the first and only time, Bert played both electric and acoustic guitars on this LP; it's also his first work to feature drumming. Some of the orchestrated numbers, especially "Woe Is Love, My Dear," were actually deemed to have potential as singles. That didn't happen (the cut "Wish My Baby Was Here" would have been a better choice in any event), but that doesn't take away from their fey period charm. *Nicola* and Jansch's 1969 release *Birthday Blues* were combined on one CD in a 1993 reissue. —*Richie Unterberger*

○ **Birthday Blues** / 1968 / Reprise 6343
It's no accident that Jansch's 1969 album sounds like a modified version of the Pentangle. Jansch was a member of the great British folk-rock group at the time of this album's release, which was produced by Shel Talmy (who also worked with the Pentangle). And he's backed by the Pentangle's sterling rhythm section of Danny Thompson (bass) and Terry Cox (drums), with occasional touches of harmonica (played by British blues singer

Duffy Power), alto sax, and flute. The affect is akin to hearing an unbalanced Pentangle, with no John Renbourn on dueling guitar or Jacqui McShee on vocals. That's not at all a bad thing— Jansch was one of the group's main motors and can still be a compelling writer and performer on his own. All of the cuts on this LP are originals, and they show Jansch leaning a little more toward bluesy styles than usual, though the mood is predominantly British folk. It's a pleasant effort, but not his best work, either as a solo performer or within a group context. *Birthday Blues* and Jansch's 1967 release *Nicola* have been combined onto one CD on a 1993 reissue. —*Richie Unterberger*

Moonshine / 1973 / Reprise 2129
Jansch covers a Ewan MacColl song, "The First Time Ever I Saw Your Face." —*Chip Renner*

Avocet / 1979 / Charisma 6
The jazz side of Jansch's music is very strong. Mandocellist Martin Jenkins takes front stage on this album, along with Jansch. —*Chip Renner*

● **Best of** / 1980 / Shanachie 99004
Arguably the finest acoustic guitarist of his generation, Bert Jansch has been heralded as the major influence on many of today's top players. This 25-track collection spans Jansch's earlier years. Tunes like the intricate solo instrumental from 1965, "Angie" (originally done by his own guitar inspiration, Davey Graham), the bluesy "Come Back Baby" (1967), and early music stylings such as "Peregrinations" and "Alman" (1971) explore a diverse musical spectrum of folk, blues, jazz, and early music in depth. Jansch possesses a voice that's startling at times, and his songs often have the dramatic impact of his instrumental prowess. "Needle of Death" sent shivers in 1965 and still does today. Some cuts feature beautiful group work with fellow Pentangle members, while others are performed solo, but the playing is brilliant throughout the disc. —*J.J. Rassler, Roundup Newsletter*

Sketches / 1990 / Temple Music 2035
With 13 cuts, this is very good. —*Chip Renner*

● **Ornament Tree** / Nov. 1990 / Capitol 71365
An influential British folksinger-guitarist of the '60s on recent recordings. —*Mark A. Humphrey*

Victor Jara

d. Sep. 14, 1973
Vocals

Victor Jara was the main proponent of the Chilean New Song movement, which brought a political consciousness to native folk music in Chile, much as the "protest" singers of the '60s did to U. S. folk music. A national figure, he was closely associated with the Allende government of the early '70s and was brutally murdered by the military junta that took over Chile in 1973. —*William Ruhlmann*

● **Unfinished Song** / 1990 / Redwood 3300
Jara's expressive, vibrant singing shows why he was the leading light of the South American New Song movement as well as a significant political figure. This compilation includes not only original political songs but also traditional Chilean folksongs and even an adaptation of Malvina Reynolds's "Little Boxes." The album's 23 tracks, taken from various sources, provide a thorough view of Jara's broad talent. (Also recommended: the Monitor Records four-volume series of Jara recordings.) —*William Ruhlmann*

Michael Jerling

Vocals, guitar

A Chicago native, Jerling has developed an urban style with the feel of country blues. He is an excellent guitar player and singer-songwriter, and his songs are full of strong imagery. "The Long Black Wall" has become one of his signature pieces. —*Richard Meyer & Chip Renner*

New Suit of Clothes / Shanachie Records Corp.
This collection has more blues-based ballads than Jerling's previous CD. The playing, including guest appearances by John Sebastian and Peter Ostroushko, is clean and unobtrusive, allowing Jerling's warm baritone to serve his sophisticated lyrics well. —*Richard Meyer*

Blue Heartland / 1970 / Moonlight

Includes "The Long Black Wall" and "Road House." —*Richard Meyer*

● **My Evil Twin** / 1992 / Shanachie 8004
Jerling has a way with words that can paint a picture in your mind's eye. "Take Me to Juarez" is a classic tale; also worthwhile are "Breakdown" and the title cut. "Before the Country Moved to Town" features Robin and Linda Williams singing nice background vocals. All in all, this is a good label debut album, with great songs and great production. —*Chip Renner*

Josh Joffen

Brooklyn-born Josh Joffen has recorded often for *The Fast Folk Musical Magazine* (1982 to the present). He released an album with songwriter David Roth (they each have one side). Joffen won the Kerrville New Folk Competition in 1987. —*Richard Meyer*

○ **Josh Joffen W/ David Roth** / 1987 / 6 of 1
Joffen highlights are "Video Arcade" and "Chain of Love." David Roth faves are "Rising in Love" and "Fireflies." —*Richard Meyer*

Crow Johnson

Songwriter
Based in Gravette, AR, Johnson is a popular songwriter in the South and West. She edits the magazine *Zassafrass Music News.—Richard Meyer*

○ **As the Crow Flies** / Zassafrass 7703

Larry Johnson

Among the postwar generation of blues artists, Larry Johnson—from Riceville, GA—is one of the most devoted to the pure delta and Texas styles of the 1920s. An excellent picker and singer he has albums out on a variety of labels, including Biograph and Spivey. —*Richard Meyer*

● **Fast & Funky** / 1974 / Blue Goose 2001
A great collection of old-time blues, including "Picked Poor Robin Clean," "Charley Stone," and "Two White Horses." —*Richard Meyer*

Prudence Johnson

Vocals
Primarily an interpreter, Minnesota-based Prudence Johnson has recorded songs for children as well as adults. —*Richard Meyer*

● **Sings the Songs of Greg Brown** / 1991 / Red House 32
A beautifully presented set of interpretations of the work of a fine Midwest songwriter. —*Richard Meyer*

Carol Elizabeth Jones

Carol has performed with the Wildcats, the Wandering Ramblers, the Green Grass Cloggers, and others. She has the most beautiful, raw mountain voice you will ever hear. Her delivery of the old songs has never been equalled by anyone. Her singing will make the hair stand up on the back of your neck! Hear her whenever you can. —*Don Stevens*

Gonna Rise Again / Rounder

Old-time Music / Marimac

On Our Knees / Yodel Ay Hee

Rambling & Wandering / Marimac

Through The Years / Rounder

Brenda Kahn

Vocals, guitar
This New Jersey singer-songwriter plays punk, thrash, blues, and folk on her maple Martin acoustic guitar. —*Chip Renner*

● **Goldfish Don't Talk Back** / 1990 / Community 3 1990
A high-energy album—part folk, part punk. The lyrics would gray the hairs on a nun's head. —*Chip Renner*

Si Kahn

Songwriter
A Southern activist and political songwriter, Kahn is known for his direct community work and also for his articulate writing. —*Richard Meyer*

○ **Home** / 1980 / Flying Fish 207

This album features songs in a mixture of styles, from gentle pastoral to hard-edged political by a singer-songwriter who is also a union organizer. —*AMG*

● **Doing My Job** / 1982 / Flying Fish 221
This album features politically aware, sensitive songs. —*AMG*

○ **Unfinished Portraits** / 1985 / Flying Fish 312

In My Heart / 1994 / Philo
A solo live recording made in concert in Holland April 1993 containing songs from his large repertoire performed with great intimacy. —*Richard Meyer*

Cindy Kallet

Vocals, guitar
Cindy Kallet is a singer-songwriter and guitarist whose songwriting mirrors her love for the New England coast. She is a fine guitarist whose musical styles vary from folk to fiddle tunes, traditional, and sea chanties. Her voice is smooth and deep, reminiscent of Joni Mitchell's. She is not consumed by her music career, which could explain the reason she is not as well known as she deserves. —*Chip Renner*

Working on Wings to Fly / 1981 / Folk Legacy
Kallet's debut album is a nice collection of songs performed acoustically, dealing mainly with the New England sea. This 1981 release is exactly what the rest of the folk community is doing in the '90s. —*Chip Renner*

● **2** / 1983 / Folk Legacy
Start out with this release. The songwriting is a little more expressive, and she plays some fine instrumentals. The music is well crafted, and the songs are from the heart. —*Chip Renner*

Dreaming Down a Quiet Line / 1989 / Stone's Throw 1
All her writing and musical talent fit together on this one. The songs are varied in content, dealing with war, politics, love, and family. The music and vocals are balanced so as not to take away from each other. —*Chip Renner*

Paul Kamm w/ Eleanore MacDonald

Group
A Nevada City, CA, duo whose songs are incisive, gentle, and beautifully performed. —*Richard Meyer*

Unbroken Chain / 1970 / Freewheel 102

● **Into the Clouds** / 1980 / Freewheel 103

Paul Kaplan

Chicago native, now resides in Amherst, MA, with his two daughters. In addition to appearing on various Folkways records and contributing songs to *Fast Folk*, Kaplan has compiled three Phil Ochs albums for that company and edited the 1982 *Fast Folk* songbook. —*Richard Meyer*

○ **Life on This Planet** / 1982 / Hummingbird
Contains his signatures, "Call Me the Whale" and "Henry the Accountant." —*Richard Meyer*

King of Hearts / 1985 / Hummingbird
A concert of new material recorded live at the SpeakEasy club in Greenwich Village in 1985. Features his beautiful song "The King of Hearts" as well as some great audience participation on "I Had an Old Coat." This album really captures the atmosphere of a more traditional New York singer-songwriter in the mid-'80s. —*Richard Meyer*

Ingrid Karklins

● **Anima Mundi** / 1994 / Green Linnet
On both of her distinctive releases, Karklins combines her Latvian background with the influence of her present home in Austin, TX. The music is swirling and earthy with a sense of dance in it supported by percussion and well-used synthesizers. Her dark voice cuts through it all. This is very emotional music. —*Richard Meyer*

Peter Keane

Vocals, guitar
Keane is a guitarist and folksinger from Boston. He plays traditional country, blues, and folk. —*Chip Renner*

○ **Goodnight Blues** / 1992 / Northeastern 5008

Keane steps out on his blues originals and is backed by Matt Leavenworth (fiddle and mandolin) and Darrell Scott on dobro. This release is very enjoyable. Keane's song "Jimmy Yancey" is wonderful and relaxed, as are his versions of John Hurt blues and the '60s chestnut, "Ruby Baby." — *Chip Renner & Ricard Meyer*

James Keelaghan

○ **My Skies** / Jan. 1993 / Green Linnet 2112
James Keelaghan might be the Canadian John Gorka. On this 1994 Juno award-winning album James Keelaghan offers lyrical portraits of regular folks and the details of their lives that make each life special, as in "Big Picture." In "Glory Bound" he tells us that each person has a mission. The production is restrained acoustic guitar-based folk & roll. — *Richard Meyer*

Robert Earl Keen, Jr.

Vocals
Keen is a Texas singer-songwriter whose songs have been covered by Nanci Griffith, and he has cowritten with Lyle Lovett. — *Chip Renner*

● **No Kinda Dancer** / 1984 / Philo 1108
A well-crafted debut, not one bad song. "Armadillo Jackal & This Old Porch," cowritten by Lyle Lovett, features Lovett and Nanci Griffith singing harmony. — *Chip Renner*

○ **Live Album** / 1988 / Sugar Hill 1024
Good sound, new material, good stories, plus audience interaction make this worthwhile. Featuring great mandolin and fiddle by Johnathan Yadkin and a nice cut of "I Would Change My Life." — *Chip Renner*

West Textures / 1989 / Sugar Hill 1028
Solid and well-produced, his storytelling has never been better. This album is as good as *No Kinda Dancer*, with Jerry Douglas on dobro and a cover of the Koller-Silverstein song "Jennifer Johnson & Me." — *Chip Renner*

Bigger Piece of Sky / Sugar Hill 1037
This album contains the radio hit "Tangled Up in Blue" soundalike song "Jesse with the Long Hair," as well as more of Keen's rough-and-tumble story songs. — *Richard Meyer*

Tom Kell

○ **One Sad Night** / 1990 / Warner Brothers 26508
More tight arrangements with commercial potential, especially "The Girl with the Single Rose." — *Richard Meyer*

● **Angeltown** / 1993 / Vanguard 79467
A Nashville-sounding band backed the singer-songwriter. "Blue Telephone" is a good one. — *Richard Meyer*

Steve Key

b. , Brooklyn, NY
Key was born in Brooklyn, NY, and raised in San Francisco, CA. He later returned to New York and joined the *Fast Folk* crowd. He hosted a radio show on WFUV-FM in New York. He now resides in Washington, DC, has issued the DC compilation *Capitol Acoustics*, and is involved in the Washington folk community. Key is a polished performer whose songs are well crafted. They are also full of deep imagery and emotion. — *Chip Renner*

Between Trains / 1970 / Local Folkel
Key's debut album is a rich collection of well-written stories that were greatly influenced by his New York lifestyle. — *Chip Renner*

○ **Record Time** / 1980 / Local Folkel 6688
Key's songs represent the best of the suburban homespun genre in contemporary folk. The title cut of this CD is a recommended example. — *Richard Meyer*

● **New Hope** / 1990 / Local Folkel 6680
This release is more upbeat than his first release. Every song is strong. The title song could be an anthem for the '60s generation. — *Chip Renner*

Kingston Trio

Group
Bob Shane (b. 1934), Nick Reynolds (b. 1933), and Dave Guard (1934-1991) formed the Kingston Trio in California in 1957. For the next ten years the group was perhaps the most popular in folk music, starting with their hit version of the traditional song

"Tom Dooley," which topped the charts in 1958. The trio adapted traditional songs and novelties to their exuberant style, which filled nightclubs and then concert halls. Critics, especially in folk music, objected to the inauthenticity of their approach, but the trio popularized folk music to millions who might never have heard it otherwise. They racked up seven gold albums by 1964 and paved the way for Joan Baez; Peter, Paul & Mary; Bob Dylan; and others. Guard left the Trio in 1961 and was replaced by John Stewart; and the trio disbanded completely in 1967, its music in popular decline. But Shane put together a new Kingston Trio in 1973, which has performed and recorded sporadically since. Much of the group's Capitol Records output from the early '60s was recently reissued on CD. — *William Ruhlmann*

Kingston Trio / 1958 / Capitol 996
The debut album of the most popular act in the folk boom of the late '50s. This contains their number one hit "Tom Dooley," Dave Guard's "Scotch and Soda," "Wreck of the 'John B'," and others. A massive hit, it spent almost four years in the bestseller charts. — *William Ruhlmann*

Kingston Trio at Large / 1959 / Capitol 1199
Perhaps the trio's bestselling album (15 weeks at number one), this contains their hilarious "M.T.A.," the lovely "Scarlet Ribbons," and several Dave Guard originals. — *William Ruhlmann*

○ **Once upon a Time** / 1969 / Tetragrammaton 5101

★ **Capitol Collectors Series** / 1990 / Capitol 92710
Here's a well-chosen 20-track compilation containing all 17 of the trio's hit singles. — *William Ruhlmann*

○ **From the "Hungry I"** / Kingston Trio / 1992 / Capitol 96748
The first two Kingston Trio albums, combined on one CD. In June 1958, a Salt Lake City DJ played "Tom Dooley" (from the debut album) to great acclaim and heavy phone action. By December the trio had a number one hit on their hands, soon to be followed by their first gold record and a Grammy award. — *Roundup Newsletter*

○ **Make Way / Goin' Places** / Jan. 6, 1992 / Capitol 96836
Make Way and *Goin' Places* are the Kingston Trio's ninth and tenth Capitol albums. This CD, which combines the two LPs, contains 24 tracks, including "Hard Travelin'," "Hangman," "The River Is Wide," "Pastures of Plenty," "It Was a Very Good Year," and "Lemon Tree." — *Roundup Newsletter*

○ **Sold out / String Along** / Jan. 6, 1992 / Capitol 96835
Sold Out and *String Along* are the fifth and sixth of the 20-odd Kingston Trio albums released on Capitol from 1958 to 1964. Remastered from original master tapes, the disc also reproduces the original photos and liner notes, plus additional new liner notes. Tunes include "El Matador," "Raspberries, Strawberries," "Bad Man's Blunder," "Leave My Woman Alone," and many more. — *Roundup Newsletter*

Kirtana

○ **Healing Rain** / 1990 / Wild Dove
This is a sweet, quiet, simple album of songs concerned with one's inner life. The music is delicately played and sung. It is available through PO Box 221 861 Carmel, CA 93922 — *Richard Meyer*

Peter Knight

Mandolin, banjo, fiddle
Knight is a Celtic musician who plays mandolin, banjo, and fiddle. He was a member of Steeleye Span in the '60s. — *Chip Renner*

○ **Ancient Cause** / 1991 / Shanachie 5001
A strong Celtic album with traces of his classical background. Bordering on new age but steeped in Celtic tradition. — *Chip Renner*

"Spider" John Koerner

b. Aug. 31, 1938, Rochester, NY
Vocals, guitar, harmonica
Koerner was a major force in the '60s folk community around Minneapolis. His Vanguard album *Running, Jumping, Standing Still*, recorded with Tony Glover and David Ray, was a seminal album of American folk and blues by urban players. — *Richard Meyer*

● **Nobody Knows the Trouble I've Been** / 1970 / Red House 12
A truly great album. The joyous playing and arrangements of
these songs, including "Leatherwing Bat," "Froggy Went a-
Courtin'," and others, are positive proof of the life that can be
brought to the great American folksong catalog in the hands of a
master. —*Richard Meyer*

○ **Raised by Humans** / 1992 / Red House 44
Produced in the same style as *Trouble*, this includes some
Koerner originals as well as driving jubilant versions of "The
Titanic," and "The Fox and the Boll Weevil." —*Richard Meyer*

Leo Kottke

b. Sep. 11, 1945, Athens, GA
Guitar
Kottke is considered (along with John Fahey) one of the finest virtuoso fingerpicking guitarists on the music scene. The two
worked closely in the '70s, playing and producing some of the
most innovative solo guitar playing of that period. Kottke and
Fahey influenced Preston Reed and Michael Hedges, both of
whom have carried on their vision in the years since. —*Chip
Renner*

Circle Round the Sun / 1970 / Symposium/Bay Street 2001
This is a good, hard-to-find record. —*Chip Renner*

Ice Water / 1974 / BGO 146
Kottke adds vocals, drums, bass, dobro, and steel guitar for a
unique Kottke sound. —*Chip Renner*

○ **Chewing Pine** / 1975 / Capitol 11446

Leo Kottke 1971-1976—Did You Hear Me? / 1976 / Capitol
21106
This album contains early and influential acoustic hot licks from
this fleet guitarist. —*Mark A. Humphrey*

Balance / 1979 / Chrysalis 21234
Good guitar work, featuring "Embryonic Journey" and Buddy
Holly's "Learning the Game." —*Chip Renner*

Guitar Music / 1981 / Chrysalis 21328
Twelve solid guitar instrumentals. —*Chip Renner*

My Father's Face / 1989 / Private Music 2050
Funky songs and staccato picking make this a very good album.
—*Mark A. Humphrey*

● **Essential** / 1991 / Chrysalis 21852
Guitarist Leo Kottke has earned a reputation as a premier fingerpicker, slide master, and 12-string virtuoso. The proof is in this 22-
track, 70-minute collection, culled from five albums released between 1976 and 1983. — *Roundup Newsletter*

○ **Great Big Boy** / 1991 / Private Music 82087
Kottke sings on this record to good effect. Features Lyle Lovett
and Margo Timmons. —*Chip Renner*

Jim Kweskin & His Jug Band

b. Jul. 18, 1940
Group
Jim Kweskin's Jug Band, including Bill Keith, Geoff Muldaur,
Maria D'Amato (later Muldaur), and others, came out of
Cambridge, MA, in 1963 with a combination of old-timey country
music, bluegrass, and ragtime, and became the major '60s propo-
nents of jug-band style. It never caught on in a big way, but it was
fun while it lasted. — *William Ruhlmann*

● **Greatest Hits** / 1990 / Vanguard 14
Washboards, kazoos, novelty songs, and general hilarity combine
to make some of the most delightful, foolish music of the '60s.
The jug-band craze was small and short-lived, but Kweskin and
his band, which included Maria D'Amato, soon to marry bandmember Geoff Muldaur, were its premier act, and this double-
disc set captures much of their whimsical style. — *William
Ruhlmann*

Peter LaFarge

b. 1931, **d.** 1965
Vocals
Singer-songwriter Peter LaFarge was the son of Pulitzer Prize-
winning author Oliver LaFarge and, like his father, a spokesman
for Indian rights. His involvement in the Korean War, where he
was decorated five times, served as the inspiration for his best-
known song, "Ballad of Ira Hayes," about a Pima Indian who was

at the battle of Iwo Jima in World War II but suffered in the postwar world. After a career as a rodeo cowboy, LaFarge turned to
folksinging in the late '50s and was part of the *Broadside* maga-
zine-Folkways Records community in New York in the early '60s,
recording several albums devoted to cowboy songs and Native
American concerns. Johnny Cash took "Ira Hayes" to number
three in the country charts in 1964. LaFarge died of a stroke the
following year. — *William Ruhlmann*

○ **As Long as the Grass Shall Grow** / 1963 /
Smithsonian/Folkways 2532
Surprisingly, this collection of songs about what we now call
Native Americans does not include LaFarge's best-known song,
"The Ballad of Ira Hayes." But the singer-songwriter, who was a
Native American himself, still manages to turn in one of the most
thorough and moving examinations of the sorry history of White
deception and aggression ever recorded. He gives his songs a dra-
matic, near-spoken delivery, making the messages all the more
convincing. — *William Ruhlmann*

● **On the Warpath/As Long As The Grass Shall Grow** / 1992 /
Bear Family 15632

Patty Larkin

Vocals, guitar
Larkin is a Boston-based singer-songwriter. After studying jazz,
she went into the acoustic folk style she is currently playing. Her
guitar work is highly respected, as is her songwriting. —*Chip
Renner*

○ **Step into the Light** / 1985 / Philo 1103
Fine debut album. —*Chip Renner*

● **Tango** / 1991 / High Street 10312
Most polished of her releases—backed by John Gorka and Darol
Anger. Very mature. —*Chip Renner*

Angles Running / 1993 / High Street Records
This lush album, produced by John Leventhal, showcases Larkin's
excellent guitar playing and expressive vocals. The first cut, "Who
Hold Your Hand" is the strongest song. Its melodic shape and
rhythmic drive are fine. The rest of the album is engaging even
when the songs are deeply introspective ballads. —*Richard Meyer*

Grey Larsen & Andre Marchand

○ **Orange Tree (Irish and French Roots), The** / 1993 / Sugar Hill
With wooden flutes, whistles, concertina, guitar feet, and vocals
this duo creates hypnotic music exploring their common roots.
Includes The "Waltz of Passing Time" and "The Wife of a
Drunken Soldier." —*Richard Meyer*

Last Fair Deal

Group
Connecticut-based bluegrass band with original songs and clean,
simple arrangements. —*Richard Meyer*

○ **Last Fair Deal** / 1989 / Bread and Butter
Be sure to check out "Spend a Little Time" and "Your Heart and
Mine." —*Richard Meyer*

Rob Laurens

○ **Honey on the Mountain** / 1993 /
San Francisco singer-songwriter Rob Laurens has a very graceful
rhythmic style. His songs are often about the expansivness of the
country and the place of the individual in it. —*Richard Meyer*

Christine Lavin

Vocals, guitar
Christine Lavin emerged out of the crowded New York City songwriter scene of the '80s with a style that distinguished her from
her peers. First of all, her songs were overwhelmingly concerned
with contemporary romantic mores (that scary, uncertain world
of "relationships" and "commitments" and "biological clocks").
Second, while her takes on this subject could sometimes be sentimental or maudlin, more often they were humorous: "If You
Need Space, Go to Utah" was the first track on her first recording,
a 1983 EP called *Husbands and Wives*, later reissued as *Another
Man's Woman*. By 1984, Lavin had managed to release her first
full-length album, *Future Fossils*, which included both her serious
and comic numbers, notably "Damaged Goods" (what people

start to feel like after enough failed relationships) and "Don't Ever Call Your Sweetheart by His Name" (how difficult it is to remember people's names after enough failed relationships). In 1986, Lavin signed to Rounder's Philo label, and since then she has recorded regularly, also touring extensively and building up a wide following.

Lavin has also made a particular point of promoting the work of her contemporaries, notably on such collections as *When October Goes* and *Buy Me, Bring Me, Take Me, Don't Mess My Hair!!! (Life According to Four Bitchin' Babes). —William Ruhlmann*

○ **Future Fossils** / 1984 / Philo 1104
A bright, wry, and earthy collection of her early songs. A great introduction. —*Bruce Eder*

● **Beau Woes (and Other Problems of Modern Life)** / 1986 / Philo 1107
From undoubtedly the sharpest wit in the contemporary folk scene, a splendidly entertaining, lively, honest, and eclectic album. Includes her clever "Biological Time Bomb"; her song for the athletically challenged, "Ballad of a Ballgame"; the more serious "Gettin' Used to Leavin'" with veteran folkie Eric Andersen; her spoof on "Camping," and other humorous and cynical vignettes. A gem. —*Ladyslipper*

○ **Good Thing He Can't Read My Mind** / 1988 / Philo 1121
Both satire and good folk music fill this album, and even a duet with Livingston Taylor. —*Ladyslipper*

Attainable Love / 1990 / Philo 1132
Ten more seriocomic songs that debunk, explore, and create the myths of contemporary (hetero) romance; includes "Shopping Cart of Love" and "Sensitive New Age Guys," as well as the somewhat more serious "Victim/Volunteer," "The Kind of Love You Never Recover From," and title. A straightforward acoustic production from this insightful observer-commentator. —*Ladyslipper*

Compass / 1991 / Philo 1142
For years, Christine's specialties have been droll commentary on the foibles of the modern world and the people in it, and what are sometimes more somber observations on heartbreak's variations. Her eye just gets sharper, and in this collection the two get mixed a bit more—irony informs the love songs, and the funny songs are just a touch more pointed than before. —*Roundup Newsletter*

Deborah Lavoy

Vocals
Deborah is a California singer-songwriter whose vocal style is similar to Patty Larkin's. Her songwriting style is serious, dealing with many of today's problems. —*Chip Renner*

○ **Hungry City** / 1991 / Lilola
Her deep rich vocals will win you over after one listen to this CD. This is mostly Lavoy and her guitar with little distraction from her songs. Highly recommended. —*Chip Renner*

Eddy Lawrence

Songwriter
This Alabama-born, New Jersey-based songwriter creates wry and insightful songs with an urban but Southern sensibility. He has three self-produced albums and is represented on the *The Fast Folk Musical Magazine. —Richard Meyer*

★ **Walker County** / 1987 / Snowplow 101
This is Lawrence's song cycle of his home county and contains some of his most arresting songs, including "Cecil's Gone," "Say It in Southern," and "Mary Lee." —*Richard Meyer*

Used Parts / 1992 / Snowplow 104
Great songs with great humor, including the title cut and "Luthor." —*Richard Meyer*

○ **Spare Parts** / 1994 / 1-800 Prime
1-800 Prime CD's release of Eddy Lawrence's fourth album is good news for fans of ironic, thoughtful country music. He takes on subjects such as Mohawk Indian steelworkers, loneliness after a suicide by a Tennessee dam, and the reckless pride of an auto junk dealer, all supported by his own great playing. A special album. —*Richard Meyer*

Will LeBlanc

○ **Relentless Pursuit...** / 1992 / Sheister Records

This collection of good time and bad times songs are played exuberantly in a folky Texas swing style by the "King of Swamp Swing." LeBlanc's straightahead vocals suit the country sentiments. "I Don't Drink" is fun, and "I've Got a Job" rocks. —*Richard Meyer*

Anne Ledermann

Fiddle, violin, mandolin, piano, Jew's Harp
Ledermann is a Canadian musician who plays fiddle, five-string violin, mandolin, piano, banjo, and jaw harp. She has played with the Ontario folk group Muddy York & the Flying Bulgar Klezmer Band. —*Chip Renner*

○ **Not a Mark in This World** / 1991 / Aural Traditions
This album is a collection of Canadian traditional music. Ledermann plays logging songs, Nova Scotia abolition songs, Ukrainian music, Yiddish folksongs, and backwoods music—a great collection. If you like old-timey, traditional folk music, you will enjoy this release. —*Chip Renner*

Katie Lee

Katie Lee is a real cowgirl. When she isn't singing by the campfire or in concert, she is running a ranch or guiding raft trips down the Colorado. Many years ago Katie was the darling of the New York crowd, singing outlandishly funny and often bawdy uptown folksongs. Today she sings outlandishly bawdy and often funny songs about the old West. She is so beautiful and has such a youthful approach to her performing—and to life, that it is hard to believe it is the same Katy Lee on her earlier recordings. She is a gem! —*Don Stevens*

● **Katie Lee Sings Love's Little Sisters** / Katydid

Brad Leftwich & Linda Higginbotham

Brad and Linda, both teachers at Augusta, are well known to Midwestern audiences. They have done as much as anyone to preserve and present traditional music in this part of the country. Brad has played with, among others, the Plank Road String Band. He learned to play the fiddle and banjo from Tommy Jarrell and other southern legends. Linda plays banjo-uke and banjo. Usually accompanied by any number of their talented friends, their recordings are just great! —*Don Stevens*

● **Leftwich, Higginbotham, & Jackson—1985 &1986 Con** / Music From Augusta

Moment In Time, A / Marimac

No One To Bring Home Tonight / County

Mark Levy

Vocals
Levy is a California singer-songwriter who uses humor and irony to show the listener how crazy life is. —*Chip Renner*

● **Sheroes Heroes** / 1980 / New-Clear
Very funny CD featuring fine guitar playing and singing. "Send a Man to Mars" is just what Bush needs. With 16 songs, it's a very nice CD. —*Chip Renner*

Take off Your Clothes / 1985 / New-Clear
Another political, humor-filled album, with "Between Iraq and a Hard Place," "Ramb. O," and "Take Off Your Clothes." —*Chip Renner*

Tom Lewis

Belfast-born and a British submarine officer for 24 years, Lewis is now based in Canada. —*Richard Pack*

● **Surfacing** / 1990 / Self-Propelled
A good collection of sea shanties and naval songs. —*Richard Pack*

Sea Dog See Dog / 1991 / Flying Fish 547
More songs and tales of the sea from this former British submarine officer. —*Richard Pack*

Gordon Lightfoot

b. Nov. 17, 1938, Orillia, Ontario
Vocals
Canadian Gordon Lightfoot first began to gain recognition as a songwriter in the mid-'60s, when his compositions "For Lovin' Me" and "Early Morning Rain" became hits for Peter, Paul & Mary, and Marty Robbins topped the country charts with "Ribbon

of Darkness." Lightfoot's own style was understated, his tasteful folk arrangements topped by a gentle burr of a voice. His albums began to appear in 1966, but it was not until the start of the '70s that he became a big success as a performer, scoring in 1970 with *Sit Down Young Stranger*, which contained his hit "If You Could Read My Mind," a song with a typically flowing melodic line and gently poetic lyrics.

Thereafter, the first half of the '70s were his. Lightfoot hit a peak in 1974 with *Sundown*, which went to number one, as did the title song when released on a single. Though he had developed a timeless style, Lightfoot was caught by the popular decline of folk-based music in the latter half of the 1970s and has performed and recorded less frequently since, sometimes trying to conform to perceived commercial trends without success. But concert appearances in the early '90s confirmed that he remains an engaging performer and that his catalog of original songs is hard to match. — *William Ruhlmann*

○ **Sit Down Young Stranger** / 1970 / Reprise 6392
Lightfoot's Reprise albums are always tastefully constructed, with their careful fingerpicking, restrained rhythm sections, and subtle string arrangements serving as a bed for the singer's sturdy baritone. What distinguishes the albums is the quality of Lightfoot's songwriting, and this one, featuring the title track, as well as "Approaching Lavender" and "If You Could Read My Mind," has the best overall selection. — *William Ruhlmann*

Summer Side of Life / 1971 / Reprise 2037
This extraordinary release doesn't have big hits on it but contains some of his finest songwriting, from the political song "Miguel," to the wistful songs about divorce, "Same Old Loverman" and "Talking in Your Sleep," and the joyous "Cotton Jenny." This is highly recommended. — *Richard Meyer*

○ **Sundown** / 1974 / Reprise 2177
Lightfoot's commercial peak came with this album, which topped the U.S. charts, containing both the number one title song and the Top Ten hit "Carefree Highway." But songs like "Somewhere U.S.A." and "High and Dry" are textured, catchy folk-rock on a par with the better-known tunes. — *William Ruhlmann*

Summertime Dream / 1976 / Reprise 2246
Due to Lightfoot's tendency to rerecord his hits when preparing compilations (the warning "caveat emptor" applies to the two volumes of *Gord's Gold*), this is the only place to find the original version of his number two "Wreck of the Edmond Fitzgerald." — *William Ruhlmann*

○ **Best of Gordon Lightfoot** / 1980 / Capitol 48396
A compilation of material Lightfoot recorded for United Artists in the '60s, this features the best of that period, including Lightfoot standards such as "For Lovin' Me," "Early Morning Rain," and "Canadian Railroad Trilogy." — *William Ruhlmann*

★ **United Artists Collection** / Oct. 5, 1993 / EMI
This double CD contains all of the Toronto singer-songwriter's 1960s studio albums (the live LP *Sunday Concert*, not included here, was also released in the '60s). On these records his resonant vocals, lyrical ambition, and melodic strengths produced as close a rival to Bob Dylan as Canada ever fashioned during that decade and foreshadowed work by other major Candian singer-songwriters of the late '60s, such as Joni Mitchell, Neil Young, and Leonard Cohen. "Early Mornin' Rain" (coverd by fellow Canadian folkies Ian & Sylvia), the folk-rock protest number "Black Day in July," the epic "Canadian Railroad Trilogy," and his cover of Ewan McColl's "The First Time Ever I Saw Your Face" are all present and are among the most popular tracks Lightfoot issued during his long career. Featuring both acoustic and folk-rock recordings, this neatly bundles Lightfoot's early work into a listenable and fairly inexpensive package. — *Richie Unterberger*

Larry Long w/ Children of Okemah

Group
Contemporary singer and songwriter Larry Long had a mission: to take Woody Guthrie's music back to the Dust Bowl balladeer's hometown. Okemah, OK, had spent about 40 years with its jaw set against its most famous native son. Decent folk there called him a Communist and said a determined "NO" when the Guthrie family proposed a kind of museum at the decaying homeplace back in the '70s. "It would just attract hippies," said the decent folk who knew this Woody was just trouble. Long's gentle subversion was to teach Guthrie's songs to the kids of Okemah and

encourage them to make up their own songs in Guthrie's kid-friendly idiom. The results were recorded at a local theater by the Flying Fish label, and now Okemah's water tower proudly proclaims the town as "Home of Woody Guthrie." — *Mark A. Humphrey*

○ **It Takes a Lot of People ...** / 1988 / Flying Fish 70508
It Takes a Lot of People (Tribute to Woody Guthrie) was recorded by Long and his young friends at the Crystal Theater in Okemah, OK, Guthrie's hometown. When they are singing Guthrie songs or reading from Guthrie's works, the tribute works beautifully. Long's own children's material is somewhat less successful. — *William Ruhlmann*

Kimberly M'Carver

Vocals, guitar
M'Carver is a Texas singer, songwriter, and guitarist who was greatly influenced by Guy Clark, Nanci Griffith, and Bev Doolittle. — *Chip Renner*

○ **Breathe the Moonlight** / Oct. 1989 / Philo 1129
M'Carver uses Stuart Duncan, Jeff White, Jerry Douglas, Roy Huskey Jr, and Dennis M'Carver as backup. "Whistle Down the Wind" and "My Way Back Home to You" are exceptional. Highly recommended. — *Chip Renner*

Rod MacDonald

b. 1949
Vocals
Connecticut-born MacDonald has performed internationally, and many of his songs have been adapted as standards by the contemporary folksong writers' community. With his pure emotive tenor and stirring, catchy tunes, MacDonald is one of the most appealing singer-songwriters to emerge in the '80s. Add to that thoughtful lyrics that touch on a variety of political and social issues, and you have a remarkable artist deserving a much wider public. MacDonald has contributed over 20 songs to *The Fast Folk Musical Magazine*, in addition to his solo releases. — *Richard Meyer & William Ruhlmann*

○ **No Commercial Traffic** / 1983 / Cinemagic
"On the Road to NY Town" should not be missed. — *Richard Meyer*

● **White Buffalo** / 1987 / Mountain Railroad 29
This, MacDonald's second album, is something of a best of, covering much of his work in the late '70s and early '80s. *White Buffalo* truly captures MacDonald's mid-'80s club sound on some of his greatest songs. — *William Ruhlmann & Richard Meyer*

Man On A Ledge / 1994 / Shanachie
Rod has put together another set of original songs with his longtime musical partner Mark Dann. They cover the wide range of romance, politics, and fun rhythm tunes. "The Song for Checkoslovakia" and "Grapes on the Vine" are two standout tracks. — *Richard Meyer*

Dave Mallett

Vocals
Mallett is a singer-songwriter whose songs often deal with New England and the working man. His "Garden Song" is a well-known standard. — *Chip Renner*

○ **Vital Signs** / 1986 / Flying Fish 373
On this, the best of several quite good albums, Mallett provides a feeling examination of the state of a generation now too old to die young. Putting aside "Midnight Madness" and "that whole James Dean thing," he embraces "solid wood and aging wine" among other long-lasting items and finds a way to look bravely into middle age. — *William Ruhlmann*

Hirth Martinez

Vocals
This East Los Angeles-born singer-songwriter released two albums, one produced by Robbie Robertson and the other by John Simon. — *Richard Meyer*

Hirth from Earth / 1975 / Warner Brothers 2867
This record was produced by Robbie Robertson. His playing, along with Garth Hudson's, gives this a sound similar to that of the Band but laid over Martinez's unusual songwriting style. An idiosyncratic but wonderful record. — *Richard Meyer*

● **Big Bright Street** / 1977 / Warner Brothers 3031
If you find this great album, don't pass it up. Especially great are the following cuts: "The Driver," "Valley of the Music," and "Nuthin' Is New." —*Richard Meyer*

John Martyn

Vocals
Scottish folksinger with a jazzy blues style, whose career dates from the late '60s. —*AMG*

Road to Ruin / 1970 / Island 1882
Martyn's wife Beverley is the vocalist. South African saxophonist Dudu Pukwana is on three tracks. This is folk mixed with new age musings. Excellent musicianship. By now it is rare, both musically and as a collector's item. —*Michael G. Nastos*

○ **Bless the Weather** / 1971 /

○ **One World** / 1977 / Island 9492
This virtuoso British guitarist and innovator mixes the music world of folk, blues, and fusion with some surprising results. Guests include Jamaican trombonist Rico, Steve Winwood, and fusioneers Hansford Rowe and Morris Pert. String arrangements are by Harry Robinson. For aficionados, a must-buy; for novices, it's a good one to try. —*Michael G. Nastos*

● **So Far So Good** / 1977 / Island 9484

David Massengill

Vocals, guitar, dulcimer
Massengill is a New York-based singer-songwriter. He is a member of the New York *Fast Folk* community. His songwriting is brilliant, and his guitar and dulcimer playing are excellent. He has just signed with the Flying Fish label. —*Chip Renner*

★ **Great American Bootleg Tape** / 1986 / Bowser Wowser
Massengill assembled this tape himself, using tracks recorded for the Stash Records *Cornelia Street* collection, *The Fast Folk Musical Magazine*, and the video of the Folk City 25th-Anniversary concert. The result is the single most impressive folk-based song collection of the decade. Massengill's lyrical facility is the most astounding to appear since that of Elvis Costello—he can be wickedly funny and deeply touching in the same line, and his imagination seems unlimited. By rights, this should be on all lists of the best albums of the '80s. (Write to David Massengill, 179 E. 3rd St., Apt. 20, NY, NY 10009.) —*William Ruhlmann*

Kitchen Tape / 1987 / Bowser Wowser
More varied and novelty-oriented than *The Great American Bootleg Tape*, this collection of demos (recorded on a Sony Walkman) nevertheless shows the range in Massengill's mastery of the English language even more extensively than the earlier tape. His guitar, dulcimer, and harmonica are clean (except for an occasional fire engine or street noise caught on the tape). —*William Ruhlmann & Chip Renner*

○ **Coming up for Air** / 1992 / Flying Fish 70590
Massengill's first studio album. He does a great job on several old songs like "Fairfax," "My Name Joe," and some new material. Producer Steve Addabbo, who has produced Suzanne Vega, manages to bring out the best in the music. Long overdue, but well worth it! —*Chip Renner*

Ian Matthews

b. Jun. 1946, Lincolnshire, England
Vocals, guitar
Ian Matthews (now spelled Iain to reflect his Celtic roots) has had a widely varied and complex recording career. He began as the lead singer for Fairport Convention after a short stint as the vocalist for the London-based surf band Pyramid in 1966. During Fairport's 1969 *Unhalfbricking* sessions, he decided to leave due to growing musical differences with the band. After making his first solo album, *Matthews Southern Comfort*, he released two albums with a band of the same name. They had a hit with a version "Woodstock."

Matthews left in 1971 for a second chance at a solo career, releasing two fine folk-rock albums for Vertigo. He then formed Plainsong while finishing the contractual obligation album, *Journeys from Gospel Oak*—one of his finest recorded moments. Plainsong released one critically acclaimed album on Elektra and then disbanded while recording the second. His stay at Elektra ended after two more acclaimed yet overlooked country-folk al-

bums. He began experimenting in different styles for the rest of the '70s, often with uninspired and unsuccessful results. He did, however, have a U.S. Top Ten hit in 1978 with "Shake It."

The '80s were a relatively slow period for Matthews. Recording intermittently, he spent a few years as an A&R man for Island and later worked for Windham Hill. He relocated permanently to the United States in the late '80s. The '90s have found him reviving his career with a return to his folk-rock roots, touring small clubs most of the year. —*Chris Woodstra*

○ **If You Saw Thro' My Eyes** / 1970 / Vertigo 1002
After leaving Southern Comfort, Matthews reunited with Fairport Convention members Richard Thompson and Sandy Denny and made one of his finest albums. Though the material and playing is superior to his previous work, it was unfortunately overlooked at the time. Now combined with his follow-up, *Tigers Will Survive* on CD (German import only), this is a must-have for fans. —*Chris Woodstra*

Tigers Will Survive / 1971 / Vertigo 1010
Recorded during two different periods of time broken up by a U.S. tour, his follow-up to *If You Saw Thro' My Eyes* lacks the focus of its predecessor. Still worthwhile if only for "Morning Star," one of Matthews's most beautiful originals. —*Chris Woodstra*

○ **Journeys from Gospel Oak** / 1972 / Mooncrest 18
Billed as a contractual obligation record by the artist, *Journeys from Gospel Oak* is easily as good as his best work. It is most assuredly a companion piece to Plainsong's *In Search of Amelia Earhart* (an album loosely based on the disappearance of Amelia Earhart), this time loosely based around the night Hank Williams died. This album includes such solid tracks as Gene Clark's "Polly," "Bride 1945" by Paul Siebel, and the haunting Jimmy Webb tune, "Met Her on a Plane". A strong but often overlooked record and well worth the effort it takes to find a copy. —*Jim Worbois*

○ **Valley Hi** / 1973 / Elektra 75061
Often regarded as his best album, *Valley Hi* finds Matthews combining his folk-rock expertise with producer Mike Nesmith's country leanings. Highlights include the Nesmith-penned "Propinquity" and Jackson Browne's "These Days." —*Chris Woodstra*

○ **Some Days You Eat the Bear Some Days the Bear Eats You** / 1974 / Elektra 75078
His final LP recorded for Elektra continues in the country spirit of *Valley Hi* with a stronger pop sensibility. Includes a brilliant rendition of Tom Waits's "Old 55" and the touching tribute to Hank Williams, "A Wailing Goodbye." —*Chris Woodstra*

Walking a Changing Line / 1988 / Windham Hill 1070
On this, the first vocal album for Windham Hill, Matthews pays tribute to the songwriting of Jules Shear. While the song selection is first rate as always, the typical Windham Hill musical indulgences take away from the enjoyment of this disc. Worthwhile for curious fans of Matthews or Shear. —*Chris Woodstra*

Pure & Crooked / 1990 / Gold Castle 71354
It's amazing, but in a career dating back to the late '60s and filled with valuable work, Matthews waited until 1990 to produce his first consistently brilliant solo album. Maybe it took all that time to develop the instrumental, lyrical, and recording mastery demonstrated on this disc, which has a thoroughly modern pop sheen (fans of Peter Gabriel and Sting will feel right at home) but at the same time maintains a folkish directness and depth of feeling. —*William Ruhlmann*

● **Best of Matthew's Southern Comfort** / 1992 / MCA 10519
A fine 16-track collection drawing from Matthews's first solo effort and the two Matthews' Southern Comfort albums. Includes the band's hit version of "Woodstock." —*Chris Woodstra*

● **Soul of Many Places** / 1993 / Asylum 61457
Soul of Many Places compiles the best moments from his recording high point for Elektra (1972-1974). Featuring selections from *Valley Hi*, *Some Days You Eat the Bear...*, and Plainsong's *The Search for Amelia Earhart*, this is the best introduction to Matthews's finest work (all currently out of print in the United States). The inclusion of non-LP tracks makes this essential for fans as well. —*Chris Woodstra*

○ **Skeleton Keys** / May 18, 1993 / Rhino
Matthews emerges from his experimental '80s period with a return to his classic acoustic country-folk sound. With his first al-

bum comprised solely of originals, he shows more focus than he has in nearly two decades. —*Chris Woodstra*

Wall Matthews

Guitar, piano, African percussion
Wall Matthews is a composer, performer, and teacher who is accomplished on guitar, piano, and African percussion. As Composer in Residence for Dance at Connecticut College, Wall has an ongoing involvement with modern dance. He has composed numerous dance scores that have been performed by the Paris Opera Ballet, the Royal Danish Ballet, the Nikolai-Louis Company, and the Limon Company. —*Chip Renner*

● **Riding Horses** / 1988 / Clean Cuts
Matthews goes from New Age to new acoustic on this release. Seven selections from his *Solo Piano and Guitar* appear on this CD. His guitar playing is up there with the best acoustic guitar players. —*Chip Renner*

Gathering the World / 1991 / Clean Cuts 712
This is not like other Matthews albums—he goes from delicate guitar work to pygmy chants to African music. Female vocals are a nice touch for a Wall Matthews album. Those with eclectic tastes will enjoy this. —*Chip Renner*

Tom May

Working out of the heartland of America, Omaha, Nebraska, Tom May hosts "River City Folk," syndicated by American Public Radio to well over 200 stations. The TV version of the show is broadcast by Americana Cable and is this country's only televised folk music program. May himself is the epitome of the balladeer, singing his own songs and those of others with warmth, humor, and accessibility. He's performed with most of this continent's better-known folk musicians and across the world from Ireland to Hawaii and Alaska to the Caribbean islands. Tom is also an accomplished guitar and Irish pennywhistle player. —*Allan Shaw*

○ **Coming Home** / Vignette
The sweep and grandeur of America captured by this quintessential balladeer. —*Mike Fleischer*

Carol McComb

Vocals
McComb is a California singer-songwriter whose music ranges from country to folk. —*Chip Renner*

○ **Tears into Laughter** / 1989 / Kaleidoscope 41
McComb's album is very compelling. The sad "Faded Dresden Blues," about the effects of Alzheimer's disease on her grandmother, touches the soul. She is backed by Nina Gerber on acoustic guitar (Kate Wolf's guitar player), Sally Van Meter on dobro (Good Ol' Persons), Laurie Lewis on vocals, and Barbra Higbie on piano. —*Chip Renner*

Ed McCurdy

b. 1919, Willow Hill, PA
Vocals
Singer-songwriter Ed McCurdy dropped out of college to make a career as a folksinger. In the late '40s, he learned guitar, put together a folk repetoire, and began performing on radio and TV in Canada. By the early '50s he was known in the United States and made New York his home in 1954. Throughout the '60s, McCurdy was a mainstay of the folk scene and a pacesetter for the younger '60s folksingers. —*Michael Erlewine*

○ **When Dalliance Was in Flower** / 195z / Elektra 170
There are four volumes to this series on which McCurdy delves into fun, racy, and indelicate songs about love. He's accompanied on some of the cuts by Alan Arkin. These are generally polite versions of ribald tunes. This set along with many similar records by Oscar Brand covers a lot of scatalogical ground. —*Richard Meyer*

● **Best of Ed McCurdy** / 1967 / Tradition 2051

Megon McDonough

Guitar, piano
McDonough is a singer-songwriter out of Des Plaines, IL, who also plays guitar and piano. Her voice is beautiful, and she can sing folk, rock, and country, all with style. —*Chip Renner*

○ **American Girl** / 1990 / Sirius 1

Megon's second release is more filled out and produced than her first (tastefully, of course), with love as a theme again, this time the personal kind, with metaphors of water and dreams a frequent image in her songs. The majority of songs are again originals and feature lovely arrangements with accompaniment on recorder, harmonica, mandolin, piano, guitar, and bass. —*Ladyslipper*

Day by Day / Singing Flower 1
As suggested by the cover, love is one of the themes on her debut release, the spiritual kind, that is . . . as well as respect for life and Mother Nature. —*Ladyslipper*

Kate and Anna McGarrigle

Group
Kate (b. 1946) and Anna (b. 1944) McGarrigle are Canadian songwriting sisters whose work first came to international recognition in 1974 when Linda Ronstadt recorded Anna's "Heart Like a Wheel" as the title song to one of her albums. The sisters were signed to Warner Brothers and recorded *Kate & Anna McGarrigle*, an album of deeply felt (sometimes deeply funny) songs with a homey, eclectic folk backing and tart, striking vocals. It was widely hailed. Its two follow-ups seemed rushed, though they contained some good songs. In 1981 the sisters (having left Warner) recorded *French Record* for Joe Boyd's Hannibal label, and it showed considerable charm. *Love Over and Over* in 1982 marked a move toward rock that cheered fans but also turned out to be their last album for almost a decade.
In the meantime, they raised families and ventured out every now and then to play a few rapturously received dates, especially in the Northeast. At one of these in the late '80s, they said they'd been working on a musical with producer Roma Baran. That project never came to fruition, but in 1990 they finally returned to the record racks with *Heartbeats Accelerating*. —*William Ruhlmann*

★ **Kate & Anna McGarrigle** / 1975 / Carthage 4401
This album was *Melody Maker*'s pick for Best Record of 1975, and it's hard to argue with that choice when you listen to the tart harmonies and solo singing on one of the best songwriting collections ever. From Anna's famous "Heart Like a Wheel" to Kate's bouncy "Kiss and Say Goodbye," the songs paint a deeply felt, highly detailed portrait of life and romance. A revelation when it was released and a classic today. —*William Ruhlmann*

Dancer with Bruised Knees / 1977 / Warner Brothers 3014

French Record / 1980 / Hannibal 1302
Many McGarrigle fans cite this as their favorite, even if they don't speak French. The Canadian-based sisters are expressively at home in the country's other language, and this may be the most musical of their albums. —*William Ruhlmann*

Love over and Over / 1983 / Polydor 1062
The first English-language record the sisters had done in several years found them rocking harder (Mark Knopfler of Dire Straits was a prominent guest star), but the layoff had also given them time to write a strong set of songs that found new things to say about love and motherhood. —*William Ruhlmann*

Heartbeats Accelerating / 1990 / Private Music 2070
Eight years later, the McGarrigles have adopted a more new age sound, with extensive synthesizer programming. The sound may be lush and modern, but the sentiments are still deeply felt and the observations remain laser-sharp. —*William Ruhlmann*

Ellen McIlwaine

Vocals
A gutsy, raw, energized purveyor of jazz, blues, rock, pop, folk, Jimi Hendrix, and Jack Bruce. Her wonderful voice commands with authority. —*Michael G. Nastos*

Honky Tonk Angel / 1972 / Polydor 5021
An album of songs by McIlwaine, Hendrix, Jack Bruce, Steve Winwood, Isaac Hayes, and Bobbie Gentry. A sweet date. One side is live, the other is a studio recording. —*Michael G. Nastos*

● **Real** / 1975 / Kot'ai 3306
Her best. McIlwaine sings and plays slide guitar in a blues-rock vein and composes prolifically. This album also includes music by Stevie Wonder, Jack Bruce, John Lee Hooker, Booker T., and Tracy Nelson. Dedicated to Jimi Hendrix. —*Michael G. Nastos*

Everybody Needs It / 1977 / Blind Pig 1081

This early '80s recording with Jack Bruce is dedicated to Professor Longhair and Tim Hardin. Half of the album features McIlwaine's own compositions. —*Michael G. Nastos*

Loreena McKennitt

○ **Mask & Mirror** / Warner Bros. Records, Inc.
On this extraordinary album McKennitt leaves behind the occasionally precious seriousness of her previous records and offers up a gypsylike mix of original songs and traditional music. She is searching for an understanding of spirit in the modern world by traveling the world musically and as the diary entries in the booklet, in person. There is no sense in the album of cultural carpetbagging. It's beautifully written and performed by all with great authority. A haunting record. —*Richard Meyer*

● **Visit** / 1992 / Warner Brothers 26880
The Visit fulfills the promise of Loreena McKennitt's first three recordings, expanding her Celtic musical and cultural influences in a fresh contemporary manner, while drawing comparisons to the work of Enya and Kate Bush. Guitar, bass, percussion, and cello provide the core accompaniment, with additional help on fiddle and uillean pipes gracefully augmenting Loreena's own harp, keyboards, and, of course, the trademark vocals in her pure, floating warble. —*Backroads Music/Heartbeats*

Elemental / Quinlan Road 101
This extremely talented musician-vocalist must have been incarnated just to bring the musics of the British Isles to life, such is the power of the images she evokes—perfectly airy, with shades of mist and surf. This 1985 album captures her magic in nine selections, ranging from poems by William Blake and W.B. Yeats set to music to traditional songs like "Banks of Claudy," "Carrighfergus," "She Moved Through the Fair." Harps, strings, and keyboards accompany her beautiful voice. —*Ladyslipper*

Parallel Dreams / Quinlan Road 103
In *Parallel Dreams*, her third release, Loreena uses elements drawn from such deep-rooted influences as the ancient Celtic tradition and the ritualism of North American first peoples. Her voice is tender and strong, delicate and haunting, soft and soaring, communicating archetypal energies that seem to radiate through her soul as she pours forth the old and the new, defying categorization. —*Backroads Music/Heartbeats*

McKinnely

○ **Next Feeding** / 1992 /
Oregonian McKinnely has an arty and effective style comparable to Jane Sibery, and Suzanne Vega. "Hallucinangels" and "Bottom of the Seas" are edgy and dreamy. —*Richard Meyer*

El McMeen

Guitar
This Connecticut-based guitarist has impeccable technique and is a sensitive interpreter of solo guitar material. —*Richard Meyer*

○ **Of Soul & Spirit** / 1974 / Shanachie 97012

Ralph McTell

b. 1944
Vocals
British singer-songwriter Ralph McTell is one of those artists whose career has been defined by the success of a single song. That song is "Streets of London," in which the narrator takes a companion complaining of loneliness through London's backstreets, pointing out the army of poor and wretched who are truly lonely. McTell recorded the song on his second album, *Spiral Staircase*, in 1969, but it wasn't until he rerecorded it in 1974 that it became a number two U.K. hit. He has continued to make albums, has become associated with the Fairport Convention family of musicians, and has appeared on British TV, especially on children's shows. —*William Ruhlmann*

★ **You Well-Meaning Brought Me Here** / 1971 / ABC 5084
You Well-Meaning Brought Me Here includes McTell's "Streets of London," which has by now become a genuine folk song—lots of people don't know he wrote it. Sadly, its portrait of what we now call the homeless is even more relevant in these times than it was in the early '70s. Happily, this album, gorgeously but simply produced by Gus Dudgeon, almost lives up to its most memorable track. —*William Ruhlmann*

Richard Meyer

Vocals
Singer-songwriter Richard Meyer has been at the center of the Greenwich Village scene since the early '80s, producing concerts and radio programs, editing the *Fast Folk Musical Magazine* for many years, and developing his strong body of work. He is a comprehensive artist, producing, arranging, and writing. —*Bill McCauly*

Laughing/Scared / 1987 / Old Forge 023
Meyer's folk-rock debut sometimes has an almost-rockabilly exuberance, even when he's dealing with the "scared" side of his lyrical dichotomy. And then there are those songs, such as "All My Ex-Girlfriends (Are Married)," in which singer and listener are laughing and shivering at the same time. Still, Meyer remains able to assure us there's "No Reason to Cry" with a song that's one of those hit-single shoulda-beens. A fine, varied collection. —*William Ruhlmann*

○ **Good Life!** / 1992 / Shanachie 8003
Meyer's second release is solid throughout. He has a very good group helping out—Rex Fowler, Mark Dann, Lucy Kaplansky, Andrew Hardin, Lisa Gutkin, Margo Hennebach, and Barry Mitterhoff. This is not the kind of CD that jumps out at you, it just grows on you. —*Chip Renner*

● **Letter from the Open Sky** / 1994 / Shanachie Records Corp.
Richard Meyer has made an artistic breakthrough with this, his third album. The curious song structures and intricate productions are well crafted. The seven-minute title cut is driven by mandolins, harp, and drums; while "Century's End" (a song of the Holocaust's last survivor) uses minor key violin lines to emphasise the lyric. Meyer is joined on "Blind October" by Katy Moffatt in a cinematic romantic travelogue duet. Meyer covers a lot of political and romantic ground in this hauntingly arranged album. —*Bill McCauly*

Walt Michael

Guitar, mandolin, harmonica, hammer dulcimer
Walt Michael is one of the premier hammer dulcimer players in the bluegrass-folk field. He is equally accomplished on guitar, mandolin, and harmonica. He is backed by Frank Orsini (fiddle), John Kirk (fiddle, guitar, banjo, mandolin, and vocals), and Mark Murphy (cello, string bass, and vocals). —*Chip Renner*

Music for Hammer Dulcimer / 1983 /
Early work. One of the finest hammer dulcimer players out there. —*Chip Renner*

○ **Good Old Way** / 1985 / FH 033
Highly recommended. —*Chip Renner*

● **Step Stone** / 1986 / Flying Fish 70480
Twelve solid songs. His best work. —*Cub Koda*

John Michaels

○ **Weather the Storm** / 1993 / Beacon Records
Former Maratime Academy alum John Michaels fits right into the regional troubador tradition. His songs about local events and people are charming. There is no musical adventure here, but the album is an uncluttered recording of what Michaels does. —*Richard Meyer*

Chad Mitchell

During the 1960s, Chad Mitchell (and the Chad Mitchell Trio) had a permanent place in the nation's Top 40 charts. Now Chad's back, and his performing has lost nothing in the years since he "retired" as an active musician. This time he's a solo, and the tunes he's chosen for his return to singing include numbers by such respected songwriters as Dave Mallett, David Massengill, Nancy Griffith, and Tom Russell. —*Allan Shaw*

● **At the Bitter End** / 1962 / Kapp 3281

Hugh Moffatt

Vocals
After leaving the Austin, TX, and Washington, DC, music scene, Moffatt moved to Nashville, TN, where he has become a respected singer-songwriter. His songs have been covered by Ronnie Milsap, Dolly Parton, Bobby Bare, Lacy J. Dalton, Jerry Lee Lewis, Alabama, and more. —*Chip Renner*

○ **Loving You** / 1987 / Philo 1111
A very good debut album. Solid songwriting. Russ Barrenberg and Jerry Douglas back up Moffatt. —*Chip Renner*

● **Troubadour** / 1989 / Philo 1127
Highly recommended. Moffat's songwriting is at its best. —*Chip Renner*

Katy Moffatt

Vocals
Moffatt is a singer-songwriter who has released three albums. She has cowritten with Tom Russell and released an acoustic album with Andrew Hardin (of the Tom Russell Band). —*Chip Renner*

○ **Walkin' on the Moon** / 1976 / Philo 1128
Moffatt's album is not overproduced. It features her on vocals and acoustic guitar and Andrew Harden on vocals and guitar. Moffatt cowrote with Tom Russell and covers three of her brother Hugh Moffatt's songs. Nice job on "Walkin' on the Moon." —*Chip Renner*

Kissin' in the California Sun / 1978 / CBS 34774
Nice album. Features Dickie Betts, Chuck Leavell (Sea Level), the Allman Brothers rhythm section, and the Muscle Shoals horn section. —*Chip Renner*

Child Bride / 1990 / Philo 1133
. . . a startling departure from last year's introspective and acoustic *Walkin' on the Moon*. — *Mark A. Humphrey, Rock & Roll Disc*

★ **Evangeline Hotel, The** / 1993 / Philo
The first thing to be aware of is that this album was briefly released with a different cover and title—*The Greatest Show on Earth*. Be assured it is the same album, and a great one it is, too. Many of the tracks were cowritten with Tom Russell, who produced the CD. Andy Hardin plays great parts as usual, and it's all held together by some of the most open and honest sounding vocals among contemporary songwriters. —*Richard Meyer*

Buddy Mondlock

Songwriter
Chicago-born and now based in Nashville, Mondlock is busy as a writer and collaborating songwriter with artists such as Janis Ian. —*Richard Meyer*

○ **On the Line** / 1987 / Sparking Gap 001
A beautiful self-produced album. Highlights are "Aunt Anna" and "Fire of Change." —*Richard Meyer*

Dave Moore

Vocals, guitar, harmonica, accordion
Dave Moore is a Midwestern singer-songwriter who plays guitar, harmonica, and button accordion. He has appeared on many of Greg Brown's albums and on "A Prairie Home Companion." —*Chip Renner*

● **Jukejoints & Cantinas** / 1956 / Red House 06
A fine collection of blues, standards, and Norteno dance music. This was not originally meant to be released as an album. —*Chip Renner*

Over My Shoulder / 1956 / Red House 34
Moore's debut as a songwriter; an outstanding release featuring Peter Ostroushko and Radislav Lorkovic. Dave steps out with "Just a Dog" (heavy Greg Brown sound), "Over My Shoulder," and "God Moves on the Water." Highly recommended. —*Chip Renner*

Jem Moore & Ariane Lydon

○ **O Susanna** / 1994 / Beacon
This versatile duo has made a crystalline album of highly ornamented instrumentals, based mostly on Moore's hammered dulcimer playing. Ariane Lydon's vocals are smokey and soothing. —*Richard Meyer*

Mae Moore

○ **Bohemia** / 1991 / Tristar Music
This beautiful album's understated arrangements provide a lush setting for Moore's dreamy lyrics of romance and self-discovery. "Arrow" and "Shape of Your Love" are good with candles. —*Richard Meyer*

Nancy Moran

Vocals
Moran is a Maryland-based singer-songwriter. Her songs are intelligent and deal with love, doubts, homelessness, and the "good old days." —*Chip Renner*

○ **Little Off Balance** / 1991 / Azalea
Moran's debut album is a collection of music that goes from bluesy saxophone to rock to delicate acoustic guitar work. The songs are very personal, and Moran lets you know it. —*Chip Renner*

Geof Morgan

Vocals
Morgan is a Washington State singer-songwriter who is known for his sensitive songs dealing with birth, AIDS, and the male-female relationship. His songs are intelligent and well crafted. —*Chip Renner*

It Comes with the Plumbing / 1970 / Nexus
An independent debut release. Shows the promise of a great career. —*Chip Renner*

Finally Letting / 1981 / Flying Fish 277
This album is ripe with promise. Good vocals and guitar playing. —*Chip Renner*

● **At the Edge** / 1984 / Flying Fish 350
A fine collection of music, including "Five Months into a Miracle," "Glad to Be a Man," "Goodbye John Wayne," and "Anna's Dance." —*Chip Renner*

○ **Talk It Over** / 1987 / Flying Fish 436
His most adventurous; moves into bolder material. —*Chip Renner*

Bill Morrissey

Vocals
Since 1984 Bill Morrissey has released four albums of original songs that have startled and delighted the following he's built up in touring around the Northeast. By the second one, *North*, he'd been picked up by the Philo division of Rounder. Morrissey sings in a surprisingly flexible deep voice (somewhat reminiscent of Leon Redbone's croak, but more supple). His songs are full of humor and pathos, expressed in keenly observed details. This is small-town life, sometimes desperate, sometimes hopeful, but always presented in new, unexpected ways. —*William Ruhlmann*

○ **North** / 1986 / Philo 1106
Morrissey's New England country accent and self-deprecating humor make it easy to miss the bite in many of his songs, which have a Hemingwayesque understatement both in their sly, sidelong observations and in their matter-of-fact presentation. In fact, Morrissey is a taste well worth acquiring for anyone seeking perceptive songwriting and the occasional dry laugh. —*William Ruhlmann*

★ **Standing Eight** / 1989 / Philo 1123
. . . his third release, may just be his best yet. If there's anything about Morrissey that becomes wearing, it may be his croak of a voice, which might be more than many can take. Still, he has a wryness and toughness of character that makes his tales of hardwon love seem so fresh and devoid of clichA and excess melodrama. *Standing Eight* may also be seen as Morrissey's super session. But this is clearly Morrissey's show from start to finish, and he's wise enough to give his famous pals the slack they need to contribute some tight, winning performances (Shawn Colvin's especially good on "She's That Kind of Mystery"). —*John Dougan, Option*

Inside / 1992 / Philo 1145
Great production, great arrangements, and perfectly honed lyrics bring a timeless sense to these short stories of rootlessness and love. "Long Gone," "Robert Johnson," and "The Man from Out of Town" are key songs. Morrissey has matured so that these songs sound as if they have always been with us. —*Richard Meyer*

○ **Night Train** / 1993 / Philo Records
His style has really matured and this album contains another solid, thoughtful set of story songs. The sound on this album is more stripped down, as basic as a Lou Reed record and just as effective. —*Richard Meyer*

Geoff Muldaur

b. Pelham, NY
Guitar
Muldaur grew up just outside New York, in Pelham, NY. He plays country-blues guitar. Muldaur was a member of Jim Kweskin's Jug Band. —*Chip Renner*

● Sleepy Man Blues / 1963 / Prestige 7727
Great covers of Blind Willie Johnson's "The Rain Don't Fall on Me," Bukka White's "Good Gin Blues," and Sleepy John Estes's "Drop Down Mama." —*Chip Renner*

Geoff & Amos / Dec. 1978 / Flying Fish 061
On this album, two artists who were prominent in folk music during the '60s sing and play a variety of lively material. —*AMG*

Blues Boy / 1979 / Flying Fish 201
This solo album features fine blues singing from Muldaur. —*AMG*

Heidi Muller

Vocals
Muller is a Washington State singer-songwriter who has been a part of the Victory Music project. Her style is reminiscent of Kate Wolf's. Her music has dealt with the Pacific Northwest and her social concerns. —*Chip Renner*

Between the Water & the Wind / 1980 / Cascadia
Muller's songwriting is strong ("Honey in My Tea," "Paradise in Puget Sound"), and her choice of cover material (Guy Clark, Bill Staines, Bob Blue) is well done. A pleasure to listen to. —*Chip Renner*

● Matters of the Heart / 1990 / Muller Music
A more mature release of 13 songs. Her song "Good Road" is a great traveler's song. "Matters of the Heart" is one of Muller's finest songs. A very good production. —*Chip Renner*

Comer "Moon" & Deborraha Mullins

Moon and Deborraha perform regularly at the Ozark Folk Center in Mountain View, AR. Usually performing as a duo, they also have a group—Sassafras. Moon has won many guitar contests. Deborraha has one of the most beautiful voices in music. She plays guitar and bowed psaltry to Moon's banjo and guitar. On their recordings, as in their performances, they make you feel as though you are sitting in their parlor. Their choice of old songs is beautiful. —*Don Stevens*

● River Of Memory / Comer Mullins

David Munyon

Vocals, guitar
David is a hard-driving guitarist and blues-based singer-songwriter. —*Richard Meyer*

○ Code Name: Jumper / Los Hermanos 0100

Mustard's Retreat

Group
The Michigan-based duo of Dave Tamuelevich and Michael Hough sings primarily original songs. —*Richard Meyer*

Home by the Morning / 1980 / Eagle 4192
Look for "Great Lakes Fishing Trade." —*Richard Meyer*

● Midwinter's Night / 1985 / Red House 20
The key song is "Jeremy Brown." —*Richard Meyer*

Fred Neil

b. 1937, St. Petersburg, FL
Vocals, guitar
Moody, bluesy, and melodic, Fred Neil was one of the most compelling folk-rockers to emerge from Greenwich Village in the mid-'60s. His albums showcased his extraordinarily low, rich voice on intensely personal and reflective compositions, sounding like a cross between Tim Buckley and Tim Hardin. His influence was subtle but significant; before forming the Lovin' Spoonful, John Sebastian played harmonica on Neil's first album, which also featured guitarist Felix Pappalardi, who went on to produce Cream. The Jefferson Airplane featured Neil's "Other Side of This Life" prominently in their concerts, and dedicated a couple of songs ("Ballad of You and Me and Pooneil" and "House at Pooneil Corner") to him. On the B-side of "Crying,"is Neil's "Candy Man"

one of Roy Orbison's bluesiest efforts. Most famously, Nilsson took Fred's "Everybody's Talkin'" into the top ten as the theme to the movie *Midnight Cowboy.* Always an enigmatic recluse, Neil retreated to his home in Coconut Grove, FL, after achieving cult success and hasn't released anything since a live album in 1971. —*Richie Unterberger*

● Bleecker & MacDonald / 1964 / Elektra 7293
Neil's Greenwich village coffeehouse roots are in strongest evidence on this album (later retitled *Little Bit of Rain*). The drummerless (but not entirely acoustic) LP is also his bluesiest recording. The uniformly strong tracks include "Other Side of This Life" and "Candy Man." —*Richie Unterberger*

Sessions / 1968 / Capitol 2862
Mostly a studio jam with five acoustic guitars and bass. Fred's basso outrageo intro to Percy Mayfield's "Please Send Me Somebody to Love" propels that timeless song into a new dimension. —*Cary Wolfson, Blues Access*

The New Christy Minstrels

b. , New York, NY
Group
A ten-member choral group organized by Randy Sparks in 1961, the New Christy Minstrels were among the most popular performers on the clean-cut, fresh-faced, earnest, fun-loving side of the folk music boom. If all those clichAs don't sound like what '60s folk music was all about, it's because the scruffy, "authentic," critical, politically oriented side of the folk music boom turned out to be more influential. But the Christys' side was initially more successful: Between 1962 and 1965, the group placed eight albums on the Top 100 bestseller charts by cheerily singing songs like "That Big Rock Candy Mountain." After that, times changed, and such original members as Barry ("Eve of Destruction") McGuire left, but the group continued till the end of the decade. Other members of the troupe at one time or another included Gene Clark and Kenny Rogers. —*William Ruhlmann*

☆ Presenting: The New Christy ... / 1962 / CBS 8672
Presenting: The New Christy Minstrels, the Christys' first album, was also the closest founder Randy Sparks came to his conception of a modern folk chorus singing such American standards as "Nine Hundred Miles" and "That Big Rock Candy Mountain." The original group contained some excellent solo and ensemble singers, and the overall impact is of full, warm harmony with an unabashedly sunny outlook. —*William Ruhlmann*

★ Ramblin' Featuring Green, Green / 1963 / CBS 8855
The Christys scored their biggest seller with their fourth album, which also contained their biggest hit single, Barry McGuire's "Green, Green." The album was also their artistic high-water mark. Their arrangements were never more stirring and their singing never lustier, as Barry Kane and McGuire made their marks as soloists. —*William Ruhlmann*

○ New Christy Minstrels' Greatest Hits / 1966 / CBS 9279
Decent folk-pop like "Green, Green" (sung by Barry McGuire), grouped with pure-pop choir versions of "Downtown." An honest anthology. —*Bruce Eder*

New Coon Creek Girls

Group
An all-female band that plays contemporary bluegrass with striking vocals. —*Chip Renner*

○ So I'll Ride / Turquoise 5075
This well-crafted album features a high energy level. Jesse McReynolds, Dempsey Young, Mike Stevens, Edgar Meyer, and Raymond McLain were guests on the album. —*Chip Renner*

New Lost City Ramblers, The

Group
During the folk boom of the late '50s and early '60s, the NLCR introduced the authentic string-band sound of the '20s and '30s, in the process educating a generation that had never heard this uniquely American sound of old-time music. While maintaining music with a social conscience, they added guts and reality to the folk movement, performing with humor and obvious reverence for the music.

Mike Seeger, John Cohen, and Tom Paley in 1958 modeled their band after groups like the Skillet Lickers, the Fruit Jar

Drinkers, and the Aristocratic Pigs, choosing a name in keeping with the past. When Tracy Schwarz replaced Paley in 1962, the Ramblers added solo songs from the Appalachian folk repertoire, religious and secular, educating a large segment of the American population about traditional music. Folkways recorded the NLCR on five albums in the early '60s, making the Ramblers famous and leading to TV appearances, successful tours, and appearances at the Newport Folk Festival. A songbook with 125 of their songs came out in 1964 and sold well.

The NLCR served at least three important purposes: They brought real folk music to a huge audience, they entertained us well with their lively acts, and they led us to rediscover the original music on which they had based their band. In the early '70s, after a long career, the group broke up. Tracy Schwarz went on the road with his wife and then his son, gradually leaning toward Cajun squeezebox music; Mike Seeger toured with his wife, Alice, and did many solo spots; and John Cohen continued playing in another string band, while making award-winning documentaries about the old music. —David Vinopal

20 Years of Concert Performances / 1978 / Flying Fish 102
Live Ramblers. —Mark A. Humphrey

20th Anniversary Concert—Live at Carnegie Hall / 1987 / Flying Fish 090
A nicely spirited celebration of a band that was longer-lived than many of its old-time role models. —Mark A. Humphrey

★ Early Years (1958-1962) / 1991 / Smithsonian/Folkways 40036
These influential revivalists of old-time string-band music played it straight, but with spirit and a keen ear for the music's inherent humor. —Mark A. Humphrey

New St. George, The

Conceived from the English folk-rock scene of the '60s that spawned Steeleye Span and The Fairport Convention and nurtured in the DC folkscene that gave the world Mary Chapin Carpenter, the New St. George is at once a look ahead at where folk music is going and a look back at where it has been. Their avant-traditional style is equally at home rocking 16th-century Breton jigs and band-member-penned originals. This award-winning band is made up of Jennifer Cutting (keyboards, accordion, arrangements), Juan Dudley (drums), Bob Hitchcock (acoustic and electric guitars, mandolin, vocals), Rico Petrucelli (bass), and Lisa Moscatiello (guitar, bouzouki, whistle, vocals). They follow in the long tradition of musicians using modern instruments with diverse musical influence to play ancient songs and melodies. It's a little jazz, a little rock, a little classical, a little folk, a little Morris dance music and a whole lot of the New St. George. —Allan Shaw

○ High Tea / Folk Era
Whirling, hard-hitting, sensual, exotic. —Mike Fleischer

Penny Nichols

b. Dec. 26, 1947
Vocals
Penny Nichols, with a background as a composer and vocal arranger, has worked as a backup singer for a wide variety of R&B and rock acts, including Jimmy Buffett, Arlo Guthrie, Art Garfunkel, Susie Quatro, and Donna Summer. She received a platinum record with Jimmy Buffett and a Grammy nomination. Nichols is one of the new lights in the modern folk scene, and her songs are living proof that all the great folk songs were not written 60 years ago. "Pioneer Woman" and "New Moon Refugees" are on their way to becoming modern folk classics. You can catch her live at any number of folk festivals, and her most recent album, All Life Is One, is mandatory listening for all folk-music fans. —Michael Erlewine

Penny's Arcade / 1968 / Buddah
This debut album sold over 50,000 copies. Hard to find. —Michael Erlewine

● All Life Is One / 1990 / Penny Nichols' Music
Includes "Pioneer Woman" and "New Moon Refugees." —Michael Erlewine

Northeast Winds

The influence of the Irish in all of New England is as strong as the sailing traditions in the state of Maine. Combine the musics of those two groups and the result is Northeast Winds, an Irish band that takes advantage of its proximity to the sea. The band's present lineup includes Taylor Whiteside, Emery Hutchins, and Allan McHale. —Allan Shaw

○ On Tour / Folk Era
A musical travelogue with plenty of frequent listener miles. —Mike Fleischer

Northern Lights

Group
Northern Lights is a New England-based bluegrass band known for its creative and distinct sound. The band consists of Taylor Armerding (mandolin and vocals), Billy Henry (guitar and vocals), Oz Barron (bass), and Mike Kropp (banjo). —Chip Renner

Can't Buy Your Way / Jun. 1991 / Flying Fish 70593
"Rainmaker," "City on a Hill," and the title track are really great. This is simply a solid band with strong material. Guest artists Vassar Clements and Matt Glaser help out. —Richard Meyer

○ Take You to the Sky / Flying Fish 70533
One of the best bluegrass albums you can buy; a nice blend of old and new sounds. Featuring guests Peter Rowan, Matt Glasen, and Alison Krauss, it's worth the price of the CD just to hear the vocal on "T for Texas." Highly recommended. —Chip Renner

Tim O'Brien

Colorado resident formerly of the band Hot Rize, Tim O'Brien has begun to make solo records that cross catagories of folk, country, and rock, all performed with enthusiam and virtuosity. —Richard Meyer

○ Take Me Back / 1988 / Sugar Hill 3766
Mollie and Tim O'Brien's vocals blend perfectly. A masterpiece. —Chip Renner

★ Away Out On The Mountain / 1994 / Sugar Hill
If you ever wished you could hear brand-new music with the conviction and flawless vocal work of the classic Everly Brothers recordings, this album by brother and sister Mollie and Tim O'Brien is for you. The cuts are mostly contemporary gospel-bluegrass tunes with an A.P. Carter and Leadbelly song tossed in. There is not a misplaced note. —Richard Meyer

○ Odd Man In / Sugar Hill 3790
This album rocks the borders of country, folk, and pop. The songs are smart and ironic. There is great playing throughout. "Lonely at the Bottom" is a really good track. —Richard Meyer

Oh Boy! O'boy! / Sugar Hill 3808
More gospel pop than Odd Man In, this record with his band the O'Boys lets us hear O'Brien run down Dylan's "When I Paint My Masterpiece," the bluegrass spiritual "Church Steeple," and the ancient "The Farmer's Cursed Wife." —Richard Meyer

Phil Ochs

b. Dec. 19, 1940, El Paso, TX, d. Apr. 9, 1976
Vocals
Depending on your point of view, you might find Phil Ochs to be an idealistic American hero or the ultimate '60s casualty. Relocating to New York City from Ohio with a college journalism background and already well versed in the emerging political left, Ochs found his niche as a topical singer-songwriter and quickly became a favorite in the Village's blossoming folk scene of the early '60s. When Bob Dylan eventually moved into the rock arena, Ochs became the folk protest movement's de facto king. By 1967 Ochs had realigned his management and record company and his music as well. He responded to the musical changes of the day with a trilogy of three heavily arranged albums that were far from the simplicity of the earlier three. These albums also graphically documented a deeply troubled life, in terms of both his personal life and the now full-blown radical politics of the period. When the left-wing movement died, evidently so did much of Ochs's muse. Ochs could never grasp why his status in the rock world never matched what he achieved in folk music. His final studio album, with the self-deprecating title, Phil Ochs's Greatest Hits, proved to be a harrowing look back at his life and a clairvoyant pointer to his short-lived future. While some music in his music have a dated air, many of the same causes ring true today, and Ochs remains one of the '60s' most fascinating characters. —Steve Aldrich

Broadside Tapes 1 /

This album of previously unreleased songs was recorded casually in the 104th St. Offices of Broadside Magazine. They were intended as demos for transcription but are in fact quite good performances. —*Richard Meyer*

All the News That's Fit to Sing / 1964 / Elektra 7269
All the News That's Fit to Sing is his bittersweet debut and is a vital and topical album of its time. —*Bruce Eder & William Ruhlmann*

○ **I Ain't Marching Anymore** / 1965 / Carthage 4422
A strident, searching, and haunting echo of the '60s. —*Bruce Eder*

Phil Ochs in Concert / 1966 / Elektra 7310
It's since been revealed that some or all of these tracks were not "in concert" at all, but recorded in the studio, with audience noise dubbed on afterward. Nevertheless, this is Ochs's finest acoustic album. As a lyricist he was moving from the singing journalist mode to more abstract symbolism, but still attacked U.S. imperialism, knock-kneed bleeding hearts, and even organized religion with an uncompromising sensitivity. Some haunting, wistful ballads transcended topical concerns entirely, including the beautiful love song "Changes" and "There But for Fortune" (a British hit for Joan Baez). —*Richie Unterberger*

★ **Pleasures of the Harbor** / 1967 / A&M 4133
Moving from his acoustic base to elaborate musical arrangements, Ochs also turns largely away from his topical material to more lyrical and poetic songs, though the caustic "Outside a Small Circle of Friends" and the apocalyptic "The Crucifixion" clearly retain his social and political focus. —*William Ruhlmann*

Tape from California / 1968 / A&M 4148
A somewhat manic production, highlighted by reasonably successful, straightforward rock (the title track) and one of the great '60s antiwar songs, "The War Is Over," a perfect combination of droll commentary with jaunty backing. Most of the rest of the tracks fall into the over-orchestrated malaise that, to a lesser degree, afflicted *Pleasures of the Harbor*. —*Richie Unterberger*

Phil Ochs's Greatest Hits / 1970 / Edsel
Not really his greatest hits (the title was intended as irony). This is his final, troubled studio album, and a good companion to *Gunfight at Carnegie Hall*. —*Bruce Eder*

○ **Gunfight at Carnegie Hall** / 1975 / Mobile Fidelity 794
Most unusual. Ochs does Elvis and Buddy Holly songs exceptionally to an angry audience and plays out his own internal conflicts at the same time. —*Bruce Eder*

○ **Chords of Fame** / 1976 / A&M 4599
A fine collection on vinyl only, but worth having for the liner notes. Note that this out-of-print double LP is the only album to combine Ochs's Elektra work (1964-1966) with his A&M work (1967-1970). The two CD samplers cover the same ground separately. —*Bruce Eder & William Ruhlmann*

Toast to Those Who Are Gone / 1987 / Rhino 70080
Fourteen previously unreleased demos, all of excellent fidelity; while no dates or sources are given for these sessions, an educated guess would put them in his earliest, most topical period, circa 1964-1965. Most of these feature just Phil and acoustic guitar, and they sound as strong as the material officially released on his first Elektra LPs. The other, equally fine cuts seem to date from a later period, and show him delving into intensely personal, nonpolitical concerns. —*Richie Unterberger*

War Is Over: The Best of Phil Ochs / 1988 / A&M 5215
Not his best by a longshot, but a cross-section of his better A&M recordings. —*Bruce Eder*

○ **There But for Fortune** / 1989 / Elektra 60832
The best of his early sides, covering his first three albums, though weighted heavily toward the third, *Phil Ochs in Concert*, probably because it's the only one not reissued by Hannibal-Cathage. —*Bruce Eder & William Ruhlmann*

○ **There and Now—Live in Vancouver** / 1990 / Rhino 70778
Definitive Ochs (along with *Gunfight at Carnegie Hall*). A "lost" 1968 concert featuring his most beloved songs. The real "best of." —*Bruce Eder*

Maura O'Connell

Vocals
Irish singer, formerly associated with the traditional group De Danann, who has turned to more of a contemporary folk-rock ap-

proach as a solo artist, interpreting the songs of Nanci Griffith, John Hiatt, and other literate songwriters on a series of albums for Warner Bros. —*William Ruhlmann*

○ **Helpless Heart** / 1989 / Warner Brothers 26016
Irish interpretive singer O'Connell has suffered from the inability of her record company to figure out whether she's a folkie, a country singer, or a pop artist. Meanwhile, she keeps singing her heart out, cherrypicking the work of such writers as Paul Brady, Nanci Griffith, Linda Thompson, and others. If you already own the albums those writers have made, maybe she's redundant. However, great songs still benefit greatly from being performed by great singers, and if you're looking for a sympathetic sampler of the best of today's songwriters, here it is. —*William Ruhlmann*

● **Blue Is the Colour of Hope** / 1992 / Warner Brothers 45063
This charmingly eclectic album may be O'Connell's best. Working with producer Jerry Douglas, O'Connell finds sympathetic accompaniment on all these songs, whether it's the piano and arco bass on the gently painful "So Soft Your Goodbye," the small-combo swing on "Love to Learn," or the full-band acoustic pop on "Still Hurts Sometimes." Though O'Connell records songs by Nashville stalwarts like Pat McLaughlin and Tom Kimmel, her ear for a wider range of material makes *Blue Is the Colour of Hope* a joy. "Bad News at the Best of Times," by rockers Paul Carrack and John Wesley Harding, is a real find, and O'Connell's cover of Mary-Chapin Carpenter's "It Don't Bring You" is simply gorgeous. —*Brian Mansfield*

Odetta (Odetta Gordon)

b. Dec. 31, 1930, Birmingham, AL
Vocals, guitar
Starting out in classical voice training, Odetta crossed over to folk just before she turned 20. Teaching herself to play the guitar, she began singing in coffee houses in the early '50s. Her appearances with Pete Seeger and Harry Belafonte helped establish her as a major talent. She began recording solo albums in the late '50s and has been active ever since. She sings in a deep, husky voice with great control and clarity. —*Michael Erlewine*

○ **And the Blues** / 1962 / Legacy 354
Odetta, one of the outstanding figures of the '60s folk boom, always featured more than a few blues songs in her vast repertoire, so this album, recorded for Riverside in 1962, was a natural step. The vocal style and instrumental backing recall the classic blues of the '20s and '30s. Twelve tunes, including "Oh, Papa," "How Long Blues," and "Make Me a Pallet on the Floor." —*Roundup Newsletter*

At Town Hall / 1962 / Vanguard 2109
This thankfully-back-in-print classic contains "Carry It Back to Rosie," "Freedom Trilogy," "Children's Trilogy," and 13 other great songs from folk, blues, spiritual, and work song repertoires . . . all grounded in dignity, strength and, resistance. —*Ladyslipper*

● **Essential Odetta** / 1989 / Vanguard 43-44
This twofer includes "No More Auction Block for Me," "If I Had a Hammer," "When I Was a Young Girl," much more. —*Ladyslipper*

Don Oja-Dunaway

Vocals
Florida-based singer-songwriter whose original historical ballads have a very strong sense of humanity. —*Richard Meyer*

○ **Kennesaw** / Dunaway
This album is a song cycle of the Civil War. The song "Paducah" is an extraordinary extended ballad. (Write to Oja-Dunaway to obtain this recording, at: 15 South Comares, St. Augustine, FL 32084.) —*Richard Meyer*

The Old-time Music Group

Group
The Old-Time Music Group from southwestern Ohio is one of the few groups still performing the old folk songs in the old-time way. Nothing pretentious, this is fun music played by a group of people just playing to entertain (to entertain us and themselves). The leader of the group, Ed Simpkins, plays banjo, guitar, and harmonica, and the rest of the band play fiddle, autoharp, dulcimer, bass, and tipple. They have played at, among many others, the Appalachia Folk Festival, and they are regulars at the

Tennessee Fall Homecoming. This is what folk music is all about! —*Don Stevens*

● **Songs At Mother's Knee, The** / Jim Dawg

Old-Time Radio Gang

Group

Based in Maine, the Old Time Radio Gang recreate the early days of electronic communication when live radio emanated from every small town station in North America, There's no homogenized "country Top-40 format" sound here, just four singers and pickers who love the music and have taken the time and trouble to recreate it in its natural setting. From novelty tunes to gospel favorites, inspirational songs to ballads, Allan "Mac" McHale, Russ Miller, Dick Monroe, and Smokey Valley have it all. —*Allan Shaw*

Country Radio Songs / 1988 / Folk Era 2062

● **When Roses Bloom Again** / 1991 / Folk Era 2071

○ **New River Train** / 1993 / Folk Era 1408

David Olney

○ **Roses** / 1977 / Philo 1137

Rhode Island-born but now a Nashville-based writer, David Olney is well respected for his fine-tuned lyrics. —*Richard Meyer*

Kristina Olsen

● **Kristina Olsen** / 1992 / Philo 1147

San Franciscan Kristina Olsen moved to Los Angeles and became one of the preeminent singer-songwriters in her community. She tours the country regularly and has been a member of the Four Bitchin' Babes. She is a dynamic performer and a writer of very personal songs. —*Richard Meyer*

Tom Ovans

Vocals

Tom Ovans is a Nashville-based, Boston-raised street rocker and song poet who is comfortable playing folk, blues, and hard-driving rock. His vocal style is eerily similar to that of Bob Dylan, with the power of Joe Ely. —*Chip Renner*

○ **Industrial Days** / 1991 / Nebula 47651

From the slow-paced "Crazy" to the hard paces of "Wild Wind Blowing" to the jazzy "Early One Morning," this CD is guaranteed to keep you interested. With Woody Guthrie lyrics and Bob Dylanlike vocals, Tom Ovans is a force to be reckoned with. —*Chip Renner*

Owner's Daughter, The

Group

○ **Owner's Daughter** / 1993 / Celtobeat Records

The Owner's Daughter is a duo made up of Valerie Price and Steve Baughman. Their collection of songs and instrumentals is unclutterd and refreshingly immediate. Unlike many American Celtic groups, they don't try to put on an ethnicity and authenticity that rings false. They simply play thieir repertoire beautifully.Recently they have expanded to a five-piece group. —*Richard Meyer*

The Oyster Band

Group

A British folk-rock band of the late '80s and early '90s, specializing in contemporary dance rhythms (played by a rock rhythm section) yet retaining a traditional English folk flavor. Members are John Jones (melodeon, accordion), Ian Telfer (fiddle, viola, concertina), Alan Prosser (guitar, mandolin), Chopper (bass), and Russell Lax (drums). —*William Ruhlmann*

Wide Blue Yonder / 1987 / Cooking Vinyl 837387

The Oysters turn in some highly political material here, leading off with "The Generals Are Born Again" and covering Billy Bragg's "Between the Wars," but the love songs are just as fervent, notably "The Oxford Girl." It all barrels along at quick tempos, with much intricate playing and full-voiced singing; this is stirring stuff. —*William Ruhlmann*

● **Ride** / 1989 / Cooking Vinyl 838400

"New York Girls" is a rollicking square-dance workout about prostitutes, which asks the musical question, "Can you dance the polka?" On the same album, the Oysters cover New Order's electro-rock "Love Vigilantes." And, somehow, it all sounds like English folk music. —*William Ruhlmann*

From Little Rock to Leipzig / Feb. 22, 1991 / Rykodisc 50098

With their infectious music and dance beats, it stands to reason the Oyster Band would be terrific live. They are and it shows here, on a collection of their best originals plus such wide-ranging covers as Phil Ochs's "Gonna Do What I Have to Do" and the old Bobby Fuller hit "I Fought the Law." —*William Ruhlmann*

Tom Paley

Everyone remembers Tom from the New Lost City Ramblers. While now living in England, Tom has continued to advance traditional music throughout the world. He has recorded with many traditional artists, including Jean Ritchie and Peggy Seeger. In recent years, Tom has added traditional Scandinavian music to his reportoire. His latest release, on Marimac, is with his son Ben. Tom, always great, is a fine source of unusual traditional music. —*Don Stevens*

Moonshine & Prohibition / Folkways

● **On A Cold Winter Night** / Marimac

Shivaree! / Elektra

Sings Songs Of The New Lost City Ramblers / Aravel

Songs From The Depression / Folkways

Sandy & Caroline Paton

Sandy and Caroline are the owners of Folk-Legacy Records. In that capacity they have brought us some of the best traditional folk musicians in America. Most of the Folk-Legacy LPs are still available. In addition to bringing us other musicians and outstanding collections like the *Golden Ring* and *Sharon Mountain Harmony* anthologies, they have made numerous terrific recordings themselves. Recording together, or with other Folk-Legacy artists, they have brought us traditional songs rarely heard in any other venue. All of these recordings should be part of any folk collection. —*Don Stevens*

● **New Golden Ring, The "Five Days Singing", Vol. 1** / Folk-legacy

● **New Golden Ring, The "Five Days Singing", Vol. 2** / Folk-legacy

○ **Sharon Mountain Harmony** / Folk-legacy

Ellis Paul

Originally from Maine, Paul is now one of the most highly regarded of the early '90s singer-songwriters to come out of the Boston area. He won the 1994 New Folk competition at the Kerrville Folk Festiville and has been a regular on the national touring circuit. His songs are finely drawn, often romantic stories. —*Richard Meyer*

○ **Say Anything** / 1993 / Black Wolf Records

Produced by Bill Morrissey, *Say Anything* provides a good introduction to Ellis Paul's music. Geoff Bartley, Johnny Cunningham, and the Story provide some of the very tasteful support. "Conversations with a Ghost," "Just the Jester Fool," and "New Light on Your Halo" are some of the key tracks on this fine debut CD. —*Richard Meyer*

★ **Stories** / 1994 / Black Wolf Records

Stories is a step forward for Ellis Paul. The lush and understated arrangements frame his detailed lyrics. Ballads like "Don't Breathe" and "Here She Is" are lovely and, placed alongside the uptempo songs, "All Things Being the Same" and "Autobiography of a Pistol," make this a strong well-balanced album. —*Richard Meyer*

Tom Paxton

b. Oct. 31, 1937, Chicago, IL

Vocals

Though he has never achieved widespread popular success, Tom Paxton has proven to be one of the most talented and certainly the funniest of the topical folksinger-songwriters who emerged in the '60s. Born in Chicago, Paxton moved to Oklahoma when he was ten. After earning a BFA at the University of Oklahoma in 1959, he joined the army, which gave him the experiences recounted in one of his best early satiric songs, "The Willing Conscript." After leaving the service, he moved to New York City and worked his way up the local Gaslight Club. His first national release was *Ramblin' Boy* on Elektra in 1965. In addition to his own renditions, his songs were recorded by a variety of fellow performers, including Peter, Paul & Mary and Judy Collins. Paxton recorded seven albums for Elektra through 1971, two of which, *The Things I Notice Now* and *Tom Paxton 6*, sold well enough to reach the charts. He then switched to Reprise Records for three albums, two of which, *How Come the Sun* and *Peace Will Come*, also made the charts. Since then he has recorded for Private Stock, Vanguard, Flying Fish, Mountain Railroad, and his own Pax label. Paxton has continued to write satiric topical material over the years, from "I'm Changing My Name to Chrysler" (an attack on the government bailout of the auto giant) to "Little Bitty Gun," which mocked Nancy Reagan. But his songs can also be scathingly serious, such as his account of "The Death of Stephen Biko," and romantically touching, such as "The Last Thing on My Mind." Recently Paxton has recorded more children's music and has written books for children as well. —*William Ruhlmann*

○ **Tom Paxton 6** / 1970 / Elektra 74066
The best of Paxton's Elektra albums came toward the end of his tenure with the label and featured an above-average collection of trenchant originals. "Whose Garden Was This" remains a masterpiece on ecology, while "Forest Lawn" is one of Paxton's funniest songs ever. —*William Ruhlmann*

Paxton Report / 1981 / Mountain Railroad 52796
An unusually high quotient of comic-political material makes this one of his most scathing collections. "I'm Changing My Name to Chrysler" nails its subject perfectly. —*William Ruhlmann*

○ **Even a Grey Day** / 1983 / Flying Fish 90280
This collection is filled with Paxton's more serious, romantic, and thoughtful songs, some of them rerecordings of '60s favorites. The overall mood is unusually somber, but the album is unusually moving, too. —*William Ruhlmann*

● **Paxton Primer** / 1986 / Pax 002
One of the frustrating things about Tom Paxton is his tendency to scatter his best material across his many albums, a couple of gems per record. This makes him a prime candidate for a "Best of," and though these are rerecordings, they are the artist's own choices, issued on his own label. This is the compilation that covers the most ground and therefore the one to look for. (74 East Park Place, East Hampton, NY 11937) —*William Ruhlmann*

Herb Pederson

b. Apr. 27, 1944, Berkeley, CA
Guitar, banjo
Pederson is a member of the Desert Rose Band. He is a skilled studio musician equally adept at the guitar and banjo. He has released several solo albums and appeared on countless musical projects. —*Chip Renner*

● **Lonesome Feeling** / 1964 / Sugar Hill 3738
A very fine blend of bluegrass and country. Sugar Hill lets Pederson shine. —*Chip Renner*

Southwest / 1976 / Epic
A solid album featuring David Lindley, Mike Post, Larry Carlton, Josh Graves, Al Perkins, Jim Gordon, and some fine backing vocals by Linda Ronstadt and Emmylou Harris. (Out of print.) —*Chip Renner*

Sandman / 1977 / Epic
The same backups as on the *Southwest* album, with the additions of Lowell George and Dolly Parton. This album is out of print, but worth the search. —*Chip Renner*

Pentangle

b. 1968
Group
A major British folk group of the late '60s and early '70s led by master guitarists John Renbourn and Bert Jansch and featuring singer Jacqui McShee, Pentangle combined traditional folk styles with contemporary songs and arrangements. —*William Ruhlmann*

Pentangle / 1968 / Reprise 6315
A thrilling debut, which saw five virtuosos creating a progressive folk album that added up to more than the sum of its parts. Divided between traditional and original material, highlights included their arrangement of "Bruton Town" and the seven-minute instrumental "Pentangling." —*Richie Unterberger*

Sweet Child / 1968 / Reprise 6334
A double album, one comprised of studio recordings, the other of a 1968 concert. No other Pentangle LP covered as much ground as this one, which included original material, Scottish folk songs, jazz, and blues, as well as instrumentals and numbers that spotlighted McShee, Jansch, and Thompson as soloists. "In Time" is a sparkling guitar duel between Jansch and Renbourn that ranks as one of the highlights in both their careers. —*Richie Unterberger*

Basket of Light / 1969 / Edsel 7
Though *Sweet Child* is usually cited as the group's high-water mark, *Basket of Light* finds them at their most progressive and exciting. Highlights of this album—which actually reached the top five in the U.K.—include the buzzing jazz dynamics of "Light Flight," their moving rendition of the traditional folksong "Once I Had a Sweetheart," their reinvention of the girl-group smash "Sally Go Round the Roses," and "Springtime Promises," one of their finest original tunes. —*Richie Unterberger*

● **Essential, Vol. 1** / 1987 / Transatlantic
● **Essential, Vol. 2** / 1987 / Transatlantic
○ **Maid That's Deep in Love** / 1987 / Shanachie 79066
Currently, only this nine-track compilation is available to remind listeners of this British traditional folk-rock quintet, which provided Fairport Convention's main competition in the late '60s and early '70s. Much of it is lovely, notably McShee's haunting singing and Jansch's fingerpicking. But a more complete picture is provided by the two volumes of *Essential Pentagle* on Transatlantic in the U.K., which may be found in U.S. record racks. —*William Ruhlmann*

Peter Paul & Mary

Group
Peter, Paul & Mary were the most popular folk group of the '60s. Put together by manager Albert Grossman in 1961, Peter Yarrow (b. 1938), Paul Stookey (b. 1937), and Mary Travers (b. 1937) carried on in the tradition of the Weavers, mixing old folksongs with newly written ones, especially those of the new crop of socially committed songwriters of the early '60s. Though their musical approach embraced clear enunciation and carefully shaded harmonies over the more "authentic" approach of other singers of the time, they were distinguished from such competitors as the Kingston Trio, the Limeliters, and the Chad Mitchell Trio by their seriousness and their ties to political causes.

They were also enormously popular, scoring 19 hit singles (6 of which hit the Top Ten) and 11 hit albums (8 of which went gold) between 1962 and 1970. Most of their songs were written by others, their biggest hits including "Leaving on a Jet Plane" (a John Denver composition that helped establish him as a solo artist), "Blowin' in the Wind," and "If I Had a Hammer" (a song written by Weavers Pete Seeger and Lee Hays), but they could also write their own, as proven by Yarrow's "Puff the Magic Dragon" and Stookey's co-composition "I Dig Rock and Roll Music." The latter was a satire that accurately described their musical dilemma as the '60s wore on (popular music was becoming much more rock-oriented than they felt comfortable with).

The group split in 1970, leading to three moderately successful solo careers. But they reformed in 1978 and have maintained a steady performing and recording schedule since. —*William Ruhlmann*

Peter, Paul & Mary / 1962 / Warner Brothers 1449
Their debut, and their purest studio album. —*Bruce Eder*

● **In Concert** / 1964 / Warner Brothers 1555
This definitive collection highlights Paul Stookey's comedic talents and features the expected hits plus "Single Girl," a surprisingly early feminist song. —*Bruce Eder*

Peter, Paul & Mary Album / 1966 / Warner Brothers 26653
1966 album produced by Albert Grossman, with supporting players including Mike Bloomfield, Al Kooper, Paul Butterfield, and others. Includes "The Other Side of This Life" and a cover of Jimmy Rodgers's 1957 hit "Kisses Sweeter Than Wine." —*Roundup Newsletter*

Late Again / 1968 / Warner Brothers 26666
A classic album from 1968, *Late Again* inspired girls to iron their hair and guys to grow goatees in emulation of their heroes: Peter,

Paul, and Mary. Songs include "Too Much of Nothing," "I Shall Be Released," and "Reason to Believe." —*Roundup Newsletter*

● **Ten Years Together—The Best of Peter, Paul & Mary** / 1970 / Warner Brothers 3105
Ten Years Together—The Best of Peter, Paul & Mary. Exactly what it says and no more. This is a good companion to *In Concert.* —*Bruce Eder*

Reunion / 1978 / Warner Brothers 3231
Much underrated, with a hauntingly beautiful version of Bob Dylan's "Forever Young." —*Bruce Eder*

Petronella

○ **Where Are You** / 1994 / FouFounette Music
This album debut by the New York-based duo Petronella contains seven songs that are by turns romantic and feminist. The instrumentation is stripped down; essentially guitar-based with occasional keyboards and recorder. Vocal harmonies are not adventurous but serve the songs well. —*Richard Meyer*

Pierce Pettis

Songwriter
An excellent songwriter who was probably first heard by most people when Joan Baez covered his "Song at the End of the Movie" on her *Blowin' Away* album in 1979. Pierce Pettis put out his independent album, *Moments,* in 1984 and has since been releasing albums on Windham Hill, the most recent of which is *Tinseltown.* —*William Ruhlmann*

○ **Moments** / 1987 / Small World 073
Containing the title cut, "Grandmother's Song," and "St. Paul's Song," this is his first album and still his best. —*Richard Meyer*

● **While the Serpent Lies Sleeping** / 1989 / Windham Hill 1087
While the Serpent Lies Sleeping. The keen observations in Pettis's songwriting gain force from the caught-in-the-throat emotionalism of his singing. As befits this record label, the instrumental settings are somewhat busy in a new age way. But where the drum and keyboard programming leave off, a strong contemporary folk album remains, especially on "Legacy," in which Pettis confronts the conflicts of his Southern heritage. —*William Ruhlmann*

○ **Chase the Buffalo** / High Street Records
Pettis comes completely into his own with this mature set of songs and performances. The production is great, and Pierce sounds really focused. His own songs are consistently good as is his cover of Mark Heard's "Nod Over Coffee." —*Richard Meyer*

Utah Phillips

Vocals, guitar
Phillips is an entertaining (and just plain fun) singer-songwriter and guitarist in the traditional style. Famous for his jokes, hobo and railroad songs, and sound effects, he is a well-known and popluar performer on the folk and concert circuit. —*Michael Erlewine*

○ **Good Though** / 1968 / Philo 1004
This 1973 Philo album includes a mix of Phillips originals with traditional tunes like "Cannonball Blues," the notorious "Moose Turd Pie" (whence comes the album's title), and "Wabash Cannonball." — *Roundup Newsletter*

El Capitan / 1969 / Philo 1016

● **I've Got to Know** / 1991 / Alcazar 114

Bruce Piephoff

○ **South** / 1993 / Flyin' Cloud
Bruce Piephoff's fourth album is a strong collection of his country-flavored songs. They deal with local subjects with mythic overtones. Instrumentation is simple guitar and bass with occasional other ornament. Piephof is a good storyteller, and these songs stand up to repeated listening. —*Richard Meyer*

Clive Pig

Vocals
A Londoner and member of the Rogue Folk movement. —*Richard Meyer*

○ **One Night in Greece** / 1985 / Pig 9

One Night in Greece with an American Tourist is acoustic punk, most notable for the title cut. —*Richard Meyer*

Tom Pirozzoli

Vocals, guitar
Based in Sunapee, NH, Pirozzoli is a very strong impressionistic acoustic guitarist and singer-songwriter. —*Richard Meyer*

● **Eyes and Footprints** / 1987 / Noumenon 103

Plainsong

Group
A quartet formed by Ian Matthews in 1972 with Andy Roberts, Bob Ronga, and Dave Richards. They released the brilliant *In Search of Amelia Earhart* the same year to critical praise but little commercial success. While working on their followup, *Plainsong III,* Ronga quit, and Matthews and Richards were unable to agree on the direction the band would take musically. They disbanded before the album's completion. In 1993, a new interest in the band inspired a new studio album, *Dark Side of the Room* as well as a BBC recording of a promotional tour from 1972. —*Chris Woodstra*

● **In Search of Amelia Earhart** / 1972 / Elektra 42120
The theme of this album is loosely based on the disappearance of Amelia Earhart and features four tunes penned by Matthews, including the spooky "For the Second Time" and "Call the Tune." Matthews also shows his ability to pick top-notch material by covering Paul Siebel's "Louise," the Jim and Jesse classic "Diesel on My Tail," and Rick Cunha's "Yo Yo Man" (a song Cunha attempted to chart with a year later). —*Jim Worbois*

Dark Side of The Room / 1993 / Line 901247
Matthews and company regrouped for this 1993 album. Though losing much of the charm of their first album, it is certainly in league with Matthews's latest work. —*Chris Woodstra*

Polka Dogs

Group
The band consists of John Millard (banjo, vocals), Tiina Kiik (accordion), Colin Couch (tuba), Ambrose Pottie (drums), and Tom Walsh (trombone). The band was formed in 1987 as the pit band for a Toronto musical (Kensington Sons et Lumieres). They play a type of polka music with a banjo. —*Chip Renner*

○ **Polka Dogs** / 1991 / Aural Traditions
A strange record: It starts out as polka and ends like rock & roll—Alabama-Starspangled-Washboard Band meets the Red Clay Ramblers. Unique release. —*Chip Renner*

Kowtow Popof

○ **Songs From the Pointless Forest** / 1993 / Wampus
Resident of Rockville, MD, Kowtow Popof- a one-man band—has created an acoustic guitar-based album that draws on the aesthetic of Euro mood bands such as Depeche Mode and succeeds. Two good dark cuts are "Scrubland," and "What Are the Wild Waves Saying?" —*Richard Meyer*

Allen Power

○ **Healing Arts** / 1993 / Beacon Records
Allen Power's album gently offers a lot of sweet songs that take on many aspects of human frailty. He runs along the border of clichA but the album produced by Anne Hills manages to steer clear. A lot of soft songs about leading a gentle life with spare, light arrangements. —*Richard Meyer*

Professor and Maryann

○ **Fairy Tale** / 1993 / Bar/None
This duo from Staten Island, NY, does an effective job of combining mainstream singer-songwriter sensibilities with jazzy guitar-based songs. Maryann's voice has the elasticity of Rickie Lee Jones with more of a whisper and articulation. She sounds perpetually heartbroken, and it's an endearing quality. The songs are carefully put together and will linger with you. This is the kind of album you will grow into. —*Richard Meyer*

Chuck Pyle

○ **Step by Step** / BF 1002

This Colorado resident is well known for his distinctive guitar playing and dramatic and lovely songs. This collection includes his signature tune, "Here Comes the Water." Contact BNF Music, Box 385, Eldorado Springs, CO 80025 —*Richard Meyer*

Jack Quigly

○ **Love Songs & Other Lies** / 1993 / IKO's Music
You get the feeling that all these songs were written just about as the bar was about to close. N. Paul Hamilton's "Marie," is sort of a hippie update on the song "Louise." Quigly gives it a weary honest treatment. His vocals are a bit ragged, but he never tries to push beyond the conversational tone that makes these songs work. —*Richard Meyer*

Danny Quinn

Vocals, guitar
Quinn is a singer-songwriter who plays Celtic and folk music. He is an accomplished guitarist who sings with a warm baritone voice. —*Chip Renner*

For Family and Friends / 1970 / Black Water
A fine debut album, featuring Eric Bogle's "And the Band Played 'Waltzing Matilda'" and Don McLean's "Vincent." The vocals are outstanding. A well-rounded album. —*Chip Renner*

○ **Overnight Success** / 1980 / Black Water
Quinn's music and songwriting matured on this release. It is more commercial than his debut but is not compromised. The title track is a good look at being an overnight success (after all the years he has put into his craft). He borrows songs from Stan Rogers, Eric Bogle, and Liam Reilly. —*Chip Renner*

● **Time for a Change** / 1990 / Black Water
Quinn uses more of his originals on this release. He and Tom Chapin do a fine version of the traditional song "The Water Is Wide." "Ordinary Man" is included, and Eric Bogle's "Leaving the Land" finishes the release. Great job! —*Chip Renner*

Raymond Gonzalez & Amy Malkoff

○ **On The Water** / 1993 / RGAM
Amy and Ray are a Boston-based duo who have been performing around the Northeast for a few years. Amy has been instrumental with various Boston folk organizations. On this, their second album, they deliver a set of songs primarily about interpersonal communication. Arrangements are simple and percussive, always based around Raymond Gonzalez's guitar parts. —*Richard Meyer*

Blind Alfred Reed

Vocals, fiddle
This West Virginia singer-songwriter and fiddler was one of Ralph Peer's discoveries on the legendary 1927 Bristol field trip that unearthed the Carter Family and Jimmie Rodgers. Reed was one of those uniquely Southern contradictions, both reactionary and progressive in his songs. "How Can a Poor Man Stand Such Times and Live?" echoed the sentiments of the rural poor, who tasted none of the Roaring 20s prosperity (a myth for all but a privileged few). "Why Do You Bob Your Hair, Girls?" invoked Biblical sanctions against flappers. Topical commentary of this sort was rare in early hillbilly recordings. Reed's contemporaries usually pruned a branch from the folk tree or swiped a page from Mom's Victorian songbook. Incongruously, Reed was a protest singer-songwriter out of time and place. Ry Cooder revived a couple of his songs in the '70s, the decade of Rounder's reissue of several Reed performances, *How Can a Poor Man Stand Such Times and Live? —Mark A. Humphrey*

○ **How Can a Poor Man ...** / 1920 / Rounder 1001
How Can a Poor Man Stand Such Times and Live? is '20s hillbilly social commentary, both reactionary ("Why Do You Bob Your Hair, Girls?") and progressive ("How Can a Poor Man Stand Such Times and Live?") from this West Virginia singer and fiddler. Austere and engaging. —*Mark A. Humphrey*

Harvey Reid

The New Hampshire musician records his albums in living stereo. He acts as producer, performer, engineer, and mixer. The all-acoustic albums are recorded direct to two-track with two mikes no matter the size of the group.The records are unusually clean, and all feature his fine songwriting and commanding instrumen-

tal. (Write Woodpecker Records, PO Box 1134 Portsmouth, NH 03802.) —*Richard Meyer*

Circles / Woodpecker Records

Overview / Woodpecker Records

● **Of Wind & Water** / Woodpecker 104

John Renbourn

Guitar
Renbourn was a founding member of Pentangle with Bert Jansch, and like Jansch, he is one of the most influential acoustic guitarists in Great Britain. Although Pentangle is best known for its revivals of traditional English folk songs, Renbourn is equally at home in blues, ragtime, jazz, and pre-classical idioms. —*Michael P. Dawson*

Faro Annie / 1972 / Reprise 2082
A bit of blues mixed in. —*Chip Renner*

Hermit / 1977 / Shanachie 97014
Exceptional acoustic guitarist John Renbourn recorded this solo release shortly after Pentangle disbanded. Inspired by lute music, it includes "Goat Island," "Caroline's Tune," the title track, and eight others. —*Roundup Newsletter*

○ **Maid in Bedlam** / 1977 / Shanachie 79004
A superb collection of traditional songs and Renaissance dances. Features the sublime voice of his Pentangle mate Jacqui McShee. —*Michael P. Dawson*

Black Balloon / 1979 / Shanachie 97009
A collection of ayres, danceries, a pastoral fantasia, and an abstract fantasia. —*Chip Renner*

Enchanted Garden / 1980 / Shanachie 79074
His followup to *Maid in Bedlam*, with multiinstrumentalist John Molineux replacing fiddler Sue Draheim. —*Michael P. Dawson*

Live in America / 1981 / Flying Fish 70103
Live in America was recorded in 1981 at the Great American Music Hall in San Francisco (so well that you might think the concert was happening in your living room). Performances feature Renbourn's distinctive vocals and accomplished guitar artistry; McShee's inimitably haunting vocals, pipes, fiddles, and tabla; and well-known favorites like "John Barley Corn Is Dead," as well as several Renbourn instrumentals. —*Erin Ryan, Roundup Newsletter*

○ **John Renbourn & Bert Jansch** / 1985 / Cambra 056

● **Live in Concert** / 1985 / Shanachie 95001
Live solos and duos with Stefan Grossman, including a couple of Charles Mingus compositions. —*Michael P. Dawson*

Three Kingdoms / 1987 / Shanachie 95006
A ragtime-jazz-folk collaboration. A very mellow guitar album. —*Chip Renner & Michael P. Dawson*

Ship of Fools / 1988 / Flying Fish 70466
Featuring flutist Tony Roberts, guitarist Steve Tilston, and singer Maggie Boyle. —*Michael P. Dawson*

Snap a Little Owl / Shanachie 97003
More ragtime-laced duets. —*Michael P. Dawson*

Malvina Reynolds

b. 1900, d. 1978
Songwriter
A topical songwriter who came to prominence in the '60s when she was at an age at which most people retire, Malvina Reynolds is best known as the author of the satirical song "Little Boxes," which was Pete Seeger's only pop singles hit in 1964. She also wrote "What Have They Done to the Rain?" a hit for the Searchers in 1965. Her songs also have been covered by Joan Baez, Judy Collins, and others. Reynolds herself recorded for Columbia (*Malvina Reynolds Sings the Truth*), Folkways (*Another Country Heard From*), and her own Cassandra label. She also wrote children's songs and material for the TV show *Sesame Street.* —*William Ruhlmann*

○ **Malvina** / 1972 / Cassandra 2807
Reynolds is best known for Pete Seeger's versions of her compositions, songs like "Little Boxes" and "What Have They Done to the Rain?" The first is included on this collection, along with 11 other uncompromisingly political songs that mark Reynolds as one of the great topical songwriters of the '60s. She has other ex-

cellent albums (including a long out-of-print Columbia LP), but this is a good place to start. — *William Ruhlmann*

Mike Rimbaud

○ **Red Light** /
One of New York's more punk antifolk artists, his lyrics are raw and edgy and his playing stripped down and direct. — *Richard Meyer*

Jean Ritchie

b. Dec. 8, 1922, Viper,KY
Vocals, dulcimer
Singer, songwriter, song collector, dulcimer player, and author, Jean Ritchie was born in the heart of the Cumberland Mountains of Kentucky and was raised in the folk music of that area. She has been active in preserving and performing traditional mountain ballads and songs. She eventually moved to the New York City area and achieved a national reputation throughout the '50s and '60s singing solo or with the mountain dulcimer. A number of Ritchie albums are still available from Smithsonian/Folkways recordings. (The address can be found in the back of the book.) — *Michael Erlewine*

● **Jean Ritchie & Doc Watson at Folk City** / 1963 / Folkways
This historic recording pairs these two great interpreters on classic songs, "The House Carpenter," "Pretty Polly," "Storms Are on the Ocean." Their unadorned harmonies lend a timeless feeling to the songs. It doesn't get more authentically beautiful than this. — *Richard Meyer*

○ **High Hills and Mountains** / Greenhays
This album is still available today. — *Michael Erlewine*

John Robert & Tony Barrand

b. Dec. 27, 1822, d. May 14, 1877
Group

Across the Western Ocean / Swallowtail 4
John Robert and Tony Barrand, a very influential duo, performing primarily traditional songs of the British Isles. — *Richard Meyer*

● **Best of Nowell Sing We Clear** / Front Hall 301
A compilation from a series of albums of Christmas music from the British Isles that Barrand and Roberts recorded in the '70s and '80s. — *Roundup Newsletter*

Maggie and Terre Roche

Group
A duet from deepest New Jersey, a pair of folkies who debuted with one well-produced record but didn't hit their stride until they found a freer sound and a third sister, forming The Roches. — *Bruce Eder*

○ **Seductive Reasoning** / 1975 / Sony 33232
A very well produced folk-rock album that is unexceptional but clearly sung and harmonized, very pleasant in its modest way. — *Bruce Eder*

The Roches

Group
Maggie, Terre, and Suzy Roche harmonize magnificently and share a quirky sense of humor that informs their songs. Most of the time it works, and their music is always interesting to listen to. — *Bruce Eder*

● **Roches** / 1979 / Warner Brothers 3298
An extraordinary debut record with ringing, soaring harmonies rubbing up against a beautiful and spare instrumental sound. A powerful piece of work. — *Bruce Eder*

Keep on Doing / 1982 / Warner Brothers 23725
This is a comeback after the bizarre misstep of their second album. — *Bruce Eder*

Another World / 1985 / Warner Brothers 25321
Their most unabashedly lyrical album. A bracing work that, alas, isn't as daring as their debut. — *Bruce Eder*

○ **Dove** / 1992 / MCA 10601
An update from the singing sisters finds them living in the urban jungle and overcoming romantic expectations in favor of self-reliance, though not without regret and not, thank God, without moments of humor and absurdity. For the most part, the trio's

folkie past has given way to a rock-pop approach on this album. — *William Ruhlmann*

Gamble Rogers

b. Jan. 31, 1937, Winter Park, FL, d. 1991
Vocals
Gamble Rogers was a singer-songwriter who was influenced by Merle Travis, Chet Atkins, Josh White, Earl Scruggs, and Doc Watson. He died trying to save a drowning person in 1991. — *Chip Renner*

○ **Sorry Is as Sorry Does** / 1989 / Flying Fish 362
Rogers was a master storyteller. His songs are witty and worth a listen. — *Chip Renner*

● **Lord Gives Me Grace (& the Devil Gives Me Style)** / Mountain Railroad 52779

Stan Rogers

b. 1949, d. 1983
Vocals, bass
Stan Rogers came from Hamilton, Ontario, a six-foot-four poet who started out as a rock bassist before turning to folk music. With his rich voice, he used his music to call to life all of the wonder and mysticism of his native Canada. His singing is occasionally mistaken for that of Gordon Lightfoot, but it's huskier and earthier than Lightfoot's, and his repertoire—made up of song cycles drawn from throughout Canada—is also more tradition-oriented and more mystical. Rogers died in a fire aboard an Air Canada flight in Cincinnati, OH, in June 1983, leaving behind a half-dozen albums. — *Bruce Eder*

From Fresh Water / 1975 / FOC 7
The final Stan Rogers album, mixed and mastered after his death, is a dazzling array of songs devoted to the Great Lakes region and the rest of inland Canada. Some of the environmental sensibilities are bitter, and the politics, as with all his work, are defiantly Canadian. — *Bruce Eder*

● **Fogarty's Cove** / 1976 / FCM 1001
A dozen songs of and about Nova Scotia, mostly about the sea and all but one written by Rogers. They successfully capture not only a people but also their sense of time and beauty, with the Rogers baritone tastefully and effectively moving through the spaces and ages of his subject, and with traditional acoustic backing (guitar, violin, flute, etc.) — *Bruce Eder*

Northwest Passage / 1981 / FCM 004
Precisely what its title indicates—a collection of material from and about the vast western expanse of Canada, all filled with robust singing and melodies that are practically part of the landscape. — *Bruce Eder*

Between the Breaks ... Live! / FCM 002
A superb concert album, without a weak moment in any of its nine songs. The highlight is Rogers's rendition of Archie Fisher's "The Witch of Westmoreland," which opens the disc, although it is hard to get past Rogers's own "The Flowers of Bermuda" without having it run through your head for days afterward as well. The upbeat, ebullient mood of the performances is also rather infectious. — *Bruce Eder*

Rooftop Singers

Group
Founded by Weaver alumnus and banjo player Erik Darling in 1962, the Rooftop Singers included guitarist Bill Svanoe and vocalist Lynne Taylor. The group, active in concerts and festivals in the early '60s, was best known for their 1963 nationwide hit "Walk Right In." — *Michael Erlewine*

Walk Right In! / 1965 / Vanguard 9123

● **Best of Rooftop Singers** / Vanguard 79457

Betsy Rose

Vocals
Betsy Rose is a California-based singer-songwriter whose songs often deal with social action or protest and the environment. — *Chip Renner*

● **Sacred Ground** / 1989 / Kaleidoscope 43
A first-class release of acoustic music. Features Nina Gerber on guitar and producer. "Kneeling at the Trains," inspired by

Vietnam veteran Brian Willson, is strong. "Read My Lips" deals with a rebellion by deaf students at Gallaudet University . All in all, it is her finest record. —*Chip Renner*

Dick Rosmini

Guitar

Dick Rosmini, a guitarist from the late '50s, early '60s folk scene, made two albums before pursuing a career of professional photography. —*Richard Meyer*

○ **Adventures for 6 & 12 String Guitar** / Elektra
This album predates much of John Fahey's work and certainly that of Leo Kottke and the other "American primitive" guitarists. Hard to find but well worth the search. —*Richard Meyer*

Sandy Ross

○ **Sessions** / 1992 / SLR Prod
Los Angeles songwriter Sandy Ross has had covers of her songs, including a big Anne Murray hit. She has continued her combination of romantic and political songs on this collection. —*Richard Meyer*

David Roth

A songwriter's songwriter, David combines a keen social sensibility with dazzling musical ability and a strong voice to produce songs that are performed by dozens of other top musicians. He's been recorded by the likes of Christine Lavin, Anne Hills, and Tom Chapin. His appearances have ranged from singing the national anthem in front of a sold-out Chicago Bulls-New York Knicks game to intimate house concerts and innumerable workshops to singing for the United Nations 40th Anniversary celebration. —*Allan Shaw*

● **Digging Through My Closet** / Folk Era
Remember the name David Roth because you'll never forget the songs. —*Mike Fleischer*

Rising In Love / Folk Era

Gail Rundlett

○ **Farther Along** / 1989 / Heartwood Records
Bostonian Rundlett's release is a homey collection of traditional songs and contemporary folksingers such as "Waltzing with Bears," and Linda Allen's "October Roses." Peaceful music. —*Richard Meyer*

Tom Rush

b. Feb. 8, 1941, Portsmouth, NH
Vocals
Tom Rush came up in the Cambridge folk scene of the early '60s, playing folk-blues on a series of albums for Prestige Records. He moved to Elektra, and by the late '60s he was interpreting the work of such upcoming writers as Joni Mitchell and James Taylor. By the early '70s, he was mixing his own songs on albums for Columbia. In recent years, Rush has become something of a folk packager, putting together road shows that include some of the newer folk performers. —*William Ruhlmann*

● **Circle Game** / 1968 / Elektra 74018
Rush managed an undistinguished career in the early '60s as a folkie who performed old blues and rock & roll tunes until he changed gears on this album and turned to the songs of a group of then-unknown contemporary songwriters: Joni Mitchell, James Taylor, and Jackson Browne. That was impressive in 1968, but even today Rush's versions of songs like "Something in the Way She Moves" and the title track hold up well against those of their now-famous composers. And Rush's own songs, among them "No Regrets," are up to their standard. —*William Ruhlmann*

○ **Wrong End of the Rainbow** / 1970 / CBS 30402
Fellow songwriters, such as James Taylor and Jesse Winchester, continue to be represented here, but the focus is on Rush's own compositions, notably the title track and "Merrimac County," and the result is one of the strongest albums in the style of the early '70s soft-rock singer-songwriters. —*William Ruhlmann*

Tom Russell Band

Group

Tom Russell is a New York-based singer-songwriter who has cowritten songs with Nanci Griffith, Peter Case, Ian Tyson, Sylvia Tyson, Katy Moffatt, and Dave Alvin. His band features Andrew Hardin (guitar), Fats Kaplin (pedal steel, fiddle, and accordion), Billy Troiani (bass), and Charles Caldarola (percussion). The sound varies from country to Tex-Mex to rock. —*Chip Renner*

○ **Road to Bayamon** / 1988 / Philo 1116
A great CD, with songs full of images. Songwriters do not get much better. This contains a great cover of Tom Waits's "Downtown Train." —*Chip Renner*

Poor Man's Dream / 1990 / Philo 1139
This CD is as good as *Road to Bayamon*. The songs might even be more polished. "Blue Wing," "Veterans Day," and "Navajo Rug" are all classics. Russell cowrites with Nanci Griffith, Kathy Moffatt, and Ian Tyson. —*Chip Renner*

Hurricane Season / 1991 / Philo 1141
The songs on this, his second Philo release, are typically diverse, ranging from Bill Haley's demise ("Haley's Comet"); to "Jack Johnson," a mythic retelling of the story of the early black heavyweight champion; to the title track, a particularly disturbing metaphor for a relationship. —*Roundup Newsletter*

Cowboy Real / 1992 / Philo 1146
A real nice cowboy-western release featuring new and old Tom Russell favorites. Russell scales down the production on "Navajo Rug," "Gallo Del Cielo," and an old Hardin and Russell song, "Zane Grey." —*Chip Renner*

Buffy Sainte-Marie

b. Feb. 20, 1941, Sebago Lake, ME
Vocals, guitar, mouth-bow
A Canadian-born, part-Native American pop-folksinger, she began in the '60s with a series of albums in which she sang bitterly about the treatment of Native Americans. Her later albums branched out into country and pop. —*William Ruhlmann*

☆ **It's My Way!** / 1964 / Vanguard 79142
This is one of the most scathing topical folk albums ever made. Sainte-Marie sings in an emotional, vibrato-laden voice of war ("The Universal Soldier," later a hit for Donovan), drugs ("Cod'ine"), sex ("The Incest Song"), and most telling, the mistreatment of Native Americans, of which Sainte-Marie is one ("Now That the Buffalo's Gone"). Even decades later, the album's power is moving and disturbing. —*William Ruhlmann*

● **Best of Buffy Sainte Marie** / 1970 / Vanguard 3
Sainte-Marie pursued a variety of musical styles, from folk to country to experimental rock, and all are represented on this wide-ranging double-record compilation. It doesn't all work, but there are some terrific songs, among them the Native American lament "My Country 'Tis of Thy People You're Dying," the romantic "Until It's Time for You to Go," and a musical adaptation of a passage from a Leonard Cohen novel, "God Is Alive, Magic Is Afoot." (Beware of the abbreviated version, Vanguard 73113.) —*William Ruhlmann*

○ **Best of, Vol. 2** / 1971 / Vanguard 33-34

Paul Edward Sanchez

○ **Home by Morning** / 1992 / Jerico
Paul Sanchez lives in Southern California and performs in the local clubs there. On *Home by Morning* Sanchez frames his family-oriented story songs in simple arrangements. He is not a great singer, but the material doesn't require it. Each of these songs reaffirms the day-to-day pleasures of the individual in a home or community without clichés. —*Richard Meyer*

Claudia Schmidt

Vocals, guitar, dulcimer, pianolin, marxolin, humorium
A folksinger with an impressive vocal range, Schmidt has recorded both as a solo artist and with Sally Rogers. —*Mark A. Humphrey*

Midwestern Heart / 1981 / Flying Fish 70241
Fine singing accompanied by dulcimer, pianolin, and guitar. —*AMG*

Claudia Schmidt / 1983 / Flying Fish 66
The debut album from this critically acclaimed songwriter and performer. —*AMG*

● **Claudia Schmidt and Sally Rogers** / 1991 / Red House
This CD features some fine dulcimer and guitar work, along with vocals that will thrill you. Many of the songs deal with social problems facing today's generation. *—Chip Renner*

David Schnaufer

Dulcimer
David Schnaufer is a transplanted Texan now residing in Nashville, TN. His mountain dulcimer playing is legendary, making him one of the premier dulcimer session men in Nashville. He has joined up with Paul Kirby, John Golemon, Will Goleman, Dave Kennedy, and Sam Polano in the band the Cactus Brothers. *—Chip Renner*

○ **Dulcimer Player** / 1989 / Smithsonian/Folkways
This is one of the finest mountain dulcimer albums you will ever find. Schnaufer goes all out with the help of Mark O'Connor and the Cactus Brothers. This album is more polished and uptempo than *Dulcimer Deluxe. —Chip Renner*

● **Dulcimer Player Deluxe** / 1990 / Smithsonian/Folkways 3
Have you ever wondered how such country standards as "Last Date," "San Antonio Rose," "Steel Guitar Rag," and Hank Williams's "I'm So Lonesome I Could Cry" would sound on dulcimer? David Schnaufer offers the answer on this 26-track showcase of his virtuosity on the fretted dulcimer. Schnaufer makes a strong case for the dulcimer as more than a parlor instrument on the rollicking "Fisher's Hornpipe" while quietly painting Stephen Foster's "Beautiful Dreamer" in appropriately sentimental hues. Fiddler Mark O'Connor and guitar "chief" Chet Atkins are among the stellar Nashville cats who abet Schnaufer in his well-crafted scheme to liberate the dulcimer from the granola ghetto on this all-instrumental set, a good one to wake up to on a frosty winter morning. *—Mark Humphrey, Roundup Newsletter*

○ **Dulcimer Deluxe** / Smithsonian/Folkways
A fine collection of old standards and traditional music. *—Chip Renner*

Schooner Fare

Group
Schooner Fare is a New England folk trio featuring Steve Romanoff, Chuck Romanoff, and Tom Rowe. Their music often reflects New England life and the sea. *—Chip Renner*

Alive / 1970 / Outer Green 8883
Recorded live at the Chocolate Factory Church. The band and audience are into the show, featuring "Rattlin' Bog" and "Mary Ellen Carter" (by Stan Rogers). *—Chip Renner*

Day of the Clipper / 1977 / Outer Green 8878
This album features Ralph McTell's "Streets of London." *—Chip Renner*

Classic Schooner Fare / 1980 / Outer Green 8891
A collection of Schooner Fare's favorite songs, recorded with the Atlantic Chamber Orchestra. *—Chip Renner*

Closer to the Wind / 1981 / Outer Green 8882
An essential Schooner Fare album, with "The King Fisher," "John Cook," and "The Ballad of Mad Jack." *—Chip Renner*

● **We the People** / 1985 / Outer Green 8885
This is the best collection, featuring "Portland Town," "We the People," "Make a Friend." The music is strong, and the vocals blend to perfection. *—Chip Renner*

First 10 Years / 1986 / Outer Green 8886
Schooner Fare recorded this double album live at the Birchmere in Washington, DC. *—Chip Renner*

Signs of Home / 1990 / Outer Green 8893
Features "Sweet Tennessee," "Golden Golden," and "Hills of Isle Au Haut." *—Chip Renner*

Steve Schuch

Vocals, fiddle
Schuch is a singer-songwriter, storyteller, and multiinstrumentalist from New Hampshire. He is a three-time winner of the New Hampshire fiddle contest. *—Chip Renner*

● **Circle of Days** / 1988 / Rare Earth
Schuch's debut album is rich in both music and vision. It features well-crafted original songs and Celtic instrumentals. His guitar and fiddle playing are flawless, with folk, classical, and Celtic flavor. A very mature release. *—Chip Renner*

Fields of Summer / 1991 / Rare Earth
Schuch uses 18 musicians to back him up. This is produced with a fuller sound than his debut CD, yet his playing is not overpowered. *—Chip Renner*

Tracy Schwarz

Tracy is one of the greatest traditional fiddlers in America. His credits run from the new Lost City Ramblers, through the Strange Creek Singers, to recordings with other traditional musicians, his family, and in more recent years with many Cajun greats. He continues to perform and explore new areas of traditional music. Any recording of his is well worth possessing. To hear him live is a great experience. *—Don Stevens*

● **Come All You Tenderhearted** / June Appal

Carla Sciacy

Vocals
Colorado-based traditionally styled singer-songwriter whose lovely interpretations have an inviting and lightly swinging feel. *—Richard Meyer*

● **In Between** / 1970 / Propinquity 1002

Under the Quarter Moon / 1980 / Propinquity 1004

Mike Seeger

b. Aug. 15, 1933, New York, NY
Vocals
Mike is the greatest musician in traditional folk music. He has done more to preserve and perpetuate old-time music than any other person. Mike has "discovered" more traditional musicians than anyone else. He has brought many traditional musicians to the world, without ever attempting to exploit them. He has mastered every old-time musical instrument. As performer, collector, teacher, lecturer, producer, and friend to so many, Mike has earned the admiration and respect of all of us. Ever gentle with those he has helped, he is a relentless taskmaster to himself. Every recording—every performance—of his is something to treasure. There are not enough adjectives or space to do him justice in this review. Take every opportunity to see and hear him. We will not see another like him in our lifetimes. *—Don Stevens*

● **Come All You Tenderhearted** / June Appal
● **Music From The True Vine** / Mercury
○ **Oldtime Country Music** / 1962 / Rounder 0278
Solo material from this multiinstrumentalist and founder of the New Lost City Ramblers. *—Mark A. Humphrey*

Peggy Seeger

b. Jun. 17, 1935, New York, NY
Vocals
The half-sister of Pete Seeger and widow of Ewan MacColl, Peggy Seeger has carved a niche for herself writing and singing folk ballads, especially with a feminist slant. Many of her albums are collaborations with her husband and other British folk artists. *—William Ruhlmann*

○ **At the Present Moment** / 1973 / Rounder 4003
This album collects some of Seeger's best topical material, some of which she sings with her husband, Ewan MacColl. The most striking song remains "I'm Gonna Be an Engineer," which encapsulates most of what the women's movement has been saying for the past 20 years. *—William Ruhlmann*

● **Folkways Years, 1955-92: Songs of Love and Politics** / 1992 / Smithsonian/Folkways 40048
For over 35 years Peggy Seeger has been a dominant figure in the folk song movement in the United States and England. As a member of the famous Seeger family, she was raised in a musical environment. This collection focuses on themes of love and politics. It includes titles that have reached millions—such as "First Time Ever I Saw Your Face" and "Gonna Be an Engineer"—and highlights Peggy's brilliant and subtle musicianship and her fine songwriting. In addition to solo work, this anthology also features Peggy's collaborations with various family members, most notably her late husband and singing partner Ewan MacColl. In her notes accompanying this release, Peggy reflects on her career

and comments on the songs, providing us with a history and context for each. —*Roundup Newsletter*

Peggy Seeger / Riverside 12-655
A beautiful collection of old songs and ballads performed solo. Part of what makes this 30-year-old LP so great is the youthful sound of Seeger's voice and her much more knowing understanding of the material, much of which has the dark overtones that make so many traditional songs haunting, such as "Waggoner's Lad." —*Richard Meyer*

Pete Seeger

b. May 3, 1919, New York, NY
Vocals, banjo

Pete Seeger probably has had a greater influence on the development of modern folk music than any other single individual. The son of musicologist Charles Seeger, he began playing the banjo in his teens, soon turning to the five-string version that would become his trademark. He hooked up with Woody Guthrie in the late '30s, and the two formed the politically oriented Almanac Singers with several other folksingers to promote unions and condemn fascism. He was a cofounder of such organizations as People's Songs and People's Artists. In 1948 he formed the folk group the Weavers, which scored massive hits with "Tzena, Tzena, Tzena," Leadbelly's "Goodnight Irene," and "On Top of Old Smokey" before losing its record contract and bookings during the Communist witchhunts of the '50s. Seeger refused to testify before the House Committee on Un-American Activities and was charged with contempt of Congress, winning his case in 1962. By that time, he had made numerous solo albums for Folkways and more Weavers albums for Vanguard. In 1961 he signed to Columbia Records, staying with the label until the end of the decade. Seeger was a major force at the Newport Folk Festivals and a promoter of upcoming talent. His marathon-length concerts included Spanish songs, African songs, Negro worksongs, new protest songs, and old folk songs, sometimes with rewritten lyrics. And he got everyone singing along, often in multipart harmony. Seeger's own songs, sometimes adaptations from other sources, became hits for others: "If I Had a Hammer" for Trini Lopez and Peter, Paul, & Mary; "Turn!Turn!Turn!" for the Byrds—but he was also known for his hit version of Malvina Reynolds's "Little Boxes," for "We Shall Overcome," "Guantanamera," and dozens more. In 1969, Seeger launched the sloop Clearwater and formed a group to help clean up the Hudson River. He maintained a busy appearance schedule, much of it given over to benefits for a variety of causes. The last time I saw him (at a shad festival in Sparkhill, NY, a few days after his 73rd birthday), Seeger didn't appear to have slowed down a bit. And when he took the makeshift stage in front of a Baptist church, he noted that the Hudson River was a lot cleaner than it had been 20 years before. —*William Ruhlmann*

○ **American Industrial Ballads** / 1957 / Smithsonian/Folkways 40058
This collection demonstrates Seeger's interest in and respect for workers of all stripes. A wonderful record. —*Richard Meyer*

○ **Broadsides Ballads, Vol. 2** / 1963 / Smithsonian/Folkways 5302
Seeger turns to the work of the new generation of topical folksingers on this follow-up to the first *Broadsides* collection, leading off with Malvina Reynolds's best-known song, "Little Boxes," and including the work of Bob Dylan, Tom Paxton, Peter LaFarge, and Phil Ochs. —*William Ruhlmann*

☆ **We Shall Overcome** / 1963 / CBS 45312
We Shall Overcome: The Complete Carnegie Hall Concert shows that Pete Seeger was at his apex as a performer and as an influential figure in the surging folk movement when John Hammond turned on the Columbia Records tape machine to capture this performance. Out flowed stories, traditional songs, covers of songs by new songwriters like Bob Dylan, and lots more. Seeger was perfectly in tune with his audience as well, and in the acoustic wonder of the hall, the harmonies were well captured. Columbia cut the tape down to a single disc in 1963, but this reissue, running over two hours on compact discs, presents the full concert for the first time. Anyone wondering what it is that has put Seeger at the forefront of folk music for the better part of his life need only hear this to understand.— *William Ruhlmann*

○ **Broadsides** / 1964 /

Pete Seeger's fearless, clearly articulated voice and spare, accurate guitar and banjo playing are presented here in the service of a collection of songs published in early editions of *Broadside*, the topical song magazine, among them Malvina Reynolds's "From Way Up Here" and the civil rights anthem "We Shall Overcome." —*William Ruhlmann*

☆ **Rainbow Race** / 1971 / Columbia 30739
For once, Pete Seeger went into the studio to make an album of mostly original songs with a few more instruments than his own accompaniment. The result is a stunning singer- songwriter collection, ranging from the topical "Last Train to Nuremberg" to the pastoral "Snow Snow" and Seeger's own wise words for the world, "My Rainbow Race." The record is a masterpiece and remains Seeger's most personal and accomplished original statement. —*William Ruhlmann*

★ **World of Pete Seeger** / 1973 / CBS 31949
An excellent two-disc compilation of Seeger's Columbia years, this album contains 20 songs, most of which will be familiar to Seeger fans and folk enthusiasts in general. There's far more valuable Seeger on Columbia, but it's good to have "Turn! Turn! Turn!" as sung by its adapter and "If I Had a Hammer" as sung by its coauthor, not to mention such Seeger concert staples as "Guantanamera" and "Last Night I Had the Strangest Dream." —*William Ruhlmann*

○ **Singalong Demonstration Concert** / 1980 / Smithsonian/Folkways 36055
Having reached his '60s, Seeger asked Folkways to document a typical concert "before my voice, memory, and sense of rhythm and pitch were too far gone." What they got is this 25-track, two-record boxed set containing the amazing variety and depth of Seeger's repertoire, from the traditional "John Henry" to the African lullaby-story "Abiyoyo" to Charlie King's antinuke tune "Acres of Clams." But what most impresses is Seeger's rapport with an audience that is willing and able to sing along on every song. —*William Ruhlmann*

Shaw Brothers

For more than 30 years twin brothers Rick & Ron Shaw have traveled the world sharing their music. As a duo and as part of The Brandywine Singers, they have appeared in every time zone in North America and in many places throughout the world. Their music is that of the balladeer and storyteller, the tunes memorable, the lyrics both entertaining and educational, the result unforgettable. —*Allan Shaw*

● **Shaw Brothers Collection** / 1986 / Folk Era 2041
Music with variety, spice, and life. —*Mike Fleischer*

Cosy Sheridan

○ **Late Bloomer** / 1991 / Fishtracks
The title song is Sheridan's ode to an aloe plant and not at all clichéA. Like all her work, love songs or funny ones, it has a simple honesty about it. Production here is understated and well played. —*Richard Meyer*

★ **Quietly Led** / 1992 / Waterbug Records
Sheridan's style is warm and engaging, and her heartfelt songs have a very comfortable sound to them. "I'd Fall for You," a loving melodic letter from mother to child is sentimental without becoming cloying for an instant. —*Richard Meyer*

Richard Shindell

b. , Lakehurst, NJ
Vocals, guitar

Born in Lakehurst, NJ, Shindell began his musical career in college in Bethlehem, PA, where he was the lead guitar player in the infamous Razzy Dazzy Spasm Band (which also included John Gorka). Shindell began writing songs in earnest in 1986. In addition to his debut album, *Sparrows Point*, he has been recorded extensively by *The Fast Folk Musical Magazine*. He was also featured on Christine Lavin's 1991 compilation *When October Goes* (Rounder). Shindell earned an MA in theology from Union Theological Seminary in 1991 but says he has no intention of joining the priesthood. —*William Ruhlmann*

○ **Sparrows Point** / 1992 / Shanachie 8002
A strong debut release "e la Eric Andersen." Shindell's songwriting is intense at times ("Sparrows Point," "The Courier," "On the

Sea of Fleur de Lis"). His "Kenworth of My Dreams" is the classic blue-collar truck-driver song, and the title song should not be missed, either. "Are You Happy Now" is the most commercial song—very strong. This is an up-and-coming artist you should check out. —*Chip Renner & Richard Meyer*

Paul Siebel

Vocals
In addition to *Live at McCabes*, this reclusive '60s singer-songwriter only made two studio albums, and they are both essential. —*Richard Meyer*

★ **Wood Smoke and Oranges** / 1970 / Elektra 74064
His classic album, which incudes "The Ballad of Honest Sam," and "Louise." —*Richard Meyer*

Jack Knife Gypsy / 1971 / Elektra 42076
Siebel's unique blend of country and folk is in peak form on his second album. A fine companion to the equally overlooked classic *Wood Smoke and Oranges*. —*Chris Woodstra*

○ **Live at McCabes** / 1981 / Rag Baby 1006
Recorded in an intimate concert setting, includes some his signature tunes such as "Louise" along with perrenials like "I'm So Lonesome I Could Cry," and "In the Jailhouse Now." —*Richard Meyer*

Dick Siegel

b. , New Jersey
Vocals
Born in New Jersey, Siegel relocated to the southern Michigan area. He is a well-known local artist who plays folk music laced with R&B, rock, and humor. He was a winner at the 1991 Kerrville Folk Festival. —*Chip Renner*

● **Snap** / 197z / Schoolkids 1562-02
A CD reissue of a late '70s, early '80s album. Siegel embraces blues, jazz, and pop structures in an interesting, arresting, and clever manner reminiscent of Mose Allison. A four-piece horn section backs up the vocal trio. The Kevin O'Connell Trio, George Bedard on guitar, and Mike Blanchard on tenor sax are featured. There are ten cuts, all Siegel originals. Standouts are "Razzle Dazzle," "Angelo's," and "What Would Brando Do?" —*Michael G. Nastos*

○ **Live** / 1990 / Schoolkids
This live release is loaded with Siegel's humor. The audience is into the show, and the sound quality is good, with more solo and low backup. Folky. —*Chip Renner*

Shel Silverstein

b. 1932, Chicago, IL
Songwriter
Silverstein originally gained fame as a cartoonist and satirist for *Playboy* magazine. His satirical songs first found a national audience with Johnny Cash's "A Boy Named Sue," Loretta Lynn's "One's on the Way," and Doctor Hook's interpretations of several of Silverstein's best, including "Sylvia's Mother" and "The Cover of the Rolling Stone." Silverstein's own recordings have earned him a deserved cult following. —*Cub Koda*

★ **Inside Folk Music** / 1962 / Atlantic 8072
A hilarious collection of folk songs by the gravel-voiced humorist. —*David Szatmary*

Shel Silverstein / 1967 / Cadet
A very strong album. —*Chip Renner*

Freakers Ball / 1972 / CBS
A very humorous and satirical collection of music. —*Chip Renner*

○ **Great Conch Train Robbery** / 1979 / Flying Fish 211
Silverstein is joined by Sam Bush, Josh Graves, John Hartford, Roy Husky, Benny Martin, Pig Robbins, Joe Stuart, and Amos Garrett. A great, funny album. —*Chip Renner*

Martin Simpson

○ **Closer Walk with Thee, A** /
Beautiful settings of gospel melodies for guitar and a small group. Very delicate. —*Richard Meyer*

● **Collection** / 1994 / Shanachie
This reissue collects tunes Simpson cut for Topic records between 1983 and 1987. His commanding, intricate guitar never overtakes

his singing of these predominently traditional songs. —*Richard Meyer*

Patrick Sky

Vocals
Patrick Sky is a singer-songwriter whose musical style ranges from folk to blues. —*Chip Renner*

○ **Patrick Sky** / 1965 / Fontana 6062
A great album. "Ballad of Ira Hayes," "Wreck of the 97," and "Separation Blues." —*Chip Renner*

Harvest of a Gentle Clang / 1966 / Vanguard 19054
A good album. —*Chip Renner*

Reality Is Bad Enough / 1968 / Verve
The change of label to Verve helps Sky on this release. Excellent songwriting. —*Chip Renner*

Photographs / 1969 / Verve 3079
Good cover of "I Like to Sleep Late in the Morning." —*Chip Renner*

Two Steps Forward One Step Back / 1976 / Leviathan 2006
A tribute to the late John Hurt. Very good. —*Chip Renner*

● **Through a Window** / 1985 / Shanachie 95003
Twelve of Sky's most influential songs. All classics. —*Chip Renner*

Fred Small

● **Heart of the Appaloosa** / 1983 / Rounder 4014
Fred's a prolific and eloquent songwriter, who has written a wealth of material in support of various progressive political movements, including feminist, environmental, peace, and disability. This album, which features the instrumental and vocal talents of folks like Betsy Rose, Sally Rogers, and Maxine Feldman, includes "Talking Wheelchair Blues"; "Face at the Window," a powerful song that deals with rape, queer-bashing, and violence, discrimination, and outlaw status awarded to minorities and "heretics" everywhere; and "Annie," about a lesbian teacher. Great songs and excellent delivery and production. —*Ladyslipper*

○ **I Will Stand Fast** / 1988 / Flying Fish 70491
This 1988 release contains a beautiful duet with Cris Williamson, "This Love"; "Scott and Jamie," the true story of two children removed from their foster home solely because the parents were two gay men; "Denmark 1943," the story of the escape of 7000 Jews from occupied Denmark to Sweden on the eve before their arrest; "If I Were a Moose," based on a true tale of moose-cow courtship; and other vignettes, each a gem of lyric, melody, and thought. Accompanists include John McCutcheon and Lorraine Duisit of Trapezoid. —*Ladyslipper*

Jaguar / Aug. 15, 1991 / Flying Fish 70570
On this 1991 release, lawyer turned folksinger-activist performs his own material that addresses everything from war to endangered wildlife to child abuse. Each song tells a story and makes a point in his inimitable manner; includes "Light in the Hall," based on the recollections and writings of an incest survivor; "Simple Living"; "All the Time in the World." —*Ladyslipper*

Everything Possible: Fred Small in Concert / Mar. 1993 / Flying Fish
A concert recording of Fred Small with a small group including Johnny Cunningham, features a set of well-played story-songs that are always carefully politically correct. —*Richard Meyer*

Lynn "Chirps" Smith

Chirps is one of those musicians, whom others beat paths to see, hear, and emulate. This honor is usually reserved for much older musicians (Chirps is just past 40). Nearly 20 years ago, he played mandolin with the Indian Creek Delta Boys. Since then he has befriended dozens of old-time musicians, both learning from, and teaching them fiddling techniques. He has played with many old-time musicians and groups, including the Volo Bogtrotters. He can best be described as a "young fogie" and a legend in his own time. He knows more Midwestern fiddle tunes than anyone else. He performs and records alone and with groups across the country. A must to see and hear. —*Don Stevens*

● **Prairie Dog & Other Fiddle Tunes From The Midwest** / Marimac

Michael Smith

Vocals

Smith lives in Chicago and is best known for writing "The Dutchman," popularized by Steve Goodman. Recent work has included the score for the Steppenwolf Theater Company's Broadway production of *The Grapes of Wrath*. Other recordings include a live coffeehouse album, the long out-of-print *Juarez*, which, strictly speaking, is not a Michael Smith album, but an electric band performing his songs with other singers—interesting. —*Richard Meyer*

Time / 1994 / Flying Fish
After years of having two excellent but short (8 songs each on LP but combined on one Flying Fish CD) Michael Smith albums containing his signature songs the "Dutchman" and "Spoon River" it's great to have a new collection to live with. This is a solo album, and so we get to hear Smith's impassioned singing and authoratative rythmic guitar playing. The songs are, like all Smith's work, detailed pieces of poetry. "Lady Susquahanna" and "Time Is Moving in the Hallways" are 2 of the 15 strong tracks. —*Richard Meyer*

● **Michael Smith & Love Stories** / Flying Fish 70404
This CD compiles Smith's two solo albums for the Flying Fish label on one disc. It has all his signature tunes, including "Three Monkies" and "Dead Egyptian Blues." A writer's writer, highly recommended. —*Richard Meyer*

Chris Smither

b., New Orleans
Vocals, guitar

Chris Smither has forged a blues-folk synthesis from his adopted hometown of Boston. Leaving the Crescent City in 1966, Smither wrote "Love You Like a Man" for Bonnie Raitt and recorded for Poppy during the '70s and Adelphi in 1984. Smither's 1991 set for Flying Fish, *Another Way to Find You*, showcases his rough-hewn vocals and slide guitar work. —*Bill Dahl*

○ **Another Way to Find You** / 1991 / Flying Fish 70568
Recorded live in the studio in Boston in 1989 with an audience of friends and guests. Smither is a very talented folk-blues singer-songwriter and a very good guitarist. He has an attractive low-key, introspective way about the blues. —*Niles J. Frantz*

● **Happier Blue** / Flying Fish
All the elements of Chris Smither's distinctive style are here: passionate vocals, his cool songs, and some covers. This is a NAIRD award-winning album. —*Richard Meyer*

The Song Project

Group

The Song Project was a group formed in the late '70s-early '80s in Greenwich Village, with various lineups through the years. During an Italian tour in 1985, the current members Lucy Kapbinsky, Tom Intondi, Martha Hogen, and Frank Christian recorded an album. They covered the work of Village writers as well as their own. —*Richard Meyer*

○ **Song Project** / 1985 / Folkstudio
The sonic quality is not state-of-the-art here, but the performances are, and the fact that this is the only Song Project material aside from the few *Fast Folk* cuts makes this an important record. Good liner notes by Dave Van Ronk. —*Richard Meyer*

Rosalie Sorrels

b. 1933, Idaho
Vocals

An important voice in American folk for the last 30 years. Sorrells is a writer and interpreter whose material has a strong political but humanistic tone. —*Richard Meyer*

○ **Always A Lady** / 1976 / Green Linnet 2110
Stories and confessions by a great and legendary folksinger. —*Richard Meyer*

○ **Travelin' Lady Rides Again** / 1978 / Green Linnet 2109
Here is an album of road songs and tales of love and lost love performed either in a honky tonk style or as country weepers. A good album of cautionary tales. —*Richard Meyer*

Be Careful There's A Baby... / 1990 / Green Linnet 2100
It's for those loved ones who are expecting a Little Person to join their household soon—they'll need to learn lullabies, soothing *and* hostile ("Baby Rocking Medley") and stories ("Mehitabel and Her Kittens"); those with children, so they can be reminded just why they had them in the first place; those who don't have any kids, and need an excuse to gloat; and yourself, because you deserve the best! Warm, alternately whimsical and serious, Rosalie introduces many of the songs with personal observations and stories (great liner notes too), and makes clear her opinion that children and motherhood *are* sacred, but to be chosen, not required. Includes an emotional reading of Marge Piercy's "Right to Life." —*Ladyslipper*

○ **Report from Grimes Creek** / 1991 / Green Linnet 2105
This 1991 release is the culmination of a career and of a remarkable   life. As reflected in thoughts and recollections of the log cabin in Utah in which she grew up and now again lives, she weaves a tale,   through song and story, of home, roots, and rural western America.   Poignant and articulate. —*Ladyslipper*

What Does It Mean to Love? / 1994 / Green Linnet
In her notes for this album Rosalie Sorrels says "This album started out to be a children's album, but in making it I have come to think of it as a conversation between an old woman . . . me and a child . . . me." A very accesable but personal record. —*Richard Meyer*

Bill & Eileen Spencer

Bill writes songs that sound like they have been handed down for generations. He has been a friend and tutor to many musicians and groups in central and southern Ohio. He and Eileen have helped get several festivals started in the area. Bill is a manufacturer of, and player on, the mountain dulcimer. A gentleman to know, see, and hear. —*Don Stevens*

● **Roses & Old Walnut** / Central Recording

Spirit of the West

Group

Geoffrey Kelly, J. Knutson, and John Mann comprise this Vancouver band. They play Celtic music mixed with strong rock & roll. —*Chip Renner*

● **Labour Day** / 1978 / Flying Fish 70475
Their finest release features high energy and well-crafted songs. "Profiteers" is a biting commentary on the people who turned out tenants to make a buck on the Vancouver World Fair. "Take It from the Source" is a great heckler song. Highly recommended. —*Chip Renner*

○ **Tripping Up the Stairs** / 1978 / Stony Plain
Reels and jigs, topical songs, Celtic rock—what an album! This music has to be heard to be believed. Outstanding. —*Chip Renner*

Go Figure / 1992 / Warner Brothers
This release is a slight departure from their other records. The band is going in a more commercial, alternative-rock direction. The addition of Vince Ditrich to the band is partly responsible. —*Chip Renner*

Spirit of the West: ... / Stony Plain
Spirit of the West: Old Material 1984-1986. A compilation of early music, featuring Dougie MacLean. Both live and studio recordings. —*Chip Renner*

Bill Staines

A popular performer, New Englander Bill Staines is known for his terrific fingerstyle guitar playing and yodeling. For over 25 years he has traveled the country performing an engaging mixture of his own songs and traditional tunes. His song "The Roseville Fair" was covered by Nanci Griffith. —*Richard Meyer*

● **Tracks and Trails** / 1991 / Philo 1134
On this studio album Staines mixes traditional songs, like "Peter Amberly," in which we get to hear the melody Dylan used in "I Pity The Poor Immigrant," with another dozen of his comforting originals enhanced by delicate arrangements —*Richard Meyer*

○ **First Million Miles** / Rounder 11560

Stampfel & Weber

Group

Peter Stampfel and Steve Weber are the founding members of the Holy Modal Rounders. Some of their albums together have been billed as "Stampfel and Weber," however, perhaps for contractual reasons, perhaps to distinguish them from the Rounders albums, which feature a larger band. — *William Ruhlmann*

○ **Going Nowhere Fast** / 1981 / Rounder 3051
Properly speaking, this is a reunion album by the Holy Modal Rounders, which is the name Peter Stampfel and Steve Weber used for their folk duo when they formed it in the early '60s. The group eventually expanded and went electric, then disbanded. This album is a return to form in more ways than one, restricted to Weber's guitar and Stampfel's banjo and fiddle, plus their squeaky, enthusiastic vocals. It blends folk standards and novelty tunes as the early Rounder albums did and, like them, is an off-the-wall gem. — *William Ruhlmann*

Peter Stampfel & the Bottle Caps

b. Oct. 29, 1938
Group
Former Holy Modal Rounder Peter Stampfel founded the Bottle Caps in 1981 to provide a folk-rock backup to his zany collection of novelty songs. They have recorded several albums for Rounder. — *William Ruhlmann*

Peter Stampfel & the Bottle Caps / 1986 / Rounder 9003
Peter Stampfel remains a folkie eccentric, and the main difference between his '80s band and his '60s one (the Holy Modal Rounders) is that the later one rocks harder and that more of the material is original. But much of the act still consists of novelties ("Surfer Angel" and "Funny the First Time," to name only two), and it's never quite clear whether Stampfel is celebrating or parodying his sources. Not that it matters. — *William Ruhlmann*

● **People's Republic of Rock 'n' Roll** / 1989 / Homestead 133
Stampfel hasn't quite turned pro on this album, but the band is a lot tighter than usual, which only makes the result funnier in songs such as "Bridge and Tunnel Girls" and "Bigfoot Stole My Wife." — *William Ruhlmann*

Jody Stecher

Jody is one of the finest musicians in the world. He has recorded with Alasdair Fraser from Scotland, Krishna Bhatt from India, and with many of America's best traditional musicians. Kate has played with many west coast groups. Jody plays mandolin, guitar, fiddle, and banjo. Kate plays banjo and guitar. Both are terrific vocalists, and as a duet are unbeatable. When Ron Thomason is at a loss of words to describe the beauty of their playing and singing, how can a mere mortal attempt to describe it. Buy *Blue Lightning*. Listen to it, and read Ron's liner notes. There is nothing I can say to add to that! You won't quit until you find all their recordings. — *Don Stevens*

● **Blue Lightning** / 1990 / Rounder 0284
This duo, based in Seattle has the ability to perform contemporary as well as traditional songs with a singular relaxed authority. They own this music, they don't just play it, as in "Blue Diamond Mines." — *Richard Meyer*

○ **Our Town** / 1992 / Rounder 304
This music breathes easily. The title song is Iris DeMent's bittersweet tune; other traditional tunes are made fresh again. — *Richard Meyer*

Steeleye Span

Group
The brainchild of Fairport Convention's Ashley Hutchings, Steeleye Span came about as a furthering vehicle for his infatuation with traditional British folk music. Hutchings succeeded in landing no less a folk deity than Martin Carthy; however, both would be gone by the time Steeleye found its great success.
In 1974, "Gaudette" (a track from their album *Below the Salt*) became a huge Christmas hit in England. Now launched into the pop charts, Steeleye discovered the volume knobs on their amps, cranking out reels with a tenacious bite. Suddenly they sported a full rock rhythm section and David Bowie was producing their records. The results were often spectacular, with Maddy Prior's pristine vocals riding on top. But by the late '70s, a realignment in the group (including a return by Carthy) saw the group slowly return to a more traditional approach and quickly lose its pop au-

dience. Still, there's rarely been a bad Steeleye Span record through the group's many phases, and they remain most excellent listening. — *Steve Aldrich*

Hark the Village Wait / 1970 / Shanachie 79052
Their debut, with a smoother and more traditional sound than later albums. The only album to feature the original lineup. — *Bruce Eder & Stephen Winick*

Please to See the King / 1971 / Shanachie 79075
The group solidifies its lineup and sharpens its sound. Fiddler Peter Knight and the well-known singer and guitarist Martin Carthy joined the band on this album. — *Bruce Eder and Stephen Winick*

Ten Man Mop / 1971 / Shanachie 79049
Ten Man Mop or Mr. Reservoir Butler Rides Again features the same lineup, with a more traditional folk sound. — *Stephen Winick*

○ **Below the Salt** / 1972 / Shanachie 79039
Fine renditions of traditional ballads, songs, and tunes. — *Stephen Winick*

Parcel of Rogues / 1973 / Shanachie 79045
Increasingly tinged with hard-rock sounds. — *Stephen Winick*

● **Now We Are Six** / 1974 / BGO 157
High-energy folk that rocks hard despite three throwaway numbers. Their best. — *Bruce Eder*

All Around My Hat / 1975 / Shanachie 79059
More rock & roll versions of folk songs. — *Stephen Winick*

Live at Last / 1978 / Chrysalis 1199
Steeleye's only live album, recorded at their farewell concert. This one features Martin Carthy and John Kirkpatrick. — *Stephen Winick*

Tempted & Tried / 1989 / Shanachie 64020
The re-formed group's most recent work. An impressive return, complete with videos; their best album since re-forming in the mid-'80s. — *Bruce Eder & Stephen Winick*

Anniversary Celebration / Shanachie 203
Steeleye Span formed in 1969 and went on to become one of the best-loved folk-rock bands in musical history. This concert, taped on their 20th Anniversary tour, contains 12 of their classic tunes, including "Sailor's Bonnet," "The Fox," "All Around My Hat," and "(Somebody's) Following Me." — *Roundup Newsletter*

John Stewart

b. Sep. 5, 1939, San Diego, CA
Vocals
John Stewart first gained recognition as a songwriter when his songs were recorded by the Kingston Trio. In 1960 he formed the Cumberland Three, which recorded three albums for Roulette. The following year, he joined the Kingston Trio, replacing Dave Guard, and stayed with them until 1967. His song "Daydream Believer" was a number one hit for the Monkees at the end of that year. Stewart traveled with Senator Robert Kennedy on his 1968 Presidential campaign, an experience that affected him deeply. In 1969 he released his classic album *California Bloodlines*, the first of seven solo albums to reach the charts through 1980. Stewart found his biggest commercial success with the Top Ten album *Bombs Away Dream Babies* and its single "Gold" in 1979. He released several of his albums and albums by others on his own Homecoming label starting in the 1980s. — *William Ruhlmann*

● **California Bloodline/Willard (minus 2)** / 1969-1970 / Bear Family 15468
This German import contains some of Stewart's most powerful work. *California Bloodlines* offers 12 original tunes backed by Nashville's finest studio musicians. *Willard Minus 2,* though not so powerful as *Bloodlines*, still features many great songs (two tracks missing from the original) and a good cast of musicians. Highly recommended. — *Chip Renner*

Lonesome Picker Rides Again / 1971 / Warner Brothers 1948
Good collection of music, with more energy than his first two records. — *Chip Renner*

Sunstorm Live 1972 / 1972 / Bear Family
Featuring Russ Kunkel, James Burton, Buddy Emmons, and brother Michael Stewart. Contains the song "Kansas Rain." A good, solid release. — *Chip Renner*

Cannons in the Rain/Wingless Angels / 1973-1975 / Bear Family 15519
In this twofer (*Cannons in the Rain, Wingless Angels*) the *Wingless Angels* release is the stronger collection of music, featuring Robert "Waddy" Wachtel on guitar and a guest appearance by John Denver. *Cannons* is a nice collection of ballads and folk-rock. —*Chip Renner*

Complete Phoenix Concerts / 1974 / Bear Family 15518
A great collection of live music covering Stewart's first five albums. —*Chip Renner*

Trancas / 1984 / Affordable Dreams 01
Stewart's electric guitar is nicely backed by touches of strings, drums, keyboards, and synthesized sounds. This album is positive in content and easy listening. —*Chip Renner*

Last Campaign / 1985 / Homecoming 0300
Influenced by Robert Kennedy's campaign for president, the songs paint a tapestry of America. Very good. —*Chip Renner*

○ **Punch the Big Guy** / 1987 / Cypress 0105
An exceptional release. Stewart stands out on his electric guitar with minimal backup. Bela Fleck, Sam Bush, and Pat Flynn (New Grass Revival), along with Rosanne Cash, Edgar Meyers, Brent Rowan, and others add just enough, but do not take away from Stewart's sound. Great job on "Runaway Trains." A classic. —*Chip Renner*

Neon Beach / 1991 / Line 9.010010
Over 60 minutes of great live music, featuring some old and new favorites: "Angels with Guns," "Lady Came from Baltimore," "Seven Angels," "Gold Medley," and "Bad Rats," to name a few. Stewart's talking between songs is insightful. —*Chip Renner*

Deep in the Neon—Live at Mc Cabe's / Jun. 1991 / Homecoming 750
Deep in the Neon—Live at McCabe's features just Stewart and Dave Batti and 16 well-performed songs. The audience is into the show, and Stewart plays an easy and relaxed quiet set. —*Chip Renner*

The Story
Group

● **Grace in Gravity** / 1992 / Green Linnet 2104
The interweaving, intuitive harmonies of the Story's Jonatha Brooke and Jennifer Kimball are mesmerizingly beautiful. Add a top-notch, sympathetic band (guitarist Duke Levine, bassist Mike Rivard, keyboardist Alain Mallet, and drummer-producer Ben Wittman) and a bunch of probing, emotional songs, and the result is this heartfelt release. Folk-pop music of the highest calibre. A great live act as well. —*Roundup Newsletter*

Angel in Our House / 1993 / Asylum 61471
More intricate harmonies from this Boston-based duo. The level of jazz influence and art music has been increased to good effect. Not as accessible as *Gravity* but quite good. —*Richard Meyer*

Tamarack
Group
From its Ontario base, Tamarack has been exploring Canada's history through song for more than 15 years. This popular trio, dubbed the "Peter, Paul, and Mary of Canada" travels the length and breadth of their northern land, singing about the fishermen and farmers, whalers and wilderness guides, trappers and tourists, immigrants and natives, and passing Americans. Tamarack is made up of founding member James Gordon, Alex Sinclair, and Carole LeClaire. The first two are from Ontario and Carole adds the rich maritime music tradition to the mix. Lots of good songs and some unusual views of the history of North America. One of Canada's cultural icons. —*Mike Fleischer*

Tamarack On The Grand / Folk Era

● **Fields of Rock & Snow** / Jul. 1993 / Folk Era Productions

Frobisher Bay / Folk Era

Jeff Tareila

○ **Dust Devil's Dance** / 1992 /
A worthwhile debut disc from one of the new generation of singer-songwriters who have used the Greenwich Village scene as thier platform. A prolific writer, Jeff takes on political and spiritual subjects, often in a wry manner. —*Richard Meyer*

Eric Taylor
Vocals
Eric Taylor is a Texas-based singer-songwriter. —*Chip Renner*

○ **Shameless Love** / 1981 / Featherbed
Every song is good on this album. The acoustic guitar blends well with Taylor's voice, and Nanci Griffith sings nice harmony on several songs. This is a highly recommended album for the Texas singer-songwriter's fans. —*Chip Renner*

Louise Taylor

○ **Looking for Rivers** / 1992 / Coyote
Louise Taylor, who makes her home in Vermont, has adopted some of the percussive and melodic devices of Shawn Colvin and infused them with the quality of her own songwriting. Her vocals are somewhat darker and less abstract; she tries her hand at more traditional sounding blues forms. Taylor is most succeful when she puts her expression to use on introspective songs such as "Fire and Brimstone," or "Endless Highway." The no-frills production of this album suits Taylor's performances well. —*Richard Meyer*

Tempest

○ **Serrated Edge** / Beacon 10100
Here is an American band in the tradition of Fairport convention during their *Leige and Leaf* sound. They play "Raggle Taggle Gypsy," "The House Carpenter," and "Tam Lin" with electric abandon. They sound like an electric Irish bar band cleaned up for the studio. —*Richard Meyer*

Art Thieme
Art is America's best-loved troubador. Many years ago, a great singer by the name of T.Texas Tyler was known as "the man with a million friends." Unfortunately, Tex is no longer with us, but that title has passed on to Art Thieme. Art is a one man skiffle band. His main instruments are his guitar and banjo, but he plays everything from the saw to the jew's harp, nose flute, and another dozen or so weird gadgets. None of them, however, is as wierd as his sense of humor. He tells the most outrageous puns and stories so well that you laugh even if you've heard them a dozen times or more. He has donated his time and talents to getting dozens of folk clubs started. He has taught children to make and play home-made instruments. He has taught other musicians, as well. He shares his songs with anyone who will listen. He has written many articles for folk publications. He has folk music radio shows. He he has performed in schools, in concert halls, at concerts, by campfires, and on riverboats. He has collected songs (and bad jokes) from hoboes, children, and other musicians while travelling across the country. Like a real balladeer, he may never sing or play a song the same way twice, but he adds new interpretations with each performance. He is a real treasure! —*Don Stevens*

○ **Out Right Bold-faced Lies** / Kicking Mule

Songs Of The Heartland / Kicking Mule

★ **On the Wilderness Road** / Folk Legacy 105
How reassuring this album sounds, how much like coming home. This is Thieme's fourth album and his best to date. It includes such gems as "The Pinery Boy" and a version of "Wabash Cannonball" that Thieme says he learned from a 93-year-old hobo he met in Chicago in 1961. The simplicity of these arrangements—one man singing, one guitar (or banjo, or 9-string guitar)—is what makes the songs so effective, despite the fact that the stories he tells are impossibly dated. Thieme is known as a "folksinger's folksinger": the kind who carries the torch, keeps the tradition alive. And he does it with no self-consciousness. Thieme performs his songs with an unabashed purity that makes the emotions spring from his stories with a new relevance. —*Kim Roberts, Option*

Aileen and Elkin Thomas
Group
A Texas-based duo who bid fair to become the South's answer to Ian and Sylvia, with a robust mix of folk and country sounds and a pair of clean, pleasing voices that meld together beautifully. —*Bruce Eder*

○ **Arise, We Must Be Growing** / Shantih 1124
A gorgeous collection of material, alternately upbeat, sentimental, and serious, with Charlie Daniels sitting in on guitar and bass. A sweet and low-keyed mid-'80s folk-country gem. —*Bruce Eder*

Sue Thompson (Eva Sue McKee)

b. 1926, Nevada, MO
Vocals, guitar
Sue Thompson was born in Nevade, MO, but she was raised in San Jose, CA. She worked on KGO-San Fransico's "Hometown Hayride" TV series while she was still a teenager. She worked with Red Foley on the "Grand Ole Opry" in the late 1950s. She was married to Hank Penny from 1953 to 1963. —*AMG*

● **Greatest Hits** / 1974 / Curb 77462

Norman / Collectables 9032

Paper Tiger / Hickory 121

Artie Traum

b. 1943
Vocals
Artie Traum is a singer-songwriter based in Woodstock, NY. Born in the Bronx, he followed his brother Happy into folk music in the New York area in the early '60s, taking guitar lessons from jazz artists. He and his brother formed the folk-rock group the Children of Paradise in the mid-'60s. After Happy's departure, they changed their name to Bear and recorded an album for Verve/Forecast. Traum moved to Woodstock in 1967 and has worked as a record producer and written film soundtracks. He has also recorded albums with his brother and with the Woodstock Mountain Revue. —*William Ruhlmann*

● **Life on Earth** / 1974 / Rounder 3014
A fine album with Pat Alger, featuring "Is There Life on Earth," "Girls of Montreal," and "Riptide." —*Chip Renner*

○ **From the Heart** / 1980 / Rounder 3039
Traum and Pat Alger are two guys who were meant to play together. Highlights include "Gambling Man," "City Lights," and "Screwin' It Up." —*Chip Renner*

○ **Cayenne** / 1986 / Rounder 3084
Artie Traum's a fine acoustic guitarist, but this 1987 release was more a showcase for his technical skills than a thoughtful or gripping effort. The 12 numbers were so short (none longer than four minutes) that frequently all Traum could do was present an opening melody, briefly improvise, and then complete the track. In addition, they were mostly on the light-impressionistic side, creating an atmosphere that often came perilously close to background caliber. Traum's too fine a player to be forgettable, but on this date he was relegated more to coloration and establishing moods than to presenting accomplished, memorable songs. —*Ron Wynn*

Happy Traum

b. 1939
Vocals
Happy Traum is a singer-songwriter based in Woodstock, NY, who served as editor of *Sing Out!* magazine for three years and currently runs Homespun Tapes, a company that sells instructional tapes narrated by well-known folk and rock musicians for aspiring musicians. Born in the Bronx, Traum attended the High School of Music and Art, where he took up music and was drawn into the folk music boom of the late '50s in the New York area. He was a member of the New World Singers and formed a folk-rock band in the mid-'60s called the Children of Paradise with his brother Artie, Eric Kaz, and others. He moved to Woodstock in 1967. Traum conducted one of the first interviews Bob Dylan granted after his 1966 motorcycle accident, and in October 1971 he recorded several tracks with Dylan that appeared on *Bob Dylan's Greatest Hits, Volume II*. He has made solo albums, records with his brother, and recordings with the Woodstock Mountain Revue. —*William Ruhlmann*

Doubleback / 1971 / Capitol 799
A nice album featuring Artie Traum, Bill Keith, Amos Garrett, Eric Kaz, Billy Sanford, and Buddy Spicher. —*Chip Renner*

○ **Hard Times in the Country** / 1975 / Rounder 3007

Artie Traum, Paul Butterfield, Roly Salley, Arlen Roth, Pat Alger, and Jim Rooney blend nicely. Great covers of "Blow Your Whistle," "Freight Train," and "Penny's Farm." —*Chip Renner*

Relax Your Mind / 1976 / Kicking Mule 110
Traditional fingerpicking guitar styles. Good covers of "John Henry" and "Worried Blues." —*Chip Renner*

● **Bright Morning Stars** / 1980 / Greenhays 703
A fine collection of music and friends make this a special album. With Pat Alger, Merle Watson, John Sebastian, Richard Manuel, Maria Muldaur, and Artie Traum. —*Chip Renner*

Bucket of Songs / 1983 / Shanachie 97002
A pleasing collection of covers and instrumentals performed along with some of the Mud Acres Gang, Andy Robinson, Pat Alger, and Rolly Sally. This is a comp from the earlier Kicking Mule LPs. The album has an enjoyable feel to it. —*Richard Meyer*

Ed Trickett

Ed is known as a "song interpeter." In his day job, he is a professor of psychology. He looks for the hidden truths in songs and sings them to us in a manner that gives old songs new meaning. Usually playing guitar and singing in a very gentle manner, Ed is also an accomplished piano player. He doesn't consider himself a "professional" musician, but he is indeed a professional in every sense of the word. The songs he has recorded alone, with Anne Mayo Muir and Gordon Bok, and with other artists are some of the most beautiful ever recorded. —*Don Stevens*

For All The Good People—A Golden Ring Reunion / Folklegacy

Lonesome Robin / Minstrel

● **On A Day Like Today** / Folk-legacy

People Like You / Folk-legacy

Turning Toward The Morning / Folk-legacy

Water Over Stone, A / Folk-legacy

Greg Trouper

This Brooklyn-based singer-songwriter has had his songs covered by many other artists, including Maura O'Connell and Tom Russell. He has found a home collaborating and writing in Nashville but remains in NY. His style is commercial but driving. It's guitar-based '60s folk rock with a '90s sensibility and thoughtfulness. He's a great performer of his own tunes. —*Richard Meyer*

○ **Everywhere** / 1992 / Black Hole
Songwriter Greg Trouper's independent CD with his band the Flatirons contains great examples of his thoughtful commercial style. Key tracks here are the title cut, "Ireland," and "Blind Spot." —*Richard Meyer*

Sylvia Tyson

From her days as half of the Canadian folk duet Ian and Sylvia to today's career as a solo performer, Sylvia Tyson has lost none of the singing power and songwriting muscle that made her a household word. Collaborations with Tom Russell, Colleen Peterson, and Shirley Eikhard have simply added to her strengths. On this, her first album in several years, Sylvia returns to her rightful spot as a respected performer and songwriter. —*Allan Shaw*

○ **Gypsy Cadillac** / Folk Era
A new vehicle for Sylvia's fans to ride in. —*Mike Fleischer*

Dave Van Ronk

b. Jun. 30, 1936, Brooklyn, NY
Vocals, guitar
One of the most important veterans of the New York folk community, Van Ronk has been active since recording his first album in the late '50s. Van Ronk began as a traditional jazz performer. His distinctive raw vocal style and his ability to incorporate elements of the blues, jazz, jug-band music, and show music allowed him to build a loyal international audience for his eclectic but still traditionally based fingerpicking guitar style. While he has composed some songs, Van Ronk is known primarily as an interpreter. His recent compilation, *The Folkways Years—1959-1961*, finds him covering Gary Davis's "Twelve Gates to the City," "Willie the Weeper," and "Come Back Baby." He is a knowledgeable performer with a fine sense of humor who never lets clinical

traditionalism get in the way of great interpretations. Van Ronk is an active participant in the folk scene in the United States and around the world. As friend, guitar teacher, and touring artist of the highest order, he has lent his support to many up-and-coming songwriters and performers, including Bob Dylan, David Massengill, and Christine Lavin. —*Richard Meyer*

Inside Dave Van Ronk / 1969 / Fantasy 24710
Van Ronk plays solo on this disc. The songs are ragged but right versions of ballads like "The House Carpenter" and "Silver Dagger." A good collection. —*Richard Meyer*

★ **Folkways Years (1959-1961)** / Smithsonian/Folkways 40041
Van Ronk's earliest recordings for Moses Asch. The coffeehouse-folksinger period captured perfectly. —*Cub Koda*

Going Back to Brooklyn / Gazell 2006
This is an album unusual in that it contains only Van Ronk originals. It's a solo album, and it's great to hear his irreverent tunes such as "Losers," "Tantric Mantra," and "Zen Koans Gonna Rise Again," as well as the bittersweet "Another Time and Place." —*Richard Meyer*

Townes Van Zandt

b. 1940, Fort Worth, TX
Songwriter
Townes Van Zandt is among the most widely admired country and folk songwriters of the last quarter century. Texas-born, Van Zandt has a dry, witty, allusive writing style that looks desolation in the eye and chuckles. Starting with Guy Clark, who became a songwriter after hearing him, Van Zandt has influenced an entire generation of artists, up to and including such current leading lights as Lyle Lovett. Van Zandt's own career has suffered from neglect, however. He began putting out albums on the tiny Poppy label in the late '60s and made one remarkable album after another until 1973 and then switched to the equally obscure Tomato label. In the early '80s his songs began to become country hits, including Emmylou Harris's version of "If I Needed You" and Willie Nelson and Merle Haggard's of "Pancho and Lefty." His *At My Window* album in 1987 was his first new effort in nearly a decade. By the '90s, Van Zandt was working on an ambitious boxed set of his songs, to be issued by a newly resuscitated Tomato. —*William Ruhlmann*

For the Sake of a Song / 1968 / Poppy 40001
The original versions of the title track, "Sad Cinderella," and "Waitin' Round to Die." An essential album for anyone interested in contemporary songwriting. —*Richard Meyer*

○ **Our Mother the Mountain** / 1969 / Tomato 269623
Small band performances and another set of Van Zandt's intimate sharp songs. —*Richard Meyer*

★ **Live at the Old Quarter (Houston, Texas)** / 1977 / Tomato 269640
Townes Van Zandt was one of the most impressive songwriters to emerge in the '70s, and his extensive catalog is sufficiently consistent to be recommended in its entirety, once the listener has acquired a taste for his spare, dry delivery and gallows humor. The place to get that taste is on this live disc (originally a two-LP set), which features the best of Van Zandt's early songs, including "If I Needed You" and "Pancho and Lefty." —*William Ruhlmann*

Flyin' Shoes / 1978 / Tomato 269624
His songs are a bit overburdened by production, but still the writing is great. —*Richard Meyer*

○ **At My Window** / 1987 / Sugar Hill 1020
Van Zandt's first album after a long layoff found him in a more accessible musical setting, courtesy of producers Jack Clement and Jim Rooney, with his striking lyrical observations intact. Van Zandt's qualities are sometimes subtle, and this is an album that gets better every time you listen to it. —*William Ruhlmann*

Live & Obscure / 1989 / Sugar Hill 1026
Recorded after returning to Nashville in 1985, this album has some of the chestnuts and some obscure material played to an adoring crowd with a cool band. —*Richard Meyer*

Roadsongs / 1994 / Sugar Hill
Here we have one of the great troubadour songwriters on the road performing the songs he admires in his own ragged but right style. Its interesting to hear how these songs sound so much like Townes Van Zandt songs when he does them. Key tracks are "Automobile Blues"; "Racing in the Streets"; and "My Starter

Won't Start," one of four Lightnin' Hopkins covers. —*Richard Meyer*

○ **First Album** / Tomato

○ **Nashville Sessions** / Tomato

Loudon Wainwright III

b. Sep. 5, 1946, Chapel Hill, NC
Vocals
Loudon Wainwright III is a singer-songwriter with a humorous, confessional style that has made him a concert favorite and a moderately successful recording artist with almost a dozen albums to his credit. He had a fluke pop hit with "Dead Skunk" in 1973. —*William Ruhlmann*

Album III / 1972 / CBS 31462
Wainwright's directly autobiographical songs are both brutally honest and extremely funny. Usually he plays alone, but here he gets a full folk-rock backup, which brings out the pop implications of his music. His fluke hit "Dead Skunk" is here, and so is "Red Guitar," about the destruction of one. —*William Ruhlmann*

○ **A Live One** / 1979 / Rounder 3050
Wainwright is well served by this collection of samples of his live work, which also doubles as the best of his '70s material, with songs like "Whatever Happened to Us," "Nocturnal Stumblebutt," and "Clockwork Chartreuse." —*William Ruhlmann*

Fame & Wealth / 1983 / Rounder 3076
Bitterness and regret become bigger factors in Wainwright's albums in the '80s. The best of these (also recommended: *I'm Alright* and *More Love Songs*), this collection shows tremendous personal insight, continuing passion for children (Wainwright may have written more about children than any contemporary singer-songwriter), and brave humor, holding out against the little defeats of middle age. —*William Ruhlmann*

○ **I'm Alright** / 1984 / Rounder 3096

○ **More Love Songs** / 1986 / Rounder 3106

○ **Career Moves** / Jan. 1993 / Virgin
As both a career summary and introduction, the live set *Career Moves* is a delight. Sparkling with the humor that drives Wainwright's concerts, the album features 24 first-class songs that prove what a witty, gifted songwriter he is. It's a blast and arguably his best album. —*Stephen Thomas Erlewine*

Little Toby Walker

Long Islander Walker really has a feel for the stretched-out old-time blues. To find his releases contact PO Box 219, Wantagh, NY 11793. —*Richard Meyer*

● **Thumbs up for The Blues** /
A solo album and probably his best. —*Richard Meyer*

Kim Wallach

Wallach is now based in New Hampshire and has released solo and group albums with the Short Sisters. —*Richard Meyer*

● **Little Gracefulness** / 1987 / Black Sox 6
With the Short Sisters. —*Richard Meyer*

Jake Walton

○ **Gloaming Grey** / 1979 / Folk Freak
This German guy sounds a lot like Donovan in his best *Gift From a Flower to a Garden* period. He plays guitar and hurdy gurdy and sings mostly traditional songs. "The Gloaming Grey" is beautifully done. —*Richard Meyer*

T. E. Kellison Warren

Vocals, guitar, banjo, steel guitar dobro
Warren is a west Texas singer-songwriter who plays a 1920 electric steel-bodied dobro, string guitar, national dobro, and banjo. He plays a blend of blues, bluegrass, country, and rock & roll. —*Chip Renner*

Wind Blown Blues / 1990 / Canadian River
A very good mix of blues, bluegrass, and country, with a dose of rock & roll to boot. "Death Drives a DeSoto" is a great song (and title), and the combination of guitar and mandolin on this album is also great. —*Chip Renner*

● **Hazardous Cargo** / 1991 / Canadian River 002

Terry Warren and sister Deborah handle all the instruments on this release, playing socially conscious ballads that are reminiscent of Woody Guthrie's music. —*Chip Renner*

Auggie the Doggie / Canadian River
A great collection of guitar instrumentals in the finest tradition. The songs are rich, well played, and a joy to hear. Highly recommended for guitar fans. —*Chip Renner*

Washington Squares

Group
New York-based folk trio formed in 1983 by Tom Goodkind, Bruce Paskow, and Lauren Agnelli, specializing in neo-Peter, Paul & Mary harmonies and song styles and (especially in concert) parodies of contemporary pop music. They broke up at the start of the '90s after two albums. —*William Ruhlmann*

● **Washington Squares** / 1987 / Gold Castle 71303
The Squares resurrect boldly sung '60s folk-pop harmonies and try to reinvoke the political spirit that went with them on such songs as "New Generation" and "You Are Not Alone." Such an ambition can't really be realized 20 years later, but in the meantime, the music is stirring. —*William Ruhlmann*

Fair & Square / 1989 / Gold Castle 71319

Watersons

Group
Superstardom seems a far cry from the cupped-ear school of a cappella folksinging, yet the Watersons were once called "the Beatles of folk music." Originally composed of sisters Lal and Norma, brother Mike Waterson, and their cousin John Harrison, the English quartet caused a stir in the folk world with their 1965 debut, *Frost & Fire*, which featured ceremonial folk songs (one, "John Barleycorn Must Die," was picked up by the band Traffic). The Watersons have produced only a handful of albums, many of the songs joined by a thematic thread. Martin Carthy replaced John Harrison in 1972, and the distinctive English country harmonies of the group have appeared in British film and television soundtracks. The Watersons guested on the acclaimed Richard and Linda Thompson album *Shoot Out the Lights*. *Four Pence and Spicy Ale* (1975) is one of their best-received efforts to date. —*Mark A. Humphrey*

● **For Pence & Spicey Ale** / 1975 / Shanachie 79056
This lovely album, almost entirly a cappella was first released by the Watersons in 1975. It is considered by many to be their finest recording and includes the participation of Martin Carty in addition to family members. This reissue also includes some later solo Waterson recordings which in fact feature others helping out. This record sounds like the back room of an old pub in its charming immediacy. You really get a sense of the fun it is to sing these old songs with affection and respect. —*Richard Meyer*

The Weavers

Group
Pete Seeger, Lee Hays, Fred Hellerman, and Ronnie Gilbert formed the Weavers in 1948 to sing folk music in harmony. The group got its big break at a two-week gig at the Village Vanguard in New York City at Christmas 1949; the gig lasted six months. The Weavers were signed to Decca and scored a double-sided hit in the summer of 1950 with "Tzena, Tzena, Tzena," which went to number two, and "Goodnight Irene," which topped the charts for 13 weeks, one of the biggest hits of the first half of the century. More hits followed through 1952, but then the Weavers fell afoul of the Communist scare of that decade, and their career declined precipitously. They came back, however, at a Carnegie Hall concert in 1955 that is remembered as the birth of the late '50s-early '60s folk boom. They then toured and recorded (for Vanguard) more successfully. Seeger left in 1958, replaced by a succession of good musicians: Frank Hamilton, Bernie Krause, and Erik Darling. In 1963 the Weavers (with Seeger and his replacements onstage) staged a reunion and farewell at Carnegie Hall. There was a final reunion and farewell of the original four at the hall in 1980. In addition to their considerable musical accomplishments, the Weavers are remembered as popularizers of folk music and as the inspiration for a whole generation of folk performers. —*William Ruhlmann*

★ **Weavers at Carnegie Hall** / Dec. 1956 / Vanguard 73101

The Weavers made a dramatic comeback from the McCarthy era at their 1955 Christmas Eve Carnegie Hall concert, immortalized here. Many of the songs were the same ones from the pop-star days—"Kisses Sweeter than Wine," "Goodnight Irene"—but backed only by guitar and banjo, they were fresh and stirring. —*William Ruhlmann*

○ **Greatest Hits** / 1957 / Vanguard 15-16
This is an excellent double-disc compilation of this group's more directly folk-related work from the mid-'50s to the mid-'60s. Note, however, that these are not the original Weavers recordings of their hits. —*William Ruhlmann*

Reunion at Carnegie Hall / 1965 / Vanguard 79161

Together Again / 1984 / Loom 1681
After years apart, the Weavers played together one last time at—where else?—Carnegie Hall in November 1980. Lee Hays was ailing (he would die the following year), but the show still transcended nostalgia, demonstrating their individual and collective talents and proving they still were a seminal folk ensemble. —*William Ruhlmann*

★ **Best of the Weavers** / 1987 / MCA 4052
The recording career of the Weavers falls into two categories: preblacklist and postblacklist. In their preblacklist days, they recorded for Decca (now MCA), and their adaptations of folk songs were backed by orchestras and choruses. Frequently these songs (notably "Goodnight Irene"), were giant pop hits. This two-album set captures 24 examples of this quasi-folk pop style, and though the group's singing is excellent, the arrangements, intended to modernize the material, now sound quaintly dated. —*William Ruhlmann*

☆ **Wasn't That a Time!** / Sep. 1993 / Vanguard
Wasn't That a Time! is a treasure for serious Weavers fans. Featuring 87 songs on its four discs, including several unreleased numbers, the box set is designed for devoted fans; the liner notes are filled with anecdotes and photos that provide a good portrait of the group. For some casual fans, it might be a bit too much, but *Wasn't That a Time* is a fitting tribute to the seminal folk group. —*Stephen Thomas Erlewine*

○ **Kisses Sweeter Than Wine** / 1994 / Vanguard/Omega
This two-CD live set is drawn from vintage concerts by the original Weavers from the early to mid-'50s. It captures them at the height of their fame and during the chilly era of McCarthyism. It's a good example of how the perceived or real political leanings of the performances color essentially neutral material. The performances themselves sound immediate and not at all dated. It's great to hear the vocal blend and commitment to a world of songwriting rarely equaled since the Weavers broke up. Ford Hellerman who compiled this album from a variety of previously unreleased sources, including concerts at Town Hall, has left in many of the songs' introductions and comments among the group. We really get to feel their enthusiam and "history in the making." The hits are here in new versions that stand up well to the "standard" versions. There are 11 songs never released in any form on Weavers records. As an added bonus and not mentioned on the package anywhere is the inclusion of a third CD of previously unreleased material by Leadbelly recorded in 1947. He performs a dozen driving blues songs including Howard Hugh's, "Hangman's Blues" and "Black Betty," and it sounds great. —*Richard Meyer*

Goodnight Irene / MCA 20201
Includes many great classics, including "Tzena, Tzena, Tzena," "Follow the Drinking Gourd," "Midnight Special." —*Ladyslipper*

Dick Weissman

Before Bela Fleck and Tony Trischka began experimenting with jazz on the banjo, Dick Weissman was a past master. He has stretched the boundaries of the folk idiom to where no ears have gone before. His most recent recording features bluegrass icons Tim & Molly O'Brien and jazz saxophonist Bob Rebholz. Truly this is music that must be heard to be believed. All originals too. —*Allan Shaw*

○ **New Traditions** / Folk Era 1400

Wellspring

Group

Features Steve Schuch (guitar, fiddle, vocals), and Odds Boskin (Celtic harp, guitar, piano, and recorder). —*Chip Renner*

○ **Live at Folkway** / 1991 / Wisdom Tree/Rare Earth
Both Steve Schuch and Odds Boskin are masters of their instruments. The duo trade off on songs (24 in all), mixing well together. Schuch's "Wale Trilogy" is wonderful, as are Boskin's "Troubadour" and "Dragon's Tales." —*Chip Renner*

Harry & Jeanie West

Years ahead of the folk revival Harry and Jeanie West were singing and recording some of the most beautiful traditional folksongs. They are as well known for their dazzling instrumentals as they are for their beautiful harmonizing and selection of songs. They specialize in the old "heart of mine" songs from aural tradition, and no one does them better. They also sing gospel in the old-time way. In addition to collecting vintage instruments, they operate an instrument business, concentrating on hand-picked vintage instruments. —*Don Stevens*

● **Smoky Mountain Ballads** / Esoteric

Cheryl Wheeler

Vocals
Wheeler is a gifted songwriter and singer. Her song "Addicted" was a hit by Dan Seals. —*Chip Renner*

● **Cheryl Wheeler** / 1986 / North Star 1
Her debut album features her hit "Addicted" and is more rock & roll than her other albums. If you like the rest, you should add this to the collection. —*Chip Renner*

○ **Circles & Arrows** / 1990 / Capitol 92063
Wheeler shines on this CD. Guests include Mark O'Connor, Jerry Douglas, Jonathan Edwards, and Billy Joe Walker. Every song is a winner, especially "Northern Girl," "Aces," and "I Know This Town." —*Chip Renner*

Half a Book / 1991 / Cypress 0107
On this 1987 release, Cheryl slows down her tempo a bit so we can really hear her beautiful acoustic guitar playing and distinctive resonant voice. Her poetic lyrics tell of growing up and of the trials and tribulations of falling in and out of love. "Tell Him Goodbye" could easily be a sequel to "Addicted," a song about codependency on her first album. —*Ladyslipper*

Driving Home / 1993 / Philo 1152
On *Driving Home* Cheryl Wheeler has finally got the natural-sounding production that her material needs. Her melodies are highly ornamented and shine through. The distinctive nature of her voice is never overshadowed by synthesized sound as on previous albums. As in the past, the material is often humorous, as in "Don't Forget the Guns"; commercially romantic, "Silver Lining"; and heart-warmingly beautiful, "Arrow." This is an excellent album. —*Richard Meyer*

Josh White

b. Feb. 11, 1908, Greenville, MS, **d.** Sep. 5, 1969
Vocals, guitar
Most blues enthusiasts think of Josh White as a folk revival artist. It's true that the second half of his music career found him based in New York playing to the coffeehouse and cabaret set and hanging out with Burl Ives, Woody Guthrie, and fellow transplanted blues artists Sonny Terry and Brownie McGhee. When I saw him in Chicago in the '60s, his shirt was unbuttoned to his waist e la Harry Belefonte and his repertoire consisted of folk revival standards such as "Scarlet Ribbons." He was a show business personality—a star renowned for his sexual magnetism and his dramatic vocal presentations. What many people don't know is that Josh White was a major figure in the Piedmont blues tradition. The first part of his career saw him as apprentice and lead boy to some of the greatest blues and religious artists ever, including Willie Walker, Blind Blake, Blind Joe Taggert (with whom he recorded), and allegedly even Blind Lemon Jefferson. On his own, he recorded both blues and religious songs, including a classic version of "Blood Red River." A fine guitar technician with an appealing voice, he became progressively more sophisticated in his presentation. Like many other Carolinians and Virginians who moved north to urban areas, he took up city ways, remaining a fine musician if no longer a down-home artist. Like several other canny blues players, he used his roots music to broaden and en-

hance his life experience, and his talent was such that he could choose the musical idiom that was most lucrative at the time. —*Barry Lee Pearson*

○ **Josh White 1933-1944** / Best of Blues 7

★ **Legendary Josh White** / MCA
This is a two-record set that has a good sampling of White's major songs. —*Michael Erlewine*

Josh White, Jr.

b. 1940
Vocals
Josh White Jr got his inspiration and start from his famous father, folk-blues singer Josh White Sr. In the late '40s and early '50s, White worked on Broadway, performing in various plays. He also did extensive work on TV from the '50s through the '70s. After his father's death, he recreated Josh White Sr's folk act in concerts across the country. He has recorded for Vanguard and is very active at major folk festivals. —*Michael Erlewine*

● **Jazz, Ballads & Blues** / 1986 / Rykodisc 10033
This is a tribute to Josh White Sr. —*Michael Erlewine*

Sing a Rainbow / Mountain Railroad 52791

Taylor Whiteside

This singer-songwriter has his feet firmly planted in the rich musical roots of his native New England, so much so that it's often hard to tell a Whiteside original from a tune that's been around for centuries. A member of the Brandywine Singers and Northeast Winds, Taylor is also in demand as a soloist and studio musician. —*Allan Shaw*

○ **Martin Greigh & Other New England Favorites** / 1992 / Folk Era 1406
Captivating! —*Mike Fleischer*

David Wilcox

Vocals
Wilcox is an up-and-coming singer-songwriter who is known for his deep, personal, well-crafted songs and smooth, rich vocals. —*Chip Renner*

Nightshift Watchman / 1987 / Song of the Wood
This debut release shows his earliest work. Worth a listen. —*Chip Renner*

● **How Did You Find Me Here** / 1989 / A&M 5275
Nice songs that, although sometimes sad, are all solid on this sophomore release. —*Chip Renner*

○ **Home Again** / 1991 / A&M 5357
A little more mature and better produced. Great songs. —*Chip Renner*

Big Horizon / Feb. 8, 1994 / A & M Records

Jeff Wilkinson

Detroit native Wilkinson now is a member of the NY folk scene. —*Richard Meyer*

● **Pitchin' Pennies** / 1987 / Blackbird 1001
This record is full of great songs—Wilkinson's songs create images that you keep long after the record is over. "C'mon Down" is a good ol' fishin' song. Wilkinson uses a nice array of mandolin, accordion, fiddle, pennywhistle, and harmonica, along with his guitar. —*Chip Renner*

Ballads in Plain Talk / 1988 / Brambus 199010
Seventeen songs, seven from his *Pitchin' Pennies* album. What an experience! Wilkinson guides you from the Triple-A ballfields of Toledo to Hoboken to Detroit. His songs are vivid and well crafted. Anyone who is into the new acoustic folk style should enjoy this CD. It's worth the import price. —*Chip Renner*

Brave and True / 1989 / Brambus 199121
A more electric album then his previous ones. Wilkinson is backed by the Navigators (at times they sound like a cross between Blue Rodeo and the Kinks). "When the River Was King" and "Henry Villard's Great Train Ride" are just two of a great collection of songs. —*Chip Renner*

Brooks Williams

Guitar

Based in central Massachusetts, a great guitarist and spiritual writer. —*Richard Meyer*

○ **North from Statesboro** / 1990 / Red Guitar 8901
"On the Rollin' Sea" and "Big Blue Wonder" are outstanding tracks. —*Richard Meyer*

○ **How the Nighttime Sings** / 1991 / Red Guitar 9102
"Jubilee" is a joyous lush song, and "Hard Love" is also excellent. —*Richard Meyer*

Inland Sailor / Sep. 1993 / Green Linnet Records
Brooks Williams has delivered another collection of expressive original songs about romance and the underlying spiritual nature of life. As we have come to expect, it is distinguished by exceptional guitar work and his carefully articulated vocals. For the sake of guitarists among his audience, Williams has noted the tuning and capo positions he uses for each song. —*Richard Meyer*

Back to Mercy / Green Linnet 2108
Williams's third album has more ambitious production, but it always serves to support his strong singing. Here are songs of hope and human renewal. —*Richard Meyer*

Dar Williams

Based in Northampton, MA, Dar Williams has previously released a number of independent tapes of her material. She is now a nationally touring artist. —*Richard Meyer*

○ **Honesty Room** / 1993 / Burning Field Music
On this, her first official release, Dar Williams's writing sucessfully explores life from unusual points of view; a child excited that the babysitter is coming, a pair of punk angels in Heaven, and Mark Rothko's paintings. While this album has some band productions, it is primarily a songwriter record. Very worthwhile. —*Richard Meyer*

Robin and Linda Williams

Group
Singers-songwriters Robin and Linda Williams were regulars on Garrison Keillor's "A Prairie Home Companion" radio show. Some of their songs have been recorded by Emmylou Harris, Kathy Mattea, and Michael Martin Murphey. Their harmonies are smooth and well matched. Their musicianship is tight and well crafted. —*Chip Renner*

Harmony / 1981 / June Appal 040
Very hard to find, but it should be in your collection. —*Chip Renner*

○ **Close As We Can Get** / 1984 / Flying Fish 327
Perfect in all ways. "The Leaving Train" is one of their best songs. As good as *All Broken Hearts*. —*Chip Renner*

Nine 'Til Midnight / 1985 / Flying Fish 359
A very good live album featuring gospel, traditional country, and contemporary songs. One of your finer live albums. —*Chip Renner*

● **All Broken Hearts Are the Same** / 1988 / Sugar Hill 1022
With top-notch songwriting and smooth vocals, this features Jerry Douglas, Stuart Duncan, and T. Michael Coleman. —*Chip Renner*

Rhythm of Love / 1990 / Sugar Hill 1027
These 12 songs are all good. Features guests Jerry Douglas and Stuart Duncan. —*Chip Renner*

Turn Toward Tomorrow / 1993 / Sugar Hill
Produced by John Jennings, this collection of primarily Robin and Linda songs is held together by great economical band arrangements. Weepers like "When the Last Tear Falls" and "Chain of Pain" are given an uptempo treatment so we don't have to get to torn up about life's hardships. "Lying to the Moon" brings the CD to a peaceful close. —*Richard Meyer*

Robin & Linda Williams & Their Fine Group Live / 1994 / Sugar Hill
Recorded while on tour in Holland, this album finds Robin and Linda Willams in a more basic band setting. It lets the strength of their vocals come through better than on some of their slicker studio records. My favorite is "The Devil Is A Mighty Wind." —*Richard Meyer*

Robin Williamson & His Merry Band

b. Nov. 24, 1943
Group

Robin Williamson was one half of the Incredible String Band from 1966 to 1974 and then went on to form His Merry Band to back up his playing of traditional Scottish music and originals in a folk style. He has released many albums on Flying Fish, including some devoted to harp music. —*William Ruhlmann*

Journey Edge / 1977 / Flying Fish 033
This album features an unusual blend of baroque, traditional, and contemporary music played by Robin Williamson, one of the founders of the Incredible String Band, and his then-current band. —*AMG*

● **American Stonehenge** / 1978 / Flying Fish 062
This album is perhaps Williamson's most generally accessible, featuring his late '70s touring band on a variety of humorous and pastoral Williamson originals. —*William Ruhlmann*

Glint at the Kindling / 1979 / Flying Fish 096
This album features a blend of rock, jazz, and Celtic music from a popular band. —*AMG*

Legacy of The Scottish Harpers, Vol. 2 / Flying Fish 358
Robin Williamson delves into his Gaelic roots for this second volume of the medieval harp music of the courts of the Scottish kings. Williamson, a founding member of the legendary '60s psychedelic folk group the Incredible String Band, plays the music of his forefathers with eloquence and skill, once again demonstrating his worthiness as a modern-day bard, a direct descendent of the harpers of old. —*Backroads Music/Heartbeats*

Kate Wolf (Kathryn Louise Allen)

b. Jan. 27, 1942, San Francisco, CA, d. Dec. 10, 1986
Piano
Wolf was born in San Francisco, CA, as Kathryn Louise Allen. She started playing piano at age 4, stopping at age 16 due to shyness. In 1969, Wolf got together with the Big Sur music community, where her music blossomed. She was a gifted guitarist and songwriter. After releasing seven records, Wolf died of acute leukemia at the age of 44. Wolf was inducted into the NAIRD Independent Music Hall of Fame in 1987. According to her wishes, material from her unreleased recordings continues to be brought to life. —*Chip Renner*

Back Roads / 1976 / Kaleidoscope 6
Recorded with friends in the living room, this record of country-folk music is remarkably well done. While some songs lean toward melancholic nostalgia, others show that it's more desire for a simpler life ahead that inspired the words of this singer-songwriter. —*Ladyslipper*

Lines on The Paper / 1977 / Kaleidoscope 7
Mostly soft country-folk music, almost all written by Kate. Her songwriting reflects feelings about life and changes. Her voice is even and well-suited to the laid-back folk sound. The second album from this northern California native. —*Ladyslipper*

Safe at Anchor / 1979 / Kaleidoscope 11
The third album by this northern California folksinger tells somehow of a woman and her strength alone. Includes "Seashore Mountain Lady " and "She Rises Like the Dolphin," all songs by Kate. —*Ladyslipper*

Close To You / 1981 / Kaleidoscope 15
A sweet collection of Kate Wolf songs . . . sweet harmonies, gentle rhythms, thoughtful lyrics . . . and this woman can sing! —*Ladyslipper*

○ **Give Yourself To Love** / 1983 / Kaleidoscope 3000
This live 1983 release of mostly previously unrecorded material features Kate's long-time colleague Nina Gerber on mandolin, harmonica, guitar, and vocals throughout the "show." Most closely resembles her concerts and includes some songs by other musicians that she enjoyed performing over the years. Compiled from three performances, in San Francisco (Great American Music Hall), Davis, and Nevada City. Includes a live version of "Redtail Hawk," and her originals "Green Eyes" and the title song. —*Ladyslipper*

Poet's Heart / 1985 / Kaleidoscope 24
Kate's sixth album, which she coproduced, features all original songs, including "In China or a Woman's Heart," "See Here She Said," and "Carolina Pines." —*Ladyslipper*

● **Gold In California** / 1986 / Kaleidoscope 3001

Kate Wolf died of leukemia on December 10, 1986. This is a retrospective that she planned before her death; she began it because she realized she might not ever record again, and finished it shortly before she became unable to work. All the songs were previously released except Alice Stuart's "Full Time Woman." A beautiful collection, it also contains "Unfinished Life," "She Rises Like the Dolphin," "Across the Great Divide," "Redtail Hawk," "Emma Rose." —*Ladyslipper*

Wind Blows Wild / 1988 / Kaleidoscope 30

This 1989 release contains all previously unreleased live and studio recordings compiled by Kate's musical associate and friend, Nina Gerber, after Kate's untimely death at age 44. It spans the period from 1979, with "Fly Away," to 1986; . . . The album radiates with Kate's heartfelt music . . . . —*Ladyslipper*

Kate Wolf /

Kate's popularity keeps increasing since her death in 1986. Her perfect blend of lyrics, voice, and music sounds like no one else. —*Backroads Music/Heartbeats*

Woodstock Mountain Revue

Group

Woodstock Mountain Revue is a loose, informal affiliation of folk-based musicians who live in the area of Woodstock, NY, and record occasionally for Rounder Records. Their first album (at which time they had not yet adopted their name) was *Mud Acres—Music among Friends*. It was recorded in 1972 and featured Happy Traum, Artie Traum, Maria Muldaur, John Herald, Eric Kaz, Jim Rooney, Bill Keith, Tony Brown, and Lee Berg. Their second album, 1977's *More Music from Mud Acres*, was credited to "Woodstock Mountains," and featured the Traums, Herald, Rooney, Keith, and Berg, plus Pat Alger, Eric Andersen, Rory Block, Paul Butterfield, Roly Salley, John Sebastian, and Paul Siebel. Their third album, 1978's *Pretty Lucky*, was the first to be credited to Woodstock Mountain Revue, which was defined as an eight-member group consisting of the Traums, Herald, Rooney, Keith, Alger, Solley, Larry Campbell, and Caroline Dutton, with special guest Cyndi Cashdollar. —*William Ruhlmann*

○ **Mud Acres—Music among Friends** / 1972 / Rounder 3001

With Happy and Artie Traum, Bill Keith, Maria Muldaur, Eric Kaz, Jim Rooney, John Herald, Tony Brown, and Lee Berg. Their first release, just sittin' and pickin'. Very informal. —*Chip Renner*

● **Woodstock Mountains** / 1977 / Rounder 3018

Woodstock Mountains (More Music from Mud Acres) features Pat Alger, Happy and Artie Traum, Eric Andersen, Lee Berg, Rory Block, Paul Butterfield, John Herald, Bill Keith, Jim Rooney, Roly Salley, John Sebastian, and Paul Siebel. This album brought it all together! Their peak. —*Chip Renner*

Pretty Lucky / 1978 / Rounder 3025

Overshadowed by the first Mud Acre album. —*Chip Renner*

Back to Mud Acres / 1981 / Rounder 3065

Featuring Happy and Artie Traum, Pat Alger, Larry Campbell, John Herald, Bill Keith, Jim Rooney, Roly Salley, Cyndi Dollar. Nice, but something was missing. —*Chip Renner*

Glenn Yarbrough

b. Jan. 12, 1930

Vocal

From his days as the singing mainstay of "The Limeliters," through a long solo career that's seen its share of hits, Glenn Yarbrough has been a respected interpreter of folk and popular music. He's had a top hit in "Baby, the Rain Must Fall," and his interpretation of "Seven Daffodils" is the benchmark against which love songs are measured. From his days in a boys choir through today, Glenn's powerful voice has rung with lusty conviction about all that he cares about. Listen to Glenn Yarbrough. He's what singing should be. —*Allan Shaw*

● **Bramble & The Rose, The** / Folk Era

With Holly Yarbrough and fingerpicking guitar champion Muriel Anderson. —*Allan Shaw*

Folk Collections

○ **Adventures in Music: Folk Sampler #7** / AIM 007

A 15-cut sampler, some good, some strange. Dan Berggren plays nice Adirondack traditional music. David Schnaufer is one of the finest mountain dulcimer players you'll ever hear. Andy Wilkenson (Texas singer-songwriter), James Mee (singer-songwriter), Savoy Doucet (Cajun), Lee Murdock (folk), Peter Leman (folk, country, bluegrass), and others make this a good way to find some new music. —*Chip Renner*

Afro-American Folk Music from Tate and Panola Counties, Mississippi / Library Of Congress 67

Fourteen songs recorded in 1942 and 1969-1971 exhibiting fine examples of the various genres and styles of Afro-American folk music coming from this limited geographical area. Includes an excellent book enhanced by powerful photographs. Edited by David Evans. —*Roundup Newsletter*

Linda Allen's Washington Notebook / 1991 / VMR 505

This album is a collection of songs written by Linda Allen and performed by 33 Northwest musicians. Allen has a way of transporting you to the Northwest when you listen to her songs. The album has a real community feel to it. After several plays, you have the feeling you know the musicians. They go to church, recycle, don't eat meat, and would not be caught dead in a McDonald's. —*Chip Renner*

○ **American Explorer Series—Selections from Debut Releases** / 1991 / Elektra 8379

American Explorer Series—Selections from Debut Releases features two tracks each from Johnnie Johnson, Jimmie Dale Gilmore, Vernard Johnson, Charlie Feathers, and Boozo Chavis. —*Chip Renner*

Angels in Daring / 1988 / Overall Music

The trio of Kallet, Ellen Epstein, and Michael Cicone performs a variety of songs a cappella and accompanied by guitar and dulcimer. It is a collection of contemporary and traditional music of the British Isles and America. Dougie MacLean's "Ready for the Storm" is powerful. Fourteen songs in all. —*Chip Renner*

Anglo-American Ballads / Library Of Congress

This album includes 15 songs recorded from 1934 to 1941. Eleven are acapella; four accompanied by guitar or banjo. Songs include "Barbara Allen," "Pretty Polly" (two versions), and two Negro worksongs, "It Makes a Long Time Man Feel Bad" and "O Lord Don't 'Low Me to Beat 'Em." Singers include Woody Guthrie, Alex Moore, and E.C. Ball. Edited by Alan Lomax. —*Roundup Newsletter*

☆ **Anthology of American Folk Music, Vol. 3** / 1966 / Smithsonian/Folkways 2953

This is an invaluable set of three double albums of songs, ballads and social music recorded in the field in the late '20s and early '30s. Clarence Ashley and the Carters are represented here, as are Dick Boggs, Blind Lemon Jefferson, and Uncle Dave Macon. Classic songs include "I Wish I Was a Mole," by Bascomb Lunsford, "Spikedriver's Blues" by John Hurt, and "The Wagoner's Lad" by Buell Kazee. The historical importance of this set issued originally in 1952 cannot be overestimated. This is folk music as heard before it became touched by the word business. These recordings are sonically primitive but have far more energy than so many modern recordings. —*Richard Meyer*

○ **Atomic Cafe** / Rounder 1034

A fine and varied compilation of '50s songs reacting to life in the atomic age. —*Mark A. Humphrey*

○ **Ben & Jerry's Newport Folk Festival—Turn of the Decade** / 1991 / Red House 36

Sixteen live cuts on a nice collection featuring Robert Earl Keen Jr, the Indigo Girls, Shawn Colvin, Luka Bloom, Richard Thompson, Greg Brown, Michelle Shocked, Cheryl Wheeler, and more. Highly recommended. —*Chip Renner*

○ **Ben & Jerry's Newport Folk Festival, Vol. 2** / 1990 / Alcazar 113

Featuring Bill Morrissey doing "Grizzly Bear," Doc Watson's "St. James Infirmary," and Richard Thompson's "Two Left Feet" and "Stands Out." Cheryl Wheeler's "I Know This Town" is also great. —*Chip Renner*

○ **Ben & Jerry's Newport Folk Festival 88** / Alcazar 105

Vanguard Records used to record the Newport Folk Festivals of the early '60s for some seminal albums displaying the quality of folk artists of the time. Alcazar has done much the same for the revived festival, and this disc spotlights a range of talent, from veterans of the '60s festival to figures who emerged during the hiatus, and to new folkies. — *William Ruhlmann*

Best of Mountain Stage Live, Vol. 1 / 1991 / Blue Plate 001
Recordings taken from the "Mountain Stage" live performance radio program. Featuring Richard Thompson, Danko and Hudson, Gregson and Collister, Loudon Wainwright III, and others. Very wide range of music. — *Chip Renner*

○ **Best of Mountain Stage Live, Vol. 2** / 1991 / Blue Plate 002
Features John Prine, Billy Bragg, Maura O'Connell, Michelle Shocked, Kathy Mattea, Jimmie Dale Gillmore, and others. Very good. — *Chip Renner*

Big Times in a Small Town—the Vineyard Tapes / 1993 / Philo
This CD has highlights of the first annual Martha's Vineyard Singer-Songwriter retreat. Sponsored by Christine Lavin, it was recorded live at the Wintertide Coffeehouse. Standout cuts are Jonatha Brooke's "Dog Dreams," Pierce Pettis's cover of Mark Heard's "Nod Over Coffee," and James Mee's title cut. — *Richard Meyer*

○ **Bread & Roses Festival 1977** / 1979 / Fantasy 79009
This two-record set chronicles the October 1977 benefit concert for Mimi Farina's Bread & Roses organization, which brings music into prisons and hospitals. A broad range of folk-related artists, including Joan Baez, Jackson Browne, Pete Seeger, and Arlo Guthrie, among many others, turns this into a brilliant songwriting showcase. — *William Ruhlmann*

○ **Bread & Roses Festival 1979** / 1980 / Fantasy 79011
The lineup for the 1979 festival was even broader than the 1977 one, including the Chambers Brothers and Chick Corea, plus the Roches, Graham Nash and David Crosby, and many more. But the folk theme still runs through all the wonderful music. — *William Ruhlmann*

○ **Broome Closet Anti-Folk Sessions** /
Compilation by members of the New York "antifolk" East Village scene, including Roger Manning, Kirk Kelly, Cindy Lee Berryhill, and others. — *Richard Meyer*

○ **Camp Cuisine Tapes: Music from the Kerrville Campgrounds** / 1991 / Agua Azul 12
These recordings of *Music from the Kerrville Campgrounds* were made at the 1989 festival on a portable DAT machine. Most of the artists are not well known, but they should be. Jon Ims does his song "She's in Love with the Boy" (number one for Trisha Yearwood). "Here Comes the Water," by Chuck Pyle, is very strong. Bob Franke has the crowd join in on "Invasion of the Money Snatchers." This record is hard to get. Write to Agua Azul, PO Box 161556, Austin, TX 78716. The crickets in the background on the CD will lull you into a trance—so will the music. — *Chip Renner*

○ **Capitol Acoustics** / 1991 / Capitol 7041
Featuring Magpie, Jane Gillman, Steve Key, Anne Louise White (formerly of Trapezoid), Hazelwood (real nice female duo), and others. The Washington area is rich in talent—traditional folk and bluegrass. This is a good way to hear some of it. — *Chip Renner*

○ **Capitol Acoustics, Vol. 2** / Impact
A less well known group than on Vol. 1, but this CD has some great music. Shady Grove and Tony Furtado play some good bluegrass. The Jon Henrys, featuring Jonathan Edwards, Henry Gross, Henry Paul, and Toulouse le Trac, are great. Cathy Fink and March Marxer also play on the CD. Here's folk, traditional, bluegrass, and contemporary on one CD. Can't wait to hear the third volume (how about Mary-Chapin Carpenter, guys?). — *Chip Renner*

○ **Circle Dance ...** / 1991 / Green Linnet 3054
Circle Dance—Hokey Pokey Charity Compilation is a well-done collection featuring the cream of British folk-rock. Many rarities. Includes Richard Thompson, Sandy Denny, June Tabor, Fairport Convention, and others. — *Michael P. Dawson*

○ **Collected Works: 15 Years of Stony Plain Music** / 1991 / Stony Plain 1166
A two-CD collection of Canada's Stony Plain artists; 2 1/2 hours, 45 artists, and 46 tunes. CD 1 features blues, Cajun, and a touch of folk with Zachary Richard, John Hammond, Robert Gray,

---

The Fast Folk Musical Magazine

At the beginning of the 80s, it would have been easy to suppose that the spark that had ignited the folk boom of the 60s was long since extinguished. The artists who abetted and benefited from that boom had gone in various directions, most of them dropped from record labels by the mid 70s, and only such minor commercial entities as the Roches and Steve Forbert had made any noise at all while using New York's Greenwich Village as a base in the late 70s. But, in fact, a whole new generation of performers was coming up, and if the record labels were going to ignore them, they were nevertheless determined to support their own community and foster songwriting themselves. Performers such as Jack Hardy, David Massengill, and Rod MacDonald set up the Songwriters' Exchange so writers would have a forum where their work could be heard by their peers. This resulted in an album released in 1980 on Stash Records. In 1981, the group formed a cooperative, which took over the booking of SpeakEasy, a Village club. And in February 1982, the cooperative launched The CooP, a combination magazine and record album featuring the work of new songwriters. A decade later, The CooP, now renamed The Fast Folk Musical Magazine, was a nonprofit corporation that had published over 70 issues and served as the springboard for such nationally recognized performers as Suzanne Vega and Tracy Chapman. The selected albums listed in this section may or may not be in print at the present time. To order any of them, write to The Fast Folk Musical Magazine, Inc., P.O. Box 938, Village Station, New York, NY 10014.

– William Ruhlmann

Aaron Neville, Jo-El Sonnier, Walter Shakey Horton, and others. CD 2 is country, folk, bluegrass, Irish, rock, and singer-songwriters with Alison Krauss, Guy Clark, Doc Watson, Ricky Skaggs, John Prine, Bonnie Raitt, Steve Goodman, Ian Tyson, Roy Rogers, Jonathan Richman, Spirit of the West, the Tom Russell Band, and others. You do not often find collections so full of talent as this. Buy it! You'll find music you never even knew existed. — *Chip Renner*

○ **Coop—April 1982** / Apr. 1982 / Coop 103
Highlights of this issue include "Small Town on the River," by Bill Morrissey, who later recorded four albums on Rounder Records; "I'm Talking to You," by Shawn Colvin, later a Grammy-winning folk artist on Columbia Records; and perhaps the most impressive song of the new folk movement of the time, David Massengill's epic "The Great American Dream." — *William Ruhlmann*

○ **Coop—February 1982** / Feb. 1982 / Coop 101
The CooP's debut issue combined the work of established folk figures such as Ed McCurdy and Dave Van Ronk (who contributed the hilarious "Jersey State Stomp") with up-and-coming performers like folk-blues guitarist Frank Christian, Ilene Weiss, David Massengill (whose "Fairfax County" turned up on a Roches album later in the year), and Suzanne Vega (whose "Cracking" would be recorded three years later for her debut album). — *William Ruhlmann*

○ **Coop—February 1983 ...** / Feb. 1983 / Coop 201
The CooP—February 1983, 1st Anniversary! Standouts here are Tom Paxton performing his Nancy Reagan parody, "Little Bitty Gun," Suzanne Vega's "The Queen and the Soldier," future editor and Shanachie recording artist Richard Meyer's "Jive Town," and then-editor Jack Hardy's Central American topical song "Porto Limon." — *William Ruhlmann*

○ **Coop—June 1982 ...** / Jun. 1982 / Coop 105
The CooP—June 1982, Traditional Music Revisited. Actually, humorous music revisited is more like it, what with the first ap-

pearance of future Philo recording artist Christine Lavin on her "Regretting What I Said . . . ," and David Massengill's "The Eunuch's Lament." Also included is Suzanne Vega's "Gypsy," later to appear on her second A&M album, five years hence. — *William Ruhlmann*

○ **Coop—June 1983: Love Songs** / Jun. 1983 / Coop 205
Suzanne Vega (who seems to have recorded much of her first two albums for *The CooP*) contributes "Some Journey," while Richard Meyer presents what will be the title track of his debut album, "Laughing/Scared." John Gorka, who now records for Windham Hill, makes his first appearance with "Downtown Tonight." — *William Ruhlmann*

○ **Coop—May 1982 ...** / May 1982 / Coop 104
The CooP—May 1982, The Political Song Revisited. A thematic album featuring Matt Jones's version of *CooP* editor Jack Hardy's Civil War story, "Incident at Ebenezer Creek," Sherwood Ross's humorous "I Sliced Pastrami for the CIA and Found God," and a duet between Steve Forbert and Jack Hardy on Woody Guthrie's "This Land Is Your Land." — *William Ruhlmann*

○ **Coop—May 1983: The Political Songs** / May 1983 / Coop 204
Appropriately, this album contains a contribution from *Broadside* magazine founder Sis Cunningham, and the other highlights include Michael Jerling's Vietnam vets song "Long Black Wall" and Fred Small's "Everything Possible." — *William Ruhlmann*

○ **Coop—September 1982** / Sep. 1982 / Coop 108
An especially strong collection recorded live at SpeakEasy and including Suzanne Vega's "Knight Moves," Rod MacDonald's "Sailor's Prayer," George Gerdes's "The Policeman Is My Friend," and Jack Hardy's "The Children." — *William Ruhlmann*

○ **Cornelia Street—Songwriter's Exchange** / 1980 / Stash
Rereleased in 1991 with additional tracks on CD. From the late '70s on, there was a weekly meeting of the many contemporary Greenwich Village songwriters. This compilation album spotlights some of the fine work from that time. A precursor to *The Fast Folk Musical Magazine.* — *Richard Meyer*

○ **Cowboy Songs from Folkways** / Smithsonian/Folkways 40043
Richly varied set, from Leadbelly to Woody Guthrie, drawn from the vast Folkways archives and dating from the early '40s to the '60s. Excellent annotations. — *Charles S. Wolfe*

○ **Don't Mourn—Organize!** / 1990 / Smithsonian/Folkways 40026
A compilation of songs by and about labor songwriter Joe Hill (turn-of-the-century labor organizer). — *Richard Meyer*

○ **Fast Folk Magazine, Vol. 1 #1** / 1984 / Fast Folk 101
This first issue of the renamed record/magazine features Eric Andersen's "The Girls of Denmark," Suzanne Vega's future Top Ten hit "Tom's Diner," John Gorka's "I Saw a Stranger with Your Hair," and Christine Lavin's "Don't Ever Call Your Sweetheart by His Name." — *William Ruhlmann*

○ **Fast Folk Magazine, Vol. 1 #2** / 1984 / Fast Folk 102
Pete Seeger turns up on this edition, as do such other folk veterans as Oscar Brand, Sammy Walker, and Jim Glover (of Jim and Jean). Among the new generation, Shawn Colvin contributes "I Don't Know Why," and Rod MacDonald sings the anthemlike "Every Living Thing." — *William Ruhlmann*

○ **Fast Folk Magazine, Vol. 1 #4** / 1984 / Fast Folk 104
Subtitled *Live at the Bottom Line.* On January 28, 1984, The Fast Folk cooperative staged the first of what would be an annual concert series presenting the best of the songs that had appeared so far on the records. The result is an essential greatest-hits album that makes the case for a folk-music renaissance in the early '80s. — *William Ruhlmann*

○ **Fast Folk Magazine, Vol. 1 #6** / 1984 / Fast Folk 106
Subtitled *The Blues.* "Traditional" is the author of the majority of these folk-blues cuts, which are performed by the likes of John Hammond, Dave Van Ronk, and some less illustrious but equally talented musicians. — *William Ruhlmann*

○ **Fast Folk Magazine, Vol. 1 #8** / 1984 / Fast Folk 108
Subtitled *Women in Song.* This exceptional album leads off with Nanci Griffith and also includes Shawn Colvin and Christine Lavin. Among the less well known names, the duo Palmer and Bragg turn in the impressive "Bayonne" and Megan McDonough contributes "A Lesson in Every Good-Bye." — *William Ruhlmann*

○ **Fast Folk Magazine, Vol. 2 #10** / 1985 / Fast Folk 210

Tom Paxton returns in this album, along with a large number of folksingers who have gone on to greater recognition, among them Pierce Pettis, David Mallett, Greg Brown, Bob Franke, Schooner Fare, and Cliff Eberhardt. All of them recorded at SpeakEasy. — *William Ruhlmann*

○ **Fast Folk Magazine, Vol. 2 #8** / 1985 / Fast Folk 208
A new batch of singer-songwriters gets their first exposure in this release, among them Lyle Lovett, Buddy Mondlock, and Cindy Lee Berryhill. — *William Ruhlmann*

Fast Folk Magazine—Songs of Tradition / 1986 / Fast Folk
This compilation is an exceptional collection of contemporary singer-songwriters who know all the traditional rules enough to enhance or break them. Josh Joffen's "Pontchartrain"-inspired "Girl from the Great Divide" is a riveting revision; Paul Kaplan's "Johnny of Hazelgreen" is lilting and delicate; Nikki Matheson turns in a haunting "Star of the County Down." One side of this album is in English; the other ranges from Italian to Yiddish. The garage-band version of "500 Miles" is a classic. — *Richard Meyer*

○ **Fast Folk Magazine, Vol. 3 #10** / 1986 / Fast Folk 310
Richie Havens is here in this release, as is Michelle Shocked (that's right, another debut). Buddy Mondlock and Fred Small return, too. — *William Ruhlmann*

○ **Fast Folk Magazine, Vol. 3 #3** / 1986 / Fast Folk 303
Lyle Lovett, Aztec Two Step, Steve Gillette, and Tom Russell are the stars of this issue, but also note Tom Intondi's stirring "Straight from the Heart" and the Folkano version of Pierce Pettis's "Moments." — *William Ruhlmann*

○ **Fast Folk Magazine, Vol. 3 #4** / 1986 / Fast Folk 304
Subtitled *Boston One.* This issue is notable for the first recorded appearance anywhere of Tracy Chapman (singing "For My Lover"), but also as a representative sampling of Boston folk music, much of it on a par with the New York scene *Fast Folk* usually chronicles. — *William Ruhlmann*

○ **Fast Folk Magazine, Vol. 3 #6/7** / 1986 / Fast Folk 7
Subtitled *Live at the Bottom Line.* Double-pocket souvenir of the third annual Fast Folk Revue show, recorded May 10, 1986, it is once again a best-of, containing the most impressive songs from *Fast Folk* over the previous year, highlights including the heartbreaking Irish emigration ballad "Kilkelly" and the sidesplitting "Railroad Bill," written and sung by Andy Breckman, whose day job is head writer for "Late Night with David Letterman." — *William Ruhlmann*

○ **Fast Folk Magazine, Vol. 4 #5/6** / 1988 / Fast Folk 6
Subtitled *The 6th Anniversary Issue.* Nicknamed "the flag album" for its cover, this double album features such *Fast Folk* regulars as David Massengill, Jack Hardy, Rod MacDonald, and Richard Meyer, plus old friends like Dave Van Ronk and Eric Andersen, new stars like Christine Lavin and Michelle Shocked, and guest Suzanne Vega, whose "The Marching Dream" is unavailable elsewhere. — *William Ruhlmann*

○ **Fast Folk Magazine, Vol. 4 #9** / 1989 / Fast Folk 409
Subtitled *Los Angeles. Fast Folk* goes bicoastal for an album featuring Peter Case, Victoria Williams, and Milo Binder. — *William Ruhlmann*

Flatpicking Guitar Festival / 1989 / Shanachie 98003
A very clean, traditional flatpicking album featuring David Bromberg, Richard Lieberson, Dick Fegy, Tom Gilfellon, and others. — *Chip Renner*

○ **Folk Classics** / 1989 / CBS 45026
Though one thinks of Elektra and Vanguard as the main record labels of the folk revival, the giant Columbia Records also made some inroads into the field, signing up not only Bob Dylan but also a wide range of folkies, from Pete Seeger to the New Christy Minstrels. This 15-track compilation delves deeper into the Columbia vault for tracks by Leadbelly and Burl Ives, but its focus is on '60s performers—the Brothers Four, Carolyn Hester, Malvina Reynolds. Many of them, like Dylan, are John Hammond signings. The focus of the album is scattered, but the selection is excellent, and Columbia was long overdue to examine its folk archives. — *William Ruhlmann*

Folk Masters / 1993 / Smithsonian/Folkways 40047
This 22-cut sampler culled from the Folk Masters radio show series reflects the openness that enhances the program; bluegrass, klezmer, classic gospel, Western swing, mountain music, blues, Cajun, and traditional jazz each are represented, as well as in-

ternational styles and conjunto. It is a quick musical education and one that should forever shatter stereotyped notions about what does and does not constitute folk music. —*Ron Wynn*

○ **Freedom Is A Constant Struggle: Songs Of The Mississippi Civil Rights Movement** / Folk Era
Developed by the Washington, DC-based Cultural Center for Social Change, this collection single-mindedly presents the music of that special historical summer. Artists who have contributed include Bob Dylan; Judy Collins; Peter, Paul & Mary; Odetta; Tom Paxton; the SNCC Freedom Singers; Sweet Honey in the Rock; Phil Ochs; and many others. The 40 songs on this two-CD set cover 2-1/2 hours, The Toledo Blade said, "Playing these two discs of 40 songs over 2-1/2 hours is like curling up with a good history book." Most songs are period recordings, some are freshly recorded for this collection, and a couple have never before been recorded. —*Allan Shaw*

○ **Fresh Oldtime String Band Music** / Rounder 0262
A Mike Seeger-compiled anthology of contemporary groups playing with the hillbilly string-band tradition. —*Mark A. Humphrey*

○ **From the New World ...** / Strange Things 5004
From the New World—Folk Rock of the 1960s is a compilation of obscure-but-cool '60s folk-rock bands. —*Richard Meyer*

Great Hudson River Revival, Vol. 1 / Flying Fish 214
This live album from 1979 contains music by Taj Mahal, John Hartford, Bernice Reagon, Pete Singer, and others and was recorded at Croton Point Park. —*AMG*

☆ **Greatest Folksingers of the '60s** / 1972 / Vanguard 17-18
Not only was Maynard Solomon's Vanguard Records one of the major folk labels of the '60s (having the prescience to pick up Joan Baez early on, and then recording the cream of the singer-songwriters thereafter), but it also had the rights to record and release material from the Newport Folk Festival, giving it access to several artists who were not signed to the label. As a result, this double-packet compilation features songs by nearly every major folk figure of the decade, from the Weavers to JosA Feliciano, with Vanguard artists such as Buffy Sainte-Marie, Eric Andersen, and Odetta sharing space with Elektra's Phil Ochs and Judy Collins and Columbia's Bob Dylan. Listen to this one record and you'll know what the '60s folk revival sounded like. —*William Ruhlmann*

○ **Greatest Songs of Woody Guthrie** / 1972 / Vanguard 35-36
This 23-track, 70-minute disc, assembled from recordings dating from the '50s and the '60s, is by now a historical document tracing the kinds of interpretations offered by the first generation of folksingers to be influenced by Guthrie, some of whom were his contemporaries. For the most part, the singers, who include the Weavers, Odetta, Ramblin' Jack Elliot, Cisco Huston, and Joan Baez, offer covers of Guthrie favorites that are sweeter and more conventional than the originals. Thankfully, they are interspersed with a handful of tunes featuring Guthrie himself. —*William Ruhlmann*

○ **Greenwich Village Folk Festival** / 1991 / Gadfly
Both the up-and-coming and the well-established perform on this CD. Five Chinese Brothers do a nice version of "My Dad's Face." Cliff Eberhardt's "When the Circus Comes to Town" is great. Tom Paxton, Jack Hardy, Guy Davis, Ilene Weiss, Dave Van Ronk, Frank Christian, Andy Breckman, Mark Johnson, and Erik Frandsen also are on this. A good collection. —*Chip Renner*

○ **Hard Cash** / 1990 / Green Linnet 3049
A talent-packed album featuring Richard Thompson, Clive Gregson and Christine Collister, Martin Carthy, June Tabor, and others. The album was for a BBC series on the theme of exploited workers. —*Chip Renner*

○ **Have Moicy!** / 1976 / Rounder 3010
The various members of the Holy Modal Rounders are a sneaky bunch of folks with a tendency to turn up on record in a variety of guises, which is only a partial explanation of why, with three artists credited on the cover, this album is really the brainchild of one who is unmentioned: Rounder cofounder Peter Stampfel. And as with his other manifestations (see the Holy Modal Rounders, Stampfel & Weber, and Peter Stampfel & the Bottle Caps), this is a collection of folk, blues, country, and rock novelties, some of which are ridiculously funny. A Rounder by any other name is still a hoot. —*William Ruhlmann*

○ **Jupiter Book of Ballads** / Smithsonian/Folkways 9890

Includes tracks from Isla Cameron, Jill Balcon, Pauline Letts, John Laurie, and others. —*Richard Meyer*

Kerrville Festival 1972-1976 / Adelphi
Kerrville Festival 1972-1976 (Texas Folk & Outlaw Music) is a first-class sampling of Kerrville, featuring Guy Clark, Willie Nelson, Jerry Jeff Walker, Townes Van Zandt, Steve Fromholz, and others. Two-record set. —*Chip Renner*

○ **Legacy: A Collection of New Folk Music** / 1989 / Windham Hill 1086
Legacy— A Collection of New Folk Music. Although only a few of them managed to break through to national attention, a generation of important folk talents appeared during the '80s, playing clubs and festivals and recording for *The Fast Folk Musical Magazine* and self-financed records sold at gigs. In 1989, Windham Hill noticed and copied the *Fast Folk* formula, presenting some of the best—David Massengill, Cliff Eberhardt, Bill Morrissey, John Gorka, and others—on this 15-track disc and even signing a few of them to contracts. The result is a stunning showcase of talent that will shock anyone who thinks good folk music disappeared around 1970. —*William Ruhlmann*

○ **On a Winter's Night** / North Star 28
Christine Lavin's compilation album, with each guest artist performing a song dealing with the theme "on a winter's night." Featuring David Wilcox, Cheryl Wheeler, Rod MacDonald, Ferron, Electric Bonsai Band, Anne Hills, Sally Fingerett, and many others. A good collection, worth looking into. —*Chip Renner*

○ **Out of the Darkness: ...** / Kaleidoscope 4001
Out of the Darkness: Songs for Survival. A fine collection of songs written and sung in the cause of peace and environmental sanity. Featuring Kate Wolf, Pete Seeger, Holly Near, Don Lange, Chris Williamson, Jesse Colin Young, Charlie King, Dick Gaughan, and Sweet Honey in the Rock. —*Chip Renner*

Resume Speed ... / 1990 / End Construction
Brian Doser, Jim Infantino, John Svetkey, and Ellis Paul perform together and with other musicians on *Resume Speed— A New Artist Compilation*, this fine CD of Boston-based acoustic singer-songwriters. This is a good look at Boston's folk-acoustic scene. —*Chip Renner*

Songs of the Civil War / New World 202
Released around the time of the PBS series on the civil war, this collection offers tunes of that period performed by Kate & Anna McGarrigle, Kathy Mattea, Richie Havens, Waylon Jennings, and Sweet Honey in the Rock. It's a celebratory but wistful-sounding collection. —*Richard Meyer*

○ **Threadgills Super Session** / 1991 / Buddy
Every Wednesday they get together and put out some of the best music in Austin. This cassette features Jimmie Dale Gilmore, Sarah Elizabeth Campbell, Champ Hood, Butch Hancock, Christine Albert, Marvin Denton, and the Threadgill Troubadors. A good selection for the Austin diehard. —*Chip Renner*

○ **Tribute to Woody Guthrie: Highlights from Concerts** / 1972 / Warner Brothers 26036
Woody Guthrie died on October 3, 1967. Tribute concerts to him were organized at Carnegie Hall in New York in January 1968 and at the Hollywood Bowl in Los Angeles in September 1970. This double-record set presents highlights from both shows and is notable for a rare Bob Dylan performance and a collection of Guthrie songs sung by others of his children (literally and figuratively): Arlo Guthrie, Judy Collins, Odetta, Richie Havens, Tom Paxton, Pete Seeger, and more. —*William Ruhlmann*

★ **Troubadours of the Folk Era, Vol. 2** / Apr. 21, 1992 / Rhino 70263
Here are some of the performers and their signature songs on which the '60s folk revival was based. Pete Seeger's rendition of "Turn,Turn,Turn" and Tim Hardin's "Reason to Believe" remind the listener that contemporary performances have a vital history. —*Richard Meyer*

★ **Troubadours of the Folk Era, Vol. 3** / Apr. 21, 1992 / Rhino 70264
These group performances represent some of the more commercial releases of the folk revival. Beginning with Leadbelly's "Goodnight Irene" performed by The Weavers and the hit "Tom Dooley" by the Kingston Trio and continuing through to recordings by Jim Kweskin's Jug Band, this collection demonstrates how "authentic" and "traditional" folk songs were sanitized and popu-

larized for mass consumption. It's an interesting reminder of how essentially neutral material can take on political weight due to the actions of the performers themselves, as in the case of the Weavers. —*Richard Meyer*

Vancouver Folk Music Festival ... / 1980 /
Vancouver Folk Musical Festival—July 1980. A real nice collection—Ferron's "Ain't Life a Brook" is good. Jim Post does a Bob Dylan soundalike ("Brain Damage"). Features Berline, Crary and Hicks, Leon Rosselson, Holly Near, the Tannahill Weavers, and Bryan Bowers. Good sound. —*Chip Renner*

○ **Victory Music: ...** / 1989 / Victory Music 504
Victory Music: 20th Anniversary Year. This is a wide-open CD featuring 21 cuts by Northwest musicians. The music ranges from singer-songwriter ballads to traditional instrumentals, blues, and back again. A strong and diverse CD done up the typical classy Victory Music way. —*Chip Renner*

Victory Sings at Sea / 1989 / Victory Music 503

This album ranges from traditional working chanties to contemporary ballads. The tight harmonies intermesh with the simple acoustic accompaniment. This collection of 19 songs is a great value. —*Chip Renner*

○ **Woody Guthrie/Leadbelly ...** / Smithsonian/Folkways 40001

Woody Guthrie/Leadbelly—Folkways Original Vision. This collection of recordings made between 1940 and 1947 was assembled as a complement to the album *A Tribute to Guthrie and Leadbelly: A Vision Shared* (Columbia OC 44034), on which various country, folk, and rock stars covered the Guthrie and Leadbelly songs. The result is an excellent sampler, made all the more potent when heard in contrast with the Columbia album. —*William Ruhlmann*

COUNTRY

Country music is facts-of-life music. It's the music of experience. More so than with other music genres (with the possible exception of the blues), country music echoes and reflects the heights and depths of the collective lives of its audience, who up into the 70s were predominantly working class, White, and rural. Willie Nelson, Waylon Jennings, Dolly Parton, Kenny Rogers, Roy Clark, and other superstars in the 70s brought country music to a new and huge audience – the middle class, the educated, and the urban listeners – in the process forever changing the direction of the music. Yet this was only another step in what has been a continuous evolution in country music. In this American music form, the older styles are revered and retained rather than discarded, so that they remain dear to their listeners, while at the same time contemporary country heads off into new territory, thus attracting a new group of listeners. It's always been this way, since the day country music went commercial with its first record in the mid 20s. Though to a degree change-resistant because of its adherence to tradition, country in fact changes as the lives of its listeners change. And this is the common bond of all these styles from the 20s to the present: it's all facts-of-life music, from the hillbilly string-bands of the 20s through the cowboys and honky-tonkers and outlaws and even the creamy country-pop sounds up to Randy Travis, Dolly Parton, the Judds, and Ricky Skaggs. Country music's singers and musicians perform music they have lived. And now, because country music has become a major force in the record industry – in fact, *the* major force, with Garth Brooks and number of records sold – it has been given the respect and attention long lavished upon jazz, blues, and rock.

When the lines of distinction between country and other genres of music begin to blur, traditional country reasserts itself, thus preventing the country sound from evolving to the point of equivalence with pop. Judge George Hay, founder of the Grand Ole Opry, said it best in the mid 20s when he admonished performers with "Keep it close to the ground, boys," if they strayed from the country style that prevailed at the time. The essence of country music has remained pretty much intact ever since. Its repertory derives from folk, minstrel, medicine show, vaudeville, and gospel music. Country's subject matter falls into some general categories: home and family, working-man blues, death and sorrow, cheatin', good love gone bad, prison, trains and trucks and travelling, disasters, booze and sorrow-drowning, and gospel songs (which can uplift with promised redemption or depress with likely damnation). Sobering material, but true-to-life: to paraphrase Hank Williams, none of us will ever get out of this world alive. And enough country music tells us of the good love and fun possible on this earth before we pass over to Canaan's land, that we keep on the sunny side of life, at least occasionally.

Kris Kristofferson says that if a song sounds country, it is. Add to this a few generalizations about instrumentation (fiddle, banjo, dobro, steel guitar, guitar, harmonica, mandolin), about vocals (pure, often stark and rough-edged, highly emotional), and about country performers (revered by and loving of their fans), and we probably know enough to stop reading and start listening to the music.

– David Vinopal

Roy Acuff (Roy Claxton Acuff)

b. Sep. 15, 1903, Maynardsville, TN, d. Nov. 23, 1992
Vocals, violin, harmonica / Traditional country
Known as the "King of Country Music," Acuff embodied the style's bedrock values from the moment he stepped onto the Grand Ole Opry stage in 1938 until his death in November 1992. He was the Opry's first national star, and for more than 50 years, he served as the radio show's best-known performer and its stylistic patriarch, advising everyone who crossed its boards to keep the music simple, honest and country. He took up the fiddle while recovering from a bad case of sunstroke and, prior to joining the Opry, worked as a traveling medicine show entertainer, which taught him "to sing real loud," he said. His first recorded song, "The Great Speckled Bird," remained a favorite throughout his career, as did such classics as "The Wabash Cannonball," "Fireball Mail" and "Wreck on the Highway." He sang in an arch, emotional, mournful voice that influenced Hank Williams, George Jones, Porter Wagoner and many others. In 1992, he became the first living performer to be elected to the Country Music Hall of Fame in 1992. His repertoire remained essentially the same over the years, and for such a crucial country figurehead, few of his albums remain in print. —*Michael McCall*

○ Fly Birdie Fly '39-41 / 1939 / Rounder 24
Recorded in 1939-1941, as he was flying high as a new star of the Opry. Not his best-known songs, but these blues and gospel songs

are rowdier than his reputation and as good as his classics. —*Michael McCall*

Songs of the Smokey Mountains / 1954 / Longhorn 3038
A nice assortment of Acuff hits, including "The Great Speckled Bird," "Wabash Cannonball," "Wreck on the Highway," and "Precious Jewel." —*Barry Lee Pearson*

The Best of Roy Acuff / 1970 / Curb 77454
Selections taken from his 1960s work for Hickory Records. Not as important as his earlier work, but powerful nonetheless. The instrumentation is slicker; the voice remains as chilling as ever. —*Michael McCall*

☆ **Columbia Historic Edition** / 1985 / CBS 39998
Includes many of his early landmark recordings, including his first recording of "Wabash Cannonball," on which he blows the train whistle and bows the fiddle though the vocals are by band member Dynamite Hatcher. Other songs do feature a few of Acuff's earliest singing. Good representation of his initial string band sound. —*Michael McCall*

☆ **Steamboat Whistle Blues** / 1985 / Rounder 23
Fine early (1936-1939) Roy Acuff band versions of blues, pop, and old-time country. —*Barry Lee Pearson*

★ **The Essential** / 1992 / CBS 48956
Acuff recorded for Columbia when he was the undisputed "King of Country Music," so these 40s gems are the ones to hear for a

taste of what so inspired the young Hank Williams and George Jones. —*Mark A. Humphrey*

Alabama

Group / Country-rock
In 1989 this foursome, with 21 straight Number 1 singles and nearly 80 major awards, received the Artist of the Decade Award from the Academy of Country Music. As you might guess, this is the most popular country group in record history, in terms of the number of records sold. Originally called Wildcountry, their country-pop material and delivery are showcased in two of their best-known hits, "My Home's in Alabama" and "Mountain Music." — *David Vinopal*

○ **My Home's in Alabama** / 1980 / RCA 6912
The album that started it all for Alabama. Their Southern rock influences are obvious but encased in a country context. The title track's sentiment is overwhelming, whether you're from Alabama or Iowa. —*Tom Roland*

○ **Feels So Right** / 1981 / RCA 3930
On their second album, Alabama is apparently more comfortable with the studio. The harmonies are tighter than in the debut, but the material selection—heavy on uptempo tunes—shows that the club mentality developed at the Bowery is still very much intact. Three hits are included, the title track, "Love in the First Degree," and "Old Flame," but nearly all the extra cuts are strong as well. —*Tom Roland*

○ **Mountain Music** / 1982 / RCA 4229
Their best effort. The group hadn't quite fallen into any formulas, and as a result, they cover the stylistic gamut pretty well. The title track practically defined what country groups have strived to accomplish, and the group slides easily from sentiment, to social relevance, to out-and-out partying. —*Tom Roland*

★ **Greatest Hits** / 1986 / RCA 7170
A batch of the hits that made them the most successful country act of the 1980s. More than the best available sampler of their much-imitated group sound, it also reflects state-of-the-art Nashville Sound the moment before Randy Travis hit. —*Dan Cooper*

Southern Star / 1989 / RCA 8587
After eight very successful years with record producer Harold Shedd, Alabama wisely opted for change. Half of this album is recorded with Josh Leo and Larry Lee, the other half with Barry Beckett, and the guys from Fort Payne attack the project with a little more energy than in some of their prior efforts. Get it on CD—three of the four "bonus" tracks are substantial. —*Tom Roland*

○ **Greatest Hits, Vol. 2** / 1991 / RCA 61040
Companion piece to the above with more emphasis on ballad material. —*Cub Koda*

American Pride / 1992 / RCA 66044
So much happened between Alabama's arrival on the scene and the country boom of the early 90s that by the time the band released *American Pride*, they were among the genre's aging veterans. As such, it was a little late to expect big surprises. So everything that Alabama's known for is here: full-group harmonies, small-town Southern virtues and common-sense patriotism. The group turned "I'm in a Hurry (And Don't Know Why)" into a big hit, but it's no surprise the best songs are about folks who settled in for the long haul, happily married parents ("Between the Two of Them"), and Richard Petty ("Richard Petty's Fans"). —*Brian Mansfield*

Cheap Seats / 1993 / RCA 66296
A charming video helped sell the way-cute title track, which offers another context for Alabama's downhome brand of nostalgia. Not to be overlooked, however, is "A Better Word for Love," a quiet, morning love song cowritten by Gary Nicholson and former NRBQ guitarist Al Anderson. —*Dan Cooper*

Deborah Allen

b. Sep. 30, 1953, Memphis, TN
Allen scored her first hits in morbid, beyond-the-grave duets with Jim Reeves, then drastically improved from there. A successful songwriter and adventurous singer, her best work blends the punched-up swamp blues of her native Memphis with aggressive country-pop. Allen scored a couple of hits in the mid-80s, but her

progressive edge led to a failed rock venture that included assistance from Prince. She came back to country with a sassy vengeance in 1993. —*Michael McCall*

● **Delta Dreamland** / 1993 / Warner Brothers 24485
Allen comes roaring back with another Van Hoy collaboration, this one produced before signing a record contract. Bluesy, sexy and intimately powerful, it rocks stronger than anything she previously offered. —*Michael McCall*

○ **All That I Am** / 1994 / Giant
Allen pushes her steamy sensuality even more to the forefront here in another strong collection. —*Michael McCall*

○ **Cheat the Night** / RCA 8514
An EP featuring her two best-known hits of the 1980s, "Baby I Lied" and "I've Been Wrong Before." Sweeter and softer-edged than her 's90s work. —*Michael McCall*

Let Me Be the First / RCA 5318
Working again with husband/producer/co-writer Rafe Van Hoy, Allen attempts an artful, electronic style of country-pop that proved too progressive for the country mainstream. —*Michael McCall*

Bill Anderson (Whispering Bill)

b. Nov. 1, 1937, Columbia, SC
Vocals / Traditional country
The nickname "Whisperin' Bill" originated from Anderson's quiet vocal delivery and his numerous recitation songs, delivered in a low-key, hushed voice. Anderson came to fame when his self-penned "City Lights" was turned into a hit by Ray Price in 1958. In the '60s he wrote and recorded numerous hits, including "Mama Sang a Song" (a narration), "Still" (his signature tune), and "I Get the Fever." In the '60s he had his own syndicated TV show and remains an Opry regular. —*David Vinopal*

● **Greatest Hits** / 1971 / MCA 013
Budget CD package of the absolute essential best, including the classic "Still." —*Cub Koda*

The Best of Bill Anderson / Curb 77436
This album includes the hit "Deck of Cards." —*AMG*

John Anderson

b. Dec. 12, 1955, Apopka, FL
Vocals, guitar / Country, big band
Growing up in Apopka, FL, John Anderson was enamored with the Beatles and the Rolling Stones, like most of his peers. But when he heard a Merle Haggard album at age 15, Anderson found his true calling. He headed for Nashville, where he showed up unannounced on his sister's doorstep. He took low-paying club jobs in Music City's Printer's Alley for experience, and worked a variety of places for money in the early '70s. In one of those jobs, he actually helped do roofing on the Grand Ole Opry House, before its opening in 1974. Signed to Warner Brothers in the late '70s, Anderson's first album hit the streets in 1980, bringing with it critical acclaim for his attention to the country tradition. Adding a vocal strain to the phrasing he picked up from Haggard and Lefty Frizzell, Anderson captured the Country Music Association's Horizon award for 1983, given to an artist who makes the most career progress. "Swingin'," which at 1.3 million in sales is the best-selling single in Warner history, also reeled in the CMA's Single of the Year trophy. Unfortunately, Anderson fell out of favor with country radio within two years and future albums failed to capitalize on his earlier momentum. With the help of producer James Stroud, Anderson's career was revitalized in 1992 with his first BNA Records release, *Seminole Wind*, and the single "Straight Tequila Night." —*Tom Roland*

John Anderson 2 / 1981 / Warner Brothers
His second album, this traditionally-minded package contrasted with the bulk of the material released in the same *Urban Cowboy*-influenced time period. His cover of Lefty Frizzell's "I Love You a Thousand Ways" shows his roots nicely, and "I'm Just an Old Chunk of Coal (But I'm Gonna Be a Diamond Someday)" is simply classic. —*Tom Roland*

Wild & Blue / 1982 / Warner Brothers 23721
The occasional use of strings in this album was probably masterminded by former Don Law protege Frank Jones, who coproduced it. Twin fiddles and steel guitar dominate, though, especially in a re-make of Ferlin Husky's "The Waltz You Saved for

Music Map **Country & Western Music**

Sources of Country Music
Minstrel, Folk, Vaudeville, Gospel – all 19th century and earlier

1920s
Hillbilly/String Band Music
Gid Tanner and the Skillet Lickers

1922:
First Country Music Recording
Fiddlin' John Carson ("The Little Old Log Cabin in the Lane")

1924:
Country's First Million-Seller
Vernon Dalhart – ("The Wreck of the Old '97")

1927
RCA-Victor scout discovers country's first superstars
Jimmie Rodgers (Blue Yodels)
Carter Family ("Wildwood Flowers," "Wabash Cannonball")
Uncle Dave Macon (The Grand Ole Opry's first star)

1950s
Nashville Country Pop
Patsy Cline – Jim Reeves – Don Gibson

Honky-Tonkers
George Jones – Webb Pierce – Hank Thompson

Chet Atkins – Country's best-known guitarist

The Louvin Brothers
Charlie and Ira Louvin
influenced the Everly Brothers and Emmylou Harris

Eddy Arnold – Country's crooner ("Cattle Call")

Faron Young – The hillbilly heartthrob

Country Women
Kitty Wells – Country's first female superstar,
leads the way ("It Wasn't God Who Made Honky-Tonk Angels")

Hank Snow – The small Nova Scotian
with a huge voice ("I'm Moving On")

Bluegrass music's classical period
Bill Monroe and His Blue Grass Boys
Jim and Jesse McReynolds
Lester Flatt and Earl Scruggs
Reno and Smiley
The Osborne Brothers

1970s
Crossover Country
Charlie Rich ("The Most Beautiful Girl")
Anne Murray ("Snowbird")
Lynn Anderson ("Rose Garden")
John Denver – Dolly Parton – Barbara Mandrell
Crystal Gayle ("Don't It Make My Brown Eyes Blue")
Mac Davis ("Don't Get Hooked on Me")
Eddie Rabbit

The Outlaws
Waylon Jennings and Willie Nelson become superstars
individually and as a duet ("Luckenbach, Texas",
"Blue Eyes Crying in the Rain")

Hee Haw continues from the 60s,
Roy Clark and Buck Owens hosting

Country Rock
Charlie Daniels Band – Hank Williams Jr.

Traditional Bluegrass
urbanized and modernized into "newgrass."

Country Groups
Alabama – Statler Brothers (continue from the 60s)
Oak Ridge Boys – Gatlin Brothers

1930s
The singing cowboy rides into town
Gene Autry – Sons of the Pioneer
(including Roy Rogers) – Tex Ritter – Patsy Montana

Decade of the duets
Blue Sky boys (Bill and Emel Bolick)
Delmore Brothers (Country boogie and blues)
Lulu Belle and Scotty– McGee Brothers

String band sound is refined
transition between hillbilly and bluegrass
Bill Monroe first appears in Grand Ole Opry in 1939

Solo stars
Jimmie Davis ("You Are My Sunshine")
Roy Acuff and the Smoky Mountain Boys (1930s to present)

Western swing
Bob Wills and His Texas Playboys
Bill Boyd and the Cowboy Ramblers
Space Cooley (West Coast)

1940s
Honky-Tonk Heroes
Hank Williams – (Country's most influential performer)
Ernest Tubb and His Texas Troubadours
Ray Price – Floyd Tillman – Lefty Frizzell

Bluegrass music
Invented by Bill Monroe,
whose classic band in the mid 40s included
Lester Flatt and Earl Scruggs
Merle Travis – a great composer ("Sixteen Tons")
and guitarist who influenced Chet Atkins
Grandpa Jones – Country's enduring comic/musician

1960s
The Bakersfield Scene
Buck Owens ("Together Again," "Act Naturally")
and Merle Haggard ("Okie from Muskogee")
these two dominate the decade

The "Saga Song"
Johnny Horton ("The Battle of New Orleans")
and Jimmy Dean ("P. T. 109," "Big Bad John")

Roger Miller – country/pop genius ("King of the Road")

Johnny Cash – the "man in black,"
reaches superstardom through TV show

Tennessee Ernie Ford continues
as king of country gospel

Charley Pride – Country's Black superstar

Country/Pop Superstars
Kenny Rogers ("Lucille");
Roy Clark ("Yesterday, When I Was Young")
Glen Campbell ("By the Time I Get to Phoenix," "Wichita Lineman")

Tom T. Hall's "Harper Valley PTA" is a hit for Jeanne C. Riley

Country Women Come of Age
Loretta Lynn ("Coal Miner's Daughter");
Tammy Wynette ("D-I-V-O-R-C-E," "Stand By Your Man,"
a duet with husband George Jones)

1980s-early 1990s
Traditional Country rebounds
Randy Travis ("On the Other Hand"),
Ricky Skaggs ("Waitin' for the Sun to Shine"),
Emmylou Harris – George Straight – John Anderson
John Conlee – ("Busted") – Vince Gill

Reba McEntire wins awards by the six-pack

The Judds
Mother Naomi and daughter Wynonna – sell billions and billions

Progressive Country explores new lands
Dwight Yoakam – k.d. lang – Lyle Lovett – Carlene Carter
Pam Tillis – Rosanne Cash – Garth Brooks

Me," featuring Emmylou Harris. Includes "Swingin'" and a new version of Lefty Frizzell's "Long Black Veil"—the very last track recorded in the legendary Columbia Studio B. —*Tom Roland*

● **Greatest Hits** / 1984 / Warner Brothers 25169
Contains his biggest and best hit, "Swingin'." —*Dan Heilman*

○ **Greatest Hits, Vol. 2** / 1990 / Warner Brothers 26304
Anderson keeps up the momentum. —*Dan Heilman*

○ **Seminole Wind** / 1992 / BNA 61029
A solid comeback album that re-established Anderson as one of the most emotionally moving stylists of his generation. The title song features pointed social commentary about the ecological destruction of his native Florida. —*Michael McCall*

Solid Ground / Jun. 1993 / BNA 66232
Lighter in theme and impact than *Seminole Wind*, but a worthy and entertaining follow-up. —*Michael McCall*

Lynn Anderson (Lynn Rene Anderson)

b. Sep. 26, 1947, Grand Forks, ND
Vocals / Country-pop
This North Dakota native became a "Lawrence Welk Show" regular in 1967, but the best was yet to come. In 1971 her "Rose Garden" was a monster hit on both the pop and country charts and led to a Grammy. Other hits include "Top of the World" and "What a Man My Man Is." —*David Vinopal*

● **Greatest Hits** / 1972 / RCA 61237
Big pipes, big production, and big hits from the mid-to-late 60s. Includes "Rose Garden." —*Mark A. Humphrey*

Eddy Arnold (Tennessee Plowboy)

b. May 15, 1918, Madisonville, TN
Vocals, guitar / Traditional country
Once known as "the Tennessee Plowboy," this Hall of Famer moved from hillbilly to the middle of the road, where through his talented voice and easy stage presence he became a highly successful crossover star. His many hits include "Bouquet of Roses," "Anytime," "Cattle Call," "Make the World Go Away," "Tennessee Stud," and "That's What I Get for Loving You." Because of his continued popularity, Eddy Arnold has sold over 70 million records. He re-signed with RCA Records in 1990 after an extended absence from the label. —*David Vinopal*

○ **Anytime/Eddy Arnold and His Guitar** / 1952 / RCA 1224
The fine, early country material ("Bouquet of Roses," "Molly Darling") featuring Little Roy Wiggins on steel guitar. —*Richard Lieberson*

○ **Cattle Call/Thereby Hangs a Tale** / 1963 / Bear Family 15441
Two LPs reissued on one CD. —*AMG*

★ **The Best of Eddy Arnold** / 1966 / Curb 77416
His smooth, lushly produced crossover hits upset the traditional crowd, but they represent some of the most romantic country recordings of the era. Features "Make the World Go Away," "Anytime," "Bouquet of Roses," "The Last Word in Lonesome is Me," and a re-recording of his classic "Cattle Call." —*Michael McCall*

Hand-Holdin' Songs / 1990 / RCA 9963
Now in his seventies, Arnold's voice remains rich, his style reserved and low-key. —*Michael McCall*

You Don't Miss a Thing / 1991 / RCA 3020
This album includes such early country hits as "Can I Put You in a Love Song," "To Have and to Hold," "A Lady Like You," and others. —*AMG*

○ **Last of the Love Song Singers: Then & Now** / 1993 / RCA 66046
A schizophrenic two-part box pairing a superficial sampling of his classic hits with a separate collection of newly recorded love songs. He deserves a more complete retrospective. —*Michael McCall*

Charlene Arthur

Texan Charline Arthur was one of the very few women singers to deliver straightup honky-tonk—in attitude as well as sound—in the 1950s. No gingham dress and home-cooking image for Arthur, she was, as she once put it, "shakin' that thing on stage long before Elvis even thought about it." Though largely overlooked by the buying public, she claimed to have been a signifi-

cant influence on such better-known rowdy women as Wanda Jackson and Patsy Cline. —*Dan Cooper*

○ **Welcome to the Club** / Bear Family 15234
Unfortunately out-of-print, this excellent compilation is culled from Arthur's 1950s recordings for RCA. Hard country, with hints of proto-rockabilly. Included is the infamous "Kiss the Baby Goodnight," a song more unforgettable than listenable. —*Dan Cooper*

Asleep at the Wheel

Group / Western swing
Tall and bearded lead vocalist Ray Benson is the only original member of this group which has kept Western swing alive and popular since the 1970s, mixed with R&B, jazz, and hard country. The style works well, and produced a Grammy in 1978 for Count Basie's "One O'Clock Jump" and another in 1987 for "String of Pearls." "I See Miles and Miles of Texas" is their signature tune. —*David Vinopal*

Asleep at the Wheel / 1974 / MCA 31281
Benson this time was revealing a romantic baritone as well as his usual sublime swing. Guest appearances by Bonnie Raitt and Willie Nelson. —*Michael McCall*

Asleep at the Wheel / 1974 / Dot 39036
Texas guitarist and singer Ray Benson started this band in the early '70s as a "longhair" tribute to Bob Wills, and they've been swinging ever since. Their first Columbia album. —*Mark A. Humphrey*

10 / 1987 / Epic 40681
Bodacious Western swing on their 10th Columbia album. —*Mark A. Humphrey*

○ **Western Standard Time** / 1988 / Epic 44213
Nicely done Western standards. —*Mark A. Humphrey*

Keepin' Me up Nights / 1990 / Arista 8550
Still swinging in the 90s. —*Mark A. Humphrey*

● **Best of** / 1992 / CEMA 57000
Features "Route 66," "Bump Bounce Boogie," "Texas, Me & You" and others. —*AMG*

● **Live & Kickin'** / 1992 / Arista 18698
A best-of that features "Jambalaya," "Route 66," "House of Blue Lights" and more. —*AMG*

○ **Tribute to the Music of Bob Wills & The Texas Playboys** / Oct. 25, 1993 / Liberty 81470
Benson and the Wheel invite a bus full of guests to pay homage to the King of Western Swing, They do so with joyful, rollicking fun. Garth Brooks, Vince Gill, George Strait, Dolly Parton, Marty Stuart and Suzy Bogguss are among the artists enjoying themselves on this exemplary album. —*Michael McCall*

Chet Atkins (Chester Burton Atkins, Mr. Nashville)

b. Jun. 20, 1924, Luttrell, TN
Guitar, fiddle / Country, guitar-pop
"Mr. Nashville himself" is how Dale Evans referred to Chet Atkins at one of the awards shows in the late '60s. For two reasons the nickname is accurate: it pays great respect to the most famous and perhaps most influential guitar-picker the business has known; and it shows how much Atkins, among many others in the music business, changed the tastes in country music with the "Nashville sound.s" This middle-of-the-road style ruled from the mid '50s through the '60s and was what music writer Chet Flippo says would be called "Country Lite" if it were a beer. This much is sure: the "sound" proved commercial and drew to country music (or to country-pop) millions of listeners who otherwise would have stayed away.

There's no controversy about Atkins the guitar player. He transformed Travis-picking into a high art, playing hardcore country—and jazz and blues and classical and whatever genre you want—as it had never been played before. He has played with them all, from Mother Maybelle Carter's band in the late 40s to a recent album with Jerry Reed, and a "Who's Who" of country giants in between. Along the way, he garnered Instrumentalist of the Year Awards as often as he changed guitar strings. As vice-president of RCA Records, a position he held until 1979 when he got back to his real love—music—Atkins discovered or guided the careers of Hank Locklin, Jerry Reed, Jim Reeves, Don Gibson,

Waylon Jennings, Bobby Bare, the Everly Brothers, and scores of other stars.

The best thing to do with Mr. Chester Atkins is to listen to one of the more than 100 albums he's recorded over a long and artistically productive career. Everyone is bound to discover some bit of beauty among those 1000 or so tracks. He's one of the greatest ever to grace country music. —*David Vinopal*

Guitar for All Seasons / 1958 / Pair 1115
Good playing, but uneven material. —*Ron Wynn*

○ **Guitar Genius** / 1963 / Capitol 753
Features "Swanee River," "Hidden Charm," "Heartbreak Hotel," "It's Now or Never" and other hits. —*AMG*

The Best of Chet Atkins / 1963 / RCA 61091
This features "Main Street Breakdown," "Blue Ocean Echo," "Meet Mr. Callaghan" and others. —*AMG*

Reminiscing / 1964 / RCA 2952
Chet Atkins with Hank Snow. —*AMG*

☆ **Pickin' My Way** / 1970 / Mobile Fidelity 787
Superior sound. Two previous Atkins albums on CD. —*Ron Wynn*

○ **Stay Tuned** / 1985 / CBS 39591
This first-rate session teams Atkins with George Benson, Earl Klugh, Larry Carlton, and Mark Knopfler. —*Ron Wynn*

The Best of Chet Atkins & Friends / 1987 / RCA 61093
Atkins and his friends play "Avalon," "Twichy," "Terry on the Turnpike," "Sweet Georgia Brown" and other standards. —*AMG*

The Best of Chet Atkins & Friends, Vol. 2 / 1987 / RCA 61092
The second volume includes "Give the World a Smile," "Yakety Axe," "Alley Cat," "Que Sera, Sera" and others. —*AMG*

★ **C.G.P.** / 1988 / CBS 44323
Great picking and guitar technique. —*Ron Wynn*

○ **Sneakin' Around** / Oct. 1991 / CBS 47873
Contains such hits as "Major Attempts at a Minor Thing," "Summertime," "Gibson Girl" and others. —*AMG*

○ **Galloping Guitar** / 1993 / Bear Family 15714
A wonderful multi-disc boxed-set retrospective of Atkins' earliest recordings. Casual fans will be surprised to hear that Chet was originally marketed as a vocalist-guitarist, much the same as then-popular Merle Travis was on Capitol. His eventual move over to strict instrumentals doesn't come until the end of this assortment, with guest vocalists flitting in and out of the picture, but Atkins' guitar is solid throughout. —*Cub Koda*

Picks on the Hits / Pair 1255
Decent starter/introduction to the Atkins sound. —*Ron Wynn*

★ **Best Selections** / RCA 41053
A fine cross-section of the best work Atkins did on RCA; unfortunately, it is probably only available as a Japanese import. —*Ron Wynn*

Street Dreams / CBS 40256
Country/fusion/countrypolitan with Tom Scott and Nancy Mason. —*Ron Wynn*

Gene Autry (Orvin Gene Autry)

b. Sep. 29, 1907, Tioga, TX
Vocals, guitar / Cowboy
In 1934, Gene Autry rode into Hollywood and became the prototypical singing cowboy—a handsome, gun-toting yodeler who came to town and set things right as he defeated the black-clad forces of evil, treated his clever horse kindly, married the prettiest girl, and found time to sing about it all. A country that was little interested in singing hillbillies flocked to the theaters to see the guitar-strumming embodiment of truth, justice, and the American way (the *western* American way) prevail over the baddies in the black hats. This romantic and fanciful image of the Golden West did much to help Americans forget the Depression and look beyond that sunset. This national fascination with that-which-never-was dominated country music in the '40s and has reappeared, from Marty "El Paso" Robbins through Michael Martin Murphey and Riders in the Sky.

The cowboy song trail had been blazed before—by real or pretend cowboys such as Carl T. Sprague, Jules Verne Allen, Goebel Reeves, and even Jimmie Rodgers—but it was Gene Autry who brought about the "country-Western" term that for nearly 50 years has been commonly used (though inaccurately) to refer to

Beginnings: Hillbilly, Old-Time, and String-Band Music

If your experience of country music has consisted of playing the latest Garth Brooks or Barbara Mandrell CD, you'll be needing to set aside considerable time to listen to and appreciate the original country music – but it *will* be time well spent. Though this music from the 20s can be an acquired taste, depending on what you're accustomed to hearing, the enthusiasm, charm, and simplicity of the music and its performers will transport you back to a decade when country music was facts-of-life music, no more and no less. The band names give a fair taste of the early performers and of their zest for playing: Gid Tanner and the Skillet Lickers, Al Hopkins and the Hill Billies, the Aristocratic Pigs, the Possum Hunters, the Fruit Jar Drinkers (Uncle Dave Macon's band), the Gully Jumpers, and the Dixie Clodhoppers, all string bands that flourished in the late 20s. The fiddle was the dominant instrument in the beginning; Texan Eck Robertson, who cut six songs for Victor in 1922 (including the classic "Sally Gooden"), is credited with the first recording in country music. The standard repertoire ranged from drinkin'-and-cuttin'-up songs to minstrel/medicine-show standards to gospel and spiritual numbers – something for everyone.

But by no means were hillbilly bands the only show in town in the 20s, nor the fiddle the only instrument: old-time music featured guitars (including the Hawaiian slide guitar), banjos, mandolins, and harmonicas, which soon backed up singers as diverse as Buell Kazee and Bradley Kincaid (folksingers) on one hand and Vernon Dalhart (a reformed opera singer) on the other. It was Dalhart who had the first country hit – "The Prisoner's Song," a 1924 million-seller. In the late 50s and early 60s, hillbilly/ old-time/string-band music was rediscovered by the folkniks who, in listening to the New Lost City Ramblers, resurrected the popularity of country music's original genre.

– David Vinopal

country music in general. Hollywood studios discovered the goldmine in the sky, personifed by Ray Whitley, Eddie Dean, Jimmy Wakely, Rex Allen, Johnny Bond, Tex Ritter, and Roy Rogers, the latter being Autry's chief rival for the affection of every red-blooded American youth through the '40s.

Autry's bit-singing role in Ken Maynard's *In Old Santa Fe* led to the gun-and-guitar hero who lives on in country music, though ebbing and flowing with the times: the horse opera is out of style but the boots are in—yodeling is corny but sequined suits are hip (thanks perhaps to Porter Wagoner alone); six-shooters frighten too many people but not those cliched cowboy hats, appendages to Garth Brooks, George Strait, Clint Black, and many contemporaries who hope the "Look" will lead them to that perfect happiness with which each cowboy movie ended. The outlaw fad and *Urban Cowboy* fallout show that at least part of the country doesn't want to let go of what Gene Autry started. To sum up Autry's philosophy in one titled sentence, "After I get back in the saddle again, I'll be riding down the canyon to see that silver-haired daddy of mine who lives south of the border, near Mexicali Rose." America and Americana were never the same after Gene Autry. —*David Vinopal*

○ **Western Classics, Vol. 1** / 195z / CBS 9001
Standards and hits. —*AMG*

○ **Country Music Hall of Fame** / 1970 / Columbia 01035

Country's first hat act, the inspiration to a generation crooning, smooth and sincere, in the Roosevelt era. —*Mark A. Humphrey*

★ **The Essential Gene Autry** / Aug. 18, 1992 / CBS 48957
The best retrospective of Autry's recordings for Columbia, *The Essential Gene Autry* features eighteen songs recorded between 1933 and 1946, including his biggest hits. —*AMG*

○ **Columbia Historic Edition** / CBS 37465
Hollywood cowboy in full trot, circa 1940. —*Mark A. Humphrey*

Hoyt Axton

b. Mar. 25, 1938, Duncan, OK
Vocals, guitar / Country
Hoyt Axton has enjoyed an amazingly diverse career as a songwriter, recording artist and movie actor. While Axton is rooted equally in the folk and country traditions, his pop smarts have enabled him to land substantial hits with numerous artists. Among the artists who have recorded Axton's songs are Three Dog Night ("Joy to the World," "Never Been to Spain"), the Kingston Trio ("Greenback Dollar"), Steppenwolf ("The Pusher," "Snowblind Friend"), and Ringo Starr ("No No Song"), as well as Waylon Jennings, Glen Campbell, Tanya Tucker, John Denver, and Commander Cody.

As an artist, Axton has released a string of remarkably consistant albums that feature his warm baritone and wry, earthy lyrical style. —*Rick Clark*

My Griffin Is Gone / 1969 / CBS 33103
One of Axton's less interesting albums—though, considering the consistent quality of this fine songwriter's work, this shouldn't deter anyone interested in it. —*Jim Worbois*

Joy to the World / 1971 / Capitol 788
Songwriter Hoyt Axton lets loose with a batch of original songs that have been heavily covered (making big hits) by artists as varied as Three Dog Night, Steppenwolf, and Waylon Jennings. Axton has a distinctive style which makes his original versions as interesting as the better-known covers. —*Jim Worbois*

● **Life Machine** / 1974 / A&M 3155
Among Axton's many albums, *Life Machine* features some of his best writing. "When the Morning Comes," and "Boney Fingers" are highlights. —*Rick Clark*

○ **Southbound** / 1975 / A&M 4510
Another solid effort. Includes "Pride of Man" and "Lion in the Winter." —*Rick Clark*

Fearless / 1976 / A&M 4571
Includes "The Devil." —*Rick Clark*

Snowblind Friend / 1977 / MCA 2263
This is the fourth in a series of enjoyable album releases. The title track is one of Axton's better-known songs, having been recorded by Steppenwolf. —*Rick Clark*

○ **Road Songs** / 1977 / A&M 3182
Another fine batch of originals including hits by Axton ("Boney Fingers") and Ringo Starr. Equally as interesting as Axton's songs are his choice of sidemen, including members of Toto, graduates of several of Elvis Presley's former bands, Cheech & Chong and the Miracles. Nice album on all counts. —*Jim Worbois*

Razzy Bailey (Rasie Bailey)

Rockabilly
Bailey's musical career got off to a slow start when sides he cut for MGM and Capricorn went virtually unnoticed. In 1976, entangled in contractual problems, he went to a psychic who told him that the contract situation would soon be settled and that another artist would record one of his songs—changing his life. Not long after that Dickey Lee recorded Bailey's "9,999,999 Tears" which went Top 5, and within two years RCA signed Bailey as an artist. By 1981, Billboard had named him "Country Singles Artist of the Year." By the time he signed with MCA in 1984, his interest in the blues was making itself evident. He had released Wilson Pickett's "In The Midnight Hour" as a single, and begun to write tunes with legendary soul guitarist Steve Cropper. —*Jim Worbois*

● **Greatest Hits** / 1983 / RCA 5973

Baillie & the Boys

Group / Country

Kathy Baillie, Alan LeBoeuf, and Michael Bonagura. Though originally from New Jersey, Kathy Baillie and Michael Bonagura met in Delaware through a friend who gave Bonagura a tape that featured Baillie's vocals. Fans of artists like the Four Tops, the Beatles, the Supremes, Linda Ronstadt and James Taylor, they developed a strong harmony—both on stage and off: they were married in 1977. Bonagura's buddy, bass player Alan LeBoeuf, joined up, and after a number of years on the Garden State's nightclub circuit, yet another friend—a driver with Allied Van Lines—persuaded them to join him on a trip to Nashville. They stayed in Music City, and in 1982 they got their first chance to appear on a record, singing backup on Ed Bruce's *My First Taste of Texas*. Bonagura cowrote Marie Osmond's single "There's No Stopping Your Heart," and the trio sang backing vocals on a number of singles for Dan Seals and Randy Travis. Ultimately, they signed with RCA Records, making their debut in 1987. After completing their second album, LeBoeuf decided their touring schedule was too hectic, and left. Baillie and Bonagura retained the original name, though "Boys" seems a bit misleading. —*Tom Roland*

○ **The Best of Baillie & The Boys** / 1991 / RCA 3118
Highlights the real strength of the act: tuneful melodies, pristine harmonies, and Kathy Baillie's infectious enunciations. Best cuts: "Oh Heart," "(Wish I Had A) Heart of Stone," "Long Shot" and "I Can't Turn the Tide." —*Tom Roland*

David Ball

b. May 3, 1959, Rock Hill,
Vocals / Country
A singer/songwriter from Rock Hill, South Carolina, David Ball formerly played with Uncle Walt's Band, which also included Walter Hyatt. He released three singles on RCA in the late '80s to little fanfare before signing with Warner Bros. in the '90s. —*Brian Mansfield*

● **Thinkin' Problem** / 1994 / Warner Brothers 45562
A hard-country album with a cerebral twist, as the title song suggests. Ball, 41 when this album came out, had a craggy Texas face and a voice to match. When he has material to match, such as "Thinkin' Problem" or the ballad "When the Thought of You Catches Up with Me," he's the kind of singer neo-traditional country fans dream about. —*Brian Mansfield*

Moe Bandy

b. Feb. 12, 1944, Meridian, MS
Vocals, guitar / Traditional country
This Mississippi native gave up rodeo riding for music. Traditionalist/honky-tonk singer Bandy has done well with "Bandy the Rodeo Clown," "Hank Williams, You Wrote My Life," and "It's a Cheatin' Situation." —*David Vinopal*

★ **The Best of Moe Bandy, Vol. 1** / 1977 / CBS 34715
A Texas honky-tonker whose unabashed paeans to the bottle were among the greatest jukebox records of the '70s. Talk about wailin' and willin'! —*Mark A. Humphrey*

○ **Greatest Hits (CBS)** / 1982 / CBS 38316
Carousing, drinking, and dodging wives are the order of the day here. "Holding the Bag" and "Tell Ole I Ain't Here, He Better Get on Home" are particularly amusing, but the biggest laughs come with the transvestite storyline of "Honky Tonk Queen." —*Tom Roland*

You Haven't Heard the Last of Me / 1987 / MCA 31224
Released nearly four years after his last previous Top 10 single, this album gave Bandy a brief return to the spotlight. Working with record producer Jerry Kennedy for the first time, Bandy maintains more command of his delivery than in any previous album. —*Tom Roland*

Many Mansions / 1989 / Curb 77283
A fine title song about homelessness, among others. —*Mark A. Humphrey*

Bobby Bare

b. Apr. 7, 1935, Ironton, OH
Vocals, guitar / Traditional country
Bobby Bare fought to secure control of his own recordings years before Waylon Jennings and Willie Nelson pulled their outlaw coup. After Johnny Cash, he was among the first country artists to look at the album as a thematic collection rather than simply a

hodge-podge of hits and throwaway tunes. In the 1960s he concentrated on folk-tinged country, and in the 1970s he mixed novelty songs, rowdy honky-tonkers and casual working-class tributes. He helped Waylon Jennings secure his first record deal, and was among the first to champion such singer-songwriters as Kris Kristofferson, Billy Joe Shaver, Guy Clark, Townes Van Zandt, Shel Silverstein and Rodney Crowell. His low-key, laid-back personality may be one of the reasons he hasn't received the recognition he deserves. —*Michael McCall*

Lullabys, Legends and Lies / 1973 / Bear Family 15683
A two-album set featuring 14 Shel Silverstein songs, all performed in a room full of rowdy friends who sing along and comment when the mood strikes. —*Michael McCall*

★ **This Is Bobby Bare** / 1973 / RCA
The best assortment of his 1960s work, including such classic hits as "Detroit City," "500 Miles from Home," and "Streets of Baltimore," as well as country-folk versions of "Four Strong Winds," "Miller's Cave," and "Long Black Veil." —*Michael McCall*

○ **Cowboys & Daddys** / 1975 / RCA
Instead of singing about outlaws and rhinestone cowboys, Bare's songs speak of the struggles and joys of those who truly make their home on the range. —*Michael McCall*

Sleeper Wherever I Fall / 1978 / Columbia
Some of Bare's best albums barely registered on the radio charts, but they're rich in unusual songs and distinct performances. Selections here include a cover of The Rolling Stones' "The Last Time" and a Rodney Crowell gem, "On a Real Good Night." —*Michael McCall*

○ **As Is** / 1981 / Columbia
Produced by Rodney Crowell, a solid collection of good songs in which Bare's sly, low-key charms shine through. —*Michael McCall*

Greatest Hits / RCA 6319
His 1970s chart songs, including the Number One hit "Marie Laveau," a sharp version of Billy Joe Shaver's "Ride Me Down Easy" and his best-known novelty song, "Dropkick Me, Jesus." —*Michael McCall*

Bashful Brother Oswald (Beecher Kirby)

b. , Sevier County, TN
Dobro, guitar, banjo / Old-time
Since 1938, Beecher Kirby's dobro has added the special sound that makes Roy Acuff's band unique, at the same time adding comedy through the Bashful Brother Oswald rube. Beecher Kirby has done much to popularize the dobro (unamplified resonator Hawaiian guitar) in mainstream country and bluegrass. —*David Vinopal*

○ **Brother Oswald** / Rounder 0013
Roy Acuff's dobroist since the '30s, in a pleasant set of Hawaiian-inspired old-time country songs. —*Mark A. Humphrey*

The Bellamy Brothers

Group / Country, easy listening, country-rock
Howard (b. Feb. 2, 1946) and David (b. Sept. 16, 1950) Bellamy. Growing up on a Florida farm that's been in the family since the Civil War, the Bellamys have an understandable interest in their roots—geographical, genealogical, and musical. The latter area is a mixed bag, evidenced in a line from "Kids of the Baby Boom": "We had sympathy for the devil and the Rolling Stones/Then we got a little older, we found Haggard & Jones." Entranced by the Beatles and Crosby, Stills, Nash & Young, the Bellamys also heard island rhythms and melodies from the migrant workers who labored in Florida. They performed as an opening act with a local R&B band that worked the same stage as Little Anthony & the Imperials and Percy Sledge, and signed up in the late 60s with Jericho, a Southern rock band that worked the same circuit as the Allman Brothers. Ultimately, David's song "Spiders and Snakes" was recorded by Jim Stafford, and the Brothers ended up in Los Angeles. Through happenstance, a producer heard Howard singing while working as a roadie for Neil Diamond, and in short order, they recorded "Let Your Love Flow," which hit Number 1 on the pop charts during 1976. Within a year they were certified has-beens in the US, though they continued to find success in Europe. Finally, they found their niche in America on the country chart in 1979 with "If I Said You Have a Beautiful Body Would You Hold

It Against Me," nominated for a Grammy. It began a series of double—entendre songs that kept them from favor with the critics, but they quietly evolved through experimentation into one of country's most daring acts. With "You're My Favorite Star" and "Get into Reggae Cowboy," they melded country with Jamaican reggae, and they matched up country and another surprising genre with the self-explanatory title "Country Rap." The Bellamys also made great strides lyrically, particularly in their thirtysomething trilogy: "Old Hippie," "Kids of the Baby Boom" and "Rebels without a Clue."
The Bellamy Brothers have racked up more Top 10 country singles than any other duo in history, yet remain one of the format's most underrated acts. —*Tom Roland*

Rip off the Knob / Intersound 9109
Features Freddie Fender and Flaco Jeminez on Staying In Love. —*Dan Cooper*

Two & Only / 1979 / Warner Brothers 337
The Bellamy's explore a number of musical styles with success. In addition to the hits, check out "May You Never," written by the outstanding British folk artist John Martyn, the bluesy "Miss Misunderstood," and "Why Did We Die So Young," with a strong early '60s pop influence. —*Jim Worbois*

You Can Get Crazy / 1980 / Warner Brothers 56777
These prolific brothers turn in another fine batch of tunes (and one non-original) for this record. Their harmonies are appealing whether on the reggae—influenced "Dancin' Cowboys" or "Let Me Waltz Into Your Heart," with not a weak track here. —*Jim Worbois*

● **Greatest Hits** / 1982 / MCA 31012
Contains such hits as "Dancin' Cowboys," "Redneck Girl," "Let Your Love Flow," "Lovers Live Longer," and others. —*AMG*

○ **When We Were Boys** / 1982 / Elektra 1982
Michael Lloyd, probably best known as the producer on Shaun Cassidy's "Da Doo Ron Ron," oversaw the brothers' cute, early country years. In this album, they were given the reins for the first time, leading to a more serious, reflective and simple approach. Also for the first time, they recorded the album at their own home studio, located on their farm in Darby, FL. —*Tom Roland*

○ **Greatest Hits, Vol. 2** / 1986 / MCA 31013
The second volume contains "Strong Weakness," "Feelin' the Feelin'," "Too Much Is Not Enough" and others. —*AMG*

Country Rap / 1987 / MCA 31306
"Kids of the Baby Boom," encapsulating images from JFK to Third World abusiveness, speaks out for an entire generation. But the album is dominated by experimental and infectious "fun stuff," including "D-D-D-D-Divorcee," "Country Rap," and their bopping group effort with the Forester Sisters, "Too Much Is Not Enough." —*Tom Roland*

Rebels Without a Clue / Sep. 19, 1988 / MCA 42224
David Bellamy shows the depth of his songwriting talents, particularly in "The Courthouse," "The Andy Griffith Show" and the autobiographical "When the Music Meant Everything." Firm images, lots of conviction. —*Tom Roland*

○ **Greatest Hits, Vol. 3** / 1989 / MCA 42298
This member of the series contains "The Center of My Universe," "Big Love," "Hillbilly Hell," "Santa Fe" and other hits. —*AMG*

Matraca Berg

b. 1964
Vocals / Contemporary country
Daughter of country songwriter/session singer Icee Berg, Matraca Berg is one of Nashville's few music figures actually born in the town. She has written songs for most of Nashville's women, among them Reba McEntire ("The Last One To Know"), Suzy Bogguss ("Hey Cinderella"), Trisha Yearwood ("Wrong Side of Memphis") and Pam Tillis ("Calico Plains"). —*Brian Mansfield*

● **Lying to the Moon** / 1990 / RCA 2066
An enchanting album from one of Nashville's best female songwriting voices, this album included two minor hits, "Baby, Walk On" and "The Things You Left Undone." The title track eventually became something of a Nashville standard, being recorded by Trisha Yearwood, Robin & Linda Williams and by Berg on *The Speed of Grace*. —*Brian Mansfield*

The Speed of Grace / Nov. 1993 / RCA 66351

After RCA Nashville refused a second album, Berg moved to the label's pop division, recording an album primarily with such L.A. studio musicians as guitarist Michael Landau and drummer Jim Keltner. The results highlighted Berg's bluesy side, but, aside from a cover of Dolly Parton's "Jolene" recorded with her Nashville buddies, lacked the acoustic Southern mysticism of *Lying to the Moon*. —*Brian Mansfield*

Clint Black

b. 1962, Long Branch, NJ

Vocals, guitar / Country

Born in New Jersey but raised in Houston, Clint Black absolutely tore up the charts following his debut in 1989—his first four singles hit Number 1. A rarity in country, Black insists on writing almost all his material with band member Hayden Nicholas. Black won the Country Music Association's Horizon Award in 1989 and was named top male vocalist a year later. Married to actress Lisa Hartman of *Knot's Landing* fame. —*Brian Mansfield*

★ **Killin' Time** / 1989 / RCA 9668

Black's accessible brand of Texas country burned up the charts upon its release, selling two million copies and yielding the hit singles "Better Man," "Killin' Time," "Nobody's Home," Walkin' Away" and "Nothing's News." — *Brian Mansfield*

Put Yourself in My Shoes / 1990 / RCA 2372

Put Yourself in My Shoes never approaches the perfection of Black's debut album, but it still produced a number of singles, including "Put Yourself in My Shoes," "Loving Blind," "Where Are You Now" and "This Nightlife." —*Brian Mansfield*

○ **The Hard Way** / 1992 / RCA 66003

Back to form, Black put some of his most exciting singles on his third album. "We Tell Ourselves" rocked without resorting to Southern boogie, and "When My Ship Comes In" contained a masterful chorus. The album also includes the hit "Burn One Down." —*Brian Mansfield*

No Time to Kill / Jul. 1993 / RCA 66239

Black's albums seem to alternate between the remarkable and the merely pretty good. *No Time To Kill*, which plays off the title of his first album, is one of the merely pretty good. All of this music is acceptable, though little matches quality of the debut album. Black does a duet with Wynonna Judd called "A Bad Goodbye." —*Brian Mansfield*

Ronee Blakley

b. Idaho

Coming from the L.A. singer/songwriter movement of the '70s, Blakley became a favorite of Bob Dylan's. The critical acclaim of her first album lead to her being cast in the film *Nashville*.

    A second album followed in 1975, after which she was asked to be part of Dylan's Rolling Thunder Review, in 1976. Afterward, a failed attempt to change musical direction resulted in her decision to pursue an acting career. —*Jim Worbois*

● **Ronee Blakley** / 1972 / Elektra 75027

A fine album by an often over looked singer-songwriter. Released three years before her appearance in Robert Altman's *Nashville*, this is all the validation one needs for her inclusion in the film. Worth the effort to find.—*Jim Worbois*

Welcome / 1975 / Warner Brothers 2890

The songwriting on this album isn't as strong as that on her self-titled album. Too bad, because the band smokes. —*Jim Worbois*

The Blue Sky Boys

Group / Old-time

In the '30s, brother duets were common in country music: among the better known were the Monroes, the Delmores, the Dixons, and the Carlisles. Bill and Earl Bolick, who in 1936 were ready to make their first recording, followed their producer's suggestion that they should be "different" by avoiding the word *brother*. From "Blue Ridge Mountains, Land of the Sky" they took two words and named their act. But the Bolicks would have been different even without the new name. Their intricate yet simple harmonies, their perfectly matching voices, and their unadorned mandolin and guitar instrumental backing set them off from the competition—so much so that two subsequent generations of duet singers echo them, some without realizing it. The Everly Brothers

and the Louvin Brothers, themselves recognized as exceptional vocal duets, acknowledge the influence of the Blue Sky Boys. In the '50s, when tastes in country music changed drastically, the Blue Sky Boys retired from music rather than forsake their love of old mountain ballads for the uptempo popularity of electric instruments, drums, and honky-tonk. In the 60s they were coaxed to come out of retirement, playing an occasional college date during the hootenanny phenomenon and recording albums in 1963, 1965, and 1976. No one in country music has done vocal duets better than the Blue Sky Boys. If your taste runs more to Conway & Loretta, George & Tammy, Wynonna & Naomi, listen to the effortless, exquisite singing of Bill and Earl Bolick—See where it all started. —*David Vinopal*

★ **There'll Come a Time ...** / 1936 / Blue Sky 1001

There'll Come a Time/Can't You Hear That Nightbird—sacred songs, weepers, and hillbilly heart-singing at its best. —*Mark A. Humphrey*

○ **Within the Circle/Who Wouldn't Be Lonely** / 1937 / Blue Tone 103

This album contains old-time recordings from 1937-1938. A genuine classic. —*AMG*

● **The In Concert '64** / Rounder 0236

An excellent "rediscovery" concert of this legendary 30s brother duo. —*Mark A. Humphrey*

Can't You Hear That Nightbird Crying? /

This album, which features "Sunny Side of Life," was recorded in 1936 in Charlotte, NC. —*AMG*

Suzy Bogguss (Susan Kay Bogguss)

b. Dec. 30, 1956, Aledo, IL

Vocals / Country-pop

Born Susan Kay Bogguss in Aledo, IL, Suzy Bogguss started singing on demos and in a Nashville ribs restaurant in 1985, but it was a gig at the Dollywood theme park in Pigeon Forge, TN, that got her a record deal. Since then, she has made her name recording commercial interpretations of songs by the likes of Nanci Griffith, Cheryl Wheeler and John Hiatt. She won the 1992 Horizon Award from the Country Music Association. —*Brian Mansfield*

★ **Somewhere Between** / 1988 / Capitol 90237

A fabulous, truly surprising debut that firmly plants one foot in the past and the other in the Nashville mainstream. The best songs here come from country legends: Merle Haggard penned the powerhouse title cut, "My Sweet Love Ain't Around" came from Hank Williams, and "I Want To Be a Cowboy's Sweetheart" was an old Patsy Montana tune. The new stuff was pretty danged good, too: "Cross My Heart," written by Verlon Thompson and Kye Fleming, was the album's highest-charting single. —*Brian Mansfield*

Moment of Truth / 1990 / Capitol 92653

Under the wing of producer and new-label head Jimmy Bowen, Bogguss relinquished her cowboy's sweetheart role and began recording more polished records that often burnished singer/songwriter material. This album didn't do so well, though: it produced only two weakly performing singles, "Under the Gun" and "All Things Made New Again." —*Brian Mansfield*

○ **Aces** / 1991 / Capitol 95847

The new strategy paid off here: Bogguss took Cheryl Wheeler's "Aces" and Nanci Griffith's "Outbound Plane" into the Top 10. She also hit with "Someday Soon" and "Letting Go." This is the album that won her the CMA's Horizon Award, five years after her first single. —*Brian Mansfield*

Voices in the Wind / 1992 / Liberty 98585

This sounds like one of those white-bread pop albums folks occasionally try to pawn off as country—until you started listening to the lyrics. *Voices in the Wind* may have been bigger on string sections than twin fiddlers, but Bogguss' choice in covers remains just off-center enough to be exciting, with Cheryl Wheeler's "Don't Wanna" and Lowell George's "Heartache." She revived John Hiatt's "Drive South" for a hit. The more risky material—especially the bleary-eyed blues of "Eat at Joe's" and the troubled alcoholic haze of Bogguss' own "In the Day"—shows why the Country Music Association gave her its Horizon Award just before the release of this album. —*Brian Mansfield*

Somethin' up My Sleeve / Sep. 13, 1993 / Liberty 8926

Includes "Hey Cinderella," which Bogguss wrote with Matraca Berg; "Just Like the Weather," which she wrote with husband Doug Crider; and "Souvenirs," a remarkably understated indictment of materialism by Gretchen Peters. The title track is a duet with Billy Dean. —*Brian Mansfield*

○ **Greatest Hits** / Mar. 8, 1994 / Liberty 28457
Ten of Bogguss' best, from "I Want to Be a Cowboy's Sweetheart" to 1993's "Heartache." It doesn't contain anything from *Something Up My Sleeve*, but it does have "Hopelessly Yours," a duet with Lee Greenwood that hadn't appeared on any of Bogguss' other albums. —*Brian Mansfield*

Larry Boone

b. , Cooper City, Florida
Vocals / Country
Floridian Larry Boone has always lagged at the back of the neo-trad country hunk parade, though some have wondered why. He's certainly a competent songwriter, writing Don Williams' "Old Coyote Town" and many of the songs on his own albums, and he's got the kind of traditional country voice radio programmers seem to love. After his 1991 album *One Way to Go* flopped, he took a year off to write and to rethink his strategy before releasing *Get in Line* in 1993. —*Brian Mansfield*

One Way to Go / 1987 / CBS 47050
Includes the singles "I Need a Miracle" and "To Be With You." —*Brian Mansfield*

○ **Larry Boone** / Dec. 1987 / Mercury 834377
Boone had had a number of small hits ("Stranger Things Have Happened," "Roses in December") when his debut album came out in the wake of such country hunks as Garth Brooks and Clint Black. Boone figured to tap into that market with his muscular voice, but didn't quite make it, though this album includes his biggest hit, "Don't Give Candy to a Stranger." —*Brian Mansfield*

Swingin' Doors, Sawdust Floors / 1988 / Mercury 836710
Contains three Top 40 hits: "I Just Called To Say Goodbye Again," "Wine Me Up," and "Fool's Paradise." —*Brian Mansfield*

Down That River Road / 1990 / PolyGram 842156
"Everybody Wants to Be Hank Williams," a brutal song about the price singers pay for commercial success, is the best thing Boone has recorded. It's also the closest thing to a hit this album produced. —*Brian Mansfield*

● **Get in Line** / Mar. 23, 1993 / Columbia 48968
Working with producer Don Cook (Brooks & Dunn, Mark Collie), Boone tried to retool his image into a tougher, leaner figure. Musically, he was fairly successful with rockers like "Call Me When the Sun Goes Down" and "I Still Got (What You Got Over)." Commercially was another matter: "Get in Line," the album's only charting single, peaked at 65 in *Billboard*. —*Brian Mansfield*

Boxcar Willie (Lecil Travis Martin)

b. Sep. 1, 1931, Sterret, TX
Vocals / Traditional country
Born Lecil Martin, this Texan has done as much as anyone to keep the hobo tradition alive in country music. Though he never had a Top10 song, his *King of the Road* album sold over three million copies through TV advertising. Long a favorite in Europe, he received a standing ovation in his 1979 debut at the Opry, where he is now a regular. —*David Vinopal*

● **Boxcar Willie** / 1976 / MCA 39052
The best-recorded and best-produced of his numerous albums. —*Charles S. Wolfe*

○ **Best Loved Favorites** / 1989 / Vanguard 8235
This album contains 11 hits, including "Six Days on the Road," "Wings of a Dove," and "Pistol Packin' Mama." —*AMG*

○ **Rocky Box: Rockabilly** / 1993 / K-Tel 3190
Country music's favorite fake hobo teams up with the Midwest's top roots music combo for a spirited, if at times surreal, outing. The Skeletons, featuring D. Clinton Thompson's excellent fretboard work, provides perfect retro backing on everything, while Boxcar is quite at home on traditional '50s boppers like "Mystery Train" and "Rockin' Bones." But the true candidate for the twilight zone is his version here of "Achy Breaky Heart," complete with his patented train whistle. It doesn't get much weirder than this in any style of music. —*Cub Koda*

Honky-Tonk

After the deification of mother, home, dead relatives, traveling, and the working man no longer bore a close-enough resemblance to reality for millions of country music listeners, a new form – honky-tonk – filled the void. This new genre didn't displace traditional country themes, but it certainly did add variety and spice by lamenting and more than occasionally celebrating the shady and seedy sides of life. When Prohibition brought booze and customers into the bars and taverns in the 30s, the patrons preferred to leave the glorification-of-home songs where they belonged, *at* home, and found a new form that better reflected a tavern's bar instead of a church's altar. And so songs about cheatin', lyin', thievin', fightin', and slippin' around – in other words, *real* life – proliferated. If something was illicit, but traditionally and conservatively illicit, there were good makings for a honky-tonk hit. The whine of a steel guitar and the beat of drums fit much better in a watering hole than in a church, and they lent themselves perfectly to this music. Whether the gin-mills' music imitated life or whether the patrons imitated the song lyrics is unclear. What is clear is that country music's love of honky-tonk themes continues unabated. Not much has changed in the forty years since Hank Thompson's complaint "I didn't know God made honky-tonk angels" (from "The Wild Side of Life") motivated Miss Kitty Wells to answer "It wasn't God who made honky-tonk angels." Then who's to blame? As Wells sings it, "From the start, most every heart that's ever broken/Was because there always was a man to blame." A classic case of both being right at the same time … "Dim Light, Thick Smoke, and Loud, Loud Music" says it all. A good place to start your honky-tonk listening is Ernest Tubb; a representative sample should include Hank Williams, Floyd Tillman, Hank Thompson, Lefty Frizzell, Webb Pierce, the early Ray Price, George Jones, Tammy Wynette, Buck Owens, Merle Haggard, Willie Nelson, and Loretta Lynn.

– David Vinopal

Truck Driving Favorites /
Features such hits as "Phantom 309," "Convoy," "Freightliner Fever," and "Whiteline Fever." —*AMG*

Jesus Makes Housecalls /
Contains such gospel favorites as "How Great Thou Art," "Swing Low Sweet Chariot," and "Somebody Touched Me." —*AMG*

Bill Boyd

b. Sep. 29, 1910, Fannin County, Texas
Vocals, guitar / Western swing
If you love Western swing, listen to Bill Boyd and his Cowboy Ramblers, a band contemporary to the more famous one of Bob Wills, but with a different sound. The Wills band often used horns and recorded many types of songs, including jazz; the Cowboy Ramblers, though, stuck to string-backing and featured western songs. Aficionados of Western swing put Bill Boyd up there with Bob Wills. —*David Vinopal*

● **Bill Boyd's Cowboy Ramblers** / RCA 5503

○ **With His Cowboy Ramblers 1934-1947** / Texas Rose 2701
Features "On the Texas Plains," "You're Just About Right," "Boyd's Blues," and more. —*AMG*

Brooks & Dunn

Group / Country
Kix Brooks and Ronnie Dunn had both had solo records (Brooks on Capitol, Dunn on the independent Churchill), but nothing really clicked for them until Arista Nashville head Tim DuBois brought them together in 1991. Both sons of Southwestern oil men, Brooks & Dunn's music captured a chip-kicker attitude tem-

pered by a fondness for California singer/songwriters like James Taylor and Jim Messina. By 1992, they had replaced the Judds as perennial Duo of the Year award winners. —*Brian Mansfield*

● **Brand New Man** / 1991 / Arista 18658
The title tale of love and redemption was a classic single for all the same reasons that made this would-be modern cowboy duo's such a winner: tightly constructed choruses; a perfect balance between romance, macho swagger, and Wild West imagery; and bracing harmonies that'll clear the trail dust out of your throat quicker than a shot of good whiskey. Four singles from *Brand New Man* topped the country charts: the title tune, "My Next Broken Heart," "Neon Moon," and "Boot Scootin' Boogie." —*Brian Mansfield*

Hard Workin' Man / 1993 / Arista 18716
As with most second albums, the successful traits started to isolate themselves on *Hard Workin' Man:* Macho stuff like "Hard Workin' Man" and "Rock My World (Little Country Girl)" rocked harder than anything on *Brand New Man,* though B&D made sure their women came off as good as they did (catch the "and women too" tag on "Hard Workin' Man"). The slower songs ("That Ain't No Way to Go," "She Used to Be Mine") tended towards the sort of evocative images that ran all through the debut. The pair never put all the elements together they way they did the first time, but they came close enough that few people noticed. —*Brian Mansfield*

Garth Brooks

b. Feb. 2, 1962, Tulsa, OK
Vocals, guitar / Contemporary country
In a word, phenomenal. After his first two albums went platinum (*Garth Brooks* and *No Fences*), Nashville knew that Garth was hot property. But no one would guess that this Oklahoma-born crooner with the big hat would sweep so many awards and end up the biggest crossover star in history. According to his press release of October 1991, his records were selling to the tune of 225,000 a week, making Tennessee Ernie Ford (and his smash "Sixteen Tons," in its time a huge crossover hit) look downright insignificant.

Brooks's 1991 *Ropin' the Wind* was the first country album to debut at the top of *Billboard*'s Pop Album chart. And that, country music fans, means money. When the pop fans think Brooks is one of theirs also and the country fans claim him as their own, he has the best of both worlds. His easy-to-listen-to style and content put him where Kenny Rogers was a decade earlier, though Brooks's fans are younger and in more of a record-buying mood. In the *Music City News* Top LPs chart of March 1992, Brooks's first three albums ranked one, two, and three, though in reverse order from when they were issued. The good old days, when country fans would argue over whether a particular singer or song is *real* country, are just that—good old days. In the DSG (days since Garth), such questions are irrelevant. —*David Vinopal*

Garth Brooks / 1989 / Capitol 90897
Brooks's first, rather modestly produced album established his mortality/preciousness-of-loved-ones themes with "If Tomorrow Never Comes" and "The Dance," both substantial country hits. —*Rick Clark*

★ **No Fences** / 1990 / Liberty 93866
This was the album that took Brooks to the top of the charts, thanks to the playfully cocky hit "Friends in Low Places," as well as "Two of a Kind, Workin' on a Full House," and the sentimental ballad "Unanswered Prayers." "The Thunder Rolls" was a controversial track that also became a big country hit. —*Rick Clark*

○ **The Chase** / 1991 / Liberty 98743
Brooks shows increasing maturity as a songwriter as he continues to mine his preciousness-of-love-and-life themes, and he again tackles a sensitive issue with "Face to Face," a song about date rape. He also includes a couple of covers, the rollicking version of the Little Feat classic "Dixie Chicken" and a swinging "Walkin' After Midnight." —*Rick Clark*

○ **Ropin' the Wind** / 1991 / Liberty 96330
Brooks expanded into more ambitious musical and thematic territory (for a country-based act) with the tracks "In Lonesome Dove" and "The River." He also covered Billy Joel's "Shameless" on this outing. —*Rick Clark*

In Pieces / Aug. 23, 1993 / Liberty 80857

After the relative commercial disappointment of *The Chase,* Brooks revamped his approach and the result was *In Pieces,* a more stream-lined and raucous album that nevertheless had its moments of ambition, like the murder ballad "The Night Will Only Know." —*AMG*

Kix Brooks

Before teaming with Ronnie Dunn to form Brooks & Dunn, Shreveport, LA native Kix Brooks wrote songs in Nashville and cut one unsuccessful album for Capitol Records. —*Brian Mansfield*

Kix Brooks / Oct. 25, 1993 / Capitol 48506
A worthy addition to the collection of any Brooks & Dunn fan, even though the album was widely ignored upon its release. ("Sacred Ground," the album's only charting single, would become McBride & the Ride's first big hit in 1992.) On his own, Brooks' bayou roots show through, and his music often sounds just as tough as Brooks & Dunn's. —*Brian Mansfield*

Brother Phelps

A duo consisting of Doug and Ricky Lee Phelps, the bassist and vocalist who left the Kentucky Headhunters following *Electric Barnyard.* —*Brian Mansfield*

Let Go / Asylum 61544
Much more low-key than most people expected, *Let Go* proves that the Phelps were the smarts behind the Headhunters. The title cut is a breezy single that recalls Buddy Holly, and elsewhere on the album the Phelps makes judicious use of Southern boogie ("Were You Really Livin'") and strings ("What Goes Around"). Not a perfect album, and not as good as the Headhunters at their peak, but *Let Go* still contains some mighty nice listening. —*Brian Mansfield*

Alison Brown

Banjo / Bluegrass
A Harvard graduate who quit a fast-track career as an investment banker to dedicate herself to her music, Brown came to prominence as a stand-out member of Alison Krauss' Union Station band, and later was musical director for Michelle Shocked. Her instrumental albums are melodic and graceful and manage to sound both accessible and adventurous. She wrote all but one song on her first three albums, and her compositions owe more to the influence of David Grisman (who produced her debut) and Bela Fleck than to Earl Scruggs or Alan O'Bryant. —*Michael McCall*

Simple Pleasures / 1990 / Vanguard 79459
Her all-instrumental debut instantly earned respect among progressive acoustic music fans. Produced by David Grisman, and feauturing guests Mike Marshall and Alison Krauss, Brown weaves cello, flute and congas into her hybrid string sound, and she maintains an innate elegance amid the tricky arranging. —*Michael McCall*

○ **Twilight Motel** / 1992 / Vanguard 79465
Produced by Mike Marshall, Brown moves in several new directions, showing off the breadth of her talent while keeping the composition at the center of her playing. Jazzier, yet also more relaxed, than her debut. Maura O'Connell provides vocals on a traditional Irish song. —*Michael McCall*

● **Look Left** / 1994 / Vanguard
Brown criss-crosses the globe sonically, taking on Cajun, Celtic, Native American and Australian Aboriginal music with characteristically relaxed proficiency. —*Michael McCall*

Jim Ed Brown (James Edward Brown)

b. Mar. 1, 1934, Sparkman, AK
Popular
A member of the Browns (along with his sisters Maxine and Bonnie), Jim Ed went solo in 1965 with "Heard From A Memory Last Night"; though the Browns continued as an act until 1967. Top 10 solo hits continued through 1974. In 1976 he teamed with Helen Cornelius and the new team hit Number 1 with their "I Don't Want to Have to Marry You". A further string of hits followed but, due to personal problems, the string ended in 1981 with "Don't Bother to Knock". —*Jim Worbois*

● **Greatest Hits** / Feb. 1992 / RCA 55979

Though probably best remembered for his work with his sisters in the Browns or his hit "Morning," this record shows how versatile a singer Brown was. Whether it's gospel flavored ("Unbelievable Love"), beer drinkin' music ("Pop A Top"), or tongue in cheek ("Broadminded Man"), Brown makes it all sound easy. —*Jim Worbois*

Junior Brown

Nothing inspires a yawn quite so fast as hearing a new hot country artist's obligatory speech about his Jones and Haggard influences. But when a singer/picker starts talking about Ernest Tubb, Jimi Hendrix, and The Ventures—and backs it up on record—better close your mouth and listen. Actually, Junior Brown (who hit the bigtime in 1993 after twenty-plus years on the Southwest roadhouse circuit) doesn't like to talk about his influences—probably because they have as much of nothing, as everything, to do with his style. A monster picker, he plays the guit-steel—a double-neck, combined electric and steel guitar of his own invention. His vocals, though sometimes shaded towards Tubb for comic effect, are always instantly recognizable as his own—and his brilliant, idiosyncratic songwriting more so. None of which really explains the complete package that is Junior Brown, honky-tonk man out of time. So-called hot country ain't nothing but a plate-warmer compared to the heat this guy turns up. —*Dan Cooper*

12 Shades of Brown / 1989 / Curb 77622
A re-issue of a 1989 self-produced cassette that Brown used to sell in Austin supermarkets. It's every bit as strong as *Guit With It*, though the accent is less on the picking and more on the songs. Then again, on hillbilly rave-ups like "Too Many Nights in a Roadhouse" and "Broke Down on South of Dallas," he pretty much has it both ways. —*Dan Cooper*

● **Guit with It** / Aug. 24, 1993 / Capitol/Curb 77622
Junior Brown's rumbling, strikingly deep voice, tasty electric and steel guitar playing, and splendid honky-tonk and Western swing songs have made him a sensation in country circles. He's a great relief for a genre overloaded with disposable folk-rock pretenders and bandwagon climbers. There's nothing phony or cliched about Brown's music; this is the genuine, untutored, undiluted article. Brown can sing with equal flair tunes requiring sincerity, ache, or irony. The CD's 12 cuts include the nearly 12-minute "Guit-Steel Blues," a sharp cover of Hank Garland's "Sugarfoot Stomp," and the bittersweet "Doin' What Comes Easy to a Fool" and "Holding Pattern." Brown is as vital and refreshing as the early John Anderson or Randy Travis, and may emerge as the head of a class anxious to keep country from losing its guts in a mad race toward mainstream supremacy. —*Ron Wynn*

Marty Brown

Vocals, guitar / Traditional country
Marty Brown, a native of the tobacco-farming community of Maceo, KY, is the kind of guy around which myths spring up. He hitchhiked into Nashville with little more than his guitar, a cheap demo tape, and a knowledge of the music industry he'd picked up from TNN (The Nashville Network). (He's said to have accosted producer Barry Beckett at a music-biz function and said "I know you! I saw you in a video!") Turned out that was enough. An unannounced visit to performing rights organization BMI led to a scramble to sign Brown to a recording deal. Brown's pinched voice is a throwback to an earlier time, sort of a Kentucky hill version of Jimmie Rodgers. —*Brian Mansfield*

○ **Cryin', Lovin', Leavin'** / MCA 11054
By his third album, Brown and producer Richard Bennett could be pretty confident they weren't going to get any radio play, so they just cut loose and made as pure an album as Brown was had in him. "You Must Be Mistakin' Me" and "Too Blue To Crow" possess a country sound so hard, they make most New Traditionalists sound like Muzak. Brown cuts Moon Mullican's "Cherokee Boogie," sings "Shameless Lies" with Melba Montgomery, shamelessly cops from Buddy Holly's "Crying, Waiting, Hoping" with the title cut, and finishes with a gorgeous duet with Joy Lynn White on "I Love Only You." —*Brian Mansfield*

○ **High & Dry** / 1991 / MCA 10330
If everything here were as pure a hillbilly distillation as the title track or the loopy "Old King Kong," Brown might come off like a simple hick with limited nostalgia appeal. But his range is surprisingly wide. Brown's ballads—"I'll Climb Any Mountain" and "Wildest Dreams"—though simple, build to stunning, emotional climaxes. "Every Now and Then" is the equal of many of the Everly Brothers' best. And "Nobody Knows" is surely one of the most lonesome wails in a long, long time. —*Brian Mansfield*

● **Wild Kentucky Skies** / 1993 / MCA 10672
One of the best things about Marty Brown's music is that it possesses the qualities that people both love and hate about country music. Brown takes a surefire hit song, "I Don't Wanna See You," then sings it in a voice that won't let folks forget just how good backwoods country music can be. Songs like "It Must Be the Rain" and "Let's Begin Again" have soaring choruses that recall the Everlys at their best. On the other hand, "No Honky Tonkin' Tonight" and "I'd Rather Fish Than Fight" put to shame the lip service some singers pay to Hank Williams Sr. and Jimmie Rodgers. With the eerie "She's Gone," Brown takes the country death ballad into territory it's never seen before, and he follows it with the sentimental "Kentucky Skies." Brown is pure country without being purist. Flatly put, he's a hillbilly—and proud of it. —*Brian Mansfield*

Milton Brown

b. Sep. 8, 1903, Stephenville, TX, d. Apr. 13, 1936
Vocal
In April, 1936, when Milton Brown was killed in a wreck on the Texas highway (his car's speedometer was found frozen at 93 mph), he was fronting a take-no-prisoners swing band every bit as popular in the Lone Star State as Bob Wills' band. In fact, Brown and Wills had been bandmates in the Wills Fiddle Band, the Alladin Laddies, and the original Light Crust Doughboys, before Brown split off to form the Musical Brownies in 1932. The latter dancehall outfit recorded for Bluebird in 1934, and for Decca in '35-36. Whether Brown, had he lived, would have attained the iconographic stature of his friendly rival Wills is anybody's guess. Certainly the music he left behind deserves wider recognition. —*Dan Cooper*

○ **Taking Off!** / 1977 / String 804
More Decca material, including a couple of 1937 cuts recorded without Brown after he died. —*Dan Cooper*

☆ **With His Musical Brownies 1934** / Texas Rose 2706
Contains the complete Bluebird recordings of 1934. Showcases fiddler Cecil Brower and pianist Fred "Papa" Calhoun on a typically wild assortment of blues, pop, jazz and fiddle tunes. —*Dan Cooper*

★ **Pioneer Western Swing Band (1935-1936)** / MCA 1509
Twelve-cut collection from Brown's brilliant Decca sessions. Same core band as on the Bluebird sides, but with the additional firepower of a second fiddle hero, Cliff Bruner, and Bob Dunn, one of the first real geniuses of the steel guitar. —*Dan Cooper*

T. Graham Brown

b. Oct. 30, 1954, Arabi, GA
Vocals / Country
Asked to describe his own music, "His T-Ness" calls it "Otis Redding meets George Jones." With the smoky timbre of rocker Chris Rea and the passionate energy of Joe Cocker, Brown possesses as much "blue-eyed soul" as Boz Scaggs or Hall & Oates. A former All-State baseball player in Georgia, Brown gave up the sport when he rode the bench on his college team. He put together a band for the Holiday Inn lounge, and in 1982 his wife Sheila convinced him it was time to head to Nashville. There, he became immersed in the world of jingles, working for McDonald's, Kraft, Coca Cola, and Taco Bell. He also sang the demo of "1982" that Randy Travis eventually recorded. His sound is a bit unusual for country music, and that's appropriate for Brown, who does nothing the same way as anyone else. Cases in point: he named his band the Rack of Spam, and named his first child Acme. —*Tom Roland*

○ **I Tell It Like It Used to Be** / 1986 / Capitol 46901
With the sessions split between Nashville's Woodland Sound Studio and Muscle Shoals, T. Graham Brown's debut often sounds affectionately like the raw, impassioned work of a garage band. Shout it out! —*Tom Roland*

Brilliant Conversationalist / 1987 / Capitol 46773

With blaring horns and bluesy growled vocals, this record has more to do with Southside Johnny than any country band one could name. That aside, there are some nice songs on here. Not a great record but if this is your type of thing, you could do worse. —*Jim Worbois*

Bumper to Bumper / 1990 / Capitol 91780
This contains "I'm Sending One Up for You," "If You Could Only See Me Now," and more. —*AMG*

● **The Best of** / 1992 / Liberty 97250
Contains "With This Ring," "Never Say Never," and "Moonshadow Road," among other hits. —*AMG*

Jann Browne

Country
An underrated singer who got lost amid the hat acts of the early 1990s, Browne is a past and future member of Asleep at the Wheel who sings honky-tonk with daring spirit and ballads with delicate, nicely phrased emotion. —*Micheal McCall*

● **Tell Me Why** / 1974 / Curb 77251
Hard-core, rollicking honky-tonk that includes a duet with Wanda Jackson. —*Michael McCall*

○ **It Only Hurts When I Laugh** / Capitol 77451
The backbeat rocks as well as swings this time. The song choices are supreme, as she covers everything from a Ray Price shuffle to progressive country by Jim Lauderdale and John Hiatt. —*Michael McCall*

The Browns

Maxine Brown (b. 4/27/31) and Jim Ed Brown (b. 4/1/34) of Sparkman, AR had been singing together for several years when, in 1954, their sister Bonnie (b. 7/31/37) joined them. Calling themselves the Browns, the sibling harmony trio struck gold in 1959 with "The Three Bells," a crossover smash that spent four weeks atop the Billboard pop chart and ten weeks at Number 1 country. They broke up in 1967, though Jim Ed Brown scored solo hits into the 1980s. —*Dan Cooper*

● **Rockin' Rollin' Browns** / 1984 / Bear Family 15104

○ **Three Bells** / 1993 / Bear Family 15665
It is a lesson in reissue absurdity that The Browns, whose popularity has warranted this attractive but expensive 8-CD boxed set, have no single disc compilation available as of mid 1994. But if you know you're a fan, you can do no better than this collection of their complete RCA recordings. —*Dan Cooper*

Ed Bruce

b. Dec. 29, 1939
Vocals / Country, rock & roll
Born in Arkansas, raised in Memphis, Ed Bruce signed first with the rockabilly-heavy Sun Records, and later with the soul-oriented Septre label. But Bruce's deep resonance and laidback approach to life were more suited to country. He was able to move to Nashville with the help of Tommy Roe's pop hit "Sheila"; Bruce wrote the B-side, and collected enough royalties when it sold a million copies to swing a new home base. A jack-of-all-trades in the business, he's done some acting (the Bret Maverick series); some radio work (on Nashville's WSM); some jingle-singing (United Airlines, Burger King, Tennessee Tourism, among many others); and some songwriting ("Mammas, Don't Let Your Babies Grow up to Be Cowboys," "Texas When I Die," and "See the Big Man Cry"). A journeyman recording artist, Bruce found brief success in the early '80s with a string of singles for MCA Records. —*Tom Roland*

● **Greatest Hits** / 1975 / MCA 27139
An album that documents the most rewarding period of Ed Bruce's recording career. Easygoing, midtempo love songs dominate, particularly with "You're the Best Break This Old Heart Ever Had," "Ever, Never Lovin' You," and "You're Leavin' Here Tonight." The reflective "After All" is permanently haunting. —*Tom Roland*

Cliff Bruner

Like his former boss, Milton Brown, ace Texas fiddler Cliff Bruner led a prewar Western swing band as steeped in jazz and blues as traditional hoedown music. Based in the Houston-Beaumont region (as opposed to Dallas-Fort Worth) his *Texas Wanderers* featured several former members of Brown's Musical Brownies, in-

cluding the immortal steel guitar man Bob Dunn. Honky-tonk singer/pianist Moon Mullican also came to prominence as a member of Bruner's band. —*Dan Cooper*

☆ **Cliff Bruner's Texas Wanderers** / 1983 / Texas Rose 2710
A fine compilation covering the years 1937-44. Beaucoups chops from the aformentioned Bruner, Dunn and Mullican, as well as Leo Raley, the first Western swinger to "plug in" a mandolin. —*Dan Cooper*

Jethro Burns

b. 1920, d. Feb. 4, 1989
Mandolin / Instrumental mandolin
Behind the country hayseed garb, the hick patter, and the outrageous parodies of popular songs lay mandolin player Kenneth "Jethro" Burns and guitarist Henry "Homer" Haynes, expert jazz musicians who for nearly four decades were country comedy's most visible duo. Their exaggerated hillbilly appearance and zany send-ups of songs belie the cleverness of their comedy and the extraordinarily high quality of their music.

Both from Knoxville, they billed themselves first as the String Dusters, but moved to comedy in 1936 when they created the Homer and Jethro characters that were intact until Haynes' death in 1971. And they made a good living from these rubes, winning a Grammy in 1959, starring in Las Vegas, and appearing regularly on TV, including "The Tonight Show." Although they canned the country corn occasionally (as in *Playing It Straight*, a 1962 album), their onstage wit and parodies of well-known songs ranging from the opera to the Opry made them famous. Regarding his "Jambalaya" being turned into "Jam Bowl Liar," Hank Williams said you know a song's good when it's been given the Homer and Jethro treatment. Other zingers include "She Was Bitten on the Udder by an Adder," "Mama, Get the Hammer (There's a Fly on Papa's Head)," and "I've Got Tears in My Ears from Lying on My Back in Bed While I Cry over You." What other act could put out a hit album titled *The Worst of Homer and Jethro?* Only these two could be so creatively, zanily bad they were excellent. Shortly after Haynes's death, in a series of swing jazz albums, Burns has shown why he's been considered the best mandolin player of a generation and, in the opinion of many, the best who has ever lived. —*David Vinopal*

☆ **Back to Back** / Kaleidoscope
The two swing giants of mandolin, Jethro Burns and Tiny Moore, are backed by guitar-great Eldon Shamblin of the Bob Wills Texas Playboys. —*David Vinopal*

Jethro Live / 1990 / Flying Fish 072
Some laughs, and much "mando-marvelosity." —*Mark A. Humphrey*

● **Tea for One** / Kaleidoscope 14
Known for cornball comedy as half of Homer & Jethro, Burns was also a deft swing-style mandolinist. This album features Jethro Burns and his mandolin and no one else. —*Mark A. Humphrey*

Carl Butler

b. Jun. 2, 1927, Knoxville, TN
Guitar, vocals, songwriter
Carl Butler had already been a successful solo artist (having recorded for both Capitol and Columbia) when in 1962 he released "Don't Let Me Cross Over," with his wife Pearl supplying harmony vocals. When it hit Number 1 they realized what a good thing they had, and continued to record as a duo throughout the '60s. —*Jim Worbois*

● **Don't Let Me Cross Over** / 1963 / CBS 2002
Butler is best remembered for the title track (a country heartbreak style song) but this album is quite versatile and, in one instance, quite inovational (check out the fuzz guitar solo on "Wonder Drug"). Butler's wife, Pearl, also joins him on several of the songs, including the title track. —*Jim Worbois*

Glen Campbell

b. Apr. 22, 1936, Delight, AR
Vocals, guitar, banjo / Country
Playing guitar on the Los Angeles session circuit, Glen Campbell got involved in such memorable releases as "Strangers in the Night," by Frank Sinatra; "I'm a Believer," by the Monkees; "Viva Las Vegas," by Elvis Presley; and "The Legend of Bonnie & Clyde,"

by Merle Haggard. Campbell also toured as Brian Wilson's stand-in with the Beach Boys. But his own recording career was hardly rewarding at the start. After several albums, he was about to give it up when a song called "Gentle on my Mind" emerged with a smattering of success. Encouraged, he continued recording, and exploded with the release of "By the Time I Get to Phoenix." A string of hits followed—not to mention the network TV show "The Glen Campbell Goodtime Hour"—and within short order, he was selling more records than his labelmates, the Beatles. But his successes didn't sustain. He tailed off in the early '70s, re-emerged with the release of "Rhinestone Cowboy" in 1975, and continued through several more up-and-down periods. Campbell's vocal range, good looks, and sense of humor all combined to make him one of country music's best-recognized personalities, even when the music didn't work commercially. —*Tom Roland*

By the Time I Get to Phoenix / 1967 / Capitol 4XL57279
Features such Campbell favorites as "Rhinestone Cowboy," "Galveston," and others. —*AMG*

The Glen Campbell Goodtime Album / 1970 / Capitol 493
A spin-off of the TV show of the same name, this album is a nice representation of what Campbell was about at the time. In addition to the hit on the album (the cover of Conway Twitty's "It's Only Make Believe"), Glen dips into the Jimmy Webb songbook for two of the tracks. —*Jim Worbois*

○ **Glen Campbell's Greatest Hits** / 1971 / Capitol 1971
Covers the most productive period of his recording career, the years in which Al De Lory's soaring string arrangements, Jimmy Webb's snapshot songs, and the identifiable low-tuned guitars vaulted Campbell to the upper strata of both the country and pop charts. You simply weren't alive if you didn't hear "Wichita Lineman," "Galveston," or "Try a Little Kindness." —*Tom Roland*

I Knew Jesus (Before He Was a Star) / 1973 / Capitol 11185
On this album, Campbell became one of the first (and only) artists to cover, and give exposure to, the talents of Kinky Freidman. Not a great album overall, but certainly an eclectic batch of songs, including some that had been recent hits by Charlie Rich, Judy Collins, and Olivia Newton-John. —*Jim Worbois*

Reunion (The Songs of Jimmy Webb) / 1974 / Capitol 11336
Glen Campbell has long been a major supporter of the work of Jimmy Webb. In fact, Webb penned several of Campbell's earliest hits. The quality of this material makes one wonder why more artists don't look to Webb for material. —*Jim Worbois*

★ **Best of** / 1976 / Capitol 11577
This record really does live up to the title. All hits and no filler, covering Campbell's career up through 1976. A nice selection of songs, and it's just right for people who know Campbell for the hits or for someone wanting to get into his music for the first time. —*Jim Worbois*

Country Gold / Jul. 22, 1991 / Liberty 94164
This contains such hits as "Your Cheatin' Heart," "Rose Garden," "Lovesick Blues," and "Help Me Make it Through the Night." —*AMG*

Somebody Like That / 1993 / Capitol 97962
Campbell has always has good taste in songwriters and sidemen, and *Somebody Like That* upholds this tradition, recruiting material from Paul Overstreet, Naomi Martin, and Billy Burnette, among others. Only a couple of ballads are given schmaltzy arrangements; for the most part the tracks choogle along in midtempo, semi-rockabilly fashion. Best bets here are "Swimming Upstream, Ain't It Just Like Love" and (especially) the chorus-kicking title track, "For Love's Old Song," in which Campbell indulges in some jazzy country-swing.
—*Roch Parisien*

Greatest Country Hits / Curb 77362
A hodge-podge of material from the mid '70s through 1989, this displays a variety of Glen Campbell approaches to country. "She's Gone, Gone, Gone" is twangy enough to do originator Lefty Frizzell justice. "Still Within the Sound of My Voice" catches Campbell at his most sensitive, and "Southern Nights" is just plain fun. —*Tom Roland*

Stacy Dean Campbell

Smooth-voiced singer originally from Carlsbad, New Mexico. —*Brian Mansfield*

● **Lonesome Wins Again** / Feb. 1992 / CBS 47872
Sexy, low-key rockabilly (like Chris Isaak but not as spooky). Includes the singles "Rosalee," "Baby Don't You Know," and "Poor Man's Rose." —*Brian Mansfield*

Paulette Carlson

Best known as the lead singer for Highway 101, Carlson writes sharply pointed songs with a strong feminine viewpoint, and she sings in a forceful rasp that breaks in all the right places. —*Michael McCall*

● **Love Goes on** / Nov. 11, 1991 / Capitol 97711
Her best songs continue the feisty, I'm-not-gonna-take-it-anymore attitude she flashed so well in Highway 101. However, the collection suffers from overly slick production and a handful of weak songs. —*Michael McCall*

Mary-Chapin Carpenter

b. Feb. 21, 1958, Princeton, NJ
Vocals, guitar / Contemporary country
Born in Princeton, NJ, Carpenter moved to Washington, D.C., in her teens and became a staple of the local folk scene. One of the first artists to break big when country music began to actively court younger listeners in the late '80s, she won the Country Music Association's Female Vocalist of the Year award in 1992 and 1993. —*Brian Mansfield*

Hometown Girl / Feb. 1987 / CBS 40758
Includes "A Road Is Just a Road," "A Lot Like Me," "Family Hands," and other Carpenter favorites. —*AMG*

○ **State of the Heart** / 1989 / CBS 44228
Carpenter, a folkie, eventually turned to the country market, especially on her third album, *Shooting Straight in the Dark.* On this, her second, she's still in transition, which makes her more thoughtful than the average country singer and catchier than the average folkie, especially on her breakthrough country hit, "Never Had It So Good." Also includes "Quittin' Time," "Something of a Dreamer," and "How Do." —*William Ruhlman*

○ **Shooting Straight in the Dark** / 1990 / CBS 46077
Carpenter's third album expands on the promise of her breakthrough, with the Searchers-style pop of "Going Out Tonight" and a guest spot from Beausoleil on the Cajun-rooted "Down at the Twist and Shout." It also holds some of her most penetrating, introspective songs, with payoff lines that would impress Elvis Costello. Contains the singles "You Win Again" and "Right Now." —*Brian Mansfield*

● **Come On Come On** / 1992 / CBS 48881
The ultra-serious *Shooting Straight in the Dark* left Carpenter in need of a breather, which she took by covering Dire Straits' "The Bug" and Lucinda Williams' "Passionate Kisses." On "I Feel Lucky," she won the lottery and flirted with Dwight Yoakam and Lyle Lovett in a bar. It's tough to say which she enjoyed more. The line about winning the lottery might have been prescience on Carpenter's part—*Come On Come On* sold more than 2 million copies and generated six hit singles, including "Not Too Much To Ask" with Joe Diffie," "The Hard Way," and the Geritol-inspired "He Thinks He'll Keep Her," her first number one, according to *Billboard.* —*Brian Mansfield*

The Carter Family

Group / Traditional country
The most influential group in country music history, the Carter Family switched the emphasis from hillbilly instrumentals to vocals, made scores of their songs part of the standard country music canon, and made a style of guitar-playing, "Carter-picking," the dominant technique for decades. For nearly 70 years the Carters' "Wildwood Flower" was first victim of most young country people learning to play the guitar. In 1970 the Original Carter Family became the first group elected to the Country Music Hall of Fame.

In a remarkable coincidence, from Aug. 1 through 4, 1927, the first two stars ("superstars" in today's inflation) were recorded in Bristol, TN, by an RCA scout looking for rural talent. One was the great Mississippi Blue Yodeler, Jimmie Rodgers; the other was a family group consisting of Alvin P. Carter, his wife Sara, and their sister-in-law, Maybelle. These three—a gaunt, shy gospel quartet member and two reserved country girls—sang a pure, simple harmony that influenced not only the numerous other family groups of the '30s and the '40s, but also Woody Guthrie, Bill Monroe, the Kingston Trio, Doc Watson, Bob Dylan, and Emmylou Harris, to mention just a few. It's unlikely that bluegrass music would have existed without the Carter family.

A.P., the family patriarch, collected hundreds of British/Appalachian folk songs and, in arranging these for recording, both enhanced the pure beauty of these "facts-of-life tunes" and at the same time saved them for future generations. The hundreds of songs the trio found around their Virginia and Tennessee homes, after being sung by A. P., Sara, and Maybelle, became *Carter* songs, even though they were folksongs and in the public domain. Among the more than 300 sides they recorded are "Worried Man Blues," "Wabash Cannonball," "Will the Circle Be Unbroken," "Wildwood Flower," and "Keep on the Sunny Side," their radio theme.

The Carter Family's instrumental backup, like their vocals, was unique. On her Gibson L-5 guitar, Maybelle played a bass-strings lead (the guitar being tuned down from the standard pitch) that is the mainstay of bluegrass guitarists to this day. Sara accompanied her on the autoharp or on a second guitar, while A.P. devoted his talent to singing a haunting though idiosyncratic bass or baritone. Although the original Carter Family disbanded in 1943, enough of their recordings remained in the vaults to keep the group current through the '40s. Maybelle, through a Flatt and Scruggs album of Carter material, found a new and younger audience in the '60s; her work on the famous three-record album *Will the Circle Be Unbroken* (under the aegis of the Nitty Gritty Dirt Band), blended old-guard country with new, restoring to her the fame of 40 years earlier. This time, though, the audience was predominantly urban and educated. *—David Vinopal*

☆ **'Mid the Green Fields of Virginia** / 1963 / RCA 1107
The Carter Family was the most important group in early country music, and this 16-track album selects some of their most notable initial recordings from the late 1920s and early '30s, among them "My Clinch Mountain Home" and their theme song "Keep on the Sunny Side." *—William Ruhlmann*

Diamonds in the Rough / 1990 / Copper Creek 107
Subtitled *Heart Songs, Hymns & Ballads as Featured on Border Radio in 1941*, this radio transcriptions reissue of the Carter Family's appearances on the legendary Del Rio border radio stations in 1938 is a fine representation of their repertoire of songs about home, hearth, and heartbreak. *—Mark A. Humphrey*

★ **Country Music Hall of Fame** / 1991 / MCA 10088
After the Depression, the Carters (originally on RCA-Victor) recorded for Decca Records. Their music was little changed from the earlier decade, though a slight Hispanic influence wafts through the lovely "You Are My Flower." This 16-track collection of 1936-1938 recordings is certainly quintessential Carter Family—simultaneously parlor delicate and oak-post solid. *—Mark A. Humphrey*

★ **Anchored in Love** / 1993 / Rounder 1064
The first volume in Rounder's chronicling of the Carter Family's complete Victor recordings starts at the beginning with the debut recordings from Bristol, TN in 1927 that changed country music forever. Including the original versions of "Keep On The Sunny Side," "Wildwood Flower," and "Little Darling Pal Of Mine," this is country music on the ground floor. *—Cub Koda*

☆ **My Clinch Mountain Home—Their Complete Victor Recordings, 1928-1929** / Oct. 1, 1993 / Rounder 1065
A.P. Carter, his wife Sara and her cousin Maybelle were now established RCA Victor recording artists by the time these 1928-1929 recordings were made. But the music is no less real, raw and compelling. Highlights include the title track, "I'm Thinking Tonight of My Blue Eyes," and "Forsaken Love." *—Cub Koda*

○ **Clinch Mountain Treasures** / County 112
These songs are treasures, but they're not among the seminal group's best-known songs. Recorded for Okeh Records in Chicago in 1940, this album captures the group's instrumentation and vocals at their most incisive. *—Michael McCall*

○ **Early Classics** / ACM 015
Features "The Cannonball," "Ain't Gonna Work Tomorrow," "Meet Me by the Moonlight," and other country standards. *—AMG*

○ **The Original Carter Family** /
Features radio transcriptions from 1936. *—AMG*

Pickin' & Singin' Together /
A.P. and Sara Carter perform Carter Family hits with A.L. and Kathleen Phipps on this reissue of an album originally recorded in 1954. *—AMG*

Carlene Carter

b. Sep. 26, 1955, Nashville, TN
Vocals / Country
Her musical pedigree (daughter of Carl Smith, a star singer and Opry standout in the '50s, and June Carter Cash, of the Carter Family and wife of Johnny Cash; and granddaughter of Mother Maybelle) made Carlene Carter the epitome of female country cool the minute she released her first record (*Carlene Carter*, Warner, 1978). She never really accepted Nashville's terms, preferring instead to record in places like London with musicians from The Rumour and Rockpile (Nick Lowe was Carter's third husband). She recorded sporadically through the '80s, with better press than sales, but she finally got it all together in 1990 with *I Fell in Love*, an across-the-board country hit. *—Brian Mansfield & David Vinopal*

Carlene Carter / 1978 / Warner Brothers 3204
This album was released in the middle of the "new wave" movement and is interesting, in part, because of the meeting of the artist with the country music background and new-wavers Graham Parker and The Rumour. Somewhat uneven but still worth owning. *—Jim Worbois*

Two Sides to Every Woman / 1979 / Warner Brothers 3375
This is Carter's second album and not as interesting as the first. Some of the songs are a bit weak and The Rumour have been replaced with studio musicians. *—Jim Worbois*

○ **Musical Shapes** / 1980 / Warner Brothers 3465
This is Carter's masterpiece to date. Great songs and production that could easily fit into today's climate of country radio. *—Cub Koda*

Blue Nun / 1981 / F Beat 12
Carter's American label passed on this one, and it's too bad. While not one of her best albums, but when she's on, she's dead on. Interesting from a historical point because it somewhat chronicles her musical associations with former husband Nick Lowe and with Paul Carrack (ex-Ace, Squeeze, Mike + the Mechanics). *—Jim Worbois*

● **I Fell in Love** / 1990 / Reprise 26139
A comeback album with a perfect mix of old (A.P. Carter's "My Dixie Darlin'") and new (guest spots from Dave Edmunds, David Lindley, and Albert Lee). If Carter hasn't come to terms with her love for rock and her duty to heritage, she's at least learned to balance them. *—Brian Mansfield*

○ **Little Love Letters** / 1993 / Giant 24499
This is the album fans always dreamed she would make. While it shows off her love of, and ability to handle, various styles of music, she never loses her direction. *—Jim Worbois*

Lionel Cartwright

Vocals / Country
Cartwright starred on The Nashville Network's TV series "Pickin' at the Paradise," and also was the songwriter, musical director, and arranger of the show. His first hit in 1988 was "You're Gonna Make Her Mine." *—AMG*

● **Lionel Cartwright** / 1989 / MCA 42276
Produced by Tony Brown and Steuart Smith (formerly Rodney Crowell's lead guitarist) Cartwright's debut disc is still his best. Includes the hits "Like Father Like Son" and "Give Me His Last Chance." *—Dan Cooper*

I Watched It on the Radio / 1990 / MCA 42336
Features "My Heart Is Set on You," "Say It's Not True," "In the Long Run," and other hits. *—AMG*

Chasin' the Sun / 1991 / MCA 10307
This album has such hits as "30 Nothin'" and "What Kind of Fool." *—AMG*

Johnny Cash

b. Feb. 26, 1932, Kingsland, AR
Vocals, guitar / Traditional country

It is almost un-American to dislike Johnny Cash. He sings songs about trains and God and farmers and Indians. And he's been around forever. Wasn't "I Walk the Line" in the '50s sometime? And wasn't he in jail for a while? No, he sang in jail—that's right! He's the guy who sang "Folsom Prison Blues." And he's still making records, right? How can you not like him?

The trick is to get past the myth and all the hype and just listen to some of the music.

Pick a period—there are lots to choose from! I'd recommend starting at the beginning, maybe with the aforementioned "I Walk the Line." Or, you might go back several months to the original version of "Folsom Prison Blues." There are no convicts shouting in the background here, but it's a mighty fine record. In fact, many of Cash's early recordings for the Sun label are about as close to perfect as one can imagine. Things couldn't get much simpler, perfectly simple, you might say.

Cash's early 45s—even his first album—feature just Johnny Cash and his two-man band, the Tennessee Two: a minimalist electric guitar and acoustic bass. You might think, "If there are just the two of them, they must do some mighty fancy picking, right?" Put it this way: the musical limitations of the Tennessee Two make Johnny Cash sound like Pavarotti. Rather than embellish Cash's strikingly sparse sound, Sun owner Sam Phillips let the band's "boom-chicka-boom" and Cash's lonely baritone vocals hang in an eerie sea of echo that, just months before, had swathed the vocals of Elvis Presley and Carl Perkins—these were friendly waters. The power of these early records (add *Train of Love* and *Big River* to the list) is unmistakable 35 years after they were made.

To his credit, Johnny Cash's recorded sound has remained almost unchanged across the decades. Like many survivors of the halcyon days at Sun Records, Cash has battled a host of demons including substance abuse and personal tragedies. He has emerged strong and fit for battle. Considering the immense amount of material in his recorded legacy, there is little to be ashamed of. There are few artists with as instantly recognizable a sound and style as Johnny Cash, and few as worthy of the attention of a whole new generation of listeners.

Johnny Cash should be approached chronologically. Stay away from his later (Polygram) work until you've digested his Columbia years (1958 through the mid '80s), and don't enter the Columbia years until you can pass a quiz on his Sun period.

By 1993, Cash felt estranged from the new country movement and successfully freed himself from Polygram to join forces with rock auteur Rick Rubin on American Records. It turned out to be an inspiring decision. —*Hank Davis*

○ **American Recordings** / American Recordings, Inc. 45520
A stark, masterful album featuring Cash and his guitar, this captures the essence of his remarkable, distinctive talent while confirming his stature as one of the most affecting artists of his time. —*Michael McCall*

The Fabulous Johnny Cash / 1958 / Sony 8122
His first Columbia album. —*Hank Davis*

○ **Now, There Was a Song!** / 1960 / CBS 8254
An outstanding album of covers of old country songs, from the familiar (Ernest Tubb, Hank Williams, George Jones) to lesser-known gems. —*Michael McCall*

Ride This Train / 1960 / Sony 8255
An early concept album detailing Cash's love of trains and Americana. —*Hank Davis*

Blood Sweat & Tears / 1963 / CBS 8730
Continuing his early 1960s focus on concept albums, this one pays tribute to the working man. Includes the hit "Busted." —*Michael McCall*

○ **Bitter Tears** / 1964 / CBS 9048
Another concept album, this one devoted to the trials of the American Indian—a bold move for a country singer in 1964. —*Michael McCall*

○ **Ballads of the True West** / 1965 / CBS 838
A two-album set of songs honoring cowboys, pioneers and western lore. Inspired by Marty Robbins, but starker than his work. —*Michael McCall*

Rockabilly Blues / 1980 / CBS 36779
Not as earth-shaking as his work with the Tennessee Two, and not really true rockabilly, but a convincing album of country-rock

songs with more depth than nearly anything else coming from Nashville at the time. —*Michael McCall*

○ **Johnny 99** / 1983 / CBS 25471
If the Springsteen tunes hadn't been included, this would still have been a good album. But Cash sinks his teeth into "Highway Patrolman" and the title tune and gives them the guts that Springsteen only dreamed of. —*Jim Worbois*

● **Up through the Years 1955-1957** / 1986 / Bear Family 15247
An excellent compilation of Cash's Sun singles. —*AMG*

★ **Columbia Years 1958-1986** / 1987 / CBS 40637
An excellent overview of Cash's middle period with all the hits (like "Ring of Fire") as well as early lonesome tracks like "I Still Miss Someone." —*Hank Davis*

○ **Come Along and Ride This Train** / 1991 / Bear Family 15563
The 4 CDs in this set contain 87 tracks originally released on 7 albums 1960-1977, all about life in the USA. Selections include "The Gettysburg Address," "Casey Jones," "From Sea to Shining Sea," "Busted," and many more. —*AMG*

○ **The Man in Black (1959-1962)** / Bear Family 15562
For the serious Cash collector. Five CDs and a book detailing all of his Sun sessions, outtakes—warts and all—and his initial Columbia work. A unique behind-the-scenes glimpse. Superbly produced. —*Hank Davis*

Rosanne Cash

b. May 24, 1955, Memphis, TN
Vocals, guitar / Contemporary country
Reba McEntire sells more records, but Rosanne Cash, the daughter of Johnny Cash, may be the greatest woman currently working in country. Her brand of art, however, has never been confined to the cut-and-dried traditions of C&W, nor can she be pigeonholed as an "outlaw" upstart. Cash works within the context of country much as did Bob Wills: by bringing her unique perspectives to the genre, she has somehow eclipsed it, changing its patterns to suit her creative needs, tailoring it to encompass the complexities of her vision.

Her first hit, the self-penned "Seven Year Ache," was a crossover smash for several reasons; the sentiments of the song contradicted the roles enforced on female country artists, and the backbeat had more in common with Bonnie Raitt than Kitty Wells. Although many of her best personality-defining songs have come from outside writers, in recent years Cash has blossomed into a clever and soul-searching songwriter. 1990's *Interiors*, produced and written entirely by Cash, uncompromisingly picked apart the disintegration of her marriage to Rodney Crowell. It remains a moody, unsettling masterpiece. At her best, Cash sounds like a meeting of Patsy Cline, Joni Mitchell, and Chrissie Hynde: she has a full-bodied vocal style reminiscent of Cline's; she manifests her emotions with the persistence of Mitchell; and she has the confidence and attitude of Hynde. —*John Floyd*

Right or Wrong / 1979 / CBS 36155
Cash's impressive debut featured a solid collection of Nashville-meets-California singer/songwriter country-rock, with occasional stylistic nods to folk and light R&B. "No Memories Hangin' 'Round" was a hit duet with Bobby Bare, and "Couldn't Do Nothin' Right" and "Take Me Take Me" also charted. Other highlights include "Man Smart Woman Smarter," "Better Start Turnin' 'Em Down," and the aching ballad "Anybody's Darlin' (Anything but Mine)," one of the finest performances of her career. —*Rick Clark*

★ **Seven Year Ache** / 1981 / CBS 36965
Cash was arguably the most important artist to emerge in country music in the early '80s, and this was her breakthrough album, which introduced a new, assertive, passionate stance to women in country and also helped foster the crossover between folk, rock, and country. Cash's songwriting (the title track and "Blue Moon with a Heartache") was first-rate, and her choices from others, notably Leroy Preston's "My Baby Thinks He's a Train," were equally strong. —*William Ruhlmann*

Somewhere in the Stars / 1982 / CBS 37570
A terrific collection, including Rodney Crowell's "Ain't No Money," and Tom T. Hall's "That's How I Got to Memphis." —*William Ruhlmann*

Rhythm & Romance / 1985 / CBS 39463

Cash expected criticism for this album, and got it but didn't deserve it. The orange hair and pink fingernails on the cover visually illustrate the musical risks she took in working with Eddie Rabbitt's former producer, David Malloy, and the result is a scorcher. Best cuts: Grammy-winner "I Don't Know Why You Don't Want Me," and "Halfway House." —*Tom Roland*

King's Record Shop / 1988 / CBS 40777
After writing most of 1985's *Rhythm & Romance*, Cash returned to largely interpretive work in this powerful collection highlighted by Eliza Gilkyson's feminist anthem "Rosie Strike Back" and her father Johnny Cash's "Tennessee Flat Top Box." —*William Ruhlmann*

Hits 1979-1989 / 1989 / CBS 45054
Ten years' worth of hits, including "I Don't Want to Spoil the Party," "Seven Year Ache," "Black and White," and others. —*AMG*

☆ **Interiors** / 1990 / CBS 46079
What makes *Interiors* brilliant isn't that Cash produced herself for the first time nor that she wrote all the songs. It's that *Interiors*—the last album Cash made for Columbia's Nashville division—meticulously chronicles the unraveling of a terribly dysfunctional relationship, namely Cash's marriage to Rodney Crowell. Cash gets at the psychology behind country's cheating and drinking themes—the emotional anesthetic of addictions, the desperate grasping for love in affairs. The arrangements are stripped as bare as Cash's soul, but *Interiors* is country at its core. —*Brian Mansfield*

○ **The Wheel** / Jan. 19, 1993 / CBS 52729
After the gloomy *Interiors*, *The Wheel* is positively sunny, full of sweet melodies and excellent playing. However, if you look beneath the surface, it becomes clear that while this is a more positive album, its cautiously optimistic, which is what makes its pleasures all the more satisfying. —*AMG*

Beth Nielsen Chapman

Vocals / Country, singer/songwriter
A Nashville-based singer/songwriter who has written several Number 1 country hits, her own work leans more toward contemporary adult pop. Her songs are melodic, her themes mostly romantic and obsessed with inner journeys. Comparable to Carole King or the earnest side of Elton John, her range covers insistent pop rock, intimate ballads, sensual soul, and solemn spirituals—all done with an undercurrent of revelation and intelligence. —*Michael McCall*

Hearing It First / 1980 / Capitol
Produced by Barry Beckett, the album reveals a young, raw talent. —*Michael McCall*

● **Beth Nielsen Chapman** / Sep. 25, 1990 / Reprise 26172
Chapman moved to Nashville in 1985, and the influence of the city's focus on songcraft helped her hone her poetic sensibilities into powerful, personal pop tunes. Includes a strong version of "Down on My Knees," a song covered by country singer Trisha Yearwood. —*Michael McCall*

○ **You Hold the Key** / Reprise 45233
The arrangements are peppier, but the subject matter as intensely internal as on her previous album. —*Michael McCall*

Mark Chesnutt

Vocals / Traditional country
The son of a country singer, Mark Chesnutt grew up in his father's footsteps. He started singing at Gilley's (the club *Urban Cowboy* made famous), at 17, and cut independent singles before signing to MCA. His debut album, 1990's *Too Cold at Home*, made him a dark-horse hit act, as he was initially overshadowed by the success of Garth Brooks and Clint Black. On his second album, the humor and personality in his delivery showed through, and Chesnutt made a name for himself with the likes of "Old Flames Have New Names" and "I'll Think of Something." —*Brian Mansfield*

○ **Too Cold at Home** / 1990 / MCA 10032
An impressive traditional country debut that often drew on George Jones and Texas swing, *Too Cold at Home* started Chesnutt off strong with the hits "Too Cold at Home," "Brother Jukebox," "Blame It on Texas," and "Your Love Is a Miracle." It also included a version of "Friends in Low Places" that came out

at almost exactly the same time Garth Brooks' did. —*Brian Mansfield*

● **Longnecks & Short Stories** / 1992 / MCA 10530
Longnecks heralded the emergence of a Texas voice that contained both the knack for humor ("Old Flames Have New Names," "Bubba Shot the Jukebox"), and the depth for heartache ("I'll Think of Something"). —*Brian Mansfield*

Almost Goodbye / MCA 10851
Weak material weighs down Chesnutt's third release, though he still sings them like the most romantic Western swinger since George Strait. "Almost Goodbye" is backed by a string arrangement as powerful as the one on "I'll Think of Something," but songs like "Texas Is Bigger" and "My Heart's Too Broke" aren't the attention-grabbers "Old Flames Have New Names" and "Bubba Shot the Jukebox" were. One of Chesnutt's biggest strengths is his casual delivery, but *Almost Goodbye* sounds too easy. "Almost Goodbye" and "It Sure Is Monday" both topped the singles charts. —*Brian Mansfield*

Circus Maximus

Group / Country
A precursor to the cosmic cowboy movement, this folk rock outfit had more than a touch of psychedelia and plenty of country. Jerry Jeff Walker got his start here. "The Wind" was a minor hit for the band. —*Bruce Eder*

● **Circus Maximus W/ Jerry Jeff Walker** / 1967 / Vanguard 79260
The psychedelic roots of progressive country music. —*Robert Gordon*

Never Land Revisited / 1968 / Vanguard 79274
If you ever wondered what the Byrds or Moby Grape might have sounded like with Jerry Jeff Walker as a member, this could be the answer. While the style is similar, the quality isn't there. Not as good as the first album. —*Jim Worbois*

Guy Clark

b. Nov. 6, 1941, Rockport, TX
Vocals, guitar / Country
Guy Clark was one of the founding fathers of the Texas singer/songwriter movement in Austin, TX, along with Waylon Jennings, Willie Nelson, Jerry Jeff Walker, and Townes Van Zandt. His musical influences have been strong, leading such musicians as Nanci Griffith, Robert Earl Keen Jr., Darden Smith, Lyle Lovett, and Hugh Moffatt to speak his praise. —*Chip Renner*

● **Old #1** / 1975 / Sugar Hill 1030
Every song is a classic. Clark is backed by Chip Young, Steve Gibson, Johnny Gimble, Rodney Crowell, Emmylou Harris, Steve Earle, and others. Start your collection here. —*Chip Renner*

Texas Cookin' / 1976 / Sugar Hill 1031
These songs are more Nashville, hitting many emotions. "Texas Cookin'," "Virginia's Reel," and "Broken Hearted" are all great songs. What a way to finish the album, as Clark and Johnny Cash sing "The Last Gunfighter Ballad." —*Chip Renner*

○ **Fool on the Roof** / 1978 / Warner Brothers 3241
This very overlooked album is more country than his first two RCA albums. Just listen to the vocals (with the Whites, Rodney Crowell, Don Everly, Gordon Payne) and the words. You'll find this album grows on you. —*Chip Renner*

The South Coast of Texas / 1981 / Warner Brothers 3381
A solid album. Check out Rosanne Cash's vocals on "Cystelle." Vince Gill, Ricky Skaggs, and Rodney Crowell give this record a real polished sound. —*Chip Renner*

Better Days / 1983 / Warner Brothers 123880
Produced by Rodney Crowell, this contains some of Clark's trademark songs, like "The Carpenter," "Homegrown Tomatoes," and the tear-jerker "The Randal Knife." —*Chip Renner*

○ **Old Friends** / 1989 / Sugar Hill 1025
Clark's finest moment. The production allows Clark to present his songs without any distractions. Sam Bush, Verlon Thompson, Michael Henderson, and Vince Gill blend with Clark perfectly, as do Rosanne Cash and Emmylou Harris. —*Chip Renner*

○ **Boats to Build** / 1992 / Elektra 61442
As unadorned and uncontrived as ever, Clark's masterful songs get to the heart of the matter and stay there. —*Michael McCall*

Roy Clark

b. Apr. 15, 1933, Meherrin, VA
Vocals, banjo, guitar, fiddle / Traditional country, country-pop
In the '70s Roy Clark symbolized country music in the United States and abroad. Between guest-hosting for Johnny Carson on "The Tonight Show" and performing to packed houses in the Soviet Union on a tour that sold out all 18 concerts, he used his musical talent and his entertaining personality to bring country music into homes across the world. As one of the hosts of TV's "Hee Haw" (Buck Owens was the other), for more than 20 years Clark picked and sang and offered kountry korn to 30 million people weekly. He is first and foremost an entertainer, drawing crowds at venues as different as Las Vegas, Atlantic City, and the Opry. His middle-of-the-road approach has filled a national void, with Clark offering music more country than Kenny Rogers but less country than Waylon Jennings. Among his numerous vocal hits are "Yesterday When I was Young" and "Thank God and Greyhound." Instrumentally he has won awards for both guitar and banjo. Multi-talented Clark co-starred on the silver screen with Mel Tillis, in the comedy *Uphill All the Way.* Roy Clark's popularity will continue as long as he wants to stay in the business. Bob Hope refers to Clark as "the consummate entertainer."
—David Vinopal

The Tip of My Fingers / 1963 / CEMA 8305
This album features "My Baby's Gone," "Silver Threads & Golden Needles," "Faded Love," and "Take Me As I Am," among others. — *AMG*

● **The Best of Roy Clark** / 1971 / Curb 77395
Compilation of Clark's earlier (pre-"Hee Haw") hits, including "Yesterday When I Was Young" and "Tips of My Fingers." *—Cub Koda*

○ **In Concert** / 1976 / MCA 37132
Nice sampling of Clark's stage show, great guitar playing, corny jokes and all. *—Cub Koda*

Patsy Cline (Virginia Patterson Hensley)

b. Sep. 8, 1932, Gore, VA, d. Mar. 5, 1963 , Camden, TN
Vocals, piano / Country-pop
Before she died in an airplane crash in 1963, Patsy Cline had the best of both worlds, country and pop. By avoiding the country & western mold and appealing to fans more accustomed to middle-of-the-road music, she changed the course of country music and ushered in a new era for country female singers—one that dominates today. Cline's quality voice was perfect for torch songs—emotional yet distant and cool at the same time. In 1957 she won an Arthur Godfrey Talent Scout TV contest, singing "Walkin' after Midnight." The single became both a country and a pop hit, creating a pattern Cline followed throughout her brief career. In 1960 she joined the Opry and saw her first smash hit, "I Fall to Pieces," a song backed by many strings and voices. Her producers continued marketing her to the pop audience, and very successfully, with similar hits to follow, including "Crazy" (written by Willie Nelson), "She's Got You," and "Leavin' on Your Mind." Even after her death, the songs were hits, among them "Faded Love," "Sweet Dreams (of You)," and "Anytime" (1969).

Oddly enough, Cline entered the country-pop market against her wishes. She liked to yodel, wore cowgirl outfits into the early 60s, and detested some of her biggest hit songs. But she has become a legend and has influenced more modern female singers than all others combined. What a great voice ... .*—David Vinopal*

Patsy Cline Showcase / 1961 / MCA 87
Pop and C&W standards plus three of her biggest hits: "I Fall to Pieces," "Crazy," and "Walkin' after Midnight." *—George Bedard*

★ **Patsy Cline's Greatest Hits** / 1967 / Decca 74854
This is the standard collection of Patsy Cline's most successful singles, containing among its 12 tracks 7 of her8 Top 10 country hits, from 1957 to 1963. Since its release, the album has sold 4 million copies. *—William Ruhlmann*

Live at the Opry / 1988 / MCA 42142
As everyone who listened to the Ryman opry knows, even a good singer can sound pretty bad live over the radio. Cline sounds simply great, with no studio effects and a sometimes pedestrian backup. *—George Bedard*

☆ **The Patsy Cline Collection** / 1991 / MCA 10421

Kitty Wells, Patsy Cline, and Country Women

In 1952, country music met its first bona fide woman star, Kitty Wells, the accepted Queen of Country Music. Patsy Montana had recorded the first million-seller by a woman ("I Want to Be a Cowboy's Sweetheart," 1935), but it was Miss Kitty who in release after release gave the male stars competition. Her first hit, "It Wasn't God Who Made Honky-Tonk Angels" (1952), an answer song to the anti-woman "Wild Side of Life," was in a sense the first women's rights song in country music; Wells and her song made it much easier for other women trying to make it in what had been a man's business. Songs sung from the woman's point of view were thereafter accepted in country music. *Billboard* voted Wells the Top Female Performer in country music from 1952 to 1965; this gives you a sense of how she dominated.

Wells's only real rival was Patsy Cline. Although only 13 years separated them in age (and Owen Bradley was producer for both of them at Decca), a gulf lay between them musically, in song content and in singing style. Wells's twang contrasts with Cline's smooth, un-rural delivery (later to be known as the "Nashville Sound"), and Kitty's honky-tonk content clashes with Cline's modern country crooning (for example, her famous version of "Crazy," a song written by Willie Nelson). Cline took the highly emotional, occasionally rough-sounding characteristics of previous female country singers and urbanized it, in the process losing much of the original soul but making country palatable to a much larger audience. Wells was at the end of the first group of country performers, the pioneers of traditional country, while Cline was at the beginning of what has proven to be modern country.

Few contemporary women singers represent Wells's group (Emmylou Harris often is true to the roots, and Reba McEntire is when she wants to be). The rest, a huge majority, have descended from Cline's camp, and distinguishing between them and pop singers is becoming increasingly difficult. Wells remains in the business she loves, as of this writing appearing frequently with her son and her husband Johnny Wright (of the Opry duet Johnny and Jack). Though Cline died in an airplane crash in 1963, her contemporary sound and two movies about her have kept her as popular now as ever, with a CD breaking the Top 20 album charts in 1992.

– David Vinopal

With 4 hours and 25 minutes of music (104 cuts), this is pretty much the definitive Cline collection. It's got all the hits, 16 previously unreleased tracks (including some live radio transcriptions), even some silliness, like "Tra Le La La La Triangle," but in only ten years of recording, Cline became the most influential female vocalist in country music—so she's worth it. *—Brian Mansfield*

Her First Recordings, Vol. 2: Hungry for Love / Rhino 70049
The second volume contains twelve more cuts, including "Just out of Reach," "Stop the World," and more. *—AMG*

Her First Recordings, Vol. 3: Rockin' Side / Rhino 70050
Twelve more performances, including "Never No More," "I Got a Lot of Rhythm in My Soul," and other numbers, some of which are tinged with rock. *—AMG*

Walkin' Dreams: Her First Recordings, Vol. 1 / Rhino 70048
Three volumes of Cline's work for the 4 Star label. The first contains "Three Cigarettes in an Ashtray," "Walkin' after Midnight" (original version), and 10 other cuts. *—AMG*

Patsy Cline / Everest 302

Another good collection with "Walkin' after Midnight," "Never No More," "Just out of Reach," and "There He Goes." No pop standards. —*George Bedard*

David Allan Coe

b. Sep. 6, 1939, Akron, OH
Vocals, guitar / Traditional country

If you want authenticity in your country singer, try David Allan Coe, who spent 20 years in reform schools and prison, gaining his release in 1967. His songwriting talent is obvious, having written "Would You Lay with Me (In a Field of Stone)" for Tanya Tucker and the workingman's anthem "Take This Job and Shove It" for Johnny Paycheck. Among his charting singles have been "Mona Lisa's Lost Her Smile" and "The Ride," which tells of an otherworldly meeting with Hank Williams. He operates a Willie Nelson and Family general store in Branson, MO. —*David Vinopal*

Longhaired Redneck / 1976 / CBS 33916
This is '70s outlaw country at its most virulent. The tattoos and biker bravado thinly conceal Coe's sentimentality. —*Mark A. Humphrey*

● **Greatest Hits** / 1978 / CBS 35627
All you need to know about this ex-con turned country conman/songwriter. One of country's more intriguing egos from the '70s. —*Mark A. Humphrey*

For the Record—The First 10 Years / 1985 / CBS 39585
An overview of Coe's Columbia sides. —*Mark A. Humphrey*

Mark Collie

Vocals / Traditional country

A native of Waynesboro, TN (between Memphis and Nashville), Collie is a country singer with a rockabilly soul. On a good day he bears a slight resemblance to a young Robert Mitchum and sings like a latter-day Eddie Cochran. —*Brian Mansfield*

Born & Raised in Black & White / 1985 / MCA 10321
The first half of Collie's second album contained some smartly written songs, including "She's Never Coming Back" and "Calloused Hands," but some of the first album's edge had been smoothed off. —*Brian Mansfield*

○ **Hardin County Line** / 1990 / MCA 42333
This honky-tonk rebel's debut evokes the heart of '50s country, with detailed and compassionate songwriting, wildcat vocals, and guitar by James Burton. One song, "Looks Aren't Everything," hit the Top 40, while two others, "Hardin County Line" and "Something With a Ring to It," didn't fare quite so well. —*John Floyd & Brian Mansfield*

● **Mark Collie** / 1993 / MCA 10658
At once a move to the mainstream and a return to Collie's West Tennessee rockabilly roots. Works fairly well, too—"Even the Man in the Moon Is Crying" and "Born To Love You" were Collie's first Top 10 hits, and "Shame Shame Shame Shame" rocks as hard as anything he's done. —*Brian Mansfield*

Unleashed / 1994 / MCA
In the same vein as *Mark Collie* but more aggressive. "It Is No Secret" followed in Collie's tradition of midtempo romantic singles, while he rocks it up elsewhere. —*Brian Mansfield*

Confederate Railroad

Originally known as The Danny Shirley Band, a six-piece Southern rock/country favorite in the Chattanooga, TN/Atlanta, GA. region. For awhile, the group worked as house band at the popular Miss Kitty's country venue in Atlanta, GA. Shirley signed to Atlantic as a solo act, adding the group persona to differentiate the act from the glut of male singers in the early '90s. The group's redneck/biker/country image has put them at home on tours with the likes of Lynyrd Skynyrd and Hank Williams Jr. —*Brian Mansfield*

● **Notorious** / Atlantic 82505
Despite its unkempt, biker image, Confederate Railroad is a country band in the tradition of Alabama. Rooted in traditional country sounds and values, both bands also have the breadth to appeal to those outside the genre, in CR's case, Southern rockers. The group rocks hardest on the funny stuff ("Elvis & Andy," "Move Over Madonna") but gets serious with some impressive ballads ("Daddy Never Was the Cadillac Kind," "Summer in Dixie," "Three Verses"). —*Brian Mansfield*

Confederate Railroad / 1992 / Atlantic 82335
Features "Queen of Memphis," "Time Off for Bad Behavior," and "She Took It like a Man," among other hits. —*AMG*

John Conlee

b. Aug. 11, 1946, Versailles, KY
Vocals, guitar / Country

Born and raised on a 200-acre farm in Versailles, KY, Conlee has continued to till the soil on his own farm in suburban Nashville, even since "hitting it big." Music was—and still is—a hobby as much as a career to him; he didn't even sign his first recording contract until age 30. Instead, he pursued work as a mortician (he still maintains his license) in Kentucky and worked as a disc jockey at a number of radio stations, including Nashville's WLAC, where he made numerous contacts on Music Row. One of his tapes attracted ABC Records, but Conlee's gruff, down-to-earth delivery wasn't an immediate success. It took a couple of years before "Rose Colored Glasses"—one of the few songs he's written himself—exploded in 1978. A self-avowed homebody, Conlee was never particularly enamored with touring, and devoted most of his career time to the recording process instead, particularly his song selection. Noted for an astute sense of quality material (he was ably assisted through the bulk of his career by record producer and former Jim Reeves sideman Bud Logan), he made albums that rarely, if ever, contained "fluff." Even when they're not commercial, Conlee's songs are always interesting. —*Tom Roland*

With Love / 1981 / MCA 1981
Nine of the ten cuts in this package came from Tree Publishing, meaning that Conlee and producer Bud Logan limited themselves unnecessarily. But Conlee is extremely convincing on "Only Oklahoma Away" and "What's Forever For," not to mention the mysterious "Miss Emily's Picture." —*Tom Roland*

● **John Conlee's Greatest Hits** / 1983 / MCA 31229
Simple, slice-of-life statements about the real world, the songs cover (in)fidelity ("She Can't Say That Anymore," "Baby, You're Something"), relationship issues ("Friday Night Blues"), and personal finance ("Busted," "Common Man"). The asylum piece, "I Don't Remember Loving You," is eternally vivid. —*Tom Roland*

Earl Thomas Conley

b. Oct. 17, 1941, Portsmouth, OH
Vocals / Country

Early in his career, ETC's music picked up the label "thinking man's country." An accurate description—Conley looks into the heart and soul of his characters, finding the motivations for their actions and beliefs. In the process, the astute listener can find fragments of him/herself in nearly any Conley creation. Born into poverty in Portsmouth, OH, Conley struggled with the limits of his social class. He aspired to be a painter or actor but found that his aspirations for music lingered after the other interests died down. Influenced by everything from Hank Williams to the Eagles, Conley delved into the details of writing, trying to learn the craft by following the rules and regulations of the Music Row songwriting community. Eventually, torn by the limits of the "law," he found his own niche by breaking many of those same rules. His public self-analysis—in both his songs and his interviews—has proven inspirational to some, bothersome to others, but Conley has evolved stylistically, even though the thinking man label continues to follow him. He's admittedly chased a more commercial sound, with a certain degree of success, but the run for the dollars also put him into a financial bind. He spent part of the late '80s and early '90s overworking himself to pay off his debts. Although he has been a hitmaker for more than a decade, his contributions to country have often gone almost unnoticed. —*Tom Roland*

Blue Pearl / 1980 / Sunbird 1980
The album that earned Conley the thinking man label. "Middle-Age Madness" and "Blue and Green" stand out as classically written profiles of people in pain. "Silent Treatment," "Fire and Smoke," and "You Don't Have to Go Too Far" possess a captivating, slick sheen that belies their raw approach. —*Tom Roland*

○ **Don't Make It Easy for Me** / 1983 / RCA 6913
Conley speaks of "programming" himself to write, and in setting the tone for this album—as well as the followup, *Treadin' Water*—he programmed "radio records" into his consciousness. The result: a driving, rock-inflected package that yielded four Number 1

singles—the first time an album did that in any format. The title track and "Your Love's on the Line" are particularly listenable, but there's not a bad cut on it. —*Tom Roland*

● **The Best of Earl Thomas Conley, Vol. 1** / 1988 / RCA 6700
As much as any of his 1980s peers, Conley might have benefited from moving his sound towards harder country. The hits he did score ("Fire & Smoke," and "Somewhere Between Right and Wrong," among the ones on this album) projected a voice ideally suited to a more Whitley-esque setting. —*Dan Cooper*

The Heart of It All / 1988 / RCA 6824
This album contains "What I'd Say," "What She Is," "We Believe in Happy Endings," "You Must Not Be Drinking Enough," and other hits. —*AMG*

○ **Greatest Hits, Vol. 2** / 1990 / RCA 2043
Conley was one of the hottest recording artists of the '80s. While this album isn't quite as strong as the first hits package, it shouldn't be ignored. Also features two new tracks. —*Jim Worbois*

Stoney and Wilma Lee Cooper

b. , Harman, West Virginia
Group / Traditional country
Stoney (b. 1918) and Wilma Lee Cooper (b. 1921), a husband-and-wife Opry act, were famed for their powerful stage presence and their authentic material that fell between mountain folk music and bluegrass. Since fiddler Stoney's death, Wilma has continued on the Opry. When she sings a song, it stays sung. —*David Vinopal*

● **Classic Early Recordings** / County
Originally recorded between 1949 and 1953, this wife-and-husband duo let it fly with passionate zeal on these old-time mountain and gospel songs. Wilma Lee could shake the coal out of the hills with her raw and full-throated voice, and she doesn't bother with nuance. —*Michael McCall*

○ **The Carter Family's Greatest Hits** /
Features "You Are My Flower," "Worried Man Blues," "Hello Central Give Me Heaven," "Wildwood Flower," and other hits. —*AMG*

Billy "Crash" Craddock

b. Jun. 16, 1959, Greensboro, NC
Vocals, guitar / Country
People often associate the "Crash" nickname with auto racing, but Craddock actually got it as a halfback in high school, crashing into linemen who were twice his size. Growing up in Greensboro, NC, he pantomimed Grand Ole Opry shows in the family's barn with a broomstick as a microphone, alternately pretending he was Hank Williams, Faron Young, or Carl Smith. But when he signed a recording contract in the late '50s, Columbia tried to mold him as a teen idol, much like Elvis Presley or Fabian. It didn't work in the United States, but "Crash" did pick up a trio of hits in Australia. Fifteen years later, he finally got his chance in country music when record producer Ron Chancey signed him onto his Cartwheel label. With a knack for making re-makes of pop hits like "Knock Three Times" and "Ruby Baby"—and for adding a certain energy to the country idiom—Craddock picked up the nickname "Mr. Country Rock." —*Tom Roland*

● **Sings His Greatest Hits** / 1978 / MCA 663
A good summation of his peak years, including the ballads "Easy As Pie" and "Broken Down in Tiny Pieces." But Craddock's at his best when he's "in the groove," as in "Ruby Baby," "Still Thinkin' 'bout You," and his staple, "Rub It In." —*Tom Roland*

Rodney Crowell

b. Aug. 7, 1950, Houston, TX
Vocals, guitar / Country-rock, contemporary country
The consummate singer/songwriter, Crowell "grew up in Houston off of Wayside Drive" (as he says in the lyrics of Waylon Jennings's "I Ain't Living Long Like This"), latching onto everything from Hank Williams to Chuck Berry and Elvis Presley. He played as a kid in his dad's local band, and packed up with friend Donivan Cowart (now a successful engineer) to move to Nashville, lured by a "promoter's" promise of an opening slot on a major concert tour with a name entertainer. Once he got there, he realized he'd been "taken," but Crowell decided to stay, and worked his way up from lounge singer to membership in

Emmylou Harris' Hot Band. From there, he earned a reputation for his evaluation of material and for his arranging "smarts," and picked up plenty of action as a songwriter and producer. His production credits include projects with now-ex-wife Rosanne Cash, Guy Clark, Bobby Bare, and Sissy Spacek, while his songwriting includes: "Leaving Louisiana in the Broad Daylight," "Somewhere Tonight," "Til I Gain Control Again," and "Shame on the Moon." Despite critical acclaim for his recording efforts, Crowell was unable to harness commercial success for a decade, but that problem ended with 1988's *Diamonds & Dirt* album. —*Tom Roland*

Aint Living Long Like This / 1978 / Warner Brothers 3228
Before Rodney Crowell began to have hits of his own, his albums were often raided by other artists for hits. This album features Crowell compositions that became hits for the Oak Ridge Boys, the Nitty Gritty Dirt Band, and Waylon Jennings. It's worth checking out to hear how they were originally done. —*Jim Worbois*

Rodney Crowell / 1981 / Warner Brothers 3587
Crowell plays down his performance on this album. Yes, he's a bit cool toward the material vocally on occasion, but the overall effect is raw, energetic, and natural, in the best garage-band tradition. A good mix of club rock & roll and country-rock, with, incidentally, his own renditions of "Till I Gain Control Again" and "Shame on the Moon." —*Tom Roland*

○ **Keys to the Highway** / 1989 / CBS 45242
Wide-ranging set, combining soul, blues, rock, and the country shuffle. Recorded shortly after the May 1989 death of Crowell's father, it's surprisingly upbeat and hopeful in its approach. Still, the two brooding songs most closely linked to James Crowell's passing, "Many a Long & Lonesome Highway" and "Things I Wish I'd Said," stand out most. —*Tom Roland*

● **The Rodney Crowell Collection** / 1989 / Warner Brothers 25965
The best of Crowell's uneven but occasionally brilliant early recordings condensed into one neat little package. Includes "Shame on the Moon," which Bob Seger rightly turned into a pop hit. This isn't *Diamonds & Dirt*, but it's a good start. —*Brian Mansfield*

○ **Diamonds & Dirt** / 1989 / CBS 44076
Record producer Tony Brown convinced Crowell to do this one quickly and not second-guess himself; the advice paid off. Leaning hard on the country shuffle, Crowell broke through with this package—live, honest, and unassuming. It yielded five hits, including the Grammy-winning "After All This Time," but the best cut might be the tantalizing "I Know You're Married." —*Tom Roland*

Life Is Messy / May 12, 1992 / CBS 47985
Features "It's Not for Me to Judge," "I Hardly Know How to Be Myself," "Lovin' All Night," and more. —*AMG*

Let the Picture Paint Itself / 1994 / MCA 11042
Since so much of Crowell's best work has been coproduced by MCA executive Tony Brown, it seemed inevitable that Crowell would wind up at MCA himself. This, the first release for his new label emphasizes Crowell the thoughtful songwriter over Crowell the neo-honky-tonk bandleader. It's a fair trade, but requires repeat listening to fully appreciate. —*Dan Cooper*

Billy Ray Cyrus

b. , Flatwoods, KY
Vocals, guitar / Contemporary country
Enamored of baseball, Billy Ray Cyrus intended to become another Johnny Bench as he grew up in Flatlands, KY. While attending Georgetown College on a baseball scholarship, he bought a guitar, and decided immediately that athletics wasn't the proper direction for his life. Instead, he formed a band called Sly Dog with his brother and gave himself a ten-month deadline for finding a place to play. One week prior to that cut-off date, the group went to work as the house band for a club in Ironton, OH, where they remained for two years. When a 1984 fire destroyed the bar—and Cyrus's equipment—he moved to Los Angeles to pursue his career. Eventually, he decided to return to Kentucky, and commuted regularly from there to Nashville in search of a record deal. Grand Ole Opry star Del Reeves got Mercury Records to take a look, and division head Harold Shedd signed him in the summer of 1990. When his first album came out in mid-1992, Cryus—with his good looks, sculpted body and the infectious

"Achy, Breaky Heart"—became an instant groundbreaking sensation. —*Tom Roland*

● **Some Gave All** / 1992 / Mercury 510635
Some Gave All became the first debut album by a country artist to enter the pop charts at Number 1 (it hit Number 1 on the country charts as well). The album's sales were fueled by the breakout single "Achy, Breaky Heart," which offered Southern-fried Rolling Stones rhythms and a goofy chorus with a hook so big it demanded a reaction. Not one to eschew the obvious, Cyrus pumped his songs full of as much rock & roll as the market would bear, so songs like "Could've Been Me" and "Never Thought I'd Fall in Love with You" appealed to young fans who had just discovered the possibilities (both musical and sexual) of country music. —*Brian Mansfield*

It Won't Be the Last / Jun. 22, 1993 / PolyGram 14758
Cyrus' followup to his smash debut, *Some Gave All*, offers more of the same—country injected with a healthy dose of rock & roll. It won't win him any new fans, but those who loved *Some Gave All* will enjoy *It Won't Be the Last*. —*AMG*

Lacy J. Dalton (Jill Byrem)

b. Oct. 13, 1948, Bloomsburg, PA
Vocals / Contemporary country
Lacy J. Dalton, who has a voice one writer described as "honey laced with whiskey," took a circuitous route to Nashville. Born Jill Byrem in Bloomsburg, PA, she attended Brigham Young University but dropped out to become folk singer. She kicked around Utah, Minnesota, Pennsylvania, and New York before winding up in front of a psychedelic rock band in San Francisco in the late '60s. She married the group's manager, who died as the result of injuries sustained in a swimming-pool accident. Dalton kept performing, and a tape of her music eventually reached producer Billy Sherrill, who signed her to Columbia in 1979. The Academy of Country Music named her Best New Female Vocalist in 1979 on the strength of her debut, "Crazy Blue Eyes." Dalton's distinct sound and far-ranging musical interests may have kept her from being the star she could have been, but her records helped open doors for new sounds in country. —*Brian Mansfield*

● **Greatest Hits** / 1983 / CBS 38883
Dalton's best songs weren't always her hits, but *Greatest Hits* is still a good sampler, including "Crazy Blue Eyes," her first hit; "Hard Times"; remakes of "Tennessee Waltz" and "Dream Baby"; and the music-biz anthem "16th Avenue." —*Brian Mansfield*

Crazy Love / 1991 / Capitol 94569
The title song is by Van Morrison, and if Dalton is not the vocalist Morrison is, she still may be the best female soul singer country offers—she's a better one than Michael Bolton, whose "Walk Away" she also covers. *Crazy Love* is an appropriate title because Dalton seems genuinely bewildered by the vagaries of the emotion—why her lover loves her ("Crazy Love"), why he leaves her ("Forever in My Heart"), and why sometimes neither marriage nor divorce makes sense. But she's a great singer, not God. —*Brian Mansfield*

Charlies Daniels Band

Group / Traditional country, country-rock
Before there was "The Devil Went Down to Georgia," there was life for Charlie Daniels in bluegrass and as a session player in Nashville (he played on Bob Dylan's *Nashville Skyline* album). In fact, before his 1979 Number 1 hit, he had success in 1975 with "The South's Gonna Do It." The Charlie Daniels Band has built a strong bridge between rock and pure country, playing both with authority. His image symbolizes the good ol' boy who loves his music and his country. His annual Volunteer Jam brings together great musicians from country, rock, jazz, and blues, and has returned to Nashville. —*David Vinopal*

☆ **Fire on the Mountain** / 1975 / Epic 44365
A great slice of country-fried boogie. —*Dan Heilman*

Saddle Tramp / 1976 / Epic 34150
This record provides more variety in song style, tempo, and subject matter than some of Daniels' other records, making it more of a find. Should be of interest to a wider audience. —*Jim Worbois*

● **A Decade of Hits** / 1983 / Epic 38795
An all-too-brief summing-up. —*Dan Heilman*

Simple Man / 1989 / Epic 45316

This album features the title track plus "Play Me Some Fiddle," "Saturday Night Down South," and other hits. —*AMG*

Renegade / 1991 / Epic 46835
Strong collection of Daniels songs rocks harder than usual, despite showing his soft side on "Little Folks" and "Fathers and Sons." Daniels practically gives a cultural history of the violin on "Talk to Me Fiddle," the album's most unusual song, and continues to extol the virtues of country living ("The Twang Factor") and patriotism ("Let Freedom Ring"). —*Brian Mansfield*

○ **At His Best** / 1992 / Hollywood 708
Features such hits as "High Lonesome" and "The South's Gonna Do It Again." —*AMG*

● **All-Time Greatest Hits** / 1993 / CBS 53743
Traces Daniel's career from his early highpoints—"Long Haired Country Boy," "The South's Gonna Do It," "The Devil Went Down to Georgia"—to the desperate attempts to revive his late career with self-referential updates ("Uneasy Rider '88") and jingoistic, red-baiting blather ("Simple Man") that was out of date before he released it. —*Michael McCall*

Gail Davies

b. Sep. 1, 1948, Broken Bow, OK
Vocals, guitar / Traditional country, country-pop
Davies, an Oklahoma native who sang jazz on the West Coast before discovering her songwriting capabilities, is an assertive, staunchly modern female singer/songwriter who created fresh country rock a decade before Wynonna, Trisha and Mary Chapin. Davies struggled against the Nashville system to produce her own records and fashion her own sound, winning out in the studio but losing when it came to promotional support. Critics loved her, but radio overlooked most of her best work. She briefly formed a band, Wild Choir, in the mid 1980s. —*Michael McCall*

The Game / 1980 / Warner Brothers 3395
Her second album, but the first in which she displayed her commanding vocals in a blend of folk-influenced ballads and punchy, melodic pop-country. —*Michael McCall*

○ **I'll Be There** / 1980 / Warner Brothers
Another consistently strong album. At a time when Barbara Mandrell and Crystal Gayle were country's biggest female stars, Davies was creating albums as distinctive and progressive as Rosanne Cash. —*Michael McCall*

○ **Giving Herself Away** / 1982 / Warner Brothers
Davies brought in such outside-of-Nashville help as guitarist Albert Lee, bassist Leland Sklar and pianist Bill Payne of Little Feat to create an excellent album that blends Southern California pop-folk with the cutting edge of modern country. Includes the hit "Hold On" as well as a popular version of Joni Mitchell's "You Turn Me On (I'm a Radio)" and "Round the Clock Lovin'," written by a then-unknown K.T. Oslin. —*Michael McCall*

What Can I Say / 1983 / Warner Brothers 23972
Lighter-hearted than her others, but even when in a playful mood Davies sounds feisty, as on "Boys Like You" and "You're a Hard Dog (To Keep Under the Porch)." Covers come from Rodney Crowell, Harlan Howard, Mark Knopfler and Ray Charles. —*Michael McCall*

○ **Where Is a Woman to Go** / 1984 / RCA
Her fiercest album as far as emotional content, and her most consistently forceful as far as musical arrangements. An unheralded classic. —*Michael McCall*

Wild Choir / 1986 / RCA
Billed as a band, Wild Choir's songs and spirit were pure Davies, but the arrangements took on mild new-wave-rock tendencies. The record proved to be too progressive at the time, and it still sounds fresher than most Nashville bands of the 1990s. "Walls" and "Never Cross That Line" rank with Davies' best compositions. —*Michael McCall*

Pretty Words / 1989 / MCA 42274
A touching combination of songs, some seeking spiritual strength, others drenched in melancholy without sinking into bathos. —*Michael McCall*

★ **Best of** / Jan. 21, 1991 / Liberty 94453
A substantial collection of radio hits and crowd favorites, including the poignant "Grandma's Song." —*Michael McCall*

Jimmie Davis (James Houston Davis)

b. Sep. 11, 1902, Quitman, LA
Vocals, guitar / Traditional country
The Jimmie Davis story, in which a white man from Louisiana cuts some of the raunchiest, double-entendre blues of the prewar country era; then, armed with a Masters degree and royalties from the original 1940 version of "You Are My Sunshine," enjoys a second career as the pious, segregationist, twice-elected governor of his home state. Along the way, he also enjoys massive (and well-deserved) hits with "Nobody's Darling But Mine" (1934), and Floyd Tillman's brilliant "It Makes No Difference Now" (1938). — *Dan Cooper*

Barnyard Stomp / 1988 / Bear Family 15285
This album features performances from the early days of Davis's career of such blues-tinged material as "Alimony Blues," "Shotgun Wedding," "Hum Dum Dinger," and more. — *AMG*

● **Country Music Hall of Fame** / 1991 / MCA 10087
1934-53 sides by this hillbilly crooner with a penchant for blues include "You Are My Sunshine." — *Mark A. Humphrey*

Linda Davis

Vocals / Country
Linda Davis has evolved through several musical and stylistic changes since the days when she sang jingles and recorded as a duet—Skip and Linda, with Skip Eaton—in the early 1980s. A talented vocalist, she seemed to lack firm direction until scoring a hit duet with her mentor and co-manager, Reba McEntire, on "Does He Love You?" Her next album found her blending torchy country ballads and swamp funk, sounding more than a little like Reba redux. — *Michael McCall*

○ **In a Different Light** / 1934 / Liberty 94829
Working with producer Jimmy Bowen, Davis created lush, MOR country rife with emotional drama. — *Michael McCall*

Linda Davis / Apr. 13, 1992 / Liberty 97868
In the same light. — *Michael McCall*

● **Shoot for the Moon** / Apr. 26, 1994 / Arista 18749
Her post-duet follow-up, the style is steamier and bluesier than her previous work, and it sounds somewhat forced. Her vocals work best on the ballads. The album does not include her duet with McEntire. — *Michael McCall*

Skeeter Davis (Mary Frances Penick)

b. Dec. 30, 1931, Dry Ridge, KY
Vocals / Traditional country, country-rock
Originally teamed with high school friend BJ (Betty Jack) Davis as the Davis Sisters, they scored mainstream C&W hits in a strong, emotive duo style. Both were involved in a car crash (BJ was killed, Skeeter seriously injured) in mid 1954. Skeeter came back in 1958 as a solo artist, joined the Grand Ole Opry, and scored nearly 20 years' worth of hits (over 40 in all), with many crossing over onto the pop charts. — *Cub Koda*

● **The End of the World** / 1962 / RCA 2699
This album includes such songs as "Angel of the Morning," "Daddy Sang Bass," and "Little Arrows." — *AMG*

○ **She Sings, They Play** / 1985 / Rounder 3092
Skeeter Davis, a prolific country singer since the '50s, teamed up with the versatile NRBQ for this delightful collaboration. Nashville with a kick. — *Jeff Tamarkin*

Billy Dean

b. Apr. 1, 1962
Vocals, guitar / Contemporary country
Billy Dean received a basketball scholarship to attend East Central Junior College in Decatur, MS, where he majored in physical education, but instead of wearing a whistle around his neck, he opted for a guitar strap. Inspired by Merle Haggard, Marty Robbins, and Dean Martin, he played the club circuit along the Gulf Coast of Florida and used national talent contests as a vehicle for his music. He made the finals of the Wrangler Country "Star Search" in 1982, then won as a Male Vocalist champ on Ed McMahon's "Star Search" program in 1988. Even before the release of his debut album, *Young Man*, he'd already gone on tour as an opening act for Mel Tillis, Gary Morris, and Ronnie Milsap. He's contributed to commercials for Valvoline, McDonald's, and

Chevrolet, and had an acting role in the brief Elvis series on ABC-TV in 1990.

His good looks are undeniable, but Dean has the talent to match—as proven when he won the Academy of Country Music's Song of the Year award for the enormously sensitive "Somewhere in My Broken Heart," cowritten with Richard ("Don't It Make My Brown Eyes Blue," "Come from the Heart") Leigh. — *Tom Roland*

○ **Young Man** / 1990 / Liberty 94302
Nashville launched so many new acts from 1989-1992 that many who deserved a shot went overlooked. Thanks in part to his own songwriting skills, and to signing with SBK Records, which had just one country act to push, Dean got a good listen and was able to capitalize on a strong debut. His vocals aren't unique, but he sings with strength and conviction, regardless of the style. You can't go wrong with "Somewhere in My Broken Heart." — *Tom Roland*

Billy Dean / 1991 / Liberty 96728
Billy Dean's second album follows the same pattern that made his first so popular: a strong emphasis on the ballads in which his supple baritone thrives. The rollicking "Hammer Down" flies in the face of everything else, but even there the message remains the same—obvious but effective. — *Brian Mansfield*

● **Greatest Hits** / Mar. 8, 1994 / Liberty 28357

Jimmy Dean

b. Aug. 10, 1928, Plainview, TX
Vocals, piano, accordian, mouth harp, guitar / Traditional country
This Texan became famous for sausages long after he made a name for himself in music via his self-penned "Big Bad John" (1961), "PT 109," and "Dear Ivan." Dean's wit and quick humor made him a natural for TV, and he had his own CBS show as well as one on ABC in the mid '60s. The syndicated "Jimmy Dean's Country Beat" did well in the '80s. Occasionally he's guest host on the Ralph Emery show, where he speaks his mind refreshingly often. — *David Vinopal*

○ **Jimmy Dean's Greatest Hits** / 1980 / CBS 9285
This contains "Big Bad John" and "PT 109." — *Dan Heilman*

● **Big Bad John** / Bear Family 13583
Features such favorites as "Sixteen Tons" and "Smoke Smoke Smoke that Cigarette." — *AMG*

Tony De La Rosa

Drum / Tex-Mex
Norteno music veteran Tony De La Rosa was one of the first bandleaders to add drums and amplification to the tradition-bound conjunto style. After a long semi-retirement, he has emerged with his no-frills Tex-Mex sound intact, applying his accordion to the ever-popular polkas and rancheras of the Texas border. — *Myles Boisen*

● **Asi Se Baila En Tejas** / Rounder 6046
Straight from the heart, old-style Tex-Mex for Saturday night border dances. — *Myles Boisen*

The Delmore Brothers

Group / Old-time, Traditional country
Alton (b. 1908 d. 1964) and Rabon (b. 1910 d. 1954) in the late '30s and '40s were famed for their matchless vocal harmony and instrumental creativity. They differed greatly from other family duets of the time because of their prolific songwriting and their use of Black-inspired material. In the '30s their sound was country blues, while in the '40s they featured songs with a boogie beat. — *David Vinopal*

● **The Best of** / 1970 / Starday 962
Terrific nasal vocal harmonies, their brisk, bubblin' tenor, and 6-string guitars and Wayne Raney's wailin' locomotive harmonica make the Delmores' late '40s King label hits the most accessible of their early brother-duo material. Sounding a mite like the amiable smalltown uncles of Elvis and the Everly Brothers, the chooglin' "hillbilly boogie" of the Delmores was just a hairpin curve away from rockabilly. — *Mark A. Humphrey*

Delmore Brothers / 1979 /
Features "Weary Lonesome Blues" and other recordings from 1930. — *AMG*

Desert Rose Band

Group / Country-rock

Founded by ex-Byrd and ex-Flying Burrito Brother Chris Hillman, the Desert Rose Band brought the country-rock tradition represented by those seminal groups to a 1980s Nashville ever more infatuated with Southern California. While Hillman was understandably the focal point of the now disbanded act, the other members—Herb Pedersen, John Jorgenson, Bill Bryson, Jay Dee Maness and Steve Duncan—all contributed too much to the overall sound for Desert Rose to have been viewed as a "Chris Hillman and..." outfit. —*Dan Cooper*

The Desert Rose Band (MCA) / 1987 / Curb 77570

For those concerned that California country might have disappeared, the mid-80s emergence of the Desert Rose Band, Southern Pacific, and Dwight Yoakam put those fears to rest. While S-Pac leaned toward country-rock, and Yoakam hits hard on the honky-tonk sound, TDRB offers just a tinge of bluegrass, lots of energy, and intriguing harmonies. The cuts "One Step Forward," "Love Reunited," and "Leave This Town" are simply stunning. —*Tom Roland*

Running / 1988 / Curb 77573

Eight solid Chris Hillman compositions are joined by a cover of a Buck Owens classic and a song John Hiatt has yet to release for a thoroughly enjoyable album. —*Jim Worbois*

● **A Dozen Roses: Greatest Hits** / 1991 / Capitol 77571

A showcase for Hillman's pop-country vocals and the considerable chops of bandmembers such as Herb Pedersen. Together they made some of the best country singles of the late '80s, all collected here. —*William Ruhlmann*

Diamond Rio

A group that began playing bluegrass at Opryland USA as the Tennessee River Boys, Diamond Rio became one of the most sudden success stories of modern country music. Diamond Rio's initial release, "Meet in the Middle," topped the charts (the first debut single by a group to do so) in 1991; the band followed with more hits and an Academy of Country Music Group of the Year award. The band's bluegrass pedigree (bassist Dana Williams is a nephew of the Osborne Brothers; other members have played for Vassar Clements and J.D. Crowe) helped establish the image of a new country band with traditional ties. The picking's hot, thanks especially to guitarist Jimmy Olander, and the sextet's tight harmonies complement Marty Roe's smooth tenor lead. —*Brian Mansfield*

● **Diamond Rio** / 1991 / Arista 8673

One of the most successful debut albums in country music, *Diamond Rio* sparked plenty of hits—"Meet in the Middle," "Mama Don't Forget To Pray for Me," "Nowhere Bound," "Norma Jean Riley"—by combining bluegrass harmonies, old-fashioned country virtues, and just enough rock to keep things moving. —*Brian Mansfield*

Close to the Edge / 1992 / Arista 18656

On "Close to the Edge," Diamond Rio took the cue of the debut's best songs and created an entire album cut from the same cloth. Diamond Rio's strongest material emphasizes the virtues of God, family and honest living—traditional stuff, no doubt influenced by the members' bluegrass background. But while most folks who'd claim divine intervention in their relationship sound sappy at best, Marty Roe comes off earnest and convincing. Unfortunately, amid hits like "In a Week or Two" and "Oh Me, Oh My, Sweet Baby," *Close to the Edge* points out such weaknesses as a penchant for bad puns ("This Romeo Ain't Got Julie Yet"—ouch!). —*Brian Mansfield*

Love a Little Stronger / 1994 / Arista 18745

Spurred by the relatively lackluster performance of *Close to the Edge* (it barely went gold to the debut's platinum), Diamond Rio explored the musical possibilities of its talents rather than digging for easy commercial success. The instrumentalists, particularly Jimmy Olander and mandolinist Gene Johnson, assume larger roles on songs like "Love a Little Stronger" and the instrumental "Appalachian Dream," but they rarely show off. The band members even tap into a acoustic jazz-rock lode for "Kentucky Mine," one of the best songs they've ever recorded. —*Brian Mansfield*

Little Jimmy Dickens

b. Dec. 19, 1925, Bold, WV

Vocals, guitar / Traditional country

At less than five feet tall (and looking much smaller with his huge Gibson guitar), Dickens' signature song is his first Top 10 single: "Take an Old Cold Tater and Wait" (1949). He's best known, though, for his crossover hit, "May the Bird of Paradise Fly up Your Nose," from 1965. Since 1949 he's appeared weekly on the Opry, entertaining fans with his boundless energy and his many novelty tunes. —*David Vinopal*

● **Columbia Historic Edition** / CBS 38905

Some '40s and '50s sides by this pint-sized hillbilly howler. One of the Opry's great characters. —*Mark A. Humphrey*

Joe Diffie

b. 1958

Vocals / Traditional country, progressive country

Joe Diffie combines musical diversity with straight country. His debut single, "Home," went to Number 1 on the charts, as did two other songs from *A Thousand Winding Roads*, his first album. Diffie can sing Hank Williams-style or progressive country with feeling. —*David Vinopal*

○ **A Thousand Winding Roads** / 1990 / Epic 46047

A likeable new country voice from Oklahoma praising home and hearth. —*Mark A. Humphrey*

● **Regular Joe** / 1992 / Epic 47477

Diffie's second album has all the cliches of country music, and all the good stuff too. If "Ain't That Bad Enough" is a run-of-the-mill song, Diffie rescues it by tearing the melody loose from its mooring. He's also willing to push the line: of all Diffie's country heroes—and you'll be able to name them after one listen—maybe only Merle Haggard would rock out as hard as Diffie does on the title track. —*Brian Mansfield*

Honky Tonk Attitude / Apr. 20, 1993 / CBS 53002

Taking a cue from some of his peers, balladeer Diffie makes a point to get rowdy on this, his most commercially successful album to date. Besides the title track, includes the hits "Prop Me Up Beside the Jukebox (If I Die)" and "John Deere Green." —*Dan Cooper*

Dixie Chicks

A charming acoustic group that combines Texas swing, upbeat bluegrass and Lennon Sister-style pop harmonies, the Dixie Chicks started as sidewalk singers in Dallas and grew to become in folk clubs across the United States and Europe. Originally a quartet, singer-guitarist Robin Lacy left after the second album. Singer-bassist Laura Lynch, fiddler Martie Erwin, and banjo player Emily Erwin continued as a trio, augmented by two instrumentalists on drums and guitar. —*Michael McCall*

Thank Heavens for Dale Evans / 1992 / Crystal Clear 9103

Their first album captures their charm and eclectic tastes in its early, amateurish stages. Ragged in spots, but gloriously enthusiastic. —*Michael McCall*

● **Shouldn't A Told You That** / 1993 / Crystal Clear

Down to a trio, the sound is more focused now, but only slightly less varied. With Laura Lynch taking lead vocals, and with help from producer Steve Fishell, the band sounds more professional and as delightful as ever. —*Michael McCall*

Little Ol' Cowgirl / Crystal Clear 9250

Their non-stop performance schedule quickly tightened the band's sound, and their musical ability leaps forward in confidence and flair. They're still willing to try anything, at least once, which results in a collection that's uneven but entertaining. —*Michael McCall*

Dave Dudley (Dave Pedruska)

b. May 3, 1928, Spencer, WI

Vocals, guitar / Traditional country

Dudley (born David Pedruska) was one of country music's biggest troubadours of trucker songs. "Six Days on the Road," a Number 2 country hit in 1963, was the first of a string of classic songs in the idiom. Between 1961 and 1980, Dudley scored 41 hits. Currently there isn't an adequate domestically available collection on compact disc. —*Rick Clark*

- **20 Great Truck Hits: Dave Dudley** / 1983 / EMI
This Swedish import collection includes a smattering of Dudley's hits like "Six Days on the Road," "Counterfeit Cowboy," and "Me and Ole C.B." —*Rick Clark*

Holly Dunn

Vocals / Contemporary country
In 1991 her single "Maybe I Mean Yes" was removed from radio playlists, at her request, after some listeners claimed the song promoted date rape. She also was interviewed for TV's "Lifestyles of the Rich and Famous." But on a musical note, catch "Daddy's Hand," her best-known single and her signature tune. —*David Vinopal*

The Blue Rose of Texas / 1989 / Warner Brothers 25939
A "nu-country-pop" belter with an occasional rock punch and a western swing and sway. —*Mark A. Humphrey*

Heart Full of Love / 1990 / Warner Brothers 26173
More of Dunn's radio-friendly songs. —*Mark A. Humphrey*

- **Milestones—Greatest Hits** / 1991 / Warner Brothers 26630
A best-of that contains "Maybe I Mean Yes," "Daddy's Hands," and other favorites. —*AMG*

Bobby Durham

Vocals / Traditional country
Bakersfield, CA, has become legendary as one of the alternatives to Nashville in country music, and Durham is one of the journeyman singers who has worked the bars there for three decades. He never attained the fame of Bakersfield's best-known sons, Buck Owens and Merle Haggard, but he did make a few good singles for Capitol in the '60s and, in the late '80s, a fine album for Hightone. —*Mark A. Humphrey*

○ **Where I Grew Up** / 1987 / Hightone 8010
Bakersfield in the late '80s, still kickin'! —*Mark A. Humphrey*

Evangeline

The New Orleans-based band blends goodtime, Bayou country tunes with sweetly sensitive balladry. The first album features a quintet headed by the smooth vocals of guitarist Kathleen Stieffel and the rowdier vocals of bassist and washboard specialist Sharon Leger. Austin keyboard vet Beth McKee also contributes vocals, lead guitarist Rhonda Lohmeyer wrote the bulk of the original songs, and Nancy Buchan filled out the sound on fiddle and mandolin. Buchan left before the recording of the second album. —*Michael McCall*

Evangeline / 1992 / MCA 10582
The Louisiana influence is subdued, except when highlighted on an obvious track like "Bayou Boy," but it does give this band a sound that separates it from most Nashville pop-country groups. —*Michael McCall*

- **French Quarter Moon** / 1993 / Margaritaille 10879
More spirited and more country than their debut, and it is aided by a better selection of songs. Their version of "The Wild One" kicks harder than Faith Hill's better-known hit. —*Michael McCall*

Exile

Group / Country-rock, country-pop
For a while this quintet gave fellow country-pop rivals Alabama a run for their money. With their material, sound, and musical arrangements, they're closer to rock than to country roots. Their "Kiss You All Over" was a 1978 pop hit before they reconstituted themselves as a country band in the mid '80s. —*David Vinopal*

- **Greatest Hits** / 1986 / Epic 40401
Pop hits, and the disco cut "Kiss You All Over." —*Bil Carpenter*

○ **Still Standing** / 1990 / Arista 8624
A fun, peppy country album. Their best. —*Bil Carpenter*

- **The Complete Collection** / 1991 / Curb 77503
Their early '80s country hits. —*Bil Carpenter*

Shelter from the Night / Epic 40901
Almost a decade removed from "Kiss You All Over," the band leans closer to Top 40 rock than country—don't read that as a complaint. The band commuted to Connecticut on off-days during a summer-long tour to record in Stamford with Bruce Hornsby producer Elliot Scheiner, and their effort is surprisingly inspired. If you can't dance to "I Can't Get Close Enough," "Just

Country Music Styles

Old-time – String-band/hillbilly music; country folk music from the 20s and 30s, including modern music in the old style (Doc Watson, Red Clay Ramblers, Uncle Dave Macon).

Traditional country – Sometimes called "hard country," as in hardcore; the main stream of country music from which these other catergories branch off; extends from Jimmie Rodgers and Roy Acuff in the 20s and 30s through George Jones, Merle Haggard, Randy Travis, George Strait, Loretta Lynn, Reba McEntire, and Ricky Skaggs.

Contemporary country – Traditional country that's been sanded and varnished, retaining most of its country soul and sound but appealing to a larger audience than its hardcore cousin (the Judds, Steve Wariner, Garth Brooks).

Progressive country – Performers who have taken country roads to new territory; highly innovative or idiosyncratic (Mark O'Connor, Willie Nelson, K. D. Lang, Lyle Lovett).

Country pop – Middle-of-the-road music with a country flavor (often imperceptible), sounding something like traditional country but modified and sweetened; crossover music – often crossing from the country to the pop charts (Kenny Rogers, Mandrell sisters, Gatlin brothers, Glen Campbell, Anne Murray).

Country rock – An amalgam – varying portions of rock and country (Charlie Daniels, Alabama, Travis Tritt, Hank Williams Jr).

Western swing – An often complex subcategory of country music; developed in the late 30s in the Southwest and incorporating many genres, including swing jazz, polkas, fiddle music, blues, cowboy songs, and what-have-you; rural rhythm's big-band sound (Bob Wills, Bill Boyd, Asleep at the Wheel).

Cowboy – Romantic songs of the Old West sung by cowboys and cowgirls dressed in rhinestones and Stetsons (Roy Rogers, Gene Autry, Patsy Montana, Sons of the Pioneers, Tex Ritter, and Riders in the Sky).

Instrumental – Self-explanatory – picking, plucking, bowing, harping, and tickling the 88s; the earliest country music featured fiddle and banjo, while contemporary country emphasizes the electric guitar and the pedal steel guitar.

Country humor – Self-explanatory; from the earliest days of country music through "Hee Haw," comedy was part of the act (Grandpa Jones, Roy Clark, Homer and Jethro, the Geezinslaws, Ray Stevens).

Gospel – Essential to country music; religious music predates other country genres and probably will outlive them all; traditionally a standard part of any performer's repertory (Tennessee Ernie Ford, the Whites, Lewis Family, bluegrass bands).

– David Vinopal

One Kiss," or "She's Already Gone," you can't dance. —*Tom Roland*

Donna Fargo (Yvonne Vaughn)

b. Nov. 10, 1949
Vocals, guitar / Country-pop
This former teacher hit the top in 1972, when her self-penned "The Happiest Girl in the Whole USA" was chosen Country Music Association Single of the Year. Over the next eight years she had fifteen Top 10 country-pop hits, among them "It Do Feel Good" and "That Was Yesterday." In 1979 she developed multiple sclerosis, but she continued with her career. —*David Vinopal*

- **The Best of Donna Fargo** / 1977 / MCA 1634

Contains "Funny Face" and "The Happiest Girl in the Whole USA." —*Dan Heilman*

Freddy Fender (Baldemar Huerta)

b. Jun. 4, 1937, San Benito, TX
Vocals, guitar / Rock & roll, traditional country, country-pop, Tex-Mex
With Johnny Rodriguez in the '70s, Freddy Fender popularized Tex-Mex music and helped to create a national interest in the genre. Born Baldemar Huerta, the son of Texas migrant farmers, Fender started in R&B, moving to country songs in which he alternated lyrics in Spanish and English. In 1975 he had three monster Number 1 hits, "Before the Next Teardrop Falls" and "Wasted Days and Wasted Nights," followed by "Secret Love." Further success eluded him for fifteen years, until he became part of the Texas Tornados. —*David Vinopal*

Before the Next Teardrop Falls / 1975 / Collectables 9135
Textbook blend of Tex-Mex and country, spiced by Fender's immortal hit. —*Ron Wynn*

○ **The Best of Freddie Fender** / 1977 / MCA 835
This contains his other classics but stops at the mid '70s. —*Ron Wynn*

● **Collection** / 1991 / Reprise 26638
This album contains some of Fender's most popular music, hits like "Vaya con Dios," "Wasted Days and Wasted Nights," and more. —*AMG*

Ray Flacke

Guitar, instrumental guitar / Guitar-pop
From England, Ray Flacke is a fingerpicking guitar whiz who is now much in demand in Nashville. He's been in Marty Stuart's touring band and is featured on a few cuts of Stuart's *Tempted* album. —*David Vinopal*

○ **Untitled Island** / Intersound 9100
This English country/rock guitarist is currently a Nashville session cat. —*Mark A. Humphrey*

Flatlanders

Group / Country
The Flatlanders became legends long after they broke up because the band's three primary members—Jimmie Dale Gilmore, Joe Ely, and Butch Hancock—each attracted a large, loyal cult following as solo performers. In 1972, when their lone album was recorded, they were part-time musicians who hooked up after each returned to their native Texas after exploring some different region of the world. The record wasn't released, and they went their separate ways, each abandoning music briefly. Their careers continued to intertwine in the ensuing decades with great results. —*Michael McCall*

● **More a Legend Than a Band** / 1990 / Rounder 34
The title refers to the status these "lost" tapes acquired as time passed and the reputations of Ely, Gilmore and Hancock grew. The music itself is odd and effective, a blend of old-time acoustic music (including a musical saw) matched with lyrics that look at the world as only modern Texas mystics could. Gilmore takes most of the lead vocals. Features the first recorded versions of two of his classics, "Dallas" and "Tonight I'm Gonna Go Downtown." —*Michael McCall*

Rosie Flores

Guitar / Country
Flories came out of the late '80s Los Angeles Western Beat scene. A gifted singer/songwriter, guitarist, and performer, her music ranges from hard country to rockabilly. —*Chip Renner*

● **Rosie Flores** / 1987 / Reprise 25626
Produced by Pete Anderson, Rosie Flores' debut made her out to be the female answer to Dwight Yoakam. Flores probably felt like that image straitjacketed her, but from a musical standpoint, it worked beautifully, incorporating Flores' San Antonio roots into Anderson's California country vision. Includes "Crying Over You," "Somebody Loses, Somebody Wins," and "Blue Side of Town," which Patty Loveless wouldn't do nearly as well the following year. —*Brian Mansfield*

After the Farm / 1992 / Hightone 8033

From start to finish, there is something special about this CD. Flores is a great guitarist, backed by Greg Liesz, David Lindley, Duane "DJ" Jarvis, and Dusty Wakeman. They rock, with some real killer slide-guitar work. If you like your country hard, you'll love this. —*Chip Renner*

Once More with Feeling / Hightone 8047
Closer to modern commercial country than *After the Farm, Once More with Feeling* doesn't have the sleekly professional touch of *Rosie Flores*, but it's not without its charms. Includes a duet with Joe Ely ("Love and Danger," which Flores wrote with Jason & the Scorchers' Jason Ringenberg). Other songs contributed by Wendy Waldman ("Ruin This Romance") and Katy Moffatt ("Real Man"). —*Brian Mansfield*

Red Foley (Clyde Julian Foley)

b. Jun. 17, 1910, Blue Lick, KY, d. Sep. 19, 1968 , Fort Wayne, IN
Vocals, guitar / Gospel, traditional country
Hall of Fame member Clyde Julian "Red" Foley was graced with a rich baritone voice and a personality that made him a natural star. In 1950 he scored with three Number 1s, "Chattanoogie Shoe Shine Boy," "Steal Away," and "Just a Closer Walk with Thee," the latter two directing him toward religious material for the rest of his career, including his signature song, "Peace in the Valley." In 1954 he hosted the "Ozark Jubilee," one of the earliest country TV shows. He continued making appearances right up to his death. —*David Vinopal*

○ **Beyond the Sunset** / 1956 / MCA 147
Foley's gospel albums ranked with Tennessee Ernie Ford's as the most popular of the era among country fans. This is his best. —*Michael McCall*

○ **Red and Ernie** / 1956 / Decca 8298
Foley recorded four albums with his good friend Ernest Tubb, whose good humor always managed to bring out the best in his partner. —*Michael McCall*

★ **Country Music Hall of Fame** / 1991 / MCA 10084
A well-chosen sampling of 1944-53 cuts. Foley is backed by some of the era's best country studio musicians. —*Richard Lieberson*

Brownie Ford

Vocals / Country
Ford was an Oklahoma-born cowboy who learned the old songs as a lad, spun a few of his own, told a few ribald tales, and offered to the world his wry take on life in a 1990 Flying Fish album, part field recording (Ford and guitar) and part recording session with an acoustic country band. Ford's wizened vocals and open spirit merited an unlikely nod from *People*, which said kind words over the sole recorded testament of an 80-something individualist. —*Mark A. Humphrey*

○ **Stories from ...** / Flying Fish 70559
Stories from Mountains, Swamps & Honky-Tonks. A delightful geezer who recalls skinny-dippin' in Oklahoma. He wails wizened folk and country to the guitar accompaniment of Dave Doucet and D.L. Menard. —*Mark A. Humphrey*

Tennessee Ernie Ford

b. Feb. 13, 1919, Bristol, TN, d. Oct. 17, 1991 , Los Angeles, CA
Vocals / Gospel, traditional country
This radio announcer quickly changed careers when "Smokey Mountain Boogie," "The Cry of the Wild Goose," "Mule Train," and his self-penned rockabilly song "Shotgun Boogie" made him a star in 1950. The best was yet to come. In 1955 he recorded Merle Travis's superb "Sixteen Tons," a grimly real song about life in the coal mines that sold more than 4 million copies over the next ten years. Ernie's TV show on NBC lasted until he grew tired of it (six years), at which time he took his warm bass voice out of the business for a while; when he returned, it was mainly to gospel, on material that was beautifully suited to his exceptional voice. His *Hymns* album is considered the first country album to sell a million. This gentleman of country music died in 1991, shortly after a television special tribute to him. —*David Vinopal*

Ernie Sings & Glen Picks / 1975 / Capitol 11389
Country ballads in an intimate guitar/bass setting. Fine guitar from Glen Campbell. —*Richard Lieberson*

★ **16 Tons of Boogie—the Best of ...** / 1990 / Rhino 70975

16 Tons of Boogie: The Best of Tennessee Ernie Ford. In his later years, Ford's little pea-pickin' heart was closely associated with gospel and patriotic music, but in earlier years he knew how to—as the album title says—boogie. This includes all the essential material from that period: "Sixteen Tons," "The Shot Gun Boogie," "Mule Train," and "Blackberry Boogie," for starters. — *Tom Roland*

○ **Country Gospel Classics, Vol. 1 And 2** / 1991 / Capitol
The 1960s followup to the previous decade's *All-Time Greatest Hymns* wasn't as overwhelmingly successful, but it holds up better. The interplay between Ford's baritone and the Jordanaires harmony support is beautiful. —*Michael McCall*

Sings Songs of the Civil War / Feb. 4, 1991 / Capitol 95705
The 1991 release combines two evocative albums of Civil War era songs that Ford recorded for that conflict's centennial remembrance in 1961. His somber style perfectly fits the subject matter. —*Michael McCall*

Red, White & Blue / Jun. 24, 1991 / Capitol 96677
Gathers together his patriotic songs, including the complete *America the Beautiful* LP from 1970. —*Michael McCall*

Capitol Collector's Series / Jul. 8, 1991 / Capitol 95291
This album contains such Ford favorites as "Sixteen Tons," "Tennessee Border," "Nine-Pound Hammer," and others. —*AMG*

○ **All-Time Greatest Hymns** / Curb 77326
His superb baritone on traditional hymns. —*Bil Carpenter*

The Forester Sisters

Group / Traditional country, progressive country
These four—and they're actually sisters—still live in their home base of Lookout Mountain, GA, and are regularly seen on TV. They started singing in church and can cover many styles, from gospel to progressive country. —*David Vinopal*

○ **The Forester Sisters** / 1985 / Warner Brothers 25314
Rock music had the Go-Gos, Motown had the Supremes, and the standard pop era had the Andrews Sisters and the McGuire Sisters. Country music finally got an all-girl vocal group with the advent of the Foresters, and their debut is surprisingly uptempo and energetic. A first album that should have received more attention. —*Tom Roland*

○ **Sincerely** / 1988 / Warner Brothers 25746
Already the possessors of a wonderful vocal harmony style, the Foresters hit a peak when they hooked up with writer/producer Wendy Waldman for this album, cutting her "Letter Home" and other strong material (note especially the shoulda-been-a-single "You Love Me," co-written by Matraca Berg). —*William Ruhlmann*

● **Greatest Hits** / 1989 / Warner Brothers 25897
A good selection of Forester singles presents the various stylistic approaches they've taken with country material, which range from good to terrific. —*William Ruhlmann*

Talkin' 'bout Men / 1991 / Warner Brothers 26500
Love songs, love-gone-wrong songs, a little bit of swing, a little bit of reggae and, oh yeah, some country, too. The novelty hit "Men" (with lines like "You can't beat 'em up, 'cause they're bigger than you/You can't live with 'em and you just can't shoot 'em") was written by two guys. —*Brian Mansfield*

I Got a Date / 1992 / Warner Brothers 26821
Somewhere along the line, some executive got the idea that this Lookout Mountain group should concentrate primarily on ballads. As a result, their non-ballad material could've been better, but that's rectified in this collection, an excellent portrayal of the humor and heartaches faced by women in modern relationships. Wide-ranging stylistically, with a strong dose of wit, particularly in the title track and "Redneck Romeo." —*Tom Roland*

Foster & Lloyd

Group / Progressive country
Radney Foster (from Del Rio, TX) and Bill Lloyd (from Bowling Green, KY) specialized in a smart synthesis of country, rock, and pop as the duo Foster & Lloyd. Between 1987 and 1990 they cut three albums for RCA, landing four Top 5 singles in the process. Unlike many Nashville acts, Foster & Lloyd wrote and produced their own recordings. Their albums, all very enjoyable listens for

their roots-rock immediacy, set them apart from their country contemporaries. —*Rick Clark*

Foster & Lloyd / 1987 / RCA 6372
This self-titled debut effort contains the duo's most recognizable radio tracks, particularly "Crazy over You," a Top 5 hit. Other hits included here are "Sure Thing," "What Do You Want from Me This Time," and "Texas in 1880." —*Rick Clark*

● **Faster & Llouder** / 1989 / RCA 9587
Foster & Lloyd's sophomore effort presented a harder, edgier collection of songs, which were even stronger than the ones found on their first album. Highlights include "Happy for Awhile," the roots-rocker "Fat Lady Sings," and the title track. Power-pop artist Marshall Crenshaw guested on "She Knows What She Wants." —*Rick Clark*

Cleve Francis

It is a dreary fact of Nashville life that any time a black artist sings country, the race issue (or as it should be, non-issue) overwhelms discussion of the music. In fact, Francis, a mainstream country singer who is black, is probably more remarkable of a story in that he released his first major label album at the age of 48, and that he gave up a successful career as a cardiologist in Washington to devote himself to singing. —*Dan Cooper*

● **Tourist in Paradise** / Mar. 16, 1992 / Liberty 96498
Album contains "You Do My Heart Good," "Love Light," "Rock Solid," and others. —*AMG*

Janie Frickie

b. Dec. 19, 1952, South Whitney, IN
Vocals, guitar / Country-pop
This versatile Indiana native made a good living writing jingles and singing backup until Nashville realized her talent as a solo star. In 1982 she had her first Number 1 with "Don't Worry About Me Baby," leading to her being named Country Music Association Female Vocalist of the Year two years running. —*David Vinopal*

It Ain't Easy / 1982 / CBS 38214
The versatility that made Frickie a jingles success might have been a liability as a solo performer. She's so adaptable that her voice might not have been distinctive enough. Here she sounds like a strong woman who's very familiar with heartache, and producer Bob Montgomery gives her some rockin' material to shout on. —*Tom Roland*

● **17 Greatest Hits** / 1986 / CBS 40235
Tenderly strident vocals on '80s country hits. —*Bil Carpenter*

David Frizzell

The younger brother of country legend Lefty Frizzell, David broke into singing as a teenage rocker touring with his famous sibling in the late 1950s. Though his first recordings date to 1959, it wasn't until 1981, the year he and duet partner Shelly West (Dottie West's daughter) hit Number 1 with "You're the Reason God Made Oklahoma," that David emerged as a full-fledged star in his own right. —*Dan Cooper*

Family's Fine, But This One's All Mine / 1982 / Warner Brothers/Viva 23688
Features "I'm Gonna Hire a Wino to Decorate Our Home," a Number 1 country novelty that's made an even bigger splash in oldies rotation. —*Dan Cooper*

● **Golden Duets(w/Shelly West)** / 1984 / Viva 25148
"You're the Reason God Made Oklahoma" (the most majestic component of the Clint Eastwood movie "Any Which Way You Can") spawned a run of duet hits by Frizzell and West. The significant ones, including "You're the Reason...," are all here. —*Dan Cooper*

Lefty Frizzell (William Orville Frizzell)

b. Mar. 31, 1928, Corsicana, TX, **d.** Jul. 19, 1975 , Nashville, TN
Vocals, guitar / Traditional country
If a singer's greatness can be measured by those he's influenced, then Lefty Frizzell is at the top, his vocal style echoing in George Jones, Merle Haggard, Willie Nelson, John Anderson, Randy Travis, Dwight Yoakam, Randy Travis, and others farther down from this summit. Frizzell took honky-tonk and vocally stretched the words and music, making them smoother and more ballad-like, wringing out the emotion in each phrase. He started out in the dance halls

and honky-tonks of West Texas, scoring his first hit with "If You've Got the Money, I've Got the Time" in 1950, which stayed on the charts for twenty weeks. In 1951 he had four singles in the Top Ten at the same time: "I Want to Be with You Always," "Always Late," "Travelin' Blues," and "Mom and Dad's Waltz." Two later hits were "Long Black Veil" (1959) and "Saginaw, Michigan" (1964). After 22 years on the Columbia label, Frizzell joined ABC in 1973 and had three hits with them: "I Never Go Around Mirrors" and "Lucky Arms" in 1974, and "Falling" in 1975, the year this ultimate honky-tonker died. —*David Vinopal*

Lefty Frizzell's Greatest Hits / 1966 / CBS 9288
The title tells the tale. —*Mark A. Humphrey*

☆ **Treasures Untold** / 1980 / Rounder 11
A wonderful selection of early performances. Rugged Texas honky-tonk delivered in a mellifluous drawl that Merle Haggard and others emulated. An archetype. —*Mark A. Humphrey*

Goes to Nashville / 1988 / Rounder 16
More early (plus some later) Columbia recordings. —*Mark A. Humphrey*

★ **The Best of Lefty Frizzell** / 1991 / Rhino 71005
These eighteen tracks cover fifteen years (1950-65) in the career of a singer whom Merle Haggard once called "the most unique thing that ever happened to country music." Included are such timeless Frizzell gems as "If You''ve Got the Money, I've Got the Time," "I Love You a Thousand Ways," "I Want To Be With You Always," "Always Late (With Your Kisses)," and "The Long Black Veil." A must-hear for anyone interested in the origins of a vocal style so influential it rules country radio to this very day. —*Dan Cooper*

○ **American Originals** / CBS 45067
The hits. —*Mark A. Humphrey*

○ **Life's Like Poetry** / Bear Family 15550
This 12-disk set contains many tracks that have been commercially released for the first time in this grouping. A 150-page booklet accompanies the release and includes a discography. —*AMG*

Chris Gaffney

Vocals, guitar, accordion / Progressive country
Austrian-born Gaffney has been playing music for two decades, based in the American Southwest. A talented songwriter with the ability to make his song's characters and locales come alive, Gaffney handles the vocals, guitar, and accordion with the 5-piece Cold Hard Facts backing him up. Gaffney seamlessly blends country, conjunto, rockabilly, zydeco, and more. Ex-Blasters guitarist Dave Alvin adds a few guitar licks to Gaffney's two releases and cowrites two songs with Gaffney on *Mi Vida Loca*. —*Dennis MacDonald*

Chris Gaffney & Cold Hard Facts / 1989 / ROM 26011
Los Angeles dock-worker, singer, songwriter, and accordionist who reflects Hispanic influences and working-class themes in songs of steely poetry. —*Mark A. Humphrey*

● **Mi Vida Loca** / 1992 / Hightone 8038
Gaffney infuses hard country with elements of Tex-Mex and pure rock & roll, coming off like a cross between Merle Haggard and the Blasters. Gaffney has a dusty voice with perfect country phrasing for ballads like "Quiet Desperation" and "Waltz for Minnie," but he's at his peak with rockers like "'68," a powerful song about a man who lost his best friend in Vietnam, and "Silent Partner," which sounds like souped-up George Jones. —*Brian Mansfield*

Hank Garland (Walter Louis Garland)

b. Nov. 11, 1930, Cowpens, SC
Guitar / Traditional country
Garland grew up outside Spartanburg, SC, listening to Arthur "Guitar Boogie" Smith and Mother Maybelle Carter on the radio as early inspirations. By his teens he had his own radio show, and his immense prowess on his instrument brought him to Nashville, where he signed as a solo artist in 1949 (as competition for the already established Merle Travis and Chet Atkins). But it was as a session player that Garland truly made his mark, playing on countless hits by Patsy Cline, Elvis Presley, the Everly Brothers, Brenda Lee, and others. Along with Ernest Tubb's guitarist, Jimmy Byrd, he codesigned the still-popular Byrdland

model for Gibson guitars in the early '50s. Garland's incredible talent was moving in a more jazz-oriented direction when an automobile accident in 1961 left his memory and coordination skills impaired, sadly putting his playing days to an end. —*Cub Koda*

○ **Jazz Winds from a New Direction** / 1960 / Columbia 8372
Garland's album was breath of fresh air and a big surprise to both jazz and country fans. It also featured Gary Burton and Joe Morello, and has been reissued on CD. —*Ron Wynn*

★ **And His Sugar Footers** / 1992 / Bear Family 15551
The best of Garland's solo sides from the early '50s, featuring his signature tune, "Sugarfoot Rag," and 19 others equally abounding with hot guitar passages. Some of country's best guitar work is right here for the listening. —*Cub Koda*

Gatlin Brothers

Traditional country, country-pop
With his brothers Rudy and Steve, strong-voiced Larry Gatlin sang gospel songs in childhood. His first break came when he worked with the Imperials in Las Vegas, as part of Jimmy Dean's show. The late Dottie West gave him a hand by recording his compositions, and Johnny Cash used some of his songs in his *Gospel Road* movie. Gatlin's first album, *The Pilgrim*, came out in 1974, and his "Broken Lady" single was a hit in 1975, leading to a Grammy. In the latter part of the '70s he had numerous Number 1s, with "I Wish You Were Someone I Love" and "All the Gold in California." In the 80s, Gatlin and his brothers were as hot as any in the business. Due to medical problems with Larry's vocal chords, the three brothers announced that at the end of 1992 they would disband. —*David Vinopal*

Night Time Magic / 1978 / Bear Family 15920
Features "Statues without Hearts," "I Just Wish You Were Someone I Love," and more. —*AMG*

● **Greatest Hits** / 1978 / CBS 36488
Both of these packages feature the best of the Gatlins' work ("All the Gold in California" being a particular standout), with the first volume showcasing the best of Larry's solo sides. —*Cub Koda*

○ **Straight Ahead** / 1979 / CBS 36250
Occasionally overstated but predominantly satisfying, a little jazz, a little gospel, a little pop, and a little country. Every country fan knows "All the Gold in California," but the best cuts are the controversial "Midnight Choir (Mogen David)" and a sweet little piece of ear candy: "Taking Somebody with Me When I Fall." —*Tom Roland*

Help Yourself / 1980 / CBS 36582
Heavy on ballads that effectively show off the Gatlins' trademark genetic harmony. As always, all ten cuts are written by Larry; "Daytime Heroes," a nod to Prince Valium and the soaps, is most inspired. The Gatlin Brothers recorded "Songwriter's Trilogy" live—whether insightful or self-indulgent depends on the listener's viewpoint. —*Tom Roland*

○ **Greatest Hits, Vol. 2** / 1983 / CBS 38923
Volume 2 features the best of the Gatlin Brothers. —*AMG*

Adios / 1991 / Liberty 95759
This album features such Gatlin favorites as "Half Moon Hotel," "Pretty Woman Have Mercy," and "Already on Fire," among others. —*AMG*

Greatest Hits Encore / 1991 / Capitol 95528
This album features such Gatlin favorites as "Love Is Just a Game," "Night Time Magic," and more. —*AMG*

Larry Gatlin

b. May 28, 1948, Seminole, TX
Popular
The eldest, and most in the spotlight, of the Gatlin Brothers, Larry was singing with the gospel group, The Imperials, in 1971 when Dottie West covered one of his songs. After a move to Nashville, Johnny Cash covered several of Gatlin's tunes and Gatlin himself, sang harmonies on Kris Kristofferson's album *Jesus Was a Capricorn*. This lead to a contract with Monument Records.

After success with both Monument and Columbia Records, a cocaine habit and some bad press nearly took its toll on Gatlin's career. But, 1993 found Larry drug free and on Broadway in the title role of the *Will Roger's Follies*. —*Jim Worbois*

• **Larry Gatlin's Greatest Hits** / Columbia 36488

Crystal Gayle (Brenda Gail Webb)

b. Jan. 9, 1951, Paintsville, KY
Vocals / Country-pop
Younger sister of Loretta Lynn, Crystal Gayle began her career when her debut single "I Cried (the Blue Right out of My Eyes)" charted high in 1970. While Lynn became a superstar with traditional country material, Gayle reached the top of her profession with songs that are more pop-oriented, for example, "Don't It Make My Brown Eyes Blue" in 1977. She's scored many Number 1 hits and collected numerous awards. —*David Vinopal*

All-Time Greatest Hits / 1974 / Curb 77360
Besides covering many of the hits that appear on *Classic Crystal*, this one also has Gayle's debut single, "I've Cried (the Blue Right Out of My Eyes,)" which was written by her sister, Loretta Lynn. —*Dan Cooper*

• **Classic Crystal** / 1979 / EMI America 46549
Of Gayle's many overlapping hits collections, this one's the best. Given her crossover success ("Don't It Make My Brown Eyes Blue," included here, hit Number 2 pop) it's interesting to note that all of these tracks were produced by Allen Reynolds, known these days for his work with Garth Brooks. —*Dan Cooper*

○ **True Love** / 1982 / Elektra 60200
When Gayle delivered the album to then-Elektra-division-head Jimmy Bowen, he complained that it rocked too much. Producer Allen Reynolds refused to make changes, so Bowen produced three new tracks that seem out of place. Yeah, the Reynolds tracks do rock. So what? Gayle gives some of her best performances ever on "Our Love Is on the Faultline" and "Deeper in the Fire." —*Tom Roland*

○ **Crystal Gayle's Greatest Hits** / 1983 / CBS 38803
Always greatly influenced by pop sounds, Gayle embraced that aspect of her musical heritage more in the late '70s and early '80s than any other period. This set covers it well ("Half the Way" is classic) and provides a nice cover photo too. —*Tom Roland*

The Best of Crystal Gayle / Aug. 25, 1987 / Warner Brothers 25622
Features "'Til I Gain Control Again," "Turning Away," "Straight to the Heart," and other hits. —*AMG*

The Geezinslaws

Group / Country humor
With a guitar, mandolin, and clever comedy act, the Geezinslaws echo Homer and Jethro on one hand, Lonzo and Oscar on the other. While they pick and sing very well, their real talent is in country humor. Son Geezinslaw doesn't talk, doesn't smile, doesn't do nothing, but he does nothing very well. Check out their *World Tour* album. In a word, they're hilarious. —*David Vinopal*

○ **World Tour** / Step One 0056
Though the best of the Geezinslaws's earlier tracks have yet to be anthologized, this album comes the closest to capturing their peculiar brand of country mayhem. —*Cub Koda*

Bobbie Gentry (Roberta Streeter)

b. Jul. 27, 1944, Chickasaw, CO
Vocals, guitar / Country-pop
Bobbie Gentry became an overnight star, moving from the Los Angeles School of Music to her smash single, "Ode to Billy Joe," a crossover hit in 1967 that led to three Grammy awards. Following this she did well on two duets with Glen Campbell, "Let It Be Me" and "All I Have to Do Is Dream." She hosted and starred on her own show for Britain's BBC in the late '60s and early '70s. —*David Vinopal*

• **Greatest Hits** / Curb 77387
Features "Fancy," "Ode to Billie Joe," "Louisiana Man," and other hits. —*AMG*

Don Gibson

b. Apr. 3, 1928, Shelby, NC
Vocals, guitar / Traditional country, country-pop
This talented singer and songwriter had numerous crossover hits in the '60s and '70s, without even trying to cross over into the pop charts. It was simply that his rich and mellow voice, combined with his exceptionally well-written songs, appealed to *many* lis-

teners, not only those in country. After failing with four different record labels early in his career, Williams was heard by Chet Atkins, who was then working as an executive for RCA. The two songs Atkins heard? "Oh, Lonesome Me" and "I Can't Stop Loving You," both of which are now country standards and which Williams wrote in a single day in 1958 in a Nashville house trailer. Williams immediately joined the Opry, giving him the regular exposure that helped his records reach the charts right into the '80s. In the '70s he had over 40 charted songs, including "Woman, Sensuous Woman," a Number 1 in 1972. His compositions have been recorded regularly by other stars, from Ray Charles ("I Can't Stop Loving You") and Ronnie Milsap ("Legend in My Time") to Emmylou Harris ("Sweet Dreams"), to mention just a few among dozens. —*David Vinopal*

★ **A Legend in His Time** / 1988 / Bear Family 15401
A superb, import-only 26-song collection of most of Gibson's best tracks and biggest hits from 1957-65. Since *All-Time Greatest Hits* is out-of-print, this is the best place to start. —*AMG*

18 Greatest Hits / 1991 / Curb 77474
Gibson's best-known hits were recorded in the late 1950s and early 1960s for RCA, with Chet Atkins producing. These recordings are drawn from his work for Hickory Records in the early 1970s. They include "Woman, Sensuous Woman," "Country Green" and several remakes of his earlier hits. —*Michael McCall*

○ **The Singer, the Songwriter (1949-1960)** / 1991 / Bear Family 15475
This four-CD set covers Gibson's RCA, MGM, Mercury, and Columbia output and includes a comprehensive booklet. —*AMG*

Vince Gill

b. Apr. 12, 1957, Norman, OK
Vocals, guitar / Traditional country
This Oklahoman with the high and pure tenor voice performed with the Bluegrass Alliance (and in the late '70s) was lead singer of Pure Prairie League. He quickly won numerous awards for his high, emotional voice, and is renowned for his guitar playing. Gill's classy material shows respect for traditional country music. He excels in three areas: singing, instrumentals, and songwriting. —*David Vinopal*

Turn Me Loose / 1983 / RCA 8517
This is one of the mini-LPs RCA, and several other labels, experimented with in the '80s. While Gill had been on the musical scene for several years, including a stint with Pure Prairie League, this is a nice sampler to display Gill's skills as both a performer and a writer. —*Jim Worbois*

The Best of Vince Gill / 1989 / RCA 9814
Some 80s RCA sides. —*Mark A. Humphrey*

• **When I Call Your Name** / 1989 / MCA 42321
"Oklahoma Swing," Gill's duet with Reba McEntire, announced his return to a rootsier sound after leaving RCA. But it was the title cut, with Patty Loveless providing the harmonies, that soared highest from car radios and announced the arrival of a major star. —*Dan Cooper*

○ **Pocket Full of Gold** / 1991 / MCA 10140
A hit album with high bluegrass vocals, traditional country arrangement, and contemporary production. —*Mark A. Humphrey*

○ **I Still Believe in You** / 1992 / MCA 10630
Lots of folks inject a shot of R&B cliches into their honky-tonk and call it country soul. Vince Gill is country's real soul man, and not because of a familiarity with black artists' catalogues (though "Nothin' Like a Woman" comes close to sounding what lovers imagine Percy Sledge's "When a Man Loves a Woman" to be). It's because Gill's voice captures pain and promise, love and loneliness—all in a distillation so smooth that you don't even notice it sneaking up to blindside you. With his high tenor harmonies on songs like "Tryin' to Get Over You" and "No Future in the Past," you might even call this bluegrass soul—and you know that's gotta be lonesome. —*Brian Mansfield*

Mickey Gilley

b. Mar. 9, 1937, Ferriday, LA
Vocals, piano / Traditional country
Like his cousin Jerry Lee Lewis, Mickey Gilley is a piano-playing singer who's at home with honky-tonk and country ballads alike.

After considerable label-hopping early in his career, his remake of George Morgan's "Room Full of Roses" put him on the music map in 1974. From then to the mid '80s he scored seventeen Number 1s, including "I Overlooked an Orchid," "Don't the Girls Get Prettier at Closing Time," and "She's Pulling Me Back Again." When *Urban Cowboy* was filmed at Gilley's club in Pasadena, TX, his career got an extra boost and a pop hit in "Stand by Me," and for a couple of years, mechanical bulls stampeded across the country. In 1990 this famous club was eventually torched by a youth "to release anger." —*David Vinopal*

Live at Gilley's / 1978 / CBS 39900
A rough and rowdy roadhouse honky-tonk performance. —*Mark A. Humphrey*

○ **That's All that Matters to Me** / 1980 / Epic 84391
This is the album that benefited most from Gilley's *Urban Cowboy* associations, and there's a perfunctory back cover shot of some cowboy riding a mechanical bull at Gilley's night club. Though Gilley the Balladeer became pretty formulaic during the progression of the '80s, it was a new wrinkle with this album, and he delivers it convincingly. Gilley says the title track is his best performance ever; we agree. —*Tom Roland*

○ **Biggest Hits** / 1982 / Epic 38320
A concise sampling of his '70s and '80s honky-tonk hits. —*Mark A. Humphrey*

● **Ten Years of Hits** / 1984 / Epic 39867
It's a shame people have such a hard time dissociating Mickey Gilley from Stepford bulls. At his best, Jerry Lee's cousin has proven himself a legitimately soulful country singer, as evidenced here on Number 1 hits like "That's All that Matters to Me" and "A Headache Tomorrow (Or a Heartache Tonight)." —*Dan Cooper*

Talk To Me / 1994 / Branson 9309

Make It Like the Fir / Be 9306

Jimmie Dale Gilmore

Vocals / Contemporary country
Jimmie Dale Gilmore's music blends the traditional with the contemporary and adds a lot of unique Gilmore. The Austin, Texas, resident's voice and vocal style have been compared to a cross between Willie Nelson's and Bob Dylan's. —*David Vinopal*

○ **Fair & Square** / 1988 / Hightone 8011
If Willie Nelson were not so mellow and were still writing good songs, he would sound a lot like this soulful Texas singer/songwriter. —*Mark A. Humphrey*

Jimmie Dale Gilmore / 1989 / Hightone 8018
More good songs from Austin. —*Mark A. Humphrey*

● **After Awhile** / 1991 / Nonesuch 61148
From the celebrated "American Explorer" series. —*Mark A. Humphrey*

○ **Spinning Around the Sun** / 1993 / Elektra 61502
Recorded in Nashville with Emory Gordy Jr. (Patty Loveless' husband and producer), *Spinning Around the Sun* contains covers of Hank Williams' "I'm So Lonesome I Could Cry" and Elvis Presley's "I Was the One." If Gilmore's nasal voice weren't so uncommercial and his songs didn't still take flight with mystical tangents, some folks might start accusing him of going mainstream. —*Brian Mansfield*

Johnny Gimble

b. 1926
Fiddle / Instrumental bluegrass, fiddle
Johnny Gimble is simply one of the greatest fiddlers who ever lived. After playing with the Bob Wills Band in the late '40s, he went back to barbering in Texas before becoming an outstanding studio fiddler, backing up Lefty Frizzell, Marty Robbins, Merle Haggard, Loretta Lynn, and Willie Nelson, to name just a few of hundreds. Pick a music style and Gimble can play it on the fiddle. He's often seen on TV, looking young and playing country, swing, or jazz as well as it's played. —*David Vinopal*

○ **Still Swingin'** / 1976 / CMH 9020
Western style, that is. —*Mark A. Humphrey*

Texas Fiddle Collection / 1981 / CMH 9027
This Texas Playboy alumnus and first-call Nashville fiddler shows how it's done in the Lone Star State. —*Mark A. Humphrey*

● **Still Fiddlin' Around** / Jun. 13, 1988 / MCA 42021

Gimble's amiable personality glows in the company of other top-drawer Nashville cats, along with the fleet bowing and pleasant vocals. —*Mark A. Humphrey*

Texas Honky-Tonk Hits / CMH 9038
Swinging doors, hardwood floors, and some tunes by which to two-step. —*Mark A. Humphrey*

Vern Gosdin

b. Aug. 5, 1934
Vocals, guitar / Traditional country
One of the best vocalists in the business, for good reason is Gosdin called "The Voice." He's been in music a while, with the Gosdin Brothers in 1960 and then as a forming partner in the Hillmen. Gosdin is a country traditionalist and a subtle singer. If you like quality vocals, listen to his award-winning *Chiseled in Stone* album. —*David Vinopal*

○ **Till the End** / 1977 / Elektra 1112
This is probably one of Gosdin's strongest records overall. Additionally, it netted him four hits. —*Jim Worbois*

○ **There Is a Season** / 1984 / Compleat 1008
Throughout the album, Emmylou Harris provides nice harmonies reminiscent of Rex Gosdin's style. Additionally, Roger McGuinn adds vocals (Background and accompanying) and the 12-string instrumental break to "Turn Turn Turn," which is very different from the Byrds' version. —*Jim Worbois*

If Jesus Comes Tomorrow / 1984 / Compleat 671011
If Jesus Comes Tomorrow (What Then) is part gospel standards, part complementary originals, all sung by a honky-tonk voice hoping for heaven. —*Brian Mansfield*

☆ **Chiseled in Stone** / 1988 / CBS 40982
The second coming of this veteran country balladeer during the late '80s. Righteous and wrenching. —*Mark A. Humphrey*

Alone / 1989 / CBS 45104
Great performances. —*Mark A. Humphrey*

The Best of Vern Gosdin / 1989 / Warner Brothers 25775
Some fine performances from the early and mid '80s, but a mite over-produced. Get his Columbia work first. —*Mark A. Humphrey*

○ **Out of My Heart** / 1991 / CBS 47051
Bold bleating from "The Voice." —*Mark A. Humphrey*

Jack Greene

b. Jan. 7, 1930, Maryville, TN
Vocals, guitar, drums / Country
Hailing from Maryville, TN, Greene got his start in the record business as a vocalist in Ernest Tubb's band, but he hardly had the same almost-on-key "twang" as his boss. In fact, Greene's smooth, pleasant sound contrasted a great deal with Tubb's blue-collar intonation. Nicknamed "the Jolly Green Giant," Greene learned guitar and drums but mined his vocal chords for a solid string of hit records from 1966 to 1969, including one with Jeannie Seely, who joined his road show and recorded duets with him for several years. A bit of trivia: In 1967, Greene became the first country artist ever to appear in the Macy's Thanksgiving Day Parade. —*Tom Roland*

● **Greatest Hits** / Decca
This basically sums up his peak years. Includes the classics: "All the Time," "There Goes My Everything," and "Statue of a Fool." —*Tom Roland*

Lee Greenwood

b. Oct. 17, 1942
Vocals, sax, piano, guitar, bass, banjo / Country-pop
Born with a good voice and a wide range, Greenwood turned it into a unique voice accidentally, by over-working it in a less-than-healthy setting. Hailing from Sacramento, he used his musical training on the casino circuit, working in the green felt jungles of Reno and Las Vegas, where he dealt cards by day and sang in dark lounges by night. The physical toll of two jobs, the vocal strain of performing six nights a week, and the damaging endeavor to sing in smoky nightclubs before the advent of smoking ordinances brought Greenwood a permanent hoarseness. He's used it to his advantage, becoming one of country music's premier balladeers. Discovered by Mel Tillis's road manager, Larry McFaden, Greenwood paid for his own ticket to fly to Nashville

and cut a few demos, and it took more than a year for that effort to payoff. When it finally did, Greenwood broke through in late 1981 with "It Turns Me Inside Out," in which his exaggerated vibrato brought frequent comparisons to Kenny Rogers.

In short order, Greenwood disposed of the "Kenny clone" image, but he continued to mine romantic material for the bulk of his hits. Occasional exceptions include "Touch and Go Crazy" and "Mornin' Ride," but the biggest exception is also his signature song, the self-written "God Bless the U.S.A.," which earned Song of the Year honors from the Country Music Association. —*Tom Roland*

● **Greatest Hits** / 1985 / MCA 5582
The extent to which Greenwood relies on ballads is fully evident here, although his departures—"Dixie Road" and "Ain't No Trick"—are most memorable. "God Bless the U.S.A." is the last track; if you're not inclined to ultra-patriotism, you can simply lift the needle or push "Stop." —*Tom Roland*

Holdin' a Good Hand / 1991 / Capitol 94153
Here you'll find performances of such songs as "Just like Me," "Enough Already," "The Moment You Were Mine," and others. —*AMG*

When You're in Love / 1991 / Capitol 95527
This album includes "Between a Rock and a Heartache," "If You'll Let this Fool Back In," and other hits. —*AMG*

American Patriot / 1992 / Liberty 98568
This album contains such patriotic selections as "America the Beautiful," the "Pledge of Allegiance," and "The Battle Hymn of the Republic." —*AMG*

Nanci Griffith

b. Jul. 6, 1953, Seguin, TX
Vocals / Progressive country, contemporary country
Nanci Griffith emerged in the '80s as perhaps the most promising folk/country singer/songwriter of her day. Kathy Mattea had a 1986 hit with "Love at the Five & Dime," and Suzy Bogguss covered "Outbound Plane" in 1991; others, including Lynn Anderson, have recorded her songs as well. A former schoolteacher from near Austin, TX, Griffith first released *There's a Light Beyond These Woods*, on her own B.F. Deal label in 1978, followed by three more albums for the folk label Philo that displayed an ear for detail and times past. 1987's *Lone Star State of Mind* was her first for the country division of MCA and included Julie Gold's soon-to-be standard "From a Distance." After three country albums, Griffith switched to MCA's Los Angeles division, where she has moved toward pop with 1989's *Storms* and 1991's *Late Night Grande Hotel*. —*Brian Mansfield & William Ruhlmann*

○ **Once in a Very Blue Moon** / 1984 / Philo 1096
After two promising albums, Nanci Griffith finally perfected her mixture of singer/songwriter folk and Texas-based country on this lovely collection, which features her own story-songs such as "Mary & Omie" and well-chosen covers such as the Pat Alger/Eugene Levine title tune. —*William Ruhlmann*

★ **The Last of the True Believers** / 1986 / Philo 1109
Griffith hit her peak as a songwriter here with classics such as "Love at the Five & Dime" and "Banks of the Pontchartrain," while singing over an always-appropriate backup provided by the '80s new bluegrass specialists Bela Fleck, Mark O'Connor, and others. The album earned her a major-label contract with MCA and provided the basis of country singer Kathy Mattea's entire career, but it is also a pivotal '80s folk album. —*William Ruhlmann*

○ **Little Love Affairs** / 1988 / MCA 42102
All of Griffith's albums have songs to recommend them; of her country/folk albums, this one has the most written by her, as well as good tunes by Harlan Howard and fellow Texan Robert Earl Keen, Jr. The first half's prime Griffith, and the second suggests that, if she'd stuck with country, she might have started outselling her press—Suzy Bogguss later turned "Outbound Plane" into a hit, and there's probably at least one more of those tucked away here. —*Brian Mansfield*

Late Night Grande Hotel / 1991 / MCA 10306
Two albums out of Nashville and Griffith doesn't even resemble the new-country/folkie role in which she was once cast. Britishers Rod Argent and Peter Van Hooke insulate Griffith with strings and moody atmospheres that complement her wallflower fantasies. She's likely partial to "Power Lines" and "Down 'n' Outer,"

both tales of folks who fall through society's cracks. Probably, come to think of it, because she identifies with them. —*Brian Mansfield*

○ **Other Voices, Other Rooms** / 1993 / Elektra 61464
Griffith pays homage to a wide cut of folk music heroes, from Woody Guthrie to Townes Van Zandt, from Bob Dylan to Kate Wolf, from Malvina Reynolds to John Prine. She sounds looser and more spirited than usual, and her earnest adoration for the songs shines through in these compellingly remakes. —*Michael McCall*

● **The MCA Years—a Retrospective** / 1993 / MCA 10914
Even though this collection features a fair number of highlights from her late '80s albums, you should hear those records in their entirety. Nevertheless, this offers a good introduction to Griffith's country-folk. —*AMG*

Merle Haggard

b. Apr. 6, 1937, Bakersfield, CA
Vocals, guitar, fiddle / Traditional country
One of Merle Haggard's best LPs is called *Someday We'll Look Back*. It's an ironic title, for in one sense Haggard has always been looking back—not just at his own troubled past, from which he has drawn so many of his lyric themes, but also at the vast tableau of American music that continually inspires his often forward-looking work. Synthesizing influences as varied as Lefty Frizzell and Emmet Miller, Bob Wills swing and Dixieland jazz, Haggard has forged a personal sound of stunning originality and a song catalog of stupendous creative wealth. Hag's life story is nearly as legendary as his music. Born the child of migrant dustbowl Okies, he was raised in a converted boxcar outside Bakersfield, California. His father died when he was nine, and though, as Merle has put it, his mama tried to raise him better, he spent much of his youth in reform school. Sent to San Quentin for a botched robbery, he did, in fact, turn twenty-one in prison. After his release, Merle started picking and singing in the red-hot early '60s Bakersfield club scene. His first singles were released on the Tally label. One of them, "(My Friends Are Gonna Be) Strangers," reached Number 10 in 1965 and earned him a contract with Capitol. It was for the latter label that Haggard recorded "I'm a Lonesome Fugitive," "Mama Tried," "Workin' Man Blues," the infamous "Okie From Muskogee," and the scores of other superb sides that defined his "poet of the working man" public identity. Through subsequent stints on MCA, Columbia and Curb, Haggard has cemented his status as unquestionably one of the handful most important figures in the history of country music. —*Dan Cooper*

☆ **Swinging Doors** / 1966 / Capitol 2585
His two best honky-tonk songs, the title track and "The Bottle Let Me Down." Also Tommy Collins's haunting "High on a Hilltop." —*George Bedard*

I'm a Lonesome Fugitive / 1967 / Capitol 2702
This early Capitol album contains the haunting "House of Memories." Haggard begins to really let his roots show on this one—see "Rough and Rowdy Ways," the Jimmie Rodgers classic. In this great early period Haggard, while seeming entirely contemporary, could evoke the Ghosts of Country Past in an absolutely convincing way without nostalgia or imitation. —*George Bedard*

○ **Branded Man** / 1967 / Capitol 2789
An out-of-print classic album. —*Richard Lieberson*

○ **Same Train, Different Time** / 1969 / Capitol 223
Haggard's loving 2-LP tribute to country pioneer Jimmie Rodgers. Lots of fine guitar from Roy Nichols and James Burton. —*Richard Lieberson*

○ **The Fightin' Side of Me** / 1970 / Capitol 451
Electrifying live Philadelphia performance. Don't let the title put you off. —*Richard Lieberson*

Okie from Muskogee / 1970 / Pair 57246
Another exciting live show. —*Richard Lieberson*

☆ **Tribute to the Best Damn Fiddle Player** / 1970 / Capitol 638
Tribute to the Best Damn Fiddle Player in the World, Haggard's salute to Bob Wills and His Texas Playboys, showcases many Playboy alumni along with Haggard's band, the Strangers. —*Richard Lieberson*

☆ **The Best of the Best** / 1972 / Capitol 91254

Includes "Today I Started Loving You Again," "No Reason to Quit," "Every Fool Has a Rainbow," "Hungry Eyes"—some of his best ballads plus the jingoistic faves "Okie from Muskogee" and "Fightin' Side of Me." A few duds, though—some of the early Capitol albums are more consistent. —*George Bedard*

Serving 190 Proof / 1979 / MCA 1645
Haggard in the midst of what he admitted was a mid-life crisis. That's no reason to dismiss this record, however, as crisis introspection served him well. Possibly the best of his MCA albums, it includes "Red Bandana," "My Own Kind of a Hat," and a brooding meditation on the emptiness of stardom called "Footlights." —*Dan Cooper*

Big City / 1981 / Epic 37593
Coming on the heels of a short-lived semi-retirement, Haggard's Epic debut is an appropriate group of songs that celebrates relaxation and expresses discontent with the situation forced on blue-collar America. Ironically, he puts plenty of energy into his work here. —*Tom Roland*

Going Where the Lonely Go / 1982 / Epic 38092
Dark, brooding package that includes some leftovers from the *Big City* sessions. Occasionally uplifting musically, but certainly a study in pain. Besides the title track, check out "Someday You're Gonna Need Your Friends Again," "Shopping for Dresses," and the Willie Nelson-penned "Half a Man." —*Tom Roland*

A Taste of Yesterday's Wine / 1982 / Epic 38203
Merle Haggard and George Jones, the two most influential country stylists of the modern country era, hook up together. Occasionally disappointing in that respect, but a case study in music to down Jack Daniels by. They take a self-deprecating poke at George Jones' former reliability problem in "No Show Jones." —*Tom Roland*

Pancho & Lefty / 1983 / Epic 37958
This album with Willie Nelson is for those curious as to why younger artists try to imitate Haggard rather than Nelson. Funny thing—though it's a duet album, they very rarely sing in harmony. Some versions spell Pancho as Poncho and are supposedly collector's items. The title track is one of the best-produced country cuts in history. —*Tom Roland*

○ **His Greatest & His Best** / 1985 / MCA 5624
Merle's tenure on MCA was brief, but productive. Highlights, all included here, were "If We're Not Back in Love By Monday," "Leonard" (a tribute to songwriter Tommy Collins), and "Misery and Gin." —*Dan Cooper*

Greatest Hits of the 80's / 1990 / MCA 5386
Features "5:01 Blues," "I Had a Beautiful Time," and other favorites, including duets with George Jones ("Yesterday's Wine") and Janie Frickie ("Natural High"). —*AMG*

☆ **More of the Best** / 1990 / Rhino 70917
Includes some of his best Capitol Records and MCA material ("Branded Man," "Mama Tried," etc.). —*Richard Lieberson*

★ **Capitol Collectors Series** / Jan. 29, 1990 / Capitol 93191
"Mama Tried," "The Bottle Let Me Down," "Workin' Man Blues," "Okie from Muskogee," and other songs from the top country artist of the '60s and '70s, with picking from the likes of Glen D. Hardin, James Burton, Roy Nichols, and Ralph Mooney. —*AMG*

Merle Haggard 1994 / Mar. 22, 1994 / Capitol/Curb 77636
After a four-year recording silence, Hag returns with his strongest record since 1981's *Big City*. The first single, "In My Next Life" (written by Max D. Barnes), is the latest entry in Haggard's incomparable registry of the unfulfilled dreams of the salt of the bitter earth. —*Dan Cooper*

Capitol Country Classics / Capitol
A British compilation that covers much of his '70s material. Sixteen hits in all, and worth finding just to make sure you own "It's All in the Movies." —*Tom Roland*

Tom T. Hall

b. May 25, 1936, Olive Hill, KY
Vocals, guitar / Country-pop
Nashville's reigning storyteller, Hall started off as a DJ and a songwriter. In the '60s his songs were recorded by Dave Dudley, Roy Drusky, and Flatt and Scruggs, but the bigtime arrived in 1968 when Jeannie C. Riley cut "Harper Valley PTA," which sold 6 million copies and led first to a movie in 1978, then to a TV se-

ries in the early '80s. Hall was phenomenally popular in the '70s, charting with many "message" songs, among them "The Year that Clayton Delaney Died," "Old Dogs, Children, and Watermelon Wine," and "Ravishing Ruby." In the '80s he became host of "Pop Goes the Country," a syndicated TV show. With his low-key singing style and his unique songs, Hall is like no one else in the business. —*David Vinopal*

☆ **In Search of a Song** / 1971 / Mercury 822500
Hall gathered his material while driving solo through rural America, and his songs are literal and compassionate—but not romantic or sentimental. Instead, he fills his heartland stories with extraordinary realism and humanity. —*Michael McCall*

○ **Greatest Hits—Vols. 1 & 2** / Mercury 810462
Combining Hall's first two *Greatest Hits* albums on one disc, this CD is the best collection of the songwriter's biggest pop hits. —*AMG*

Emmylou Harris

b. Apr. 2, 1949, Birmingham, AL
Vocals, guitar / Traditional country, progressive country, country-rock, contemporary country
It's difficult to label Emmylou Harris, except to say everyone agrees that her voice is exceptionally, achingly beautiful. Her career, now heading toward the quarter-century mark, spans many types of music and at the moment rests in traditional country—sort of. In fact, Harris, who came to country with a hip and rock image, is now one of the most vocal proponents of pure country. In a decade that has begun with a mania for singers with over-sized Stetsons, she has the taste and the credentials to suggest that maybe George Jones and Merle Haggard ought to be given a good listen, too.

Her career began with folk music in the late '60s in NYC and around the Washington, DC, area, where she met Gram Parsons, formerly of the Byrds. It was Parsons who fine-tuned her appreciation for country music, particularly songs that featured heart-tugging harmony work, a la Louvin Brothers and Everly Brothers. During a brief spell Harris and Parsons worked together in his band the Fallen Angels. After his death in 1973, Harris went solo, pursuing a sound that melded strains of pure country with elements of singer/songwriter folk and acoustic-flavored rock into her sound.

It was with her second album, (*Elite Hotel*), that Harris achieved some real success. *Elite Hotel* blended country standards and country rock and yielded three Number 1 hits, including a remake of a Don Gibson song, "Sweet Dreams."

Later on in her career, the traditional *Blue Kentucky Girl* brought Harris a Grammy. Another album, *Roses in the Snow*, reinforced her reputation as a superb interpreter of traditional country. In the '80s, she teamed up with Dolly Parton and Linda Ronstadt on *Trio*, a great commercial success and the only country album of that decade to reach the pop Top 10. As a live performer, Harris has enjoyed a reputation for assembling stellar road bands, which have included British guitar ace Albert Lee and bluegrass journeyman Ricky Skaggs.

Given her versatility and broad musical taste, it's difficult to predict what kinds of albums we'll see from Emmylou Harris through the '90s; but whether it's country-rock or blues, ballads or bluegrass, you can be sure it will be done right—memorably right. —*David Vinopal*

☆ **Elite Hotel** / 1975 / Reprise 2286
Picking up the torch from her late partner, Gram Parsons, Emmylou Harris defined the country-rock hybrid of the '70s and '80s. Here she presents her own versions of the Parsons classics "Sin City" and "Wheels," gives a boost to up-and-comer Rodney Crowell, and even covers the Beatles, all in her heartbreaking voice and backed by a group of session stars soon aptly named "The Hot Band." —*William Ruhlmann*

○ **Pieces of the Sky** / 1975 / Reprise 2284
With a feathery voice that could knock people over, and a taste for vintage country music nurtured by Gram Parsons, Harris' career persona was already fully in place on this, her remarkable major label debut. Included is "Boulder to Birmingham," one of Harris' rare original tunes, and a performance that could give a dead man chicken skin. —*Dan Cooper*

★ **Profile (The Best of Emmylou Harris)** / 1978 / Warner Brothers 3258

A greatest hits collection featuring "Together Again," "One of These Days," "Two More Bottle of Wine," and nine other cuts. — *AMG*

★ **A Quarter Moon in a Ten Cent Town** / 1978 / Warner Brothers 3141
Harris' albums of the period are uniformly strong, and the choices made here are predicated more than usual on personal taste. This album gets the nod largely for its definitive versions of the Crowell songs "Leaving Louisiana in the Broad Daylight" and "I Ain't Living Long like This." — *William Ruhlmann*

○ **Roses in the Snow** / 1980 / Warner Brothers 3422
The record label questioned Harris' decision to release an album featuring hybrid bluegrass—understandably, since it wasn't exactly in vogue. But Harris had Ricky Skaggs in her corner, and pulled it off with her usual flair. — *Tom Roland*

Evangeline / 1981 / Warner Brothers 3508
This rock-heavy package moves gracefully to bluegrass, folk, and jazz-inflected tracks as well. Thanks to contractual agreements, this is the only place you'll find the version of "Mister Sandman" that features Dolly Parton and Linda Ronstadt. — *Tom Roland*

○ **The Ballad of Sally Rose** / 1985 / Warner Brothers 25205
Harris switched gears on this album, cowriting with Paul Kennerley a semi-autobiographical song cycle that makes you wonder why she had spent so much time interpreting the work of others. The album is unique in her catalog, but it's a successful attempt to try something different. — *William Ruhlmann*

Bluebird / 1988 / Reprise 25776
Some of Harris's favorite hits, including "Heaven Only Knows," "Lonely Street," and "Heartbreak Hill." — *AMG*

○ **At the Ryman** / 1992 / Reprise 26664
The album debut of the Nashville Ramblers, her acoustic backing band featuring Sam Bush and Roy Huskey, Jr., recorded over three nights in the former home of the Grand Ole Opry. Harris's choice of songs strikes a balance between hillbilly classics and folk-influenced rock, with Bill Monroe receiving heaviest tribute but sharing space with Tex Owens, Bruce Springsteen, and John Fogerty. — *Brian Mansfield*

○ **Cowgirl's Prayer** / 1993 / Asylum
An collection of reflective, wholly adult songs set to exquisitely austere arrangements. — *Michael McCall*

John Hartford
b. Dec. 30, 1937, New York, NY
Fiddle, banjo, guitar, Vocals / Old-time, traditional country, progressive country, country-rock
"Gentle on My Mind," counterculture's think-I'll-be-movin'-along song, became Hartford's first hit when Glen Campbell covered it in 1967, leading to three Grammys and fame for its multi-talented composer. Soon Hartford appeared on TV's "Smothers Brothers Comedy Hour" and then became a regular on the "Glen Campbell Goodtime Hour." After touring with his own band for a while, Hartford created a spell-binding solo act, which he continues to the present. His long-time love of riverboats is seen in many of his songs and was the basis of a TV special in the 1980s. With his fiddle and banjo, Hartford is first and foremost an exceptional entertainer and is famous for his riveting and memorable solo performances. — *David Vinopal*

○ **Mark Twang** / 1976 / Flying Fish 70020
His first and one of his best, with Hartford as solo artist. — *Charles S. Wolfe*

● **Me Oh My, How the Time Does Fly** / 1982 / Flying Fish 70440
The CD version of *Me Oh My, How the Time Does Fly—A John Hartford Anthology* includes an additional ten tracks. — *AMG*

○ **Gum Tree Canoe** / 1987 / Flying Fish 289
Best rounded of all the Flying Fish albums—everything from bluegrass to Civil War songs. — *Charles S. Wolfe*

Hartford & Hartford / 1991 / Flying Fish 70566
Hartford's son, Jamie, a fine mandolin player, joins his father for this album. — *Charles S. Wolfe*

Hawkshaw Hawkins (Harold Hawkins)
b. Dec. 22, 1921, Huntingdon, WV, d. Mar. 5, 1963
Vocals, guitar / Country

Born Harold F. Hawkins, Hawkshaw is a country singer, guitarist, songwriter, and entertainer. A large man (6 ft. 6 in.) with a deep singing voice, Hawkins was an immensely popular performer in country music for many years without the benefit of big record success. He started on radio, becoming a regular on WWVA's "Wheeling Jamboree" by 1946 and making his first records for the King label around that time. By 1953 he signed with RCA Victor and became a regular member of the Grand Ole Opry by 1955. Described as "the man with eleven and a half yards of personality," Hawkins was a warm and engaging performer both onstage and on records, able to pull off a wide variety of material from maudlin weepers to uptempo novelties. His label-jumping from Columbia by the late '50s and back to King by the early '60s moved his material closer to commercial mainstream country, but his time in the spotlight ran out when he perished in the same plane crash as Cowboy Copas and Patsy Cline. — *Cub Koda*

● **Vol. 1** / 1988 / Deluxe 587
A good single disc collection of many of Hawkins' best songs. — *AMG*

○ **Hawk 1953-61** / 1991 / Bear Family 15539
An excellent three-CD boxed set. All the RCA-Victor and Columbia recordings, with superlative sound and liner notes. — *Cub Koda*

Jimmy Heap & the Melody Masters
Guitar, vocals, bandleader / Country
Texas-born bandleader Heap put together the Melody Masters after WWII and quickly became an attraction on the roadhouse/dancehall circuit, mining similar turf to that of other Western swing bands of the area. Quite popular from the late '40s through early '50s, Heap & the Melody Masters are generally credited with one of the earliest versions of the country classic "Release Me," as well as several other hits such as another country standard, "The Wild Side of Life." — *Cub Koda*

○ **Release Me** / 1992 / Bear Family 15617
A great 30-track, single-disc compilation of Heap's earliest and best sides. Includes the title track, "Let's Do It Just Once," "It Takes a Heap of Lovin'," and "Ethyl in My Gas Tank (No Gal in My Arms)." This is great Western swing-style material in transition. — *Cub Koda*

Michael Henderson
b. Jul. 7, 1951, Yazoo City, MS
A behind the scenes star-of-all-trades for years, Henderson had done everything but put out a solo album prior to joining RCA. A Missouri native, he once led a club band, the Bel-Airs, based in Columbia. After moving to Nashville, he became an in-demand session guitarist and mandolinist, a road musician backing up Kevin Welch and Tracy Nelson (among others), and leader of a couple of the toughest bar bands in Music City (The Bluebloods, The Snakes). He also enjoyed success as a songwriter—his hits include "Powerful Stuff" by the Fabulous Thunderbirds. — *Michael McCall*

● **Country Music Made Me Do It** / Mar. 15, 1994 / RCA 66324
Pure roadhouse honky-tonk, stoked with bent notes, twisted humor and a couple of tough, bittersweet ballads. — *Michael McCall*

Don Henry
Guitar / Progressive country
Don Henry came to prominence when Kathy Mattea's version of "Where've You Been" (cowritten with Mattea's husband Jon Vezner) won every award in sight in 1990 and 1991. Henry grew up in suburban San Jose, CA, and moved to Nashville in 1979, where he spent four years copying tapes for publisher Tree International (now Sony/Tree) and then became a staff songwriter there. He wrote tunes for Mattea, John Conlee, T.G. Sheppard, and Conway Twitty and won Tree's Writer of the Year award in 1990 before recording his first album. — *Brian Mansfield*

○ **Wild in the Backyard** / 1991 / Epic 46034
Henry's debut album can only be classified country because of its high moral sense (which it actually gets from folk) and from the styles of the session players. With its malls and Mercedes, *Wild in the Backyard* isn't country—it's suburban. Henry's a singer/songwriter capable of drama and humor within the same song. But

his real strength is his ability to create honest humanity, a trait equally present in "Harley," about a boy named after a chopper, and "Half a Heart," a touching tale of unfulfilled promise. —*Brian Mansfield*

Joe Henry

California singer-songwriter who North Carolina upbringing gives him strong country roots. He's also Madonna's brother-in-law, but he doesn't like to talk about it. —*Brian Mansfield*

Fireman's Wedding / Mammoth 0067
CD-5 containing title track (originally from *Kindness of the World*) and four live recordings, including versions of A.P. Carter's "Hello Stranger" and Merle Travis' "Dark as a Dungeon." —*Brian Mansfield*

Shuffletown / 1990 / A&M 5315
Moody, jazzy, primarily acoustic album produced by T-Bone Burnett. —*Brian Mansfield*

● **Short Man's Room** / Jun. 16, 1992 / Mammoth 0037
○ **Kindness of the World** / 1993 / Mammoth 0057
More strong songs, some with definite country leaning towards. Henry covers Tom T. Hall's "I Flew Over Our House Last Night," and he wrote "She Always Goes" with George Strait in mind. —*Brian Mansfield*

Highway 101

Group / Country-Rock, Country-Pop
This country-pop quartet formed in Los Angeles in 1986 and a year later had a #4 hit with "The Bed You Made for Me." They won Group of the Year honors from two of the awards associations before lead singer Paulette Carson left for a solo career. —*David Vinopal*

● **Highway 101** / 1987 / Warner Brothers 25608
The main thing that this country-rock quartet had going for it was lead singer Paulette Carlson, who approximated the throaty, torn vocal style of Stevie Nicks, but with a Southern accent. The group was heard best on its debut album, which included such characteristic hits as "Whiskey, If You Were a Woman" and "The Bed You Made for Me." —*William Ruhlmann*

Highway 101, Vol. 2 / 1988 / Warner Brothers 25742
This second volume includes "Desperate Road," "All the Reasons Why," and other hits. —*AMG*

Faith Hill

Raised in Star, Mississippi, by adoptive parents, Faith Hill grew up idolizing Reba McEntire. She even worked briefly for McEntire's Starstruck Entertainment before signing her first record deal. Hill's debut single, "Wild One," spent four weeks atop the country singles chart in 1993, making her one of the most important female voices to emerge that year. —*Brian Mansfield*

● **Take Me As I Am** / Warner Brothers 45389
Whether she's singing songs associated with Janis Joplin ("Piece of My Heart") or Maura O'Connell ("I Would Be Stronger Than That"), Faith Hill sounds every bit like the new-generation Reba McEntire heir that her press makes her out to be. Hill sings with a natural tear in her voice that recalls McEntire without ever mimicking her. Hill sounds like a star on all 10 cuts, whether she's fronting minimal acoustic accompaniment on "Just Around the Eyes" or rocking out on "Wild One." —*Brian Mansfield*

Chris Hillman

b. Dec. 4, 1944, Los Angeles, CA
Mandolin, bass / Progressive country, country-rock
This Californian has been perhaps the greatest influence on the country-rock/folk genre that's taken for granted today. He began as the mandolin player of the Scottsville Squirrel Barkers, a group which turned into the Hillmen, a bluegrass-oriented group based in California. Then came the Byrds, a legendary country-rock quintet that recorded Bob Dylan's "Mr. Tambourine Man" (in 1965) and the pioneer country-rock album *Sweetheart of the Rodeo*, with Gram Parsons. Hillman and Parsons then formed the Flying Burrito Brothers in 1969. In the '70s Hillman performed as a solo act. In the '80s Hillman formed the Desert Rose Band and has been touring with them. —*David Vinopal*

○ **The Hillmen (Chris Hillman)** / 1971 / Together 1012

Recorded approximately two years before Hillman joined the Byrds, this album does as much to explain his background as the Byrds' *Sweetheart of the Rodeo* album. This fine bluegrass band also featured the Gosdin brothers, who not only had country hits during the '70s and '80s, but also made a fine record with Gene Clark. Worth looking for—some fine music. —*Jim Worbois*

Slippin' Away / 1976 / Asylum 1062
Having recently departed Souther, Hillman, & Furay, this album more heavily reflects his association with Manassas than anything he did with SH&F. —*Jim Worbois*

● **Morning Sky** / 1982 / Sugar Hill 3729
A back-to-the-roots album (of sorts), Hillman has given up the bass in favor of the mandolin and acoustic guitar for this mostly acoustic album of other people's tunes. The band is made up of people with whom Hillman has worked over the years, and it's obvious they are comfortable together. Listening to this album is almost like eavesdropping on a group of friends making music in their living room. —*Jim Worbois*

○ **Desert Rose** / 1984 / Sugar Hill 3743
Bluegrass, country, and country-rock, Hillman played mandolin on this album, but his main instrument (with the Byrds and Desert Rose Band) is bass. —*Mark A. Humphrey*

Becky Hobbs

Hobbs is a piano-pounding honky-tonker who performs cheeky country boppers and hard-bitten ballads. An Oklahoma native, she had some success as a songwriter in Los Angeles providing songs for Helen Reddy and Jane Olivor before moving to Nashville. —*Michael McCall*

● **All Keyed Up** / 1988 / RCA 9770
Originally released on MTM Records, her contract and album were picked up by RCA after MTM's demise. It was her sixth label in a decade, and getting a second chance with this worthy album didn't help much. She deserves better. —*Michael McCall*

Homer & Jethro

Country comedy
Henry "Homer" Haynes and Kenneth "Jethro" Burns remain country music's most famous comedy team, as well as one its most enduring duos, more than 20 years after Homer's death ended their partnership. Their stock-in-trade was parodies of other songs, as well as cornball comic tunes, and their humor was supported by deft musicianship and great timing. Late in their career, they recorded several solid instrumental albums as the Nashville String Band. After Haynes' passing, Burns went on to record several albums highlighting his influential mandolin style. —*Michael McCall*

● **The Worst of Homer & Jethro** / 1957 / RCA 1560
Their best early parodies, including the hilarious "How Much Is that Hound Dog in the Window?" and "Jam Bowl Liar," a recasting of Hank Williams' "Jambalaya." —*Michael McCall*

○ **Playing It Straight** / 1962 / RCA 2459
Showing off their instrumental talents. —*Michael McCall*

● **The Best of** / 1992 / RCA 61088
Their latter favorites, including their version of the Beatles' "I Want to Hold Your Hand," and "The Battle of Kookamonga," based on Johnny Horton's "The Battle of New Orleans." —*Michael McCall*

Johnny Horton

b. Apr. 3, 1929, Tyler, TX, d. Nov. 5, 1960
Vocals / Traditional country
Horton is remembered mainly for his popular historical "saga" songs such as "The Battle of New Orleans," "North to Alaska," "Johnny Reb." However, during his brief career (he was killed in a car wreck in 1960 at the height of his popularity), he also produced a body of work that influences country singers today. Exemplified by songs like "Honky Tonk Man" (covered by Dwight Yoakam), "I'm Comin' Home," and "One Woman Man" (recently a hit for George Jones), this style bridged the gap between honky-tonk and rockabilly, with the chugging, twangy, picked-close-to-the-bridge guitar of Grady Martin perfectly complementing and answering Horton's vibrant and expressive singing. Horton has a fine voice with a huge range, versatile enough to adapt to almost any kind of song. On his

(Honkyabilly? Rock-a-tonk?) sides he swoops effortlessly from low notes to high, adding just the right growling edge when needed, and the most effective use of the vocal "break" or "tear" since Hank Williams. —*George Bedard*

● **Johnny Horton's Greatest Hits** / 1961 / CBS 8396
Though best remembered for his historical songs (and they're all here), this album shows another side of Johnny Horton. "Honky-Tonk Man," "Whispering Pines," and "All For The Love Of A Girl" clearly show that Horton had far more talent than his novelty songs would indicate. —*Jim Worbois*

● **Rockin' Rollin' Johnny Horton** / 1981 / Bear Family 15543
This album features re-releases of tracks originally recorded for Columbia during the '50s. —*AMG*

★ **American Originals** / 1989 / CBS 45071
This album contains "The Battle of New Orleans," "Sink the Bismark," "Honky Tonk Man," and other hits. —*AMG*

☆ **1956-1960** / 1991 / Bear Family 15470
From the first note recorded at Columbia, to the last hotel room demo, a superb in-depth look at Horton's later career. These four CDs are a collector's dream. —*Hank Davis*

David Houston
b. Dec. 9, 1938, Shreveport, LA
Vocals, guitar / Country
Houston apparently came from good stock: his lineage includes Sam Houston and Gen. Robert E. Lee. Born and raised in Bossier City, LA, Houston became a regular on the Louisiana Hayride as a teenager. Apparently his soaring tenor voice wasn't totally appreciated; he found trouble getting work in the music business, and ended up as an insurance underwriter. But record producer Billy Sherrill brought Houston into the fold when Epic Records was still a young label (the early '60s), and Houston brought the company its first real hit with "Mountain of Love." In 1966 he broke through to major status with "Almost Persuaded," which netted a pair of Grammy awards and brought pop recognition as well. A member of the Grand Ole Opry since 1971, he racked up 28 hit records over a decade, including duets with Tammy Wynette and Barbara Mandrell. —*Tom Roland*

● **American Originals** / 1989 / CBS 45074
Houston's soaring falsetto is well represented in this greatest-hits collection on CD. "Almost Persuaded," "Baby Baby (I Know You're a Lady)," "Mountain of Love," and "My Elusive Dreams" (duet with Tammy Wynette) are all here—though, sad to say, "Livin' in a House Full of Love" is missing. —*Tom Roland*

Ferlin Husky
b. Dec. 3, 1927, Flat River, MO
Vocals, guitar / Traditional country
This performer made a name for himself—in fact, three names for himself—over the years. As Terry Preston, in 1953 he dueted with Jean Shepard on "A Dear John Letter" ("Forgive Me John" was soon to follow); two years later, as Ferlin Husky, he had his first hit with the novelty song "I Feel Better All Over"; and in the comic philosopher guise, Simon Crum, Ferlin had success with "Country Music Is Here to Stay." Ferlin is best-known for his Number 1 hit "On the Wings of a Dove." —*David Vinopal*

● **Capitol Collectors Series** / 1989 / Capitol 91629

Frank Ifield
b. Nov. 30, 1937
Vocals / Country
This English-born, Australian-reared balladeer with a unique yodeling style was highly successful during the early '60s, with a string of pop/country hits, which includes "I Remember You," "I'm Confessing that I Love You" and "Lovesick Blues." —*Hank Davis*

● **The Best of Frank Ifield** / 196z / Curb 77453
Combines a hillbilly yodel with slick pop stylings. —*Hank Davis*

○ **The Emi Years** / Capitol
A generous 20-track sampler of his biggest hits (circa 1960), including "I Remember You." —*Hank Davis*

Alan Jackson
b. Oct. 17, 1958, Newnan, GA
Vocals, guitar / Traditional country

A lanky, quiet-spoken Georgian with an understated sense of direction and intelligence, Jackson was the first artist signed when Arista opened its Nashville divison in 1988. A singer with a strong feel for traditional country, he has steadily built his career rather than become an overnight sensation. He started strong with *Here in the Real World*, and each of his first three albums sold more than the one before. Between 1990 and 1993 he had seven Number 1 singles, more than any other act except Garth Brooks (he co-wrote a good many of those songs.) He joined the *Grand Ole Opry* cast in 1991. —*Brian Mansfield*

○ **Here in the Real World** / 1990 / Arista 8623
"I'd Love You All Over Again" was Jackson's fifth single but his first Number 1. But any country fan of the time would also recognize the title track and "Chasin' That Neon Rainbow." —*Brian Mansfield*

Don't Rock the Jukebox / 1991 / Arista 8681
The album art's really ugly, but the music isn't—"Don't Rock the Jukebox," "Someday," "Love's Got a Hold on You," and "Dallas" all hit the top of the singles charts. And "Midnight in Montgomery," which details a ghostly encounter with Hank Williams' spirit, became a video classic. —*Brian Mansfield*

★ **A Lot About Livin' (& A Little 'bout Love)** / 1992 / Arista 18711
By this third album—when many artists start to run out of ideas—Jackson sounds like he's just starting to hit his stride with songs like "Tonight I Climbed the Wall," "She's Got the Rhythm (And I Got the Blues)" (cowritten with Randy Travis), and "Chattahoochee," one of country's great summer singles. He also continues a proud tradition of country artists covering blues tunes by singing "Mercury Blues" by a minor Bay Area bluesman named K.C. Douglas. —*Brian Mansfield*

○ **Who I Am** / 1994 / Arista 18759
The huge singles aren't as readily apparent here, but Jackson begins to reveal more of himself with his album. "Gone Country" is a subtly brilliant jab at people who discover country music only when there's money to be made. The joke is that Jackson leads the album with Eddie Cochran's teenage-angst anthem "Summertime Blues." Jackson pulls out chesnuts from the catalogs of Con Hunley and the Kendalls, and writes "Job Description" to explain to his daughter why daddy is never home. In a time when even artists had trouble telling all the young hat acts apart, a personal statement like *Who I Am* was possibly the smartest move Jackson could have made. —*Brian Mansfield*

Stonewall Jackson
b. Nov. 6, 1932, Tabor City, NC
Vocals, guitar / Traditional country
Stonewall Jackson (and this is his real name) probably thought he was doing well when his "Life to Go" was a big country hit in 1958. A year later, though, he had a career-maker in "Waterloo," a crossover that reached the top in the country and pop charts. As a result, he starred on Dick Clark's "American Bandstand," the TV show that usually featured pop and only pop. He also had luck with his self-penned "I Washed My Hands in Muddy Water" and with "Stamp out Loneliness." —*David Vinopal*

○ **The Dynamite Stonewall Jackson** / 1959 / Sony 8186
Collection of early hits—"Waterloo," "George Jones," "Life to Go," "Smoke Along the Track," "Why I'm Walking"—almost all good songs, delivered in his powerful, homely, but engaging voice. —*George Bedard*

● **American Originals** / 1989 / CBS 45070
A re-packaging of many of Jackson's best-known songs, including the great "Don't Be Angry," "A Wound Time Can't Erase," and "Smoke Along the Tracks," the latter revived by Dwight Yoakam. For some unfathomable reason, "I Washed My Hands in Muddy Water" is missing. These kinds of omissions were standard place in this half-hearted oldies series. —*Michael McCall*

Sonny James (Jimmy Loden, the Southern Gentleman)
b. May 1, 1929, Hackleburg, AL
Vocals, guitar / Country-pop
Known as the Southern Gentleman, he had sixteen consecutive records between 1967 and 1971 that reached Number 1. His rich and mellow voice helped make him a crossover artist, starting with "Young Love," a pop hit in 1956. Even when his material was country, James presented it in a pop form acceptable to a large

audience. Among his many hits are "Running Bear," "You're the Only World I Know," and "Take Good Care of Her." In the '60s he also appeared in the movies, including *Hillbilly in a Haunted House* with Lon Chaney, Jr. and *Las Vegas Hillbillies* with Jayne Mansfield. —*David Vinopal*

American Originals / 1989 / CBS 45066
The best of James's Columbia hits. —*Mark A. Humphrey*

● **Capitol Collector's Series** / 1990 / Capitol 91630
Features 20 of James's most popular cuts. —*AMG*

Waylon Jennings

b. Jun. 15, 1937, Littlefield, TX
Vocals, guitar / Traditional country, progressive country
The ultimate outlaw, Waylon Jennings squeezed a lot of recording and a lot more living into the years between touring as Buddy Holly's bass player and recording the *Highwayman II* album in 1991. And all the time he fought against the lush but sterile Nashville sound and against the Nashville establishment record labels that produced this sameness of sound. With fellow Texan and close friend Willie Nelson, Jennings changed the way things were done in Music City, including insisting on recording with their own bands rather than with homogenized studio musicians of the Nashville feudal system.

In the early '60s, Jennings and his band the Waylors were doing well out of Phoenix. Chet Atkins learned about the talented singer and offered him a contract. Jennings's first singles did well enough ("Anita You're Dreaming," for example), but the husky, powerful voice, the faded-jeans image, and the raw and emotional material delivered with a rock beat scared some people in Nashville. He enjoyed moderate success through the '60s, recording and touring and building up an enthusiastic audience (*cult* would be accurate) for this unique sound.

In spite of all the talent, Jennings wasn't to become a major star until the '70s brought such influential albums as *Good Hearted Woman* (1972) and *Honky-Tonk Heroes*, (1973). Then came the landmark album that sold millions, *Wanted: the Outlaws* (1976), that featured Jennings, Jessi Colter (his wife), Tompall Glaser, and Willie Nelson, performing eleven previously released songs. Jennings was a superstar and the outlaws had won. As further proof, in 1978 the *Waylon & Willie* album was a runaway hit, remaining on the country and pop charts for over a year. His singles did as well as the albums, with such hits as "Luckenbach, Texas," "The Wurlitzer Prize," "I've Always Been Crazy," and "Amanda." Meanwhile, the Outlaw clones proliferated, leading (thanks to the mechanical bull rodeo) to the *Urban Cowboy* fad, and prompting Jennings to pen and record "Don't You Think this Outlaw Bit's Done Got out of Hand." But Jennings had racked up eight consecutive gold albums while keeping his musical integrity, and the direction of country music had been changed.

With his superstar status intact, Jennings recorded regularly in the '80s, but his popularity slipped a notch or two, having in fact nowhere to go but down. In 1985, Jennings, Willie Nelson, Johnny Cash, and Kris Kristofferson produced their *Highwayman* album, a best-seller that spawned a Number 1 single of the same title. Jennings, having done his music his way, has earned the right to rest on his laurels, should he choose to. —*David Vinopal*

Good Hearted Woman / 1972 / RCA 4647
Waylon's career really began to take off with this album, which featured two hits. Still holds up well. —*Jim Worbois*

☆ **Honky Tonk Heroes** / 1973 / Pair 1110
As Waylon himself once noted, the "outlaw bit" got out of hand pretty fast. It's no accident that this, his defining outlaw-era album, hit the streets before the term ever did. Nine of the ten songs are from the pen of then-unknown Billy Joe Shaver, a gritty Texas songwriter from whom more would definitely be heard. —*Dan Cooper*

Early Years / 1979 / RCA 9561
Pre-outlaw Waylon, though "Only Daddy That'll Walk the Line" is as tough as any of his 1970s work. —*Dan Cooper*

★ **Greatest Hits** / 1979 / RCA 3378
Jennings' career dates back to his days as a Cricket in the 50s, but it wasn't until the 70s that he began to define a particular hard-edged subgenre of country music with his rock shuffles and his deep, sardonic voice on songs like "Lonesome, On'ry and Mean" and "Luckenbach, Texas," the best of which are included here. (A

second volume, released in 1984, is also recommended.) —*William Ruhlmann*

Will the Wolf Survive / 1985 / MCA 31102
Moving to MCA after a long stay at RCA brought Jennings a new producer in Jimmy Bowen and a fresh approach. This resulted in one of his better albums, typified by his version of the Los Lobos title track and a cover of Steve Earle's tailor-made "The Devil's Right Hand." —*William Ruhlmann*

○ **Greatest Hits, Vol. 2** / 1985 / RCA 5325
This second volume contains Jennings's "Theme from the Dukes of Hazzard," "America," "I Ain't Living Long like This," and more. —*AMG*

● **Only Daddy That'll Walk the Line** / 1993 / Camden 10306
You wouldn't think that two CDs with 40 cuts could adequately summarize a career as important as Jennings's, but quite the opposite is true. If anything, this box set highlights more than we might want to know of Waylon's creative rise, peak, and artistic decline. The first disc, covering the years 1965-74, will be as a revelation to anyone unfamiliar with his luminous early work. On cuts like "Stop the World (and Let Me Off)" and "Just to Satisfy You" his struggle to free himself of the suffocating Nashville Sound is palpable. On "Lonesome, On'ry and Mean" and "I'm a Ramblin' Man," his success at doing the same is vicariously liberating. Disc two picks up in the midst of the revolution ("Are You Sure Hank Done It this Way," "Bob Wills is Still the King") and carries on through the Napoleonic expansion ("Luckenbach, Texas," a Top-40 pop hit). But the last quarter of the set is really quite depressing, as the performances become more and more self-consciously outlaw. Call "Theme From the Dukes of Hazzard" Waterloo, if you will. The one gem from the 1980s, Jessi Colter's lovely "Storms Never Last," can be taken more than one way. —*Dan Cooper*

Santiago Jimenez, Jr.

d. Jun. 22, 1984
Vocals, accordion / Tex-Mex
The namesake of one of the pioneers of Norteno music, this singer and accordionist takes a more traditional approach than that of his celebrated brother, Flaco. Santiago favors the two-row button accordion, and many of his recordings offer the basic two voices, accordion, and guitar presentation of Tex-Mex music. In addition to recording extensively for local San Antonio labels, Santiago has recorded for Arhoolie and Rounder and has appeared in the documentary film, *Chulas Fronteras*. —*Mark A. Humphrey*

Familia Y Tradicion / 1989 / Rounder 6033
The songs on this album were mostly rigid, though spirited, emphasizing the polka and midtempo beat and sung in Spanish. Jimenez played the two-row button accordion, and his riffs and solos were fluidly expressed and superbly played, while his singing was intense and earnest. The instrumental "Daddy's Polka" displayed his accordion skills, while "El corrido de Santiago Jimenez" paid homage to his father's accomplishments and struggles, and "Ester" was a tribute to his wife. Only on "You Are My Sunshine" did Jimenez veer away from strict ethnic traditions to do a fun/throwawy piece. Otherwise, these were topical and/or vintage numbers that celebrated the conjunto sound with vigor and love. —*Ron Wynn*

● **El Mero Mero De San Antonio** / Nov. 1990 / Arhoolie 317
More traditional than his *hermano* Flaco, singer and accordionist Santiago plays Norteno music much the same as his celebrated father did in the '40s. —*Mark A. Humphrey*

El Gato Negro / Rounder 6044
Santiago Jimenez, Jr.'s trademarks are the two-row button accordion and passionate, fiery singing in the classic conjunto mode. That was the menu on this session that featured 14 tracks, with Jimenez doing polkas, rancheros and boleros, but no pop or rock covers. His band included Jesse Castillo on bajo sexto, with bassist Robert Ramos and drummer Cookie Martinez. The short numbers (none longer than four and a half minutes) were structured to give Jimenez's vocals and accordion bursts maximum space, while the backing players tightly filled in underneath him. This was contemporary conjunto with an authentic and vintage sensibility, performed by one of the idiom's major stars. —*Ron Wynn*

Johnnie & Jack

Somewhat like the Delmore Brothers and Louvin Brothers, the brothers-in-law Johnnie & Jack (Johnnie Wright, b. May 13, 1914; and Jack Anglin, b. May 13, 1916, d. Mar. 8, 1963) connected the prewar Appalachian harmony era to the postwar commercial country era. To add an additional twist, their two most memorable hits, "Poison Love" and "Ashes of Love," were bluegrass-styled numbers propelled by a latin beat. In 1937, Johnnie married Muriel Deason, better known by her stage name, Kitty Wells. In 1963, Jack died in a car wreck, allegedly en route to Patsy Cline's funeral, though some say he was heading the opposite direction. —*Dan Cooper*

○ **And the Tennessee Mountain Boys** / 1958 / Bear Family 15553
As usual, Bear Family is way ahead of the game. While domestic RCA has not been moved to provide country fans with so much as a single-disc Johnnie & Jack compilation, the German indie has gone ahead and produced this lavish boxed set comprised of six CDs and a book. The collection covers their complete RCA recordings from 1947-1962. —*Dan Cooper*

Michael Johnson

b. Aug. 8, 1944
Vocals, guitar / Progressive country
Pinpointing Michael Johnson on the musical scale of style is a difficult chore. As a teenage guitar player, he took notes from seminal rocker Chuck Berry and jazzman Charlie Byrd. At age 21 he spent a year in Barcelona, studying under classical guitarist Graciano Tarrago; once he'd returned to the United States, he signed up for a one-year folk tour as a member of the Mitchell Trio, where his fellow musicians included John Denver. To complicate matters, when he first made inroads in the record business, he did it in pop, racking up hits with "Bluer Than Blue," "Almost Like Being in Love," and "This Night Won't Last Forever." He hadn't yet covered polka music, or country, but he tackled the latter idiom after signing with RCA Records in the winter of 1985. His pleasant intonation, relaxed phrasing, and unusual pronunciations blend well with his usual acoustic arrangements, although Johnson's never quite earned the level of recognition his talents deserve. —*Tom Roland*

● **Wings** / 1987 / RCA 9501
Johnson's first country album didn't stray far from the formula that gave him pop hits. The band on *Wings* is essentially the same as on "Bluer Than Blue," but Johnson leaned toward songs by Nashville writers. And what songs they were! *Wings* yielded two Number 1 singles, "Give Me Wings" and the ultra-romantic "The Moon Is Still over Her Shoulder." Those are the hits, but the quality songwriting runs as deep as any country album of the time. —*Brian Mansfield*

David Lynn Jones

b. , Bexar, Arkansas
Vocals, guitar / Progressive country
A talented singer/songwriter who released his debut in 1987, Jones has received plenty of critical acclaim but little action on the charts. —*AMG*

● **Mixed Emotions** / 1992 / Liberty 97251
After two albums for Mercury that left his promise unfulfilled, David Lynn Jones switched labels and recorded an album in his home studio in Bexar, AR. Like a saved man flirting with sin, Jones forsakes Nashville wisdom and takes his cues from renegade American rockers like Leon Russell and Robbie Robertson. In his heart he's still country, but he revs the tempos, cranks the guitars, and lays on the horns as he takes off screaming into the Arkansas Delta. —*Brian Mansfield*

George Jones

b. Sep. 12, 1931, Saratoga, TX
Vocals, guitar / Traditional country
A singer's singer, George Jones is likely to appear on anybody's list of the top male singers in country music history, along with Hank Williams and Lefty Frizzell. Like the other two, Jones interprets the country archetypes—broken love, human failings, sweet dreams gone sour—through personal experience; unlike the other two, he has somehow managed to reach age 60 despite the excesses encountered over the decades in coping with the music

business, the road, and life. And his unsurpassed voice remains unscathed after 40 years of artistic heights and the self-destructive depths that led to his nickname of "No-Show" Jones. By singing about what they have lived, he and Williams and Frizzell are the ultimate interpreters of honky-tonk.

In 1955 Jones made his first record on the Starday label, charting with the self-penned "Why Baby Why." From the start he showed his versatility by singing rockabilly and his trademark torch songs with equal ease. Immediately he signed with the Louisiana Hayride, moving on to the Opry in less than four months. More of his uptempo rollicking hits followed, among them "White Lightning" (his first Number 1) and "The Race Is On." In the '60s the hits kept coming, Jones scoring with the slow, emotion-draining sad songs that no one has done better, among them "Window up Above," "She Thinks I Still Care," and "We Must Have Been out of Our Minds," the latter recorded with Melba Montgomery, who travelled with Jones's show and whose voice blended with his perfectly. Though the heavy drinking was getting out of control, the hits continued in the mid '60s, with "Walk through This World with Me" and "If My Heart Had Windows," just two of those that charted.

In 1967 Jones met Tammy Wynette, and they became the king and queen of country music, the two recording hits, both solo and together. Their duet "We're Gonna Hold On" (1973) brought Jones one half of a Number 1, the first he had since 1967. "Golden Ring" and "Near You" came out after the two had agreed on a divorce. In the '80s the awards came for Jones, including an Grammy for best country male vocalist. His life apparently had straightened out; Jones no longer was called "No-Show," and he was busy with collaborations (Merle Haggard and Ray Charles) and solo efforts, including "If Drinking Don't Kill Me Her Memory Will," "Yesterday's Wine," and "Who's Gonna Fill Their Shoes." As of this writing, this master singer is in perfect voice, bending notes and interpreting phrases in his inimitable way. His influence on other singers is obvious: when you listen to many of the contemporary singers, in a sense you're listening to Jones, for they graduated from his school, by listening to him in person or to one of the 100 albums he has recorded since 1956. The "legend in his own time" cliche seems much too weak to describe George Jones. —*David Vinopal*

George Jones Salutes Hank Williams / 1960 / Mercury 822646
Country's greatest singer performs the songs of country's greatest writer. Liner notes by Elvis Costello. (The 1984 release is a 10-song abridged version of a longer, earlier set, Mercury SR 60257.) —*William Ruhlmann*

George Jones Sings Bob Wills / 1962 / United Artists 6221
Rather than try to ape the Wills arrangements, producer Pappy Daily sets Jones up in front of a honky-tonk combo and lets the Ol' Possum rip. The combo rips, too, on a couple of instrumentals. —*Dan Cooper*

○ **Greatest Hits** / 1962 / Mercury 20621
A 10-song compilation of Jones's Mercury years including the Top-10 hits "Treasure of Love," "White Lightning," "Who Shot Sam," "The Window up Above," and "Tender Years," plus the song that started it all, "Why Baby Why." —*William Ruhlmann*

I Get Lonely in a Hurry / 1965 / United Artists 3388
Includes his big hit "The Race Is On" and the haunting "Book of Memories." —*George Bedard*

☆ **Trouble in Mind** / 1965 / United Artists 6408
One of his best albums. There are sappy vocal choruses on some of the tunes, but they can't diminish George. A few that don't—"You Done Me Wrong" (written by George) and "It's a Sin"—are among the best things he's ever recorded. Also included are great versions of a couple of Hank Williams songs and a couple of truly definitive songs: "My Tears Are Overdue" and "Sometimes You Just Can't Win." Essential for anyone interested in Jones, country music, or American folk-based popular music in general. —*George Bedard*

☆ **Burn the Honky-Tonk Down** / 1970 / Rounder 15
Good collection of songs from the Musicor era, including the beautiful and hard-to-find "Beneath Still Waters." The liner notes go to great length to carp about the overproduction of Jones's records over the years. Ironically, some of the more elaborate Musicor productions such as "Good Year for the Roses" are included here. A bit too much is made of this—fans of '60s mainstream country learn how to tune out sappy vocal choruses and

such. In any case, this and the other Rounder selection, *Heartaches & Hangovers*, have the great advantage of being stuff from Jones's peak period that may actually be available for purchase. —*George Bedard*

○ **The Best of Sacred Music** / 1971 / Gusto 0136
Country gospel classics like "I'll Fly Away" plus a great song cowritten by Jones, "Small Time Laboring Man." Also "Family Bible." Highly recommended. —*George Bedard*

George Jones & Melba Montgomery / 1974 / Musicor 3259
Great duets with Tennessee beauty Melba Montgomery—her voice suits Jones's better than Wynette's. Includes the eerie "Long as We're Dreaming" and "Long Walk Off a Tall Rock." Lots of dobro. Not for the countrypolitan. —*George Bedard*

My Very Special Guests / 1979 / Epic 35544
Jones duets with some expected country contemporaries (Tammy Wynette, Johnny Paycheck), some outlaws (Waylon Jennings, Willie Nelson), and, most interestingly, some up-and-coming and pop-oriented guests (Emmylou Harris, Linda Ronstadt, Elvis Costello), often to beneficial effect for both. —*William Ruhlmann*

○ **I Am What I Am** / 1980 / Epic 36568
If this album contained only George's classic performance on "He Stopped Loving Her Today," it would be worth getting. Fortunately, that's not the only good performance here. —*Jim Worbois*

Still the Same Ole Me / 1981 / Epic 37106
Recorded at the peak of his popularity, this album is sometimes restrained, and sometimes finds Jones at his uncontrollable best. Predominantly honky-tonk ballads; best cuts (besides the obvious hits) include "Good Ones and Bad Ones," "Together Alone," and the raucous "You Can't Get the Hell out of Texas." —*Tom Roland*

○ **Encore—George Jones & Tammy Wynette** / 1981 / Epic 37348
One album in an entire series of greatest-hits releases for CBS artists, this package documents the very best singles by George Jones and Tammy Wynette, an act that was once country music's top running soap opera. The sad hitch in Wynette's voice, and the greasy slides in the Possum's, make for an interesting contrast. They sound just as good after their 1975 breakup ("Golden Ring," "Two Story House") as before ("We're Gonna Hold On," "Near You"). —*Tom Roland*

★ **Anniversary—Ten Years of Hits** / 1982 / Epic 38323
Choosing "the greatest country record of all time" is the sort of fundamentally stupid game no fan can ever resist. Often as not, the top vote-getter is George Jones's "He Stopped Loving Her Today." Between it and "The Grand Tour," both of which appear on this truly essential collection, you could probably draw tears from the Terminator. Also includes "Bartender's Blues," a duet with James Taylor, and "If Drinkin' Don't Kill Me (Her Memory Will)." —*Dan Cooper*

☆ **White Lightning** / 1984 / ACE 13(10')
Uptempo material from the Starday and Mercury eras—includes the rockabilly experiments from Starday. —*George Bedard*

☆ **The Lone Star Legend** / 1985 / ACE 139
Mostly Mercury material, with a couple of Starday cuts. Emphasis is on the ballads, including previously unissued songs. Includes the great "Hearts in My Dreams" and the incredible "Mr. Fool," one of the most masterful pieces of country singing ever recorded. Along with *White Lightnin'*, a good portrait of the '50s Jones. —*George Bedard*

One Woman Man / 1989 / Epic 44078
One of Jones's best Epic albums, despite two previously released songs being tagged on to fill it out. One of those is "Radio Lover," a bizarre cheating tale. Things get even stranger with "Ya Ba Da Ba Do (So Are You)," in which Jones gets drunk and talks to a Fred Flintstone glass and an Elvis Presley wine decanter (it also sparked legal action by Hanna-Barber). Beyond that, it's quality Jones honky-tonk and weepers, including a first-rate remake of "Just out of Reach (Of My Two Empty Arms)." —*Brian Mansfield*

★ **Hard Core Honky-Tonk—the Best of George Jones** / 1991 / Mercury 848978
This album contains reissues of recordings Jones made for Mercury in the earlier days of his career. —*AMG*

★ **The Best of (1955—1967)** / 1991 / Rhino 70531
This album contains the tracks from Jones's years at Mercury, United Artists, Musicor, and Starday that influenced every coun-

try artist after him, from Buck Owens to Sammy Kershaw. These songs aren't just songs—Jones makes them sound as if he's talking about someone real each time. The album contains "She Thinks I Still Care," "The Race Is On," "White Lightning," "Just One More," and others. —*AMG*

And Along Came Jones / 1991 / MCA 10398
Jones ended a long association with Epic and producer Billy Sherrill in 1990 when he jumped ship to MCA and Kyle Lehning. His MCA debut wasn't a masterpiece, but it was stronger than almost everything he'd done in the '80s. The abandoned house in "Where the Tall Grass Grows" is yet another symbol for the unchecked memories of Jones' mind, and the Post-it Notes in "You Couldn't Get the Picture" are the kind of trivial detail he loves. The Cajun remake of "You Done Me Wrong" (cowritten in 1960 with Ray Price) works, and the only moment of true silliness is "Heckel and Jeckel." —*Brian Mansfield*

High-Tech Redneck / 1993 / MCA 10910
George Jones' third MCA album is a 10-track, pure country outing. Despite the digital sound and short running time (less than 32 minutes), it is produced in classic fiddle/steel instrumental glory. Jones sounds steely on the title cut, and such songs as "I've Still Got Some Hurtin' Left to Do" and "Tear Me Out of the Picture" are the type of earnest, unsophisticated heartache songs that define country. He concludes things with a tribute to the departed Conway Twitty, an urgent "Hello Darlin'" that rivals any version Twitty ever issued. —*Ron Wynn*

George Jones & T. Wynette: Concert / Epic 34716
The President and First Lady take one of country music's great tabloid love afairs into the studio. Includes "Golden Ring," "Take Me," and "(We're Not) The Jet Set" ("We're the...Jones and Wynette Set"). —*Dan Cooper*

Book of Memories / United Artists 21002
Haunting title tune plus "There's No Justice" and one of his best drinking laments, "Warm Red Wine." —*George Bedard*

Cold Cold Heart / Pickwick 6108
Great collection of Mercury honky-tonk featuring "You're Still on My Mind" and "Talk to Me Lonesome Heart." —*George Bedard*

☆ **Heartaches & Hangovers** / Rounder 17
Excellent collection of some of his best Musicor sides, and some of the best country singing ever recorded by anyone. The liner notes do an excellent job of describing Jones' style and importance. An absolute must for anyone interested in country music, or American music in general. —*George Bedard*

Grandpa Jones (Louis Marshall Jones)

b. Oct. 20, 1913, Niagra, KY
Vocals, banjo, guitar / Old-time, country humor

Louis Marshall "Grandpa" Jones is one person who has aged right into his makeup. His nickname reportedly was given to him by hillbilly crooner Bradley Kincaid when Jones was about 23 years old. His geezer image has thus been with him for over 55 years. In the early '40s, Jones, Merle Travis, and the Delmore Brothers formed the Brown's Ferry Four, an influential group. After the war, Jones joined the Opry, where he has appeared regularly ever since, often with his wife Ramona. Jones is among the last of the Uncle Dave Macon school of banjo picking and all-round entertaining. His years on "Hee Haw" made him even more famous; he was elected to the Country Music Hall of Fame in 1978. —*David Vinopal*

○ **Grandpa Jones Story** / 1976 / CMH 9007
The "Hee Haw" banjo comic in a pleasant folksy setting with Ramona. —*Mark A. Humphrey*

Family Album / 1979 / CMH 9015
This album features 25 classic old-time songs. —*AMG*

● **Country Music Hall of Fame Series** / 1992 / MCA 10549
The banjo player's entire recorded output for Decca Records between 1956 and 1959, including a live performance and previously unreleased tracks. Jones sings about dogs and trains, rerecords some previous hits for King Records, and parodies Johnny Cash's "Don't Take Your Guns to Town." —*Brian Mansfield*

Wynonna Judd (Christina Ciminella)

b. May 30, 1964, Ashland, Kentucky
Vocals, guitar / Contemporary country

Wynonna Judd, who recorded under simply "Wynonna," became an even bigger star on her own after her mother, Naomi, retired from recording and touring. Her first two solo albums each sold more than 2 million copies, making them among the first by a female country artist to do so. —*Brian Mansfield*

Wynonna / 1992 / Curb 10529
Daughter Judd stakes out her own territory. It's probably safe to say that she had more in her than most people guessed. From the tender "She Is His Only Need" to the Southern rock & soul of "No One Else on Earth," Wynonna sings with a smoldering sensuality that pulsed beneath the surface of the duo's best records—even "Live With Jesus" sounds sexy. After a few more albums like this, folks may not even remember the Judds. Also includes "I Saw the Light" and "My Strongest Weakness." —*Brian Mansfield*

● **Tell Me Why** / May 11, 1993 / MCA 10822
Wynonna's second album features the strongest and most consistent music she has made, even if it is slicker and more pop-oriented than her debut. —*AMG*

The Judds

Group / Contemporary country
Between their first single, "Had a Dream," in 1983 and their farewell concert in Murfreesboro, TN, in December of 1991, mother Naomi and daughter Wynonna had quite a ride. They had dozens of hits, including "Mama He's Crazy," "Change of Heart," "Grandpa," and "Guardian Angels," and won numerous awards along the way, including two Grammys in 1992, one for vocal duo/group and another for "Love Can Build a Bridge" as the best country song of the year.
    Because of incurable hepatitis, Naomi retired from the business. Wynonna continues solo. The Judds were *the* dominant duo in the '80s. —*David Vinopal*

The Judds (Wynonna & Naomi) / 1983 / RCA 8402
The debut for this mother/daughter duo who became one of country's leading lights in the '80s. —*Mark A. Humphrey*

○ **Why Not Me?** / 1985 / RCA 5319
Their second album. Wynonna establishes herself as a fearsome and sultry belter. The production is built around an essentially acoustic base. —*Mark A. Humphrey*

★ **The Greatest Hits** / 1988 / RCA 8318
These singles document the rise of Naomi and Wynonna Judd, a mother-daughter team who seemed, at times, to be singing for every bank teller, teacher, and struggling single mama in every small town in America. Songs like "Why Not Me," "Mama He's Crazy," and "Girl's Night Out" were more than country hits; they're like validation for every woman brave enough to believe in innocence even when she knows better. —*Dan Cooper*

Love Can Build a Bridge / 1990 / RCA 2070
Their final album together. —*Mark A. Humphrey*

○ **Greatest Hits, Vol. 2** / 1991 / RCA 61018
While songs like "Young Love" and "Love Can Build a Bridge" continue to emphasize The Judds's warm and fuzzy middle-American sensibilities, several other hits—"Let Me Tell You About Love," for instance—showcase the side of Wynonna that admires Bonnie Raitt. —*Dan Cooper*

Kieran Kane

Country folk
Formerly one-half of the O'Kanes, this New York native returned to a solo career after a four-year break. His solo work continues the sparse, casual, evocative style of the O'Kanes. If anything, Kane is more austere on his own, supplementing insistent but unobtrusive rhythms with fragmentary lyrics that are seductively idealistic and sometimes haunting. —*Michael McCall*

○ **Find My Way Home** / Atlantic 82547
Kane quietly and effectively examines his relationships and decisions in songs that are as acutely accurate as they are minimally drawn. —*Michael McCall*

Bill Keith

b. 194?, MA
Banjo / Instrumental bluegrass
Boston-born Bill Keith is a highly innovative five-string banjo player who first mastered the Scruggs style and then invented his own. His chromatic style departed from the Scruggs approach,

which lay down right-sounding notes around the melody, but with only some of those notes carrying the melody. Keith's system allows the picker to play intricate melody lines, note for note, fiddle-like. He has played with numerous major-league bands, including Bill Monroe and the Blue Grass Boys and Red Allen. Just as Scruggs re-invented the banjo, Bill Keith re-invented it again. —*David Vinopal*

○ **Something Auld, Something Newgrass, Something Borrowed** / 1976 / Rounder 0084
Catch Tony Rice, David Grisman, Jim Rooney, Tom Grey, Vassar Clements, Ken Kasek, and Al Jones on this album. The bluegrass is top-notch, and Bill Keith struts his stuff. —*Chip Renner*

The Kendalls

b. , St. Louis, MO
Group / Traditional country
When father Royce and daughter Jeannie saw their "Leavin' on a Jet Plane" reach the charts in 1970, Royce put his barber's clippers away and left Missouri for Nashville. Not until 1977 did they find real success, with the B-side "Heaven's Just a Sin Away," which climbed to Number 1 and brought awards to the father and daughter. Another chart-topper came in 1984, "Thank God for the Radio." —*David Vinopal*

16 Greatest Hits / 1988 / Deluxe 1005
This represents the bulk of their best work, with those cut-to-the-quick harmonies fully omnipresent. One sad note: Royce and Jeannie claim they don't receive a dime for this stuff, thanks to (il)legal wranglings when the original label, Ovation, went under. —*Tom Roland*

● **20 Favorites** / Epic 45249
Jeannie Kendall had a winsome hillbilly soprano. Daddy Royce sang hand-in-glove harmony. Here daddy and daughter delivered some of the best cheatin' anthems of the late '70s and early '80s. —*Mark A. Humphrey*

Kennedy Rose

Group / Country-Rock, contemporary country
Pam Rose and Mary Ann Kennedy, otherwise known as Kennedy Rose, have provided back-up singing for artists like Emmylou Harris, Dan Fogelberg and Sting. Their songs have been covered by Reba McEntire, Art Garfunkel, and Restless Heart. As artists, this Nashville-based duo has fashioned a distinctive hard acoustic pop/rock sound that has showcased their fine vocal sound to great effect. —*Rick Clark*

● **Hai Ku** / 1989 / IRS 13011
Kennedy and Rose's decision to turn to performing resulted in this debut, which reprises familiar songs of theirs, such as "Love Like This" and "The Only Chain." The production is deep and echoey, with sharply record acoustic instruments, and the swinging is as forceful as the writing. —*William Ruhlmann*

Walk the Line / Feb. 8, 1994 / IRS 13202
Working with co-producer Ray Kennedy, an unrelated country singer with a few offbeat hits, Kennedy Rose created a tighter, leaner sound for *Walk the Line*. The duo's spacious music resonates with possibilities, and guest appearances by Emmylou Harris and David Lanz suggest that Kennedy Rose is in the process of creating a New Age alternative to country. —*Brian Mansfield*

Kentucky Headhunters

Group / Country
You won't confuse this group with any others—not in sound, not in image. These two brothers, a cousin from Kentucky, and two brothers from Missouri have been making music for over 20 years. Their debut, *Pickin' on Nashville*, turned some heads—and some ears—by adding Southern metal boogie to the likes of "Walk Softly on This Heart of Mine." When appearing at the Grammy show to pick up their Best Country Vocal Group award in 1990, they dressed in their normal outfits, but the overalls didn't fit in so well among all the tuxedos. The group split in 1992 when lead singer Ricky Lee Phelps and his brother Doug decided to pursue a more mainstream country direction; they were replaced by Anthony Kenney and Mark Orr, who had previously played with the three remaining HeadHunters. —*David Vinopal & Brian Mansfield*

● **Pickin' on Nashville** / 1989 / Mercury 838744
As their album title suggests, the Headhunters aren't entirely comfortable with the country tag, which seems appropriate when you hear their guitar-heavy, rambunctious music. The vocals have that twang, but these good old boys are often closer to Lynyrd Skynyrd than they are to Merle Haggard—and all the better for it. — *William Ruhlmann*

Electric Barnyard / 1991 / Mercury 848054
The Kentucky HeadHunters aren't a remarkable country mutation, just a top-notch Southern rock band with a sense of humor. "The Ballad of Davy Crockett" is the kind of clever novelty that won't work twice; "Big Mexican Dinner" is a novelty that doesn't even work the first time. Once again, the country and bluegrass covers—"Only Daddy That'll Walk the Line," "With Body and Soul"—are the highlights, and most of the originals (the Beatlesque shuffle "Always Makin' Love" aside) are offbeat, adequate filler. — *Brian Mansfield*

Sammy Kershaw

Traditional country
The third cousin of fiddler Doug Kershaw ("Louisiana Man"), Sammy Kershaw doesn't owe much to Cajun music. Instead, he's a disciple of George Jones and Mel Street, with maybe a touch of Lynyrd Skynyrd thrown in for that all-important youth audience. He's unabashedly corny, but that's part of his charm. — *Brian Mansfield*

Don't Go Near the Water / 1991 / Mercury 510161
"Cadillac Style," Kershaw's first single, started him off strong. This album, which made Kershaw's Jones influence explicit with a cover of "What Am I Worth," also produced the hits "Don't Go Near the Water," "Yard Sale" and "Anywhere But Here." — *Brian Mansfield*

● **Haunted Heart** / 1993 / PolyGram 514332
The more you know about Sammy Kershaw, the more there is to like about his albums. Though Kershaw doesn't write his songs, he makes some of the most autobiographical albums to come from Music Row. If you know that Kershaw quit performing for a year and a half when it threatened his marriage, "Still Lovin' You" assumes greater significance. Even a song as strange as "Queen of My Double Wide Trailer" makes more sense when you learn that Kershaw still owns a trailer in Louisiana, "in case things don't work out." Sure, he still sounded a lot like George Jones with a South Louisiana accent. But *Haunted Heart* showed that Kershaw's was coming into his own as a vocalist. Just as important, he was choosing songs that set him apart from the pack. If some of those were as offbeat as "Double Wide" and "Neon Leon," well, that's just part of what made him distinctive. — *Brian Mansfield*

Clark Kessinger

Fiddle / Instrumental bluegrass
One of the greatest of old-time fiddlers, Kessinger and his nephew Luches were billed as the Kessinger Brothers and recorded for the Brunswick company in the late '20s, producing records that greatly influenced other fiddle players around the South. When Kessinger was "rediscovered" during the folk revival of 1960, he appeared on the Opry, giving two encores because of audience demand. He entered many of the better-known fiddle contests, winning first place and the title as World's Champion Fiddler at the 47th Annual Union Grove, when he was in his mid-eighties. — *David Vinopal*

☆ **Clark Kessinger—Fiddler** / 1966 / Smithsonian/Folkways 2336
Tunes played with incredible drive. — *Charles S. Wolfe*

★ **Clark Kessinger (Old-Time Music w/ Fiddle & Guitar)** / 1984 / Rounder 0004
A West Virginian who began recording in 1928, Kessinger was rediscovered in the '60s and made several "comeback" albums, of which this is one of the best. — *Charles S. Wolfe*

Hal Ketchum

Vocals / Country-pop
This country-pop singer was raised in upstate New York and started off in rock. His "Small Town Saturday Night" debut single went to Number 1 on the charts. — *David Vinopal*

○ **Past the Point of Rescue** / 1991 / Curb 77450

An unassuming album that doesn't try to pass plain-guy Ketchum off as a country hunk or honky-tonk hero. "Small Town Saturday Night" introduced him to the masses, but Ketchum's voice carries more weight when dealing with matters of the heart in "Past the Point of Rescue" and "Somebody's Love." Ketchum worked up a cover of the Vogue's 1965 hit "Five O'Clock World" to surprise producer Allen Reynolds, who wrote the song—it turned out to be such a gem they recorded it. — *Brian Mansfield*

Sure Love / 1992 / Capitol 77581
Ketchum was surprised by the success of his major-label debut, and he followed up with a slicker, peppier album. The melodies are stout, and he's at his best when on the working-class tributes "Mama Knows the Highway" and "Daddy's Oldsmobile." — *Michael McCall*

● **Every Little Word** / 1994 / Curb
Ketchum reconciles the thoughtfulness of his folkie heart with the verve of modern country, tapping into the directness and earthiness that ties them together. His most country album, and his most consistent. — *Michael McCall*

Claude King

b. Feb. 5, 1933, Shreveport, LA
Vocals / Traditional country
Although "The Burning of Atlanta" and "Big River" made everyone in the business think that Claude King was the next big star, this wasn't to be. Tastes changed, and the Louisiana native with the big voice had one more hit in him, but it was a *huge* hit: "Wolverton Mountain," which told the story of Clifton Clowers and his unfriendly welcome toward any and all suitors who came a-courtin' his daughter. In one of the great songs of the '60s is the memorable line, "Her tender lips were sweeter than haw-nee." — *David Vinopal*

● **American Originals** / CBS 45075
"Wolverton Mountain" and other '60s hits from Johnny Horton's pal. — *Mark A. Humphrey*

Fred Koller

Vocals / Country
Fred Koller is a Nashville songwriter whose songs have been covered by Kathy Mattea (three Number 1 hits), the Jeff Healey Band, Nanci Griffith, Peter Rowan, New Grass Revival, the Forester Sisters, and Lacy J. Dalton. Koller has collaborated with such artists as John Prine, Tom Paxton, John Hiatt, Shel Silverstein, John Gorka, Bill Staines, and others. He is the author of a book on songwriting, *How to Pitch and Promote Your Songs*. Koller has developed a cult following who appreciate his deep rough-edged vocals and powerful, often humorous songwriting. — *Chip Renner*

Night of the Living Fred / 1989 / Alcazar 108
Accentuates his broad humor and biting irony—instead of lingering in the shadows, here his wit hogs the spotlight. — *Michael McCall*

○ **Songs from the Night Before** / 1989 / Alcazar 107
His first solo album, it portrays the eclectic character of Koller's colorful insights and his balance of troubling observations, hard-eyed irony, and sentimental yearnings. "Life As We Knew It" recalls a friendlier, slower America, while "This Hell We Created" and "Showbizness" wonderfully spoofs modern relationships and entertainment. — *Michael McCall*

● **Where the Fast Lane Ends** / 1990 / Alcazar 112
Koller's versions of his songs "Goin' Gone" and "Lone Star State of Mind" are here, but he has a deep, bluesy voice that puts a very different spin on these familiar tunes. — *William Ruhlmann*

Kris Kristofferson

b. Jun. 22, 1936, Brownsville, TX
Vocals, guitar / Traditional country, progressive country, singer/songwriter
The '70s was a decade ripe and waiting for rebels. The Nashville establishment, though, which had sold a lot of records with the bland "Nashville Sound," wasn't quite ready for this songwriting former soldier who, with long beard and dressed in jeans, in 1970 walked on stage at the Country Music Association awards and got his award for "Sunday Morning Coming Down," a song that friend Johnny Cash had made a hit. When in the next year Janis

Joplin sold a million with "Me and Bobby McGee," he was on his way, anti-establishment or not. Then Sammi Smith's version of "Help Me Make It through the Night" was a hit on both the country and the pop charts, also in 1971; suddenly Kristofferson's creative lyrics and memorable music made the establishment forget about his image and created a cult following.

In 1973, the year he and singer Rita Coolidge married, *The Silver Tongued Devil and I* went gold. Meanwhile, his duets with Coolidge sold well and produced two Grammys for them. It was at about this time that his record sales began to dip, so he stepped up a film acting career. Role followed role, among them *Cisco Pike*, *Pat Garrett and Billy the Kid* (co-starring Bob Dylan), *Alice Doesn't Live Here Anymore*, *Blume in Love*, *Rollover*, etc. Critics liked his work on the silver screen, writing that Kristofferson had real talent, that he wasn't only a singer who might sell tickets. He charted again, right into the '80s, but nothing like his phenomenal sales of the previous decade, though his collaboration with Johnny Cash, Willie Nelson, and Waylon Jennings on *Highwayman* (1985) produced another Number 1 album. This gifted songwriter, performer, and actor made success easier for subsequent musicians who, like him, don't fit into the mold. — *David Vinopal*

○ **Kristofferson** / 1970 / Monument 18139
Classic first album from Kristofferson showcasing his versions of songs made famous by others. While he sometimes went to extremes to get these songs heard in the first place (landing a helicopter in John Cash's yard in an effort to get the singer to hear his songs), this album should not be missed by anyone who's ever liked any of these songs. Once Monument realized what a talent they had, they reissued this record as *Me And Bobby McGee*. — *Jim Worbois*

★ **Me & Bobby Mcgee** / 1971 / Monument 44351
In the late '60s and early '70s, Kris Kristofferson's adult, reality-based songs were the most shocking thing to hit Nashville in a long time, and what's more, they were hits. This album contains his own versions of some of the best, including the title song, "Help Me Make It through the Night," and "Sunday Mornin' Comin' Down." — *William Ruhlmann*

○ **The Silver Tongued Devil and I** / 1971 / Monument 44352
This second album from Kristofferson continues where the first one left off: with more great songs that were readily snapped up and made into hits by other artists. In addition to original versions of songs that were hits by Bobby Bare and Ray Price, this album also features the first appearance of Rita Coolidge on one of Kris' albums (billed as The Lady.) — *Jim Worbois*

○ **Border Lord** / 1972 / Monument 31302
While the quality of the song writing remains high on this album, the overall feel of the record is more "down." Monument seemed to be showing some faith in Kristofferson as an artist by releasing "Josie" as a single. Unfortunately, it wasn't a hit. Still, this album should not be missed. — *Jim Worbois*

Jesus Was a Capricorn / 1972 / Monument 47064
After a visit to the church of Jimmy Snow, Kristofferson was inspired to write the song that was his first hit as a performer: "Why Me." This is also the first time Kristofferson covered a song by another writer. — *Jim Worbois*

○ **The Songs of Kristofferson** / 1977 / Monument 44350
A greatest hits collection featuring most of the songs he wrote but that others turned into hits, including "Sunday Morning Coming Down," "The Pilgrim Number 33," "For the Good Times," "Help Me Make It Through the Night," and "Why Me." His idiosyncratic versions aren't pretty, but they're intimate and often powerful. — *Michael McCall*

Singer/Songwriter / 1991 / CBS 48621
An interesting concept: a two-disc set, one featuring Kristofferson's version of 17 of his songs, the other featuring covers of the same songs by Ray Price, Janis Joplin, Bob Dylan, Johnny Cash and others. — *Michael McCall*

k. d. lang

Vocals / Progressive country, contemporary country
Katherine Dawn, from Alberta, Canada, won a Grammy for Best Vocal Collaboration in her duet with Roy Orbison on his hit "Crying." She's famous for her unisex look and her powerful voice. — *David Vinopal*

Angel With a Lariat / 1987 / Sire 25441
On her debut album, big-voiced k.d. lang took a rockabilly approach, with Dave Edmunds as her perfect producer choice. Edmunds brought out the sharp, rhythmic aspects of her band the Reclines, and lang wailed over them. The record, which was underappreciated at the time of its release, was an amazingly confident first effort. — *William Ruhlmann*

○ **Shadowland** / 1988 / Sire 25724
Rebuffed commercially, lang turned to veteran Nashville producer Owen Bradley for this genre exercise, which recreates the kind of country diva style of Patsy Cline. It was an accomplished, if puzzling, effort that broke lang through to the country market, at least temporarily. — *William Ruhlmann*

● **Absolute Torch and Twang** / 1989 / Sire 25877
As the title suggests, lang's third (and last country) album combines the best qualities of the first two—the affected-but-original country songwriting of *Angel with a Lariat* and the soaring, Patsy Cline-influenced vocals of *Shadowland*. — *Brian Mansfield*

Ingenue / 1992 / Warner Brothers 26840
Ingenue marked k.d. lang's switch from country to an adult contemporary market. Although some of her old fans might balk, the album is an example of all of the best qualities of adult contemporary pop music; nearly all the songs are as well-crafted as the hit "Constant Craving." It also provided lang with her first genuine hit—*Ingenue* sold over a million copies. — *AMG*

Jim Lauderdale

Country
North Carolina-born Jim Lauderdale is a Nashville-based songwriter whose big influences were Gram Parsons, George Jones, Buck Owens, Hank Williams, and Merle Haggard. He considers himself a country artist with rock, soul, and blues influences thrown in. — *Chip Renner*

○ **Pretty Close to the Truth** / Atlantic
Lauderdale's outstanding debut received little support from the country establishment, so he transferred to the New York office of Atlantic and created another compelling, authoritative album that more freely roams through his various roots influences. — *Michael McCall*

● **Planet of Love** / 1991 / Reprise 26556
Jim Leventhal and Rodney Crowell produced and helped out on this release and Shawn Colvin and Emmylou Harris provide great vocal support. Great debut—an example of the new singer/songwriter "traditionalist" coming out in country music today. — *Chip Renner*

Chris LeDoux

Vocals / Cowboy
This cowboy-and-western singer knows what he's singing about, having been a champion bronc-rider. — *David Vinopal*

○ **Rodeo Songs "Old & New"** / 1973 / Liberty 96594
The title tells the tale. — *Mark A. Humphrey*

Powder River / 1990 / Liberty 96871
Ledoux performs his own compositions. — *AMG*

Radio & Rodeo Hits / 1990 / Liberty 96593
Contemporary cowboy singer/songwriter. — *Mark A. Humphrey*

Western Underground / Jul. 22, 1991 / Liberty 96499
After nearly 20 years and as many self-produced albums, LeDoux found himself attracting attention as the rodeo singer mentioned in Garth Brooks' first hit, "Much Too Young (To Feel this Damn Old)." Brooks' company soon offered the cowboy his first major label contract. Here, his producers try to turn him into a conventional Nashville hat act. — *Michael McCall*

○ **Whatcha Gonna Do with a Cowboy** / Jul. 20, 1992 / Liberty 98818
Brooks helps out his new friend again by joining him for a duet on the title cut, and LeDoux flashes more of his own personality and gritty charm. — *Michael McCall*

● **Best of Chris Le Doux** / Mar. 8, 1994 / Liberty 28458

Brenda Lee

b. Dec. 11, 1944, Lithonia, GA
Vocals / Country-pop, rock-pop

This country, rockabilly, and rock & roll singer was born Brenda Mae Tarpley. One of the most popular female vocalists of her time, with fifty Hot 100 entries between 1957 and 1973. The classic little girl with the big voice, Lee started as a child prodigy on the radio in her native Georgia at the age of five and began recording and appearing on television by 1955. Few can jump from rockabilly to country to novelty rockers to world-weary ballads as well as she. Lee went back to recording country by the early '70s, with consistent hits in that marketplace ever since. The voice and style of Brenda Lee continue to be an American music treasure. —*Cub Koda*

○ **Brenda Lee** / 1960 / Warner Brothers 26439
Brenda Lee at 15—her nickname was "Miss Dynamite" and it's no lie. Some of her early hits—"Sweet Nothin's," "That's All You Gotta Do," plus "I'm Sorry," a great rocking reworking of "Weep No More My Lady," the bluesy "Be My Love Again," and "Just Let Me Dream." —*George Bedard*

● **The Brenda Lee Story (Her Greatest Hits)** / 1974 / MCA 4012
Contains "Thanks a Lot," "You Always Hurt the One You Love," "Johnny One Time," "I Want To Be Wanted," and other hits. —*AMG*

☆ **Anthology—Vols. 1 & 2 (1956-1980)** / 1991 / MCA 10384
A 40-song, two-CD collection that proves Lee was the best White female rock singer of the pre-Beatles '60s. By the time she turned 18, Lee had hit the pop Top 10 11 times. All of those cuts are here, from the innocently salacious "Sweet Nothin's" to the string-laden "I'm Sorry" and her remake of Earl "Fatha" Hines's "You Can Depend on Me." Her best country singles "Johnny One Time" and "Big Four Poster Bed" are also included. The compilers wisely passed over some minor hits in favor of obscure sides like the odd rockabilly "Let's Jump the Broomstick," a cover of Edith Piaf's "If You Love Me (Really Love Me)," and "Is It True?" a middling hit from 1964, which features guitarist Jimmy Page (who is 11 months older than Lee). *Anthology* thoroughly traces Lee's development as a vocalist, from early-childish exuberance to mature, graceful phrasing. —*Brian Mansfield*

Johnny Lee (John Lee Harn)

b. Jul. 3, 1946, Texas City, TX
Vocals, guitar / Country
Like many his age, Johnny Lee grew up on the music of Chuck Berry, Elvis Presley, and Jerry Lee Lewis. Raised on a dairy farm in Alta Loma, TX, he formed his first band, Johnny Lee & the Road Runners, during high school. He tricked his way into playing on stage with Mickey Gilley at a Houston club called the Nesadel, and that shot brought him a long-term run at Gilley's clubs. When *Urban Cowboy* was shot at Gilley's, record executive Irving Azoff offered Lee an opportunity to sing in the picture, and he ended up with a song that more than 20 artists had previously rejected. In his hands, that song—"Lookin' for Love"—became a million-seller and the musical centerpiece of the movie. Stardom occurred practically overnight for Lee, but it was a mixed bag. He and Gilley toured steadily; Lee got a substantial string of hits for about three years and ended up marrying Dallas starlet Charlene Tilton. But the marriage soured, he found his name constantly in the tabloids, and he was forced to record a large amount of same-sounding material. Nevertheless, Johnny Lee had an important role in a huge era for country music, and his easygoing vocal style still makes him very listenable. —*Tom Roland*

● **Greatest Hits** / 1983 / Full Moon 23967
Lots of midtempo love songs, much in the vein of "Lookin' for Love." Too bad Lee couldn't break out of that mold a little sooner—"Sounds like Love" and "Hey Bartender" show some real teeth. —*Tom Roland*

The Lightcrust Doughboys

Originated in 1931 as a trio consisting of Bob Wills, Milton Brown and Herman Arnspiger, the Light Crust Doughboys were just as famous for their association with announcer "Pappy" W. Lee O'Daniel, later a hugely controversial Texas politico and a man to whom Wills did not particularly cotton. —*Dan Cooper*

Light Crust Doughboys 1936-39 / 1982 / Texas Rose 2704
Sixteen sides that catch the band long after Wills and Brown left, but still laying down solid, bluesy licks. "Pussy, Pussy, Pussy" is simply not to be believed. —*Dan Cooper*

● **1936-1939** /
Features "Just Once Too Often." —*AMG*

Hank Locklin

b. Feb. 15, 1918, McLellan, FL
Vocals, guitar / Traditional country
When you hear Hank Locklin's high, sweet tenor, you'll know why he has been popular in Ireland for so many years. He's recorded two country classics: his self-penned "Send Me the Pillow that You Dream On" (1959) and "Please Help Me I'm Falling," a blockbuster Number 1 in 1960. Though his hits slowed down, Locklin toured internationally in the '70s and played to packed houses. —*David Vinopal*

● **Hank Locklin** / 1962 / Wrangler 31004
One of the most perfect early country albums ever recorded; heart-wrenching songs sung in Locklin's perfect tenor—before the hits. It does not get any better than this hard-to-find, but quintessential album. —*Michael Erlewine*

Valerio Longoria Sr

Accordion / Tex-Mex
Valerio is a Tex-Mex accordion veteran, one of the first to update the conjunto sound by adding drums. His music retains a strong "old school" sound and is always danceable, particularly when he breaks into a polka or Colombian cumbia rhythm. —*Myles Boisen*

○ **Caballo Viejo** / Nov. 1989 / Arhoolie 336
Roots-conscious border music from a pioneer of the genre, excelling here on the catchy "cumbia" rhythm. —*Myles Boisen*

The Louvin Brothers

Group / Traditional country
From the close-harmony brother acts of the '30s evolved Charlie (b. 1927) and Ira (Loudermilk) Louvin (b. 1924—d. 1965), ranking among the top duos in country music history. With Ira's incredibly high, pure tenor and Charlie's emotional and smooth melody tenor, they learned well from the Bolick brothers (the Blue Sky Boys), the Monroe Brothers, the Delmore Brothers, and other major family duos of the previous generation, preserving the old-time flavor, while bringing this genre into the '50s, when country music moved to a newer sound. Whatever type of songs they recorded—gospel, folk, hillbilly, or '50s pop—those songs became the Louvins. Add to the list the many Louvin compositions (for example, "If I Could Only Win Your Love," Emmylou Harris's first hit), and you have an act that is outstanding in country music history. Their career took a while to get going, partly because of interruptions from WWII and the Korean War. In the early '50s, after making a reputation for unexcelled gospel singing, the Louvins broadened their repertoire, recording "The Get Acquainted Waltz" (with Chet Atkins adding another guitar to Charlie's and to Ira's mandolin), a fair hit that showed success was reachable with non-religious music. The electric guitar, with the duo's unique harmony and Ira's exceptional tenor, created a sound that fans asked for in increasing numbers. In 1955, after ten unsuccessful auditions, they finally joined the Opry, where they performed to great acclaim until 1963, when they broke up. They had a number of hits, including the much-covered "When I Stop Dreaming." Ira continued on with a solo career. Charlie has remained with the Opry to this day, where his excellent voice has only improved with the years, scoring a major hit with "See the Big Man Cry, Mama." Driving home from a performance one night in 1965, Ira's car was struck in a head-on collision, killing probably the most exceptional high tenor country music has ever known. —*David Vinopal*

☆ **Tragic Songs of Life** / 1956 / Rounder 12
A reissue of their first Capitol album. A sort of tribute album to the country duos that preceded them, it's the Louvins at their best. —*George Bedard*

★ **Louvin Brothers (JS)** / 1957 / JS 6165
The best of their later non-sacred recordings, including "When I Stop Dreaming" and "My Baby's Gone." Probably the ultimate expression of country music's brother-duet tradition. Essential, not only for country fans, but for anyone interested in American music. Previously released on Capitol. —*George Bedard*

☆ **The Family Who Prays** / 1958 / Capitol 1061

All-sacred album, all songs written by the brothers themselves, with one exception ("Swing Low Sweet Chariot"). Country duos just don't come any better. —*George Bedard*

○ **Songs That Tell a Story** / 1981 / Rounder 1030
Arguably the greatest duet and brother act in country history, Ira and Charlie Louvin made remarkably moving, yet simply performed songs about their faith and lives. They did these with only guitar and mandolin backing, plus their voices, and reflected the values of country with more sincerity and genuine feeling than hundreds of elaborately produced and packaged dates have since. Rounder issued these numbers on album in the late '70s, and reissued them on CD in 1991. The digital backdrop doesn't drain the authority from their voices; instead, it simply reaffirms the glory and splendor of the Louvins on 15 short, but brillant gospel numbers. —*Ron Wynn*

★ **Radio Favorites 1951-57** / 1987 / Country Music Foundation 009
Here are 14 live performances of gospel and secular music, released here for the first time. The album includes "I Wish You Knew," "They've Got the Church Outnumbered," and more. —*AMG*

○ **Close Harmony** / 1992 / Bear Family 15561
For the serious country collector, *Close Harmony* is absolutely essential—eight discs of prime Louvin Brothers material, featuring 219 tracks in all. It includes all of their greatest tracks and reaffirms their stature as greats. For casual listeners, start with the single disc collections and work your way up to this splendid set. —*AMG*

Louvin Brothers (Rounder) / Rounder 07
Mostly sacred songs from three MGM recording sessions. This includes the original recording of "Weapon of Prayer," their first successful record. A fine example of their early work. —*George Bedard*

Patty Loveless

Vocals / Country-rock
Loveless came to Nashville from Pikeville, KY, at age 14 and was eventually signed by the Wilburn Brothers to replace her cousin Loretta Lynn as the band's singer. Her sound ranges from rock to progressive country sound. She sings with emotion. —*David Vinopal*

○ **If My Heart Had Windows** / 1988 / MCA 42092
Fine songs by Steve Earle, Dallas Frazier, and others. —*Dan Heilman*

Honky Tonk Angel / 1988 / MCA 42223
The song subjects hardly classify Loveless as a honky-tonk angel, at least by Hank Thompson's definition. But this was the album that established Loveless as a major presence, and it includes two of her biggest singles, "Chains" and "Timber I'm Falling in Love," and two of her best, "Blue Side of Town" and "Don't Toss Us Away," the latter, a duet with Rodney Crowell. —*Brian Mansfield*

On Down the Line / May 15, 1990 / MCA 6401
Features the hits "The Night's Too Long," "I've Got to Stop Loving You (And Start Living Again)," and "Blue Memories," among others. —*AMG*

Up against My Heart / 1991 / MCA 10336
Loveless gets a little more adventurous with each album, though she never forgets to include sure-fire hits like "Hurt Me Bad (In a Real Good Way)" and "Jealous Bone." This time she invites comparisons to Patsy Cline with "Can't Stop Myself from Loving You" and implies that God is female by switching the pronouns in Lyle Lovett's "God Will." —*Brian Mansfield*

○ **Only What I Feel** / 1993 / CBS 53236
Loveless underwent throat surgery and switched labels before creating this album, and both helped. She sounds stronger and more impassioned than she had in years, and her artistic drive seemed more confident and determined. "Nothin' But the Wheel" ranks with her best ballads. —*Michael McCall*

● **Greatest Hits** / May 11, 1993 / MCA 10653

Bob Luman

b. Apr. 15, 1937, Nacogdoches, TX, d. Dec. 27, 1978
Vocals, guitar / Country-Rock, Rockabilly

Bob Luman started out as a rockabilly in the Elvis Presley mold. His first break came when he replaced Johnny Cash on Shreveport's Louisiana Hayride. Then came Las Vegas bookings and soon after a national name resulting from "Let's Think about Living," a crossover hit in 1960. After some success in following years, he recorded *Alive and Well*, an album produced by friend Johnny Cash. He died a year later. —*David Vinopal*

● **American Originals** / 1984 / CBS 45078
A likable '60s country/pop singer. —*Mark A. Humphrey*

Loretta Lynn (Loretta Webb)

b. Apr. 14, 1935, Butcher's Hollow, KY
Vocals, guitar / Traditional country
Because of her 1980 biographical movie, *Coal Miner's Daughter*, this native of Butcher's Hollow, KY, is country music's most famous rags-to-riches story. In the late '60s and early '70s, her country voice, quality material (much of which she wrote), and winsome personality combined to make her Nashville's most prolific female star. Most of her singles reached the charts, including "Don't Come Home A-Drinkin'," "Coal Miner's Daughter," and the controversial "The Pill." With Conway Twitty she recorded numerous duet hits; "Louisiana Woman, Mississippi Man" was probably the best-known. Paying a compliment to two country woman greats who preceded her, Lynn says that Kitty Wells' singing and Patsy Cline's personality have been her biggest influences. —*David Vinopal*

Hymns / 1965 / MCA 5
Features such gospel hits as "The Third Man," "I'd Rathr Have Jesus," and "Everybody Wants to Go to Heaven." —*AMG*

★ **Loretta Lynn's Greatest Hits** / 1968 / MCA 31234
Lynn had a big hand in raising Nashville's perception of women as capable and competent (although the city still has a way to go). "Don't Come Home A-Drinkin'" and "You Ain't Woman Enough" are particularly representative: sassy, honest, and aggressive. —*Tom Roland*

○ **Loretta Lynn's Greatest Hits, Vol. 2** / 1974 / MCA 932
In the liner notes, Pete Axthelm cites "the range of her personality," and that range is in evidence here: reflective ("Coal Miner's Daughter"), feisty ("Fist City"), humorous ("One's on the Way"), and sentimental ("Love Is the Foundation"). —*Tom Roland*

★ **Country Music Hall of Fame** / 1991 / MCA 10083
Few greatest-hits packages pack the wallop of these 16 performances (1961-1976). This album includes duets with Ernest Tubb and Conway Twitty, men who knew to stand clear when Lynn wailed "Your Squaw Is on the Warpath" or "Fist City." —*Mark A. Humphrey*

○ **Here's Loretta Lynn** / CBS 20056
A collection of her earliest recordings, made for the Zero label (unfortunately not including "Honky Tonk Girl," her first hit). Good, bluesy honky-tonk, with Lynn already in top form and a very swinging band. —*George Bedard*

Shelby Lynne

b. 1969, Alabama
Vocals, fiddle / Country
Born in Quantico, VA, and raised in Alabama, Shelby Lynne is a countrified torch singer with a passionate growl who sings from her own pain. (Her father murdered her mother, then killed himself. Lynne raised her sister and had a broken teenage marriage.) Lynne won fiddling contests that led to an appearance on Ralph Emery's *Nashville Now*. The day after she appear on the show in 1987, she received four recording contract offers. After three albums on Epic, she made a break with mainstream Nashville, recording the big-band *Temptation*. —*Bil Carpenter, David Vinopal & Brian Mansfield*

Soft Talk / 1976 / Epic 47388
Defiant, emotionally dranching country. Contains "The Very First Lasting Love," a duet with former Exile member Les Taylor. —*Bil Carpenter & AMG*

Sunrise / Jan. 1976 / Epic 44260
Lynne's debut album, released when she was barely out of her teens. It contained a duet with George Jones called "If I Could Bottle This Up." —*Brian Mansfield*

● **Tough All Over** / 1989 / Epic 46066

Contains "Things Are Tough All Over," her most successful single, as well as covers of Johnny Cash's "I Walk the Line" and Duke Ellington's "Don't Get Around Much Anymore". —*Brian Mansfield*

Temptation / Jul. 6, 1993 / Morgan Creek 2959
An album of big-band country swing produced by Brent Maher (the Judds). "Feelin' Kind of Lonely Tonight" had limited success as a single. —*Brian Mansfield*

Uncle Dave Macon

b. Oct. 7, 1870, Smart Station, TN, **d.** Mar. 22, 1952, Readyville, TN
Group / Old-time
David Harrison Macon, born in Smartt Station, TN, didn't perform professionally until he was past 50, but he became one of the first superstars of country music. A talented banjoist and comic (and sometimes preacher and farmer), Uncle Dave Macon was the Grand Ole Opry's first major star and an audience favorite from 1925 until his death in 1952. He derived much of his repertoire and stage patter from vaudeville and minstrel shows, but his songs reflected on a wide variety of subjects from political corruption to current events like the advent of the automobile. His presence affected country music like none before it; even today a three-day festival, Uncle Dave Macon Days, is held in Murfreesboro, TN, the site of the National Old-Time Banjo Championship. —*Brian Mansfield*

● **Country Music Hall of Fame Series** / 1992 / MCA 10546
"Shout if you are happy!" Uncle Dave Macon exclaims during "Tom and Jerry" as Mazy Todd saws away at her fiddle. "Kill yo'self!" That's the kind of enthusiasm Macon brings to these 16 fine examples of string-band music, recorded between 1926 and 1934 for the Vocalion, Brunswick, and Champion labels. Macon, who was 55 at the first of these recording sessions, frequently starts the songs with a spoken anecdote (including a plug for his Macon Midway Mule and Wagon Transportation Company). This collection is essentially an expanded version of *Uncle Dave Macon: First Featured Star of the Grand Ole Opry*, a retrospective issued in 1966, after his posthumous election to the Country Music Hall of Fame. —*Brian Mansfield*

Maddox Brothers & Rose Maddox , The

Group / Traditional country
The Maddox Brothers (Cliff, Cal, Fred, Don, and "friendly Henry, the working girl's friend") and their sister Rose called themselves "America's Most Colorful Hillbilly Band." They weren't kidding. It wasn't just a matter of hillbilly couture—though with their matching Turk suits and spangles the family had style in spades. But colorful described their sound, as well. Throughout the 1940s and '50s, they tore down the honky-tonks from the Pacific Northwest to the Gulf Coast with slap-bass boogie and an iconoclastic attitude towards the stiffer mores of conventional country. In other words, they rocked the house.

It all started in 1933, when the Maddox family—Charlie and Lula, and five of their seven children—hitchhiked and rode the rails from Boaz, Alabama to California, where they worked in the migrant labor camps of the San Joaquin Valley. Fred Maddox quickly tired of picking fruit and wrangled a radio spot for his intensely musical family (which featured 11-year old Rose on decidedly raw lead vocals). On the air in Modesto by 1937, the group made their first records, for the 4-Star label, in 1946. From 1951 till 1956, they recorded for Columbia. At that point, the family act broke up, though Rose maintained a successful solo career for many years after. She still performs occasionally. —*Dan Cooper*

☆ **Maddox Brothers & Rose: "Their Original Hits** / Arhoolie 209
Same material as above, except more of it. Only available on cassette, it combines the out-of-print Arhoolie LPs 5016 and 5017. —*Dan Cooper*

○ **Rose Maddox Sings Bluegrass** / 1962 / Capitol 1779
Of the many fine (and now rare) LPs that Rose cut for Capitol, this humdinger is the best one to break your neck trying to find. Bluegrass sung with honky-tonk fire. Sparks do fly. —*Dan Cooper*

○ **Columbia Historic Edition** / CBS 39997
A too short lived (and too brief) LP, this sampler from their Columbia years further showcases their relentless chops and outrageous sense of humor. Though the Bear Family LPs draw from the same source, a full CD collection of the Maddox's Columbia work is desperately needed. —*Dan Cooper*

● **Maddox Brothers & Rose on the Air, Vol. 1 & Vol. 2** / Arhoolie 222
A fascinating document, this double-length cassette (formerly the Arhoolie LPs 5028 and 5033) includes radio broadcasts from as early as 1940 (six years before the Maddox's cut their first record) and on into the early 1950s. Not the place to find out if you're a Maddox family fan, but if you are one already, this collection (which includes their only appearance on the Grand Ole Opry) will give you a sense of what it must have been like to hear Rose wreak havoc with 1950s gender roles by taking the lead on a cover of Hank Snow's "The Gold Rush Is Over. —*Dan Cooper*

★ **Maddox Brothers & Rose, 1946-1951, Vol. 1** / Arhoolie 5016
Consisting of twenty-seven cuts from the years 1946-51, this disc is indespensable to anyone seeking a dose of vintage country music at its most hedonistically raucous. Though the archaic sound quality may make an audiophile cringe, the musical vitality of these boogie, blues and ballad recordings is absolutely astonishing. So is the degree of nerve they show with their winking versions of "Whoa Sailor" and "Sally Let Your Bangs Hang Down." —*Dan Cooper*

Barbara Mandrell

b. Dec. 25, 1948, Houston, TX
Vocals, steel guitar / Country-pop
A show-biz veteran of over thirty years, this country-pop superstar is the first artist to win the Country Music Association Entertainer of the Year award two consecutive years. She started early, touring with Johnny Cash when she was thirteen. Her first hit was with Otis Redding's "I've Been Loving You Too Long" in 1969. Among her many Number 1 records are "Sleepin' Single in a Double Bed," "I Was Country When Country Wasn't Cool," "Years," and "One of a Kind Pair of Fools." She and her sisters Louise and Irlene have received much TV play through their national show, on which each shows her versatility on lots and lots of instruments. Her biography, *Get to the Heart: My Story*, recounts how her near-fatal auto accident of 1984 changed her life. —*David Vinopal*

Moods / 1978 / MCA 1677
Includes "Sleepin' Single in a Double Bed." —*Bil Carpenter*

○ **The Best of Barbara Mandrell** / 1979 / MCA 31107
Classic Southern twists on '60s R&B. —*Bil Carpenter*

● **Greatest Hits** / 1985 / MCA 31302
Hank definitely didn't do it this way. Nevertheless, "I Was Country When Country Wasn't Cool" summed up a lot of folks' feelings as the Travolta crowd tried to claim Hank as their own. Also includes the Number 1 "Sleeping Single in a Double Bed," "(If Loving You is Wrong) I Don't Want to Be Right," and "Years." —*Dan Cooper*

Best of Barbara Mandrell / 1992 / Liberty 98491
Features "I'll Be Your Jukebox Tonight," "Tall Drink of Water," "Feed the Fire," and more. —*AMG*

Joe Maphis

b. May 12, 1921, Suffolk, VA
Guitar / Instrumental bluegrass
Joe and Rose Maphis were a popular husband-and-wife act in the late '40s and early '50s, singing traditional material backed by the amazing instrumental talent of Joe, who played everything with strings on it, especially the twin-neck guitar. The honky-tonk anthem "Dim Lights, Thick Smoke (And Loud, Loud Music)" was their big hit. Until his death in 1986, Joe was a sessions instrumentalist, backing such stars as Rick Nelson, Tex Ritter, and Wanda Jackson. —*David Vinopal*

● **Flat-Picking Spectacular** / 1982 / CMH 9030
These are later recordings made by this '40s-era sessionman and singer. —*Charles S. Wolfe*

Kathy Mattea

b. 1959
Vocals, guitar / Country-pop
A former tour guide at Nashville's Country Music Museum, Kathy Mattea scored her first Number 1 country hit with "Eighteen Wheels and a Dozen Roses." Another hit was "Where've You Been," which brought awards her way. Give a listen to *Time Passes By*, country with a folk flavor. —*David Vinopal*

Walk the Way the Wind Blows / 1986 / Mercury 830405
An injection of brash, bluegrass-style energy gave her music a
needed lift. This is her strongest collection, matching her folkie
sensitivity with an innocent verve that is truly catchy. Includes
her hit version of Nanci Griffith's "Love at the Five and Dime." —
Michael McCall

Untasted Honey / Sep. 28, 1987 / Mercury 832793
Features one of her best uptempo tunes, "Untold Stories," and
one of her most wistful ballads, "Life As We Knew It." —*Michael
McCall*

Willow in the Wind / 1989 / Mercury 836950
Contains "Where Have You Been," 'Burnin' Old Memories,"
"Come from the Heart," and more. —*AMG*

● **A Collection of Hits** / 1990 / Mercury 842330
Kathy Mattea has risen to near the top of the Nashville ranks because of a haunting, soulful voice, well-produced recordings that
have a simple, folkie directness, and, most especially, an amazing
talent for picking the best songs being written for the country
market, among them "Eighteen Wheels and a Dozen Roses,"
"Goin' Gone," and the heartbreaking "Where've You Been." —
William Ruhlmann

Time Passes By / 1991 / Mercury 846975
On her most ambitious album, Mattea gets impeccably chosen
songs (as usual) and strong supporting performances (from
Emmylou Harris, Dougie MacLean, and the Roches). She doesn't
write her own stuff, so she may not be the romantic dreamer of
"Asking Us to Dance," but she sure sounds like it. Songs like
"Time Passes By," cowritten by husband Jon Vezner, suggest
there's more honesty here than image. She can even make the
half-baked "From a Distance" convincing. —*Brian Mansfield*

○ **Lonesome Standard Time** / 1992 / Mercury 512567
The title cut is an out-and-out bluegrass blazer with drums, and a
couple of the ballads rank with her best. Unfortunately, Mattea's
commercial status seemed to be slipping just as she was creating
her best music. —*Michael McCall*

○ **Walking Away a Winner** / Oct. 1993 / Mercury 518852
Tired of having critics rave while radio programmers yawned,
Mattea enlisted contempo-country producer Josh Leo to help
brighten her sound for commercial consumption. It worked. The
title cut was a hit right out of the box. —*Dan Cooper*

The Mavericks

Group / Country-rock
This Miami quartet cut its teeth playing country music in Florida
rock clubs. Lead singer and main songwriter Raul Malo is of
Cuban descent and has a serious jones for rockabilly; he's also got
a haunting tenor that promises to become one of country most
distinctive voices. —*Brian Mansfield*

Mavericks / 1990 / Y&T 1
The group's first indie release. Includes early versions of four
songs recut for *From Hell to Paradise*: "The End of the Line,"
"This Broken Heart," "A Better Way," and "Mr. Jones." —*Brian
Mansfield*

● **From Hell to Paradise** / 1992 / MCA 10544
In spite of Malo's Cuban heritage and the band's Miami roots—*be-
cause* of them, in fact—the Mavericks understand outsiders like
Buck Owens and Hank Williams (both of whom the group covers)
better than most of country's recent comers. And originals like "I
Got You," "This Broken Heart," and the scathing title track about
Malo's aunt's escape from Cuban oppression, are so good the cov-
ers don't really matter. —*Brian Mansfield*

○ **What a Crying Shame** / 1994 / MCA 10961
Superb, highly accessible follow-up to *From Hell to Paradise* included songs that made overt comparisons between Raul Malo
and Roy Orbison ("I Should Have Been True," Jesse Winchester's
"O What a Thrill"). Those who didn't realize the power of Malo's
voice knew after these songs, when he didn't come off looking
like a fool. Plenty of hot rockabilly shuffles, and the title track,
with its Byrdsian guitar hook and bittersweet melody, became the
first single by an "alternative" country act since Dwight Yoakam
to break radio's Top 30. —*Brian Mansfield*

Mac McAnally

Born in rural Mississippi and based in Muscle Shoals, AL,
McAnally scored a huge radio hit, "It's a Crazy World," as a 19-

year-old in 1977. Since then, he's recorded primarily what he
refers to as "unintentional collectors items." They all feature his
distinctively optimistic slant on James Taylor-style acoustic pop,
and they've all slipped through the cracks for one reason or another. He's been enjoying greater success as a country songwriter
lately. —*Michael McCall*

○ **Mac McAnally** / 1977 / Ariola
McAnally's debut revealed uncommon wisdom and spiritual re-
flection for such a young singer/songwriter. Features the favorite,
"It's a Crazy World." —*Michael McCall*

Simple Life / Feb. 13, 1990 / Warner Brothers 26136
McAnally has an ability to inject exceptional compassion into
mannered country-pop songs. The album features well-crafted
lyrics, fastidious acoustic-pop arrangements, and his unremarkable voice. —*Michael McCall*

● **Live & Learn** / 1992 / MCA 10543
Writing songs packed with gentle emotions and hard-earned life
lessons seems to come easy for McAnally. However, hits don't—at
least not when he's singing. —*Michael McCall*

Martina McBride

A Kansas native who can sing with power and tenderness,
McBride started out in a more traditional vein, then kicked up the
beat and the tempo with her second album. Her song selection is
consistently strong, making her one of the more promising young
Nashville singers. —*Michael McCall*

The Time Has Come / 1992 / RCA 66002
Her bold debut, blending traditional country ("Cheap Whiskey,"
"That's Me") with acoustic rave-ups, as in the title song. —*Michael
McCall*

● **The Way That I Am** / 1993 / RCA
McBride revamps her image, flashing a new haircut and a more
forceful, uptempo style. She matches the music with a feisty, daring collection of distinguished songs, including the hit "My Baby
Loves Me" and the remarkable "Independence Day," about an
abused wife who takes justice into her own hands. —*Michael
McCall*

Charly McClain (Charlotte Denise McClain)

b. Mar. 26, 1956, Memphis, TN
Vocals / Country
Originally named Charlotte, Charly McClain was given her masculine moniker by neighborhood friends in Memphis, and she
also used it when she started playing hotel lounges. Epic Records
decided it was more "catchy" than Charlotte, and it became a permanent professional banner. Her father had tuberculosis when
she was eight, and, since she was under age for visitation rights
at the hospital, she had to communicate with him through a tape
recorder. That inspired her interest in recording, and by age 17
she was a regular on the club circuit. Signed to her first recording
contract in 1976, McClain's distinct vocal sound provided an edge
in recognizability—as did her appearance. She hit country's Top
10 fairly regularly from 1978-1985, both as a solo artist, and in
duets with Mickey Gilley and former soap star Wayne Massey,
whom she married in 1984. —*Tom Roland*

○ **Greatest Hits** / 1982 / Epic 38313
McClain's Southern heritage is very much in evidence in her vo-
cal style. No other woman sounds as simultaneously tough and
feminine as she does; this is simply McClain at her best—"Men,"
"Sleepin' with the Radio On," "Who's Cheatin' Who," and "The
Very Best Is You." —*Tom Roland*

● **Biggest Hits** / 1985 / Epic 40186
Basically an interchangeable repackaging with "10 Year
Anniversary" and "Greatest Hits." One isn't any better than the
other. —*Rick Clark*

Del McCoury

Vocals, guitar / Traditional bluegrass
Del McCoury was guitarist and lead singer in one of Bill
Monroe's great bands in the early '60s. He went on to form high-
quality traditional bluegrass bands, including the Dixie Pals, a
band he organized with his brother Jerry in 1969. Del McCoury is
well-known for his exceptional vocal leads. —*David Vinopal*

○ **Don't Stop the Music** / 1990 / Rounder 0245

The title track is a Geroge Jones song. The album includes diverse and often bluesy material and fine performances. —*Mark A. Humphrey*

○ **Blue Side of Town** / May 15, 1992 / Rounder 0292
Named for his version of the Patty Loveless hit "The Blue Side of Town," McCoury covers Steve Earle's "If You Need a Fool" and Arthur "Big Boy" Crudup's "That's Alright Mama." When it comes to song choice, he may be the most well-rounded man in bluegrass. —*Brian Mansfield*

☆ **Deeper Shade of Blue** / 1993 / Rounder 0303
A classic from the word go, McCoury's love affair with blues is never more explicit than here, where songs with the titles like "Cheek to Cheek With the Blues," "A Deeper Shade of Blue," and "The Bluest Man in Town" are the order of the day. Never a purist when it comes to songs, McCoury covers Kevin Welch's "True Love Never Dies," Willie Nelson's "Man With the Blues," and the Jerry Lee Lewis hit "What Made Milwaukee Famous." His version of Lefty Frizzell's "If You've Got the Money Honey" is downright piercing. —*Brian Mansfield*

★ **Classic Bluegrass** / Rebel 1111
Rebel label recordings from the '70s by the man who sometimes sounds more like Bill Monroe than Monroe himself. Stunning, pure, high-lonesome pipes and mountain bluesy songs. Beautiful. —*Mark A. Humphrey*

I Wonder Where You Are Tonight / Arhoolie 5006
McCoury's first album (the CD reissue includes a number of previously unreleased cuts). A favorite of purists, but McCoury hadn't developed the vocal style that would make him great in the '90s. —*Brian Mansfield*

Neal McCoy

Vocals / Country
Part Irish, part Filipino, Neal McCoy (real name: Hubert Neal McGauhey, Jr.) grew up in Jacksonville, Texas. He released a single, "That How Much I Love You," under the name Neal McGoy on 16th Ave. Records in 1988. —*Brian Mansfield*

Where Forever Begins / 1992 / Atlantic 82396
Includes the singles "Where Forever Begins," "There Ain't Nothin' I Don't Like About You," and "Now I Pray for Rain." —*Brian Mansfield*

● **No Doubt About It** / 1994 / Atlantic
This Barry Beckett-produced disc was the first to capture the rock-influenced sound of McCoy's stage show (which usually included a rap version of *The Beverly Hillbillies* theme). Though McCoy had never had a single chart above Number 21, the album gave the singer his first two Number 1 hits: "No Doubt About It" and "Wink." —*Brian Mansfield*

At This Moment / Atlantic 82171
This debut's most notable song is its title track, a country version of the Billy Vera prom-night pop hit. —*Brian Mansfield*

Mel McDaniel

b. Sep. 6, 1942, Checotah, OK
Vocals, guitar, trumpet / Country
Born in Checotah, OK, he decided at age 14 that he had to pursue music, inspired by seeing Elvis Presley on TV. After establishing himself on the Tulsa club circuit, he moved briefly to Nashville, then headed off to Anchorage, AK, where he refined his stage skills. Once he returned to Music City, he signed his first recording deal in 1976 with Capitol Records, but it took five years for him to first hit the Top 10. He had sporadic success thereafter, but his signature song, "Baby's Got Her Blue Jeans On," invited a bevy of recognition, including multiple nominations for Grammy and Country Music Association awards. —*Tom Roland*

● **Greatest Hits** / 1987 / Capitol 46867
He is gravelly-voiced and has a limited range, but McDaniel gets the most out of his talents by concentrating on songs with the proper "groove." "Louisiana Saturday Night" and "Baby's Got Her Blue Jeans On" are staples; "Stand Up" and "Big Ole Brew" are pretty damn good. —*Tom Roland*

Ronnie McDowell

b. Mar. 26, 1950
Vocals, guitar / Country

Raised in rural Portland, TN, north of Nashville, McDowell didn't take performing seriously until he was stationed in the Philippines with the navy. The first song he performed in public, "It's Now or Never," was appropriate, since Elvis Presley has had a huge impact on his career. McDowell wrote his first hit, "The King Is Gone," the day that Elvis died. Enough people shared his grief that a reported three million copies were sold. McDowell did all the Elvis vocal imitations for a 1979 Elvis TV movie, starring Kurt Russell, and he began to take on the image of an Elvis imitator. However, McDowell consciously distanced himself from those comparisons, which became easier when record producer Buddy Killen took over the reins of his career, bringing in solid uptempo material that consistently showcased McDowell's strong (though a bit nondescript) vocal talents. Now comfortable with his reputation, he's returned on occasion to more "Elvis" work, providing the vocal parts for the short-lived ABC series "Elvis" in 1990. —*Tom Roland*

● **Older Women and Other Greatest Hits** / 1987 / Epic 40643
McDowell fell into this "clone" thing for a couple of years where he re-made his own hits; and all three soundalikes ("Older Women," "Wandering Eyes," "Watchin' Girls Go By") are curiously placed back-to-back. His later material is the most emotive, especially "I Dream of Women Like You," "In a New York Minute," and "Love Talks," recorded with Exile. —*Tom Roland*

Reba McEntire (Reba Nell McEntire)

b. Mar. 28, 1954, Chockie, OK
Vocals, guitar / Traditional country, contemporary country
With her powerful, versatile voice, this Chockie, OK, native can sing traditional country as well as it's sung. Like Dolly Parton before her, talented Reba McEntire has moved sideways out of hard country into songs that appeal to a broader, more popular palate, following the path of so many contemporary country performers. And again like Parton, McEntire is on the silver screen. She ably plays a desert girl in the sci-fi comedy *Tremors*, in which the subsand critters are lured to their death by vibrations of the non-musical kind. Before moving toward the middle of the road, she cut *My Kind of Country*, a traditionalist's delight, and from this album came the hit single "How Blue," which led to the Country Music Association's Female Vocalist of the Year Award in 1984. McEntire's awards haven't stopped since. She's a natural talent who can sing country or pop or anything in-between with power and beauty. In 1990, seven of her band members and her road manager died in a plane crash on a California mountain. —*David Vinopal*

○ **The Best of Reba McEntire** / 1985 / Mercury 824342
A compilation of her late '70s and early '80s Polygram hits. Reflections of future triumphs on MCA. —*Mark A. Humphrey*

○ **My Kind of Country** / 1986 / MCA 31108
McEntire's celebration of the back-to-basics movement in country. Many country shuffles here. Her purest country performances and most straightforward production. —*Mark A. Humphrey*

○ **Whoever's in New England** / 1986 / MCA 31304
The album that elevated McEntire from pretty-good-country-singer to megastar. A number of the melodies have pop sensibilities, but the production is decidedly country. —*Tom Roland*

The Last One to Know / 1987 / MCA 42030
Recorded as McEntire went through the process of divorce from first husband Charlie Battles. Understandably heavy on songs about breakups and the uncertainty of the future, "The Stairs"—about domestic violence—is particularly moving. Despite her personal pain, she still holds out hope in "Love Will Find Its Way to You." —*Tom Roland*

★ **Greatest Hits** / 1987 / MCA 5979
Overview of her late '80s MCA hits. Powerful pipes. —*Mark A. Humphrey*

☆ **For My Broken Heart** / 1991 / MCA 10400
Only the quietly moving "If I Had Only Known" might be considered a tribute to the members of McEntire's band who died in a 1990 plane crash, but the tragedy creeps into McEntire's voice and her song selection. Throughout the album, McEntire dwells on regrets, unvoiced feelings, and missed chances. The best songs aren't the hits "For My Broken Heart" and "Is There Life out There," but a group of evocative story-songs that unfold slowly, leaving loose threads and developing complex emotional under-

currents. *For My Broken Heart* may be the strongest album of McEntire's career; it's certainly her most heartbreaking. —*Brian Mansfield*

Tim McGraw

The son of former major-league pitcher Tug McGraw, Tim McGraw grew up in Start, Louisiana, moving to Nashville the day Keith Whitley died. His first album, *Tim McGraw* didn't leave much of a mark, but his second, *Not a Moment Too Soon*, contained a controversial song called "Indian Outlaw" that took him to the top of the country charts and to the upper levels of the pop charts too. —*Brian Mansfield*

Tim McGraw / 1993 / Capitol 77603
Three songs—"Welcome to the Club," "Memory Lane," and "Two Steppin' Mind"—appeared on the bottom half of the *Billboard* singles chart, which suggested McGraw had some talent but wasn't anything special. During a year that introduced Clay Walker and Doug Supernaw, hardly anybody noticed this young hot act. —*Brian Mansfield*

● **Not a Moment Too Soon** / Mar. 22, 1994 / Capitol/Curb 77659
"Indian Outlaw," with its controversy and its resemblance to the Raiders' "Indian Reservation," made McGraw a star, and the ballad "Don't Take the Girl" reinforced the image. *Not a Moment Too Soon* contained better hooks than its predecessor, but it also belabored the obvious with songs like "It Don't Get Any Countrier Than This" and "Give It to Me Strait." —*Brian Mansfield*

Frankie Miller

Vocals / Country-rock
Reclusive Texas-based singer who recorded in the late '50s and early '60s in an anachronistic Hank Williams style. Enjoyed one major hit ("Black Land Farmer") before drifting into obscurity. Many of his records are highly collectable. —*Hank Davis*

● **Rockin' Rollin'** / 1983 / Bear Family 15128
A stunning 18-track selection of tracks cut for the Nashville Starday label between 1959 and 1963. Distinctive and haunting music. —*Hank Davis*

Hey! Where You Going? / 1984 / Bear Family 15082
A complete collection of this country "groaner's" early 1954-1956 Columbia sides. —*Hank Davis*

Roger Miller

b. Jan. 2, 1936, Fort Worth, TX
Vocals, guitar
A native Texan and a legendary free-spirited songwriter from the salad days of Nashville's Music Row, Miller woke up one morning in 1965 with five Grammies in his possession. He owed them, for the most part, to the improbable "Dang Me," which spent six weeks at Number 1 country and reached Number 7 pop. And it wasn't half the hit "King of the Road" was. The latter song, as good as any ever written in Nashville, is still the one with which Miller's name is most closely associated, though his catalog of country standards is truly astounding in scope. In his later years, Miller enjoyed a career resurgence as songwriter for the hit Broadway musical "Big River," and as a bemused father figure to New Traditionalists rediscovering his early work. —*Dan Cooper*

★ **Golden Hits** / 1965 / Smash 826261
Years before Waylon and Willie grew their hair long, Miller took country to the counterculture with these hipster twists on the Nashville sound. No tunesmith in Music City had ever tossed off songs like "Dang Me," "King of the Road," "Chug-A-Lug," and "Engine Engine Number 9." No one has since. —*Dan Cooper*

☆ **Best of Roger Miller, Vol. 1: Country Tunesmith** / 1991 / Polygram 848977
Downplays Miller's humorous muse in favor of showing off his skill as a straight-ahead country writer. Twenty-one tracks (including some strongly Ray Price-influenced fare from 1957) either written or cowritten by Miller. Well worth the money to hear his own versions of such standards as "Invitation to the Blues," "Half a Mind," and "Don't We All Have the Right." —*Dan Cooper*

☆ **The Best of Roger Miller, Vol. 2—King of the Road** / Aug. 4, 1992 / Mercury 512646
A more comprehensive, but also more diffuse version of Smash Hits. —*Dan Cooper*

More Golden Hits / Smash 835332
Miller's lesser late '60s hits. —*Dan Heilman*

Ronnie Milsap

b. Jan. 16, 1944, Robbinsville, NC
Vocals, piano / Country-pop
Born blind, Milsap formed his first band at the State School for the Blind in North Carolina. His first release was R&B, and he was able to sing blues and jazz with equal ease. In the early '70s he changed to country-pop and since has had many Top 10 hits, including "A Legend in My Time," "Daydreams about Night Things," "No Gettin' Over Me," and "Still Losing You." He has won many awards, including the Country Music Association Entertainer of the Year. —*David Vinopal*

● **Greatest Hits** / 1980 / RCA 8504
A solid, albeit random assessment of Milsap's first seven years in country music. Mainstream country, with "Pure Love" and "(I'm A) Stand by My Woman Man," but Milsap really shines on the elaborate and challenging arrangements of "(I'd Be) A Legend in My Time," "It Was Almost like a Song," and "Let's Take the Long Way around the World." One previously unreleased track: "Smoky Mountain Rain." —*Tom Roland*

One More Try for Love / 1984 / RCA 5016
In his effort to expand the boundaries of country, Milsap pushes the edge harder here than in any other album. The electronically altered vocals in the tracks "She Loves My Car" and "Suburbia" have a winning effect—tasteful, not overdone. —*Tom Roland*

○ **Greatest Hits, Vol. 2** / 1985 / RCA 5425
Juxtaposed to the first *Greatest Hits* package, this one nicely displays the evolution of a motivated risk-taker. Milsap re-defines the outer limits of the commercial country format with his soul-and/or rock-inflected singles "(There's) No Gettin' over Me," "Lost in the Fifties Tonight," and (most dramatically) "Stranger in My House." —*Tom Roland*

True Believer / Jun. 7, 1993 / Liberty 80805
If only the whole album had the energy of the John Hiatt title track (not to mention the wit of the Hoss Allen intro), Milsap's Liberty debut would have been a record to reckon with. —*Dan Cooper*

Patsy Montana (Ruby Blevins)

b. Oct. 30, 1914, Hot Springs, AK
Vocals / Cowboy
Born Rubye Blevins in Arkansas, Patsy Montana is the first woman in country music to have a million-seller, "I Want to Be a Cowboy's Sweetheart" in 1935. For more than 25 years she was a mainstay on Chicago's WLS National Barn Dance. In the '30s and '40s she was the sweetheart of many a cowpoke, appearing in numerous Westerns on the silver screen. Boy, could she yodel. —*David Vinopal*

Precious Memories / 1977 /
Features "O Lord I Am not Worthy," "When It's Prayer-Meetin' Time in the Hollow," and other gospel songs. —*AMG*

● **The Cowboy's Sweetheart** / 1988 / Flying Fish 459
Late recordings by this Western radio star. The title track, from 1935, was the first million-selling female country vocal performance. —*Mark A. Humphrey*

Tiny Moore

b. 1920, Hamilton County, TX
Electric mandolin / Instrumental bluegrass
Three of the greatest mandolin players of all time (and probably the greatest) only obliquely played country music, devoting their time instead to swing and jazz. Dave Apollon and Jethro Burns are covered elsewhere in this book, and Tiny Moore is the third. Tiny played lead mandolin with Bob Wills' Texas Playboys in the '40s. In the '50s he invented a five-string electric mandolin that he has played while touring with Merle Haggard's band, the Strangers, a group famed for its instrumental excellence. Moore's virtuosity is a joy to listen to. —*David Vinopal*

George Morgan

b. Jun. 28, 1925, Waverly, TN, d. Jul. 7, 1975
Guitar / Traditional country

Morgan started his career as a smooth country crooner and grew more down-home country as the years passed. He enjoyed his greatest success early, when he scored seven chart hits in 1949. He was a Grand Ole Opry mainstay until his death, and introduced his daughter Lorrie to the stage. —*Michael McCall*

● **American Originals** / 1977 / CBS 45076

All of his famous hits, including "Candy Kisses" and "Room Full of Roses," are featured, although not necessarily in their original form. Contrary to the album title, a few of these songs are 1959 remakes of earlier hits. —*Michael McCall*

Lorrie Morgan

b. 1960

Vocals / Traditional country, contemporary country

Loretta Lynn Morgan, daughter of Opry star George Morgan ("Candy Kisses") and widow of bluegrass and country star Keith Whitley, appeared on the Opry at 13, becoming its youngest member in 1984. Her white-blonde hair and striking good looks are appropriate for her country-pop songs and torch delivery. Her 1991 album *Something in Red* yielded her biggest hit, "A Picture of Me without You," the video of which got considerable TV play. —*David Vinopal*

○ **Leave the Light on** / 1987 / BNA 9594

"Trainwreck of Emotion" and other belters. Hailed by some as the "new Tammy Wynette." —*Mark A. Humphrey*

Something in Red / 1991 / RCA 3021

Morgan backs off the sad songs for her second album—a wise move. (She went through the first part of her life known as George Morgan's daughter; she wouldn't want to spend the rest of it as Keith Whitley's widow.) Instead she concentrates on laid-back country and ballads like the title track, which is about the dress colors during different stages of a woman's life. Dolly Parton duets on "Best Woman Wins." —*Brian Mansfield*

● **Watch Me** / Oct. 1992 / BNA 66047

Morgan's second and third albums each improved on the last. *Watch Me* contains more good songs than the first two combined, including "I Guess You Had to Be There" and "From Our House to Yours" but not "What Part of No" or the remake of Bonnie Tyler's 1978 hit "It's a Heartache." —*Brian Mansfield*

Gary Morris

b. Dec. 7, 1948, Fort Worth, TX

Vocals / Country

An artist who refuses to be categorized, Morris has explored a variety of country sounds—acoustic folk, rock-edged commercial songs, romantic ballads—but also accepted a couple of roles on Broadway, including the physically demanding part of Jean Valjean in *Les Miserables*. Born and raised in Texas, Morris got his "break" by working on Jimmy Carter's 1976 election campaign. For his efforts, he got a chance to play for some influential members of the Country Music Association at a Presidential function, and when his demo tape crossed the desk of Warner's executive Norro Wilson, Wilson remembered him immediately and signed him to a recording deal. Frustrated by the restrictions inherent in the marketing of modern music, Morris refuses to compromise his musical integrity, and some of his work has thus fallen between the cracks. But few country artists—if any—have been able to match Morris for his vocal strength and clarity. —*Tom Roland*

● **Hits** / 1987 / Warner Brothers 25581

Morris may have the best "pipes" in country music, but he works so hard at showcasing them that most of his studio albums are bogged down by ballads. This collection includes the best of those ballads ("The Love She Found in Me," "100% Chance of Rain"), plus his best overall material ("I'll Never Stop Loving You," "Baby Bye Bye," "Velvet Chains"), which he seemingly undervalues. For those who appreciate such things, it also includes a sampling of his Broadway work, with a song from *La Boheme*. —*Tom Roland*

These Days / 1990 / Liberty 94103

Contains the hit "Miles across the Bedroom" and other Morris favorites. —*AMG*

Moon Mullican

b. Mar. 29, 1909, Corrigan, Polk County, TX, **d.** Jan. 1, 1967, Beaumont, TX

Piano / Instrumental bluegrass, traditional country

A piano-pounding honky-tonk man, born and raised deep in the heart of East Texas, Aubrey "Moon" Mullican is said to have had a significant musical influence on Jerry Lee Lewis, among others. Throughout the Depression and war years, he cut his ivory teeth on western swing, most notably as vocalist and piano player in Cliff Bruner's Texas Wanderers. In 1946, he signed with the emerging independent powerhouse King Records. A performer of wide-ranging tastes, Mullican was comfortable singing straight country, treacly pop or white-boy boogie. Indeed, many of his King sides, cut with black producer Henry Glover, jumped to the beat of hardcore R&B. —*Dan Cooper*

○ **Seven Years to Rock: The King Years, 1946-56** / Western 2001

Not a hits compilation, but a good sampling of Moon in his boogie phase. His take on Tiny Bradshaw's "Well, Oh Well" is required listening for anyone who thinks Elvis invented the hillbilly/R&B cover. —*Dan Cooper*

● **Sings His All-Time Greatest Hits** / 1958 / King 555

On CD, it's a budget-line reissue, but includes "I'll Sail My Ship Alone," "Pipeliner's Blues," and "Cherokee Boogie." —*Dan Cooper*

★ **Moonshine Jamboree** / 1993 / ACE 458

The best available compilation, this import CD includes "I'll Sail My Ship Alone," the one bona fide smash hit of Mullican's underappreciated career, and twenty-two lesser successes or hits that never were. —*Dan Cooper*

Moon's Rock / Bear Family 15607

Draws from Mullican's later years, after his career had gone into commercial decline. —*Dan Cooper*

Anne Murray

b. Jun. 20, 1946, Spring Hill, NS

Vocals, ukelele / Country-pop

Nova Scotia-born Anne Murray built her musical influences from the pop sounds that her parents listened to (Rosemary Clooney, Perry Como) and the Top 40 sounds that AM New York radio stations piped into Canada (Buddy Holly, Elvis Presley, Brenda Lee).

Originally she intended to work as a physical education instructor, but she continued to pursue an interest in music. Turned down for a spot on a national TV show called "Singalong Jubilee," she received a call from the show's producer two years later. He offered her a chance to make records, and when she agreed, she found herself with a million-selling crossover single in 1970, "Snowbird."

Murray was frequently at odds with the trappings of success—she even performed barefoot in Las Vegas—and when she got married in 1975, she seemingly dropped out of the business. With her family established, she started working in 1978 with a new producer, Jim Ed Norman, who returned her to prominence with "Walk Right Back" and the million-selling followup "You Needed Me."

Throughout the late '70s and early '80s, Murray successfully walked the line between country and pop with a rich alto voice and a knack for romantic material. Admirably, she continues to insist that no matter how high or low her career goes, her family in Toronto is her top priority. —*Tom Roland*

● **Greatest Hits** / 1980 / Liberty 46058

Covers Murray's first decade in the international limelight, beginning with "Snowbird" and concluding with "Could I Have This Dance," a track from the 1980 movie *Urban Cowboy*. Ranges from the folky "Danny's Song" to her cover of the Beatles' "You Won't See Me," but the middle-of-the-road approach is quite obvious. —*Tom Roland*

○ **Greatest Hits, Vol. 2** / 1989 / Liberty 92072

With her country base firmly established, Murray grew restless in the early and mid '80s, very much desirous of conquering the pop market. It never quite happened, though she made a nice stab at it in her duet with Dave Loggins, "Nobody Loves Me like You Do." She may not be country in the classic sense, but good music is good music and it's hard not to like "Time Don't Run Out on Me" or "Now and Forever (You and Me)." —*Tom Roland*

Willie Nelson

b. Apr. 30, 1933, Abbott, TX
Vocals, guitar, bass / Traditional country, progressive country
A lot of people, including lovers of country music, hadn't heard of
Willie Nelson until 1975, the year that an old Roy Acuff song titled "Blues Eyes Crying in the Rain" made him famous to the
multitudes and led to the first of his five Grammy awards.
During the two previous decades, though, he had written hundreds of quality songs, played thousands of honky-tonks, and perfected his vocal style, which many think ranks among the best of
any kind of popular American music. His "outlaw" and anti-establishment image, which now seems old hat, less than 20 years
after its creation, was not an act but the real thing. His abundance
of talent allowed him to back up this image; there's only one
Willie Nelson.

After a stint as a country DJ on a Ft. Worth radio station,
Nelson played bass with the Ray Price band, and Price recorded
his "Night Life," now a country standard. Faron Young then cut
"Hello Walls" and Patsy Cline, "Crazy" and "Funny How Time
Slips Away": Nelson had made his reputation as a premier songwriter. (Though he never sang them as such, many of his songs
are natural crossovers. Frank Sinatra, Perry Como, Stevie Wonder,
and Bing Crosby are a few of the stars who have recorded his
songs.) He then borrowed members of Price's band and started on
the road. Despite reasonable success, only when he moved back
to Texas from Nashville did his singing start getting the attention
it deserved. In this period before "Blue Eyes Crying in the Rain,"
he recorded three albums, including *Shotgun Willie* and *Phases
and Stages*, a concept album about a broken marriage, telling the
point of view of both the husband and the wife. Nelson had ignored the prevalent "Nashville sound" lushness, and succeeded.

Starting in 1975, Nelson reached the top, in the process melding country and "hip" music while turning millions of younger
listeners into fans. His *Red-Headed Stranger*, a concept album
about the Old West, hit Number 1, as did *Wanted: The Outlaws*,
with Waylon Jennings, Jessi Colter, and Tompall Glaser. The
Outlaws' national tour following this album created an explosion
of interest in country music. Nelson, now a superstar, recorded a
number of hit singles ("Remember Me," "Good-Hearted Woman,"
and others) before joining with Waylon Jennings in 1978 for
Waylon and Willie, an album that quickly sold a million and
locked both singers into the outlaw image for years. *Stardust*, a
hit album of popular songs, showcased Nelson's versatility.

In 1979, Nelson showed his acting talent in the well-received
movie, *Electric Horseman* (with Robert Redford and Jane Fonda);
Honeysuckle Rose was released a year later, drawing praise for
Nelson's acting. The film's soundtrack album was another hit. The
early '80s brought more superstardom, with "On the Road Again"
and "Angel Flying Too Close to the Ground."

Nelson's contributions to country music are enormous. His unsurpassed vocal style, his tasteful and subtle guitar playing, his
introduction of country music to millions of new listeners, his sophisticated yet real song compositions: these all show us what a
unique and incomparable talent is Willie Nelson. And his Farm
Aid benefits show us that his heart is where his music is. *—David
Vinopal*

☆ **Red Headed Stranger** / 1975 / CBS 33482
Recorded in Texas, Willie's sparsely-produced concept album
about the old West subverted the old ways in Nashville and made
country converts of hippies everywhere. In fact, it did more than
that, as "Blue Eyes Crying in the Rain" became one of the most
unlikely Top 40 hits in pop music history. *—Dan Cooper*

To Lefty from Willie / 1977 / CBS 34695
A fine tribute to Lefty Frizzell. *—Dan Heilman*

☆ **Stardust** / 1978 / CBS 35305
The record label didn't want Nelson to do this project, inspired
partially by the death of pop crooner Bing Crosby. Standard ma-
terial—"Moonlight in Vermont," "All of Me," "Don't Get Around
Much Anymore"—arranged by Booker T. Jones and recorded in
Nelson's inimitable style in Emmylou Harris' house. *—Tom
Roland*

Sings Kris Kristofferson / 1979 / Columbia 36188
No one does it better, Janis Joplin notwithstanding. *—Michael
McCall*

San Antonio Rose / 1980 / CBS 36476

Willie joined by his former bandstand boss, Ray Price, for remakes of "Crazy Arms," "Night Life," and a gorgeous version of
"Faded Love." *—Dan Cooper*

★ **Greatest Hits (& Some that Will Be)** / 1981 / CBS 37542
Greatest Hits (And Some that Will Be). Capsulizes Nelson's first
five years in the spotlight, with lots of classics: "On the Road
Again," "Blue Eyes Crying in the Rain," "Heartbreak Hotel" (a
duet with Leon Russell), as well as the smartly produced "My
Heroes Have Always Been Cowboys." *—Tom Roland*

Half Nelson / 1985 / CBS 39990
An appropriate collection, since Nelson has recorded more duets
with more fellow performers than any other country singer in
history. This runs the gamut, from traditional country singers
Merle Haggard and George Jones, to soulman Ray Charles, to
Latin lover Julio Iglesias, and the rock band Santana. Even has a
duet with the late Hank Williams, arranged through modern studio recording technology. *—Tom Roland*

★ **Nite Life ...** / 1989 / Rhino 70987
Nite Life—Greatest Hits & Rare Tracks (1959-1971). The best of
Nelson, the Nashville songwriter. *—Dan Heilman*

○ **Who'll Buy My Memories...** / 1992 / CBS 52981
Better known as the "IRS Tapes," this 25-song collection of solo
voice and guitar numbers is equal parts dark and scintillating;
but all parts unadorned Willie. *—Dan Cooper*

○ **Across the Borderline** / 1993 / CBS 52752
Nelson took a bold move by going into the studio with a hot rock
producer, Don Was, and it resulted in a strikingly artistic album,
the equal of *Stardust* and *Red Headed Stranger*. It includes duets
with Sinead O'Connor, Bonnie Raitt and Paul Simon. *—Michael
McCall*

○ **Willie Nelson—the Early Years** / May 3, 1994 / Liberty 28077
Struggling songwriter Willie performing his own material in a
clasic Ray Price mode. *—Dan Cooper*

☆ **Shotgun Willie/Phases & Stages** / Mobile Fidelity 581
This disc features Willie's entire Atlantic output. This was a
golden period for Willie artistically (if not financially), and these
are two of his very best albums. *—Jim Worbois*

Mickey Newbury

b. May 19, 1940, Houston, TX
Vocals, guitar / Progressive country
This talented songwriter moved to Nashville in the mid '60s, with
Elvis Presley, Ray Charles, and Jerry Lee Lewis recording some of
his emotional songs. He wrote "Just Dropped In (To See What
Condition My Condition Was In)," which was covered by Kenny
Rogers and the First Edition. In his "American Trilogy" (1972),
Newbury combined three Civil War songs, creating an interna-
tional hit. His songs are intricate and well crafted. *—David
Vinopal*

● **Frisco Mabel Joy** / 1971 / Elektra 74107
Elvis Presley took Newbury's "American Trilogy" as his own, but
the deeply felt original is here, along with some other excellent
songs by a songwriter who has long deserved far more recognition than he has received, and who turns out to be an affecting
singer as well. *—William Ruhlmann*

Jimmy C. Newman

b. Aug. 27, 1927, Big Mamou, LA
Vocals / Traditional country
This native of Big Mamou left Cajun country for Shreveport's
"Louisiana Hayride," proving ground of many country greats, and
graduated to the Grand Ole Opry in 1956 after the success of
"Cry, Cry Darling" and other Dot label hits. The "C" in his name
stands for Cajun, his stage suit is covered in rhinestone alligators,
and the cry in his voice comes from his Cajun background, but
Newman's material is essentially '50s Nashville. A notable excep-
tion was a fine 1963 Decca album, *Folk Songs of the Bayou
Country*. *—Mark A. Humphrey*

○ **Jimmy C. Newman & Cajun Country** / 1986 / Dot 39047
A collection of Newman's country/Cajun hits. *—Jeff Hannusch*

● **Bob a Hula-Diggy Liggy Lo** / 1990 / Bear Family 15469
This two-fer contains all the material recorded by Newman for
Dot Records, 47 tracks in all. *—AMG*

Juice Newton

b. Feb. 18, 1952, Virginia Beach, VA
Vocals, guitar / Country-rock
This country-rocker moved from Virginia to Northern California in the late '60s, when she formed Dixie Peach with Otha Young, an electric band. In the mid '70s she moved to Los Angeles and formed the Silver Spur Band, which mixed rock and pop with country. Her *Juice* album yielded two Number 1 singles, "Angel of the Morning" and "Queen of Hearts" (1981). Throughout the '80s she moved closer to rock and farther from country. *—David Vinopal*

● **Greatest Hits** / 1984 / Capitol 46489
Her countrified pop hits of the '80s. *—Bil Carpenter*

The Nitty Gritty Dirt Band

Group / Country-rock
In their 25 years together, the Nitty Gritty Dirt Band has recorded music that ranges from rock to pop to country. Under their aegis the three-disc *Will the Circle Be Unbroken* album in 1972 brought together many country music greats (including Earl Scruggs, Doc Watson, Roy Acuff, and Jimmy Martin) and brought national recognition to the NGDB. Their *WTCBU Vol. 2* (1989) won a Grammy. Through their music they have introduced country to millions of city and suburban listeners. *—David Vinopal*

○ **Uncle Charlie & His Dog Teddy** / 1970 / Liberty 7642
The album that gave them a career. Their laid-back mix of country and California folk gave a breezy feel to well-selected songs, including their million-selling version of Jerry Jeff Walker's "Mr. Bojangles." *—Michael McCall*

★ **Will the Circle Be Unbroken ...** / 1972 / EMI America 46589
The influence of this two-disc set, which brought the previously pop-oriented Dirt Band together with some of the seminal names in country music, is incalculable. Mother Maybelle Carter, Earl Scruggs, Doc Watson, Roy Acuff, and others sat down with a bunch of longhairs, found common ground on the best of old-time country music, and changed the direction of popular music. Two decades on, it still sounds great. *—William Ruhlmann*

○ **20 Years of Dirt ...** / 1986 / Warner Brothers 25382
20 Years of Dirt: The Best of the Nitty Gritty Dirt Band. This album traces the development of the Nitty Gritty Dirt Band from a pop outfit with folk and country edges into a contemporary country band. Their version of "Mr. Bojangles" remains memorable, as does "American Dream;" other tracks are sturdy, middle-of-the-road, '80s Nashville. *—William Ruhlmann*

○ **More Great Dirt (Best, Vol. 2)** / 1989 / Warner Brothers 25830
Tight harmonies and infectious arrangements are the staple of this compilation. "I've Been Lookin'," "Fishin' in the Dark," and "Baby's Got a Hold on Me" are the musical equivalent of a good book—you can't put 'em down. *—Tom Roland*

Will the Circle Be Unbroken, Vol. 2 / 1989 / Universal 12500
Easily won the Country Music Association's Album of the Year Award, thanks to a stellar cast that includes John Denver, Johnny Cash, the Carter Family, Bruce Hornsby, Ricky Skaggs, Chris Hillman, Roger McGuinn, Rosanne Cash, Steve Wariner, Roy Acuff, Chet Atkins ... you get the message. Tracks were all recorded in one "take," with no overdubs, making the outstanding musicianship particularly noteworthy. *—Tom Roland*

Acoustic / May 31, 1994 / Liberty 28169
Mighty professional sounding when compared to *Uncle Charlie*, but after more than 25 years as music pros, they still sound best when at their most casual, as they are here. *—Michael McCall*

The Oak Ridge Boys

Group / Gospel, country-pop
The Oaks (as they prefer to be called) started out as an award-winning gospel quartet, and each of the four singers worked for other gospel groups before forming the present band composed of Duane Allen, lead singer; Joe Bonsall, tenor; Richard Sterban, bass; and Steve Sanders, guitarist. In the mid '70s they swung toward country-pop, where they have remained. A break came when Johnny Cash asked them to open for him in Las Vegas. Subsequent country-pop groups such as Alabama owe a lot to the Oaks. Among their many hits are "Elvira" and "Y'All Come Back Saloon." William Lee Golden, who has country's longest (and

grayest) beard, left the group after singing baritone for two decades, because of an "image problem." *—David Vinopal*

● **Greatest Hits** / 1980 / MCA 42294
Earliest package of hits, with gospel roots showing on material like "Y'All Come Back Saloon." *—Cub Koda*

○ **Fancy Free** / 1981 / MCA 5209
Their best-selling album, thanks to the presence of "Elvira." Each of the Oaks gets a turn at the lead part, although Duane Allen is easily best suited to that role. Includes some quasi-folk and straightahead country, but the best track is the obligatory gospel tune "I Would Crawl All the Way (To the River)." *—Tom Roland*

○ **Greatest Hits, Vol. 2** / 1984 / MCA 5496
Covers the Oaks at their peak, with repetitive, singalong choruses predominating in "American Made," "Love Song," and "Everyday." The delicate "I Guess It Never Hurts to Hurt Sometimes" is a nice change of pace, but why did MCA hold out "Bobbie Sue" until *Greatest Hits 3*? *—Tom Roland*

Monongahela / 1987 / MCA 42205
Though *Heartbeat* was recorded after the dismissal of William Lee Golden, this is the first album in which replacement Steve Sanders was involved from beginning to end in the recording process. Harmonies are understandably more soulful—and more in tune—and the project is generally more uplifting. Includes "Gonna Take a Lot of River." *—Tom Roland*

Sensational Oak Ridge Boys / 1987 / Starday 356
Solid collection of their early gospel recordings. Interesting to compare to their secular success. *—Cub Koda*

Greatest Hits, Vol. 3 / 1989 / MCA 42294
Contains "Gonna Take a Lot of River," "Take Pride in America," "This Crazy Love," and others. *—AMG*

Mark O'Connor

b. Aug. 5, 1961
Fiddle / Instrumental bluegrass, progressive country
Born and raised in Seattle, O'Connor was always a bit out of sync with his teenage peers. Understandably—he was winning fiddle contests and had even mapped out a sketchy career path. O'Connor moved to Nashville in 1983, already a former sideman for jazz violinist Stephane Grappelli, a job that allowed him to play the stage at Carnegie Hall. At the time O'Connor arrived in Music City, the post-*Urban Cowboy* era—fiddle was hardly in vogue, and it took a couple of years for him to make his mark. Finally, in 1985, the Nitty Gritty Dirt Band used him in its single "High Horse"; and thanks to that work, O'Connor's phone number became a popular one with country record producers. Over the next five years he played on 450 albums, including such stellar projects as *Trio* by Dolly Parton, Linda Ronstadt, and Emmylou Harris; *Always & Forever* by Randy Travis; *Killin' Time* by Clint Black; and *Loving Proof* by Ricky Van Shelton. Despite his success, O'Connor gave up session work to concentrate on his own solo career, in the process providing a new focus on Nashville's studio players while simultaneously building a reputation for himself with the general public. *—Tom Roland*

Soppin' the Gravy / 1981 / Rounder 0137
Good collection of mainly traditional Texas fiddle music. *—Brian Mansfield*

On the Mark / 1989 / Warner Brothers 25970
Featuring James Taylor, Jerry Douglas, and Michael Brecker (one of my favorites). Great sax on "Get Set, Go." A must-have for O'Connor fans. *—Chip Renner*

○ **Championship Years** / 1990 / Country Music Foundation 015
O'Connor at his earliest and most traditional, these recordings were made during his National Fiddling Championships competitions between 1975 and 1984. *—Brian Mansfield*

○ **The New Nashville Cats** / 1991 / Warner Brothers 26509
Incredible lineup of Nashville's very best musicians. This package covers a wide range of musical territory, from bluegrass to the blues, with plenty of stellar "pickin'." Ironically, this mostly instrumental album won a vocal Grammy when Vince Gill, Ricky Skaggs, and Steve Wariner teamed with O'Connor on "Restless." *—Tom Roland*

False Dawn / Rounder 0165
New-age acoustic music. A turning-point album in which O'Connor comes of age. *—Chip Renner*

Mark O'Connor / Rounder 0046
An early album. Raw. —*Chip Renner*

● **Retrospective** / Rounder 11507
Chronological overview of O'Connor's first six Rounder albums. —*Brian Mansfield*

○ **Heroes** / Warner Brothers 45257
O'Connor performs with his favorite fiddlers from a variety of styles, including Jean-Luc Ponty, Johnny Gimble, Vassar Clements, Pinchas Zukerman, and L. Shankar, among others. Features "The Devil Comes Back to Georgia," a sequel to Charlie Daniels 1979 hit "The Devil Went Down to Georgia." —*Brian Mansfield*

O'Kanes

Group / Country
During their relatively brief time together, Kieran Kane and Jamie O'Hara, otherwise known as the O'Kanes, produced three albums of absolutely superb country music. The self-titled, first, and arguably strongest effort contains everything that is best about the O'Kanes' sound. It is rich in country music's finest traditions, yet it is by no means a nostalgia album. It is sparse in instrumentation, yet richly textured. Most of all, it contains direct, honest music, whose emotional intensity stays with the listener long after the sound waves have stopped.

The O'Kanes' vocals recall the best of country harmony. Some critics liken them to the Louvin Brothers. Others, because of the more driving sound of their backing, compare them to the Everlys. The instrumental sound ranges from bluegrass (prominent mandolin) to the tense drive of Sun rockabilly (their hit "O Darlin'" is evidence of this). The addition of an accordion adds both Tex-Mex and unmistakably bluesy feels to the proceedings. This is truly hybrid music.

Kane and O'Hara's best songs ("O Darlin'," "Can't Stop My Heart," and "This Isn't Love") explore the lonely, desperate, and occasionally obsessive side of love. Whether they continue to record or not, the O'Kanes reflect and contribute to the renaissance of solid, unaffected country music that has spawned the success of stars like Dwight Yoakam and Randy Travis and heralds a welcome return to basics. —*Hank Davis*

The O'Kanes / 1987 / CBS 40459
Introspective lyrics and occasional guitar/mandolin jams make an interesting concept from Music City before the "hat" proliferation of 1990. —*Mark A. Humphrey*

● **Tired of the Runnin'** / 1988 / CBS 44066
A strong title song, austerely folkish, represents this short-lived duo at its best. —*Mark A. Humphrey*

K. T. Oslin

b. 1942
Vocals / Country-pop
As a veteran of a '60s folk trio, commercials, and successful songwriting, Kay Toinette Oslin was in her mid-forties when her debut album, *80s Ladies*, sold platinum and led to many awards in 1987-1988. Her country-pop flavor found a receptive audience of middle-aged single women. —*David Vinopal*

○ **80's Ladies** / 1987 / RCA 2193
A pop-turned-country belter with anthems meant for thirtysomething women. —*Mark A. Humphrey*

This Woman / 1988 / RCA 8369
Album features the hits "Didn't Expect It to Go Down this Way," "Hold Me," and "This Woman," among others. —*AMG*

○ **Love in a Small Town** / 1990 / RCA 2365
Oslin built this loosely defined concept album from 10 years of song, including the first one she wrote. Oslin sings of the guises romance wears in the small-town South: Nelda Jean Prudie waxes nostalgic about weekend dances of her Texas youth; a young girl enthuses about a pick-up-driving Romeo named Cornell Crawford; and people searching for perfect partner wind up lonely. *Love in a Small Town* also contains a low-key version of the 1946 standard "You Call Everybody Darling" and a cover of Mickey and Sylvia's "Love Is Strange." Oslin's coyness isn't always flattering, and the arrangements sometimes border on a new countrypolitan, but those moments are rare. On most of *Small Town*, Oslin displays her best assets: her worldly sensibility and complex maturity. —*Brian Mansfield*

● **Greatest Hits** / Apr. 27, 1993 / RCA

Paul Overstreet

b. 1929
Vocals / Gospel, contemporary country
This songwriter-turned-performer has helped pen "On the Other Hand" and "Forever and Ever, Amen," both huge hits for Randy Travis. A born-again Christian, he emphasizes basic values in his music and is also found on the gospel charts. His hits include "Heroes" and "Ball and Chain." —*David Vinopal*

○ **Sowin' Love** / 1989 / RCA 9717
A pleasant nonregional mix of country and gospel. —*Bil Carpenter*

Heroes / 1991 / RCA 2459
Features "Love Lives On," "Ball & Chain," "She Supports Her Man," and other songs. —*AMG*

● **The Best of Paul Overstreet** / Feb. 1994 / RCA 66350
The ultimate New Traditionalist factory songwriter, Overstreet's best work is the series of hits he wrote (usually with Don Shlitz) for Randy Travis in the 1980's. On his own, as evidenced by this colection, he's a bit too obsessed with convincing everybody that he's a good Christian man who just can't wait to get home to his wife. There's more to life—and music—than family values, no matter how you define them. —*Dan Cooper*

Buck Owens (Alvis Edgar Owens)

b. Aug. 12, 1929, Sherman, TX
Vocals, guitar, saxaphone, trumpet / Traditional country
In 1992 Alvis Edgar "Buck" Owens retired from performing, after 26 consecutive Number 1 hits in the 1960s and the creation of the "Bakersfield sound" that continues to influence contemporary honky-tonk singers, including Dwight Yoakam. With the Buckaroos, his band of exceptional musicians, Owens sang his gritty, real-life songs, which changed the direction of country music. When Route 66 led Owens from his Texas home to Arizona and finally to Bakersfield, he began as a guitar player, singing (against his own wishes) only when the band's usual lead singer lit out for Hollywood. The crowds in the honky-tonks kept asking for more Owens, so Owens the guitarist became Owens the singer. His first chart song was "Second Fiddle" (1959), followed by "Under Your Spell Again," "Excuse Me (I Think I've Got a Heartache)," and "Fooling Around"; and he was a star. Duets with Rose Maddox brought him more fame. Throughout the '60s he scored hit after hit, including "Act Naturally" (covered by the Beatles), "I've Got a Tiger by the Tail," "Waiting in the Welfare Line," "Love's Gonna Live Here," "Tall Dark Stranger," and "Together Again."

In the early '70s, the hits continued with "I Wouldn't Live in New York City" and "Ruby (Are You Mad?)." His glory days came to an end after years at the top, except for a "Play Together Again, Again" duet with Emmylou Harris and his appearance on Dwight Yoakam's *Streets of Bakersfield* album more than ten years later. As co-host (with Roy Clark) of "Hee Haw," TV's long-running country-music/country-corn series, Owens kept in the public eye until 1986, after having spent 17 years on the program. Owens has left us with years of beautiful music and an enduring honky-tonk/rockabilly influence. —*David Vinopal*

I Don't Care / 1964 / Capitol 2186
Studio album version of Owens and the Buckaroos' mid-60s stage show—Owens plays "Buck's Polka." Doyle Holly and Don Rich are featured—also "Loose Talk," a duet with Owens and Rose Maddox. —*George Bedard*

Together Again/My Heart Skips a Beat / 1964 / Capitol 1489
Includes his covers of "Truck Drivin' Man," "A-11," and "Hello Trouble." —*George Bedard*

○ **I've Got a Tiger by the Tail** / 1965 / Capitol 2283
The title track, plus some great ballads including "Cryin' Time." These '60s Capitol albums are not just mish-mashes like many C&W albums of the period—they're well thought-out, usually including a vocal or two by Don Rich (one of C&W's unsung heroes) or the deep-voiced bass player Doyle Holly and a fiddle or steel-guitar instrumental by Don or Tom Brumley, respectively. —*George Bedard*

○ **Roll out the Red Carpet** / 1966 / Capitol 2443

Mostly written or cowritten by Owens, this is Owens and the boys at their peak. —*George Bedard*

☆ **Live at Carnegie Hall** / 1989 / Country Music Foundation 12
This album contains 21 tracks, the debut concert (Mar 25, 1966) of Buck & the Buckaroos in its entirety, and features such songs as "Waitin' in Your Welfare Line," "I've Got a Tiger by the Tail," and more. Here is Owens at his best. —*AMG*

★ **All-Time Greatest Hits, Vol. 1** / 1990 / Curb 77342
The 12 cuts on this album contain some of Owens' best-loved songs from the '60s. —*AMG*

★ **The Buck Owens Collection (1959-1990)** / 1992 / Rhino 71016
A glorious three-disc collection featuring nearly every great track Buck Owens ever recorded. —*AMG*

Country Hit Maker #1 / Starday 324
Pre-Capitol material, half of this album consists of Owens' very early recordings like "Sweethearts in Heaven" and "There Goes My Love" (covered later by Highway 101), which show his developing vocal style. A little more down-home than his later stuff. The other half consists of covers of Owens' later material by other artists. —*George Bedard*

Lee Roy Parnell

Guitar / Rock, country
Texas country-rocker with strong R&B roots, who wrote songs for Johnny Lee, Marcia Ball, and others before getting his own recording deal. He was the second artist, behind Alan Jackson, signed to Arista Records' Nashville division when the label opened shop in the late '80s. —*Brian Mansfield*

○ **Lee Roy Parnell** / 1990 / Arista 8625
Hard-rocking country soul, complete with horn section. Produced by Barry Beckett, whose experiences at Muscle Shoals mean he knows how to make this kind of record. —*Brian Mansfield*

● **Love without Mercy** / 1992 / Arista 18684
For his second album, Parnell dropped the horns and gave his slide guitar a bigger role. He was still a Texas rocker disguised by a pedal steel, but the album produced three Top 10 hits—"Love Without Mercy," "What Kind of Fool Do You Think I Am," and "Tender Moment." —*Brian Mansfield*

On the Road / Oct. 26, 1993 / Arista 18739
More roots-rocking road music, though not as perfectly realized as *Love Without Mercy*. The title track and "I'm Holding My Own" were hits, and Parnell sang with Brooks & Dunn's Ronnie Dunn on the Hank Williams standard "Take These Chains From My Heart." —*Brian Mansfield*

Dolly Parton

b. Jan. 19, 1946, Locust Ridge, TN
Vocals, guitar, banjo / Traditional country, contemporary country
It's difficult to find a country performer who has moved from country roots to international fame more successfully than Dolly Parton. Her autobiographical single "Coat of Many Colors" shows the poverty of growing up one of 12 children on a run-down farm in Locust Ridge, TN. At 12 years old she was appearing on Knoxville television; at 13 she was recording on a small label and appearing on the Grand Ole Opry; at present she has to her credit hit albums, hit singles, hit movies, and a TV variety show.

Her 1967 hit "Dumb Blonde" (and she's not) caught Porter Wagoner's ear, and he hired Parton to appear on his television show, where their duet numbers became famous. By the time her "Joshua" reached Number 1 in 1970, Parton's fame had overshadowed the boss's and she'd struck out on her own, though still recording duets with him. Between those duets and her recent one with Ricky Van Shelton came a lot of stardom.

Parton's debut on the silver screen was in the 1980 hit *9 to 5* with co-stars Lily Tomlin and Jane Fonda; Parton's *9 to 5 and Odd Jobs* album was released with the film. *The Best Little Whorehouse in Texas* brought further fame, or notoriety, two years later; in 1984 she and Sylvester Stallone starred (and in fact sang a duet) in *Rhinestone*. "Tennessee Homesick Blues," from the film's soundtrack, earned Parton another Grammy nomination. Since then she has appeared in *Steel Magnolias* as a small-town gossipy beautician, and in *Wild Texas Wind*, a made-for-TV thriller-melodrama co-starring Ray Benson, leader of Asleep at the Wheel, a Western-swing band.

The critics have told us that she can act, but can Parton sing? Yes, and very well, in spite of her reputation created by her movies, her cheesecake image, and her many forays into pop music. She can still be pure country when she wants, all tinsel aside. Try listening to "Coat of Many Colors," "Jolene," "But You Know I Love You," and "Tennessee Homesick Blues." Parton is a woman of considerable talents, country singing chief among them. —*David Vinopal*

○ **Just Because I'm a Woman** / 1968 / RCA 3949
It's a measure of how impressed producer Bob Ferguson must have been with Dolly that he (and possibly Porter Wagoner in the background) made no attempt to crowd her with strings or choruses on her first RCA album. In fact, it's almost frightening to hear how fully realized her talent was in 1968. —*Dan Cooper*

The Best of Dolly Parton / 1975 / RCA 5146
Dolly projects an admirable child-like sense of hope and positivism, which is matched to some degree by her thin, girlish vocal quality. It translates well in her pre-Hollywood, unencumbered productions, notably "Coat of Many Colors," "Love Is like a Butterfly," and "The Bargain Store." —*Tom Roland*

9 to 5 and Odd Jobs / 1980 / RCA 3047
Dolly Parton has never been an albums artist, and RCA has always been adept at shoving poorly organized products onto the market (look how they've treated Elvis Presley). Hence, though she is an important country figure, most of Parton's albums are hard to recommend. This one contains the title hit, plus a few other Parton originals and a version of Woody Guthrie's "Deportee" among its eight tracks. But that's enough to put it a notch above most of Parton's RCA catalog. —*William Ruhlmann*

● **Greatest Hits** / 1982 / RCA 8505
A good sampling of Parton's work in the first few years that she deliberately chased a crossover career in Hollywood. The country-pop stuff might offend purists, but it still gets the toe tappin'. "Hard Candy Christmas" and her updated version of "I Will Always Love You" (both from *The Best Little Whorehouse in Texas*) show her growth as an interpreter. —*Tom Roland*

★ **Collector's Series** / 1985 / RCA 5471
This is a well-programmed selection of Parton's RCA hits, among them "Jolene," "Coat of Many Colors," and "Me and Little Andy." —*William Ruhlmann*

Real Love / 1985 / RCA 85414
A lot of critics would push this one aside, perhaps with good reason since she turned over much of the creative control on the project to David Malloy. But Malloy set out to highlight the bright, bubbly facet of her personality, and he succeeded. —*Tom Roland*

○ **White Limozeen** / 1989 / CBS 44384
Parton moved to Columbia in the late '80s and started paying more attention to her recordings, the best of which is this album. It's produced by Ricky Skaggs, who brought in such fast-picking cronies as Bela Fleck and Jerry Douglas and used more of Parton's own songs than usual. The result is an unusual consistency and a musical revitalization for the singer. —*William Ruhlmann*

Eagle When She Flies / 1991 / CBS 46882
She confirms that she's fully returned to the country fold, and is rewarded with her first million-selling album that wasn't a greatest hits package. The title song is a powerful female anthem. —*Michael McCall*

★ **RCA Years 1967-1986** / 1993 / RCA 66127
The long-overdue box set turns out to be a cursory two-CD set that cheats on her better early years in favor of latter-day hits. Still, it's the best retrospective available, and it emphasizes her stature as a truly significant songwriter, which is easy to forget in the shadow of her Daisy Mae in Hollywood image. —*Michael McCall*

○ **The World of Dolly Parton, Vol. 1** / Monument 44361
Captures young Dolly on Monument Records circa 1967, just before she hooked up with Porter. "Just because I'm blonde, don't think I'm dumb," she sings on "Dumb Blonde." We don't, Dolly, we don't. —*Dan Cooper*

○ **The World of Dolly Parton, Vol. 2** / Monument 44362
More from the Monument catalog. —*Dan Cooper*

Johnny Paycheck (Don Eugene Lytle, Donny Young)

b. May 31, 1938, Greenfield, OH
Steel guitar, Vocals, bass, guitar / Traditional country, country-rock

The first that many people ever heard of Johnny Paycheck was in 1977, when his "Take This Job and Shove It" inspired one-man wildcat strikes all over America. The next time was in 1985, when he was arrested for shooting a man at a bar in Hillsboro, OH. That Paycheck is remembered for a fairly amusing novelty song and a violent crime (for which he spent two years in prison) is a shame, for it just so happens that he is one of the mightiest honky-tonkers of his time.

Born Donald Lytle in Greenfield, OH, he was performing in talent contests by the age of nine, and riding the rails as a drifter by the time he turned fifteen. After a Navy stint landed him in the brig for two years, he arrived in Nashville, where he performed in the bands of Porter Wagoner, Faron Young, Ray Price and George Jones. He recorded several singles under the name Donny Young, then, in 1965, cut his first sides as Johnny Paycheck for the Hilltop label. A year later, he and gadfly producer Aubrey Mayhew started the Little Darlin' label, for which Paycheck recorded his greatest work. Marked by Lloyd Green's knockout steel guitar and Paycheck's broad, resonant vocals (not to mention his rounder's sense of humor) his Little Darlin' records of the 1960s have since become cult favorites.

After splitting with Mayhew (and after running his life into the gutter) Paycheck made a celebrated comeback on Epic in the 1970s. "Take This Job and Shove It" was the most famous result, though ballads like "She's All I Got" and "Someone to Give My Love To" are far more indicative of his stylistic range. —*Dan Cooper*

○ **Johnny Paycheck at Carnegie Hall** / 1966 / Little Darlin' 8001
Ha ha. Despite the title and the photo of Paycheck in black-tie garb, his debut album is actually a Nashville studio product. But what a hopped-up product it is. Makes most mid '60s honky-tonk sound like Jim Nabors with steel guitar. —*Dan Cooper*

○ **Jukebox Charlie** / 1967 / Little Darlin' 4006
One of the all-time great honky-tonk singers before his bad habits got the better of him. Includes two of the greatest country songs ever—"Apartment #9" and "Touch My Heart," both written by Paycheck. —*George Bedard*

Again / 1970 / Certron 7002
Post-Little Darlin', but still Mayhew-produced, Paycheck keeps right on kicking. Includes "Living the Life of a Dog," a hilarious romp that probably had multiple meanings for Johnny. —*Dan Cooper*

Take This Job & Shove It / 1978 / Laserlight 15483
His big '70s novelty hit and an uneven selection of tunes, but worth having for "Colorado Kool-Aid"—a sort of Red Sovine-from-hell recitation on the subject of barroom etiquette. —*George Bedard*

Bars, Booze & Blondes / 1979 / Little Darlin'
More repackaged '60s classics, with the memorable "I Drop More Than I Drink" and "The Pint of No Return." —*Michael McCall*

○ **Extra Special** / 1982 / Accord
A budget-line release featuring a handful of characteristically bizarre honky tonk recorded in the 1960s around the same time he was recording for Little Darlin'. —*Michael McCall*

● **Biggest Hits** / 1983 / Epic 38322
Heavy on the late '70s outlaw sound, this is where to find the original "Take This Job and Shove It" on CD. —*Dan Cooper*

Minnie Pearl (Sarah Ophelia Colley)

b. Oct. 25, 1912, Centerville, TN

Among the Grand Ole Opry's most beloved longterm members, comedienne Minnie Pearl got her first Opry laughs in 1940. She was born Sarah Ophelia Colley in the middle Tennessee town of Centerville. The actress daughter of a sawmill owner, she was, in real life, by no means the cornpone hillbilly—price tag hanging from her straw hat—that she played on stage. Rather, it's a credit to her comedic skill that plain folks not only bought her man-hungry, downhome sister act, but ultimately took her closer to their hearts than any Opry star except Roy Acuff. Poor health has kept her inactive of late, but her motherly presence remains. —*Dan Cooper*

● **The Best of Minnie Pearl** /
Features "Gossip from Grinder's Switch," "The Party Kissing Game," and others. —*AMG*

Webb Pierce

b. Aug. 8, 1926, West Monroe, LA, **d.** Feb. 24, 1991
Vocals, guitar / Traditional country

A Louisiana native, Webb Pierce first found fame on Shreveport's KWKH, home of the Louisiana Hayride, where he quickly became a popular performer, recording two hits during this period, "Wondering" and "Back Street Affair," the latter prompting an answer song from Miss Kitty Wells, "Paying for That Back Street Affair." Quickly he moved on to the Opry, where (with his high and nasal tenor) he gained fame for singing honky-tonk songs that stayed sung. "Slowly," a 1954 hit, is the first to feature a pedal guitar (played by Buddy Isaacs). In 1955 he had three Number 1s, and a year later "Why Baby Why," a duet with Red Sovine, charted high. Though Pierce charted in 1982 in a duet with Willie Nelson that covered "In the Jailhouse Now" (by Jimmie Rodgers), changes in music taste left a lot of lean years after the heights he reached in the '50s. When he died in 1991, he left a legacy of authentic, well-done honky-tonk music, many of the songs having been written by Pierce himself. Though Pierce never quite managed to be what people expected—the next Hank Williams—he had enough success (32 hits from his debut record to 1960) to be fondly remembered by fans who like their music gritty and sparse in instrumentation. His "There Stands the Glass" of 1952 remains the beer-drinker's anthem. And he really did have a guitar-shaped swimming pool, with bridge, sound hole, and strings visible on the bottom. —*David Vinopal*

○ **Greatest Hits** / 1960 / MCA 120
Contains "There Stands a Glass," "If the Back Door Could Talk," "In the Jailhouse Now," "Wondering," and other hits. —*AMG*

Walking the Streets / 1960 / Decca 74079
Good weepers, including "Drinkin' My Blues Away." —*George Bedard*

Webb with a Beat! / 1960 / Decca 74015
Includes "I Ain't Never" (cowritten by Mel Tillis) and "In the Jailhouse Now." The title is a bit misleading, but "I Ain't Never" definitely rocks. —*George Bedard*

☆ **The Wondering Boy (1951-1958)** / 1990 / Bear Family 15522
For the devout, Germany's Bear Family offers a four-CD boxed set of Pierce's primal honky-tonk. A total of 113 songs by one of the seminal post-War country artists, including duets with Kitty Wells, Red Sovine, and the Wilburn Brothers. The best sound quality and presentation available of this influential music. —*Mark A. Humphrey*

★ **Webb Pierce: King of the Honky-Tonk** / 1994 / Country Music Foundat 0019
No one ever accused Pierce of being a singer's singer, nevertheless, his classic country oeuvre is totally individualistic, which is really more important. Any fan of 1950s fiddle-and-steel honky-tonk will want this collection, which features such Pierce immortals as "There Stands the Glass," "Slowly," a rollicking 1954 remake of Jimmie Rodgers' "In the Jailhouse Now," and the to-the-point "Honky Tonk Song." The latter is one of several cuts from the pen of a young Mel Tillis. —*Dan Cooper*

○ **Sands of Gold/Sweet Memories** / Mobile Fidelity 750
Oo-ooh, what a little remastering can do. Two Nashville Sound LPs from the downside of Pierce's career, with Webb singing more of other people's hits than his own. But reissued Mofi-style, Pierce and the echo chamber sound great. —*Dan Cooper*

○ **That Wondering Boy** / Decca 8295
Includes "Slowly," "There Stands the Glass," and "Back Street Affair." —*George Bedard*

Pinkard & Bowden

Group / Country humor

Sandy Pinkard and Richard Bowden are in the Lonzo-and-Oscar/Homer-and-Jethro tradition of spoofing hit songs. Two of their parodies are "Driving My Wife Away" (a sendup of "Driving My Life Away") and "Blue Hair's Driving in My Lane" ("Blue Eyes Crying in the Rain"). Bowden is a former member of Emmylou Harris's Hot Band. —*David Vinopal*

○ **Live in Front of a Bunch of Dickheads** / 1990 / Warner Brothers 26057
Nashville's wiseacres and country parodists in their element, such as it is. —*Dan Heilman*

Pirates of the Mississippi

Group
Six-piece band consisting of lead singer Bill McCorvey, guitarist Rich Alves, drummer Jimmy Lowe, bassist Dean Townson, and steel player Pat Severs. A rock-influenced group who debuted with a cover of Hank Williams' "Honky Tonk Blues," the Pirates hit the charts a couple of months after the Kentucky HeadHunters, which, considering the similarities in the names, probably wasn't the best timing. The Pirates won the Academy of Country Music's Top New Vocal Group award in 1991. —*Brian Mansfield*

○ **Pirates of the Mississippi** / Jun. 18, 1990 / Capitol 94389
The Pirates made their name with their third single, "Feed Jake," which had a video that became country music's version of *Old Yeller*. The rest of the debut is a cross between Alabama country and Southern rock. (The album starts with a speeded-up version of "Honky Tonk Blues," if that's a hint at what's to come.) There's a few twists, though, namely a Guy Clark song ("I Take My Comfort in You") and a surf-country instrumental. —*Brian Mansfield*

Walk the Plank / Sep. 30, 1991 / Capitol 95798
As country, the Pirates' Allman Brothers cops are more exciting than their stone-country material, although that's certainly competent enough. The white-country-soul "Till I'm Holding You Again"—which tries to rock out when you're not looking—is probably the best of all. —*Brian Mansfield*

A Street Man Named Desire / Sep. 28, 1992 / Liberty 98781
"Street Man Named Desire" may not be the most clear-cut metaphor given the phrase's origins, but if you're gonna make literary allusions, you can do worse than Tennessee Williams. While that's the title tune, the Allman and Doobie Brothers influences in the instrumental "Mystery Ship" tell more about the band—namely, that they're a tamed biker band. The Pirates are good-natured renegades, but they never take the image too far. So "Mississippi Homegrown" is about music, not marijuana (and contains another Williams reference), "The Hard Side of Love" only hints at the Southern boogie the guys might have in them, and "All Your Eyes Can See" is a tender love song for the ladies. Powerful in spots, pedestrian in others. —*Brian Mansfield*

Dream You / Oct. 11, 1993 / Liberty 80379
Basically a party album containing songs like "Save the Wild Life," "Pop From the Top," "The Night They Rocked the Grand Ole Opry," and a full-tilt cover of Hank Thompson's "The Wild Side of Life." —*Brian Mansfield*

● **Best of the Pirates of The Mississippi** / Mar. 8, 1994 / Liberty 28089
Beyond the video for "Feed Jake," the Pirates of the Mississippi never found great success (five Top 40 hits in four years, none making the Top 10). Even so, they were a pretty decent singles band, as this collection shows, especially when they nail the fast stuff (like "Rollin' Home" and "Speak of the Devil"). *Best of* also includes dance mixes of two tunes from *Dream You*: "Dream You" and "Pop From the Top." —*Brian Mansfield*

Ray Price

b. Jan. 12, 1926, Perryville, TX
Vocals, guitar / Traditional country,country-pop
Ray Price has covered—and kicked up—as much musical turf as any country singer of the postwar era. He's been lionized as the man who saved hard country when Nashville went pop, and villified as the man who went pop when hard country was starting to call its own name with pride. Actually, he was—and still is—no more than a musically ambitious singer, always looking for the next challenge for a voice that could bring down roadhouse walls.

Born in tiny Perryville, TX, Price spent most of his youth in Dallas. It was there, circa 1949, that he cut his first record for Bullet at the famous Jim Beck studio. In 1951, he was picked up by Columbia, the label for which he would record for more than twenty years. After knocking around in Lefty Frizzell's camp for six months or so (his first Columbia single was a Frizzell composition) Price befriended Hank Williams. The connection brought

him to the Opry and profoundly effected his singing style. After Hank died, Price starting stretching out more as a singer and arranger. His experimentation culminated in the 4/4, bass-driven "Crazy Arms," the country song of the year for 1956. The intensely rhythmic sound he discovered with "Crazy Arms" would dominate his—and much of country in general's—music for the next six years. To this day, people in Nashville refer to a 4/4 country shuffle as the "Ray Price beat." Heavy on fiddle, steel, and high tenor harmony, his country work from the late 1950s is as lively as the rock & roll of the same era. Price tired of that sound, however, and started messing around with strings. His lush 1967 version of "Danny Boy," and his 1970 take on Kris Kristofferson's "For the Good Times," were, in their crossover way, landmark records. But few of his old fans appreciated the fact. For the last 25 years, Price's career has been an often awkward balancing act in which twin Texas fiddles are weighed against orchestras. —*Dan Cooper*

○ **Talk to Your Heart** / 1958 / CBS 1148
Great collection of "weepers," honky-tonk, and Western swingy numbers from the '50s. Several songs by Floyd Tillman. Features "I'll Keep on Loving You," "Deep Water," "I Gotta Have My Baby Back," and "I'm Tired." A real "Texas-flavored" record by a honkytonk master. —*George Bedard*

Night Life / 1963 / CBS 8771
Probably the first country & western "concept" album. Willie Nelson penned the title track plus other 3 AM classics—tied together by the masterful steel guitar of Buddy Emmons. —*George Bedard*

○ **The Best of Ray Price** / 1976 / CBS 34160
This compilation presents the highlights of Price's string-laden years. "For the Good Times" is simply one of the most mature singles ever recorded. "She's Got to Be a Saint" has somehow gotten lost over the years. —*Tom Roland*

Greatest Hits, Vol. 4 (By Request) / 1988 / Step One 0050
The fourth volume in the series contains "April's Fool," "Twenty Fourth Hour," "I've Got a New Heartache," and other Price favorites. —*AMG*

Just Enough Love / 1988 / Step One 0033
Features "I'd Do it All Over Again," "Big Ole Teardrops," and other Price hits. —*AMG*

★ **The Essential Ray Price (1951-1962)** / 1991 / CBS 48532
A not-completely-accurate title, as this 20-track compilation excludes a few later necessities like "Night Life" and "For the Good Times," but the important stuff from Price's hard-country heyday is all here, from the teetering rise-and-fall of "Crazy Arms" (the first of a thousand country songs to employ a walking bassline and modified swing beat, which became known as the "Ray Price shuffle") to Harlan Howard's "Heartaches by the Number." The fake stereo that marred earlier reissues of his '50s material is happily absent here. Essential country music. —*Brian Mansfield & Mark A. Humphrey*

Honky-Tonk Years (1951-1953) / Rounder 22
Early, Hank Williams-inspired material, some backed by Hank's Drifting Cowboys. —*Mark A. Humphrey*

Charley Pride (Country Charley)

b. Mar. 18, 1938, Sledge, MS
Vocals, guitar / Traditional country
With thirty-six Number 1 hits under his belt, Charley Pride, who is black, has helped prove how little race matters to the majority of country music fans. It's taken a long time to understand that, though. His first single, "Snakes Crawl at Night," was released without publicity photos, as some in the industry feared listeners would automatically reject a black country singer. Since then, according to the *Book of Lists*, Pride's 12 gold albums in the US, combined with 30 gold and 4 platinum internationally, place him in the top 15 all-time record sellers. His easygoing singing style and easy-to-listen-to voice show why these honors have come his way.

From picking cotton in his native Mississippi, Pride ended up working in a smelting plant in Montana, after a stint as a semipro baseball player. At the suggestion of Red Sovine, Pride moved to Nashville, where he was signed by Chet Atkins of RCA. In 1966, "Just Between You and Me" brought Pride a Grammy nomination and national fame. At the end of the 60s and the early part of the '70s, he had five Number 1s in a row, including "All I Have to Offer Is Me" and "Is Anybody Goin' to San Antone?" Numerous awards came in 1971 and 1972, with many more hits following, among them "She's Too Good to Be True," "Kiss an Angel Good Mornin'," and "Night Games."

Pride's warm baritone voice and relaxed style made him the highest-selling act for RCA since Elvis Presley. His Number 1 album in 1980, *There's a Little Bit of Hank in Me*, showed why he is called "Country Charley." —*David Vinopal*

● **The Best of Charley Pride** / 1969 / Curb 77471
Pride sang in a Hank Williams-influenced voice that yielded some of the best country performances of the late '60s and early '70s. —*Mark A. Humphrey*

○ **The Best of Charley Pride, Vol. 2** / 1972 / RCA 8448
Perhaps because RCA wanted to leave no doubts about Pride's country heritage, his early career mined the standard three-chord structure almost exclusively. As with the first volume, this set does that, but in "Kiss an Angel Good Mornin'" and "Is Anybody Goin' to San Antone?" his performance is a notch or two above the previous package. —*Tom Roland*

The Best of Charley Pride, Vol. 3 / 1977 / RCA
To be honest, Pride sounds a bit bored with some of this material. But "Mississippi Cotton Pickin' Delta Town" is practically a page out of his life. By the way, the cover art, with its rope script and blue-jeans-and-patches sports suit, is so '70s, it's camp. —*Tom Roland*

○ **Greatest Hits #2** / 1981 / RCA 6917
Pride seems a little uninvolved with some of the material, but when he lets loose—as in "When I Stop Leaving (I'll Be Gone)" or "A Whole Lotta Things to Sing About"—he's absolutely convincing. —*Tom Roland*

○ **Charley Sings Everybody's Choice** / 1982 / RCA
Dumb title, but an excellent album. Producer Norro Wilson revitalized Pride's career by bringing out the Memphis soul that rests in the shadows of his country veneer. —*Tom Roland*

Eddie Rabbitt (Edward Thomas)

b. Nov. 27, 1941, Brooklyn, NY
Vocals, guitar / Country-pop
One of country music's most innovative artists during the late '70s and early '80s, Rabbitt has made contributions to the format that have often gone overlooked. Especially in songs like the R&B-inflected "Suspicions" and the rockin' "Someone Could Lose a Heart Tonight," Rabbitt challenged the commonly recognized creative boundaries of the idiom.

Hailing from Brooklyn and New Jersey, Rabbitt moved to Nashville in 1968. Though it took a few years to get his recording career off the ground, he paid the rent through songwriting, authoring Elvis Presley's "Kentucky Rain" and Ronnie Milsap's "Pure Love."

Signing with Elektra Records' newly established country division in 1975, Rabbitt made recordings that were decidedly country—mostly uptempo material, like "Two Dollars in the Jukebox" and "Drinkin' My Baby (Off My Mind)"—with thick, inimitable harmonies, most of them overdubbed by Rabbitt himself.

Driven in part by then-associates David Malloy and Even Stevens, Rabbitt's records became "progressively progressive," well into the late '80s. At that time, his country shuffle on "On Second Thought" demonstrated a return to more traditional sounds. —*Tom Roland*

○ **The Best of Eddie Rabbitt** / 1979 / Elektra 235
Strong melodies enhanced by Rabbitt's searing harmonies. The instruments are "hotter" in the final mix than in other productions from the same period, so even the mainstream country fare is a little different from that of his mid '70s contemporaries. —*Tom Roland*

Loveline / 1979 / Elektra 181
Fellow reviewers will cringe at this choice, but it displays Rabbitt at his most daring. Lots of R&B influence—even a bit of a "disco" feel on a couple of tracks—inspired melodies and unusual chord progressions throughout. Lyrically lightweight, but hey, this is music not poetry. —*Tom Roland*

Horizon / 1980 / Elektra 276
Rabbitt's rockabilly release. "I Love a Rainy Night" and "Drivin' My Life Away" set the pace for Side 1: Sun-inspired, guitar-based

productions, heavy on the echo. Side 2 is a bit ballad-heavy, though most of the tracks stand up well individually. "That's Just the Way it Is" is something of a forerunner for "Someone Could Lose a Heart Tonight." —*Tom Roland*

○ **Greatest Hits, Vol. 2** / 1983 / Warner Brothers 23925

★ **All Time Greatest Hits** / Mar. 12, 1991 / Warner Brothers 26467
Covers Rabbitt's most commercially productive period. "Drivin' My Life Away," "I Love a Rainy Night," and "Step By Step" were all Top 10 pop hits, in addition to hitting Number 1 country. "Drivin'" and "Rainy," in fact, were million-sellers. —*Dan Cooper*

Boots Randolph (Homer Louis Randolph III)

b. 1925, Paducah, KY
Sax, trombone / Rock & roll, instrumental bluegrass, country-pop
Tenor saxophonist Randolph has been a very influential instrumentalist within the country field, with his peak years in the '60s. Randolph switched from trombone to tenor sax in high school, and played in local combos in Evansville in the '40s and '50s. He scored with "Yakety Sax," a novelty work cowritten by James Rich, and was signed to RCA by Chet Atkins. His playing was and is quite simple; pleasant melodies, catchy themes, and occasional use of vocal effects have made up his signature style. He became a featured session musician and did many "countrypolitan" (country MOR) dates, placing 13 albums on the charts in the '60s and '70s. —*Ron Wynn*

○ **Boots Randolph's Yakety Sax** / 1963 / Monument 18002
Nashville session tenor saxman doing what he does best. A rocking set. —*Bill Dahl*

The Yakin' Sax Man / 1964 / Capitol 825
This album contains such hits as "So Rare," "Teach Me Tonight," "Bongo Band," and "Sleep Walk." —*AMG*

Country Boots / 1972 / Monument 44358
Randolph is a fine country saxist. —*Ron Wynn*

● **Greatest Hits** / 1988 / Monument 44355
This country saxman shows his versatility. —*Bill Dahl*

Eddy Raven

b. Aug. 19, 1945, LA
Vocals / Country-pop
Born Edward Garvin Futch, it's no wonder that his name was changed by a record executive to Raven on his very first single, released on tiny Cosmos Records in the the late '60s. Numerous influences have made his music almost indescribable: the Cajun sounds of his native Louisiana, the blues influence from working with Johnny Winter, the rock and roll of his idol Elvis Presley, and the pure country of the Grand Ole Opry. Befriended by Jimmy C. Newman, Raven made the first of many trips to Nashville in 1970, though he didn't move there permanently for a couple of years. Signed to a publishing deal with Acuff-Rose (the same company that owns the Hank Williams songwriting catalog), he wrote songs for Don Gibson and Roy Acuff, among others, and started making records himself in 1974. Despite the acclaim of his peers, Raven didn't actually earn a hit record as a recording artist until 1981, with the release of his *Desperate Dreams* album. After he lost his recording contract in a 1983 consolidation involving Elektra and Warner, Raven took the next year to realign his business. The Oak Ridge Boys earned a hit at that time with his song "Thank God for Kids," and Raven came out of his forced vacation strong, signing with RCA and gaining his first Number 1 single with "I Got Mexico." For the next half-dozen years, Raven remained a consistent staple of country radio: frequently adventurous, always listenable. —*Tom Roland*

Desperate Dreams / 1981 / Elektra
Raven had more creative control than in previous efforts and developed a tough-sounding album. Heavy on rhythm guitar, long on bravado. —*Tom Roland*

● **The Best of Eddy Raven** / 1988 / Liberty 98480
After his 1983 layoff, Raven put together a string of some of the best "in-the-groove" records Nashville had to offer. Many of them—"I Got Mexico," "Shine, Shine, Shine," "Sometimes a Lady," among others—are here, plus his refried Cajun effort, "I'm Gonna Get You." —*Tom Roland*

○ **Temporary Sanity** / 1989 / Liberty 90289
Successfully merges elements of the Cajun sound into the mainstream country format. Snaps, crackles, and pops! —*Tom Roland*

Collin Raye

Country

A native of Arkansas, Collin Raye (born Floyd Collin Wray) recorded as a member of the Wrays, who released four minor country hits in the 1980s. After that group disbanded, he played Reno clubs for a number of years before making his solo country debut in 1990 with *All I Can Be.* —*Brian Mansfield*

● **Extremes** / Epic 53952
Tired of the balladeer image "Love, Me" and "In This Life" had tagged him with, Raye set out to show that he was made of stronger material. The first single, the rollicking "That's My Story," was a Lee Roy Parnell tune that Raye roared through. *Extremes,* as its title suggested, caromed recklessly from that type of song to, of course, ballads—but "Little Rock," about a recovering alcoholic, and "Dreaming My Dreams with You," earlier cut by Waylon Jennings, were two of the most powerful recordings of Raye's career. —*Brian Mansfield*

All I Can Be / Dec. 1990 / Epic 47468
Many people compared Raye to Vince Gill, especially since Gill sang harmony on the album's lead track and first single, "All I Can Be (Is a Sweet Memory)." Raye hit the top of the charts with the three-hankie "Love, Me," which his fans sometimes play at funerals. —*Brian Mansfield*

In This Life / Aug. 25, 1992 / Epic 48983
The soft-focus-yet-rugged album art helps establish Raye as the heartthrob his silky smooth tenor makes him out to be. Inside, it's an even smoother mix than *All I Can Be,* with Raye indulging his tendencies at every turn, including a revival of the Everly Brothers' make-out classic "Let it Be Me." The hit "I Want You Bad (And That Ain't Good)" put some sweat and muscle into Raye's image, but even the trucker song, "Latter Day Cowboy," sounds like it was written for the women back home. Also includes "In This Life," a Number 1 hit; "Somebody Else's Moon;" and "That Was a River." —*Brian Mansfield*

The Red Clay Ramblers

Group / Old-time

One of the most authentic of the string-band revival groups, the RCR perform traditional Appalachian folk music, contemporary compositions, and mixed genres with considerable talent and authority. For years they have been considered among the best of the modern revivalists of string-band music. —*David Vinopal*

Stolen Love / 1976 / Flying Fish 009
The Ramblers hit on all cylinders: old-timey, jazz, country, fiddle tunes, and blues. —*Chip Renner*

It Ain't Right / 1986 / Flying Fish 334
A good mix of music. —*Chip Renner*

● **Merchant's Lunch** / Flying Fish 055
One of their top three albums. Flying Fish features *Merchant's Lunch* and *Twisted Laurel* on one CD. —*Chip Renner*

Jerry Reed (Jerry Reed Hubbard)

b. Mar. 20, 1937, Atlanta, GA

Guitar / Rock & roll, instrumental bluegrass, progressive country

Before there were *Smokey and the Bandit I & II, Gator, W. W. and the Dixie Dance Kings,* and *BAT 21,* there was Jerry Reed—a guitarist and singer/songwriter whose musical talents have now been overshadowed by his roles on the silver screen. Reed first made his reputation as a hot studio guitarist. More fame came when Elvis Presley made hits of two Reed compositions, "Guitar Man" and "US Male." In 1970 his "Amos Moses" reached Number 1, resulting in a Grammy. Three other Reed singles reached Number 1: "When You're Hot, You're Hot," "Lord, Mr. Ford," and "She Got the Goldmine (I Got the Shaft)." His fast-playing, fast-talking performances have shown Reed to be a man of many talents. —*David Vinopal*

○ **When You're Hot You're Hot** / 1971 / RCA 4506
Wild and loose, this is Reed's best album. —*Dan Heilman*

● **Best of Jerry Reed** / 1972 / RCA 4729
Features several key hits ("Amos Moses," "Guitar Man," "When You're Hot, You're Hot") and some crackling instrumentals. Alimony-payers looking for "She Got the Goldmine (I Got the Shaft)" will be disappointed, however. It's not here. —*Dan Cooper*

East Bound & Down / 1977 / RCA 58450

The title song was Reed's last sizable hit. —*Dan Heilman*

Jim Reeves (James Travis Reeves)

b. Aug. 20, 1924, Galloway, Panola County, TX, d. Jul. 31, 1964 , Outside Nashville

Vocals, guitar / Country-pop

Gentleman Jim Reeves was perhaps the biggest male star to emerge from the Nashville Sound. His mellow baritone voice and muted velvet orchestration combined to create a sound that echoed around his world and has lasted to this day. Detractors will call the sound country-pop (or plain pop), but none can argue against the large audience that loves this music. Reeves was capable of singing hard country ("Mexican Joe" went to Number 1 in 1953). From 1955 ("Bimbo") through 1969, Reeves was without exception in the charts, country and/or pop—an amazing fact in light of his untimely death in an airplane accident in 1964. "Four Walls" (1957) and especially "He'll Have to Go" in 1957 solidified the reputation of Reeves as the Crooner of Country. After his death a near-cult developed, and songs of his released after his death actually outsold his previous hits, with six Number 1s coming in a three-year period following his burial. (These include "I Guess I'm Crazy," "Is It Really Over?" and "Blue Side of Lonesome.") Hits in the '70s continued, with "Angels Don't Lie" and "Don't Let Me Cross Over." Through technical wizardry he had duet hits in the early '80s: "Take Me in Your Arms and Hold Me" (with Deborah Allen) and "Have You Ever Been Lonely?" with his smooth-singing female counterpart of the plush Nashville sound, Patsy Cline, who also perished in an airplane crash, in 1963. —*David Vinopal*

☆ **He'll Have to Go & Other Hits** / 1960 / RCA 52301
There may have been other country crooners as smooth, but no one else in his era had the hand-in-glove marriage of great songs and appropriate "countrypolitan" production. —*Mark A. Humphrey*

Live at the Opry / 1987 / Country Music Foundation 008
Here's a fascinating glimpse of Gentleman Jim Reeves in performance. —*Mark A. Humphrey*

★ **Four Walls (The Legend Begins)** / Aug. 1991 / RCA 2493
A golden throat and melifluous moroseness. Includes "Then I'll Stop Loving You," "Anna Marie," "Mexican Joe," and other hits. —*Mark A. Humphrey*

★ **Welcome to My World: The...** / 1993 / RCA 66125
A fine two-CD set that features most of Reeve's biggest hits. —*AMG*

○ **Gentleman Jim 1955-1959** / Bear Family 15439
This four-CD set, which contains 110 tracks, has Reeves' first ventures into pop as well as some of his best country performances of such favorites as "Am I Losing You," "Just Call Me Lonesome," "According to My Heart," and others. —*AMG*

Restless Heart

Group / Country

The origins for Restless Heart are a bit unusual. Songwriter Tim DuBois couldn't find an outlet for some of his material—"too pop" for many Nashville acts, "too country" for Los Angeles—and he sought out some of his friends to help work up the songs for demo tapes.

He pulled in five musicians he already knew (John Dittrich, Dave Innis, Greg Jennings, and Paul Gregg), and as fate would have it, the combination worked better than anyone expected. The group pursued a recording deal, and signed with RCA Records in 1983. Just as they started to work on the first album, lead vocalist Verlon Thompson had second thoughts, and Larry Stewart was brought in as his replacement.

Often compared to the Eagles in their early days, Restless Heart displayed a strong reliance on tenor harmonies, working country/rock territory. Despite a resurgence in traditional country, the band was able to consistently place its hybrid sound on country radio. At the end of 1991, Stewart left the group for a solo career. —*Tom Roland*

○ **Wheels** / 1986 / RCA 5648
The guys found their niche with this project. Big, overpowering sound, heavy backbeats, and very tight harmonies. In contrast, the ballads "I'll Still Be Loving You" and "New York (Hold Her Tight)" are incredibly sensitive. —*Tom Roland*

Fast Movin' Train / 1989 / RCA 9961
This album has "Long Lost Friend," "Dancy's Dream," and other hits. —*AMG*

● **The Best of** / Oct. 1991 / RCA 61041
Features "Fast Movin' Train," "You Can Depend on Me," and other favorites. —*AMG*

Big Iron Horses / 1992 / RCA 66049
Down to a quartet, the guys in Restless Heart still have the highest Eagles rating in country music—they get the vocals right almost every time, and "Blame It on Love" evokes memories of the likes of "Witchy Woman." Musically, not much changed for the members of the band: they still like a good train song, and they're more likely to show the influence of Bruce Hornsby ("Meet Me on the Other Side") and Creedence Clearwater Revival ("Born in a High Wind") than any of country's honky-tonk heroes. Another song, "When She Cries," became one of the biggest crossover hits of 1992. Paul Gregg, John Dittrich and Dave Innis (who left the group after the album's release, reducing Restless Heart to a trio) trade lead vocals—they blend well from song to song, though Dittrich sounds the most like Don Henley—but it's definitely those harmonies that make *Big Iron Horses* run smooth. —*Brian Mansfield*

Charlie Rich

b. Dec. 14, 1932, Forest City, AK
Vocals, piano / Progressive country, country-pop, rockabilly
It is doubtful that any artist in the *AMG* presents more of a challenge to pigeonhole than Charlie Rich. Rich, who would have initially been happy arranging and playing piano for Stan Kenton's band, spent his first professional years in the late '50s as a singer, songwriter, and session pianist at Sun Records. His gospel-rock hit "Lonely Weekends" (1960) remains a classic of the genre. Following Sun, Rich moved to RCA where he recorded persuasively in a variety of styles ranging from country to blues and pop/jazz. If you can survive "River Stay Away from My Door," you're probably immune to Rich's brand of hybrid soul. He next recorded two highly acclaimed R&B albums for Smash, which included the hit single "Mohair Sam" (1965). A brief tenure with the Memphis Hi label yielded, among other things, some startlingly good White soul music.
It wasn't until Rich joined forces with Sun alumnus Billy Sherrill at Epic Records that country hits like "Behind Closed Doors" (1973) started to occur. But a procession of albums for Epic and UA became increasingly formulaic and tepid, until Rich was virtually phoning in his vocals and all but his bedrock fans had departed.
Charlie Rich currently lives in semi-obscurity in Memphis. Periodic rumors surface about a definitive Charlie Rich album worthy of his talent. The man has never been captured at his soulful, hybrid best for an entire album, although there are glimpses here and there, and they are stunning to say the least.
Charlie Rich epitomizes Memphis music. His roots stretch across racial boundaries and genres in a totally unselfconscious way. When his voice and piano are on, there is no finer and more impassioned Memphis artist. Whether the music is country, soul, R&B, or jazz is strictly academic.
The listener who has never sampled beyond Rich's slick country hits is strongly encouraged to dig more deeply into the early roots of this formidable and reclusive talent. —*Hank Davis*

○ **Behind Closed Doors** / 1973 / Epic 32247
Classic early '70s country schmaltz. Laidback vocals and great chintzy production by Billy Sherrill. —*Mark A. Humphrey*

○ **Greatest Hits** / 1976 / Epic 81478
Focuses on Rich's biggest hits ("Behind Close Doors," "The Most Beautiful Girl") though not necessarily his most representative work. Ignore the cheesy production, however, and you'll hear his vocals as utterly sublime. —*Dan Cooper*

○ **American Originals** / 1989 / CBS 45073
Essentially the same material as the Epic *Greatest Hits*, but with the addition of an almost claustrophobically intimate version of "Since I Fell For You." —*Dan Cooper*

★ **The Complete Smash Sessions** / Aug. 4, 1992 / Mercury 512643
Not a hits package by any stretch. Nevertheless, these mid '60s recordings, produced in a pop-rock vein by Jerry Kennedy, have aged better than some of Rich's more popular work. —*Dan Cooper*

☆ **Original Hits & Midnight Demos** / Charly 10
All the Sun singles plus rare glimpses of informal jam sessions on this import CD. Country, blues, jazz, and boogie demos from the multi-talented Rich. Do not confuse this with *Rebound*, also on Charly (CD-52), which is missing virtually all the "midnight demos." —*Hank Davis*

Riders in the Sky

Group
Since 1979 this trio (who named themselves after a classic Vaughan Monroe/Sons of the Pioneers song) has been mildly satirizing the standard Roy Rogers-Gene Autry "B" Westerns from the '40s and '50s, in the process creating a mini-cult among young urbanites. Their act is part yodel, part genuine love of the material, and a larger part good-natured spoof. Their short-lived Saturday morning CBS show appeared in 1991. —*David Vinopal*

The Best of the West / 1988 / Rounder 11517
Western cowboy song standards. —*Mark A. Humphrey*

Live / Mar. 15, 1992 / Rounder 186
Square-but-hip comedy with songs crooned in lush Sons of the Pioneers-style western harmony. —*Mark A. Humphrey*

○ **Cowboys In Love** / 1994 / Epic
Putting the skits aside for the time being, the Riders focus largely on their under-rated musical ability. Ranger Doug shows off his sublime baritone on several Western-style love songs, including an exquisite duet with Emmylou Harris on "One Has My Name, the Other Has My Heart." The instrumentals, especially Woody Paul's expert fiddling, are superb, as is the spirited take with guests Asleep at the Wheel on "I'm a Ding Dong Daddy from Dumas." —*Michael McCall*

● **Best of the West Rides Again** / Rounder 11524
More faves. Twenty-five tracks culled from their first five Rounder albums, over an hour's worth of music in all. —*Mark A. Humphrey*

Jeannie C. Riley (Jeanne Stephenson)

b. Sep. 19, 1945, Anson, TX
Vocals / Gospel, country-pop
Tom T. Hall's song about small-town hypocrisy did a lot for his reputation, but it absolutely made Jeannie C. Riley a star. "Harper Valley P.T.A." sold 6 million copies, went gold as far away as Australia, and in 1968 brought a Grammy to its singer. Other hits followed, including "The Girl Most Likely," but nothing was going to match her initial success. Riley eventually moved to gospel. —*David Vinopal*

● **Harper Valley P.T.A. & Other Greatest Hits** / Rhino 70344
Late '60s hot pants and go-go country. —*Mark A. Humphrey*

Tex Ritter (Woodward Maurice Ritter)

b. Jan. 12, 1905, Murval, TX, d. Jan. 2, 1973 , Nashville, TN
Vocals, guitar / Traditional country, cowboy
Father of TV's John Ritter ("Three's Company"), Woodward Maurice "Tex" Ritter was a college-educated Broadway performer long before he rode into the sunset as a singing cowboy of the silver screen. *Song of the Gringo* in 1936 started a movie career that was to last through nearly 60 horse operas. As one of the first artists to sign with the newly-created Capitol label, in 1942 Ritter recorded enough hits ("There's a New Moon over My Shoulder," "Deck of Cards," "Boll Weevil") to make him one of the better-selling country singers in the '40s. Nothing before or after matched the theme song of *High Noon*, starring Gary Cooper. This movie did what all the "B" Westerns couldn't—it made Ritter a national star. —*David Vinopal*

○ **Country Music Hall of Fame** / 1991 / MCA 10188
Pure Texan, Ritter was grittier than most of Hollywood's singing cowboys and nearer the roots of western song. His 1935-1939 sides are here. —*Mark A. Humphrey*

● **Capitol Collectors Series** / Feb. 17, 1992 / Capitol 95036
Ritter spent more than three decades with Capitol, and the 25 songs (including the great "Rye Whiskey" and "Blood on the Saddle") on this well-annotated set feature Ritter's yelping theatricality at its best. —*Michael McCall*

Dennis Robbins

Slide guitarist and former member of Detroit blues-rock band The Rockets and country songwriter supergroup Billy Hill. Writer of Garth Brooks' "Two of a Kind, Workin on a Full House" and Shenandoah's "Church on Cumberland Road." —*Brian Mansfield*

● **Man with a Plan** / Jun. 16, 1992 / Giant 24458
Redneck rock that lives and dies by the slide guitar, like Hank Williams, Jr. with a sneakier sense of humor. Tracy Lawrence found "Paris, Tennessee" here, and Confederate Railroad got "I Am Just a Rebel" (which Robbins had earlier recorded with Billy Hill). Robbins broke the Top 40 with the slice-of-life "Home Sweet Home." —*Brian Mansfield*

Marty Robbins (Martin David Robbins)

b. Sep. 26, 1925, Glendale, AZ, **d.** Dec. 8, 1982 , Nashville, TN
Vocals, guitar / Country
No artist in the history of country music has had a more stylistically diverse career than Marty Robbins. Never content to remain just a country singer, Robbins performed successfully in a dazzling array of styles during more than 30 years in the business. To his credit, Robbins rarely followed trends, but often took off in directions that stunned both his peers and fans.

Plainly Robbins was not hemmed in by anyone's definition of country music. Although his earliest recordings were unremarkable weepers, by the mid '50s Robbins was making forays into rock music, adding fiddles to the works of Chuck Berry and Little Richard. By the late '50s, Robbins had pop hits of his own with teen fare like "A White Sport Coat." Almost simultaneously, he completed work on his *Hawaiian Songs of the Islands* album. In 1959, Robbins stretched even further with the hit single "El Paso," thus heralding a pattern of "gunfighter ballads" that lasted the balance of his career.

Robbins also enjoyed bluesy hits like "Don't Worry," which introduced a pop audience to fuzztone guitar in 1961. Barely a year later, Robbins scored a calypso hit with "Devil Woman." Marty Robbins also left a legacy of gospel music and a string of sentimental ballads, showing that he could croon with nary a touch of hillbilly twang. Although it is fashionable to criticize such diversity, Robbins was not simply a dabbler. The truth is he was possessed of a superb voice and the ability to adapt it to an unprecedented range of styles. It also didn't hurt that most of Robbins' biggest hits were his own compositions. Robbins literally established trends; then, while others swarmed in to capitalize, he moved on to other pursuits. If you already know some of Robbins's music, choose a different phase to sample. There is bound to be some aspect you haven't heard. If you are unfamiliar with any of it, the new CBS sampler covers more than a quarter of a century of his career and can be used as a smorgasbord to help define your preferences. There is a lot to enjoy here. —*Hank Davis*

Lost & Found / Columbia 57695
Previously unreleased material and a studio-manufactured duet with Michael Martin Murphey in "Big Iron." —*Dan Cooper*

○ **Gunfighter Ballads & Trail Songs** / 1959 / CBS 116
This landmark 1959 collection featuring "El Paso," was a trendsetter. —*Hank Davis*

Hawaii's Calling Me / 1963 / Bear Family 15568
Take a complete look at Robbins's Hawaiian period on these 28 tracks. —*Hank Davis*

☆ **Rockin' Rollin' Robbins** / 1985 / Bear Family 15046
The jewel of Bear Family's exhaustive Robbins re-issue project, the title does not lie. Marty shakes and rattles in fine style on "That's Allright," "Maybelline," "Singing the Blues," and 14 other good rockin' numbers. Much of this material appeared on a 1956 album of the same name, which is many country LP collectors' Holy Grail. —*Dan Cooper*

★ **The Essential Marty Robbins: 1951-1982** / 1991 / CBS 48537
Beware of greatest-hits compilations by Marty Robbins. He had a long and unusually varied career. There are certain phases that might not be to everyone's taste (e.g., early hillbilly era 1951-54; pop/rock & roll 1954-58; gunfighter ballads; calypso; sentimental ballads). This collection contains 50 tracks on 2 CDs or cassettes, including 16 digitally remastered songs that hit Number 1. —*Hank Davis*

○ **Country 1951-1958** / 1991 / Bear Family 15570

Listeners charmed by his pre-*El Paso* country have a motherlode to explore in this five-CD boxed set filled with dewy-eyed weepers (his earliest recordings), his rockabilly (he cut the first cover of "Maybellene"), ancient country/folk accompanied solely by acoustic guitar ("The Dream of the Miner's Chill"), Hawaiiana ("Aloha Oe"), and a handful of his country-pop outings arranged by Ray Conniff. —*Mark A. Humphrey*

○ **Ruby Ann: Rockin' Rollin' Robbins, Vol. 3** / Bear Family 15569
The best of his bluesy rockers from the early '60s. —*Hank Davis*

Jimmie Rodgers

b. Sep. 8, 1897, Meridan, MS, **d.** May 26, 1933 , New York, NY
Vocals, guitar, banjo / Traditional country
In 1927 Ralph Peer, an RCA talent scout, placed an ad offering auditions for local hillbilly talent. The results exceeded his wildest expectations: on August 1 and 2 he recorded the Carter Family; and two days later, a gaunt, ex-railroad man, Jimmie Rodgers. A brass plaque in the Country Music Hall of Fame reads, "Jimmie Rodgers' name stands foremost in the country music field as *the man who started it all*." This is a fair assessment. The "Singing Brakeman" and "Mississippi Blue Yodeler," whose six-year career was cut short by tuberculosis, became the first nationally known star of country music and the direct influence of many later performers from Hank Snow, Ernest Tubb, and Hank Williams to Lefty Frizzell and Merle Haggard. Rodgers sang about rounders and gamblers, bounders and ramblers—and he knew what he sang about. At age 14 he went to work as a railroad brakeman, and on the rails he stayed until a pulmonary hemorrhage sidetracked him to the medicine show circuit in 1925. The years with the trains harmed his health but helped his music. In an era when Rodgers' contemporaries were singing only mountain and mountain/folk music, he fused country (hillbilly), gospel, jazz, blues, Appalachian soul, pop, cowboy, and folk; and many of his best songs were his compositions, including "TB Blues," "Waiting for a Train," "Travelin' Blues," "Train Whistle Blues," and his thirteen blue yodels. He was the first musician inducted into the Hall of Fame, in 1961.

Although Rodgers wasn't the first to yodel on records, his style was distinct from all the others. His yodel wasn't merely sugarcoating on the song, it was as important as the lyric, mournful and plaintive or happy and carefree, depending on a song's emotional content. His instrumental accompaniment consisted sometimes of only his guitar, while at other times a full jazz band (horns and all) backed him up. Country fans could have asked for no better hero—someone who thought what they thought, felt what they felt, and sang about the common person honestly and beautifully. In his last recording session, Rodgers was so racked and ravaged by TB that a cot had to be set up in the studio, so he could rest before attempting that one song more. No wonder Jimmie Rodgers is to this day loved by country music fans. —*David Vinopal*

★ **First Sessions** / 1991 / Rounder 1056
The opening volume in Rounder's mammoth eight-disc Jimmie Rodgers reissue series presents his earliest and in some cases most tentatively performed material from 1927 and 1928. Rodgers quickly makes the leap from raw, if engaging, singer to emphatic, distinctive artist—and midway through has established a singular sound and riveting delivery, with his trademark yodel and mastery of blues inflection and sensibility in place. These cuts include the signature track "Blue Yodel," plus other classics such as "In the Jailhouse Now," "Treasures Untold," and "Memphis Yodel," as well as "The Brakemen's Blues." Things would never be the same for Rodgers, and these were the songs that helped make him an institution. —*Ron Wynn*

☆ **Last Sessions, 1933** / 1991 / Rounder 1063
Illness ravaged Jimmie Rodgers during his final days, as he attempted to record as much as possible. There's an eerie quality to such tunes as "The Yodeling Ranger," "Years Ago" and "Somewhere Down The Line," and it's evident Rodgers was far from top vocal form. But despite the shortness of breath, lack of range, and weak quality, he could still deliver emotionally gripping performances while approaching death. —*Ron Wynn*

☆ **No Hard Times, 1932** / 1991 / Rounder 1062
Though he was nearing the end, Jimmie Rodgers kept going in 1932, turning out several sterling numbers—among them the dynamic "Blue Yodel No. 10" and riveting "No Hard Times" and

"Long Tall Mama Blues" (with Oddie McWinders on banjo). Rodgers also displayed his affection for his mother in "Mother, the Queen of My Heart" and the interesting confessional number "I've Only Loved Three Woman." Rodgers teamed effectively with guitarist Slim Bryant on "Prairie Lullaby," "Miss the Mississippi and You" and "In the Hills of Tennessee"; and he once more sang frankly and movingly about his illness on "Whippin' that Old T.B.," though it wasn't as triumphant as "The T.B. Blues." *—Ron Wynn*

○ **The Early Years 1928-29** / 1991 / Rounder 1057
The second disc in the Jimmie Rodgers series covers 1928 and 1929, the years in which Rodgers solidified his stature as a premier performer. These 16 tracks saw him doing both his brilliant solo yodeling blues and also working with bands on some cuts. "Desert Blues" featured Rodgers backed by a group with cornet, clarinet, tuba, and piano among the instrumentation. Steel guitarist John Westbrook provided tingling accompaniment on "I'm Lonely and Blue," "My Carolina Sunshine Girl," and "Blue Yodel No. 4." But once more it's such cuts as "Daddy and Home," "You and My Old Guitar" and "Never No Mo' Blues" that are the triumphs, with Rodgers simply wailing, singing and yodeling, displaying the emotional clout and memorable style that turned these numbers into anthems. *—Ron Wynn*

☆ **On the Way up 1929** / 1991 / Rounder 1058
This third Jimmie Rodgers disc in the eight-CD line covers what was arguably his greatest year, 1929. Rodgers scored huge hits doing popular novelty cuts like "Frankie and Johnny" and railroad numbers like "Train Whistle Blues," and he continued cutting yodeling tunes as well as cowboy songs and bawdy blues. The 17 cuts include the marvelous "Everybody Does It in Hawaii" with Weldon Burkes on ukulele and Joe Kapo on steel, and the memorable "Hobo Bill's Last Rides." The session also contains alternate takes of "The Land of My Boyhood Dreams" and "Frankie and Johnny" among its 17 tracks. Rodgers was now ably mixing identities and personnas, alternating between the yodeling blues singer, the railroad narrator, and the carefree cowboy. *—Ron Wynn*

☆ **Riding High 1929-1930** / 1991 / Rounder 1059
Jimmie Rodgers was enjoying the fruits of his labors and success in 1929 and 1930, the years covered on this fourth CD in Rounder's historic eight-disc retrospective series. The 17 numbers highlighted here were done either during his final 1929 session or in Hollywood the next year. They're primarily yodeling blues tunes, with Rodgers backed by guitarist Billy Burkes. There's two versions of "Anniversary Blue Yodel (Blue Yodel No. 7)," "Mississippi River Blues," and "Why Did You Give Me Your Love?," as well as stark, marvelous numbers like "She Was Happy 'Till She Met You," "A Drunkard's Child," and "Why Should I Be Lonely." *—Ron Wynn*

☆ **America's Blue Yodeler 1930-31** / 1991 / Rounder 1060
This fifth set of vintage Jimmie Rodgers performances included some spectacular collaborations. While neither sounded fully comfortable, the meeting of Rodgers and Louis Armstrong on "Blue Yodel No. 9" was (and is) a landmark date in music annals, two immortals finding a way to make seemingly disparate styles mesh on a short tune. Armstrong's wife at the time, Lil Hardin, accompanied the pair on piano. Rodgers also teamed frequently with Lani McIntire's Hawaiians on this set, often on throwaway tunes that Rodgers' vocals made enjoyable. There's another collaboration with a blues artist, this time Clifford Gibson on "Let Me Be Your Side Track," a great bawdy/innuendo number. Rodgers was paired with the Carter Family on two wonderful classic country numbers, the heartbreak tune "Why There's A Tear In My Eye" and the gospel song "The Wonderful City." *—Ron Wynn*

○ **Down the Old Road 1931-32** / 1991 / Rounder 1061
This CD features songs with Jimmie Rodgers working in fresh formats as producer Ralph Peer attempted to break a sales slump. Rodgers recorded with the Louisville Jug Band on "My Good Gal's Gone Blues" and teamed with the Carter family again in both Kentucky and Texas in 1931. They made four songs together, but three were unissued until after Rodgers' death. They're pleasant, often nicely sung, but not among either artists' finest dates. Rodgers teamed with steel guitarist Cliff Carlisle and guitarist Wilber Ball on three songs in which Rodgers added ukulele backing. The final four cuts saw Rodgers return to his trademark rail-

road numbers and yodeling blues in 1932. These weren't for the most part great tunes, and they show Rodgers experimenting, then finally opting to do comfortable, familiar material rather than keep trying new things. *—Ron Wynn*

○ **The Singing Brakeman** / Bear Family 15540
This six-CD set of one of the most important artists in the early history of the genre contains a very informative booklet with a discography and thorough liner notes. *—AMG*

Johnny Rodriguez

b. Dec. 10, 1952, Sabinal, TX
Vocals, guitar / Traditional country, country-pop
Johnny Rodriguez was a singing stagecoach driver at the Alamo Village when Bobby Bare and Tom T. Hall heard him, brought him to Nashville, and made him one of Hall's Storytellers. His "Pass Me By" (1972) entered the chart Top 10, and he followed up with 20 consecutive Number 1s, including "You Always Come Back (To Hurting Me)," "Riding My Thumb to Mexico," and "That's the Way Love Goes." With his good looks and easy-to-listen-to voice, he has done well enough right through the '80s, after solving a drug problem. With Freddy Fender, he blended English and Spanish lyrics, creating a Tex-Mex craze. *—David Vinopal*

● **Greatest Hits** / 1976 / PolyGram 826271
A comprehensive overview of a Latino country singer who never achieved the stardom he merited. *—Ron Wynn*

Kenny Rogers

b. Aug. 21, 1938, Houston, TX
Vocals, guitar, bass / Country-rock, country-pop
Kenny Rogers was a star before he was Kenny Rogers. As a member of the First Edition (and the New Christy Minstrels before that), he shared in some million-sellers, among them "Reuben James" and "Ruby, Don't Take Your Love to Town," an excellent Mel Tillis song about a disabled veteran. But superstardom lay ahead for this Texan with the mellow rasp. If superstardom can be counted, then count 48 major music awards, one at a time, and he's still not done.

His experience with the two previous pop groups had prepared him well: he knew the easy-listening audience was out there, and he supplied them with well-done middle-of-the-road songs with a country flavor. Having gone solo, in 1976 Rogers charted with "Love Lifted Me." But it was with an outstanding song by writer Don Schlitz, "Lucille," that his star shot upward. The rest (as they say) is history: award-winning duets with Dottie West and Dolly Parton, 12 TV specials, another song-of-the-year with "The Gambler," "Daytime Friends," "Coward of the County," "We've Got Tonight," "Crazy," "Lady" (his first pop Number 1), etc., etc., etc.

And that's just the *music side* of Kenny Rogers. In 1980 the made-for-TV movie *The Gambler* blasted the competition, followed quickly by *Coward of the County*, then enough sequels to *The Gambler* to get him to Roman numeral IV. In music and in television and in movies, Kenny Rogers puts the *super* back in superstar, enough so as to have his own private 18-hole golf course on his spread outside Nashville. *—David Vinopal*

Every Time Two Fools Collide / 1978 / United Artists 30170
Country-pop with Dottie West. *—Bil Carpenter*

○ **The Gambler** / 1978 / EMI America 48404
Plaintive Southern storytelling. *—Bil Carpenter*

Duets / 1984 / Capitol 46595
Duets Kim Carnes, Sheena Easton, and others. *—Bil Carpenter*

○ **25 Greatest Hits** / 1987 / EMI America 46673
This two-CD set includes much the same material as *Greatest Hits*, but also has "Daytime Friends," "Love or Something like It," and "Love Will Turn You Around." *—Dan Cooper*

● **Greatest Hits** / SND 56
Shows off both Rogers the storyteller ("Lucille," "The Gambler," "Coward of the County") and Rogers the hero of easy listeners ("She Believes in Me," "Lady"). *—Dan Cooper*

Roy Rogers (Leonard Slye)

b. Nov. 5, 1911, Cincinnati, OH
Vocals, guitar / Acoustic blues, electric blues, guitar-pop

Roy Rogers (born Leonard Slye in southern Ohio, 1912) eventually outdrew Gene Autry, his fellow Republic Studio star, at least at the box office. Autry won the battle of the records (his *Silver-Haired Daddy of Mine* alone sold over 5 million copies). Rogers, in spite of his excellent voice and superior yodel, is perhaps best known musically as the founder of what's generally considered to be among the best, if not the best, vocal group ever to grace country music—The Sons of the Pioneers. Rogers, Bob Nolan, and Tim Spencer began as a trio (The Pioneers) in 1933, and changed to their more famous name a year later, when Hugh Farr, with his swing-style fiddle and bass voice, joined. When Rogers, who was to become known as "King of the Cowboys," left for the silver screen in 1938, the six-piece group in a sense went with him, appearing in scores of his movies through 1949.

Over the years, The Sons of the Pioneers recorded hundreds of Western-flavored songs, many of which other Western groups also recorded (for example, "Ghost Riders in the Sky," "Empty Saddles"), but two classic songs written by Bob Nolan, "Cool Water" and "Tumblin' Tumbleweeds," elevated the Sons above the competition. In addition, because of the sophisticated musical arrangements, the intricate instrumentals, and the complicated vocal harmonies, The Sons of the Pioneers have for the past 60 years remained at the top of the scale, against which all subsequent country vocal groups must measure themselves. Happy trails to you, Dale and Roy. —*David Vinopal*

Roy Rogers Tribute / 1991 / RCA
At 79, Rogers' voice wasn't as sure as it was in his heyday. But Richard Landis gave him sympathetic production, and none of his guests sound like paid hands or hired guns. Everyone involved—from Rogers' son Dusty to the Kentucky Headhunters—sounds more committed to making a good record than to adding star power. The material has been chosen accordingly, a good blend of old and new. The tribute's best when young singers repay an obvious debt (the duets with Ricky Van Shelton, Clint Black and Randy Travis), but even when K.T. Oslin and Restless Heart join in The Sons of the Pioneers' theme, "Tumbling Tumbleweeds," they bring new life to an old workhorse. And Rogers' yodel is still in great shape. —*Brian Mansfield*

● **Country Music Hall of Fame Series** / 1992 / MCA 10548
When Gene Autry got into a contract dispute with Republic Pictures in 1937, the studio replaced him with Sons of the Pioneers member Len Slye, whose name they changed to Roy Rogers. These Decca tracks, which range from 1934 to 1942, cover Rogers' output just before he became "King of the Cowboys" with the release of *Ridin' Down the Canyon.* Two of these cuts were recorded with The Sons of the Pioneers; the rest are solo. —*Brian Mansfield*

Billy Joe Royal

b. 1945
Vocals / Country-pop, rock-pop
It's been a varied career for Billy Joe Royal. He started as pure pop: "Down in the Boondocks" was a huge hit in 1965, and as a teen idol he toured with Dick Clark's "Cavalcade." He's jumped from pop to country and back ever since, along the way hitting 12 consecutive Top 25 singles. "A Ring Where a Ring Used to Be" was his sixth consecutive Number 1 video. —*David Vinopal*

● **Greatest Hits** / 1964 / CBS 45063
Can't go wrong with this one, featuring his two biggies, "Down in the Boondocks" and "Cherry Hill Park." —*Cub Koda*

Run C&W

Former Eagle Bernie Leadon, former Amazing Rhythm Ace Russell Smith, and Nashville songwriters Vince Melamed and Jim Photoglo formed this novelty act in Nashville clubs, playing soul music "the way it ought to be played—bluegrass style." —*Brian Mansfield*

● **Into the Twangy-first Century** / 1993 / MCA 10727
If you don't believe bluegrass versions of soul classics is an inspired gag, listen to the beginning of Run C&W's "Stop in the Name of Love" and imagine the possibilities. The quartet also rewrote Arthur Conley's "Sweet Soul Music" to poke fun and Lee Greenwood and Tanya Tucker, among others, and parodied Billy Ray Cyrus' "Achy Breaky Heart" with "Itchy Twitchy Spot." —*Brian Mansfield*

Sawyer Brown

Group / Country, rock & roll
This is a group formed in Nashville in the late '70s by Mark Miller and Bobby Randall. The band included Gregg "Hobie" Hubbard on keyboards, Jim Scholten on bass, and "Curly" Joe Smyth on the drums. The group was originally named Savanna, but it was re-named after streets in Nashville, Tennessee. —*AMG*

Buick / Jan. 7, 1991 / Liberty 94260
More songs about girls and cars—or, better yet, girls in cars. "The Walk" did so well as a single, the group included it on the next album, too. —*Brian Mansfield*

● **Cafe on the Corner** / 1992 / Capitol 77574
By *Cafe on the Corner*, the members of Sawyer Brown had essentially (i.e., for recording purposes at least) given up on being rock & rollers and revealed themselves to be a pretty decent country band. "Cafe on the Corner" paints a graphic picture of small-town desolation, but these guys are smart enough to avoid preaching: Most of the album reflects the marvels of love. The rock & roll sneaks back in on the last two cuts, but by then it's too late to matter. Good stuff in the case of Mac McAnally's "All These Years"—even great. —*Brian Mansfield*

The Dirt Road / Jan. 6, 1992 / Liberty 95624
The band's robust work ethic makes it into these songs about simple life and small-town values, and Mark Miller controls a tendency to over-sing them, maybe because he believes them. Miller's heart is still filled with cliches like "Burning Bridges (On a Rocky Road)," but the sleaze in his voice is convincing on "Ruby Red Shoes," which has to be a song of lust for Judy Garland. —*Brian Mansfield*

Jack Scott (Jack Scafone, Jr.)

b. Jan. 24, 1936, Windsor, Ontario
Guitar / Rock & roll, rockabilly
Jack Scott sounded tough, like someone you wouldn't want to meet in a dark alley unless he had a guitar in his hands. When he growled "The Way I Walk," wise men (and women) stepped aside. Despite his snarling rockabilly attitude, Scott hailed from Ontario, Canada, and grew up near Detroit, developing a love for hillbilly music along the way. His first sides for ABC-Paramount in 1957 exhibited a profound country-rock synthesis, and after moving to the Carlton label, Scott hit the charts the next year with the tremulous ballad "My True Love," backed by his vocal group, the Chantones. Flip it over, however, and you have the hauling rocker "Leroy," all about some wacked-out tough guy who's content to remain behind the bars of his local jail.

Scott's pronounced emphasis on acoustic guitar distinguishes atmospheric rockers like "Goodbye Baby," "Go Wild Little Sadie," "Midgie," and "Geraldine." But his principal pop success came with tears-in-your-beer country-based ballads—"What in the World's Come Over You" and "Burning Bridges" were massive smashes on Top Rank in 1960, and he recorded an entire album's worth of Hank Williams covers for the firm the same year.

Scott continued to vacillate between cowboy crooner and rough-edged rocker throughout the '60s, recording for Capitol and Groove. He still occasionally turns up on the oldies circuit, and he still looks and sounds like a man you seriously don't want to mess with. —*Bill Dahl*

● **Greatest Hits** / Curb 77255
This collects the cream of Scott's late '50s hits. —*Dan Heilman*

Dan Seals

b. 1948
Vocals, guitar / Country-rock, country-pop
Country-pop singer/songwriter Dan Seals was half of England Dan & John Ford Coley. Some of their hits during the '70s include "We'll Never Have to Say Goodbye Again" and "Nights Are Forever without You." The first of nine consecutive Number 1s was "Meet Me in Montana," a duet with Marie Osmond. —*David Vinopal*

● **The Best of Dan Seals** / 1987 / Liberty 48308
All the hits ("Bop," "Big Wheels in the Moonlight," etc.) collected up in one nice, solid package. —*Cub Koda*

○ **Rage on** / 1988 / Liberty 46976
On *Rage On*, Seals tells stories woven around traditional country themes while rarely resorting to country cliches. "Addicted,"

"They Rage On," "Five Generations of Rock County Wilsons"—these are tales of quiet desperation, and the empathy in Seals' voice makes their impact devastating. Almost as good as his *Best*. —*Brian Mansfield*

On Arrival / Nov. 1990 / Liberty 91782
This is the product of a man very much in touch with his emotions. In "Bordertown," "A Heart in Search of Love" and "Wood," he works the listener's heart with the skill of a surgeon. At the same time, "Good Times" and "Love on Arrival" are incredibly celebratory. —*Tom Roland*

Dawn Sears

Dawn Sears owns a brash, emotionally convincing voice that grabs a song with impressive authority—she's sort of a modern Wanda Jackson with just a touch of polish, or a Brenda Lee with more honky-tonk feeling. Her excellent debut didn't receive much of a chance from her record company, but she recently signed with Decca Records after a couple of years of singing harmony in Vince Gill's band. —*Michael McCall*

● **What a Woman Wants to Hear** / Oct. 15, 1991 / Warner Brothers 26442
Her powerful debut, produced by Barry Beckett, reveals her ability with a forceful country rocker ("Good Goodbye") as well as a touching ballad ("Till You Come Back to Me") —*Michael McCall*

Jeannie Seely

b. Jul. 16, 1940, PA
A Pennsylvanian who started performing on the radio at age 11, Jeannie Seely is associated almost as strongly with her duet partners—Porter Wagoner, Ernest Tubb, and Jack Greene—as she is with her own music. Her first single, "Don't Touch Me," won her a Grammy in 1967, and she continued to have charting hits for the next 11 years. Most of her material came from her fellow country songwriter (and eventually husband) Hank Cochran. A cast member of the Grand Ole Opry since 1967. —*Brian Mansfield*

● **Greatest Hits on Monument** / 1993 / CBS 52426
Seely recorded her hits for four labels—Decca, MCA, Columbia, and Monument—and much of that material is currently out of print. These Monument recordings document only about the first three years of her career, but they include some great records, especially "Don't Touch Me," "I'll Love You More (Than You Need)," and the brutally fatalistic "It's Only Love." —*Brian Mansfield*

Billy Joe Shaver

b. , Corsicana, TX
Shaver is a rough-hewn Texan with a rounder's sensibilities, a prophet's humility, and a poet's tongue. He first arrived in Nashville during the freewheeling 1970s, when he fell under the influence of ambitious songwriters like Kris Kristofferson. He combined their artful earthiness with his own colorful way of looking at the world, and came up with a string of honky-tonk classics that express the uncommon yearnings of common people. Waylon Jennings' classic *Honky Tonk Heroes* album consists solely of Shaver originals, and Willie Nelson, Johnny Cash, John Anderson, and others enjoyed hits with his songs. Despite several exceptional, critically acclaimed albums, he never found the larger audience he deserved. *Tramp On Your Street*, however, gave his late-blooming career a much-deserved lift. —*Michael McCall*

○ **Old Five & Dimers Like Me** / 1973 / Monument 32293
His hillbilly charm glows on the autobiographical title tune and the rest of his one-of-a-kind songs. —*Michael McCall*

When I Get My Wings / 1976 / Capricorn 0171
Proof that his blend of sawdust-floor honkers and spiritually endowed ballads were in place from the start. —*Michael McCall*

○ **I'm Just an Old Chunk of Coal** / 1981 / CBS 37078
Again, he combines straight-from-the-soul spirituals like the title cut, with some of the most colorful honky-tonk ever written—including "Fit to Kill and Going Out In Style" and "Saturday Night"—as well as an astounding "Ragged Old Truck," in which he begins by contemplating suicide before deciding all he needs is a good, hard night on the town. —*Michael McCall*

Billy Joe Shaver / 1982 / CBS 37959

As with the title, this is his most straightforward collection of Texas soul music. It includes a few remakes of earlier classics. —*Michael McCall*

★ **Tramp on Your Street** / Aug. 10, 1993 / Zoo Entertainment 11063
His rawest, rockingest setting comes courtesy of his guitarslinging son, Eddie Shaver, who gooses his old man in all the right places. Then, on the more introspective tunes, the father dispenses his hard-earned wisdom in unforgettable fashion. A true classic. —*Michael McCall*

Ricky Van Shelton

b. 1952
Vocals, guitar / Contemporary country
This talented baritone's debut album, *Wild-Eyed Dreams*, yielded three Number 1 songs, making him an instant star and producing a ton of awards in 1988-1989. Subsequent hits have included "I Am a Simple Man" from his *Backroads* album. He and Marie Osmond cohosted the "Music City News Country Songwriters Awards" in 1992. —*David Vinopal*

Wild-Eyed Dream / 1987 / CBS 40602
The debut of this country hunk balladeer, with occasional thumpin' at the hop. Contains "Working Man Blues," "Crime of Passion," and more. —*Mark A. Humphrey*

○ **Loving Proof** / 1988 / CBS 44221
Here are stabs at rockabilly, alongside the ballads at which Shelton excels. Some of the songs on the album are "From a Jack to a King" and "Hole in My Pocket." —*Mark A. Humphrey*

RVS 3 / 1990 / CBS 45250
The third album puts out more sounds in the winning Shelton formula, such as "I Still Love You," "I've Cried My Last Tear for You," "Oh Pretty Woman," and more. —*Mark A. Humphrey*

○ **Backroads** / 1991 / CBS 46855
When he's not trying to be Roy Orbison (as he was on 1990's *RVS III*), it's easy to see that Van Shelton's a fine singer. And this is a fine record—so fine, it's tempting to hunt for signs of listener manipulation. But Van Shelton balances the self-pity of songs like "After the Lights Go Out" with the up-tempo punch of stuff like "Call Me Up." So even though Van Shelton recycles "Rockin' Year"—the duet from Dolly Parton's *Eagle When She Flies*—just call it good taste, sit back, and enjoy. —*Brian Mansfield*

● **Greatest Hits Plus** / 1992 / CBS 52753
Despite rocking hits like "Wild Man" and "I Am a Simple Man," or even the new cover of Elvis Presley's "Wear My Ring Around Your Neck," Ricky Van Shelton's greatest-hits collection shows that he's made his best records as a balladeer raised on stone-country gospel. For proof, listen to "Just As I Am," "I'll Leave This World Loving You," or "Keep It Between the Lines." —*Brian Mansfield*

Shenandoah

Group / Country
The five founding members of Shenandoah (Mike McGuire, Ralph Ezell, Marty Raybon, Jim Seales, and Stan Thorn) were all associated in some way with the small, but mighty musical community in Muscle Shoals, AL. They performed locally on occasion—calling themselves the MGM Band—simply for the chance to play live. But songwriter Robert Byrne caught their act one night, and persuaded producer Rick Hall to let him work up some demo tapes with the group. Shortly thereafter, they signed with Columbia Records, which gave them the name Shenandoah.
By their third single, in 1987, they hit the Top 10 with "She Doesn't Cry Anymore." Their next, "Mama Knows," became a signature song. Strong lead vocals by Marty Raybon, and a high level of musicianship, have propelled Shenandoah in sensitive ballads and often-inspired uptempo singles.
The groups' name came into dispute in the courts, and they filed for bankruptcy while still signed to Columbia. They re-emerged in 1992 with RCA. —*Tom Roland*

Shenandoah / 1987 / CBS 40783
Contains "What She Wants," "She Doesn't Cry Anymore," "She's Still Here," and other songs. —*AMG*

○ **The Road Not Taken** / 1989 / CBS 44468
Blue-collar romance. The songs mix the day-to-day struggles of everyday Joe with a steady respect for love, personal roots, and

family. It doesn't hurt to have six bona fide hits on it, either. — *Tom Roland*

Long Time Comin' / 1992 / RCA 66001
This album contains such hits as "Same Old Heart," "Rattle the Windows," and "Rock My Baby." — *AMG*

● **Greatest Hits** / Mar. 31, 1992 / CBS 48885
This album features some of their most popular music, songs like "Two Dozen Roses," "The Moon over Georgia," "Any Ole Stretch of Blacktop," and "Ghost in This House." — *AMG*

Jean Shepard

b. Nov. 21, 1933, Pauls Valley, OK
Vocals, bass
Few country singers working since the 1950s—let alone female country singers—have produced a large body of work as enduring as Jean Shepard's. Her voice is pure country—accent on both words. Born in Oklahoma, she grew up in Southern California, where Hank Thompson discovered her. She had her first Top-10 hit in 1953, and her last almost exactly 20 years later. In between, she cut one great record after another, mostly on Capitol Records. Nearly all of them crackle—no matter the topic—with honky-tonk angel spunk. Of course, good luck finding them. — *Dan Cooper*

○ **This is Jean Shepard** / 1959 / Capitol 1253
One of her earlier LPs, strong on Jean's voice and steel-friendly West Coast production. Includes her spry, proto-feminist "Two Whoops and a Holler." — *Dan Cooper*

● **Best of** / 1963 / Capitol 1922
A good compilation of her first wave of hits ("A Dear John Letter," "A Satisfied Mind"), this is also the LP that shows up most often in used-record bins. Someday this stuff has got to make it to CD. — *Dan Cooper*

Dear John / 1981 / Laserlight 12112
A reissue of material recorded in 1981. — *Dan Cooper*

T. G. Sheppard (Bill Browder [real name], Brian Stacy)

b. Jul. 20, 1944, Humboldt, TN
Vocals, guitar / Country
A native of Humboldt, TN, Bill Browder (his name at birth) headed off to Memphis after high school, getting involved in the record business on several different levels. He tried recording as a pop artist, and even signed with Atlantic Records under the name Brian Stacy, opening shows for the Beach Boys. A few years later, he took a job with a Memphis record distributor, then ended up in record promotion, where the job entailed calling radio stations and trying to persuade them to play his company's records. Working in that capacity for RCA, he helped break Elvis Presley's "Suspicious Minds," Perry Como's "It's Impossible," and John Denver's "Take Me Home Country Roads." After "going independent," he came across a demo tape of "Devil in the Bottle." He tried to talk a number of artists into doing the song, and when no one was interested, he decided to do it himself. Then a number of record labels said no as well, although Motown's fledgling country division, Hitsville Records, said yes. Primarily a recitation, "Devil" went to Number 1 in 1975—but within three years, the company folded, and Sheppard's career was in limbo. Connecting with record producer Buddy Killen, he signed with Warner; and over a four-year period starting in 1979, the two churned out some of country's best-crafted singles.

Sheppard gradually moved away from recitations, and grew significantly as a vocalist, though the press often ignored his achievements. He changed producers several times in the mid '80s and, after a divorce in 1987, took a couple of years off for personal reflection. When Sheppard returned, he found it difficult to regain his earlier momentum. — *Tom Roland*

Slow Burn / 1983 / Warner Brothers
This album has its weak moments, but Sheppard's performance is stronger than in previous albums. He's more confident, probably understands the craft of singing a little better, and—in this first outing with record producer Jim Ed Norman—the arrangements don't bury T.G. — *Tom Roland*

● **The Best of** / 1992 / Curb 77545
You'll have to look for this one at used-record stores. A sampler released only to radio, it covers the half-dozen years up to and including "I Loved 'Em Every One." Some of the performances are a little stiff, but it lends appreciation for his improved, later work. — *Tom Roland*

Ricky Skaggs

b. Jul. 18, 1954, Cordell, KY
Vocals, guitar, mandolin, fiddle, banjo / Traditional bluegrass, traditional country, progressive country
For someone still in his thirties, Kentuckian Ricky Skaggs has already produced a career's worth of music. At age seven he appeared on TV with Flatt and Scruggs; at 15 he was a member of the legendary Ralph Stanley's bluegrass band (with fellow teenager, the late Keith Whitley). None of the contemporary stars, male or female, has better credentials than Ricky. The term "multi-talented" lacks enough power to characterize this extraordinary singer and instrumentalist. Not only can he sing and pick with the best in progressive country, but his broad and deep experience in traditional music separates him from the crowd. In the estimation of many, he is without peer as a combination vocalist and intrumentalist (guitar, mandolin, fiddle, banjo). After playing with Ralph Stanley for three years, Ricky moved on to progressive bluegrass bands—the Country Gentlemen and J. D. Crowe and the New South. With his own band, Boone Creek, he mixed the old and the new, adding Django Reinhardt. Ricky took Rodney Crowell's place in Emmylou Harris's Hot Band in 1977, and the band's excellent *Roses in the Snow* album showcased Ricky's versatility. Two Number 1 hits came out of his self-produced *Waiting for the Sun to Shine* album (1981), and the awards started arriving.

Skaggs is largely responsible for a back-to-basics movement in country music. He showed many that a bluegrass tenor with impeccable taste and enormous talent can sell traditional country, at a time when pop music had invaded the land of rural rhythm. His remake of Bill Monroe's "Uncle Pen," for example, was the first bluegrass song since Flatt and Scruggs' the "Ballad of Jed Clampett" to reach Number 1 in the charts. — *David Vinopal*

○ **Sweet Temptation** / 1979 / Sugar Hill 3706
With guest vocals by then-boss Emmylou Harris, Skaggs's first solo effort (not counting the Boone Creek project) is equal parts bluegrass and Harris-styled new traditionalism. — *Dan Cooper*

Waitin' for the Sun to Shine / 1981 / Epic 37193
Skaggs's first album after signing with Epic Records, this one took him into the mainstream—in effect beginning the new-traditionalist movement. Simple, mountain approach, with lots of remakes and Skaggs's mournful vocal tones. The best cut is the plaintive title track. — *Tom Roland*

○ **Highways & Heartaches** / 1982 / Epic 37996
Long a sideman or supporting vocalist in previous situations, Skaggs wasn't totally comfortable with his role as a lead vocalist when he signed with Epic Records. Thanks to a year of touring, and greater support from his record label , he had greater confidence vocally the second time around. (When Epic signed him, the company honestly didn't think he'd sell more than 100,000 copies of his debut for them.) And the material's more upbeat. — *Tom Roland*

Family & Friends / 1982 / Rounder 0151
Skaggs' last breath of pure bluegrass, recorded with help from the Whites, guitarist Peter Rowan, dobroist Jerry Douglas, and others. Two songs by Carter Stanley, one by Bill Monroe, and some fine examples of Appalachian gospel, including a stunning a cappella trio vocal on "Talk About Sufferin." — *Brian Mansfield*

○ **Country Boy** / 1984 / Epic 39410
Every one of Ricky Skaggs's albums is a pickin' festival and a country delight. This one no exception, and it also includes Bill Monroe's "Wheel Hoss" with Monroe himself picking along on mandolin—which earns it a listing here. If you like this album, you'll probably like every other one Skaggs has made. — *William Ruhlmann*

Favorite Country Songs / 1985 / Epic 39409
Contains such hits as "Sweet Temptation," "Nothing Can Hurt You," and others. — *AMG*

● **Live in London** / 1985 / Epic 40103
This is the one Skaggs album to own if you can only own one. Because it's a live recording, the picking is just that much more exciting, and the album serves as an unofficial best-of—its highlights including "Heartbroke," "Uncle Pen," and a version of

"Don't Get Above Your Raising" that features noted country fan Elvis Costello. —*William Ruhlmann*

My Father's Son / 1991 / Epic 47389
A concept album about families, *My Father's Son* is the Skaggs album that owes the least to bluegrass. Skaggs is concerned with the legacies fathers leave their sons, both the wisdom ("Father Knows Best") and the limitations (the title track). He also sees materialism for the distracting, destructive force it is. His duet with Waylon Jennings on "Only Daddy that'll Walk the Line" fits neatly, though perhaps not the way the writer intended. And because Skaggs's background is bluegrass rather than honky-tonk, every father image is inextricably bound to God. —*Brian Mansfield*

Carl Smith

b. Mar. 15, 1927, Maynardsville, TN
Vocals, guitar / Traditional country
For the first five years of the '50s, this Opry headliner was one of country's biggest stars, going on to rack up nearly three dozen hits in the decade. Although he could sing great honky-tonk, Smith's country ballads sold so well that he soon specialized in them. His second release for Columbia, "Let's Live a Little," was a huge hit, followed by "If Teardrops Were Pennies" and "Mr. Moon."
   In 1953, three singles reached Number 1: "Hey Joe," "Satisfaction Guaranteed," and "Trademark." He branched out from Nashville with two movies, and his "Country Music Hall" TV program was broadcast coast-to-coast in Canada in the mid '60s. In his quarter-century with the Columbia label, Smith sold over 15 million records. He and his wife Goldie Hill (also an Opry star) retired early to their horse farm in Tennessee. Smith was "Mr. Country" in the '50s. —*David Vinopal*

Old Lonesome Times / 1988 / Rounder 25
This album features such guest artists as Ray Price and Lefty Frizzell, in recordings made in the early '50s. Included are such favorites as "Loose Talk" and "Hey Joe." —*AMG*

★ **The Essential Carl Smith (1950-1956)** / 1991 / CBS 47996
Twenty tracks, including his early hits, from this smooth and soulful country vocalist. If you like Hank Williams and Lefty Frizzell and the '50s fiddle and steel sound, give this a try. —*Richard Lieberson*

Connie Smith

b. Aug. 14, 1941, Elkhart, IN
Vocal, guitar / Christian rock, country
You rarely hear the name Connie Smith mentioned in the same breath with Patsy Cline, Loretta Lynn, Tammy Wynette or Dolly Parton. But poll Nashville's old guard as to who the great female country singers of all time have been, and Connie's name will show up near the top every time. Listening to Smith can be emotionally exhausting. One song blows you off your barstool, the next tears a hole in your heart, and the third sends you crying to the chapel. A Cinderella story to boot, young housewife Smith was discovered by Bill Anderson in 1963 at a talent contest in small-town Ohio. Her debut RCA single, released a year later, was the Anderson-penned "Once A Day." A Number 1 smash, it made Smith an instant superstar, the one thing the shy singer has never really wanted to be. In the late 1970s, she dropped out of the business completely, but has recently re-emerged on the Nashville scene, her pipes as strong as ever. —*Dan Cooper*

Soul of Country Music / 1968 / RCA Victor 3889
More of the same unearthly sound, but with Connie covering—at times burying—other singers' hits. Her version of Rex Griffin's "The Last Letter" is almost literally to die for. —*Dan Cooper*

○ **Back in Baby's Arms** / 1969 / RCA 4229
If any Thomas ever doubted Smith's religious convictions (which are as much a part of her story as her voice is), one listen to this LP's "How Great Thou Art" should take care of that mistrust. —*Dan Cooper*

Live In Branson, MO, USA / 1993 / Laserlight 12138
Includes a 10-minute medley of her early hits. —*Dan Cooper*

○ **Greatest Hits on Monument** / CBS 52962
Connie in the '70s with too much syrupy production. —*Dan Cooper*

★ **Connie Smith** / RCA Victor 3341

Cut in Music City, Smith's first LP (which includes "Once a Day") features her blowing through the Nashville Sound production like a downhome Streisand fronting the Lennon Sisters. —*Dan Cooper*

Darden Smith

Vocals / Blues-rock, contemporary country
Named for a local rodeo rider, Darden Smith grew up in Austin, TX, and placed two singles, "Little Maggie" and "Day after Tomorrow," on the country charts in 1988. In 1989 he teamed up with British songwriter Boo Hewerdine of the Bible rock band, to record *Evidence*, which expanded his following beyond the country market. —*William Ruhlmann*

Native Soul / 1986 / Watermelon 1009
A fine debut album. Nanci Griffith sings harmony vocal on "Two Dollar Novels." Lyle Lovett sings harmony on five songs. This one's a gem. Smith is just breaking out and developing his style. —*Chip Renner*

● **Darden Smith** / 1988 / Epic 40938
Darden's big-label debut, featuring three cuts off his *Native Soul* album. This time the production is better, with strings and extra vocals. Nanci Griffith and Lyle Lovett back him, along with Roland Denney and Paul Pearcy. All of his songs are strong, and the playing is dead-on. It's a keeper. —*Chip Renner*

Trouble No More / 1990 / Columbia 45289
A strong album, not as diverse as *Darden Smith*, but as good. Contains "Midnight Train," "Frankie & Sue," "Trouble No More," "Fall Apart at the Seams," and the list goes on. With two songs cowritten with buddy Boo Hewerdine. —*Chip Renner*

Hank Snow (Clarence Eugene Snow)

b. May 9, 1914, Liverpool, Nova Scotia
Vocals, guitar / Traditional country
Canada's greatest contribution to country music, for over 40 years Hank Snow has been famous for his "traveling" songs. It's no wonder. At age twelve he ran away from his Nova Scotia home and joined the Merchant Marines, working as a cabin boy and laborer for four years. Once back on shore, he listened to Jimmie Rodgers records and started playing in public, building up a following in Halifax. His original nickname, the Yodeling Ranger, was modified to the Singing Ranger when his high voice changed to the great baritone it is today. And great his voice is—great enough for him to record on the same label, RCA, for 45 years. In 1950, the year he became an Opry regular, his self-penned "I'm Moving On" (the first of his many great travelling songs) became a smash hit, reaching Number 1 and remaining on the charts for 40 weeks. "Golden Rocket" (also 1950) and "I've Been Everywhere" (1962), two other hits, show his life-long love for trains and travel. But he was as much at home with two other styles, the ballad and the rhumba/boogie. Among his many great ballads are "Bluebird Island" (with Anita Carter of the Carter Family), "Fool Such As I," and "Hello, Love," a hit when Snow was 60 years old.
   Still appearing regularly on the Opry, Snow shows that his incredible voice has suffered no loss of quality over the last half-century. And he still proves what a tasteful, understated guitar stylist he is. To show you his impact on the business, in 1963 the nation's disk jockeys voted *I'm Moving On* as their favorite all-time country record. With small stature and huge voice, Snow is a country traditionalist who has given much more to the business than he's taken. His output of over 100 albums gives a sense of his importance to country music history. —*David Vinopal*

○ **The Singing Ranger: 1949-1953** / 1989 / Bear Family 15426
This five-CD collection, with discography and notes, contains recordings Snow made from 1949 to 1953. Some of the 105 tracks in this collection include "Spanish Fire Ball," "Just Keep a'Movin'," "I'm Movin' On," and "The Rhumba Boogie." —*AMG*

★ **I'm Movin' On & Other Country Hits** / 1990 / RCA 9968
Rockabilly couldn't have happened without him. Train songs with hillbilly rumbas and more. —*Mark A. Humphrey*

○ **The Singing Ranger, Edition 2** / 1990 / Bear Family 15476
This is the second volume containing four CDs with recordings made by Snow until 1958, including 23 previously unavailable performances, and a rare single that Snow recorded especially for his Canadian fans. —*AMG*

○ **The Thesaurus Transcriptions** / 1991 / Bear Family 15488
This five-CD set contains 138 of Snow's songs recorded for RCA
in the early '50s, which have been released for the first time here.
Some of the songs in the set include "Wreck of the Old 97," "Blue
Eyes Crying in the Rain," "My Rough and Rowdy Ways," and
"Sally Goodin." —*AMG*

Collector's Series / RCA 52279
A nasal Canadian crooner, a crisp flat-top picker, and one of the
most influential country artists of the early 50s. Snow is relaxed
and driving at the same time. —*Mark A. Humphrey*

Jo-El Sonnier

Vocals, guitar, accordion / Progressive country, Cajun
In the late '80s, when the folks in Nashville realized country consisted of more than the Tennessee-Texas axis, they started looking
for new sounds. One of the best was that of Cajun accordionist Jo-
El Sonnier, who had kicked around for a number of years, gaining a reputation as a "musician's musician." Sonnier initially
caused a major fuss in Nashville and a minor one elsewhere,
though his songs—a blend of Cajun music, twangy guitars, and
New Orleans R&B—briefly added a touch of spice to country radio. —*Brian Mansfield*

Cajun Life / 1975 / Rounder 3049
Jo-El Sonnier, like Jimmy C. Newman, has found a comfortable
middle ground between traditional Cajun and contemporary
country music, working both styles and achieving a measure of
commercial and aesthetic success in each. This album accents the
Cajun side, though it includes competent pop/country material as
well—like the rollicking cover of "Jambalaya," and more interesting "Louisiana Blues." Besides the autobiographical title track,
Sonnier demonstrated his roots facility on "Les Yeux Bleu," "Jolie
Blon" and "Les Grands Bois." Sonnier has since gone on to become a bigger name in country, but this earlier date will appeal
both to lovers of vintage material and to those unaware of his
solid Cajun skills and background. —*Ron Wynn*

● **Come on Joe** / 1987 / RCA 6374
Sonnier's French-Cajun accent brings new life to songs by Randy
Newman, Richard Thompson, Moon Martin, and Dave Alvin.
Steve Winwood takes an organ solo on a cover of Slim Harpo's
"Raining in My Heart." Cajun-tinged contemporary country, with
a rock edge and intelligent songs. The best of Sonnier's Nashville
work. —*Brian Mansfield & Mark A. Humphrey*

Have a Little Faith / 1990 / RCA 9718
The emphasis here lies more heavily on ballads, as Sonnier dis-
covers John Hiatt and delivers penetrating versions of his "Have
a Little Faith" and "I'll Never Get Over You." Also includes a remake of Iry LeJeune's 1945 "Evangeline Special" and a straight-
country single in "If Your Heart Should Ever Roll This Way
Again." —*Brian Mansfield*

Tears of Joy / 1991 / Liberty 95684
In the Cajun/pop/country mold of his RCA albums. —*Mark A.
Humphrey*

● **The Complete Mercury Sessions** / 1992 / Mercury 512645
Fifteen fine '70s country songs, including the aching "Blue Is Not
a Word." —*Mark A. Humphrey*

The Sons of the Pioneers

Group / Cowboy
See the biography under Roy Rogers. —*AMG*

Cool Water / 1959 / RCA 58406
Later '50s material, but still smooth and fine. —*Mark A.
Humphrey*

☆ **Columbia Historic Edition** / 1982 / CBS 37439
This group wrote the book on dreamy, close-harmony crooning to
panoramic vistas. Leader Bob Nolan supplies poetic lyrics, and
Hugh and Karl Farr provide the Django Reinhardt/Stephane
Grappelli-inspired accompaniment. Archetypal sounds from the
'30s. —*Mark A. Humphrey*

The Sons of the Pioneers / 102
Features '40s transcriptions of such songs as "I Wonder if She
Waits for Me Tonight," "When Payday Rolls Around," "The
Howlin' Pup," and others. —*AMG*

● **Vol. 1** / Bear Family 15202

Music originally recorded by the group's original members for
RCA between 1945 and 1956. —*AMG*

○ **Vol. 2** / Bear Family 15252
Sixteen songs recorded in 1946-1947. —*AMG*

○ **Vol. 3** / Bear Family 15253
Sixteen more cuts, recorded in 1947. —*AMG*

○ **Vol. 4** / Bear Family 15254
This final volume in the series contains 16 tracks recorded at the
end of the '40s, some of which are released here for the first time.
—*AMG*

★ **Country Music Hall of Fame** / MCA 10090
Decca recordings from the '30s to the early '50s. —*Mark A.
Humphrey*

○ **Empty Saddles** / MCA 1563
All of the Pioneers '30s-era compilations are fine, but this in-
cludes Bob Nolan's darkest and most beautiful song, "Blue
Prairie." —*Mark A. Humphrey*

Southern Pacific

Group / Country
Stu Cook, John McFee, Tim Goodman, David Jenkins, and Kurt
Howell formed this group in mid-1983. Southern Pacific's rock &
roll past constantly dogged the group's reputation. Keith Knudsen
and John McFee were former members of the Doobie Brothers
(McFee had also played alongside Huey Lewis in a band called
Clover), original lead vocalist Tim Goodman had recorded a solo
album, and Stu Cook performed in Creedence Clearwater
Revival. Even when Goodman left the band, they replaced him
with another ex-rocker, former Pablo Cruise vocalist David
Jenkins. They did have one member with strong country roots:
Kurt Howell played keyboards for Crystal Gayle.
    Southern Pacific signed with Warner and released a strong de-
but album in 1985, though the media continually questioned the
band's commitment to country. The group plied a very danceable
brand of country, and hit a high point with their 1988 album
Zuma, which included their biggest single, "New Shade of Blue."
    Eventually, Southern Pacific left country music, intending to
pursue a pop career. —*Tom Roland*

● **Greatest Hits** / 1991 / Warner Brothers 26582
Why this group never quite made "the big time" remains a mystery. The material is sometimes two-step-able, sometimes kick-
ass, and in "New Shade of Blue," they out-Eagle the Eagles. —*Tom
Roland*

Red Sovine (Woodrow Wilson Sovine)

b. Jul. 17, 1918, Charleston, WV, d. Apr. 4, 1980 , Nashville, TN
Vocals, guitar / Traditional country
Sovine is regarded as the king of truck-driving songs. Between
1955 and 1980, Sovine scored 31 country hits, including
"Phantom 309," a song about a truck-driving ghost. "Teddy Bear,"
a maudlin story about a crippled boy who talked to friendly
truckers with his CB radio, was a Number 1 hit. Other chart suc-
cesses included "Giddyup Go" and several duets with Webb
Pierce on "Why Baby Why," "Little Rosa," and "Hold Everthing."
Sovine died in an automobile accident in 1980. —*Rick Clark*

● **The Best of Red Sovine** / Starday 952
This set includes some of Sovine's big hits, but a definitive collection still isn't available domestically. Among the tracks present
are "Phantom 309," "Giddyup Go," and "I Know You Are Married,
But I Love You Still." —*Rick Clark*

Buddy Spicher

Fiddle / Instrumental bluegrass
Since playing with the progressive country band Area Code 615
in the late 60s, Buddy has been a much-in-demand session fiddler. He has recorded with the Pointer Sisters and Henry Mancini,
along with making albums of his own. —*David Vinopal*

American Sampler / 1988 / Flying Fish 021
Varied dates with fine playing by Spicher. —*Ron Wynn*

● **Fiddle Classics** / 1988 / Flying Fish 278
A high-caliber acoustic session by Spicher, showcasing country,
folk, and blues influences. —*Ron Wynn*

Me & My Heroes / 1990 / Flying Fish 065
A nice folk/jazz/country mixture. —*Ron Wynn*

The Statler Brothers

Group / Traditional country

Brothers Harold and Don Reid (Phil Balsey and Jimmy Fortune round out the present quartet) have been the kings of country groups since the mid 60s. The brothers, who began as a gospel quartet in 1955, made it big in 1965 with "Flowers on the Wall," a pop and country hit. In spite of competition from other groups over the years (the Oak Ridge Boys, Alabama, the Judds), the Statler Brothers have pretty much remained in the traditional country mold while winning every award in sight, over 400 in all. Their distinct sound is unmistakable, nostalgic, and unique. Hits include "You Can't Have Your Kate and Edith Too," "Elizabeth," "Class of '57," and "I'll Go to My Grave Loving You." In 1991, their television show quickly became the highest-rated weekly series on TNN. —*David Vinopal*

○ **Big Hits** / 1967 / CBS 9519
This gathers all their '60s Columbia hits. —*Ron Wynn*

○ **Oh Happy Day** / 1969 / CBS 9878
Another "roots" effort, this one from the '60s. —*Ron Wynn*

○ **Bed of Roses** / 1971 / Mercury 826247
Their first Mercury album. —*Ron Wynn*

○ **Country Music Then & Now** / 1972 / Mercury 826260
From the early '70s. A bit rougher and less slick than some '80s dates. —*Ron Wynn*

★ **The Best of the Statler Brothers** / 1975 / Mercury 822524
Gathers past hits for the label, including "Flowers on the Wall" and "Carry Me Back." —*Ron Wynn*

○ **Holy Bible—Old & New Testament** / 1979 / Mercury 826264
CD twin disc of great single country gospel albums. —*Ron Wynn*

○ **The Best of the Statler Brothers, Vol. 2** / 1980 / Mercury 822525
A followup to their prior greatest-hits release. —*Ron Wynn*

○ **Today** / 1983 / Mercury 812184
An excellent prototype session. —*Ron Wynn*

○ **Atlanta Blue** / 1984 / Mercury 818652
A tremendous title track, with marvelous singing. —*Ron Wynn*

Radio Gospel Favorites / 1986 / Mercury 826710
This harks back to their roots as a spiritual ensemble. Heated vocals. —*Ron Wynn*

The World of the Statler Brothers / CBS 31557
An overview of mid '60s material; duplication with earlier albums. —*Ron Wynn*

Gary Stewart

b. May 28, 1945, Letcher County, KY

Piano, guitar, bass / Traditional country, country-rock

Gary Stewart's versatility allows him to cover rockabilly and honky-tonk material equally well. After playing piano for Charley Pride's band, he had a 1974 hit with "Drinking Thing," a honky-tonker's delight. —*David Vinopal*

☆ **Out of Hand** / 1975 / Hightone 8026
His debut, and a rowdy 'n' rough honky-tonk classic. Stewart not only offers a first-person look at the tortured lifestyle of an emotional drinker, he also exposes how it tends to magnify jealousy and guilt. His voice keens with passion barely contained. —*Michael McCall*

Brand New / 1988 / Hightone 8014
Stewart ends a lengthy recording hiatus, showing a newfound maturity while tackling songs that are still rife with tortured self-revelation. His voice has lost little of its edge. —*Michael McCall*

★ **Gary's Greatest** / 1992 / Hightone 8030
An excellent collection of Stewart's hits from 1973-1990. —*Dan Heilman*

I'm a Texan / Oct. 15, 1993 / Hightone 8050
More impassioned than ever, Stewart continues to excel at raw-boned honky tonk and revved-up country rock. The songs don't all live up to his treatment, but when they do, as on "Honky Tonk Hardwood Floor" or the inviting "Come On In," he reveals the timidity that undercuts the new traditionalists of the modern country era. —*Michael McCall*

Doug Stone

Vocals / Traditional country

Doug Stone's sensitive Deep South baritone has made him one of country's premier romantic balladeers. This Georgian can sing hard traditional country and easy country with equal ease. For years, diesel mechanics was his day job, and he hated it. This dissatisfaction carries over into his music and his stage presence, which presents him as distant and alone; he knows what he's singing about. With the release of his first album, his record company announced the dawning of a new "Stone Age." They weren't far off, as acceptance from country's female-dominated audience was almost immediate; his second album, 1991's *I Thought It Was You*, overdid the self-pity but yielded a couple of hits, including the title cut. "I'd Be Better Off (In a Pine Box)" was his breakthrough song. Shortly before the release of his third album, *From the Heart*, in 1992, 35 years of Southern-fried food sent Stone under the surgeon's knife for quadruple bypass surgery. —*Brian Mansfield & David Vinopal*

○ **Doug Stone** / 1990 / Epic 45303
"I'd Be Better Off (In a Pine Box)" is a towering expression of self-pity that most singers could spend a career trying to top. If Stone never bested his performance on his debut, he came close with ballads like "In a Different Light" and "My Hat's off to Him," becoming a genuine heartthrob in the process. —*Brian Mansfield*

I Thought It Was You / 1991 / Epic 47357
Self-pity has always played an integral role in country music, but it's more effective a song at a time, not spread over an entire album. Unlike some harder-voiced honky-tonkers who funnel their emotions into cathartic country blues, Stone seems to wallow in sorrow. His ex is showing him up; his kid's growing up too fast; his new wife's walking out on him and telling him to shut up as he slams the door. This guy's favorite honky-tonk even gets turned into a fern bar. —*Brian Mansfield*

More Love / Epic 57271
With "Addicted to a Dollar," balladeer Stone stakes his claim for "hot country" status alongside all his Nashville peers. —*Dan Cooper*

The Stoneman Family

Group / Old-time, traditional country

The Stonemans are literally the first family of country music. Patriarch E.V. "Pop" Stoneman recorded "The Sinking of the Titanic" in 1925 and watched it become one of the biggest-selling country records of the decade. With fiddler Hattie Stoneman, his wife, he toured widely until the Depression cut into recording and personal appearances. In the '50s, when the 13 kids had taught themselves the family music, the Stonemans became a popular act, appearing on the Opry in 1962 and at numerous folk festivals. The spots on national TV, combined with their albums for Starday and Folkways, gave them coast-to-coast exposure. When "Pop" died in 1966, the family kept going, making them the longest continuous act in country music. —*David Vinopal*

○ **First Family of Country Music** / 1981 / CMH 9029
New recordings by members of this classic group whose patriarch began recording in 1924. Bluegrass-flavored old-time country. —*Charles S. Wolfe*

George Strait

b. May 18, 1952, Pearsall, TX

Vocals, guitar / Traditional country, Western swing, contemporary country

The fact that *People* magazine named George Strait one of the 50 most beautiful people in the world might mislead you: he can still sing pure country, as witnessed by his twenty-two Number 1 singles, ten gold albums, and four platinum. On the debit side, he may have unwittingly started the "hat act" fad, singers with Stetsons as big as (and sometimes bigger than) their voices. But from his *Strait Country* debut album in 1981, country listeners have found pleasure in his rich, unadorned voice and his straightahead delivery. Neither his songs nor his style is varnished or gussied-up, a breath of fresh air in modern country. He reintroduced twin fiddles and a tasteful steel guitar accompaniment, perfectly matching his voice and his Western-swing style. He's earned his rewards, including Vocalist of the Year and Album of the Year (1985) for *Does Fort Worth Ever Cross Your Mind*. If you like listening to Merle Haggard, and you ought to, give George Strait a serious listen as well. —*David Vinopal*

Right or Wrong / 1983 / MCA 31068

The title track is vintage Bob Wills, and much here draws from similar swinging Southwestern roots. —*Mark A. Humphrey*

Strait Country/Strait from the Heart / 1983 / MCA 5871
Two early albums in one. The first and arguably the best of the '80s crop of Haggard-indebted hats, Strait has never much wavered from a Western-swing-tinged, honky-tonk base. —*Mark A. Humphrey*

☆ **Does Fort Worth Ever Cross Your Mind** / 1984 / MCA 31032
Hardcore country shuffles, sudsy weepers, and swinging stompers. This is '80s "nu-traditional" country at its finest and most heartfelt. —*Mark A. Humphrey*

○ **Something Special** / 1985 / MCA 5605
Schmaltzier than some, but consistent with Strait's work. —*Mark A. Humphrey*

★ **Greatest Hits** / 1986 / MCA 5567
A good overview of Strait's early MCA chartbusters. Includes "Right or Wrong," "Amarillo by Morning," "You Look So Good in Love," and more. —*Mark A. Humphrey*

#7 / 1987 / MCA 5750
No frills 'n' fine. —*Mark A. Humphrey*

○ **Greatest Hits, Vol. 2** / 1987 / MCA 42035
More chartbusters from the Texan in the white hat, including such favorites as "All My Exes Live in Texas" and "Ocean Front Property." —*Mark A. Humphrey*

If You Ain't Lovin' (You Ain't Livin') / 1988 / MCA 42114
A great cover of the old Faron Young title song, and other swingin' tonkers. —*Mark A. Humphrey*

Chill of an Early Fall / 1991 / MCA 10204
A hit album. Strait holds his own despite a plethora of new hats in the decade since his debut. —*Mark A. Humphrey*

Marty Stuart

Vocals, mandolin / Traditional bluegrass, country-rock
For someone who started at the top—as a 13-year-old mandolin-playing phenomenon touring with Lester Flatt's band—a lot of time passed before Marty reached his later successes. At home with bluegrass, country-rock, or rockabilly, Marty's biggest hit to date is "Hillbilly Rock." His rhinestone Nudie suits are second only to Porter Wagoner's in the shimmer awards. —*David Vinopal*

Hillbilly Rock / 1989 / MCA 42312
Like the title says, contemporary rockabilly from this singer/guitarist. —*Mark A. Humphrey*

● **Tempted** / 1991 / MCA 10106
No song here is less than memorable, and the best are better than that. If *Tempted* rates any gripes, it's that the disc doesn't go on long enough. Upbeat contemporary country with rockabilly roots. —*Mark A. Humphrey*

This One's Gonna Hurt You / 1992 / MCA 10596
Stuart starts by relating how he received Hank Williams, Sr.'s blessing in a dream. With covers of Charlie Pride's "Just Between You and Me" and Ola Mae Belle's "High on a Mountain Top," he makes you believe. But the most retro stuff gets too hamfisted to keep *This One's Gonna Hurt You* on the same level as *Tempted*. —*Brian Mansfield*

Doug Supernaw

New country hat act who combines mild honky-tonk with tender balladry. —*Michael McCall*

● **Red and Rio Grande** / 1993 / BNA 66133
Includes his initial mainstream country hits, "Reno," and the anthem for divorced fathers, "I Don't Call Him Daddy." —*Michael McCall*

Sweethearts of the Rodeo

Group / Contemporary country
By winning the Wrangler Country Showdown with "Gotta Get Away," California sisters Kristine Arnold and Janis Gill (wife of singer Vince Gill) received a Columbia contract. They've done well with "Blue to the Bone" and "Midnight Girl," and have been nominated for Best Vocal Duo awards. —*David Vinopal*

● **Sweethearts of the Rodeo** / 1986 / CBS 40406

Californian sisters gone to Music City. Good vocal harmony on contemporary rock-tinged country. —*Mark A. Humphrey*

Rodeo Waltz / 1993 / Sugar Hill 3819
This duos album is refreshingly open sounding. The soft Nashville production provides a fine background for the sweet vocal harmonies. "Jenny Dreamed of Trains," "Get Rhythm," and "Broken Arrow" are standout cuts. —*Richard Meyer*

Sylvia (Sylvia Kirby Allen)

b. Dec. 9, 1956, Kokomo, IN
Vocals / Country
Growing up in Kokomo, IN, Sylvia moved to Nashville around Christmas of 1975 with a definite gameplan: get a job as a secretary, get to know influential people in town, and build a career as a recording artist.

The plan worked. She picked up a job as the receptionist for Pi-Gem Music, headed by record producer Tom Collins. She started singing on demo sessions, and Collins helped her secure a recording contract with RCA. Since she'd never performed live before, Sylvia ended up learning to do concerts at the same time she was making hit records.

With an engaging voice, a bubbly personality, and a beautiful appearance, Sylvia was practically a marketing dream, and Collins built her sound around catchy melodies and strong backbeats. The material was often lyrically shallow, however, and Sylvia grew increasingly frustrated. She left Collins and recorded a pair of albums with record producer Brent Maher. The second was never released. Sylvia, instead, was dropped by RCA in 1987.

She used the opportunity for personal growth (she had toured almost constantly during the height of her career and was emotionally drained) and for development as a songwriter. In 1992, she re-emerged as a touring artist and pursued a recording deal with self-penned material that was inner-directed and uplifting. —*Tom Roland*

Just Sylvia / 1982 / RCA 4312
Producer Tom Collins plays around with Sylvia's vocals a lot, altering them electronically for effects that range from ever-so-slight to overbearing. But the material's predominantly sassy, and as catchy as a virus. The honesty in "You Can't Go Back Home" really hurts. —*Tom Roland*

● **Greatest Hits** / 1987 / RCA 5618

Gid Tanner & His Skillet Lickers

b. Jun. 6, 1885, **d.** May 13, 1960
Group / Old-time
This influential string band of the '20s and '30s featured three major figures of early country music: Gideon "Gid" Tanner, fiddler Clayton McMichen (b. 1900—d. 1970), and Blind Riley Pucket (b. 1894—d. 1946) on guitar. Tanner's band, the Skillet Lickers, featured fiddle breakdowns, folk material, and comedy skits dealing with moonshine. This high-spirited band broke up in 1934. —*David Vinopal*

○ **Kickapoo Medicine Show** / 1988 / Rounder 1023
A '20s string band plays raucous and rippin' old-time music on this album. —*Mark A. Humphrey*

B. J. Thomas (Billy Joe Thomas)

b. Aug. 7, 1942, Houston, TX
Vocals / Gospel, country-pop, rock-pop
Billy Joe Thomas began as a rocker but had his first Top 10 with Hank Williams' "I'm So Lonesome I Could Cry" in 1966. In 1969 "Raindrops Keep Fallin' on My Head," the theme song from the movie *Butch Cassidy and the Sundance Kid*, made a country-pop star of him. After years of substance abuse he found Christianity and rose again to the top with gospel albums, with *Home Where I Belong* winning him a Grammy. He now mixes gospel and secular country-pop with equal success. —*David Vinopal*

● **B.J. Thomas' Greatest Hits** / 1991 / Rhino 70752
A fine eighteen-song collection that features all of Thomas' greatest hits, from "I'm So Lonesome I Could Cry" through "Hooked on a Feeling" to "(Hey Won't You Play) Another Somebody Done Somebody Wrong Song." —*Stephen Thomas Erlewine*

Hank Thompson

b. Sep. 3, 1925, Waco, TX

Vocals, guitar / Traditional country, Western swing
Country Hall of Famer Hank Thompson has had chart hits in five different decades. Between Bob Wills and Asleep at the Wheel, there was Thompson with his Brazos Valley Boys, keeping the sound of Western swing alive. His swing music and well-written honky-tonk songs produced 21 Top 20 charters from 1949 and 1958. His signature song, "The Wild Side of Life" (1952), was his biggest hit, prompting Miss Kitty Wells to defend bar-life females in "It Wasn't God Who Made Honky Tonk Angels." Much of his best music was set in the dim lights and thick smoke of the honky-tonk, with such hits as "Hangover Tavern," "On Tap, in the Can, or in the Bottle," "Smokey the Bar," "A Six-Pack to Go," and "Honky-Tonk Girl." While music tastes changed during his career, he kept on touring world-wide with his band, keeping true honky-tonk and western swing in the public's ear. He's often seen on Ralph Emery's "Nashville Now" TV show. —*David Vinopal*

○ **A Six Pack to Go** / 1961 / Capitol 11881
Beer-drinkin' music and honky-tonk from the '50s. Great band, including Merle Travis on guitar on some cuts. —*George Bedard*

● **Capitol Collector's Series** / 1989 / Capitol 92124
A fine collection that features twenty of Thompson's greatest hits. —*AMG*

○ **Country Music Hall of Fame Series** / 1992 / MCA 10545
1968-1978 recordings from Dot Records, when Thompson was past his prime but still capable of turning out good singles when the Nashville sound didn't smother him. —*Brian Mansfield*

Marsha Thornton

Vocals / Country
Thornton is one of the new Nashville thrushes. Her two MCA albums are 1989's *Marsha Thornton*, produced by the legendary Owen Bradley, and 1991's *Maybe the Moon Will Shine*. Like many of her contemporaries, Thornton is labelled a "new traditionalist" and is stylistically indebted to Emmylou Harris. —*Mark A. Humphrey*

● **Maybe the Moon Will Shine** / 1991 / MCA 10142
Pleasant pipes and Emmylou Harris-style production. —*Mark A. Humphrey*

Mel Tillis

b. Aug. 8, 1932, Pahokee, FL
Vocals, guitar / Traditional country
Though he stutters when he speaks, Mel Tillis is downright eloquent in his singing and superb songwriting ("Ruby, Don't Take Your Love to Town" and "Detroit City," a huge hit for Bobby Bare). Over 500 of his songs have been covered by the likes of Faron Young, Kenny Rogers, folksinger Burl Ives, and Webb Pierce. Among his recordings that hit Number 1 are "Good Woman Blues," "Heart Healer," "Coca-Cola Cowboy," and "Southern Rains." As an actor he's appeared in *W. W. and the Dixie Dance Kings* and *Uphill All the Way* (1986) with Roy Clark. His winning personality and sense of humor lead him to regular TV appearances. —*David Vinopal*

M-M-Mel Live / 1980 / MCA 789
Tillis the showman heard working a crowd. —*Mark A. Humphrey*

○ **American Originals** / 1989 / CBS 45079
Good '60s shuffles in a Ray Price vein. —*Mark A. Humphrey*

● **The Best of Mel Tillis** / MCA 4091
Fine '60s hard-country singer/songwriter with Ray Price shuffles, etc. —*Mark A. Humphrey*

Pam Tillis

b. 1957
Vocals / Contemporary country
Daughter of country singer and actor Mel Tillis, Pam Tillis flirted with rock and free jazz before returning finally to the Nashville fold in 1991. She appeared with her dad at the Ryman Auditorium when she was eight, but later worked furiously to establish herself a separate identity. Her compositions have been recorded by Ricky Van Shelton and Conway Twitty. She's married to songwriter Bob DiPiero, a former member of Billy Hill. —*David Vinopal & Brian Mansfield*

○ **Put Yourself in My Place** / 1991 / Arista 8642
The album that established Tillis as a performer in her own right has a traditional country base cut with bluegrass, folk and rock. It

all creates the same sort of mixed breed she sings about in "Melancholy Child": "You take a black Irish temper, some solemn Cherokee, a Southern sense of humor, and you got someone like me." Her characters are the awkward dancers of "I've Seen Enough to Know": bruised, tentative, and needing to be cajoled back to love. Even the throwaway songs are of a high standard; the best ones ("Maybe It Was Memphis," "Don't Tell Me What to Do") are truly enticing. —*Brian Mansfield*

Homeward Looking Angel / 1992 / Arista 18649
Tillis had an enviable challenge with *Homeward Looking Angel*—topping *Put Yourself in My Place*, which spawned four Top 10 singles, including "Don't Tell Me What To Do." Tillis' pure, full-bodied country voice can be both a boon and a burden. Some tracks on *Angel* reek with cliche, her twang exaggerated to the verge of annoyance, for instance, on the retro "Do You Know Where Your Man Is." Others work an original magic, including the sly and sexy "Shake the Sugar Tree" and the wry and telling "Cleopatra, Queen of Denial." These songs, along with "Let That Pony Run," had no trouble finding their way to the chart heights of their predecessors. —*Roch Parisien*

Pam Tillis Collection / 1994 / Warner Brothers
Before hitting big with Arista Records and "Don't Tell Me What To Do," Tillis had recorded rock-influenced country for Warner Bros. She had minor success with the likes of "There Goes My Love" and "These Memories of You," but what makes *Collection* interesting is early versions of "One of Those Things" and "Maybe It Was Memphis" as well as a version of "Five Minutes," later a hit for Lorrie Morgan. —*Brian Mansfield*

● **Sweetheart's Dance** / Apr. 26, 1994 / Arista 18758
Producing herself for the first time (along with Steve Fishell), Tillis found the magic blend of Nashville Sound, California country-rock and post-Beatles pop. She released the heady "Spilled Perfume" as her first single, but the riches of *Sweethearts Dance* go much deeper: the Bo Diddley/Tejano rhythms of "Mi Vida Loca (My Crazy Life)," the lilting waltz of "In Between Dances," and a playfully romantic title cut. A charming album without a bad cut, *Sweethearts Dance* ranks with the best of Trisha Yearwood, Wynonna Judd and Carlene Carter. —*Brian Mansfield*

Floyd Tillman

b. Dec. 8, 1914, Ryan, OK
Vocals, guitar / Traditional country
This Hall of Famer is probably best known for writing "It Makes No Difference Now," a country classic that he sold to Jimmie Davis for $300 in 1938, only to watch it become a hit for Davis, Bob Wills, Bing Crosby, Gene Autry, and others. In the late '40s he had recording hits with his self-penned "Slippin' Around" and "I Love You So Much It Hurts." His Western swing/honky-tonk mixture and his easy vocal delivery have made him a much-imitated performer, and for good reason. —*David Vinopal*

● **Country Music Hall of Fame Series** / 1991 / MCA 10189
Tillman had his biggest hits in the late '40s while recording for Columbia, but these WWII-era sides for Decca show him as a leader of a Texas dance band that's not afraid to mix it up with some jazz playing. Moon Mullican plays piano on a number of these sides. —*Brian Mansfield*

☆ **The Best of Floyd Tillman** / CBS 34334
Contains his classics, such as "Slippin' Around" and "Gotta Have My Baby Back." Wait for this one; with Columbia reissuing much of its vintage country material, this stuff has got to appear on CD in some form. —*Richard Lieberson*

Aaron Tippin

b. 1958
Vocals / Traditional country
A South Carolina singer influenced by Jimmie Rodgers, Hank Thompson, and Lefty Frizzell, Aaron Tippin had an incredible twang in his voice that sounded somewhat out of place among the clean-cut honky-tonkers of the early '90s. Before debuting with his own single, "You've Got To Stand for Something," in 1991, he had written songs for country singers Mark Collie and Charley Pride and gospel groups the Kingsmen and the Mid South Boys. —*Brian Mansfield*

● **You've Got to Stand for Something** / 1991 / RCA 2374

Exciting hardcore country from a man whose previous blue-collar experience as a farm hand, welder, pilot, and truck driver made him a publicist's dream. Includes the singles "You've Got to Stand for Something," "I Wonder How Far It Is Over You," and "She Made a Memory Out of Me." *—Brian Mansfield*

○ **Read between the Lines** / 1992 / RCA 61129
A good follow-up by this popular hatless hillbilly. Contains "There Ain't Nothin' Wrong with the Radio," "I Wouldn't Have It Any Other Way," "My Blue Angel," and more. *—Mark A. Humphrey*

Call of the Wild / Aug. 1993 / RCA 66251
Though he was still capable of singing up a storm and cranking out great grooves, some of Tippin's song choices were hillbilly silly. Of course, they were also the singles, which had names like "Honky Tonk Superman" and "Working Man's Ph.D." *—Brian Mansfield*

Karen Tobin

Vocals / Country
Tobin worked in the Los Angeles-area country bars in the late '80s as half of the country duo Crazy Hearts (cf. Enigma's *A Town South of Bakersfield II* anthology) before signing a solo deal with Atlantic in 1991. Her debut album offers contemporary traditional-country tunes. *—Mark A. Humphrey*

○ **Carolina Smokey Moon** / 1991 / Atlantic 82323
An impressive debut from this California-based traditional country singer. *—Mark A. Humphrey*

Merle Travis

b. Nov. 29, 1917, Rosewood, KY, **d.** Oct. 20, 1983 , Tahlequah, OK
Guitar / Instrumental bluegrass
As a guitarist and songwriter, Travis is unsurpassed in the business; he's one of the few to have an instrumental style named after him—"Travis picking"—putting him in the elite company of Earl Scruggs and the Carter Family. Travis learned his distinctive three-finger-style guitar from fellow Kentuckians Mose Rager and Ike Everly (father of Phil and Don), and he transferred the banjo roll to the guitar. Travis style uses the thumb to play the bottom notes of a chord individually, while playing the melody on the higher strings with the index finger and occasionally the third finger. The result is a constant motion and flow of the lower notes, while the melody floats on the top. The influence of this style can't be overstated: super-picker Chet Atkins has acknowledged his debt to Travis.

Before the war, Travis was a member of two important bands: the Georgia Wildcats and the influential Browns Ferry Four, with Grandpa Jones and the Delmore brothers, Alton and Rabon. After his discharge from the Marine Corps, he had numerous hits, self-written or with others, including "Divorce Me C.O.D.," "So Round, So Firm, So Fully Packed," "Smoke, Smoke, Smoke That Cigarette," "Dark as a Dungeon," and "Sweet Temptation." In 1947 he wrote and recorded "Sixteen Tons" and watched Tennessee Ernie Ford eight years later make it perhaps the blockbuster hit in the history of country music. Country music is so much richer thanks to multi-talented Merle Travis. *—David Vinopal*

☆ **Walkin' the Strings** / 1960 / Capitol 1391
Mostly instrumental. A classic of fingerstyle guitar. *—Richard Lieberson*

○ **Songs of the Coal Mines** / 1963 / Capitol 1956

○ **Travis Pickin'** / 1981 / CMH 6255
Until his Capitol Records instrumental recordings become available again, this is the one for guitar buffs to go for. *—Richard Lieberson*

★ **Merle Travis Story—24 Greatest Hits** / 1989 / CMH 9018
This collection emphasizes Travis' trailblazing guitar work, making it the place to start. *—AMG*

☆ **The Best of Merle Travis** / 1990 / Rhino 70993
The emphasis here is on Travis's novelty vocals and songwriting, rather than his guitar. *—Richard Lieberson*

Unreleased Radio Transcriptions 1944-1949 / Rounder 0009
This album contains 22 tracks of performances originally broadcast on such shows as "Hollywood Barn Dance," "Melody Roundup," and the "Grand Ole Opry," among others. *—AMG*

Randy Travis (Randy Traywick)

b. May 4, 1959, Marshville, NC
Vocals, guitar / Traditional country, contemporary country
Like the Beatles in rock, Randy Travis marks a generational shift in country music. When his *Storms of Life* came out in 1986, country music was still wallowing in the post-*Urban Cowboy* recession, chasing elusive crossover dreams. Travis brought the music back to its basics, sounding like nothing so much as a perfect blend of George Jones and Merle Haggard. He became the dominant male voice in country until the rise of "hat acts" like Garth Brooks and Clint Black, releasing seven consecutive Number 1 singles during one stretch. He won the CMA's Horizon Award in 1986 and was the association's Male Vocalist of the Year in 1987 and '88. *—Brian Mansfield*

★ **Storms of Life** / 1986 / Warner Brothers 25435
His first and best album. Astonishing Lefty Frizzell-style pipes, excellent material, and sympathetic production. Easily the most impressive country debut of the '80s. Features "1982," "On the Other Hand," "Diggin' Up Bones," and "No Place Like Home." *—Mark A. Humphrey*

○ **Always & Forever** / 1987 / Warner Brothers 25568
This one stayed at the top of the country charts for 10 months and sold 5 million copies. Well, of course he was huge. If you had songs as good as "Forever and Ever, Amen" you'd be a star too. *—Brian Mansfield*

○ **Old 8x10** / 1988 / Warner Brothers 25738
Almost on a par with *Storms of Life, Old 8x10* lacks the monster hits of his debut but wears just as well. When Travis sings of love, he doesn't mean romance; there's a permancence in his voice that sounds like settling down. Contains "Honky Tonk Moon," "Deeper Than the Holler," and "Is It Still Over?" *—Brian Mansfield*

○ **No Holdin' Back** / 1989 / Warner Brothers 25988
Features "Hard Rock Bottom of Your Heart," "Somewhere in My Broken Heart" and "He Walked on Water." *—AMG*

Heroes and Friends / 1990 / Warner Brothers 26310
A duets album that includes the obvious influences (George Jones, Conway Twitty, Tammy Wynette) as well as a few surprises (B.B. King, Clint Eastwood). The Jones song, "A Few Ole Country Boys," and the title track were hit singles. *—Brian Mansfield*

High Lonesome / 1991 / Warner Brothers 26661
With young whippersnappers like Clint Black and Garth Brooks breathing down his neck, Travis realized he needed to be more than just a pretty voice. On *High Lonesome* he proved he could write, too, helping pen 5 of the album's 10 songs, including "Forever Together" for his manager-turned-wife Lib Hatcher, and the country-gospel "I'm Gonna Have a Little talk," sung a cappella with Take 6. Includes "Better Class of Losers," written with Alan Jackson. *—Brian Mansfield*

Wind in the Wire / 1992 / Warner Brothers
An album of Western cowboy music, some old and some new, made to go with a TV show of the same name. *—Brian Mansfield*

★ **Greatest Hits, Vol. 1** / Sep. 15, 1992 / Warner Brothers 45044
When Travis finally got around to releasing a greatest-hits collection, he realized he had almost enough material for two albums. So, adding two new songs to each, he put them out simultaneously. Volume one gets the edge for including those first two hits, "1982" and "On the Other Hand'; the best of the new songs, "If I Didn't Have You"; and the shattering "Reasons I Cheat," which proved as early as 1986 that Travis could write 'em as well as sing 'em. *—Brian Mansfield*

☆ **Greatest Hits, Vol. 2** / Sep. 15, 1992 / Warner Brothers 45045
Eleven more Travis classics, among them "Diggin' Up Bones," "Forever and Ever, Amen" and a fabulous remake of Brook Benton's "It's Just a Matter of Time." New songs: "Look Heart, No Hands" and "Take Another Swing at Me." *—Brian Mansfield*

○ **This Is Me** / 1994 / Warner Brothers 45501
The vanity project *Wind in the Wire* excepted, Travis hadn't released an album of new music in three years, and some people were wondering what had happened to the man who started the neotraditionalist boom. *This Is Me*, which included the wildly funny "Before You Kill Us All" and a stunning song called "Whisper My Name" that synthesized countrypolitan with gospel, silenced most of the questioners and showed the young

whippersnappers what all the fuss had been about in the first place. —*Brian Mansfield*

Travis Tritt

b. 1963
Vocals, guitar / Traditional country
Southern rock and outlaw country found common ground in Travis Tritt, a native of Marietta, GA. A singer with acting ambitions, he starred with Kenny Rogers in the made-for-TV *Rio Diablo* and had a cameo in the 1994 Woody Harrelson film *The Cowboy Way*. He won the CMA's Horizon Award in 1991 and joined the Grand Ole Opry in 1992. —*Brian Mansfield*

Country Club / 1990 / Warner Brothers 26094
Tritt proclaimed his influences early with "Put Some Drive in Your Country," which paid homage not only to Roy Acuff and George Jones but to Hank Williams, Jr. and Duane Allman as well. It was the lowest-charting single off Tritt's debut, but it sold him a ton of albums. Radio programmers preferred the ambitious "I'm Gonna Be Somebody" and the ballads "Help Me Hold On" and "Drift Off to Dream." —*Brian Mansfield*

● **It's All About** / 1991 / Warner Reprise 38246
Better production means ballads like "Anymore" sound bigger and rockers like "Bible Belt" (with Little Feat) and a cover of bluesman Buddy Guy's "Homesick" rock harder. Tritt brought in Marty Stuart for a duet on "The Whiskey Ain't Workin'" and revived "Here's a Quarter (Call Someone Who Cares)" as a catchphrase. —*Brian Mansfield*

T-r-o-u-b-l-e / 1992 / Warner Brothers 45048
Travis' covers of Buddy Guy ("Leave My Girl Alone") and Elvis Presley ("T-R-O-U-B-L-E") are nice touches and show deeper roots than the Gary Rossington cowrite ("Blue Collar Man") or the last album's Little Feat remake. Beyond that, *T-R-O-U-B-L-E* is almost indistinguishable from *It's About to Change*: a good novelty song masquerading as more, a couple of ballads with big flourishes, and a large helping of Southern. That's a good formula, granted, but it still sounds like a formula. —*Brian Mansfield*

Loving Time of the Year / May 1992 / Warner Brothers 45029
The harder Tritt rocks on *Loving Time of the Year,* the better he sounds. His Southern-boogie versions of "Winter Wonderland" and "Silver Bells" make a perfect antidote to sleigh-bell burnout. When he tries to be an "interpretive singer" on "Have Yourself a Merry Little Christmas," he falls flat on his face. Elsewhere, Tritt writes the title track while covering two by Buck Owens and one by Sonny James. —*Brian Mansfield*

○ **Ten Feet Tall & Bulletproof** / 1994 / Warner Brothers 45603
Tritt's most personal album, and the one in which he feels most comfortable with his Southern rock/outlaw mantle. ("Outlaws Like Us," in fact, features the voices of Hank Williams, Jr. and Waylon Jennings.) Tritt poked fun at his own foibles in the title track and cowrote "Wishful Thinking" and "No Vacation from the Blues" with Lynyrd Skynyrd's Gary Rossington. "Wishful Thinking" and "Foolish Pride" are ballads that rival "Anymore" for power and Skynyrd and Bob Seger for production values. —*Brian Mansfield*

Ernest Tubb (Ernest Dale Tubb, Texas Troubadour)

b. Feb. 9, 1914, Crisp, TX, d. Sep. 6, 1984 , Nashville, TN
Vocals, guitar / Traditional country
The incomparable Ernest Tubb ("E. T." to all who knew him) became a legend as much for what he was personally as for the half-century career that stretched from his first radio date in 1932 to his death in 1984. Though other singers with better voices and more raw musical talent have come and gone, none has inspired greater love of the fans over six decades. Along with such performers as Jimmie Rodgers, Roy Acuff, Bill Monroe, Hank Williams, Lefty Frizzell, and George Jones, E.T. is country music personified. Tubb was among the first of the honky-tonk singers and the first to achieve national recognition. His first recording was "The Passing of Jimmie Rodgers," a tribute to his hero. His long association with Decca began with "Blue Eyed Elaine" in 1940. Three years later his self-penned "Walkin' the Floor over You," a country classic, was a hit, leading to the Opry, movie roles, and stardom.

In 1947 he opened his Nashville record store and began the "Midnight Jamboree," which followed the Opry on WSM and advertised the shop while showcasing stars and those on the rise.

Over the years, Tubb toured widely with his Texas Troubadours, pressing the flesh with fans after shows that featured his many hits, including "Slippin' Around," "Two Glasses Joe," "Tomorrow Never Comes," "Drivin' Nails in My Coffin," "Rainbow at Midnight," "Let's Say Goodbye Like We Said Hello," and "Driftwood on the River." In 1975, after 35 years with Decca/MCA, he was let go, the allegiance of company executives not matching that of his multitude of fans.

Because of a lung disease Ernest Tubb had to rest in pain on a cot between takes, ending his career just as his hero Jimmie Rodgers had fifty years earlier. Quoting one of his album titles, Tubb left a legend and a legacy. —*David Vinopal*

The Importance of Being Ernest / 1959 / Decca 78834
A good album representative of his later ('50s and '60s) sound. Above-average song selections. —*George Bedard*

Honky Tonk Classics / 1983 / Rounder 11
A nicely varied selection of early Tubb recordings (not necessarily hits) from 1940-1954. —*Mark A. Humphrey*

★ **Country Hall of Fame** / 1987 / CDL 8078
A great chronological retrospective that includes the original 1941 "Walkin' the Floor over You" and Tubb's Jimmie Rodgers imitation on "Mean Mama Blues," then moves up through the '40s and '50s. Great bands, featuring (among others) Billy Byrd and Leon Rhodes on guitar and Buddy Charlton on steel. —*George Bedard*

○ **Let's Say Goodbye Like We Said Hello** / Bear Family 15498
This five-CD boxed set of Tubb's 1947-1953 recordings (all 115 of them) is arguably "most of the best" of E.T., including his hillbilly jive exchanges with Red Foley. —*Mark A. Humphrey*

Tanya Tucker (Tanya Denise Tucker)

b. Oct. 10, 1958, Seminole, TX
Vocals / Country-rock, contemporary country
In 1972 13-year-old Tanya Tucker had a hit with "Delta Dawn"; more than 20 years later this woman with the husky voice is a veteran of country, rock, and all that lies in between. With over 30 Top 10 hits and a few movie roles (*Jeremiah Johnson* and *Hard Country*), she sings with conviction and great experience. From the start, a renegade/bad-girl label was pinned on her, reinforced by her controversial material—"Would You Lay with Me (In a Field of Stone)" is an example—and her brush with rock music. Fans welcomed her return to mainstream country, where her unique voice and powerful stage presence have led to albums and singles that regularly reach the charts. —*David Vinopal*

★ **Greatest Hits** / 1978 / MCA 1698
No matter how far Tanya's come the last 20 years, it all comes back to "Delta Dawn," "What's Your Mama's Name," and the other hillbilly-gothic hits of her youth. Producer Billy Sherrill is best known for his work with George Jones and Tammy Wynette, but how he turned an underage, waifish Southwestern homegirl into a singer to make old boys sweat is surely his most notable, if unsettling, career achievement. —*Dan Cooper*

T.N.T. / 1978 / MCA 31152
Tucker rocks out on this steamy album. —*Mark A. Humphrey*

The Best of Tanya Tucker / 1982 / MCA 31166
Later '70s material for the blooming of a belter—honky-tonk style. —*Mark A. Humphrey*

Girls Like Me / 1986 / Capitol 12474
A bad girl tries to go good in the '80s on a new label. —*Mark A. Humphrey*

○ **Love Me Like You Used To** / 1987 / Liberty 46870
A fully mature artist, uncompromisingly gritty in the sanitized new Nashville. —*Mark A. Humphrey*

○ **Greatest Hits (Liberty)** / 1989 / Liberty 91814
Tanya's second coming as commercial country queen, here with her 1986-1991 hits. —*Mark A. Humphrey*

Tennessee Woman / 1990 / Liberty 91821
Here's one Tennessee singer who is more fiery than most Nashville divas. —*Mark A. Humphrey*

Can't Run from Yourself / Sep. 28, 1992 / Liberty 98987
Edgier and more consistent than *What Do I Do with Me, Can't Run from Yourself* runs the range of Tucker's abilities, from the slow-blues burn of Marshall Chapman's "Can't Run from Yourself" to the wistful melancholy of Hugh Prestwood's "Half the

Moon." A rollicking duet with Delbert McClinton on "Tell Me About It" is matched by the fine romance of "Two Sparrows in a Hurricane," and which one you like best will depend strictly on personal preferences. Switch one song on each side, and you've got a side of rockers and a side of ballads. —*Brian Mansfield*

Conway Twitty (Harold Lloyd Jenkins)

b. Sep. 1, 1933, Friars Point, MS, d. Jun. 5, 1993 , Branson, MO
Vocals, guitar / Traditional country
Adored by his fans and respected by his peers in Music City, Conway Twitty was in many respects the consummate country star. Though (with his rhinestones and sideburns he never looked the part), he was also something of a modernist. His knack for singing in a downhome voice laced with bedroom intimacy allowed adult themes to enter country music, without offending conservative listeners. Conway made "going country" sound like growing up. Born Harold Lloyd Jenkins, in Friar's Point, Mississippi, he did most of his real-life growing up across the river in Helena, AK. Drafted by Uncle Sam and the Philadelphia Phillies both, he started singing in earnest while stationed in Japan. Back home, he knocked around the local nightclubs, mostly singing Elvis-type rockabilly. He changed his name to Conway (after Conway, Arkansas) Twitty (after Twitty, Texas), cut a few unissued sides for Sun, and a few that were issued by Mercury. Finally, in 1958, his immortal MGM recording of "It's Only Make Believe" blasted to the top of the pop charts and made Conway Twitty a rock & roll star. After the usual round of followup hits, Bandstand appearances, teen exploitation flicks, and waning popularity, Twitty officially "went country" in 1965. Three years later he scored the first of his more than fifty Number 1 country hits with "Next in Line." Another chart-topper, released in 1970, was "Hello Darlin'," the song that would forever be known as his signature tune. An unstoppable hitmaker, both on his own and through his famous duets with Loretta Lynn, Twitty was still going strong when he died at the age of 59. His sudden passing, sad though it was, was nowhere near as depressing as the ugly estate battle that ensued. —*Dan Cooper*

Super Hits / Epic 57841
One of early rock & roll's most soulful and dramatic singers—inspired by Elvis Presley, but with a country/gospel edge all his own. This includes his biggest hits, the self-penned "It's Only Make Believe," along with "Lonely Blue Boy" and the great gospel-tinged "I'll Try." —*George Bedard*

○ **Hello Darlin'** / 1970 / Decca 75209
Twitty's finest hour as a country singer and songwriter. The great title track, plus "Up Comes the Bottle" and "I'm So Used to Loving You." He's at his C&W vocal peak on this one, and almost all of the material is good—even forgive the inclusion of "Rocky Top." —*George Bedard*

★ **Greatest Hits, Vol. 1** / 1972 / MCA 31239
Not all of these songs were hits, but this 1972 package goes a long way to explain Conway's appeal. There's not a weak track on this record and non-hits like "I Wonder What She'll Think About Me Leaving" and "Image of Me" are every bit as good as the monster hits. —*Jim Worbois*

☆ **The Very Best of Conway & Loretta** / 1979 / MCA 937
Lust and guilt, and stunning soulful harmonizing by Twitty and Loretta Lynn from the early to mid '70s. Stupendous country vocalizing in a honky-tonk vein. —*Mark A. Humphrey*

○ **Number One's (MCA)** / 1982 / MCA 1488
After moving from rock & roll to country, Twitty remained sensitive to criticism that he might not be serious, and rarely deviated from the standard three-chord country song for about his first decade in the format. This package, which selects material almost randomly from 1975-1981, does a good job of showing a Twitty more willing to experiment, particularly with the soulful "Don't Take It Away" and the dramatic "I May Never Get to Heaven." —*Tom Roland*

○ **Number One's—the Warner Brothers Years** / 1988 / Warner Brothers 25777
Conway Twitty's Number 1's: The Warner Bros. Years. This greatest-hits set shows (with the exception of "The Rose") an artist in command of his own performance, with a clear grasp on quality

material and a strong sense of powerful arrangements. Diverse and engaging. —*Tom Roland*

★ **Silver Anniversary Collection** / 1990 / MCA 8035
25 hits from Twitty's work for MCA and Warner Bros. are contained on this album, from "Guess My Eyes Were Bigger than My Heart" (1966) to "She's Got a Single Thing in Mind" (1989). —*AMG*

★ **Best of, Vol. 1: Rockin' Years** / 1991 / PolyGram 849574
The best collection available of Twitty's days as a rock & roller, featuring "It's Only Make Believe." —*AMG*

Final Touches / 1993 / MCA 10882
Produced by Don Cook, Final Touches has its moments, but seems a less fitting swan song for Twitty than his princely duet with Sam Moore on the *Rhythm Country and Blues* album. —*Dan Cooper*

The Final Recordings of His Greatest Hits, Vol. 1 / Nov. 2, 1993 / Capitol/Curb 77641

The Final Recordings of His Greatest Hits, Vol. 2 / Nov. 2, 1993 / Capitol/Curb 77642

Ian Tyson

Vocals / Country
The male half of the early 1960s folk group Ian & Sylvia, Tyson had retreated from performing and recording in the 1970s to become a rancher in the foothills of southern Alberta, Canada. He quietly returned to music-making in the 1980s, releasing a series of albums that dwelled on highly detailed songs about the concerns of the working cowboy. —*Michael McCall*

○ **I Outgrew the Wagon** / 1989 / Stony Plain 1131
The best of his series of homegrown album on what he calls "cowboy culture." Simple, unadorned songs affectionately yet unromantically examining rural life on the Canadian plains, as well as a couple of philosophical offerings. —*Michael McCall*

● **Eighteen Inches of Rain** / 1994 / Vanguard 79745
Tyson emerges from Canada to record an album with producer Jim Rooney in Nashville. The basic charms and wise observations remain, but are brought into focus without detracting from the raw appeal of Tyson's purposefully casual style. —*Michael McCall*

Rick Vincent

A singer who came by his Bakersfield sound honestly. Born in San Bernadino, he grew up in Bakersfield. —*Brian Mansfield*

○ **A Wanted Man** / 1993 / Capitol 77586
Vincent draws on the legacies of hometown heroes like Buck Owens and Merle Haggard without ever trying to sound just like them. He doesn't need to: Vincent, who wrote or cowrote all 10 of these songs, writes thoughtful and literate lyrics (he alludes to John Steinbeck and *Casblanca*). And whether he's shuffling into drunken despair in "Hello, She Lied" or comparing his marriage to an abandoned railway in "Ain't Been a Train through Here in Years," he's got a voice as big and warm as the San Joaquin Valley. —*Brian Mansfield*

Porter Wagoner

b. Aug. 12, 1927, West Plains, MO
Vocal / Popular
Porter Wagoner, the Thin Man from West Plains, Missouri, is a case of an artist often ahead of his time who has always appeared hopelessly behind the times. He's among the most immediately recognizable figures in country music, largely due to his exploiting TV—and flashy costumes—a good twenty years before the video boom. And while he's forever perceived as the man who tried to hold Dolly Parton back from pop success, he was also responsible, in many ways, for putting her in a career position where the issue could even arise. As for his music, since signing with RCA in 1952 he has produced a wealth of superb hard country, and just as much of the most wretchedly oversentimentalized tripe you'll ever want to hear. The latter, of course, is half the reason we love him. —*Dan Cooper*

○ **Satisfied Mind** / 1956 / RCA Victor 1358
A common vinyl sampling of Porter's raw-boned early sound. The title cut, from 1955, was his first Number 1 hit. It also has "Company's Comin'," in which Porter makes the arrival of dinner

guests sound as exciting in the current context as logging onto the Internet. —*Dan Cooper*

○ **The Thin Man from West Plains** / 1965 / RCA Victor 3389
Seems a little snooty, this otherwise exemplary four-CD box set. One can't help noticing that it cuts off at approximately the same time Porter was getting famous for hawking laxative on TV. —*Dan Cooper*

● **The Best of Porter Wagoner** / 1966 / RCA 61089
The Wagonmasters could drive hard as any backup band of the day, and this set shows it on cuts like "Y'all Come (You All Come)." Meanwhile, good ol' Porter could be as morbid as any singer of his day. Witness "Misery Loves Company," "Green, Green Grass of Home," and "Skid Row Joe." —*Dan Cooper*

○ **Confessions of a Broken Man** / 1966 / RCA Victor 3593
Not the coolest of the cool among you can hear the aformentioned "Skid Row Joe" without a lump rising in your throat to interrupt your laughter. —*Dan Cooper*

The Cold Hard Facts of Life / 1967 / RCA Victor 3797
Good, straight-ahead country is one reason to hunt for this LP. The other reason is the album cover—a near-consensus choice as the hillbilly graphics howler of all time. Write to your congressman to get this back in print as is. —*Dan Cooper*

● **Pure Gold** / 1991 / RCA 1991
This low budget-produced CD is the pick title until RCA sees fit to give Wagoner a legitimate reissue set. Actually, it's a pretty decent glimpse at the many moods of career-peak Porter. And yup, its got "Skid Row Joe." —*Dan Cooper*

Sweet Harmony / Pair 1013
Another poor budget excuse for a reissue. And again it's better than it appears. The 20 tracks will give you a pretty strong sense of the weird tension that drove the duo's work, and ultimately drove them apart. —*Dan Cooper*

Frank Wakefield

Mandolin / Instrumental bluegrass
One of the chief experimenters with the mandolin, Frank Wakefield played straight bluegrass with a number of well-known bands, including Red Allen and the Greenbriar Boys. Based in Saratoga Springs, NY, he remains one of the all-time innovators on the mandolin. —*David Vinopal*

Frank Wakefield / Flying Fish 049
Top-notch bluegrass with the Good Ol' Boys. —*Chip Renner*

● **Frank Wakefield with Country Cooking** / Rounder 0007
A fine bluegrass album. Wakefield is backed by Country Cooking, featuring Peter Wernick, Tony Trischka, Russ Barenberg, and Kenny Kosek. Hear them before they became known. —*Chip Renner*

○ **Pistol Packin' Mama** / Round 109
Wakefield and David Nelson (New Riders) give a more San Francisco sound to this album, with Jerry Garcia producing "Ashes of Love," "Dim Lights, Thick Smoke," and "Glendale Train." All excellent. —*Chip Renner*

Billy Walker

b. Jan. 14, 1929, Ralls, TX
A native of West Texas, active on the Grand Ole Opry to this day, Billy Walker emerged from the talent-rich Dallas scene of the late 1940s and early '50s. After a brief stint on Capitol, he was signed to Columbia in 1951 at almost exactly the same time as Ray Price. For awhile, Walker, Price, and Lefty Frizzell were all recording at the legendary Jim Beck studio in Dallas, which did for 1950s honky-tonk what the Sun Studio in Memphis did for rockabilly. Nevertheless, Walker enjoyed his greatest success ten years later in Nashville, where the studio sound was perhaps more suited to his smooth tenor voice. —*Dan Cooper*

○ **Billy Walker's Greatest Hits, Vol.II** / Columbia 9798
Noteworthy for "Cross the Brazos at Waco," Walker's 1964 quasi-sequal to Marty Robbins's "El Paso," and a terrific version of the Harlan Howard/Walker tune "Down To My Last Cigarette." —*Dan Cooper*

● **Billy Walker's Greatest Hits** / 1963 / Columbia 8735
Early '60s Nashville Sound, though always with Walker's voice agreeably front and center. Contains "Charlie's Shoes" and a 1961

take on Willie Nelson's "Funny How Time Slips Away." —*Dan Cooper*

○ **Cross the Brazos at Waco** / 1993 / Bear Family 15657
The usual exhaustive, prestigious, and expensive package (six CDs and a book) from Germany's Bear Family, the best roots music reissue company in the world. Covering the years 1949 to 1965, the set chronicles Walker's career from his initial, tentative Capitol cuts through his entire career on Columbia. —*Dan Cooper*

Greatest Hits on Monument / CBS 52963
Not Walker's most compelling material, but does include "A Milion to One," a Number 2 hit for him in 1966. —*Dan Cooper*

Jerry Jeff Walker (Paul Crosby)

b. Mar. 16, 1942, Oneonta, New York.
Vocals, guitar / Progressive country
Born Paul Crosby in upstate New York, Walker travelled the country in the '60s, playing folk music, and finally settled in Austin. In 1966 he formed Circus Maximus, a rock group. He went solo, writing "Mr. Bojangles," a song that hit the Top 10 for the Nitty Gritty Dirt Band in 1970. His good-natured approach to country-style music has created a loyal following. —*David Vinopal*

○ **Driftin' Way of Life** / 1969 / Vanguard 73124
A beautifully simple album of country-flavored original songs, mostly from the point of view of the sentimental roustabout. This great record sounds as though the players just went in, knocked it off, and hit the road. Classic. —*Richard Meyer*

○ **Jerry Jeff Walker** / 1972 / Decca 75384
Kind of folksy, featuring David Bromberg. —*Robert Gordon*

○ **Viva Terlingua** / 1973 / MCA 919
The Lost Gonzo spirit settles in. —*Robert Gordon*

● **Great Gonzos** / 1991 / MCA 10381
The best available compilation of Walker's material. —*AMG*

Monte Warden

A popular Austin, TX, singer since his teens, Warden was the lead vocalist for the Wagonners before striking out on his own. —*Brian Mansfield*

○ **Monte Warden** / 1993 / Watermelon 1015
Imagine finding a long-lost Buddy Holly album—not outtakes, but the real thing. Then start playing *Monte Warden* just about anywhere—"Don't Know a Thing," "It's Amazing," "All I Want Is You," or even the ballad "Just to Hear Your Voice." You won't feel let down. —*Brian Mansfield*

Steve Wariner

b. Dec. 25, 1954, KY
Vocals, bass, guitar / Contemporary country
One of country's most versatile performers, Wariner's gone seemingly unnoticed for each of his skills: as a vocalist, guitarist, and songwriter. Wariner grew up in suburban Indianapolis, interested in the Beatles on the radio, and Chet Atkins and George Jones, the artists his father listened to most frequently. He started playing music in his dad's band, and by his high school years, he was playing local clubs. At age 17, Wariner caught the ear of Dottie West, who persuaded him to join her band; in that position, he ended up playing bass on her classic "Country Sunshine." Wariner moved on to work as a sideman for Bob Luman and signed with RCA Records in 1976. His career developed slowly—he didn't put out an album until 1982—and in the beginning, the low-tuned guitars and wide range of his singles brought frequent comparisons to the early Glen Campbell hits. Gradually, Wariner took more personal direction in his recording career, and his albums became progressively more guitar-oriented as well as more adventurous musically and more insightful lyrically. —*Tom Roland*

● **Steve Wariner** / 1982 / RCA 5970
RCA waited until they had a veritable greatest-hits package before releasing Wariner's first album. Bright arrangements with lots of dovetailing instruments. And Wariner shows off a substantial vocal range. —*Tom Roland*

○ **It's a Crazy World** / 1987 / MCA 31299
Wariner's in charge vocally, and seems to glide through the album with no effort. He's received more responsibility for his own

direction, and—with one or two exceptions—has upgraded every aspect of his record, particularly in song selection and musicianship. —*Tom Roland*

Laredo / 1990 / MCA 42335
After nine years and nine Number 1 singles, Wariner had basically established himself as Mr. Consistency. *Laredo* proved, again, that he could sing any type of country well—swing ("L-O-V-E, Love"), rock ("The Domino Theory"), and heartbreak ballads conveying genuine pain ("She's in Love," "There for Awhile"). — *Brian Mansfield*

○ **I Am Ready** / 1991 / Arista 18691
Wariner, a master of the subtle touch, builds this album's impact quietly and methodically, with songs like Bill Anderson's "The Tips of My Fingers" and Wariner's own "Like a River to the Sea." "Leave Him out of This" is a masterpiece of smoldering intensity, its raging anger and pain barely held in check. The only time Wariner lets it loose is at the end, where he locks his guitar in mortal combat with Mark O'Connor's fiddle in the cathartic "Crash Course in the Blues." —*Brian Mansfield*

Doc Watson (Arthel Watson)

b. Mar. 2, 1923, Deep Gap, NC
Guitar, banjo, vocals / Old-time, traditional country
In this half of our century there have been three preeminently influential guitar players: Merle Travis, Chet Atkins, and Arthel "Doc" Watson, a flat-picking genius from Deep Gap, NC. Unlike the other two, Watson was in middle age before gaining any attention. Since 1960, though, when Watson was recorded with his family and friends in Folkways' *Old Time Music at Clarence Ashley's*, people have remained in awe of this gentle blind man who sings and picks with a pure and emotional authenticity. The present generation, folkies and country pickers alike, including Ricky Skaggs, Vince Gill, the late Clarence White, Emmylou Harris, and literally hundreds of others, acknowledge their great debt to Watson. Watson has provided a further service to country/folk by his encyclopedic knowledge of many American traditional songs. While Merle Travis and Chet Atkins started on acoustic guitars and moved to electric, during Watson's "discovery" during the folk revival in the early '60s, he played electric in a local all-purpose band that played current rock, swing, country, and of course folk music. He gained recognition gradually, first from the *Clarence Ashley* album, which led to a rave performance at the Newport Folk Festival in 1963. Folkways soon recorded an album of Watson, followed in 1964 by a series of albums by Vanguard, nearly one a year through the decade. No sooner had interest in folk music waned than Watson was back in great demand because of the three-disc *Will the Circle Be Unbroken*, a watershed album in 1972 that was created by the Nitty Gritty Dirt Band. It featured Watson, Merle Travis, Roy Acuff, and a who's-who of country greats. Watson's son, Merle, a talent in his own right, began appearing with him and they won two Grammys for traditional music, in 1973 and 1974. Father and son played beautiful music together for over 15 years, until Merle died on the family farm in 1985, the sad victim of a tractor accident.

Watson continues with his appearances, showcasing his beautiful voice, his great instrumental talent, and his mastery of traditional material. He is an American treasure. —*David Vinopal*

★ **The Doc Watson Family** / 1963 / Smithsonian/Folkways 40012
The most traditional performances of Watson and such family members as fiddler Gaither Carlton. This is as authentic as country music gets. —*Mark A. Humphrey & David Vinopal*

☆ **Doc Watson** / 1964 / Vanguard 79152
His first Vanguard album, ca. 1964. Warm vocals, influential guitar, harmonica, and old-time banjo. —*Mark A. Humphrey*

○ **Treasures Untold** / 1964 / Vanguard 77001
Newport Festival performances, including four guitar duets with Clarence White. —*Mark A. Humphrey*

☆ **Southbound** / 1966 / Vanguard 79213
Watson's second Vanguard album and the debut of son Merle on second guitar. —*Mark A. Humphrey*

Ballads from Deep Gap / 1967 / Vanguard 6576
Fine traditional songs, old ballads, and more. —*Mark A. Humphrey*

The Essential Doc Watson / 1974 / Vanguard 45-46
Fine '60s Newport Festival performances. —*Mark A. Humphrey*

Riding the Midnight Train / 1984 / Sugar Hill 3752
A bluegrass album with Nashville super-pickers Sam Bush, Mark O'Connor, and Bela Fleck. These are the last recordings of Merle Watson. —*Mark A. Humphrey*

○ **Watson Family Tradition** / Rounder 0129
Austere beauty, ancient ballads, and rough string-band sounds. Joining in are mother Annie Watson, wife Rosa Lee Watson, father-in-law Gaither Carlton, brother Arnold Watson, and son Merle Watson. The unpolished roots of Doc Watson. —*Mark A. Humphrey*

Gene Watson

b. Oct. 11, 1943, Palestine, TX
Vocals, guitar / Traditional country
Though he can sing honky-tonk, Gene Watson has made a reputation for soulful ballads in the classical country tradition. After working as an auto-body man, he finally had success with "Love in the Hot Afternoon," which as a single and as his debut album did well in 1975. His hits have been steady since then, with "Farewell Party," "Got No Reason Now for Going Home," "Nothing Sure Looked Good on You," and "Memories to Burn." Watson is a vocal stylist of considerable talent. —*David Vinopal*

● **Greatest Hits** / 1986 / Curb 77393
Solid collection of '70s hits by this unpretentious, terribly underrated country singer. The key track is "Farewell Party," a deceptive, near-trance-inducing honky-tonk number that delivers an emotional knockout at precisely the moment many country songs wimp out. —*Dan Cooper*

Back in the Fire / 1989 / Warner Brothers 25832
His comeback album, rife with Watson's trademark hard balladeering. —*Mark A. Humphrey*

Kevin Welch

Vocals / Country
This singer/songwriter from Oklahoma made his name as a writer of hits for the Judds, Ricky Skaggs, Gary Morris, Moe Bandy, Don Williams, and others before bringing the fully realized characters of his songs to his own recordings in 1990. Though based in Nashville, Welch's music claims kinship with the songwriting style of Texans like Joe Ely and Butch Hancock. — *Brian Mansfield*

● **Kevin Welch** / 1990 / Reprise 26171
Welch's songs sprawl out like great, open flatlands, mixing elements of folk, country, and rock in a captivating way. Welch himself—half-singing, half-speaking songs such as "Hello, I'm Gone" and "Some Kind of Paradise"—comes off as a cross between a renegade storyteller and a heartland romantic. —*Brian Mansfield*

Western Beat / 1991 / Reprise 26823
Contains "Sam's Town," "Same Old Rain," "Train to Birmingham," "Early Summer Rain," and other songs. —*AMG*

Kitty Wells (Muriel Deason)

b. Aug. 30, 1918, Nashville, TN
Vocals, guitar / Traditional country
One of the few country stars born in Nashville, Kitty Wells (born Muriel Deason) had a string of hits from the '50s to the early '70s that earned her the title "Queen of Country Music." She made her radio debut on Nashville's WSIX, where she met her future husband, Johnnie Wright of Johnnie and Jack. She began touring as part of Johnnie and Jack's show; Wright gave her the stage name, taken from a folk song called "I'm A-Goin' to Marry Kitty Wells." Wells recorded unsuccessfully for RCA before switching to Decca, where she hit with 1952's "It Wasn't God Who Made Honky Tonk Angels," a response to Hank Thompson's "The Wild Side of Life." Its controversial pre-feminist lyrics, which blamed unfaithful men for creating unfaithful women, paved the way for Loretta Lynn and Tammy Wynette and established Wells as the first major female country star. Wells recorded a number of answer songs and remakes, but she got top-notch original material as well, including some of Harlan Howard's earliest hits. She joined the Grand Ole Opry in 1952 and was elected to the Country Music Hall of Fame in 1976. —*Brian Mansfield*

★ **Country Music Hall of Fame Series** / 1991 / MCA 10081
This 16-track overview is hardly complete (Wells issued more than 400 singles for MCA between 1952 and 1973), but it's got the

essentials: "It Wasn't God Who Made Honky Tonk Angels," "I Can't Stop Loving You," "Heartbreak U.S.A.," etc., all sung with the thin Tennessee vibrato that made Wells famous. —*Brian Mansfield*

Dottie West

b. Oct. 11, 1932, McMinnville, TN, **d.** Sep. 4, 1991
Vocals, guitar / Country-pop
Dottie West had a successful career singing music that ranged from traditional to country-pop to TV commercials. "Here Comes My Baby" was a huge hit for her in 1964 and led to a Grammy. She appeared in movies, wrote more than 400 songs, made commercials, recorded hit duets with Jim Reeves, Don Gibson, and Kenny Rogers ("A Lesson in Leaving"), and was a country beauty queen. In 1991, while en route to the Opry, where she was a member of the regular cast, she was killed in an auto accident. For the two previous years, she had gone through personal bankruptcy and had seen her belongings auctioned off by the IRS. A happier end should have come to this veteran performer. She is missed. —*David Vinopal*

○ **A Legend in My Time** / 1971 / RCA 7043
Sparse instrumentation on a 1970 reissue of sad ballads: "Don't You Ever Get Tired of Hurting Me" and "There Goes My Everything." —*Bil Carpenter*

Special Delivery / 1979 / United Artists
With her career revitalized by the duets with Kenny Rogers, West takes a new tack. Her "Country Sunshine" is replaced with country-funk and a touch of melancholy. —*Tom Roland*

● **Greatest Hits** / 1992 / Capitol 77555

○ **Collector's Series** / RCA 7047
Features such songs as "Would You Hold It against Me," "Paper Mansions," and more. —*AMG*

Speedy West

b. 1924, MS
One of the greatest virtuosos that country music has ever produced, Speedy West bridged the western swing and rockabilly eras with eye-popping steel guitar. Besides contributing to literally thousands of country sessions, West cut many of his own instrumentals, as a solo act and with his guitarist partner Jimmy Bryant. Adept at boogie, blues, and Hawaiian ballads, West played with an infectious joy and daring improvisation that, at its most adventurous, could be downright experimental. It's doubtful whether anyone could collect all of Speedy's solos under one roof, but it was his sessions of the 1950s and early 1960s—especially those with Jimmy Bryant—that found his genius at its most freewheeling and dazzling. —*Richie Unterberger*

● **Two Guitars Country Style** / 1954 / Capitol 520

Joy Lynn White

Born in Arkansas, raised in Mishawaka, IN. White moved to Nashville at 19, playing clubs and singing on demos before getting her record contract. —*Brian Mansfield*

○ **Between Midnight & Hindsight** / Apr. 1992 / CBS 48806
White's rousing country-rockers singles "Little Tears" and the Marty Stuart-penned "True Confessions" didn't rip up the charts, but the accompanying videos and White's flaming red hair made her a cult favorite among those into pumped-up, hardcore honky-tonk. White's wild vibrato added intensity to her ballad weepers, too. —*Brian Mansfield*

● **Wild Love** / 1994 / Columbia
White added a middle name, but didn't change her sound much. On the Springsteenian rave-up "Wild Love," her hillbilly vibrato left the impression of passion about to spin out of control. Her version of the redneck-pride anthem "I Am Just a Rebel" (earlier recorded by Billy Hill, Dennis Robbins and Confederate Railroad) added toughness to her image (as though she needed it), and the likes of "Too Gone to Care" and "On and On and On" showed she could rock out even while singing hard country. —*Brian Mansfield*

Lari White

Who would've thought The Nashville Network's *You Can Be a Star* could discover such a talent? Florida-born Lari (pronounced "Laurie") White, a product of the University of Miami, won the

talent show in 1988. Turned out she was an incredibly expressive singer with a knack for acting (she appeared in a number of Nashville theater productions) and songwriting (she wrote or cowrote 80% of the songs on her first two albums). Rodney Crowell, for whom she toured in 1991, produced her debut. —*Brian Mansfield*

○ **Lead Me Not** / 1993 / RCA 66117
White's amibitious debut covered a lot of musical territory, from straight country ("Where the Lights Are Low") to torch ballad ("Just Thinking"), from Latin-flavored pop ("Made to Be Broken") to fervid gospel ("Good Good Love"). The breadth of her talent turned out to be something of a problem. Since nobody could get a handle on her, none of the album's three singles ("What a Woman Wants," "Lead Me Not," and "Lay Around and Love on You") broke the Top 40. —*Brian Mansfield*

● **Wishes** / Jun. 1994 / RCA 66395
Produced by Garth Fundis (Trisha Yearwood, Keith Whitley), *Wishes* focused White's abilities into something more palatable to the country mainstream. The first single, "That's My Baby," sounded like a companion piece to Yearwood's breakthrought "She's in Love With the Boy." But where Yearwood turned her back on those kind of small-town, teen-passion songs, White made a whole album of them. *Wishes* is filled with charm, playfulness, and nifty hooks, especially on a thrilling duet with Hal Ketchum, "That's How You Know." —*Brian Mansfield*

Keith Whitley

b. 1955, **d.** 1989
Vocals / Traditional country, progressive country
Keith Whitley and Ricky Skaggs started at the top in show business when, as teenagers, they went on the road with Ralph Stanley's bluegrass band. Whitley could sing pure country and honky-tonk. He lived the fast life and died young. Wife Lorrie Morgan and he sang together. "Till a Tear Becomes a Rose" was a posthumous creation, with Whitley's voice layered over Morgan's. —*David Vinopal*

○ **Hard Act to Follow** / 1984 / RCA 8525
A lighthearted album of honky tunes that revealed his talent but didn't exactly indulge in it. —*AMG*

L.A. to Miami / 1986 / RCA 5870
Whitley's first RCA and mainstream country album. Nice, but not as strong as his later work. —*Mark A. Humphrey*

Don't Close Your Eyes / 1988 / RCA 6494
More heartfelt. Artist and producer focus on good songs and piquant performances. —*Mark A. Humphrey*

★ **I Wonder Do You Think of Me** / 1989 / RCA 9809
Recorded shortly before his death, the bounty of drinking songs provides a morbid weight to a generally excellent collection. —*Mark A. Humphrey*

Greatest Hits / 1990 / RCA 2277
Whitley started singing bluegrass with Ralph Stanley, drew great inspiration from Lefty Frizzell and Merle Haggard, and developed an incomparably smooth, melismatic vocal style. The best balladeer of his generation. —*Mark A. Humphrey*

Kentucky Bluebird / 1991 / RCA 3156
A posthumous collection of previously unreleased performances. —*Mark A. Humphrey*

Slim Whitman (Otis Dewey Whitman Jr)

b. Jan. 20, 1924, Tampa, FL
Vocals, guitar / Easy listening, traditional country
Otis Dewey "Slim" Whitman became popular nationwide in the early '80s with his cable TV ads featuring his remarkable voice. Extraordinarily popular in England ("Rose Marie" was Number 1 for eight straight weeks in 1955), he specializes in slow, romantic songs showcasing his flexible voice that changes easily to falsetto. He may be the only contemporary yodeler who sells scads of records. —*David Vinopal*

● **The Best of Slim Whitman (1952—1972)** / 1990 / Rhino 70976

The Wilburn Brothers

Group / Traditional country
As members of the larger Wilburn Family group (mother, father, elder brothers, sister), 9-year-old Teddy (b. 1931) and 10-year-old

Doyle (b. 1930—d. 1982) appeared on the Opry in 1940; 13 years later, when they had grown up, they became part of the Opry's regular cast. With Jim and Jesse McReynolds and Bobby and Sonny Osborne, the Wilburns continue the tradition of brother duets in country music. Their wide choice of material is shown by the traditional "Knoxville Girl," a hit in 1959, and the more modern sound of "Hurt Her Once for Me" (1966). —*David Vinopal*

Carefree Moments / 1962 / VL 3691
Their sometimes slick "Nashville sound" recordings and tendency to double-track the vocals sometimes obscure the fact that these guys are one of the great brother duets in C&W. When they keep it straight, as in the rockabilly-esque "Cry Baby Cry," they can hold their own with anyone. —*George Bedard*

● **Retrospective** / MCA 25990
A nice overview of the Wilburn Brothers' smooth Decca hits of the '50s and '60s, featuring 12 songs. —*Mark A. Humphrey*

Don Williams

b. May 27, 1939, near Plainview, TX
Vocals, guitar / Traditional country
Known as the "gentle giant," Don Williams is known for the trademark rolled-brim hat that was a prop he used when appearing in *W. W. and the Dixie Dance Kings* (1975). His easygoing personality and laidback baritone vocals have produced many hits, among them "You're My Best Friend," "'Til the Rivers All Run Dry," "Amanda," "Some Broken Hearts Never Mend," and "I Believe in You," the last becoming a hit on the pop charts. His songs are among the prettiest and easiest-to-listen-to in country music. —*David Vinopal*

○ **Volume One** / 1972 / MCA 1474
Don Williams first album as a country singer was originally released on Cowboy Jack Clement's JMI label before being snapped up by ABC-Dot the following year. There were four hits on this record; not a small feat for any artist, much less on the first try. Over the years Williams has made some fine records but none better than this. —*Jim Worbois*

I Believe in You/Especially for You / 1981 / MCA 6941
Two early (1980-1981) collections for the price of one. Contains the gem "Lord, I Hope This Day Is Good." —*Hank Davis*

Prime Cuts / 1981 / Capitol 91444
Williams released four greatest-hits albums for MCA, so this is the fifth of his career. The R&B flavor of "Heartbeat in the Darkness" shakes up his approach. Much of the remainder is a thing of sparsely scored beauty. —*Tom Roland*

Cafe Carolina / 1984 / MCA
Williams has a very identifiable core sound, but occasional subtle differences can seem like major alterations. Here he recruits sax player Jim Horn, and while Horn doesn't play on every track, his mere presence provides a fresh change. —*Tom Roland*

● **20 Greatest Hits** / 1987 / MCA 5944
The best thing about Don Williams is that it's so hard to peg him against this, that or the other country music era. Hits like "Amanda," "You're My Best Friend," "I Believe in You," and "Good Ole Boys Like Me," all present in this collection, are so understated it's as if they float on top of Nashville history. —*Dan Cooper*

○ **Best of Don Williams, Vol. 2** / 1988 / MCA 31172
This album is so good, it will whet ones appetite for all the records from which these songs were taken. Williams has a laid back sound that no one has been able to imitate or copy. —*Jim Worbois*

Currents / 1992 / RCA 61128
Contains such hits as "Catfish Bates," "The Old Trail," "Too Much Water," and more. —*AMG*

Hank Williams (Hiriam King Williams, the Hillbilly Shakespeare)

b. Sep. 17, 1923, Mount Olive, AL, **d.** Jan. 1, 1953 , Oak Hill, WV
Vocals, guitar / Traditional country
It is impossible to overstate the importance of Hank Williams to country music. Incredibly, that statement is as true today as it was during the peak of his career more than 40 years ago. Both as a composer and a recording artist, Hank Williams has few peers. This is doubly impressive when one realizes that Williams was dead before his 30th birthday and his entire recording career

spanned barely 6 years. It is easy to lose sight of this in terms of the sheer number of "greatest hits" left in his wake. Virtually every noteworthy country artist for the past 40 years has recorded an album of Hank Williams songs, while tunes like "Your Cheatin' Heart" and "Cold Cold Heart" have frequently crossed musical boundaries and enriched the careers of distinctively non-hillbilly artists such as Tony Bennett and Ray Charles.

Hank Williams' music is noteworthy for the quality of his songs and the emotional intensity of his performances. Both are truly timeless. Throughout the years, owners of the Hank Williams catalog have subjected it to a variety of indignities, such as vocal and instrumental overdubbing, to tart up the recordings for the marketplace. Undoubtedly, Williams' records work best just as they were made, which, after many years, is how they are again being released. It is perhaps in his midnight home recordings, which feature only vocal and acoustic guitar, that one best hears the harrowing emotional intensity of his work. Williams came by it honestly. His short life was filled with physical pain, substance abuse, and enough backwoods pathos to fuel a dozen TV movies.

There is perhaps no greater indication of Hank Williams' appeal to new audiences than that virtually every song he recorded remains in Polygram's active catalog. The label continues to spend as much time repackaging and promoting his music as it does their hottest country acts, whose names will be lost in the mists of time while the Hank Williams catalog is being transferred to DAT, or whatever technology changes the 21st century brings. —*Hank Davis*

★ **40 Greatest Hits** / 1978 / PolyGram 821233
The ideal starting place; the title says it all. —*Hank Davis*

○ **Lovesick Blues** / 1985 / PolyGram 825551
Volume two of the chronological series features "Lovesick Blues," the song that made Hank a superstar. —*Dan Cooper*

On the Air / 1985 / PolyGram 827531
Collectors only. Radio show performances 1949-1952. —*Hank Davis*

☆ **I Ain't Got Nothin' But Time (12/46-4/47)** / 1986 / PolyGram 825548
In 1985, after years of cheesy overdubs and haphazard hits compilations, Polydor, with the aid of Colin Escott and Hank Davis, made a commitment to present Hank's music in its original form and in chronological order. The result was an eight-volume series, each volume of which includes a mixed bag of hit singles, outtakes, demos and/or radio transcriptions. If the Hillbilly Shakespeare has worked his way into your blood, you'll want all eight volumes. If you're content with the performances that made him famous, this and the seven companion pieces will probably seem like overkill. In any case, this first volume includes "Honky Tonkin'" and "Move It On Over," and a spooky gospel number called the "Battle of Armageddon." —*Dan Cooper*

The First Recordings / 1986 / Country Music Foundation 007
The underside of the Hank Williams legend. An eye-opener, but get to know the hits first. —*Hank Davis*

☆ **I'm So Lonesome I Could Cry, Vol. 4 (3/49-8/49)** / 1986 / PolyGram 825557
By this point, Hank's revealing the fissures in his soul through songs like "I'm So Lonesome I Could Cry," "I Just don't Like this Kind of Living," and a chilling demo number called "We're Getting Closer to the Grave Each Day." —*Dan Cooper*

○ **Lost Highway (12/48-3/49)** / 1986 / PolyGram 825554
The third in this series, with his 1948-1949 material. —*Hank Davis*

○ **Hey, Good Lookin' (12/50-7/51)** / 1987 / PolyGram 831634
Volume six, 1950-51. —*Hank Davis*

☆ **I Won't Be Home No More (6/52-9/52), Vol. 8** / 1987 / PolyGram 833752
The last volume in the chronological series is almost painfully poignant in its sense of desolation. It includes "Take These Chains From My Heart," "You Win Again," and "Your Cheatin' Heart." —*Dan Cooper*

○ **Let's Turn Back the Years** / 1987 / PolyGram 833749
Volume seven, 1951-52. —*Hank Davis*

○ **Long Gone Lonesome Blues** / 1987 / PolyGram 833633
Volume five, 1949-50 —*Hank Davis*

○ **Rare Demos—First to Last** / 1990 / Country Music Foundation 67
This CD features 24 publisher's demo recordings containing Williams's earliest performances originally released on *The First Recordings* and *Just Me and My Guitar*. —*AMG*

☆ **Original Singles Collection ... Plus** / 1992 / PolyGram 847194
A three-CD collection of all original singles as issued during his lifetime. Plus an undubbed solo version of "Tears in My Beer" without Hank Williams, Jr's voice. —*Hank Davis*

○ **Health & Happiness Shows** / PolyGram 517862
An exceptional two-disc set of eight radio performances from the late 40s. —*AMG*

Hank Williams, Jr. (Randall Hank Williams)

b. May 26, 1949, Shreveport, LA
Vocals, guitar / Traditional country, country-rock
Hank Williams, Jr's 1966 recording of "Standing in the Shadows (Of a Very Famous Man)" told us how tough it is to be the son of country music's greatest legend. Up to this point, this enormous talent in his own right had made something of a career doing his father's old songs, and doing them well. When in the mid '70s he embarked on his own musical journey, with his own sound of country, country/rock, and rockabilly, he attracted a following that would have astonished even his famous father.

In 1975 he left Nashville for Alabama to prepare the *Hank Williams, Jr. and Friends* album, the first of his unique Southern-rock albums. In spite of a terrible climbing accident in Montana, Williams went on to bigger and more frequent hits. When "My Rowdy Friends" reached Number 1 in 1981, it was his sixth chart-topper.

In the late '80s he was the biggest draw of any country music star or act, packing them in coast to coast, to the degree that he had eight albums on the *Billboard* charts simultaneously. Like his father, Williams is a cult figure, enjoying the limelight created by his own talent and opening for Monday Night Football over the past three years. —*David Vinopal*

☆ **Hank Williams, Jr. & Friends** / 1975 / PolyGram 831575
The breakthrough record of Williams's career. On his first mature record (made in his mid '20s), Williams teamed with Southern rockers Charlie Daniels, Toy Caldwell (Marshall Tucker Band), and Chuck Leavell (Allman Brothers Band), among others, for a session that opened his musical vistas to folk, blues, and rock, and incidentally introduced his mature persona in songs like "Stoned at the Jukebox" and "Living Proof." —*William Ruhlmann*

○ **14 Greatest Hits** / 1976 / PolyGram 825091
Williams was a good, if conventional, country singer during the early years covered in this anthology (1966-1974). It includes 11 of his first 12 Top 10 hits, among them the Number 1s "Eleven Roses" and "All for the Love of Someone." —*William Ruhlmann*

Family Tradition / 1979 / Warner Brothers 194
Williams returned to the upper reaches of the country charts with this album, his "outlaw" image, and songs like the title track, a Number 4 hit. —*William Ruhlmann*

Rowdy / 1981 / Warner Brothers 330
In 1981, Hank Williams, Jr. was one of the hottest acts in country music, starting the year with this album, which spawned the Number 1 hits "Texas Women" and "Dixie on My Mind" and the striking "Are You Sure Hank Done It This Way." —*William Ruhlmann*

★ **Hank Williams, Jr.'s Greatest Hits** / 1982 / Warner Brothers 60193
The biggest hits of Hank Williams, Jr., 1979-1982, are among the best country music of the time: hard, tough, and (in the manner of one of country's great eccentrics) weird. —*William Ruhlmann*

Major Moves / 1984 / Warner Brothers 25088
Williams topped the country charts with this album, largely on the strength of the raucous "All My Rowdy Friends Are Coming over Tonight," though the title track and the caustic "Attitude Adjustment" were also hits. —*William Ruhlmann*

○ **Greatest Hits, Vol. 2** / 1985 / Warner Brothers 25328
A well-chosen hits collection covering 1983 to 1985, including "Leave Them Boys Alone" and "All My Rowdy Friends Are Coming Over Tonight." —*William Ruhlmann*

○ **Greatest Hits, Vol. 3** / 1989 / Warner Brothers 25834

This chronicles Williams's ongoing '80s success, 1985-1989, featuring the Number 1 hits "I'm for Love," "Ain't Misbehavin'," "Mind Your Own Business," and "Born to Boogie." —*William Ruhlmann*

America (the Way I See It) / 1990 / Warner Brothers 26453
Williams plays political commentator on this, a collection of his best revenge fantasies, reasons for America's problems, and the theme from Monday Night Football. Includes the survivalist anthem "A Country Boy Can Survive" and "Don't Give Us a Reason," an open letter to Saddam Hussein. —*Brian Mansfield*

Lone Wolf / 1990 / Warner Brothers 26090
Features "Man to Man," "Big Mamou," and other hits. —*AMG*

Maverick / Oct. 1991 / Capricorn 26806
Williams' first album for the revived Capricorn label rocks harder than usual, even while he's evangelizing for country music. A good chuck of *Maverick* sounds like a cross between a roaring drunk and a *Penthouse* letter. There's also a great ghost story ("Cut Bank, Montana") and a really dumb novelty song ("Fax Me a Beer"). There's probably not a soul on earth who could pull off "Come on Over to the Country" but Hank—it's corny and obvious about everything country music wishes it was. But every time the slide guitar kicks in, he makes it all come true. —*Brian Mansfield*

○ **The Bocephus Box: Hank Williams, Jr. Collection '79-'92** / 1992 / Capricorn 45104
A boxed set covering much the same turf as the Warner Brothers greatest hits volumes, though with additional outtakes and live cuts for the completist to enjoy. —*Dan Cooper*

○ **The Best of Hank Williams, Jr. Vol. 1—Roots & Branches** / Aug. 4, 1992 / Mercury 849575
The title is a bit of a ringer here, as these are the songs Hank, Jr. charted with through the mid '60s to mid '70s, before his reincarnation as Bocephus, the outlaw country rocker, brought him mega-success. However, this 20-track compilation makes for interesting listening to hear how he evolved to his present style. —*Cub Koda*

Kelly Willis

Vocals / Progressive country
Virginia-born singer who ran off with her boyfriend when she was a teenager to start a band in Texas. Signed to MCA in 1990 on the recommendation of Nanci Griffith, Willis charmed male country fans looking for a female singer who knew how to rock. She appeared in the 1992 Tim Robbins film *Bob Roberts*. —*Brian Mansfield*

Well Travelled Love / 1990 / MCA 6390
On her debut, this Austin country-rocker sings Texas-steel tunes and roisterous rockers with spirited assurance, but there's a natural tremble in her voice that makes her sound dangerous yet vulnerable. Willis is one of the few country singers with the disarming beauty to become a true sex symbol, and if she's the feminine response to all the hat acts, that's fine. —*Brian Mansfield*

● **Bang Bang** / 1991 / MCA 10141
Willis' idea of country comes from female rockabillys like Janis Martin and Wanda Jackson and from the blues-influenced Texas crowd she runs with in Austin. *Bang Bang* reflects that influence in the blistering tempos of "Too Much to Ask" and "Standing by the River," the Tex-Mex groove of "The Heart that Love Forgot," and an absolutely incendiary version of Joe Ely's "Settle for Love." —*Brian Mansfield*

○ **Kelly Willis** / MCA
Where Willis first two albums occasionally turned into showcases for her musicians, *Kelly Willis* emphasizes concise, twangy pop songs over barn-burners. Willis sings a mandolin-propelled cover of Marshall Crenshaw's "Whatever Way the Wind Blows" and blends her voice with two members of Jellyfish on "One More Night." She also dips into Nashville back catalog with a version of the Kendalls' 1977 "Heaven's Just a Sin Away." —*Brian Mansfield*

Bob Wills & His Texas Playboys (James Robert Wills)

b. Mar. 6, 1905, Kosse, TX, d. May 13, 1975
Group / Western swing
While he may not have invented Western swing (Milton Brown, Leon Selph, Ted Daffan, and Bill Boyd deserve some credit), Bob Wills defined the genre. Take fiddle-based old-time string-band music from the '20s and '30s, move it to a city such as Tulsa or Ft.

Worth, add jazz and blues and pop and sacred music, back it with strings and horns played by a dozen or so musicians, add an electric steel guitar along the way, and you have Western swing; and when you talk Western swing, you start with Bob Wills. Though the sound began in the '30s, the '40s were its heyday, with Bob Wills and his Texas Playboys filling dancehalls across the South. Wills picked his musicians carefully: bluesy crooner Tommy Duncan was the vocal lead, Leon McAuliffe played electric steel guitar (doing much to popularize it country-wide), and the great Eldon Shamblin played lead guitar. Wills, a fiddler himself, always featured one or two of the hottest around, including the incredible Johnny Gimble. One of country's best-known songs, "San Antonio Rose," was written by Wills and sold a million in 1940.

Wills and his Texas Playboys sold so well that they appeared in eight movies, Westerns in which the solitary singing cowboy was replaced by a hot-playing swing band. Superstardom was brief. The mania for Western swing ended by the '50s, and though Wills played dates (including Las Vegas) right through the '60s, and recorded occasionally, the heights of the '40s were never again reached.

In 1973, Wills called together a group of his best Playboys (plus Merle Haggard, one of his greatest fans) for one last recording session. In a wheelchair, Wills was present for the first day only—he suffered a stroke and never regaining consciousness. This final album was titled *For the Last Time*. —*David Vinopal*

For the Last Time / 1974 / United Artists 216
Wills and the Texas Playboys reunited for the last swinging session of Wills's life. Sitting in on fiddle and vocals is one of Bob's biggest fans: Merle Haggard. —*Dan Cooper*

○ **Tiffany Transcriptions, Vol.5** / 1986 / Kaleidoscope 25
★ **Tiffany Transcriptions, Vol. 2** / Sep. 1986 / Kaleidoscope 19
○ **Tiffany Transcriptions, Vol. 3** / Sep. 1986 / Kaleidoscope 20
○ **Tiffany Transcriptions, Vol.4** / Sep. 1986 / Kaleidoscope 21
☆ **Tiffany Transcriptions, Vol.6: Sally Goodin'** / 1987 / Kaleidoscope 27
The bluesy stuff is here. It's a good place to start with this series for an understanding of their range. —*Mark A. Humphrey*

○ **Tiffany Transcriptions, Vol.7: Keep Knockin'** / 1987 / Kaleidoscope 29
○ **Tiffany Transcriptions, Vol.8: More of the Best** / 1988 / Kaleidoscope 32
○ **Tiffany Transcriptions, Vol.9: 1946-47** / 1991 / Kaleidoscope 35
★ **Anthology (1935-1973)** / 1991 / Rhino 70744
A good overview of several decades of Wills's music. —*Mark A. Humphrey*

○ **Country Music Hall of Fame Series** / 1992 / MCA 10547
This set contains Western swing recordings made by Wills 1955-1967, including such hits as "With Tears in My Eyes," "Cornball Rag," "Texas Two Step," and many more. —*AMG*

○ **Longhorn Recordings** / 1993 / Bear Family 15689
Mid 1960s Dallas sessions featuring Wills in both large band and small rootsy combo settings. —*Dan Cooper*

★ **Anthology** / Sony 32416
These 24 essential songs from the '30s and '40s, in chronological order, show the evolution of one of American pop's most eclectic and adventuresome dancebands, the Texas Playboys. A cornerstone of any inclusive pop collection. —*Mark A. Humphrey*

Fiddle / Country Music Foundation 010
A fascinating document of a range of fiddle styles, from Celtic-inspired "frontier" tunes to the genuinely swingin' stuff. —*Mark A. Humphrey*

☆ **Tiffany Transcriptions, Vol. 1** / Kaleidoscope 16
A series of radio transcriptions from post-WWII San Francisco. Looser than their studio recordings and presenting the hottest-ever Playboys in full gallop. All volumes of this series are uniformly excellent. Wills enthusiasts will want them all. —*Mark A. Humphrey*

Johnnie Lee Wills

b. 1912, Texas, **d.** 1984
Banjo / Western swing
Johnnie Lee Wills was younger brother to legendary Bob Wills and a member of the original Texas Playboys, the most famous Western swing band in history. Wills was a talent in his own right, playing tenor banjo in the Light Crust Doughboys, which became the Playboys and finally the Texas Playboys. When business was good, Bob Wills started a satellite band called Johnnie Lee Wills and his Boys. They had two hits, "Rag Mop" and "Peter Cottontail." And when business got bad, Johnnie Lee Wills retired and operated Tulsa's Stampede as well as a popular Western clothing shop. —*David Vinopal*

○ **Reunion** / 1978 / Flying Fish 069
Bob Wills' brother remained in Tulsa in the '30s and led a band that became a training ground for dozens of Western swing sidemen; many of the best are reunited here, in what were to be Wills' last recordings. —*Charles S. Wolfe*

Curtis Wright

Pennsylvania native Curtis Wright was a member of the Super Grit Cowboy Band and sang backup for Vern Gosdin, but he probably made more money as the writer of hits like Shenandoah's "Next to You, Next to Me" and "Rock My Baby." He and frequent co-writer Robert Ellis Orrall formed Orrall & Wright duo in 1994. —*Brian Mansfield*

○ **Curtis Wright** / Jul. 6, 1992 / Liberty 97825
Wright's singles, the utterly charming "Hometown Radio" and "If I Could Stop Lovin' You," hardly dented the charts, but his only solo album did get heard: Clay Walker turned "What's It to You" into a number-one hit in 1993, and Daron Norwood recorded "Phonographic Memory" and "If I Ever Love Again." —*Brian Mansfield*

Michelle Wright

b. Jul. 1, 1961
Vocals / Country
A native of Ontario, Canada, Michelle Wright grew up listening to the sounds of '60s soul from nearby Detroit radio stations. Both her parents were country musicians. and Wright followed in their footsteps as a teenager. A major star in Canada (she replaced k.d. Lang as the nation's favorite native female country singer), she has yet to rise to those heights in the United States. —*Brian Mansfield*

● **Michelle Wright** / 1990 / Arista 8627
With her husky, cigarette-deep voice, Wright sounds like nothing so much as a young Lacy J. Dalton on her American debut. There's some straight country here ("The Dust Ain't Settled Yet"), but more often than not, Wright's singing R&B material with steel guitars. Not only does she sing the stuff, she knows how: Drop her voice two octaves on "Not Enough Love to Go 'Round," and she's Barry White. —*Brian Mansfield*

Now & Then / 1992 / Arista 18685
Wright made a mainstream move with *Now & Then*, downplaying the R&B and remaking herself as a sleek, sultry version of Lorrie Morgan. It paid off, too: She had her first real hits in the US with "Take It Like a Man" and "He Would Be 16," a tear-jerking ballad dealing with the regrets of giving an illegitimate child up for adoption. Her Nudie jackets and black bodysuits made her a video favorite, too. The music's not as distinctive here as on *Michelle Wright*, but the hits hold up nicely. —*Brian Mansfield*

Tammy Wynette (Virginia Wynette Pugh)

b. May 5, 1942, Tupelo, MS
Vocals, guitar / Traditional country
One of the major voices in country history, Tammy Wynette has had 11 Number 1 albums and 35 Number 1 singles (21 in a row) in a career that has produced at least two country standards: "Stand by Your Man" and "D-I-V-O-R-C-E," both from 1968. She and the great Loretta Lynn alternated in the '60s and early '70s as country music's most popular female singer. Along the way Wynette married George Jones, the singer's singer, resulting in duets as great as have been sung, including "We're Gonna Hold On," "Near You," and "Golden Ring." In spite of these song titles, Mr. and Mrs. Country Music labored through a turbulent relationship, beautiful harmony coming in the songs only, and were divorced in 1975. (A 1982 film, *Stand by Your Man*, tells of Wynette's heartaches.) Wynette remains in demand: she appears on a 1991 album by the British techno duo KLF. Her exceptional voice is as good as it's ever been. —*David Vinopal*

○ **Your Good Girl's Gonna Go Bad** / 1967 / Epic 26305
Her unmatched first album proves why she's the greatest female C&W "heart" singer. —*George Bedard*

★ **Greatest Hits** / 1969 / Epic 26486
Follows Wynette's trail of tears right out of the chutes on classics like "Stand By Your Man" and "D-I-V-O-R-C-E." Producer Billy Sherrill's less-than-light touch never found a better instrument to work with than Tammy's voice. —*Dan Cooper*

Kids Say the Darndest Things / 1973 / Epic 31937
Wynette and Sherrill join forces for a concept album. Includes "Listen, Spot," "My Daddy Doll," "Buy Me a Daddy," and "Too Many Daddies." Sound funny? It is. Except "Too Many Daddies" will still rip your heart out. —*Dan Cooper*

Greatest Hits, Vol. 3 / 1975 / CBS 33396
The best reason to include this package is to simply say that one greatest-hits album from Wynette just isn't enough. The lyrical and musical themes here are much the same as in the first package, but the quiet determination of "'Til I Get It Right" and the pure celebration of "My Man (Understands)" help broaden the picture of Wynette just a little. —*Tom Roland*

★ **Anniversary: 20 Years of Hits** / 1987 / Epic 40625
"Stand By Your Man" and "D-I-V-O-R-C-E" speak for themselves. But not to be overlooked are the less honored likes of "Apartment #9," her debut hit, written by Johnny Paycheck; and "Your Good Girl's Gonna Go Bad," in which Tammy's freedom (instead of little J-O-E's tears) are at stake. Also includes three duets with George Jones. —*Dan Cooper*

Trisha Yearwood

Vocals / Contemporary country
One of the first artists to benefit by association with Garth Brooks, not that she wouldn't have made it on her own. The product of Monticello, GA, Yearwood came to Nashville to study the music business at a local university before graduating to record-company receptionist, demo singer, and backup singer (for Brooks, among others). Her first single, "She's in Love With the Boy," went straight to Number 1, and she's hardly slowed down since. Frequently evokes comparisons to Linda Ronstadt for her singing style and choice of material. —*Brian Mansfield*

○ **Trisha Yearwood** / 1991 / MCA 10297
An impressive debut that brought everybody to lend a hand: Vince Gill, Mac McAnally, keyboardist Al Kooper, and others. Garth Brooks cowrote two songs and helped sing one, the tentatively tender "Like We Never Had a Broken Heart." Yearwood's more at home with blue-collar romance than sweltering Texas nightlife, but her big Georgia range lets her sing just about anything, from the ballad "When Goodbye Was a Word" to Pat McLaughlin's saucy "That's What I Like About You." —*Brian Mansfield*

★ **Hearts in Armor** / Sep. 1, 1992 / MCA 10641
Take away the bluesy hit "Wrong Side of Memphis," and this is practically an emotional diary of Yearwood's divorce (which happened just as she hit the big time). In light of that event, "Nearest Distant Shore" and "Hearts in Armor" assume devastating significance and the cover of Emmylou Harris's "Woman Walk the Line" couldn't be more appropriate. As before, she's got the big-name backup singers—Harris, Don Henley, Vince Gill, and Garth Brooks—but not one steals the spotlight. *Hearts in Armor* is strictly Yearwood's show, and she's marvelous in it. —*Brian Mansfield*

Dwight Yoakam

b. 1956, Pikeville, KY
Vocals, guitar / Traditional country, country-rock
His highly successful debut album, *Guitars, Cadillacs, Etc., Etc.,* a re-packaging (with four new cuts) of a 1984 Oak album, showed the listening public that somebody different had arrived. Outspoken and self-assured, Yoakam mixes country oldies ("Ring of Fire" and a reprise of Johnny Horton's "Honky Tonk Man," his first Top 10 single) with his own country/rock and hard-country compositions. Platinums and golds and numerous chart-toppers later, he's still marching to his own drum while paying respect to his heroes along the way. He and Buck Owens collaborated on "Streets of Bakersfield," a song that gives you an accurate sense of what Dwight Yoakam's all about. —*David Vinopal*

○ **Guitars, Cadillacs, Etc., Etc.** / 1986 / Reprise 25372
Who would have guessed when this album was released, with its uncompromisingly basic, honky-tonk approach, that it would not only be a success but would help move the country music industry back from its crossover ways of the early '80s to a new renaissance based on its most traditional sounds? Maybe Yoakam, who doggedly stuck to that approach and wrote a bunch of songs that fit in with covers like Johnny Horton's "Honky Tonk Man." —*William Ruhlmann*

Hillbilly Deluxe / 1987 / Reprise 25567

○ **Buenos Noches from a Lonely Room** / 1988 / Reprise 25749
The first five cuts constituted a cold-blooded cycle that ran from possessive love to murderous rage with alarming quickness. The rest was subsequently a letdown but still gave Yoakam a couple of big hits in "I Sang Dixie" and "Streets of Bakersfield," a duet with Buck Owens. —*Brian Mansfield*

★ **Just Lookin' for a Hit** / 1989 / Reprise 25989
A strong singles collection with a typically sarcastic title, paced by duets with K.D. Lang on Gram Parsons' "Sin City" and with Buck Owens (a match made in heaven) on "Streets of Bakersfield." —*William Ruhlmann*

☆ **If There Was a Way** / 1990 / Reprise 26344
Yoakam's strongest studio album to date, with 14 songs (Nashville's standard is 10). Includes the classic Yoakam/Roger Miller collaboration "It Only Hurts When I Cry." —*Brian Mansfield*

○ **La Croix D`Amour** / 1992 / Reprise 45136
An international-only compilation, *La Crois D'Amour* is worth searching out for its rarities: two songs that appeared on other collections (Elvis Presley's "Suspicious Minds" and the Grateful Dead's "Truckin'") and four new tracks, among them covers of the Beatles' "Things We Said Today" and Them's "Here Comes the Night." —*Brian Mansfield*

☆ **This Time** / 1993 / Warner Brothers 45241
Heartbroke fool that he is, Dwight Yoakam knows all the words for loneliness. He doesn't let up once he starts on the self-pity binge of *This Time:* He begins as the devastated lover and winds up 11 songs later the desolate loner. A musical traditionalist, he knows all the styles, too, from Buck Owens' Bakersfield country ("This Time") to Gene Pitney's mini-soundtracks ("A Thousand Miles from Nowhere") to rock's spite fantasies ("Fast as You"). He knows so many that *This Time* sounds more like a collection of individual songs that the single-minded work that it is. He understands them, too—that's why Yoakam gets good mileage out of campy gimmicks like the ooh-wah background vocals on "Pocket of a Clown." There's plenty of hardcore country here ("This Time," "Home for Sale," "Lonesome Road") but the best stuff allows for Yoakam's pop roots, too. —*Brian Mansfield*

Faron Young

b. Feb. 25, 1932, Shreveport, LA
Vocals, guitar / Traditional country
Faron Young is versatile. In his younger days known as "the Hillbilly Heart-throb," he has managed to remain in the public eye for nearly 40 years, due to his musical talent, his entertaining personality, his numerous TV appearances (especially on Ralph Emery's "Nashville Now" show), and his many side interests, which have included movie acting and publishing. Young began *Music City News*, country music's dominant monthly magazine.

In 1951 Young signed with Capitol, and because of two quick hits ("Have I Waited Too Long" and "Tattle Tale Eyes") he became an Opry regular within the year. The next two years he spent in the army, entertaining the troops at home and abroad. His first major success came with "I've Got Five Dollars and It's Saturday Night" (1956), rounding out the '50s with "Sweet Dreams" and "Country Girl" (1959). In 1961 "Hello Walls," a Willie Nelson composition, became Young's best-known hit. He continued to sell well, singles and albums alike, through the '60s and '70s, with "Wine Me Up," "Another You," and "Crutches."

Young's strong, clear voice has been a perfect vehicle for his upbeat, let's-have-some-fun material. He's in the same league as Jimmy Dean in wit, candor, and downright entertainment as a guest on TV talk shows. The audience gets the feeling that in his life Young has followed the suggestion of "Live Fast, Love Hard, and Die Young" (a 1955 hit for him), except for the dying part, though no doubt he'd come up with some pun about even that, too. —*David Vinopal*

★ **All-Time Greatest Hits** / 1990 / Curb 77334
Although it's way too brief with only ten tracks, there's no better availble Faron Young collection than *All-Time Greatest Hits*, which features his absolute biggest hits. —*AMG*

○ **The Classic Years 1952-62** / Bear Family 15493
Swashbuckling Louisiana honky-tonk, much of Faron Young's early work on Capitol is marked by an undertone of grinning lasciviousness. That's not a bad thing, given how many of his industry pals completely hid their wolfishness behind apple pie lyrics. In any case, Bear Family has here collected the entirety of Young's Capitol output on five CDs. Besides the swaggering stuff ("If You Ain't Lovin'," "Live Fast, Love Hard, Die Young," and the amazing "Alone With You") one can hear the hit version of "Sweet Dreams" he cut seven years before Patsy Cline's. Comes with a beautiful 48-page book. —*Dan Cooper*

Steve Young

b. Jul. 12, 1942, Georgia
Vocals, guitar / Progressive country, contemporary country
Alabama-raised singer/songwriter Young is best known as the writer of "Seven Bridges Road," a pop success for the Eagles in 1980. Since his acclaimed 1972 A&M debut, *Rock Salt & Nails*, Young has recorded a meager handful of albums, which garnered him cult status (Waylon Jennings called him "the second-best country singer, after George Jones"). "Lonesome, On'ry, and Mean" was the title track of a 1973 Waylon Jennings album, and writer Young was one of the leading poetic spirits of the "outlaw" alternative folk/country movement of the '70s. —*Mark A. Humphrey*

Seven Bridges Road / 1972 / Rounder 3058
The title tune is this folkie's best work. —*Hank Davis*

Honky Tonk Man / 1975 / Rounder 3087
Early sides by this Colorado folkie, surrounded by stellar, largely acoustic backing. A good album—a four-year layoff helped him hone his trade. —*Hank Davis & Chip Renner*

○ **Renegade Picker** / 1976 / RCA 11759
A very good album featuring Tracy Nelson, Johnny Gimble, and Buddy Emmons. Features his hit "Tobacco Road." —*Chip Renner*

○ **No Place to Fall** / 1977 / RCA 12510
Critically acclaimed album—this one and *Renegade Picker* were forerunners of the progressive country movement. —*Chip Renner*

● **Solo/live** / Mar. 1991 / Watermelon 1004
Passionate singer-songwriter Steve Young is known in acoustic circles for penning "Seven Bridges Road", a song included on his Watermelon debut *Solo/Live*. —*Roch Parisien*

Country Collections

Sixteen Country Hits from the 1940s /
Features the "Tennessee Waltz" and other traditional favorites. —*AMG*

20 Great Truck-Driving Songs /
Features such artists as Convoy, Duanne Eddy, the Wills Brothers, and others. —*AMG*

● **25 Years of Studio B Hits** / 1982 / CMF 001
Features Waylon Jennings's "Honky Tonk Heroes," Dolly Parton's "The Seeker," and other hits recorded at the recording studio that saw the emergence of the Nashville sound. —*AMG*

○ **60 Years of Grand Ole Opry** / 1986 / RCA 9507
A carefully selected collection of vintage RCA cuts by many key Opry stars from 1928 to the present. —*Charles S. Wolfe*

Are You from Dixie?—Great Country Brother Teams of the 1930s / RCA 8417
This contains 18 classic tracks from such legendary country brother groups as the Delmore Brothers, the Monroe Brothers, the Blue Sky Boys, and more. Good sound, considering the age of the recordings. —*AMG*

Best of Texas Country Music /
This album includes such artists as George Jones, Jeannie C. Riley, Cowboy Copas, Billy Walker, and Tex Ritter. —*AMG*

Best of Today's Country Love Songs / Capitol 4XL58997
Features Marie Osmond & Dan Seals' "Meet Me in Montana," Michael Martin Murphy's "What's Forever For," T. Graham Brown's "Hell and High Water," and others. —*AMG*

● **Best of the West** / Rounder 11517

○ **Billboard Top Country Hits: 1989** / 1989 / Rhino 70693

○ **Billboard Top Country Hits: 1959** / 1990 / Rhino 70680
Each volume of this series contains the Top 10 country hits of that year. This volume contains Johnny Cash's "Don't Take Your Love to Town," George Jones's "White Lightning," Johnny Horton's "The Battle of New Orleans," and more. —*AMG*

○ **Billboard Top Country Hits: 1960** / 1990 / Rhino 70681
Features Jim Reeves's "He'll Have to Go," Marty Robbins's "El Paso," Hank Locklin's "Please Help Me, I'm Falling," and other hits. —*AMG*

○ **Billboard Top Country Hits: 1961** / 1990 / Rhino 70682
Features Patsy Cline's "I Fall to Pieces," Jimmy Dean's "Big Bad John," and other Top 10 hits from 1961. —*AMG*

○ **Billboard Top Country Hits: 1962** / 1990 / Rhino 70683
Features Patsy Cline's "She's Got You," Hank Snow's "I've Been Everywhere," Claude King's "Wolverton Mountain," and other top hits from 1962. —*AMG*

○ **Billboard Top Country Hits: 1963** / 1990 / Rhino 70684
Includes Johnny Cash's "Ring of Fire," Buck Owens's "Act Naturally," and Ned Miller's "From a Jack to a King," among other early '60s favorites. —*AMG*

○ **Billboard Top Country Hits: 1964** / 1990 / Rhino 70685
This volume in the series includes George Jones's "The Race Is On" and Roger Miller's "Dang Me," among other hits. —*AMG*

○ **Billboard Top Country Hits: 1965** / 1990 / Rhino 70686
Features Eddy Arnold's "Make the World Go Away" and Roger Miller's "King of the Road." —*AMG*

○ **Billboard Top Country Hits: 1966** / 1990 / Rhino 70687
This volume includes David Houston's "Almost Persuaded," Loretta Lynn's "You Ain't Woman Enough," and Jack Greene's "There Goes My Everything." —*AMG*

○ **Billboard Top Country Hits: 1967** / 1990 / Rhino 70688
Includes David Houston and Tammy Wynette's duet "My Elusive Dream" and Wynn Stewart's "It's Such a Pretty World." —*AMG*

○ **Billboard Top Country Hits: 1968** / 1990 / Rhino 70689
This volume contains such hits from 1968 as Merle Haggard's "Mama Tried," Tammy Wynette's "Stand By Your Man," Jeanne C. Riley's "Harper Valley PTA," and Johnny Cash's "Folsom Prison Blues." —*AMG*

○ **Billboard Top Country Hits: 1990** / 1990 / Rhino 70694

☆ **The Bristol Sessions** / 1991 / Country Music Foundation 11
It's common knowledge that Ralph Peer's open recording session in Bristol, TN, launched the careers of the Carter Family and Jimmie Rodgers, but as this double CD proves, they weren't the only worthwhile musicians to turn up. In fact, Peer recorded 21 other acts, including the Stoneman Family and Blind Alfred Reed, in what turns out to be an amazing display of rural talent and the birth of country music. —*William Ruhlmann*

☆ **Columbia Country Classics, Vol. 2: Honky Tonk Heroes** / 1984 / CBS 46030
The second volume in the series contains 27 songs performed by Stonewall Jackson, Floyd Tillman, Lefty Frizzell, Marty Robbins, Carl Butler, Carl Smith, Little Jimmy Dickens—13 performers in all. —*AMG*

Columbia Country Classics, Vol. 5: New Tradition / 1988 / CBS 46033
The final volume in the set contains music from today, both established artists and up-and-coming ones, like Larry Gatlin, Asleep at the Wheel, Willie Nelson, Sweethearts of the Rodeo, the O'Kanes, and more. —*AMG*

☆ **Columbia Country Classics, Vol. 1: Golden Age** / CBS 46029
This 5-volume set contains 128 of the greatest country music recordings in Columbia's vaults, which span the genre from its beginnings. Each volume (available separately or as a set) contains major country artists. This first volume contains 27 landmark recordings by the artists that made them famous, such as the late Roy Acuff's "Wabash Cannonball" and the Carter Family's "Will the Circle Be Unbroken"—16 artists in all.—*AMG*

○ **Columbia Country Classics, Vol. 3: Americana** / CBS 46031
Eighteen artists—top country musicians like Billy Walker, Willie Nelson, the Statler Brothers, Johnny Cash, Jimmy Dean, the Highwaymen, and Merle Haggard—on 25 tracks. —*AMG*

○ **Columbia Country Classics, Vol. 4: Nashville Sound** / CBS 46032
The fourth volume in the series contains hits from Tammy Wynette, Charlie Rich, Johnny Cash, Johnny Paycheck, June Carter, George Jones, and others. —*AMG*

Country Comedy /
Contains some of the most popular work of such artists as Minnie Pearl, Lonzo & Oscar, and Archie Campbell, among others. —*AMG*

○ **Country Duos** / Bear Family 14740
Contains hit country duets like George Jones and Tammy Wynette's "Never Ending Song of Love" and Johnny Cash and June Carter's "If I Were a Carpenter." —*AMG*

○ **Country Hicks—Vols. 1 & 2** / Bark Log 1
A 2-volume compilation of obscure humorous country songs, apparently from the late '50s and early '60s. —*Richard Meyer*

Country Hits of the '40's / Curb 77346
Features country standards from Merle Travis, Tex Ritter, Tennessee Ernie Ford, and nine others. —*AMG*

Country Hits of the '50's / Curb 77330
Features the work of such major country artists as Sonny James, Tex Ritter, Slim Whitman, and eight others. —*AMG*

Country Hits of the '60's / Curb 77343
Contains the work of 11 top country legends, such as Bobby Goldsboro, Glen Campbell, and Merle Haggard. —*AMG*

Country Hits of the '70's / Curb 77344
Contains the work of 11 country artists like Hank Williams, Jr., Merle Haggard, and Crystal Gayle. —*AMG*

Country Hits of the '80's / 1992 / CEMA 57418

○ **Early Roanoke Country Radio** /
Features music recorded between 1920 and 1959 from early country radio broadcasts. The collection was compiled by the Blue Ridge Institute. —*AMG*

○ **Fiddler's Hall of Fame** / CMH 9037
This double album features such artists as Johnny Gimble and Buddy Spicher playing classic old-time bluegrass and swing hits; 28 in all. —*AMG*

Golden Country Jukebox Favorites / Jun. 10, 1991 / Capitol 95916
Features such hits as Billie Jo Spears' "Your Good Girl's Gonna Go Bad," Tennessee Ernie Ford's "Sixteen Tons," and Ferlin Husky's "The Waltz You Saved for Me." —*AMG*

Greatest Country Hits of the '90's, Vol. 2 / 1991 / CBS 48603
Contains Mary-Chapin Carpenter's "You Win Again," Willie Nelson's "Ain't Necessarily So," Ricky Van Shelton's "I Meant Every Word He Said," and other hits. —*AMG*

○ **Hello Operator... This Is Country Gazette** / Flying Fish 70012
This is a compilation of tracks contained on albums released by Flying Fish between 1976 and 1987, and contains music by Sam Bush, Alan Munde, David Grier, and others. —*AMG*

☆ **Hillbilly Music—Thank God!, Vol. 1** / 1989 / Bug 91346
An excellent double-disc compilation of country music from the late '40s to the mid '50s, featuring Buck Owens, Merle Travis, Faron Young, Tennessee Ernie Ford, and more. —*William Ruhlmann*

☆ **The King-Federal Rockabillys** / 197? / 1041
Features such artists as Charlie Feathers, Hank Mizell, Mac Curtis, and others on rare cuts originally recorded for the Federal and King labels during the '50s. —*AMG*

★ **Legends of Guitar—Country, Vol. 1** / Rhino 70718
Part one of an astutely compiled pair that showcases the kings of country guitar from the '30s to the '70s. Includes work from Jimmy Bryant, Speedy West, Chet Atkins, and Joe Maphis. Good liner notes on both sets. —*John Floyd*

☆ **Legends of Guitar—Country, Vol. 2** / Rhino 70723
Part two of this well-done collection. —*John Floyd*

The New Tradition Sings the Old Tradition / Aug. 8, 1989 / Warner Brothers 25949

Features music played by Dwight Yoakam, Emmylou Harris, Hank Williams, Jr., and others. —*AMG*

○ **The Okeh Western Swing** / Columbia Special Products 37324
Recordings from the early days of Western swing, featuring such legends as Hank Penny, Adolf Hofner, the Light Crust Doughboys, Bob Wills, and others. —*AMG*

○ **Old-Time Harmonica Classics** /
This LP contains classic country harmonica tracks that were recorded between 1923 and 1937 by such virtuosos of the instrument as Henry Whitter, DeFord Bailey, and more. —*AMG*

☆ **Ragged But Right** / RCA 8416
This seminal collection of early country highlights all influences and spotlights premier string bands from the '30s. Marvelous sound. —*Ron Wynn*

☆ **Rounder Old-Time Music** / 1988 / Rounder 11510
The Chicken Chokers, the Louvin Brothers, and others, 26 tracks in all. —*AMG*

○ **Songs of the West** / 1993 / Rhino
A lovingly assembled four-CD box celebrating cowboy songs throughout the years, *Songs of the West* is a treasure for serious country and western fans. A majority of the tracks are from movies and television or Gene Autry and Roy Rogers, but there is enough variety and rarities to keep the set from becoming stale. And the full-color, detailed book is worth the price alone. —*David Jehnzen*

● **Tender Lovin' Country** / Priority 53707
Features Tammy Wynette's "Good Lovin'," Johnny Cash's "Daddy Sang Bass," and more. —*AMG*

○ **Town South of Bakersfield, Vol. 1 & 2** / Restless 72575
Thanks to the likes of Buck Owens and Merle Haggard, Bakersfield has long played an important part in country music. This disc features some of the new generation. A few of the artists (like Rosie Flores and Katy Moffatt) have been around for a long time but have never received the recognition they deserve. The variety of styles on this disc ensure that there is something for everyone. —*Jim Worbois*

○ **Town South of Bakersfield, Vol. 3** / Mar. 18, 1992 / Restless 72592
Not as generous as the first disc but still worth the price, this one features more of the music and artists that may not otherwise have been heard but deserve to be. Let's hope there are more to follow. —*Jim Worbois*

☆ **Uncle Art Satherly—American Originals** / CBS 46237
This pioneering A&R man recollects the recording of several early country standards, making this a fine best-of '30s and '40s vintage Columbia label country. Includes "San Antonio Rose" by Bob Wills and "I Want to Be a Cowboy's Sweetheart" by Patsy Montana, among others. —*Mark A. Humphrey*

☆ **Urban Cowboy (Soundtrack)** / 1980 / Asylum 90002
Includes Joe Walsh, Bob Seger, Boz Scaggs, and Dan Fogelberg, so it's obviously not strictly a country album. But the soundtrack is important because it symbolizes the country trend that grew, then faded, in the early '80s (a case can be made that J. R. Ewing had a lot more influence on the fad than the film *Urban Cowboy*). Most of the country tracks here lean toward MOR. —*Tom Roland*

● **Western Swing, Vol. 1** / Old Timey 105
Includes such artists as Bob Wills, Harry Choates, Bill Boyd, Milton Brown, and the Lightcrust Doughboys, among others. —*AMG*

○ **Western Swing, Vol. 2** / Old Timey 116
This second volume features Jimmie Revard, the Tune Wranglers, W. Lee O'Daniel, and others, including several artists who appeared on the first album. —*AMG*

○ **Western Swing, Vol. 3** / Old Timey 117
This album features several artists who appeared in the preceding volumes, plus such additions as the Modern Mountaineers, Brown's Brownies, and Spade Cooley. —*AMG*

○ **Western Swing, Vol. 4** / Old Timey 119
This member of the series features Ted Daffan, Milton Brown, the Washboard Wonders, Jimmie Revard, Hank Penny, the Crystal Ramblers, Claude Casey, Shelly Lee Alley, and several other artists old and new to the series. —*AMG*

○ **Western Swing, Vol. 5** / Old Timey 120

This album features music recorded during the '30s by the Universal Cowboys, Buddy Jones, Bob Skyles, Ocie Stockard, the Farr Brothers, the Nite Owls, and others. —*AMG*

○ **Western Swing, Vol. 6** / Old Timey 121

Features Buddy Duhon & Harry Choates, Johnny Tyler, Don Churchill, Johnnie Lee Wills, T. Texas Tyler, Pee Wee King, Jerry Irby, Easy Adams, Webb Pierce, and other '40s and '50s stars. —*AMG*

○ **Western Swing, Vol. 7** / Old Timey 122

This volume also features music recorded between 1940 and 1960, this time by such artists as Ole Rasmussen, Hoyle Nix, T. Texas Tyler, Bob Wills, Arkie Shibley, Tommy Mooney, Glynn Duncan, Tommy Duncan, Tex Williams, Rocky Billy Ford, and others. —*AMG*

○ **Western Swing, Vol. 8** / Old Timey 123

More from the '40s and '50s, this time by Jimmy Walker, Jack Rhodes & Al Petty, the Maddox Brothers & Rose, Hawkshaw Hawkins, T. Texas Tyler, Big Jim DeNoone, Tommy Duncan, and others. —*AMG*

○ **When I Was a Cowboy** / Morningstar 45008

A compilation of classic original cowboy songs. —*Richard Meyer*

Hi Tone Poppa / Collectables 5330

This album contains guest performances by such artists as Claude King, Teddy Wilburn, and Tex Grimsley, among others. —*AMG*

BLUEGRASS

Of all the sub-styles within country music, bluegrass is the most distinctly different. The average country music fan who might listen to five average country songs – one each from honky-tonk, country rock, Western swing, country pop, and bluegrass – most likely would label the first four generically as "country" while specifying the last as "bluegrass." Despite common roots, bluegrass and mainstream country diverged during WWII, bluegrass following a path of tradition that has changed relatively little in the last half-century, in sharp contrast to country music's many paths that over the years have continually led into numerous and often far-from-home musical territories.

In the early 40s, country and bluegrass parted company, country moving on to honky-tonk, Western swing, rockabilly, and electrified instruments, with bluegrass remaining closer to its roots, especially to the string-band music of the 20s and 30s. Among these traditional string bands (at the time called "hillbilly") were Gid Tanner and the Skillet Lickers, the Possum Hunters, the Georgia Wildcats, and many others, most of which played traditional music in bands of three to six performing on guitars, fiddles, banjos, mandolins, and unamplified steel guitars (dobros) – instruments that were eventually adopted as the standard bluegrass configuration. While it's clear that bluegrass evolved from these bands, it remained for the great Bill Monroe (accurately called the "Father of Bluegrass"), with his band the Blue Grass Boys, to refine the old sound. The music itself does a much better job than words in showing how Monroe transformed this old music from a Model T to the bluegrass Cadillac V-8, with overdrive: no listener can mistake Mainer's Mountaineers, Roy Hall and His Blue Ridge Entertainers, or any other early 40s string band with Bill Monroe's Blue Grass Boys of the same period.

In 1945 Monroe formed the classic bluegrass band: Lester Flatt, guitar and vocal lead; Earl Scruggs, instrumental lead with the reinvented banjo; Chubby Wise, fiddler and cowriter of "Orange Blossom Special"; Cedric Rainwater, standup bass; and Bill. "Kentucky Waltz" and "Footprints in the Snow" were hits, and Monroe and his Boys were wildly popular. Though the term bluegrass wasn't commonly used until ten years later, the bluegrass sound attracted enough attention among country musicians to create numerous competitors to the Blue Grass Boys, by 1950 including Flatt & Scruggs (they had left Monroe after three years), Reno and Smiley, the Stanley brothers, Jim & Jesse, the Osborne brothers, and the Lilly brothers, to name only the prominent bluegrass bands from the "classical" period. Though none of

these bands were Monroe soundalikes, they shared characteristics that have come to define bluegrass: the standard instruments (listed above) played acoustically, with the five-string banjo dominating; alternating instrumental solos (as in jazz bands); close harmony, whether with two, three, or four parts; and a tempo generally much faster than mainstream country's. These are only general characteristics, though, not rules, and they often have been ignored, even by the most conservative of traditional bluegrass bands; Bill Monroe allowed an accordion in early recordings, and that music was still bluegrass. Further, it's difficult to specify a characteristic content of bluegrass songs. To cite two extreme examples, Jim and Jesse in 1965 recorded an album of Chuck Berry songs (*Berry Pickin'*), while the Boston-based Charles River Boys bluegrassed the Fab Four in *Beatles Country*, also in the 60s. And both albums sound bluegrass – not classical bluegrass, but bluegrass nonetheless. Bluegrass and country often have shared the same song repertory, though bluegrass bands have shown more reticence at accepting the latest musical fads than have many of their country cousins.

But like mainstream country, bluegrass itself has evolved into sub-styles. These changes were all but assured when urban audiences discovered bluegrass during the urban folk-revival of the late 50s and early 60s. The nation may not have been prepared for Jethro Bodine, Granny, Ellie May, and TV's "Beverly Hillbillies," but they positively embraced the Flatt & Scruggs background music, as witnessed by "The Ballad of Jed Clampett" in 1963 becoming the first bluegrass song to hit #1 in the country charts. Then followed "Foggy Mountain Breakdown" by Earl Scruggs in the popular *Bonnie and Clyde* movie and "Dueling Banjos" in *Deliverance*. Bluegrass music, and especially the five-string banjo, had become so popular with a new and huge and urban audience that traditional bluegrass had to make way for variations. Bluegrass was divided: traditional bluegrass remained, for the lovers of the pure, original sound; and progressive bluegrass (often called "newgrass") was created. The rules for newgrass were more relaxed, allowing electric instruments, rock songs, and whatever else creatively fit within the confines of this new and malleable term. Newgrass doesn't mean worse, it just means different. The top-notch newgrass bands (Seldom Scene, Country Gentlemen, J. D. Crowe and the New South, New Grass Revival) by and large are vocally and instrumentally on the same plane as the traditional bluegrass bands. There's room for both.

– David Vinopal

Eddie Adcock

Traditional, progressive bluegrass.

Among the major-league talent that emerged from the folk music scare of the late '50s were the Country Gentlemen, a DC-based quartet that introduced bluegrass to a generation of city folks and college students, people who had never heard of Flatt and Scruggs or Bill Monroe or the Stanley Brothers. The Gentlemen,

in playing the old bluegrass standards but playing them "different," were in a sense the first newgrass group. Adcock became their banjo player in 1959, and a player of distinction, whose style was as innovative as Don Reno's. Adcock's considerable talent spread to other country instruments when he left the Gentlemen in 1970. He has continued to perform his unique music to the present day, in the II Generation and other groups. *—David Vinopal*

And His Guitar / 1975 / CMH

Just Eddie and his guitar, no backup, and a very clean sound. Chet Atkins and Merle Travis-influenced. —*Chip Renner*

○ **Talk of the Town** / CMH
Backed by four women, Eddie is at his best here. The album features nice vocals. —*Chip Renner*

Paul Adkins & the Borderline Band

Traditional bluegrass.
They are a top-notch bluegrass band featuring Paul Adkins (guitar, vocals), Ron Pennington (mandolin, guitar), Ned Luberecki (banjo, guitar, bass, vocals), Fred Travers (dobro, vocals), and Robin Smith (bass vocals). They are fine musicians and deliver strong harmonies. —*Chip Renner*

○ **Reflections of Love** / Rebel
Everything on this CD is first-class. Fourteen songs dealing with all aspects of love. —*Chip Renner*

Mike Auldridge

Instrumental bluegrass.
Formerly of Cliff Waldron's New Shades of Grass, Mike Auldridge has earned a well-deserved reputation as one of the great contemporary dobro players. In addition to cutting albums under his own name, he was featured in the Seldom Scene, a newgrass/traditional supergroup formed in 1971 by former Country Gentlemen mandolin player John Duffy. —*David Vinopal*

Mike Auldridge / 1976 / Flying Fish
On this one, the bluegrass dobroist is joined by apt accompanists. —*Mark Humphrey*

○ **High Time** / Sugar Hill
This great dobro picker plays here with Lou Reid and Michael Coleman. —*Mark Humphrey*

Treasures Untold / Sugar Hill
More bluesy barrin'. —*Mark Humphrey*

Austin Lounge Lizards

Progressive bluegrass.
The Austin Lounge Lizards are a country bluegrass band out of Austin. The Lizards are Hank Card (guitar, vocals), Conrad Deisler (guitar, mandolin), Tom Pittman (banjo, pedal steel, vocals), Michael Stevens (bass, vocals), and Tim Wilson (mandolin, fiddle, vocals). After the first album, Paul "Tex" Sweeney (mandolin) and Kirk Williams (bass, vocals) replaced Stevens and Wilson. They are known for the humor in their songs and live shows. —*Chip Renner*

○ **Creatures from the Black Saloon** / 1984 / Watermelon
This good, humorous record features "The Car Hank Died In" and "Anahuac," with Jerry Jeff Walker singing some vocals. The band plays a good blend of country and bluegrass. —*Chip Renner*

Highway Cafe of the Damned / 1988 / Watermelon
Another good, solid, humor-packed CD featuring "The Highway Cafe of the Damned," "Industrial Strength Tranquilizer," "Ballad of Ronald Reagan," and more. —*Chip Renner*

Lizard Vision / 1991 / Flying Fish
This very funny album was a Grammy nominee. It features the hit, "Jesus Loves Me." —*Chip Renner*

Butch Baldassari

Traditional bluegrass.
Butch Baldassari is a member of the bluegrass band Weary Hearts. He is one of the better mandolin players in his field. —*Chip Renner*

○ **Old Town** / 1990 / Rebel
One of the finer bluegrass albums of 1990—Butch Baldassari has five originals on the CD, plus strong material by Alison Krauss and Bill Monroe. Tom Adams (banjo) and Stuart Duncan (fiddle) are very good in support. —*Chip Renner*

E. C. and Orna Ball

Old-time, gospel.
This fine old-time gospel singer and guitarist, Estil C. Ball (b 1913–d 1978) hailed from Rugby, VA and performed with his wife Orna (b 1907) and the Friendly Gospel Singers. First recorded for the Library of Congress in 1938, Ball was recorded extensively in his later years by the County and Rounder labels.

The Banjo

With the possible exception of pedal steel guitar, the banjo is that one instrument most identified with country music, especially bluegrass music. Beginning as a four-stringed fretless instrument, the banjo became much more versatile with an added fifth string (the shorter "drone" string). In the South after the Civil War, banjos of many configurations – some with four strings (the tenor and plecctrum banjo), others with five strings (since the 20s *the* country banjo) – were plentiful; in fact, in the 20s the banjo/fiddle combination formed the basis of country music instrumentals.

Uncle Dave Macon, the first real star of the Opry, in the 20s played five-string in the old style, often called frailing, clawhammer, or simply "thumping." In this style, the backs of the fingernails pick out the melody, while the thumb catches the drone string, thus creating a regular beat and rhythm. (Grandpa Jones is no doubt the most famous living player of the frailing banjo.)

Although the banjo didn't die out in the 30s, the many guitar/mandolin duets put it on the back burner for the decade. String bands, precursors to Bob Wills and other Western swing bands of the 40s, used the tenor banjo for volume and rhythm. Meanwhile, a banjo picker from North Carolina, Charlie Poole, had developed his own style of playing, three-finger picking instead of frailing; he was in fact paving the way for another North Carolinian, Earl Scruggs, who may not have invented the banjo but certainly reinvented it. Bill Monroe's Blue Grass Boys, formed in 1939, were without a five-string banjo until 1942, when Dave "Stringbean" Akeman added his frailing style to the band. But it wasn't until 1945, when Earl Scruggs joined the Blue Grass Boys, that what is now known as bluegrass banjo was invented.

It's nearly impossible to overstate the effect of Earl Scruggs on banjo playing. Live audiences gaped and gasped in disbelief when hearing the flood of careful notes that rolled off Earl's fingers. Many banjo pickers who rose to prominence admit to giving up the old style the same night they heard the new "Scruggspicking" style on the Grand Ole Opry. This new sound absolutely dominated, in large part because of Scruggs's signature songs "Foggy Mountain Breakdown" (recorded with Flatt and the Foggy Mountain Boys around 1951 and later the chase music for the movie *Bonnie and Clyde*) and "The Ballad of Jed Clampett" (on TV's "Beverly Hillbillies"). Further reinforcement came in the form of "Dueling Banjos" in the weirdly memorable version from the 1973 film *Deliverance*.

Though Earl Scruggs will rightly be remembered as the reinventor of the banjo, other musicians, all beholden to Earl, have taken the instrument in yet different directions: Buck Trent electrified it; Bill Keith invented the chromatic/melodic style; and Bela Fleck adds jazz, classical, and other difficult-to-label influences.

– David Vinopal

His lively, Travis-style guitar was an unusual element in traditional gospel singing. —*Mark Humphrey*

○ **E. C. Ball** / Rounder
This is old-time mountain gospel as good as it gets. Estil's guitar virtuosity and powerful baritone blend beautifully. —*David Vinopal*

Banjo Dan & the Mid-Nite Plowboys

Traditional bluegrass.
Traditional bluegrass band featuring Alan Davis (guitar, vocals), David Gusakov (fiddle, vocals), Dan Lindner (banjo, lead guitar,

vocals), Peter Riley (bass vocals), and Andy Sacher (mandolin). —*Chip Renner*

○ **Banjo Dan ... / 1990 / Greener Pastures**
Banjo Dan & the Mid-Nite Plowboys is a good traditional bluegrass CD recorded in one take: 19 songs all solid and well played. This band might be unknown, but they're well worth checking out. —*Chip Renner*

Russ Barenberg

Progressive bluegrass.
Russ Barenberg is a guitarist who played with the bluegrass band Country Cooking. He later went solo, playing a blend of jazz, funk, Latin, and bluegrass. —*Chip Renner*

Behind the Melodies / 1983 / Rounder
A very good cast: Tony Trischka, Andy Statman. —*Chip Renner*

○ **Halloween Rehearsal / 1987 / Rounder**
Combines his *Cowboy Calypso* and *Behind the Melodies.* —*Chip Renner*

Moving Pictures / 1988 / Rounder
The second choice, after *Halloween Rehearsal.* —*Chip Renner*

Cowboy Calypso / Rounder
A good album w/ Andy Statman and Jerry Douglas. —*Chip Renner*

Bashful Brother Oswald

Instrumental bluegrass.
Since 1938, Beecher Kirby's dobro has added the special sound that makes Roy Acuff's band unique, at the same time adding comedy through the Bashful Brother Oswald rube. Beecher Kirby has done much to popularize the dobro (unamplified resonator Hawaiian guitar) in mainstream country and bluegrass. —*David Vinopal*

○ **Brother Oswald / Rounder**
Roy Acuff's dobroist since the '30s, in a pleasant set of Hawaiian-inspired old-time country songs. —*Mark Humphrey*

Byron Berline

194?
Instrumental bluegrass.
This prodigy won his first fiddle contest at age ten. A much-in-demand session man, he appeared on the Dillards's *Pickin' and Fiddlin'* in 1964, an album that brought bluegrass to a new, urban audience. Byron Berline cofounded the Los Angeles-based Country Gazette, an influential bluegrass band, in the early '70s. He left the Gazette to form another group, Sundance. —*David Vinopal*

● **And the L.A. Fiddle Band / 1980 / Sugar Hill**
Put together three fiddles and some great acoustic bluegrass music and you have *Byron Berline & the L.A. Fiddle Band*, a great album. Guests are Vince Gill and John Hickman. —*Chip Renner*

Outrageous / 1980 / Flying Fish
Berline has a strong cast featuring Dan Crary, Albert Lee, James Burton, and John Hickman. —*Chip Renner*

○ **Berline, Hickman, Crary / 1981 / Sugar Hill**
Nice songs: "Bonapart's Retreat," "Turkey in the Straw." —*Chip Renner*

Night Run/ 1984 / Sugar Hill
Fine bluegrass. Pistol Pete, Forked River, Berline, Dan Crary, and John Hickman will knock you out. —*Chip Renner*

B-C-H / 1986 / Sugar Hill
Eclectic. This one's my favorite. —*Chip Renner*

○ **Double Trouble / 1986 / Sugar Hill**
Berline and John Hickman feed off each other's talents. Very smooth. —*Chip Renner*

Now They Are Four / 1989 / Sugar Hill
You'll love "Kodak 1955." A must-have for Berline fans. —*Chip Renner*

Nancy Blake

Old-time.
Nancy Blake has released albums with husband Norman Blake and solo. She is an accomplished musician whose musical styles include bluegrass, traditional, and classical. —*Chip Renner*

Blind Dog / 1988 / Rounder
Nancy and Norman Blake on traditional songs like "Wreck of the Old 197," "Black Mountain Rag," and a good cover of Woody Guthrie's "Grand Coulee Dam." —*Chip Renner*

Just Gimme Somethin' I'm Used To / 1992 / Shanachie
More pleasant parlottunes by Norman and Nancy Blake. Fine guitar from both, plus Norman's fiddle and Nancy's cello. —*Mark Humphrey*

○ **Grand Junction / Rounder**
A good debut album featuring Nancy Blake and her many instruments. —*Chip Renner*

Norman Blake

1938
Old-time.
Tennessee-born and Georgia-raised, Norman Blake is an unassuming vocalist, but an impressive multi-instrumentalist (guitar, mandolin, fiddle, dobro) who came to prominence in the '70s as one of the outstanding acoustic flatpickers of the Doc Watson school.
Beginning at the age of 16 with the Dixie Drifters, he quickly established a reputation for his instrumental skills and has worked with the banjoist Bob Johnson as the Lonesome Travelers, as a member of June Carter's touring band, as session player on Bob Dylan's *Nashville Skyline* (1969), in Kris Kristofferson's '70s road group, with John Hartford, and with the Nitty Gritty Dirt Band on *Will the Circle be Unbroken* (1973). Norman also performs with wife Nancy. —*Mark Humphrey & ED*

Back Home in Sulphur Springs / 1972 / Rounder
Norman Blake and Tut Taylor (dobro), basic and pure. —*Chip Renner*

Blackberry Blossom / 1974 / Flying Fish
Norman and Nancy Blake. A little less bluegrass with the addition of Nancy Blake's cello. —*Chip Renner*

○ **Fields of November / 1974 / Flying Fish**
A first-class album. Tut Taylor, Charlie Collins, and Nancy Short come in real strong. Features "Greycoat Soldiers," "Last Train to Poor Valley," and "The Fields of November." —*Chip Renner*

Live at McCabe's / 1976 / Takoma
Very good recofeatures "Nine Pound Hammer" and "Arkansas Traveler." Good sound. —*Chip Renner*

Whiskey Before Breakfast / 1976 / Rounder
Blake's best. He and Charlie Collins let their guitars do the talking. Perfect. —*Chip Renner*

Norman Blake and Red Rector / 1976 / County
On these 12 cuts, Blake and Red Rector (on mandolin) are backed by Charlie Collins and Roy Huskie Jr. —*Chip Renner*

Full Moon on the Farm / 1981 / Rounder
This album features Norman Blake and the Rising Fawn String Ensemble—James Bryan, Charlie Collins, and Nancy Blake. It has a nice, well-rounded feeling. —*Chip Renner*

Nashville Blues / 1984 / Rounder
Blake's vocals give this one more of an old-timey bluegrass feel. —*Hank Davis*

Lighthouse on the Shore / 1985 / Rounder
Norman teams up with Nancy Blake, James Bryan, and Tom Jackson. Features "Hello Stranger," "President's Garfield's Hornpipe," and "Wildwood Flower." —*Chip Renner*

● **Original Underground Music / Rounder**
Original Underground Music from the Mysterious South includes deceptively simple acoustic string music featuring multiple mandolins, mandolas, cellos, fiddles, and guitars for a hauntingly beautiful yet old-timey feel. —*Hank Davis & Chip Renner*

Rising Fawn String Ensemble / Rounder
More memorable acoustic instrumental work. —*Hank Davis*

Slow Train through Georgia / Rounder
Modern and soulful bluegrass sound. —*Hank Davis*

Norman Blake w/Tony Rice

Traditional bluegrass.
This duo represents two of the most important influences in the bluegrass revival of the '70s. Both Blake (b 1938) and Rice have been in-demand session players and represent near-perfection on

their instruments—Rice on flat-top guitar and Blake on the guitar, mandolin, dobro, and fiddle. Blake's Rising Faun String Ensemble shows a love and refined taste for the old-time music. —*David Vinopal*

○ **Blake & Rice** / 1987 / Rounder
Underrated but sprightly. Two fleet-fingered acoustic guitar flat-pickers flex their chops in these 14 cuts. —*Mark Humphrey*

Blake & Rice #2 / Rounder
More hot licks and backporch singing. —*Mark Humphrey*

Blue Rose

Traditional bluegrass.
This band features the talents of Laurie Lewis, Cathy Fink, Marcy Marxer, Molly Mason, and Sally Van Meter. —*Chip Renner*

○ **Blue Rose** / 1972 / Sugar Hill
This is the women's bluegrass version of Blind Faith. Cathy Fink, Laurie Lewis, Marcy Marxer, Molly Mason, and Sally Van Meter combine for a fantastic sound. This was a supergroup. Highly recommended! —*Chip Renner*

The Bluegrass Album Band

Traditional bluegrass.
This group features an all-star lineup including Tony Rice (guitar), J. D. Crowe (banjo), Doyle Lawson (mandolin), Bobby Hicks (fiddle), Todd Phillips (bass), and Jerry Douglas (dobro). —*ED*

○ **Bluegrass Album—Vol. 1** / Rounder
The debut from this superstar bluegrass band. —*Chip Renner*

Bluegrass Album—Vol. 2 / 1973 / Rounder
A good followup. Perfection. —*Chip Renner*

Bluegrass Album—Vol. 3 / Rounder
They just do not put out a bad album. —*Chip Renner*

Bluegrass Album—Vol. 4 / Rounder
They get tighter as they go along. Any one of these records is gonna get you movin'. —*Chip Renner*

Bluegrass Compact Disc / Rounder
A full, classic bluegrass album. —*Chip Renner*

Bluegrass Compact Disc—Vol. 2 / Rounder
A collection of the group's first four releases. There are 21 songs in all. —*Chip Renner*

Bluegrass Cardinals

Traditional bluegrass.
Before founding the Cardinals, Kentucky banjo player Don Parmalee played with a California band, the Hillmen, and for nine years played background banjo for the "Beverly Hillbillies" TV show. The Bluegrass Cardinals are noted for their intricate harmonies and for Parmalee's exceptional picking. —*David Vinopal*

Livin' in the Good Old Days / 1978 / CMH
Twelve solid songs. —*Chip Renner*

Cardinal Soul / 1979 / CMH
Early sound. Good. —*Chip Renner*

○ **Live & on Stage** / 1980 / CMH
The double album has 29 songs. —*Chip Renner*

Sunday Mornin' Singin' / 1980 / CMH
One of your better gospel albums. —*Chip Renner*

Cardinal Class / 1983 / Sugar Hill
A very good, solid, tight album. The Cardinals at their best. Highly recommended. —*Chip Renner*

Home Is Where the Heart Is / 1984 / Sugar Hill
A good mix of music. Jerry Douglas guests. —*Chip Renner*

Shining Path / 1986 / Sugar Hill
My favorite of their gospel releases. —*Chip Renner*

Welcome to Virginia / Rounder
Great vocals. —*Chip Renner*

Ginger Boatwright

Progressive bluegrass.
Ginger Boatwright is a singer/songwriter and guitar player. Her musical style leans toward bluegrass with a country-rock influence. She was an original member of the Red, White & Blue(grass) band. —*Chip Renner*

○ **Fertile Ground** / Flying Fish
An excellent album. Ginger Boatwright brings her great vocals from the Red, White & Blue(grass) band. She gets better with age. —*Chip Renner*

Boone Creek

Traditional bluegrass, progressive bluegrass.
After playing with bluegrass bands that varied from ultraconservative (Ralph Stanley's) to more progressive (Country Gentlemen, J. D. Crowe & the New South), instrumental wizard Ricky Skaggs formed Boone Creek in 1977, a band that blended the traditional with the new. —*David Vinopal*

Boone Creek / Rounder
A fine album with great picking. —*Chip Renner*

○ **One Way Track** / Sugar Hill
Jerry Douglas and Ricky Skaggs are outstanding. Tight, well-played bluegrass, including "In the Pines." —*Chip Renner*

Alison Brown

Bluegrass.
Alison Brown is a fine picker of the banjo. She plays for Alison Krauss and Union Station, and she has released a record with Stuart Duncan. —*Chip Renner*

○ **Simple Pleasures** / 1990 / Vanguard
A fine, well-produced CD featuring David Grisman, Mike Marshall, and Alison Krauss, plus some great banjo from Brown on this all-instrumental album. —*Chip Renner*

James Bryan

Traditional bluegrass.
Bryan, from north Alabama, is considered to be the best traditional Southern fiddler playing today. —*Charles Wolfe*

☆ **First of May** / Rounder
This set includes a variety of unusual local tunes and old favorites. —*Charles Wolfe*

Pat Burton & the Bray Brothers

Traditional bluegrass.
Pat is a guitar player who teamed up with Nate and Harley Bray to play a country/bluegrass brand of music. —*Chip Renner*

○ **We've Been Waiting for This** / Flying Fish
Burton teams with John Hartford, Vassar Clements, Harley Bray, and Frances Bray for some great bluegrass sounds. Pat tries for a "hit" on this album. —*Chip Renner*

Cache Valley Drifters

Progressive bluegrass.
The Cache Valley Drifters are an eclectic bunch who are comfortable playing boogie, bluegrass, country, Grateful Dead, folk, and old timey music. Cyrus Clarke (guitar, vocals), Bill Griffin (mandolin, vocals), Tom Lee (string bass), and David West (guitar, vocals) are the members. —*Chip Renner*

New Cache Valley Drifters / Flying Fish
Their debut album combines bluegrass with rock for a great sound. —*Chip Renner*

○ **Step Up to Big Pay** / 1980 / Flying Fish
A great sophomore album. Good vocals and playing, with nice covers of John Prine's "Hello in There" and the Grateful Dead's "Cumberland Blues." —*Chip Renner*

Tools of the Trade / Flying Fish
There is a lot of energy on this live album from McCabe's Guitar Shop. Very good! —*Chip Renner*

The Chicken Chokers

Progressive bluegrass.
The Chicken Chokers are a highly energetic band that plays music from string band to synthesizer. Chad Crumm (fiddle, synthesizer), Jim Reidy (banjo, ukelele, mandolin), Stefan Senders (banjo, guitar), Chip Taylor Smith (guitar, steel guitar), and Paul Strother (bass) make up this band. —*Chip Renner*

○ **Shoot Your Radio** / 1987 / Rounder
Old-time instrumentation, a pseudo-punk bad attitude, and a hilarious title-track rap from this short-lived but fun band from Boston. —*Mark Humphrey*

Old Time Music / Rounder
On this album, two avant-garde/old-time bands, the Chicken Chokers and the Horseflies, pushed the envelope of the new/old-time styles. —*Mark Humphrey*

Vassar Clements

1928
Instrumental bluegrass.
In the company of Johnny Gimble and Mark O'Connor, Vassar Clements has been among the elite of contemporary sidemen fiddlers. He started in mainstream country and bluegrass, playing for Bill Monroe, Faron Young, and Jim and Jesse. With his virtuosity, he moved occasionally to progressive country, including a stint with the Earl Scruggs Revue. His technique and versatility are astounding. —*David Vinopal*

Crossing the Catskills/ 1987 / Rounder
Tasty fiddling from one of the finest. —*Mark Humphrey*

○ **Hillbilly Jazz** / 1987 / Flying Fish
Wonderful '70s swing (western and otherwise). W/ Vassar Clements, David Bromberg on guitar, and D. J. Fontana on drums, plus many more on this loose session. —*Mark Humphrey*

Grass Routes / 1991 / Rounder
This recent album shows why Clements is one of the greatest fiddlers in modern country music. —*Mark Humphrey*

The Bluegrass Session / Flying Fish
The title tells the truth. —*Mark Humphrey*

Bill Clifton

1931
Traditional bluegrass, traditional country.
A pioneer in bluegrass and traditional music, Bill Clifton was a prime mover in starting the Newport Folk Festival and the bluegrass festival phenomenon. Since the mid '50s he has assembled the best musicians on album after album. His sound over four decades has remained pretty much the same, uniquely and beautifully Clifton. —*David Vinopal*

○ **Bill Clifton & the Dixie Mountain Boys** / County

The Country Gazette

Progressive bluegrass.
In 1972, when the Flying Burrito Brothers broke up, the bluegrass segment of the band re-formed, creating the influential Country Gazette. At their many festival shows, this California group performed a blend of traditional bluegrass and newgrass, gaining a reputation for vocal harmonies and instrumental excellence. Their *Traitor in Our Midst* album, their first, remains perhaps their best. —*David Vinopal*

Keep on Pushing / Flying Fish
Fourteen great bluegrass cuts with Alan Munde. The Country Gazette's 20th year. —*Chip Renner*

The Country Gentlemen

Traditional bluegrass, progressive bluegrass.
In 1957, when the Country Gentlemen formed in the Washington, DC, area, their sound expanded the definition of "bluegrass"; they were progressive bluegrass before the term existed. The Gentlemen came along with the first wave of the folk-music revival and quickly made a name for themselves as a band who could not only play traditional material straight but who also brought Bob Dylan and contemporary country material into the genre. Because of their exceptional singing and virtuoso instrumentals, the Gentlemen attracted a broad audience, ranging from traditional country/bluegrass fans to folk and soft-rock lovers. Their earlier albums featured the remarkable quartet of Charlie Waller, guitar and lead vocal; Eddie Adcock, banjo; John Duffey, mandolin; and Tom Gray, bass. —*David Vinopal*

★ **Country Songs Old & New** / 1960 / Folkways
This is a reissue of the 1960 Folkways album that launched their career. Includes "The Little Sparrow," "The Long Black Veil," "Under the Double Eagle," and 13 other classic cuts. A magic album. —*Michael Erlewine*

One Wide River / 1987 / RB
Nice, but not so energetic or ambitious as other releases. —*Ron Wynn*

○ **Folk Songs & Bluegrass** / 1988 / Folkways
Another essential '60s release. —*Ron Wynn*

☆ **Sit Down Young Stranger** / 1988 / Sugar Hill
A tremendous date; brilliant playing by Mike Aulridge. —*Ron Wynn*

○ **River Bottom** / 1989 / Sugar Hill
Great solos and harmonies, excellent compositions. —*Ron Wynn*

○ **Award Winning** / RB
Outstanding session. —*Ron Wynn*

Sound Off / RB
Good, with a more contemporary sound. —*Ron Wynn*

Dan Crary

Progressive bluegrass.
Crary is among the "sons of Doc" who emerged in the '70s, taking Doc Watson's flatpicked guitar style a step further. The Kansas native was among the founders of the Bluegrass Alliance, and subsequently pursued a solo career while teaching speech communications in California. Recording for Sugar Hill and similar labels, Crary has carved a niche for himself as a distinctive interpreter of traditional material for acoustic '6- and 12-string guitars. He also records original compositions. He may be best known for his work with "Fiddler" Byron Berline and "Banjoist" John Hickman, who combined with Crary in a bluegrass-and-beyond trio that has been active for more than a decade. —*Mark Humphrey*

○ **Guitar** / 1983 / Sugar Hill
The title leaves the erroneous impression that this is a solo set. Instead, it's an exciting blowing session featuring the cream of the new generation of bluegrass players who emerged in the '80s—Sam Bush, Mark O'Connor, and Bela Fleck. But on selections ranging from a "Bill Monroe Medley" to a transcribed Mozart piano sonata, Crary and his guitar more than hold their own. —*William Ruhlmann*

J. D. Crowe & the New South

Progressive bluegrass.
In the late '50s, bluegrasser Jimmy Martin attracted a number of highly talented musicians to his Sunnysiders. One is J. D. Crowe, a Kentucky native who quickly made a reputation on the five-string banjo, initially as a first-rate interpreter of traditional bluegrass and then, with his band the New South, as a highly respected proponent of progressive—a blend of the old with modern country and rock, sometimes with electrified instruments. Rounder's 1975 album *J. D. Crowe and the New South* greatly influenced other progressive bluegrass groups. The band's personnel, in addition to the stellar picking of Crowe, included guitarist Tony Rice, Ricky Skaggs on mandolin and fiddle, and dobro player Jerry Douglas, all of whom went on to make big names in the business. —*David Vinopal*

☆ **J. D. Crowe & the New South** / 1975 / Rounder
A trailblazing album of "young blood" in bluegrass, with Ricky Skaggs and Tony Rice. Very influential. —*Mark Humphrey*

My Home Ain't in the Hall of Fame / 1978 / Rounder
Crowe, on banjo and baritone, moves closer to country in the company of Keith Whitley and Doug Jernigan. —*Mark Humphrey*

Somewhere Between / 1981 / Rounder
A hard-country album. Lovely ballads, with Lefty Frizzell-style vocals from Keith Whitley. —*Mark Humphrey*

Live in Japan / 1982 / Rounder
Spirited performances with Keith Whitley and the great mandolinist Jimmy Gaudreau. —*Mark Humphrey*

Straight Ahead / 1986 / Rounder
More or less traditional bluegrass, with Sam Bush on mandolin and Jerry Douglas on dobro. —*Mark Humphrey*

Crowe-Rice-Lawson-Hicks-Phillips

Traditional bluegrass.
J. D. Crowe, Tony Rice, Doyle Lawson, Bobby Hicks, and Todd Phillips, along with Jerry Douglas, have teamed up to produce several bluegrass albums that are of the highest caliber. All members of the band are considered the tops in their field. —*Chip Renner*

○ **Bluegrass Album** / 1986 / Rounder
A good, straightforward bluegrass album. —*Chip Renner*

Dillard & Clark

Traditional bluegrass.
This duo consisted of ex-Byrd Gene Clark and Doug Dillard of the Dillards. —*Kenneth M. Cassidy*

☆ **Expedition/Through the Morning** / Mobile Fidelity
Good writing, singing, and playing on one CD containing two of their albums. These songs have been covered by Linda Ronstadt, the Eagles, and others. —*Kenneth M. Cassidy*

Doug Dillard

1937
Traditional bluegrass.
See the listing for the Dillards. —*ED*

What's That? / 1974 / Flying Fish
A solid album. —*Chip Renner*

○ **Jackrabbit** / 1979 / Flying Fish
A live album from the Telluride Bluegrass Festival, with guests Sam Bush and Byron Berline. —*Chip Renner*

Heaven / 1979 / Flying Fish
A gospel album featuring Dan Crary, Byron Berline, John Hartford, Herb Pedersen. It includes an excellent cover of "Turn Your Radio On." —*Chip Renner*

Rodney Dillard

1942
Progressive bluegrass.
See the listing for the Dillards. —*ED*

○ **At Silver Dollar City** / 1988 / Flying Fish
A very Dillard-like album. It must be those trademark vocals. Includes a good cover of "Caney Creek." —*Chip Renner*

The Dillards

Progressive bluegrass.
Remember the Darling family, the hillbillies who now and again came down to Mayberry to visit sheriff Andy Griffith? The Darlings were the Dillards, a progressive West Coast bluegrass band with brothers Doug and Rodney as the nucleus. The band regrouped in 1987 for the TV movie *Return to Mayberry*. The brothers are still making music, though separately, with Doug heading up his own band. —*David Vinopal*

Homecoming & Family Reunion / 1979 / Flying Fish
A pleasant album of several Dillard generations live at a picnic. —*Mark Humphrey*

Let It Fly / 1990 / Vanguard
Recordings produced by Herb Pedersen of the Desert Rose Band. —*Mark Humphrey*

○ **There Is a Time** / Vanguard
A 29-track retrospective of their 1963-1970 Elektra recordings. Influential urban bluegrass. —*Mark Humphrey*

Jerry Douglas

Traditional bluegrass.
Jerry Douglas is considered the premier dobro player on the Nashville music scene. He plays on most sessions and often teams up with Sam Bush, Mark O'Connor, Bela Fleck, and Edgar Meyer to form the group Strength in Numbers. —*Chip Renner*

Fluxology / 1979 / Rounder
A good bluegrass album with Tony Rice, Darol Anger, Todd Phillips, and Ricky Skaggs. —*Chip Renner*

Fluxedo / 1982 / Rounder
A smoother sound, which has become his trademark with Strength in Numbers. Featuring Sam Bush, Bela Fleck, the Whites, Mark Shatz, and Russ Barenberg. —*Chip Renner*

Under the Wire / 1986 / MCA
MCA gave Douglas total control on this album featuring Sam Bush, Bela Fleck, Russ Barenberg, Edgar Meyer, and Mark O'Connor. It's a shame they could only fit ten songs on the CD. Buy it! —*Chip Renner*

○ **Everything Is Gonna Work Out Fine** / 1987 / Rounder
Fluxology and *Fluxedo* on one CD—a great value from the master of the dobro. —*Chip Renner*

● **Slide Rule** / 1992 / Sugar Hill

His finest release hits the jackpot. Featuring Sam Bush, Alison Krauss, Tim O'Brien, Maura O'Connell, Stuart Duncan, Artie McGlynn, and others, this album is produced to perfection. Highly recommended. —*Chip Renner*

Plant Early / MCA

Dry Branch Fire Squad

Traditional bluegrass.
This southern Ohio bluegrass group is fronted by Ron Thomason, a mandolin player, comic, and philosopher who says that "*Lonesome* (the essential word in bluegrass music) is a car up on blocks." Now that's a traditional value country fans can appreciate ... —*David Vinopal*

Antiques & Inventions / 1966 / Rounder
Kenny Baker and Hazel Dickens give this a nice flavor. —*Chip Renner*

Long Journey / 1972 / Rounder
Old timey—in a modern way. Very good. —*Chip Renner*

Born to Lonesome / 1979 / Rounder
Good. Featuring Kenny Baker, Bobby Osborne. A nice cover of "Brand New Tennessee Waltz." —*Chip Renner*

Fannin' the Flames / 1982 / Rounder
Very nice album. —*Chip Renner*

Fertile Ground / 1983 / Rounder
Very good. "Devil Take the Farmer" and "Bonaparte Crossing the Rhine." —*Chip Renner*

○ **Good Neighbors** / 1985 / Rounder
Tight mountain harmonies on 14 cuts. A must-have. —*Chip Renner*

Golgotha / 1986 / Rounder
A nice gospel album. —*Chip Renner*

Buddy Emmons

Instrumental bluegrass.
A much-in-demand session man, Buddy Emmons is credited with bringing the pedal steel guitar to prominence and great popularity, so much so that the instrument is no longer considered "country" only, having been accepted by rock and nearly every other form of popular music. Earlier in his career he played in the road bands of Little Jimmy Dickens, Roger Miller, Ernest Tubb, and others. He and fellow steel player Shot Jackson founded the Sho-Bud steel guitar company, which made numerous innovations in the instrument. —*David Vinopal*

○ **Buddy & Lenny** / Flying Fish
Country meets jazz as two super-pickers, Buddy Emmons and Lenny Breau (pedal steel and electric guitar), collide. A very creative and innovative album. —*Hank Davis*

Glenda Faye

Traditional bluegrass.
Glenda Faye is one of the top guitar (flatpicker) players in the bluegrass field. —*Chip Renner*

○ **Flat Pickin' Favorites** / Flying Fish
Faye shines on her debut album. Bill Monroe and Jesse McReynolds give the album a nice sound. —*Chip Renner*

Lester Flatt

1914-1979
Traditional bluegrass.
After Lester Flatt and Earl Scruggs parted ways in 1969, Flatt reassembled many of the Foggy Mountain Boys, renamed the group Nashville Grass, and toured very successfully until his death in 1979. Unlike Scruggs, who with his sons moved on to music that was only marginally country, Flatt and the Grass stuck to traditional bluegrass material. Even without Scruggs, the band shone, and Flatt's vocals, musical direction, and taste received the credit they had so long deserved. —*David Vinopal*

Live—Bluegrass Festival / 1986 / CM
A bluegrass veteran in concert in the '70s. —*Mark Humphrey*

○ **Vol. 1—Greatest Bluegrass Hits** / CM
A good overview of Flatt's post-Scruggs recordings with Nashville Grass, a band that included a young Marty Stuart on mandolin. —*Mark Humphrey*

Flatt & Scruggs

Traditional bluegrass.
Probably the most famous bluegrass band of all time was Flatt and Scruggs and the Foggy Mountain Boys. They made the genre famous in ways that not even Bill Monroe, who pretty much invented the sound, ever could. Because of a guitar player and vocalist from Tennessee named Lester Flatt and an extraordinary banjo player from North Carolina named Earl Scruggs, bluegrass music has become popular the world over and has entered the mainstream in the world of music.

Like so many other bluegrass legends, Flatt and Scruggs were graduates of Bill Monroe's Blue Grass Boys. Because of the unique sound they added ("overdrive," one critic called it), Monroe felt let down after Flatt's quality vocals and Scruggs's banjo leads left in 1948. Quickly the two assembled a band that in the opinion of many was among the best ever, with Chubby Wise on fiddle and Cedric Rainwater on bass; a later band, with Paul Warren on fiddle and Josh Graves on dobro, was equally superb. With so many extraordinary musicians and the solid, controlled vocals of Flatt, it's no wonder the Foggy Mountain Boys was the band that brought bluegrass to international prominence. From 1948 until 1969, when Flatt and Scruggs split up to pursue different musical directions, they were *the* bluegrass band, due to their Martha White Flour segment at the Opry and, especially, their tremendous exposure from TV and movies.

TV's preeminent hillbilly sitcom, "The Beverly Hillbillies," helped Flatt and Scruggs (and bluegrass) immensely. In the early '60s this top-rated show not only featured Flatt and Scruggs singing and playing "The Ballad of Jed Clampett," the show's theme song and the first bluegrass song to reach #1 in the country charts, it occasionally presented the two in cameo appearances, year after year. Further, in the early '60s the folk revival, then in its glory, made Flatt and Scruggs popular to a different audience, one that was educated and urban. In 1967 the movie *Bonnie and Clyde* was a huge hit, and with it came even more exposure for Flatt and Scruggs, whose "Foggy Mountain Breakdown" was the chief background music, making that song the most well known of all bluegrass instrumentals. Listeners who never had warmed up to straight country music grew hot for bluegrass, and festivals proliferated nationwide.

What made Flatt and Scruggs so famous, when numerous other excellent bluegrass groups of high quality (Jim and Jesse, the Stanley Brothers, the Osborne Brothers, Reno and Smiley, the Lilly Brothers) remained relatively unknown? One reason is that they always attracted the talent and their 1948 sound was way ahead of the others. More important, the Foggy Mountain Boys had Earl Scruggs, who reinvented the banjo with his three-finger picking (forever after known as "Scruggs picking") of mile-a-minute syncopated notes. The banjo was never the same after Earl Scruggs, whose presence at that time would have made *any* country band unique. They were elected to the Country Music Hall of Fame in 1985. *—David Vinopal*

Mercury Sessions #1 / 1948 / RS
1948-1950 recordings by the banjo whiz and baleful vocalist who took Bill Monroe's music a step further. *—Mark Humphrey*

At Carnegie Hall / 1962 / CBS
A highly influential "folk-boom" concert album . *—Mark Humphrey*

☆ **20 All-Time Great Recordings** / 1983 / CBS
Three-part gospel-style harmonies, breakneck banjo, flinty Americana, and "a bubblin' crude" are the cornerstone collection of bluegrass at its best. *—Mark Humphrey*

Columbia Historic Edition / Columbia
Wonderful '50s recordings, including some rarities. *—Mark Humphrey*

Don't Get Above Your Raisin' / RS
Flatt's song became a back-anthem when Ricky Skaggs waxed it ca. 1981. The original is here, along with other greats from the '50s. *—Mark Humphrey*

Golden Era 1950-55 / Rounder
Classic Columbia performances. *—Mark Humphrey*

Greatest Hits / CBS
A concise sampler for those who don't want their *20 All-Time Great Recordings* album. *—Mark Humphrey*

Mercury Sessions #2 / RS

More great 1948-1950 recordings, including the original "Foggy Mountain Breakdown." *—Mark Humphrey*

Songs of the Famous Carter Family / CBS
Depression-era country/folk performed bluegrass style. *—Mark Humphrey*

The World of Flatt & Scruggs / CBS
Another good Columbia sampler. *—Mark Humphrey*

Bela Fleck & the Flecktones

Progressive bluegrass.
A highly original banjo stylist, Fleck has played traditional bluegrass, newgrass (with the New Grass Revival), and his own innovative material. He has been in high demand as a session player. *—David Vinopal*

○ **Bela Fleck & the Flecktones** / 1990 / Warner
After disbanding New Grass Revival, Bela Fleck began recreating the role of the banjo in the same way Charlie Parker redefined the role of the saxophone. But Fleck may be the least innovative member of this quartet: Howard Levy gets chromatics from his blues harp, Victor Wooten picks banjo rolls on his bass, and Roy "Future Man" Wooten plays a Frankenstein- monster drum machine/guitar synthesizer. For all the Flecktones's flash, there's little pretense; the group's astonishing musicianship keeps an "aw-shucks" accessibility that lets everybody follow the melody while they marvel. *—Brian Mansfield*

Flight of the Cosmic Hippo / 1991 / Warner
The Flecktones owe more to bebop than bluegrass, and here the group finally names its style "blu-bop." Which is why *Cosmic Hippo* topped the jazz, not the country, chart. The Flecktones continue to make it look easy, adding banjo power chords to "Turtle Rock" and reworking Lennon/McCartney's "Michelle." *—Brian Mansfield*

Tony Furtado

Progressive bluegrass.
Tony Furtado is a highly regarded banjo player who hits all styles of banjo music: bluegrass, old-timey, swing, and jazz style. *—Chip Renner*

○ **Swamped** / Rounder
A very good album, featuring Laurie Lewis, Darol Anger, and Todd Phillips. *—Chip Renner*

Josh Graves

Traditional bluegrass.
Burkett "Josh" Graves has been probably the most influential dobro player in history, with Pete Kirby (Brother Oswald of Roy Acuff's band) in the running. Graves at least is responsible for making the dobro so popular in bluegrass music. He played for years with the Flatt & Scruggs band, his energetic playing beautifully complementing Scruggs on the banjo. In the '70s he played with the Earl Scruggs Revue and since then has has been active in recording work and on TV. Graves did much to bring the dobro out of the hillbilly and into the mainstream. *—David Vinopal*

○ **The Puritan Sessions** / Rebel
Longtime fiddler Kenny Baker appears in an uncharacteristic role as a fingerstyle guitarist in a delightfully low-key set of tunes and songs with dobroist (and sometime-singer) Josh Graves. *—Mark Humphrey*

○ **King of the Dobro** / CMH
The man who created bluegrass-style dobro with his bluesy hound-dog slide playing. *—Mark Humphrey*

David Grier

Traditional bluegrass.
David Grier is a top-notch guitar player who has played with some of the best bluegrass musicians in the business. *—Chip Renner*

○ **Freewheeling** / Rounder
David Grier is backed here by Stuart Duncan, Roland White, Sam Bush, Wyatt Rice, and Mark Shatz. *—Chip Renner*

David Grisman

1945
Instrumental bluegrass.

Grisman began as a bluegrass mandolin player, working with Red Allen, Don Stover, and others. Greatly influenced by mandolin superplayer Jethro Burns, Grisman played briefly in Earth Opera, a rock band, and in the non-country Great American Music Band, while continuing to experiment with new approaches for the mandolin. This new sound, which echos the past but includes many other music genres, has become known as "dawg." —*David Vinopal*

Rounder Album / 1976 / Rounder

○ **The David Grisman Quintet** / 1976 / Rounder
Creative and adventurous sessions by this jazz/bluegrass group. —*Hank Davis*

Hot Dawg / Mobile Fidelity / 1979
W/ Stephane Grappelli and a Django-esque sound. —*Hank Davis*

Early Dawg / 1985 / Sugar Hill
Bluegrass meets jazz. —*Hank Davis*

Hot Dawg 90 / 1987 / A&M

>**Here Today** / 1988 / Rounder
Hot mandolin-led newgrass with guests Pedersen, Gill, and Buchanan. —*Hank Davis*

Home Is Where the Heart Is / 1988 / Rounder

Mandolin Abstractions / 1988 / Rounder
Modern mandolin playing in a variety of acoustic settings. At times hot and driving, other times melodic and haunting, and occasionally abstract and eerie. This is challenging yet pleasant music with guest Andy Statman. —*Hank Davis*

Svingin' with Svend / Zebra
A Django-esque sound, with Svend Asmussen on violin. —*Hank Davis*

The Hillmen

Progressive bluegrass.
An early '60s, West Coast bluegrass band with Chris Hillman, Vern and Rex Gosdin, and Dan Parmley (later a Bluegrass Cardinal), which evolved from the Scottsville Squirrel Barkers. —*Mark Humphrey*

○ **The Hillmen** / 1970 / Sugar Hill
Traditional bluegrass plus Dylan covers. —*Mark Humphrey*

Hot Rize

Traditional bluegrass, progressive bluegrass.
This Colorado progressive bluegrass band can also play traditional, jazz, and rock. As part of their stage act they become Red Knuckles and the Trail Blazers and, in good fun, parody hardcore '50s country music. —*David Vinopal*

Hot Rize / Flying Fish
Debut album. Very good. Featuring Tim O'Brien and Pete Wernick. —*Chip Renner*

Radio Boogie / Flying Fish
No sophomore high jinks on this release. Solid album, highly recommended. —*Chip Renner*

○ **Untold Stories** / Sugar Hill
It all comes together on this CD. Tim O'Brien's swan song. —*Chip Renner*

Jim & Jesse (McReynolds)

Traditional bluegrass.
One of the great bluegrass bands in history, brothers Jim (b 1927) and Jesse (b 1929) and their Virginia Boys have remained at the top by changing with the times. Starting as a traditional brothers duet, Jim on guitar and Jesse on mandolin showed their versatility by following country's changing tastes, moving to country/folk when necessary to keep a road band going. Whatever style they played (including *Berry Pickin' in the Country*, an album of bluegrass versions of Chuck Berry tunes), they retained a pure country core, due in no small part to Jim's pure, high tenor and Jesse's virtuoso mandolin playing. Opry regulars since 1964, they have recorded hit singles over the years, among them "Johnny B. Goode," "Diesel on My Tail," "Better Times A-Comin'," Jesse's "Cotton Mill Man," and a well-known version of John Prine's "Paradise." Jim's exquisite voice and Jesse's innovative cross-picking style of mandolin are well worth the price of admission. —*David Vinopal*

○ **Music among Friends** / 1991 / Rounder
A celebration of this bluegrass duo's 25 years on the Grand Ole Opry, with guest appearances by Bill Monroe, Emmylou Harris, Porter Wagoner, and others. —*Mark Humphrey*

Jim & Jesse: 1952-1955 / 1992 / Bear Family
Twenty stunning performances for the Capitol label (their first label) featuring hand-in-glove harmonies and Jesse's unique banjo-influenced mandolin. —*Mark Humphrey*

★ **Bluegrass Special** / Epic
A bluegrass classic. Many of their most popular songs. —*Richard Lieberson*

Jim & Jesse Saluting the Louvin Brothers / Epic
The best of the duo's recordings, with electric country rather than bluegrass accompaniment. —*Richard Lieberson*

Jim & Jesse Story / CMH
Remakes of some of their best-known tunes. —*Richard Lieberson*

Johnson Mountain Boys

Traditional bluegrass.
From the band's formation in 1978 until its breakup in 1988, the Johnson Mountain Boys were the salvation of bluegrass traditionalists, the hardcore who prefer the pure to progressive bluegrass and newgrass. Led by guitarist/vocalist Dudley Connell, the Washington, DC-based band echoed the classic bands of the '50s, instrumentally and vocally. They left a void. —*David Vinopal*

Let the Whole World Talk / 1987 / Rounder
More great wailin'! —*Mark Humphrey*

Requests / 1987 / Rounder
An eclectic album by this short-lived but brilliant quintet. —*Mark Humphrey*

At the Old School House / 1988 / Rounder
Wonderful live and traditional bluegrass from their farewell tour. —*Mark Humphrey*

☆ **Working Close** / Rounder
Dudley Connell's chilling, high-lonesome lead vocals were only one of the delights of this militantly traditional, young bluegrass band. Any of their albums are among the best bluegrass of recent decades. —*Mark Humphrey*

Bill Keith

Instrumental bluegrass.
Boston-born Bill Keith is a highly innovative five-string banjo player who first mastered the Scruggs style and then invented his own. His chromatic style departed from the Scruggs approach, which lay down right-sounding notes around the melody, but with only some of those notes carrying the melody. Keith's system allows the picker to play intricate melody lines, note for note, fiddle-like. Bill Keith has played with numerous major league bands, including Bill Monroe and the Blue Grass Boys and Red Allen. Just as Scruggs reinvented the banjo, Bill Keith reinvented it again. —*David Vinopal*

○ **Something Bluegrass** / 1976 / Rounder
Catch Tony Rice, David Grisman, Jim Rooney, Tom Grey, Vassar Clements, Ken Kasek, and Al Jones on this album. The bluegrass is top-notch, and Bill Keith struts his stuff. —*Chip Renner*

The Kentucky Colonels

Traditional bluegrass.
Evolving from the Country Boys in 1962, the California-based Kentucky Colonels quickly garnered a national following. Members Clarence White (guitar), his brother Roland (mandolin), Billy Ray Latham (banjo), Roger Bush (bass), and Leroy Mack (dobro) brought their traditional/progressive sound to a young urban audience. —*David Vinopal*

☆ **Appalachian Swing** / 1964 / World Pacific
With bluegrass guitarist Clarence White. —*Richard Lieberson*

★ **Long Journey Home** / 1964 / Vanguard
Fiersome recordings from a 1964 live performance at the Newport Folk Festival, with Clarence White and many others, including duets with Doc Watson. —*Richard Lieberson & Mark Humphrey*

Alison Krauss

Traditional bluegrass, progressive bluegrass.

With a Grammy in her hand, this excellent fiddler with the high, fragile voice has made it, after years of small jobs on the road, paying her dues. With all the TV coverage she's had at the beginning of the '90s, this folk/bluegrass traditionalist should continue her great success with Union Station, her band. —*David Vinopal*

Two Highways / 1989 / Rounder
Earlier recordings of a fine young singer and fiddler, this time with Union Station. —*Mark Humphrey*

○ **I've Got That Old Feeling** / 1990 / Rounder
A sweet voice, fine fiddling, and a tight plaintive band on this breakthrough bluegrass/country/pop album that produced the first music video for bluegrass. —*Mark Humphrey*

Doyle Lawson & Quicksilver

Traditional bluegrass.
After first making a name as a mandolin player and guitarist for J. D. Crowe's band, in 1971 Doyle Lawson moved to the Country Gentlemen, another well-known band that played traditional bluegrass with a progressive touch. In the late '70s he formed his own band, Quicksilver, which quickly drew raves for its inspired gospel singing. —*David Vinopal*

● **Gospel Collection #1** / 1987 / Sugar Hill
The best way to have their gospel music is with this collection. Highly recommended. —*Chip Renner*

○ **Rock My Soul** / 1991 / Sugar Hill
Not a flaw on the album. —*Chip Renner*

○ **My Heart Is Yours** / Sugar Hill
As good as *Rock My Soul.* First-class bluegrass. —*Chip Renner*

Laurie Lewis

Progressive bluegrass.
Laurie Lewis is a fine violinist and vocalist in bluegrass music and is the leader of the Grant Street String Band. She also performs with Blue Rose and Lewis & Kallick. —*Chip Renner*

Love Chooses You / 1989 / Flying Fish
A followup in the spirit of the first, with a good choice of material. —*Mark Humphrey*

○ **Together—Lewis & Kallick** / 1990 / Kaleidoscope
Laurie Lewis and Kathy Kallick perform some really fine duets on this long-awaited collaboration. Lewis's violin playing is first-rate and her vocals are always a joy to listen to. Kallick's songwriting is spotlighted, along with her strong rhythm guitar work. —*Chip Renner*

● **Restless Rambling Heart** / Flying Fish
The first solo album from this Bay Area singer and fiddler. Sweet but not saccharine, this is a mix of old-time, bluegrass, and rootsy contemporary folk. —*Mark Humphrey*

The Lilly Brothers

Traditional bluegrass.
Starting in 1962, for 18 years West Virginians Everett (b 1923) and Bea Lilly (b 1921) turned downtown Boston into an oasis for music lovers in New England. With their extraordinary banjo player, Don Stover, they played nightly at the Hillbilly Ranch, a watering hole in Boston's "Combat Zone," bringing their pure and traditional mountain bluegrass to an audience of sailors, sailors' companions, other denizens of the night, and many lovers of the real thing. For whatever reason (and in spite of recording a number of albums), the Lilly Brothers and Don Stover never got the acclaim they deserved. —*David Vinopal*

☆ **Early Recordings** / RB
Driving, late-50s performances with breathtaking banjo from Don Stover and hand-in-glove vocal harmonies. One of the best bluegrass albums ever. —*Mark Humphrey*

Bluegrass Breakdown / Rounder
Great 1964 performances. —*Mark Humphrey*

Joel Mabus

Traditional bluegrass.
Based in Michigan, Mabus has released albums over the years on his Fossil Record label and on Flying Fish. —*Richard Meyer*

Fairies and Fools / Flying Fish

Firelake / Fossil

Settin' the Woods on Fire / Flying Fish

● **Fortunes** / Fossil

Jimmy Martin

Traditional bluegrass.
Blessed with a great tenor voice, this traditional bluegrass singer and guitarist mastered his craft as lead vocalist for Bill Monroe's Blue Grass Boys for much of 1949-1951 and again in 1952-1953. Martin's vocals and his dynamic guitar playing both complemented Monroe perfectly, and in the opinion of many, he was the finest lead singer and guitarist Bill Monroe ever had. In 1951, between stints with Monroe's band, Martin joined with the Osborne Brothers, forming the Sunny Mountain Boys. Though this association lasted only until 1955, Martin has used this band name up to the present. In keeping up such high standards over the years, Martin has hired numerous major-league musicians, including banjo players J. D. Crowe, Bill Emerson, Vic Jordan, and Alan Munde, and mandolin player Paul Williams, all of whom subsequently made it big in bluegrass. Jimmy Martin is required listening for anyone with more than a passing interest in bluegrass. —*David Vinopal*

☆ **You Don't Know My Mind (1956-1966)** / Rounder
A Monroe band veteran with astonishing high pipes and a penchant for blending bluegrass and honky-tonk. Great bands, great songs, and classic 1956-1966 Decca sides. —*Mark Humphrey*

The McCoury Brothers

Traditional bluegrass.
Del and Jerry McCoury pursued individual careers in bluegrass before the Pennsylvania-born siblings teamed up for the 1987 Rounder album, *The McCoury Brothers.* Older brother Del played banjo before switching to guitar and singing lead with Bill Monroe's Blue Grass Boys in 1963-1964. He subsequently led his Dixie Pals and recorded for both Rounder and Rebel. Jerry sang and played bass with Red Allen and the Kentuckians, as well as with Don Reno and Bill Harrell. The McCoury Brothers' sole album together to date is a wonderful close-harmony exposition of bluegrass, rooted in the "brother duo" tradition. —*Mark Humphrey*

○ **The McCoury Brothers** / Rounder
Jerry and Del McCoury fit together like hand-in-glove on these fine performances. —*Mark Humphrey*

Del McCoury

Traditional bluegrass.
Del McCoury was guitarist and lead singer in one of Bill Monroe's great bands in the early '60s. He went on to form high-quality traditional bluegrass bands, including the Dixie Pals, a band he organized with his brother Jerry in 1969. Del McCoury is well known for his exceptional vocal leads. —*David Vinopal*

Don't Stop the Music / 1990 / Rounder
The title track is a George Jones song. The album includes diverse and often bluesy material and fine performances. —*Mark Humphrey*

○ **Classic Bluegrass** / RB
Rebel label recordings from the '70s by the man who sometimes sounds more like Bill Monroe than Monroe himself. Stunning, pure, high lonesome pipes and mountain bluesy songs. Beautiful. —*Mark Humphrey*

High on a Mountain / Rounder
More grand bluegrass. —*Mark Humphrey*

Bill Monroe

1911
Traditional bluegrass.
Bill Monroe invented bluegrass music and reinvented the mandolin, two of the many reasons he's in the Country Music Hall of Fame. He has for decades been a tower in country music, as influential as the Carter Family, Jimmie Rodgers, and Hank Williams. His band, the Blue Grass Boys, has yielded graduates who make up a Who's Who in bluegrass history, including Flatt and Scruggs, Reno and Smiley, Mac Wiseman, and Carter Stanley. No one has shown greater love for the music, nor done more to promote it, than Bill Monroe. From 1927, when he and his brothers got a band together, up to the present, Bill Monroe has toured

and played in schools and cellars and tents and auditoriums and in the open; as of this writing, he has been on the road for over 55 years. And he obviously loves what he does at least as much now as when he started. He'll perform his beloved bluegrass until he dies. It's difficult to imagine any type of music having a stronger advocate.

With Bill on mandolin, Charlie on guitar, and Birch on fiddle, in 1934 the Monroe Brothers played on a Chicago radio station, then moved to the Carolinas, where Bill and Charlie cut some records in 1936. The duo's sound was much closer to the prevailing duet sounds at the time than to what evolved into bluegrass. Two years later the band separated, with Bill moving on to an Atlanta radio station and forming the first of his many Blue Grass Boys configurations. By October 1939, when he debuted on the Opry with "Mule Skinner Blues" (a Jimmie Rodgers song), he had already established his trademarks—the high, pure tenor and the powerful instrumental leads on the mandolin. In 1945 Earl Scruggs and his banjo entered the band, and the bluegrass sound was complete. When Earl Scruggs left three years later, Bill Monroe replaced him with the first of a long succession of Scruggs-style banjo pickers. As band members came and went, the Monroe sound stayed intact.

As country music tastes have changed over the last half-century, so have most of the acts, with performers understandably trying to make a better living from prevailing musical fads. But not Bill Monroe and his Blue Grass Boys. In feast or famine, Bill's sound has remained the same—that high and lonesome tenor, the mastery of the mandolin, and that unyielding determination to protect and preserve the bluegrass music he so loves. —*David Vinopal*

○ **Bill Monroe—Bluegrass** / Bear Family
1950-1958. This superb 4-CD boxed set from Bear Family (import) offers the most comprehensive collection of Bill Monroe ever assembled. The liner notes are beautifully done—pictures, discography, the works. A second box covering the period from 1959 on is also available. —*Michael Erlewine*

Mule Skinner Blues / 1940 / RC
On these 1940-1941 recordings of the earliest and loosest bluegrass band, Monroe is wearing his blues, old-time, and even swing influences on his sleeve. —*Mark Humphrey*

☆ **The Essential Bill Monroe (1945-1949)** / 1992 / Sony
A 2-CD set of all the "classic" Blue Grass Boys material (the band with Flatt and Scruggs). This is the music that defined bluegrass. —*Mark Humphrey*

★ **Country Music Hall of Fame** / MCA
A brilliant overview of one of the great originators and synthesists of 20th-century music on these 16 selections from 1950-1988. Classic music with a consistent vision and varied accompanists. —*Mark Humphrey*

★ **The Music of Bill Monroe from 1936 to 1994** / MCA 11048
A wonderful 4-CD boxed set covering Monroe's entire career from his earliest recordings with the Monroe Brothers in 1936 to a previously unreleased live performance from January 1994. This beautiful package, complete with comprehensive liner notes and photos, gives the best overview of Monroe's legacy available in this country. —*Chris Woodstra*

Lynn Morris Band

Traditional bluegrass.
Lynn Morris is a well-respected vocalist and guitar player. Her band consists of Tom Adams (banjo), David McLaughlin (mandolin), Stuart Duncan (fiddle), and Marshall Wilborn (bass and vocals). They play a blend of bluegrass, folk, and country music. —*Chip Renner*

The Bramble and the Rose / 1992 / Rounder
A solid release, with great vocals and a good cover of "Blue Skies and Teardrops." Another fine effort. Lynn Morris and Marshall Wilborn's harmonies are very good. Stuart Duncan stands out on fiddle. —*Chip Renner*

○ **Lynn Morris Band** / Rounder
Great sound, great vocals, and outstanding bluegrass. It includes "Enjoy Black Pony" and "Come Early Morning." —*Chip Renner*

The Nashville Bluegrass Band

1984

Traditional bluegrass, progressive bluegrass.
This veteran group got together in 1984 and plays traditional bluegrass, sometimes in a more progressive style. Guitarist Pat Enright is the bandleader. Their video received considerable airplay in 1992, unusual for a bluegrass band. —*David Vinopal*

My Native Home / 1985 / Rounder
A flawless album. One of their best. —*Chip Renner*

Idletime / 1986 / Rounder
This hits on all cylinders with 12 tight songs. Has the classic "The Train Carryin' Jimmie Rodgers Home." —*Chip Renner*

To Be His Child / 1987 / Rounder
A gospel album. Good. —*Chip Renner*

○ **The Boys Are Back in Town** / 1990 / Sugar Hill
Very well performed, highly recommended. These vocals are on the mark. Produced by Jerry Douglas. —*Chip Renner*

New Grass Revival

Progressive bluegrass.
The Revival, formed in 1972 by four former members of the Bluegrass Alliance, was named by leader Sam Bush and flourished in the decade when numerous groups took traditional bluegrass and changed it to varying degrees. Bush's group was successful enough to have the group's name become a generic label: "newgrass." The band's image, with long hair and occasionally electrified instruments, as well as its musical material, contrasted greatly with standard (traditional) bluegrass like that played by Bill Monroe, Ralph Stanley, the Lilly Brothers, and Lester Flatt's band. In terms of longevity, popularity, and exposure, the Revival, with its hip reputation, was perhaps the most successful in competition against II Generation, Seldom Scene, the Country Gentlemen, and others. In personnel, the Revival's best-known band includes Bush, John Cowan, Bela Fleck, and Pat Flynn. They have covered material from Leon Russell, Bob Marley, and Curtis Mayfield. —*David Vinopal*

Fly through the Country / 1975 / 1975 / Flying Fish
This first version of New Grass was not so polished as their second era, but they had good chemistry. You've gotta love "These Days," "Skippin'," "All Night Train," and "Fly through the Country." —*Chip Renner*

Too Late to Turn Back Now / 1977 / Flying Fish
Recorded live at Telluride, CO, with guests J. Hartford and Peter Rowan, this one has a good-time feel. —*Chip Renner*

Barren County / 1979 / Flying Fish
The first incarnation of this band was never better than on this one. Strong songs and vocals. —*Chip Renner*

○ **Commonwealth** / 1981 / Flying Fish
The best of their newer era, with guests Leon Russell, Sharon White, and Kenny Malone. The cover of Hartford's "Steam Powered Aereo Plane" is great. —*Chip Renner*

Live / 1984 / Sugar Hill
Includes a 19-minute version of "Sapporo." Buy this one after checking the rest of their material. —*Chip Renner*

New Grass Revival / 1986 / Emi-Usa
A solid release, and a great cover of Peter Rowan's "Revival." Pat Flynn shows some good songwriting on "In the Middle of the Night," "Lonely Rider," "Sweet Release," and "How Many Hearts." Sam Busit and John Cowan come together well on T. Moore's "Saw You Runnin'." —*Chip Renner*

Hold to a Dream / 1987 / 1987 / Capitol
A good use of drums on this one. It worked. Standout tracks include "Looking Past You," "Unconditional Love," "Metric Lips," and the title track. —*Chip Renner*

On the Boulevard / 1988 / Sugar Hill
An overlooked CD with a couple of standout tracks. Played beginning to end, this one will leave you fulfilled. —*Chip Renner*

Friday Night in America / 1989 / Capitol
Their last album covers John Hiatt's "Angel Eyes," Jesse Winchester's "Let's Make a Baby King," and Bela Fleck's "Big Foot." Hot! These guys will be missed. —*Chip Renner*

Mark O'Connor

Progressive country, instrumental bluegrass.
Even the fiddling contests Mark O'Connor was winning while still a kid didn't prepare listeners for how good he would become, and

he's barely into his thirties now. He started out playing pure country, but the fact that he has been a sideman on over 400 albums tells us that he's incredibly versatile. Lots of fiddlers are more "pure country," but only a handful (if that) can match his technique. He's a virtuoso. His *New Nashville Cats* album (with 53 guest musicians and a variety of music styles) won a Grammy in 1992 and made him famous. He's also the music director of TNN's "American Music Shop." — *David Vinopal*

○ **The New Nashville Cats** / 1991 / Warner
A fine collection of friends on this CD. Slick country featuring Sam Bush, Jerry Douglas, Bela Fleck, Vince Gill, John Cowan, Ricky Skaggs. This CD won two Grammy Awards. As good as they come! — *Chip Renner*

Championship Years / Country Music Foundation
These are good-quality early recordings from his championship days. — *Chip Renner*

Elysian Forest / Warner
More in the new-age frontier. Mark O'Connor's fiddle turns into a violin right in front of your ears, if you know what I mean. — *Chip Renner*

False Dawn / Rounder
New-age acoustic music. A turning-point album in which O'Connor comes of age. — *Chip Renner*

Mark O'Connor / Rounder
An early album. Raw. — *Chip Renner*

Markology / Rounder
An acoustic-guitar album. — *Chip Renner*

On the Mark / Warner
Featuring James Taylor, Jerry Douglas, and Michael Brecker (one of my favorites). Great sax on "Get Set, Go." A must-have for O'Connor fans. — *Chip Renner*

On the Rampage / Rounder
New-age. — *Chip Renner*

Pickin' in the Wind / Rounder
Bluegrass, newgrass. — *Chip Renner*

Retrospective / Rounder
A good all-around sampler of O'Connor's Rounder catalog. — *Chip Renner*

Soppin' the Gravy / Rounder
Good Texas fiddle music. — *Chip Renner*

Stone from Which the Arch Was Made / Warner
R&B featuring Bela Fleck, Jerry Douglas, John McCutheon, and Maura O'Connell. Very nice; more rock and electric. — *Chip Renner*

Old & in the Way

Progressive bluegrass.
Jerry Garcia (banjo and vocals), Peter Rowan (guitar and vocals), David Grisman (mandolin and vocals), Vassar Clements (fiddle), and John Kahn (acoustic bass). — *Chip Renner*

○ **Old & in the Way** / 1975 / Rykodisc
This release was one of the greatest things to happen to bluegrass music, in that it exposed a whole new audience to bluegrass music and acoustic music. — *Chip Renner*

The Osborne Brothers

Traditional bluegrass, progressive bluegrass.
From Hyden, KY, Bobby (b 1931) and Sonny (b 1937) Osborne for the last 40 years have been one of country music's most successful bluegrass bands. As music tastes changed, so did the Osbornes, remaining true to Bobby's mandolin and Sonny's five-string banjo, though modifying traditional music to make it more palatable to current tastes and adding songs from other genres. Their swings into and out of progressive bluegrass and electrified instruments worked—the Osbornes have not only survived but thrived over all these years, maintaining their insistence on quality and their unique sound.
In 1956 they became regulars on WWVA's Wheeling Jamboree (the Opry's chief competitor) and developed, with guitarist Benny Birchfield, their trademark trio-singing which was intricate and modern and traditional at the same time. In 1959, in the heat of the folk revival, they became the first bluegrass band to play a college date (at Antioch College in Ohio). In 1964 the brothers joined the Opry, where their progressive sound alienated some

purists; but even the detractors admitted that, with musical tastes aside, the Osbornes were vocally and instrumentally unsurpassed. Bobby's highest-of-the-high tenor and his exceptional mandolin playing combined beautifully with Sonny's vocal harmony and dynamic banjo playing.
In 1968 the Osbornes had a hit with the song that has become their signature tune, "Rocky Top." Their many albums offer material from traditional bluegrass to newgrass, and the many variations in between. — *David Vinopal*

Singing Shouting Praises / 1988 / Sugar Hill
Nice bluegrass gospel. — *Mark Humphrey*

Bobby & His Mandolin / CMH
An album featuring sprightly mandolin renditions of traditional fiddle tunes. Nice. — *Mark Humphrey*

Greatest Bluegrass Hits / CM
A good "favorites" collection. — *Mark Humphrey*

☆ **The Osborne Brothers** / RS
Great vocal harmonies and tightly woven banjo-mandolin conversations. The best early material from 1959-1963. — *Mark Humphrey*

Best of the Osborne Brothers / MCA
Their 1963-1967 Decca hits blend smooth bluegrass with then-contemporary country production. A unique sound, radical for its time. — *Mark Humphrey*

Peter Rowan

Progressive bluegrass.
Rowan has been a high-profile figure in American popular music since the '60s, among a group of Bostonians (including Jim Rooney and Bill Keith) who helped bluegrass grow big in northern cities. After a stint as a Blue Grass Boy, Rowan played with various progressive country bands, and with David Grisman and Bill Monroe. He has been a founding member of the bands Seatrain, Earth Opera, and Old & in the Way. — *David Vinopal & Richard Meyer*

Walls of Time / 1982 / Sugar Hill
This release is hard to put a finger on. The music takes on a feel more like that of the Old & in the Way band, yet seems to be missing the "something special" that project had. — *Chip Renner*

Red Hot Pickers / 1984 / Sugar Hill
Peter Rowan is backed by Richard Greene (fiddle), Tony Trischka (banjo), Andy Statman (mandolin), and Roger Mason (bass). This is a lively, well-played album. — *Chip Renner*

First Whippoorwill / 1985 / Sugar Hill
A good album. Rowan stacks the deck with Sam Bush, Bill Keith, Richard Greene, Buddy Spicher, and Roy Huskey Jr. — *Chip Renner*

○ **New Moon Rising** / 1988 / Sugar Hill
Tight album. Rowan is backed by the Nashville Bluegrass Band. Maura O'Connell sings harmony vocals on "Meadow Green" and Jerry Douglas is featured on dobro. This release set the tune for some real good music. — *Chip Renner*

Dust Bowl Children / 1990 / Sugar Hill
A very good album. It is all acoustic featuring Peter Rowan alone on guitar, mandola, and vocals. This grows on you. — *Chip Renner*

All on a Rising Day / 1991 / Sugar Hill
An all-around fine release. Rowan picks up where he left off on *Dust Bowl* but improves on the idea with some great backup musicians—Stuart Duncan, Sam Bush, Jerry Douglas, Alison Krauss, Roy Husky Jr, Alan O'Bryant, Edgar Meyer. Twelve solid songs. Highly recommended! — *Chip Renner*

The Rowans

Progressive bluegrass.
Formed in the mid '70s, the group consists of brothers Peter, Chris, and Lorin Rowan. The Rowans produced three albums of original songs and rich harmonies. This was a turning point for Peter Rowan away from his more rock efforts. — *Chip Renner*

○ **The Rowans** / 1975 / Asylum
The Rowans put out a strong album featuring killer songs of Peter's—"Midnight Moonlight," "Thunder on the Mountain," and "Beggar in Bluejeans." The album also features Lorin's "On the Ground" and Chris's "Here Today and Gone Tomorrow." First-class album. — *Chip Renner*

Jubilations / 1977 / Asylum
The final Rowans album. Peter steps back, only producing three songs. —*Chip Renner*

Sibling Rivalry / 1978 / Asylum
Not so good as their debut album. Includes Peter and Lorin's "Tired Hands" and "Mongolian Swamp/Kings Men." —*Chip Renner*

Earl Scruggs

1924
Traditional bluegrass.
Earl Scruggs is to the five-string banjo what Paganini was to the violin. After more than twenty years with the Foggy Mountain Boys, forming the most famous band in bluegrass history, Scruggs and Lester Flatt parted company in 1969 because of artistic differences, with Flatt pursuing more traditional sounds and Scruggs forming the Earl Scruggs Revue with his two sons. The Revue appealed more to a young and urban audience and, with dobro player Josh Graves, played rock and other non-country music. Scruggs has made many albums since his parting with Flatt (including *The Storyteller and the Banjoman* with Tom T. Hall in 1982) and is seen on TV, often for reunion appearances. —*David Vinopal*

○ **Dueling Banjos** / 1984 / Columbia
A classic album. Scruggs shines on this one. —*Chip Renner*

Family Portrait / Columbia
Scruggs and family put out a nice, well-crafted album. —*Chip Renner*

Live from Austin City Limits / Columbia
The crowd enjoys this live show—you will too. —*Chip Renner*

Seldom Scene

Progressive bluegrass.
Mandolin-great John Duffey, formerly of the Country Gentlemen, formed the Seldom Scene newgrass band in 1971 in the Washington, DC, area. He surrounded himself with major-leaguers, including Mike Auldridge on dobro, Ben Eldridge on banjo, John Starling as guitarist/lead singer, and Tom Gray (another Country Gentleman alumnus) as bass player. They are at (or near) the top of newgrass bands. —*David Vinopal*

Act Two / 1973 / RB
They cover some good songs by Gene Clark and B. Lead on "Train Leaves Here," Norman Blake's "Last Train," and Hank Williams's "House of Gold." —*Chip Renner*

Old Train / 1974 / RB
Catch this album featuring Duffy, Starling, Eldridge, Auldridge, and Gray, plus Linda Ronstadt, Ricky Skaggs, Paul Craft, and Bob Williams. Includes a good cover of "Pan American." —*Chip Renner*

Live at the Cellar Door / 1975 / RB
A two-record set of a very good live show, with covers of "City of New Orleans," "Raw Hide," and "If I Were a Carpenter." —*Chip Renner*

○ **New Seldom Scene Album** / 1976 / RB
Duffey, Starling, Auldridge, Eldridge, and Gray put out one of the best bluegrass albums ever. Linda Ronstadt sings with them on one song. It doesn't get much better than this. —*Chip Renner*

Act Four / 1978 / Sugar Hill
Features a good cover of Bob Wills's "San Antonio Rose." —*Chip Renner*

Baptizing / 1978 / RB
An enjoyable gospel album, with guest Ricky Skaggs. —*Chip Renner*

After Midnight / 1981 / Sugar Hill
Good vocals, with covers of Eric Clapton's "Lay Down Sally" and J. J. Cale's "After Midnight." —*Chip Renner*

15th Anniversary Celebration / 1981 / Sugar Hill
A 20-song live CD with Duffey, Auldridge, Mike Reid, Eldridge, and Gray. A must for fans, with special guests galore—Emmylou Harris, Ricky Skaggs, Linda Ronstadt, John Starling, Tony Rice, Jonathan Edwards, and others. —*Chip Renner*

Change of Scenery / Sugar Hill / 1988
Their vocal sound is changed here, but this is a first-class CD. Check out "West Texas Wind." —*Chip Renner*

○ **Blue Ridge** / Sugar Hill
Songwriter and vocalist Jonathan Edwards ("Sunshine") teams with the Seldom Scene's flawless playing. Featuring Edwards, John Duffey, Mike Auldridge, Phil Rosenthal, Ben Eldridge, Tom Gray, Robbie Magruder, and Kenny White. —*Chip Renner*

Best of Seldom Scene—Vol. 1 / RB
A good collection from the Rebel label. —*Chip Renner*

Shady Grove Band

Traditional bluegrass.
This band plays traditional bluegrass with an old-timey feel. —*Chip Renner*

Mulberry Moon / Flying Fish
Same level as *On the Line*. —*Chip Renner*

○ **On the Line** / Flying Fish
A good, solid bluegrass album. —*Chip Renner*

Sidesaddle

Progressive bluegrass.
Sidesaddle is a bluegrass band that has country, Western, Irish, and folk influences. The band features Kim Elking (mandolin), Lee Anne Caswell (fiddle), Sheila McCormick (guitar), Jackie Miller (guitar), and Sonia Shell (banjo). —*Chip Renner*

○ **Daylight Train** / Turquoise
Sidesaddle's unique sound sets it apart from other bluegrass bands. The vocals blend nicely, with an Irish feel at times. These are also first-class musicians. An exciting album. —*Chip Renner*

The Red Rose Saloon / Turquoise
A very good record—nominated for Best Bluegrass Album (NAIRD). —*Chip Renner*

Skyline

Progressive bluegrass.
Featuring banjoist Tony Trischka, Skyline helped pioneer the newgrass sound in the '80s, combining a bluegrass/country blend with strong songs and tight harmonies. —*Chip Renner*

Skyline Drive / Flying Fish
A strong project with great harmonies. —*Chip Renner*

Late to Work / 1979 / Flying Fish
Skyline's debut album. Strong songs. Trischka's band blends vocals to perfection. —*Chip Renner*

Fire of Grace / 1979 / Flying Fish
Rachel Kalen replaced DeDe Wyland on this record. —*Chip Renner*

○ **Stranded in the Moonlight** / Flying Fish
The band hits its stride on this very rich album. Tight harmonies and great original compositions. —*Chip Renner*

Southern Rail

Traditional bluegrass.
Southern Rail is a bluegrass band that plays traditional and original material. They consist of Jim Muller (guitar, vocals), Jim Rohrer (mandolin, bass vocals), Sharon Horovitch (bass, tenor vocals), and Dave Dick (banjo, baritone vocals). —*Chip Renner*

○ **Drive by Night** / Turquoise
Good solid bluegrass. Clean, with rich vocals and first-class playing. —*Chip Renner*

Larry Sparks

Traditional bluegrass.
One of the finer lead singers in contemporary bluegrass, Sparks filled in with Ralph Stanley's band after the great Carter Stanley died in 1966. He went on to head the Lonesome Ramblers, an excellent traditional band popular on albums and at festivals right through the '80s. —*David Vinopal*

The Best of Larry Sparks / Rebel
A fine traditional bluegrass singer. —*Mark Humphrey*

○ **Larry Sparks Sings Hank Williams** / Rebel
A minor classic. Honky-tonk meets bluegrass. —*Mark Humphrey*

The Special Consensus

Traditional bluegrass.

The current band features Greg Cahill (banjo), Dallas Wayne (bass), Marty Marrone (guitar), and Al Murphy (fiddle). They are a highly respected bluegrass band that also plays gospel, covers, and original material. *—Chip Renner*

○ **Hey, Y'All** / Turquoise
This great album features Elvis Presley's "Viva Las Vegas," "When the Walls Come Tumblin' Down," "I Can't Sit Down," and others. Some of the better bluegrass music around. *—Chip Renner*

The Stanley Brothers

Traditional bluegrass.
If you even *think* you know bluegrass, you have to know Ralph (b 1927)and Carter Stanley (b 1925), the Stanley Brothers. Parallel to Flatt and Scruggs and Bill Monroe's Blue Grass Boys, though not with their renown, were Virginians Ralph and Carter, mountain boys who took those mountains and their traditions and their songs and wove them into a traditional bluegrass sound of utter purity, simplicity, and astonishing beauty. Their first band, formed around 1947, played more of a mountain/folk music reminiscent of the old string bands, changing to their style of ultra-traditional bluegrass when Bill Monroe's band became popular. Even on their recordings in the early '50s, the Stanleys' unmistakable sound is there, with guitarist Carter singing lead and banjo player Ralph singing tenor harmony. In the opinion of many, Carter possessed the best lead voice in bluegrass history—rich, emotional, and (in the best sense of the word) lonely. He took a happy song and sang it sad; he took a sad song and sang it sadder. And Ralph's unworldly mountain tenor matched his brother's voice perfectly, soaring above and often lightening the emotional load of the lyrics, creating a duet unsurpassed in country history.
The great Carter Stanley died in 1966. In spite of numerous personnel changes over the last quarter-century, Ralph Stanley has retained the original sound with the Clinch Mountain Boys, his high tenor and tasteful banjo playing preserving the legacy of the inimitable Stanley Brothers. *—David Vinopal*

Stanley Series—Vol. 2 #1 / 1956 / Copper Creek
Live recordings and wonderful performances of several Stanley standards. *—Mark Humphrey*

Stanley Series—Vol. 3 #3 / Copper Creek
More fine live performances. *—Mark Humphrey*

Hymns and Sacred Songs / 1960 / King
King-label sacred sides. Lovely. *—Mark Humphrey*

Long Journey Home / Rebel
From the '60s, and great as always. *—Mark Humphrey*

☆ **Columbia Sessions 1949-1950 #1** / Rounder
Beautiful vocal harmonies and piquant songs. Bluegrass poetry at its purest. *—Mark Humphrey*

Columbia Sessions #2 / Rounder
More wonderful early performances. *—Mark Humphrey*

★ **The Stanley Brothers (1949-1952)** / Bear Family
All 22 of the their Columbia recordings, superbly remastered, including the issued and alternate takes of two classics, "The Fields Have Turned Brown" and "Little Glass of Wine." Carter Stanley's dramatic story songs are underpinned by chilling vocal harmonies and an ensemble sound that bore their unique signature. *—Mark Humphrey*

Ralph Stanley

Traditional bluegrass.
After brother Carter died in 1966, Ralph Stanley was quick in hiring talented Larry Sparks (to handle Carter's leads) and fiddler Curly Ray Cline. In the years since, the Clinch Mountain Boys have undergone numerous changes in band personnel, but Stanley has kept his standards high, over the years hiring Ricky Skaggs, Keith Whitley, Roy Lee Centers, Jack Cooke, and others. As of this writing, the band is still much in demand, with a full schedule year-round. *—David Vinopal*

Pray for the Boys / 1990 / Rebel
Sacred performances with the Clinch Mountain Boys. *—Mark Humphrey*

☆ **Bound to Ride** / Rebel

This legendary singer and banjoist's most atavistic performances, with claw-hammer banjo and terrific wailing Baptist banshee vocals on old-time songs. *—Mark Humphrey*

Star-Spangled Washboard Band

Progressive bluegrass.
A hilarious washboard band that features humor and high-energy bluegrass in their shows. *—Chip Renner*

○ **Collector's Item** / 1978 / Flying Fish
A very funny, oddball bluegrass band. This album brings out the best of their live show, "Radarbeems." *—Chip Renner*

John Starling

Progressive bluegrass.
A US Army surgeon, guitarist, and singer, Starling played with the Seldom Scene progressive bluegrass band from 1971 until 1977. After playing with various other groups in the '80s, he recently rejoined Seldom Scene. *—David Vinopal*

○ **Long Time Gone** / Sugar Hill
This is the kind of album you play over and over again. Featuring Lowell George, Emmylou Harris, Tony Rice, and Ricky Skaggs. Highly recommended. *—Chip Renner*

Waitin' on a Southern Train / Sugar Hill
Another strong effort. Mike Auldridge, Sam Bush, and John Cowan back up John. Good selection of songs; "New Delhi Freight Train" stands out. *—Chip Renner*

Andy Statman

Progressive bluegrass.
Andy Statman is a talented mandolin player who plays all styles of mandolin music. *—Chip Renner*

Flatbush Waltz / Rounder
A good album featuring Kenny Kosak, Russ Barenberg, Matt Glaser, and others. *—Chip Renner*

○ **Nashville Mornings, New York Nights** / Rounder
An excellent display of mandolin artistry, featuring Bela Fleck, Tony Trischka, Jerry Douglas, Vassar Clements, Russ Barenberg, and Kenny Kosek. *—Chip Renner*

Carl Story

1916
Traditional bluegrass, gospel.
Carl Story could rightly be called the father of bluegrass gospel. Though from the late 30s he has recorded much secular material, it's with the sacred-quartet material with bluegrass instrumentation that he's gained his reputation. His falsetto voice is his trademark. *—David Vinopal*

○ **Mighty Close to Heaven** / Starday

Strength in Numbers

Progressive bluegrass.
Strength in Numbers consists of Sam Bush (fiddle and mandolin), Jerry Douglas (dobro), Bela Fleck (guitar and banjo), Mark O'Connor (guitar and mandolin), and Edgar Meyer (bass). Each is a recognized as a highly influential master of his instrument. After working together in various combinations through the '80s on each other's solo albums, they became known as the Telluride All Stars for their outstanding performances at the Telluride Bluegrass Festival in Telluride, CO. All the members are involved in other endeavors and consider this a fun project. *—Chip Renner*

○ **Telluride Sessions** / Mca
Bush, Fleck, Douglas, O'Connor, and Meyer. Each song is a collaboration by two members of the group. These guys just don't put out a bad record. Bluegrass to newgrass to jazz-grass! *—Chip Renner*

Tony Trischka

Progressive bluegrass.
An influential banjo player with Country Cooking (a Syracuse University-based band that recorded progressive bluegrass for Rounder Records in the '70s), Trischka has moved further from bluegrass into jazz and other non-traditional styles. *—David Vinopal*

Hill Country / 1991 / Rounder

A traditional bluegrass album. —*Chip Renner*

○ **Dust on the Needle** / Rounder
A good collection of Trischka's six Rounder albums, featuring Sam Bush, Marc O'Connor, and David Grisman. —*Chip Renner*

Robot Plane Flies over Arkansas / Rounder
An early release that spotlights Trischka's banjo skills. A progressive album. —*Chip Renner*

Sally Van Meter

Traditional bluegrass.
Sally Van Meter is one of the top dobro players in the bluegrass field. She has played with Blue Rose and the Good Ol' Persons. —*Chip Renner*

○ **All in Good Time** / Sugar Hill
Sally Van Meter's debut album is a chance for her dobro to stand out, and it does. She gets help from Mike Marshall, Todd Phillips, Tony Furtado, and John Pederson. —*Chip Renner*

Rhonda Vincent

Progressive bluegrass.
Rhonda Vincent is one of the finest vocalists in bluegrass today. Her voice is clear and rich. She is also a respectable fiddler and mandolinist. —*Chip Renner*

○ **Timeless and True Love** / 1991 / Rebel
Rhonda Vincent's vocals shine on this release, cementing her place as one of the finest vocalists in bluegrass. This CD features 12 solid cuts, and she is backed by Darrin Vincent, Bela Fleck, Alison Brown, Randy Kohrs, Scott Sanders, Kenny Malone, Sonny Louvin, and Hargus "Pig" Robbins. —*Chip Renner*

Clarence White

1944-1973
Traditional bluegrass.
With his brother Roland, guitar'Clarence White began his career in bluegrass and first gained fame with the influential Kentucky Colonels on the West Coast in the early '60s. In 1965, after the Colonels had recorded two albums, White left to become a much-in-demand session guitaris, working with Ricky Nelson, the Everly Brothers, and others. White joined the Byrds full-time in 1968, becoming famous as a country-rock guitarist, before he died accidently in 1973. —*David Vinopal*

○ **And the Kentucky Colonels** / 1964 / Rounder
Clarence White & the Kentucky Colonels includes 1964-1967 live performances that are musts for bluegrass guitar enthusiasts. White was a member of the Byrds and a session player for Linda Ronstadt and the Everly Brothers. —*Richard Lieberson*

Live in Sweden 1973 / Rounder
A good live show. Clarence White is at his best, performing with the White Brothers. —*Chip Renner*

Mac Wiseman

1925
Traditional bluegrass.
If a poll were conducted to find the most popular bluegrass artists, on the list would be a number of groups but only one name unassociated with a particular band. And that would be Mac Wiseman, who over the years has been famous for his clear and mellow tenor voice. Though Wiseman has with many of the great bands, including those of mountain singer Molly O'Day, Flatt and Scruggs, Bill Monroe, and the Osborne Brothers, his great voice has always kept a separate identity of its own. His material has ranged from the old ("Jimmy Brown the Newsboy," "I'll Be All Smiles Tonight") to the new ("You're the Best of All the Leading Brands," "A Million Million Girls," "If I Had Johnny's Cash and Charley's Pride"). Wiseman's command of traditional material makes him much in demand by bluegrass and folk fans alike. —*David Vinopal*

Essential Bluegrass Album / 1969 / CM
Classics on a double album. These old salts play like spring chickens. Highly recommended. —*Chip Renner*

Songs that Made the Jukebox Play / 1974 / CM
A nice album. —*Chip Renner*

Mac Wiseman Sings Gordon Lightfoot / 1979 / CM
Well done. Belongs in the collection of any Gordon Lightfoot fan. —*Chip Renner*

Classic Bluegrass / 1987 / RB
Very good. Bluegrass at its best. —*Chip Renner*

Greatest Bluegrass Hits / 1989 / CM
A good collection. —*Chip Renner*

Country Music Memories / CMH
This has a slightly different sound than other albums; more country than bluegrass. —*Chip Renner*

Grassroots to Bluegrass / CMH
Grammy finalist with 22 songs. —*Chip Renner*

○ **The Mac Wiseman Story** / CM
The best of Mac Wiseman. A good place to start. —*Chip Renner*

Bluegrass Collections

○ **Bluegrass Class of 1990** / 1990 / Rounder
An excellent sampler, featuring Ricky Skaggs, Tony Rice, Alison Krauss, Lynn Morris, Sam Bush, and J. D. Crowe. A good way to start your bluegrass collection. —*Chip Renner*

○ **Country Cooking: 14 Instrumentals** / Rounder
Country Cooking: 14 Bluegrass Instrumentals is a good collection of instrumentals. —*Chip Renner*

○ **Country Cooking: 26 Instrumentals** / Rounder
The best place to start. *Country Cooking: 26 Bluegrass Instrumentals* is packed with music. —*Chip Renner*

○ **Early Mandolin Classics—Vol. 1** / Rounder
A fascinating glimpse into multi-ethnic mandolin music in the '20s and '30s. Recordings from ragtime and blues to Ukrainian bands and, of course, hillbillies. —*Mark Humphrey*

○ **Flatpicking Guitar Festival** / 1989 / Shanachie
A very clean, traditional flatpicking album featuring David Bromberg, Richard Lieberson, Dick Fegy, Tom Gilfellon, and others. —*Chip Renner*

○ **Mountain Music—Bluegrass Style** / Folkways
This classic reissue features performances by Don Stover, Earl Taylor, Chubby Anthony, Tex Logan, and others. —*Richard Meyer*

○ **Rounder Banjo** / Rounder
An extensive catalog of banjo music featuring Snuffy Jenkens, J. D. Crowe, Bela Fleck, Tony Trischka, and many more. —*Chip Renner*

○ **Rounder Bluegrass—Vol. 1** / Rounder
Highly recommended. The best bluegrass money can buy! —*Chip Renner*

Rounder Bluegrass—Vol. 2 / Rounder
A collection of fine music. —*Chip Renner*

○ **Rounder Fiddle** / Rounder
A loaded album featuring a wide range of fiddle music by Ricky Skaggs, Eddie Stubbs, Alison Krauss, Vassar Clements, and Byron Berline. More than '60 minutes of music. —*Chip Renner*

○ **Rounder Guitar—Acoustic Guitar** / Rounder
Rounder Guitar—Collection of Acoustic Guitar is a fine compilation of flat- and finger-pickin' acoustic guitar featuring Tony Rice, Mark O'Connor, Norman Blake, Dan Crary, and others. —*Chip Renner*

○ **Rounder Sampler—Traditional Music** / Rounder
A good collection of traditional music. Start your collection here and discover some new artists. —*Chip Renner*

☆ **Twenty-Four Greatest Bluegrass Hits** / CMH
The bluegrass greats, ranging from Bill Monroe to Flatt and Scruggs and the Osborne Brothers. —*David Vinopal*

RAP MUSIC

No one who heard the Sugarhill Gang's "Rapper's Delight" when it was released in 1979 could have guessed that rap would become the most important and incendiary music of the 80s and 90s. Certainly there wasn't much in the song to suggest such grandiose notions: Over a bass groove borrowed from Chic's "Good Times," Big Bank Hank, Master Gee, and Wonder Mike offered a series of humorous boasts in a drawling fashion that wasn't quite spoken-word but definitely wasn't conventional singing. The pumping music was rooted in the house-party traditions of the Bronx, where DJs mixed throbbing funk records through massive sound systems. Although people snapped the record up, most critics thought the song was an intriguing novelty hit and left it at that.

But that silly novelty tune introduced the masses to a challenging new facet of R&B. By the time Grandmaster Flash and the Furious Five released "The Message" in 1982, rap had established itself as the next link in the chain that connects Delta and urban blues, R&B, soul, funk, and disco. "The Message" was a stark, shocking cry from the ghetto, centered around Melle Mel's warning, "Don't push me 'cause I'm close to the edge." By expanding the still-young genre's musical and lyrical boundaries, "The Message" opened the doors to a new form of expression. Coupled with the low-cost equipment needed to make the music – a couple of mikes, a PA, a turntable, and some source records – rap became accessible to anyone who had a way with words and a clever DJ who could cut records on the turntable.

By 1984 rap had exploded, with dozens of grassroots independent labels releasing bold new records (mostly singles) by the likes of Kurtis Blow, Run-D.M.C., the Fat Boys,

LL Cool J, and countless other young artists. Run-D.M.C.'s third album, Raising Hell, was a massive crossover hit in 1984, thanks in part to their collaboration with Aerosmith's Steven Tyler and Joe Perry on "Walk This Way." LL Cool J's 1985 debut (Radio) established him not only as one of the genre's greatest lyricists but also as rap's first sex symbol.

The contrast between "Rapper's Delight" and "The Message" continues today, with rap offering dance-floor novelties like Digital Underground's "Humpty Dance," explicit boasts of sexual potency à la Luke Campbell's 2 Live Crew, and the trenchant, militant wail of Public Enemy, N.W.A., and Ice Cube. Unlike punk rock, to which rap has always been compared, the genre has continually evolved, taking advantage of electronic innovations such as digital samplers (through which DJs can lift the riffs from old records and rework them around their own beats and soundscapes) and expanding and elaborating on the themes introduced in "The Message." There are nearly as many varieties of rap as there are of rock & roll.

Rap has come under constant attack from Black radio programmers, hostile White rock fans, and music censors. In the late 80s and 90s, the censors attacked everyone from N.W.A., Ice Cube, and 2 Live Crew to Public Enemy and the Geto Boys on the grounds that their music was vulgar and lewd. But the music has retained its vitality throughout these assaults, as suggested by new acts such as De La Soul, Brand Nubian, Arrested Development, and PM Dawn, who have taken the music farther than the Sugarhill Gang could have ever dreamed.

– John Floyd

Above the Law

Group / Rap, dance

Los Angeles crew of the Cold 187um (Gregory Hutchinson), KM.G the Illustrator (Kevin Dulley), Go Mack (Authur Goodman), and Total K-oss (Anthony Stewart) blend hard-hitting tales of urban violence with explicit sex talk and commentary. They shared the mike for one cut with Eazy-E on their 1990 debut *Livin' Like Hustlers*. Their last release *Black Mafia Life* wasn't the heralded outing its proponents anticipated; instead, it was pro forma gangsta rap, some of it expertly done, but little you couldn't hear elsewhere. —*Ron Wynn*

Livin' Like Hustlers / 1990 / Ruthless 46041

Prototype gangsta rap. —*Ron Wynn*

○ **Vocally Pimpin' Ep** / 1991 / CBS 47934

Improved production and studio techniques, and sharper quips. — *Ron Wynn*

● **Black Mafia Life** / 1993 / Warner Brothers 24477

While the controversy rages on over gangsta rap and its role and responsibility in the violence plaguing America's inner cities, such groups as Above the Law keep issuing sordid, offensive collections chronicling their misadventures. Here, as usual, their narratives are heavily obscene and often sexist, sprinkled throughout

with violent imagery. But unlike some others, there's no humor or absurdist logic operating as a counterbalance to the constant refrain of guns and "hoes." One could argue, of course, that groups like Above the Law aren't glamorizing the brutal, ugly lifestyle depicted in "Never Missin' a Beat" or "Pimpology 101" but relating it; certainly the cold, callous tone and complete disrespect for life expressed on "V.S. O.P." and "Process of Elimination (Untouchakickamurdaqtion)" speak far more effectively about the urgency of the situation than tons of strident anti-gangsta rhetoric. —*Ron Wynn*

Afros

Group / Rap

The Afros are a trio with a penchant for sight gags linked to huge bushy hairstyles from the same decade (two members, Hurricane and Koot Tee, are clean-shaven, while DJ Kippy-O has an extensive Afro). The group also has a good pedigree; Hurricane is a former DJ for the Beastie Boys and a rapper for Davy D. Their material is more in a mode of parody/satire than confrontation, with a couple of political-consciousness and cultural-awareness cuts added to spice up the menu. —*Ron Wynn*

○ **Kickin' Afrolistics** / 1990 / Ral 46802

A wacky trio combines a love for '70s blaxploitation films and comedy with occasional inspired political commentary and witty repartee. —*Ron Wynn*

Amg

Rap

Select recording artist AMG has not made much hip-hop impact thus far. His tough-talking, prototype gangsta rap was featured on two discs for Select in 1991. *Bitch Betta Have My Money* charted, peaking at 63 on the pop albums chart. —*Ron Wynn*

Give a Dog Bone / 1991 / Select 61209

Sullen, cold, and occasionally provocative commentary from AMG that doesn't shed much light on any situation, social, political, or romantic. The production is acceptable, and the rapping and rhymes are mildly amusing, but there's little here that's inspirational, compelling, or worth hearing more than once. —*Ron Wynn*

● **Bitch Betta Have My Money** / 1992 / Select Street 21642

A flood of recordings similiar to this one triggered the ongoing '90s furor over sexist language. It's debatable whether the tone and sentiments expressed by AMG are tongue in cheek, but the steady stream of vulgarities and the message that women's roles are exclusively those of sexual surrogate and cash cow will certainly strike many as indefensible. The rap style is fluid enough, though the rhymes are more repetitious than clever. —*Ron Wynn*

Antoinette

Vocals / Rap

Introduced via hip-hop producer Hurby "Luv Bug" Azor's compilation disc *Hurby's Machine*, self-styled "Gangstress of Rap" and Queens native Antoinette has matured from a tough-talking mama into a more unpredictable, sometimes fresh, sometimes alluring, and sometimes defiant rapper whose musical surroundings are equally divided among funk, go-go, hip-house, and hardcore sampler and production snippets. —*Ron Wynn*

Who's the Boss / 1989 / Next Plateau 1015

Sturdy debut by the "Gangstress of Rap." —*Ron Wynn*

● **Burnin' at 20 Below** / 1990 / Next Plateau 1021

A substantial improvement, venturing into hip-house, go-go, and funk. —*Ron Wynn*

Arabian Prince

Rap

Arabian Prince was a founding member of N.W.A. and also a member of Bobby Jimmy & the Critters. He went solo in 1988, but his self-titled debut for Orpheus bombed. —*Ron Wynn*

Brother Arab / Sep. 1989 / Orpheus 75614

Hard-hitting hip-hop with an unrepentant gangsta tone. Arabian Prince angered some in the middle-class community with this unrelenting condemnation of inner city life. It was vicious and vulgar but delivered with the kind of cold, harsh slant that made it convincing. —*Ron Wynn*

● **Tha Underworld** / 1992 / EMI America 96419

Arabian Prince doesn't discuss anything that other gangsta types haven't talked about numerous times, but his commentaries on drugs, violence, sex, and such are done in such a deadpan yet defiant and angry manner that you're hooked even as you're disgusted by a litany of hopelessness and injustice. —*Ron Wynn*

Arrested Development

Group / Rap, dance, urban

An innovative conglomeration from Brownsville, TN, fusing blues and southern soul with the hip-hop innovations of De La Soul and PM Dawn. With group leader Speech's intelligent, insightful lyrics and laidback delivery, as well as the clever turntable techniques and creative self-production of their debut, *3 Years 5 Months & 2 Days in the Life of . . .*, Arrested Development became the hip-hop success story of 1992, sweeping year-end critical polls and going multiplatinum.

Two years later, after gangsta rap had reemerged as the dominant commercial force in rap, Arrested Development released *Zingalamaduni*, its second album, which had favorable reviews but slightly sluggish initial sales. —*John Floyd & Stephen Thomas Erlewine*

★ **Three Years, Five Months & Two Days in the Life of . . .** / 1992 / Chrysalis 21929

A crew who's become one of 1992's sensations by infusing hip-hop with blues sensibility on their debut, *Three Years, Five Months & Two Days in the Life of . . .*, especially on the single "Tennessee." —*Ron Wynn*

Unplugged / 1993 / Capitol 21994

Basically a live rerecording of *3 Years* (minus their breakthrough hit, "Tennessee"), *Unplugged* breaks no new ground for Arrested Development. Eight of the 11 songs on the album are from their debut, and the three new tracks are slight. The album is filled out with remixes of seven tracks, which are the instrumental tracks with the vocals turned down (they are still slightly audible). Only hardcore fans will need to hear this more than once. —*Stephen Thomas Erlewine*

Zingalamundi / 1994 / Chrysalis

Arrested Development's proper follow-up to their smash hit debut doesn't stray too far from the rootsy southern hip-hop that made *3 Years* a hit, yet it doesn't ignite as frequently as its predecessor. While its best tracks—like "Mister Landlord" and "Prasin' U"—are the equal of "Mr. Wendal" and "People Everyday," there is no statement of purpose on the level of "Tennessee." The album is too unfocused to be as impressive as the debut, yet *Zingalamundi* shows that the group is more than a one-hit wonder. —*Stephen Thomas Erlewine*

Audio Two

Group / Rap

Milk and Gizmo Dee (both of whom are sons of First Priority president Nat Robinson and brothers of MC Lyte) are a Brooklyn-based duo who offer unflinching, sometimes repelling outlooks on inner-city living and hustling, sandwiched around often good studio/production efforts. Their forte is exaggerated (even for hip-hop) claims of sexual potency and rapping proficiency. Their second release pushed the bounds of taste with the inclusion of bathroom sounds. Occasionally sexist and homophobic, they nonetheless have netted several minor hits. Their most recent release is 1992's *One Dead Indian* with MC Lyte in 1992.—*John Floyd & Ron Wynn*

○ **What More Can I Say** / 1988 / Atlantic 90907

Contains their moment of glory, "Hickeys on My Neck." —*Dan Heilman*

● **I Don't Care—The Album** / 1990 / First Priority 91358

Crisper, tighter production and harder raps, with one hard-edged antidrug tract, "Get Your Mother Off the Crack." Only a distasteful homophobic cut "Whatcha Lookin' At" keeps this from being a classic. —*Ron Wynn*

First Dead Indian / 1992 / First Priority 92145

Afrika Bambaataa

x / Rap, dance, urban

Some call him the godfather of rap; others put him in the category of genre creator. Bronx disc jockey Afrika Bambaataa's record "Planet Rock," cowritten by John Robie and produced by Arthur Baker, was the seminal presentation of scratching, electronic additions, high-tech beats, and highly processed vocals. The single and its followers like "Looking for the Perfect Beat" and "Renegades of Funk" opened the door for the '80s electro-funk movement. Later, his collaboration with James Brown on "Unity" and his joint vocals with John Lydon on "World Destruction" furthered the link between hip-hop, funk, soul, and rock. He's also done other work as a member of the group Shango, but it's as a producer, compositional force, rapper, influence, and father figure that Africka Bambaataa rules within the hip-hop nation. —*Ron Wynn*

☆ **Looking for the Perfect Beat** / 1982 / Tommy Boy 831

Producer Arthur Baker proved the real star on this seminal 1982 album, adding what were then state-of-the art studio effects and mixing gimmicks to balance often repetitive rhythms. This was a milestone record, despite what sounds like limited rap skills by '90s standards. —*Ron Wynn*

★ **Planet Rock** / 1986 / Tommy Boy 823

All the important early 12-inchers from 1982 to 1984 are here, including "Planet Rock" and "Looking for the Perfect Beat," plus three previously unreleased tracks (recorded with Soulsonic Force). —*John Floyd*

○ **Beware (The Funk Is Everywhere)** / 1987 / Tommy Boy 1008

Another stunning assortment of singles, with heavier beats, thicker rhythms, and a blistering cover of the MC5's "Kick out the Jams." —*John Floyd*

1990-2000: The Decade of Darkness / Jun. 1991 / EMI America 97777

After several lackluster albums, Bambaataa came back with a record that explored modern-day dance trends without losing his signature sound. Fueled by a righteous social commentary throughout all the songs, the record showed that he wasn't creatively spent. It wasn't as innovative as his groundbreaking singles from the early '80s, yet it was far from being an embarrassment. —*Stephen Thomas Erlewine*

Rob Base

Vocals / Rap, dance, indie
This New York-based DJ caused a stir with his clipped cadences and straightahead raps contrasted by choruses lifted from classic soul songs, notably Frankie Beverly and Maze's "Joy and Pain," which he neglected to credit. He had a partner, DJ E-Z Rock, on his first release, *It Takes Two.* He did the second on his own and continued the practice, this time using as his base (no pun intended) music from Edwin Starr, Marvin Gaye, Tammi Terrell, and Native American rockers Redbone. —*Ron Wynn*

● **It Takes Two** / 1988 / Profile 1267
His wildly successful debut album from 1988 contains the excellent title cut and "Joy and Pain," which lifts from the Maze hit of the same name. Base is joined by DJ E-Z Rock. —*John Floyd*

Incredible Base, The / 1989 / Profile 1285
On this good follow-up to his hit debut release, Base makes first-rate party raps and utilizes surging samples, rhythms, and grooves. He also makes a good plea for resolving rap rivalries on a reworking of the Edwin Starr/Temptations classic "War." —*Ron Wynn*

Beastie Boys, The

b. 1979
Group / Rap, hip-hop
When they were terrorizing America in 1987 with *Licensed to Ill,* nobody imagined that seven years later the Beastie Boys would still be recording, let alone be respected and release a series of consistently creative albums. But that is what happened. The Beasties have managed to tie together the two largest underground musical movements of the '80s—hip-hop and punk/post-punk—into one wildly eclectic mix, borrowing from any genre they can get their hands on.

Originally, the Beastie Boys were a hardcore New York punk band in the early '80s, releasing a couple of weak EPs before becoming infatuated with the burgeoning rap underground. By that time, there were three Beastie Boys: Adam Yauch (MCA), Mike Diamond (Mike D), and Adam Horovitz (Ad-Rock). The trio hooked up with Rick Rubin, one of the cofounders of Def Jam Records, who produced the group's first full-length album, *Licensed to Ill,* which was released in late 1986. A brutal and hysterical amalgam of hard rock, hip-hop, and satiric macho posturing, *Licensed to Ill* followed the footsteps of Run-D.M.C.'s groundbreaking commercial breakthrough *Raising Hell,* becoming the first rap album to reach number one; it eventually sold over four million copies and scored a number-seven single with "(You Gotta) Fight for Your Right (to Party)."

After a tour that wallowed in its own decadence, the group became embroiled in a vicious fight with Def Jam that prevented them from releasing new material for a couple of years. In 1989 the Beastie Boys reappeared on Capitol Records with *Paul's Boutique,* an album that was radically different from their debut. Although it was a commercial failure, it was a surreal, brilliantly inventive record that foreshadowed many hip trends of the early '90s.

After another three-year absence, the Beastie Boys emerged with *Check Your Head* in 1992. The Beastie Boys had returned to playing live instruments to create a sloppy, inspired album that featured equal doses of Stax soul, hardcore punk, '70s funk, reggae, and '90s hip-hop beats. It was as bold of a departure from *Paul's Boutique* as that album was from *Licensed to Ill,* except this time it sold. The Beastie Boys emerged as cultural icons for the new alternative audience and continued as such with their

follow-up, 1994's *Ill Communication,* a record that refined the innovations of *Check Your Head.* —*Stephen Thomas Erlewine*

☆ **Licensed to Ill** / 1986 / Def Jam 40238
Some of the album sounds dated, but its impact in 1987 was about as subtle as a brick through a window. It was the first number-one hip-hop album, selling four million copies, and the first album from a White rap group. From the opening kick of John Bonham's drums and Tony Iommi's guitar, the Beasties proceed to "steal" from every record they can get their hands on and "rhyme" about an absurd array of macho fantasies. Sure, it's obnoxious, but it's an act, and an insanely humorous one at that. Even if the album sounds a bit dated today, the sheer force of the music and the bold, smart-assed rhymes make it worth hearing. —*Stephen Thomas Erlewine*

★ **Paul's Boutique** / 1989 / Capitol 91743
Endlessly complex and relentlessly innovative, *Paul's Boutique* is the Beastie Boys' masterpiece, dense with samples from nearly every genre of music and clever, literate, absurd lyrics that drop references from Jack Kerouac to "Dragnet." *Paul's Boutique* is a virtual catalog of pop culture, deeply rooted in the '70s. As rappers, the Beasties have grown immeasurably, writing lyrics that are both smart-assed and smart. Musically, the album is much richer than *Ill,* covering everything from funk and pop to country and hip-hop, with several layers of samples and beats on each track. *Paul's Boutique* is a brilliant, visionary album that hasn't aged a day since its release five years ago. —*Stephen Thomas Erlewine*

☆ **Check Your Head** / 1992 / Capitol 98938
Check Your Head returned the Beastie Boys to the spotlight, although in the most unlikely manner possible. Refashioning themselves as a loose and gritty groove band, the Beasties picked up their instruments again and made an album of dirty Stax and New Orleans funk, tripped-out reggae, hard hip-hop, blistering hardcore punk, and scores of pop-culture references and jokes. In its own way, *Check Your Head* is as trailblazing as *Paul's Boutique;* with its inspired amateurishness, it acknowledges no boundaries or limitations, creating a post-post-punk world where Eddie Harris, Bob Dylan, Cheap Trick, Groove Holmes, Spoonie Gee, and Biz Markie exist together, as one music. And, strange as it may sound, it works. —*Stephen Thomas Erlewine*

Some Old Bullshit / 1994 / Capitol
Sadly, the title is accurate. Even for die-hard Beastie fans, the early hardcore punk of *Pollywog Stew* wears thin quickly, and "Cookie Puss," while fairly interesting, only hints at their future inventiveness, leaving *Some Old Bullshit* for completists only. —*Stephen Thomas Erlewine*

○ **Ill Communication** / May 23, 1994 / Grand Royal
More of a refinement and restatement of *Check Your Head* than a bold departure, *Ill Communication* still finds the Beastie Boys in prime form, adding more elements of jazz to their dense, surrealistic sound. From the scores of wah-wah guitars to the short hardcore punk songs, *Ill Communication* is firmly entrenched in '70s worship, without ever once sounding like it's recycled. It may offer the same thing as *Check Your Head,* but *Ill Communication* never sounds formulaic or tired. —*Stephen Thomas Erlewine*

Big Daddy Kane (Antonio Hardy)

Vocals / Rap, dance
Brooklynite Big Daddy Kane (*Kane* is an acronym for "King Asiatic Nobody's Equal") has been able to nicely balance his image as the ultimate hipster with the air of solemnity, indignation, and anger necessary to creditably deliver messages of Afrocentric awareness and Muslim reverence. He's done alternately inspirational, prophetical, ridiculous, and scandalous raps over his career and has also managed to include duets with the maestro of love, Barry White, and legendary comedian Rudy Ray Moore, aka Dolemite, who laid waste to Kane in a dozens (insult-swapping) classic.

Big Daddy Kane has been a high-profile figure the past couple of years. Not only has he appeared in such films as *Posse* and *Gunmen,* but he also posed in Madonna's controversial photo book *Sex,* and issued a defiant disc *Looks Like a Job For* that offered no apologies for past actions and ridiculed unnamed individuals he claimed were fronting as gangsters. —*Ron Wynn*

★ **Long Live the Kane** / 1988 / Cold Chillin' 25731
Kane's debut was his hottest. —*Dan Heilman*

○ **It's a Big Daddy Thing** / 1989 / Cold Chillin' 25941
A good application of funk sentiments and influence within a
hip-hop context, particularly "I Get the Job Done." But Kane also
veers into homophobic and sexist territory, notably on "Pimpin'
Ain't Easy." —*Ron Wynn*

Taste of Chocolate / 1990 / Cold Chillin' 26303
Worth the purchase price for the exchange between Kane and
Rudy Ray Moore (Dolemite), longtime champion of the under-
ground Black comic circuit. Moore lays waste to Kane with relish.
—*Ron Wynn*

Prince of Darkness / 1991 / Cold Chillin' 26715
On *Prince of Darkness*, Kane is more soul-based than on his previous records and also changes his rapping style to suit the sound,
bringing a faster, twisting wordplay to his rhymes. When the
change in style works—as in "I'm Not Ashamed"—the record is
deadly, but when it doesn't it is deadly boring; unfortunately,
most of the record doesn't work. —*Stephen Thomas Erlewine*

Looks Like a Job for Big Daddy / May 25, 1993 / Warner
Brothers
Looks Like a Job for Big Daddy was a solid comeback record by
Kane, bringing him back to the harder beats of his earlier albums.
His rapping hadn't lost its spark, and the music was sparse and
funky, but it didn't have the same flair or innovation of *Long Live
the Kane* and *It's a Big Daddy Thing*, and it quickly fell off the
charts. —*Stephen Thomas Erlewine*

Black Sheep

b. , USA
Dance
Bronx rapper Andre "Dres" Titus and William "Mista Lawnge"
McLean scored a big hit with the debut *A Wolf in Sheep's
Clothing* for Mercury in 1991. The disc went gold, with the single
"Choice Is Yours" scoring on the R&B charts and getting extensive
pop exposure as well. —*Ron Wynn*

○ **Wolf in Sheep's Clothing, A,** / 1990 / Mercury 848368
Bronx rappers Black Sheep scored with the single "Choice Is
Yours," a song featuring the catchphrase "you can get with this or
you can get with that." But while this hit and "Strobelite Honey"
were satirical, the album also included the biting "Black with N.V.
(No Vision)" and "To Whom It May Concern," message tracks that
harshly criticized successful Blacks who turned their backs on the
inner city. —*Ron Wynn*

Kurtis Blow

b. Aug. 9, 1959, New York, NY
Vocals / Rap
Arguably rap's first crossover star, at least from a chart standpoint, New Yorker Blow emerged in the early '80s doing both social protest/Afrocentric material and apolitical, boasting, and
asexual posturing material, though not to the degree that has
since become commonplace. His landmark recording "The
Breaks" was an eye-opener for its time in terms of pace, verbal
dexterity, and rhythm track. Blow was also a big-time producer at
one point, using the likes of Bob Dylan and George Clinton in
guest stints and incorporating bits from television shows and cartoons in his production. Blow was finally overhauled by new-
school producers and rappers in the late '80s; his early work now
sounds quite dated by comparison. —*Ron Wynn*

○ **Kurtis Blow** / 1980 / Mercury 6337137
Kurtis Blow exploded onto the fledgling rap scene with "The
Breaks," still one of the rawest, most hypnotic bits of rhythm and
oral narrative ever issued. Blow's defiant, posturing rap, punctuated by drums that seemed to signify an invading army, surprised, shocked, and amazed listeners totally unprepared for anything so stark. An edited version got only mild pop response, but
the complete single was a huge hit among Black and club audiences. The song was so definitive it rendered everything else on
the LP irrelevant, even the good second single "Hard Times." —
Ron Wynn

○ **Deuce** / 1981 / Mercury 4020
Things cooled quickly for Kurtis Blow following the success of
"The Breaks" in 1980. He was unable to get any single from this
1981 record on the charts, even though "Rockin'" and "It's Gettin'
Hot" were well produced and competently delivered. But rap was

still far from being a mainstream phenomenon, and this album
did very poorly commercially. —*Ron Wynn*

○ **Party Time?** / 1983 / Mercury 812757
An ahead-of-its-time collaboration between Kurtis Blow and EU
that was really a five-song EP rather than a full-length album.
Rap meets go-go in a rousing, nicely performed set that deserved
more attention but didn't generate much action in 1983. —*Ron
Wynn*

Ego Trip / 1984 / Mercury 822420
Kurtis Blow briefly returned to the spotlight with the single
"Basketball" from this 1984 LP. His brand of sparse, electro-funk
rap was fading, and it was clear Blow's skills were in production
rather than performance. "Eight Million Stories" was a decent cut
inspired by the old "Naked City" television series, while "Fallin' in
Love Again" was among his better romantic efforts; but Blow's albums were always erratic propositions, and this one proved no
different. —*Ron Wynn*

America / 1985 / PolyGram 826141
Consistent rap beats with poignant social commentary. —*Bil
Carpenter*

★ **Best of Kurtis Blow** / 1994 / Mercury
While he made many groundbreaking singles, Kurtis Blow was
never a consistent album artist, making this "best of" collection
his definitive artistic statement. Throughout the early '80s Blow
helped define what rap could do, and these tracks confirm his status as one of hip-hop's legendary acts. —*Stephen Thomas
Erlewine*

Blowfly (Clarence Reid)

Vocals / Comedy
Soul singer Clarence Reid found fame in a different setting with
vividly explicit (though also mostly comical) sex material and outrageous commentary. Reid issued several albums as Blowfly, an
adult comedian in the Redd Foxx and Dolemite (Rudy Ray
Moore) tradition. His albums were issued on tiny southern independents and sold mostly in the Black community. —*Ron Wynn*

○ **Oldies but Goodies** / 1978 / Weird World 2026
Here are raunchy-beyond-belief sendups of "American
Bandstand," with every song you ever loved from the '50s raped,
pillaged, and plundered in the bargain ("Ten Commandments of
Sex," "F***k Around the Clock," etc.). —*Cub Koda*

Twisted World of Blowfly, The / 1990 / Oops! 3007
Some inspired philosophy, delivered in terms ranging from confused to bizarre to obscene. Longtime urban/ghetto comedian
Blowfly entered the '90s in style. Suddenly he was getting publicity from the same image-conscious types who'd once relegated his
humor to the underground. He even appeared on a Big Daddy
Kane record, and people suddenly realized that a host of Black
comics never got a chance to practice their wares in comedy clubs
or for major labels. —*Ron Wynn*

● **Blowfly's Party (X-Rated)** / Weird World 2034
Blowfly actually reached the pop charts with this 1980 LP that
blended adult humor, vividly explicit sexual commentary, and
material ranging from clever to tasteless to insipid. —*Ron Wynn*

○ **For President** / Oops! 3006
The sheer lunacy of X-rated comedian Blowfly running for any
political office, let alone the presidency, provides an entertaining
hook for this often outrageous release. —*Ron Wynn*

Fresh Juice / Oops! 101
Blowfly's albums enjoyed renewed popularity in the '80s, but
while they had bite and humor, they weren't as ribald or on the
edge as his underground albums in the '70s. Still, hearing
Blowfly's frank, explicit, and vulgar stories is interesting in light
of current discussions about sexism and images. The material is
certainly tasteless; it's also frequently hilarious. —*Ron Wynn*

Bobby Jimmy & The Critters

Rap
Bobby Jimmy formed his Los Angeles comic rap group Bobby
Jimmy & the Critters in the late '80s. One of the Critters was
Arabian Prince. Bobby Jimmy's 1986 Macola album spent one
week at the very bottom of the LP charts. —*Ron Wynn*

Roaches: The Beginning / Macola 933

This album included the tasteless "We Like Ugly Women" and "Big Butt," which wasn't as humorous or as clever as Jimmy Castor's "Bertha Butt." Other songs included "New York Rapper," a decent swipe at East Coast macho posturing, and "Bag Bobby Jimmy Jam," the one number that had the charm and outrageousness necessary to be a good novelty tune. —*Ron Wynn*

Boo-Yaa T.R.I.B.E.

b. Los Angeles, CA
Group / Rap
A six-piece assemblage of Samoan-American brothers who boast a full-band live sound not unlike that of Stetsasonic and augment their sound with surprisingly tasty horn charts. —*John Floyd*

○ **New Funky Nation** / 1990 / Fourth & Broadway 444017
Boo-Yaa T.R.I.B.E. came onto the scene in top form with *New Funky Nation*, a hard-bitten collection of surly, edgy raps delivered over music supplied by an equally animated live band. This is one of the more underpublicized fine album statements done in 1990. —*Ron Wynn*

Boogie Down Productions

Group / Rap, hip-hop, dance, soul
Formed in 1986 by Laurence Krisna Parker and Scott Sterling, Boogie Down Productions (BDP) quickly became one of the most influential and important hip-hop groups. Parker adopted the name KRS-One (an acronym for "Knowledge Reigns Supreme over Almost Every One"), and Sterling became DJ Scott LaRock. They released an independent single, "Crack Attack," in 1986. BDP's groundbreaking 1987 debut; *Criminal Minded*, full of blunt, matter-of-fact tales of life on the mean streets, was a prototype for gangsta rap. As the album was building to a massive underground success, LaRock was shot to death in the South Bronx as he tried to settle an argument. Instead of calling it quits, KRS-One continued BDP with his brother Kenny Parker and D-Nice as DJs and released *By All Means Necessary* the following year. KRS-One began calling himself "the Teacher," promoting self-awareness and education in his rhymes. KRS-One began touring colleges on the lecture circuit around 1989, and some of his writings appeared in the *New York Times*. It became evident that KRS-One had taken his role as the Teacher too far on 1990's *Edutainment*, where most tracks were lectures pasted over lackluster beats.

KRS-One obliterated all concerns that he sold out on 1992's *Sex and Violence*, where he sounds angrier and stronger than he has in years, but the album wasn't the commercial blockbuster it could have been. The following year, KRS-One released his first solo album, *Return of the Boom Bap*, which was even better; many hip-hop critics equated it with the seminal *By All Means Necessary*. But by early 1994 it had already dropped off the R&B and hip-hop charts. —*Stephen Thomas Erlewine*

★ **Criminal Minded** / 1987 / Sugar Hill Rap 5255
Classic early-gangsta rap work, *Criminal Minded* was the only time the contributions of DJ Scott LaRock were featured on a Boogie Down Productions recording as he was murdered shortly after this was issued. The toughest, hardest-hitting BDP effort. —*Ron Wynn*

☆ **By All Means Necessary** / 1988 / Jive 1097
Boogie Down Productions' first album since the death of Scott LaRock finds KRS-One keeping his hardcore, proto-gangsta stance and strengthening it with socially conscious rhymes. All the while the beats and samples are richer than the first record, creating a dense urban landscape for KRS-One's fiercely intelligent raps. —*Stephen Thomas Erlewine*

☆ **Ghetto Music: The Blueprint of Hip Hop** / 1989 / Jive 1187
On BDP's third album, KRS-One strips the beat down to the basics, concentrating his efforts on his rhymes. KRS-One has called himself the teacher, and teach he does on *Ghetto Music*. From hip-hop to heritage, not a single subject slips by him. Sadly, *Ghetto Music* would prove to be the last time that he would be able to completely capture the imagination of the hip-hop audience; it remains one of BDP's finest efforts. —*Stephen Thomas Erlewine*

Edutainment / 1990 / Jive 1358
Some speculated that KRS-One might be getting a bit soft with this one despite his lengthy expositions on the impact of poverty, drugs, and violence on his life. Parker emphasized a "humanist" tone on most of the material. —*Ron Wynn*

Live Hardcore Worldwide / 1991 / Jive 1425
The Teacher sounds explosive on stage, tearing into BDP's greatest tracks and destroying the myth that live hip-hop is bland and unnecessary. In fact, the pure energy of this album can be offputting at first—the group jumps around their catalog, playing fragments of their classics and complete tracks from their latest, *Edutainment*, and the audience sings along with almost every track. *Live Hardcore Worldwide—Paris, London & NYC!* may not be the first live hip-hop album (2 Live Crew released one a couple of months before BDP), but it is certainly the best. —*Stephen Thomas Erlewine*

○ **Sex and Violence** / 1992 / Jive 41470
KRS-One demolishes any idea he's losing his clout or anger. *Sex and Violence* is his most chilling, slashing, and effective overall statement since *Criminal Minded*. —*Ron Wynn*

Brand Nubian

Group / Rap
One of the better Islam-oriented groups that popped up in the early part of the '90s. Their religious fervor never dissipates into ranting, exclusionary dogma; the beats are seriously funky.
Brand Nubian has since undergone some changes, the most notable being the departure of dynamic lead rapper Grand Puba. Their 1993 album *In God We Trust* was quite controversial for the single "Punks Jump Up to Get Beat Down," a song that was enormously popular while it earned them charges of homophobia. —*John Floyd*

○ **One for All** / 1990 / Elektra 60946
Post-De La Soul, daisy-age rappers here wrap their Islamic-slanted lyrics around challenging, clever, and hard-hitting beats and samples. —*John Floyd*

● **In God We Trust** / 1993 / Elektra 61381
Love Me or Leave Me Alone / 1993 / Asylum 64661

Bushwick Bill (Richard Shaw)

Rap
Bushwick Bill, born in Jamaica, gained early hip-hop notoriety as a member of the Geto Boys. He made his solo debut in 1992 with *Little Big Man*, a disturbing and extremely graphic CD that included an account of him losing his right eye in a shooting incident. —*Ron Wynn*

Little Big Man / 1992 / Priority 57189
Bushwick Bill went solo on this 1992 release and made an effective debut album that chronicled in, graphic detail, the shooting incident that cost him an eye. While the Geto Boys sessions were more disgusting than incisive, he actually turned in some coherent message tracks, notably "Letter from KKK" and "Stop Lying." Of course, it wouldn't have been a Bushwick Bill disc without some disgusting tracks, and "Ever So Clear" and "Call Me Crazy" certainly fit that description. —*Ron Wynn*

Candyman

Rap
Los Angeles rapper Candyman was featured backing Tone-Loc before he earned his own solo stint. His 1990 debut *Ain't No Shame in My Game* scored a Top Ten pop hit with "Knockin' Boots." The next year he followed that with another less successful LP for Epic, *Playtime Is Over*. His most recent release was *I Thought U Knew* for I.R.S. in 1993, which also failed to click. —*Ron Wynn*

● **Ain't No Shame in My Game** / 1990 / Epic 46947
Although this scored a huge crossover hit with "I Got a Man," the rest of the record didn't prove whether the single was a fluke or not; the jury was still out. —*Ron Wynn & Stephen Thomas Erlewine*

Playtime Is Over / 1991 / Epic 48679
A decent follow-up, but it lines up in the pop-gimmick camp despite occasionally interesting raps and production. —*Ron Wynn*

Cash Money & Marvelous

Group / Rap
Philadelphia rappers Cash Money & Marvelous made only one album in the late '80s. *Where's the Party At?*, produced by Joe "The Butcher" Nicolo, was undeservedly ignored. —*Stephen Thomas Erlewine*

○ **Where's the Party At?** / 1988 / Sleeping Bag
Undernoticed, undervalued work, boasting a nice mix of juvenile humor, funk-tinged hip-hop, and excellent production. —*Ron Wynn*

Neneh Cherry

b. Mar. 10, 1964, Stockholm, Sweden
Vocals / Dance-pop
A one-time member of Rip Rig + Panic and of the punk group the Slits, she had a massive 1989 hit with "Buffalo Stance," which masterfully balanced hip-hop sensibilities with the crisp, accessible bounce of high-tech R&B. Cherry is the stepdaughter of jazz trumpeter Don Cherry.
　　After several years of inactivity, Cherry returned in 1992 with the critically acclaimed *Homebrew,* which failed to capture the same sales as her debut but proved that she remained artistically innovative.—*John Floyd*

☆ **Raw Like Sushi** / 1989 / Virgin 91252
Cherry's wonderful debut, produced by British dancemaster Bomb the Bass, offers a brash, sassy portrait of a contemporary feminist, unwilling to take shit from a lip-flapping homeboy and confident enough to tackle thorny issues, both political and sexual. —*John Floyd*

★ **Homebrew** / 1992 / Virgin 86516
Despite the absence of a knockout single like "Buffalo Stance," *Homebrew* is a stronger album than Neneh Cherry's debut, *Raw Like Sushi.* On *Homebrew,* Cherry's melding of hip-hop and R&B is so complete that no seams show—*it doesn't belong to either genre; it stands on its own. It takes a couple of plays before it starts to sink in, but after some time even Michael Stipe's rap on "Trout" seems completely natural.* —Stephen Thomas Erlewine

Chill Rob G (Rob Frazier)

Vocals / Rap
Queens native Chill Rob G is an excellent rapper whose version of "The Power" was unfortunately obliterated by the hit rendition done by the duo Snap over the same music. Chill Rob G's original rap was done on a song called "Let the Words Flow," and German producers Benito Benites and John Garrett II added new musical trappings to it, renaming it "The Power." G's fine album *Ride the Rhythm* likewise didn't enjoy the commercial success it merited. —*Ron Wynn*

○ **Ride the Rhythm** / 1990 / Capitol 97545
Powerful raps with underrated percussion, production, and rhythm tracks. —*Ron Wynn*

Chubb Rock (Richard Simpson)

Vocals / Rap, hip-hop, dance, urban
Weighing in at around 250 pounds, Chubb Rock often evokes images of a hip-hop Barry White (with whom he dueted on *And the Winner Is . . .*). Chubb Rock had a group while he was a teenager in New York but started his career in earnest after he dropped out of college. After three singles from his first album went nowhere, his second album *And the Winner Is . . .* was released to greater commercial and critical acclaim, thanks to a remixed single version of "Caught Up" that was released prior to the album. —*Stephen Thomas Erlewine*

Featuring Hitman Howie Tee / 1988 / Select 21624
Interesting and entertaining raps, witty quips, and good samples from disco and funk works. —*Ron Wynn*

● **And the Winner Is . . .** / 1989 / Select 21631
Sharp humor with first-rate samples and production, plus insightful commentary on ghetto violence and the ignorance of the National Academy of Recording Arts and Sciences. —*Ron Wynn*

One, The / 1991 / Select 21640
Rock still raps hard, but uneven production and mixes sometime slow the momentum. —*Ron Wynn*

Compton's Most Wanted

Group / Rap
Interracial quartet who walk the same turf as hood mates N.W.A. and Ice Cube, with similarly tough, swaggering grooves. Intricate production makes their best work stand out among the gangsta-rap pack. —*John Floyd*

It's a Compton Thang / 1990 / Capitol 75627

More tense, defiant, and obscene gangsta commentary (also available in a censored version). —*Ron Wynn*

○ **Straight Checkn 'em** / 1991 / Orpheus 47926
Compton's Most Wanted's second CD got more sullen, combative, and sexist in its language and themes than the debut. Where "Duck Sick" and "It's a Compton Thang" at least had some swagger and a taste of humor to offset the posturing, "Can I Kill It?" and "Compton's Lynchin'" were more surly, "Gangsta Shot Out" and "Growin' Up in the Hood" were fatalistic, and "Raised in Compton" was despairing rather than informative. Only "Mike T's Funky Scratch" sounded a lighter note, and that was because it's a declaration of rap prowess rather than street superiority. —*Ron Wynn*

● **Music to Driveby** / Jun. 1992 / Orpheus 52984
This third and commercially most successful album by Los Angeles rappers Compton's Most Wanted contained such terse narratives as "Dead Men Tell No Lies" and "Hit the Floor." If there hadn't been such an abundance of similar material in the early '90s, these tales might have triggered intense scrutiny and analysis. Instead, the most common response is that M. C. Eiht's raps aren't quite as loose or expressive as those of Spice 1, Ice Cube, Nas, or many others telling identical stories. —*Ron Wynn*

Cypress Hill

Group / Rap
With their lazily menacing hip-hop, Cypress Hill became one of the biggest hip-hop groups of the early '90s. Powered by the slow, stoned production of DJ Muggs, the group's self-titled debut album became a sleeper sensation in 1991. B-Real's whiny vocals were balanced by the more straightforward rapping of Sen Dog, yet the lyrics of both were severely warped, whether they were telling surreal gangsta tales or celebrating marijuana. With its deliberate bass and beats, Cypress Hill's music sounded stoned, and it was one of the most unique, creative sounds to hit hip-hop since the Bomb Squad. While preparing the group's second album, DJ Muggs produced a number of best-selling acts, including House of Pain and Funkdoobiest. All the while the group earned notoriety by continuing to campaign for the legalization of marijuana.
　　Cypress Hill's second album, 1993's *Black Sunday,* was an even bigger hit than their debut, selling over a million copies and earning a crossover hit with "Insane in the Brain." —*Stephen Thomas Erlewine*

★ **Cypress Hill** / 1991 / Ruffhouse 47987
With its slow, heavily stoned funk, surrealistic gangsta fantasies, and whining delivery, *Cypress Hill* was a landmark hip-hop album of the early '90s, ushering in an era of marijuana and lazy funk. But it wasn't all good times; "How I Could Just Kill a Man" and "Hand on the Glock" were positively terrifying when delivered in such a slow, blunted fashion. —*Stephen Thomas Erlewine*

○ **Black Sunday** / 1993 / Columbia
It doesn't matter if *Black Sunday* follows the same formula as *Cypress Hill,* because it is so intoxicatingly convincing. Bolstered by the splendid singles "We Ain't Goin' Out Like That," "When the Sh— Goes Down," and "Insane in the Brain," *Black Sunday* is a surreal, stoned vision of contemporary hip-hop culture that is as funny as it is frightening. —*Stephen Thomas Erlewine*

D-Nice (Derrick Jones)

Vocals / Rap, dance
D-Nice, the former DJ for Boogie Down Productions, left the group in 1990, releasing his debut album *Call Me D-Nice.* —*Stephen Thomas Erlewine*

● **Call Me D-Nice** / 1990 / Jive 1202
The former KRS-One/Boogie Down Productions associate made a strong impact with his first solo outing. —*Ron Wynn*

○ **To Tha Rescue** / 1991 / Jive/Novus 41466
On his second CD former Boogie Down Productions member D-Nice rapped hard, straight, and true on such cuts as "Check Yourself" and "Straight from the Bronx." He didn't score any hits, but he certainly demonstrated his rhyming acumen and fluidity. —*Ron Wynn*

Da Lench Mob

Rap

Ice Cube produced this West Coast rap trio's 1992 project *Guerillas In Tha Mist,* featuring T-Bone, J-Dee, and Shorty. The title track proved to be an R&B and rap hit, and a video loosely modeled on the film *Predator* included an appearance by Cube. —*Ron Wynn*

○ **Guerillas in Tha Mist** / 1992 / Atco 92206
Not surprisingly, Da Lench Mob has some similarities to their mentor and producer Ice Cube: they elaborate on Cube's hardcore fantasies with their group sound and contribute their own dose of scathing politics and controversy. —*AMG*

Dana Dane

Vocals / Rap
Though a New York rapper, Dana Dane broke from the customary "hard" East Coast mode and forged an alternative style, spinning yarns and presenting his stories with a bemused British accent and often other-worldy tone. His songs "Nightmares" and the huge hit "Cinderella" took hip-hop through territory it seldom ventured into before (or since). Dane was also a rap fashion maven, opening a store to sell apparel long before it became almost mandatory for hip-hop artists to hawk clothing lines. —*Ron Wynn*

● **Dana Dane with Fame** / 1987 / Profile 1233
Humorous, more pop-oriented rap, with a dose of reggae. —*Ron Wynn*

Dana Dane 4 Ever / 1990 / Profile 1298
Geared toward those who prefer hip-hop with a light touch. Good production. —*Ron Wynn*

Das EFX

Group / Rap
With their first album, Das EFX caused a minor revolution with their speedy, quick-tongued stuttering; it helped that they backed their rhymes with thick, funky tracks. The album was a major success, scoring a Top 40 pop single and going gold. On their second LP, *Straight Up Sewaside,* the duo of Drayz and Skoob Effect slightly altered their approach, downplaying their high-speed stuttering though continuing with the intense rhyming and confrontational themes that made their debut so memorable. —*AMG*

● **Dead Serious** / 1992 / East West 91827
Their raps are often lightweight, but this album has made an immediate and substantial impact in the hip-hop community. —*Ron Wynn*

Straight Up Sewaside / 1993 / East-West
It may not be as revolutionary or immediately memorable as *Serious Business* and its twisting rhymes, but *Straight Up Sewaside,* with its harder-edged styles, has enough slamming rhythms and rhymes to satisfy most fans. —*Stephen Thomas Erlewine*

Willie Dee (William Dennis)

Rap
Willie Dee was an original member of the Houston rap ensemble the Geto Boys. Dee's 1990 debut *Controversy* certainly incited some with the track "F—- Rodney King," a no-holds-barred attack on King for purportedly selling out when he made his famous "Can't we all just get along?" comment. Dee followed that with *I'm Going Out Like a Soldier.* —*Ron Wynn*

● **Controversy** / 1992 / Priority 57133
Former Geto Boy Willie Dee started his own controversy when he lit into Rodney King on this album. "F—- Rodney King" was a blistering indictment and denunciation depicting King as a sell-out, traitor, and collaborator for asking his now-famous "Can't we all just get along?" question during the LA riots. Unfortunately, the rage Dee felt toward King or America in general wasn't effectively communicated, either on that cut or the rest of the album. The raps were unfocused, the beats predictable, and the rhymes seldom catchy or inventive. —*Ron Wynn*

Def Jef

Vocals / Rap, dance, house music
This California rapper entered 1989 with a strong debut that elaborated on the minimalism of hip-hop and highlighted both his quick-tongued delivery and his unique twists on Afrocentrisms. —*John Floyd*

● **Just a Poet with Soul** / 1989 / Atlantic 92199
The title just about sums it up. —*Dan Heilman*

Soul Food / 1991 / Atlantic 92174
The sophomore jinx apparently affected Def Jef, as his second album lacked both the wit and the energy of his debut. The raps sounded forced, often delivered with little sincerity, and the poetry and rhymes were tepid. —*Ron Wynn*

Del Tha Funkee Homosapien

Rap
An emerging rap star, Del Tha Funkee Homosapien is Ice Cube's cousin. His debut *I Wish My Brother George Was Here* was less topical and more unfocused than anticipated, but the follow-up *No Need for Alarm* was a harder, sharper, and more coherent release. Del's rapping was also more fluid and wittier, and had more edge and bite. —*Ron Wynn*

● **I Wish My Brother George Was Here** / 1991 / Elektra 61133
This was a little more cutesy than expected, especially because Del Tha Funkee Homosapien was sometimes on the verge of making some credible political points. But making good novelty and message songs at the same time can be difficult, and the split focus made this release difficult to comprehend and tough to follow. Still, he displayed enough potential to suggest that better days lie ahead. —*Ron Wynn*

De La Soul

Group / Rap, dance
This trio of Long Island rappers consists of Posdnous (*sound sop* spelled backwards, born Kelvin Mercer), Trugoy (*yogurt* spelled backwards, born David Jolicoeur), and Mase. Their albums are lyrically keen and idiomatically diverse, sampling cuts from both the Coasters and the Turtles (the latter got them in some legal hot water), while espousing viewpoints that put them in the Afrocentric pocket yet don't wed them to any hard-and-fast religious or political position. Some have called them hip-hop's first hippies; more to the point, they're among rap's sharpest and savviest performers.

De La Soul challenged detractors who claimed they lacked edge and relevance with *Buhloone Mind State* in 1993, skewering gangsta rap for its obsession with hardness and posturing. —*Ron Wynn*

★ **Three Feet High & Rising** / 1989 / Tommy Boy 1019
A remarkable debut, with the hit "Me Myself and I," that runs the gamut from absurdity ("Jenifa Taught Me" and "Plug Tunin'") to hard-hitting social commentary ("Ghetto Thang" and "Say No Go"). De La Soul's inventiveness shines—not many rappers would be able to pull funky beats from Steely Dan and Turtles tracks. Throughout the album a mock game show is interspersed between the songs, giving the entire recording a bizarre, humorous feel. *Three Feet High & Rising* would be incoherent if it weren't for the trio's sizable rhyming and musical talents. —*Stephen Thomas Erlewine*

○ **De La Soul Is Dead** / 1991 / Tommy Boy 1029
The title and cover (a picture of a broken pot of daisies) illustrate the degree De La Soul wishes to debunk their myth and shed the attention that their debut album earned them. For the most part, the songs on the album are considerably less lighthearted than the ones on the debut, yet they are no less impressive. "Millie Pulled a Pistol on Santa" is one of the most chilling tales of child abuse ever recorded. *De La Soul Is Dead* is not easy to assimilate on the first listen, but the rewards are great. —*Stephen Thomas Erlewine*

Buhloone Mindstate / 1993
Departing from the serious, introspective *De La Soul Is Dead,* De La Soul returns to the lighter, more irreverent territory of their debut, *Three Feet High and Rising* without sacrificing their wit or conscience. —*Stephen Thomas Erlewine*

Digable Planets

Urban
One of the hottest hip-hop jazz groups to emerge in the '90s, Digable Planets combined a witty, loose rapping style, similar to old "beat" poetry, with improvisational backing to score a commercial and aesthetic success with their debut CD, *Reaching: a New Refutation of Time & Space.* —*Ron Wynn*

● **Reachin': A New Refutation** . . . / 1993 / Pendulum 61414
Digable Planets' debut album was one of the more successful fusions of jazz and rap, blending the two genres into a funky, seamless, stylish sound without losing the integrity of jazz or the street credibility of hip-hop. —*Stephen Thomas Erlewine*

Digital Underground

Group / Hip-hop, dance
Nearly every rap posse from the '80s and '90s has borrowed from George Clinton's mountain of P-Funk, but this San Francisco Bay Area conglomerate has mutated Clinton's boogie into the heaviest funk-fueled sound in rap. And their sense of humor is always dead on-target.
Although the Digital Underground haven't been able to continue the commercial success of their debut, their music has remained consistently strong, even if it all sounds a bit similar. —*John Floyd*

★ **Sex Packets** / Jan. 1990 / Tommy Boy 1026
A pulsating and wiggy debut, powered by the two instant classics "The Humpty Dance" and "Doowutchyalike." It's sometimes spotty but worthwhile for aficionados. —*John Floyd*

This Is an Ep Release / Feb. 1990 / Tommy Boy 964
Two decent remixes from their debut pad this half-hour mini opus. The new stuff ("Same Song," "Nuttin' Nis Funky") attests to the Underground's devotion to funk and to their staying power. —*John Floyd*

○ **Sons of the P** / 1991 / Tommy Boy 1045
Their devotion to brother George Clinton mutates into a full-blown sort of concept album. No truly great singles, but as a whole this is their best album. —*John Floyd*

Body Hat Syndrome, The / Tommy Boy
With their third album, the Digital Underground don't change their style much at all, but that isn't bad. Instead, *The Body-Hat Syndrome* is a goofily endearing mess of P-Funk-inspired hip-hop, with enough good humor and beats to satisfy their fans. —*Stephen Thomas Erlewine*

Disposable Heroes of the Hipoprisy

Urban
Michael Franti's deep and defiant tones were the lure for this short-lived group who didn't bill themselves as a rap band. Franti's resemblance in style, tone, and timbre to Gil Scott-Heron, plus his willingness to tackle targets ranging from television to fellow rappers, won them immediate attention. There were charges that the Disposable Heroes of Hipoprisy were themselves engaging in hypocrisy themselves by not identifying with rappers yet cashing in on the genre's popularity. They issued only one album before disbanding. —*Ron Wynn*

● **Hypocrisy Is the Greatest Luxury** / 1992 / Fourth & Broadway 444043
Hard-hitting political rap that is excellent on the rhetoric and lyrics but a bit weak on the grooves; closer to Gil Scott-Heron than Public Enemy. —*AMG*

DJ Jazzy Jeff & the Fresh Prince

Group / Rap
If you're looking for bubble-gum rap, these guys are your best bet. The Fresh Prince spins his teen-suburban tales in a pleasant if facile fashion, and Jeff isn't bad on the turntable. Don't look for anything gritty or street-smart: when Jeff boasts that he can beat Mike Tyson, that's about as menacing as it gets.
Will Smith, the Fresh Prince, starred in the early '90s TV sitcom, "The Prince of Bel Air," appeared in the film *Six Degrees of Separation*, and also tried to expand his hip-hop horizons enough to offset the talk that his raps had become hopelessy whitebread and irrelevant. In 1991's *Homebase*, including "Dog Is a Dog" and the Top Ten pop hit "Summertime," Smith's rap is done in a leaner, harder fashion even if the lyrics were pretty much family hour. But by *Code Red* in 1993 it seemed Smith had made peace with his image and was back to laidback, pop-oriented material such as "Boom! Shake the Room," "I Wanna Rock," and "Can't Wait to Be with You," which had a guest stint from Christopher Williams. —*John Floyd*

Rock the House / 1987 / Jive 1026
A ten-song work originally issued on Pop Art Records and later picked up by Jive, it contained the hit "Girls Ain't Nothing but

Trouble," which launched them as the kings of teen/clean rap. It had maximum crossover appeal yet retained a large following among the core hip-hop audience. —*Ron Wynn*

● **He's the D.J. I'm the Rapper** / 1988 / Jive 1091
Their commercial breakthrough contains their number-12 hit, "Parents Just Don't Understand," and other good-time raps. —*Dan Heilman*

And in This Corner . . . / 1989 / Jive 1188
More wit and whim from Jeff and the Prince, this time with assistance from saxes, flutes, and trumpets. Though not as commercially successful as its predecessors, it's actually a more faithful rap work. —*Ron Wynn*

○ **Homebase** / 1991 / Jive 1392
After enduring a temporary sales slump, DJ Jazzy Jeff and the Fresh Prince roared back with *Homebase*. They scored a huge pop and R&B hit with "Summertime," using Kool & the Gang's "Summer Madness" single for the music base while Will Smith rapped about romantic hopes and community barbeques. He landed another Top 20 single with "Ring My Bell," this time reworking Anita Ward's '70s oldie on his double-entendre take. Undoubtedly helped by the success of "The Prince of Bel Air," this album returned the duo to platinum status, even as Smith showed once more (protests to the contrary notwithstanding) that he was an accomplished pop rapper, not hardcore. —*Ron Wynn*

Code Red / Oct. 12, 1993 / Jive
After years of proclaiming that he wouldn't do gangsta rap, the Fresh Prince finally succumbs to a harder-edged style on *Code Red*. Surprisingly, he pulls it off well, thanks to sharp production and his endearing personality. —*Stephen Thomas Erlewine*

DJ Quik

Dance
Compton rapper DJ Quik made a strong debut as a 20-year-old in 1991 with his debut *Quik Is the Name* on Profile. The single "Jus Lyke Compton" was an R&B hit, and both it and "Tonite" got some mild pop response. The second LP *Way 2 Fonky*, which peaked at 14 on the pop albums chart in 1992, was even more explicit and vulgar than its predecessor. —*Ron Wynn*

● **Quik Is the Name** / 1991 / Profile 1402
DJ Quik was 20 years old when he came roaring out of the chute in 1991 with the single "Tonite." While it was a mild hit, "Quik's Groove," "Born and Raised in Compton," and "Deep" were more appropriate for establishing him as another in the continuing line of West Coast hard rappers. The recordings overdosed on the sexist references, but Quik's furious pace and flippant style signaled that he was a hip-hop force, at least for the moment. —*Ron Wynn*

○ **Way 2 Fonky** / 1992 / Profile 1430
DJ Quik proved his mettle with "Jus Lyke Compton," a definitive bit of regional touting that proclaimed West Coast rap the style setter and all others followers. Whether or not you bought the line, you were hooked by the rap. Nothing else on the disc matched this single's intensity and wit, but it helped him earn a second straight gold LP. —*Ron Wynn*

DJ Red Alert

Rap
A hip-hop pioneer, DJ Red Alert currently hosts a weekly hip-hop show in New York on WRKS-FM. He was one of the early disc jockeys who participated in house parties and pioneered the technique of extemporaneously speaking over sequenced beats that evolved into rapping. He's also compiling classic raps for anthology packages and planning to issue a new release shortly. —*Ron Wynn*

☆ **We Can Do This** / 1988 / Next Plateau 1016

The D.O.C.

Group / Rap, dance
After the release of his debut album, the career of Texas-born rapper the D.O.C. was shattered by a car crash that almost took his life. Although he could then no longer rap like he used to, his former producer Dr. Dre featured him on the groundbreaking album *The Chronic*, which built on the foundation laid by the D.O.C.'s *No One Can Do It Better;* he was also featured on Snoop Doggy Dogg's *Doggystyle*. —*Stephen Thomas Erlewine*

★ **No One Can Do It Better** / 1988 / Ruthless 91275

This Texas-born rapper hooks up with Dr. Dre of N.W.A. fame to make an effective effort fusing funk, hip-hop, soul, and reggae, along with some tough, taut commentary and raps. Guest spots from Eazy-E, Miche'le, and MC Ren. —*Ron Wynn*

○ **Straight from the Basement of Kooley High** / Def Jam 44470
This rambling, wildy erratic session contained enough mildly amusing elements for a good record but lacked coherence and focus. It seemed a work-in-progress, and the raps fluctuated from clever to silly to boring. The same held true for the production and rhymes. —*Ron Wynn*

Dr. Dre (Andre Young)

Urban

Hip-hop's reigning star and sales giant, "Dr. Dre" was originally a member of World Class Wreckin' Cru along with DJ Antoine "Yella" Carraby. They left that group to join Eric "Eazy-E" Wright, Lorenzo "M.C. Ren" Patterson, and Oshea "Ice Cube" Jackson in creating N.W.A. Their 1989 album *Straight Outta Compton* shocked many observers with its explicit vulgarity and sexism, but it immediately shot them to the top, eventually becoming a double platinum record. N.W.A. stayed in the spotlight a couple of years; then they splintered because of internal strife and the defection of Ice Cube and Eazy-E. Eazy-E, Ice Cube, and Dr. Dre also had a falling out over fiscal matters involving their former label Ruthless Records and ex-agent Jerry Heller.

Dre emerged as the head of his own organization and a solo star as a rapper-producer in 1993; his protégé Snoop Doggy Dogg became an equally huge star, rapping in a lower key, in off-rhythm fashion. Dre's commanding, brusque, and menacing cadences, coupled with his skillful adoption of Parliament/Funkadelic and classic funk beats made *The Chronic* a rap juggernaut. Despite his indefensible physical attack on hip-host Dee Barnes, which resulted in a criminal conviction, Dr. Dre maintained his status in 1994 as the rapper many love to hate and hate to love. —*Ron Wynn*

☆ **Chronic, The** / 1993 / Priority 57128
With its deeply funky George Clinton-inspired grooves, whining synthesizers, female backing vocals, and romantic gangster tales, *The Chronic* redefined hip-hop for the '90s. Dr. Dre's genius lies in how he keeps the funk loose but concise, creating perfect singles like "Down Wit Dre Day," "Let Me Ride," and "Nuthin' but a 'G' Thang." For all his musical genius, Dr. Dre remains an unremarkable rapper, which is what makes Snoop Doggy Dogg all the more remarkable. Snoop raps as much as Dre throughout *The Chronic*, and his surreally menacing drawl shows the reality that lies behind the stylized portraits of sex and violence. —*Stephen Thomas Erlewine*

Tim Dog (Tim Blair)

Urban

Bronx rapper Tim Dog fired fresh shots in the long-simmering hip-hop coastal warfare with his 1991 album *Penicillin on Wax*. His single "F—- Compton" triggered answers and comebacks in West and East Coast circles and helped his album become an underground sensation, though not a major hit. Tim Dog's alternately leering and fiery tone, his confrontational diatribes, and cutting beats were even more vigorous on the follow-up *Do or Die* in 1993. —*Ron Wynn*

● **Penicillin on Wax** / 1991 / CBS 48707
Bronx rapper Tim Dog informed the world about what he thought of West Coast types with the single "F—- Compton." It was the definitive composition on his debut album, setting the stage for a series of angry, often vicious and sneering taunts, challenges, boasts, and putdowns. —*Ron Wynn*

Do or Die / 1993 / Ruffhouse 53237
Bronx rapper Tim Dog fired more shots in the constant East versus West Coast war. His second CD was just as defiant and disrespectful as his debut. Dog once more refused to moderate his chip-on-the-shoulder attitude, the results being mildly amusing sometimes, extremely offensive at others. —*Ron Wynn*

Domino

Rap

Domino's *Sweet Potato Pie* was a pop and R&B hit from his self-titled debut LP. —*Ron Wynn*

○ **Domino** / Dec. 1993 / Mocity Music 131313
Rapper Domino's scattershot/stuttering rhyming (a near-flawless imitation of early Das EFX) yielded a big hit with "Getto Jam" and is the hook for his self-titled CD. "Do You Qualify" offers a comic (if not comical) spin on a tale of mistaken identity and consensual sex, while "Money Is Everything" and "Sweet Potato Pie" provide Domino's insights into materialism and sexual conquest; "Raincoat" is his safe-sex lecture. He's not fully a gangsta, satirist, or protester; Domino's songs are delivered in a deadpan, half-sung, half-spoken fashion, and he's aided by tight production from DJ Battlecat and smart samples of Kool & the Gang and the Ohio Players that fortify "Do You Qualify" and "That's Real." —*Ron Wynn*

Dream Warriors

Group / Rap, dance
New York rappers King Lou and Capital Q formed Dream Warriors, a crew that is pioneering the fusion of jazz and hip-hop. —*Stephen Thomas Erlewine*

○ **And Now the Legacy Begins** / 1991 / Fourth & Broadway 444037
A great example of the burgeoning jazz/hip-hop coalition, plus clever incorporation of TV themes and punk tidbits. —*Ron Wynn*

Eazy-E (Eric Wright)

Vocals / Rap, dance
The whiny-voiced member of N.W.A. has also hit paydirt as a solo act. His 1988 debut, believe it or not, is even more caustic than the work of his Compton posse.
After disbanding N.W.A. in 1992, Eazy-E found himself in the limelight through much of 1993 and 1994. He was targeted by Dr. Dre as a traitor and sellout. Not only was he repeatedly attacked on *The Chronic* CD, but he was also parodied and abused in the subsequent video through the use of a lookalike. Easy-E shot back, calling Dr. Dre a fraud and phony and ripping him in his EP *It's On (Dr. Dre 187 UM) Killa*. Eazy-E was also criticized for making statements on behalf of Officer Theodore Bresnio, one of the police officers involved in the Rodney King beating. Eazy-E appeared as a guest at a Republican fundraiser and even participated in a national discussion on gangsta rap lyrics on "Larry King Live" with writer James Bernard and the Reverend Jesse Jackson. None of these things compensated for the hollow lyrics, pallid rapping, and absence of originality and creativity on his EP. —*Ron Wynn & John Floyd*

● **Eazy-Duz-It** / 1988 / Priority 57100
N.W.A.'s mouthpiece should feel lucky that he hasn't been assassinated: his debut has something to offend just about everyone, regardless of leftist or rightist leanings or vehemence regarding issues of feminism. But at its best, *Eazy-Duz-It* is a fiery piece of hip-hop menace, marred only by E's incessant whine of a voice and his rampant sexism. Play at your own risk. —*John Floyd*

It's On (Dr. Dre 187UM) Killa / 1993 /
Eazy-E fires back in the unending war of words with former N.W.A. comrade Dr. Dre on his most recent EP. The only problem is that Eazy-E has already lost credibility in hip-hop circles for appearances with Republicans and one of the officers involved in the Rodney King incident. Thus his charges that Dre is a fraud lack consistency and weight. In addition, his raps throughout the disc sound tired and lame. Where Eazy-E was once cocky, funny, and often intriguing, now he sounds merely bitter. Besides the usual sexist and sexual posturing, he even reprises N.W.A.'s debut single "Boyz in Tha Hood" again. The song was once an entertaining manifesto, but now it's just dated, "G" mix and all. The same holds true for Eazy-E. —*Ron Wynn*

Ed O. G. & Da Bulldogs

Dance
Ed O. G. (born Edward Anderson) penned a poignant and brilliant message track on his 1991 CD *Life of a Kid in the Ghetto*. "Be a Father to Your Child" was a much more effective plea for parental responsibility than the scores of political rhetoric spewed by left- and right-wing types. The entire disc was a disturbing, evocative, and wonderfully produced and performed look at inner-city life that neither glorified nor minimized the tragedy or understated the triumphs inherent in surviving the madness. The follow-up *Roxbury 02119* wasn't quite as captivat-

ing but was still miles ahead of many more heavily hyped and promoted hip-hop releases in 1993. —*Ron Wynn*

● **Life of a Kid in the Ghetto** / 1990 / PWL America 848326
Ed O. G. made a signature song with "Be a Father to Your Child," arguably 1991's finest message song, a no-nonsense plea to men to support their children regardless of circumstance. It was the finest cut on an above-average concept album that contained several searing, insightful tunes that presented dilemmas but neither glorified nor made them seem unsolvable. "Gotta Have Money (If You Ain't Got Money You Ain't Got Jack)" sounded a rather pessimistic note, but it was balanced by "Stop (Think for a Moment)." "Dedicated to the Right Wingers" was a smartly conceived challenge to the "conservatives" to address problems in a real rather than rhetorical/symbolic manner. ED O. G. & Da Bulldogs deserved much more recognition and praise for this effort. —*Ron Wynn*

Roxbury 02119 / Jan. 18, 1994 / Chemistry Records
This second ED O. G. album wasn't quite as ambitious nor as satisfying as his debut. It didn't have any standout singles, and ED O. G.'s rapping lacked the power, conviction, and satirical clout he'd previously displayed. The production wasn't as varied nor the rhymes and stories as gripping. But it was still much better than much of the prototype gangsta material flooding the marketplace. —*Ron Wynn*

Egyptian Lover

Group / Rap, urban
A one-man electronic band who followed the techno-dance-rap lead of Arthur Baker, adding the love-man pose of Barry White. —*John Floyd*

● **On the Nile** / 1985 / Egyptian Empire 663
This gets more attention for its concept and thematic slant than for its execution. —*Ron Wynn*

Filthy / Priority 9723
Lover tries to gain wider exposure by taking an obscene tack. —*Ron Wynn*

King of Ecstasy—Best of Egyptian Lover / DMSR 883
Some good tunes, but overall of minimal importance. —*Ron Wynn*

EPMD

Group / Rap
Long Island rappers Erick Sermon and Parrish Smith (EPMD stands for "Erick & Parrish Making Dollars") have confounded some observers by achieving monumental success despite minimal production and rapping skills. The deadpan, almost mushmouth rapping style and simplistic insertion of samples and snippets throughout their three albums notwithstanding, such cuts as "You Gots to Chill" and "Rampage" have been hits. The duo are also accomplished producers and preside over the Hit Squad, a combine of rap acts including Redman, K Solo, and Das EFX.

Sermon and Smith were unable to reconcile artistic differences and personality conflicts and dissolved their formerly successful partnership in 1993. Sermon issued his own CD, *No Pressure*, later that same year. —*Ron Wynn*

★ **Strictly Business** / 1988 / Priority 57135
In reality a collection of singles, EPMD's debut turns some clever samples (Steve Miller, Kool & the Gang, Bob Marley, Otis Redding) into an overpowering funk assault. "You Gots to Chill" is a classic. —*John Floyd*

○ **Unfinished Business** / 1989 / Priority 57136
Although this doesn't hit as hard as their debut, it does contain some good jabs at the quiet-storm, Black, upwardly mobile crowd and also some slams at their doubters. —*Ron Wynn*

Business as Usual / 1991 / Def Jam 47067
A little to the processed side production-wise, but it boasts one good collaboration with LL Cool J on "Rampage." —*Ron Wynn*

○ **Business Never Personal** / Jul. 28, 1992 / Ral 52848
EPMD's terse, thick-tongued rapping style was back on point with their fourth album. Although behind-the-scenes turmoil finally split up Erick Sermon and Parrish Smith, they were together and cooking on this 1992 record. They scored their final signature single with "Crossover," a dead-on commentary directed at rappers putting pop hopes ahead of hip-hop values.

"Headbanger" and "Can't Hear Nothing but the Music" were other sterling tracks from their last great album. —*Ron Wynn*

Eric B & Rakim

Group / Rap, hip-hop, funk
The Queens, NY, duo has the distinction of being the first of dozens of ensembles to construct a sound around James Brown samples. The rapid-fire boasts of Eric B & Rakim's inventive turntable techniques make their entire catalog worth investigating.

This once-formidable duo, whose biting, sullen style was among the tightest and most influential during the '80s, called it quits in 1993.—*John Floyd*

★ **Paid in Full** / 1987 / Fourth & Broadway 444005
Their debut contains new mixes of early singles ("I Ain't No Joke," "Eric B. Is President") and adds some prime stuff, including the monumental "Paid in Full," which became a heavily sampled item in the late '80s. —*John Floyd*

☆ **Follow the Leader** / 1988 / UNI 3
No immediate standouts, but Rakim's tongue-twisting boasts are sharper, and Eric B. is still a monster at the turntable. —*John Floyd*

Let the Rhythm Hit 'em / 1990 / MCA 6416
This subdued set works its magic more subtly, but the title is no joke. —*John Floyd*

○ **Don't Sweat the Technique** / MCA 10594
While it doesn't match their trailblazing work of the late '80s, *Don't Sweat the Technique* is a solid effort from this influential duo. —*Stephen Thomas Erlewine*

The Fat Boys

Group / Rap, dance
More a comedy troupe than a rap posse, the Fat Boys marketed their obesity and goofiness with true savvy during the early '80s. Most of the songs dealt with their prodigious food intake, and Buff the Human Beat Box was always good for at least one laugh. The music ain't bad, and, in 1984, they made a novelty for the ages: "Jailhouse Rap." —*John Floyd*

○ **Fat Boys** / 1984 / Sutra 1015
This rotund rap trio featuring Darren "The Human Beat Box" Robinson, Mark "Prince Markie Dee" Morales, and Damon "Kool Rock-ski" Wimbley tipped the scales at 750 pounds. Their heft and Robinson's verbal skills were the hook that helped the Fat Boys land a gold record with their self-titled debut album. Even the lack of a standout single couldn't prevent the album from being a steady seller nor limit the group's popularity. Such singles as "Human Beat Box" and "Jail House Rap" helped them quickly build a solid following that they retained until the end of the decade. —*Ron Wynn*

Big & Beautiful / 1986 / Sutra 1017
The train began derailing for the Fat Boys with their third album. It was their first that failed to go gold, and such songs as "Beat Box Is Rockin'," "Breakdown" and "Go for It" were indications that their novelty tunes and party rapping were becoming passe. They would make a brief comeback the next year fueled by the film *Disorderlies*, but the end was nearing for this overweight trio. —*Ron Wynn*

● **Best Part of the Fat Boys, The** / 1987 / Pair 103
Everything you need by rap's fattest trio can be found on this concise sample of their first three albums. Includes "All You Can Eat," "Jailhouse Rap," and "Stick 'Em." —*John Floyd*

○ **Crushin'** / 1987 / PolyGram 831948
The Fat Boys enjoyed their biggest year in 1987. Their film *Disorderlies* proved much more commercially resilient than anticipated, and this LP earned their only platinum certification though it was the only Fat Boys album to make the pop Top Ten (peaking at eight). They also landed a Top 20 single with an updated version of "Wipeout." —*Ron Wynn*

Coming Back Hard Again / 1988 / Tin Pan Apple 835809
The last Fat Boys LP to make any noise, this sixth Sutra release proved their second most successful album, peaking at 33 and earning them their last gold record. It piggybacked on the success of "Louie Louie," their last chart single. They did try to adjust to changing audience demands, cutting "Rock the House, Y'All" and "Powerlord," but the Fat Boys' strength remained in novelty num-

bers; weight-based raps like "Big Daddy" and "Pig Feet" had lost almost all their popularity. —*Ron Wynn*

Father MC

Vocals / Rap, hip-hop, dance
Father MC straddles the line between hip-hop and new-jack-swing, which resulted in a number-20 hit, "I'll Do 4 U," from his debut album *Father's Day*. Nearly two years after his debut, Father MC followed it with *Close to You*. Its success was almost guaranteed by Father MC's appearance on the CD *Uptown MTV Unplugged*. Father MC was formerly a dancehall reggae performer, so there is always some reggae influence interspersed with his sentimental love lyrics and hip-hop production. —*Ron Wynn & Stephen Thomas Erlewine*

● **Close to You** / 1992 / Uptown 10542
Bronx rapper Father MC faked folks out on both sides of the style line when he released this 1990 debut. Those expecting 100 percent hardcore blanched at hearing sentimental love themes and straight R&B; others who thought he was strictly a new-jack-swinger were caught sleeping when the booming beats of the title track were cranked up on the box and when Father MC matched one-liners with Lady Kazan on "I've Been Watching You." —*Ron Wynn*

Everything's Gonna Be Alright / MCA 54524
Nearly two years after his debut and a few months after a successful number on the *Uptown MTV Unplugged* CD, Father MC rolled in with his second disc. Things weren't nearly as varied nor as successful as the debut, though he maintained his niche among new-jack types thanks to some creative production support. —*Ron Wynn*

Doug E. Fresh & the Get Fresh Crew

Group / Rap
New Yorker Doug E. Fresh (born Doug E. Davis), got his initial notoriety for being the "human beatbox," able to approximate and imitate a rhythm machine. He had a string of hit singles with his then-partner Ricky Dee in the early and mid '80s, notably "The Show (Oh, My God)" in 1985, which included guest stints from veteran jazz trumpeter Jimmy Owens and synthesizer player Bernard Wright. Fresh had a long absence from the scene after 1988's *The World's Greatest Entertainer* and has just resurfaced with a new release on a small independent label. —*Ron Wynn*

○ **Oh My God!** / 1985 / Reality 9649
Zany rhymes, slashing beats, with bits and pieces of everything from reggae to gospel to funk. —*Ron Wynn*

● **World's Greatest Entertainer, The** / 1988 / Reality 9658
With the exception of the monster hit "Keep Rising to the Top," Fresh trimmed the religious zealotry and increased the lyrical and rhythmic potency. —*Ron Wynn*

Fu-Schnickens

Rap
This Brooklyn rap trio, among the better humor-oriented hip-hop groups, devised their name by combining the letters *F* and *U* (For Unity) with *Schnicken*, a term they invented to convey coalition. Their 1992 debut *F.U. "Don't Take It Personal"* on Jive didn't yield any big hits, but the group hit paydirt when they collaborated with NBA star Shaquile O'Neal on the single "What's Up Doc." It got them widespread visibility and exposure, and their follow-up album was eagerly anticipated. —*Ron Wynn*

○ **F.U.-Don't Take It Personal** / Feb. 25, 1992 / Jive 41472
What makes the Fu-Schnickens' debut album special is not their beats, but their impressive verbal facility. Not only are they blindingly fast, but their lyrics are clever and inventive; the excitement of their rhyming makes the rote backing tracks invigorating. —*Stephen Thomas Erlewine*

Full Force

Rap
During the late '80s, Full Force was the dominant production, compositional, and performing ensemble in rap, though they were never hardcore rappers. The three George brothers—B-Fine, Paul Anthony, and "Bowlegged" Lou—teamed with cousins Gerry "Baby" Charles, Junior "Shy Shy" Clark, and "Curt-T-T" Bedeau.

Besides writing and producing hits for Lisa Lisa and Cult Jam, U.T.F.O., Cheryl "Pepsi" Riley, and many others, the group issued three albums on its own. But none of them came close to equaling the success they earned producing other acts. After they appeared in both Hudlin brothers' films, *House Party* and *House Party 2*, things cooled considerably for the Brooklyn combine. —*Ron Wynn*

Full Force / 1985 / CBS 40117
Though they were among the hottest production and performance combines on the scene in the mid and late '80s, Full Force was never able to translate that magic to their own albums. This 1986 debut included the mildly entertaining "Alice, I Want You Just for Me!," but was mostly uneventful love tunes, haphazard novelty pieces, and unfocused, formulaic quasi-raps. —*Ron Wynn*

○ **Guess Who's Comin' to the Crib?** / 1987 / CBS 40894
Full Force's third album did only marginally better than the first two; it peaked a little higher on the low end of the pop albums chart. They tried everything in their creative arsenal, from the bittersweet sentiments of "Love Is for Suckers (Like Me and You)" to the naughty double-entendre notions expressed on "Low Blow Brenda" and even a traditional soul number "Take Care of Homework." Nothing clicked, and it probably didn't help matters that the album included the justifiable but shrill diatribe "Black Radio." —*Ron Wynn*

Don't Sleep! / Aug. 31, 1992 / Capitol 96292
Full Force tried a comeback in '92, teaming with longtime James Brown confidant and vocal partner Bobby Byrd on *Don't Sleep*. A lot of folk evidently thought Full Force was in retirement as the album failed to get even a cursory glance from urban contemporary radio, and hip-hop/rap audiences weren't interested in '80s legends. This was their first release for Capitol; there hasn't been another thus far. —*Ron Wynn*

● **Get Busy 1 Time** / CBS 40395
The second Full Force release was a little better than the first, but still far from the levels they were scoring with Lisa Lisa and Cult Jam. Once more they were unable to get any breakout or chart singles, and while songs like "Body Heavenly" and "Old Flames Never Die" may have contained potentially catchy lyrics, they lacked defined vocals, attractive arrangements, or interesting production. —*Ron Wynn*

Funkdoobiest

Rap
Thanks to the production efforts of DJ Muggs from Cypress Hill, Funkdoobiest became a hot cult item in 1993 with their critically acclaimed debut album. —*Stephen Thomas Erlewine*

○ **Which Doobie U B?** / 1993 / CBS 53212
Thanks to producer DJ Muggs, Funkdoobiest has the same spaced-out funk as Cypress Hill and House of Pain, only with an engaging, surrealistic point of view that keeps their album original, not a retread. —*Stephen Thomas Erlewine*

Gang Starr

Group / Rap, dance
Brooklyn rappers near the top among hip-hop artists influenced by jazz. In 1989 longtime jazz and Black-pop publicist Elliot Horne placed a poem he wrote with them, and the group used it as the foundation for the song "Jazz Music" on their debut *No More Mr. Nice Guy*. That track was later included on the soundtrack for Spike Lee's *Mo Better Blues*. The group has also used saxophonist and "Tonight Show" bandleader Branford Marsalis and included acoustic as well as electric instruments on their follow-up release *Step in the Arena*. They've also discussed the jazz/rap connection in such magazines as the *Source* and the *Wire*. They did make a big gaffe on one cut though, crediting Dizzy Gillespie with playing the saxophone rather than the trumpet.

Both Gang Starr and their main man Guru have been in the limelight in 1993 and 1994. Guru teamed with old and new jazz types Donald Byrd, Roy Ayers, and Ronnie Foster, as well as vocalist N'Dea Davenport and other guest stars for the session *Jazzmatazz*. He later did some New York club dates with some of the same musicians. Gang Starr issued *Hard to Earn* in March 1994; it debuted on the *Billboard* R&B charts at number two.—*Ron Wynn*

No More Mr. Nice Guy / 1989 / EMI America 98709
Plenty of attitude although not so strong otherwise. —*Ron Wynn*

Step in the Arena / 1991 / Chrysalis 21798
It has its moments. —*Ron Wynn*

● **Daily Operation** / 1992 / Chrysalis 21910
Arguably the best example of the hip-hop/jazz coalition, Gang
Starr's latest continues the trailblazing path. —*Ron Wynn*

○ **Hard to Earn** / Mar. 8, 1994 / Chrysalis Records
After a couple of side projects, Gang Starr returns with a harder
album that never loses sight of their innovative jazz/hip-hop fusion. —*Stephen Thomas Erlewine*

Gerardo

Vocals / Rap

A rap performer whose Latino-flavored macho posturings (he frequently performs bare-chested with his pants unzipped) made
him a minor sensation on both the dance and pop scene in 1991
with "Rico Suave" and "We Want the Funk." —*Cub Koda*

● **Mo' Ritmo** / 1991 / Interscope 91619
A hard mix of soul and Latin music, with guest George Clinton.
—*Bil Carpenter*

Geto Boys

Group / Rap, urban

Houston rappers who've at times rivaled Public Enemy, 2 Live
Crew, and Ice-T for their ability to generate controversial publicity. Among the most outrageous, outlandish, and frequently offensive gangsta rap crews, they have released songs that include
violent and perverse subject matter that some may find distasteful. They've also had problems with stores refusing to stock their
albums and even, in some cases, labels refusing to distribute
them. The future of the group is now in doubt; Scarface's single
album has been a big hit, Willie Dee has split to do a solo release,
and the remaining Geto boys are working on their own projects.
The inevitable greatest-hits album appeared in 1993, which was
an indication that there wouldn't be any fresh Geto Boys material for a long time, if ever. —*Ron Wynn*

○ **Grip It! on That Level** / 1990 / Def American 24306
The Geto Boys hit the national spotlight with this '90 debut that
disgusted many, frightened a few others, and won them a niche
in hip-hop's growing gangsta constituency. From the sheer repul-
siveness of "Let a Ho Be a Ho" and "Do It Like a G.O." to the
frightening nihilism of "Mind of a Lunatic" and "Life in the Fast
Lane," here was one group definitely uninterested in pop/main-
stream approval. The rapping ranged from surly to sleazy; the
beats were sometimes popping, other times slashing; and even
the most loyal fan would have a tough time finding something
good to say about "Trigga Happy Nigga" or "Scarface." —*Ron
Wynn*

○ **We Can't Be Stopped** / 1991 / Rap-A-Lot 57161
Contains their best song, the disturbing "Mind Playing Tricks on
Me." —*Dan Heilman*

● **Geto Boys the Best Uncut Dope** / 1992 / Rap-A-Lot 57183
With various members opting for solo projects and the group disintegrating, Rap-A-Lot Records primed the pump one last time
with what was essentially a greatest-hits CD. It wasn't totally a
retrospective because it included "Damn It Feels Good to Be a
Gangsta," the ultimate genre definition piece and the last significant Geto Boys composition. "And My Word," "Actions Speak
Louder than Words," and "The Unseen" were other fresh jams
that joined Geto Boys anthems "Mind Playing Tricks on Me,"
"Assassins," "Scarface," and "Mind of a Lunatic," among others.
The old/new menu made this the one to grab if all you need is
one Geto Boys CD. —*Ron Wynn*

Till Death Do Us Part / Rap-A-Lot 57191
The Geto Boys' last album finds them expanding on the success
of "Mind Playing Tricks on Me" with "Six Feet Deep," but more
frequently it keeps to their standard, grotesque gangsta rap with
"Murder Ave." and "This Dick's for You." On these tracks the
whole shock formula seems like a worn-out trick and points the
way to their eventual disbanding. —*Stephen Thomas Erlewine*

Grand Puba

Rap

The former lead rapper for Brand Nubian came out roaring on
his own with *Reel to Reel* in 1992. It contained everything from
unrelenting Nation of Islam propaganda to one number that
seemed like an updated "My Ding-a-Ling" with its shameless
touting of Puba's sexual prowess. But overall, it showed he had
the skills to flourish on his own. —*Ron Wynn*

○ **Reel to Reel** / 1992 / Elektra 61314
Grand Puba's first solo album is an angry, righteous record,
which is saved by his lyrical inventiveness, not his rhetoric. —
Stephen Thomas Erlewine

Grandmaster Flash (Joseph Saddler)

b. Jan. 1, 1958
Group / Rap, hip-hop, dance

Grandmaster Flash and the Furious Five—*Cowboy (Keith
Wiggins), Melle Mel (Melvin Glover), Kidd Creole (Danny Glover),
Mr. Ness (Eddie Morris), and Rahiem (Guy Williams)*—were the
most important group in the early days of rap music and, in fact,
developed certain crucial aspects of the genre. Saddler was the
DJ, providing the musical bed by manipulating records on turntables, scratching them, repeating particular instrumental sections,
and thus creating new music out of collages of existing recordings. The most important such work was the single "The
Adventures of Grandmaster Flash on the Wheels of Steel," released in 1981.
Most of the group's records, however, featured the interlocking
raps of the five rappers, and the most significant of these was
"The Message" (1982), led primarily by Melle Mel, which turned
away from the party subjects of many current rap records to focus on urban social issues.
The group had split by 1984, with Melle Mel going off on his own,
but re-formed in 1987.
Grandmaster Flash resurfaced in the public consciousness in late
1993, thanks to interviews done in *Rolling Stone* and the *Source*
and Rhino reissues featuring such legendary tracks as "White
Lines" and "The Adventures of Grandmaster Flash on the Wheels
of Steel." A comeback session was announced for sometime later
in 1994, though no producers or record label were announced. —
William Ruhlmann

☆ **Message, The** / 1984 / Sugar Hill 1007
Grandmaster Flash and the Furious Five merged the Afrocentric
consciousness expressed by such early rappers as Gil Scott-Heron
and The Last Poets with b-boy production to create "The
Message," an all-time rap anthem. It was the focal point of this LP
that also included "It's Nasty" and "Scorpio," two other strong cuts
that might have been winners on their own. Unfortunately, rather
than a starting point, this album proved to be their ultimate peak.
—*Ron Wynn*

Source, The / 1986 / Elektra 9604761
Grandmaster Flash's follow-up album to *The Message* was his
first minus the Furious Five. Things weren't the same from a
compositional or performance standpoint, as his raps seemed
weaker and his rhymes almost devoid of crispness, humor, or insight. Only "Ms. Thang" and "Street Scene" offered any hint of the
incisiveness or vision depicted in "The Message." —*Ron Wynn*

○ **Greatest Hits** / 1987 / Sugar Hill Rap 5246
Flash was the DJ and the Furious Five were the best multiple rappers around, moving from the music's low-rent dance origins (it
was Flash who began cutting in repeated portions of other
records) and party spirit to the "message" approach that took over
in the mid '80s, prefigured in "The Message." Much of what came
later started here. —*William Ruhlmann*

★ **Message from Beat Street: The Best of** / 1994 / Rhino
Grandmaster Flash was one of the most groundbreaking rap
artists of the early '80s, and all of his most important records—
recorded with and without Melle Mel and the Furious Five—are
collected on this essential 11-track disc; includes the classic tracks
"The Message" and "White Lines (Don't Don't Do It)." —*Stephen
Thomas Erlewine*

Guru

Rap

The main cog behind Gang Starr, rapper-composer Guru stepped
out on his own in 1994 with the album *Jazzmatazz*. He enlisted
support from the hip-hop and jazz communities, getting everyone
from Roy Ayers and Donald Byrd to N'Dea Davenport of the

Brand New Heavies. Guru later did selected club dates with some of the *Jazzmatazz* personnel before returning to straighter hip-hop on *Hard to Earn.* —*Ron Wynn*

○ **Jazzmatazz, Vol. 1** / 1993 / Chrysalis 94632199829
Gang Starr's Guru has put together the best hip-hop/jazz outing issued yet, at least on these shores. Instead of merely wedding rap to recycled jazz samples, Guru and a cast of jazz, fusion, and R&B stars actually converge performance-wise, with the jazz musicians playing and the rappers and vocalists singing fresh material. The results are never less than enjoyable and are occasionally inspirational. Guru's deadpan rap style works, as does N'Dea Davenport's sultry vocals; Roy Ayers, Donald Byrd, and Lonnie Liston Smith sound more convincing on these songs than they have on any recent releases of their own. —*Ron Wynn*

Hammer

Vocals / Rap
Considered either the ultimate success story or consummate fraud, Oakland's MC Hammer, a onetime jack-of-all-trades for the Oakland Athletics baseball team, dominated the charts in 1990 with *Please Hammer Don't Hurt 'Em.* The single "U Can't Touch This," despite a rather feeble rap and recycle job on Rick James's single "Superfreak," was an enormous crossover smash. Hammer puts on a fine show as far as dancing, sound, light effects, production, and such are concerned; but from a technical standpoint, everything, from his rhymes to his enunciation, qualifies as the ultimate in "wack" (weak) performance. He does have great taste in cover songs, picking choice items from Marvin Gaye, B. B. King, the Chi-Lites, and Prince, among others. He's since dropped the *MC* from his name.
After staying in the limelight as a race-horse owner and Evander Holyfield's promoter, Hammer returned to the rap wars in 1994 with *The Funky Headhunter.* It featured a leaner, harder sound, with assistance and material provided by gangsta rap producers, and Hammer sporting a more "street" look. He previewed the new style on Arsenio Hall's show early in the year and then issued the CD in March. It debuted at number two on *Billboard's* R&B charts, then dipped the next week to six. Skeptics voiced their doubts about the new Hammer, especially in the hip-hop press. —*Ron Wynn*

Let's Get It Started / 1988 / Capitol 90924
MC Hammer's debut effort established him as a hip-hop superstar, with its energetic dance tracks on its pop-tinged choruses, highlighted by the single "Turn This Mutha Out." —*Stephen Thomas Erlewine*

★ **Please Hammer Don't Hurt 'em** / 1990 / Capitol 92857
MC Hammer's second album stands as the pinnacle of pop-rap crossover, with its hit singles "U Can't Touch This," "Have You Seen Her," and "Pray" forming its core. Hammer relied on pop choruses as much as hip-hop beats, which is what made the album sell more than ten million copies and stay on the top of the charts for 21 weeks. —*Stephen Thomas Erlewine*

Too Legit to Quit / 1991 / Capitol 98083
Hammer responded to hip-hop credibility charges by dropping the *MC* from his name and releasing *Too Legit to Quit,* an album recorded with a live band. Although it sold over three million copies and had hits in the title track and "This Is the Way We Roll," the results were more well intentioned than successful. —*Stephen Thomas Erlewine*

○ **Funky Headhunter, The** / Mar. 1, 1994 / Giant Records
The once and former MC Hammer resurfaced with a new musical identity and rap approach on this 1994 album. Getting help from new-school producers and debuting a video on Arsenio Hall's show, Hammer sounded leaner, his rapping tougher and more fluid, and his subject matter harder and less humorous. The results seemed to have worked; *Funky Headhunter* peaked at number two on the R&B list, went gold, and remained in the Top 30 midway through the year. —*Ron Wynn*

Heavy D & the Boyz

Group / Rap, hip-hop, dance, disco
Jamaican-born Heavy D (born Dwight Myers) may have a 260-pound frame, but he can move and dance with agility and verve. He wisely chose sensitivity, rather than obesity or verbosity, as his framework, and many of his lyrics emphasize his search for a

mate of similar qualities. He's also done good cover songs and penned cultural-awareness tunes and tributes to Black women. Heavy D has managed perhaps the ultimate balancing act. He's remained a "positive" figure, maintains close ties to his mother, and is arguably the most admired male rap figure among African-American feminists. At the same time he's been willing to take chances musically, never embracing hardcore gangsta rap, but yet is able to include snatches of pop, R&B, reggae, and funk in his music without being assaulted with cries of "sellout." He's even survived the tragic death of longtime friend and original Boyz member Troy Dixon, aka T-Roy, in 1990. *Blue Funk* in 1993 is his most recent release. —*Ron Wynn*

Living Large / 1987 / MCA 5986
This offers his first hit, a smartly done remake of "Mr. Big Stuff," plus charming romantic entries, though he sometimes overdoes the "overweight lover" routine. —*Ron Wynn*

○ **Big Tyme** / 1989 / Uptown 42302
Heavy D's commercial breakthrough and best album. —*Dan Heilman*

● **Peaceful Journey** / 1991 / Uptown 10289
A continuation of the fine direction cemented in *Big Tyme,* this includes a first-rate rendition of the O'Jays/Third World hit "Now That We Found Love," plus strong message and romance cuts. —*Ron Wynn*

Blue Funk / 1992 / Uptown 10734
Although it didn't have a big hit, *Blue Funk* was another solid album of pop-oriented, R&B-tinged rap from Heavy D. —*AMG*

House of Pain

Rap
This Irish rap ensemble headed by former Rhythm Syndicate member Everlast vaulted into national stardom in 1992 with "Jump Around" from their self-titled debut LP. After weathering criticism about their hip-hop integrity, they returned in 1994 with harder, funkier *Same As It Ever Was.* —*Ron Wynn*

● **House of Pain** / 1992 / Tommy Boy 1056
It would be hard for nearly anyone to top the explosive, insanely catchy "Jump Around," so it is no great surprise to find that House of Pain isn't up to the task. At times HOP comes close to duplicating the intoxicating power of their slamming single, but for the most part their debut album is a repetitive circle of similar beats, misogyny, racism, and posturing lyrics. But the perfection of "Jump Around" almost makes up for the numerous faults. —*Stephen Thomas Erlewine*

○ **Same As It Ever Was** / 1994 / Tommy Boy
House of Pain's second album finds the group getting harder, adding elements of jazz and dirty, street-oriented funk to their sound. *Same As It Ever Was* may not have a hit the size of "Jump Around"—and it may be plagued by misogynist lyrics—but it's a more focused, impressive effort.

Ice Cube (Oshea Jackson)

Vocals / Rap, dance
Through his detailed, unflinching lyrical stance and his inventive phrasing, this former N.W.A. writer and rapper has become the finest mouthpiece gangsta rap has produced. His posse, the Lynch Mob, constructs sonic backdrops that kick with the force of the best Public Enemy. Ice Cube is a controversial but major figure in comtemporary pop and has recently begun an acting career in films, including 1991's *Boyz 'n the Hood.*
Ice Cube has arguably become rap's most controversial and widely known figure in the '90s. He's topped R&B, pop, and rap charts with his releases *AmeriKKKa's Most Wanted, The Predator,* and *Lethal Injection.* Cube has been the cover boy for every magazine from *Vibe* to the *Source,* and also joined the Nation of Islam. He currently ranks alongside Ice-T as perhaps the most feared personality in rap circles.
Whispers abounded that marriage and his decision to join the Nation of Islam were responsible for Ice Cube's weakest CD as a solo act. *Lethal Injection* went platinum, but the rage was more unfocused, the rhymes less fluid and thoughtful, and the rapping less striking than on any other Ice Cube session. While his interviews sounded just as fierce, some think that Ice Cube may have peaked as a creative force in hip-hop. —*John Floyd*

☆ **AmeriKKKa's Most Wanted** / 1990 / Priority 57120

Cube gets some production help from Public Enemy's Bomb Squad and comes up with a stark and gripping portrait of life in America's inner cities. If you can get past the sexism, you'll find this debut to be one of rap's most unflinching bursts of rhythmic and political fury. —*John Floyd*

★ **Death Certificate** / 1991 / Priority 57155
His sexism is becoming even more repugnant, and his racism is sometimes misdirected, but this one perfectly articulates Cube's frustration with, and outrage at, American injustice. —*John Floyd*

○ **Kill at Will** / 1991 / Priority 7230
A few remixes from the debut bog this one down, but the title track, which examines the emotional facets of gangland murder with brutal nakedness and accuracy, is Cube's best moment. —*John Floyd*

Predator, The / 1992 / Priority 57185
Although Ice Cube makes a lot of noise throughout *The Predator*, he never actually says anything. For the most part *The Predator* is Ice Cube by numbers, spouting his standard line about women, police, drugs, and gangsters. But the album doesn't sound weak at all; it's full of strong beats and muscular rhymes. Das EFX invigorate "Check Yo Self," "Wicked" is a classic single, and the '70s-funk groove of "It Was a Good Day" proves that Ice Cube doesn't need hardcore beats to succeed. If Ice Cube had only said something, instead of blustering grandiosely, *The Predator* might have ranked among his previous efforts. —*Stephen Thomas Erlewine*

Lethal Injection / 1993 /
Ice Cube's now a family man with two children and a renewed commitment to Islam. That's the reason some observers are using to explain the dip in quality that plagues his most recent CD. Where Cube was once among hip-hop's most acerbic, gripping rappers, his voice sounds unconvincing and devoid of fury on such ostensibly political numbers as "Cave Bitch" and "Ghetto Bird." He takes repeated cheap shots at Christianity, but his pitch for Islam on "When I Get to Heaven" doesn't convey any sense of that religion's alternative views or allegedly superior stances. It's only on such standard gangsta tracks as "Make It Ruff, Make It Smooth" with K-dee and "You Know How We Do It" that Cube comes close to resembling the incendiary figure that made *Kill at Will* and *AmeriKKKa's Most Wanted*. It's hard to believe, but could Ice Cube possibly be running out of things to say after only four solo albums? —*Ron Wynn*

Ice-T

Vocals / Rap, dance
Los Angeles-based rapper and ex-con Ice-T was one of the first to establish the West Coast as a rival to the East Coast posses. Along the way he's become one of the genre's most intelligent (albeit sometimes sexist) gangsta rap advocates.

Things turned sour for Ice-T in 1993. The ongoing controversy over the single "Cop Killer" from the *Body Count* album finally resulted in the song getting removed from the album and Ice-T's departure from Warner Brothers. While both sides claimed the move was an amicable and mutual decision, there was widespread doubt that it was voluntary. The much-anticipated and - awaited *Home Invasion* also proved a disappointment. Ice-T rebounded a bit in 1994, at least in the eyes of the hip-hop faithful, with his book *The Ice Opinon*. Rhino also issued an anthology of early Ice-T material, *The Classic Collection*. —*John Floyd*

Rhyme Pays / 1987 / Sire 25602
Ice-T made his inital pop impact with this 1987 album. It earned him his first gold record, and while there were still lighter numbers like "I Love Ladies" it was also an early indication that the graphically violent images and sexist language of such songs as "Squeeze the Trigger," "Sex," and "Pain" would appeal across racial and economic lines. Ice-T was also trimming and tightening his rap approach, putting more menace in his tone and more edge in his rhymes. —*Ron Wynn*

☆ **Iceberg, Freedom of Speech . . . Just Watch What You Say, The** / 1989 / Sire 26028
The Iceberg is a brutal, occasionally brilliant condemnation of censorship, drug use, and societal injustice, marred only by a few conflicting ideals and Ice-T's own sexism. —*John Floyd*

○ **Power** / 1989 / Sire 25765
His second release is a quantum-leap improvement over his debut—better samples, a more pronounced and developed rapping

style, and smarter material. Ice-T does marvelous homage to Curtis Mayfield with an excellent adaption of "I'm Your Pusherman" from the vintage *Superfly* soundtrack. —*Ron Wynn*

★ **O. G. Original Gangster** / 1991 / Sire 26492
T's masterpiece. An ambitious, sprawling examination of gangsta rap culture that confronts all the relevant issues and even offers a few alternatives and solutions. It's also Ice-T's most musically visceral outburst. —*John Floyd*

Body Count / 1992 / Sire 26878
Ice-T's excursion into heavy metal brought him a firestorm of controversy; yet the album is a tepid collection of '80s-styled arena metal that never sounds dangerous. Frequently, it's hard to tell if Ice takes this stuff seriously; tracks like "Body Count" and "Cop Killer" are invigorating stabs at social criticism, but most of the album is filled with stupid attempts at being threatening, like "KKK Bitch" and "Mama's Gotta Die Tonight." Maybe the humor was intentional, but too frequently the record sounded embarrassing. When "Cop Killer" was pulled from the album, a version of "The Iceberg," recorded with Jello Biafra, replaced it.—*Stephen Thomas Erlewine*

Classic Collection, The / 1993 / Rhino 71170
A good collection of Ice-T's early tracks for various rap groups and labels, before he recorded his gangsta rap classics. Historically it's interesting but most fans will prefer *Iceberg* or *O. G. Original Gangster*. —*Stephen Thomas Erlewine*

Home Invasion / 1993 / Priority 53858
Given that most of *Home Invasion* was recorded during and after the "Cop Killer" media firestorm, it comes as no surprise that the album is an uneven, muddled affair, not the clean, focused attack of *O. G. Original Gangster*. Instead of producing an album that illustrates his confusion through the music (like Public Enemy's claustrophobic "Welcome to the Terrordome"), Ice-T has made a confused album, unsure in its musical and lyrical direction. *Home Invasion* does have some flashes of brilliance (about a third of the album, particularly the tribute to the gang truce, "Gotta Lotta Love"), but it takes a little digging to find the best material. —*Stephen Thomas Erlewine*

Intelligent Hoodlum (Percy Chapman)

Vocals / Rap, dance
While New York rapper Intelligent Hoodlum served 20 months on Riker's Island for robbery in 1988, he used the experience to immerse himself in African-American culture and the theology of the Nation of Islam. That combination underscores all his work and makes his songs radiate with righteousness, anger, indignation, and frustration. It doesn't hurt that ace producer Marley Marl supplies the undergirding as well. —*Ron Wynn*

○ **Intelligent Hoodlum** / 1990 / A&M 5311
A great social commentary. "Arrest the President" is a great rap. —*Robert Gordon*

● **Tragedy—Saga of a Hoodlum** / Jun. 22, 1993 / A&M 215389
Onetime Riker's Island prisoner Intelligent Hoodlum speaks with genuine insight about inner-city hell and chaos. His second album wasn't laden with posturing rhetoric and wasn't presented in an ambitiously produced package. Instead, it was a chilling, unapologetic chronicle of brutal, ugly, and negative experiences relayed by someone neither celebrating nor regretting what he's seen and heard. There was no attempt to entertain, impress, or amuse in his rapping or rhymes; this was just the straight dope. —*Ron Wynn*

Jungle Brothers

Group / Rap, hip-hop, dance
An endlessly funky New York trio who've collaborated with like minds such as De La Soul and A Tribe Called Quest. Their love of James Brown goes deeper than mere sampling.
Although the Jungle Brothers have received an enormous amount of critical acclaim, they have not yet been able to score a commercial success as large as either De La Soul's or Tribe's. —*John Floyd*

● **Straight out the Jungle** / 1988 / Warlock 2704
The trio's debut is powered by muscular funk riffs underpinned by an Afrocentric sensibility and a sharp sense of humor. —*John Floyd*

○ **Done by the Forces of Nature** / 1989 / Warner Brothers 26072

By injecting some vocal delicacy and some clever samples into their moderately militant message, they made a second album that elaborates on their own winning formula. —*John Floyd*

J. Beez Wit the Remedy / Jun. 22, 1993 / Warner Brothers
Nearly four years after *Done by the Forces of Nature*, the Jungle Brothers return with a hazy, funky album filled with their brand of literate hip-hop. Although they've made some stylistic progressions since the last record, they weren't enough to make this a completely groundbreaking release, nor was it commericial enough to break them out of their critically acclaimed cult status. Instead, it was another solid, inventive album that didn't receive the attention it deserved. —*Stephen Thomas Erlewine*

Just Ice

Rap
New York rapper Just Ice has been one of the least-publicized, hardest East Coast artists. His 1993 release *Gun Talk* has just as much explicit language and sexist commentary and just as many violent scenarios and apocalyptic visions as much more publicized and controversial releases from bigger-name groups. He's been unable to generate much response or attention outside of New York. —*Ron Wynn*

○ **Gun Talk** / 1993 / Savage 50211
As pessimistic and fatalistic as anything coming out of the East Coast, Just Ice minced no words and offered little hope to anyone wondering if rappers saw anything in the future except pointless death and violent confrontation. In Just Ice's vision, survival's the thing, by any means necessary. —*Ron Wynn*

● **Desolate One, The** / Fresh 82010
East Coast rapper Just Ice's often brusque blend of reggae-inflected hip-hop production, angry raps, and cutting beats was strictly for the hardcore. The lack of thematic variety sometimes made things ponderous, but for searing, to-the-point gangsta commentary, Just Ice is one of the better proponents. —*Ron Wynn*

K Solo (Kevin Madison)

Rap
New York rapper K Solo was a childhood friend and associate of Parrish Smith's. They worked together in a rap group before Madison formed K Solo (Kevin Self Organization Left Others) in the early '90s. His 1992 debut, *Times Up*, attracted scant attention, but K Solo got better notices for his performances on tour with EPMD. —*Ron Wynn*

○ **Time's Up** / 1992 / Atlantic 82388
Despite the lack of a standout single, K Solo turned a few heads on the hip-hop trail with this 1992 debut. A longtime friend of Parrish Smith's (EPMD), K Solo displayed a good rap style and the versatility to credibly deliver on message tracks like "Premonition of a Black Prisoner" and "Long Live the Fugitive" as easily as on "Household Maid" and "I Can't Hold It Back." —*Ron Wynn*

Kid 'n Play

Group / Rap, dance
They've recorded several decent albums with the aid of producer Hurby "Luv Bug" Azor, but this duo is best known for their starring roles in the *House Party* film series. The movies helped Kid 'n Play's infectious pop-flavored hip-hop to cross over into the mainstream without losing much street credibility. —*John Floyd*

● **2 Hype** / 1988 / Select 21628
A solid debut with snatches of house, dance, and go-go. Despite minimal rapping abilities, the duo quickly captured a chunk of the hip-hop audience. —*Ron Wynn*

House Party (Soundtrack) / 1990 / Motown
Not strictly or even mainly their album, it does contain the singles "Funhouse" and "Kid vs. Play (The Battle)." Its prime importance was as the soundtrack from an extremely successful film of the same name, which launched the duo into cinematic stardom. —*Ron Wynn*

Kid 'n Play's Fun House / 1990 / Select 21638
One of two releases from the twosome in 1990, this has new cuts with funkier, looser foundations and more ambitious adult lyrics and rapping style. —*Ron Wynn*

Kid Frost

Vocals / Rap
Frost expanded rap's vocabulary by flaunting his Latin heritage and celebrating its culture. The fusion is fascinating, both lyrically and musically. —*John Floyd*

● **Hispanic Causing Panic** / 1990 / Virgin 91377
Frost's debut brings his Latin heritage into the arena of rap, not just with the Spanish language, but also with his convincing and clever street dramas. A masterful and long-overdue fusion of funk and salsa samples. —*John Floyd*

King Sun

Vocals / Rap, hip-hop, dance
One of the first and most successful Afrocentric hip-hop prophets. —*John Floyd*

● **Righteous but Ruthless** / 1990 / Profile 1299
Noteworthy Afrocentric/Islamic rap. —*Ron Wynn*

○ **XL** / Zakia 1270
A prominent player in the political rap movement. —*Ron Wynn*

King Tee

Rap
West Coast rapper King Tee was born in Los Angeles but gained early experience in Houston as a mixer at radio stations KTSU and KYOK. He made his performance debut on Capitol in 1989 with *Act a Fool*. He followed that with *At Your Own Risk* in 1990. Both blended boasts with comic and novelty material that wasn't hard or gangsta oriented, which may explain why they barely scraped the lower end of the pop albums chart. —*Ron Wynn*

● **Act a Fool** / Nov. 16, 1988 / Capitol 90544
Alternately defiant, angry, confrontational, and bemused raps from King Tee on this late '80s rap release. While there's some blustering and macho/sexual posturing, there are also many moments when Tee's comments deserve close scrutiny. The production isn't as relentless as many other recent hip-hop releases in the number of fragments, samples, and snippets it contains, nor is it as intricately edited. —*Ron Wynn*

○ **At Your Own Risk** / Sep. 24, 1990 / Capitol 92359
Compton rapper King Tee's second album again blended humorous jibes, novelty cuts, and some message cuts, but it was far different from most of what was coming from Compton by 1990. Such songs as "Do Your Thing," "Jay Fay Dray," and "On the Dance Tip" were light-years away from N.W.A.-styled gangsta rap. Even the more serious cuts like "At Your Own Risk" were more reflective than combative or prophetic, and Tee's rapping was a mix of clowning, taunting, and mocking, rather than declaring and challenging. —*Ron Wynn*

Tha Triflin' Album / 1993 / Capitol 99354
Sometimes titles can be quite accurate, and this one reflected the general attitude the hip-hop audience took toward King Tee's third CD. He'd never been that much in the spotlight, and now his rhymes and lighter rap approach sounded dated and far off the mark. —*Ron Wynn*

Kool G Rap & DJ Polo

Group / Rap
A young Big Apple duo chaperoned by production wiz Marley Marl. —*John Floyd*

● **Road to Riches** / 1989 / Cold Chillin' 25820
Their debut contains some bright moments. —*Dan Heilman*

○ **Wanted: Dead or Alive** / 1990 / Cold Chillin' 26165
Their second album is a relevant and musically sumptuous collection. —*John Floyd*

Kool Moe Dee

Vocals / Rap, dance
One old-school rapper who's managed to thrive by mixing it up with new-school types. Kool Moe Dee was a member of the Harlem trio the Treacherous Three in the early '80s that was spotted by music veteran and producer Bobby Robinson. The trio eventually split from Robinson and joined rival Sugarhill Records, then disbanded when their contract there expired. Dee hooked up with producer Teddy Riley, now the king of new-jack-swing efforts, and hit instant gold with the single "Go See the

Doctor," an amazing safe-sex story that combines a cautionary message with a frenetic, hypnotic beat. Since then, Dee has had a lengthy, disturbing sexist slant. He engaged fellow rapper LL Cool J in a continuing battle of words that was interesting for a while but degenerated into a stock formula.

Kool Moe Dee's past was celebrated in 1993 with the release of a greatest-hits LP. He has also talked about a Treacherous Three reunion, though no firm plans had been announced as of summer 1994. —*Ron Wynn*

I'm Kool Moe Dee / 1986 / Jive 1025
A commanding debut, especially the smashing tune "Go See the Doctor," one of the best and most pointedly cautionary sex songs ever. —*Ron Wynn*

○ **How Ya Like Me Now** / 1987 / Jive 1079
The title track was a big smash, and it marked the beginning of the lengthy Kool Moe Dee versus LL Cool J rap war. The second hit,"Wild, Wild West," was also a masterpiece; the album's greatness overcomes its forays into sexism on "Stupid." —*Ron Wynn*

★ **Greatest Hits** / 1989 / Sequel 623
Kool Moe Dee was an early hip-hop/rap pioneer and a founding member of the Treacherous Three. As much as any single performer he epitomized rap's rise from an East Coast underground genre to a national youth sound and has been unceasing in his demands for respect and recognition. Dee was also among the first to bring social significance to his material without being pedantic, and his songs (with the exception of "They Need Money") weren't littered with sexist and misogynistic rhetoric. This 15-song collection covers his biggest recordings, from novelty-type fare ("Wild, Wild West" and "Whosgotdaflava") to the safe-sex number "Go See the Doctor," cultural battle cries like "Rise 'N' Shine" and "No Respect," and his "war" with LL Cool J that peaked with "Death Blow" and "How Ya Like Me Now." Dee's role in rap's explosion is documented on this compilation, and it's instructive to hear how his rhythming style, elocution, and pacing differs from those of the '90s gangsta mode. —*Ron Wynn*

Knowledge Is King / 1989 / Jive 1182
Another brilliant hit with "They Want Money," though Dee expands on a disturbing antifemale line. But it's balanced by a stirring antidrug, Afrocentric philosophy and a rap methodology that puts him near the top among hip-hop purists. —*Ron Wynn*

Funke Funke Wisdom / 1991 / Jive 1388
The single "Rise and Shine" was a summit meeting of rap theorists, with Dee joined by Chuck D from Public Enemy and KRS-One. Unfortunately, an overreliance on sexual posturing and macho imagery had begun to set in, weighing down an otherwise notable effort. —*Ron Wynn*

Kriss Kross (Kris Kross)

Group / Rap
Rap successes come in the strangest packages. Kriss Kross are two 13-year-olds from Atlanta who, with the help of 19-year-old producer Jermaine Dupri, released a gimmick-laden but fairly charming debut that promptly outsold nearly all its competition in the summer of 1992. Whether they can turn their success story into a career remains to be seen.

While it wasn't a disaster, their 1993 follow-up, *Da Bomb*, didn't match the levels of their debut, mainly because it didn't have a single as strong as "Jump" or "Warm It Up." —*John Floyd*

● **Totally Krossed Out** / 1992 / Ruffhouse 48710
The hottest rap duo of summer 1992, thanks to their penchant for wearing their clothes backward and the single "Jump," which crossed over to pop and R&B markets. —*Ron Wynn*

Da Bomb / 1993 /
Da Bomb sounds nearly identical to Kriss Kross's debut, but there are no singles that are as clever or catchy as either "Jump" or "Warm It Up." —*AMG*

Kwame & A New Beginning

Group / Rap
Kwame's nice-guy personality—alternately humble and intelligent, outspoken and easy-stepping—offers a refreshing break from the usual bad-boy posturing of most of the rap pack. —*John Floyd*

● **Day in the Life: A Pokadelick Adventure** / 1990 / Atlantic 82100

Day in the Life is a strange but fun hip-hop journey. —*Dan Heilman*

○ **Featuring a New Beginning** / 1990 / Atlantic 81941
Queens rapper Kwame stepped out with this 1989 debut, exhibiting a competent rap style and erratic but sometimes catchy compositions. "Boy Genius" and "Mic Is Mine" were good boasting numbers and the best vehicles for his evolving rap style. "Pushthe panicbutton!!" and "U Gotz 2 Get Down" were less successful, sounding like Biz Markie or Marley Marl outtakes. —*Ron Wynn*

Nastee / 1992 / Atlantic 82356
Tasha Lambert joined Kwame on his third album, but the union didn't generate much compositional fruit. The raps were unconvincing, the production a mish-mash of funk and soul snippets underpinning rhymes that were neither fluidly presented nor cleverly composed.—*Ron Wynn*

L'Trimm

Group / Rap
Miami-based female rappers Tigra and Bunny D. were 18 when they scored a mild hit with "Cars with the Boom" in 1988. For a brief period their CD *Grab It!* stayed on the charts after Atlantic leased it from Time-X, but they were unable to get another single to maintain the momentum, and kiddie-pop gradually lost its audience. —*Ron Wynn*

● **Grab It!** / 1988 / Atlantic 81925
Miami teen rappers L'Trimm enjoyed a little pop mileage with "Cars with the Boom," a 1988 single reflecting the days when hip-hop was less serious and novelty/comic tunes could still get sizable audiences. The duo sounded cute and eager, but when they tried to show that they could also handle "adult" material, the credibility gap nearly swallowed them.—*Ron Wynn*

L.A. Star

Rap
In 1990, L.A. Star provided a woman's perspective on the gangsta life at a time when there weren't many female rappers willing to operate in that arena. At the same time, she also included some material with a romantic side, though she couldn't afford to juxtapose vulnerability and combativeness too closely. *Poetess* was a decent debut on Profile, but so far there hasn't been a follow-up. —*Ron Wynn*

○ **Poetess** / 1990 / Profile 1290
Good debut work from this South Bronx rapper; a frank, distressing portrait of inner-city life and times. —*Ron Wynn*

Latin Alliance

Group / Rap, dance
A one-off collaboration by Latino rappers Kid Frost, Mellow Man Ace, and MC A.L.T. —*John Floyd*

○ **Latin Alliance** / 1991 / Virgin 91625
Hip-hop with an Afro-Latin/dance edge. —*Ron Wynn*

Leaders of the New School

Rap
Uniondale, New York, rappers MC Charlie Brown, MC Dinco D., MC Busta Rhymes, and Cut Monitor Milo issued *A Future without a Past* for Elektra in 1991 as Leaders of the New School. They combined Afrocentric message tracks with comic/novelty throwaways and got a little attention for "Teachers, Don't Teach Us Nonsense!" They followed it with *T.I.M.E.* in 1993. —*Ron Wynn*

○ **Future without a Past** / Elektra 60976
Hard-edged political rap; good message but standard presentation. —*Ron Wynn*

LL Cool J (James Smith)

Vocals / Rap, hip-hop, dance
The importance of LL Cool J (his moniker stands for "Ladies Love Cool James") in rap cannot be exaggerated. By fusing the beatbox minimalism of Run-D.M.C. with the b-boy snarl of his defiant lyrics, LL Cool J pushed the music into new terrain, opening the door for numerous hip-hop contenders and becoming a superstar in the process.

Since the across-the-boards success of *Mama Said Knock You Out*, LL Cool J's had trouble reclimbing the mountain from which he once stood tall. He predicted *14 Shots to the Dome* would be the ticket, and it did respectably, but it lacked both the resonance and the power of *Mama Said.* —*John Floyd*

☆ **Radio** / 1986 / Def Jam 40239
LL Cool J's debut, produced by Rick Rubin, is a brilliant mix of hardcore street anthems ("I Can't Live without My Radio," "Rock the Bells") and updated twists on the dozens ("That's a Lie"), with a couple of ballads thrown in. —*John Floyd*

Bigger and Deffer / 1987 / Def Jam 40793
On his second album, LL Cool J's ego goes to his head, resulting in a weak album of mild beats and inflated bragging, only partially saved by his first successful ballad, the syrupy "I Need Love." —*Stephen Thomas Erlewine*

☆ **Walking with a Panther** / 1989 / Def Jam 45172
A sprawling follow-up to his stinko second album, and his most ambitious. LL Cool J not only regroups the strengths that made his debut a winner, but also shows a musical expansion of his art that bodes well for the future. Includes "I'm That Type of Guy," "Going Back to Cali," and "Big Ole Butt." —*John Floyd*

★ **Mama Said Knock You Out** / 1990 / Def Jam 46888
The future, LL Cool J 1990-style. He's mixing house and hip-hop into his minimalist backdrops, and he's finally come up with some decent love songs. With "The Boomin' System," he's created yet another essential rap anthem. Includes "Around the Way Girl," "6 Minutes of Pleasure," "Jingling Baby," and the title track. — *John Floyd*

14 Shots to the Dome / CBS 53325
It's not the tour de force of *Mama Said Knock You Out,* but *14 Shots to the Dome* is a solid effort that finds LL Cool J maturing gracefully and strongly, without selling out. *Fourteen Shots* may not have sold as well as *Mama,* either; yet at least half of the album ranks with his best work. —*Stephen Thomas Erlewine*

Main Source

Rap
New York rappers Main Source exploded into the hip-hop universe with *Breaking Atoms* for Wild Pitch in 1991. It featured the Large Professor's cutting, often cynical narratives about everything from police brutality to betrayal by friends. The onetime cohort of Producer Paul C., the Large Professor, was joined by twin disc jockeys K-Cut and Sir Scratch. The single "Lookin' at the Front Door" proved a sizable hit, and Main Source seemed on its way. But nearly three years later no second LP had been issued and the group was rumored to be disbanding. —*Ron Wynn*

● **Breaking Atoms** / 1991 / EMI America 97543
Sparkling raps, snazzy production, and an energetic set. —*Ron Wynn*

F—K What You Think / Mar. 22, 1994 / Wild Pitch Records, Ltd.

Mantronix

Group / Rap, hip-hop
Electro-rap funk duo led by DJ Mantronix and Bryce Luvah. — *John Floyd*

● **Album, The** / 1985 / Sleeping Bag 6
This intriguing mid '80s debut remains Mantronix's finest album. Curtis "Mantronik" Kahleel and rapper MC Tee scored with what was then an imaginative and unusual mix of dance and hip-hop production styles and sensibility with soul and R&B vocals. They weren't house, nor rap, nor urban contemporary, but a wonderful hybrid of all these and more, among them dancehall reggae, even pop and funk. The album had two fine singles in "Bassline" and "Ladies" and made Mantronix a hot property. —*Ron Wynn*

This Should Move Ya / 1987 / Capitol 94479
Mantronik switched labels in the late '80s, moving from the independent Sleeping Bag to the major label Capitol. This was their second Capitol album, and it worked out fine. Though the lineup had now changed, with Bryce Luvah and D.J.D. on board rather than MC Tee, the group had another strong single in "Got to Have Your Love," and Capitol was providing Curtis "Mantronik" Kahleel with a bigger push and sharper production and sound. But the underground spirit that permeated Mantronix's Sleeping Bag albums was missing, as was the quirky air that marked their past singles. —*Ron Wynn*

In Full Effect / 1988 / Capitol 48336

The Capitol debut for Curtis "Mantronik" Kahleel and the final album featuring rapper MC Tee. This album skirted the lower regions of the pop charts; had a less abrasive, smoother sound though the patented dance/hip-hop/urban contemporary fusion hadn't been affected. But it wasn't overall as quite as risky or spirited as their Sleeping Bag dates, which may have been the reason Tee departed. —*Ron Wynn*

Incredible Sound Machine, The / Mar. 18, 1991 / Capitol 94570
Things had changed for the production-songwriting duo Mantronix by the early '90s. Curtis "Mantronik" Kahleel was still aboard doing remixes and production, but now the vocalists were Jade Trini and Bryce Luvah. They had one mildly interesting single with "Don't Go Messin' with My Heart"; but otherwise the formerly inspired mix of hip-hop/dance production and soul/R&B vocals wasn't as exuberant or as catchy. The studio work was equally as sharp, but they didn't generate as much attention in the dance, hip-hop, or urban contemporary market. —*Ron Wynn*

Marky & the Funky Bunch Mark

Rap
Few suspected that Marky Mark, the younger brother of New Kids on the Block vocalist Donnie Wahlberg, would still be around in the mid '90s when New Kids on the Block would be history. But Marky Mark has survived through high-profile underwear ads and low-grade but popular enough pop-rap. He's even overcome a homophobic controversy and scored a number-one hit with "Good Vibrations" from his debut *Music for the People;* that single has been his high point. Even though the second LP *You Gotta Believe* peaked at 14, it didn't duplicate the platinum status of the debut. —*Ron Wynn*

● **Music for the People** / 1991 / Interscope 91737
On the strength of the number-one hit "Good Vibrations" and the Top Ten follow-up "Wildside," Marky Mark & the Funky Bunch Mark's first album became a pop sensation. Unfortunately, the rest of the album couldn't match the catchy, pop-oriented rap of the singles, making the entire record a hit-and-miss affair. — *Stephen Thomas Erlewine*

You Gotta Believe / 1992 / Interscope 92203
Marky Mark tried to keep riding the wave he enjoyed with *Music for the People,* but failed to score any pop or R&B hit. He'd topped the charts with "Good Vibrations," but discovered the second time around that finding another hit to scavenge or maintain a gimmick is much harder. He eventually enjoyed a moderate success with "You Gotta Believe," but a combination of some ill-timed homophobic remarks in an interview and rather limp material like "Bout Time I Funk You" and "I Run Rhymes" extinguished whatever fires Marky Mark had previously lit. —*Ron Wynn*

Biz Markie

Vocals / Rap
A productive member of Marley Marl's posse, Markie is a contemporary master of comedic rap. He doesn't have much to say, but songs such as "Picking Boogers" are worthy of the Fat Boys, and "Spring Again" is a classic summer single.
Biz Markie managed to dodge a potential career-ending bullet when a controversy involving a sample from Gilbert O'Sullivan's "Alone Again Naturally" was resolved. Markie had allegedly used the sample without permission, triggering a lawsuit. He gave his own spin to the controversy with the 1993 release *All Samples Cleared.* —*John Floyd*

☆ **Goin' Off** / Feb. 23, 1988 / Warner Brothers 25675
Biz Markie's debut album introduced his absurdly comical and extremely inventive musical style. While he talked about "Pickin' Boogers," hanging out at "Albee Square Mall," and made music with his mouth, the Biz never kept the music similar; and with Marley Marl's production covering all of the bases, he concentrated on a goofy funky R&B/dance beat. It was a funny, surrealistic minor masterpiece. —*Stephen Thomas Erlewine*

★ **Diabolical Biz Markie—the Biz Never Sleeps** / Oct. 10, 1989 / Cold Chillin' 26003
Biz Markie's madcap humor was effectively utilized on this 1989 release. Markie relied on puns, quips, bad jokes, and his disjointed rap style, creating material that was quite different from the hard-edged fare that now rules hip-hop. Some of it was funny, some of it stupid, but none of it was vicious or offensive. The al-

bum contained the hits "Just a Friend" and "Spring Again." —*Ron Wynn*

○ **I Need a Haircut** / Aug. 27, 1991 / Cold Chillin' 26648
While others rapped about gang strife, inner-city turmoil, their proficiency on the mike, or their sexual prowess, Biz Markie discussed bad haircuts and other such weighty matters on his 1991 release. This might be what the Coasters would sound like if they'd grown up during the rap era. Sadly, there aren't many people on the '90s hip-hop scene interested in absurdist humor. —*Ron Wynn*

All Samples Cleared / 1993 / Cold Chillin'
Biz Markie made sure he had permission for every sample featured on this album. Unfortunately, it appears that the effort to get clearances took its toll on the creative process. The bizarre humor that made his earlier releases so entertaining was much less evident, as now Markie strained for results and mostly came up short. —*Ron Wynn*

Marley Marl

Vocals / Rap, Hip-hop, dance
Ace producer Marl has worked with the likes of Roxanne Shante, Biz Markie, Big Daddy Kane, MC Shan, and Master Ace. His style maintains its roots in old-school hip-hop while pushing the music to new, often blatantly accessible levels. —*John Floyd*

● **In Control, Vol. 1** / 1988 / Cold Chillin' 25783
Marl shows off his greatest stars, including Roxanne Shante and Big Daddy Kane. —*Dan Heilman*

In Control, Vol. 2 (For Your Stee / 1991 / Cold Chillin' 26257
Though the date carried his name, this was really a showcase for various rappers produced by Marley Marl. Everyone from Chuck D, LL Cool J, and Heavy D to Chubb Rock, Def Jef, and King Tee made an appearance on his second Cold Chillin' CD. Unfortunately, this all-star lineup didn't hit any home runs, and the LP struck out. —*Ron Wynn*

Master Ace

Vocals / Rap, dance
He's young, but Master Ace is a smart cookie. He expounds on such things as racial unity and the need for education, and Marly Marl fits him with thick grooves that suggest possible crossover appeal. —*John Floyd*

○ **Take a Look Around** / 1990 / Cold Chillin' 26179
Ace's throbbing Marley Marl-produced debut mixed the loopy humor of Biz Markie (who shares a cut here) with the urgency of the best LL Cool J. Best cut: "Music Man." —*John Floyd*

MC Brains (James De Shannon)

Rap
Michael Bivins discovered Cleveland-born MC Brains in 1992. With Bivins's assistance and encouragement, MC Brains debuted on Motown with *Lovers Lane*. The single "Oochie Coochie" just missed the pop Top 20, while *Brainstorming* was a respectable follow-up. MC Brains's style was pop crossover rather than hard or gangsta, but he showed enough potential the first time out to indicate a second release would be justified. —*Ron Wynn*

○ **Lover's Lane** / 1992 / Motown 6342
MC Brains was discovered by former New Edition and current Bell Biv Devoe member Michael Bivins. He was 17 when this 1992 CD was released. Thus it seemed appropriate that the teen angst/new-jack number "Oochie Coochie" would be the lone hit, peaking at 21 on the pop charts. There was nothing confrontational or angry about this one, the MC moniker nothwithstanding. If there were any questions about MC Brains's (and Bivins's) intentions, tracks like "Strawberry Lane" and "G-String" thoroughly answered them. —*Ron Wynn*

MC Breed (Eric Breed)

Rap
Flint, Michigan, rapper MC Breed came out hard, tough, and fast on his 1991 debut *MC Breed & DFC*. "Ain't No Future in Yo' Frontin'" set the tone for a collection of confrontational, at times almost paranoid Afrocentric and/or gangsta tracks with occasional reggae flavoring. DFC were nowhere to be found on the 1992 follow-up *20 Below*. It opted to be even more explicit, angry, and offensive than the debut, though such tracks as "Little Child

Running Wild" and "Flash's Groove" provided some variety. Breed then issued *The New Breed* for Wrap in 1993. He came back strong with *Funkafied* in 1994, hitting the Top Ten on the R&B charts. It was also for Wrap, a label distributed by Atlanta-based Ichiban. —*Ron Wynn*

○ **MC Breed & DFC** / 1991 / SDEG 4103
MC Breed was 19 when he and DFC made their debut in 1991. Things got started on a positive front with the defiant cut "Ain't No Future in Yo' Fronting," a tough-talking, nicely rapped, and rhymed assault on hypocrisy. "Black for Black" and "I Will Excel" were also worthy message cuts, while "Get Loose" and "Job Corp" added more good material. It was a solid but low-selling first album, one that suggested that the rap audience should more closely notice MC Breed. —*Ron Wynn*

● **20 Below** / 1992 / Wrap/Ichiban 8109

MC Breed came out even harder and more combative on his second CD than he did on his debut. "Jealous Pimp" and "Ain't to Be F– With" set the agenda squarely in gangsta territory, though he hedged his bets with "Life of a Flintstone" and "Whenever You Want Me." But apparently audiences were also unsure whether MC Breed wanted to brandish a gun or hang out with Bugs Bunny. —*Ron Wynn*

Funkafied / Jun. 7, 1994 / Wrap/Ichiban Records

New Breed, The / Wrap/Ichiban 8120
MC Breed was alone and rapping with fire and fury on this 1993 album. He continued changing his image to that of a seasoned, prophetic gangsta commentator, rather than alternating between hard and light material. Breed's raps weren't always fluid, but his rhymes were frequently compelling. —*Ron Wynn*

MC Lyte

Vocals / Rap
Though she's turned a bit in the pop direction on her latest release, Brooklyn rapper MC Lyte has done some inventive, distinctive material on her two prior releases. She's provided some of the better comebacks and putdowns aimed at out-of-control male egos and libidos, and she's also quite funny. It is to be hoped that the pop tinges on *Act Like You Know* are merely an alternative, rather than a primary, direction.
MC Lyte responded to fans questioning her direction on *Ain't No Other*, her 1993 album. This marked a return to the tough-talking, fat beats and no-nonsense persona that had characterized her most successful material. —*Ron Wynn*

Lyte as a Rock / 1988 / First Priority 90905
The debut of this femme rapper thrusts a middle finger toward the sexism of the male-dominated rap turf, through clever rhymes and a sharp sense of humor, ensuring that her feminism never exhausts and always enlightens. —*John Floyd*

○ **Eyes on This** / 1989 / First Priority 91304
This expands on the promise of her debut, both musically (the samples are more dense) and lyrically (witness "Shut the Eff Up! (Hoe)" and the winningly arty "Cuppucino"). —*John Floyd*

Ain't No Other / 1993 / First Priority Music

MC Ren (Lorenzo Patterson)

Rap
MC Ren joined the list of N.W.A. members gone solo in 1992 with *Kizz My Black Azz*. It peaked at number 12 and eventually went platinum despite being thoroughly unplayable on even the most underground radio station. The follow-up, *Shock of the Hour*, briefly topped the pop charts but didn't have lasting power. On both releases, Ren has showed surprising facility and fluidity as a rapper. The rhymes haven't been anything special, though, nor have the beats. —*Ron Wynn*

○ **Kizz My Black Azz** / Jun. 30, 1992 / Priority 53802
Dismissing MC Ren's obsessively violent and sexist lyrics would be easier if his music weren't so tight and menacing. Taken on purely musical terms, *Kizz My Black Azz* is thrilling; when it's analyzed more deeply, the simplistic, disturbing lyrics unravel the achievements of the music. However, the production and beats are so deeply funky that they almost lift Ren's debut solo EP out of the swamp of violent, misogynist gangstas. Almost. —*Stephen Thomas Erlewine*

● **Shock of the Hour** / 1993 / Ruthless

N.W.A. charter member MC Ren has been one of rap's overlooked practitioners. He's gifted with nearly as commanding a voice as Dr. Dre, and he recently became another of the considerable number of hip-hop types who've joined the Nation of Islam. His second EP's uneven but at least presents a consistent lyric vision when it's not spewing out familiar, tired sexist clichés about Black women. Ren highlights American hypocrisy with a vengeance, and the title track foresees the nation's fiery end in an apocalyptic fury enabling Black people to finally achieve justice. Both this tune and "Attack on Babylon" come closest to presenting a coherent, effective philosophy. Another provocative track is "Same Old S," a song that strips away any pretense of glamour around the gangsta lifestyle and outlines the brutality, paranoia, and violence that are at its core. These tracks display MC Ren's potential as a hip-hop theorist; the others just fill out the CD. —*Ron Wynn*

MC Serch (Michael Berin)

Rap
MC Serch was half of the White rap duo 3rd Bass, still the most insightful and "authentic" of the Caucasian hip-hoppers. When 3rd Bass disbanded, Serch began rapping on his own. He had a sizable hip-hop hit with "Here It Comes *from his 1992 release* Return of the Product *on Def Jam.* —Ron Wynn

○ **Return of the Product** / 1992 / Def Jam 52964
MC Serch's first album after the breakup of 3rd Bass was a stripped-down, surprisingly melodic album that suffers from a lack of sharp production. Even so, Serch's skillful rhymes overcome most of the weaknesses of the record. —*Stephen Thomas Erlewine*

MC Shy D (Peter Jones)

Rap
MC Shy D is the Bronx-born cousin of Afrika Bambaataa. He began on Luther Campbell's label in 1987 with *Got to Be Tough.* After a lean period, he rebounded with *The Comeback* in 1993. This was his most artistically ambitious release to date, with more contemporary production and a lean, refined rapping style. —*Ron Wynn*

Mellow Man Ace

Vocals / Rap, hip-hop, house music
The Los Angeles-based rapper from Havana works the same terrain as Kid Frost: he has a penchant for novelty numbers and the usual hip-hop boasts and brings Hispanic culture to American hip-hop. —*John Floyd*

★ **Escape from Havana** / 1990 / Capitol 91295
A landmark hip-hop/Afro-Latin merger. —*Ron Wynn*

○ **Brother with Two Tongues, The** / May 25, 1992 / Capitol 94608
African-American/Latino rapper Mellow Man Ace's second Capitol release continued his merger of hip-hop and Afro-Latin musical, linguistic, and political elements. Unfortunately, he didn't create anything quite as commercially viable as "Mentirosa," but his beats and rhymes ranged from average to intriguing while the rap style was again inspirational in its appeal to a multicultural audience. —*Ron Wynn*

Monie Love (Simone Wilson)

Vocals / Rap, urban
London-born Simone Wilson was featured on Queen Latifah's single "Ladies First" while still a teen. Her CDs as a leader have been erratic, often suggesting much more than they delivered, though they've usually contained at least one strong single. After *Down to Earth,* Love issued *In a Word or Two* in 1993. —*Ron Wynn*

○ **Down to Earth** / 1990 / Warner Brothers 26358
The mood moves through vibrant, concerned, bemused, and resigned. Nice samples and good production. —*Ron Wynn*

● **In a Word or 2** / 1993 / Warner Brothers 45054
Monie Love's second CD was more ambitious than her first and took a harder, less pop tone and approach. She spoke frankly and with clarity about such topics as promiscuity and self-esteem, while her rapping was more focused, her beats starker and more forceful, and the rhymes less gimmicky. —*Ron Wynn*

Movement Ex

Group / Rap
Afrocentrism at its sharpest, from Lord Mustafa Hasan Ma'd and DJ King Born Khaaliq. The thick, intricate production of their 1990 debut expands on the Bomb Squad's work with Public Enemy. Ex's Five Percent Nation of Islam outlook is uncompromising and rightfully hostile. —*John Floyd*

○ **Movement Ex** / 1990 / Columbia 46894
A forthright Islamic/Afrocentric outing, with tight studio production support. —*Ron Wynn*

Naughty by Nature

Group / Rap, dance
One of the finest new rap posses received some help from Queen Latifah on their 1991 debut and landed a huge hit with the naggingly incessant "O.P.P." Naughty by Nature scored another huge hit with their next release, *19 Naughty III,* which featured "Hip Hop Hooray," rivaling "O.P.P." as a crossover smash and national catchphrase in 1993. —*John Floyd*

● **Naughty by Nature** / 1991 / Tommy Boy 1044
This leering trio's first single, "O.P.P.," dominated the airwaves in fall 1991 on the strength of its home-truth bedroom message and its butt-hugging beat. Fans of the single will find plenty more in NBN's rollicking debut album. —*John Floyd*

○ **19 Naughty III** / 1993 / Tommy Boy 1069
With its slamming beats and infectious hooks (exemplified by the hit single "Hip Hop Hooray"), *19 Naughty III,* Naughty by Nature's second album, proves they are not a one-hit-wonder group. Although the music is terrific, their lyrical posturing and misogyny can grow tiring. —*Stephen Thomas Erlewine*

Nice & Smooth

Rap
New York City rap duo Gregg Nice (born Gregg Mays) and Smooth Bee (born Daryl Barnes) had an underrated 1991 debut release *Ain't a Damn Thing Changed.* It included the biting, nicely written, and bitterly performed "Sometimes I Rhyme Slow," which was a sizable hit on the R&B and hip-hop circuit. —*Ron Wynn*

○ **Ain't a Damn Thing Changed** / 1985 / Ral 47373
New York City rappers Gregg Nice and Smooth Bee composed one of 1991's most powerful message tracks with the title cut of this album. Oddly, that wasn't the jam that got them over. Instead, it was the softer, more melancholy but equally effective "Sometimes I Rhyme Slow," which was accompanied by a killer video. —*Ron Wynn*

NWA (Niggers with Attitudes)

Group / Rap
This Compton, CA, ensemble once held the title of "most controversial rap act," but in recent months others have surfaced to share some of the heat. The original posse, including Ice Cube, Eazy-E, Arabian Prince, MC Ren, and the D.O.C., made their first release in 1987. *N.W.A. and the Posse* was mainly a party/fun record but cuts like "Boyz 'n the Hood" and "Dope Man" should have been a warning to alert ears of what was coming. Anyone who missed the debut was certainly caught by surprise when the 1988 follow-up *Straight Outta Compton* came along. The stark, brutal depictions of gang strife and urban warfare; the coarse, obscene language; and the complete amoral tone—*plus the antiauthority number "F**k Tha Police"*—earned N.W.A. scorn from middle-class types of all colors and also FBI attempts to get retailers not to stock it. Since that high point, N.W.A. has really become less an entity and more an amalgam of solo acts. Ice Cube, Eazy-E, Arabian Prince, the D.O.C., and MC Ren have all done separate projects; Cube has not only left the group but also has engaged in bitter, heated public feuds; and the D.O.C. suffered a near-fatal car crash that took him out of circulation for quite some time. The EP *100 Miles and Runnin'* (1990) was halfhearted, and the group's 1991 release *Efil4zaggin* ("Niggaz4Life" backwards) elicited some controversy but nothing close to past albums.

Amidst gargantuan clashes of egos, N.W.A. dissolved the following year, leaving behind an enormously influential body of work. —*Ron Wynn*

○ **N.W.A. and the Posse** / 1987 / Priority 57119
A hodgepodge of early singles from N.W.A. and some of their Compton contemporaries (including the D.O.C.). The highlights are N.W.A.'s "Boyz-N-the-Hood" and "Dope Man." —*John Floyd*

★ **Straight Outta Compton** / 1989 / Priority 57112
A scalding, relentless, and always jolting look at life in the ghettos of south-central Los Angeles You may not agree with their relish of violence or the rampant sexism, but this series of inflammatory and bruising vignettes is a visceral landmark on a par with the MC5 or the Sex Pistols. —*John Floyd*

100 Miles and Runnin' / 1990 / Priority 7224
After the revolutionary (in more than one sense of the word) *Straight Outta Compton*, N.W.A. could hardly go any farther, especially with the departure of Ice Cube, the most gifted rapper of the crew. *100 Miles and Runnin'* was released as a stopgap while N.W.A. was preparing their next full-length release. It reprises all of the gangsta/bitch fantasies of *Compton*, yet with no insight or humor and very little reality. —*Stephen Thomas Erlewine*

Efil4zaggin / Ruthless/Priority
Unfortunately, this desultory effort may ultimately stand as N.W.A.'s final project. Internal dissension and creative stagnation were the major culprits in this feeble effort. They sounded like a stumbling caricature rather than the defiant Compton ensemble who forced you to pay attention to their work, no matter how offensive you found it. —*Ron Wynn*

Onyx

Rap
The hip-hop trio Onyx ushered in a new development in 1993: rap in the mosh pit. Their shouting, in-your-face brand of high-volume rapping didn't sit well with everyone, but their debut CD *Bacdafucup* had a huge crossover smash with "Slam." —*Ron Wynn*

○ **Bacdafucup** / 1993 / CBS 53302
With its simple, brutal production and shouted rhymes, Onyx's debut album was a menacing, threatening record that relied more on sheer aggression than musical competence. Still, that aggression could produce undeniably classic tracks, like their breakthrough single "Slam." —*Stephen Thomas Erlewine*

Paris

Vocals / Rap, dance
This San Francisco rapper debuted in 1990 with *The Devil Made Me Do It* for Tommy Boy; then he moved to the independent Scarface label with *Sleeping with the Enemy* in 1992. His fiercely Afrocentric themes were reminiscent of the Last Poets or Gil Scott-Heron but didn't generate as much response as anticipated. They did cause lots of controversy in other circles, however, leading to allegations of "reverse" racism. —*Ron Wynn*

★ **Sleeping with the Enemy** / 1993 / Scarface 100
It took several months and a change of record labels before it was released, but Paris's *Sleeping with the Enemy* was the most incendiary political hip-hop album released since Ice Cube's *Death Certificate* in 1991. Paris's production may rely on beats that have come before, but in no way does that detract from the strength of his militant rhymes or the controlled, vicious anger of the music. —*Stephen Thomas Erlewine*

○ **Devil Made Me Do It** / Tommy Boy 1030
San Francisco rapper Paris's debut album featured several angry, Afrocentric numbers (the CD included four selections that didn't make it onto the vinyl LP and two that weren't on the cassette either). Little here was designed to make anyone feel good. It was Paris, not Sister Souljah, who effectively described racism's impact on the psyche of oppressed people with his composition "Hate That Hate Made." —*Ron Wynn*

Pharcyde

Rap
Among the better absurd/comic rap outfits, the Pharcyde made significant inroads with *Bizarre Ride to the Pharcyde* in 1992; they followed that with *Bizarre Ride II* in 1993. Their biggest hit thus far was the single "Passing Me By." —*Ron Wynn*

● **Bizarre Ride to the Pharcyde** / 1992 / Atlantic 92222
A wild ride through the Pharcyde's warped, surrealistic world. Their first album is filled with uneasy and absurd humor as well

as skewered, funky production. It's by no means a consistent record; yet the depth of their vision—beneath their humor lie some serious themes—makes it a rewarding record. —*Stephen Thomas Erlewine*

PM Dawn

Group / Rap, dance, urban
The Cordes brothers put the daisy-age principles of De La Soul into sharper focus. —*John Floyd*

★ **Of the Heart, of the Soul and of the Cross: The Utopian ExperienceB>** / 1991 / Gee Street 510276
Of the Heart is a standout release, sandwiching psychedelic tinges, political/social discourse, and invigorating raps and production. Includes the hit "Set Adrift on Memory Bliss." —*Ron Wynn*

○ **Bliss Album?, The** / 1993 / PolyGram 514517
Calling PM Dawn a hip-hop band is inaccurate because their sensibility lies with smooth ballads and mellow soul; they only use hip-hop to underscore their songs. In many ways, *The Bliss Album?* is a more focused album than their debut, containing such brilliant ballads as "I'd Die without You" and "Looking through Patient Eyes." When Prince Be tries to go harder, such as on "Plastic," the results are well intentioned but seriously flawed—they don't have the strength or power to pull off hardcore material. But when they stick to their pop-friendly R&B, PM Dawn is often quite remarkable; *The Bliss Album?* was the rare second album to expand on the achievements of the debut, not duplicate them. —*Stephen Thomas Erlewine*

Poor Righteous Teachers

Group / Rap, dance
This Trenton, NJ, trio brings Islam Five Percent theories to ripping, inventive riffs and samples. —*John Floyd*

● **Holy Intellect** / 1990 / Profile 1289
A sharp session, squarely in an Afrocentric groove. —*Ron Wynn*

Pure Poverty / 1991 / Profile 1415
An even tougher, harder lyric thrust, but not quite as strong or varied musically. —*Ron Wynn*

○ **Black Business** / 1993 / Profile
The Poor Righteous Teachers offered more Islamic and Afrocentric raps on this 1993 album, sometimes becoming overly pedantic but also keeping the raps and rhymes flowing and the beats moving. Their material's propagandistic tone was offset to some extent by the use of reggae and funk influences, but few groups are more open about their religious and political affiliations and beliefs. —*Ron Wynn*

Positive K

Rap
Positive K's debut LP *Da Skills Dat Pay Da Bills* on Island landed a hit with the single "I Got a Man." The CD was a mix of sexual one-upmanship and Afrocentric, Islamic rhetoric that retained a sense of humor even in the midst of the propaganda. —*Ron Wynn*

● **Da Skills Dat Pay Da Bills** / 1992 / Island 514057
Positive K scored one of 1992's few nonpolitical rap hits with the amusing "I Got a Man," a song exploring all the shadings of the age-old game of sexual pursuit. The remaining cuts ranged from predictable Afrocentric and gangsta posturing to decent pop-flavored ditties and boasts. —*Ron Wynn*

Prime Minister Pete Nice & Daddy Rich

Rap
The original lineup for the rap ensemble 3rd Bass featured White rappers Pete Nice (born Pete Nash) and MC Serch as well as DJ Richie Rich (born Richard Lawson), the group's lone African-American. When Serch split in 1992, Nice and Rich tried it as a duo. Their 1993 debut *Dust to Dust* failed to equal the success of 3rd Bass. —*Ron Wynn*

○ **Dust to Dust** / Apr. 27, 1993 / Def Jam/Columbia 53454
When 3rd Bass disbanded, Prime Minister Pete Nice & Daddy Rich tried to regroup with this 1993 album. It contained some competent message tracks and hard-edged commentary but failed to recapture the niche or audience that 3rd Bass previously enjoyed. —*Ron Wynn*

Professor Griff (Richard Griffin)

Vocals / Rap

Professor Griff was the "minister of information" for Public Enemy until June 1989. He gave a controversial interview to the *Washington Post* that included comments deemed anti-Semitic by many. In the ensuing furor, Chuck D eventually fired him from Public Enemy and even briefly disbanded the group, only to re-form them. Griff formed his own band, the Asiatic Disciples. The results have been mixed, the slant predictably Islamic and Afrocentric. —*Ron Wynn*

● **Pawns in the Game** / 1990 / Luke 91653

A respectable showing from Griff in the face of negative expectations. —*Dan Heilman*

Kao's II Wiz-7-Dome / Luke 91721

Professor Griff tried again with this 1991 release on Luther Campbell's Luke label. But like his previous effort, *Pawns in the Game*, Griff failed to realize that advocacy alone, regardless of the justness of his message, couldn't overcome pedestrian production, unconvincing rhymes, and a stiff, leaden rap style. Rather than threatening, the net effect was boring. —*Ron Wynn*

Professor X

Rap

After leaving the militant X-Clan, Professor X made a series of equally strong political records in the early '90s. —*Stephen Thomas Erlewine*

Puss 'n Boots (The Struggle Continues . . .) / Jun. 22, 1993 / Polydor 519360

The second Professor X album was even more unrelenting than the first in its Islamic and Afrocentric slant. There was little thematic variety, and the production was very much just a background prop to the propaganda, which was quite heavy. —*Ron Wynn*

● **Years of the 9 on the Blackhan** / Fourth & Broadway 444033

Brooklyn rapper Professor X offered his own Islamic and Afrocentric observations on this date done outside the auspices of X-Clan. Otherwise, the rap and rhyming style, production, outlook, and scope were quite similiar to what was expressed on X-Clan releases. —*Ron Wynn*

Public Enemy

Group / Hip-hop

Without question the most talked-about rap group ever and among the most controversial and publicized bands of its day in any genre. Carlton Ridenhour, a Long Island college student and former radio disc jockey, has parlayed a booming voice, a congenial yet forceful personality, and the articulation skills necessary to cogently present often inflammatory viewpoints into a hugely successful performance, marketing, and proselytizing empire. As Chuck D, Ridenour is Public Enemy's theorist, lyricist, and head rapper. He's quoted constantly, seen on television around the world, and idolized by legions of Black and White youth. Through three albums, Public Enemy has served as the hip-hop vanguard, rapping about issues of race, rage, and inequality without lapsing (too often) into vicious sexism or homophobia, though the group has been tagged with charges of anti-Semitism. Public Enemy did eventually cut loose former minister of information Professor Griff following a flap about comments he made in an interview, but the group has been able to ride out storms over lyric content and maintain its popularity without any stylistic compromise. Hank Shockless, Terminator X, Flavor Flav, and the rest of the Bomb Squad and crew also deserve praise, especially Shockless and Terminator X, whose dynamite production keeps things anchored through hard-hitting, rapid-fire snippets and impressive studio techniques. Flav's absurdist raps and on-stage antics provide some welcome levity and comic relief.

After laying low for nearly three years, the reaction was swift and mostly unfavorable when Public Enemy's first new full-length album since *Apocalypse 91* was unveiled in 1994. Extensive reviews in *Rolling Stone* and the *Source* turned thumbs down on *Muse Sick N Hour Mess Age*, with critics labeling it dated and irrelevant. —*Ron Wynn*

☆ **Yo! Bum Rush the Show** / 1987 / Def Jam 40658

When their debut was released in 1987, very few rap groups even approached Public Enemy's musical or political stance. In retro-

spect, only a few of the songs are actually political—the sheer force of the sound fools the listener into thinking Chuck D is saying more than he actually is. Still, "Megablast," "Public Enemy No. 1," and "Miuzi Weighs a Ton" carry a small amount of political rhetoric. Much sparer than later releases, the album is carried over the top by Chuck D's bulldozer roar. —*Stephen Thomas Erlewine*

★ **It Takes a Nation of Millions to Hold Us Back** / 1989 / Def Jam 44303

Arguably the best hip-hop album ever made, *It Takes a Nation of Millions* was a huge leap forward, not only for Public Enemy, but also for all of hip-hop. PE's signature sound—a barrage of found sounds, densely woven samples, and noisy tape loops—was evident for the first time, courtesy of the Bomb Squad. Chuck D's lyrics, full of revolutionary rhetoric yet managing to avoid being hysterical, matched the aural onslaught. The group's political stance would be meaningless if the music didn't put it over the top throughout, and on "Black Steel in the Hour of Chaos," "Night of the Living Baseheads," "Rebel without a Pause," "Dont Believe the Hype," and "Bring the Noise" in particular. There's no time for relaxation on the album, and there's not a weak moment. A landmark recording. —*Stephen Thomas Erlewine*

☆ **Fear of a Black Planet** / 1990 / Def Jam 45413

Nothing could quite match the pure, concentrated fury of *It Takes a Nation of Millions*, and Public Enemy wisely didn't try to replicate it on their third album. *Fear of a Black Planet* is much more experimental than its predecessor, boasting an impressive array of textures from pseudo-reggae to crushing hip-hop. Chuck D's phrasing and vocalization have matured; on "Pollywanacraka" he even sounds seductive. The basic theme of *Fear of a Black Planet* is an exploration of American racism, concentrating on interracial relationships and White injustice. The relative lack of heavy beats and the wall of rage caused some to cry sellout, but *Fear* is hardly a sellout. —*Stephen Thomas Erlewine*

☆ **Apocalypse 91 . . . The Enemy Strikes Black** / 1991 / Def Jam 47374

In response to accusations that *Fear of a Black Planet* was a sellout, Public Enemy lashed back with *Apocalypse 91 . . . The Enemy Strikes Black*, an album of hard, noisy funk, much closer to *Millions* than to *Fear*. Having dealt with White racism on their previous album, Public Enemy turns their sights on correcting the problems in the Black community. On "1 Million Bottlebags," "Nighttrain," "Shut 'Em Down," and "By the Time I Get to Arizona," Chuck D offers some of his hardest-hitting rhymes matched to equally hard rhythm tracks. Public Enemy offers solutions on a few tracks, a rarity in the rap world. Although the Imperial Grand Ministers of Funk have replaced the Bomb Squad (who are listed as executive producers) as the main production team, Public Enemy's sound has not changed drastically. —*Stephen Thomas Erlewine*

Greatest Misses / Sep. 15, 1992 / Chaos 53014

For the first time in their career, Public Enemy sounds unsure of their music's direction. *Greatest Misses* is half original tracks, half remixes, and consequently sounds muddled. Public Enemy sounds like they are treading water throughout the new songs; none of the tracks are particularly bad, but unlike all of their previous material, none of it is groundbreaking. "Tie Goes to the Runner," "Air Hoodlum," and "Hazy Shade of Criminal" are good, solid songs but strongly recall earlier, more inventive tracks like "Can't Truss It," "Welcome to the Terrordome," and "Don't Believe the Hype." None of the remixes are awful, but they are neither revelatory nor insightful and often miss the original intent of the song. —*Stephen Thomas Erlewine*

Queen Latifah (Dana Owens)

Vocals / Rap, hip-hop

The New Jersey-born Queen Latifah (*Latifah* is an Arabic word meaning sensitive and delicate) has almost singlehandedly opened the doors for female rappers in the '90s, belying the sexism that permeates the male side of the genre. Her versatility suggests she'll be around for a long while.

Queen Latifah's moved into television as part of the cast on Fox's hit situation comedy "Living Single." While there was far from universal praise for the series, even its detractors had positive things to say about her portrayal of a magazine editor. She moved to Motown from Tommy Boy; her CD *Black Reign* was her finest since *All Hail the Queen*. —*John Floyd*

★ **All Hail the Queen** / 1989 / Tommy Boy 1022
Her genius is twofold. She preaches Afrocentrism through clever, versatile, and educated raps, and they're coming from a clever, versatile, and educated feminist. The whole shebang is funky beyond belief. —*John Floyd*

Nature of a Sista' / 1991 / Tommy Boy 1035
Her feminism becomes even more focused on this follow-up. With an equally diverse and creative set list, Latifah is becoming the female voice in a male-dominated genre. —*John Floyd*

○ **Black Reign** / Nov. 16, 1993 / Motown

Shabba Ranks

Reggae, rap
The 1992 reggae Grammy winner, this dancemaster is noted for his lewd and leering lyrics that represent the polar opposite of reggae's spiritual and unifying concerns. Hugely popular, with major-label support, Ranks is Jamaica's DJ emissary to the weird world of the '90s.
In the wake of his Grammy triumph, the CDs kept coming from Shabba Ranks, each one seemingly more lewd than its predecessor. *Love Punanny Bad* was perhaps prototype "slack" Ranks on King Jammy in 1993, while *Volume II* continued the adventures begaun on *X-tra Naked* in 1992. —*Roger Steffens*

● **As Raw As Ever** / 1991 / Epic 47310
This is an X-rated hip-hop reggae crossover that won a Grammy. —*Roger Steffens*

○ **Rough & Ready, Vol. 1** / Jul. 14, 1992 / Epic 52443
Shabba Ranks kept the "slack" dancehall coming with this 1992 follow-up to *As Raw As Ever*. His thick, patois-laced delivery scored a pop hit with "Mr. Loverman," a song that basically defined the CD. If you didn't get it the first time around, after hearing "Bad & Wicked," "Ca'an Dun," and "Gal Yuh' Good," you sure understood it later. —*Ron Wynn*

○ **X-tra Naked** / Oct. 6, 1992 / Epic 52464
Shabba Ranks landed another pop hit on his third album to hit the charts over a two-year span. "Slow and Sexy" peaked at 33 and provided ample momentum for another collection of sex cuts and come-ons. Ranks did include "Rude Boy" and "Two Breddrens," but otherwise the focus stayed completely in the bedroom. —*Ron Wynn*

Rough & Ready, Vol. 2 / Epic Records
Yet another sex-heavy dancehall collection from Shabba Ranks, whose super-lewd material rivals the pedantic ramblings of X-Clan and other Islamic/Afrocentric rappers in its utter lack of thematic variety. Not only were almost all the songs alike, but it also seemed that Ranks was recycling the raps and beats as well. —*Ron Wynn*

The Real Roxanne

Vocals / Rap, dance, soul
Not to be confused with the other rap Roxannes, this New York spitfire released one near-perfect album in 1988 (produced by Jam Master Jay and Howie "Hitman" Tee) but hasn't been heard from since. Too bad. —*John Floyd*

○ **Real Roxanne, The** / 1988 / Select 21627
With the aid of Jam Master Jay, Howie Tee, and Full Force, this Puerto Rican whipped up a stunning debut that highlights her inimitable skills as a rapper and lyricist, as well as her band's way with the funk. —*John Floyd*

Redman

Rap
New Jersey rapper Redman made his initial impact with *Whut? Thee Album* in 1992. He blended reggae and funk influences with topical commentary and displayed a terse though fluid rap style that was sometimes satirical, sometimes tough, and sometimes silly. —*Ron Wynn*

☆ **Whut? Thee Album** / Sep. 22, 1992 / Chaos 52967
Redman's debut album is a minor masterpiece, fueled by the thick, P-Funk-influenced production of Erick Sermon. Redman's rhyming is forceful and intelligent, and he's never afraid of lightening his rhetoric with humor. The deeply funky grooves that

form the core of the album never grow tiresome or repetitive. —*Stephen Thomas Erlewine*

Pete Rock & C. L. Smooth

Rap
In 1992 Pete Rock, a producer and disc jockey, and rapper C. L. Smooth emerged from Mt. Vernon, NY, both as a powerhouse performance duo and as prolific producers. Their album *Mecca and the Soul Brother* was a solid hit, notably the cuts "They Reminisce over You (T.R.O.Y.)" and "Straighten It Out." They later collaborated with Mary J. Blige for a remix of her song "Reminisce," which effectively merged the two tracks in a reedited hit. They've since done many productions for both hip-hop acts and urban contemporary artists like Johnny Gill. —*Ron Wynn*

○ **All Souled Out** / 1991 / Elektra 60948
A strong debut release that combines jazz and hip-hop to an impressive effect. —*AMG*

★ **Mecca and the Soul Brother** / 1992 / Asylum 60948
C. L. Smooth's clever raps and Pete Rock's snazzy production put this duo into the hip-hop big time with their second album. There were tremendous message cuts and attractive general material; it was simply an excellent album on every level. Includes the hit single "They Reminisce over You (T.R.O.Y.)." —*Ron Wynn*

Lots of Lovin' / 1993 / Asylum 64662

Rodney O.

Rap
Los Angeles rap trio Rodney Oliver, Joe Cooley, and "General" Jeff Page debuted in 1989 with *Me and Joe*. Though not a sales hit, they scored enough underground attention with such singles as "Everlasting Bass" and "Cooley High" to land a deal with Atlantic. Their label debut was *Three the Hard Way* in 1990, but it didn't do much better. They also issued a Nastymix album *Get Ready to Roll*. —*Ron Wynn*

Three the Hard Way / 1990 / Atlantic 82082
Moving from Egyptian Empire to Atlantic, Rodney O.'s Joe Cooley tried again for hip-hop stardom with this 1990 album. It again mostly avoided gangsta-styled material, though "Three the Hard Way" did try to tap into the "hood" ethic. But the problem wasn't so much the production as the fact that cuts like "Party" and "See Ya" weren't very interesting. —*Ron Wynn*

● **Me & Joe** / Egyptian Empire 777
The Los Angeles rap trio Rodney Oliver, Joe Cooley, and "General" Jeff Page made a competent, if commercially limp, 1989 debut. The direction was mostly nonpolitical, humorous material like "Cooley High," "Everlasting Bass," and "Give Me the Mic." The raps and rhymes were neither disastrous nor especially attractive, while the production was standard and derivative. —*Ron Wynn*

Run-D.M.C.

Group / Rap, hip-hop, dance
The most famous exports from Hollis, Queens, NY, expanded the boundaries of rap in ways Grandmaster Flash could only imagine. Through their early singles they built up a devoted street following and, without ever diluting their music, managed to bust their grooves into the White pop mainstream. They've lost their edge in the '90s, but their influence is still felt.
Run-D.M.C. bounced back from the aesthetic graveyard in 1993 with *Down with the King*. The album linked them with the hip-hop generation that had grown up admiring them, and the trio also sported a new look (shaved heads) and philosophy (they had become born-again Christians). The title track was a huge hit, and the disc ended speculation that they were finished on the hip-hop scene. —*John Floyd*

☆ **King of Rock** / 1985 / Profile 1205
Run-D.M.C. scored their first platinum LP and roared into pop consciousness with this 1985 LP. Such cuts as "King of Rock," "Rock the House," and "Can You Rock It Like This" were definitive; and their tough tone, clipped style, and posturing attitudes set the hip-hop agenda for several years. —*Ron Wynn*

☆ **Run-D.M.C.** / 1985 / Profile 1202
Their album debut features all the early singles, including "It's Like That" and "Rock Box," which stripped rap down to the bare

essentials and introduced slews of innovations, lyrically and musically. —*John Floyd*

☆ **Raising Hell** / 1986 / Profile 1217
The collaboration with Steven Tyler and Joe Perry on "Walk This Way" made this the most successful rap album of its time, but the blistering title track, the pulsating "You Be Illin'," kept it in the Top Ten. A masterful and important release, not just for rap but for modern music as well. —*John Floyd*

Tougher Than Leather / 1988 / Profile 1265
After the epic *Raising Hell*, it was almost a drop in the bucket for Run-D.M.C. to get merely a platinum LP for *Tougher Than Leather*. While it included the mild hit "Mary Mary," the album indicated that all was not well with the trio creatively. There was an ominous quality to "I'm Not Going Out Like That," and cuts like "Miss Elaine" and "Beats to the Rhyme" signaled that their nonstop run to the top was in its final stages. —*Ron Wynn*

★ **Together Forever: Greatest Hits** / 1991 / Profile 1419
A few necessary items are missing, but this provides a great introduction to the most influential posse in rap. —*John Floyd*

Down with the King / May 4, 1993 / Profile 1440
After 1990's lackluster *Back from Hell*, most hip-hop fans thought that Run-D.M.C. was no longer capable of delivering a solid record. *Down with the King* proved those doubters wrong. Although it didn't burn up the charts like *Raising Hell* or wasn't as innovative as their first album, *Down with the King* showed that they remained strong and talented; it also didn't hurt that several of the '90s' most talented artists—*Public Enemy, Pete Rock, Naughty by Nature, and Q-Tip*—provided the production. —*Stephen Thomas Erlewine*

Salt-N-Pepa

Group / Rap, dance
Queens, NY, rappers Sandy Denton, Cheryl James, and DJ Dee Dee Roper have been prime female stars since 1986, when *Hot, Cool & Vicious,,* with its single smash "Push It" made them stars. Salt-N-Pepa have been able to shift gears at will, sometimes being naughty, other times nice, letting the beat propel their rhymes on one song, and then slicing their exchanges off it on the next. They've done numbers that were feminist in their viewpoints and then turned around and echoed the conventional wisdom about male/female relationships in another number. But contradictions aside, they're among the tighter, most accomplished rap acts active, and their records have held up well. Salt-N-Pepa made the pop big time with *Very Necessary* in 1993. The huge hit "Whatta Man" teamed them with En Vogue. They became walking billboards for the benefits of vigorous daily exercise with a personal trainer; did commercials for the NBA and various products; and found themselves the rap act of choice for the upper class. At the same time, they recaptured the Black audience that they'd previously lost with more lightweight material like *A Salt with a Deadly Pepa*. The group also took more control over their image and production, wresting the reins from longtime producer Hurby Azor. —*Ron Wynn*

○ **Hot, Cool & Vicious** / 1987 / London 828363
One of the earliest female rap groups, they hit the big leagues with this debut that includes the pulsating "Push It" and the salacious "Tramp." —*John Floyd*

○ **Salt with a Deadly Pepa, A,** / 1988 / London 828364
A concept album musically if not lyrically. This one fleshes out one terrific single, "Shake Your Thing," with a sharpening of the trio's sensibilities and talents. —*John Floyd*

★ **Blacks' Magic** / 1990 / London 828362
Another concept album. This time the themes celebrate Black education and awareness, with some concise feminism included. —*John Floyd*

○ **Very Necessary** / 1993 /
Driven by the ferociously sexy "Shoop" and "Whatta Man," Salt-N-Pepa's latest album matches the drive of that hit as well as the best of their earlier classics, making it one of the best albums of their successful career. —*AMG*

Hits Remixed, The / Next Plateau 41025
As remix albums go, Salt-N-Pepa's is fine, but their hit singles lose a bit of their magic in these extended forms. —*Stephen Thomas Erlewine*

Scarface (Brad Jordan)

Rap
Scarface Akshen was an original member of the Houston rap group the Geto Boys. He became the latest Geto Boy to go solo with *Mr. Scarface Is Back* in 1993. His CD had some impact, but other than Bushwick Bill, most of the Geto Boys did better together than apart. —*Ron Wynn*

● **Mr. Scarface Is Back** / 1991 / Rap-A-Lot 57182
Scarface became the latest Geto Boy to try it solo with this 1991 album. He also created a memorable message track in "A Minute to Pray and a Second to Die," a song that should have been a crossover sensation. Few gangsta numbers have more vividly and effectively chronicled the litany of hopelessness and violence plaguing the nation's inner cities. Other cuts—"Body Snatcher," "Born Killer," and "Diary of A Madman"—were less compelling and more chilling. —*Ron Wynn*

○ **World Is Yours, The** / Rap-A-Lot/Priority
The second album from former Geto Boys cohort Scarface didn't contain any single cut as moving or hypnotic as "A Minute to Pray and a Second to Die," but it proved more popular. It also was an indication that the Geto Boys were kaput, as everyone continued cutting solo dates and talk of a proposed new Geto Boys album went from probable to possible to the backburner. —*Ron Wynn*

Schoolly D (Jesse B. Weaver Jr.)

Vocals / Rap
Opinion about the merits of Philadelphia rapper Schoolly D's music has been widely mixed. Long before the debate about gangsta rap lyrics became an easy way to get national newsprint there was outrage over Schoolly D's explicit and undiluted narratives on inner-city strife. *Saturday Night* in 1987 and *Smoke Some Kill* in 1988 had city officials openly endorsing removal of the albums from record stores. He's continued in the same vein, with *Am I Black Enough for You*, his most recent release in 1993. Schoolly D's rather lackluster rapping style and repetitive material don't place him in the forefront of hip-hop creators, but he does merit mention (or blame, depending on your perspective) for being an early gangsta proponent. —*Ron Wynn*

● **Adventures of Schoolly D, The** / 1987 / Rykodisc 20050
This collects his early singles, cut before his bad-ass rep subverted whatever creativity he had left. —*John Floyd*

○ **Saturday Night** / 1987 / Jive 1066
Philadelphia rapper Schoolly D functions better as an absurdist commentator exploring the netherworld of inner-city chaos than as a political philosopher or Afrocentric advocate. This 1987 album was among his best precisely because he chose to be bizarre rather than prophetic and kept things freewheeling instead of didactic. —*Ron Wynn*

○ **Welcome to America** / 1994 / Ruffhouse/Columbia
Schoolly D returns with a spare, dark attempt to recapture the gangsta audience he helped create back in the '80s; it helps that the record contains the best music he has ever recorded, although the best moments can't hide the fact that Schoolly D doesn't have the lyrical grace of the rappers that followed in his footsteps. —*Stephen Thomas Erlewine*

Second II None

Rap
Los Angeles cousins Tha D and KK attended high school in Compton with DJ Quik before landing a record deal with Profile. Their debut *2nd II None* had two strong compositions in "Be True to Yourself" and "If You Want It," both of which did respectably. —*Ron Wynn*

○ **2nd II None** / 1991 / Profile 1416
Los Angeles cousins Second II None made a better-than-expected 1991 debut album, aided by the solid cuts "If You Want It" and "Be True to Yourself." Though not the most fluid or creative rappers, they compensated by varying their material, utilizing some great beats, and not relying solely on gangsta posturing for salvation. —*Ron Wynn*

Roxanne Shante (Lolita Goodeh)

Vocals / Rap
Roxanne Shante was walking outside a New York housing project called the Queensbridge when she heard three men talking about

how the trio U.T.F.O. had canceled their appearance at a show they were promoting. Shante offered to make a rap record that would get back at U.T.F.O., who'd previously recorded "Roxanne, Roxanne," a song about a woman too stuck up to notice them. The three, Tyrone Williams, disc jockey Mister Magic, and producer Marley Marl, took her up on the idea, with Marl producing "Roxanne's Revenge." The song was confrontational, sneering, boastful, and even borderline obscene, and it spawned 102 additional answer records. Since then she's had two albums. The original "Roxanne's Revenge" was issued by Pop Art. Eventually U.T.F.O. threatened to sue Shante for using their B-side as the musical foundation. She settled with them and recut the song with a different, though related track.

Roxanne Shante's fortunes have been thin since the heyday of the "Roxanne, Roxanne" rush. She did share a number-one R&B and Top Ten pop hit with Rick James in 1986, "Loosey's Rap," but has otherwise found the going tough. Her last release was *Go Down but Don't Bite It*, a 1992 album that proved much less interesting, alluring, or sensual—*and even less offensive*—than its title would suggest. —*Ron Wynn*

● **Bad Sister** / 1989 / Cold Chillin' 25809
Her debut album doesn't quite live up to the promise of her early singles, which can be found on various rap compilations. —*Dan Heilman*

Shinehead (Carl Aiken)

Vocals / Rap
Though born in London, Shinehead was raised in both Jamaica and the Bronx. His divided birthplaces were reflected in his knowledge of reggae, rock, and rap, all of which he incorporated into his debut *Unity* for Elektra in 1988. Neither it nor the 1990 follow-up, *The Real Rock*, were able to generate much momentum, but they were forerunners to the hip-hop/reggae convergence later exploited by Shabba Ranks, the Mad Cobra, and others. *Sidewalk University*, issued in 1992, was his most recent release. —*Ron Wynn*

● **Unity** / 1988 / Elektra 60802
A promising, original album. —*Dan Heilman*

○ **Real Rock, The** / 1990 / Elektra 60890
Fine follow-up to *Unity*, with Shinehead sandwiching together melodies from classic R&B with rock and reggae inflections, and adding his own wild originals as well. —*Ron Wynn*

Sir Mix-A-Lot

Vocals / Rap, soul, urban
Sir Mix-A-Lot put Seattle on the rap map in the late '80s with catchy, comedic dramas drenched in b-boy culture and punctuated by his whiny vocals.

Sir Mix-A-Lot vaulted into the spotlight and into controversy with the single "Baby Got Back." Not only was it an enormous pop and R&B hit, but it also triggered a backlash against what was widely viewed as both sexist and racist lyrics, since on it he celebrated rear ends and put down women who lacked them. It helped make the *Mack Daddy* album one of 1992's biggest. —*John Floyd*

Swass / 1988 / Def American 26970
Sir Mix-A-Lot's debut album fluctuated between heavy bass tracks, like 2 Live Crew's, and heavy metal/rap fusions, like a heavier version of Run-D.M.C. At this point he hadn't perfected his goofy, almost satiric, take on gangsta rap, although some tracks pointed the way toward his finest album, 1992's *Mack Daddy*. —*Stephen Thomas Erlewine*

● **Mack Daddy** / Apr. 1991 / Def American 26765
Sir Mix-A-Lot scored a huge sleeper hit with his ridiculous paean to large buttocks, "Baby Got Back," in summer 1992. For those who want it, the rest of *Mack Daddy* offers more of the same—skeletal raps that verge on the point of parody. Sir Mix-A-Lot can barely rap, and his lyrics are full of posturing tales that never have a dose of reality. But this is the very element that makes *Mack Daddy* fun, because Sir Mix-A-Lot tries so hard and sounds so silly. —*Stephen Thomas Erlewine*

Sister Souljah

Rap
Then-presidential candidate Bill Clinton helped turn a little-known rapper, Sister Souljah, briefly into a celebrity when he at-

tacked her album *360 Degrees of Power*. During an interview Souljah called for African-Americans to stop destroying their own property and turn their efforts on the White power brokers instead. Clinton accused her of appealing to hatred and urging blacks to randomly target and kill whites. The resulting controversy didn't sell many copies of her record but did get her onto numerous talk shows and into many general-interest magazines. She was eventually dropped by Epic when the record bombed. —*Ron Wynn*

○ **360 Degrees of Power** / Jan. 1992 / Epic 48713
Seldom has something so mundane generated more controversy. Candidate Bill Clinton garnered some cheap positive publicity when he attacked Sister Souljah for allegedly encouraging African-Americans to blindly strike against Whites. If he'd actually heard the CD, he'd know Sister Souljah's raps and rhymes were so unappealing and delivered so flatly that few hip-hoppers, let alone any adults, would be paying much attention after the first few minutes. —*Ron Wynn*

Slick Rick (Ricky Walters)

Vocals / Rap
Born in London and raised in the Bronx, Ricky Walters carved himself a niche with his debut album, *The Great Adventures of Slick Rick*, which featured a sly, drawling delivery and detailed and inventive storybook raps. The onetime partner of Doug E. Fresh, Slick Rick eventually wound up in jail following a shooting incident and has been charged with attempted murder. —*John Floyd & Ron Wynn*

★ **Great Adventures of Slick Rick, The** / 1988 / Def Jam 40513
Superb slices and excellent rap technique on this fast-paced release. —*Ron Wynn*

○ **Ruler's Back, The** / 1991 / CBS 47372
A fine follow-up from a troubled soul. —*Ron Wynn*

Snoop Doggy Dogg

Rap
Rap's reigning superstar, Snoop Doggy Dogg made his debut on Dr. Dre's *The Chronic*. His laconic, low-volume rap style struck a nerve with hip-hop audiences, and his debut release, *Snoop Doggy Dogg*, became the first album by a new artist ever to make its initial entry onto the pop albums chart at number one. The album had sold over four million copies by the midpoint of 1994 and also generated plenty of controversy over its sexist and homophobic tendencies and explicit language. The record did shine the spotlight on some neglected acts and music from the '70s, notably the Dramatics, who appeared in one of Dogg's videos and backed him on one single. —*Ron Wynn*

☆ **Doggystyle** / 1993 /
Snoop Doggy Dogg became a hip-hop superstar last year as the laconic second rapper to Dr. Dre's booming leads on *The Chronic*. His debut entered the charts at number one and has proven equally popular even though there's little departure musically or production-wise from Dre's release. *Doggystyle* features more of Dogg's part drawl, part spoken-word narratives, but expresses a vision more paranoid than confident. Throughout the disc Dogg has dreams (nightmares) about being killed and spends most of his time either defaming women or getting out of conflicts. The single "Who Am I (What's My Name)" uses nearly the identical samples and bass lines as "Nuthin but A G Thang," as only Dogg's lean, almost casual sneers and rejoinders differentiate it from Dre's prior recording. He also throws a few darts at Eazy-E, but otherwise this is prototype gangsta rap with Dogg's signature rapping style as its major hook. —*Ron Wynn*

Snow

Rap
Canadian rapper Snow scored one of 1993's biggest hits with the single "Informer." His patois-laced song soared up the pop and R&B charts, even though only hardcore reggae listeners could understand it without a lyric translation sheet. The album *12 Inches of Snow* also did well, with the second single, "Girl I've Been Hurt," becoming a hit. —*Ron Wynn*

○ **12 Inches of Snow** / 1993 / East West 92207
Canadian reggae-rapper Snow became a celebrity when his patois-laced single "Informer" soared to the top of the charts in

1993. The song shattered the myth that pop audiences wouldn't embrace any tune whose lyrics weren't in pristine English; when his video was released, it included a rolling translation at the bottom. Unfortunately, the rest of this album was mildly pleasant, instantly forgettable pop reggae delivered in a manner that made Shabba Ranks sound like U-Roy. —*Ron Wynn*

Son of Bazerk

Group / Rap

A blazing five-piece posse recalls the late '60s sound of James Brown and combines it with the dense, intense caterwaul of Public Enemy. —*John Floyd*

○ **Bazerk Bazerk Bazerk** / 1991 / Soul 10028
By enlisting Public Enemy's Bomb Squad for the musical muscle, this six-piece aggregation concocted an abrasive (but rhythmic) debut that stands as one of the genre's finest. —*John Floyd*

Special Ed

Vocals / Rap, dance

In 1989 this 16-year-old released a technically dazzling debut album that highlighted his rapid-fire delivery and the ace production of hip-hop mastermind Howie "Hitman" Tee. —*John Floyd*

Youngest in Charge / 1989 / Profile 1280
The debut from this hugely confident teenage rapper with a very adult, mature rapping style and boastful, though effective lyrics and themes. —*Ron Wynn*

● **Legal** / 1990 / Profile 1297
Release number two by Special Ed marks his turning 18 and has a more varied, less excessive production approach. Ed also moves smoothly between topical and romantic material, as well as serious and satirical tones. —*Ron Wynn*

Spice 1

Rap

Too Short discovered rapper Spice 1, who'd been born in Texas and moved to California. His self-titled debut was as vivid and fatalistic a gangsta album as possible, and his hard-edged, angry, and pessimistic rapping style and tone only added to the despair emanating from the disc. He followed it with an even more bitter and nihilistic release, *187 He Wrote*, in 1993, complete with simulated gunfire. —*Ron Wynn*

Spice 1 / May 12, 1992 / Jive 41495
The sheer vulgarity, anger, coarseness, sexism, and horror unveiled, celebrated, and presented on Oakland rapper Spice 1's debut release can be frustrating and saddening. But it should not be ignored. Spice 1 has done what gangsta rap's detractors should want; he's stripped away even the slightest veneer of glamour around the atmosphere of casual violence, sexual exploitation, and drug selling/pimping that he's examining on such selections as "Welcome to the Ghetto" and "Money or Murder." His style, an appropriate mix of irony, disdain, acceptance, and confusion, never succumbs to the situation and seeks to justify or downplay the sense of impending doom. —*Ron Wynn*

● **187 He Wrote** / Sep. 28, 1993 / Jive
Spice 1 continues his bleak, stripped-down version of gangsta rap with *187 He Wrote*, an album that is alternately harrowing and appalling. Throughout the record, the spare, funky production keeps the music engaging, making the disturbing lyrics cut even deeper. —*Stephen Thomas Erlewine*

Spoonie Gee

Rap, urban

Spoonie Gee was one of the top old-school performers in New York in the early '80s. —*AMG*

● **Godfather . . . Rap** / Tuff City 5551
Spoonie Gee was among the earliest old-school rappers, performing in a coarse, terse style over funk beats. He was never a great rapper, but he was an effective one, and this album showcased his functional approach on material ranging from straight come-ons to microphone challenges and message cuts. —*Ron Wynn*

Steady B (Warren McGlone)

Rap

Philadelphia rapper Steady B made his debut in 1987 with *What's My Name*. It blended confrontational boasting with some

gangsta narrative but wasn't as pessimistic or as solemn as many similar releases. The 1988 follow-up, *Let the Hustlers Play*, took a harder, harsher tone. He followed those with *Going Steady* and *Steady B V* but has been unable to land a breakout or crossover hit. —*Ron Wynn*

○ **What's My Name** / 1987 / Jive 1060
Philadelphia rapper Steady B made his debut in 1987 with this disc, which included a prophetic number "Gangster Rockin'," plus decent old-school material in "Don't Disturb This Groove" and "Believe Me Das Bad." Changes were looming on the hip-hop horizon, and this session shows why they were necessary; rappers were overdosing on microphone challenges, novelty fare, and sex/innuendo material. They didn't progress much on the sex front, but inevitably a demand arose for harder, more socially conscious rap lyrics (though it's debatable if that's what the audience is getting from most gangsta content). —*Ron Wynn*

● **Bring the Beat Back** / Jive 1020
This was prototype pre-gangsta rap. Steady B demonstrated a fluid, often energetic approach, and his compositions were about nonstop partying and loving, along with an occasional political or nationalistic or antidrug comment. He was more concerned about proclaiming his superiority on the mic than giving a dissertation on racism or police brutality. —*Ron Wynn*

○ **Going Steady** / Jive 1284
This contained good, occasionally clever raps and rhymes in a mostly apolitical tone by Steady B. Hip-hop hadn't yet been overrun by gangstas, so lightweight party material and microphone challenges were still the dominant compositional terrain. —*Ron Wynn*

Stereo MC's

Rap, dance, house music

For a number of years, Stereo MC's were one of the top rap/dance outfits in the UK before they broke big in America in 1993 with their single "Connected." —*AMG*

○ **Supernatural** / 1990 / Fourth & Broadway 444032
The only thing that separates *Supernatural* and its hit follow-up *Connected* is that *Connected* had a hit. Otherwise, the albums are nearly identical and are equally enjoyable. —*AMG*

● **Connected** / 1993 / PolyGram 514061
Stereo MC's' American breakthrough is an energetic, club-oriented collection of colorful, funky dance tracks. The raps almost seem like an afterthought, yet that doesn't distract from the sheer pleasure of their sound. —*AMG*

Stetsasonic

Group / Rap, hip-hop

This Brooklyn-based rap group established a unique sound by using real instruments in addition to the twin-turntable techniques of Prince Paul and Wise. Prince Paul has become a formidable producer, working with the likes of 3rd Bass, De La Soul, and Queen Latifah, among others. —*John Floyd*

On Fire / 1986 / Tommy Boy 1012
Stetsasonic was quite unique on the pop front in 1986 because not many bands utilized a hip-hop format in the mid '80s. While their subject matter was invariably light and their raps now sound hopelessy tame and effete, they were groundbreaking at the time and retain a certain charm. —*Ron Wynn*

● **In Full Gear** / 1988 / Tommy Boy 1017
They're not "the world's only hip-hop band" anymore, but this seven-piece group (real drums even!) paved the way. Their second disc documents their innovative best, culminating in the anthemic "Talkin' All That Jazz." —*John Floyd*

Sugarhill Gang, The

Group / Rap, hip-hop, dance

The Sugarhill Gang—Master Gee (born Guy O'Brien, 1963), Wonder Mike (born Michael Wright, 1958), and Big Bank Hank (born Henry Jackson, 1958)—were the first group to record rap music, releasing the popular single "Rapper's Delight" in 1979. —*William Ruhlmann*

★ **Rapper's Delight** / 1980 / Sugh 5242
The Sugarhill Gang's 1979 hit "Rapper's Delight" is arguably the first true rap song to gain widespread recognition and, as such,

the progenitor of one of the major musical genres of the '80s. No
wonder it doesn't sound dated yet. —*William Ruhlmann*

8th Wonder / 1992 / Sugar Hill 249
The Sugarhill Gang enjoyed their final moments in the spotlight
with this 1982 LP. They scored two moderate hits with the title
cut and "Apache" while continuing the old-school approach that
initally gained mainstream attention and exposure for rap. —*Ron
Wynn*

○ **Greatest Hits** / Sugar Hill 9122
The Sugarhill Gang were among rap's founding fathers and exemplified much of what was great about the early hip-hop material. It was irreverent, had a sense of humor, featured different
thematic material, and wasn't yet enough of a pop phenomenon
to generate controversies or dictate trends. The production, raps,
and rhymes seem simple next to today's elaborate and sophisticated efforts, but they also had a charm and innocence that's lacking in much contemporary hip-hop. —*Ron Wynn*

Terminator X & the Valley of the Jeep Beats

Vocals / Rap
Terminator X (born Norman Rogers), Public Enemy's DJ extraordinaire, strikes out on a solo project in 1991. —*John Floyd*

○ **Terminator X & the Valley of the Jeep Beats** / 1991 / Ral 46896
Public Enemy's turntable whiz takes center stage on a debut that
spans the gamut of contemporary Black pop, from scalding hip-
hop to reggae. —*John Floyd*

3rd Bass

Group / Rap
Along with the Beastie Boys, 3rd Bass stands as the rare White
hip-hop act that's actually won respect and credibility among the
rap hardcore. Pete Nice, onetime English major at Columbia
whose radio program "Top of the Hip-hop" was unceremoniously
canceled by the purportedly progressive WKCR-FM, teamed with
MC Serch to offer devastating putdowns of the hip-hop lifestyle
and worldview. They have since disbanded, but their two albums
were definitive, if at times uneven. —*Ron Wynn*

● **Cactus Album, The** / 1989 / Def Jam 45415
With their first album, 3rd Bass turned in a surrealistically funky
record of uproarious jokes, cutting social criticism, and eclectic
music, drawing from Stax and Blood, Sweat and Tears. —*Stephen
Thomas Erlewine*

○ **Derelicts of Dialect** / 1991 / Def Jam 47369
After countless false starts and a filler remix EP, 3rd Bass finally
issued their second album. It was an impressive statement, with
a devastating attack on Vanilla Ice via the cut "Pop Goes the
Weasel." —*Ron Wynn*

Three Times Dope

Rap, dance
Philadelphia rappers Duerwood Beale, Walter Griggs, and Robert
Walker formed Three Times Dope and issued their debut
Original Stylin', in 1989. It was filled mainly with boasting, self-
promoting narratives and comic/novelty material, though the
"What's Going On" medley attempted to address social issues.
Their second release was *Live from Acknikulous Land* in 1990,
which tried to be a more serious "concept" work. —*Ron Wynn*

● **Original Stylin'** / 1989 / Arista 8571
Three Times Dope made their debut with this 1989 record that
was still in an old-school mode. They spent much of the album
proclaiming their microphone superiority, though the "What's
Going On" medley offered some good social commentary and
"Once More You Hear the Dope Stuff" was a good boasting number. —*Ron Wynn*

Live from Acknickulous Land / 1990 / Arista 8615
Things weren't so dope for Philly rappers Three Times Dope on
their second album. The implied fantasy concept translated into a
rather lame reality as the trio came up short in the compositional,
production, rapping, and rhyme departments. —*Ron Wynn*

Tone-Loc (Tony Smith)

Vocals / Rap
Tone-Loc soared from obscurity into pop stardom in 1989 when
his hoarse voice and unmistakable delivery made the song "Wild
Thing" (using a sample from Van Halen's "Jamie's Cryin") a mas-

sive hit. The song was cowritten by Marvin Young, better known
as Young MC, as was the second single smash "Funky Cold
Medina." The album *Loc-ed After Dark* became the second rap release to top the pop charts.
Tone-Loc expanded his horizons into acting in 1992 and 1993, appearing a few times on the Fox network program "Roc." He was
also in the film *Posse*. —*Ron Wynn*

● **Loc'ed After Dark** / 1990 / Delicious Vinyl 4000
An engaging debut that contains both "Wild Thing" and "Funky
Cold Medina." —*Dan Heilman*

Cool Hand Loc / 1992 / PolyGram 510609
Tone-Loc's second album didn't generate widespread pop appeal
or quiet the rumblings and disdain he'd earned from the hardcore
audience for his double-platinum smash *Loc-ed After Dark*. In
fact, things were so commercially uneventful that Loc began
putting more energy into acting, securing television and film
roles with relish. —*Ron Wynn*

Too Short (Todd Shaw)

Group / Rap, dance
Oakland, CA, rapper Too Short has become a huge star without
getting any pop airplay or crossover support. He's mined the
mack (pimp) routine effectively, turning out albums routinely
loaded with plenty of X-rated sexual escapades and commentary
or variations on a day in the life of a player-pimp. He did score
one classic sociopolitical number, his take on "The Ghetto," and
has also done a good anticensorship bit with Ice Cube on "Ain't
Nothin' but a Word to Me."
Too Short's eighth release, *Get in Where You Fit In,* had plenty of
pimping, explicit language and commentary on players. To those
who protested that his language demeaned African-American
women, Short was unrepentant. He established headquarters in
Atlanta, building a studio and home there. —*Ron Wynn*

○ **Greatest Hits, Vol. 1—The Player Years, 1983-1988** / In-A-
Minute Records
If you have never read the collected works of Chester Himes or
Iceberg Slim, simply run through this Too Short anthology and
you'll get the general idea. Though never an inventive rapper or
clever composer of rhymes, Too Short was smart enough to find
his niche and stay in it. Most people who continually mined the
pimp arena quickly became merely tedious; Too Short became
both tedious and profitable. —*Ron Wynn*

Born to Mack / 1988 / Jive 1100
A breakout release. —*Ron Wynn*

○ **Life Is . . . Too Short** / 1988 / Jive 1149
Essential, bawdy, and often offensive and troubling. —*Ron Wynn*

● **Short Dog's in the House** / 1990 / Jive 1348
A tremendous combination of outrage, anger, and morbid outlook. —*Ron Wynn*

A Tribe Called Quest

Group / Rap, dance
The junior part of the Native Tongues—the prolific Afrocentric
family from New York that also includes the Jungle Brothers and
De La Soul—this foursome displayed intriguing subject variety
on their debut, covering everything from social ills to the adventures of a shaggy dog and problems with lice. Their second effort,
The Low End Theory, reflected through arrangements and sensibility the influence of an emerging jazz/rap stylistic coalition and
yielded a huge hit in "Scenario."
A Tribe Called Quest modified their jazz ties with *Midnight
Marauders* in 1993. Though it still had an improvisational undergirding, the raps were tougher, the production tighter, and the
beats more unpredictable and varied. —*Ron Wynn*

○ **People's Instinctive Travels and the Paths of Rhythm** / 1990 /
Jive/Novus 1331
People's Instinctive Travels is a brilliant concept with jazzy edges
and tense, biting narratives. It's a visionary release blending the
improvisatory force of jazz with the technological wizardry and
verbal inventiveness of hip-hop. —*Ron Wynn*

★ **Low End Theory, The** / 1991 / Jive 1418
Excellent raps and production. —*Ron Wynn*

○ **Midnight Marauders** / 1993 /
Midnight Marauders was an intriguing and smartly paced collection that ranged from descriptive verbal essays on city life to con-

frontational taunts, comic expositions, denunciations, and even quasi-religious theorizing. While their celebrated hip-hop/jazz roots were often evident, the group also utilized fusion, Urban Contemporary, Afro-Latin, and funk samples, while Q-Tip's rap style was alternately cool and deadpan, reflective, analytical, satirical, and disgusted and angry. There was precious little gangsta posturing or sexist rhetoric, and such numbers as "Sucka Nigga," "God Lives Through," "Electric Relaxation," and "Award Tour" were cleverly delivered and brilliantly arranged and composed. Here's an ensemble that deserves much recognition both inside and outside of rap's arena. —*Ron Wynn*

2 Live Crew

Group / Rap, hip-hop
Luther Campbell, a promoter, record-label owner, and rapper created this Florida rap band in 1986 as an updated version of old-time X-rated party performers. Campbell's production consists of heavy doses of booming synthesized bass, scratching effects, samples, and explicit sex raps and leers. The notoriety of Campbell and the group grew in direct proportion to the lewdness of the material, and as their songs attained more national prominence, Campbell has become part of a national controversy involving censorship and lyrics. He's issued two solo records.

In the '90s 2 Live Crew hasn't found the going quite as smooth as it was in the late '80s. They've continued recording for Luke Records but haven't scored as much success with such releases as *Move Somethin'* and *Sports Weekend*. Luther Campbell issued both clean and dirty versions in an effort to defuse criticism, but 2 Live Crew's detractors have moved on to gangsta rap, and the group's most recent releases have been almost ignored. They resurfaced in 1994 as the New 2 Live Crew and were prominently featured on *Back at Your Ass for the Nine 4*. The disc did well briefly, peaking at number nine on the R&B chart. But their brand of X-rated humor seemed almost tame compared to the mix of explicit sex and violence available on more hardcore gangsta rap sessions, while the Jamaican toasters like Shabba Ranks and the Mad Cobra outdistanced them in creative lewdness. —*Ron Wynn*

2 Live Crew Is What We Are / 1986 / Luke 91648
The record that launched the whole phenomenon. If the puerile language and vulgarity had been allowed to run its course without censorship attempts, this lunacy might have ended right here. The production does provide good examples of Miami "bass" music. —*Ron Wynn*

Move Somethin' / 1987 / Luke 101
Luther Campbell hits on the ingenious idea of issuing clean and dirty versions simultaneously in an ill-fated attempt to take the censorship heat off. The clean version lacks guts; the dirty version lacks taste. —*Ron Wynn*

○ **As Nasty As They Wanna Be** / 1990 / Luke 91651
Not only did it cause all the legal controversies, but *As Nasty As They Wanna Be* is the quintessential 2 Live Crew album, showing all their tasteless, bass-driven glory. —*AMG*

Banned in the USA / 1990 / Atlantic 91424
This offers an interesting, if somewhat perverse version of Springsteen's "Born in the USA" as the title track and underlying theme. The rest is an erratic, meandering blend of X-rated sexual comments and quasi-political rhetoric. —*Ron Wynn*

● **Greatest Hits** / 1992 / Luke 122
Full of the low-minded humor that made this Miami outfit notorious throughout the country, *Greatest Hits* does contain the best material 2 Live Crew ever recorded; it is all the 2 Live Crew most will ever need to hear. —*Stephen Thomas Erlewine*

Two pac

Rap
Rapper Tupac Amaru Shakur threatened to supplant Luther Campbell and Ice-T as the most demonized figure in hip-hop. The former Digital Underground member became a solo performer with *2Pacalypse Now;* his status soared following a critically acclaimed performance in *Juice.* His follow-up album also earned a hit with "Keep Your Head Up." But far outweighing these successes, Shakur generated a great deal of negative publicity from several incidents that resulted in criminal charges and an assault conviction for attacking the Hughes brothers, who'd fired him from the film *Menace II Society.* All this didn't stop his acting ca-

reer; there were appearances in the films *Poetic Justice* with Janet Jackson and *Above the Rim.* —*Ron Wynn*

○ **2pacalypse Now** / 1992 / Interscope 91767
Few expected former Digital Underground member Tupac Amaru Shakur to become hip-hop enemy number one when he made his solo debut with this 1992 album. Sure, songs like "Crooked Ass Nigga" and "Tha' Lunatic" might have hinted at storm clouds on the horizon, but there were also excellent advocacy numbers like "Words of Wisdom" and "Young Black Male." The album didn't make him a celebrity, but it did put him on the road to stardom. —*Ron Wynn*

● **Strictly 4 My N.I.G.G.A.Z.** / Atlantic 92209
Tupac Shakur became a crossover acting and singing success with this release. The disc yielded a couple of hits, with the fiery message track "Keep Your Head Up" particularly outstanding. Unfortunately, he also found himself on police blotters coast to coast and the designated demon of antirap forces nationwide. Several ugly personal incidents, among them a public physical fight with film directors the Hughes brothers and allegations of violent attacks on an off-duty police officer and sexual misconduct threaten to derail a promising multimedia career. —*Ron Wynn*

U Krew

Rap
Portland, OR, rappers the Untouchable Krew later shortened their name to U Krew. Drum programmer Larry Bell and vocalist Kevin Morse signed with Enigma and released *The U-Krew* in 1990. The single "I U Were Mine" cracked the pop Top 30, while "Let Me Be Your Lover" also did moderately well. But their focus was on light romanticism and occasional confrontational rap, and their style quickly became passé. —*Ron Wynn*

U-Krew / Enigma 73524
Portland rappers U-Krew landed a Top 30 pop hit with their 1990 *The U-Krew.* "If U Were Mine" was among the last romantic/love-styled singles to make much headway on the hip-hop scene, and a moderately successful follow-up single "Let Me Be Your Lover" helped get the album onto the lower reaches of the pop albums chart. Of course, Kevin Morse's sentimental vocals probably had more to do with this than the raps or production. —*Ron Wynn*

Urban Dance Squad

Group / Rap, dance
An unlikely Dutch rock/rap aggregation, they won well-deserved raves for their debut album, *Mental Floss for the Globe.* —*Dan Heilman*

○ **Mental Floss for the Globe** / 1990 / Arista 8640
A heady brew of dense hip-hop, featuring the great hit single "Deeper Shade of Soul." —*Dan Heilman*

● **Life 'n Perspective of a Genuine Crossover** / 1991 / Arista 18672
Dutch hip-hop/dance rockers the Urban Dance Squad followed their mildly successful debut LP with an even more advanced second set production-wise. Though rapper Rudeboy's accent and outlook were more jive than jam, the excellent funk beats and techno-backing made this a lot more interesting than anticipated. Sales-wise, it didn't make anyone stand and holler, but it showed that the group was worth more scrutiny. —*Ron Wynn*

US3

Rap
Perhaps the finest of the hip-hop/jazz ensembles, US3 emerged as a hit act in 1994. Their adaptation of Herbie Hancock's "Cantaloupe Island" into the single "Cantaloop" became a hit, and the group's 1993 *Hand on the Torch* album made the pop, R&B, and rap hit lists. They were also unusual in that they weren't a rap ensemble integrating jazz samples into their compositions, but a band—saxophonists Steve Williamson and Ed Jones, trumpeter Gerald Presencer, keyboardists Mel Simpson and Matthew Cooper, trombonist Dennis Rollins, and special guest guitarist Tony Remy interacting live with rappers Kobie Powell, Rahsaan, Tukka Yoot, and DJ Geoff Wilkinson. The album got so much response that Blue Note later issued a companion CD highlighting the original tracks from which they sampled the backing material. —*Ron Wynn*

● **Hand on the Torch** / 1993 / Blue Note
Hip-hop jazzers US3 have forged the most elaborate union between the styles since the early days of Gang Starr and A Tribe Called Quest. Blue Note's vast catalog gives them a huge advantage over several similar groups in terms of source material, and classic sounds by Art Blakey, Horace Silver, and Herbie Hancock add zest and fiber to their narratives. Indeed, when things falter, it's because the raps aren't always that fat or creative. They are serviceable, sometimes catchy, but too often delivered without the snazzy touches, gripping tones, or distinctive skills that make Tribe's and Gang Starr's material topnotch. But when words and music mesh, as on "Cantaloop" and "The Darkside," US3 show how effectively hip-hop and jazz can blend. *—Ron Wynn*

U.T.F.O.

Group / Rap
Doctor Ice, the Kangol Kid, and the Educated Rapper (later joined by Mix-Master Ice), the Untouchable Force Organization (U.T.F.O.), dreamed up a tune about a gorgeous woman oblivious to their charms and appeals. "Roxanne, Roxanne" dominated the airwaves for much of 1984 and 1985, yielding eventually more than 100 answer versions. Their first albums included the hit single plus "Roxanne Part 2" and "The Real Roxanne." The Brooklyn group's popularity and influence waned as the Roxanne fad peaked, and subsequent releases had limited appeal. *—Ron Wynn*

● **Utfo** / 1985 / Elektra 21614
The Brooklyn production/performance combine U.T.F.O. shot to fame in the mid '80s with their story about Roxanne, Roxanne. It generated a flood of answer songs, started the careers of both Roxanne Shante and the real Roxanne, and for a moment put U.T.F.O. into the thicket of hip-hop and urban contemporary music. Unfortunately, they really weren't that gifted, as they showed on such singles as "Bite It," "Beats and Rhymes" and "Lisa Lips." They're now rightly regarded as the ultimate novelty/one-hit wonders. *—Ron Wynn*

Skeezer Pleezer / 1986 / Elektra 21616
Reality began to set in for U.T.F.O. with their second album in 1986. They got a little buzz from the single "We Work Hard" but were essentially already in stylistic retreat as the gimmick tag they picked up from the success of "Roxanne, Roxanne" was proving difficult to shake. It didn't help that songs like "Bad Luck Barry" and "House Will Rock" didn't exactly inspire generations of aspiring rappers. *—Ron Wynn*

Vanilla Ice

Vocals / Rap, dance
This White 1990 pop-rap sensation enjoyed his "15 minutes of fame" with "Ice, Ice Baby" (using a riff from the David Bowie/Queen song "Under Pressure").
　　Vanilla Ice attempted to return to the hip-hop spotlight in 1994 with his second release, *Mind Blowin',* on SBK. It didn't surprise anyone, except that it was even more devoid of originality, inspiration, and content than anticipated.*—AMG*

● **To the Extreme** / 1990 / SBK 95325
On the strength of the incessantly catchy single "Ice Ice Baby," *To the Extreme* was an enormous success, holding the number-one slot for 16 weeks and selling over seven million copies in America. Apart from that single and a cover of Wild Cherry's "Play That Funky Music," the album was unmemorable, with limp beats and tepid rhymes. *—Stephen Thomas Erlewine*

Mind Blowin / 1994 / Sbk Records
Four years after *To the Extreme,* Vanilla Ice comes back with a refashioned and modern sound, borrowing from the blunted Cypress Hill, the deep funk of Dr. Dre, the quick-tongued rapping of Das EFX—basically, anything that's been popular since his first album. While he spends an obscene amount of time dissing 3rd Bass, he counters all charges about being a sellout by stating that he's sold over 11 million records. There's not a single moment that establishes a distinct musical identity, and the whole thing is rather embarrassing. Not surprisingly, the record dropped out of sight almost a month after its release. *—Stephen Thomas Erlewine*

Whodini

Group / Rap, hip-hop, soul, funk

The influential Brooklyn, NY, rap group Whodini was one of the better groups to merge straight R&B with pop-fueled hip-hop. Whodini started recording in 1983 and broke up in 1988, scoring hits with "Magic's Wand" and "Freaks Come out at Night." *—John Floyd*

Whodini / 1983 / Jive 10
More singers than straight rappers, Jali Hutchins and Ecstasty made a successful conversion to hip-hop, scoring two hits on their debut with "Rap Attack" and "The Haunted House of Funk," a reworking of "The Monster Mash." *—Ron Wynn*

○ **Escape** / 1984 / Jive 1226
Their best release, containing "Friends," "Freaks Come Out at Night," and "Big Mouth." Memorable tunes and state-of-the-art (for that time) production. *—Ron Wynn*

Back in Black / 1986 / Jive 1227
Signs of stagnation and decay are evident, though the cut "Funky Beat" forestalled the decline for a short while. *—Ron Wynn*

★ **Greatest Hits** / 1990 / Jive 1340
A worthwhile compilation that shows what all the fuss was about regarding this unit in the early '80s. *—Ron Wynn*

World Class Wreckin' Cru

Rap
This was a West Coast pop-funk band whose ranks at one time included Dr. Dre, Michele, and Arabian Prince. Though their records never made much headway, they did have one Top 30 R&B single "Turn Off the Lights" in 1988. The group was mainly a footnote until one of their tracks appeared on a Rhino anthology in 1994 and Eazy-E brought up the group as part of a campaign to declare Dr. Dre a fraud. *—Ron Wynn*

● **Turn Off the Lights** / Creative Funk 7006

Wrecks-N-Effect

Rap
Wrecks-N-Effect earned a huge crossover smash with the single "Rump Shaker" off their 1992 album *Hard or Smooth.* The accompanying video with its array of shapely women following the directions of the lead singer generated nearly as much heat as Sir Mix-A-Lot's "Baby Got Back." It also helped the group secure a platinum certification, something it hardly seemed they'd earn from their Motown debut *Wrecks-N-Effect* in 1990. Markell Riley, brother of super producer Teddy Riley, was part of the rap ensemble along with Aquil Davidson and Brandon Mitchell; Mitchell was killed in a '90 shooting. *—Ron Wynn*

● **Wrecks-N-Effect** / 1991 / Atlantic 81860
Striking mix of go-go funk and new-jack-swing, highlighted by the "New Jack Swing," an anthem for the new beat. Produced by Teddy Riley, who created that new beat with Guy. *—John Floyd*

○ **Hard or Smooth** / 1992 / MCA 10566
Although nothing on *Hard or Smooth* compares to the monster groove of "Rump Shaker," the rest of the album offers enough beats to satisfy most fans of the hit singles. *—AMG*

X-Clan

Group / Rap
Out of all the militant Afrocentric rappers X-Clan was the most radical. Although their first album was only known inside hip-hop circles, X-Clan's second release *Xodus* peaked at 31 on the pop charts and got them much more attention than the debut, *To the East, Blackwards.* The Brooklyn-based group's ranks included Professor X—*Lumumba Carson, the son of extremely controversial activist Sonny Carson. There were charges during New York City's 1993 mayoral campaign that X-Clan was doing unsolicited campaign work for David Dinkins. The charge didn't hurt X-Clan, but it probably didn't help Dinkins either.* —Ron Wynn

○ **To the East Blackwards** / 1990 / Fourth & Broadway 444019
An uncompromising Islamic session with frequently powerful raps. *—Ron Wynn*

● **X Odus** / 1992 / Polydor 513225
Even more Afrocentric and Islamic-oriented than their previous effort, and better produced. *—Ron Wynn*

Yo-Yo (Yolanda Whitaker)

Vocals / Rap, dance

Yo-Yo has been among the most sophisticated and unpredictable female rappers around. She doesn't take an overtly feminist tack but urges young women to show sexual restraint and use their minds as well as their bodies. She's released two records as a leader.

Yo Yo came out less embracing and more confrontational on *You Better Ask Somebody*, her 1993 album. There was little compromising or demure about her rapping or the record's mood. Where before she'd sometimes seemed conciliatory, this time she was stark and combative, particularly in her demands for respect. — *Ron Wynn*

○ **Make Way for the Motherlode** / 1991 / East West 91605
Intelligent, forceful, and affirmative rap from a woman whose cadence, tone, and delivery are as hard as those of any man on either coast and anywhere in between. —*Ron Wynn*

● **Black Pearl** / 1992 / East West 92120
Yo-Yo's positive (but not simplistic or naive) messages about female sexuality, self-esteem, and achievement were grounded in hard raps and thudding beats on this album, still her most complete and effective production. Unfortunately, it seemed that only cutesy material like "You Can't Play with My Yo-Yo," from her first release, could get the widespread support and attention necessary to get a hit. —*Ron Wynn*

Young MC (Marvin Young)

Rap, dance
Although his good looks and pop appeal would suggest he's beaten LL Cool J to the crossover punch, Young MC has pumped his own personality into some of rap's greatest across-the-board hits. "Bust a Move" and "Principal's Office," among others, hit harder than the similar work of DJ Jazzy Jeff & the Fresh Prince, and the jokes last longer than the ones you'll find in the Fat Boys catalog. He also wrote Tone-Loc's smash single, "Funky Cold Medina," and cowrote "Wild Thing."

Despite his enormous pop success, Young MC tried for a more hardcore effect on *What's the Flavor*. The results were mixed, but the general reaction was that he was much better with light material. —*John Floyd*

Brainstorm / 1989 / Capitol 96337
While *Brainstorm* was not a bad record, it didn't capture the energetic spark of his debut; consequently, the album wasn't the across-the-boards smash of *Stone Cold Rhymin'*, even though it sounded a lot like it. —*Stephen Thomas Erlewine*

● **Stone Cold Rhymin'** / 1989 / Delicious Vinyl 842375
Young MC's first album was a major hit, featuring such pop-rap crossover classics like "Bust a Move" and "Principal's Office." With his friendly, clever rhyming and a warm, funky production dominating the album, *Stone Cold Rhymin'* was not only Young MC's most popular album—*it was also his best.* —Stephen Thomas Erlewine

What's the Flavor? / 1993 / Capitol
On his third album, Young MC was trying to recapture his audience, adding elements of jazz-rap—thanks to the production of A Tribe Called Quest's Ali Shaheed—to his pop-oriented style. While it didn't rocket him back to the top of the charts, the results were agreeable and likeable, with only a couple of embarrassing tracks. —*Stephen Thomas Erlewine*

Rap Collections

○ **2 Nasty 4 Radio** / Nov. 27, 1990 / Cold Chillin' 26441
A worthwhile collection of naughty and street raps that were left off the airwaves because of the language they contained. Solid content. —*Ron Wynn*

Bass That Ate Miami, The / 1991 / Pandisc 8801
A collection spotlighting various artists performing in the Miami bottom-heavy bass hip-hop style. —*Ron Wynn*

○ **Bass Waves, Vol. 3: Rap's Biggest Hits of the 90s** / Luke 91598
Bass Waves, Vol. 3 is a good collection of recent rap hits. —*Ron Wynn*

Battle of the Boom / Jam City 2000
A loose aggregation of contemporary rap/bass tunes. —*Ron Wynn*

Battle of the D.J.'s / Jive 1112

A good hip-hop anthology covering material from Eric B & Rakim, DJ Jazzy Jeff & the Fresh Prince, Run-D.M.C., Steady B, Cash Money & Marvelous, Whodini, Grandmaster Flash, Kurtis Blow, Schoolly D, and Too Short. —*Ron Wynn*

☆ **Compton Compilation** / Kru Cut 1013
An overview of the school from whence came N.W.A., Ice Cube, and P & 91. —*Ron Wynn*

Cut It Up Def—Bass Jams / 1991 / Cut-it-up-def 0101
A collection of extended grooves and bass cuts, more of interest to rap completists. —*Ron Wynn*

★ **Def Jam Classics, Vol. 1** / Def Jam 45035

☆ **Def Jam Classics, Vol. 2** / Def Jam 46801
A useful overview of the seminal rap label, including its best artists and some sumptuous rarities. —*John Floyd*

Detroit's Most Wanted—Tricks of the Trades / Bryant 30010
A Midwest spin on the gangsta equation. —*Ron Wynn*

○ **East Vs. West—Rap Battle Royale** / 1991 / K-Tel 60012
An entertaining contrast between hard-edged pop and gangsta crew: Run-D.M.C., Kool Moe Dee, MC Lyte, and others. —*Ron Wynn*

○ **Explicit Rap** / 1990 / Priority 7993
A caustic compilation directed to the PMRC and delivered by the likes of Ice Cube, 2 Live Crew, and the Geto Boys. —*John Floyd*

○ **First Priority Music Family—Basement Flavor, The** / Atlantic 91046
First Priority Music Family is a sampler aimed at new rap listeners. —*Ron Wynn*

○ **Fresh Rap** / K-Tel 685
This budget compilation does contain a representative crop of recent hits and typical K-Tel sound. —*Ron Wynn*

○ **Gangsta Rap** / Priority 8656
This sampler introduces proponents of urban fantasies and raw street chants. —*Ron Wynn*

○ **Great Hits of the Street—Rappin' & Scratchin'** / Priority 9469
Great Hits of the Street is a better-than-usual collection of uncut, non-pop rap. —*Ron Wynn*

☆ **Greg Mack Compilation—What Does It All Mean?** / Motown 6279
Assembled by onetime major rap disc jockey Mack, *Greg Mack Compilation* gives a comprehensive portrait of raps he once aired. —*Ron Wynn*

★ **Hip Hop Greats: Classic Raps** / Rhino 70957
A decent overview of rap's salad days, including the Sugarhill Gang's "Rapper's Delight" and Grandmaster Flash's best singles ("White Lines," "The Message"), plus "Jam on It" from Newcleus. A nice place to start your education. —*John Floyd*

☆ **Hip Hop Heritage, Vol. 1** / 1987 / Jive 1291
Pioneering cuts from Grandmaster Flash, Spoonie Gee, and others. —*Ron Wynn*

Hip House / 1989 / Quality 15141
Worthwhile because of the number of cuts that were previously hits only in Europe. —*Ron Wynn*

○ **Kings of Rap** / Priority 9264
This entertaining anthology is loaded down with easily obtainable cuts. —*Ron Wynn*

☆ **Miami Bass Express** / 1986 / Pandisc 8806
The one to grab for an adequate portrait of bass music. —*Ron Wynn*

Miami Bass Machine / 1986 / Jamarc 9002
Strictly for fans. —*Ron Wynn*

Miami Bass Wars II / 1986 / Pandisc 8813
Another aimed wholly at the converted. —*Ron Wynn*

Miami Bass Waves, Vol. 2 / 1986 / Luke 5001
Dense, snappy production but little else. —*Ron Wynn*

☆ **Mixmasters** / Jul. 23, 1991 / MCA 42184
A good collection of tricky, intricate arrangements. —*Ron Wynn*

○ **Mr. Magic's Rap Attack** / Profile 1213
Great series. Chronicles what is essentially a single genre. —*Dan Heilman*

Power Rap / Priority 9363
Standard rap cuts with little unavailable elsewhere. —*Ron Wynn*

○ **Pump That Bass** / Gucci 3317
This has hearty sound and production. *—Ron Wynn*

○ **Queens of Rap** / Priority 7916
The women get the spotlight. *—Ron Wynn*

R-Rated Rap / Priority 9701
A cross-section of cuts, heavy on the four-letter words. *—Ron Wynn*

○ **Rap Beat from the Street** / K-Tel 6070
A solid collection of some of 1991's harder-edged hip-hop without any profanity or overt political messages. That doesn't mean the music is lacking, as proved by Public Enemy's "Shut 'Em Down," Cypress Hill's "The Phuncky Feel One," and the Geto Boys' incredible "Mind Playing Tricks on Me." *—Stephen Thomas Erlewine*

☆ **Rap Beginnings, Vol. 1** / K-Tel 316
Sound notwithstanding, these are a good look at early and tangential rap on a budget compilation. *—Ron Wynn*

○ **Rap Miami Style** / 1990 / Pandisc 8811
Bass and Florida influences integrated into hip-hop. *—Ron Wynn*

○ **Rap the Beat** / Priority 9753
A collection of pretty familiar rap cuts. *—Ron Wynn*

★ **Rap's Biggest Hits** / 1990 / K-Tel 315
A strong collection of some of hip-hop's biggest and most important singles from 1986 to 1989, including Tone-Loc, Public Enemy, Run-D.M.C., and Rob Base,. and D.J. E-Z Rock. A good introduction to hip-hop. *—Stephen Thomas Erlewine*

○ **Rap's Greatest Hits—Vols. 1-3** / Priority
Well-known commonplace pop and crossover tunes. *—Ron Wynn*

○ **Rap's Most Wanted** / 1991 / K-Tel 60262
Riding on the strength of Biz Markie's "Just a Friend," Candyman's "Knockin' Boots," Eric B & Rakim's "Let the Rhythm Hit 'em," and LL Cool J's "Around the Way Girl," *Rap's Most Wanted* is a very good collection of hip-hop's pop crossovers of the early '90s. *—Stephen Thomas Erlewine*

○ **Rap's New Generation** / Profile 1259
A good sampler showcasing up-and-coming stars. *—Ron Wynn*

○ **Rap's Next Generation—Hard as Hell** / Profile 1251
Crisp, often compelling cuts from new-school rappers. *—Ron Wynn*

○ **Rap: Today's Greatest Hits** / K-tel International 6081
A good collection of some of the best mainstream hip-hop from the early '90s, including Eric B & Rakim's terrific "Don't Sweat the Technique," Snap's "Rhythm Is a Dancer," Main Source's "Fakin' the Funk," and Digital Underground's "No Nose Job." It's by no means a complete picture of hip-hop in 1992, but it is a thoroughly enjoyable singles collection. *—Stephen Thomas Erlewine*

☆ **Rapmasters, Vol. 1: Best of the Jam** / Priority 7951
An ambitious and exhaustive historical survey of rap from the early days up to yesterday. The categorical divisions of each volume don't mean much, and each one contains at least four songs that are essential to any rap collection. Mix 'em, match 'em, or buy 'em all. *—John Floyd*

○ **Doo Hop Legacy, The** / 1991 / A&M 75021-5341

Terse and often edgy nationalistic material with interesting variations on the hip-hop mode. *—Ron Wynn*

○ **Raps Street** / Par 2005
Recent hits from current and rising stars. *—Ron Wynn*

Sex in the Hood / Connoisseur 5
Shows off the steamy side of house music. *—Ron Wynn*

○ **Straight from the Basement of Kooley High** / 1988 / Def Jam 44470
This entertaining, mainly comedic and dance-oriented album from a collection of Long Island rappers and disc jockeys is rap to amuse rather than inform, except for a couple of antiracism and antiviolence tracts. —Ron Wynn

○ **Straight from the Hood** / 1991 / Priority 7063
Street rap available with and without obscenities. *—Ron Wynn*

★ **Street Jams—Electric Funk** / 1992 / Rhino 70575
This is an excellent four-volume series of rare 12-inch mixes of pioneering dance and hip-hop records from the early '80s. All four volumes are essential to any funk, rap, or dance collection. *—AMG*

★ **Street Jams—Hip-Hop from the Top** / 1992 / Rhino 70577
This terrific four-volume series offers rare 12-inch mixes of influential hip-hop and rap records from the early '80s. Many of the tracks aren't available anywhere else, making all four discs essential to any comprehensive rap collection. *—AMG*

☆ **This Is Bass** / Gucci 3312

○ **This Is Bass, Vol. 2** / Hot Prod. 3319
The first is a good introduction to bottom-heavy bass music; Volume 2 is a thorough follow-up. *—Ron Wynn*

☆ **Tommy Boy's Greatest Hits** / Tommy Boy 1005
An excellent overview of '80s-era hits from the pioneering hip-hop label. Includes the finest work of Arthur Baker, Afrika Bambaataa, and many others. *—John Floyd*

Vs. West Coast / Jive 1132
A fine late '80s rap collection with such East Coast acts as Run-D.M.C., Kool Moe Dee, Boogie Down Productions, and others, matched against West Coast types Ice-T., Too Short, and Kid Frost. *—Ron Wynn*

☆ **West Coast Rap: The First Dynasty, Vols. 1-3** / 1992 / Rhino 70590
Rhino's three-volume *West Coast Rap: The First Dynasty* is an excellent collection of groundbreaking rap from the early and middle '80s. *—AMG*

☆ **West Coast Rap: The Renegades** / 1992 / Rhino 71039
A sequel to the *First Dynasty* series continues the fine form of the original three discs, spotlighting the prototype gangstas and other mavericks. *—AMG*

○ **Yo! MTV Raps!, Vol. 1** / Jive 1201

Yo! MTV Raps!, Vol. 2 / 1991 / Jive 1420
Basic collections of rap hits featured on the groundbreaking MTV program. *—Stephen Thomas Erlewine & Ron Wynn*

JAZZ

Jazz is a music with a history and a heart. Born in the rich melting pot of New Orleans after the turn of the century, jazz has grown into a vast and deep current of American musical culture. Historically and culturally, it is a music that had to happen. Though it is undoubtedly Black America's gift to the world, it is culturally a profound integration of musical factors: African rhythms and tonalities, the sensibilities of Blues and Gospel expression, European styles and instrumentation, and the creative energy of America's expansive and tumultuous early 20th century. Important battles against racism were won in the jazz era as bands and audiences began to integrate by virtue of sharing the music. Thus jazz is both historically and musically a very deep expression of American culture. We achieved in this music what we couldn't - and have yet to - achieve in our social environment: a true and harmonious integration of the diverse streams of human culture that converged in America. Even more than rhythm & blues or rock & roll, jazz has become a melting pot, absorbing and integrating the musical styles of the whole world, which is in fact our cultural legacy.

The types of jazz are many, ranging from blues-based styles drenched in feeling to the more airy styles of jazz that are almost indistinguishable from modern classical music. Your own favorite kind of jazz is in there somewhere; you just have to find it. What is important is to hear the different styles of jazz and find ones that work for you.

And chances are you that may already be somewhat of a jazz expert. If you like movies or watch TV, you are already hearing all-kinds of jazz. Many soundtracks and almost all the background music used for movies and many TV shows is popular jazz. Whether its a Woody Woodpecker cartoon, an old Laurel & Hardy bit, or the latest full-length movie, jazz is the predominant music behind the video that we watch.

For all this cultural significance, jazz is remarkably easy to listen to, with an unpretentious, spontaneous feeling, and a wide emotional range. It has tremendous diversity in its styles and historical eras, and the richness of recorded jazz (recorded music started about the same time as jazz itself) makes it a wonderful project for long-term enjoyment and learning. Most of us who listen to jazz have found one or two favorite types of jazz that we can really get into. We work outward from there.

Jazz is synonymous with improvisation - the spontaneous and unrehearsed expression of musical ideas. Once common in classical European music (Bach and Mozart were awesome, among others) improvisation was gradually eliminated from music education. Jazz brought it back to us with a vengeance. Although jazz is largely instrumental, jazz melody and rhythm are deeply influenced by vocal music, especially by the early tradition of African-American vocal music. In turn, many jazz vocalists have been heavily influenced by instrumental jazz.

– Michael G. Nastos, JME, DNM

Ahmed Abdul-Malik (Sam Gill)

b. Jan. 30, 1927, New York, NY
Bass, oud, Asian instruments / Hard bop, world fusion
A Brooklyn-born bassist whose father is from Sudan, Ahmed Abdul-Malik also plays oud. He played with Art Blakey and Randy Weston and spent a particularly fruitful two years (1957-1958) with Thelonious Monk. —*Michael G. Nastos*

☆ **Jazz Samba** / Oct. 1958 / Riverside 287
○ **East Meets West** / Mar. 16, 1959+Mar. 31, 1959 / RCA 2015
★ **Music of Ahmed Abdul-Malik, The** / May 23, 1961 / New Jazz 8266

Ahmed Abdullah

b. 1947, New York, NY
Trumpet / Modern creative
This New York-based trumpeter is best known for working in the '70s loft jazz scene. He led a group known as the Solomonic Quintet in the '80s, and has also worked with Chico Freeman, Malachi Favors of the Art Ensemble, and Charles Brackeen. Abdullah played for many years with Sun Ra. An aggressive, striking soloist, Abdullah has recorded for such independent labels as Silkheart and Cadence Jazz. —*Ron Wynn*

○ **Live at Ali's Alley** / Apr. 24, 1978 / Cadence
Trumpeter Ahmed Abdullah featured French horn and cello in his instrumental configuration, while working alongside tenor saxophonist Chico Freeman on this 1978 date. It's symbolic of the decade's "loft" jazz, a free-wheeling date with uneven but often compelling solos, as well as periods of rambling, unproductive, and ragged ensemble work. Freeman's blistering tenor sax is uniformly inspired, and Abdullah's solos are aggressive and energetic. Vincent Chancey's French horn and Muneer Abdul Fataah's cello contributions provide interesting contrast, while bassist Jerome Hunter and drummer Rashied Sinan are competent and effective, though not memorable. —*AMG*

★ **Life's Force** / 1978-1979 / About Time 1001
Progressive trumpeter with sextet in an all-original program. Includes Jay Hoggard on vibes and Vincent Chancey on French horn. —*Michael G. Nastos*

John Abercrombie (John L. Abercrombie)

b. Dec. 16, 1944, Port Chester, NY
Guitar / Early jazz rock, modern creative
One of the most sensitive and virtuosic of the fusion guitarists, John Abercrombie was influenced by solid mainstream jazz players such as Jim Hall and Bill Evans and tenor sax giants Sonny Rollins and John Coltrane. His organ trio days with Johnny Hammond gave him a solid grounding in blues-based styles. Abercrombie worked with many top players in 70s progressive jazz and fusion, such as Jack DeJohnette, Gato Barbieri, Billy Cobham, and Gil Evans. He has recorded in a variety of creative settings. A high point was Abercrombie's Gateway Trio sessions with Dave Holland and DeJohnette. They achieved a powerful rhythmic sound while retaining a chamber jazz aesthetic with great spontaneity. Generally Abercrombie's recordings exemplify the "ECM sound," a coloristic wash of sounds played by well-trained musicians with eclectic influences. He uses electronic effects from the rock world; more importantly, he absorbs sounds, techniques, and musical ideas from virtuoso rock solo styles. *Sargasso Sea* with Ralph Towner is a gem of guitar duet work.

His more recent recordings have emphasized electric guitar synthesizer explorations. —*David Nelson McCarthy*

★ **Timeless** / Jun. 21, 1974-Jun. 22, 1974 / ECM 829114
Guitarist John Abercrombie debuted on ECM in 1974 working in a trio setting, a format that would become familiar. Jan Hammer on synthesizer, organ, and piano and drummer Jack DeJohnette accompanied him on a date that included crisp, taut riffs and solos from Abercrombie, sparse and tasty fills and licks by DeJohnette, and a bonus in long stretches of first-rate organ work by Hammer, minus the rock gimmicks that eventually plagued his keyboard work. —*AMG*

☆ **Gateway—Vol. 1** / Mar. 1975 / ECM 829192
The first of two fine trio albums that matched guitarist John Abercrombie, bassist Dave Holland, and drummer Jack DeJohnette, managed the trick of being both reflective and dynamic, thanks to Abercrombie's intelligent, finely crafted solos, and DeJohnette's first-rate, sympathetic rhythms. Though Holland didn't play with his usual vigor, he remained enough of a force to interact successfully with Abercrombie and DeJohnette. —*AMG*

☆ **Sargasso Sea** / May 1976 / ECM 835015
A nice session, though not as spectacular as anticipated, matches guitarists John Abercrombie and Ralph Towner, who also plays piano. Towner's 12-string solos are stronger than his classical ones, which are frequently beautiful but don't make much of an impression contrasted with Abercrombie's more energetic improvisations. The title track's the best cut; the others are more decorative than intriguing. —*AMG*

○ **Straight Flight** / Mar. 19, 1979-Mar. 20, 1979 / Jam 5001

★ **Night** / Apr. 1984 / ECM 823212
Spirited original featuring Jan Hammer (k). Favorable group setting for guitarist Abercrombie and timeless trio. Michael Brecker (ts). Definitive. —*Michael G. Nastos*

Works / i. Jan. 25, 1991 / ECM 837275
A good 1989 compilation of past Abercrombie selections on various ECM releases, spotlighting his versatility and proficiency. Songs featuring his fluid guitar in introspective mainstream and free contexts, as well as everything from new age-tinged originals to covers of standards, are presented. —*Ron Wynn, AMG*

Muhal Richard Abrahms

b. Sep. 19, 1930, Chicago, IL
Piano, composer, cello, clarinet / Early free, progressive big band, modern creative
Abrams was a founding member of the Association for the Advancement of Creative Musicians (AACM) and is a premier player, arranger, conductor, and writer. In 1961 he formed the Experimental Band, whose lineup included Eddie Harris, Donald Garrett, and Roscoe Mitchell. A cooperative designed to help Chicago musicians promote and present their music, it evolved into a major force within the Chicago Black music community, holding festivals and concerts and starting a school for young musicians. As a pianist, Abrams's style incorporates everything from stride and ragtime to bop and free, and his compositions seamlessly blend vintage and current idioms. He has influenced countless musicians, been a confidant to such players as George Lewis and Joseph Jarman, and gained some measure of long-deserved recognition in the last few years thanks to a series of outstanding albums issued by the Black Saint/Soul Note family, plus CD reissues of his landmark Delmark '60s sessions. —*Ron Wynn*

★ **Levels and Degrees of Light** / Jun. 7, 1967 / Delmark 413
This was one of Muhal Richard Abrams's early gems, a 1967 session that included him playing both piano and synthesizer and heading a quartet with Anthony Braxton on clarinet, Thurman Barker on drums, and Gordon Emmanuel on vibes. Abrams superbly interspersed free, hard bop, and blues elements, while Braxton's solos and the intriguing frontline and contrasts provided by vibes and drums rather than bass resulted in some unusual and striking compositions. This has been reissued on CD. —*AMG*

☆ **Young at Heart, Wise in Time** / Jul. 2, 1969+Aug. 20, 1969 / Delmark 423
In his work for solo piano, "Young at Heart," Muhal Richard Abrams weaved a gossamer expression, opening to the receptive listener the utter fullness of his heart in a manner defiant of analysis or description. No, it wasn't "jazz"—but then nothing is,

now. No other man could build this in such delicate beauty, nor should any wish to. "Wise in Time" is also appropriate. —*Barry Tepperman, Coda*

○ **Duet 1976** / i. 1976 / Black Saint
This was not Muhal Richard Abrams's session, but Anthony Braxton's, and was issued on Arista under his name. The duo teamed for intriguing, sometimes intense, and other times more introspective performances on material ranging from Braxton's numerical compositions to their unusual version of "Maple Leaf Rag." Braxton played alto and soprano saxophones, plus contrabass clarinet and sax and standard clarinet, while Abrams concentrated on piano and added everything from bop riffs to stride accents and ragtime and blues lines. —*AMG*

☆ **Lifea Blinec** / Feb. 1978 / Novus 3000
Muhal Richard Abrams headed one of his finest small combos on this intense quintet session from 1978. Joseph Jarman provided riveting bass saxophone and bassoon contributions in addition to playing alto clarinet, flute, soprano sax, and percussion and providing vocals. His multiple contributions were matched by Douglas Ewart on an equal array of reed instruments, including bass and soprano clarinet, bassoon, alto and tenor sax, and percussion. Abrams divided his time between keyboards, conducting, and percussion, while Amina Claudine Myers added vibrant, bluesy riffs and statements. Thurman Barker took care of drum duties and doubled on percussion. —*AMG*

○ **Blues for Ever** / Jul. 20, 1981-Jul. 27, 1981 / Black Saint 0061
Tremendous large orchestra session with Abrams heading a crew that includes the cream of '70s and '80s improvisers plus some '60s survivors. Though not every arrangement clicks, the band romps and stomps successfully through enough cuts to show the big band sound doesn't just mean "ghost" groups recreating dusty numbers from the '30s and '40s. —*Ron Wynn, AMG*

★ **Rejoicing with the Light** / Jan. 8-25, 1983 / Black Saint 0071
Rejoicing with the Light recalled the episodic, "watch what happens" serialism of Muhal Richard Abrams's and Anthony Braxton's initial waxings on Delmark circa the late 1960s, a period of sentimental value for me because it marked my introduction to new music. On side one, duet and a cappella "events" for soprano voice, percussion, strings, brass, and clarinets were alternated with controlled, somberly weighted textures from 15-piece band. During "Bloodline"—dedicated to Fletcher Henderson, Don Redman, and Benny Carter—the proceedings showed signs of life, albeit nothing special compared to the elan of former Abrams collaborator Henry Threadgill's takes on "the tradition." —*Peter Kostakis, Downbeat*

☆ **Roots of Blue** / Jan. 7, 1986 / RPR 1001
Roots of Blue is equivalent to hard-won success that needn't have been so difficult. It pales by comparison to Abrams's '70s masterstroke *Sight Song* (which featured bassist Malachi Favors), though this was not because the participants were not up to the previous standards...Abrams soloed imaginatively during the course of the whole album. The upshot isn't so much the way he approached the compositions (after all they are his own), but the way they didn't seem to allow bassist McBee room to get off. —*Ludwig Van Trikt, Cadence*

○ **Colours in Thirty-Third** / Dec. 19, 1986 / Black Saint 0091
Muhal Richard Abrams constantly varied the lineups on the seven numbers that comprised this 1986 session, alternating between trio, quartet, quintet, and sextet pieces. The title track and "Introspection" featured the entire group and were the most striking works, though the trio tunes offered the most musically challenging material. John Purcell on soprano and tenor sax and bass clarinet provided several stirring solos, while violinist John Blake was a solid contributor on several selections and the rhythm tandem of bassist Fred Hopkins and drummer Andrew Cyrille were also consistent and engaging, particularly Cyrille. Abrams as usual was an inspiring force as an instrumentalist and conceptualist. —*AMG*

George Adams (George Rufus Adams)

b. Apr. 29, 1940, Covington, Georgia, d. 1992
Tenor sax, flute, bass clarinet / Blues & jazz, modern creative
Tenor saxophonist, flutist, bass clarinetist, and sometime singer George Adams was a dynamic, aggressive player whose style reflected both sizable blues/R&B influence and the vocal effects and spiraling solo tendencies of avant-garde players. He played

with such notables as Howlin' Wolf, Lightnin' Hopkins, and Bill Doggett and backed singers like Sam Cooke and Hank Ballard. Adams came to New York from Georgia in 1968. He established his jazz reputation through a stint with Art Blakey and later played with Roy Haynes and Gil Evans. A major gig came with Charles Mingus in the '70s. Adams co-led with pianist Don Pullen the George Adams-Don Pullen quartet, one of the top small combos of the '70s and '80s. His last group was Phalanx with Blood Ulmer in the mid '80s. (*also see* Don Pullen) —*Ron Wynn*

○ **Suite for Swingers** / Jul. 28, 1976 / Horo 3
Extended compositions, with Don Pullen. One of the great jazz quartets of the last two decades. All albums worthwhile. —*Michael G. Nastos*

★ **Don't Lose Control** / Nov. 2-03, 1979 / Soul Note 1004
George Adams (tenor sax, flute, vocals) contributed three pieces and Don Pullen (piano) two pieces to this session for Black Saint's mainstream affiliate (Soul Note). Of the Adams lines, the lilting, pristine "Autumn Song" was the most winning. —*Milo Fine, Cadence*

○ **Hand to Hand** / Feb. 13-14, 1980 / Soul Note 1007
What we had here, in essence, was an abbreviated Mingus Dynasty playing its members' own compositions rather than Charles Mingus's. —*Francis Davis, Cadence*

● **America** / May 24, 1989-Jul. 1989 / Blue Note 93896
Saxophonist George Adams was nearing the end of his creative road on 1989's *America*, so it was appropriate for him to go back to his roots and play some blues. He alternates between terse, rippling solos and impassioned, almost serene ones, something that puzzled many critics when this was released. Pianist Hugh Lawson, bassist Cecil McBee, and drummer Marc Johnson took their cues from Adams, mostly playing it straight in their roles and when in the spotlight keeping things simple and restrained, except when Adams himself turned up the intensity. —*Ron Wynn, AMG*

○ **Old Feeling** / Mar. 11-12, 1991 / Blue Note 96689
Old Feeling ranks as one of George Adams's most exciting and happily eccentric sessions. Unlike some other avant-gardists who seem to lose their personality and purpose when they play standard material, George Adams turns even overplayed songs into his own inventive devices; three standards get the "Adams treatment" on this CD. —*Scott Yanow, Cadence*

Pepper Adams (Pepper Park Adams III)

b. Oct. 8, 1930, Highland Park, MI, **d.** Sep. 10, 1986, New York, NY
Baritone sax / Bop, hard bop
Pepper Adams was born Park Adams in Highland Park, MI, and came to prominence in the late '50s as a hard bop baritone saxophonist with a big sound and multinoted attack. Adams was coleader of a group with Detroit trumpeter Donald Byrd (late '50s-early '60s) and a member of the first Thad Jones-Mel Lewis Band beginning in late 1965. He was active in New York studios and played with many freelance groups until the mid '70s, when he devoted himself full-time to jazz. Adams made many recordings as a leader and sideman; among his best are *Ephemera* (Spotlite), *Encounter* (Prestige), *Plays Charles Mingus* (Workshop), *Urban Dreams* (Palo Alto), and *The Master* (Muse). —*Bob Porter*

● **10 to 4 at the 5-Spot** / Apr. 5, 1958 / Riverside 031
The best example of the bebop baritone saxophonist from Detroit. Includes a young Donald Byrd (tpt) and pianist Bobby Timmons. —*David Szatmary*

★ **Reflectory** / Jun. 14, 1978 / Muse 5182
Pepper Adams—of the gritty tone and redoubtable spirit—was among the foremost exponents of the baritone sax, after Harry Carney and Gerry Mulligan, and his mettle as a section man soloist was tested and found true during a 13-year charter tenure with the Thad Jones/Mel Lewis Orchestra...The humors Adams expresses here are more phlegmatic and even melancholic than his often fiery, brittle work with the big band, a not surprising shift for this freed spirit and interior individual. Each side opens with intriguing minor musings from Adams's own pen that involve ringing, long-toned solos by bassist George Mraz, a perfect companion for deep note philosophizing. Other Mraz and Adams duos crop up in a eulogy for Harry Carney ("Lady") and a brisk

Mutt-and-Jeff scamper ("Etude"). Mraz's soloing first on five of the six tunes speaks of Adams's modesty, ability to set mood, and attention to procedural niceties. Drummer Billy Hart neatly inserts choruses on either side of pianist Roland Hanna's fleet three on "Etude" and rattles along alone under Adams's first on "That's All. —*Fred Bouchard, Downbeat*

Cannonball Adderley (Julian Edwin Adderley)

b. Sep. 15, 1928, Tampa, FL, **d.** Aug. 8, 1975, Gary, IN
Alto sax, bandleader / Hard bop, soul jazz
Few saxophonists combined popularity and artistry better than Cannonball Adderley. A music teacher from Fort Lauderdale, he moved to New York in 1955. Arriving shortly after the death of Charlie Parker, he forged a sound that displayed aspects not only of Bird but also of Benny Carter, Louis Jordan, and Eddie Cleanhead Vinson. Adderley had a full, rounded tone and could play beautiful ballads or swirling, blistering tempos. In later years his band became very popular through his incorporation of blues, R&B, and gospel elements, but Cannonball Adderley was above all a champion of melody and one of the greatest ballad stylists ever. He co-led a band with his brother Nat from 1956 to 1957, then joined Miles Davis from 1957 to 1959, appearing on some of Davis's greatest masterpieces of the era, including *Kind of Blue* and *Milestones*. From 1959 until his death he again co-led groups with his brother. His bands included such distinguished alumni as Yusef Lateef, Charles Lloyd, Sam Jones, Joe Zawinul, and George Duke. The 1967 song "Mercy, Mercy, Mercy" was a sizable pop hit. —*Ron Wynn*

○ **Spontaneous Combustion** / Jul. 14, 1955 / Savoy 70816
These are Cannonball's first recordings. W/ Donald Byrd (tpt), Horace Silver (p), Paul Chambers (b), Kenny Clarke (d), Nat Adderley (cnt), and Jerome Richardson (ts, fl). —*Michael Erlewine*

★ **Somethin' Else** / Mar. 9, 1958 / Blue Note 46338
Shortly after Cannonball Adderley broke up his original quintet and joined Miles Davis's sextet, he recorded this LP with Miles in the rare role of a sideman. Actually Davis dominates several of the selections (including "Autumn Leaves," "Love For Sale," and "One For Daddy-o"), but both hornmen (backed by pianist Hank Jones, bassist Sam Jones, and drummer Art Blakey) sound quite inspired by each other's presence. —*Scott Yanow*

☆ **Portrait of Cannonball** / Jul. 1, 1958 / Riverside 361
This was Cannonball Adderley's debut (7/1/58) on Riverside, and it was a good one, if you like hard open blowing dates. The quintet (Bill Evans, piano; Sam Jones, bass; Philly Joe Jones, drums) included Blue Mitchell, whose Brownielike attack was derivative, but quite a nice contribution, giving balance to the front line, although on the opening themes they did not always appear together. The rhythm section grinds away nicely as a unit, with particularly nice prodding from Jones, though the entire group seemed to have ideas and energy in reserve. —*Bob Rusch, Cadence*

☆ **Things Are Getting Better** / 1958 / Riverside 032
Vibist Milt Jackson turned up in the company as a guest with alto saxophonist Cannonball Adderley on this 10/28/58 date, which was also issued previously as part of a twofer set. The funk blues was the common point here, and *this* would have been the setting for Horace Silver, though pianist Wynton Kelly was an excellent part of the rhythm backup (bassist Percy Heath, drummer Art Blakey). One does not always get what one expects based on packaging; here the ingredients were pure, natural, and preserving. —*Bob Rusch, Cadence*

○ **Cannonball Adderley Quintet in Chicago** / Feb. 3, 1959 / Mercury 20449

☆ **Cannonball Adderley Quintet in San Francisco** / Oct. 18+20, 1959 / Original Jazz Classics 35
Live date with Bobby Timmons (p), Nat Adderley (cnt), Sam Jones (b), and Louis Hayes (d). Contains the classic and soulful "This Here." —*Hank Davis*

○ **Coast to Coast** / Oct. 18, 1959+Jan. 12, 1962 / Milestone 47039
Tracks taken from two popular Adderley albums: *Cannonball Adderley Quintet in San Francsico* and *The Cannonball Adderley Sextet in New York.* —*AMG*

Cannonball Adderley Collection—Vol. 1: Them Dirty Blues / Feb. 1, 1960 / Landmark 1301

Jazz Styles

Ragtime – A piano-based music style that is classically derived and rhythmically bouncy. Main proponents: Scott Joplin, Eubie Blake, Joe Lamb.

New Orleans Traditional – The original jazz style; band music for celebrations and funerals. Tuba and clarinet are prominent. Main proponents: the Dodds Brothers, Louis Armstrong, King Oliver, Preservation Hall Jazz Band(s), Papa Celestin, Sidney Bechet, Jelly Roll Morton, Jimmy Noone, Buddy Bolden.

Dixieland – Riverboat shuffles, emphasizing banjo and brass; uptempo, happy music. Major proponents: Bob Scobey, Al Hirt, Pete Fountain, Dukes of Dixieland, World's Greatest Jazz Band, Bix Beiderbecke.

Harlem Stride – Piano music. More heavily rhythmic than ragtime, and more nimble. Major proponents: Fats Waller, Meade Lux-Lewis, Albert Ammons, James P. Johnson, Willie "The Lion" Smith.

Boogie & Blues Piano – Rollicking, no-holds-barred music, with train rhythms prevalent. Major proponents: Pete Johnson, Jimmy Yancey, Little Brother Montgomery, Roosevelt Sykes, Tuts Washington, Professor Longhair, James Booker, Mr. B.

Swing Era – American popular songs played instrumentally. Musical films of this era were a great promoter for these songs and bands. It was immensely popular concert music as well. Major proponents: Bobby Hackett, Jack Teagarden, the Quintet of The Hot Club of France, Benny Goodman, Lester Young, Coleman Hawkins, Buck Clayton, Art Hodes, Earl Hines.

Big Band Era – Jazz orchestras playing swing-oriented music. Used for dancing primarily; very popular on radio. Major proponents: Artie Shaw, the Dorsey Brothers, Jimmie Lunceford, Fletcher Henderson, Glenn Miller, Duke Ellington, Boyd Raeburn, Erskine Hawkins, Cab Calloway, Billy Eckstine, Count Basie.

Bop – The artistic evolution of swing produced this quick, harmonically intricate, virtuoso music. Bop marked the departure of jazz from mainstream pop music, as many didn't like or understand it, but it was the source of (or at least influence on) all later jazz styles. Major proponents: Thelonious Monk, Dizzy Gillespie, Charlie Parker, Kenny Clarke, Bud Powell, Max Roach, Miles Davis, Fats Navarro, Billy Eckstine, Sonny Stitt.

Hard-Bop – A return to a bluesier, earthier sound than bop, while retaining and evolving its highly virtuosic instrumental styles. Major proponents: Lee Morgan, Art Blakey, Jackie McLean, John Coltrane, Miles Davis, Clifford Brown, Sonny Rollins.

Post-Bop – Less reliance on popular-song forms and more open-ended harmonies brought new possibilities for extended improvisation. Early exploration of world music influences. "Modal Jazz" is also used to describe much of this music. Major proponents: John Coltrane, Donald Byrd, Gigi Gryce, Max Roach, Wayne Shorter, McCoy Tyner, Kenny Dorham.

Cool-Jazz – A reaction to the hyper-kinetics of bop which emphasized a restrained feel, softer colors, and purposefully limited dynamics. Originating in the famous "Birth of the Cool" sessions, it developed as primarily a West Coast phenomenon. Major proponents: Chet Baker, Gerry Mulligan, Miles Davis, Paul Desmond, Stan Getz.

Blues/Jazz – Blues rhythms incorporated into a swinging context. Also the vestiges of rhythm & blues. Major proponents: Louis Jordan, Big Jay McNeeley, Dave Bartholomew, Slim Gaillard, Mose Allison, Jay McShann, Ray Bryant.

Ballads & Blues Vocals – Classic singers interpreting American popular songs and new originals. Major proponents: Lena Horne, Billie Holiday, June Christy, Anita O'Day, Dinah Washington, Joe Williams, Billy Eckstine, Mel Torme, Eddie Jefferson, Sarah Vaughan, Ella Fitzgerald, Sheila Jordan.

Soul Jazz/Original Funk – Blues-based but with modern

W/ Bobby Timmons (p), Nat Adderley (cnt), Barry Harris (p), Sam Jones (b), and Louis Hayes (d). The first studio recording by Cannonball's new quintet. Features two takes of Nat's new tune "Work Song"—a jazz classic. —*Michael Erlewine*

★ **Cannonball Adderley Collection—Vol. 4: The Poll Winners** / May 21, 1960-Jun. 5, 1960 / Landmark 1304
The "Poll Winners" at the time of this recording were altoist Cannonball Adderley, guitarist Wes Montgomery, and bassist Ray Brown; together with Victor Feldman doubling on piano and vibes and drummer Louis Hayes, they cut this excellent quintet date. This was the only meeting on records by Adderley and Wes and, although not quite a classic encounter, the music (highlighted by "The Chant," "Never Will I Marry," and two takes of "Au Privave") swings hard and is quite enjoyable. —*Scott Yanow*

Know What I Mean? / Jan. 27, 1961-Feb. 21, 1961 / Riverside 105
Great album. W/ Bill Evans (p), Percy Heath (b), and Connie Kay (d). Recorded at Bell Sound Studios in NYC. —*Michael Erlewine*

Quintet Plus / May 11, 1961 / Riverside 306
Recorded just after Adderley's group returned from a very successful European tour. The band is tight. The "Plus" is Wynton Kelly (p). Also Victor Feldman (p, vib), Nat Adderley (cnt), Sam Jones (b), Ron Carter (b), and Louis Hayes (d). —*Michael Erlewine*

In New York / Jan. 12+14, 1962 / Riverside 142
Live date at The Village Vanguard in NYC. W/ Nat Adderley (cnt), Yusef Lateef (ts, fl), Joe Zawinul (p), Sam Jones (b), and Louis Hayes (d). —*Michael Erlewine*

○ **Lush Side of Cannonball, The** / i. Mar. 1962 / Mercury 60652

Cannonball Adderley Collection—Vol. 7: Cannonball in Europe / Aug. 4+05, 1962 / Landmark 1307

Live concert at the International Jazz Festival, Comblain-La-Tour, Belgium—over 30,000 people. W/ Nat Adderley (cnt), Yusef Lateef (ts, fl), Joe Zawinul (p), Sam Jones (b), and Louis Hayes (d). —*Michael Erlewine*

○ **Sextet, The** / Sep. 21, 1962-Jul. 19, 1963 / Milestone 9106
Some argue that the early-'60s Cannonball Adderley sextet was his finest group. That point can be argued; what can't be disputed was that Yusef Lateef, on tenor, oboe, and flute, gave the band an instrumental push and urgency that its more popular soul-jazz material never matched. Both Cannonball and Nat Adderley were often pushed to the limit, and that competitive spirit extended to the rhythm section as well. —*Ron Wynn, AMG*

Cannonball Adderley Collection—Vol. 3: Jazz Workshop Revisited / Sep. 21, 1962 / Landmark 1303
Return to San Francisco for the second live "Lighthouse" recording with Cannonball's (now-seasoned) sextet. This album reached #11 on the charts! W/ Nat Adderley (cnt), Yusef Lateef (ts, fl), Joe Zawinul (p), Sam Jones (b), and Louis Hayes (d). —*Michael Erlewine*

○ **Best of the Capitol Years** / 1962-1969 / Curb 77399
Contains "Mercy, Mercy, Mercy" and Adderley's most successful jazz/gospel/pop fusion work with Joe Zawinul (k). —*Hank Davis*

★ **Mercy, Mercy, Mercy! Live at 'the Club'** / Jul. 1966 / EMI 5007
Quintet. This is a great live performance with Nat Adderley (cnt), Victor Gaskin (b), Roy McCurdy (d), and Joe Zawinul (p) at the Club in Chicago. "Mercy, Mercy, Mercy" was a pop hit. —*Michael Erlewine*

☆ **Black Messiah** / 1970 / Capitol 846
This is an outstanding two-record set from 1970 that found Cannonball Adderley playing explosive, bluesy alto and soprano

harmonies, usually with a back beat. Strong Gospel influence. Organ and guitars are prevalent. Major proponents: Horace Silver, Jimmy Smith, Ramsey Lewis, Lee Morgan, Jack McDuff, Jimmy McGriff, Grant Green, the Adderley Brothers, Lou Donaldson, Hank Crawford, Stanley Turrentine, Shirley Scott.

Early Free Jazz – The original improvisers who changed the face of jazz in the late 50s to late 60s, doing away with fixed harmonic and rhythmic structures in lieu of spontaneous feelings. Major proponents: Ornette Coleman, Cecil Taylor, Archie Shepp, Bill Dixon, Sam Rivers, John Coltrane, Don Cherry, Pharoah Sanders, the A.A.C.M., Bobby Bradford, John Carter, Albert Ayler, Sonny Sharrock, the Art Ensemble of Chicago.

Progressive Big Band – This is music for listening, with denser, more modernistic arrangements than the earlier, more dance-oriented big-band styles, and more room to improvise. Major proponents: Gil Evans, Stan Kenton, Toshiko Akiyoshi, Cal Massey, Frank Foster, Carla Bley, George Gruntz, David Amram, Sun Ra, Duke Ellington.

Latin-Jazz – Latin rhythms melded to jazz melodies, with heavy emphasis on hot beats, horn charts, and choral lyrics in Spanish. Major proponents: Dizzy Gillespie, Machito, Chano Pozo, Tito Rodriguez, Noro Moralez, Tito Puente, Ray Barretto, Mario Bauza, Eddie Palmieri, Poncho Sanchez, Cal Tjader, Mongo Santamaria.

Early Jazz/Rock Fusion – A melding of rock rhythms with jazz solo techniques, prevalent in 1968-1974. Major proponents: Miles Davis, Larry Coryell, John McLaughlin, Herbie Hancock ("Mwandishi"), Chick Corea (Return to Forever), Passport, Frank Zappa, Weather Report, Santana, Brand X, Bill Bruford, Gong, National Health, Jean-Luc Ponty.

World Fusion – Combining a wide variety of world music rhythms and melodies into improvisation-based instrumental music. Major proponents: John McLaughlin ("Shakti"), Oregon, Airto, Flora Purim, Don Cherry, David Amram, Ronald Shannon Jackson, M'Boom, Abdullah Ibrahim.

New-Age – Atmospheric, cerebral, spiritual, and earthy music used for meditation, relaxation. Major proponents: Windham Hill artists, George Winston, Andreas Vollenweider, Eno, Tangerine Dream, Paul Winter, Suzanne Ciani, Terry Riley.

Instrumental Pop – Commercial music with minimal improvisation or creative risks. Generic, short in duration, simple themes. Major proponents: Herb Alpert, Chuck Mangione, Kenny G, Acker Bilk, Boots Randolph, George Benson.

Neo-Bop – A new generation of young players taking bop and other influences and creating traditional acoustic jazz. Sidestepping rock/fusion/electric influences, they are diligent students of earlier styles, often with spectacular results.They may not all be innovators, but often try to stretch the parameters. Major proponents: Wynton Marsalis, Kenny Garrett, Bob Berg, Terrence Blanchard, Brian Lynch, Courtney Pine, Roy Hargrove, Benny Green.

Contemporary Funk – Dance-oriented 4/4 music, slow or mid-tempo. No swing, little blues. Major proponents: Grover Washington Jr, David Sanborn, Joe Sample and the Crusaders, Bob James, George Howard, Gerald Albright.

M-Base/Avant Fusion – Combining some creative music precepts with funky dance rhythms. Major proponents: Steve Coleman, Greg Osby, Charnett Moffitt, Jamaaladeen Tacuma, Geri Allen.

Modern Creative – Continuing the tradition of the 50s-to-60s Free-jazz mode. Musicians may incorporate free playing into structured modes, or play ... well, anything. Major proponents: John Zorn, Henry Kaiser, Eugene Chadbourne, Tim Berne, Bill Frisell, Steve Lacy, Cecil Taylor, Ornette Coleman, Ray Anderson.

– Michael G. Nastos

---

sax, heading a band that included his brother Nat on cornet, pianist George Duke doing some of his most intense and energetic jazz-based soloing, and bassist Walter Booker and drummer Roy McCurdy. Special guests included guitarist Mike Deasey and on one number New Orleans clarinetist Harold Batiste. Airto Moreira added sympathetic percussion, and the group's extended numbers included "Dr. Honouris Causa," "The Chocolate Nuisance," and the title cut. There was also plenty of Cannonball Adderley's witty asides and excellent support from the rhythm section and Nat Adderley's blistering cornet solos. Cannonball Adderley had some of his hottest recorded soprano sax improvisations and his customary biting and bluesy alto solos. –*Ron Wynn*

Nat Adderley (Nathaniel Adderley)

b. Nov. 25, 1931, Tampa, FL
Cornet / Hard bop, soul jazz
Nat is the brother of Julian "Cannonball" Adderley. He was a trumpeter before switching to cornet. He had some success playing with Lionel Hampton prior to joining Cannonball for a short stint in the '50s, then rejoined Adderley in 1959 after periods with Woody Herman and J. J. Johnson. From 1959 to 1975, when Cannonball died, the Adderleys were the dominant soul-jazz group, making records with popular appeal that retained a jazz/improvisational base and integrity. Nat Adderley has led various bands since the mid '70s.–*Ron Wynn*

● **Work Song** / Jan. 25+27, 1960 / Riverside 363
Guitarist Wes Montgomery was also aboard for *Work Song,* a Nat Adderley date with Bobby Timmons (piano), Louis Hayes (drums), Sam Jones, and Ketter Betts or Percy Heath (cello, bass). This was, of course, Nat Adderley's date, and Montgomery's role

was not so much that of guitarist extraordinaire as of one of the plucked strings that give this date its particular ambience...A thoughtful and varied date with a multidimensional personality, this has been previously issued as part of a twofer. –*Bob Rusch, Cadence*

★ **Little New York Midtown Music,** A / Sep. 18-19, 1978 / Galaxy
Cornetist Nat Adderley is a fine jazzman who has gotten better as the years roll on, but on this date he was pretty well upstaged by the solo work of tenor saxophonist Johnny Griffin, pianist Victor Feldman, and bassist Ron Carter...Just listening to the recording without a view of the leader's name on the album cover would lead one to think this was Griffin's date. –*Shirley Klett, Cadence*

Air

b. 1975, **d.** 1986
Modern creative
This fine trio formed in Chicago during the early '70s. The group consisted of multisaxophonist Henry Threadgill, bassist Fred Hopkins, and percussionist Steve McCall. They became skilled at blending spontaneous creation, theatrical flair, and a gritty blues underpinning during their years as members of the Association for the Advancement of Creative Musicians (AACM). The trio moved to New York in 1975 and made a stunning debut album in 1977. They continued until McCall left in 1983 and made other good albums as New Air from 1983 to 1986. Threadgill currently heads his own groups and often works with Hopkins. McCall died several years ago. –*Ron Wynn*

☆ **Teilweise Kacke.. Aber Stereo** / i. 1973 / Eigenbau 12

○ **Air Song** / Sep. 10, 1975 / India Navigation 1057

Originally released on Why Not (Japan) Records, this Air excursion was one of their strongest vinyl documents, if not the strongest. —*Milo Fine, Cadence*

○ **Live Air** / Jul. 1, 1976 / Black Saint 0034
This was vintage Air, recorded in 1977 less than a month before *Air Time*, their initial U.S. release. Side one was mainly Henry Threadgill's flute, beginning with a dramatic, elegiac piece dedicated to the late AACM bassist Charles Clark. Threadgill spun out angular oriental lines, and the overall image was of a wind-blown bluff; the wind itself was bassist Fred Hopkins hovering just behind with tense, delicate vibrato blowing, while drummer Steve McCall touched down here and there like the occasional shaft of sunlight glancing off the rocks. —*Brent Staples, Downbeat*

★ **Air Time** / Nov. 17-18, 1977 / Nessa 12
Air's roots were in the controlled instrumental extremes, with their earnest intellectual tastes showing through in their esoteric explorations of the Great Black Music avant-garde. Tension in the three extended Henry Threadgill pieces arose from detailed textural and dynamic juxtapositions and was sometimes resolved as mysteriously as clouds dispersed. Drummer Steve McCall's opening ballad and bassist Fred Hopkins's folkish, warm, sonorous vamp ("G.v.E."), the shorter tracks, were flawlessly structured. —*Howie Mandel, Downbeat*

○ **Open Air Suite** / Feb. 21-22, 1978 / Novus 3002
(Air) was not your typical soloist with accompaniment trio—the rhythm section was equal to the horn in the creation of cooperative sound sculptures. Reedman-composer Henry Threadgill's writing was full of elliptical twists and turns, eerie empty spaces, surprising stop-and-go interplay, and wide vocalized intervallic leaps. His flute playing was glassy and, well, airy, while his saxophones were glassy and guttural...Bassist Fred Hopkins had a resilient time feel and a big woody tone. Drummer Steve McCall was a master of dynamics and tuning. He was able to maintain group continuity even as he kept turning the beat around with surging authority; he was playing pulse, not time. —*Chip Stern, Downbeat*

★ **Air Lore** / May 11-12, 1979 / Bluebird 6578
Three of the compositions here dated from the first decade; Scott Joplin's "Weeping Willow Rag" (1903) and "Ragtime Dance" (1906) and Jelly Roll Morton's "King Porter Stomp" (1905). Air did not re-create these works but reacted to them in light of 80 years of jazz "lore." What resulted was a carefully conceived and flawlessly executed set of chamber pieces. Air didn't mess with the original tunes. Consequently, much of this music was outrageously tonal; its rhythms hopelessy regular, its harmonies shockingly simple. Yet it came as no surprise that the music never sounded dated. —*Douglas Clark, Downbeat*

○ **Air Mail** / Dec. 28, 1980 / Black Saint 0049
The Chicago trio Air was at a high point on this 1980 date, thanks in part to remarkable percussive foundations provided by the late Steve McCall and his interaction with bassist Fred Hopkins, plus the amazing solos and versatility of nominal leader Henry Threadgill. Besides alto and tenor sax, flute and bass flute, Threadgill plays his own unique instrument called the hubkaphone and makes it just as memorable a weapon as the other horns. —*Ron Wynn, AMG*

○ **80 Degrees Below '82** / Jan. 23-24, 1982 / Island 1007
Air moved to Antilles for the release of their ninth LP; it was one of the group's more straightahead records. The four selections were highly structured variations on blues themes and rarely ventured off into freer spaces. There was more emphasis on individual solos than on group improvisation. *80 Degrees Below 82* may seem a bit conservative to some listeners, but they will undoubtedly appreciate the good musicianship. —*Richard Kamins, Cadence*

○ **Air Show No. 1** / i. Jul. 1987 / Black Saint 0099
Air Show No. 1 was the second album by *New* Air; drummer Steve McCall had been replaced by Pheeroan AkLaff. Fred Hopkins's bass was the dominant force on this album, reverberating majestically throughout every minute of the music. —*Krin Gabbard, Cadence*

Toshiko Akiyoshi

b. Dec. 12, 1929, Dairen, China

Piano, composer, bandleader / Big band, bop, progressive big band
Toshiko Akiyoshi is a Japanese-born, Bud Powell-influenced jazz pianist. Akiyoshi's a progressive-minded composer and arranger, mostly in a big band format, but she also works with a trio. She's used her heritage to create expansive, orchestral voicings, and is a most influential presence for modern jazz in the '70s and '80s. —*Michael G. Nastos*

★ **Long Yellow Road** / Apr. 4, 1974-Mar. 4, 1975 / RCA 1350
Toshiko Akiyoshi's approach, like Duke Ellington's, was to write solo and ensemble parts tailored to each band member's individual strengths. Her woodwind voicings were especially effective. On "Quadrille, Anyone?," for example, the rich baritone sax intro of Bill Perkins ended with a dramatic upward line that was taken to its lofty summit by Lew Tabackin's piccolo. After the full band roared, excellent solo voyages were taken by Gary Foster on soprano and Tabackin on tenor...The most outstanding of the band's many strengths included Lew Tabackin's eclectic, electric soloing on tenor and flute (Tabackin was simply incredible!); Akiyoshi's exotic, kaleidoscopic colors and textures; the band's spirited ensemble work; and the fine improvisations of such gifted players as Gary Foster, Bobby Shew, and Bill Perkins. —*Chuck Berg, Downbeat*

○ **Tales of a Courtesan** / Dec. 1-03, 1975 / RCA 10723
Tales of a Courtesan was the second Toshiko Akiyoshi-Lew Tabackin big band album under the RCA banner, and it was every bit as good as its predecessor *Long Yellow Road*. —*Bill Gallagher, Cadence*

○ **Road Time** / Jan. 30, 1976-Feb. 8, 1976 / RCA 2242
Toshiko Akiyoshi juggled her big band forms and capable soloists brilliantly on this two-LP set, recorded during the band's early '76 Japanese tour following the surprise success of their first album, *Kogun*. Coleader and then-husband Lew Tabackin shared the blowing space with a brace of contrasting altoists, a competitive brass section, and thoughtful slide specialists. But it was the particular achievement of Akiyoshi, who cracked the all-male echelon of composing bandleaders, that made this assemblage sound like no other. —*Howie Mandel, Downbeat*

★ **Finesse** / May 8, 1978 / Concord Jazz 4069

○ **Carnegie Hall Concert** / i. Sep. 17, 1992 / Columbia 48805

Joe Albany (Joseph Albani)

b. Jan. 24, 1924, Atlantic City, NJ, d. Jan. 11, 1988, New York, NY
Piano / Bop
Pianist Joe Albany is a solid bop soloist and accompanist with a fine blues sensibility. He was a prolific player in the prebop era, then made the transition despite a strong personality that led to creative differences with many players (notably Charlie Parker). Albany continued playing from the '50s through the '80s, doing a variety of things from backing singers to trios and solo dates. —*Ron Wynn*

★ **Right Combination** / Sep. 1957 / Riverside 1749
The only early documentation of the swinging bebop pianist. Features Warne Marsh (ts). —*David Szatmary*

Gerald Albright

Vocals, sax / Instrumental pop
A fusion and pop-jazz saxophonist, Albright is among the most popular artists on Atlantic's current roster. His 1991 live album, recorded at Birdland West, demonstrates his improvisational skills and ability to play mainstream jazz in an effective fashion. His other releases have been primarily instrumental pop, though he's a gifted soloist even in a restrictive format.—*Ron Wynn*

○ **Dream Come True** / Nov. 6, 1990 / Atlantic 82087
Albright, among the most popular instrumental pop-fusion saxophonists around, plays both high octane uptempo tunes and slick covers of urban contemporary hits. It's well produced, with a minimum of improvisational content, but should attract those who like lite jazz. —*Ron Wynn, AMG*

★ **Live at Birdland West** / 1991 / Atlantic 82334
Saxophonist Gerald Albright seems and sounds fearless on this issue of half standards and half originals, with bonus points for assembling a fine coterie of sidemen. —*Patricia Myers, Jazz Times*

Howard Alden

b. 1958, Newport Beach, CA
Guitar / Swing
Among the best swing-influenced small combos of the '80s, the Howard Alden Trio was anchored by this guitarist, one of a group of young '70s and '80s players whose muse wasn't bop but swing. His first date was a 1989 Howard Alden Trio effort on Concord with Lynn Seaton and the late Mel Lewis. Alden's own prominent career on Concord has included recordings with quartets and strings. He has also co-led the Howard Alden-Dan Barrett (tb) Quintet. —*Ron Wynn*

○ **Howard Alden Trio Plus Special Guests Ken Peplowski & Warren Vache** / Jan. 1989 / Concord Jazz 4378
Guitarist Howard Alden showed not only taste but also wide knowledge of the traditions in his selection of two seldom-heard Duke Ellington tunes ("Gazelle" and "Your Love"), a pair of Django Reinhardt gems ("Douce" and "Tears"), pieces by Charlie Parker such as "Back Home," Thelonious Monk's "Reflections," and Fats Waller's "Keep A Song"—all tunes that were not from the obvious top of the jazz stockpile. In its sources of inspiration, Alden's playing was as eclectic as his choice of material, nicely unified in its style, which, for lack of a better term, could be described as modern mainstream with swing era tributaries and bop outlets. —*Doug Ramsey, Jazz Times*

★ **Thirteen Strings** / Feb. 1991 / Concord Jazz 4464
W/ George Van Eps. Alden's six-string and Van Eps's seven-string make the 13. Long overdue for George Van Eps. Excellent. —*Michael G. Nastos*

Monty Alexander (Montgomery Bernard)

b. Jun. 6, 1944, Kingston, Jamaica
Piano / Bop, world fusion
A capable pianist, one of a group from the Caribbean who utilized their background and interspersed it through a jazz focus. Alexander came to Florida in 1962, then went to New York eight years later. He's been a prolific contributor throughout the '70s, '80s, and '90s, though his best albums are solos or trios. —*Ron Wynn*

☆ **Triple Treat I** / Mar. 1982 / Concord Jazz 4193
This particular trio worked together before and were well integrated (guitarist Herb Ellis and bassist Ray Brown, of course, had long experience with pianist Oscar Peterson)...Just straightahead middle-of-the-road jazz, very professionally played with a nice "Body and Soul," a good "Triple Treat Blues" on which Ray Brown stood out, and a "But Not For Me" in which Alexander was not up to the remainder of the session but in which Herb Ellis was especially good. —*Shirley Klett, Cadence*

Duke Ellington Songbook / Mar. 29, 1983 / Verve 821151

★ **River, The** / Oct. 1985 / Concord Jazz 4422
Monty Alexander added three appropriate compositions of his own to this wide- ranging and sympathetic program of music from the church. —*Shirley Klett, Cadence*

☆ **Triple Treat II** / Jun. 1987 / Concord Jazz 4338

☆ **Triple Treat III** / Jun. 1987 / Concord Jazz 4394
While the menu of well-worn show tunes, standards, and an occasional Alexander original isn't overwhelming, the participants' taste and artistry elevate things beyond the realm of another good date among old friends. —*Ron Wynn, Rock & Roll Disc.*

Rashied Ali (Robert Patterson)

b. Jul. 1, 1935, Philadelphia, PA
Drums / Early free, modern creative
Drummer and percussionist Rashied Ali emerged in the '60s as a premier player and figure among drummers when he joined, then eventually supplanted, Elvin Jones in the John Coltrane group. Ali's mother sang with the Jimmie Lunceford orchestra, and his initial experiences were with R&B bands in Philadelphia. Following a 1963 visit to Japan with the Sonny Rollins group, Ali moved to New York and became a prolific contributor to the evolving free-experimental movement. He worked with Pharoah Sanders, Don Cherry, Paul Bley, Bill Dixon, Archie Shepp, Marion Brown, and Sun Ra. When Coltrane decided he wanted a second drummer and a looser rhythmic setting, he contacted Ali in 1965. Ali eventually became the principal percussionist after Jones departed. He worked for a time with Alice Coltrane after her hus-

band's death in '67, then began heading his own bands. During the '70s, Ali participated in assisting musicians' efforts to improve their economic situation. He helped organize the New York Musicians Festival in the summer of 1972, formed Survival Records in 1973, and opened his own club, Ali's Alley, operating it until 1979. He has been less visible in the '80s and '90s. —*Ron Wynn*

● **Rashied Ali Quintet** / 1973 / Survival 102
These were more titles from the gig at the Loa in Santa Monica and...even better than the first. On that one (*Triple Threat II*), I felt that the trio itself was in exceptional form, but that violinist John Frigo (a member, like guitarist Herb Ellis, of the Soft Winds group of some years ago) was deficient in jazz chops...Frigo sounded more with it on the selections on this LP than on the earlier one. Frigo came close to making the violin swing and contributed some good improvisations to this CD. This was an excellent issue with Concord's usual good production and liners. —*Shirley Klett, Cadence*

Geri Allen

b. Jun. 12, 1957, Pontiac, MI, raised in Detroit.
Piano, composer / M-base, modern creative
Pianist and composer Geri Allen has been one of the prime stars of the '80s and '90s. She's been a major participant in Steve Coleman's controversial M-base movement in Brooklyn. She emerged in the free, mainstream, hard bop, and R&B-funk arena in the early '80s as a sparkling soloist whose style was eclectic, yet compelling. She's played with Paul Motian, Charlie Haden, and Coleman, and led her own groups, recording mainly on JMT and Blue Note. She is a player to watch in the '90s, as a composer-player and bandleader. —*Ron Wynn*

☆ **Printmakers, The** / Feb. 8-09, 1984 / Minor Music 001
For her debut disc, released on a new label from Germany—Minor Music—pianist Geri Allen chose two excellent sidemen in bassist Anthony Cox and percussionist Andrew Cyrille. Chances are the listener will first be grabbed by Cox's melodic phrasing and rock-solid attention to the rhythm or by Cyrille's brilliant flair...Cox and Cyrille provided most of the sparks, but Allen did a decent job. This was an interesting debut. —*Richard B. Kamins, Cadence*

★ **Open on All Sides in the Middle** / Dec. 1986 / PolyGram 850013
Pianist Geri Allen focuses on her rock-funk-pop heritage on her third LP...Fronting the band half the time was Shahita Nurallah, whose voice was high and clear and light—so light it seemed almost disembodied, in the high soprano range where Allen placed her. Hypnotic Latin-derived (but not textbook) rhythms drove several of these pieces; Allen pounded out attractive if static syncopated patterns. —*Kevin Whitehead, Cadence*

○ **In the Year of the Dragon** / Mar. 1989 / PolyGram 834428
Throughout *In the Year of the Dragon*, whether the music was classic bop or very free, this trio was creative, colorful, and right on the mark. The musical communication between these three musicians seemed telepathic; each of them obviously possessed large ears. —*Scott Yanow, Cadence*

☆ **Twylight** / 1989 / Verve 841152
Twylight, which looks from its cover as if it could be a reggae session, was actually a strong example of her originality. The opener, "When Kabuya Dances," was the longest (8:42) and most memorable selection of this date. Starting off as a new age-type ballad, this performance (which could easily serve as background music for a creative dancer) gradually became freer and its repetitions more intense, until it approached the fury of a Cecil Taylor before working its way back to its new age beginnings. —*Scott Yanow, Cadence*

○ **Nurturer, The** / Jan. 5-06, 1990 / Capitol 95139

☆ **Segments** / i. 1990 / DIW 833

○ **Maroons** / i. 1992 / Capitol 99493
On "Mad Money," one of pianist Geri Allen's 13 original compositions on *Maroons*, don't even bother keeping track of the beat. Just lie back and listen to her sail by with trumpeter Wallace Roney...She revels in off-kilter meters and the harmonic intricacies of "Dolphy's Dance." On "Laila's House," abrupt time changes just click into place...Allen's compositional chops are in order, too...Repeated patterns anchor her compositions even when they veer into abstraction...Trumpeter Marcus Belgrave, her mentor

from Detroit days, sounds especially attuned to her. He weaves and she bobs in perfect choreography on Lawrence Williams's "Number Four." —*Elaine Guregian, Downbeat*

☆ **Live at the Village Vanguard** / DIW 847

☆ **Etudes—Geri Allen-Haden-Motian** / Soul Note

Henry Allen (Henry James Allen, Jr.)

b. Jan. 7, 1908, New Orleans, LA, d. Apr. 17, 1967, New York, NY
Trumpet / New Orleans traditional
The son of the leader of the Allen Brass Band of Algiers, LA, "Red" Allen is often characterized as a "swing" trumpeter in the Armstrong mode. He initally played with his father's band, and worked with several other New Orleans brass bands before joining King Oliver's Dixie Syncopators in St. Louis in 1927. He built a reputation as a featured soloist, gradually becoming one of the most influential big band trumpeters. Allen played with the Luis Russell band in 1937 (which was then backing Louis Armstrong), and made recordings with Jelly Roll Morton and Sidney Bechet after 1940. He gravitated once again toward the mainstream after 1943, forming bands that included such sidemen as Coleman Hawkins, Buster Bailey, and Pee Wee Russell. Red Allen's stylistic proficiency tended to lead to comparisons with Louis Armstrong, and like Armstrong, he adapted his playing to suit the particular bands and periods in which he participated. True to his New Orleans roots, he liked to keep his audiences guessing, wondering what he might play next. As a soloist and singer, Allen was a consummate entertainer who knew how to have fun with his music and how to communicate that spirit to the audience. —*Bruce Boyd Raeburn*

● **Henry Allen Collection—Vol. 1 (1929-1930), The** / 1929-1930 / JSP 332

○ **Henry Allen Collection—Vol. 2 (1929-1930), The** / 1929-1930 / JSP 333

★ **World on a String** / Mar. 21, 1957-Apr. 10, 1957 / Bluebird 2497
Red Allen with J. C. Higginbotham (tb), Coleman Hawkins (sax), Buster Bailey (cl), and others—a collaboration that shines on "I Cover the Waterfront," tickles on "Ride, Red, Ride." —*Bruce Raeburn*

○ **Henry Red Allen Meets Kid Ory** / i. 1960 / Verve 6076

○ **Red Allen Plays King Oliver** / Nov. 1960 / Verve 1025

○ **Mr. Allen** / Jun. 5, 1962 / Swingville 2034

Mose Allison (Mose John Allison, Jr.)

b. Nov. 11, 1927, Tippo, Mississippi
Piano, vocals, composer, trumpet / Cool, blues & jazz
Among the most understated yet distinctive pianists and vocalists in either jazz or blues, Mose Allison combines wry humor, exceptional timing, and a marvelous vocal approach. He's fused the rhythmic intensity of an improvising singer with the storytelling acumen of a country blues artist. Allison honed his skills playing around the South after leaving Louisiana State University in the '50s, then moved to New York in 1956. He worked with Stan Getz, Gerry Mulligan, Al Cohn, and Zoot Sims, then formed his own trios and played both in New York and overseas in Paris, Stockholm, and Copenhagen. Through the '60s, '70s, '80s, and '90s, he has toured frequently, playing either with his own groups or pickup bands at various stops. A list of his great songs includes "Hello There, Universe," "I Don't Worry about a Thing," and "Parchman Farm." —*Ron Wynn*

○ **Seventh Son, The** / Mar. 7, 1957-Feb. 13, 1959 / Prestige 3003
This is a compilation of cuts from Allison's albums from 1957 to 1959: *Back Country Suite, Local Color, Young Man Mose, Ramblin' with Mose, Creek Bank,* and *Autumn Song.* —*AMG*

○ **Greatest Hits** / Nov. 8, 1957-Feb. 13, 1959 / Prestige 6004

Autumn Song / Feb. 13, 1959 / Prestige 7189
Fine trio outing with the witty, always engaging Mose Allison in good vocal form and also adding sparkling piano accompaniment and solos. He's backed by Addison Farmer (Art's brother) on bass and Ronnie Free on drums. Set includes early version of signature song "Eyesight to the Blind." —*Ron Wynn, AMG*

Creek Bank / Aug. 15, 1959 / Prestige 24055
Similar themes, performance levels, and musical lineup as for *Autumn Song.* The tunes were recorded a few months before and include more definitive Allison, including his brillant "Seventh

Son" and dazzling version of "Yardbird Suite." This has been reissued on CD. —*Ron Wynn*

★ **I Love the Life I Live** / Jun. 28, 1960-Sep. 9, 1960 / Columbia 8367

○ **I Don't Worry about a Thing** / Mar. 15, 1962 / Atlantic 1389

○ **Best of Mose Allison** / i. 1962-1982 / Atlantic 1542

★ **Western Man** / Feb. 2, 1971-Mar. 4, 1971 / Atlantic 1584

○ **Your Mind Is on Vacation** / Apr. 5-09, 1976 / Atlantic 1691

○ **Middle Class White Boy** / Feb. 2-03, 1982 / Elektra 52391

○ **Allison Wonderland: Anthology** / i. 1994 / Rhino
Only Dave Frishberg and possibly Mark Murphy can rival Mose Allison when it comes to creative use of irony in lyric writing, and neither compares as an instrumentalist. He's a fine bop pianist able to play challenging instrumentals and eclectic enough to integrate country blues and gospel elements into his style. Allison's unique mix of down-home and uptown styles has made him a standout since the '50s. He's one of the few jazz musicians on Atlantic's roster ideally suited for the two-disc anthology format. Allison recorded so many different kinds of songs and was always as much, if not more, a singles than an album artist. In addition, Rhino thankfully sequenced titles chronologically. Allison does reflective duo and trio pieces, moves into uptempo combo numbers with a jump beat, then returns to the intimate small group sound. His ability to highlight key lyrics, delivery, timing, and pacing is superb. The set includes such classics as "Back Country Blues," "Parchman Farm," "Western Man," and "Ever Since the World Ended," plus definitive covers of Willie Dixon's "The Seventh Son" and Rice Miller's (Sonny Boy Williamson II) "Eyesight to the Blind." Hopefully, Rhino will issue Allison's entire Atlantic catalog; meanwhile, here's an essential beginning. —*Ron Wynn*

Laurindo Almeida

b. Sep. 2, 1917, Sao Paulo, Brazil
Acoustic guitar, composer / Latin jazz, world fusion
Acoustic guitarist and composer Laurindo Almeida is another Brazilian instrumentalist who migrated to America and became a significant figure on the U.S. jazz scene. He arrived in America in 1947. After a stint with Stan Kenton he formed his own trio. He has frequently played with Bud Shank and recorded with West Coast players. Almeida's made successful Latin-jazz and classical albums, and won a Grammy award. He was among the most prolific players during the '60s bossa nova craze. *See* the L.A. Four. —*Ron Wynn*

● **Brazilliance—Vols. 1 & 2** / Apr. 15-22, 1953 / World Pacific 96339
W/ Bud Shank (as, fl) on both albums. W/ Gary Peacock (b) and Chuck Flores (d) on the second album. It is almost possible to hear the birth of the bossa nova in these albums. —*Michael Erlewine*

○ **Delightfully Modern** / i. 1957 / Jazztone 1264

○ **Broadway Solo Guitar** / i. Jun. 1964 / Capitol 2063

○ **Tango: Laurindo Almeida and Charlie Byrd** / Aug. 1985 / Concord Jazz 4290

Barry Altschul

b. Jan. 6, 1943, New York
drums / World fusion, modern creative
Barry Altschul has been among the better percussionists and drummers in both free and mainstream circles since the '60s, when he was a member of the Jazz Composers Guild. Altschul began playing drums at 11 and later studied with Charlie Persip. He went to Europe in 1968, where he worked with Carmell Jones, Leo Wright, and Johnny Griffin before returning to America in 1969. Altschul was a member of the premier group Circle, with pianist Chick Corea, bassist Dave Holland, and multisaxophonist Anthony Braxton from 1970 to 1972. Since then he's frequently played with Braxton and other free and avant-garde musicians, such as saxophonist Sam Rivers, as well as heading his own band and working with more conventional jazz musicians, such as Art Pepper. His extensive experience in free circles notwithstanding, Altschul has the facility, skill, and rhythmic dexterity to excel in any situation. He's studied African, Indian, Afro-Latin, and

Caribbean music and integrated elements of these styles into his music. —*Ron Wynn*

★ **You Can't Name Your Own Tune** / Feb. 8-09, 1977 / Muse 5124
Barry Altschul's *You Can't Name Your Own Tune* jumped right out and grabbed you with its authoritative swing and probing free horn lyricism. Altschul has a unique sound. His setup is a throwback to 1930s big band drummers (via Harry Partch), combining the best aspects of an incidental percussionist and a small group drummer. On his first outing as a leader, Altschul's musical collaborators were all leaders and virtuosic innovators of the first rank...The improvising on this session was emotional and cohesive, and Altschul's compositions reflected a most cheerful disposition. —*Chip Stern, Downbeat*

Franco Ambrosetti

b. Dec. 10, 1941, Lugano, Switzerland, **d.** 1990
Trumpet, flugelhorn, composer / World fusion
Trumpeter, flugelhorn player, and composer Franco Ambrosetti is a good brass player from Switzerland. A onetime classical pianist, Ambrosetti switched to trumpet in the early '60s and taught himself the instrument's rudiments. A fiery, well-regarded soloist, he has led groups with both European and American players and also worked with George Gruntz and Daniel Humair in the George Gruntz Concert Jazz Band since the early '70s. Appearances at various festivals, plus occasional recordings, keep his profile visible to U.S. jazz critics and fans. —*Ron Wynn*

★ **Movies Too** / Mar. 22-23, 1988 / Enja 79616
Brilliant playing from Swiss-born trumpet/flugelhorn player. W/ Geri Allen (p) and all-star cast. "Superman," "Angel Eyes," "Peter Gunn." —*Michael G. Nastos*

○ **Music for Symphony & Jazz Band** / 1990 / Enja 79670
Involved, often sprawling work that seeks to link symphonic, improvisational traditions, plus work in guest stars and a national radio orchestra. Things do hold together, and alto saxophonist Greg Osby adds some torrid licks when he gets space. —*Ron Wynn, AMG*

Albert Ammons (Albert C. Ammons)

b. Sep. 23, 1907, Chicago, **d.** Dec. 2, 1949, Chicago, IL
piano / Boogie-woogie
A founding father of boogie-woogie, Albert Ammons was a remarkable soloist and driving, galvanizing performer. He started playing at the age of ten and became a national figure when the boogie-woogie rage dominated the country in the late '30s. Ammons worked in Chicago clubs during the '20s, then played with territory bands and orchestras in the early '30s, before heading his own group in Chicago from 1934 to 1938. He made some incredible records for Decca in 1936 with trumpeter Guy Kelly and bassist Israel Crosby among others. Ammons moved to New York for a Carnegie Hall concert in 1939, then made regular appearances at Cafe Society, sometimes with Pete Johnson, and other times in a trio with Meade "Lux" Lewis. He continued performing and recording into the '40s, making his final records with Mercury in 1949. —*Ron Wynn*

★ **Complete Blue Note Albert Ammons** / Jan. 6, 1939 / Mosaic
This is everything you thought you knew about the Albert Ammons-Meade Lux Lewis Blue Note recordings plus eight previously unissued sides. This was a three-record set, on which producers Mike Cuscuna and Charlie Lourie had a limited run of 5,000 copies...Ammons played his music, poised with excitement, but paced by a rich blues as swampy as it was concrete, while Lux Lewis, with frumpy deliberativeness, was pounding out poetry on the piano. —*Bob Rusch, Cadence*

○ **First Day** / 1939 / Blue Note 98450

○ **King of Boogie Woogie (1939-1949)** / **i.** 1939-1949 / Blues Classics 27
Classic early-'30s, '40s boogie-woogie from a giant in the genre. Albert Ammons began emulating the style of Pinetop Smith, then gradually developed his own voice to the point where he was a master player. These cuts include both solos and duets between Ammons and Meade Lux Lewis and are seminal cuts. —*Ron Wynn, AMG*

○ **Boogie Piano Stylings** / **i.** 1950 / Mercury 25012
○ **Boogie Woogie Classics** / **i.** 1951 / Blue Note 7017
○ **8 to the Bar** / **i.** 195? / RCA 9

○ **Master of Boogie** / Milan 35628
○ **Giants of Boogie Woogie** / Wolf 10
○ **Boogie Woogie Trio—Vol. 3** / Storyville 4006
Albert Ammons, Meade Lux Lewis (p), and Pete Johnson (p). Not a trio, but separate cuts (one duo) from 1939-1949. —*Michael Erlewine*

Gene Ammons (Eugene Ammons)

b. Apr. 14, 1925, Chicago, IL, **d.** Aug. 6, 1974, Chicago, IL
Tenor sax, bandleader / Bop, soul jazz
The son of boogie-woogie pianist Albert Ammons, Gene Ammons came to prominence as a teenage tenor saxophonist with Billy Eckstine's big band (1944-1946), and later with Woody Herman (1949). He led his own combos from 1947 to 1955 featuring Sonny Stitt as coleader (1950-1952), and his recordings for Mercury (1947-1949) included the big hit "My Foolish Heart." Ammons began recording with Prestige in 1950 and (except for 1952-1953) continued with this label until his death in 1974. Highlights include tenor battles with Stitt ("Blues Up And Down") and small combo singles to 1955; hi-fi jam sessions and album contests (1955-1958); and small group dates with occasional guests (1960-1962). Later recordings (1969-1974) resumed after a lengthy prison sentence for narcotics violations and involve a whole spectrum of settings.
Always a popular jazz artist, Ammons recorded dozens of albums. His most creative period was the early '60s, when almost anything he recorded is worth hearing. There have been album collections of his complete Mercury output, complete Chess recordings, and a whole spate of Prestige reissues. His work is highlighted by a hard-driving mixture of bebop and R&B devices delivered with a tone as big as a house. One of the great ballad players of any era, he has been widely hailed as a great interpreter. —*Bob Porter*

○ **Gene Ammons Story: The 78 Era** / Mar. 5, 1950-Nov. 4, 1955 / Prestige 24058
A two-record anthology that gathers Ammons's 78 recordings made in the early and mid-'50s. Despite the often short length, the power and energy Ammons displays is impressive, as are the twin-tenor battles with Sonny Stitt. Ammons also occasionally played baritone or did vocals on some selections. —*Ron Wynn, AMG*

○ **Woofin' and Tweetin': Gene Ammons All Star Session** / Mar. 5, 1950 / Prestige 7050

○ **Blues up and Down—Vol. 1** / Mar. 5, 1950-Jul. 27, 1950 / Prestige 7823

★ **All Star Sessions** / 1950-1955 / Original Jazz Classics 014

◇ **Golden Saxophone** / Nov. 18, 1952-Apr. 15, 1953 / Savoy 14033

☆ **Happy Blues, The** / Apr. 23, 1956 / Prestige 013

○ **Funky** / Jan. 11, 1957 / Prestige 244
A blues-oriented bop album that is not "funky" in the soul-jazz sense of that word. An exception is the title cut, a bluesy tune with Kenny Burrell (g). W/ Jackie McLean (as), Art Farmer (tpt), Mal Waldron (p). Recorded in New York City. —*Michael Erlewine*

○ **Blue Gene** / May 3, 1958 / Prestige 192
This is a wonderful blues date, with great support from Pepper Adams (bs), Mal Waldron (p), Art Taylor (d), Doug Watkins (b), Idrees Sulieman (tpt), and Ray Barretto (conga). —*Ron Wynn*

○ **Boss Tenor** / Jun. 16, 1960 / Prestige 297
The relaxed, warm, narrative tenor of Gene Ammons took over on *Boss Tenor*. This was a 6/16/60 date with Tommy Flanagan (p), Doug Watkins (b), Art Taylor (d) and Ray Barretto (conga). —*Bob Rusch, Cadence*

○ **Gene Ammons Story: Organ Combos** / Jun. 17, 1960-Nov. 28, 1961 / Prestige 24071
These Gene Ammons dates were good ones on several counts. Jug's presence on these recordings, alone, could serve as a possibly holy book for all saxophonists from the rhythm and blues stylists to the loft jazz set. His musicianship and saxophone conception was just that basic. —*Spencer R. Weston, Cadence*

Gene Ammons Story: Gentle Jug / Jan. 26, 1961-Apr. 13, 1962 / Prestige 24079
Two classic albums from 1961-1962: *Nice N' Cool* and *Gene Ammons* —*Michael Erlewine*

★ **Boss Tenors—Straight Ahead from Chicago 1961** / Aug. 27, 1961 / Verve 837440

There are perhaps no better tenors, no better jazz. Definitive. W/ Sonny Stitt. —*Michael G. Nastos*

○ **Brother Jack Meets the Boss** / Jan. 23, 1962 / Prestige 7228

On *Brother Jack Meets the Boss*, one of the fathers of Chicago tenor, Gene Ammons, teamed with Jack McDuff in a quintet setting (Harold Vick, tenor sax; Eddie Diehl, guitar; Joe Dukes, drums) for the usual blues-based romp. Here McDuff was in particularly good form, and Jug maneuvered with as much subtlety and changes as the genre and drummer allowed. —*Bob Rusch, Cadence*

○ **Soulful Moods of Gene Ammons** / Apr. 14, 1962 / Moodsville 28

○ **Blue Groove** / Apr. 27, 1962 / Prestige 2514

Blue Groove is a long-forgotten date full of Gene Ammons's sour mash, pinched tone. Four of the eight selections employed Clarence Anderson on organ that varied from late cocktail lounge to early soap opera filler. Ammons work was strident and startlingly fresh—especially on "It Never Goes Away" as Anderson slowed and tempered his often brutal attack. —*Christopher Kuhl, Cadence*

David Amram (David Werner Amram III)

b. Nov. 17, 1930, Philadelphia, PA
Composer, French horn / World fusion

David Amran is a multiinstrumentalist most prominent on French horn. Originally from Philadelphia, and classically trained, he played with Charles Mingus, Sonny Rollins, Lionel Hampton, and Oscar Pettiford in the '50s. Amram scored for TV and Broadway in the '60s, and carved a singular identity by combining world rhythms, especially those found in Cuban music. He's also a fine orchestrator, most notably with Betty Carter. —*Michael G. Nastos*

★ **Havana New York** / 1977 / Flying Fish 70057

A landmark 1977 recording with Amram, Thad Jones, Pepper Adams, and Irakere. —*Ron Wynn*

Arild Anderson

b. Nov. 27, 1945, Lillestrom, Norway
Bass / World fusion, new age

Among Europe's finest bassists, Arild Anderson actually majored in electrical engineering in college, studying music privately with theorist/composer George Russell. He spent six years playing with Jan Garbarek's quartet and trio and also worked with vocalist Karin Krog. He was a featured member of Sam Rivers's and Paul Bley's groups in the mid '70s, when he was living in America. He later formed his own group with Scandinavian musicians. Anderson worked in a pair of all-star groups in 1979 and 1981, then co-led a quintet with drummer Jon Christensen in 1983. He was voted Musician of the Year in Norway in 1969 and the top European bassist by *Jazz Forum* in 1975. —*Ron Wynn*

★ **Sagn** / Aug. 1990 / ECM 849647

Recent release putting bassist Anderson in company with percussionist Nana Vasconcelos. Music ranges from lightweight to exciting and deserves hearing for array of colors Vasconcelos can create, plus the usual bright ECM production and sound. —*Ron Wynn, AMG*

Cat Anderson (William Alonzo Anderson)

b. Sep. 12, 1916, Greenville, SC, **d.** Apr. 29, 1981, Norwalk, CA
Trumpet, flugelhorn / Swing, big band

An outstanding trumpeter, especially in the upper register, and long-time member of Duke Ellington's orchestra, Cat Anderson grew up in a South Carolina orphanage, where he learned music playing in its student bands. He formed the Carolina Cotton Pickers, a touring student ensemble, in the early '30s. Anderson played in big bands led by Claude Hopkins and Lionel Hampton before joining Ellington in 1944. He left Ellington in 1947 to head his own band until 1949. Anderson rejoined Ellington in 1950, and stayed until 1959. He was a formidable contributor to several suites. Anderson again returned in 1961, playing infrequently with the orchestra until 1971. From that point until his death Anderson played with the Ellington band only for special occasions, also doing various West Coast dates.—*Ron Wynn*

● **Plays W.C. Handy** / i. Jun. 1977+May 1978 / Black & Blue 591632

Ernestine Anderson (Ernestine Irene Anderson)

b. 1928, Houston, TX
Vocals / Big band, blues & jazz, ballads & blues

Ernestine Anderson is a fine singer in the jazz vein. She's been active since the '40s, and scored a hit with "K. C. Lover" while a member of Shifty Henry's band in 1947. Anderson was the *DOWN BEAT* Critic's Poll New Star winner in 1959, but basically dropped out of sight ten years later, after singing a number that was included in the soundtrack of Sidney Poitier's film *The Lost Man*. She did selected dates in the Northwest until bassist Ray Brown became her manager in the mid '70s, and secured her a Concord Records post in 1976. She's been quite busy ever since. —*Ron Wynn*

★ **Big City** / Feb. 1983 / Concord Jazz 4214

With sublime Hank Jones (p) and fine vocals. Solid, swinging arrangements. —*Ron Wynn*

○ **Be Mine Tonight** / Dec. 1986 / Concord Jazz 4319

Backed by a fine rhythm section (pianist Marshall Otwell deserves a date of his own) and assisted by Benny Carter's alto on several selections, Anderson sounded as if she really enjoyed this session. Best were a rare vocal version of "In a Mellotone" and a Dinah Washington-inspired treatment of "Christopher Columbus," the two most jazz-oriented tracks on this well-rounded album. —*Scott Yanow, Cadence*

Ray Anderson

b. 1952, Chicago
Trombone, cornet, tuba, slide trumpet / Hard bop, Soul jazz, Modern Creative

Trombonist, cornetist, slide trumpeter and tuba player Ray Anderson is one of the best contemporary players and also very knowledgeable of traditional and swing styles. An active player since childhood, he began attending AACM concerts and blues shows in Chicago as a teenager. Anderson played in funk bands during the early 70s and came to New York in 1972. Early stints with Mingus led to gigs with Barry Altschul and Anthony Braxton, plus many session dates in Latin-jazz bands. He has been a bandleader since the late 70s and won the 1981 *DOWN BEAT* Critic's Poll in the category of Talent Deserving Wider Recognition. —*Ron Wynn*

★ **Blues Bred in the Bone** / Mar. 27-28, 1989 / Gramavision 79445

Trombonist Ray Anderson's *Blues Bred In The Bone* paid homage, stylistically, to such pioneer plumber's helper bonemen as Tricky Sam Nanton and Vic Dickenson. With guitarist John Scofield and drummer Johnny Vidacovich, Anderson proved an uncommonly sensitive interpreter of Billy Strayhorn's "A Flower Is a Lonesome Thing" as well as an intrepid voyager into largely uncharted sonic seas. — *W. Royal Stokes, Jazz Times*

Lil Armstrong (Lillian Armstrong)

b. Feb. 3, 1898, Memphis, TN, **d.** Aug. 27, 1971, Chicago, IL
Piano, vocals, composer / New Orleans traditional

Pianist and vocalist Lilian Armstrong was an underrated pianist and classically trained musician but is better known as reportedly the person who advised Louis Armstrong to break away from King Oliver. She's reputed to have told him she didn't want to be married to "no second trumpet player." Whether this story is true or not, the former Lillian Hardin married Armstrong in 1924, and he played in her band after leaving Fletcher Henderson in 1924. But professional and personal tensions caused the marriage to unravel, and the two divorced in 1938. Lillian Hardin eventually successfully sued Armstrong for unpaid royalties on songs they co-wrote, and at one point was billing his replacement in her band, Jonah Jones, as "Louis Armstrong the Second." She later worked with both all-male and all-female groups, was Decca's house pianist in 1936, and moved to Chicago in 1940. She opened a restaurant there and was a busy club pianist until her death. She suffered a heart attack while participating in a memorial service for Louis Armstrong. —*Ron Wynn*

● **Lil Hardin Armstrong** / Sep. 7, 1961 / Riverside 401

Louis Armstrong (Louis Daniel Armstrong)

b. Aug. 4, 1901, New Orleans, LA, **d.** Jul. 6, 1971, New York, NY
Trumpet, bandleader, vocals / New Orleans traditional

Known variously as "Pops" to most musicians and "Satchmo" to the public, Louis Armstrong is considered by many critics the most important and influential figure in jazz history. Any writer who deals with Armstrong soon realizes that all the superlatives that might be applied to his musical contributions have long ago been exhausted, but the current trend is to assign equal importance to his dual roles as artist and entertainer, thus opening up the entirety of his extensive recorded output to serious consideration. From his *Hot Five* rendition of "Heebie Jeebies" (often identified as the first recorded example of "scat" singing) to the All Stars "Hello Dolly" (which displaced the Beatles at the top of the charts in 1964), there is literally something for everyone in the Armstrong discography. Small wonder that his "What A Wonderful World" was recently used to advertise a variety of products—its appeal is truly universal.

Attempts to explain Armstrong's virtuosity on cornet and trumpet in terms of influences usually focus on Joe "King" Oliver (and sometimes Bunk Johnson), but it is more likely he drew on the entire range of styles available to him while a precocious youth in New Orleans (including Buddy Petit, Chris Kelly, Henry "Kid" Rena, and Manuel Perez, as well as Oliver and Johnson), creating a synthesis that was intensely personal and compelling. Historians now credit him as the pioneer figure in the development of extended solo improvisation with his *Hot Five* recordings, effectively transcending the collective improvisational techniques that were the hallmark of the early New Orleans jazz bands. His singing style was no less creative, setting the standard for virtually every major jazz vocalist who followed him. Throughout his long career, Armstrong maintained a down-to-earth quality that made him accessible to his audiences; considering his meteoric rise from the Waif's Home to superstar status by the mid '20s, this was a remarkable achievement in its own right. As a symbol for the aspirations of African-Americans, "Pops" offered the world a vision of harmony that was more than strictly musical. This fact was not lost on the State Department: Armstrong's All Stars became the group of choice for "good will" tours designed to win over Third World countries with the escalation of the Cold War in the '50s.

During the course of his recording career, Louis Armstrong was affiliated with virtually every major label in the United States, and a complete sampling of his oeuvre requires a dedicated sense of commitment from the listener because of the sheer enormity of the undertaking. For those who are up to the task, what soon becomes apparent is Armstrong's adaptability—he followed (or led) every trend from the "hot" jazz of the '20s through the swing era, but eventually drew the line at "modern" jazz (bebop), at which point he returned to a "traditional" format with the formation of the All Stars in 1946. In a sense, he came full circle, returning to his roots and the intimacy of a small-band setting populated with a succession of close musical friends. What held all these bands together, what gives Armstrong's work continuity, is his personality, a gift that he offered modestly and sincerely. The sweat-soaked handkerchief and the "Satchmo" smile said it all: It's easy to work hard when you love what you do. This simple message to a complex world is precisely what Louis Armstrong was all about. *—Bruce Boyd Raeburn*

☆ **Louis Armstrong and King Oliver** / i. Apr. 5, 1923-Dec. 22, 1924 / Milestone
This set has the same 25 selections by Oliver's Creole Jazz Band and the Red Onion Jazz Babies plus the two King Oliver-Jelly Roll Morton cornet-piano duets of 1924, both of which are now available on Morton Milestone CD. In one form or another, this music is essential. *—Scott Yanow*

○ **Jazz Classics: Great Original Performances 1923-1931** / 1923-1931 / Mobile Fidelity 597

○ **Hot 5's & 7's 1925-1928** / 1925-1928 / Laserlight 15721

★ **Hot Fives—Vol. 1** / i. Jun. 23, 1926-May 13, 1927 / CBS 44049
Eight apiece from Louis Armstrong's Hot Fives and Sevens with some stunning trumpet on "Willie The Weeper" and "Potato Head Blues" and Johnny Dodds' very distinctive clarinet at its best during "Weary Blues." Classic and very influential New Orleans jazz. *—Scott Yanow*

★ **Hot Fives and Sevens—Vol. 2** / May 13, 1927-Jun. 28, 1928 / Columbia 44253
The last (and some of the best) of the Hot Sevens and Fives with Armstrong in brilliant form and followed closely by clarinetist Johnny Dodds and guest guitarist Lonnie Johnson. Armstrong is wonderful on "Struttin' With Some Barbeque," "Hotter Than That," and (with his new pianist Earl Hines) "A Monday Date." *—Scott Yanow*

● **Hot Fives and Sevens—Vol. 3** / May 1927-1928 / Columbia 44422
Earl Hines (p) makes his presence felt, and Baby Dodds (d) joins the hit parade, yielding "A Monday Date," "Struttin' With Some Barbecue," "S.O.L. Blues," "Savoy Blues," and "Hotter Than That." A brilliant collaboration and soloing. *—Bruce Raeburn*

● **Louis Armstrong Collection—Vol. 4: Louis Armstrong and Earl Hines, The** / i. 1928 / Columbia 45142
Louis Armstrong was at his most advanced at the time of these timeless recordings with pianist Earl Hines. Hines constantly challenged Satch to stretch himself. Their duet "Weather Bird" is futuristic for 1928, their version of "Basin Street Blues" was that standard's earliest recording, and the stunning "West End Blues" was Armstrong's personal favorite recording ever. *—Scott Yanow*

☆ **Louis Armstrong Collection—Vol. 5: Louis in New York** / i. Mar. 5, 1929-Nov. 26, 1929 / CBS 46148
By 1929, Louis Armstrong had switched from New Orleans jazz to fronting a variety of larger orchestras, widening his repertoire to include pop tunes but always leaving room for closing trumpet solos. This set includes all known versions (including a few new alternates) of his recordings of this era including appearances backing singers Seger Ellis and Victoria Spivey. Highpoints include "Mahogany Hall Stomp" and "Ain't Misbehavin'." *—Scott Yanow*

☆ **Louis Armstrong Collection—Vol. 6: St. Louis Blues** / i. Dec. 10, 1929-Oct. 9, 1930 / CBS 46996
Using different big bands purely as a backdrop by 1930, Louis Armstrong was free to stretch out with flashy virtuosic trumpet solos and often scat-filled vocal choruses. "St. Louis Blues," "Body and Soul," and "'Tiger Rag" are classics, but his rendition of "I'm A Ding Dong Daddy" (which has a solo that gradually builds to a tremendous finish) is a true gem. *—Scott Yanow*

☆ **V.S.O.P.—Vol. 1** / i. Nov. 3, 1931-Mar. 11, 1932 / Epic 22019
Louis Armstrong fronted Zilner Randolph's orchestra for these 16 selections, alternating some exhibitionistic solo showcases with expressive ballads. Armstrong is the star throughout, really excelling on two versions of "Stardust," "Chinatown," and "Lawd, You Made the Night Too Long." Not as essential as his recordings of a few years earlier but enjoyable enough in their own right. *—Scott Yanow*

○ **1934-1936** / i. Oct. 1934-Feb. 4, 1936 / Classics 509
This valuable CD includes Louis Armstrong's often riotous Paris session from 1934 ("St. Louis Blues" and "Tiger Rag" almost get out of control!) and then Satch's first 17 Decca recordings, smooth renditions of pop tunes that he turns into classic jazz. Duplicates and exceeds Decca's *Rhythm Saved The World*. *—Scott Yanow*

☆ **Rhythm Saved the World** / Oct. 3, 1935-Feb. 4, 1936 / GRP 602
The first and so far only domestic volume on CD of Louis Armstrong's swing era recordings for Decca in chronological order. Joined by the musical, but by then somewhat anonymous, Luis Russell orchestra, Armstrong's melodic variations turn these pop tunes into hot jazz, even "La Cucaracha!" The 14 selections find Louis Armstrong in consistently smooth form with his warm vocals as notable as his melodic trumpet. *—Scott Yanow*

★ **Rare Items** / i. Dec. 19, 1935-Aug. 9, 1944 / Decca 9225
This particular LP is actually much rarer now than its music. A fine cross-section of Louis Armstrong's big band years with such highpoints as "Thanks A Million," "Swing That Music," "Jubilee," and "I Double Dare You" among its highpoints. Possibly the best single LP of this productive (but much maligned) period in Louis Armstrong's career. *—Scott Yanow*

☆ **1936-1937** / i. Feb. 4, 1936-Apr. 7, 1937 / Classics 512
Continuing the complete chronological reissue of Louis Armstrong's output for Decca during the swing era, this set finds Satch at his most exhibitionistic (hitting dozens of high notes on "Swing That Music"), fronting Jimmy Dorsey's orchestra, doing a "Pennies from Heaven" medley with Bing Crosby, joining in for

two collaborations with the Mills Brothers and, on four selections, even making charming (if weird) music with a group of Hawaiians! Not essential but quite enjoyable. — *Scott Yanow*

★ **Pops: 1940's Small Band Sides** / Sep. 6, 1946-Oct. 16, 1947 / RCA 6378
Recorded at the time Louis Armstrong was in the film *New Orleans*, broke up his orchestra and formed his very popular "All-Stars," these 20 tracks feature Satch in prime form whether playing relaxed standards or New Orleans gems or duetting with trombonist-vocalist Jack Teagarden. Highpoints include a reunion with his old boss, trombonist Kid Ory; five selections from his classic 1947 Town Hall concert (including definitive versions of "Ain't Misbehavin," "Rockin' Chair," and "Back O'Town Blues"); sharing the spotlight with Jack T. on "A Song Was Born" and "Please Stop Playing Those Blues, Boy"; and taking one of his greatest ever solos on "Jack-Armstrong Blues." An outstanding set. — *Scott Yanow*

☆ **California Concerts** / i. Jan. 30, 1951-Jan. 21, 1955 / GRP 613
This four-CD set contains two nearly complete concerts by Louis Armstrong's All-Stars, giving one a very good idea of the type of performance the great trumpeter-vocalist put on every night. Some dated comedy aside, Satch is in exciting form, assisted by trombonists Jack Teagarden and Trummy Young, clarinetist Barney Bigard and (for the earlier concert) pianist Earl Hines. Actually it is the later session (which takes up most of the last three CDs) that is quite spirited and lively, with Armstrong enthusiastically leading his All-Stars through time-worn but fresh Dixieland standards. — *Scott Yanow*

☆ **Louis Armstrong Plays W.C. Handy** / Jul. 12, 1954-Jul. 14, 1954 / Columbia 40242
This is considered, along with his Fats Waller tribute, Louis Armstrong's most rewarding recording of the 1950s, but Columbia, when they reissued it in 1986, thought they were doing collectors a favor by substituting alternate takes on six of the songs for the originals. If they had merely augmented the set with the extra material it would have increased its value, but instead the original (and superior) versions of many of these songs are out of print! The result is an interesting but flawed tribute with Armstrong's monumental version of "St. Louis Blues" replaced by an imposter! — *Scott Yanow*

○ **Chicago Concert** / i. Jun. 1, 1956 / Columbia 236426
Originally out on a double-LP, this is a definitive set of the Louis Armstrong All-Stars of 1956. The music and many of the solos will be familiar to longtime Armstrong fans, but whether it be "Struttin' With Some Barbecue," "Basin Street," or Louis's new hit "Mack The Knife," the spirit and enthusiasm of this music is irresistible. The best live set of Louis Armstrong in the 1950's. — *Scott Yanow*

○ **Satchmo: A Musical Biography** / i. 1956-1957 / Decca 8604
During 1956-1957 Louis Armstrong revisited many of the highpoints of his career, re-recording his classics from the 1920s and '30s while backed by augmented members of his All-Stars. Decca made a big production out of it, adding some slightly earlier All-Star performances; the result was a superb four-LP box set that is very much in need of being reissued on CD. — *Scott Yanow*

☆ **Definitive Album by Louis Armstrong, The** / i. Aug. 3, 1959-Aug. 5, 1959 / Audio Fidelity 6241
Louis Armstrong recorded two sessions with the Dukes of Dixieland, the fine New Orleans band led by trumpeter Frank Assunto. Although undoubtedly in awe of Armstrong, the Dukes fare very well on this LP, and Louis is in often-stunning form, for perhaps the last time in his career really nailing some high notes. Well worth searching for. — *Scott Yanow*

☆ **Complete Sessions** / i. 1961 / Roulette 93844
An album with Duke Ellington. This is a joyful collaboration by two of the greatest names in jazz. Tunes include "Mood Indigo," "Black and Tan Fantasy," and other Ellington pieces. Sideman Barney Bigard (cl) adds particular charm to "It Don't Mean a Thing." — *Bruce Boyd Raeburn*

☆ **Armstrong/Ellington: Together for the First Time/The Great Reunion** / i. Apr. 3, 1961-Apr. 1961 / Mobile Fidelity 514
Formerly available as a two-LP set, and also put out on CD by Roulette, these 17 selections are the entire results of the only meeting in the studios by Louis Armstrong and Duke Ellington. Although it might have been preferable to have Armstrong per-

form with Duke's orchestra, Ellington's performance as pianist with Satch's All-Stars is quite satisfying. The all-Ellington program gave Armstrong a rest from his usual repertoire and permitted him an opportunity to work his magic on fresh material. Lots of surprises, some sensitive vocalizing, and fine supporting work from trombonist Trummy Young and clarinetist Barney Bigard. A gem. — *Scott Yanow*

☆ **Hello, Dolly!** / i. Dec. 3, 1963-Apr. 18, 1964 / Kapp 3364
This wonderful album has not only the original hit version of "Hello Dolly" but also a great rendition of "A Kiss to Build a Dream On," and Louis Armstrong's last extended trumpet solo during a hot version of "Jeepers Creepers." No matter how many times one hears "Hello Dolly," it is still a joy. — *Scott Yanow*

○ **Giants of Jazz: Louis Armstrong** / i. Feb. 1979 / Time Life 1P31
The three records here took us through Louis Armstrong's career from 1923 with King Oliver's Creole Jazz band to 1950 with his own All Stars…The first three sides of this set (from "Dippermouth Blues" to "Mahogany Hall Stomp" in 1929) offered a well-structured, if quite incomplete, study of Armstrong's sustained growth as a musician and as an influence. Time-Life's *Giants of Jazz* was, however, perfect for the informed jazz aficionado who might enjoy the convenience of so many recordings under one roof, as well as the clear sound transfers achieved. — *Linda Prince, Downbeat*

☆ **Genius of Louis Armstrong, The** /
This two-album set, which, despite the title, contains recordings made between 1924 and 1932, is out of print, but that's the only reason it is denied the highest possible recommendation. Containing 29 tracks, it traces Armstrong's evolution from sideman to his Hot Fives and Hot Sevens and is the best one-album look at his early years. — *William Ruhlmann*

Art Ensemble of Chicago

Group / Early free, modern creative
The most famous group to emerge from the AACM (Association for the Advancement of Creative Musicians), its origins dating back to the Windy City in 1965, this quintet consists of Lester Bowie (trumpet and other brass instruments), Joseph Jarman and Roscoe Mitchell (reed instruments), Malachi Favors (b), and Don Moye (d). In addition to these main instruments, all five also double on a variety of sound-producing devices, ranging from vibes and banjo to whistles, conch shells, sirens, and so on. The AEC started in Paris in 1969 (Moye joined in 1970) and made 11 albums in Europe. After returning home in 1971, AEC members have been involved in many other ventures, singly or together, but the group's remained intact for concerts, festivals, and other major engagements. Their motto, "Great Black Music—Ancient to the Future," describes their eclectic approach, based in free jazz but ranging widely over the spectrum of jazz and contemporary improvised music. Costumes, masks, makeup, pantomime, and other forms of theatrics have been an AEC trademark from the start. The group performs its own music exclusively; after more than two decades together, its members have reached a remarkable degree of spontaneous yet disciplined interaction. — *Dan Morgenstern*

Jackson in Your House / Aug. 1969 / Affinity 9
Vitality was the key to the success of the Art Ensemble of Chicago's *A Jackson in Your House* which reissued the material from the BYG LP of the same name. This was recorded with just the quartet of Lester Bowie, Roscoe Mitchell, Joseph Jarman, and Malachi Favors (Philip Wilson (drums) had left, and Don Moye had yet to link up.) — *Bob Rusch, Cadence*

○ **Live at Mandel Hall** / Jan. 15, 1972 / Delmark 432
A sonic barrage recorded live. The Art Ensemble don't give concerts, they present multimedia spectacles, and this one proved no different. There are lengthy, relentless dialogues and solos, then short, snappy interludes and silly comments, all integrated into one seamless, nonstop show. — *Ron Wynn, AMG*

★ **Bap-Tizum** / Sep. 9, 1972 / Atlantic 1639
Recorded at Ann Arbor Blues & Jazz Festival. Essential. Improvised music. — *Michael G. Nastos*

☆ **Jazzlore: Fanfare for Warriors—Vol. 12** / Sep. 6, 1973 / Atlantic 1651
Fanfare for Warriors, recorded in Chicago in September of 1973, established a mood similar to the group's previous Atlantic re-

lease *Bap-Tizum,* only *Fanfare* had two distinct advantages; first, it was cut in the studio, while *Bap-Tizum* was recorded at the mercy of the Ann Arbor Blues & Jazz Festival PA system; second, it solicited the aid of the AACM's spiritual leader, pianist Muhal Richard Abrams...As usual, the Art Ensemble gleaned the essence from the back-to-the-roots form and, in the process, transformed it into something of a more transcendental nature. *—Ray Townley, Down Beat*

○ **Great Black Music** / **i.** 1978 / Affinity 9

☆ **Nice Guys** / May 1978 / ECM 827876
The Art Ensemble's album *Nice Guys* was their first for Manfred Eicher's ECM label. Though not their best album, *Nice Guys* was possibly their most representative, a variegated showcase illustrating much of what they do best. Each of the six compositions displayed a distinct personality and musical profile...The finale, Jarman's "Dreaming of the Master," was more than an act of homage to one of the AEC's influential ancestors, the Miles Davis Quintet; it was a haunting reminder that great art transcends temporal and spatial boundaries. It was not important that Bowie could recreate, note for note, Davis' cool modal insouciance, or that Jarman could echo John Coltrane's feverishly explosive tenor torments in such a ghostly fashion; it was the spirit that instigates and informs each note that remained universal, direct, and affecting, and the Art Ensemble was a living testimonial to the glories of the past and the promises of the future. *—Art Lange, Down Beat*

○ **Live Part One** / **i.** 197z / BYG 2401
Live combines confrontational juxtapositions and stretches of seamless fluidity, yet compared to later concert recordings, *Live* is not as dynamically paced and proportioned. Still, there is a lot of engaging material—a relentless opening barrage that segues into one of their patented, pungently humored themes: some fine solos, particularly from bassist Malachi Favors and trumpeter Lester Bowie; a funky strut of a closer. *—Bill Shoemaker, Down Beat*

○ **Full Force** / Jan. 1980 / ECM 829197
The Art Ensemble of Chicago's first go-round with ECM's Manfred Eicher found them on their best (well, almost) collaborative behavior: they brought a little fire to his ice; he focused their heat into clear blue flame...Short, frenzied solos (Roscoe Mitchell's tenor, Joseph Jarman's soprano) spiced "Dance," on which drummer Don Moye and bassist Malachi Favors exchanged wild twos; flute and small-horn snippets skittered through "Full Force." The one major sax contribution was Roscoe Mitchell's solemnly, stridently ringing but brief theme statement over Favor's intriguing vamp on "Magg." *—Fred Bouchard, Down Beat*

○ **Dreaming of the Masters Suite** / **i.** Jan. 1990-Mar. 1990 / DIW 854

Dorothy Ashby (Dorothy Jeanne Ashby)

b. Aug. 6, 1932, Detroit, MI, **d.** 1986
Harp / Bop
Detroit jazz harp player Dorothy Ashby merged blues and gospel roots, classical notions, and swinging rhythms, taking the synthesis to its height on an unlikely instrument. She sometimes ventured into syrup and original funk, but for the most part played purely jazz. *—Michael G. Nastos*

○ **Jazz Harpist** / **i.** Mar. 21, 1957 / Regent 6039
Dorothy Ashby was at the top of a very small and select circle, jazz harpists. Rather than simply providing atmosphere and colors, Ashby improvised on the instrument and exploited it to the fullest, regardless of the song or context. This now deleted '57 album has some incredible passages, songs that not only anticipate but in some ways exceed things later done by Alice Coltrane and others. *—Ron Wynn, AMG*

★ **Hip Harp** / Mar. 21, 1958 / Prestige 7140

○ **Fantastic Jazz Harp of Dorothy Ashby, The** / May 3-04, 1965 / Atlantic 1447
Detroiter Ashby is the premier player on her instrument. With horns and percussion from Richard Davis (b), Grady Tate (d), Willie Bobo (per). *—Michael G. Nastos*

Harold Ashby (Harold Kenneth Ashby)

b. Mar. 27, 1925, Kansas City, MO

tenor sax / Swing, big band
Harold Ashby is a tenor saxophonist and longtime member of the Duke Ellington Orchestra. He worked with Tommy Douglas and vocalist Walter Brown in Kansas City before moving to Chicago in the early '50s and working with several blues bands. Ashby relocated to New York in 1957, playing with Milt Larking and Mercer Ellington, as well as occasionally with Duke Ellington. He did sessions with Ben Webster, Johnny Hodges, Paul Gonsalves, and Lawrence Brown between 1958 and 1965, then joined the Ellington orchestra permanently in 1968, remaining with them until 1975. Since then he has been a freelance and session musician, playing at festivals in both America and Europe. Ashby presented a concert of his music in 1984 at St. Peter's Church in New York through an NEA grant. He has recently recorded as a leader for Stash and has also done sessions for Progressive. *—Ron Wynn*

● **Born to Swing** / Oct. 9, 1959+Feb. 27, 1960 / Master Jazz 8122

Svend Asmussen

b. Feb. 28, 1916, Copenhagen, Denmark
Violin, Vocals / Swing
Violinist and occasional vocalist Svend Asmussen has been playing the violin since he was seven and shows no signs of ever losing the vitality and flashy skills that have stamped his playing ever since. Asmussen left the Academy of Arts in Copenhagen, Denmark, when his father died and he was forced to find a job. He made his professional debut in 1933 at Copenhagen's version of the Apollo Theater. By 1934 he'd formed his own band along the lines of Joe Venuti's Blue Four. Asmussen joined the Mills Brothers and Fats Waller when they came through Denmark but then disbanded his group to pursue an acting and comic career in 1943. Asmussen returned to music when World War II concluded but was unable to pursue lucrative opportunities in America due to strict immigration laws during the period he was most eager to come ('50s). He became a huge star in Europe, playing violin and singing in groups led by Alice Babs on three occasions, as well as working with Ulrik Neumann. His collaborative efforts with violinists Stuff Smith and Stephane Grappelli were acclaimed examples of superb technique, joyous and tasteful, yet exuberant performances. He also appeared on the masterful album *Duke Ellington's Violin Summit.* *—Ron Wynn*

● **Hot Fiddle** / **i.** Jul. 29, 1953 / Brunswick 58051

Roy Ayers (Roy E. Ayers, Jr.)

b. Sep. 10, 1940, Los Angeles, CA
Vibes, vocals, piano / Soul jazz, instrumental pop
A talented vibist, Ayers was among the top jazz players of the '60s. He had speed, technique, and the good fortune to appear on several high-profile Herbie Mann albums. He turned almost exclusively to R&B and funk in the '70s. His group Ubiquity started playing jazz-based R&B, then shifted to R&B-funk. Ayers was essentially an R&B bandleader in the late '70s, with eight albums making the Billboard charts in 1976-1979. During the '80s and '90s, he's split bandleading, performing, writing, and producing duties. Ayers issued *Love Fantasy* in 1980, then toured Africa the next year, performing with Nigerian Afrobeat king Fela Anikulapo-Kuti. Kuti appeared on Ayers's 1981 LP *Africa, Center of the World.* He departed Polydor after 1982's *Feeling Good,* which contained the single "Turn Me Loose." Ayers formed Uno Melodic Records and worked with Bobby Humphrey, Eighties Ladies, and Sylvia Striplin. He co-wrote "Turned on to You" with Edwin Birdsong for Eighties Ladies and produced "Give Me Your Love" for Striplin, as well as recording and issuing his own *Lots of Love* LP for Uno Melodic. Ayers signed with Columbia in 1984 and landed one Top 20 R&B single in 1986, "Hot," while cutting a number of LPs. He began recording with Ichiban in 1989. Ayers has also returned to jazz, recording a live LP at Ronnie Scott's in 1991, and making a guest appearance on the hip-hop/jazz release *Jazzamatazz* in 1993. The session was produced by Gang Starr's Guru, and Ayers has also done New York club dates with Guru and Donald Byrd. His Ubiquity LPs are being reissued on CD.*— Ron Wynn*

○ **West Coast Vibes** / Jul. 1963 / United Artists 6325

Virgo Vibes / Mar. 6, 1967 / Atlantic 1488

★ **Mystic Voyage** / 1975 / Polydor 6057
Nice outing, though there's minimal jazz content. Ayers, once a Down Beat New Star winner, decided at the end of the '60s to

forego the rigors of straight jazz life and investigate the world of funk and R&B. He would (and still does) dabble in light soul-jazz, but has become far more known for his funk and R&B releases like this one. —*Ron Wynn, AMG*

Albert Ayler

b. Jul. 13, 1936, Cleveland, OH, **d.** Nov. 1970, New York, NY
Tenor sax / Early free
Albert Ayler is remembered by many as the epitome of the'60s fire-breathing saxophonists. He was a quirky, genre-crossing tenorist whose raw, bluesy tone combined the archaic vibrato of early New Orleans jazzmen with the reed-splitting multiphonics of the R&B screamers. In his day he was dismissed as a primitive, fake, destroyer of jazz, and, paradoxically, a sell-out when, on his final albums, he shifted his attention to blues and rock grooves (anticipating Miles Davis's more successful fusion efforts). He got his start touring as a teenager with blues harpist Little Walter and later traveled to California and then Europe, trying in vain to find musicians and an audience for his evolving ideas. His first recordings were made in Scandinavia in 1962-1963, using local musicians, During those years he was encouraged by Cecil Taylor, Don Cherry, Sonny Rollins, and John Coltrane. What little literature exists about Ayler often assigns a mentor role to Coltrane, and while Coltrane may have been responsible for getting Ayler a contract with Impulse Records, the musical evidence suggests a mutual relationship, with Coltrane benefiting mainly from the liberating influence of their association.

During Ayler's most fertile period (1964-1966), he did several domestic sessions for Debut, ESP, and Impulse, and toured Europe, with many live recordings resulting. His midsized ensembles followed a simple, almost formulaic approach: concise sing-along melodies reminiscent of nursery rhymes, hymns, and brass band material would segue abruptly into wild collective improvisation, with Albert's evocative tenor playing the role of a Pied Piper gone mad. This was the time for music of emancipation and catharsis, and Ayler's fresh conception, freed of jazz clichés and delivered with sweat-drenched intensity, was certainly timely. In the late '60s his output decreased, although he seemed more willing than ever to experiment—singing, playing bagpipes, and adding White rock musicians and soul singers to his band. One of these vocalists was his companion Mary Parks (aka Mary Maria), who seemed to dominate the last few efforts before his death by drowning in 1970. Few figures have generated as much controversy and mystified speculation as Ayler, but whatever label you choose to apply—conservative, radical, folk musician, or jazz revolutionary—he created his own unique sound, and that sound is still relevant today. In the CD era, unissued material continues being released, and his best albums are also being reissued, sparking a long overdue critical reappraisal of his importance. —*Myles Boisen*

○ **Witches and Devils** / Feb. 24, 1964 / Freedom 741018
This 1964 date was also issued as *Spirits* on Debut label and *Mothers and Children* on Black Lion. Regardless of title, it was a fierce, free-wheeling, and often poignant session with Ayler, trumpeter Norman Howard, bassist Earle Henderson, and drummer Sunny Murray. One cut used two bassists. —*Ron Wynn, AMG*

★ **New York Eye and Ear Control** / Jul. 17, 1964 / ESP 1016
A summit meeting of the New York jazz avant-garde. W/ Don Cherry (tpt), John Tchicai (as), Roswell Rudd (tb), Gary Peacock (b). —*Myles Boisen*

○ **Hilversum Session, The** / Nov. 9, 1964 / Osmosis 6001
Hilversum, Holland, in June 1964—the scene of Eric Dolphy's *Last Date* concert—was five months later the location for Albert Ayler's no less great radio performance. This was the essential year in Albert Ayler's music when he finally found freedom through ensembles of players willing to join him in inventing his fantastic idiom. This album was well-recorded, unlike the ESP's, so the listener can appreciate the group's responses to the chaos that threatened from Ayler's unearthly sounds and tornado energy. —*John Litweiler, Down Beat*

○ **Bells** / May 1, 1965 / ESP 1010
Album-length live piece, with a quintet including Charles Tyler (as). Dan Morgenstern's insightful notes give a contemporary account of this ensemble's archaic sound and wild humor. —*Myles Boisen*

● **Spirits Rejoice** / Sep. 23, 1965 / ESP 1020

Peak Ayler, with the saxophonist churning, wailing, and soaring over the beat. He's so energetic and combative that things threaten to implode constantly, yet he keeps right on going. —*Ron Wynn, AMG*

○ **Albert Ayler: The Village Concerts—Vol. 7** / 1967 / ABC/Impulse 9336
This release consisted of all unreleased material recorded at the Village Theatre (2/26/67) and the Village Vanguard (12/18/66)...If you still haven't been swept up by Ayler's spiritual jazz, this is the track to approach first. —*Carl Brauer, Cadence*

○ **Love Cry** / Aug. 31, 1967 / GRP 108
The 1967-1968 *Love Cry* is good introductory Albert Ayler, less loose and forbidding than his earlier, writhing trio classics. Half these pieces are under four minutes, the singsong-martial themes crisp ("Universal Indians" is his masterstroke of economical writing: two notes in a repeating phrase). Like the brass band, Ayler seems to spring from everywhere. With his bellyful slow vibrato, and an acute if rarely acknowledged time sense—dirges float like driftwood, the dances shout with an urgency more civic than spiritual—Ayler has enough in common with now-digested late John Coltrane to be accessible at last. —*Kevin Whitehead, Down Beat*

○ **Volume 2** / i. Jun. 1970 / Shandar 10004

○ **Nuits De La Fondation Maeght—Vol. 1** / Jul. 25-27, 1970 / Shandar 10000
These recordings were previously available as separate volumes and now are packaged together as a double set. These concerts were recorded after Albert Ayler's attempts at more commercial efforts and shortly before his death...This was a historically important recording without a doubt, and if not given concentrated attention, very satisfying in many ways. —*Bob Rusch, Cadence*

Roberto Baden-Powell (Roberto Baden-Powell de Aquino)

b. Aug. 6, 1936, New York, NY,˙**d.** Aug. 1, 1966, New York, NY
Guitar / World fusion
He's among Brazil's finest, most expressive guitarists, perhaps the strongest rhythmic player to emerge from the blend of Iberian baroque and West African-Latin influences. Powell's albums have had authenticity, beauty, and transcendent elegance, and he's demonstrated complete command of guitar and a thorough knowledge of jazz, flamenco, and classical styles. —*Ron Wynn*

● **Solitude on Guitar** / i. Dec. 10-11, 1971 / Columbia 32441

Benny Bailey (Ernest Harold Bailey)

b. Aug. 13, 1925, Cleveland, Ohio, US
Trumpet / Bop, hard bop
Trumpeter Benny Bailey played with Teddy Edwards and toured with Jay McShann. He later worked with Dizzy Gillespie and Lionel Hampton. He made his home in Europe in 1953 and over the years has recorded with Stan Getz, Eric Dolphy, Les McCann, and George Gruntz. An exciting soloist. —*Michael Erlewine*

★ **Big Brass** / Nov. 25, 1960 / Candid 79011
Septet with trumpeter-leader Bailey, Phil Woods (as, bass cl), Julius Watkins (French horn), Les Spann (fl, g), and Tommy Flanagan (p) Trio. Well-known standards and two originals. Extensions from Quincy Jones Big Band, that is, large sound from seven pieces. Fine document. —*Michael G. Nastos*

Buster Bailey (William C. Bailey)

b. Jul. 19, 1902, Memphis, TN, **d.** Apr. 12, 1967, New York, NY
Clarinet, sax / Swing, big band
A virtuoso player, clarinetist Buster Bailey was among the first musicians to be attacked for overemphasizing technique and not emphasizing soul and heart as much as tone and facility. He played in W.C. Handy's orchestra as a teen in Memphis, then moved to Chicago in 1919. During his five years there, Bailey worked with Erskine Tate and King Oliver before relocating to New York in 1924 to join Fletcher Henderson's orchestra. His speed, clean solos, and overall skill resulted in Bailey being featured frequently on Henderson's recordings from '24 until '37. Bailey also worked with many others in that period, among them Noble Sissle and the Mills Blue Rhythm Band. After leaving Henderson, Bailey played with John Kirby another 11 years, where his smooth, almost flawless tone were a marked contrast to the more earthy, rugged wailing of such great players as

Sidney Bechet and Johnny Dodds. Bailey later played with Wilbur De Paris, Red Allen, and Big Chief Moore, spending two stints with Allen. He ended his career in two stages. He worked initally with Wild Bill Davison, then spent the last two years with Louis Armstrong. —*Ron Wynn*

All About Memphis / Feb. 13, 1958 / Felsted 7003

Derek Bailey

b. Jan. 29, 1932, Sheffield, England
Guitar / Early free, modern creative
Guitarist Derek Bailey has been a champion of free and spontaneously improvised music since the mid-'60s, and ranks among that genre's most recorded performers. His grandfather was a professional pianist and banjo player, and his uncle a guitarist. Bailey studied guitar and music with C. H. C. Biltcliffe and John Duarte, and played in numerous settings and contexts from '52 to '65. These included clubs and concert halls, studios and broadcasts for radio and television, and orchestras and dance halls. As the '60s continued, Bailey became known for explosive, frenetic solos, with often spectacular runs, effects, phrases, and distortion. He formed Incus Records, Britain's first independent record label, with Evan Paker and Tony Oxley in 1970. Parker also created the Spontaneous Music Ensemble in the '60s, and Company, an ensemble with rotating personnel in the '70s, but he eventually opted to specialize in solo performances with an occasional duo date. Bailey actually received a Grammy nomination for the album *View from 6 Windows* in 1982, and wrote a book on the history of improvisation that's been translated into Italian, French, Japanese, and Dutch. —*Ron Wynn*

● **Yankees** / **i.** 1982 / Celluloid 5006

Mildred Bailey (Mildred [Née Rinker] Bailey)

b. Feb. 27, 1907, Tekoa, WA, **d.** Dec. 12, 1951, Poughkeepsie, NY
Vocals, piano / Swing, ballads & blues
A premier vocalist, Mildred Bailey was renowned for caustic outbursts and a wildly changeable personality, especially in regard to her principal rival Billie Holiday. She would often profess professional admiration for Holiday, then refer to her in ugly, coarse language that often skirted racism. Bailey's distinctive timbre and swinging ability were the hallmark of her finest recordings. When she died in 1951 of liver and heart failure, Bailey was penniless, despite all the money she'd made for record companies and the fame she'd amassed in her career. —*Ron Wynn*

★ **Her Greatest Performances (1929-1946)** / 1929-1946 / Columbia 3L22
A superb three-record set that contains the finest performances from the acclaimed female singer many critics considered the finest white woman jazz vocalist ever. Bailey had a distinctive high-pitched range and excellent phrasing; she also had a penchant for making comments that would be deemed racist even in an unenlightened area. This anthology gives the cream of the crop from 1929—1946 and is out of print. —*Ron Wynn, AMG*

☆ **Uncollected Mildred Bailey** / 1944 / Hindsight 133

○ **M.B.** / Mar. 5, 1946-1947 / Savoy 12219

○ **Rockin' Chair Lady, The** / **i.** 1953 / Decca 5387

Chet Baker (Chesney Henry Baker)

b. Dec. 23, 1929, Yake, OK, **d.** May 13, 1988, Amsterdam
Trumpet, vocals / Cool
Baker came to prominence as a trumpet player with Charlie Parker (briefly), then Gerry Mulligan in Los Angeles 1952. He began to record as a leader in 1953 and formed his first quartet with pianist Russ Freeman. Baker's initial vocal recordings also date from 1953, and his early recordings for Pacific Jazz define his essence as a light, middle-range-dominant trumpet player and a singer of similar characteristics. These formative recordings have an innocence rarely captured in his later, more technically assured work. The Prestige albums from 1965 are also fine examples of small combo playing without vocals. Dogged by a narcotics habit throughout his adult life, Baker spent much of his professional career in Europe. The recordings from Europe vary widely in quality but, in general, the earlier the better. The subject of a film, *Let's Get Lost*, he recorded right up until his death in 1988. —*Bob Porter*

★ **Complete Pacific Jazz Live Recordings** / 1953-1957 / Mosaic 113
Also includes a session from October 1954. Studio recordings. 1953-1957. W/ Chet Baker Quartet and Russ Freeman. Chet Baker at the height of his powers. —*Michael Katz*

★ **Chet Baker with Strings** / **i.** Feb. 20, 1954 / Columbia 46174
Chet Baker with Strings was a reissue (with three "new" takes) of the music that Chet Baker recorded *instrumentally* when he was just past his 24th birthday. The charts for the nine strings and the jazzmen (Zoot Sims, tenor sax; Bud Shank, alto sax, flute; Russ Freeman, piano; Joe Mondragon, bass; Shelly Manne, drums) were by the likes of Marty Paich, Johnny Mandel, Jack Montrose, and Shorty Rogers, and the arrangements generally avoided getting sickly sweet...Sims, Shank, and Freeman helped out on the more swinging material, but the emphasis was on Baker's soft sound. —*Scott Yanow, Cadence*

○ **Chet Baker Sextet** / Sep. 9+15, 1954 / Pacific Jazz 15

○ **Chet in Paris—Vol. 1** / Oct. 1955 / Verve 837474

○ **Chet in Paris—Vol. 3: Cheryl** / Dec. 1955-Mar. 1956 / Verve 837476

★ **Chet Baker in New York** / Sep. 1958 / Riverside 207
There was much to listen to here in the parts (not all pleasant), but as a whole this LP pulls in different directions and never gives the listener a sense of resolve from either the group or the music. —*Bob Rusch, Cadence*

○ **Chet (The Lyrical Trumpet of Chet Baker)** / Dec. 30, 1958+Jan. 19, 1959 / Riverside 087
This was a lovely record subtitled *The Lyrical Trumpet of Chet Baker*. Recorded in the late '50s, it presented in different settings Baker with Herbie Mann, Pepper Adams, Bill Evans, Kenny Burrell, Paul Chambers, Connie Kay, or Philly Joe Jones over nine tracks. A placid ambiance permeated all the music, and while this now appears to be an all-star date, the all-stars were really only in a coloring supporting role, though their sound jazz instincts gave the extra meaning even in understatement. It was Baker's date all the way, though when Pepper Adams (baritone sax) was present, his powerful contributions made themselves obvious. —*Bob Rusch, Cadence*

○ **Chet Baker with Wolfgang Lackerschmid** / **i.** Nov. 1979 / Inakustik 8571
This was a record not so much of rhythm as of tonal coloring, pitch, and reverberation. This was also an avant-garde Chet Baker, without gimmicks, just meeting an interest to expand and further develop: to invent, expand, create. This was also very beautiful creativity; art for art's sake. Wolfgang Lackerschmid played vibes in a manner owing more to Red Norvo and Gary Burton than to Milt Jackson and proved himself to be a creator and artist in his ebb and flow with the trumpeter. Bravos for both artists. —*Bob Rusch, Cadence*

○ **Improviser, The** / Aug. 15+30, 1983 / Cadence 1019
These 50 minutes were fairly bustling with drama and tension. As Per Husby's meticulous liner notes point out, trumpeter Chet Baker sounded "beautifully relaxed" on Tadd Dameron's "Gnid" and Hal Galper's "Night," improvising at length and phrasing with the laconic lyricism that was his trademark. And, happily, we have here another Baker essay on Sam Rivers's plaintive "Beatrice," wherein the rhythm section played with amazing responsiveness. —*Alan Bargebuhr, Cadence*

○ **Chet's Choice** / Jun. 25, 1985 / Criss Cross 1016
The brief liner notes to this record speak of Chet Baker's trumpet playing as being "pure poetry," which wasn't too inappropriate a description of most of this record. Baker's somewhat low-key and melodic attack provided for some nice listening on this set of ballads and bop tunes. The lack of percussion on this trio recording provided a somewhat spare setting, which perhaps highlighted Baker's lyricism. The trio played with sufficient heat to prevent this date from being too contemplative and chamberlike. —*Ronald B. Weinstock, Cadence*

○ **My Favourite Songs, Vols. 1 and 2: The Last Great Concert** / **i.** Nov. 1, 1991 / Enja 79600

Shorty Baker (Harold J. Baker)

b. May 26, 1914, St. Louis, MO, **d.** Nov. 8, 1966, NYC
Trumpet / Swing, big band

Trumpeter Shorty Baker was an elegant, careful but always impressive player, someone who made an impression whether doing simple melodies or accompaniment. Baker switched from drums to trumpet in the '20s, playing for a time in a band led by his brother. Baker had a steady slate of appearances and jobs in the '30s; these included periods with Fate Marable, Erskine Tate, Don Redman, the first interlude with Duke Ellington and Teddy Wilson. Baker joined Andy Kirk in 1940 and met pianist Mary Lou Williams, whom he married in 1942. After years of freelance gigs, Baker rejoined Wilson in 1952, then worked in Johnny Hodges' orchestra in 1954-1955. From 1959 through the last part of his career, Baker recorded with Doc Cheatham and Bud Freeman, headed a quartet andd played as a sideman at the Metropole. —*Ron Wynn*

● **Shorty & Doc** / Jan. 17, 1961 / Prestige 2021

Burt Bales (Burton Frank Bales)

b. Mar. 20, 1916, **d.** Oct. 26, 1989
Piano / New Orleans traditional
Although known primarily as a pianist, Burt Bales was also accomplished on mellophone and baritone horn. He began his career with dance bands after 1934, but soon responded to the "traditional" New Orleans jazz revival that hit the Bay Area in the early 40s. He played with Bunk Johnson during the trumpeter's triumphal visit to San Francisco in 1944 and led his own band in 1945-1949. He also maintained a working relationship with Lu Watters and Turk Murphy, then later with Bob Scobey and Marty Marsala in the '50s. He worked primarily as a solo pianist from 1954 to 1959, becoming a local favorite as a regular feature at the Washington Square Bar & Grill in the North Beach section of San Francisco. His love of ragtime and early jazz piano style (especially Jelly Roll Morton) was clearly evident throughout his career, but most reviewers felt Bales added a special sensitivity and subtlety to the music all his own. Often described as playing with a "rocking" style, Burt Bales was a specialist at reviving "old" music.—*Bruce Boyd Raeburn*

★ **They Tore My Playhouse Down** / **i.** 1953 / Good Time Jazz 12025
Burt Bale's testament to Jelly Roll Morton, with numbers such as "Wild Man Blues," "New Orleans Joys," and "Midnight Mama," backed with Paul Lingle's mixed bag of W.C. Handy and Jelly Roll blues and stomps, including "Memphis Blues" and "Black Bottom Stomp" (1953). —*Bruce Raeburn*

Billy Bang (William Vincent Walker)

b. Sep. 20, 1947, Mobile, Alabama, US
Violin / Modern creative
An excellent violinist, Billy Bang grew up in Spanish Harlem and briefly studied violin as a youngster. He examined the music of Ornette Coleman and John Coltrane, and it influenced his later compositions and playing. Bang began playing violin again in 1968, and was working in New York studios in the early '70s. He also studied with Leroy Jenkins. After completing a European concert in 1977, Bang did his initial solo concert. He began visiting Europe annually, and formed the String Trio of New York with guitarist James Emery and bassist John Lindberg in 1977, leading it until 1986. He's also played in Ronald Shannon Jackson's Decoding Society and in Material with guitarist Sonny Sharrock. —*Ron Wynn*

● **Distinction without a Difference** / **i.** Jan. 1981 / Hat Hut 04
Billy Bang's solo violin recital was a gem. Here he displayed not only an accomplished technique but also a fertile imagination that made the 40-minute performance seem more like half that length. —*Carl Brauer, Cadence*

○ **Outline No. 12** / Jul. 1982 / Celluloid 5004
Fine, animated, but tough-to-find album featuring violinist Billy Bang, arguably the most striking to emerge on the jazz scene since Leroy Jenkins. The songs on this set weren't gentle, demure, or bluesy; they were explosive, searching, and combative and as such were ideal for Bang's sawing effects and sweeping solos. —*Ron Wynn, AMG*

○ **Live at Carlos 1** / Nov. 1986 / Soul Note 121136

Paul Barbarin (Adolphe Paul Barbarin)

b. May 5, 1899, New Orleans, LA, **d.** Feb. 17, 1969, New Orleans, LA
Drums / New Orleans traditional
A member of one of New Orleans' most renowned musical dynasties, Paul Barbarin developed his drumming style on the streets of the Crescent City as a teen playing with bands like Buddy Petit's Young Olympians. He left home to find work in the Chicago stockyards in 1917 but soon found more satisfying employment playing with transplanted homeboys like King Oliver and Jimmie Noone, as well as several Chicago outfits. Barbarin maintained a strong association with New Orleans artists throughout his career, working with Oliver's Dixie Syncopators in the mid '20s before joining Luis Russell's Orchestra in 1928, a move that afforded opportunities to play with Jelly Roll Morton and Louis Armstrong in the '30s. Barbarin returned to New Orleans in 1939, but was back in Chicago by 1942-1943 when he joined Red Allen's Sextet. The following year he began playing with Sidney Bechet. After World War II he stayed in his hometown, performing with several small combos and brass bands, including the Onward Brass Band (formed in 1960 and named after the original Onward, which his father Isidore had led at the turn of the century). Barbarin became affiliated with many of the musicians who worked at Preservation Hall during the last decade of his life. These included Sweet Emma Barrett, with whom he recorded. During this period he also made several recordings as a leader for Atlantic, Nobility, and Southland. His death occurred while leading the Onward for a street parade in 1969, concluding his career as it first began. As a drummer, Paul Barbarin excelled in the simple, straightforward approach associated with New Orleans, reflecting the parade beats that pervade the city's festival traditions. His forte was the press roll, and he required no more than a basic kit of snare, bass drum, tom tom, and wood block to present his message effectively. He primarily used cymbals to accent the upbeat on "out choruses" and almost never engaged in extended drum solos. His approach, like that of Warren "Baby" Dodds, was to play for the band, provide just enough swing and lift to hold the group together, and inspire the front-line soloists. Less was always more for players like Barbarin. In addition to his contributions as a "rhythm man," Paul was also known for several musical compositions that have become standards among New Orleans jazz bands, both on the street and in dance halls. These include "Bourbon Street Parade" and "The Second Line."—*Bruce Boyd Raeburn*

★ **And His New Orleans Jazz** / Jan. 7, 1955 / Atlantic 90977
W/ Danny Barker (g), Willie Humphrey, Lester Santiago, and others, romping through traditional New Orleans favorites such as "Eh La Bas" and Barbarin's own "Bourbon Street Parade." Milt Hinton fits in nicely. —*Bruce Boyd Raeburn*

Chris Barber

b. Apr. 17, 1930, Welwyn Garden City, Hertfordshire, En
Trombone, bandleader / New Orleans traditional, blues & jazz
Trombonist-bandleader Chris Barber was active in England's "trad" jazz boom during the '60s, served as a blues promoter, and has recorded for Decca, Columbia, Black Lion, Tempo, and Marmalade among others. He studied trombone at London's Guildhall School and began leading bands in the late '40s. Barber organized a group in the '50s that was initally led by Ken Colyer. Barber became its leader in 1954. Besides promoting concerts bringing Muddy Waters and the Brownie McGhee-Sonny Terry duo to England in the '60s, he restructured his band, changing its name to Chris Barber's Jazz & Blues band. Barber did dates with rock guest stars John Slaughter and Pete York and recorded with Louis Jordan in the '70s. He participated in an "Echoes Of Ellington" tour with Russell Procope and Wild Bill Davis in the '70s and a "Take Me Back To New Orleans" show with Dr. John in the '80s. —*Ron Wynn & Michael G. Nastos*

○ **Louis Jordan Sings** / **i.** 1962 / Black Lion 30175

★ **Live in East Berlin** / Nov. 26, 1968 / Black Lion 760502
Spirited live trad jazz set cut in Berlin in 1968. Barber's music is always enjoyable and catchy, though it's also very derivative and predictable. They tried to change things a bit here by not sticking strictly to trad with the inclusion of "Mercy, Mercy, Mercy." —*Ron Wynn, AMG*

○ **Chris Barber & Lonnie Donegan** / **i.** 1973 / Boulevard 4110

○ **Echoes of Ellington** / **i**. 1978 / Black Lion 001
○ **Creole Love Call** / **i**. 1983 / Timeless 3

Gato Barbieri (Leandro J. Barbieri)

b. Nov. 28, 1934, Rosario, Argentina
Tenor sax, composer / Latin jazz, world fusion, instrumental pop, modern creative
Tenor saxophonist and composer Gato Barbieri ranks among the most popular Latin-jazz players ever. He has had a complete career turnaround since the mid '60s when he was a screaming avant-garde player under the influence of Pharoah Sanders. Born in Argentina, Barbieri made an early impact in Lalo Schfrin's band in 1953. He traveled through Europe, meeting Don Cherry in Paris in 1956 and recording with him in New York in 1966. Barbieri made a splash in 1969 by mixing Latin American rhythms with free-music influences and techniques. During the early '70s, he made some substantial records with sweeping, blazing solos, but he switched to a lush, romantic style in 1972 with the Grammy-winning *Last Tango in Paris* soundtrack. Despite cutting adventurous albums with Latin musicians during the '70s, his sensual sessions with strings became the most popular and best remembered recordings.—*Ron Wynn*

○ **Gato Barbieri and Don Cherry** / 1965 / Inner City 1009
Great duo record with Barbieri and Cherry at their most adventurous and outside. This record is miles away from the heavily orchestrated, quasi-pop soundtracks and mood music that Barbieri's had hits with in the '70s and '80s, and also much different from Cherry's international material. —*Ron Wynn, AMG*

★ **Fenix** / Apr. 27-28, 1971 / FD 10144
The manic album that won him fame on college campuses in the early '70s. Still his greatest record on all levels. Nana Vasconcelos is tremendous on percussion. —*Ron Wynn*

● **Last Tango in Paris** / Nov. 20-25, 1972 / United Artists 29440
An incredibly popular soundtrack, dreamy and lush. Still sounds great 20 years later. Grammy-winning, sensual soundtrack to the controversial film. —*Ron Wynn*

☆ **Chapter 1: Latin America** / **i**. 1973 / MCA 39124
A major statement of Latin Jazz. Barbieri with a cast of Argentinian musics. He later toured with them in the USA to overflow crowds in several places. —*Ron Wynn*

☆ **Caliente** / 1976 / A&M 3247

Danny Barker (Daniel Moses Barker)

b. Jan. 13, 1909, New Orleans, LA
Guitar, banjo, vocals, composer / New Orleans traditional
Composer, historian, guitarist, and banjoist Danny Barker's career covered the whole of jazz history, particularly traditional New Orleans music. His single-string technique and chordal style on guitar and banjo were featured on numerous recordings and live dates, including albums made with Red Allen and Blue Lou Barker (his wife). He wrote many revered songs, among them "Save The Bones for Henry Jones" and "Don't You Make Me Feel High." Barker played and/or toured with Little Brother Montgomery, The Boozan Kings, Willie Pajeaud, Sidney Bechet, Fess Willliams, James P. Johnson, Lucky Millinder, Benny Carter, Albert Nicholas, Mutt Carey, Bunk Johnson, and Cab Calloway among others. He was a regular at Ryan's in New York, was featured on the '40s radio series "This Is Jazz" and served as curator of the New Orleans Jazz Museum for over a decade. Barker was also grand marshal of the Onward Brass Band in the '60s and '70s, founder of the Fairview Baptist Church Brass band, co-author with Jack Buerkle of "Bourbon Street Black" and author of "A Life In Jazz" in 1986. He died in 1994. —*Ron Wynn and Michael G. Nastos*

★ **Save the Bones** / 1988 / Orleans 1018

Charlie Barnet (Charles Daly Barnet)

b. Oct. 26, 1913, New York, NY, **d**. Sep. 4, 1991
Bandleader, vocals, sax / Swing, big band
Charlie Barnet was a fine swing-era bandleader and alto player of musical and political importance. He headed bands from age 16 until his death at 78. He was a master talent evaluator, spotting Lena Horne, Buddy De Franco, and Dodo Marmarosa, among many others, in their early stages. He had some big hits in the '30s and '40s, particularly "Cherokee" in 1939. He was also

among the first White bandleaders to hire Black musicians in the '30s, without the fanfare given some others. —*Ron Wynn*

★ **Barnet—Vol. 1 (1935-1939)** / 1935-1939 / EPM
An excellent reissue of late and mid-'30s swing cuts. —*Ron Wynn*

○ **Complete Charlie Barnet—Vol. 2** / **i**. 1939 / RCA 5577
One in a series devoted to late-'30s swing recordings of Charlie Barnet. The songs, solos, arrangements, and mood are mostly joyous, and if you're a big band devotee, these are essential cuts. But you're better served getting a complete multidisc package rather than yearly sets. —*Ron Wynn, AMG*

○ **Clap Hands, Here Comes Charlie** / **i**. 1939-1941 / Bluebird 6273
This sampler had 21 of Barnet's best recordings (62:46), tracing his band from Jan. 20, 1939 to Aug. 14, 1941, its prime period. Barnetophiles will desire his six twofer sets, but this CD is the definitive single package. —*Scott Yanow, Cadence*

○ **Rockin' in Rhythm** / **i**. 1954 / RCA 3062

Joey Baron

Drums / M-Base, modern creative
A slashing, excellent drummer who's worked with several of the '80s and '90s most eclectic instrumentalists, and led his own bands. Baron's recorded with Tim Berne, Hank Roberts, Steve Swallow, and Ellery Eskelin, while also playing with Jim Hall and Toots Thielemans. He's also worked, recorded, and toured frequently with alto saxophonist and composer John Zorn. His compositions range from free and collective unison works to funk, fusion, rock, and reggae. Baron's also recorded in trios with Enrico Pieranunzi and Marc Johnson and with Charlie Haden and Fred Hersch. Baron's done sessions on JMT and Soul Note. He has dates available on CD. —*Ron Wynn*

○ **RAIsedpleasuredot** / **i**. 1993 / New World 80449
Drummer Joey Baron has played with such unorthodox types as John Zorn, Wayne Horovitz, and Tim Berne, so it's not surprising his own sessions are equally diverse and ambitious. This '93 date presents an unusual instrumental lineup and a free-wheeling, constantly changing musical menu. Baron heads a trio with trumpet and trombone; the absence of bass, keyboards, or guitar results in intriguing voicings, and the pieces are solely dependent on the interaction of his drumming with Ellery Eseklin's saxophone and Steve Sewell's trombone contributions. There are meaty unison passages, segments with shuddering sax, thrashing trombone, and crashing drums, and others that emphasize complementary playing. Though it is a collective work, Baron's drumming and vision set the pace throughout the 17 pieces. Elements of free jazz, contemporary funk, Afro-Latin, and even modern classical are incorporated into the mix, and it's an outstanding example of Joey Baron's scope and range as a composer, bandleader, and player. —*Ron Wynn*

Dan Barrett

b. Dec. 14, 1955, Pasadena, California, US
Brass, trombone / Swing
Another of the contemporary swing-influenced musicians, Barret played in many small combo settings for Concord Records in the '80s and '90s. The octet made one acclaimed album in 1987. Barrett co-led another group with guitarist Howard Allen. He's an accomplished, very capable brass player. —*Ron Wynn*

● **Strictly Instrumental** / Jun. 1987 / Concord Jazz 4331
Individually, pianist Dick Wellstood and trombonist Dan Barrett were the stars. To have theme statements made by trombone again was very welcome indeed. —*Stanley Dance, Jazz Times*

Ray Barretto

b. Apr. 29, 1929, Brooklyn, NY
Composer, conga, percussion, bandleader / Latin jazz, world fusion
Barretto ranks among the greatest, most influential percussionists of all time. He brought Latin rhythms into the jazz mainstream and has been exhaustively recorded since the early '50s. He's also done numerous R&B and rock dates and many salsa sessions. Born in Brooklyn, Barretto played with jazz musicians in New York. He made his way up the ladder and eventually replaced Mongo Santamaria in Tito Puente's band, working with him for four years. Barretto made his first Latin-jazz album for Riverside in 1965 and has been active ever since as a player, ses-

sion man, and producer. He rivals Mongo and Puente as the best-known Latin-jazz instrumentalist. —*Ron Wynn*

● **Other Road, The** / 1973 / Fania 00448
With Billy Cobham on drums and Arthur Webb adding lilting flute inflections, this album was a conscious attempt by Ray Barretto to overstep the merely ethnic appeal. With a nod to old times on "Round Midnight" (which featured an intriguing arrangement by Dick Mesa), a journey into the more electronic sounds of tomorrow on "Oracion (The Prayer)," and a rock-energized tune like "Lucretia The Cat," the album contained an unusual variety of material. —*Ray Townley, Down Beat*

Bill Barron (William Barron, Jr.)

b. Mar. 27, 1927, Philadelphia, PA, **d.** Sep. 21, 1989
Tenor sax, soprano sax, flute, composer / Hard bop
The brother of pianist Kenny Barron, tenor saxophonist Bill Barron had a sturdy tone and resourceful style. He was adaptable enough to record in bop and hard bop contexts, yet also work with Cecil Taylor and colead a band with Ted Curson. Barron played with Jimmy Heath and Red Garland in Philadelpia before moving to New York in 1958. Barrron directed the Muse Jazz Workshop at the Children's Museum in Brooklyn and taught at City College in the '60s and '70s, then served as chairman of Wesleyan University's Music Department in the mid-'80s. He recorded for Savoy, Audiophile, and Muse among others. —*Ron Wynn*

● **Variations in Blue** / Aug. 23-24, 1984 / Muse 5306
Fine release by Bill Barron, a 1983 quintet set, with him playing in familiar, warm manner, able to either shift into more animated pace or move into interpretative, somber ballad style with ease. Steady, consistent contributions from trumpeter Jimmy Owens, pianist Kenny Barron, bassist Ray Drummond, and drummer Ben Riley. —*Ron Wynn, AMG*

Kenny Barron (Kenneth Barron)

b. 1943, Philadelphia, PA
Piano, composer / Hard bop
Kenny Barron's professional career as a pianist began at 15 with an R&B band in his native Philadelphia. He then worked with Philly Joe Jones, Yuseff Lateef, and Jimmy Heath. Barron came to New York in 1961 and joined Dizzy Gillespie's group a year later, staying until 1966. Stints with Freddie Hubbard, Stanley Turrentine, Buddy Rich, Ron Carter, and many others followed. He became one of jazz's most prolific recording artists. Barron made his first album as a leader in 1974, a year after he'd been appointed to the faculty of Rutgers University. He co-led the group Sphere (dedicated to the music of Thelonious Monk) and has fronted his own trios and quintets. In the early '90s, Barron teamed with saxophonist Stan Getz, who made his final live recording (*People Time*) a duo date with Barron. A marvelous player with his own distinctive touch, Barron's adaptable to any situation.—*Ron Wynn*

○ **1 + 1 + 1** / Apr. 23-24, 1984 / Blackhawk 506
1+1+1 presented pianist Kenny Barron in the company of either Michael Moore or Ron Carter, two of the world's finest bassists. Both were superb partners who provided such self-sufficient harmonic and rhythmic support that additional instrumentation would seem superfluous. —*A. David Franklin, Cadence*

○ **Scratch** / Mar. 11, 1985 / Enja 4092
Here pianist Kenny Barron took on a too-infrequent lead date with two of Europe's leading lights (English bassist Dave Holland and Swiss drummer Daniel Humair) and the sparks flew! —*Fred Bouchard, Jazz Times*

★ **Live at Maybeck Recital Hall—Vol. 10** / Dec. 3, 1990 / Concord Jazz 4466

○ **Quickstep** / Feb. 18, 1991 / Enja 79669
Kenny Barron Quintet. Composer Barron's best group effort. "Big Girls" is a big composition. —*Michael G. Nastos*

Gary Bartz (Gary Lee Bartz)

b. Sep. 26, 1940, Baltimore, MD
Alto sax, soprano sax, composer / Hard bop
Alto saxophonist Gary Bartz reclaimed his reputation as a solid hard bop and mainstream soloist in the '80s and '90s after some erratic late '70s recordings. He played as a teen in his father's

Baltimore jazz club, and spent two years at Juilliard, where his associates included Grachan Moncur III and Lee Morgan. Bartz's inital mark was made with Max Roach and Abbey Lincoln in the mid-'60s. He was in Art Blakey's Jazz Messengers in 1965 and 1966 before forming the NTU Troop in 1967. Bartz recorded with Max Roach and Charles Tolliver as well as McCoy Tyner in the late '60s. He played with Miles Davis in 1970 and 1971, recorded with Woody Shaw, Pharoah Sanders, Jackie McLean, and Lee Konitz and toured Europe. Bartz continued recording with Tyner until the late '70s. He's done sessions as a leader for Milestone, Prestige, Steeplechase, Capitol, and Candid among others. —*Ron Wynn*

○ **Another Earth** / Jun. 19, 1968 / Milestone 9018
The album that brought alto saxophonist Gary Bartz close to stardom in the late '60s. It's got lengthy songs; intense, sometimes dramatic solos; and a guest spot from Pharoah Sanders. When he turned in less challenging directions in the early '70s, many were puzzled and disappointed. —*Ron Wynn, AMG*

○ **Libra** / May 31, 1969+Jun. 15, 1967 / Milestone 9006
Excellent compositions and playing in mainstream mode. Features Kenny Barron on piano and Jimmy Owens on Trumpet. This is the more lyrical side of Bartz. —*Michael G. Nastos*

○ **I've Known Rivers and Other Bodies** / Jul. 7, 1974 / Prestige 66001
I've Known Rivers was the Ntu Troop's complete performance (with some editing) at the 1973 Montreaux Jazz Festival. Side one and two of the double disc package, in fact, were totally uncut. The first two sides were nonstop music beginning with the blues "Majick Song," Bartz's device for freeing the audience from any evil thoughts they may have brought with them, and evolved naturally through "Zote," "Jujuman," "Baptist," "Feeling," and "Mama's Soul." "Jujuman," for example, was based on John Coltrane's "Love Supreme" theme, while "Feeling" found drummer Howard King and pianist Hubert Eaves in a rock groove. "Rivers," which opened side three, was based on a Langston Hughes poem, and the melody was beautiful. Bartz's vocal, his best, was warm and infectious. *I've Known Rivers and Other Bodies* was music for everybody, happy, honest, and exciting. It was a celebration. —*Herb Nolan, Down Beat*

★ **West 42nd Street** / Mar. 31, 1990 / Candid 79049
Another fine recent release by Gary Bartz, who seems determined not to let his reputation slip in the '90s. From burning hard bop to convincing blues with a touch of funk, this is someone with something to say, rather than another instrumentalist confused and plugging into the latest trends. —*Ron Wynn, AMG*

Count Basie (William Basie)

b. Aug. 21, 1904, Red Bank, NJ, **d.** Apr. 26, 1984, Hollywood, CA
Bandleader, piano / Swing, big band
One of the towering figures in big-band jazz, Count Basie was a leader from 1935 until his death. His lean piano style was like a signature, and he was a master at setting tempos and making a rhythm section swing. Born in New Jersey, Bill Basie learned his piano craft from James P. Johnson and Fats Waller and was touring on the vaudeville circuit while still a teenager. Stranded in Kansas City in 1927, he settled there, joined Walter Page's Blue Devils (the hottest KC band), and then Bennie Moten's Orchestra (the most successful KC band). He took over when Moten died suddenly in 1935 but then scaled the group down to a smaller band, the Barons of Rhythm, at the Reno Club in KC. Talent spotter John Hammond heard them on his car radio and zoomed out to hear the band live. He got them a record deal, and made Basie expand for a national tour. With such soloists as Lester Young and Herschel Evans on tenors, Buck Clayton and (a bit later) Harry Edison on trumpets, and a rhythm section of Freddie Green, guitar, former boss Walter Page, bass, and Jo Jones, drums, the streamlined swing of Basie & Co. captivated both jazz fans and dancers and made the band part of jazz royalty. Though he briefly was forced to lead a sextet (1950-1951), Basie was soon back at the helm of a 16-piece crew; this "new testament" band (as it was dubbed by Basie biographer Albert Murray) became a jazz institution, notably after singer Joe Williams joined, and continues today as the Count Basie Band led by Frank Foster, one of Count's most distinguished post-1952 alumni. In the history of jazz, no name is more synonymous with swinging big-band jazz. —*Dan Morgenstern*

● **Complete Roulette Live Recordings of Count Basie and His Orchestra (1958-1962), The** / Mosaic 135

Count Basie is one jazz musician that was amply recorded throughout his career and has been the subject of numerous domestic and foreign reissue lines. Yet Mosaic has managed to release Count Basie material in a valuable fashion. This eight-disc set contains Basie recordings for the Roulette label from 1959 to 1962. It is the first of a two-part series covering his full Roulette output. These are live recordings; the studio sessions are coming via their own set. They were recorded in Miami at Birdland and in Sweden. The menu includes the familiar standards "One O'Clock Jump,""Lil' Darlin'," "Moten Swing," and "Jumpin' at the Woodside." There are plenty of blues, relaxed swingers, and superb vocals provided by a roster of singers that includes Joe Williams, Sarah Vaughan, Jon Hendricks, and O.C. Smith. The regular lineup is augmented on the Swedish sessions by guest instrumentalists trumpeter Benny Bailey and trombonist Ake Persson.

There is nothing revolutionary about this music. But its consistency and celebratory fiber remains impressive through every disc. Basie's band contained such musical veterans as Frank Wess, Billy Mitchell, Al Grey, Freddie Green, Marshall Royal, and Sonny Payne. They were pros who played every night with wit, humor, precision, and charm; could truly play the blues; and never wasted energy or emotion. Their songs were short, steady, and always delightful.

While eight discs is a lot of time for one band no matter how great (and they do frequently repeat some songs like "One O'Clock Jump" and "Lil' Darlin'") the set provides a chance to replicate the experience of life on the road for a touring band. Basie fanatics probably already have this and are eagerly awaiting the follow-up; those who are not should still get this set. *—Ron Wynn*

☆ **Basie's Basement** / Oct. 23, 1929-Dec. 13, 1932 / Bluebird 61065

W/ Jimmy Rushing. The genesis of the Count Basie band can be heard in these recordings by Bennie Moten's Kansas City Orchestra. With Count on piano, trumpeter Hot Lips Page, tenorsaxophonist Ben Webster, and such future Basieites as trombonist-guitarist Eddie Durham, baritonist Jack Washington, bassist Walter Page, and the great singer Jimmy Rushing, there are times when Moten's orchestra almost sounds like Count's. Eight selections from the 1929- 1930 period are followed by eight numbers recorded at Moten's last and greatest sesssion (from Dec. 13, 1932). Such tunes as "Moten's Swing," "Lafayette," and "Blue Room" are prime examples of early swing. *—Scott Yanow*

○ **Count Basie in Kansas City** / 1929-1932 / Camden 514

☆ **Essential Count Basie—Vols. 1 and 2** / Oct. 9, 1936-Jun. 24, 1939 / Columbia 40061

Rather than release all of Count Basie's studio recordings (as Decca recently has or as French Columbia did in two large LP sets over a decade ago), CBS has put together three samplers that contain some (but not all) of the essential Basie recordings from the 1939-1941 period. This first volume has Lester Young's great solo on 1936's "Lady Be Good," the classics "Rock-a-Bye Basie" and "Taxi War Dance," and fine examples of the Basie orchestra throughout 1939. *—Scott Yanow*

☆ **Best of Count Basie, The** / i. 1937-Feb. 2, 1939 / MCA 4050

This two-LP set contains the best of Basie's Decca years, 24 prime selections including the five mentioned in the review for *The Complete Decca Recordings*. A fine general collection, although most collectors will opt for the much more complete three-CD package. *—Scott Yanow*

★ **Complete Decca Recordings (1937-1939), The** / 1937-Feb.· 4, 1939 / GRP 36112

This magnificent three-CD set has the first 63 recordings by Count Basie's orchestra, all of his Deccas. The consistency is remarkable (with not more than two or three turkeys), and the music is the epitome of swing. With such soloists as Lester Young and Herschel Evans on tenors, trumpeters Buck Clayton and Harry "Sweets" Edison, the great blues singer Jimmy Rushing, and that brilliant rhythm section of Basie, guitarist Freddie Green, bassist Walter Page, and drummer Jo Jones, the music is timeless. It's all here: "One O'Clock Jump," "Sent for You Yesterday," "Blue and Sentimental," "Jumpin' at the Woodside," "Jive at Five," and many others. This is the first Count Basie collection to acquire and should be in every jazz collection. *—Scott Yanow*

○ **Golden Years Vol. 1 (1938), The** / 1938 / EPM 5502

○ **Golden Years Vol. 2 (1938), The** / 1938 / EPM 5510

○ **Essential Count Basie—Vol. 2** / Aug. 4, 1939-May 31, 1940 / Columbia 40835

A fine sampler of the 1939-1940 Count Basie orchestra with such classic performances as "Dickie's Dream," "Lester Leaps In" and "Tickle Toe." Lester Young and fellow tenor Buddy Tate, trumpeters Buck Clayton and Harry Edison, and trombonist Dickie Wells all have their chances to star; they can't help swinging with that light but solid Basie rhythm section! Count's Columbia recordings deserve to be reissued in full (with all of the alternate takes) but until CBS gets around to it, this is a good introduction to that period. *—Scott Yanow*

☆ **Blues by Basie** / i. 1939-1950 / Columbia 901

Because Count Basie streamlined his piano style down to the bare basics, it is often forgotten how strong a pianist he could be when he was inspired. This intriguing LP features live performances taken from a variety of settings and time periods (dating from 1941-1967), all of which put the focus on Basie's piano. Not too surprisingly most of the numbers are blues, but Basie is in consistently fine form and there is enough variety to keep one's interest throughout this excellent set. *—Scott Yanow*

☆ **Essential Count Basie—Vol. 3** / Aug. 8, 1940-Apr. 10, 1941 / Columbia 44150

The third and thus far final volume in a sampler series picking out some of the highpoints of Count Basie's 1939-1942 period on Columbia. Lester Young's departure in December 1940 robbed the orchestra of their top soloist, but the band still outswung all of its competitors and the personnel was consistently outstanding. Coleman Hawkins' guest appearance on "9:20 Special" and "Feedin' the Bean" round out this enjoyable all-round set, but when is Columbia going to reissue all of their Count Basie recordings instead of always recycling the same ones? *—Scott Yanow*

○ **Count Basie (1940-1941)** / i. Nov. 1940-Apr. 1941 / Classics 623

○ **Brand New Wagon: Count Basie 1947** / Jan. 3, 1947-Dec. 12, 1947 / Bluebird 2292

While French RCA put out a three-LP set documenting 48 of Count Basie's recordings for that label during 1947-1950, its American counterpart just reissued 21 of those sides (all from 1947) on this highly enjoyable CD. Best are the octet and nonet recordings of May 20-21, but none of these tracks are weak. Trumpeter Harry "Sweets" Edison, the tenors of Paul Gonsalves and Buddy Tate, and the long underrated baritonist Jack Washington star, along with vocalist Jimmy Rushing and the rhythm section. Even during what is sometimes written off as a declining period, the Basie orchestra was near the top in quality, if not popularity. *—Scott Yanow*

☆ **Class of '54** / Sep. 2, 1954-Sep. 7, 1954 / Black Lion 760924

This fine CD consists of two radio airchecks from 1954, featuring Count Basie with a nonet and his full orchestra. The smaller group also has trumpeter Joe Newman, trombonist Henry Coker, and the tenors of Frank Wess and Frank Foster well featured, while the big band tracks (which mostly sport Neal Hefti arrangements) finds the orchestra on the brink of great success. *—Scott Yanow*

☆ **Count Basie Swings, Joe Williams Sings** / i. Jul. 17, 1955-Jul. 26, 1955 / Verve 825770

Joe Williams's debut on records with the Basie orchestra was so successful in every way that the band's future was secure for the next few decades. Included on this essential set are the classic versions of "Every Day I Have the Blues," "The Comeback," "Alright Okay, You Win," "In the Evening," and "Teach Me Tonight," hits that Williams and Basie would have to perform nightly for the remainder of the 1950s. Highly recommended. *—Scott Yanow*

☆ **April in Paris** / Jul. 26, 1955-Jan. 5, 1956 / Verve 825575

A true classic, this studio album includes Count Basie's hit versions of "April in Paris," "Shiny Stockings," and "Corner Pocket," three tunes that have remained in the Basie band's repertoire ever since. Actually all ten selections are very enjoyable, and this exciting and of course swinging record is definitive of 1950's Count Basie. *—Scott Yanow*

★ **Swings with Joe Williams** / i. 1955 / PolyGram 825770

W/ Joe Williams. Simply glorious after all these years. Williams was the greatest singer in this style in 1955, at least among males. —*Ron Wynn*

○ **Basie Roars Again!** / **i.** 1956 / Clef 723

○ **King of Swing, The** / **i.** 1956 / Clef 724

○ **Basie Rides Again!** / **i.** 1956 / Clef 729

○ **Basie Bash** / **i.** 1956 / Columbia 2560

☆ **Greatest! Count Basie Plays...Joe Williams Sings Standards, The** / **i.** Apr. 28, 1956 / Verve 833774
W/ Joe Williams. Joe Williams never wanted to be typecast as just a blues singer, so on his second full album with Count Basie he concentrated on standards. The swinging treatments given to songs such as "Thou Swell," "My Baby Just Cares for Me" and even "Singin' in the Rain" works quite well even if the band is mostly confined to a supporting role. —*Scott Yanow*

☆ **Count Basie in London** / Sep. 7, 1956 / Verve 833805
The original of this session's title is a bit of a mystery since this album was actually recorded live in Sweden! The Count Basie orchestra plays its usual repertoire (including "Jumpin' at the Woodside," "Shiny Stockings," and "Corner Pocket") with enthusiasm, concise solos, and typical Basie swing. Joe Williams takes a few vocals, and this CD is rounded by three previously unreleased performances. —*Scott Yanow*

☆ **Count Basie at Newport** / Sep. 7, 1957 / PolyGram 833776
At the 1957 Newport Jazz Festival the music was consistently inspired and often historic. Count Basie welcomed back tenor great Lester Young and singer Jimmy Rushing for part of a very memorable set highlighted by "Boogie Woogie" and "Evenin'"; Young plays beautifully throughout, and Rushing is in prime form. An exciting full-length version of "One O'Clock Jump" features Young, Illinois Jacquet, and trumpeter Roy Eldridge; the Basie band stretches out on "Swingin' at Newport"; and five previously unreleased selections (put out for the first time on this CD) include four Joe Williams vocals. A great set of music. —*Scott Yanow*

○ **Atomic Mr. Basie** / Oct. 21, 1957-Oct. 22, 1957 / Roulette 1309
Known as the Atomic album due to the cover picture of an A-Bomb exploding, this is one of the great Count Basie records, ranking with *April in Paris*. The 1957 edition of the Basie orchestra romps through "The Kid from Red Bank" (a superlative feature for its leader)," "Whirly Bird" and "Lil' Darlin'" among others; everything works on this essential album. —*Scott Yanow*

☆ **Sing Along with Basie** / May 26, 1958-Sep. 3, 1958 / Roulette 95332
The extraordinary jazz vocal group Lambert, Hendricks, and Ross had debuted in 1957 with *Sing a Song of Basie*, during which they recreated Count's orchestra with their overdubbed voices. That album was so successful that the following year they were able to actually team up with the Basie band. Frank Foster put down on paper the original head arrangements of the '30s and '40s for the orchestra, leaving space for the vocalists to recreate the original solos. The result is a colorful and swinging set. Best is a version of "Goin' to Chicago Blues" that has Joe Williams taking his original vocal while L., H. & Ross sing around him. —*Scott Yanow*

☆ **One More Time (Music from the Pen of Quincy Jones)** / Dec. 18, 1958-Jan. 24, 1959 / Roulette 97271
For this studio album from late 1958 and early 1959, the Count Basie orchestra performs ten Quincy Jones compositions; he also contributed all of the arrangements. "I Needs to Be Beed With," "For Lena and Lennie," and "The Midnight Sun Never Sets" all caught on and Jones's charts helped expand the Basie sound without altering it. An excellent CD. —*Scott Yanow*

☆ **Basie Swings, Bennett Sings** / Jan. 1959 / Roulette 93899
W/Tony Bennett (v). Dynamic meeting of the great singer and great band. —*Ron Wynn*

☆ **Everyday I Have the Blues** / Sep. 24, 1959 / Roulette 52033
W/ Joe Williams. One of Joe Williams's most rewarding recordings with Count Basie. On this set of blues-oriented material, Williams does a fine remake of "Everyday I Have the Blues" and a classic version of "Going to Chicago," but all ten selections are quite enjoyable. —*Scott Yanow*

☆ **Kansas City Suite: The Music of Benny Carter** / Sep. 1960 / Roulette 94575

These two 1960 sessions gave Benny Carter a unique chance to write a full program for Count Basie's orchestra. Arranged as a type of suite, the ten originals pay tribute to the various Kansas City clubs that were active in the 1930s when Basie was a resident. The band swings throughout as usual, with concise solos adding color to this memorable modern session. —*Scott Yanow*

☆ **First Time! the Count Meets The Duke** / Jul. 6, 1961 / Columbia 40586
This session was an impossible dream come true, the teaming up of the entire Count Basie and Duke Ellington orchestras, including the principals on joint pianos. Whether it be "Take the 'A' Train," "Jumpin' at the Woodside," or "Until I Met You," everything works on this album, and somehow the ensembles avoid sounding overcrowded. This version of "Segue in C" is the outstanding performance of a unique and highly enjoyable set. —*Scott Yanow*

○ **Basie at Birdland** / Jul. 28, 1961 / Capitol 59039
The Count Basie orchestra was very much at home at New York's Birdland in the 1950s and early '60's, frequently playing there several months a year. This spirited set has swinging versions of such Basie classics as "Segue in C," "Blues Backstage," and "Little Pony" with Jon Hendricks's guest vocal on "Whirly Bird" taking honors. —*Scott Yanow*

☆ **Count Basie and the Kansas City 7** / Mar. 21, 1962 / MCA 5656
One of Count Basie's few small-group sessions of the 1960s and his best. With trumpeter Thad Jones and the tenors of Frank Foster and Eric Dixon filling in the septet, Basie is in superlative form on a variety of blues, standards, and two originals apiece from Thad Jones and Frank Wess. Small group swing at its best. —*Scott Yanow*

☆ **Ella and Basie!** / Jul. 15, 1963-Jul. 16, 1963 / Verve
It is hard to believe considering how often they would work together in future years, but at the time of this 1963 session, Ella Fitzgerald had never recorded with Count Basie's orchestra. Their first collaboration was a happy one with Quincy Jones providing arrangements to such swingers as "Honeysuckle Rose," "Them There Eyes" (one of two numbers played by a small group from Basie's big band), "Tea for Two," and "On the Sunny Side of the Street." Other than "Shiny Stockings," most of the repertoire is not strictly from Basie's book, but the results are quite pleasing. —*Scott Yanow*

☆ **Basie's Beat** / Oct. 7, 1965-Feb. 15, 1967 / Verve 8687
During an era when the Count Basie orchestra was often being used as a mere prop behind other singers, this album was quite refreshing. With the exception of trombonist Richard Boone's two eccentric vocals, this is an instrumental date with arrangements provided by bandmembers past and present and concise solos contributed by quite a few talented players. —*Scott Yanow*

○ **Our Shining Hour** / 1965 / Verve 8605

☆ **Jazz Fest Masters—Count Basie** / Jun. 1969 / Jazz Masters 75245
If one judged them by their studio albums of the 1963-1970 period, it might seem that Count Basie's orchestra was in its decline, but this recently released live CD proves otherwise. Recorded at the 1969 New Orleans Jazz Festival, the Basie band swings such tunes as "Whirlybird," "Corner Pocket," "Cherokee" (an Eddie "Lockjaw" Davis feature), and "April in Paris" with enthusiasm and power. A fine session. —*Scott Yanow*

☆ **Afrique** / Dec. 22, 1970-Dec. 23, 1970 / Doctor Jazz 39520
Possibly the most unusual album by Count Basie and certainly the most modern. For this session Oliver Nelson arranged eight recent songs, including avant-gardist Albert Ayler's "Love Flower" and Pharoah Sanders's "Japan," giving the Basie band a more "contemporary" setting (utilizing electric bass on half the songs) while not altering its basic sound. Nelson's "Kilimanjaro" and "Hobo Flats" are highlights of this very successful but never repeated "experiment." —*Scott Yanow*

○ **Basie Jam at Montreux '75** / Jul. 19, 1975 / Pablo 2310750
On one of the earliest and best of the Count Basie jams for Pablo, Basie sounds very happy pushing the combative trumpeter Roy Eldridge, tenor-saxophonist Johnny Griffin, and vibraphonist Milt Jackson on two blues and a lengthy version of "Lester Leaps In." Plenty of sparks fly. —*Scott Yanow*

○ **88 Basie Street** / May 11-12, 1983 / Pablo 2310901
One of Count Basie's final albums, the very appealing title cut seems to sum up Basie's career, a lightly swinging groove with a strong melody. Two small group performances with guest Joe

Music Map

Jazz Bass, Double-Bass, Contrabass

1890s Ragtime Orchestras & String Bands – Tub & stick
Billy Marrero (1874) – Henry Kimball

Early Jazz Bass – Classic Jazz Era
Bill Johnson (1872-1972) – Steve Brown
John Lindsay (1894-1950) – Wellman Braud (1891-1966)

Early Rhythm Section
Pops Foster (1892-1969) – Al Morgan (1908-1974)

Billy Taylor (1906-1986) – Hayes Alvis (1907-1972)
Grachan Moncur II (1915) – George Kelly (1915-1985)

1930s Players
Walter Page (1900-1957)
John Kirby (1908-1952)
Jimmy Blanton (1918-1942)

1940s Players
Ray Brown (1926)
Milt Hinton (1910)
Tommy Potter (1918-1988)
Red Callender (1916-1922)
Charles Mingus (1922-1979)
Oscar Pettiford (1922-1960)
Slam Stewart (1914-1987)

Sing Along with Instrument
Slam Stewart (1914-1987) – Major Holley (1924)

1950s Players
Wilbur Ware (1923-1979)
Ray Brown (1926)
Charles Mingus (1922-1979)
Red Mitchell (1927)
Scott LaFaro (1936-1961)
Gary Peacock (1935)
Eddie Gomez (1944)

Mainstream
Sam Jones (1924) – Doug Watkins (1934-1962)
Bob Cranshaw (1932) – Paul Chambers (1935-1969)
Ron Carter (1937) – Walter Booker Jr. (1933)
Jimmy Garrison (1934-1976)– George Mraz (1944)
Harvey Swartz (1948)

Major Players
Charlie Haden (1937)
Dave Holland (1946)
Barre Phillips (1934)
Arlid Andersen (1945)
Miroslav Vitous (1947)
Niels Henning-Ørsted Pedersen (1946)
Bary Guy (1947)
Henry Grimes (1935)
Alan Silva
Cecil McBee (1935)
Chris White (1936
Clint Houston (1946)
Israel Crosby (1919-1962)
Bill Crow (1927)
Isla Eckinger (1939)
David Izenon (1932-1979)
Gene Ramey (1913-1984)

Electric Bass
Steve Swallow (1940)
Eberhard Weber (1940)
Jamaaladeen Tacuma (1956)
Alex Blake
Alphonso Johnson (1951)
Albert MacDowell
Jymie Merritt (1926)
Chuck Rainey (1940)
Stanley Clarke (1951)
Monk Montgomery (1921-1982)
Jaco Pastorius (1951-1987)

1980s-1990s
Mark Johnson
Eddie Gomez (1944)
Ratso Harris
Christian McBride
Reginald Veal
Charnett Moffitt
Robert Hurst
Rodney Whitaker
Ray Drummond
Rufus Reid (1944)
Charles Fambrough

Sirone (1940) – Ron McClure (1941)

Pass on guitar and the tenor of Kenny Hing add variety to a particularly strong set. —*Scott Yanow*

☆ **Legend—the Legacy** / May 16, 1989-May 17, 1989 / Denon 73790
Three years after Frank Foster had become leader of the Count Basie Orchestra, the group continued to place very well in jazz polls; few big bands were in its class. This fine CD finds Foster extending the tradition of Count Basie with new arrangements and features for both veterans (including trumpeter Sonny Cohn, altoist Danny Turner, and the tenors of Kenny Hing and Eric Dixon) and the newer members (such as trumpeter Byron Stripling and pianist Ace Carter). With Carmen Bradford proving to be the band's best vocalist since Joe Williams, Frank Foster had succeeded at not only reviving the Count Basie orchestra but also restoring it to its prime. The lengthy "Count Basie Remembrance

Suite," "Booze Brothers," and a new version of Neal Hefti's "Whirly Bird" are among this enjoyable CD's highlights. —*Scott Yanow*

Alvin Batiste

b. 1937, New Orleans, Louisiana

Clarinet / New Orleans traditional bop, hard bop blues & jazz
He's among New Orleans's most respected musicians, yet clarinetist Alvin Batiste has neither a huge public profile nor an extensive recorded legacy. Batiste played with Ed Blackwell while in high school. Following army duty, he met and befriended Ornette Coleman, playing with him in jam sessions in Los Angeles in the mid-'50s. Upon returning to New Orleans, Batiste did freelance studio work, where his dipping, darting runs and

soulful wails earned plaudits from musicians. He toured in Ray Charles's band in 195 but gained more recognition during the late '60s and throughout the '70s and early '80s as an educator. Batiste directed a jazz course at Southern University from 1969 to the mid-'80s. This work prevented him from completing a project with Cannonball Adderley, though he did appear on two Adderley albums, including the final Cannonball session *Lovers* in '75. Batiste also appeared at the Montreaux Jazz Festival with Billy Cobham and was part of the excellent early '80s group Clarinet Summit. The '85 album *Musique d'Afrique Nouvelle Orleans* featured his work as a leader, composer, and player, as did the '89 India Navigation release *Bayou Magic*. He finally got a major label shot, the '93 Columbia CD *Late.—Ron Wynn*

● **Musique D'afrique Nouvell Orleans** / 1984 / India Navigation 1065

Mario Bauza

b. Apr. 28, 1911, Cayo Hueso, Havana, Cuba, **d.** 1993
Oboe, clarinet, trumpet / Latin jazz
A child prodigy, Mario Bauza was a seasoned oboe and clarinet player by age 16. He left Cuba for New York in April 1930. Bauza played jazz trumpet for Chick Webb, Don Redmond, and Cab Calloway before joining Machito and the Afro Cubans as musical director in December 1940. While in the U.S. Army, Bauza composed "Tangat" on May 29, 1943, and Latin jazz was created. Machito died in 1984, but his tradition continued through the music of Mario Bauza and his legendary vocalist Graciella until Bauza's death in 1994. Dr. Bauza composed "Mambo Inn" and "Sambia," two of the most recorded tunes.—*Max Salazar*

○ **Ahora Mismo, Guateque De Chombo, Simale, Contigo La D** / **i.** 1976 / Lamp

○ **Mambo Inn, Quedate, El Marelito & Cubanola** / **i.** 1986 / Caiman

● **Tanga Suite, The** / **i.** 1992 / Messidor
A swinging orchestra conducted by the redoubtable Mario Bauza and featuring such exceptional soloists as Paquito D'Rivera on alto sax, Victor Paz on trumpet, Pablo Calogero on baritone sax, and Marcus Persiani on piano, plus the sophisticated arrangements and songwriting genius of Chico O'Farrill and Ray Santos make *Tanga* a Cuban jazz classic...Everything on this disc is of a high order. —*Marcela Breton, Jazz Times*

Sidney Bechet (Sidney Joseph Bechet)

b. May 14, 1897, New Orleans, LA, **d.** May 14, 1959, Paris, France
Clarinet, soprano sax / New Orleans traditional
New Orleans-born clarinetist and soprano saxophonist Sidney Bechet was a prodigy who turned pro at 13 and left home three years later. He was in Europe with composer Will Marion Cook's Southern Syncopated Orchestra by 1919. Bechet returned home in 1924, making his first records. They showed he had no peers when it came to soloing; soon he was teamed on disc with another New Orleanian, Louis Armstrong, then the only player who could hold his own with him. Soon Bechet went back to Europe, touring as far afield as Russia, where he was lionized. The '30s found him home again; his 1932 sides with his New Orleans Feetwarmers are classics. After some years in Noble Sissle's Society Dance Band, Bechet was rediscovered and became a fountainhead of the traditional jazz revival. He returned to Europe after World War II, settling in France in 1951 and becoming one of that country's biggest stars. Though he never abandoned the clarinet, Bechet concentrated on the soprano sax, of which he was the first and greatest master, from 1920 through the rest of his career. His tone was as powerful as a trumpet's, and he took the lead in any group he played with. His autobiography, *Treat It Gentle*, is one of the most moving books about jazz. — *Dan Morgenstern*

○ **Complete 1923-6 Clarence Williams Sessions: 1, The** / **i.** Jul. 1923-Oct. 1923 / EPM 5197

○ **Chronological Sidney Bechet, 1923-1936, The** / Oct. 1923-Mar. 1936 / Classics 583
The first in a series of Classics CDs focusing on the recordings of Sidney Bechet, this disc features the clarinetist-soprano saxophonist on two early titles with blues singer Rosetta Crawford, his torrid 1932 session with the New Orleans Feetwarmers (which also features trumpeter Tommy Ladnier and is high-

lighted by "Shag" and "Maple Leaf Rag"), and sides from Noble Sissle's somewhat commercial orchestra. Fortunately Sissle was wise enough to give Bechet plenty of solo space on some of his selections, most notably "Polka Dot Rag." Even with a few indifferent vocals, this CD is recommended to those not already owning this music. —*Scott Yanow*

★ **In New York** / **i.** 1923-1925 / Smithsonian

○ **Giants of Jazz** / **i.** 1923-1958 / Time Life 09
A great retrospective package that contained some of everything Sidney Bechet recorded from the beginning to the end and in the middle. It was part of a Time-Life anthology series, was brillant mastered and intelligently sequenced, and contained scholarly notes and text. This series has sadly been discontinued. —*Ron Wynn, AMG*

☆ **Legendary, The** / **i.** 1932-1941 / Bluebird 6590
For those not fortunate enough to own *Master Musician, The Legendary* contains some excellent examples of Sidney Bechet's driving soprano, along with good moments from Tommy Ladnier, Earl Hines, and Charlie Shavers among others, and it includes Bechet's historic "one-man band" performance of "Sheik of Araby" (although not "Blues for Bechet") on which Bechet (via overdubbing) played clarinet, soprano, a weird sounding tenor, piano, bass, and drums. —*Scott Yanow, Cadence*

★ **Master Takes: Victor Sessions (1932-1943)** / 1932-1943 / Bluebird 2402
This three-CD set is perfect in all respects except that it leaves out the very interesting alternate takes from Sidney Bechet's Victor sessions. Consisting of 60 selections (mostly from 1939-1941), this release finds soprano saxophonist and clarinetist Sidney Bechet in his prime, making traditional jazz sound modern during the height of the swing era. A true individualist, Bechet is heard romping with the New Orleans Feetwarmers in 1932, dominating a Tommy Ladnier-Mezz Mezzrow session, starring with Jelly Roll Morton in 1939, and creating classic after classic with the all-star groups he headed. Highpoints include "Indian Summer," "Nobody Knows the Way I Feels Dis' Mornin'," "Stompy Jones," "Egyptian Fantasy," and his one-man band, overdubbed performance of "The Sheik of Araby." A package that is essential for jazz collectors who do not already possess the French RCA twofer series. — *Scott Yanow*

○ **Chronological Sidney Bechet, 1937-1938, The** / Apr. 1937-Nov. 1938 / Classics 593
The second in a series of CDs reissuing recordings featuring Sidney Bechet has quite a bit of variety. The unique soprano saxophonist is heard with Noble Sissle's show band, dominating a small group sponsored by Sissle, backing blues singer Trixie Smith and the team of Grant & Wilson, and leading his own session with a sextet that includes baritonist Ernie Caceres and on "Hold Tight" a vocal by "The Two Fish Mongers"! Enjoyable if not quite essential music. —*Scott Yanow*

○ **1938-1940** / **i.** Nov. 28, 1938-Feb. 5, 1940 / Classics 608
This entry in Classics' chronological reissue of the master takes of Sidney Bechet's early recordings finds the soprano great playing with trumpeter Tommy Ladnier and Mezz Mezzrow on the famous "Really the Blues" session, performing a hit version of "Summertime," overshadowing the other members of the all-star Port of Harlem Seven, and recording "Indian Summer" and a hot version of "One O'Clock Jump" in a 1940 session for Victor. However half of this CD is taken up by an odd and surprisingly restrained marathon date with pianist Willie the Lion Smith in which they perform Haitian folk songs! An interesting if not essential set. —*Scott Yanow*

★ **Complete Blue Note Recordings** / **i.** 1939-1953 / Mosaic
Mosaic, a mail order company, has compiled a series of remarkable box sets that feature the complete recordings of various immortal musicians at the peak of their careers. This limited edition six-LP set (get it while you can!) has all of Sidney Bechet's recordings for Blue Note, including three songs with the Port Of Harlem Seven (climaxed by his hit version of "Summertime"), two blues with guitarist Josh White, and Bechet's sessions from 1940, 1944, 1945, 1946, 1949, 1950, 1951, and 1953 in which he shares the frontline with such trumpeters as Sidney DeParis, Max Kaminsky, Bunk Johnson, Wild Bill Davison, and Jonah Jones. The music ranges from hot swing to exuberant Dixieland, and Bechet somehow always sounds inspired. —*Scott Yanow*

○ **Port at Harlem Jazzmen** / **i.** 1939 / Blue Note 7022

○ **1940** / **i.** Mar. 7, 1940-Jun. 4, 1940 / Classics 619
Classics' chronological reissue of Sidney Bechet's recordings (at least the regular takes) continues with a pair of songs made with blues singer Josh White, eight very enjoyable performances cut with a quartet consisting of cornetist Muggsy Spanier, guitarist Carmen Mastren, and bassist Wellman Braud, and a pair of Bechet's Victor sessions. One of the strongest entries in this valuable series. —*Scott Yanow*

○ **1940-1941** / **i.** Sep. 6, 1940-Oct. 14, 1941 / Classics 638
Classics' Sidney Bechet series continues with this CD, a generous set full of the soprano's prime Victor recordings, including appearances by cornetist Rex Stewart and pianist Earl Hines, Bechet's guest shot with the Chamber Music Society of Lower Basin Street, and his innovative "one-man band" recordings of "The Sheik of Araby" and "Blues of Bechet." Timeless music. —*Scott Yanow*

○ **La Legende De Sidney Bechet** / **i.** Oct. 14, 1949-Jul. 4, 1958 / Vogue 600245
This CD features has a cross-section of soprano great Sidney Bechet's 1950s European recordings. A national hero in France during this time, although relatively unknown to the general public in the United States, Bechet really dominates this set. The music ranges from his 1949 hit "Les Oignons," an early version of "Petite Fleur," and a passionate "Summertime," to romping jams on "Royal Garden Blues" and "When the Saints Go Marchin' In." A fine introduction to late period Bechet, one of the true giants of jazz history. —*Scott Yanow*

○ **Jazz Classics—Vol. 1** / **i.** 1950 / Blue Note 7002

○ **Jazz Classics—Vol. 2** / **i.** 1950 / Blue Note 7003

○ **New Orleans Style, Old and New** / **i.** 1952 / Commodore 20020

○ **Immortal Performances** / **i.** 1952 / RCA 31

○ **Olympia Concert, Paris** / **i.** 1954 / Blue Note 7029

○ **Creole Reeds** / **i.** 1956 / Riverside 12-216

● **When a Soprano Meets A Piano** / **i.** 1957 / Inner City 7008
One of Sidney Bechet's final recordings was this relatively modern quartet session, which also features pianist Martial Solal. This LP finds Bechet playing melodically and with invention on superior swing (rather than Dixieland) standards, meeting the modern 25-year old pianist halfway. Bechet's sound was still beautiful, even at this late stage. —*Scott Yanow*

Bix Beiderbecke (Leon Bix Beiderbecke)

b. May 10, 1903, Davenport, IA, **d.** Aug. 6, 1931, New York, NY
Cornet / New Orleans traditional
Dead at 28 of alcohol abuse, Bix Beiderbecke is one of jazz's great romantic legends—an icon of the "jazz age." In fact, Beiderbecke was an enormously gifted "natural" who took to the new musical language of jazz as if to the manner born. His cornet sound ("like a girl saying 'yes,'" in Eddie Condon's words) was a thing of beauty, and it survives on a few dozen records, none of which give him much room. But he could tell a story in 8 or 16 bars. Also an accomplished pianist, he recorded his most famous composition, "In a Mist," on that instrument. He reached the peak of his career as a member of Paul Whiteman's orchestra (1927-1929), then at the pinnacle of the popular music world, but though Whiteman loved his playing, he had to let him go. The whole sad story of Bix's short life is told in rich detail by Dick Sudhalter et al., in *Bix: Man and Legend.*"—*Dan Morgenstern*

○ **And the Wolverines** / **i.** 1924 / Riverside 1050

○ **Complete Bix Beiderbecke, The** / **i.** 1924-1930 / Everest 317

○ **Bix Beiderbecke (1924-1930)** / 1924-1930 / BBC 601
By 1927, Bix Beiderbecke had jumped to New York, but his Gang's Three Midwesterners were its more consistent swingers. But the whole sextet lifts off by the end of "Since My Best Girl Turned Me Down," once Adrian Rollini gets his bass sax up to speed. (That track shows off Beiderbecke's nice cornet tone and supple bent notes, too.) —*Kevin Whitehead, Down Beat*

★ **And the Chicago Cornets** / Jan. 26, 1925 / Milestone 47019
All the Wolverines recordings were on this release, including two alternate takes and two with Jimmy McPartland replacing Beiderbecke. The faults of the 21-year-old avant-gardist's mates were obvious; the most remarkable was a tuba player who single-handedly dragged the whole band's tempo at the slightest excuse.

But as historian Max Harrison said, it was a creatively explosive time for Beiderbecke, crackling with excitement in the February 1924 sides, growing in detail by May (the "off" attack and a perfect slur on "Riverboat Shuffle"). In June he was capable of a truly lovely improvisation on the "Tiger Rag" changes, a total performance, incidentally, that most groups of the period would have been proud of (Beiderbecke's lead was inspired). . . . Both the exalted lyricism of Beiderbecke and the classic formulations of Armstrong were soon to be realized, in works that affected jazzmen a half century later. —*John Litweiler, Down Beat*

○ **Early Bix** / **i.** Jan. 26, 1925 / Riverside 1023

○ **Bix and Tram** / Feb. 1927-Sep. 1927 /

★ **Bix Beiderbecke—Vol. I: Singin' the Blues** / Feb. 1927-Sep. 1927 / Columbia 45450

○ **Bix Beiderbecke Story—Vol. 1, The** / **i.** Jul. 7, 1928 / Columbia 844

● **Giants of Jazz** / **i.** 192z / Time Life 04
This Time-Life Giants of Jazz collation gave the listener a thorough primer on a brief (1927 and 1928) but crucial period in Bix Beiderbecke's career. . . . Beiderbecke was among the first important players in jazz to bring a sense of artistic consciousness to his work. He was schooled in the classics, had a decent foundation in theory, and was articulate enough to talk intelligently about what he played. Whereas Louis Armstrong fulminated with instinctive brilliance and urgent power, Beiderbecke found it possible to create in a bold but circumspect manner. Of the 40 selections included on the three LPs, 34 were from the 1927-1928 period. No significant Beiderbecke landmarks were ignored, and some lesser efforts were included, too, including "Crying All Day," which was to Beiderbecke's "Singin' the Blues" as Coleman Hawkins' "Rainbow Mist" was to his "Body and Soul," and "Humpty Dumpty," with its insinuations of "Charleston Alley" and modest Beiderbecke solo presence. But we get "I'm Coming Virginia," "Jazz Me Blues," the driving and harmonically alert "Lonely Melody" with Paul Whiteman, and many other gems. —*John McDonough, Down Beat*

○ **Whiteman Days, The** / **i.** 192z /

Richie Beirach (Richard Beirach)

b. May 23, 1947, New York, NY
Piano / Early jazz rock world fusion modern creative
Pianist Richie Beirach's style reflects the influence of Keith Jarrett, Chick Corea, and Bill Evans. Trained in both jazz and classical, Beirach studied at Berklee and the Manhattan School of Music, where he earned his bachelor's degree in the early '70s. He was a member of David Liebman's Lookout Farm band in the mid-'70s, then formed his own trio after they disbanded. Beirach played in John Abercrombie's quartet in the '80s, and also coformed Quest with Liebman. Quest made a number of recordings and also toured in the '80s and '90s. Besides a duo recording with George Coleman, Beirach's done dates for Magenta, Owl, Storyville, Concord, CMP, Triloka, and Blue Note. —*Ron Wynn*

○ **Forgotten Fantasies** / **i.** 1975 / A&M 709
This features brilliant duets with longtime partner David Liebman (flute and sax) on the creative side. Beirach wrote three of the six cuts and shows his original approach to jazz. —*Michael G. Nastos*

○ **Eon** / Nov. 1976 / ECM 1054
Richie Beirach's well-programmed set began with an intense reworking of Miles Davis's "Nardis." The introductory rhythm vamp, through its numerous reappearances, functioned as an *idee fixe* thereby allowing Beirach to fragment the tune's melodic and harmonic components so that space and the piano's overtonal timbres interacted (along with melody and harmony) as coequal musical elements. Dave Liebman's "Places" was a poignant solo essay capturing echoes and images of bittersweet remembrances. Throughout, Beirach was ably assisted by the excellent musicianship of his colleagues from Lookout Farm, bassist Frank Tusa and percussionist Jeff Williams. —*Chuck Berg, Down Beat*

○ **Continuum** / Jul. 5, 1983 / Eastwind 704
Another in the solo piano series Bierach cranked out in the '80s. This was done for the Japanese Baybridge label, and like predecessors and successors it was mostly originals, though this time he did the title track (Tadd Dameron) and also covered "Some Other Time" and "Round Midnight." —*Ron Wynn, AMG*

○ **Common Heart** / Sep. 28-29, 1987 / Owl 79243
Alternately stunning and uneven solo piano work from 1987, with Bierach covering originals, spinning out melodies, pacing the set, and trying something different besides conventional theme-solo-theme arrangements. This has been reissued on CD. —*Ron Wynn, AMG*

★ **Convergence** / Nov. 10-11, 1990 / Triloka 185
Great communications. Pianist Richard Beirach and tenor saxophonist George Coleman. —*Michael G. Nastos*

○ **Chant** / i. 1991 / Creative Music Prod. 40

○ **Self Portraits** / i. 1992 / CMP 51
Recently issued set of solo piano originals by Bierach, done in manner that gives autobiographical context to the session and pacing and definition to the compositions. —*Ron Wynn, AMG*

Marcus Belgrave

b. 1936
Trumpet / Hard bop
A capable, versatile player with great range and a strong and distinctive sound, trumpeter Marcus Belgrave has worked in several contexts, ranging from Ray Charles's combos to groups led by Charles Mingus, McCoy Tyner, Geri Allen, and George Gruntz. A lack of dates as a leader and a generally low profile have kept Belgrave from being better known to the general jazz audience. But his crisp, inventive solos can be heard on numerous releases. —*Ron Wynn*

★ **Gemini Ii** / 1975 / Tribe 4004
Nonet with master trumpeter. Sometimes funky, spacy, or swinging, but always potent. With Roy Brooks, Wendell Harrison, Harold McKinney, and Phil Ranelin. The band sounds twice its size due to the expansive compositional stance of the leader. —*Michael G. Nastos*

Louie Bellson (Luigi Paulino Alfredo Francesco Antonion Balassoni)

b. Jul. 26, 1924, Rock Falls, IL
Drums / Swing big band
A first-rate, swing-based stylist and soloist, drummer Louis Bellson participated in and presided over many major sessions. He's known for his flamboyant, yet disciplined support and pinpoint mastery of two pedal-controlled bass drums. Bellson's also an underrated composer. His works include "Marriage Vows," a 1962 jazz ballet, "The Hawk Talks," which was included on the 1951 Duke Ellington LP *HiFi Ellington*, and "I Need Your Key" for James Brown's *Soul on Top* LP in 1970. The winner of a national contest sponsored by Gene Krupa as a teen and a member of Benny Goodman's orchestra at 17, Bellson's reputation was earned during stints with Goodman, Tommy Dorsey, Harry James, Count Basie, and Ellington, plus a long tenure as Pearl Bailey's music director (he was also her husband). His relationship with Ellington was so special that Bellson periodically returned to the fold for such recordings as *A Drum Is a Woman* and the first sacred concert. Alumni of various Bellson bands include Conte Candoli, Bobby Shew, George Duvivier, John Heard, Cat Anderson, Don Menza, and Joe Romano. Bellson's recorded for such labels as Concord, Pablo, and Musicmasters among many others. —*Ron Wynn and Michael G. Nastos*

○ **Louis Bellson with Wardell Gray** / i. 1954 / Norgran 14

○ **Concerto for Drums** / i. 1956 / Norgran 1095

● **150 M.P.H.** / i. May 25, 1974 / Concord Jazz 36

★ **Airmail Special: A Salute to the Big Band Masters** / Feb. 15-16, 1990 / Music Masters 5038
A Salute to the Big Band Masters. Powerhouse salute to big band masters. —*Ron Wynn*

Satima Bea Benjamin

b. Oct. 17, 1936, Cape Town, South Africa
Vocals / Ballads & blues world fusion
An enchanting, evocative vocalist, Satima Bea Benjamin has made several recordings as a leader since establishing herself in Abdullah Ibrahim's (her husband) band during the '70s. Benjamin's performed and recorded show tunes and standards, traditional South African and African music, and has improvised on her originals and other jazz pieces. The two met in South Africa at the end of the '50s. After leaving their homeland, they met Duke Ellington in Switzerland in the early '60s. He invited them to Paris for a recording session. Though only Ibrahim's date was issued, Benjamin eventually sang with Ellington's orchestra at Newport in 1965. She recorded an Ellington tribute album in 1979, and has since done sessions for Blackhawk and Enja. Ricky Ford, Buster Williams, Billy Higgins, and Kenny Barron are some other musicians who've played and worked with Benjamin. —*Ron Wynn*

○ **Windsong** / Jun. 17, 1985 / Black Hawk 50206

★ **Love Light** / Sep. 5, 1987 / Enja 79605

David Benoit

b. 1953, Bakersfield, CA
Piano / Instrumental pop
A consistently popular pianist, David Benoit's been among the most commercially dominant players of the '80s and '90s. He's best known for his GRP sessions, though he's also recorded for AVI and Spindletop. Other than the CD *Waiting for Spring*, where he demonstrated a commendable command of mainstream and traditional jazz styles, Benoit's done heavily arranged, tightly produced "lite" jazz dates. He's played with Dave Valentin, Stanley Clarke, Brandon Fields, and Eric Marienthal among others. —*Ron Wynn*

● **Waiting for Spring** / Feb. 1989-May 1989 / GRP 9595

○ **Letter to Evan** / i. 1992 / GRP 9687

George Benson

b. Mar. 22, 1943, Pittsburgh
Guitar, vocals / Blues & jazz soul jazz instrumentalpop hard bop
George Benson ranks among jazz's most talented guitarists and vocalists, although he's scored his greatest commercial successes with his least (artistically) ambitious music. His initial recognition came as a vocalist. He recorded for a tiny R&B label as an 11-year-old. Benson began guitar studies shortly afterward and joined Jack McDuff's group as a teen, playing with him from 1962 through1965. He led his own band with organist Lonnie Smith, then won fame for his participation in a 1967 Spirituals to Swing anniversary concert. He moved into lighter, pop-influenced crossover material in the late '60s on A&M, which was enjoying success with Wes Montgomery in a similar vein. Benson hit the big time in 1976 with *Breezin'* (a Top Ten hit), a collection of easy-listening, heavily orchestrated numbers whose breakout single was a vocal rendition of Leon Russell's "Masquerade." After a string of hit albums that mined this formula, Benson returned to jazz in 1990, recording with the Count Basie orchestra. His fluidity, relaxed yet dynamic vocal presence, and overall skills make almost anything Benson records at least interesting, and he periodically flashes his considerable skills in live performance or special recording sessions. Benson's most recent entry, 1993's *Calling You*, didn't equal past fusion-pop smashes like *Breezin.—Ron Wynn*

○ **Benson, George/Jack Mc Duff** / Apr. 23, 1964+Oct. 19, 1965 / Prestige 24072
Here's another in the series of specially priced, two-record sets that Prestige issued in the '70s. This featured guitarist George Benson and organist Jack McDuff from the time when Benson was a member of various McDuff groups. It was better-than-average guitar-tenor sax-organ dates from 1964 and 1965. —*Turner Martin, Cadence*

★ **New Boss Guitar** / May 1, 1964 / Prestige 461

○ **Benson Burner** / i. 1965-1966 / CBS 33569
Hot, soulful mid-'60s organ combo material when George Benson was playing with bluesy abandon and reflecting considerable influence of Grant Green. Anyone hearing these songs shouldn't be surprised at his eventual crossover success, but these weren't as overproduced and orchestrated as either his A&M or his Warner Bros. recordings. —*Ron Wynn, AMG*

☆ **Cookbook** / Aug. 1, 1966-Oct. 19, 1966 / Columbia 9413
Simmering interplay, fueled by guitarist Benson and baritone saxophonist Ronnie Cuber make this early-'60s effort one to savor. Six Benson originals, four standards. Produced by John Hammond. Lonnie Smith (organ), Bennie Green (tb). —*Michael G. Nastos*

○ **Blue Benson** / i. 1967-1968 / Polydor 2486272

Another sampler spotlighting his bluesy, funky material, this time taken from his brief period on Verve when he recorded with the Sweet Inspirations and also played in quintet with Herbie Hancock and Ron Carter. It's fine material but not as strong as the Columbia or Prestige fare that preceded it. —*Ron Wynn, AMG*

★ **Beyond the Blue Horizon** / Feb. 1971 / CBS 40810

☆ **White Rabbit** / Nov. 1971 / CBS 40685

○ **Best of George Benson (On Cbs)** / i. 1971-1976 / Columbia 45225
This 1989 compilation covers Benson's tenure at CTI Records, 1971-1975 and presents his best as a pure jazz guitarist, prior to his move to singing and the pop-jazz approach found in "Breezin'" and later albums. —*William Ruhlmann*

☆ **Good King Bad** / Jul. 1975+Dec. 1975 / Columbia 45226
This is a good place to hear Benson playing at his jazz best rather than his commercial best. —*Michael Erlewine*

● **Breezin'** / Jan. 6-09, 1976 / Warner Brothers 3111
This was the definitive Benson album commercially; counterpart to Wes Montgomery's pop works of the '60s. Platinum album. —*Ron Wynn*

Bob Berg (Robert Berg)

b. Apr. 7, 1951, New York, NY
Tenor sax, soprano sax / Hard bop, m-base
Bob Berg is one of many modern sax players (tenor and soprano) whose career has been affected by his time with Miles Davis. Berg became a more orthodox hard-bop soloist in the '70s than he was in the '60s, then joined Miles Davis in the mid-'80s and got the fusion-electric conversion. He's very solid technically, with his solos distinguished by his big sound. Lately Berg's releases have had balanced traditional and contemporary elements. —*Ron Wynn*

★ **New Birth** / May 12, 1978 / Xanadu 159
New Birth displayed plenty of enthusiasm—occasionally too much, as on "Pauletta," where Bob Berg's doubletiming and gangly phrasing confused the pleasant changes, added unwanted tension, and never totally meshed with the rhythm section. . . . He seemed most comfortable on the funky, uncomplicated changes of "Shapes." Luckily, trumpeter Tom Harrell and pianist Cedar Walton satisfied with their less frantic, less cluttered stylings. —*Art Lange, Downbeat*

○ **In the Shadows** / i. Feb. 26, 1992 / Denon 6210
On his third Denon release Berg ventures into a few jazz standards while maintaining a strong hold on his fusion roots. Jim Beard is featured on keyboards. —*Paul Kohler*

Karl Berger (Karl Hans Berger)

b. 1935, Heidelberg, Germany
Piano, vibes, composer, percussion / Modern creative
One of the more prolific players during the '60s and '70s, Karl Berger has been more prominent as an educator than as a musician in recent years. But he's one of the great vibes players and was a daring, explosive soloist and ambitious composer heading and/or playing with several interesting and intriguing bands from the mid '60s through the '70s. Berger earned a doctorate in musicology and sociology from the University of Heidelberg in 1963, switching from piano to vibes on the advice of French vibist Michel Hausser, with whom he played in Germany and Paris. Berger moved to Paris in 1965, where he met trumpeter Don Cherry and played with him for 18 months. He then worked a month with soprano saxophonist Steve Lacy in 1966, before leaving for New York with Cherry. Berger played with (among others) trombonist Roswell Rudd and saxophonist Marion Brown during the late '60s and the early '70s. He founded the Creative Music Foundation with Ornette Coleman in 1971, then moved to Woodstock, NY, in 1973; established the Creative Music Studio; and began full-time classes in various musical departments. Berger continues to tour, perform, and record periodically. —*Ron Wynn*

○ **Live at the Donaueschingen Festival** / Oct. 1979 / MPS 68250
Definitive Berger originals done live in Germany with the Woodstock Workshop Orchestra, a combination of Creative Music Studio students and instructors. —*Michael G. Nastos*

★ **Transit** / Aug. 25-16, 1988 / Black Saint 92

○ **Around** / Black Saint 112

Bunny Berigan (Rowland Bernart Berrigan)

b. Nov. 2, 1908, Hilbert, WI, d. Jun. 2, 1942, New York, NY
Trumpet, vocals / Swing
Trumpeter and vocalist Bunny Berigan was another of early jazz's tragic figures alongside fellow White trumpet star Bix Beiderbecke. A wonderful player, Berigan was noticed in the late '20s while playing in a college band. He joined the CBS studio band in 1931, then became a member of Paul Whiteman's group as a late replacement for Beiderbecke, but left to join Benny Goodman in 1935. Berigan's most famous for recording is the definitive version of "I Can't Get Started." —*Ron Wynn.*

★ **Complete Bunny Berigan—Vol. 1, The** / i. Apr. 1, 1934-Oct. 7, 1937 / Bluebird 5584
The Bunny Berigan groups did contain George Auld (sounding much like Charlie Barnet on tenor sax), Arnold Fishkin, and George Wettling. The tune Berigan seemed to own at the time, "I Can't Get Started," got its steam after the vocal when Berigan played around a group of sustained chords, which was very exciting then. "A Study in Brown" and "Mahogany Hall Stomp" were some pieces that are worth a hearing. —*Jerry Atkins, Cadence*

○ **Bunny Berigan and His Boys** / Apr. 13, 1936-Jun. 9, 1936 / Epic 16006

○ **Sing! Sing! Sing!—Vol. 1: 1936-1938** / Jul. 1936-Jun. 1938 / Vintage Jazz 627

○ **Bunny Berigan & His Orchestra (1937-1938)** / 1937-1938 / Hindsight 239

○ **Devil's Holiday—Vol. 2: 1938** / 1938 / Vintage Jazz 638

Tim Berne

b. 1954, Syracuse, NY
Alto sax / Modern creative
Experimentation and eclecticism are primary elements of alto saxophonist Tim Berne's musical approach. His albums have included strains of free jazz, hard bop, rock, pop, fusion, various international, and even contemporary classical elements. Berne's solos sometimes incorporate odd rhythms and tonal colors; move from poignant melodies to explosive phrases; and include vocal effects, screams, squawks, blues motifs, and soulful statements. Though he didn't begin playing alto until 19, Berne proved a quick study. He was greatly helped by studies with Anthony Braxton and Julius Hemphill. Berne established his own label and made his first two recordings on the West Coast before moving to New York. He's worked with Vinny Golia, Alex Cline, Roberto Miranda, Olu Dara, Ed Schuller, John Zorn, Marilyn Crispell, and Paul Motian among others. Berne's recorded for Soul Note, Columbia, and JMT and also headed the group Minature with Hank Roberts and Joey Baron. —*Ron Wynn*

○ **7x** / Jan. 8, 1980 / Empire 36
With the exception of "Water People," a tiring AACM-type exotic percussion and reed "atmosphere" piece, the material on alto saxohonist Tim Berne's record was all very good, with the pastoral "A Pearl In the Oliver C" and zigzagging "Chang" examples of particularly well-delineated lines. Berne's tone was like a marriage of Ornette Coleman and Anthony Braxton's, and his best solos— "Flies," for example, or "Showtime,"—displayed a nice balance of passion and logic. . . . Trombonist John Rapson added a feisty voice to this group on three titles, and bassist Roberto Miranda and drummer Alex Cline listened well to the soloist and to each other. —*Francis Davis, Down Beat*

○ **Songs and Rituals in Real Time** / Jul. 1, 1981 / Empire 60K2
Here Berne's pieces were stretched to accommodate plenty of solo space, the lion's share of which went to the leader. Berne the composer of shapely melodies was most obviously represented by the dirgelike "rituals," "San Antonio," "Shirley's Song," and "The Ancient Ones." But the two-sax heads of the "songs" made use of the same long notes and appealing plain-interval consonances and subtle dissonances as the rituals did. —*Kevin Whitehead, Cadence*

○ **Ancestors** / Feb. 1983 / Soul Note 1061
Tim Berne's playing on *Ancestors* was fluid and warm and conveyed a relaxed levity. For this live recording Berne enlarged his regular quartet (Mack Goldsburg, tenor sax, soprano sax; Ed Schuller, bass; Paul Motian, percussion) to include Herb Robertson (trumpet) and Ray Anderson, perhaps the finest trombonist of the past five years. As usual, the tunes were all Berne

originals and displayed the sectional and harmonic structures that so much of his music seems to exhibit. —*Bob Rusch, Cadence*

○ **Mutant Variations** / Mar. 5-06, 1983 / Soul Note 1091
Definitely not part of the new traditional scene, alto saxophonist Tim Berne keeps moving forward. This '84 quartet set of all originals at times was reminiscent of mid-'50s Ornette Coleman, notably due to Herb Robertson's pocket trumpet solos and the dynamics generated by Berne and Robertson's interaction with bassist Ed Schuller and percussionist Paul Motian. —*Ron Wynn, AMG*

★ **Fulton Street Maul** / 1986 / Columbia 40530
On the surface at least *Fulton Street*—produced by ex-Beefheart guitarist Gary Lucas—is his least jazzy effort; overdubs abound; improvisation, Berne says, is secondary; the churning rhythm section is more relentless than swinging ("Unknown Disaster," "Federico") caught up in an urban tribal dance.... *Fulton Street Maul's* not Tim Berne's best, but it's certainly no flop—his keening alto sound and appealingly melancholy writing rise above the carefully plotted din. —*Kevin Whitehead, Cadence*

Warren Bernhardt

b. Nov. 1938, Wausau, WI
Piano, keyboards / Modern creative
Adaptability and the influence of modal playing are the main attributes displayed by pianist and keyboardist Warren Bernhardt. He studied classical piano and gave his first concert at nine. Bernhardt began playing jazz dates while attending college in Chicago, then spent three years in Paul Winter's sextet in the early '60s. During that time Bernhardt toured South America with Winter's band. He moved to New York in 1963 and did sessions, studio, and recording dates with Gerry Mulligan, Clark Terry, George Benson, Jeremy Steig, Tim Hardin, Richie Havens, Liza Minnelli, and Carly Simon, among others. A career turning point came when he toured and recorded with Jack DeJohnette's group in 1976. Bernhardt worked in several duos and trios from '75 to '86, including ensembles with bassists Dave Holland and Eddie Gomez and drummers Peter Erskine and Jimmy Cobb. He headed Steps Ahead, one of the better '80s fusion bands, in '84 and '85; composed film scores; taught jazz piano courses; and did some solo recording. —*Ron Wynnbetter*

● **Blue Montreux** / i. 1979 / Arista 4224

Chu Berry (Leon Brown Berry)

b. Sep. 13, 1910, Wheeling, WV, **d.** Oct. 30, 1941, Conneaut, OH
Tenor sax / Swing, big band
Chu Berry was a wonderful tenor saxophonist whose contributions tended to be underrated due to the domination of Coleman Hawkins during his era. While his sound was smoother than Hawkins's, Berry had a deep, dark tone and, on uptempo numbers, shined with great breath control and a harmonic intensity that never sacrificed intensity or swing in his solos. Berry played with Benny Carter, Teddy Hill, and Fletcher Henderson in the '30s and was in Cab Calloway's orchestra until his death in a car crash. He led the Stompy Stevedores in 1937, a "little jazz" group featuring Roy Eldridge in 1938, and an ensemble in 1940 with Hot Lips Page. Berry recorded with Charlie Ventura in 1941. Some of his most famous solos were on "Krazy Kapers" with The Chocolate Dandies, "Hot Mallets" with Lionel Hampton and "Blues in C# Minor" with Teddy Wilson. He was featured on recordings for Commodore, Columbia, and Variety. —*Ron Wynn & Michael G. Nastos*

★ **Indispensable** / i. 1936-1939 / RCA 89481
1936-1939. A wide variety of sessions from an immortal stylist. W/ Gene Krupa (d), Lionel Hampton (vib), Cab Calloway (vocals), Fletcher Henderson (leader), and Wingy Manone's bands. —*Michael G. Nastos*

○ **Memorial** / i. 1954 / Commodore 20024
☆ **Chu** / i. 1955 / Epic 3124
☆ **Chu Berry** / i. 1959 / Commodore 30017

Gene Bertoncini

b. Apr. 6, 1937, New York, NY
Guitar / Swing, bop

Guitarist Gene Bertoncini is a wonderful, fluid player equally impressive on electric or acoustic guitar, and at home in mainstream, Latin, or swing situations. He began playing at 7 and was featured on television at 16. He studied architecture at Notre Dame for a while, then returned to his New York hometown and joined a small combo headed by Buddy Rich, with other members including Sam Most and Mike Mainieri. He was busy throughout the '60s and '70s, playing with Clark Terry, Paul Winter, Nancy Wilson, Wayne Shorter, and Charles McPherson, among others, plus making frequent appearances on the Tonight Show. He formed a duo with Mike Moore in the late '70s and also had a trio with Moore and Michael Urbaniak in 1981. Bertoncini's led many workshops in recent years and taught at the Eastman school. —*Ron Wynn*

O Grande Amor / 1986 / Stash 258
Strollin' / i. 1987 / Stash 272
Art of the Duo / 1987-1987 / Stash 6
Two in Time / Chiaroscuro 308

Andy Bey (Andrew W. Bey)

b. 1939, Newark, NJ
Vocals / Hard bop, ballads & blues, soul jazz
Despite some erratic sessions with Horace Silver, vocalist Andy Bey has a rich, full voice and good command of blues and bop mechanics. He played piano and sang in Newark as a child and appeared at the Apollo with Louis Jordan in the late '50s. Bey teamed with his sisters Salome & Geraldine in a group during the '50s, '60s, and '70s. They toured and recorded in Europe and then recorded for Atlantic in the '70s. Bey also recorded with Max Roach (his finest jazz work), Duke Pearson, Gary Bartz, and Stanley Clarke in the '60s and '70s, plus multiple stints with Silver. Bey later sang with the Thad Jones-Mel Lewis orchestra and Bobby Vidal in the '70s. —*Ron Wynn*

★ **Now Hear** / Aug. 17+20, 1964 / Prestige 7346
Expressive vocalists hook up w/ Jerome Richardson (sax and fl), Kenny Burrell (g) for expansive treatments of jazz. —*Michael G. Nastos*

Ed Bickert (Edward Isaac Bickert)

b. Nov. 29, 1932, Hochfeld, Manitoba, Canada
Guitar / Swing, cool
Canadian Ed Bickert is a sleeper in the world of jazz; he lacks a big reputation but is quite simply one of the finest guitarists currently active. He's been a steady presence in the Toronto studio and club scene since the '50s. His first major recording was with clarinetist Phil Nimmons in 1961. An affinity for working with horn players recurs in his recordings with Rob McConnell's Boss Brass and Paul Desmond. Bickert thrives playing a hard-swinging traditionalist jazz that sidesteps bop angularity altogether, while at the same time employing a modern, sophisticated harmonic sense. As a chordal player, Bickert has few if any equals. His relaxed sense of melody and gentle tone, joined with his evident rapport in ensembles, makes for very accessible and listenable music—virtuoso jazz without the pretenses. —*David Nelson McCarthy*

● **At Toronto's Bourbon Street** / Jan. 1983 / Concord Jazz 216

Barney Bigard (Albany Leon Bigard)

b. Mar. 3, 1906, New Orleans, LA, **d.** Jun. 27, 1980, Culver City, CA
Clarinet / New Orleans traditional, swing
The great New Orleans teacher Lorenzo Tio had many pupils, but none became more successful than clarinetist and tenor saxophonist Barney Bigard. A jam session master, Bigard's ragged, squiggly lines and marvelous tone were heard in many first-rate groups, among them King Oliver's and Duke Ellington's. Bigard also played fine tenor sax alongside Albert Nicholas in a duo at Tom Anderson's cafe early in his career. Both he and Nicholas joined Oliver in the '20s; then Bigard was part of Ellington's first Cotton Club season orchestra. He remained with Ellington until 1942. Bigard helped restart Kid Ory's career, recording with him and appearing in the film *New Orleans*. Then came five years with Louis Armstrong and his All-Stars. Bigard left for a time, worked with Ben Pollack and Cozy Cole, then returned to Armstrong in 1960. He left again in 1961, and finally stopped playing music full-time in 1965. But he'd periodically return for

touring, guest shots, and radio and television dates until his death. —*Ron Wynn*

● **Bucket's Got a Hole in It** / Delmark 211
In January 1968, a Chicago television station flew Barney Bigard (clarinet) in from Los Angeles to take part in one of pianist Art Hodes's television shows. Bob Koester took the opportunity to record him with a trio consisting of Hodes, Rail Wilson (bass), and Barrett Deems (drums) and then in another session adding Nap Trottier (trumpet) and Georg Brunis (trombone). As Koester pointed out in his very informative and personal liner notes, Hodes had been collecting great clarinetists since he started recording. These were his first sessions with Bigard. . . . All of the quartet sides were truly wonderful, with "Sweet Lorraine" having the kind of breath-taking beauty that marked the very greatest of Bigard's playing, "Hesitation Blues" marking again his mastery of the blues form, and "Three Little Words" epitomizing his swing. —*Ron Anger, Coda*

Walter Bishop Jr ()

b. Apr. 10, 1927, New York, NY
Piano / Bop, hard bop
A fine bop and hard bop pianist and the son of songwriter Walter Bishop, Walter Bishop Jr. has been an effective bandleader, composer, and educator. He played with Art Blakey in the late '40s; with Charlie Parker, Miles Davis, and Oscar Pettiford in the '50s; and with Curtis Fuller in 1960 before forming his own trio with Jimmy Garrison and G.T. Hogan. Bishop toured with Terry Gibbs in the mid-'60s and studied with Hall Overton at Juilliard. He combined studies and recording after moving to the West Coast in 1969, cutting dates with Supersax and Blue Mitchell. Bishop became an instructor before he moved back to New York in the '70s. He wrote a book on jazz theory in 1976, was in Clark Terry's big band in the late '70s, and toured Switzerland while leading various bands. He taught at the University of Hartford in the early '80s and had a solo Carnegie Hall concert in 1983. Bishop's recorded for DIW, Prestige, Black Lion, Seabreeze, Muse, and Red and Black Jazz, among others. —*Ron Wynn*

○ **Bish Bash / i.** Aug. 1964+May 1968 / Xanadu 114
● **Coral Keys** / 1971 / Black Jazz 2

Eubie Blake (James Hubert Blake)

b. Feb. 7, 1883, Baltimore, MD, **d.** Feb. 12, 1983, New York, NY
Piano, composer / Ragtime
Blake was one of ragtime's most noted performers and an American institution. As a child, he started playing hymns but heard the sounds of the then-new form all around him in Baltimore, from brass bands to saloons to dance halls. Blake picked up his technique by playing for everything from performing in medicine shows to backing vocalists to appearing in gaming houses. He wrote his first major number, "The Charleston Rag," in 1899. He teamed with Noble Sissle in 1915 for a vaudeville appearance, and the duo eventually made it to Broadway in 1921 with the musical *Shuffle Along*. Blake subsequently became a prolific composer for shows, among them the famous *Blackbirds Review*, then left the field to study the Schillinger system at New York University after World War II. He became a celebrity on the strength of a 1969 album, *86 Years of Eubie Blake*, and made an acclaimed appearance at the 1970 New Orleans Jazz Festival. He was given the James P. Johnson award in 1970 and the Duke Ellington Medal in 1972, and collaborated with Terry Waldo on the comprehensive book *This Is Ragtime* in 1976. The 1976 Broadway show *Eubie* was a memorable overview of his career, which was capped by his receiving the Presidential Medal of Honor in 1981. —*Ron Wynn*

● **Blues and Ragtime (1917-1921)** / 1917-1921 / Biograph 1011
Collection featuring vintage tunes done by ragtime and early jazz great Eubie Blake. The feeling and energy he generates is tremendous, and even when the solos aren't impressive, Blake's attitude and personality keep things moving. —*Ron Wynn, AMG*

○ **Blues & Spirituals (1921)** / Mar. 1921-Dec. 1921 / Biograph 1012
More classic songs from pianist Eubie Blake, whose 100-year lifespan kept him in the public eye through much of the 20th century. He reflected that experience through his playing, which rocks, sways, and rips at times, then is appropriately mournful or reverent. —*Ron Wynn, AMG*

○ **Golden Reunion in Ragtime** / 1962 / Stereoddities 1900
○ **Live Concert** / May 22, 1973 / Eubie Blake Music 5
Live Concert, recorded at the Yesteryear Museum's "annual salute to show business nostalgia," was regrettably heavy on both show business and remembrances. . . . Nevertheless, there was also some good music. "Tricky Fingers," one of Blake's best and most difficult compositions, had a really clever right hand line, brighter and crisper than anything in the Scott Joplin catalog. Blake's playing reminds us that East Coast ragtime was a style much flashier and crisper than the Sedalia school of this genre. —*Jon Balleras, Down Beat*

Ran Blake

b. Apr. 20, 1935, Springfield, Mass.
Piano, keyboards, composer / Modern creative
While many musicians have either avoided the "Third Stream" school or deplored it, Ran Blake has long been one of its champions. His style blends devices from contemporary classical music, gospel rhythms, and influences from film scoring. Blake teamed with vocalist Jeanne Lee during the late '50s and early '60s for a series of duets that were essentially vocal and piano improvisation, with little or no structure in the classic jazz sense. He became a staff member at the New England Conservatory of Music in the late '60s, and was named the head of the Third Stream Department in 1973. He's also worked extensively with saxophonist Ricky Ford and vocalist Eleni Odoni.—*Ron Wynn*

○ **Blue Potato** / Apr. 1970 / Milestone 9021
Pianist Ran Blake's selection of material for this album ranged from an original composition dedicated to three revolutionary heroes to Italian folk melody to popular American songs. His style was as eclectic as his taste. Sources and influences spanned the history of music. The life in his hands and feet drew the piano to the task of playing events and feelings. The instrument assumed priority over the demands of tunes, which for him existed only as nameable starting points and figural references. —*Alan Offstein, Coda*

○ **Breakthru** / Dec. 2+05, 1975 / Improvising Artists 373842
Excellent, haunting melodies and compositions, delivered in a piano style that's completely distinctive and personal. Ran Blake is one of the few Third Stream pianists who never deserted or abandoned the concept or the style; yet his playing is never rhythmically vapid or harmonically predictable. He's also great at building and varying moods in his pieces. —*Ron Wynn, AMG*

○ **Duke Dreams** / Sep. 1982 / Soul Note 1027
Ran Blake's tribute to Billy Strayhorn and Duke Ellington, *Duke Dreams*, was recorded 5/27 and 6/2/81. Now a tribute to these men might appear to be an "in-the-tradition" gambit, but Blake's realization of his own tribute (the title cut), Dave Brubeck's "The Duke," and the other material was a glance backward actually looking toward the present-future. Some of the very familiar tunes were given a most creative reworking. None of the original intent-feeling was destroyed . . . but instead developed and distilled through this unique artist whose quirky voicings, rhythms, and lines make everything he does unmistakably Blake. —*Bob Rusch, Cadence*

○ **Suffield Gothic** / Sep. 28-29, 1983 / Soul Note 1077
His best concept album, with introspective, teeming melodies and alternately limp and joyful rhythms. Ran Blake's piano solos don't bowl anyone over with their speed or intensity, nor are they filled with clever counterpoint or multiple rhythms or constant reworking of pop tunes. They're dialogues that shift and evolve according to Blake's vision of the moment; this requires listeners to simply respond, rather than to anticipate. —*Ron Wynn, AMG*

○ **Painted Rhythms: The Compleat Ran Blake—Vol. 2** / Sep. 1983 / GM 3008
Vol 1. of *Painted Rhythms*, from the same sessions as its partner, was an excellent introduction to pianist Ran Blake's style, for it included his reharmonizations of a variety of jazz standards and obscurities. Vol II ranges from Blake's often-scary originals ("Shoah!"/Babbit/Storm Warning") to 1,000-year-old melodies written by Spanish Jews and a fourth reinterpretation of "Maple Leaf Rag" (the first three were on Vol. I). Throughout, Blake was quite concise (only "Shoah!" exceeded four minutes and seven other sketches were under two), very expressive and, as usual, totally individual. —*Scott Yanow, Cadence*

○ **Painted Rhythms: The Compleat Ran Blake—Vol. 1** / Dec. 1985 / GM 3007

First in a projected series dedicated to the work of pianist-composer Ran Blake, a genuine iconclast. His songs can be moving, muddled, dense, or aggressive, but they're never dull. His playing is the same way; always changing, seldom flashy, and usually rewarding for listeners with open ears. —*Ron Wynn, AMG*

☆ **Short Life of Barbara Monk** / Aug. 26, 1986 / Soul Note 1127

Interesting concept work, with Blake's love of Third Stream (jazz and modern classical concepts merging) and film noir uniting in a series of related, yet divergent compositions. Blake's lines, phrasing, rhythms, and voicings defy easy analysis or fixed patterns. They're as diffuse and diverse as his interests, making every Blake album both a challenge and a delight. —*Ron Wynn, AMG*

★ **You Stepped out of a Cloud** / Aug. 11, 1989 / Owl 79238

Pianist Blake and vocalist Jeanne Lee's first record since the mid-'60s. —*Michael G. Nastos*

☆ **Epistrophy** / **i.** 1991 / Soul Note 121177

Art Blakey (Abdullah ibn Buhaina)

b. Oct. 11, 1919, Pittsburgh, **d.** Oct. 16, 1990
Drums / Hard bop

As much as any one person can be called the creator of a style, Art Blakey looms as a hard bop founder. His emphatic playing manner, with its bombastic snare drum licks, slashing beats, and amazing array of rhythms behind soloists, was always easily identifiable and at the core of numerous brilliant units. Blakey actually began as a pianist and was heading his own band at 15. When Erroll Garner proved a more substantial pianist, Blakey switched to drums. He was part of Mary Lou Williams's first New York group in the early '40s, then played with Fletcher Henderson and Billy Eckstine's pioneering big band. He had an early aggregation called the 17 Messengers and made an intriguing album for Blue Note in 1947. He also worked with Thelonious Monk, Charlie Parker, Miles Davis, Horace Silver, Lucky Millinder, Buddy DeFranco, and the Tadd Dameron-Fats Navarro band in the late '40s and early '50s. A 1954 studio date that was supposed to spotlight Horace Silver eventually led to the creation of the Jazz Messengers, featuring Blakey, Silver, trumpeter Kenny Dorham, saxophonist Hank Mobley, and bassist Doug Watkins. By 1956 the Messengers had become the signature name for all Blakey units, and it ranked as jazz's premier repertory and talent development unit until Blakey's death. The alumni list includes Johnny Griffin, Wayne Shorter, Jackie McLean, Lee Morgan, Curtis Fuller, Slide Hampton, Bobby Timmons, Cedar Walton, and John Gilmore, to cite just a few, as well as both Branford and Wynton Marsalis and three super Memphis pianists, Mulgrew Miller, James Williams, and Donald Brown. Blakey also made some impressive contributions outside the Messengers arena throughout his career, among them seminal dates with Sonny Rollins, Milt Jackson, Cannonball Adderley, Hank Mobley, James Williams, and a year-long stint with the Giants of Jazz in 1971-1972. —*Ron Wynn*

● **Complete Blue Note Recordings of Art Blakey's 1960 Messengers, The** / Mosaic 141

Drummer Art Blakey led many great editions of the Jazz Messengers from the inaugural mid-'50s sessions until his death in the '90s. While arguments rage regarding which was his "best," there is no doubt the 1960-1961 unit figures in the debate. The lineup included several players recruited by former music director Benny Golson in the late '50s: trumpeter Lee Morgan, bassist James "Jymie" Merritt, and pianist Bobby Timmons. Golson left in '59 when Blakey opted for a less arranged, looser sound than Golson wanted. Wayne Shorter eventually replaced him, and Timmons returned after temporarily leaving to play with Cannonball Adderley. This wonderful six-disc set, notated with care and painstaking detail by Bob Blumenthal, covers studio and live sessions from March 6, 1960, to May 27, 1961, with the same personnel on all but two songs that were recorded on February 18, 1961, when Walter Davis had replaced Timmons. Producer Michael Cuscuna used only first issue dates, and while he included some alternate takes, he did not litter the discs with second-rate vault material. They smoothly detail Blakey's evolution, cohesion, and maturation. This set, as with all Mosaic boxes, goes beyond essential. Get it posthaste. —*Ron Wynn*

○ **Africaine: Art Blakey and His Jazz Messengers** / **i.** Nov. 10, 1950 / Blue Note 1088

On this Art Blakey session, trumpeter Lee Morgan was in consistent good form, tenor saxophonist Wayne Shorter was presentable with strong moments, pianist Walter Davis was too laid back, but Blakey was in rhythm glory and contributed one of his lengthy solo features on "Haina," along with generally keeping things swinging. The strongest cuts were "Lester Left Town" and the title track. —*Bob Rusch, Cadence*

★ **Art Blakey and the Jazz Messengers** / Oct. 31, 1953 / Birdland 110

○ **Art Blakey Quintet—Vol. 2** / Feb. 21, 1954 / Blue Note 5038

○ **Hard Bop** / Dec. 12, 1956+Dec. 13, 1956 / Columbia 1040

While not a particularly "classic" recording, the album was a strong example of drummer Art Blakey's driving, swinging style of jazz (the title was certainly applicable). —*Carl Brauer, Cadence*

○ **Art Blakey and the Jazz Messengers Live** / Jul. 29, 1957 / Calliope 3008

★ **Moanin': Art Blakey and the Jazz Messengers** / Oct. 30, 1958 / Blue Note 46516

With The Jazz Messengers. Here is a superb session. W/ Lee Morgan (tpt) and Bobby Timmons (p). —*Hank Davis*

○ **At the Jazz Corner of The World—Vols. 1 and 2** / Apr. 15, 1959 / Blue Note 4016

○ **Paris Concert: Art Blakey and the Jazz Messengers** / Nov. 15, 1959 / Portrait 44120

☆ **Like Someone in Love** / Aug. 7, 1960 / Blue Note 84245

○ **Meet You at the Jazz Corner of The World—Vol. 1** / Sep. 14, 1960 / Blue Note 84054

○ **Meet You at the Jazz Corner of The World—Vol. 2** / Sep. 14, 1960 / Blue Note 84055

☆ **Mosaic** / Oct. 2, 1961 / Blue Note 46523

☆ **Caravan** / Oct. 23-24, 1962 / Riverside 038

Same band as *Ugetsu*. Shorter writes "Sweet 'n Sour" and "This Is for Albert," two of his lesser-known but great compositions. His best work. —*Michael G. Nastos*

○ **Ugetsu** / Jun. 16, 1963 / Riverside 090

Blakey's best sextet with Wayne Shorter (sax), Freddie Hubbard (tpt), and Curtis Fuller (tb). Cedar Walton is prominent as music director, arranger, and composer. Live at Birdland, NYC. Famous tunes "One by One," "On the Ginza," and title track. Among his best work. —*Michael G. Nastos*

☆ **Jazz Message, A** / Jul. 10, 1963 / MCA 5648

Art Blakey Quartet. Not the Jazz Messengers, but featuring McCoy Tyner (p), Sonny Stitt (ts). Extraordinary version of "Cafe." —*Michael G. Nastos*

☆ **Kyoto** / Feb. 20, 1964 / Riverside 145

Prime examples of blowing dates can usually be found on Art Blakey recordings, of which *Kyoto* was an example. This was a 2/20/64 date with the Messengers of that time: Wayne Shorter (tenor sax), Freddie Hubbard (trumpet), Cedar Walton (piano), Reggie Workman (bass). On one ("Wellington's Blues") of the five tracks is a vocal by Wellington Blakey, a cousin to Art Blakey (drums/bandleader). "Wellington Blues," credited to Blakey, was notable in that it was one of the infrequent times he struck out. —*Bob Rusch, Cadence*

○ **In My Prime—Vol. 1** / Dec. 29, 1977 / Timeless 114

Blakey, without a doubt a massive wielder of percussive pronouncements was nevertheless thoroughly within the dictates of good taste when he prodded with merciless insistence even the most sheltered of his younger charges. For the most part, they responded vigorously to the drummer's initiatory challenges. —*Jack Sohmer, Cadence*

○ **Live at Montreux and Northsea** / Jul. 13+17, 1980 / Timeless 150

The Jazz Messengers big band album on Timeless was culled from tapes recorded in July 1980 at the Montreaux and NorthSea jazz festivals, and boasted the additional virtue of more similarly striking soloists. In actuality, the big band was more of an extended sextet than it was an orchestra, for the charts (three originals by alto saxophonist Bobby Watson, one by pianist James Williams, and one standard) served as almost exclusively stepping stones for the many featured soloists. All were in top-notch shape, with trumpeter Valerie Ponomarev and trombonist Robin

Eubanks being the most exceptional of those not already mentioned. —*Jack Sohmer, Down Beat*

★ **Keystone 3** / Jan. 1982 / Concord Jazz 4196
Art Blakey's Messengers band with trumpeter Wynton Marsalis is destined to be remembered in a league with those incorporating Lee Morgan, Clifford Brown, and Kenny Dorham. All the more reason to savor *Keystone 3*, which came from a live date at San Francisco's Keystone Korner. Marsalis didn't dominate *Keystone 3*, a near classic because Blakey achieved a tremendous balancing act with the headstrong talents of three disparate front-liners (including the scholarly Wynton and freewheeling saxophonist Branford Marsalis). —*R. Bruce Dold, Down Beat*

☆ **Oh, By the Way** / May 20, 1982 / Timeless 165
Oh, By the Way, recorded four months and three personnel changes after *Keystone 3*, lacked the overwhelming strength of the Marsalis-fed Messengers, yet was an impressive album, showing how Art Blakey could in a short time begin to meld musicians with dynamics different from their predecessors into another powerful group. The new band on *Oh, By the Way* lacked the discipline and singularity of purpose of its predecessor but suggested that the voices were developing, the cohesion was finding a groove. Trumpeter Terence Blanchard, 19 at the time of the recording, avowed a love for Miles Davis and unabashedly emulated Davis on "My Funny Valentine." Johnny O'Neal added a quite different piano color than Donald Brown. O'Neal had an airy, flowing style that got a workout on "Tropical Breeze," a trio number that was the best chance on either record to hear Blakey's style. —*R. Bruce Dold, Down Beat*

○ **I Get a Kick out of Bu** / Nov. 11, 1988 / Soul Note 121155
○ **History of Jazz Messengers** / i. 1992 / Blue Note 97190
Three-disc anthology that covers various editions of the Messengers from the beginning to the end. It contains such classics as "Moanin'" and does a good job of showing how much talent passed through the Blakey organization over the decades. It's particularly valuable as an introductory tool but is not comprehensive enough to substitute for what should come from the label; a true multidisc boxed set featuring his full recordings for the Blue Note label. —*Ron Wynn, AMG*

Terence Blanchard

b. Mar. 13, 1962, New Orleans, LA
Trumpet / Neo-bop
Trumpeter Terence Blanchard was one of several fine New Orleans prodigies to emerge in the '80s. He became a star member of Art Blakey's Messengers in the early '80s and was a musical partner with fellow Crescent City musician Donald Harrison for a long period. The duo made a string of glittering, though musically conservative, releases for Concord and CBS before going their separate ways. Blanchard has it all: range, tone, ideas, facility, and confidence. *See* Donald Harrison. —*Ron Wynn*

○ **Fire Waltz- Eric Dolphy and Booker Little Remembered** / i. Oct. 3, 1986-Oct. 4, 1986 / Projazz 681
Terence Blanchard and Donald Harrison continued their homage to the Eric Dolphy-Booker Little duo with a second set of performances recorded at Sweet Basil. They featured *Fire Waltz* and *Bee Vamp*, two more tunes the duo immortalized during their Five Spot performances. Their versions of these as well as of *Number Eight* are well intentioned, frequently exciting, and superbly played. But they are not transcendent for the simple reason that Harrison lacks Dolphy's fluency on either alto sax or bass clarinet, and Blanchard does not possess Little's command of the upper register or his embouchure. That is not a knock; they certainly clicked with the identical rhythm section of pianist Mal Waldron, bassist Richard Davis, and drummer Ed Blackwell, who did play on the originals. They spur them on, interact well, and chime in with nicely constructed, thoughtful solos when necessary. Both these volumes are highly recommended, but once you finish them, if you have not heard the originals, do whatever it takes to get them. —*Ron Wynn*

★ **Crystal Stair** / i. 1987 / Columbia 40830
● **Black Pearl** / i. 1988 / Columbia 44216
Blanchard-Harrison. The best by trumpeter Blanchard and saxophonist Donald Harrison, especially the title track. —*Michael G. Nastos*

○ **Simply Stated** / 1991 / Columbia 48903
Nice date from the youthful New Orleans prodigy, one of his first done after he and onetime alto sax partner Donald Harrison parted. Blanchard was battling embouchure problems, but still manages some compelling solos. Antonio Hart makes a fine replacement for Harrison on alto and a good second solo voice. —*Ron Wynn, AMG*

☆ **Terence Blanchard** / 1991 / Columbia 47354

Carla Bley (Carla [Née Borg] Bley)

b. May 11, 1938, Oakland, CA
Piano, composer, bandleader / Progressive big band, modern creative
A wonderful composer, pianist, madcap personality, and arranger, she married pianist Paul Bley in 1957 and built a career as a songwriter and an active participant in the '60s free movement. She cofounded the Jazz Composers' Guild, the Jazz Composers' Orchestra, and the Jazz Composers' Orchestra Association. Later she started Watt records, divorced Bley, and married Michael Mantler. Her output has been huge, and her influence considerable, most notably as a bandleader and composer. She is a quirky, unorthodox piano player whose wit and charisma communicate a genuine depth of musicality. —*Ron Wynn*

★ **Genuine Tong Funeral, A** / i. 1967 / RCA 42766
○ **Escalator over the Hill** / Nov. 1968-Jun. 1971 / ECM 839310
☆ **European Tour (1977)** / Sep. 1977 / ECM 831830
European Tour 1977 was a studio recording made in Munich. "Rose and Sad Song" was a sort of mambo, highlighted by two trombone solos (which were separated by one very dull organ solo)... "Spangled Banner Minor" was the major work on the album, a 20-minute opus with Carla Bley as Charles Ives. It began with a marvelous orchestration of "The Star Spangled Banner" in a minor key, played with mock seriousness. Then drummer Andrew Cyrille went into a march cadence, and we got a polytonal mixture of "La Marseillaise," "Yankee Doodle," and other patriotic favorites. Another grave and ghostly reference to the national anthem led into a long section where the band solemnly intoned a dark hymn while Gary Windo went mad on tenor. —*Douglas Clark, Down Beat*

☆ **Musique Mecanique** / Aug. 1979-Dec. 1978 / ECM 839313
Musique Mecanique began with "440," a composition using the standard A as a tonal center. After stating the rolling melodic theme the band got into a rock riff reminiscent of the Rolling Stones circa 1970, complete with a Bobby Keys-styled tenor solo. At first it sounded thin without the electric instruments, but then it found its own groove with a breathtaking solo by altoist Alan Braufman, a sassy Rosewell Rudd trombone chorus, and a stately one by John Clark on French horn. "Musique Mecanique" was a 23-minute, three-part composition taking up all of side two. The title referred to machines like music boxes and calliopes, and so in Part I we got machines imitating musicians. Part II had a lyric, rendered by Rudd with appropriate theatrics, which twisted in on itself like a mobius strip or an Escher print. Part III could have been the music for some grotesque ballet, where freaks danced crooked steps. At several points Bley wrote the score to sound like a stuck record. You might curse the disc at first, but it was a trick, like so much of this music: a prank, a sleight of hand. —*Douglas Clark, Down Beat*

☆ **Duets: Carla Bley and Steve Swallow** / 1988 / ECM 837345
Despite the coy packaging of this set, there was more *music* here than Carla Bley had offered in many a document, including a healthy revisit to "Batteriewoman" from her investigative days of yesteryear. With the exceptions of the static "Utviklingssang" and "Tango," her work throughout showed a mature voice embracing spare lyricism; sly, subtle dissonance; and inventive phrasing. —*Milo Fine, Cadence*

☆ **Very Big Carla Bley Band** / Oct. 29-30, 1990 / ECM 847942
Her best LP of the last decade. Best cut is the Latin-tinged *Lo Ultimo*." —*Michael G. Nastos*

Paul Bley

b. Nov. 10, 1932, Montreal, Quebec
Piano / Early free, modern creative
A fine supportive pianist who's always been better in a cooperative rather than individual spotlight situation. He left Montreal

for New York, went back to Canada briefly, then returned to New York full-time in 1954. His first recordings came as a member of a trio with Charles Mingus and Art Blakey. He has since worked with cutting-edge avant-gardists like Ornette Coleman and is looking forward. His best bands and recordings are trio dates with an emphasis on interaction. At times, his music has a spacey quality, but it never loses its guts or edge. —*Ron Wynn*

○ **Live at the Hillcrest Club (1958)** / Oct. 1958 / Inner City 1007
A classic avant-garde (or free or outside if you prefer) from 1958. This was considered Ornette Coleman's album for years, but Bley was the actual leader. The sound quality on the original vinyl album was poor at best, but Coleman's searing, jagged solos and Bley's furious answering lines more than compensated. The CD cleans things up a bit, though it's still a sonic nightmare. —*Ron Wynn, AMG*

○ **Floater Syndrome, The** / Aug. 17, 1962+Sep. 12, 1963 / Savoy 1148
1962 & 1963. Trio sessions were with Steve Swallow (b) and Pete La Roca (d). Paul and Carla Bley and Ornette Coleman wrote the music for this dense and wide-ranging trio. —*Michael G. Nastos*

★ **Paul Bley with Gary Peacock** / Apr. 13, 1963 / PolyGram 843162

☆ **Syndrome** / Sep. 12, 1963 / Savoy 1175
The followup to *Floater* features more music from Carla Bley. The Savoy albums really introduced her work (through her then husband) to the world. —*Michael G. Nastos*

☆ **Paul Bley Quartet** / Feb. 9, 1964 / ECM 835250
Free jazz proponent Paul Bley's album here consisted of original compositions by each of his sidemen, as well as two by Bley. Bley's compositions, "Interplay," and the solo piano piece, "Triste," started and ended the album. —*Robert Iannapollo, Cadence*

○ **Closer** / Dec. 18, 1965 / ESP 1021
On *Closer*, the setting for pianist Paul Bley was the more familiar trio format (Barry Altschul, percussion; Steve Swallow, bass). . . . This LP was much more characteristic of the Paul Bley style—understated, probing, and occasionally passionately percussive, but always with a gently searching ambiance. —*Bob Rusch, Cadence*

○ **Mr. Joy** / May 11, 1968 / Limelight 86060
There were eight issues: six by Annette Peacock along with Bley's "Only Lovely" and Ornette Coleman's "Ramblin." These recordings and one made in December 1968 for RCA were some of Bley's best and last (during that period) acoustic work. Bley utilized a full range of the piano's tonal qualities, expressing thought and emotions with economy, but played with an almost Thelonious Monklike deliberation. —*Cadence*

○ **Copenhagen and Harlem** / i. Oct. 1975 / Arista 1901
Copenhagen and Harlem, recorded and released in Europe in 1965 and 1966, presented Paul Bley's classic trio running through seven short and two long musical pieces. . . . He and his companions seemed to envision music as pure *design*. Nothing here was programmatic or didactic. He thought in melodic shapes and rhythmic thrusts, rather than in key signatures, meters, and conventional harmonic cadences. The result was an anthology of intricate, if somewhat dry, musical patterns. —*Jon Balleras, Down Beat*

○ **Ramblings** / i. 1980 / Affinity 37
In many ways this was typical of Bley's original piano style, but it seemed even more exaggerated in his use of silence and empty space than some of his better-known and more concise efforts. There were times here when Bley's "hold your breath" approach went past the stretch of continuity. It was Bley's show and Mark Levison (bass) and Barry Altschul (drums) gave perfect support. —*Bob Rusch, Cadence*

○ **Bebopbebopbebopbebop** / Dec. 22, 1989 / Steeple Chase 31259
A surprising album from Bley, long considered an outside player with little, if any, affinity for straight bop. He shatters that myth on this set, going through a dozen songs, including such anthems as "Ornithology" and "The Theme," with vigor, harmonic distinction, and rhythmic edge. He's brilliantly backed by bassist Bob Cranshaw, providing some of his best, less detached playing in quite a while, and drummer Keith Copeland, navigating the tricky changes with grace. —*Ron Wynn, AMG*

○ **Memoirs** / i. Jul. 1990 / Soul Note 121240
Memoirs serves as a tidy summation of Paul Bley's gifts as an individual and musical conversationalist. It helps that he converses with old friends. Paul Motian is, roughly, to the drums what Bley

is to the piano, capable of sculpting icy, paradoxical emotions on a moment's notice, they can venture "out" where tonal centers and rhythmic pulses are not invited. And there, always, is the fundamental Charlie Haden, who demonstrates how a few well-placed notes and well-observed silences can lock a group texture into place. —*Josef Woodard, Down Beat*

Jane Ira Bloom

b. 1955, Newtown, MA
Soprano sax / Modern creative
A progressive and original composer, Jane Ira Bloom plays soprano saxophone and uses electronics creatively in her live performances. She's composed music for NASA, and performs highly rhythmic material that can be simple or complex. Her work is for the challenged listener. —*Michael G. Nastos*

○ **Second Wind** / Jun. 1980 / Outline 138
Here soprano and alto saxophonist Jane Ira Bloom stretched out a little, varied her formats, portioned out additional blowing space, controlled yet joyous, to other thoughtful colleagues as well, either needling vibraphonist Dave Friedman or spare pianist Larry Karush. The firm groundwork of bassist Kent McLagan anchored each track, but drummer Frank Bennett added kit colors. We hear more of Bloom's spacious, dynamic soprano, but the last track on each side showed her pearly, rounded, yet "straighter" alto. —*Fred Bouchard, Down Beat*

○ **Modern Drama** / Feb. 1987 / Columbia 40755
On the opening cut, "Overstars," you can hear her tone is extended (with the use of an octave divider). . . . Purists may blanche at the use (or misuse) of the soprano sound, but this is not a sellout album. You can hear that these musicians have played alongside each other many times. . . . A variety of sounds await the listener and, if your ears and mind are open, you cannot help but enjoy Jane Ira Bloom's fine achievement. —*Richard B. Kamins, Cadence*

★ **Slalom** / Jun. 6+09, 1988 / Columbia 44415
At times her soprano takes on the sonic characteristics of a chromatic harmonica. At her most playful, Bloom darts in between the rhythmic cracks of percussionist Tom Rainey. As with her previous album *Modern Drama* and the tracks "Overstars" and "Vario," Bloom digs down deep on "Drums Like Dancing" and shows a boppish edge. . . . This is not a hard-swinging date. It is a well-crafted, artistic statement and perhaps Bloom's most diverse, definitely most listenable, album so far. —*Michael G. Nastos, Cadence*

Hamiet Bluiett

b. 1940, Lovejoy, IL
Baritone sax, clarinet / Modern creative
A premier player, and one of the finest improvisers to emerge during the '70s and '80s, baritone saxophonist Hamiet Bluiett has a deep, robust tone, facility, and imagination, and has combined the swing savvy of a Harry Carney with the range and fluidity of a Pepper Adams or Serge Chaloff. He's a charter member of the World Saxophone Quartet, was also a member of Clarinet Summit, and has recorded several albums as a leader. —*Ron Wynn*

★ **Endangered Species** / Jun. 19, 1976 / India Navigation 1025
Baritone saxophonist Hamiett Bluiett wrote the four compositions on this session, but trumpeter Olu Dara got more solo space and used it to good advantage with some impassioned improvisations. —*Carl Brauer, Cadence*

○ **Dangerously Suite** / i. Apr. 1981 / Soul Note 1188
This session was recorded on 4/9 and 4/17/81 and tried a bit too hard to cover all the "Black music" bases from ballads to swing to blues to gospel to funk. The group played well, but only a few surface levels of feeling-commitment seemed to be explored. —*Milo Fine, Cadence*

○ **Clarinet Family, The** / Nov. 1984 / Black Saint 0097

○ **Ebu** / 1984 / Soul Note 1088
Pianist John Hicks was featured on baritonist Hamiett Bluiett's *Ebu* with bassist Fred Hopkins and drummer Marvin "Smitty" Smith. Hicks's presence was indicative of the album's neotraditional leanings. On the riff tunes "New Bones" and "Gumbo (Vegetarian Style)," Bluiett let more than a touch of R&B honking seep into his playing, exploiting the baritone's power. —*Kevin Whitehead, Cadence*

○ **Live in Berlin with the Clarinet Family** / Black Saint 0097

Arthur Blythe (Arthur Murray Blythe)

b. Jul. 5, 1940, Los Angeles, CA
Alto sax, soprano sax / Hard bop, modern creative
Misinformation, false perceptions, and hype have hurt the career of alto and soprano saxophonist Arthur Blythe, who has always been an excellent player. In the '70s he was nicknamed "Black Arthur," leading to the exaggerated notion that he was a Black nationalist-activist. He joined Columbia in the '70s after relocating to New York from LA and was the victim of a senseless hype campaign calling him the "greatest saxophonist in the world." From his days with Stanley Cowell and Chico Hamilton to his present involvement with the World Sax Quartet and his groups, his work has been consistently high caliber and thoughtful. Blythe is a superb uptempo improviser who has become equally adept at ballads and composition over the years. —*Ron Wynn*

★ **Metamorphosis** / Feb. 26, 1977 / India Navigation 1038
This album from India Navigation (alto saxophonist Arthur Blythe's second on that bold New York label) used nearly as traditional foundations as his *In the Tradition* LP, but in "outer" guise. Blythe's writing, as clear and articulate as his playing, was firmly grounded in blues, often limned in gritty riffs. . . . In his solos, Blythe effectively used repetition, shouts, Dolphian figures, and—dig this for traditionalism—melodic variation. . . . Even the free sections swung, and Blythe's spirit prevailed. —*Fred Bouchard, Down Beat*

☆ **Lenox Avenue Breakdown** / 1978 / Columbia 84152
Producer Bob Thiele not only rounded off the starker edges in the tone of Blythe, as well as flutist James Newton; he also rounded off the music. The arrangements were glitzy and monolithic; for that matter, Blythe's music was to some degree codified. Still, everyone got solo space here; Newton had one grand break on the title tune, guitarist Blood Ulmer recreated the trumpet role on *The Grip* in his fragmented solos, and tuba player Bob Stewart benefited from the superior Columbia recording quality. Drummer Jack DeJohnette was uniformly excellent, enlivening the island vamp of the sprightly "Down San Diego Way" with sudden and inexplicable sunbursts of cymbals. On the title track, Blythe sounded too straightfowardly Tranelike for so true an originator, but he played hard and wild on the last two cuts. —*Neil Tesser, Down Beat*

Willie Bobo (William Correa)

b. Feb. 28, 1934, New York, NY, **d.** Sep. 15, 1983, Los Angeles, CA
Percussion, bandleader / Latin-jazz
Percussionist Willie Bobo helped Latin rhythms become a familiar part of many groups in the '50s, '60s, and '70s. His father was a cuatro (10-string guitar) player, and Bobo started on bongos at 14. He eventually learned congas, timbales, and trap drums as well. Bobo was a band boy for Machito's Afro-Cubans in the '40s and was tutored by Mongo Santamaria in 1948. He played with Mary Lou Williams's group in '50; she's credited with giving him his nickname of "Bobo" (his name's actually William Correa). Bobo's first major recognition came when he joined Tito Puente in 1954; he was with Puente during his "Mambo King" period, and teamed with Puente and Mongo Santamaria to form an amazing rhythm section within Puente's orchestra. Bobo played timbales during Puente's vibes solos. Bobo also played briefly with George Shearing in the '50s and appeared on albums in that same period with Cal Tjader and Mongo Santamaria. Bobo joined Santamaria's band in 1961, then formed his own group and made several topflight Afro-Latin albums over the years. —*Ron Wynn*

● **New Dimension, A** / Dec. 1968 / Verve 8772

○ **Spanish Grease** / Verve 8631
Bobo, a prolific percussionist, enjoyed some pop attention with this session. The album was a wonderful mix of R&B, Latin, and jazz elements and had both open-ended, frentic jams and catchy, hook-filled songs. —*Ron Wynn, AMG*

Joe Bonner (Joseph Leonard Bonner)

b. 1948
Piano / Modern creative
Another contemporary pianst whose phrasing and conception reflect McCoy Tyner's sizable influence, Joe Bonner's been featured on several dates as a leader and session player since the '70s. He studied at Virginia State College and then played in Roy Haynes Hip Ensemble in the '70s. He also worked with Freddie Hubbard, Pharoah Sanders, and Billy Harper, touring with Harper in '78 and '79. Bonner made solo, duo, trio, and combo recordings for Muse, Steeplechase, and Theresa in the '70s and '80s. He also played with Johnny Dyani and Billy Higgins. —*Ron Wynn*

○ **Angel Eyes** / Oct. 1974 / Muse 5114
Pianist Joe Bonner's second album for Muse could almost be called schizophrenic, what with its diversity of musical settings. —*Carl Brauer, Cadence*

★ **Lifesaver, The** / Nov. 1974 / Muse 5065
Pianist Joe Bonner's primary influence was McCoy Tyner, as he gladly acknowledges. Traces of Bill Evans also appeared, particularly on "Native Son," where both the symmetrical, whimsically innocent line and some of the improvisation recall Evans's delicacy, if not his inventiveness. One could also hear Charles Mingus the pianist in here and even some Debussy and Moussorgsky. —*Alan Heineman, Down Beat*

○ **Impressions of Copenhagen** / 1981 / Evidence 22024
Pianist Joe (then known as Joseph) Bonner turned in an intriguing variation on the shopworn concept of jazz artist recording with strings. He conceived a set mixing piano, brass, chimes, woodwinds, and a string quartet, generating an array of enticing backgrounds, frameworks, and delightful sounds around and behind his own lush, sentimental solos. The results were a gentle, enchanting '81 session that Evidence has reissued with an extra track on a '92 CD. *Lush Life* is a fine bonus, and the full date spotlights Bonner's tremendous piano and chimes. Great remastering brings the blend of strings, brass, and keyboards to the center, augmented by the bass-drum interplay of Paul Warburton and J. Thomas Tilton (who also produced) and the trumpet and trombone playing of Eddie Shu and Gary Olson. —*Ron Wynn*

Lester Bowie

b. Oct. 11, 1941, Frederick, MD
Trumpet, flugelhorn, composer / Modern creative
Trumpeter, flugelhorn player, and composer Lester Bowie is a maverick player, humorist, and charter member of the Art Ensemble of Chicago. He's shown it's possible to be on the edge musically without being solemn or pompous. His solos are alternately complex and simple, crisp and full of blues licks and tricks. His constant shifting between outside and inside reflects his eclectic background. He has played with the Art Ensemble, backed his ex-wife Fontella Bass in gospel, and led jazz-rock and trumpet repertory and experimental duos. Comparisons are made to Cootie Williams due to his use of growls, slurs, and high-octane solos. —*Ron Wynn*

○ **Numbers 1 & 2** / Aug. 11, 1967+Aug. 25, 1967 / Nessa 1

★ **5th Power, The** / Apr. 12+17, 1978 / Black Saint 0020
1978 quintet w/ Arthur Blythe (as), Amina Myers (p). Creative jazz and a progressive gospel segment. Bowie at his eclectic best. Essential. —*Michael G. Nastos*

☆ **Twilight Dreams** / Apr. 1987 / Venture 90650

○ **Works** / 1989 / PolyGram 837274
1980-1985 anthology with Art Ensemble of Chicago, Brass Fantasy, Stanton Davis, Rasul Siddik, Vincent Chancey, Steve Turre, Frank Lacy, Phillip Wilson, and Bob Stewart. —*AMG*

Charles Brackeen

b. 1940, White's Chapel (renamed Eufaula), OK
Tenor sax, trumpet / Modern creative
Tenor saxophonist and trumpeter Charles Brackeen is an explosive, powerful soloist and composer whose best recordings were done for the Strata-East label in the '70s. He also recorded for Silkheart in the '80s. He was married to pianist Joanne Brackeen, who's gone on to attain a measure of stardom. —*Ron Wynn*

★ **Rhythm X** / 1973 / Strata East

Joanne Brackeen (JoAnne [Née Grogan] Brackeen)

b. Jul. 26, 1938, Ventura, CA
Piano / Hard bop
Essentially a self-taught pianist, Joanne Brackeen's solos and compositions are distinguished by their thematic variety and her facility and use of complex harmonies. While a student at Los Angeles Conservatory, Brackeen listened to pianist Frankie Carle,

then directly imitated his solos. She later played with Teddy Edwards, Harold Land, Dexter Gordon, and Charles Lloyd in Los Angeles during the late '50s. After moving to New York with then husband Charles Brackeen in the '60s, she played with Art Blakey's Messengers before joining Stan Getz in the late '70s. The acclaim from that stint led to her getting the chance to be a leader. Since then, Brackeen's led several trios, done solo and combo dates, and had recordings issued on Choice, Ken Music, Concord, and Columbia. Terence Blanchard, Branford Marsalis, Jack DeJohnette, Eddie Gomez, Cecil McBee, and Al Foster are among musicians who've worked with Brackeen. —*Ron Wynn and Michael G. Nastos*

★ **Tring-A-Ling** / Mar. 20, 1977 / Choice 1016
Brilliant pianist-composer with powerful modern modal music (all originals). With Michael Brecker on sax plus two bassists. —*Michael G. Nastos*

○ **Havin' Fun** / Jun. 1985 / Concord Jazz 4280
Good trio session by the underrated pianist Joanne Brackeen. She's extended and complimented by bassist Cecil McBee and drummer Al Foster and shows rhythmic verve and harmonic strength, plus good solo technique throughout the album. This has been reissued on CD. —*Ron Wynn, AMG*

○ **Where Legends Dwell** / Sep. 3+04, 1991 / Ken Music 021
Extraordinary trio with Eddie Gomez on bass and Jack DeJohnette on drums, this is her best work of the past decade. The 12 tracks are all originals. Over 70 minutes of incredibly ingenious jazz included. This is easy to dig into. —*Michael G. Nastos*

○ **Dr. Chu Chow** / Pathfinder 8851

Bobby Bradford (Bobby Lee Bradford)
b. Jul. 19, 1934, Cleveland, OH
Cornet, trumpet, composer / Early free, modern creative
Trumpeter and cornetist Bobby Bradford is a truly distinctive player who's never made enough recordings or gotten the widespread acclaim his talent merits. Outside of Don Cherry, no one else from the '60s free school has been more of a trailblazer on trumpet and cornet. Bradford played with future greats Cedar Walton and David "Fathead" Newman in high school and college. His first major work came with Buster Smith. Bradford moved from Dallas to Los Angeles in 1953, where he met and began working with Ornette Coleman. He also played with Wardell Gray, Gerald Wilson, and Eric Dolphy before going into military service. Following that, he began music studies, but then went to New York and replaced Cherry in Coleman's band in 1961. Unfortunately none of the work that the group did during Bradford's two-year tenure was recorded. He returned to the West Coast in 1965 and played the next six years with John Carter. The Bradford-Carter group made several exciting records throughout the '60s and early '70s. Bradford visited Europe four times in the '70s and '80s, each time recording with John Stevens, while also teaching in Los Angeles and heading his own bands. He appeared on Coleman's '71 releases *Science Fiction* and *Broken Shadows*. Bradford was part of the Little Big Horn workshop with Carter, Arthur Blythe, James Newton, and others from 1976 to 1978. During the '80s, he spent two years in the David Murray Octet and also worked with Charlie Haden's Liberation Music Orchestra, Stevens' Freebop, and his own group the Mo'tet. His son was a founding member of the band Jeff Lorber Fusion in 1979. —*Ron Wynn*

● **With John Stevens and the Spontaneous Music Ensemble, Vol 1** / i. Dec. 1971 / Nessa 17
This set was recorded in England in 1971; the jazz avant-garde there was still relatively new then, and John Stevens's series of Spontaneous Music Ensembles were among its most notable exponents. It was their good fortune to meet the American Bobby Bradford, who along with Don Cherry, had invented and defined the trumpet's role in the evolving new music while with Ornette Coleman's early groups. It was Bradford's good fortune to meet five skilled players so enthusiastically moved by the philosophical tenets of Coleman's music, and it was certainly our good fortune to have one of the rare recorded appearances of this master trumpeter. —*John Litweiler, Down Beat*

○ **One Night Stand** / Nov. 1986 / Soul Note 1168
A melodic player with a healthy sense of humor who has become more expressive through the years, Bobby Bradford really got a

chance to stretch out on this fine session. Although pianist Frank Sullivan is essentially a bop player, he did a good job of keeping up during the more adventurous performances. Bassist Scott Walton (who has learned from the innovations of Charlie Haden) and drummer Billy Bowker were excellent in support. "Ashes" (a calypso version of "I Got Rhythm") and the mysterious "Woman" were the highpoints of this highly recommended disc. —*Scott Yanow, Cadence*

○ **Comin' On** / i. Feb. 1990 / Hat Art 6016
An uneven 1988 date that still contains some glorious moments, mostly when Bradford and longtime cohort clarinetist John Carter play together. Bradford's solos aren't as universally sharp or focused as usual, but he doesn't totally falter. Drummer Andrew Cyrille and bassist Richard Davis dominate in the rhythm section. —*Ron Wynn, AMG*

Ruby Braff (Reuben Braff)
b. Mar. 16, 1927, Boston, MA
Cornet / New Orleans traditional, swing
When cornetist and trumpeter Ruby Braff came to New York from his native Boston in 1953, he was considered an oddball because he modeled his playing on Louis Armstrong and Lester Young rather than bebop. But he was received with open ears by the older mainstream jazzmen and soon was recording prolifically and working with Benny Goodman and other luminaries. There was a long association with the Newport All Stars and, later, an interesting quartet co-led with guitarist George Barnes. More recently, Braff's done fruitful work with pianist Dick Hyman—their duets are special. As a stylist, Braff is an original; his exploration of the cornet's lower register and his approach to melody make his work stand out. He's gone from young iconoclast to revered elder statesman. —*Dan Morgenstern*

○ **Inventions in Jazz (Volume 2)** / i. 1955 / Vanguard 8020
○ **Adoration of the Melody** / Mar. 17-18, 1955 / Bethlehem 6043
Back in the mid-'50s when *Adoration of the Melody* was made, Ruby Braff had a unique sound of great distinction and character. It was thick and fat, and Braff could fine-tune its vibrato with a master's touch. He could taper his notes, hold them on perfect pitch, then drift into a warm, broad vibrato that swung with as much grace and relaxation as his best phrases. The album's best blends were on "Lucky Guy," "Easy Living," "I'll Be Around," "It's Easy," and above all "When You're Smilin'," which contained an exquisite ensemble orchestration of Lester Young's classic "triplet" solo of 1937. —*John McDonough, Down Beat*

● **Two by Two: Ruby and Ellis Play Rodgers And Hart** / Oct. 14, 1955 / Vanguard 8507
○ **Two Part Inventions in Jazz—Vol. 1** / i. Nov. 2, 1955 / Vanguard 8019
○ **Two Part Inventions in Jazz—Vol. 2** / i. Nov. 2, 1955 / Vanguard 8020
● **Ball at Bethlehem** / Dec. 31, 1955+Jan. 1, 1955 /
○ **Magic Horn of Ruby Braff, The** / May 28, 1956 / RCA 1332
○ **Ruby Braff Octet with Pee Wee Russell And, The** / Jul. 5, 1957 / Verve 8241
○ **This Is My Lucky Day** / i. Aug. 19, 1957-Dec. 26, 1957 / Bluebird 6456
On the Berrigan tributes, the four-horn front line gave the ensemble a sound almost too fat and generous, giving "It's Been So Long" an almost glib air. Braff's own plump sound radiated the joy of living and Beriganesque romanticism, evoking Berrigan's balladry on "I Can't Get Started" (natch) and the Duke Ellington. —*Kevin Whitehead, Cadence*

○ **Easy Now** / Aug. 11+19, 1958 / RCA 1966
★ **With the Newport All Stars** / Oct. 28, 1967 / Black Lion 760138
W/ Buddy Tate (ts), George Wein (p), Jack Lesberg (b), and Don Lamond (d). Both Tate and Braff are in top form on this one. —*Michael Erlewine*

○ **Ruby Braff-George Barnes Quartet, The** / 1973 / Chiaroscuro 121
This album by the Ruby Braff-George Barnes quartet was a thing of beauty. . . . Wayne Wright was a fine rhythm guitarist who knew just how to play behind Braff and Barnes. John Giufridda (later replaced by Mike Moore) provided a solid bass backing. The two soloists were in sterling form. Braff never sounded freer, hap-

pier, or more imaginative; he glided through the air with acrobatic ease. . . . The Braff-Barnes record is indispensable. —*Tom Piazza, Down Beat*

○ **Mr. Braff to You: The Ruby Braff Quintet** / Dec. 15, 1983 / Phontastic 7568
Braff set the mood for this record with his cozy cornet tone. Tenor saxist Scott Hamilton got equal solo time and outplayed the leader. He'd edged a little closer to Lester Young than he once had, with a lighter tone and gracefully flowing linear ideas that hinted at "Pres"-ian ancestry. Pianist John Bunch was mainly an accompanist here, tying the solos together with his accomplished backing. —*Doug Long, Cadence*

○ **Music from "South Pacific"** / i. Jun. 12, 1990-Jun. 13, 1990 / Concord Jazz 4445

○ **Ruby Braff & His New England Songhounds—Vol. 1** / Oct. 25, 1991 / Concord Jazz 4478

Anthony Braxton

b. Jun. 4, 1945, Chicago, IL
Sax, composer / Cool, modern creative
After jazz achieved total freedom of expression in the mid-'60s, where could it go next? Saxophonist Anthony Braxton devised a brilliant solution beginning with his first Delmark album (1968). Working closely with members of the Art Ensemble of Chicago and the Association for the Advancement of Creative Musicians (AACM), Braxton staged his own quiet revolution with written structures that could accommodate compositional complexity alongside improvisational liberation. In essence, his debut *Three Compositions of New Jazz* turned the oft-publicized extremes of free-jazz inside out, favoring silence and quiet sounds, purposefully excluding the usual rhythm section, and substituting small and unusual instruments to reinforce his frameworks of spacious tension. At the same time, he built an impressive repertoire of solo alto sax works and, like many of his Chicago peers, reintroduced forgotten members of the saxophone and clarinet family to jazz audiences. His early influences included both cold and hot reedmen—Paul Desmond, Warne Marsh, Charlie Parker, John Coltrane, Ornette Coleman, Eric Dolphy—as well as advanced European composers like Stockhausen. But the most obvious inspiration for Braxton's highly theoretical approach came from the senior members of the AACM cooperative, many of whom, like Muhal Richard Abrams, Leroy Jenkins, Roscoe Mitchell, Steve McCall, and Joseph Jarman, were his earliest collaborators. Following a period of European self-exile and work with the Circle Trio (with Dave Holland and Chick Corea) in the early '70s, Braxton's music has moved in manifold directions, incorporating the best of American jazz, free improvisation, and the European vanguard. He has consistently played with his own quartets or quintets, performing his labyrinthine "creative music" compositions in standard jazz instrumentation, as well as expanding his multiinstrumental mastery in solo and ensemble settings. Improvised duos with diverse and challenging partners have been a staple over the years, and more recently Braxton has recorded entire albums of jazz standards. As a player his scope and facility are unsurpassed; as a composer he is as prolific as he is imaginative. His compositions, all bearing graphic titles instead of names, run into the hundreds and cover almost every musical ensemble imaginable, from solos to large orchestras. His more adventuresome pieces involve theater, dance, opera, and multiple orchestras performing simultaneously in different locations—even on different planets! He's now a tenured full-time professor at Wesleyan. Many of his best recordings are on import labels and can be found in major record stores along with out-of-print copies of his many U.S. Arista label albums from the 70s. —*Myles Boisen*

★ **For Alto Saxophone** / Oct. 1968 / Delmark 420-421

★ **In the Tradition—Vol. 1** / May 29, 1974 / Steeple Chase 1015
This session showed another side of Anthony Braxton from his Arista recordings as he eschewed his own compositions for a series of jazz classics. The critics who think Braxton isn't a jazz musician (if that's really important) should finally have been silenced. His alto playing on "Marshmallow" and "Just Friends" had his unmistakable stylings, but on "Lush Life" he was at his most traditional similar to "Nickie" on his *Duets 1976* album. —*Carl Brauer, Cadence*

☆ **In the Tradition—Vol. 2** / May 29, 1974 / Inner City 31045

Braxton's set of vintage bop and mainstream songs, done with reverence and, for the most part, extreme competence. These seemed to be Braxton's answer to those who claimed he knew little about jazz tradition and even less about how to present it on album. Reaction to both albums was strong; fellow alto saxophonist Bob Mover even cut an album in answer to them. —*Ron Wynn, AMG*

○ **Duo—Vols. 1 and 2** / Jun. 30, 1974 / Emanem 601
These two albums were originally issued as a double album on Emanem and were the results of a concert given June 30, 1974, in London (the rehearsal extract was recorded the preceding day). The music here went to the furthest borders where the line between sound and music became most abstract. —*Bob Rusch, Cadence*

○ **19 (Solo) Compositions (1988)** / Jun. 1974-Apr. 1988 / New Albion 23

○ **Creative Orchestra Music (1976)** / Feb. 1976 / Arista 4080
This was Anthony Braxton's music in an orchestral framework. To perform these six varied compositions Braxton assembled some seminal creative improvisers including multiinstrumentalist Roscoe Mitchell, trumpet and cornet player Leo Smith, and pianist, arranger, composer, and bandleader Muhal Richard Abrams in addition to those musicians who then made up his regular group. —*Carl Brauer, Cadence*

★ **Seven Standards (1985)—Vol. 1** / Jan. 30-31, 1985 / Magenta 0203
Saxophonist plays straightahead with the Hank Jones (p) Trio. Very enjoyable. Vol. 2 also excellent. —*Michael G. Nastos*

○ **Five Compositions (1986)** / Jul. 2-03, 1986 / Black Saint 0106
When Anthony Braxton installed a piano in his quartet, his music increasingly echoed the classic group Circle, in which, circa 1970, he worked with Chick Corea. Braxton, of course, never turned his back on heady concepts like those Circle limned; his artistic progress has always relied on refining elements first set forth over two decades ago. And while the compositional strategies he employed grew ever more familiar, his sidefolk executed his thorny themes ever more smoothly. —*Kevin Whitehead, Cadence*

○ **Six Monk's Compositions (1987)** / Jun. 30, 1987+Jul. 1, 1987 / Black Saint 1201161
This may be Braxton's finest straight jazz release, and it's among his best in any style. Bassist Mal Waldron and bassist Buell Neidlinger are fully equipped to handle Monk's tricky passages, chord structures and movements, while Braxton displays an affinity for Monk's work that his legion of detractors would find astonishing. Drummer Bill Osborne isn't intimidated by Neidlinger or Waldron and drives the session effectively. —*Ron Wynn, AMG*

○ **Vancouver Duets (1989)** / Jun. 30, 1989 / Music & Arts 611
Blistering, compelling duets that are intense, effective, and often frightening in style, volume, and energy. There's little hard bop, mainstream, or even straight bop; just searing, surging alto sax and piano. —*Ron Wynn, AMG*

○ **Tristano Compositions (1989)** / Dec. 10-12, 1989 / Hat Art 6052
Braxton tackles works by another keyboard genius—Lennie Tristano, and shows he's just as able to handle his pieces as those of Monk. Bassist Cecil McBee and drummer Andrew Cyrille threaten, but don't overwhelm, baritone saxophonist John Raskin and pianist Dred Scott. The album is dedicated to Warne Marsh, a saxophonist whose influence resounds in much of Braxton's work. —*Ron Wynn, AMG*

Lenny Breau (Leonard Breau)

b. Aug. 5, 1941, Auburn, ME, d. Aug. 12, 1984, Los Angeles, CA
Guitar / Swing, bop
An outstanding finger-style jazz guitarist who performed on both acoustic and electric guitars. Breau's right hand drew on classical, flamenco, and country (Travis-Atkins) finger-picking techniques. He was among the first guitarists to digest the impressionistic, postbop chord voicings of pianist Bill Evans. Breau developed the ability to simultaneously comp chords and improvise single-string melodies, creating the illusion of two guitarists playing together. His facility with artificial harmonics remains the envy of many guitarists. Late in his career, Breau began using a seven-string guitar that extended the instrument's range in the upper register. Breau's early RCA recordings are eclectic and technically

dazzling. His later work is less flashy but communicates on a deeper level. —*Richard Lieberson*

★ **Five O'clock Bells** / Oct. 1977-Jan. 1978 / Genes 5006
1977 & 1978. Solo guitar and vocals. This includes five Breau originals, two standards, and McCoy Tyner's "Visions." Guitar students, this is your homework—find this album. —*Michael G. Nastos*

○ **Mo' Breau** / 1977-1978 / Adelphi 5012
1977 & 1978. The companion to *5 O'Clock Bells* features solo versions of four of Breau's originals, one melded to McCoy Tyner's "Ebony Queen" and three nice standards, including "Emily." —*Michael G. Nastos*

Michael Brecker

b. Mar. 29, 1949, Philadelphia
Tenor sax, soprano sax, flute, piano / Modern creative
Versatility has been saxophonist Michael Brecker's strong suit, as he's forged a career in both jazz and rock. His father was a pianist; Brecker studied under Vince Trombetta and Joe Allard in the mid '60s. After one year at Indiana University in 1970, Brecker joined his brother Randy in New York. His style, a mix of intense Coltrane-influenced licks and blues-funk tinges, has become among the most recognizable of his generation. He started with organist-vocalist Edwin Birdsong in 1970, then was in the excellent but commercially ill-fated band Dreams. The two Breckers formed their own band in the mid '70s, a musically top-flight jazz-rock ensemble that managed to inject some quality into songs that were often predictable and stilted. Prior to that, Michael Brecker had worked with James Taylor, Horace Silver, Billy Cobham, and Yoko Ono. After the Brecker Brothers disbanded, he joined Steps, which later became Steps Ahead.
In 1986 Brecker's belated debut album as a leader, "Michael Brecker," topped the jazz charts for months, finally establishing him as a solo star. On that and subsequent albums, Brecker used both conventional horn and the EWI (Electronic Wind Instrument), a synthesizer activated by blowing. His use of the EWI has helped establish it and other synthesized instruments as valid jazz tools. In 1980 Brecker embarked on a world tour with Paul Simon, and he had a featured solo spot in each show. —*Ron Wynn*

○ **Cityscape** / **i.** 1983 / Warner Brothers 3698

★ **Don't Try This at Home** / 1988 / MCA 42229
Good follow-up to Brecker's 1987 debut for the revived Impulse label, though it wasn't quite as energized or as passionate as his debut. He had another excellent supporting cast, but the songs didn't seem as interesting, and the session at times sounds like merely a less intense continuation of its predecessor. —*Ron Wynn, AMG*

○ **Now You See It . . . Now You Don't** / 1990 / GRP 9622
For *Now You See It*, Brecker's third recording as a leader, the tenor great used different personnel on most of the selections, but played consistently well. Jim Beard's synthesizers were used for atmosphere, to set up a funky groove or to provide a backdrop for the leader. Some of the music sounded like updated John Coltrane (Joey Calderazzo's McCoy Tyner-influenced piano helped) but other pieces could have almost passed for Weather Report, if Wayne Shorter rather than Joe Zawinul had been the lead voice. Most of the originals (either by Brecker, Jim Beard, or producer Don Grolnick) projected moods rather than featured strong melodies, but Michael Brecker's often-raging tenor made the most of every opportunity; his intensity on the ironically named "Peep" could have easily challenged Courtney Pine. —*Scott Yanow, Cadence*

Randy Brecker

b. Nov. 29, 1945, Philadelphia, PA
Trumpet / Modern creative
This trumpeter has played jazz, funk, fusion, and rock with Horace Silver, Dreams, Larry Coryell, Jack DeJohnette, and Frank Zappa. He collaborates frequently with his wife, Brazilian keyboardist/vocalist Eliane Elias. He's also a very capable straightahead player, one of the best. —*Michael G. Nastos*

★ **In the Idiom** / Oct. 19-25, 1986 / Denon 1483
Just how strong a trumpeter Brecker could be was demonstrated well on "Little Miss P," a freeish cooker that wound down into

near orgasmic playing between trumpet, bass, and drums. . . . But while suggestive of a bygone era, the music—or perhaps more accurately—the playing was fresh. —*Bob Rusch, Cadence*

Willem Breuker

b. Nov. 4, 1944, Amsterdam, Netherlands
Sax, clarinet, composer / Progressive big band, modern creative
Bandleader and multireed player Willem Breuker is a champion of Europe's avant-garde community, and someone who's never wavered in his commitment to establishing a tradition and sound influenced by, but in many ways different from, American jazz. Breuker was a founder of the Instant Composers Pool, a nonprofit organization sponsoring performances and recordings by Dutch avant-garde musicians. He's played with the Globe Unity Orchestra since 1965, working with a host of leaders and musicians. Some alumni or members include Alexander Von Schlippenbach, Gunter Hampel, Peter Brotzmann, Misha Mengelberg, and Han Bennik. He formed the Willem Breuker Kollektief in 1974, and they've toured America, Europe, and Canada in the '70s and '80s. This group rivals the Art Ensemble for intriguing multimedia performances, mixing theater, free and Latin music, satire, and even classical strains. Breuker was awarded the Dutch National Jazz Prize in 1970 and the West German Music Critics Jazz Prize in 1976. —*Ron Wynn*

● **Live in Berlin** / **i.** Nov. 1975 / FMP 06
This was one of reedman Willem Breuker's works for larger group, and while there was an obvious set of structures within these, it was quite open. —*Bob Rusch, Cadence*

○ **De Klap** / **i.** 1985 / BVHaast 068

○ **Metropolis** / Jan. 1989-Apr. 1989 / BVHaast 8903

○ **To Remain** / **i.** Jan. 1989-Apr. 1989 / BVHaast 8904
This album was a retrospective of sorts, exploring Willem Breuker's compositions and arrangements from the late '70s through the late '80s. —*Michael Rosenstein, Cadence*

○ **Bob's Gallery** / BVHaast 8801

Cecil Bridgewater (Cecil Vernon Bridgewater)

b. Oct. 10, 1942, Urbana, IL
Trumpet, arranger, composer / Hard bop
Trumpeter, arranger, and composer Cecil Bridgewater is a fine soloist and underrated composer who's performed frequently with various Max Roach groups. He's the brother of tenor saxophonist Ron Bridgewater, and he studied music at the University of Illinois from 1960 to 1964 and again in 1968-1969. Bridgewater performed with and wrote arrangements for the school band, touring with them in Europe and the Soviet Union in '68 and '69. The Bridgewater brothers had their own band for a while in '69, then Cecil Bridgewater moved to New York and joined Horace Silver's quintet. He was a member of the Thad Jones-Mel Lewis Orchestra from 1970 to 1976, and accompanied them on tours of Europe, Japan, Russia, and America. During the mid-'70s and through the '80s, Bridgewater played often with Max Roach and also recorded and played with Art Blakey, Randy Weston, Harold Vick, Jimmy Heath, Joe Henderson, Sam Rivers, Roy Brooks, Dizzy Gillespie, Abdullah Ibrahim, Charles McPherson, Frank Foster, and Klaus Weiss. He's also maintained an active teaching career. —*Ron Wynn*

● **I Love Your Smile** / **i.** Dec. 4, 1992 / Blue Moon 78187
In his 20 years with Max Roach, Cecil Bridgewater has been a model sideman, more craftsman than creator, distinguished by his rich tone and quirky way with a blue note. He's lined up a topflight crew for this solo outing, which sparkles with ensemble empathy and communal high spirits. Horn men Antonio Hart, Roger Byam, and Steve Turre toss off sleek, fluid hard-bop runs as Hanna comps with masterly ease, leaving Bridgewater, with his slightly off-kilter attack, the odd man out. But it's Roach, playing on only two tracks, who makes the most distinctive mark.—*Larry Birnbaum, Down Beat*

Dee Dee Bridgewater (Dee Dee [Née Garrett] Bridgewater)

b. May 27, 1950, Memphis, TN
Vocals / Ballads & blues
Dee Dee Bridgewater is a supremely talented jazz singer whose records have not always been indicative of her skills. Her best

work came with the Thad Jones-Mel Lewis big band. She can sing loud or soft; do brassy upbeat tunes, blues, or sentimental ballads; and became popular overseas in the late '70s for her one-woman show, "Lady Day." She is always on the edge of superstardom. —*Ron Wynn*

★ **Live in Paris** / Nov. 24-25, 1986 / MCA 6331
Bridgewater shows her roots in both Carmen McRae and Sarah Vaughan but brings a new sense of maturity and fullness to her singing; she can now be, and is, in command. And the surroundings on this live recording are loose enough to allow the entire group to blow. —*Bob Rusch, Cadence*

○ **In Montreux** / **i**. Jan. 7, 1992 / Verve 511895
Dee Dee Bridgewater moved herself years ago to Paris and is now reappearing on disc. Her flamboyant, energetic, wide-ranging style projects well at Montreux, where she envelopes an adoring audience in a bear hug of brilliant surface emotions, sheer Sassian skill, and deeply thriling vibrato. A Horace Silver medley is pure xenon, Billie Holiday's "Strange Fruit" an untouchable tribute. —*Fred Bouchard, Down Beat*

Nick Brignola (Nicholas Thomas Brignola)

b. Jul. 17, 1936
Sax / Bop, postbop
An outstanding baritone saxophonist, Nick Brignola also plays tenor, soprano, alto, flute, and clarinet. He demonstrates extensive range and control in either the upper or lower register and is a very capable ballad stylist as well. Though he studied theory at Berklee and Ithaca College, Brignola's primarily a self-taught improviser. He played and recorded with Reese Markewich in the late '50s and Herb Pomeroy in Boston, as well as on the West Coast with the Mastersounds and Cal Tjader. He moved to Albany in 1959 and formed his own band. Brignola worked and recorded with Woody Herman and Sal Salvador in the mid-'60s, and toured Europe with Ted Curson in 1967. Brignola later formed his own label, recorded with fellow baritone players Ronnie Cuber, Cecil Payne, and Pepper Adams in the late '70s and made several recordings through the '80s. He's been featured on Beehive, Interplay, Priam, Discovery, Night Life, and Trend releases. —*Ron Wynn and Michael G. Nastos*

★ **Baritone Madness** / Dec. 22, 1977 / Bee Hive 7000
While evidencing considerable imagination in planning and attentive care in production, *Baritone Madness* was fundamentally a blowing date but one, it should be emphasized, that produced striking results. Three of its five cuts offered the spark-producing pairing of veteran Pepper Adams and the then- younger Nick Brignola, their two baritone saxophones joined on "Billie's Bounce" and "Marmeduke" (sic) by Ted Curson, playing trumpet on the former and flugelhorn on the latter. —*Pete Welding, Down Beat*

○ **Northern Lights** / Jul. 3, 1984 / Discovery 917

○ **Raincheck** / Sep. 1988 / Reservoir 108
Nick Brignola's baritone packs a powerful punch, but Brignola prefers the high register to the low, often darting to harmonics well above the horn's written range.... This album gave Brignola plenty of elbow room, and he proved he could play the hell out of a standard. —*Mark Stryker, Cadence*

Bob Brookmeyer (Robert Brookmeyer)

b. Dec. 19, 1929, Kansas City, MO
Valve trombone, arranger, piano / Cool
Though well known as a premier valve trombonist, Bob Brookmeyer actually began professionally as a pianist in the early '50s. He established himself on valve trombone in later years, particularly in the '70s, when his blend of swing phrasing and sound variations plus humor proved appealing. He started in the bands of Stan Getz, Gerry Mulligan, and Jimmy Giuffre. He co-led a fine early-'60s group with Clark Terry and was a founding member of the Lewis-Jones big band. A prolific session player and arranger throughout the '70s, he is still active. —*Ron Wynn*

○ **Bob Brookmeyer with Phil Urso** / Apr. 30, 1954 / Savoy 15041

○ **And Friends** / May 25-27, 1964 / Columbia 36804
Cool was not dead in 1964; valve trombonist Bob Brookmeyer and friends here captured that school's careful restraint, and a touch of its wimpiness. As a front line, the mellow tone qualities

of the leader's valve trombone and Stan Getz's tenor were well-matched. —*Kevin Whitehead, Cadence*

★ **Bob Brookmey Small Band—Vols. 1 and 2** / Jul. 28-29, 1978 / Gryphon 4042
Live at Sandy's in Beverly, MA in 1978. With Michael Moore (b), Jack Wilkins (g), Joe LaBarbera (d). Mostly standards, some music of Andy Laverne. Two Brookmeyer originals. All arrangements by Brookmeyer. Fine group effort. —*Michael G. Nastos*

Roy Brooks

b. Sep. 3, 1938, Detroit, MI
Drums, percussion / Hard bop
Both a powerful soloist and a compelling accompanist, drummer Roy Brooks rhythmically fortifies any situation. He got his start with Yusef Lateef and has since worked with numerous groups and leaders, among them Pharoah Sanders, James Moody, Wes Montgomery, Sonny Stitt, Dexter Gordon, Charles Mingus, Jackie McLean, Horace Silver, and M'Boom. Brooks formed a center in Detroit for bringing jazz instruction to young people in 1976, and started the Aboriginal Percussion Choir, which performed at the 1980 Detroit-Montreaux Jazz Festival. He's recorded as a leader for Muse, Enja, and Bayside, and his '70 LP *The Free Slave* is a classic. —*Ron Wynn and Michael G. Nastos*

★ **Free Slave, The** / Apr. 26, 1970 / Muse 5003
Recorded at the Left Bank Jazz Society in Baltimore, MD, this all-star quintet features George Coleman (ts), Woody Shaw (tpt), Hugh Lawson (p), Cecil McBee (b), and Brooks (d/per). There are four originals, all extended, with room to stretch for musicians. Wild club date. —*Michael G. Nastos*

Tina Brooks (Harold Floyd Brooks)

b. Jun. 7, 1932, Fayetteville, NC, **d**. Aug. 13, 1974, New York, NY
Tenor sax / Hard bop, postbop, soul jazz
A criminally overlooked and underrated player, tenor saxophonist Tina Brooks evolved from being an interesting R&B player with Sonny Thompson and Amos Milburn into a solid, engaging soloist and writer. He could play fine blues, funk and soul jazz, or hard bop. His tenure with Jimmy Smith was especially noteworthy, where his warm, robust sound filling in spaces was striking. His albums mixed soul-jazz rhythmic foundations and ambitious compositions. All his albums are available in a Mosaic boxed set. —*Ron Wynn*

★ **Blue Note Recordings** / 1958-1961 / Mosaic 106
1958-1961. Tenor saxophonist with four different bands, including Lee Morgan, Freddie Hubbard, Blue Mitchell, and Johnny Coles (trumpets). Also Jackie McLean. Trios led by pianists Sonny Clark, Duke Jordan, and Kenny Drew. 15 Brooks originals, seven standards. Brooks is an unsung hero. His work deserves your investigation. —*Michael G. Nastos*

○ **True Blue** / Jun. 25, 1960 / Blue Note 4041

○ **Back to the Tracks** / Sep. 1, 1960+Oct. 20, 1960 / Blue Note 84052

Peter Brotzmann

b. Mar. 6, 1941, Remscheid, Germany
Tenor sax / Progressive big band, modern creative
A longtime champion of Europe's avant-garde, and a self-taught tenor saxophonist famous for animated, swirling solos and lengthy, twisting dialogues, Peter Brotzmann initally played in local Dixieland bands in Germany. He was an early member of the Fluxus movement and began playing free jazz by 1964. A year later, Brotzmann, Peter Kowald, and Seven-Ake Johannsson formed a group. Brotzmann toured Europe in 1966 with a quintet that included Mike Mantler and Carla Bley. He also began working with the Globe Unity Orchestra, and continued with them until 1981. Brotzmann was a founder of the cooperative FMP in 1969, an organization that sponsors and issues free jazz releases. He also founded a trio with Han Bennink and Fred Van Hove that became extremely influential through its blend of European theater and folk music and African rhythms. Van Hove left the group in 1976 but continued playing with Bennink until 1979. Brotzmann's associations during the '80s and '90s have included Harry Miller, Louis Moholo, Willie Kellers, Andrew Cyrille, the Alarm Orchestra, Cecil Taylor, and Last Exit. —*Ron Wynn*

○ **For Adolphe Sax** / **i**. Jun. 1967 / FMP 0080

○ **Balls** / **i.** Aug. 1970 / FMP 0020

○ **Brotzmann, Van Hove, Bennink** / **i.** Feb. 1973 / FMP 0130

○ **Outspan No. 1** / **i.** Apr. 1974 / FMP 0180

○ **Outspan No. 2** / **i.** May 1974 / FMP 0200

○ **The Nearer the Bone, The Sweeter The Meat** / **i.** Aug. 1979 / FMP 0690

○ **Alarm** / **i.** Nov. 1981 / FMP 1030

For most of two (now three) decades, saxman Peter Brotzmann has been a principal catalyst in Europe's free music activity. *Alarm* was by a nine-piece band of, again, Europe's finest. It began with long unison siren wails; solos followed, both unaccompanied and over a violently charging rhythm section, as horn screaming moved in and out and collective improvisations appeared. As the wailing and moaning continued, the amazing (then) East German trombonist Johannes Bauer trilled, bubbled, and chattered a wayward line that climaxed as the band swelled to screams. Saxmen Brotzmann and Willem Breuker dueted, unaccompanied, in a pleasant fugue. Drummer Louis Moholo and pianist Alexander Schlippenbach were among the other participants in *Alarm's* madness. It was loud, happy, wild music, packed with event and structured for maximum visceral impact, an ingenious form to enhance energy music materials. — *John Litweiler, Down Beat*

● **Andrew Cyrille Meets Peter Brotzmann in Berlin** / **i.** Mar. 1982 / FMP 1000

Clifford Brown

b. Oct. 30, 1930, Wilmington, DE, **d.** Jun. 26, 1956, PA
Trumpet / Bop, hard bop
Clifford Brown's unarguably one of the greatest trumpet players of all time. The bulk of his work was for Emarcy 1954-1956 and can be found in a definitive ten-CD set *Complete Emarcy Recordings* in which there is a preference for studio group sessions co-led with Max Roach over the wonderful *Clifford Brown with Strings* material. Studio jam sessions and live jams for this label yield much excellent Brown playing but bog down somewhat in lengthy solos by lesser lights. While there is no Clifford Brown not recommended, one to avoid because of very poor audio is the double Columbia album *Live at the Bee Hive* (Columbia), while *Daahoud* (Mainstream) is a pirate release of Emarcy material despite what the album notes say. Other domestic recordings can be found on Prestige, which also includes Swedish recordings from 1953, 1954 concert recordings on GNP, Blue Note and Pacific Jazz combined in the recommended five-album box *The Complete Blue Note/Pacific Jazz Clifford Brown* (Mosaic) which feature him in a sideman's role for the most part. The French Vogue recordings from 1953 have been issued on a number of US labels—Prestige and GNP among others. One convenient way to have them is a three-album box *Clifford Brown/Paris Collection* (Japanese Vogue).

There are bits and pieces of live jams on Ingo, Hall of Fame Elektra/Musician, and Xanadu releases, but the quintessential Clifford Brown is the album *The Beginning and the End* (Columbia), which combines his earliest work as an R&B band sideman with three lengthy jams recorded shortly before his death. — *Bob Porter*

★ **Beginning and the End, The** / 1952-1956 / Columbia
Clifford Brown Sextet. Side one has his earliest recordings of some Caribbean-influenced R&B material; side two is a live recording of his last performance, the night before he died. Includes the famous "Donna Lee" solo. A touching tribute album. — *David Nelson McCarthy*

○ **Clifford Brown Quartet in Paris** / **i.** 1953 / Prestige 357
This session was one of the poorer Clifford Brown recordings from his prime period. . . . It would be unfair to say that it was a bad session, mind you—the original takes of the various titles are excellent, but the little errors of improvisation that creep in here and there and the totally monotonous effect of the original-alternate takes being juxtaposed combined to remove the impact of the music if you try and listen to it all at once. — *Barry Tepperman, Coda*

★ **Complete Blue Note-Pacific Jazz** / Jun. 9, 1953-Oct. 15, 1953 / Mosaic
The Complete Blue Note and Pacific Jazz Recordings of Clifford Brown documented six sessions recorded over a period of 14 months. The first nine tracks were from a June 9, 1953, date . . . .

The last four LP sides were culled from a live performance recorded on the evening of February 21, 1954, at Birdland in New York City. . . . The notes on the sessions, by Ira Gitler, were informative without being pedantic. — *Bob Rusch, Cadence*

○ **Brownie Eyes** / Aug. 28, 1953 / Blue Note 267
The original Blue Note *Clifford Brown Memorial Album* used five of the six sides done at each of two summer 1953 dates; this collection retained four from Brown's first date as a leader and two from a Lou Donaldson session. An added song from each session appeared here, new to 12-inch LP, which meant the label retired four Brown titles from general circulation. . . . His art could include the fire of Gillespie, the brilliance of Navarro, and sometimes even a lyricism almost as personal as Davis's. But Brown had a special sweetness of spirit, and now, 21 years (1975) after these tracks were recorded, we understand why they were so influential. — *John Litweiler, Down Beat*

○ **Clifford Brown Sextet in Paris, The** / Oct. 8, 1953 / Original Jazz Classics 358
These sessions were recorded in 1952 when Clifford Brown and his friend Gigi Gryce were traveling through Europe as members of the Lionel Hampton band. American expatriate Jimmy Gourley was on guitar; Frenchman Henri Renaud, piano; Pierre Michelot, bass; and Jean-Louis Viale on drums rounded out the sextet. Altoist Gryce contributed five compositions to the album including such interesting pieces as "Minority," "Blue Concept," and "Salute to the Bandbox.". . . Michelot and Viale provided intelligent rhythmic support throughout the LP. It was Brown, though, who clearly stole the show. His clear-toned flowing trumpet solos were a joy to behold. — *Peter Friedman, Coda*

○ **Clifford Brown in Paris** / Oct. 8+15, 1953 / Prestige 24020
Though he's not playing with equals, Clifford Brown's exquisite solos and general trumpet execution make his every note on this 1953 date worth hearing. Pierre Michelot on bass was the best among the European rhythm section. — *Ron Wynn, AMG*

○ **Clifford Brown Quartet** / Oct. 15, 1953 / Blue Note 5047
Simply brillant playing by Brown and his comrades, notably Max Roach. The Brown-Roach unit had everything; they played as a cohesive group, yet everyone could also spin out majestic solos, and in pianist Richie Powell, Clifford's brother, there was a third fantastic soloist. This is essential, as are most Brown recordings. — *Ron Wynn, AMG*

○ **Clifford Brown & Max Roach** / **i.** 1954 / PolyGram 814645
This recording came from the beginning of the Max Roach-Clifford Brown association. Actually, this was two sessions . . . . The earlier set was a bit rough, both in audio and ensemble. Even with its raggedness there were moments when the supreme excitement of Brownie's trumpet work bit through and when that happened, even if it was just for a chorus or two, it made a recording impossible to ignore. — *Bob Rusch, Cadence*

○ **Clifford Brown and Max Roach—Vol. 1** / Aug. 6, 1954 / Emarcy 36036

● **Brownie: The Complete Emarcy Recordings Of** / **i.** 1954-1956 / PolyGram 838306
Comprehensive, multidisc set that contains Clifford Brown's output for the Emarcy label. This is wonderful material, particularly the sessions by the quartet Brown co-led with Max Roach. But he's also heard here with big bands, backing Dinah Washington, and on other occasions outside the quartet. Brown's tone, speed, command, and phrasing were immaculate and amazing; had he lived past his mid-20s, he'd certainly have become an icon, and he has influenced hosts of players anyhow. — *Ron Wynn, AMG*

○ **Live at the Bee Hive** / Nov. 7, 1955 / Columbia 35969
This long-buried session was a welcome addition to the skimpy legacy left by trumpeter Clifford Brown, and for several reasons. There was the obvious: that *any* new material featuring Brownie, who was unarguably the finest trumpet player of the hard-bopping '50s, has a place waiting for it on the record shelf. But this November 1955 session, recorded at the now defunct Bee Hive in Chicago, also offered the first documentation of the Brown-Max Roach unit featuring young Sonny Rollins. . . . This was raw, unfettered jazz, played by men interested in pushing their creativity a little further (and a lot longer) than commercial recording limitations would allow. — *Neil Tesser, Down Beat*

○ **Jam Sessions—Vol. 1** / Emarcy 814640

○ **Daahoud** / Mobile Fidelity 00826

Donald Brown

b. 1954, Memphis, TN
Piano / Hard bop
This Memphis-born pianist is one of the top contemporary players, arrangers, and writers. Like many Memphis pianists, he's a former member of Art Blakey's band. His knowledge of blues and soul reflects both his background working in the '70s Stax scene and his love for all styles. A fluid, often exuberant soloist, Brown has a busy career as a producer (Kenny Garrett, Donald Byrd) and performer and is also a music professor at the University of Tennessee at Knoxville. —*Ron Wynn*

○ **Early Bird** / Jan. 4-05, 1987 / Sunnyside 1025
The Buhainian influence was unmistakable on these young musicians even if they frequently adopted a studied posture of laid-back modality. The album's strongest elements were the free-wheeling, Eric Dolphyesque exuberance of Donald Harrison and the sturdy bass work of Bob Hurst, who took an amazing, lightning fast solo on "Bassically Simple."... This was a well-produced, often enjoyable example of the facile, often dreamy neobop that has captured the imagination of so many young jazz musicians. —*Krin Gabbard, Cadence*

★ **Sources of Inspiration** / Aug. 11, 1989 / Muse 5385
Pianist Donald Brown wrote all the tunes on this session, which includes two ballads ("Do We Have to Say Goodbye?," "Phineas"), two midtempo numbers ("Overtaken by a Moment," "New York") and two impassioned tunes with political overtones ("Capetown Ambush" and "The Human Impersonator"). There was a nice swing to Brown's compositions, a bit of a mid-'60s Blue Note feel about them. —*Tim Smith, Cadence*

Marion Brown (Marion Brown, Jr.)

b. Sep. 8, 1935, Atlanta
Alto sax, flute / Early free, modern creative
Though he's best known as a free or avant-garde player, saxophonist Marion Brown's roots are in swing and blues. He played with Johnny Hodges in the '50s before moving to New York, where he worked with Archie Shepp and the Jazz Composers Orchestra before starting his own group in 1965. Brown appeared on many landmark '60s releases, including *Ascension*, and co-led a duo with trumpeter Leo Smith in the '70s. Pungent lines, sometimes frenetic solos balanced by tender melodies, and expressive lines are Brown's trademark on alto. His '70s releases have reflected his absorption and interest in African and African-American folk music and traditional rhythms and songs. —*Ron Wynn*

○ **Marion Brown Quartet** / Dec. 1, 1966 / ESP 1022

★ **Three for Shepp** / Dec. 1, 1966 / Impulse 9139

☆ **Geechee Recollections** / Jun. 4-05, 1973 / Impulse 9252
Geechee Recollections was a somewhat conscious evocation of the spirit of African music.... Marion Brown stretched out hauntingly on both alto and soprano sax on parts of the "suite" that comprised the second side ("Introduction-Tokalokaloka-Ending"), and Leo Smith essayed an occasional statement on trumpet, but it was those ferocious drummers—and, to almost as great an extent, James Jefferson's firm and sensitive bass work behind them—that captured my attention. Marion Brown created an album that was evocative and challenging. Taken on its own terms, *Geechee Recollections* was a hell of a record. —*Peter Keepnews, Down Beat*

○ **Vista** / Feb. 18-19, 1975 / Impulse 9304
There was nothing at all wrong with this album. It was relaxing, skillfully played, and pretty and featured a vocal on Stevie Wonder's "Visions." The whole first side was in a slow, dreamy vein. The vocal on "Visions" was the kind of thing you'd hear on a Quincy Jones album, but it harks back to Earl Coleman. The solos didn't stand out, but blended into the rhythm section. Most of the songs took a great deal of time to state the melody and a short space to improvise off of it. —*Ira Steingroot, Down Beat*

Ray Brown (Raymond Matthews Brown)

b. Oct. 13, 1926, Pittsburgh, PA
Bass / Swing, big band, bop
Ray Brown has long been considered among jazz's finest bass players. He's been featured on countless recording sessions as a sideman. His own albums began with Verve in 1956 and contin-

ued on an occasional basis through 1965 as he made six LPs for the label, including two co-led with Milt Jackson. Several of these were orchestral and less dependent on Brown's own contributions than on the arrangers' writing. Of the small band items, *This Is Ray Brown* (Verve) is a relaxed session involving Oscar Peterson and Herb Ellis, while *Much In Common* (Verve) has Kenny Burrell and Hank Jones as well as gospel singer Marion Williams on some titles along with Jackson. Of the big-band albums, *Ray Brown with the All Star Big Band* (Verve) involves arrangements by Al Cohn and Ernie Wilkins and New York personnel whose playing truly fulfills the album title. He began recording for Concord Records in 1975, again on an occasional basis, often with pianists Jimmy Rowles, Monty Alexander, or Gene Harris. Brown continues to contribute to dozens of Concord recordings. If the quality of some sessions is less than others, it's never Brown's fault. One recording apart from the Concord sessions that demands mention is *Super Bass* (Capri), which features Brown with his protAgA and most likely successor, John Clayton. This contains masterful bass playing throughout and is an ideal example to demonstrate Ray Brown's lasting brilliance.—*Bob Porter*

○ **Ray Brown with Milt Jackson** / Jan. 4-05, 1965 / Verve 8615

★ **As Good As It Gets** / Dec. 22, 1977 / Concord Jazz 66
In this well-balanced pairing with bassist Ray Brown, pianist Jimmy Rowles predictably came up with the unexpected: to wit, a James P. Johnson-like interpretation of "Like Someone in Love," in which this seldom played '40s tune was transformed into a timeless classic.... Rowles's artistry may be unfamiliar to many, but followers of both Teddy Wilson and Thelonious Monk will find much to admire in this musician's talents. —*Jack Sohmer, Cadence*

○ **Something for Lester** / Jun. 22-24, 1979 / Contemporary 412
The splendid *Something for Lester* was only bassist Ray Brown's second album as a leader (*Brown's Bag* for Concord Jazz was the first), all the others having been as a sideman or coleader. Pianist Cedar Walton and drummer Elvin Jones were apropos partners-in-sound for the superlative bassist, having worked together in J.J. Johnson's hot band of the late '50s, alongside Freddie Hubbard; their intuitive understanding of each other's playing, combined with Brown's obvious talents, let the music flow unencumbered. —*Zan Stewart, Down Beat*

● **This One's for Blanton** / i. 1982 / Pablo 2310721
Bassist Jimmy Blanton died at the premature age of 21 after serving with the Duke Ellington band in the early '40s. This album was dedicated to him. Ellington (piano) and Ray Brown (bass) excelled on the original Blanton showcase tune "Pitter Panther Patter," where both exhibited their complete control of their instruments.... It was superbly recorded with clear surfaces—an album not to be missed. —*Bill Gallagher, Cadence*

☆ **Live at the Loa—Summer Wind** / Jul. 1988 / Concord Jazz 426
Brown's trio with Gene Harris (k) and Jeff Hamilton (d). Perhaps Brown's very best. —*Michael G. Nastos*

○ **Super Bass** / i. Dec. 10, 1990 / Capri 74018

Dave Brubeck (David Warren Brubeck)

b. Dec. 6, 1920, Concord, CA
Piano, bandleader / Cool
One of the best at using odd time signatures, pianist and bandleader Dave Brubeck began at age 13, playing with bands in Concord, CA. His studies with Milhaud were a lasting influence on the construction of his solos and compositions. During the '50s and '60s, his groups were the most popular in the world, especially on college campuses. He was the most popular "cool" stylist of all time from an exposure standpoint. He and alto saxophonist Paul Desmond were precise, sparing players whose every note seemed measured, and they seldom pushed or rushed any tempos. Brubeck employed a host of things from the classical world—block chording, counterpoint, and fugues—and made them palatable. He's been a huge seller since 1954 and remains immensely popular. —*Ron Wynn*

○ **Dave Brubeck Trio, The** / Sep. 1949-Nov. 1950 / Fantasy 24726
Early, seminal music by the pianist who made jazz history in the '50s. This trio featured Cal Tjader in his pre-Latin impresario days playing either drums or percussion, while Ron Crotty was the bassist. There are glimmers of what Brubeck would later make his signature sound; classical devices interspersed with a modi-

fied stride technique, and odd time signatures. —*Ron Wynn, AMG*

○ **Cal Tjader with the Dave Brubeck Trio—Vol. 1** / i. 1949-1950 / Fantasy 3331

★ **Greatest Hits from the Fantasy Years (1949-1954)** / 1949-1954 / Fantasy 4528

A nice overview of his material in the years before he crossed over and became a celebrity. —*Ron Wynn*

☆ **Dave Brubeck and Paul Desmond** / Sep. 1952-Feb. 1953 / Fantasy 24727

This is a set of various live recordings of the Brubeck quartet on the eve of national prominence, *Time* magazine covers and the ridiculous controversy concerning "cool" jazz and East Coast blues. The listener can trace the genesis of Brubeck's music as he molded "new" fragments in search of the trademark: Paul Desmond's unexplicable, ethereal, and cutting reed-thin alto voice and Brubeck's charging, spirited, and shifting jazz pianism. —*Christopher Kuhl, Cadence*

○ **Jazz at Storyville** / Oct. 1952-Feb. 1953 / Fantasy 8

○ **Brubeck & Desmond at Wilshire-Ebell** / Jun. 20, 1953 / Fantasy 3249

○ **Featuring Paul Desmond in Concert** / i. Jun. 1953 / Fantasy 013

○ **Jazz at the Blackhawk** / Sep. 1953 / Fantasy 210

★ **Jazz at the College of the Pacific** / Dec. 14, 1953 / Fantasy 047

This was one of two live concerts featuring the Dave Brubeck quartet on college campuses in 1953. Pianist Brubeck's quartet was unique and was soon to become the rage with white America. . . . It was equally hip (and has remained so) for critics to say Brubeck didn't swing and suggest that Desmond was wasting his talents. . . . Nonsense. This group did swing, had emotional depth and great humor. —*Bob Rusch, Cadence*

○ **Stardust** / i. 1954 / Fantasy 24728

○ **Old Sounds from San Francisco** / i. 1954 / Fantasy 16

★ **Jazz Goes to College** / Mar. 1954 / Columbia 45149

One of the great Dave Brubeck recordings, *Jazz Goes to College* found the pianist's three-year-old quartet in its early prime. Bassist Bob Bates and drummer Joe Dodge offered quiet and steady support throughout; a perfect backing for the consistently creative and highly original playing of Brubeck and altoist Paul Desmond. . . . The piano solos have held up very well throughout the years ("Take the "A" Train" has a gem) and offer more variety in moods than the typical bop solo of the time. *Jazz Goes to College* ranks in the top five among Dave Brubeck's recordings. —*Scott Yanow, Cadence*

○ **Brubeck Plays Brubeck** / Mar. 12, 1956-Apr. 19, 1956 / Columbia 878

○ **Dave Brubeck Quartet in Europe, The** / Mar. 5, 1958 / Columbia 1168

★ **Time Out** / Jun. 25, 1959-Aug. 18, 1959 / Columbia 40585

Time Out helped launch a series of "time" records, which for awhile became a minor fad in jazz and had a number of musicians, mainly drummers, demonstrating how adroitly they could play in various exotic, or at least nonstandard, time signatures. . . . Not surprisingly, the record that ignited the fad, *Time Out*, was one of the most successful. Its program featured six solid Dave Brubeck originals and the classic Paul Desmond original, "Take Five." —*Bob Rusch, Cadence*

○ **All Night Long** / i. 1960 / Epic 17032

○ **Brubeck and Rushing** / Aug. 4, 1960 / Columbia 8353

○ **Take Five** / Sep. 6, 1961 / Sony Special Products 9116

○ **Brubeck in Amsterdam** / Dec. 3, 1962 / Columbia 9897

This was an odd little album; "little" because it was almost an antithesis of pianist Dave Brubeck's then hyperambitious LPs, filling a crevice in Brubeckia whose existence had not occurred to me. Of the eight tracks, six were tunes from "The Real Ambassadors," Brubeck's "musical" that was committed to wax at various times throughout 1961 (this concert was recorded December 3, 1962). The Ambassadors were Louis Armstrong, Carmen McRae, and the vocal trio of Lambert, Hendricks, and Ross, and it is interesting, if scarcely thrilling, to hear their songs performed as instrumentals. —*Wayne Jones, Coda*

○ **At Carnegie Hall** / Feb. 22, 1963 / Columbia 826

The quartet does its usual mix of standards and originals in a live setting before faithful admirers. There are few surprises; Brubeck goes through his alternately subdued and lively piano work, while Desmond has his normal swoops and shimmering slow ballads, and the Wright/Morello team works off them impressively. —*Ron Wynn, AMG*

☆ **Jazz Impressions of New York** / Jun. 18, 1964-Aug. 21, 1964 / Columbia 46189

Jazz Impressions of New York is not what people would expect from its title—a collection of tunes having something to do with New York. In 1964, Dave Brubeck wrote the music for a now-forgotten TV series called "Mr. Broadway." The 11 themes on this disc were not merely cues or incidental music, but full-length performances by Brubeck's quartet from which the show's soundtrack was drawn. Although none of these individual pieces caught on, the quality was generally high with cross-rhythms, waltz time, and a variety of options being explored. —*Scott Yanow, Cadence*

○ **Time In** / Jun. 14-15, 1966 / Columbia 2512

○ **Bravo! Brubeck!** / i. Dec. 1967 / Columbia 2695

○ **Compadres** / Apr. 1968 / Columbia 9704

○ **Brubeck on Campus** / i. Apr. 1973 / Columbia 31298

☆ **All the Things We Are** / Jul. 17, 1973 / Atlantic 1684

Has cuts with Braxton (sax), Lee Konitz (sax), and others. Very different from regular Brubeck. —*Ron Wynn*

● **Time Signatures: A Career Retrospective** / i. Nov. 17, 1992 / Columbia 52945

Time Signatures samples 46 albums, not limited to Dave Brubeck's Columbia catalog, but including work from his years at Fantasy, Atlantic, Concord, and MusicMasters. This ambitious package invites consideration of Brubeck's place in jazz cosmology. . . . Brubeck's controversial inspiration was a conception of jazz that focused on improvisation but allowed room for nontraditional devices and influences, including classical studies and impressions of world music. Brubeck's conception was brainy but not highbrow, complex but not intimidating, and always melodic. It enticed millions who might otherwise have closed their minds to jazz. —*Jon Andrews, Down Beat*

Ray Bryant (Raphael Bryant)

b. Dec. 24, 1931, Philadelphia, PA
Piano / Bop, hard bop, blues & jazz, soul jazz
Ray Bryant's one of the greatest pianists of the post-World War II period. His professional career started with Tiny Grimes in the late '40s. He worked in Philadelphia with singers and visiting soloists until the mid '50s, and became the favorite sideman of many small combo leaders. He was featured on dozens of albums as a sideman from the mid to late '50s. Bryant also had his own recordings for Epic, Prestige, New Jazz, and Signature in either solo or trio context. His '60s associations with Columbia (1960-1962), Sue (1963-1965), and Cadet (1966-1969) are variable. There are commercial attempts mixed in with straight jazz dates, but in general the quality is solid. The Columbia period produced his biggest hit, "Madison Time," a dance featuring calls by a Baltimore DJ over tasty mainstream jazz, with such players as Al Grey, Sweets Edison, and Buddy Tate involved! The Atlantic (1970-1972) period produced a fine solo album, *At Montreux* (Atlantic), but the remaining items are failed commercial attempts. A return to Cadet was disappointing but an album recorded for French Black & Blue, *Hot Turkey*, in 1975, is recommended. Late-'70s recordings for Pablo are all fine, as are late-'80s recordings for Emarcy. —*Bob Porter*

○ **Con Alma** / Nov. 25, 1960-Jan. 26, 1961 / Columbia 44058

This definitive early Ray Bryant album includes "Cubano Chant." —*Michael G. Nastos*

○ **Alone at Montreux** / Jul. 1972 / Atlantic 1626

Ray Bryant's a true two-fisted pianist, seemingly ambidextrous, tripping knowledgeably across the keys. Unlike Keith Jarrett's slightly melancholy stance, Bryant is a solo humorist who sounds as though he, more than being wrapped up inside himself as are so many solo artists, spreads himself outwardly. —*Willard Jenkins Jr., Cadence*

○ **Solo Flight** / Dec. 21, 1976 / Pablo 798

Tremendous collection of standards, blues, and ballads from Ray Bryant. He shows his knowledge of early tunes like "Blues in de

Big Brass Bed," while ripping through "Moanin'," and nicely re-working "Take the "A" Train" and "St. Louis Blues." —*Ron Wynn, AMG*

○ **All Blues** / Apr. 10, 1978 / Pablo 820
This set was an absolute pleasure from beginning to end, chock-ful of witty, engaging, buoyant and always resourcefully imagina-tive pianism by one of the underappreciated masters of the mu-sic. The choice of material was intelligently varied and was undoubtedly a major factor in the program's success, as was the firm, sympathetic, impeccable support furnished by bassist Sam Jones and drummer Grady Tate. —*Pete Welding, Down Beat*

★ **Ray Bryant Trio Today** / Feb. 13-14, 1987 / Emarcy 832589
W/ Ray Bryant Trio. Loaded with standards and two Bryant clas-sics: "Tonk" and "Slow Freight". Recommended. —*Michael G. Nastos*

★ **Plays Basie and Ellington** / Feb. 15-16, 1987 / Emarcy 832 235

Milt Buckner (Milton Brent Buckner)

b. Jul. 10, 1915, St. Louis, Missouri, d. Jul. 27, 1977
Piano, organ, arranger / Swing, soul jazz
Milt Buckner was among the prime innovators who helped pop-ularize the organ, as well as an excellent arranger and the younger brother of alto saxophonist Ted (not Teddy) Buckner. He played and arranged for several Detroit bands in the '30s, notably McKinney's Cotton Pickers, then became a star with swirling, dashing riffs and phrases during two stints in the '40s and '50s with Lionel Hampton. Between Hampton periods, Buckner had his own 17-piece (later 10-piece) group, which he eventually paired down to a trio in the early '50s. He teamed with saxo-phonist Illinois Jacquet in the '70s. —*Ron Wynn*

★ **Rockin' Hammond** / Feb. 22, 1956-Mar. 15, 1956 / Capitol 722
Classic organ combo with a master. From blues to ballads. A fine representation of Buckner's brilliance. —*Michael G. Nastos*

○ **Play Chords** / i. Jun. 1973 / MPS 20631

○ **Green Onions** / Feb. 21, 1975 / Inner City 141
With French rhythm section, guitarist Roy Gaines, drummer Panama Francis. Funky and groove-laden. —*Michael G. Nastos*

Dave Burrell (Herman Davis Burrell)

b. Sep. 10, 1940, Middletown, Ohio
Piano, composer / Modern creative
Pianist Dave Burrell has been active in musical, educational, and cultural circles, particularly in the '70s. He received degrees from Berklee and the Boston Conservatory, and later taught for two years at Queens College. He's among the more percussive, dy-namic pianists, is a good ballad stylist and bandleader, as well as an underrated soloist, accompanist, and composer. His first re-lease was on the Douglas label in the mid-'60s, and he later recorded for Affinity and other European and Japanese labels. —*Ron Wynn*

★ **Jelly Roll Joys** / 1991 / Gazell 4003

Kenny Burrell (Kenneth Earl Burrell)

b. Jul. 31, 1931, Detroit, MI
Guitar / Bop, hard bop, postbop, soul jazz
Guitarist Kenny Burrell came to New York from his native Detroit as part of the wave of important musicians from the Motor City in 1956. Soon he was in demand for record dates with practically everybody in modern jazz (but also with such veterans as Buck Clayton and Benny Goodman) and led his own studio and working groups. One of the most versatile and musical jazz guitar stylists, Burrell has never flirted with rock or pop, stead-fastly remaining a pure jazz guitarist. He can be heard on literally hundreds of albums.—*Dan Morgenstern*

○ **After Hours: Prestige Classic Jam Sessions—Vol. 1** / i. Dec. 28, 1956-Jan. 4, 1957 / Prestige 24107

○ **Blue Moods** / Feb. 1, 1957 / Prestige 7308
Smooth, cool yet musically impressive late '50s date that has both blowing session fervor and soulful undergirding. Burrell's fluid guitar voicings and Cecil Payne's robust baritone make nice part-ners, while Tommy Flanagan adds his usual sparkling piano riffs and solos, and bassist Doug Watkins teams with Elvin Jones, who shows he can drive a date without dominating things on drums. —*Ron Wynn, AMG*

● **Kenny Burrell Quintet with John Coltrane, The** / Mar. 7, 1958 / Prestige 7532
This was where aesthetic and historical concerns intersected. It is true there is plenty of both guitarist Burrell and tenor saxophon-ist Coltrane's material available (and from this period, 1957-1958), so it might seem, since this wasn't exceptional music from either, that reasons for reissue were weak. Of course what is exceptional from both Burrell and Coltrane would be sensational from others. —*Joel Ray, Cadence*

☆ **Blue Lights—Vol. 1** / May 15, 1958 / Blue Note 81596
I would certainly not overlook this pair of small-combo gems. Burrell deftly juggles blues, ballads, and soul-jazz. Tina Brooks (sax), Art Blakey (d), Junior Cook (ts), and others shine on both sets. These are 1989 CD reissues. —*Ron Wynn*

○ **Blue Lights—Vol. 2** / May 15, 1958 / Capitol 81597
Tina Brooks (sax), Art Blakey (d), Junior Cook (ts), and others shine on both sets. These are 1989 CD reissues. —*Ron Wynn*

☆ **Night at the Vanguard, A** / Sep. 17, 1959 / Chess 9316

○ **Midnight Blue** / Jan. 7, 1963 / Blue Note 46399
Best of the Blue Note period, with Stanley Turrentine (ts), Major Holley (b). Solid album. —*Michael G. Nastos*

Guitar Forms / Dec. 4, 1964+Apr. 1965 / Verve 825576
An experimental "artsy" record arranged by Gil Evans that has become a classic. However, don't look for the usual bluesy format. —*Michael Erlewine*

○ **Both Feet on the Ground** / Feb. 15-19, 1973 / Fantasy 9427

○ **Up the Street, 'round The Corner Down The Block** / Jan. 1974-Feb. 1974 / Fantasy 9458

★ **Ellington Is Forever—Vol. 1 & 2** / Feb. 4-05, 1975 / Fantasy 79005
While Kenny Burrell certainly possessed the credentials to make an album of Ellingtonia that featured his guitar as the principal voice, he also commanded better taste than to weaken such an endeavor by occupying the spotlight too much. Instead, he en-listed a large cast of diverse musicians who shared a common bond of devotion and cared deeply about their purpose. As a re-sult, even in the large ensemble numbers, no one's psyche got in the way of the music. —*Mikal Gilmore, Down Beat*

Gary Burton

b. Jan. 23, 1943, Anderson, IN
Vibes / Postbop, early jazz rock
Gary Burton is a world-class vibraphonist and developer of the four-mallet technique. He's also well known as a jazz theoretician and instructor. Burton worked in early period fusion groups, then attained his own group sound. He's equally effective at atmos-pheric, lilting ballads or steady rolling jazz. He's been an impor-tant presence in the past 30 years.—*Michael G. Nastos*

○ **New Vibe Man in Town** / Jul. 6, 1961 / RCA 2420

○ **Artist's Choice** / 1963-1968 / Bluebird 6280
This session traces vibist Gary Burton's musical evolution during 1963-1968 with selections taken from eight of Burton's 13 RCA LPs. . . . Burton was among the very first to incorporate elements of rock, pop, and freer forms of jazz into his own music without trivializing any of the styles. . . . *Artist's Choice* is a fine retro-spective of the early Gary Burton, although I wish that these ses-sions were available in full rather than piecemeal. —*Scott Yanow, Cadence*

○ **Time Machine, The** / Apr. 5+06, 1966 / RCA 3642

★ **Duster** / Apr. 18-20, 1967 / RCA
Prophetic session with references to everything from country to rock. Suggested new directions for jazz musicians. —*Ron Wynn*

○ **Gary Burton in Concert** / i. 1968 / RCA 3985

★ **Gary Burton and Keith Jarrett** / Jan. 12, 1971 / Atlantic 1577
It was not surprising that this album by Gary Burton and Keith Jarrett quickly settled in that warm spot listeners reserve for their favorite musical experiences; not because it was an exceptional and rare piece of jazz, but because the beat and the lyric were so well met in the kind emotions these two players shared during their collaboration. —*Alan Offstein, Coda*

○ **Turn of the Century** / Jun. 19, 1971 / Atlantic 2321

☆ **Passengers** / Nov. 1976 / ECM 835016

Gary Burton Quartet. Includes some stirring originals w/ Pat Metheny (g), Eberhard Weber (b). —*Michael G. Nastos*

Billy Butler

b. Dec. 15, 1925, Philadelphia, PA, **d.** Mar. 20, 1991
Guitar / Blues & jazz, soul jazz
As part of organist Bill Doggett's combo, guitarist Billy Butler brought a strong Charlie Christian jazz influence to '50s R&B grooves. Coaxing a warm fat tone from a hollow-bodied electric guitar, Butler played tasty and deceptively simple solos and fills that have become staples of the R&B guitar vocabulary. Doggett's "Honky Tonk," featuring Butler, is perhaps the classic R&B guitar instrumental. "Ram-Bunk'-Shush" and "Big Boy" are other highlights of Butler's his work with Doggett. He also turned in fine performances on Charles Brown's 1986 Alligator recordings.— *Richard Lieberson*

○ **Guitar Soul!** / Sep. 1969 / Original Jazz Classics 334
★ **This Is Billy Butler** / Dec. 16, 1969 / Prestige 7622

Billy Butterfield (Charles William Butterfield)

b. Jan. 14, 1917, Middletown, OH, **d.** Mar. 18, 1988, North Palm Beach, FL
Trumpet, flugelhorn / Swing, big band
A first-rate trumpet soloist, with tremendous range, versatility, and taste, plus a gifted sight reader, Billy Butterfield worked in Andy Anderson and Austin Wylie's band in the '30s before joining Bob Crosby's orchestra in 1937. He was spotlighted on many of the band's most popular recordings, but Butterfield joined Artie Shaw's band in 1940. He was supposed to play on the soundtrack for the film *Second Chorus* but instead gained popularity for his playing on "Star Dust." He also played with the Gramercy Five before leaving to join Benny Goodman in 1941; he departed Goodman for Les Brown's band in 1942. Prior to military service in '44 and '45, Butterfield played regularly in the NBC and CBS radio orchestras. He led a big band from 1945 to 1947 and then became head of the house band at the New York club Nick's in 1947. During the '50s, Butterfield returned to studio work and also made several college tours heading groups. He was a member of the World's Greatest Jazz Band from 1968 to 1972 and continued performing and doing studio sessions through the '80s. —*Ron Wynn*

● **Uncollected Billy Butterfield & His Orchestra (1946)** / 1946 / Hindsight 173

Jaki Byard (John A. Byard, Jr.)

b. Jun. 15, 1922, Worcester, MA
Piano / Hard bop, progressive big band, bop
Pianist Jaki Byard's proven an excellent soloist in several styles and a first-rate bandleader. His compositions are known for their humor, and he's headed the Apollo Stompers, a sorely underrated aggregation, in Boston and New York. After playing trumpet and piano as a child, Byard learned trombone while in the army. After touring and recording stints with Earl Bostic during the '40s and '50s, Byard moved to Boston. He had stints as a saxophonist in Herb Pomeroy's big band and a pianist with Maynard Ferguson during the '50s and '60s, as well as being a solo pianist. Byard's been featured in the bands of such major figures as Charles Mingus, Eric Dolphy, Don Ellis, Booker Ervin, and Charlie Mariano and appeared on many recordings with Ron Carter, Rahsaan Roland Kirk, Ray Nance, and Elvin Jones, among others. Some of his dates were later reissued under Kirk's name. Byard's also been prominently involved in jazz education, teaching at several schools, notably the New England Conservatory of Music. He's done several recordings for Muse and Soul Note, plus duet LPs with Earl Hines in the '70s and Ran Blake in the '80s. —*Ron Wynn and Michael G. Nastos*

○ **Out Front!** / May 21, 1964 / Prestige 7397
○ **Live! at Lennie's—Vol. 1** / Apr. 15, 1965 / Prestige 7419
☆ **With Strings** / Apr. 2, 1968 / Prestige 7573
Top-notch recording for the brilliant pianist with George Benson (g), Ray Nance (tpt), Ron Carter (b), Richard Davis (b), and Alan Dawson (d). —*Michael G. Nastos*
○ **Solo Piano** / Jul. 31, 1969 / Prestige 7686
★ **There'll Be Some Changes Made** / Dec. 27, 1972 / Muse 5007

○ **Family Man** / Apr. 28, 1978-May 1, 1978 / Muse 5173
W/ Major Holley on bass. Includes excerpts from "Family Suite." Challenging listening. —*Michael G. Nastos*
○ **Live at Maybeck Recital Hall—Vol. 17** / Sep. 8, 1992 / Concord Jazz 4511
A dynamic, topflight piano soloist and bandleader gets a chance to present his complete package in another superb Maybeck set. Byard employs stride, shuffle, and hard bop rhythms, playing with a density and controlled force that make each selection a treasure. —*Ron Wynn, AMG*

Don Byas (Carlos Wesley Byas)

b. Oct. 21, 1912, Muskogee, OK, **d.** Aug. 24, 1972
Tenor sax / Swing
Byas is a classic example of a superb tenor saxophone stylist who was influential and harmonically innovative. He played in the swing bands of Don Redman, Lucky Millinder, Andy Kirk, and Count Basie. Byas knew all the tricks of the trade: he employed overblowing effects and a huge tone and was an incredible blues and ballad player. Some view him as a transitional figure between swing and bop, but his later releases were neatly balanced between those styles, and he had no problem fitting in with new players like Monk and Max Roach. He left America for Holland in the '50s and died there in 1972. —*Ron Wynn*

★ **Savoy Jam Party** / Aug. 17, 1944 / Savoy 2213
○ **Don Byas in Paris** / Oct. 18, 1946-Jan. 5, 1949 / Prestige 7598
Bluesy, often explosive blues, ballads, and standards cut in Paris by the great swing tenor saxophonist Don Byas. His huge tone, expressive phrasing, and hard blowing were ideal for this collection, which is heavy on standards and includes a sterling rendition of "Body and Soul." The backing band proves capable, if unexciting, keyed by pianist Billy Taylor. —*Ron Wynn, AMG*
★ **On Blue Star** / **i.** 1950-1952 / PolyGram 833405
Don Byas on Blue Star is a collection of 23 sides cut in Paris between January 13, 1947, and March 1952. . . . The material on this CD is gracious and generally mellow, and fans of the mainstream tenor of Byas will have good reason to acquire it. —*Bob Rusch, Cadence*
○ **Don Byas** / Feb. 1954 / Inner City 7018
○ **Anthropology** / Jan. 13, 1964 / Black Lion 160
This session was recorded live in Copenhagen with a superior European rhythm section, and, as the tunes indicate, it was a bop-conscious, high-voltage evening. Pianist Brent Axen was a talented Bud Powell disciple who comped beautifully, but got off fine solos. Bassist Niels-Henning Orsted Pedersen was strong, and drummer William Schiopffe was adequate. Highlights were the title track and "Don't Blame Me.". . . For a sampling of late Byas, this was certainly a valuable issue. —*Gary Giddins, Down Beat*
○ **Ballads for Swingers** / **i.** Nov. 1966 / Polydor 623207

Charlie Byrd (Charles L. Byrd)

b. Sep. 16, 1925, Chuckatuck, VA
Guitar / Cool, Latin-jazz
A guitarist best known for his mastery of Latin forms, Byrd began as a classical and light jazz player. He learned the rudiments of the instrument during studies with Segovia in the '50s, as well as an awareness of the guitar's romantic, sentimental qualities. Byrd played with Woody Herman in 1959 and then toured Latin America for the State Department. He and Stan Getz helped launch the samba-bossa nova craze in the '60s when he suggested they record Antonio Carlos Jobim tunes. He has been busy ever since and has made many nice recordings with Bud Shank.—*Ron Wynn*

○ **Guitar Artistry of Charlie Byrd, The** / 1960 / Riverside 9451
★ **Byrd at the Gate** / May 9+10, 1963 / Riverside 262
Byrd at the Gate presented the unique jazz guitar approach of Charlie Byrd and his trio (Keter Betts, bass; Bill Reichenbach, drums) live at the Gate. The program was also joined by the guesting of Clark Terry (trumpet) and Sheldon Powell (tenor sax) on five of the tracks. —*Bob Rusch, Cadence*
○ **Brazilian Byrd** / **i.** 1965 / Columbia 9137
○ **Great Guitars** / 1974 / Concord Jazz 4004

Donald Byrd (Donaldson Toussaint L'Ouverture Byrd II)

b. Dec. 9, 1932, Detroit, MI

Trumpet / Hard bop, soul jazz, instrumental pop, contemporary funk

Though he initally gained fame as an accomplished trumpeter and solid soloist, Donald Byrd moved from jazz to urban contemporary and instrumental pop in the '70s. He was a Jazz messenger in the '50s, and his biting, dynamic lines and crackling sound were featured on many top Blue Note LPs. But Byrd scored his biggest successess in the mid-'70s with enormously popular, heavily produced dates like *Black Byrd* and *Street Lady*. This continued until the early '80s, though Byrd earned a doctorate and became Howard University's Black Music chairman during this era. He returned to hard bop in the late '80s, and has juggled jazz and pop in the '90s, recording mainstream LPs and making appearances on the hip-hop-jazz circuit.—*Ron Wynn*

● **House of Byrd** / Aug. 3, 1956+Nov. 2, 1956 / Prestige 24066
It was slightly inaccurate to have released this Donald Byrd twofer under his leadership, as on the two LPs reissued here he shared the billing with trumpeter Art Farmer on one and alto saxophonist Phil Woods on the other. The point seems especially moot since Byrd's playing held one's attention less well than either of his coleaders. —*Joel Ray, Cadence*

○ **Chant** / Apr. 17, 1961 / Blue Note 991
Trumpeter Donald Byrd and baritone saxophonist Pepper Adams recorded and played together for a long time. This unissued material was both a surprise and a winner. It may have been pianist Herbie Hancock's first recording date, and he and bassist Doug Watkins made it a solid quintet with a good but little known drummer (Eddy Robinson) who handled the tempos well. "I'm an Old Cowhand" was used before as a jazz vehicle and its structure seemed weak, but Pepper roared as always. . . . This was first rate Blue Note material. —*Jerry L. Atkins, Cadence*

○ **Groovin' for Nat** / Jan. 12, 1962 / Black Lion 760134
Solid early-'60s session with Byrd meshing alongside Duke Pearson and Bob Cranshaw. Johnny Coles makes effective appearances. —*Ron Wynn*

● **Blackjack** / Jan. 9, 1967 / Blue Note 84259
Perhaps his very best of many recordings with Sonny Red (as), Hank Mobley, (ts), and Cedar Walton (p). —*Michael G. Nastos*

☆ **Electric Byrd** / May 15, 1970 / Blue Note
Pivotal release with Byrd using a 12-piece group. Duke Pearson on electric piano. The arrangements and mood are harbingers of Byrd's shift into pop, funk, and R&B. —*Ron Wynn*

○ **City Called Heaven, A** / Jan. 1991 / Landmark 1530

Don Byron

Clarinet / World fusion, modern creative

Don Byron is an exciting player now widely regarded as arguably the finest contemporary clarinet soloist. He is well versed in everything from bop to free but has stayed away from "young lion" hype and the hard bop scene. His *Tuskegee Experiments* album on Elektra was a critical smash; the recent ('93) release of klezmer music proved a less unanimous success, though Byron remains determined to play any- and everything, including klezmer. He also plays bass clarinet.—*Ron Wynn*

★ **Tuskegee Experiments / i.** 1992 / Nonesuch 79280
The album that helped introduce clarinet sensation Don Byron to a wider audience. Byron's twisting, soaring solos and impressive command of numerous styles had already made him a critical favorite, and he got rave reviews for this release. It contained a mix of social commentary and explosive playing and was expertly produced and mastered. —*Ron Wynn, AMG*

George Cables (George Andrew Cables)

b. Nov. 14, 1944, New York, NY

Piano / Hard bop

A favorite pianist of saxophonists from Art Pepper to Frank Morgan, Cables has been in demand as a session regular since the mid '60s. After studying at Mannes College, he worked with premier drummers Max Roach and Art Blakey in both the '60s and the '70s. Cables was Sonny Rollins's pianist in 1969 and spent two years with Joe Henderson, two with Dexter Gordon, and six in two stints with Freddie Hubbard. He made two acclaimed duet works with Art Pepper and worked with him in the final three years of Pepper's career. Cables is an exciting, very rhythmically potent player, a first-rate accompanist, and a delightful soloist. —*Ron Wynn*

○ **Circles** / Mar. 27-28, 1979 / Contemporary 14015
Aggressive date with robust solos from Joe Farrell (ts), decisive playing by Cables. —*Ron Wynn*

★ **Phantom of the City** / May 14-15, 1985 / Contemporary 14014
This LP featured strong interplay between the musicians. Bassist John Heard has a big tone and a strong rhythmic feel. Tony Williams played well on this record—his tasty fills on the title cut were perfect, while his drive was most important to "You Stepped Out of a Dream.". . . Cables plays his melodies with a flourish, almost a swagger, as displayed on the Chick Corea-like "Blue Nights." He also has a bluesy side, which was best heard on the standard "Old Folks." There were no weak moments on either side, and these cuts really swing. —*Richard B. Kamins, Cadence*

☆ **By George** / Feb. 27, 1987 / Contemporary 14030
Pianist George Cables's tribute to George Gershwin was a zebra of a different stripe: various rhythms were used as methods of diversification on the well-known standards, and the leaner instrumentation was varied to a small extent. It took a certain amount of courage to tackle these overdone songs, but Cables, who also doubled as producer, explained in his brief notes that these were some personal favorites, and he met the self-challenge with inventiveness and versatility. —*Larry Hollis, Cadence*

○ **Night and Day / i.** May 1991 / DIW 606

Red Callender (George Sylvester Callender)

b. 1916, Haynesville, VA, **d.** Mar. 8, 1992, Los Angeles, CA

Bass, tuba / Swing, big band, bop, cool

Red Callender is a legendary West Coast session bassist who also played tuba. He was a most dependable musician, who could do it in his sleep. He was a true unsung hero worldwide. —*Michael G. Nastos*

★ **Swingin' Suite / i.** 1956 / Modern 1201

Cab Calloway (Cabell Calloway)

b. Dec. 25, 1907, Rochester, NY

Vocals, bandleader / Swing, big band

Cab Calloway is an incredibly energetic performer, vocalist and bandleader. He's best known as the zoot-suited, hip-talking, scat-singing "Highness of Hi-De-Ho," but Calloway's influence on all Black performers who followed him is incalculable. He began in Baltimore, eventually coming to New York and forming his first band. He followed Duke Ellington into the legendary Cotton Club, leading the house band, and it was there that he made his reputation as the hippest musician in all of Harlem, becoming a national phenomenon through live radio broadcasts from the club. With an act chock full of wild physical energy, his long black hair flying, he made "hi-de-ho" a national catchphrase when "Minnie the Moocher" became a hit in 1930. Hollywood beckoned, and Cab's manic, visual style and excellent orchestra were put to good effect in such films as *Stormy Weather, Manhattan Merry-Go-Round,* and *The Big Broadcast of 1932,* among others. He kept performing in his familiar, affable style throughout the intervening decades, coming to the attention of a whole new audience with his appearance in *The Blues Brothers* in 1980. He still actively performs today and shows no signs of slowing down.—*Cub Koda*

○ **Cab Calloway (1930-1931) / i.** Jul. 1930-Jun. 1931 / Classics 516

★ **Jazz Heritage: Mr. Hi-De-Ho (1930-1931)** / 1930-1931 / MCA 1344
A budget compilation of Calloway's early-'30s cuts. A good starter set despite the uneven sound. —*Ron Wynn*

○ **Cab Calloway (1931-1932) / i.** Jul. 1931-Jun. 1932 / Classics 526
From the start Calloway's style was fully-formed, and it is particularly interesting to hear his interpretations of tunes associated with others, especially "Happy Feet" (Paul Whiteman), "The Viper's Drag" and "I'm Crazy 'bout My Baby" (Fats Waller), and several Duke Ellington hits. A real rarity was "Yaller" on which Calloway bemoaned the difficulties of being a light-skinned black. . . . Cab Calloway made up for his lapses of taste with excitement and zaniness; one can fully understand from these fun recordings why he became such a popular celebrity. —*Scott Yanow, Cadence*

○ **Cab Calloway (1932)** / **i.** Jun. 1932-Dec. 1932 / Classics 537

○ **Cab Calloway (1932-1934)** / **i.** Dec. 1932-Sep. 1934 / Classics 544

○ **Cab Calloway (1934-1937)** / **i.** Sep. 1934-Mar. 1937 / Classics 554

○ **Cab Calloway (1937-1938)** / **i.** Mar. 1937-Mar. 1938 / Classics 568

○ **Cab Calloway (1938-1939)** / **i.** Mar. 1938-Feb. 1939 / Classics 576

○ **Cab Calloway (1939-1940)** / **i.** Mar. 1939-Mar. 1940 / Classics 595

○ **Cab Calloway (1940)** / **i.** Mar. 1940-Jul. 1940 / Classics 614

○ **Minnie the Moocher** / MCA Special Products 20366

★ **Kicking the Gong Around** / ASV 5013

Cab's naughtier side, with the virtues of substance use imbuing the lyrical text of several tunes included here. If you thought drug songs didn't start until the late '60s in rock music, be prepared for a shock. —*Cub Koda*

Michel Camilo

b. Apr. 4, 1952
Piano / Bop, Latin-jazz
An extremely fast pianist known for playing stunning solos and being an above-average melodic interpreter, Michel Camilo's reputation preceded his recording debut. While the subsequent releases haven't been as consistent or exciting as anticipated, they did contain several stretches of imaginative playing interspersed with lengthy periods of expertly played, routine hard bop and Afro-Latin material. He's worked with Dave Weckl, Anthony Jackson, Mongo Santamaria, Phillip Mossman, D.K. Dyson, Ralph Bowen, and Marc Johnson, and has recorded for Electric Bird, Portrait, and Epic. —*Ron Wynn and Michael G. Nastos*

○ **Why Not** / Feb. 25, 1985-Feb. 2, 1985 / Evidence 22002

Pianist Michel Camilo made his recording debut as a leader with this '85 session for the Japanese King label. Camilo was anxious to show everything, and did so on such cuts as "Thinking of You" and the title track. He'd rip through phrases, add powerhouse chords and rippling lines, switch tempos and meters, or move from a hard bop feel to an Afro-Latin groove in the middle of a piece. His intensity and energy were impressive, but at times he'd try too much and stumble getting back to the melody.... It wasn't an unflawed debut, but Camilo showed he'd be a pianist to be reckoned with down the line. —*Ron Wynn*

★ **On Fire** / **i.** 1989 / Epic 45295

○ **On the Other Hand** / **i.** Oct. 16, 1991 / Epic 46236

Conte Candoli (Conte [Secondo] Candoli)

b. Jul. 12, 1927, Mishawaka, IN
Trumpet / Bop, Cool
Trumpeter Conte Candoli is well known for his work on the "Tonight Show" with Doc Severinsen, and has played with other fine leaders including Woody Herman, Stan Kenton, Charlie Barnet, and Howard Rumsey's LightHouse All Stars. He also worked with Shelly Manne and was a member of Supersax.— *Michael Erlewine*

★ **Conte Candoli Quartet** / Jul. 1957 / Mode 109

Harry Carney (Harry Howell Carney)

b. Apr. 1, 1910, Boston, MA, **d.** Oct. 8, 1974, New York, NY
Baritone sax / Swing big band
Baritone saxophonist and bass clarinetist Harry Carney was the rock-solid foundation and bottom of the Duke Ellington Orchestra for decades, and he was also one of the finest baritone soloists and players in any style. He explored the horn's full range, could switch from honking fire to serene beauty, and was also a pioneer in using circular breathing, a technique allowing the soloist to hold notes for inordinate periods. Carney first played piano, then clarinet and alto sax, before switching full-time to baritone. He started playing professionally as a teen in Boston, moved to New York in 1927, and began the association with Duke Ellington that continued throughout his career. Carney also achieved almost equal fame for being Ellington's driver and confidant. —*Ron Wynn*

● **Harry Carney with Strings** / Dec. 14, 1954 / Clef 640

Terri Lyne Carrington (Terri Lynne Carrington)

b. 1962
Drums / Instrumental Pop, Modern Creative
Carrington is a thoroughly accomplished drummer grappling with questions of direction and musical integrity. A one-time protege of Alan Dawson at Berklee in Boston, Carrington was a figure in Boston clubs and jazz functions as a child and a teen. She became a national fixture through exposure on the Arsenio Hall Show during its first year, before leaving to establish her solo career. So far she's done both creditable and disappointing dates. — *Ron Wynn*

● **Real Life Story** / 1989 / Verve/Forecast 837697

Baikida Carroll (Baikida E. J. Carroll)

b. Jan. 15, 1947, Saint Louis, MO
Trumpet, flugelhorn / Modern creative
Trumpeter and flugelhorn player Bakida Carroll became known for his work with the Black Artists Group (BAG), a St. Louis organization similiar to Chicago's AACM, in the mid-'70s. He played in Europe with BAG members in 1973, and made his recording debut in Paris the next year. He's played with many major New York and Chiago avant-garde musicians, among them Oliver Lake, Michael Gregory Jackson, Muhal Richard Abrams, Jack DeJohnette, and David Murray, and has also composed several film soundtracks and scores. —*Ron Wynn*

● **Shadows and Reflections** / **i.** May 1983 / Soul Note 1023

Trumpeter Baikida Carroll was once again in the company of alto saxophonist Julius Hemphill for a January 1982 recording with pianist Anthony Davis, bassist Dave Holland, and drummer Pheeroan Ak Laff for Soul Note called *Shadows & Reflections*. The material here sounded like it could have been a late Blue Note recording; in fact, there were times when the horns brought back flashbacks of the Jackie McLean-Charles Tolliver front line of the '60s. And for all their avant-garde credentials, this group sounded very comfortable and at home with the squirrelly free bop displayed here. —*Bob Rusch, Cadence*

Benny Carter (Bennett Lester Carter)

b. Aug. 8, 1907, New York, NY
Alto sax, composer, bandleader / Swing big band
Billed in the '40s as "The Amazing Man of Music," that title holds true for alto saxophonist Benny Carter even more so today—he's vitally active as a player, writer, and leader in his eighth decade of musical activity. Born and raised in New York City, Carter led his own first big band in 1928. After working with Charlie Johnson and other leaders, he joined Fletcher Henderson. Carter had his own band again in 1933-1935, then spent three years in Europe, where he wrote for the BBC in London, led an integrated band in Holland, and made history in the Paris recording studios. Back home, Carter introduced a new band at Harlem's Savoy Ballroom. He continued to lead big bands until the late '40s, but from 1943 on he was also active in the Hollywood studios, scoring for many feature films as well as appearing on screen; later he also wrote for TV. While he continued to play in the '50s and '60s, including tours abroad with Jazz at the Philharmonic and the direction of many fine albums, he became fully active as a leader and player again from the mid-'70s on. Carter was one of jazz's pace setters at the dawn of the swing era, both as an alto sax stylist (rivaled only by Johnny Hodges) and as an arranger (his scoring for saxophones, especially, was—and is—state of the art). And he is still at the top today—truly an amazing man. — *Dan Morgenstern*

○ **Chronological Benny Carter (1929-1933), The** / **i.** Sep. 1929-May 1933 / Classics 522

○ **Chronological Benny Carter (1936), The** / **i.** Apr. 1930-Oct. 1936 / Classics 541

○ **Chronological Benny Carter (1933-1936), The** / **i.** May 1933-Apr. 1936 / Classics 530

○ **Chronological Benny Carter (1937-1939), The** / **i.** Jan. 1937-Jun. 1939 / Classics 552

○ **Chronological Benny Carter (1940-1941), The** / **i.** May 1940-Oct. 1941 / Classics 631

● **Complete Benny Carter on Keynote** / Apr. 22, 1946 / PolyGram 830965
Here's a fine representative sampling of prime Carter '40s cuts. With Arnold Ross Quintet, his own LA group at the time. —*Ron Wynn*

○ **Swing 1946** / 1946 / Prestige 7604
The first session in this album was by the Chocolate Dandies for which Benny Carter used Al Grey, Sonny White, and John Simmons from his big band, along with Buck Clayton, Ben Webster, and Sid Catlett. . . . The next session was by Gene Sedric's Orchestra, an actual working band that included, besides the leader, two other Fats Wallerites, Al Casey and Slick Jones. . . . The third session was by Jonah Jones and his Cats, a group made up entirely of Cab Calloway sidemen (except for drummer Kansas Fields). These must be among Jones's finest records, and to hear them is worth the price of the album alone. His playing was soaring, brillant, daring, and subtle, by turns. . . . There was an informative liner by Stanley Dance and full discographical details, and the recording quality was good despite the phony stereo. —*Ron Anger, Coda*

★ **Swingin' the Twenties** / Nov. 2, 1958 / Contemporary 339
Alto saxophonist Benny Carter received top billing on this album, but Earl Hines didn't exactly assume the role of mere sideman. With Carter, Hines was an equal. These contemporaries obviously enjoyed their first recording session together. The tempos were playful; so were the tones. Their fondness for the material (classics from the '20s) showed, as did a penchant for producing tidy solos that began, grew, climaxed, resolved, and ended. On *Swingin' the '20s* Hines gave an exhibition of what jazz piano was, is, and will be. The light, airy right hand on "If I Could Be with You (One Hour Tonight)" is a favorite device of Ramsey Lewis. The thumping chords of "Sweet Lorraine" point to Errol Garner. The spurts of flamboyance decorating "Who's Sorry Now" have been appropriated by Oscar Peterson. The flip stridish echoes in "Mary Lou's" opening cadenza recall Fats Waller. —*Cliff Radel, Down Beat*

○ **Fabulous Benny Carter, The** / i. 1959 / Audio Lab 1505

○ **Jazz Calendar** / i. 1960 / United Artists 5080

★ **Further Definitions** / Nov. 13+15, 1961 / MCA 5651
This is classic, a masterpiece of arranging, playing, and composing. Carter duplicated the instrumental setting and included some cuts from a landmark session he'd done back in Paris during the '30s. Still sounds wonderful 31 years later, though the vinyl album is superior to the MCA reissue. —*Ron Wynn*

○ **B.B.B. & Co.** / i. 1962 / Prestige 758
This is a 4/10/62 session served up with class and decorum by Benny Carter (as/tpt), Ben Webster (ts), Barney Bigard (cl), Shorty Sherock (tpt), Jimmy Rowles (p), Dave Barbour (g), Leroy Vinnegar (b), and Mel Lewis (d). If you like the slow drag blues, the highlight here will be the anchor track "You Can't Tell," which stretches out over 12 minutes and keeps the pressure but never breaks its tension or sweat. —*Bob Rusch, Cadence*

☆ **Additions to Further Definitions** / Mar. 2, 1966 / Impulse 9116
Additions to Further Definitions was a beautiful, timeless date featuring the writing, arranging and playing of alto saxophonist Benny Carter on ten tracks. Fans of mainstream or modern will find rewards in this music. —*Bob Rusch, Cadence*

● **Carter, Gillespie, Inc.** / Apr. 27, 1977 / Pablo 682
Producer Norman Granz deserved much applause for returning alto sax master Benny Carter to vinyl on a regular basis in the '70s. Here he was teamed with the bubbly trumpeter Dizzy Gillespie, a pair seemingly made for each other. Carter is primarily a swing-era survivor, while Gillespie was the quintessential bopper. The feelings were meshed together for an album of real pleasure. —*Willard Jenkins Jr., Cadence*

● **Gentleman and His Music, A** / Aug. 3, 1985 / Concord Jazz 4285
On "Lover Man," and the tribute to George Duvivier, Benny Carter gets to stretch out as the front line solos are divided between Carter and Joe Wilder (tpt)—no Scott Hamilton—with Ed Bickert (g) and Gene Harris (p) getting a spot before and after. Hamilton (ts) takes his turn on each of the remaining titles, being particularly good on Carter's "A Kiss for You," despite having just been introduced to it at the session. —*Shirley Klett, Cadence*

○ **Harlem Renaissance** / Nov. 7+09, 1992 / Music Masters 65080

Though an elder statesman, alto saxophonist Benny Carter still has a vigorous, emphatic sound and can play with zest on up-tempo wailers or slow, churning blues and ballads. He conducted a combined orchestra blending his own big band with the Rutgers University group. Guest stars Frank Wess, Ralph Bowen, Virgil Jones, and others played on several cuts, then joined the students. —*Ron Wynn, AMG*

Betty Carter (Lorraine Carter)
b. May 16, 1930, Flint, MI
Vocals / Bop, ballads & blues
Betty Carter is among the few genuine jazz singers and vocal improvisers. She has her own style and communicative approach, is an amazing interpreter, and does several of her own arrangements. She turned professional in 1946 after studying piano at the Detroit Conservatory and then winning an amateur contest. Using the moniker "Be-Bop" in the first phase of her career, she toured with Lionel Hampton, Miles Davis, Sonny Rollins, and others before forming a trio that became a college fixture in the '70s. The distinctiveness and individuality of her albums (few short songs, scatting) and her refusal to compromise have led to the inability to secure recording dates on major labels, and she has issued and distributed her own recordings since the '70s. A new pact with Verve in the late '80s has given her widespread fresh exposure, as did an appearance on "The Cosby Show." —*Ron Wynn*

○ **I Can't Help It** / i. 1958 / GRP 114
Late-'50s session with Carter honing her skills, backed by both a moderate-sized group and the Richard Wess Orchestra. The group includes Kenny Dorham, Melba Liston, Wynton Kelly, and Benny Golson. Carter was still building a reputation, and was then more in standard scat/hard bop mode than in the interpretative style she later patented. —*Ron Wynn, AMG*

★ **Modern Sound of Betty Carter** / Aug. 18, 1960 / ABC (Import) 363

☆ **Ray Charles and Betty Carter** / 1961 / ABC (Import)
The session with Betty Carter has been an elusive treasure for many, having only a brief reappearance as a bootleg after its original removal from the ABC catalog. Here the program was augmented by three other Ray Charles items from the back catalog. The collaboration with Betty Carter has become a legendary session. . . . Marty Paich's arrangements are memorable. In this setting Ray Charles is the balladeer and moves back toward his Nat King Cole/Charles Brown roots. —*Bob Rusch, Cadence*

☆ **'round Midnight** / Dec. 6, 1969 / Atlantic 80453
This was recorded live in 1969; it was splendid. Carter has a breathy, distorted voice capable of twisting and bending in a manner not unlike Sarah Vaughan's. Unlike Vaughan, at least on this recording, she was never affected or presumptuous. She managed to evoke tension and emotion rather than a condescending hipness. She's also capable of great humor in her singing, but she always swings, and an eight-minute outing of "Surrey with the Fringe on Top" was the epitome of this always-present ability. —*Doug Shaw, Cadence*

☆ **What a Little Moonlight Can Do** / i. 1976 / Impulse
The material on this two-record set is a reissue of material that originally appeared on Progressive Records around 1958 and a 1960 ABC recording. This recording, in relation to other Betty Carter material, was not her best, although there were moments. —*Bob Rusch, Cadence*

★ **Audience with Betty Carter** / Dec. 6-08, 1979 / Verve 835684
This live recording showed Betty Carter at her liveliest and most compelling. Response among all parties was exceptionally alert: Carter's animated, emotionally charged performance received an enthusiastic reception that encouraged her to bait the delighted audience further—with witticism and, apparently some visual gesturing—and the sidemen flattened her idiosyncracies, anticipating and following her infallibly. Standards and new tunes split the bill here. —*Elaine Guregian, Down Beat*

○ **It's Not About the Melody** / i. 1992 / Verve 513870
Contemporary Betty Carter session in which her deep, sometimes weary and often swaying voice sounds defiant as she moves through both uptempo selections and declarative ballads. Carter has become the top jazz vocalist on the scene, and her treatments

don't follow any formula or adhere to any set principles other than her own. —*Ron Wynn, AMG*

John Carter (John Wallace Carter)

b. Sep. 24, 1929, Forth Worth, Texas, **d.** Mar. 31, 1991
Clarinet, alto sax / Modern creative
An ambitious composer and superb clarinet player who was never able to get the widespread exposure he deserved, even in jazz circles, Carter played with Ornette Coleman and Charles Moffett in the '40s and '50s. He formed a critically acclaimed quartet with Bobby Bradford in 1965 and then led his own groups from 1973 until he joined James Newton's woodwind quintet in 1980. He was also a vital member of the original Clarinet Summit in the mid '80s and composer of a critically acclaimed series of pieces celebrating the progress of African-Americans.—*Ron Wynn*

○ **West Coast Hot** / **i.** 1969 / Novus 3107
The first recordings in 1969 of the quartet co-led by clarinetist John Carter and trumpeter Bobby Bradford undermined the stereotypes of West Coast jazz and challenged the New York fire-music establishment's exclusive franchise. Material from two Flying Dutchman sessions has been reissued on *West Coast Hot*. Despite the easy comparison, the assets of Carter and Bradford's quartet were markedly different from Ornette Coleman's. Carter, who displays equal facility on alto, tenor, clarinet, and flute on these early recordings was, unlike Coleman, a true multiinstrumentalist. Bradford was by far the most lyrically swinging, postbop trumpeter of the day. . . . Additionally, Coleman's patented lexicon was only one of many compositional tools Carter and Bradford employed. It's a stretch to call them derivative. —*Bill Shoemaker, Down Beat*

○ **Self-Determination Music** / 1969-1970 / Flying Dutchman 128
○ **Dauwhe** / Feb. 25, 1982-Mar. 8, 1982 / Black Saint 0057
This recording brought together some of the best of the West (cornetist Bobby Bradford; flutist James Newton; soprano saxophonist, clarinetist, and oboe player Charles Owens; bassist Roberto Miranda; drummer Williams Jeffrey; and percussionist-waterphone player Luis Peralta) for a set of five John Carter compositions. The title track was brilliant both in its open construction and in solos executed by the leader, Bradford, and Newton. In fact, this was arguably Newton's most inspired work. —*Bob Rusch, Cadence*

★ **Castles of Ghana** / Feb. 1985 / Gramavision 79423
John Carter's *Castles of Ghana* was a suite dealing with the crucible of slavery and its devastating consequence on African civilization. It was performed magnificently, attesting to a composer who created a body of work that added graceful formality and personal signature while never losing sight of the art of individual improvisation. This was an ensemble of brilliantly paired voicings and inspired soloists. . . .*Castles of Ghana* stands as one of the seminal works of the '80s, both for the way it enlivened history and because it was in and of itself one more example of the Black Diaspora. —*Ludwig Van Trikt, Cadence*

Ron Carter (Ronald Levin Carter)

b. May 4, 1937, Ferndale, MI
Bass, cello, bass guitar, composer / Hard bop, postbop, early jazz rock
An extremely talented bassist and cellist whose skills extend to violin, clarinet, trombone, and tuba, Ron Carter started on cello at ten and was soon giving concerts. He switched to bass in high school in Detroit, and later graduated from the Eastman School of Music in 1959. Carter played and recorded with the Eastman Philharmonic Orchestra before joining Chico Hamilton in 1959. From 1960 until the present, the list of greats Carter has worked with includes Eric Dolphy, Miles Davis, McCoy Tyner, Lena Horne, the New York Bass Choir, the New York Jazz Quartet, and many others. His huge tone, sense of time, rhythmic pulse, imagination, and ability to provide whatever's necessary in any musical situation have enabled Carter to do everything from solos to duos to trios, and even work with rappers. He formed his own quartet in 1976, and his exchanges with fellow bassist Buster Williams, plus his use of the piccolo bass, were breathtaking. Carter's legacy runs over 500 albums. —*Ron Wynn*

○ **Out Front** / **i.** 1966 / Prestige 7397

● **Uptown Conversation** / Oct. 6, 1969 / Atlantic 521
Arguably his best release. A 1989 reissue of an Embryo album that featured some rangy, vibrant Carter solos. —*Ron Wynn*

★ **Piccolo** / Mar. 26+27, 1977 / Milestone 55004
This was a finely crafted recording, abounding in a pleasing variety of cleverly voiced ensemble passages in a wide range of styles and densities. "Saguaro," for example, walked into a light, quasi-string quartet interlude and featured thoughtful rhythmic diversity throughout, from back beat to double-time swing. On tracks like these Ron Carter came close to transcending his instrument's idiosyncrasies and indeed almost capitalized on them. . . . Pianist Kenny Barron received ample solo space and as always used it wisely and wittily, and the other members of this quartet (bassist Buster Williams and drummer Ben Riley) loaned their equally sympathetic support to this provocative if not entirely successful experiment. —*Jon Balleras, Down Beat*

☆ **Third Plane** / Jul. 13, 1977 / Milestone 754

Michael Carvin

b. Dec. 12, 1944, Houston, TX
Drums / Hard bop
A marvelously gifted drummer, Michael Carvin's been a prolific contributor on the contemporary jazz scene. Whether driving a group, doing a solo or interacting with the rhythm section, Carvin's demonstrated outstanding technique and sensitive accompanying skills. His father was a drummer who taught him the basics before Carvin joined Earl Grant's big band in the mid-'60s. After a tour of duty in Vietnam, Carvin played with B. B. King. Later came stints with Freddie Hubbard, Pharoah Sanders, Lonnie Liston Smith, McCoy Tyner, Jackie McLean, and Clive Stevens' Atmospheres band during the '70s, plus recordings with Mickey Bass and Charles Davis in the '80s. Carvin's done his own recordings for Muse and Steeplechase in the '70s, '80s, and '90s. —*Ron Wynn*

★ **Between Me and You** / Sep. 27, 1988 / Muse 5370

Al Casey (Albert Aloysius Casey)

b. Sep. 15, 1915, Louisville, KY
Guitar / Swing
Guitarist Al Casey became a major jazz force while teaming with Fats Waller for a tremendous string of sessions. They made over 230 recordings and served as their era's equivalent of Count Basie and Freddie Greene. Casey nicely blended single-string and chordal approaches on acoustic and later developed an equally distinctive style on electric. He began working with Waller while still a teen and later recorded with Frankie Newton during a 1939 session organized by French critic and author Hughes Panassie. Billie Holiday, Teddy Wilson, Earl Hines, Big Sid Catlett, Buster Harding, and Chu Berry were other jazz greats Casey played with in the '30s and '40s, while also leading his own trio. When he began on electric, Casey became part of the R&B revolution in the late '50s, teaming with King Curtis. But he returned to basic blues and jazz in the '70s and '80s, playing with Helen Humes and the Harlem Blues and Jazz Band. He recorded for Moodsville, Fantasy, and JSP. —*Ron Wynn and Michael G. Nastos*

★ **Buck Jumpin'** / Mar. 7, 1960 / Prestige 675
Quintet sides w/ Herman Foster Trio and reedman Rudy Powell. Nine tracks, mostly old timey and bluesy, sweet and mellow. Two previously unreleased tracks. —*Michael G. Nastos*

Philip Catherine

b. Oct. 27, 1942, London, England
Guitar / World fusion, modern creative
Philip Catherine is a Belgian guitarist and contributor to many acclaimed sessions in the '70s, '80s, and '90s. Catherine worked with Lou Bennett in the late '50s and then played for Belgian radio stations in the '60s. He joined Jean-Luc Ponty's group in 1970, staying until 1972. Then he came to America, enrolled at the Berklee School of Music, and established the band Pork Pie with Charlie Mariano and Jasper van't Hof. They recorded one 1974 LP. He began working extensively with bassist Niels-Henning Orsted Pedersen in the mid-'70s, and they continued their relationship through the '80s. Catherine was dubbed "Young Django" by Charles Mingus, and he's worked in a trio with fellow guitarists Larry Coryell and Bireli Lagrene, while also recording with Mingus and Stephane Grappelli. —*Ron Wynn*

● **I Remember You** / Oct. 1990 / Criss Cross 1048

Serge Chaloff

b. Nov. 24, 1923, Boston, MA, d. Jul. 16, 1957
Baritone sax / Bop

Few have better exploited the richness and depth of the baritone sax than Serge Chaloff, who began playing with big bands as a teenager. He bridged the swing and bebop eras, absorbing the changes in theory and execution and then brilliantly incorporating them into his work. Harry Carney and Jack Washington were two prime influences, though as a self-taught baritone player, Chaloff forged his own direction. He played with Boyd Raeburn, Georgie Auld, and Jimmy Dorsey before he joined Woody Herman in 1947. Chaloff spent two years with Herman and another with Basie before returning to Boston. He did some teaching and made a few releases as a leader before his death, which was caused by complications from spinal paralysis. Despite a rather slim discography, Chaloff's commanding style and formidable sound have seldom been equaled on his instrument. —*Ron Wynn*

○ **New Stars-New Sounds—Vol. 2** / Mar. 10, 1949 / Mercer 1003
○ **Serge Chaloff and Boots Mussulli** / **i.** 1954 / Storyville 310
○ **Boston Blow-Up** / Apr. 4+05, 1955 / Capitol 6510
Another swinging, boppish session from a musician who was once a mainstay of Woody Herman's band. —*David Szatmary*

★ **Blue Serge** / Mar. 4, 1956 / Capitol 742
An indispensable session from one of the great underrated baritone sax players, featuring Sonny Clark (p) and Philly Joe Jones (d). —*David Szatmary*

Joe Chambers (Joseph Arthur Chambers)

b. Jun. 25, 1942, Stoneacre, Virginia
Drums, piano / Modern creative

Drummer Joe Chambers has the ability to be both commanding and sensitive, on top of the beat or slightly behind it. He moved to New York in 1963, where he became a regular on the scene, working with Eric Dolphy, Freddie Hubbard, and Andrew Hill, among others. He spent five years with Bobby Hutcherson from 1965 to1970 and has worked since 1970 with Max Roach's M'Boom, as well as doing several sessions as a freelancer. —*Ron Wynn*

★ **Almoravid, The** / Oct. 8, 1973-Nov. 1, 1973 / Muse 5035
This set offered glimpses of quite a few facets of Joe Chambers. The tracks with horns (which date from 1971) were reminiscent of Miles Davis's *Filles De Kilimanjaro* set: long, languid lines, generally reflective soloing, and a gradual realization that the drummer, crisp and cryptic, was at the center of things, the smoldering fold to all that sublime coolness. "Catta," by contrast, found Chambers in the driver's seat of a rather Caribbean juggernaut, directing the rhythmic energy with a calm, casual, half-time cymbal line. Only on the last track did the leader really step out front, erupting from a rock beat to speak his piece on the fragmentary "Gazelle Suite," then careening ominously around the foreboding landscape of the enigmatic "Jihad." —*Steve Metaliz, Down Beat*

○ **Double Exposure** / Nov. 16, 1977 / Muse 5165
Double Exposure was a suite of related themes and moods that featured percussionist Joe Chambers, mostly on acoustic piano, in tandem with the late organist Larry Young. It was not your typical drummer's date, but then Joe Chambers is not your typical drummer. He made his mark during the '60s as much for his tasteful composing as for his drum fury. And this was a fully realized, touching work. One could not say enough good things about Larry Young. His work on the first side of *Double Exposure* was largely supportive, but his embellishments were so driven and subtle that it was like being caught up in a whirlpool of rhythm and harmony—circles of sound. —*Chip Stern, Down Beat*

Paul Chambers (Paul Laurence Dunbar Chambers, Jr.)

b. Apr. 22, 1935, Pittsburgh, PA, d. Jan. 4, 1969, New York, NY
Bass / Hard bop

Paul Chambers was one of the great bass players of the '50s and '60s. He was a member of Miles Davis's working groups, 1955-1963, after which he formed a cooperative trio with pianist Wynton Kelly and drummer Jimmy Cobb. This group frequently

backed Wes Montgomery in the mid '60s, recording with him and also guitarist Kenny Burrell for Verve. While these albums are solid items—and the Montgomery *Smokin' at the Half Note* much more than that—the best Chambers release as a leader is on Blue Note. Any of his Blue Note albums are highly recommended, and his Vee Jay sessions are just a slight cut beneath the Blue Note ones. As a soloist Chambers was noted for his bowed solos and is heard to great advantage in the trio of pianist Red Garland on many Prestige and Prestige Moodsville albums, recorded 1955-1959. An active freelance recording musician around New York, he was featured on dozens of albums, and his presence added a little extra quality to any setting. —*Bob Porter*

★ **Bass on Top** / Jul. 14, 1957 / Blue Note 46533
Extraordinary bassist. Highly recommended. A definition for modal-jazz expression. —*Michael G. Nastos*

Teddy Charles (Theodore Charles Cohen)

b. Apr. 13, 1928, Chicopee Falls, Mass
Vibes, composer / Cool, progressive big band

Vibist and composer Teddy Charles's conception and approach have changed considerably from his early days of working with big bands led by Benny Goodman, Chubby Jackson, Artie Shaw, and Buddy DeFranco. Charles began trying newer things and playing more aggressively in his own groups, and as a producer and sideman in the '50s. He created groups for recordings that matched three trumpets and a rhythm section or a tenor and two baritones; his solos on vibes were far-reaching and an influence on the current styles of such players as Jay Hoggard or Steve Nelson. —*Ron Wynn*

★ **Tentet (Jazzlore 48)** / Jan. 6-17, 1956 / Atlantic 90983
This session from 1956 found vibraphonist Teddy Charles creating new music beyond bop. As with Jimmy Giuffre, Charles's recordings were not particularly influential, but in both cases the individuality of the style made for a timelessness that kept the 33-year-old (1989) music from sounding dated. Charles' tentet, which only existed for this record, was a pioneering third-stream unit that utilized classical dissonances in the many arranged sections, even behind soloists. Giuffre, Mal Waldron, Gil Evans (then emerging from obscurity), and George Russell contributed an original each (with each arranging their own songs), but it was Charles's three charts (especially the multithemed "The Emperor") that were most memorable. This is an album that rewards repeated listenings. —*Scott Yanow, Cadence*

★ **Live at the Verona Jazz Festival (1988)** / Jun. 1988 / Soul Note 1183
Concert date with Harold Danko trio. Highlight is the Mingus composition "Nostalgia in Times Square." —*Michael G. Nastos*

Doc Cheatham (Adolphus Anthony Cheatham)

b. Jun. 13, 1905, Nashville, TN
Trumpet / Swing, big band, bop

A jazz legend and elder statesman, trumpeter Doc Cheatham remains a formidable, exciting soloist and performer in his eighties. His ability to hit high notes; play with fire and zip; excel at ballads, blues, or bop; and be a dominating figure on the bandstand has continued over several decades. Cheatham came to Chicago in the mid '20s and played and recorded with Ma Rainey. He was in Wilbur de Paris's orchestra from 1927 to 1928 and went to Europe the next year with Sam Wooding's ensemble. Cheatham played with Cab Calloway for six years in the '30s, taking time off at various times to work with Teddy Wilson and Benny Carter. He later spent two years in Fletcher Henderson's orchestra and played with Eddie Heywood and Marcelino Guerra in the '40s. Cheatham displayed his proficiency in Afro-Latin and Latin-jazz in the '50s, spending a year with Perez Prado and touring during the summers with Calloway's band. He reunited with de Paris in the '50st and led his own band in New York City at International on Broadway from 1960 to 1965. Cheatham spent a year with Benny Goodman's group in 1966, and made several delightful recordings for independent labels during the '70s and '80s. Doctor George Butler signed Cheatham to Columbia in the '90s as part of the "Legends" series, and he issued a recording in '93.—*Richard Meyer*

★ **Black Beauty** / Oct. 31, 1979 / Sackville 3029
A Salute to Black American Songwriters. Classic music duet w/ pianist Sammy Price. Mostly pre-'40s music. Trumpet and piano

in perfect harmony—truly a great album to start a collection with. —*Michael G. Nastos*

○ **At the Bern Jazz Festival** / Apr. 1983-Jan. 1985 / Sackville 3045
Veteran trumpeter Doc Cheatham and soprano saxophonist Jim Galloway colead these three separate live sessions. The sextet (which also includes trombonist Roy Williams) explores a variety of standards, including "Cherry," "Love Is Just Around the Corner," "Swing That Music," and a ballad medley. Everyone is in fine form on this small-group swing CD. —*Scott Yanow*

Don Cherry (Donald Eugene Cherry)

b. Nov. 18, 1936, Oklahoma City
Trumpet, piano, organ, wooden flute, vocals / Early free, world fusion, modern creative

Don Cherry began as an experimental trumpeter and gradually expanded his interest and involvement with ethnic and international music until it's become his primary mode. He played piano in an R&B band with drummer Billy Higgins in his teens, and both joined Ornette Coleman in the late '50s. Cherry's pungent, rippling trumpet provided an ideal contrast to Coleman's sprawling, bluesy, and greatly misunderstood alto sax leads. Cherry and Coleman spent the summer of 1959 at the Lenox School of Music. Coleman made his controversial New York debut that autumn with bassist Charlie Haden and Higgins. Cherry stayed two years with Coleman, then freelanced with John Coltrane, Steve Lacy, and Sonny Rollins before becoming a founding member of the short-lived but invigorating New York Contemporary Five. Cherry, Archie Shepp, John Tchicai, and others toured and recorded in Europe and then disbanded in 1964. Cherry continued working with Albert Ayler, Gato Barbieri, and George Russell and gradually became immersed in world music. He lived in Sweden in the '70s and then returned to New York. He started working with a group of Coleman alumni that blossomed into the group Old and New Dreams in 1976. The band played several Coleman classics, while also doing compositions by Cherry and Haden. Cherry received a grant from the National Endowment for the Arts in 1982 and has reemerged as a jazz player in recent years thanks to excellent albums on A&M. —*Ron Wynn*

★ **Complete Communion** / Dec. 24, 1965 / Blue Note 4226
The tracks "Complete Communion" and "Elephantasy" each occupy one side of the record. In a compositional sense, they both have the same basis. That is to say they are both suites divided into four continuous subsections, each part with its own title. It is not necessary to separate the subsections into single tunes, for Cherry's music, as always, is a collective musical experience being expanded from points of departure that enter by chance, or so it would appear, rather than arranged to stop and start. —*Bill Smith, Coda*

○ **Don Cherry** / i. May 1977 / Horizon 717
What made this record worth your attention were the other two pieces [other than "Brown Rice" and "Degi-Degi"]. "Malkauns" opened with a fairly long Charlie Haden bass solo acompanied by Moki's tamboura. Then Cherry and drummer Billy Higgins enter, and when you hear that shining trumpet tone reverberating through the air, you can't help but be moved. —*Carl Brauer, Cadence*

★ **El Corazon with Ed Blackwell** / Feb. 1982 / ECM 829199
Cherry spent many years as a wandering minstrel, traveling to Europe, Africa, and points beyond all the while immersing himself in the native music. On trumpet his attack was strong and his tone hard, but not brittle. When he moved to piano, there was a folklike quality to the notes he chose to play. His gospellike chords on Thelonious Monk's "Bemsha Swing" brought to mind the playing of Abdullah Ibrahim. His solo trumpet piece closed the LP—the echo on his horn broadened his tone and lengthened the notes . . . . The composition was like a prayer and a fitting close to the album. —*Richard B. Kamins, Cadence*

☆ **Art Deco** / Aug. 27-30, 1988 / A&M 5258
Don Cherry's *Art Deco* not only offered a reunion of old friends, but a thoroughly pleasurable outing by musicians who revolutionized jazz by mastering its traditions. The ever-unpredictable Cherry reunited his pre-Ornette Coleman bandmates for a relaxed set of standards, solo features, and three of Coleman's tunes. —*Steven Hahn, Jazz Times*

Billy Childs

Piano / Bop, hard bop
Pianist Billy Childs is a capable player and good interpreter whose style is strongly influenced by Herbie Hancock. He's among the rare mainstream and hard bop players who've recorded extensively for Windham Hill. Childs has played or recorded with Eddie Daniels, Freddie Hubbard, Bruce Forman, and Bunky Green, among others.—*Ron Wynn*

★ **Take for Example This...** / 1988 / Hip Pocket 0113

○ **Portrait of a Player** / i. 1993 / Windham Hill 10144
On his fourth outing for Windham Hill, pianist Billy Childs delivers an excellent collection of interpretations of jazz and pop standards as well as two originals, the reflective "End of Innocence" and a spirited tribute to Tommy Flanagan ("Flanagan"). Childs gets strong rhythmic support from his bass-drum team (Tony Dumas and Billy Kilson), freeing him to fly through John Coltrane's hard-boppin' "Satellite" and the vibrant "It's You or No One." —*Dan Ouellette, Down Beat*

Chocolate Dandies

b. , USA
Group / Swing, big band
There were several different bands named The Chocolate Dandies. The title was taken from the title of an extremely successful 1924 show co-written by Eubie Blake and Noble Sissle. The earliest Chocolate Dandies ensemble was directed by Don Redman and recorded for Okeh in 1928 and 1929. Recordings Redman supervised for McKinney's Cotton Pickers were also issued under that name. There were several groups under Benny Carter's leadership called Chocolate Dandies during the early '30s. The most famous were the ones with Coleman Hawkins in 1930; but others who were featured in subsequent editions included Max Kaminsky, Floyd O'Brien, and Buck Clayton, plus members of both Carter's and Fletcher Henderson's bands. —*Ron Wynn*

★ **Chocolate Dandies (1928-1933)** / 1928-1933 / Disques Swing 8448
Pivotal cuts by early jazz greats like Benny Carter, Coleman Hawkins, and the like. —*Ron Wynn*

Charlie Christian (Charles Christian)

b. Jul. 29, 1916, Texas, d. Mar. 2, 1942, New York
Guitar / Bop
He made his first records in the fall of 1939 and was hospitalized for TB in the summer of 1941; though he didn't live to see another spring, the music he had recorded—live and in the studio—immortalized Charlie Christian and influenced everyone who picked up a guitar in his wake. The Texas-born genius was a pioneer of amplified guitar and set the style for playing jazz on what was, in effect, a new instrument. A master of the blues and sophisticated harmonic "changes," he was a tireless and creative improviser who loved playing in jam sessions. Recommended to John Hammond by Mary Lou Williams, Christian was brought to Benny Goodman's attention by Hammond, hired after a single hearing, and featured in a new Goodman Sextet. His solos were of necessity short on the 78 rpm discs of the day. Fortunately he was also captured jamming in Harlem (at Minton's and Monroe's), so we can hear him "stretching out." Every note he left us is a gem. —*Dan Morgenstern*

○ **Solo Flight (1939-1941)** / Aug. 19, 1939-Jun. 1941 / Stash 1021
Although not the very first electric guitarist, Charlie Christian was its first major soloist. During the 19 months between debuting with the Benny Goodman sextet and being stricken with tuberculosis (which killed him less than a year later), Christian played such an appealing and virtuosic style (playing the guitar with the force and logic of a horn rather than as a barely audible part of the rhythm section) that he remained the major influence on virtually all jazz and popular guitarists (whether they realized it or not) until the emergence of rock in the mid-to-late 1960s, 25 years after his death! *Solo Flight* collects many of Christian's most exciting radio appearances with the Benny Goodman Sextet (which started out with Lionel Hampton and Fletcher Henderson and by 1941 featured trumpeter Cootie Williams and tenorman Georgie Auld), along with five selections from a very rare (and at

the time unreleased) session with Goodman, Count Basie, Buck Clayton, and Lester Young. Classic music! —*Scott Yanow*

★ **Genius of the Electric Guitar** / 1939-1941 / Columbia 40846
This set contains some of guitarist Charlie Christian's greatest recordings (although he did not live long enough to record any bad ones!). Christian is heard with the Benny Goodman Sextet on famous versions of "Seven Come Eleven," "Benny's Bugle," and "Air Mail Special"; is showcased with Goodman's orchestra on "Solo Flight"; and jams with the members of the Sextet (minus their leader) on "Blues in B" and a fascinating ad-lib "Waitin' for Benny." This important release belongs in every jazz collection and contains a great deal of essential music. —*Scott Yanow*

○ **Immortal Charlie Christian, The** / i. 1939-1941 / Legacy 373

☆ **With the Benny Goodman Sextet and Orchestra** / Feb. 7, 1940-Nov. 7, 1940 / Columbia 652

○ **Solo Flight with the Benny Goodman Sextet, Septet & Orches** / Nov. 7, 1940 / Columbia 62581

Pete Christlieb (Peter Christlieb)

b. Feb. 16, 1945, Los Angeles, CA
Tenor sax / Bop, cool
Though he's a West Coast player, tenor saxophonist Pete Christlieb has demonstrated on "The Tonight Show" and various recordings a power and authority that's quite hot. An especially rousing soloist on uptempo numbers, Christlieb's also displayed his facility with blues and ballads. He played with Si Zentner, Chet Baker, and Woody Herman in the '60s and then established a musical relationship with Louis Bellson that continued into the '90s. Christlieb also has extensive studio experience, appearing on various film and television projects since the late '60s. He was in the backing bands of Della Reese and Sarah Vaughan, among other vocalists, and both headed a quartet and began a record label in the '80s. Christlieb's done sessions with numerous musicians, among them Count Basie, Quincy Jones, and Mel Lewis. One of his finest albums was a '70s duet date with Warne Lewis. —*Ron Wynn and Michael G. Nastos*

★ **Apogee** / 1978 / Warner Brothers 3236
This music swung hard from note one to the very end. Aside from that, the album was unusual in several ways. For one thing, the featured soloists were both tenor players; for another, both were highly experienced but not terribly well known. Warne Warsh had been active since he played with Lennie Tristano in the '50s. Pete Christlieb was a busy session man who also played in the Tonight Show band. Also of interest, the album was produced by Walter Becker and Donald Fagen, AKA Steely Dan. There was fire on every cut. Christlieb and Marsh seemed to inspire each other, helped along by a good choice of material and Joe Roccisano's charts. The rhythm section provided plenty of support. Some of the most exciting moments occurred when Christlieb and Marsh soloed simultaneously, egging each other on. —*Douglas Clark, Down Beat*

○ **Mosaic** / Feb. 16, 1990 / Capri 74026
Recorded at Portland Inn. Christlieb and Bob Cooper swing dual tenors. —*Michael G. Nastos*

Sonny Clark (Conrad Yeatis Clark)

b. Jul. 21, 1931, Herminie, Pennsylvania, d. Jan. 13, 1963, New York, NY
Piano / Hard bop
A topflight player who was both wonderfully inventive and extremely funky, Sonny Clark made some wonderful records during an unfortunately short career. He was especially known for his right-hand lines and rhythmic drive. Clark moved to California from the East Coast in the early '50s, and settled eventually in Los Angeles after a brief period in San Francisco working with Vido Musso and Oscar Pettiford. He cut his first sessions with Teddy Charles's West Coasters and later did stints with Buddy DeFranco and Dinah Washington's trio. His late '50s dates, such as *Dial S for Sonny, Cool Struttin',* and *Sonny's Crib* are acknowledged classics. Clark's finest dates were for Blue Note, but he also had sessions issued by Time, Xanadu, and Bainbridge. Clark worked and recorded with Sonny Rollins, Hank Mobley, John Jenkins, Curtis Fuller, Clifford Jordan, and Bennie Green. A heart attack claimed Clark long before his productivity had diminished. —*Ron Wynn*

★ **Sonny's Crib** / Oct. 9, 1957 / Blue Note 46819
Striking sextet performances. Memorable efforts from John Coltrane (ts), Curtis Fuller (tb), and Donald Byrd (tpt). 1987 CD reissue has three fine bonus cuts. —*Ron Wynn*

● **Leapin' and Lopin'** / Nov. 13, 1961 / Blue Note 84091
Mainstream, mostly uptempo jazz with a slight taste of funk. One of Clark's best albums as a leader. The CD has two extra tracks. —*Michael Erlewine*

Kenny Clarke (Kenneth Spearman Clarke)

b. Jan. 9, 1914, Pittsburgh, PA, d. Jan. 26, 1985, Paris, France
Drums, vibes, composer / Bop
You could initiate a good argument over whether Kenny Clarke or Max Roach should be deemed the founder of bop drumming. Clarke was surely among the style's seminal figures, with his steady work on the snare and bass, plus unflappable beats and pulse. He was also among the few equally capable of spearheading a large group or a small combo. He made his initial impact with Roy Eldridge in 1935 and joined the Edgar Hayes group in 1937. He did some dates as a leader and then worked with Claude Hopkins and Teddy Hill in the early '40s. Clarke participated in many sessions as part of the Minton's house band. He was among the experimenters whose jam sessions and woodshedding culminated in the modern jazz revolution of the mid- and late '40s. Clarke worked with Dizzy Gillespie's big band in 1946 and 1948, going with them to Europe in 1948. He stayed a few months in Paris and then joined Tadd Dameron, returning to Paris with him in 1949. Clarke worked with Billy Eckstine and Milt Jackson in 1951. He was also featured that year backing Charlie Parker and in a trio with pianist John Lewis. Clarke was an original member of the Modern Jazz Quartet before leaving in 1955. Clarke settled in France in 1956 and was a busy studio and session musician there the remainder of his life. —*Ron Wynn*

○ **Paris Bebop Sessions, The** / Oct. 9, 1950 / Prestige 7605
Good, though somewhat stiff, sessions done in Paris by Clarke with a French bassist and pianist. Tenor saxophonist James Moody certainly isn't stiff however, and it's his exuberant, bluesy solos, coupled with Clarke's spinning beats, that keep the date from bogging down, especially when pianist Ralph Schecroun takes the spotlight. —*Ron Wynn, AMG*

★ **Klook's Clique** / Feb. 6, 1956 / Savoy 12083
An indispensable session by the bop pioneer, with John LaPorta (sax) and Donald Byrd (tpt). —*David Szatmary*

○ **Kenny Clarke Meets the Detroit Jazzmen** / Apr. 30, 1956+May 9, 1956 / Savoy 1111
Sensational mid-'50s date that exemplifies the Detroit hard bop sound. Clarke rides herd on a great band that includes baritone saxophonist Pepper Adams, pianist Tommy Flanagan, guitarist Kenny Burrell, and bassist Paul Chambers. This has been reissued on both domestic and import CDs. —*Ron Wynn, AMG*

○ **Sax No End** / Jun. 18, 1967 / PA/USA 7097

○ **Let's Face the Music** / May 13-14, 1968 / Prestige 7699

★ **Pieces of Time** / i. 1983 / Soul Note 1078
Standout session late in his career, with fellow drummers Andrew Cyrille, Milford Graves, and Don Moye. —*Ron Wynn*

Stanley Clarke (Stanley M. Clarke)

b. Jun. 30, 1951, Philadelphia, PA
Bass, composer / Early jazz rock, instrumental pop, contemporary funk
Stanley Clarke pioneeered many of the now-established techniques used by contemporary electric bassists in the '70s. A one-time violinist and cellist from Philadelphia, Clarke approached bass like a guitar, making dazzling, rapid patterns his specialty. Clarke's rock background and amazing skill made him a favorite on both acoustic and electric bass. He was initially a prolific contributor in hard-bop circles, then a pivotal member of Return to Forever (in both its acoustic and electric phase) with Chick Corea. He finally hit the R&B bigtime coleading The Stanley Clarke/George Duke Project and reaped rock dividends with Jeff Beck and the New Barbarians. He's become a successful film composer in the '80s and '90s and is one of the greats of his generation. —*Ron Wynn*

★ **Stanley Clarke** / i. 1974 / Epic 36973

The music on this album moved logically with thematic direction and covered an unusually wide range of colors and emotions. At the top, there was Bill Connors's articulately soaring electric guitar work, along with Jan Hammer's keyboard and shrewdly applied Moog; at the bottom, bassist Stanley Clarke and drummer Tony Williams were in melodic and rhythmic tandem. These four might have been constant in the mathematics of structure and stress, but this was music of energy, spirit, and imagery that was open and moving—no fixed rules applied. —*Herb Nolan, Down Beat*

○ **3 / i.** 1990 / Epic 46012

Both an accomplished acoustic player and a pioneering electric bassist, Stanley Clarke found new success in two other areas during the '80s and '90s. One was scoring films, the other cutting urban contemporary hits with George Duke. This was their third venture, and it continued in the path of its predecessors; short songs, little solo space, double-tracked background vocals and lots of wah-wah and synthesizer effects. —*Ron Wynn, AMG*

○ **Funny How Time Flies** / Portrait 08051

James Clay

b. Sep. 8, 1935
Tenor sax / Bop, hard bop, soul jazz
James Clay is an underrated tenor saxophonist whose career has enjoyed a publicity rebirth in the '90s. Clay played honking sax and blues in the Southwest during the '50s and was an early partner of Ornette Coleman. Clay was a featured member of the Ray Charles Orchestra during the '60s, and cut a superb album with Fathead Newman before seeming to drop out of sight. He resurfaced on Antilles and Caravan of Dreams recordings that showed his always-moving tenor playing had grown more evocative with time, and the blues were never far behind. He's a genuine jazz survivor. —*Ron Wynn*

● **Sound of the Wide Open Spaces** / Apr. 26, 1960 / Riverside 257
W/ David Newman. Dueling Texas tenors on an album recorded by Cannonball Adderley. Definitive music. —*Michael G. Nastos*

★ **I Let a Song Go out of My Heart** / Jan. 29, 1989 / Antilles 848279
Although he made his early mark on the jazz scene working with Ornette Coleman and Don Cherry, he's far more of a traditional blues-and-ballad stylist than an explosive experimentalist.—*Ron Wynn, Rock & Roll Disc.*

Buck Clayton (Wilbur Dorsey Clayton)

b. Nov. 12, 1911, Parsons, KS, **d.** Dec. 8, 1991
Trumpet, arranger / Swing, big band
Buck Clayton was a wonderful swing-era trumpeter who began heading a band in the '30s. He enjoyed seven stellar years with Count Basie in the '30s and '40s, while serving as a keen arranger for Basie, Goodman, Harry James, and others in swing's peak period. He led small combos throughout the '50s. He was forced to give up active playing in the '60s but was active as a composer, arranger, and educator until his death in 1991. He was a striking trumpeter—a truly great muted player—and thoroughly versed in vintage Kansas City stomping jam-mode. —*Ron Wynn*

○ **Singing Trumpets** / Feb. 4, 1953 / Jazztone 1267

● **Complete Cbs Buck Clayton Jam Sessions** / i. 195? / Mosaic 144
In the 1950s George Avakian and John Hammond produced a series of all-star mainstream jam sessions for Columbia under the leadership of Buck Clayton. A typical session involved 10 to 12 participants, including the likes of Buddy Tate, Woody Herman, Joe Newman, and Al Cohn. . . . Give credit to this boxed set's producer Michael Cuscuna, for going back to the original sessions whenever possible and issuing unedited performances, including a few never before released. . . . The production of this six-disc boxed set in virtually every category—from sound quality to annotation—is first-rate. —*Chip Deffa, Jazz Times*

★ **Olympia Concert (22 April 61)** / Apr. 22, 1961 / Vogue 30
A splendid set with vintage sensibility and a jam session atmosphere. Buddy Tate (ts) and Sir Charles Thompson (p) are on the money. —*Ron Wynn*

○ **Passport to Paradise** / May 15-16, 1961 / Inner City 7009

Jimmy Cleveland (James Milton Cleveland)

b. May 3, 1926, Wartrace, TN, **d.** Feb. 9, 1991
Trombone / Bop, hard bop
Trombonist Jimmy Cleveland is a tremendous player with an instantly recognizable tone and style, no matter the material or arrangement. Cleveland began playing trombone at 16, performing first in his family's band and then with the Tennessee State University orchestra. He worked for three years in the early '50s with Lionel Hampton, his first major job. Then came stints with Oscar Pettiford, Lucky Thompson, James Moody, Johnny Richards, and Gerry Mulligan from 1954 up to 1960. Cleveland was among the most recorded trombonists in history from the '50s through the '80s, partly due to his long relationship with Quincy Jones. He did several Jones film and television soundtracks in New York and later California, and played in many Broadway pit bands. Sessions with groups led by Dizzy Gillespie, Donald Byrd, Jimmy Smith, Miles Davis, Oliver Nelson, Jimmy Smith, Wes Montgomery, Kenny Burrell, and Stanley Turrentine are only part of Cleveland's immense recorded legacy. —*Ron Wynn*

● **Cleveland Style** / Dec. 12+15, 1957 / Emarcy 36126

Arnett Cobb (Arnette Cleophus Cobb)

b. Aug. 10, 1918, Houston, TX, **d.** Mar. 24, 1989
Tenor sax / Swing
One of the original and finest "honking" tenor saxophonists, Cobb was a contemporary of Illinois Jacquet and assumed the star tenor's chair when Jacquet left Lionel Hampton's band in 1942. These reedsmen had many interesting parallels—both spent early years in Houston, played in trumpeter Milton Larkins's "territory bands" in the '30s, and subsequently formed their own orchestras in the late '40s. In the heady postwar period, tenor "battles" and extroverted showmanship were the rage, ushering in the uninhibited music (and uncontrollable capacity crowds) of the R&B/ rock & roll era. These were Cobb's best years, before health problems knocked him from the top of the heap. Sporadic but generally top-notch recordings of his straightahead jazz blowing have been made and sporadically reissued since the '50s (mostly for Prestige/ OJC). Cobb's contributions to the superb *Atlantic Honkers* compilation (Atlantic) reveal his truly great stature, as do the albums listed here. —*Myles Boisen*

★ **Go Power!** / Jan. 9, 1959 / Prestige 7835
Madcap exchanges with Eddie "Lockjaw" Davis (ts). If you find it, savor the purchase. —*Ron Wynn*

☆ **Smooth Sailing** / Feb. 27, 1959 / Original Jazz Classics 323
Noteworthy appearance from undervalued Buster Cooper (tb). Textbook soul power; exemplary sax technique from Cobb. —*Ron Wynn*

○ **More Party Time** / Feb. 16, 1960 / Prestige 7175

★ **Arnett Cobb Is Back** / Jun. 27, 1978 / Progressive 7037
Arnett Cobb Is Back was recorded in June 1978. The material was safe and solid—standards and blues—and Cobb played with authority. Cobb was a master of tonal effects and unexpected quotations, and his playing retained the hard-swinging power that made him a major star when he came charging out of Lionel Hampton's orchestra in the 1940s. —*Jim Roberts, Down Beat*

Billy Cobham (William C. Cobham)

b. May 16, 1946, Panama
Drums, composer, bandleader / Early jazz rock
From the age of eight, when he sat in with his pianist father, Billy Cobham has been a prime drummer. He spent time in the army during the '60s, where he met Billy Taylor. He made a shift from a standard timekeeper in a hard-bop context to a dashing, flamboyant anchor with Miles Davis, Dreams, and the Mahavishnu Orchestra, where he became a rock idol. At one time his combination of bombastic power and rhythmic clarity made him THE drummer, and his barrages accented John McLaughlin's equally brilliant guitar on the '70s jazz-rock scene. Cobham's 1976 group Spectrum included George Duke and John Scofield. Cobham became an active educator in the late '70s and '80s and continues doing clinics and living mostly overseas.—*Ron Wynn*

● **Spectrum** / 1973-1974 / Atlantic 7268

Music Map

Jazz Clarinet

Sopranino E-Flat Clarinet

First Used in Brass Bands
New Orleans Players – John Casimir – Polo Barnes
George Lewis – Sammy Rimington

Soprano Clarinet

Creole Musicians
Lorenzo Tio Family (1893-1933) – Alphonse Picou (1878-1961)

Vaudeville Use
Wilbur Sweatman (1882-1961) – Ted Lewis (1892-1971)
Jimmy O'Bryant (1896-1928) – Wilton Crawley (1900-1948)

Dixieland
Pete Fountain (1930) ✓

Pupils Lorenzio Tio, Jr.
Sidney Bechet (1897-1959) – Barney Bigard (1906-1927)
Albert Nicholas (1900-1973)

Bechet's Pupil: Jimmie Noone (1895-1944)
Influenced These White Players:

Alcide "Yellow" Nunez (1884-1934)
Larry Shields (1893-1953) – Jimmy Dorsey (1904-1957)
Benny Goodman (1909-1986) – Artie Shaw (1910)
Leon Rappolo (1902-1943)

Major Early Players
Edmond Hall (1901-1967) – Pee Wee Russell (1906-1969)
Frank Teschemacher (1906-1932)
Early Lester Young (1909-1959) – Ernie Caceres (1911-1971)
Bob Wilber (1928) – Kenny Davern (1935)
Albert Nicholas (1900-1970) – Omer Simeon (1902-1959)
Garvin Bushnell (1902)

The rise of the Saxophone limits Clarinet use

Benny Goodman Tradition
Peanuts Hucko (1918) – Alvin Batiste (1937)
Sol Yaged (1922) – Aaron Sachs (1923) – Bob Wilber (1928)
Stan Hasselgard (1922-1948) – Jimmy Hamilton (1917)

Bass Clarinet
Eric Dolphy (1928-1964)
Bennie Maupin (1940)
Roscoe Mitchell (1940)
Hamiet Bluiett (1940)
Howard Johnson (1941)
Gunther Hampel (1937)
Kalaparusha Maurice McIntyre (1936)
David Murray (1955)
Mario Bavza (1911-1993)
Harry Carney (1910-1974)

Contrabass Clarinet
Anthony Braxton (1945)
Rahsaan Roland Kirk (1936-1977)

Flutists
Sam Most (1930)
Paul Horn (1930
Herbie Mann (1930)

Free Players
John Carter (1929)
Perry Robinson (1938)
Gunter Hampel (1937)
Anthony Braxton (1945)

Sax Players
Art Pepper (1925-1982)
Buddy Tate (1915)
Kim Cusak

Modern Stylists
John La Porta (1920)
Rolf Kuhn (1929)
Jimmy Giuffre (1921)
Tony Scott (1921)
Buddy DeFranco (1923)
Bill Smith (1926)
Rahsaan Roland Kirk (1936-1977)

1980s John Carter's Clarinet Quartet

Clarinet Summit

Classical Soloist Richard Stolzman

1980s-1990s
Eddie Daniels (1941)
Richard Stoltzman
Don Byron
Wendell Harrison

Al Cohn (Alvin Gilbert Cohn)

b. Nov. 24, 1925, New York, NY, **d.** Feb. 15, 1988, Stroudsburg, PA
Tenor sax, arranger / Bop
A rousing swinger, Al Cohn's music always made listeners happy. He and longtime friend and musical partner Zoot Sims were two tenors directly influenced by Lester Young, and their approaches contained stylistic tendencies known as "cool," but there was never anything dry or detached about Cohn's solos. Few in any style have ever played more joyously. Cohn worked with Joe Marsala in the early '40s and then played and wrote arrangements for Georgie Auld. Among his numerous playing engagements and stints, the two most famous were his time with Woody Herman in the "Four Brothers" section and the decades-long association with Sims that led to periodic reunions from the '50s to the early '80s. Artie Shaw and Elliot Lawrence were two other extensive Cohn engagements. He was also on countless recordings

for multiple labels; these include RCA, Epic, Decca, Savoy, Coral, Muse, Sonet, Timeless, Xanadu, Gazell, Concord, Prestige, and Gemini. He was also principal arranger for the musicals *Raisin; Music, Music, Music;* and *Sophisticated Ladies.* Cohn provided solos on the soundtrack for the film *Lenny* and made many festival appearances and as many club dates in his distinguished career. —*Ron Wynn and Michael G. Nastos*

○ **Cohn's Tones** / Jul. 29, 1950 / Savoy 12048

★ **Natural Rhythm** / May 14, 1955 / RCA 45164
Wonderful mid-'50s date with Freddie Green (g) stepping outside Basie's orchestra; Joe Newman accenting things on trumpet. —*Ron Wynn*

★ **Al and Zoot** / Mar. 27, 1957 / MCA 31372
Red-letter duet date with the Al Cohn Quintet. Al Cohn, Zoot Sims (ts) dates here are memorable, though you can't say the same thing for MCA's mixes and remastering. W/ Mose Allison. —*Ron Wynn*

○ **Jazz Legacy** / i. 1968 / Inner City 7022

○ **Body and Soul** / Mar. 23, 1973 / Muse 5356
W/ Zoot Sims. Immortal tenor pair with Jaki Byard (p), plus George Duvivier (b) and Mel Lewis (d). Can't miss. —*Michael G. Nastos*

★ **True Blue** / Oct. 22, 1976 / Xanadu 136
Excellent reissue of mid-'70s duo, quintet, and septet sessions. High-quality pairing of Cohn with Dexter Gordon (ts). —*Ron Wynn*

○ **Silver Blue** / i. Oct. 1976 / Xanadu 137

★ **Standards of Excellence** / Nov. 1983 / Concord Jazz 4241
Accurate title. Confident veterans going through their paces with a minimum of flash and a maximum of talent. Herb Ellis (g) shines. —*Ron Wynn*

Dolo Coker (Charles Mitchell Coker)

b. Nov. 16, 1927, Hartford, CT, **d.** Apr. 13, 1983, Los Angeles, CA
Piano / Bop
Dolo Coker was a fine pianist who worked with many major figures in the '50s, '60s, and '70s. Coker played in Philadelphia with Ben Webster, Kenny Dorham, Sonny Stitt, Gene Ammons, Lou Donaldson, Philly Joe Jones, and Dexter Gordon between 1946 and 1961. He made his recording debut with Stitt in the mid-'50s. Coker formed his own trio when he moved to Los Angeles in 1961. He played with Supersax in the '70s, as well as with Herb Ellis, Blue Mitchell, Red Rodney, Lee Konitz, and Stitt. He and Sonny Criss gave a series of public school concerts in 1973 and 1974. Coker recorded as a leader in the late '70s and with Harry Edison in 1977. —*Ron Wynn*

● **Dolo!** / i. Feb. 1978 / Xanadu 139
Amazingly, this was pianist Dolo Coker's debut album as a leader. Like most Don Schlitten-Xanadu projects, the session featured straightahead blowing by compatible pros who obviously respected and enjoyed each others' musical company. Stylistically, Coker was a product of the bop era. Within that grind, his zesty improvisations spun out of a fluent technique and an inventive approach to melody, harmony, and rhythm. So did his compositions. Three of his lines included here, originally from the 1959 L.A. production of Jack Gelber's play *The Connection* ("Dolo," "Affair in Havana," and "Field Day"), are puckish bop-based tunes that neatly set the course for the soloists. Especially attractive was the exotic "Affair in Havana" with its smoky, mysterious south-of-the-border atmosphere. —*Chuck Berg, Down Beat*

Cozy Cole

b. Oct. 17, 1906, East Orange, NJ, **d.** Jan. 29, 1981, Columbus, OH
Drums / Swing, big band
Drummer Cozy Cole was a swing and big band era mainstay, both a crowd-pleasing, flashy stylist and a steady, dependable rhythm section anchor. He started his career with Wilbur Sweatman in 1928 and shortly thereafter was leading his own bands. He recorded in 1930 with Jelly Roll Morton and during that decade played in the bands of Blanche Calloway, Benny Carter, Willie Bryant, and Stuff Smith. Cole became a star in the late '30s, playing with Cab Calloway's orchestra. He studied at Juilliard in the early '40s, eventually becoming a percussionist in studio and theater ensembles while continuing to head his own quintet and septet. Cole resumed touring in 1949, becoming a

member of Louis Armstrong's All-Stars until 1953. Cole was featured in a number of films in the '40s and '50s, among them *Make Mine Music,* and *The Glenn Miller Story.* He also played on the soundtrack for *The Strip* in 1951. Cole left Armstrong's group to manage a New York drum school in partnership with Gene Krupa. He scored the biggest single hit of his career in 1958 with recording of "Topsy." He led his own band until end of the '60s, when he joined Jonah Jones's quintet. He did freelance work through the '70s, touring Europe in 1976 with Benny Carter's quartet as part of Barry Martyn's show *A Night in New Orleans.* —*Ron Wynn*

● **Concerto for Cozy** / Mar. 13, 1944-May 1, 1944 / Savoy 12197

Nat King Cole (Nathaniel Adams Cole)

b. Mar. 17, 1919, Montgomery, AL, **d.** Feb. 15, 1965
Piano / Swing, ballads & blues
Nat "King" Cole formed an instrumental jazz trio with guitarist Oscar Moore (b Dec 25, 1912-d Oct 8, 1981) and bassist Wesley Prince (later replaced by Johnny Miller) in 1939. The group established itself in jazz circles with a series of successful recordings. Then came a date in Hollywood when they were harrassed by a drunk asking Cole to sing "Sweet Lorraine," launching the pianist on a singing career that came to overshadow the trio and the jazz music it played.
The Cole Trio signed to the then-tiny Capitol label in Los Angeles and by 1944 was scoring such hits as "Straighten Up and Fly Right," "Get Your Kicks on Route 66," "(I Love You) For Sentimental Reasons," and "The Christmas Song." In 1948, accompanied by an orchestra, Cole recorded "Nature Boy" and saw it top the charts for eight weeks. Cole maintained the trio until 1951, though his biggest successes came with more elaborate accompaniment. He then embarked on a career as a solo singer that made him one of the best-loved entertainers of the '50s and early '60s and a star on television and in the movies. (Another edition of the trio featuring guitarist John Collins and bassist Charlie Harris performed with Cole from 1952 to 1961.) Cole died of lung cancer in 1965. —*William Ruhlmann*

★ **Complete Capitol Trio Recordings** / i. 1939-1951 / Mosaic 138
The definitive (18 full CDs!) collection. These are the trio recordings to listen to, with Nat playing and singing throughout. Lovely music for the jazz purist and everyone else as well. —*Michael Erlewine*

○ **Jumpin' at Capitol** / i. 1939-1951 / Rhino 71009
For those who cannot afford or get hold of the magnificent Mosaic 18-CD box set, this single CD offers a fine sampling of Nat King Cole's talents as a pianist and jazz singer with his popular trio in the 1940s. These 16 selections (highlighted by "Straighten Up and Fly Right," "Sweet Lorraine," and "Route 66") are still quite enjoyable a half-century later. —*Scott Yanow*

Hit That Jive Jack: The Earliest Recordings / i. Dec. 1940-Oct. 1941 / MCA 42350

○ **Nat Cole at J.A.T.P.—Vol. 1** / Jul. 2, 1944 / Verve 14

○ **Nat Cole at J.A.T.P.—Vol. 2** / Jul. 2, 1944+1946 / Verve 25

● **Anatomy of a Jam Session** / Jun. 1945 / Black Lion 760137
Nat King Cole is heard on this quintet session purely as a pianist, costarring with trumpeter Charlie Shavers and tenor saxophonist Herbie Haymer; bassist John Simmons and drummer Buddy Rich play mainly in support. The quintet actually performs only five songs but seven alternate takes fill in the program, and it is very interesting hearing the musicians gradually form the shape of their solos. Fine late period swing. —*Scott Yanow*

○ **King Cole Trios Live: 1947-1948, The** / i. Mar. 1947-Mar. 1948 / Vintage Jazz Classics 1011
This excellent CD contains five of the King Cole Trio's radio shows for NBC during 1947-1948. There are some guests (singer Clark Dennis, the Dinning Sisters, Pearl Bailey, Woody Herman, and Duke Ellington) for a song apiece, but the focus is on the trio with occasional vocals from Nat King Cole. This historical music is enjoyable, although the performances (many around the two-minute mark) are sometimes frustratingly brief. Still worth acquiring. —*Scott Yanow*

○ **Big Band Cole** / 1950-1958 / Blue Note 96259
Outstanding early-'50s session with Cole showing his tremendous piano skills, backed by big band. His playing was still loose, bluesy, and exciting at this juncture, and the arrangements were

designed to give him full exposure yet also have the orchestra really punctuating his solos instead of just accompanying them. The original album was reissued on CD in 1991 with six bonus cuts. —*Ron Wynn, AMG*

○ **In the Beginning** / i. 1956 / Decca 8260

● **Complete After Midnight Sessions, The** / i. Aug. 15, 1956-Sep. 24, 1956 / Capitol 7483282
This 1956 session featured his trio with a host of distinguished guest stars. The excellent digital remastering, plus a menu of 17 numbers and some of Cole's less sugary vocals, make this one of the few Cole items equally valued by pop and jazz fans alike. — *Ron Wynn, Rock & Roll Disc.*

○ **Capitol Collectors Series** / i. 1990 / Capitol 93590
Most of Nat King Cole's biggest hits and best-known songs are here on this terrific 20-track compilation of his solo Capitol work. Includes "Mona Lisa," "The Christmas Song," "Send for Me," "Ramblin' Rose," and "Unforgettable." —*Stephen Thomas Erlewine*

○ **Unforgettable Nat King Cole, The** / i. 1992 / Capitol 99230
A '92 reissue designed to take advantage of the success Cole's daughter Natalie had with a reworked version of "Unforgettable" that featured her doing duet with her father via digital technology. The album offered Cole doing the original and other selected songs in same vein. —*Ron Wynn, AMG*

○ **Jazz Encounters** / i. Apr. 13, 1992 / Blue Note 96693
Nice anthology presenting Cole in instrumental and vocal outings matched with numerous jazz and some pop artists, among them Dizzy Gillespie, Stan Kenton, Benny Carter, Coleman Hawkins, Woody Herman, Charlie Barnet, Max Roach, Jo Stafford, Kay Starr, Johnny Mercer, and Buddy De Franco. —*Ron Wynn, AMG*

Richie Cole (Richard Cole)

b. Feb. 29, 1948, Trenton, NJ
Alto, tenor, and baritone sax / Bop, hard bop
Alto, tenor, and baritone saxophonist Richie Cole's studies as a teen with Phil Woods have never been forgotten. He's influenced as much by Woods's conception as some have accused Woods of being under Charlie Parker's. At times Cole's phrasing and tone are identical to Woods's, but he's largely succeeded in creating his own sound. His playing never lacks passion or energy. His releases are seldom poor but have yet to get beyond the (admittedly highly virtuosic) Parker-Woods influence. —*Ron Wynn*

★ **New York Afternoon-Alto Madness** / Oct. 13, 1976 / Muse 5119
While this album clearly showed alto saxophonist Richie Cole's formidable talents as a soloist in the Phil Woods tradition, none of the music was particularly memorable (all but two selections were by Cole). The tunes merely served as jumping-off points for the soloists, which in itself wasn't necessarily bad, but except for Cole and a few fleeting moments from guitarist Vic Juris, the solos were quickly forgettable. On the two tunes featuring Eddie Jefferson's vocals, "Waltz for a Rainy Bebop Evening" and "It's the Same Thing Everywhere," Cole fared better. Jefferson also added short vocals to "Alto Madness" and Juris's "You'll Always Be My Friend." —*Carl Brauer, Cadence*

○ **Keeper of the Flame** / Sep. 6, 1978 / Muse 5192
A straightahead date, Cole's follow-up to the acclaimed *Hollywood Madness*. He contributed his usual sparkling, energized alto sax, backed by virtually the same personnel as on the previous release, except he used only one bassist. Pianist Harold Mabern again took second soloist honors, while guitarist Vic Juris, drummer Eddie Gladden, and percussionist Ray Mantilla handled the rhythm section responsibilities. —*Ron Wynn, AMG*

☆ **Hollywood Madness** / Apr. 15, 1979 / Muse 5207
Unusual instrumental configuration and lineup for this '79 session. Cole headed a band with two bassists, a drummer, a pianist, a percussionist, and vocalists Eddie Jefferson and the Manhattan Transfer. This was a part concept vehicle, part blowing session, but other than Cole on alto sax, no one else was as decisive. Jefferson and the Manhattan Transfer provide bluesy, flashy singing. —*Ron Wynn, AMG*

○ **Side by Side** / Jul. 1980 / Muse 6016
What we had here was a standard live blowing date, and a quite predictable one, too. This sort of predictability has its postive sides though, as it goes without saying that when players of this

caliber play as one would expect them to do, some good music is bound to come out. As with most sessions of this type, the musical output tended to be uneven. When the session caught fire, as it did on "Scrapple from the Apple," it was very good. —*Per Husby, Cadence*

○ **Alto Annie's Theme** / Jul. 31, 1982 / Palo Alto 8036
This was recorded in 1982 while this group was working at the Keystone Korner (in San Francisco). This, however, was a studio recording; it had to be to get all the effects and over-dubbing used to allow Richie Cole to play all the saxophones (alto, tenor, baritone). —*Jerry Atkins, Cadence*

George Coleman

b. Mar. 8, 1935, Memphis, TN
Tenor sax / Hard bop
A resolute blues and ballad stylist and one of jazz's most fluid tenor saxophonists, George Coleman has been an exceptional player since the '50s, when he departed Memphis for Chicago. His background was in blues and R&B, and he had two stints in B.B. King's band during the early and mid-'50s. He left Memphis with trumpeter Booker Little in 1957, and the duo joined Max Roach's quintet in 1958. Coleman remained until 1959 and then worked in several bands during the '60s. These included Miles Davis's quintet, as well as groups led by Lionel Hampton, Lee Morgan, Elvin Jones, Shirley Scott, and Cedar Walton. Coleman's been a leader since the late '60s, heading quintets, quartets, and octets, and he's also included alto, soprano, and keyboards in his instrumental arsenal. Coleman's recorded for many labels, among them Theresa, Timeless, Catalyst, and Verve. —*Ron Wynn and Michael G. Nastos*

★ **Amsterdam After Dark** / Nov. 2-03, 1977 / Timeless
Legendary tenor saxophonist blows up a storm with the Hilton Ruiz Trio. This has been reissued on CD. Best cut is "New Arrival." —*Michael G. Nastos*

○ **At Yoshi's** / Aug. 1987 / Evidence 22021
George Coleman's animated, anguished tenor sax solos are the hook on this seven-track live set done at Yoshi's in Tokyo during 1989. Coleman offered lush, sensitive playing during *Soul Eyes* and *Good Morning Heartache* but much of the time ripped through chord changes, expanding through the upper register and burning. Drummer Alvin Queen and bassist Ray Drummond wisely gave Coleman extensive space, spreading and splitting the beat while he roared about. Pianist Harold Mabern added a contrasting element, nice bluesy, passionate solos or sensitive, subtle understatements that followed and reaffirmed Coleman's emphatic lines. It is a fine live date, and one that is superbly remastered. —*Ron Wynn*

○ **Eastern Rebellion** / Impulse 33102

Ornette Coleman

b. Mar. 9, 1930, Fort Worth, TX
Alto sax, trumpet, violin, composer / Early free
Alto saxophonist, trumpeter and violinist Ornette Coleman is a soft-spoken, unassuming man whose music reflects playful, almost childlike simplicity and fascination with melody. Contrary to his sweet nature, Coleman has provoked more critical schizophrenia and outright hatred than almost any other jazz figure. Anecdotes about his formative years are the stuff of tragicomic legend—receiving physical threats on the bandstand, having his horn confiscated and destroyed by an angry mob, or being left behind in Los Angeles after an ill-fated tour out West with bluesman Pee Wee Crayton. Legends aside, it is true that a progressive underground existed in Los Angeles when Coleman arrived, and he made his first record there for Contemporary in 1958. This was the beginning of the free-jazz movement, and immediately critics were split into two warring camps. Some proclaimed him the most important stylist since Charlie Parker, to whom he was indebted stylistically (and perhaps also for his use of a plastic alto); others found his music unlistenable or boring or dismissed it as a novelty. With the help of admirer John Lewis of the Modern Jazz Quartet, Coleman soon found himself recording for Atlantic Records and playing an extended engagement at the prestigious Five Spot in New York. Coleman's most sympathetic bandmates during these years were also his students back in Los Angeles, where he first devised his revolutionary concept of melodic and harmonic improvisation without the use of pre-

arranged chord changes. Trumpeter Don Cherry, bassist Charlie Haden, drummer Billy Higgins, and (later) bassist Scott La Faro and drummer Ed Blackwell have contributed to many of his best performances over the past three decades. All the aforementioned, plus multireedist Eric Dolphy and trumpeter Freddie Hubbard, recorded the landmark *Free Jazz* album in December 1960; this album-length piece documented the "Double Quartet" improvising collectively in the studio without written music. Many forward-thinking musicians seized on the free-jazz concept, and this influential work sounds tame today when compared to the many varieties and extremes of freedom it propagated. But after *Free Jazz* and a handful of other records on Atlantic, Ornette's career faltered, and his output of the next few years was inconsistent. There were more advances and outrages in the mid 60s—new ensembles, pieces for classical chamber groups, challenging film soundtracks, recordings with his preteen son Denardo, and unschooled solos on trumpet and violin. Coleman seemed to pick up steam again in the late '60s, reuniting with his former bandmates and discovering a sympathetic new voice in tenorist Dewey Redman, who joined him on two Blue Note sessions with Coltrane alumni Elvin Jones and Jimmy Garrison. His classical ensemble writing continued to thrive into the '70s—his orchestral masterpiece *Skies of America* was premiered at the Newport Jazz Festival on the 4th of July 1972. This triumph was followed by more years of relative inactivity and the emergence of Coleman's theories of harmonic, melodic, and rhythmic improvisation, called "harmolodics." The exact meaning of harmolodics varies from one interpreter to the next, but this approach to pantonal collective improvisation has been a major feature of Ornette's music since the mid '70s. Various incarnations of the Prime Time band, typically an electric rock sextet of drums, bass, and guitar pairings, ply their high-density harmolodics on hip young audiences, further polarizing both fans and critics. But despite the endless debate, or because of it, his music lives on—in his own occasional projects; in the acoustic jazz homages of Old and New Dreams; through younger sidemen like Ronald Shannon Jackson, Jamaaladeen Tacuma, and James Blood Ulmer; and in the efforts of Coleman converts like Pat Metheny. —*Myles Boisen*

● **Beauty Is A Rare Thing: Complete Atlantic Recordings** / Rhino 71410
Nearly 34 years after his initial session, Atlantic (in conjunction with Rhino) has finally done justice to Ornette Coleman's music. They have issued a mammoth six-disc set with exhaustive liner notes by Robert Palmer, presenting Ornette Coleman's entire album output for Atlantic including *To Whom Keeps a Record,* the Japanese date. There are six previously unissued selections, some of them originally issued on the LP *John Lewis Presents Contemporary Music: Jazz Abstractions—Gunther Schuller & Jim Hall.* The discs are mostly in chronological order, although things are switched on the sixth disc with the final Coleman combo dates in 1961 in front of the orchestral sets recorded in 1960.

This set spotlights every Coleman facet at Atlantic: amazing free sessions with a double quartet, pieces with large orchestra and numerous controversial combo sessions. The fierce, anguished, and spiraling solos taken from such albums as *The Art of the Improvisers* and *Ornette on Tenor* are not for the faint-of-heart or novices. It is sax playing that rivals John Coltrane's most vivid, energized, and shattering late '60s work and was equally reviled. The booklet compiles numerous quotes from other musicians about Coleman and details his philosophy and insights. His playing and concepts were so progressive that they are still intriguing, debated, and scaring many people. The mastering is superb; never has Coleman's alto been so well recorded or his group's interactions documented so effectively. Whether you are a Coleman fan or think he's a fraud, don't bypass this set. —*Ron Wynn*

○ **Coleman Classics—Vol.1** / Oct. 1958-Nov. 1958 / Improvising Artists 373852
Basically, this was a seminal edition of the Ornette Coleman Quartet that outraged and transmuted the jazz world of the early '60s, but with the addition of pianist Paul Bley, which, of course, made it not a quartet at all, but a quintet. Atypical of jazz ensembles—and of jazz notions altogether—up to that time, the harmonic and percussive latitude traditionally afforded by keyboards only served to bridle Coleman's aims. But still, the Coleman-Bley pairing of 1958 was an invigorating and amiable

one, and a particularly productive interval for Coleman. —*Mikal Gilmore, Down Beat*

○ **Tomorrow Is the Question!** / Jan. 16, 1959-Mar. 10, 1959 / Contemporary 342
More early explorations of his second Contemporary label date. The affinity between Coleman and Don Cherry (tpt) is more obvious here, but the music is still hampered by a less-than-ideal rhythm section. —*Myles Boisen*

☆ **Shape of Jazz to Come** / May 22, 1959 / Atlantic 1317
Another phrophetic title, and Coleman's first recording with his own band, including Charlie Haden (b). This New York session marks the beginning of his most innovative period and contains the jarring "Congeniality". —*Myles Boisen*

Twins / May 22, 1959 / Atlantic 8810
Later release of early Coleman. Features the first take of his classic "Free Jazz." —*Michael Erlewine*

☆ **Change of the Century** / Oct. 8-09, 1959 / Atlantic 81341
Coleman's roots in New Orleans jazz ("Ramblin'") and Charlie Parker ("Bird Food") are still audible here, with the title cut indicating the way of the future. Drummer Ed Blackwell enlives the whole affair. —*Myles Boisen*

○ **Art of Improvisers, The** / 1959 / Atlantic 90978
1959-1961. From six early Atlantic sessions. Close-to-definitive group interplay. Extraordinary musicianship. —*Michael G. Nastos*

● **This Is Our Music** / Jul. 19+26, 1960 / Atlantic 1353

★ **Free Jazz (A Collective Improvisation)** / Dec. 21, 1960 / Atlantic 1364
An across-the-board definitive album. Must-buy. Only for open ears. —*Michael G. Nastos*

☆ **Ornette on Tenor** / Mar. 22+27, 1961 / Atlantic 1394
Coltrane bassist Jimmy Garrison joins Ed Blackwell (d), Don Cherry (tpt), and Coleman. A fascinating date, and his only one on the tenor sax—"Cross Breeding" is an 11-minute tour de force. —*Myles Boisen*

○ **At the "Golden Circle" in Stockholm—Vol. 2** / Dec. 3-04, 1965 / Blue Note 84225
Historic trio sessions from Ornette Coleman cut at the Golden Circle. Coleman was playing at an inspiring, feverish pace, working off patterns and arrangements he was constructing almost on the spot. His assistants were bassist David Izenon and drummer Charles Moffett. Both volumes are essential. —*Ron Wynn, AMG*

○ **At the "Golden Circle" in Stockholm—Vol. 1** / Dec. 3-04, 1965 / Blue Note 84224
Vol. 1 & 2. At Stockholm. More trio recordings (without the string quartet)—very edgy and uncompromising, with energy to spare. Ornette's violin and trumpet make fine appearances here. —*Myles Boisen*

○ **Love Call** / Apr. 29, 1968+May 7, 1968 / Blue Note 84356
Ornette's trumpet work goes south sometimes, but his violin and alto sax are always striking. CD has three bonus cuts. Dewey Redman makes his points as well. —*Ron Wynn*

New York Is Now / Apr. 29, 1968-May 7, 1968 / Blue Note 84287
Another excellent representation of Coleman's creative brilliance. With Dewey Redman (ts), Jimmy Garrison (b), and Elvin Jones (d). —*Michael G. Nastos*

○ **Ornette at 12** / Jun. 16, 1969 / Impulse 9178
This album was a recapitulation on and a summation of Ornette Coleman's last three recordings (*The Empty Foxhole* and *New York Is Now* being the previous two). Certainly Ornette Denardo Coleman (drums) had improved considerably technically, and now had a much better understanding of and capacity to cope with the demands his father's music made of him and his instrument.... If you have any feeling at all for the new music, you cannot possibly go untouched by Coleman's alto playing; he leaves you with mouth agape, thinking he's played it all ... and then he comes right back in to show you how wrong you were. His interpretations, on both the impassioned dirge of "New York" and the up "C.O.D.," were masterful, complete. His downfall here, though, lay in his other instruments. The trumpet vehicle, "Rainbows," was perhaps a more pointed solo than some of his other brass excursions; but his chops just weren't in shape for it, and he muffed too much that he attempted. "Bells and Chimes," like the remainder of Coleman's violin work, was flyweight by comparison with the rest of his output. —*Barry Tepperman, Coda*

● **Dancing in Your Head** / Jan. 1973 / A&M 0807
Seminal album that outlined Ornette Coleman's "harmolodic" concept in its full glory. Besides Coleman's blend of sanctified-blues-honking alto sax, his band included the slashing drummer Ronald Shannon Jackson, plus formidable bassist Jamalaadeen Tacuma, and various guitarists. The music sizzles, shakes, and explodes, never starting or ending the way you'd expect. —*Ron Wynn, AMG*

Virgin Beauty / 1988 / Portrait 44301

Steve Coleman

b. Sep. 20, 1956, Chicago, IL
Sax, composer / M-Base
Alto saxophonist and composer Steve Coleman is a Brooklyn-based theorist whose ideas about merging jazz, funk, reggae, and R&B into a seamless mix lead some to sing his praises and others to proclaim him a charlatan. Coleman has talked for years about a multiple musical approach (M-Base), and his Five Elements work includes many top players from the current generation. His own playing, while rooted in funk and blues, is also solidly in the hard-bop tradition, something that's more evident when he makes guest appearances. —*Ron Wynn*

Motherland Pulse / Mar. 1985 / JMT 834401
This shows the jazz side of Coleman. W/ Geri Allen (p), Lonnie Plaxico (b), Graham Haynes (tpt). —*Michael Erlewine*

On the Edge of Tomorrow / Jan. 1986+Feb. 1986 / JMT 834405
Modern soul music. This is real contemporary funk, most of it danceable. W/ Geri Allen (synth) and Cassandra Wilson (v). —*Michael Erlewine*

★ **World Expansion** / Nov. 1986 / JMT 834410
W/ Geri Allen (k), Robin Eubanks (tb). Not his jazziest release, but a lot of good clean funk. —*Michael Erlewine*

Rhythm People (The Resurrection of Creative Black / Nov. 1990 / Novus 3092
Coleman & the Five Elements. *Rhythm People (the Resurrection of Creative Black Civilization.* Funky, creative improvisations along the lines of Ornette Coleman's harmolodic music. W/ Dave Holland (b), Robin Eubanks (tbn). —*Michael Erlewine*

Johnny Coles (John Coles)

b. Jul. 3, 1926, Trenton, NJ
Trumpet, flugelhorn / Hard bop
Trumpeter and flugelhorn player Johnny Coles is a mostly self-taught, sparing stylist who's always eschewed high-note antics or bending, twisting maneuvers. His forte is squeezing the most into a few notes, reminiscent of Miles Davis. He has worked with Philly Joe Jones, James Moody, Gil Evans, George Coleman, Herbie Hancock, Ray Charles, Charles Mingus, and Duke Ellington. The impressive list displays his ability to fit into a large orchestra or a tight, small combo. Very few of his own albums are available. —*Ron Wynn*

○ **Warm Sound, The** / Apr. 13, 1961 / Epic 16015

★ **Little Johnny** / Aug. 9, 1963 / Blue Note 4144
The best of this hard-bop trumpeter, w/ Leo Wright (as) and Joe Henderson (sax). —*David Szatmary*

Buddy Collette (William Marcell Collette)

b. Aug. 6, 1921, Los Angeles, CA
Sax, clarinet, flute, composer / Bop, cool
An excellent jazz flutist, Buddy Collette helped popularize that instrument, though he also displayed fine skills on other saxophones. Collette worked with Les Hite in the early '40s, before joining the Navy and leading a dance band during World War II. Lucky Thompson, Edgar Hayes, Louis Jordan, Benny Carter, Gerald Wilson, and Charles Mingus were some of the musicians Collette played and recorded with in the late '40s. He had several radio and television dates in the '50s, before gaining prominence for his playing in Chico Hamilton's mid-'50s quintet. He's led various groups and recorded several albums featuring primarily his compositions. Collette's prolific career also included a period of extensive film scoring and soundtracks, playing with Stan Kenton's Neophonic Orchestra, traveling to Japan with Benny Carter, and cofounding and serving as president of Legend Records. A collection of Collette compositions was published in 1985, and three years later he recorded with James Newton and

Geri Allen. Contemporary, Soul Note, Specialty, ABC/Paramount, Dootone, and Legend are among the labels that have issued Collette recordings. —*Ron Wynn*

★ **Man of Many Parts** / Feb. 13, 1956-Apr. 17, 1956 / Contemporary 239
This is material from three 1956 sessions that made up Buddy Collette's first LP as a leader and seemed designed to display his multiinstrumental approach. —*Bob Rusch, Cadence*

Alice Coltrane

b. Aug. 27, 1937, Detroit, MI
Piano, vibes, harp, organ / Early free
A pianist, vibist, and harpist, the former Alice McLeod incurred the wrath of some jazz fans when she replaced pianist McCoy Tyner in her husband John Coltrane's famous group. Some claimed she influenced her husband to disband the group, but that assessment doesn't carry much historical weight as it's more likely that Coltrane's musical direction and decisions were responsible. They were married in 1966. Her background was as a member of the Terry Gibbs Quartet, plus backing vibist Terry Pollard. She and drummer Rashied Ali changed the sound and scope of Coltrane's band, shifting the front line focus onto Coltrane's and Pharoah Sanders's energized dialogs. After Coltrane's death, she led bands in the late '60s and the '70s. Her ethereal harp playing was the most striking part of her repertoire. —*Ron Wynn*

★ **Ptah the El Daoud** / Jan. 26, 1970 / Impulse 9196
Alice Coltrane's album *Ptah the El Daoud* was a portrait of this woman's deep spiritual nature, in addition to her fine talents as a musician. Coltrane, who said that Bud Powell was her biggest influence, created a style of playing that combined the quick, melodic, bop-rooted (in the tradition of Powell) phrasings of her right hand in conjunction with a uniscale, broad spectrum, flowing sound of her left, a style obviously influenced by her close association with John Coltrane. Her album featured four of her compositions, three of which included Pharoah Sanders and Joe Henderson (tenor sax, flute). In addition, Ron Carter on bass and Ben Riley on drums were featured throughout the album. —*Robert Rouda, Coda*

○ **Universal Consciousness** / Apr. 6, 1971-Jun. 19, 1971 / Impulse 9210

John Coltrane (John William Coltrane)

b. Sep. 23, 1926, Hamlet, NC, **d.** Jul. 17, 1967, New York, NY
Tenor sax, soprano sax, composer, bandleader / Bop, hard bop, postbop
Few musicians of the postbebop era have enjoyed such fame and endured such controversy as John William Coltrane, the major saxophone stylist of an age when the saxophone reigned supreme. During the late '40s and early '50s he developed his urgent tenor style with the rhythm & blues bands of Eddie "Cleanhead" Vinson and Earl Bostic, as well as jazz heavyweights Dizzy Gillespie (where he made his recording debut, on alto), and Johnny Hodges. Like all young players of his generation, Coltrane profited from the advances of Charlie Parker, but he showed little direct influence of Bird in his mature style—this is an important difference between his playing and that of his major contemporary (and friendly rival) Sonny Rollins. It was in the acclaimed Miles Davis Quintet of 1955 that "Trane" really came into his own as a pure-toned sideman and independent, often brash soloist. Soon afterward he became a sought-after session participant and, inevitably, a leader in his own right, featured on dozens of recordings for the leading jazz labels Prestige and Blue Note during the last half of the '50s. He worked periodically with Davis up through 1960, perfecting his cascading "sheets of sound" technique and exploring the modal structures of pieces like Miles's classic "So What" as a foundation for future innovations. During this period he also honed his chops with three of the most challenging and idiosyncratic pianists of the day, Thelonious Monk, Mal Waldron, and Cecil Taylor, and threw down the gauntlet in good-natured "cutting contests" with saxophone stars Johnny Griffin, Hank Mobley, Sonny Rollins, and others. Besides being a top-notch technician and superb at ballads, Coltrane was always seeking new levels of expression, practicing obsessively and listening attentively to the insurgent efforts of the new jazzmen. Around 1960 he was associating with Los Angeles renegades

Ornette Coleman, Don Cherry, and Eric Dolphy, and his final recordings with Davis demonstrate, in lengthy volcanic phrases, that Coltrane had moved beyond the hard bop conventions he had helped to establish a few short years before. At the beginning of the most turbulent decade in jazz, Coltrane was winning *Down Beat* polls and alienating conservative critics at the same time; he had also begun assembling the quartet that accompanied him throughout the first half of the '60s—pianist McCoy Tyner, bassist Jimmy Garrison, and drummer Elvin Jones.

On the Atlantic and Impulse labels, the classic Coltrane quartet ushered in a new era of musical freedom, typically along modal lines (although not as controlled and austere as Miles Davis) with dense, interwoven harmonic and rhythmic webs underpinning lengthy solo statements. These were the years featuring albums with side-long compositions, exotic Afrocentric themes, the introspective spirituality of *A Love Supreme*, the resurrection of the soprano sax as a lead instrument, and what many regard as the greatest performances of his productive and multifaceted career. Never content to rest on his laurels, Coltrane kept pushing on, recording with the newest of the New York revolutionaries and bringing some of them into his band, prompting the eventual departure of Tyner and Jones. Jimmy Garrison stayed with Coltrane as he pursued the emotive and often frenzied extremes of his final free-jazz phase, spurred on by saxophonist Pharoah Sanders, pianist Alice Coltrane (his second wife), and drummer Rashied Ali. The Coltrane-Ali duo album *Interstellar Space* indicated yet another new direction in Coltrane's unceasing development, but liver cancer overtook him soon afterward, and he died in July 1967. Ornette Coleman and Albert Ayler played at his funeral, and since that day, musicians of all persuasions have paid tribute to the diverse and significant achievements John Coltrane brought to the most volatile epoch of jazz. —*Myles Boisen*

○ **John Coltrane Plays for Lovers** / Oct. 26, 1956-Dec. 26, 1958 / Prestige 7426

○ **On a Misty Night** / Oct. 26, 1956 / Prestige 24084
This John Coltrane twofer was originally released as *Tenor Conclave* and *Mating Call* (the latter under Tadd Dameron's name). *On a Misty Night* was an uneven affair with the first record being relatively unsatisfying. Since the session was a standard "blowing date" the arrangements were minimal and most of the tunes were given over to straightahead blowing. . . . The Dameron date provided an unadorned look at the John Coltrane of the mid-'50s. And, as Andrew White's liner notes attested, one could hear a good example of Trane's "post-bebop lyricism" (on tenor). —*Carl Brauer, Cadence*

Dakar / Apr. 20, 1957 / Prestige 393
Releasing *Dakar* under tenor saxophonist John Coltrane's name was more of a marketing decision than a musical one. In point of fact, it could just as easily have been released under pianist Mal Waldron's name since he appeared on all the tracks and also wrote 5 of the 11 compositions. The album consists of reissues of three Prestige dates: the first six cuts were released as *Dakar*, Jimmy Heath's "C.T.A." was released under Art Taylor's name on *Taylor's Wailers* and was played by a quartet of Coltrane, Waldron, bassist Paul Chambers, and Taylor (drums); the final four tracks were released as *Interplay for 2 Trumpets and 2 Tenors.* —*Carl Brauer, Cadence*

☆ **Lush Life** / Aug. 16, 1957 / Prestige 131
Fine session in which Coltrane stripped away his usual surrounding sound and recorded in a trio format. He's backed only by bassist Earl May and drummer Art Taylor, working in the pianoless format championed by Sonny Rollins. The extra space seems to benefit him, as his solos on these cuts are emphatic and exuberant. —*Ron Wynn, AMG*

★ **Blue Train** / Sep. 15, 1957 / Blue Note 46095
A landmark album—stunning. This is Coltrane's only Blue Note recording as a leader, and he never made a better album in this particular hard-bop style. A must-hear for all jazz fans, Blue Train includes Coltrane's most impressive early composition, "Moment's Notice." With outstanding performances from sidemen Lee Morgan (tpt), Curtis Fuller (tb), and Kenny Drew (p). —*Michael Erlewine*

● **John Coltrane: The Prestige Recordings** / i. 1957-1958 / Prestige 4405
Coltrane was *the* major sax stylist in a decade when the tenor saxophone reigned supreme, and his 1955-1958 recordings for

Prestige live on as marvels of jazz invention . . . . The complete set of 31 albums he made as leader and sideman—that's 125 slices of jazz genius on 16 CDs. The Rudy Van Gelder studio recordings are warm and clear, simply state of the art. —*Myles Boisen, Roots & Rhythm*

☆ **Soultrane** / Feb. 7, 1958 / Prestige 021
Coltrane works with the Red Garland trio, a busy unit during this period. He tackles these standards with a quiet confidence, sometimes extending his solos, other times merely expanding the original melody. Garland was an excellent soloist on standards and ballads, while Paul Chambers on bass and drummer Art Taylor provided their own sterling counterpoint. —*Ron Wynn, AMG*

○ **Black Pearls** / May 23, 1958 / Prestige 352
W/ Donald Byrd (tpt), Red Garland (p), Paul Chambers (b), and Art Taylor (d). —*Michael Erlewine*

Bahia / Dec. 26, 1958 / Original Jazz Classics 415
Steady, often excellent hard blowing and blues date featuring Coltrane in his busiest recording period. He cut numerous sessions during the late '50s for Prestige to satisfy a commitment to the label and move to Atlantic. Most were done with the same rhythm section: pianist Red Garland, bassist Paul Chambers, and drummer Art Taylor. All were present here, plus trumpeter Wilbur Harden. —*Ron Wynn, AMG*

★ **Giant Steps** / May 4, 1959 / Atlantic 1311

○ **Art of John Coltrane: The Atlantic Years, The** / 1959-1961 / Atlantic 313
Good anthology collecting several good tracks from Coltrane's Atlantic period, among them the earliest "My Favorite Things" and other standards and originals. Though these songs weren't as transcendant as the Impulse period, they were an important indicator of future directions. —*Ron Wynn, AMG*

☆ **Avant Garde** / Jun. 20, 1960-Jul. 8, 1960 / Atlantic 90041
W/ Don Cherry (tpt). This meeting of the titans doesn't sound so "out" nowadays. Influenced by Ornette Coleman. —*Michael G. Nastos*

● **My Favorite Things** / Oct. 24-26, 1960 / Atlantic 1361
Classic early Coltrane. The title cut is most beautiful and contains unforgettable piano by McCoy Tyner. —*Michael Erlewine*

Coltrane Plays the Blues / Oct. 24, 1960 / Atlantic 1382
Single session. Great tunes like "Mr. Day" and "Mr. Knight". A much neglected, but important Coltrane album. —*Michael G. Nastos*

Coltrane's Sound / Oct. 24, 1960 / Atlantic 1419
Wonderful early-'60s date, with Coltrane playing standards and extending them, straining at times, other times just playing wondrous melodies. The quartet lineup was not yet in place, but McCoy Tyner on piano and Elvin Jones on drums were slowly locking into the Coltrane concept. Bassist Steve Davis did his best to assist things. —*Ron Wynn, AMG*

○ **Africa Brass Sessions—Vol. 1 & 2** / May 23, 1961+Jun. 7, 1961 / MCA 42231
This two-volume recording features the orchestral Coltrane. Important recordings, available on one CD. —*Michael G. Nastos*

☆ **Ole Coltrane** / May 25, 1961 / Atlantic 1373
When *Ole Coltrane* first came out in 1961, Eric Dolphy played under the pseudonym George Lane for contractual reasons. The reissue gets the names right in a session that featured Coltrane, Dolphy, Freddie Hubbard, McCoy Tyner, Reggie Workman, Art Davis, and Elvin Jones. The original had only three extended tunes, "Ole," "Dahomey Dance," and "Aisha." The reissue has a bonus. It is the lovely Billy Frazier tune "To Her Ladyship," which was called "Original Untitled Ballad" when first released on *The Coltrane Legacy.* —*Ken Franckling, Jazz Times*

○ **Africa Brass Sessions—Vol. 2** / Jun. 7, 1961 / Impulse 42
Alternate takes, previously unissued titles and some leftovers comprised this anthology featuring material from the early '60s. Coltrane was steadily heading toward the outside, playing with a searing intensity and probing fury that indicated he'd soon be moving beyond established musical frontiers. Eric Dolphy did the arrangements and conducted the orchestra on the main track. —*Ron Wynn, AMG*

○ **Other Village Vanguard Tapes** / Nov. 1-05, 1961 / Impulse 9325
Even if you have John Coltrane's *Live at the Village Vanguard* and *Impressions*, don't think that just because "Spiritual," "India,"

and "Chasin' the Trane" are on those recordings, there's no need to have these versions. You'd be making a big mistake for this is great Coltrane. This version of "Chasin' the Trane" can't match the *Live at the Village Vanguard* one for sheer exuberance and breathtaking intensity, but it does have a very good Eric Dolphy solo on alto between Trane's two sorties. —*Carl Brauer, Cadence*

★ **Live at the Village Vanguard** / Nov. 2-03, 1961 / MCA 39136
Coltrane's first eye-opening Vanguard release, parts of which featured him in ambitious, relentless songs with partner Eric Dolphy. The others are a superb rendition of "Softly, as in a Morning Sunrise," set up by McCoy Tyner's passionate piano solo, and the other is a furious version of "Impressions." —*Ron Wynn, AMG*

○ **Live in Stockholm (1961)** / Nov. 1961 / Charly 117

○ **European Impressions** / i. Nov. 1961 / Bandstand 1514

Ballads / 1961 / MCA 5885
Partly to counter the ridiculous accusation of being an "angry tenor" and partly for variety's sake, John Coltrane decided to stick to standard ballads for this album and, if anything, he was too respectful to the melodies. Trane's tone was frequently gorgeous here, easily the main joy of the album. —*Scott Yanow, Cadence*

○ **Coltrane** / i. Jun. 1962 / MCA 5883
Coltrane was a well-rounded set that is a perfect introduction to the classic quartet. The 14-minute "Out of This World" (penned by Harold Arlen and Johnny Mercer) got an intense improvisation that would have shocked its composers. "Soul Eyes" was one of Trane's most beautiful ballad performances, "The Inch Worm" was quite playful (especially for Coltrane), "Tunji" sounded dead serious in the same vein as "Alabama," and the boppish "Miles Mode" was such a strong tune that it is surprising how obscure it remains. —*Scott Yanow, Cadence*

○ **Paris Concert** / Nov. 17, 1962 / Pablo 2308-217
The John Coltrane quartet was formed in 1961, and its impact on jazz and popular music was immediate. Coltrane found in pianist McCoy Tyner, bassist Jimmy Garrrison, and drummer Elvin Jones musicians with the ability not only to play what he wanted but to nightly inspire and stimulate him in his search for musical nirvana. Although the quartet was in its infancy on these sessions, its emergence can be heard throughout the 26-minute performance of "Mr. P.C." Coltrane searches through the intervals and choruses and throughout his solo for alternative ways to express himself, while the Tyner-Garrison-Jones section keeps altering, reshaping, and evolving underneath. Some of Coltrane's Pablo output has been spotty, but here is one that is not in the least. —*Ron Wynn*

○ **Best of John Coltrane** / i. 1962 / Pablo 2405-417
Sessions done for the Pablo label, most of them featuring the great Coltrane quartet. McCoy Tyner on piano, Jimmy Garrison on bass, and Elvin Jones on drums were the ultimate rhythm section for Coltrane; they could provide dynamic support, each was a wonderful soloist, and they could interact with brillance. Not every Coltrane solo during this period was superb, but each one was compelling. —*Ron Wynn, AMG*

○ **Retrospective—Impulse** / i. 1962-1967 / GRP 119
A *John Coltrane Retrospective* is an admirable attempt to encapsulate the seemingly boundless scope of John Coltrane's creativity during his six years with Impulse! . . . Given that three CDs is barely enough space for a cursory survey of this historic body of work, producer Michael Cuscuna makes a well-constructed case for Coltrane as an artist who reconciled the various facets of his music with a voice of overriding power and clarity. . . . Cuscuna has made a detailed survey that retails at about $25, which should attract new and young listeners. And that's a worthy cause. —*Bill Shoemaker, Jazz Times*

○ **Bye Bye Blackbird** / 1962 / Pablo 681
In 1962, probably in Stockholm, the John Coltrane quartet offered these two concert performances. The quartet's complementary qualities had been long established by this time, and if McCoy Tyner was not quite the original he soon would become, his soloing was bright and ever mobile; Jimmy Garrison was big-toned, and the two provided the setting for the powerful interplay of Elvin Jones, whose drumming was especially combustible, and Coltrane. Coltrane's opening solo in "Blackbird" was one of his very finest middle-period performances, not for its modernity of

sound and harmony so much as for a rhythmic variety that seldom entered his playing after 1957. —*John Litweiler, Down Beat*

○ **European Tour, The** / 1962 / Pablo 2308-222
This is not the best available material by *the quartet*—but it is still inspirational, which, if you are not yet familiar with John Coltrane's power, might give you some idea of just how formidable Coltrane's artistry was and is. This has not become inspiring . . . years after it was recorded because the Coltrane mystique has grown and touched so many. This *was* inspiring at the time, as those fortunate enough to hear it during its own time can attest. And those hearing it now for the first time can share almost the same fortune, for this accurately represents what could have been any one of countless nights of average playing. —*Bob Rusch, Cadence*

☆ **John Coltrane and Johnny Hartman** / Mar. 7, 1963 / MCA 5661
This session featured six romantic ballads cradled by Johnny Hartman's silky deep baritone vocals, accompanied by the John Coltrane quartet. Trane revealed that he, too, knew how to read a lyric. —*Alan Bargebuhr, Cadence*

☆ **Impressions** / Apr. 29, 1963 / MCA 5887
A three-minute blues ("Up Against the Wall") and a pretty, but far from maudlin ballad ("After the Rain") balance out the two passionate Village Vanguard performances here by John Coltrane's group. While "India" was quite spiritual (and highlighted by Eric Dolphy's wonderful bass clarinet), the roaring version of "Impressions" displayed John Coltrane's ability to break through new musical boundaries. Antijazz indeed; this was the true spirit of jazz. —*Scott Yanow, Cadence*

○ **Live at Birdland** / Oct. 8, 1963 / MCA 33109

○ **Afro Blue Impressions** / Oct. 1963 / Pablo 101
Intensity was the keynote of this two-disc set recorded by Norman Granz in 1962 at Stockholm and Berlin. John Coltrane attacked the repertory with the kind of probing vigor characteristic of this period in his career. That vigor, however, was somewhat mellowed by a sense of joy coming from the saxophonist's pleasure at his audiences' warm reaction. Throughout the album one was impressed by the extraordinary chemistry of the Coltrane, McCoy Tyner, Jimmy Garrison, and Elvin Jones unit. In the history of jazz, this was one of the landmark groups. Especially noteworthy here were the energizing dialogues between Trane and Jones. Unquestionably, Jones was the sparkplug that constantly fired Coltrane's pistons. —*Chuck Berg, Down Beat*

○ **Crescent** / Apr. 27, 1964+Jun. 1, 1964 / MCA 5889
Crescent finds the classic John Coltrane quartet in prime form in 1964, although none of the five originals they played caught on as standards. There was not enough Coltrane on this album for it to be an essential acquisition. Much of "Lonnie's Lament" was a bass solo (Jimmy Garrison's were always an acquired taste) and "The Drum Thing" was a feature for Elvin Jones. Much more memorable were the intense "Crescent," the spiritual "Wise One" (foreshadowing the upcoming *Love Supreme*) and the happy, straightfoward "Bessie's Blues." —*Scott Yanow, Cadence*

★ **Love Supreme, A** / Dec. 9, 1964 / MCA 5660
A most powerful statement. His most acclaimed and definitive recording. —*Michael G. Nastos*

○ **Selflessness** / i. 1965 / Impulse 9161
I have no hestitations about hailing the 1963 Newport sides from the *Selflessness* album as two further masterpieces of the John Coltrane quartet era. Certainly, "My Favorite Things" ranked with Coltrane's best recordings of the time, and it is to me the definitive version of this standard. . . . "I Want to Talk about You" is a deeply moved version, played with obvious affection and dedication to the thought of the line, culminating in a spread-winged a cappella cadenza of total personal lyricism, of transferring the musician's love to a single linear utterance. —*Barry Tepperman, Coda*

● **Ascension** / Jun. 28, 1965 / Impulse 95

☆ **Major Works of John Coltrane, The** / Jun. 1965-Oct. 1965 / GRP 113
There is no question that these works are major in length. The two versions of "Ascension" run about 40 minutes each and "Om" runs 29 minutes. Beyond a doubt, they had major impact on the avant-garde of the free jazz movement of the 1960s. Whether they were among John Coltrane's major contributions will be a function of the listener's appreciation of the music made during

the final years of the saxophonist's search. . . . These examples remain as exhibition pieces from the late career of a man driven to perpetually seek. However little they may be listened to, they cannot be disregarded because John Coltrane was one of the most important musicians of the second half of the century. —*Doug Ramsey, Jazz Times*

New Thing at Newport / Jul. 2, 1965 / GRP 105
One of the earliest examples of Coltrane moving in a newer, freer direction. Archie Shepp (sax) made an immediate impression. —*Michael G. Nastos*

○ **Live in Paris** / Jul. 1965 / Charly 87

Om / Oct. 1, 1965 / MCA 39118
Perhaps Coltrane's only major release of questionable quality, this was reportedly recorded on his first (and only) LSD trip. Featuring screechy playing and moaning vocals, this is for true believers and historical interest only. —*David Nelson McCarthy*

Meditations / Nov. 23, 1965 / MCA 39139
A perfect companion to *A Love Supreme*. As powerful and pure in spiritual content and intent. Long, extended, embellished passages in hymnlike prayer session. W/ Pharoah Sanders (ts), Elvin Jones (d), Rashied Ali (d), McCoy Tyner (p), and Jimmy Garrison (b). —*Michael G. Nastos*

○ **Live in Antibes (1965)** / i. 1965 / France's Concert 119
This session was a remarkable, often stormy and disquieting transitional one. The classic John Coltrane quartet was clearly in its final days, and you can hear Coltrane on such songs as "Impressions," "Blue Waltz," and "Afro Blue" searching for new things to say, starting, breaking, and restarting statements and expressing frustration in midsolo. He also played many incredible passages on soprano and tenor, but the most instructive cut was the version of "My Favorite Things," one of the least smooth and turbulent renditions available on record. McCoy Tyner's piano forays were equally arresting and uneven, while the bass-drums interplay of Jimmy Garrison and Elvin Jones remained unified and stimulating. Despite occasional engineering problems and even with the tension, this was a pivotal date in the Coltrane legacy. It's one fans should listen to closely; they can hear the shattering of the quartet's musical bonds. —*Ron Wynn*

○ **Live at the Village Vanguard Again!** / May 28, 1966 / Impulse 9124
Live. Shattering, piercing, and unforgettable. Coltrane and Sanders (ts) blast off to places unforeseen. —*Michael G. Nastos*

○ **Concert in Japan** / Jul. 22, 1966 / Impulse 9246
Concert in Japan didn't unveil any new facets of John Coltrane's last musical phase, except for the fact that on at least one occasion both he and Pharoah Sanders played the Yamaha saxophone, whatever that is. But it was another example, and a rather beautiful one, of the kind of searing, soaring, fiercely spiritual sounds he was putting out at this point in his life. Late period Trane is not everybody's trip, but anyone who has taken the time to make the trip knows how rewarding it can be. —*Peter Keepnews, Down Beat*

Expression / Feb. 15, 1967-Mar. 1967 / Impulse 9120
His final recording session. Features more flute than any other of his recordings. —*Michael G. Nastos*

● **Interstellar Space** / Feb. 22, 1967 / GRP 110
Posthumous, free-wheeling date by Coltrane with drummer Rashied Ali in series of slashing, complimentary, and explosive duets. Coltrane was now playing more rhythms than anything else, having leaped beyond notions of chord changes, structure, and melody. Ali sometimes supported him, sometimes challenged him, and held things together as best he could. —*Ron Wynn, AMG*

○ **Last Giant: Anthology** / i. Jun. 15, 1993 / Rhino
Rhino's Jazz Gallery series is highlighted by the release of *The Last Giant: The John Coltrane Anthology*, a 19-track, two-CD set concentrating on his Atlantic recordings, including four previously unreleased performances. The set is housed in a clothbound slipcase with an extensive booklet with new essays from Joel Dorn and Amiri Baraka and unreleased photos. All in all, *The Last Giant* is a very beautiful set. —*AMG*

Eddie Condon (Albert Edwin Condon)
b. Nov. 16, 1905, Goodland, IN, d. Aug. 4, 1973, New York, NY
Banjo, guitar / Dixieland

Eddie Condon was a self-taught musician, first on ukelele, then on banjo and guitar. Condon helped define what is often referred to as "classic Chicago style" jazz in the McKenzie-Condon Chicagoans, a recording group cofounded with Red McKenzie in 1927. Moving to New York in 1929, he became close with several musicians with whom he maintained long associations, including Max Kaminsky, Jack Teagarden, Sid Catlett, Pee Wee Russell, and Bud Freeman. In 1938 he helped to launch Milt Gabler's Commodore label with a series of small-band recordings. He worked during the '40s with such players as George Wettling, Billy Butterfield, and Bobby Hackett, using them at various gigs around New York and on the famous Town Hall concerts, which were broadcast to servicemen in World War II. Condon also started his own nightclub in the Village in 1945, where he continued to promote integration of the bandstand—an idea to which he was fully committed. He continued to perform, albeit infrequently, at Condon's in the '50s and also made tours to Europe and the Orient 1957-1964.

As a promoter and entrepreneur of small-band jazz, he effectively used his music and wit to expand appreciation of the music he loved. In addition to the groups he led, Condon performed as a sideman with a wide array of jazz talents, including Fats Waller, Artie Shaw, Red Nichols, Miff Mole, and Wild Bill Davison. —*Bruce Boyd Raeburn*

★ **In Japan** / Mar. 1964-Apr. 1964 / Chiaroscuro 154
Trumpeter Buck Clayton appeared in an active role on *Eddie Condon in Japan*, a concert performance recorded in 1964. This was pure Condon. Clarinetist Pee Wee Russell, saxophonist Bud Freeman, Dick Cary, Cliff Leeman, and trombonist Vic Dickenson joined Clayton for some delightful sparring. It was particularly good to hear Clayton in top form. The sound was excellent concert-hall quality. —*John Mcdonough, Down Beat*

★ **Commodore Years, The** / i. Mar. 1974 / Atlantic 2309
The first two sides of this two-record set offered some of the best recorded evidence available of the mature white Chicago style at a period when it had fully emerged from its New Orleans roots and had not yet been perverted into that middle-aged, middle-brow, supreme mediocrity known as Dixieland. But the real musical treasure was unearthed on the second disk of this two-record set. It featured Bud Freeman's lithe but meaty tenor accompanied only by piano and drums—a setting untypically intimate for the period (1938). On these tracks, Freeman proved to be not only one of the premier saxophone stylists of his day, but, interestingly, a precursor of saxophone styles to come. These two albums were important as artifacts and as pure music. They were a throwback to a time when the playing of jazz was first and foremost a fun thing to do. The important thing to keep in mind is that the records were a delight. —*Peter Keepnews, Down Beat*

○ **Real Sound of Jazz, The** / i. Mar. 1990 / Pumpkin 116

○ **Jazzlore: That Toddlin' Town—Chicago Jazz Revisited—Vol. 23** / Atlantic 90461

○ **Town Hall Concerts—Vol. 5** / Jazzology 10

○ **Town Hall Concerts—Vol. 1** / Jazzology 1001
May 27, 1944, marked the first of a year-long series of weekly concerts at Town Hall that were transcribed onto 16-inch discs by the Armed Forces Radio Service and sent over the world for broadcast to servicemen. . . . As collectors of the AFRS series know, the half-hour concerts were a little short on playing time for a 16-inch disc, and usually another title from another concert was tacked on after Fred Robbins's closing announcements and the fadeout. In this case it was "Ballin' the Jack," with Grauso on drums, which itself faded out. This title and the preceding blues jam opened side two of this release; the remainder of the side was part of the 6/24/44 concert, consisting of "I've Found a New Baby". . . . The transfer was decent, if a little boomy, and near true pitch. —*Wayne Jones, Coda*

○ **Town Hall Concerts—Vol. 2** / Jazzology 1003

○ **Town Hall Concerts—Vol. 3** / Jazzology 6

○ **Town Hall Concerts—Vol. 4** / Jazzology 8

○ **Ballin' the Jack** / Commodore 7015
Eddie Condon & Band. Set-piece Condon, as old and conservative as ever. —*Michael G. Nastos*

Chris Connor
b. Nov. 8, 1927, Kansas City, MO

Vocals / Ballads & blues, cool
Chris Connor was the prime "torch" singer of the '50s. She first studied clarinet but began singing at the University of Missouri in a band led by Bob Brookmeyer. She was a member of Claude Thornhill's vocal quintet The Snowflakes before going solo. Later, she was in the Kenton big band, where she became known for a cool, tantalizing style that had its romantic and alluring side but was far from bawdy or bluesy. Connor was a star in the '50s and '60s, made a comeback in the late '70s, and remained active through the '80s. *—Ron Wynn*

★ **Cocktails and Dusk** / Apr. 1955 / Bethlehem 6010
Fine album. Unsung vocalist of the '50s. Lots of Cole Porter, with J.J. & Kai (tb), Ralph Sharon (p), Matt Hiaton (b). *—Michael G. Nastos*

○ **Sings Gershwin** / Feb. 7, 1957-May 1, 1957 / Atlantic 601
This is a double CD, with 34 tracks and ten different instrumental groupings, in which she was backed by everything from trios to a large band in sessions recorded between 1957 and 1961. She was smokey when the song warranted it and kicked things up a few notches when the mood was right, particularly when backed by Maynard Ferguson's hot band on the final two tracks, "Strike Up the Band" and "Summertime." *—Ken Franckling, Jazz Times*

★ **Chris Craft** / Apr. 8, 1958+May 23, 1958 / Atlantic 1290

★ **Portrait of Chris, A** / Dec. 5, 1960-Jan. 23, 1961 / Atlantic 8049

Bill Connors (William A. Connors)

b. Sep. 24, 1949, Los Angeles, CA
Guitar / Early jazz rock, modern creative
Guitarist Bill Connors has been successful in jazz-rock, fusion, instrumental pop, free, and more conventional jazz settings. He played electric with Mike Nock and Steve Swallow in San Francisco during the early '70s and toured and recorded with Return to Forever in 1973 and 1974. Later came a solo ECM date, a session with Stanley Clarke, and recordings with Gary Peacock, Jan Garbarek, and Jack DeJohnette later in the '70s. He alternated between acoustic and electric and then played primarily electric as a member of Jan Garbarek's band in the '80s, while also making a straight rock release in the mid-'80s. *—Ron Wynn and Paul Kohler*

● **Theme to the Guardian** / Nov. 1974 / ECM 829387
An album of terrific solo acoustic guitar from a former member of Return to Forever. *—Paul Kohler*

☆ **Swimming with a Hole in My Body** / Aug. 1979 / ECM 1158
Brilliant solo acoustic guitar with some overdubs. Required listening. *—Paul Kohler*

☆ **Step It!** / Jun. 12, 1984-Oct. 15, 1984 / Pathfinder 8503
Superb instrumental fusion album with Connors on electric guitar. Strong compositions. A must! *—Paul Kohler*

Junior Cook (Herman Cook)

b. Jul. 22, 1934, Pensacola, FL, d. Feb. 4, 1992
Tenor sax / Hard bop
Junior Cook's playing has been steady, usually reliable, and enjoyable, though he wasn't a groundbreaking soloist or top composer. Cook spent ten years with two groups, the Horace Silver and Blue Mitchell quintets, which intermingled several members. Later he co-led two fine '70s groups with Louis Hayes and Bill Hardman. He's the kind of forthright jazz musician who has never been well known outside the jazz workd, yet is invaluable. *—Ron Wynn*

○ **Stablemates** / i. Nov. 1977 / Affinity 766

★ **Somethin's Cookin'** / 1982 / Muse 5470
Something's Cookin' represents tenor saxophonist Junior Cook at his prime, a period that lasted for his entire career. Indeed, consistency marked Cook's work. He was, right up through his last session, a soulful storyteller. He fills every phrase with meaning and emotion, especially on the ballad "Detour Ahead." *—David Dupont, Cadence*

○ **Place to Be, The** / Nov. 1988 / Steeple Chase 31240

○ **On a Misty Night** / i. Jun. 1989 / Steeple Chase 31266

Jerome Cooper (Jerome D. Cooper)

b. Dec. 14, 1946, Chicago, Il
Percussion / Modern creative

A progressive percussionist and former Revolutionary Ensemble member, Cooper is a tour de force solo performer. *—Michael G. Nastos*

★ **Unpredictability of Predictability** / Jul. 6, 1979 / About Time 1002
Jerome Cooper's concert was not the standard virtuoso percussion display (of which he is certainly capable) but a series of speculative compositional situations for a one-man band. Some of them worked and some didn't; that is, while all of them realized their ambitions, some of them were more interesting to contemplate than they were to hear. *—Francis Davis, Cadence*

Chick Corea (Armando Anthony Corea)

b. Jun. 12, 1941, Chelsea, MA
Electric piano, acoustic piano / Postbop, early free, Latin-jazz, early jazz rock
An electric and acoustic pianist, composer, and bandleader, Corea played free jazz and Latin-jazz early in his career. He carved his identity as a premier fusion innovator with the group Return to Forever. He plays lovely acoustic piano when the mood strikes. Corea's a melodic genius, though some of his later fusion is not as potent. His work is, in general, of good quality. He's a true hero of improvised-based music, and his work provides a good starting point for the novice. *—Michael G. Nastos*

○ **Tones for Joan's Bones** / Nov. 30, 1966-Dec. 1, 1966 / Atlantic 50302
Youthful Corea makes quick splash. This is an extremely rare album. *—Ron Wynn*

★ **Now He Sings, Now He Sobs** / Feb. 26, 1968 / Blue Note 90055
Now He Sings, Now He Sobs summarized Corea's fresh melodic and harmonic vocabulary for an entire generation of jazz musicians. Young jazz pianists learned these solos note-for-note. The album soon became a staple in the record collections of musicians everywhere. The Miroslav Vitous bass solos were greeted as the most impressive since Scott LaFaro's recordings with Bill Evans in 1961. And this album offers the best Roy Haynes drumming on record. Corea sparkles as he effortlessly darts through his compositional and improvisational innovations at high speed atop the crisp, responsive sounds of Haynes and facile bass of Vitous. *—Mark C. Gridley*

○ **Chick Corea** / Mar. 14, 1968-Apr. 7, 1970 / Blue Note 39542
This 2-album set contains cuts from four sessions: two early sessions in 1968 and 1969, and tracks from two sessions that resulted in the album *Song of Singing.* *—AMG*

○ **Is** / Jun. 30, 1969 / Solid State 18055
Side one of *Is* was the title track. In the beginning there was peace (?) with tubular bells, finger cymbals, clacking bits of wood, gongs, bass lines going "boing" with flute overlays, and on into loud, noisy chaos.... The quartet without the horns was the highlight of the record ... Chick Corea (piano), David Holland (bass), and drummer Jack DeJohnette (the Miles Davis rhythm section at the time) with the addition of Horace Arnold's percussion had a beautiful collective sound, and it was a great shame that Woody Shaw (trumpet) and Hubert Laws (flute) had to keep intruding on it. *—Bill Smith, Coda*

○ **Sundance** / 1969 / People 09

○ **Early Circle** / Apr. 3, 1970 / Blue Note 84465
Corea in his most experimental, outside period. He was part of the musically advanced group Circle with multiinstrumentalist Anthony Braxton, bassist Dave Holland, and drummer Barry Altschul. These sessions and others won critical acclaim but attracted little commercial attention. Corea also played vibes and marimba, Holland occasionally played guitar, and Altschul played some marimba along with drums. Braxton's arsenal included alto and soprano sax, clarinet, and contrabass clarinet. *—Ron Wynn, AMG*

★ **Paris Concert** / Feb. 21, 1971 / ECM 843163
This music was constantly changing, was concerned more at times with sound than melody, and strained at its restrictions. A good deal of this cooked—"Nefertitti" started off at breakneck speed. *—Richard B. Kamins, Cadence*

★ **Return to Forever** / Feb. 2-03, 1972 / ECM 811978
The first and by far the best and most appealing edition. Flara Purim sings wistfully; Stanley Clark dominates on bass; Corea is a sharp, creative pianist. *—Ron Wynn*

☆ **Light As a Feather** / Sep. 1972 / Polydor 827148

☆ **Crystal Silence** / Nov. 6, 1972 / ECM 831331
Debut on ECM with Corea (k). The first of many successful pairings of the two. —*Ron Wynn*

☆ **Inner Space** / i. 1974 / Atlantic 305
Formative dates from the late '60s reissued as a comprehensive CD anthology. Hubert Laws (fl) at his most ambitious. Woody Shaw (tpt), Joe Farrell (ts), and Ron Carter (b) are also on hand. —*Ron Wynn*

Where Have I Known You Before / Jul. 1974-Aug. 1974 / PolyGram 825206
Crackling electric Return to Forever. Includes one killer composition, but marks the beginning of the end if you are looking for a jazz influence.. —*Ron Wynn*

☆ **Romantic Warrior** / Feb. 1976 / Columbia 34076

○ **Chick Corea and Gary Burton in Concert** / i. Oct. 23+25, 1978 / ECM 821415

○ **3 Quartets** / i. 1981 / Warner Brothers 3552
The Quartets featured dark, pensive lines—more functional than memorable—and exploited nuances of nearly subliminal orchestration and texture: etudes exploring the possibilities of varied instrumental groupings, shadings, and densities rather than the pure song form. —*Jon Balleras, Down Beat*

● **Trio Music—Live in Europe** / Sep. 1984 / ECM 827769
An expert trio date that includes impeccable ensemble interaction and solos from Corea, Miroslav Vitous (b), and Roy Haynes (d). —*Ron Wynn*

○ **Light Years** / 1987 / GRP 9546

○ **Eye of the Beholder** / 1988 / GRP 9564
Corea and his band venture into new territory this time around. Much of this recording sounds as if it could be used with motion pictures. Beautiful soundscapes created by Corea's synthesizers and piano backed by his very capable band makes this album the band's finest work. Recommended. —*Paul Kohler*

Larry Coryell

b. Apr. 2, 1943, Galveston, TX
Guitar / Early jazz rock, world fusion
A former journalism student at the University of Washington, guitarist Larry Coryell has a long background in rock and jazz. He was on the ground floor of the jazz-rock tradition with the Gary Burton Quartet and the band Free Spirits, and his solos with Chico Hamilton in 1965 suggested the coming of a new era. Corea later played in the jazz-rock and fusion groups Foreplay and Eleventh House. Coryell's been an excellent improviser on acoustic and electric guitar and has made outstanding jazz, Latin, and classical releases.—*Ron Wynn*

● **Essential Larry Coryell** / i. 1968-1975 / Vanguard 75-76

○ **Basics (1968-1969)** / 1968-1969 / Vanguard 79375

★ **Barefoot Boy** / 1971 / Philips 6369407
Larry Coryell's band on this recording might be considered to have two main parts. As one section, we had three drummer-percussionists—Roy Haynes, Lawrence Killian, and Harry Wilkinson—locked into a rhythm machine of fantastic richness and drive, one that you would do well to make it your business to hear. On the other hand, we had two horns and Coryell (guitar) and Steve Marcus (tenor and soprano sax). Both hornmen are primarily riff players—musicians who mostly function in a strongly delineated rhythmic framework, developing the substance of their solos as embellishments of increasing elegance on and around basically simple ideas. —*Barry Tepperman, Coda*

☆ **Just Like Being Born** / 1984 / Flying Fish 337
With Brian Keane (g). Soothing acoustic guitar duets by two excellent players. —*Paul Kohler*

○ **Larry Coryell—Don Lanphere** / i. 1990 / Hep 2048

Eddie Costa (Edwin James Costa)

b. Aug. 14, 1930, Atlas, PA, d. Jul. 28, 1962, New York, NY
Vibes, piano / Bop
Vibist and pianist Eddie Costa was among the first to pursue an aggressively percussive piano style. He was known for using the lower half of the keyboard for his rippling lines. After playing with Joe Venuti in 1949, he gained fame through dates with Kai

Winding and finally Tal Farlow and Woody Herman in the '50s, before forming his own trio. Costa recorded with Sal Salvador and was a 1957 Down Beat Poll winner on vibes and piano. His trio with Henry Grimes and Paul Motian were among the more intriguing of the late '50s trios, and he recorded for Jubilee, Mode, and Coral. Costa's career ended when he was killed in a 1962 car crash.—*Ron Wynnan*

★ **Quintet** / Jul. 13, 1958 / Mode 118
A classic bop session with Art Farmer (tpt) and Phil Woods (as). —*David Szatmary*

Curtis Counce (Curtis Lee Counce)

b. Jan. 23, 1926, Kansas City, MO, d. Jul. 31, 1963, Los Angeles, CA
Bass / Hard bop
Curtis Counce was a first-rate accompanist and great proponent of the "walking" bass style—a floating, yet propulsive way of articulating and phrasing notes to create the effect of the bassline walking along underneath the soloist and the other players. Counce worked with many of the best West Coast players of the '50s, among them Wardell Gray and Shorty Rogers; led some fine groups; and also did a lot of film work and private teaching.—*Ron Wynn*

○ **Sonority** / Jan. 1956 / Contemporary 7655
Curtis Counce Group. A relaxed, yet vibrant date, with Harold Land (ts) and Carl Perkins (p) as standouts. —*Ron Wynn*

★ **Landslide** / Oct. 8+15, 1956 / Contemporary 606
Curtis Counce Group. This is the same lineup as *Sonority*, and the music swings just as hard. —*Ron Wynn*

○ **Counceltation—Vol. 1** / Oct. 15, 1956 / Contemporary 1007539

○ **Counceltation—Vol. 2** / Apr. 15, 1957-Sep. 3, 1957 / Contemporary 7539
This second volume of the three recorded by the Curtis Counce quintet in 1956, '57 and early '58 appeared as a reissue, although the packaging was different from that of the original release, which was known as *You Get More Bounce with Curtis Counce*. It was a welcome reminder of what a tight and joyous group it was, and what losses to the music were the early deaths of bassist Counce and the excellent pianist Carl Perkins. —*Doug Ramsey, Down Beat*

☆ **Carl's Blues** / Aug. 29, 1957-Jan. 6, 1968 / Contemporary 423
The Curtis Counce (bass) group was a working group when they recorded *Carl's Blues*. This album, with its cool-hot late night ambiance was a sleeper when it was first released and remains so years later. —*Bob Rusch, Cadence*

Stanley Cowell (Stanley A. Cowell)

b. May 5, 1941, Toledo, OH
Piano, composer / Bop, hard bop
Originally from Toledo, Ohio, Stanley Cowell was classically trained in piano at the University of Michigan, becoming a leader in jazz and creative improvised music. An outstanding composer and arranger, he also worked with the Heath Brothers. Cowell sometimes leads piano-choir ensembles but mostly plays in a trio or solo format. He's noted for pretty and probing melodies and is one of the best overall pianists.—*Michael G. Nastos*

○ **Blues for the Viet Cong** / Jun. 5, 1969 / Freedom 41032
This album was recorded in London during 1969, when Stanley Cowell was working with Music, Inc. This was a trio perfectly fit to reflect the style of their leader, a rolling, gently fierce, modal keyboard attack, a methodical, schooled approach that worked well with artists as varied as Max Roach and Marion Brown. The material here was decidely *not* avant-garde, postdating a brief period with the likes of Brown and Joseph Jarman of the AACM. As always, the right hand was most active, rocking and swinging on "Departure," reverting to block-chording near the end as the ferocious bass drums of Jimmy Hopps ushered the theme out. The continuous and plentiful examples of dexterous ability on both sides attested to the high standards of quality. —*Arnold Shaw, Down Beat*

★ **Back to the Beautiful** / Jul. 1989 / Concord Jazz 4398
A good session, with Steve Coleman (reeds) in an unusual mainstream role. —*Ron Wynn*

Hank Crawford (Bennie Ross (Jr) Crawford)

b. Dec. 21, 1934, Memphis, TN

Alto sax, baritone sax, piano, composer / Blues & jazz, soul jazz
Alto and baritone saxophonist, pianist, and composer Hank Crawford's initial fame came as a member of the Ray Charles groups of the late '50s. He ascended through the ranks to musical director before leaving in 1963. Blues-drenched, soulful jazz has been the Memphis-born Crawford's specialty ever since. His Atlantic albums were generally great, his CTI '70s sessions primarily commercial fusion. He's returned to more blues and conventional jazz in the late '70s, '80s, and '90s on Milestone. —*Ron Wynn*

★ **After Hours** / 1965-Jan. 14, 1966 / Atlantic 82364
Soul-jazz and blues with ensembles of varying size from trio up to octet. Detroiters Ali Jackson and Wendell Harrison appear, as well as stalwarts Howard Johnson, Wilbert Hogan, and Joe Dukes (drums), and John Hunt and Fielder Floyd (trumpet). Four standards including the title track. Originals by Bennie Golson, Ben Tucker, Stanley Turrentine, and the leader. —*Michael G. Nastos*

○ **Double Cross** / Nov. 20, 1967 / Atlantic 1503

Marilyn Crispell

b. Mar. 30, 1947, Philadelphia, PA
Piano / Modern creative
Marilyn Crispell is a dynamic pianist and leader who's emerged as an exciting personality and someone to watch in '90s. She hasn't attained the profile of a Geri Allen due to recording for independent labels, but her solos are propulsive and distinctive, and she's held her own working with dominating drummers like Andrew Cyrille. —*Ron Wynn*

○ **Spirit Music** / May 15, 1981+Jan. 13, 1982 / Cadence 1015
Pianist Marilyn Crispell's music takes some getting used to. It's experimental in the now-familiar manner of players like Cecil Taylor and Anthony Braxton. Crispell plays as if her life depended on it. On *Spirit Music* (recorded live) the group headed toward a trademark sound, but things didn't quite jell; ragged spots broke up the flow. One strong point that became more apparent after repeated hearings was Crispell's ability to shape a piece with well-defined contours. "ABC," dedicated to Anthony Braxton, was the most impressive example of this control. Clocking in at 23 minutes, it generated—and sustained—the kind of lunatic energy you'd find in a tune by Carla Bley. The performances were never short on excitement. The intensity was ultimately overpowering. —*Elaine Guregian, Down Beat*

● **Concert in Berlin, A** / Jul. 2, 1983 / Free Music 46
Pianist Marilyn Crispell was close to the Cecil Taylor model on *Live In Berlin,* recorded with violinist Billy Bang, drummer John Betsch, and bassist Peter Kowald. In place of the lean, contrapuntal style she favors elsewhere, her dissonant-and-percussive-as-ever playing here was thicker and more cluttered. —*Kevin Whitehead, Cadence*

○ **Live in Zurich** / Apr. 1989 / Leo 122
Crispell keeps cranking out furious, aggressive free dates for the European market. They're devoid of any devices now in vogue on the jazz circuit; no standards, electronics, hard bop, adult contemporary, strings, or fusion. If you enjoy hearing spirited dialogues between Crispell, bassist Reggie Workman, and drummer Paul Motian, this one's for you. —*Ron Wynn, AMG*

○ **Images** / i. Aug. 1991 / Music & Arts 634
The current piano favorite among the new generation of outside players, Crispell doesn't tone down the intensity until she concludes the session. Her approach, attack, tone, and phrasing have often been compared to her mentor Cecil Taylor, but she's not quite as percussive (no one is). However, this is as close as any living being can get to duplicating his energy and power. —*Ron Wynn, AMG*

Sonny Criss (William Criss)

b. Oct. 23, 1927, Memphis, TN, d. Nov. 19, 1977, Los Angeles, CA
Alto sax, soprano sax / Hard bop
Although alto saxophonist Sonny Criss was a devoted Charlie Parker disciple, he also developed a personalized style and sound that allowed him to do more than mirror Parker's influence. He moved from Memphis to the West Coast in the '40s and was a key figure in the California Black jazz scene of the '50s. He had a three-year gig with Buddy Rich in the '60s and spent time in Europe. During the '70s, Criss toured Europe again. Criss did

many dates for Prestige, Xanadu, Muse, and Impulse. Wardell Gray, Sonny Clark, Billy Eckstine, Gerald Wilson, Parker, Stan Kenton, Howard Rumsey's Lighthouse All-Stars, and Buddy Rich were among the people and bands Criss played with during his career, which ended with his suicide in the late '70s.—*Ron Wynn*

● **Sonny Criss Plays Cole Porter** / 1956 / Imperial 9024
○ **Sonny Criss at the Crossroads** / Mar. 1959 / Peacock 91
○ **I'll Catch the Sun** / Jan. 20, 1969 / Prestige 7628
Torrid uptempo pieces and equally moving ballads from a topflight saxophonist who never got the credit he deserved while alive. Sonny Criss was as fine a hard bopper and blues-based alto player as anyone in his generation, and this quartet date was ample evidence. Hampton Hawes on piano, Monte Budwig on bass, and Shelly Manne made a capable, supportive rhythm section. —*Ron Wynn, AMG*

● **Saturday Morning** / Mar. 1, 1975 / Xanadu 105

Crusaders

b. , USA
Group / Blues & jazz, soul jazz, contemporary funk
Formerly the Jazz Crusaders, this combo was among the finest soul-jazz and populist bands of the '60s and '70s. Saxophonist-bassist Wilton Felder, keyboardist Joe Sample, trombonist Wayne Henderson, and drummer Stix Hooper (and early in their tenure saxophonist-flutist Hubert Laws) deftly mixed blues, funky instrumentals, pop covers, and originals into a style that was danceable and entertaining, but also had improvised segments that highlighted Felder's blues sound and Sample's keyboard skills. The longtime friends' chemistry made their Pacific Jazz LPs very successful, but they were often criticized for emphasizing more pop than jazz in their material. They dropped "Jazz" from their name in the early '70s, but kept making reliable, if less ambitious, music until Henderson's departure caused a change. He'd been a vital part of the core sound, and they never replaced his voice. Now the balance shifted to more heavily produced pop rather than bluesy, jazz-tinged fare. They enjoyed a huge hit with "Street Life" in the '80s, but when Hooper left the group was essentially finished, though Felder and Sample kept things going until the end of the decade with a parade of various contributors. —*Ron Wynn*

● **Freedom Sounds** / i. Apr. 1969 / Atlantic 1512
★ **I** / i. 1970 / Chisa
Their finest modern soul-jazz date. Wilton Felder burns on tenor, and the arrangements meld funk beats and jazz licks to maximum success. —*Ron Wynn*

☆ **Second Crusade** / i. 1972 / Chisa
○ **Golden Years, The** / i. 1992 / GRP 5007
Anthology containing several Crusaders' hits and representative songs from their greatest years. It focuses on their '70s records, which were both their most popular and finest. The group's sound began to decline after trombonist Wayne Henderson left and they deserted their patented formula that seamlessy mixed blues, R&B, funk, and soul-jazz. This set features them at their best. —*Ron Wynn, AMG*

☆ **Southern Comfort** / MCA 6016

Ronnie Cuber (Ronald Edward Cuber)

b. Dec. 25, 1941, New York, NY
Baritone sax / Hard bop, Latin-jazz
One of New York's busiest baritone sax session players in the '70s and '80s, Ronnie Cuber's equally versed in Latin-jazz and mainstream. Thick, booming sound and a knowledge of salsa and Latin styles made him a perennial favorite of Latin-jazz bandleaders. When not in the Latin groove, he cuts nice hard-bop and mainstream sessions. Cuber's played in bands led by George Benson, Slide Hampton, Maynard Ferguson, Lee Konitz, Nick Brignola, and Mickey Tucker among others, and also recorded with the Xanadu All-Stars. He's also led his own groups, and recorded for Xanadu, Fresh Sound, and Fantasy. Cuber issued his most recent release in 1994.—*Ron Wynn*

★ **Cuber Libre** / Aug. 20, 1976 / Xanadu
Baritone sax often sounds awkward in phrasing, lacking flow, with an absence of range, characterized by a squawky sound in the bottom register. Ronnie Cuber's work here had some of those

shortcomings, but even when he overcame them he often was at a loss for ideas during his solos. He seemed strongest as an improviser at medium tempos and when he followed good solos by pianist Barry Harris, as on "Tin Tin Deo" and "Sudwest Funk." — *Jerry De Muth, Cadence*

Ted Curson (Theodore Curson)

b. Jun. 3, 1935, Philadelphia, PA
Trumpet, piccolo trumpet, flugelhorn / Hard bop, modern creative
After attending Granoff Music Conservatory and taking private lessons with Jimmy Heath, Ted Curson moved from Philadelphia to New York, where he worked with Mal Waldron, Red Garland, Philly Joe Jones, and Cecil Taylor and then Charles Mingus and Eric Dolphy. An aggressive, often stirring trumpet and flugelhorn soloist, Curson's first recordings came with Mingus; he then co-led a band with Bill Barron, played with Max Roach, and fronted his own groups. Curson spent most of the late '60s and '70s in Europe. An ambitious, challenging player, Ted Curson's recordings have never broken him out to a general audience. He's done sessions for Inner City, India Navigation, Chiaroscuro, Interplay, and EMI, among others.—*Ron Wynn*

★ **Tears for Dolphy** / Aug. 1, 1964 / Arista
Recorded in Paris, this 1964 session documented Ted Curson's first quartet as a leader. While reflecting his collaborations with Charles Mingus and Cecil Taylor, Curson's approach here was closer to the spirit of the mainstream. Eschewing the more radical techniques of the free approach, Curson and reedman Bill Barron etched tough but highly melodic lines above the steady and crisp rhythmic substructure ably provided by bassist Herb Bushler and drummer Dick Berk. — *Chuck Berg, Down Beat*

★ **Jubilant Power** / Oct. 16+17, 1976 / Inner City 1017
Slashing, dynamite exchanges, and an intense approach make this the Curson to grab. — *Ron Wynn*

Andrew Cyrille (Andrew Charles Cyrille)

b. Nov. 10, 1939, New York, NY
Drums / Early free, modern creative
Drummer and percussionist Andrew Cyrille's among the finest rhythm players of his generation. He's extremely disciplined and never excessive or flashy. Cyrille played in a drum and bugle corps at 11 and at 15 was in a trio with guitarist Eric Gale. He enrolled at Juilliard in 1958 but by the early '60s was amassing a host of credits working in groups. Some of the people he played with during this period were Mary Lou Williams, Roland Hanna, Rahsaan Roland Kirk, Illinois Jacquet, Coleman Hawkins, Junior Mance, Walt Dickerson, and Howard McGhee. Cyrille began his move into less conventional jazz in 1964, when he replaced Sunny Murray in Cecil Taylor's group. He stayed with Taylor until 1975 and eventually became as important a part of the leader's music as Taylor. Cyrille also worked with many other major figures in the free school, such as Marion Brown, Grachan Moncur III, and even Jimmy Giuffre. He recorded a solo album in Paris in 1969 and participated with Rashied Ali and Milford Graves in a Dialogue of the Drums series of mid-'70s concerts. After leaving Taylor, Cyrille headed the group Maono from 1975 to 1980. Some Maono members included David Ware, Sonny Smith, Ted Daniel, Lisle Atkinson, and Nick DiGeronimo. In the '80s Cyrille played in two fine bands; the Group (with Billy Bang, Fred Hopkins, Sirone, Ahmed Abdullah, and Marion Brown) and Pieces of Time (with Don Moye, Kenny Clarke, and Milford Graves). He did sessions with Muhal Richard Abrams and John Carter and headed his own band. He's recorded recently with Sony/DIW and also done many other dates for independent or foreign labels.—*Ron Wynn*

● **Metamusicians' Stomp** / Sep. 1978 / Black Saint 0025
Metamusicians Stomp was the group Maono's best recorded documentation to date, featuring strong solos, interesting compositional structures, and excellent sound quality. If Maono occasionally took on an ensemble sensibility reminiscent of Tony Williams's early Blue Note sessions, it was because of drummer-leader Andrew Cyrille's stylistic flexibility and fastidiousness, forcing his cohorts through a wide range of textural and emotional situations. — *Art Lange, Down Beat*

○ **Nuba** / 1979 / Black Saint 0030
The interplay between vocalist Jeanne Lee and alto saxophonist Jimmy Lyons was perfectly offset by the balancing force of drum-

mer Andrew Cyrille. . . . Lyons's dry tone virtually suggested the desert for "Nuba" (in both its versions) the most fully-conceptualized composition on the album. Cyrille's repetitious rhythms visualized the caravan bouncing along through the sands Lyons conjured; Jeanne Lee's vocal became the very oasis she sang of. — *Mike Cornette, Cadence*

○ **My Friend Louis** / Nov. 18+19, 1991 / Columbia 52957
Fiery, rampaging session with drummer Andrew Cyrille anchoring a stirring set featuring the dynamic tenor saxophonist David S. Ware. This is uncompromising, exciting material, far from sedate standards or derivative hard bop recitations. —*Ron Wynn, AMG*

Meredith D'Ambrosio

b. 1941
Vocals / Ballads & blues, modern creative
Vocalist Meredith D'Ambrosio is a soft, yet engaging vocalist who's particularly effective on ballads. She's written lyrics for such works as John Coltrane's "Giant Steps" and Dave Brubeck's "Strange Meadowlark," while adding sparse piano accompaniment. Interpretation and performance skills and material selection are her other strong points. —*Ron Wynn and Michael G. Nastos*

○ **Little Jazz Bird** / 1982 / Palo Alto 8019
Fine '82 combo session in which D'Ambrosio shows her ability to handle a variety of songs supplied by composers as diverse as harpist Deborah Henson-Conant and vocalist David Frishberg. Phil Woods heads a capable backing band and supplies his customary heated alto sax solos, while Hank Jones lends some flair on piano. —*Ron Wynn, AMG*

★ **Love Is Not a Game** / Dec. 19+20, 1990 / Sunnyside 1015
With husband Eddie Higgins's Trio. Dreamy, soft-voiced D'Ambrosio makes a definitive emotional statement. Of the 15 tracks, 9 are standards (three adapted or modified by D'Ambrosio)and 5 are written by her. Nice twisting on "I Love You/You I Love," "Oh, Look at Me Now/But Now Look at Me," and "Lament/This Lament." —*Michael G. Nastos*

Paquito D'Rivera

b. Jun. 4, 1948, Havana, Cuba
Alto sax, clarinet / Latin-jazz, world fusion
A flamboyant alto saxophonist with a spiraling, hard-edged sound and a good clarinetist, Paquito D'Rivera gained his initial fame as a member of the Cuban band Irakere. He departed Cuba in the '80s while on tour, leaving his family behind. D'Rivera's rubbery, frenetic alto solos have been the high point of his albums, and he's proven equally proficient at hard bop and Afro-Latin material, blending originals, jazz classics, and standards. He's played with David Amram, Dizzy Gillespie, and McCoy Tyner, as well as heading his own combos and larger groups. D'Rivera's recorded for Columbia, Chesky, and Messidor.—*Ron Wynn*

○ **Blowin' / i.** 1981 / CBS
Despite the overly slick production (thankfully with no strings)—including that "magic" touch of reverb—a raw genuine feeling still shines through. It was especially present in D'Rivera's fiery, bop-oriented (with obvious Latin subtitles) stylings, which often climaxed with effective honks and squeals, as well as in bassist Eddie Gomez's solo work on "Waltz for Moe" and "Basstronaut". . . . —*Milo Fine, Cadence*

★ **Mariel** / 1982 / Columbia 38177
With pianists Hilton Ruiz and Jorge Dalto. Becoming more funky. Also includes "Moment's Notice." Funk and jazz from Cuban fire-spitter. —*Michael G. Nastos*

○ **Why Not** / Jun. 19-21, 1984 / Columbia 39584
Cuban expatriate Paquito D'Rivera issued a commercially viable, yet fairly musically challenging album with *Why Not.* . . . By combining infectious percussion work, accessible funk-inspired rhythms, and impassioned solo statements, D'Rivera was able to get airplay on "adult contemporary" radio stations without compromising his musical integrity. The date consisted of eight tunes that highlighted D'Rivera's alto and clarinet work. —*Carl Brauer, Cadence*

○ **Who's Smoking?!** / May 21-22, 1991 / Candid 79523

Hot, surging Afro-Latin set by alto saxophonist Pacquito D'Rivera, matching him with both celebrated veterans and established session stars. D'Rivera doesn't falter through any of these pieces and gets strong assistance from special guest James Moody and super trumpet solos by Claudio Roditi. The percussive backgrounds supplied by Danilo Perez and Al Foster are varied and constantly shifting and changing. —*Ron Wynn, AMG*

Albert Dailey (Albert Preston Dailey)

b. Jun. 16, 1938, Baltimore, MD, **d.** LATE
Piano, composer / Postbop, hard bop
Albert Dailey was a pianist and an outstanding contributor to several '70s jazz combos and also released a couple of fine albums as a leader. He never attained widespread attention but was a favorite accompanist and session man for many musicians, including Stan Getz. Dailey died in the late '70s. —*Ron Wynn*

★ **Textures** / 1981 / Muse 5256
One of only two in-print releases featuring the engaging, striking piano work of Albert Dailey. This 1981 session had him working with a pianoless trio keyed by saxophonist Arthur Rhames (who reportedly killed himself over bad reviews), plus bassist Rufus Reid and drummer Eddie Gladden. Dailey was a particular favorite of Stan Getz's and was especially strong doing uptempo material. —*Ron Wynn, AMG*

Tadd Dameron (Tadley Ewing Peake Dameron)

b. Feb. 21, 1917, Cleveland, OH, **d.** Mar. 8, 1965, New York, NY
Composer, arranger, bandleader, piano / Bop
Pianist and composer-arranger Dameron was the master melodist of the bebop era. He was an arranger for many groups, but is best known for his Royal Roost quintet of 1948, which featured Fats Navarro, Allen Eager, Curly Russell, and Kenny Clarke. Several recordings by this group have been reissued under Navarro's name on Blue Note, Savoy, and Riverside/Jazzland, while others for Prestige have been reissued by sidemen such as Clifford Brown or John Coltrane. His orchestral approach is best displayed on his Capitol recordings from 1949 and a 1956 Prestige album *Fontainebleau*, although more personnel would have helped each session. A big band recording for Riverside in 1962 suffers from a lack of rehearsal time. While not highly regarded as an instrumentalist, Dameron's compositions are held in the highest regard by the entire bebop fraternity. His arrangements for vocalists such as Carmen McRae (Decca) and Sarah Vaughan (Musicraft) are models of their kind. —*Bob Porter*

○ **Classics of Modern Jazz—Vol. 1: Fats Navarro** / Aug. 28, 1948-Nov. 13, 1948 / Jazzland 950

○ **Classics of Modern Jazz—Vol. 4: The Tadd** / Aug. 28, 1948-Nov. 13, 1948 / Jazzland 968

○ **Fontainebleau** / Mar. 9, 1956 / Prestige 055
Fontainebleau put greater emphasis on arrangements and those who might have hoped for a blowing date with Kenny Dorham, Henry Coker, Sahib Shihab, Joe Alexander, Cecil Payne, John Simmons, and Shadow Wilson would be advised to look elsewhere. . . . It was mostly for the arranging that one would pick this up, for it did offer some nice examples of the floating, suspended heat that marked this arranger's touch. —*Bob Rusch, Cadence*

★ **Mating Call** / Nov. 30, 1956 / Prestige 212

Eddie Daniels (Edward Kenneth Daniels)

b. Oct. 19, 1941, New York, NY*
Clarinet, tenor sax / Postbop
A technically wondrous contemporary clarinetist who has emerged as a fusion star, thanks to GRP recordings, Eddie Daniels also had an extensive period as a mainstream tenor saxophonist in such big bands as The Thad Jones-Mel Lewis Orchestra. Daniels's always impressive solos feature as clean and fluid a tone and sound as possible on clarinet, while his tenor playing is often bluesy and exuberant. Some question whether his clarinet work has the soulfulness or is as ambitious and varied as that of Don Byron or Perry Robinson, but it's certainly every bit as well played. His GRP releases have been his most successful, while an earlier Daniels date was recently reissued by Fantasy.—*Ron Wynn*

○ **Memos from Paradise** / Dec. 1987-Jan. 1988 / GRP 9561

Excellent, soaring clarinet solos by Eddie Daniels help overcome occasional compositional defects on this late-'80s set. Daniels emerged during this decade as the clarinet's reigning soloist, and showed why with plenty of spiraling, exhaustive contributions. The orchestrations sometimes got sappy, and Roger Kellaway's piano playing was more nice than exuberant. But the disc was very popular with the light jazz and adult contemporary audience. —*Ron Wynn, AMG*

★ **To Bird with Love** / 1987 / GRP 9544
This clarinetist's best solid and swinging studio date, w/ Fred Hirsch (p) and Al Foster (d). —*Michael G. Nastos*

○ **Nepenthe** / Dec. 1989 / GRP 9607

Kenny Davern (John Kenneth Davern)

b. Jan. 7, 1935, Huntington, NY
Soprano sax, clarinet / Dixieland
A top traditional jazz soprano saxophonist and clarinetist, Kenny Davern's been a fine player for many years. Though his style and approach are quite conservative, his sound and tone are superb, and he's dazzled listeners and critics alike thanks to a sophisticated and impressive solo style. Davern was a professional at 16 and made his recording debut with Jack Teagarden. He played in New York with Phil Napoleon, Pee Wee Ervin, Red Allen, Buck Clayton, and Jo Jones after Teagarden moved to California. Davern joined the Dukes of Dixieland in 1962 and 1963 after leading a band at Nick's. Later Davern was part of both Soprano Summit with Bob Wilber and the Big Three with Dick Wellstood and Bobby Rosengarden. He appeared at several European jazz festivals and has played with such musicians as Howard Alden, Phil Flanigan, Bob Haggart, Giampaolo Biagi, Eddie Condon, and Ruby Braff. He's recorded for many labels, among them Atlantic and Musicmasters. —*Ron Wynn and Michael G. Nastos*

★ **Soprano Summit** / **i.** Mar. 1976 / Concord Jazz 29
Live at the Concord Festival with Bob Wilber and quintet. Two Wilber originals, one by guitarist Marty Grosz. A fine representation of two artists in Dixie-early-swing mode with blues and a touch of Ellington. —*Michael G. Nastos*

○ **Playing for Kicks** / Nov. 1985 / Jazzology 197

Walter Davis Jr

b. Sep. 2, 1932, Richmond, VA, **d.** Jun. 2, 1990
Piano / Bop
Walter Davis Jr was an accomplished hard bop and bop pianist who made several solid dates ranging from his early sessions in the '50s to trio dates in the '60s. He worked frequently with Max Roach, Charlie Parker, Sonny Rollins, and Art Blakey and later did sessions with Sonny Criss, Jackie McLean, Archie Shepp, and Kenny Clarke, among others. Davis didn't make many records on American labels, didn't have a wide profile outside the jazz community, and at one point he even left the music business temporarily to run his tailoring shop. But he returned to the music world and enjoyed a few more years in the spotlight. He was a particularly invigorating solo pianist. —*Ron Wynn*

★ **Davis Cup** / Aug. 2, 1959 / Blue Note 4018
Propulsive hard bop with Donald Byrd (tpt) and Jackie McLean (as).—*David Szatmary*

○ **In Walked Thelonious** / **i.** Apr. 1991 / Mapleshade 512631
Some spectacular solo playing by Walter Davis Jr, a severly underrated pianist. He did 15 Monk classics, among them complex works like "Trinkle, Tinkle" and "Panonica," and made them his own. All the songs were complete first takes, and there was no overdubbing or multitracking, just Davis displaying his brillance on each cut. —*Ron Wynn, AMG*

Anthony Davis

b. Feb. 20, 1951, Paterson, NJ
Piano, composer / Modern creative
Anthony Davis is a pianist and composer whose music is as singular as any. It featurs very dense passages, free improvisations, and textures unlike any other. It's an acquired taste but one that reaps great rewards. He's made several solo piano recordings and group efforts and also composed material for dancers and some operatic works. Dream motifs have proven a great inspiration. Davis's work is for the intellectual and open-minded.—*Michael G. Nastos*

○ **Of Blues and Dreams** / Jul. 30-31, 1978 / Sackville 3020
Of Blues and Dreams was largely given over to a suite in three movements based on the fantasy writings of pianist-composer Anthony Davis's wife, Deborah Atherton. The title track, a neo-romantic rhapsody in somber hues, set the stage for a voyage to the planet "Lethe," whose gray mists and phosphorescent waters were conjured up by the swirling, ominous interplay of violin and cello over Davis's brooding piano. An eerie, insistent vamp erupted from amid the fog before unraveling into controlled cacophony, whereupon the ensemble descended to the frightening depths of "Graef," a forbidden drug, which foretold the user's death. . . . The suite concluded with the journey of Atherton's protagonist, "Madame Xola," through her interplanetary travels. The lengthy, morose explanation fused jumpy omnirhythms with a dark Schoenbergian serialism, until at last Jenkins broke into a nostalgic swing lament that Stuff Smith might have appreciated. —*Larry Birnbaum, Down Beat*

★ **Song for the Old World** / Jul. 1978 / India Navigation 1036
Anthony Davis, then known in the New York as a young pianist-composer from the left side or avant-garde, presented us with his first group record, *Song for the New World* and what I think was a distinct return to melody. "Song for the Old World" was a collection of musical folk fragments from Asia, Africa (Ghana), and southern America (New Orleans). The beauty of this composition was in the musical harmonic transitions that floated over a very fine percussion line by Ed Blackwell. Generations of string instruments that were from the African hunting bow and also centuries of percussive devices that dated from before Christ were but a few of the "interior" musical elements. This was a gentle record, and it took time for one to hear the beauty and indeed to *feel* the melody. A great deal of musical history was covered, and it was done not only in a lyrical way but also in an honest way. —*Bradley Parker-Sparrow, Down Beat*

○ **Mystic Winds, Tropic Breezes** / i. Nov. 1982 / India Navigation 1049

○ **Undine** / Mesa Blue Moon 8612

Charles Davis

b. 1933
Baritone, tenor sax / Hard bop
Baritone and soprano saxophonist Charles Davis was one of the better baritone players to emerge in the '60s, and a contributor to several fine groups and bands on soprano as well. He attended DuSable High School in Chicago and the Chicago School of Music from 1948 to 1950. Davis worked with Jack McDuff, Ben Webster, Billie Holiday, and Dinah Washington in the mid- and late '50s, before spending three years in Kenny Dorham's group, a period that helped establish his reputation. Davis also had an extensive musical relationship with Sun Ra, first working with him in 1954. He was a full-time Arkestra member for two years and would periodically perform, record, and tour with Ra in the '80s. Davis played with John Coltrane, Illinois Jacquet, and Lionel Hampton in the early '60s and formed his own band in 1965 and 1966. Davis performed for ten years with the Jazz Composer's Orchestra. During that same period, he played in other bands, among them Artistry in Music, the Louis Hayes Sextet, Clark Terry's Big B-A-D Band, and, in 1978, the Thad Jones-Mel Lewis Orchestra. Davis formed the Baritone Saxophone Retinue, a baritone sextet plus rhythm section, in 1974. He was equally prolific in the '80s, working with Barry Harris, Dameronia, the Philly Joe Jones quartet, and Abdullah Ibrahim and also serving as music director for various bands. —*Ron Wynn*

Dedicated to Tadd / i. Jul. 1980 / West 54 8006
This album featured some very adventurous, inventive modern mainstream jazz. Like the music of Tadd Dameron, to whom one assumed this date was dedicated, this music won through its honesty, its beauty, and its artfulness. —*Zan Stewart, Down Beat*

Reflections / i. 1990 / Red 123247

Eddie Lockjaw Davis (Edward Davis)

b. 1922, New York, NYy, **d.** Nov. 3, 1986, Culver City, CA
Tenor sax / Bop, hard bop
Eddie "Lockjaw" Davis was a popular tenor sax star his entire professional career. He made his first recordings with Cootie Williams (1944) and also played with Andy Kirk, Lucky Millinder, and other big bands. Popular in Harlem, Davis worked regularly

in clubs there throughout the '40s and '50s. He recorded for many small labels in the '40s, while his '50s recordings for Roost, King, Roulette, and Prestige often included an organist (Bill Doggett, Doc Bagby, or, most frequently, Shirley Scott). The Davis trio with Shirley Scott was the first of many organ-tenor sax combos in the '50s and '60s. He was a unique tenor sax stylist, employing rasps and squeals often associated with R&B players but filtered through his own highly original harmonic conception. Davis joined the Count Basie Orchestra in 1952 and maintained a long relationship with that band, being in and out of it for the next 20 years. His longest unbroken tenure with Basie was 1966-1973. He also co-led a quintet with saxophonist Johnny Griffin (1960-1962) and actually retired from music for a period in 1963 when he worked as a booking agent. Davis was a prolific recording artist and participated in many all-star jam sessions. He was often featured in a group with trumpeter Harry Edison during the '70s. Davis also recorded frequently in Europe. His recordings were rarely dull but also rarely inspired. His "Cookbook" series for Prestige with Shirley Scott is worthy of note and the best collaboration with Griffin was the live material from Minton's, also on Prestige. —*Bob Porteralso*

○ **Jaws N' Stitt at Birdland** / i. 1954 / Roulette 97507

○ **Cookbook—Vols. 1, 2 & 3, The** / Jun. 20, 1958-Dec. 15, 1958 / Original Jazz Classics 652-653-756
A pair of new reissues featuring the late '50s group, with Davis and Shirley Scott (organ) riding herd on the band. —*Ron Wynn*

Jaws in Orbit / May 1, 1959 / Original Jazz Classics 322
Includes Shirley Scott on the Hammond organ. This is early Scott, not yet all that funky. Traditional swinging, uptempo music. —*Michael Erlewine*

○ **Tough Tenors** / Nov. 4+10, 1960 / Philips 821293
A rugged workout with Johnny Griffin (ts); w/ Francy Boland (p), and Kenny Clarke (d) in the rhythm section. —*Ron Wynn*

★ **Live at Minton's** / Jan. 6, 1961 / Prestige 24099
This duo (tenor saxophonists Eddie Lockjaw Davis and Johnny Griffin) made about a dozen LPs together, most for Jazzland and Prestige, and they are all worth investigating. They had a special affinity for pianist Thelonious Monk's music, and while there were other sets that emphasize that better, the Monk pieces ("Straight No Chaser," "In Walked Bud") included in the program on this live set were among the highlights. —*Bob Rusch, Cadence*

○ **Live! the Midnight Show** / Jan. 6, 1961 / Prestige 7330

○ **Live! the Breakfast Show** / Jan. 6, 1961 / Prestige 7407

○ **Lookin' at Monk** / Feb. 7, 1961 / Jazzland 939

○ **Singin' 'til the Girls Come Home** / i. Mar. 1976 / Steeple Chase 31058
This was almost as fine an Eddie "Lockjaw" Davis album as you could want. . . . Jaws followed a pattern of cool to hot as he advanced through a tune, immediately leading to crescendoes of gruff, macho, Ben Websterish vibrato on tenor, stopping just short of excessive romanticism. —*Bob Rusch, Cadence*

○ **Eddie Lockjaw Davis** / i. Feb. 1981 / Enja 3097

○ **Simply Sweets** / i. 1982 / Pablo 2310806

○ **Toughness Tenors** / i. 1986 / Milestone 8212932

★ **Stolen Moments** / Prestige 7834

Jesse Davis

Tenor sax, alto sax / Neo-bop
Jesse Davis is a 20-something tenor sax star who got his start through a recommendation by jazz critic Ira Gitler, who was teaching a class on the history of music and was impressed with Davis. Davis's debut Concord session shows he has much promise as a player and writer. He's continued recording for that label, made appearances on other sessions, and is a spirited, resourceful player, whose compositions reflect his knowledge of the jazz tradition, as well as a personalized approach. —*Ron Wynn*

○ **Horn of Passion** / i. 1989 / Concord Jazz 4465
Solid debut from saxophonist who once was in a class taught by Ira Gitler. Decent originals and exuberant performances. CD version has two bonus cuts. —*Ron Wynn*

● **Young at Art** / i. Mar. 1993 / Concord Jazz CCD-4565
Davis's third release features his alternately poignant, intense, and introspective treatments of such classics as Cole Porter's *I*

Love Paris, Thelonious Monk's *Ask Me Now,* and his own originals *Brother Roj, Georgiana,* and *One for Cannon.* He is backed by some youngsters who play with more drive and less relaxed, steady precision, such as guitarist Peter Bernstein, pianist Brad Mehldau, bassist Dwaye Burno, and drummer Leon Parker. Burno's bass lines are big and prominently mixed into the arrangements, while Parker's drumming has plenty of kick, and Bernstein's accompaniment is tasty and reserved. Davis's hard blowing statements add the final ingredient to a date that demonstrates Concord's openness to acts who are not within their usual stylistic sphere but are nonetheless deserving of substantial exposure. —*Ron Wynn*

Miles Davis (Miles Dewey Davis III)

b. May 25, 1926, Alton, Illinois, **d.** Sep. 25, 1991

Trumpet, keyboards, composer, flugelhorn / Bop, cool, early jazz rock

Trumpeter Miles Davis was the master of understatement and one of the rare jazz musicians to enjoy widespread acclaim and recognition across the spectrum of popular music. Davis defied clichés, trends, and norms and refused to remain static or stagnant at any point in his life or career. He often scandalized or angered fans who preferred he remain in a particular phase rather than forge ahead. Receiving a trumpet from his father for his 13th birthday, he later played (in the early '40s) in his high school band and, as a student, with Eddie Randall's Blue Devils—a St. Louis R&B group. He had early encounters with Clark Terry, Dizzy Gillespie, and Charlie Parker before he went to New York in 1944 to study at the Juilliard School of Music. Davis left there shortly to learn in a less formal setting: the laboratory of 52nd Street. He became a member of Charlie Parker's group before he was 20 and worked with them from 1946 to 1948. He later helped assemble an innovative unit that offered a stylistic alternative to the bop approach. The idea for a nonet, culled from discussions that had been held in Gil Evans's apartment in New York, resulted in the *Birth of the Cool* sessions as well as a short-lived band featuring Davis, Gerry Mulligan, Lee Konitz, Evans, and others. Davis endured hard times personally and professionally from 1949 (following a stint at the Paris Jazz Festival) until 1954, when he reemerged and began to forge the remarkable sound and style that would stamp him forever as a musical giant. During the '50s Davis's crisp, concise, and often unforgettable solos showed one could make an impact through intelligent use of space and time as much as speed and flash. His work with arranger Gil Evans was equally influential in its ability to blend a dynamic ensemble around Davis—a captivating lead player. Davis introduced the metal Harmon mute (minus the stem) and utilized the flugelhorn as a legitimate alternative brass instrument.

His great combos of the mid- and late '50s, with pianists Red Garland or Bill Evans, saxophonists John Coltrane and Cannonball Adderley, bassist Paul Chambers, and drummers Philly Joe Jones or Jimmy Cobb were seminal in their impact inside and outside jazz. The *Kind of Blue* album in 1959 popularized modal jazz, with its improvisations based on a series of scales rather than chord sequences, a technique that generated more thought and creativity along melodic lines. During the '60s and '70s, Davis continued to break ground, with his mid-'60s band being among the most fluid and revolutionary of its era. This band, with pianist Herbie Hancock, bassist Ron Carter, and drummer Tony Williams, plus saxophonist Wayne Shorter, worked with written themes but no prearranged harmonies. This allowed both the soloist and the answering rhythm section players to choose whatever notes or chords they desired after the initial theme statement. From the late '60s and on into the '70s, Davis opted for longer pieces without composed structures. He used rock as the rhythmic foundation, employed Indian and Asian instrumentation along with standard jazz pieces, and went electric, yet his trumpet solos remained as definitive and clear as in earlier, acoustic periods. But a debilitating illness, plus other personal problems, resulted in Davis taking a break from 1975 to 1980. Through the '80s, Davis's playing seemed to get stronger and more interesting, especially his use of the middle and lower registers, but controversy raged around his albums. He steadily moved more and more into funk and R&B, although he also made an appearance at the 1991 Montreux Jazz Festival and had allegedly talked about doing a reunion Birth of the Cool date. The

most recent posthumous Davis release features his always expressive trumpet work over hip-hop arrangements. —*Ron Wynn*

○ **Prebirth of the Cool / i.** 1949 / Jazz Live 8003
This Italian LP featured the first release of these two important broadcasts, although this music has since been reissued on CD. Miles Davis's "Birth of the Cool" nonet recorded a dozen influential performances during 1949-1950 but actually appeared in public for only one gig: a two-week stint in 1948 as the intermission band at the Royal Roost for Count Basie's orchestra. This set features nine performances taken from radio broadcasts and are near-classic. This version of the nonet features Miles Davis, baritonist Gerry Mulligan, altoist Lee Konitz, pianist John Lewis, and drummer Max Roach in addition to French horn, tuba, trombone, and bass. Other than getting to hear "new" and extended versions of some of the nonet's studio sides, this set offers otherwise unrecorded arrangements of "Why Do I Love You" and "S'il Vous Plait." —*Scott Yanow*

★ **Capitol Jazz Classics—Vol. 1 (Complete Birth of the Cool) /** Jan. 21, 1949 / Capitol 16168
This LP contains the great Miles Davis 1949-1950 nonet records. It's called *The Complete Birth of the Cool* because, in addition to the 11 tracks originally issued on Davis's American Capitol LP, it includes "Darn That Dream," a piece featuring Kenny Hagood's singing, which was previously unavailable on an American LP. These performances are extraordinarily important; they mark a turning point in the history of jazz, an evolution from bop into a more restrained, writer-oriented music. Davis and altoist Lee Konitz soloed superbly, but the stars here were the guys who provided the charts: Gil Evans, Gerry Mulligan, John Lewis, and John Caris. The ensemble sound that Davis's groups produced was unique. This was due in part to the instrumentation; it wasn't common in those days for jazz bands to employ tuba and French horn. Combined with baritone sax and trombone, they gave the group a soft, bottom-heavy, ensemble sound. The softness of the ensemble textures tended to mask the harmonically advanced quality of the writing. There was dissonance aplenty here. The compositions were excellent, ranging from the bop pieces "Move" and "Budo" to the standard "Moon Dreams." . . . There are all sorts of forecasts of things to come in the charts. The greater emphasis on jazz writing in the '50s was stimulated in part by these records. —*Harvey Pekar, Coda*

★ **Miles Davis: Chronicle—the Complete Prestige Recordings (1951-1956) /** 1951-1956 / Prestige 012
The complete Prestige recordings. This is an unbelievable eight-disc set of 93 performances containing everything on the Prestige label. —*Ron Wynn*

○ **Miles Davis Featuring Sonny Rollins /** May 19, 1953+Mar. 15, 1954 / Prestige 161

☆ **Bags Groove /** 1954 / Prestige 245
& Modern Jazz Giants. Sterling sessions with Miles and Monk (p), Milt Jackson (vib), Sonny Rollins (ts), and Horace Silver (p). —*Ron Wynn*

Walkin' / 1954 / Prestige 213
Miles Davis All Stars. This may well be his best single Prestige date. A wonderful session with Lucky Thompson (sax), Horace Silver (p), Percy Heath (b). —*Ron Wynn*

○ **Miles Davis & The Modern Jazz Giants /** Dec. 24, 1954 / Prestige 347
Good anthology featuring Miles Davis in sessions with Thelonious Monk, Milt Jackson, John Coltrane, Red Garland, Kenny Clarke, and others. Some are just the Miles Davis mid-'50s quartet that also included Paul Chambers and Philly Joe Jones, others were specific studio dates. This has been reissued on CD. —*Ron Wynn, AMG*

Dig / 1955 / Original Jazz Classics 5
Tenor saxophonist Sonny Rollins was present as a member of the Miles Davis sextet (alto saxophonist Jackie McLean, pianist Walter Bishop, bassist Tommy Potter, drummer Art Blakey) on *Dig,* which was part of a 10/5/51 session, all of which was also on a twofer. —*Bob Rusch, Cadence*

Miles & Monk at Newport / 1955 / CBS 8978
Outstanding sessions recorded at Newport Festival. Monk's portion rivals the Miles group. —*Ron Wynn*

☆ **Round About Midnight /** Oct. 27, 1955-Sep. 10, 1956 / Columbia 40610

Miles Davis's first Columbia album is a classic. His quintet (with tenor-saxophonist John Coltrane, pianist Red Garland, bassist Paul Chambers, and drummer Philly Joe Jones) was quickly becoming one of the pacesetters in jazz, and each of these six performances are memorable. In addition to the definitive nonMonk rendition of "'Round Midnight," one hears the quintet making such diverse songs as "Ah-Leu-Cha," Cole Porter's "All of You," "Tadd's Delight," and "Dear Old Stockholm" sound as if they were all written for the group. Their version of "Bye Bye Blackbird" is the ultimate in cool sophistication. Essential music. —*Scott Yanow*

☆ **Workin'** / 1956 / Prestige 296

☆ **Steamin'** / 1956 / Prestige 391
Miles Davis Quintet. This is a landmark '50s work. Both vinyl and CD reissue are topflight. —*Ron Wynn*

☆ **Cookin'** / 1956 / Prestige 128
Classic moments were turned in on *Cookin',* a 10/26/56 date with Miles Davis (trumpet), John Coltrane (tenor sax), Red Garland (piano), Paul Chambers (bass), and Philly Joe Jones (drums) on five tracks. Everything on the date was right, but perhaps special mention should be made of Red Garland, whose solos and comping have for some become an integral part of these compositions. —*Bob Rusch, Cadence*

☆ **Relaxin' with the Miles Davis Quintet** / May 11, 1956-Oct. 26, 1956 / Prestige 190

● **Miles Davis: The Columbia Years 1955-1985** / i. 1956-1986 / CBS 4K45000
(This set) spans his three decades of activity at the company by splitting the 35 featured tunes into five categories: blues, standards, originals, moods, and electric. Columbia has answered critics of this approach by saying this collection wasn't intended for sophisticated or knowledgeable fans but was designed for novices and casual collectors. Assuming that's true, this set doesn't fully serve that audience either. These criticisms don't in and of themselves mean the set is worthless. There are many memorable and notable selections. Still, these four discs don't give a comprehensive accounting of Davis's Columbia years. —*Ron Wynn, Rock & Roll Disc*

'58 Sessions Feat. Stella by Starlight / Mar. 4, 1958-May 26, 1958 / Columbia 47835
Some recorded May 26, 1958. Rare sessions, never available before. Well worth it. —*Michael G. Nastos*

☆ **Miles & Coltrane** / May 17, 1958-Apr. 2, 1959 / Columbia 44052
In addition to two selections ("Little Melonae" and "Budo") from Miles Davis's first session for Columbia, this CD contains his complete performance at the 1958 Newport Jazz Festival. When one considers that Davis's sextet at the time included such giants as tenor-saxophonist John Coltrane, altoist Cannonball Adderley, pianist Bill Evans, bassist Paul Chambers, and drummer Jimmy Cobb, it is not surprising that fireworks resulted. Still, the power and drive of this intense version of "Ah-Leu-Cha" is a revelation, and the band really swings and stretches out on "Straight, No Chaser," "Fran Dance," "Two Bass Hit," and "Bye Bye Blackbird." Brilliant music by some of the giants. —*Scott Yanow*

☆ **Porgy & Bess** / 1959 / Columbia 40647
Porgy and Bess was one of the perfect collaborations between Miles Davis and Gil Evans. This was recorded at a time (July/August '58) when America was having a renaissance with "Porgy & Bess," during which numerous jazz interpretations, most of them quite excellent, were released. This *pan genre* effort was amazingly successful in satisfying the joys of both orchestration and improvisation, and it did it in deceptively simple, straightforward terms. For this program Davis was used first as a colorist with great improvisatory skills. —*Bob Rusch, Cadence*

☆ **Milestones** / 1959 / Columbia 40837
A heart-stopping session—wonderful Miles, Coltrane (ts), and Cannonball Adderley (as). Again, get the vinyl if you can find it, though this CD reissue isn't as bad as some others. —*Ron Wynn*

★ **Kind of Blue** / Mar. 2, 1959+Apr. 22, 1959 / CBS 40579
Kind of Blue came from 1959 (3/2 & 4/22) and offered up a program that cemented the move to modal playing that had been developing the previous few years. Here the mood was pensive and the playing from the group (Cannonball Adderley, alto sax; John Coltrane, tenor sax; Wynton Kelly, Bill Evans, piano; Paul Chambers, bass; Jimmy Cobb, drums; Miles Davis, trumpet) su-

perb. Many consider this one of the most essential jazz recordings. . . . It was certainly one of the most influential and really put the cap on an evolutionary development going back to the *Birth of the Cool* sides of ten years earlier. It also brought to a close the Davis-Coltrane-Evans group, Bill Evans having actually left the group in '58. —*Bob Rusch, Cadence*

★ **Sketches of Spain** / i. Nov. 20, 1959 / CBS 40578
The third and final of the great Miles Davis-Gil Evans collaborations of 1957-1959 was also their most ambitious. This set finds Davis in the forefront improvising on two numbers associated with Spanish music and three Evans compositions in that idiom. Much of the music is quite dramatic and emotional (notably "Saeta") and Miles plays at his best throughout, really stretching the boundaries of jazz. —*Scott Yanow*

○ **Legendary Concert, Stockholm, March 22, 1960, The** / Mar. 22, 1960 / Natasha 4011

○ **Someday My Prince Will Come** / 1961 / Columbia 40947
These are transitional, alternately great and uneven 1961 sessions. Coltrane on his way out, and Hank Mobley struggling in vain to replace him and satisfy Miles. —*Ron Wynn*

☆ **Miles Ahead** / 1962 / Columbia 40784
Miles Davis's first collaboration with arranger Gil Evans since the Birth of the Cool recordings of 1949-1950 resulted in this classic album. The advantage that this CD reissue has over the LP is that since the music was recorded as a continuous suite, this way there is no break between the fifth and sixth songs. Miles's trumpet (backed by Evans's 19-piece orchestra) is heard at its best on such selections as "The Duke," "My Ship," "Miles Ahead," "Blues for Pablo" and "I Don't Wanna Be Kissed." Although a bit brief (just 36 minutes) this set is highly recommended. —*Scott Yanow*

At Carnegie Hall / 1962 / CBS 8612
Transitional early-'60s sessions. Hank Mobley (sax) tries hard, but doesn't really fill Coltrane's shoes. W/ good Gil Evans orchestra cuts. —*Ron Wynn*

Sorcerer / Aug. 21, 1962-May 24, 1967 / Columbia 9532
This vigorous 1967 session has nonmusical significance: Miles put Cicely Tyson's face on the album cover, which scored points for visual impact and the image of black women. —*Ron Wynn*

☆ **Quiet Nights** / 1962-1963 / CBS 8906

○ **Miles in Tokyo** / Jul. 14, 1964 / Columbia 162

★ **My Funny Valentine** / 1965 / CBS 9106
Originally issued as two individual records, one of mostly ballads, the other, cookers, these releases chronicle 1965 sessions at a benefit concert held in New York's Philharmonic Hall at Lincoln Center. Tenor saxophonist George Coleman turns in some inspired playing (according to Miles Davis, his best), particularly on "My Funny Valentine" and Davis's "All Blues." Pianist Herbie Hancock, bassist Ron Carter, and drummer Tony Williams all perform with grace, poise, and fire. But it's Davis who plays some of his most impassioned trumpet on record. Gone is the need for formal statements, adherence to melodic shape and contour. Williams's drum solos remain free of the pulse as he chooses to extend the drums' range as a *musical* instrument. The '60s avant garde impinges in subtle, delightful ways, providing clues to this transitional band's method of deconstruction. —*John Ephland, Down Beat*

Cookin' at the Plugged Nickel / 1965 / Columbia 40645
This session is a CD's worth of more material from the *Live at the Plugged Nickel* sessions recorded at the end of 1965. It has additional songs culled from the club date that featured Miles Davis on trumpet, Herbie Hancock on piano, bassist Ron Carter, saxophonist Wayne Shorter, and drummer Tony Williams. There's also a Japanese import version available *Complete Live at Plugged Nickel 1965.* —*John Ephland, Down Beat*

○ **E.S.P.** / Jan. 20-22, 1965 / Columbia 46863
One of numerous mid-'60s standout albums by the great band w/ Wayne Shorter (sax), Herbie Hancock (p), Ron Carter (b), Tony Williams (d). Get the vinyl album if at all possible; Columbia's new reissue leaves a lot to be desired. —*Ron Wynn*

☆ **Four & More** / 1966 / CBS 9253
Good material from mid-'60s period. Herbie Hancock (p) has fine solos. —*Ron Wynn*

Miles Smiles / 1966 / Columbia 48849

With a simpler, drier, more austere (and relatively pianoless) sound, the unrehearsed rough *Miles Smiles* holds up so well because it was more of a *jazz* record, spontaneous warts and all. — *John Ephland, Down Beat*

Nefertiti / 1967 / Columbia 46113
This tremendous late-'60s cut gives you transcendent Wayne Shorter (sax). Can't say the same about lackluster Columbia remastering of the new reissue. — *Ron Wynn*

Miles in the Sky / May 15-17, 1968 / Columbia 48954
This suggestive, prophetic date is clearly inching toward *In a Silent Way* and *Bitches Brew* territory. — *Ron Wynn*

Filles de Kilimanjaro / Jun. 20+21, 1968 / Columbia 46116

☆ **In a Silent Way** / 1969 / Columbia 40580
In a Silent Way brought Miles Davis together with members of his brillant group of the '60s (Herbie Hancock, Wayne Shorter, Tony Williams) and emerging musical spirits (Chick Corea, Dave Holland, Joe Zawinul, John McLaughlin) who would launch Davis into the *Bitches Brew* era. On *In a Silent Way*, Davis was moving away from "tunes" while utilizing more electric instrumental coloring and rockish patterns and splicing to manufacture the music—ideas that seemed to take hold a year after his stunning *Plugged Nickel* recordings. Here the music continued to show the distinct Davis use of suspension and space, but it was more amorphous and no longer seemed rooted in a clear, direct emotion, but was rather indirectly emotional in an illusive sense of reality. — *Bob Rusch, Cadence*

★ **Bitches Brew** / 1970 / Columbia 40577
No jazz collection is complete without this double LP (which has since been reissued as a double CD). This very influential set was one of the first successful attempts to form a new music (soon termed fusion) by combining jazz solos with rock rhythms. "Miles Runs the Voodoo Down" is the most memorable of the six lengthy selections, featuring a fascinating ensemble with Davis's trumpet; Wayne Shorter's soprano; Bennie Maupin's bass clarinet; guitarist John McLaughlin; the keyboards of Chick Corea and Larry Young (Joe Zawinul is on some of the other selections); Dave Holland and Harvey Brooks on basses; drummers Jack DeJohnette, Charles Alias, and Lenny White; and percussionist Jim Riley. Not for the close-minded, this music brought many rock listeners into jazz and gave jazz musicians new possibilities to explore. — *Scott Yanow*

● **Tribute to Jack Johnson** / Feb. 18, 1970 / Columbia 47036
Superior soundtrack-tribute. Arguably better than any pop-,R&B-, rock-tinged set, even *Bitches Brew*. Recently reissued on disc. W/ John McLaughlin (g), Herbie Hancock (k), Steve Grossman (ss), Billy Cobham (d), and Michael Henderson (b). — *Ron Wynn*

On the Corner / 1973 / CBS 31906

Big Fun / 1974 / One Way 21398
While *Big Fun* is far from prime Davis, it's arresting, sometimes entertaining, and in its own way quite representative of his overall work. (two-disc set) — *Ron Wynn, Rock & Roll Disc.*

Agharta / 1975 / Columbia 46799
CD reissue of a pivotal rock-oriented date. W/ rambling, extensive solos with a loose feel. Miles plays keyboards as well as trumpet. Funk backings with torrid sax by Sonny Fortune and explosive guitar by Pete Cosey. Jazz purists were scandalized. — *Ron Wynn*

Pangaea / i. Feb. 1, 1975 / CBS 46115
There are only two cuts on [it], both over 40 minutes in length, and the results are at once intriguing, chaotic, inspired, and maddening. (two-disc set) — *Ron Wynn, Rock & Roll Disc.*

○ **Heard 'round the World** / i. Apr. 1984 / Columbia 238506
Either trying to impress his Japanese audience or simply feeling grand, Miles Davis opened what has long been known as *Miles in Tokyo* fast and happy. The classy young rhythm trio he'd had for a year immediately ignited—Tony Williams a sizzle on his cymbals, bassist Ron Carter so low as to seem subliminal but dependably *there*, pianist Herbie Hancock chording cautiously as though to tend a small blue flame. Then Sam Rivers's tenor burst forth, scorching the changes and threatening to flare out of control. He didn't. The trio rose to his pitch, and after three quick choruses in which Rivers singed the edge, regrouped behind Hancock, who simmered prettily, like Red Garland. They laid back, under Davis's second, unhurried turn. Davis dared much, trying tempo suspensions, extending his personal technique,

sense of harmony, and intonation throughout both the Tokyo and *Miles in Berlin* concerts included in this album. But he insisted the second horn, like the rhythm section, underline *his* directions. While Rivers was masterly, emotional, and to the point, there was a hint of friction—at least, the sparks were flying. When Wayne Shorter took over (on sides three and four) the quintet still sounded inspired—and, overall better balanced. — *Howard Mandel, Down Beat.*

Aura / Jan. 1985 / Columbia 45332
This is a very different type of Miles record: A ten-part suite in which he weaves in and out. The moods, feel, and sound keep shifting, thanks to Palle Mikkelborg's compositions and arrangements. — *Ron Wynn*

Ballads / i. 1989 / Columbia 44151
These are beautiful, timeless pieces, but they should really be heard in their original, intact sessions. This is aimed at the casual Davis listener, novices, or new fans. — *Ron Wynn*

Richard Davis

b. Apr. 15, 1930, Chicago, IL
Bass / Bop, hard bop
This multitalented instrumentalist could have been a symphonic rather than a jazz player. Richard Davis has kept a foot in both worlds, playing in symphony orchestras as well as jazz combos and groups from the '50s on to the present. His mastery of the bass is self-evident; he can drive or break up the beat, plays marvelously with both bow and fingers, and constantly varies his approach. Davis began with Ahmad Jamal and Don Shirley, later played with Charlie Ventura, Sarah Vaughan, Kenny Burrell, Eric Dolphy, Jaki Byard, and the Thad Jones-Mel Lewis big band. He's also done session work in both classical and jazz veins.—*Ron Wynn*

○ **Philosophy of the Spiritual** / 1971 / Cobblestone 9003

★ **Harvest** / May 3, 1977 / Muse 5115
Premier bassist with groups of varying size. Most interesting listening for the adventurous jazz lover. — *Michael G. Nastos*

Wild Bill Davis

b. 1918
Organ, piano / Swing, big band
A fine organist, pianist, and arranger who's worked with many big bands and major figures. Davis learned music from his father, a professional singer. He studied music at Tuskegee and Wiley College and then moved to Chicago. Davis played guitar and wrote arrangements for Milt Larkin in the late '30s and early '40s. Then he provided arrangements for Earl Hines and Louis Jordan in the '40s, also playing piano for Jordan. During the '50s, Davis began playing organ and heading his own groups, mostly trios. He also kept writing arrangements, among them one for "April in Paris" by Count Basie in 1955. Davis recorded with Johnny Hodges and Ella Fitzgerald among others in the '60s and then toured and recorded with Duke Ellington from 1969 to 1971. He served as an arranger, organist, and second pianist. Davis toured extensively in the '70s, recording in Paris with Buddy Tate, Al Grey, Slam Stewart, and Illinois Jacquet. He worked with Lionel Hampton in the late '70s and early '80s, led his own group in Europe and has played several festivals in the '80s and '90s. — *Ron Wynn*

○ **Wild Bill Davis at Birdland** / Mar. 21, 1955 / Epic 3118

Wild Bill Davison (WIlliam Stephen Davis)

b. Jan. 5, 1906, Defiance, OH, d. Nov. 14, 1989
Cornet / Dixieland
Cornetist Wild Bill Davison, a traditional jazz mainstay, became a fixture on the jazz scene in the late '20s and had his own band by 1931. He overcame a lip injury in 1939 and came to New York in 1941. A re-creation of the Original Jazz Band for the Katherine Dunham Show resulted in a 1944 recording session and paved the way for a switch from a Chicago-style approach to a New Orleans traditional approach. He joined Eddie Condon in 1945 and became a fine lead player and charismatic personality. His skills were and are centered in a very active style, with lots of grunts, grimaces, long tones, and crackling leads. — *Ron Wynn*

★ **Jazz A-Plenty** / Nov. 27+30, 1943 / Commodore 7011

● **Individualism Of....** / Nov. 7, 1951 / Savoy 2229

1951 sessions at Eddie Condon's in Boston. Features Cutty Cutshall (tb), Ed Hall (cl), George Wein (p), Buzzy Drootin (d). Sextet and septet recordings with two different groups. Dixie to swing standards by the master cornetist. 23 cuts. —*Michael G. Nastos*

○ **Blowin' Wild** / Feb. 14, 1965 / Jazzology 18

○ **"Wild" Bill Davison/Papa Bue's Viking Jazz Band** / i. Feb. 1974 / Storyville 4029

○ **Together Again** / Storyville 4027

Blossom Dearie

b. Apr. 28, 1926, East Durham, NY
Vocals / Bop, ballads & blues
Despite a tiny voice, Blossom Dearie's become an American music icon through her controlled, often exaggerated attack, distinctive delivery, unique sound, and highly individualistic performance style. Her professional career began with The Blue Flames, a vocal unit contained within Woody Herman's orchestra. She later sang with The Blue Reys, an ensemble that was part of Alvino Rey's band. She recorded "Moody's Mood for Love" in 1952, but her version was buried by King Pleasure's. That same year she performed in Paris with Annie Ross. Dearie formed the Blue Stars, and received instrumental backing from jazz musicians like Fats Sadi and Roger Guerin. They landed a hit with "Lullaby in Birdland" sung in French. Both The Double Six Quartet of Paris and Swingle Singers were spawned by The Blue Stars. Dearie recorded for Barclay in 1954, before returning to America in 1956. Dearie played with Herb Ellis, Ray Brown, and Jo Jones on a mid-'50s Verve LP, and formed her own label, Daffodil Records, in the '70s. She was the first recipient of the Mabel Mercer Foundation Award in 1985. —*Ron Wynn and Michael G. Nastos*

★ **Blossom Dearie** / i. 1956 / Verve 837934

Joey Defrancesco

b. 1971
Organ, piano, synthesizer, trumpet / Bop, soul jazz
Like Charles Earland, Jimmy McGriff, and countless other Hammond B-3 organists, the young DeFrancesco hails from Philadelphia. He's got their chops, but is less than half their age, and his material is more jazz-oriented. His Columbia recordings have thrust him into the spotlight as one of the new young jazz players to watch in the coming years. This Miles Davis protAgA, who's in his early 20s but began playing when he was just four, has a maturity and dexterity in his playing that goes far beyond his years. —*Richard Skelly*

★ **All of Me** / 1989 / Columbia 44463

○ **Reboppin'** / i. 1992 / Columbia 48624
Recent release by the youthful organ sensation. His powerhouse riffs, solos, and soulful phrasing have made DeFrancesco the top mainstream stylist. This set includes contributions from his father and brother on one cut, and a good backing band despite the absence of major names or stars. —*Ron Wynn, AMG*

Buddy DeFranco (Boniface Ferdinand Leonardo DeFranco)

b. Feb. 17, 1923, Camden, NJ
Clarinet, bass clarinet, alto sax / Swing, big band, bop
An exceptional clarinetist, good alto saxophonist, and fine bass clarinetist, Buddy DeFranco had extensive training and nurturing while playing with Charlie Barnet, Tommy Dorsey, Gene Krupa, and Count Basie in the '40s and early '50s, before establishing his own group. While a member of the Basie band in the '50s, he was not allowed to be shown in a filmed short with the otherwise all-Black band. DeFranco made his recording debut as a label in 1949 and has been featured on Capitol, MGM, Norgran, Verve, Advance Guard, Mercury, Vee Jay, Hep, Palo Alto, Pablo, even a Saturn date with Sun Ra. DeFranco's also worked with many great pianists, among them Art Tatum, Oscar Peterson, and Sonny Clark. The group he co-led with Clark was probably his finest. DeFranco was a full-time instructor during the '70s, but returned to the world of club dates, recording sessions, and tours in the '80s, while coleading a group with Terry Gibbs at one point.— *Ron Wynn*

○ **Buddy Defranco with Strings** / i. 1954 / MGM 253

○ **Buddy Defranco Quartet, The** / i. 1954 / Clef 149

★ **Complete Verve Recordings of Buddy De Franco with Sonny Clark** / Apr. 1954-Aug. 1955 / Mosaic 5117

○ **Cooking the Blues** / 1956-1957 / Verve 8221

○ **Sweet and Lovely** / 1956-1957 / Verve 8224

○ **Closed Session** / Oct. 30, 1957-Nov. 1, 1957 / Verve 8382

★ **Like Someone in Love** / Mar. 11, 1977 / Mosaic
Simply incredible in every way! Sonny Clark offers moving, heated piano, and this is some of DeFranco's most sumptuous, engaging, and accomplished playing. With majestic Tal Farlow guitar work. —*Ron Wynn*

Jack DeJohnette

b. Aug. 9, 1942, Chicago, IL
Drums, piano, melodica / Hard bop, modern creative
A classical piano student for over a decade and an American Music Conservatory graduate, Jack DeJohnette ended up with drums rather than keyboards as his instrument of choice . His background in R&B, free, and various styles earned him regular work in Chicago before he moved to New York in 1966. His playing with the Charles Lloyd Quartet in the late '60s provided a final break after prior stints with John Patton, Jackie McLean, Abbey Lincoln, and Betty Carter. DeJohnette is unmatched as a timekeeper and anchor and has led jazz-rock, hard-bop, and many other types of groups. He's made numerous recordings as a leader and sideman, doing duets, trios, combos, and larger group sessions for ECM, Columbia, and other labels. He also plays melodica.—*Ron Wynn*

★ **Have You Heard?** / Jul. 4, 1970 / Epic 64692

★ **Special Edition** / Mar. 1979 / ECM 827694
Arguably his finest small combo. David Murray and Arthur Blythe light up the sky. —*Ron Wynn*

○ **Tin Can Alley** / Sep. 1980 / ECM 1189
Tin Can Alley suggested a tonal history of jazz—from the earthy, layered, African rhythmic buildup of Jack DeJohnette's solo feature "The Gri Gri Man" to the ducal sonorities of the drummer's "Pastel Rhapsody." Bassist and cellist Peter Warren's "Riff Raff" completed the circle with a primal collective ad-lib. The leader's title track was boppish and angular. "I Know" danced to a backbeat while the multitracked horns riffed and composer DeJohnette soul-shouts. . . . DeJohnette on this record scored again with some of the most coherent, timbrally compelling, multidirectional music around. Rich combinations abounded among these exceptional players. —*Owen Cordle, Down Beat*

Barbara Dennerlein

b. 1965
Organ / Soul jazz, modern creative
Barbara Dennerlein's a fast-rising organist whose methodology combines the best of soul-jazz and a more outside, ambitious style championed by Larry Young. Since she's recorded for small independents and done more work in Europe than America, Dennerlein's much better known by critics than the general audience. But she's been playing organ since age 11 and worked in the '80s and '90s with Ronnie Burrage, Ray Anderson, Mark Mondesir, and Andy Sheppard, among others.—*Ron Wynn*

★ **Straight Ahead** / Jul. 1988 / Enja 79608
Organ-fired and guitar-laced modern jazz from this up-and-coming keyboardist. A solid album throughout. —*Michael G. Nastos*

Sidney DeParis (Sidney De Paris)

b. May 30, 1905, Crawfordsville, IN, **d.** Sep. 13, 1967, New York, NY
Trumpet, tuba / New Orleans traditional
Trumpeter and tuba player Sidney DeParis was a controversial figure in traditional jazz circles for his use of vocal effects and showmanship. He worked successfully in both the traditional and swing style. He studied music with his father, then worked in Charlie Johnson and Don Redman's bands in the '20s and '30s, as well as recording with Jelly Roll Morton in 1939. DeParis worked with Zutty Singleton from 1939 to 1941 and played with Benny Carter, Art Hodes, Roy Eldridge, Claude Hopkins, and Sidney Bechet in the '40s. But he was best known for playing with his

brother Wilbur DeParis from 1943 until 1967 in various traditional groups.—*Ron Wynn*

● **Original Blue Note Jazz—Vol. 2** / Mar. 18, 1944-Oct. 26, 1944 / Blue Note 6506

○ **Sidney Deparis' Blue Note Stompers** / Jun. 14, 1951 / Blue Note 7016

Wilbur DeParis (Wilbur De Paris)

b. Jan. 11, 1900, Crawfordsville, IN, **d.** Jan. 3, 1973, New York, NY
Bandleader, trombone / New Orleans traditional
Trombonist and bandleader Wilbur DeParis was a prominent figure in New Orleans jazz circles from the '20s to the '70s. He started as an alto horn and played with his father's circus band. While visiting New Orleans in 1922, DeParis played C-melody saxophone with Louis Armstrong and worked with A. J. Piron. During the mid-'20s he led bands in Philadelphia before going to New York in 1928. There he recorded and performed with LeRoy Smith, Dave Nelson, Edgar Hayes, and Noble Sissle, with whom he toured Europe in 1931. DeParis made another European tour in 1936-1937 with Teddy Hill's band, and also recorded with the Mills Blue Rhythm Band in 1937. When Armstrong called in 1937, DeParis answered the summons and remained with the band till 1940. After that, DeParis headed up his own groups and also worked with Ella Fitzgerald. De Paris was a member of Duke Ellington's orchestra from 1945 to 1947 and recorded with Sidney Bechet in 1946, 1949, and 1950. There was an 11-year stint for DeParis at Ryan's in New York; he led a house band that included his brother Sidney and Omer Simeon. DeParis also made a State Department-sponsored trip to Africa in 1957, and worked as both a leader and arranger until 1972.—*Ron Wynn*

● **New Orleans Blues** / Oct. 31, 1957 / Atlantic 1266

Paul Desmond (Paul Emil Desmond)

b. Nov. 25, 1924, New York, NY, **d.** May 30, 1977, New York, NY
Alto sax / Cool
Alto saxophonist Paul Desmond forged a great career as perhaps the prime embodiment of the "cool" alto sax style. No one did more with a short-breath approach. Desmond studied clarinet in high school and college and joined Dave Brubeck's octet in 1948, where he stayed until 1950. He left, returned to Brubeck's group from 1951 to 1967, and periodically came back in the last decade of his life for tours. Desmond was emphatic and appealing in his own way and could swing, despite the shortness of his lines. He was among the finest alto players of the early '50s, using the instrument's upper harmonics. Besides Lester Young, another prime influence on Desmond's style was Benny Carter. He had a lovely luminous tone. Desmond's best recordings were with Gerry Mulligan and Jim Hall. But he also played with many others, among them the Modern Jazz Quartet, Herbie Hancock, Airto, Jack DeJohnette, Ed Bickert, Don Thompson, and Jerry Fuller. Desmond did albums for Warner Bros., CTI, RCA, A&M, and Finnesse among others.—*Ron Wynn & Michael Erlewine*

○ **Paul Desmond/Gerry Mulligan Quartet** / **i.** Sep. 2, 1952 / Fantasy 273
Paul Desmond Quintet/Gerry Mulligan Quartet. Lovely. Four dates, from 1952 to 1954. —*Michael Erlewine*

○ **Quintet/Quartet** / **i.** 1954 / Original Jazz Classics 712

★ **Paul Desmond—Jim Hall Recordings** / **i.** 1959-1965 / Mosaic
Incredible music! A six-disc boxed set of recordings from 1959-1965 featuring Desmond with Jim Hall. Desmond plays flawless sax, and Jim Hall likewise on guitar. In brief, these are classic cuts; the best. Whether you're a beginning listener or a jazz expert, this is satisfying music. Mosaic does it again. —*Michael Erlewine*

○ **Take Ten** / Jun. 5, 1963-Jun. 25, 1953 / RCA 66146
Early-'60s sessions reissued on recent Bluebird CD. The title refers not to a song but the number of cuts that Desmond, guitarist Jim Hall, and others recorded. Bassist Percy Heath and drummer Connie Kay also participated. These sessions were partially reissued on CD before; this is the full date. —*Ron Wynn, AMG*

○ **Polka Dots & Moonbeams** / 1963-1964 / Bluebird 61066

★ **Bridge over Troubled Water** / 1969 / A&M 51204

★ **Paul Desmond Quartet Live, The** / Oct. 25, 1975-Nov. 1, 1975 / A&M 10
Here were four sides of stylish, rich music performed at Bourbon Street in Toronto by four pros. Everyone had a chance to stretch out (all the pieces were between 7 and 12 minutes) in a setting that was obviously comfortable and yet stimulating. The recording was excellent for a club date. —*Joel Ray, Cadence*

Vic Dickenson (Victor Dickenson)

b. Aug. 6, 1906, Xenia, OH, **d.** Nov. 16, 1984, New York, NY
Trombone / New Orleans traditional
Vic Dickenson was a superb trombonist and one of the finest traditional jazz players, as well as a good mainstream stylist. He played with Midwestern bands in the '20s and '30s and then with Blanche Calloway, Claude Hopkins, Benny Carter, Count Basie, and Frankie Newton from 1933 to 1943. Dickenson was in Eddie Heywood's band from 1943 to 1946 and worked on the West Coast in 1947 and 1948. Dickenson moved to Boston and headed a band until the mid-'50s before settling in New York. He played with Red Allen in 1958 and was a co-leader with Red Richards of the group Saints and Sinners in the '60s. He toured with George Wein's All-Stars, played with Wild Bill Davison, and worked regularly at Eddie Condon's club. Dickenson toured Asia and Australia with Condon in 1964 and visited Europe as a soloist in 1965. He co-led a quintet with Bobby Hackett from 1968 to 1970 and performed frequently with the World's Greatest Jazz Band in the '70s. Dickenson freelanced through the late '70s and into the early '80s. —*Ron Wynn*

○ **Vic's Boston Story** / 1956-1957 / Storyville 920

○ **Mainstream** / Oct. 28, 1958 / Atlantic 1303

○ **Vic Dickenson Quintet** / Storyville 4021

● **Plays Bessie Smith: "Trombone Cholly"** / Gazell 1011
If all the material here was not blues, trombonist Vic Dickenson certainly turned it into the feeling of the blues. Producer Sam Charters wisely picked this classic trombonist material that was mid- and slow tempo. Dickenson worked well in these tempos and with a controlled vibrato, was able to steer away from some of the Dixie bits he found himself in over the years. —*Geoff Millerman, Cadence*

Walt Dickerson

b. 1931, Philadelphia, PA
Vibist / Hard bop, modern creative
A probing soloist, vibist Walt Dickerson uses only two sticks and hardens them with a special solution. He developed a very individualistic sound during the '60s before he abruptly stopped playing in 1965. A Down Beat "New Star" winner in '62, Dickerson teamed with Sun Ra on the '65 recording *Impressions of a Patch of Blue*, based on an arrangement Dickerson had made for the music in Jerry Goldsmith's film *A Patch of Blue*. After a ten-year hiatus, Dickerson returned, but he has mainly worked in Europe. He recorded again with Sun Ra on Steeplechase in the late '70s and also did a duo date with Pierre Dorge. He's since made other recordings on Steeplechase and Soul Note, among them a duet session with Andrew Cyrille. —*Ron Wynn and Michael G. Nastos*

○ **Relativity** / Jan. 16, 1962 / New Jazz 8275

★ **Jazz Impressions of "Lawrence Of Arabia"** / 1963 / Dauntless 6313
Jazz Impressions: Lawrence of Arabia. This effort from the vibraphonist stretches the parameters of Maurice Jarre's themes. Rare, but great to have. —*Michael G. Nastos*

○ **Unity** / Mar. 5, 1964 / Audio Fidelity 6131
Vibist Walt Dickerson's intense, circling, John Coltrane-inspired vibes contrasted with pianist Walter Davis's more lighthearted, bop-rooted, locked-hands approach. This contrast was even more evident on "High Moon.". . . Dickerson was clearly heading into new territory at this time, both as vibist and leader. It is a shame that his name stopped appearing on record jackets not long after this album was first issued. —*Tom Bingham, Cadence*

Al DiMeola (Al Di Meola)

b. Jul. 22, 1954, Jersey City
Guitar, bandleader, composer / Early jazz rock, world fusion
Guitarist Al Di Meola earned his early fame as a member of Return to Forever, but he's a versatile player equally capable play-

ing jazz, blues, rock, Latin, or classical. He started playing as a nine-year-old and began on the steel-string guitar at 15. Di Meola attended Berklee in Boston in the mid '70s, and joined Return to Forever in 1974. Follwing that sint, Di Meola's led various bands, including the Al Di Meola Project, and has toured and recorded with John McLaughlin and Paco De Lucia. He's a gifted electric and acoustic stylist.—*Ron Wynn*

Casino / 1977 / Columbia 47482

Guitarist Al DiMeola was in his electronic fusion phase when this was recorded in the late '70s. He played frenetic, flashy riffs and solos and was assisted on a variety of keyboards by Barry Miles, electric bassist Anthony Jackson, and drummer Steve Gadd, who added a steady array of rock and funk beats. —*Ron Wynn, AMG*

● **Splendido Hotel** / 1979 / Columbia 46117

On *Splendido Hotel*, Al DiMeola combined tight electronic ensemble playing with acoustic forays, some in characteristic territory, and some elsewhere. He maintained a Latin Mediterranean tone through much of the album, and his emphasis was on composition more than improvisation. —*Robin Tolleson, Down Beat*

☆ **World Sinfonia** / **i.** 1991 / Tomato 79750

○ **Kiss My Axe** / **i.** Feb. 26, 1992 / Tomato 79751

Dirty Dozen Brass Band

Group / New Orleans traditional

The appearance of the Dirty Dozen Brass Band in 1975 (emerging, like a phoenix, from the kazoo and drum corps of "secondliners") signalled a new phase of development in traditional New Orleans music, which was both popular and controversial. While they retained parts of the traditional repertoire, they also added titles associated with modern jazz and rhythm and blues—a departure that did not always sit well with other brass bandsmen. But the public loved it! From modest beginnings at neighborhood bars, the Dirty Dozen soon became local celebrities, opening doors that have since led to international celebrity on the festival circuit. The band's success ushered in a renaissance in the New Orleans brass band field, attracting young musicians who formed bands of their own, such as the Rebirth. In retrospect, the Dirty Dozen has done more to revitalize the New Orleans brass band tradition than to endanger it. Their music is vibrantly attractive for its often stunning virtuosity and the sort of infectious street rhythms that practically compel dancing. —*Bruce Boyd Raeburn*

★ **My Feet Can't Fail Me Now** / **i.** 1984 / George Wein Collection 43005

The Dirty Dozen's 1984 debut paved the way for a new generation of New Orleans street music—traditional brass band instrumentation meets modern jazz and funk. The Dozen had a number of secret weapons to set them off from the competition, including veteran baritone player Roger Lewis, a member of Fats Domino's band; Kirk Joseph, the greatest tuba player in jazz, and the ultra-funky Jennell Marshall on snare drum and vocals. This CD, while not as gutsy in the recording quality as their later efforts, is highlighted by the Dozen's versions of "Blue Monk" and an early signature tune of theirs, their cover of Dave "Fat Man" Wilson's "I Ate Up the Apple Tree." —*Roundup Newsletter*

Voodoo / Aug. 1987-Sep. 1987 / Columbia 45042

Guest stars Dizzy Gillespie (tpt), Dr. John (p), and Branford Marsalis (ts) fit right in with the band's masterful ensemble work. —*Bruce Raeburn*

New Orleans Album / Dec. 1989 / Columbia 45414

This time, veteran Orleanians Danny Barker, Eddie Bo, and Dave Bartholomew join in, plus Elvis Costello—the fun quotient runs off the meter with plenty of solos and absolutely infectious rhythms. —*Bruce Raeburn*

○ **Open up—Whatcha Gonna Do for the Rest of Your Life?** / Jan. 1991-Apr. 1991 / Columbia 47383

Jelly / **i.** 1993 / CBS 53214

On the whole this is joyous, energetic, and celebratory music. —*Bart Grooms, Option*

Bill Dixon (William Robert Dixon)

b. Oct. 5, 1925, Nantucket, MA

Trumpet, composer, flugelhorn, piano / Early free, modern creative

Trumpeter, composer, and teacher Bill Dixon is a criminally neglected, overlooked player and theorist, as well as a champion for

musicians' rights to control and properly profit from their work. Dixon's solo style includes plenty of things that set him apart, among them creative uses of distortion, vibrato, and very distinctive phrasing and articulation. Dixon studied painting at Boston University and became part of the '60s free movement, working with Archie Shepp in 1962 and 1963. He promoted and presented a series of concerts at the Cellar Cafe in New York in 1964 that gave forums to then largely unknown players such as Roswell Rudd, Milford Graves, Paul Bley, and Dixon's own group, plus those who always needed exposure, like Sun Ra. At the end of '64 Dixon organized the Jazz Composers Guild, a collective that would support musicians independently of clubs and booking agents. Though the idea had widespread support and Collective members included Cecil Taylor, Mike Mantler, Rudd, John Tchicai, Sun Ra, and both Carla and Paul Bley, it didn't last. Dixon began a ten-year collaboration with dancer Judith Dunn in 1965; they presented multimedia events including free jazz and dance concerts at the 1966 Newport Jazz Festival. Dixon has taught at Bennington College since 1968 and eventually helped found a department of black music. His compositions have been presented at prestigious jazz festivals internationally since 1976. Though he's never made a lot of recordings, he's recently done dates for Soul Note.—*Ron Wynn*

● **Jazz Artistry of Bill Dixon, The** / Oct. 10, 1966 / RCA 3844

Baby Dodds (Warren Dodds)

b. Dec. 24, 1898, New Orleans, LA., **d.** Feb. 14, 1959, Chicago, IL

Drums / New Orleans traditional

Baby Dodds is the premier, most influential drummer in New Orleans style jazz history. Dodds's playing approach, even his equipment, set the standard for many other drummers, and he directly influenced both Dave Tough and Gene Krupa, who absorbed everything from his rhythmic patterns to his showmanship. Dodds played in New Orleans with Bunk Johnson, Papa Celestin, and others before joining Fate Marable's riverboat band from 1918 to 1921. His reputation grew, and he was invited to join King Oliver's band in 1922. They were in San Francisco at that time. The following year they relocated to Chicago and began recording. Dodds stayed in Chicago for over two decades, making seminal records with Louis Armstrong and Jelly Roll Morton and also working with his equally gifted brother Johnny in small groups. During the '40s, Dodds kept working with groups led by Jimmie Noone, Sidney Bechet, and Bunk Johnson. He was a frequent guest on radio broadcasts in 1947, and he toured Europe with Mezz Mezzrow in 1948. Dodds battled health problems but kept playing until 1957, two years prior to his death. —*Ron Wynn*

○ **Baby Dodds Drum Method: Trio** / Jan. 31, 1944 / American Music 2

● **Footnotes to Jazz—Vol. 1** / Jan. 10, 1946 / Smithsonian/Folkways 2290

Johnny Dodds (John M. Dodds)

b. Apr. 12, 1892, New Orleans, LA, **d.** Aug. 8, 1940, Chicago, IL

Clarinet / New Orleans traditional

In the early years of recorded jazz music, ensemble work was the main measure of a band's merit. Solo statements were often confined to short unaccompanied breaks, and bandleaders were not always known for producing exciting (or even competent) melodic improvisation. Louis Armstrong was one of jazzdom's first brilliant soloists; clarinetist Johnny Dodds was another. His birthplace—was New Orleans—was the birthplace of jazz, and in that city the clarinet has always reigned supreme, due at least in part to Dodds's formative work with Kid Ory, and '20s sessions with King Oliver, Jelly Roll Morton, Armstrong, and many more. Dodds was not a technical giant on the clarinet, but his audience wasn't concerned with embouchure and fingering patterns—they were amazed (as are listeners to this day) at his freedom of spirit, impressive soaring lines, and confident, even brash, expression. Many early jazz players made ends meet by accompanying vocalists, and Dodds's work with blues singers Ida Cox, Lovie Austin, and others was time well spent. He was an excellent blues player; his wide creole vibrato, throaty tone, and commanding aural presence (that has all the hallmarks of the ranking female blues vocal) with a jazz clarinet was not revolutionary, but his ability to make the instrument sing was, and jazz hasn't been the same since. Note: Affinity 1023 is a three-CD box just released (U.K.) that has many of Dodd's landmark recordings from 1926-1927. This is volume one; more are anticipated to trace his career up to his death in 1940. —*Myles Boisen*

○ **Jazz Classics: Great Performances (1923-1929)** / 1923-1929 / Mobile Fidelity 00603

○ **Chronological Johnny Dodds: 1926, The** / i. May 1926-Dec. 1926 / Classics 589

○ **Johnny Dodds and Kid Ory** / i. 1926-1928 / Epic 16004

○ **King of the New Orleans Clarinet (1926-1938)** / 1926-1938 / Brunswick 58016

○ **Chronological Johnny Dodds: 1927-1928, The** / i. Jan. 1927-Oct. 1927 / Classics 603

★ **South Side Chicago Jazz** / 1927-1929 / MCA 42326
1927-1929. Dodds in various combinations, from his Trio through the Black Bottom Stompers to Jimmy Blythe's Washboard Wizards and the Beale Street Washboard Band. "Wild Man Blues" shows one of many reasons Dodds was one of the most individual and celebrated clarinetists from New Orleans. —*Bruce Raeburn*

Eric Dolphy (Eric Allan Dolphy)

b. Jun. 20, 1928, Los Angeles, CA, d. Jun. 29, 1964, Berlin
Alto sax, bass clarinet, flute / Hard bop, early free
Alto saxophonist, bass clarinetist, and flutist Eric Dolphy, like many '60s jazz innovators, spent his formative years in the creative cauldron of '50s Los Angeles, nourished on a diet of Charlie Parker and other bop visionaries. Also like so many others, his career was cut short by the rigors and self-neglect of the jazz life. He apprenticed with an R&B band, drummer Roy Porter's big band, and navy bands, and had numerous opportunities to try out his ideas in jam sessions with many prominent Los Angeles progressives. His associations with major figures like John Coltrane, Charles Mingus, Oliver Nelson, George Russell, Ornette Coleman, Booker Little, Max Roach, Gunther Schuller, and many others were always satisfying, vitalized by Eric's relentless search to expand the role of the alto sax, the flute, and the somewhat obscure bass clarinet. In Dolphy's hands each of these instruments gained new personalities and produced absolutely stunning unaccompanied solos; in ensembles his playing had the controlled invention of Parker, but with all the smooth edges broken off and discarded. Dolphy is remembered as an iconoclast, but his performances with Chico Hamilton's easy-going 1958-1959 group, various Latin-jazz dates, Oliver Nelson's blues-flavored projects, bebop jams, and the third-stream constructions of Schuller and John Lewis demonstrate the versatility and traditional grounding of this gentle multiinstrumentalist. It is tragic that Dolphy, a well-loved figure throughout the modern jazz community, had to endure the "antijazz" epithets of reactionary critics and pursue his career with pickup bands in Europe, where he died of diabetes in 1964. His *Out to Lunch* still stands as a definitive statement of the mid-'60s "new thing" avant-gardists. —*Myles Boisen*

☆ **Outward Bound** / Apr. 1, 1960 / New Jazz 022
Expansive, compelling, and excellent Dolphy with strong Freddie Hubbard and even better Jaki Byard. —*Ron Wynn*

○ **Here and There** / Apr. 1, 1960-Sep. 8, 1961 / Prestige 673

☆ **Out There** / Aug. 15, 1960 / New Jazz 023
Dolphy at his evocative best, with wonderful support from Ron Carter and Roy Haynes. —*Ron Wynn*

Candid Dolphy / Oct. 20, 1960-Apr. 4, 1961 / Candid 79033
From 1960-1961. This is an excellent collection of small-combo sessions with numerous luminaries such as Ted Curson (tpt), Kenny Dorham (tpt), and Abbey Lincoln (v). —*Ron Wynn*

★ **Far Cry** / Dec. 21, 1960 / New Jazz 400
This marks Dolphy's departure from standard jazz repertoire playing, with originals and exciting Parkerisms.—*Myles Boisen*

★ **Live! at the Five Spot—Vol. 1** / Jul. 16, 1961 / New Jazz 133
The first of the immortal Dolphy live dates, with incredible interaction between Dolphy and Booker Little (tpt). Awesome alto sax and bass clarinet, with feverish tempos. —*Ron Wynn*

★ **Live! at the Five Spot—Vol. 2** / Jul. 16, 1961 / Prestige 247
Just as vital as its predecessor. Wondrous solos and compositions. 1987 reissues of a landmark concert. —*Ron Wynn*

○ **Eric Dolphy and Booker Little** / Jul. 16, 1961 / Prestige 7334

☆ **Great Concert of Eric Dolphy, The** / Jul. 16, 1961 / Prestige 34002
The complete Five Spot concert recordings in a three-album package. It may be unavailable now. —*Ron Wynn*

○ **Eric Dolphy Memorial Album** / Jul. 16, 1961 / Prestige 7334
This and *Eric Dolphy 1928—1964* are exactly the same LP, just packaged differently. . . . The music was from Eric Dolphy's highly regarded 1963 Douglas sessions, at which he was surrounded with fellow avant acolytes. . . . *Eric Dolphy 1928—1964* lists full personnel for each track and has sensible liner notes (by Leonard Feather). *The Eric Dolphy Memorial Album* boasts neither of those assets. —*Alan Bargebuhr, Cadence*

Copenhagen Concert / Sep. 8, 1961 / Prestige 24027
Remarkable, soaring alto sax, bass clarinet, and flute from the incomparable Eric Dolphy, featured in concert from Copenhagen, Denmark, in 1961. Dolphy was so transcendent that he dominates the European rhythm section and renders their contributions, both accompanying him and solo, nearly meaningless. This has been reissued on CD. —*Ron Wynn, AMG*

Stockholm Sessions / Sep. 25, 1961-Nov. 10, 1961 / Enja 79647
Dolphy is typically amazing. Borderline European players and material. 1990 CD issue has a bonus cut. —*Ron Wynn*

Vintage Dolphy / Mar. 14, 1963-Apr. 18, 1963 / GM 3005
A collection of early-'60s Dolphy recordings that veer everywhere stylistically. Worth having. —*Ron Wynn*

★ **Out to Lunch** / Feb. 25, 1964 / Blue Note 46524
His classic. Daring structures and startling solos from a quintet who would all go on to star status. W/ Freddie Hubbard (tpt), Bobby Hutcherson (vib). —*Myles Boisen*

☆ **Last Date** / Jun. 2, 1964 / PolyGram 822226
The best of Eric's European sessions, with inspired backing and outstanding solo spots.—*Myles Boisen*

Lou Donaldson

b. Nov. 1, 1926, Badin, NC
Alto sax, vocals / Bop, blues & jazz, soul jazz
Alto saxophonist Lou Donaldson came to prominence in the early '50s via Blue Note recordings of his own as well as sessions with Art Blakey and Jimmy Smith. He has been a bandleader based in New York from that point until today. Originally associated with bebop, he combines a thorough knowledge of bebop harmony, a fondness for little-known songs, and a genuine feeling for the blues. His work was on Blue Note until 1964, when he began a six-album contract with Chess/Cadet. He returned to Blue Note in 1967 and achieved some of his greatest success in the late '60s. His '70s work features an electric saxophone, and his Blue Note and Atlantic/Cotillion releases from this period are commercial departures from what he does best. In general his '50s work is either in the hard bop vein—though Donaldson is not a hard bopper—or comfortable mainstream-modern albums where he is usually the only horn. His '60s work features organ more often than not, and Donaldson becomes a talent scout here, providing major breaks for the likes of Grant Green, John Patton, Charles Earland, and Melvin Sparks. A return to straightahead jazz marked his '80s work, and he recorded frequently in Europe and Japan, where he is a major star. His work has often featured blind pianist Herman Foster in recent years. One Muse album *Sweet Poppa Lou* is recommended, while his '90s Milestone releases are his most recent domestic output. He is still touring nationally and internationally. —*Bob Porter*

● **With Clifford Brown** / Jun. 9, 1953 / Blue Note 5030

○ **Wailing with Lou** / Jan. 27, 1955 / Blue Note 1545

○ **Lou Takes Off** / Dec. 15, 1957 / Blue Note 1591

● **Blues Walk** / Jul. 28, 1958 / Blue Note 46525
Alto saxophonist Lou Donaldson recorded with all manner of groups during his two long stays with Blue Note. Herman Foster, Peck Morrison, Dave Bailey, and Ray Barretto may not have had the hippest reputations vis-e-vis some other Blue Note rhythm players, but on *Blues Walk* they certainly got the job done. Donaldson was in his finest form here. Just how well-remembered the album is is best exemplified by the fact that several of the tunes here are among his most requested. —*Bob Porter, Jazz Times*

○ **Lou Donaldson with the Three Sounds** / Feb. 12-18, 1959 / Blue Note 4012

○ **Possum Head** / 1964 / Argo 734

★ **Lush Life** / Jan. 20, 1967 / Blue Note 84254

Kenny Dorham

b. Aug. 30, 1924, Fairfield, TX, **d.** Dec. 5, 1972, New York, NY
Trumpet, composer / Hard bop
Trumpeter and composer Kenny Dorham was a youthful prodigy who played piano at seven. He combined a seemingly fragile, brittle style with subtlety, melodic dexterity, and a creative, sparse approach. He was also among the rare jazz musicians to be a published critic. He was a superb blues player whose lyricism enlivened the tritest ballad. He began with Billy Eckstine, Lionel Hampton, and Dizzy Gillespie in the '40s and replaced Miles Davis in the Charlie Parker quintet in 1948. A charter member of Art Blakey's Jazz Messengers in the '50s, he was very prolific in the '50s and '60s. Dorham was also a brilliant composer. —*Ron Wynn*

★ **Afro-Cuban** / Jan. 30, 1955-Mar. 29, 1955 / Blue Note 46815

☆ **2 Horns, 2 Rhythms** / Nov. 13, 1957 / Riverside 463
Quartet. Includes the brilliant Ernie Henry (as), who has been sadly overlooked, plus more excellent Dorham. —*Ron Wynn*

○ **But Beautiful** / Feb. 18, 1959 / Milestone 47036

○ **Showboat** / Dec. 9, 1960 / Bainbridge 1043
Superb quintet date from 1960, with Dorham's bright, crackling trumpet contrasted by the smooth, yet vibrant tenor sax of Jimmy Heath. A dynamic rhythm section featuring pianist Kenny Drew, bassist Jimmy Garrison, and drummer Art Taylor not only complemented and supported the front line, but frequently spurred and even subtly challenged them during ensemble passages. This has been reissued on CD. —*Ron Wynn, AMG*

○ **Whistle Stop** / Jan. 15, 1961 / Blue Note 4063

○ **Osmosis** / Oct. 1961 / Black Lion 760146

○ **Inta Somethin'** / Nov. 1961 / Pacific Jazz 41

★ **Una Mas** / Apr. 1, 1963 / Blue Note 46515

★ **Trompeta Toccata** / Sep. 4, 1964 / Blue Note 84181
The composer-trumpeter's finest hour. A quintet with Joe Henderson (ts). —*Michael G. Nastos*

Jimmy Dorsey (James Dorsey)

b. Feb. 29, 1904, Shenandoah, PA, **d.** Jun. 12, 1957, New York, NY
Clarinet, alto sax, trumpet, baritone sax / Swing, big band
Clarinetist, alto saxophonist, and trumpeter Jimmy Dorsey, Tommy Dorsey's younger brother, was a featured member in his older brother's group in the '30s. He previously worked in many bands, including Paul Whiteman's. After their famous 1934 fight over the tempo of a song, Jimmy replaced his brother at the band's helm, and continued with many other successful orchestras. He reunited with his brother in 1953, and again took over the band's leadership for a brief time upon Tommy's death.—*Ron Wynn*

○ **The Early Years** / **i.** Oct. 10, 1935-Dec. 22, 1941 / Bandstand 7104
Jimmy Dorsey was best-known during the swing era for leading a rather commercial big band dominated by vocals, so a jazz-oriented retrospective such as this LP was quite welcome. The 16 performances (10 of which are instrumentals) includes many rarities, such as "Serenade to Nobody in Particular," "Stop! and Reconsider," "Bar Babble" and "Mutiny in the Brass Section." These selections show that, despite its public image, the older Dorsey's orchestra could be a strong jazz band when called upon. —*Scott Yanow*

● **Contrasts** / **i.** Jul. 7, 1936-Oct. 7, 1943 / Decca 626
This CD, virtually the only example of Jimmy Dorsey's orchestra currently available on CD, puts the emphasis on JD's jazz sides rather than the vocal bestsellers. Popular singer Helen O'Connell does make three appearances (including on the hit "Tangerine"), but most of these selections are instrumentals with Dorsey's alto and clarinet in outstanding form (it was easy to forget how talented an instrumentalist he was during these commercial years). Most of the other fine soloists are lesser names although they include future bandleaders Ray McKinley (on drums) and pianist Freddie Slack. Highlights are "Parade of the Milk Bottle Caps," "I Got Rhythm," "John Silver," "Dusk in Upper Sandusky," Dorsey's

theme "Contrasts," and "King Porter Stomp," although there isn't a weak track on this release. Recommended, Dorsey's definitive set. —*Scott Yanow*

☆ **Greatest Hits** / **i.** 1940-1944 / MCA 252
Sampler containing jazzy pop and big band songs done by Jimmy Dorsey band in period immediately after he left Tommy's orchestra. It's a decent introduction to his music, but far from comprehensive. —*Ron Wynn, AMG*

○ **Featuring Maynard Ferguson** / **i.** Mar. 1949-May 1949 / Big Band Archives 1216
The 1949 Jimmy Dorsey Orchestra was one of the most interesting if overlooked big bands of the era. Although Dorsey had mostly played commercial music earlier in the decade, he had never lost his love for jazz. By 1949 he had hired some bebop musicians and was playing some modern charts, but at the same time was also performing dixieland with a small group from his orchestra. This LP of radio broadcasts not only features Dorsey's alto and clarinet and the Dixielandish trumpet of Charlie Teagarden but the outstanding high-note trumpet of Maynard Ferguson, heard a year before he became famous playing with Stan Kenton. Since Ferguson was not with Dorsey long enough to record with him commercially, these radio airchecks are particularly valuable historically in addition to being enjoyable musically. —*Scott Yanow*

Tommy Dorsey (Thomas Dorsey)

b. Nov. 19, 1905, Shenandoah, PA, **d.** Nov. 26, 1956, Greenwich, CT
Trombone, bandleader / Swing, big band
Trombonist and bandleader Tommy Dorsey worked with his younger brother from the '20s until the 1934 argument that split them. After that, he took over Joe Haymes's orchestra. His efforts to woo big stars with huge (for the era) salaries helped his orchestra become prominent. The best-known member was vocalist Frank Sinatra. Dorsey kept up with changes by adding a string section in 1942 and Charlie Shavers in 1945. A 1947 film *The Fabulous Dorseys* fancified their lives. The brothers reunited in 1953. Tommy Dorsey billed himself "The Sentimental Gentleman of Swing." —*Ron Wynn*

○ **Music Goes Round and Round** / Dec. 1935-Feb. 1947 / Bluebird 3140
In 1935, Tommy Dorsey first jammed with musicians from his big band in a Dixieland format, calling the little band the Clambake Seven. He recorded frequently with the unit until 1939 and then rarely until 1950. This particular CD has 21 of the Clambake's better performances, and, although it would have been preferable to reissue all of the group's recordings, this is a strong introduction to their music. With such soloists as trumpeters Yank Lawson, Max Kaminsky, and Pee Wee Erwin, clarinetists Johnny Mince and Joe Dixon, tenorman Bud Freeman, and TD himself, this music was quite joyous and spirited. Edythe Wright ably sings on many of the songs, which are highlighted by the title cut, "At the Codfish Ball," two versions of "The Sheik of Araby," and "When the Midnight Choo-Choo Leaves for Alabam." These are Dixieland recordings that predated the New Orleans revival of 1940. —*Scott Yanow*

● **Seventeen Number Ones** / **i.** 1935-1942 / RCA 9973

○ **Complete Tommy Dorsey—Vol. 1 (1935)** / 1935 / RCA 5521
The most complete series of Tommy Dorsey reissues was a twofer LP program that succeeded in issuing in chronological order all of TD's recordings from the beginnings of his big band in September 1935 up to March 1939, eight volumes in all before corporate indifference brought the program to a halt at its halfway mark. Since Dorsey led a dance band that performed novelties and commercial vocal features in addition to jazz, not all of their recordings were classics. General collectors might be more satisfied with samplers rather than getting everything. Volume I in this series has as its highpoints "Weary Blues," Dorsey's theme "I'm Getting Sentimental over You," and the first sides by TD's Clambake Seven including "The Music Goes Round and Round." —*Scott Yanow*

○ **Complete Tommy Dorsey—Vol. 2 (1936)** / 1936 / RCA 5549
The second of eight twofer LP's that trace complete and in chronological order all of Tommy Dorsey's recordings from 1935 up to March 1939, this set like the others includes gems and duds. During 1936 Dorsey's band was popular enough to keep going

but had not broken through to the bigtime yet. With trumpeter Max Kaminsky, clarinetist Joe Dixon, and the great tenor Bud Freeman contributing solos and Edythe Wright and the commercial singer Jack Leonard heard on vocals, the music ranges from pop schlock to some big band swing (such as "Royal Garden Blues," "That's a Plenty" and "After You've Gone") and two songs by Dorsey's Clambake Seven. —*Scott Yanow*

○ **Complete Tommy Dorsey—Vol. 3 (1936-1937)** / 1936-1937 / RCA 5560
The third LP twofer in this "complete" series (which died after the eighth volume when Bluebird lost interest), this set is the most essential of the bunch because it includes the 18 selections that the great trumpeter Bunny Berigan cut with Dorsey. These include not only the major hits "Marie" and "Song of India" (which made Tommy Dorsey into a household name) but also memorable solos on "Mr. Ghost Goes to Town," "Melody in F," "Liebestraum," and "Mendelssohn's Spring Song." Not all of the other songs cut directly before and after Berigan's stint were classics, but there are superior versions of "Keepin' Out of Mischief Now," "Black Eyes," and "Jammin'." —*Scott Yanow*

○ **Complete Tommy Dorsey—Vol. 4 (1937)** / 1937 / RCA 5564
The post-Berigan era found Tommy Dorsey heading one of the most popular of all big bands, rivaling Benny Goodman's. This fourth of eight LP twofers has all of TD's recordings that were cut during a three-month period, including 15 selections by Dorsey's Clambake Seven (which was now featuring trumpeter Pee Wee Erwin, Bud Freeman's tenor, and clarinetist Johnny Mince in addition to singer Edythe Wright) and a variety of big band titles, most memorably "Satan Takes a Holiday," "Beale Street Blues," and a truly bizarre version of "Am I Dreaming." Recommended. —*Scott Yanow*

○ **Complete Tommy Dorsey—Vol. 5 (1937)** / 1937 / RCA 5573
The fifth in Bluebird's superb series of LP twofers that trace the "complete Tommy Dorsey" up until 1939 is highlighted by 11 performances by his Dixielandish Clambake Seven, along with "Night and Day" and "Once in a While" from his big band. As with the others in this admirable series, there plenty of novelties and forgettable vocals are included, but Dorsey fanatics should go out of their way to get all of these highly appealing sets. —*Scott Yanow*

○ **Complete Tommy Dorsey—Vol. 6 (1937-1938)** / 1937-1938 / RCA 5578
The sixth out of the eight volumes in "The Complete Tommy Dorsey" series of twofer LPs has only two Clambake Seven performances and no major hits, but, even with the large amount of so-so Jack Leonard vocals, there are also many examples of first-class dance music and swing from the very versatile orchestra. Worth picking up by those Dorsey fans who are wise enough to search for all eight volumes. —*Scott Yanow*

○ **Complete Tommy Dorsey—Vol. 7 (1938)** / 1938 / RCA 5582
The seventh in this series of eight LP twofers contains all of the recordings made by Tommy Dorsey's orchestra during a five-month period in 1938. Seven commercial Jack Leonard vocals are compensated for by seven performances from TD's Clambake Seven, a Dixieland outfit taken out of his big band. With such tunes as "Music, Maestro Please," "Panama," "Chinatown, My Chinatown," "The Sheik of Araby," and the big hit "Boogie Woogie," this set (along with all the others in this valuable series) is recommended to all true Tommy Dorsey fans. —*Scott Yanow*

○ **Complete Tommy Dorsey—Vol. 8 (1938-1939)** / 1938-1939 / RCA 5586
The eighth and unfortunately the final volume in this superb LP twofer series closed the program of Tommy Dorsey recordings partway through the session of March 8, 1939, thanks to the indifference of RCA Records. This very worthy series reissued all of Tommy Dorsey's studio recordings during the four years after he formed his own band, and, although it necessarily included both gems and duds, the former generally outnumbered the latter! Volume 8 is highlighted by "Tin Roof Blues," "Hawaiian War Chant," the two-part "Milenberg Joys," and the Clambake Seven's "You Must Have Been a Beautiful Baby." All of the volumes in this increasingly hard-to-find series are recommended to serious swing fans. —*Scott Yanow*

○ **Yes, Indeed!** / Jun. 1939-Jun. 1945 / Bluebird 9987
This CD includes many of Tommy Dorsey's very best recordings from 1939-1942 along with four selections dating from 1944-

1945. During this period the sound of Dorsey's orchestra had changed from the earlier days, thanks in large part to Sy Oliver's arrangements and the hard-driving drums of Buddy Rich. With such soloists as trumpeter Ziggy Elman, tenor-saxophonist Don Lodice, and clarinetist Johnny Mince (in addition to Dorsey's trombone), this orchestra could play jazz with the best of their contemporaries, although many of their other recordings (not included here) actually showcased vocals and dance music. Highlights of this recommended disc include "Well, All Right," "Stomp It Off," "Quiet Please," "Swing High," "Swanee River," "Deep River," and "Well, Git It!" while the later tracks include "Opus #1'," the Charlie Shavers feature "At the Fat Man's," and a guest appearance by Duke Ellington on "The Minor Goes Muggin'." —*Scott Yanow*

● **All-Time Greatest Dorsey/Sinatra Hits—Vol. 1—4** / **i.** 1940-1942 / RCA 8324
When RCA decided to issue its early '40s Tommy Dorsey recordings containing Frank Sinatra vocals on compact disc, it abandoned the chronological sequencing found on the Grammy-winning album series *The Dorsey/Sinatra Sessions* and instead jumped back and forth through the catalog. This first volume of four contains some of the biggest hits, notably "I'll Never Smile Again" and "I'll Be Seeing You," and thus is the best selection for beginners. But be sure to move on to Vol. 2 and Vol. 3 and, especially, Vol. 4, which contains Sinatra's first solo session. —*William Ruhlmann*

Ray Draper (Raymond Allen Draper)

b. Aug. 3, 1940, New York, NY, **d.** Nov. 1, 1982, NYC
Tuba / Hard bop
Ray Draper was among the few notable jazz tuba soloists. He attended the High School of Performing Arts and Manhattan School of Music, made his first entry into the jazz world playing with Jackie McLean in 1956 and 1957, and later played with Donald Byrd and John Coltrane. Draper was part of Max Roach's group in 1958 and 1959. He spent a brief period with Don Cherry in 1962 and then played with Big Black and Horace Tapscott. Draper led the jazz-rock ensemble Red Beans and Rice in 1968 and 1969. He moved to England in '69, and played with Kenneth Terroade and Archie Shepp, as well as Dr. John. Draper returned to America in 1971, recording with Jack McDuff and briefly teaching at Wesleyan. His final stint was with the group Gravity, led by Howard Johnson. Draper never overcame severe drug problems and spent three years in prison during the early '60s. He was killed in 1982.—*Ron Wynn*

● **Tuba Sounds** / Mar. 15, 1957 / Prestige 7096

Kenny Drew (Kenneth Sidney Drew)

b. Aug. 28, 1928, New York, NY, **d.** 1993
Piano / Hard bop
From his formative years as an accompanist for Lester Young and Buddy DeFranco, Kenny Drew developed into a masterful soloist and accompanist. He was a keyboard giant whose specialty among many other technical skills was long lines in the right hand; he was a dynamic soloist, and his albums displayed his versatility and facility in many styles and musical situations. From his first session with Howard McGhee in 1949 through numerous dates that featured him with Coleman Hawkins, Lester Young, Art Blakey, Dinah Washington, Buddy Rich, Charley Parker, and Milt Jackson, and numerous others, Drew's legacy was making tasteful, swinging, and inventive contributions to numerous groups and recordings. Drew joined with bassist Niels-Orstead Henning Pedersen for over 20 years as part of the house rhythm section at the Montmarte, appearing on countless recordings during that time. He also made his own albums for Blue Note, Timeless, Riverside, Fantasy, and Soul Note, among others. Kenny Drew was certainly among jazz's most prolific pianists of all time.—*Ron Wynn*

This Is New / Mar. 28, 1957+Apr. 3, 1957 / Riverside 483
★ **Undercurrent** / Dec. 11, 1960 / Blue Note 84059

Ray Drummond

Bass / Hard bop
A topflight contemporary jazz bassist, Ray Drummond stayed busy on many hard bop sessions in the '80s and '90s. He's recently done trio projects with Hank Jones and Billy Higgins and

a duo session with John Hicks. He's been a frequent partner with drummer Marvin "Smitty" Smith. Drummond's appeared often on Criss Cross, DMP, and Teresa (Evidence) releases but has hardly been restricted to those labels.—*Ron Wynn*

● **Essence, The / i.** 1991 / Digital Music 480
The third album with premier bassist Ray Drummond stepping out from the rhythm section to serve as leader. But this trio session seems more a cooperative venture, as pianist Hank Jones, Drummond, and drummer Billy Higgins zipped through the program of standards and originals sounding almost like one player. —*Ron Wynn*

George Duke

b. Jan. 12, 1946, San Rafael, CA
Keyboards, producer / Early jazz rock, instrumental pop, contemporary funk
Keyboardist George Duke has enjoyed several successful careers. He's done jazz and jazz rock in the '60s and '70s, playing with Cannonball Adderley and Frank Zappa as well as coleading a band with Billy Cobham in the mid '70s. Later came hits as a pop producer and the rise of his own urban contemporary and fusion group The Stanley Clarke-George Duke Project. This band has enjoyed urban contemporary and pop hits, and Duke has also done independent productions for various artists. He's periodically returned to jazz and fusion dates as a sideman.—*Ron Wynn*

● **Solo Keyboard Album (1976)** / 1976 / Epic 25021

Ted Dunbar (Earl Thodore Dunbar)

b. Jan. 17, 1937, Port Arthur, TX
Guitar / Hard bop, modern creative
A fine player in multiple styles and a serious student of his instrument who's published several books on guitar technique, Ted Dunbar is a self-taught musician. He led a dance band while in high school, and played trumpet and guitar while studying pharmacy at Texas Southern University in the late '50s. He also played with Arnett Cobb, Don Wilkerson, and Joe Turner. Dunbar moved to Indiana in the early '60s, where he played and studied with Dave Baker for two years and occasionally filled in for Wes Montgomery. Dunbar moved to New York in 1966 and stayed busy during the remainder of the '60s and through the '70s. He performed and recorded with Gil Evans, Tony Williams' Lifetime, Frank Foster, Sonny Rollins, Ron Carter, Billy Harper, Roy Haynes, Billy Taylor, McCoy Tyner, the New Jazz Repetory Company, and the National Jazz Ensemble. Dunbar joined the music faculty at Livingston College, Rutgers, in 1972. He's continued doing sessions and recordings.—*Ron Wynn*

Opening Remarks / i. Jan. 1978 / Xanadu 155

Secundum Artem / i. Jun. 1980 / Xanadu 181

Jazz Guitarist / i. Jul. 1982 / Xanadu 196

Johnny Dyani (Johnny [Mbizo] Dyani)

b. Nov. 30, 1945, **d.** Jul. 11, 1986
Bass, piano / World fusion, modern creative
A commanding bassist with a stalwart, deep tone, Johnny Dyani was part of a sizable South African expatriate community living and working in England. He arrived there with pianist Chris McGregor's Blue Notes band, and subsequently played with McGregor's The Brotherhood of Breath, the Spontaneous Music Ensemble, Musicians Co-op, and Steve Lacy. Dyani later recorded with Lacy, Enrico Rava, and Louis Moholo, as well as touring South America in the late '60s. He moved to Copenhagen in the early '70s and did several recordings in various European locales. He worked with Don Cherry, John Tchicai, Dudu Pukwana, Makaya Ntshoko, Joseph Jarman, and David Murray and also led his own groups. After Mongezi Feza's death in 1975, Dyani returned briefly to England and played on McGregor's album *Blue Notes for Mongezi.* —*Ron Wynn and Michael G. Nastos*

○ **Mbizo** / Feb. 1981 / Steeple Chase 1163

★ **Afrika** / Oct. 1, 1983 / Steeple Chase 1186
The South African bassist, pianist, composer with septet. Well-respected as a musician worldwide. A unique amalgam of styles. —*Michael G. Nastos*

Allen Eager

b. Jan. 27, 1927, New York, NY

Tenor sax, alto sax / Bop
Tenor saxophonist Eager began as a swing-era player with Tommy Dorsey as a teen, but he made the switch to bop in the '40s and remained proficient at swing as well. He worked with Buddy Rich and Tadd Dameron in the late '40s and '50s, then made infrequent appearances through the mid and late '50s both abroad and in America. He made a brief jazz return in the '80s. —*Ron Wynn*

★ **Tenor Sax** / Mar. 22, 1946-Jul. 15, 1947 / Savoy 15044

Charles Earland

b. May 24, 1941, Philadelphia, PA
Organ, soprano sax / Hard bop, blues & jazz, soul jazz
Originally a saxophonist from Philadelphia, Earland started out working with Jimmy McGriff and was leading his own band by the early '60s. Unable to keep organists in his group, he switched to the Hammond organ in 1963 and later played that instrument with Lou Donaldson. Forming his own organ trio, he recorded *Black Talk* in 1969, a commercial success. A groove player, Earland went on to make many albums in the soul-jazz vein. —*Michael Erlewine*

○ **Black Talk** / Dec. 15, 1969 / Prestige 335
The punchy organ-based music moves along nicely from a group that keeps in the vernacular and also manages to play engagingly on a program of stretchers. —*Bob Rusch, Cadence*

★ **Leaving This Planet** / Dec. 11-13, 1973 / Fantasy 66002
Great stints by Joe Henderson (sax), Eddie Henderson (tpt), and Freddie Hubbard (tpt). His most ambitious album. —*Ron Wynn*

☆ **Front Burner** / Jun. 27, 1988 / Milestone 9165
Recorded at Englewood Cliffs, NJ. Comeback for veteran organist. "Mom & Dad" (in 10/4 time) is infectious. —*Michael G. Nastos*

Bill Easley

Multireeds / Hard bop, modern creative
One of the most versatile reed players among contemporary stylists, Easley plays alto, tenor, baritone, clarinet, and flute with equal fire and skill. During the '60s, he moved to Memphis from the East Coast and attended MSU. Easley played in Stax and Isaac Hayes bands in the '70s. Since the mid '70s, he has been a busy session man and periodic bandleader. Easley's worked with Roland Hanna, James Williams, Mulgrew Miller, Grady Tate, Victor Gaskin, and Billy Higgins, among others, and has recorded for Sunnyside and Milestone.—*Ron Wynn*

★ **Wind Inventions** / Sep. 1988 / Sunnyside 1022
Premier clarinetist in a neo-contemporary setting. Very attractive music. —*Michael G. Nastos*

Billy Eckstine (William Clarence Eckstine)

b. Jul. 8, 1914, Pittsburgh, PA, **d.** Mar. 8, 1993
Vocals, bandleader, trumpet, valve trombone / Swing, big band, bop
He could have been a great trombonist or trumpeter; instead Billy Eckstine parlayed his rich, deep voice and suave looks into a career as a romantic idol. He had a great big band in the '40s, which he had to disband due to economics. A careful shift from a strict jazz-based style, where the instrumentalist reigns, to lush MOR ballads made him a superstar, and he remained among the most popular for sentimental fare throughout his lifetime. Eckstine had 12 songs reach the Top 30 between 1949 and 1952, among them "My Foolish Heart" and "I Wanna Be Loved." He secured a lucrative five-year deal from MGM, and while the hit run ended in the '50s, Eckstine maintained his appeal and popularity for many years afterward.—*Ron Wynn*

○ **I Want to Talk about You / i.** Feb. 1940-Mar. 1945 / Xanadu 207
I Want to Talk about You was a find for fans of the Earl Hines orchestra as well as admirers of singer Billy Eckstine, since most of the titles were taken from the Hines recordings of 1940 and 1941. . . . "If That's the Way You Feel," "I Want to Talk about You," and "Without a Song" were from Air Force Radio Service transcriptions of the Eckstine band, and are dated March 4, 1945. . . . The sound is satisfactory. —*Shirley Klett, Cadence*

★ **Mister B and the Band** / 1945 / Savoy 4401
1945-1946. Landmark recordings whence bop partly (maybe fully) emerged. Album has incredible personnel and great vocals. —*Ron Wynn*

Music Map

Jazz Drums

African, Caribbean Drummers	Military Marches	Avant-Garde

Avant-Garde
Ed Blackwell (1929)
Paul Motian (1931)
Rashied Ali (1935)
Beaver Harris (1936)
Sunny Murray (1937)
Andrew Cyrille (1939)
Barry Althschul (1943)
Famoudou Don Moye (1946)
Tani Tabbal
M'Boom Ensemble (1970)
Steve McCall (1933-1989)
J.C. Moses (1936-1977)
Clifford Jarvis (1941)

Early Jazz Drummers
Baby Dodds (1898-1959)
Tony Sbarbaro (1897-1969)
Jasper Taylor (1894-1964)

Ragtime Drummers
William Reitz
James Lent
Budd Gilmore

Chicago & New York
Ben Pollack (1903-1971)
Frank Snyder
Vic Berton (1896-1951)
Dave Tough (1907-1948)
Bob Consulman
Paul Kettler
George Stafford–Barrett Deems (1914)
Wayne Jones–Slick Jones (1907-1969)

New Orleans
Baby Dodds (1898-1959)
Zutty Singleton (1898-1975)
Paul Barbarin (1899-1969)

Milton Graves (1941)
Charles "Bobo" Shaw(1947)

Swing Era
Sonny Greer (1895-1982)
Cozy Cole (1906-1981)
Dave Tough (1907-1948)
Gene Krupa (1909-1973)
Chick Webb (1909-1939)
Big Sid Catlett (1910-1951)
Buddy Rich (1917-1987)
Jo Jones (1911-1985)
Kaiser Marshall (1899-1948)

Jazz-Rock
Bobby Colomby (1944)
Billy Cobham (1944)
Tony Williams (1945)
Alphonze Mouzon (1948)
Lenny White (1949)
Bill Bruford (1949)
Peter Erskine (1954)
Simon Phillips (1973)

Solos
Lionel Hampton (1909)
Chick Webb (1901-1939)
George Wettling (1907-1968)
Ray Baudic (1909-1988)

Bop Drumming
Art Blakey (1919-1990)
Philly Joe Jones (1923-1985)
Max Roach (1924)
Roy Haynes (1926)
Kenny Clarke (1929-1985)
Dannie Richmond (1935-1988)

Cool Jazz
Shelly Manne (1920-1984)
Joe Morello (1928)

Roy Brooks (1938)
Dennis Charles (1933)
Jerome Cooper (1946)
Joe Chambers (1942)

Post Bop
Sam Woodyard (1925) – Elvin Jones (1927)
Arthur Taylor (1929) – Louis Hayes (1937)
Roy McCurdy (1936) – Mickey Roker (1932)
Al Foster (1944)
Alan Dawson (1929)
Jimmy Cobb (1929)
Billy Higgins (1936)
Pete LaRoca (1938)

1980s-1990s
Jeff Watts
Jack DeJohnette (1942)
Omar Hakin (1959)
Adam Nussbaum (1955)
Cecil Brooks III
John Vidacovich
Cyndi Blackman
Terri Lyne Carrington
Marvin Smitty Smith (1961)

● **MGM Years** / **i.** 1947-1957 / PolyGram 19442

○ **Mister B with a Beat** / **i.** 1955 / MGM 3176

☆ **Mr. B** / **i.** 1960 / Audio Lab 1549

○ **No Cover, No Minimum** / 1960 / Capitol 98583
An outstanding '60 live set, with Eckstine backed by a good combo doing classics like "Lush Life" and "Moonlight in Vermont." The intimate nightclub setting, coupled with Bobby Tucker's simple, yet effective arrangements, make this perhaps Eckstine's best album outside his prime '40s and early '50s dates. It has been reissued on CD with 12 previously unissued cuts. — *Ron Wynn, AMG*

☆ **At Basin St. East** / Oct. 1961 / Mercury 832592
A 1990 reissue of a fine live date with Quincy Jones leading the orchestra and writing the tracks. —*Ron Wynn*

★ **Billy Eckstine Sings with Benny Carter** / Nov. 17, 1986-Nov. 18, 1986 / Verve 832011
Billy Eckstine Sings with Benny Carter coupled the master balladeer with the great altoist (who played trumpet on one cut) for a recorded first. There were delicious vocalizations, impeccable

accompaniments, and the bonus of Helen Merrill's voice joining Eckstine's on two tracks. — *W. Royal Stokes, Jazz Times*

○ **Stardust** / Polydor 525

Harry Edison (Harry "Sweets" Edison)

b. Oct. 10, 1915, Columbus, OH

Trumpet / Swing

Few players deserve the description of being "natural" players, but trumpeter Harry "Sweets" Edison merits it. An early Louis Armstrong disciple, Edison began in territory bands before coming to New York in the '30s. He joined Basie in 1938 and stayed until 1950. He worked in the studios and, in the early '50s, began an association with Frank Sinatra. Through the '50s, '60s, and '70s, he stayed busy on all fronts: touring, bandleading, and recording. Edison was once a mercurial, rampaging trumpeter, but later became a reserved, elegant stylist. He revolutionized the use of the mute and was a skilled soloist.—*Ron Wynn*

★ **Sweets** / Sep. 4, 1956 / Clef 717

☆ **Gee Baby, Ain't I Good to You?** / Mar. 5, 1957+Mar. 30, 1957 / Verve 8211

★ **Jawbreakers** / Apr. 18, 1962 / Riverside 487
Solid, inviting duo work, matching Edison with Eddie "Lockjaw" Davis (ts). —*Ron Wynn*

○ **Ben Webster and Sweets Edison** / Jun. 6, 1962-Jun. 7, 1962 / Columbia 1891

○ **Simply Sweets** / Sep. 22, 1977 / Pablo 2310-806
Another giant of swing trumpet who bridged the gap successfully, Harry Edison reunited with his old partner, tenor saxophonist Eddie "Lockjaw" Davis, for a tour through what turned out to be primarily blues terrain. . . . Davis offered little that was unexpected, but he did it so damned well that few could fault him. — *Jack Sohmer, Cadence*

★ **For My Pals** / Apr. 18, 1988-Apr. 19, 1988 / Pablo 2310-934
Trumpeter Edison never sounded better than on this studio date. Highly recommended. —*Michael G. Nastos*

○ **Harry Sweets Edison and Eddie Lockjaw Davis—Vol. 1** / Storyville 4004

○ **Harry Sweets Edison and Eddie Lockjaw Davis—Vol. 2** / Storyville 4025

Teddy Edwards (Theodore Marcus Edwards)

b. Apr. 26, 1924, Jackson, MS
Tenor sax / Bop
A very good tenor saxophonist, Teddy Edwards's role in the West Coast movement has been underrated by everyone except jazz historians and musicians. His skill on blues and ballads, as well as a soloist, is evident on the '40s recordings Edwards made as a leader and sideman. He moved to Los Angeles in 1945, after having played in Ernie Fields's orchestra. Edwards played with Roy Milton, Benny Carter, Howard McGhee, Howard Rumsey, and the Max Roach-Clifford Brown quintet in the '40s and '50s but earned special notoriety for his participation in tenor battles with Dexter Gordon, where Edwards' robust tone and aggressive playing made their mark. Edwards played with Gerald Wilson, Jimmy Witherspoon, and Billy Higgins in the late '50s and made some fine recordings for Contemporary in the early '60s. He's subsequently recorded for Muse, Steeplechase, and Antilles, and appeared on Xanadu, as well as a Verve session with Jimmy Smith and an Impulse date with Milt Jackson. Benny Goodman, Wilson, Sarah Vaughan, and Tom Waits, who helped him gain entry to Antilles, are other musicians with whom Edwards has worked or recorded during his career. —*Ron Wynn*

○ **Together Again!** / May 15+17, 1961 / Contemporary 424
Dynamite pairing with Howard McGhee (tpt). Incredible piano by Phineas Newborn Jr. (p) —*Ron Wynn*

★ **Feelin's** / Mar. 25, 1974 / Muse 5045
Teddy Edwards, who had not had a leader's date for more than seven years, far too long for so capable a musician, perhaps tried a little too hard. Of his four originals, "Tracks" and "April Love" were excellent, "Eleven Twenty Three" and "The Blue Sombrero" routine. "Ritta Ditta Blues" by Brown was very good indeed, and "Georgia on My Mind" was the famous standard. . . . Working out of a Gene Ammons bag, Edwards invested "Tracks" with plenty of tenor soul; the strategically placed low note was a catchy device. On the pretty bossa "April," his approach was much smoother but equally convincing, and he displayed humor and dexterity on "Ritta." Trumpeter Conte Candoli, more relaxed than with Supersax, was in a very lyrical groove on "April" and bopped the blues on "Ritta." Pianist Dolo Coker, long absent from recording studios, was not featured, but when he got a chance, as on "Tracks," he showed that he had not lost his Bud Powell-inspired chops. Bassist Ray Brown was beautifully recorded and was simply masterful. This is solid mainstream fare and, at times, more. —*Dan Morgenstern, Down Beat*

Marty Ehrlich

Sax / Modern creative
Marty Ehrlich's compositions cover not only musical concerns but also sociopolitical ones. He is a gifted saxophonist whose work tries mightily to embrace many idioms. Ehrlich plays several saxophones and has worked in free, ethnic, hard bop, and large group situations. B-flat and bass clarinet; various flutes; and alto, tenor, and soprano saxophones are part of his extensive instru-

mental arsenal. Ehrlich's played with Anthony Cox, Frank Lacy, Wayne Horovitz, and Pheeroan Ak Laff, among others, and has appeared on recordings by Christy Doran, Julius Hemphill, Muhal Richard Abrams, Leroy Jenkins, and John Zorn. He's recorded as a leader for Sound Aspects, Muse, and Enja.—*Ron Wynn*

○ **Eight Bold Souls** / i. 1986 / Sessoms 0002

○ **Pliant Plaint** / i. Apr. 1987 / Enja 5065

★ **Falling Man** / 1990 / Muse 5398
An intriguing, though sometimes disjointed, duo outing between multiinstrumentalist Marty Ehrlich and bassist Anthoy Cox. They venture into free, fusion, funk, and rock territory, and while all their duets are exceptionally played, the compositions aren't uniformly interesting. The best cut is their emphatic duet "You Don't Know What Love Is," which was a signature song for Eric Dolphy. —*Ron Wynn, AMG*

Roy Eldridge (David Roy Eldridge)

b. Jan. 30, 1911, Pittsburgh, PA, d. Feb. 26, 1989
Trumpet / Swing, big band
Dubbed "Little Jazz," the compact bundle of energy that was Roy Eldridge was all jazz. No one loved playing more or was more competitive. He took the innovations of Louis Armstrong a step higher and faster and added harmonic daring that captured the ear of young Dizzy Gillespie, who idolized him. As a soloist in many big bands, including those of Teddy Hill (with whom he made his first important records in 1935) and Fletcher Henderson, and on many great small-group sides with Billie Holiday and Teddy Wilson (1935-1941), Eldridge's style was studied by every trumpeter of the day, but it was his sensational flights with his own swinging little band in 1937 that really showed what this "Wizard of the Trumpet" could do. In 1941, he became the first Black musician to join an otherwise White band (Gene Krupa's) not just as a featured attraction or singer, but as a regular member of the section. He played the same role with Artie Shaw a few years later. After 1945, he strictly led his own bands, big or small, though he joined other stars in *Jazz at the Philharmonic*, of which he was a mainstay from the '40s through the '70s. In JATP, he was often teamed with Coleman Hawkins; these two giants also worked a lot together on their own. A 1980 heart attack put an end to Roy's trumpeting, but he was a fine singer and continued to perform occasionally in that role until his death. He was one of the most exciting players in the history of the music. —*Dan Morgenstern*

○ **Little Jazz** / i. Feb. 1935-Apr. 1940 / CBS 465684

★ **After You've Gone** / 1936-1946 / GRP 605
Roy Eldridge was a complex trumpet artist, and it is no shame that *After You've Gone* includes several failed attempts to recapture the glory of his 1941 epic-tragic ballad, "Rocking Chair." The other dominant mood here is the hot, screaming, high-note Eldridge. Most satisfying are the less forced, more modest works, usually at medium tempos, displaying the warmth and rasp of his sound. These are mostly big-band works from 1943-1946 and contain brief, vivid moments by the likes of tenorist Tom Archia and altoist Porter Kilbert, showing bop rearing its lovely head even in this late-swing setting. —*John Litweiler, Down Beat*

★ **On Keynote** / i. 1944 / PolyGram 830923
A very good collection of '40s Eldridge done for Keynote. The Coleman Hawkins quintet sides are particularly tasty. —*Ron Wynn*

☆ **Dale's Wail** / Apr. 20, 1953+Dec. 1953 / Clef 705
The expansion of Roy Eldridge's trumpet sonority made all the difference in the world. The bravura passages, as in "Rocking Chair" and "Wrap Your Troubles in Dreams," echoed rather than rang. Muted or open, his horn's inflections impressed this character on his lines. Eldridge, the third great trumpeter of the generation of Red Allen and Cootie Williams, was and is an emotional player, and the growth of his skill with dynamics finally unified the often disparate elements of his soloing. You could hardly wish for a more complete portrait of an artist than this album. —*John Litweiler, Down Beat*

★ **Little Jazz** / i. 1954 / Columbia 45275
Roy Eldridge was at the top of his form in Paris in June 1950; these sessions showed him in magnificent mettle. The rhythm sections were both first-rate as Dick Hyman and Ed Shaughnessy

took the piano-drum honors on side one, Gerry Wiggins and Kenny Clarke were on side two, and the ubiquitous Pierre Michelot, who appeared on six Jazz Legacy LPs, was the bassist on all cuts. The idea of adding Zoot Sims to the first session was useful; Sims's warm, bubbling tenor was a perfect foil for Eldridge's bristling, room-shaking trumpet. Even Eldridge's vocal talents were put to good use here; his singing was as expressive and individualistic as his trumpet playing. —*Lee Jeske, Down Beat*

○ **Trumpet Battle** / Oct. 29, 1954 / Clef 730
Though titled *The Trumpet Battle 1952,* this date devoted only seven minutes of its total to any such activity. Side one was entirely taken up with "Jam Session Blues" employing Roy Eldridge and Charlie Shaves on trumpet. . . . Side two spent 11:07 on the "Ballad Medley," another Norman Granz JATP convention, wherein Young played "I Can't Get Started," Shavers essayed "Summertime," Phillips did "Sweet Lorraine," Eldridge performed "It's the Talk of the Town," and Benny Carter capped it off with "Cocktails for Two," all marred by some of the worst recorded sound I've had the misfortune to hear. . . . The poor sound extended right into the so-called "Trumpet Battle," distorting what sounded like some fine Benny Carter alto, preceding the Shavers and Eldridge derring-do. —*Alan Bargebuhr, Cadence*

★ **Mexican Bandit Meets Pittsburg Pirate** / i. Aug. 24, 1973 / Fantasy 9646
Mexican Bandit Meets Pittsburgh Pirate. Interesting title for this wonderful collaboration between Eldridge and Paul Gonsalves (ts); a delightful date. —*Ron Wynn*

○ **I Remember Harlem** / i. 1976 / Inner City 7012
This was primarily a showcase for the dynamic trumpet style of "Little Jazz." Roy Eldridge played the blues with so much strength, resilience, and fun that it was difficult not to get caught up in the excitement. Whether singing the blues in French or playing piano, his music was extremely infectious. —*Spencer R. Weston, Cadence*

Duke Ellington (Edward Kennedy Ellington)

b. Apr. 29, 1899, Washington, DC, **d.** May 24, 1974, New York, NY
Composer, bandleader, piano / Swing, big band
One of the greatest composers of the 20th Century and leader for 50 years of a band that became the greatest of all jazz orchestras, Ellington is, alongside Louis Armstrong, the dominant figure in jazz history. He began his career in his native Washington, DC, and came to New York in 1924. His first group was a sextet; by the time his became the resident band at New York's Cotton Club in late 1927, it had grown to 11 pieces; by 1933, when it made its first visit to Europe, it had stabilized at 14 men. By that year, Ellington had reached his first peak as creator of the most original and personal big-band music in jazz. Throughout the '30s and into the first two years of the next decade, the band enjoyed remarkable stability of personnel, enabling Ellington to use it as his "instrument." A remarkable group of soloists interpreted the music he wrote for them: trumpeter Cootie Williams; cornetist Rex Stewart; trombonists Lawrence Brown and "Tricky Sam" Nanton; clarinetist Barney Bigard; alto saxist Johnny Hodges; baritone saxist Harry Carney; and Duke himself at the piano. In 1939, tenorist Ben Webster and the sensational young bassist Jimmy Blanton joined. The 1940-1942 band is considered by some to have been Ellington's greatest; coarranger and composer (and sometime pianist) Billy Strayhorn had also come on board by then. But Ellington continued to write great music and lead great bands until the final days. Such works as, for example, the suite *Such Sweet Thunder* (1957) equal anything in Ellingtonia. Among the musicians who starred in later editions of the band, trumpeter Clark Terry; cornetist and violinist Ray Nance; tenorist Paul Gonsalves; and clarinetist, arranger, and sometime tenorist Jimmy Hamilton must be noted. Key rhythm section players included pioneers Sonny Greer (drums) and Wellman Braud (bass), and, later Louis Bellson and Sam Woodyard (drums) and Oscar Pettiford (bass). Ellington's output was extraordinary, ranging from short pieces to suites, film scores, "sacred concerts," and all-time hits like "Mood Indigo," "Solitude," "Sophisticated Lady," and "Satin Doll." Ellington made more records, including wonderful small-group things and piano features, than any other single performer in jazz, and treasures continue to be uncovered. —*Dan Morgenstern*

☆ **Okeh Ellington** / Mar. 22, 1927-Nov. 8, 1930 / Columbia 46177
★ **Sophisticated Ellington** / i. 1927-1966 / RCA 4098
This is a wonderful two-record set of material ranging from the '20s to the '60s. —*Ron Wynn*

☆ **Braggin' in Brass: The Immortal 1938 Years** / 1938 / Portrait 44395

○ **Webster—Blanton Years, The** / i. 1939-1942 / RCA/Bluebird 5659
Fine three-disc anthology of late '30s, early '40s Ellington material covering contributions by pioneer bassist Jimmy Blanton. It includes full orchestra selections, plus bass-piano duets and small combo sessions. While much of this material is also available on more costly packages, this is a good domestic package. —*Ron Wynn, AMG*

☆ **1940 Fargo Concert** / Nov. 7, 1940 / Jazz Society 5201
One winter night in late 1940, Jack Towers (then a young Ellington fan) received permission to record Duke's orchestra on his portable disc cutter at a dance in Fargo, North Dakota. Little did he know that it was a historic night (as trumpeter Ray Nance made his debut with the band) and that the band would be in inspired form. Decades later the music came out on LP and now this double CD includes every scrap of music that has survived. The Duke Ellington orchestra was at one of its peaks during this period, overflowing with distinctive and unique soloists, and propelled by the top bassist in jazz (Jimmy Blanton). With the accelerated writing activity of Ellington and his new musical partner Billy Strayhorn, there was no better orchestra at the time, and rarely since. Tenor-saxophonist Ben Webster is heard in top form on "Star Dust"; cornetist Rex Stewart, trombonists Tricky Sam Nanton and Lawrence Brown, clarinetist Barney Bigard, and altoist Johnny Hodges also have some very strong moments; and Ray Nance does his best to fit in: many in the band were hearing him for the first time. It is indeed very fortunate that Jack Towers was present for what would have been a forgotten one-night stand. —*Scott Yanow*

○ **Take the "A" Train: The Legendary Blanton-Webster** / Jan. 15, 1941-Dec. 3, 1941 / Vintage Jazz Classics 1003
During 1941, one of Duke Ellington's peak years, not only did Ellington record frequently in the studios but he made this CD's worth of transcriptions for radio. Of the 26 selections on this generous set, eight of the songs were never recorded commercially and six others are heard here in their earliest versions, including Duke's theme "Take the 'A' Train" and "Perdido." The all-star orchestra is propelled by the great bassist Jimmy Blanton. Highly recommended. —*Scott Yanow*

○ **Duke Ellington (1943)** / Nov. 9, 1943 / Circle 103
The third of nine volumes in this collector's series featuring Duke Ellington's transcriptions from 1943 and 1945. Best are strong versions of "Caravan" and "Ain't Misbehavin" (featuring trumpeter Harold "Shorty" Baker). —*Scott Yanow*

○ **Golden Duke, The** / Oct. 23, 1946-Nov. 1950 / Prestige 24029
This double LP contains some very valuable Duke Ellington studio recordings that have since been reissued as separate sessions. The 13 titles from late-1946 include the hot "Jam-a-Ditty," a classic trumpet battle on "Blue Skies," Ray Nance's colorful vocal on "Tulip or Turnip," and the original version of "Happy- Go-Lucky Local," which Jimmy Forrest would "borrow" a few years later and rename "Night Train." The second half of this twofer features piano duets by Duke Ellington and Billy Strayhorn (the radical-sounding "Tonk" is very memorable) and four showcases for Oscar Pettiford's cello. This music is recommended, in one form or another. —*Scott Yanow*

○ **Carnegie Hall Concerts (December 1947)** / Dec. 27, 1947 / Prestige 24075
The final 1947 Carnegie Hall concert featured the premier performance of "Liberian Suite." Although this was called an extended work, the term is misleading. "Liberian" was merely a series of short pieces, no different from any of Ellington's other conventional charts and without any cumulative momentum. The composer's interest seemed focused much more on rhythmic than on harmonic structures. But then this was a program piece celebrating Liberia's 100th year of independence. Dance number three was the best of the group of five, a dark absorbing melody played by Ray Nance and Harry Carney. "Cotton Tail" featured exciting Al Sears, apparently bitten by the JATP bug. Sonny Greer

was boisterous. "Blue Serge" by Mercer Ellington had echoes of 1941. "Triple Play" was a longish piece for Johnny Hodges, Carney, and Lawrence Brown that failed to develop any momentum. Harold Baker was lively on Cootie Williams's piece, "Harlem Airshaft." The rarely played "East St. Louis" was played in tribute to Bubber Miley, responsible more than any other musician perhaps, including Duke, for putting the band on the track to its unique sound. "Basso Profoundo" gave off a whiff on "Now's the Time" before being taken over by Raglin and Pettiford. "Echoes of Harlem" and a Hodges medley were beautiful. —*John Mcdonough, Down Beat*

○ **Carnegie Hall Concerts (November 1948)** / Nov. 13, 1948 / Vintage Jazz Classics 25
The sixth and final of Duke Ellington's acclaimed Carnegie Hall concerts, this two-CD set allows one to hear the largely undocumented 1948 orchestra, which was kept off record because of a musicians union strike. With Ben Webster temporarily back in the band and such solo stylists as altoist Johnny Hodges, Al Sears on tenor, clarinetist Jimmy Hamilton, and trumpeters Ray Nance and Shorty Baker, the Ellington orchestra performs both newer material (such as "The Tattooed Bride" and several obscurities) and some surprising older compositions, including a revival of "Reminiscence in Tempo" and a "hits medley." An oddity is one of the very few Ellington performances of Billy Strayhorn's classic "Lush Life." —*Scott Yanow*

☆ **Piano Reflections** / Apr. 1953-Dec. 1953 / Capitol 92863
These trio dates from 1953 not only accent the Duke's formidable stride background and rhythmic dexterity but also range from introspective pieces to mournful blues and soulful ballads. —*Ron Wynn, Rock & Roll Disc.*

○ **Drum Is a Woman, A** / Sep. 1956-Dec. 1956 / Columbia 951

★ **Duke Ellington—Vols. 1-10** / i. 1956 / Atlantic 91041
1956-1970. This essential series came from his private collection; many brilliant cuts and well worth having. Hard to separate any of the individual volumes. Studio and dance sessions—suites. —*Ron Wynn*

○ **Ella Fitzgerald/The Duke Ellington Songbook** / Jun. 25, 1957-Sep. 1957 / Verve 2535
The first lady of song meets the genius of jazz on this delightful two-LP set. Unlike many other albums in which a singer is backed by a big band, there are many spots for Ellington's sidemen to shine; in fact the four-part "Portrait of Ella Fitzgerald" is purely instrumental until the final movement. It is wonderful to hear Ella sing such songs as "Drop Me Off in Harlem," "Rockin' in Rhythm," and "Perdido" along with the ballads. Recommended. —*Scott Yanow*

○ **All Star Road Band—Vol. 2** / Jun. 1957 / Doctor Jazz 39137

☆ **Ellington Indigos** / Sep. 9, 1957-Oct. 10, 1957 / Columbia 44444

○ **Girl's Suite and the Perfume Suite, The** / Dec. 9, 1957-Aug. 20, 1961 / Columbia 38028
Recorded in 1962 but first released 22 years later, this was a rather unusual studio session for Duke Ellington because he chose to allocate all of the solo sections on eight of his standards to tenor-saxophonist Paul Gonsalves, even numbers such as "C Jam Blues" and "Jam with Sam," which generally served as features for a variety of players. Obviously those listeners who most enjoy Gonsalves' harmonically advanced and unpredictable style will have to pick this up. This disc can also remind more general Ellington collectors just how power-packed Duke's lineup really was, for Ellington could have given the same treatment to at least six of his other sidemen! —*Scott Yanow*

○ **Black, Brown and Beige (1944-1946 Band Recordings)** / Feb. 5, 1958-Feb. 12, 1958 / Bluebird 6641
Outstanding three-disc set that collects his somewhat controversial mid- and late-'40s concert recordings into one nice package. —*Ron Wynn*

○ **Blues Summit** / Aug. 14, 1958-Feb. 20, 1959 / Verve 8822
Partly reissued on CD, this very enjoyable double LP includes two related sessions. The main one is both unusual and delightful, for it features altoist Johnny Hodges and trumpeter Harry "Sweets" Edison leading a sextet that found Duke Ellington on piano. The repertoire is inspired, a variety of jam tunes, including several by W.C. Handy, and both Sweets and Hodges are heard at their most expressive. The remainder of this twofer teams Hodges and trombonist Lawrence Brown with tenor great Ben Webster and the ex-

citing trumpeter Roy Eldridge; this time Billy Strayhorn is on piano, and the music is almost as memorable. Highly recommended in one form or another. —*Scott Yanow*

☆ **Side by Side** / **i.** 195z / Verve 821578
W/ Johnny Hodges. Joyous 1986 reissue of magnificent late-'50s small-group material. —*Ron Wynn*

○ **Duke Ellington-Louis Armstrong Years, The** / Apr. 3, 1961-Apr. 4, 1961 / Roulette 108
Although Duke Ellington and Louis Armstrong were jazz music's most famous and acclaimed musicians, their only meeting on record (other than a couple of isolated selections in the 1940s) is the music contained on this two-LP set (since reissued on CD). Rather than have Armstrong sit in with Ellington's orchestra, Duke temporarily became a member of Satch's All-Stars. In this all-Ellington program, Louis is inspired by the fresh repertoire and his vocals are often jubilant. With strong assistance from trombonist Trummy Young and clarinetist Barney Bigard (a former Ellington bandmember then travelling with Armstrong), Pops and Duke created a very memorable and quite unique program of classic music. —*Scott Yanow*

○ **Great Tenor Encounters, The** / **i.** Aug. 18, 1962-Sep. 26, 1962 / Impulse 9350
The Great Tenor Encounters was unique because it contained the only sides Duke Ellington ever recorded with Coleman Hawkins (sides one and two) and John Coltrane (sides three and four). Both sessions took place in 1962. Hawkins should have recorded more with the Duke. His sound and style were perfectly suited to the band. He was surrounded here by the Ellington elite, a septet including Johnny Hodges, Ray Nance, Harry Carney, and Lawrence Brown, and he fit right in. Most of these arrangements were not elaborate and were meant to give everyone room to blow. Some cuts were better than others, but none failed. "Mood Indigo," with Hawkins taking five choruses, and "Solitude," with Nance on violin, have rarely sounded better. Pairing Ellington and Coltrane was an odd idea. Ellington wisely kept the group down to a quartet. Duke's team appeared on side three with Aaron Bell on bass and Sam Woodyard on drums and Trane's team on side four with Jimmy Garrison on bass and Elvin Jones on drums. The ballads worked best because Trane played them very straight, very beautifully. But even the cuts that did not work were interesting. Rarely did old meet new in such a startling and revealing manner. —*Douglas Clark, Down Beat*

○ **Reevaluations: The Impulse Years** / **i.** Aug. 18, 1962-Jan. 10, 1966 / ABC/Impulse 9256
This two-LP set is an excellent sampling of Duke Ellington's music as originally released on Impulse. In addition to selections featuring Ellington in small groups with Coleman Hawkins and John Coltrane, there are performances of Duke's music by groups led by Johnny Hodges, McCoy Tyner, Ben Webster, Earl Hines, Clark Terry, Lawrence Brown, and Paul Gonsalves. Careful selection resulted in the most exciting recordings being included. A fine introduction to Ellington's legacy, as mostly heard through the interpretations of others. —*Scott Yanow*

★ **Money Jungle** / Sep. 17, 1962 / Blue Note 46398
In 1962 Duke Ellington was teamed on record with a trio consisting of bassist Charles Mingus and drummer Max Roach. The setting may have seemed "modern" for a pianist from Duke's generation, but one should realize that he was a major influence on both Thelonious Monk and Cecil Taylor. Ellington, one of the few veterans of the 1920s to make a smooth transition to the relatively modern era, is in superlative form on this date, even when challenged on "Money Jungle" by the potentially combative Mingus. This LP version includes four selections not on the original release; the later CD also added a couple of "new" alternate takes. Well worth acquiring. —*Scott Yanow*

● **Duke Ellington and John Coltrane** / Sep. 26, 1962 / MCA 39103
W/ John Coltrane. Jazz immortals collaborate. Mostly pristine music. —*Michael G. Nastos*

★ **Great Paris Concert, The** / Feb. 1, 1963-Feb. 23, 1963 / Atlantic 304
A definitive look at the early 1960s edition of the Duke Ellington orchestra, this live two-LP set contains many highlights: fresh versions of "Rockin' in Rhythm," "Concerto for Cootie" (featuring Cootie Williams), and "Jam with Sam"; extended renditions of "Suite Thursday" and the "Harlem Suite"; and a few newer selections. Without counting the pianist-leader, 11 soloists are heard

from in memorable settings, including both Cootie Williams and Ray Nance. Highly recommended music, either as this twofer or on CD. —*Scott Yanow*

☆ **My People** / **i.** Aug. 20, 1963-Aug. 28, 1963 / Red Baron 52759
In 1963 Duke Ellington wrote the music for a short-lived show titled *My People*, which was a sort of combination of his early 1940s *Jump for Joy* play along with some of the music from his "Black, Brown and Beige" suite. Using an orchestra comprised of Ellingtonians past, present, and future, along with a few compatible outsiders, and featuring a variety of vacalists that include Joya Sherrill, Jimmy Grissom, and Lil Greenwood, Duke created music whose message of racial harmony remains timeless. Due to the high quality of the "Black, Brown and Beige" suite and the shorter originals, this interesting set is more enjoyable than one might expect. —*Scott Yanow*

○ **Duke Ellington—Vol. 5** / **i.** Nov. 6, 1968-Jun. 15, 1970 / Atlantic 91045
One of the most interesting of the ten volumes released in The Private Collection series, this CD contains "The Degas Suite" (music for a soundtrack of an art film that was never produced) and a ballet score titled "The River." Ellington is mostly the lead voice but his star sidemen are heard from on these formerly very rare and somewhat unusual performances. Clearly Duke's genius was strong enough to fill three lifetimes full of new music, and this CD contains some melodies that might have been more significant if he had lived long enough to find a place for them! —*Scott Yanow*

○ **Duke Ellington—Vol. 9** / **i.** Nov. 23, 1968-Dec. 3, 1968 / Atlantic 91233
The ninth of ten volumes of music from Duke Ellington's "Private Collection" of unknown tapes, this CD captures Duke in 1968 shortly after clarinetist Jimmy Hamilton left the band and tenor-saxophonist Harold Ashby joined up. Even after 30 years of playing some of these standards, Ellington found new ways to rearrange such songs as "Sophistcated Lady," "Mood Indigo," and "Just Squeeze Me." In addition, there are a few new obscurities such as "Knuf" (which finds Jeff Castleman switching to electric bass), "Reva," and the somewhat dated Trish Turner vocal on "Cool and Groovy." Lots of surprises on this fine CD. —*Scott Yanow*

○ **Giants of Jazz** / **i.** Oct. 1979 / Time Life 02
There is nothing seriously amiss in this collation. The 40 selections agreed upon by the consulting experts John S. Wilson, Stanley Dance, Michael Brooks, and Richard Spottswood are unquestionably among the Ellington band's greatest. Moreover, the consistency of the sound quality achieved in remastering was especially commendable in that the material was drawn from at least eight different original labels. Featured in the first eight selections, those predominantly in the "jungle style" were Bubber Miley, Sam Nanton, Barney Bigard, and Johnny Hodges, but there were also notable solos from Duke Ellington, Wellman Braud, Jabbo Smith, Louis Metcalf, and guest star Lonnie Johnson. The band's next phase was marked by Cootie Williams's replacement of Miley and the subsequent emergence of increasingly more sophisticated compositions. Outstanding solos and orchestrations abounded throughout the selections in the '30s, a fruitful period often eclipsed by the even greater years ahead. The universally praised 1940 band, which was defined by the dual presence of Jimmy Blanton and Ben Webster, produced an unprecedented cornucopia of sound and inspired the composer-leader to conceive, write, and record some of the most enduring works of his career. That band recorded some 75 titles in two years, not counting alternate takes, and the list of airchecks and documented concerts and dances is still growing. For those who feel, as I do, that the entirety of listenable Ellington should be made generally available in perpetuity, the reduction of the complete 1940-1942 oeuvre to only 13 titles seems the unkindest cut of all. But the intention of the selection committee must be read as an inducement to further study, for no panel of conscionable jazz savants could ever feel thoroughly confident that it had indeed made an infallible decision where music of this kind is concerned. —*Jack Sohmer, Down Beat*

Mercer Ellington (Mercer Kennedy Ellington)

b. Mar. 11, 1919, Washington, DC
Trumpet, composer, bandleader / Swing, big band

Trumpeter, composer, and bandleader Mercer Ellington is the son of Duke Ellington and current leader of the surviving Ellington orchestra. Mercer Ellington has held jobs such as arranger and section trumpeter within the Ellington empire, and he also wrote a biography of his famous father in 1978. He studied music in Washington and then in New York at the Institute of Musical Art. Ellington worked in and around New York in the late '20s and early '30s before forming his own band. The group included such musicians as Clark Terry, Cat Anderson, and Carmen McRae. He contributed some works to the Ellington library, among them "Blue Serge," and "Things Ain't What They Used to Be." While in the army in the mid-'40s, Ellington played in a band under Sy Oliver's leadership. From that point on Ellington led his own groups and did such odd jobs as disc jockey, sales representative, and record company executive before becoming Cootie Williams's manager and section trumpeter. He joined his father's band in those same two capacities in 1965. Mercer Ellington took the reins of the Ellington orchestra in 1974. He directed the musical "Sophisticated Ladies" from 1981 to 1983. —*Ron Wynn*

● **Digital Duke** / **i.** 1987 / GRP 9548
This was the new Mercer Ellington record. You wouldn't know that from looking at the front cover, which boasted the "Duke Ellington orchestra"—the flanking words in tiny letters and Duke's name in huge ones. . . . There were a number of Duke alumni aboard—Clark Terry, Britt Woodman, Chuck Connors, Norris Turney, and Louis Bellson. But the standout among the guests, oddly enough, was Branford Marsalis, roaring through the Ducal bop of "Cottontail," coming back for a Ben Webster-informed ride on "Take the 'A' Train." . . . The playing wasn't sloppy, but the vets seemed to miss the direct encouragement of their flattering, encouraging, wicked taskmaster. —*Kevin Whitehead, Cadence*

Don Ellis (Donald Johnson Ellis)

b. Jul. 25, 1934, Los Angeles, CA, **d.** Dec. 17, 1978, Hollywood, CA
Trumpet, composer, bandleader / Big band, early jazz rock, modern creative

Don Ellis was an innovative composer/trombonist/trumpeter. His early period 50s recordings show a progressive bent, while the albums in the 60s were on the electric side. A fine improviser, Ellis is better known for inventing split meter time signatures. He worked in the progressive big band format for the most part. —*Michael G. Nastos*

★ **New Ideas** / May 11, 1961 / New Jazz 431
The original thinking-jazz-lover's music. Quintet with unsung vibist Al Francis, and the Jaki Byard Trio. All originals by Ellis, who has a lot to say with combos like this. Variations, nay mutations, of familiar themes crop up, along with staggered and fractured time signatures. Very innovative musician, especially for jazz. —*Michael G. Nastos*

Herb Ellis (Mitchel Herbert Ellis)

b. Aug. 4, 1921, Farmersville, TX
Guitar / Swing, bop

Ellis began as a banjo player in his childhood and learned the rudiments of guitar on his own before attending North Texas State College with Jimmy Giuffre and Gene Roland. He got his start in the mid '40s with the Casa Loma Orchestra and Jimmy Dorsey band. In 1947 he formed the Soft Winds trio, a unit that echoed the influence of the Nat King Cole trio right down to Ellis's guitar lines underneath pianist Lou Carter's leads and bassist John Frigo's accompaniment. The trio stayed together until 1952 and had the successful song "Detour Ahead" recorded by Billie Holiday. Ellis replaced Barney Kessel in Oscar Peterson's group in 1953 and attained stature and stardom. He has worked extensively with Ray Brown since the '70s. Exhaustive studio and session and recording work hasn't dulled his passion. He is a prototype jazz guitarist in the Charlie Christian tradition. —*Ron Wynn*

★ **Herb Ellis Meets Jimmy Giuffre** / Mar. 26, 1959 / Verve

● **Seven Come Eleven** / Jul. 29, 1973 / Concord Jazz 4002
W/ Joe Pass. Concord's second record. Titans clash. Great music. Good on CD. First-rate band doing prototype arrangements. —*Ron Wynn*

★ **Doggin' Around** / Mar. 1988 / Concord Jazz 4372

Certainly a pair of time-tested veterans can't go wrong. The CD has two bonus cuts. —*Ron Wynn*

○ **Roll Call** / **i.** 1992 / Justice 1001
Well-done recent release with Ellis backed by a solid lineup of session and studio pros, among them trumpeter Jay Thomas and violinist Johnny Frigo. They play mix of blues, traditional jazz stomps and standards, with organist Mel Rhyne adding soulful support, alongside drummer Jake Hanna. —*Ron Wynn, AMG*

○ **After You've Gone** / **i.** Mar. 13, 1992 / Concord Jazz 4006

James Emery
Guitar / Modern creative
An outstanding electric guitarist, James Emery was a member of the original String Trio of New York with Billy Band and John Lindberg. He made six albums with the String Trio in the '70s and has since gone on to record for Lumina and Knitting Factory Works. He made a duo record with violinist Leroy Jenkins and one record heading the James Emery/Illiad Quartet. —*Ron Wynn*

● **Exo Eso** / **i.** Oct. 1987 / FMP 59

Peter Erskine
b. Jun. 5, 1954, Somers Point, NJ
Drums / Modern creative
Peter Erskine is a drummer who started with bands of Stan Kenton and Maynard Ferguson, then joined Weather Report. His ability is unquestioned—he can swing hard or play dance rhythms. One of the most well rounded drummers in contemporary music, Erskine's solo albums range from neo-bop to futuristic-fusion. —*Michael G. Nastos*

★ **Peter Erskine** / Jun. 22-23, 1982 / Contemporary 610
First release by a first-rate drummer and lots of New York friends. "All's Well That Ends" is a winning track, as is "Leroy St." —*Michael G. Nastos*

○ **Sweet Soul** / Mar. 1991 / Novus 63140
A terrific date featuring John Scofield (g), Joe Lovano (s), Bob Mintzer (s), Kenny Werner (p). Erskine's abilities as a composer are quite evident on this recording. —*Paul Kohler*

Booker Ervin (Booker Telleferro Ervin II)
b. 1930, Denison, Texas, **d.** Jul. 31, 1970
Tenor sax / Hard bop, blues & jazz
A marvelous robust tenor saxophonist and a prime example of the huge "Texas Tenor" style, Ervin played trombone as a child and later studied tenor and music theory at Berklee. He played in the Air Force Band in 1951-1952 and toured from 1954 to 1958 in Ernie Fields's R&B band. From the late '50s and often throughout the '60s, Ervin worked with Charles Mingus's Jazz Workshop groups, where his honking, funky sound was ideal for those compositions that featured a pronounced gospel or blues tone. Ervin also worked with Randy Weston, Dexter Gordon, Horace Parlan, and Ted Curson in the '60s, while making a number of marvelous albums as a leader, among them *The Book Cooks, That's It,* and *Exultation,* plus *The Blues Book* and *The Space Book.* —*Ron Wynn*

○ **Soulful Saxes** / **i.** Jun. 1960 / Affinity 758

★ **Book Cooks, The** / Jun. 1960 / Affinity
Robust, earthy Ervin throughout. This tremendous combo date was originally on Bethlehem. —*Ron Wynn*

○ **Cookin'** / Nov. 26, 1960 / Savoy Jazz 150

☆ **Back from the Gig** / Feb. 15, 1963+May 24, 1968 / Blue Note 488
Tenor saxophonist Booker Ervin's *Back from the Gig* was a perplexing volume. Perplexing because it took Blue Note nearly seven years after Ervin's untimely death to release these valuable and infectious recordings. Apparently both sessions, one recorded under the tutelage of pianist Horace Parlan, whom Michael Cuscuna thoughtfully documented in his liner notes, were scheduled for release years ago but never materialized. The Parlan sextet (1963) was a tough, no-nonsense blues unit. Ervin, trumpeter Johnny Coles, and guitarist Grant Green were the lead voices and were sly, raw, and often dirty. Ervin, in particular, played with an inciting bounce and masterful range, lean and to the core. His own 1968 recordings, in cahoots with saxophonist Wayne Shorter and pianist Kenny Barron, were more expansive, envincing a knack for melding his blues romanticism to modal foundations

and professing some plain big band-inspired truths. —*Mikal Gilmore, Down Beat*

★ **Freedom and Space Sessions** / Dec. 3, 1963+Oct. 2, 1964 / Prestige 7386
While Byard, Davis, and Dawson pushed the music into the future, Ervin's tenor reached beyond the blues (which he intensely dug into on "Grant's Stand") back to the field holler. If his uptempo excursions were shouts, then his ballads were cries. On the slow numbers he liked long notes with strong terminal vibrato, and he hit some notes a little flat to add to the pathos. . . . This reissue contained the complete *Freedom Book* and *Space Book* sessions and one extra cut from each session, "Stella by Starlight" and "The Second #2", both of which originally appeared on Ervin's *Groovin' High.* —*Kevin Whitehead, Cadence*

○ **Groovin' High** / Jun. 30, 1966-Oct. 30, 1962 / Prestige 7417
Exuberant quartet date from 1964, with Ervin again playing bluesy, often searing tenor solos. He's supported by an ace rhythm section that includes pianist Jaki Byard, bassist Richard Davis, and drummer Alan Dawson. This has been issued on vinyl as part of a two-record set titled *The Freedom and Space Sessions* as well as a single album under the original title. It's not available on domestic CD but on a Japanese disc. —*Ron Wynn, AMG*

Kevin Eubanks (Kevin Tyrone Eubanks)
b. Nov. 15, 1957, Philadelphia, PA
Guitar, electric guitar / M-Base, modern creative
A fusion guitarist who has concentrated on funk, but is also capable of playing excellent jazz, Kevin Eubanks is an adept neoclassicist as well. His early albums show great potential, and he's a good improviser with a readily identifiable sound. Eubanks is now a member of Branford Marsalis's "Tonight Show with Jay Leno" orchestra.—*Michael G. Nastos*

● **Turning Point** / **i.** 1992 / Blue Note 98170
Recent Blue Note session in which Eubanks disproves those who've questioned his jazz and improvising credentials. There are only four cuts, and they're designed for intense solos and exacting ensemble interaction. Besides Eubanks on electric and acoustic guitar, the cast features alto flutist Kent Jordan, bassist Dave Holland, and drummer Marvin "Smitty" Smith. —*Ron Wynn, AMG*

Robin Eubanks
b. 1959
Trombone, keyboards / M-Base, modern creative
The trombone-playing brother of Kevin. His use of multiphonics, overdubbing, and teaming with other trombonists shows his willingness to experiment. He's a promising young contemporary jazz player who should do great things. —*Michael G. Nastos*

○ **Different Perspectives** / **i.** 1988 / JMT 834424
Exceptional first album from this trombonist. A great listening album with many components, mostly in a progressive vein. —*Michael G. Nastos*

★ **Dedication** / Apr. 1989 / JMT 834433
W/ Steve Turre. Two trombonists live up to their reputations with much vital music. —*Michael G. Nastos*

Bill Evans (William John Evans)
b. Aug. 16, 1929, Plainfield, New Jersey, **d.** Sep. 15, 1980
Piano / Cool
Arguably the most lyrical and expressionistic of all jazz pianists, Bill Evans was an extraordinary player and soloist from his first album as a leader in 1956 until his death. He did his best work by far in the trio mode, where his touch, technique, facility, phrasing, and imagination were at their peak. He was a member of the pivotal Miles Davis unit that helped popularize modal jazz, and even his detractors had to admire Evans's skill while they bemoaned the alleged lack of energy and vitality in his solos. Evans worked for a time with Tony Scott and also spent eight months with Miles Davis but otherwise led his own groups. He had important collaborations during his career with Charles Mingus, Philly Joe Jones, and George Russell; still, his solo and trio releases are his most intriguing and memorable. His interplay with bassists Scott LaFaro and later Eddie Gomez was very distinctive, especially the range Evans displayed and the answering lines and directions LaFaro and Gomez crafted. He also proved a wonder-

ful partner to singer Tony Bennett and guitarist Jim Hall and made Grammy-winning releases through clever incorporation of multitracking. His complete Riverside and Fantasy recordings have been compiled and released in two huge boxed sets. —*Ron Wynn*

★ **Complete Riverside Recordings (1956-63)** / 1956-1963 / Riverside 018
12 CDs. Fantasy/1985. All the marvelous Evans one could ever want is on this incredible 18-disc boxed set. It is a wonderful, comprehensive collection of superb performances, with some of his most majestic trio and solo dates. —*Ron Wynn*

○ **Peace Pipe and Other Pieces** / Jan. 19, 1959 / Milestone 47024
Half of *Peace Pipe and Other Pieces* was a reissue of Bill Evans's second Riverside album, *Everybody Digs Bill Evans*. Recorded in 1958 after Evans left the Miles Davis Sextet, it contained some of the most memorable ballads on record. The remainder of the twofer was cut in 1959, save for one track recorded in 1962. Six of the previously unissued tracks were recorded with two members of that auspicious Davis sextet, Philly Joe Jones, and Paul Chambers.... The music was straightahead jazz, precise and austere, yet also spirited and brimming with lyric warmth. —*Steve Marks, Down Beat*

★ **Undercurrent** / May 15, 1959 / Blue Note 90583
A must-have reissue of a brilliant date with Jim Hall (g). —*Ron Wynn*

○ **More from the Vanguard** / Jun. 25, 1961 / Milestone 9125
Material recorded live at the Village Vanguard during several sessions with arguably the finest Bill Evans trio; pianist Evans, bassist Scott LaFaro, and drummer Paul Motian. They did enough tracks to fill several albums; these were sessions not included on the original *Live at the Village Vanguard* dates. —*Ron Wynn, AMG*

○ **Sunday at the Village Vanguard** / Jun. 25, 1961 / Riverside 140
This represents one of the best known sessions from the Village Vanguard and most of the material from this 6/25/61 date was on a previous twofer. Simply put, it sounds like pianist Bill Evans, bassist Scott LaFaro, and drummer Paul Motian, and it sounds like Sunday. —*Bob Rusch, Cadence*

Interplay / Jul. 16, 1962 / Original Jazz Classics 308
Quintet. A dazzling small-group date with top-flight Freddie Hubbard (tpt). 1987 reissue. —*Ron Wynn*

○ **Empathy / a Simple Matter of Conviction** / Aug. 14, 1962+Oct. 11, 1966 / PolyGram 837757
Empathy was a collaboration between drummer Shelly Manne and pianist Bill Evans and came almost a year after their first pairing. On this date Monty Budwig was the bassist. This set was a bit uneven as there were times when the creative lines taken by Manne and Evans did not really interplay and Budwig tended to straddle between the two. On the other hand, there were individually fine moments and one particular cut, "Washington Twist," matched Manne and Evans equally in creative interplay and involvement. —*Bob Rusch, Cadence*

Conversations with Myself / Jan. 1963-Feb. 1963 / Verve 821984
These stunning multiple-tracked piano solos won a Grammy in a rare acknowledgment of amazing achievement. Great playing and admirable use of multitrack technology. —*Ron Wynn*

☆ **Bill Evans at Town Hall** / Feb. 21, 1966 / Verve 831271

★ **Intermodulation** / Apr. 7, 1966 / Verve 833771

○ **Simple Matter of Conviction, A** / Oct. 11, 1966 / Verve 8675
What separated this from the average good Bill Evans date was the inclusion of Shelly Manne on drums, who inventively pushed and took unexpected chances. This was, I believe, Eddie Gomez's (bass) debut release with Evans (piano) and it was quite impressive. There were numerous takes at this session and judging from Chuck Briefer's liners it might be interesting to hear them released. —*Bob Rusch, Cadence*

○ **California Here I Come** / Aug. 17-18, 1967 / Verve 22545
California Here I Come by pianist Bill Evans was not a reissue but previously unreleased material from two nights (8/17 & 18/67) at the Village Vanguard. This was first-class material, with textbook Evans and drummer Philly Joe Jones pushing the trio (bassist Eddie Gomez) along quite nicely, especially on the up-tempos. —*Bob Rusch, Cadence*

☆ **At the Montreux Jazz Festival** / Jun. 15, 1968 / Verve 827844

A superb trio date. Eddie Gomez (b) and Jack DeJohnette (d) are brilliant in accompanying roles. —*Ron Wynn*

★ **Complete Fantasy Recordings** / 1973-1979 / Fantasy 1012
This gorgeous boxed set is a collection of his '70s selections. It covers everything in all contexts and is a must-have for piano fans. —*Ron Wynn*

Intuition / Nov. 7-08, 1974 / Fantasy 470
This is a wonderful pairing of musically attuned comrades Bill Evans and Eddie Gomez (b). —*Ron Wynn*

○ **Tony Bennett/Bill Evans Album, The** / Jun. 10-13, 1975 / Original Jazz Classics 439
Exquisite collaboration between a great romantic vocalist and a tremendous melodic interpreter. Bennett and Evans mesh as though they'd been working together for years, never having any problems with tempo, pacing, or mood. This has been reissued on CD. —*Ron Wynn, AMG*

○ **Alone (Again)** / Dec. 16-18, 1975 / PolyGram 833801
Includes moving, appealing, and expansive solos. The CD issue has two bonus cuts. —*Ron Wynn*

☆ **You Must Believe in Spring** / Aug. 23-25, 1977 / Warner Brothers 3504
Recorded in the fall of 1977, shortly before bassist Eddie Gomez and drummer Eliot Zigmund left Bill Evans's trio, this posthumous release attested to the continuity and clarity of Evans' musical means and ends. Indeed, much of the trio's work looked backwards to those vintage Riverside sessions, *Moonbeams* and *Sunday at the Village Vanguard*, both impressionistic collections of haunting mood pieces. For example, here Evans's own "B Minor Waltz" simply floated along, interspersed with melodic motifs straight from *Moonbeams*. In the work of lesser players, such deliberate self-quotation lapses easily into self-parody; in the work of a musician of Evans's stature, the melodic permutations of his earlier work simply reaffirmed the continuity of his craft and his commitment to it. —*Jon Balleras, Down Beat*

○ **Paris Concert, Edition Two** / Nov. 26, 1979 / Elektra 60311
Recorded less than a year before his death (Sept. 1980), this album and its companion volume show us that Evans had at last found a bassist and drummer that fit his particular concept of rhythmic interplay without sacrificing intensity or energy (as seemed to be the case with some of the '70s trios). —*Peter Leitch, Cadence*

○ **The Brilliant** / i. Aug. 1980-Sep. 1980 / Timeless 329

☆ **Conception** / Milestone 47063
This two-record set was most welcome since it combined a reissue of pianist Bill Evans's first trio album released in 1956 with one alternate take and some previously unissued solo tracks from 1958 and 1962. The original album was *New Jazz Conceptions* (Riverside) and was probably the only Evans album never recorded in stereo. This trio developed before the idea of interplay with the bassist, and Evans was very much into a bebop bag. —*Jerry L. Atkins, Cadence*

☆ **Spring Leaves** / Milestone 47034

Bill Evans (Sax)

b. 1958
Saxophone, keyboards / Early jazz rock, modern creative
Tenor, soprano saxophonist, keyboardist, and composer Bill Evans has made his own mark in the jazz world, though not at the same level as his pianist namesake. But they share one similarity; both worked for Miles Davis, with saxophonist Evans being in his band longer than the pianist. Evans has a tough, taut, and funky-bluesy sound, with a full and authoritative tenor tone and thin but assertive soprano style. While he's been associated with jazz-rock, fusion, and instrumental pop, Evans can also play sterling standards and ballads, handles himself well on blues and has written some interesting compositions. He was prominently featured in Davis's early and mid-'80s bands, and was viewed in many quarters as the finest instrumentalist in some of those units. Davis himself was once quoted saying "he's one of the greatest musicians I've ever come upon." Evans was featured with the Davis group on several major American, European, and Japanese tours. He began playing piano as a child, then studied tenor. Evans had both university and conservatory training before studying privately with David Liebman. He moved to New York in 1978, and joined Davis in 1980, receiving widespread acclaim

before going solo in the mid-'80s. Evans recorded with Elements, the band co-led by Mark Egan and Danny Gottlieb in 1982, then debuted as a leader the next year. Evans later worked with the reformed Mahavishnu Orchestra and John McLaughlin, as well as doing more sessions with Elements and playing with Herbie Hancock. He began studying and playing keyboards in the mid-'80s, and his album *The Alternative Man* on Blue Note featured Evans using multiple synthesizers, drum machines, and signal processors. He's since done several albums for Jazz City, playing with Chuck Loeb, Marc Johnson, Gottlieb, Gil Goldstein, Jim Beard, Mitch Forman, Victor Bailey, Dennis Chambers, and Richie Morales. A pair of these albums were recorded live in Tokyo, and they combine fusion, vintage jazz-rock and instrumental pop, funk, and rock elements with some straight bebop. Evans also had an early '80s session for the Paddle Wheel label with Hank Jones and Red Mitchell that's almost totally a traditional work, with the trio recording several standards. He was featured on Davis's '80s albums *The Man with the Horn*, *We Want Miles*, and *Star People*. His American label debut as a leader was *Living on the Crest of a Wave* for Elektra/Musician. The Paddle Wheel release preceded it, but was mainly available in Japan. His next release was issued on Blue Note. —*Ron Wynn*

● **Alternative Man** / Jan. 19, 198585 05 / Blue Note 46336

Gil Evans (Ian Ernest Gilmore Green)

b. May 13, 1912, Toronto, Ontario, **d.** Mar. 20, 1988, Cuernavaca, Mexico

Arranger, composer, piano, bandleader / Cool, progressive big band

Best known for his marvelous collaborations with Miles Davis, the self-taught arranger and reluctant pianist formed his first band in Stockton, California, at 21. Singer Skinnay Ennis fronted the band in 1938, and Claude Thornhill came in as pianist and co-arranger. When Thornhill started his own band in 1941, he hired Evans. By the late '40s, Evans started to incorporate the ideas of Charlie Parker and Dizzy Gillespie into his scores and was one of the leading thinkers behind the *Birth of the Cool* recordings of Miles Davis, with whom he forged a lifelong friendship. When Davis signed with Columbia, he was able to bring Evans into the studios with a large ensemble, and the finished albums—*Miles Ahead* (1957), *Porgy and Bess* (1958), *Sketches of Spain* (1959)—became milestones in both men's careers. Because he was a perfectionist, with little regard for record company budgets, Evans did not work as much as he might have, but there were some fine albums in the '60s, and occasional big band club and concert work. In the next decades, Evans became more consistently visible and was able to keep fairly stable personnel together for long stretches of time; musicians wanted to work with him even when jobs and money were skimpy. Evans experimented with electronics and free-jazz improvisatory principles; he toured Europe with the band, and in his last years of life did some film scoring, was reunited with Miles in the studios, and visited Brazil. Insatiably curious about new musical ideas until the end, Gil Evans was a man who followed his own star. Miles Davis's final public appearance was in a tribute to Gil. —*Dan Morgenstern*

○ **Gil Evans and Ten** / Sep. 6, 1957-Oct. 10, 1957 / Prestige 346
Excellent arrangements, with a lineup and compositions that are of high quality. —*Ron Wynn*

○ **New Bottle, Old Wine** / Aug. 9, 1958-May 26, 1958 / EMI 46855
Early, intriguing Gil Evans orchestra material, one of the sessions that established his reputation as an arranger and bandleader. The band, which included Johnny Coles, Cannonball Adderley, Paul Chambers, and Art Blakey, did rousing, fresh versions of vintage songs like the "St. Louis Blues" and "King Porter Stomp." This material has also been issued as vinyl album and CD under title *Pacific Standard Time* and as a CD under the same title. —*Ron Wynn, AMG*

○ **Great Jazz Standards** / 1959 / Blue Note 46856

★ **Out of the Cool** / Nov. 18, 1960-Nov. 30, 1960 / MCA 5653
Out of the Cool offered Gil Evans fresh from triumphs with Miles Davis pursuing his orchestral muse with a couple of originals, an attractively odd John Benson Brooks song, a Brecht-Weil number from *Happy End*, and a George Russell composition wherein the Lydian concept met the 12-bar blues. The orchestrations were characteristically rich, layered, slow to unfold. Johnny Coles as-

sumed the Miles Davis role to some effect, and there were other soloists of interest, foremost of which was Jimmy Knepper, whose trombone was featured on "Flamingos." —*Alan Bargebuhr, Cadence*

● **Individualism of Gil Evans, The** / Sep. 1963-Apr. 1964 / Verve 833804

○ **Live at Sweet Basil—Vols. 1 and 2** / Aug. 20, 1984-Aug. 2, 1984 / Evidence 22026
Gil Evans ran into his share of would-be defenders of his "tradition" when he began experimenting with rock songs and electronic instruments in the '70s and '80s. One of jazz's greatest arrangers was suddenly viewed as a charlatan in certain circles, and a band loaded with great players was now being dismissed as a crew of frauds. But the records disproved anyone foolish enough to accept that wisdom. This second volume of songs done live during the band's long run as Sweet Basil's regular Monday night attraction proves decisively that neither Evans nor his band lost anything. Their rendition of Hendrix's *Voodoo Chile* includes some riveting tuba and baritone sax work by Howard Johnson, a splintering collective reading of the melody by the band and strong individual solos all around. The versions of Wayne Shorter's *Parabola* and Herbie Hancock's *Prince of Darkness* are multifaceted and compare favorably with almost anything done by any previous Evans aggregation. Adam Nussbaum proved a solid rhythm asset during his tenure, and the solos of trumpeter Hannibal Marvin Peterson, saxophonists George Adams, Chris Hunter, and Johnson or guitarist Hiram Bullock were always on the money. It may not have been "cool," but it was most assuredly great jazz. —*Ron Wynn*

★ **Arrangers' Touch** / Prestige 24049
Here was an excellent reissue from Prestige featuring lesser-known work from two seminal figures in modern jazz, Gil Evans and Tadd Dameron. The Evans material dated from 1957, with Evans as pianist,leader, and arranger, heading a medium-sized group filled with outstanding musicians. The beauty of these seven selections was in the balance between ensemble and solo work, all within the boundaries of Evans' disarmingly low-key musical ideas. Tadd Dameron's music *moved* much more than Evans's although he was concerned with delicacy and musical beauty as much as his colleague. —*Leonard Maltin, Down Beat*

Jon Faddis (Jonathan Faddis)

b. Jul. 24, 1953, Oakland, CA
Trumpet, flugelhorn / Bop
The charge of being a Dizzy Gillespie clone has dogged Jon Faddis during much of his career. He began trumpet studies at 8 and was a regular with R&B bands at 13. After some early-'70s stints with Lionel Hampton, Gil Evans, Charles Mingus, and the Jones-Lewis big band, he began guesting with Gillespie in 1974, recording and playing with him and Oscar Peterson. Faddis's upper-register fireworks and a tendency to construct solos and play in a manner similar to Gillespie generated controversy for many years. Faddis retreated into the studios for a while in the '80s and then reappeared as an active player in 1985 at the Chicago Jazz Festival. He's recorded as a leader for Pablo, DCC, Concord, and Columbia. Faddis was prominently featured in many tributes and special programs after Gillespie's death in 1993.—*Ron Wynn*

★ **Youngblood** / Jan. 8-09, 1976 / Pablo 2310765
☆ **Legacy** / Aug. 1985 / Concord Jazz 4291
A tremendous mainstream session to which Harold Land (ts) and Kenny Barron (p) make excellent contributions. —*Ron Wynn*

○ **Hornucopia** / i. 1990 / Epic 46958
This is his best release. He works with his idol Dizzy Gillespie (tpt), and makes a case for his own voice and style as well. —*Ron Wynn*

Charles Fambrough

b. 1950
Bass / Hard bop
This New Orleans-born bassist was prominent with McCoy Tyner and Art Blakey in the '70s. He is a solid musician and composer, mostly in modern mainstream style, though he has played some fusion. He's recently played with Grover Washington, Kenny Garrett, Kenny Kirkland, Wynton Marsalis, Roy Hargrove, Jeff

Watts, and Abdullah Ibrahim, among others, and recorded as a leader for CTI.—*Michael G. Nastos*

● **Proper Angle** / **i**. 1991 / CTI 79476
Excellent bassist Charles Fambrough steps into the spotlight with his debut album as a leader. While his compositions are straight foward hard bop, he's recruited an impressive guest list. The lineup includes both Wynton and Branford Marsalis, Roy Hargrove, Kenny Kirkland, Jeff Watts, Jerry Gonzalez, and Steve Berrios. —*Ron Wynn, AMG*

Tal Farlow (Talmage Holt Farlow)

b. Jun. 7, 1921, Greensboro, NC
Guitar / Bop, cool
A leading early bop guitarist, Tal Farlow helped define the modern jazz guitar style with his great speed, technique, and flow of ideas. A self-taught, nonreading musician, he began playing the instrument at a fairly late age and learned Charlie Christian solos by heart from records. Early performances with Red Norvo and Artie Shaw earned him acclaim as an inventive player; he won the *Down Beat* critics "New Star Award" in 1954. Farlow uses a special shorter fingerboard for looser tuning and softer sound. He was also an early explorer of artificial harmonics. In what may well be a positive testimony on his character, he never much liked the business side of the music world and life on the road. Returning to his native North Carolina and working as a sign painter, he has been rather reclusive for many years, emerging only occasionally for recording and performances. —*David Nelson McCarthy*

○ **Tal Farlow Album, The** / Apr. 11, 1954-Jul. 5, 1955 / Verve 2584
This album featured two groups working with guitarist Tal Farlow; bassist Oscar Pettiford, pianist Barry Galbraith and drummer Joe Morello were on several numbers, and bassist Red Mitchell and pianist Claude Williamson were on the others. Both it and its companion *Tal* are highly recommended. —*Bob Rusch, Cadence*

○ **Fascinating Rhythm** / Jan. 17, 1955 / Norgran 1101

○ **Recital by Tal Farlow, A** / Apr. 25, 1955-May 4, 1955 / Norgran 1030

★ **Tal** / Mar. 1956 / PolyGram 829580
This was recorded in 1956 with Eddie Costa on piano and vibes and Vinnie Burke on drums. Tal Farlow is a most listenable guitarist, accessible without compromising either technical brilliance or depth of content. —*Bob Rusch, Cadence*

○ **Fuerst Set** / Dec. 18, 1956 / Xanadu 109
Recorded in 1956 at the home of Ed Fuerst, this was almost 50 minutes of relaxed jamming. The group was working together at the time, and they were obviously comfortable not only in the setting but with themselves. —*Bob Rusch, Cadence*

○ **Second Set** / Dec. 18, 1956 / Xanadu 119
Like its predecessor *Fuerst Set*, this LP of four extended performances recorded in late 1956 at the New York City apartment of jazz fan Ed Fuerst continued the documentation of the remarkable trio Tal Farlow led from 1956 to 1958 and that most frequently performed at the Composer in that city. The rapport between Farlow, pianist Eddie Costa, and bassist Vinnie Burke, was exemplary and this, coupled with their individual strengths as players, made for performances of great musicality, intelligence, sensitivity, vigorous creativity, and an interactivity of conception and execution that placed the trio among the finest small groups of the period. —*Pete Welding, Down Beat*

○ **This Is Tal Farlow** / Jun. 1958 / Verve 8289

○ **Guitar Artistry of Tal Farlow, The** / 1959-1968 / Verve 8370

Art Farmer (Arthur Stewart Farmer)

b. Aug. 21, 1928, Council Bluffs, IA
Trumpet, flugelhorn / Hard bop
Among the most lyrical players ever as a trumpeter, Art Farmer helped popularize the flugelhorn when he turned to it in the '60s and '70s. He now plays flugelhorn almost exclusively. Farmer began making inroads on the Los Angeles jazz scene when he moved there with his twin brother Addison in 1945. He played in bands led by Horace Henderson, Floyd Ray, Benny Carter, Gerald Wilson, and Lionel Hampton and later worked with Johnny Otis, Joe Turner, Teddy Edwards, Sonny Criss, and Frank Morgan before moving to New York in 1954. Later came stints with the

group New Directions and Charles Mingus, Teo Macero, Teddy Charles, Horace Silver, and Gerry Mulligan, plus coleading a group with Gigi Gryce and recording with George Russell. Farmer recorded with Quincy Jones twice in the '50s, did combo dates for Contemporary and small and large group sessions for United Artists. He was a cofounding member of the Jazztet with Benny Golson in 1960-1962, co-led a group with Jim Hall, and did a big band date with Oliver Nelson. Farmer has maintained an active career since the '60s, making many recordings that feature sensitive, often beautiful flugelhorn solos, though he's also a solid uptempo and hard bop player. He's periodically revived the Jazztet with Golson and Curtis Fuller and has also done studio work in Europe with various orchestras. Farmer played with Clifford Jordan, Cedar Walton, Art Pepper, and Chico Freeman, among others, in the '70s, '80s, and '90s. Concord, Contemporary, Mainstream, and Soul Note have been some of the labels that have issued Farmer recordings. —*Ron Wynn*

○ **Early Art** / Jan. 20, 1954+Nov. 9, 1954 / New Jazz 8258

★ **Farmer's Market** / Nov. 23, 1956 / New Jazz 398
Quintet. A top release from the '50s, with precise, deftly played solos, compositions, and arrangements. It has a wonderful all-star lineup and is one of the rare occasions where Farmer worked on record with his brother Addison. —*Ron Wynn*

★ **Meet the Jazztet** / Feb. 6-10, 1960 / Chess 91550
W/ Benny Golson. The first Jazztet recording and definitive ensemble jazz. Featuring McCoy Tyner (p) and Curtis Fuller (tb). —*Michael G. Nastos*

☆ **Art** / Sep. 1960 / Argo 678

○ **Jazz at the Smithsonian** / **i**. 1965 / PolyGram 1272

○ **From Vienna with Art** / Sep. 7, 1970 / MPS 741
Thoughtful introspective solos are Farmer's forte, and he gave us some nice ones here that came as an oasis in the desert of free playing and rock-oriented screamers. Jimmy Heath, who'd been a longtime associate of Farmer, completed the front line. Heath is a solid, mature tenor saxophonist who added the soprano sax and flute to his bag of instruments. He handled both with professional acumen. —*Peter Friedman, Coda*

○ **Homecoming** / Jul. 1971 / Mainstream 332

★ **Gentle Rain** / **i**. 1971-1972 / Mainstream 716

○ **On the Road** / Jul. 26-28, 1976 / Contemporary 478
Comparing this to Farmer's 1979 C.T.I. work, and the like, is similar to listening to Sidney Bechet in the '30s and early '40s and then later in the '50s with those French bands. The magic was always somewhere, but it became little more than reflex motion. —*Bob Rusch, Cadence*

☆ **Maiden Voyage** / Mar. 1983 / Denon 7071

○ **Jazztet, The: Moment to Moment** / **i**. May 1983 / Soul Note 1066
Two decades down the road, the reactivated Jazztet still reveres the old values. Would that every hard bop group working now shared this sextet's high level of commitment and aversion to falling into ruts. On *Moment to Moment* Benny Golson's tenor was particularly arresting, with its post-Lester Young drive, a rapid vibrato under Coleman Hawkins's wing, and a chocolate syrup tone. —*Kevin Whitehead, Cadence*

☆ **Blame It on My Youth** / Feb. 4-08, 1988 / Contemporary 14042
The group was no hastily thrown-together unit. Saxophonist Clifford Jordan, a longtime colleague, continued to deepen his expression, James Williams (piano) had long since picked up the jazz torch with skill and authority, Rufus Reid (bass) was the very pillar of swing society, and drummer Victor Lewis struck the perfect balance between pulse and volume. His solos were terse, witty, and well-ventilated. The album's repertoire was intelligently varied. The two classic standards that opened and closed the set were respectively Oscar Levant's "Blame It on My Youth" and Alec Wilder's "I'll Be Around", both quartet numbers. —*Ira Gitler, Jazz Times*

○ **Summer Knows** / Inner City 6004
The Summer Knows was a set of pop tunes that were easy listening in the best sense, soothing and mellow but never dull or sticky. Art Farmer's understated, almost effortless flugelhorn style blended perfectly with Cedar Walton's more busy, down-to-earth piano approach, and they were both complemented by an adventurous rhythm team. Bassist Sam Jones reached high on the neck

and bent notes at will, while drummer Billy Higgins fired off tom-tom rolls and cymbal flourishes that always fit right in. All four had free reign, but no one was in a hurry, and the set glided smoothly from one number to the next. —*Ben Sandmel, Down Beat*

Joe Farrell (Joseph Carl Firrantello)

b. Dec. 16, 1937, Chicago Heights, IL, **d.** Jan. 10, 1986, Los Angeles, CA

Tenor sax, flute, alto sax, oboe / Bop, Latin-jazz, early jazz rock
Tenor saxophonist and flutist Joe Farrell was an excellent soloist and reliable musician who squeezed in work as a big-band performer, octet contributor, and small-combo session man, plus jazz-rock and R&B dates. He began with Ira Sullivan in Chicago and moved to New York in 1960 to join Maynard Ferguson. His biggest break was as a founding member of the Thad Jones-Mel Lewis big band and also as part of the Elvin Jones '70s groups. During the '70s, Farrell's flute solos enhanced the first and last editions of "Return to Forever." He returned to mainstream jazz in his final years. Farrell was both a superb uptempo player and a thoughtful, capable soloist who could play with precision and passion and creatively condense his statements. —*Ron Wynn*

★ **Follow Your Heart** / Jul. 1+02, 1970 / CTI 6003
○ **Joe Farrell Quartet** / i. Jul. 1+02, 1970 / Columbia 40694
Quartet. Early CTI recordings for this West Coast transplant. Farrell's flute and sax are well represented. This must-buy also includes John McLaughlin (g) and Chick Corea (p). Includes "Follow Your Heart." —*Michael G. Nastos*
☆ **Moon Germs** / Nov. 21, 1972 / Columbia 40929
Another early CTI recording. Farrell's flute and sax are well represented. A must-buy, though a bit electric. —*Michael G. Nastos*

Victor Feldman (Victor Stanley Feldman)

b. Apr. 7, 1934, London, England, **d.** May 12, 1987, Los Angeles, CA

Piano, vibes / Cool
Victor Feldman was a British pianist-vibist who found a home in the United States, coming to join Woody Herman in 1955. A prodigy who started playing at age eight, he'd been active on the English scene before leaving there. Feldman was most prolific through the '50s and '60s, especially with Cannonball Adderley and Miles Davis, for whom he wrote "Seven Steps to Heaven." He refused Davis's offer of a permanent gig to stay with his wife, becoming a busy studio musician in the '70s and '80s. Rockers may remember his contributions to Steely Dan records from the mid '70s to 1980. —*Ron Wynn*

● **Arrival of Victor Feldman, The** / Jan. 1959 / Contemporary 268
This date proclaimed the beginning of Victor Feldman's American recording career as a leader. This January 1958 recording had some strong jazz performances on its program but not a particularly strong personality. Feldman reached back and forth between vibes and piano, making clear, rich, unequivocating pronouncements on both instruments. —*Bob Rusch, Cadence*
★ **Artful Dodger** / Jan. 26, 1977 / Concord Jazz 4038
This album brought pianist Victor Feldman back to the recording studio with the standard trio format. His accompanists, Monty Budwig on bass and Colin Barlay on drums, established an easy rapport with the Feldman style, which was very much out front and on top of the beat and just about everything else. —*Spencer R. Weston, Cadence*

Maynard Ferguson

b. May 4, 1928, Verdun, Quebec
Trumpet, bandleader / Cool, progressive big band
A dazzling trumpet stylist with incredible range, Maynard Ferguson's initial fame came through stints with Boyd Raeburn and Stan Kenton in the late '40s and early '50s. He had his own band from 1957 to 1965 and began a gradual shift into jazz-rock and pop with the M. F. Horn group. He increased, then trimmed the size of his band, and alternated between rock and big-selling film soundtracks, then returned to jazz. He's recently done mainstream dates and at his best can blow paint off the roof and then make you sit up and notice his ballad skills. —*Ron Wynn*

○ **Maynard Ferguson Octet** / Apr. 25, 1955 / Emarcy 36021
Birdland Dreamband, The / i. Sep. 1956 / Bluebird 6455

★ **Maynard** / Mar. 1961 / Capitol 93900
○ **Blues Roar** / Dec. 1+11, 1964 / Mainstream 717
○ **Maynard Ferguson's Horn—Vol. 2** / Jar. 1972 / Columbia 31709
○ **Maynard Ferguson's Horn—Vol. 4: Live at Jimmy's** / 1973 / Columbia 32732
○ **Maynard Ferguson's Horn—Vol. 3** / 1973 / Columbia 32403
○ **Big Bop Nouveau** / 1989-1990 / Intima 73390
Recent session featuring Maynard Ferguson's latest big band. He's returned to conventional jazz material, though the volume remains loud and the mood aggressive. But Ferguson does a wide range of material rather than just ear-splitting high-note theatrics, and the band plays the arrangements well. There's no great second soloist, but Ferguson's presence helps compensate. —*Ron Wynn, AMG*

Firehouse Five Plus Two (Firehouse Five + Two)

Jazz ensemble / Dixieland
One of the most prolific and accomplished traditional jazz bands. The original Firehouse Five dates back to the '40s, while the Firehouse Five + Two made several good albums for the Good Time Jazz label in the '50s and '60s. —*Ron Wynn*

○ **Firehouse Five Plus Two Crashes a Party** / Sep. 29, 1958-Nov. 10, 1959 / Good Time Jazz 10038
★ **16 Dixieland Favorites** / i. 195z / Good Time Jazz 60008

Clare Fischer

b. Oct. 22, 1928, Durand, MI
Keyboards / Progressive big band, Latin-jazz
An accomplished keyboardist and graduate of Michigan State University, Clare Fischer is well-versed in Latin music, and also a skilled arranger and composer. He's been a major contributor to the LA scene for many years. He was an arranger and accompanist for the Hi-Los and later did arrangements for a Dizzy Gillespie LP *Portrait of Duke Ellington* in 1960. Fischer recorded some of the earliest bossa nova dates in America, has doubled as an organist, and has mixed bop and Afro-Latin on many recordings.—*Michael G. Nastos*

☆ **America the Beautiful** / i. 1974 / Discovery 786
★ **Machacha** / May 16-17, 1979 / Discovery 835
Salsa picante at its instrumental best. Latin jazz-hots with Rick Zunigar (g), Gary Foster on saxophone and flute, and Alex Acuna and Poncho Sanchez on percussion. —*Michael G. Nastos*

Ella Fitzgerald

b. Apr. 25, 1918, Newport News, VA
Vocals / Swing, ballads & blues
Ella Fitzgerald ranks as perhaps the most accomplished jazz singer alive and certainly among the best of the century. After winning an amateur contest in 1934, she was hired by bandleader Chick Webb and began scoring hits by 1936. Her recording of "A-Tisket, A-Tasket" topped the charts for ten weeks in 1938, becoming one of the first records to sell really well since the start of the Depression. After Webb's death in 1939, Fitzgerald took over leadership of the Webb orchestra and then went solo in 1942. Among her major hits in the '40s were "I'm Making Believe" and "Into Each Life Some Rain Must Fall," the latter with the Ink Spots.

Fitzgerald began issuing a series of two-record "songbooks," each devoted to a different songwriter or songwriting team in the '50s. The first was *Ella Fitzgerald Sings the Cole Porter Song Book*, and others were devoted to Rodgers and Hart and George and Ira Gershwin. Fitzgerald's flawless performances were marked by clear enunciation and a light, warm tone that made her renditions near-definitive. She has continued to perform regularly into the '90s. —*William Ruhlmann*

○ **Ella Fitzgerald 1935-1937** / i. Jun. 1935-Jan. 1937 / Classics 500
○ **Ella Fitzgerald 1937-1938** / i. Jan. 1937-May 1938 / Classics 506
○ **Ella Fitzgerald 1938-1939** / i. May 1938-Feb. 1939 / Classics 518
○ **Ella Fitzgerald 1939** / i. Feb. 1939-Jun. 1939 / Classics 525
○ **Ella Fitzgerald 1939-1940** / i. Aug. 1939-May 1940 / Classics 566
○ **Lullabies of Birdland** / Oct. 4, 1945-Mar. 19, 1947 / Decca 8149

★ **Sings the Cole Porter Songbook (Complete), The** / Feb. 7, 1956-Mar. 27, 1956 / Verve 821990

○ **Ella and Louis Together** / i. Aug. 18, 1956 / Laserlight 15706
The master and one of his greatest pupil-trainees, Ella Fitzgerald. —*Ron Wynn*

★ **Sings the Rodgers and Hart Songbook** / Aug. 1956 / Verve
Ella Fitzgerald's *The Rodgers and Hart Songbook* was a winner. A complete musician with the ability to plumb each song's emotional-dramatic core, Fitzgerald forcefully communicated the sophisticated urbanity of Rodgers and Hart. As for the composer and lyricist, a checklist of their many gems should suffice. "Lover," "I Could Write a Book," "Blue Moon," "My Funny Valentine," "Little Girl Blue," "Mountain Greenery,"—they just don't write songs like that anymore. The wit of Larry Hart, the sophistication of Richard Rodgers, the consumate artistry of Ella Fitzgerald—it was a triumvirate that conquered all obstacles. —*Chuck Berg, Down Beat*

○ **Songbooks, The** / i. 1956-1964 / Verve 823445

★ **Ella & Louis Again** / Jul. 22-23, 1957 / Verve 4006
W/ Louis Armstrong. This is excellent material and wonderful vocals. —*Ron Wynn*

○ **Porgy & Bess** / Aug. 18, 1957-Oct. 15, 1957 / Verve 6040
This version of *Porgy and Bess* (recorded in 1957) with Ella Fitzgerald singing all the female parts and Louis Armstrong singing all the male parts was as good as any version so far released. . . . If you're into *Porgy and Bess*, by all means buy this album, but if you are only interested in Ella Fitzgerald and Louis Armstrong, there is much better material available. —*Carl Brauer, Cadence*

○ **Ella Fitzgerald at the Opera House** / Oct. 19, 1957+Oct. 25, 1957 / Verve 6026

○ **Sings the Irving Berlin Songbook** / Mar. 13+19, 1958 / PolyGram 829534
This was a great period for Ella Fitzgerald; Norman Granz was her producer, and she was in great voice and projection. . . . It was seamless great American music and well suited to Fitzgerald ambiance. This set included all the 32 titles, in the same sequence, as the original issues. There is, however, one extra track that did appear on a "Playboy" collection. —*Bob Rusch, Cadence*

★ **Ella in Rome: The Birthday Concert** / Apr. 1958 / Verve 835454
The singer was in peak form here in Rome on her 40th birthday. . . . After Norman Granz's introduction, she came on with an effervescent "St. Louis Blues," and then offered immediate contrasts with "These Foolish Things" and "Just Squeeze Me." Lengthy public recitals of this kind often compel unwelcome emphasis on variety in programming, but beyond the scatting and hornlike improvising in which she excels and humor, as in her affectionate Louis Armstrong salute, her ability to convince and enchant when singing a lyric straight with minimal variation of the melody helps very much to make her the greatest. —*Stanley Dance, Jazz Times*

○ **Sings the George & Ira Gershwin Songbook [box]** / i. 1959 / Verve 825024

○ **Ella Returns to Berlin** / Feb. 1961 / Verve 837758
This is a new release of a concert that Ella Fitzgerald gave on February 11, 1961, in Berlin. This CD has a little of the blues and ballads—and a great deal of swinging and scatting on such fare as "Take the 'A' Train." —*Leslie Gourse, Jazz Times*

★ **Sings the Jerome Kern Songbook** / Jan. 5-07, 1963 / Verve 825669
This double album featured the works of two of the greatest composers of the American ballad or song form. Actually more than two composers, as on the second side lyricist Johnny Mercer collaborated with such giants as Harold Arlen, Hoagy Carmichael, and Sammy Cahn. Included in the first album were several infrequently heard Jerome Kern pieces which are minor classics: "I'll Be Hard to Handle," "You Couldn't Be Cuter," and "She Didn't Say Yes." The second album's material was probably better known, and there were some short solo gems from Buddy DeFranco (clarinet) and Willie Smith (alto sax). All the songs were given perfect settings by Nelson Riddle, long a master of orchestration and accompaniment. —*Peter Leitch, Cadence*

○ **Sings the Johnny Mercer Songbook** / Oct. 20, 1964 / Verve 823247

○ **Ella Fitzgerald** / i. Jun. 1965 / Living Era 55

○ **Ella at Duke's Place** / Nov. 1965 / Verve 4070
Ella at Duke's Place was recorded in LA in October '65 with the full accompaniment of the Ellington band and a full Ellingtonia program. There was some real controlled beauty to some of the performances, but overall the Ellingtonness of the performance was held somewhat in check. —*Bob Rusch, Cadence*

○ **Newport Jazz Festival: Live at Carnegie Hall** / Jul. 5, 1973 / Columbia 32557
This two-record set chronicled a series of thoroughly polished vocal performances, ranging in mood from the melancholoy "Good Morning Heartbreak" to the ebullient "I've Gotta Be Me." Along the way, Fitzgerald also romped through a wide range of a dozen or so standards, 14 extemporaneous choruses of a blues (posttitled "Any Old Blues") and a little known bop classic, George Wallington's "Lemon Drop." The selection of material was judicious, tasteful, and refreshingly free from any jazzed-up versions of current pop tunes that a lesser singer might have been tempted to throw in to please the multitudes. Fitzgerald here was backed by musicians in a wide variety of musical contexts, ranging from piano only to quartet, to full dance band; and this musical variety was one of the album's chief virtues. —*Jon Balleras, Down Beat*

○ **Montreux '77** / 1977 / Pablo 376
Ella Fitzgerald was in excellent voice in a program of generally blue chip standards. "My Man" was built with the mastery of a great actress. "Billie's Bounce" was a solid scat line from beginning to end. The voice sounded as strong and commanding as ever. No exceptional peaks were struck, but this was satisfying Fitzgerald on stage. —*Douglas Clark, Down Beat*

☆ **Classy Pair, A** / Feb. 15, 1979 / Pablo 2312-132

○ **Early Years—Part 1, The** / i. 1992 / GRP 618
In her first years as a songstress, Ella Fitzgerald projected a sunny, winning personality through clear articulation, flawless intonation, and assured grasp of swing rhythm. Chick Webbs's utterly professional dance band framed her with attention to the dynamics of their riff-based charts, but Fitzgerald carried the tunes she performed from age 17 on. —*Howard Mandel, Down Beat*

Tommy Flanagan (Tommy Lee Flanagan)

b. Mar. 16, 1930, Detroit, MI
Piano / Bop
Pianist Tommy Flanagan is a marvelous, often undervalued artist who quickly established his reputation as a Detroit teenager. He first recorded with Dexter Gordon in 1945, moved to New York in 1956, and later worked many years with Ella Fitzgerald. His tenure with her and Tony Bennett established the standard for backing vocalists without losing your playing identity. Flanagan is not only one of jazz's finest accompanists, but an equally amazing soloist, with great facility on bop, blues, and ballads and a delicate touch that is immediately identifiable. —*Ron Wynn*

○ **Cats, with John Coltrane and Kenny Burrell** / Apr. 18, 1957 / New Jazz 079
Tenor saxophonist John Coltrane was part of a 4/18/57 blowing session along with Idrees Sulieman (trumpet), Kenny Burrell (guitar), Doug Watkins (bass), Louis Hayes (drums), and the obvious leader, though uncredited, Tommy Flanagan (piano). This set was also present on a twofer. —*Bob Rusch, Cadence*

○ **Complete `overseas'** / i. Aug. 1957 / DIW 25004

○ **Jazz...Its Magic** / Sep. 5, 1957 / Regent 6055
A late '50s quintet date, one of the earliest that established pianist Tommy Flanagan as a tremendous soloist and leader. He headed a superior group, with alto saxophonist Sonny Red, bassist George Tucker, trombonist Curtis Fuller, and drummer Louis Hayes. It preceded by two years the sessions he cut with Coltrane that became the *Giant Steps* album and was done the same year he and Coltrane had recorded for Prestige. Though he wasn't yet as accomplished on ballads, his harmonic brillance was already evident. —*Ron Wynn, AMG*

○ **Plays the Music of Rodgers & Hammerstein** / Sep. 1958 / Savoy 4429

☆ **Montreux 1977** / Jul. 13, 1977 / Pablo 372
Pianist Tommy Flanagan doesn't suffer in the least from traditionalism; whatever bop's drawbacks may be as a style, it doesn't

yet sound old-fashioned. But then there was an air of skilled conventionalism about this record that made the contents somewhat passive. The rhythm section (bassist Ketter Betts and drummer Bobby Durham), although together for several years as the accompanying pulse of Ella Fitzgerald, served Flanagan effectively but without high style. —*Douglas Clark, Down Beat*

★ **Alone Too Long** / Dec. 8, 1977 / Denon 7260

☆ **More Delights with Hank Jones** / Jan. 28, 1978 / Galaxy 5152
These were flawless performances from two absolute masters. This recording consists of alternate takes and other selections recorded at the same session that produced the previously released *Our Delights*. The material was all familiar—Tadd Dameron and Thelonious Monk were treated especially lovingly. —*Peter Leitch, Cadence*

☆ **Our Delights** / Jan. 28, 1978 / Galaxy 752
Pianists Tommy Flanagan and Hank Jones are not really of the same generation, yet they play so much alike that it is difficult to tell them apart. Flanagan's solo lines tend to be a bit more boppish and convoluted, but there are plenty of passages where even this does not hold true. Jones's accompaniment is smooth, and steady, like a guitar quietly strumming along with a walking bass, while Flanagan's accompaniment is choppier, punchier. This music aged well . . . . Like two dazzling dancers, they knew when to step out and when to lend support, when to walk and when to fly. It was a masterful demonstration of mainstream piano. —*Douglas Clark, Down Beat*

○ **Magnificent Tommy Flanagan** / Jun. 2, 1981 / Progressive 7059
Producer Gus Statiras of Progressive allowed the trio on *The Magnificent Tommy Flanagan* two days to record eight tunes. The extra time and polish was evident with this trio working on reasonably familiar ground. —*Jerry L. Atkins, Cadence*

○ **Giant Steps** / Feb. 17+18, 1982 / Enja 79646
Pianist Tommy Flanagan's playing seems to be more direct, edited, and stronger as he gets older; certainly his reemergence in the mid-'70s as a solo artist produced his strongest work. *Giant Steps*, was a February '82 tribute to John Coltrane with super backing from bassist George Mraz and drummer Al Foster. . . . This set was particularly inventive; it was Coltrane's music, but it drinks of its own spirit. You won't listen for the familiar Trane solos, but you will listen! —*Bob Rusch, Cadence*

★ **Thelonica** / Nov. 30, 1982-Dec. 1, 1982 / Enja 79615
Thelonica was again a thematic effort, this time exploring the work of Thelonious Monk. Sandwiched by two takes of the title tracks were six Monk originals. . . . This, as might be expected, was a reflective-introspective set. That is not to say it was soft or withdrawn. It swung handily and did not remove itself as far from the Monkisms of the music as one might expect. —*Bob Rusch, Cadence*

○ **Jazz Poet** / Jan. 1989 / Timeless 301

○ **Beyond the Blue Bird** / Apr. 1990 / Timeless 350
Tommy Flanagan, the gentle genius from Detroit, draws upon boplicity and blues for this effort. Special guest homeboy Kenny Burrell adds his string-proud lilt to the proceedings to turn the corner on what might have been viewed as just another piano date (as if anything Flanagan does is just routine). —*Willard Jenkins, Jazz Times*

○ **Trinity** / Inner City 1084
Pianist Flanagan never sounded better playing material from himself, Thelonious Monk, George Gershwin, Benny Carter, Tadd Dameron, and two others . . . . This was all very well rehearsed and tightly played, with only drummer Roy Haynes's heavy and very busy work sometimes distracting from the good mood transmitted throughout. —*Jerry L. Atkins, Cadence*

Bob Florence (Robert C. Florence)

b. May 20, 1932, Los Angeles, CA
Arranger, piano, bandleader / Swing, big band, bop, cool
Bob Florence is a West Coast studio musician and big-band leader, one of the few still able to record and tour in the '80s and '90s. Florence was a pianist and arranger for Si Zenter in the '50s and '60s and also did arrangements for Sergio Mendes, Frank Capp, and Bud Shank in the '60s. Florence was also a pianist in Capp and Shank's bands. He's been an active bandleader since 1958, and Herb Geller, Bill Perkins, Shank, and Bob Cooper have been some of his featured musicians. Florence has also recorded

in Dave Pell's octet and issued albums as a bandleader on the Trend and Discovery labels. —*Ron Wynn*

○ **Westlake** / Mar. 3, 1981 / Musicraft 832

○ **Soaring** / Oct. 1982 / Bosco 3

○ **Magic Time** / Nov. 29+30, 1983 / Trend 536

○ **Trash Can City** / i. 1984 / Musicraft 545

★ **State of the Art** / i. 1988 / USA Music Group 589
Bob Florence Limited Edition. Five standards, four Florence originals. W/ 20-piece big band. Cool as a breeze for these West Coast veterans. —*Michael G. Nastos*

○ **Treasure Chest** / i. 1990 / USA Music Group 680

Chris Flory

Guitar / Swing
A guitarist and the son of saxophonist Med Flory, Chris Flory plays in a swing-influenced style and has been associated with Concord Records during the '80s and '90s. He's backed vocalists Rosemary Clooney and Maxine Sullivan, and played with Scott Hamilton as well as recording as a leader for Concord.—*Ron Wynn*

● **For All We Know** / Jan. 1988 / Concord Jazz 4403

Ricky Ford (Richard Allen Ford)

b. Mar. 4, 1954, Boston, MA
Tenor sax / Hard bop, modern creative
There was no young-lion hype for tenor player Ricky Ford to exploit in the '70s when, as a 20-year-old, he was debuting with Gunther Schuller and working with Jaki Byard and Ran Blake. His style, which blended swing-era volume, bop discipline, and harmonic knowledge, matured with the Charles Mingus group in the late '70s. During the '80s, he penned charts for Lionel Hampton and the Mingus Dynasty, toured and recorded as a leader, and was part of a wonderful Afro-jazz group led by Abdullah Ibrahim. Ford continues to be a highly valuable asset on the jazz scene and recently recorded for Candid. —*Ron Wynn*

○ **Tenor for the Times** / Apr. 6, 1981+Jul. 1, 1981 / Muse 5250
Here and there Ricky Ford's reedy tenor flirted with the standard commercial sax sound, though there wasn't a hint of trendiness in the backup. More often, Ford was closer to the languid relaxation of Dexter Gordon. These originals were given mostly laid-back renditions, with rare double-timing and John Coltrane flurries from Ford; a bopping uptempo break on "Saxaceous Serenade" broke up the lazy pattern. —*Kevin Whitehead, Cadence*

○ **Future's Gold** / Feb. 9, 1983 / Muse 5296
Tenor saxophonist Ricky Ford's musical lineage has been traced to Coleman Hawkins, and indeed there's a good helping of Bean's robust tone and extroversion in his playing. But Ford's work also has more than a touch of Sonny Rollins, minus Rollins's sly sarcasm. For instance, on "A-Flat Now," a bright, show-type tune, Ford breezed through the snappy head as his fat tone toyed with the opening motif, rippling through nimble runs. His soloing was marked by a feeling of sustained, forward-driving momentum and a seemingly unshakable confidence in the improvisational course he was plotting. —*Jon Balleras, Down Beat*

★ **Ebony Rhapsody** / Mar. 1989-Jun. 2, 1990 / Candid 79053
Among his most recent, a high-level date with Jaki Byard immense on piano. —*Ron Wynn*

○ **Hard Groovin'** / 1989 / Muse 5373
Drummer Jeff Watts and bassist Robert Hurst animated tenor saxophonist Ricky Ford's *Hard Groovin'.* Ford's fifth Muse release found him in the company of several distinguished younger peers: Geoff Keezer on piano and Roy Hargrove on trumpet. —*Bret Primack, Jazz Times*

○ **Hot Brass** / i. 1992 / Candid 79518
Nice recent session matching tenor saxophone standout Ricky Ford with a crew of fiery trumpet and trombone players, plus bassist Christian McBride, drummer Carl Allen, and percussionist Danilo Perez. Ford was a young lion back in the '70s when there was no hype. He's now an experienced, skilled veteran, and teams superbly with trumpeters Lew Soloff and Claudio Roditi and trombonist Steve Turre. —*Ron Wynn, AMG*

○ **Manhattan Blues** / i. May 11, 1992 / Candid 79036

Music Map

Jazz Flute

Little jazz flute before late 1920s

Alberto Soccarras
Bennett's Swamplanders (1930)

First True Jazz flutists
Wayman Carver w/Benny Carter, Chick Webb (from 1932)
Harry Klee w/Ray Linn (1944)
Jimmie Lunceford (1902-1947)

Jazz composers writing for flute (1950s)
Pete Rugolo (1915)
Shorty Rogers (1924)
Marty Paich (1925)

Flute Important Element in Latin American Music
Johnny Pacheco (1935)

1950s–Major Jazz Flutists Emerge
Frank Wess (1922)–Count Basie's band
Also:
Jerome Richardson (1920)
Buddy Collette (1921)
James Moody (1925)
Bud Shank (1926)
Frank Foster (1928)
Eric Dolphy (1928-1964)
Moe Koffman (1928)–Canada
Paul Horn (1930)

Gil Evans began to arrange for flute (1950s)

1956 *Down Beat* Award established for best flutist

More Flutists
Bobby Jaspar (1926-1963)
Herbie Mann (1930)

Jazz/Jazz-Rock
Jeremy Steig (1943)
Dave Valentin
Alexander Zonjic
Bobbi Humphrey

Sing/Hum/Speak into Flute
Sam Most (1930)
Sahib Shihab (1925)
Yusef Lateef (1920)
Rahsaan Roland Kirk (1936-1977)

Major Influence
Rahsaan Roland Kirk (1936-1977)
James Newton (1953)

Saxophone Crossovers
James Moody (1925)
John Coltrane (1926-1967)
Eric Dolphy (1928-1964)
Paul Horn (1930)
Sam Rivers (1930)
Charles Lloyd (1938)
Pharoah Sanders (1940)
Lew Tabackin (1940)

Piccolo
Marshall Allen (1924)
Joseph Jarman (1937)
Hubert Laws (1939)
Roscoe Mitchell (1940)
Anthony Braxton (1945)
Douglas Ewart (1946)

More Major Flutists
Ira Sullivan (1931)
Bob Downes (1937)
Chris Hinze (1938)
Hubert Laws (1939)
A.A. Webb
Simeon Shterev

Ethnic Flutes
Yusef Lateef (1920)–wood/bamboo flutes
Rahsaan Roland Kirk (1936-1977)–nose flute
Don Cherry (1936)
Joseph Jarman (1937)
Roscoe Mitchell (1940)
Douglas Ewart (1946)

Holly Hoffman – Byard Lancaster (1942)

Bruce Forman

b. 1956

Guitar / Swing, bop

A fusion and contemporary jazz guitarist, Bruce Forman has also done good solo work. He plays mostly electric, with potent melodic content. Forman's done sessions on Concord and Kamei and has recorded with Richie Cole, Bobby Hutcherson, and George Cables.—*Michael G. Nastos*

○ **Bash, The** / Nov. 2, 1982 / Muse 5315

Good mid-'80s date by guitarist Bruce Forman, with pianist Albert Dailey, bassist Buster Williams, and drummer Eddie Gladden. Forman, a mainstream stylist solidly in the Jim Hall-Herb Ellis-Joe Pass school, plays with a precise, delicate mastery. —*Ron Wynn, AMG*

★ **Full Circle** / May 1984 / Concord Jazz 251

Guitarist Bruce Forman has a wealth of major playing experience behind him. While his ability to sustain lengthy single note guitar lines at top speed is formidable, he is aware of the enhancing effect of restraint.... Every track on this LP had something of interest, and the entire LP, minor warts and all, repays close study. This was not an "easy" listen, but a rewarding one. —*Shirley Klett, Cadence*

○ **Forman on the Job** / i. 1992 / Kamei 7004

Recent album by guitarist Bruce Forman with his current band. He's moved more toward swing, though he also includes some Caribbean flavor on some cuts with guest Andy Narrell on steel drums. Forman uses alternating personnel, and gets great contributions from pianist Mark Levine and saxophonist Joe Henderson, among others. —*Ron Wynn, AMG*

Jimmy Forrest (James Robert Forrest)

b. Jan. 24, 1920, St. Louis, MO, **d.** Aug. 26, 1980, Grand Rapids, MI
Tenor sax / Swing, big band, blues & jazz, soul jazz
Tenor saxophonist Jimmy Forrest didn't invent the term or style, but he was among the all-time great honking, sax-soul, jazz players. Forrest worked with many St. Louis bands as a teen and joined Jay McShann in 1942. He later played with Andy Kirk and Duke Ellington before heading his own group and later working with the Harry Edison quintet. He was with Count Basie in the late '70s. Forrest had an immortal version of "Night Train" that fused the Ellington tunes "That's the Blues, Old Man" and "Happy-Go-Lucky Local." Such techniques as smears and slurs, expert projection of lines, and a great thick tone helped him become a soul-jazz master. —*Ron Wynn*

★ **Night Train** / 1951-1953 / Delmark 435
This is tremendous early '50s material from Forrest's days on the pioneering United label. The label was owned by a Black postman and was one of the earliest Black-owned record companies in the nation. The title cut was a huge jukebox and R&B hit. —*Ron Wynn*

○ **All the Gin Is Gone** / Dec. 10-12, 1959 / Delmark 404
An excellent reissue of a wonderful set featuring Grant Green, Harold Mabern, and Elvin Jones (among others). Super work from Forrest. —*Ron Wynn*

Black Forrest / Dec. 10-12, 1959 / Delmark 427
Bop. From the same session as *All the Gin Is Gone.* Includes the lovely "But Beautiful," featuring Grant Green (g), with Forrest sitting this tune out. Recorded in Chicago. —*Michael Erlewine*

☆ **Forrest Fire** / Aug. 9, 1960 / Original Jazz Classics 199
This Jimmy Forrest date from 8/9/60 is a more common set. Forrest was backed here by Larry Young (organ), Thornel Schwartz (guitar), and Jimmy Smith (drums), all of whom worked quite handily together to produce a solid blowing sax-organ-guitar date. —*Bob Rusch, Cadence*

○ **Out of the Forrest** / Apr. 18, 1961 / Prestige 097
This was a 4/18/61 date with Joe Zawinul (piano), Tommy Potter (bass), and Clarence Johnston (drums) backing Jimmy Forrest on eight tracks. This was an honest and rewarding big tenor date with a touch of Lester Young. . . . excellent smokey soulful tenor playing that I think has probably been overlooked by many. —*Bob Rusch, Cadence*

○ **Most Much** / Oct. 19, 1961 / Prestige 350

Sonny Fortune (Cornelius Fortune)

b. May 19, 1939
Alto sax, flute, percussion / Hard bop, early jazz rock
At times as passionate and inspired a soprano and alto saxophonist as any on the current scene, Sonny Fortune's also endured some substantial recording droughts. But at his best, as evidenced on recordings with Miles Davis and McCoy Tyner, there are few players better able to combine a lyrical sound, extensive range, and explosive possibilities. A onetime contributor to Philadelphia R&B bands, Fortune later backed Carolyn Harris on jazz dates before moving to New York in 1967. He's since played with Elvin Jones, Mongo Santamaria, and Buddy Rich, in addition to Tyner and Davis. There were also fusion and jazz-rock stints in the '70s, though he returned to mainstream material in the '80s and '90s. Fortune has recorded as a leader for Strata-East, Horizon, and Atlantic. —*Ron Wynn and Michael G. Nastos*

● **Waves of Dreams** / Mar. 22+23, 1976 / Horizon 711
Waves of Dreams was a pleasant mainstream LP with a definite commercial intent that was slightly alluded to in the liners. It was not a sellout type of trip as the music really stayed in a jazz mold with swinging rhythms and nonpop tunes, yet the solos and overall drive seemed held back." —*Milo Fine, Cadence*

☆ **Serengeti Minstrel** / Apr. 6-08, 1977 / Atlantic 18225
Studio date from this virile Philadelphia saxophonist-flutist, who tackles the Coltrane legacy in fine fashion with Woody Shaw (tpt) and Kenny Barron (p). —*Michael G. Nastos*

○ **It Ain't What It Was** / Konnex 5033

Frank Foster (Frank Benjamin Foster III)

b. Sep. 23, 1928
Sax, arranger, composer, bandleader, flute / Swing, big band

Frank Foster's writing and arranging skills have been so keen, some people have forgotten what a sharp, complete saxophone soloist he's been. Foster played with Wardell Gray and Elvin Jones in the '40s. After two years in the army during the '50s, he joined Count Basie for 11 memorable years. He was highly active in the '60s and '70s as an arranger, member of the Elvin Jones and Thad Jones-Mel Lewis groups, and a bandleader. He co-led an '80s group with Frank Wess and took over leadership of the Basie band in 1986. His best-known composition is "Shiny Stockings." —*Ron Wynn*

★ **Two Franks Please!** / Oct. 13, 1957 / Savoy 2249
High-quality hard-bop set with trumpeter Donald Byrd. —*Ron Wynn*

★ **Frankly Speaking** / Dec. 1984 / Concord Jazz 4276
One of Foster's many sparkling collaborations with his longtime friend, fellow Basie bandmate Frank Wess. Outstanding rhythm section as well. —*Ron Wynn*

○ **Shiny Stockings** / Denon 8545

Pete Fountain (Peter Dewey Fountain, Jr.)

b. Jul. 3, 1930, New Orleans, LA
Clarinet / Dixieland
Clarinetist Pete Fountain's roots extend back to the '40s in New Orleans music, where he worked with Monk Hazel, the Junior Dixieland Band, Phil Zito, and others. He spent four years with the Basin Street Six, then hit the jackpot with Lawrence Welk. Hit records and television appearances followed. Many tourists have continued to identify New Orleans music with either Fountain or Al Hirt since the '60s, and Fountain was also a regular for many years on "The Tonight Show" during Johnny Carson's reign as host. He has undeniable gifts, especially his tone. —*Ron Wynn*

★ **Best of Pete Fountain—Vols. 1 & 2** / MCA 4032

Panama Francis (David Albert Francis)

b. Dec. 21, 1918, Miami, FL
Drums / Swing, big band, bop
Among the last of the top swing drummers, Francis learned his craft playing in his church in Miami at revivals before joining George Kelly's band. He moved to New York in 1938, and in 1939 he became part of Roy Eldridge's band. He got his nickname from wearing a Panama hat. The glory years came with Lucky Millinder's band at the Savoy. His bombastic style, complete with riveted Chinese cymbal, galvanized audiences through the mid-'40s, and Francis keeps reforming various editions of the Savoy Sultans. He later had a lucrative studio career as an R&B session player, laying down similar beats and keeping the groove going. By the '70s he'd gotten back into playing jazz as well as backing vocalists, and he once again formed a version of his beloved Savoy Sultans. —*Ron Wynn*

★ **All-Stars 1949** / 1949 / Collectables 5313

○ **Savoy Sultans** / Classic Jazz 149
Several of the arrangements of this extremely well recorded album (licensed from French Black and Blue) reenacted Al Cooper's originals; the others were by band members Francis, tenor saxophonist George Kelly, and Norris Turney (alto sax, clarinet). Within their styles, the soloists were all very good, especially Turney, whose lingering pre-Charlie Parker vibrato disguised some surprisingly modern harmonic notions, and Kelly, a model of droll virility. —*Francis Davis, Cadence*

Bud Freeman (Lawrence Freeman)

b. Apr. 13, 1906, Chicago, IL, **d.** Mar. 15, 1991
Tenor sax / Dixieland
Tenor saxophonist Bud Freeman was a master of vintage Chicago-style jazz, and an innovator in his genre. His lush, witty style was absorbed by generations of White tenor players. Freeman began in the '20s with C-melody sax, then switched to tenor in 1925. He spent nine years with the cream of Chicago-based leaders, including Red Nichols and Eddie Condon. Freeman moved to New York and joined Ray Noble in the '30s and attained major popularity with Tommy Dorsey. He appeared on Broadway in a musical with Louis Armstrong and Maxine Sullivan in the late '30s. Freeman kept the cause of traditional jazz alive from the '40s on, through associations with Condon or on his own, though his playing never calcified or lost its charm. He was a founder of

the World's Greatest Jazz Band in 1968 and returned to Chicago in 1970. —*Ron Wynn*

● **Commodore Years (1938-1939), The** / 1938-1939 / Commodore
An anthology-overview of his most influential material from the late '30s. —*Ron Wynn*

★ **All Stars with Shorty Baker** / May 13, 1960 / Prestige 183
Authentic was the word that best described these musicians. They were among the best of the white mainstream jazz players of the prebop days. Their mixed associates here all represent an era of jazz that wasn't exactly Dixieland and preceded Bird and Dizzy. Even after the entry of bop they continued to do their own thing and avoided almost completely any influence of bebop licks. Bud Freeman had a style and sound on tenor that only a handful of players ever followed, and it leaves you with a feeling that he never tried to alter it. . . . This album represented a style connected with Eddie Condon followers and was very typical of club playing in the early '40s. —*Jerry L. Atkins, Cadence*

○ **Compleat Bud Freeman, The** / Dec. 10+12, 1969 / Monmouth 7022

○ **Bucky and Bud** / i. 1975 / Flying Dutchman 1378

Chico Freeman (Earl Lavon Freeman, Jr.)

b. Jul. 17, 1949, Chicago, IL
Tenor sax / Hard bop, modern creative
The son of venerable Chicago tenor saxophonist Von Freeman, Chico began studying tenor while at Northwestern University. His studies with Muhal Richard Abrams and Joe Daley, plus a Masters degree in composition, gave him both formal and practical training. He settled in New York in the '70s and became known as a player whose sound had power, appeal, and flexibility. He was grounded in swing and bop but was also able to work creatively in an avant-garde framework. One of the first concerts billed as a "young lions" event in the early '80s had him on a bill with Wynton Marsalis. He also recorded with his father in the '80s. Freeman's been featured as a leader on recordings for many labels, including Contemporary, Black Saint, Blackhawk, Columbia, and Musician/Elektra. He's played and worked with Henry Threadgill, Bobby Hutcherson, Billy Hart, Wallace Roney, Lester Bowie, Kirk Lightsey, and Kenny Kirkland, among others.—*Ron Wynn*

★ **Beyond the Rain** / Jun. 21-23, 1977 / Contemporary 479
With the Hilton Ruiz Trio, featuring the compositions of M. R. Abrams and Freeman's hard-charging playing. —*Michael G. Nastos*

○ **Chico** / 1977 / India Navigation 1031
A standard for creative tenor saxophonists to live up to. W/ Cecil McBee, Muhal Richard Abrams, and Steve McCall. —*Michael G. Nastos*

★ **Spirit Sensitive** / Sep. 1979 / India Navigation 1045
On *Spirit Sensitive* tenor saxophonist Chico Freeman made a valiant attempt at taking on the standards, something the younger players other than Arthur Blythe, Air, and Anthony Braxton have shied away from. "Autumn in New York" was beautifully handled as a Cecil McBee-Freeman bass-tenor duet, but on Horace Silver's "Peace," which was a pace or two slower, the open space and the absence of the upbeat percussion left Freeman a bit too out in the open. Freeman was occasionally overmiked, perhaps in an attempt to accomplish that ravishing vibrato characteristic of Ben Webster and the old-style tenor players. The B side did the job of partial vindication: "Don't Get Around Much Anymore" was particularly bouncy and achieved the old style. —*Brent Staples, Down Beat*

○ **Peaceful Heart, Gentle Spirit** / Mar. 6-07, 1980 / Contemporary 14005
Good use was made on *Peaceful Heart, Gentle Spirit* of varied voicings from the various personnel; for example, "Heart and the Gentle Spirit" opened with a bass figure and the other instruments slowly entered—alto flute, piano, vibes, percussion. The sound remained open and airy, in keeping with the tune's gentle, lilting feel. James Newton (bass flute, c-flute) took flight with a warm, full c-flute tone darting through the air. Following a piano solo that brought things back to earth, Chico Freeman tenderly nudged the piece along with his alto flute. —*Jerry de Muth, Down Beat*

Russ Freeman (Russell Donald Freeman)

b. May 28, 1926
Piano / Cool
Pianist Russ Freeman, an impressive and swinging soloist, played with West Coast bop groups in the late '40s, including Howard McGhee, Dexter Gordon, Art Pepper, Wardell Gray, and Shorty Rogers. He also studied classical piano as a child. Freeman had very profitable musical relationships with Chet Baker in 1954, and began a longtime association with Shelly Manne in 1955. He's worked in television and films as a music director and pianist since the mid '60s.—*Michael Erlewine*

★ **Trio with Richard Twardzik** / Oct. 1953-Aug. 1957 / Pacific Jazz 46861

● **Freeman/Baker Quartet** / Nov. 6, 1956 / Pacific Jazz 1232

Von Freeman (Earl Lavon Freeman, Sr.)

b. Oct. 3, 1922, Chicago
Tenor sax / Swing, bop
Von Freeman's a masterful veteran and another in a long line of jazz greats who attended Chicago's Du Sable High School and studied under Capt. Walter Dyett. His huge, quickly recognizable tone, articulation, proficiency on ballads, and great timing have made him an admired player. Freeman's insistence on spending most of his career in Chicago certainly kept him from gaining wider recognition. He played with Horace Henderson, Sun Ra, and Charlie Parker and recorded in the early '50s with Andrew Hill. His infrequent (but always enjoyable) albums have had a great mix of blues, ballads, and bop. He finally got some degree of the spotlight when he recorded on Columbia with his son Chico for half of the delightful *Fathers and Sons* album in 1981. He later teamed with Chico in a two-tenor group for a European tour. Besides his son, there are other musician brothers, George Freeman (guitar) and Bruz Freeman (drums). —*Ron Wynn*

★ **Serenade and Blues** / Jun. 11, 1975 / Nessa 11
To devotees of Ornette Coleman and Albert Ayler, tenor saxophonist Von Freeman's quirky phrasing, rubbery vibrato, microtonal melodies, and abrupt changes of register and timbre raised no hackles, but to some mainstreamers, past revelation became present dogma, provoking puzzled reactions that *Serenade & Blues* was "sour," "off key," and so on. In this case, Thelonious Monk's dictum that "wrong is right" was precisely applicable, for Freeman projected more creativity and emotional truth through his novel approach to tradition than a whole wax museum full of revivalist clones. There was certainly nothing peculiar in Freeman's choice of material: a Glenn Miller ballad, a Jule Styne/Sammy Cahn standard, and a pair of unpretentious blues. The rhythm section never strayed far from orthodox canons, but there was no dearth of swing in the inexhaustible reservoirs of John Young's Art Tatum-Bud Powell piano stylings or Wilbur Campbell's ever-tasty drumming. Freeman's sax, however, was a horn of another color, transmuting familiar melodies into startling, though recognizable abstractions. —*Larry Birnbaum, Down Beat*

○ **Young and Foolish** / Aug. 12, 1977 / Daybreak 002
Von Freeman's *Young & Foolish*—recorded "live" at Laren in 1977—was probably the best tenor saxophone album issued in 1981. It was another testament to dues paying, being only Freeman's fourth LP in a career even longer than Jimmy Knepper's. Like Knepper, Freeman is a uniquely individual stylist with such a personal way of juxtaposing even the smallest number of notes that he is always instantly recognizable. It said much for the coherence of his invention that the 25-minute "I'll Close My Eyes" (well-chosen, unhackneyed material), which filled side one, rarely fell short of being thoroughly inspired. Unusually for Freeman, there were no blues tunes here, yet they pervaded every chorus in inflection and mood. They were the unseen hand guiding the unaffected, almost naked emotional directness of his playing, be it on the wailing "Eyes," the singing "Foolish," or the intense "Bye, Bye, Blackbird." —*Chris Sheridan, Down Beat*

Don Friedman (Donald Ernest Friedman)

b. May 4, 1935, San Francisco, CA
Piano, composer / Modern creative
A veteran pianist and composer from San Francisco, Don Friedman has a fine lyrical touch and piano style, often incorpo-

rating classical and free jazz elements in his playing and compositions. He's been mostly heard as a sideman, but played bop with the masters. Friedman also played with the Clark Terry Big Band. Friedman recorded with Buddy Collette and played alongside Chet Baker, Ornette Coleman, and Pepper Adams, as well as forming his own trio and recording as a leader. Friedman was later in the Jimmy Giuffre Three and played with Atilla Zoller. He taught jazz piano at New York University in the '70s and has done sessions for Owl, Riverside, Progressive and Lime Tree.—*Michael G. Nastos*

★ **Day in the City, A** / Jun. 12, 1961 / Riverside 1775
Don Friedman's 6/12/61 trio (Chuck Israels, bass; Joe Hunt, drums) recording is titled *A Day in the City*. This was six jazz variations on a theme. The theme in this case was "The Minstril Boy," and Friedman used it as a springboard for each part of the city's day. The mode here was a familiar one and the impressionism in a direction you might expect. . . . But there was nothing predictable about the actual improvised music. Friedman was not afraid here to mix his attacks from Bill Evansish lyricism to dissonant blocks more associated with Cecil Taylor. This was fine cerebral jazz that remains totally contemporary more than 20 years later. —*Bob Rusch, Cadence*

○ **Dreams and Explorations** / 1964 / Riverside 485
○ **Metamorphosis** / Feb. 22, 1966 / Prestige 7488

David Friesen

b. May 6, 1942, Tacoma, WA
Bass / New age, modern creative
David Friesen is a strong, talented bassist who has worked in both straight jazz and more chamberlike settings. His most exciting playing came in sessions with Mal Waldron and Ted Curson, where his skills were extended and he was a forceful contributor to the rhythm section. His own albums have become increasingly mood- and environment-centered—well-done background music without a strong jazz presence. Friesen's played with John Handy, Marian McPartland, Joe Henderson, Billy Harper, Ted Curson, Ricky Ford, Paul Horn, John Stowell, and Duke Jordan among others. He's done sessions for Global Pacific, Steeplechase, Palo Alto, Muse, Golden Flute, and Inner City.—*Ron Wynn*

● **Amber Skies** / Jan. 1983+Apr. 1983 / Palo Alto 8043
Bassist Dave Friesen has marvelous technical skills, but doesn't always stick to jazz context. This '83 date has him doing quasi-classical, light pop and more conventional jazz; the compositions are erratic, but his bass solos and skills are consistently impressive. —*Ron Wynn, AMG*

Bill Frisell (William Richard Frisell)

b. Mar. 18, 1951, Baltimore, MD
Guitar / Early jazz rock, modern creative
Guitarist Bill Frisell studied with Jim Hall and at the Berklee College of Music. His influences include Jim Hall, Wes Montgomery, and Jimi Hendrix. His many ECM recordings have made him a sort of house guitarist for that label, doing successful work with Jan Garbarek and percussionist Paul Motian. He has also recorded duets with Tim Berne and John Scofield. Frisell blends jazz, rock, and avant-garde influences in an exuberant and unpredictable style. Perhaps his most distinctive quality as a guitarist is creative and tasteful use of synthesizers and electronic effects, creating sonorities like wind instruments and organs. — *David Nelson McCarthy*

★ **Rambler** / Aug. 1984 / ECM 825234
Frisell's a slick harmonist (more than ever now that he's using a guitar synthesizer), but a playful one, tweaking accepted tonalities. Together, he and the disruptive timekeeper Paul Motian, who's employed the guitarist for years, feed off each other's comic streaks, and that's something the easy-rolling tubaist Bob Stewart readily picks up on playing the tongue-in-cheek march "Music I Heard." —*Kevin Whitehead, Cadence*

☆ **Lookout for Hope** / Mar. 1987 / ECM 833495
"Country and Eastern" music with Frisell's distinct guitar sound. Constantly challenging listening. —*Michael G. Nastos*

David Frishberg (David L. Frishberg)

b. Mar. 23, 1933, St. Paul, MN
Songwriter, vocals, piano / Blues & jazz, ballads & blues

This singer and pianist is best known for writing and singing funny, witty songs with a distinctive delivery. He's a special individual, with a one-of-a-kind style. Frishberg's a baseball fan and astute observer of society. —*Michael G. Nastos*

★ **Getting Some Fun out of Life** / Jan. 25-26, 1977 / Concord Jazz 37

○ **Dave Frishberg Classics** / 1982-1983 / Concord Jazz 4462
This hits collection reissued almost all of his best-known tunes. A must-buy. —*Michael G. Nastos*

★ **Live at Vine Street** / Oct. 1984 / Fantasy 9638
Vocalist-pianist David Frishberg didn't perform this program in anyone's living room or family room, but it very well could have been. Such was the feeling of integral relaxation and informality generated by an artist who makes it all sound deceptively simple, if not easy. —*Alan Bargebuhr, Cadence*

Tony Fruscella

b. Feb. 4, 1927, d. 1969
Trumpet / Swing, bop, cool
A promising trumpeter who never totally fulfilled the promise displayed on some early recordings, Tony Fruscella's style was very close to Chet Baker's, though not as compelling. After stints in an army band, Fruscella played with Lester Young and Gerry Mulligan and recorded and performed with Stan Getz in 1955. There were also occasional dates with fellow trumpeter Don Joseph, but Fruscella was dead by 1969. His finest LP was a mid-'50s session for Atlantic.—*Ron Wynn*

Debut / i. Dec. 1948-1953 / Spotlite 126
Fru 'n Brew / i. 1953 / Spotlite
● **Tony Fruscella** (Jazzlore # 25) / i. 1955 / Atlantic 90463
I'll Be Seeing You / Mar. 29, 1955+Apr. 1, 1955 / Atlantic 1220
A brilliantly bopish session by this little-recorded trumpeter, with Allen Eager (ts). —*David Szatmary*

Curtis Fuller (Curtis Dubois Fuller)

b. Dec. 15, 1934, Detroit, MI
Trombone / Hard bop
Curtis Fuller ranks near the top among bop trombonists. He's one of the '50s Detroit jazz class, studied music in high school, and played with Cannonball Adderley in the U.S. Army Band. Fuller moved to New York in 1957. He is almost as fast and technically flawless as his main influence, J. J. Johnson, though not so fond of vocal effects and less flamboyant. A master at slow, lyrical pieces and not quite as creative or imaginative on faster tunes, Fuller's played on numerous great sessions and been part of such groups as the Jazztet and Art Blakey's Jazz Messengers. Cannonball Adderley, Yusef Lateef, Kenny Burrell, Benny Golson, Art Farmer, Dizzy Gillespie, Kai Winding, Cedar Walton, and Count Basie are among the major artists with whom Fuller's recorded or played. He's recorded as a leader for Mainstream, Warwick, Smash/Trip, Epic, Impulse, Timeless, and Bee Hive, among others.—*Ron Wynn*

○ **Opener, The** / Jun. 16, 1957 / Blue Note 1567
○ **Blues-Ette** / May 21, 1959 / Savoy Jazz 127
A powerhouse session with Fuller leading a stalwart group. Benny Golson (ts) and Tommy Flanagan (p) are sublime. —*Ron Wynn*

● **All-Star Sextets** / Aug. 25, 1959+Dec. 17, 1959 / Savoy 2239
Combos led by trombonist Fuller, members of the Jazztet and Coltrane ensembles. Essential jazz-postbop. Seminal material from a brilliant trombonist. Features Lee Morgan (tpt), Wynton Kelly (p), McCoy Tyner (p), and others. —*Ron Wynn*

○ **Smokin'** / 1974 / Mainstream 370
☆ **Four on the Outside** / Sep. 18, 1978 / Timeless 124
Curtis Fuller's LP was nearly stolen by Pepper Adams (baritone sax). Not that Fuller was any slouch in the soloing department, but . . . Adams romped through several sections of "Suite-Kathy" with particular elan and had a grand time elsewhere. James Williams (piano) had some excellent solo spots. Most of the originals here seemed to be fragments of melody from various standards reworked into a new whole. "Suite-Kathy" was a lengthy example of a reworking using a number of different time signatures and other attractive variations. Everyone bit into "Hello,

Young Lovers" and turned it into the highlight of a good album. —*Shirley Klett, Cadence*

Kenny G (Kenneth Gorelick)

b. 1959, Seattle, WA
Soprano sax, reeds / Instrumental pop
It's amazing that someone whose music is so melodic and soothing could generate such controversy. Love him or hate him, Kenny G (born Kenneth Gorelick) has garnered a wide audience for his light jazz-pop music since his 1982 self-titled solo debut. His smooth alto sax melodies can also be found on albums by Whitney Houston, Aretha Franklin, and Natalie Cole, and his presolo career included stints with Barry White's Love Unlimited Orchestra and the Jeff Lorber Fusion band.

Despite (or because of?) his million-selling, Top Ten success, music critics usually withold any praise, while jazz aficionados bristle at the thought of including him in the realm of jazz. But it is clear that his music has found a niche with millions of fans who aren't concerned with such labels. —*AMG*

Kenny G / **i.** 1982 / Arista 8036
Although he hadn't perfected his stylish amalgam of pop melodies and jazz improvisation, Kenny G's first album is worthwhile to his fans; parts of *Kenny G* may be rough, yet it shows the roots of his massive success. —*AMG*

Duotones / **i.** 1986 / Arista 8496
Kenny G's breakthrough effort featured the hit "Songbird," which is the definitive example of the saxophonist's smooth, lyrical playing; the rest of the album is nearly as good, highlighting his melodic jazzy pop. *Duotones* remains his best effort. —*AMG*

● **Silhouette** / **i.** 1988 / Arista 8457
Following the breakthrough success of 1986's *Duotones*, Kenny G was at the top of his form with *Silhouette*, turning in a set of smooth, melodic sax that cemented his position as America's favorite jazzy pop instrumentalist; Smokey Robinson's lead vocal on "We've Saved the Best for Last" was a particular highlight. —*AMG*

Kenny G Live / **i.** 1989 / Arista 8613
Like most live albums, *Kenny G Live* functions as a greatest hits of sorts, picking the best and most popular tracks from his multimillion selling albums. Thankfully, the disc isn't a stale photocopy of the original recordings; instead, Kenny G offers a fresh perspective on his standards, making it an album that fans will cherish. —*AMG*

Steve Gadd

b. 1945
Drums / blues & jazz, soul jazz, contemporary funk
While much of what Steve Gadd has played is either quasi-jazz or straight pop, R&B, and funk, few question Gadd's drumming credentials. He's emerged after Billy Cobham and prior to Dave Weckl as one of the main drum stylists in jazz-rock, widely imitated in both his kit tuning and rhythmic approach. Gadd played with Dizzy Gillespie as an 11-year-old. He studied at the Eastman school and later served in the army. After playing in a Rochester big band, Gadd formed a trio and moved to New York in the early '70s. He quickly became a prolific presence in the studios. Gadd played and recorded jazz sessions with Chick Corea, Al DiMeola, and Carla Bley, and pop and soul with Aretha Franklin, Barbra Streisand, Stevie Wonder, Steely Dan, and Paul Simon. His work with David Sanborn fell into the stylistic cracks. Gadd was a coleader of the highly touted session band Stuff, with Eric Gale, Cornell Dupree, and Richard Tee. While all were acknowledged studio greats, Stuff's albums stiffed in America. They did much better in Japan. Gadd later teamed with Eddie Gomez and Ronnie Cuber to form the Gadd gang. They recorded in the late '80s, cutting a date that mixed Bob Dylan and Bill Doggett compositions. Gadd later recorded for Projazz with Tee, Cuber, and other guest stars. His Gadd Gang later recorded for Columbia. —*Ron Wynn*

○ **Best of Steve Gadd** / Projazz Records 662

Slim Gaillard (Slim Bulee Gaillard)

b. Jan. 4, 1916, **d.** Feb. 25, 1991
Guitar, vocals / Swing, bop
A highly entertaining, witty entertainer and underrated musician, Slim Gaillard's success at inventing and interpolating "vout," his

own vocalese-code, has often overshadowed his skill as a bassist. Gaillard also played piano and guitar and even tap danced earlier in his career. He initially teamed with fellow bassist Slam Stewart in 1938, and their "Slim and Slam" musical and verbal routine and act became a national sensation featured on New York's WNEW-AM. At the height of his popularity, Gaillard was featured in films and even did some stints as an emcee. He later had a role in the television miniseries "Roots—The Next Generation," playing guitar and piano and singing. Besides the long-running "Slim and Slam," Gaillard recorded with Bucky Pizzarelli and Major Holley, did sessions on his own, and made many club and festival appearances. —*Ron Wynn and Michael G. Nastos*

★ **Opera En Vout** / 1947 / Verve 554
A variety of sessions from 1946, 1947, 1951, and 1952 from Gaillard. A perfect representation of Gaillard's musical and comedic mastery. —*Michael G. Nastos*

○ **Original 1938 Recordings—Vol. 1** / Tax 1
○ **Original 1938 Recordings—Vol. 2** / Tax 2

Larry Gales (Lawrence Bernard Gales)

b. 1936
Bass / Hard bop
While he gained his highest profile from being Thelonious Monk's bassist in the '50s and '60s, Larry Gales played dependably with several other groups and in many situations. These included stints with J.C. Heard, the Eddie "Lockjaw" Davis-Johnny Griffin quintet, Herbie Mann, Junior Mance, and Joe Williams. Gales played with Monk from 1964 until 1969 and was a pivotal part of the musical equation. He later moved to the West Coast, where he joined Erroll Garner. Gales was featured on recordings with Blue Mitchell, Jimmy Smith, Sonny Criss, Clark Terry, Dave Frishberg, Kenny Burrell, and Joe Turner, while playing with Willie Bobo, Red Rodney, Harold Land, Harry Edison, and Bill Berry during the '70s. He also toured extensively both domestically and abroad with Benny Carter. He's led his own bands during the '80s and '90s. —*Ron Wynn and Michael G. Nastos*

★ **Message from Monk, A** / Jun. 1990 / Candid 79503
Larry Gales, longtime bassist for Thelonious Monk, pays tribute to his former boss, heading a band that includes another Monk veteran in drummer Ben Riley. The other band members are accomplished players, although tenor saxophonist Junior Cook has uneven time. Trombonist Steve Turre and trumpeter Claudio Roditi fill the gap. —*Ron Wynn, AMG*

Hal Galper (Harold Galper)

b. Apr. 18, 1938, Salem, MA
Piano / Bop, modern creative
Pianist Hal Galper has been influenced by fellow virtuosos McCoy Tyner and Oscar Peterson. He worked with many of New York's finest modern ensembles, playing primarily bop and postbop. Galper played with Tony Williams, Chet Baker, the Brecker Brothers, and in Herb Pomeroy's big band, while also accompanying vocalists Anita O'Day and Joe Williams. He played in Cannonball Adderley's group for two years and was a member of the Phil Woods Quintet for a decade. Galper's bands are great, displaying him at his best. He's recorded as a leader for Steeplechase, Enja, and Contemporary. —*Michael G. Nastos*

○ **Now Hear This** / **i.** Feb. 1977 / Enja 2090
Pianist Hal Galper played churning, high-energy music that sounded quite a bit like McCoy Tyner. Listen to Galper's left hand and you'll see how close to Tyner this came. Two exceptions were "Shadow Waltz," a dreamy ballad, and Thelonious Monk's "Bemsha Swing." . . . Bassist Cecil McBee and drummer Williams (first name not listed) didn't disappoint, playing with what had become their customary verve and inventiveness. —*Carl Brauer, Cadence*

★ **Speak with a Single Voice** / Feb. 1978 / Enja 4006
First quintet recording, with the Brecker Brothers, at Rosie's in New Orleans. Essential. —*Michael G. Nastos*

○ **Hal Galper Quartet** / **i.** Jun. 23, 1992 / Enja 3053

Ganelin Trio

Modern creative

Russian free-jazz improvisers; they are the premier band of this style. They constantly switch instruments, on occasion playing each other's. —*Michael G. Nastos*

★ **Concerto Grosso** / i. 1978 / Melodiya
Ganelin-Tarasov-Checkasin. Russian trio of wildly pure improvisers. A must-buy for the challengable listener. —*Michael G. Nastos*

Jan Garbarek

b. Mar. 4, 1947, Mysen, Norway
Tenor sax, soprano sax, flute / New age, modern creative
Tenor saxophonist Jan Garbarek is a Norwegian jazz artist. Garbarek's early influences included John Coltrane, and he played with and studied George Russell's tonal system. He also played with Terje Rypdal, Keith Jarrett, and Don Cherry. His music combines elements of free-jazz, jazz-rock, folk music, and European avant-garde, all within a very introspective and personal improvisation process. An ECM recording artist, his contemplative sound epitomizes that label's style of high-quality improvisational art music. His recordings range from extremely avant-garde to spacious mood music and include highly successful collaborations with artists such as Keith Jarrett (*Nude Ants*). Garbarek has also composed for TV, theater, and film. As a European who is not merely an imitator of American jazz, he incorporates classical influences such as great sensitivity and contrast of dynamics, along with a compositional sense of progression and sharp changes of density and mood. His European stylistic influences range from traditional church and folk harmonies to the acerbic minimal gestures of 20th-century classicism. His music is often slower, more moody, and more spacious than the dense textures of urban jazz, but his powerful tone and fluid technique, influenced by the intense and searching sound of Coltrane, places him squarely in the jazz tradition. Garbarek practices what is truly an international jazz style, yet without contradiction it can be said to be completely personal as well. —*David Nelson McCarthy*

★ **Afric Pepperbird** / Sep. 22-23, 1970 / ECM 843475

● **Witchi-Tai-To** / Nov. 27-28, 1973 / ECM 833330
The Jan Garbarek-Bob Stenson group was certainly one of the most versatile nonelectric ensembles playing anywhere in the world at this time (1973). Frankly, *Witchi-Tai-To*—superbly recorded from a technical standpoint—provided a clear, refreshing respite from the surfeit of wah-wahs, electric quirks, and merely funky posturings that were so prevalent on turntables at the time. Each member of this group deserved his own niche in the higher echelons of music polls, and the quartet *in toto* should have been recognized for its direct blowing, varied and smooth dynamic transitions, and intense emotional fervor. —*Charles Mitchell, Down Beat*

○ **I Took up the Runes** / Aug. 1990 / ECM 843850

○ **Star** / Jan. 1991 / ECM 849649
For saxophonist Jan Garbarek, *Star*'s approach is jazzier, more ethereal and less earthy than 1991's *I Took Up the Runes*. There were even instances on three tunes where, when stating the melody, he somehow used electronics. The effect was to lift the music heavenward. In an all-originals program (Garbarek penning the lilting title track, bassist Miroslav Vitous with four, including the bouncy "Jumper," drummer Peter Erskine with two, "Snowman" being a tripartite offering), there was a simple beauty to the melodies. —*John Ephland, Down Beat*

Red Garland (William M. Garland)

b. May 13, 1923, Dallas, TX, d. Apr. 23, 1984, Dallas, TX
Piano / Bop, postbop
Pianist Red Garland was influenced by Count Basie and Nat King Cole, as well as modernists such as Bud Powell and Art Tatum. Garland played with the great horn players of his era, including Charlie Parker, Coleman Hawkins, and Lester Young. His greatest recognition came as part of the famous Miles Davis rhythm section with Paul Chambers and Philly Joe Jones. He led his own trio, but functioned mostly as a sideman, exemplifying the many fine jazz musicians who never became huge stars in their own right, but played with all the greats. Garland was a fine ensemble player, who made several recordings for Prestige and Galaxy. —*David Nelson McCarthy*

● **Soul Junction** / Nov. 15, 1957 / Prestige 481

Quintet. More Donald Byrd (tpt), John Coltrane (ts), Red Garland. Solos from Coltrane and Byrd are better than on *High Pressure*. —*Ron Wynn*

○ **Red in Bluesville** / Apr. 17, 1959 / Original Jazz Classics 295

○ **Red Garland Live!** / Oct. 2, 1959 / New Jazz 8326

★ **Red Alone** / Apr. 2, 1960 / Moodsville 3

○ **Solar** / Jan. 30, 1962 / Jazzland 755
W/ Les Spann (g, fl), Sam Jones (b), and Frant Gant (d). This is easy-listening, cocktail-lounge-style jazz. —*AMG*

○ **When There Are Grey Skies** / Oct. 9, 1962 / Prestige 704
Good early '60s standards and originals date featuring pianist Red Garland in trio with bassist Wendell Marshall and drummer Charlie Persip. Garland roams, explores, and reworks pieces, at times creating alternate melodies, other times working back till he returns to the original. The CD reissue has one bonus cut. —*Ron Wynn, AMG*

★ **Crossings** / Dec. 1977 / Galaxy 472
Tremendous update. An example of Garland's ability to heave and create in a trio setting, this time with Ron Carter (b) and Philly Joe Jones (d). —*Ron Wynn*

○ **Jazz Junction** / Prestige 24023

○ **Misty Red** / Timeless 179

Erroll Garner (Erroll Louis Garner)

b. Jun. 15, 1921, Pittsburg, PA, d. Jan. 2, 1977, Los Angeles, CA
Piano / Swing
One of the most original piano stylists in all of jazz, Garner never learned to read music but conceived of the piano as a big, swinging band in which he was both melody voice and rhythm section. He used his left hand almost like Count Basie's sterling guitarist Freddie Green, and in the trio setting he preferred (with bass and drums just keeping steady time), he could outswing most bands and combos at the middle and up tempos he mastered. On ballads, he adopted a heavily arpeggiated, romantic approach that contrasted with the impish humor he brought to his swinging style. Garner also liked to keep his listeners in suspense with elaborate solo introductions that were little masterpieces in themselves. Though he never said a word on stage, he could hold the largest audience spellbound just with his music, which was filled with joy and life. Like Louis Armstrong, he transcended the jazz category and had fans of all ages and musical persuasions. Also like Armstrong, he was one of the first (and few) jazz performers to establish himself as a concert attraction. A prolific recording artist, he left behind a legacy from which treasures continue to be culled. His most famous composition, of course, is "Misty." —*Dan Morgenstern*

○ **Complete Savoy Sessions—Vol. 1, The** / Jan. 30, 1945 / Savoy 70521

○ **Erroll Garner—Vol. 1** / Feb. 17, 1947+Jun. 10, 1947 / Dial 205

★ **Elf, The** / Mar. 29, 1949 / Savoy 4408
The lion's share of these Erroll Garner recordings was done in 1949. There were also four tunes done in 1945. These earlier recordings were clearly those of a pianist strongly influenced by jazz; but to refer to Garner's playing here as "jazz piano" is simply not correct, or at least not fair to the many keyboardists who were more seriously investigating the resources of the idiom. He was, at the time, a lush, influential stylist but a limited improviser. The 1949 tracks loosen up considerably more, but the similar tempos and stylings, while lovely, don't have the lean strength or compelling swing that would emerge a bit later. Everything here was a trio recording, and that, of course, compounded the problem. —*Neil Tesser, Down Beat*

Long Ago and Far Away / Jun. 28, 1950-Jan. 1, 1951 / Columbia 40863
1950-1951. This is great Garner. Unfortunately, the remastering is not as great. —*Michael Erlewine*

○ **Gone-Garner-Gonest** / Jan. 11, 1951-Mar. 30, 1953 / Columbia 617

○ **Gems** / Jan. 11, 1951 / Columbia 6173

○ **Solo Flight** / Feb. 29, 1952 / Columbia 6209

★ **Erroll Garner Plays Misty** / i. 1954 / Emarcy 824892

★ **Original Misty** / i. 1954 / Mercury 834910

This is a reissue of the first Garner version of Misty made in the early '50s. —*Ron Wynn*

Afternoon of an Elf / Mar. 14, 1955 / Mercury 826457
Spectacular, frenzied solo piano from Erroll Garner, done in 1955. Sometimes he'd probe and pick apart and then reconstruct standards. Other times he'd race through a song, varying the tempo, pulse, and pace with each solo. This has been reissued on CD. —*Ron Wynn*

★ **Concert by the Sea** / Sep. 19, 1955 / Columbia 40589
Concert by the Sea was arguably the finest record pianist Erroll Garner ever made, and he made many—a few outstanding—many good recordings. But this live recording (9/19/55) with his trio (Eddie Calhoun, bass; Denzil Best, drums) presented a typical Garner program; it was a mixture of originals, show biz, and pop standards delivered with his unique delivery and enthusiasm. The rhythms and brilliant use of tension and release was perfectly captured. And while for many jazz listeners, Garner's deliberate structures were too orchestrated, there was an equal spontaneity in the propulsion of these orchestrations that swung as well as anything. —*Bob Rusch, Cadence*

○ **Most Happy Piano, The** / Jun. 7, 1956-Sep. 11, 1956 / Columbia 939

○ **Paris Impressions—Vol. 1** / Mar. 27, 1958+May 11, 1958 / Sony Special Products 9
This Garner, while not his best, was still fine Garner. The big drawbacks on this double set was his work on the harpsichord, an instrument that may have knocked him out but has never adapted well to jazz that I know of. Garner made no concessions to the instrument and played it in the same style he played the piano, a style that clashed on the harpsichord. —*Bob Rusch, Cadence*

○ **Paris Impressions—Vol. 2** / Mar. 27, 1958+May 11, 1958 / Columbia 1217

○ **Plays Gershwin and Kern** / Aug. 1964-Feb. 1968 / Emarcy 826224
Erroll Garner Plays Gershwin and Kern is a reissue of material previously issued in Europe on Bulldog, MPS, and Polydor.... the material is quite excellent, often adventuresome and some of his best studio sides. Included here from 2/5/68 and never issued before is a brief "Nice Work If You Can Get It" with Garner singing along to himself—it's a wonderful gem of a private moment. Backup is Eddie Calhoun or Ike Isaacs on bass, Kelly Martin or Jimmy Smith on drums and Jose Mangual, congas. This was the first domestic issue of this material. —*Bob Rusch, Cadence*

That's My Kick / Nov. 1967 / MGM 4463
Hot piano and excellent bass by Milt Hinton, with a guest stint by Johnny Pacheco (fl, v, per). —*Ron Wynn*

○ **Magician** / i. Oct. 1974 / London 640
All of Erroll Garner's familiar trademarks . . . remained intact here. Added were a couple of new tricks: some funky left hand rhythms and a rhythm section that played fluently in straight eighth-note rhythms. The Latin-rock treatments of "Someone to Watch Over Me" and "Yesterdays" owed much to mainstream Ramsey Lewis. But while Garner updated his style in places, his basic style remained intact. And the outlines of Garner's style had more to do with emotion—especially the comic emotions—than with technique. —*Jon Balleras, Down Beat*

○ **Body and Soul** / i. Mar. 18, 1991 / Columbia 47035

○ **Erroll Garner Collection—Vols. 4 & 5: Solo Time!** / i. Nov. 16, 1992 / Verve 511821

○ **Savoy Sessions** / Savoy 4408

Kenny Garrett

Alto sax, tenor sax, flute / Hard bop, neo-bop
Garrett is a nice alto and tenor saxophonist who has become a major figure among the "young lion" corps. He is a former member of OTB, a band that originated under the auspices of Blue Note. He has played with Miles Davis and recorded on Atlantic. A fiery altoist, his runs and vibrant tone echo Cannonball Adderley and harken back (though not directly) to Charlie Parker. —*Ron Wynn*

● **African Exchange Student** / i. 1990 / Atlantic 82156

Larry Gelb

b. 1952
Piano / Postbop, neo-bop
Larry Gelb is a composer-lyricist, jazz pianist-teacher, and author. Aside from albums, he has written film scores, off-Broadway musicals, and the book "The Geometry of Melody." Born in Scranton, PA on February 25, 1952, Gelb began playing piano at age 7, started composing seriously at age 11, and recorded his first album at 13. At 14 he won the Yamaha International Young Composer competition. As a teenager, he formed his own trio and toured with Buddy DeFranco and the Glenn Miller Orchestra. A student of Margaret Chaloff's (mother of Serge Chaloff), he attended the Berklee School of Music in Boston, and taught history of jazz at the University of California in the '70s. With his first major jazz album *New Souls*, released in 1980, Gelb established a worldwide reputation. His first two albums featured Kim Parker, stepdaughter of Charlie Parker. An expert on the pianist Bill Evans, Gelb operates a music publishing company entitled Imagin Action Music.—*Ron Wynn and Michael G. Nastos*

★ **New Souls** / 1979 / ESSENE 7001

☆ **Language of Blue, The** / Jun. 1980+Sep. 1, 1981 / Cadence 1012
What a unique record by composer-lyricist-player Larry Gelb featuring the seemingly endlessly flexible voice of Kim Parker. The only completely instrumental track was "Kim, When I Close My Eyes." Everything else was written for Kim, daughter of Charlie Parker. You've got to follow the lyrics, which were all included on the back cover, and then you've got to be a bit amazed at how she handled such intervals to match endless and reasonably unfamiliar changes laid down by Gelb (piano). The additional bonus was beautiful accompaniment by Doug LeFebvre (saxes). He and trumpeter Tiger Okoshi never played on the same tracks but were probably at the same sessions. —*Jerry L. Atkins, Cadence*

Herb Geller (Herbert Geller)

b. Nov. 2, 1928, Los Angeles, CA
Alto sax / Cool
Herb Geller's a good saxophonist whose style reflects extensive harmonic knowledge, and he is a smooth, reliable, if not particularly intriguing soloist. He's played with Billy May's orchestra and with Maynard Ferguson, Shorty Rogers, Bill Holman, Benny Goodman, and Louis Bellson. He traveled with Goodman to Brazil at the peak of bossa nova mania. He moved to Berlin in the early '60s, and lived there for a while running a nightclub and playing in the orchestra of a radio station. Geller headed a bop quartet in the '80s and has recorded for EmArcy, Jubilee, Nova, Circle, Enja, and Discovery. Geller overcame the tragic death of his wife Lorraine, with whom he'd co-led a group and recorded during the '50s. —*Ron Wynn*

★ **American in Hamburg** / **View from Here** / **i.** Jan. 13, 1975 / Nova 28332

Stan Getz (Stanley Getz)

b. Feb. 2, 1927, Philadelphia, PA, **d.** Jun. 6, 1991
Tenor sax / Bop
Stan Getz went on the road with Jack Teagarden's band at 16 and never looked back. The most gifted and famous of the Four Brothers—tenormen who emulated Lester Young and most of whom were alumni of Woody Herman's Second Herd—Getz established himself with a beautiful solo on Herman's "Early Autumn" (1948). Though his personal life had its ups and downs, his music was consistently brilliant. Highlights include his association with guitarist Jimmy Raney; his great success with the bossa nova (in the '60s, when there was no other instrumental music on the hit charts); his wonderful collaboration with Eddie Sauter on *Focus,* a unique composition created for Stan; and his final triumph over a debilitating illness in the duets with pianist Kenny Barron (*People Time*). Getz was above all a supreme melodist, who could make even a mediocre song sparkle, but he was also a marvelous improviser and master of high-speed invention. As a saxophonist he was without peers. —*Dan Morgenstern*

○ **Complete Recordings of the Stan Getz Quartet with Jimmy Raney** / Yazoo 1082

○ **Quartets** / Jun. 21, 1949-Apr. 14, 1950 / Original Jazz Classics 121

This was Prestige Records' second 12-incher and presented quartet sides from 6/21/49, 1/6/50, and 4/14/50 with backing from Al Haig or Tony Aless (piano); Stan Levey, Roy Haynes, or Don Lamond (drums); and Gene Ramey, Tommy Potter, or Percy Heath (bass). These were short sides, concisely stated with Stan Getz at times as close to Lester Young as he ever got. Some songs were previously issued on twofer sets. —*Bob Rusch, Cadence*

○ **At Carnegie Hall** / **i.** Dec. 1949-Nov. 1952 / Fresh Sound 1003

○ **Split Kick** / Dec. 10, 1950 / Roost 423

○ **Sounds of Stan Getz, The** / Dec. 10, 1950 / Roost 2207

○ **Chamber Music** / Aug. 15, 1951 / Roost 417

○ **Jazz at Storyville—Vol. 3** / Oct. 28, 1951 / Roost 420

○ **Modern World** / Oct. 28, 1951 / Roost 2255

○ **Moonlight in Vermont** / Mar. 11, 1952 / Roost 2251

○ **Birdland Sessions** / **i.** Apr. 1952-Aug. 1952 / Fresh Sound 149

○ **Getz Age** / Dec. 5, 1952 / Roost 2258

○ **Stan Getz and the Cool Sounds** / Apr. 16, 1953-Aug. 19, 1955 / Verve 8200

○ **Stan Getz Plays Blues** / Aug. 15, 1953-Oct. 10, 1957 / Verve 31

★ **Diz and Getz** / Dec. 9, 1953 / Verve 8141
This is prime material with two giants playing bop and old time standards with characteristic verve and wit. John Lewis (p) and the Oscar Peterson quartet join the masters. —*Michael G. Nastos*

○ **West Coast Jazz** / Aug. 15, 1955 / Norgran 1032

○ **For Musicians Only** / Oct. 16, 1956 / Verve 837435
This has plenty of great players and lots of amazing music. Getz, Dizzy Gillespie (tpt), and Sonny Stitt (as) are great, as are John Lewis (p) and Herb Ellis (g). —*Ron Wynn*

○ **And the Oscar Peterson Trio** / Oct. 10, 1957 / Verve 8251
W/ Oscar Peterson Trio. Getz shines while Peterson (p) keeps the trio whipped to a frenzy behind him. —*Ron Wynn*

○ **At the Opera House** / Oct. 1957 / Verve 831272

○ **Jazz Giants '58** / Aug. 1, 1958 / Verve 8248
Tenor saxophonist Stan Getz, baritone saxophonist Gerry Mulligan, and trumpeter Harry Edison headlined a 1957 recording called *Jazz Giants '58*. Backing the horns were pianist Oscar Peterson's trio (guitarist Herb Ellis, bassist Ray Brown) plus drummer Louis Bellson. This was a typical Norman Granz superjazz session; they are rarely "poor" and occasionally truly outstanding—this was "good." —*Bob Rusch, Cadence*

★ **Focus** / Jul. 1961-Oct. 1961 / Verve 821982
This 1961 recording put tenor saxophonist Stan Getz in the hired gun role for an album written and arranged by Eddie Sauter, conducted by Hershy Kay, and originally produced by Creed Taylor. It was a classic example of how successfully inventive pop-semi-classical scoring and jazz horn could be paired. Sure it was *pretty*, it was meant to be, and the strings and woodwinds ensured that ambiance, but it was also imaginative. —*Kevin Whitehead, Cadence*

○ **Stan Getz and Bob Brookmeyer** / Sep. 12-13, 1961 / Verve 8418

★ **Jazz Samba** / Feb. 13, 1962 / Verve 810061
This recording was not just a laidback treasure but a really major milestone: the 1962 album that introduced the bossa nova to the United States. Byrd conceived it, Getz got a Grammy off one cut, "Desafinado." So much silliness ensued that the whole idiom's importance has been downplayed, but it was the beginning of a permanent Brazilian tinge in jazz —*John Storm Roberts*

Big Band Bossa Nova / Aug. 27-28, 1962 / Verve 825771
This is an essential part of his bossa nova period. W/ Gary McFarland; this album was one of his biggest sellers. —*Ron Wynn*

☆ **Bossa Nova Years (Girl from Ipanema)** / 1962-1964 / Verve 823611
1962-1964. The five Getz bossa albums in a boxed set: *Jazz Samba, Big-Band Bossa Nova, Jazz Samba Encore, Getz/Gilberto,* and *Getz/Almeida*. In a word: great music for young and old, even non-jazz buffs. Each of these discs is jam-packed with classic Getz tracks. Highest recommendation. —*Michael Erlewine*

○ **Getz and Gilberto Featuring Antonio Carlos Jobim** / Mar. 18-19, 1963 / Verve 810048

The huge hit with Getz, Joao (g), and Astrud Gilberto (v). "The Girl from Ipenema" was an international smash. Gold album. —*Ron Wynn*

○ **Stan Getz Years, The** / **i.** 1964 / Roost 103

○ **Chick Corea / Bill Evans Sessions** / May 5, 1964-Mar. 30, 1967 / Verve 823242
Taken from one session with Evans, and two sessions with Getz and Corea. —*AMG*

Getz Au Go Go Featuring Astrud Gilberto / Aug. 19, 1964 / Verve 821725
W/ Joao Gilberto. Landmark release. Getz completed a run in 1964 of hit albums that were both popular and influential. Astrud Gilberto (v) was sensual, dynamic, and unforgettable while with Getz. It will always sound wonderful. Jobim adds extra spice. —*Ron Wynn*

★ **Sweet Rain** / Mar. 30, 1967 / Verve 815054
From someone who made so many classics, this might be his best romantic work overall. —*Ron Wynn*

Dynasty / Jan. 11, 1971-Mar. 17, 1971 / Polydor 839117
Amazing playing from Getz in this date cut in London, partly at Ronnie Scott's. —*Ron Wynn*

★ **Captain Marvel** / Mar. 3, 1972 / Columbia 32706
This brilliant mainstream date w/ Chick Corea (p), Stanley Clarke (b), Tony Williams (d), and Airto (per) got lost in publicity fever over the rise of jazz-rock. It came out three years after it was done in 1972. —*Ron Wynn*

Best of Two Worlds / May 21, 1975 / Columbia 33703
An outstanding set, with Getz doing both mainstream and bop work and then backing Joao Gilberto. —*Ron Wynn*

Another World / Sep. 13, 1977 / Columbia
Andy Laverne makes a good impression on piano. Getz again is amazing. —*Ron Wynn*

Dolphin, The / May 10, 1981 / Concord Jazz 4158
An underrated date. Getz is superb, with a sympathetic trio backing him. —*Ron Wynn*

☆ **Anniversary!** / Jul. 6, 1987 / Polydor 838769
A brilliant, rousing date, with Kenny Barron (p) in peak form. Getz is enthused, animated, and intense. —*Ron Wynn*

Complete Roost Sessions—Vol. 1, The / Vogue 600128

Complete Roost Sessions—Vol. 2, The / Vogue 600174

Terry Gibbs (Julius Gubenko)

b. Oct. 13, 1924, New York, NY
Vibes, drums / Bop
Vibist Terry Gibbs won a radio amateur contest at 12 and was a professional drummer before joining the army during World War II. He apprenticed with Tommy Dorsey, Chubby Jackson, Buddy Rich, and Woody Herman in the '40s, and with Louie Bellson and Benny Goodman in the '50s, before getting his own group. Gibbs didn't play with the vitality or inspired flair of Milt Jackson, but he could provide highly charged solos or accompaniment in a more swing-era mode than straight bop. Many feel his '40s big band, which often had Mel Lewis on drums, was a forerunner to the Thad Jones/Mel Lewis big band. Gibbs remains active currently and has recorded several dates for Contemporary. He's done sessions for Brunswick, Savoy, Verve, Limelight, Dot, and Palo Alto, among others.—*Ron Wynn*

★ **El Nutto** / Apr. 15, 1963 / Limelight 82005
From the vibist and quartet with pianist Alice McLeod, featuring all originals. —*Michael G. Nastos*

○ **Holiday for Swing** / **i.** Jul. 1987-Aug. 1988 / Contemporary 14047

Astrud Gilberto

b. 1940, Bahia, Brazil
Vocals / World fusion
It's doubtful anyone outside her native city of Rio had ever heard of vocalist Astrud Gilberto before 1963. Then, in response to a request to sing the English lyrics to a song titled "The Girl from Ipanema," she made history. Despite (or perhaps, in part, because of) a deadpan and childlike vocal style, she and the song were a smash. Gilberto toured frequently through the years with Getz; the 1964 album *Getz A-Go-Go* was a chart-topper and has recently been reissued. —*Ron Wynn*

★ **Look at the Rainbow** / i. 1966 / Verve 821556
This was a beautiful bossa nova record of Astrud Gilberto's vocal stylings. . . . All the material here, with the exception of "Learn to Live Alone" and "Pretty Place," which were arranged by Al Cohn, were arranged by Gil Evans. —*Bob Rusch, Cadence*

Dizzy Gillespie (John Birks Gillespie)

b. Oct. 21, 1917, Cheraw, SC, **d.** Jan. 7, 1993
Trumpet, conga drums, piano, bandleader / Bop

Dizzy Gillespie was bop's pioneering trumpeter, kindred spirit, virtuoso, and beloved personality. Gillespie shattered notions about the trumpet's limitations and showed artistry and entertainment need not be mutually exclusive. Only his collaborator Charlie Parker ever understood the music's nuts and bolts as well as Gillespie. His solos could be blistering or poignant, and the portrait of Gillespie's inflated cheeks and bulging veins in his neck was among the most striking in any musical idiom. Gillespie was also a longtime advocate of Afro-Latin music; he learned congas and played with such bandleaders and musicians as Chano Pozo, Mario Bauza, and Chico O'Farrill, as well as Arturo Sandoval. Lalo Schfrin was once his music director. He was also quite competent on piano. Gillespie got his early professional education in Frankie Fairfax's band in the '30s, where he learned several Roy Eldridge solos from Charlie Shavers. He also earned his nickname from various on and off stage antics. Gillespie earned a job in Teddy Hill's big band in the late '30s, in part because he sounded so much like their former player Eldridge. A couple of years later, Gillespie was working in Cab Calloway's band, where he met and developed a friendship with Mario Bauza. He met Charlie Parker in 1940 while on tour in Kansas City. The two began playing in after-hours jam sessions in New York clubs, one of them being Minton's Playhouse. The jam sessions involved such players as drummers Kenny Clarke and Max Roach and pianist Thelonious Monk. After his famous dismissal from Calloway's band, Gillespie had short stints with many groups in the early '40s. He recorded while with Lucky Millinder what many consider the first bop solo, on "Little John Special" in 1942. The initial bop session was done with Coleman Hawkins in 1944, then he and Parker made some seminal small group dates in 1945, recording among other things "Hot House," "Salt Peanuts," and "Shaw Nuff." From there until his death in 1993, Gillespie did virtually everything that any one person could do in jazz. He recorded constantly, served as a goodwill ambassador on various State Department tours, played at every type of venue from Carnegie Hall to one-nighters in tiny cities and small clubs to big city engagements. He led big bands and small combos, fronted his own bands and headed special ensembles. Gillespie was an internationally beloved musician, and among the few whose profile outside jazz may have been even greater than inside it. —*Ron Wynn*

★ **Development of an American Artist** / i. 1940-1946 / Smithsonian 004
1940-1946. A thorough compilation of Gillespie's formative '40s dates. Available by mail order only from the Smithsonian. —*Ron Wynn*

○ **Dizzy Gillespie with Charlie Christian** / May 1941 / Esoteric 4

★ **Shaw 'nuff** / Feb. 1945-Nov. 1946 / Musicraft 53
Formative sessions cut for the Musicraft label when trumpeter Dizzy Gillespie was just beginning to hone the style that would ultimately emerge as bop. They include one of his earliest hits, plus other solos and vocals. —*Ron Wynn, AMG*

○ **In the Beginning** / May 11, 1945-Nov. 12, 1946 / Prestige 24030
Finally, all the seminal Dizzy Gillespie Musicraft-Guild dates from 1945-1946 collected under one roof—and it never rains but it pours! If you consider yourself any sort of jazz person, this album belongs in your collection. The seven pieces with Bird (Charlie Parker) and Dizzy, in particular, are among the key recordings in jazz—and aside from that, just lovely music. The two great cocreators of bebop didn't record together all that much, but every time they did come together, there was fire. The sparks are still flying. Take "Shaw 'Nuff," for instance; at the furious tempo, which scared everybody then, the two horns breathed together in perfect unison, as one single-double voice. And the solos! If you wanted a quick definition of bebop (2 minutes and 55 seconds), this was it. Everything else is commentary. Ralph Gleason's notes were warmly personal, and the sound, despite the

poor surfaces of the original 78s, is excellent. —*Dan Morgenstern, Down Beat*

○ **Modern Trumpets** / Feb. 7, 1946 / Dial 212

★ **Dizziest** / i. 1946-1949 / Bluebird 5785
The titles on *Dizziest* pretty much speak for themselves. The first four selections were from one of Dizzy Gillespie's most satisfying small group dates of the 1940s despite their briefness. . . . The remainder was the complete output of Dizzy Gillespie's orchestra for Victor (excepting the rare alternate of "Dizzier and Dizzier"). . . . This overflows with classics (especially "Cubana Be/Cubana Bop," "Manteca," "Two Bass Hit," and "Jumpin' with Symphony Sid") that contain plenty of dazzling solos from the leader's trumpet and such players as James Moody, Cecil Payne, J.J. Johnson, the young Yusef Lateef, and Chano Pozo. This orchestra helped alter the course of jazz, and the arrangments still sound a bit futuristic today, over 40 years later. This set belongs in every serious jazz collection. —*Scott Yanow, Cadence*

○ **Dizzier and Dizzier** / Aug. 22, 1947-Jul. 6, 1949 / Victor 1009

○ **Champ, The** / Apr. 16, 1951+Jul. 18, 1952 / Savoy 12047

★ **Dee Gee Days (The Savoy Sessions)** / i. 1951 / Savoy 4426
Dizzy Gillespie: Dee Gee Days documented the rise and fall of trumpeter Dizzy Gillespie's attempt at producing records for his own company in 1951 and 1952. These sides featured little Gillespie trumpet and lots of vocals, some good by Joe Carroll, some pedestrian by Melvin Moore, a Billy Eckstine imitator. Milt Jackson did a lot of piano work on these sessions, even playing organ and singing on one. —*Jon Goldman, Cadence*

○ **In Paris** / i. 1952 / Vogue 600047

○ **Dizzy's Diamonds: The Best of Verve Years [box]** / i. 1953-1968 / Verve 513875
Good, multidisc package featuring fine performances by trumpeter Dizzy Gillespie in various decades and situations and with an assortment of performers. It's not a greatest hits, more a retrospective collection covering his years on the Verve label. —*Ron Wynn, AMG*

One Night in Washington / Mar. 13, 1955 / Elektra 60300
A superb live date that Elektra reissued for a short while and then deleted. —*Ron Wynn*

○ **Groovin' High** / 1956 / Savoy Jazz 152
This disc spans small groups, including a couple of cuts with Bird and big bands featuring the John Lewis-Milt Jackson (piano and vibes, respectively) rhythm section that would later mutate into the personnel and format we have known for four decades as the Modern Jazz Quartet. —*Gene Santoro, Jazz Times*

○ **Modern Jazz Sextet, The** / Jan. 12, 1956 / Verve 12533
Producer Norman Granz was a near-genius at matching jazz musicians in such a way that they would stimulate each other to play above their heads. He always loved jam sessions, but it did not take too much insight to realize that putting trumpeter Dizzy Gillespie and altoist Sonny Stitt together with a strong rhythm section would result in some explosive music. The fireworks really fly on this LP during versions of "Tour de Force," "Dizzy Meets Sonny," "Mean to Me" and "Blues for Bird," with time out taken for a ballad medley. Bebop at its best. —*Scott Yanow*

○ **Dizzy in Greece** / May 18, 1956-Apr. 8, 1957 / Verve 8017

○ **World Statesman** / May 18-19, 1956 / Norgran 1084

○ **School Days** / i. 1957 / Savoy Jazz 157

○ **Dizzy Gillespie and His Big Band** / i. 1957 / GNP 23
The Dizzy Gillespie big band was the most innovative jazz orchestra of 1946-1949, proof that bebop was not exclusively a small group music. All of its recordings are well worth acquiring and this particular CD gives one a well-rounded picture of the orchestra at a concert before an enthusiastic crowd. With prominence given James Moody's tenor, Cecil Payne on baritone, and Chano Pozo on congas (he was killed a short time after this performance), in addition to the remarkable leader-trumpeter, the Dizzy Gillespie orchestra is heard at its absolute prime. Versions of "Good Bait," "One Bass Hit," and "Manteca" are among the highlights of this recommended CD. —*Scott Yanow*

○ **Bird's Works** / Apr. 8, 1957 / Verve 8222

○ **Dizzy Gillespie-Stuff Smith** / Apr. 17, 1957 / Verve 8214

★ **At Newport** / i. Jul. 6, 1957 / PolyGram 513754

Super late '50s set featuring trumpeter Dizzy Gillespie with pianist Wynton Kelly, trumpeter Lee Morgan, trombonist Melba Liston, tenor saxophonist Benny Golson, and pianist Mary Lou Williams among others at the Newport Jazz Festival in spirited jam session and exchanges. The CD reissue contains three bonus cuts. —*Ron Wynn, AMG*

○ **Dizzy Gillespie at Newport** / Jul. 6, 1957 / Verve 6023
Dizzy Gillespie's "world statesman" big band of the '50s was one of his best, and this live set found the aggregation and its fearless leader at the peak of their creative prowess. With arrangements by the leader, Quincy Jones, and Ernie Wilkins played by such rugged individualists as Wynton Kelly (piano), Benny Golson (tenor sax), Al Grey (trombone), Charlie Persip (drums), and Lee Morgan (at 18, the youngest member), the band absolutely smoked. —*Bret Primack, Jazz Times*

○ **For Musicians Only** / Oct. 16, 1957 / Verve 8198

○ **Dizzy Gillespie Duets** / Dec. 11, 1957 / Verve 8260

○ **Sonny Rollins / Sonny Stitt Sessions** / Dec. 11+19, 1957 / Verve 22505
This two-LP set (whose contents have since been reissued on CD) contains a couple of the very best Norman Granz studio sessions. Dizzy Gillespie is matched with the great tenor Sonny Rollins on two selections, Sonny Stitt (sticking to tenor) takes Rollins's place for a couple of other songs and then the two Sonnys team up with Dizzy for four remarkable selections. Dizzy sings "On the Sunny Side of the Street" with good humor and "After Hours" is given a fine treatment, but it is Rollins's ferocious stoptime solo on "I Know That You Know" and the pure fire that is felt on a rapid "The Eternal Triangle" that makes this set truly memorable. —*Scott Yanow*

○ **Jazz Portrait of Duke Ellington, The** / Apr. 27+28, 1960 / Verve 8171072

☆ **An Electrifying Evening with the Dizzy Gillespie** / Feb. 9, 1961 / Verve 8401

○ **Night in Tunisia** / i. Jun. 1966 / VSP 7

★ **Swing Low Sweet Cadillac** / May 25-26, 1967 / MCA 33121

○ **Reunion Big Band** / Nov. 7, 1968 / MPS 15207
The full range of trumpeter Dizzy Gillespie came across on *The Dizzy Gillespie Reunion Big Band*, which was recorded live at the Berlin Jazz Fest. As one might expect from the title, the music was somewhat familiar; however, it was played with a renewed freshness for its time, but, alas, also in contrast with many of the post-'60s Gillespie recordings. —*Bob Rusch, Cadence*

○ **Dizzy Gillespie and the Dwike Mitchell-Willie Ruff Duo** / 1971 / Mainstream 325
Trumpeter Dizzy Gillespie sounds quite comfortable playing in an intimate setting with pianist Dwike Mitchell and Willie Ruff (who plays bass and occasional french horn). Dizzy explores a couple of recent collaborations with his sidemen plus "Con Alma," "Woody 'n You" and Ruff's "Bella Bella." This is one of Gillespie's stronger sets of the 1970s; he was 54 at the time. —*Scott Yanow*

★ **Afro-Cuban Jazz Moods** / Jun. 4+05, 1975 / Pablo 447
Combining one of the foremost Afro-Cuban jazz musicians, Dizzy Gillespie, with percussionist Machito and his fiery orchestra seems so natural that one wonders why it took so long to do it. Throw in the compositions and arrangements of Chico O'Farrill, and you have the makings for a classic album—almost. If it weren't for a couple of problems with O'Farrill's compositions, I wouldn't have hesitated to heap plaudits on this record. As it was, the playing of both Gillespie and the orchestra was outstanding. —*Carl Brauer, Cadence*

○ **Bahaina** / Nov. 19+20, 1975 / Pablo 708
The results on this double LP set constituted a respectable entry in the Dizzy Gillespie discography. Gillespie played with the easy control of one who knew precisely what he was doing and was in complete and unchallenged command. Gillespie fashioned some cleverly intricate splashes of invention, but they were little more than dabs of color on a generally monochromatic canvas. Supporting musicians Roger Glenn on flute and vibes, and guitarists Mike Howell and Al Gafa provided compatible balance without becoming an opposing center of musical gravity. Drummer Mickey Roker and percussionist Paulinho De Costa were firm but predictable. —*John Mcdonough, Down Beat*

John Gilmore (John E. Gilmore)

b. 1931, d. 1991
Tenor sax / Early free, modern creative
John Gilmore was among the most versatile and dynamic tenor saxophonists of all time, though he spent most of his career contributing to the Sun Ra Arkestra. He was extremely effective performing hard bop, fluid solos, and freer, high-energy material with upper register effects and fireworks. He was also the Arkestra's auxiliary drummer. Gilmore played tenor and clarinet in high school during the '40s and later in an army band. He spent one year with the Earl Hines band in 1952 and then began working almost exclusively with Sun Ra from 1953 until his death, with the exception of one year in the mid '60s with Art Blakey. —*Ron Wynn*

★ **Blowing in from Chicago** / Mar. 3, 1957 / Blue Note 1549

Egberto Gismonti

b. Dec. 5, 1947, Carmo, Brazil
Guitar, composer / World fusion
This brilliant, prolific composer, guitarist, and multiinstrumentalist has in effect created his own genre of music, with elements from the entire spectrum of Brazilian styles as well as classical and jazz influences. —*Terri Hinte*

○ **Danca Das Cabecas** / i. Nov. 1976 / ECM 827750
The initial American release features extended pieces for guitarist and percussionist Nana Vasconcelos. Side 1 is a tour de force, with the pieces segueing together beautifully. —*Michael G. Nastos*

★ **Sol Do Meio Dia** / Nov. 1977 / ECM 829117
Guitarist Egberto Gismonti's *Sol Do Meio Dia* was very colorful, involved music. . . . The music on this recording was dedicated to the Xingu Indians of the Amazon. Each song was a dedication to the various deities that are part of the Xingu cosmology. The music was folkloric, and Gismonti's talents gave it a deep spiritual quality. —*Spencer R. Weston, Cadence*

○ **Solo** / i. 1985 / ECM 827135

Jimmy Giuffre (James Peter Giuffre)

b. Apr. 26, 1921, Dallas, TX
Clarinet, tenor sax, baritone sax / Cool
Composer, clarinetist, tenor, and baritone saxophonist Jimmy Giuffre is a genuine multitalent who's never failed to turn in a quality performance, no matter the context or instrument. From his student days at North Texas State, Giuffre moved to the big bands of Jimmy Dorsey, Buddy Rich, and Woody Herman, where he penned "For Others." He ventured into experimental circles in the '50s but fell somewhere between avant-garde and total chaos. His work in the '70s and '80s saw him emphasize supreme tonal quality on all instruments. At times he incorporated the swing style of his youth, at other times he again employed unconventional devices. —*Ron Wynn*

★ **Jazzlore: the Jimmy Giuffre Three, Vol. 46** / Dec. 3-24, 1956 / Atlantic 90981

○ **Lee Konitz Meets Jimmy Giuffre** / May 12-13, 1959 / Verve 8355
A simply amazing collaboration. Extra spice comes from Hal McKusick (as), Warne Marsh (ts), and Bill Evans (p). —*Ron Wynn*

○ **1961** / Mar. 1961-Aug. 1961 / PolyGram 849644
Excellent '92 reissue of a pivotal set featuring multiinstrumentalist Jimmy Giuffre with bassist Steve Swallow, pianist Paul Bley. It's actually two separate, compelling albums issued as one CD, *Fusion* and *Thesis*. The three interacted so completely there was more emphasis on mood, sound, and texture than on individual voices. —*Ron Wynn, AMG*

○ **Tenors West** / i. Feb. 1978 / GNP 9040
The ensemble passages on this album were very tight, the "Four Brothers" blend was excellent, the arrangements were thoughtful if a little corny. Significantly, the best cuts on the album were Billy Strayhorn's "Take the 'A' Train" and Count Basie's "Shorty George." Marty Paich's best number was the title tune, which was light, but swinging. Jimmy Giuffre was the best soloist, naturally, bringing a little personality into an otherwise faceless lineup. —*Douglas Clark, Down Beat*

★ **Dragonfly** / Jan. 14-15, 1983 / Soul Note 1058

Jimmy Giuffre, he of the intellectual cool and the composer behind the Four Brothers, went electric on this album. The new direction of *Dragonfly* shouldn't have been that startling to anyone who closely followed Giuffre's career. Beyond his Woody Herman experience, Giuffre took part in some unique trios. Yet the dynamics of *Dragonfly* were likely to catch even longtime Giuffre fans at least a little by surprise. First, there was the tone on saxes—it was more sinewy, aided by a slight electric echo that might be unsettling to fans of Giuffre's usually spare, dry tone. . . . For the most part, the ensemble was well attuned to Giuffre (longtime colleague percussionist Randy Kaye was sympathetic to the moods of the electronics, sometimes shattering the sublime with chimes or shimmering along with cymbals). —*R. Bruce Dold, Down Beat*

Globe Unity Orchestra

Group / Progressive big band, modern creative

Pianist Alexander von Schlippenbach founded the Globe Unity Orchestra in 1966 to perform his composition "Globe Unity" at the Berlin Festival. It was a work for 14 players that the Festival commissioned for him. The group developed into an international forum for free-jazz musicians, attracting players from Germany, England, Italy, and America. The roster has included trombonists Albert Mangelsdorff and Paul Rutherford , trumpeters Kenny Wheeler and Manfred Schoof, and saxophonist Evan Parker. Globe Unity Orchestra performed at the World Exhibition in Osaka, Japan, in 1970, but worked mostly in Germany until 1974. It appeared at the 1975 Rheims festival with special guests Anthony Braxton and Enrico Rava and made a ten-day tour of England in 1977. It's subsequently appeared at concerts and festivals in France, Switzerland, India, and the Far East. The orchestra has made several recordings for the FMP label, as well as Po Torch and Japo. They're available via mail order but aren't sold in many record outlets except in big-city super stores. —*Ron Wynn*

★ **Live in Wuppertal 73** / **i.** 1973 / FMP 0160
○ **Evidence—Vol. 1** / **i.** Mar. 1975 / FMP 0220
○ **Pearls** / Nov. 25+27, 1975 / FMP 0380
  Free-jazz big band with a cast of stars: Enrico Rava, Albert Mangelsdorff, Anthony Braxton, and many others. —*AMG*
○ **Hamburg '74** / FMP 0650

Benny Golson

b. Jan. 25, 1929, Philadelphia, PA
Tenor sax, composer, arranger / Hard bop

Tenor saxophonist, composer, and arranger Benny Golson is another jazz veteran with strong R&B ties. He began with Bull Moose Jackson in the early '50s and then worked with Lionel Hampton and Johnny Hodges and later with Earl Bostic. A two-year period with Dizzy Gillespie helped his arranging and composing skills flower, and he became an in-demand writer. Along with Art Farmer, he cofounded the Jazztet in 1959 and kept it going until 1962. After the Jazztet folded, Golson decided to be a writer exclusively and spent the remainder of the decade writing for recording sessions, television series, and commercials. He began playing again in the late '70s and re-formed the Jazztet in 1982 for periodic engagements. A good, distinctive stylist and soloist with a big tone and warm sound. His best-known composition is "Killer Joe." —*Ron Wynn*

○ **Other Side of Benny Golson, The** / **i.** 1958 / Riverside 1750
  This session put the emphasis on the tenor playing of Benny Golson as opposed to his writing and arranging skills (though those are present as well, including a very nice Golson original, "Are You Real?"). Joining Golson on the program previously reissued on a twofer were a compatible group consisting of Curtis Fuller (trombone), Barry Harris (piano), Jymie Merritt (bass), and Philly Joe Jones (drums). . . . Golson was the highlight, and he took a number of nice, steady, slightly John Coltraneish solos. —*Bob Rusch, Cadence*

○ **Free** / Dec. 26, 1962 / Argo
★ **California Message** / Oct. 20-22, 1980 / Baystate 8013
  Here the isolation of instrumental sounds, bass amplification, and an electric piano that oscilliated wildly between channels (earphone users should check their Dramamine supplies) conspired against a potentially solid reunion session of the Benny Golson-

Curtis Fuller band. Turning hastily to the featured artists we found trombonist Fuller in gruffer, less fluid form but not substantially changed from his younger self. Golson's case was more interesting, for he'd acquired a slight quaver to his tenor tone, and this, coupled with an increased graininess, a burrowing lower register, and a more balanced sense of construction, suggested that the new phase of his development might be quite distinctive. —*Terry Martin, Down Beat*

Eddie Gomez (Edgar Gomez)

b. Oct. 4, 1944, San Juan, Puerto Rico
Bass / Cool, Latin-jazz

This Puerto Rican bassist is able to do everything from free to fusion jazz and is especially good in trio settings and when backing pianists. Gomez was raised in New York and joined the Newport Jazz Festival Band at 14. His early experiences with Rufus Jones, Marian McPartland, and Gary MacFarland were instructive, but his year-long stint with Paul Bley was monumental—he began to expand his ideas about the range and style of his playing. Gomez's repertoire truly grew during an 11-year stay with pianist Bill Evans. He became known for his forays into the bass's upper register and for his melodic adventurousness. He later brought that same flashy technique to the electric bass, though he mostly preferred playing amplified acoustic in fusion sessions. Since 1977 he has been very busy, and he helped found the group Steps (later Steps Ahead) in 1979. —*Ron Wynn*

★ **Gomez** / Jan. 1984-Feb. 1984 / Denon 7189

Paul Gonsalves (Paul [Mex] Gonsalves)

b. Jul. 12, 1920, Boston, MA, d. May 14, 1974, London, England
Tenor sax / Swing, big band

Paul Gonsalves is among the most expressive, frenetic tenor players in jazz history. Indeed, his exciting, polyrhythmic technique enabled Gonsalves to get away with a rather fragile, thin tone. He played with Sabby Lewis and Count Basie in the '40s and with Dizzy Gillespie briefly in 1949-1950, but it was his 24 years with Duke Ellington that cemented Gonsalves's fame. Gonsalves was a competitor who was seldom bested in jam-session battles. His incredible, 20-plus chorus solo on "Diminuendo and Crescendo in Blue" at the 1956 Newport Jazz Festival is a musical high point and helped put the Ellington band on the cover of *Time* magazine. —*Ron Wynn*

★ **Cookin'** / Aug. 6, 1957 / Argo 626
○ **Just A-Sittin' and A-Rockin'** / Aug. 28, 1970+Sep. 3, 1970 / Black Lion 760148
  The title here was apt. This was a very relaxed, gently swinging session, almost self-effacing in the musicians' insouciant refusal to call attention to themselves, other than by the obvious merit of their art. It was particularly welcome because we rarely get to hear, on records, Paul Gonsalves outside of the Ellington band or Ray Nance at all. —*Gary Giddins, Down Beat*

★ **Mexican Bandit Meets Pittsburgh Pirate** / **i.** 1973 / Fantasy 751
  While Roy Eldridge (trumpet) was in good form on this date, Paul Gonsalves was not, although choruses reminiscent of his best could be heard on the ballads and "C Jam Blues." He was not in good health in his last years (he died ten days before Ellington). Despite his poor health and the consequent effect on his solo work, his sense of humor shone through in appropriate spots. —*Shirley Klett, Cadence*

Jerry Gonzalez

b. 1949
Conga drums, trumpet, bandleader / Latin jazz, world fusion

A first-rate conga player and trumpeter, Jerry Gonzalez has headed one of the best contemporary Latin-jazz groups, the Fort Apache Band. A New Yorker, his music merges traditional Afro-Cuban rhythms, salsa, funk, rock, jazz, and pop with an urban sensibility and improvisational framework. Gonzalez has recorded for American Clave, Enja, and Sunnyside, among others.—*Ron Wynn*

○ **Ya Yo Me Cure** / Jul. 1980-Aug. 1980 / Pangaea 6242
  An often spectacular, breakout Afro-Latin album by conga player, bandleader, composer and sometime pianist Jerry Gonzalez. He merged Latin jazz, salsa and Afro-Cuban rhythms, producing an

album that had both multiple textures and plenty of explosive improvising. —*Ron Wynn, AMG*

● **River Is Deep, The** / Nov. 1982 / Enja 79665
Powerhouse group (Fort Apache Band); strong material. A sparkling session that helped cement Gonzalez's status among the new crop of Latin-jazz stars. —*Ron Wynn*

○ **Rhumba Para Monk** / i. Oct. 27-28, 1988 / Sunnyside 1036
Great production by Jim Anderson on eight Monk standards. Stripped to quintet with Carter Jefferson, the tenor sax foil. Very intriguing concept, melding Latin rhythms to Monk's off minorisms. —*Michael G. Nastos*

○ **Obatala** / Nov. 6, 1988 / Enja 79665
& The Fort Apache Band. Explosive Afro-Latin and Latin-jazz with a hard edge. CD bonus cut. —*Ron Wynn*

○ **Earthdance** / i. Oct. 2-03, 1990 / Sunnyside 1050
Red-hot modern Afro-Latin and Latin-jazz, with driving grooves, great playing, and up-to-the-minute rhythms. —*Ron Wynn*

Benny Goodman (Benjamin David Goodman)

b. May 30, 1909, **d.** Jun. 13, 1986
Clarinet, composer, bandleader / Swing, big band
By the time he formed his first big band in 1934, Benny Goodman had been a pro for a decade. Born into a large and poor family in Chicago (of which he became the main support after his father's death in 1926), he joined drummer Ben Pollack's band at 16, came to New York with it in 1928, and soon was one of the Big Apple's most in-demand recording and radio studio musicians. His clarinet style, influenced at first by Jimmie Noone and Frank Teschemacher, was fluent and swinging and was widely imitated during the Swing Era, which he helped ring in. As a bandleader, Goodman was a demanding taskmaster. He lived for music and expected others to be as dedicated; this often caused friction, but the personnel of his bands, which he led full-time until 1948 and sporadically thereafter, nevertheless was quite stable. Dubbed "King of Swing," a title he neither invented nor invited but felt no need to refuse, Goodman helped break down racial barriers in popular music by hiring pianist Teddy Wilson, vibist Lionel Hampton, guitarist Charlie Christian, trumpeter Cootie Williams, and other Black stars-to-be, first for his small "bands-within-the-band," and then for the full orchestra. His choice of arrangers, chief among them Fletcher Henderson (though Jimmy Mundy was the most productive), also bespoke his admiration for Black musical creativity. Goodman helped launch the band-leading the careers of Gene Krupa, Harry James, and Hampton, among others. He liked to perform classical music and commissioned compositions from Béla Bartok, Paul Hindemith, Aaron Copland, and Leonard Bernstein. Though he periodically went into semiretirement, Goodman could never stay away from his beloved clarinet for long; at the very end of his life, he was once again leading a big band that specialized in Fletcher Henderson arrangements. Until the end, the number of his fans was legion. —*Dan Morgenstern*

● **Complete Capitol Small Group Recordings** / Mosaic
Benny Goodman took some stylistic chances during his 11-year tenure with Capitol. He listened closely to, then flirted with, bebop during this time, not altering his own swing-based playing but inserting it into a bop framework. Goodman worked with such players as pianist Mel Powell, trumpeter Fats Navarro, tenor saxophonist Wardell Grey, guitarist Mundell Lowe, and bassists George Duvivier and Red Callendar. He also played traditional swing in various small groups, working with longtime comrades pianist Teddy Wilson and drummer Dave Tough, and teaming with others like pianist Jimmie Rowles, guitarist Al Hendrickson, vibist Red Norvo, and bassists Harry Babasin or Art Shapiro. The sessions covered on this most recent Mosaic four-disc (six-album) set were originally issued on a number of 10- and 12-inch albums, as well as prior CDs *BG in Hi Fi* and *The Benny Goodman Story*, a Japanese issue with bonus tracks. It covers a valuable and often overlooked part of the Goodman musical equation, showing him mixing and matching idioms, retaining his own style and vision, and ultimately opting to return to the music he felt most comfortable making and playing. The date also includes a previously unissued 1947 session that reunited Goodman with Peggy Lee and Dave Barbour and featured Lee's excellent vocal on "I Never Knew (I Could Love Anybody)." Despite some variation in sound quality caused by the problem of transferring music origi-

nally issued on 16-inch acetate discs, the performance quality certainly compensates for occasional technical problems, and the discographical information and session histories are as exhaustive as possible. —*Ron Wynn*

○ **Benny Goodman and the Giants of Swing** / i. Apr. 18, 1929-Oct. 23, 1934 / Prestige 7644
This excellent CD collects some of Benny Goodman's best early recordings, all cut at least a few years before he became known as the King of Swing and also costarring the great trombonist-singer Jack Teagarden. BG is heard during 1929-1931 with Red Nichols's Five Pennies (whose eight selections include "Indiana," "Dinah," and Teagarden's famous vocal on "The Sheik of Araby"), the 1930 session by Irving Mills's Hotsy Totsy Gang that included an ailing Bix Beiderbecke, an Adrian Rollini date from 1934, and four gems by the Joe Venuti-Eddie Lang All-Star Orchestra in 1931. Throughout, Goodman (just barely out of his teens) and Teagarden, along with other talented jazzmen then earning a living as studio musicians, seem overjoyed to be able to play jazz. This is highly enjoyable music that serves as a fine introduction to early preswing jazz. —*Scott Yanow*

○ **B.G. & Big Tea in Nyc** / Apr. 1929-Oct. 1934 / GRP 609
CD reissue of some early '30s material that doesn't feature clarinetist Benny Goodman in a leadership role. Instead, he's in bands under the direction of Red Nichols, Arthur Rollini, and Irving Mills. Yet, he's the star soloist, along with trombonist Jack Teagarden. —*Ron Wynn, AMG*

★ **Birth of Swing, The** / Apr. 4, 1935-Nov. 5, 1936 / Bluebird 61038
This three-CD set includes all of the Benny Goodman big band's recordings from April 1935 through November 1936, a period when the orchestra became the most popular and influential in the world, making both swing and Benny Goodman into household words. Augmented by some alternate takes, this set shows just how solid and musical a unit Goodman had from the start. Key soloists include trumpeters Bunny Berigan and Ziggy Elman, pianist Jess Stacy, and the band's excellent singer Helen Ward, but BG usually emerges as the main star with the tight and swinging ensembles being a close second. In addition to the hits ("King Porter Stomp," "Sometimes I'm Happy," "When Buddha Smiles," "Stompin' at the Savoy," and "Goody-Goody") even the lesser-known numbers and pop tunes have their strong moments. This music is essential to any serious jazz collection. —*Scott Yanow*

☆ **Original Benny Goodman Trio and Quartet Sessions—Vol. 1: After You've Gone** / Jul. 13, 1935-Feb. 3, 1937 / Bluebird 5631
Although Benny Goodman came to fame as leader of a big swinging orchestra, from nearly the beginning he always allocated some time to playing with smaller groups. On July 13, 1935, the Benny Goodman Trio debuted (featuring drummer Gene Krupa and pianist Teddy Wilson) and 13 months later vibraphonist Lionel Hampton made the unit a quartet. The first interracial group to appear regularly in public, this outlet gave BG an opportunity to stretch out and interact with his peers. The CD *After You've Gone* contains the first ten trio recordings and the initial 12 studio performances by the quartet. Helen Ward contributes two fine vocals, but the emphasis is on the close interplay between these brilliant players. A gem. —*Scott Yanow*

○ **Stompin' at the Savoy** / Jul. 1935-Feb. 1938 / Bluebird 61067

○ **Complete Benny Goodman—Vol. 2 (1935-1936)** / Nov. 22, 1935-Jun. 16, 1936 / RCA 5562
The second two-LP set in this eight-volume series has all of Benny Goodman's Victor studio sides that were recorded during a seven-month period when the orchestra consolidated and built on its unexpected success. In addition to such popular recordings as "When Buddha Smiles," "Stompin' at the Savoy," and "Goody-Goody" there are six selections by the Benny Goodman Trio, many enjoyable vocals from Helen Ward (the best of BG's many singers), and four hot numbers by a combo under Gene Krupa's leadership that matched the clarinetist with trumpeter Roy Eldridge and tenor great Chu Berry. Essential music in one form or another. —*Scott Yanow*

☆ **After You've Gone—Vol. 2** / i. 1935-1957 / RCA/Bluebird 2273
The complete trio and quartet sides (along with 'Volume 1') for Victor. Great sound. —*Cub Koda*

★ **Legendary Performer** / i. 1935-1937 / RCA 2470
A valuable collection of mid-'30s sides, now available in new, better-mastered collections. —*Ron Wynn*

○ **Complete Benny Goodman—Vol. 3 (1936)** / Aug. 13, 1936-Dec. 9, 1936 / RCA 5532
The third of eight two-LP sets reissuing all of Benny Goodman's Victor recordings from the swing era, this twofer has such "killer dillers" as "Down South Camp Meeting," "St. Louis Blues," and two versions of "Bugle Call Rag," in addition to performances by the Benny Goodman Trio and his new quartet (with vibraphonist Lionel Hampton), Ella Fitzgerald as a guest vocalist, and trumpeter Ziggy Elman's first recordings with the band. In all there are 32 performances on this set that prove that Benny Goodman really did deserve the title "The King of Swing." —*Scott Yanow*

○ **Complete Benny Goodman—Vol. 8 (1936-1939)** / Dec. 2, 1936-May 4, 1939 / RCA 5568
The final volume of this definitive series of Benny Goodman's Victor studio recordings not only contains his recordings from April and May 1939 but also digs up a variety of alternate takes (most of them previously unissued) from the 1936-1939 period. It is fascinating to hear "new" versions of such songs as "Stompin' at the Savoy," "Sing, Sing, Sing," "Avalon," and "Sugarfoot Stomp," especially when one is familiar with the original released renditions. In addition, this twofer has the two recordings (and one alternate) cut by the Metronome All-Star Band, which in 1939 (with such musicians as Bunny Berigan, Jack Teagarden, and Tommy Dorsey) allowed Goodman to reunite with some of his associates from the earlier days. A fitting ending to an essential series. —*Scott Yanow*

○ **Complete Benny Goodman—Vol. 4 (1936-1937)** / Dec. 30, 1936-Oct. 22, 1937 / RCA 5537
The fourth of eight volumes (all are two-LP sets) documenting Benny Goodman's highly influential Victor studio sides, the 1936-1937 period covered by this set found BG's amazing popularity still on the rise (he was now a household name), Harry James joining the orchestra, and Martha Tilton settling in as the band's regular vocalist. Among the many memorable recordings are "Sing, Sing, Sing," the BG Quartet's "Avalon," and "Sugarfoot Stomp." —*Scott Yanow*

● **On the Air 1937-1938** / i. Mar. 25, 1937-Sep. 20, 1938 / Columbia/Legacy 48836
In the early 1950s, after the unexpectedly large sales of Benny Goodman's 1938 Carnegie Hall Concert, Columbia came out with a two-LP set of broadcasts from 1937-1939 that also sold well. This recent double-CD set not only includes the music on the original LPs but also adds 14 tracks previously put out only on collector's labels. *On the Air* really captures the Benny Goodman big band (along with some examples of the trio and quartet) at its peak and shows why the original swing orchestras (as opposed to the weak nostalgia bands that are currently around) were so popular with younger people in the '30s and '40s. These performances are still exciting! —*Scott Yanow*

○ **Complete Benny Goodman—Vol. 5 (1937-1938)** / Oct. 29, 1937-Apr. 8, 1938 / RCA 5557
It was during the period covered by this twofer that Benny Goodman played his famous Carnegie Hall concert and his orchestra reached its peak. This fifth of eight two-LP sets documenting Benny Goodman's Victor recordings of the 1930s has more than its share of memorable performances, including "Don't Be That Way," "One O'Clock Jump," and two versions of "Life Goes to a Party," plus the last recordings of the Benny Goodman Quartet before Gene Krupa (after a dispute with BG) left the band to form his own orchestra. Other sessions include an unusual one that found some of Count Basie's sidemen (including tenor great Lester Young) sitting in, and there is also a quartet date with Dave Tough sitting and performing ably in the departed Krupa's place. As with all of the twofers in this series, this one is highly recommended and deserves to be reissued in full on CD. —*Scott Yanow*

☆ **Complete 1937-38 Jazz Concert No. 2** / i. 1937-1938 / Columbiua 180
This two-LP series was quickly released after the big success of Benny Goodman's bestselling 1938 Carnegie Hall Concert set. Labelled "No. 2," these excellent aircheck performances have no relation to the Carnegie Hall concert except for the time period. The Benny Goodman orchestra and small groups often sounded much more exciting live in concert than on their studio recordings, and one can really tell from these performances why drummer Gene Krupa was so popular, and a thorn in BG's side. With

Harry James, Ziggy Elman, and Chris Griffin forming a classic trumpet section, the Benny Goodman orchestra (with its clean ensembles and hard-swinging sound) had its own distinctive and well-loved style. This double-LP (since reissued with additional tracks on CD) contains essential music; listen to Harry James on "St. Louis Blues" for proof of the band's excitement. —*Scott Yanow*

● **Benny Goodman Carnegie Hall Jazz Concert** / i. Jan. 16, 1938 / Columbia 160
One of the great concerts ever captured on record and in itself a turning point in the way jazz is judged by outsiders. Never before had a full jazz concert been held at Carnegie Hall; it is hard to believe that tapes of this momentous event were kept in a closet, forgotten until rediscovered by accident in 1950! There are many highpoints including exciting versions of "Don't Be That Way" and "One O'Clock Jump," a tribute to the 20 years of jazz that were then on record, a jam session version of "Honeysuckle Rose" that found sidemen of the orchestras of Duke Ellington and Count Basie interacting with Goodman's stars, exciting performances by the trio and quartet, and of course "Sing Sing Sing" with Gene Krupa's creative (if not too subtle) drumming and Jess Stacy's remarkable ad-lib piano solo. Fortunately this program has been reissued in full on CD, and it belongs in every serious music library, capturing Benny Goodman and the swing era in general at its height. —*Scott Yanow*

○ **Complete Benny Goodman—Vol. 6 (1938)** / Apr. 8, 1938-Oct. 13, 1938 / RCA 5566
This sixth of eight two-LP sets documenting Benny Goodman's Victor studio recordings finds BG in his post-Gene Krupa era. The classic trumpet section of Harry James, Ziggy Elman, and Chris Griffin was still intact, but after the Carnegie Hall concert there must have been a feeling of these performances being anticlimatic. Still, there are lots of memorable moments on these big band and quartet tracks with a liberal amount of Martha Tilton vocals, pop tunes (although superior ones), and jazz standards. The rhythm was now much more subtle (with Dave Tough on drums), but the BG sound in 1938 was not that much different than in 1937 and the music is well worth acquiring. —*Scott Yanow*

○ **Complete Benny Goodman—Vol. 7 (1938-1939)** / Oct. 13, 1938-Apr. 7, 1939 / RCA 5567
The seventh two-LP set in this eight-volume series continues the documentation of Benny Goodman's influential studio recordings for Victor in the 1930s. Highpoints of this fine twofer include a version of "Ciribiribin" that predates Harry James's famous recording, the unusual "Bach Goes to Town," a memorable "I Cried for You" by Goodman's quintet (with John Kirby on bass), "Sent for You Yesterday" (featuring a Johnny Mercer vocal), and the big Ziggy Elman hit "And the Angels Sing." Recommended. —*Scott Yanow*

○ **Eddie Sauter Arrangements** / i. Dec. 18, 1940-Mar. 17, 1945 /
Here is an LP crying to be reissued on CD. Eddie Sauter was Benny Goodman's most advanced arranger. His writing for BG in the early 1940s was much more unpredictable than Fletcher Henderson's and often full of surprises and unusual colors. A dozen of Sauter's greatest arrangements (including "Moonlight on the Ganges," "La Rosita," "Superman" and a remarkable reworking of "Love Walked In") are heard on this set, and they really challenge Benny Goodman to come up with fresh ideas. A classic album. —*Scott Yanow*

● **Way Down Yonder (1943-1944)** / Dec. 9, 1943-Jan. 1946 / Vintage Jazz Classics 1001
This valuable CD contains performances from 1943-1946 originally recorded for World War II servicemen. VJC has fleshed out the original recordings with alternate takes and breakdowns, which, due to the high quality of the music, makes this CD even more interesting. Gene Krupa is heard with Goodman's 1943 big band and in a trio with pianist Jess Stacy, while the bulk of this set features the BG Quintet with vibraphonist Red Norvo during 1944, including an early version of the classic "Slipped Disc." —*Scott Yanow*

○ **For the Fletcher Henderson Fund** / i. 1954 /

○ **B.G. In Hi/Fi** / i. Nov. 8, 1954-Nov. 16, 1954 / Capitol 92864
On this excellent all-round CD, Benny Goodman performs a dozen selections (mostly Fletcher Henderson arrangements) with a big band filled with sympathetic players in 1954 and eight

other numbers with a pair of smaller units that also feature pianist Mel Powell and either Charlie Shavers or Ruby Braff on trumpets. Although the big band era had been gone for almost a decade, Benny Goodman (then 46) plays these swing classics with enthusiasm and creativity and shows that there was never any reason for anyone to write him off as "behind the times." —*Scott Yanow*

★ **Yale Recordings, Vols. 1-6** / Mar. 26, 1955-Jun. 28, 1967 / Music Masters 5000

In his will, Benny Goodman gave to Yale not only all of his band arrangements (over 1,500) but also 400 ten-inch master tapes of unreleased studio and concert recordings. Some of the more rewarding sessions have now been issued by Music Masters, and this particular boxed set includes the first five volumes (and a 40-page booklet), six CD's in all (since Vol. 5 had two CD's by itself), which are also available separately. The music dates from 1955-1984 (the second half of Benny Goodman's career) and is taken from quite a few sessions, including a full CD of material by his excellent septet of 1955 (featuring trumpeter Ruby Braff and Paul Quinichette on tenor), big band performances from 1958 with several vocals by Jimmy Rushing, and many selections from a 1959 engagement with a nonet featuring trumpeter Jack Sheldon, trombonist Bill Harris, and tenorman Flip Phillips. Although no longer a pacesetter, Benny Goodman remained one of the jazz world's most brilliant performers, making this set well worth acquiring. —*Scott Yanow*

★ **Together Again! (1963 Reunion with Lionel Hampton, Teddy Wilson & Gene Krupa** / Feb. 13, 1963-Aug. 27, 1963 / Bluebird 6283

In 1963, almost exactly 25 years after Gene Krupa left Benny Goodman's orchestra, the Benny Goodman Quartet recorded together for the first time in a quarter-century. This CD, a straight reissue of the original LP, finds BG, Lionel Hampton, Teddy Wilson, and Gene Krupa clearly happy to be back together, not so much revisiting their older "hits" as having a good time playing songs that they missed the first time around. One can feel the absence of a bass (the more primitive recording quality of the 1930s helped cover it up originally) but the music is so joyful and swinging that one does not mind. —*Scott Yanow*

Mick Goodrick

b. Jun. 9, 1945, Sharon, PA
Guitar, instructor / Early jazz rock, modern creative
A technical genius on the guitar, Mick Goodrick's music is well worth study. He is also a fine teacher. His limited recordings show an individuality that defies easy description, though a "postfusion" label might work. Goodrick recorded with Woody Herman early in his career and also played with Alan Broadbent, Rick Laird, and Pat Metheny, as well as Jack DeJohnette, Joe Williams, Astrud Gilberto, and Eddie Gomez. Goodrick also recorded with Charlie Haden and John Surman.—*Michael G. Nastos*

★ **Biorhythms** / Oct. 1990 / CMP 46

Dexter Gordon (Dexter Keith Gordon)

b. Feb. 27, 1923, Los Angeles, CA, d. Apr. 26, 1990
Tenor sax / Bop
The leading bebop tenor stylist, Dexter Gordon's personal amalgam of Lester Young, Charlie Parker, and himself set the tenor pace until the maturity of Sonny Rollins, who was influenced by Dexter. Even more so was John Coltrane, whose earliest recorded solos are pure Gordon. Dexter—six feet, three inches, filled with charm—had periodic bouts with drugs that interrupted his career (which took off after early work with the bands of Lionel Hampton, Louis Armstrong, and Billy Eckstine). He settled in Denmark in 1962. There he found steady work and a stable lifestyle, and when he returned to the United States in 1976, he was at the top of his playing form and enjoyed the greatest success of his career. In 1986 he starred in the French film *Round Midnight*, for which he got an Oscar nomination. At his best, Gordon could play chorus upon chorus without repeating himself, notably on the blues or rhythm changes; he was also a master of the ballad. —*Dan Morgenstern*

○ **Dexter Rides Again** / Oct. 30, 1945-Dec. 11, 1947 / Savoy Jazz 120

○ **Master Takes: The Savoy Recordings** / **i.** 1945-1947 / Savoy 1154

These are some of tenor saxophonist Dexter Gordon's earliest recordings—he was just 22-24 years old at the time of these dates, and already a respected and influential stylist on his instrument. This album shows some of his early development. —*Doug Long, Cadence*

Doin' Alright / May 6, 1961 / Blue Note 84077
A high-quality Blue Note date with touches of soul-jazz and African-American slang influence in the title. —*Ron Wynn*

○ **Landslide** / May 9, 1961-Jun. 25, 1962 / Blue Note 1051
Dexter Gordon's entry (*Landslide*) was also notable for the contributions of his sidemen, most specifically, pianists Kenny Drew and Sonny Clark, bassists Paul Chambers and Ron Carter. Unfortunately, though, the trumpeters (Tommy Turrentine and Dave Burns) fared less well, and the over-modulated clattering of the cymbals undoubtedly proved a distraction to many. That shouldn't have been a deterrent, however, for Gordon's work alone was ample compensation for these minor flaws. Playing in that lean, brittle manner so long a fabric of his art, he quite literally rose above it all. —*Jack Sohmer, Down Beat*

Go! / Aug. 27, 1962 / Blue Note 46094
With the Sonny Clark (p) Trio. Classic Dexter repertoire included, like "Cheese Cake" and "Love for Sale." Rhythm section a monster. —*Michael G. Nastos*

○ **Our Man in Paris** / May 23, 1963 / Blue Note 46394
This is a tremendous album done in Paris w/ Bud Powell (p), Kenny Clarke (d), and Pierre Michelot (b). 1987 reissue, CD version. —*Ron Wynn*

○ **Cheesecake** / Jun. 1964 / Steeple Chase 6008
Cheesecake, previously unissued, was made in 1964 during Dexter Gordon's three-month stay at Copenhagen's Montmarte Jazzhus. In contrast to his usual reserved studio approach, Gordon played with a searing intensity, most notably on the title track—an intensity missing in many of his other recordings. The European rhythm section, while lacking the confidence and experience of Blue Note's group, more than made up for it with their spontaneous enthusiasm and willingness to take liberties with the format at hand. "Second Balcony Jump" showed Gordon's cutting edge. Pianist Tete Montoliu was particularly hot on "Manha de Carnival," taken as a fast bossa. Dynamically, he tended to stay at the same level throughout this recording, but swung as hard as most American pianists, if not harder. —*Arthur Moorehead, Down Beat*

★ **Tower of Power** / Apr. 2+04, 1969 / Prestige 299
With James Moody on tenor as well, the two stretch out on one tune "Montmartre." Barry Harris Trio shines throughout. —*Michael G. Nastos*

○ **More Power** / Apr. 2+04, 1969 / Prestige 7680
More Power! was from the same dates (April 2 and 4, 1969) as *The Tower of Power* and once again James Moody was added on two tracks, although he only soloed on Tadd Dameron's lovely "Ladybird." This was a very enjoyable set, and Gordon was comfortable and relaxed. . . . Gordon roared through these catchy pieces literally chewing up the changes. He got strong support, of course, from Barris Harris (piano), Buster Williams (bass), and drummer Al "Tootie" Heath (and Moody, in the ensembles only, on "Sticky Wicket"). There was nothing very cerebral about this album, but it was head and shoulders above the average blowing session. —*Don Brown, Coda*

○ **Shadow of Your Smile, The** / Apr. 1971 / Steeple Chase 1206

○ **Generation** / Jul. 22, 1972 / Prestige 10069
Good quintet set, one of three that Gordon recorded in '72. He's ably backed by trumpeter Freddie Hubbard, whose bent notes, slurs, and crackling solos keep the tension going when Gordon's not playing. Gordon mixed things up, sometimes soloing with bluesy force, other times light and easy. —*Ron Wynn, AMG*

○ **Ca' Purange** / 1972 / Prestige 10051
The second quintet session that Dexter Gordon cut in '72, and this one was probably the most inconsistent. It contains some fabulous Gordon tenor solos, which are then followed with some rather routine compositions. But it's worth getting, though it's proven the least distributed of the three. —*Ron Wynn, AMG*

○ **More Than You Know** / Feb. 1975-Mar. 1975 / Steeple Chase 31030
This Dexter Gordon with orchestra session was another one of those albums that did not involve the soloist in the arrangements.

The orchestra was merely a backdrop. "Tivoli," though, had Idrees Sulieman (flugelhorn) soloing from out of the context of the orchestra, linking tenor saxophonist Gordon with the orchestra. Both "Tivoli" and "Bernie's Tune" effectively blended in and out the full orchestra with a small group, sometimes only Gordon and bass. —*Jerry De Muth, Cadence*

★ **Stable Mable** / Mar. 10, 1975 / Inner City 2040
Dexter Gordon usually managed to put his best foot forward on record dates. *Stable Mable*, his third LP for Steeplechase, was no exception. Gordon sounded relaxed and slick, blowing nary a line that didn't make sense. Horace Parlan delivered a typically percussive, yet near-elegant series of performances, and acoustic bassist Niels-Henning Orsted Pedersen knows no peer on his instrument. Though the listener will rarely get the impression that any limits were being tested on this collection of tunes by Charlie Parker, Benny Golson, Duke Ellington, Miles Davis, and Erroll Garner (the standard "Just Friends" was also included), taste and swing prevailed. —*Charles Mitchell, Down Beat*

○ **Something Different** / Sep. 13, 1975 / Steeple Chase 1136
What made tenor saxophonist Dexter Gordon's album *Something Different* something special was its lack of *planned* novelty. The album was made in a day, culminating a 22-day, four-album spree for Gordon in 1975. And, title and absence of a piano aside, it showcased the excellence that any great artist must summon under ordinary conditions. More than anything else, *Something Different* presented Gordon the interpreter, the stylist. Rather than accede to composer's designs, he stamped each selection with suaveness. His urbanity, so typified in long, lush notes, unified his approach to all the songs. —*Sam Freedman, Down Beat*

★ **Bouncin' with Dex** / Sep. 14, 1975 / Inner City 2060
These sides were recorded in Copenhagen in 1975. It was a re-union date, the quartet having played together often since the early '60s. The musicians' familiarity with one another was immediately apparent. They had no trouble finding a groove and staying in it. Tete Montoliu is a fine Spanish pianist who was only beginning to become known in this country, although he was well known in Europe. His style drew inspiration from Bud Powell, Thelonious Monk, and McCoy Tyner and was embossed by a touch that was almost classic in its lightness. Billy Higgins matched Montoliu in lightness, yet his crisp drumming never failed to swing. Niels-Henning Orsted Pedersen had as full a sound as any bassist and impeccable time; he was ever-solid on these tunes. With such fine sidemen, Gordon was free to enjoy himself. His tenor sax playing was supremely relaxed but never sloppy, often taking unexpected but fitting turns. —*Douglas Clark, Down Beat*

○ **Lullaby for a Monster** / Jun. 15, 1976 / Steeple Chase 1156
On "Born to Be Blue" Dexter Gordon stretched out his lazy sound even more than usual in a languorous conversational tone. Gordon's familiar fat, rubbery sound and leisurely attacks set a relaxed mood. On his composition "Nursery Blues," which took children's songs as its compositional springboard, his playing was especially smooth and assured. He mixed clichés and new lines as if embellishing an old story with adventures. —*Elaine Guregian, Down Beat*

☆ **Bitin' the Apple** / Nov. 1976 / Steeple Chase 31080
Even if you obtained tenor saxophonist Dexter Gordon's *Swiss Nights* first, you may want *Bitin' the Apple* because of the presence of pianist Barry Harris and bassist Sam Jones, who are masterful bop gyrostabilizers and added a timeless performance to the date. —*Bob Rusch, Cadence*

★ **Homecoming—Live at the Village Vanguard** / Dec. 11-12, 1976 / Columbia 46824
This is the set that welcomed Gordon back to the States. His return was a major event in the late '70s, as was his signing with Columbia. In retrospect this isn't his best work, but it's probably his top Columbia session of the period. —*Ron Wynn*

○ **Swiss Nights—Vol. 1** / i. Nov. 1977 / Inner City 2050
Recorded at the 1975 Zurich Jazz Festival by Steeplechase and released in America by Inner City, this was Dexter Gordon perfectly matched with a rhythm section that fully understood and appreciated the saxophonist's approach. Pianist Kenny Drew, bassist Niels-Henning Orsted Pedersen, and drummer Alex Riel really listened and responded with faultless supportive commentary. Combined with the warm encouragement of the Festival goers,

Swiss Nights emerged as one of the truly magical efforts in the Gordon discography. —*Chuck Berg, Down Beat*

○ **King Neptune** / i. Jun. 1984 / Steeple Chase 6012
○ **Love for Sale** / i. Jul. 1984 / Steeple Chase 6018
○ **Both Sides of Midnight** / i. Jun. 17, 1992 / Black Lion 760103
Dexter Gordon appeared with the familiar rhythm section that egged him on for so many years in Copenhagen: pianist Kenny Drew, bassist NHOP (Niels Pedersen), and drummer Al "Tootie" Heath. Gordon, somewhere between those rambunctious and full-blooded Blue Note Years and the raggedy, slouching postexile decline before his "'Round Midnight" revival, was showing the tawny tones of mellowing graciously. —*Fred Bouchard, Jazz Times*

○ **Tangerine** / Prestige 10091
Working out the mainstream tradition of bop and blues, Dexter Gordon spun a set of strong virile performances, which were cushioned by two fine rhythm sections. On the title track, Gordon deftly mixed cascading sheets of 16th notes; notes of longer duration that revealed his potent sound, which blended both metallic and woody resonances; and his penchant for dipping back into a tune's melodic contours for slightly shaded variations. As with Gordon's two blues renderings ("August Blues" and "What It Was"), there were tasty, low-key solos by both Thad and Hank Jones and the superb Stanley Clarke. —*Chuck Berg, Down Beat*

○ **Apartment, The** / Steeple Chase 1025
While this Steeple Chase reissue didn't capture the 1977 edition of Dexter Gordon, it certainly captured the inspired, creative genius that was Dexter Gordon. This was, to put it mildly, a marvelous recording. Everyone was "on" for the quartet date ("Old Folks" was a Gordon-Pederson(bassist) duet) with the intensity and inventiveness never flagging. And at the same time the music seemed too relaxed and unhurried. There was never a hint of uneveness or pressure. And always above everything else soared that warm, rich, broad tenor saxophone of Mr. Gordon. Joyous music. —*Carl Brauer, Cadence*

Stephane Grappelli (Stephane Grappelly)

b. Jan. 26, 1908, Paris, France
Violin / Swing
The sole survivor of the first generation of accomplished European jazz musicians, Grappelli in his 80s is as elegant and smooth on the fiddle as ever. A chance encounter with the great Gypsy guitarist Django Reinhardt led to the formation of the unique Quintet du Hot Club de France in 1934. Despite extreme differences in temperament and character, the musical partnership continued until 1939, when Grappelli decided to stay in Great Britain for the duration of World War II. After the war, they worked together again for about a year but then went their separate ways. Grappelli's international career blossomed in the '70s, the decade during which he established his popularity in the United States with many festival, club, and concert appearances, and on records with his collaborations with Yehudi Menuhin. Grappelli has a beautiful tone, perfect intonation, and a flair for making a melody swing and sing. —*Dan Morgenstern*

Feeling + Finesse = Jazz / Mar. 7-09, 1962 / Atlantic 1391
Fine early '60s set from violin veteran Stephane Grappelli, who still plays in the "hot" swing style that he championed back in the '30s. This is CD reissue of the album. —*Ron Wynn, AMG*

○ **I Remember Django** / Jun. 23-24, 1969 / Black Lion 105
○ **Limehouse Blues** / Jun. 23-24, 1969 / Black Lion 760158
● **Meets Barney Kessel** / Jun. 23-34, 1969 / Black Lion 760150
○ **Venupelli Blues** / Oct. 22, 1969 / Charly 73
○ **Just One of Those Things** / Jul. 4, 1973 / Angel 69172
○ **Parisian Thoroughfare** / Sep. 5+07, 1973 / Black Lion 760132
For *Parisian Thoroughfare*, violinist Stephane Grappelli was teamed with the 1973 rhythm section of the Thad Jones-Mel Lewis band, pianist Roland Hanna, bassist George Mraz, and, of course, drummer Lewis. It was a magical blend of superb musicianship and sparkling camaraderie. Grappelli's bow-finger coordination was awesome. Grappelli skated and slid through the melody and changes on Bud Powell's "Parisian Thoroughfare" with gusto and abandon. Equally impressive was bassist Mraz. His empathy with Grappelli was extraordinary. Listen, for example, to their arco doubling of Hanna's "Perugia" and pizzicato trac-

ing of the pianist's "Too Cute." Hanna, too, was superb. His solo and support work were the ultimate in taste and perception. On drums, Lewis kept the fire stoked with his characteristic low-key burn. —*Chuck Berg, Down Beat*

○ **Steff and Slam** / Mar. 25, 1975 / Accord 233076

○ **Reunion, with George Shearing, The** / Apr. 11, 1976 / PolyGram 21868
A high-caliber reissue of a delightful date with George Shearing (p). —*Ron Wynn*

○ **Stephane Grappelli / Bill Coleman** / i. Jun. 1977 / Classic Jazz 24
Trumpeter Bill Coleman was 69 when he made these recordings and was playing in the same lovely legato style that was his forte for many years. Certainly violinist Stephane Grappelli respected him, and his own work accordingly was never crowding and almost always used the spirit of Coleman's work to develop his own solos. This was a splendid set of swing evergreens that had just enough tartness to avoid the saccharine. —*Geoff Millerman, Cadence*

★ **Young Django** / Jan. 19-21, 1979 / Verve 815672
Young Django was violinist Stephane Grappelli's album first, guitarist Phillip Catherine's second, and then guitarist Larry Coryell's, but Coryell's role was not inconsiderable. Collecting seven classic Django Reinhardt/Grappelli compositions from the late '30s, plus an original each from the two guitarists, the excellent music here kept an emphasis on *le jazz hot*. Grappelli, of course, was still in his prime, delivering memorable solos on "Sweet Chorus," "Minor Swing," and elsewhere. But his equally young cohorts managed to keep up with the pace, jumping in together on the skittish "Swing Guitars," doing nice things to "Sweet Chorus," and playing with the whimsical "Are You in the Mood?" —*Bob Henschen, Down Beat*

★ **Stephane Grappelli and Hank Jones—a Two-Fer!** / Jul. 20, 1979 / Muse 5287

○ **Stephane Grappelli and David Grisman Live** / Sep. 20, 1979 / Warner Brothers 3550
Recorded at the Berklee Center for the Performing Arts in Boston and San Francisco's Great American Music Hall, *Live* is guaranteed to reawaken even the most moribund. Whether it was because he was surrounded with enthusiastic musicians many years his junior or he just felt inspired, Stephane Grappelli's playing was nothing short of brilliant. Lithe and nimble, Grappelli's violin work shined with class and distinction. —*Carl Brauer, Cadence*

○ **Together at Last** / i. 1984 / Flying Fish 421

○ **Paris Encounter** / Atlantic
Thoughtful at times, funky in spots. Gary Burton (vib) proves a fine partner. —*Ron Wynn*

Milford Graves

b. Aug. 20, 1941, New York, NY
Drums / Early free, modern creative
Milford Graves has been among the flashiest drummers in the free mode, known for skillful inclusion of Asian and African rhythmic ingredients into his solos. His style is extremely fluid and mobile. He's a masterful accompanist who's worked smoothly in many multiple percussion situations. Graves has been among the most outspoken proponents of all jazz, free and otherwise, being performed in communities rather than clubs or arenas. He studied Indian music extensively, including learning the tabla from Wasantha Singh. He has unfortunately not recorded much in recent years, especially on American labels. Graves played congas as a child, then switched to trap drums at 17, before his tabla studies with Singh. During the '60s Graves worked with Giuseppi Logan and the New York Art Quartet. He recorded on ESP in the early '60s with Logan and was an original member of the Jazz Composers' Orchestra Association. Graves also played with Hugh Masekela and Miriam Makeba in the early '60s. His appearance in the Bill Dixon-sponsored concert series "The October Revolution in Jazz" helped introduce Graves to a wider audience. He did two albums of duets with pianist Don Pullen at Yale in 1966. Graves worked regularly with Albert Ayler in 1967 and 1968, performing at the '67 Newport Festival. He also played with Hugh Glover, and worked in a duo with Andrew Cyrille. During the '70s Graves participated in a series of mid-'70s concerts called "Dialogue of the Drums" with Cyrille and Rashied Ali, including several shows in

black neighborhoods. Graves taught at Bennington College alongside Bill Dixon in the '70s, and toured Europe and Japan. During the '80s, he played in percussion ensembles with Cyrille, Kenny Clarke, and Don Moye. Philly Joe Jones later replaced Clarke. Graves's only listed in-print date on CD is the quartet percussion session on Soul Note in 1983. —*Ron Wynn*

● **Graves Pullen Duo, The** / Apr. 30, 1966 / Pullen Graves Music 286

Wardell Gray

b. Feb. 13, 1921, Oklahoma City, OK, **d.** May 25, 1955, Las Vegas, NV
Tenor sax / Bop
Tenor saxophonist Wardell Gray was on his way to being a jazz giant when he died under mysterious, still-unresolved circumstances. He toured with the Earl Hines band from 1943 to 1945 after working locally in Detroit. He then settled on the West Coast and had his first session as a leader in 1946. Later he worked twice with Benny Carter and had brief stints with Benny Goodman, Count Basie, and Tadd Dameron in 1948, with subsequent second stays with Goodman and Basie in 1949 and 1950-1951. But it was his remarkable recording sessions in 1946-1950, especially those with Dexter Gordon, that made his reputation. He had the same combination of lyricism, blues fervor, and facility as Lester Young, a major influence, but was also able to incorporate bop techniques, resulting in a sound that was his own and quite striking. —*Ron Wynn*

○ **Wardell Gray Tenor Sax** / Nov. 11, 1949+Apr. 25, 1950 / Prestige 115

● **Central Ave.** / i. 1949-1952 / Prestige 24062
Landmark West Coast jazz recordings from a neglected figure who was definitely not part of the dominant cool school. Wardell Gray was a superb soloist, particularly when involved in combative jam sessions with fellow players such as Dexter Gordon. These late '40s and early '50s recordings were among the finest done by black jazz musicians playing bop in hostile territory. They were rereleased as part of Prestige's two-record reissue line in the '70s and are now available on compact disc. —*Ron Wynn, AMG*

○ **Wardell Gray Memorial—Vol. 2** / Aug. 27, 1950+Jan. 21, 1952 / Prestige 051
Both this and the first volume were originally paired together in the '60s as one of the first twofers initiated by Prestige. It was a terrific bargain then, a great bargain again almost ten years later, when it was included in another twofer, and now in single album incarnation the music remains fine. The material here all came from between 11/49 and 12/51 and contained almost all of Gray's (tenor sax) Prestige material and some classics. —*Bob Rusch, Cadence*

○ **Wardell Gray's Los Angeles Stars** / Jan. 21, 1952 / Prestige 147

○ **Wardell Gray / Stan Hasselgard** / i. Oct. 1978 / Spotlite 134
This album was a mixture of moods. Most satisfying were the three Howard McGhee Sextet concert performances. Wardell Gray was surrounded here by an electrifying Howard McGhee on trumpet and some slashing alto by Sonny Criss ("Bebop"). But his jog through the changes of Cole Porter's "What Is This Thing Called Love" (via "Hot House") was the ultimate marriage of jazz's physical and intellectual elements, i.e., swing and ideas. Six Count Basie tracks featured Gray in numbers of varying interest and quality. Tempos were lickety split all the way and the sound was on the murky side, but none was without at least some interesting Gray, especially "The King," a reworking of "Jumpin' at the Woodside." —*John Mcdonough, Down Beat*

Benny Green (Trombone)

b. 1923, **d.** 1977
Trombone, critic / Bop
A capable bebop soloist with swing era roots, Chicago trombonist Bennie Green was influenced by Dizzy Gillespie. He worked with Earl Hines in the early and late '40s and early '50s and also played with saxophonists Coleman Hawkins, Gene Ammons, and Charlie Ventura. Green recorded as a leader for Prestige, Blue Note, Vee-Jay, and Time, among others, and was a bop to postbop leader. —*Michael G. Nastos*

★ **Walkin' Down** / Jun. 29, 1956 / Prestige 1752

Benny Green (Piano)

b. 1963
Piano / Neo-bop
A young jazz pianist, Benny Green made an early mark with Art Blakey and Betty Carter, then began leading a trio and also recording as a leader. His work reflects the influences of Thelonious Monk, Bud Powell, and McCoy Tyner. He's been a Blue Note artist since 1990. —*Michael G. Nastos*

○ **Prelude** / Feb. 1988 / Criss Cross 1036

★ **Lineage** / Jan. 30, 1990-Feb. 1, 1990 / Blue Note 93670
Debut work, with this former Jazz Messenger forging his identity as a leader. —*Ron Wynn*

○ **In This Direction** / Mar. 1990 / Criss Cross 1038
Good set from ranking young jazz lion pianist, along with Geoff Keezer. Green, a former Messenger, plays anything from standards to originals with flair, and his solos are always inventive and nicely crafted. —*Ron Wynn, AMG*

○ **Testifyin'!: Live at the Village Vanguard** / i. 1992 / Blue Note 98171
Pianist Benny Green seems intent on continuing the great groove-piano trio tradition in performances such as his title tune, bassist Christian McBride's "McThing," and the traditional "Down by the Riverside." But all is not funk. The ballads—"Beautiful Moons Ago" (by Nat King Cole, surely one of Green's models as a trio pianist) and "I Should Care"—illustrate the pianist's ability to embroider a pretty melody. —*Owen Cordle, Down Beat*

Bunky Green

b. 1935
Sax, instructor / Swing, big band, bop
Bunky Green is a good saxophonist, though much of his recorded output seems to have disappeared. He's done lots of session work and is a solid blues and ballads player and a reliable improviser whose best instrument is alto. —*Ron Wynn*

○ **Places We've Never Been** / Feb. 21+22, 1979 / Vanguard 79425
With Randy Brecker (tpt), Al Dailey Trio. Modal "East & West" shows alto saxophonist at his improvisational best. —*Michael G. Nastos*

★ **Healing the Pain** / Dec. 1989 / Delos 4020
With Billy Childs Trio, sharp drummer Ralph Penland, and the great bassist Art Davis. All standards save two are Bucky's originals. A bright alto voice shines through. —*Michael G. Nastos*

Freddie Green (Frederick William Greene)

b. Mar. 31, 1911, Charleston, SC, d. Mar. 1, 1987, Las Vegas, NV
Rhythm guitar / Swing, big band
Freddie Green was the consummate rhythm guitarist, a player who proved you could be as vital to a band's success as any front line brass or reed soloist. He didn't even use an amplifier and never stepped out front, yet his lines, phrases, and riffs were always a vital ingredient in the Basie orchestra mix. John Hammond heard him at the Black Cat Club in Greenwich Village and later recommended him to Basie as a replacement for Claude Williams. He auditioned for Basie in his dressing room at the Roseland Ballroom in 1937 and remained with the band until his death. Many consider the rhythm section of Green on guitar, bassist Walter Page, and drummer "Papa" Jo Jones to be the greatest trio in big-band and swing history. —*Ron Wynn*

★ **Natural Rhythm** / i. Dec. 18, 1955-Feb. 3, 1955 / Bluebird 6465
Green's *Mr. Rhythm* & Al Cohn's *Natural Seven* albums combined. A wonderful collaboration between Freddie Green (away from the Basie band) and Al Cohn (ts). —*Ron Wynn*

Grant Green

b. Jun. 6, 1931, St. Louis, MO, d. Jan. 31, 1979, New York, NY
Guitar / Bop, hard bop, postbop, blues & jazz, soul jazz
Grant Green is one of the great unsung heroes of jazz guitar. Green always claimed that he listened to horn players and not other guitar players, and it shows. No other player has this kind of single-note linearity (he avoids chordal playing). There is very little of the intellectual element to Green's playing, and his technique is always at the service of his music. And it is music, plain and simple, that makes Green unique. Green recorded during the late '50s and early '60s with players like Jimmy Forrest and Lou Donaldson and with many organ combos, including those of Jack McDuff and Larry Young. Although he shared time and space with the very popular Wes Montgomery, Grant Green remained his own man. His music is immediately recognizable—perhaps more than any other guitarist's. The greatest example of Green's work can be found in the Blue Note boxed set—a treasure. Green has been almost systematically ignored by jazz buffs with a bent toward the cool side, and he has only recently begun to be appreciated for his incredible musicality. Perhaps no guitarist has ever handled standards and ballads with the brilliance of Grant Green. Note: Also see Ike Quebec and Larry Young. —*Michael Erlewine*

○ **Green Blues** / Mar. 15, 1961 / Muse 5014
This album was released under drummer Dave Bailey's name in 1961 on the Jazztime label. The company and the album quickly disappeared. Now that listener appreciation for this kind of unpretentious modern mainstream music has grown, the tasteful playing of guitarist Grant Green, bassist Ben Tucker, Bailey, and the underappreciated tenor saxophonist Frank Haynes should find a welcome audience. Gardner's piano work was a notch below the general level; his automated comping would have been an irritant if there hadn't been such interesting things going on around him. Bailey's marvelously loose, relaxed, and propulsive drumming, for example, and Green's simple but thoughtful and swinging guitar lines. Also, Tucker's big sound and easy drive, and Haynes's round tone and architectural sense of what a solo should be. —*Doug Ramsey, Down Beat*

Reaching Out / Mar. 15, 1961 / Black Lion 760129
Green is in fine form, as is pianist Gardner (better known as an organist), but the album is perhaps most valuable for the contributions of the obscure tenorman Frank Haynes who died in 1965; his sound will remind some a little of Stanley Turrentine. —*Scott Yanow, Cadence*

Grantstand / Aug. 1, 1961 / Blue Note 46430
This is his third album for Blue Note. A quartet session with Yusef Lateef (ts, fl) and vintage Jack McDuff on the Hammond organ. The 15-minute "Blues in Maude's Flat" is very nice indeed, and "My Funny Valentine" (with Lateef on flute) is just plain lovely. No one does standards like Green. —*Michael Erlewine*

○ **Born to Be Blue** / Dec. 11, 1961+Mar. 1, 1962 / Blue Note 84432
Marvelous 1961-1962 dates, with splendid playing by Ike Quebec (sax), Sonny Clark (p), and Green. CD has three bonus cuts. —*Ron Wynn*

● **Complete Blue Note with Sonny Clark** / 1961-1962 / Mosaic 133
W/ Sonny Clark. 1961-1962. Includes Blue Note albums *Gooden's Corner, Nigeria, Oleo, Born to Be Blue* (w/ Ike Quebec), plus unissued tracks. Some of the best bluesy jazz in existence, with the guitarist at the top of his form. Great liner notes. Just incredible music. —*Michael Erlewine*

○ **Nigeria** / Jan. 13, 1962 / Blue Note 1031
Annotator Ben Sidran perceptively characterizes Green as "kind of corny at times, but very hip." The guitarist's blues-imbued style retains something of a country twang, and even exploiting the sustain and reflex capacities of his hollow-body electric, he sounds perfectly natural. The familiar tunes all elicit winning solos from Green, but on the sanctified "Necessarily" he is especially good. —*Francis Davis, Cadence*

○ **Latin Bit, The** / Apr. 26, 1962 / Blue Note 4111

○ **Idle Moments** / Nov. 4, 1963+Nov. 11, 1963 / Blue Note 84154
Excellent album, with Green in good form. Bobbi Hutcherson (vib) in the group produces a somewhat different sound than the usual Green album, so make a note of that. Joe Henderson (ts) is hot. —*Michael Erlewine*

Solid / Jun. 12, 1964 / Blue Note 990
Green's solos are crisp and clean single-note executions, and Joe Henderson (ts) comes through with some fine moments. . . . What one gets is the by-now standard Blue Note recording of that era: solid, straightahead jazz with no frills. —*Carl Brauer, Cadence*

○ **I Want to Hold Your Hand** / Mar. 31, 1965 / Blue Note 4202

★ **Matador** / May 20, 1965 / Blue Note 84442
With Coltrane sidemen McCoy Tyner (p) and Elvin Jones (d)—still with Coltrane at the time. Green tackles the Coltrane hit "My Favorite Things" and pulls it off in his own style. This is a fine album. —*Michael Erlewine*

Iron City / 1967 / Muse 5120
Visions / 1971 / Blue Note 84373
Main Attraction, The / Mar. 1976 / Kudu 29

Al Grey (Albert Thornton Grey)

b. Jun. 6, 1925, Aldie, VA
Trombone / Big band, swing
Al Grey was a crowd-pleasing trombone stylist who became a major name in the late '50s due to his role in the Count Basie orchestra. He became so identifiable there that few remember he also played with Benny Carter, Lucky Millinder, Jimmie Lunceford, Arnett Cobb, Lionel Hampton, and Dizzy Gillespie, plus a navy band, all before Basie. Grey's use of the mute, humor, swing, and rhythmic verve, plus his teamwork in the Basie section and exchanges with Eddie "Lockjaw" Davis made him a world-class hero until he left in the early '60s. Grey did lots of studio work, *Jazz at the Philharmonic,* and George Wein All-Star dates in the '60s. He toured regularly in the '70s with Jimmy Forrest, and in the '80s, after Forrest's death, he worked often with Buddy Tate. He has also returned often for guest stints, records, and appearances with the Basie band. —*Ron Wynn*

★ **Having a Ball** / Jan. 29, 1963 / Argo 718
○ **Featuring Arnett Cobb and Jimmy Forrest** / Jul. 11, 1977 / Black & Blue 233143

Johnny Griffin (John Arnold Griffin III)

b. Apr. 24, 1928, Chicago, IL
Tenor sax / Bop, hard bop
Griffin is an amazingly fast, extremely aggressive tenor saxophonist, whose style and technique weld the fervor of swing, the lowdown grit of blues, and the harmonic mastery of the bop era, with a nod toward the freewheeling tendencies of avant-garde, though he's never ventured too far out of the mainstream. A member of Lionel Hampton's Orchestra at 17, Griffin then became a mainstay on the R&B circuit with a breakaway group headed by trumpeter Joe Morris. He had brief stints with Arnett Cobb and Jo Jones in the early '50s, and spent three years in Hawaii, returning to his Chicago hometown in the mid-'50s. He led his own group and had career-turning tenures with Thelonious Monk and Art Blakey. During the '60s and '70s, Griffin led his own smashing two-tenor group with Eddie "Lockjaw" Davis and was a featured soloist in the Kenny Clarke-Francy Boland big band. He remains active. —*Ron Wynn*

○ **Chicago Calling** / Apr. 17, 1956 / Blue Note 1533
○ **A Blowing Session** / Apr. 6, 1957 / Blue Note 1559
This Johnny Griffin date had a young Lee Morgan on trumpet; good, flowing 1957 Hank Moble;, John Coltrane's melodies sometimes even better; and more Art Blakey on drums. The hero was Griffin, in a ferociously joyous mood, offering a big sound and utterly wild, disorganized, long, gorgeous solos. The chases were outrageous, and "Smoke Stack" was certainly not for the faint of heart. —*John Litweiler, Down Beat*

☆ **Johnny Griffin—Vol. 2: A Blowin' Session** / Apr. 6, 1957 / Blue Note 81559
Half of this session features Griffin. The other half included fellow tenors Coltrane, Eddie "Lockjaw" Davis, Clifford Jordan, and John Gilmore. —*Michael G. Nastos*

○ **Tough Tenor Favorites** / i. Jan. 1963 / Jazzland 76
○ **Salt Peanuts** / i. Aug. 1964 / Black Lion 60121
○ **Blues for Harvey** / Jul. 4-05, 1973 / Inner City 2004
On this live session recorded in 1972 at Jazzhus Montmarte, Copenhagen, tenor saxophonist Johnny Griffin plunged into each tune with virtuosic abandon. Griffin's exuberance was obviously contagious for both rhythm section and audience. Pianist Kenny Drew—as in many of Inner City's Steeplechase releases—came through in dazzling style. His rich harmonic palette and melodic inventiveness were expressed with a virtually faultless technique. Bassist Mads Vinding commanded a large resonant sound, impressive technical facility, and a resilient rhythmic sense. Drummer Ed Thigpen, a master of controlled intensity, drove the proceedings with finesse. —*Chuck Berg, Down Beat*

● **Live in Tokyo** / Apr. 23, 1976 / Inner City 6042
It was an indication of the high level of creativity of Johnny Griffin that one of the long tracks on this two-record set (on

which all tunes but the 3:46 minute "Wee" were between 16:34 and 19:19 minutes) was a ballad that was always taken at a slow tempo, and which the saxophonist wrote. Further, although "The Man I Love" was taken at the traditional, for jazz, fast tempo, Griffin slowed things down for a long cadenza that captured the wistful sadness of the Gershwin original. It was one of two long cadenzas on this set, and each underlined the effective way Griffin used both dynamic and rhythmic shading in his phrasing. —*Jerry De Muth, Down Beat*

★ **Return of the Griffin** / Oct. 17, 1978 / Galaxy 5117
Return of the Griffin defied notetaking. So much happened so fast and was so good it almost annulled the ability and reason to criticize. *Return* amounted to a history lesson about Johnny Griffin. Start with the standards—"Autumn Leaves" and "I Should Care." Griffin played the hell out of them, attacking as if he first read them just yesterday. "A Monk's Dream" paid homage to pianist Thelonious, in whose group Griffin replaced John Coltrane. On tenor, Griffin played both the inscrutable voice of Monk and his own bolting style. The funky "The Way It Is" sounded like an ode to Griffin's barnstorming partner of the early '60s, Eddie "Lockjaw" Davis. But the Griffin of 15 years later left space for Ronnie Mathews's tinkling piano, Ray Drummond's extended bass notes, and Keith Copeland's hi-hat pacing. The sound was consummate barroom in the finest jazz definition. —*Sam Freedman, Down Beat*

○ **Bush Dance** / Oct. 18-19, 1978 / Galaxy 5126
Bush Dance was a studio recording with more premeditation. Tenor saxophonist Johnny Griffin headed a sextet—and in addition to sounding somewhat hastily put together, the recording included studio concessions. This version of "The Jams Are Coming" was under seven minutes and stood in sharp contrast to the longer, relaxed segments that showed the range of Griffin's strengths and sensibilities. Here, when Griffin lost his roomy spaces, he was greatly restrained. The lead "A Night in Tunisia" was interesting, its intro framed by a pleasant enough African motif, and the head itself extended in a swaggering blues approach. —*Brent Staples, Down Beat*

○ **Griff and Lock** / i. 1987 / Original Jazz Classics 264
This session presented another two-sax front line, this a sometimes working group that made a series of excellent records. Jaws and Griff approached the two-tenor format more in harmony than in battle. Both sax men were *blowers,* both had personally identifiable styles, and one could rely on a certain level of projection and swing from any of their combined efforts. —*Bob Rusch, Cadence*

○ **Toughest Tenors** / Milestone 47035
Eddie "Lockjaw" Davis and Johnny Griffin had big fun burning each other up for the most part on these sessions, but there was clearly a sense of kinship within these grooves. . . . The results were gratifying. One side with three Thelonious Monk tunes, kicked off by a medium tempo romp through "Epistrophy" and ending with a humorous run-through of "I Mean You" was highly rewarding. As usual the Fantasy/Prestige/Milestone packing, liner notes and recording info was impeccable. —*Willard Jenkins Jr., Cadence*

Henry Grimes (Henry Alonzon Grimes)

b. Nov. 3, 1935, Philadelphia, PA
Bass / Early free
A superb player who simply walked away from music, Henry Grimes was a topflight bassist during the '50s and '60s. He evolved from a straight bebop stylist taking mostly a supporting role to a freewheeling, driving and dashing player, mixing stunning arco and plucked solos, adding droning effects and countermelodies. Grimes played violin, tuba, and double bass in his teens and attended Juilliard. He toured with Arnett Cobb and Willis Jackson. During the '50s Grimes worked with Bobby Timmons, Lee Morgan, and Tootie Heath, and in the late '50s he played with Sonny Rollins, Anita O' Day, Charles Mingus, and Gerry Mulligan. He was featured at the 1958 Newport Jazz Festival working with Lee Konitz, Tony Scott, Thelonious Monk, and Rollins and later appeared with Monk in the celebrated "Jazz on a Summer's Day" film made of the festival. Grimes played with Lennie Tristano in 1958 and toured Europe with Rollins in 1959. He was among the busiest bassists in free music for a period in the early and mid-'60s, recording and playing with Steve

Music Map

Jazz Guitar

The Beginning
Lonnie Johnson (1889-1970) (Blues)
Eddie Lang (1902-1933) (Classical)

Early Jazz Guitar
Django Reinhardt (1910-1953)
George VanEps (1913)
Al Casey (1915)
Dick McDonough (1904-1938)
Carl Kress (1907-1965)

Gibson Electric Guitar: 1936
Charlie Christian (1916-1942)
Floyd Smith (1917-1982)
George Barnes (1921-1977)

Brazilian Style Jazz
Laurindo Almeida (1917)
Charlie Byrd (1925)
Luiz Bonfa
Bola Sete (1923-1987)
Baden Powell (1937)
Egberto Gismonti (1947)
João Gilberto (1931)

Cool Jazz
Billy Bauer (1915)

Django Reinhardt Style 1950s/1960s
Les Paul (1915)
Gabor Szabo (1936-1982)
Attila Zoller (1927)
Arthur Smith
Birelli Lagrene (1966)
Phillip Catherine (1942)

Swing & Bop
Oscar Moore (1912-1981)
Tal Farlow (1921)
Herb Ellis (1921)
Barney Kessel (1923)
Jim Hall (1930)
Joe Pass (1929)
Kenny Burrell (1931)
Ed Bickert (1932)
Linc Chamberlain
Joshua Breakstone
Jimmy Raney (1927)

1950s Experimenters
Lou Mecca
Joe Cinderella

1960s Guitar
Wes Montgomery (1923-1968)
Jimmy Raney (1927)
Howard Roberts (1929)
Grant Green (1931-1979)

Acoustic Jazz
Bill Harris (1925)
Ralph Towner (1940)
Lenny Breau (1941-1984)
John McLaughlin (1942)
Larry Coryell (1943)
Earl Klugh (1954)
Al DiMeola (1954)
Paco DeLucia
Gene Bertoncini (1937)
Bucky Pizzarelli (1926)
John Pizzarelli
Howard Alden

Rock: Major Impact
Jimi Hendrix (1942-1970)
Vernon Reid

Keyboard-Like
Stanley Jordan (1959)

Jazz-Fusion
Frank Zappa (1940-1993)
Sonny Sharrock (1940)
John McLaughlin (1942)
Larry Coryell (1943)
George Benson (1943)
John Abercrombie (1944)
Carlos Santana (1947)
Allan Holdsworth (1948)
John Scofield (1951)
Kazumi Watanabe (1953)
Pat Metheny (1954)
Al DiMeola (1954)
Earl Klugh (1954)
Kevin Eubanks (1957)
Mike Stern (1954)
Bill Connors (1949)
John Tropea (1948)
Lee Ritenour (1952)
Larry Carlton

Modern Jazz
Pat Martino (1944) – Emily Remler (1957) – Jack Wilkins

Avant-garde
James Blood Ulmer (1942)
Sonny Sharrock (1940)
Derek Bailey (1932)
Eugene Chadbourne (1954)
Bill Frisell (1951)
Fred Frith
Ted Dunbar (1937)
Raymond Boni
Jean-Paul Bourelly

Soul Guitar
Melvin Sparks
Phil Upchurch (1941)
Wah-wah Watson
Grant Green (1931-1979)
Billy Butler (1924)
Cornell Dupree
Eric Gale (1938)
George Freeman
Freddie Robinson

Steel Guitar
Buddy Emmons – Doug Jernigan

Lacy, Cecil Taylor, Perry Robinson, Rollins, Albert Ayler, Archie Shepp, Frank Wright, Mose Allison, and Don Cherry, with whom he made three albums. Then Grimes quit in 1967, for reasons that remain unclear. He appeared on many classic works, among them Taylor's *Unit Structures*. As might be expected, there are no sessions featuring Grimes as a leader cited anywhere. —*Ron Wynn*

● **Henry Grimes Trio** / **i.** 1965 / ESP 1026

Tiny Grimes (Lloyd Grimes)

b. Jul. 7, 1916, Newport News, VA, **d.** Mar. 4, 1989
Guitar / Bop, blues & jazz
Guitarist Tiny Grimes is a unique musician's musician, a veteran performer on the four-string tenor guitar whose playing touches on the best of blues, vintage R&B, and small-group swing jazz. He has been an accomplished session man throughout his life (including many recordings with Charlie Parker), a frequent jam-session participant, and a danceband leader in the '40s and '50s, whose popular Rocking Highlanders wore kilts and tams onstage! —*Myles Boisen*

★ **Profoundly Blue** / Mar. 6, 1973 / Muse 5012
The album's title track was a profound dedication by young guitarist Tiny Grimes to Charlie Christian's science of guitar playing. It came out as a heartfelt tribute and extension of the original, because Grimes wasn't that modern a player, but . . . there was nothing in Grimes's work on this track that couldn't have been played by Christian. Other cuts hearkened back to Grimes's sessions as a sideman with the late Ike Quebec ("Tiny's Exercise"). Throughout were evidences of the wry humor that marked his work with pianist Art Tatum, though he didn't go the famous quotations route the way he did then. —*Joe Klee, Down Beat*

Steve Grossman (Steven Grossman)

b. Jan. 18, 1951, New York, NY
Tenor and soprano sax / Early jazz rock, modern creative
While many of the saxophonists influenced by John Coltrane turned to hard bop or free jazz, Steve Grossman initially worked in jazz-rock and fusion, though he later played more conventional jazz material. Grossman began studying alto sax in the late '50s and moved to Pittsburg from New York in the mid-'60s. He returned to New York in 1967 and began playing soprano and later tenor. Grossman worked with the Jazz Samaritans, which also included Lenny White and George Cables, and led his own bands. He was studying at Juilliard in 1969 when he got the opportunity to record with Miles Davis. A year later, Grossman replaced Wayne Shorter but only stayed about six months. He played with Lonnie Liston Smith, Elvin Jones, and Gene Perla's Stone Alliance through the mid-'70s. During the '80s and '90s, Grossman's led his own groups, playing with Cedar Walton, Fred Henke, Billy Higgins, Charles Bellonzi, Junie Booth, Joe Chambers, and Gilbert Rovere, among others. He's also worked and recorded with the Jazz Tribe, whose members include Jack Walraith and Bobby Watson. Grossman's recorded for PM, Horo (Italy), Atlantic, Red, Timeless, and DIW. He has several sessions available on CD. —*Ron Wynn*

○ **Steve Grossman Quartet—Vol. 1** / **i.** Nov. 1985 / DIW 8007
○ **Steve Grossman Quartet—Vol. 2** / **i.** Nov. 1985 / DIW 8008
● **My Second Prime** / **i.** 1990 / Red 123246

George Gruntz (George Paul Gruntz)

b. Jun. 24, 1932, Basel, Switzerland
Piano, composer, arranger, bandleader / Progressive big band
The Swiss-born pianist, composer-arranger, and bandleaderhas worked mostly with extremely large all-star progressive big bands. He makes complex melodic statements, but the harmonic content is most impressive and he's able to bring out the best in his cohorts. Musically he's a contemporary of Gil Evans. —*Michael G. Nastos*

★ **George Grunst Concert Jazz Band** / **i.** Sep. 22, 1978 / MPS 62305
21-piece band. Stunning music by ensemble. Soloists include Elvin Jones (d), John Scofield (g), Lew Tabackin (sax). Other players, like Woody Shaw (tpt), Jimmy Knepper (tb), and Bennie Wallace (ts), make this band special. —*Michael G. Nastos*

○ **Serious Fun** / **i.** Nov. 1, 1991 / Enja 79659

○ **Blues 'n Dues Et Cetera** / **i.** Nov. 17, 1992 / Enja 79673
Blues 'N Dues Et Cetera gets high marks for high-spirited compositions, a high level of musicianship, and sheer enthusiasm. George Gruntz's playfulness erupted in the compositions. Who else would let trombonist Ray Anderson "Rap for Nap" (Napolean, that is); combine guitarist John Scofield, Chris Hunter's Dave-Sanbornish alto, and a scratchin' DJ on a tune called "Q-Base" (a trendy nudge at the M-Basers?); or weave warm atonal variations around "In a Sentimental Mood?" Soloists like trumpeters Jon Faddis, Wallace Roney, and pianist Gruntz himself don't hurt either. —*Art Lange, Down Beat*

○ **First Prize** / Enja 79606
George Gruntz Concert Jazz Band live in Zurich. Pianist Gruntz with four compositions, originals by saxophonist Larry Schneider, trumpeters Franco Ambrosetti and Kenny Wheeler, and trombonist Ray Anderson. Standout is Gruntz's "Gorby-Chief." 18-piece band, horn and brass-heavy, with dynamite rhythm section of Gruntz, Mike Richmond (b), Adam Nussbaum (d). —*Michael G. Nastos*

Dave Grusin

b. Jun. 26, 1934, Denver, CO
Piano, arranger, composer, producer / Progressive big band, instrumental pop
Producer, performer, composer, label executive, and arranger Dave Grusin's been a prolific film and television soundtrack artist. Grusin played with Terry Gibbs and Johnny Smith while studying at the University of Colorado. He was an assistant music director and pianist with Andy Williams in the late '50s and '60s and also played with Benny Goodman and Milt Hinton, as well as Sarah Vaughan, Quincy Jones, and Carmen McRae. He and his partner Larry Rosen began Grusin-Rosen Productions in the '70s; it evolved into GRP Records, one of the top fusion, "lite" jazz, and instrumental pop companies. Initially a separate operation, they were later acquired by Arista. They're now part of an impressive MCA operation that also includes Decca and Impulse reissues. Grusin's continued recording and done many soundtracks, among them "The Fabulous Baker Boys." He's also done recordings for Columbia, Sheffield Labs, and Polygram and has done projects with his brother Don, plus conducted the GRP big band and worked with symphony orchestras. Never a great soloist, Dave Grusin's nonetheless a major name on the contemporary jazz circuit.—*Ron Wynn*

★ **Discovered Again** / **i.** Aug. 1977 / Sheffield Lab 5
○ **Sticks and Stones** / **i.** 1987 / GRP 9562
○ **Gershwin Collection** / 1991 / GRP 2005

Gigi Gryce (Basheer Quism)

b. Nov. 28, 1927, Pensacola, FL, **d.** Mar. 17, 1983, Pensacola, FL
Alto sax, arranger, composer, flute / Bop, hard bop
Gigi Gryce was once a successful alto saxophonist as well as a prolific composer but later opted to emphasize writing and arranging end rather than playing. He was a great admirer of Tadd Dameron, and his writing and voicings reflected that influence. Gryce studied composition in Boston and played with local bands there in the mid-'40s. He won a Fulbright scholarship to Paris in the early '50s and later worked with Max Roach and Dameron, played with Oscar Pettiford, and then began heading his own bands. Gryce co-led the Jazz Lab Quintet with Donald Byrd in the mid- and late '50s, and did arrangments for Clifford Brown and Art Farmer. Later came recording sessions with Thelonious Monk, Lee Morgan, and the Lab Quintet before he took a sabbatical from playing in the early '60s. Among Gryce's best-known works is "Nica's Tempo," which has become an established standard. —*Ron Wynn*

○ **Gigi Gryce / Donald Byrd** / **i.** 1963 / Josie 3500
★ **Rat Race Blues, The** / 1984 / New Jazz 081

Bobby Hackett (Robert Leo Hackett)

b. Jan. 31, 1915, Providence, RI, **d.** Jun. 7, 1976, Chatham, MA
Cornet, trumpet, arranger, bandleader / Dixieland
Cornetist, arranger, and bandleader Bobby Hackett was a master accompanist who had a wonderful, immediately recognizable sound and such knowledge of harmony he could truly be said to have never played a bad note. Elegant, tasteful, and striking,

Hackett managed to make memorable music, playing in light-weight '40s bands like Glenn Miller and the Casa Loma Orchestra. He became a staff player at ABC in the late '40s and a regular at Eddie Condon's club, and he was the musical director and second cornetist for Louis Armstrong's historic 1947 Town Hall concert. He became famous in the '50s for contributions to Jackie Gleason albums and dates with Jack Teagarden and his Hudson Hotel band. During the '60s, he worked with Benny Goodman, Ray McKinley, and Tony Bennett. Late in his career, Hackett did guest stints with the World's Greatest Jazz Band and with Dave McKenna. —*Ron Wynn*

★ **Hackett Horn, The** / i. 1930 / Sony Special Products 22003
This set of 16 songs has been reissued intact several times, most notably on this LP. It includes 12 of the first 16 songs cut at dates led by cornetist Bobby Hackett, featuring a pair of hot combos and a larger big band (why are the other four rewarding sides always left out?) along with two Bix-associated songs recorded under the sponsorship of bandleader Horace Heidt and a pair of jams from a set led by critic Leonard Feather. Throughout Hackett, then barely in his mid-20s, shows why his original reputation as "the new Bix" never quite fit. Even this early in his career his pretty tone was distinctive. Among the other stars of these swing-trad performances are trombonists George Brunies and Brad Gowans, and clarinetists Pee Wee Russell and Joe Marsala. Fun and still highly enjoyable music. —*Scott Yanow*

● **Featuring Vic Dickenson at the Roosevelt Grill** / i. Apr. 1970 / 1970 / Chiaroscuro CR 161
The Bobby Hackett-Vic Dickenson quintet of 1969-1971 was one of Hackett's favorite bands of his career. The cornet-trombone front line worked together very well as did a rhythm section led by pianist Dave McKenna. This particular LP, released long after the group had become history, differs from the previous releases in that all of the songs are Dixieland (rather than swing) favorites but, no matter, the band's sly wit and subtle creativity remained at a high level. —*Scott Yanow*

Charlie Haden (Charles Edward Haden)

b. Aug. 6, 1937, Shenandoah, IL
Bass / Early free, modern creative
Charlie Haden's name will always be linked to Ornette Coleman due to this magnificent bassist's pivotal role on Coleman's classic Atlantic albums and continued association with the alto saxophone rebel. But Haden is not just an important sideman; he is an important and inimitable stylist who is credited with shaping the sound of Pat Metheny, Keith Jarrett, Old & New Dreams, Geri Allen, and more, as well as leading his own Liberation Music Orchestra and Quartet West. His upright bass technique is deceptively simple, sometimes characterized as a "folk" approach, using pedal tones and insistent double-stop chording much like a country or blues guitarist. Haden is often cited for the economy of his playing and for making each note function as a foundation for the ensemble—no small feat, considering the freely improvisational and often atonal settings he works in. Haden's status as an in-demand studio player (especially for ECM) and critic's favorite seems to be at odds with his eclectic modernist leanings. But in many ways his playing thrives on very traditional merits—he is almost always rhythmically steady, tonally centered, and adept at carrying a tune. He is to be commended for carrying the acoustic bass (literally and figuratively) into the '90s, while the vast majority of bassists have gone electric. Charlie is also involved in progressive political causes, with a special interest in Latin and South American issues, inspiring his leadership of the Liberation Music Orchestra projects. —*Myles Boisen*

★ **Liberation Music Orchestra** / 1969 / MCA 39125
One of the few message-protest jazz vehicles that works on every level. It has brilliant compositions, arrangements, playing, and lineup, plus passionate material. Recently reissued on MCA. —*Ron Wynn*

○ **As Long As There's Music** / Jan. 25, 1976 / Artists House 4
This duo date by bassist Charlie Haden and pianist Hampton Hawes was done in two studio sessions on January 25 and August 21, 1976, when Hawes returned from commercialism. Of course it wasn't like the old days, but he had that bluesy feel on "Irene," and "What Is This Thing" briefly returned him to his bop roots. . . This does require serious listening, and if that doesn't bother

you, then you'll find a lot of beauty and rapport here. —*Jerry L. Atkins, Cadence*

★ **Closeness** / Jan. 26, 1976+Mar. 21, 1976 / A&M 710
This one is absolutely essential. One duet apiece with Ornette Coleman (sax), Alice Coltrane (p), Keith Jarrett (p), Paul Motian (d). —*Michael G. Nastos*

★ **Quartet West** / i. Dec. 22-23, 1986 / Verve 831673
Fine quartet material, with Ernie Watts (d) far more aggressive and animated than usual. —*Ron Wynn*

○ **First Song** / i. Apr. 1990 / Soul Note 1222

Dialogues / i. 1991 / Antilles 849309
Jazz bassist Haden meets Portuguese guitarist. Stangely beautiful. —*Michael G. Nastos*

○ **Haunted Heart** / 1992 / Verve 513078
Bassist Charlie Haden, always among the finest accompanists around, has become a first-rate bandleader as well with his Quartet West. The lineup, with tenor saxophonist Ernie Watts, pianist Alan Broadbent, and drummer Lawrence Marable, makes cooperative, stunning sessions in which each player expresses himself fully yet never destroys the group balance. That's the key on their recent release, which mixes vocal inserts by guest singers taken from classic films and supported by their playing. —*Ron Wynn, AMG*

Al Haig (Allan Warren Haig)

b. Jul. 22, 1924, Newark, NJ, d. Nov. 16, 1982, New York, NY
Piano / Bop
A sorely-underrated, overlooked pianist much of his life, Al Haig was among the earliest players able to master bop's techniques and forge his own style. Though not in Bud Powell's league, Haig had first-rate skills. His flexibility and harmonic knowledge enabled him to respond quickly and inventively regardless of tempo. He was a masterful accompanist and played with everyone from Charlie Parker to Fats Navarro and Stan Getz. While he seldom got much space, he crammed decisive ideas and statements into concise, crisp solos. Haig played in Coast Guard bands during the early '40s and worked with several Boston groups before joining Dizzy Gillespie's band in 1945. He was soon a fixture on 52d Street, playing in many different groups. Besides Parker and Gillespie, Haig played with Charlie Barnet and Fats Navarro. There were sessions for Prestige and dates with Stan Getz, Wardell Gray, Coleman Hawkins, John Hardee, Zoot Sims, and Allen Eager. He played with Getz, Gray, and Chet Baker during the '50s, but wound up essentially frozen out of the recording and playing scene in a situation that remains among the most controversial in modern jazz history. Haig is one of the players around whom the "Crow Jim" controversy eventually emerged. As a white player who'd been generally accepted during bebop's early days, Haig found he wasn't able to get opportunities during the '50s and the '60s with many black bandleaders. Many white critics maintained this was simply "reverse" racism, while black observers said these claims were exaggerated and that black bandleaders were simply moving toward racial solidarity and ensuring chances for black musicians in an establishment still totally controlled by whites. Regardless of the reasons, Haig's unplanned obscurity robbed him of some productive years and was an unfortunate, unfair situation out of his control. Happily, his skills hadn't diminished when he returned to recording in the mid-'70s. A nice 1974 trio date with Kenny Clarke and guitarist Jimmy Raney, plus a series of records on Trio, Seabreeze, Inner City, Interplay, Musica, and Spotlite reaffirmed Haig's prowess. He cut duets and solos; played acoustic and electric piano; and played Ellington and Jerome Kern compositions, bop anthems, and originals. There were more Al Haig albums recorded and issued between 1974 and his death in 1982 than in the rest of his professional career combined. Many are still available, while his classic accompaniment on Parker, Gillespie, and Gray albums provides positive proof that excellence has no color. —*Ron Wynn*

○ **Al Haig Meets the Master Saxes—Vol. 1** / i. 1948 / Spotlite 139

○ **Al Haig Meets the Master Saxes—Vol. 2** / i. 1948 / Spotlite 140

○ **Al Haig Meets the Master Saxes—Vol. 3** / i. 1948-1951 / Spotlite 1430

○ **Piano Moderns** / Feb. 27, 1950 / Prestige 175

○ **Al Haig Trio and Quintet** / Mar. 13, 1954 / Prestige 7841

Trio and quartet sessions from the final period before pianist Al Haig would drop out of the jazz scene for several years. These dates are quite uneven, as would be expected, almost mirroring the difference between when Haig was physically functioning and when he wasn't. —*Ron Wynn, AMG*

○ **Al Haig Trio** / Mar. 13, 1954 / Esoteric 7
○ **Special Brew** / i. Nov. 1974 / Spotlite 8
○ **Interplay** / Nov. 16, 1976 / Sea Breeze 1005
Fine duets featuring pianist Al Haig during a busy period in the mid-'70s. He'd overcome personal problems and was cranking out albums left and right for both domestic and foreign labels. These were cut for Interplay, a small West Coast firm, but then were mostly issued in Japan. They are mostly excellent examples of Haig's surging bop style. —*Ron Wynn, AMG*
○ **Ornithology** / Jul. 22, 1977 / Progressive 7024
★ **Stablemates** / i. Sep. 1977 / Spotlite 11
☆ **I Remember Bebop** / Nov. 3-05, 1977 / Columbia 235381
○ **Expressly Ellington** / i. Oct. 1978 / Spotlite 20
○ **Bebop Live** / i. May 1982 / Spotlite 23

Edmond Hall

b. May 15, 1901, New Orleans, LA, **d.** Feb. 11, 1967, Boston, MA
Clarinet / New Orleans traditional
An outstanding clarinetist famed for his exuberant, rough-edged solos, Edmond Hall also played baritone sax and was part of a musical family in New Orleans. His brothers included clarinetist Herbie Hall and saxophonist Clarence Hall, who played at one time with Fats Domino. His father, Edward Hall, was a member of the Onward Brass Band. Hall worked in several New Orleans bands, among them groups led by Jack Carey, Lee Collins, and Kid Thomas, before going to New York in 1928. He began working with Claude Hopkins in 1930, and remained with him until 1935. Hall joined Red Allen's band in 1940 and played with Teddy Wilson's sextet in 1941 and was featured on their radio broadcasts and recordings of the period. He recorded for Blue Note in the early and mid-'40s and had his own group from 1944 to 1946. This band had a residency at Cafe Society. He later spent four years in Boston before joining Eddie Condon in 1950. Hall played with Condon until 1955 and then joined Louis Armstrong's All-Stars, where he worked from 1955 to 1958. He returned to Condon's band in 1960 and stayed with him until his death in 1967. Another in the long line of outstanding Mosaic sets, the four-disc, six-album *The Complete Edmond Hall/James P. Johnson/Sidney De Paris/Vic Dickenson Blue Note Sessions* features Hall's finest dates for Blue Note. —*Ron Wynn*

☆ **Complete Edmond Hall/James P. Johnson/Sidney De Paris/Vic Dickenson Blue Note Sessions,** / Mosaic 109
○ **Celestial Express** / Feb. 5, 1941-Jan. 25, 1944 / Blue Note 6505
○ **Jamming in Jazz Hall** / Nov. 29, 1943 / Blue Note 7007
● **Original Blue Note Jazz—Vol. 1** / Nov. 29, 1943 / Blue Note 6504
○ **Edmond Hall in Copenhagen** / i. Dec. 1966 / Storyville 6022

Jim Hall (James Stanley Hall)

b. Dec. 4, 1930, Buffalo, NY
Guitar / Cool
Admired, even revered, by guitarists and jazz sophisticates for his purity of tone, imagination, and elegant taste in melody and harmony, guitarist Jim Hall remains as respected a presence in jazz today as when he emerged in the '50s. His early work with Chico Hamilton and Jimmy Giuffre led to many fine small-group recordings with the likes of Bill Evans, Sonny Rollins, and Paul Desmond. *Intermodulation* with Evans stands out as a gem of the empathetic duet playing of two masters in their prime, while the sessions with Paul Desmond show him in quartet work at his best. His recordings often have a chamber music feel, but his deep immersion in the blues and swing make his music pure jazz. Later recordings with Ron Carter, George Shearing, and even classical violinist Itzhak Perlman point out his effectiveness in small groups. His recordings with younger players such as Don Thompson and Terry Clarke show him moving in a more modern direction while keeping his strong sense of melodic beauty. Highly influential on a whole generation of guitarists, Hall's presence in the world of jazz has been a bit like one of his solos: un-

derstated, gentle, and expressing real musical values. —*David Nelson McCarthy*

○ **Jazz Guitar** / Jan. 10+24, 1957 / Pacific Jazz 1227
Trio. Topflight session. Features a brilliant Carl Perkins (p). Hall is a marvel on guitar. —*Ron Wynn*
★ **Alone Together** / Aug. 4, 1972 / Milestone 467
★ **Jim Hall Live!** / Apr. 1976 / Horizon 705
Jim Hall is a musician's musician. His hallmark is a terse, witty combination of large chords and pithy single-note lines, given life by an incredibly rich, warm sound. In the company of two fine Canadian musicians—bassist Don Thompson and drummer Terry Clarke—Hall's playing had an exuberance and energy that was somewhat of a departure from his usually more introspective-reflective orientation. Listen, for example, to the high intensity of "Scrapple from the Apple." The individual forays melded together in an exciting set of constantly developing episodes. One immediately sensed the musicians' warm respect for one another and their desire to communicate with each other, the audience at the club, and us. —*Chuck Berg, Down Beat*
○ **Live at Town Hall—Vols. 1 and 2** / i. Jun. 26, 1990 / Music Masters 5050

Chico Hamilton (Forestorn Hamilton)

b. Sep. 21, 1921, Los Angeles, CA
Drums / Cool
A former clarinet player, drummer Chico Hamilton got a head-start to musical glory in high school in Los Angeles, where he played with fellow students Dexter Gordon, Charles Mingus, Ernie Royal, and Buddy Collette. He subsequently worked with Floyd Ray, Lionel Hampton, and Slim Gaillard and then spent four years in the army, where he studied (among other things) drums with Jo Jones. Brief encounters with Lester Young, Jimmy Mundy, and Count Basie led to his first established gig, a seven-year stint with Lena Horne, during which he frequently toured. He also worked with Gerry Mulligan in the early '50s before forming his own quintet. The self-styled chamber-jazz unit used flute, clarinet, and cello. It had an intimate sound and elements of "cool" and symphonic music. Never as aggressive as many drummers, Hamilton has been among the best at spotting and debuting new talent. The list of major names who started with him includes Buddy Collette, Jim Hall, Paul Horn, Eric Dolphy, Ron Carter, Charles Lloyd, Gabor Szabo, John Abercrombie, and Arthur Blythe. Hamilton is still active and recording regularly. —*Ron Wynn*

○ **The Chico Hamilton Quintet with Strings Attached** / Oct. 26-27, 1958 / Warner Brothers 1245
○ **Chico Hamilton Special, The** / Nov. 29-30, 1960 / Columbia 1619
● **Passin' Thru** / Sep. 18+20, 1962 / Impulse
One of Hamilton's best groups, with Charles Lloyd (reeds) and Gabor Szabo (g). —*Ron Wynn*
○ **Different Journey, A** / Jan. 19-31, 1963 / Reprise 6078
★ **Dealer, The** / Sep. 9, 1966 / MCA 39137
This groundbreaking session heralded the coming of jazz-rock in 1966 and introduced Larry Coryell (g) to the jazz world. —*Ron Wynn*
○ **Reunion** / Jun. 1989 / Soul Note 1191
This 1989 date by the original Chico Hamilton Quintet recreates the unique chemistry of the pianoless quintet Hamilton led from '55 to '61. Fred Katz's bowed cello adds an intriguing texture, while John Pisano, who replaced Jim Hall in the second edition of the original quintet, plays the elegant, fluid plectorist. But the real standout is Buddy Collette, who blows velvety alto ("Ain't Nobody Calling Me"), pungent clarinet ("Delightful, Charming and Cool"), and brisk flute lines ("Magali"). The improvised duets between Hamilton and Collette on "Brushing with B" and "Conversation" are classic examples of listening and reacting. High point is the daring group improv "Five Friends." —*Bill Milkowski, Down Beat*

Jimmy Hamilton (James Hamilton)

b. May 25, 1917, Dillon, SC
Clarinet / Swing, big band
A talented clarinetist, Jimmy Hamilton's most closely associated with Duke Ellington. He sports a swinging, laugh-laden tone, and

is the logical extension of Benny Goodman. Before joining Ellington, Hampton played with Lucky Millinder and Teddy Wilson in the early '40s. He was also a member of Clarinet Summit. He was featured on such band numbers as "The Mooche" and "Flippant Flurry."—*Michael G. Nastos*

● **Benny Morton and Jimmy Hamilton Blue Note Swingtets** / Mosaic

★ **Swing Low Sweet Clarinet** / Jul. 1960 / Everest 5100

Scott Hamilton

b. Sep. 12, 1954, Providence, RI
Tenor sax / Swing, bop
Tenor saxophonist Scott Hamilton was a prototypical young traditionalist, though his preference was for swing rather than hard bop. He became famous in New England circles in the '70s, moved to New York, and was recommended to Benny Goodman by John Bunch. He met a frequent collaborator, cornetist Warren Vache, in a club. His tenure with Goodman led to a contract with Concord Records and widespread (overdone) publicity that he was the leader of a swing revival. Hamilton has persevered, gradually developing his own stirring, distinctive sound. He still reflects the timbre, tone, and vocabulary of swing-era greats Coleman Hawkins, Ben Webster, Lester Young, and Don Byas, but his solos and phrases are now his, not just theirs recycled. —*Ron Wynn*

○ **Good Wind Who Is Blowing Us No Ill** / Mar. 1, 1977 / Concord Jazz 4042
Tenor saxophonist Scott Hamilton's 1977 debut as a leader astounded the jazz world at the time. Unlike the '80s and '90s generation, whose muses are '50s hard boppers, Hamilton took his inspiration from the lusty swing sound of the '30s—Coleman Hawkins particularly, but also Ben Webster and Lester Young. —*Ron Wynn, AMG*

○ **Scott Hamilton and Warren Vache (With Scott's Band in New York)** / Jun. 26, 1978 / Concord Jazz 70
Despite the fact that this was a Scott Hamilton-Warren Vache album, the standouts were trombonist George Masso and Vache (cornet, flugelhorn). Everyone was given several solo opportunities except Harold Ashby (tenor sax), Phil Flanagan (bass), and Chuck Riggs (drums). Masso had three turns in the spotlight, and all of them were outstanding. The best of the three was "Nancy's Fancy," but he was also the standout on "Lightly and Politely" and "Love You Madly." He also contributed three of the arrangements, while Nat Pierce did the remaining in his Count Basieish approach. —*Shirley Klett, Cadence*

● **Scott's Buddy** / Aug. 1980 / Concord Jazz 148
Tenor saxophonists Scott Hamilton and Buddy Tate played together for several years whenever an engagement came up that both were able to fit into their schedules. This LP was recorded directly after one such engagement in Los Angeles. . . . this was a good solid session of swing tenor saxophone, with plenty of solo space for both men, plus Nat Pierce's piano, as well as a number of opportunities for chase sequences. One thing that characterized encounters between these two was their sense of fun and good humor, and both were present here in abundance. —*Shirley Klett, Cadence*

○ **Major League** / May 1986 / Concord Jazz 4305
A baseball motif underlines this good set in which Dave McKenna (p) and Jake Hanna (d) share the spotlight with Hamilton. —*Ron Wynn*

★ **Scott Hamilton Plays Ballads** / Mar. 1989 / Concord Jazz 4386
This was a refreshing album not only for the Scott Hamilton tenor sax, but also because the ballads were far from the usual, "In a Sentimental Mood" excepted. Even the latter Duke Ellington title is not recorded all that often. —*Shirley Klett, Cadence*

Jan Hammer (Jan Hammer, Jr.)

b. Apr. 17, 1948, Prague, Czechoslovakia
Keyboards, composer / Early jazz rock, world fusion, modern creative
A pianist and drummer as a child, Jan Hammer played in a trio with Alan and Miroslav Vitous during his high school years in Prague, Czechoslovakia. He studied classical composition and piano at the Prague Conservatory and won a 1966 international music competition and a scholarship to Berklee. Hammer left his

homeland for the United States in 1968, following the Soviet invasion. He worked with Sarah Vaughan and Jeremy Steig during the early '70s, before meeting John McLaughlin. His work with the Mahavishnu Orchestra and Billy Cobham's Spectrum established him as an excellent acoustic and electric pianist, one of the rare synthesizer players able to present the instrument as a musical asset rather than electronic bombast. The first Mahavishnu Orchestra suggested the possibility of a fertile form emerging that truly blended rock dynamics and jazz sensibility. Hammer enjoyed new fame in the '80s as the first composer for the "Miami Vice" TV show. —*Ron Wynn*

○ **Make Love** / i. Aug. 30, 1968 / MPS
An album with a wonderful title and an excellent example of real jazz-rock. —*Ron Wynn*

○ **Like Children** / i. 1974 / Atlantic 50092
The keyboardist and violinist Jerry Goodman away from Mahavishnu. They play all instruments (overdubbed). "Country and Eastern Music" and "Steppings Tones" were high water marks for this new breed (at the time). —*Michael G. Nastos*

★ **Oh Yeah** / i. 1976 / Nemperor 50276
This is an album of fusion at its best. "Magical Dog" and "Red & Orange" are definitive statements. This was the first exposure for violinist Steve Kindler. David Earle Johnson is on congas. —*Michael G. Nastos*

Gunter Hampel (Gunther Hampel)

b. Aug. 31, 1937, Gottingen, Germany
Vibes, clarinet, sax, flute, piano, composer / Progressive big band, modern creative
Gunther Hampel's a genuine multi-instrumentalist who plays vibes, clarinet, bass clarinet, flutes, piano, and various saxophones. He's also a composer and bandleader. Hampel's performed numerous free sessions, as well as written music for films. He's best known for a series of recordings and duets with such musicians as Anthony Braxton and vocalist Jeanne Lee (his wife). His compositions range from introspective and abstract to intense and usually features many collectively improvised sections. Hampel studied music and architecture and began heading his own band in 1958, touring Europe and Germany. During the '60s, he turned to free music almost exclusively and toured for the Goethe Institute in Africa, Asia, and South America. Hampel founded Birth Records in 1969 and started the Galaxie Dreams Band in the early '70s. He performed solo concerts at the 1972 Munich Olympic Games and at that year's Berlin Jazz Festival. Hampel has recorded several albums on Birth, among them sessions with Braxton, Willem Breuker, Enrico Rava, and other European and American free musicians. They can be obtained on CD by mail order or from international sources. —*Ron Wynn*

● **All the Things You Could Be If Charles Mingus Was Your Daddy** / i. Jul. 1980 / Birth 0031

○ **Fresh Heat: Live at Sweet Basil** / Feb. 1985 / Birth 39

Lionel Hampton

b. Apr. 12, 1909, Louisville
Vibes, drums, piano / Swing, big band
Vibist Lionel Hampton's a legend as a player, bandleader, entertainer, and inspirational figure. His role in revolutionizing the vibes as a jazz instrument cannot be overstated; his solos were rhythmically and harmonically creative, often astonishing and spectacular, and remain among the finest in modern jazz history. Hampton also played drums and piano and even did vocals. After a stint in Les Hite's band, Hampton gained international fame during his years with Benny Goodman in the mid-'30s and early '40s. Later he had many popular records in the swing era, and his band's rousing performances, particularly on a song he wrote titled "Flying Home," were among those that laid the groundwork for the development of R&B. Hampton has appeared in several films, among them *The Benny Goodman Story*, had his own record label and management firm, and continued performing and touring right into the '90s. —*Ron Wynn*

☆ **Complete Lionel Hampton, The** / Feb. 8, 1937-Apr. 8, 1941 / RCA 65536
Although this six-LP boxed set is now out-of-print, it is so definitive that it deserves the highest rating. Consisting of all of the sessions led by vibraphonist Lionel Hampton prior to the formation

of his popular big band, these hot swing sides feature a who's who of jazz greats from the 1930s, including trumpeters Ziggy Elman, Cootie Williams, Jonah Jones, Harry James, Rex Stewart, Red Allen, and Dizzy Gillespie; altoists Benny Carter, Johnny Hodges, and Earl Bostic; tenors Herschel Evans, Chu Berry, Coleman Hawkins, and Ben Webster; guitarist Charlie Christian; and the Nat King Cole Trio, among many others. With Hamp on vibes, two-fingered piano, and occasional vocals, this set is overflowing with classic performances. It should have been reissued in complete form on CD instead of in the piecemeal fashion that it has thus far partially reappeared. This box has yet to be matched! —*Scott Yanow*

○ **Stompology** / Feb. 8, 1937-08 1 / RCA 575

○ **Lionel Hampton (1937-1938)** / i. Feb. 1937-Jan. 1938 / Classics 524

★ **Lionel Hampton's Jumpin' Jive—Vol. 2** / Feb. 1937-Oct. 1939 / Bluebird 2433
The All-Star Groups. The second volume of topflight late-'30s material, with exuberant solos from Johnny Hodges (as), Benny Carter (as), and Dizzy Gillespie (tpt). —*Ron Wynn*

○ **Lionel Hampton (1938-1939)** / i. Jan. 1938-Jun. 1939 / Classics 534

○ **Lionel Hampton (1939-1940)** / i. Jun. 1939-May 1940 / Classics 562

○ **Steppin' out (1942-1944)** / 1942-1944 / MCA 1315
Released as part of MCA's Jazz Heritage series in the early 1980s, this LP contains 14 of the 16 selections from Lionel Hampton's 1942-1944 sessions, including two versions of "Flying Home" (featuring the contrasting tenor-sax solos of Illinois Jacquet and Arnett Cobb) and the original recording of "Hamp's Boogie-woogie." This is classic music played in an exuberant swing style that Hampton has continued to keep alive for the half-century since. —*Scott Yanow*

● **Flyin' Home (1942-1945)** / 1942-1945 / MCA 42349
An excellent compilation of similar material. A great big band, plus some driving vibes solos. —*Ron Wynn*

○ **Jazz Heritage: Steppin' out (1942-1944)** / 1942-1944 / MCA 1351

○ **Original Stardust, The** / Aug. 4, 1947 / Decca 74194
Lionel Hampton's classic live version of "Star Dust" at this "Just Jazz" concert is rightfully acclaimed and remains one of the highpoints of his long career. Oddly enough Hampton does not appear on the other three selections included on this LP (which has since been reissued on CD), but these fine renditions of "One 'O'Clock Jump," "The Man I Love," and "Lady Be Good" do benefit from excellent solos by trumpeter Charlie Shavers, altoist Willie Smith, Corky Corcoran on tenor, and bassist Slam Stewart. Highly recommended. —*Scott Yanow*

○ **Lionel Hampton Quartet, The** / Sep. 2, 1953-Apr. 12, 1954 / Clef 142

○ **Lionel Hampton Quintet, The** / Apr. 12, 1954 / Clef 628

○ **Swingin' with Hamp** / Apr. 12, 1954+Sep. 15, 1954 / Clef 736

○ **Hamp's Big Four** / Apr. 12, 1954-Sep. 13, 1954 / Clef 744

○ **Tatum-Hampton-Rich...Again** / Aug. 1, 1955 / Pablo 775
Missing from the Art Tatum Group Masterpieces set were the previously issued "Body and Soul" from the Tatum-Hampton-Rich date, plus six unissued titles. Here they are at last, with two takes of "Love for Sale" for good measure. This was a fascinating set, at its best fully the equal of the original issue. —*Shirley Klett, Cadence*

● **Hampton-Tatum-Rich Trio, The** / Aug. 1, 1955 / Clef 709

○ **Hamp in Hi Fi** / May 1-02, 1956 / Harmony 7115

○ **You Better Know It** / Oct. 26-29, 1964 / Impulse 78

Slide Hampton (Locksley Wellington Hampton)

b. Apr. 21, 1932, Jeannette, PA
Trombone, tuba, arranger / Hard bop
Slide Hampton's known for being not only one of the rare left-handed trombonists but also among the fastest, most fluid players. Hampton played with Lionel Hampton, Maynard Ferguson, and Buddy Johnson in the '50s before forming his own octet in 1959. He was musical director for R&B/blues singer Lloyd Price and did freelance arranging in the '60s before joining Woody

Herman in 1968. He toured Europe and resettled there. Hampton returned to New York in 1977 and began heading his 12-piece band, the World of Trombones. He's been an activist in jazz education in the '80s, and still does occasional recording sessions. —*Ron Wynn*

● **His Horn of Plenty** / Oct. 1959 / Strand 1006

★ **World of Trombones** / Jan. 8-09, 1979 / Black Lion 760113
Ambitious project with nine trombonists merging their skills under the leadership of Slide Hampton. The list includes both established veterans like Curtis Fuller and Steve Turre and emerging newcomers Janice Robinson and Afro-Latin star Papo Vasauez. Hampton's arrangements are excellent, but there's more emphasis on performance style than real solo development. Pianist Albert Dailey and bassist Ray Drummond were also outstanding. —*Ron Wynn, AMG*

Herbie Hancock (Herbert Jeffrey Hancock)

b. Apr. 12, 1940, Chicago, IL
Keyboards / Hard bop, cool, blues & jazz, early jazz rock, contemporary funk
Herbie Hancock is a premier jazz keyboardist who has been a superb player in a variety of styles, from the '60s, when he worked with Miles Davis, to several groundbreaking albums for Blue Note, the jazz-rock and fusion of the '70s and beyond, which have seen him regularly invade the pop charts. Hancock moved from Chicago to New York in 1961 and worked with a variety of jazz stars before joining Davis's quintet in 1965, a unit that also included Ron Carter, Tony Williams, and Wayne Shorter and ranks among the finest bands of Davis's career. In addition to the memorable music the group made (some of it written by Hancock), the pianist also had his own pact with Blue Note for a series of solo albums, starting with *Takin' Off* in 1962. Hancock scored the film *Blowup* in 1966, which made the pop charts. After he left Davis in 1968, Hancock began to divide his time between acoustic piano work and electric playing, and he became a major star in both genres. His "straight" jazz dates included the V.S.O.P. group (which was the old Davis quintet with Freddie Hubbard substituting for Davis) and albums with fellow keyboardist Chick Corea. His jazz-rock and fusion albums included the gold-selling 1974 release *Head Hunters*. In all, he charted 11 albums during the '70s, amazing for a jazz musician. Of course, there are few who like all of Hancock's work. This became even more true when Hancock scored on the dance floor and singles chart with "Rockit," a hip-hop track with a successful video that went gold in 1983. Since then, Hancock has continued to move back and forth between the worlds of purist-jazz and outright pop. —*Bill Ruhlmann*

○ **Best of Herbie Hancock: The Blue Note Years** / May 1962-Mar. 1968 / Blue Note 91142
The Blue Note years. A good compilation to start with. Many of his best works. —*Michael G. Nastos*

○ **My Point of View** / Mar. 19, 1963 / Blue Note 84126
Tremendous compositions and playing in an all-star date that helped make Hancock a star. —*Ron Wynn*

○ **Empyrean Isles** / Jun. 17, 1964 / Blue Note 84175
1985 reissue of one of Hancock's seminal releases. Freddie Hubbard (tpt) is daring and aggressive. Ron Carter (b) and Tony Williams (d) are squarely in the pocket. —*Ron Wynn*

★ **Maiden Voyage** / Mar. 17, 1965 / Blue Note 46339
The definitive Blue Note Herbie with an ensemble. You can't go wrong with this one. —*Michael G. Nastos*

○ **Speak Like a Child** / Mar. 9, 1968 / Blue Note 46136
A simply beautiful title cut, plus wondrous arrangements and playing throughout. —*Ron Wynn*

★ **Fat Albert Rotunda** / Mar. 10, 1969+Dec. 8, 1969 / Warner Brothers 1834
Herbie plays Fender Rhodes with Joe Henderson (ts). Featuring "Tell Me a Bedtime Story." —*Michael G. Nastos*

● **Mwandishi** / 1970 / Warner Brothers
A forerunner of Africentric sentiment. One of Hancock's finest electric, jazz-rock outings. —*Ron Wynn*

★ **Headhunters** / 1973 / Columbia 47478

○ **Live under the Sky** / i. 1976 / Columbia 875
Despite the overwhelming individual virtuosity, these five talents came together as a true *band*, passing the severest test; even their

most intricate arrangements (and this was no mere jamming band) sounded spontaneous. Consider the wonderful empathy of trumpeter Freddie Hubbard's "One of Another Kind," with its subtle ensemble rubato and tight give-and-take between soloist and hard-charging accompaniment. And hear the way Hubbard burned and soared, constructing a solo, not merely linking flashy runs, while Wayne Shorter showed how to handle an inclement-weather affected horn (wet pads, swollen reed, etc.) and still create an intriguing outing through a disintegrating line with shorter and shorter fragments, squeezed and wrung out of a soggy soprano. —*Art Lange, Down Beat*

○ **V.S.O.P. Quintet** / Jul. 16, 1977-Jul. 18, 1977 / Columbia 34976
This often stunning quintet set was done live at Newport. Hancock again confounds cynics who insist he's lost his jazz roots. —*Ron Wynn*

○ **Quartet** / i. 1981 / Columbia 38275
A fine mainstream set that showed detractors Hancock hadn't lost his jazz chops. Wynton Marsalis (tpt) (then reaping a wave of prodigy-discovery headlines) is in the group. —*Ron Wynn*

Village Life / i. 1985 / Columbia 39870
An arresting mix of Hancock's jazz concept with African Foday Suso's rhythmic innovations. —*Ron Wynn*

○ **V.S.O.P.—Vol. 2** / Columbia 40015

○ **Evening with Chick Corea and Herbie Hancock, An** / Polydor 6238
This double album, recorded in concert, began with two standards. In "Someday My Prince Will Come" the melody was nearly smothered beneath the garlands of ornaments and runs. Chick Corea and Herbie Hancock did not always maintain a strict division of labor. In "Someday" there was a wonderful two-chorus embrace where you could not tell the dancer from the dance. In the other standard, George Gershwin's "Liza," Corea and Hancock traded a few conventional choruses, but then they went loco and took "Liza" to places she had never been before. Sides two and three were taken up by two loosely structured pieces performed with both virtuosity and self-indulgence. Side four was a jewel. On Hancock's classic "Maiden Voyage," both pianists played fine solos to equally fine accompaniment, although the double solo that followed did not fare as well as others on the album. —*Douglas Clark, Down Beat*

John Handy (John Richard Handy III)

b. Feb. 3, 1933, Dallas, TX
Alto sax, flute, tenor sax / Bop, hard bop
Alto saxophonist John Handy is not to be confused with "Captain" John Handy, the traditional jazz player. He's a self-taught reed specialist who later studied theory in college. He moved from Dallas to New York in 1958 and joined Charles Mingus in 1959. His flexible, bluesy, and hard-edged alto style, which was a cross between classic bop and free, emerged in his work with Mingus and his own band in the late '50s and '60s. A quintet he co-led with violinist Michael White in 1965 was another of those bands whose work suggested the coming jazz-rock marriage. They were a huge hit at Monterey that year. In 1968 Handy played with Mike Nock, White, and Ron McClure in another ahead-of-its-time group that later became Fourth Way. Handy repeatedly experimented with jazz-Indian collaborations and symphony compositions, served as an educator, and played numerous festivals during the '70s and '80s. He had a hit with the album *Hard Work* in the late '70s, and he resurfaced heading an otherwise-all-female group in 1989. —*Ron Wynn*

○ **No Coast Jazz** / 1961 / Roulette 52058

★ **Live at Monterey** / Sep. 18, 1965 / Columbia 2462

○ **Second John Handy Album, The** / Apr. 27, 1966-Jul. 26, 1966 / Columbia 2567

○ **John Handy** / Sep. 18, 1966 / Columbia

Sir Roland Hanna (Sir Roland P. Hanna)

b. Feb. 10, 1932, Detroit, MI
Piano / Bop
An extremely versatile pianist who also excels at solo performances, Sir Roland Hanna's lyricism and touch are among jazz's finest. Hanna worked with both Benny Goodman and Charles Mingus in the late '50s before joining Sarah Vaughan in 1960. He led a trio at the Five Spot in the mid-'60s before joining the Thad

Jones-Mel Lewis orchestra in 1966. He remained with them until 1974 and over that time became as familiar to jazz audiences as any of their featured horn soloists. Hanna was also in the New York Jazz Sextet and Quartet of the '60s and '70s alongside Frank Wess, Ben Riley, and Ron Carter. An underrated composer, Hanna's finest work, "A Child Is Born," was actually credited to Thad Jones for many years. He's done many recording dates as a leader since leaving the Jones-Lewis orchestra, among them sessions for Black & Blue, Blackhawk, DIW, and Enja. —*Ron Wynn*

○ **Sir Elf** / Apr. 1974-May 1974 / Choice 1003
Pianist Roland Hanna puts so much music into each song that the listener must be especially prepared to devote every bit of attention in order to keep up. . . . Solo piano demands great arrangements as well as great performances, and Hanna's treatments were novel and captivating, although he occasionally tinkled the ivories for one or two choruses too many. But there was plenty of meat on those bone chips. —*Neil Tesser, Down Beat*

★ **Perugia** / Jul. 2, 1974 / Freedom 741010
Recorded live at the 1974 Montreux Jazz Festival, this, Sir Roland Hanna's second solo piano album, gave a revealing cross-section of his abilities. Basically a mainstream jazz player in the tradition of Erroll Garner and Oscar Peterson, Hanna opened here with two Ellington-associated tunes, memorializing the bandleader's then recent death. "Take The 'A' Train," with its gutsy walking bass lines and Oscar Peterson-style licks, seemed to please this pianist as much as it did his audience. "I Got It Bad and That Ain't Good," punctuated by some telling grunts and groans in its free-flowing inventive prowess that suggested that anything might happen next, was tinged by the spirit of Garner himself. In performing his originals Hanna came into his own. "Time Dust Gathered" pulsed with high tension chords and was graced by percussive, interlocking keyboardlines. "Perugia" broods with romanticism and mysticism. His playing was marked with a fine melodic sense throughout, and as the concert continued, his keyboard textures became more daring and inventive. —*Jon Balleras, Down Beat*

○ **Persia My Dear** / i. Aug. 1987 / DIW 8015

Wilbur Harden

b. 1925
Trumpet / Hard bop
Besides being one of the first jazz trumpeters to convert to flugelhorn, Wilbur Harden was among hard bop and bebop's more lyrical, melodic stylists. His flugelhorn solos greatly reflected that tendency; Harden played soothing, lush middle register statements and subtle embellishments and melodic adjustments. He was an R&B player in bands led by Ivory Joe Hunter and Roy Brown during the '50s. Harden played in a navy band before moving to Detroit. His transition to jazz was greatly aided by Yusef Lateef, with whom he played in 1957. He recorded with Lateef on Savoy and then made several marvelous dates with John Coltrane on that same label; though these were Harden's sessions, three of the four were later issued as Coltrane records. Illness ended Harden's active career in 1959. His albums on Savoy are currently unavailable on CD under his name; they're available as Coltrane reissues. Harden can also be heard on a Lateef reissue. —*Ron Wynn*

● **Tanganyika Suite** / May 13, 1958 / Savoy 13005

Bill Hardman (William Franklin Hardman, Jr.)

b. Apr. 6, 1933, Cleveland, OH, d. Dec. 1990
Trumpet, flugelhorn / Hard bop
Trumpeter and flugelhornist Bill Hardman became one of the finer soloists of the '50s and '60s, working with Charles Mingus, Art Blakey, Horace Silver, and Lou Donaldson. His longest stint was with Lou Donaldson (seven years), though he had four different periods with Art Blakey. Hardman also led his own group, the Brass Company, in the late '60s and was with Junior Cook in the late '70s and early '80s. —*Ron Wynn*

Saying Something / i. Oct. 18, 1961 / Savoy 1164
An album with topflight blowing from Sonny Red (sax). This is perhaps Hardman's best date; among his most memorable. —*Ron Wynn*

Home / Jan. 10, 1978 / Muse 5152

Trumpeter Bill Hardman's *Home* was a straightahead bebop session by a journeyman trumpet player, best known for his work with drummer Art Blakey and bassist Charles Mingus. The playing was competent if not exceptional, and anyone who likes bebop would appreciate it. —*Sam Little, Cadence*

Politely / Jul. 7, 1981 / Muse 5184

This Bill Hardman date was interesting because of his nice trumpet playing, both open and with a mute, and also because he and Junior Cook on tenor sax were such a great team. Hardman's highlight had to be "Love Letters." —*Jerry Atkins, Cadence*

Roy Hargrove

b. 1970
Trumpet / Neo-bop

Hargrove is among the high-profile young lions. This 20-something trumpeter recently moved to Verve from RCA in a move that was chronicled in many general music magazines as well as the jazz press. He's been in the spotlight since his late teens, when word surfaced about a dynamic, exciting player from the East Coast. Hargrove's sound and technique, as well as his tone, have continued to impress even as he's matured almost nightly on the bandstand and in the recording studios.—*Ron Wynn*

★ **Diamond in the Rough** / Dec. 1989 / Novus 3082

The Harper Brothers

Neo-bop

Brothers Winard and Phillip Harper were once a duo identified as part of the young-lion, hard-bop movement, but in recent months opted to go their separate ways. The drums/trumpet duo were once in a group whose sound reflected the huge influence of Art Blakey's Messengers. They earned critical respect and admiration for their decision to stick to genuine jazz. They later explored the blues and worked with vocalists to broaden their audience.—*Ron Wynn*

★ **Remembrance** / **i.** Mar. 1990 / Verve 841723

Billy Harper (Billy R. Harper)

b. Jan. 17, 1943
Sax / Hard bop

An often animated, slashing soloist, tenor saxophonist, and flutist, Billy Harper has been in the jazz limelight since the mid-'60s. After moving from Houston to New York in 1966, Harper toured California with Gil Evans, played in Art Blakey's Jazz Messengers, and worked with Elvin Jones in 1970. Later came periods with Max Roach, the Thad Jones-Mel Lewis Orchestra, and Lee Morgan. Harper began heading his own band in 1973 but maintained ties with Roach until 1978, and with Evans into the '80s. Harper has recorded as a leader for Strata-East, Denon, Black Saint, and Soul Note. —*Ron Wynn*

★ **Black Saint** / Jul. 21-22, 1975 / Black Saint 001

An important document and the first album for the Italian Black Saint label. A potent quartet, with Harper's most familiar themes. This is essential listening in the modal jazz idiom. —*Michael G. Nastos*

Tom Harrell

b. Jun. 16, 1946, Urbana, IL
Trumpet, flugelhorn / Hard bop

An outstanding trumpeter, Tom Harrell's one of the top hard bop soloists. After touring with Stan Kenton in 1969 and Woody Herman in 1970 and 1971, Harrell spent four years with Horace Silver. He also performed and recorded with Chuck Israel's National Jazz Ensemble and played with Arnie Lawrence, Cecil Payne, Bill Evans, and Lee Konitz's nonet. Harrell worked with George Russell in 1982 and then joined Phil Woods in 1983, helping expand his basic group from a quartet to a quintet. Harrell's done his own sessions for Adamo, Palo Alto, and Contemporary. —*Ron Wynn and Michael G. Nastos*

★ **Sail Away** / **i.** Mar. 22 23, 1989 / Contemporary 14054

Spirited originals and his best effort to date. Featuring Dave Liebman (ss) and Joe Levano (ts). A must-buy. —*Michael G. Nastos*

Joe Harriott (Joe Arthurlin Harriott)

b. Jul. 15, 1928, Kingston, Jamaica, **d.** Jan. 2, 1973, London, England
Alto sax, clarinet / Hard bop, world fusion

Until Courtney Pine emerged, Joe Harriott had the distinction of being the most prominent Jamaican jazz figure in British history. He came to England in 1951, having played in dance bands and studied clarinet at a boys' school. He worked in various combos during the '50s, touring with the Modern Jazz Quartet in 1959. Harriott became famous in the '60s for forging a sound that merged elements of Indian and Asian music with jazz. He was also among the first musicians anywhere in the world to play free jazz.—*Ron Wynn*

Free Forms / 1960 / Jazzland 49/949

Swings High / **i.** 1967 / Cadillac 12

Indo Jazz Fusions: The Joe Harriott-John Mayer Do / Jul. 1968 / Atlantic 1482

Barry Harris (Barry Doyle Harris)

b. Dec. 15, 1929, Detroit, MI
Piano / Bop

Barry Harris is one of the finest of all bebop pianists and a first-class interpreter of Bud Powell and Thelonious Monk. His national reputation began in Cannonball Adderley's group in 1960, and he moved to New York, working frequently with Coleman Hawkins, Yusef Lateef, and Charles McPherson, as well as heading his own groups. He made many sideman appearances in the '60s and '70s, while making his debut as a leader for Riverside and Prestige ('60s). He recorded frequently for Xanadu in the '70s, with one-shot album appearances for a variety of labels. There are no bad albums by this artist, but in general his later work is his most interesting, with the Xanadu albums being his finest. —*Bob Porter*

○ **Barry Harris at the Jazz Workshop** / May 15-16, 1960 / Riverside 208

Barry Harris has been remarkably consistent over the years. *At the Jazz Workshop* captured him live in 1960 with Sam Jones (bass) and Louis Hayes (drums). Adding to the expected pleasures of Harris was the slick work of Sam Jones's active bass and the powerful (as in accomplished) drumming of Louis Hayes. —*Bob Rusch, Cadence*

○ **Preminado** / Dec. 21, 1960+Jan. 19, 1961 / Riverside 486
○ **Newer Than New** / Sep. 28, 1961 / Riverside 413
○ **Chasin' the Bird** / May 31, 1962+Aug. 23, 1962 / Riverside 9435
○ **Bull's Eye** / Jun. 4, 1968 / Prestige 7600
★ **Live in Tokyo** / Apr. 1, 1976 / Xanadu
○ **Bird of Red and Gold, The** / **i.** Sep. 1989 / Xanadu 213
○ **Live at Maybeck Recital Hall—Vol. 12** / Mar. 1990 / Concord Jazz 4476

In this CD, Barry Harris joins the succession of pianists recorded by Concord in solo performances at Maybeck Recital Hall in Berkeley, California. His leisurely opening piece, "It Could Happen to You," finds him reflecting on Art Tatum, with an incorporation of the master's articulated runs and bursts of swing inside the basic tempo. When Harris is playing, Bud Powell is never far away, and in "All God's Chillum Got Rhythm," after a bow toward Thelonious Monk, the pianist gives the first of several demonstrations in this recital of his absorption of Powell's style into his own. —*Doug Ramsey, Jazz Times*

Beaver Harris (William Godvin Harris)

b. Apr. 20, 1936, Pittsburgh, **d.** Dec. 22, 1991
Drums / Progressive big band, modern creative

Drummer Beaver Harris also played baseball in the Negro Leagues and blended sports and music for a while. He played in an army band and then moved to New York in 1963. Harris worked with Sonny Rollins, Thelonious Monk, Joe Henderson, and Freddie Hubbard before joining Archie Shepp in 1966. He had stints with Shepp, Sonny Stitt, Dexter Gordon, and Clark Terry before forming a cooperative band with trombonist Grachan Moncur III in 1969. The 360 Degree Experience did free music with zest and flair, anchored by Harris's rollicking, inspired, but always steady drumming. Harris continued playing with Shepp in the '70s and also appeared in pit bands for some plays. He toured Japan with a Newport Jazz Festival Tour in the mid-'70s, and recorded with Steve Lacy, Pharoah Sanders, Gato Barbieri, and Albert Ayler in the '70s. —*Ron Wynn*

★ **In: Sanity** / Mar. 8-09, 1976 / Black Saint 7
Recording with 360-Degree Music Experience. Improvisational music with world-music touches from percussionist Harris and pianist Dave Burrell. An essential purchase for the adventurous listener. —*Michael G. Nastos*

○ **Live at Nyon** / Jun. 14, 1979 / Cadence 1002
This set, recorded by Bob Rusch, editor-publisher of *Cadence* magazine, contained a long swinger, two shorter ballads for quartet and duo, and a long sizzler. Harris, a team player, gave himself little solo space. Yet his ensembles pushed along the rhythm team joyously, and his mesh with old Army pal pianist Ron Burton, probing and positive throughout, and bassist Cameron Brown cut a clean, happy groove all the way. —*Fred Bouchard, Down Beat*

○ **Negcaumongus** / Dec. 7, 1979 / Cadence 1003
Brilliant septet cuts. Ricky Ford (ts) and Don Pullen (p) are magnificent. —*Ron Wynn*

○ **Well Kept Secret with Don Pullen** / 1984 / Hannibal
This edition of the 360 Degree Experience walked the line between inside and outside playing as well as any unit around at the time; they covered a lot of ground, and swung from a light to heavy-handed approach in no time, while rarely letting the transitions and juxtapositions sound forced. . . . [The] sound on this studio recording was many times better than on the live *Negcaumongus*, yet for some reason the group failed to attain the same high excitement. —*Kevin Whitehead, Cadence*

Craig Harris

b. Sep. 10, 1954, Hempstead, NY
Trombone / Soul jazz, modern creative
Craig Harris is a strong contemporary trombonist capable in multiple styles from New Orleans and "tailgate" to bop and free. He has been prominent on the jazz scene through the '80s and '90s as a session man, bandleader, and composer. Harris's dates have ranged from covering James Brown tunes in a group of equally eclectic players, to recording songs using an Australian instrument similar to the trombone, and playing Afro-Latin and hard-bop.—*Ron Wynn*

★ **Blackout in the Square Root of Soul** / Dec. 1986-Nov. 1987 / PolyGram 34415
A first-rate example of a fresh direction in jazz that blends improvisatory zeal, funk, and R&B references. —*Ron Wynn*

○ **Cold Sweat Plays J.B.** / i. 1989 / JMT 834426
Great gutbucket R&B and populist jazz played with fire, zeal, and grit. The Godfather would be proud. — *Ron Wynn, Rock & Roll Disc.*

Eddie Harris

b. Oct. 20, 1934, Chicago, IL
Tenor sax, electric sax, trumpet, keyboards / Bop, hard bop, blues & jazz, instrumental pop
A popular tenor saxophonist of the '60s and '70s, Harris burst into national prominence with his version of "Exodus," which reached Top 40 pop single status in 1961. His Vee Jay recordings from 1961-1964 displayed a light-toned saxophone approach over a gently funky rhythm section, usually featuring guitar. He seemed to have found a popular group sound. He came to Atlantic in 1965 and, after a couple of straightahead jazz albums, turned to the electronic saxophone and a more funk-oriented approach. This resulted in "Listen Here," a pop/R&B success from 1968, and a hit album *The Electrifying Eddie Harris.* From this point forward, his work became more commercial and more involved with a variety of electronics, to the point where his mid-'70s work was virtually devoid of any jazz content. A live album, co-led with pianist-vocalist Les McCann (*Swiss Movement*), provided a jazz hit with "Compared to What" in 1970. After an almost endless series of commercial attempts, Harris returned to jazz and made some fine straightahead jazz albums in the '80s. —*Bob Porter*

○ **Exodus to Jazz** / Jan. 17, 1961 / Vee Jay 3016
Once past the phlegmatic movie theme ("Exodus"), which was a bit of a hit for Eddie Harris (but in abbreviated form), *Exodus to Jazz* proved to be a surprisingly sturdy LP. It was the tenorist's

first and found him in a somewhat Stan Getzian mood and mode. Joe Diorio's guitar, at the same time, reminded me of Jimmy Raney's. The rhythm trio (Willie Pickens, piano; William Yancey, bass; Harold Jones, drums) was supple and propulsive, and the originals, four by Harris, two by Pickens were diverse, and never less than interesting, with "A.T.C.," "Velocity," and "W.P." the clear winners. The recital was topped off by Harris's restrained, but fervent, reading of Rodgers and Hart's "Little Girl Blue." —*Alan Bargebuhr, Cadence*

○ **Mighty Like a Rose** / Apr. 14, 1961 / Vee Jay 3025

○ **Jazz for "Breakfast at Tiffany's"** / 1961 / Vee Jay 3027

○ **"In" Sound, The** / Aug. 9, 1965 / Atlantic 1448

○ **Best Of, The** / i. Sep. 1965-Dec. 1973 / Atlantic 1545
A skeletal anthology of some of Harris's Atlantic cuts. It leans toward hits but does contain "Listen Here" and "Theme from Exodus." A good introductory album to his work. —*Ron Wynn*

★ **Electrifying Eddie Harris** / 1967 / Atlantic
The birth and fruition of Harris's use of varitone and electronics on tenor as a legitimate technique. —*Ron Wynn*

★ **Swiss Movement** / Jun. 1969 / Atlantic 50405
W/ Less McCann. Evergreen! Contains the monster hit "Compared to What." A must-buy, if you don't have it already. — *Michael G. Nastos*

☆ **Second Movement** / 1971 / Atlantic 1583
W/ Less McCann. The followup to *Swiss Movement* didn't sell so well but still has plenty of fine music. —*Ron Wynn*

○ **Eddie Who?** / Feb. 1986 / Impulse 33104

○ **There Was a Time (Echo of Harlem)** / May 9, 1990 / Enja 79663
Eddie Harris Quartet. This is a fine retrospective and mainstream date. CD bonus cut. —*Ron Wynn*

○ **Lost Album Plus the Better Half, The** / i. 1993 / Vee-Jay 913
An excellent blues, soul jazz, and bop player when he exerts himself, Harris has also issued several woeful albums, recording sessions of standup comedy, and other filler that wasted his skills. That was not the case on these eight cuts culled from early '60s Vee Jay dates. The first four blend soul jazz and straight bop with Ira Sullivan sparkling on trumpet and Harris dueling with alto saxophonist Bunky Green. The other two feature Harris wailing the blues alongside organist Melvin Rhyne, Sullivan, Green, and guitarist Joe D'Orio. They recall the glory days of steamy, funky organ combos, with drummer Gerald Donovan keeping the backbeat steadily in the groove. —*Ron Wynn*

○ **Artist's Choice: Anthology** / i. 1994 / Rhino
Eddie Harris has long been a jazz enigma; he's a skilled improviser who's enjoyed significant hits and made some superb albums, but he has also issued puzzling, inferior releases featuring vocals, standup comedy, and oddities. His tenure at Atlantic in the '60s and '70s was most productive, yet until recently it was represented only by a pair of single-album greatest hits collections. Now a fine two-disc anthology containing selections chosen by Harris and his comments fully covers his Atlantic years. The discs include his huge singles "Exodus" and "Love Theme from *The Sandpiper* ("The Shadow of Your Smile"), plus soul-jazz numbers like "Get on Down," "Funkaroma," and "1974 Blues"; his most famous single composition "Freedom Jazz Dance"; and his remakes of "Giant Steps" and "Love for Sale." Harris has creatively utilized the varitone attachment on his saxophone and the reed trumpet, while constructing and playing his blues, soul, and funk solos with zest and a modicum of gimmickry. This set equals the Dr. John, Rahsaan Roland Kirk, and David "Fathead" Newman collections as the most representative and inclusive of the Atlantic packages issued thus far. —*Ron Wynn*

○ **Excursions** / Atlantic
A very underrated, two-record live set with some of Harris's best acoustic and electric sax solos. —*Ron Wynn*

Gene Harris (Eugene Harris)

b. Sep. 1, 1933, Benton Harbor, MI
Piano / Hard bop, blues & jazz
Pianist Gene Harris has been undervalued because of a lack of flash, hype, or reputation. A tasty, blues-influenced player, he formed the Sounds in 1957 and was an immediate hit, with a string of nice albums on Blue Note and Verve. The group became the Three Sounds in 1958 and were a precursor to other, more

lightweight groups like the Ramsey Lewis Trio. They performed and recorded standards, pop-R&B, and soft-jazz. Harris had other credentials besides the Three Sounds, recording with Nat Adderley, Lou Donaldson, and Stanley Turrentine. Harris has continued doing trio and small-combo dates for Concord in the '80s and '90s. He's an inventive and resourceful player, fine accompanist, and above-average soloist. —*Ron Wynn*

● **Feelin' Good** / **i.** 1959 / Blue Note
Prototypical Three Sounds release. Elements of funk, soul-jazz, and blues merge into a workable jazz concept. —*Ron Wynn*

★ **Live at Otter Crest** / Apr. 24, 1981 / Bosco 4
Underrated latter-period Harris on piano with trio. Great extended "Battle Hymn," Basie's repertoire represented in "Shiny Stockings" and "Ate" and your reliable Harris's "A Little Blues There" included. —*Michael G. Nastos*

○ **At Last** / May 1990 / Concord Jazz 4434
Harris-Hamilton Quintet. A wonderful teamup of Gene Harris with Scott Hamilton's band. CD version has two bonus cuts. —*Ron Wynn*

○ **Black and Blue** / **i.** Oct. 25, 1991 / Concord Jazz 4482
Pianist Gene Harris's church-oriented funk and rhythmic stamp is on everything, whether musician's tunes—a half dozen here—or standards. He straight-fours Stevie Wonder's "Another Star" and funk-a-fies the Fats Waller classic "Black and Blue." Guitarist Ron Eschete gets a particularly good airing on "C.C. Rider," the traditional line, done medium up, but no less soulful. —*Arnold Jay Smith, Jazz Times*

Donald Harrison (Donald "Duck" Harrison)

b. Jun. 23, 1960, New Orleans
Alto, soprano sax / Neo-bop
One of the stalwart talents among the "young lions" class, saxophonist Donald Harrison emerged while a member of Art Blakey's Jazz Messengers in the '80s. Harrison studied under Ellis Marsalis and Alvin Batiste in New Orleans and went to Berklee in 1979. He played with Roy Haynes from 1980 to 1981 and with Jack McDuff in 1981 and then spent four years with Art Blakey from 1982 to 1986. Harrison worked in tandem with fellow New Orleans musician trumpeter Terence Blanchard from the mid-'80s until 1991. His best instrument is alto sax, but he's also become proficient on soprano and clarinet. Harrison's recorded lately for Candid.—*Ron Wynn*

● **For Art's Sake** / Nov. 1990 / Candid 79501
A tribute album to great drummer Art Blakey from onetime Jazz Messenger alto saxophonist Donald Harrison. This was one of the first sessions after Harrison and longtime partner trumpeter Terence Blanchard went their separate ways, and Harrison was working with new trumpeter Marlon Jordan and other young lions pianist Cyrus Chestnut, bassist Christian McBride, and drummer Carl Allen. The results would have made Blakey smile. —*Ron Wynn, AMG*

Antonio Hart

Sax / Neo-bop
Alto saxophonist Antonio Hart is part of the class of the '90s. He's recorded for RCA/Novus and also teamed with trumpeter Roy Hargrove. His playing shows the influence of Eric Dolphy and Cannonball Adderley and has power, confidence, and authority. Hart still needs seasoning but has shown more growth with recent releases, as well as a distinctive sound.—*Ron Wynn*

● **Don't You Know I Care** / **i.** 1992 / Novus 63142
Some beautiful ballads and surging uptempo songs done by alto saxophonist Antonio Hart on his '92 follow-up release to his '91 debut as a leader. Hart has the tone, style, and skill to be a star, and he hasn't succumbed to "young lion" publicity hype. He's aided by a cast that blends new players such as Gregory Hutchinson and Rodney Whitaker with veterans like Gary Bartz. —*Ron Wynn, AMG*

Billy Hart (William W. Hart)

b. Nov. 29, 1940, Washington D.C.
Drums / Hard bop
Drummer Billy Hart's been a strong contributor to many sessions in jazz-rock, mainstream, and even free situations. A self-taught player who made his debut with Shirley Horn, Hart has worked

with Jimmy Smith, Wes Montgomery, Eddie Harris, Pharoah Sanders, and Marian McPartland and spent three years in Herbie Hancock's band during the early '70s. Hart also played extensively with Stan Getz in the '70s and has either done recordings or performed with Miles Davis, Jimmie Rowles, Hal Galper, Clark Terry, Niels-Henning Orstead Pedersen, Lee Konitz, Chico Freeman, and many others. He coformed Colloquium III with fellow drummers Horacee Arnold and Freddie Waits and led percussion workshops at the New York Drummers' Collective. He's recorded as a leader for A&M and Gramavision. —*Ron Wynn and Michael G. Nastos*

● **Enchance** / Feb. 24, 1977-Mar. 3, 1977 / A&M 0818
A recording just at the edge of all-out. Powerful, pretty, and potent. All originals. An important document. —*Michael G. Nastos*

Johnny Hartman (John Maurice Hartman)

b. Jul. 3, 1923, Chicago, IL, **d.** Sep. 15, 1983, New York, NY
Vocals / Ballads & blues
A classic love-ballad and standards singer and heartthrob vocalist, Hartman studied piano and sang as a child, earning a vocal scholarship in 1939. He gained his first fame with Earl Hines in the '40s and then worked with Dizzy Gillespie before becoming a solo star. He never attained the notoriety of similar types like Billy Eckstine or Arthur Prysock, though his glorious voice was equal to theirs. His amazing early '60s collaboration with John Coltrane didn't get the fame it merited at the time. —*Ron Wynn*

★ **I Just Dropped by to Say Hello** / Oct. 9, 1963+Oct. 17, 1963 / MCA 39105

○ **Once in Every Life** / Aug. 11, 1980 / Bee Hive 7012
Johnny Hartman was the best, or certainly one of the best, mellow jazz singers. Considering all of Hartman's LPs made previous to this Bee Hive recording, he made two great ones: one with John Coltrane and Impulse, and another for Perception Records called *Today*. This record ranked with his best. It was vocal honey and beyond words. —*Bob Rusch, Cadence*

Hampton Hawes

b. Nov. 13, 1928, Los Angeles, CA, **d.** May 22, 1977, Los Angeles, CA
Piano / Hard bop
Pianist Hampton Hawes was a major member of the '50s West Coast movement. Hawes had his initial R&B experience with Big Jay McNeely as a teen, plus a brief time with Charlie Parker. He emerged as a prime player in a '50s trio with Red Mitchell, where his combination of crisp, precise solos and gospel-blues riffs and patterns paralleled the rise of funk sound in hard-bop. In the early '70s he took up electric piano and actually got more attention in session endeavors and tours with people like Joan Baez than among the jazz audience. Hawes made some brillant trio dates for Contemporary, and after his death Artists House released some poignant and exceptional duets he made with Charlie Haden.—*Ron Wynn*

○ **East/West Controversy, The** / Sep. 22, 1951 / Xanadu 104

○ **Hampton Hawes—Vol. 1** / Jun. 28, 1955 / Original Jazz Classics 638
Mid-'50s trio dates, with pianist Hampton Hawes in peak, robust form. He was then an invigorating soloist, whose runs, phrases, and lines were often remarkable and whose inventiveness and creativity as a composer were beginning to be noticed. —*Ron Wynn, AMG*

○ **All Night Session!—Vols. 1-3** / Nov. 12-13, 1956 / Contemporary 638
Hampton Hawes Quartet. Some wondrous, invigorating playing from everyone included, especially Hawes and Jim Hall (g). —*Ron Wynn*

○ **Four! Hampton Hawes!!!!** / Jan. 27, 1958 / Contemporary 165

★ **Seance, The** / Apr. 30, 1966-May 1, 1966 / Contemporary 455
There was an uneasy feeling given by pianist Hampton Hawes as he made little rips in his blues out of which tumbled skittering runs. Hawes's playing here proved more than a backdrop for one's thoughts and action; it drew one's attention to its ideas and body. This set was recorded live, over two days, at Mitchell's Studio Club, where the group had been gigging for most of a year. Hawes's trio and music with bassist Red Mitchell and drummer Don Bailey really had everything going for it, including a solid program of standards and excellent originals; superior sup-

port, especially from Mitchell; and swinging improvisation that was both inventive and accessible. —*Bob Rusch, Cadence*

★ **Challenge, The** / May 7-12, 1968 / Storyville 1013

☆ **Key for Two** / Jan. 1969 / Affinity

○ **Live at the Montmartre** / Sep. 2, 1971 / Arista 1020
What came across when Hampton Hawes played piano was his genuineness. And as this record indicated, he was still vital and changing. He did not create his own language in jazz, but he was a native and fluent speaker of the music, as were bassist Henry Franklin and drummer Michael Carvin. They recorded these five numbers in 1971 at Copenhagen's Cafe Montmartre and most of it sounded like a conversation in rhythm and melody between three friends. The influence of Coltrane and especially McCoy Tyner was present, but not in a mimicking way. Some of what Hawes was attempting then on acoustic piano oddly presaged what he was soon to implement on the Rhodes. —*Ira Steingroot, Down Beat*

★ **Blues for Walls** / Jan. 16-18, 1973 / Prestige 10060
Good, early '70s set with pianist Hampton Hawes mixing acoustic and electric keyboard numbers, playing with passion, although the material is uneven. He's backed by electric bassist Carol Kaye and tries to find a balance between the bop and West Coast style numbers he'd done in the past and more contemporary material. —*Ron Wynn, AMG*

○ **Live at the Jazz Showcase in Chicago** / Jun. 1973 / Enja 3099
Vol. 1. As fine as any trio set Hawes ever made, with Cecil McBee (b) and Roy Haynes (d). —*Ron Wynn*

Coleman Hawkins (Coleman Randoph Hawkins)

b. Nov. 21, 1904, St. Joseph, MO, **d.** May 19, 1969, New York, NY
Tenor sax / Swing, big band
After starting on piano and cello, Hawkins took up the saxophone at nine; seven years later, singer Mamie Smith picked him from a Kansas City theater pit band to join her touring Jazz Hounds, with whom he made his first records. In New York he was part of a group of freelance musicians who chose Fletcher Henderson to front them for an audition in 1923; they landed the job, and Hawkins stayed with Fletcher for a decade, becoming the leading stylist on his instrument in jazz—the first to create a viable vocabulary for the tenor. In 1934 British bandleader and promoter Jack Hylton invited him to Europe; he stayed until the late summer of 1939 and influenced a generation of European musicians. Back home, he recorded his two-chorus variations on "Body and Soul" and immediately reestablished his supremacy, which had been challenged by such comers as Chu Berry, Hershel Evans, and, notably, Lester Young. Hawk, or "Bean," as he was nicknamed, formed his own big band, but it was not a success, and he soon reverted to small groups. Among the musicians he hired on 52d Street before there was such a term as *bebop* were Thelonious Monk, Howard McGhee, and Dizzy Gillespie. Hawkins was the premier champion of the young modernists among established players, and they in turn admired and respected him. He was an early and permanent member of *Jazz at the Philharmonic* and often teamed with another JATP regular, Roy Eldridge, during the last two decades of his life. Not until his health began to deteriorate in the late '60s was Hawk ever less than a commanding presence on the bandstand, his tone alone a thing to marvel at, his harmonic knowledge unbeatable. —*Dan Morgenstern*

● **In Europe 1934/39** / **i.** Nov. 18, 1934-May 26, 1939 / Jazz Up 318-319
In 1934 Coleman Hawkins, after 11 years as the star soloist with Fletcher Henderson's pioneering jazz big band, was looking for other worlds to conquer. To satisfy his curiosity he traveled to Europe, and for the next five years he was a major celebrity overseas, returning to the United States only when World War II was about ready to start. This magnificent three-CD set contains every recording that the great tenor-saxophonist made in Europe, 71 in all (including alternate takes). Whether featured in London, Switzerland, Paris, or Holland, Hawkins dominates these recordings, which find him in a variety of settings, from duets with pianist Freddie Johnson to medium-sized bands. Benny Carter and Django Reinhardt also make a few notable appearances. This perfectly done set is highly recommended. —*Scott Yanow*

○ **Hawk in Holland** / **i.** Feb. 4, 1935-Apr. 26, 1937 / GNP 9003

This enjoyable LP finds Coleman Hawkins guesting with the Ramblers, a fine Dutch swing group, in 1935 and 1937. While pianist Freddie Johnson is the only other distinctive soloist (although Annie de Reuver contributes two haunting vocals), the Ramblers do an excellent job of accompanying their American guest on a variety of standards and a couple of Hawk's originals. The closer, "Something Is Gonna Give Me Away," finds the tenorman romping with just the rhythm section and is quite memorable. This material has since been reissued on CD. —*Scott Yanow*

● **Body and Soul** / **i.** Oct. 11, 1939-Jan. 20, 1956 / RCA Bluebird 5658
Much of the material on this two-LP set has since been reissued on CD but, one way or the other, this music (particularly the first 16 tracks) belongs in every serious jazz collection. In 1939 Coleman Hawkins returned to the United States after five years in Europe, and it took him very little time to reassert his prior dominance as king of the tenors. This set starts off with the session that resulted in Hawk's classic version of "Body and Soul," teams him with Benny Carter (on trumpet) for some hot swing (including a memorable rendition of "My Blue Heaven"), and then finds him using younger musicians (including trumpeter Fats Navarro and trombonist J.J. Johnson) on some advanced bop originals highlighted by "Half Step Down Please." The remainder of this set is also good but less historic with Hawkins' being well showcased with three larger groups in 1956, culminating in a remake of "Body and Soul." —*Scott Yanow*

○ **Commodore Years: The Tenor Sax** / May 25, 1940-Aug. 12, 1954 / Atlantic 2306
Coleman Hawkins was one of the first great jazz saxophonists and one of the undisputed giants in the music's history, a timeless musical Gibraltar. Hawkins's cuts on this anthology, which also included a number of tracks by saxophonist-flutist Frank Wess, were never less than excellent and often monumentally great on "I Surrender Dear," "I Can't Believe," and "Boff Boff." Everything was in evidence, including Hawkins's big, full tone, his aggressive attack, his harmonic and melodic genius, and his innate sense of structure. In addition, he was surrounded on both sides of this record (the first recorded in 1940, the second three years later) by brilliant sidemen. —*Peter Keepnews, Down Beat*

☆ **Big Three, The** / **i.** 1943-1946 / Doctor Jazz 40950
An album with Lester Young and Ben Webster. This is a 1990 reissue that spotlights classic '40s cuts of the three featured tenor stars. —*Ron Wynn*

● **Rainbow Mist** / **i.** Feb. 16, 1944-May 22, 1944 / Delmark 459
Coleman Hawkins was always an open-minded musician. A very advanced player even when he first emerged with Fletcher Henderson's orchestra in the 1920s, by the 1940s he may have been technically middle-aged but remained a young thinker. For his recording session of February 16, 1944, the great tenor invited some of the most promising younger players (including trumpeter Dizzy Gillespie, bassist Oscar Pettiford, and drummer Max Roach), and the result was the very first bebop on records. During their two sessions the large ensemble recorded six selections, including Gillespie's "Woody'n You," Hawk's "Disorder at the Border," and a new treatment of "Body and Soul" by the tenorman, which he retitled "Rainbow Mist." Also on this highly recommended CD are four titles matching the tenors of Hawkins, Ben Webster, and Georgie Auld (with trumpeter Charlie Shavers included as a bonus) and a session from Auld's big band, highlighted by Sonny Berman's trumpet solo on "Taps Miller." —*Scott Yanow*

○ **Bean and the Boys** / Oct. 19, 1944-Dec. 21, 1949 / Prestige 24124
This Prestige reissue collects Coleman Hawkins sessions from 1944, 1946, and 1959. The first seemingly bids farewell to the swing era with Jonah Jones, Walter Thomas, Hilton Jefferson, and Cozy Cole in a nicely homogeneous group. The second, also made for the Joe Davis label, introduced most of us to Thelonious Monk. The third, originally made for Sonora, puts Hawkins with Fats Navarro, J.J. Johnson, Milt Jackson, and Max Roach. The last was made by the Prestige Blues Swingers, an idiomatically mixed bunch notable for Ray Bryant on piano and, of course, the tenor player. The set is valuable in showing how Hawkins met challenges of the '40s and '50s. —*Stanley Dance, Jazz Times*

★ **Coleman Hawkins on Keynote** / 1944 / PolyGram 830960

○ **Hollywood Stampede** / i. Feb. 23, 1945-Mar. 9, 1945 / Capitol 92596

Coleman Hawkins led one of his finest bands in 1945, a sextet with the fiery trumpeter Howard McGhee that fell somewhere between small-group swing and bebop. This CD contains all of that group's 12 recordings, including memorable versions of "Rifftide" and "Stuffy"; trombonist Vic Dickenson guests on four tracks. This CD concludes with one of Hawkins' rarest sessions, an Aladdin date from 1947 that finds the veteran tenor leading a septet that includes 20-year-old trumpeter Miles Davis. Recommended. —*Scott Yanow*

○ **Hawk in Paris** / i. Jul. 9, 1956-Jul. 13, 1956 / Bluebird 51059

This CD is a major surprise. Coleman Hawkins had always wanted to record with a large string section, and he got his wish on the majority of these 12 romantic melodies, all of which have some association with Paris. The surprise is that Hawkins plays with a great deal of fire (his double-timing on "My Man" is wondrous), and that Manny Albam's arrangements mostly avoid being muzaky and quite often are creative and witty. What could have been a novelty or an insipid affair is actually one of Coleman Hawkins's more memorable albums. Recommended. —*Scott Yanow*

○ **Hawk Flies High, The** / Mar. 12+15, 1957 / Riverside 027

The Hawk Flies High found tenor saxophonist Coleman Hawkins in the front line company of the boppers J.J. Johnson, Idrees Sulieman, Hank Jones, Oscar Pettiford, Jo Jones, and Galbraith (no first name given). While perhaps not at his most distinctive, he was neverthelesss up to any demands and received from Johnson and Sulieman inspired performances. The entire session was also issued as part of a twofer set. —*Bob Rusch, Cadence*

○ **High and Mighty Hawk** / i. Feb. 18, 1958-Feb. 19, 1958 / Affinity 163

Although Coleman Hawkins had been a major tenor stylist for over 35 years by the time of this recording, he had never felt all that comfortable playing blues, preferring to dig his harmonic talents into more complicated material. For one of the first times on the lengthy "Bird of Prey Blues" that opens this LP, Hawkins showed that at last he had mastered the blues. His honking and roaring improvisation, although more sophisticated than the usual solos by R&B tenors, captured its spirit and extroverted emotions perfectly. It is the highlight of this otherwise excellent (if more conventional) quintet session with trumpeter Buck Clayton and pianist Hank Jones. —*Scott Yanow*

★ **In a Mellow Tone** / 1958-1961 / Prestige 6001

A superior session with Hawkins, Eddie "Lockjaw" Davis (ts), and others. —*Ron Wynn*

○ **At the Bayou Club** / i. Jan. 1959 / Honeysuckle Rose 5002

Coleman Hawkins teams up with his frequent musical partner trumpeter Roy Eldridge for a fairly heated set of music. On the first of two LPs from this particular gig, Hawk and Roy jam on "Bean and the Boys," "How High the Moon," "Basin Street Blues," "Vignette," and a ballad medley. The two veterans always brought out the best in each other, and this fine LP has its share of explosive moments. —*Scott Yanow*

○ **At the Bayou Club, Vol. 2** / i. Jan. 1959 / Honeysuckle Rose 5006

The second of two LPs from this particular engagement once again teams the great veterans Coleman Hawkins and trumpeter Roy Eldridge. Tenor legend Hawkins explores "Body and Soul" again (his many interpretations were always different from the previous ones), and the duo (backed by a fine local rhythm section) jams happily on such numbers as "Blue Lou," "Soft Winds," and "Just You, Just Me." Although no longer pacesetters, Hawkins and Eldridge remained creative and exciting until the end; they were still in their prime for this fine session. —*Scott Yanow*

○ **Dali** / i. 1959-May 1962 / Stash 538

This Stash CD, despite some silly graphics on the liners, has quite a bit of rewarding music. There are three examples of the fireworks that generally occurred when tenor-saxophonist Coleman Hawkins and trumpeter Roy Eldridge met (taken from a live session in 1959), while the remainder of this disc finds Hawk playing in Brussels in 1962. The veteran tenor is particularly strong on "Disorder at the Border" and "Rifftide" but the highpoint is a rare unaccompanied solo on "Dali," the fourth and final time that Hawkins recorded an improvisation by himself. It is a pity that he never recorded an entire album like that! —*Scott Yanow*

○ **Duke Ellington Meets Coleman Hawkins** / Aug. 18, 1962 / Impulse 26

Amid the recent flood of reissues, this is an album to be savored. It took roughly 20 years for jazz giants Duke Ellington and Coleman Hawkins to get into the studio together from the time Ellington first proposed this small group session until it happened in 1962. It was worth the wait. Hawkins's swinging, full-bodied tenor added to the Ellington ensemble sound, his distinctive tone fitting like a warm glove. —*Ken Franckling, Jazz Times*

★ **Desafinado: Bossa Nova and Jazz Samba** / Sep. 12+16, 1962 / MCA 33118

This set seems to have the word *fad* written all over it, but surprisingly it is a major success. During the era when everyone was trying to cash in on the popularity of bossa nova, tenor great Coleman Hawkins recorded eight selections with a group consisting of two guitars, bass, and three percussionists. In addition to a classic version of "O Pato" and such typical songs as "Desafinado" and "One Note Samba," Hawkins and company even turn "I'm Looking over a Four Leaf Clover" into a strong bossa. Although this straight CD reissue of a former LP is a bit brief, the music is highly enjoyable. —*Scott Yanow*

○ **Wrapped Tight** / i. Feb. 22, 1965-Mar. 1, 1965 / Impulse 109

Coleman Hawkins's last strong recording finds the veteran tenor saxophonist, 43 years after his recording debut with Mamie Smith's Jazz Hounds, improvising creatively on a wide variety of material on this CD, ranging from "Intermezzo" and "Here's That Rainy Day" to "Red Roses for a Blue Lady" and "Indian Summer." Best is an adventurous version of "Out of Nowhere" that shows that the veteran tenor-saxophonist was still coming up with new ideas in 1965. —*Scott Yanow*

○ **Re-Evaluations: The Impulse Years** / Impulse 9258

Anthology album containing selections by tenor sax great Coleman Hawkins from albums he cut for the Impulse label in the early and mid-'60s. It includes performances with Duke Ellington, Oliver Nelson, and Benny Carter, plus Afro-Latin and bossa nova tracks. —*Ron Wynn, AMG*

Erskine Hawkins (Erskine Ramsey Hawkins)

b. Jul. 26, 1914, Birmingham, AL, d. 1993
Trumpet, bandleader / Swing, big band

Erskine Hawkins was a trumpeter and bandleader of one of the greatest Southern swing bands. Hawkins, who began playing trumpet at 13 and was an immediate Louis Armstrong devotee, formed a band from a college group based at Alabama State Teacher's College. The orchestra, which came to New York in 1934 and eventually replaced Chick Webb's band at the Savoy after Webb's death, was a textbook romping, stomping swing aggregation, with crowd-pleasing songs and top performances. They traveled throughout the South from their New York base during the '40s and recorded for Vocation from the mid '30s. Their big hits included "Tuxedo Junction," "Tippin' In," and "Somebody's Rocking My Dreamboat." Hawkins, a ferocious, accomplished trumpeter, continued as a combo leader and player into the late '70s. —*Ron Wynn*

☆ **Jazz Heritage: Tuxedo Junction** / i. 1950-1960 / MCA 1361

This includes 1950 big-band and 1960 quintet recordings. Contrast the title track between the two groups. —*Michael G. Nastos*

Louis Hayes (Louis Sedell Hayes)

b. May 31, 1937, Detroit, MI
Drums / Hard bop

A topflight hard bop drummer who's been a vital member of many major bands, Louis Hayes numbers just below Art Blakey and Philly Joe Jones in the genre's pantheon. He's especially adept at pushing the beat and driving a combo. He was a bandleader in Detroit by 16 and, after moving to New York, replaced Art Taylor in Horace Silver's quintet in 1956. Hayes joined Cannonball Adderley in 1959, remaining until 1965, when he succeeded Ed Thigpen in Oscar Peterson's trio. After a two-year stint, Hayes began heading his own groups. He also played with Joe Henderson, Freddie Hubbard, and James Spaulding before rejoining Peterson in 1971. A year later, Hayes formed a sextet that was co-led initially by Junior Cook and later by Woody Shaw. Hayes continued as group leader after Shaw's departure. He's maintained a full schedule as a session player through the '80s and '90s. —*Ron Wynn and Michael G. Nastos*

★ **Real Thing, The** / **i.** May 20, 1977 / Muse 5125
His best band, with Woody Shaw (tpt), Rene McLean (sax), and Slide Hampton (tb). All originals, all excellent. —*Michael G. Nastos*

Tubby Hayes (Edward Brian Hayes)

b. Jan. 30, 1935, London, England, **d.** Jun. 8, 1973, London
Tenor sax, flute, vibes, composer / Swing, bop
Tenor saxophonist Tubby Hayes was among the finest European jazz musicians of all time. He was a professional at 15, working in various big bands led by Kenny Baker, Vic Lewis, and Jack Parnell, among others. Hayes toured England with his own octet in the mid-'50s. He started playing vibes a year later and co-led the Jazz Couriers with Ronnie Scott from 1957 to 1959. During the early and mid-'60s, he became a featured soloist at several clubs in America and had a regular television show in England from 1961 to 1963. A superior soloist and arranger, Hayes made two recordings heading American bands that included the likes of Clark Terry, Rahsaan Roland Kirk, and James Moody. —*Ron Wynn*

★ **New York Sessions** / Oct. 3-04, 1961 / Columbia 45446
Tubby Hayes (U.K. tenor man) blows strong with Clark Terry (tpt). A sleeper. —*Michael G. Nastos*

○ **Tubby the Tenor** / Oct. 3-04, 1961 / Epic 16023

○ **Introducing Tubbs** / **i.** Mar. 1962 / Epic 16019

○ **For Members Only** / **i.** Jan. 1967-Oct. 1967 / Mastermix 10

Roy Haynes (Roy Owen Haynes)

b. Mar. 13, 1926, Roxbury, Mass.
Drums / Bop, hard bop
Sometimes a light sound can be as attention-grabbing and definitive as a bombastic one, and that's been Roy Haynes's trademark as a drummer. Though he's every bit as inventive, steady, and capable as any other percussionist, Roy Haynes has not played with the volume or power of other well-known bop stars such as Max Roach or Art Blakey. Haynes worked in Boston with the Sabby Lewis band, as well as with Frankie Newton and Pete Brown in the '40s, before touring with Luis Russell from 1945 to 1947 and the Lester Young sextet from 1947 to 1949. After stints with Kai Winding and Bud Powell, Haynes joined Charlie Parker's band from 1949 to 1950 and later worked with Wardell Gray and Stan Getz. He was Sarah Vaughan's regular drummer for five years in the mid-'50s and spent time with Miles Davis, Lee Konitz, and Thelonious Monk before heading his own bands. In the '60s, Haynes split time between his groups and periods with George Shearing, Lennie Tristano, Kenny Burrell, Getz, John Coltrane, and Gary Burton. Perhaps his most heralded band in recent years was the wonderful Hip Ensemble of the early '70s, whose roster included George Adams on tenor sax and Hannibal Marvin Peterson on trumpet. —*Ron Wynn*

★ **We Three** / Nov. 14, 1958 / New Jazz 196
A wonderful session, with spectacular piano by Phineas Newborn and great bass from Paul Chambers. —*Ron Wynn*

★ **Out of the Afternoon** / May 16+23, 1962 / Impulse 23
Definitive creative music with Roland Kirk (reeds) and Tommy Flanagan (p). —*Michael G. Nastos*

★ **Hip Ensemble** / 1971 / Mainstream
This explosive session helped cement the reputations of George Adams (ts) and Hannibal Marvin Peterson (tpt). —*Ron Wynn*

J.C. Heard (James Charles Heard)

b. Oct. 8, 1917
Drums / Swing, big band
An influential and excellent swing drummer, J.C. Heard was featured in many Jazz at the Philharmonic sessions and worked with numerous musicians and groups during the '40s and '50s. A one-time dancer and vaudeville performer, Heard moved from Detroit to New York in 1919 and later joined Teddy Wilson's big band. Heard subsequently played in Wilson's sextet and worked with Benny Carter and Coleman Hawkins. He played in Cab Calloway's band in the mid-'40s and participated in early bebop sessions. Heard also played with Erroll Garner. Besides the JATP duties, Heard performed in Japan, Australia, and Europe in the

'50s. He returned to Detroit in 1966 and still works there, playing and leading a combo and drumming in a big band. Heard's also done many festivals. —*Ron Wynn and Michael G. Nastos*

★ **This Is Me, J.C.** / 1958 / Argo 633

○ **Some of This, Someof That** / **i.** 1986 / Hiroko 187
Master drummer leads 13-piece band. Loads of blues and modern jazz along with some goofy fun and solid musicianship. Fine "Nica's Dream" and "Sweet Love of Mine, Sweet Samantha." Heard vocalizes frequently on this album, which features trumpeter Walt Szymanski. —*Michael G. Nastos*

Jimmy Heath (James Edward Heath)

b. Oct. 25, 1926
Sax, flute / Bop, hard bop
Tenor, alto, and soprano saxophonist and flutist Jimmy Heath's nickname "Little Bird" is a tip-off to his array of talents. A superb soloist whose facility rivals his creativity, Heath actually stopped playing alto for much of his career to establish a reputation and style on tenor, where he's one of the great hard bop players. Yet he played alto with Nat Towles and Howard McGhee in the '40s, led his own big band in Philadelphia in 1948-1949, and joined Dizzy Gillespie in 1949-1950. A gifted writer and arranger, Heath penned tunes for Miles Davis, Chet Baker, and Art Blakey in the '50s and later arranged for Milt Jackson, Davis, Kenny Dorham, Art Farmer, and Gil Evans in the late '50s and '60s. In addition, he cut his own dates. He formed the Heath Brothers group with bassist Percy and drummer Albert. He continues to be successful as a player, composer and arranger.—*Ron Wynn—-*

○ **Nice People** / Dec. 1959-1964 / Riverside 6006

★ **Gap Sealer, The** / Mar. 1, 1972 / Cobblestone
Some of Heath's finest, most aggressive playing. He is a standout on soprano, flute, and tenor. —*Ron Wynn*

★ **Peer Pleasure** / Feb. 1987 / Landmark 1514
A smooth session with sharp work from Heath. As usual, it has fine compositions. The CD has a bonus cut. —*Ron Wynn*

Neal Hefti

b. Oct. 29, 1922, Hastings, NE
Composer, arranger, trumpet / Swing, big band
An acclaimed arranger, Neal Hefti wrote and arranged numerous songs for Count Basie and many other bands. He's known for inventive, catchy charts that manage to be both popular and challenging, never losing their swinging quality, yet avoiding clichés. Hefti wrote his first arrangements in high school, and later worked as both trumpeter and arranger for Charlie Barnet, Earl Hines, Charlie Spivak, and Horace Heidt before joining Woody Herman in the mid-'40s. He updated their "Woodchopper's Ball" themes and also arranged "The Good Earth," "Wildroot," and "Northwest Passage," among others. After doing arrangements for Charlie Ventura and Harry James, Hefti joined Basie in 1950 and remained over a decade, contributing numerous classic charts. He worked for both the octet and big band; some Hefti gems include "Little Pony," "Lil' Darlin," "Splanky," and virtually everything from the album *The Atomic Mr. Basie.* Hefti, a trumpeter and pianist in addition to being an arranger and composer, led his own bands at times and served as music director for his wife, Frances Wayne. During the '60s, Hefti did some studio work, contributing to the 1962 Frank Sinatra Reprise sessions, some with Basie. He later became a successful television arranger, writing the themes for the "Barefoot in the Park" and "Odd Couple" shows (as well as the films) and "Batman." Hefti toured and gave lectures through the '70s. He recorded a few albums as a leader for Jazz Scene, Coral, and Epic. His arrangements and compositions are heard on many landmark Count Basie and Woody Herman discs. —*Ron Wynn*

● **Neil Hefti** / RCA 3573

Julius Hemphill

b. 1940, Forth Worth, TX
Alto sax / Modern creative
A topflight alto saxophonist from Fort Worth, TX, Hemphill got his start in St. Louis in the late '60s, when he was a member of the Black Artists Group (BAG). He played with Anthony Braxton and became known for a pungent, soaring alto style with equal parts blues, free, bop, and soul during the '70s. He was a co-

founder of the World Saxophone Quartet in 1977 and has done other types of recording in eclectic formats. His big band included many top players and jumped all over the stylistic board in a manner similar to most Hemphill sessions. Though plagued by health problems in recent years, Hemphill continues composing and has done some conducting and occasional recordings when possible. —*Ron Wynn*

★ **Dogon A.D.** / **i.** Feb. 1972 / Freedom 1028
Between the moment cellist Abdul Wadud and drummer Phillip Wilson interlocked to establish the slow, portentous rhythm of "Dogon A.D." and the last fluted notes of the lovely, gravely dancing theme of "The Painter," there were nearly 40 minutes of magical music. Magical because it is at once exhilirating and peaceful. Every bit as remarkable as the compositional synthesis (and related to it) was the merging of these four players into one. —*Joel Ray, Cadence*

○ **Coon Bid'ness** / **i.** Jan. 29, 1975 / Freedom 1012
Side one of this album was recorded in 1975 and found Julius Hemphill's interests lying elsewhere, borrowing somewhat from Anthony Braxton. The four tracks actually broke quite easily into a pair of two-section pieces, both of which explored the careful dissection of ensemble writing through the gradual prismification of textures and harmonies. Hemphill's major label debut struck a rich balance between his modern, somewhat academic concepts and the rarefied funk of years past. —*Neil Tesser, Down Beat*

★ **Roi Boye and the Gotham Minstrels** / **i.** Mar. 1, 1977 / Sackville 15
Psychotheater drama in the form of the free African-American creative-jazz movement at its height. —*Michael G. Nastos*

○ **Raw Materials and Residuals** / **i.** 1977 / Black Saint 0015

○ **Georgia Blues** / Aug. 1984 / Minor Music 003

★ **Julius Hemphill Big Band** / Feb. 1988 / Elektra 60831
A 16-piece progressive big band with lots of saxophones. Good dose of Bill Frisell and Jack Watkins on guitar. Trumpets Rasul Siddik and David Hines are outstanding. —*Michael G. Nastos*

○ **Fat Man and the Hard Blues** / **i.** Jul. 1991 / Black Saint 1201152
The Fat Man and the Hard Blues is a selection of sax-sextet shorties that includes one piece from *Long Tongues*, his saxophone opera, several from a collaboration with choreographer Bill T. Jones, the classic Julius Hemphill gemstone "The Hard Blues," and plenty more. —*John Corbett, Down Beat*

○ **Live from the New Music Cafe** / **i.** 1992 / Music & Arts 731

Fletcher Henderson (Fletcher Hamilton Henderson, Jr.)

b. Dec. 18, 1897, Cuthbert, GA, **d.** Dec. 29, 1952, New York, NY
Bandleader, arranger, piano / Swing, big band
Though he came to New York from Georgia to do graduate work in chemistry, Henderson's aptitude at the piano led him into a musical career, first as house-band leader for Black Swan (the first African-American-owned record label), then as accompanist for singer Ethel Waters. He was chosen by a group of recording musicians to front them for an audition. Henderson presided over an array of musical talent that remained unmatched during the '20s: Louis Armstrong, Coleman Hawkins, Benny Carter, Don Redman, Jimmy Harrison, Buster Bailey, Rex Stewart, and many others graced his band, which made its home at the Roseland Ballroom in Manhattan and recorded hundreds of sides. Though his main reputation is as an arranger, Fletcher did not begin to write until the early '30s; before that, Redman and Carter, among others, created the band's book. Once he took pen in hand, however, Fletcher quickly mastered the new idiom of swing and had a major role in the success of Benny Goodman's newly formed band. (In 1934, when Goodman started, Fletcher's men deserted him, and he was without a regular band for six months.) Though his arrangements were noted for their difficult keys, they were phrased in a manner that practically made the notes swing. Fletcher's last great band, in 1936, had much of its book written by his younger brother Horace, who also was a better pianist. It included such new stars as Roy Eldridge, Chu Berry, and Sid Catlett. By 1939 Fletcher was staff arranger and band pianist for Goodman, who helped him start another band in 1941; he hung in until the end of the decade. By 1949 Fletcher led a sextet. In his best charts, such as "King Porter Stomp" and "Sometimes I'm Happy," Fletcher Henderson gave big-band swing a very special lilt. —*Dan Morgenstern*

★ **Study in Frustration, A** / **i.** Aug. 7, 1923-May 28, 1938 / Columbia
Although still available only as a four-LP set, this is easily the definitive Fletcher Henderson package. Between 1923 and 1938, Henderson's orchestra was one of the finest swing bands in the world, and during 1923-1927 (until Duke Ellington's emergence) it was the first and the best. The arrangements of Don Redman in the early days set the pace for jazz; Benny Carter and Horace Henderson also wrote some important charts before Fletcher himself finally developed into a major arranger in 1932. This Columbia set is not "complete" but it includes 64 selections, at least 60 of them gems! This essential box (which contains three wonderful versions of "King Porter Stomp") belongs in everyone's jazz collection. —*Scott Yanow*

○ **Henderson Pathes** / **i.** Nov. 1923-Feb. 1925 / Fountain 112

☆ **Fletcher Henderson and the Dixie Stompers 1925-1928** / **i.** Nov. 23, 1925-Apr. 6, 1928 / Swing
One of the main pseudonyms that Fletcher Henderson used while recording illegally for rival record labels was The Dixie Stompers, and all of their 33 recordings are included on this superlative two-LP set. —*Scott Yanow*

○ **Fletcher Henderson (1925-1926)** / Nov. 23, 1925-Apr. 14, 1926 / Classics 610
The Classics series has undergone the admirable task of reissuing on CD in chronological order every selection (although no alternate takes) of Fletcher Henderson's orchestra. This set finds the post-Armstrong edition of this pacesetting big band swinging hard on a variety of standards and obscurities. With cornetist Joe Smith, trombonist Charlie Green, clarinetist Buster Bailey, and tenor great Coleman Hawkins contributing many fine solos and Don Redman's often-innovative arrangements inspiring the musicians, at this period Fletcher Henderson's orchestra had no close competitors among jazz-oriented big bands. Even the weaker pop tunes (like "I Want to See a Little More of What I Saw in Arkansas") have their strong moments. —*Scott Yanow*

☆ **Fletcher Henderson (1926-1927)** / Apr. 14, 1926-Jan. 22, 1927 / Classics 597
This CD, in Classics' chronological series, which captures the Fletcher Henderson orchestra at its peak, is overloaded with classics: "Jackass Blues," "The Stampede" (which has a very influential tenor solo by Coleman Hawkins), "Clarinet Marmalade," "Snag It," and "Tozo," among others. In addition to Coleman Hawkins, Tommy Ladnier emerges as a major trumpeter, and Fats Waller drops by for his "Henderson . . . Stomp." Eight years before the official beginning of the swing era, Fletcher Henderson's orchestra was outswinging everyone. —*Scott Yanow*

☆ **Complete Fletcher Henderson (1927-1936), The** / Mar. 11, 1927-Aug. 4, 1936 / RCA/Bluebird 5507
Complete is in this case a relative term, meaning every recording by Fletcher Henderson's orchestra owned by RCA/Bluebird rather than every record he made during this period. A perfectly done two-LP set, these 34 songs include three from 1927 (featuring trumpeters Tommy Ladnier and Joe Smith at their best), 12 varying sides from 1931-1932 (during which tenor-saxophonist Coleman Hawkins and trumpeters Rex Stewart and Bobby Stark make even the most commercial material into worthwhile music), a session from 1934 with trumpeter Red Allen, and 15 numbers from 1936 that costar trumpeter Roy Eldridge and Chu Berry on tenor. Throughout the consistent high quality of the solos and the musicianship (even with some off moments) makes one regret that this classic orchestra was not more commercially successful. —*Scott Yanow*

☆ **Fletcher Henderson (1927)** / Mar. 11, 1927-Oct. 24, 1927 / Classics 580
Fletcher Henderson's orchestra was at the peak of its powers during this period, as can be heard on such torrid recordings as "Fidgety Feet," "Sensation," "St. Louis Shuffle," and "Hop Off"; even the overly complex Don Redman arrangement "Whiteman Stomp" (which Paul Whiteman's musicians apparently had trouble learning) is no problem for this brilliant orchestra. Classics' chronological reissue of Henderson's valuable recordings on this CD covers the many highpoints of the peak year of 1927; only Duke Ellington's orchestra was on the level of this pacesetting big band. —*Scott Yanow*

○ **Hocus Pocus: Classic Big Band Jazz** / **i.** Apr. 27, 1927-Aug. 4, 1936 / RCA 9904

Highpoints include "St. Louis Shuffle," "Variety Stomp," "Sugar Foot Stomp," the swinging title cut, examples of early Roy Eldridge trumpet, and "Strangers," which contrasts a horrendous vocal with some inspired Coleman Hawkins tenor. —*Scott Yanow*

○ **Fletcher Henderson (1927-1931)** / Nov. 4, 1927-Feb. 5, 1931 / Classics 572

With its high musicianship and many talented soloists (including trumpeters Rex Stewart and Bobby Stark, trombonist Jimmy Harrison, Coleman Hawkins on tenor, and altoist Benny Carter), the Fletcher Henderson should have prospered during this period, but unaccountably its leader (never a strong businessman) seemed to be losing interest in the band's fortunes and made several bad decisions. The result is that by 1931 Henderson's orchestra was struggling, while Duke Ellington's was becoming a household name. This Classics CD, in covering over three years, demonstrates how few recordings this band was making (only four songs apiece in both 1929 and 1930) although the quality largely makes up for the quantity. The original band version of "King Porter Stomp" and an explosive "Oh Baby" are the highpoints of this satisfying collection. —*Scott Yanow*

○ **Fletcher Henderson (1929-1937)** / **i.** May 1929-Sep. 1937 / BBC 682

☆ **Fletcher Henderson (1931)** / Feb. 5, 1931-Jul. 31, 1931 / Classics 555

Even with such strong players as trumpeters Bobby Stark and Rex Stewart, trombonist Benny Morton, and tenor saxophonist Coleman Hawkins, the fortunes of Fletcher Henderson's orchestra were slipping during 1931. With the departure of Don Redman several years earlier, the group's arrangements were less innovative, and the pressure was on to perform commercial songs for the Depression audience. Even the jazz standards (such as "Tiger Rag" and "After You've Gone") are less interesting than those of their competitors, although this new version of "Sugar Foot Stomp" is a classic, and the strong solos by the all-star cast makes this CD well worth acquiring. —*Scott Yanow*

☆ **Fletcher Henderson (1932-1934)** / Dec. 9, 1932-Sep. 12, 1934 / Classics 535

Although the Fletcher Henderson orchestra was struggling and missing opportunities during this era, its recordings greatly improved from the ones in 1931. Henderson had finally developed into a top arranger (as can be heard on "Honeysuckle Rose" and "Wrappin' It Up"), the band was full of top soloists (trumpeter Bobby Stark has his greatest moments on "The New King Porter Stomp"), and even if Coleman Hawkins chose to move to Europe (after starring on "It's the Talk of the Town") the band should have been poised to flourish in the swing era. These recordings (from Classics' complete chronological program) prove that swing did not begin with Benny Goodman in 1935. —*Scott Yanow*

○ **Big Bands (1933), The** / 1933 / Prestige 7645

○ **Fletcher Henderson (1934-1937)** / Sep. 25, 1934-Mar. 2, 1937 / Classics 527

In early 1935 Fletcher Henderson broke up his classic orchestra, but a year later, with the success of so many other big bands, he formed a new ensemble. This Classics CD includes four songs from 1934, Henderson's entire output from 1936, and his first recording of 1937. The main difference between the two units is that the later one boasted the trumpet of Roy Eldridge and tenor solos from Coleman Hawkins's potential successor Chu Berry. "Christopher Columbus" became a hit, as did the band's new theme song ("Stealin' Apples"), but the brief bit of glory would not last. However Henderson's brand of swing music still sounds fresh today, and this CD is easily recommended. —*Scott Yanow*

Joe Henderson (Joseph A. Henderson)

b. Apr. 24, 1937, Lima, Ohio
Tenor, soprano sax, flute, composer / Bop, hard bop

Tenor saxophonist Joe Henderson hit the big time in the '90s. He's been long admired by musicians but was generally unknown outside the jazz sphere for many years. Henderson's looping lines; mournful, passionate ballad playing; and often fiery solos with strategic wails and cries are always done tastefully and with swing and verve. Henderson's initial fame came when he headed a band with trumpeter Kenny Dorham from 1962 to 1963. He was then part of Horace Silver's band from 1964 to 1966 and co-

led the Jazz Communicators with Freddie Hubbard from 1967 to 1968. Henderson was in Herbie Hancock's sextet from 1969 to 1970 and then had a highly publicized but short-lived stint with Blood, Sweat & Tears in 1971. Since then he's mainly headed his own bands and also has been active as an educator. He was part of the group who helped relaunch Blue Note Records in 1985, but his 1992 album *Lush Life* thrust him into the spotlight. —*Ron Wynn*

○ **Our Thing** / Sep. 9, 1963 / Blue Note 84152

A wonderful 1986 reissue of a prime 1963 date. The lineup is amazing, with Andrew Hill (p) and Kenny Dorham (tpt). CD has a bonus cut. —*Ron Wynn*

○ **In 'n Out** / Apr. 10, 1964 / Blue Note 46510

An early '60s Blue Note classic by tenor saxophonist Joe Henderson. This was one of his first albums as a leader, and it was distinguished by numerous swirling, dynamic solos, the usual first-rate engineering job by Rudy Van Gelder, and fine compositions and arrangements. —*Ron Wynn, AMG*

○ **Inner Urge** / Nov. 30, 1964 / Blue Note 84189

A 1989 reissue of another in his line of great Blue Notes from the '60s. —*Ron Wynn*

★ **Mode for Joe** / Jan. 27, 1966 / Blue Note 84227

☆ **Elements, The** / Oct. 15+17, 1973 / Milestone

Ambitious concept work gets an ethereal feeling via Alice Coltrane's harp. —*Ron Wynn*

Barcelona / Jun. 2, 1977 / Enja 3037

Recently released, tremendous, frenzied trio date by tenor saxophonist Joe Henderson, with bassist Wayne Darling and drummer Ed Soph. After many years of obscurity, Henderson has become famous in the last few years. But the whirling lines, huge tone, and astonishing solos that he routinely offers on this album have been prized by jazz fans since the early '60s. —*Ron Wynn*

○ **Mirror, Mirror** / Jan. 1980 / PA/USA 7075

Even when tenor saxophonist Joe Henderson's approach was low key, his array of ideas was stunning. Pianist Chick Corea, bassist Ron Carter, and drummer Billy Higgins provided sympathetic support throughout but did not really ignite until "Keystone," Carter's goofy, Thelonious Monkish blues, and "Bolero." —*Arthur Moorehead, Down Beat*

○ **Live at the Village Vanguard—Vol. 2: State of The Tenor** / Nov. 14-15, 1985 / Blue Note 46296

Comparison with Sonny Rollins's *A Night at the Village Vanguard*, recorded in 1957, is inevitable. Rollins is more melody oriented, Henderson more rhythm oriented. Where Rollins bursts into bel canto, Henderson becomes a drummer. . . . This album goes down better in small doses—one tune at a time, and then take a break. Otherwise, you could overdose on tedium. It's a heavy album. The state of the tenor is a drum kit. No tenorman matches Henderson's rhythmic variety. —*Owen Cordle, Jazz Times*

○ **Evening With, An** / Jul. 1987 / Red 123215

Recorded at the 1987 Genoa Jazz Festival (and well reproduced on that country's Red Record label), tenor saxophonist Joe Henderson's full-bodied, go-for-broke approach was still intact on *An Evening with Joe Henderson*. . . . Bassist Charlie Haden (Al Foster, drums) got some marvelously long outings as well and moved things along with finesse and flair. This album makes a fine companion to the Blue Notes and on that basis alone can be recommended. —*Miles Jordan, Jazz Times*

○ **Standard Joe, The** / Mar. 1991 / Red 123248

Joe Henderson breathes new life, ferocity, and humor into the familiar repertorial turf of "Blue Bossa," "Take The 'A' Train," and "Round Midnight. " He serves up 25 minutes worth of spontaneous observations on that tenor saxist's chestnut "Body and Soul" and realizes the meaning of the title of his own classic, "Inner Urge." —*Josef Woodard, Down Beat*

★ **Lush Life** / **i.** 1992 / Verve 511779

With his first recording for the Verve label, tenor saxophonist Joe Henderson performs the music of Duke Ellington's composer-collaborator Billy Strayhorn. This date, one of Henderson's best, shows him at his most intimate, virtuosic, and romantic. —*Eugene Holley Jr., Jazz Times*

○ **So Near So Far** / **i.** 1993 / Verve

Discs like *So Near, So Far (Musings for Miles)* will shift the focus onto Miles Davis's richly varied compositions. Tenor saxophonist Joe Henderson, a Davis album by virtue of four weekend gigs in '67, is masterful throughout this well-sequenced program, toasting sublime lyricism on "Miles Ahead," invoking Iberian mysteries on "Flamenco Sketches," and summoning fire on "Side Car." Yet, he is not the dominant voice in this quartet. Guitarist John Scofield, bassist Dave Holland, and drummer Al Foster make defining contributions on each track. —*Bill Shoemaker, Down Beat*

Jon Hendricks (John Carl Hendricks)

b. Sep. 16, 1921, Newark, OH
Vocals / Ballads & blues
Vocalist and self-taught drummer Jon Hendricks used the radio as an early inspiration and reference. He sang on broadcasts in Toledo as an 11-year-old. One of 17 children in his family, he studied law for a time after high school, but became a full-time professional musician at Charlie Parker's behest. He moved to New York in 1952 and had his song "I Want You to Be My Baby" recorded by Louis Jordan. He put lyrics to "Four Brothers," "Cloudburst," and some George Russell songs on his *New York, New York* album in the late '50s. His backup group was initially the Dave Lambert Singers and ultimately became Lambert, Hendricks, and Ross. This trio was a dominant jazz vocalese unit from the late '50s to the mid '60s, adding lyrics to a host of tunes by Count Basie, Horace Silver, Miles Davis, and Art Blakey. Hendricks has had a solid solo career as a performer, writer, and jazz critic for the *San Francisco Chronicle*. He was briefly reunited with Annie Ross and Georgie Fame in 1968.—*Ron Wynn*

★ **New York, N.Y.** / **i.** Nov. 26, 1959 / Decca 79216

★ **Tell Me the Truth** / 1975 / Arista 4043
Aided by a resurgent interest in the scat vocal styles of Dave Lambert and others, Jon Hendricks took the opportunity to record his first album for an American label in years, *Tell Me the Truth.* Special credit went to Ben Sidran for sitting back, keeping things clutter-free and letting Hendricks work his magic. Not surprisingly, that magic came across better on the uptempo and soulful material, particularly Slim Gaillard's "Flat Foot Floogie" and Hubert Laws's "No More." —*Mikal Gilmore, Down Beat*

○ **Freddie Freeloader** / **i.** 1990 / Denon 6302
Tour-de-force recording with Bobby McFerrin (v), George Benson (v), Al Jarreau (v), and Manhattan Transfer (v). —*Michael G. Nastos*

○ **Jon Hendricks** / Enja 4032

Ernie Henry (Ernest Albert Henry)

b. 1926, NYC, **d.** Dec. 29, 1957, NYC
Alto sax / Hard bop
Ernie Henry was a tremendous performer on alto, despite a brief career. Though he only played about a decade, his work with Tadd Dameron, Dizzy Gillespie, Charles Mingus, and Thelonious Monk (along with a few sessions with Illinois Jacquet) cemented his importance. He was a searing, attention-getting saxophonist, whose phrasing and intensity were matched by his ideas and expressiveness. —*Ron Wynn*

○ **Presenting Ernie Henry** / Aug. 23, 1956 / Riverside 102
This presents an artist who died right at the beginning of his solo career and whose promise has continued to interest listeners ever since. Part of that interest comes from the company he kept on his few recordings; on this 1956 date it was Kenny Dorham (trumpet) and Kenny Drew (piano) with Art Taylor and Wilbur Ware on drums and bass respectively.... This was imperfect, and the interplay and exchange between the leader and the group was less than smooth, at times almost awkward. Yet there was music, solos in particular, here that was rewarding and plenty of what must be heard as the spontaneous creating of jazz to be enjoyed. —*Bob Rusch, Cadence*

★ **Last Chorus** / Aug. 1956-Nov. 1957 / Riverside 086
Last Chorus presented the final recordings of Ernie Henry, who died 12/29/57 at the age of 30. Henry's alto playing combined the exigency of the hard alto sound with the big, scooping delivery more associated with the tenor sax and players like Sonny Rollins; a more deliberate sound than fleet register runs. This record, not a totally convincing sample, found him leading his own groups or in the company of Kenny Dorham or Thelonious Monk. —*Bob Rusch, Cadence*

Woody Herman (Woodrow Charles Herman)

b. May 16, 1913, Milwaukee, WI, **d.** Oct. 29, 1987
Clarinet, alto and soprano sax, bandleader / Swing, big band, bop
Bandleader, clarinetist, and alto and soprano saxophonist Woody Herman fought the good fight to keep a big band active for several decades. Neither changes in audience tastes and preferences nor the dire economic consequences altered Herman's determination to keep his band viable, and he maintained an active touring and recording schedule right until the end. Not a great player, Herman was an effective soloist within the orchestral framework, sometimes capable of surprise. His earliest experience came playing in the bands of Tom Gerun and Harry Sosnik. After working in the bands of Gus Arnheim and Isham Jones, Herman formed his first orchestra with several leftovers from Jones's disbanded ensemble. He had his initial hit with the first version of "Woodchopper's Ball" in 1939. The list of distinguished Herman alumni reads like a jazz Hall of Fame; it includes Zoot Sims, Stan Getz, Al Cohn, Chubby Jackson, Gene Ammons, and Serge Chaloff. Despite having to disband and reform twice in the '40s, Woody Herman kept a band performing from the '30s until the '80s, with the peak period being from 1937 to 1952. Herman enjoyed several Top Ten pop hits in the '40s, and won a Grammy in '73. The end finally came in 1987, when Herman died. Prior to that, his band established a legacy comparable with that of the Ellington and Basie orchestras. —*Ron Wynn*

★ **Blues on Parade** / Apr. 26, 1937-Jul. 24, 1942 / GRP 606
This single CD gives one a definitive look at Woody Herman's first orchestra, the Decca ensemble he led during 1936-1942 that was billed "The Band That Plays the Blues." Although Herman also recorded many vocal ballads during this era, the emphasis here is on hot swing with such highlights as the original version of "Woodchopper's Ball," "Blue Prelude," "Blue Flame," the humorous "Fan It," and two takes of "Blues on Parade." Also heard are performances by Herman's early small combos (the Woodchoppers and the Four Chips) along with a Dizzy Gillespie composition-arrangement ("Down Under") that hints at Woody Herman's future. Highly recommended. —*Scott Yanow*

○ **Thundering Herds 1945-1947** / **i.** Feb. 19, 1945-Dec. 27, 1947 / Columbia 44108
Since the definitive three-LP boxed set *Thundering Herds* is out of print, this single CD is the best place for listeners to go when starting to explore the music of Woody Herman. There are 14 selections from what was arguably Woody Herman's best band, his First Herd, and two numbers (including the original version of "Four Brothers") by the Second Herd. A few rarities (such as "A Jug of Wine" and "The Blues Are Brewing") are mixed in with such classics as "Apple Honey," "Northwest Passage," "Your Father's Mustache," and a new version of "Woodchopper's Ball," but there is unavoidably a lot missing from this single disc, a set that will have to suffice until a more complete reissue series comes along. —*Scott Yanow*

★ **Thundering Herds** / Feb. 19, 1945-Dec. 27, 1947 / Columbia 44108
This now out-of-print three-LP boxed set is still the best compilation to date of Woody Herman's First and Second Herds. These 48 selections (the cream of Herman's Columbia recordings) include many classics such as "Apple Honey," "Caldonia," "Northwest Passage," "Bijou," "Your Father's Moustache," eight numbers from Woody Herman's Woodchoppers, "Let It Snow," a new rendition of "Woodchopper's Ball," the four-part "Summer Sequence," and the original version of "Four Brothers." Even the lesser items on this set are memorable, making this the number one Woody Herman release to own. Why hasn't it been reissued in total on CD yet? —*Scott Yanow*

○ **Herd Rides Again** / **i.** Jul. 30, 1958-Aug. 1, 1958 / Evidence 22010
This CD contains a better-than-expected reunion of Woody Herman's First Herd. Actually many of the key players from that classic band (such as tenorman Flip Phillips and trombonist Bill Harris) were not on this date, while some of the musicians who did participate were Hermanites from a later era or (in the case of trombonist Bob Brookmeyer and tenor-saxophonist Sam Donahue) had never been part of Woody's bands before. Because

the music was generally only a decade old, the results are quite satisfying, with fresh solos and spirited ensembles giving new life to such numbers as "Northwest Passage," "Caledonia," and "Blowin' Up a Storm," among others. Certainly Brookmeyer's playing on "Bijou" will not remind anyone of Bill Harris. —*Scott Yanow*

○ **Herman's Heat & Puente's Beat** / **i.** Sep. 1958 / Evidence 22008
By 1958 Woody Herman's Third Herd was history and he was back to working with small groups. For the sessions that comprise this CD, Herman used two separate studio orchestras filled with musicians (and some alumni) familiar with his music. In addition to the fine straightahead charts (which include a new version of "Woodchopper's Ball," "Lullaby of Birdland," and "Midnight Sun"), Woody added Tito Puente's five-piece Latin rhythm section to six selections, bringing variety and strong rhythmic excitement to this fine set. —*Scott Yanow*

○ **Live at Monterey** / Oct. 3, 1959 / Atlantic 90044
Woody Herman returned to the big band wars in 1959 with these two very successful appearances at the Monterey Jazz Festival. His new band featured such major players as trumpeter Conte Candoli; trombonist Urbie Green; acoustic guitarist Charlie Byrd; and a sax section comprised of tenors Zoot Sims, Bill Perkins, and Richie Kamuca, Don Lanphere on alto and tenor, and baritonist Med Flory, in addition to Woody himself. The all-star orchestra romps happily through "Four Brothers," "Monterey Apple Tree," and "Skoobeedoobee," and Urbie Green is well featured on the ballad "Skylark" and "The Magpie." Excellent music that signalled a "comeback" for Woody Herman. —*Scott Yanow*

○ **Woody's Winners** / Jun. 28, 1965-Jun. 30, 1965 / Columbia 2436
Of the many exciting recordings by Woody Herman's Swinging Herd of the 1960s, this is the definitive set. With such soloists as trumpeters Bill Chase, Dusko Goykovich, and Don Rader and tenors Sal Nistico, Andy McGhee, and Gary Klein, this orchestra rarely had any difficulty raising the temperature. Recorded live at Basin Street West in late-June 1965, this set finds the enthusiastic band featuring a three-way trumpet battle on "23 Red," reworking "Northwest Passage" (highlighted by Sal Nistico's long tenor solo), and romping on a lengthy version of "Opus De Funk" in addition to interpreting a few ballads and blues. This is a very memorable LP that deserves to be reissued on CD so it can be in every jazz collector's library. —*Scott Yanow*

☆ **Woody and Friends at the Monteray Jazz Festival** / Sep. 1979 / Concord Jazz 4170
1992 reissue of a fine set with Herman featuring people he seldom played with, such as Woody Shaw (tpt) and Slide Hampton (tb). —*Ron Wynn*

○ **At Carnegie Hall** / Verve 2317

○ **Keeper of the Flame: Complete Capitol Recordings** / Blue Note 98453
Subtitled *The Complete Capitol Recordings of the Four Brothers Band*, this CD contains 19 selections from Woody Herman's Second Herd, including three songs never before released. Topheavy with major soloists (including trumpeters Red Rodney and Shorty Rogers; trobonist Bill Harris; tenors Al Cohn, Zoot Sims, Stan Getz, and Gene Ammons; not to mention Herman himself) this boppish band may have cost the leader a small fortune, but they created timeless music. Highlights include "Early Autumn" (a ballad performance that made Stan Getz a star), the riotous "Lemon Drop," and Gene Ammons's strong solo on "More Moon." A gem. —*Scott Yanow*

Vincent Herring

b. 1964
Alto sax, composer / Neo-bop
Alto saxophonist and composer Vince Herring has earned praise for his hard-bop writing and loose, exuberant, and sometimes funky style that reflects the influence of many modern altoists, particularly Cannonball Adderley and Charlie Parker. He has several good sessions as a leader for such labels as Fantasy and Musicmasters, and has also done several sessions on other albums.—*Ron Wynn*

★ **Evidence** / **i.** 1990 / Landmark 1527
A much sharper, clearer statement than his other release. The compositions are better, and the music is more dynamic. —*Ron Wynn*

Fred Hersch

Piano / Modern creative
A fine pianist whose work blends introspective and energetic elements and is strongly influenced by Bill Evans, Fred Hersch has gotten quite a bit of publicity over the last few years for being HIV-positive. He's done benefit concerts and several interviews on the subject, but Hersch's playing deserves just as much attention. He smartly mixes free, hard bop, and contemporary classical voicings and elements, and his originals are probing and unpredictable. Hersch has played with Marc Johnson, Joey Baron, Charlie Haden, Mike Formanek, Steve Laspina, and Jeff Hirshfield, among others. He's recorded as a leader for Chesky, Sunnyside, Concord, Angel, and Red. —*Ron Wynn and Michael G. Nastos*

○ **Heartsongs** / Dec. 1989 / Sunnyside 1047

★ **Forward Motion** / **i.** 1991 / Chesky 55
Fred Hersch Group. This is a release that has components of jazz, chamber, and new-age. The playing is better and more consistent than the material. —*Ron Wynn*

John Hicks

b. 1941, Atlanta, GA
Piano / Hard bop, modern creative
Hicks is a busy modern pianist whose initial reputation was built on probing trio sessions and accompaniment for Betty Carter. He has done traditional trio and small-combo dates, played in the Power Trio doing more adventurous rock and free improvisation, made a dazzling solo record, and made some critically acclaimed recordings for the DIW label. His playing approach has some elements of McCoy Tyner, but he's far from an imitator—he is a dynamic interpreter and a striking soloist in complete command of the instrument. —*Ron Wynn*

★ **After the Morning** / Jan. 5-06, 1979 / West 54 8004
Pianist John Hicks hurtled headlong through five of the eight tracks here, slowing long enough to get his teeth into the splendid Tex Allen tune "Night Journey", with its sinuous vamp and moist minor harmonies, as well as Frieda Herzog's evocative gem "Some Other Spring," and a wisp of Dave Brubeck's "Duke." Sometimes his ideas, usually pretty, florid ones coming from Bill Evans as much as McCoy Tyner, came just a hair too fast for his hands, but he was certainly challenging himself and the listener. —*Fred Bouchard, Down Beat*

○ **Eastside Blues** / **i.** 1991 / DIW 828
His most recent excursion into the trio vein, this album is explosive and substantive, with Curtis Lundy and Victor Lewis. —*Ron Wynn*

J.C. Higginbotham (Jay C. Higginbotham)

b. May 11, 1906, Social Circle, GA, **d.** May 26, 1973
Trombone / New Orleans traditional
An exuberant, entertaining trombonist, J.C. Higginbotham was a delightful soloist whose style included plenty of rough, voicelike smears and slurs, as well as humorous refrains and choruses. He was influenced by Jimmy Harrison but added his own flourishes. Higginbotham played in various Southern and Midwestern bands as a youngster and moved to New York in the '20s. He joined Luis Russell in 1928 and worked with Fletcher Henderson, Chick Webb, and Benny Carter during the '30s. His solos in Russell's orchestra, which were featured during the era when Louis Armstrong was also in the band, earned him widespread fame. During the '40s, Higginbotham played with many traditional jazz combos, including groups led by Henry "Red" Allen and Sidney Bechet, as well as his own group. Higginbotham was part of the excellent trombone section on the Henderson reunion album in the late '50s, teaming with Benny Morton and Dicky Wells. He led groups in the '60s and appeared at the 1963 Newport Jazz Festival. He recorded for Okeh, Jazzology, and Prestige, with Bechet, Coleman Hawkins, Carter's Chocolate Dandies, Jelly Roll Morton, and Tiny Grimes. He currently has one session available as a leader on CD, and is featured on other reissues by Carter, Bechet, and Hawkins. —*Ron Wynn*

● **Higgy Comes Home** / **i.** Nov. 1967 / Cable 126601

Billy Higgins

b. Oct. 11, 1936, Los Angeles, CA, **d.** May 26, 1973
Drums / Hard bop, early free, modern creative

"Smilin' Billy" Higgins is, next to J. C. Heard and Art Taylor, the most recorded jazz drummer of the last 40 years. His unflagging time, consistent virtuosity, and innate ability to listen and contribute to a group sound keep him in demand. He's truly one of the all-time greats. The list of players Higgins has worked with runs from Amos Milburn to Ornette Coleman and covers every facet of jazz, as well as blues, R&B, and even pop.—*Michael G. Nastos*

★ **Bridgework** / Apr. 23, 1980 / Contemporary 14024
A rare Higgins album, with conservative arrangements and compositions, plus outstanding technique and percussive foundations. —*Ron Wynn*

○ **Mr. Billy Higgins** / i. Apr. 12, 1984-May 2, 1984 / RIZA 104
One of jazz's greatest session drummers got a rare date as a leader on this '84 set, yet it was tough to tell that it was Billy Higgins's album. He was in his usual place, driving and pacing the session on drums, while soprano and tenor saxophonist Gary Bias took the spotlight on such songs as "Morning Awakening" and "Humility." —*Ron Wynn*

Andrew Hill

b. Jun. 30, 1937, Port Au Prince, Haiti, raised Chicago
Piano / Postbop, early free, modern creative
A visionary, percussive pianist who evolved from R&B and mainstream roots into one of the more advanced theorists and players on the '60s scene. Hill worked with everyone in Chicago, from Paul Williams and Dinah Washington to Von Freeman and Gene Ammons, before moving first to Los Angeles and then to New York in the '60s. He has varied his approach and his harmonic and rhythmic tendencies, has utilized Caribbean textures, and has played very outside at times and at other times quite conventionally. His '60s Blue Note albums and his playing with Joe Henderson were models of balance between complexity and simplicity. His latest albums have seen him again carefully mixing experimental and traditional elements. —*Ron Wynn*

☆ **Black Fire** / Nov. 8, 1963 / Blue Note 84151
Haiti's gift to jazz piano of the '50s and now. For adventurous listeners. —*Michael G. Nastos*

☆ **Point of Departure** / i. Mar. 31, 1964 / Capitol 84167
A 1989 reissue of a remarkable session that still has an avant-garde quality today. Eric Dolphy (sax) and Joe Henderson (sax) break barriers with their splendid solos. —*Ron Wynn*

○ **Andrew!** / Jun. 25, 1964 / Blue Note 84203

★ **Compulsion** / Oct. 8, 1965 / Blue Note

○ **One for One** / Aug. 1, 1969+Jan. 23, 1970 / Blue Note
These are previously unreleased sessions from 1969 and 1970. Group efforts, at times with a string quartet. Hefty solos from B. Maupin, P. Patrick, J. Henderson, F. Hubbard, and C. Tolliver. —*Michael G. Nastos*

★ **From California with Love** / Oct. 12, 1978 / Artists House
This solo piano release contained two long musical epistles, each penned in a stunning variety of moods and techniques. Again, paradox seemed one of Andrew Hill's principal organizational strategies. . . . In his dense probing of limited thematic material, this large-form pianist never seemed at a loss for a new nuance of expression or a new twist on an old formula. —*Jon Balleras, Down Beat*

★ **Verona Rag** / Jul. 1986 / Soul Note 121110
Pianist Andrew Hill long ago established himself as one of the most creative of postbebop improvisors on his instrument. His solo *Verona Rag* richly displayed the vast spectrum of sources this gifted artist draws upon, from rags and spirituals to the standard song book to bebop and beyond, not to mention his Caribbean roots. — *W. Royal Stokes, Jazz Times*

Earl Hines (Earl Kenneth Hines)

b. Dec. 28, 1903, Dusquesne, PA, **d.** Apr. 22, 1983, Oakland, CA
Piano / New Orleans traditional, boogie-woogie, swing
Known as "Fatha," Hines is the progenitor of modern jazz piano style; he took the instrument on a new road when he applied the rhythmic and harmonic discoveries of Louis Armstrong (his closest musical associate in Chicago in 1927-1928) and his own daring ideas to the keyboard. He was the first to give the piano a real voice within a band, with his ringing right-hand clusters and uncanny sense of timing. After his seminal collaborations with

Armstrong, Hines formed his own big band in 1929; its stay at Chicago's Grand Terrace Ballroom lasted ten years. Among the band's notable alumni in that first decade were Omer Simeon, Budd Johnson, Trummy Young, Ray Nance, and Billy Eckstine; in 1943 Hines had both Dizzy Gillespie and Charlie Parker in his ranks, as well as Sarah Vaughan. By 1947 Hines threw in the towel; the next year he'd joined his old friend Armstrong's All-Stars. But he soon was on his own again, eventually settling in San Francisco and nearly forgotten by the jazz audience until two New York concerts (coproduced by this writer) launched him on a new and vital career as a soloist, mainly fronting trios but adding a horn and a singer when the budget allowed, and making tons of records, many of them superb examples of his undimmed vitality and inventiveness. —*Dan Morgenstern*

● **Earl Hines (1937-1939)** / i. 1937-1939 / Classics 538

○ **Earl Hines (1939-1940)** / i. Oct. 1939-Dec. 1940 / Classics 567

○ **Earl Hines Plays Fats Waller** / i. 1953 / Brunswick 58035

★ **Monday Date, A** / i. Sep. 1961 / Riverside 1740
Earl Hines, one of jazz's greatest pianists, was a modern stylist who broke up the usual stride piano pattern of the 1920s with unexpected accents and an uncanny ability to play successfully with time; he had the trickiest left hand in the business. After his orchestra disbanded in 1947 and he spent a few unfulfilling years as a sideman with the Louis Armstrong All-Stars, Hines entered a decade of critical neglect and indifference in which his talents were pretty well forgotten; he found himself playing Dixieland in San Francisco for several years. This particular LP is a decent Dixieland set with trumpeter Eddie Smith, trombonist Jimmy Archey, and clarinetist Darnell Howard. Still, Hines's abilities are somewhat wasted on tunes such as "Bill Bailey," "Yes Sir, That's My Baby," and "Clarinet Marmalade." His renaissance was still three years in the future. —*Scott Yanow*

○ **In Concert** / Mar. 7, 1964 / Focus 335

○ **Blues in Thirds** / Apr. 1965 / Black Lion 760120
This Black Lion CD has two alternative takes and "Black Lion Blues" added to what was on the original LP. For someone who always discounted his own ability as a blues player, Earl Hines had a remarkable gift for coming up with fresh, pleasing blues ideas, as he showed in the reworking of his 1928 "Blues in Thirds," in "Blues after Midnight" and "Black Lion Blues." — *Stanley Dance, Jazz Times*

○ **Once upon a Time** / Jan. 10-11, 1966 / Impulse 9108
Pianist Earl Hines's *Once Upon a Time* will be great fun for Duke Ellington and Hines fans. The January date paired Hines with many Ellingtonians such as Johnny Hodges, Paul Gonsalves, Clark Terry, Larry Brown, Bill Berry, Cat Anderson, Ray Nance, Sonny Greer, Harold Ashby, Jimmy Hamilton, Buster Cooper, and Aaron Bell, along with clarinetist Pee Wee Russell and drummer Elvin Jones. Actually, Hines fans expecting the usual may have been surprised to hear how much he remained the pianist here, even on the small group cuts. —*Bob Rusch, Cadence*

○ **Quintessential Recording Session** / i. Mar. 15, 1970 / Halcyon 101
Pianist Earl Hines's later solo work was even freer of stylistic restriction, and Hines wielded ever-larger palettes with consummate ease, as seen in this version of "Deep Forest," against which earlier versions, however admirable, seem almost incomplete. There were many solo Hines recordings in his later years, but few matched this session's dramatic, sweeping statements and none its consistency. —*Chris Sheridan, Cadence*

○ **Earl Hines Plays Duke Ellington** / Jun. 1, 1971-Dec. 10, 1971 / Master Jazz 8114
This was the fourth record in a series of unaccompanied Duke Ellington compositions featuring pianist Earl Hines, and according to the liner notes, Hines did not know any of these tunes before the session. It did not matter; we heard Hines, not Ellington, and each tune became a very personal statement. —*Tom Everett, Cadence*

○ **Hines Plays Hines** / i. Jul. 1972 / Swaggie 1320

☆ **Hines Does Hoagy** / i. 1972-1973 / Audiophile 113
Earl Hines pays tribute to composer Hoagy Carmichael on this inventive set of solo piano. Highpoints of this fine LP include a ten-minute version of "Stardust," "Skylark," and "Ole Buttermilk Sky." Pity that Hines did not tackle "Riverboat Shuffle," but he chose to stick mostly to Carmichael's classic ballads. One of three

albums recorded by the great pianist in a two-day period, this is one of about 50 recommended Hines sets! —*Scott Yanow*

★ **Earl Hines at the New School** / Mar. 1973 / Chiaroscuro 157
Even though it is not yet available on CD, this LP gets a + rating because it features pianist Earl Hines at the absolute peak of his powers. Nine years after his renaissance began, Hines seemed to still be getting more daring in his playing. This version of "I've Got the World on a String" is somewhat miraculous (the chances he takes are breathtaking), and the Fats Waller medley (which features six songs) is definitive. The inclusion of "When the Saints Go Marching In" might not have been necessary, and "Boogie Woogie on the St. Louis Blues" is a bit exhibitionistic but those are minor complaints about a definitive and classic session by a true jazz master. —*Scott Yanow*

● **Giants of Jazz** / i. Mar. 1981 / Time Life 11
The task of paring hundreds of hours of pianist Earl Hines's music down to three significant albums for a workable anthology was a prodigious one, and critic Stanley Dance went about it with commendable thoroughness and a dedication that exceeded mere professionalism, going to the source himself, looking over short-listed tracks, and involving Hines in the decision making. The notes were thus full of Hines's wincing, wonderment, rich anecdotes and wry asides. The selections included here divided fairly evenly into solo, small group, and big band performances.... This collection was an indispensable document of one of the most formidable American musicians of our century. —*Fred Bouchard, Down Beat*

○ **Earl Hines and Budd Johnson** / Black & Blue 233084

★ **Partners in Jazz** / MPS 61172
W/ Jaki Byard (p). Piano duets from masters of two styles and generations. Definitive. —*Michael G. Nastos*

Milt Hinton (Milton John Hinton)

b. Jun. 23, 1910, Vicksburg, MS
Bass / Swing, bop
A legendary bassist, Milt Hinton has been working in combos, making records, and touring since the '30s, and he remains a formidable figure. One of the greatest timekeepers ever among bassists who have a huge, magnificent sound, Hinton's worked with numerous vocalists as well as instrumentalists. He's also an outstanding photographer who's had several exhibitions of his work, and a book of his jazz photos, *Over Time*, was published in 1991. He conducted several interviews with such noted musicians as Danny Barker, Teddy Wilson, Quentin Jackson, and Jo Jones through National Endowment for the Arts grants during the '70s and '80s. These are now collected at the Institute for Jazz Studies at Rutgers. Nicknamed "The Judge," Hinton began playing professionally in Chicago during the '30s with Body Atkins, Tiny Parham, and Jabbo Smith. He also worked with Eddie South, Erskine Tate, and Zutty Singleton, among others, before joining Cab Calloway's band in 1936. He remained with Calloway until 1951, when he became a freelancer, and he has remained among the most in-demand session bassists ever since. Hinton has played with everyone from Bing Crosby to Louis Armstrong and Count Basie, as well as Joe Newman, Lionel Hampton, Terry Gibbs, Jimmy Rushing, Branford Marsalis, Buddy DeFranco, and many others. The 1988 book *Bass Line*, co-written by David Berger and Hinton, covers his life and times in the jazz world. Hinton's also recorded a few albums as a leader for such labels as Progressive and Chiaroscuro. He has a couple of sessions available on CD. —*Ron Wynn*

● **Basses Loaded!** / Feb. 1, 1955 / Victor 1107

Al Hirt (Alois Maxwell Hirt)

b. Nov. 7, 1922, New Orleans, LA
Trumpet / Dixieland
A classically trained trumpeter, Al Hirt (best known as "Jumbo" to his friends in New Orleans) picked up jazz licks by listening to the recordings of Harry James and Roy Eldridge in the '40s. He began his professional career working with the swing bands of Tommy and Jimmy Dorsey, but when he returned to New Orleans in the latter '40s he gravitated toward the "traditional" jazz format. In 1955 he formed a combo that included Pete Fountain, and over the next five years worked on attracting national recognition. His greatest popularity, however, came in the mid-'60s, when he had back-to-back hits with "Java," and "Cotton Candy," tunes that were perhaps closer to a popularized country-music style than to Dixieland. During the '70s, he operated his own nightclub on Bourbon Street. After a hiatus of several years, in the early '90s he returned to Bourbon Street, where he is still active. Al Hirt's substantial popularity stems from his genuine technical virtuosity and powerful delivery. —*Bruce Boyd Raeburn*

★ **That's a Plenty** / i. 1988 / Pro Arte 659
Jumbo with Peanuts Hocko, Bobby Breaux, Dalton Hagler, and others pouncing on New Orleans favorites like "Royal Garden Blues," "Bourbon Street Parade," and "Saints." —*Bruce Raeburn*

Art Hodes (Arthur W. Hodes)

b. Nov. 14, 1904, Nikoliev, Russia, **d.** Mar. 4, 1993
Piano / New Orleans traditional, blues & jazz
A fine traditional jazz and blues pianist, Art Hodes came to America when he was six months old and grew up in Chicago. His rollicking style was honed playing dances at Hull House and working with Chicago bands, as well as playing in New York on 52d Street in the late '30s. Hodes made his debut on record in 1928 with Wingy Manone and has recorded periodically ever since. Most of his releases are solo, but his activities in music are not limited to the performing arena. Hodes was editor of the magazine *Jazz Record* from 1943 to 1947. He was a disc jockey and eventually became an educator and lectured extensively. He moved back to Chicago in 1950 and became a resident at Bob Scobey's nightclub in 1959, while also writing for *Down Beat* and hosting a television series that won him an Emmy. Hodes has toured Europe frequently, and he resurfaced in New York in the early '80s. His albums are available as reissues from GHB, Delmark, Audiophile, and Jazzology, while his latter-day material has been released on Sackville and Muse. —*Ron Wynn*

● **Complete Blue Note Art Hodes Sessions** / Mosaic

○ **Art Hodes' Hot Five** / Oct. 12, 1945+Oct. 12, 1945 / Blue Note 7005

○ **Chicago Rhythm Kings** / i. 1953 / Riverside 1012

★ **Albert Nicholas** / i. Jul. 1959 / Delmark 207

○ **Hodes' Art** / Oct. 22, 1968 / Delmark 213
Playing in the context of three different groups here, he showed his indebtedness to Jelly Roll Morton and James P. Johnson in his playing as well as in the selection of some tunes by those same greats. On the first three tracks, Hodes played only with bass (Truck Parham) and drums. Under his fingers, "Winin' Boy Blues" became a relaxed, almost pretty blues, while in "Old Fashioned Love," Hodes played in a busy, hard-driving stride style. —*Jerry De Muth, Cadence*

○ **Friar's Inn Revisited** / 1968 / Delmark 215
The central idea around which this release was built was that of the New Orleans Rhythm Kings, who played Friar's Inn. Both trombonist George Brunis and clarinetist Volly De Faut were, of course, members of this historic group, Brunis originally, and De Faut later. The titles were also closely associated with, or originated by, the NORK. —*Shirley Klett, Cadence*

○ **Someone to Watch over Me** / Feb. 27, 1981 / Muse 5252
More than many of the (1920s) crop of white Chicago musicians, Hodes really soaked in the blues but developed a style uniquely his own. This rediscovery LP was well recorded, the piano of high quality and the audience both attentive and appreciative.... The title track was outstanding, with "St. Louis Blues," "Georgia on My Mind," and "Plain Ol' Blues" the best of the remainder. —*Shirley Klett, Cadence*

○ **Just the Two of Us** / Aug. 26, 1981 / Muse 5279
Here, the 78-year-old pianist was truly at his best, performing well-honed classics to the accompaniment of the finest traditional bass player still alive. While it is unarguably true that the presence of a Baby Dodds, Zutty Singleton, or George Wettling on drums would have added that much more to the overall impact of Hodes's and Hinton's music, we must be grateful for what we still had. —*Jack Sohmer, Cadence*

● **Selections from the Gutter** / i. Mar. 1983 / Storyville 4057
Wonderful blues, traditional jazz, and stride numbers by jazz pianist and critic Art Hodes, who cut many superb records for small independents during an extensive career. These were done in mid-'80s. —*Ron Wynn, AMG*

○ **Live from Toronto's Cafe Des Copains** / i. 1988 / Music & Arts 610

○ **Pagin' Mr. Jelly** / Nov. 198z / Candid 79037

○ **Up in Volly's Room** / Delmark 217

Johnny Hodges (John Hodges)

b. Jul. 25, 1907, Cambridge, MA, d. May 11, 1970
Alto and soprano sax / Swing, big band
Perhaps the most influential alto saxophonist until Charlie Parker arrived, and one of the most beloved musicians ever, Johnny Hodges brought a lyrical beauty and relaxed majesty to the instrument that has seldom been equalled and never surpassed. Hodges grew up on Hammond Street in Boston with such neighbors as Harry Carney, Toots Mondello, and Charlie Holmes. He was privileged to get saxophone lessons from the great Sidney Bechet, who taught him the soprano. He later worked at the Club Bechet in New York and played some duets with the master. Duke Ellington signed him in 1928 to replace Otto Hardwicke, and he became the saxophone section's director for the next 22 years. Hodges eventually stopped playing soprano because Ellington was penning so many pieces that accented his alto, which he played with a flawless tone and impressive, yet seemingly easy technique. For a time Johnny Hodges and His Orchestra were a small-group unit within the Ellington combine. Such masterpieces as "Jeep's Blues," "The Jeep Is Jumpin'," "Empty Ballroom Blues," and "Warm Valley" were showcase pieces for Hodges. He finally left the Ellington nest in 1951 and headed his own group until 1955, when he returned to Ellington's orchestra to stay. Hodges was set to play the soprano sax on a recording again for the first time since he'd stopped in 1940, when he died in 1970, shortly after being featured on the "Blues for New Orleans" cut from *New Orleans Suite*. Several of the Hodges small-group Ellingtonian sessions, as well as his own small-group material from the '50s, have been reissued. —*Ron Wynn*

● **On Keynote with Rex Stewart** / i. 1946 / PolyGram 30926
A thorough collection of sides from Keynote, spotlighting Ellingtonians Hodges and Rex Stewart (cnt). —*Ron Wynn*

● **Complete Johnny Hodges Sessions (1951-1955)** / 1951-1955 / Mosaic 6126

★ **Big Sound, The** / Jun. 26, 1957+Sep. 3, 1957 / Verve 8271
No surprises, but the session was as good as one might hope. Gathered here was the Ellington band with Billy Strayhorn at the piano. While it was not an Ellington record, the band brought its solid qualities in backing and the occasional solo to all the fine Hodges features. This was an integrated unit, not some detached studio band for Hodges to blow over, under, around, and through. It was wonderful Hodges and fine Ellington. —*Bob Rusch, Cadence*

Jay Hoggard

b. Sep. 24, 1954, New York, NY
Vibes / Modern creative
Jay Hoggard emerged as a major voice on vibes in the '70s and '80s. His use of counterpoint and his ambitious compositions, solo ability, and participation in some cutting-edge sessions stamped him as a prime jazz figure. Lately he's done fewer recordings. Hoggard also moved into pop and fusion for a time during the '80s.—*Ron Wynn*

○ **Little Tiger, The** / i. Jun. 10, 1990 / Muse 5410
An album with the vibist at his best. The title track is worth the price alone. W/ Benny Green. —*Michael G. Nastos*

○ **Fountain, The** / i. 1992 / Muse 5450
The Fountain is a contemporary recording that pairs Jay Hoggard with virtuoso guitarist Kenny Burrell, and their vibes-guitar interplay is superb. . . . The program is rich and varied, showcasing Hoggard's facility with the full range of the tradition, with pieces from Ellington to Monk and Mingus, as well as the "freer" title track. —*Sid Gribetz, Jazz Times*

★ **Mystic Winds, Tropical Breezes** / India Navigation 1049
Strong, free-wheeling date by vibist Jay Hoggard, done in the late '70s. He was working with a topflight group, among them pianist Anthony Davis, bassist Cecil McBee, Drummers Billy Hart and Don Moye, and Dwight Andrews on various saxophones. The

compositions were loosely structured and extended, and solos were fierce. —*Ron Wynn*

Billie Holiday (Eleanora Fagan)

b. Apr. 7, 1915, Baltimore, MD, d. Jul. 17, 1959, New York, NY
Vocals / Swing, big band, ballads & blues
Vocalist Billie Holiday became a stylist—and a great one—whose unhappy personal life (drug addiction, wrong male partners) was reflected in her art. There were still happy moments, among them the recordings made for Norman Granz with great players like Benny Carter, "Sweets" Edison, and Ben Webster, and her appearance in the 1957 TV show "The Sound of Jazz," which reunited her (for a minute) with Lester Young. Her death was a tragic example of the inhumanity and stupidity of our drug laws. The film and plays purportedly based on her life would have made her throw up, but it is a sad fact that Billie Holiday is more famous and appreciated in death than she ever was in life—if not always for the right reason: her indelible artistry. —*Dan Morgenstern*

★ **Billie Holiday: The Legacy Box 1933-1958** / 1933-1958 / Columbia 47724
Most welcome; the best overview of her many fine Columbia sessions, from the very first to the last. Great sound quality, high-caliber booklet. —*Ron Wynn*

★ **Quintessential Billie Holiday—Vols. 1—9, The** / i. 1936-1942 / CBS
In-depth material on Columbia. Nine CDs. Excellent. —*Michael Erlewine*

★ **Complete Decca Recordings** / i. 1944-1950 / GRP 601
An outstanding two-record set of Holiday's Decca cuts from the '40s and '50s. Some of her most pop oriented dates, but excellent remastering, annotation, and comprehensive collection. —*Ron Wynn*

★ **Complete Billy Holiday on Verve, The** / i. 1945-1959 / Verve 833765
It took the earlier LP version of the ten-CD *The Complete Billie Holiday on Verve 1945-1959* to convince Buck Clayton, who performed with Holiday for both Columbia and Verve, that the Verve recordings were Holiday's greatest. After the 12-hour immersion required to hear this splendidly packaged collection of all-star studio sessions, concert recordings, and revealing rehearsal tapes, it is impossible not to agree. Norman Granz's genius in producing Holiday was returning her to the small-group context. Not only was she inspired by her collaborators, but she also had a minimal load on her shoulders. Granz was wise to surround her frequently with musicians she had known in better times, such as Clayton, Roy Eldridge, and others. The camaraderie of old friends and the energies of younger musicians such as Oscar Peterson, Barney Kessel and Ray Brown provided the necessary spark for Holiday. —*Bill Shoemaker, Down Beat*

○ **Lady in Autumn: The Best of The Verve Years** / Apr. 1946-Mar. 1959 / Verve 849434
The Best of the Verve Years is a selection of 24 such sides, plus 11 nondefinitive live takes on Holiday standards like "I Cover the Waterfront," "Strange Fruit," and a '58 "Lover Man." Most are from mid-'40s JATP shows, have slightly wobbly sound and do not measure up to the studio tracks where the sound is okay. — *Kevin Whitehead, Down Beat*

☆ **Billie Holiday Sings** / i. 1950 / Columbia 6129

☆ **Favorites** / i. 1950 / Columbia 6163

○ **Billie Holiday at Storyville** / Oct. 1951-Oct. 1953 / Black Lion 760921

○ **Jazz at the Philharmonic** / i. 1954 / Clef 169

★ **Lady in Satin** / 1958 / Columbia 40247
An unforgettable date, with Holiday clearly at the end of the line, yet still sounding hypnotic. —*Ron Wynn*

○ **Stay with Me** / i. 1959 / Verve 511523
A '91 reissue from late in vocalist Billie Holiday's career. She was fading but hadn't lost the dramatic quality in her delivery or her ability project and tell a shattering story. She's backed by trumpeter Charlie Shavers, pianist Oscar Peterson, guitarist Herb Ellis, bassist Ray Brown, and drummer Ed Shaughnessy. The CD reissue has three bonus cuts. —*Ron Wynn*

○ **Billie Holiday, Al Hibbler and the Blues** / i. 1962 / Imperial 9185

○ **Giants of Jazz** / **i.** Mar. 1980 / Time Life 03

For reasons not cheerfully accepted by the jazz purists, the Billie Holiday set on Time-Life probably enjoyed wider currency than any other in this admirably conceived series. . . . there can still be no overlooking the consistently high quality of musicianship abounding in this collection. It is not possible to even approach an understanding of this complex and changing artist unless one is first familiar with the entirety of her musical achievements. This set was only a prelude. —*Jack Sohmer, Down Beat*

☆ **I Like Jazz: The Essence of Billie Holiday** / **i.** Nov. 21, 1991 / Columbia 47917

○ **Billie's Blues** / **i.** Aug. 19, 1992 / Bulldog 1007

○ **God Bless the Child** / MCA 60003

☆ **Strange Fruit** / Atlantic 1614

This out-of-print LP contains all 16 selections recorded by Billie Holiday for Commodore; four titles from 1939 and the remainder from 1944. Whether it be the searing "Strange Fruit," "Billie's Blues," "Fine and Mellow," or optimistic versions of "I'll Get By" and "On the Sunny Side of the Street," Lady Day's voice is in peak form on these sessions; pianist Eddie Heywood costars on the 1944 numbers. Fortunately all of this essential music has since been reissued on CD. —*Scott Yanow*

Lady Day / Columbia 637

A fine single-disc compilation that has five cuts with Lester Young (ts). —*Ron Wynn*

Dave Holland (David Holland)

b. Oct. 1, 1946, Wolverhampton, England
Bass / Early jazz rock, modern creative

It seems ironic that Dave Holland, one of today's most respected and virtuosic acoustic bassists, got much of his fame playing in Miles Davis's *Bitches Brew*-era electric fusion band. After backing Miles, Chick Corea, Anthony Braxton, and other boundary-extending jazzmen, Holland came out with his brilliant *Conference of the Birds* album. On this highly regarded debut he achieved a rare mixture of spontaneity, structure, and widely varied moods, setting the tone for his many ECM recordings to come. Over the years he has evolved as a writer and a technician, known for tricky composing in small groups that display his jaw-dropping solo talents alongside equally proficient young players. Though Holland has always kept in touch with the iconoclastic sentiments of the European free improvisers he grew up with, his music usually avoids the extremes of the avant-garde. He is at his most exploratory on his very satisfying solo albums (on bass as well as cello), and also contributed unconventional bass techniques to various small-label recordings with tenor saxophonist Sam Rivers in the '70s. But he also knows the tradition inside and out and, like Charlie Haden, has been a major contributor to the diverse offerings on the ECM label, among others. —*Myles Boisen*

○ **Music for Two Basses** / Feb. 15, 1971 / ECM 1011

★ **Conference of the Birds** / Nov. 30, 1972 / ECM 829373

Dave Holland Quartet. This English bassist's finest hour. Definitive progressive music, with Sam Rivers (ts), Anthony Braxton (reeds), and Barry Altschul (d). —*Michael G. Nastos*

○ **Dave Holland—Vol. 1** / Feb. 18, 1976 / Improvising Artists 373848

○ **Dave Holland—Vol. 2** / Feb. 18, 1976 / Improvising Artists

★ **Emerald Tears** / Aug. 1977 / ECM 1109

Bassist Dave Holland's rich, varnished tone and throbbing percussive sensitivity are compounded with keen intelligence and a brooding streak of romantic melancholy. An anxious classicism haunted his somber constructions, but the buoyant pulse of his rhythmic imagination drove him through the abstract, often arid landscape of his intellect. Employing a full panoply of modern effects, Holland pursued his sober visions with masterful deftness and aplomb, occasionally bogging down with portentous weightiness on the bowed material. —*Larry Birnbaum, Down Beat*

☆ **Razor's Edge** / Oct. 1983-Feb. 1987 / ECM 833048

Brisk, edgy work with some top "young lion" types, notably Steve Coleman. —*Ron Wynn*

Major Holley (Major Quincy Holley, Jr.)

b. Jul. 10, 1924, Detroit, MI, **d.** Oct. 25, 1990

Bass / Swing, big band, bop

A fine bassist who's also gifted at accompanying his bowed playing with wordless, bluesy vocalisms, Major Holley has been a busy session contributor since 1950. His combination bowing-vocals and occasional addition of humorous lyrics is now quite familiar, and bolsters his tremendous bass playing. Holley began on violin and tuba, then started on bass in the navy. He joined Dexter Gordon after his discharge, and then played with Charlie Parker and Ella Fitzgerald before making his recording debut in a duo with Oscar Peterson. Holley moved to London to work as a studio musician with the BBC in the mid-'50s. He joined Woody Herman's orchestra for a South American tour in 1958 and then returned to America and worked with the Al Cohn-Zoot Sims band in 1959 and 1960. Holley did many studio sessions in the '60s, and also played with Kenny Burrell, Coleman Hawkins, and Duke Ellington. He was an instructor at Berklee from 1967 to 1970 and then played in New York clubs; toured Europe with Helen Humes and the Kings of Jazz; and recorded with Roy Eldrige, Lee Konitz, and Roland Hanna. During the '80s Holley made many appearances at European festivals. He recorded on the Black & Blue label as a leader in the mid-'70s and can be heard on CD reissues featuring the Cohn-Sims band, Woody Herman, Teddy Wilson, and Coleman Hawkins. —*Ron Wynn*

● **Featuring Gerry Wiggins** / Black & Blue 233074

Red Holloway

b. 1927

Tenor sax, alto sax / Swing, bop, blues & jazz

A veteran alto and tenor saxophonist and top sideman and session man, Holloway plays swing to bop, soul jazz with an R&B edge, and blues as well as any, better than most. He's a legendary collaborator with Sonny Stitt. —*Michael G. Nastos*

● **Locksmith Blues** / **i.** 1989 / Concord Jazz 4390

Gutbucket blues, stately show tunes, and high-caliber originals from a sextet co-led by two great musicians who don't try to impress anyone with their dexterity, yet dazzle with every effort. —*Ron Wynn, Rock & Roll Disc.*

○ **The Early Show—Vol. 1: Blues in the Night** / Fantasy 9647

Christopher Hollyday

Hard bop

Christoper Hollyday's searing, hard-edged, and biting alto style, which reflected the influence of Charlie Parker and Phil Woods primarily as well as Jackie McLean, has ripened and grown more into his own voice over the past few years. Hollyday began recording for RCA/Novus in the late '80s, and continued into the '90s. He's recorded with Wallace Roney, Cedar Walton, David Williams, Billy Higgins, Scott Coltney, Kenny Werner, Larry Goldings, John Clark, Mark Feldman, and several others. —*Ron Wynn*

● **Oh, Brother** / **i.** Jun. 1987 / Jazzbeat 102

Groove Holmes

b. 1931, **d.** 1991

organ / Blues & jazz, soul jazz

A great jazz organist, Groove Holmes taught himself organ and developed a strongly swinging style with powerful bass lines and a superb harmonic and melodic edge, something that reflects Holmes's ability to play acoustic bass and the influence of saxophonists on his approach. He worked in local New Jersey clubs for a number of years. Holmes had successful albums with such guests as Les McCann, Ben Webster, Gene Ammons, and Clifford Scott (using the alias Joe Splink) in the early '60s. Though Holmes played well, these sessions got more exposure due to their illustrious guests. He did more trio settings in the mid-'60s and also got better-quality recordings. Holmes scored a huge pop hit with his version of "Misty." His late '60s releases yielded neither hits nor memorable efforts, while his early '70s sessions, particularly those with Jimmy McGriff in a pair of organ battles, were good. Holmes turned in several fine efforts from the late '70s through the late '80s, often working with Houston Person. But Holmes also experimented with various electronic keyboards during the '70s on dates that are short of his best work. He recorded as a leader for Pacific Jazz (twice), Prestige, Groove Merchant, Muse, and Blue Note. Holmes has some sessions available on CD. —*Ron Wynn and Bob Porter*

Groove / Mar. 1961 / Pacific Jazz 94473
A 1990 reissue of an interesting meeting between Groove Holmes and Ben Webster (ts). Webster shows he's capable of adapting his robust soul to a soul-jazz context. —*Ron Wynn*

Groovin' with Jug / Aug. 15, 1961 / Pacific Jazz 92930
Recorded live at The Black Orchid and at the Pacific Jazz Studio earlier that afternoon. Ammons at his peak of popularity, Holmes just about to become well-known—the only date they ever played together. Both players are on. Holmes, also a bassist and famous for his organ bass lines, can be heard to good advantage on "Morris the Minor." —*Michael Erlewine*

● **Soul Message** / Aug. 3, 1965 / Prestige 329
Recorded in New York, NY. This early Holmes album contains his biggest hit "Misty." —*Michael Erlewine*

Living Soul / Apr. 22, 1966 / Prestige 7468
Recorded at Basie's in NYC. —*AMG*

Misty / Jul. 7, 1966+Aug. 12, 1966 / Original Jazz Classics 724
Groove Holmes ranks among the finest soul-jazz organists of all time, and he scored his biggest hit with the title track from this 1966 session. It was done in more blues-oriented vein than the original, and came close to making Top 40. His band included Gene Edwards and Jimmie Smith (the drummer, not the organist). This has been reissued on CD. —*Ron Wynn, AMG*

★ **That Healin' Feelin'** / Aug. 26, 1968 / Prestige 7601
Rusty Bryant smokes on tenor, as does Richard "Groove" Holmes on organ. —*Ron Wynn*

Comin' on Home / 1974 / Blue Note
Funky and nice. —*Ron Wynn*

Shippin' Out / Jun. 1977 / Muse 5134
There is a lot of fine music here—all of it funky, spacious, clear. This album feels good. It has some of that soul-jazz magic. —*Michael Erlewine*

Good Vibrations / Dec. 19, 1977 / Muse 5167
Recorded at Englewood Cliffs, NJ. An album of uptempo cookers from his middle period. W/ Houston Person (ts). —*Michael Erlewine*

Broadway / Dec. 2, 1980 / Muse 5239
W/ Houston Person (ts). Tight band. Later, uptempo but slick. It lacks the space that his early small-combo funk albums have. —*Michael Erlewine*

Blues All Day Long / i. Feb. 24, 1988 / Muse 5358
W/ Houston Person (ts), Jimmy Ponder (g). Respectable, and enjoyable later effort by Holmes. Slightly uptempo, but funky. Very nice album. —*Michael Erlewine*

● **Hot Tat** / Sep. 5, 1989 / Muse 5395
One of the last recordings of "Groove" Holmes. W/ Houston Person (ts), Cecil Bridgewater (tpt), and Jimmy Ponder (g). The album is bit uneven, but it's good to know that someone is still playing this old-style funk. There is some good guitar by Jimmy Ponder. —*Michael Erlewine*

Elmo Hope ([St.] Elmo Sylvester Hope)

b. Jun. 27, 1923, New York, NY, d. May 19, 1967, New York, NY
Piano / Hard bop
An excellent pianist in the bop tradition, with fast, rippling runs, exemplary harmonic knowledge, and a keen rhythmic sense, Hope was also a good composer, well grounded in the vocabulary of R&B and blues plus jazz. He started in the Joe Morris R&B band in the late '40s and then worked with Sonny Rollins and Clifford Brown before forming his own group. He relocated to Los Angeles in 1957 and spent three years there playing with Harold Land and Lionel Hampton. —*Ron Wynn*

○ **Elmo Hope Trio, The** / May 1953-Jun. 1953 / Contemporary 7620

☆ **Elmo Hope—Vol. 2** / May 9, 1954 / Blue Note 5044

☆ **New Faces-New Sounds: Elmo Hope Quintet—Vol. 2** / May 9, 1954 / Blue Note 5044

○ **Elmo Hope Memorial Album, The** / Jul. 28, 1955 / Prestige 7675

★ **Hope Meets Foster** / Oct. 1955 / Prestige 1703
This, Elmo Hope's second date as a leader for Prestige, was not one of his quirkier recordings; he played in a fleet manner very much out of Bud Powell. Three tunes were by a quartet with Frank Foster (tenor sax), John Ore (bass), and Art Taylor (drums)

and three by a quintet with the addition of Foster's Wilberforce University bandmate, the accomplished if little-known trumpeter Freeman Lee. The standout here was "Georgia on My Mind," as it was played at an uncommonly brisk clip. . . . This was honest, hard-swinging music. —*Kevin Whitehead, Cadence*

○ **High Hope** / 1961 / Beacon 401

● **All Star Sessions, The** / Feb. 1977 / Fantasy 47037
Includes two sessions, from 1956 and 1961. A gathering of greats, supervised and sparked by Hope on piano. The list includes Coltrane (ts), Donald Byrd (tpt), and Jimmy Heath (sax). —*Ron Wynn*

Claude Hopkins (Claude Driskett Hopkins)

b. Aug. 24, 1903, Alexandria, VA, d. Feb. 19, 1984, New York, NY
Piano, bandleader / Swing, big band, blues & jazz
A rollicking pianist, arranger, and bandleader, Claude Hopkins was an exceptional musician who was underrated due to his success as a conductor and arranger. He had extensive harmonic knowledge, was a fine melodic interpreter, and played energetic, joyous uptempo tunes and steady blues and ballads. His parents were on the faculty at Howard University, where he studied music and medicine and obtained his degree. Hopkins's bands included such players as Jabbo Smith, Vic Dickenson, and Edmond Hall. He played with Wilber Sweatman in the '30s. Sweatman then led the band that accompanied Josephine Baker on her European tour in the mid-'20s. Hopkins led bands in New Jersey, New York, and Washington DC and then took over the Charlie Skeet band in 1930. They were featured at the Savoy and Roseland ballrooms and the Cotton Club. They also appeared in the films *Dance Team, Wayward, Barber Shop Blues*, and *Broadway Highlights* in the '30s. Orlando Robertson's vocal on "Trees" turned the song into a huge hit. Hopkins disbanded the orchestra in 1940, moved to the West Coast, and divided his time between conducting and arranging. He returned to New York in the mid-'40s and formed another band that played at the Zanzibar club. During the '50s Hopkins first led a combo in Boston and then went back to New York and the Zanzibar club in 1951. He worked with groups led by Henry "Red" Allen, Wild Bill Davison, and others. During the '70s Hopkins made solo records on the Chiaroscuro and Sackville labels. —*Ron Wynn*

○ **Singin' in the Rain** / Oct. 18, 1935 / Jazz Archives 27
The Claude Hopkins orchestra's light textures and even-handed attack were tailored for dancing. Solo strength was minor save for Hopkins, whose virtuosity exceeded his originality. —*John Mcdonough, Down Beat*

● **Soliloquy** / May 13, 1972 / Sackville 3004

Shirley Horn

b. May 1, 1934, Washington, DC
Vocals, piano, bandleader / Bop, ballads & blues
Vocalist, pianist, and bandleader Shirley Horn has been a star in Washington, DC since the '80s and now enjoys national attention and acclaim. She studied at Howard University and was helped early in her career by Miles Davis and Quincy Jones. She's among a select handful of artists whose vocal and piano skills are equal. Horn's a fine singer in the cabaret mode and prefers intimate ballads, show tunes, and standards. She's also a first-rate pianist with masterful solo and accompanying skills. Her late '80s and '90s records, as well as the now-sizable stream of reissues from earlier periods, have garnered critical raves. —*Ron Wynn*

★ **I Thought about You** / 1987 / Verve 833235
The art of comping behind oneself requires from a singer-pianist a combination of rare skills: an unerring sense of time, the ability to fill gaps without disturbing the lyrical flow, and intense concentration. Shirley Horn has mastered the dual role so effectively that she is able to lay back and play "catch up" with herself vocally, reharmonize what she plays creatively, and at times swing so confidently that she manages to goose her rhythm section. It could all be heard on her album *I Thought about You*. The vocal tricks and the free-wheeling swing seemed to come automatically. —*Harvey Siders, Jazz Times*

● **You Won't Forget Me** / Jun. 1990-Aug. 1990 / Verve 847482
The set that finally got her some attention. Miles Davis (tpt) and Wynton (tpt) and Branford Marsalis (ts) are part of the guest cast. Great piano and delightful vocals. —*Ron Wynn*

George Howard

Sax / Instrumental pop
George Howard is a top-selling instrumental pop and fusion sax-ophonist, among the biggest names on the "lite" jazz circuit of the '80s and '90s. Howard was formerly in Palo Alto's TBA division. He's been featured on several MCA/GRP releases. Howard performs instrumental covers of urban contemporary and R&B tunes. His songs are heavily produced, with background vocalists, a dominant backbeat, and minimal improvisation.—*Ron Wynn*

Nice Place to Be / i. 1977 / MCA 5855
More jazz content than usual, but still far from what Howard is capable of doing. —*Ron Wynn*

Steppin' Out / i. 1984 / GRP 9686

Dancing in the Sun / 1985 / TBA 205

Personal / i. Aug. 14, 1990 / MCA 335

Love Will Follow / i. Dec. 30, 1991 / GRP 9659

Do I Ever Cross Your Mind? / i. 1992 / GRP 9669
Unlike most of the soprano blowers out there in the pop-jazz market, Howard avoids the "Fuzak" plague, and keeps a strong hold on his R & B roots. At the same, time, Howard's latest stays away from the vocal-dominated tracks, which pop up all the more frequently in this genre. A solid, masterful set of funk-fusion. — *Steve Aldrich*

○ **Reflections** / MCA 42145

Very Best of George Howard, Vol. 1 / TBA 233

○ **When Summer Comes** / 80449

Freddie Hubbard (Frederick Dewayne Hubbard)

b. Apr. 7, 1938, Indianapolis
Trumpet, flugelhorn, piano, composer / Hard bop
Only occasional lapses in taste and material mar the otherwise glorious reputation and record of trumpeter Freddie Hubbard, a legitimate jazz giant. Hubbard began playing with the Montgomery Brothers in Indianapolis and at a Chicago club with Bunky Green, Frank Strozier, and Booker Little. He moved to New York in the late '50s and roomed with Eric Dolphy for 18 months. Hubbard played and worked with Sonny Rollins, Slide Hampton, and J. J. Johnson. He played with Quincy Jones from 1959 to 1961 and then joined Art Blakey's Jazz Messengers. This stint earned Hubbard widespread recognition, a *Down Beat* New Star Award in 1961, and validation of his driving, high-note, often acrobatic trumpet style. His work with Blakey, freelance appearances on a host of '60s gems from Ornette Coleman's *Free Jazz* to Coltrane's *Ascension*, and his own releases showed Hubbard's other trumpet gifts. These included a wonderful full tone, extensive range in the upper register and overblowing effects, his ability to excel in structured or free situations, and a dynamic, individualistic approach. Hubbard became a crossover star of sorts in the '70s: his albums *Red Clay* and *Straight Life* sold well outside the jazz world and his 1972 album *First Light* won a Grammy. Hubbard flirted with fusion and jazz-rock, but was largely unsuccessful from both an artistic and a financial standpoint. He reunited with Herbie Hancock, Wayne Shorter, Ron Carter, and Tony Williams in 1977. Calling themselves VSOP, the band had an acclaimed worldwide tour and equally praised recordings. Hubbard also participated in the relaunching of Blue Note Records in 1985. The bulk of his releases in the late '70s and throughout the '80s and '90s have been in the mainstream or hard-bop tradition, though not on the cutting edge like his '60s releases.—*Ron Wynn*

★ **Artistry of Freddie Hubbard** / Jul. 2, 1962 / MCA 33111
A misleading title, but a good attempt to compile Hubbard's best cuts from his '60s stint on Impulse. —*Ron Wynn*

○ **Caravan** / Jul. 2, 1962 / Impulse 27

★ **Hub-Tones** / Oct. 10, 1962 / Blue Note 84115

○ **Body and Soul, The** / Mar. 8+11, 1963 / Impulse 38

○ **Hub of Hubbard, The** / Dec. 9, 1969 / MPS 15267
Trumpeter Freddie Hubbard had a short stint on Verve Records during the '60s. The songs on this disc are taken from a quintet he led and recorded with in the late '60s. Hubbard worked with pianist Roland Hanna, tenor and clarinetist Eddie Daniels, bassist Richard Davis, and drummer Louis Hayes. The date was tightly

and professionally produced, and the performances were good. — *Ron Wynn*

★ **Red Clay** / Jan. 27+29, 1970 / CBS 40809
With his best-known composition, it stands the test of time. Done with Joe Henderson (ts). —*Michael G. Nastos*

★ **Straight Life** / Nov. 16, 1970 / CTI 8022
The second of his two best early '70s releases. Joe Henderson (ts) is amazing, and Hubbard is in top form, plus George Benson (g). —*Ron Wynn*

○ **First Light** / Sep. 1971 / CBS 40687
This is overarranged (as is usual with CTI) but has wonderful Hubbard solos. —*Ron Wynn*

○ **Live at the Hague (1980)** / 1980 / Pablo 2620113

○ **Sweet Return** / Jun. 13-14, 1983 / Atlantic 80108
Sweet Return was another all-star session, but what a difference! This band, assembled by George Wein to play festival dates in 1983, was simply outstanding. They spurred Freddie Hubbard into some of his most inspired and meaningful playing in years, and the result was his best album since *Super Blue* (1978). —*Jim Roberts, Down Beat*

★ **Double Take** / Nov. 21, 1985 / Blue Note 7462942
Other than their joint appearance as sidemen on Benny Golson's *Time Speaks* in 1983, Freddie Hubbard and Woody Shaw had never recorded together before *Double Take*. . . . At this point in their evolution, Hubbard still gets the edge (his range is wider and he cannot be surpassed technically). Although Shaw tended to play more harmonically sophisticated lines and is remarkably inventive, they are both trumpet masters. Their meeting on *Double Take* was more of a collaboration than a trumpet battle; in fact, the brass giants only trade off briefly on "Lotus Blossom." —*Scott Yanow, Cadence*

○ **A Hub of Hubbard / i.** 1988 / Polydor 8259562

☆ **Bolivia** / Dec. 1990-Jan. 1991 / Music Masters 5063
A set with good contributions by Ralph Moore (ts), Cedar Walton (p), and Billy Higgins (d). —*Ron Wynn*

○ **Live at Fat Tuesday / i.** 1991 / Music Masters 65075
Recent live date for trumpeter Freddie Hubbard, cut at Fat Tuesday's nightclub in New York. He's got a super group on this session, with pianist Bennie Green, bassist Christian McBride, drummer Tony Reedus, and excellent saxophonist Javon Jackson. The songs are peformed with enthusiam, and the solos are torrid. —*Ron Wynn*

Helen Humes

b. Jun. 23, 1913, Louisville, KY, **d.** Sep. 9, 1981, Santa Monica, CA
Vocals / Swing, big band, blues & jazz, ballads & blues
Though she often swore she wasn't a blues player, there was plenty of low-down soul in Helen Humes's best vocals. She recorded four songs for Okeh at 14 and worked steadily with Stuff Smith and Jonah Jones, Vernon Andrade, and Al Sears in the '30s. When Count Basie selected her to replace Billie Holiday in 1938, she spent three years with his orchestra. Humes was a popular participant in many package shows during the '40s. A move to the West Coast and her associations with Norman Granz and John Hammond helped Humes shift to the R&B circuit. She became a powerhouse vocalist in that style, while keeping her jazz roots through stints with Red Norvo. Humes lived in Australia during the early '60s, returned when her mother became ill in 1967, and resurfaced in triumph at the 1973 Newport Jazz Festival. She enjoyed great success for a long period in the '70s. —*Ron Wynn*

★ **E-Baba-Le-Ba** / Nov. 20, 1944-Nov. 20, 1950 / Savoy 1159
The rhythm and blues years. 1986 reissue of 1944 and 1950 sessions. Stomping, lusty cuts with Humes at her most down and dirty. Though she said she didn't sing blues, this is sure close to it. —*Ron Wynn*

○ **Tain't Nobody's Biz-Ness If I Do** / Jan. 5, 1959-Feb. 10, 1959 / Contemporary 453
This Helen Humes date will lock in one's mind—because she was one of the immediately identifiable jazz stylists and because it was an excellent example, perhaps one of the best post-Count Basie days examples, of her work. Emotion, open, warm, and swinging is what you've got here. —*Bob Rusch, Cadence*

○ **Helen Humes / i.** Jul. 1960 / Contemporary 3571

○ **Helen Humes: Talk of the Town** / Feb. 18, 1975 / Columbia 33488

This Columbia session, done in 1975, came much closer to challenging Helen Humes, due largely to the sensitivity of producer John Hammond, who truly understood Humes's musical element. Her "Talk of the Town" was among the most memorable treatments of the tune since Coleman Hawkins's 1954 version for Vanguard. "Good for Nothing Joe" and "You've Changed" were nearly as impressive. Her renderings were straightforward and totally unaffected, characteristics shared by the handful of great vocalists today. What gave them their unique mark, however, was the lilting innocence with which she graced even the most poignant lyric, lyrics that could sound self-pitying in lesser hands. —*John Mcdonough, Down Beat*

Bobby Hutcherson (Robert Hutcherson)

b. Jan. 27, 1941, Los Angeles
Vibes, marimba / Hard bop, modern creative
Vibist and marimba player Bobby Hutcherson's been an exceptional soloist and charismatic bandleader since the '60s, when his angular solos were heard on some of Blue Note's most challenging dates. His playing was distinguished by dazzling harmonic maneuvers using four mallets, blazing tempos, unusual voicings, and explosive solos. Hutcherson's albums gradually moved more to the center, but they remain delightful as he's done Afro-Latin, hard bop, soul-jazz, sessions with strings, and variations on all the above. He turned to vibes after being inspired by hearing a Milt Jackson recording. Hutcherson studied briefly with Dave Pike. He moved to New York from the West Coast in the early '60s. Hutcherson played with Jackie McLean, Grachan Moncur III, Charles Tolliver, Archie Shepp, Eric Dolphy, Andrew Hill, Tony Williams, and Herbie Hancock on many pivotal '60s dates. Later he co-led an influential and popular band with Harold Land in the late '60s and early '70s. Since then he's led various combos and done many sessions for such labels as Blue Note, Columbia, Landmark, Contemporary, and Timeless. —*Ron Wynn*

● **Dialogue** / Apr. 3, 1965 / Blue Note 46537
An album that was a landmark work in its time, this still has an edgy, avant-garde feeling, thanks to Sam Rivers (ts) and Andrew Hill (p). —*Ron Wynn*

★ **San Francisco** / 1971 / Blue Note 84362
Variety seemed to be the keynote of this collection of the Bobby Hutcherson-Harold Land quintet. The six compositions, which came from the members of the quintet, ranged from a fairly heavy rock sound ("Night in Barcelona") to dirty funky bluesy ("Ummh!") to bossa nova to a shimmering, static reflective effort by pianist Joe Sample. To further extend the range of sounds, the group made the most of its instrumentation—Sample played electric as well as acoustic piano (he got some weird twanging sounds on "Ummh!"); Land played tenor sax, oboe, and flute; Hutcherson used vibes and marimba. —*Jack McCaffrey, Coda*

☆ **Cirrus** / Apr. 17+18, 1974 / Blue Note
On *Cirrus* Bobby Hutcherson often favored the marimba for improvised solos and the vibraphone in the ensemble passages like a second piano. The album itself was one of strong rhythmic melodies laced with a variety of colors. All the music, except "Rosewood," was written and arranged by Hutcherson, and it ran an emotional scale from the tender ballad "Even Later," with its rich flute-trumpet harmonies and blend of acoustic piano and vibes, to the tense and dramatic "Zuri Dance." . . . Simply put, *Cirrus* was a musically exciting and emotionally satisfying album. —*Herb Nolan, Down Beat*

★ **Knucklebean** / 1977 / Blue Note 789
For this number Hutcherson brought in old pal trumpeter Freddie Hubbard, a mate for the Blue Note salad days, whose music at the time had gone to seed. Fortunately the huge Hubbard chops were still stimulated by an adventurous romp. He was truly resounding when helping a friend's album, even when giving the listener some sweet mute work on Hutcherson's updated "Little B." "Sundance" found him opening what became a roaring furnace with a beautiful unaccompanied prelude. —*Willard Jenkins Jr., Cadence*

○ **Solo / Quartet** / 1981 / Contemporary 425
This record had a split personality. One side, besides sharing the same vinyl, seemed unrelated to the other. On the solo side, Hutcherson played unaccompanied with some token assistance

from producer John Koenig on bells on "The Ice Cream Man." Side two was a quartet (pianist McCoy Tyner, bassist Herbie Lewis, drummer Billy Higgins) featuring the same group that collaborated in 1968 on Hutcherson's Blue Note record *Stick Up.* —*Gordon F.X. Allen, Cadence*

Dick Hyman (Richard Roven Hyman)

b. Mar. 8, 1927, New York City
Synthesizer, piano, organ, clarinet, composer / Ragtime, stride, boogie-woogie, swing
Dick Hyman has done valuable work as a jazz player, critic, and advocate. He collaborated with critic-journalist Leonard Feather on a series of "History of Jazz" concerts and did several major historical concerts with the New York Jazz Repertory Company, recreating the music of Louis Armstrong, James P. Johnson, Jelly Roll Morton, and Scott Joplin in the '70s. He recorded a number of technically wondrous albums of vintage and classic jazz piano in the '80s and recorded programs for British television. Hyman was a trailblazer in using synthesizers in jazz, and *The Electric Eclectics of Dick Hyman* was a '60s sensation. He remains an active and vital player, continuing to play vintage American pop and classic jazz and jazz-based styles.—*Ron Wynn*

○ **Live at Maybeck Recital Hall—Vol. 3: Music of 1937** / 1937 / Concord Jazz 4415

○ **Some Rags, Some Stomps, and a Little Blues** / Dec. 3, 1973 / Columbia 32587

○ **Satchmo Remembered** / Nov. 8, 1974 / Atlantic 1671

★ **Themes and Variations on "A Child Is Born"** / Oct. 11-12, 1977 / Chiaroscuro 198
Dick Hyman took "A Child Is Born" and beat it to death by playing it not only in his style, but also in the style of 11 other pianists (Scott Joplin, Jelly Roll Morton, James P. Johnson, Fats Waller, Earl Hines, Teddy Wilson, Errol Garner, George Shearing, Cecil Taylor, Art Tatum, and Bill Evans). —*Bob Rusch, Cadence*

○ **Charleston** / i. 1977 / Columbia 33706
A selection of the composed works of James P. Johnson was the focus of this recording issued on Columbia Masterworks. . . . Hyman fashioned orchestrations following note for note the models of Johnson's piano rolls, recordings, and sheet music. The voicings, which were Hyman's own, were faithful to the period, and the impeccable performances made the music superior to any other modern retrospective of the '20s that comes to mind. —*John Mcdonough, Down Beat*

○ **Music of Jelly Roll Morton** / Feb. 26, 1978 / Smithsonian 006
This live recording was from a concert at the Smithsonian. As the program proceeded, the musicians warmed up before an attentive and appreciative audience, and the performances became looser and began to lose their mechanical quality. "King Porter Stomp" and "Wolverine Blues" were scored by James Dapogny rather than pianist Dick Hyman, and the former title was the only full septet title on side one that achieved some impression of spontaneity. —*Shirley Klett, Cadence*

○ **Manhattan Jazz** / i. Dec. 2, 1985 / Music Masters 5031
W/ Ruby Braff. A wonderful, if very dated, example of vintage swing-era material. It's not traditional, simply a classic approach. —*Ron Wynn*

★ **Blues in the Night** / i. 1990 / Music Masters 5021

○ **Runnin' Ragged** / i. 1991 / Pro Arte 652

○ **Stride Piano Summit** / i. Nov. 6, 1991 / Milestone 9189

○ **Jelly and James—Music of "Jelly Roll" Morton And James P. Johnson** / i. Dec. 22, 1992 / Sony 52552

○ **Face the Music: A Century of Irving Berlin** / Music Masters 5002

Abdullah (Dollar Brand) Ibrahim
(Adolph Johannes Brand)

b. Oct. 9, 1934, Cape Town, South Africa
Piano, composer / World fusion
Although this pianist-composer's recordings are plentiful (on Enja primarily, and also Black Lion, Japo, Sackville, Plane, and others), he is not always easy to find in stores. One reason for this is that he started performing and recording as Dollar Brand (born Adolph Johannes Brand) and, to make matters worse for record store clerks, he is a South African artist who usually includes

African references in his album titles. But once located, his works are uniformly satisfying and consistently jazz-based, with unconcealed affinity for the music of Duke Ellington and Thelonious Monk. Ibrahim left South Africa in 1962, but before expatriation he left a legacy of lasting impact, in the form of recordings with Hugh Masekela, Kippy Moeketsi, and other forward-looking jazzmen. And he has never neglected his roots, maintaining the trademark "marabi" township sound in an ever-changing mix of solo, small group, large-band, straight jazz, and his own original compositions. His eclecticism and '60s influences often get him lumped in with the avant-garde, but his style is consistently melodious, and in recent years he has gravitated toward simpler African forms and mellow reflection, with breathy flute as his second instrument. Abdullah is the subject of a video entitled "A Brother with Perfect Timing", offering an engaging look into his personal blend of politics, spirituality, and world music. —*Myles Boisen*

○ **Fats Duke and the Monk** / i. 1973 / Sackville 3048

○ **Sangoma** / Feb. 1973 / Sackville 3006
Here Abdullah Ibrahim knitted African, Christian, and jazz themes into a cloak of identity that the pianist-composer hadn't before worn on album. Dramatic, somber rubato movements contrasted with folkish tunes and stylized single note and stride bass lines. The result was a weave detailing the past times and places of this far-traveled musician. —*Howie Mandel, Down Beat*

○ **African Space Program** / Nov. 7, 1973 / Enja
With this release of his first recording with a large group, he revealed his talents as an arranger. "Tintiyana, First Part" was enough to establish Ibrahim's credentials as an orchestrator of the first order. He wrote in colors, not sections, piling layer upon layer of muted dissonance, worthy of one of his mentors, Duke Ellington. "Tintiyana, Second Part" was mainly a series of remarkably coherent solos by all hands except, unfortunately, Ibrahim himself. His orchestral backgrounds encouraged and reinforced the soloists. This passionate, at times violent music, was uncompromisingly personal, deeply felt, and marked by complete musical integrity. —*Jon Balleras, Down Beat*

★ **Echoes from Africa** / Sep. 7, 1979 / Enja 79620
Echoes from Africa was, first and foremost, mood music. An atmosphere was immediately established in an African dialect, by Abdullah Ibrahim and Johnny Dyani. This led into a simple, repeated piano vamp, with the voices continuing, almost as added instruments. Despite the foreign words, one felt an eloquent story was being told, at times moaning, at other times distinctly conversational, and then moving into a crescendo of joy. —*Frankie Nemko-Graham, Down Beat*

○ **African Marketplace** / i. Dec. 1979 / Elektra
The title cut on *African Marketplace* was decidely non-Western, with African drums rolling through the piece and horn pairings that had a Middle Eastern flavor. Except for the drums, this depicted a marketplace anywhere in the Third World. Abdullah Ibrahim took a happy yet restrained soprano sax solo here; it was one of the few chances to hear him on that instrument rather than as a voice in horn pairings. . . . The finest moments on the record were found in those compositions most firmly rooted in the hymns and chants of Ibrahim's social-spiritual background, and it was encouraging to see how that environment more and more dominated his musical conceptions. —*R. Bruce Dold, Down Beat*

☆ **Zimbabwe** / May 29, 1983 / Enja 79632
This was a nicely blended, somewhat mellow, and seemingly quite finished recording by Abdullah Ibrahim with Carlos Ward (alto sax, flute), Essiet Okun Essiet (bass), and Don Mumford (drums). Interspaced with nonoriginals were four Ibrahim compositions, most of which were inspired by the imagery from Ibrahim's South African roots. —*Bob Rusch, Cadence*

☆ **Ekaya** / Nov. 17, 1983 / Ekapa 005
This studio date with septet is a must-buy. Extraordinary ensemble music. —*Michael G. Nastos*

☆ **Mantra Mode** / i. 1991 / Enja 79671
The sensual, reflective mergings of jazz, gospel, and South African-based music we have come to expect from Abdullah Ibrahim over the years are once again in full flower on *Mantra Mode*, recorded in January 1991 after he returned to his native Cape Town. *Mantra's* seven selections, recorded with a septet

comprising all South African musicians, will not surprise listeners acquainted with Ibrahim's stateside recordings with the aggregation he dubbed Ekaya (home). —*Reuben Jackson, Jazz Times*

Chuck Israels (Charles H. Israels)

b. Aug. 10, 1936, New York, NY
Bass, educator / Cool
A stirring, aggressive, and technically impressive bassist, Chuck Israels was not only an outstanding player in various free situations but also a capable and challenging accompanist for Bill Evans. He later formed a repertory group that performed and recreated traditional jazz arrangements. Israels had formal training in both America and Europe before making his jazz recording debut with Cecil Taylor in the late '50s. He joined George Russell's sextet in 1959, recording with him, Eric Dolphy, and Paul Horn in the early '60s. Israels replaced Scott LaFaro in Evans' trio in 1961 and remained until 1966. Israels also worked and recorded with J.J. Johnson, Herbie Hancock, Gary Burton, Stan Getz, and Hampton Hawes during that period. He formed the National Jazz Ensemble in the mid-'70s. This group recreated and performed arrangements and solos originally done by such giants as Jelly Roll Morton, Louis Armstrong, Duke Ellington, and Thelonious Monk. Tom Harrell, Jimmy Maxwell, Jimmy Knepper, Sal Nistico, and Bill Goodwin were among its members during the ensemble's five-year tenure. They recorded for Chiaroscuro in 1975 and 1976. Israels recorded with Rosemary Clooney in the mid-'80s.—*Ron Wynn*

● **National Jazz Ensemble** / i. 1976 / Chiaroscuro 151

Milt Jackson (Milton Jackson)

b. Jan. 1, 1923, Detroit
Vibes, marimba, piano / Bop
Arguably the greatest vibes player of the modern jazz era, Milt Jackson has become the epitome of class, skill, and mastery on his instrument by varying his approach on vibes, emphasizing longer notes, and playing in a subtle, careful fashion. *See* Modern Jazz Quartet. —*Ron Wynn*

○ **Milt Jackson** / i. Jun. 1948-Apr. 1952 / Blue Note 7815092

○ **Milt Jackson** / Aug. 18, 1951 / Blue Note 81509
W/ Thelonious Monk Quartet, this is the best early Milt away from the Modern Jazz Quartet. —*Michael G. Nastos*

○ **Quartet, The** / Aug. 1951-Apr. 1952 / Savoy 12046

○ **All-Star Bags** / Apr. 17, 1952 / Blue Note 590
All-Star Bags delineated a crucial transition period in Milt Jackson's journey, when he was converting his bop fluency into a more strident coinage, the reassuring tonal web that has been described as "Bags's Groove." The earliest tracks here—including pianist John Lewis, drummer Kenny Clarke, and bassist Percy Heath—featured Lou Donaldson's rich tenor foil. The tonal and spiritual catalyst of the saxophone often extracted the most aggressive and inventive sides of Jackson, and these vernal examples bore that out. The subsequent 1957 recordings with saxophonist Hank Mobley, pianist Horace Silver, and drummer Art Blakey were less interactive. —*Mikal Gilmore, Down Beat*

○ **First Q, The** / Apr. 1952-Aug. 24, 1952 / Savoy 1106
Very early Milt Jackson material from his formative period, some of it featuring him playing vibes with future Modern Jazz Quartet colleagues pianist John Lewis and bassist Percy Heath, plus the Quartet's first drummer, Kenny Clarke. These sessions have been reissued on CD. —*Ron Wynn*

○ **Meet Milt Jackson** / Oct. 28, 1955 / Savoy Jazz 172
Meet Milt Jackson unites cuts from '56 (Wade Legge replacing Hank Jones; best is the lengthy "Soulful"); "Telefunken Blues" from '55 arranged by Ernie Wilkins (Bags is credited for piano and vibes); Bags crooning "I've Lost Your Love" from a '54 session (without the listed horns); and three septet cuts stirred by drummer Roy Haynes from '49.—*Howard Mandel, Down Beat*

○ **Atlantic Years, The** / Jan. 17, 1956-Feb. 24, 1960 / SD 2319

○ **Ballads and Blues** / Jan. 17, 1956 / Atlantic 1242

★ **Jazz Skyline, The** / Jan. 23, 1956 / Savoy 410
This session has interest as an example of Milt Jackson's mid-'50s work in a non-Modern Jazz Quartet context. And despite the many critical assertions that the vibist was restrained by pianist

John Lewis's direction, his playing here revealed no marked changes. The overall feel of the group (Lucky Thompson, tenor sax; Hank Jones, piano; Wendell Marshall, bass; Kenny Clarke, drums; Jackson, vibes), however, was somewhat more dynamic than that of the MJQ, as Clarke and Jones generally achieved a greater sense of forward momentum than Connie Kay or Lewis. —*Bob Rusch, Cadence*

○ **Plenty, Plenty Soul** / Jan. 5, 1957 / Atlantic 1269
Not only did it capture vibist Milt Jackson in a straightahead jazz date, but it also offered some fine contributions from the likes of alto saxophonist Cannonball Adderley, tenor saxophonist Frank Foster, pianist Horace Silver, and trumpeter Joe Newman. . . . All in all there wasn't a weak track on this refreshing recording. —*Carl Brauer, Cadence*

★ **Soul Brothers** / i. 1958 / Atlantic 1279
Both this and Milt Jackson-Ray Charles releases are essential. The perfect marriage of blues, jazz, soul, and elegance. —*Ron Wynn*

☆ **Bags and Trane** / Jan. 15, 1959 / Atlantic 1368
Exceptional meeting of minds between Jackson and John Coltrane (ts). —*Ron Wynn*

○ **Impulse Years, The** / 1962-1969 / Impulse 92822
Retrospective containing songs cut by vibist Milt Jackson during his tenure at Impulse. This included quartet, quintet, sextet, and big band albums recorded between 1962 and 1969, most done in the studio, but two recorded live. They also feature several numbers done with non-Modern Jazz Quartet players, among them bassists Paul Chambers and Ray Brown, as well as pianist Hank Jones. —*Ron Wynn*

○ **Milt Jackson Big Four, The** / Jul. 17, 1975 / Pablo 2310753

○ **Big Three, The** / Aug. 25, 1975 / Pablo 757
Recorded on August 25, 1975, in Los Angeles, this contained some breezy solos that lifted the standard of the music above that of run-of-the-mill competence. The program selection varied and the rhythm propelled as melodic cohesion. —*Bill Gallagher, Cadence*

○ **Milt Jackson in London (Memories of Thelonious Monk)** / Apr. 28, 1982 / Pablo 235
Commemorative concert for piano great Thelonious Monk done by vibist Milt Jackson in the early '80s. Jackson transferred Monk's intricate, complex compositions to vibes perfectly, getting both the flavor and the difficult harmonic structures down easily. —*Ron Wynn*

● **Memories of Thelonious Sphere Monk** / Apr. 1982 / Pablo 235
"Django" held up well for its 10+ minutes; "Groundhog" boasted one of those nice blues grooves that Bags (Milt Jackson) digs into so nicely. One expected a certain standard from these veterans (pianist Monty Alexander, bassist Ray Brown, drummer Mickey Roker) and you got it; look for an average couple of night club sets (Ronnie Scott's), don't expect more, and you'll not be disappointed. —*Bob Rusch, Cadence*

★ **Harem, The** / i. 1991 / Music Masters 5061

Ronald Shannon Jackson

b. Jan. 12, 1940, Fort Worth, TX
Drums / Early jazz rock, modern creative
Ronald Jackson is in the top echelon of contemporary drummers. He played in Dallas bands as a teen with legendary figures James Clay and Leroy Cooper. Later he got a music scholarship in New York, cut free records with Charles Tyler, and played with Albert Ayler, Betty Carter, and others. By the mid-'70s, Jackson was at the center of a pulsating, cutting-edge, "harmolodic" band, playing drums in Ornette Coleman's group. He also worked with Cecil Taylor and later "Blood" Ulmer and then formed Last Exit with Sonny Sharrock and Bill Laswell. He is a master at unifying seemingly chaotic sessions with his crisp, attacking drumming, varying the beat and the pulse. —*Ron Wynn*

○ **Nasty** / i. Mar. 1981 / Moers 01086

○ **Street Priest** / Jun. 13-16, 1981 / Moers 01906
Chronologically, *Street Priest* preceded *Man Dance*, and differed by the latter having a wider sonic latitude as Henry Scott on trumpet replaced Lee Rozie's reeds after the band returned to America. Otherwise the band personnel remained the same, featuring the two-bass team of Melvin Gibbs and "Rev" Bruce Johnson with guitarist Vernon Reid and saxist Zane Massey

alongside the leader's drums. So much of the music entered into the realm of sheer sound, as instruments slipped in and out of synch to the beat. Themes were stated, disappeared, and resurfaced again slightly changed. *Street Priest* was a jewel that combined the fire of a live performance and the finish of a studio album. —*Jim Brinsfield, Down Beat*

○ **Mandance** / Jun. 1982 / Antilles 846397
The compositions, with two exceptions, had a frenetic quality, with the group building a wall of sound that was thick and sometimes impenetrable. Yet there was such a positive feeling to the music that it did not come off as overkill. The two bassists never clashed —Bruce Johnson had a smoother style, accentuated by his use of fretless bass, while Melvin Gibbs had more of a trebly tone. —*Richard B. Kamins, Cadence*

★ **Barbeque Dog** / Mar. 1983 / Antilles 848817
The most memorable songs were "Gossip" and "Harlem Opera." Jackson said the former was "like being in the middle of a New York disco and an African village at the same time." Both places were infested with vicious prattle, and the Decoding Society, with motormouth guitar, brazen horns, and alternating outspoken and private passages, did its damnedest to parody the nuances of idle talk. "Harlem Opera" was an elegy for a fallen cultural center; the blue four-note melodic theme was made all the more dolorous by the inclusion of voices. Saxophonist Zane Massey, who was submerged in the record mix elsewhere, added some tortured cries. Jackson's songs were infused with intricate rhythmic ideas. African, Central European, and Eastern influences—rhythmic or otherwise—stirred drummer and band. —*Frank-John Hadley, Down Beat*

☆ **Red Warrior** / i. 1990 / Axiom 510149
Sprawling drums and guitar highlight this recent session. Produced by Bill Laswell. —*Ron Wynn*

Willis Jackson (Willis "Gator" Jackson)

b. Apr. 25, 1932, Miami, FL, d. Oct. 25, 1987, New York, NY
Sax / Swing, blues & jazz, soul jazz
Saxophonist Willis Jackson is a soul-jazz giant. He invented the "gator" horn, a long sax with a ball-shaped bell and small opening with a sound between alto and soprano. An established professional at 14, Jackson got his nickname when he cut the original "Gator Tail" while playing with Cootie Williams. From the 50s to the 80s, Jackson was superb playing with a funky, blues-based, and soulful style. His approach included lots of honks, moans, and vocal effects—never anything outside or fancy, but it was very popular and appealing. Jackson also had a busy schedule of R&B dates in the '50s and was married for a time to Ruth Brown. Soul-jazz was his menu from the '60s till the end of his career. —*Ron Wynn*

○ **Cool Gator** / May 25, 1959-Nov. 9, 1959 / Prestige 220
Willis Jackson (tenor sax) was one of the prime exploiters of the commercial funk exposure of the late '60s. *Cool Gator*, however, was a reasonably restrained LP made up of three dates. —*Bob Rusch, Cadence*

★ **Together Again** / May 25, 1959-Aug. 16, 1960 / Prestige 7364

○ **Cookin' Sherry** / Nov. 9, 1959-Aug. 16, 1960 / Prestige 7211

○ **Thunderbird** / Mar. 31, 1962 / Prestige

★ **Shuckin'** / Oct. 30, 1962 / Prestige
His second great album that year. All-star lineup included Kenny Burrell (g), Tommy Flanagan (p). —*Ron Wynn*

○ **In the Alley** / 1976 / Muse 5100
Solid soul-jazz from a tenor sax master of the style. Willis Jackson never tried to play intricate or elaborate solos; he relied on intensity, blues feeling, and simplicity to communicate his soulful messages. —*Ron Wynn*

★ **Bar Wars** / Dec. 1977 / Muse 6011

○ **Single Action** / Apr. 1978 / Muse 5179
The best piece was six lean and mean minutes of boiling, double-timed blues that featured a delightfully frenzied Jackson and the taut Wes Montgomeryisms of guitarist Pat Martino. —*Bill Shoemaker, Cadence*

Illinois Jacquet (Jean Baptiste Illinois Jacquet)

b. Oct. 31, 1922, Boussard, LA
Tenor sax / Swing, big band, bop, soul-jazz

Jean Baptiste Illinois Jacquet, one of the great tenor saxophonists of all time, was raised in Houston and began his professional career while in high school with the Milt Larkin band. He moved to Los Angeles in 1939 and came to prominence in the Lionel Hampton band. With Hampton, he recorded the "Flying Home" solo (1942), among the most famous tenor sax solos ever. He did more big band work with Cab Calloway (1943-1944) and Count Basie (1944-1946) and was active in the California jam session scene that resulted in the first *Jazz at the Philharmonic* concert (July 1944)recorded. Though the records took almost two years to be issued, they created a sensation via Jacquet's screaming tenor work. The records were the first live jazz on record. Of his JATP solos, "Blues Part 2" was the most famous. He made national tours with JATP (1946-1948, 1951 and 1955-1957) and was a frequent participant on JATP recordings ("Perdido"). His own small band was formed in the mid-'40s, and he recorded for Apollo, Alladin, and RCA (1945-1950). Of these, the Apollos have a slight edge on the Alladins, with the RCAs some distance behind, but all contain his driving, sensual tenor work in combos of varying size, utilizing a swing-bop-jump combination typical of the '40s. He began recording for Mercury/Clef (later Verve) in 1951. "Port of Rico" was a big hit featuring the tenor-organ sound. His albums began in 1955, and there are many good ones on Verve, Roulette, Epic, and Prestige (*Bottoms Up, The Blues, That's Me* are especially good). European and Japanese recordings from the '70s and '80s are variable, but his best in many, many years was *Jacquet's Got It* (Atlantic), devoted to his big band (formed in 1983) and showing him still in top form. —*Bob Porter*

★ **Black Velvet Band** / i. 1947-1950 / Bluebird 6571
Prime eight- and ten-piece group cuts from 1947-1950, plus one cut from the 1967 Newport festival. —*Ron Wynn*

○ **Illinois Jacquet Jam Session** / i. 1951 / Apollo 104

○ **Illinois Jacquet** / Sep. 16, 1955 / Clef 676

○ **Port of Rico** / i. 1956 / Clef 701

○ **King, The** / Aug. 20, 1968 / Prestige 7597

★ **Blues from Louisiana** / Jul. 7, 1973 / Classic Jazz
This was an odd record, taken either from different live sessions or as part of a bigger all star bash.... "On a Clear Day" was open, loose, and swingingly pushed by Jacquet's big throaty vibrato on tenor; "Marlow's La. Blues" was a slow d-r-a-w-n out funky teaser worried to death by organist Milt Buckner and Jacquet. —*Bob Rusch, Cadence*

● **Cool Rage, The** / Verve
The Cool Rage reissued by tenor saxophonist Illinois Jacquet was culled from various Verve sessions. The two-record set included tracks from 4/21/58 with Wild Bill Davis (organ), Kenny Burrell (guitar), and Johnny Williams (drums).... The music was a mixture of *Jazz at the Philharmonic* wailings, after-hours blues, and relaxed Lestorian (Young) blowing. There were some nice tastes of Basie organ, an organist even for those who do not like organ. This was a nice look at '50s Jacquet. —*Bob Rusch, Cadence*

Ahmad Jamal (Fritz Jones)

b. Jul. 2, 1930, Pittsburgh, PA
Piano / Bop
Pianist Jamal was amazingly influential, though far from being an Art Tatum or Bud Powell. His left hand voicings and teasing right hand contrasts, plus a liberal inclusion of block chords and particularly concept of space, got an enormous boost through the embrace and utilization of various Jamal techniques by Miles Davis. Jamal formed his first band in 1949 after leaving the George Hudson group and scored a hit with a new arrangement of "Billy Boy." He adopted his textbook trio formula in the '50s when he replaced the guitar with drums and upgraded bassist Israel Crosby's role. He predated other popular trios like Ramsey Lewis, though he was a superior stylist. Jamal remains active and has recorded extensively for Cadet/Chess, Impulse, Atlantic, and Telarc, among others.—*Ron Wynn*

● **Poinciana** / i. Oct. 25, 1952-1955 / Chess 31266

○ **Chamber Music of New Jazz** / May 23, 1955 / Argo 602

○ **Ahmad Jamal Trio** / Oct. 25, 1955 / Epic 3212

○ **Count 'em—88** / Sep. 27, 1956+Oct. 4, 1956 / Argo 610

★ **At the Pershing / But Not for Me** / i. Jan. 16, 1958 / Chess 9108

Recorded at Pershing Club, Chicago, IL. A twofer. Third album (includes hit "Poinciana") was the turning point in his career. His liberal use of silence influenced many jazz musicians, including Miles Davis. —*Michael Erlewine*

Ahmad Jamal Trio—Vol. 4 / Sep. 5-06, 1958 / Argo 636
One of his most popular albums ever in its original issue. Fine, if a bit to the pop side. —*Ron Wynn*

○ **Listen to the Ahmad Jamal Quintet** / Aug. 15-16, 1960 / Argo 673

○ **Piano Scene** / i. Apr. 1965 / Epic 634

○ **Live at the Montreux Jazz Festival** / i. Feb. 1986 / Atlantic 81699
Shimmering, attacking style at times. Still the master of space and pauses. —*Ron Wynn*

☆ **What's New** / Telstar 3604
Giants of Jazz series. 17 hits from a variety of his original Chess recordings. Includes "Poinciana." —*Michael Erlewine*

Khan Jamal

b. Jul. 23, 1946, Jacksonville, FL
Vibes / Modern creative
Though not a widely known vibist, Khan Jamal has been a proficient soloist whether playing free material, jazz-rock and fusion, hard bop, or bluesy fare. He's also an outstanding marimba player and percussionist. Jamal's mother was a stride pianist, and he began on vibes in the mid-'60s. Jamal was in the Cosmic Forces in the late '60s, then coformed the Sounds of Liberation with Byard Lancaster in the early '70s. He studied vibes and percussion at Combs College of Music and then performed and recorded with Sunny Murray's Untouchable Factor in the late '70s. Jamal played with Ronald Shannon Jackson's Decoding Society and in bands led by Joe Bonner and Billy Bang and headed his own groups in the '80s and '90s. Jamal has recorded as a leader for Philly Jazz, Steeplechase, Stash, Gazell, and Storyville among others. He's played with Bill Lewis, Monette Sudler, Dwight James, and Jamaaladeen Tacuma, among others. Jamal has some sessions available on CD. —*Ron Wynn*

● **Infinity** / i. Dec. 1982-Mar. 1984 / Stash 278

Bob James (Robert James)

b. Dec. 25, 1939, Marshall, MO
Piano, composer, producer / Early jazz rock, instrumental pop
Pianist and composer Bob James took a turn toward fusion in the early '70s and never returned to straight jazz. James worked for Maynard Ferguson in the '60s and then spent five years with Sarah Vaughan. He amassed a lot of studio credits as a composer-arranger until 1973, when he hit the jackpot with CTI/Kudu. Since then he has specialized in making instrumental pop albums with catchy melodies, heavy beats, and little jazz content. —*Ron Wynn*

One / i. 1974 / Columbia 36835
The first in a string of hugely successful albums from pianist-composer Bob James in the '70s. James joined the CTI label in 1973 and became their exclusive arranger; the next year he signed a separate recording deal as an artist. This was his debut, and he scored a hit with an interpretation of Moussorgsky's "Night on Bald Mountain." —*Ron Wynn, AMG*

Lucky Seven / i. 1979 / Columbia 36056
Successful fusion album by a superstar in the genre. James made an art form of short solos, pop-tinged instrumentals, and multi-tracked vocals by guest stars. This album utilized all those elements. —*Ron Wynn, AMG*

○ **Two of a Kind** / i. 1982 / Capitol 12244

★ **Grand Piano Canyon** / i. 1990 / Tappan Zee 26256

Harry James (Harry Hagg James)

b. Mar. 15, 1916, Albany, GA, d. Jul. 5, 1983, Las Vegas, NV
Trumpet, bandleader / Swing, big band
In 1942, Harry James had the most popular band in the United States, broke Benny Goodman's attendance record at New York's Paramount Theater, and made more money than any living musician. He was married to Betty Grable, the number one pinup of the Armed Forces, and appeared in feature films himself. It was this great fame, little remembered today, that enabled James to

carry on as leader of a big band long after most others had quit—indeed, only Count Basie, Duke Ellington, Woody Herman, and Stan Kenton joined him in that select circle. James came to stardom with Benny Goodman's band, which he joined at 20. The son of a circus band leader and a sometime contortionist, he was raised under the big top; his first instrument was drums. At ten, he took up trumpet and soon was winning contests; at 17, he hit the road. His idol was Louis Armstrong, but it was with a piece of "schmaltz," "You Made Me Love You," that his struggling big band finally hit the jackpot. From then on, he had to provide liberal doses of sweet stuff but remained loyal to his jazz muse. (He also was Mr. Nice, letting the unknown singer he'd been first to hire, Frank Sinatra, go on to bigger bucks with rival Tommy Dorsey). Harry had integrated bands; altoist Willie Smith of Lunceford fame was with him for decades. He liked good drummers: Buddy Rich and Louis Bellson both spent time with him. And he loved the Count Basie sound, hiring Ernie Wilkins, Thad Jones, and Neal Hefti to write for him. When he wanted to, Harry could play jazz trumpet with the best of them, and more often than not, he did. —*Dan Morgenstern*

★ **Harry James and Dick Haymes** / 1941 / Circle

○ **Uncollected Harry James & His Orchestra—Vol. 1 (1943-1946)** / 1943-1946 / Hindsight 102

○ **Uncollected Harry James & His Orchestra—Vol. 2 (1943-1946)** / 1943-1946 / Hindsight 123

○ **Uncollected Harry James & His Orchestra—Vol. 4 (1943-1946)** / 1943-1946 / Hindsight 141

○ **Uncollected Harry James & His Orchestra—Vol. 5 (1943-1953)** / 1943-1953 / Hindsight 142

○ **Uncollected Harry James & His Orchestra—Vol. 6 (1947-1949)** / 1947-1949 / Hindsight 150

○ **Uncollected Harry James & His Orchestra—Vol. 3 (1948-1949)** / 1948-1949 / Hindsight 135

○ **Young Man with a Horn** / i. 1950 / Columbia 582
Soundtrack from a well-intentioned, inaccurate film portrait of Bix Beiderbecke. —*Ron Wynn*

Joseph Jarman

b. Sep. 14, 1937, Pine Bluff, Arkansas
Reeds, flute, clarinet, piccolo, percussion, composer / Early free, modern creative
Saxophonist Joseph Jarman was a founding member of the Art Ensemble of Chicago and an early participant with Muhal Richard Abrams and Roscoe Mitchell in an experimental band that led to the formation of the Association for the Advancement of Creative Musicians (AACM). He studied drums in high school and learned sax and clarinet while in the army, before taking additional courses at the Chicago Conservatory. He and Mitchell were members of Abrams's experimental band, later teaming up with trumpeter Lester Bowie, bassist Malachi Favors, and drummer Don Moye to form the Art Ensemble of Chicago, a band that performed everything from meticulously structured pieces to freewheeling statements incorporating aspects of theater and makeup. Jarman also headed his own bands in the late '60s, including poetry and programmed selections during his performances, as well as premiering theatrical pieces. —*Ron Wynn*

★ **Song For** / Oct. 20, 1966-Dec. 16, 1966 / Delmark 410
The ensemble the now criminally underrecorded Joseph Jarman put together for *Song For* is nothing less than legendary: trumpeter Bill Brimfield; tenor godfather Fred Anderson; the late, great drummer Steve McCall; and the late, destined-to-be-great bassist, Charles Clark; pianist Christopher Gaddy; and drummer Thurman Barker. Additionally, all of the tenets of Jarman's music were already in place, such as fanfares floating over drum swells, elongating into themes tinged with bop and serialism; adagios with a hallowed, hymnal feel, catalysing impassioned solos; and a more pointed integration of auxilliary percussion and poetry than practiced by his collegues. No wonder, then, that *Song For* has retained its edge and its cogency. —*Bill Shoemaker, Down Beat*

● **As If It Were the Seasons** / 1968 / Delmark 417
A textbook '60s Chicago free-jazz album from a founding member of the AACA, multiinstrumentalist Joseph Jarman. He employs his full array of horns and is joined by several mainstays, among them pianist Muhal Richard Abrams, bassist Charles

Clark, drummer Thurman Barker, and tenor saxophonist John Stubblefield. This is not compromising material; songs are long, and everything from bells to whistles to shakers to energized sax screaming comprises the music. —*Ron Wynn*

○ **Magic Triangle** / Jul. 24-26, 1979 / Black Saint 0038
Though *The Magic Triangle* was ostensibly equilateral, the pianist (Don Pullen) was the dominant player. Don Moye's "J.F.M. 3-Way Blues" began with his solo parade drums, soon joined by fellow Chicago Art Ensemblist Joseph Jarman's piccolo for a little Fourth of July fife-and-drum. —*Kevin Whitehead, Cadence*

○ **Black Paladins** / i. Dec. 1979 / Black Saint 0042
The teaming of South African bassist Johnny Dyani with Art Ensemble of Chicago stalwarts Joseph Jarman and Don Moye resulted here in an absorbing album. This was a program of well-fired, articulate performances, in both individual and collective terms. *Black Paladins* was roughly divided between pieces of a marked Third World flavor and those more squarely implanted in the jazz tradition. —*Bill Shoemaker, Cadence*

Keith Jarrett

b. May 8, 1945, Allentown, PA
Piano, composer / Cool, early jazz rock, world fusion
Pianist Keith Jarrett has been a prolific contributor and often controversial figure since his days with the Charles Lloyd quartet. His playing, with its frenetic left hand rhythms, equally intense and linear right hand runs, and his swing and subdued blues feeling, is among the most readily identifable in recent history. His classical playing lacks the emotional impact of his best jazz work but is usually immaculately performed. Jarrrett's been extremely well served by his ECM albums, especially the solo works. He's also done duets with Jack DeJohnette, led one of the more acclaimed combos of the '70s, made many trio and concept dates, even written guest New York Times pieces. Jarrett's been quite critical of contemporary tastes and culture and in recent times has been embroiled in his own flap regarding critics who've attacked his tendency to accompany his piano solos with vocal effects (something many find charming and others disturbing or irritating). His live dates are never dull and can often be unforgettable; likewise, his best albums are spectacular triumphs, his worst self-indulgent beyond anyone's worst nightmares. —*Ron Wynn and Michael G. Nastos*

☆ **Life Between the Exit Signs** / May 4, 1967 / Vortex 2006

★ **Expectations** / Oct. 1971 / Columbia 46866
Two-record set with lots of experimental, high energy moments. 1991 reissue. —*Ron Wynn*

☆ **Facing You** / Nov. 10, 1971 / ECM 827132
Keith Jarrett, a stunningly original musician, disavows having *any* premeditated approach to improvisation. He also formulated what amounts to a partially Platonic musical aesthetic, one that suggests he was simply allowing music from a higher source to flow through himself. This record was so inspired that it was tempting to believe this was actually happening. Indeed, dividing the music here into eight "tunes" would be highly arbitrary and, in fact, incorrect. What we were listening to was simply the music in Jarrett, whatever it's ultimate source. —*Jon Balleras, Down Beat*

☆ **Fort Yawuh** / Feb. 1973 / MCA 33122
Pianist Keith Jarrett's biggest contributions on this album came on the two more reflective numbers. The title cut was something of a gem. Jarrett expanded his atmospheric (if slightly melodramatic) line with sensitivity and boldness; he, bassist Charlie Haden, and drummer Paul Motian weren't afraid to vary their individual and collective pulses, with some nice results. . . . "Still Life" had two sets of romantic feeling to it; the solo piano intro was expressive within a severe, almost metronomic rhythm, while the tune itself had a looser, lusher ballad sound. —*Steve Metaliz, Down Beat*

☆ **Solo Concerts—Bremen and Lausanne** / Mar. 20, 1973+Jul. 12, 1973 / ECM 827747
The musical commingling of beauty, strength, and precision can be most elusive. When it is accomplished by one man on one instrument without sacrifice or compromise, it can be an act of total interaction between player and listener. And when it is done by an artist (though he avoids the term) of pianist Keith Jarrett's inventiveness and commitment—and done over the course of a three-record, two-hours-plus album— he emotional sharing can

be an *incredible* experience. In fact, the word *incredible* is an understatement here. The music was lyrical without being soft or fragile. It was at once a crystalline and flowing beauty, a music with the pastoral grace of Bach and the heart of the blues. It was heart-swelling and head-swinging. And it was totally devoid of vacant impressionism and gushing romanticism. — *Will Smith, Down Beat*

☆ **Belonging** / Apr. 1974 / ECM 829115
"Spiral" was a good introduction to this session, serious but not sober. Keith Jarrett set up a left hand drone and played off right hand figures against it; the melody—surprisingly, given the drone effect—evoked the days of hard bop. A similiar astonishment surfaced on "Long As." The setting, performed by the piano trio, was nearly gospel, but the melody contained some Caribbean flavoring and some fascinatingly unexpected accents, sliding between bar lines in a most ungospelish manner. But "Blossom" was the best thing on the album, 12 minutes of inspired improvisation. — *Alan Heineman, Down Beat*

○ **Luminessence** / Apr. 1974 / ECM 839307
Keith Jarrett's *Luminessence* was a musical enterprise that totally transcended the convenient labels that are used by the music industry, the public, and the critics. Probing deep into his own personal musical cosmos, Jarrett brought back a chilling and singular achievement that stands as a landmark in the musical landscape of the '70s. The musicianship was excellent. Jan Garbarek's amazingly harnessed high energy and the superb ensemble playing of the Sudfunk Symphony Orchestra's string section provided an outstanding performance. — *Chuck Berg, Down Beat*

★ **Backhand** / i. Oct. 9-10, 1974 / Impulse 9305
Landmark quintet with Dewey Redman (ts), Charlie Haden (b), Paul Motian (d), Guilherme Franco (per). Any recording by this band is worthwhile. — *Michael G. Nastos*

☆ **Koln Concert** / Jan. 24, 1975 / ECM 810067
Keith Jarrett recorded this concert in Koln, Germany, which emerged as the pinnacle of his solo art. Jarrett not only distilled and refined the broad concept and specialized technique of his earlier *Solo-Concerts;* he also broke through the potential limitations of the solo idiom—and of his own choices in length and form—to erect magnifying mirrors of his clear vision. The fingers were often startling, the melodies infectious, the piano arranging richly diverse, the self-propulsive rhythmic stomp sections glorious in their vibrancy; and still, the most enduring quality of these performances was their breathtaking intimacy. — *Neil Tesser, Down Beat*

○ **Shades** / 1975 / Impulse 9322
[The music] was direct and to the point with none of the aimlessness that tended to mar *Death and the Flower* and *Backhand.* Pianist Keith Jarrett and tenor saxophonist Dewey Redman immediately grabbed the listener on "Shades" with their unison lines. A brisk Jarrett solo followed with him humming along a la Erroll Garner. After Redman's solo and a brief theme restatement, the piece segued into "Southern Smiles," a gospel tune with a calypso-styled beat. Not once was the listener left daydreaming. Unfortunately "Rose Petals" failed to sustain the excitement, but then "Diatribe" ripped things apart. — *Carl Brauer, Cadence*

○ **Silence** / 1975 / GRP 117
Tremendous mid-'70s quartet session headed by pianist Keith Jarrett. Jarrett was in the midst of an impressive recording and touring string with this group, which included tenor saxophonist Dewey Redman, bassist Charlie Haden, and drummer Paul Motian. Almost every release they issued was superb; this one was no different. It has been reissued on CD. — *Ron Wynn, AMG*

○ **My Song** / Oct. 31, 1977-Nov. 1, 1977 / ECM 821406
My Song showcased Keith Jarrett's maximizing his European-Romantic insights at the expense of his incredibly powerful rhythmic and blues roots. Jarrett's focus here seemed to be on creating little melodic miniatures and interludes. The playing was refined and idealized the recording (as expected on ECM). It was flawless, but at times the concept seemed a shade too languid. — *Chip Stern, Down Beat*

○ **Nude Ants** / May 1979 / ECM 829119
Nude Ants was the first live album pianist-composer Keith Jarrett made with his quartet featuring the Scandinavian mafia, saxophonist Jan Garbarek, bassist Palle Danielson, and drummer Jon

Christensen. It was also the pianist's second in-concert recording at the Village Vanguard. While they were able players—Garbarek's haunting tone and Christensen's subtle backbeats were quite enticing—they were at a disadvantage in dealing with Keith Jarrett, vintage 1980. He was now a star. Notoriety canonized his technique and creative powers. Working with him became a lesson in inhibition. So it was for Garbarek, Danielsson, and Christensen. They played well, but they held back—Jarrett came forth. Thus, *Nude Ants* became a document of his growth as a composer and pianist since the days of *Fort Yawuh.* —*Cliff Tinder, Down Beat*

○ **Standards—Vol. 1** / Jan. 1983 / ECM 811966
The approach on this record extended the trio concept initiated by pianist Bill Evans, bassist Scott LaFaro, and drummer Paul Motian circa 1960. Keith Jarrett guided, but Gary Peacock and Jack DeJohnette were free to follow their own instincts in pursuing the collective goal. And Jarrett left plenty of room for their explorations. The pianist accumulated fragments into longer lines, punctuating with sparsely placed chords. Only "God Bless the Child" received a different transport—funky, gospel chords and a semirock beat. —*Owen Cordle, Down Beat*

○ **Standards—Vol. 2** / Jan. 1983 / ECM 825015
(*Standards, Vol. 2*) was almost on a par with the free-wheeling *Changes* from the same trio sessions. This was one of Jarrett's better trio dates; it was not up to the high water mark of his Vortex album *Somewhere Before* with Charlie Haden (bass) and Paul Motian (drums), but then Jarrett wasn't the playfully exuberant pianist he was in 1968. Still, here he neither strained for effect nor attempted to build a cathedral every time out. —*Kevin Whitehead, Cadence*

○ **Standards Live** / Jul. 2, 1985 / ECM 827827
Standards Live, from 1987, continued at the same high level of previous *Standards Vol. 1 & 2* with pianist Keith Jarrett often recalling his early influence, Bill Evans. The well-integrated trio (w/ Gary Peacock, bass and Jack DeJohnette, drums) played three frequently performed tunes and three obscurities. The interplay between the players was constantly impressive. —*Scott Yanow, Cadence*

○ **Foundations: Anthology** / i. 1994 / Rhino
Pianist Keith Jarrett didn't attain stardom or international acclaim while an Atlantic artist; that came when he moved first to Impulse and then to ECM, where label head Manfred Eicher turned him loose to do anything he desired. That resulted in numerous releases ranging from shimmering solo sets to classical concerts; quartet, quintet, and trio dates; even organ works. Jarrett polished his skills during his Atlantic tenure, doing dates as a sideman with vibist Gary Burton, working in Art Blakey's Jazz Messengers, as a member of the Charles Lloyd Quartet, and with Miles Davis. He'd later form a group with bassist Charlie Haden, drummer Paul Motian, and tenor saxophonist Dewey Redman that evolved into a phenomenon during the '70s. This two-disc anthology presents formative Jarrett material from the late '60s and early '70s; it doesn't have the depth, emotional intensity, imagination, or charm of his Impulse or ECM releases, but it still contains some fine tracks. These include two superb songs with Burton (also available on the reissued *Gary Burton/Keith Jarrett* CD), plus a cut with Blakey's Messengers, others with the Lloyd group, and some odds and ends from unrelated dates. One has Jarrett playing in a reflective, at times self-effacing manner in a group with drummer Bob Moses, bassist Steve Swallow, and tenor saxophonist Jim Pepper. This was for an LP that was never issued, but Pepper's tone and style are remarkably similiar to how Jarrett's longtime saxophone colleague Jan Garbarek sounded years later. The second disc includes three '71 tunes by the Jarrett unit with Haden, Motian, and Redman. At this time, the foursome wasn't fully comfortable or used to each other, and there are uncertain, tentative stretches balanced by other periods with all four interacting smoothly and playing exuberantly. Jarrett is regarded now as an enigma by some and a genius by others; these songs are reminders of a less assured, but in some ways less predictable and wary pianist who's now a star. —*Ron Wynn*

Bobby Jaspar (Robert B. Jaspar)

b. Feb. 20, 1926, Liege, Bel., d. Feb. 28, 1963, New York, NY
Tenor sax, flute / Postbop

Tenor saxophonist and flutist Bobby Jaspar was a topflight European musician, especially on flute. He made his reputation playing at U.S. Army bases and in Europe during the early '50s. Jaspar moved to New York in the mid-'50s with his wife, Blossom Dearie, and had a long string of fine dates with J. J. Johnson, Miles Davis, Donald Byrd, Bill Evans, and Chris Connor before a final tour in the '60s with Rene Thomas. A good tenor player, Jaspar's long lines and fluid melodies and solos on flute were often magnificent. —*Ron Wynn*

★ **Bobby Jaspar in Paris** / **i.** Dec. 27+29, 1955 / Disques Swing 8413

Wonderful 1986 reissue of prime Jaspar small-combo dates from mid-'50's. Tommy Flanagan (p), Elvin Jones (d), Milt Hinton (b) among the crew. —*Ron Wynn*

○ **Memory of Dick** / Dec. 1955 / Verve 837208

Carter Jefferson

Tenor sax / Hard bop

A good, if conservative in tone and style, tenor saxophonist, Carter Jefferson recorded as a leader for Timeless and did sessions with Barbara Donald, Clint Houston, and Jack Walraith, among others. He was never a bombastic soloist, but he was a very effective one.—*Ron Wynn*

● **Rise of Atlantis, The** / **i.** Apr. 1980 / Muse 309

Carter Jefferson, possibly best known for his association with Woody Shaw (who produced *The Rise of Atlantis*), may not have been an original, but he synthesized his sources well. The first side of his album took on an Impressionistic hue, especially the mellow samba-ish tint of "Why" and "Wind Chimes." Jefferson's soprano articulation and sweet tone was noteworthy, both here and on the vibrantly John Coltrane-styled outing, "Blues for Wood." "Changing Trains," was his stab at a "Giant Steps"-type vehicle, and his fluid, warm work was convincing and dramatic. Jefferson shared his front line alternately with trumpeters Terumasa Hino and Shunzo Ono, both of whom were sparse and unadventurous. —*Art Lange, Down Beat*

Eddie Jefferson (Edgar Jefferson)

b. Aug. 3, 1918, Pittsburgh, PA, **d.** May 9, 1979, Detroit, MI
Vocals / Ballads & blues

Eddie Jefferson was a real vocal improviser, who, like Jon Hendricks, created lyrics to fit songs rather than specializing in scatting. Jefferson and King Pleasure appeared at virtually the same time in 1952. Jefferson was a big member of James Moody's group in the late '50s. Supplanted in popularity by Lambert, Hendricks, and Ross in the late '50s, Jefferson spent a decade in obscurity before returning as a dancer in 1967 and rejoining Moody in 1968. This reignited his career and he worked his last few years with Richie Cole. —*Ron Wynn*

○ **There I Go Again** / Feb. 1953-Aug. 1969 / Original Jazz Classics 503

This material was taken, with the exception of the '53, '54, and '55 tracks, from vocalist Eddie Jefferson's releases on Riverside and Prestige. Some of it, especially the Prestige session suffered poor recording sound, balance, and a piano no doubt infamous to the unfortunate pianists made to suffer at its keys. However, this was a most satisfying collection for the joys of jazz singing and Eddie Jefferson. —*Bob Rusch, Cadence*

☆ **Letter from Home** / Dec. 18, 1961-Feb. 8, 1962 / Riverside 307

1961 and 1962. Definitive vocalese from the man! —*Michael G. Nastos*

★ **Body and Soul** / 1968 / Prestige 396

Body and Soul was an open-hearted loving testament to the greatest tenor saxophonist of the age. It told about Americans and Europeans, about Coleman Hawkins, born to play the tenor. . . . There were other people. James Moody (reeds), Dave Burns (trumpet), Barry Harris (piano), Steve Davis (bass), and Bill English (drums). But there was only one Eddie Jefferson. The composer of "Moody's Mood for Love." The teacher of bop history. The balladeer of modern jazz. He bridged the gap between music and feeling with meaningful and fanciful lyrics. Eddie Jefferson spoke for himself to anyone who wanted to listen. —*Alan Offstein, Coda*

Leroy Jenkins

b. Mar. 11, 1932, Chicago, IL
Violin, composer, bandleader / Modern creative

A former school teacher, Leroy Jenkins turned the violin and viola into sawing, percussive weapons of the avant-garde. Another graduate of DuSable High School in Chicago, Jenkins abandoned the alto sax for the violin in the early '60s and worked in both Alabama and Chicago. He became involved with the AACM in the '60s and went to Europe in 1969 with Anthony Braxton and Leo Smith. He was back in the United States in 1970 and moved to New York with Braxton later that year. Jenkins worked with many free-jazz luminaries during the '70s. He formed the invigorating Revolutionary Ensemble with Sirone on bass and trombone and Jerome Cooper on drums and piano in 1971. They stayed together six years, a marvelous band that played in every conceivable style. They mixed classical and improvisational, structured and free, serene and chaotic. Jenkins later toured with Andrew Cyrille and Anthony Davis and has recorded as a leader for Black Saint and Tomato. —*Ron Wynn*

★ **Solo Concert** / Jan. 11, 1977 / India Navigation

○ **Lifelong Ambitions** / Mar. 11, 1977 / Black Saint 0033

Violinist Leroy Jenkins and pianist Muhal Abrams's more than 30-minute duet session was recorded in performance at Washington Square Church in 1977. "Happiness" involved inner piano box pluckings, choked string picking, and raspy scratching. "The Blues" was a Jack Benny riff extended by some classical figures and bluesy modulations, mostly at Abrams's insistence. Frenzied bowing described "The Weird World," and lengthier lines of the same frenzy characterized "The Father, the Son, the Holy Ghost." —*Howard Mandel, Down Beat*

○ **Mixed Quintet** / Mar. 22-23, 1979 / Black Saint 0060

Budd Johnson (Albert J. Johnson)

b. Dec. 14, 1910, Dallas, TX, **d.** Oct. 20, 1984, Kansas City, MO
Tenor sax, arranger / Swing, big band

Budd Johnson was a jazz mainstay who brilliantly played both swing and bop. His roots dated back to a Texas group led by Terrence Holder, then Louis Armstrong's '30s band in Chicago, followed by nine years with Earl Hines. Johnson was one of the first musicians influenced by Lester Young. He was a busy arranger and participant in various swing bands through the '40s and became part of the rock revolution of the '50s, arranging and producing several records as well as publishing songs. He helped Alan Freed by putting together huge bands for his shows. Toward the end of the '50s, Johnson's playing picked up again, and he worked with Benny Goodman, Gil Evans, Quincy Jones, and Count Basie. He reunited with Earl Hines often in the '60s and later formed his own group with Hines's personnel. Johnson did repertory work, guest stints, and many tours in the '70s. Throughout his career, Johnson was among the warmest, most humorous, and enticing ballad and blues players, as well as a great interpreter. —*Ron Wynn*

○ **Rock 'n' Roll Stage Show** / May 1954-Jun. 1955 / Mercury 20209

○ **And the Four Brass Giants** / Sep. 22, 1960+Sep. 6, 1960 / Riverside 209

This was one of Budd Johnson's finest leadership moments; he not only wrote charts that did a marvelous job of setting up his gems, but he also made particularly clever use of four distinctive trumpeters. Cannonball Adderley produced this date. . . . This was a mercurial effort with the pacing and talent to make boredom impossible. —*Bob Rusch, Cadence*

★ **Let's Swing** / Dec. 2, 1960 / Prestige 1720

○ **Ole Dude and the Fundance Kid, The** / Feb. 4, 1984 / Uptown 2719

This album was a straightahead swinger, and unlike some record session pairings, Budd Johnson (tenor sax) and Phil Woods (alto sax) *really* did play together. Not a song went by that they didn't either duet, pass the solo back and forth, or play contrapuntally off each other. . . . Although Johnson was making records two years before Woods was born, they were stylistically compatible. Charlie Parker provided the main stylistic link—an early influence for Woods, a later one for Johnson. —*Doug Long, Cadence*

Bunk Johnson (William Geary Johnson)

b. Dec. 27, 1889, New Orleans, **d.** Jul. 7, 1949

Trumpet / New Orleans traditional

One of the seminal trumpeters in the traditional New Orleans style, Bunk Johnson as a youngster played with such heralded players as Adam Olivier, Bob Russell, and Buddy Bolden. He became known as a superb second trumpet player, someone especially keen at playing behind the beat, while also a marvelous blues stylist and interpreter. Johnson left New Orleans in 1915 and toured the South working in every type of traveling show and theatrical troupe. Johnson enjoyed a flurry of activity from 1942 to 1945, making nearly 100 sides while recording sessions mainly produced by David Stuart. These records helped spur a traditional jazz resurgence and garnered Johnson a little national acclaim, though it didn't exactly make him a star. Harold Drob, a former GI, helped Johnson assemble another band near the end of his life, one that recorded in 1947 and gave him some final attention as a genuine early jazz marvel. *—Ron Wynn*

★ **Bunk and Lu** / Feb. 1944 / Good Time Jazz 12024
This put together two sessions. The first was from 12/19/41 and was recorded on Watters' 30th birthday at a gathering with Bob Scobey (cornet), Turk Murphy (trombone), Ellis Horne (clarinet), Wally Rose (piano), Clancy Hayes, Russ Bennett (banjo), Dick Lammi (tuba), and Bill Dart (drums) to play and pay tribute to the traditional jazz of the "past.". . . The other session here was from spring of 1944 and featured Bunk Johnson's spirited, sometimes sour, but strong 66-year-old trumpet with Hayes, Murphy, Horn, Pat Patton (bass), Squire Girsback (bass), and Sister Lottie Peavey (vocal on two cuts) on eight tracks. *—Bob Rusch, Cadence*

○ **Bunk Plays the Blues—The Spirituals** / Aug. 2, 1944 / American Music 638

○ **Bunk Johnson (1944)** / 1944 / American Music 3

○ **Bunk Johnson & His New Orleans Jazz Band—New York (1945)** / 1945 / Folklyric 9047

○ **Last Testament of a Great Jazzman** / i. 1947 / Columbia 520

Howard Johnson (Howard William Johnson)

b. 1941, Boston, MA
Baritone sax, alto sax, tuba / Progressive big band, early jazz rock, modern creative

Arguably the most influential tuba player to emerge in the modern era, Howard Johnson's fluency, range, and skill changed perceptions about how to utilize the instrument not only in jazz but also in modern popular music. Johnson's also a gifted baritone saxophonist but has accomplished his greatest feats on tuba. A self-taught musician, Johnson started on baritone at 13 and moved to tuba at 14. He was a merchant seaman and met John Surman in England. Johnson came to New York in the mid-'60s, and worked with Charles Mingus, Hank Crawford, and Archie Shepp before meeting Gil Evans in 1966. He and Evans formed a musical bond that was maintained well into the '80s. Johnson formed Substructure in 1966, a band that at one time included four tubas and backed Taj Mahal. He wrote arrangements for Maria Muldaur, Paul Butterfield, and B. B. King while working with Mahal. Johnson was conductor of the Saturday Night Live band in the late '70s, and formed a second tuba band Gravity. They performed in New York and toured Europe. Johnson recorded with Jack DeJohnette's Special Edition, Jimmy Heath, and Crawford again in the '80s and has continued doing sessions and heading bands into the '90s. He can be heard on numerous discs of both recent and vintage material by everyone from Mingus to DeJohnette, Gil Evans, Mahal, and Crawford. *—Ron Wynn*

Keepin' Love New / A&M 4895

J.J. Johnson (James Louis Johnson)

b. Jan. 22, 1924, Indianapolis, IN
Trombone, composer / Hard bop

The first great bebop trombonist, J.J. Johnson's abilities were astonishing. His speed and facility were so incredible he was accused of playing a valve rather than a slide trombone. His solos both were harmonically sophisticated and rhythmically exciting. He played intricate compositions with ease and incorporated swing and classical influences into his sound and writing. Johnson began playing trombone at 14 and gained his early experience in the bands of Clarence Love and Isaac Russell, but particularly that of Benny Carter in the '40s. Johnson was in the first

Jazz at the Philharmonic concert, played with Count Basie in 1945, and moved to New York in 1946. He toured with Illinois Jacquet in the late '40s and from the '50s to the present has been a magnificent player as well as bandleader, composer, and arranger. Johnson played with trumpet giants Miles Davis and Clifford Brown, co-led two trombone groups with Kai Winding, played in four- and six-trombone ensembles, penned orchestral works, and has done sessions for many labels, including Blue Note, Columbia, Pablo, Concord, and Verve. *—Ron Wynn and Michael G. Nastos*

○ **Mad Bebop** / Jun. 26, 1946 / Savoy 2232
Seminal material from 1946-1954. Pivotal dates pairing Johnson with movers and shakers like Sonny Rollins (ts), Charles Mingus (b), Bud Powell (p). *—Ron Wynn*

○ **Early Bones** / May 26, 1949 / Prestige 24067
These groups, especially those led by trombonists J.J. Johnson and Kai Winding, showed some of the important writing styles and soloists creating new music at the end of the '40s. The most fascinating group, Johnson's 1949 sextet, unfortunately had only four cuts. *—Tom Everett, Cadence*

○ **Eminent Jay Jay Johnson—Vol. 2, The** / Jun. 1953-Jun. 1955 / Capitol 81506

☆ **Eminent Jay Jay Johnson—Vol. 1, The** / Sep. 24, 1954 / Capitol 81505

○ **Jay and Kai** / Dec. 3, 1954 / Prestige 195

○ **J.J. Johnson, Kai Winding, Bennie Green** / Dec. 3, 1954 / Prestige 7030
All of this album was also issued on a previous twofer set in 1981. The material comes from three dates: 5/26/49, 8/23/49, and 10/5/51. The trombonists are represented this way: Johnson's on the earliest cuts, Winding the middle, and Green the '51 sessions. *—Bob Rusch, Cadence*

★ **Blue Trombone** / i. 1956 / Columbia

○ **Jay and Kai Octet** / i. 1958 / Columbia

★ **Great Kai and J.J.** / Oct. 3, 1960-Nov. 9, 1960 / MCA 42012
w/ Kay Winding. Definitive work for two trombonists, plus Bill Evans (p), Paul Chambers (b), Art Taylor (d). *—Ron Wynn*

○ **Pinnacles** / Sep. 17, 1979 / Milestone 9093

★ **Quintergy—Live at the Village Vanguard** / i. Jul. 1988-1986 / Antilles 848214
This live album is excellent—top-notch J. J. Highly recommended. *—Michael G. Nastos*

James P. Johnson (James Price Johnson)

b. Feb. 1, 1894, New Brunswick, NJ, **d.** Nov. 17, 1955, New York, NY
Piano, composer / Stride, boogie-woogie

The "father of stride piano," James P. Johnson was a great player in many prejazz forms. These included rags, reels, blues, novelty tunes, originals, even spirituals. Johnson's sweeping right hand lines, neatly crafted bass lines, and steady rhythms were extremely influential. Johnson's achievements included directing music for Bessie Smith's film short "St. Louis Blues," writing plays, composing a symphony, cutting piano rolls, writing Broadway scores, and playing on various circuit in the late '30s and early '40s. *—Ron Wynn*

★ **Carolina Shout** / i. 1917-1925 / Biograph 105
James P. Johnson's piano playing here covers an interesting phase from ragtime to stride. The piano roll and the march elements of ragtime seem to have been made for one another, but it is impossible to tell how free to express himself the "first Negro composer to cut his own rags" really was. But on his "Carolina Shout," "Harlem Strut," "Eccentricity," and "Charleston" are routines and ideas that must have influenced many early jazz pianists. *—Stanley Dance, Jazz Times*

○ **Snowy Morning Blues** / 1930+1944 / GRP 604
Snowy Morning Blues begins with the very great pianist, composer, *and* songwriter James P. Johnson in his prime, in 1930; mixing rhythmic urgency, restless reharmonizing, lacy decoration, and fresh melodies. Some of the intensity, though not the interpretative subtlety, is gone by the 1944 dates that make up the bulk of this disc; by then Johnson had suffered a stroke, and the discreet drumming of Eddie Daugherty proves helpful. *—John Litweiler, Down Beat*

○ **James P. Johnson Plays Fats Waller Favorites** / **i.** 1950 / Decca 5228

★ **Giants of Jazz** / **i.** Oct. 1982 / Time Life 18

☆ **Father of the Stride Piano** / Columbia

Lonnie Johnson (Alonzo Johnson)

b. Feb. 8, 1889, New Orleans, LA, **d.** Jun. 16, 1970, Toronto, Canada
Vocals, guitar, piano, violin, harmonium / Blues & jazz
Guitarist and vocalist Lonnie (born Alonzo) Johnson's career spanned over 40 years. He worked with everyone from Louis Armstrong to Duke Ellington and may have been the most durable of all bluesmen. Certainly, few even approached his versatility. With jazz orchestras, small groups, piano-guitar duos, and solo, Johnson recorded everything from low-down blues and the then-popular hokum style to duets with jazz guitarist Eddie Lang. Johnson's backup work behind vocalists or as part of a larger group (he soloed on one of the earliest versions of "Stardust") is as interesting as any of his better-known solo sides. His execution and knowledge of his instrument was a major influence on a young Robert Johnson (some of whose more obscure numbers are virtual homages to his namesake) and other Delta bluesmen, and he was lauded as a well-known recording star. Lonnie Johnson was primarily noted for the cleanly picked, highly intricate patterns used on his turnarounds. Though his recording career goes as far back as 1925, Johnson had an R&B hit with the self-penned ballad "Tomorrow Night" in 1948. He recorded for folk labels in the '60s, mostly using an electric guitar, as durable and versatile as ever. —*Cub Koda*

Pete Johnson (Peter Johnson)

b. Mar. 25, 1904, Kansas City, MO, **d.** Mar. 23, 1967, Buffalo, NY
Piano / Boogie-woogie
Pete Johnson was another great boogie-woogie pianist whose impact extended beyond his genre. His rumbling, energetic phrases and rollicking rhythms, whether in combative sessions with other players or accompanying longtime friend and robust shouter Big Joe Turner, were emphatic and majestic. Johnson played drums and piano as a teen in Kansas City. He worked with vocalist Edna Taylor at the Hole in the Wall Club and Jazzland and then, while backing Turner at the Sunset Cafe, was heard by John Hammond. Johnson moved to New York in the late '30s, playing in 1936 at the Famous Door. He and Turner joined many other jazz greats at the 1938 Carnegie Hall concert "From Spirituals to Swing," which Hammond organized. In December of that year, Johnson played with fellow greats Albert Ammons and Meade "Lux" Lewis in the Boogie-Woogie Trio. The threesome appeared the next year at Cafe Society. Johnson worked regularly with Ammons over the next decade and made some appearances with Lewis, while also playing as a soloist. Johnson moved to Buffalo in 1950; toured with Lewis, Art Tatum, and Errol Garner in 1952; and toured Europe and performed at the Newport Jazz Festival in 1958. A stroke later that year left him partly paralyzed and virtually ended his career other than a nostalgic appearance at Hammond's "Spirituals to Swing" concert in 1967. —*Ron Wynn*

☆ **Pete Johnson/Earl Hines/Teddy Bunn Blue Note Sessions, The** / Mosaic 119

● **Boogie Woogie Boys, The** / **i.** Feb. 1939-Jan. 1953 / Storyville 229

○ **Boogie Woogie Trio** / **i.** Sep. 1939-Oct. 1930 / Storyville 4094

○ **Boogie Woogie Trio—Vol. 3** / **i.** Oct. 1939-Sep. 1954 / Storyville 4006

○ **Pete's Blues** / **i.** 1946 / Savoy 14018

○ **Cozy Cole All Star Swing Groups** / **i.** 1946 / Savoy 2218

○ **Pete's Blues** / **i.** 1958 / Savoy 414

○ **All Star Swing Groups** / Savoy 2218

● **Central Avenue Boogie** / Delmark 656
Pete Johnson's *Central Avenue Boogie* justly celebrates one of the truly authentic barrelhouse pianists, but his 1949-1950 output for Apollo was so slender that of his 11 tracks for this CD, three are previously unissued alternate takes of "Hollywood Boogie." Of the remainder, the stride-based "Margie" (sic: should read "Marie"), "66 Stomp," and "Minuet Boogie" speak the most, primarily because they disclose another dimension of Johnson's Kansas City

roots. Fleshing out the disc are three boogie solos by the obscure Arnold Wiley. —*Jack Sohmer, Down Beat*

Pete Jolly (Peter A. Ceragioli)

b. Jun. 5, 1932, New Haven, CT
Piano, accordion / Cool
A rare jazz accordionist, Pete Jolly achieved much greater fame as a powerful pianist. He had a mild hit with "Little Bird" in the '50s. Jolly started accordion and piano studies at eight. He moved from the East Coast to Los Angeles in the early '50s and played with Georgie Auld, Shorty Rogers, and Buddy DeFranco before beginning his own groups. Jolly recorded with Red Norvo, Richie Kamuca and Chet Baker, Buddy Collette, DeFranco, Gibbs, Rogers, and Art Pepper in the '50s and early '60s. He also cut sessions for RCA, AVA, Charlie Parker, and Atlas. Jolly's done extensive studio work for films and television since the '60s and '70s and recorded a quartet album with Pepper in 1980.—*Ron Wynn*

○ **Gems** / **i.** 1990 / Holt 3303

Bobby Jones

b. Oct. 30, 1928, Louisville, KY, **d.** Mar. 6, 1980, Munich, Germany
Tenor sax, flute, alto sax, clarinet / Hard bop
Tenor saxophonist and clarinetist Bobby Jones had an original conception and vital sound that made him an important part of some Charles Mingus groups in the '60s. Prior to going into the army, Jones had been in big bands. He played some rockabilly after his discharge, then joined the Glenn Miller Orchestra under Ray McKinley's direction as a tenor saxophonist in 1959. He played with Woody Herman's orchestra in 1963, and worked as a clarinetist with Jack Teagarden. Jones joined Mingus in 1970, and played with him until 1972, touring Japan and making two visits to Europe. He opted to stay in Europe after the second visit, and eventually settled in Munich. But a chronic emphysema problem that cut short his tenure with Mingus was aggravated by Munich's climate, and Jones eventually became a nonplaying arranger. But his solos and playing on *Let My Children Hear Music* especially displays his virtues. He recorded as a leader for Cobblestone and Enja. —*Ron Wynn and Michael G. Nastos*

★ **Arrival of Bobby Jones, The** / Jul. 12, 1972 / Cobblestone 9022
This is a studio session from this highly original reed-flute player, plus Charles McPherson (as), Jaki Byard (p); a must-buy. —*Michael G. Nastos*

Carmell Jones (WIlliam Carmell Jones)

b. Jul. 19, 1936, Kansas City, KS
Trumpet / Bop, hard bop
An appealing, warm and big-toned trumpeter, Carmel Jones was a solid bop soloist. There were rarely any technical flaws in his playing. Jones began playing at 11 and was greatly influenced by Clifford Brown. After participating in the collegiate jazz festival at Notre Dame in 1959, Jones led a group in Kansas City and then moved to California in 1960. He played with Bud Shank, Harold Land, Gerald Wilson, and Curtis Amy in the early '60s, before touring and recording with Horace Silver in the mid-'60s on such popular releases as *Song for My Father*. Jones spent many years in Europe and played for the SFB orchestra. He returned to America in 1980, and issued *Carmell Jones Returns* in 1982 on Revelation. —*Ron Wynn and Michael G. Nastos*

○ **Remarkable Carmell Jones, The** / Jun. 1961 / Pacific Jazz 29
The Remarkable Carmell Jones was the debut for this trumpeter and found him in the strong company of Harold Land (tenor sax), Frank Strazzeri (piano), Gary Peacock (bass), and Leon Pettis (drums) for six tracks. This was an unspectacular whole with some very nice parts in its program and solos. —*Bob Rusch, Cadence*

Elvin Jones (Elvin Ray Jones)

b. Sep. 9, 1927, Pontiac, MI
Drums, bandleader / Hard bop, early free
The youngest of the famed Jones brothers (which include pianist Hank and trumpeter Thad), drummer Elvin Jones became a member of the jazz "who's who" during his influential half-decade with the John Coltrane Quartet. Jones's status is further underlined by his earlier work with Coltrane's rival in the Sonny Rollins Trio. With Coltrane (from 1960 to 1965) he did not make himself conspicuous with volume or flashiness; instead he pur-

sued a subtle percussive density that balanced pianist McCoy Tyner's web of sound and Coltrane's long solo lines. He obscured the beat with carefully placed accents, but rarely abandoned pulse, and in so doing inspired the coming generation of free-jazz percussionists. After leaving Coltrane (an unfortunate departure provoked by the addition of second drummer Rashied Ali), Jones's career has been hit-and-miss. Most of his many albums as leader (on Blue Note, Impulse, Enja, and others) lack the edge and excitement of his earlier years, but his two albums under Ornette Coleman's leadership worked very well. And recently he teamed with former bandmate Pharoah Sanders and guitarist Sonny Sharrock for the excellent *Ask the Ages* recording (Axiom 422 848 957), proving that there are still many good things to come from this drumming master. —*Myles Boisen*

● **Illumination** / Aug. 8, 1963 / Impulse 49
Sextet w/ Jimmy Garrison (b), Prince Lasha (as), Sonny Simmons (as), Charles Davis (bar sax), and McCoy Tyner (p). All originals in progressive stance. A jewel. Must-find. —*Michael G. Nastos*

★ **Dear John C** / Feb. 23+25, 1965 / Impulse

○ **Prime Element, The** / Mar. 14, 1969-Jul. 26, 1973 / Blue Note 506
These 1973 sessions placed Elvin Jones in the center of an 11-piece ensemble (including saxophonists Frank Foster, Steve Grossman, and Pepper Adams; bassist Gene Perla; guitarist Cornell Dupree; and keyboardist Jan Hammer), an uncontainable group with a permutable vocabulary. The sensual horn mating and slight funky and Cubano rhythmic undertow suggested a re-casting of Charles Mingus's *The Black Saint and the Sinner Lady* in Santana and Frank Zappa settings. The earlier sextet cuts (featuring the horns of George Coleman, Joe Farrell, and Lee Morgan) were a more linear project, although every bit as combustible. The soloists solo rather than mingle, hoot, and banter. Throughout, Jones was typically magnificent, always the consummate percussionist. —*Mikal Gilmore, Down Beat*

○ **Live at the Lighthouse—Vol. 2** / Sep. 9, 1972 / Blue Note 84448

○ **Elvin Jones Is on the Mountain** / 1975 / PM 005
Elvin Jones Is on the Mountain was a keyboard trio date featuring Jan Hammer on electric piano and Moog synthesizer, quite different from Jones's past recordings. (Hammer plays acoustic piano on "Namuh" and "London Air"). On Gene Perla's "Destiny" there was an intriguing Hammer-Jones duet that was a structural gem. Perla, who along with Hammer, wrote all the material for *Mountain* and was Jones' bassist for a number of years, possesses a stalwart style with considerable tonal depth. His work in this trio setting was topflight. Jones in this somewhat different environment seemed subdued—laid back—constructing his rhythmic circle in an almost delicate fashion. —*Herb Nolan, Down Beat*

○ **Elvin Jones Live at the Town Hall** / i. May 1976 / PMR 004
Elvin Jones Live was taken from a John Coltrane Memorial Concert performed at New York's Town Hall, September 12, 1971, and featured his group at that time, Frank Foster on soprano and tenor saxes, Chick Corea's piano, Joe Farrell's sax and flute, and Gene Perla's bass on two extended compositions. . . . These were five strong individual artists giving exceptionally of themselves, bringing forth a record where the dynamics of the whole were equal to the sum of the parts, making for an exceptional and truly beautiful record. —*Bob Rusch, Cadence*

○ **Elvin Jones Jazz Machine in Europe, The** / Jun. 1991 / Enja 79675

Hank Jones (Henry Jones)

b. Jul. 31, 1918, Vicksburg, MS
Piano / Bop
The elder brother of Thad and Elvin Jones, Hank Jones is one of the founding members of the extraordinary "Detroit school" of pianists. He has a reserved, careful approach that doesn't mean he's not a brilliant player. He is a first-rate accompanist and highly effective soloist. He moved to New York in 1944 and worked with Hot Lips Page, Andy Kirk, Coleman Hawkins, and Ella Fitzgerald in the '40s and '50s. Since the early '50s, he has made multiple records as a leader and been featured in countless settings (solo, trio, combo, backup for vocalists, etc.). —*Ron Wynn*

● **Trio** / Aug. 4, 1955 / Savoy
Seminal stuff from Hank Jones, with Kenny Clarke (d), Wendell Marshall (b). —*Ron Wynn*

○ **Bluebird** / Aug. 1955-Nov. 1955 / Savoy 1193

Kenny Clarke drums with pianist Hank Jones on a satiny trios-plus-guests set called *Bluebird* with guests including Donald Byrd and Joe Wilder on trumpets, Herbie Mann on snoozy flute, Jerome Richardson on better flute and tenor sax. —*John Corbett, Down Beat*

★ **Bop Redux** / Jan. 18-19, 1977 / Muse 5444
This album was unique because pianist Hank Jones played only Bird's (Charlie Parker) and Thelonious Monk's tunes. His mastery of this material was most evident on the sensitive approach to Monk's ballads: "Ruby My Dear" and "'Round Midnight".. . . He has a special finesse and said some really beautiful things. His partners bassist George Duvivier and drummer Ben Riley made this a superior session. —*Jerry L. Atkins, Cadence*

○ **Oracle, The** / Mar. 1989-Apr. 1989 / Emarcy 846376
W/ Dave Holland, Billy Higgins. Includes three different generations of jazzmen. A very nice album. —*Michael G. Nastos*

○ **Live at Maybeck Recital Hall—Vol. 16** / i. 1992 / Concord Jazz 4502
A high point in the career of distinguished pianist Hank Jones was being among the artists tabbed for a solo release in the Maybeck series. While he's always been known as a great accompanist and good trio contributor, his solo skills have sometimes been undervalued. But after hearing him work in this unaccompanied setting, there should be no doubt Hank Jones is a superb soloist along with all his other talents. —*Ron Wynn*

Jo Jones (Jonathan Jones)

b. Oct. 7, 1911, Chicago, IL, **d.** Sep. 3, 1985, New York, NY
Drums / Swing, big band
"Papa" Jo Jones is considered by many to be the finest swing-era drummer of all, superior to even Gene Krupa and Buddy Rich, but he didn't compare to them in power, flash, or speed. Instead, he was the preeminent timekeeper, quite fast enough but especially skilled at driving the beat and punctuating the pulse. He had a lengthy apprenticeship with various territory bands but became a star with Count Basie in 1934. Jones spent 12 years with Basie in two different stints and helped establish the percussive vocabulary for swing drummers and beyond. He did plenty of session work in the '50s but was taken out of the mainstream by the changing tastes of the '60s. But he continued to be a strong presence on drums into the '80s.—*Ron Wynn*

★ **Main Man, The** / Nov. 29-30, 1976 / Pablo 799
This date w/ Harry Edison (tpt), Roy Eldridge (tpt), Vic Dickerson (tb), and others is sterling silver. —*Michael G. Nastos*

Jonah Jones (Robert Elliott Jones)

b. Dec. 31, 1909, Louisville, KY
Trumpet / Swing, big band
Both a popular and a talented trumpeter, Jonah Jones could be flashy, spectacular, and sometimes excessive, but he was always a masterful player. Jones played in riverboat bands early in his career and worked with Horace Henderson in the late '20s and with Stuff Smith and Jimmie Lunceford in the early '30s. Smith and Jones did a combination music-comedy act. Jones worked in Mckinny's Cotton Pickers in the mid-'30s and played with Fletcher Henderson and Benny Carter in the early '40s before joining Cab Calloway in 1941. He remained with Calloway until 1952. Jones was the culprit in the famous spitball incident that got Dizzy Gillespie tossed from the band. Jones recorded often with Teddy Wilson and Billy Holiday in this period. He played with Earl Hines in the early '50s and was in the pit band for the Broadway production of "Porgy and Bess." Jones toured Europe as a solo act and then formed a club band. He became a hot property in the '50s, playing muted trumpet and doing vocals. Jones had a string of albums make the Top 20 in the late '50s, among them *Muted Jazz* and *Jumpin' with Jonah* on Capitol. He later recorded for Decca, Motown, and Chiaroscuro.—*Ron Wynn*

○ **Jonah Jones Sextet** / Dec. 9, 1954 / Bethlehem 1014

○ **Jazz Kaleidoscope** / i. 1956 / Bethlehem 4

○ **Jonah Jones at the Embers** / Feb. 14, 1956-Feb. 29, 1956 / Groove 1001

○ **Muted Jazz** / Feb. 22-25, 1957 / Capitol 839

★ **Jazz Legacy** / Inner City 7021

○ **Jonah Jones with Dave Pochonet and His All Stars** / Disques Swing 8408

Philly Joe Jones (Joseph Rudolph Jones)

b. Jul. 15, 1923, Philadelphia, PA, **d.** Aug. 30, 1985, Philadelphia, PA
Drums / Hard bop
Philly Joe Jones was among the most influential drummers ever in the bop genre. His technique of "rim" shots, use of wire brushes, and accompaniment behind soloists have become part of the modern jazz rhythm vocabulary. Jones got his nickname from the many years he worked in Philadelphia, his hometown, before leaving to tour with Joe Morris's R&B band. After a short stint with Ben Webster in 1949, he moved to New York and was an active freelancer until 1953. During the mid '50s, he became part of the Miles Davis group and worked with him in 1952-1955, 1955-1957, 1958, and 1962. He worked extensively with both Gil and Bill Evans in the '60s and moved to England in 1967. Jones worked and taught all over Europe until returning to Philadelphia in the mid-'70s. His last extended engagement was heading the repertory band Dameronia, playing Tadd Dameron's compositions, from 1981 to 1985. Jones's final group was Pieces of Time for a few months in 1985. *—Ron Wynn*

★ **Blues for Dracula** / Apr. 2, 1959 / Riverside 230
The program opened with the title track and a too-long and unamusing monologue by the leader spoken in the style of Bela Lugosi and largely borrowed from Lenny Bruce. This, of course, made the record memorable but not good. Over the program each member of the sextet (Nat Adderley, Julian Priester, Johnny Griffin, Tommy Flanagan, Jimmy Garrison) all had their moments (and this was a prime period for Griffin, arguably one of the most distinct and strongest bop tenors in the late '50s). *—Bob Rusch, Cadence*

☆ **Drum Song** / Oct. 10-12, 1978 / Galaxy 5153
There was a definite "Blue Note" ambiance to the music on this session, what with the likes of trumpeter Blue Mitchell (the album was dedicated to him), trombonist Slide Hampton, tenor saxophonist Harold Land, and pianist Cedar Walton being kicked along by the drums of Philly Joe Jones. . . . This was music with no pretense to being anything other than inspired jazz played with skill and feeling by musicians dedicated to their art form. *— Carl Brauer, Cadence*

★ **To Tadd with Love** / Jul. 11, 1982 / Uptown
The Dameron material contained here was not generally the compositions you'd hear most . . . . One of the album's brightest moments was Sickler's great trumpet on "Misty Night." Johnny Coles (trumpet) also played well on the opener, "Philly Joe." Frank Wess (alto sax) did his chores on "Soultrane," which came from the record originally done with John Coltrane. . . . Jones's drumming was tasteful, and it was natural that he be the one to fulfill this project. *—Jerry Atkins, Cadence*

○ **Mean What You Say** / Sonet 735
Philly Joe Jones led a quartet (pianist Mickey Tucker, Charles Bowen on soprano and tenor saxes, bassist Mickey Bass) and quintet (add trumpeter Tommy Turrentine) on an April 1977 date called *Mean What You Say.* This was a nice blowing date for Bowen, who at the time had an R&B background and had never before recorded a jazz album. . . . Mickey Tucker was very strong on this set and at times almost seemed to be the leader with Jones seemingly pushing to assert his position. Still, this was an enjoyable recording with just that little extra added personality to give it an edge. *—Bob Rusch, Cadence*

Quincy Jones (Quincy Delight Jones, Jr.)

b. Mar. 14, 1933
Trumpet, composer, arranger / Swing, big band, progressive big band, instrumental pop, contemporary funk
Trumpeter, composer, arranger, and record label executive Quincy Jones is such a big name in pop circles today his jazz background has almost been forgotten. But Jones was a major figure among jazz musicians, spending two-and-a-half years in the early '50s with Lionel Hampton, who recorded several Jones pieces. Later he was Dizzy Gillespie's musical director. He spent 18 months in France and Scandinavia studying composition and working for Barclay Records in 1957-1958, and formed his own all-star big band for the European opening of the show *Free and*

Easy. This band played for two years, while Jones also wrote compositions for albums by Count Basie and recorded arrangements for Sarah Vaughan, Dinah Washington, and Billy Eckstine. A fine trumpeter particularly known for his use of chords built in fourths, Jones was also a terrific arranger and writer. He expanded into film soundtracks in the '60s and was also an executive at Mercury Records, where he enlarged his interests and reached into the pop market. Jones has produced the biggest selling album of all time, Michael Jackson's *Thriller,* won Grammy awards for his own albums, been a consultant for the Montreaux Jazz Festival, and recently expanded his activities into publishing with the hip-hop magazine "Vibe." He's also part of the production team for the hit television show "Fresh Prince of Bel-Air." His most recent release was *Live at Montreaux* with Miles Davis. Warner Bros. has also issued the film biography "Listen Up: The Lives Of Quincy Jones."*—Ron Wynn*

★ **Birth of a Band—Vol. 1, The** / Jun. 16, 1959 / Mercury 8224692
Though a far cry from the arrantly commercial results of his later labors, this music from the late '50s, taken as a whole, could be seen to lean away from the adventurous or risky and toward the safe and sure. This is not to say that the writing (to which such as Melba Liston, Nat Pierce, and Al Cohn contributed) was dull; within the limits observed, it was frequently exciting, certainly always sturdy enough to serve a bevy of first line horn players. . . . For those just edging into an interest in jazz, it could serve as an entry window of sorts. *—Alan Bargebuhr, Cadence*

○ **Great Wide World of Quincy Jones: Live!, The** / Nov. 4-09, 1961 / Mercury 822613

★ **Walking in Space** / 1969 / A&M 0801
A Grammy-winning work that marked the beginning of Jones's shift into R&B and pop. *—Ron Wynn*

○ **Gula Matari** / Mar. 25-26, 1970 / A&M 0820
A superb followup that might have been better than *Walking in Space* overall. *—Ron Wynn*

Sam Jones (Samuel Jones)

b. Nov. 12, 1924, Jacksonville, FL, **d.** Dec. 15, 1981, New York, NY
Bass, cello / Hard bop, postbop
A wonderful accompanist equally skilled at bass or cello, Jones made being in the rhythm section an art form. He moved from Florida to New York in the '50s, working first with Tiny Bradshaw and then with Illinois Jacquet and Kenny Dorham. His first major impact was as a member of Cannonball Adderley's early quintet from 1956 to 1957, followed by time with Dizzy Gillespie and Thelonious Monk. Jones stayed in the re-formed Adderley group from 1959 to 1966 and then spent three years with the Oscar Peterson trio. For the rest of his career Jones was an active session player, plus he led a 12-piece band part-time. *—Ron Wynn*

★ **Soul Society, The** / Mar. 8, 1960 / Riverside 1789

☆ **Down Home** / Aug. 15, 1962 / Riverside

○ **Cello Again** / Jan. 5, 1976 / Xanadu
Combining the warmth and guts of a guitar and bass, cellist Sam Jones really put a splendid session together with everybody concerned tight and bending in harmony together. Some of the music here ("In Walked Ray," "Scorpio") sounded very much like the early 1950 recording with Stan Getz and Doug Raney from Storyville. *—Carol Ober, Cadence*

○ **Something New** / Jun. 4, 1979 / Sea Breeze 2004

Thad Jones (Thaddeus Joseph Jones)

b. Mar. 28, 1923, Pontiac, MI, **d.** Aug. 20, 1986, Copenhagen
Trumpet, cornet, arranger, composer / Bop, hard bop
A wonderful soloist and gifted arranger, Thad Jones was hard bop's most harmonically daring trumpeter. His playing was clean, direct, and striking, with a very lyrical sound and great tone. His compositions were quite versatile, covering jazz, jazz-rock, blues, even waltz rhythms. He began on trumpet in his teens and turned professional at 16, playing with his pianist brother Hank and Sonny Stitt. Jones played with his other drummer brother Elvin in Billy Mitchell's band during the early '50s and was in Charles Mingus's Jazz Workshop in 1954 and 1955. After a nine-year stint with Count Basie's orchestra, Jones had several other engagements before joining Mel Lewis to form their Orchestra. These included working with CBS, playing with Thelonius Monk, and being in a group with Gerry Mulligan. Jones also co-led a quintet

with Pepper Adams and Mel Lewis that evolved into the Orchestra. Jones stayed with the Orchestra from the mid-'60s to the mid-'70s. Later came some European dates, some recordings, a new band, and his final stint heading the Count Basie orchestra in the '80s. —*Ron Wynn*

○ **Thad Jones—Billy Mitchell Quintet** / **i.** 1953 / Dee Gee 4009

★ **Magnificent Thad Jones** / Jul. 14, 1956 / Blue Note 46814

○ **Fabulous Thad Jones** / **i.** 1958 / Debut 625

○ **After Hours** / **i.** Mar. 1958 / Prestige 7118

☆ **Mean What You Say** / Apr. 26, 1966-May 9, 1966 / Milestone 464

★ **Thad Jones and the Mel Lewis Quartet** / **i.** May 1979 / A&M 0830

Patience and care were the hallmarks of this album. This was evident in the sound, which was clean and live. Most important, it was evident in the music itself. The musicians nursed the tunes lovingly, giving them time to develop. This means that, in spite of a few slow moments, the music was *alive*. The fact that the music was recorded live—at Miami's Airliner Lounge in September 1977—contributed to the organic feeling of this session. —*Douglas Clark, Down Beat*

Scott Joplin

b. Nov. 24, 1868, **d.** Apr. 1, 1917
Piano, composer / Ragtime

Ragtime's greatest composer, Scott Joplin's lifelong ambition (some would say obsession) was seeing ragtime treated as "serious" music. Joplin loathed hearing his rags being played at a faster pace than written, and he was a stickler for detail and accuracy. But he was also able to adhere to the genre's rigid structure and still pen expressive works. Joplin sold his first works in 1895 and his first rags in 1899. He wrote "The Guest of Honor," a ragtime opera in 1903, and continued pushing experimental, extended works. His opera "Treemonisha" debuted in Harlem at his own expense in 1911 but was a rousing flop. Joplin never recovered from this debacle. Many years later Joplin received a posthumous Pulitzer, something that still rankles many jazz fans since Duke Ellington didn't receive a similar award despite the unanimous recommendation of the music committee. —*Ron Wynn*

○ **Ragtime—Vol. 2 (1900-1910)** / 1900-1910 / Biograph 1008
Classic Scott Joplin ragtime compositions ranging from early in his career to near the end. Despite the restrictive form (which Joplin rigidly followed) he managed to find ways to rework themes creatively and vary his sound a bit. —*Ron Wynn*

○ **Ragtime—Vol. 3 (Early 1900's)** / 1900 / Biograph 1010
The third volume of digitally remastered classic piano rags by Scott Joplin from the early 1900s. If you're a diehard ragtime lover or piano student, you'll be enthralled by hearing this much ragtime. Others may find it a bit wearing, especially since there's almost no variation in arrangements, pacing, or voicings, only in the player's intensity. —*Ron Wynn*

○ **Joplin, Scott—1916 (Classic Solos from Piano Rolls)** / 1916 / Biograph 1006
More vintage ragtime taken from piano rolls. Scott Joplin was incensed whenever he heard someone playing his rags too fast, so he tried to put them down on piano rolls himself to keep them from being speeded up. These were transferred digitally from rolls. —*Ron Wynn*

○ **King of Ragtime Writers** / **i.** Feb. 28, 1992 / Biograph 110

★ **Elite Syncopations: Classic Ragtime from Rare, The** / Biograph 102
If you want to hear exactly how ragtime should be played, here's the real thing from a founding father. These vintage Scott Joplin rags were transferred to digital from piano rolls and are the way he wanted his rags to sound. —*Ron Wynn*

Clifford Jordan (Clifford Laconia Jordan, Jr.)

b. Sep. 2, 1931, Chicago, IL, **d.** 1993
Tenor sax / Hard bop, postbop

Tenor saxophonist Clifford Jordan was a mainstay in the Chicago jazz school, along with friends and classmates Johnny Griffin and Richard Davis. Jordan switched from tenor to tenor sax at 14. He started his career playing in local R&B bands before hitting the road in jazz groups led by Max Roach and Horace Silver. He briefly replaced Sonny Rollins in Roach's 1957 group. He was also

a member of J. J. Johnson and Kenny Dorham's ensembles before he reunited with Roach for three more years in the mid '60s. After a short period with Charles Mingus, Jordan spent several years as a soloist and arranger in Europe before becoming an established figure in New York during the '70s. His style, with its big tone and full sound, mixed blues references and total harmonic and melodic control. He never adopted any of the nuances of the free or avant-garde stylists, yet he recorded many memorable solos over the years. He was an excellent player solidly in the mainstream. —*Ron Wynn*

○ **Clifford Jordan in the World** / Mar. 1969 / Strata East 19721
Tenor saxophonist Clifford Jordan was impressive here on every count, as composer, soloist, and leader. Pianist Wynton Kelly was heard in a more avant-garde context than customarily. None of his essential qualities were altered, but the high-energy surroundings inspired him to solos on "Vienna," "Ouagoudougou," and "Prelude" that were superb even by the standards of his best work. Trumpeter Kenny Dorham had a beautfully developed statement on "Ouagoudougou," the kind of minor key invention at which he was incomparable. . . . Really quite a lovely record, produced, not incidentally, by Jordan. —*Doug Ramsey, Down Beat*

★ **Glass Bead Game** / Oct. 29, 1973+Oct. 29, 1973 / Strata East
Even with two quartets and compositions by each of the six musicians, this set had a unity of conception and feeling that realized the sense of family that Strata-East recordings often strived for; there was a relaxed easiness among the players and a clear sense of pleasure in playing together. —*Joel Ray, Cadence*

○ **Dr. Chicago** / **i.** Jan. 1988 / Bee Hive 7018

○ **Live at Condon's, New York/Down through the Years** / **i.** Apr. 24, 1992 / Milestone 9197

Duke Jordan (Irving Sidney Jordan)

b. Apr. 1, 1922, New York, NY
Piano / Bop, hard bop

Consistency has not been Jordan's strong suit, but whenever he's been active, he's been a solid, enjoyable pianist. He played with a sextet that won an amateur competition at the 1939 World's Fair and worked with both swing and bop groups during the '40s, playing with Coleman Hawkins and the original Savoy Sultans at one time and later with Charlie Parker. He spent nine months in a group led by Stan Getz in 1952. Jordan was among the rare pianists in the '40s and '50s able to display a personalized approach different from the dominant one created by Bud Powell. He was neither as fast nor as complex in his solo structure as Powell, but his phrasing and statements were just as convincing and emphatic. During the '50s Jordan was quite active in recording sessions. Then he went to Europe in 1959, where he wrote music for the French film *Les Liaisons Dangereuses* using the name Jack Murray. Jordan seemed to disappear at times during the '60s and '70s and then resurface with a flurry. In addition to being a highly respected player and arranger, Jordan's a gifted composer. Many of his songs have been recorded by other musicians, with "Jordu" now a modern jazz anthem. —*Ron Wynn*

● **Flight to Jordan** / Aug. 4, 1960 / Blue Note 46824
Bucking the Bud Powell tide, Duke Jordan's playing on this disc was subtle and economical. He was nearly flawless in gracefully expressing his melodic feelings, whether with single notes or chorded solos. His roots were in bop and also swing; not surprising, considering that he played for a year with the Savoy Sultans prior to his association with Charlie Parker. Cecil Payne (baritone sax) teamed with Jordan occasionally for several years. He showed why here—his sensitive playing complimented Jordan well. —*Doug Long, Cadence*

○ **Thinking of You** / **i.** Oct. 1979 / Steeple Chase 1165
The Duke Jordan set (pianist Jordan, bassist Niels-Henning Orstead Pedersen, drummer Billy Hart) swings nicely in an underplayed fashion. "Foxie Cakes" was taken solo and was interesting for its mix of piano techniques like Thelonious Monk; one began to feature a more pronounced stride element in his playing. —*Bob Rusch, Cadence*

○ **Tivoli One** / **i.** Oct. 1985 / Steeple Chase 1189
This presented pianist Duke Jordan in a trio setting (Wilbur Little, bass; Dannie Richmond, drums) recorded live. It was an enjoyable session consisting of four Jordan originals and three standards. It

was good bop piano from one of its first-generation exponents. —
Peter Leitch, Cadence

○ **Tivoli Two** / **i.** Oct. 1985 / Steeple Chase 1193
This recording, like its predecessor *Tivoli One*, documented a performance at Jazzhus Slukefter, Tivoli Gardens, in Copenhagen. . .
. Jordan's playing on the album certified his status as one of the strongest pure bop pianists ever and accentuated the extent to which his presence on the American jazz scene had been missed. The basic style was still unchanged from the '40s, but the passing years saw the more frequent surfacing of additional influences; alternating with fleet, extended, Bud Powell-like lines would be the almost awkward-sounding angular skips and jagged phrases of a Thelonious Monk. —*A. David Franklin, Cadence*

Louis Jordan

b. Jul. 8, 1908, Brinkley, AR, **d.** Feb. 4, 1975, Los Angeles, CA
Sax, vocals, bandleader / Swing, big band, blues & jazz
In his youth, Louis Jordan had a reputation among musicians as a great jazz clarinetist, but it was as a singer and showman that he climbed to the very top of show business, with several million-selling records to his credit when that kind of figure still meant something. In 1938, Jordan left Chick Webb's big band and debuted a sextet, Louis Jordan and his Tympany Five (his drummer featured tympany), at a small Harlem club, the Elk's Rendezvous. This swinging little group mixed jazz and jive in a manner that appealed to both dancers and listeners and communicated well on records (Jordan had a Decca contract from the start and recorded steadily). Its big hits didn't come until the early '40s. Much of the group's success came from Jordan's terrific sense of time and pacing; he could put on a show with the best of them. On records, he could almost make you see him as he preached mock sermons ("Beware"), told funny stories ("Five Guys Named Mo"), or just sang the blues with a message that all could absorb ("Early in the Morning") . Sometimes the story took both sides of a 78 to tell ("Saturday Night Fish Fry"), and sometimes the story was even romantic ("Don't Let the Sun Catch You Cryin'"). Nat Cole, Ray Charles, B. B. King—they all learned from Louis Jordan. Not forgotten, Jordan has been celebrated on records and on stage, most recently with *Five Guys Named Mo*, first in London, then on Broadway in 1992. —*Dan Morgenstern*

○ **At the Swing Cats' Ball** / **i.** Jan. 1937-Nov. 1939 / JSP 330
○ **Let the Good Times Roll: The Complete Decca Recordings 1938-54** / **i.** 1938-1954 / Bear Family 15557
With nine CDs and a 48-page color bio-discography full of fabulous photographs, this boxed set of *all* of Louis Jordan's Decca recordings asks the musical question, "How much jive can the human body stand?" Plenty! The collection chronicles Jordan's career from his first jokey swing novelties of 1939 to wartime smash hits like "What's the Use of Gettin' Sober" and "Is You Is Or Is You Ain't (My Baby)." From there, Jordan picked up speed, delivering one of the most productive, influential, and successful careers in American popular music. It's hard to imagine another artist of Jordan's commercial stature with so few duds in his past. . . . The enclosed book is a classy, sympathetic measure of both the man and his career. —*Tom Smith, Roundup Newsletter*

○ **Five Guys Named Moe: Original Decca Recordings, V.2** / **i.** 1939-1955 / MCA 10503
Eighteen Decca sides, 1942-1952, from the king of jump 'n jive. Ten of the selections are used in the Broadway revue about Jordan, *Five Guys Named Moe*. This set includes Jordan's biggest hit (Number One on both the R&B and pop charts), "G.I. Jive," as well as other hits, "Boogie Woogie Blue Plate," "Open the Door Richard," and more. —*Roundup Newsletter*

Jazz Heritage: Greatest Hits—Vol. 2 (1941-1947) / 1941-1947 / MCA 1337
Another package of Louis Jordan's R&B hits, this one covering the early and mid-'40s. Jordan was among the biggest stars in the nation during this period, and not only did he have smash songs for himself, others like Woody Herman, Ella Fitzgerald, and even Pearl Bailey and Moms Mabley covered his material. —*Ron Wynn, AMG*

☆ **Best of Louis Jordan, The** / 1942-1945 / MCA 4079
This is the best domestic collection of seminal Jordan cuts. In many ways, it's foundation music for the creation of R&B and can be linked to rap as well. Funny lyrics, superior arrangements, amazing material from the '40s and '50s. —*Ron Wynn*

★ **Louis Jordan and His Tympany Five** / **i.** 1944 / Circle
Wondrous cuts that combined hip vocals, robust solos, and inventive lyrics into a sound that was later called R&B. These are also available in other collections on Charly and Jukebox Lil. —*Ron Wynn*

Five Guys Named Moe, Vol II / 1948-1949 / Decca 10503
The second volume of '40s hits featuring R&B legend Louis Jordan. Jordan, formerly in Chick Webb's band, took the swing principles he'd learned there and mixed them with comedic energy and wit. The results helped fuel a musical revolution, and these are among the songs that played a vital role in it. —*Ron Wynn, AMG*

○ **One Guy Named Louis** / **i.** 1954 / Blue Note 96804
Twenty-one tracks recorded for the Aladdin label in 1954, nearly three years after the end of Jordan's hit-making decade with Decca. The first single from these sessions—"Whiskey, Do Your Stuff"—was penned by bass player Shifty Henry, who was later immortalized in song by Leiber and Stoller ("Jailhouse Rock"). More fine jump blues and novelty tunes include "Dad Gum Ya Hide, Boy" and "Fat Back and Corn Liquor." — *Roundup Newsletter*

○ **Complete Aladdin Sessions, The** / **i.** Jan. 1954 / EMI 7965672
○ **I Believe in Music** / Nov. 6, 1973 / Evidence 26006
Nice early '70s date with alto saxophonist and vocalist Louis Jordan doing more conventional blues and jazz material, very little comedy. Jordan's instrumental prowess took a back seat as he became a celebrity to his quips and monologues. But this time the music reigned. —*Ron Wynn*

○ **Reed Petite and Gone** / **i.** 1983 / Krazy Kat 414
★ **Look Out!** / Charly
Just Say Moe! Mo' Best of Louis / Rhino 71144
Rhino's *Just Say Moe!* covers Jordan's entire career, including some material from his peak years at Decca and a song from the Broadway musical, *Five Guys Named Moe*, based on his life. A good compliment to MCA's *Best of Louis Jordan.* —*AMG*

Sheila Jordan (Sheila Jeanette Jordan)

b. Nov. 18, 1928, Detroit, MI
Vocals, songwriter / Ballads & blues, modern creative
There's something at once esoteric, yet eminently accessible about vocalist Sheila Jordan. She sounds so unlike anyone else that it can be hard to get a handle on her at first listening. She is one of the idiom's most personal, intense, and emotionally direct vocalists. Her singing is infused with intelligence, musicianship, and deep feeling. A jazz singer from the word go, she eschews all the trappings of show biz glitz without becoming aloof to her audience. You'll never hear a glib or facile lick thrown on to demonstrate how hip, soulful, or technically adept she is. Yet, she has plenty of chops. She is not afraid to take chances, especially in her scat singing, which she infuses with a whimsical humor. Jordan's current partnership with bassist Harvie Swartz has yielded some of her finest moments. She's a greatly under-appreciated artist. —*Richard Lieberson*

○ **Portrait of Sheila Jordan** / Sep. 1962-Oct. 1962 / Blue Note 89002
Innovative date w/ Barry Galbraith (g), Steve Swallow (b), and Denzil Best (d). The one to get —*Richard Lieberson*

○ **Playground** / Jul. 1979 / ECM 1159
A studio date with the Steve Kuhn Trio. The most distinctive voice in modern jazz. Some of Jordan's best work. —*Michael G. Nastos*

★ **Last Year's Waltz** / ECM 1213
Live at Fat Tuesdays in NYC with the Steve Kuhn Trio. Sheila at her best. —*Michael G. Nastos*

Stanley Jordan

b. Jul. 31, 1959, Chicago, IL
Guitar / Instrumental pop, neo-bop, contemporary funk
Guitarist Stanley Jordan created an uproar in the '80s with his unusual tuning and technique. Jordan used the "hammering-on" approach, playing the guitar like a keyboard. Both hands played melody lines through his tapping the strings rather than strumming or using a pick. Jordan's ability to play melodies in the right hand and chords and bass lines in the left were acknowledged as

remarkable even by his detractors. He was discovered playing on the street, but was soon doing comfortably with a major label contract. Jordan's albums have been uneven affairs, but his live dates are more enjoyable and give him more room to fully display his skills. —*Ron Wynn*

★ **Magic Touch** / 1985 / Blue Note 46092
The debut album by a musician who helped redefine how a guitar is played. A must! —*Paul Kohler*

○ **Stolen Moments** / i. 1991 / Somethin' Else 97159
Guitarist Stanley Jordan's acclaimed technique, in which he roams over the fretboard strumming and gliding rather than picking, has earned him both plaudits and brickbats. His albums have been inconsistent affairs, but he quieted critics with this '91 session. He took standards and anthems that had been done to death and made them sound fresh through invigorating, explosive guitar solos. —*Ron Wynn*

Max Kaminsky

b. Sep. 7, 1908, Brockton, MA
Trumpet / Dixieland
An assertive, often delightful trumpeter, Max Kaminsky is one of the more concise, swinging traditional players whose tone and style echo the influence of King Oliver, Freddy Keppard, and Louis Armstrong. He's performed since the late '20s, and has done both swing and traditional jazz. Kaminsky worked in Boston in the '20s before moving to Chicago in 1928. He played with George Wettling and Frank Teschemaker at the Cinderella Ballroom and then with Red Nichols in New York for a short stint in 1929. During the '30s Kaminsky played with dance bands, while recording with Eddie Condon, Benny Carter, and Mezz Mezzrow. He worked with Tommy Dorsey and Artie Shaw in the late '30s and recorded with Bud Freeman in both 1939 and 1940. Kaminsky teamed with Shaw again from 1941 to 1943, playing in Shaw's navy band that toured the South Pacific. He later participated in early '40s New York concerts at Carnegie Hall and Town Hall organized by Condon and played traditional jazz in the '40s with Sidney Bechet, Georg Brunis, Art Hodes, Joe Marsala, Willie "The Lion" Smith, and Jack Teagarden. Kaminsky toured Europe with Teagarden and Earl Hines's All Stars in the late '50s and played at Ryan's periodically from the late '60s until 1983. He also made appearances at the Newport Jazz Festival and New York World's Fair in the mid '60s. Kaminsky recorded some fine material for Commodore in the '40s and did some stellar material in the '70s for the Fat Cat's Jazz label. —*Ron Wynn*

● **Chicago Style** / 1954 / Jazztone 1208

Richie Kamuca (Richard Kamuca)

b. Jul. 23, 1930, Philadelphia, PA, **d.** Jul. 22, 1977, Los Angeles, CA
Tenor sax / Cool
An outstanding ballad stylist and ardent Lester Young disciple, tenor saxophonist Richie Kamuca had a wonderful sound and tone. Kamuca played with Roy Eldridge while a teen and joined Stan Kenton's orchestra in the early '50s. He was principal soloist for Woody Herman from 1954 to 1956, and played with Cy Touff, Chet Baker, Art Pepper, Maynard Ferguson, and Shelly Manne in the '50s and early '60s, before moving from California to New York. There were reunion gigs with Eldridge, and Kamuca later became part of Merv Griffin's studio orchestra. He returned to California when Griffin moved there in 1970. Kamuca played with Bill Berry's L.A. band in the mid- and late '70s. Cancer cut Richie Kamuca's career prematurely short, but he left behind plenty of fine music. —*Ron Wynn and Michael G. Nastos*

○ **Tenors Head On** / Jul. 1956 / Liberty 3051

★ **West Coast Jazz in Hi Fi** / 1959 / Hi Fi 1760
A worthy reissue. A good West Coast-style effort. Limited-edition release. —*Ron Wynn*

○ **Richard Kamuca (1976)** / 1976 / Jazz 104

○ **Richie** / 1977 / Concord Jazz 41
Kamuca's ideas and his playing here was some of his best on record. The choice of tunes was as pleasing as his companions on this date (guitarist Mundell Lowe, bassist Monty Budwig, drummer Nick Ceroli). His ballads "Some Other Spring," "Say It Isn't So," and "Tis Autumn" were all essential to lovers of the tenor saxophone, and it's comforting to have his vocal interpretations preserved on the final track. —*Jerry L. Atkins, Cadence*

○ **Charlie** / 1978 / Concord Jazz 96
A little-known facet of tenorman Richie Kamuca's musical personality was his love for the alto, an instrument he associated almost exclusively with Charlie Parker and which he himself enjoyed playing, but only "for fun." Alternatively, had he devoted more of his time to the smaller horn, his chops would have been in better shape for this date; but as it was, ill-aligned mouthpiece grip and all, he did surpassingly well. —*Jack Sohmer, Cadence*

Geoff Keezer

b. 1970
Piano / Neo-bop
Geoff Keezer is an emerging piano star on the East Coast. His speed, facility, creativity, and flash have already stunned several East Coast critics, and he's become a prime "young lion." He has also played with Roy Hargrove, Antonio Hart, and many others. He's a member of the Contemporary Piano Ensemble, along with James Williams, Donald Brown, Harold Mabern, and Mulgrew Miller, plus bassist Christian McBride and drummer Tony Reedus. Their debut release was issued in '94 on Columbia. —*Ron Wynn*

○ **Curveball** / Jun. 1989 / Sunnyside 1045

★ **Here and Now** / Oct. 1990 / Blue Note 96691
Best album from Wisconsin pianist. More to come from Keezer. With Steve Nelson on vibes. Excellent version of Harold Mabern's "There But for the Grace of . . ." —*Michael G. Nastos*

○ **World Music** / i. 1992 / Columbia 52958
The most recent release by critically acclaimed pianist Geoff Keezer. Despite the title, there's as much American hard bop as anything, but the set also shows Keezer's knowledge of Afro-Latin rhythms and pulse. He's working with a new group featuring James Genus, Tony Reedus, and Rudy Bird. —*Ron Wynn*

Roger Kellaway

b. Nov. 1, 1939, Newton, MA
Piano, composer, arranger / Bop
A well-known accompanist, Roger Kellaway plays everything from rumbling boogies to bop. He's written the scores for such films as "Paper Lion," "A Star Is Born," and "Breathless," had the ballet "PAMTGG" commissioned by George Balanchine in 1971 and the orchestral work "Portraits of Time" by the Los Angeles Philharmonic in 1983. His piano solos were featured for many years as part of the television show "All in the Family." Kellaway actually spent time as a bassist with Jimmy McPartland and then played piano with Kai Winding. He was in groups co-led by Zoot Sims and Al Cohn and the bands of Clark Terry and Bob Brookmeyer in the mid-'60s. He also recorded with Ben Webster, Maynard Ferguson, Wes Montgomery, and Sonny Rollins, later joining Don Ellis's big band after moving to Los Angeles. He was Bobby Darin's music director for two years in the late '60s. Besides being busy in the studios doing television soundtracks, Kellaway also found time in the '70s and '80s to record with everyone from Joni Mitchell to Mundell Lowe. He's recorded as a leader for Prestige, A&M, Dobre, Concord, All Art, Voss, Regina, and Stash, among others. —*Ron Wynn*

○ **Ain't Misbehavin'** / i. 1986 / Bainbridge 6833
Kellaway showed off his command of the piano on a medium-tempo "How Deep Is the Ocean" and although "Blue in Green" wandered a bit, "Skylark" was very explorative, almost atonal in spots. Despite its weak beginning, Ain't Misbehavin was one of Kellaway's best jazz records to date. —*Scott Yanow, Cadence*

★ **Live at Maybeck Recital Hall—Vol. 11** / Mar. 1991 / Concord Jazz 4470
Recent view of Kellaway's style. Melodic yet driving. Strong stride-piano influence. —*Hank Davis*

○ **Roger Kellaway Meets Gene Bertoncini and Michael...** / Chiaroscuro 315

Wynton Kelly

b. Dec. 2, 1931, Jamaica, **d.** Apr. 12, 1971, Toronto, Canada
Piano / Hard bop, postbop, soul-jazz
Wynton Kelly was one of the great pianists of the post-World War II era. Originally influenced by Nat Cole, Kelly began in small bands around New York in the late '40s. Working with Lester Young and Dizzy Gillespie, he soon became the favorite session pianist in New York, featured with Miles Davis (1959-1963), in a

cooperative trio with Paul Chambers and Jimmy Cobb (1964-1967), and often with Wes Montgomery. He appeared as a sideman on dozens of recordings (the albums from the '50s and early '60s are good), though the mantle of leadership was not worn easily by Kelly. His Verve recordings from the mid-'60s tended to be more commercial. Any time he recorded with Chambers and a good drummer (Cobb, Blakey, PJ Jones, etc.) as a rhythm section, is a listener's delight. —*Bob Porter*

○ **Wynton Kelly** / **i.** Jan. 31, 1958 / Riverside 1540
This was a satisfyingly low-keyed trio date from June 1961, with Paul Chambers and Sam Jones alternating on bass and Jimmy Cobb on drums. Yes (in anticipation of the next question), with Chambers on bass, this trio was the Miles Davis rhythm section of the time. Two fine Kelly originals were offset by six standards. Throughout the set, Kelly's uncluttered melodic swing held sway. —*Alan Bargebuhr, Cadence*

★ **Kelly Blue** / Feb. 19, 1959-Mar. 1959 / Riverside 033
Recorded at Reeves Sound Studios in New York. Small group. Classic Kelly. Bluesy, bright, nice. There is magic in this album. — *Michael Erlewine*

☆ **Kelly Great** / Aug. 12, 1959 / Vee Jay 907
This presents pianist Wynton Kelly from 2/19/59 and 3/10/59 with trumpeter Nat Adderley, saxophonists Bobby Jaspar and Benny Golson, bassists Paul Chambers and Sam Jones, and drummer Jimmy Cobb. Adderley, Jaspar, and Golson played only on the 2/19/59 tracks (two), and Kelly was accompanied by just the rhythm trio on the remaining four cuts. The sides with horns were the best; Nat Adderley was in especially good form. The trio sides were solid, if not particularly explosive or individualistic. The entire LP was also issued as part of a twofer. —*Bob Rusch, Cadence*

☆ **Best of Wynton Kelly, The** / **i.** 1963 / Vee Jay 1086

○ **Blues on Purpose** / Jun. 25, 1965+Aug. 17, 1965 / Xanadu
Fidelity may not be as high as some may wish on this mono disk, but the level of playing *is*, and the sound is quite good enough to document the bristling excitement these three soulmates could generate, whether playing the blues at various tempos or giving Tadd Dameron's "If You Could See Me Now" an elegantly burnished treatment. —*Bob Rusch, Cadence*

★ **Smokin' at the Half Note** / Jun. 1965+Sep. 22, 1965 / Verve 829578
Some recorded September 22, 1965, at Englewood Cliffs, NJ. Wynton Kelly Trio w/ Wes Montgomery (g). Slow to midtempos—very listenable. Both Wynton and Wes are in fine form. A rare chance to hear Montgomery in a small-group setting. — *Michael Erlewine*

☆ **Someday My Prince Will Come** / Vee Jay 902
Wynton Kelly was perhaps the most rhythmically energetic and intense soloist among the session pianists who were in demand during the '50s. He and Red Garland did numerous dates, with Garland's block chords and relaxed pacing the stylistic opposite of Kelly's faster, more linear approach. This 15-cut session contains four bonus cuts: one number with Wayne Shorter and Lee Morgan, and the other tunes trio dates with Kelly's often raging piano contrasted by Paul Chambers' strong, big-toned bass and Philly Joe Jones resolute fills. —*Ron Wynn*

Stan Kenton (Stanley Newcomb Kenton)

b. Dec. 15, 1911, Wichita, KS, d. Aug. 25, 1979, Los Angeles, CA
Piano, arranger, composer / Cool, progressive big band
Stan Kenton, along with Duke Ellington, Count Basie, and Woody Herman, persevered the longest in maintaining his big band. Unlike the other three, there's much less general acclaim accorded the Kenton orchestra. Kenton tried many unusual things with instrumentation and musical concepts. Kenton tried to blend (maybe even sandwich) symphonic and jazz elements; he headed groups with as many as 40 members. There were also several suites, Afro-Latin pieces, rock, pop, and other things. Jimmie Lunceford's orchestra was a prime influence, and Kenton got his start writing and arranging for Benny Goodman, Vido Musso, and Gus Arnheim in the '30s. He founded the 14-piece Artistry in Rhythm Orchestra in 1941 and made his debut recordings for Decca in 1941 and 1942. The list of distinguished Kenton alumni include Stan Getz, Lucky Thompson, Lennie Niehaus, Art Pepper,

and Kai Winding, plus vocalists June Christy, Anita O'Day, and Chris Connor. —*Ron Wynn*

● **Complete Capitol Recordings of the Bill Holman** / Mosaic

○ **Kenton Era** / 1941-1955 / Creative World 1030
A limited edition, four-record set that covers the Stan Kenton orchestra in its formative period from 1941 to 1955. It includes a four-page booklet with Kenton's biography, and shows how the controversial composer moved from being strictly a swing era leader into his wide-ranging blend of jazz, Afro-Latin, and classical. —*Ron Wynn*

○ **Christy Years** / May 4, 1945-1947 / Creative World 1035
A 1977 anthology covering hits turned out when June Christy was the Kenton Orchestra's lead vocalist from 1945 to 1947. There's also some material with the Pied Pipers vocal group. —*Ron Wynn*

○ **Innovations in Modern Music** / Feb. 3-04, 1950 / Creative World 1009
A pivotal Kenton album from 1950, one of the first in which he displayed the controversial unorthodox time signatures, huge brass sections, and bombastic sound. —*Ron Wynn*

○ **Artistry in Rhythm** / Sep. 4, 1950 / Creative World 1043
Probably Stan Kenton's most jumping band was this mid-'40s group. Anita O'Day not only established the style in which June Christy and Chris Connor followed less successfully, but she also practically marked the way for every girl jazz singer to come along in the '40s and '50s. Eddie Sofranski's bass reflected Jimmy Blanton, as did Gene Englund's on "5 O'Clock Drag," "Southern Scandal," "Painted Rhythm" (with Vido Musso), and "Artistry Jumps" were all fairly standard late-swing-era pieces. —*John Mcdonough, Down Beat*

★ **New Concepts of Artistry in Rhythm** / Sep. 8-10, 1952 / Capitol 386

○ **Kenton Showcase** / 1953 / Creative World 1026
A '66 release of material that was originally recorded in 1953 and 1954. This was among Kenton's finest bands ever, especially due to such soloists as Frank Rosolino, Lee Konitz, and both Conte Candoli and Maynard Ferguson in the trumpet section. —*Ron Wynn*

○ **By Request—Vol. 5 (1953-1960)** / 1953-1960 / Creative World 1066
The fifth volume in the series dedicated to the Kenton orchestra cutting a variety of material, some of it their own, some their interpretations and reworkings. This one covered the mid '50s to 1960. —*Ron Wynn*

○ **By Request—Vol. 2 (1953-1960)** / 1953-1960 / Creative World 1040
The second of a series by the Kenton orchestra doing everything from standards to originals. This covered1953 to 1960, and was the first of two devoted to this time frame. —*Ron Wynn*

○ **Kenton in Hi-Fi** / Feb. 11-12, 1956 / Blue Note 98451
A '92 reissue of a '56 album that was early Kenton orchestra release in stereo. It's otherwise a pretty routine release, but it was interesting to hear the imbalance as engineers had a difficult time balancing the huge Kenton brass section. —*Ron Wynn*

○ **Cuban Fire—Vol. 1** / May 22-24, 1956 / Blue Note 96260

○ **Cuban Fire—Vol. 2** / May 22-24, 1956 / Creative World 1008

○ **Stan Kenton and His Innovations Orchestra** / **i.** 1992 / Laserlight 15770
A '92 anthology featuring bandleader Stan Kenton and his orchestra from 1951, with their experimental orchestral recordings. Kenton's unorthodox time signatures and rhythms were always controversial, and never more so than on these recordings, which presented even more unusual orchestrations. —*Ron Wynn*

★ **Retrospective** / **i.** 1992 / Blue Note 97350
Anthology covering the Kenton orchestra from its early years into the '70s. A good introductory or sampler, though not really a greatest-hits presentation. —*Ron Wynn*

☆ **Comprehensive Kenton** / Capitol 12016

☆ **Stan Kenton** / Mosaic 136
The Holman and Russo Charts. Four-CD set contains all 72 works that Russo and Holman wrote or arranged for Kenton. Long unavailable. This is the high-water mark of Kenton's career as one

of the chief innovators in experimental big-band jazz. —*Michael Erlewine*

Freddie Keppard

b. Feb. 27, 1890, New Orleans, LA, **d.** Jul. 15, 1933, Chicago, IL
Cornet / New Orleans traditional
A lack of recorded evidence hasn't diminished Freddie Keppard's reputation for musicians and critics who heard him validate his ability. Keppard's approach was quite close to ragtime in its staccato style, but his few recordings (only one as a leader) show a soaring melodic quality and sound. Unfortunately, by the time he got a chance to record extensively, his health was failing. Keppard studied mandolin, violin, and accordion and began playing professionally as a cornetist in 1906 with his band the Olympia Orchestra and other New Orleans groups. Keppard became a national sensation in 1914, when he went to California to join the Original Creole Band. The band did a "white-tie, all-musical act" sans blackface mugging and minus comedic quips. They were so beloved Keppard had a chance to record with Victor in 1916, but he turned it down because he didn't want other bands copying the group's style. They toured the Orpheum vaudeville circuit and then Keppard settled in Chicago after a brief period with King Oliver. In Chicago he played with his own groups and those of Doc Cook, Erskine Tate, Ollie Powers, and Charlie Elgar. Keppard's lone date as leader had him heading a quintet with Johnny Dodds and trombonist Eddie Vincent. He also recorded with Doc Cook's Dreamland Orchestra and Erskine Tate. —*Ron Wynn*

○ **Red Onion Jazz Babies / Cook's Dreamland Orchestra/ Freddie Keppard's Jazz Cardinals** / i. Jan. 1924-Sep. 1926 / Fountain FJ-107

Barney Kessel

b. Oct. 17, 1923, Muskogee, OK
Guitar / Bop, cool
Barney Kessel is a very influential jazz guitarist. He picked up the torch from Charlie Christian and was a major presence on electric guitar by the mid-'40s. Prior to Kessel, most jazz guitarists had specialized in either single-string or chord-melody solos. Kessel became a complete jazz guitarist by incorporating both approaches into his aggressive, hard-swinging, bluesy style. As a sideman, Kessel gained a reputation through his work with Artie Shaw's Gramercy Five, the Oscar Petersen Trio, and Charlie Parker, among others. His '50s albums with bassist Ray Brown and drummer Shelly Manne put the guitar trio format on the map, revealing the electric guitar as a fully formed jazz voice. He's continued working and recording.—*Richard Lieberson*

○ **Easy Like** / Nov. 14, 1953-Dec. 19, 1953 / Original Jazz Classics 153
This presents the first two sessions guitarist Barney Kessel recorded for Contemporary: 11/14/53 and 12/19/53. These were pleasant, somewhat easy swinging dates with backing from Bud Shank (alto sax, flute), Arnold Ross (piano), Harry Babasin (bass), and Shelly Manne (drums). They were originally released as a ten-incher. They blend well with the 2/23/56 date that fills out the 12-inch LP. —*Bob Rusch, Cadence*

○ **Kessel Plays Standards** / Jun. 4, 1954-Jul. 1, 1954 / Contemporary 238
Guitarist Barney Kessel and the great American standard were the program on *Plays Standards*, the ringer being "Barney's Blues," the one Kessel original. Recorded in three sessions between June 4, 1954, and September 12, 1955, the personnel included Bob Cooper, Claude Williamson, Monty Budwig, Shelly Manne, Hampton Hawes, Red Mitchell, and Chuck Thompson. — *Bob Rusch, Cadence*

○ **Music to Listen to Barney Kessel By** / Aug. 6, 1956-Oct. 15, 1956 / Contemporary 746
Kessel's guitar with five woodwinds and a rhythm section. 12 songs w/ Buddy Collette (fl), Andre Previn (p), Shelly Manne (d), Jimmy Rowles (p), Red Mitchell (b), Buddy Clark (b), and others. —*AMG*

● **Poll Winners with Ray Brown and Shelly Manne** / Mar. 18-19, 1957 / Contemporary 156
While this wasn't as powerful as *Feeling Free*, it did succeed, and again, the drummer must get equal credit. There was a comfortable conversational tone about this recording, a fact also men-

tioned by Nat Hentoff in his liners. This kind of effort will always sound good, familiar, yet with enough meat and thinking to sustain concentrated listening. —*Bob Rusch, Cadence*

★ **Poll Winners Ride Again, The** / Aug. 1958 / Contemporary 607

★ **Some Like It Hot** / Mar. 30-31, 1959 / Contemporary 168
Here was one of two sessions guitarist Barney Kessel recorded in the middle of his ten-year exclusive Contemporary period ('53-'62). It was a 1959 (3/30, 3/31, 4/3) date that included Art Pepper (clarinet, alto saxophone), Joe Gordon (trumpet), Jimmy Rowles (piano), Jack Marshall (rhythm guitar), Monty Budwig (bass), and Shelly Manne (drums). It was somewhat contained by ten air-play length cuts. This had moments from the leader, Pepper and Gordon, but it really only visited the listener. —*Bob Rusch, Cadence*

○ **Guitar Workshop** / Nov. 5, 1967 / Saba

☆ **Straight Ahead** / i. 1975 / Contemporary 7635

○ **Red Hot and Blues** / Contemporary 14044
Kessel was at his best on *Red Hot and Blues* for which he was joined by an all- star cast of vibraphonist Bobby Hutcherson, pianist Kenny Barron, bassist Rufus Reid, and drummer Ben Riley. —*W. Royal Stokes, Jazz Times*

Steve Khan

b. Apr. 28, 1947, Los Angeles, CA
Guitar / Early jazz rock, neo-bop
Steve Khan, son of songwriter Sammy Cahn, is a well-known session guitarist who has amassed a large number of credits doing mainly fusion-style material, though he's a good straightahead jazz player. He has been ranked alongside Cornell Dupree and Eric Gale as the most versatile studio players, but lacks the blues facility of the other two. He has made some records as a leader but has done better as accompanist to a host of pop/R&B big names, among them Sheila Jordon, Chaka Khan, Bob James, and Grover Washington Jr. —*Ron Wynn*

★ **Evidence** / Jul. 1980 / Novus 3074

○ **Eyewitness** / i. 1981 / Antilles 848821
Eyewitness was a straightforward, simple, yet challenging LP. The guitarist changed his compositional approach from earlier albums like *Arrows* and *Tightrope*. There was no more playing the head, soloing over the changes, repeating the head, and out. Khan allowed much of the music here to happen as it would. There was very little flaunting of chops here. Khan left a lot of space for his bandmates (bassist Anthony Jackson, drummer Steve Jordan, percussionist Manolo Badrena), and used his guitar to suggest ideas and textures for the band to explore and to create unusual washes. —*Robin Tolleson, Down Beat*

☆ **Let's Call This** / Blue Moon 79168
This tenacious trio of jazz heavyweights put together a fine compilation of tunes; spontaneous, yet relaxed, with that nightclub feel. Throughout, guitarist Steve Khan offers his smooth and silky feather-light fingerwork on the frets. —*Scott Thompson, Jazz Times*

John Kirby

b. Dec. 31, 1908, Baltimore, MD, **d.** Jun. 14, 1952, Hollywood, CA
Bass, tuba, bandleader, arranger / Swing
John Kirby led one of the finest small combos of the '30s and '40s. He was a disciplined, technically proficient bassist and leader whose band played a popular brand of jazz that came close to being a forerunner of the "lite" music currently favored on adult contemporary radio stations. They were a finesse group that avoided exuberant displays and hard-hitting, bluesy solos for melodically enchanting, swinging music that lacked fire but was brilliantly played. The group was known for "jazzin' the classics." Kirby had earlier played trombone and tuba, before settling on bass. He played with Fletcher Henderson in the early '30s, joined Chick Webb in the mid '30s, and returned to Henderson. After a stint with Lucky Millinder, Kirby began his own band. Saxophonist Pete Brown and trumpeter Frankie Newton were originals. The group's popularity zoomed when it settled on the lineup of trumpeter Charlie Shavers, clarinetist Buster Bailey, saxophonist Russell Procope, pianist Billy Kyle, and drummer O'Neill Spencer. Shavers contributed arrangments and played lots of muted trumpet, while Kirby's wife at the time Maxine Sullivan did vocals. They did dates at whites-only hotels and even

were featured on a 1940 radio show, "Flow Gently, Sweet Rhythm." But when Sullivan left to go solo, Shavers joined Tommy Dorsey, and Kyle went into the army, the group disbanded. A Carnegie Hall reunion concert with Big Sid Catlett on drums was a commercial failure. Kirby later died of diabetes. The survivors staged a quasi-reunion on the Bethlehem date *The Complete Charlie Shavers with Maxine Sullivan* in 1953. Their finest work was reissued on a Smithsonian collection *John Kirby: The Biggest Little Band 1937-1941*. There are also reissued CDs on Circle and Classic Jazz. —*Ron Wynn*

○ **John Kirby** / **i**. 1938 / Columbia 502

● **Biggest Little Band, The** / Oct. 28, 1938-Jan. 15, 1941 / Smithsonian 013

Andy Kirk (Andrew Dewey Kirk)

b. May 28, 1898, Newport, KY, **d**. 1992
Baritone sax, bass, bandleader / Swing, big band
A decent saxophonist and tuba player, Andy Kirk was a better bandleader and presided over one of the great territory bands. A student of Paul Whiteman's father at Wilberforce, Kirk began playing bass sax and tuba in George Morrison's orchestra in 1918 and moved to Dallas in 1925. He joined Terrence Holder's band and assumed the leadership role in 1929. Kirk's band gained some national attention in 1936, thanks to Pha Terrell's high note vocals. Pianist Mary Lou Williams, Fats Navarro, Don Byas, and Howard McGhee were other prominent members. They scored some hits in the late '30s with songs like "Until the Real Thing Comes Along," and later teamed with the Jubilaries for more hits in the '40s. Kirk occasionally led a West Coast band and also managed a New York City hotel in the '50s and toured Europe in the '60s. —*Ron Wynn and Michael G. Nastos.*

○ **March 1936** / Mar. 1936 / Mainstream 399
A neat bonus, this: five Mary Lou Williams solo pieces and 13 tracks by what proved the most commercially successful of the legendary Kansas City bands, nicely packaged and with useful Charles Fox liners. These were the Decca recordings that began Andy Kirk's most popular period, and if you missed the deleted Kirk reissue on Decca, you'll find six of the best pieces here. —*John Litweiler, Down Beat.*

○ **Jazz Heritage: Instrumentally Speaking (1936-1942)** / 1936-1942 / Decca 9232

○ **Jazz Heritage—Lady Who Swings the Band (1936-1938)** / 1936-1938 / MCA 1343

★ **Andy Kirk (1944)** / 1944 / Hindsight 227

Rahsaan Roland Kirk (Ronald T. Kirk)

b. May 15, 1936, Columbus, Ohio, **d**. Dec. 5, 1977
Tenor sax, multireeds / Bop, hard bop
His incredible musicianship, vibrant onstage personality, and fondness for creating sometimes-outlandish instruments led some in the jazz world to mistakenly downplay Rahsaan Roland Kirk's immense skills. But Kirk was an amazing improviser, a musician completely knowledgeable of the entire jazz spectrum, and a cultural advocate who was displeased that both he and the music he loved were often viewed with disdain or ignored. He could swing; play fiercely or with serenity; handle blues, bop, or free; interpret the anthems; or make up his own songs and lyrics on demand. Kirk was blinded shortly after birth and studied at the Ohio State School for the Blind. He was playing sax and clarinet at 12 and was heading his own dance band in 1951, while doing freelance work with other groups as well. He began his technique of playing three instruments at once at 16, going into a music store and finding two long-forgotten saxophones that had been used in turn-of-the-century Spanish marching bands: the manzello and the stritch. He found a way to play these two plus the tenor at the same time, and generated some unforgettable moments on record and in concert over the years. Kirk was also a master of circular breathing, a means of holding notes and sustaining them while still finding a way to breathe. Kirk's 1956 debut release didn't get much attention, but when Ramsey Lewis got him a date with the Cadet label, detractors dismissed him as a showman and charlatan. In 1961 he played on the Mingus album *Oh Yeah*, obliterating much of the early criticism. He toured with Mingus as well, going with his band to Europe and appearing at a festival in West Germany. From 1963 until his death, Kirk

headed his own bands and was never unwilling to buck the odds or sound off in print or on television about the plight of jazz and African-American musicians. —*Ron Wynn*

Does Your House Have Lions: The Rahsaan Roland Kirk Anthology / Rhino R2-71406
The Atlantic/Rhino anthology line has delighted novices and angered purists who have balked at what they deem questionable inclusions and exclusions, plus nonchronological sequencing and liners with plenty of personal anecdotes but limited musical analysis. None of these things are corrected with this CD of Rahsaan Roland Kirk material, which does raise the question: who are these intended for anyhow? If they are designed to interest a newcomer in the artist, they do the job. The 31 selections range from 1961 to 1976 and cover Kirk originals, covers, straight jazz, pop-soul, gospel-backed, and hard bop workouts and feature both live and studio segments. While it is a bit jarring to hop from the early '60s to the '70s and back, series compiler Joel Dorn opted for stylistic organization rather than session exactness. It is not the way I would personally do it, but it is not the hanging crime some imply. Since no one is claiming that this series is supposed to resemble Mosaic's climactic boxed line, it is hard to understand what the fuss is all about. Any hardcore Kirk fan will want the individual albums the label is reissuing. Otherwise, the anthology serves its purpose, which is to spotlight a brillant player and make you want to hear more. —*Ron Wynn*

★ **Rahsaan—Complete on Mercury** / 1961-1964 / Mercury 846630

☆ **We Free Kings** / Apr. 1962 / Mercury 826455

○ **Reeds & Deeds** / Aug. 1963 / Mercury 20800

○ **Rip, Rig and Panic / Now Please Don't ...** / Jan. 13, 1965-Apr. 1967 / Emarcy 832164
1965 & 1967. Also: *Now Please Don't You Cry, Beautiful Edith*. A couple of Kirk's more popular '60s albums combined. —*Ron Wynn*

○ **Now Please Don't You Cry, Beautiful Edith** / Jul. 1968 / Verve 68709
This April 1967 recording with Lonnie Smith (piano), Ronnie Boykins (bass), and Grady Tate (drums) presented a solid display of Rahsaan Roland Kirk's talents on tenor, manzello, whistle, stritch, and flute in what was perhaps typical of the cornucopia of musical roots and messages that became part of his statements from the '60s until his death. —*Bob Rusch, Cadence*

Inflated Tear, The / Nov. 1968 / Atlantic 90045
Recorded in November 1967 with pianist Ron Burton, bassist Steve Novosel, drummer Jimmy Hopps, and trombonist Dick Griffin, it was in many ways a typically planned date to display the 360 degrees of Rahsaan Roland Kirk. —*Bob Rusch, Cadence*

★ **Volunteered Slavery** / Jan. 1970 / Atlantic 1534
There seems to be no expression that Rahsaan Roland Kirk couldn't elicit from his arsenal of horns, individually or in multiples. . . . "Three for the Festival" was just wild grunts, groans, shouts, smashings, and whistles, and did I hear "We Shall Overcome" in the melee? It sounded like a coda for "One Ton" and took the record out the same way it came in. Side two was recorded at the Newport Jazz Festival in 1968. Kirk delighted the audience and the crowd. . . . This portion of the disc was a really powerful side of Kirk's unique personality. The Newport episodes were entertaining enough to warrant purchasing the album for the studio cuts. —*Alan Offstein, Coda*

☆ **Rahsaan / Rahsaan** / May 11-12, 1970 / Atlantic 1575
This session consisted of a repetition of Rahsaan Roland Kirk's nightclub patter, a medley of references to jazz history—Charlie Parker, New Orleans, Duke Ellington—and a couple of new items of minimal interest. . . . The second medley found Kirk soloing on a new saxophone that allowed him to play two melody lines simultaneously. The effect was one of playing two different melodies simultaneously. —*Alan Offstein, Coda*

☆ **Bright Moments** / Jun. 8-09, 1973 / Atlantic 907
Rahsaan Roland Kirk was a trip in himself, and this live recording, done at Todd Barkan's Keystone Korner, showed why. Whether stretching into well-used solo space or spinning out his hand-woven, Rahsaanized philosophy, he gripped an audience via the sincerity and exuberance of his sayings and playings. . . . The audience was ready for him this night, and Kirk was as "on" as they were. That was why *Bright Moments* was so engrossing

and absorbing: Kirk's musical fanaticism and sheer joy drew you into the world seen only by his inner eye, and when you left, you were exhausted but fulfilled. He took you on the trip he promised—and then some. —*Neil Tesser, Down Beat*

○ **Vibration Continues, The** / Atlantic 1003

This is a compilation from 1968-1974. Excellent introduction to a virtuoso. —*Michael G. Nastos*

Kenny Kirkland (Kenneth David Kirkland)

b. Sep. 28, 1955, Newport, NY
Piano, synthesizer / Postbop, neo-bop
Pianist Kenny Kirkland's a member of Branford Marsalis's "Tonight Show with Jay Leno" band and was formerly a prime contributor to Wynton Marsalis's group. He's also played with such rock musicians as Sting and has been a fine soloist on acoustic and electric. Kirkland's an excellent bop and hard bop player but is eclectic enough to handle any situation, part of the reason he was tabbed for the Tonight show orchestra. Herbie Hancock's a prime influence, and Kirkland played with Miroslav Vitous, Terumasa Hino, Elvin Jones, and Michael Urbaniak, among others. He's recorded for GRP as a leader. —*Ron Wynn*

★ **Kenny Kirkland** / i. 1991 / GRP 9657

This is a good set with Afro-Latin and hard-bop influences mixed. —*Ron Wynn*

John Klemmer

b. Jul. 3, 1946, Chicago, IL
Sax / Bop, early jazz-rock
A saxophonist who's seemed on the verge of stardom since the early '70s, John Klemmer never made the definitive album that would establish his credibility. He was very influenced by Coltrane in his early years, but experimented successfully with the echoplex on some Impulse recordings in the '70s. The mid-'70s release "Waterfalls" remains his finest work. —*Ron Wynn*

★ **Waterfalls** / Jun. 17+22, 1972 / MCA 33123

☆ **Nexus for Duo and Trio** / i. 1978 / Novus 23500

Nexus was a return for tenor saxophonist John Klemmer to the solid jazz he was "weaned on" long ago. The shadows of John Coltrane and Sonny Rollins loomed over a highly spontaneous session that was recorded live (unoverdubbed) in the studio with, Klemmer related, no preparation or prior discussion of the music to be played. Carl Burnett was particularly noteworthy in both the trio (first two sides) and sax-drums duo format. He was a dynamo of energy, but like Elvin Jones with Trane, his polyrhythmic subtleties offered an impressive range of color and constant change. —*Bob Henschen, Down Beat*

○ **Solo Saxophone II: Life** / 1981 / Elektra 566

This album was almost totally echoplexed. . . . Klemmer's extreme mastery of his tenor sax often was turned into glibness, rhythmic ideas lost impact, and much musical personality was lost in a dreamy whole. Closer listening revealed that Klemmer is a talented player with a lot to say on his own. There are moments on this record where truly original and creative passages managed to cut through the seemingly endless sea of reverberation and echo, like on "The Journey" and "The Celebration." —*Per Husby, Cadence*

Eric Kloss

b. Apr. 3, 1949, Greenville, PA
alto sax / Bop, hard bop, postbop, neo-bop
A blind alto saxophonist with an exuberant, intense style and biting tone, Eric Kloss has never been a superstar, but he's made some fine recordings for independent labels, particularly Muse. Kloss has recorded or played with Cedar Walton, Kenny Barron, Chick Corea, Dave Holland, Bob Cranshaw, Leroy Vinnegar, and Billy Higgins, among others. He also studied with Lee Konitz, Sonny Stitt, and James Moody. Other dates have been for Prestige and Omnisound.—*Ron Wynn*

★ **Celebration** / Jan. 6-07, 1979 / Muse 5196

Good, sometimes strong alto sax solos by Eric Kloss are the lure for this otherwise routine blend of fusion, soul-jazz, and funk with decent production, arrangements, and compositions. —*Ron Wynn*

Earl Klugh

b. Sep. 16, 1954, Detroit, MI
Guitar / Early jazz rock, new age, instrumental pop, contemporary funk
Self-taught guitarist Earl Klugh claims to have been inspired by Chet Atkins, George Van Eps, and Laurindo Almeida and was recording with Yusef Lateef at 15. He worked with George Benson and Chick Corea's Return to Forever and was selected by George Shearing for one of his tours. Klugh plays acoustic, nylon-stringed guitar and has resisted efforts to go electric. Although not strictly jazz, almost all his albums have been commercial successes in the pop-instrumental market. He is noted for his deft solos and subtle phrasing. —*Michael Erlewine*

★ **Earl Klugh** / i. 1976 / EMI 46553

○ **Heart String / Late Night Guitar** / i. 1983 / Liberty 183439

Heartstring offered a round of friendly little Earl Klugh originals that all stayed within a slow to medium tempo range featured the guitarist's fluently melodic style. Stripped of extremities and intensities, the album's sound was as mood-controlled and mood-conducive as a piece of Muzak, but it was saved from being entirely a commodity article by Klugh's quiet yet engaging warmth and by the swinging pulse of the backing. —*Lars Gabel, Down Beat*

Wishful Thinking / 1983 / Capitol 46030

Recorded at Media Sound, NYC/A&M Studios, LA. Jazz light. With some heavyweight sidemen mixed in, the sound is light, relaxing, jazz-space music. Pleasant stuff. —*Michael Erlewine*

Soda Fountain Shuffle / 1984 / Warner Brothers 25262

Recorded at A&M Recording Studios, Hollywood, CA. Synthesizer, drum machine backgrounds. Easy-listening programmed light jazz with a touch of space music. One of his most popular. —*Michael Erlewine*

○ **Solo Guitar** / i. 1989 / Warner Brothers 26018

Earl Klugh's long-awaited solo album showcased his pretty sound on the acoustic guitar, giving two- to three-minute melodic readings of superior standards. Some of the pieces (notably "I'm Confessin") found Klugh playing a relaxed "stride" similar to some of the guitarists of the '30s. . . . it was Earl Klugh's most rewarding album to date. —*Scott Yanow, Cadence*

○ **Earl Klugh Trio—Vol. 1, The** / i. 1991 / Warner Brothers 26750

Jimmy Knepper (James M. Knepper)

b. Nov. 22, 1927, Los Angeles
Trombone, arranger / Bop, hard bop
Among the rare trombonists able to forge a direction blending elements of both modern and vintage jazz, Jimmy Knepper has combined a fluid, rapid-pace technique with the slurs, growls, and smears of so-called "tailgate" players. Knepper began playing professionally in the '40s with a band co-led by Dean Benedetti and Chuck Cascales. He toured with Freddie Slack in 1947 and alto saxophonist Johnny Bothwell in 1948 and worked in Roy Porter's band alongside Eric Dolphy in 1948-1949. He worked in other big bands in the '50s before relocating to New York, where he replaced Willie Dennis in Charles Mingus's Jazz Workshop band in 1957-1958. Knepper had a lengthy but often turbulent relationship with Mingus, working with him in the late '50s and early '60s, then reuniting with him in 1976 and 1977. Knepper became a member of the Thad Jones-Mel Lewis big band in 1967 and remained with them until 1973. He joined Lee Konitz's nonet from 1975 to 1979. He's been involved with the Mingus Dynasty as both a player and musical director since 1979 and has also issued recordings as a leader on various independent labels. —*Ron Wynn*

○ **Idol of the Flies** / Sep. 1957 / Bethlehem

Idol of the Flies was trombonist Jimmy Knepper's second album, and it featured a surprisingly reticent drummer Danny Richmond and a still-verdant pianist Bill Evans. Evans' formative subtlety was notable for the fine tension between his percussive propensities and his ruminative, dissonant breaks. Like Donald Byrd, Knepper's solo style favored "vocalisms" (another trumpet trait), with wry, rolling intonations. Tellingly, he relaxed and flaunted his lyricism more readily in the presence of trumpeter Gene Roland, particularly on "Gee Baby, Ain't I Good to You," featuring Roland's riveting, ghostly vocal. —*Mikal Gilmore, Down Beat*

★ **Pepper-Knepper Quintet** / i. 1958 / MGM

★ **Cunningbird** / Nov. 8, 1976 / Steeple Chase
Quintet w/ Al Cohn (ts), Sir Roland Hanna (p), George Mraz (b), Dannie Richmond (d). A tremendous date. —*Ron Wynn*

○ **Tell Me...** / Aug. 14, 1979 / Daybreak 001
Knepper's is a uniquely conversational style, full of asides, questions, and a witty rhetoric that is never empty. It is expressed in a gruff, opaque tone whose vocal nature is obtained by subtle variations of inflection and timbre.... The album was ... dominated by Knepper's rubbery lyricism, with its surprising twists and turns—nowhere better demonstrated than on his former employer's "Ecclesiastics" or on the duet with piano, dedicated to Billie Holiday, "I Thought about You." His work on "Home," the impishly-titled "Nearer My God in C," and the title track were of an equally high standard, so comparison becomes sterile. —*Chris Sheridan, Down Beat*

○ **Dream Dancing** / i. Apr. 1986 / Criss Cross 1024
Tenor sax player Ralph Moore has played with Horace Silver, and his contribution to this date was mostly to provide additional color since his solo work was relatively limited. Truthfully, his best moments were when he was providing counterpoint, floating in and around Knepper's solos. Dick Katz (piano), George Mraz (bass) and Mel Lewis (drums) provided all the support that Knepper could want accentuating the floating quality of the music. —*Carl Brauer, Cadence*

Lee Konitz

b. Oct. 13, 1927, Chicago, IL
Alto sax / Postbop, cool
Born in Chicago, young Lee Konitz there met the unique and Svengalilike pianist-teacher Lennie Tristano, with whom he studied. He made his recording debut with Claude Thornhill's band (featured on Gil Evans's bop arrangements) and participated in the famous *Birth of the Cool* sessions. During these activities, he also worked with Tristano's groups, notably the sextet including tenorist Warne Marsh, with whom he fashioned unique, sinuous lines in unison and counterpoint. Tristano also pioneered a kind of aleatory group improvisation (*Intuition*, 1949). On his own early recording dates, Konitz used Miles Davis and played music by George Russell. From 1952 to 1954, Konitz toured with Stan Kenton's band, in which he was a very effective voice, then he led his own groups, also working with Gerry Mulligan and Gil Evans. Unlike most altoists of his generation, Konitz did not attempt to play like Charlie Parker (whom he admired) but fashioned his own unique style, rooted in a firm belief in improvisation. From the '60s on, Konitz spent much time in Europe and Japan and made many records in a wide variety of playing situations, from duets to his own nonet. In 1992 he was awarded the prestigious Danish Jazzpar prize, and he continues to fearlessly explore the musical horizon. —*Dan Morgenstern*

★ **Konitz Meets Mulligan** / i. 1953 / Capitol 46847
W/ Gerry Mulligan Quartet. A simply wonderful pairing of idiosyncratic talents. —*Ron Wynn*

○ **Inside Hi-Fi** / Sep. 26, 1956+Oct. 16, 1956 / Atlantic 90669

★ **Motion** / Aug. 29, 1961 / Verve 2563
Lee Konitz's August 29, 1961, set with Elvin Jones (drums) and Sonny Dallas (bass) issued on Verve as *Motion* was not overall a superb example of the Konitz art, but like almost all of his recordings was music of interest and certainly deserves reissue every decade or so. —*Bob Rusch, Cadence*

○ **Peacemeal** / Mar. 20-21, 1969 / Milestone 9025
The music on this session was much less cerebral than one might expect. This, of course, was due to the quiet simplicity and relaxed personalities of the players on this particular date. Lee Konitz's (alto sax) touch was masterful. His tone was pure and ideally suited to the lyrical nature of the Bela Bartok numbers. Marshall Brown (arranger-bassist) was careful and selective, a calm and flawless musician whose easy approach molded well to the others.... A very high standard of musicianship was set and maintained throughout this mature and satisfying LP. —*Alan Offstein, Coda*

★ **Altissimo** / Jul. 15, 1973 / West Wind 2019

○ **Figure and Spirit** / Oct. 20, 1976 / Progressive 7003
Alto and soprano saxophonist Lee Konitz sounded very good on this date and it was good to hear pianist Albert Dailey and tenor saxophonist Ted Brown, two talents that were underrecorded and

overlooked. Brown sounded a bit like Konitz on tenor and there was more than once when the flow of the record distinctly reminded me of the Stan Getz-Gerry Mulligan Verve date. However, this was no nostalgia trip, but vital and lasting music of the moment. —*Bob Rusch, Cadence*

☆ **Seasons Change** / Oct. 29, 1979 / Circle 291079

○ **First Sessions (1949-1950)** / Prestige 24081
First Sessions is a collection of early sessions from the New Jazz, Birdland, and Prestige labels. The first session features a quintet that includes pianist Lennie Tristano, alto saxophonist Lee Konitz, and guitarist Billy Bauer. The four cuts by this group transcend time, and when listening to them there are few clues that they were recorded in 1949, so fresh and bright is the sound. —*Sam Little, Cadence*

○ **Jazzlore: Lee Konitz / Warne Marsh** / Atlantic 90050

Dave Koz

Alto sax, flute / Instrumental pop
The latest contender for the instrumental pop saxophone throne, Dave Koz came out of nowhere after his self-titled 1990 release made it onto the Billboard Contemporary Jazz charts and stayed there several weeks. He has more fire and intensity in his work than Kenny G., and often sounds like a reworked David Sanborn. Koz also played on Arsenio Hall's show, which increased his popularity among the urban contemporary, light jazz, and pop audience. Koz plays instrumental pop covers and some upbeat tunes and generally sticks to the fusion production formula; background vocalists, synthesizers, and drum machines; a minimum amount of solo space; and so on.—*Ron Wynn*

Dave Koz / i. 1990 / Capitol 91643
A decent, though highly derivative, player. —*Ron Wynn*

Roy Kral and Jackie Cain

b. 1921
Ballads & blues
The duo of Roy Kral and Jackie Cain (1928) was particularly popular in the '40s and '50s. They mixed vocalese, humor, and show business patter, with Cain also being a good ballad and interpretative vocalist. Kral met Cain in Chicago while he was playing piano in a quartet. They worked with Charlie Ventura in the late '40s, with Kral doubling as Ventura's pianist and supplying some arrangements. The duo left Ventura, married in 1949, and began a sextet. They had their own television show temporarily in Chicago in the early '50s. They played with Ventura again briefly in the mid-'50s and became a successful nightclub act in the late '50s and early '60s, playing in New York, Los Angeles, and Las Vegas. They moved to New York in 1963. Kral penned several commercials featuring the duo in the '60s, among them a famous Plymouth ad, and they've continued recording and performing into the '90s. They've recorded for Brunswick, Storyville, ABC-Paramount, Columbia, Audiophile, Discovery, Fantasy, Verve, CTI, and Concord.—*Ron Wynn*

● **Jackie and Roy in the Spotlight** / i. May 14, 1959 / Paramount 267

Gene Krupa

b. Jan. 15, 1909, Chicago, IL, **d.** Oct. 16, 1973, Yonkers, NY
Drums, bandleader / Swing, big band
One of the great swing era drummers, Krupa came to prominence with Benny Goodman (1935-1938), playing in the big band as well as trios and quartets from within the band. His flashy solo style focused attention on the drummer for the first time. Krupa led his big band off and on from 1938 to 1951, and his own combos after that. He was often featured with *Jazz at the Philharmonic*. His '30s and '40s big-band recordings reveal an exciting, thoroughly musical organization at all times. Early stars included Sam Donahue, Roy Eldridge, and vocalist Anita O'Day, while his mid-'40s band gave major exposure to Red Rodney, Charlie Ventura, and arranger Gerry Mulligan. The Columbias are mostly very good, while the RCAs (1950-1951) should be avoided. The small groups for Mercury/Clef, beginning in 1952, are fine until the late '50s, when the soloists' quality begins to dip. A reunion with Ventura from 1964 is an exception. There are several studio big-band projects for Verve (1956-1961), of which

Drummin' Man and *Plays Gerry Mulligan Arrangements* are recommended. —*Bob Porter*

★ **Drummer Man / i.** 1956 / Verve 827843
Roy Eldrige (trumpet) got the featured billing (along with vocalist Anita O'Day) he deserved on *Drummer Man*, a 2/12/56 date featuring Gene Krupa fronting a big band. This was a reunion of sorts, but one that worked well, better in some cases than the original. The title's a bit misleading, for although Krupa's propulsions were clearly heard, his soloing was limited to a few features. Still, any drummer or fan of drumming will respond to the ambiance of this date. —*Bob Rusch, Cadence*

☆ **Gene Krupa, His Orchestra and Anita O'Day / i.** Apr. 1974 / Columbia 32663

○ **That Drummer's Band / i.** 1985 / Columbia 22027
Anthology from 1988 featuring the biggest hits by drummer Gene Krupa heading his own band in 1940. This was period directly after Krupa left the Benny Goodman orchestra and formed his own big band, which included tenor saxophonist Charlie Ventura and used arrangements from a young baritone saxophonist named Gerry Mulligan. —*Ron Wynn*

○ **Gene Krupa and Buddy Rich / Echo Jazz 14**
On the title track the two drummers squared off in somewhat contrived fashion, and, as the sound was original mono, the spatial dimension was totally lost. Buddy Rich's playing throughout was all speed and precision. . . . Krupa was a more subtle drummer than Rich by a mile, and that's never been more clear than here. —*Kevin Whitehead, Cadence*

Steve Kuhn (Stephen Lewis Kuhn)

b. Mar. 24, 1938, Brooklyn
Keyboards, piano, composer / Postbop, neo-bop
Steve Kuhn often gets more attention for being one of the pianists to precede McCoy Tyner in John Coltrane's group than for his own fine playing and writing abilities. Kuhn began taking lessons at five, and he was accomplished enough to earn stints with Coltrane, Kenny Dorham, and Stan Getz by 1959. He was a member of the Art Farmer Quartet from 1964 to 1966. Kuhn moved to Sweden in 1967, living there until 1971 and heading his trio throughout Europe from his Stockhom base. He returned to New York that year, heading a quartet, and since then he's recorded and toured frequently, appearing at festivals throughout America and Europe. —*Ron Wynn*

○ **October Suite / Nov. 1, 1967 / Impulse 9136**

★ **Playground / Jul. 1979 / ECM 1059**
With Sheila Jordan (v), Harvie Swartz (b), Bob Moses (d). Intense group interplay with Jordan's deep tones. Very emotional music, especially "The Zoo" and "Deep Tango." A record for the ages. —*Michael G. Nastos*

○ **Porgy / i.** Dec. 1988 / Jazz City 66053012

○ **Live at Maybeck Recital Hall—Vol. 13 / i.** Oct. 25, 1991 / Concord Jazz 4484

Steve Lacy (Steven Morman Lackritz)

b. Jul. 23, 1934
Soprano sax, composer / Dixieland, postbop, early free, modern creative
Other than Sidney Bechet and arguably Wayne Shorter and John Coltrane, no musician has been more singlehandedly identified with the soprano sax than Steve Lacy. Though he began on piano and later played clarinet, Lacy's squeaks, tortured lines, squiggly solos, and vocal effects have been a jazz delight since the late '50s. He also went from one extreme to another, getting his initial inspiration from traditional jazz but ultimately turning into a champion of spontaneous improvisation. Lacy studied with Cecil Scott and attended both the Schillinger School of Music (now Berklee) and the Manhattan School of Music. After his early immersion in vintage New Orleans music, Lacy began working and playing with Cecil Taylor, a shift that took him to the far reaches of composition and playing. Lacy worked for a while in the late '50s with Gil Evans, Mal Waldron, and Jimmy Giuffre and began studying the works of Thelonious Monk. He spent four months in Monk's quartet in 1960 and then formed his own group with trombonist Roswell Rudd and drummer Dennis Charles, playing almost exclusively Monk material. Lacy left that group in 1965, worked in Denmark with pianist Kenny Drew, formed a group in

Italy with trumpeter Enrico Rava, and toured South America. He subsequently returned to New York and started another group, though Rava remained a member. Finally in 1967, Lacy returned to Europe to live with his wife, Irene Aebi. He spent three years in Rome, studying electronics and sound extensively. He moved to Paris in 1970 and two years later started giving solo soprano sax recitals. Throughout the '70s and '80s, he worked with some of Europe's most individualistic players, such as guitarist Derek Bailey and saxophonist Steve Potts. —*Ron Wynn*

○ **Soprano Sax / i.** Apr. 1958 / Prestige 7125
This was the first of three recordings soprano saxophonist Steve Lacy made for Prestige, and this 11/1/57 session was his first as a leader. . . . There was a controlled tension to this date, like everybody's trying to play, carefully, to a common goal. It's almost as if someone were present to make sure everybody stayed within obvious perimeters. —*Bob Rusch, Cadence*

★ **Reflections: Steve Lacy Plays Thelonious Monk / Oct. 17, 1958 / New Jazz 063**
Enamored of Thelonious Monk, Lacy stretches out on challenging harmonic material with the Mal Waldron trio. —*Michael G. Nastos*

○ **Evidence / Nov. 14, 1961 / New Jazz 1755**
Evidence found soprano saxophonist Steve Lacy in nettle fettle with Ornetteans—incisive, prancing, right on Thelonious Monk's funny money. Every note was just ducky, each rest neatly timed, phrase after lucid phrase precisely right. Trumpeter Don Cherry, too, was in wryly inspired form, his chicken-scratchings approach containing a quivering fullness vis-e-vis Lacy's limpid fishhorn. —*Fred Bouchard, Down Beat*

● **Straight Horn of Steve Lacy, The / i.** Aug. 1962 / Candid 8007
Soprano saxophonist Steve Lacy, who now works exclusively in a "free-jazz" context was at this time heavily involved with pianist Thelonious Monk and his music. Though there were two tunes by pianist Cecil Taylor and Bird's "Donna Lee," it was the Monk themes that were the meat and potatoes of this session. It was a real pleasure to hear "Played Twice" and "Criss Cross" executed so easily by Lacy and baritone saxist Charles Davis. This was a pianoless group in which there was a lot of spaciousness, so much in fact, one wished to hear a pianist at times—perhaps Monk himself. —*Spencer R. Weston, Cadence*

○ **Forest and the Zoo / i.** 1966 / ESP 1060
A brillant mid-'60s album by soprano saxophonist Steve Lacy that's textbook free work; virtually no structure; roaring, screaming solos from Lacy and comrades, including trombonist Roswell Rudd. This was poorly recorded, but the playing more than compensated for the sonic flaws. —*Ron Wynn*

○ **Scraps / Feb. 18+21, 1974 / Sravah 10049**
Its finest single track was "Torments," Steve Potts's unaccompanied alto sax solo. He featured an unusually full, resonant tone throughout all ranges, particularly noticeable in the lower octaves. It augments a rather Roscoe Mitchell-like sensitivity to sound detail and timing, and indeed, Potts's sense of structure and linear purpose sustained tension throughout this work's five minutes. "Obituary" was an instance of Dada wedged between two long and uneventful communal blow-outs, though a third collective improvisation, "The Wire," was nicely done, with a sounds-against-silence sequence. —*John Litweiler, Down Beat*

○ **Sidelines / Sep. 1, 1976 / Improvising Artists 123847**
Soprano saxophonist Steve Lacy and pianist Michael Smith worked well together and no doubt succeeded admirably in what they set out to do, but the controlled, deliberate manner in which they played got oppressive after two whole sides. All but two of the compositions were Lacy's, so the blame must fall on him. Certainly his playing couldn't be faulted—his command of the full range of the soprano sax was outstanding. —*Carl Brauer, Cadence*

○ **Stamps / Feb. 22, 1981 / Hat Hut**
One disc of *Stamps* was recorded at the jazz festival in Willisau in 1977, the other at Jazz au Totem in Paris in 1978. Soprano saxophonist Steve Lacy's timbral effects were as important as the melodic and rhythmic styles in giving the music a contemporary feel. In "Names," Lacy's tone was Eastern in color: nasal and turgid, like a primitive oboe, a drone in the bass circles with a ringing pulsation. The bass's (Kent Carter) timbre was raw with overtones and well matched to Lacy's, as was Steve Potts's saxo-

phone sound. Lacy was just as comfortable here as he was when running changes or squealing. —*Elaine Guregian, Down Beat*

○ **Flame, the** / **i.** Jan. 1982 / Soul Note 1035

○ **Regeneration** / **i.** 1982 / Soul Note 1054
The consensus album of the year in 1983, it includes one side of Monk's and the other of Herbie Nichols's music. Includes Roswell Rudd (tb), Misha Mengleberg (p), Kent Carter (b), and Hans Bennik (d). —*Michael G. Nastos*

★ **Momentum** / May 1987 / Novus 3021
This record, soprano saxophonist Steve Lacy's first on an American label in a decade, was surprisingly lyrical. Only the title cut, an accelerating three-note motif based on the syllables and intervals of the word *momentum*, was dissonant. . . . The group interacted like minimalists at times, pouring over each detail. But then it opened up, and liberation music followed from logic. —*Owen Cordle, Jazz Times*

○ **Window, The** / Jul. 1987 / Soul Note 121185
This purified distillation of soprano saxophonist Steve Lacy's extensive improvisational experience emitted a cool, yet warm glow nourishing body and soul as well as mind. Shedding his usual sextet format for the intimacy of a trio, Lacy and his soprano weaved their way through sensitive backdrops spun by bassist Jean-Jacques Avenel and drummer Oliver Johnson. —*Chuck Berg, Jazz Times*

☆ **Live at Sweet Basil** / **i.** 1991 / Novus 63128
Recorded live in a New York club with a sextet. Includes many familiar themes. Soprano saxophonist with regular band: Steve Potts on alto and soprano sax, Irene Aebi on violin and vocal, Jean Jacques Avenel on bass, Bobby Few on piano, and John Betsch on drums. —*Michael G. Nastos*

Tommy Ladnier (Thomas J. Ladnier)

b. May 28, 1900, Florence, LA, **d.** Jun. 4, 1939, Geneva, NY
Trumpet / New Orleans traditional
Though he didn't have a lengthy career, Tommy Ladnier made some important contributions as a trumpeter in the '20s and '30s. An excellent swinging soloist, Ladnier was a melodic conservative, but brilliantly used the cackling mute timbre that was in vogue at the time. He was strongly influenced by King Oliver's phrasing and often adapted musical elements similar to those of blues pianists, such as double-time. Ladnier blended compelling energy with lyrical, relaxed precision. He moved to Chicago from Louisiana in 1917, and worked with such bandleaders as Ollie Powers, Fate Marable, and Oliver in the early '20s. Ladnier recorded with several blues vocalists, among them Ma Rainey. He toured Europe with Sam Wooding and worked with Billy Fowler before becoming Fletcher Henderson's principal soloist in the mid-'20s. Ladnier returned to Europe with Wooding in 1928 and 1929, also working there with Benny Peyton, heading his own band, and playing with Noble Sissle in 1930 and 1931. Ladnier worked with Sissle in both Europe and America and then became a coleader with Sidney Bechet of the New Orleans Feetwarmers in the early '30s. They briefly ran a tailor shop in New York and then Ladnier led his own group in New Jersey, worked and taught in Connecticut, and played in New York State. He recorded with Bechet and Mezz Mezzrow in 1938. Ladnier had a heart attack in Mezzrow's apartment in 1939. His work with Rainey, Henderson, and Bechet was often magnificent. He made no sessions as a leader for Bluebird, but one date he did with Mezzrow later had four songs split off and released as *Tommy Ladnier and His Orchestra*. He has no sessions available on CD. —*Ron Wynn*

● **Tommy Ladnier** / **i.** 1954 / 'X' 3027

Bireli Lagrene

b. Sep. 4, 1966, Saverene, France
Guitar / Early jazz rock, modern creative
There's a refreshing maturity in the recent work of guitarist Bireli Lagrene, who once was known for rambling, often amazing but also unfocused, displays. Now there's thought, scope, completeness, and form to his rigorous journeys over the frets, and much less flash. As would be expected, there's sizeable Django Reinhardt influence on Lagrene's style, but he's always had his own voicings and approach. Both his father and grandfather were guitarists, providing him a good foundation. He began recording

for Antilles in 1980 and has worked with Larrry Coryell, Miroslave Vitous, and Jaco Pastorius. Lagrene's also recorded for Jazzpoint and Blue Note. —*Ron Wynn and Michael G. Nastos.*

○ **Fifteen** / **i.** Feb. 1982 / Antilles 848814
This early, inconsistent album by guitarist Bireli Lagrene showed his enormous potential despite its problems . At this stage, Lagrene was so intent on displaying his complete arsenal that he roamed all over the fretboard on every song, throwing in extraneous lines and elaborate licks where they weren't necessary. But the album presented an early portrait of a player who's gone on to fulfill his promise. —*Ron Wynn*

★ **Foreign Affairs** / Aug. 1988 / Blue Note 90967
From the gentle opening tune, "Timothee" to the cool and mysterious "Josef" and the blistering "Senegal," the listener just keeps getting more facets of this jewel. Guitarist Bireli Lagrene demonstrates some remarkable versatility here. On Herbie Hancock's "Jack Rabbit," he plays some thrilling acoustic leads. On "Foreign Affairs," he is a rock-fusion stylist of the highest degree. On "Passing Through the Night," he even runs his lead through a voice box gadget and manages to make it sound tasteful. At each turn, the music is riveting, fun, and even pleasant. —*Denny Townsend, Jazz Times*

Oliver Lake (Oliver Eugene Lake)

b. 1942, Marianna, AR
Alto sax, soprano sax, flute, synthesizer / Early free, world fusion, contemporary funk, modern creative
Oliver Lake is an alto and soprano saxophonist, flutist, and synthesizer player who's also been consistently among the finest players of his generation. A founding member of the Black Artists Group (BAG), a St. Louis ensemble similar in scope to the Chicago-based AACM, Lake's technique seamlessy combines bop, free, funk, and blues influences into a coherent, seamless sax and compositional style. He has worked in such bands as Jump Up, which has pronounced rhythmic pieces, and the adventurous World Saxophone Quartet. An explosive, spirited saxophonist, fully knowledgeable in bop and hard bop, Lake is able to go outside easily and then return and play standards with authority. He's done sessions for Arista/Freedom, Sackville, Black Saint, Gazell, and Blue Heron.—*Ron Wynn*

○ **Ntu: The Point from Which Freedom Begins** / 1971 / Arista 1024

★ **Shine** / Oct. 30-31, 1978 / Novus 3010
Shine! was a sort of Oliver Lake sampler: on side one, which focused on his composing, Lake used his version of a string quartet (three violins and a cello and no basses at all) to augment his regular trio; the remaining two pieces were recorded at a concert by that energetic threesome in late 1978. It was here that Lake's broad and authoritative instrumental saxophone vocabulary was heard to best advantage; his sound alone, be it one- or three-dimensional, gutturally rough or Parker-pretty, helped him mold a conversational style of great virtuosity. —*Neil Tesser, Down Beat*

★ **Expendable Language** / Sep. 17-20, 1984 / Black Saint
Oliver Lake is one of the few post-free structuralists to record much with electric guitarists. . . . Kevin Eubanks was the picker on *Expandable Language*. . . . Here his tone was a compromise between rock distortion and mainstream jazz muffling, and he didn't bring the same assurance to Lake's roving interplay that Michael Gregory Jackson did. . . . Lake's own solos are full of coiled tension, and his tunes are sleek, despite their Eric Dolphian angles. —*Kevin Whitehead, Cadence*

○ **Gallery** / Jul. 1986 / Gramavision 8609
This quartet recording features pianist Geri Allen. An A+ album of angular saxophony. The cover artwork is as fascinating as the music. —*Michael G. Nastos*

○ **Boston Duets** / **i.** 1989 / Music & Arts 732
Here Oliver Lake works in a duet with a classically trained pianist, Donal Fox, trying out some fascinating improvisational ideas. Fox's spartan playing can run along the keyboard in the customary post Cecil Taylor fashion, but he never aims for Taylor's critical mass. . . . He is very interesting, but his partner is brilliant. Whether blowing long, serpentine melody lines or squalling and squeaking like Jimmy Lons, [Lake] and Fox have a grand time. . . . This is an exhausting and stunning CD. It is a dazzling workout even for Oliver Lake. —*Jerome Wilson, Cadence*

○ **Again and Again** / Apr. 1991 / Rhino 79468
Again and Again, a collection of eight original ballads, might be the perfect gift for that cynical friend who considers the World Saxophone Quartet, of which Oliver Lake is a member, little more than a collection of aural anarchists committed to razing the more traditional approaches to the music. *Again*'s titles are—at their finest—a sublime mix of light and shadow. —*Reuben Jackson, Jazz Times*

Byard Lancaster (William Byard Lancaster)

b. Aug. 6, 1942, Philadelphia, PA
Sax, flute / Hard bop, early free, modern creative
Though he has a low profile in terms of active recordings, alto saxophonist and flutist Byard Lancaster's a thoroughly respected player who's made inroads on the mainstream and free jazz scene. Lancaster played briefly with J.R. Mitchell as a teen and formally studied music at Troy University, Boston Conservatory, Berklee, and Howard. Lancaster played and recorded periodically with Sunny Murray in both America and Europe from the mid-'60s to the '80s. He played with Bill Dixon, Sun Ra, McCoy Tyner, and Ra again in his '60s and '70s, and also worked with Memphis Slim in Paris during the '70s. Lancaster's sessions for Vortex/Atlantic and Bellow seem to have disappeared. —*Ron Wynn*

★ **It's Not up to Us** / Dec. 19, 1966 / Vortex 2003
Byard Lancaster played both flute and alto on this album, and the flute tracks were the more interesting. His shrill sound was quite attractive, but for depth and any fulfilled creative improvisation, jazz lovers will have to look elsewhere. Sonny Sharrock (guitar) had little of the solo space. —*Bill Smith, Coda*

Harold Land (Harold de Vance Land)

b. Dec. 18, 1928, Houston
Tenor sax, flute, oboe / Hard bop, postbop
A steady, always invigorating player, Harold Land has been a jazz mainstay since 1949 when he made his first recording. Land moved to Los Angeles in 1954 and for a time was part of the landmark Max Roach-Clifford Brown Quartet, though he had the misfortune of leaving before the band became a sensation (he was replaced by Sonny Rollins). He was part of Curtis Counce's group from 1956 to 1958 and also played with Gerald Wilson and Shorty Rogers's group before cofounding a band with bassist Red Mitchell in 1961-1962. There were sessions with Wes Montgomery and Kenny Dorham and dates of his own in the '60s, but the group that did get Land some overdue recognition was one he co-led with vibist Bobby Hutcherson from 1969 to 1971. It was among the finest small combos of the period and introduced his son Harold Land Jr on piano. Land reunited with Hutcherson in 1983 for a European tour. —*Ron Wynn*

● **Fox, The** / Aug. 1959 / Contemporary 343
This Harold Land session, originally issued in 1960, has four Elmo Hope tunes (only "Little Chris" and "The Fox" are by the leader) and except for "Mirror-Mind Rose" were uptempo. Pianist Hope's ascending ("Rose") and descending ("One Down") chord changes helped shape the solos, and he played in his quirky, modernist style. —*Kevin Whitehead, Cadence*

☆ **Mapenzi** / Apr. 14, 1977 / Concord Jazz 4044
W/ Mitchell Quintet. W/ Kirk Lightsey (p), Blue Mitchell (tpt). Near-essential album. —*Michael G. Nastos*

Eddie Lang (Salvatore Massaro; Blind Willie Dunn)

b. Oct. 25, 1902, Philadelphia, PA, **d.** Mar. 26, 1933, New York, NY
Guitar / Blues & jazz
If you struggled to learn to play jazz or pop music on guitar in the '20s or early '30s, Eddie Lang was the man you listened to. Lang was an exciting, propulsive rhythm player and a superb, imaginative accompanist with a knowledge of the fingerboard that was unheard of at that time. As a soloist, he was the first to express the era's harmonic and melodic vocabulary on the guitar. During his brief career, Lang recorded with countless vocalists, dance bands, and small jazz combos. He is prominent on many recordings by Bing Crosby, the Boswell Sisters, Red Nichols, and with the Jean Goldkette and Paul Whiteman bands. His most celebrated recordings are his collaborations with violinist Joe Venuti and a small number of band dates with Bix Beiderbecke and Frankie Trumbauer. One should also hear Lang's duets with Lonnie Johnson. Lang's full, pianistic guitar accompaniments provide the perfect foil for the blues guitarist's fluid solo lines. —*Richard Lieberson*

★ **Jazz Guitar** / 1925-1932 / Yazoo 1059
Lang's solo features, plus duets with guitarists Lonnie Johnson and Carl Kress. To get the complete picture of Lang hear this recording in conjunction with the Joe Venuti-Eddie Lang duets (*see* Joe Venuti). —*Richard Lieberson*

☆ **Stringing the Blues** / **i.** Mar. 1963 / Columbia 2124

Ellis Larkins (Ellis Lane Larkins)

b. May 15, 1923, Baltimore, MD
Piano / Stride, boogie-woogie, swing
The pianist of choice among many vocalists, Ellis Larkins is also an excellent soloist, and he has made some good albums with instrumentalists as well as singers. Larkins studied at Juilliard in the '40s and then worked in many New York clubs before playing with Coleman Hawkins and Dicky Wells. He began to make his mark accompanying Mildred Bailey; he's subsequently worked with Larry Adler, Joe Williams, Ella Fitzgerald, Chris Connor, Ruby Braff, Tony Middleton, and Sylvia Sims, among others. —*Ron Wynn*

★ **Blues in the Night** / Jun. 21, 1951-Jan. 9, 1952 / Decca 5391
Stomping blues, charming ballads, and dazzling interpretations of standards by pianist Ellis Larkins, one of the most underrated players from the swing era still active. This album was done in the early '50s, when Larkins was making more animated releases than he does today. —*Ron Wynn*

○ **Live at Maybeck Recital Hall—Vol. 22** / **i.** 1992 / Concord Jazz 4533

Pete LaRoca (Peter Sims)

b. Apr. 7, 1938
Drums / Hard bop, Latin-jazz
When Pete LaRoca left the music world for a gig as a lawyer, it wasn't due to a decline in his skills. He was just as capable a soloist and accompanist; he simply didn't want to play the music he felt was becoming dominant at the time, jazz-rock. LaRoca studied classical percussion at the High School of Music and Art and at the Manhattan School of Music. He's changed his name from Pete Sims to Pete LaRoca earlier to facilitate things when he played timbales in various Latin groups. LaRoca was in demand during the '50s and '60s; he played with Jackie McLean, Slide Hampton, Tony Scott, John Coltrane, Marian McPartland, Art Farmer, Charles Lloyd, Paul Bley, Steve Kuhn, and Sonny Rollins. Besides being house drummer at Boston's Jazz Workshop in 1963 and 1964, LaRoca also led his own groups. He did some releases for Blue Note and Douglas in the '60s. —*Ron Wynn and Michael G. Nastos*

★ **Basra** / May 19, 1965 / Blue Note 84205

Yusef Lateef (William Evans)

b. Oct. 9, 1920, Chatanooga, TN
Reeds, composer / Hard bop, world fusion, new age
Before there was something called "worldbeat," Yusef Lateef was experimenting with Chinese and African instruments, playing Indian scales, and integrating jazz with the music of other cultures. Lateef began on alto in high school and then moved to tenor, oboe, and other flutes and began making his own instruments. He played with Lucky Millinder and Dizzy Gillespie in the '40s and began his own group in the mid '50s. He left Detroit for New York in the '60s and worked there with Charles Mingus, Olatunji, and Cannonball Adderley for two years. Lateef was never comfortable with the tag "jazz musician" and was seeking a fuller concept in the early '60s. As a saxophonist, he's basically a prototype hard-blowing, bop-centered soloist; his flute work and his use of oboe, argol, and other less Western instruments have been more exciting, with long lines and enticing melodies and vocal effects. He's made many recordings for Atlantic, Fantasy, Prestige, Milestone, and Impulse. —*Ron Wynn*

○ **Morning** / Apr. 5, 1957 / Savoy 2205
This collection compressed the material originally issued on three Savoy LPs onto two records—modern technology, and so on—but would be well worth the price even if it didn't. ... By the time of this date (1957), Lateef's interest in the music of the

Middle and Far East had already led him to skirt with modality; his flute work, making its debut on these sessions, was generally considered to have helped pioneer that instrument's jazz development; and "Happyology" was alive with Lateef's stylized African vocalizations. Yet on "Yusef's Mood" he cooked on tenor through a jump band riff-jam. This set was panoramic and an important part of an unusual musician's past. —*Neil Tesser, Down Beat*

○ **Prayer to the East** / Oct. 10, 1957 / Savoy 12117

○ **Yusef Lateef** / Oct. 11, 1957-Dec. 29, 1961 / Prestige 24007
This double record set was a reissue of selected material originally found on three New Jazz albums entitled *Other Sounds, Cry Tender,* and *Into Something.* . . . Lateef's main appeal seemed to be his use of instruments such as the flute, oboe, and argol, as well as his Eastern-influenced compositions. . . . Lateef's playing is imbued with his individual character and is readily identifiable. —*Peter Friedman, Coda*

☆ **Angel Eyes** / Jun. 11, 1959 / Savoy 2238
Outstanding late '50s jazz with Lateef not yet in his pioneering worldbeat-international music phase. —*Ron Wynn*

★ **Cry! / Tender** / Oct. 16, 1959 / Prestige 482
First-rate '50s works cover a diversity of jazz standards, European folk, and blues, with Yusef on tenor, flute, and oboe fronting a mid-sized group. —*Myles Boisen*

○ **Many Faces of Yusef Lateef, The** / May 1961-Jun. 1961 / Milestone 47009

☆ **Eastern Sounds** / Sep. 5, 1961 / Prestige 612
Asian sounds abound here, as well as a couple of movie themes, with accompaniment by Barry Harris on piano and bass and drums. —*Myles Boisen*

○ **Into Something** / Dec. 29, 1961 / New Jazz 700

○ **Live at Pep's** / Jun. 29, 1964 / Impulse

☆ **Golden Flute, The** / Jun. 15-16, 1966 / Impulse

★ **Blue Yusef Lateef, The** / 1968 / Atlantic 82270

○ **Re-Evaluations: The Impulse Years** / i. Jun. 1974 / Impulse 92592
Spanning the years 1963-1966 these cuts find Yusef Lateef working out on several different instruments, most of which at the time were simply unheard of in the jazz world. If the recordings at hand don't sound revolutionary today, it's probably because they didn't really sound that way then either. Lateef shared with a handful of other musicians the gift of transmuting standard sow's ears into silken purses of jazz. His selections ranged from the exotic to the excruciatingly familiar, while his compositions (over half of these tunes are originals) combined theories native to jazz—bop, ballad form, and lots and lots of blues—with just enough atonality, Orientalisms, and rhythmic experimentation to produce an alloy both scintillating and durable. —*Steve Metaliz, Down Beat*

○ **1984** / 1984 / Impulse 84

○ **Every Village Has a Song: Anthology** / i. 1994 / Rhino
Yusef Lateef has been both a pioneer and versatile stylist; he was exploring fusions of jazz and international styles many years before the emergence of a "world" music industry; Lateef utilized instruments from other nations and broadened the role of flutes and non-Western items in an improvisational vein. He displayed his facility with hard bop, blues, and ballads and his compositional skills while working with several distinguished bands and musicians prior to becoming an established bandleader. This good two-disc set covers his tenure at Atlantic as well featuring some formative material from early sessions for Transition, Prestige/Moodsville, Riverside, Impulse, Blue Note, and Savoy. The discs show Lateef honing a thick, bluesy, and expressive tenor tone in the beginning, evolving into a superior straight jazz player and expanding his repertoire and choice of instruments and contexts. His flute playing became arguably superior to his tenor, while his solos on oboe, shenai, and other previously unheard of or little-known instruments enabled Lateef to create arresting, fresh, and ultimately significant music. While the sampler approach can't fully showcase or document his contributions, it outlines how he and his music changed over the years and is a solid introduction for those unfamiliar with his output. —*Ron Wynn*

Hubert Laws

b. Nov. 10, 1939, Houston, TX
Flute, tenor sax / Postbop, early jazz rock, instrumental pop
Though a virtuoso flute player whose solos are remarkably clean and his tone beautiful, there's little soul or fire in Hubert Laws playing. However, he attained great success in the '70s doing "jazzy classics." As a teen, Laws was a member of the early Jazz Crusaders, playing with childhood friends Joe Sample, Wilton Felder, Stix Hoooper, and Wayne Henderson. He also studied and played classical music in Houston. Laws recorded for Atlantic in the '60s and was one of CTI's big acts in the '70s. HIs LPs *Afro-Classic* and *The Rite of Spring* were huge hits. Laws also played with the New York Philharmonic and Metropolitan Opera Orchestra and was a member of the New York Jazz Sextet. He worked with Jean-Pierre Rampal in the '80s and did some fusion, "lite" jazz, and instrumental pop dates with Columbia before taking a hiatus from recording. He returned with a Musicmasters CD in 1993. —*Ron Wynn*

★ **Afro Classic** / Dec. 1970 / Columbia 44172
This is by far the best solo work Laws has on record. He sets the standard for classical-influenced modern jazz. —*Ron Wynn*

○ **Rite of Spring** / Jun. 1971 / Columbia 40693

○ **Wild Flower** / Jan. 27, 1972 / Atlantic 1624
A nice date from an earlier Laws period with a harder tone and more traditional jazz direction. —*Ron Wynn*

○ **In the Beginning** / i. Sep. 1974 / CTI 3+3
The amazing thing about flutist Hubert Laws's music was that it could appeal to a broad range of musical tastes without making any sort of commercial concessions. How did Laws accomplish this? First, he gathered a crack rhythm section. . . . Ron Carter's time and giantic tone probably need little description, but the playing of drummer Steve Gadd might. His accents uncannily anticipated and complemented Carter's bass lines; his bass drum patterns were incredible; he seemed comfortable in everything from free music to sanctified 12/8. . . . Bob James, who did most of the keyboard work on the album, was another musician to watch for. He contributed several cohesive, facile, and well-structured solos. Laws himself was in little danger of being upstaged by his sidemen. He'd become a master improviser who weaved logical musical statements while never sounding mathematical or premeditated. —*Jon Balleras, Down Beat*

Hugh Lawson (Richard Hugh Jerome Lawson)

b. Mar. 12, 1935, Detroit, MI
Piano, composer, arranger / Bop, hard bop
A compelling bebop piano stylist, especially on standards, Hugh Lawson has quietly but superbly played on many topflight sessions since the mid-'50s. Despite being an excellent soloist and possessing skills the equal of anyone currently active, Lawson doesn't have as much name recognition as several other equally worthy but not superior stylists. He was very influenced by Bud Powell, but has developed his own voicings, phrasing, and approach. Lawson worked with Yusef Lateef in the mid-'50s and '60s, both in Detroit and New York. He also recorded with Harry Edison and Roy Brooks in the '60s, as well as with Lateef again. Lawson continued recording in the '70s, this time with Kenny Burrell and Brooks again. He gained some fame for his role in helping form the Piano Choir, a group of seven keyboardists that recorded for Strata East. Lawson toured Europe with Mingus in the mid- and late '70s, then made his own Middle East tour in the early '80s. Lawson recorded with Charlie Rouse and cut trio sessions in the late '70s and early '80s, then worked with former Mingus group members George Adams and Dannie Richmond in Italy. He taught composition and jazz improvisation at the Henry Street Settlement in New York. Lawson's done sessions for Soul Note and Storyville, and currently has a couple of dates available on CD. —*Ron Wynn*

Yank Lawson (John Rhea Lawson)

b. May 3, 1911, Trenton, MO
Trumpet / Dixieland
Another sterling veteran whose roots date back to the '30s, Yank Lawson began playing trumpet as a teenager and played with college bands before joining first Wingy Manone and then Ben Pollack. He left Pollack's band in 1935 after Pollack reportedly re-

fused to spotlight Lawson's girlfriend. He came to New York and eventually joined Bob Crosby's band, staying there from 1935 to 1938. He worked a time with Benny Goodman and then became a staple in the New York studios and clubs from 1942 to 1968. Ragged lines, marvelous mute technique, and a moving blues and swing feel are always exemplified in Lawson's solos. He helped form the great trad group The World's Greatest Jazz Band in 1968, and his work with comrades such as Bob Haggart or Billy Butterfield had a classic sound but a modern warmth and appeal. —*Ron Wynn*

★ **Live** / **i.** 1970 / Atlantic 90982

Jeanne Lee

b. Jan. 29, 1939, New York, NY
vocals / Early free, modern creative
Among the most breathtaking and unpredictable vocal improvisers in jazz history, Lee is best known for upper-register percussive singing with pianist Ran Blake or clarinetist Gunther Hampel. She can do straight singing but is far more provocative and compelling with her array of loops, screams, yells, and other devices. —*Ron Wynn*

★ **Legendary Duets** / Nov. 15, 1961-Nov. 16, 1961 / Bluebird 6461
W/ Ran Blake. It's an appropriate title. A must-buy for creative music listeners. Jeanne Lee does vocals; Ran Blake is on piano. —*Ron Wynn*

Michel Legrand

b. Feb. 24, 1932, Paris, France
Arranger, composer / Progressive big band, instrumental pop
A well-known composer of pop music, Michel Legrand works mainly with symphonies. There's not much connection to jazz, but jazz players appreciate his melodies. —*Michael G. Nastos*

○ **I Love Paris (Features Miles Davis)** / **i.** 1954 / Columbia 555

★ **Legrand Jazz** / 1957-1958 / Philips 830074
Michel Legrand's "Southern Routes" on *Le Jazz Grand* was a suite based on his soundtrack for the film *Les Routes de la Sud*—a work of evolving lines and shifting moods with fine solos by alto saxophonist Phil Woods, baritone saxophonist Gerry Mulligan, and trumpeter Jon Faddis backed by a 16-piece band whose sounds ranged from driving brass to delicate harp. Sometimes harp strings were stroked in a series of breaks during blazing trumpet, alto, and baritone solos. Legrand's orchestrations made effective use of his forces, from a single instrument to a full brass section. —*Jerry de Muth, Down Beat*

○ **Michel LeGrand at Shelly Manne's Hole** / Jan. 1968 / PolyGram 834827
A good upbeat mainstream session. Legrand shines as an improviser. —*Ron Wynn*

○ **After the Rain** / May 28, 1982 / Pablo 139

○ **Castles in Spain** / Columbia 888
Finely produced, orchestrated, and arranged work by a master of moods and textures. —*Ron Wynn*

George Lewis

b. 1952, Chicago, IL
Trombone, electronics
Born in Chicago, trombonist George Lewis has been among the most adventurous soloists and conceptualists. The holder of a BA in philosophy from Yale, Lewis began playing trombone at nine and played with pianist Anthony Davis when the two were attending college. He entered the AACM school in 1971, taking music theory courses from pianist, composer, and conductor Muhal Richard Abrams. Lewis is the most advanced proponent of the technique of multiphonics (playing more than one note simultaneously) on the trombone since European stylist Albert Mangelsdorff, and he also includes the array of growls, slurs, and vintage New Orleans vocal effects in his energetic playing. Lewis has played classical and electronic music, although he also spent two months with Count Basie's band in 1976. He's worked frequently with Anthony Braxton since 1976, as well as with guitarist Derek Bailey, bassist Dave Holland, and pianist Randy Weston. —*Ron Wynn*

● **Solo Trombone Album** / **i.** 1976 / Sackville 3012

John Lewis (John Aaron Lewis)

b. May 3, 1920, La Grange, IL
Piano, composer, arranger / Bop, cool
Piano, composer, arranger John Lewis has been said to be one of the few people who really understand the similarities between jazz and classical and helps bridge gaps between these disciplines. Kenny Clarke recommended Lewis to replace Thelonious Monk in Dizzy Gillespie's band in the late '40s. After the band's demise, Lewis and Clarke stayed in Paris. Lewis was a steady freelance player and arranger in the late '40s and early '50s, working with Illinois Jacquet, Charlie Parker, Miles Davis, and Lester Young. The longtime Modern Jazz Quartet had its beginnings in the Milt Jackson quartet of the early '50s. The MJQ began in 1954 and was augmented in 1955 when Connie Kay replaced Kenny Clarke. That's been the main vehicle for Lewis ever since, though he's done film soundtrack work, been a professor of music at City College since 1977, and was the cofounder and conductor of the American Jazz Orchestra in the late '80s. What either delights or irritates fans about Lewis is the sparseness of his playing; there's none of the volume, power, or rhythmic intensity normally associated with jazz. Instead he ambles along, seeming to prefer subtlety and suggestion to energy or verve. But some of his compositions (notably "Django") are legendary, and his contrast with Milt Jackson's bluesy, often funky, vibes make the MJQ sound a jazz staple. —*Ron Wynn*

○ **Afternoon in Paris** / Dec. 4, 1956 / Atlantic 1267

● **Kansas City Breaks** / **i.** May 25+26, 1982 / Disques Swing 8430
Has the interesting instrumentation of a flute, violin, guitar, and piano trio. All selections are Lewis originals, including the especially famous "Django," "Milano," and "Sacha's Mardi." A sweet session. —*Michael G. Nastos*

★ **Chess Game—Vols. 1 & 2, The** / **i.** 1987-1988 / Verve 832015

Meade "Lux" Lewis (Meade Anderson Lewis)

b. Sep. 4, 1905, Chicago, IL, **d.** Jun. 7, 1964, Minneapolis, MN
Piano, composer / Boogie-woogie
Two of the greatest boogie-woogie pianists ever, Meade Lux Lewis and Albert Ammons, the father of Gene Ammons, played around Chicago in the '20s and sorted out their ideas on a piano owned by the taxi firm that employed them. The 1928 composition "Honky Tonk Train Blues" eventually was heard by record producer John Hammond, who started looking for Lewis. Hammond found Ammons and then Lewis and eventually paired them with Pete Johnson in the immortal 1938 "Spirituals to Swing Carnegie Hall" concert that made them international stars. The exciting, pounding boogie style has seldom been performed with more artistry and craft than by Meade Lux Lewis. —*Ron Wynn*

★ **Complete Blue Note Recordings** / Jan. 6, 1939-Aug. 22, 1944 / Mosaic
W/ Meade Lux Lewis. 1939-1944. A wonderful, comprehensive compilation of stamping, romping boogie-woogie piano by the masters. —*Ron Wynn*

Mel Lewis (Melvin Sokoloff)

b. May 10, 1929, Buffalo, NY, **d.** 1990
Drums / Big band, bop, postbop, progressive big band
The son of a professional drummer, Mel Lewis was a full-time player at 15. He did combo work with Frank Rosolino and Hampton Hawes in the '50s and played in big bands led by Boyd Raeburn and Stan Kenton in the '40s and '50s. He started his own band in 1958 and then worked in the Los Angeles studios during the early '60s, while also touring with Gerry Mulligan, Benny Goodman, and Dizzy Gillespie. He moved back to his New York hometown in 1963 and two years later coformed a band of top East Coast studio pros with trumpeter Thad Jones. The Jones-Lewis orchestra began as a once-a-week venture and became a staple on the jazz scene from 1965 through the '70s, continuing even after Jones left in 1978. Lewis also did some session work in the late '70s and '80s, continuing to shine in his role as the anchor of any situation. Lewis was a star at spurring and heading a big band and was very underrated as a soloist and small group leader. —*Ron Wynn*

★ **Suite for Pops** / **i.** 1975 / A&M

An album of spry, invigorating, and memorable Jones-Lewis recordings. —*Ron Wynn*

○ **Mel Lewis and Friends** / Jun. 8-09, 1976 / A&M 0823
This was a fine straightahead blowing bop date, with the only electricity being that produced by the players themselves. This was trumpeter Freddie Hubbard's best recorded effort in nearly five years, and he deserved support for his work here.... The trio also shone on "Wind Flower," a John Lewis-type loper by Sarah Cassey on which the horns sat out; Hank Jones, Ron Carter and Lewis all had outstanding feature spots.... This was a faultless date with many high moments of musical substance. —*Bob Rusch, Cadence*

★ **Mel Lewis Plays Herbie Hancock** / Jul. 16, 1980 / MPS

○ **Lost Art, The** / Apr. 11-12, 1989 / Music Masters 5023
Sextet. This is the definitive small-group album, with pianist Ken Werner. —*Michael G. Nastos*

Ramsey Lewis (Ramsey Emmanuel Lewis, Jr.)

b. May 27, 1935, Chicago, IL
Piano, keyboards, synthesizer, composer / Soul-jazz, instrumental pop
Ramsey Lewis has been active as a pianist, keyboardist, synthesizer player, composer, and now host of a weekly show on Black Entertainment Television (BET). He led one of the most popular instrumental groups of the '50s and '60s, the Ramsey Lewis Trio. Lewis and friends (bassist Eldee Young and drummer Red Holt) had played in teenage bands. They started recording for Argo in 1956. Though he also worked with Sonny Stitt, Max Roach, and Clark Terry, the trio format served Lewis well. He was originally a good (though not great) soloist in the traditional bop mode, but he gradually scaled down his stylistic flair, opting for simple melodic statements with occasional flourishes or fancy phrases. The trio scored a huge hit with "The In Crowd," a remaking of a Dobie Gray pop song in 1965. Since then, some 30 Lewis albums have charted, and he had two Top 20 albums and 13 singles on the Top 100 in the '60s alone. He also scored well in the '70s, with duets backing Earth, Wind and Fire and Nancy Wilson. Original trio members Young and Holt left in 1966 and were replaced by Cleveland Eaton and Maurice White. White left in 1970 to lead Earth, Wind and Fire and was replaced by Maurice Jennings. Lewis reunited with Holt and Young in 1982. He remains very popular on urban-R&B radio stations among those who like easy-listening jazz, and now has a television following with his weekly cable show. He's one of the creative forces behind BET founder Robert Johnson's proposed jazz channel, which was slated to begin operation in the fall of '94. —*Ron Wynn*

○ **Lem Winchester and the Ramsey Lewis Trio** / Oct. 1958 / Argo 642

★ **In Crowd, The** / 1965 / Chess 9185
The In Crowd was the Ramsey Lewis Trio's big hit of the time. The title track typified part of the Lewis style, but helped commercially lock it in to a narrow style. Recorded in May 1965 at the once hip Bohemian Caverns in Washington, DC, it remains a pleasant easy listen. —*Bob Rusch, Cadence*

○ **Upendo Ni Pamoja** / 1972 / CBS 31096

★ **Sun Goddess** / 1974 / Columbia 33194
Teo Macero and Maurice White (of Earth, Wind and Fire) did an excellent job in putting together this package of almost a dozen odd musicians who were called in to supplement and perhaps rejuvinate the Ramsey Lewis trio. Richard Evans's string and brass arrangements provided pretty background filler, and the whole thing clicked along as precisely as a Swiss timepiece. —*Jon Balleras, Down Beat*

David Liebman

b. Sep. 4, 1946, New York, NY
Tenor sax, soprano sax, flute, piano, drums / Postbop, early jazz rock, neobop, modern creative
Tenor and soprano saxophonist, flutist, pianist, and drummer Davis Liebman is a well-educated, versatile player. He studied with such musicians as Bob Moses, Joe Allard, Charles Lloyd, and Lennie Tristano, while gaining a degree in history from NYU and a teaching diploma in the late '60s. Liebman began in the rock-jazz band Ten Wheel Drive in 1970. He's since divided his time between jazz stints with Elvin Jones; playing with Miles Davis;

leading critically acclaimed groups Lookout Farm, Open Sky, and Quest; and working with two European and Japanese musicians. His eclectic background has made it easy for Liebman to play any and everything; rock, R&B, hard bop, free, and a variety of Eastern and African styles have been filtered through his work. He's a very animated, intense player, a consistent soloist, and a good composer. —*Ron Wynn*

★ **Lookout Farm** / Jun. 12, 1975 / Jugoton 6132
Lookout Farm was Dave Liebman's working quartet augmented by a percussion ensemble, voice, and the omnipresence of John Abercrombie's guitar.... Liebman handled the tenor like an early Trane or a Cannonball Adderley playing alto on the historic session. Signatures took root and then were broken up. No firm melodic line was sustained. An exquisite mood was established by Don Alias on congas and Badal Roy on tablas. Beirach played around with the strings of his piano, and then Liebman returned, only this time with full, commanding tone associated with Gato Barbieri. —*Ray Townley, Down Beat*

○ **Forgotten Fantasies** / Nov. 18-20, 1975 / Horizon 709

○ **Quest II / i.** Apr. 17, 1986 / Storyville
Quartet set with Liebman, Richie Beirach (p), Ron McClure (b), and Billy Hart (d). —*Ron Wynn*

○ **Tree, The** / Apr. 1990 / Soul Note 121195
A strong set of solo free improvisations on loosely predetermined material relating to a very loose arborescent theme. Each piece is announced unceremoniously by Liebman, the entire suite played frontward, then back.... The two takes of harsh, multiphonic "Leaves" are great, and both "Twigs" are fine, static studies in breath and trill, riding close to the line of intonation and occasionally dropping out into the toneless zone. Liebman owes much to the two solo soprano masters, Steve Lacy and Evan Parker. —*John Corbett, Down Beat*

Kirk Lightsey

b. Feb. 15, 1937, Detroit, MI
Piano / Hard bop, modern creative
A driving soloist and excellent accompanist, pianist Kirk Lightsey's been a fine addition to many groups and also backed several vocalists. Lightsey played with Melba Liston and Ernestine Anderson in New York in the early '60s and backed such singers as Damita Jo, O.C. Smith, and Lovelace Watkins in Detroit and California. He recorded with Sonny Stitt in 1965 and made five LPs that same year with Chet Baker. Lightsey worked extensively with Dexter Gordon in the '70s and early '80s and recorded with Jimmy Raney and Clifford Jordan in the mid-'80s. Later dates included a Jazzfest Berlin engagement with Jabbo Smith and Don Cherry in 1986 and frequent engagements with The Leaders band in the late '80s and the '90s. Lightsey's recorded as a leader for Sunnyside, Criss Cross, and Lime Tree. —*Ron Wynn and Michael G. Nastos*

○ **Isotope / i.** Feb. 1983 / Criss Cross 1003

○ **Lightsey Live** / Jun. 28, 1985 / Sunnyside 1014
For this solo concert Lightsey played one original along with works by Tony Williams, Thelonious Monk, Rodgers & Hart, Wayne Shorter, and Cole Porter, a rather distinct group of composers. Even so, all the music here became a collaboration with the pianist whose individual style composes itself on the music as well. —*Bob Rusch, Cadence*

★ **Everything Is Changed** / Jun. 4-05, 1986 / Sunnyside 1020
This was Kirk Lightsey's fourth album for Sunnyside, but his first as a group leader for the label. And what a group he chose. Eddie Gladden (drums) was Lightsey's partner in the Dexter Gordon rhythm section of the early '80s. Santi Wilson DiBriano (bass) was a solid resilient anchor for the group. But the real standout on this LP was trumpeter Jerry Gonzalez. —*Robert Iannapollo, Cadence*

○ **From Kirk to Nat** / Nov. 1990 / Criss Cross 1050
That Detroit native Kirk Lightsey chose to utilize a trio format in tribute to the very same elegant and subtly swinging facet of the late Nat King Cole's career should not trouble listeners; *From Kirk to Nat* is not some stale but well-meaning replication of Cole favorites like "Sweet Lorraine." For one thing, the pianist-leader's personnel (bassist Rufus Reid, guitarist Kevin Eubanks) practically guarantees a healthy technique-feeling ratio, and in an appropriately low-key sort of way they deliver urgency when he and

his fellow musicians dig into "Appointment in the North Country".
—Reuben Jackson, Jazz Times

Abbey Lincoln (Anna Marie Wooldridge)

b. Aug. 6, 1930, Chicago, IL
Vocals / Ballads & blues, modern creative
Vocalist Abbey Lincoln (later called Aminata Moseka) has enjoyed a career rebirth these last few years, after being away from both the music and acting scenes for quite a while. Lincoln began singing in dance bands as a teenager in Chicago and moved to the West Coast in 1951. Her sultry looks earned her brief notoriety as the "Black Marilyn Monroe," and she even appeared in the 1957 film, *The Girl Can't Help It*. But after meeting drummer Max Roach, Lincoln changed her image and became a serious vocalist and political activist. Their *Freedom Now Suite*, released in 1960, was one of the harbingers of changing sentiments in the Black community. Lincoln made many superb releases with top jazz names like Sonny Rollins as well as Roach during the '50s and '60s. She changed her name to Aminata Moseka in 1975. There was a period of inactivity in the early '80s, but she's resurfaced with a vengeance in the '90s. Lincoln is an intuitive, often-compelling singer who manages to overcome occasional problems with intonation and range. She is among the most striking vocalists ever from the standpoint of delivery, and few can match her effectiveness in communicating lyrics and moods. *—Ron Wynn*

☆ **Freedom Now Suite** / **i.** 1960 / Candid
Definitive social protest and jazz. Lincoln and her then-husband Max Roach were a great team. *—Ron Wynn*

★ **Straight Ahead** / Feb. 22, 1961 / Barnaby 31037
Lincoln wrenches out her tough soul in her steadfast, determined ways with an all-star cast led by her then-husband drummer Max Roach. *All-star* is not used loosely here: Coleman Hawkins (tenor) intoned gruffly in measured authority on the title track; Eric Dolphy (alto) and Mal Waldron (piano) were superb in support; and trumpeter Booker Little, whose brilliant candle was snuffed much too soon, played bittersweet throughout. *—Fred Bouchard, Jazz Times*

★ **People in Me** / Jun. 23, 1973 / Inner City 6040
As good as she gets on this recording. A perennial favorite for many. W/ David Liebman (soprano/tenor and fl.), Al Foster (d), Mtume (per), and two Japanese musicians. "Living Room," "Africa," "Naturally," and the title track stand out. Proud music. *—Michael G. Nastos*

○ **Golden Lady** / **i.** Mar. 1982 / Inner City 1117
Early-'80s material by the neglected vocalist Abbey Lincoln. Her intonation, delivery, phrasing, and style are unique and sometimes so distinctive they seem wrong for a song. But Lincoln makes every number come alive, giving even overly familiar lyrics fresh, vibrant treatments. *—Ron Wynn*

○ **You Gotta Pay the Band** / 1991 / Verve 511110
Studio date featuring Stan Getz one last time and the Hank Jones Trio. Maxine Roach on viola for two cuts. Six cuts feature either words or music written by Moseka. She has lost absolutely none of her brilliance or passion for singing, interpreting, and creating. *—Michael G. Nastos*

○ **Abbey Sings Billie—Vol. 2** / **i.** 1992 / Enja 7037
The Billie Holiday disc is recorded live, recorded in New York in 1987, featuring a strong rhythm section and tenorman Harold Vick. In fact, the two concerts took place just a few days before the saxophonist died. . . . There's no better place to observe the differences and likenesses of Billie Holiday and Abbey Lincoln than on Lincoln's less-eerie "Don't Explain," or her lovely version of "For All We Know." *—John Corbett, Down Beat*

John Lindberg (John Arthur Lindberg III)

b. Mar. 16, 1959, Royal Oak, MI
Bass / Modern creative
A steady, sympathetic accompanist and solid soloist, bassist John Lindberg's best known for his work in the String Trio of New York. Lindberg studied music in Ann Arbor, MI, before moving to New York in 1977. He played and recorded in the Human Arts Ensemble with Joseph Bowie and Bobo Shaw in the late '70s and worked with Anthony Braxton from 1978 to 1985. They performed in both Europe and America. Lindberg was a founding

member of the String Trio of New York in 1979 and remains with the ensemble. He also worked in a trio with Jimmy Lyons and Sunny Murray in 1980. Lindberg lived and worked in Paris from 1980 to 1983, leading small combos, playing solo, and working in a group led by Murray that also featured John Tchicai. Lindberg has recorded as a leader for Cecma, Black Saint, West Wind, ITM, and Sound Aspects. *—Ron Wynn*

● **Trilogy of Works for Eleven Instrumentalists** / **i.** Sep. 1984 / Black Saint 0082

Melba Liston (Melba Doretta Liston)

b. Jan. 13, 1926, Kansas City, MO
Trombone, arranger / Bop, hard bop, progressive big band
A heralded arranger and fine trombonist, Melba Liston was achieving notoriety long before women's rights were an issue in jazz circles. Liston's range, flexibility, and skills as an improviser, equaled by her abilities as an arranger, were evident early in her career. She's been active since the '40s and has worked in bands and orchestras as diverse as those of Quincy Jones and Randy Weston. She and Weston have done many collaborations in recent years. Liston joined Gerald Wilson's big band in 1943 and also began writing arrangements. She later recorded with Dexter Gordon's band. Liston played with Dizzy Gillespie's band, and toured with Billie Holiday, but quit music for a while in the '50s. After being a clerk and an extra in such films as "The Prodigal" and "The Ten Commandments," Liston rejoined Gillespie for State Department tours in 1956 and 1957 and played in Jones's band during the European tour of the show *Free and Easy*. Liston taught at the Jamaica School of Music for six years during the '70s and then returned to America. Her most recent collaboration with Weston was *Volcano Blues* for Verve in 1993. *—Ron Wynn*

★ **And Her Bones** / Dec. 22-24, 1958 / Metrojazz 1013

Booker Little (Booker Little, Jr.)

b. Apr. 2, 1938, Memphis, TN, **d.** Oct. 5, 1961
Trumpet / Hard bop
His premature death kept Booker Little from being one of the most consistently arresting players of the '60s, but his short ouput was still riveting and attention grabbing. Little had one of the sharpest, most vibrant sounds of any trumpeter and could stretch and bend the fabric of a composition without destroying the harmonic framework or losing clarity or tone. He grew up in Memphis but began to make his mark after moving to Chicago in 1957. He joined drummer Max Roach in 1958 and stayed with him for most of his remaining career, though he's best known for some incendiary sessions with Eric Dolphy at the Five Spot in 1961. He also played with Mal Waldron and John Coltrane. Little died of uremia, a rare blood disorder. *—Ron Wynn*

☆ **Booker Little 4 and Max Roach** / 1958 / Bainbridge 1041
A tremendous showcase of early '60s sessions that has exceptional musicians and wonderful compositions. Everyone from Phineas and Calvin Newborn to George Coleman and Max Roach. *—Ron Wynn*

○ **Out Front** / Mar. 1961-Apr. 1961 / Candid 79027
Trumpeter Booker Little was the principal soloist on this date. He played a trumpet that was sometimes as sweet as (Clifford Brown) Brownie's but often tinged with acidity. Undoubtedly, if Little had survived, he would have been a major trumpet voice. *—Spencer R. Weston, Cadence*

★ **Victory and Sorrow** / Aug. 9, 1961 / Affinity 124
Booker Little's *Victory and Sorrow* was also the last statement of an auspicious vision in mid-bloom, recorded approximately one month before his death in the fall of 1961. Like Clifford Brown (his major influence), Little was an astonishingly protean stylist and composer who reconciled the structures and temperament of bop to fit his own pointedly lyrical vistas. This final winging offered Little at his most assertive and museful, careening generally in a supple, honeyed voice, but rising up hard on the right occasion for a metal-line exclamation. *—Mikal Gilmore, Down Beat*

Charles Lloyd

b. Mar. 15, 1938, Memphis, TN
Tenor sax, flute / Hard bop, early jazz rock, world fusion
Among the more engaging tenor saxophonists and daring flutists, Charles Lloyd played in R&B and blues bands with B. B. King and

Bobby "Blue" Bland before moving from Memphis to the West Coast in 1956. He later worked with Chico Hamilton and Gerald Wilson and toured with Cannonball Adderley before forming his own group in the mid-'60s. His late '60s group (that also included pianist Keith Jarrett) enjoyed both jazz and pop notoriety, thanks to a 1967 concert his quartet played at the Fillmore. His tenor has the warm, bluesy sound associated with Southern and Southwestern stylists, although Lloyd also weaves vocal effects, honks, and upper-register careening into his solos. His flute lines, wavery phrases, and over-blowing are more energetic. —*Ron Wynn*

★ **Forest Flower** / Sep. 8, 1966+Sep. 18, 1966 / Atlantic 1473

Joe Lovano

b. 1952
Tenor sax / Postbop, neo-bop, modern creative
Joe Lovano's huge sound, sweeping phrases, and overall tenor sax facility have made him an in-demand player and major name in the '90s. He's played with Marc Johnson, Bill Frisell, John Scofield, and Joshua Redman among others, the Lovano-Redman album was one of the finest issued in '94. —*Ron Wynn*

○ **One Time Out** / **i.** Sep. 1987 / Soul Note 1224

★ **Village Rhythm** / Jun. 7-09, 1988 / Soul Note 182.1
Quintet w/ Tom Harrell (tpt) and Ken Werner (p). This Cleveland saxophonist at his best. —*Michael G. Nastos*

○ **From the Soul** / **i.** 1992 / Blue Note 98636
A '92 release by acclaimed tenor saxophonist Joe Lovano. He's heading a different lineup from his most recent releases, with pianist Michel Petrucciani, bassist Dave Holland, and the late drummer Ed Blackwell. It's hard-edged, explosive playing all around, with Blackwell laying down his patented bombs while Petrucciani and Holland converge behind Lovano's dynamic solos. —*Ron Wynn*

Frank Lowe

b. Jun. 24, 1943, Memphis, TN
Tenor sax / Early free, modern creative
Another saxophonist forging an alliance of R&B, soul, and free music, Frank Lowe's high-energy style has been heard on '60s and '70s sessions. Though his tone sometimes seems to flatten out, his array of screams, shrieks, octave leaps, and bursts is always attention grabbing, if occasionally chaotic. Lowe began on tenor at 12 and studied briefly at the University of Kansas and with Donald Garrett in San Francisco. He played with Sun Ra in New York during the late '60s; returned to study classical music at San Francisco Conservatory; and played with Alice Coltrane, Rashied Ali, Archie Shepp, Milford Graves, and Don Cherry in New York in the early '70s. He's been a leader since the mid-'70s, recording on Survival, ESP, Cadence Jazz, Musicworks, and Soul Note, among others. Lowe has played with Lester Bowie, Bobo Shaw, Joseph Bowie, Anthony Braxton, and many others. He currently has several dates available on CD. —*Ron Wynn*

● **Fresh** / **i.** Apr. 1976 / Arista 1015
The album's title, *Fresh,* aptly described the music. Instead of focusing on improvisations based on the traditions of Western harmonic practice, Frank Lowe's group centered on the emotive ramifications of color and texture. . . . Lowe and both trumpeter Lester and trombonist Joseph Bowie produced an incredible array of sound, which, in the manner of John Cage's prepared piano, extended the boundaries of their respective instruments past the canons of conventional technique and taste. —*Chuck Berg, Down Beat*

○ **Skizoke** / **i.** Nov. 1982 / Cadence CJR
This was an enjoyable album documenting tenor saxophonist Frank Lowe's conception of the mainstream, which appears to be a very fertile place for him. All the tunes, save for "Close to the Soul," are in a medium tempo bag (though the title cut and "Some Do, Some Don't" featured heads that moved from a medium to a slow tempo and then back again). —*Milo Fine, Cadence*

○ **Decision in Paradise** / Sep. 24+28, 1984 / Soul Note 1082
Lowe's *Decision in Paradise* is a meeting of first, second, and fourth wave avant-gardists—Don Cherry, pocket trumpet; Grachan Moncur III, trombone; Geri Allen, piano, ringer; Charnette Moffett, bass; Charles Moffett, drums—and if the mu-

sic's not quite as explosive as the lineup promises, it's still quite fine: robust, sinewy blowing music in a relatively straightahead vein. —*Kevin Whitehead, Cadence*

Jimmie Lunceford (James Melvin Lunceford)

b. Jun. 6, 1902, Fulton, MS, **d.** Jul. 12, 1947, Seaside, OR
Reeds, conductor, arranger / Swing, big band
Jimmie Lunceford's orchestra achieved the ideal balance of showmanship and artistry. Their distinctive sound was directly attributable to the arrangements of Sy Oliver, a master of incorporating unusual elements into his pieces. "Organ Grinder Swing," for example, included wood blocks, celeste, and saxes playing in an exaggerated, vocal manner. He was also known for imaginative interplay between soloists, brass, and reed sections and for his endings. Two-beat swing at medium tempos was the Lunceford orchestra's forte. Lunceford insisted on elegance in dress and perfection in performance, though with high entertainment value. The Lunceford orchestra was credited with 22 hits between 1934 and 1946, putting them behind only Duke Ellington and Cab Calloway among black swing bands. "Rhythm Is Our Business," "Blues in the Night," and "I'm Gonna Move to the Outskirts of Town" were their signature songs. Lunceford died suddenly in 1947. The band continued for a short time afterward and did a reunion album for Capitol in the mid-'50s. —*Ron Wynn*

○ **Jimmie Lunceford (1930-1934)** / **i.** Jun. 1930-Nov. 1934 / Classics

○ **Stomp It Off** / **i.** Sep. 1934-May 1935 / MCA 16082
If craftsmanship is its own reward, there is much to admire in this Decca set, which collects Jimmie Lunceford's early 1934-1935 recordings in chronological order, skipping a half-dozen mediocrities and some alternates. Reed players Willie Smith and Joe Thomas deliver smart solo work. And the ensembles are precise, sometimes to the point of pickiness, not just in their attacks but in the shadings and dynamics that only a leader's vision can bring to a score. —*John McDonough, Down Beat*

○ **Jazz Heritage—Jimmie's Legacy (1934-1937)** / 1934-1937 / MCA 1320
A detailed anthology covering the mid-'30s Jimmie Lunceford band. It's more detailed and annotated, as well as better remastered and sequenced than most other Lunceford sets. The three years covered (1934-1937) were pivotal, as Lunceford's whole conception of light, bouncy blues swing was honed during this time. —*Ron Wynn*

○ **Jazz Heritage—Harlem Shout (1935-1936)** / 1935-1936 / MCA 1305
Unlike Fletcher Henderson's band, Jimmie Lunceford did not have the all-star lineup, alto saxophonist Willie Smith being a notable exception, but the almost instant polish and advanced sophisticated arrangements certainly made this a modern hip band of its day. It was also, to a great extent, the base on which many of the jazzy dance bands that were to come along, even into the '70s, were built. —*Bob Rusch, Cadence*

○ **Jazz Heritage—for Dancers Only (1936-1937)** / 1936-1937 / MCA 1307
The first in a series dedicated to the late '30s recordings of the Jimmie Lunceford orchestra, among the greatest swing bands ever. It covers 1936 and 1937, their earliest years on Decca, and predates most of their big hits. It's a nicely packaged collection and remains one of the better Lunceford anthologies. —*Ron Wynn*

★ **Jazz Heritage—Last Sparks (1941-1944)** / **i.** 1941-1942 / MCA 1321
Recorded 1941-1942. Arrangements here are by Ed Wilcox, Horace Henderson, Roger Segure, Tadd Dameron, Pee Wee Jackson, and Billy Moore Jr. These are another 12 great tracks. —*Michael G. Nastos*

○ **Rhythm Is Our Business** / Living Era 5091
This is the earliest of several Jimmie Lunceford reissues made in the early '80s by MCA. These sessions covered the period from 9/4/34 to 12/17/34 and included "Rose Room," "Black and Tan Fantasy," "Stomp It Off," and the title track. The six Lunceford albums originally issued in the set covered 80 tracks over a ten-year stretch. —*Cadence*

Jimmy Lyons

b. Dec. 1, 1933, Jersey City, NJ, **d.** May 19, 1986, New York, NY
Alto sax, soprano sax / Early free, modern creative
He was mainly known for his long and fertile association with
Cecil Taylor, but Jimmy Lyons deserved just as much praise for
his abilities as an alto saxophonist outside that union. A bebop
player who juxtaposed that style atop Taylor's avant-garde works,
Lyons had a dynamic, energetic, and searing style, which was necessary considering the aggressive quality of Taylor's music. But
there was also a lyrical, introspective air in Lyons's solos, a softness that balanced the fury. Lyons was given an alto sax by Buster
Bailey as a teen and was aided by Elmo Hope, Bud Powell, and
Thelonious Monk. He studied with Rudy Rutherford and began
his long tenure with Taylor in the early '60s. Lyons sometimes did
other jobs, working in the early '70s for a time teaching music at
a New York drug treatment center. He was an artist-in-residence
with Taylor and Andrew Cyrille at Antioch College and served
with Bill Dixon at Bennington College as director of the Black
Music Ensemble in 1975. But until the late '70s, Lyons's poignant,
fiery alto solos were the other familiar part of Taylor's music.
They recorded for many labels, and Lyons adjusted to constant
personnel changes, sometimes playing with other saxophonists
like Sam Rivers, other times with violinists, multiple drummers,
or trumpeters. Lyons and Taylor made their recording debut in
1962, and Lyons was on every Taylor record until he began heading his own bands. His late '70s and '80s groups usually included
his wife, bassoonist Karen Borca, and drummer Paul Murphy
with assorted guest stars. Lyons also worked in a trio with vocalist Jeanne Lee and Andrew Cyrille, and in duos with Cyrille and
Sunny Murray. Lyons recorded for Byg, Hat Hut, and Black
Saint.—*Ron Wynn*

● **Jump Up / What to Do About** / Aug. 30, 1980 / Hat Hut 21
Jimmy Lyons's trio recording with Sunny Murray (drums) and
John Lindberg (the bassist in the String Trio of New York and the
Anthony Braxton quartet) was a real gem. Lyons's prior Hat Hut
three-record set *Push Pull*, with his regular group, suffered from
poor recording quality, but this performance at the 1980 Willisau
Jazz Festival was very well recorded. . . . Like his recordings with
pianist Cecil Taylor, Jimmy Lyons maintained a high level of in-
tensity and inspiration from the first note to the last. —*Carl
Brauer, Cadence*

○ **Something in Return** / 1981 / Black Saint 1201251
○ **Burnt Offering** / i. 1982 / Black Saint 120130

M'Boom

Group / World fusion, modern creative
A group of diverse percussionists and drummers started by Max
Roach in the '70s. The lineup has grown as large as 14 at times,
with the players alternating on conventional trap drums, congas,
African talking drums, cowbells, marimbas, and other percussion
instruments, playing mainly original, extended compositions. —
Ron Wynn

○ **Live at S.O.B.'s New** / i. 1992 / Blue Moon 79182
Exciting percussion duels, multiple rhythms, and teeming
arrangements and performances by the conglomeration of drummers known as M'Boom. This recent release included founding
member Max Roach, plus Roy Brooks, Joe Chambers, Omar Clay,
Fred King, Ray Mantilla, Warren Smith, and Freddy Waits performing live at the celebrated New York club S.O.B.'s. —*Ron
Wynn*

★ **M'Boom** / Columbia 36247

Harold Mabern (Harold Mabern, Jr.)

b. Mar. 20, 1936, Memphis, TN
Piano / Hard bop
Harold Mabern is a veteran jazz pianist from Memphis. He's a
straightahead swinger who has gotten down on his share of
blues-funk or original soul. He was primarily a sideman with
MJT+3, Lionel Hampton, Miles Davis, Jazztet, J.J. Johnson, and
has also backed many singers. Mabern played with Lee Morgan
in the '60s and early '70s and is currently a member of the
Contemporary Piano Ensemble.—*Michael G. Nastos*

★ **Rakin' & Scrapin'** / Dec. 23, 1968 / Prestige 330
Any old Mabern album is great. The Memphis pianist is now in
New York. —*Michael G. Nastos*

Teo Macero

b. Oct. 30, 1925
Tenor sax, arranger, bandleader, producer / Cool
Teo Macero's accomplishments include both bandstand and production studio. He was a progressive saxophonist who studied at
Juilliard in the late '40s and early '50s and recorded on the
Charles Mingus-Max Roach Debut label. His LP *Explorations* featured Macero playing two tenors and two altos via multitracking,
something that was quite unusual in that era. Macero's much better known as a producer. He produced albums for Charles
Mingus and Thelonious Monk and was Miles Davis's producer
during most of Davis's sojourn, beginning with *Kind of Blue*. In
later years, Macero has recorded for American Clave and produced a Mingus anthology and a Loose Tubes release. —*Ron
Wynn and Michael G. Nastos*

★ **Acoustical Suspension** / i. 1984 / Doctor Jazz 40111
○ **Best of Teo Macero, The** / i. Aug. 1990 / Stash 527
Interesting anthology with super producer Teo Macero presented
during his playing days in various lineups. Guests include Art
Farmer, Bill Evans, Lee Konitz, Ed Shaughnessy, Mal Waldron, Al
Cohn, and Charles Mingus. —*Ron Wynn*

Machito (Frank Grillo)

b. 1912, Havana, Cuba, **d.** Apr. 15, 1984, London, England
Vocals / Latin-jazz, world fusion
Machito left Cuba for New York in October 1937. He sang with
several groups before organizing his orchestra in 1940. The
Decca 78s "Sopa de Pichon," "La Paella," "Nague," "Tingo
Talango," and "Chacumbele" enabled his orchestra to enjoy top
billing status by 1943. It was the WOR radio remotes from La
Conga Club in midtown Manhattan that enabled the band to be
heard coast to coast. During its 44 years, the Machito band
recorded for several major labels. —*Max Salazar*

○ **Dizzy Gillespie/Charlie Parker** / i. 1948 / Verve
A selection of prime Latin-jazz cuts w/ both Parker and Diz plus
Machito. —*Ron Wynn*

★ **Machito and His Afro-Cuban Salseros** / i. 1948 /
○ **Afro-Cuban Jazz Suite** / Dec. 21, 1950 / Clef 505
★ **Latin Soul Plus Jazz** / 1957 / Charly 149
This band, under Machito's sizzling baton, blows up a storm that
could wipe Cuba right off the map! Sitting in are jazz heavy-
weights Cannonball Adderly, Curtis Fuller, Joe Newman, Herbie
Mann, Johnny Griffin, Candido Camero, and others. —*Myles
Boisen, Roots & Rhythm*

○ **Machito at the Crescendo** / 1960 / GNP 58
Excellent 1960 sessions made in Hollywood with a great dance
and Latin-Jazz band. —*Ron Wynn*

★ **Afro-Cuban Jazz Moods** / i. Jun. 4-05, 1975 / Pablo
○ **Machito & His Salsa Big Band** / i. 1982 / Impulse 33106
This was the recording that won Machito a Grammy in 1983. A
dynamite band with Chocolate Armenteros in the trumpet section and Macho's daughter as lead female vocalist and a fine mix
of well-known and less-familiar numbers, including "El
Manicero" and a Machito warhorse, "Quimbombo." A worthy
memorial indeed. —*John Storm Roberts*

☆ **1983 Grammy Award Winner** / i. 1983 / MCA 33106
& His Salsa Big Band. Showing the band is still vital, this live
recording in Holland is hot. —*Michael G. Nastos*

Adam Makowicz (Adam Matyszkowicz)

b. Aug. 18, 1940, Cesky Tesin, Czech.
Piano / Bop
Pianist Adam Makowicz began playing professionally in 1962 in
Cracow and moved to Warsaw in 1965. He headed his own trio
and toured extensively through Europe, Cuba, India, and around
the world. Makowicz began writing both music and music criti-
cism, as well as arranging in 1971. He joined violinist Michael
Urbaniak's group the same year, spending three years with
Urbaniak and his wife Urzula. He began working with the
Tomasz Stanko trio and later formed a band with Stanko in 1975.
Makowicz's reputation in Europe eventually spread to America,
where critics began to recognize his fluency, rhythmic verve, and
dazzling technique. His subsequent albums haven't always been

consistent affairs but have shown at times Makowicz's great ability and his debt to Art Tatum.—*Ron Wynn*

★ **Adam** / 1977 / Columbia 35320

Polish pianist Adam Makowicz's debut American release was definitely a tour de force from a traditional-technical point of view. The variety of colors in his improvisations, as well as the cliché hook of pure speed in his runs, made this an enjoyable album. —*Milo Fine, Cadence*

○ **Naughty Baby** / **i.** 1987 / Novus 3022

An all-Gershwin program with two bassists, Dave Holland and Charlie Haden. Essential. —*Michael G. Nastos*

Junior Mance (Julian Clifford Mance, Jr.)

b. Oct. 10, 1928, Chicago, IL

Piano / Hard bop, blues & jazz, soul-jazz

Junior Mance is among the best funk, blues, and soul-jazz pianists. He began in the Chicago scene of the late '40s and moved to New York and joined Lester Young's group in 1949. He played with the Sonny Stitt-Gene Ammons band in 1950-1951 and then spent three years in the army. Mance became Dinah Washington's accompanist for a year after that and worked with Cannonball Adderley's first quintet in 1956-1957. Subsequently, Mance played with Dizzy Gillespie's group and the Eddie "Lockjaw" Davis-Johnny Griffin group. Mance then formed his own trio and since then has done mostly trio recordings, though he has also been quite prolific as a session player. Though some would place him alongside Ramsey Lewis or Ahmad Jamal, Mance's recordings have been more aggressive and less introspective than those of Jamal and contained more mainstream jazz content than most of Lewis's. —*Ron Wynn*

○ **Junior Mance Trio at the Village Vanguard** / Feb. 22-23, 1961 / Jazzland 204

This session presented the Junior Mance trio (Ben Riley, drums; Larry Gales, bass) in a live program from 2/22/61-2/23/61. Mance was one of the first crop of funk cum soul cum funky pianists of the '60s to follow in the lineage developed by Horace Silver in the '50s. And, like his West Coast contemporary Les McCann, he made his best records at a time before commercial considerations put his playing under the looking glass and a purity and naturalness were lost. When this record was cut, funk was merely hip, not yet hype. —*Bob Rusch, Cadence*

★ **Truckin' & Trakin'** / Dec. 13, 1983 / Bee Hive 7015

Recorded by a quartet with pianist Mance and saxophonist David Newman. Produced by Bob Porter. Includes one Mance original, Hank Crawford's "Truckin," and four standards. The group really comes together for the blues-jazz legend. —*Michael G. Nastos*

○ **Mance's Special** / Sep. 1986-Nov. 1988 / Sackville 3043

Fine '86 set with pianist Junior Mance running through romping blues, intricate originals, and moving standards and ballads in a solo set. While he's best at blues-tinged material, Mance shows the versatility necessary to do other material and doesn't substitute clichés and gimmicks for ideas and substance. —*Ron Wynn*

Albert Mangelsdorff

b. Sep. 5, 1928, Frankfurt, Germany

Trombone, composer / Early free, progressive big band, modern creative

Mangelsdorff is the master of multiphonics, the trombone technique of playing more than one note simultaneously. He's also among the prime veterans in the European free-improvisation school, though his roots date back to the late 40s, when he was playing bop. He appeared in America as a member of the Newport International Band in 1958. He then played with a specially assembled band called the European All Stars and toured Western Europe and Yugoslavia with his own band in the early '60s. He recorded with pianist John Lewis in 1962 and toured Asia in 1964. Enchanted by the sound of Indian music, Mangelsdorff began to work ragas into his own music and recorded a song by Ravi Shankar. Later visits to Japan and Eastern and Western Europe, plus his involvement with the Globe Unity Orchestra beginning in the '60s, moved Mangelsdorff into free improvisation. Through the '70s, '80s, and '90s, Mangelsdorff has recorded with symphony orchestras, done solo concerts, worked with trios and duos, and been voted many times Europe's "Musician of the Year." —*Ron Wynn*

○ **Tromboneliness** / Jan. 1976-Mar. 1976 / Sackville 2011

Tromboneliness came on like a swarm of boppish bees; buzz, flying, aerobatics, focus, sting—but underlying all was as strong a sense of form and organization as in a hive, and as much care and workmanship as in a honeycomb. Forty-four minutes of raw trombone may sound insufferable, but Albert Mangelsdorff blew miracles. . . . Mangelsdorff utilized his chordal capabilities nearly all the time, for haunting motifs ("For Peter"), basslines ("Mark Suetterlyn's Boogie," under his sped-up flugelly overdub), whole pieces ("Questions to Come"), call-and-response to single lines ("Creole Love Call"), and dazzlingly quick display (title track). . . . A landmark album for solo trombone. —*Fred Bouchard, Down Beat*

★ **Trilogue** / Nov. 6, 1976 / PA/USA 7055

Live trio recording for virtuoso German trombonist. Startling sounds! With Jaco Pastorius (b). —*Michael G. Nastos*

Chuck Mangione (Chuck ii Mangione)

b. Nov. 29, 1940, Rochester

Trumpet, flugelhorn, keyboards, composer / Early jazz-rock, instrumental pop

Mangione was among the first superstar instrumentalists who went from playing traditional bop to scoring huge hits with lightweight material far removed from his jazz roots. Mangione went to the Eastman School of Music in Rochester from 1960 to1964. He co-led the Jazz Brothers with his brother Gap, then moved to New York City in 1965 and played for short periods with Woody Herman, Kai Winding, and Maynard Ferguson. He spent two years working with Art Blakey's Jazz Messengers and then was the director of the jazz ensemble of the Eastman School of Music from 1968 to 1972. He started his own group in 1968 and in 1970 recorded the live album *Friends and Love* with the Rochester Philharmonic Orchestra. A single from that album, "The Hill Where the Lord Hides," was a hit, and the album seamlessy mixed jazz, rock, folk, and classical elements. He scored another hit album with *Land of Make Believe* in 1972, working with the Hamilton Philharmonic of Ontario, Canada. He formed his own recording label in 1974, and his compositions have been done by many artists, among them Cannonball Adderley, Herb Alpert, and Mark Murphy. In later years, Mangione has had massive success in the pop arena, writing songs for commercials and the Olympics among other ventures, though his work has increasingly moved away from improvisation and harder-edged sounds. —*Ron Wynn*

○ **Recuerdo** / Jul. 31, 1962 / Jazzland 495

W/ Wynton Kelly (p), Sam Jones (b), Lou Hayes (d), and Joe Romano (fl, as). The is the real jazz Mangione. Recommended. —*Michael G. Nastos*

○ **Alive!** / Aug. 1972 / Mercury 1650

○ **Together** / 1972 / Mercury 7501

★ **Bellavia** / 1975 / A&M 3172

Bellavia followed the same popular formula Chuck Mangione adopted for his *Chase the Clouds Away*: a warm phase-shifted electric piano lightly outined the chords, the rhythm section and orchestra formed sweeping underlayers for the horn vamps, and the brass section immodestly punctuated the break points, which served as transitions for the soloing instrument. . . . Mangione's proficiency for powerhouse arrangements was truly staggering, and his music was undeniably friendly. —*Mikal Gilmore, Down Beat*

Feels So Good / 1977 / A&M 3219

Recorded at Kendun Recorders, Burbank, CA. Small group. Pop/jazz yes, but it is too pretty not to enjoy. Platinum album. —*Michael Erlewine*

○ **An Evening of Magic, Live at the Hollywood Bowl** / Jul. 16, 1978 / A&M 66701

An extremely popular late-'70s date done at the Hollywood Bowl by trumpeter Chuck Mangione. —*Ron Wynn*

Herbie Mann (Herbert Jay Solomon)

b. Apr. 16, 1930, New York, NY

Flute, tenor sax, bass clarinet / Bop, early jazz-rock, world fusion, instrumental pop

No instrumentalist was more popular, or more eclectic, in the '60s and early '70s than Herbie Mann. Mann began to investigate and record bossa nova music in 1961 and had his first hit single and album in 1962. Through the late '50s and early '60s, Mann had been a fairly conventional mainstream-bop saxophonist, but the switch to flute made him a superstar in the '60s. Mann's simple melodies and incorporation of international elements, R&B, blues, and rock backbeats, clicked with record buyers. He played in Brazil and Japan and regularly topped magazine listener-reader polls throughout the '60s. His late '60s release *Memphis Underground* was a monster smash and early jazz-rock-fusion document. Mann moved into reggae and disco; had his own label for a while; and produced sessions by Ron Carter, Miroslav Vitous, and Attila Zoller in the '70s. Mann's popularity waned in the '80s, and he'd never been a critical favorite. But he continued recording, both on his own label and later with Chesky. Reissues have shown he's made many respectable albums along with the more commercial and pop dates, notably *Nirvana* in 1961 with Bill Evans.—*Ron Wynn*

○ **Yardbird Suite** / Nov. 14, 1957 / Savoy 12108

★ **Nirvana** / Dec. 8, 1961 / Atlantic 1426

○ **Impressions of the Middle East** / Mar. 7, 1966-Nov. 9, 1966 / Atlantic 1475

★ **Memphis Underground** / Aug. 21-23, 1968 / Atlantic 1522
Mann's best pop-R&B recording has been enormously popular and is still somewhat influential. W/ Roy Ayers (vib), Larry Coryell (g), and Sonny Sharrock (g). —*Ron Wynn*

Evolution of Mann: Anthology / i. 1994 / Rhino
Herbie Mann's populist jazz made him an enormously popular performer during the '60s and '70s and the most publicized flutist in jazz history. Mann's strong points include his adaptability and love for many musical genres, particularly Afro-Latin and Brazilian material. He was also a competent bop and swing soloist, and scored hits playing R&B and soul, rock, funk, disco, and open-ended jams. This two-disc anthology doesn't cover his bop or swing origins, instead concentrating on Mann's evolution from the '60s to the '90s. The first disc has more interest for jazz fans; it includes the influential "Memphis Underground" and "Coming Home Baby" and shows his early flirtations with Latin and African music, as well as live workouts and Southern sessions. The second date documents Mann's move into straight pop and light instrumentals, though near its conclusion he's returned to the groove-oriented Afro-Latin music of his earlier days. This disc concludes with a rousing "Amazing Grace." While there are questionable inclusions, especially the inferior live version of "Hold On I'm Coming" on the second disc rather than the definitive rendition from *Memphis Underground,* this set offers a good overview of a controversial but consistent musician. —*Ron Wynn*

Shelly Manne (Sheldon Manne)

b. Jun. 11, 1920, New York, NY, d. Sep. 26, 1984, Los Angeles, CA
Drums / Cool
A tremendously swinging drummer and much more versatile than his reputation might lead you to believe, Shelly Manne was gifted enough to cut recordings with both Andre Previn and Ornette Coleman. He was the West Coast's most prolific percussive stylist during the '50s and '60s, and though he wasn't a flashy soloist, Manne was a gifted one. He had a father and two uncles who were also drummers, and Manne was a saxophonist before turning to drums at 18. He substituted for Dave Tough in Benny Goodman's band and later replaced him in Joe Marsala's group. Manne was in the bands of Will Bradley, Raymond Scott, and Les Brown during the '40s, and played on Coleman Hawkins's historic "The Man I Love" recording in 1943. Later came stints with Stan Kenton, Johnny Bothwell, George Shearing, Charlie Ventura, Bill Harris, Woody Herman, and a Jazz at the Philharmonic tour. Among groups he participated in was the Poll-Winners trio with Ray Brown and Barney Kessel; Previn's trio; the L.A. Four; and The Gentlemen of Swing with Benny Carter, Teddy Wilson, and Milt Hinton. Manne did many film scores and television parts, had an appearance in "The Man with the Golden Arm" and did many recordings for Contemporary, Concord, Trend, and Atlas, among others. —*Ron Wynn and Michael G. Nastos*

○ **Here's That Manne** / Nov. 12, 1951 / Dee Gee 1003

○ **Shelly Manne and His Men** / i. 1953 / Contemporary 2503

○ **Shelly Manne—Vol. 2** / Dec. 8, 1953-May 17, 1954 / Contemporary 2511

○ **Shelly Manne—Vol. 3** / Sep. 10, 1954 / Contemporary 2516

○ **Shelly Manne & His Friends—Vol. 1** / Feb. 1956 / Contemporary 240
From the sometimes torturous testifying of the Jazz Workshop to the mercurial music of Andre Previn (piano), Leroy Vinnegar (bass), and Shelly Manne (drums) on this date was quite a contrast. Not much can be said about this 2/11/56 session that hasn't been said about most other Shelly Manne and his friends' dates with Previn. The program was neither the epitome of hip jazz that the socialites of the upper middle class would have you believe nor the epitome of sterile jazz cliché that the elitists would have you believe. It was just light, unpretentious, and swinging music. —*Bob Rusch, Cadence*

● **At the Blackhawk—Vols. 1-5** / Sep. 22-24, 1959 / Contemporary 660
This series was taped at San Francisco's now-defunct Black Hawk club in September, 1959 under the direction of Lester Koenig, Contemporary's founder and guiding light. The five artists played extensively and with intensity, feeling and thought on a tasteful variety of material. —*Zan Stewart, Downbeat*

○ **Essence** / Jul. 5-06, 1977 / Galaxy 5101
This Shelly Manne album was a straightahead session featuring Lew Tabackin's strong tenor saxophone and liquid flute, with material by Duke Ellington, Jerome Kern, and George Gershwin. With strong support from pianist Mike Wofford and bassist Chuck Domanico, Manne and Tabackin got down to some hard swinging on tunes like "What Am I Here For?" and "Take the Coltrane." —*Herb Nolan, Down Beat*

☆ **Double Piano Jazz Quartet at Carmelo's—Vol. 2** / Sep. 12-13, 1980 / Trend 527
Drummer Shelly Manne's *Double Piano Jazz Quartet,* recorded in performance at a California club, was headed by a competent piano duo. Alan Broadbent and bassist Bill Mays had little trouble negotiating tunes like "The Night Has a Thousand Eyes" and that musical obstacle course "Lennie's Pennies." There was a happy kicky version of Horace Silver's "Strollin'," as well as a casually intertwining reading of "Sweet and Lovely." —*Jon Balleras, Down Beat*

☆ **Double Piano Jazz Quartet at Carmelo's—Vol. 1** / Sep. 12-13, 1980 / Trend 526
An unusual 1980 session with drummer Shelly Manne heading a group that includes pianists Bill May and Alan Broadbent and bassist Chuck Domanico but no brass, reeds, or woodwinds. Manne's crisp, steady drumming teams with Domanico's consistent bass to set the rhythmic foundation, while pianists Mays and Broadbent alternate solos and either interact with, complement, or contrast with Manne and Domancio. —*Ron Wynn*

★ **At the Manne-Hole—Vols. 1 and 2** / Contemporary
'92 reissue of a '61 live release by drummer Shelly Manne's quintet. Trumpeter Conte Candoli, tenor saxophonist Richie Kamuca, pianist Russ Freeman, and bassist Chuck Berghofer join Manne for program of swing, cool, and mainstream fare that's nicely played. —*Ron Wynn*

Charlie Mariano (Charles Hugolie Mariano)

b. Nov. 12, 1923, Boston, MA
Alto sax / Bop, postbop, early jazz-rock, world fusion
Alto saxophonist Charlie Mariano began working in the Boston area with Jaki Byard, Sam Rivers, Herb Pomeroy, and others. Mariano spent two years with Stan Kenton in the '50s and nearly three years working with Los Angeles players like Fran Rosolino, Shelly Manne, and others. He co-led a group with his wife Toshiko Akiyoshi in the early '60s and also played briefly with Charles Mingus in 1962. He lived in Japan with Akiyoshi during 1963 and 1964 and returned to America in 1965. He also toured extensively with Astrud Gilberto. Mariano lived in Europe during the '70s and '80s, working with many groups and leading several bands. Mariano began as a bop advocate, though Johnny Hodges was also an early influence. In subsequent years, his sound grew more lyrical and the impact of Asian and Eastern themes quite identifiable. He's been among jazz's most powerful, penetrating soloists. —*Ron Wynn*

○ **Boston All Stars** / 1951-1953 / Prestige 1745

★ **Helen 12 Trees** / May 6-08, 1976 / BASF 22941

In *Helen 12 Trees* one heard an amalgam of Charlie Mariano's varied experiences—the bop inflections of the Charlie Parker school, the Indian/Asian overtones, and the driving pulse of rock. Because of Marian's unifying and uncompromising musical vision, the synthesis worked well. —*Chuck Berg, Down Beat*

Dodo Marmarosa (Michael Marmarosa)

b. Dec. 12, 1925, Pittsburgh, PA
Piano / Bop
A wonderful melodic interpreter and soloist, Dodo Marmarosa was another among a handful of important white bop pianists. He was a gifted rhythmic improviser, who skillfully adapted swing elements for bop tunes, proving a reliable and engaging ensemble contributor. Marmarosa's style was also partly derived from contemporary classical music in the mid- and late '40s. He has been forgotten due to a lack of available material and an illness that took him off the scene in his prime. Marmarosa retired in the early '60s. Though he started studying classical piano, Marmarosa was interested in the keyboard techniques of Art Tatum and Teddy Wilson. He joined Gene Krupa's band in 1942 after playing in Pittsburgh groups. Marmarosa worked with Tommy Dorsey for part of 1944 and with Artie Shaw for the remainder of that year and the next, cutting some outstanding records with Shaw's big band and quintet. A 1946 move to Los Angeles, coupled with his growing interest in the new bop sounds, resulted in Marmarosa's style evolving. He became house pianist for Atomic Records and recorded with Boyd Raeburn. But the pivotal event was meeting and playing with Charlie Parker. These sessions won Marmarosa widespread acclaim. But an illness in 1948 took him away from clubs and studios for nearly ten years, except for brief tours with vocalist Johnny "Scat" Davis and Shaw. Marmarosa made a nice comeback album in 1961, *Dodo's Back*, and also recorded around that same time with Gene Ammons. The following year he appeared in concert at the University of Chicago. But that was it for his return. Marmarosa retired to Pittsburgh and hasn't recorded since. —*Ron Wynn*

● **Dodo's Back** / May 9-10, 1961 / Argo 4012

Branford Marsalis

b. Aug. 26, 1960, Breaux Bridge, LA
Tenor, soprano, and alto sax / Postbop, neo-bop
The current leader of the new "Tonight Show" band, Branford Marsalis hasn't been as controversial or as high-profile (until recently) as his brother Wynton. A member of jazz's best-known family, Branford Marsalis began as an alto player, replacing Bobby Watson in Blakey's Jazz Messengers in 1981. He switched to tenor and soprano and joined his brother's band in 1982, staying until 1985. The group toured extensively nationally and internationally and won critical applause, while selling vast numbers of recordings for jazz releases. After leaving his brother's band a couple of years later, Marsalis was heading his own band and has since become a major player in his own right. His swooping, huge-tone, supple phrasing and witty licks have links to Wayne Shorter, Sonny Rollins, and even Coleman Hawkins or Ben Webster, but Marsalis has developed his own voice and has also shown a willingness to record in many styles, from blues to a 1994 hip-hop-jazz date. —*Ron Wynn*

★ **Scenes in the City** / Apr. 18, 1983-Nov. 29, 1983 / Columbia 38951
The title cut of this album was a well-staged, smoothly narrated bit of Charles Mingus theater, older than most of these musicians. The remaining material was mainstream modern; three tunes in the John Coltrane-McCoy Tyner mold, a run at Sonny Rollins ("No Backstage Pass"), and a piece ("Parable") so pensive it almost disappeared. The material may have been routine; the playing wasn't. The album was an exposition of young lions that augured health for the '80s. —*J.B. Figi, Down Beat*

Royal Garden Blues / Mar. 1986-Jul. 1986 / Columbia 40363
Quartet sessions that feature some outstanding piano by Kenny Kirkland. —*Ron Wynn*

○ **Renaissance** / i. 1987 / Columbia 40711
Marsalis's best ensemble with Kenny Kirkland (p), Bob Hurst, and Tony Williams (d). Four standards, two of Tony's originals, and one of Branford's. A very solid album. —*Michael G. Nastos*

Beautyful Ones Are Not Yet Born / 1991 / Columbia 46990

Trio. An exciting pianoless session, plus a cut with guest star British tenor saxophonist Courtney Pine. Intense, deeply personal, and searing pianoless trio sessions for the '90s. —*Ron Wynn, Rock & Roll Disc*

I Heard You Twice the First Time / i. 1992 / Columbia 46083
A first-rate recent release by tenor saxophonist Branford Marsalis. This was his "blues" date and included songs or performances by B.B. King, Joe Louis Walker, Linda Hopkins, and John Lee Hooker, plus a guest stint by Wynton Marsalis and contributions from Kenny Kirkland, Jeff Watts, Robert Hurst III, and, of course, Brandford Marsalis on tenor and soprano. He and the rest of the cast fill their roles well, but it's the least self-conscious performers, like vocalist Linda Hopkins, who steal the show. —*Ron Wynn, AMG*

Ellis Marsalis

b. Nov. 14, 1934
Piano / New Orleans traditional, postbop
The pianist elder of the Marsalis clan, Ellis Marsalis is its least-known member, but he has finally begun to get notice for his own accomplishments. He is an experienced and outstanding pianist, whose experiences include playing in a Marine Corps band; working with Al Hirt; and training a host of familiar names, including Terence Blanchard, Donald Harrison, Harry Connick Jr, and Kent Jordan, as well as famous sons Branford and Wynton. He's well-versed in traditional New Orleans music and blues, bop, and hard bop. His style is precise and disciplined, yet engaging and swinging. Ellis Marsalis never rushes or seems ill-prepared in his solos, playing with verve and feeling. —*Ron Wynn*

★ **Father and Sons** / i. 1982 / CBS
The side with sons Wynton and Branford are worth the price. They swing very hard. —*Michael G. Nastos*
☆ **Piano in E-Solo Piano** / 1984 / Rounder 2100
○ **Heart of Gold** / 1991 / Columbia 47509
Of his few recordings, this is a gem. With Ray Brown (b), Billy Higgins (d)—none finer for rhythm mates. All standards save one by Ellis, two by his son and producer Delfeayo. This album shows the pianist's depth in perception of the entire jazz spectrum. —*Michael G. Nastos*

Wynton Marsalis

b. Oct. 18, 1961, New Orleans, LA
Trumpet, flugelhorn / Postbop, neo-bop
Jazz's most honored trumpeter, multiple Grammy winner Wynton Marsalis is the top star and biggest celebrity of the '80s and '90s. He has drawn lots of heat for supposedly being an imitator; his antirock and antirap diatribes and jibes at eclecticism have also earned him derision in some sectors. But few dispute his obvious technical attributes; his crisp, crackling notes and full, pure sound have gotten warmer and tighter, and he's proven, via forays into the blues, traditional jazz, and (lately) composition—that he's open to experimentation and change within the hard-bop format. Marsalis got his first trumpet at the age of 6 from fellow trumpeter Al Hirt and began studying both jazz and classical music at 12. He joined Blakey's Jazz Messengers as an 18-year-old. Besides making several albums in the late '70s and early '80s with Blakey, he recorded with Herbie Hancock in 1981 and signed with Columbia a little over a year later. His subsequent Columbia debut won a Grammy, triggering a run of multiple awards, and in 1984 he became the first artist ever to win simultaneous Grammys for jazz and classical, repeating this feat in 1985. Marsalis continued to try new things as the '80s closed and the '90s began, doing suites, commissioned works for ballet, and the blues. He was also artistic director for the Lincoln Center in New York, where he became part of an ongoing controversy regarding artist selection and program direction. —*Ron Wynn*

★ **Wynton Marsalis** / i. Oct. 11, 1980 / Columbia 37574
Wynton Marsalis's eagerly awaited debut recording found him in fine form and in fine company. He dug in on "Father Time"; his sure-toned trumpet commented with authority while following the tune's metrical shifts. Marsalis's cannily shaped phrases (reference point: Miles Davis) were buoyed by his brother Branford's saxophone—when the older Marsalis blows we hear the influence of Wayne Shorter. . . . On these tracks pianist Kirkland, drummer Jeff Watts, and alternately Charles Fambrough or Clarence Seay on bass—all impressive young players—aided and abetted the

brothers with active concern. Venerable Miles Davis alumni Herbie Hancock, Ron Carter, and Tony Williams (with whom Wynton Marsalis toured in 1981) were on hand for several numbers. —*Frank-John Hadley, Down Beat*

○ **Think of One** / 1983 / Columbia 38641
Think of One was Wynton Marsalis's second Columbia effort as leader—the first to use only the Marsalis brothers' working band. From "Knozz-Moe-King," which opened side one, through pianist Kenny Kirkland's "Fuchsia," the standard "My Ideal," bassist Ray Drummond's "What Is Happening Here (Now)?," the title track by Thelonius Monk, Wynton Marsalis's two originals ("The Bell Ringer" and "Later"), and Duke Ellington's "Melancholia," the Marsalis quintet appropriated with little embellishment the sophisticated and occasionally explosive sound of Miles Davis's mid-'60s combo. —*Howard Mandel, Down Beat*

Hot House Flowers / Mar. 30-31, 1984 / Columbia 39530

Black Codes (from the Underground) / Jan. 11-14, 1985 / Columbia 40009

○ **Live at Blues Alley** / Dec. 1986 / Columbia 40675
This offering by the brillant Wynton Marsalis quartet, recorded several months after *Marsalis Standard Time, Vol 1*, bolstered the case of those who hold Marsalis to be the one of the most important young musicians in jazz.... Disarming at first to the unsuspecting listener, his unorthodox manipulation of normal flow by forcing accents on other than expected beats, all the while keeping his place in the form and, most importantly, maintaining the swing, is masterful and arresting. —*David Franklin, Jazz Times*

○ **Carnival** / i. 1987 / CBS 42137
This was a dandy on which a maturing Wynton Marsalis traded his trumpet for cornet and paid homage to some of the great music made and popularized by wind bands throughout America from the 1860s through the 1930s. Marsalis's tone and coloring were impeccable here. This performance was highlighted by a fast and dazzling rendition of Rimsky-Korsakov's "The Flight of the Bumblebee," thanks to circular breathing, and a soulful interpretation of "Sometimes I Feel Like a Motherless Child." —*Ken Franckling, Jazz Times*

Standard Time—Vol. 2: Intimacy Calling / Sep. 1987-Aug. 1990 / Columbia 47346

○ **Majesty of the Blues, The** / 1989 / Columbia 45091
A more appropriate title for this album would be one word: "Homecoming"—for Wynton Marsalis returned to his New Orleans roots in this album. Yet it was a homecoming with a difference, with an appreciation for where he's been and all of those values along with those he'd carried from home. Marsalis had matured. He appreciated what Louis Armstrong was doing; his solo efforts were more concise and lyrical here than ever—with the *Hot House Flowers* ballads as exceptions. —*Rhodes J. Spedale Jr., Jazz Times*

Standard Time—Vol. 3 / i. 1990 / CBS 46143
1987-1990. Subtitled: *The Resolution of Romance*. Wynton, with his father Ellis on the piano. Very traditional and very nice listening. —*Michael Erlewine*

Thick in the South—Soul Gestures In Southern Blue, Vol. 1 / i. 1991 / Columbia 47977
The best of the three-part series, with Joe Henderson (ts) dead center. —*Ron Wynn*

Uptown Ruler—Soul Gestures in Southern Blue, Vol. 2 / i. 1991 / Columbia 47976

Levee Low Moan—Soul Gestures in Southern Blue, Vol. 3 / i. Nov. 1991 / Columbia 47975

○ **Blue Interlude** / i. 1992 / Columbia 48729
Good '92 session with trumpeter Wynton Marsalis's latest combo doing his hard bop and mainstream compositions. The lineup includes pianist Marcus Roberts, saxophonists Wessell Anderson and Todd Williams, bassists Reginald Veal and Herlin Riley, and drummer Wycliffe Gordon. —*Ron Wynn*

○ **Citi Movement** / i. Dec. 18, 1992 / Columbia 53324
Written for Wynton Marsalis's septet as the score for Garth Fagen's Bucket Dance Theater's modern ballet, *Griot New York*, this collection tells a story—of the history of mankind, of life in the teeming metropolis, of the tenacity of the human spirit— through music that is intricately written and expertly performed.

The best sections occur when the band is swinging, as it does mightily and joyfully throughout a broad range of expressions— traditional New Orleans brass band, '60s modal jazz, big-band swing, calypso, even circus music. —*Suzanne McElfresh, Down Beat*

Warne Marsh

b. Oct. 26, 1927, Los Angeles, CA, **d.** Dec. 18, 1987, Hollywood, CA
Tenor sax / Cool
Never a big name outside jazz circles, Warne Marsh was a creative, fluid saxophonist noted for surprising, often unorthodox phrases and vivid, rapid-paced solos. He started with the Hoagy Carmichael group in the mid-'40s and then went into the army. He toured in 1948 with Buddy Rich but met Lennie Tristano a year earlier while in the service. Tristano's influence remained with Marsh throughout his career, especially in the construction of his sax statements and in his writing. Marsh often collaborated with another Tristano disciple, Lee Konitz. Marsh made many vital recordings during the '60s and '70s. —*Ron Wynn*

○ **Live in Hollywood** / i. Dec. 1952 / Xanadu 151
It had been about three years since tenor saxophonist Warne Marsh had recorded those famous Capitols with alto saxophonist Lee Konitz and pianist Lennie Tristano. His sound was much the same and his amazing ideas were a pleasing contrast to pianist Hampton Hawes's bebop phrases. —*Jerry Atkins, Cadence*

○ **Warne Marsh Quintet** / i. 1956 / Storyville 4001

★ **Music for Prancing** / Sep. 1957 / Mode 125

● **Warne Marsh & Lee Konitz (Live at Club Montmartre)** / Dec. 1975 / Storyville 4026
State-of-the-art throughout. Blues, ballads, uptempo, and standards. —*Ron Wynn*

○ **Warne Marsh and Lee Konitz—Vol. 3** / i. Dec. 1975 / Storyville 4096

○ **How Deep, How High** / Apr. 25, 1977-Aug. 8, 1979 / Discovery 863

○ **Warne Marsh Meets Gary Foster** / i. 1982 / Ewd 90024

Pat Martino (Pat Azzara)

b. Aug. 25, 1944, Philadelphia, PA
Guitar / Postbop, early jazz-rock, neo-bop
A professional guitarist from an early age, Pat did a lot of performing on the "chitlin' circuit" with organists such as Jimmy Smith, Jack McDuff, and Jimmy McGriff. Moving to a more mainstream jazz style, he played with John Handy and led his own groups, which included Cedar Walton, Richard Davis, and Billy Higgins. A fluid and tasteful improviser with great speed and technique, Martino remains an important influence on advanced guitarists. —*David Nelson McCarthy*

○ **East!** / Jan. 1968 / Prestige 248
East! was a thematic production and also somewhat reflected a period of growing interest in the East. The title track was a lengthy piece for which the quartet (Eddie Green, piano; Ben Tucker, bass; Lenny McBrown, drums) was augmented by bassist Tyrone Brown (Tucker moved to tambourine for this piece). The mood here was meditative, circular, and repetitive, with lengthy solos by Pat Martino (guitar) and Eddie Green.... The rest of the program was more idiomatically bop, quite nice, but exposing both the piano's and Green's limitations. —*Bob Rusch, Cadence*

○ **Live!** / Sep. 1972 / Muse 5026

★ **Consciousness** / Oct. 7, 1974 / Muse 5039
Martino on the way up. Mostly quartet recordings for the brilliant guitarist. "Willow," a dark, understated gem. Contains seven tracks, three by Martino, three standards, and Joni Mitchell's "Both Sides Now." Guitar students should study this one. — *Michael G. Nastos*

○ **We'll Be Together Again** / Feb. 13-17, 1976 / Muse 5090

Hugh Masekela (Hugh Ramopolo Masekela)

b. Apr. 4, 1939
Trumpet, flugelhorn, vocals / World fusion
Trumpeter, flugelhorn player, occasional vocalist, and keyboardist Hugh Masekela is perhaps the best-known South African expatriate instrumentalist. Masekela heard both township music and vintage swing and bop in his teens, and the African, African-

American mix has been retained in Masekela's own music. In the early '60s, he left South Africa after John Dankworth and Harry Belafonte got him a passport. During the '60s, Masekela had a steady career recording for Mercury, MGM, and later his own label, Chisa, while living in London and New York and on the West Coast. He even had a number one pop hit with "Grazing in the Grass" in 1968. But a 1970 trip to Lagos and a concert with Fela Kuti rekindled his interest in African music, and he moved to London in 1972 to work and record with other expatriates. He returned to America in 1977 but went back to Africa in 1980, this time to Zimbabwe and Botswana, and toured with his ex-wife Miriam Makeba on Paul Simon's Graceland tour in the late '80s. Masekela has found a middle ground between commercialized Afro-funk, Afro-jazz, and true township music. —*Ron Wynn*

★ **Masekela / i.** 1969 / UNI 73041
It all comes together here. Magic synthesis of trumpet-led African sounds, jazz, and R&B. —*Hank Davis*

○ **Grrr / i.** 196z / Mercury 61109
Masekela as a young trumpeter from the mid-'60s. Rare, but clearly his best format and playing. —*Michael G. Nastos*

★ **Home Is Where the Music Is** / Jan. 1972 / Blue Thumb
An outstanding blend of Afro-pop and jazz with strong work by Dudu Pukwana. (as) —*Ron Wynn*

Cal Massey

b. 1928, **d.** 1972
Keyboards, composer / Hard bop, progressive big band
There's some doubt about the birthdate of composer and trumpeter Cal Massey, with some accounts having him born in 1928. But there's no question about his ability as a composer; Massey wrote some poignant and compelling material, and had works recorded by John Coltrane, Freddie Hubbard, Jackie McLean, Lee Morgan, Philly Joe Jones, and Archie Shepp, among others. Some Massey numbers that were recorded include "Bakai" by Coltrane, "Fiesta" by Jones, "Assunta, Father and Son" by Hubbard, "Message from Trane" by McLean, and "Cry of My People" by Shepp. Massey studied trumpet with Freddie Webster and worked in big bands led by Jay McShann, Jimmy Heath, and Billie Holiday. Massey then opted to concentrate on composing and didn't do much playing the rest of his career, though he did lead an ensemble that included Jimmy Garrsion, McCoy Tyner and Tootie Heath in the late '50s. This group played Massey's compositions and had periodic guest appearances from Coltrane and Donald Byrd. Massey worked and toured with Archie Shepp from 1969 until his death in 1972, and he also worked with Romulus Franchini, cofounding the Romas Orchestra, which also performed Massey compositions. His musical play "Lady Day: A Musical Tragedy" was Massey's final work.—*Ron Wynn*

● **Blues to Coltrane** / Jan. 1961 / Candid 79029

Bennie Maupin

b. Aug. 29, 1940, Detroit, MI
Sax, flute, bass clarinet / Hard bop, soul-jazz, early jazz-rock
A powerful tenor saxophonist, good bass clarinetist, and flutist and soprano saxophonist, Bennie Maupin's been a member of several fine Herbie Hancock groups and played in Lee Morgan's band during the '70s. Maupin's rumbling bass clarinet was also heard on Miles Davis's *Bitches Brew* sessions. Maupin attended the Detroit Institute for the Arts and began playing tenor in high school. He worked with Yusef Lateef, Barry Harris, Alice McLeod (Coltrane), and Hugh Lawson before leaving Detroit for New York in 1963. Maupin played and recorded with Marion Brown; worked with Pharoah Sanders; and did various dates with organ combos, soul singers, R&B and rock bands, and even calypso ensembles before playing with Roy Haynes and Horace Silver in the late '60s. Maupin also did dates with McCoy Tyner, Chick Corea, Jack DeJohnette, and Morgan before replacing Joe Henderson in Hancock's band. He stayed there through the jazz-rock and *Headhunters* period. Maupin recorded with Woody Shaw and Sonny Rollins in the '70s and did his own dates as a leader for ECM and Mercury but didn't remain as prolific afterward. —*Ron Wynn and Michael G. Nastos*

★ **Jewel in the Lotus, The** / Mar. 1974 / ECM 1043
Detroit multiinstrumentalist with other members of Herbie Hancock's Mwandishi. Early-period progressive fusion. —*Michael G. Nastos*

Lyle Mays (Lyle David Mays)

b. 1953
Keyboards / Early jazz-rock, modern creative
Keyboardist Lyle Mays is best known for a long musical relationship with Pat Metheny. Mays won prior acclaim for composing and notating an album for the North Texas State University Lab Band, which became the first by a college band to get a Grammy nomination in 1975. That same year, he met Pat Metheny, beginning their association. Mays worked exclusively with Metheny through the '70s and early '80s. His background was in classic bop, and his occasional forays on acoustic piano reveal those roots, but it's his array of colors, sounds, textures, and electronic support on synthesizer that has earned him respect with Metheny. Mays has released recordings as a leader on ECM since the mid-'80s. —*Ron Wynn*

★ **Lyle Mays / i.** 1986 / David Geffen Co. 24097
His best as a leader. Contemporary multikeyboardist with an original concept. —*Michael G. Nastos*

Cecil McBee

b. May 19, 1935, Tulsa, OK
Bass / Modern creative
A powerful, though not flashy bassist, Cecil McBee has been among jazz's most prolific players since the '60s. He's a highly talented accompanist, whose rich, superb lines and strong tone make their presence felt, though he's usually in the rhythm section and background. When McBee does take the spotlight, he offers an amazing array of speedy licks, bowed or plucked lines, and furious tones. McBee played clarinet before turning to bass at 17. He attended Central State University, but at various times in both the '50s and '60s, sandwiching this around a two-year stretch in the service from 1959 to 1961 and a stint with Dinah Washington in 1959. While in the army McBee played in a trio with Kirk Lightsey and Rudy Johnson and also conducted the Fort Knox band. He moved to Detroit in 1962, where he played with Paul Winter, and then moved to New York in 1964. McBee's schedule was full through the '60s. It included performances or recording sessions with Grachan Moncur III, Jackie McLean, Wayne Shorter, Charles Tolliver, Charles Lloyd, Yusef Lateef, Sam Rivers, Pharoah Sanders, and Alice Coltrane. During the '70s McBee had extended stints with Abdullah Ibrahim and Chico Freeman that lasted into the '80s. He worked with Ibrahim in combo and large band settings, and, when he started doing his own recordings in the mid-'70s, they usually included Freeman. He also worked with Sanders, Coltrane, Sonny Rollins, and Art Pepper in the '70s. His own sessions were for Strata-East, Enja, and India Navigation. McBee worked with McCoy Tyner, Mal Waldron, James Newton, and Joanne Brackeen in the '80s. In 1984 he joined the Leaders, with whom he's continued playing into the '90s. He played at the 1985 Kool Jazz Festival with Harry Edison and Buddy Tate.—*Ron Wynn*

● **Mutima** / May 8, 1974 / Strata East 7417

Les McCann (Leslie Coleman McCann)

b. Sep. 23, 1935, Lexington, KY
Piano, vocals / Blues & jazz, soul-jazz
Pianist and vocalist. A prime player in the soul-jazz and pop-jazz arenas, McCann got his first major exposure as a member of the Gene McDaniels backing band in 1959, following a stint in the navy. He formed his own trio in 1960 and has been consistently popular ever since. A fine, earthy singer who has also done well with romantic ballads and occasional protest songs, McCann has done a lot with limited instrumental gifts. A dependable player in terms of establishing grooves or setting up rhythms, he is not renowned as a great soloist or technician. Instead, he lets others like the Jazz Crusaders, Eddie Harris, or Rahsaan Roland Kirk do the work when they collaborate. —*Ron Wynn*

○ **The Les McCann Anthology** / i. 1960-1971 / Rhino/Atlantic 271279
Keyboardist-vocalist Les McCann ranked among jazz's more successful populists, injecting healthy doses of blues, soul, and R&B vocals and feeling into his work, without neglecting the improvisational end. McCann made hits, but didn't plug into any formula, moving back and forth between short, pop-centered arrangements and longer, looser funk jams. The 21 tracks on this two-CD set range from trio works to complex, multiartist suites and in-

clude two songs from his tenure with Eddie Harris, plus collaborations with the Jazz Crusaders, Grove Holmes, Ben Webster, the Gerald Wilson orchestra, Stanley Turrentine, and Lou Rawls. The most ambitious piece—the layered, ethereal "The Lovers"—offers a fitting climax to a set showcasing an undervalued, underrated performer. —*Ron Wynn*

★ **Les McCann Sings** / Aug. 1961 / Pacific Jazz
A super set with Ben Webster (ts) and Groove Holmes on organ. Soul-jazz and blues at their best. —*Ron Wynn*

★ **Invitation to Openness** / Nov. 1972 / Atlantic 1603

Ron McClure (Ronald Dix McClure)

b. Nov. 22, 1941, New Haven, CT
Bass, composer / Modern creative
Bassist Ron McClure has been an effective contributor in several major groups. He played in the Charles Lloyd Quartet and Fourth Way, and was also in groups led by Wynton Kelly, Buddy Rich, Marian McPartland, Mose Allison, Jack DeJohnette, Dave Liebman, Thelonious Monk, and Tony Bennett. A tremendous rhythmic player, McClure's recorded with Jerry Hahn, Julian Priester, Cal Tjader, and the Pointer Sisters and spent three years with Blood, Sweat and Tears. He's also done sessions and played with George Russell, Tom Harrell, John Scofield, John Abercrombie, Richie Bierarch, and Vincent Herring. He's recorded as a leader for Ode, Bellaphon, EPC, Steeplechase, and Ken Music. —*Ron Wynn and Michael G. Nastos*

★ **Tonight Only** / i. 1991 / Steeple Chase 31288
After decades as a sideman, the bassist leads a truly first-rate album. W/ Randy Brecker (tpt), John Abercrombie (g), Adam Nussbaum (d). Five McClure originals—mostly in postbop, neo-contemporary vein—and three nice standards. A great record. —*Michael G. Nastos*

Rob McConnell (Robert Murray Gordon McConnell)

b. Feb. 14, 1935, London, Ontario
Trombone, bandleader / Swing, big band, progressive big band
One of the most widely respected big band leaders, Rob McConnell has led various edtions of the Boss Brass big band over 20 years. The Canadian trombonist and arranger has kept the band going as it evolved from basically a pop aggregation into an improvising organization with over 20 members playing both jazz standards and originals. McConnell played valve trombone in Toronto during the '50s and early '60s, studying with Gordon Delamont while working in various dance bands. He played and recorded with Maynard Ferguson in New York during the mid-'60s and then played with Phil Nimmon's group Nimmon 'n' Nine Plus Six in the mid- and late '60s in Toronto, while also doing studio work. The Boss Brass was initially a pop ensemble, but it had grown and changed direction by the mid-'70s. They've since done sessions for Sea Breeze, Unisson, and Concord and have backed vocalist Mel Tormé. —*Ron Wynn and Michael G. Nastos*

★ **Boss Brass & Woods** / Mar. 11-12, 1985 / MCA 5982
& Boss Brass. Potent solos by Phil Woods (as), excellent playing by Canada's premier big band. Four standards, one each by saxophonist Rick Wilkins and Quincy Jones, two by leader. 23 pieces working as one. Great solos from Guido Basso, Jan McDougal, and Ed Bickert. —*Michael G. Nastos*

Susannah McCorkle

Vocals / Ballads & blues
Vocalist. Susannah McCorkle has made a sizable impact in a relatively brief period. While in Paris, McCorkle was captivated by the music of Billie Holiday. She's earned a Grammy nomination and published several short stories and articles in the New Yorker. McCorkle has a clear and striking voice and never picks bad or unsuitable material. She's established herself as a topflight performer and has done a number of albums for Concord.—*Ron Wynn*

○ **Over the Rainbow** / Jan. 11, 1980-Feb. 19, 1980 / Inner City 1131
More classy standards and prerock pop from jazz vocalist Susannah McCorkle, whose rendition of the title track wisely doesn't try to imitate other, higher-pitched vocalists but instead works off her strengths: pacing, enunication, dramatic tension, and delivery. —*Ron Wynn*

○ **Songs of Johnny Mercer, the** / i. Aug. 1981 / Inner City 1101
A first-rate interpretive and standards vocalist tackles the classic songs written by a compositional master. The results are just what you'd expect: magical and outstanding. McCorkle's timing, instincts, and lyric readings are exceptional, as are her choices of Mercer material. —*Ron Wynn*

★ **No More Blues** / Nov. 1988 / Concord Jazz 4370
○ **How Do You Keep the Music Playing?** / PA/USA 7195
The lightweight title song aside, here's another expertly done album showcasing the swinging skills of jazz vocalist Susannah McCorkle, among the finest contemporary singers around. Her timing, delivery, and sound, even on disposable fodder, is consistently impressive, and she's an outstanding lyric interpreter as well. —*Ron Wynn*

○ **Thanks for the Memory (Songs of Leo Robin)** / PA/USA 7175
While several of these songs aren't strictly jazz or even necessarily pop, Susannah McCorkle makes them all worth hearing. That's because she's a marvelous lyric interpreter who also has an easy, swinging style and excellent delivery. She makes you pay attention to whatever she's singing, whether you understand it or not (or even care about it). —*Ron Wynn*

Jack McDuff (Eugene McDuffy)

b. Sep. 17, 1926, Champaign, IL
Organ / Blues & jazz, soul-jazz
Organist Jack McDuff is one of the great jazz organists and combo leaders. McDuff began as a bassist and switched to organ in the mid '50s. He first gained attention via the Willis Jackson group (1958-1960). His Prestige recordings with Jackson are of the highest quality in organ-tenor sax collaboration. McDuff's own debut recordings were for Prestige, beginning in 1960. These early dates find him in a studio pickup group with tenor saxophonist Jimmy Forrest. They cut two albums, *Tough Duff* and *The Honeydripper*, and both are outstanding. McDuff formed his own group in 1961 with saxophonist Harold Vick and drummer Joe Dukes. His big breakthrough came in summer 1963 with a quartet that included Dukes, tenor sax man Red Holloway, and young guitarist George Benson. The group had a number of best-selling albums (1963-1965), and any music this group made is worth hearing. This is the best McDuff music. Later groups lacked the fire of this one, and Atlantic (1966-1967) and Chess/Cadet (1968-1969) albums never quite reached the same level. More recordings for Verve and Cadet again had moments but generally were, at best, good. Much of the '70s found McDuff getting more involved with electronic keyboards and sacrificing much of his identity in the process. *Cap'n Jack* (Muse) from 1988 finds him back on the right track. A versatile organist, McDuff is also a capable arranger and bandleader whose groups are well rehearsed and thoroughly conversant with his methods. McDuff's recorded for Concord in the '90s. —*Bob Porter*

● **Brother Jack Meets the Boss** / Jan. 23, 1962 / Prestige 326
W/ Gene Ammons. Exceptional organ/tenor sax meetings from the early '60s. A looser, more relaxed McDuff than his subsequent Prestige recordings, yet equally good. w/ Harold Vick (ts). —*Bob Porter*

○ **Live!** / i. Jun. 5, 1963 / Prestige 7274
★ **Heating System, The** / i. 1972 / Cadet

Bobby McFerrin

b. Mar. 11, 1950, New York, NY
Vocals, piano / Ballads & blues, early jazz-rock
Bobby McFerrin is a true vocal improviser. His ability to stretch and strain his voice, produce rhythmic patterns, use his entire body like a drum, and make notes by breathing in and then out made McFerrin an '80s pop icon. Jon Hendricks saw McFerrin, encouraged him, and later sang some duets with him. McFerrin began doing solo performances in 1983. He later scored a huge pop hit with "Don't Worry, Be Happy" and became a huge attraction. Over the years, his song content and performance approach have veered away from jazz, but he's an awesome stylist and a compelling vocalist. —*Ron Wynn*

Bobby McFerrin / 1982 / Elektra 60023
McFerrin's debut, which shocked, rocked, and amazed everyone. He's more of a vocal improviser than a performer of strictly jazz. —*Ron Wynn*

● **Voice, The** / Mar. 17, 1984-Mar. 26, 1984 / Elektra 60366
The Voice was a milestone in jazz history; it was the first time a jazz singer had recorded an entire album solo, without accompaniment or overdubbing, for a major label. Bobby McFerrin's amazing ability to switch back and forth between bass notes and falsetto, along with his talent for jumping octaves made this record quite a virtuoso showcase.... For those interested in the potential of the human voice and in an important jazz talent, *The Voice* is recommended without reservations. —*Scott Yanow, Cadence*

Spontaneous Inventions / 1986 / Blue Note 46298
More superb vocal gymnastics. Takes on everyone from the Beatles to Dizzy Gillespie. —*Hank Davis*

★ **Simple Pleasures** / 1988 / EMI 48059
The breakthrough album. Contains the megahit "Don't Worry, Be Happy" and other gems like "Drive My Car." Platinum album. —*Hank Davis*

Howard McGhee (Howard B. McGhee)

b. 1918, **d.** 1987
Trumpet, composer / Bop, hard bop, postbop
Howard McGhee was among bop's finest pure trumpeters, gifted with great range, taste, sensitivity, harmonic knowledge, and skill. McGhee played with Lionel Hampton in 1941; then, through the rest of the decade, worked with Andy Kirk, Charlie Barnet, and Georgie Auld, before coming under the musical spell of bop. His debut as a leader with Charles Mingus in 1945 (for Modern) was an indication that McGhee's style had made the transition. He later recorded for Dial, Blue Note, Bethlehem, and Savoy, working with such players as Milt Jackson, Fats Navarro, Pepper Adams, and Tina Brooks. He continued into the '60s and '70s. —*Ron Wynn*

○ **Howard McGhee's All Stars** / Oct. 11, 1948-Jan. 23, 1950 / Blue Note 5012

● **Maggie** / i. 1948-1952 / Savoy 2219
Maggie was a two-disc set of trumpeter Howard McGhee's work during the late '40s and early '50s.... In 1948 he put together a sextet with alto-baritone saxophonist Jimmy Heath, vibist Milt Jackson, pianist Will Davis, bassist Percy Heath, and drummer Joe Harris. The 1948 session was a bop-inspired unit of considerable energy. Maggie (McGhee) was a gutsy, full-toned player whose innate sense of lyrical swing enabled him to extract the best from ballads, standards, and burning blues.... The McGhee dates of 1952 included trombonist J.J. Johnson, tenorist Rudy Williams, guitarist Skeeter Best, bassist Oscar Pettiford, and drummer Charlie Rice. —*Chuck Berg, Down Beat*

○ **McGhee-Navarro Sextet (With Fats Navarro), The** / i. 1952 /

○ **Return of Howard McGhee, The** / Oct. 22, 1955 / Bethlehem 42

★ **Maggie's Back in Town** / Jun. 26, 1961 / Contemporary 693
Trumpeter Howard McGhee's date was a rather common outing made interesting because of the quality of the individuals. Maggie (McGhee) was in good command; his rumpled style of playing always seemed to have direction and purpose and rarely dipped into predictable phrasing. Bassist Leroy Vinnegar and drummer Shelly Manne were as you would expect—solid. The added plus was pianist Phineas Newborn, whose quixotic playing provided a strong second voice adding unexpected zing. —*Bob Rusch, Cadence*

Chris McGregor

b. Dec. 24, 1936, Umtata, South Africa, **d.** May 26, 1990
Piano, bandleader / Progressive big band, world fusion
Pianist and bandleader Chris McGregor combined African rhythmic and classic swing principles in a special, distinctive fashion. He studied music four years at Cape Town College of Music, where he mixed classical training with nightly experience in local jazz clubs. He formed the Blue Notes with Dudu Pukwana, Mongezi Feza, Nick Moyake, Johnny Dyani, and Louis Moholo in 1962. The group eventually ran afoul of apartheid laws that banned live performances by mixed groups. They left the country for good in 1964, when they were invited to play at the French Antibes festival. They were helped by compatriot Abdullah Ibrahim, who got them jobs in Europe. McGregor gradually incorporated elements of free music into his repertoire after hearing Albert Ayler, Archie Shepp, and Cecil Taylor while his group

was working alongside them at the Montmarte in Copenhagen. McGregor created a larger group, the Brotherhood of Breath, in 1970, which became a favorite on the international circuit. He toured Africa with the group in the early '70s and continued to lead them through the decade, although he moved to the southwest of France and commuted to dates. He also did several solo piano concerts. —*Ron Wynn*

★ **And the Brotherhood of Breath** / i. 1971 / Neon 2
Studio release with excellent compositions, particularly "The Bride." —*Michael G. Nastos*

○ **Live at Willisau** / i. 1974 / Ogun 100
The pianist-leader w/ an 11-piece band of South African expatriates and English free-jazz men. Explosive. —*Michael G. Nastos*

☆ **Country Cooking** / Venture 90998

Jimmy McGriff (James Harrell McGriff, Jr.)

b. Apr. 3, 1936, Philadelphia, PA
Organ, bandleader / Blues & jazz, soul-jazz
McGriff is one of the great jazz organists. His first record, *I Got a Woman* (Sue Records), was a Top 20 hit in 1962. Followups *All about My Girl* and *Kiko* were also hits in 1963-1964. McGriff joined Solid State records in 1966, beginning a long relationship with producer Sonny Lester, who also recorded McGriff on Blue Note, Capitol, Groove Merchant, and LRC. "The Worm" was a hit in 1968-1969. McGriff's '60s work, while R&B-oriented, is top-quality organ jazz. Of special interest is *The Big Band* (Solid State), which is a marvelous tribute to Count Basie. McGriff's '70s work found him alternating between small-combo organ jazz (including a couple of organ battles with Richard "Groove" Holmes) and more commercial attempts utilizing a battery of electronic keyboards. In general, the earliest Groove Merchants are the best, and LRC titles should be avoided. 1980s recordings (JAM, Milestone) find him back in his jazz bag, and all of these can be recommended. Among them are three collaborations with Hank Crawford and *Blue to the Bone* with trombonist Al Grey. McGriff considers himself a blues organist, and he is the very best at that, but his jazz abilities are considerable and should not be overlooked. Two recordings from 1990 and 1991 (Headfirst Records) find him alternating between the electronics and organ jazz. *See* Hank Crawford. —*Bob Porter*

★ **At the Apollo** / i. 1963 / Collectables 5126

☆ **I've Got a Woman** / 1963 / Collectables 3062

○ **Movin' Upside the Blues** / i. Apr. 1982 / Jazz America 005
There are few better combinations for producing after-hours funk than organist Jimmy McGriff and guitarist Jimmy Ponder. Irrepressibly swinging McGriff is always in spitting distance of those down-home or South Side blues. Ponder compliments with a lightness that brings an appealing optimism to the realities.... If you haven't had a taste yet, start here; if you have had a taste and have room for more in your diet, this is a tasty dish. —*Bob Rusch, Cadence*

● **Starting Five, The** / 1986 / Milestone 9148
Best of the last decade for one of the better Hammond B-3 organists. —*Michael G. Nastos*

○ **State of the Art** / i. 198z / Milestone 9135
Organist Jimmy McGriff's *State of the Art* was, according to the liner notes, an attempt to "bring the sound of the organ group into today."... Actually, this was a fairly self-conscious effort to graft "new" sounds, meaning synthesizers, onto an "old" sound, meaning the organ trio. —*Neil Haverstick, Cadence*

○ **On the Blue Side** / i. May 1990 / Milestone 9177
An updated version of the vintage McGriff formula; bluesy, soulful organ fare with a balance struck between jazz sensibility and a funk-R&B groove. McGriff has wisely decided to play more organ and less synthesizer and has also mostly scrapped the quasi-fusion and gone back to pretty straight soul-jazz. —*Ron Wynn*

○ **Toast to Golden Classics** / Collectables 5125

Kalaparush Maurice McIntyre (Maurice McIntyre)

b. 1936
Sax / Early free, modern creative
A very creative, energetic, and forceful saxophonist, Kalaparusha Maurice McIntyre's solos mix the intensity of R&B with the abandon of free jazz and the earnestness of blues and gospel. His

comparative lack of albums have kept his profile lower than that of many Chicago counterparts, but McIntyre's every bit as compelling a player as any of the AACM members. A founding participant in 1965, McIntyre recorded with Muhal Richard Abrams, played with Jerome Cooper, and made his debut LP *Humility in the Light of the Creater* in 1969. He took the name Kalaparusha, moved to New York, and began playing with Warren Smith. He worked in both Chicago and New York during the '70s and '80s, playing with Cooper, Warren Smith, Sonelius Smith, and Wilber Morris. McIntyre recorded for Trio, Black Saint, Delmark, Cadence, and Karma. —*Ron Wynn and Michael G. Nastos*

● **Ram's Run** / i. 1981 / Cadence 1009
Ram's Run documented a concert at New York's Soundscape, capturing the spontaneity of a live performance at some cost to its recorded presence. Malachi Thompson's agile, flat-toned trumpeting complemented Maurice McIntyre's grainy tenor contortions, but Julius Hemphill's alto, distinguishable by its smoother contours, was largely overhadowed. Drummer J.R. Mitchell laid down an appropriately open-ended barrage, but the absence of a bass imparted a slightly arid quality to the set. —*Larry Birnbaum, Down Beat*

Ken McIntyre (Kenneth Arthur McIntyre)

b. Sep. 7, 1931, Boston, MA
Alto Sax, piano, instructor / Postbop, early free
Both a longtime instructor and capable soloist who recorded with Eric Dolphy, Ken McIntyre has combined playing and teaching for many years. McIntyre, whose style mixes hard bop and free influences, began playing alto at 19. He studied with Andrew McGhee, Gigi Gryce, and Charlie Mariano, attended Boston Conservatory and eventually earned an MA in composition. After more studies at Brandeis, McIntyre formed a band in Boston and made his debut recording for Prestige. After moving to New York he met Eric Dolphy in 1960. Following a New Jazz release, McIntyre decided to become a full-time professor. But he's since moved back and forth between the two worlds, displaying a multiinstrumental fluency that's seen him play flute and oboe on his recordings as well as alto. McIntyre's recorded with Bill Dixon, Thierry Bruneau, Cecil Taylor, and the Jazz Composers Guild Orchestra. He's done sessions for Steeplechase and Inner City among others. —*Ron Wynn and Michael G. Nastos*

★ **Looking Ahead** / Jun. 28, 1960 / New Jazz 252
Eric Dolphy (alto sax, bass clarinet, flute) had a featured role on Ken McIntyre's date *Looking Ahead* (6/28/60), which also included Walter Bishop (piano), Sam Jones (bass), and Art Taylor (drums). McIntyre's alto playing was marked by an original tone (sort of an unresolved thrust that seemed bent on trailing away into the outward bounds). —*Bob Rusch, Cadence*

Dave McKenna (David McKenna)

b. May 30, 1930, Woonsocket, RI
Piano / Stride, swing, bop
A veteran pianist, McKenna is especially appealing in solo format due to his ability to utilize both classic and contemporary keyboard styles. McKenna can play "stride," blues, or conventional bop and is known for brisk, romping solos that include aggressive passages, strong right hand rhythmic accompaniment, excellent statements, and quick, unpredictable harmonies. McKenna began working with Charlie Ventura in 1949 and spent 1950-1951 with Woody Herman. McKenna worked with Gene Krupa, Stan Getz, Zoot Sims, and Ventura during the '60s and started a string of club dates in Cape Cod in 1967. He returned to the touring circuit in the '70s and began a run on Concord in the '80s. Since then he's worked with small combos, done several solo releases, and appeared with the label's big Superband. During the early '70s, McKenna led a quartet with Zoot Sims, Major Holley, and Ray Mosca, whose 1974 album was reissued last year by the Chiaroscuro label. He's continued recording into the '90s.—*Ron Wynn*

○ **This is the Moment** / i. 1959 / Portrait 44091

○ **Dave McKenna Quartet Featuring Zoot Sims** / Oct. 1974 / Chiaroscuro 136
W/ Zoot Sims. Quartet. A 1990 reissue of a delightful date that's hotter than usual, thanks to Zoot Sims (ts) and Major Holley (b). —*Ron Wynn*

○ **Giant Strides** / May 1979 / Concord Jazz 99

There is a singlemindness to Dave McKenna's piano playing that is unique. The engine that powers it is his right hand, which flicks off long, assertive strings of eighth notes in an immaculate pulsation of even accents. The pattern is uninterrupted by arpeggios, frills, triplets, octaves, chords, silences, and dynamic variations. Tunes like "Dreams Come True" and "Lulu" from the *Giant Strides* solo album were typical. McKenna underpinned himself with a rolling 4/4 pulse for a chorus or two before falling suddenly into an almost cathartic two-beat stride gait. And if Charlie Parker boptized swing staples like "I Got Rhythm" and "Honeysuckle Rose," McKenna reversed the process just as effectively by recasting a bebop anthem like "Yardbird Suite" in a pure swing idiom. —*John McDonough, Down Beat*

○ **Left Handed Complement** / Dec. 1979 / Concord Jazz 4123
Look again at the title of pianist Dave McKenna's album. That's not *compliment*, but *complement*, as in McKenna's left-hand acts as an entire rhythm section or as in McKenna's left hand complements what the right is doing. . . . There are at least three, often four levels of activity going on at any given time—melody, right-hand comping, left-hand bass line, or left hand comping. Add to that fills and embellishments from either hand, and you've got incredible amounts of piano playing and musical thinking from two hands and one brain! —*Tom Bingham, Cadence*

★ **No Bass Hit** / 1979 / Concord Jazz 4097
The bassless trio with Scott Hamilton on tenor sax and Jake Hanna on drums was a nice idea. All selections are early period standards. McKenna is an undisputed master. —*Michael G. Nastos*

○ **Piano Mover** / Apr. 1980 / Concord Jazz 146
On this LP, the best of Dave McKenna's piano was heard on "Cottontail," where McKenna threw caution to the winds and ignored the presence of bassist Bob Maize while producing a roaring and furious solo. Elsewhere the presence of Maize's bass took a little something away from the McKenna style. "Nobody Else But Me" illustrated the results of putting a bass with McKenna, as Maize was attempting to stay out of McKenna's way, while McKenna was simplifying his left hand in order to give the bassist some room. —*Shirley Klett, Cadence*

○ **Dave McKenna Trio Plays Music of Harry Warren** / Aug. 1981 / Concord Jazz 174

○ **Celebration of Hoagy Carmichael** / May 1983 / Concord Jazz 227

○ **Keyman, The** / Aug. 1984 / Concord Jazz 261
This LP by Dave McKenna is recommended to all lovers of good piano. All musicians, or their producers, are hard put to find material that is new to their recorded works and provides variety and interest. This particular program was an excellent example of a successful solution to this problem. Where McKenna was concerned, no rhythm section assistance was needed; in fact, it would detract from the enjoyment. —*Shirley Klett, Cadence*

○ **Dancing in the Dark** / Aug. 1985 / Concord Jazz 4292

○ **My Friend the Piano** / Aug. 1986 / Concord Jazz 4313
Pianist Dave McKenna filled *My Friend the Piano* with constant surprises; rhythm, tempo, and key changes that somehow seemed logical after the fact. There was a slight emphasis on ballads, but one's attention rarely wandered, for the music, although tasteful, was never entirely predictable. —*Scott Yanow, Cadence*

○ **No More Ouzo for Puzo** / Jun. 1988 / Concord Jazz 4365
Recorded by a quartet with guitarist Gray Sargent. The title piece was written by McKenna; the rest are all standards treated with tender loving care. —*Michael G. Nastos*

○ **Live at Maybeck Recital Hall—Vol. 2** / Nov. 1989 / Concord Jazz 4410

○ **Shadows 'N Dreams** / i. 1990 / Concord Jazz 4467
As usual, McKenna's playing ranges from good to great. CD version has two bonus cuts. —*Ron Wynn*

John McLaughlin

b. Jan. 4, 1942, Yorkshire, England
Guitar, bandleader / Early jazz-rock, world fusion
By the time Miles Davis introduced John McLaughlin to American audiences, the guitarist was already dazzling the British jazz crowd with his fluid technique, suggesting a schooled jazz player, unafraid to reflect rock influences. McLaughlin

prominently guested on Miles's first two transitional fusion albums, *In a Silent Way* and *Bitches Brew* (ultimately others as well), while hooking up with Davis's drummer, Tony Williams, in the highly volatile Lifetime band.

McLaughlin soon put together his own group, Mahavishnu Orchestra, an exciting combination of rock and jazz players, one of the few groups to live up to the potential of the fusion revolution. Unfortunately, that group was to be short-lived, and in its place came a ponderous outfit with the same name, the main purpose of which seemed to be spreading McLaughlin's religious ideology. This group did not last long either. What came next was Shakti, in which McLaughlin teamed with musicians from India, and which featured a return to acoustic guitar. While Shakti lasted no longer than the previous outfits, McLaughlin would largely concentrate on the acoustic from this time on. Although McLaughlin's popularity has never regained the stature he enjoyed with the original Mahavishnu Orchestra, he has continued to record many fine albums, and his trio efforts with Trilock Gurtu rank among the highlights of his career. —*Steve Aldrich*

★ **Extrapolation** / Jan. 18, 1969 / Polydor 841598
The success of this album was very hard to separate into nice neat clichéed boxes, but a good deal of it had to do with the extraordinary talents of John Surman. Surman played baritone and soprano sax on this recording, but it was more than apparent that baritone was his horn. He appeared to have rejected the premise that the baritone is an unwieldy instrument and just played it however he wanted. His control, from the conventional range of the horn to the several false octaves, was all done with apparent ease. And he swung like hell. Surman, John McLaughlin (guitar), Brian Odges (bass), and Tony Oxley (percussion) succeeded in completely moulding all their independent talents into one large collective one. —*Bill Smith, Coda*

☆ **Devotion** / 1970 / Restless 72656
John McLaughlin's Devotion may very well have been to Jimi Hendrix on this reissue of a Douglas recording of 1970. Along with the Band of Gypsies rhythm section (Billy Cox, bass; Buddy Miles, drums), Larry Young (organ) was added. McLaughlin was at his rawest, blues-rock-oriented state, much different from his work on, say, *My Goals Beyond*, the Mahavishnu Orchestra, or much later Shakti. The music was more reminiscent of his work with Tony Williams's Lifetime. It had a real '60s psychedelic garage band feel to it and put McLaughlin into perspective in terms of his gravitation to more refined modal reflections of North and South Indian classical music. —*Brian Auerbach, Cadence*

★ **My Goals Beyond** / 1970 / Rykodisc 10051
A reissue of an original Douglas/CBS album. A landmark recording. One side is solo guitar, the other is the first Mahavishnu Orchestra. A must-buy. —*Michael G. Nastos*

● **Shakti with John McLaughlin** / Jul. 5, 1975 / CBS 46868

○ **Passion, Grace and Fire** / 1983 / CBS 38645
There's a lot to be said for athletic muscle, and on *Passion, Grace & Fire*, guitarists John McLaughlin, Paco De Lucia, and Al Di Meola flexed a lot of it. Every solo had an edge of danger here, a sense that the artist was putting himself on the line. And they communicated that danger with a reckless passion, carrying you to the edge with them. —*John Diliberto, Down Beat*

Live at the Royal Festival Hall / i. Nov. 27, 1989 / JMT 834436
Trio recording with Kai Eckhart (b) and Trilok Gurtu (per). His best of the last decade. —*Michael G. Nastos*

○ **Jazz—Vol. 2** / i. 1991 / Rhino 270722

Jackie McLean (John Lenwood McLean, Jr.)

b. May 17, 1932, New York, NY
Alto sax / Hard bop
A remarkably intense and furious alto saxophonist, Jackie McLean's albums in the '50s and '60s were hard bop classics. A biting player greatly influenced by both Charlie Parker and Ornette Coleman, McLean studied briefly with Foots Thomas and Cecil Scott before he began working with Sonny Rollins in the late '40s. McLean made his recording debut with Miles Davis in the early '50s and played with Paul Bley, George Wallington, and Charles Mingus later in the decade. Later came a three-year stint with Art Blakey's Jazz Messengers before McLean began heading a quintet in 1958. Since that time, he's made many brillant

recordings for Prestige, Status, New Jazz, Blue Note, Steeplechase, RCA, East Wind/Inner City, Antilles, and Verve. McLean also became active in jazz education. He eventually became head of the music department at the University of Hartford. His son Rene's also a fine saxophonist and a bandleader, and the two have recorded and played together frequently. —*Ron Wynn*

● **Complete Blue Note 1964-1966** / Mosaic
Alto saxophonist Jackie McLean was among hard bop's most invigorating, challenging players during the '60s. He crafted an impressive and distinctive sound with a bluesy underpinning and fervor that was also harmonically and melodically challenging. McLean's mid-'60s Blue Note albums embraced both inside and outside elements, with selections that ranged from covers of classic soul jazz tunes like "Dat Dere" to blistering originals. This four-disc (six-LP) Mosaic collection covers sessions originally issued on McLean albums *It's Time, Right Now, Action, Jackknife,* and *Consequences*. It features him heading either quintets or quartets and working in alternating configurations with various bands. The lineups include trumpeters Charles Tolliver or Lee Morgan; pianists Harold Mabern, Herbie Hancock, or Larry Willis; bassists Cecil McBee, Bob Cranshaw, Don Moore, Larry Ridley, or Herbie Lewis; drummers Billy Higgins, Roy Haynes, Clifford Jarvis, or Jack DeJohnette; and vibist Bobby Hutcherson. The stylistic contrasts and shifts in direction among the various units proves quite instructive. Tolliver's angular, somber thrusts were effective, but Morgan's fiery, frequently spectacular bursts were magnificent. Willis displayed more versatility and flair on these tracks than on many sessions that followed them; while DeJohnette was already an emerging star; and Higgins, McBee, Haynes, and Mabern were crafty, experienced veterans who smoothly followed McLean's biting forays. The sound, annotation, and discographical information is first-rate as Mosaic continues its tradition of brilliant remastering and packaging. —*Ron Wynn*

○ **Jackie McLean Quintet, The** / i. 1956 / Jubilee 1064

Jackie's Pal / Aug. 31, 1956 / Original Jazz Classics 1714
Here was Bill Hardman, who he introduced into a quintet with Mal Waldron (piano), Paul Chambers (bass), and Philly Joe Jones (drums). Hardman's hot breaking tone sounds a bit less forceful than on his (soon-to-be) later work with the Messengers, but it was already identifiable. . . . Chambers has some exciting bowed spots, Mal Waldron was a bit bland, and while Jones' drumming fills the role, it missed the push Art Taylor's drumming seemed to invite so often with McLean. So, not as I might have planned it, but I wouldn't change a note on this program, which has aged so well. —*Bob Rusch, Cadence*

★ **Alto Madness** / i. May 3, 1957 / Prestige 1733
All of this material except "Bird Feathers" was originally issued on Prestige and later reissued on Status. For the first time, the entire session was available on one LP. . . . The music is what you would expect from the two altoists, since Bird (Charlie Parker) had only been dead a couple of years. The performances were rather raw, using Bird's many inflections, licks, and other creations, which were being used by almost everybody. —*Jerry L. Atkins, Cadence*

○ **Jackie's Bag** / Jan. 18, 1959-Sep. 1960 / Blue Note 46142

★ **Fickle Sonance, A** / Oct. 26, 1961 / Blue Note 84089
A remarkable merger of new-thing, avant-garde leanings and hard-bop fluidity and feelings. —*Ron Wynn*

○ **It's Time** / Aug. 5, 1964 / Blue Note 4179

○ **Jacknife** / Apr. 12, 1966 / Blue Note 457
A twofer w/ Lee Morgan (tpt), Charles Tolliver (tpt), Larry Willis (p), and Jack DeJohnette (d). Potent. —*Michael G. Nastos*

★ **New and Old Gospel** / Mar. 24, 1967 / Blue Note 84262

○ **Demon's Dance** / Dec. 22, 1967 / Blue Note 84345

★ **Meeting, The** / Jul. 20+23, 1973 / Steeple Chase 31006
This set with tenor saxophonist Dexter Gordon and alto saxophonist Jackie McLean was less a "meeting" than a date on which both appeared and soloed. There was little sign of having worked anything out in advance. . . . This was generally good Gordon, but not much of a meeting. —*Jerry De Muth, Cadence*

☆ **Source, The** / i. Jul. 20+23, 1973 / Steeple Chase
The feeling that alto saxophonist Jackie McLean had for tenor saxophonist Dexter Gordon was warmly stated in McLean's closing remarks on this, the second volume of the McLean-Gordon

Montmarte recordings (Vol. 1 was *The Meeting*). What was captured on this recording is the essence of jazz: the instantaneous creation of moving and stimulating music. You could hear ideas being developed, cast off, and new ones forming. —*Carl Brauer, Cadence*

☆ **New Wine, Old Bottles** / Apr. 6-07, 1978 / Inner City 6029
A superb quartet date w/ Hank Jones (p), Ron Carter (b), and Tony Williams (d). —*Ron Wynn*

Rene McLean

b. 1946
Sax and flute / Hard bop, world fusion
Multisaxophonist Rene McLean's established his own legacy, despite being the son of the great Jackie McLean. He's played African, Afro-Latin, and Caribbean music as well as jazz, and gotten the benefit of private studies with Sonny Rollins as well as his father. McLean once played baritone and alto sax with Tito Puente and also worked with Sam Rivers, Lionel Hampton, and Doug Carn. He co-led the Cosmic Brotherhood with his father, played with Tyrone Washington and in the Woody Shaw-Louis Hayes quintet, and has headed his own bands. He's recorded as a leader for Steeplechase and Triloka. —*Ron Wynn and Michael G. Nastos*

★ **Watch Out** / Jul. 9, 1975 / Inner City 2037
Jackie McLean's then 30-year-old son, appeared as a leader himself on *Watch Out* with a hard driving, Art Blakeyesque sextet. . . . Despite the solid support and big sound, it was McLean's show all the way. He is a forceful, mature instrumentalist of excellent taste and convincing expressive range on the three upper-register saxes and flute. —*Charles Mitchell, Down Beat*

Marian McPartland (Marian Margaret McPartland)

b. Mar. 20, 1920, Windsor, England
Piano / Swing, bop
Few have combined performing, writing, and broadcasting more effectively than Marian McPartland, who has been an active pianist since the '40s. She came to America from England in 1946, one year after marrying Jimmy McPartland, a trumpeter in the classic Chicago vein. The two had met in Belgium in 1944 and played for Eisenhower in 1946. McPartland formed her own trio in 1959 and was also a house pianist at several clubs in the '50s and '60s. She formed her own label in 1969 and made a triumphant return to active club and concert work in the '70s. She began her Peabody-award-winning show "Piano Jazz" in 1979. Since then she has made extensive radio and television appearances, served on jazz boards, written critically praised essays, and made some outstanding albums. —*Ron Wynn*

○ **Great Britain's Marian McPartland / George Shearing** / Dec. 22, 1952 / Savoy 12016

○ **Solo Concert at Haverford** / Apr. 12, 1974 / Halcyon 111
Wide in stylistic scope, her program began with a trenchant, tone-setting blues, running a conventional pattern with most unconventional chord substitutions, melodic digressions of singular eloquence, strong bass lines, and smoothly flowing rhythm shifts. On ballads such as "Send in the Clowns" and "Killing Me Softly with His Song," McPartland let her melodies stand with little embellishment; she preferred instead to employ advanced chord support and unexpected turns of rhythm. Yet she didn't come off as fickle; each mood and tempo was thoroughly established before new changes set in. —*Charles Mitchell, Down Beat*

○ **Concert in Argentina** / Nov. 1974 / Jazz Alliance 10008
This document of a 1974 concert in Buenos Aires showcases four wonderfully personable piano stylists in solo recital. Marian McPartland's portion of the show is highlighted by a reverent, if reserved, medley of Ellingtonia, though she does pick up steam and take a few more chances on "It Don't Mean a Thing." —*Bill Milkowski, Down Beat*

○ **Willow Creek and Other Ballads** / Jan. 1985 / Concord Jazz 4272
The exemplary solo playing on this album helped embellish the new-star status won through her "Piano Jazz" series on National Public Radio. —*Ron Wynn*

★ **Marian Mcpartland Plays the Benny Carter Songbook** / i. Oct. 1990 / Concord Jazz 4412

This is McPartland's finest work in quite some time and includes wonderful interpretations of great compositions by Benny Carter—a spry, exciting alto soloist, in his eighth decade as a player! CD has two bonus cuts. Good support comes from John Clayton and Harold Jones. —*Ron Wynn*

Charles McPherson

b. Jul. 24, 1939, Joplin, MO
Alto sax, tenor sax / Bop, hard bop
Alto saxophonist Charles McPherson's blend of lyricism and spirit reflects his prime influences, Johnny Hodges and Charlie Parker. An outstanding alto player, he's also capable on tenor and is a fine bop soloist. His professional career began at 17 in Detroit with such players as Barry Harris and Lonnie Hillyer. He moved to New York in 1959 and periodically worked with Charles Mingus workshop editions until 1974, appearing on some seminal Mingus recordings and in the '68 documentary film "Mingus." McPherson recorded as a leader for Mainstream, Discovery, and Xanadu and also played with the Uptown Express in the '80s. His son Chuck was among the Uptown Express's members, along with trumpeter Tom Harrell. —*Ron Wynn and Michael G. Nastos*

○ **Be-Bop Revisited** / Nov. 20, 1964 / Prestige 710
This is one of his first strong dates as a leader outside the Charles Mingus Jazz Workshop fold. Includes fine contributions from Barry Harris on piano and Carmell Jones on trumpet. —*Ron Wynn*

○ **Charles McPherson Quintet Live!, The** / Oct. 13, 1966 / Original Jazz Classics 1804
Some frenetic trumpet solos from Lonnie Hillyer, recorded live at the immortal Five Spot. —*Ron Wynn*

○ **Live in Tokyo** / Apr. 14, 1976 / Xanadu
"Tokyo Blues" was a perfunctory blues with everyone (pianist Barry Harris, bassist Sam Jones, drummer Leroy Williams) feeling things out. McPherson was the lone soloist on "East of the Sun," and now he was extending himself. When he let loose on "Desafinado," all the cobwebs had been totally eradicated. From there on the music sparkled. —*Carl Brauer, Cadence*

★ **Free Bop!** / Oct. 23, 1978 / Xanadu
There were some good moments, especially Charles McPherson's tenor on "Chuck-A Luck" and "Estrellita." Charles McPherson Jr. (drums) played extremely well, but he and Kevin Jones (percussion) put forth an awfully busy backing. . . . The introduction to guitarist Peter Sprague and McPherson's good tenor were the highlights. —*Jerry Atkins, Cadence*

Carmen McRae

b. Apr. 8, 1920, New York NY
Vocals / Ballads & blues
Many consider Camen McRae the greatest pure jazz vocalist currently active. She has remarkable interpretive ability, a striking delivery, and the kind of timing and musicality one would expect from a former pianist. McRae wrote the song "Dream of Life" for Billie Holiday when she was 16. She worked with Benny Carter's band in 1944 and also had a brief period with Count Basie. She sang for a year with Mercer Ellington's band in 1946-1947 as Carmen Clarke, while she was married briefly to drummer Kenny Clarke. After a stint as an intermission pianist and singer at various clubs in the early '50s, McRae began making records in the mid-'50s. She had two songs hit the pop charts in 1956 and 1957 and became internationally known through tours and festival appearances as well as several acclaimed records. Her trio has had such famous pianists as Ray Bryant, Norman Simmons, and Duke Pearson. Her 1990 album *Carmen Sings Monk*, an incredible recasting of Monk songs into amazing lyric performances, was nominated but failed to win a Grammy. —*Ron Wynn*

○ **Lover Man** / 1962 / Columbia 8530

★ **Great American Songbook, The** / i. Oct. 1972 / Atlantic 904
A wonderful two-disc set, with McRae showing her complete music vocabulary and interpretive talents. —*Ron Wynn*

○ **Greatest of Carmen McRae, The** / i. Oct. 1977 / MCA 24111
A misnomer, but a decent attempt at presenting '60s and '70s Carmen McRae material. It's is impossible to cover such a varied career in one record, and this one is even more limited since it doesn't extend to her formative years in the '50s. —*Ron Wynn*

★ **You're Lookin' at Me (A Collection of Nat King Cole Songs)** / Nov. 1983 / Concord Jazz 4235
This album had a subtitle—*A Collection of Nat King Cole Songs*—and Carmen McRae added John Collins (guitar) to her regular supporting trio to enhance the tribute to Cole. Collins was Nat Cole's regular guitarist from 1951 on. —*Shirley Klett, Cadence*

● **Carmen Sings Monk** / Jan. 30, 1988-Feb. 1, 1988 / Novus 3086

Jay McShann (James Columbus McShann)

b. Jan. 12, 1916, Muskogee, OK
Piano / Boogie-woogie, swing, big band, blues & jazz
Pianist Jay McShann is one of the great personalities of jazz and the embodiment of the Kansas City style of jazz and blues. He came to prominence in the late '30s with the last of the Kansas City big bands. His sidemen included alto saxophonist Charlie Parker, bassist Gene Ramey, drummer Gus Johnson, and vocalist Walter Brown. His Decca recordings (1941-1943) show the excellence of the band, but the emphasis on blues material probably gives less than a true picture of the band's overall abilities. The big band broke up in 1944, and McShann spent the rest of the decade in Los Angeles leading small blues-based combos and recording for Philo/Alladin, Mercury, Capitol, and DownBeat/Swingtime, among others. Sadly, except for the latter group on a Black Lion album, none of McShann's Los Angeles recordings have been properly collected. He returned to Kansas City in 1950 and has been based there since. He recorded for Vee Jay (1955-1956) and backed Priscilla Bowman on her big hit, "Hands Off," for that label. His return to records in 1966 resulted in an excellent Capitol album *McShann's Piano*, and rekindled interest in his work at home and, especially, in Europe, where he quickly became a star touring attraction. He has many European recordings, notably for French Black & Blue, Danish Storyville, and English JSP. His recordings for the Canadian Sackville label have presented him in solo and duo settings as well as a more customary band setting. This intermittent association began in 1971 and continued through the '80s. American albums of special interest are *Last of the Blue Devils* (Atlantic) and *Goin' to Kansas City* (Master Jazz). McShann often appears in all-star groups and has also become a frequent and engaging vocalist over the past 25 years. *Paris All-Star Blues* (Music Masters) finds him at the helm of a big band, revisiting much of his old book to good effect. —*Bob Porter*

★ **Early Bird—Charley Parker, The** / Nov. 30, 1940-Mar. 27, 1944 / Spotlite 120
1940-1943 airchecks. W/ Charley Parker (as), Paul Quinichette, and Gus Johnson. —*Michael Erlewine*

○ **Jazz Heritage—Early Bird Charlie Parker (1941-1943)** / 1941-1943 / MCA 1338
Until the '92 release of another, better-prepared reissue package, this single album reissue was the only domestic Jay McShann covering this vital early-'40s period in print. As such, if you can't find or don't want the more recent release, it's worth having. It was inexpensive and reasonably comprehensive for the times, though it's not as well engineered as the current material. —*Ron Wynn*

○ **Confessin' the Blues** / Mar. 28, 1969 / Classic Jazz 128
Confessin' the Blues, recorded in 1971 and first issued on the European Black and Blue label, paired McShann with a small jump band containing two adequate accompanists and an outstanding one, T-Bone Walker. "Our Kinda Blues" was a slow-bounce kicker with laidback triples and some fresh guitar-piano interplay. In the teasing "Stompin' in K.C.," a slow blues, interlacing piano treble figures gave way to tight, taut runs and block chords e la Red Garland, and there was a snappy "After Hours" with bouncing chordal punctuation. —*Jon Balleras, Down Beat*

○ **Big Apple Bash, The** / Aug. 3-10, 1971 / New World 358
Most of this all-star get-together was more mainstream oriented than the opener ("Crazy Legs and Friday Strut"). Still, this was primarily the jazz Jay McShann rather than the blues McShann, though the latter did get his licks in. —*Tom Bingham, Cadence*

○ **Man from Muskogee** / Jun. 24, 1972 / Sackville S3005
One of McShann's finest recordings. W/ Claude Williams (violin). —*Michael Erlewine*

○ **Crazy Legs and Friday Strut** / Jul. 1, 1976 / Sackville 3001

On this recording, pianist Jay McShann's playing was closer in many ways to Earl Hines and Teddy Wilson than to what I know as McShann. McShann was even a little Erroll Garnerish on "Crazylegs," with touches of Randy Weston and Mal Waldron. Certainly McShann's work on "Crazylegs" will fascinate his fans. —*Bob Rusch, Cadence*

○ **Paris All-Star Blues—A Tribute** / i. 1979 / Music Masters 5052
A '91 tribute album (recorded in '89) to Charlie Parker by a great cast of veteran and recent jazz musicians, under the leadership of pianist Jay McShann, who conducted the band that gave Parker his start. The lineup runs from Benny Carter, Al Grey, and James Moody to Terence Blanchard. —*Ron Wynn, AMG*

○ **Swingmatism** / Oct. 1982 / Sackville 3046

Pat Metheny (Patrick Bruce Metheny)

b. Aug. 2, 1954, Lees Summit, MO
Guitar / Early jazz-rock, modern creative
Only a few guitarists in every generation achieve the kind of popular and artistic success that Pat has seen. He was an impressive virtuoso at an early age, and formed a beneficial early association with vibraphone innovator Gary Burton. Metheny studied and taught at Berkelee College of Music and University of Miami. He has had many successful albums from the beginning. He brings a bit of the mystique and allure of the rock star to his image, but his popularity centers on his compelling and polished performance style. Later collaborations, such as *Song X* (with Ornette Coleman) and *80/81* (with Charlie Haden and others), show a highly accomplished and versatile jazz artist. Though he has great instrumental technique and speed, he has developed a very accessible style, with great lyrical ability and a fine melodic sense, working for simplicity rather than flash. He was an early and tasteful explorer of electronic effects, such as chorus boxes, and one of the first to use guitar synthesizer effectively. He has also written music for films. Some later albums have tended toward a rather ethereal sort of Latin-influenced mood music. —*David Nelson McCarthy*

Bright Size Life / Dec. 1975 / ECM 827133
First album, with Jaco Pastorius (b) and Bob Moses (d). Excellent original material. —*Michael G. Nastos*

★ **Pat Metheny Group** / Jan. 1978 / ECM 825593
Pat Metheny played a 12-string and 6-string guitar during this period and combined with what was then his regular band; Lyle Mays (on piano, autoharp, and Oberheim Synthesizer; Mark Egan, bass; and Dan Gottlieb, drums. Metheny's guitars and the synthesizer gave this music a decidedly electric feel. —*Spencer R. Weston, Cadence*

American Garage / Jun. 1979 / ECM 827134
This is the session that marked Metheny's coming of age; better songs, more intense playing, and more variety in arrangements. —*Ron Wynn*

● **1980-1981** / May 1980-1981 / ECM 843169
The album that showed jazz purists Metheny's guitar chops extended beyond fusion rock. Extensive crisp performances. The CD issue contains two bonus cuts. —*Ron Wynn*

○ **Rejoicing** / Nov. 29-30, 1983 / ECM 817795
Rejoicing showed the gifted guitarist playing with a scope and maturity only hinted at on *Bright Size Life*. Backed by the sublime accompaniment of bassist Charlie Haden and drummer Billy Higgins, kindred spirits from their days together in the revolutionary Ornette Coleman Quartet of the late '50s, Metheny seemed especially inspired on this outing. Throughout side one the guitarist's playing was imbued with the spirit of Wes Montgomery and Jim Hall. . . . Side two was a whole other story. After a mournful acoustic guitar ballad, Metheny's "Story from a Stranger," he pulled out the high-technology weapons and launched into a frenzied ten-minute manifesto for the guitar synthesizer. This triumphant freak-out session entitled "The Calling," was as daring and full of tension as anything he'd recorded—an extension of his dissonant excursions on the title cut from *Offramp*. —*Bill Milkowski, Down Beat*

★ **Song X** / Dec. 1985 / David Geffen Co. 24096
W/ Ornette Coleman. Metheny pays tribute to a surprising influence, teaming with Ornette Coleman in a collaboration that shocked everyone with its musical effectiveness. —*Ron Wynn*

☆ **Question and Answer** / Dec. 1989 / David Geffen Co. 24293

A great trio. Metheny stretches out. This is highly recommended. —*Michael G. Nastos*

Glenn Miller

b. 1904, **d.** 1944
Swing, big band
Bandleader, trombone. Glenn Miller was the most popular bandleader of the last part of the swing era, starting in 1939 with "In the Mood" and other hits. He led a military band during the war and was lost over the English Channel on his way to Paris. More biographical details are included in the reviews below. —*William Ruhlman*

Legendary Performer / 1938 / RCA
The 22 live performances found here, taken from 1939-1942 airchecks, demonstrate that, in performance, the Miller band's notorius precision could give way (slightly) to electric excitement. If any demonstration were needed for the band's success, these tracks provide it.—*William Ruhlman*

Army Air Force Band 1943-1944 / 1943 / RCA
'40s recordings. -Ron Wynn

Major Glenn Miller. . . . / 1943 / Bluebird
Recorded 1943-1944. W/The Army Air Force Band. At what turned out to be the end of his career, Glenn Miller led a very big band, playing martial arrangements of often military-oriented material at bond rallies around the country. This collection preserves the gaudy, uplifting style of Miller's last music —*William Ruhlman*

○ **Moonlight Serenade & Other Hits** / RCA
1990 release of familiar items. —*Ron Wynn*

○ **Pure Gold** / RCA
1988 reissue of familiar recordings. —*Ron Wynn*

○ **Chatanooga Choo Choo - #1 Hits** / RCA
1991 release that spotlights some of his biggest songs. —*Ron Wynn*

Collectors Choice-Vintage Glen / CBS
An attempt to put his career in perspective. —*Ron Wynn*

Complete Glenn Miller - Vols. 1-13 / RCA
The 13-disc boxed set. —*Ron Wynn*

Memorial 1944-1969 / RCA
Two-record set from '80s. —*Ron Wynn*

★ **Popular Recordings** / RCA
Of the many compilations of Glenn Miller hits, this three-disc set strikes the best balance between comprehensiveness and economy. More casual listeners might want to try Pure Gold, while true scholars will have to have the Complete Glenn Miller, but this 60-track collection contains the best of the most popular bandleader of the last part of the swing era. —*William Ruhlman*

Mulgrew Miller

b. Aug. 13, 1955, Greenwood, MS
Piano / Postbop, neo-bop
Arguably the most prolific and accomplished pianist among the contemporary generation, Miller is an outstanding soloist, especially in the trio setting, and he has been able to adapt his style to any context from big band to solo to sextet or quintet. After attending Memphis State University and moonlighting in Memphis clubs during the '70s, Miller worked with Johnny Griffin and Woody Shaw. He spent three years with Mercer Ellington and another with Betty Carter. After working with Blakey's Messengers in the early '80s, Miller recorded with the Terence Blanchard-Donald Harrison group and has been a leader since the mid-'80s. He continues to work with numerous other groups, notably Tony Williams's. —*Ron Wynn*

★ **Work** / Apr. 1986 / Landmark 1511
Memphis pianist Miller with trio (Teri Lyne Carrington on drums). Excellent. —*Michael G. Nastos*

○ **Time and Again** / i. 1992 / Landmark 1532
A recent release by pianist Mulgrew Miller, this time featuring him in a trio format playing primarily his own compositions from '91. He's backed by bassist Peter Washington and drummer Tony Reedus, and this constitutes his most intimate, distinctive set as a leader. —*Ron Wynn*

○ **Landmarks** / i. Feb. 12, 1992 / Landmark 1311

○ **Trio Transition** / DIW 808

Charles Mingus (Charles Mingus, Jr.)

b. Apr. 22, 1922, Nogales, AZ, **d.** Jan. 5, 1979, Cuernavaca, MX
Bass, composer, bandleader, piano / Bop, hard bop, postbop, early free, progressive big band
Charles Mingus was arguably the greatest bass player in the history of jazz, both as a virtuoso and as an innovator. He brought the bass from primarily a rhythm instrument to the forefront as a melodic instrument, not only for himself but for all bass players to follow. He looms equally large as a composer, combining composition and improvisation seamlessly to achieve a seminal new sound. He also strongly supports the European perception of jazz as modern classical music. Mingus had a reputation as a stern and even unreasonable leader, demanding that his musicians pay total attention to the music they were playing and that they sound "like themselves." Yet he consistently elicits performances from his musicians that surpass any of their efforts elsewhere.

Almost any Mingus album is instantly recognizable as his, even if he is not himself playing at the time. This is not background music, and his music is not relaxing but energizing and exciting. If you would like to glimpse the essentially kind, humorous, and big presence of Mingus, both the film *Mingus 1968* and his autobiography, *Beneath the Underdog*, are highly recommended.

There are many ways to categorize Mingus's music. A simple but useful way is to separate it into four categories: His formative years—anything up to *Pithecanthropus Erectus*; his standards—original studio versions of his live-performance repertoire; his live performance recordings; and his compositions—usually one-time performances of a Mingus composition and arrangement.

Any Mingus album is worth owning. If you have never listened to Mingus, I would recommend, as a great starting point, *Mingus at Antibes* (live performance). This is Mingus with perhaps his strongest group, at the height of his powers, and is certainly some of the hottest live jazz ever recorded. —*Michael Katz*

Thirteen Pictures / i. 1952-1977 / Atlantic/Rhino 271402
Even on a loving two-disc anthology, it's impossible to accurately or fully convey the accomplishments of Charles Mingus, arguably jazz's finest modern bassist-composer. *Thirteen Pictures* tries to outline his career achievements by spotlighting his most famous works and showcasing his abilities. But the set does it in a curious manner; the sequencing is particularly odd, with songs hopping all over the place from decade to decade and the older things coming near the end rather than the beginning. They also jump from intricate suites with huge groups to solo works to combo dates. Still, there are many essential Mingus pieces here, from the sprawling "Cumbia & Jazz Fusion" to seminal "Goodbye Pork Pie Hat," "Pithecanthropus Erectus," and "Better Git It in Your Soul." The absence of "Fables of Faubus" is puzzling, and the inclusion of only one track featuring Eric Dolphy bizarre, but for the Mingus newcomer to whom this set was obviously directed, it fulfills its basic goal of introducing a genius's work. —*Ron Wynn, AMG*

○ **Mingus at the Bohemia** / Dec. 23, 1955 / Debut 045
This date came from a particularly fertile period for Mingus (the whole session was on a previous Prestige twofer set). The music here was not as dynamic as the soon-to-come Atlantic recordings, but Eddie Bert (trombone) and George Barrow (tenor sax) were more pastel players and closer to some of the chamber jazz that seemed to interest Mingus during the period just prior to this. This was adventuresome music, and Mingus was heard to good advantage. —*Bob Rusch, Cadence*

○ **Plus Max Roach** / Dec. 23, 1955 / Fantasy 440
The Mingus-Roach-Mal Waldron dialogs overcome the ordinary stylings of Eddie Bert and George Barrow. —*Ron Wynn*

○ **Charles Mingus** / Dec. 23, 1955 / Prestige 24010

● **Pithecanthropus Erectus** / Jan. 30, 1956 / Atlantic 8809
The year was 1956 and Dwight Eisenhower *was* president, but Mingus, like the musical revolutionary and visionary he was, was forecasting—still reachin', still teachin'. This is music that gets in yo' soul. This is a historic recording; an essential! —*Bob Rusch, Cadence*

☆ **Clown, The** / Feb. 13, 1957 / Atlantic 90142

A wonderful date that has bitter, reflective, and poignant Mingus compositions. The album marked the first appearance on vinyl of trombonist Jimmy Knepper. —*Ron Wynn*

★ **New Tijuana Moods** / Jul. 18, 1957-Aug. 6, 1957 / Bluebird 5644
Thanks to RCA's revitalized Bluebird reissue program, not only is the *Tijuana Moods* album available again, but also it is accompanied by a second LP of alternate takes. More accurately, producer Ed Michel has used base takes to carry previously unissued solos. When the solos are of the quality of those recorded in two eventual days by Clarence Shaw (trumpet), Shafi Hadi (alto sax), Jimmy Knepper (trombone), Bill Triglia (piano), and Charles Mingus (bass), there is reason to celebrate.... The combination of raw rhythmic passion and lyrical improvisation was all but unequaled in the work of Mingus or anyone else. He called it "the best record I ever made." ... This was amazing music in every respect. —*Doug Ramsey, Jazz Times*

○ **East Coasting** / Aug. 6, 1957 / BCP 6019
Same group as in *Tijuana Moods*. Really a Clarence Shaw session. Cool jazz that sounds like Miles Davis in spots. Easy listening. With Bill Evans (p). —*Michael Katz*

● **Complete 1959 CBS Charles Mingus Sessions** / i. 1959 / Mosaic 143
Mingus assembled powerhouse bands for the Columbia sessions, but in true clueless fashion the label never issued the music in the manner his bands recorded it. They released *Mingus Ah Um* in 1959, *Mingus Dynasty* in 1960, then *Better Get It in Your Soul* as a double album and *Nostalgia In Times Square* as a reissued special, never bothering to explain what they were doing. Mosaic has finally issued the music the right way on this wonderful four-album (no CDs) boxed set, intact and in chronological order.

This set is exquisitely mastered, and Mingus biographer Brian Priestly provides background and historical information, while Sy Johnson gives a musical analysis of the sessions. The original liner notes from *Mingus Ah Um* by Diane Dorr-Dorynek and *Mingus Dynasty* by Mingus himself are included. Grab this quickly; there is no telling how long Columbia will let Mosaic retain the license once they realize how dumb they were not to issue this boxed set from the start. —*Ron Wynn*

☆ **Blues and Roots** / Feb. 4, 1959 / Atlantic 1305
A great Mingus album of gospel church music. Exciting, high-energy music. —*Michael Katz*

☆ **Mingus Ah Um** / May 5, 1959 / Columbia 40648
Many think this is Mingus's best studio album. All the selections are top notch: there are no letdowns on this album. Similar in feel to *Blues and Roots*, but more fully realized. If you could have only two Mingus albums, this and *Mingus at Antibes* would be the two. —*Michael Katz*

★ **Mingus at Antibes** / Jul. 13, 1960 / Atlantic 90532
This never-before-heard two-record set of performances was recorded live at the Antibes Jazz Festival on July 13, 1960, a scant three months before the classic Candid session *Charles Mingus Presents Charles Mingus*, which utilized the same personnel (minus saxophonist Booker Ervin and pianist Bud Powell of course). Two works from that date, "What Love" and "Folk Forms I," appear in still-formulating arrangements here, though trumpeter Ted Curson's long, tumbling, rhapsodically reflective solo in the former was easily one of the concert's high points. And while any chance to hear Mingus and Eric Dolphy in collaboration was one to be cherished, the presence of Booker Ervin's booting Texas tenor attack seemed to inspire Dolphy even more. —*Art Lange, Down Beat*

★ **Complete Candid Recordings** / Oct. 20, 1960-Nov. 11, 1960 / Mosaic 111
Studio sessions with a particularly strong group that had been playing at the same club together for a year. Mingus at his most avant-garde. Beautiful solo work by all throughout. Many Mingus standards. Incredible packaging (always the case with Mosaic). Limited edition, so *buy it while you can!* —*Michael Katz*

Charles Mingus Presents Charles Mingus / Oct. 20, 1960 / Candid 79005
A roaring, magnificent session from '60 with bass legend Charles Mingus heading a band that included Booker Ervin and Eric Dolphy playing complex, intricately layered, yet also soulful and animated compositions. This was reissued on vinyl in the '70s and then issued on CD in '90. —*Ron Wynn, AMG*

○ **Reincarnation of a Lovebird** / Oct. 31, 1960-Nov. 27, 1960 / Candid 79026
A vastly different counterpoint was happening in the music of Charles Mingus in 1960, as demonstrated by *Reincarnation of a Lovebird*, which contains four reissued performances and one previously undiscovered alternate take. It shows the stylistic counterpoint of Swing era veterans Roy Eldridge and Jo Jones, boppers Jimmy Knepper and Tommy Flanagan, and bop extenders Eric Dolphy and Mingus and the blues-rooted, Ellingtonlike, jazzed orchestral development of the title cut and "Bugs." —*Owen Cordle, Jazz Times*

☆ **Oh Yeah** / Nov. 6, 1961 / Atlantic 90667
This album has a bluesy, New Orleans feel. Mingus plays piano and sings (no bass). Roland Kirk is featured on the siren and other instruments. A spirited, fun album. Very droll. There is a bonus 25-minute interview of Mingus by Nesuhi Ertegun that makes this a must-have for the Mingus fan. —*Michael Katz*

○ **Money Jungle** / i. 1962 / United Artists 15017

Mingus Plays Piano / i. 1963 / Mobile Fidelity 783
Mingus's range, ideas, touch, and technique are sonically outlined to their ultimate glory. — *Ron Wynn, Rock & Roll Disc.*

☆ **Black Saint and the Sinner Lady** / Jan. 20, 1963 / MCA 5649
A remarkable work that showcases both Mingus the composer and Mingus the bandleader. A six-piece suite, the session showed the influence and impact of Ellington on Mingus as an arranger. —*Ron Wynn*

☆ **Mingus, Mingus, Mingus** / Jan. 1963-Sep. 20, 1963 / MCA 39119
Somewhat similar in feel to "Black Saint and the Sinner Lady". More driving and spontaneous sounding, without the pervading sound of Charles Mariano's sax. A solid album, worth owning. —*Michael Katz*

○ **Mingus in Europe—Vol. 2** / Apr. 26, 1964 / Enja 3077

○ **Mingus in Europe—Vol. 1** / Apr. 26, 1964 / Enja 3049
The tour from which this album was drawn was Eric Dolphy's last with Charles Mingus—Dolphy stayed in Europe and was dead two months later. Mingus and drummer Dannie Richmond were telepathic musical blood brothers, and the greatest joys here were their playing together and their obvious pleasure in driving Dolphy to his limits. The album contains a 38-minute "Fables of Faubus" and a Mingus-Dolphy duet on "I Can't Get Started." Mingus was particularly light in his long exploration, but didn't seem to catch fire until Dolphy danced in for one of his famous conversations with the leader. —*Lee Jeske, Down Beat*

Mingus at Monterey / Sep. 20, 1964 / VDJ 1572
At the Monterey Jazz Festival. Has attained legendary status. Some of his other live performances seem stronger. Good performance of his and Ellington's material. —*Michael Katz*

○ **Great Concert of Charles Mingus, The** / i. 1964 / Prestige 34001

Let My Children Hear Music / Sep. 23, 1971 / Columbia 48910
Some of his strongest later compositions. Can get a little tedious at times ("The Chill of Death"), but Mingus merely follows his muse. If you weren't told this was jazz, you might think it was modern classical music. —*Michael Katz*

Shoes of the Fisherman's Wife.... / i. Sep. 23, 1971-Nov. 1, 1959 / Columbia 44050
The Shoes of the Fisherman's Wife Are Some Jive Ass Slippers. Most of the *Mingus Dynasty*, which features the same lineup as *Mingus Ah Um* and has a similar feel but is less driving. Inexplicable inclusion of "Shoes of the...." from *Let My Children Hear Music*, recorded 12 years later. All great music. —*Michael Katz*

Mingus Moves / Oct. 29-31, 1973 / Atlantic 1653
It took forever, but Atlantic (through Rhino) has finally had the good sense to reissue on CD the outstanding sessions of Charles Mingus's last great Jazz Workshop band, his early '70s unit. Pianist Don Pullen, the twisting, swaying tenor saxophonist and flutist George Adams, and drummer Dannie Richmond subsequently formed three-fourths of the Pullen-Adams quartet, a powerhouse late '70s and early '80s combo. While Rhino previously rereleased *Changes One* and *Changes Two*, here is the fiery date that preceded them and is slightly better. That is due to the propulsive solos of Adams and Pullen, each percussive, angular, and dynamic as they constructed remarkable solos on "Wee," "Opus 4," and the title cut. —*Ron Wynn*

Mingus at Carnegie Hall / Jan. 19, 1974 / Atlantic 1667
A live set with only two compositions. Rahsaan Roland Kirk steals the show with explosive, extensive tenor-sax solos. —*Ron Wynn*

★ **Changes One** / Dec. 27-30, 1974 / Atlantic 1677
Spotlighting the last of his great small bands, heralding the forerunner of the George Adams-Don Pullen quartet that became a preeminent '80s jazz quartet. —*Ron Wynn*

○ **Changes Two** / Dec. 27-30, 1974 / Atlantic 1678
The second of a pair that heralded the forerunner of the George Adams-Don Pullen quartet that became a preeminent '80s jazz quartet. —*Ron Wynn*

Cumbia and Jazz Fusion / Mar. 31, 1976+Apr. 1, 1976 / Atlantic 8801
Japanese issue. His strongest late recording. Somewhat of a departure for him. Big ensemble, exotic sound effects. Worthwhile. —*Michael Katz*

☆ **Epitaph** / i. 1990 / Columbia 45428
A tribute. Memorial orchestra directed by Gunther Schuller playing the late bassist's works. A magnum opus. —*Michael G. Nastos*

★ **Complete Debut Recordings** / Debut 4402
1951-1958. Early recordings. All of the sessions on which Mingus played for the label he and Max Roach founded. If you are a Mingus fanatic, you need this set to trace his development. If not, you can get the highlights by getting *Mingus at the Bohemia* and *Jazz at Massey Hall*. —*Michael Katz*

Debut Rarities-Vol 1 / Original Jazz Classics 1807
The Charles Mingus Octet cuts from '53 that make up the first half of *Debut Rarities, Volume 1* are ambitious, but are polite by Mingus's later standards, particularly the impressionistic balladry of "Blue Tide," and the cool-hued bop of "Pink Topsy" and "Miss Bliss." Only "Eclipse," which features singer Janet Thurlow, has the provocative edge of Mingus's mature work, as the svelte lyricism of the song collides with the bold orchestral interludes scored by the date's arranger, pianist Spaulding Givens (aka Nadi Qamar). —*Bill Shoemaker, Down Beat*

Debut Rarities-Vol 2 / Original Jazz Classics 1808
Debut Rarities, Volume 2 features Charles Mingus in '51 duets with Spaulding Givens, a florid, facile pianist, and in '53 trios rounded out by Max Roach. This is a comparatively soporific collection, though Mingus's numerous solos make it suggested listening for students of Mingus the virtuoso. —*Bill Shoemaker, Down Beat*

Blue Mitchell (Richard Allen Mitchell)

b. Mar. 13, 1930, Miami, FL, **d.** May 21, 1979, Los Angeles, CA
Trumpet / Hard bop, blues & jazz
Trumpeter Richard Allen Mitchell was accurately nicknamed. He was an expressive, dynamic player whose style was easily adapted to either R&B or jazz. Mitchell worked with Paul Williams, Earl Bostic, and Red Prysock's R&B groups in 1951-1955. He became a major figure on the jazz scene during his five years with Horace Silver (1958-1964), where his pungent lines and assured, emphatic solos were a welcome part of the Silver hard-bop, gospel, Caribbean rhythms axis. Mitchell used similar instrument and group concepts when he formed his own group in 1964, using Chick Corea to fill the role Silver had previously occupied. Mitchell's final years were spent back in an R&B and blues setting, as he worked first with Ray Charles and then John Mayall before doing lots of session work. —*Ron Wynn*

○ **Big Six** / Jul. 2, 1958-Apr. 2, 1959 / Riverside 615
An outstanding date, with above-average solos from Johnny Griffin (ts), Curtis Fuller (tb), and Mitchell. The rhythm section of Wynton Kelly (p), Wilbur Ware (b), and Philly Joe Jones (d) aren't slouches, either. —*Ron Wynn*

★ **Thing to Do, The** / Jul. 30, 1964 / Blue Note 84178
W/ Chick Corea, Jr. Cook (ts), and Al Foster (d). Recommended for jazz/trumpet lovers. —*Michael G. Nastos*

○ **Down with It** / Jul. 14, 1965 / Blue Note
One of Mitchell's least-recognized sessions, this has some fervent trumpet pieces, plus nice piano from a still-emerging Chick Corea. —*Ron Wynn*

Red Mitchell (Keith Moore Mitchell)

b. Sep. 20, 1927, New York, NY, **d.** 1992
Bass / Cool
Though viewed more as a rhythm-section mainstay than an innovative player, Red Mitchell has been in the forefront of expanding the bass's potential as a lead instrument. He took a horn-like approach to playing bass, varying his technique and articulation and reaching notes and playing in a dashing, distinctive fashion. Mitchell began as a pianist with Chubby Jackson in 1949 and became a bassist with Charlie Ventura that same year. After two years with Woody Herman, Mitchell's personalized bass approach came to fruition during stints with Red Norvo and Gerry Mulligan. Mitchell became part of the Hampton Hawes trio for two years (1955-1957). He also had his own quartet for a year in 1957 and then played with Andre Previn and Shelly Manne for four years while simultaneously becoming a busy studio musician. After coleading a group with Harold Land in 1961-1962, he reunited with Hawes in 1965-1966. —*Ron Wynn*

○ **Hear Ye!** / 1989 / Atlantic 1376

★ **Talking** / i. 1989 / Capri 74016
A piano-drum-bass date with Kenny Barron and Ben Riley, Red Mitchell's *Talking* is especially companionable. On the deepest level, you'd be hard-pressed to find a trio swing with more conviction or spirited interplay than these old mates from Bradley's (University Place, Manhattan). They speak with warmth, pointedness, and occasional ("Locomotive") hilarity. Their swing, more often implied than bared, gets around to all sorts of cutting, curving, joshing. —*Fred Bouchard, Down Beat*

Roscoe Mitchell (Roscoe Edward Mitchell, Jr.)

b. Aug. 3, 1940, Chicago, IL
Reeds, composer / Early free, modern creative
Reed player and composer Roscoe Mitchell has achieved recognition in two different (though not mutually exclusive) capacities within the jazz sphere. He's a founding member and major participant in the Art Ensemble of Chicago, and he's also issued several stunning releases as a leader. A versatile improviser and exceptional soloist, Mitchell has recorded with distinction on alto, soprano, and bass saxes and a wealth of percussion and miscellaneous instruments. He played in both high school and the army and worked in a small combo with Henry Threadgill before joining Muhal Richard Abrams's experimental band that ultimately led to the creation of the Association for the Advancement of Creative Musicians (AACM) in the '60s. He's an underrated composer whose writing has creatively explored interesting uses of sound, space, and rhythm. His finest releases, especially *Sound* from 1966 and *Nonaah* from 1976, have brilliantly mixed elaborate, dense compositions and expansive, often outrageous solos.— *Ron Wynn*

○ **Sound** / 1966 / Delmark 408
Mitchell's first significant statement as a leader has ambitious pieces, amazing solos, and unorthodox arrangements. —*Ron Wynn*

● **Old** / **Quartet** / May 18-19, 1967 / Nessa 5

○ **Roscoe Mitchell Solo Saxophone Concerts, The** / Oct. 22, 1973+Nov. 2, 1973 / Sackville 2006
Roscoe Mitchell's solo work had often been ignored, which made this brilliantly vigorous Sackville LP all the more welcome. Like Cecil Taylor, Mitchell here thought in highly structured outlines, though his extraordinary concept of rhythm often made for delightfully odd forms. —*John Litweiler, Down Beat*

★ **Nonaah** / Aug. 23, 1976-Feb. 22, 1977 / Nessa 10
1976-1977. This is arguably Mitchell's best solo statement. It includes a full-side treatment of the title cut, solo works, duos, and an incredible alto number with Mitchell, Henry Threadgill (as), Joseph Jarman (reeds), and the undervalued Wallace McMillan (b). —*Ron Wynn*

○ **Snurdy Mcgurdy and Her Dancin' Shoes** / Jun. 1982 / Nessa 20
This album is more upbeat and humorous, less dense and intense than some past Mitchell dates, but the music's just as ferocious. —*Ron Wynn*

Hank Mobley (Henry Mobley)

b. Jul. 7, 1930, Eastman, GA, **d.** May 30, 1986, Philadelphia, PA
Tenor sax / Hard bop

A consistently swinging tenor saxophonist, Hank Mobley crafted solos with a precise, yet steadily rhythmic vigor. He played in Paul Gayten's R&B band in the early '50s and then worked with Max Roach and Dizzy Gillespie. A founding member of Art Blakey's Jazz Messengers in 1954, Mobley stayed with them until 1956. He played in Horace Silver's quintet and with Dizzy Reece as well as another stint with Blakey. He played with Miles Davis in the early '60s and did several sessions as a leader for Blue Note, Savoy, and Prestige. Mobley played with John Coltrane, Jackie McLean, Paul Chambers, Johnny Griffin, Blue Mitchell, Cedar Walton, Donald Byrd, Ron Carter, Wynton Kelly, Philly Joe Jones, and Lee Morgan, among others. After touring Europe in the late '60s and early '70s, Mobley had to abandon music for health reasons. He appeared in a nonplaying capacity at the '85 concert that relaunched Blue Note and did one last short date with Duke Jordan in 1986, not long before his death of double pneumonia. —*Ron Wynn*

☆ **Peckin' Time** / Feb. 9, 1958 / Blue Note 81574
One of the best by this prolific yet underrated tenor. With Lee Morgan (tpt) and Wynton Kelly (p). —*David Szatmary*

★ **Soul Station** / Feb. 7, 1960 / Blue Note 46528
Another good Blue Note date that languished until its reissue in 1987. —*Ron Wynn*

○ **Roll Call** / Nov. 13, 1960 / Blue Note 46823

○ **Workout** / Mar. 26, 1961 / Blue Note 84080

★ **Another Workout** / Mar. 1961-Dec. 1961 / Blue Note 84431
A wonderful session that remained in the Blue Note vaults until 1985. —*Ron Wynn*

○ **Straight No Filter** / Jul. 7, 1963-Feb. 4, 1965 / Blue Note 84435
Straight No Filter consists of the last remaining unissued Hank Mobley-led Blue Note recordings. The first half of this disc was often superb with several brillant solos from Mobley, McCoy Tyner (piano), and the still underrated Lee Morgan (trumpet). —*Scott Yanow, Cadence*

○ **Flip, The** / Jul. 12, 1969 / Blue Note 84329
This collection was recorded in Paris on July 12, 1969, with young Vince Benedetti (piano) and Frenchman Alby Cullaz (bass) the other members of a stylish quintet. The five tunes were all Hank Mobley originals and served their purpose as springboards for explosive jazz excitement. . . . There were no slow ballads on this fiery set, which went out with a blazing "Early Morning Stroll." Once more Jones appears to be challenging Mobley to let go—if he dare! He pushed the soloists and makes all of them move. In this mood Jones was a complete rhythm section and woe betide the slouchers. This was a really good blowing session in the best tradition of Blue Note. —*Mark Gardner, Coda*

Modern Jazz Quartet

b. 1951
Cool
The Modern Jazz Quartet is the longest-lived small combo in jazz and one of the most important. The group was formed by pianist John Lewis, vibraphonist Milt Jackson, bassist Percy Heath, and drummer Kenny Clarke in January 1952, although the four had played together in various configurations prior to that. From 1952 to 1955 they recorded for Prestige Records, turning out such records as *Concorde* and *Django*.

In 1955 Clarke left the MJQ and was replaced by Connie Kay, and the lineup has not changed since. The same year, the group switched affiliations to Atlantic Records. *Fontessa*, released in 1956, was the first of 27 albums recorded for the label over 32 years.

The MJQ's repertoire consisted mainly of Lewis compositions, and the pianist proved an ambitious writer, notably scoring the film *No Sun in Venice* (also called *One Never Knows*) in 1958, and in 1959 and 1960 taking the MJQ into the hybrid field of third-stream music, a confluence of jazz and classical music, on *Third Stream Music* and *MJQ and Orchestra*.

The MJQ broke up officially in 1974, though it continued to play concerts on an irregular basis until an official reunion in 1981. Its most recent album at this writing is the 1988 *For Ellington*, though Atlantic released a four-disc boxed set retrospective, *MJQ40*, in 1991. —*Bill Ruhlmann*

○ **Modern Jazz Quartet Plays Jazz Classics, The** / Dec. 22, 1952-Jul. 2, 1955 / Prestige 7425

An early work that laid out the essence of the Modern Jazz Quartet; a unit that brought both jazz sensibility and classical precision to anything they played. This time they performed classical material with improvisational backdrop, something that pianist John Lewis particularly loved. Vibist Milt Jackson also executed his parts smoothly, while bassist Percy Heath and drummer Connie Kay were consistently supportive and steady. —*Ron Wynn*

○ **Modern Jazz Quartet** / Dec. 22, 1952-Jul. 2, 1955 / Savoy Jazz 111
First works from early '50s with drummer Kenny Clark. Quintessential MJQ. Rare Prestige recordings. —*Michael G. Nastos*

★ **MJQ—40 years [Boxed Set]** / 1952-Feb. 3, 1988 / Atlantic 82330
Recent set gathers a variety of styles from 40 years of recording. —*Michael Erlewine*

★ **No Sun in Venice** / Apr. 4, 1957 / Atlantic 1284
An adventurous John Lewis score for the Roger Vadim film of the same name. —*Ron Wynn*

○ **Collaboration with Almeida** / Jul. 21, 1964 / Atlantic 1429
W/ Laurindo Almeida. Lush and romatic, very much a product of the early '60s Latin craze. Almeida makes a sympathetic collaborator. —*Ron Wynn*

★ **Complete Last Concert** / Nov. 25, 1974 / Atlantic 81976
At the time, this two-record set was viewed as the end of an era. Now it only represents the climax of phase one. It's an excellent set, though- among their best live efforts. —*Ron Wynn*

○ **More from the Last Concert** / Nov. 25, 1974 / Atlantic 8806
When the Modern Jazz Quartet got together in 1974 to do what was thought to be their final recording, it was a historic occasion. So much worthwhile material was done, there was enough for a second album. Fortunately, it turned out not to be the end for the band, but this second album from the '74 date is still well worth hearing. —*Ron Wynn*

○ **For Ellington** / Feb. 1988 / East West 90026
For Ellington was a salute to Duke's genius, but it seemed to tightrope the effete and tepid in the Modern Jazz Quartet's response with moments of musical excitement. . . . But this collection did have its moments of brillance and glory. Even "Prelude" was full of tenderness, and on "Ko-Ko," pianist John Lewis played Harry Carney's figure to vibist Milt Jackson's response with the melody, and Ellington would have appreciated Lewis's percussive texture on the solo here. —*Ron Weilburn, Jazz Times*

○ **Modern Jazz Quartet with Sonny Rollins, The** / Atlantic 1299

Louis Moholo (Louis T. Moholo)

b. Mar. 10, 1940, Cape Town, South Africa
Drums, cello, percussion, vocals / World fusion
Drummer Louis Moholo has been among the most dynamic and prolific of the expatriate South African musicians. His vibrant, crisp rhythm work has fueled many pivotal ensembles, and he's been a contributor in a variety of styles from mainstream to outside to rock. Moholo taught himself the drums before founding a big band called the Chordettes in 1956. He later joined the Blue Notes, a band led by pianist Chris McGregor. After playing at the Antibes Festival, they arrived in England in 1965, settling in London. Moholo spent a year on tour in South America with saxophonist Steve Lacy in 1966. He also worked with trombonist Roswell Rudd and saxophonists Archie Shepp and John Tchicai, He returned to England in 1967, where he performed with McGregor's Brotherhood of Breath and many other groups, led by such European musicians as saxophonist Peter Brotzmann and Mike Osborne. During the late '60s and throughout the '70s and '80s, Moholo has done extensive freelancing and recording and has headed his own groups such as Moholo's Unit, Spirits Rejoice, Culture Shock, and the African Drum Ensemble. —*Ron Wynn*

★ **Spirits Rejoice** / Jan. 24, 1978 / Ogun 520
The South African drummer with the Blue Notes and Brotherhood of Breath leads an octet. This is a great album, a must-buy. —*Michael G. Nastos*

Grachan Moncur III

b. 1937
Trombone / Early free, modern creative
A premier trombonist among the most fluid of his generation, Grachan Moncur III is the son of Grachan Moncur, a fine bassist

who was a member of the original Savoy Sultans and recorded with (among others) Billie Holiday and Mildred Bailey. Grachan Moncur III studied formally at the Manhattan School of Music and Juilliard in the early '60s, before touring with Ray Charles from 1961 to 1963. He also spent a year with the Art Farmer-Benny Golson group in 1962. He settled in New York and became a familiar name on many records of the '60s, playing with Jackie McLean, Sonny Rollins, and Archie Shepp, and later becoming part of drummer Beaver Harris's 360 Degree Music Experience. He became a member of the Jazz Composers Orchestra Assocation in the '70s, writing the song "Echoes of Prayer" for the group. He returned to Newark later in the '70s and became an educator and activist, though he recorded with organist Big John Patton in 1983. He toured Europe with the second edition of the Paris Reunion Band in 1986. —*Ron Wynn*

○ **Evolution** / Nov. 21, 1963 / Blue Note 84153
Easily recommended Blue Note date from the '60s with Lee Morgan (tpt) and Jackie McLean (as). —*Michael G. Nastos*

○ **Echoes of Prayer** / Apr. 11, 1974 / JCOA 1009
The 1974 *Melody Maker Jazz Album of the Year*. Progressive and thought-provoking. A legendary recording, with the Jazz Composers Orchestra. —*Michael G. Nastos*

Thelonious Monk (Thelonious Sphere Monk)

b. Oct. 10, 1917, Rocky Mount, NC, **d.** Feb. 17, 1982, Weehawken, NJ

Piano, composer, bandleader / Bop, postbop

Only Duke Ellington and arguably Charles Mingus are the equals of Thelonious Monk as a composer. His works forced musicians to exert themselves to their fullest, put a premium on surprise, and demonstrated a harmonic knowledge and musical sophistication that fooled those who'd tabbed him a witless recluse or just an eccentric personality. His piano playing was just as subtle and unpredictable, with odd phrases, unexpected pauses, tempo changes, and melodic quirks that always came together at the end to make a coherent, memorable statement. Monk began playing piano at 11, backing his mother's vocals in church, and he became a professional in the late '30s, gaining the job of house pianist at Minton's in 1939. He worked with many in the emerging bop generation, laying down what would become the vocabulary of the '40s. He was part of the group hired by Coleman Hawkins in 1944 to make some of the earliest bop recordings. But his career was plagued by personal and political problems. He made many superb recordings with Atlantic, Savoy, Verve, Blue Note, and Riverside but didn't debut on a so-called major label until 1962, when he was signed by Columbia. His stint there was a stormy one, and the label in fact didn't issue most of his finest live material until he died. Toward the end of his career, Monk became a celebrated elder statesman, and he was honored in 1978 at a Jazz Party held at the White House by President Jimmy Carter. Several Mosaic sets issued since his death chronicle his greatness, while artists from McCoy Tyner to NRBQ's Terry Adams hail his genius. —*Ron Wynn*

○ **Complete Genius, The** / Oct. 15, 1947-May 30, 1952 / Blue Note 579
It's no longer necessary to grope around the random selections of Monk tracks on Blue Note's various albums because they were all collected on this double LP (including the two issued alternate takes). And if that wasn't enough, there were also two items that were only previously on a 78. For some strange reason, they were not presented in chronological order, but all the pieces from each session were grouped together, and that was the most important thing on such a reissue. This reissue included superlative examples of Monk *the* pianist (if he didn't have technique as has been claimed, how come no one could imitate him?), Monk *the* composer (22 of his best tunes were performed), and the lesser known Monk *the* arranger (hear especially how he transformed the hypermaudlin "Carolina Moon" into a masterpiece for jazz quintet). —*Martin Davidson, Cadence*

○ **Genius of Modern Music—Vol. 1** / Oct. 15, 1947-Nov. 21, 1947 / Capitol 81510

★ **Complete Blue Note Recordings** / 1947-1952 / Mosaic 101
Here's everything you ever wanted to know about pianist-composer-bandleader Thelonious Monk's Blue Note recordings, but were afraid to ask. These 1947 through 1952 sessions were his first as a leader and prime mover. Replete with alternate takes,

they showed him to have been an iconoclast from the start, a unique jazz composer with such a special sense of accent, rhythm, and dour melody that his compositions, even when under hands other than his, always bore his distinctive stamp. —*Alan Bargebur, Cadence*

○ **Genius of Modern Music—Vol. 2** / Jul. 23, 1951-May 30, 1952 / Capitol 81511

Monk / Nov. 13, 1953-May 11, 1954 / Prestige 016
These fine '50s quintet dates include particularly strong solos from tenors Sonny Rollins and Frank Foster, plus typically unusual and odd Monk piano solos. —*Ron Wynn*

★ **Thelonious Monk and Sonny Rollins** / 1953 / Original Jazz Classics 59
This date contained "The Way You Look Tonight" from the *Moving Out* session, plus titles from 11/13/53 and 9/22/54. The latter two were pianist Thelonious Monk's dates with tenor saxophonist Sonny Rollins, Julius Watkins (French horn), Percy Heath (bass), and Willie Jones (drums) or Heath and Art Blakey (drums on the 9/22/54 cuts). For me, the standout here was the wonderfully effervescent handling of "The Way You Look Tonight." Rollins attacked it with a *major* spirit and played with a euphoria rarely matched in recorded jazz. —*Bob Rusch, Cadence*

★ **Complete Black Lion and Vogue** / 1954-1971 / Mosaic
This serves two important purposes. It cleans up the mess that had been made of the 1954 Paris session, which had been sloppily reissued on a variety of irresponsible labels. . . . This Thelonious Monk box also offered what turned out to be the pianist's last recordings as a leader. . . . There was much to enjoy and study here, the opportunity to compare the Paris material with its Blue Note and Prestige forerunners, even the opportunity to make comparisons between the Paris and London sessions. —*Alan Bargebuhr, Cadence*

Plays Duke Ellington / Jul. 21+27, 1955 / Riverside 024
One genius tackles the music of another. Superb trio recordings spiced by Oscar Pettiford (b) and Kenny Clarke (d). —*Ron Wynn*

☆ **Brilliant Corners** / Dec. 17-23, 1956 / Riverside 026
A recording feat. Clark Terry (tpt), Sonny Rollins (ts), and Max Roach (d). Excellent version of the title tune. —*Hank Davis*

★ **Complete Riverside Recordings** / 1956-1960 / Riverside 022
1955-1960. Priceless Monk, 15 CDs and worth every cent. Essential. —*Michael Erlewine*

○ **Round Midnight** / Apr. 5, 1957 / Milestone 47067
Round Midnight contains all the complete takes from the two-day session for *Mulligan Meets Monk*. . . . it seemed aimed more at a specialty audience than at casual listeners. —*Kevin Whitehead, Cadence*

○ **Art Blakey's Jazz Messengers with Thelonious Monk** / May 14-15, 1957 / Atlantic

○ **New York with Johnny Griffin** / May 14-15, 1957 / Atlantic

☆ **Monk's Music** / Jun. 25-26, 1957 / Riverside 084
Superb septet with tenor greats Coltrane and Coleman Hawkins. —*Hank Davis*

● **Thelonious with John Coltrane** / Jun. 25-26, 1957 / Original Jazz Classics 39
Tenor saxophonist John Coltrane was present on a spring of '58 date as part of the Thelonious Monk quartet on a session that made up half of *Thelonious Monk with John Coltrane*. The remainder was a 6/12/57 date with Trane, Coleman Hawkins, Gigi Gryce, Ray Copeland, Ware, and Art Blakey, and Monk solo piano on "Functional." The material has been scattered around; most of it was on a previous twofer. It was great music—Trane, Hawk, Blakey . . . . This presented classic encounters and lasting music. —*Bob Rusch, Cadence*

☆ **At the Five Spot** / Aug. 7, 1958 / Milestone 47043
A landmark live date by a legendary pianist and composer. Monk was just starting to emerge as a dynamic, highly distinctive, and unorthodox player, while his compositions were getting equal acclaim both for their unusual structure and their overall brilliance. He headed a group that included at various times tenor saxophonist John Coltrane, drummer Shadow Wilson, and bassist Wilbur Ware. —*Ron Wynn*

Mysterioso / Aug. 7, 1958 / Riverside 206
Additional sessions with the Johnny Griffin (sax), Ahmed Abdul-Malik (b), Roy Haynes (d) group. —*Ron Wynn*

○ **In Person** / Feb. 28, 1959 / Milestone 47033
This Thelonious Monk session was a reissue of his Riverside "Town Hall" (Feb. 1958) and "Black Hawk" (Apr. 1960) albums with an additional previously unissued version of "Little Rootie Tootie" added. The dilution of the jazz group into larger ensembles usually results in very dull music. However, the strength of Monk's compositions and the ideal arrangements that he put together shed a new light on the material without really either adding or detracting anything. —*Martin Davidson, Cadence*

Five by Monk by Five / Jun. 1-02, 1959 / Riverside 362
Quintet. The music proves as intriguing as the title. Excellent trumpet solos from Thad Jones. CD has bonus cuts. —*Ron Wynn*

Alone in San Francisco / Oct. 21, 1959 / Original Jazz Classics 231
Solo piano. Exacting, distinctive renditions of such Monk classics as "Blue Monk," "Pannonica," and "Reflections." Bonus CD cuts. —*Ron Wynn*

At the Blackhawk / Apr. 29, 1960 / Riverside 305
Special guests Harold Land (ts) and Joe Gordon (tpt) make this a great sextet. Monk's playing is daring and energized. The CD version includes the complete "Epistrophy." —*Ron Wynn*

○ **Two Hours with Thelonious Monk—Vol. 1** / Apr. 18+21, 1961 / Riverside 9460

○ **Two Hours with Thelonious Monk—Vol. 2** / Apr. 18+21, 1961 / Riverside 9461

○ **April in Paris** / Apr. 18, 1961 / Milestone 47060
This was originally a Riverside limited edition, two-record set called *Two Hours with Thelonious* and made up of concert material (April 1961) from Italy and France. On this reissue, Milestone cut it down to 82:17 with Monk and quartet (tenor saxophonist Charlie Rouse, bassist John Ore, and drummer Frankie Dunlop) by eliminating the Italian concert material. —*Bob Rusch, Cadence*

Monk's Dream / Oct. 1962-Nov. 1962 / Columbia 40786
Quartet with Charlie Rouse (ts). Monk is in superb form on his debut Columbia album. —*Hank Davis*

Criss-Cross / Feb. 26-28, 1963 / CBS 48823
This is as fine a quartet recording of Monk's early '60s work as exists in the Columbia catalog. —*Ron Wynn*

Solo Monk / Oct. 31, 1964 / CBS 47854

● **Underground** / Dec. 14, 1967-Feb. 14, 1968 / Columbia 40785
An excellent latter-period Monk group. "Green Chimneys" is a prime cut. Charlie Rouse is on tenor sax. —*Michael G. Nastos*

☆ **London Collection—Vol. 1, The** / Nov. 15, 1971 / Black Lion 760101
This 1971 London recording was a delightful collection of his singularity. There were extended incursions into Monkland as well as introspective, brief commentary on other vistas of his original compositions ("Trinkle Tinkle," "Crepuscle with Nellie," "Little Rootie Tootie," and "Jackieing"). The blues ("Blue Sphere") sounded like James P. Johnson in spots. The ballads were some of Monk's finest later ruminations, especially the seven-minute previously unreleased "Lover Man." —*Rhodes Spedale, Jazz Times*

Standards / Columbia 45148
A sparkling solo and good quartet performances culled from Columbia dates. —*Ron Wynn*

J. R. Monterose (Frank Anthony Monterose, Jr.)

b. 1927, d. 1993
Sax / Bop, hard bop, postbop
Detroit-born tenor saxophonist J.R. Monterose worked frequently in the Catskills of upstate New York. He a bop and postbop innovator. (Not related to fellow Detroiter Jack Montrose and not to be confused with him.) He played with Charles Mingus's Jazz Workshop and Kenny Dorham's Jazz Prophets, among others. Monterose recorded as a leader for Xanadu, Jaro, and Uptown; he died in 1993. —*Michael G. Nastos*

○ **J. R. Monterose** / Oct. 21, 1956 / Blue Note 1536

★ **Message, The** / Nov. 24, 1959 / Jaro 5004

○ **Straight Ahead** / i. Nov. 24, 1959 / Xanadu 126
Even though the music was magnificent, it wouldn't matter to Monterose fanatics. The added treat were the liner notes which filled us up on where Monterose had been (Europe) and what he

was into (playing sax and guitar). This record was a reissue of the phantom Jaro disc, *The Message*, recorded on November 24, 1959. ... Throughout this set Monterose played with great ease and authority. Certainly there was never a played-out quality in the improvised work, which came with an ease of breath, nor did the improvising become static. It was always inventive and warm. —*Bob Rusch, Cadence*

○ **A Little Pleasure** / Apr. 6-07, 1981 / Uptown 2706
This was intimate and somewhat stimulating, quiet, clublike music. Pianist Tommy Flanagan's fluency as he spread improvised melodic lines effortlessy over the bar lines was a wonder to hear as were his lush chordal voicings. Tenor and soprano saxophonist J. R. Monterose was more noteworthy for the sincere feeling inherent in his playing than for technical skills. Together they were an interesting pair, playing off one another with sensitivity and grace. —*Milo Fine, Cadence*

Montgomery Brothers

b. 1930
Postbop, soul-jazz
This trio was originally known as the Mastersounds in 1957-1960, then as the Montgomery Brothers in 1960-1962. The group consisted of Wes Montgomery on guitar, Monk Montgomery on bass, and Buddy Montgomery on vibes. They made several fine albums that blended easy-listening, standards, blues, and originals. —*Ron Wynn*

★ **Groove Yard** / Jan. 3, 1961 / Riverside 9362
Indianapolis brothers in their heyday together. Essential listening. —*Michael G. Nastos*

Wes Montgomery (John Leslie Montgomery)

b. Mar. 6, 1925, Indianapolis, IN, d. Jun. 15, 1968, Indianapolis, IN
Guitar / Hard bop, instrumental pop
A highly respected, loved, and widely imitated musician, Wes Montgomery was acknowledged as the most influential jazz guitarist after Charlie Christian. He expanded the resources of guitar in all its main functions—chordal, melodic, and rhythmic. Originally from Indianapolis, he had a long musical association with his brothers Monk and Buddy. Wes played the guitar with his thumb instead of a pick, and achieved a warm, controlled sound with great rhythmic feel—very melodic and accessible. He also mastered the use of parallel-octave style in soloing, giving a thicker, more penetrating punch to his brilliantly straightforward and unerring melodic style. Unfortunately, some of his records were pop-jazz compromises under commercial pressure, but these brought him widespread acceptance and success, including a Grammy award in 1965 for *Goin' Out of My Head*. The recordings that have stood the test of time are his small group efforts with many of the jazz greats of his time, such as Tommy Flanagan, Hank Jones, Wynton Kelly, Paul Chambers, and Johnny Griffin. These recordings, which include albums such as *Full House* and *Movin' Along*, also feature his fine original compositions. Seemingly set for a long and celebrated career in the jazz world, Wes appeared on the cover of *Down Beat* only a week before his premature death of a heart attack at 43. —*David Nelson McCarthy*

○ **Beginnings** / Apr. 18-22, 1958 / Blue Note 531
This Wes Montgomery grouping was a hodge-podge of early groups, in a period when all maintained he was at his best. Gifted at blues and bop, his reputation rests on such works as "Montgomeryland Funk." Certainly his rhythmic vigor was distinctive in a period of less forceful guitarists. His mastery of construction in those days was his most noted feature: He built his forms in a classic way, with a deceptively relaxed versatility and an attractive tone. Harold Land appears on seven of these tracks to make the point: The tenorist lacked many of Montgomery's virtues, yet was joyously articulate, playing lovely arpeggios, the best music on the records. —*John Litweiler, Down Beat*

★ **Complete Riverside Recordings [Box Set], The** / Oct. 5, 1959-Nov. 27, 1963 / Fantasy 4408

○ **Yesterdays** / Oct. 5-06, 1959 / Milestone 47057
(1959-1963). Compilation from *Wes Montgomery Trio* (6 cuts), *Boss Guitar* (5 cuts), *Portrait of Wes* (3 cuts), and four cuts previously unissued. —*Michael Erlewine*

○ **Pretty Blue** / 1959-1963 / Milestone 47030
(1959-1963). A double album that includes the complete *Fusion* album, plus cuts from *Wes Montgomery Trio* (3), *Boss Guitar* (2), *Portrait of Wes* (3), and *Guitar on the Go* (2). —*Michael Erlewine*

● **Incredible Jazz Guitar of Wes Montgomery** / Jan. 26+28, 1960 / Riverside 036
Considered by many to be his best album. "West Coast Blues" is considered a classic jazz guitar piece. This album won Montgomery the *1960 Down Beat Critic's New Star* award. Recorded in New York. —*Michael Erlewine*

○ **Groove Brothers** / Oct. 11, 1960-Dec. 1961 / Milestone 47051
A compilation from *The Montgomery Brothers* (3 cuts), The Montgomery Brothers in Canada *(4 cuts), and* Groove Yard (8 cuts—whole album). —Michael Erlewine

Movin' Along / Oct. 11, 1960 / Riverside 089
This is especially noteworthy for the presence of James Clay (ts). Solid Montgomery guitar. —*Ron Wynn*

So Much Guitar / Aug. 4, 1961 / Riverside 233
Includes an unaccompanied guitar solo on "While We're Young" in a chordal style, and the down-home "One for My Baby." —*Michael Erlewine*

Full House / Jun. 25, 1962 / Riverside 106
Ranks with *Incredible Jazz Guitar of Wes Montgomery* as one of Montgomery's best albums. —*Michael Erlewine*

Movin' / Jun. 25, 1962 / Milestone 47040
This is a two-LP set containing the Montgomery albums *Movin' Along* and *Full House*. —*Michael Erlewine*

★ **Boss Guitar** / Apr. 27, 1963 / Riverside 261
Tart, stinging Montgomery guitar and good suppport from Jimmy Cobb on drums. —*Ron Wynn*

Guitar on the Go / Oct. 10, 1963+Nov. 27, 1963 / Riverside 489
One of his last two albums on the Riverside label (the other being "A Portrait of Wes"), which were released without the artist's approval. —*Michael Erlewine*

○ **Small Group Recordings** / Jun. 1965-Sep. 22, 1965 / Verve 833555
(1965-1966). A compilation of cuts from *Smokin' at the Half Note, Further Adventures of Jimmy [Smith] and Wes*, and *Willow Weep for Me* (cuts released in original form, without orchestration). —*Michael Erlewine*

★ **Smokin' at the Half Note** / Jun. 1965-Sep. 22, 1965 / Verve 829578

Goin' Out of My Head / Dec. 7-22, 1965 / Verve 825676
Creed Taylor produced this Grammy Award winning album that marked the beginning of Montgomery's pop success. Large band with arrangements by Oliver Nelson. —*Michael Erlewine*.

Tequila / Mar. 17, 1966-May 18, 1966 / Verve 831671
Produced by Creed Taylor. W/ Ron Carter (b), Grady Tate (d), Ray Baretto (conga), and strings. The title track has real jazz content. —*Michael Erlewine*

Day in the Life, A / Jun. 6-26, 1967 / A&M 0816
One of Montgomery's biggest pop-hit albums. His playing is excellent. It's the inspiration behind similar George Benson efforts. Gold album. —*Ron Wynn*

Tete Montoliu (Vincente Montoliu)
b. Mar. 28, 1933, Barcelona, Spain
Piano / Bop, world fusion
One of the fastest and most compelling European pianists, Montoliu has become an international star without resettling permanently in America. Blind since birth, Montoliu became interested in jazz by hearing Duke Ellington records. He accompanied many visiting American musicians, recording with Lionel Hampton, Rahsaan Roland Kirk, and Anthony Braxton, among others, in the '50s, '60s and '70s. He's made many outstanding releases on European and independent labels, with his best work coming in either solo or trio settings. —*Ron Wynn*

○ **That's All** / i. Sep. 1971 / Steeple Chase 1199
Pianist Tete Montoliu is a brillant technician at the keyboard, yet he never overpowers or bores one, probably due to his tone and the uniqueness of his rhythmic and harmonic ideas, which, while remaining within the mainstream, are nevertheless quite personal. . . . The program consisted of very well known pieces and

he made them all come alive and maintained interest. —*Peter Leitch, Cadence*

○ **Lush Life** / i. Sep. 1971 / Steeple Chase 1216

○ **Tete!** / May 28, 1974 / Inner City 2029
On this trio disc (bassist Niels-Henning Orsted Pedersen and drummer Albert Heath) Tete Montoliu demonstrated a tradition in stride piano that is almost lost in the contemporary jazz scene. The sound here owed more to a slightly later school that included Bud Powell, Oscar Peterson, and Wynton Kelly yet possessed a more modern sense of tonality. Heath and Pedersen helped propel this record to a status somewhat above a tribute album. The album contained spirited versions of John Coltrane's "Giant Steps," Tadd Dameron's "Hot House," and the standard "Body And Soul." —*David Less, Down Beat*

★ **Lunch in L.A.** / Oct. 22, 1980 / Contemporary 14004
Fine two-piano set from the early '80s, with the flamboyant Spanish pianist Tete Montliu dueting with fellow pianist Chick Corea. Their exchanges, sometimes combative, sometimes complementary, and always engaging and gripping, are brillant. —*Ron Wynn, AMG*

○ **Music I Like to Play—Vol. 2, The** / i. Dec. 1986 / Soul Note 1200

○ **Music I Like to Play—Vol. 1, The** / Dec. 1986 / Soul Note 121180
The first in a four-part series that featured pianist Tete Montliu doing his favorite material, much of it standards, but also bop and mainstream pieces, ballads, and an occasional blues. —*Ron Wynn*

James Moody

b. Mar. 26, 1925, Savannah, GA
Alto sax, tenor sax, flute / Bop
Alto and saxophonist-flutist James Moody was among the first tenor players to master bop's demanding vocabulary, although he scored a huge hit on alto with the 1949 song "I'm in the Mood for Love." Moody was in the Air Force band in 1943-1946 and worked with Dizzy Gillespie in 1946-1948, touring Europe with him during that stint. He was in Paris in 1948-1951, even while "I'm in the Mood for Love" was burning up jukeboxes. The song was a hit again in 1952, when King Pleasure wrote words to fit his solo and turned it into "Moody's Mood for Love." Moody added flute to his arsenal in the '50s, co-led a septet in 1951-1962, and was in a three-tenor unit with Sonny Stitt and Gene Ammons in 1962. He rejoined Gillespie in 1963-1968. He's been a leader ever since and worked in Las Vegas in the late '70s. He is currently recording on Novus with a new band that includes young lion Todd Coleman and old pro Kenny Barron. —*Ron Wynn*

○ **New Sounds** / i. 1948 / Blue Note 84436

○ **Beginning and End of Bop, The** / Oct. 19, 1948 / Blue Note 6503
This James Moody recording was basically two different groups. The first five selections on side one found Moody (tenor sax) with Max Roach (drums), Kenny Dorham (trumpet), Al Haig (piano), and Tommy Potter (bass). While the recording quality left something to be desired, the music itself was hot and often inspired. —*Carl Brauer, Cadence*

○ **Moodsville** / May 21, 1951-Jan. 8, 1954 / Emarcy 26040

★ **Moody's Mood for Love** / Dec. 14, 1956 / Argo
A strong version of the "Moody's Mood for Love," with a vocal by the late Eddie Jefferson (v). —*Ron Wynn*

○ **Great Day** / Jun. 17-18, 1963 / Chess 91522
Some good, sometimes excellent sax and flute work from the always reliable James Moody. This was period in which he was dabbling sometimes in soul-jazz, other times hard bop, but mostly played mainstream, straightahead originals, standards, and ballads. —*Ron Wynn*

★ **Don't Look Away Now** / Feb. 14, 1969 / Prestige

★ **Everything You've Always Wanted to Know About Sax** / i. Mar. 1972 / Cadet 60010
Everything You've Always Wanted To Know About Sax. Twofer date with Eddie Jefferson (v) on some tracks. Also with Tom McIntosh (tb), Howard McGhee (tpt), Hank Jones (p), and Kiane Zawadi (euphonium/tb). —*Michael G. Nastos*

○ **Jazz Legacy** / i. 1980 / Inner City 7020

○ **Sweet and Lovely** / Mar. 1989 / Novus 3063

Saxophone veteran James Moody stages an impromptu reunion with his longtime friend and onetime leader Dizzy Gillespie on this '89 session. Their interaction hasn't been dulled by their time apart; they still anticipate each other and mesh effectively. Moody's own solos are mellow, well constructed, and superbly played. The backing band wisely defers to the giants, though keyboardist Marc Cohen has a few good passages. —*Ron Wynn*

○ **Honey** / Oct. 1990 / Jive/Novus 3111
The selections on this recent album are eratic, but he and veteran Kenny Barron (p) uphold things. It is certainly not a classic, but it's worth having. —*Ron Wynn*

Ralph Moore

b. Dec. 24, 1956
Tenor sax / Neo-bop
This exemplary young-lion tenor saxophonist moved to the West Coast from England in the '80s. He is a driving, exciting soloist and a versatile stylist who has managed to find work in every setting from big band to small combo. He has recorded for Landmark since 1989 and has solo albums on the German Criss-Cross label as well. —*Ron Wynn*

★ **Furthermore** / Mar. 3-05, 1990 / Landmark 1526
One of the best among the young-lion tenor saxophonists makes an aggressive, explosive statement. —*Ron Wynn*

Airto Moreira (Airto Guimorva Moreira)

b. Aug. 5, 1941, Itaiopolis, Brazil
Percussion, vocals / Latin-jazz, early jazz-rock, world fusion
Arguably the greatest Brazilian percussionist ever, and certainly the most famous, Airto Moreira was working in bands at age 12, having studied acoustic guitar and piano as a child. He was a familiar figure in Brazil's night clubs and spent three years on that circuit. He later worked with, then co-led, a group with Hermeto Pascoal. During extensive travels throughout Brazil, Moreira collected 120 different instruments. He left Brazil for America in 1968 with his wife Flora Purim, and in 1970 he joined Miles Davis, where he instantly got widespread attention. After a brief 1971 stint with Lee Morgan, Moreira was part of the first edition of Weather Report and later the initial Return to Forever. Besides heading his own band, Moreira was the most in-demand percussionist of the '70s. He also worked in Purim's bands and recorded with Cannonball Adderley, Stan Getz, and many others. He hasn't been quite as active in the '80s and '90s, but still appears on many albums. He paved the way for the introduction of unusual Latin instruments and sounds into the jazz vernacular. —*Ron Wynn*

○ **Seeds to the Ground** / i. 1970 / Buddah 5085
★ **Free** / Apr. 1972-May 1972 / Columbia 40927
Includes first version of "Return to Forever." With Chick Corea (k), Keith Jarrett (p), Stanley Clarke (b), and Joe Farrell (ts). A great album. —*Michael G. Nastos*

Joe Morello (Joseph A. Morello)

b. Jul. 17, 1928, Springfield, MA
Drums, composer, arranger, bandleader / Cool
Joe Morello is a quicksilver drummer, most closely associated with the classic Dave Brubeck Quartets. He is also a fine arranger, composer, and bandleader. —*Michael G. Nastos*

★ **Joe Morello Sextet** / Jan. 3, 1956 / Intro 608
○ **Joe Morello** / i. 1961 / Bluebird 9784
It's About Time featured ten songs with the word *time* in their titles. Of these, five of the six quintet selections (starring Phil Woods and a young Gary Burton) and two of the four other songs (with the quintet augmented by a brass section) are on this, along with a totally unreleased big band session from the following year.... With Manny Albam contributing the arrangements, *It's About Time* was a happy surprise, a hard-driving set of swinging music. —*Scott Yanow, Cadence*

Frank Morgan

b. Dec. 23, 1933, Minneapolis, MN
Alto sax / Bop
Currently a hero to many young lions, the alto saxophonist overcame severe drug problems and two stretches in prison to become a viable, popular performer. In his 20s, Morgan was one of

the leading lights on the West Coast scene, but was imprisoned in the '50s, right at the peak of his powers. He moved to California at the age of 14, heard Charlie Parker for the first time as a teen, and began playing professionally in the early '50s. He made his first recordings in 1955, then went to jail for a year. Morgan was in and out of prison often in the '60s and '70s and was once in the same San Quentin band as Art Pepper. After going to Synanon in 1974, Morgan was sent back to prison and then got paroled. In solo structure, tone, phrasing, and approach, he's among the closest to Parker of any living alto player. —*Ron Wynn*

○ **Frank Morgan** / i. 1955 / GNP 12
Recorded in 1955, this reissue was more than another period piece. For one thing, it marked the rediscovery of a very talented alto player in Frank Morgan. For another, it was Wardell Gray's last recording. Moreover, it was a worthwhile period piece because it caught so many of the currents swirling through jazz in 1955. —*Douglas Clark, Down Beat*

○ **Introducing Frank Morgan** / 1955 / GNP 904
○ **Bebop Lives!** / Dec. 1986 / Contemporary 14026
Live date at the Village Vanguard in NYC, with this veteran alto saxophonist on top of things. Prime bop, not to be missed. —*Michael G. Nastos*

★ **Yardbird Suite** / Nov. 1988 / Contemporary 14045
Excellent piano from Mulgrew Miller, bass from Ron Carter, and drums from Al Foster. Morgan is sharp and authoritative as a leader and player. —*Ron Wynn*

○ **A Lonesome Thing** / i. 1992 / Antilles
Displays the other side of Morgan's personality, as he turns to sentimental numbers and old favorites like "When You Wish upon a Star" and "Ten Cents a Dance." There's also the demanding "Pannonica," where Morgan gets to stretch out a bit more, but mostly he's doing light, impressionistic fare here, albeit doing it with his customary flair and fire. —*Ron Wynn, Rock & Roll Disc*

Lee Morgan

b. Jul. 10, 1938, Philadelphia, PA, **d.** Feb. 19, 1972, New York, NY
Trumpet / Hard bop
This amazing trumpet firebrand was in the top echelon among hard bop players. Besides his great range, Morgan's lines and solos were bristling and intense. He often utilized slurs or bent notes and delivered retorts and rhythmic phrases that were unforgettable. Morgan joined Dizzy Gillespie's big band as an 18-year-old in 1956. Two years later he became one of Art Blakey's Jazz Messengers during a pivotal era, when Benny Golson was the music director. Morgan's elastic, exuberant solos made him a headliner. He got some pop action with the 1964 hit "The Sidewinder," his most popular composition. He became a consistent attraction on Blue Note in the '60s and early '70s before being killed by an ex-girlfriend at a night club. —*Ron Wynn*

○ **Introducing Lee Morgan** / Nov. 5, 1956 / Savoy 12091
Even at 19, on *Introducing Lee Morgan,* trumpeter Morgan was astounding. He hadn't completely honed the trademark slurs, but his remarkable control and bright, inventive phrasing make this a great listen—not to mention tenor saxophonist Hank Mobley, pianist Hank Jones, bassist Doug Watkins, and drummer Art Taylor, all playing in top form. —*John Corbett, Down Beat*

○ **Cooker, The** / Sep. 29, 1957 / Blue Note 1578
● **Best of Lee Morgan** / 1957-1965 / Blue Note 91138
☆ **A-1** / i. 195z / Savoy 1104
A collection of cuts from the group Morgan co-led with Hank Mobley (sax) in the '50s. —*Ron Wynn*

● **Sidewinder, The** / Dec. 21, 1963 / Blue Note 84157
★ **Search for the New Land** / Feb. 15, 1964 / Blue Note 84169
W/ Grant Green. Absolutely gorgeous compositional jazz. Near essential. —*Michael G. Nastos*

★ **Live at the Lighthouse** / Jul. 10-12, 1970 / Blue Note 89906
Twofer of a great live club date with extended versions and Bennie Maupin (sax), Harold Mabern (p), Jymie Merritt (b), and Mickey Roker (d). —*Michael G. Nastos*

Butch Morris (Lawrence Morris)

b. 1940, Los Angeles, CA
Cornet, composer, conductor / Progressive big band, modern creative

Once a promising cornetist and familiar figure in the avant-garde, Morris had been almost exclusively a composer and conductor in the '70s, '80s, and '90s, working extensively with David Murray. He's done some playing in Murray's big band, but prefers conducting and premiering his works for large orchestra. A one-time member of the Black Artists Group in St. Louis, Morris was an acclaimed free-style player in the '70s before switching almost totally to conducting. —*Ron Wynn*

○ **Current Trends in Racism in Modern America** / i. Feb. 1985 / Sound Aspects 4010
There are overemphasized, rather-too-sharp turns in direction (dynamics, time, texture) during *Current Trends* that suggest cues from the conductor; often they sound more jarring than organically developed. . . . Morris does exercise real control; he may not call individual notes, but he shapes the performance in a real if not always desirable way. The piece has textural sweep, but sometimes the results are ambiguous: The sing-song rhythm at the start of side two is amusing, yet also kinda crude. But there are also obvious fruits of conduction—like the descending cascades that precede Marclay's heavy rap-record cameo—that sound okay. —*Kevin Whitehead, Cadence*

★ **Dust to Dust** / i. Nov. 18-20, 1990 / New World 80408
A fine large-group recording. The ensemble has several top players, including Wayne Horvitz (k), Marty Ehrlich (reeds), and John Purcell (reeds). Morris conducts and supervises with his usual skill. —*Ron Wynn*

Jelly Roll Morton (Ferdinand Joseph Lemott)

b. Oct. 20, 1890, New Orleans, LA, **d.** Jul. 10, 1941, Los Angeles, CA

Piano, composer / New Orleans traditional
Pianist and composer Ferdinand "Jelly Roll" Morton is widely regarded as the first great composer in the jazz idiom, witnessed especially in his Red Hot Peppers recordings made for Victor in 1926-1930. A Creole pianist who was extremely proud of his French heritage, he earned the disapproval of his family by beginning his career in the bawdy houses of Storyville, the famed Red Light district of New Orleans, where he is said to have earned $100 a night entertaining the patrons of places such as the Hilma Burt House while still in his teens. Jelly's early years were spent traveling the nation solo and with various tent shows and vaudeville troupes. During World War I he settled in Chicago, where he began to assemble bands to record his compositions and other traditional New Orleans fare. In 1923 he participated in recording sessions with the New Orleans Rhythm Kings (NORK— a White outfit) for the Gennett label, located in Richmond, IN. At that time Indiana was the scene for a resurgence of Ku Klux Klan activity, and integrated recording sessions were risky business. According to NORK trombonist George Brunies, Jelly was passed off as a Spaniard—apparently accepted without question because of the diamond inlay that the pianist flashed with his broad smile. For the next five years Morton toured with various outfits from his home base in Chicago, including stints with Fate Marable, W. C. Handy, and The Alabamians. He also worked as a staff writer for the Melrose Publishing House, which covered many of his most famous compositions. For the Red Hot Peppers sessions he recruited a number of talented New Orleans sidemen, including Omer Simeon, Kid Ory, and the Dodds brothers. By 1930, however, it seemed that changing fashions (and a depressed recording market) had passed Jelly Roll by, and he was dropped from the Victor roster. As was the case for many of the older New Orleans players, the Depression years were unkind to Morton, and by the end of the decade he was living in obscurity in Washington, DC, waiting tables at a shoe-box nightclub called the Band Box. A series of oral history recordings made by Alan Lomax for the Archive of American Folksong at the Library of Congress in 1938 returned Jelly to national attention for a time (especially among a cadre of "hot" record collectors), but his death in 1941 ended his illustrious career before he was able to benefit from the New Orleans revival of the '40s.

Morton was certainly one of the most colorful characters in jazz history. His bravura and penchant for self-promotion (including the claim that he personally invented jazz) may have won some friends but also made him many enemies. As a solo pianist, he was capable of milking the instrument completely, with the ability to make a piano sound like an entire band. As a composer, arranger, and bandleader, he demanded absolute adherence to his

vision of the principle of traditional collective improvisation. The Red Hot Peppers records especially drew on a wide variety of musical elements, simultaneously restating themes from ragtime and presaging the syncopated section work that later became the hallmark of the swing era. —*Bruce Boyd Raeburn*

○ **Jelly Roll Morton (1917-1921)** / 1917-1921 / Biograph 1003
○ **Jelly Roll Morton (1923-1924)** / Apr. 1923-Jun. 1924 / Milestone 47018
Landmark stomps, blues, Afro-Latin tinged romps and early versions of anthems "King Porter Stomp" and "Wolverine Blues" make this pivotal work essential by a jazz legend. Morton probably didn't invent jazz as he claimed, but he certainly had a lot to do with it. This material was issued on a two-record vinyl set in '75, and the sound quality is dubious. This set has been supplanted by CD reissues on both domestic and import labels. —*Ron Wynn*

● **Piano Solos (1923-1924), The** / i. Jul. 1923-Jun. 1924 / Fountain 104
Jelly Roll Morton's crucial years were 1923-1928. They see him in the process of putting spring in his slightly stiff step of formal piano ragtime, synthesizing it orchestrally to the point of becoming preeminent as a bandleader in 1926, before taking his first steps toward becoming an anachronism. The piano solos demonstrated that Morton was by no means a faultless technician—he sometimes rushed tempos and stiffened under pressure at speed. He preferred a medium tempo, which gave him the freedom to swagger spryly and the space to deploy those personal pianistic characteristics he added to the piano's vocabulary. —*Chris Sheridan, Cadence*

Blues and Stomps: Rare Piano Rolls / Sep. 1924-Dec. 1924 / Biograph 111
1924-1926. These are just immaculate classic rolls, seminal piano cuts. —*Ron Wynn*

☆ **Jelly Roll Morton** / i. 1926-1938 / Bluebird 6588
A more-manageable selection of Morton's Red Hot Peppers, well-suited to the beginner. —*Bruce Raeburn*

★ **Jelly Roll Morton Centennial: His Complete Victor Recording** / 1926-1939 / Bluebird 2361
1926-1929. The ultimate Morton collection for the specialist, although all possible Victor takes are not included and some appear twice. Even so, a splendid range of Mortonia from the Red Hot Peppers through Jelly Roll Morton and his New Orleans Jazzmen. —*Bruce Raeburn*

○ **Library of Congress Recordings Vol. 1, The** / i. May 1938-Jun. 1938 / Classic Jazz 1
A fascinating mixture of music and reminiscence. Jazz history from the Morton perspective. —*Bruce Raeburn*

○ **Library of Congress Recordings Vol. 2, The** / i. May 1938-Jun. 1938 / Classic Jazz 2
○ **Library of Congress Recordings Vol. 3, The** / i. May 1938-Jun. 1938 / Classic Jazz 3
○ **Library of Congress Recordings Vol. 4, The** / i. May 1938-Jun. 1938 / Classic Jazz 4
○ **Library of Congress Recordings Vol. 5, The** / i. May 1938-Jun. 1938 / Classic Jazz 5
○ **Library of Congress Recordings Vol. 6, The** / i. May 1938-Jun. 1938 / Classic Jazz 6
○ **Library of Congress Recordings Vol. 7, The** / i. May 1938-Jun. 1938 / Classic Jazz 7
○ **Library of Congress Recordings Vol. 8, The** / i. May 1938-Jun. 1938 / Classic Jazz 8

○ **Jelly Roll Morton: Rediscovered Solos** / i. 1953 / Riverside 1018
○ **Mr. Jelly Lord** / i. 1956 / Tomato 70384
● **Complete Vols. 1 and 2, The** / i. Jun. 1980 / RCA 42405
The Complete Jelly Roll Morton, a double album contained—chronologically for the first time—all the pianist-composer-bandleader's Chicago recordings of 1926-1927. Their importance as initial organizing and formalizing instruments, creating structure within the music, had often been stressed, though this neglected the extent to which they formed the basis for future developments. In "Black Bottom Stomp,"—the first, and ironically, unsurpassed Morton masterpiece, we had a pre-echo, not merely of Kansas City swing, but of later methods like Horace Silver's brand

of hard bop. Time and again, in performances like "Dead Man Blues," "Steamboat Stomp," "Grandpa's Spells," "Doctor Jazz," "The Pearls," or "Wolverine Blues," we were given evidence of Morton's ability to vary rhythm or to spin secondary and tertiary themes from the masterial as a means of unifying the improvisations. And even in a saccharine piece like "Someday Sweetheart" there was a concern for texture that, albeit comparatively unsophisticated, remained neglected outside the Ellington milieu until most modern times, finding sympathy in such diverse ambiences as those of Charles Mingus, the Art Ensemble of Chicago, and Air. One final point is that "Dead Man Blues" appeared for the first time on LP in unexpurgated form. —*Chris Sheridan, Down Beat*

Sam Most (Samuel Most)

b. Dec. 16, 1930, Atlantic City, NJ
Sax, flute / Bop
Sam Most is a saxophonist from the West Coast cool school who's also one of the few truly great jazz flute players. He's a perfect role model for future generations. Any of his albums on the Xanadu label are worth hearing. —*Michael G. Nastos*

○ **Bebop Revisited—Vol 3** / **i.** Dec. 1953 / Xanadu 172
This album presented a nice cross-section of known and unknown artists—a second generation of bop. Everyone accounted for themselves well, with Tony Fruscella's trumpeting being a real ear-opener and the arrangements for most selections cleary charting ideas or forms for the future. The music swings in that traditional manner and Mark Gardner's comprehensive notes complement the aural experience very well. —*Milo Fine, Cadence*

★ **Mostly Flute** / May 27, 1976 / Xanadu
W/ Duke Jordan Trio and Tal Farlow on guitar. Two Sam Most originals, five standards. Great interplay between Most and Farlow. —*Michael G. Nastos*

○ **Flute Flight** / **i.** Dec. 1976 / Xanadu 141
Flutist Sam Most's beautiful vibrato and duo with pianist Lou Levy on "It Might as Well Be Spring" made this a great track. The album surprise was in the last three tracks. "Last Night When We Were Young" was a magnificent tune, and this had to be a classic rendition. —*Jerry Atkins, Cadence*

○ **But Beautiful** / 1976 / Catalyst 7609
Sam Most was among the early exponents of the jazz flute. He played with people as diverse as Henry Mancini, Charles Mingu,s and Oscar Pettiford, occasionally wandering off into the wilderness of Las Vegas, Palm Springs, and Los Angeles. With a subdued rhythm section of drummer Will Bradley, George Muribus on piano, and Patrick "Putter" Smith on bass, Most drifted through standards like "But Beautiful" and "There Is No Greater Love." His interpretation of "I've Grown Accustomed to Your Face," featuring a passage with flute and bass, was stunning. Most also played some tenor sax on this date, but his flute was the most compelling component. —*Herb Nolan, Down Beat*

★ **From the Attic of My Mind** / Apr. 25, 1978 / Xanadu
Flutist Sam Most had it all here: a distinctively dark, breathy tone, technique to spare, a varied batch of original tunes, an able backup crew, even a hilarious album title. Most's clean, pressive articulation recalled Rahsaan Roland Kirk (who of course followed Most onto the scene); he explicity evoked Kirk on the hum-and-blow choruses of the irresistibly danceable "Keep Moving," which featured some gracefully choppy funk. —*Kevin Whitehead, Cadence*

○ **Flute Talk** / Jan. 23-24, 1979 / Xanadu 173
Sam Most's *Flute Talk* broke no new ground in the sense of setting standards by which all jazz flutists were judged. Primarily a high-spirited straightahead session, this record nevertheless filled the void for those who like the sound of jazz flute, yet are disenchanted with the peppy muzak of Herbie Mann, Dave Valentin, and Hubert Laws. —*Arthur Moorehead, Down Beat*

Bennie Moten (Benjamin Moten)

b. Nov. 13, 1894, Kansas City, MO, **d.** Apr. 2, 1935, Kansas City, MO
Piano, bandleader / Swing
Pianist and bandleader Bennie Moten was a prime personality in the '20s. He began as a trio leader playing ragtime and traditional New Orleans jazz. Moten built his band to six pieces by 1925 and

added more members three years later to build the orchestra to a full group. Moten emphasized dance-oriented compositions and was a precursor to the classic '30s Kansas City swing bands. He built his orchestra by raiding Walter Page's Blue Devils, forcing Page to dismantle his band and join Moten. His early '30s bands included Ben Webster, Eddie Barefield, Herschel Evans, and Lester Young. His band reached its peak in popularity in 1935. At his death, Moten's band became the Count Basie Band. —*Ron Wynn*

○ **Benny Moten Complete—Vols. 1 and 2** / **i.** 1926 / RCA 42410
1926-1928. Chicago recordings for pianist's Kansas City orchestra. —*Michael G. Nastos*

★ **Basie Beginnings (1929-1932)** / 1929-1932 / Bluebird 9768
Bennie Moten's orchestra, arguably the top territory band at the time Count Basie joined as second pianist in 1929, had been reasonably well represented on records since 1923. . . . This does have the cream of Moten's 1929 and 1930 sessions, plus seven of the ten songs cut at their superb December 13, 1932, date. Moten himself never again appeared on records after Basie joined. —*Scott Yanow, Cadence*

Paul Motian (Stephen Paul Motian)

b. Mar. 25, 1931, Philadelphia, PA
Drums, percussion, composer / Cool, modern creative
Not a bombastic, dazzling, or powerful percussionist, Paul Motian has become a formidable drummer through his ability to interact with group members and vary or break up the beat, rather than keep a steady, throbbing pulse. His best work has been done in loose outside or free contexts, rather than conventional hard bop, mainstream, or swing. He began recording in the mid '50s. He worked with vocalist Bob Dorough and Miles Davis in the '50s before joining Bill Evans in 1959. He stayed until 1963 and then played with Paul Bley and many others before joining Keith Jarrett for two long stretches (1966-1969 and 1971-1975). Motian was part of the Jazz Composers Orchestra Association and worked in Charlie Haden's Liberation Orchestra as well. During the '70s and '80s, he led small combos, worked in solo and trio situations, and reunited with Paul Bley on two excellent late '80s releases. —*Ron Wynn*

○ **Conception Vessel** / Nov. 25-26, 1972 / ECM
This is Motian's debut as a leader. It includes ambitious cuts with guitarist Sam Brown and also features pianist Keith Jarrett. —*Ron Wynn*

★ **Dance** / Sep. 1977 / ECM
Excellent solos by saxophonist Charles Brackeen and above-average writing and ensemble work. —*Ron Wynn*

☆ **Monk in Motian** / Mar. 1988 / JMT 834421
A top tribute, with sterling work by Frisell (g) and Dewey Redman (ts). —*Ron Wynn*

★ **Paul Motian on Broadway—Vol. 1 (with Bill Frisell, Charlie Haden, Joe Lovano & Paul M** / Nov. 1988-Sep. 1989 / JMT 834430

○ **Paul Motian on Broadway—Vol. 2** / Nov. 1988-Sep. 1989 / JMT 834440

○ **Bill Evans: Tribute to the Great Post-Bop Pianist** / May 1990 / JMT 834445
An excellent quartet date featuring sensational guitar by Bill Frisell and nice tenor sax from Joe Lovano. —*Ron Wynn*

Famoudou Don Moye

b. May 23, 1946, Rochester, NY
Drums, percussion / Early free, modern creative
A member of the Art Ensemble of Chicago, Moye has been one of the drummers of choice among the '60s-and-beyond free generation, along with Ed Blackwell and Sunny Murray. He took percussion classes at Wayne State University in 1965-1966 and played with a group called Detroit Free Jazz, touring Europe with them in 1968. He worked with saxophonist Steve Lacy in Europe, also playing with the Gospel Messenger Sisters, guitarist Sonny Sharrock, pianist Dave Burrell, saxophonists Gato Barbieri and Pharoah Sanders, and trumpeter Alan Shorter before joining the Art Ensemble of Chicago in Paris in 1969. He's been a member of the ensemble ever since and has also made some freewheeling, ambitious records as a leader. —*Ron Wynn*

Percussionist w/ Art Ensemble of Chicago. A powerhouse multiinstrumentalist, as scary musically as he can be subtle. — *Michael G. Nastos*

○ **Sun Percussion** / **i.** Jan. 1979 / AECO 001
Quintessential solo recording (all percussion) from an Art Ensemble standout. —*Michael G. Nastos*

★ **Black Paladins** / **i.** 1981 / Black Saint
Adventurous concept pieces, excellent percussive foundations, and adept playing. —*Ron Wynn*

Idris Muhammad (Leo Morris)

b. Nov. 13, 1939, New Orleans, LA.
Drums / Hard bop, soul-jazz, contemporary funk, modern creative

Though consistency has not been a strong point, drummer Idris Muhammad has turned in some outstanding performances on hard bop and soul-jazz dates. His own albums as a leader have been another matter; they have been mostly undistinguished at best. Muhammad's strengths include his ability to provide rhythmically dynamic backgrounds and smoothly vary a session's tempo and pace. Muhammad began playing drums at 8, and worked in jazz groups at 16. He backed soul vocalists Sam Cooke and Jerry Butler in the early and mid-'60s, as well as the Impressions. Muhammad played with Lou Donaldson in the mid- and late '60s, and was in the pit band for the musical *Hair* from 1969 to 1973. He was Prestige's house drummer in the early '70s and anchored several rocking soul-jazz dates, while cutting some not-so-rocking ones as a leader. He played with Roberta Flack in the early '70s, led his own bands, and played with Johnny Griffin in 1978 and 1979 and Pharoah Sanders in 1980. Muhammad's continued his odd recording pattern in the '80s and '90s with such tepid releases as *Black Rhythm Revolution* and *My Turn*. He's recorded as a leader for Prestige, Theresa, and Lipstick, among others. Muhammad has a couple of sessions available on CD. — *Ron Wynn*

● **Kabsha** / **i.** Nov. 1981 / Theresa 110
Much more jazz oriented than some of the session drummer's releases, this '81 date included guest stint by Pharoah Sanders and had Muhammad playing far more aggressively and anchoring the date. —*Ron Wynn, AMG*

Gerry Mulligan (Gerald Joseph Mulligan)

b. Apr. 6, 1927, New York, NY
Baritone sax, arranger / Cool

Now an elder statesman of the cool sound, Gerry Mulligan is arguably the best-known baritone saxophonist in jazz. He grew up in Philadelphia and got some early recognition as a writer. Mulligan's never had any problems with the cumbersome baritone sax—getting a rich, full sound, and displaying great range, tone, and ideas. He had songs recorded by Gene Krupa in 1947 and Claude Thornhill in 1948, and he also played in both bands on alto. He joined the Miles Davis band in 1948, switched to baritone, and was one of the participants in the seminal cool recordings that proved extremely influential in forging an alternative to bop. He led groups similar to the Davis orchestra in 1951, 1953, and 1972 and spent a year writing for Stan Kenton in 1953. But he attained his reputation for his work with a number of quartets in the '50s, particularly his 1952-1953 group with trumpeter Chet Baker, plus other groups he led with Jon Eardley, Bob Brookmeyer, and Zoot Sims. Mulligan led a 12-piece unit for three years in the early '60s and spent four years with the Dave Brubeck band. As a composer and arranger, Mulligan was famous for writing pieces that didn't include the piano and for leading ensembles that lacked either piano or guitar. His arrangements emphasized precision, swing, and a mild sound, with Mulligan usually opting for either two or three trumpets in his brass section, rather than the customary four. He's also made some extraordinary albums working with people he wouldn't normally be stylistically linked with, such as alto saxophonist Johnny Hodges and tenor saxophonist Ben Webster. —*Ron Wynn*

○ **Mulligan Plays Mulligan** / Sep. 27, 1951 / Prestige 003
A standout date, with Mulligan doing his own songs and top-echelon playing by Allen Eager (ts). —*Ron Wynn*

★ **Pacific Jazz and Capitol Recordings** / Jun. 10, 1952-May 20, 1953 / Mosaic 203(l)

Complete Pacific Jazz and Capitol Recordings of the original Gerry Mulligan Quartet and Tentette with Chet Baker. Virtually the entire '50s output of the superb Mulligan-Baker small and large groups (except their Fantasy dates). —*Ron Wynn*

○ **Lee Konitz Plays with the Gerry Mulligan Quartet** / Jan. 30, 1953-Feb. 24, 1953 / Pacific Jazz 2

○ **Pleyel Concert (June 1954)** / Jun. 1-07, 1954 / Vogue 655610
Recorded at the Third Paris Jazz Festival, the album captured this particular Gerry Mulligan unit on an inspired occasion. The main attraction of the music was the interplay between Mulligan (baritone sax) and Bob Brookmeyer (valve trombone), which gave the music substantial depth. —*Carl Brauer, Cadence*

○ **Arranger, The** / 1957 / Columbia 34803
As the title announced, this was a notable attempt at documenting the status and evolution of Gerry Mulligan's first love: orchestral arrangement. It made available, for the first time, a handful of Mulligan's primal, formative arrangements for Gene Krupa and Elliot Lawrence's orchestras, as well as several extensive blowing sessions from his own late '50s orchestra with Bob Brookmeyer, Lee Konitz, and Zoot Sims, which predated his imperial Concert Jazz Band. Actually, the signature of Mulligan's style changed little over the 11 years documented here. He consistently favored a seamless theme line underscored with a smooth sax bedding, stated often in terms of simple counterpoint and gentle contrary sweeps. But it was from the timing of those lines, the way they stretched around and overlapped one another, and the percussive texture of whole sections, that he derived his resilent and elegant sense of tension. —*Mikal Gilmore, Down Beat*

○ **Mulligan Meets Monk** / Aug. 12-13, 1957 / Riverside 12247

○ **Gerry Mulligan Meets Stan Getz** / Oct. 22, 1957 / Verve 8535

★ **Gerry Mulligan Meets Ben Webster** / Nov. 3, 1959-Dec. 2, 1959 / PolyGram 841661
Gerry Mulligan Meets Ben Webster was a classic confrontation of two of the mellowest, most virile, and most expressive of saxophonists. . . . Mulligan's renowned adaptability complements rather than idolizes Webster, and the two proved boon companions (like genial sumo wrestlers sparring), be it blowing heads at full sail or cracking fours with drummer Mel Lewis. Mutual respect inspired them and never faded into obeisance, and the rhythm supported admirably (keyed by the sprightly, canny Jimmy Rowles on piano) with never a thought to obtruding on the dialog—practically unimaginable today! —*Fred Bouchard, Down Beat*

☆ **Holiday with Mulligan** / Apr. 10-17, 1961 / DRG 5191
Baritone-saxophonist Gerry Mulligan and actress Judy Holliday were an "item" around the time of this recording. Their one meeting on record features Holliday doing some effective singing on 11 songs, mostly lesser-known standards plus four songs cowritten by the two leaders. Unfortunately Mulligan's Concert Jazz Band is largely wasted, being restricted to anonymous accompaniment of Holliday, making this CD of greater historical value than of interest to jazz listeners. —*Scott Yanow*

☆ **Jeru** / Jun. 8, 1962-Aug. 13, 1962 / RCA Victor 2624

★ **Lonesome Boulevard** / **i.** 1990 / A&M 5326
The 1989 Gerry Mulligan quartet (with pianist Bill Charlap, bassist Dean Johnson, and drummer Richie De Rosa) is well featured on this enjoyable set, performing "Splendor in the Grass" and nine recent Gerry Mulligan compositions including "Lonesome Boulevard," "The Flying Scotsman," and "Good Neighbor Thelonious." Baritonist Mulligan deserves great credit for the consistency of his recordings during the previous '40 years. This CD is easily recommended, for the leader remained very much in his prime. —*Scott Yanow*

○ **Re-Birth of the Cool** / Jan. 1992 / GRP 9679
Baritone saxophonist Gerry Mulligan fulfilled a long dream in '92 with a rerecording of the sessions in the late '40s that launched the "cool" era. He'd wanted to do it with trumpeter Miles Davis, but Davis died before the project could reach fruition. So trumpeter Wallace Roney took his spot and did an admirable job. Gil Evans is the other principal who'd died, but pianist John Lewis, alto saxophonist Phil Woods, and vocalist Mel Tormé helped rekindle the original feeling. —*Ron Wynn, AMG*

Jimmy Mundy (James Mundy)

b. Jun. 28, 1907, Cincinnati, OH, **d.** Apr. 24, 1983, NY
Arranger, tenor sax / Swing, big band
One of the swing era's finest arrangers, Jimmy Mundy was a vital contributor to sessions by everyone from Earl Hines to Count Basie in the '30s and '40s. Mundy trained as a classical violinist and toured with an evangelist's orchestra while a teen, playing violin and tenor sax. He developed his arranging skill working in Washington during the mid-'20s. Mundy worked in the early and mid-'30s for Earl Hines, providing for him "Cavernism" and "Copenhagen," among others. He also played tenor sax and recorded while with Hines. Mundy arranged "Swingtime in the Rockies," "Jumpin' at the Woodside," "Solo Flight," and "Air Mail Special" while serving as staff arranger for Benny Goodman in the mid-'30s. "Swingtime in the Rockies" and "Solo Flight" were also Mundy compositions. Gene Krupa also recorded Mundy arrangements in the '30s. He recorded for Varsity in 1937 and led his own big band briefly in 1939. Mundy supplied several arrangements to Count Basie in the '40s, among them "Super Chief," "Queer Street," and "Blue Skies." He also had arrangements recorded by Dizzy Gillespie in the '40s. Mundy didn't do much in jazz from the '50s on, though he occasionally wrote arrangements for and led studio orchestras backing various jazz and pop musicians. He served as music director for Barclay Records in France in the late '50s and early '60s and then returned to New York and did more freelance studio arrangements. Vintage Basie and Goodman reissues feature stunning Mundy arrangements and compositions. —*Ron Wynn*

Mark Murphy (Mark Howe Murphy)

b. Mar. 14, 1932, Syracuse, NY
Vocals / Ballads & blues
Mark Murphy is a New York-born, California-based jazz vocalist, who was championed by Steve Allen in the '50s. He's a great singer of ballads, blues, and bop, and an incredible scat singer. His distinctive voice is used well in all ranges. Murphy was influenced by Charlie Parker and inspired by Jack Keroac. He's a hipster. —*Michael G. Nastos*

○ **That's How I Love the Blues** / 1962 / Riverside 367

☆ **Bop for Kerouac** / Mar. 12, 1981 / Muse 5253
On *Bop for Kerouac*, alto saxophonist Richie Cole played Bird (Charlie Parker) to vocalist Mark Murphy's Miles Davis. You got the vividly hot and detached cool intensity of the music. Kerouac captured the feeling in his writing, and it was charted lovingly here in keyboarder Bill Mays's nostalgic yet exultantly contemporary settings. The makeup inspired solos that were on target and dancing. The singer's thoroughly masculine timbre coarsened or cracked for dramatic emphasis. His vibrato swaggered or glided. *Bop for Kerouac* was a great album for romance. —*Owen Cordle, Down Beat*

★ **Artistry of Mark Murphy** / Apr. 2-03, 1982 / Muse 5286
Includes a stunning medley of "Babe's Blue," "Little Niles," and "Dat Dere." Recorded with Tom Harrell (tpt), Gene Bertoncini (g), and Ben Aranov (p) in a larger-group setting. —*Michael G. Nastos*

☆ **Beauty and the Beast** / 1983-1986 / Muse 5355
This is really good Murphy, arranged by Bill Mays. McCoy Tyner's "Effendi" is a highlight, as is "Doxy" and "I Can't Get Started." —*Michael G. Nastos*

☆ **Kerouac Then and Now** / Nov. 1986 / Muse 5359

Turk Murphy (Melvin Edward Alton Murphy)

b. Dec. 16, 1915, Palermo, CA, **d.** May 30, 1987, San Francisco, CA
Trombone, bass clarinet, bandleader / New Orleans traditional
Trombone, bandleader. Along with Lu Watters, Turk Murphy was instrumental in the revival of New Orleans-style jazz in San Francisco during World War II. He was the trombonist with Watters's Yerba Buena Jazz Band until 1947, when he decided to forge out on his own. The Turk Murphy Jazz Band made numerous recordings from 1950 to 1980; headquartered in San Francisco at Earthquake McGoon's for many years, it became a major influence on the Bay Area traditonal jazz scene. In the mid-'70s Murphy's band toured Australia and Europe, and in 1987 it performed at Carnegie Hall. Playing in a full-bodied tailgate style, like Ory, Murphy used the trombone to achieve a spectrum of

emotional coloring from humor to pathos. One of the adjectives most often applied to his playing was "gutsy," and considering the fact that Turk Murphy continued to make music until the final days of his life (despite a long illness), in this case the style can be said to define the man. —*Bruce Boyd Raeburn*

○ **Favorites / i.** 1949-1951 / Good Time Jazz 60011
Turk Murphy Jazz Band. A good introduction to the Turk Murphy style. —*Bruce Raeburn*

○ **San Francisco Jazz—Vol. 1** / Jan. 19, 1950 / Good Time Jazz 12026

● **Turk Murphy's Jazz Band** / May 8, 1950 / Good Time Jazz
Turk Murphy is a Kid Ory-inspired trombonist and was featured prominently in the revivalist era. This record (and Vol. 2) is a classic of sorts (historical more than musical). It rates high in enthusiasm, and for Bob Scobey's trumpet, but low for finesse and subtlety and repeated and extended listenings become a bit weary. —*Bob Rusch, Cadence*

○ **San Francisco Jazz—Vol. 2** / May 8, 1950-Jul. 10, 1951 / Good Time Jazz

○ **Music of Jelly Roll Morton** / Aug. 29, 1953-Sep. 14, 1953 / Columbia 559

David Murray (David Keith Murray)

b. Feb. 19, 1955, Berkeley, CA
Tenor sax, bandleader / Early free, modern creative
Tenor sax and bandleader David Murray has, simply put, presented himself in a variety of settings with more success than any other saxophonist of his time. While suggesting a strong link to the work of Sonny Rollins, Murray's music is steeped in the church (check out the DIW release *Spirituals* if there are any doubts) and in R&B, yet Murray is one of jazz's most uninhibited improvisers.

While the majority of raves have come in favor of Murray's octet dates, emphasizing Murray's considerable voicing skills, one should not neglect the many excellent small-group settings, particularly the more recent DIW sets. Murray's big-band outings rank among his most challenging work and are worth investigation. And did we mention Murray's work with the esteemed World Saxophone Quartet? Any of these attributes would be distinguished enough on their own, and Murray has so skillfully negotiated them as to give cause for strong argument that he could be one of the most formidable jazz musician of our era. —*Steve Aldrich*

★ **Flowers for Albert** / Jun. 26, 1976 / India Navigation
A common link to all four pieces of this live recording from the Ladies' Fort in New York City was a relaxed restraint. Nobody was trying to dazzle the listener with speed or technique; there were no ego trips. The best example was drummer Phillip Wilson's contributions. He was so unobtrusive that one might overlook his importance to the overall mood and sound. —*Carl Brauer, Cadence*

○ **Live at the Lower Manhattan Ocean Club—Vol. 1 & 2** / Dec. 31, 1977 / India Navigation 1032

○ **Murray's 3d Family** / Sep. 3, 1978 / Hat Art 6020
This particular two-record set captured tenor saxophonist David Murray and his trio in performance at the '78 Willisau Jazz Festival. From the opening high-energy tenor exorcisms of "In Memory of Jomo Kenyatta" to the final quiet ending of "Shout Song" this trio was in total command of its music. Murray's most outside playing was found on the opening track, but he never fell over into random noise or into the trap of running out of ideas. —*Carl Brauer, Cadence*

★ **Ming** / Jul. 25+28, 1980 / Black Saint 120045
Murray rose so impressively to the occasion as a triple-threat composer, arranger, and soloist that his budding legend was given new credibility. Confirming Murray's importance as a post-Ayler traditionalist, *Ming* may very well prove to be his first indispensable recording. Murray galvanized this sterling unit with a diverse program culled, in large measure, from previously recorded material. —*Bill Shoemaker, Down Beat*

○ **Home** / Oct. 31, 1981+Nov. 1, 1981 / Brass Star 0055
Tenor saxophonist David Murray regrouped the same octet that recorded *Ming* and released *Home*. . . . There was not a weak solo moment on the set, and it was that combination of arrangements

and ensemble strength that made this more than just another date. —*Bob Rusch, Cadence*

☆ **Murray's Steps** / Jul. 19, 1982 / Black Saint 120065
David Murray's octet stands as the premier ensemble in contemporary jazz, and this, their third album, was an effervescent, swinging, joyous piece of work. Henry Threadgill, Butch Morris, Steve McCall, and Wilber Morris were still in tow from previous Murray Octet albums, with Craig Harris (trombone), Bobby Bradford (trumpet), and Curtis Clark (piano) replacing, respectively George Lewis, Olu Dara, and Anthony Davis. It was hard to single out soloists or solos here. . . . What was important to point out was that this was a group effort, but the combined voice was very much that of David Murray. He proved himself, at age 28, a fully-developed writer and bandleader and a still-growing soloist. —*Lee Jeske, Down Beat*

○ **Live at Sweet Basil—Vol. 2** / Aug. 24-26, 1984 / Black Saint 95
The second of two marvelous big band dates featuring the Murray big band recorded at Sweet Basil's. The band included the cream of '70s and '80s jazz, with Murray roaring and spearheading things on tenor and bass clarinet, with Butch Morris conducting. —*Ron Wynn, AMG*

○ **Live at Sweet Basil—Vol. 1** / Aug. 24-26, 1984 / Black Saint 0085

Ming's Samba / i. Jul. 20, 1988 / Portrait 44432
Recorded at CBS Studios in New York, this album is named after David Murray's wife Ming. It includes some nice work, in particular the very lovely cut "Spooning." —*Michael Erlewine*

○ **Special Quartet** / 1990 / Columbia 52955
A simply magnificent Murray quartet session from '90, among the first issued under a joint Columbia/DIW deal. His roaring tenor sax was the focal point for some excellent compositions, which were punctuated by pianist McCoy Tyner, bassist Fred Hopkins, and drummer Elvin Jones. Here's one group that most definitely should record again. —*Ron Wynn, AMG*

○ **David Murray Big Band, Conducted by Lawrence "Butch" Morris** / Mar. 1991 / Columbia 48964
The triptych of tenor homages (Ben Webster, Lester Young, Paul Gonsalves) is an invigorating reassessment of David Murray's roots, with an unavoidable touch of Duke Ellington and Charles Mingus in the orchestration. Nice solos sliced in by the likes of trumpeter Hugh Ragin, trombonist Craig Harris, clarinetist Don Byron, and alto saxophonist James Spaulding, too. Conductor Butch Morris's "Calling Steve McCall," for the late AACM drummer, acts as a memorial coda. —*Art Lange, Down Beat*

Black and Black / i. 1992 / Red Baron 48852
A powerhouse '92 session by the prolific tenor saxophonist and bass clarinetist David Murray. He heads a strong quintet with trumpeter Marcus Belgrave, pianist Kirk Lightsey, bassist Santi Debriano, and drummer Roy Haynes through some bristling up-tempo originals, mixed with a couple of nice mid-tempo and ballad pieces for contrast. —*Ron Wynn*

○ **MX** / i. Dec. 21, 1992 / Red Baron 53274
MX takes David Murray about as far inside as he goes. Dedicated to Malcolm X, *MX* is no dirge. Murray contributes three memorable new tunes, ranging from an exotic processional ("Icarus") to uptown R&B ("Harlemite"). Murray shares solo space with John Hicks, Bobby Bradford, and Ravi Coltrane on tenor. The kid competently handles everything thrown at him, including Murray's high-speed blues,"El Hajj Malik El-Shabazz." —*Jon Andrews, Down Beat*

Sunny Murray (James Marcellus Arthur Murray)
b. Sep. 21, 1937, Idabel, OK
Drums, percussion / Early free, modern creative
A rampaging, fiery drummer, Sunny Murray has propelled some of the hottest free and outside jazz dates of the '60s and '70s. A self-taught player, Murray went to New York in 1956 and worked with Henry Allen and Willie "The Lion" Smith, playing rather traditional jazz, until he moved on to Jackie McLean and Ted Curson. But his 1959 meeting with Cecil Taylor changed Murray's professional life. Taylor's percussive, attacking, and slashing musical style resulted in a change in Murray's approach to the drums. He went to Europe with Taylor in 1963 and then joined a memorable trio with bassist Gary Peacock and saxophonist Albert Ayler, where his playing became even more energetic, loose, and frenetic than with Taylor. He later worked with (among

others) Don Cherry, John Coltrane, and Ornette Coleman before returning to France in 1968, where he played for a time with Archie Shepp and Grachan Moncur III. He was featured on a number of wonderful but poorly distributed and recorded albums for BYG in the late '60s. His group, The Untouchable Factor, did some recording in the '70s and appeared at the Wildflowers Festival in 1976, probably the high-water mark for the "loft jazz" movement. —*Ron Wynn*

○ **Hard Cores** / i. 1968 / Philly Jazz

★ **Never Give a Sucker an Even Break** / Nov. 22, 1969 / Affinity
Free rhythm, resuscitations, and spiritual quaverings made up an LP of music that sprang directly from the Albert Ayler-John Coltrane roots. It was a solid effort in structured freedom, rather even-handed and with no great peaks or insights revealed. —*Bob Rusch, Cadence*

Amina Claudine Myers

b. Mar. 1943, Blackwell, AR
Piano, organ, vocals / Modern creative
Amina Claudine Myers, a pianist and organist, has an extremely lovely voice. She plays blues, gospel, and her own witty originals that look to avant-garde musings. —*Michael G. Nastos*

★ **Song for Mother E** / i. 1979 / Leo 100
Duets with percussionist Pheeroan Aklaff. Sounds like a bigger group. Excellent. —*Michael G. Nastos*

☆ **Salutes Bessie Smith** / i. 1980 / Leo 103
It was ironic that the kind of majestic emotional power that would benefit a tribute to blues singer Bessie Smith was achieved by Amina Claudine Myers not in her renditions of blues originated by Smith, but on "African Blues," the 15-minute cry that finished the album. Before "African Blues," however, Myers interpreted some well-known Bessie Smith material and her own traditional composition "The Blues (Straight to You)." Myers voice itself came across as the wrong instrument, lacking the force or sheer guts with which Smith carved out her powerful lyrics and stately tunes. Instrumentally, though, the salute succeeded. Myers' spirited gospel and blues-based piano, Cecil McBee's graceful bass, and Jimmy Lovelace's discrete drumming provided the four Smith tunes with an elastic sound, sophisticated yet respectful. —*Lars Gabel, Down Beat*

Najee

Tenor and soprano sax / Instrumental pop
A popular multiinstrumentalist whose style is very similar to that of Kenny G., Dave Koz, and George Howard. His releases feature heavily produced, tightly arranged covers of urban contemporary songs; often include appearances by R&B vocalists; and have very limited solos and improvisational space. A saxophonist, flutist, and occasional keyboardist, Najee makes no claims to being a jazz musician, but his releases are marketed as "contemporary" jazz, and he's aired on lite jazz stations. He's recorded several sessions for EMI and Manhattan; all are available on CD. —*Ron Wynn*

Ray Nance (Ray Willis Nance)

b. Dec. 10, 1913, Chicago, IL, d. Jan. 28, 1976, New York, NY
Trumpet, cornet, violin, vocals / Swing, big band
A versatile trumpeter, violinist, vocalist, and dancer, Ray Nance brought both high artistic and great entertainment values to the Duke Ellington orchestra. His violin solos, replete with plucked string segments, broken lines, and bluesy phrases were crowd pleasers, while his ringing, superbly played trumpet solos were equally well appreciated, as were the occasional vocals. Nance wasn't as accomplished on mutes as predecessor Bubber Miley, but could provide exaggerated, voicelike effects and tonal colors. Nance even sometimes added some dance excitement. He began on piano at six, and took lessons on violin while teaching himself trumpet. Nance was a drum major in high school and led a sextet in Chicago in the early and mid-'30s. He worked with Earl Hines and Horace Henderson mostly as a trumpeter in the late '30s. Nance performed solo for a few months in 1940 and then joined the Ellington orchestra, where he was free to showcase his entire repertoire. Nance remained with Ellington until 1963, taking only a few brief periods off during the 23-year run. His violin was featured on such cuts as "Moon Mist" and "Come Sunday," while his wa-wa trumpet embellished an early '40s version of

"Take the 'A' Train." Nance later switched to cornet in the '60s. After leaving the Ellington orchestra, Nance played at the mid-'60s World's Fair with Paul Lavelle's orchestra and with Sol Yaged in the late '60s and Brooks Kerr in 1973. He toured England with Chris Barber in 1974 and then worked New York clubs. Nance can be heard on numerous Ellington recordings. He also recorded with Paul Gonsalves on Solid State, Black Lion, and MPS/BASF. They are currently not available on CD. —*Ron Wynn*

● **Body and Soul** / **i.** Apr. 1969 / Solid State 18062

Fats Navarro (Theodore Navarro)

b. Sep. 24, 1923, Key West, FL, **d.** Jul. 7, 1960, NYC
Trumpet / Bop
The trumpeter whose big, brawny tone set the stage (along with Dizzy Gillespie and Miles Davis) for the rise of bebop, Fats Navarro is another great artist whose career was cut short by tuberculosis, edged on by narcotics use. He did scant recording between the mid-'40s and his death in 1950. He was notable for his quick attack and Spanish-tinged phrasings. —*Michael G. Nastos*

☆ **Fat Girl** / Sep. 6, 1946-Dec. 5, 1947 / Savoy 2216
Landmark Navarro Savoy sessions with Howard McGhee (tp), Ernie Henry (as), and others. —*Ron Wynn*

☆ **Fabulous Fats Navarro—Vol. 1, The** / Jan. 29, 1947-Nov. 29, 1948 / Blue Note 81531
1947-1948. Here are brilliant trumpet solos from the sadly neglected trumpet master Fats Navarro. Blue Note may have deleted this completely by now. It has six bonus cuts featuring the equally undervalued Tadd Dameron. —*Ron Wynn*

○ **Fats Navarro with Tadd Dameron** / **i.** Jan. 29, 1947 / Milestone 47041
1989 reissue. Simply sublime sessions spotlighting the radical innovations of the great Fats Navarro, plus Tadd Dameron's creative arrangements. —*Ron Wynn*

★ **Prime Source** / Sep. 26, 1947-Aug. 9, 1949 / Blue Note
1947, 1948, and 1949 recording dates. Navarro as featured soloist with the Tad Dameron Sextet and Septet, the Howard McGhee-Navarro Boptet, and Bud Powell's Modernists. Reissue compilation of Navarro's prime early work. —*Michael G. Nastos*

○ **Fabulous Fats Navarro—Vol. 2, The** / Sep. 1947-Aug. 1949 / Blue Note 81532
The importance of this follow-up volume is equal to that of the first one. —*Ron Wynn*

Buell Neidlinger

b. Mar. 2, 1936, NYC
Bass / Early free, modern creative
Bassist Buell Neidlinger has played with distinction in free-jazz, traditional jazz, and bluegrass bands. He studied piano, trumpet, and cello as a child and in his early professional years played traditional and mainstream jazz in New York with Rex Stewart, Eddie Condon, and Vic Dickenson, among others. During the '50s he was part of Cecil Taylor's explosive group and worked with him from 1955 to 1960. In fact the great album *New York City R&B* was actually a Neidlinger session for Candid that wasn't issued until 11 years after it was recorded (and then under Taylor's name). Neidlinger also worked in the '50s with Steve Lacy and later did session work on electric as an R&B player. He switched styles again in 1960, spending two years playing part-time with the Houston Symphony Orchestra while also doing some club work playing soul jazz with Arnett Cobb. Then came rock sessions and dates with Frank Zappa and jazz-rock-fusion with Jean-Luc Ponty. He eventually formed his own K2B2 label and made jazz and contemporary music recordings, while doing freelance bluegrass and classical work. —*Ron Wynn*

○ **New York City R&B** / **i.** Jan. 9+10, 1961 / Candid 79017
W/ Cecil Taylor. This is actually Neidlinger's date. It is currently issued under Cecil Taylor's name. —*Ron Wynn*

○ **Buellgrass (Swingrass)** / **i.** 1980 / KZBZ

★ **Locomotive** / Jun. 1987 / Soul Note 121161
Virtuoso bassist and Marty Krystall on tenor sax. Fine music written by Monk and Ellington. —*Michael G. Nastos*

Oliver Nelson (Oliver Edward Nelson)

b. Jun. 4, 1932, St. Louis, MO, **d.** Oct. 27, 1975, Los Angeles, CA

Composer, arranger, alto sax, tenor sax, flute / Postbop, soul-jazz, progressive big band
Composer, arranger, alto and tenor saxophonist, and flutist Oliver Nelson was also a superb arranger and composer and a highly underrated soloist. Nelson was an incisive, frequently compelling alto player and quite accomplished on his other horns and flute. He came from a musical family and began playing publicly as a child. He worked in territory bands around St. Louis in the late '40s and joined Louis Jordan's big band in 1951. After serving in the military and studying music formally, Nelson moved to New York. He had stints with Erskine Hawkins, Wild Bill Davis, and Louis Bellson in California, and was with Quincy Jones in 1960-1961. Nelson began to build his reputation with some vital recordings from the early and mid-'60s, including his first big-band recording as well as small-group releases and works with Eric Dolphy. Nelson's arranging greatness became evident in the '60s as well, and he began arranging for Jimmy Smith, Billy Taylor, Wes Montgomery, and many others. From the mid-'60s until 1975, Nelson was quite busy with studio and television work, arrangements, recordings, and tours. —*Ron Wynn*

○ **Screamin' the Blues** / May 27, 1960 / New Jazz 080
Oliver Nelson and Eric Dolphy (alto sax, bass clarinet, flute) collaborated on some classic material and while *Screamin' the Blues* may not be classic, it did have bite, and excellent solos from a band that also included Richard Williams (once again producing stronger trumpet work as a sideman than he did as a leader), Richard Wyands (piano), George Duvivier (bass), and Roy Haynes (drums). —*Bob Rusch, Cadence*

★ **Soul Battle** / Sep. 9, 1960 / Prestige 325
Recorded at Englewood Cliffs, NJ. Oliver Nelson with King Curtis and Jimmy Forrest . . . called a *Soul Battle*, but it's really just a straightahead blowing date by three saxmen with distinct styles representative of different eras and genres. None of the saxes concede or compromise. This is King Curtis's most compelling jazz work . . . and makes one wonder just how big his talent was. —*Bob Rusch, Cadence*

● **Blues and the Abstract Truth** / 1961 / MCA 5659
This LP offered six substantial Oliver Nelson originals that allowed for exciting solo work by young Freddie Hubbard (trumpet), Eric Dolphy (alto sax, flute), and Nelson himself (tenor sax, alto sax). Bill Evans (piano) soloed, but not with the impact of the horns noted. The ensemble was completed by George Barrow (baritone sax), Paul Chambers (bass), and Roy Haynes (drums). This was inventive jazz that still sounded fresh years after it was recorded. —*Alan Bargebuhr, Cadence*

○ **Straight Ahead** / Mar. 1, 1961 / New Jazz 099
Oliver Nelson and Eric Dolphy were a formidable pair. . . . This date was also issued on another twofer. . . . Maybe it was too *straight ahead* rather than letting the muses go where they might naturally take themselves at this point in time. However, as usual Dolphy's playing was rewarding. The program had Richard Wyands (piano), George Duvivier (bass), and Roy Haynes (drums) as the rhythm section. —*Bob Rusch, Cadence*

☆ **Main Stem** / Aug. 25, 1961 / Prestige 1803
This is a laudable small-group date with solid piano by Hank Jones. W/ Joe Newman. —*Ron Wynn*

☆ **Stolen Moments** / Mar. 6, 1975 / Inner City 6008

● **More Blues & Abstract Truth** / Impulse
More Blues and the Abstract Truth was an excellent blues-oriented date that included plenty of bright moments, both from the colorful charts and the soloists, especially Adams and Roger Kellaway. —*Scott Yanow, Cadence*

Steve Nelson

Vibes / Modern creative
Steve Nelson has developed into a consistently outstanding vibes soloist and session musician. He's recorded as a leader for Sunnyside and Red, and played with such musicians as Mulgrew Miller, Bobby Watson, Kirk Lightsey, Ray Drummond, Donald Brown, Victor Lewis, and others. Nelson has also backed vocalists; worked in large and small combos; and played hard bop, bebop, blues, and free settings. He has some sessions available on CD. —*Ron Wynn*

● **Communications** / Oct. 1989 / Criss Cross 1034

Phineas Newborn (Phineas Newborn, Jr.)

b. Dec. 14, 1931, Whiteville, TN, d. 1989
Piano / Hard bop, postbop

Phineas Newborn was one of jazz's great technicians, gifted with incredible harmonic and rhythmic skills and imagination, plus remarkable facility and speed. Unfortunately, health problems caused frequent absences from playing and cut short his productive years. The Memphis-born Newborn worked in various local bands during the '40s and joined Lionel Hampton in the '50s. He played with Hampton in '50 and '52, spending '53-'55 in the service, and then moving to New York in 1956. Hampton had a duo with Charles Mingus in 1958, and toured Europe in '58 and '59. He made some highly praised recordings for Atlantic, RCA, Prestige, Roulette, and United Artists in the late '50s that established his reputation. One was a trio date with Roy Haynes and Paul Chambers. There were more fine sessions for Contemporary in the '60s, but then Newborn began suffering from injuries and illness that caused long absences from the music scene. He resumed a limited performance schedule in the early and mid-'70s, making the brilliant *Solo Piano* for Atlantic. Newborn recorded sonatas by Alexander Scriabin for VSOP in 1987. He died in Memphis in 1989. —*Ron Wynn*

○ **Here Is Phineas** / May 3-04, 1956 / Atlantic 1235

○ **While My Lady Sleeps** / 1957-1958 / Bluebird 61100
Some late-'50s cuts by piano great Phineas Newborn, then at the peak of his powers. Newborn could totally pick apart and rework any standard, while his own works were often so full of tricky phrases and dazzling devices they astonished even other great players. These were done in 1957 and 1958, and the CD features two bonus cuts. —*Ron Wynn, AMG*

● **Great Jazz Piano of Phineas Newborn Jr, The** / Nov. 21, 1961-Sep. 12, 1962 / Contemporary 388
Pianist Phineas Newborn Jr. could hardly restrain himself on this trio disc. Both rhythm sections (bassist Leroy Vinnegar, drummer Milt Turner first five songs; bassist Sam Jones, drummer Louis Hayes the last four) were at his service and didn't get a chance to step out; Newborn had so many ideas there was hardly room for anyone else; even when he was comping he was in a hurry, and he shifted between left-hand chording and two-handed octave unison work without apparent effort. —*Kevin Whitehead, Cadence*

○ **Newborn Touch** / Apr. 1, 1964 / Contemporary 270

○ **Harlem Blues** / Feb. 12-13, 1969 / Contemporary 662
In 1969, when this date was recorded, Phineas Newborn was an awesome pianist, having combined the dark, mahogany-rich sound and dazzling technique of Art Tatum with the fertile linear imagination of Bud Powell into an individual style that was passionate and explosive. There was nothing in jazz beyond his reach; his uptempos were full of vivid, polished ideas, brought off with the utmost confidence; he could swing hard enough to make you put your foot through the floor, and his ballad renditions evoked images of quietude and grandeur. Although Newborn had most of the solo space, *Harlem Blues* comes off as an integrated trio date. —*Zan Stewart, Down Beat*

○ **Please Send Me Someone to Love** / Feb. 12-13, 1969 / Contemporary 7622
Fabulous piano technique by the late Phineas Newborn, one of jazz's finest pure soloists. His amazing harmonic knowledge and masterful playing were ideal for the standards he performed on this album, especially the title track. —*Ron Wynn, AMG*

★ **Back Home** / 1976 / Contemporary 57648

○ **Look Out—Phineas Is Back** / Dec. 7-08, 1976 / Pablo 801
Pianist Phineas Newborn's playing twists in new directions on each tune, such as the touch of stride in "Salt Peanuts," which suddenly leads into runs in octaves. His various influences—James P. Johnson, Art Tatum, Bud Powell—were well knitted together with his own brillant ideas and approaches. —*Jerry De Muth, Cadence*

David "Fathead" Newman

b. Feb. 24, 1933, Dallas, TX
Tenor sax, flute / Blues & jazz, soul-jazz

Tenor saxophonist and flutist David Newman picked up his "Fathead" nickname from a childhood music teacher. He started in local groups around Dallas and then worked in blues bands led by Lowell Fulson and T-Bone Walker. In 1954 he joined Ray Charles and became the personification of tasteful but expressive and bluesy sax playing. He stayed until 1964, played with King Curtis in 1966, rejoined Charles in 1970-1971, and worked with Herbie Mann from 1972 to 1974. Throughout the '50s, '60s, and '70s, Newman's Atlantic solo albums had lots of funk, some blues and ballads, plus an occasional more-daring piece that showed Newman could also play bop. He moved farther into the straight jazz vein in the early '80s, but since 1985 has been doing more soul-jazz and funk. He recently appeared on James Clay's second Antilles album. —*Ron Wynn*

Fathead: Ray Charles Presents David Newman / Nov. 5, 1958 / Atlantic 1304

★ **Lonely Avenue** / Nov. 2-04, 1971 / Atlantic

Resurgence / Sep. 1980 / Muse 5234
Newman shows bop talents heading a fine ensemble and supported by Cedar Walton on piano. —*Ron Wynn*

○ **Still Hard Times** / Apr. 1982 / Muse 5283
The original intent of the David "Fathead" Newman session was to recreate a Ray Charles reunion band, but scheduling conflicts prevented that. Nevertheless, this septet admirably captured the spirit of the Charles band even if solos were relatively straight-forward. —*Carl Brauer, Cadence*

Fire! Live at the Village Vanguard / Dec. 22-23, 1988 / Atlantic 81965
A nice outing that matches Newman with Stanley Turrentine (ts) and Hank Crawford (as). —*Ron Wynn*

○ **Blue Head** / Sep. 1989 / Candid 79041
An excellent '90 session by tenor saxophonist and flutist David Newman, done without fanfare or flash. Newman plays big-toned, bluesy tenor and more introspective flute. He's backed by some top players, among them guitarist Ted Dunbar, tenor saxophonist Clifford Jordan, and Buddy Montgomery on piano. —*Ron Wynn*

○ **House of David Newman -David "Fathead" Anthology** / i. 1993 / Rhino 271452
There have not been many saxophonists and flutists more naturally soulful than David "Fathead" Newman. His tenor has honking resiliency; a deep, mournful tone; and the compelling qualities that define soul, plus he knows the blues inside out. Newman's playing in Ray Charles's great combos, with such leaders as Herbie Mann, and either as a lead act or with James Clay, was both simple and shattering. This two-disc set may be the best of all Rhino's anthologies, for it does capture Newman at his best. He has never really been an album artist, though he has done lots of LPs. Each one has had its nuggets, and that is what this captures. It is almost a greatest hits record. There is Newman wailing the blues, then stretching out in the Charles band. He covers a Beatles tune, then an Aaron Neville number. He backs Aretha Franklin and pays homage to the great Buster Cooper. The sound, as on all the Rhino sets, is breathtaking, as is Newman's shimmering sax and flute. Here is one anthology that can be recommended without hesitation, because you are not going to get many complete Newman albums coming down the reissue pike. —*Ron Wynn*

Joe Newman (Joseph Dwight Newman)

b. Sep. 7, 1922, New Orleans, LA, d. Jul. 5, 1992
Trumpet / Swing, big band

Trumpeter and veteran New Orleans musician Joe Newman was born into a musical family. He took lessons from David Jones, a noted multiinstrumentalist and then joined the band at Alabama State College. That band later toured under his leadership. Newman joined Lionel Hampton in 1941 and then joined Count Basie two years later, where he remained until 1947. He played for five years with Illinois Jacquet and then with J. C. Heard before rejoining Basie in 1952-1961. He has made several excellent albums, written extended pieces, and toured the international scene. —*Ron Wynn*

★ **Good N' Groovy** / Mar. 17, 1961 / Prestige 185
This was the second of Joe Newman's three dates he led under the Swingville banner. For this 3/17/61 session he was in the very fine company of Frank Foster (tenor sax), Tommy Flanagan (piano), Eddie Jones (bass), and Bill English (drums). The two horn-men have had their share of recorded mismatches, but on this set

they were in the vernacular in which they both excelled. —*Bob Rusch, Cadence*

○ **Featuring Shirley Scott** / MCA 1380

Frankie Newton (William Frank Newton)

b. Jan. 4, 1906, Emory, VA, **d.** Mar. 11, 1954, New York, NY
Trumpet / New Orleans traditional
A fine trumpeter who often used a buzz-wow mute for contrast, Frankie Newton had a singular, entertaining approach and was a highly respected player. Though his career was repeatedly interrupted by illness, he had a sizable impact during those periods when he was active. Newton moved to New York after having toured the West Coast in the early and mid-'20s. He played with Cecil Scott, Chick Webb, Elmer Snowden, Charlie Johnson, Garland Wilson, and Sam Wooding in the late '20s and early '30s and then recorded in the '30s with Bessie Smith and Mezz Mezzrow. Newton was in John Kirby's small group in 1937 and with Lucky Millinder in both 1937 and 1938. He formed a band in 1939 that played at the Cafe Society, Kelly's Stable, and other clubs. Newton continued heading both large bands and small combos in the '40s. He also worked with such players as James P. Johnson in the mid-'40s. Newton eventually stopped playing except for occasional appearances and devoted himself to painting. He'd made some recordings for Vocalion and other labels but is probably better known for his solos on Bessie Smith's "Gimme a Pigfoot" or Mezz Mezzrow's "Mutiny in the Parlor." Newton is not currently represented on CD as a leader but can be heard on anthologies featuring Smith, Mezzrow, and Johnson. —*Ron Wynn*

● **At the Onyx Club** / **i.** Mar. 1937-Oct. 1937 / Tax 8017
Like many of his contemporaries he found himself in recording situations that, given the commercial considerations of the period, teamed him with singers that were rarely better than second rate—often they were not as good as that. This has lent his surroundings a somewhat dated air, disguising the more lasting value of his own work, and that of certain key associates—the altoists Pete Brown and Tab Smith and the clarinetist William "Buster" Bailey. Though a fine melodist, it was his often sharp variation in timbre that catches the ear and seems to direct the emotional expressiveness of a performance. —*Chris Sheridan, Cadence*

James Newton

b. May 1, 1953, Los Angeles, CA
Flute / Modern creative
James Newton is the most gifted flutist to emerge since Hubert Laws and is among the few able to play flawlessly, yet with soul and passion. He began as a bassist playing in rock and R&B bands while in high school and then moved to alto sax and bass clarinet before finally choosing the flute. He studied music at California State College, where he was inspired by the work of fellow-flutist Eric Dolphy. He played in both jazz and classical bands in college and then moved to New York with saxophonist David Murray and drummer-writer Stanley Crouch in 1975 after he received his degree. He decided to concentrate on flute in 1977 and, by using special fingerings, became a virtuoso and master in playing the flute and using his voice simultaneously. His ability to improvise a melody while also singing it was a revelation to critics hearing it for the first time. He's made a number of first-rate recordings and also composed and played classical music. —*Ron Wynn*

○ **Crystal Texts** / **i.** Nov. 1978 / Moers 01048

★ **Mystery School** / 1979 / India Navigation
James Newton, who composed these three pieces for wind quintet, is a talented flutist, and he assembled a team of skilled players who had no trouble making the transitions from composed to improvised sections and back again. "The Wake" (which was written in tribute to the late composer Dr. Howard Swanson) strung together some pretty phrases in a loose counterpoint that showed Newton's classical orientation. But since the phrases were much longer than is normal in classical music, the ensemble work still sounded like a collection of jazz riffs. —*Joel Rothstein, Down Beat*

○ **James Newton** / Oct. 1982 / Gramavision 8205
Features three Newton originals for pianists Anthony Davis and Billy Strayhorn. W/ Jay Hoggard (vib) and Slide Hampton (tb). Excellent, creative music. —*Michael G. Nastos*

○ **Portraits** / 1982 / India Navigation

○ **Luella** / 1983 / Gramavision 8304
An ambitious, intricately composed and structured album from flutist James Newton that blends improvised and set pieces played by eight-piece group. The lineup includes vibist Jay Hoggard, pianist Kenny Kirkland, violinists John Blake and Gayle Dixon, cellist Abdul Wadud, bassist Cecil McBee, and drummer Billy Hart. —*Ron Wynn, AMG*

○ **Water Mystery** / Jan. 1985 / Gramavision 8407
Some soothing, some entrancing, and some astonishing flute performances from James Newton on this album—one of his finest ever from both a performance and a compositional standpoint. —*Ron Wynn, AMG*

○ **African Flower, The** / Jun. 1985 / Blue Note 46292
On *The African Flower* flutist James Newton explored the music of Billy Strayhorn and his mentor Duke Ellington; the results were a fresh reappraisal of timeless music. —*Scott Yanow, Cadence*

○ **Romance and Revolution** / **i.** 1987 / Blue Note 46431
Flutist James Newton's brillantly written and performed pieces for octet were featured on this '87 session. Trombonists Steve Turre and Robin Eubanks, vibist Jay Hoggard, and pianist Geri Allen along with Newton were among solo stars. —*Ron Wynn, AMG*

Albert Nicholas (Albert [Nick] Nicholas)

b. May 27, 1900, New Orleans, LA, **d.** Sep. 3, 1973, Basle, Switzerland
Clarinet, Sax / New Orleans traditional
A remarkable clarinetist and one of the great blues improvisers, Albert Nicholas played wonderful low-register tunes, offering rich, gritty inflections and phrases during his solos. A nephew of Wooden Joe Nicholas, he studied with Lorenzo Tio, Jr. Nicholas played with Buddy Petit, King Oliver, and Manuel Perez while still a teenager. He spent three years in the Merchant Marine and then joined Perez's band in 1922. Nicholas led his own group at Tom Anderson's New Cabaret and Restaurant in 1923 and then worked with Oliver in Chicago for two years. He toured internationally with various groups, appearing in China, Egypt, and Paris from 1926 to 1928 before returning and joining Luis Russell's orchestra. He stayed with Russell until the early '30s and then spent the next several years playing with several major figures. These included Rex Stewart, Chick Webb, John Kirby, and Louis Armstrong. Nicholas also periodically led his own bands. He lived and toured in Europe from 1953 until his death in 1973, returning to America in 1959 and 1960 for recording sessions and concerts. Nicholas appeared on Vocalion, Jazztet, and Okeh records as a sideman, and on Circle and Delmark as a leader. He can be heard on anthologies featuring Oliver, Stewart, and Russell. —*Ron Wynn*

○ **Albert Nicholas Quartet** / Jul. 19, 1959+Jul. 27, 1959 / Delmark 207
The Albert Nicholas Quartet is part of the venerable and diversified Delmark's *Art Hodes Notebook* series. While the clarinetist and the pianist come from different regions, cliques, and cultures, they're delightfully and effortlessly compatible, finding common home ground in the blues. —*Kevin Whitehead, Cadence*

● **All Star Stompers** / Jul. 30-31, 1959 / Delmark 209

Herbie Nichols (Herbert Horatio Nichols)

b. Dec. 3, 1919, New York, NY, **d.** Apr. 12, 1963, New York, NY
Piano, composer / Bop
Pianist and composer Herbie Nichols was involved in the startup of the new bop music, but shied away from the jazz scene itself. Instead he worked through the '40s and mid-'50s in swing and Dixieland bands. His recordings are very few. He recorded three times for Blue Note in 1955 and 1956, and the Mosaic set is the result of those sessions. Almost everything he recorded was of his own composition.

This is remarkable music. It is very listenable and at the same time sounds a wake-up call. It has an internal consistency and integrity that reminds one of both Thelonious Monk and the modern European classical tradition, in particular the music of Erik Satie. This is not "cool" music. It has humor and warmth. Perhaps every generation has a couple of "sleepers"—great music that, not heard when it was played, suddenly is found. The exquisite music of Herbie Nichols fits this description. —*Michael Erlewine*

○ **Third World, The** / May 6, 1955-Apr. 19, 1956 / Blue Note 142
1955 & 1956. Trio session. Many of his best numbers. Part of the Mosaic box. —*Michael G. Nastos*

○ **Art of Herbie Nichols, The** / 1955-1956 / Blue Note 99176
An anthology collecting some pieces by the neglected and overlooked pianist Herbie Nichols. Nichols had one of the truly unique styles in all jazz piano history, and didn't really borrow or imitate anyone. This single disc doesn't match either an earlier Blue Note two-record set, now deleted, or the outstanding Mosaic set, but it's a fine introduction to Nichols's music. —*Ron Wynn, AMG*

★ **Complete Blue Note** / 1955-1956 / Mosaic 118
1955-1956. This is just great stuff . . . desert island material. The notes are informative, the sound superb, but it is the music that will make you return time and again. This material is best described as intelligent yet emotional music. It has its roots in the blues and postbop. —*Richard B. Kamins, Cadence*

○ **Thelonious Monk and Herbie Nichols** / i. 1956 / Savoy 1166
Nichols is like a bridge from the outside world to Monk. His dissonance is not as stark as Monk's, nor does he rely on it as much. And those who find Monk's technical abilities limited will find Nichols much more impressive. —*Doug Long, Cadence*

○ **Bethlehem Session, The** / Nov. 1957 / Affinity 759
Nichols was an unrequited master who was pitifully underrecorded and overlooked while alive. —*Williard Jenkins, Cadence*

Red Nichols (Ernest Loring Nichols)

b. Aug. 5, 1905, d. Jun. 28, 1965
Cornet / Dixieland
Overrated in Europe in the early 1930s when his records (but not those of his black contemporaries) were widely available and then later underrated and often unfairly called a Bix imitator, Red Nichols was actually one of the finest cornetists to emerge from the 1920s. An expert improviser whose emotional depth did not reach as deep as Bix or Louis Armstrong, Nichols was in many ways a hustler, participating in as many recording sessions (often under pseudonyms) as any other horn player of the era, cutting sessions as Red Nichols and his Five Pennies, the Arkansas Travelers, the Red Heads, the Louisiana Rhythm Kings, and the Charleston Chasers among others, usually with similar personnel! Nichols studied cornet with his father, a college music teacher. After moving from Utah to New York in 1923 Nichols, an excellent sightreader who could always be relied on to add a bit of jazz to a dance band recording, quickly became in great demand. His own sessions at first featured trombonist Miff Mole and Jimmy Dorsey on alto and clarinet, playing advanced music that utilized unusual intervals, whole-tone scales, and often the tympani of Vic Berton, along with hot ensembles. Later on in the decade his sidemen included such young greats as Benny Goodman, Glenn Miller, Jack Teagarden, Pee Wee Russell, Joe Venuti, Eddie Lang, Adrian Rollini, Gene Krupa, and the wonderful mellophone specialist Dudley Fosdick among others; their version of "Ida" was a surprise hit. Although still using the main name The Five Pennies, Nichols's bands were often quite a bit larger, and by 1929 he was alternating sessions featuring bigger commercial orchestras with small combos. At first Nichols weathered the depression well with work in shows, but by 1932 his long string of recordings came to an end. He headed a so-so swing band up until 1942, left music for a couple of years and for a few months in 1944 was with Glen Gray's Casa Loma orchestra. Later that year he reformed the Five Pennies as a Dixieland sextet and, particularly after bass-saxophonist Joe Rushton became a permanent member, it was one of the finer traditional jazz bands of the next 20 years. Nichols recorded several memorable hot versions of "Battle Hymn of the Republic," the best being in 1959. That same year that a highly enjoyable if rather fictional Hollywood movie called The Five Pennies (and featuring Nichols's cornet solos and Danny Kaye's acting) made Red into a national celebrity at the twilight of his long career. Nichols's earlier sessions are just now being reissued on CD in piecemeal fashion but none of his later albums are in print yet. —*Scott Yanow*

● **Red Nichols 1925-28** / i. Nov. 1925-Sep. 1928 / Fountain 110

○ **Jazz Classics (1925-1930)** / 1925-1930 / Mobile Fidelity 00664
○ **Red Nichols—Vol. 2** / i. Jun. 1927-Mar. 1928 / Classic Jazz 25
○ **Red Nichols—Vol. 3** / i. Mar. 1928-May 1928 / Classic Jazz 27
○ **Red Nichols—Vol. 4** / i. Jun. 1928-Jan. 1929 / Classic Jazz 28
○ **Red Nichols—Vol. 5** / i. Feb. 1929-Apr. 1929 / Classic Jazz 30
○ **Syncopated Chamber Music—Vol. 1** / i. 1953 / Audiophile 7

Lennie Niehaus (Leonard Niehaus)

b. Jun. 1, 1929, Saint Louis, MO
Alto sax, composer, arranger / Cool
Though he's won a lot of contemporary notice for his work on Clint Eastwood films, Lennie Niehaus was among the finest West Coast saxophonists to emerge in the '50s. Though his sound was relaxed and his solos smooth rather than intense, his phrasing, technique, and swing were remniscent of such players as Benny Carter and Charlie Parker. But Lee Konitz was Niehaus's primary influence. Niehaus worked with Jerry Wald in the early '50s and then joined Stan Kenton. After an army stint, Niehaus rejoined Kenton, where he won praise and fame for his playing on several sessions through the '50s. He then moved into film and television work and has remained there. Niehaus has appeared on such Eastwood films as *Bird, Unforgiven,* and *Play Misty for Me.* A few of his Contemporary albums have been reissued on CD. —*Ron Wynn*

○ **Lennie Niehaus—Vol. 2: The Octet—Part 1** / 1954 / Contemporary 2517
★ **Lennie Niehaus—Vol. 1: The Quintet** / Nov. 17, 1954 / Contemporary 2513
○ **Lennie Niehaus—Vol. 3: The Octet—Part 2** / Jan. 11, 1955-Feb. 1, 1955 / Contemporary 1767
This music stretches, squeezes, and in general turns figure eights on itself, and glides through the whole like a well-oiled eel. —*Bob Rusch, Cadence*

Sal Nistico (Salvatore Nistico)

b. Apr. 12, 1940, Syracuse, NY, d. 1991
Tenor sax / Bop
A powerful, aggressive soloist, Sal Nistico demonstrated his fiery bebop skills many times with Woody Herman. His playing had energy and soulfulness, as well as harmonic invention and rhythmic vitality. Nistico began playing alto at the end of the '40s and switched to tenor in the mid-'50s. He worked in Syracuse R&B bands until the late '50s and then played in the Jazz Brothers group co-led by the Mangione Brothers. Nistico made his first recordings with them. He made his first stop with Herman in the mid-'60s, and continued to work with him periodically into the '80s. Nistico played briefly with Count Basie in 1965 and then lived in Sweden. Nistico returned to Herman's band for a 1966 African tour. He worked again with Herman in the late '60s and in 1971. Nistico lived briefly in Los Angeles and played briefly with Don Ellis. Following another short stint in Boston, Nistico moved to New York. He played with Buddy Rich in 1974 and the National Jazz Ensemble under Chuck Israels in the mid- and late '70s, and headed his own groups. Nistico had his final stint with Herman in the early '80s. He recorded a couple of sessions for Jazzland and Bee Hive. Nistico currently has no dates as a leader available on CD, but can be heard on Herman reissues. —*Ron Wynn*

● **Empty Room** / i. 1988 / Red 123222

Red Norvo (Kenneth Norville)

b. Mar. 31, 1908, Beardstown, IL
Vibes / Swing, big band
During the first part of his long career, Red Norvo employed the xylophone, an instrument commonly dismissed as "the woodpile," on which he made exquisite music, in particular at the helm of a "little" (12-piece) big band from 1936 to 1939, with arrangements by himself and Eddie Sauter and vocals by his then-wife, the fine singer Mildred Bailey (they were known as "Mr. & Mrs. Swing"). In 1943 Norvo switched to vibes, which he plays with some of the same delicacy as the xylophone. After stints with Benny Goodman and Woody Herman, he formed a trio with guitarist Tal Farlow and bassist Charles Mingus; it was a special kind of modern jazz chamber group. Since then Norvo has performed

in a wide variety of settings, always in the best of taste, but health problems, including deterioration of his hearing, have caused him to be largely inactive in the '90s. —*Dan Morgenstern*

★ **Featuring Mildred Bailey** / **i.** 1933 / Portrait 44118
1933-1938. This neglected gem features Norvo with Mildred Bailey (v), Bunny Berigan (tpt), and Charlie Barnet (sax) on superb '30s swing cuts with excellent mastering. It's probably deleted by now. —*Ron Wynn*

○ **Time in His Hands** / **i.** May 1945-Aug. 1945 / Xanadu 199
The music on *Time in His Hands* was definitely in the swing category, but it was tinged with the influence of bop. Actually none of these sessions were led by Norvo; the first two showcased bassist Slam Stewart, and the August 22 sides were put together by entrepreneur Timmie Rosenkrantz. —*Scott Yanow, Cadence*

○ **Fabulous Jam Session** / Jun. 1945 / Spotlite 127
Cream-of-the-crop recordings pairing this vibes great with Charlie Parker (as), Dizzy Gillespie (tpt), and friends. A high-caliber reissue. —*Ron Wynn*

★ **Red Norvo Trio with Tal Farlow and Charles Mingus at the Savoy** / 1950-1951 / Savoy 2212
Trio. This excellent two-record set highlights Norvo in peak playing form with Tal Farlow (g) and Mingus (b). Thoughtful yet aggressive playing. —*Ron Wynn*

○ **Fabulous Jazz Session** / **i.** 1951 / Dial 903

○ **Move! (With Tal Farlow and Charlie Mingus)** / **i.** 1951 / Savoy 12088

○ **Red Norvo Trios, The** / 1953-1955 / Prestige 24108
Fine two-record set from the mid-'50s featuring sessions led by vibist Red Norvo, with trio members guitarists Jimmy Raney or Tal Farlow and bassist Red Mitchell. They made both chamber jazz and light swing recordings. —*Ron Wynn, AMG*

☆ **Red Plays the Blues** / Jan. 28, 1958+Mar. 6, 1958 / RCA 1792

○ **Live at Rick's Cafe Americain** / 1978 / Flying Fish 079
A joyful, exuberant, and loose session led by vibist Red Norvo and recorded in 1978 at Rick's. Besides Norvo's swinging, propulsive vibes there's also Buddy Tate's lusty tenor and Urbie Green's resilient trombone, with pianist Dave McKenna adding his own stride and boogie riffs. The four are so relentless it's easy to forget about the absence of bass and drums. —*Ron Wynn, AMG*

Anita O'Day (Anita Belle Colton)

b. Oct. 18, 1919, Kansas City, MO
Vocals / Big band, bop
Anita O'Day is a legitimate jazz legend and diva. She was in Chicago dance marathons as a teenager and sang with Max Miller's combo in 1939. Her sizzling delivery and sound, along with her unmatched phrasing and timing, stood out during her years with Gene Krupa in the '40s, though she wasn't so successful with Stan Kenton in 1944-1945. O'Day was dominant in the swing era, working with Benny Goodman, Duke Ellington, Will Bradley, Ralph Burns, Benny Carter, and many others, and scoring several hits. She was equally prolific in the '50s, heading her own combos, recording frequently, and still having smash hits. She began a comeback in the '70s with albums on her own label and others for small independent companies. O'Day is still active, albeit on a reduced schedule. —*Ron Wynn*

● **Cool Heat** / Apr. 6-08, 1959 / Verve

○ **Jimmy Giuffre Arrangements** / Apr. 6-08, 1959 / Verve 8312

★ **Anita O'Day and the Three Sounds** / Oct. 12-15, 1962 / Verve 8514

○ **In a Mellow Tone** / **i.** 1989 / DRG 5209
A good '89 session with singer Anita O'Day doing her familiar jazz-based prerock standards and ballads, backed by a quintet with some different names. A particular change is the appearance of harpist Corky Hale, plus Pete Jolly and Gordon Brisker. —*Ron Wynn, AMG*

○ **At Vine St.—Live** / Sep. 1991 / DRG 8435
Recent live recordings by vocalist Anita O'Day done in intimate setting as part of the Vine Street series. O'Day's voice has lost some luster and shine over the years, but she compensates with great timing, delivery, and tone, which help overcome some loss of range. —*Ron Wynn, AMG*

Chico O'Farrill (Arturo O'Farrill)

b. Oct. 28, 1921, Havana, Cuba
Arranger / Latin-jazz, world fusion
Chico O'Farrill was the architect of the full-flowered Latin-jazz charts of the Machito-Chano Pozo-Dizzy Gillespie ground-breaking dates of the '40s and '50s. He was also an adept pop arranger. —*Michael G. Nastos*

★ **Chico O'Farrill Jazz** / Aug. 7, 1951-Mar. 24, 1952 / Clef 132
Chico with Flip Phillips (ts), Nick Travis (tpt), and Roy Eldridge (tpt). —*Michael G. Nastos*

○ **Afro-Cuban** / 1951 / Clef 131

Old and New Dreams

Group / Modern creative
This was Ornette Coleman's '60s combo without Ornette—Dewey Redman (ts), Don Cherry (tpt, p), Charlie Haden (b), Ed Blackwell (d). Playing out of Ornette's harmolodic bag, they were tuneful but challenging and never dull. They were one of the most important ensembles of the last two decades. —*Michael G. Nastos*

○ **Old and New Dreams** / Oct. 1976 / ECM 829379
Debut. Fully realized. Quintessential. Modern jazz supreme from Don Cherry (cnt), Dewey Redman (ts), Charlie Haden (b), and Ed Blackwell (d). —*Michael G. Nastos*

● **Old and New Dreams** / Aug. 1979 / ECM 1154
Great music from Ornette Coleman's band, playing with his verve and creative spirit. —*Michael G. Nastos*

King Oliver (Joe Oliver)

b. May 11, 1885, New Orleans, LA, **d.** Apr. 8, 1938, Savannah, GA
Cornet, bandleader / New Orleans traditional
Cornetist and bandleader Joe "King" Oliver is often remembered today as the man who gave Louis Armstrong his first big break, but his tremendous influence on the development of early jazz as a cornetist and bandleader requires a deeper examination of his contributions. He is credited with pioneering the use of mutes to achieve vocal effects on cornet and with being the prime influence in the development of "hot" cornet styles, departing from the approach represented by Buddy Bolden and Freddie Keppard, which they described as closer to ragtime and "corny" by comparison. As a member of the Kid Ory band before relocating to Chicago in 1918, Oliver enjoyed widespread popularity and picked up tips on how to manage musicians to best effect from Manual "Hoss" Manetta, the straw boss of the band. Between 1918 and 1923 he built the Creole Jazz Band into one of the most celebrated "hit" units in jazz history, adding Armstrong and dual cornet breaks as a finishing touch. Also present were the Dodds brothers (Johnny on clarinet and "Baby" on drums), musicians who knew how to integrate virtuosity into a collectively improvised concept that demanded "playing for the band." After the band began to record in April 1923, the cooperative spirit within the group started to crumble, largely because several of the members felt that King Joe had become too dictatorial.

Oliver's next project was the Dixie Syncopators, a larger ensemble. But Oliver's fortunes were in decline, especially after he took the band to New York, where he passed up an offer to become the featured act at the Cotton Club (the job went to Duke Ellington instead). As his career continued to decline, the Depression wiped out his savings, his teeth were lost to gum disease, and he abandoned the band business in 1937, a forgotten hero. He died the following year in obscurity, just barely in advance of the onset of the New Orleans revival that renewed interest in the Creole Jazz Band recordings. The tragic implications of Oliver's life story have attracted considerable attention, but the music he made was buoyant and joyful, a triumph of sorts over the adversity that plagued his final years, and a testament to a spirit that never lost its musicality. —*Bruce Boyd Raeburn*

☆ **King Oliver—Vol. 1 (1923-1929)** / **i.** Apr. 1923-May 1929 / BBC 787

★ **King Oliver—Louis Armstrong** / **i.** 1923-1924 / Milestone 47017
1923-1924. Classic renditions of "Snake Rag," "Dipper Mouth Blues," and "Canal Street Blues" by the hottest band of its day, Oliver's Creole Jazz Band. Also includes Oliver duets with Jelly Roll Morton. —*Bruce Raeburn*

○ **King Oliver (1926-1928)** / **i.** Mar. 1926-Jun. 1928 / Classics 618

○ **Jazz Heritage: Papa Joe (1926-1928)** / 1926-1928 / Affinity 1025

And His Dixie Syncopators. Recorded from 1926 to 1928. Mid-'20s jazz with Oliver leading a coterie of New Orleans stars like Omer Simeon (cl), Kid Ory (tb), Barney Bigard (cl), Luis Russell (p), and Paul Barbarin (d) on tunes such as "Snag It," "Sugar Foot Stomp," and "Farewell Blues." —*Bruce Raeburn*

○ **Sugar Foot Stomp** / **i.** 1926-1927 / GRP 616

Vintage, historically vital early jazz, featuring the King Oliver orchestra that also included Kid Ory, Albert Nicholas, Luis Russell, and Barney Bigard. The title track later became a swing era staple when it was adapted by the Fletcher Henderson orchestra. This is the first time these sessions have been available on a domestic release, and the mastering makes it possible to hear them better than ever before. —*Ron Wynn, AMG*

★ **New York Sessions (1929-1930)** / **i.** 1929-1930 / RCA 9903

1929 and 1930. The King in the final chapter of his recording career with an excellent selection of titles, showcasing his abilities as a bandleader more than as a soloist. —*Bruce Raeburn*

○ **King Oliver's Jazz Band** / **i.** May 1976 / Smithsonian 001

(The King Oliver sides with Louis Armstrong) are certainly cornerstone recordings in any jazz collection, and they are among the most finished and polished specimens of a form that was becoming obsolete even as they were made. . . . they were the first important black jazz records. . . . There are masterpieces here ("Chattanooga Stomp," "Dipper Mouth Blues," "I Ain't Gonna Tell Nobody"), derived primarily from the perfection of the ensembles. —*John Mcdonough, Down Beat*

Sy Oliver (Melvin James Oliver)

b. Dec. 17, 1910, Battle Creek, MI, **d.** May 28, 1988, New York, NY
Arranger, trumpet / Swing, big band

Sy Oliver's arrangements for the Jimmie Lunceford band blended simplicity and sophistication with exuberance, helping Lunceford's orchestra temporarily challenge the giants like Ellington, Basie, and Goodman, for whom he also did arrangements. Oliver learned trumpet and played in local bands in Ohio. He worked with Zack Whyte's Chocolate Beau Brummels in the late '20s and early '30s and played for a short time with Alphonso Trent. He moved to Columbus and worked as a freelance arranger and teacher. Oliver joined Lunceford in 1933 and remained until 1939. He wrote arrangements and compositions, played trumpet, and sometimes sang. Such tunes as "Stomp It Off-My Blue Heaven," "Organ Grinder's Swing," and "On the Beach at Bali-Bali" were hits for the Lunceford orchestra thanks to Oliver. He also wrote arrangements for Goodman from 1934 until 1939 and then joined Tommy Dorsey as a vocalist and arranger. After completing army service, Oliver led his own band for a time and then served as a music director and supervisor to various record labels and led his own band. Oliver toured extensively during the '60s and '70s, directing a band in Paris during 1968 and 1969. He resumed playing trumpet and led a nonet that played at several New York clubs. Oliver worked with Money Johnson, Bobby Jones, Mousey Alexander, and Chris Woods, among others. They played Oliver's arrangements and worked into the '80s. Oliver also recorded for the Black and Blue label in 1973. Recent Lunceford and Goodman reissues spotlight several Oliver arrangements and compositions. —*Ron Wynn*

Take Me Back / **i.** Jan. 1973 / Flac 1 2572

Oregon

Jazz chamber ensemble / World fusion, modern creative, new age

Paul McCandless (oboe, English horn, bass clarinet, saxophones), Glen Moore (bass, violin, piano flute), Ralph Towner (classical and 12-string guitars, piano, and brass instruments), Colin Walcott (percussion, especially tabla, sitar, clarinet). All of Oregon's members were members of the Paul Winter Consort; the group formed in 1970. Although usually categorized as jazz, Oregon breaks all the boundaries. The genuine virtuosity and versatility of group members helped the group achieve an unprecedented level of integration of cultural and stylistic influences, somehow managing to make their wide range of influences work artistically and reach a large audience. Influences include classical music (including 20th-century), world music (especially Indian), jazz (including group improvisation concepts from free jazz), all within a very sensitive, melodic aesthetic. The group accomplished highly

disciplined ensemble recordings, including many fine compositions by Towner and other group members. The death of Collin Walcott in an accident in Europe in 1984 was a terrible blow, but Oregon re-formed with percussionist Trilok Gurtu and is still touring and recording. Considered a seminal influence for much of the eclectic, new-age, and world-music efforts to follow, Oregon has never been surpassed for artistic standards and integrity in that genre. —*David Nelson McCarthy*

★ **Distant Hills** / Jul. 2-05, 1973 / Vanguard 79341

This is one of the first releases to click from this group that knows how to make soothing, acoustic fare without becoming boring or wimpy. —*Ron Wynn*

☆ **Music of Another Present Era** / 1973 / Vanguard 79326

A 1989 reissue of an outstanding release that blows most similar ECM albums out of the water. —*Ron Wynn*

☆ **Winter Light** / Jul. 16, 1974-Aug. 7, 1974 / Vanguard 79350

Here are some simply brilliant, feathery compositions. Marvelous playing. —*Ron Wynn*

Original Dixieland Jazz Band

Group / Dixieland

The Original Dixieland Jazz Band in many ways was at the foundation of a long-running, still simmering feud in jazz over origins and authenticity. The Original Dixieland Jazz Band was a five-member, five-piece, white New Orleans ensemble. They played in Chicago in 1916, then moved to New York. They got a great reception from appearances at Reeisenweber's Restaurant in 1917, and because they were the first jazz band to make phonograph recordings they got enormous exposure and a reputation their skills didn't merit. They disbanded in the mid-'20s and then regrouped briefly in 1936. It cannot be denied that they were the first to record the historical importance of cornetist Nick LaRocca, clarinetist Larry Shields, trombonist Eddie Edwards, drummer Tony Sbarbaro, and pianist Henry Ragas (later replaced by J. Russel Robinson). Nor can it be discounted that in 1917 a white jazz band would certainly be picked ahead of any black jazz band to cut the first recordings. When black jazz bands got their shot, it was immediately evident the ODJB was outclassed. Some see this as the first example of white imitators capitalizing on black innovations, though the group's sound was radically different from anything else on record. Their defenders argue that the group provided a service by exposing the music to audiences who'd otherwise never hear it, and it also spurred interest in the genuine item (a familiar argument recycled in other jazz, blues, R&B, and even reggae and Latin situations). LaRocca further inflamed things by insisting his band played a vital role in "inventing" jazz during the early 1900s, a claim thus far lacking either hard or soft evidence. They were responsible for popularizing the Dixieland style in parts of Europe and America. —*Ron Wynn*

● **Original Dixieland Jazz Band** / **Louisiana Five** / **i.** Aug. 1917 / Retrieval 101

Kid Ory (Edward Ory)

b. Dec. 25, 1890, La Place, LA, **d.** Jan. 23, 1973, Honolulu, Hawaii
Trumpet, bandleader, trombone / New Orleans traditional

The dean of New Orleans Creole "tailgate" trombonists, Ory led the first Black jazz band to record for the Nordskog label in Los Angeles in June 1921. As a sideman with Armstrong's Hot Five and King Oliver's Dixie Syncopators in the mid '20s, Ory recorded extensively in Chicago before returning to the West Coast to reform his own band. He reclaimed national attention in the mid-'40s as a result of the New Orleans revival. Along with Bunk Johnson and George Lewis, he became widely regarded as an example of how jazz sounded in its earliest years. Observers of Ory in his New Orleans days recalled that he blew "the most foul" trombone ever heard (intended as a compliment). Of special interest are the songs he sings in Creole dialect—a rarity even among New Orleans artists. Members of Ory's generation were arguably the last to rigorously maintain creole customs—including the spoken patois—and these tunes provide an important glimpse of the kind of "good time" music that filled dancehalls in New Orleans so many years ago. His masterful style conveys the sense of playful fun and revelry associated with New Orleans dance music. Ironically, Ory's most famous composition, "Muskrat Ramble," became the basis for one of the most pervasive protest songs of the Vietnam era—Country Joe MacDonald's "Feel Like I'm Fixin' to Die." —*Bruce Boyd Raeburn*

○ **Kid Ory (1944-1945)** / 1944-1945 / Good Time Jazz 12022
Mid-'40s traditional jazz by trombonist Kid Ory, a New Orleans legend. Ory's trombone mastery was second only to Jack Teagarden's among traditional players, so his solos and sound provide the album's hook. The material for the most part is well played but very similiar throughout. —*Ron Wynn*

★ **Creole Jazz Band at Club Hangover** / May 9-16, 1953 / Storyville 4070
The Kid with Don Ewell (p), Albert Burbank (cl), Ed "Montudie" Garland (b), and others, captured in remote broadcast. Specialties include "South Rampart Street Parade," "High Society," and "Milneberg Joys." Ewell and Burbank offer some inspired soloing and ensemble work. —*Bruce Raeburn*

○ **Legendary Kid** / Nov. 22-25, 1955 / Good Time Jazz 12016
Ory's Creole Jazz Band delivering traditional favorites such as "Mahogany Hall Stomp," "Snag It," and "Pallet," with sidemen Alvin Alcorn (tpt), Phil Gomez, Wellman Braud (b), and Minor Hall (d). —*Bruce Raeburn*

○ **This Kid's the Greatest!** / i. 195? / Good Time Jazz 12045

Greg Osby

Alto sax / Modern creative
Osby is a highly regarded alto saxophonist and one of the few young lions in the '90s to take an alternative approach to the hard bop revival. He has led his own band; played with the Black Rock Coalition and with Steve Coleman's groups; and done session work in R&B, funk, and jazz contexts. He currently appears on Andrew Hill and Jack DeJohnnette recordings and has been on the JMT label since 1987. —*Ron Wynn*

★ **Greg Osby and the Sound Theatre** / Jun. 1987-Jun. 1987 / JMT 834411
This is Osby's most-accomplished ensemble, especially with Michele Rosewoman on piano. —*Ron Wynn*

Makoto Ozone

b. Mar. 25, 1961, Kobe, Japan
Piano / World fusion, modern creative
A premier jazz musician in Japan, Ozone has made a successful transition to America, where he became equally prominent in this nation's improvisational community. He began on organ at four and took up piano as a teenager. He went to Berklee in 1980 and studied composing and arranging. He was noticed by Gary Burton and later recorded with him and was part of his band. Ozone's striking ability (especially on midtempo pieces) and impressive technique made him a big hit at the Kool Jazz Festival. His 1984 debut recording featured Burton and bassist Eddie Gomez. It was a stunning example of complete knowledge and mastery of the full jazz piano spectrum. Ozone later worked with European pianist Michel Petrucciani and spent extensive time studying classical music. —*Ron Wynn*

○ **Makoto Ozone** / Jun. 23-24, 1981 / CBS 26198
Produced by Gary Burton. Solo piano in light-jazz to edges of new-age. Bright, but not shining. —*Michael G. Nastos*

★ **Starlight** / 1990 / JVC 3323

Hot Lips Page (Oran Thaddeus Page)

b. Jan. 27, 1908, Dallas, TX, **d.** Nov. 5, 1954, New York, NY
Trumpet, vocals / Swing, big band
Oran "Hot Lips" Page loved jam sessions. He thrived in the competitive, unpredictable heat of battle, where his on-the-edge style was at its best. Page could ad lib, construct marvelous hot blues or begin ripping through fiery phrases. He was an excellent blues vocalist, though he sometimes put so much intensity into his singing that it became overbearing. Page made a tactical error in the late '30s, leaving the Basie orchestra, where he was principal soloist, to go out on his own. Page took the advice of Louis Armstrong's manager, Joe Glaser; he enjoyed a good career, but that still doesn't seem like a wise choice. Page was a professional musician as a teen in Texas during the '20s, and was part of Ma Rainey's backing band on the old chitlin' circuit. They also accompanied Bessie Smith and Ida Cox, and Page maintained this was where he learned how to sing the blues. He worked with Walter Page's Blue Devils in the late '20s and early '30s and then

joined Bennie Moten's band in Kansas City. Page led his own band in New York in 1937 and worked with Artie Shaw in 1941 and 1942. He worked in combos in the mid- and late '40s and became mainly a solo act after 1950. Page made a number of recordings from the late '30s until the mid-'50s, working with Earl Bostic, Ben Webster, Don Byas, and J.C. Higginbotham, among others. He recorded for Savoy, Bluebird, and V-discs. Page has some sessions available on CD. —*Ron Wynn*

☆ **Chronological Hot Lips Page (1938-1940), The** / i. Mar. 1938-Dec. 1940 / Classics 561

● **After Hours in Harlem** / i. Oct. 1973 / Onyx 307

Marty Paich (Martin Louis Paich)

b. Jan. 23, 1925, Oakland, CA
Arranger, bandleader, composer / Cool, progressive big band
An arranger, big-band leader, and composer who made his best jazz recordings in the '50s. At one time, Paich led a band that included Art Pepper and Russ Freeman. He later became a successful studio and session musician and also did television and film soundtrack work. —*Ron Wynn*

★ **Picasso of Big Band Jazz** / i. Jun. 7-08, 1957 / Candid 79031
West Coast mainstream . . . . These arrangements create a light, airy feeling punctuated by a crisp (Mel Lewis) beat. —*Paul B. Matthews, Cadence*

○ **Moanin'** / i. Jul. 22, 1992 / Discovery 962

Charlie Palmieri

b. 1927, New York, NY, **d.** 1988
Piano / Latin-jazz
Palmieri began piano studies at 6, was sitting in with bands at dances at 14, and was a full-time musician at 16. He formed his group, El Conjunto Pin Pin, in 1948. He played piano for Pupi Campo, Tito Puente, Tito Rodriquez, Bicentico Valdes, and Pete Terrace before forming his Charanga Dubonney group in 1958. —*Max Salazar*

Eddie Palmieri

b. Dec. 15, 1936, New York, NY
Vocals, piano / Latin-jazz
Eddie Palmieri started out as a vocalist and was influenced by elder brother Charlie to study piano. Eddie Palmieri is the only Latin bandleader to win five Grammies and is a tremendous record seller. He started with the neighborhood band of Orlando Marin and made his professional debut in 1955 with Johnny Sequi's orchestra. After stints with Vicentico Valdes, Pete Terrace, and Tito Rodriguez, he formed Conjunto La Perfecta in 1962. —*Max Salazar*

Charlie Parker (Charles Parker, Jr.)

b. Apr. 29, 1920, Kansas City, **d.** Mar. 12, 1955, New York, NY
Alto and tenor sax, composer / Bop
If any single person might be deemed the father of "modern" jazz, Charlie Parker could legitimately qualify. No saxophonist has been more influential, and Parker's legacy towers over jazz and modern music to this day. As a player his skills were unsurpassed, especially his ability to constantly invent melodies in his solos, and he was also a harmonic genius. He was able to modulate from any key to another key, play in any register, and provide endless surprises whether doing originals, shopworn show tunes, ballads, or blues. At times, Parker and his cohort Dizzy Gillespie would even turn practice compositions upside down and play them that way for relief. Sadly, a lifelong addiction to drugs, plus other personality problems, not only prevented him from living beyond 34 but certainly limited the amount of time he was effective on the bandstand. Despite all this, Parker's talent and greatness emerged on scores of records and through accounts from musicians and fans who heard him.
Parker grew up in Kansas City and started on alto as a child. He played baritone in a school band but dropped out at 15, and shortly afterward he began his tragic involvement with drugs. His early influences were local players Buster Smith and Lester Young, and Parker got his first significant tenure in Jay McShann and Harlan Leonard's bands in the late '30s. He moved to New York in 1939 and spent three months washing dishes at a club where Art Tatum worked. During a job in Harlem, Parker began making his mark on the jazz scene, improvising on the upper in-

tervals of the chords in the song "Cherokee" rather than the lower ones, creating a new harmonic framework. He later recorded with McShann in 1941, following his return to Kansas City for his father's funeral. After leaving McShann and returning to New York, he began appearing at the historic jam sessions at Minton's, while also playing in the bands of Noble Sissle, Earl Hines, Cootie Williams, Andy Kirk, and Billy Eckstine. In 1944 he made some combo dates with Tiny Grimes and worked a year later in a quintet with Dizzy Gillespie. He changed locales in late 1945, going to Los Angeles and playing with a band that included Gillespie, Milt Jackson, Al Haig, and others. But following a record session for Dial, Parker had a mental breakdown and was confined for six months in Camarillo State Hospital. He made some more recordings for Dial in 1947 and then returned to New York, heading various groups and continuing to make incredible solo performances when he could physically appear at the date. During the '50s, Parker played Afro-Latin jazz with Machito and Gillespie, made many remarkable dates for Verve, participated in a legendary concert in Canada at Massey Hall with several other notables, and also made a controversial recording with a string orchestra. During the '40s and '50s he also wrote a number of seminal tunes, among them "Ornithology," "Scrapple from the Apple," "Parker's Mood," and "Yardbird Suite." Continued abuse of drugs and alcohol, plus other drug-induced escapades, eventually resulted in his death. Still, some 37 years later, Charlie Parker's music remains immense. —*Ron Wynn*

○ **Complete "Birth of Bebop", The** / May 1940-Nov. 1953 / Stash 535
A more comprehensive '91 CD update of formative Charlie Parker sessions from the label that originally issued an edited version in the '80s. Stash reworked this compilation, including more alternate takes and also more complete liner notes. As a result, while the original release was vital, this new one is essential. —*Ron Wynn*

○ **Early Bird (1940-1944)** / 1940-1044 / Stash 542

Bird/The Savoy Recordings (master takes) / i. 1944-1948 / Savoy 8801
Foundation recordings by alto sax giant Charlie Parker, which have been reissued in many other forms. These are remastered versions taken directly from the master tapes. Parker was making history at this point, playing with a speed, harmonic brilliance, and creativity that hadn't been imagined before, particularly on alto sax. —*Ron Wynn, AMG*

○ **Charlie Parker on Dial—Vol. 5** / Jun. 1945-Nov. 1947 / Spotlite 105
On Volume 5, pianist Duke Jordan was in a better mood; Miles Davis, open horn for a change, was more coherent; drummer Max Roach was at his best. "Bird Feathers" was excellent for everyone. ... Bird's wealth of emotion extended far beyond the pretty confines of "Don't Blame Me," the opening four measures of his bridge were incredible—and maybe the only reason he made momentary "Don't Blame Me" theme fragments was to show how his rhythmic and tonal variety completely transcended the original. Three versions of "Out of Nowhere" seemed preoccupied with where to place a slurred descending decorative phrase. —*John Litweiler, Down Beat*

● **Complete Studio Sessions, The** / i. 1945-1948 / Savoy 5500
A three-disc compendium of virtually everything Charlie Parker did for Savoy. ... It includes a 24-page booklet with specific compositions transcribed, breakdowns of individual solos and collective instrumentation, interviews, and commentary. The discs cover his 1944 sessions with the Tiny Grimes Quintet and continue through dates with Parker's groups the Reboppers and All-Stars, and his work with the Miles Davis All-Stars. Savoy Jazz's painstaking care and diligence in compiling the whole of Parker's work, rather than making assumptions about what should and should not be inserted, provide a service to the music and one of its most important participants. — *Ron Wynn, Rock & Roll Disc.*

○ **At the 1946 JATP Concert** / May 27, 1946 / Verve 513756
A no-holds-barred, exciting jam session with several all-time greats going after each other in instrumental battle. This 1946 date featured Charlie Parker, Lester Young, Dizzy Gillespie, Coleman Hawkins, Buck Clayton, and Buddy Rich, among others, taking turns showing their mettle. The '92 CD reissue brings things up front with some glorious remastering. —*Ron Wynn*

☆ **Bird & Pres** / i. 1946 / Verve 2518

Jazz at the Philharmonic. More in LA from Lester and Lee Young, Dizzie Gillespie, Charlie Parker, Buck Clayton, Willie Smith, Mel Powell, Howard McGhee, and Charlie Ventura. It is the ultimate melding of swing era and bop musicians. —*Michael G. Nastos*

★ **Bird: Complete on Verve** / 1946-1954 / PolyGram 837141
If you want one good boxed set, get this one. It contains 51 unissued selections—over 11 hours of engrossing, majestic music thematically and chronologically assembled to reflect Parker's peak 1946-1954 period on Verve. An exhaustive 36-page booklet is included. —*Ron Wynn*

○ **Charlie Parker on Dial—Vol. 1: West Coast Days, The** / i. 1947 / Stash 23

☆ **Charlie Parker on Dial—Vol. 2: New York Days, The** / i. 1947 / Stash 25

○ **Charlie Parker on Dial—Vol. 3** / Feb. 1947 / Spotlite 103
Volume 3, recorded only a week after Volume 2, was curious. Parker was extremely relaxed, not at all inclined to smash bar lines or chord barriers, expansive or decorative or powerfully expressive phrases absent, each improvised strain beginning on the beat or laid back. The result was, as the liners say, "floods of melody," the very lyrical, happy Bird at work. —*John Litweiler, Down Beat*

● **Dean Benedetti Recordings of Charlie Parker, The** / Mar. 1947-Jul. 1948 / Mosaic 129

○ **Charlie Parker on Dial—Vol. 4** / Oct. 1947 / Spotlite 104
Volume 4 was New York Charlie Parker, eight months after recording Volume 3, and the change was terrific. "Dexterity," B, was the great Parker, the virtuoso of structured emotion. "Bongo Bop," A, was remarkable for the satiric quality inherent in the bold staging of his blues phrases, and the staged quality persisted in the first chorus of B, pain, then sorrow emerging as the work progressed (note the easy, flowing Miles Davis). ... Throughout the LP, Miles Davis's evolving style hinted at individuality in medium tempos, still in Dizzy Gillespie's shadow at fast and slow, irritatingly frivolous in "Embraceable You," A. —*John Litweiler, Down Beat*

★ **Dial Masters—Vol. 1** / i. Dec. 1947 / Stash 23
This contains 25 of the master takes from Charlie Parker's Dial sessions. The Dials have always been a bit underrated compared to the better distributed Savoys, but they are of equal value, with Miles Davis, Lucky Thompson, Dodo Marmarosa, Howard McGhee, Erroll Garner, Wardell Gray, and J.J. Johnson making important contributions. Dizzy Gillespie is on "Diggin' Diz." These are ideal for general listeners and CD collectors. —*Scott Yanow, Cadence*

★ **Dial Masters—Vol. 2** / i. Dec. 1947 / Stash 25
This contains the remaining ten masters from Charlie Parker's Dial sessions (25 were on Vol. I), 9 of the 57 alternate takes and the complete *Home Cooking* private session, including a pair of poorly recorded (but previously unissued) minute-long blues. —*Scott Yanow, Cadence*

○ **Charlie Parker on Dial—Vol. 6** / Dec. 1947 / Spotlite 106
Volume 6 highlighted Charlie Parker's new Selmer saxophone with a richer sound, super blues solo, especially "Bongo Beep," C ... "Quasimado," A, reflected a bit of "Embraceable You" a month later, but B was more vigorous and emotionally contained. "Charlie's Wig," B, solo, was perhaps the best of the three here, though a wonderful phrase entered his improvised bit in the theme of D.... These volumes came from the peak of Parker's career, chronologically simultaneous with Savoy and JATP Parker. —*John Litweiler, Down Beat*

○ **Bird at the Roost—Savoy Years** / i. Sep. 4, 1948-1949 / Savoy 4411
Vols. 1-4. 1948-1949. Absolute must-buys, every volume. Live at the Royal Roost in the late '40s. —*Michael G. Nastos*

○ **Live at Carnegie Hall** / i. 1949 / CP 2

○ **Genius of Charlie Parker—Vol. 4: Bird and Diz, The** / Jun. 6, 1950 / PolyGram 831133
Sharp date with T. Monk (p) and Buddy Rich (d) is a nice introductory vehicle for Parker novices. It has three bonus cuts on disc. —*Ron Wynn*

Verve Years (1950-1951) / 1950-1951 / Verve 821684
1950-1951. This authoritative twin set nicely compiles and covers two prime Parker years. —*Ron Wynn*

Verve Years (1952-1954) / 1952-1954 / Verve 827154
1952-1954. This is the continuation of twin anthologies covering
the Verve years. —*Ron Wynn*

○ **One Night in Washington** / i. 1953 / Elektra 60019
In spectacular form, even by his own amazingly high standards,
Parker was almost everywhere in evidence. Obviously eschewing
the need for any lead sheet cues that might have been provided
for him, he played wherever and whenever he wanted, searing,
soaring, and literally ripping asunder any preconceived notions
some may have entertained about the proper role of a big band
soloist. In the words of Bill Potts, "Bird plays straight through sectional solis, full band tuttis and even the modulations. Some of
the key changes are abrupt and without a modulation, but this
bothered him none." —*Jack Sohmer, Down Beat*

○ **Jazz at Massey Hall** / i. May 15, 1953 / Original Jazz Classics 044
This is a Charlie Parker (as) and Dizzy Gillespie (tpt) album, with
Charles Mingus on bass. —*Michael Katz*

★ **Live at Carnegie Hall** / i. Mar. 27, 1965 / PolyGram 26985
Tenth Memorial concert. Not Parker himself. Immortal sessions
with various artists celebrating the Bird. —*Michael G. Nastos*

○ **Summit Meeting at Birdland** / i. Feb. 1978 / Columbia 34831
Here Charlie Parker, Dizzy Gillespie, and Bud Powell were heard
in their only recorded meeting aside from the Massey Hall concert. The time was 1951. The place, Birdland. The sound quality,
sparkling. Everything fell into place flawlessy. The music rolled
with a smooth, well-oiled sense of control. Even at such tripham-
mer tempos as "Anthropology," no detail or nuance was lost. —
John Mcdonough, Down Beat

Bird with Strings / i. Feb. 1978 / Columbia 34832

☆ **Very Best Bird, The** / Warner Brothers 3198
Despite a confusing and misleading title, this is a good two-
record set of Parker cuts, covering songs he is best known for. It's
not comprehensive, but it's a good introduction. —*Ron Wynn*

Leo Parker

b. Apr. 18, 1925, Washington, DC, **d.** Feb. 11, 1962, New York, NY
Baritone sax / Hard bop
This overlooked baritone saxophonist made some good hard bop
recordings in the '60s. He was a fluent, formidable soloist and a
strong accompanist and bandleader, as well as an above-average
composer. Parker has gotten fresh exposure, thanks to '80s and
'90s reissues on Blue Note and Collectables. —*Ron Wynn*

○ **Back to Back Baritones** / i. 1948-1950 / Collectables 5329
1948-1950 recordings. Baritone sax work in early R&B-honker
style with some jazz leanings. Small combo backing. Album's use
of multiple and alternate takes will be of particular interest to
musicians and collectors. —*Hank Davis*

★ **Baritone Great (1951-1953), The** / 1951-1953 / Chess 413
His best, with Sahib Shihab (fl/sax) and Red Saunders (d). One to
seek. —*Michael G. Nastos*

○ **Rollin' with Leo** / Oct. 12+20, 1961 / Blue Note 84095
Rollin' with Leo was the better-late-than-never first release for
the baritone saxophonist. It was a typical Parker date, finding
him in the company of hard-working journeymen and improvising on blue minor ballads and jump tunes based on the hoariest
of riffs—precisely the kind of surrounding where he emerges
transcendent by rolling up his sleeves and pitching in. —*Francis
Davis, Cadence*

Horace Parlan (Horace Louis Parlan)

b. Jan. 19, 1931, Pittsburgh, PA
Piano / Hard bop
A pianist discovered by Charles Mingus, Parlan has overcome disability and made it an asset. His right hand was partially crippled
by polio when he was a child, yet he has made kinetic, rhythmic
right-hand phrases part of his attack, contrasting them with striking left-hand chords. Parlan filters blues and R&B influences
through solos that are stark, sometimes somber, but never dull or
lifeless. Parlan began playing in R&B bands during the '50s,
moved from Pittsburgh to New York, and joined Mingus's group
from 1957 to 1959. He worked with Booker Ervin in 1960-1961
and was a regular pianist with the Eddie "Lockjaw" Davis-Johnny
Griffin quintet in 1962. He played with Rahsaan Roland Kirk
from 1963 to 1966. Parlan had a string of strong Blue Note releases in the '60s, but encountered tough times near the end of

the decade. He left America for Copenhagen in 1973, and during
the '70s and '80s he gained international recognition for some superb releases on Copenhagen, including a pair of stunning duet
sessions with Archie Shepp. —*Ron Wynn*

○ **Back from the Gig** / Feb. 15, 1963 / Blue Note
This was later issued under Booker Ervin's name, but it was truly
Parlan's date. Ervin's lusty tenor and Parlan's shimmering piano
are impressive. —*Ron Wynn*

★ **Happy Frame of Mind** / Feb. 15, 1963 / Blue Note 84134
Expatriate pianist on a reissue of one of his best albums, with
Booker Ervin (ts). Search for others. —*Michael G. Nastos*

★ **Going Home** / i. Apr. 25, 1979 / Steeple Chase

○ **Pannonica** / Feb. 11, 1981 / Enja 4076
Good early '80s trio session with pianist Horace Parlan working
alongside bassist Reggie Johnson and drummer Alvin Queen. The
material—mostly standards, some originals and ballads—isn't
overly ambitious, but Parlan's dense, strong blues-influenced solos and good interaction among the three principals keeps things
moving. —*Ron Wynn*

Joe Pass (Joseph Anthony Passalaqua)

b. Jan. 13, 1929, New Brunswick, NJ, **d.** 1994
Guitar / Bop, cool
Joe Pass emerged in the early '60s after years of drug problems,
displaying an astounding technical ability and overall mastery of
the guitar. He recorded and toured in the '60s with many major
jazz artists such as George Shearing, Sara Vaughan, and Carmen
McRae, but was not well known until his first solo album,
Virtuoso, on Pablo in 1973. This set of personal improvisations on
standard tunes, featuring bass lines, chord solos, and lightning-
fast melodic soloing, often with several of the above happening at
the same time, established a new level of guitar mastery in mainstream jazz. He went on to several successful collaborations with
artists such as Oscar Peterson, Ella Fitzgerald, and Herb Ellis and
has released several solo recordings in addition to extensive live
performing as a solo artist. Joe s many contributions to jazz guitar include bringing its contrapuntal resources into the mainstream in new ways and showing that high-energy bebop
melodies can stand on their own in solo guitar settings. He is musically a traditionalist, and the power and energy of his spontaneous improvisations make for exciting listening. He died in
1994. —*David Nelson McCarthy*

○ **Joe Pass at Akron University** / i. 1974 / Pablo 2308-249
Most of the material on this concert was familiar but remained
fresh. Of the newer work, "Bridgework" was a blues with a
bridge, "Tarde" a Milton Nascimento ballad, and "Time In," a key-
switching blues . . . . Joe Pass retains his position as one of the
masters of the jazz guitar with this album. —*Scott Yanow,
Cadence*

○ **Live at Dante's** / Dec. 1974 / Pablo 114
Over the four sides of this set guitarist Joe Pass treated us to some
stunning playing. Despite having been a regularly working
group, Pass, bassist Jim Hughart, and drummer Frank Severino
achieved a more prosaic type of interaction. If the bassist and
drummer had risen to the soaring levels of Pass's playing, the results would have been spectacular. As it was, they were merely
excellent. —*Pete Welding, Down Beat*

★ **Virtuoso—Vol. 2** / Sep. 14, 1976-Oct. 26, 1976 / Pablo 2310-788
Guitarist Joe Pass dealt with material ranging from Chick Corea's
near-standard "Miles High," to everybody's pop hit "Feelings,"
with that impeccable tone and warm approach that have made
him worthy of the mantle "Virtuoso." The music was played at an
easy pace that made it particularly great late night music . . . .
There aren't many guitarist who could handle the solo idiom as
well as Joe Pass. —*Willard Jenkins Jr., Cadence*

● **I Remember Charlie Parker** / Feb. 17, 1979 / Original Jazz
Classics 602
This is a worthy reissue of Pass's late '70s tribute to Charlie
Parker. —*Ron Wynn*

○ **Northsea Nights** / Jul. 1979 / Pablo 221
Despite there being only two players present who both played at
all times, these were not really duets. The guitarist and bassist
embraced but never entwined. No, this live concert was all solo
plus rhythm, with Pass chording for the bassist and Niels-

Henning Orsted Pedersen often achieving behind Pass the status of a rhythm guitar. —*Francis Davis, Cadence*

○ **Virtuoso—Live!** / **i.** 1991 / Pablo 2310948
A continuation of the virtuoso series spotlighting guitarist Joe Pass's skills differed from the others in that this time he was recorded live. The extra ingredient seemed to make Pass play with even more brilliance; he executed difficult runs, octave jumps, and phrases with verve, while his interpretations of standards and harmonic maneuvers were often amazing. —*Ron Wynn*

○ **All Too Soon** / Original Jazz Classics 450
Solid, nicely played standards, originals, blues, and ballads by guitarist Joe Pass. He seldom plays in exuberant fashion, preferring a smooth, relaxed, yet intricately crafted solo approach. His full notes and elaborate voicings are technically impressive, though sometimes a lack of thematic variety results in his albums all sounding the same. —*Ron Wynn*

○ **Virtuoso—Vol. 4** / Pablo 102
The fourth in the series that gave guitarist Joe Pass a forum to show things that weren't always evident on his many studio dates. Everything, from the elaborate and sophisticated solos to his choices of material, reflected his commitment to excellence, and every release he made for the line was superb. —*Ron Wynn*

Jaco Pastorius (John Francis Pastorius)

b. Dec. 1, 1951, Norristown, PA, **d.** Sep. 21, 1987, Fort Lauderdale, FL
Bass / Early jazz-rock
An incredible electric bassist, Jaco Pastorius was ultimately undone by personal demons. But before that he established an incredible body of work as a player, notably for Weather Report. Pastorius approached his instrument as a lead rather than rhythm section one; his lines and tone had so much depth and form that they dominated any arrangement. His solos were performed with a remarkable fluidity and speed. But Pastorius knew how talented he was, and he could cause thorny problems, particularly when egged on by alcohol. After playing with Blood, Sweat & Tears and recording with Ira Sullivan, Paul Bley, Joni Mitchell, and Pat Metheny, Pastorius joined Weather Report in 1976. He stayed with them several years and then toured with his own group Word of Mouth from 1980 to 1983. Pastorius suffered from depression and endured several financial setbacks. He died as a result of injuries suffered in a 1987 club incident after which the club's manager was arrested for assault. —*Ron Wynn*

● **Jaco Pastorius** / **i.** Aug. 1976 / Epic 33949
Studio group date and first album from this late, great electric bass guitar genius. A must-buy. —*Michael G. Nastos*

○ **Jaco** / **i.** 1978 / Improvising Artists 373846
This was the recording debut for both electric bassist Jaco Pastorius and electric guitarist Pat Metheny and, not too surprisingly, the biggest seller in IAI's history. An electric session with creative but dated sounding keyboards (Paul Bley), Metheny searching for his sound, and an already very distinctive bassist, the music rewards repeated listening. After *Jaco* was released in 1976, Bley gave up electronics. —*Scott Yanow, Coda*

○ **Word of Mouth** / **i.** Dec. 1981 / Warner Brothers 3535
Word of Mouth was Jaco Pastorius' first release under his own name since his Epic debut, *Jaco*, in 1976. . . . On one hand, the album was largely derivative and unresolved; on the other, it contained some overwhelming and amazing moments. —*Lars Gabel, Down Beat*

Don Patterson (Donald B. Patterson)

b. Jul. 22, 1936, Columbus, OH, **d.** Feb. 10, 1988
Organ / Blues & jazz, soul-jazz
A pianist, Patterson took up the Hammond organ in 1956 after hearing Jimmy Smith and made his professional debut in 1959. He worked in and around Chicago with Eric Kloss (1965-1966), Pat Martino, Eddie "Lockjaw" Davis (1963), Gene Ammons (1962), and, most of all, Sonny Stitt (throughout the '60s). From 1981 onward, he often played with Al Grey. He is noted for a pianistic style, his individual style, and understatement. Although Patterson (along with Shirley Scott) is not well-known to the public, he is the organist of choice for many experienced jazz buffs. —*Michael Erlewine*

○ **Exciting New Organ of Don Patterson, The** / Dec. 1964 / Prestige 7331

○ **Genius of the B-3, The** / Oct. 30, 1972 / Muse 5443
A fine album (fast and slow) with Patterson in excellent form. There is some very nice music here. CD clocks out at 43 minutes. —*Michael Erlewine*

★ **These Are Soulful Days** / Sep. 17, 1973 / Muse 5032
Quartet with this great Hammond B-3 organist, Jimmy Heath (sax), Pat Martino (g), and A. Heath (d). —*Michael G. Nastos*

Cecil Payne (Cecil McKenzie Payne)

b. Dec. 14, 1922, Brooklyn
baritone, alto sax, flute / Bop, hard bop
Baritone saxophonist Cecil Payne has simply been a consistently first-rate contributor to a number of fine jazz dates since making his debut on record in 1946 on alto playing with J. J. Johnson. Payne worked with Dizzy Gillespie in 1947-1948 and toured Europe with him. He later played with James Moody, Tadd Dameron, and others before spending two years in the early '50s with Illinois Jacquet. He had some lean periods before he worked again with Randy Weston in the late '50s. He continued working regularly in the '60s, spending time with Woody Herman's Orchestra, plus Machito and Weston. He formed the Jazz Zodiac Quartet for a time and then joined the New York Jazz Repertory Orchestra in 1974, touring with them and recording an album with his vocalist sister Cavril. Payne also did some R&B session work in the '50s and has continued to record for Muse and Spotlite, though not as regularly as his talents merit. —*Ron Wynn*

○ **Patterns** / May 1956 / Savoy 1167
Fine late '50s hard bop session featuring baritone saxophonist Cecil Payne. This was one of two strong albums that matched Payne with pianist Duke Jordan, who was then establishing his own reputation as an aggressive soloist and good accompanist. These are mostly short, tartly played, and well-written and arranged pieces. —*Ron Wynn*

★ **Zodiac** / **i.** 1969 / Strata East
Outstanding quintet date featuring Kenny Dorham (tpt), but hard to find. —*Ron Wynn*

○ **Brooklyn Brothers** / Mar. 16, 1973 / Muse 5015
Brooklyn Brothers was a pleasant, unpretentious set of performances notable mainly for the craftsmanlike consistency and easy familarity the coleaders brought to the assignment. Payne and Jordan worked well in tandem, and the music coursed along effortlessy if unadventurously, the two winding their solo ways through the changes with the practiced ease and agility of past masters running through their paces on home ground. —*Pete Welding, Down Beat*

☆ **Bird Gets the Worm** / Feb. 2, 1976 / Muse 5061
Some of Payne's most vibrant, expressive playing. Good ensemble and compositions. —*Ron Wynn*

Gary Peacock

b. May 12, 1935, Burley, ID
Bass / Modern creative
Gary Peacock is a world-class improvising bassist with an unusual approach. He has a highly individual sound and is able to inspire great, creative collective music. Peacock has played with many greats from Albert Ayler to Keith Jarrett. —*Michael G. Nastos*

★ **Tales of Another** / Feb. 1977 / ECM 827418
W/ Keith Jarrett (p) and Jack DeJohnette (d). Their playing interweaves tightly, with many lines going on at once. Each musician strengthens rather than just supports the other. —*Jerry De Muth, Cadence*

Duke Pearson (Columbus Calvin Pearson, Jr.)

b. Aug. 17, 1932, Atlanta, GA, **d.** Aug. 4, 1980, Atlanta, GA
Piano, composer, arranger / Bop, hard bop
Duke Pearson is a pianist, composer, and arranger and has served as an A&R man for Blue Note. The Atlanta-born player has also accompanied many singers. He's a musician's musician who's at his best when leading a midsize ensemble, where his harmonic genius comes shining through. His music is classic postbop jazz of the '60s and is true group music. —*Michael G. Nastos*

★ **Dedication** / Aug. 2, 1961 / Prestige

This is among Pearson's finest '60s sessions. Includes sterling solos by Freddie Hubbard (tpt) and Pepper Adams (sax). —*Ron Wynn*

○ **Wahoo** / Nov. 24, 1964 / Blue Note 84191
From this late pianist, composer-arranger, and A&R man. Many others by him are as excellent. Find this one and as many others as you can. —*Michael G. Nastos*

☆ **Introducing Duke Pearson's Big Band** / Dec. 1967 / Blue Note 84276

☆ **Now Hear This!** / Dec. 2-03, 1968 / Blue Note

Niels-Henning Orsted Pedersen

b. May 27, 1946, Osted, Denmark
Bass / Swing, modern creative
Along with Eberhard Weber, Miroslav Vitous, and Palle Danielsson, Denmark's Niels-Henning Orsted Pedersen is a premier European bassist who's played superbly in free, bebop, or swing situations. Pedersen's tone, bow or plucked skills, counterpoint, and accompaniment, as well as solo talents are in the virtuoso stage and have been since he was a teen. Pedersen's won numerous European magazine polls as the continent's top bassist and has done well in similar polls conducted by American music publications. His mother was a church organist, and Pedersen studied piano, but he was such a great bassist that he began playing with groups at 14. Count Basie wanted to recruit him at 17. Pedersen was the house bassist at the Club Montmarte and a member of the Danish Radio Orchestra. He worked with numerous musicians during the '60s and '70s, among them Sonny Rollins, Bill Evans, Rahsaan Roland Kirk, Albert Ayler, Dexter Gordon, Anthony Braxton, and many others. Pedersen recorded two duo albums with Kenny Drew, was featured on many Pablo sessions recorded at the 1975 Montreuux festival, and was a regular member of the Oscar Peterson Trio for many years. He hosted a British jazz show in the early '80s. Pedersen has recorded in groups with Monty Alexander and Grady Tate, Claudio Fasoli, Drew, and Barry Altschul. He currently has a couple of sessions as a leader available on CD, and is featured on records by numerous jazz musicians. —*Ron Wynn*

● **Jaywalkin'** / i. Sep. 1975+Dec. 1975 / Steeple Chase 1041

Ken Peplowski

b. 1959
Sax, clarinet / Swing
Ken Peplowski is a Cleveland saxophonist and clarinetist who's a revisionist of swing and light-bop traditions. He's well known as a session man and sideman and has been featured on many sessions for Concord, both as a leader and playing in various groups. —*Michael G. Nastos*

○ **Double Exposure** / Dec. 1987 / Concord Jazz 4344
Good swing-influenced small combo set by alto, tenor sax, and clarinetist Ken Peplowski. While Peplowski's solos are conservative in their range and style, they're well played and done with good taste. He's backed by a group whose members all reflect his values in their own playing; guitarist Ed Bickert, pianist John Bunch, bassist John Goldsby, and drummer Terry Clarke. —*Ron Wynn*

○ **Sonnyside** / Jan. 1989 / Concord Jazz 4376
Quintet. Another tasteful, restrained mainstream date, though Dave Frishberg (p) isn't for everyone. Extra cut on CD issue. —*Ron Wynn*

★ **Mr. Gentle and Mr. Cool** / Feb. 1990 / Concord Jazz 4419
Quintet. This tasty swing-mainstream date has exciting piano by Hank Jones and excellent drumming from Alan Dawson. The CD boasts two bonus cuts. —*Ron Wynn*

○ **Illuminations** / Nov. 20-21, 1990 / Concord Jazz 4449
Quintet. A conservative but well-played small-combo set with swing influences. Junior Mance brings some blues fervor on piano. The CD has two bonus cuts. —*Ron Wynn*

○ **Natural Touch, The** / i. 1992 / Concord Jazz 4517
A '92 session done in saxophonist Ken Peplowski's usually restrained, sophisticated fashion. His material, solo approach, and ensemble style can either be called conservative or derivative, depending on one's slant. He picks supporting players who also don't get overly aggressive or animated in either their solos or their reponses. The CD has three bonus cuts. —*Ron Wynn*

Art Pepper (Arthur Edward Pepper, Jr)

b. Sep. 1, 1925, Gardenia, CA, **d.** Jun. 1, 1982
Alto sax / Cool
Though often lumped in with the cool school because of his status as a West Coast saxophonist, Art Pepper could burn with the hottest of the boppers. At his peak, Pepper played with a passion, harmonic Alan, and zeal that echoed his devotion to Charlie Parker, while swinging with an ease and flow that also reflected a love and knowledge of Lester Young's style. Pepper played with Gus Arnheim's band as a teenager but also spent lots of time working with Black bands on Central Avenue in Los Angeles. He had two stints with Stan Kenton in the early '50s, sandwiched around some time in the army. His '50s output included many superb dates with Chet Baker, Shorty Rogers, Carl Perkins, Hampton Hawes, Sonny Clark, Russ Freeman, and Warne Marsh, as well as the landmark 1957 album *Meets the Rhythm Section*, where Pepper worked with Miles Davis's great trio of pianist Red Garland, bassist Paul Chambers, and drummer Philly Joe Jones. He continued his run of fine releases in the early '60s, but finally ran afoul of the law due to his drug addiction. Pepper was off the recording scene through most of the '60s and then made a stirring comeback. During the '70s Pepper made several majestic releases and also issued a no-holds-barred autobiography titled *Straight Life*. He was also the subject of an excellent 1981 film, *Notes from a Jazz Survivor*. —*Ron Wynn*.

☆ **Complete Pacific Jazz Small Group Recordings of Art Pepper, The** / Mosaic 105

○ **Way It Was, The** / Nov. 1956-Nov. 1960 / Contemporary 389
The first four tracks on this album are from Art Pepper's first Contemporary date, November 1956; three include an ideal partner, Warne Marsh. The others are additions from the famous 1957 to 1960 Pepper dates. The saxophone playing was beautiful throughout, almost as fine as Pepper's great *Smack Up*. Pepper and Marsh were an even hipper team than the classic Marsh-Lee Konitz pairings, and it's a sin they didn't work together frequently. —*John Litweiler, Down Beat*

● **Meets the Rhythm Section** / Jan. 19, 1957 / Original Jazz Classics 338
This Art Pepper album was, according to producer Lester Koenig, beset with problems, but the results were a marvel of inventive blowing. *The* rhythm section of course was Miles Davis's (pianist Red Garland, bassist Paul Chambers, drummer Philly Joe Jones). ... As a unit they had a great gift. This was one of Pepper's finest mid-'50s efforts; it was at the end of a period when Paul Desmond, Lee Konitz, and Pepper had pretty much established the West Coast alto sound. Pepper had the hardest tone and as one can hear was brilliantly imaginative. —*Bob Rusch, Cadence*

★ **Smack Up** / Oct. 24-25, 1960 / Contemporary 176
It is notable that by 1960 alto saxophonist Art Pepper had picked up on Ornette Coleman, the composer, and on *Smack Up* he included Coleman's "Tears Inside" as part of the program. On this record, Pepper was backed by Jack Sheldon (trumpet), Pete Jolly (piano), Jimmy Bond (bass) and Frank Butler (drums). —*Bob Rusch, Cadence*

○ **Living Legend** / Aug. 9, 1975 / Contemporary 408
This session featured an excellent rhythm section with alto saxophonist Art Pepper out in front for a whole LP. Art Pepper had a piercing quality to his playing (as does Jackie McLean) that broke the surface and attacked the absolute heart of the music. —*Peter S. Friedman, Cadence*

○ **Trip, The** / Sep. 15+16, 1976 / Contemporary 410
With the George Cables Trio and Elvin Jones (d). One of his strongest quartet efforts in his final ten years. —*Michael G. Nastos*

○ **No Limit** / Mar. 1977 / Contemporary 411
No Limit, in fact, was less successful than its predecessors, but nonetheless remained an essential item for Art Pepper devotees. The reasons for this were both on the second side of the album. The high point of the record was attained on the modal ballad "My Laurie," which was a superb example of the dialectics of grace and pain typical of his post-1960 style. The sober line was broken by Jackie McLean-like shrieks (the McLean of *Let Freedom Ring* and *Right Now*); there were also of course those entirely distinctive marks of Pepper's personality in the abun-

dance of timbral alterations, provocative silences, and control of time. —*Terry Martin, Down Beat*

○ **Live at the Village Vanguard** / Jul. 28, 1977 / Contemporary 400-7642-3

Alto saxophonist Art Pepper recorded several albums during an extended stint at the Village Vanguard in 1977. They were originally issued as *Live at the Vanguard, volumes 1-4*, then reissued using various weeknights as the reference. Either way, all are exceptional, with burning Pepper solos, outstanding secondary solos by pianist George Cables, and equally fine work from bassist George Mraz and drummer Elvin Jones. This was rereleased on CD as *Thursday Night at the Village Vanguard. —Ron Wynn, AMG*

○ **Friday Night at the Village Vanguard** / Jul. 29, 1977 / Contemporary 695

'92 CD reissue of one among several superb sets done live at the Village Vanguard in the late '70s. Pepper was playing furious, twisting, and energized alto sax solos, while pianist George Cables was showing his empathy with Pepper's style, and bassist George Mraz and drummer Elvin Jones were finding ways to fit themselves into the dialogues. The CD has one bonus cut. —*Ron Wynn, AMG*

○ **Saturday Night at the Village Vanguard** / Jul. 30, 1977 / Contemporary 696

The fourth and final release in the series recorded at the Village Vanguard in 1977. It was issued originally as *Live at the Village Vanguard, Vol. 4* on vinyl, then reissued on CD under the *Saturday Night at the Village Vanguard* title. But no matter, it was riveting material, keyed by the surging Pepper alto sax. There was also pianist George Cables, bassist George Mraz, and drummer Elvin Jones, all of whom were just as remarkable. —*Ron Wynn, AMG*

★ **Complete Galaxy Recordings** / 1977-1982 / Galaxy 1016

This massive 16-disc set covers almost everything in the last phase of Pepper's career. Exquisite piano throughout by George Cables; invaluable liner notes by Gary Giddins. It has 58 unissued tracks, plus alternate takes. —*Ron Wynn*

○ **Artworks** / Mar. 1979 / Galaxy 5148

An exceptional quartet date from '79, with Pepper having just established what became a regular working relationship with pianist George Cables, who plays with passion and conviction. He hadn't yet hired a bassist and drummer, so Charlie Haden and Billy Higgins were used for the occasion . Pepper was certainly inspired by what they contributed; his alto sax solos are intense and often jubilant. —*Ron Wynn, AMG*

★ **Straight Life** / Sep. 1979 / Galaxy 475

Authoritative, statesmanlike Pepper on alto, while Tommy Flanagan proves a distinguished second soloist on piano. —*Ron Wynn*

☆ **Winter Moon** / Sep. 3-04, 1980 / Galaxy 677

Art Pepper's *Winter Moon* featured a full complement of strings plus guitarist Howard Roberts, in addition to the usual rhythm trio. The combo, including bassist Cecil McBee and pianist Stanley Cowell, provided firm but understated support, which could not be said for the often obtrusive fiddles. Still, as string productions go, this one was a success; the dreamy charts of Bill Holman and Jimmy Bond enhanced the altoist's accessibility at not too great a cost to his bittersweet purity. —*Larry Birnbaum, Down Beat*

○ **One September Afternoon** / Sep. 5, 1980 / Galaxy 678

Yet another first-rate early '80s Art Pepper album, this one featuring pianist Stanley Cowell, guitarist Howard Roberts, bassist Cecil McBee, and drummer Carl Burnett. It has a few more midtempo numbers and a generally more upbeat feel than most Pepper sessions from this period. The CD reissue contains two bonus cuts. —*Ron Wynn, AMG*

○ **So in Love** / i. Jul. 1981 / Artists House 9412

Of the new releases issued under Art Pepper's name in 1980, *So in Love* was overall the finest. The altoist stretched out on a program of standards and blues here, backed by alternating rhythm sections from the East and West Coast. —*Francis Davis, Cadence*

○ **Art Lives** / Aug. 1981 / Galaxy 5145

Nice live '81 set from alto saxophonist Art Pepper, who was still playing with fire and fury despite being in poor health. Pianist George Cables had become a Pepper favorite by this time and of-

fered some sparkling solos, while bassist David Williams and drummer Carl Burnett gave the duo the room and space to roam and then delivered when they were called to take the spotlight. —*Ron Wynn*

○ **Rediscoveries** / i. Mar. 1987 / Savoy 1170

More early '50s Pepper material culled from Savoy's vaults and issued in the late '80s as part of what was at the time the most recent Savoy reissue series. Since Denon now owns the label, hopefully at some point they will put all the Pepper tracks into one well-done package, rather than have them floating all over the place. —*Ron Wynn*

○ **Among Friends** / Musicraft 837

Excellent late '70s set by alto saxophonist Art Pepper, one of several that made this as productive a period for Pepper as the early '50s. He worked here with longtime friend and associate pianist Russ Freeman, plus bassist Bob Magnusson and drummer Frank Butler, on some vigorous, dynamic numbers. —*Ron Wynn*

○ **Modern Jazz Classics** / Mobile Fidelity 805

Another outstanding Art Pepper late '50's album, though in a different style. Pepper was backed by an 11-piece orchestra and applied his torrid solos to works that were arranged by Marty Paich. This has been issued both as *Modern Jazz Classics* on CD and as *Modern Jazz Classics: Art Pepper Plus Eleven* on vinyl. —*Ron Wynn*

Bill Perkins (William Reese Perkins)

b. Jul. 22, 1924, San Francisco, CA
Tenor sax, bandleader / Cool

Tenor saxophonist and bandleader Bill Perkins is a "Tonight Show with Johnny Carson " orchestra veteran. He's a fine player who's recorded with his own ensembles and big bands. Perkins is a former member of the Woody Herman orchestra.—*Michael G. Nastos*

○ **Jazz Origin—2 Degrees East, 3 Degrees West** / i. 1956 / PA/USA 9019

★ **Quietly There** / Nov. 23-30, 1966 / Riverside 1776

Quintet. A very-overlooked West Coast saxophonist in one of his better sessions. Reissue of 1966 album as compact disc. —*Ron Wynn*

Carl Perkins (Jazz)

b. 1928, **d.** 1958

Not the rockabilly-rock star, but a fine pianist whose potentially great career was cut short by drug problems. Carl Perkins's left hand was slightly crippled by polio, but he overcame that and inserted superb blues inflections into his work with that same hand. An excellent bebop and hard bop soloist, Perkins initially worked with Tiny Bradshaw and Big Jay McNeely. After moving from the Midwest to the West Coast, Perkins was in an early edition of the Max Roach-Clifford Brown quintet. He was later in the Clifford Counce quintet, and played and recorded with Harold Land, Art Pepper, Chet Baker, and Jim Hall, among others. He began recording for Savoy as a leader in 1949 and issued the outstanding *Introducing Carl Perkins* on Dootone in 1956. He made another session the next year with Red Mitchell and Hall; drum tracks were later overdubbed. Sadly, Perkins was dead at 29. His composition "Grooveyard" remains a jazz anthem. Perkins has a couple of sessions available on CD. —*Ron Wynn*

○ **Introducing Carl Perkins** / Apr. 4, 1956 / Dootone 211

Recorded two years before the legendary West Coast pianist's death. W/ Leroy Vinnegar (b), Lawrence Marable (d). Six Perkins originals make this an important document. He was an important sideman. Here as a leader he shows his true worth. A must-find/buy. —*Michael G. Nastos*

Charlie Persip (Charles Lawrence Persip)

b. Jul. 26, 1929, Morristown, NJ
Drums / Swing, big band, bop, progressive big band

Drummer Charli Persip has publicity stated he'd rather play bop with larger bands than small combos, despite the fact its been a long-established cliché that bop's a combo rather than large group sound. But while his slashing style has certainly clicked in big bands, Persip's been equally effective in quartet and quintet, even trio settings. He played with Tadd Dameron and recorded with Dizzy Gillespie in the '50s. Persip joined Harry Edison's group and played briefly with Harry James before founding the Jazz Statesmen with Freddie Hubbard and Ron Carter in 1960. He did many sessions in the '50s and '60s, working or recording with Dinah Washington, Kenny Dorham, Zoot Sims, Don Ellis, Eric Dolphy, and others. He toured with Billy Eckstine, serving as drummer and conductor from the mid-'60s to the early '70s, and he was the Jazzmobile's principal drum instructor in the mid-'70s. Persip played with Archie Shepp, Frank Foster, and Rahsaan Roland Kirk in the late '70s, and co-led the Superband with trumpeter Gary La Furn in the early '80s. He also was in a trio with Eddie Gomez and Jack DeJohnette (piano). Persip later reformed the Superband, recording with this second edition. He's also done recordings for Bethlehem, Stash, and Soul Note as a leader. —*Ron Wynn and Michael G. Nastos*

● **Charles Persip and the Jazz Statesmen** / Mar. 1961 / Bethlehem 6046
At the time of this recording, most of this group's members were in their early 20s, except for the leader (drummer Charlie Persip), who was a relative veteran at 31. This probably explains the fact that this record had a certain air of immaturity to it. The good moments belonged mostly to Persip and trumpeter Freddie Hubbard, who already at this stage was a quite personal soloist. —*Per Husby, Cadence*

○ **Superband** / Jul. 1982 / Stash 209

Houston Person

b. Nov. 10, 1934, Florence, SC
Tenor sax / Blues & jazz, soul-jazz
This solid, big-toned tenor saxophonist has made many good sessions in the soul-jazz, blues, and ballads vein through the '70s, '80s, and '90s. He often works with vocalist Etta Jones. He doesn't play in relentless, experimental, or innovative fashion but offers nice, pleasing solos and interpretations. An '80s duet album with bassist Ron Carter opened some eyes to his ability to stretch out and go beyond the norm; he's still best in uptempo situations with funk, blues, or soul-jazz arrangements and foundation. — *Ron Wynn*

★ **Goodness!** / Aug. 25, 1969 / Prestige 332
This is the first album of Person's that was a real hit. Here is one of the best examples of his late '60s-early '70s style. Small organ combo with that funky sound. Perhaps too formulaic but still nice. Includes the hypnotic tune "Jamilah." —*Michael Erlewine*

○ **Stolen Sweets** / Apr. 29, 1976 / Muse 5110
First-rate soul-jazz, funk, blues, and ballads by tenor saxophonist Houston Person. Vocalist Etta Jones wasn't on this session, so things were mostly uptempo and cooking, with plenty of robust tenor from Person, tasty guitar by Jimmy Ponder, swirling organ riffs and support from Sonny Phillips, and percussion and rhythmic assistance from Frankie Jones and Buddy Caldwell. —*Ron Wynn*

○ **Big Horn** / May 20, 1976 / Muse 5136
Reliable soul-jazz, nicely played ballads, and good standards are tenor saxophonist Houston Person's forte, and he demonstrates that repeatedly on this '76 quintet set. Pianist Cedar Walton's the type of no-nonsense, consistent player whose skills are often taken for granted, while bassist Buster Williams, and drummer Grady Tate are equally unassuming veterans. —*Ron Wynn*

○ **Party, The** / Nov. 1989 / Muse 5451
Good recent soul-jazz and blues session, with young lion organist Joey DeFrancesco providing the funky undercurrent to tenor saxophonist Houston Person's thick, authoritative solos, and Randy Johnston and Bertell Knox filling the spaces on bass and drums, plus Sammy Figueroa adding some Afro-Latin fiber for additional support. —*Ron Wynn*

○ **Why Not!** / Oct. 5, 1990 / Muse 5433
Organ-tenor-trumpet session. Person's most-recent album includes hot contributions by young lions Phillip (d) and Winard Harper (tpt). W/ Joey DeFrancisco on the Hammond organ. —*Ron Wynn*

Hannibal Marvin Peterson

b. Nov. 11, 1948, Smithville, TX
Trumpet, composer / Progressive big band, modern creative
Exciting high-note trumpeter who first surfaced as a member of Roy Haynes's Hip Ensemble in the early '70s. He later worked

with Pharoah Sanders and Gil Evans and has also made some recordings as a leader. —*Ron Wynn*

○ **Hannibal** / Jul. 1-02, 1975 / MPS 22669
Trumpeter Marvin "Hannibal" Peterson's musical vocabulary ranges from the sharp staccato runs of Clifford Brown to a breathy impreciseness like Miles Davis, each used in the appropriate setting. The compositions provided varied formats in which the musicians soloed, from the slow changes of "Misty" to the modal repetition of "Revelation." —*Kevin Yatarola, Cadence*

★ **In Antibes** / Jul. 20, 1977 / Inner City 3020
Marvin "Hannibal" Peterson combines superior technique with emotional intensity to produce a sound totally satisfying to anyone even remotely attracted to the trumpet. While this album didn't showcase Peterson at his best, it was sufficient to whet the listener's appetite for this remarkable musician. —*David Less, Down Beat*

● **Visions of a New World** / i. 1989 / Atlantic 781973
High note hijinks, verbal forays, superb percussion, and alternately gripping and confusing lyrics combine to keep things unpredictable, intense, and sometimes infuriating. — *Ron Wynn, Rock & Roll Disc.*

☆ **Kiss on the Bridge** / i. 1990 / Ear Rational 882454909

Oscar Peterson (Oscar Emmanuel Peterson)

b. Aug. 15, 1925, Montreal, Quebec
Piano / Swing, bop, hard bop
Canadian virtuoso pianist Oscar Peterson started out on classical piano and by his teens was playing on a weekly radio show. In the mid-'40s he was playing with the Johnny Holmes Orchestra in a style reminiscent of Teddy Wilson, Erroll Garner, and Art Tatum. He was discovered by Norman Grantz and invited to appear at a Jazz at the Philharmonic concert in Carnegie Hall in 1949. This was his real start. He then formed a trio using piano, guitar, and bass after the style of Nat "King" Cole. His most famous trio, including Herb Ellis (g) and Ray Brown (b), was together from 1953 to 1958, and he worked with other trio members until 1965. After 1970, Peterson concentrated on solo piano performances, and has worked with symphony orchestras since the mid-'70s. Next to Art Tatum, Peterson is considered by musicians and critics as the greatest virtuoso jazz pianist. He has recorded extensively, issuing as many as six albums a year. — *Michael Erlewine*

○ **Oscar Peterson Plays Cole Porter** / Nov. 25, 1951-Dec. 1952 / Mercury 603

○ **Oscar Peterson Plays Jerome Kern** / Dec. 1952-Dec. 31, 1953 / Clef 623

○ **Oscar Peterson Plays Duke Ellington** / Dec. 1952 / Mercury 606

○ **Oscar Peterson Plays George Gershwin** / Dec. 1952 / Mercury 605

○ **Oscar Peterson Trio at the Concertgebouw, The** / Apr. 12, 1958 / Verve 8268

★ **Very Tall** / Sep. 1961 / Verve 827821

☆ **Night Train—Vol. 1** / Dec. 15-16, 1962 / PolyGram 821724

○ **We Get Requests** / Oct. 19, 1963 / Verve 810047

○ **Oscar Peterson Trio Plus One** / i. Nov. 1964 / Mercury 20975
A first-rate early '60s release in which the usual Oscar Peterson trio got a nice addition via trumpeter Clark Terry. Terry's trademark humor, tart trumpet solos, and general upbeat personality helped pump some life into Peterson and his crew, and he also gave a contrasting solo voice and options to the selections. This has been reissued on CD. —*Ron Wynn*

○ **Reunion Blues** / Jul. 1971 / PolyGram 817490
Fine early '70s set with pianist Oscar Peterson working in a different situation from the characteristic trios, solos, or duos. He's featured in a quartet with vibist Milt Jackson, bassist Ray Brown, and drummer Louis Hayes, who's much more wide open and groove-oriented than most who've worked with Peterson. The results are looser, with more blues sensibility and rhythmic punch. —*Ron Wynn*

○ **History of an Artist—Vol. 1** / Dec. 27, 1972 / Pablo 702
The first of a two-part anthology collecting Peterson material from his years on Verve. It's solo, trio, and combo sessions, with numerous interpretations of standards, blues, ballads, and vari-

ous other things. Excellent playing throughout; the only problem is that if you're not a piano lover, the lack of diversity can become troubling. —*Ron Wynn*

○ **Oscar Peterson Feat. Stephane Grappelli** / Feb. 22+23, 1973 / Prestige 24041

★ **Trio, The** / May 16-19, 1973 / Pablo 2310-70
The Nat Cole piano, guitar, bass lineup Oscar Peterson used here represented not a departure but a somewhat nostalgic return to the format he perfected in the company of such musicians as Ray Brown, Barney Kessel, and Herb Ellis. The result, recorded live at Chicago's London House, was gratifying. Peterson was as loquacious and polished as ever; only a cursory listening to, say, "Blues Etude" (a kind of microhistory of blues piano from barrelhouse to stride to bop) confirmed that Peterson could effortlessy realize just about everything on piano —*Jon Balleras, Down Beat*

○ **Oscar Peterson and Roy Eldridge** / Dec. 8, 1974 / Pablo 739
This was generally a good Eldridge album, considering his limitations at the time. He acquitted himself well indeed on less frantic pieces such as "Little Jazz," "Sunday" (with a walking bass line by Oscar Peterson on organ), and "Blues for Chu," in which a few brief high note thrusts are brought off nicely. When muted (on more than half the LP), he was incisive and reasonably articulate. His open horn was clean, round, and characteristically rugged. If it wasn't a landmark record, it was certainly far from being a disappointment. —*John Mcdonough, Down Beat*

○ **Oscar Peterson & Jon Faddis** / Jun. 5, 1975 / Pablo 743
Jon Faddis started off this album with a sullen "Things Ain't What They Used to Be," which growled through several muted choruses and climaxed with several rounds of economical high note work that suggested Harry Edison more than Dizzy Gillespie, who is considered Faddis's mentor. The energy level was high throughout this LP, as high as the keys in most cases.... Oscar Peterson's piano seemed particularly inspired. But the most satisfying tract was "Lester Leaps In," simply because it was the most swinging. —*John Mcdonough, Down Beat*

○ **Oscar Peterson Big Six, The** / Jul. 16, 1975 / Original Jazz Classics 496
Fine live set with piano wizard Oscar Peterson leading a sextet at the 1975 Montreux Festival. Peterson is a longtime favorite of Norman Granz, who's issued numerous Peterson recordings over the years on many labels. The piano solos are rigorous and intricately constructed and executed, while the ensemble work and solos from other participants are equally impressive, especially those from guitarist Joe Pass and vibist Milt Jackson. —*Ron Wynn*

○ **Oscar Peterson and Clark Terry** / i. 1975 / Pablo 742
Pianist Oscar Peterson was in excellent company with Clark Terry on what was the first of the Pablo label's piano-trumpet records. Terry's nimble attack served him well, even though neither musician really rose to any unexpected heights. —*John Mcdonough, Down Beat*

○ **Montreux (1977)** / Jul. 15, 1977 / Original Jazz Classics 385
Peterson takes the harmonic and solo spotlight. Nice assistance by Ray Brown (b) and Niels-Henning Orsted Petersen (b). —*Ron Wynn*

○ **Exclusively for My Friends [Boxed Set]** / i. 1992 / PolyGram 513830
The music here, originally released on six MPS LPs, has been reissued as *Exclusively for My Friends,* a four-CD set that awesomely reconfirms the opinion expressed by Oscar Peterson that these were the best recordings he ever made. —*Owen Cordle, Down Beat*

Ralph Peterson

Drums / Neo-bop
This top drummer is rapidly becoming a star in the '90s jazz scene. He's a stirring accompanist, aggressive soloist, and intriguing composer and bandleader, who has managed to attract some of the best players around to record with him and play in his groups. Signed to Blue Note in the late '80s, he has made trio, small-combo, and large-group sessions. His fotet (4 pieces) release in 1991 was among the year's best recordings. —*Ron Wynn*

★ **Triangular** / Aug. 21-22, 1988 / Blue Note 92750

○ **Volition** / Feb. 1989 / Blue Note 93894
Quintet. Excellent session; wondrous lineup. Pianist Geri Allen and trumpeter Terence Blanchard are masterly. —*Ron Wynn*

○ **Fo'tet Ornettology** / Aug. 1990 / Somethin' Else 98290
An outstanding hard bop session by drummer Ralph Peterson, with him heading a band that includes many top modern players, among them Don Byron on clarinet and Melissa Slocum and Bryan Carroll. The compositions are mostly originals, and though arranged in a vintage style have a contemporary flavor. —*Ron Wynn*

Michel Petrucciani

b. Dec. 28, 1962, Orange, France
Piano / Cool, neo-bop
Pianist Petrucciani has made a strong impact in the jazz world. At age 15, he was playing with Kenny Clarke and doing guest stints with Clark Terry. He toured California in the early '80s, following a visit to New York, and moved to America in 1982. He was part of Charles Lloyd's comeback band in 1982, recording and touring Europe with him and made a heralded appearance at the Kool Jazz Festival in 1984. He subsequently recorded with Wayne Shorter, Jim Hall, and Lloyd and cut many albums as a leader. Petrucciani is an accomplished technician whose solos show a masterfully harmonic talent. —*Ron Wynn*

○ **100 Hearts** / Jun. 1983 / George Wein Collection 3001
If it's possible to fault pianist Michel Petrucciani's playing, it's only in that his considerable technique and expansive imagination sometimes lead him to pack too much into one piece, to journey down every possible improvisational byway, to play more than necessary. But such exuberance is nonetheless fascinating to contemplate. Consider the approach Petrucciani took to Ornette Coleman's *Turn Around.* He addressed this gutsy, side-slipping blues line with brittle excursions into inside and outside tonalities supported by a hefty walking bass line spiced with witty twists. —*Jon Balleras, Down Beat*

○ **Live at the Village Vanguard** / Mar. 16, 1984 / George Wein Collection 43006
Comparisons to the great Bill Evans trios may seem premature; they are not unwarranted. More than the setting, format, and drummer Eliot Zigmund's presence suggest them. Michel Petrucciani's sure-handed swing and soft lyricism, the balance of interpretations and original material, and most of all, the interplay between Petrucciani, bassist Palle Danielsson, and Zigmund, recall another set of trio performances recorded at the Vanguard. —*Eric Shepard, Cadence*

○ **Cold Blues** / Jan. 1985 / Owl 79224
A '91 CD reissue featuring the outstanding pianist Michel Petrucciani in duets with bassist Ron McClure. While some accuse Petrucciani of too much flash and not enough soul, his expressive phrasing and often dazzling solos reflect a complete knowledge and mastery of the keyboard, while bassist McClure adds enough depth and bottom to keep things from getting too spacy. —*Ron Wynn*

★ **Pianism** / Dec. 20, 1985 / Blue Note 46295
The virtuosic pianist Michel Petrucciani was at his best throughout this dazzling set. Although frequently recorded in recent years, *Pianism* ranked among Petrucciani's most satisfying releases because he emphasized emotion over his remarkable technique. —*Scott Yanow, Cadence*

☆ **Power of Three** / Jul. 14, 1986 / Blue Note 46427
It was logical that Michel Petrucciani (piano) and Jim Hall (guitar) would eventually play together. Both are masters of chordal improvisation and possessors of harmonically rich and introverted styles.... At the 1986 Montreux Jazz Festival the pair worked together perfectly, sounding as one on the altered blues "Careful" (where their comping behind each other's solos was exquisite) and on a lengthy and well-constructed version of "In a Sentimental Mood." —*Scott Yanow, Cadence*

Oscar Pettiford

b. Sep. 30, 1922, Okmulgee, OK, **d.** Sep. 8, 1960, Copenhagen
Bass, cello / Bop
Pettiford is one of the most exemplary bassists and cellists of the '50s. He was born on a Native American reservation and played in a family band with ten musical siblings that was quite popular in the Midwest. He worked with Charlie Barnet in 1942 and went to New York and joined Roy Eldridge in 1943. He did several sessions in the mid-'40s with Coleman Hawkins, Earl Hines, and Ben Webster. He co-led a group with Dizzy Gillespie in 1944 and had

his own combos and big band in 1945. Pettiford relocated on the West Coast to work with Hawkins in 1945 and then spent three years with Duke Ellington's orchestra. After that he usually led his own bands, with the exception of a year with Woody Herman in 1949 and another year with Charlie Shavers and Louie Bellson's band in 1950. Pettiford was a marvelous improviser and pioneered the art of playing the pizzicato style on cello. His technique and intonation have been absorbed by nearly every bassist from the early '50s on, and such pieces as "Bohemia After Dark" and "Laverne Walk" are modern masterpieces. —*Ron Wynn*

○ **Oscar Pettiford Memorial Album** / Mar. 10, 1949+Mar. 13, 1954 / Prestige 7813
Stunning bass and cello playing from Oscar Pettiford (the bass parts are multitracked) showing his technical prowess both with bow and plucked. Phenomenal showcase for Pettiford's work and for bass and cello in general. —*Ron Wynn*

○ **Discoveries** / Feb. 21, 1952-Oct. 1957 / Savoy 1172
1952-1957. A stunning early work by the bass and cello great. Has some duets with Charles Mingus (b), plus other examples of his stirring cello technique. —*Ron Wynn*

★ **New Oscar Pettiford Trio, The** / Dec. 29, 1953 / Debut 112
A wonderful set. Pettiford is in prime form as a bassist and composer. —*Ron Wynn*

○ **O.P.'s Jazz Men (The Oscar Pettiford Orchestra)** / i. 1958 / Paramount 227

○ **Montmartre Blues** / Black Lion 760124

Flip Phillips (Joseph Edward Filipelli)

b. Mar. 26, 1915, New York, NY
Tenor sax / Swing, bop
Tenor saxophonist Flip Phillips is one of the legitimate living masters of swing. He first played alto sax and clarinet in Brooklyn groups in the '30s and then played clarinet exclusively for Frankie Newton in 1940-1941. He turned to tenor and worked with Benny Goodman, Wingy Manone, Red Norvo, and Woody Herman in the early and mid-'40s. But it was a ten-year tenure on the *Jazz at the Philharmonic* tours that earned him his jazz spurs. Phillips was a prime crowd-pleaser in these jam sessions, playing with energy and flash and adding honks, squalls, and vocal effects, plus possessing rhythmic vitality and sizzle. But he was (and is) also an excellent ballad stylist, and his albums in later years spotlighted that aspect of his talents. After leaving the JATP circuit, he moved to Florida, where he worked with Bill Harris and Woody Herman, toured Europe with Benny Goodman in 1959, and headed his own groups for 15 years. He returned to New York in 1975 and made another European tour in 1982. —*Ron Wynn*

● **Melody from the Sky, A** / i. 1944-1945 / Doctor Jazz 39419
An album of 1944-1945 sessions from New York with a good, swinging sound. —*Michael G. Nastos*

○ **Rock with Flip** / Sep. 13, 1954 / Clef 740

○ **Flip in Florida** / i. May 1974 / Onyx 214
This recording, made in 1963 and issued briefly, showed Flip Phillps in familiar territory. The tenor saxophonist and bass clarinetist played a program of standards ("Sweet Georgia Brown"), jazz classics ("Round Midnight"), Ellingtunes ("Satin Doll"), and lovely ballads ("Nuages") backed by a rhythm section. —*Joe Klee, Down Beat*

○ **Claw—Live at the Floating Jazz Festival, The** / i. 1986 / Chiaroscuro 314

○ **Sound Investment, A** / Mar. 1987 / Concord Jazz 4334
W/ Scott Hamilton (ts). An excellent, sympathetic collaboration. A standout pairing of this top swing-era stylist and a modern disciple. —*Ron Wynn*

★ **Real Swinger** / May 1988-Jun. 1988 / Concord Jazz 4358
W/ Howard Alden (g), Butch Miles (d), and this veteran saxophonist on his most recent album. Still swinging after all these years. Highly recommended. —*Michael G. Nastos*

○ **Small Herd on Keynote** / i. Aug. 15, 1991 / Verve 830968

Bill Pierce (William Pierce)

b. Sep. 25, 1948, Hampton, VA
Multi-instruments / Hard bop, postbop, neo-bop

A multiinstrumentalist and session player who's recorded for Sunnyside. A hard bop-mainstream soloist, not to be confused with traditional jazz artist Billie Pierce. —*Ron Wynn*

★ **William the Conqueror** / May 29-30, 1985 / Sunnyside 1013
It is the powerful tenor of Billy Pierce that makes this a highly recommended album. —*Scott Yanow, Cadence*

Courtney Pine

b. Mar. 18, 1964, London, England
Tenor sax, soprano sax / Hard bop, world fusion
Tenor and soprano saxophonist Courtney Pine is arguably the greatest British jazz musician of his generation, Pine first worked in reggae bands and funk groups. He formed a 21-piece Jazz Warriors orchestra in 1985, as well as a support alliance to promote the arts in Britain. His 1986 debut attracted international attention, and subsequent releases include hard bop, reggae, and funk-influenced compositions. Pine has extensive gifts: a robust tone, extensive knowledge of jazz history, and the ability to play in a frenzied, aggressive manner, especially on soprano. —*Ron Wynn*

○ **Journey to the Urge Within** / Jul. 1986-Aug. 1986 / Antilles 842687
Pine was consistently strong in a loose foursome with pianist Julian Joseph; Gary Crosby, bass; and Mark Mondesir, drums. London-born but Jamaica-bred and with reggae experience, Pine didn't push the island "riddims" that snagged Oliver Lake; he played mostly pretty ballads, or alert, slighty outward-moving postbop that betrayed subtle Latin tinges. —*Kevin Whitehead, Cadence*

★ **Destiny's Song and the Image of Pursuance** / i. 1988 / Antilles 842772
English young lion Courtney Pine has heart and soul but sometimes lacks ideas and taste. —*Ron Wynn*

Bucky Pizzarelli (John Paul Pizzarelli, Sr.)

b. Jan. 9, 1926, Paterson, NJ
Guitar / Swing, big band
Better-known as Bucky than John, Pizzarelli is a self-taught player and well known for using a seven-string guitar and emphasizing touch, delicacy, and restraint instead of speed, aggression, or high volume. Pizzarelli started with Joe Mooney's combo and became a studio musician with NBC in 1954. He switched to ABC in 1966 and played on the "Dick Cavett Show." Then Pizzarelli expanded his horizons in the '70s, doing more jam-session and freelance work and building his reputation as a versatile musician who could contribute in small combos, duos, or big bands or work with strings and support vocalists. His recordings have also been eclectic, ranging from solo acoustic to quartet and duo dates. Since the '80s, Pizzarelli has virtually dropped the "John" to avoid confusion with his son John Jr., who's also a fine acoustic and electric guitarist. The two have even recorded together since 1985. —*Ron Wynn*

○ **Buck and Bud** / i. Feb. 1977 / Flying Dutchman 11378

● **Complete Guitar Duos** / 1991 / Stash 536
Fine guitar vehicle for Bucky Pizzarelli and John, Jr. They team on both uptempo and slow tunes, some originals, mostly interpretations of both jazz and nonjazz items. This is wonderful for guitar devotees; others may have problems with the lack of variety and generally sedate production and sound. —*Ron Wynn*

○ **Rhythm Encounters with Red Norvo and Slam Stewart** / Stash 18

King Pleasure (Clarence Beeks)

b. Mar. 24, 1922, Oakdale, TN, d. Mar. 21, 1981, Los Angeles, CA
Vocals / Pop, ballads & blues
Born Clarence Beeks, King Pleasure is perhaps the inventor, and certainly the first popularizer of vocalese, the process of setting lyrics to instrumental solos. His first hit was "Moody's Mood for Love" (Prestige) in 1952, and he followed that with "Red Top" (Prestige) in 1953. His Prestige work was collected on the album *Moody's Mood for Love*. Later sessions for Jubilee (1955) and Alladin (1956) are collected on the Blue Note CD also called *Moody's Mood for Love*, along with an album recorded in 1962 for Untitled Artists. One last recording session for HiFi Jazz (*Golden Days*) was done in 1960. Vocalese requires a bit of get-

Jazz Piano

Keyboards from Europe

Ragtime
Scott Joplin (1868-1917)
Joe Lamb (1887-1960)

Early Jazz Piano
Eubie Blake (1883-1983)
Jelly Roll Morton (1890-1941)
Earl Hines (1903-1983)

Stride Piano
Lucky Roberts (1887-1968)
Willie "The Lion" Smith (1897-1973)
James P. Johnson (1894-1955)
Fats Waller (1904-19430

Major Influence
Art Tatum (1909-1956)

Boogie-Woogie
Jimmy Yancey (1898-1951)
Pinetop Smith (1904-1929)
Pete Johnson (1904-1967)
Meade Lux Lewis (1905-1964)
Little Brother Montgomery (1906-1985)
Albert Ammons (1907-1949)
Memphis Slim (1915)
Art Hodes (1904)

1930s Experimental
Clarence Profit (1912-1944)

Swing Piano
Count Basie (1904-1986)
Jess Stacy (1904)
Teddy Wilson (1912-1986)
Erroll Garner (1921-1977)
Ralph Sutton (1922)

Transition to Bop
Thelonious Monk (1917-1982)

Bop Piano
Mary Lou Williams (1910-1981)
Lennie Tristano (1919-1978)
Bud Powell (1924-1966)
Al Haig (1924)
Oscar Peterson (1925)
Barry Harris (1929)
Hank Jones (1918)
Tommy Flanagan (1930)
Duke Jordan (1922)
Walter Bishop, Jr. (1927)
Elmo Hope (1923-1967)
Kenny Drew (1928)
Dodo Marmarosa (1925)

Cool Piano
Lennie Tristano (1919-1978) – John Lewis (1920)
Bill Evans (1929-1980) – Dave Brubeck (1920)

Post Bop
Herbie Nichols (1919-1963)
Red Garland (1923-1984)
Randy Weston (1926)
Horace Silver (1928)
Phineas Newborn (1931)
Wynton Kelly (1931-1971)
Bobby Timmons (1935-1974)
McCoy Tyner (1938)
Hal Galper (1938)
George Cables (1944)
Horace Parlan (1931)
Hugh Lawson (1935)
Joanne Brackeen (1938)
Sonny Clark (1931-1963)

Free Style
Sun Ra (1915)
Cecil Taylor (1929)
Alex Von Schilippenbach (1938)
Yosuke Yamashita (1942)
Marilyn Crispell (1947)
Don Pullen (1944)
Horace Tapscott (1934)
Muhal Richard Abrams (1930)
Dave Burrell (1940)

Experimental
Mal Waldron (1926)
Andrew Hill (1937)

Keith Jarrett (1945)
Michel Petrucciani (1962)
Hilton Ruiz (1952)
Tete Montoliu (1933)

Electric
Joe Zawinul (1932)
Herbie Hancock (1940)
Chick Corea (1941)
Lonnie Liston Smith (1940)

Soul and R&B Piano
Ramsey Lewis (1935)
Junior Mance (1928)
Gene Harris (1933)
Joe Sample (1939)
Les McCann (1935)

Revival
Jim Dapogny (1940)
Judy Carmichael
Mr. B.
Dick Wellstood (1927-1987)
Dick Hyman (1927)
Roger Kellaway (1939)
Reginald Robinson

New Players
Mulgrew Miller (1955)
Renee Rosnes
Geri Allen (1957)
Marcus Roberts (1963)
Michele Rosewoman(1953)
Stephen Scott
Kenny Kirkland (1957)
James Williams
Donald Brown
Kenny Drew, Jr.
Geoff Keezer
Benny Green

Jacki Byard (1922), Marian McPartland (1926), Ellis Larkins (1923)

ting used to, but Pleasure's recordings are some of the very best in the idiom. Pleasure could also handle a straight lyric with equal ability. —*Bob Porter*

★ **Source** / Feb. 19, 1952-Dec. 7, 1954 / Prestige 24017
1952-1960. A twofer of essential material from the essential master of vocalese. —*Michael G. Nastos*

○ **King Pleasure Sings with Annie Ross** / 1952-1954 / Prestige 217

○ **Moody's Mood for Love** / i. 1992 / Blue Note 84463

Daniel Ponce

b. 1953
Percussion / Latin-jazz, world fusion
Daniel Ponce is a Latin percussionist whose presence and magnetism is inspirational of its own accord. He's primarily a conga player who leads contemporary Latin-jazz dance oriented bands. Ponce is a premier, in-demand sideman. —*Michael G. Nastos*

Jean Luc Ponty (Jean-Luc Ponty)

b. Sep. 29, 1942, Avranches, France
Violin / Early jazz-rock
Jean Luc-Ponty began his career as a classically trained violinist from France; he was influenced by Stephane Grappelli. He worked with Grappelli, George Duke, Frank Zappa, and John McLaughlin in the '60s and formed his own band in fusion format in the mid '70s. He created four albums of original music before turning more toward instumental formula rock. He's worked recently with African percussionists. —*Michael G. Nastos*

★ **Violin Summit** / i. Sep. 30, 1966 / Verve 821303
Violin Summit featured Stuff Smith, Stephane Grappelli, Svend Asmussen, and Jean Luc-Ponty (with pianist Kenny Drew, bassist Niels-Henning Orsted Pedersen, drummer Alex Riel) in concert (9/30/66). . . . The music came off quite well, in large part probably because the four violinists were paired in different sets with all four actually featured together on only one take, "It Don't Mean a Thing If It Ain't Got That Swing." —*Bob Rusch, Cadence*

○ **Canteloupe Island** / Mar. 1969 / Blue Note 632
The late '60s experiments that violinist Jean Luc-Ponty recorded with Frank Zappa were resurrected here on "Cantaloupe Island." Thematically it was Zappa's show, from compositions to arrangements, but Ponty played with a fervor and imagination that was fresh to the rock idiom, if that generic term could be applied here. —*Mikal Gilmore, Down Beat*

○ **New Violin Summit** / i. 1972 / MPS 8

○ **Upon the Wings of Music** / Jan. 1975 / Atlantic 18138
Violinist Jean Luc-Ponty put together a well-paced, unified, and sweet-tempered LP in the high-energy vein, and it was eminently listenable. —*Neil Tesser, Down Beat*

Odeon Pope

b. Oct. 24, 1938, Ninety six, SC
Trumpet, bandleader / Hard bop
A dynamic, hard-driving tenor sax soloist noted for his work with Max Roach, Odean Pope's among the most fiery of contemporary players. His muscular tone, thrusts, honks, and vocal cries make every Pope solo memorable. Pope learned saxophone and harmony from Ray Bryant while growing up in Philadelphia. Jymie Merrit introduced him to Roach, and Pope toured Europe with his quartet in the late '60s and also accompanied Vi Redd during a London recording session. He formed Catalyst in 1971, a band that made four good jazz-rock and hard bop albums in the early '70s. Pope organized the Saxophone Choir in 1977, a band featuring eight saxes and a rhythm section. He headed the group until 1979, when he rejoined Roach for another European tour. Pope made four recordings with the Roach band in the '80s. He also led the Saxophone Choir again and recorded with a trio. Pope has a couple of dates available on CD. —*Ron Wynn*

○ **Saxophone Shop, The** / i. Sep. 1987 / Soul Note 1129
Pope is one of the few saxophonists to use multiphonics without sounding self-conscious (it is, in fact, the basis of his style). "Elixir" and "Almost Like Me, Part 2" demonstrate this aptly. Philadelphia composers have always been deft musical portraitists. The vibrancy and edge of the streets can be heard in McCoy Tyner's "Blues on the Corner" or Lee Morgan's "The Rump Roller." —*Ludwig Van Trikt, Cadence*

★ **Out for a Walk** / i. Oct. 1990 / Moers 02072

○ **Ponderer, The** / i. May 19, 1992 / Soul Note 121229

Bud Powell (Earl Powell)

b. Sep. 27, 1924, New York, NY, d. Jul. 31, 1966, New York, NY
Piano, composer / Bop
The greatest pianist to emerge from the bop tradition, Bud Powell was another instrumental genius plagued during his lifetime with personal demons. A superior composer, Powell played in a frenetic rhythmic fashion and was as remarkable a harmonic and melodic inventor as Charlie Parker. Only Art Tatum and arguably Oscar Peterson have ever been more suited for the trio format, and his accompaniment behind the soloists was often better than what was being played upfront. Powell studied classical music in his youth and then became immersed in the bop revolution in the early '40s. He joined the Cootie Williams band in 1943-1944 and made his debut on records with them. He later worked with Charlie Parker on 52d Street, before being hospitalized in 1945, allegedly as a result of police brutality. Later in the '50s, Powell would suffer attacks during performances and have to be helped off stage. When lucid, he was a marvel at the piano. He made memorable sessions for Blue Note in the '40s and '50s and was part of the immortal Massey Hall concert in 1953 with Charles Mingus, Max Roach, Dizzy Gillespie, and Charlie Parker. Influenced early on by Teddy Wilson, Nat King Cole, Tatum, and the underrated and undervalued Billy Kyle, Powell was a legitimate innovator, and his rhythmic right hand lines are famous among pianists. —*Ron Wynn*

● **Complete Bud Powell Blue Note Recordings** / Mosaic 116

○ **Shaw Nuff** / i. 1945-1960 / EPM 5167
An anthology with performances by pianist Bud Powell from three periods. Some songs were done in 1945 (the best), others in 1959 and 1960. Powell's work was in its formative stages in the '40s, but was exploding and maturing. He'd become an established star in the late '50s and on the '59 and '60 tracks plays with an easy confidence and relentless skill that's technically superior to the '40s material, but lacks the same passion. —*Ron Wynn*

○ **Alternate Takes** / Aug. 9, 1949-May 23, 1963 / Mainstream 724
Various alternate or unissued takes by the great hard bop pianist Bud Powell recorded in the late '40s. These were gathered on an album and issued by Blue Note in the late '60s. While the playing's mostly excellent, there's really nothing here that hasn't been surpassed on other Powell releases. However, it's still good to hear almost any Powell piano. —*Ron Wynn*

★ **Amazing Bud Powell—Vol. 1** / 1949-1953 / Blue Note 81503

☆ **Bud Powell's Moods** / Jul. 1950-Feb. 1951 / Mercury 610

★ **Genius of Bud Powell—Vol. 2, The** / Jul. 1950-Feb. 1951 / Verve 827901

★ **Genius of Bud Powell—Vol. 1, The** / Jul. 1950-Feb. 1951 / PolyGram 827901
These trio sides represented pianist Bud Powell at his very best. Particularly stunning were the uptempo tracks such as "Tempus Fugit," "Sweet Georgia Brown," and "Just One of Those Things," in which he created a continuously brilliant, yet highly emotional line, that moved at breathtaking speed. —*Martin Davidson, Cadence*

● **Amazing Bud Powell—Vol. 2, The** / May 1951-Aug. 1953 / Blue Note 81504

○ **Charles Mingus Trios** / i. Mar. 1953 / Jazz Door 1213

○ **Legacy, The** / i. Mar. 1953-1964 / Jazz Door 1204

○ **Jazz at Massey Hall—Vol. 2** / May 15, 1953 / Debut
This is the less famous half of the 5/15/53 Massey Hall concert. These are the trio (Charles Mingus, bass; Max Roach, drums) sides that were also on a prior Prestige twofer. . . . On the record as a whole, the brillance comes overwhelmingly from Powell. —*Bob Rusch, Cadence*

○ **Jazz at Massey Hall—Vol. 1** / May 15, 1953 / Original Jazz Classics

★ **Amazing Bud Powell—Vol. 3, The** / 1956 / Blue Note 81571

○ **Groovin' at the Blue Note (1959-1961)** / i. 1957-Jan. 1961 / Mythic Sound 6005

○ **Amazing Bud Powell—Vol. 4: Time Waits** / May 1958 / Blue Note 46820

The fourth volume in a series featuring hard bop piano legend Bud Powell during extensive series of recordings for Blue Note in the early '50s. These are items that weren't included in either the first three volumes or the CD reissue that covered the first volumes. —*Ron Wynn*

Scene Changes / Dec. 29, 1958 / Blue Note 46529
This late '80s Blue Note reissue is uneven but has plenty of Powell fireworks. —*Ron Wynn*

Time Waits / May 25, 1959 / Blue Note 46820
A bonus cut in the 1987 reissue. Good sound and exceptional Powell solos. —*Ron Wynn*

○ **Cookin' at Saint Germain (1957-1959)** / i. Nov. 1959 / Mythic Sound 6003

○ **Bud in Paris** / Jun. 15, 1960 / Xanadu 102
Pianist Bud Powell had his on and off moments during his last years, but on this recording, recorded 3 1/2 years before his death, he was very much *on*, lucid and direct. The tormented brilliance that became characteristic of his later work was not present here; here was a young, alert, and futuristic personality. —*Bob Rusch, Cadence*

○ **Relaxin' at Home (1961-1964)** / i. 1961-1964 / Mythic Sound 6004

○ **Return to Birdland (1964)** / i. Sep. 1964 / Mythic Sound 6009

○ **Award at Birdland (1964)** / i. Oct. 1964 / Mythic Sound 6010

○ **Invisible Cage, The** / i. Sep. 1974 / Black Lion 153
Recorded in Paris in July 1964, two years to the day before Bud Powell's death and only several weeks before what was to be his last return from Europe to the States, this album gave us a sober picture of the artist in his declining years. Some brighter spots came on the delightful "Like Someone in Love." —*Jon Balleras, Down Beat*

○ **Bud Powell Trio at the Golden Circle Vol.1** / i. Jan. 1980 / Steeple Chase 6001
For students and serious collectors of pianist Bud Powell recordings, this first volume of previously unissued masters is a must. These sessions were recorded when Powell's loneliness and depression seemed to blossom as in a garden of moonless, windless darkness. The importance of these sides was the fact that they are "living transcriptions" of Powell's music, vintage bop in slow motion. —*Bradley Parker-Sparrow, Down Beat*

Mel Powell (Melvin Epstein)

b. Feb. 12, 1923, New York, NY
Piano, composer / Swing
Pianist and composer Mel Powell was a Pulitzer Prize winner in 1991, and his career exemplifies extraordinary achievement in both jazz and classical circles. Though he hasn't made many records, his incredible technique and masterly solo approach, along with his flexibility, put him in the forefront of modern keyboard artists. As a teen, he was in Muggsy Spanier's big band, and he auditioned for Benny Goodman in 1941. He became a staff musician at CBS in 1942 and worked with Glenn Miller in 1943 and 1944, going with him to England and eventually being featured on the BBC's "Piano Party" show. After returning to America, Powell dropped out of the jazz world, going first to Hollywood to work in the studios and then to Yale to study composition with Paul Hindemith and piano with Nadia Reisenberg. Powell later taught music theory at Queens College and composition at Yale and was awarded a Guggenheim fellowship in 1959. During the '70s and '80s, Powell split his time between being Dean of Music at the California Institute of Arts and doing occasional jazz dates on cruises and with Bobby Hackett. An exceptional 1989 release on Concord with Benny Carter alerted a new corps of listeners to Powell's amazing talents. —*Ron Wynn*

★ **World is Waiting, The** / Feb. 4, 1942 / Commodore 543

○ **Columbia Special Products** / i. Dec. 1979 / XFL 14943

Andre Previn (Andreas Ludwig Priwin)

b. Apr. 6, 1929, Berlin, Germany
Piano, conductor / Cool, swing, bop
Andre Previn has amassed some solid credentials in the jazz and pop world to go along with his extensive classical accomplishments. He took piano lessons in his native Berlin as a child but had to endure being booted from the conservatory in a shameful

anti-Semitic incident. His family moved to Paris and then Los Angeles. Previn played piano and did the score for a Jose Iturbi film at 16. He began dividing his time and interests between jazz, classical, and film scores, and has continued doing this ever since. Previn scored the Oscar-winning films *Gigi, Porgy & Bess*, and *My Fair Lady*, among others, and issued over 20 trio albums in the '50s, '60s, and '70s. His most popular trio included bassist Leroy Vinnegar and drummer Shelly Manne. Previn also had best-selling albums such as *Like Love* and *A Touch of Elegance* in the '60s. He's continued maintaining his jazz ties, working with Niels-Henning Orstead Pedersen, Ray Brown, Mundell Lowe, and many others in the '80s and '90s. —*Ron Wynn and Michael G. Nastos*

★ **Double Play!** / May 11, 1957 / Original Jazz Classics 157
This was a two-piano (Andre Previn and Russ Freeman) with rhythm (drummer Shelly Manne) date with a baseball theme. The thematic perspective didn't get in the way of the music, and the two pianists worked more in harmony and counterpoint than in juxtaposition. —*Bob Rusch, Cadence*

○ **Old Friends** / Aug. 1991 / Telarc 83309
Superb trio recordings that marked the return of well-known classical conductor Andre Previn to intimate jazz recording. He teamed with bassist Ray Brown and guitarist Mundell Lowe, and the three complemented each other expertly, while their solos were tasteful and concise. —*Ron Wynn*

Bobby Previte

Drums, bandleader / Modern creative
Bobby Previte is a progressive-creative drummer and bandleader who presents a unique perspective in modern improvised music. Third World influences creep in, and he handles free music capably. —*Michael G. Nastos*

★ **Claude's Late Morning** / i. 1989 / Gramavision 79448
The daring drummer doesn't tailor his work to conventional jazz tastes. Excellent playing, erratic compositions. —*Ron Wynn*

○ **Weather Clear Track Fast** / i. 1991 / Enja 79667

○ **Pushing the Envelope** / Mesa Blue Moon 79449

Julian Priester (Julian Anthony Priester)

b. Jun. 29, 1935, Chicago
trombone, synthesizer / Hard bop, modern creative
He's not as adventurous as a George Lewis, but Julian Priester has been among the rare trombonists with a bop background who have embraced the synthesizer technology of the '70s and beyond. He spent five productive years in the mid-'50s working with Lionel Hampton, Dinah Washington, and others in Chicago before he moved to New York in 1958. Priester was in the bands of Max Roach and Slide Hampton for a time and played with Eric Dolphy, Clifford Jordan, and Booker Little in Roach's fine early '60s group. He worked with numerous bands in the '60s, among them a six-month period in Ellington's orchestra. Priester got national attention for his stint with Herbie Hancock's group from 1970-1973. During that period he began to include synthesized effects in his performances, something he continued upon leaving Hancock's band. Priester stayed active in the '80s, working with Dave Holland's band until 1985. He's continued doing session and studio work. —*Ron Wynn*

○ **Keep Swinging** / Jan. 11, 1960 / Riverside 316
Quintet. W/ Jimmy Heath (sax), Tommy Flanagan (p), and Elvin Jones (d). Excellent. —*Michael G. Nastos*

★ **Love, Love** / Jun. 28, 1974-Sep. 12, 1974 / ECM 1044
Trombonist Priester is electrified; setting is extended. Hardhitting. —*Michael G. Nastos*

Russell Procope

b. Aug. 11, 1908, New York, NY, **d.** Jan. 21, 1981, New York, NY
Alto sax, clarinet / Swing, big band
A consistently solid section contributor and dependable, if not intriguing, soloist, Russell Procope was a longtime Ellingtonian and also part of the John Kirby band of the '30s, one of the more popular small combos with whom he displayed a vital and highly original alto sax style. Procope studied violin eight years before turning to clarinet and alto sax as a teenager. He played clarinet with Jelly Roll Morton in the late '20s and worked with the big bands of Benny Carter, Chick Webb, Fletcher Henderson, and Teddy Hill in the late '20s and the '30s, touring Europe with the

Hill orchestra. Procope enjoyed stardom in the Kirby band from 1938 to 1943. He played in shows while stationed in New York during his tour of army duty. He rejoined Kirby in 1945 and then joined Ellington the next year. He remained there until 1974, never a star but someone who could be counted on night in and night out to play the music with energy and accuracy. Procope worked in New York with Brooks Kerr in the musical "Ain't Misbehavin'" following Ellington's death. He also led the group Ellingtonia. Procope can be heard playing on countless Ellington dates from the mid-'40s to the '70s. —*Ron Wynn*

● **Persuasive Sax of Russell Procope, The** / i. 1956 / Dot 3010

Arthur Prysock

b. Jan. 2, 1929
Vocals / Blues & jazz, ballads & blues
Vocalist Arthur Prysock's commanding, robust, and deep baritone have made their impression through smash R&B, blues, and jazz-flavored recordings, as well as commercials and radio spots. Arthur Prysock became famous in Buddy Johnson's band in 1944-1952, having a number of big R&B hits, as did his sister Ella Johnson. He gained even more notoriety as a romantic ballad specialist in the '50s and '60s. During the '70s Prysock did mainly club dates, but he resurfaced in 1985 with some superb recordings. —*Ron Wynn*

○ **Like Who? Like Basie** / i. 1959 / United Artists 5024
○ **Basie Reunion (With Buck Clayton)** / i. 1962 / Swingville 2037
● **Arthur Prysock and Count Basie** / i. Dec. 13-21, 1965 / Verve 827011
Seven saxes are led by Lockjaw Davis in a big band that drives Prysock. Eleven songs, the best of which are, "I Could Write a Book" and "Don't Go Fo' Strangers." —*Michael G. Nastos*

★ **Rockin' Good Way** / Jul. 29, 1985-Aug. 2, 1985 / Milestone 9139
Great comeback on records that helped reestablish Prysock among some who'd forgotten his '50s & '60s material. —*Ron Wynn*

○ **Silk and Satin** / i. 19zz / Polydor 28901
☆ **Songs That Made Him Famous** / Decca
Good compilation of R&B and jukebox hits from '40s and '50s, some featuring his sister Ella Johnson. —*Ron Wynn*

Tito Puente

b. Apr. 20, 1923, New York, NY
Percussion, piano, vibraphone, timbales / Latin-jazz
Tito Puente is a first-rate Latin-jazz vibraphonist, timbales player, and bandleader. He's known for his showmanship and incorporates many styles of Latin music, melded with jazz standards. A stalwart in this idiom, Puente has been extensively recorded for the last four decades. —*Michael G. Nastos*

Puente Goes Jazz / 1956 / RCA 66148
On this mid-50s reissue, the king of Latin music strays into the realm of straightahead big-band jazz. These guys swing hard! With the full dynamic range you'd expect from the best big-band. —*Len Paterson, Roots & Rhythm*

○ **Top Percussion** / i. 1957 / Bmgi 3264
A stunner from Puente's golden age, this 1957 recording brought together Tito, Mongo, Willie Bobo, Aguabella, and Julito Collazo on percussion with vocalists that included Mercedita Valdez, in seven wonderful cuts of traditional and (then) contemporary Afro-Cuban skin-on-skin. Then as an unexpected gift, there is a seven-minute Latin-jazz suite featuring Puente's considerable jazz-arranger head and a powerful band with (Ripley, though, should still be living at this hour) Doc Severinson on lead trumpet. —*John Storm Roberts*

● **Dance Mania** / i. 1958 / BMG 72252
What a treasure! We'd long despaired of finding anything from the days of Puente's young prime, and here's one of his two best albums reissued in CD! This was Puente's big band at the height of its powers, one of the great documents of New York Latin music and the sort of thing that established the man's claim to be one of the creators of big-band mambo. —*John Storm Roberts*

○ **On Broadway** / Jul. 1982 / Concord Jazz 4207
On this LP in Concord's Picante series, Ray Gonzales (trumpet) was added to the regular group and enhanced the group to good effect in several places, notably as an echo to Jimmy Frisaura

(trumpet, trombone) on "First Light," a feature for the latter trumpeter. —*Shirley Klett, Cadence*

★ **El Rey** / May 1984 / Concord Jazz 4250
☆ **Un Poco Loco** / i. Jan. 1987 / Concord Jazz 4329
One of his best for the label. Puente's playing in both large and small contexts. —*Ron Wynn*

○ **Salsa Meets Jazz** / i. 1988 / Concord Jazz 4354
& Latin Ensemble. Excellent, maybe his best on the label. Phil Woods (as) joins the party and soars. —*Ron Wynn*

○ **Goza Me Timbal** / i. 1990 / Concord Jazz 4399
The songs . . . mix Sonny Rollins and Miles Davis landmarks with topical Puente numbers, extending both bop and Latin horizons. —*Ron Wynn, Rock & Roll Disc*

○ **Mambo King, The** / i. 1991 / RMM 80680
Puente's 100th album is a celebration of that fact, with a procession of vocalists, most of whom—like Celia Cruz—were professionally associated with him at one time or another. That doesn't make for a very tight concept, but recordings by musicians of Tito's generation didn't have concepts, they had music. So does this one, including a minor riot with Celia Cruz riding a big, burly mambo arrangement by a band full of just everybody, and a wonderful "El Bribon del Aguacero" with Chocolate Armenteros on trumpet. —*John Storm Roberts*

○ **Mambo of the Times** / i. 1992 / Concord Jazz 4499
A '92 CD session showing that the great Afro-Latin and Latin-jazz master Tito Puente continues to churn out tremendous music. This is his current band, and they're all first-rate jazz players and execute the tricky Latin clave beat easily. The CD version contains two bonus cuts. —*Ron Wynn*

Dudu Pukwana

b. Jul. 18, 1938, Port Elizabeth, South Africa, **d.** 1990
Piano, sax / World fusion
Alto saxophonist Dudu Pukwana left South Africa in 1964 to play in a freer environment. Originally from Walmer, Port Elizabeth, he started on the piano at the age of six. He was semiprofessional during secondary school. Dudu was influenced by Kippie Moeksetsi, Mackay Davashe, and Nick Moyake. He worked with various bands in the late 1950s, including his own Jazz Giants with Dollar Brand. Dudu was a saxophonist of the year in 1962. He played with Chris MacGregor's Blue Notes. They did record a LP, but the conditions were difficult for the band to survive. The Blue Notes moved to Europe and with the help of Ronnie Scott, they became the Brotherhood of Breath. Later in 1969, Dudu formed Spear. Pukwana's most recent band was Zila, with Lus mocky Ranku on guitar and Pinise Saul on vocals. —*AMG*

● **Diamond Express** / i. Oct. 1978 / Freedom 41044
An early '70s recording of this saxophonist, with the late trumpeter Mongezi Feza, in their last meeting before Feza died of pneumonia. Squeaky sax and ensemble in an unabashed mood. South African free-jazz. —*Michael G. Nastos*

Don Pullen (Don Gabriel Pullen)

b. 1941, Roanoke, Virginia
Piano, organ, composer / Hard bop, modern creative
One of the most percussive pianists in jazz, Don Pullen's razor-sharp phrasing and intense right hand clusters were especially noteworthy during his tenure as coleader of the Pullen-Adams quartet of the late '70s and '80s. Pullen studied with Muhal Richard Abrams and Giuseppe Logan before making his recording debut in 1964. He had his own groups and also worked with drummer Milford Graves as well as playing organ in R&B groups. He worked a year with Nina Simone in 1970-1971 and briefly with Art Blakey in 1974. But it was his stint with Charles Mingus in 1973-1975 that got Pullen substantial attention, as well as his teaming with saxophonist George Adams, who was also in the group. He and Adams teamed up in 1979, following several European tours Pullen had made with his own bands. The Pullen-Adams group was a staple on the '80s jazz scene until they disbanded. He's recently recorded with saxophonist David Murray. —*Ron Wynn*

○ **Jazz a confonto** / Mar. 21, 1975 / Horo 21
○ **Tomorrow's Promises** / 1976-1977 / Atlantic 1699

A certain hesitancy and stodginess aside, the fine moments here were fine indeed. —*Mikal Gilmore, Down Beat*

★ **Earth Beams with George Adams Quartet** / **i**. 1980 / Timeless

★ **Sixth Sense, The** / Jun. 1985 / Black Saint 0088
Don Pullen's singular warp-speed keyboard blurs—again on display here—can make one forget how deep his soul-jazz roots are. *The Sixth Sense* was a refresher course. The cooking Latin-funk 5/4 title track could well occupy the kickoff spot on a late '60s Blue Note LP. —*Kevin Whitehead, Cadence*

☆ **Breakthrough** / **i**. Apr. 30, 1986 / Blue Note 46314
W/ George Adams Quartet. Pianist Don Pullen and sax-flute-vocalist George Adams (both ex-Mingus players) with drummer Dan Richmond at their creative zenith. —*Michael G. Nastos*

○ **Kele Mou Bana** / **i**. May 7, 1992 / Blue Note 98166
On *Kele Mou Bana*, pianist Don Pullen's third release as a leader for Blue Note, his percussive tendencies culminate in an album of Afro-Brazilian tunes. —*Suzanne McElfresh, Down Beat*

Ike Quebec (Ike Abrams Quebec)

b. Aug. 17, 1918, Newark, NJ, **d**. Jan. 16, 1963, New York, NY
Tenor sax / Swing, hard bop, soul-jazz
Perhaps the greatest "populist" sax player ever, this longtime people's choice was seldom recognized by the critics. Quebec began as a pianist in the early '40s, switched to tenor in 1942, and quickly became celebrated for a raw, rough, and forceful style that had roots in the swing era but was ideal for the emerging honking sax, R&B, and soul-jazz sounds of '50s and '60s. Quebec worked in Chicago and New York during the remainder of the '40s, making his debut as leader on Blue Note in 1944. His song "Blue Harlem" was a huge hit. Quebec recorded sporadically for Blue Note in the '40s, played with Lucky Millinder and Cab Calloway from 1949 to 1953 and then departed the business for a while due to a combination of personal problems and lack of opportunity. Quebec was a close friend of Blue Note's Alfred Lion and urged him to give chances to many top players who would go on to make the label a premier jazz outlet in the '50s and '60s. Quebec was prolific from 1959 to 1962, working with Sonny Clark, Dodo Green, and Jimmy Smith, plus heading some wonderful sessions, several of which yielded singles that were breakout jukebox hits. For a number of years he doubled as Blue Note's musical director. —*Ron Wynn*

○ **Tenor Sax Album: The Savoy Sessions, The** / **i**. Aug. 1945 / Savoy 70812

★ **Complete Blue Note 45 Sessions** / 1959-1962 / Mosaic
A wonderful three-disc collection of Quebec's 1959-1962 songs that packed jazz punch, had R&B appeal, and were originally recorded for and designed as singles for jukeboxes. —*Ron Wynn*

○ **Blue and Sentimental** / Dec. 1961 / Blue Note 84098
Hot, lusty, and wonderful. Quebec was a rare jazz musician who never lost his appeal in the R&B community. W/ Sonny Clark (p), Grant Green (g), Paul Chambers (b), Philly Joe Jones (d). —*Ron Wynn*

Congo Lament / Jan. 20, 1962 / Blue Note 1089

Easy Living / **i**. 1962 / Blue Note 46846

★ **Complete Blue Note Recordings** / Mosaic
This is an essential compilation of virtually all the laudable Quebec jazz dates. —*Ron Wynn*

Alvin Queen

b. Aug. 16, 1950, NYC
Drums / Hard bop
A drummer, producer, and record label owner, Alvin Queen is an expatriate living in France. He's capable of being either a powerhouse or subtle and is also a fine composer. —*Michael G. Nastos*

★ **In Europe** / **i**. 1980 / Nilva 3401
Quintet with drummer Queen at the helm. Mainstream, bordering on progressive. —*Michael G. Nastos*

Gene Quill (Daniel Eugene Quill)

b. Dec. 15, 1927, Atlantic City, NJ
Alto sax, clarinet / Bop, cool
A consistent alto saxophonist whose style changed from straight bebop to a milder, more mellow sound, Gene Quill initially played with fire and exacting fluidity. He gradually smoothed the

edges off his solos and opted for a relaxed, introspective approach. Quill started on saxophone in his childhood and was a professional at 13. He worked in big bands during the '50s and '60s, playing and recording with Buddy DeFranco, Claude Thornhill, Gene Krupa, Quincy Jones, Johnny Richards, Manny Albam, Johnny Carisi, Bill Potts, and Gerry Mulligan. Quill also played in the combos of Mundell Lowe and Jimmy Knepper, led his own bands, and memorably teamed with Phil Woods. He did some session work, but his career was tragically cut short when he suffered partial paralysis following brain damage. Quill's sessions with Woods for Prestige and RCA, but not their Epic dates, have been reissued on CD. His own dates for such labels as Dawn and Roost haven't been reissued on CD. —*Ron Wynn*

● **Three Bones and a Quill** / 1958 / Roost 2229

Paul Quinichette

b. May 17, 1916, Denver, CO, **d**. Jun. 2, 1983, New York, NY
Tenor sax / Swing, big band
Tenor saxophinst Paul Quinichette is an excellent player with a powerful, appealing tone and excellent technique. He got pegged in some quarters as little more than a Lester Young imitator, a reputation he shed through years of recording and performing. Quinichette worked in territory bands in the '40s, among them Jay McShann, Nat Towles, and Ernie Fields. He was in Johnny Otis's band in 1945 and then relocated to New York from West Coast and played with Louis Jordan, Lucky Millinder, Red Allen, and Hot Lips Page. Quinichette played with Count Basie for a year and had even briefer stints with Benny Goodman, Nat Pierce, and Billie Holiday while heading his own bands. After taking a sabbatical from music that lasted from the '60s until 1973, he resurfaced playing vibrant, swing-influenced music with Sammy Price and Buddy Tate, among others. —*Ron Wynn*

● **Pres Meets Vice-Pres** / **i**. 1954 / Emarcy 26021

★ **On the Sunny Side** / May 1957 / Original Jazz Classics 76
A standout late '50s blowing date led by tenor saxophonist Paul Quinichette with trombonist Curtis Fuller, alto saxophonists John Jenkins and Sonny Red, pianist Mal Waldrons, bassist Doug Watkins, and drummer Ed Thigpen. This was simply straightahead blues, ballads, and standards, with Jenkins in particular taking some torrid solos. —*Ron Wynn*

Doug Raney

b. 1957
Guitar / Bop
The son of legendary guitarist Jimmy Raney, Doug has understandably being heavily influenced by his father. He's an impressive soloist and utilizes almost identical full tones, crisp chording, and fluid voicings. He made his first recording with his father and Al Haig in the mid-'70s and did duo dates with his dad in the late '70s. Raney recorded for Steeplechase in the '70s and '80s and for Criss Cross in the '80s. He's recorded with Chet Baker and Bernt Rosegren and played in Horace Parlan's band. Raney has a couple of sessions available on CD. —*Ron Wynn*

● **Meeting the Tenors** / Apr. 29, 1983 / Criss Cross 1006

Jimmy Raney (James Elbert Raney)

b. Aug. 20, 1927, Lousiville, KY
Guitar / Bop
Jimmy Raney is one of the most fluid, melodic, and enjoyable guitarists directly connected to the bop tradition, and he's also a superior accompanist. As a teen Raney worked in local groups in both Chicago and New York, and he joined Woody Herman for a short stay in 1948. Raney played with a host of groups in the late '40s and early '50s, among them Al Haig, Buddy DeFranco, Artie Shaw, and Terry Gibbs, and he was a member of Stan Getz's quintet in 1951-1952 and replaced Tal Farlow in Red Norvo's trio in 1953-1954. Raney then spent six years with pianist Jimmy Lyon and rejoined Getz in 1962-1963. During the remainder of the '60s and the '70s, Raney did various gigs, from backing vocalists to session work. Reissues from the late '80s spotlight Raney's ability to interact with players as diverse as Sonny Clark, Sam Jones, and Billy Higgins. —*Ron Wynn*

○ **Introducing Phil Woods** / **i**. 1953 /

○ **Jimmy Raney—A** / Feb. 18, 1955 / Original Jazz Classics 1706

The '54 sides with Hal Overton (piano), Teddy Kotick (bass), and Art Madigan (drums) were brilliant. On parts Raney overdubbed himself and in effect became the Stan Getz to his own Raney. The music was smooth, hip, felt, and swinging. On the later dates Nick Stabular replaced Madigan, and John Wilson's trumpet was added. Wilson's dry trumpet counterpointed well with the guitarist's lines, but it was used mostly in themes. —*Jimmy Raney, Cadence*

○ **Jimmy Raney Featuring Bob Brookmeyer** / Dec. 12, 1956 / Paramount 129

★ **Two Jims and Zoot** / Sep. 1964 / Mobile Fidelity 833

○ **Complete Jimmy Raney in Tokyo, The** / Apr. 12+14, 1976 / Xanadu 5157
Guitarist Jimmy Raney's album was brilliant from start to finish. ... You could listen to "Darn That Dream," "Anthropology," "Stella by Starlight," and the rest over and over, and each time hear nuances that might have been overlooked previously. —*Carl Brauer, Cadence*

○ **Jimmy and Doug Raney Quartet** / Apr. 19, 1979 / Steeple Chase 31118

○ **Wisteria** / Dec. 1985 / Criss Cross 1019

Enrico Rava

b. Aug. 20, 1943, Trieste, Italy
Trumpet, flugelhorn / World fusion, modern creative
Enrico Rava ranks among Europe's top players. His mother was a classical pianist, and Rava taught himself the trumpet by listening to jazz records, though he began on trombone. He later studied in New York with Carmine Caruso. He made his initial splash in 1964 with the Gato Barbieri quintet and then played three years with Steve Lacy, touring in Europe, South America, and the United States. From 1969 to 1972 he was a member of Roswell Rudd's group as well as the Jazz Composer's Orchestra Association (JCOA) and Bill Dixon. Rava formed his own band in 1975 and has continued to head his own groups ever since, working with many of America's and Europe's best players. He also performed with Gil Evans in 1982 and toured Europe with Cecil Taylor in 1984. —*Ron Wynn*

★ **Il Giro Del Giorno in 80 Mondi** / Feb. 1972 / Black Saint 0011
A recording that is "out" and sometimes funky, with guitarist Bruce Johnson. —*Michael G. Nastos*

○ **Pilgrim and the Stars, The** / Jun. 1975 / ECM 1063
Among the most impressive of Rava's originals was "Parks," a decepitvely simple duet built around Rava's mellow, smoke-toned trumpet and Abercrombie's subtle fluctuations between Barney Kessell and samba-comping styles. This brief duet effectively captured the open and expansive qualities we associate with parks. Also striking was "By the Sea." It created a sultry, low-burn atmopshere charged with a tense sensuality due to the careful placement of Abercrombie's high-pitched erotic jabs in the background. —*Chuck Berg, Down Beat*

○ **Plot, The** / Aug. 1976 / ECM 1078
Enrico Rava's trumpet tone and technique are straighter, cleaner than Miles Davis's. With the exception of the pensive "On the Red Side of the Street," a kind of anatomy of morosity, Rava's stance was less oblique and introverted, more fluid and impressionistically romantic. —*Jon Balleras, Down Beat*

Sonny Red (Sylvester Kyner)

b. Dec. 17, 1932, Detroit, MI, d. Mar. 20, 1981, Detroit, MI
Alto sax, bandleader / Hard bop
An alto saxophonist from Detroit, whose bluesy, intense style made him a popular figure in the '50s and '60s, Sonny's full name was Sylvester Red Kyner. He played with Barry Harris, Curtis Fuller, Art Pepper, Donald Byrd, and Kenny Dorham, among others. —*Ron Wynn*

○ **Two Altos** / i. 1959 / Blue Note 6069

☆ **Sonny Red** / i. 197z / Mainstream 324

Freddie Redd

b. May 29, 1927, New York, NY
Piano, composer / Hard bop
Freddie Redd is a recently resurfaced pianist who had a double impact in the late '50s and the '60s as musician and actor. A surg-

ing, demonstrative player and penetrating soloist, Redd was a member of the more progressive West Coast jazz community, and worked with Hampton Hawes, George Tucker, John Ore, and others during the '50s. After a long absence, Redd returned to recording in 1990, with a fine live trio date. He's since issued a strong combo work. —*Ron Wynn*

☆ **Piano East—Piano West** / Feb. 1955 / Prestige 7067
A deluxe session with Redd and Hampton Hawes dominating the piano. Limited edition set. —*Ron Wynn*

○ **San Francisco Suite for Jazz Trio** / Oct. 2, 1957 / Riverside 1748

★ **Complete Blue Note Freddie Redd, The** / Feb. 15, 1960-Jan. 17, 1961 / Mosaic
Freddie Redd has been recording since 1951, but his works have been conspicuously absent from the bins and displays of most record and CD stores for some time. ... This is a three-LP Blue Note blast from the past by Mosaic. Redd's splayed angularity and percussive drive place him solidly on the Thelonious Monk to Bud Powell continuum. —*Alan Bargebuhr, Cadence*

☆ **Shades of Redd** / Aug. 13, 1960 / Blue Note 4045
Quintet with Tina Brooks on tenor sax and Jackie McLean on alto sax plays all Redd originals with flair and bluesy poignancy. —*Michael G. Nastos*

○ **Everybody Loves a Winner** / 1990 / Milestone 9187
There is a sextet on *Winner*, but it is not a matter of the individual performances contained here. Redd composed and arranged all the tracks and he *plays* the arrangements. They are not headsolos-lines. The chart is adhered to with under-solo riffing. That is not to say the horns are not exemplary or that the rhythm simply supports. It is just that you get a feeling of unity, a sense of beginning-middle-end. —*Arnold Jay Smith, Jazz Times*

○ **Lonely City** / Uptown 2730
Freddie Redd, an aggressive, emphatic hard bop pianist, has had an erratic recording career due to personal and drug problems that forced him off the scene. He shows on this session the swinging style, distinctive phrasing, and consistently impressive solo skills that made his Blue Note and Prestige dates so popular during the late '50s. —*Ron Wynn*

Dewey Redman (Walter Dewey Redman)

b. May 17, 1931, Fort Worth, Texas
Reeds, composer / Early free, modern creative
Dewey Redman is a rambling, often electrifying saxophonist and frequent companion of Ornette Coleman. Redman's splintering, swirling forays have been heard in the groups of Keith Jarrett; Coleman; and Old and New Dreams, a Coleman-influenced band. Redman played for the first time with Coleman, as well as Charles Moffett and Prince Lasha, in a high school marching band. He moved to the West Coast in 1959 after finishing his college education, working with Pharoah Sanders and Wes Montgomery, among others, before moving to New York in 1967. He spent the next seven years working with Coleman and then worked with Charlie Haden's Liberation Orchestra, Carla Bley, and Rosewell Rudd before joining Keith Jarrett's group in the late '70s. During the '80s, he worked extensively with Don Cherry in Old and New Dreams and also made a surprising record with Pat Metheny. —*Ron Wynn*

★ **Look for the Black Star** / i. Jan. 4, 1966 / Arista
This was an album full of the intensity, humor, and excess that was the earmark (literally) of the New Music—a music in its fullest flower in 1966 when this was recorded. Its most immediate quality was its rawness. —*Bill Adler, Down Beat*

★ **Ear of the Behearer, The** / i. Jan. 1974 / Impulse
Much of the music here (or "sounds" if you prefer) was difficult to get into at first. One must make the prior decision to take that extra effort needed to realize Dewey Redman's brooding, dark world. For, despite the melodic similiarities to Ornette Coleman, the music contained little of Coleman's lyrical brightness. —*Ray Townley, Down Beat*

○ **Musics** / i. Mar. 1980 / Galaxy 5118
Though on *Musics* tenor saxophonist Dewey Redman sacrificed much of his expansive instrumental palette, he gained a measure of warmth and lyrical understatement, especially evident on his sentimental but uncloying version of "Alone Again (Naturally)." —*Art Lange, Down Beat*

○ **Struggle Continues, The** / Jan. 1982 / ECM

His best. Shows great teamwork from bassist Mark Helias, drummer Ed Blackwell, and pianist Charles Eubanks. It's a record to make you say "wow." "Turn Over Baby" is a good boogie, and "Joie de Vivre" is one of Redman's best vehicles for improv. — *Michael G. Nastos*

☆ **Living on the Edge** / Sep. 1989 / Black Saint 120123
A first-rate late-'80s date by tenor saxophonist Dewey Redman. He's working alongside the excellent pianist Geri Allen, and the compositions are rigorously played. As the only horn player, Redman gets extensive space and offers his patented twisting, slashing solos. Bassist Cameron Brown and drummr Eddie Moore prove equally adept at adjusting to the Redman-Allen team. — *Ron Wynn*

Don Redman

b. 1900, **d.** 1964
Bandleader, tenor sax / Swing, big band
A pioneer arranger, Don Redman premiered many things in the Fletcher Henderson orchestra that became established procedures. His first arrangements mixed ensemble passages with solos in an improvised manner and incorporated breaks, horn chases, and call-and-response patterns between sections or individual players into arrangements. Redman was a child prodigy who eventually mastered nearly every instrument. As a high school senior he was already writing arrangements. He graduated from Storer College at 20 with a music degree. He worked in Piedmont for a year and then worked with Billy Paige's Broadway Syncopators, a Pittsburgh band. Redman played clarinet and saxophones and wrote arrangements. He met Henderson while on tour in New York and joined him on recording sessions. When Henderson formed his orchestra, Redman was one of his first members. He played clarinet and saxophones and wrote arrangements. When Armstrong joined as their jazz specialist, Redman increasingly made the arrangements more imaginative and looser to reflect Armstrong's impact. They moved away from rigidly structured dance music and into hot jazz. Redman left Henderson to join McKinney's Cotton Pickers in 1927. His influence transformed them into a topflight jazz orchestra. Redman's arrangements were more sophisticated, and he was also playing alto sax solos and singing. Redman formed his own band in 1931, with Benny Morton and Harlan Lattimore among others. His song "Chant of the Weed" was a major work. The band was quite popular at the start of the '40s, appearing on radio and making several records for Victor and Brunswick, among others. Redman later composed and wrote arrangements for radio, television, and big bands in the '40s. He provided scores for Count Basie and Jimmy Dorsey. Redman led a big band on a post-World War II European tour, and became Pearl Bailey's music director in 1951. He issued a few recordings at the end of the '50s but during his final years didn't do much playing, preferring to write. Redman's arrangements can be heard on CD reissues of the Henderson band. — *Ron Wynn*

○ **Shakin' the African** / i. Sep. 1931+Oct. 1931 / Hep 1001
○ **Doin' the New Low Down** / i. Sep. 1931-Apr. 1933 / Hep 1004
○ **For Europeans Only** / i. Sep. 1946 / Steeple Chase 6020
● **Chronological Don Redman, 1931-1933, The** / Classics 543

Dizzy Reece (Alphonso Son Reece)

b. Jan. 5, 1931, Kingston, Jamaica
Trumpet / Bop, world fusion
Until Courtney Pine began getting headlines a few years ago, Dizzy Reece had the distinction of being the best-known jazz musician with a Jamaican heritage. Reece came to Europe in 1948. He moved to London in 1954 and five years later came to America. During the late '50s, his strong trumpet solos were heard on albums with Ronnie Scott, Tubby Hayes, Hank Mobley, and Donald Byrd. In the '60s, Reece worked with Joe Farrell, Cecil Payne, and John Gilmore. He got some wider attention in the '70s with recordings pairing him with Clifford Jordan and Ted Curson. Reece played in the Paris Reunion Band in 1985. — *Ron Wynn*

○ **Asia Minor** / 1958 / New Jazz 1806
W/ Cecil Payne (bar sax), Hank Jones (p) Trio. Fine document. — *Michael G. Nastos*
★ **Blues in Trinity** / Aug. 24, 1958 / Blue Note 84006

Tony Reedus

b. 1959
Drums / Neo-bop
A dynamic, very aggressive and animated, yet disciplined drummer, Tony Reedus initially gained attention as a member of Woody Shaw's early '80s band. Since then he's done other session work with such players as James Williams and Mulgrew Miller and also led sessions for Jazz City and Enja in the '80s and '90s. His dates are still available on CD. — *Ron Wynn*

● **Incognito** / Dec. 1989 / Enja 6058

Rufus Reid (Rufus L. Reid)

b. Feb. 10, 1944, Sacramento, CA
Bass / Bop
A prolific, busy bassist, one of the top session players, particularly for hard-bop and mainstream dates. He's also made some solid releases as a leader on the Sunnyside label. — *Ron Wynn*

★ **Perpetual Stroll** / Jan. 27, 1980 / Theresa 111
Rufus Reid's album represented a logical modern extension of the classic jazz piano trio—a format that flourished in the 1950s and reached a transcendent pinnacle in the work of Bill Evans, Scott LaFaro, and Paul Motian. The music here swung hard, and the compositions (three of them written by Reid) were firmly rooted in bebop harmonies. — *Jim Roberts, Down Beat*

○ **Seven Minds** / i. 1984 / Sunnyside 1010
Live at William Patterson College, NJ. Premier bassist Reid with pianist Jim McNeely and drummer Teri Lyne Carrington. Extraordinary playing, approaching telepathic. — *Michael G. Nastos*

☆ **Yours and Mine** / i. Sep. 1990 / Concord Jazz 4440
Rufus Reid (b) and Akira Tana (d). Effective session with strong help from young lions Ralph Moore (ts) and Jesse Davis (as). CD version has two bonus cuts. 1991 release. — *Ron Wynn*

Django Reinhardt (Jean Baptiste Reinhardt)

b. Jan. 23, 1910, Liberchies, Belgium, **d.** May 16, 1953
Guitar / Swing
Born in a Gypsy caravan in Belgium and raised on the outskirts of Paris, Django received his first informal lessons from an uncle who was a banjo virtuoso. At 12 he was playing with some of the best local bands in working-class bars and at dances; he made his first records in 1928, the year in which he was gravely injured in a fire, losing the use of two fingers on his fret hand. With tremendous determination, he taught himself a new system of fingering and took up guitar. Introduced to jazz via Louis Armstrong records in 1931, Reinhardt was also influenced by Eddie Lang; he became the favorite accompanist of singer Jean Sablon, and, after a chance backstage meeting during which they jammed on "Dinah," formed the Quintet of the Hot Club of France with violinist Stephane Grappelli. It consisted of violin, solo guitar, bass, and two rhythm guitars. A born improviser, with a rhythmic drive to rival the best American players and an exceptional melodic gift, Django was the greatest jazz guitarist before Charlie Christian, whom he influenced; others who listened carefully to his records were Wes Montgomery and B. B. King. His brief visit to the United States in 1946, during which he performed in concert with Duke Ellington's orchestra, was not a success, but during World War II he was the toast of Paris. After the war he picked up electric guitar and listened to Christian and the boppers, but his harmonic ear had always been ahead of the pack. His compositions, among them "Nuages," "Django's Castle," and the haunting "Bolero," show the introspective side of his mercurial personality. Django was a unique musical phenomenon whose records continue to intrigue and inspire guitarists and fans. — *Dan Morgenstern*

☆ **Djangologie—Vol. 2** / i. 1930 / Disques Swing 8424-26
A terrific two-CD set of '30s sides. Django is heard in small groups with Rex Stewart (cnt), Benny Carter (as), Eddie South (violin), as well as with Stephane Grappelli (violin) and The Hot Club Quintet. — *Richard Lieberson*

○ **Django '35-'39** / 1935-1939 / GNP 9019
○ **Djangologie—Vol. 1** / i. 1935-1938 / Disques Swing 8421-23
  Swingin' with Django / i. 1935-1940 / Pro Arte 549
○ **Swing Guitar** / Oct. 1945-Mar. 1946 / Vintage Jazz 628

A '91 CD reissue featuring mid-'40s material with guitarist Django Reinhardt and his American Swing Big Band. This was the guitarist's attempt at expanding his frontiers, and it worked fairly well considering Reinhardt was much more comfortable in small surrouninding. These were an experiment that didn't totally work, but wasn't a complete failure either. —*Ron Wynn*

Swing De Paris / Jul. 1947-Nov. 1947 / Arco 110

★ **Quintette of the Hot Club of France, The** / i. 1947 / GNP 9053
A new set featuring his mid- and late '40s dates with Hot Club. Wondrous playing by Reinhardt and Grappelli (violin). —*Ron Wynn*

Djangology (1949) / Jan. 1949-Feb. 1949 / Bluebird 9988
Django and Stephane Grappelli (violin) with an Italian rhythm section in 1949. A cooler, more harmonically advanced Django with a pronounced bop influence. —*Richard Lieberson*

○ **Django Reinhardt and the American Jazz Giants** / i. 1969 / Prestige 7633
Here's one Django Reinhardt package that's *not* like all the others. Reinhardt got together during the '30s with some major American jazz stars for some special sessions. The roster included both Benny Carter and Coleman Hawkins, and the resulting material ranked alongside the quintet dates Reinhardt did with violinist Stephane Grappelli. Prestige put this out on vinyl in 1969; unfortunately they're still available only that way. —*Ron Wynn*

★ **Djangologie/USA—Vols. 1-7** / i. Jun. 1988 / Swing 842026
This is a definitive collection that contains a high and truly representative proportion of Django Reinhardt's greatest music. The really dedicated Reinhardt fan will, of course, know of still other admirable performances on labels not available to E.M.I., but the essence of the guitarist's art is here.... All these are indispensable recordings in any serious collection, and they are very conveniently gathered together in this box. —*Stanley Dance, Jazz Times*

○ **First Recordings** / Prestige 7614
Exactly what the title says, sessions done in the very earliest stages of guitarist Django Reinhardt's career. This album's value has been reduced by the release of a boxed set by Affinity that includes 144 Reinhardt tracks over the years 1936–1940. It has most of this, and with more information. —*Ron Wynn*

○ **Legendary Django** / GNP 9039
A decent, though not comprehensive, anthology of '30s and '40s cuts by Django Reinhardt. It tries to cover every aspect and doesn't aim to be anything except a sampler. In that regard, it accomplishes its goal. —*Ron Wynn*

○ **Parisian Swing** / GNP 9002
Delightful, often energetic session with the great guitarist Djano Reinhardt displaying his jam session and combative nature. Reinhardt plays with force, joy, and creativity, while incorporating some blues licks and feeling into his fleeting solos. —*Ron Wynn*

○ **Solos/Duets/Trios** / Inner City 1105
An interesting concept work; pulling and issuing selected sessions from guitarist Django Reinhart either alone or playing with just a bassist or a drummer. His solos are striking in their simplicty and beauty, while his duets are intimate and attractive, the trio sessions faster, more competitive, and among the least satisfying, at least on this release. —*Ron Wynn*

Emily Remler

b. Sep. 18, 1957, NYC, d. 1990
Guitar / Postbop, neo-bop
Guitarist Emily Remler's first interests were folk music and rock, but she was introduced to jazz via records by Charlie Christian and Wes Montgomery and graduated from Berklee at 18. Encouraged by Herb Ellis, she played with him at the Concord Jazz Festival in 1978 and the following year began to record for Concord Jazz, also forming her own group and accompanying Astrud Gilberto. She made her first album as a leader in 1981; by then she'd established herself as one of the most interesting new voices on her popular instrument. Her tasteful conception, exceptional swing, and attractive sound combined to make her special. She was also an excellent teacher. Her death during a tour of Australia robbed jazz of a more than promising talent. —*Dan Morgenstern*

★ **Firefly** / Apr. 1981 / Concord Jazz 4162
Guitarist Emily Remler's album started slowly with the first three cuts presenting little more than perfunctory albeit quality play-

ing. However, starting with the title cut, things really picked up and remained on a solid level for the second side. —*Milo Fine, Cadence*

☆ **Retrospective—Vol. 2** / 1981-1988 / Concord Jazz 4463
Excellent compositions from this late guitarist. You don't want to miss this. —*Michael G. Nastos*

○ **Catwalk** / Aug. 1984 / Concord Jazz 4265
Guitarist Emily Remler at the time of *Catwalk* was rapidly developing her chordal style to add to her single string work, and the variety achieved, when combined with her fertile imagination, enhanced her solos and comping even more. —*Shirley Klett, Cadence*

Revolutionary Ensemble

Group / Early free, modern creative
This trio formed in 1971, and was primarily a free-jazz ensemble, with the unusual instrumentation of Leroy Jenkins (violin), Sirone (b), and Jerome Cooper (per). —*Myles Boisen*

★ **People's Republic, The** / Dec. 4-06, 1975 / A&M 708
The People's Republic was a powerful argument for group improvisation. The trio shifted through textures with individual brilliance while retaining the ensemble blend. Horizon included some of the scores, providing the listeners with the material from which the artists worked. —*Kevin Yatarola, Cadence*

Buddy Rich (Bernard Rich)

b. Sep. 30, 1917, New York, NY, d. Apr. 2, 1987, Los Angeles, CA
Drums, vocals, bandleader / Swing, big band
Virtuoso drummer Buddy Rich began his entertainment career (at 18 months of age) as Traps, the Drum Wonder in his parent's vaudeville act. At the age of six he became a headliner, and his parents dropped out of the act to manage his career. Buddy gained national attention as a drummer when he joined Bunny Berigan (1938), Artie Shaw (1939), and the volatile Tommy Dorsey Orchestra with Frank Sinatra and the Pied Pipers (1939-1942). After two years in the Marines, Buddy rejoined Dorsey until 1946, when he left to form the first of many bands he would lead throughout his career.

With the exception of Harry James, whom he would join, quit, and rejoin several times (the last time as the world's highest paid sideman), Buddy would alternate between leading his own small groups, recording, and touring with Norman Grant's Jazz at the Philharmonic. During this period he played with virtually every great jazz musican around, including Art Tatum, Lionel Hampton, Dizzy Gillespie, Charlie Parker, Oscar Peterson, and Count Basie. In 1966, he put together a new big band, which had great success in clubs, concerts, and college campuses. From that point until his death, he would contine to tour successfully with his big band both nationally and broad. —*Buz Overbeck*

● **This One's for Basie** / Aug. 18+25, 1956 / Verve 817788
A classic! Marty Paich, Buddy, and top Los Angeles studio musicians play Basie. —*Buz Overbeck*

★ **Rich Versus Roach** / Apr. 1959 / Mercury 826987
Definitive battle of the drummers from 1959. CD has four bonus cuts. —*Ron Wynn*

★ **Rich in London** / Dec. 6-08, 1971 / RCA

☆ **Swings and Swings and Swings** / RCA
Textbook album by drummer Buddy Rich. It features the characteristic uptempo arrangements and sweeping ballad treatments. The horn and brass solos are good, the rhythm section competent, and Rich, as usual, dominates from the drum position. —*Ron Wynn*

Jerome Richardson (Jerome C. Richardson)

b. Nov. 15, 1920, Sealy, TX
Sax, flute / Big band, bop, hard bop, postbop, progressive big band
Jerome Richardson is a famed studio musician and sideman, as well as a peerless saxophonist and flute player. He is so much in demand for TV, radio, and movies that he rarely ventures outside those areas anymore. He's an unsung hero in the strictest sense. —*Michael G. Nastos*

○ **Midnight Oil** / i. 1958 / Original Jazz Classics 1815

★ **Roamin' with Richardson** / Oct. 21, 1959 / New Jazz 8226

Dannie Richmond (Charles D. Richmond)

b. Dec. 15, 1935, New York, NY, **d.** Mar. 15, 1988, New York, NY
Drums, tenor sax / Bop, hard bop, progressive big band, early jazz rock

Dannie Richmond was a marvelous drummer, accomplished at anchoring a song, interacting with the rhythm section, or putting a flourish on a tune. He was best known for being the favorite drummer of Charles Mingus from 1956 until his departure. Though he played tenor sax as a teen, Richmond made his debut on drums with Mingus on Atlantic in early 1957, and also made some fine trio releases in the '50s, backing Hampton Hawes. Richmond was quite eclectic; when not working with Mingus, he recorded with Chet Baker, Jimmy Knepper, Herbie Nichols, the Mark-Almond Band, Joe Cocker, Elton John, and Johnnie Taylor, and he published a celebrated drum method book in 1965 in Germany. After Mingus's death, Richmond was musical director of the Mingus Dynasty repertory band and later was a founding member of the Adams-Pullen quartet. He also made a number of fine albums as a leader, most of them in the '80s, though he also recorded under his own name in the '60s and '70s. —*Ron Wynn*

★ **In Jazz for the Culture Set** / 1965 / Impulse 98
W/ pianist Jaki Byard and harmonicist Toots Thielemans. Andy Warhol soup can cover art. Great record. —*Michael G. Nastos*

☆ **Ode to Mingus** / Nov. 23-24, 1979 / Soul Note 1005
A super tribute to his longtime employer and musical comrade. The set should have made the jazz world notice Bill Saxton on tenor sax. —*Ron Wynn*

○ **Quintet** / Sep. 24, 1980 / Gatemouth 1004
Projecting an insight that only Mingus's closest musical associate could possess, drummer Dannie Richmond captured more of the Mingus gift and genius than all the Dynasties (even those he was a part of) or Joni Mitchells put together, and in addition offered an entire side of rich material composed by band members. — *Cliff Tinder, Down Beat*

☆ **Dionysius** / May 30, 1983 / Red Record
An album played by ex-Mingusites, this is one side of originals and one side of Charles Mingus's music. Features Jack Walrath (tpt), Ricky Ford (ts), Bob Neloms (p), and Cameron Brown (b). — *Michael G. Nastos*

Lee Ritenour (Lee Mack [Captain Fingers] Ritenour)

b. Nov. 1, 1952, Hollywood, CA
Guitar, banjo, mandolin / Early jazz-rock, instrumental pop, contemporary funk

Guitarist, banjo, and mandolin player Lee Ritenour taught classical guitar at USC and has been a premier Los Angeles studio player since the mid '70s. Ritenour's knowledge of jazz, international, and pop styles is impressive, and his speed, facility, phrasing, and technique are always flawless. He sometimes has been criticized for his choice of material and a penchant for fusion and commercial music. He has issued rock-dominated releases, instrumental pop, light Brazilian, and film soundtracks, plus one or two rare sets where he's been able to stretch out and play with flair, distinction, and individuality. —*Ron Wynn*

Captain Fingers / **i.** 1977 / Epic 34426
A great player shows how easily he can handle trite pop. Wonderful Mobile Fidelity mastering job. —*Ron Wynn*

Captain's Journey / **i.** 1978 / Elektra 136
Guitarist Lee Ritenour had just switched labels from Epic to Elektra when he cut *Captain's Journey* in 1978. It was a follow-up to the successful crossover work *Captain Fingers* and used a similar strategy: tight, hook-laden arrangements; polished production; and minimal solo space. What individual things it has are dominated by Rietnour, a supremely talented guitarist who doesn't display that much of it with these arrangements. —*Ron Wynn, AMG*

● **Wes Bound** / **i.** 1993 / GRP 9697
On *Wes Bound*, Lee Ritenour pays homage to Wes Montgomery, the last great jazz guitarist of the prefusion era. Ritenour does an uncanny job of recreating Montgomery's hollow-body Gibson L-5 sound and flowing octave melody lines on standards such as "Road Song" and "West Coast Blues." —*Rick Mitchell, Request*

Sam Rivers (Samuel Carthorne Rivers)

b. Sep. 25, 1930, El Reno, Okla

Tenor and soprano sax, flute, composer / Early free, modern creative

Arguably the greatest unknown saxophonist around, Sam Rivers has never gotten any exposure outside limited jazz circles, despite amassing some extremely impressive credentials. He's been associated with the free school exclusively, but his style actually reflects the entire jazz spectrum, while being one of the most individualistic around. He's at his best on tenor but is also an invigorating flute player and a good soprano and piano soloist. He began his career with area musicians like Herb Pomeroy, Jaki Byard, and Gigi Gryce. He also accompanied Billie Holiday on tour during 1955. Rivers returned to Boston in 1958, working with the Pomeroy big band and leading his own quartet with an unknown 13-year-old named Tony Williams on drums. Before going on a tour of Japan with Miles Davis in 1964, Rivers led a Boston band that backed guest artists coming to town in every genre from jazz to blues and R&B. He played with Cecil Taylor from 1968 to 1973. Rivers also made several pivotal albums in the early '70s—extremely personal, ambitious, and powerful recordings—among them a pair of duets with Dave Holland, trios, combos, and even one big-band date. In 1975 he was guest soloist with the San Francisco Symphony Orchestra, and his music was presented in glorious fashion at Carnegie Hall for the 1978 Newport in New York festival. A year later, a Rivers work for 32 musicians was presented at New York's Public Theater. He's continued to record, though no major American label has featured him since the '70s. —*Ron Wynn*

○ **Fuschia Swing Song** / Dec. 11, 1964 / Blue Note 84184
Mid-'60s date with Jaki Byard (p). All Rivers originals and his best period album. —*Michael G. Nastos*

★ **Contours** / May 21, 1965 / Blue Note

○ **New Conception, A** / Oct. 11, 1966 / Blue Note 4249

○ **Involution** / Mar. 17, 1967 / Blue Note 4261
Six emotion-titled pieces that resulted from a session led by pianist Andrew Hill were released on Sam Rivers's *Involution*—Rivers played as part of Hill's quartet—along with a major and truly remarkable sextet session Rivers led in 1967. Hill's playing at this time was forcefully directed. His compositions, though, stemmed from different sources than on earlier releases; "Lust" and "Desire" were less lyrical in any traditional sense, and the aptly named "Violence" was an uncompromised avant-garde performance owing at least something to Cecil Taylor. —*Neil Tesser, Down Beat*

★ **Streams—Live at Montreux** / Jul. 6, 1973 / MCA 39120
Streams featured Sam Rivers as the lead voice on the album-long "Streams," a lengthy multisectioned free improvisation recorded at the Montreux Jazz Festival (7/6/73). With support from the brillant bassist Cecil McBee and subtle drumming for the predisco Norman Connors, Rivers took a powerful solo on tenor, sang through his flute, rambled a bit on piano, and concluded with a strong dosage of his soprano. . . . *Streams* remains one of Sam Rivers's strongest recordings. —*Scott Yanow, Cadence*

○ **Crystals** / 1974 / Impulse 9286

☆ **Sam Rivers and Dave Holland** / Feb. 18, 1976 / Improvising Artists 373843
Vols. 1 & 2. Excellent, experimental duets between a great bassist and a superior improviser. Unfortunately, it's hard to find. —*Ron Wynn*

○ **Sam Rivers—Vol. 2** / Feb. 18, 1976 / Improvising Artists 373843
"Ripples" found Sam Rivers on flute, along with the tenor saxophone. . . . The music proceeded along a multitude of paths: There was a swinging, bluesy section; a *muy rapido* section with a maniacal walking pattern from bassist Dave Holland; an Eastern-tinged section with a rhythm-guitar-like ostinato pattern from Holland; and a free-form section with Holland simultaneously bowing and plucking his bass. This was a classic performance. "Deluge" was the more abstract of the two pieces due to Rivers's piano stylings. —*Carl Brauer, Cadence*

Max Roach (Maxwell Roach)

b. Jan. 10, 1924, New Land, NC
Drums, marimba, composer, bandleader / Bop

Though he could rightfully sit back and bask in well-deserved glory as an elder statesman of bop, Max Roach could still offer riveting, blistering drum solos at 68. Roach began playing the drums at 12 and worked with Charlie Parker as a teenager. He was part of the Minton's (jazz club) bop laboratory, though he was at that time very much under the influence of fellow drummer Kenny Clarke. After a brief stint with Duke Ellington, Roach joined the Benny Carter band and later recorded with Coleman Hawkins. But his amazing timing and rhythmic style became the percussive centerpiece for the bop revolution. He recorded with both Miles Davis and Charlie Parker in the late '40s, going with Parker to Paris in 1949. He went to Europe with one of Norman Granz's *Jazz at the Philharmonic* shows in 1952, and two years later was part of Howard Rumsey's Lighthouse shows. He co-led a quintet with trumpeter Clifford Brown that was among the most popular and influential in jazz. Roach continued heading great groups with such players as Sonny Rollins and Kenny Dorham in the '50s, and he was also a partner in Charles Mingus's ill-fated Debut Records label. In the early '60s, Roach had another great group with a wonderful trumpeter who died prematurely, Booker Little. Roach and then-wife Abbey Lincoln made a watershed album in the '60s, *Freedom Now Suit,* a work that got them lots of heat and controversy from right-wing types. He's also maintained a progressive musical front, recording with gospel choirs, string quartets, and renegades like Cecil Taylor and Anthony Braxton, as well as performing the bop he's well known for championing. *—Ron Wynn*

★ **Max Roach Plus Four** / Oct. 12, 1956 / Emarcy 36098
This is great. Roach with Sonny Rollins (ts), Kenny Dorham (tpt), Hank Mobley (ts), and more. *—Ron Wynn*

☆ **Jazz in 3/4 Time** / Mar. 18-21, 1957 / Mercury 826456

○ **Max Roach Plus Four on the Chicago Scene** / Jun. 1958 / Emarcy 36132

○ **Max Roach Plus Four at Newport** / Jul. 6, 1959 / Emarcy 80010

Deeds, Not Words / Sep. 4, 1959 / Riverside 304
A late '50s classic, one of many that Roach released in this period with some pointed sociopolitical album titles. This was cut for Riverside with group that included Ray Draper on tuba, George Coleman on tenor sax, and Booker Little on trumpet. There's a brillant, incendiary drum solo to conclude the set. *—Ron Wynn*

● **Freedom Now Suite** / Aug. 31, 1960+Sep. 6, 1960 / Columbia 36390
The *Freedom Now Suite* dates from 1960, just as the first sit-in demonstrations ushered in a decade of racial upheaval. Roach's then-wife Abbey Lincoln gave voice to the lyrics of Oscar Brown Jr., articulating concerns that Roach continued to espouse: the African-American heritage, pan-African musical culture, the travails of slavery and discrimination, and the ongoing liberation struggles in South Africa. Roach's Charles Minguslike compositions represented the culmination of the new musical revolution waiting in the wings. *—Larry Birnbaum, Down Beat*

○ **Max Roach, Sonny Clark, George Duvivier** / i. 1962 / Bainbridge
This was really more of a Sonny Clark (piano) recording and showed how tragic his death at such an early age was. All eight selections were Clark originals showcasing his formidable composing talents. With its trio format (George Duvivier was the bassist) the music took on a lean and intimate quality, drawing the listener into the center. *—Bob Rusch, Cadence*

○ **Max Roach Trio, Featuring the Legendary Hasaan, The** / Dec. 4+07, 1964 / Atlantic 82273
Hassan was an East Coast pianist reputed to be among the greatest, but who made precious few recordings and disappeared from the jazz world long ago. Max Roach was among the few ever to perform with him, and this session verifies Hassan's credentials while also showing how masterful a percussionist and combo leader Max Roach always has been. *—Ron Wynn*

○ **Force—Sweet Mao—Suid Africa '76** / Jul. 1976 / BASE 28976
Duets with Archie Shepp (sax). Extended pieces from two virtuosos. Quintessential. *—Michael G. Nastos*

○ **Long March, The** / Aug. 30, 1979 / Hat Hut 2R13
The Long March found its antecedent in earlier pairings of drummer Max Roach with Anthony Braxton. Roach's approach was by no means trendy; he merely carried the best of "old" stylings to the nth degree. He constructed the entire 26-minute title selection around a series of drum rolls so fast and focused as to evoke in sound blurred vision. *—Sam Freedman, Down Beat*

○ **Historic Concerts** / Dec. 15, 1979 / Soul Note 11001

This 80-minute portion of drummer Max Roach and multiinstrumentalist Anthony Braxton's 1979 duet concert bears out the press's initial lionizing of Roach for his magnetolike role. Taylor proved himself to be an especially responsive pianist, employing Bud Powell-like sprinting when Roach quickened the pulse, or laying into tangy left hand figures when Roach coaxed a Latin tinge from his toms. Conversely, Taylor elicited from Roach a daring departure from his usually classic narrative style. *—Bill Shoemaker, Down Beat*

○ **Scott Free** / May 1984 / Soul Note 1103
Steady, consistently urgent mid-'80s quartet session by drummer Max Roach, who was regularly recording, thanks to foreign labels that recognized and welcomed his talent. This one wasn't much different from others he did for the Soul Note/Black Saint label; the arrangements and songs were tight, the solos were expressive, and his drumming was always crackling and intense. *—Ron Wynn*

○ **Bright Moments** / i. Sep. 1987 / Soul Note 1159
A great late-'80s album as drummer Max Roach, with roots going back to the bop days, keeps growing and changing with the times. He uses the double quartet, his regular group with long-time trumpeter Cecil Bridgewater plus the explosive saxophonist Odean Pope, and pairs them with a string quartet that includes his daughter Maxine on viola. The results are stimulating, unpredictable, and exciting. *—Ron Wynn*

★ **To the Max** / 1991 / Blue Moon 79164
Showcases Roach working solo; with his own quartet and double quartet; with the M'Boom percussion delegation; and with a string section, singers, and full orchestra. It's a great two-disc set, one that highlights Roach's percussive talents and versatility, plus his compositional verve. At 68, he's still an invigorating, amazing player. *—Ron Wynn, Rock & Roll Disc*

Marcus Roberts

b. 1963
Piano / Neo-bop
Exciting New Orleans pianist and former pivotal member of Wynton Marsalis's group. His keen piano solos, probing lines, and steady rhythmic contributions made a sizeable impact in Marsalis's unit when he replaced Kenny Kirkland. He now records as a leader and recently has been exploring classic New Orleans, stride, and gospel via unaccompanied recordings, as well as bop and hard-bop. *—Ron Wynn*

○ **Deep in the Shed** / Aug. 9, 1989-Dec. 10, 1989 / Jive/Novus 3078
His second solo project accents the blues, with nicely arranged compositions and a full band that sometimes swells to include alto and tenor sax, trumpet, and trombone, plus bass and drums. *—Ron Wynn, Rock & Roll Disc.*

★ **Alone with Three Giants** / Jun. 3, 1990-Sep. 22, 1990 / Novus 3109
15 tracks of solo piano from the young, blind pianist from Jacksonville, FL. Repertoire of Monk, Ellington, and Jelly Roll Morton. Fares best on the Monk, and there are five of them. *—Michael G. Nastos*

○ **Prayer for Peace** / i. 1991 / Jive/Novus 63124
Outstanding piano solos, so good that even those who loathe holiday music might find it hard to ignore if they give it a listen. Roberts's solo dates have moved more and more back to early styles like stride, ragtime, and boogie-woogie, but here he's more contemporary and introspective than reflective. *—Ron Wynn*

○ **As Serenity Approaches** / i. Dec. 18, 1991 / Novus 63130
Pianist Marcus Roberts' penchant for florid blues-ragtime or stride variations isn't what's so enticing about *Serenity;* his pensive collaborations with tenor saxophonist-clarinetist Todd Williams, trumpeter Wynton Marsalis, and trombonist Ronald Westray are. *—Reuben Jackson, Jazz Times*

○ **If I Could Be with You** / i. Dec. 21, 1992 / Novus 63149

Perry Robinson (Perry Morris Robinson)

b. Aug. 17, 1938, New York, NY
Clarinet / Early free, modern creative
A postbop-to-progressive clarinetist with technique to burn and ideas to match, Robinson is a neglected kindred spirit to his instrument. *—Michael G. Nastos*

★ **Funk Dumpling** / 1962 / Savoy 1180

○ **Traveler, The** / 1978 / Chiaroscuro 190
The Traveler was an honest effort and not some kind of commercial token. It was a freewheeling, rough-edged reflection of Perry Robinson's multifaceted abilities and wry sense of humor. —*Milo Fine, Cadence*

Betty Roche (Mary Elizabeth Roche)

b. Jan. 9, 1920, Wilmington, DE
Vocals / Ballads & blues
Betty Roche sang prominently with Duke Ellington in 1944. She made several good records, showing a pristine voice. —*Michael G. Nastos*

★ **Singin' & Swingin'** / Mar. 1961 / Prestige 1718
Backed soulfully by a quintet . . . her free use of tempos and warm, distinct sound is nicely captured on this record. —*Bob Rusch, Cadence*

Red Rodney (Robert Chudnick)

b. Sep. 27, 1927, **d.** 1994
Trumpet / Bop
Trumpeter Red Rodney was one of the last living links to Charlie Parker and the bop era. He got big-band experience as a teen playing with Gene Krupa, Claude Thornhill, and Woody Herman, and he made his first recordings as a leader at 19. He was Parker's trumpeter from 1949 to 1951 and came under his spell in every way, absorbing Parker's love for music. He made some fine records in the late '40s and early '50s, including a sensational session with Ira Sullivan in 1955. Rodney made yet another triumphant comeback with a superb 1973 album matching him with Charlie McPherson. He had a series of fine releases in the '70s and '80s and toured in 1987 with Australian phenom James Morrison. Recognized as a prime bop stylist, Rodney's fiery licks, harmonic knowledge, and crackling solos put him in the upper echelon among '50s players. Rodney died in 1994. —*Ron Wynn*

★ **Early Bebop on Keynote** / Jan. 29, 1947 / Mercury 830922
W/ Hefti. A good 20-track overview of Rodney's mid-'40s cuts on Keynote. Both his own band and his stints with others are covered. —*Ron Wynn*

☆ **Red Arrow, The** / i. 1957 / Onyx 204
W/ Ira Sullivan (tpt/sax) and Tommy Flanagan Trio. Historic early meeting between Rodney and Sullivan. Two by Rodney, one by bassist Oscar Pettiford, three standards. —*Michael G. Nastos*

○ **Live at the Village Vanguard** / May 8, 1980-Jul. 7, 190 / Muse 5209
With Ira Sullivan (tpt/sax) and quintet. Three Jack Walrath originals, three standouts. This is one of the most together jazz bands of the '80s. A perfect vehicle for Red and Ira to blow. Sullivan plays saxes, flute, and flugelhorn. —*Michael G. Nastos*

○ **Night and Day** / Jun. 15-16, 1981 / Muse 5274
Trumpeter Red Rodney has worked with multi-instrumentalist Ira Sullivan since the '50s. Their friendship carries over into their musical relationship. This '81 dates sometimes has Rodney dominating a song with Sullivan supporting him; then they switch roles, and sometimes they're dueling or complementing each other. They carry the album, for everything else, from backing musicians to songs and production, is competent but nothing more. —*Ron Wynn*

○ **Spirit Within** / Elektra 60020
The first of two early '80s albums reuniting frequent collaborators trumpeter Red Rodney and multi-instrumentalist Ira Sullivan. Sullivan plays second trumpet and a variety of saxophones and provides a challenging and complementary presence to Rodney, who sometimes plays in restrained, easy fashion, and sometimes turns up his own playing a notch in response to Sullivan. —*Ron Wynn*

Shorty Rogers (Milton M. Rajonsky)

b. Apr. 14, 1924, Great Barrington, MA
Trumpet, composer, arranger, bandleader / Cool
A fine trumpeter, Shorty Rogers has been an important arranger and performer since the '50s. He played with Will Bradley, Red Norvo, and Woody Herman in the '40s and Stan Kenton in the '50s. Rogers recorded with Art Pepper, Shelly Manne, Jimmy Giuffre, and others in the '50s and '60s, before turning almost completely to arranging for film and television from the '60s to

the early '80s. He began recording and leading bands again during the mid-'80s. —*Ron Wynn*

★ **Short Stops** / 1953-1954 / Bluebird 5917
1953-1954. A thorough reissue that covers his first three RCA albums. For some strange reason, the CD has only 20 of 32 cuts. —*Ron Wynn*

○ **Martians, Stay Home** / Nov. 3, 1955 / Atlantic 50714
The quintet for this trumpeter, from the West Coast via Massachusetts and New York, includes Jimmy Giuffre (cl), Pete Jolly (p), Curtis Counce, Shelly Manne, (d) and others. There are six Shorty originals and three standards. These are nice groups with Rogers's sensitive trumpet leading in a nonthreatening, mainstream groove. —*Michael G. Nastos*

○ **Afro Cuban Influence** / Jun. 19, 1958 / RCA 1763

○ **Jazz Origin: Shorty Rogers / Stan Kenton / June Christy / i.** Mar. 1984 / PA/USA 9016

● **Complete Atlantic and EMI Jazz Recordings, The / i.** Aug. 1989 / Mosaic 6125
Another exhaustive Mosaic boxed set, this one devoted to the complete material trumpeter Shorty Rogers cut for EMI and Atlantic in the '50s, including both cool-influenced material and concept "Martians" albums. Art Pepper is featured on some cuts on alto sax, also Shelly Manne, Jimmy Giuffre, and Curtis Counce. —*Ron Wynn*

Sonny Rollins (Theodore Walter [Newk] Rollins)

b. Sep. 7, 1930, New York, NY
Tenor, soprano sax, composer / Hard bop, bop
He's considered by many the greatest living saxophonist, and Sonny Rollins has crafted numerous unforgettable recordings since the '50s. His solos are crammed with ideas, are executed flawlessy, and often dazzle with their combination of song fragments, chord changes, and harmonic maneuvers. Rollins is also a remarkable calypso jazz player. He did his first recordings with Babs Gonzales in 1948 and then played with J.J. Johnson, Thelonius Monk, Art Blakey, Bud Powell, Tadd Dameron, and Miles Davis. Rollins's famous LPs in the '50s and '60s included landmark sessions at the Village Vanguard, his famous pianoless trios, a guest stint with the Modern Jazz Quartet, and many others. He has also become famous for periodic sabbiticals. Rollins added soprano to his arsenal in the '70s and remains quite active in the '90s. —*Ron Wynn*

★ **Complete Prestige Recordings** / 1949-1956 / Prestige 4407
Sonny Rollins on Prestige—a seven-CD boxed set covering the years 1949-1956 (90 selections). Includes his early work as a sideman plus all of his solo albums for Prestige. About every jazz great appears somewhere in this compilation, from Charlie Parker and Miles Davis to Clifford Brown and John Coltrane. The liner notes are superb. This set is a treasure. —*Michael Erlewine*

○ **Work Time** / Dec. 2, 1955 / Prestige 007
Worktime presents an entire Sonny Rollins session from 12/2/55 with pianist Ray Bryant, drummer Max Roach, and bassist George Morrow. There was nothing tentative about this performance, and fans of Rollins and Roach should find many joyful encounters with it. —*Bob Rusch, Cadence*

Sonny Rollins Plus 4 / Mar. 22, 1956 / Prestige 7038
A wonderful outing that was among the last for the Clifford Brown-Max Roach group. —*Ron Wynn*

☆ **Tenor Madness** / May 24, 1956 / Prestige 124
Just a gigantic session with the Miles Davis rhythm section and a wonderful duet with Coltrane (ts) on the title cut. Rollins emerges as his own man in style. —*Ron Wynn*

★ **Saxophone Colossus and More** / Jun. 22, 1956 / Original Jazz Classics 291
Superb. Reissue of a seminal late '50s Rollins session. Max Roach crackles on drums. —*Ron Wynn*

★ **Way out West** / Mar. 7, 1957 / Contemporary 337
A remarkable masterpiece. Explosive Rollins gets steady support from Ray Brown (b) and Shelley Mann (d). —*Ron Wynn*

★ **Newk's Time** / Sep. 22, 1957 / Blue Note 84001
W/ Wynton Kelly (p) and Philly Joe Jones (d). Blue Note. Just a super quartet date; excellent reissue with original cover and notes. —*Ron Wynn*

☆ **Night at the Village Vanguard—Vol. 1** / Nov. 3, 1957 / Blue Note 46517
One of two incendiary live dates from Vanguard in the late '50s. The pianoless trio steps forth and claims its fame. —*Ron Wynn*

☆ **Night at the Village Vanguard—Vol. 2** / Nov. 3, 1957 / Blue Note 46518

○ **Freedom Suite** / Feb. 11, 1958+Mar. 7, 1958 / Riverside 067
By the time *Freedom Suite* was recorded, Sonny Rollins's influences were well integrated into a mature, individual style. The *Freedom Suite* was much heralded, and the title can arguably be interpreted both musically and socially. An extended piece not yet usual for jazz recordings, it held up well over its entire run. This was a tribute not only to Rollins's technical and imaginative power but also to Oscar Pettiford (bass) and Max Roach (drums), who completed the trio and were "up" for the entire 19 minutes. —*Bob Rusch, Cadence*

★ **Bridge, The** / Jan. 30, 1962-Apr. 5, 1962 / Bluebird 61061
Rollins makes a shattering return from sabbatical. He's joined by the youthful Jim Hall (g), who makes a great partner. —*Ron Wynn*

○ **What's New?** / Apr. 25, 1962-May 14, 1962 / RCA
Some early '60s cuts featuring tenor saxophonist Sonny Rollins leading a pianoless quartet with Jim Hall on guitar. These were songs taken from the landmark session on RCA that marked Rollins's return from a sabbatical in 1962. They weren't included on *The Bridge* album but were done by the same personnel. —*Ron Wynn*

All the Things You Are / Jul. 15, 1963-Jul. 2, 1964 / Bluebird 2179
1963-1964. Super 1990 reissue. It includes stints by Coleman Hawkins (ts) and Herbie Hancock (k). —*Ron Wynn*

Sonny Meets Hawk! / Jul. 15, 1963+Jul. 18, 1963 / RCA
W/ Coleman Hawkins (ts). The grand master teams with the still relatively young master for a moving, evocative session. Available mainly in a two-record reissue with *The Bridge* by French RCA. —*Ron Wynn*

★ **East Broadway Run Down** / May 9, 1966 / MCA 33120
The title cut is exceptional. Freddie Hubbard (tpt) is also great, as are Elvin Jones (d) and Jimmy Garrison (b). —*Ron Wynn*

☆ **Cutting Edge, The** / Jul. 6, 1974 / Milestone 468
"The Cutting Edge" and "First Moves" had Sonny Rollins improvising on the rhythmic character of the themes, the latter a very good Rollins tune. The best part, though, and the most significant moment on the record, was when Rollins played "To a Wild Rose" unaccompanied, breaking time, dissecting the theme, lightly embellishing it, adding cadenzas and bits of extraneous material—it wasn't quite the spiritual freedom he often proved in his a cappella works, but it was certainly engaging. —*John Litweiler, Down Beat*

Don't Stop the Carnival / Apr. 1978 / Milestone 55005
Majestic. A fiery calypso beat on the title track and first-rate Rollins throughout. —*Ron Wynn*

○ **Vintage Sessions** / Prestige 24096
Early '50s sessions featuring the formative Sonny Rollins tenor style, which at this point is still emerging from a synthesis of Coleman Hawkins, Lester Young, and Charlie Parker, plus his own contributions. —*Ron Wynn*

Wallace Roney

b. 1960
Trumpet / Neo-bop
First-rate young lion trumpeter very much in basic hard-bop mode. Roney, still in his 20s, has made some vibrant sessions for Muse and showed his knowledge of jazz standards and command of the trumpet. Especially good at upper-register statements, he also plays very commendable ballads. He's still growing as a composer and bandleader. —*Ron Wynn*

★ **Obsession** / 1990 / Muse 5423
The latest from this trumpet whiz boasts excellent songs supplied by both Roney and pianist Donald Brown. —*Ron Wynn*

○ **Seth Air** / i. Oct. 14, 1992 / Muse 5441
Seth Air is not only Wallace Roney's first recording after the 1991 Montreux gig with Miles Davis and tour with his '60s quintet, but it was recorded on the day Davis passed, the news of which reportedly reached the musicians in midsession. It's a solid album,

leavening the muscular modal blowing and vaguely Wayne Shorteresque expositions with engaging interpretations of Gershwin's "Gone," which is hinged on nimble trumpet-drums exchanges, and Burt Bacharach's loopy waltz, "Wives and Lovers." —*Bill Shoemaker, Down Beat*

Michele Rosewoman

b. 1953
Piano / World fusion, neo-bop
Michele Rosewoman is a pianist who plays a lot of music, including modal, Monkish melodic, harmolodic, Latin jazz, and creative. She works mostly in small ensemble format or with New Yoruba Latin Band. —*Michael G. Nastos*

★ **Contrast High** / Jul. 1988 / Enja 79607

Renee Rosnes

b. 1962
Piano / Neo-bop
Renee Rosnes is an excellent pianist from Canada who's established herself on New York scene. Rosnes has worked with Joe Henderson, O.T.B., and led her own group, showing equal skills on acoustic keyboard, electric, and synthesizer. A percussive, driving soloist, excellent accompanist, and emerging jazz star. —*Ron Wynn*

★ **Renee Rosnes** / Apr. 18, 1988-Feb. 4, 1989 / Blue Note 93561
High-caliber duet and quartet sessions. Rosnes proves captivating in any context. Guests include Wayne Shorter (sax) and Branford Marsalis (sax). —*Ron Wynn*

○ **For the Moment** / Feb. 15-16, 1990 / Blue Note 94859
The better of her two albums. Four Rosnes originals, four others from Monk, Woody Shaw, Walt Weiskopf, and the Warren-Dubin team. Joe Henderson is featured on seven of the eight cuts. —*Michael G. Nastos*

○ **Without Words** / i. 1993 / Blue Note 98168

Frank Rosolino

b. Aug. 20, 1926, Detroit, MI, d. Nov. 26, 1978, Los Angeles, CA
Trombone / Bop, big band
Frank Rosolino was a brilliant Detroit-born trombonist, who lived and worked in Los Angeles. He played with Gene Kupa, Stan Kenton, Lighthouse All Stars, and many West Coast postbop ensembles and studio sessions. He was also an occasional big-band member. Rosolino was known for his natural lyrical sense and was an uncanny balladeer. —*Michael G. Nastos*

○ **Frankly Speaking** / May 4-05, 1955 / Affinity

○ **I Play Trombone** / May 1956 / Bethlehem 26

★ **Frank Rosolino Quintet** / Jun. 1957 / VSOP 107
This brilliant trombonist, with a quintet including Richie Kamuca (sax) and Vince Guaraldi (p), plays three Rosolino originals and five standards, including Bill Holman's "Fallout." —*Michael G. Nastos*

☆ **Free for All** / i. Dec. 22, 1958 / Specialty 1763
Top Rosolino session with Harold Land (ts) and Leroy Vinnegar (b). Outstanding CD reissue is a limited edition. —*Ron Wynn*

☆ **Thinking About You** / Apr. 21+23, 1976 / Sackville 2014
Recorded live at Bourbon Street in Toronto with Ed Bickert (g), Don Thompson (b), and Terry Clarke (d), this album includes four long standards. With room to stretch, the whole band is up to the task. This is on the mellow side. —*Michael G. Nastos*

Charlie Rouse (Charles Rouse)

b. Apr. 6, 1924, Washington, DC, d. Dec. 1988
Tenor sax / Bop
Tenor saxophonist Charlie Rouse was a wonderful, underrated musician, but his fame has nevertheless stemmed mainly from his longtime association with Thelonious Monk. Rouse worked with Billy Eckstine, Dizzy Gillespie, Tadd Dameron, and Fats Navarro in the '40s and joined Duke Ellington in 1949-1950. For almost the entire decade of the '50s Rouse was a freelancer, but he joined Monk in 1959 and remained with him until 1970. No saxophonist better anticipated Monk's quirks, twists, tempo shifts, and textures, and his own understated, quirky, yet emphatic style filled in the gaps nicely. He formed a repertory band with Mal Waldron in the early '80s; the band Sphere gradually expanded

their repertoire from just Monk to originals and other standards. Rouse gained a measure of well-deserved publicity and recognition near the end of his career; he was a marvelous soloist and accompanist. —*Ron Wynn*

○ **Chase Is On, The** / **i**. 1957 / Bethlehem 6021
If you associate the term *chase* with a cutting contest, this album had quite a misleading title. The character of the session was rather that of friendly interplay, and the result was a thoroughly relaxed and enjoyable affair. All hands worked well, in a mood that was kind of low-keyed Al Cohn and Zoot Simsish, with a sprinkle of Count Basie added for taste. —*Per Husby, Cadence*

★ **Two is One** / 1974 / Strata East
○ **Moment's Notice** / Oct. 1977 / Storyville 4079
This quartet features pianist Hugh Lawson, bassist Bob Cranshaw, and drummer Ben Riley. Rouse, a model tenor saxophonist, plays with melodic wit and sense of purpose throughout. —*Michael G. Nastos*

Jimmy Rowles (James George Rowles)

b. Aug. 19, 1918, Spokane, WA
Piano / Swing
Jimmy Rowles has long been known as a steady, relaxed, and confident pianist and master accompanist for vocalists. His style includes elements of stride and boogie-woogie, and he's flexible enough to handle any situation from solo to duo to small combo to large orchestra. Rowles moved to Los Angeles from Spokane, WA, in 1940, and worked with Slim Gaillard, Lester Young, Benny Goodman, and Woody Herman before going into the army in 1942. After finishing his tenure there, Rowles worked again with Goodman and Herman as well as Les Brown and Tommy Dorsey, while cutting a number of records as a freelance studio player. Rowles moved to New York in 1973, and has been a busy contributor ever since, appearing on a host of excellent sessions in mainstream and swing-influenced mode. —*Ron Wynn*

☆ **Special Magic of Jimmy Rowles, The** / Apr. 7, 1974 / Halcyon 110
This album includes duets with Rusty Gilder on bass. Solo, Rowles shows he can do it alone, and with Gilder sparks occasionally fly. Mostly this is laid back. They play lots of Duke Ellington. There is a good version of Carl Perkin's "Grooveyard." —*Michael G. Nastos*

★ **Grandpaws** / Mar. 1976 / Choice 1014
The trio for this pianist includes Buster Williams on bass and Billy Hart on drums. They play two by Rowles, the others are standards. They do an exquisite medley of "Lush Life," " 'A' Train," " I Love You," " I Hadn't Anyone 'Till You," "Margie," " Chicago," and "Desert Fire." Rowles shows his ballad skills best. —*Michael G. Nastos*

○ **Plays Ellington and Billy Strayhorn** / Jun. 1981 / Columbia
Jimmie Rowles divided his entry in half, with side one being devoted to compositions by Duke Ellington (although "Jumpin' Punkins" was actually written by his son, Mercer) and side two to some of Billy Strayhorn's less frequently heard tunes. There were well-worn items on both sides, to be sure, but in Rowles's hands they took on a freshness due only in part to the pianist's deep understanding of the various compositional methods involved. — *Jack Sohmer, Cadence*

Gonzalo Rubalcaba

Piano / Bop, Latin-jazz, world fusion
Gonzalo Rubalcaba is a Cuban pianist in modern jazz idiom whose career is just beginning to flower. He's shown on his early releases overwhelming technique and dense chordal ideas. — *Michael G. Nastos*

● **Blessing** / Blue Note 97197
Pianist Gonzalo Rubalcaba is capable of playing a flurry of notes, and he does so on the opening tune "Circuito." The surprise of where he will go next is what holds the interest of the listener, not his virtuosity. He can suggest his influences from Cecil Taylor on "Circuito," to Bill Evans on "Blue in Green." —*Shaukat Husain, Coda*

○ **Mi Gran Pasion** / **i**. Apr. 1989 / Messidor 15999
Cuba's most celebrated musical prodigy, Rubalcaba is presently busy becoming a major jazz pianist, having expanded his activities well outside Cuba. This album, recorded in Germany with a

Cuban band, is a masterpiece: his salute to danzon, the music Rubalcaba's father (Guillermo Rubalcaba) still plays in Havana. Modernist, and at the same time an elegant essay on how to play this most decorous of musical forms. —*Ned Sublette*

○ **Discovery—Live at Montreux** / Apr. 1991 / Blue Note 95478
○ **Images: Live at Mt.Fuji** / **i**. 1992 / Somethin' Else 99492
A powerhouse live session from the dynamic Cuban pianist Gonzalo Rubalcaba. It was recorded live for Blue Note and is a trio date with bassist John Patitucci and drummer Jack DeJohnette. Patitucci, normally heard in either a fusion or an instrumental pop setting, shows his facility and versatility as he smoothly adjusts to Rubalcaba's upbeat, unorthodox style and meshes with DeJohnette. —*Ron Wynn*

Roswell Rudd (Roswell Hopkins Rudd, Jr.)

b. Nov. 17, 1935, Sharon, CT
Trombone / Early free, modern creative
Rosell Rudd is an innovative trombonist and composer and stick-to-your-ribs progressive, with a dash of soul and humor. He began playing Dixieland and then advanced into the free and experimental worlds. He's played with Herbie Nichols, Steve Lacy, Bill Dixon, and Dennis Charles, and was a founding member of the New York Art Quartet in the '60s. Rudd is the real thing. — *Michael G. Nastos*

★ **Everywhere** / Sep. 1966 / Impulse 9126
W/ legendary flutist-bass clarinetist Giuseppi Logan and two bass players. All originals. —*Michael G. Nastos*

○ **Flexible Flyer** / Mar. 1974 / Freedom 1006
Date for creative trombonist who fell in the cracks when Ray Anderson arrived. A solid album, with Sheila Jordan (v). —*Michael G. Nastos*

★ **Regeneration** / Jun. 25-26, 1982 / Soul Note 1054
One of many intriguing collaborations pairing Rudd and Steve Lacy (ss). —*Ron Wynn*

Hilton Ruiz

b. May 29, 1952, New York, NY
Piano / Bop, Latin-jazz, world fusion
Hilton Ruiz is a bop-influenced Latin pianist. He's equally comfortable as a Latin or jazz player. Ruiz is an in-demand sideman and solo pianist. His later-period recordings stray more into funk, but his style reflects McCoy Tyner-Chick Corea-Herbie Hancock. —*Michael G. Nastos*

○ **Piano Man** / Jul. 10, 1975 / Inner City 2036
Pianist Hilton Ruiz got a rhythmic boost from the ever-reliable bassist Buster Williams and the ever-impeccable drummer Billy Higgins on this interesting selection of tunes, including two originals and pieces by Duke Jordan, John Coltrane, Mary Lou Williams, and Charlie Parker (an unfortunately awkward, overlong "Big Foot.") —*Charles Mitchell, Down Beat*

★ **Cross Currents** / Nov. 1984 / Vintage Jazz 19
These trio and quintet performances helped cement Ruiz's status in the Afro-Latin and jazz communities. —*Ron Wynn*

○ **Moment's Notice, A** / Feb. 1991-Mar. 1991 / Novus 3123
Pianist Hilton Ruiz mixes Afro-Latin, Latin-jazz, and bop on this '91 session. Flutist Dave Valentin has stronger, more dynamic solos here than on his own records, while saxophonists George Coleman and Kenny Garrett are hot and consistently outstanding. —*Ron Wynn*

○ **Manhattan Mambo** / **i**. Jul. 30, 1992 / Telarc 83322
As on his previous series of albums on Novus, pianist Hilton Ruiz emphasizes his Latin roots on this one. Working with a nonet (three horns, six rhythm), he ranges from a Perez Prado mambo of the '50s to a Horace Silver-tinged original called "Home Cookin'" to John Coltrane's "Impressions." He's a firm, rhythmically enticing pianist, and when he breaks loose, as he does on "Impressions," he can dazzle. —*Owen Cordle, Jazz Times*

Howard Rumsey

b. Nov. 7, 1917, Brawley, CA
Bass, piano, drums / Cool
Howard Rumsey began on piano and switched to drums. He began work in Vido Musso's band with pianist Stan Kenton, and was later a founding member of Kenton's first big band. Rumsey

did a lot of freelance work in West Coast groups in the '40s, and started some jam sessions at the Lighthouse in Hermosa Beach, CA, in 1949. The sessions evolved into a who's who of West Coast jazz, and Contemporary began recording a series of albums done at the Lighthouse. Rumsey was a steady presence and unifying figure able to get contrasting, sometimes vastly differing personalities to mesh smoothly in studio-jam environment. The All-Stars series was a profitable one for Contemporary in the '50s, and some six volumes have been reissued by Fantasy. Rumsey went on to head various combos and big bands and spearhead a Concerts by the Sea series in the '60s and '70s. —*Ron Wynn*

★ **Sunday Jazz a la Jazzhouse** / Feb. 21, 1953 / Original Jazz Classics 151
Rumsey made numerous LPs for Contemporary in the '50s and this was the first. This was live and captured the hip jams that took place every Sunday from noon till night. People would sit in and drop out, and the changing personnel reflected that. The playing was intense and enthusiastic though imperfect and at times ill-constructed; the frontier ambiance came through. —*Bob Rusch, Cadence*

○ **Howard Rumsey's Lighthouse All-Stars—Vol. 3** / Oct. 20, 1953 / Contemporary 266
This was a set of three dates put together by entrepreneur and bassist Howard Rumsey. The 7/22/52 session on four tracks boasted crowded arrangements and not very distinct solos. . . . [On the 10/20/53 date] there was a heavy Latin tinge to some of this music, but, overall, it was largely undistinguished. The last date opened things up a bit more with a smaller group on three tracks and had the most extended blowing and clearest projection, along with some nice solos from Shank and Rosolino in particular. —*Bob Rusch, Cadence*

○ **In the Solo Spotlight—Vol. 5** / Mar. 12, 1956 / Contemporary 3517

○ **Music for Lighthousekeeping** / i. Oct. 2-16, 1956 / Contemporary 636
The title of this Howard Rumsey date referred to the Lighthouse jazz club where Rumsey (bass) was a regular with his various Lighthouse All-Stars. —*Bob Rusch, Cadence*

★ **In the Solo Spotlight** / Mar. 12, 1957 / Contemporary 451

○ **Jazz Invention** / i. Feb. 12, 1989 / Contemporary 14051

Jimmy Rushing (James Andrew Rushing)

b. Aug. 26, 1903, Oklahoma City, OK, **d.** Jun. 8, 1972, New York, NY
Vocals / Swing, big band, blues & jazz
Jimmy Rushing was one of the great singers of the Swing Era. He was a member of the Count Basie band from 1935 to 1950 and vocalist on dozens of Basie recordings from this period. Among his classics with Basie were "Outskirts of Town," "Sent for You Yesterday," "Evenin'," and "Boogie Woogie." His own recordings began in 1945 when he made his first album for Vanguard. Two subsequent Vanguard albums are complemented by five Columbia albums (1956-1960). All these, with the exception of the Columbia album with accompaniment by the Dave Brubeck Quartet, are highly recommended. Rushing was a master of Kansas City blues and jazz, and the Vanguards have a strong blues emphasis. Later albums on Colpix and ABC Bluesway have good moments, and his last recording from 1971, "The You and Me That Used to Be," (RCA) is excellent. —*Bob Porter*

★ **Essential Jimmy Rushing, The** / 1954-1957 / Vanguard 65-66
Fine anthology collecting material done by the great blues shouter for Vanguard during the mid-'50s. Songs included remake of "Going to Chicago," plus other combo dates, and he was backed by such Basie comrades as Jo Jones and Buddy Tate. This has been reissued on CD. —*Ron Wynn*

☆ **And the Big Brass** / i. 1958 / Columbia 1152

○ **Dave Brubeck and Jimmy Rushing** / i. 1961 / Atlantic

○ **Blues and Things** / i. 1967 / Master Jazz
Blues and Things is a remarkable collection. Combining vocalist Jimmy Rushing with the Earl Hines quartet (Budd Johnson, Bill Pemberton, and Oliver Jackson) was a stroke of genius, and the empathy between all concerned was marvelous to hear. This particular version of the Hines quartet was a landmark in the pianist's career. —*John Norris, Coda*

○ **Gee, Baby, Ain't I Good to You** / i. Jan. 1969 / Master Jazz 8104
This certainly looked good on paper—the accompanying musicians were Buck Clayton, Julian Dash, Dickie Wells, Sir Charles Thompson, Gene Ramey, and Jo Jones. On top of that, the session took place in a recording studio (which means good sound) but was turned into a jazz party—the idea being to remove the clinical sterility of most studio sessions. The results were somewhat less exciting than the promise. —*John Norris, Coda*

George Russell (George Allan Russell)

b. Jun. 23, 1923, Cincinnati, OH
Composer, piano, theorist, drums / Progressive big band, modern creative
Composer, pianist, and theorist George Russell's father was a professor of music at Oberlin University, so it's not surprising that George Russell became a prime educator and theorist. He sold his first big-band composition to Benny Carter and Dizzy Gillespie in 1945. Russell wrote for Earl Hines in the mid-'40s and also for some shows in Chicago before moving to New York. After overcoming an illness, Russell penned "Cubana Be, Cubana Bop" for Gillespie and premiered it in Carnegie Hall in 1947 by his big band with Chano Pozo. Russell became a widely published composer in the late '40s and '50s, having songs recorded by Buddy Defranco, Charlie Ventura, Artie Shaw, Claude Thornhill, Lee Konitz, Jimmy Giuffre, and Charles Mingus. He taught at the School of Jazz in Lennox, MA, in 1959-1960; formed and led his own group from 1960-1965; and played at the landmark 1962 Washington, DC, Jazz Festival. He spent several years in Europe after 1964, and also made many remarkable big-band and large-group works after 1959 with *New York, New York* on through the '60s, '70s, and '80s. His 1972 work *Living Time* featured a collaboration with Bill Evans, while his 1983 *The African Game* was one of the first releases on the newly revived Blue Note label. —*Ron Wynn*

○ **Jazz Workshop** / Dec. 1956 / Bluebird 6467
A CD reissue of an intriguing release from '56 by George Russell. This was a superb late '50s album, marked by brilliant playing and provocative compositions. Russell spearheads everything and occasionally helps out on piano. The band includes another brilliant player in pianist Bill Evans, plus Hal McKusick on alto sax and flute; Art Farmer on trumpet; guitarist Barry Galbraith; bassists Milt Hinton and Teddy Kotick; and Joe Harris, Osie Johnson, or Paul Motian on drums. —*Ron Wynn*

● **New York, New York** / 1959 / MCA 31371
This is a landmark of conceptual, arranging, production, and playing magnificence. John Coltrane (ts), Max Roach (d), Bill Evans (p), Jon Hendricks (v) all soar. —*Ron Wynn*

☆ **George Russell in Kansas City** / Feb. 1961 / Decca 74183

☆ **Ezz-Thetic** / 1962 / Riverside 070
The sextet on this 1961 Riverside date—pianist-leader George Russell; Eric Dolphy, whose "'Round Midnight" solo alone was worth the album price; trumpeter Don Ellis; Dave Baker on trombone; bassist Steve Swallow (this was his first record session); and drummer Joe Hunt—linked Russell's compositional concepts and the brand of on-top-of-the-chords improvisation he traced to Lester Young. —*Bill Shoemaker, Cadence*

★ **Electronic Sonata for Souls Loved by Nature 1968** / i. Apr. 1982 / Soul Note 1009
Electronic Sonata for Souls Loved by Nature covered more than 50 minutes, filling an entire album. The sextet consisted of composer-pianist George Russell, tenor saxophonist Jan Garbarek, guitarist Terje Rypdal, drummer Jon Christensen, bassist Red Mitchell, and German trumpeter Manfred Schoof, plus an electronically treated tape with fragments of different styles of music. The performance, recorded live in concert, was powerful. Russell's compositional genius shone through the freedom of the performers and the catalytic inclusion of the prerecorded tape. —*Michael Cuscuna, Down Beat*

Luis Russell (Luis Carl Russell)

b. Aug. 6, 1902, Careening Clay, Panama, **d.** Dec. 11, 1963, New York, NY
Bandleader, arranger, piano / New Orleans traditional
Luis Russell led some outstanding big bands in the late '20s and early '30s, though he was overshadowed by the Ellington and Basie orchestras. His bands mixed comic vocals, stomping

arrangements, and elements of traditional New Orleans with swing, making delightful and popular tunes while enabling some emerging players to sharpen their skills. Russell was born in Panama and used the winnings from a lottery ticket to move his mother and sister with him to New Orleans. He played with King Oliver in New York and, after working with some other groups, formed a band in Chicago. They recorded four songs in 1926. The Heebie Jeebie Stompers included Darnell Howard and Barney Bigard. They appeared at Harlem's Saratoga Club with a lineup including Henry Allen, Bill Coleman, Albert Nicholas, Charlie Holmes, and Paul Barbarin, later adding J.C. Higginbotham, Dicky Wells, and Teddy Hill. The band recorded more than 30 songs between 1929 and 1934 for various labels, and backed Louis Armstrong on "Song of the Islands" in 1930. They made such popular tunes as "Call of the Freaks," "Saratoga Shout," "Jersey Lightning," and "On Revival Day," with songwriter Andy Razaf doing lead vocals. Louis Armstrong's manager Joe Glaser took the group over in 1935, following two days when they'd supported Armstrong at the Savoy. This move effectively destroyed their identity. Russell served as Armstrong's musical director until 1943. The coming of bop drove Russell, unable to make the adjustment, out of music. He was a businessman for a time and then became a piano teacher and later a chauffeur. Russell died in 1963. His work has not gotten the widespread exposure it merits through reissue mania as yet. —*Ron Wynn*

● **Luis Russell Collection (1926-1934), The** / 1926-1934 / Collector's Classics 7

○ **Luis Russell and His Louisiana Swing Orchestra** / **i.** Apr. 1974 / Columbia 32338

Forgotten by all but specialists and collectors, the Luis Russell band in its prime (1929—1931) was one of the greatest of pre-Swing era big bands. . . . On this overlapping sampling of the band's growth, development, and beginning decline, the great stuff is on tracks 10 through 26. . . . Of the masterpieces from the important period, "Jersey Lightning" is perhaps the most perfect; it could be by Jelly Roll Morton, certainly Russell's chief influence, both as pianist and arranger, but it is more successful than Morton's own attempts to adapt to the larger instrumentation. Nearly as fine are "Panama," "Doctor Blues," "Saratoga Shout" (an interesting combination of the "The Saints" and the minor blues), "High Tension," and "Feelin' the Spirit." —*Dan Morgenstern, Down Beat*

Pee Wee Russell (Charles Ellsworth Russell)

b. Mar. 27, 1906, St. Louis, MO, **d.** Feb. 15, 1969, Alexandria, VA
Clarinet / Dixieland
Born in Oklahoma, Pee Wee Russell played piano and violin before taking up clarinet; he was a pro at 15. In 1924 he worked with the legendary pianist Peck Keily in a band that also included Jack Teagarden, who became his lifelong friend. In 1925 he played with Bix Beiderbecke in Frank Trumbauer's band, and in 1927 he settled in New York, recording frequently in all-star groups assembled by Red Nichols but also working in dance bands, doubling on tenor, alto, and soprano.

In 1935 he joined Louis Prima's band on 52d Street and went to California with the trumpeter. Back in New York, he was a key member of the musical fraternity around Eddie Condon; with the guitarist, he was a fixture at Nick's and later at Condon's own clubs, playing in a style that always was unclassifiable and totally original, with a tonal palette that ranged from whispers to raspy shouts. Near death in 1951, he recovered and began to lead his own groups, mostly made up of young musicians, such as Ruby Braff. In 1963 he formed a quartet with valve trombonist Marshall Brown that featured a repertoire including pieces by John Coltrane and Ornette Coleman; in that same year, he performed with Thelonious Monk at Newport and finally began to receive the critical attention he'd so long deserved. Late in life he also took up painting, for which he showed as natural a gift as for music, though he didn't develop it. —*Dan Morgenstern*

★ **Individualism of Pee Wee Russell, The** / **i.** 1952 / Savoy
In December 1950 clarinetist Pee Wee Russell nearly died from the effects of years of excessive drinking and limited eating. By the time of the Boston engagement that resulted in this double-LP, Russell was 90 percent recovered. Leading a strong sextet that boasted fine solos from trombonist Eph Resnick and the great young trumpeter Ruby Braff, Russell mostly performs veteran Dixieland standards during these extended workouts, avoiding

clichés and playing his typically unique ideas with spirit and enthusiasm. —*Scott Yanow*

○ **We're in the Money** / 1953-Oct. 2, 1954 / Black Lion 70909
The unique clarinet style of Pee Wee Russell is featured on this CD with two overlapping groups, both of which include trombonist Vic Dickenson and pianist George Wein. One band has Pee Wee matching wits with the brilliant trumpet of Wild Bill Davison, while the other date showcases the more mellow horn of Doc Cheatham, heard in a rare solo spot in the mid-1950s. This music mostly avoids the old warhorses and features superior swing standards by some of the top Condonites. —*Scott Yanow*

○ **Jazz Reunion** / Feb. 23, 1961-Mar. 8, 1961 / Candid 79020
The reunion that took place in this 1961 session was between clarinetist Pee Wee Russell and tenor great Coleman Hawkins. They had first recorded one of the songs ("If I Could Be with You") back in 1929! Both Hawk and Pee Wee had remained modern soloists and on this unusual but very satisfying date (which also features trumpeter Emmett Berry and trombonist Bob Brookmeyer) they explore such numbers as a pair of Ellington classics ("All Too Soon" and "What Am I Hear For"), two Pee Wee originals, and even the boppish "Tin Tin Deo." Timeless music. —*Scott Yanow*

○ **Ask Me Now!** / **i.** May 1966 / Impulse 96
After a lifetime spent playing unusual and unpredictable clarinet solos in Dixieland settings, Pee Wee Russell late in life broke out of the stereotype and played in more modern settings. This Impulse LP (which is begging to be reissued on CD!) has Russell's clarinet placed in a pianoless quartet with valve trombonist Marshall Brown, playing tunes by John Coltrane, Thelonious Monk, and Ornette Coleman, along with some classic ballads. It is a remarkable and very lyrical date that briefly rejuvenated the career of this veteran individualist. A classic of its kind. —*Scott Yanow*

○ **Spirit of '67, The** / 1967 / Impulse 9147

★ **Memorial Album** / **i.** 1969 / Prestige 7672
Teaming trumpeter Buck Clayton with clarinetist Pee Wee Russell in 1960 was a logical move. Both of these individual stylists had been stuck often in Dixieland settings in the 1950's, yet they were really highly distinctive swing soloists. Joined by a modern rhythm section led by pianist Tommy Flanagan, Buck and Pee Wee are in top form on six fine standards, making one wish that they had teamed up in this type of setting more often. —*Scott Yanow*

○ **Giants of Jazz** / **i.** Jan. 1982 / Time Life 18
Regrettably, this three-LP box set is out of print, for it is a fine introduction to the unique clarinetist Pee Wee Russell. The 40 selections that are included here span a 35-year period and are highlighted by early sides with Red Nichols, many encounters with Eddie Condon's bands (including some real classic performances), a few numbers from Russell's mid-1930s association with Louis Prima, and later recordings with his own pickup groups. Along with an excellent booklet, this box is an excellent tribute to a truly individual stylist. —*Scott Yanow*

○ **Pied Piper of Jazz, The** / **i.** Sep. 1982 / Commodore 16440

Terje Rypdal

b. Aug. 23, 1947, Oslo, Norway
Guitar, flute, soprano sax, composer / Early jazz-rock, world fusion, new age, modern creative
Guitarist, flutist, soprano saxophonist, and composer Terje Rypdal has played rock, blues, and jazz. He became a member of Jan Garbarek's group in the late '60s. Rypdal later played with George Russell's sextet and big band, closely studying and absorbing Russell's Lydian chromatic concept. After working with Lester Bowie in 1969, he was featured on Garbarek's first two ECM releases and formed his own trio and group. He had a band with Palle Mikkelborg and Jon Christensen from the late '70s into the '80s. Rypdal's rock background is reflected in his liberal use of electronics, distortion, and synthesized backgrounds, and he has written many compositions for jazz combos and large orchestras, plus many symphonic works. —*Ron Wynn*

★ **Works** / 1974-1981 / ECM 825428
Excellent sampler of Rypdal's music, including two cuts from his superb (but currently unavailable) early '70s albums. —*Michael P. Dawson*

○ **Odyssey** / Aug. 1975 / ECM 835355

Jazz Saxophone *Music Map*

| **1900: Classical sax players** |
| Little Jazz Influence |

| **1916 Vaudeville** |
| Rudy Wiedoeft used the C-melody sax in vaudeville performances. |

| **1920s Jazz and Commercial Dance Music** |

| **1930s Jazz Instrument Ensembles** |

Most Significant Soloists
Sidney Bechet (1897-1959)–soprano
Coleman Hawkins (1904-1969)–tenor
Lester Young (1909-1959)–tenor
Johnny Hodges (1907-1970)–alto, soprano
Charlie Parker (1920-1955)–alto
John Coltrane (1926-1967)–tenor and soprano
Sonny Rollins (1930)–tenor
Ornette Coleman (1930)–alto, tenor
Harry Carney (1910-1974)–baritone
Adrian Rollini (1904-1956)–bass

Sal Salvador

b. Nov. 21, 1925, Monson, MA
Guitar / Bop
A guitarist and educator who played with Stan Kenton and Maynard Ferguson in the '50s and '60s, Sal Salvador later headed his own combos. He's a good player in a traditional jazz, Brazilian, Afro-Latin, or big-band context, well versed in the classic jazz guitar style of Django Reinhardt and Charlie Christian. — *Ron Wynn*

○ **World's Greatest Jazz Standards** / Nov. 1983 / Stash 234
As guitarist Sal Salvador pointed out in the liner notes, the idea of this session was to do an album of songs that had been overplayed in the past.... There were a few different twists—"Misty" as a waltz, "Cherokee" as a samba—but the program was basically straightahead. Salvador was a good soloist in an older bebop style, and he had the lion's share of the solo space here. — *Peter Leitch, Cadence*

★ **Sal Salvador and Crystal Image** / Stash 17
W/ Ted Macero (s), Barbara Oakes (v). Very enjoyable and unusual in its instrumentation and approach. —*Shirley Klett, Cadence*

Joe Sample (Joseph Leslie Sample)

b. Feb. 1, 1939, Houston, TX
Piano, composer / Blues & jazz, soul-jazz, instrumental pop, contemporary funk
Pianist Joe Sample formed a group with some Texas comrades in the late '50s that played an aggressive brand of funky blues and instrumental R&B with jazz touches that they called the "Gulf Coast Sound." When the group moved to Los Angeles in 1960, they changed their name to the Jazz Crusaders. Though he also worked with some other musicians in the '60s, among them Tom Scott and the Harold Land-Bobby Hutcherson group, the main unit (Sample on keyboards, Wayne Henderson on trombone, Wilton Felder on tenor sax, and Stix Hooper on drums) were unparalleled at playing R&B-infused soul-jazz. The group dropped the Jazz part of their name in the '70s, became the Crusaders, and gradually began doing less ambitious, markedly lighter material without the strong blues and R&B backing. Sample got more involved in the production in '70s and '80s, and his most recent releases have been heavy on studio touches, weaker on content. — *Ron Wynn*

○ **Fancy Dance** / Apr. 1969 / Gazell 1016
A different, and rather strong session for keyboardist Joe Sample from '69. Rather than the fusion, blues, and funky instrumentals he's done both with and without his fellow Crusaders, this is a mainstream trio session with Sample, bassist Red Mitchell, and drummer J.C. Moses. While there are two spry blues pieces, there are also some demanding bop and standards in which Sample shows he can execute the chord changes and perform conventional jazz with conviction, even if it's not what he does today. — *Ron Wynn*

○ **Rainbow Seeker** / 1978 / MCA 31067
Joe Sample's solo effort *Rainbow Seeker* epitomized some of the strengths and weaknesses of contemporary fusion. At the core of Sample's music is still a deep gospel resonance. "In All My Wildest Dreams" had a gentle churchy ambience, and Sample's transparent electric piano had a sing-song blues quality. . . . "Islands in the Rain" was a Latin cooker that showcased Sample's acoustic piano talents, while the unaccompanied "Together We'll Find a Way" found him involved in more reflective musings that mixed '50s style block chords with romantic melodies. —*Chip Stern, Down Beat*

★ **Carmel** / 1979-1981 / MCA 37210

Edgar Sampson (Edgar Melvin Sampson)

b. Aug. 31, 1907, New York, NY, d. Jan. 16, 1973, Englewood, NJ
Sax, violin, composer, arranger / Swing, big band
While he was a first-rate violinist and versatile saxophonist, Edgar Sampson's greatness came as a composer and arranger. His works include "Stompin' at the Savoy," "Don't Be That Way," "Blue Minor," "If Dreams Come True," "Blue Lou," "Lullaby in Rhythm," and many others, plus numerous arrangements. He began playing violin as a child and took up alto sax as a teen. He started his professional career with Joe Coleman in 1924 and worked with Duke Ellington in 1925. Later came stints with Bingie Madison, Billy Fowler, Arthur Gibbs, Charlie Johnson, and Alex Jackson. Sampson joined Fletcher Henderson in 1931, remaining until 1933. He played with Chick Webb from '33 until '37, and began writing arrangements with Rex Stewart while in Webb's band. Sampson was a prolific freelance arranger during the swing era's heyday, providing them for Webb, Benny Goodman, Artie Shaw, Red Norvo, and Teddy Wilson. He played baritone sax with Lionel Hampton in 1938 and became Ella Fitzgerald's music director in 1939. Sampson played alto and baritone sax for Al Sears in 1943 and then started his own bands. During the late '40s and '50s, Sampson played in many Afro-Latin bands, including those of Marcellino Guerra, Tito Puente, and Tito Rodriquez. He continued heading bands through the '60s and died in 1973. —*Ron Wynn*

● **Jazz Heritage: Sampson Swings Again** / MCA 1354

David Sanborn (David William Sanborn)

b. Jul. 30, 1945, Tampa, FL
Alto sax / Blues & jazz, instrumental pop
Alto saxophonist David Sanborn has moved back and forth between the musical worlds of jazz and pop as if there were no difference between them. He is, however, an outstanding jazz alto player in either a hard bop or more outside mode. Since 1975 he has made a series of popular fusion albums under his own name, and he is also an in-demand session player. —*Bill Ruhlmann*

★ **Taking Off** / 1975 / Warner Brothers 2873
Alto saxophonist David Sanborn's debut album for Warner Bros. was a polished, toe-tappin', finger-poppin', jazz-flavored rhythm and blues outing, infectious in nature. Working out of the tradition of such R&B saxophonists as Jr. Walker and King Curtis, Sanborn convincingly engaged the tight, funky charts of David Matthews, Howard Johnson, Don Grolnick, and Randy Brecker. — *Chuck Berg, Down Beat*

David Sanborn / i. Feb. 1976 / Warner Brothers 2957

Heart to Heart / Jan. 1978 / Warner Brothers 3189

○ **Another Hand** / 1990 / Elektra 61088
Return by Sanborn to his real, true love: unadorned (or only partly adorned) jazz. —*Ron Wynn*

○ **Upfront** / 1991 / Elektra 61272
Despite an array of session musicians and some heavily arranged material, alto saxophonist Dave Sanborn cuts long with his most

The Tenor Saxophone

Music Map

Tenor Sax Early Influences Prince Robinson (1902-1960) Happy Caldwell (1903-1978) Stump Evans (1904-1928)	**Sonny Rollins influenced by** Charlie Parker Coleman Hawkins Dexter Gordon
Coleman Hawkins (1901-1969) **First Major Early Tenor Soloist**	**Sonny Rollins (1930)** **Major Saxophone Soloist**
Major influence on: Charlie Barnet (1913-1991) Tex Beneke (1914) Chu Berry (1908-1941) Vido Musso (1913-1982) Ben Webster (1909-1973) Herschel Evans (1909-1939) Dick Wilson (1911-1941)	**Influenced:** Joe Henderson (1937) Rahsaan Roland Kirk (1936-1977) Yusef Lateef (1920) Barney Wilen (1937) Branford Marsalis(1961) Ricky Ford (1954) David Murray (1955) Junior Cook (1934-1992)
Bud Freeman (1906-1991)–First Major White Tenor Player Eddie Miller (1911-1991) Babe Russin (1911-1984) Boomie Richman (1921)	**John Coltrane Influenced by:** Earl Bostic (1913-1965) Big Nick Nicholas (1922) John Gilmore (1931) w/Sun Ra Dexter Gordon (1923-1990) Stan Getz (1927-1991)
Arnett Cobb (1918-1990) Illinois Jacquet (1922) Ike Quebec (1918-1963) Jimmy Forrest (1920-1980) Hal Singer (1919) Buddy Tate (1915) Don Byas (1912-1972)	**John Coltrane (1926-1967)** **Major Saxophone Soloist**

Influenced:

Mike Brecker (1949)	Dave Young (1912)
Bob Berg (1951)	George Coleman (1935)
Steve Grossman (1951)	Joe Farrell (1937-1986)
John Klemmer (1946)	Charles Lloyd (1938)
Booker Ervin (1930-1970)	Sonny Fortune (1939)
Bill Evans (1957)	Pharoah Sanders (1940)
Azar Lawrence (1953)	Dave Liebman (1946)

Lester Young influenced by: Frank Trumbauer	Wayne Shorter (1953)
Lester Young (1909-1959) **Major Saxophone Soloist**	**Free Jazz** Albert Ayler (1936-1970)
Influenced: Budd Johnson (1910-1984) Jerry Jerome (1912) Paul Quinichelte (1916-1983) – Al Klink (1915-1991) Charlie Parker (1920-1955)	**Other Free Jazz:** David Murray (1955) – Joseph Jarman (1937) Archie Shepp (1937) – Frank Lowe (1943) Willem Breuker (1944) – Rev. Frank Wright (1935) Peter Brotzmann (1941) – Jan Garbarek (1947) Sam Rivers (1930) – Gato Barbieri (1934) Kalaparusha Maurie McIntyre (1936) George Adams (1940-1993)

Later influence on:

Gene Ammons	Jackie McLean
Al Cohn	Warne Marsh
John Coltrane	James Moody
Allen Eager	Art Pepper
Stan Getz	Herbie Stewart
Wardell Gray	Zoot Sims
Lee Konitz	Sonny Stitt
Dexter Gordon	

expressive, joyous playing in many years. That's partly due to Marcus Miller's bass work, which is fluid and backbeat-oriented, while others, like trumpeter Herb Robertson and organist Richard Tee, lay in some perfect riffs in support of Sanborn's earnest solos. *—Ron Wynn*

Poncho Sanchez

b. Oct. 30, 1951, Laredo, Texas
Flute, guitar, percussion / Latin-jazz
Born to Mexican parents, Poncho Sanchez studied flute and guitar in junior high school and later took up percussion. He gigged

with Gary Foster, Mark Levine, Willie Bobo, and Luis Gasca until he joined Cal Tjader's Combo on December 31, 1975. When Cal Tjader died, Sanchez inherited the group. The Sanchez aggregation is hot property—it is always in demand, has great drawing power, and is a top record seller. *—Max Salazar*

★ **Gauiota** / **i.** 1980 / Discovery

○ **Papa Gato** / **i.** 1986 / Concord Jazz 4310

Poncho Sanchez continues to turn out fine recordings. Justo Almario took over the reeds (alto, tenor, flute) with the remaining personnel veterans of this popular group. Almario had a good showcase (along with pianist Charlie Otwell) on the title song, but was, of course, much in evidence elsewhere. —*Shirley Klett, Cadence*

○ **Fuerte** / **i**. 1987 / Concord Jazz 4340
Features an octet with standout pianist-composer Charlie Otwell, who wrote the title track and two other cookers. Saxophonist Ken Goldberg wrote two others. Because of these two, this stands as a prime Sanchez album, aside from the group's hot playing. —*Michael G. Nastos*

☆ **Night at Kimball's East, A** / **i**. 1990 / Concord Jazz 4472
Recorded at Kimball's East, this live performance starts out warm and finishes smoking. The final cut, Charlie Otwell's "La Familia," is a pulsating showstopper with everyone doing something to blow the roof off. . . . This was clearly a night to remember. —*Marcela Breton, Jazz Times*

Pharoah Sanders (Farrell Sanders)

b. Oct. 13, 1940, Little Rock, AR
Tenor sax / Early free, modern creative
After his first solo album on the radical ESP label, tenor saxophonist Pharoah Sanders joined John Coltrane in 1965 for his ground-breaking *Ascension* album, playing alongside such dynamic young modernists as Archie Shepp, John Tchicai, Marion Brown, Freddie Hubbard, and others. This was a time of great transition for John Coltrane, and the addition of Sanders to his newly enlarged recording and touring group signalled the leader's commitment to the musical freedom and egoless Eastern spirituality of his final phase. In the weighty sound-mass of what was essentially a free-jazz unit, Pharoah alternated long linear solos or engaged his boss in fiercely heated horn duets that marked this group's most explosive climaxes. His was an equal voice to Coltrane's, and he often exhibited superior expressiveness on tenor as well as other wind instruments, going all the way out in shrieking and gutteral ranges, unfettered by the vestiges of bop and modal structures.

After Coltrane's death, Pharoah recorded a string of acclaimed records for Impulse, consistently developing his freedom of expression in a deeply spiritual and often introspective setting. Like many of his peers, he began incorporating African, Asian, and other musical forms into his work in the late '60s, and he maintains a global focus, recently including a Moroccan traditional musician in his group. Infrequent collaborations with Don Cherry, the Jazz Composer's Orchestra, Sonny Sharrock, and a few others are noteworthy, but by and large he has followed his muse in expansive small groups, ably furthering the legacy of the '60s on a handful of small record labels. —*Myles Boisen*

○ **Journey to the One** / Evidence 22016
Journey to the One confirmed that Pharoah Sanders continued to command one of the richest, loveliest, and fiercest tenor sax sounds in all of jazz. The immediacy and almost tactile intimacy of his tone and intonation again were stunningly employed to serve the awesome emotional power that is Sanders' ultimate contribution. *Journey* also confirmed, however, the static nature of the saxophonist's musical concept built on religious mysticism and his somewhat banal sense of dynamics, which constantly balanced fervor against lyricism. As a whole, this double album represented a more traditionalist approach for Sanders. —*Lars Gabel, Down Beat*

★ **Karma** / Feb. 14, 1969-Oct. 20, 1969 / MCA 39122
Karma was a real rarity, an avant-garde "hit." One could almost call it "free jazz for the masses." Pharoah Sanders, who in 1966 would have easily won a poll for "least likely to succeed commercially" by 1969 was out on his own featuring his Jekyll and Hyde tenor (alternately peaceful and screaming) over rhythmic vamps. With Leon Thomas singing and yodelling, the 33-minute atmospheric "The Creator Has a Master Plan" caught on and received quite a bit of airplay on jazz stations at the time. —*Scott Yanow, Cadence*

★ **Love in Us All** / Sep. 13-14, 1973 / ASD 9280
Side one, "Love Is Everywhere," which Pharoah Sanders does regularly in concert in foot-stomping style, was here a crudely-spliced, 20-minute exercise in rhythmic entropy where Sanders was heard just once, very briefly, on soprano sax. To be just, side two, "To John," was music high as an elephant's eye, as Sanders, an anonymous trumpet player, and another anonymous tenor

player all conspired to make this an intensely gratifying tribute. —*Bill Adler, Down Beat*

Arturo Sandoval

b. Nov. 6, 1949, Artemisa, Cuba
Trumpet, piano, composer / Latin-jazz, world fusion
Trumpeter Arturo Sandoval is a former Irakere member acknowledged as perhaps the premier trumpeter in Latin-jazz and Afro-Cuban circles. Sandoval first attracted attention in the States when Irakere performed during a 1977 State Department-sponsored jazz concert in Cuba, where he caught the eye of Dizzy Gillespie. Sandoval later traveled internationally with Irakere, recorded by special arrangement with Gillespie overseas, and eventually defected. Releases he did for German Messidor label both on his own and with former Irakere cohort Paquito D'Rivera are sparkling ensembles of his brassy, flashy, high-register style. —*Ron Wynn*

★ **To a Finland Station** / **i**. 1982 / Pablo 889
W/ Dizzy Gillespie (tpt) in Helsinki. Excellent interplay. Lots of good feeling on this session. —*Michael G. Nastos*

○ **Breaking the Sound Barrier** / **i**. 1983 / CCAA 8301
Live made in Chicago from Cuban standpoint. Cuban trumpeter plays it straight in jazz and Latin veins. No funk. His best. —*Michael G. Nastos*

○ **Tumbaito** / Messidor 15974
A tremendous session with dynamic trumpeter Arturo Sandoval mixing things up with an all-star lineup. It was originally available only overseas but has now been issued in America through Messidor. —*Ron Wynn*

Mongo Santamaria

b. Apr. 7, 1922, Jesus Maria, Havana, Cuba
Percussion / Latin-jazz
Mongo Santamaria plays congos, bongos, and various percussion instruments and has been a longtime bandleader. He's the greatest Cuban percussionist since Chano Pozo, and certainly the most dominant of his generation. Santamaria's grandfather was born in Africa; he originally studied the violin but switched to drums and dropped out of school in Cuba to play the congas. Santamaria established himself playing in clubs during the years prior to Castro's takeover; he left Cuba for Mexico City in 1948 with his cousin Armando Peraza. They came to New York in 1950 and were billed as the Black Cuban Diamonds. Santamaria's first American gig came with Perez Prado; he stayed with him three years and then spent seven glorious years with Tito Puente, where their multiple percussion barrages and rhythmic assaults made Latin-jazz history. Santamaria helped bring traditional African and Afro-Cuban music to the forefront in the '50s by cutting a series of albums featuring songs derived from Afro-Cuban religious groups and ceremonies. He also played Latin-jazz, and switched to Cal Tjader's group in 1958, cutting several great albums with him while staying for three years. He did some work with Dizzy Gillespie and Jack McDuff, while also cutting his own albums in the late '50s and throughout the '60s, many of them for Latin labels. During the '70s and '80s Santamaria also began to do more pop-oriented and fusion releases, harnessing, often subverting his impressive rhythmic skills and instead merely supporting limp, lightweight melodies and arrangements. But during the '80s Santamaria also made some outstanding works in vintage Latin-jazz and Afro-Cuban style, including an 1987 date with Charlie Palmieri. He's best known generally for the 1963 hit song "Watermelon Man," but no one, including Airto or Olatunji, has been a more consistent representative of the link between African, Latin, African-American, and jazz concepts. —*Ron Wynn*

○ **Afro-Roots** / **i**. 1958-1959 / Prestige 24018
Mongo Santamaria made a pair of superb Latin-jazz albums for Fantasy in the late '50s. These were subsequently reissued ona two-record set on vinyl in the '70s and then repackaged for CD. The disc contains full albums *Yambu* and *Mongo,* each one brilliant. —*Ron Wynn*

○ **Skins** / 1962 / Milestone 47038
This twofer (originally *So Mongo* and *Mongo Explodes* on Riverside) includes many compositions by trumpeter Marty Sheller. Guests include Hubert Laws, Chick Corea, and Jimmy Cobb. Every track is vital. —*Michael G. Nastos*

Music Map

The Alto Saxophone

Early Alto Players:
Otto Hardwick (1904-1970) w/Duke Ellington
Johnny Hodges (1907-1970) w/Duke Ellington
Charles Holmes (1910-1985) w/Luis Russell
Earl Warren (1914) w/Count Basie – Benny Carter (1907)

Alto Players of the 1920s
Jimmy Dorsey (1904-1957) – Frank Trumbauer (1901)

Influenced: Lester Young (1909-1959)

Alto Players of the 1930s
Hilton Jefferson (1903-1968) – Woody Herman (1913-1987)
Buster Smith (1904) – Pete Brown (1906-1963)
Tab Smith (1909-1971) – Eddie Barefield (1909)
Earl Bostic (1913-1965) – Don Stovall (1913-1970)
Louis Jordan (1908-1975) – Scoops Carry (1915-1970)
Willie Smith (1910-1967) – Benny Carter (1907)

Bop Alto Sax Players
Charlie Parker (1920-1955)

Influenced:
Charlie Mariano (1923) – Sonny Stitt (1924-1982)
Lou Donaldson (1926) – Sonny Criss (1927-1977)
Eric Dolphy (1928-1964) – John Jenkins (1931-1994)
Ornette Coleman (1930) – Jackie McLean (1932)
Cannonball Adderley (1928-1975) – Phil Woods (1931)
Sonny Red (1932-1981) – Gene Quill (1927)
Charles McPherson (1939)

Lester Young's Influence on Alto Players:
Lee Konitz (1927)
Art Pepper (1925-1982)
Paul Desmond (1924-1977)

Free Jazz Alto Saxophone Player
Ornette Coleman (1930)

Influenced:
John Tchicai (1936)
Marion Brown (1935)
Roscoe Mitchell (1940)
Henry Threadgill (1944)
Anthony Braxton (1945)
Vladimir Chekasin (1947)
Ray Nathanson
John Zorn (1953)

Free Jazz Players
Jimmy Lyons (1933-1986)
Gary Bartz (1940)
Roscoe Mitchell (1940)
Julius Hemphill (1940)
Oliver Lake (1944)
Arthur Blythe (1940)
Marshall Allen (1924)
James Spaulding (1937)
Ken McIntyre (1931)
Greg Osby
Ken McIntyre (1931)
Sonny Simmons (1933)

★ **Mongo at the Village Gate** / **i.** 1963 / Riverside 490
This is a nonet with Pat Patrick, Bobby Capers, Marty Sheller, and Chihuahua Martinez—a Latin, jazz, and soul combo. Emceed by Symphony Sid, it is startlingly fresh for its era. It still sounds fresh. —*Michael G. Nastos*

○ **Bravo, el** / **i.** 1966 / CBS

○ **Mongo at Montreux** / **i.** 1971 / Atlantic

○ **Amanecer, Gabrielle** / **i.** 1977 / Vaya

○ **Bomboro, Asiha, Guajiro, Nada Mas** / **i.** 1978 / Vaya

★ **Live at Jazz Alley** / **i.** 1990 / Concord Jazz 4427

Gunther Schuller (Gunther Alexander Schuller)

b. Nov. 11, 1925, Jackson Heights, NY
French horn, composer, author / Early free, progressive big band
Gunther Schuller has written comprehensive, extensive works on early jazz and the swing era and is an authority on both jazz and classical. He's also a musician who played with Miles Davis in 1949-1950 and in many symphony orchestras around the nation. He was an early advocate of third-stream music, and recorded albums in that style for Columbia and Verve in the '50s and Atlantic in the '60s. The president of the New England Conservatory, Schuller also formed a ragtime ensemble, made a hit ragtime album in 1973, and formed the New England Conservatory Jazz Repertory Orchestra to play classic arrangements of vintage tunes by Ellington and other greats. His landmark books, one on early jazz and the other on the swing era have been reprinted in paperback. —*Ron Wynn*

★ **John Lewis Presents** / 1960 / Atlantic 1365

○ **Jumpin' in the Future** / **i.** May 1990 / GM 3010CD43:5
A historic big band session led by composer-conductor Gunther Schuller. The band performed Schuller compositions that had

never been recorded covering the years 1947-1966. The band included such musicians as Howard Johnson. —*Ron Wynn*

Diane Schuur

Vocals / Ballads & blues
West Coast jazz and blues vocalist Diane Schuur burst into the national spotlight in the mid-'80s with a number of critically acclaimed albums for GRP Records. Her recent album, *Pure Schuur*, consists of a range of songs that includes jazz, pop, and contemporary. Her appeal in performance and on record goes beyond a straight jazz audience, though, and she has been making inroads in the pop and contemporary music worlds of late. Schuur remains a singer with one foot firmly planted in the jazz world, but one who has great crossover potential. —*Richard Skelly*

○ **Timeless** / **i.** 1986 / GRP 9540

● **Collection** / **i.** 1986-1989 / GRP 9591

○ **And the Count Basie Orchestra** / **i.** 1987 / GRP 1039

Bob Scobey (Robert Alexander Scobey)

b. Dec. 9, 1916, Tucumcari, NM, **d.** 1963
Trumpet / Dixieland
Trumpeter Bob Scobey was an energetic, always crowd-pleasing stylist who was among the most popular players in the '50s and '60s traditional jazz school. Bob Scobey played in pit bands, dance orchestras, and clubs during the '30s, meeting Lu Watters in 1938. He spent most of the '40s playing second trumpet to Watters' first in the Yerba Buena Jazz Band, taking off four years for army duty. Scobey left Watters in '49 to form his own band, and was a beloved leader, soloist, and performer the rest of his life. His group made many recordings on the Good Time Life label, were headliners at most traditional festivals, and had a three-year residency at two clubs in Oakland. Scobey opened his own club in

Chicago in 1959, while making regular trips with his group to New York, Las Vegas, and San Francisco on off weeks. —*Ron Wynn*

● **Scobey's Story—Vol. 1 and 2** / Nov. 6, 1951-Apr. 12, 1952 / Good Time Jazz
Bob Scobey Frisco Band. First-rate traditional date with veterans like Albert Nicholas (cl) and George Probert (sax) in lineup. —*Ron Wynn*

○ **Scobey and Clancy** / Jul. 6-07, 1955 / Good Time Jazz 12009

John Scofield

b. Dec. 26, 1951, Dayton, OH
Guitar / Early jazz-rock, modern creative
Electric guitarist John Scofield has played with people as diverse as his influences—Charles Mingus, Jack DeJohnette, Jay McShann, and Miles Davis. A steely tone and fluid lines earmark his distinctive style. His early fusion material is good, but the later period neo-bop and contemporary improvised music is even better. He's hitting his stride these days. —*Michael G. Nastos*

○ **Shinola** / Dec. 12-13, 1981 / Enja 79656
Trio set reissued in 1991. Dense, prickly, and lots of space for guitar work. —*Ron Wynn*

○ **Time on My Hands** / Nov. 1989 / Blue Note 92894
His best contemporary album. Excellent playing and writing. A must-buy for jazz-contemporary music listeners. —*Michael G. Nastos*

★ **Meant to Be** / Dec. 1990 / Blue Note 95479
Quartet. Just about as good as *Time on My Hands*, maybe a little better in terms of composition. —*Michael G. Nastos*

○ **Grace under Pressure** / Dec. 1991 / Blue Note 98167
Guitarist John Scofield leads a topknotch group on this '91 session. It's a pianoless band, with Scofield's nimble guitar lines contrasted by those of second guitarist Bill Frisell. They team up with trombonist Jim Pugh, bassist Charlie Haden, and drummer Joey Baron, plus Randy Brecker on flugelhorn and John Clark on French horn. —*Ron Wynn*

Hazel Scott (Hazel Dorothy Scott)

b. Jun. 11, 1920, Port of Spain, Trinidad, d. 1981
Piano, vocals / Postbop, cool
Pianist and vocalist Hazel Scott had a laidback style. But closer listening to her piano trio sounds revealed an advanced harmonic sense. —*Michael G. Nastos*

★ **Late Show** / May 6, 1953 / Capitol 364

○ **Relaxed Piano Moods** / Jan. 21, 1955 / Debut 1702
Definitive piano trio with Charles Mingus (b) and Max Roach (d). A must-buy. Three bonus tracks on the CD. —*Michael G. Nastos*

Shirley Scott

b. Mar. 14, 1934, Philadelphia, PA
Organ / Blues & jazz, soul-jazz
One of the top organists of the '50s and '60s. Scott came to prominence in the trio of saxophonist Eddie "Lockjaw" Davis in 1955 and recorded with him for King, Roulette, and Prestige. Her own first recordings (1958) were for Prestige, including many with bass and drums accompaniment. Beginning in 1961, she started a long series of recordings with saxophonist Stanley Turrentine. Their collaborations for Prestige, Blue Note, Impulse, and Atlantic were very consistant organ combo jazz. Many of these sessions are under Turrentine's name. After a marital breakup with Turrentine in 1971, Shirley Scott's recordings became less frequent. In general her work over the past 20 years has not equalled the quality of her earlier work. —*Bob Porter*

★ **Great Scott! / For Members Only** / May 27, 1958-1963 / MCA 33115
Compilation blends two prime Scott albums (1958 & 1963); some cuts arranged and conducted by Oliver Nelson. —*Ron Wynn*

★ **Sweet Soul** / Dec. 5, 1962 / Prestige 7360
Reissued from the "Happy Talk" session this features Earl May on bass and Roy Brooks on drums. It includes a nice "Jitterbug Waltz." All are standards. —*Michael G. Nastos*

☆ **Blue Flames** / Mar. 31, 1964 / Prestige 328
Recorded at Englewood CLiffs, NJ. W/ Turrentine, Stanley. This is exactly the kind of straightahead funky music you would expect

from the Scott-Turrentine combination. No disappointments. —*Michael Erlewine*

○ **Great Live Sessions, The** / Sep. 23, 1964 / ABC/Impulse 9341
Double record live date from the '60s, with then-husband Turrentine, is impressive in its solid tasty swing and Scott's restraint in building a burning intensity. Turrentine's tenor is brimming with confidence and is wonderful to hear in such a sparse setting. Ms. Scott hasn't been exactly overrecorded in recent years, and her playing here is stunning in its logic and swing. —*Ronald B. Weinstock, Cadence*

○ **Queen of the Organ** / Dec. 2, 1964 / GRP 123
A steamy, hot mid-'60s soul-jazz session with the soulful, bluesy organist Shirley Scott providing some booming, funky solos. This was one of several combo works she cut, usually with saxophonist Stanley Turrentine, who was her husband at the time. Anything Scott recorded from this period is worth hearing. —*Ron Wynn*

○ **One for Me** / Nov. 1974 / Strata East 7430
The record is a beauty with Harold Vick, perhaps the most suited and sensitive horn player Ms. Scott has worked with. . . . [a] thoroughly enjoyable album of bop stream music, and while it is nothing overly heavy or deep, it's thoughtfully and sensitively produced and of its kind an almost perfect album. —*Bob Rusch, Cadence*

Stephen Scott

b. 1944
piano / Neo-bop
Another highly publicized young lion pianist from New York. He's recently worked with Joe Henderson on his acclaimed album *Lush Life* and also released his own debut session. A captivating soloist despite being only in his 20s, and his debut reveals considerable expertise as a composer. Certainly still in developmental stage, but someone to watch in the '90s. —*Ron Wynn*

★ **Something to Consider** / i. 1991 / Verve 849557
Young lion roars out of the box with impressive piano debut, aided by both old stars like Joe Henderson (sax) and fellow brats like Roy Hargrove (tpt). —*Ron Wynn*

Tony Scott

b. Jun. 17, 1921, Morristown, NJ
Clarinet / Cool, big band, postbop
One of the more eclectic players, Tony Scott studied at Juilliard and spent three years in army bands from 1942-1945. After leaving the service, Scott worked with Tommy Dorsey, Charlie Ventura, Claude Thornhill, and Earl Bostic (among others) before heading his own groups. He worked with a number of great jazz singers as well, among them Billie Holiday, Carmen McRae, and Sarah Vaughan. He was Harry Belafonte's musical director in 1955, and during international tours he made in 1957 and from 1959 to1965 Scott became quite knowledgeable about ethnic music, especially Asian and Indian styles. His recordings date back to a 1946 session on Gotham with Vaughan and include several notable '50s and '60s works. His *Music for Zen Meditation* and *Music for Yoga Meditation* in 1964 and 1967 respectively are seen in some quarters as percursors for the new-age sound of the '80s. In recent years he's recorded with Indonesian groups and done albums paying homage to Africa. —*Ron Wynn*

○ **Scott's Fling** / i. 1955 / RCA

★ **Complete Tony Scott, The** / i. Oct. 3, 1957 / RCA Victor 1452
Best from a series of mid-'50s recordings showcasing Scott in quartet, big band, and combo situations. —*Ron Wynn*

★ **Golden Moments** / 1959 / Muse 5230
Recorded in 1959, just after pianist Bill Evans had finished a stint with Miles Davis, this record showed Evans with his Bud Powell influences intact. The pianist had worked with clarinetist Tony Scott several times over the prior two years and was accustomed to his freewheeling style. . . . Scott's playing was a revelation— here was a player who had gone beyond the stylistic influences of Benny Goodman and Pee Wee Russell and forged his own sound out of bebop. Scott sounded more like Charlie Parker and Lester Young, two musicians to whom he listened and from whom he learned. —*Richard B. Kamins, Cadence*

○ **Music For Zen Meditation (and Other Joys)** / i. 1964 / Verve

The Soprano Saxophone

Music Map

The Baritone Saxophone

Older Sax Players
Dexter Gordon (1923-1989)
Budd Johnson (1910-1984)
Oliver Nelson (1932-1975)
Jerome Richardson (1920)
Sam Rivers (1930)
Lucky Thompson (1924)
Cannonball Adderley (1928-1975)
Sonny Rollins (1930)
Zoot Sims (1925-1985)

Soprano Saxophone
Sidney Bechet (1897-1959)

Influenced:
Bob Wilber (1928) – Johnny Hodges (1907-1970)
Don Redman (1900-1964) – Charlie Barnet (1913)
Woody Herman (1913-1987)
Emmett Mathews (1902)

European Soprano Players inspired by Sidney Bechet
Jeann-Pierre Bonnel
Claude Luter (1923)
Wally Fawkes (1924)

Free Jazz Soprano Sax
Steve Lacy (1934)
Evan Parker (1944)
Jan Ira Bloom (1953)

Early Baritone Sax
Harry Carney (1910-1974)
Jack Washington (1910-1964)
Ernie Caceres (1911-1971)

1950s
Bob Gordon (1928-1955)
Gerry Mulligan (1927)
Lars Gullin (1928-1976)

Also:
Serge Chaloff (1923-1957)
Leo Parker (1925-1962)
Cecil Payne (1922)
Doc Holladay

Pepper Adams (1930-1987)
Nick Brignola (1936)

Coltrane's Influence
Charles Davis (1933)
Hamiet Bluiett (1940)
John Surman (1944)
Pat Patrick (1929)
Ronnie Cuber (1941)
Charles Tyler (1941)

1960s Dixieland
John Barnes (1932)

This elegant, contemplative set of pieces was conceived during one of the jazz artist's trips to Japan when Scott had the opportunity to record with a shakuhachi flutist and a koto player. Though ears unaccustomed to oriental styles might assume it's a performance of traditional Japanese music, the album is actually a set of finely wrought improvisations merging Eastern and Western sensibilities. —*Linda Kohanov*

○ **African Bird: Come Back! Mother Africa** / 1981-1984 / Soul Note 1083
Clarinetist as a world music pacemaker. Removed from his early jazz and meditative phases, while combining aspects of both with African rhythms and Charlie Parker inflections. "African Bird Suite" is a modal stunner. —*Michael G. Nastos*

Doc Severinsen

b. Jul. 7, 1927, Arlington, OR
Trumpet, bandleader / Big band, bop, progressive big band
Trumpeter Doc Severinsen was the longtime "Tonight Show" bandleader and Johnny Carson foil. He spent several years playing in bop groups and jazz clubs before attaining his high visibility, big-paying television gig. He worked with Charlie Barnet, Sam Donahue, and Tommy Dorsey during the '40s, and did several sessions in studios. His studio reputation got him a chance to work at NBC, and he played in the bands for Steve Allen shows and other programs. He became a member of the Tonight Show orchestra, and assembled a first-class aggregation that often included many top players from major swing and big bands. Severinsen in the '80s has led his own big band and small combo when away from the Tonight Show and won a Grammy in 1986. He's often been a guest soloist and conductor with various symphony orchestras, and he can hit high notes and play ballads and standards with ease. —*Ron Wynn*

★ **Once More, with Feeling!** / Amherst 94405

Bud Shank (Clifford Everett Shank, Jr.)
b. May 27, 1926, Dayton, OH
Alto sax, flute / Cool
Though he's a good, sometimes inspiring saxophonist, Bud Shank deserves more recognition and credit for enhancing and expanding the role of the flute in the jazz context. He was among the first bop players to utilize the instrument as a legitimate lead, rather than a supportive or decorative one, and to explore its range and present it in its fullest improvising capacity. Shank started on clarinet at 10, changed to sax at 14, and moved to the West Coast in 1947. He spent a year with Charlie Barnet and played with Stan Kenton from 1950 to 1951. He was a featured member of the Lighthouse All-Stars group from 1953 to 1956 and began making albums as a leader in 1954. He became a prominent studio and session player in the '60s and was a founding member of the LA 4 in 1974. He's made several tours of Europe and played with Frank Morgan and Shorty Rogers (among others) in the '80s and '90s. —*Ron Wynn*

○ **This Bud's for You** / Nov. 11, 1984 / Muse 5309
Arguably his best quartet date ever, and certainly among the top three. Alto saxophonist Bud Shank took a page from Art Pepper's book, and decided to work with a set rhythm section. Bassist Ron Carter, pianist Kenny Baron, and drummer Al Foster kicked into gear on the opening song and never faltered. Shank soared, playing more aggressively and showing more conviction in his solos than at any time since the '50s. —*Ron Wynn*

★ **Serious Swingers** / i. Feb. 2-04, 1986 / Contemporary 14031
○ **That Old Feeling** / Feb. 1986 / Contemporary 14019
The presence on this session of George Cables (piano) suggests that Bud Shank had the feel of a latter-day Art Pepper session in mind, and the playing exhibited a Pepper date's energy and fleet fecundity. Shank didn't attempt to steal Pepper's sound, but the si-

miliarities were there: The once wispy West Coast alto now shouted. —*Kevin Whitehead, Cadence*

☆ **Doctor Is In, The** / i. 1991 / Candid 79520

Good '91 session featuring the steady cool and bop-tinged alto sax solos of Bud Shank in a combo setting. He's backed by pianist Mike Wofford, bassist Bob Magnusson, and drummer Sherman Ferguson. They tackle familiar standards and a few originals, and make satisfying, if unchallenging, music. —*Ron Wynn*

Sonny Sharrock (Warren Harding Sharrock)

b. Aug. 27, 1940, Ossining, NY, d. 1994
Guitar, slide guitar / Early jazz-rock, modern creative
Sonny Sharrock carved his own unique niche in the world of jazz and jazz-based rock. Sharrock studied at Berklee at 21, took four months of composition, and in 1965 began playing with Olatunji, Pharoah Sanders, Sunny Murray, and Don Cherry. His amazing solos creatively included lots of feedback, distortion, clusters and raking, and shattering phrases and notes, but all of it done in a very coherent, rhythmically and harmonically consistent fashion. He achieved his greatest notoriety as a member of various groups led by Herbie Mann from 1967 to1973. He formed his own group in 1973 and did some tours and recording with his wife Linda. Sharrock later joined the group Last Exit in 1985 and made both avant-garde and rock-R&B releases as a leader. He died in 1994. —*Ron Wynn*

★ **Ask the Ages** / 1991 / Axiom 848957

Across-the-board acclaim for this splendid power-drunk band. Sharrock's guitar still espouses new and fresh sounds. With Pharoah Sanders (ts) and Elvin Jones (d). Six pieces written by Sharrock. Need wide-open ears, and they may implode. Revolutionary and revelatory. —*Michael G. Nastos*

Charlie Shavers (Charles James Shavers)

b. Aug. 3, 1917, New York, NY, d. Aug. 8, 1971, New York, NY
Trumpet / Swing, big band
Charlie Shavers was a topflight trumpeter, particularly effective with high note flurries. He was extremely fluid and flexible and provided memorable, exciting solos at impressive tempos. His tone was warm, rich, and inviting, and he often elevated routine, below-par music through his playing. Shavers's father was also a trumpeter and a distant relative of Fats Navarro. But Shavers initially played piano and banjo. He started in the bands of Tiny Bradshaw and Lucky Millinder and earned his reputation during a lengthy stint with the John Kirby sextet. This was the premier "chamber" and small jazz combo of the day, and Shavers's compositions "Pastel Blue" and "Undecided" earned him additional fame. "Undecided" became a hit for Ella Fitzgerald, Benny Goodman, and the Ames Brothers. Shavers stayed with Kirby until 1944. He later played with Tommy Dorsey and co-led a sextet with Terry Gibbs and Louis Bellson. Shavers later toured with Jazz at the Philharmonic (where he had some exciting trumpet battles with Roy Eldridge) but mostly stayed buried, if well treated and occasionally featured, in Tommy Dorsey's orchestra, staying even after Dorsey's death. He had recording sessions with Coleman Hawkins, Bellson, Goodman, Georgie Auld, Charlie Ventura, and Lionel Hampton. A mid-'50s album he made with vocalist Maxine Sullivan for Bethlehem rekindled interest in the Kirby band. His only fault was unfailing loyalty. He worked for years with a Dorsey ghost band fronted by Sam Donahue and eventually toured with it as a vocalist; by this time the name had been changed to the Frank Sinatra Jr. show. Fortunately, his earlier work more than overwhelms this period and material. —*Ron Wynn*

● **Girl of My Dreams** / Oct. 10, 1959 / Everest 1070

○ **Here Comes Charlie** / Jul. 1960 / Everest 108

○ **Like Charlie** / Oct. 1960-Nov. 1960 / Everest 1127

○ **Charlie Shavers at Le Crazy Horse** / Jun. 1964 / Everest 5225

Artie Shaw (Arthur Jacob Arshawsky)

b. May 23, 1910, New York, NY
Clarinet, bandleader, composer, arranger / Swing, big band
One of the swing era's biggest stars, Shaw was a successful studio musician in New York but hardly known to the public until he performed a number with a string quartet at the first so-called Swing concert in 1936. Later that year he formed his first band,

incorporating the strings; it was a flop, and Shaw reorganized along conventional lines. His playing, however, was anything but conventional; like his archrival Benny Goodman, he was a musical perfectionist, but he didn't emulate Benny—his sound and style on the instrument were his own. A huge hit record, *Begin the Beguine*, launched Shaw to stardom in 1938, but tired of the showbiz nonsense that came with fame, he suddenly disbanded in 1939. To fulfil his record contract he made *Frenesi* with a studio group in 1940 and scored another monster hit. He then reformed his own band, eventually hiring the great black trumpeter and singer Hot Lips Page and featuring strings once again. He enlisted in the Navy in 1942 and led a first-rate service band in the Pacific Theater; in late 1944 he started a new civilian band with Roy Eldridge and a rhythm section with guitarist Barney Kessel and the gifted young pianist Dodo Marmarosa. By 1953 he was leading a sextet that had Hank Jones on piano and Tal Farlow's guitar, but the next year he gave up the clarinet for good. He had already written his autobiography, *The Trouble with Cinderella*, and went on to publish a novel; he also pursued various nonmusical enterprises, including film distribution. In 1983 he again fronted a big band playing his vintage library and some new arrangements; it had Dick Johnson on clarinet, but Shaw was clearly the musical director. The band has performed on and off since then. A highly intelligent, mercurial man (who was married to, among others, Lana Turner and Ava Gardner), Shaw's bands were consistently interesting and often outstandingly so; his own clarinet playing places him at the top of the all-time poll. —*Dan Morgenstern*

★ **Free for All** / i. 1937 / Portrait 44090

☆ **Complete Artie Shaw—Vol. 1: 1938-39, The** / 1938-1939 / RCA 5517

This two-record set contains, in chronological order, all the titles that clarinetist and bandleader Artie Shaw recorded for Victor between July 24, 1938, and January 23, 1939, commencing with "Begin the Beguine" and continuing through "Carioca." —*Bill Gallagher, Cadence*

☆ **Complete Artie Shaw—Vol. 2 (1939)** / 1939 / RCA 5533

The second of seven two-LP sets released by RCA Bluebird in the late 1970s (still the best Artie Shaw series ever) traces Shaw's orchestra throughout 1939, the year that they were the most popular in the land. Among the 32 studio sides are "Deep Purple," "One Night Stand," and "Traffic Jam." In addition to the leader-clarinetist, the main soloists include Georgie Auld on tenor, trumpeter Bernie Privin, and pianist Bob Kitsis, while Helen Forrest and Tony Pastor provide vocals on half of the songs. Shaw would lead stronger orchestras, but this band remains the best loved. —*Scott Yanow*

☆ **Complete Artie Shaw—Vol. 3 (1939-1940)** / 1939-1934 / RCA

The third of seven two-LP sets in Bluebird's definitive Artie Shaw series consists of the last 18 recordings by his very popular 1939 orchestra (riding on the success of "Begin the Beguine"), Shaw's two orchestral sessions of 1940 (recorded after the clarinetist's return from his celebrated flight to Mexico), and three of the four selections performed by his new small group, the Gramercy Five in September 1940. The 1939 orchestra (featuring Georgie Auld's tenor, Buddy Rich's drums, and vocals from Helen Forrest and Tony Pastor) is at its best on "Lady Be Good" and "I Surrender Dear." Artie Shaw's first session after his return yielded his second biggest hit ("Freseni") and some fascinating classical-influenced pieces with a full string section. The initial Gramercy Five date included yet another major bestseller in "Summit Ridge Drive." Artie Shaw just could not avoid success at this time despite his best efforts! —*Scott Yanow*

☆ **Complete Artie Shaw—Vol. 7 (1939-1945)** / 1939-1945 / RCA 5580

The final volume in this definitive series of two-LP sets covers Artie Shaw's 1945 orchestra, a band that boasted the playing of trumpeter Roy Eldridge, pianist Dodo Marmarosa, and guitarist Barney Kessel; all three also joined Shaw and the rhythm section in his Gramercy Five. The band often hints strongly at bop and has moments of excitement, but the end of the swing era brought its demise. All seven volumes in this series should be acquired if they can still be found! —*Scott Yanow*

★ **Complete Gramercy Five Sessions, The** / 1940-1945 / Bluebird 7637

This set marks the first time in at least 20 years or more that the classic small group Gramercy Five . . . material has been available. . . . The playful, sophisticated, and hot interplay between Shaw and his sidemen made this what it is. —*Rich Kienzle, Rock & Roll Disc*

☆ **Complete Artie Shaw—Vol. 4 (1940-1941)** / 1940-1941 / RCA 5572

Of the six main orchestras that Artie Shaw formed and broke up during 1936-1949, his third, the "Stardust" band, was arguably his greatest. He had a strong variety of soloists in trumpeter Billy Butterfield, trombonist Jack Jenney, tenor-saxophonist Jerry Jerome, and pianist Johnny Guarnieri, in addition to a string section. Such arrangers as William Grant Still, Lennie Hayton, Jerry Gray, and Ray Conniff were employed, and the writing was as creative as the solos, with the string section easily uplifting the music instead of weighing it down. The results, as heard on this twofer, include such classics as "Temptation," "Prelude in C Major," "Moonglow," "Love of My Life," and particularly "Concerto for Clarinet" and the best-ever version of "Stardust." As a bonus this set also has five of the eight recordings made by Shaw's original Gramercy Five (with Johnny Guarnieri heard on harpsichord). —*Scott Yanow*

☆ **Complete Artie Shaw—Vol. 5 (1941-1942)** / 1941-1942 / RCA 5576

Despite his success with his "Stardust" band, Artie Shaw broke up the orchestra and took time off in early 1941. This fifth in a highly recommended (but increasingly hard to find) series of two-LP sets documents Shaw's activity during the remainder of 1941. The clarinetist led a very successful if unusual orchestral session with such guests as trumpeter Red Allen, trombonist J.C. Higginbotham, altoist Benny Carter, and singer Lena Horne, and then later in the year formed his fourth big band. The new orchestra had an even larger string section than its predecessor and such alumni as trombonist Jack Jenney, Georgie Auld on tenor, and pianist Johnny Guarnieri, in addition to the great trumpeter-singer Hot Lips Page. Unfortunately Shaw impulsively broke it up shortly after Pearl Harbor, but, as can be heard on this very enjoyable set, it also had a personality of its own. Highpoints include "Blues in the Night," "Beyond the Blue Horizon," "St. James Infirmary Blues," and several classical-oriented pieces. Fascinating if relatively obscure recordings from another of Artie Shaw's great orchestras. —*Scott Yanow*

☆ **Complete Artie Shaw—Vol. 6 (1942-1945)** / 1942-1945 / RCA 5579

The sixth in a seven volume of twofer LPs that reissue all of clarinetist Artie Shaw's recordings for Victor during 1938-1945, after including the last session by his fourth orchestra, concentrates on his fifth big band, a modern swing outfit from 1944-1945 that featured trumpeter Roy Eldridge, pianist Dodo Marmarosa, and guitarist Barney Kessel, among others. Quite a few of the arrangements are memorable; among the classics are Jimmy Mundy's "Lady Day," Eddie Sauter's "Summertime," Buster Harding's "Little Jazz," and Ray Conniff's "'S Wonderful." It is difficult to believe that, with one brief exception, this was Artie Shaw's last regularly working big band. Recommended. —*Scott Yanow*

○ **1949** / 1949 / Music Masters 65026

In 1949 the swing era was already in the past, and the public's enthusiasm for bebop was quickly receding. No matter, Artie Shaw decided that it was time to put together a modern big band. The venture lasted only three months but the largely forgotten music that it performed was quite rewarding. This Musicmasters CD consists of private recordings of the barely documented orchestra, valuable performances that feature the always-modern clarinetist with an outfit that included trumpeter Don Fagerquist, a great saxophone section with the tenors of Al Cohn and Zoot Sims, and guitarist Jimmy Raney. It is a real pleasure to hear Artie Shaw stretching out in this setting and a real pity that this band could not have lasted! —*Scott Yanow*

○ **More Last Recordings** / i. Feb. 1954-Mar. 1954 / Music Masters 65101

The second two-CD set of recordings by Artie Shaw's final Gramercy Five is comparable to the first. Shaw would give up his clarinet permanently shortly after this band broke up, but the musical evidence shows that he was still very much in his prime and growing as an improviser, making his retirement a tragedy for jazz. With pianist Hank Jones, vibraphonist Joe Roland, and

guitarist Tal Farlow contributing strong solos and inspiration for Shaw, this cool bop music (which even has updated performances of "Begin the Beguine," "Frenesi," and "Stardust" that owe surprisingly little to the original hit versions) is quite enjoyable and creative. —*Scott Yanow*

○ **Last Recordings—Vol. 1: Rare and Unreleased, The** / 1954 / Music Masters 65071

The first of two double-CD sets contains a healthy share of the recordings that clarinetist Artie Shaw made with his final Gramercy Five, a unit that included pianist Hank Jones, either Tal Farlow or Joe Puma on guitar and usually Joe Roland's vibes. Unlike his long-time competitor Benny Goodman, Artie Shaw felt perfectly comfortable with younger modernists. In fact his own clarinet playing had evolved through the years, and sometimes he hints strongly at Buddy DeFranco without losing his own musical personality during these 20 performances. This is very rewarding music that makes one especially regret that Artie Shaw chose to give up the clarinet after this band ran its course. —*Scott Yanow*

○ **This Is Artie Shaw—Vols. 1 and 2** / RCA 5096

Fine introductory volume to his RCA/Bluebird output. —*Ron Wynn*

Charles Bobo Shaw ()

b. Sep. 5, 1947, Pope, MS
Drums, leader / Modern creative

An outstanding free drummer who's also able and willing to get funky at any time, Charles "Bobo" Shaw's playing is rhythmically diverse and alternately intense or relaxed, frenetic or steady. Shaw studied drums with Ben Thigpen and briefly doubled on trombone and bass. He was one of the founders of the St. Louis-based Black Artists Group in the '60s. Shaw and other BAG members went to Europe later in the '60s, and Shaw played free jazz in Paris for a year with Anthony Braxton, Steve Lacy, Frank Wright, Alan Silva, and Michel Portal. He returned to St. Louis in the '70s and recorded there with Oliver Lake in 1971. He led the Human Arts Ensemble in the mid-'70s, recording with Lester and Joseph Bowie, Julius Hemphill, Lake, and others. Shaw worked and did sessions with Lester Bowie, Frank Lowe, Hamiett Bluiett, and Lake in the mid-'60s. After touring with the Human Arts Ensemble in Europe during the late '70s, Shaw recorded with Billy Bang in the mid-'80s. He's recorded as a leader for Moers and Black Saint, among others. Shaw has one session currently available on CD. —*Ron Wynn*

● **Bugle Boy Bop** / Feb. 5, 1977 / Muse 5268

Woody Shaw (Woody Herman Shaw II)

b. Dec. 24, 1944, Laurinburg, BC, d. 1989
Trumpet / Hard bop

Trumpeter Woody Shaw was a wonderfully lyrical, sparkling trumpeter who never achieved the kind of widespread recognition or publicity now routinely given to the young lion generation. Shaw was influenced by Clifford Brown, and his solos often took the same aggressive fashion, while his ballad playing had a similarly sensitive, almost innocent fashion. He and Freddie Hubbard had similiarities in their style as well, something very evident when they played together, though each also had his own special tendencies. Shaw began on bugle and switched to trumpet at 11. He played with Willie Bobo and Chick Corea while working with Eric Dolphy in the '60s. Dolphy wanted Shaw to join him in Paris in 1964, but he died before Shaw could leave America. Shaw went on to play with Nathan Davis, Johnny Griffin, and Kenny Clarke, while also recording for London and Berlin. Later came sessions with Jackie McLean, McCoy Tyner, and Andrew Hill, as well as periodic dates with Max Roach and some stints in Broadway orchestras and New York studios. Shaw began heading sterling bands in the '70s, playing with Joe Henderson and signing with Contemporary and Muse. Miles Davis's efforts earned him a deal at Columbia, from which came some wonderful albums that didn't earn enough dollars from the label's perspective to keep Shaw on the roster. Shaw also played in Art Blakey's Jazz Messengers in '71 and '72 and then co-led groups with Bobby Hutcherson and Louis Hayes. He played with Dexter Gordon during Gordon's historic return to America in the '70s. He recorded for Enja, Muse, Timeless, Elektra, and Red in the '80s.—*Ron Wynn*

● **Complete CBS Studio Recordings of Woody Shaw, The** / Mosaic 142

Woody Shaw was among the finest trumpeters in the hard bop tradition, yet he never attained the recognition he earned or deserved. The bulk of his great sessions were recorded for small jazz independents, ensuring them widespread critical evaluation but little audience except with the hardcore faithful. But things seemed about to change in the late '70s when Miles Davis suggested to Columbia that they record Shaw's group. They actually took his suggestion and signed Shaw. He issued a string of remarkable but low-selling records, and Columbia cut him loose after four years and four albums, an eternity for a conglomerate such as Columbia. They compounded the crime by deleting the records shortly after Shaw departed. Mosaic has corrected that slight with another of their marvelously produced and comprehensively notated and packaged boxed sets. This three disc collection covers Shaw's Columbia sessions. . . . While it is sad that Shaw's stay at Columbia was not more personally benefical, it was musically productive. Thanks to Mosaic for returning into circulation great music that its first label could not or would not give the treatment it merited. —*Ron Wynn*

○ **In the Beginning... /** i. 1965 / Muse 5298

Some interesting, uneven, but worth hearing '65 material from trumpeter Woody Shaw. He was still fresh on the jazz scene and had only recently recovered from the death of mentor Eric Dolphy. Shaw played with tenor saxophonist Joe Henderson, pianist Herbie Hancock, and bassists Ron Carter or Paul Chambers on these cuts. His potential certainly emerges, as does the fact that he was a tentative, unsure soloist at this juncture. —*Ron Wynn*

☆ **Blackstone Legacy** / Dec. 8-09, 1970 / Contemporary

☆ **Little Red's Fantasy** / Jun. 29, 1976 / Muse 5103

Shaw was at the top of his game for the '76 Muse date. His tone was rounder, his ideas more developed, his involvement total. That was the real Woody Shaw. Shaw's foil up front was Frank Strozier, a remarkable altoist who deserved to be heard more often. In back, pianist Ronnie Matthews, bassist Stafford James, and drummer Eddie Moore listened and supported with tasteful zest. . . . Whether on a tough burner like "Tomorrow's Destiny," a gritty bossa like "Sashianova," or a reflective outing like "Jean Marie," the ensemble and solos here crackled with emotion, drama, and virtuosity. —*Chuck Berg, Downbeat*

○ **Woody Shaw Concert Ensemble at the Berliner Jazztage** / Nov. 6, 1976 / Muse 5139

Trumpeter Woody Shaw and drummer Louis Hayes worked together in a dynamic quintet during the mid-'70s that also included the considerable talents of reedman Rene McLean, pianist Ronnie Mathews, and bassist Stafford James. For the 1976 Berlin Jazz Festival, however, Shaw augmented the quintet by adding the voices of saxophonist Frank Foster and trombonist Slide Hampton. The result was a dynamic set of performances that attested to Shaw's growth as both a player and an arranger. —*Chuck Berg, Down Beat*

★ **Rosewood** / Dec. 15-19, 1977 / CBS

This album offered the two presentational modes Woody Shaw worked with for four years during the '70s. The first of these was the quintet. This, however, was the *new* five-piece dynamo featuring saxophonist Carter Jefferson, pianist Onaje Allan Gumbs, bassist Clint Houston, and drummer Victor Lewis. Their compact intensity made the brisk "Rahsaan's Run" and tasty "Theme for Maxine" tautly coiled forays. For the other tracks it was the Woody Shaw Concert Ensemble. . . . Overall, *Rosewood* presented contemporary acoustic playing at its best. —*Chuck Berg, Down Beat*

Stepping Stones / Aug. 5-06, 1978 / Columbia

This is as fine a major-label jazz album as possible in the late '70s. —*Ron Wynn*

Woody III / 1978 / Columbia

Third consecutive wonderful album for Columbia, which responded by cutting him loose. —*Ron Wynn*

☆ **Night Music** / i. 1984 / Elektra 60299

This album was the second one culled from a 1982 recording session at the Jazz Forum in New York City, with Bobby Hutcherson featured as a "guest artist.". . . Trumpeter Woody Shaw's distinctive music mixed elements of bebop and modal playing into a style

that might be called "modern mainstream.". . . The three originals here—one each by Shaw, trombonist Steve Turre, and pianist Mulgrew Miller—were all taken at somewhat relentless tempos, and the solos sounded like a relay race after a while. "All the Things You Are" finally slowed the pace and gave Shaw a chance to develop some of his darkly glowing, lyrical lines. —*Jim Roberts, Down Beat*

George Shearing (George Albert Shearing)

b. Aug. 13, 1919, London, England
Piano / Bop, cool, Latin-jazz

Among England's most distinguished jazz pianists, Shearing studied classical piano at a school for the blind, and learned jazz from hearing records. He started playing professionally in the late '30s with the Ambrose dance band and appeared at hotels and did radio work while playing with Harry Parry and Stephane Grappelli in the early '40s. Shearing left London for America in 1946 and settled here permanently in 1947. He formed a quintet using vibes, guitar, bass, drums, and piano in 1949 and it was an extremely popular, extensively recorded group until 1967. The Shearing style, which incorporates elements of boogie-woogie, bop, Latin, and even blues and gospel, plus a tasteful use of block chords and unison lines, has retained its popularity for many decades. During the '70s, '80s, and '90s Shearing has led trios and duos and made some acclaimed recordings with vocalists Carmen McRae and Mel Torme, with his 1983 date winning a Grammy. Shearing's vintage sessions with Nat King Cole, Dakota Staton, and Nancy Wilson have begun reappearing via reissues. —*Ron Wynn*

○ **Lullaby of Birdland** / i. 194z / Polydor 827977

His classic and best-known cuts, plus lots of other seminal music in this 1986 reissue of late '40s and '50s material. —*Ron Wynn*

★ **I Hear Music** / i. 1952 / Metro 534

★ **George Shearing and the Montgomery Bros.** / Oct. 9-10, 1961 / Original Jazz Classics 40

Recorded 10/9-10, 1961, this had pianist George Shearing joining the Montgomery Brothers (guitarist Wes, vibist Buddy, and bassist Monk) and Walter Perkins (drums, plus Latin percussion). —*Bob Rusch, Cadence*

★ **Nat King Cole Sings / Shearing Plays** / i. 1961 / Capitol

○ **Reunion, The** / Apr. 11, 1976 / PA/USA 7049

A wonderful duo release from '76 with pianist George Shearing collaborating with violinist Stephane Grappelli. Shearing's sessions are usually more introspective and light than upbeat and hot, but Grappelli's soaring, exuberant violin solos seem to put a charge into Shearing, who responds with some of his hotter playing in many years. —*Ron Wynn*

○ **Two for the Road** / Jun. 1980 / Concord Jazz 4128

W/ George Shearing. Shearing (p) is smooth. McRae's hot at times and reflective or probing at others. —*Ron Wynn*

★ **Alone Together** / Mar. 1981 / Concord Jazz 4171

With these two players it should be almost unnecessary to say that this album represents a thoroughly relaxed, tasteful, and professionally executed set. —*Per Husby, Cadence*

☆ **Breakin' Out** / May 1987 / Concord Jazz 4335

Marvin "Smitty" Smith's chuckling drums bring out fresh qualities and rhythmic verve in old master Shearing. —*Ron Wynn*

○ **I Hear a Rhapsody—Live at the Blue Note** / i. 1992 / Telarc 83310

Jack Sheldon

b. Nov. 30, 1931, Jacksonville, FL
Trumpet, bandleader, comedian / Bop, cool

West Coast trumpeter Jack Sheldon was quite active in the '50s West Coast scene. Due to his comic, flashy personality, some forget his '50s recordings in which he displayed a vibrant, sometimes exciting approach and good technique, though he wasn't an adventurous soloist. —*Ron Wynn*

★ **Stand by for Jack Sheldon** / Mar. 1983 / Concord Jazz 229

Listeners to this recording may perhaps discern some Chet Baker in the way of a wistful tone (or some early Miles Davis, for that matter) but they would be hard pressed to find other comparisons except with Sheldon's own work. —*Shirley Klett, Cadence*

Archie Shepp (Archie Vernon Shepp)

b. May 24, 1937, Fort Lauderdale, FL

Sax / Hard bop, early free, modern creative

Once the embodiment of the free, experimental, and often enraged generation, Archie Shepp has evolved into one of the revered and respected elders of jazz. Shepp studied piano, clarinet, and alto as a child before switching to tenor and soprano. He worked as a teen in R&B bands, and many attribute his fondness for poetic inclusions and spoken monologs in his music to the fact that Shepp has a degree in drama. Shepp worked with Cecil Taylor in 1960 and then got involved with Bill Dixon and a short-lived but excellent group called the New York Contemporary Five, with John Tchicai and Don Cherry. Shepp later worked and recorded with John Coltrane and had a series of albums in the '60s on Impulse that featured lengthy, spiraling solos, slashing rhythms, and Black Nationalist themes. In the '70s and '80s, Shepp's playing, which always had a swing-mainstream grounding, became warmer and often more engaging, though he could still offer furious lines and phrases when so moved. But his best work in the '70s and '80s has been in a bluesy or ballad setting, where his thick, lush tone, and sentimental side are best presented. His more stark Impulse releases are being slowly reissued. —*Ron Wynn*

○ New York Contemporary 5 in Europe / i. 1963 / Delmark 9409
Originally released by Delmark in 1967, this recording came about from an agreement with Sonet Records (1979), which recorded the New York Contemporary Five in 1962 at the Jazzhus Montmarte. . . . There really was no call for releasing this under his name, for he had no more solo space than anyone else. Besides the NYCF was a cooperative unit in the strictest sense of the term. Terry Martin's usual well-thought-out and informative liner notes placed this short-lived group in the proper historical perspective while giving the music a brief interpretation. At turns the music was sloppy, powerful, imperfect, moving, irritating—but always alive and distinctly human. —*Carl Brauer, Cadence*

★ Four for Trane / Aug. 10, 1964 / Impulse 71

New Thing at Newport / Jul. 2, 1965 / Impulse 97

Live in San Francisco / Feb. 19, 1966 / Impulse
Includes some wonderful trombone by Roswell Redd, intense Shepp solos. —*Ron Wynn*

★ Magic of Ju-Ju / Apr. 26, 1967 / Impulse

○ Live at the Donaueschingen Music Festival / Oct. 21, 1967 / Saba 15148

○ In Europe / i. Jun. 1968 / Delmark 409
Some brilliant moments and some uncertain, tentative sections on this late '60s work recorded in Europe by tenor saxophonist Archie Shepp. He was working with the New York Contemporary Five, a brilliant band that didn't stay together long because it had absolutely no commercial future. The songs were played with fire and intensity. Besides Shepp, trumpeter Don Cherry and alto saxophonist John Tchicai were outstanding. —*Ron Wynn*

○ Three for a Quarter: One for a Dime / i. Sep. 1969 / Impulse 9162

○ Live at the Pan-African Festival / i. 196? / Affinity
Archie Shepp probably led more BYG recordings than anyone else. The first of his BYG's has been reissued as *Live at the Pan African Festival*. The Pan African Festival in Algiers served as a great realization of art and culture for many of the participants, and on this recording we heard Shepp, Clifford Thornton, and Grachan Moncur III in an impromptu jam ("Brotherhood at Ketcha") with various native Algerian percussionists and "horn" men. . . . Any study of Shepp makes listening to all of his BYG recordings essential. —*Bob Rusch, Cadence*

○ Kwanza / i. 1974 / Impulse 9262
This album showed once again why tenor saxophonist Archie Shepp deserved to be regarded as one of the leaders of the avant-garde. The beat on all these compositions was distinctively and repetively enunciated in a manner that was often rocklike. In fact, until he soloed you'd swear you were listening to yet another anonymous jazz-rock band. Despite the dangers inherent in heavy and repetitious beat enunciation, Shepp and his partners made that element a *constituent* of the compositions. And their solos as well as the ensemble section were as "out" as if they were

played on top of beats only arbitrarily insinuated. —*Gordon Kopulous, Down Beat*

Steam / May 14, 1976 / Enja

★ Goin' Home / Apr. 25, 1977 / Steeple Chase
Tenor and soprano saxophonist Archie Shepp and pianist Horace Parlan recorded this selection of traditional spirituals in a reverential yet contemporary context. The repertoire was a familiar one, as familiar as "Swing Low, Sweet Chariot" and "Go Down Moses," but Archie Shepp did his best to kindle the spark of spontaneity, even in the hoariest classics. —*Larry Birnbaum, Down Beat*

On Green Dolphin Street / Nov. 28, 1977 / Denon 7262

Duo Reunion / i. 1979 / L & R Music 5003
W/ Horace Parlan. One of the better, more moving sax-piano duos of the '70s reunites effectively. —*Ron Wynn*

☆ Attica Big Band / i. 1979 / Inner City 1001

☆ Trouble in Mind / Feb. 6, 1980 / Steeple Chase 31139

Soul Song / Dec. 1, 1982 / Enja 4050
W/ Ken Werner (p), Santi Di Briano (b), Smitty Smith (d). Powerful statement. —*Michael G. Nastos*

Splashes (Tribute to Wilbur Little) / May 1987 / L & R Music 5005
Bluesy, aggressive, typically expressive. W/ Horace Parlan (p), Harry Emmery (b), and Clifford Jarvis (d). —*Ron Wynn*

Sahib Shihab (Edmund Gregory)

b. Jun. 23, 1925, Savannah, GA

Alto sax, baritone sax, soprano sax, flute / Bop

A strong baritone player and above-average alto soloist who's also added soprano and flute to his arsenal in recent years, Sahib got his initial experience working in territory bands and went to Boston from Georgia in 1941 for formal music studies. He toured with Fletcher Henderson in 1944-1945 on alto and was a member of the Roy Eldridge band in 1946. He went to New York in 1947, and worked with Art Blakey, Thelonious Monk, and Tadd Dameron for the remainder of the '40s and the early '50s. Shihab resurfaced in 1953, playing baritone with Dizzy Gillespie. Baritone proved his best instrument. His sturdy tone; facility in both the upper and lower registers; and ability to play with speed, clarity, and distinction on uptempo and slow pieces distinguished him as a premier baritone stylist. During the '50s Shihab worked with Illinois Jacquet, Oscar Pettiford's big band, Dakota Staton, and Quincy Jones's orchestra, plus led his own group. He settled in Europe following a Jones tour in 1959-1960 and remained there 12 years, becoming a regular member of the Kenny Clarke-Francy Boland Big Band from 1961 to 1972. His prime recordings for Savoy and Chess have begun turning up as reissues. —*Ron Wynn*

● All Star Sextets / Jul. 11, 1957-Sep. 7, 1957 / Savoy 2245
This excellent reissue spotlights great groups Sahib worked with in the late '50s. Phil Woods (as), Bill Evans (p), others on hand. —*Ron Wynn*

Wayne Shorter

b. Aug. 25, 1933, Newark, NJ

Tenor sax, soprano sax, composer / Bop

Tenor and soprano saxophonist Wayne Shorter's among the greats of his generation. His deftly articulated, thoughtful tenor solos were impressive from his days as a leader on Vee-Jay and his tenure in Art Blakey's Jazz Messengers, where he served as music director. Shorter was in Miles Davis's great mid-'60s group and also in the early electric band, where he began doubling on soprano. Shorter later co-led arguably the last great jazz-rock band of the '70s, Weather Report with Joe Zawinul. Until he and Zawinul tired of the pace and began having conflicts, Weather Report was an unpredictable, musically exciting unit that knew how to mix jazz sophistication and rock-pop-funk energy. Shorter's also made some fine Afro-Latin recordings, working with Milton Nascimento and Djavan, among others. He was instrumental in helping discover and get work for drummer Terri Lyne Carrington in the late '80s, and though his most recent material lacks the distinction of his prior work, he remains always capable of tasteful, intelligent, and striking music.—*Ron Wynn*

☆ Blues e la Carte / i. Nov. 10, 1959 / Affinity

★ **Some Other Stuff** / Jul. 6, 1964 / Blue Note 84177
Red-hot dates, with Moncur and Wayne Shorter (sax) swapping licks and keying the session. —*Ron Wynn*

○ **JuJu** / Aug. 3, 1964 / Blue Note 46514
His best single album composition. The playing is extraordinary. With McCoy Tyner (p). —*Michael G. Nastos*

Night Dreamer / Aug. 3, 1964 / Blue Note 84173
1988 reissue of prime '60s lineup: Lee Morgan (tpt), McCoy Tyner (p), Reggie Workman (b), Elvin Jones (d). —*Ron Wynn*

☆ **Speak No Evil** / Dec. 24, 1964 / Blue Note 46509

○ **Best of Wayne Shorter** / 1964-1967 / Blue Note 91141
A very well done compilation. Good for beginners and aficionados. —*Michael G. Nastos*

☆ **Etcetera / i.** Jun. 4, 1965 / Blue Note 1056
As with so many of these Blue Note discoveries, the question naturally arises: Why wasn't this music issued soon after it was recorded in 1964? No doubt the answer lies in Wayne Shorter's prolificacy back then, for he led one fine recording session after another, and particularly in Grachan Moncur III's *Some Other Stuff* (recorded soon after *Etcetera*), tested again the limits of his mastery. In general, these musicians' triumph was twofold. —*John Litweiler, Down Beat*

★ **Adam's Apple** / Feb. 24, 1966 / Blue Note 46403
This is a galloping romp, one of Shorter's best '60s dates. Great record. —*Ron Wynn*

Super Nova / Aug. 29, 1969+Sep. 2, 1969 / Blue Note 84332
1988 reissue of careening, eventful date; has Chick Corea (k), John McLaughin (g), Jack DeJohnette (d). —*Ron Wynn*

☆ **Odyssey of Iska** / Aug. 26, 1970 / Blue Note 84363
An album that is alternately daring and sentimental. Wonderful soprano solos. —*Ron Wynn*

★ **Native Dancer** / Dec. 1974 / Columbia 46159

Alan Silva

b. 1939
Bass, cello / Early free, modern creative
A consistently strong acompanist and bassist, Alan Silva played on several recordings during the '60s and '70s, working with many top groups and players. He's a strong soloist, particularly with the bow, and an assertive stylist. Silva studied piano and violin in his youth and later attended the New York College of Music. He began playing bass in the early '60s. Silva teamed with Burton Greene in the Free Form Improvisation Ensemble and participated in the October Revolution in Jazz concert series. He played with Cecil Taylor, Sun Ra, Albert Ayler, Sunny Murray, and Archie Shepp in the late '60s and early '70s before settling in Europe. Silva formed the Celestrial Communication Orchestra, a group with rotating personnel, and also played with Frank Wright, Bobby Few, and Muhammad Ali (drums). He lived and worked in both Paris and New York during the '70s and '80s, playing and recording with Taylor, Bill Dixon, Andrew Hill, and the Globe Unity Orchestra. He recorded as a leader for BYG and Sun. Silva has no sessions available as a leader but can be heard on Taylor and Ayler CD reissues. —*Ron Wynn*

● **Seasons** / Dec. 29, 1970 / BYG 529342

Horace Silver (Horace Ward Martin Tavares Silver)

b. Sep. 2, 1928, Norwalk, CT
Piano, bandleader, composer / Hard bop
Hard bop's greatest composer and an all-time jazz great as a pianist, Horace Silver continues making music into the '90s. No one's ever blended gospel, blues, jazz, and Caribbean elements in a more inspired manner. Silver was a founding member of Art Blakey's Jazz Messengers and crafted many releases that were widely popular while also being musically challenging. Some premier compositions include "Song for My Father," "The Preacher," Doodlin'," and "Sister Sadie." The list of great players who've been in his bands includes Joe Henderson, Carmell Jones, Stanley Turrentine, Randy Brecker, Kenny Dorham, and many others. Though his constant desire to write lyrics has sometimes resulted in less-than-memorable, pop-tinged works, Silver's also issued so many classics no one counts the occasional stumbles. He was on Blue Note for over 25 years but in later years issued material on either independents or his own label. Silver signed

with Columbia in the early '90s, and *You've Got to Be Funky* was released in 1993. He remains a compelling player. —*Ron Wynn*

Horace Silver Trio—Vol. 1: Spotlight on Drums / Oct. 23, 1952 / Capitol 81520
Most Silver albums are with a mid-'60s combo (quintet etc.). It is refreshing and clarifying to listen to his trio work. Includes the classic "Opus De Funk." —*Michael Erlewine*

★ **Best of Horace Silver—Vol. 1** / 1953-1959 / Blue Note 91143
The Blue Note Years Vol 1 & 2. Excellent compilation on CD. Two volumes. —*Michael G. Nastos*

○ **Horace Silver and the Jazz Messengers** / Nov. 13, 1954 / Capitol 46140
Horace Silver and the Jazz Messengers contains a lot of memorable music. Some of the melodies here have been overdone ("Doodlin'," "The Preacher"), while some others ("Room 608," Hank Mobley's "Hippy") deserve wider exposure. Yet this tight-knit quintet of stars sounded *so* good on almost everything! Kenny Dorham (trumpet), Hank Mobley (tenor sax), Horace Silver (piano), and Doug Watkins (bass) all benefitted substantially from the association. —*Bob Porter, Jazz Times*

★ **Six Pieces of Silver** / Nov. 10, 1956 / Blue Note 81539
Quintet. Hard-bop, gospel-tinged jazz gem. 1988 reissue, CD has three bonus cuts. —*Ron Wynn*

○ **Sterling Silver** / Nov. 10, 1956-Jan. 28, 1964 / Blue Note 945
Sterling Silver was a classic compilation of previously unissued (at least on LP) material from the period 1956 through 1964, selected by Horace Silver himself. Featuring mainly the Blue Mitchell, Junior Cook, Gene Taylor, Roy Brooks, Silver quintet, the album spotlighted Silver on piano, demonstrating again that feeling and taste need not take a back seat to technical bravura. —*Larry Birnbaum, Down Beat*

Finger Poppin' with the Horace Silver Quintet / Feb. 1, 1959 / Blue Note 84008
W/ The Horace Silver Quintet. State-of-the-art late '50s Silver gospel, Caribbean-influenced jazz. —*Ron Wynn*

Blowin' the Blues Away / Aug. 10, 1959 / Blue Note 46526
Standout Silver jazz-cum-blues and gospel from the late '50s, 1985 reissue. —*Ron Wynn*

Horace-Scope / Jul. 9, 1960 / Blue Note 84042
Quintet. 1990 reissue of another Silver masterpiece. Includes the famous piece "Nica's Dream." —*Ron Wynn*

Doin' the Thing (At the Village Gate) / May 19-20, 1961 / Blue Note 84076
Quintet. 1989 reissue of standard live set with Silver super, Blue Mitchell (tpt), Junior Cook (ts) in the groove. —*Ron Wynn*

● **Song for My Father** / Oct. 26, 1963+Oct. 1964 / Blue Note 84185
Silver's most successful and popular album. Includes three additional tracks. Two sessions, two different bands. Aside from famous title track, includes quintet and trio versions of "Que Pasa." Essential —*Michael Erlewine*

★ **Cape Verdean Blues** / Oct. 1-22, 1965 / Blue Note 84220
By late 1965 Horace Silver's quintet featured trumpeter Woody Shaw and tenor-saxophonist Joe Henderson, and, on half of this set, the great trombonist i.i. Johnson sits in. "The Cape Verdean Blues," "Pretty Eyes," and Henderson's "mo' Joe" are among the highlights of this high-quality set of funky hard bop by one of the pacesetting groups. —*Scott Yanow*

☆ **Serenade to a Soul Sister** / Feb. 23, 1968+Apr. 29, 1968 / Blue Note 84277
One of the final classic albums by the Horace Silver quintet, this set finds Silver using such sidemen as trumpeter Charles Tolliver, either Stanley Turrentine or Bennie Maupin on tenors, and, on half of the tracks, the young drummer Billy Cobham. The six Silver compositions include "Psychedelic Sally" and "Serenade to a Soul Sister." This music is both timeless and very much of the period. —*Scott Yanow*

☆ **In Pursuit of the 27th Man** / Oct. 6, 1972+Nov. 10, 1972 / Blue Note 054
Quintet. 1969-1970 recording with the Brecker Brothers (sax & tpt). Very good. —*Michael G. Nastos*

☆ **Silver 'n Percussion** / Nov. 12-30, 1977 / Blue Note 853
On this album pianist-composer Horace Silver mixed African and Native American chants with his own distinctive sound and style. It was a highly successful mix, coupling jazz, the American folk

form, and the stylized folk traditions of tribal music. The voices established theme and feeling for each piece, but it was the playing of tenor saxophonist Larry Schneider, trumpet and flugelhorn player Tom Harrell, Silver, bassist Ron Carter, and drummer Al Foster that was the dominant factor. This was music of exceptional quality and imagination, another variation on the Horace Silver style—straightahead, cooking, and occasionally funky. — *Herb Nolan, Down Beat*

Omer Simeon (Omer Victor Simeon)

b. Jul. 21, 1902, New Orleans, LA., **d.** Sep. 17, 1959, New York, NY
Clarinet / New Orleans traditional

Omer Simeon was another early clarinetist skilled in lower-register solos, as well as being a warm, often delightful improviser in the traditional style. Simeon began to play clarinet when his family moved from New Orleans to Chicago in 1914. Lorenzo Tio, Jr. gave him lessons from 1918 to 1920. Simeon played in his brother Al's band briefly, then worked with Charlie Elgar's Creole Orchestra in Chicago and Milwaukee in the mid- and late '20s. He recorded with Jelly Roll Morton in 1926 and was featured on "Black Bottom Stomp." Simeon joined King Oliver in 1927, touring with him in St. Louis and New York. He also worked with Luis Russell in New York and recorded with Morton again in 1928. Simeon worked in Chicago with Erskine Tate in the late '20s and early '30s and with Earl Hines in the early and mid-'30s, Horace Henderson in 1938, Walter Fuller in 1940, and Coleman Hawkins in 1941. He became a member of Jimmie Lunceford's orchestra in 1942. Simeon also recorded with Kid Ory in 1944 and 1945 in Hollywood. He stayed with the Lunceford band after the leader's death until 1950 and then worked in New York the remainder of his life. Simeon played and recorded with Wilbur de Paris from 1951 until 1959. He made a few recordings as a leade, mostly for Brunswick. Simeon was featured on Victor, Crescent, and Atlantic, working with Morton, Jimmie Noone, and de Paris, among others. He has one CD of vintage recordings available on CD, though others can probably be obtained via import. Simeon can also be heard on Morton reissues. —*Ron Wynn*

● **Omer Simeon Trio with James P. Johnson / i.** 195? / Disc 748

Zoot Sims (John Haley Sims)

b. Oct. 29, 1925, Inglewood, CA, **d.** 1985, New York, NY
Tenor sax, bandleader / Cool

The California-born Sims made his debut in 1941 and played with various "name" bands, including Benny Goodman's, until he was drafted. He briefly rejoined Goodman but made his mark with his next leader, Woody Herman; in this band, he struck up a friendship with fellow tenorist Al Cohn that would last for life and result in wonderful music whenever they got together. Sims toured frequently with Jazz at the Philharmonic, was often hired by Goodman for various gigs, including the famous tour of the Soviet Union (1962), and freelanced in clubs and on records in a variety of settings. No matter what the surroundings, Sims was consistently swinging and inventive; the music just seemed to flow from him in the most natural way, and he never played a meretricious note. —*Dan Morgenstern*

★ **Brother in Swing / Jun. 26, 1950 / Inner City 7005**
This was a Jazz Legacy album in 1950. Recorded by a quartet with Gerald Wiggins on piano, Pierre Michelot on bass, and Kenny Clarke on drums. Great rhythm section stokes Sims's fire. Album includes five Sims originals, some with alternate takes. It was recorded in Paris, and the liner notes by Herb Wong are very informative. —*Michael G. Nastos*

○ **Zootcase / Sep. 16, 1950+Jul. 16, 1954 / Prestige 24061**
While not greatly exciting, these sesssions do swing well throughout, and the variety of groups backing Sims (there are four) makes for some useful comparisons. —*Joel Ray, Cadence*

☆ **Zoot! / Oct. 12, 1956 / Riverside 228**
The arrangements of George Handy made their mark on *Zoot*, a December 1956 recording under the leadership of Zoot Sims and also nicely featuring the reaching trumpet work of Nick Travis. Unfortunately, here the arrangements tend to diminish and hold in check the essential *zootness* which Sims blew so well. —*Bob Rusch, Cadence*

○ **Zoot Sims Plays Four Altos / Jan. 11, 1957 / Paramount 198**
Zoot Sims Plays 4 Altos was not from the Impulse catalog but a multitracked ABC date of 1/11/57. The material here was all by

George Handy and its construction was very similiar to another Handy-Sims collaboration of November 1956. To further confuse things, MCA put the liners, personnel, and dates to that record on this record. Both dates had Knobby Totah (bass), while the '57 date had Handy (piano) and Nick Stabulas (drums) rounding out the quartet. The novelty to this date was the multitracking of Sims on four altos; the earlier date had him on tenors and baritone as well. —*Bob Rusch, Cadence*

★ **Down Home / Jul. 1960 / Bethlehem 6051**
Down Home, recorded in 1970, with bassist George Tucker, drummer Dannie Richmond, and pianist Dave McKenna, was widely considered to be one of Sims's strongest efforts. He was in a jouncier swing of mind here than on the Booker Ervin *The Book Cooks* album, shaking the tail of his notes firmly but lovingly, and emoting hardest in his gossamer upper range, where he pushed his tone as close as one could get to brittle and still stay safe. —*Mikal Gilmore, Down Beat*

○ **Zoot Plays Soprano / Jan. 8-09, 1976 / Pablo 770**
A masterpiece, perhaps the best single record Zoot Sims made for Pablo. He'd never done a full record on soprano only, so the idea resulted in him really extending himself and exploring the instrument rather than just treating it as an alternative voice. His rhythm section, with pianist Ray Bryant, bassist George Mraz, and drummer Grady Tate, responded as well. —*Ron Wynn*

○ **Hawthorne Nights / Sep. 20-21, 1976 / Pablo 783**
Tenor saxophonist Zoot Sims recorded almost constantly for the Pablo label in the '70s, the final phase of his career. This was a pleasant session with Sims heading a mid-sized band playing charts provided by Bill Holman. There weren't any fireworks, but Sims played with his usual mix of blues and swing, and the backing band gave him enough support to keep things interesting. — *Ron Wynn*

★ **Just Friends / Dec. 18+20, 1978 / Pablo 499**

Sirone

b. 1940
Bass / Early free, modern creative

Once a member of the Revolutionary Ensemble along with Leroy Jenkins and Jerome Cooper, Sirone is a first-rate bassist, either as an accompanist or a soloist, playing with the bow or his fingers. He played with Cecil Taylor after the Ensemble disbanded. —*Ron Wynn*

○ **Artistry / Jul. 5, 1978 / Of The Cosmos 801**
On this, his first recording since the dissolution of the Revolutionary Ensemble, bassist Sirone attempted to surround himself with a familiarly constructed ensemble consisting of a companion string instrument and experienced members of the new musicianship. . . . It was clear throughout that Sirone was in search of another string partner with whom to renew the empathetic relationship he had with RE violinist Leroy Jenkins—the comparison was unfortunate, but unavoidable. —*Brent Staples, Down Beat*

★ **Live / Jul. 11, 1980 / Serious 1000**

Jabbo Smith (Cladys Smith)

b. Dec. 24, 1908, Pembroke, GA, **d.** Jan. 16, 1991
Trumpet, trombone / Swing, big band

One of the '20s greatest and most exceptional trumpeters who was gifted with exemplary all-round skills, Jabbo Smith possessed great range and wonderful tone. He was a fine singer and could play both striking uptempo tunes and nicely evocative ballads. Smith played longer and more complex lines than most trumpeters during the late '20s and was among the most advanced musicians of his day. He was also a decent trombonist and pianist. Smith learned music at the Jenkins Orphanage in Charleston. He was a professional at 16, and worked in the mid- and late '20s in Charlie Johnson's band. He recorded with Duke Ellington's orchestra in 1927, soloing on "Black and Tan Fantasy." Smith toured with James P. Johnson in *Keep Shufflin'* in 1928 and then worked in Chicago during the late '20s and early '30s with Carroll Dickerson, Earl Hines, Erskine Tate, Charlie Elgar, Tiny Parham, and Fess Williams. He also led his own bands in the Midwest. Smith played with Claude Hopkins's band in the late '30s and led his own groups in the '40s. He cut back his appearances to only part-time after that, but received universally positive notices for his appearance in the show *One Mo' Time* during the '70s. He continued to appear as a vocalist in the '80s, despite erratic health. He appeared at festivals in 1983 and 1986. Smith currently has only one selection available on CD. *—Ron Wynn*

★ **Jabbo Smith—Vol. 1** / **i.** Mar. 1928-Feb. 1929 / Retrieval 131
☆ **Jabbo Smith—Vol. 2** / **i.** Mar. 1929-Feb. 1938 / Retrieval 132
○ **Jazz Heritage—Ace of Rhythm** / 1929 / MCA 1347
○ **Sweet 'n' Lowdown** / **i.** Mar. 1987 / Affinity 1029

Jimmy Smith (James Oscar Smith)

b. Dec. 8, 1925, Norristown, PA
Organ / Postbop, soul-jazz
Hammond organist Jimmy Smith is one of the greatest instrumentalists in jazz history. He revolutionized the sound of the Hammond organ in 1955 and began recording for Blue Note the following year. His Blue Note period (1956-1963) is highly recommended, although his jam-session recordings contain lengthy solos by players who are sometimes not up to the task. Any collaborations with Kenny Burrell are among his finest work. There are many trio recordings with guitar and drums and only the length of some tracks brings down the overall rating for Smith in this setting. His Verve period (1963-1972) tends to find him with big-band backing more often than not, but these recordings were some of the biggest-selling albums (regardless of the type of music) in the '60s. Especially memorable are Oliver Nelson's arrangements for Smith. As with the Blue Note recordings, the Verve period is all recommended until 1968. After that, Smith begins to flirt with rock music and in general there is a long downhill slide throughout much of the '70s. A return to Blue Note in 1985 brought a welcome return to jazz and those recordings plus his sessions for Milestone in 1991 can compare with some of his best work from the '50s and early '60s. *—Bob Porter*

New Sound, a New Star, A / Feb. 13+18, 1956 / Blue Note 1512
Recorded in New York. This is his debut album with his original trio. *—Michael Erlewine*

☆ **Greatest Hits—Vol. 1** / Mar. 27, 1956-Feb. 8, 1963 / Blue Note 89901
○ **Best of Jimmy Smith, The** / Feb. 12, 1957-Jan. 3, 1986 / Blue Note 91140
1958-1986. Small group setting. Selections from some of Smith's best Blue Note albums, such as: *The Sermon, Go For Whatcha Know, Midnight Special, Back at the Chicken Shack, A New Sound,* and *At the Organ. —Michael Erlewine*

Jimmy Smith at the Organ—Vol. 1: All Day Long / Feb. 12, 1957 / Blue Note 81551
W/ K. Burrell (g), Art Blakey (d), Donaldson (as). Bluesy, yet driving. *—Hank Davis*

Jimmy Smith at the Organ—Vol. 2 / Feb. 13, 1957 / Blue Note 1552
○ **House Party** / Aug. 25, 1957 / Blue Note 46546
W/ Tina Brooks (ts), Lee Morgan (tpt), Kenny Burrell (g), Art Blakey (d). Mid-sized band. All up-tempo pieces. Studio jam session for nonregular sideman. With this many sidemen, the group is a little too large for that classic Smith sound. *—Michael Erlewine*

Confirmation / Aug. 25, 1957+Feb. 25, 1958 / Blue Note 992
Smith has the best playing companions. Art Blakey (d) contains himself . . . playing a subdued and excellent supportive role. Kenny Burrell's solo work . . . on "Cherokee" are heavy highlights . . . Lee Morgan (tpt) makes this album essential. . . . Bop lovers have to have this. *—Jerry L. Atkins, Cadence*

★ **Groovin' at Small's Paradise—Vols. 1 and 2** / Nov. 14+18, 1957 / Blue Note 1586
● **Sermon** / Feb. 25, 1958 / Blue Note 46097
Recorded in Manhattan Towers, NY. Small group. Studio jam sessions (also two from August 25, 1957) featuring Lou Donaldson (sax), Lee Morgan (tpt), Kenny Burrell (g) that produced this album, *Houseparty,* and *Confirmation. —Michael Erlewine*

☆ **Cool Blues** / Apr. 7, 1958 / Blue Note 84441
Live album at the legendary Harlem club Small's Paradise—where Smith was first discovered by Blue Note in 1956. Mono recordings with Tina Brooks and Lou Donaldson. *—Michael Erlewine*

Home Cookin' / 1958-1959 / Blue Note 84050
Recorded at Hackensack, NJ. Trio recording. Bluesy, intense. Nice title track, good soul-jazz set. *—Ron Wynn*

☆ **Crazy! Baby** / Jan. 4, 1960 / Blue Note 84030
Recorded at Englewood Cliffs, NJ. Classic Smith trio. Includes hit single "When Johnny Comes Marching Home." *—Michael Erlewine*

Open House / Plain Talk / Mar. 22, 1960 / Blue Note 84269
Recorded at Hackensack, NJ. Studio session featuring Blue Mitchell (tpt), Ike Quebec (ts), and Jackie McClean (as). This is essentially a jam session without Smith's regular sidemen. More mainstream than most, but very nice tracks—fast and slow. This is an excellent album. *—Michael Erlewine*

★ **Back at the Chicken Shack** / Apr. 25, 1960 / Blue Note 46402
○ **Midnight Special** / Apr. 25, 1960 / Blue Note 84078
Recorded at Englewood Cliffs, NJ. Small group. This was recorded at the same session as *Back at the Chicken Shack,* and it is almost as fine—that is, magical! This is a must-have for jazz organ fans. W/ Stanley Turrentine (ts). *—Michael Erlewine*

Bashin' the Unpredictable Jimmy Smith / Mar. 26+28, 1962 / Verve 823308
Debut session for Verve, his first with big-band backing. Featuring Oliver Nelson, his orchestra, and "Walk on the Wild Side" (a hit single). Smith's first album with a bass player! Three cuts are with small combo. *—Michael Erlewine*

☆ **Prayer Meetin'** / Feb. 8, 1963 / Blue Note 84164
With Stanley Turrentine. Fine Album. Small group. Smith's last Blue Note album until 1986 (*Go for Whatcha Know*). Also, last two cuts from June 13, 1960, were released in Japan on the album *Special Guests. —Michael Erlewine*

Cat, The / Apr. 27-29, 1964 / Verve 810046
Recorded at Englewood Cliffs, NJ. Large band. Conducted and arranged by Lalo Schifrin. This is perhaps his best-known album featuring the big-band sound. A Grammy Award winner. *—Michael Erlewine*

☆ **Organ Grinder Swing** / Jun. 14-15, 1965 / Verve 825675
Recorded at Englewood Cliffs, NJ. W/ Kenny Burrell (g). Trio album by Smith after much big-band success. This is reminiscent of Smith's early small-combo work. In other words, he cooks on this one. *—Michael Erlewine*

Got My Mojo Workin' / Dec. 16-17, 1965 / Verve 8641
Recorded at Englewood Cliffs, NJ. Smith in his large-band context. With Oliver Nelson and his orchestra. *—Michael Erlewine*

★ **Dynamic Duo, The** / Sep. 21+28, 1966 / Verve 821577
This may or may not have needed the big band setting for some of the tracks, but Oliver Nelson's tight, hard arranging and conducting gives the music the same added attraction he gives to Sonny Rollins' Alfie date. . . . This is a pairing of giants, and, while the music is broadly accessible, it needs no apology. Good listening. *—Bob Rusch, Cadence*

○ **Further Adventures of Jimmy and Wes** / Sep. 21+28, 1966 / Verve 68766
Respect / Jun. 2+14, 1967 / Verve 8705
Recorded in New York. Superb solos, soul-jazz with class. Prototype Smith. *—Ron Wynn*

Boss, The / Nov. 20, 1968 / Verve 8779
Recorded at Paschal's La Carousel, Atlanta, GA. Lots of fine solos. George Benson (g) does best soul-jazz work since McDuff days. *—Ron Wynn*

○ **Bluesmith** / 1972 / Verve 8809
☆ **Fourmost** / Nov. 16-17, 1990 / Milestone 9184
Recent material, Smith still wails on organ. Stanley Turrentine (ts), Kenny Burrell (g) in top form. *—Ron Wynn*

Leo Smith

b. Dec. 18, 1941, Leland, MS
Trumpet, flugelhorn / Modern creative
While an ambitious, unpredictable composer, Leo Smith's trumpet playing has leaned more toward the reflective, introspective side. His tone, approach, and sound emphasize lyricism and a calm, pleasing style rather than an energized, exuberant approach. Smith began on mellophone and French horn before turning to trumpet. He played in R&B bands and in the service

following his high school graduation. He became a member of the Association for the Advancement of Creative Musicians (AACM) in 1967 and co-founded the Creative Construction Company with Leroy Jenkins and Anthony Braxton later that year. They played and recorded in Europe and with other AACM members in New York during the late '60s before disbanding in 1970. Smith teamed with Marion Brown to make the documentary film *See the Music* in 1970, then formed the New Dalta Ahkri in New Haven. The group's personnel ranged from two to five members, including at various times Henry Threadgill, Anthony Davis, Oliver Lake, and Dwight Andrews. Smith began the Kabell record label in 1971 and studied ethnomusicology in the mid-'70s at Wesleyan. He played with Braxton again in the late '70s and recorded with Derek Bailey's group Company in London. Smith also led a trio with Peter Kowald and Gunther Sommer. He's recorded for Kabell, Moers, ECM, Nessa, Black Saint, and Sackville in the '70s and '80s. Smith has a couple of sessions available on CD. —*Ron Wynn*

● **Rastafari / i.** Feb. 1985 / Sackville 3030
Here was American trumpeter Leo Smith in Canada, with the Bill Smith group. In free improvisation smallest ensembles are best, otherwise lines and textures become obscured and direction dispersed. On *Rastafari*, the problem was generally solved by one or more players dropping out of the ensemble from passage to passage. Extensive, very sober improvisation was the content of three tracks—the trumpeter providing the music's warmth. —*John Litweiler, Down Beat*

Lonnie Smith (Organ)

Organ / Blues & jazz, soul-jazz
Dr. Lonnie Smith is a Philadelphia based Hammond B-3 organist who preceded Lonnie Liston Smith. He was a longtime sideman for saxophonist Lou Donaldson and among the better soul-jazz players. —*Michael G. Nastos*

★ **Mama Wailer** / Jul. 14-15, 1971 / Kudu

Lonnie Liston Smith (Lonnie Liston Smith, Jr.)

b. Dec. 28, 1940, Richmond, VA
Keyboard / Early jazz-rock, instrumental pop, modern creative
Lonnie Liston Smith was among the more influential keyboard players of the '70s, with his cluster style and keyboard colorations being featured on albums by Pharoah Sanders and Gato Barbieri. Smith played with Betty Carter in 1963-1964 and with Rahsaan Roland Kirk the next year, and then he worked with Art Blakey and Joe Williams before joining Pharoah Sanders in 1969. He stayed with Sanders for four years and wrote the title song for Sanders's album *Jewels of Thought*. He spent one year with Miles Davis in the mid '70s and then had a string of his own albums from the late '70s through the '80s, many of which had new-age sensibility in their lyrics and arrangements. —*Ron Wynn*

○ **Think / i.** 1923 / Blue Note 84290
W/ Lee Morgan (tpt). This is an excellent 1986 reissue of a fine soul-jazz Blue Note date by organist Lonnie Smith. —*Ron Wynn*

○ **Astral Travelling** / 1973 / Flying Dutchman 0163

★ **Expansions / i.** 1975 / Flying Dutchman 0934

☆ **Reflections of a Golden Dream** / Sep. 1976 / RCA 1460
There was an innate sensuality here, with the haunting echoes of electric piano, the mooing vocals of Lonnie Liston and Don Smith, and the weird melange of space sounds. —*Arnold Shaw, Down Beat*

Marvin Smith (Marvin "Smitty" Smith)

b. Jun. 24, 1961, Waukegan, IL
Drums, percussion / Hard bop
Drummer Marvin "Smitty" Smith is in the top rung of current jazz drummers and percussionists. He's a sometimes spectacular soloist and tremendous player capable of consistently driving a date, stepping back and keeping time or dominating the session. He's made some fine releases as a leader in hard-bop mode and has backed both young lions and old vets. —*Ron Wynn*

○ **Keeper of the Drums** / Mar. 1987 / Concord Jazz 4325

☆ **Road Less Traveled** / Feb. 1989 / Concord Jazz 4379
Fine 1989 date with strong piano from James Williams. CD version has two bonus cuts. —*Ron Wynn*

★ **Carryin' On** / Concord Jazz 325
Good, nicely played date with a harder edge than usual for Concord material. —*Ron Wynn*

Stuff Smith (Hezekiah Leroy Gordon Smith)

b. Aug. 14, 1909, Portsmouth, OH, **d.** Sep. 25, 1967, Munich, Germany
Violin / Swing
Violinist Stuff Smith was an extraordinary player, who had among other things the opportunity to record with Nat "King" Cole. His wide vibrato, frenetic rhythmic sense, unique intonation, and ambitious style are only part of the story; he was among the best at inspiring other musicians during performance, and Dizzy Gillespie has often credited Smith with showing him artistry and entertainment could be combined. Smith studied music with his father and performed with the family band as a child, eventually winning a scholarship to Johnson C. Smith University. Then at 15, Smith joined a touring revue. He performed for two years with Alphonso Trent and briefly with Jelly Roll Morton, but returned to Trent because he felt he couldn't be heard in Morton's band. After spending several years in Buffalo, Smith moved to New York in 1936. He led a quintet at the Onyx Club with Jonah Jones and Cozy Cole and there began playing an amplified violin. His group mixed music and comedy performances, sometimes nearly crossing the line between risquéA humor and lamentable stereotype. They recorded a novelty song "Tse A Muggin'" in 1936. They did 15 more songs for Vocalion and five for Decca. Smith added clarinetist Buster Bailey and pianist Clyde Hart for the Decca sessions, then recorded with a group he called Stuff Smith and His Orchestra in 1939 and 1940 for the Varsity label. When Fats Waller died in 1943, Smith was chosen to lead his band. Norman Granz recorded several exceptional sessions with Smith on Verve in the late '50s, and he toured extensively in the '60s. He recorded during this decade with Nat King Cole, Dizzy Gillespie, Ella Fitzgerald, Stephane Grappelli, Svend Asmussen, and the Oscar Peterson Trio. Smith resettled in Copenhagen in 1965, and died there two years later. —*Ron Wynn*

○ **Swingin' Stuff** / Mar. 23, 1956 / Storyville 4087
One of two mid-'60s sessions that violinist Stuff Smith recorded with a mostly foreign band, plus expatriate pianist Kenny Drew. He plays with his characteristic fervor, punctuating his rippling phrases with blues licks, smears, and slurs, plus some dazzling phrases. Bassist Niels-Henning Orsted Pedersen emerges as the dominant rhythm section member besides Drew, while drummer Alex Riel mainly follows their lead. —*Ron Wynn*

● **Live at the Montmartre** / Mar. 1965 / Storyville 4142

Tab Smith (Talmadge Smith)

b. Jan. 11, 1909, Kinston, NC, **d.** Sep. 17, 1971, St. Louis, MO
Sax, alto sax / Swing, big band, blues & jazz
Alto and C-melody saxophonist Tab Smith was a honking-R&B-swing master. Tab Smith began on C-melody, switched to alto, and eventually became a giant within his genre. Smith had lots of experience in territory bands during the '30s, achieved his first real fame with Lucky Millinder from 1936-1939. Later came stints with Frankie Newton, Red Allen, Teddy Wilson, and Eddie Durham, before he joined Count Basie in 1940. He returned to Millinder in 1942 and stayed until 1944, after which he led his own groups, sometimes with singer Wynonie Harris. His explosive, torrid solos were tailor-made for the swing-derived, jumping material that comprised vintage R&B, and during the '50s Smith cut many songs for tiny independent labels that were huge hits in the black community and on jukeboxes. He retired from the music business in the '60s and became involved in real estate, often playing the organ in clubs for fun. His finest sessions are now reappearing on both domestic and import reissue packages. —*Ron Wynn*

★ **I Don't Want to Play ... / i.** 1944-1945 / Saxophonograph
1944-1945. *I Don't Want to Play in the Kitchen*. Great honking sax, swing-inflected solos. —*Ron Wynn*

☆ **Because of You** / 1951-1957 / Delmark 429
Tab Smith, a reedman with Lucky Millinder and Count Basie, had a hit with the title tune of this collection. It was a very sweet ballad, oozing from Smith's sax to drench the laidback band support. So the cry of Smith's alto was urbane, rather than raunchy, and

some of the material he chose reflected overly cautious taste. —
Howie Mandel, Down Beat

○ **Jump Time** / 1951-1952 / Delmark 447

Alto and tenor saxophonist Tab Smith recorded several dozen
tunes for United between '51 and '57, 20 of which (including five
hitherto unreleased) show up in this Delmark collection. They're
a mixed bunch, reflecting the practice then of appeasing buyers
by placing sweet numbers back-to-back with swinging ones. . . . A
proficient soloist, he shakes and bounces over his fit little band
without going over the top, ennobling "Slow Motion," "Dee Jay
Special," "Wig Song," "Boogie Joogie." —*Frank-John Hadley,
Down Beat*

Willie the Lion Smith
(William Henry Joseph Bonaparte Bertholoff Smith)

b. Nov. 25, 1897, **d.** Apr. 18, 1973
Piano, composer, vocals / Stride

Pianist, composer, and vocalist Willie "The Lion" Smith was without question one of jazz's greatest exaggerators and self-promot-
ers, but he could back up all he said with his playing. Smith
started during the ragtime era. He was an influence on Duke
Ellington and a cohort of James P. Johnson and Fats Waller. Smith
played on the first blues record released by Mamie Smith in the
'20s. From the '30s until his death in the '70s, Smith was a storytelling, entertaining, dueling piano madman and performer. He
wrote over 70 songs, recorded with a host of groups and bands,
did duets with Jess Stacy and Joe Bushkin. His approach seamlessly incorporated all keyboard developments from rag, boogie-
woogie, and stride through swing up to bop, with plenty of blues
mixed in as well. Not to be confused with alto saxophonist and
singer Willie Smith. —*Ron Wynn*

★ **Snooty Fruity** / **i.** 1944-1955 / Columbia 45447

Hot Willie "The Lion" Smith. 1944-1955. Nice collaboration with
Harry James that has more form than many of James's cuts. —
Ron Wynn

☆ **Willie the Lion Smith** / Dec. 1, 1949-Jan. 29, 1950 / Inner City
7015

Part of the Jazz Legacy series, these 1949-1950 sessions with
Wallace Bishop on drums include some solos and some combo ef-
forts with Buck Clayton on trumpet, Claude Luter on clarinet, and
Bishop on drums. Ten Smith numbers and eight standards.
Includes Smith's classic "Echoes of Spring." —*Michael G. Nastos*

○ **Relaxin' After Hours** / **i.** 1954 / Emarcy 26000

The material on this album was recorded a short time after the
sessions that produced *Live at Blues Alley*, and except for the addition of a drummer, little was changed. Smith's piano work was
as infectious as ever. He strutted and stomped his way through
the equivalent of two sets, granting solo space to the drummer,
and above all, conveying a spirit of good times. —*Jack Sohmer,
Cadence*

★ **Legend of Willie Smith, The** / Aug. 21, 1957+Sep. 19, 1957 /
Grand Award 368

○ **Memoirs of Willie the Lion Smith** / Apr. 25-28, 1967 / RCA 6016

Mike Lipskin had a good idea here that didn't quite come off, but
we should have more failures like this. The Lion was a great pianist, an excellent composer, a very good raconteur with a memory to go with that talent, and a god-awful singer. Lion was one of
the last of the magnificent Harlem pianists, a school perhaps
more pianistic than anything done in jazz since their time. The
Lion illustrates the style perfectly by playing Scott Joplin's "Maple
Leaf Rag" and then showing how a Harlem pianist would change
the stiff rhythms and set phrases of "classical" ragtime into loose,
driving "stride." —*Ron Anger, Coda*

Elmer Snowden (Elmer Chester Snowden)

b. Oct. 9, 1900, Baltimore, MD, **d.** May 14, 1973, Philadelphia, PA
Guitar, banjo, sax, bandleader / Swing, big band

A great banjo player and versatile musician who could also play
excellent sax and guitar, Elmer Snowden was a rarity in the early
jazz era: a trained player who could read in any key and also a
smart businessman. Snowden played banjo and guitar as a child,
worked with Eubie Blake in a dance school in 1915, and played
in a trio with Duke Ellington in 1919. Snowden took a band to
New York from Washington in 1923, planning to use Fats Waller.
When that didn't materialize, Snowden sent for Ellington, and the

group became the Washingtonians. Snowden ran several bands
in the mid- and late '20s and early '30s. He headed his own bands
for three decades, before moving to California in 1963 to teach at
Berkeley. He began touring Europe for George Wein in 1967.
Snowden declined an offer to rejoin Ellington's orchestra in the
late '60s. A fine quartet album he recorded for Fantasy in 1960
has recently been reissued. —*Ron Wynn*

★ **Harlem Banjo** / Dec. 9, 1960 / Riverside 1756

Elmer Snowden Quartet. The legendary banjo player, with the
Cliff Jackson (p) Trio, plays standards with the emphasis on old-
time swing, including some Ellington. This is a unique album,
one every jazz fan should get to know. —*Michael G. Nastos*

Martial Solal

b. Aug. 23, 1927, Algiers
Piano, composer / Postbop

Pianist and composer Martial Solal's remarkable prowess and
technical talents, plus his willingness to utilize and display them
on record, has sometimes earned him critical displeasure. His
vast harmonic knowledge, tendency to assault the listener with
rippling phrases and complex passages, and sometimes relentless
pacing, turns off as many people as it impresses. Solal settled in
Paris in the late '40s and worked with expatriate American musicians like Kenny Clarke and Don Byas while recording with
Sidney Bechet, Lee Konitz, and Hampton Hawes. He's led his own
trios, done extensive session work since 1959, and become internationally famous through a 1963 visit to New York and subsequent Newport festival appearances. He's also done substantial
film score work in Europe. Solal doesn't have an overabundance
of available recordings in print but just recently issued a session
with European sax group. —*Ron Wynn*

★ **Martial Solal** / **i.** 1961 / Blue Note 10261

○ **Trio in Concert** / **i.** 1962 / Liberty 3335

Paris concert by this Algerian pianist, with Guy Pederson on bass
and Damiel Humaia on drums. An excellent album to find. —
Michael G. Nastos

☆ **Four Keys** / May 1979 / PA/USA 7061

The Lee Konitz-Martial Solal disc was rewarding, due primarily
to Konitz's increasingly refined approach to organization in his
solos and Solal's carefully constructed arrangements and means
of presentation. There was a particularly attractive balance to the
material, too: The first side featured some programmatic, chamberlike pieces, and the accompaniment seemed more designed
and less felt. —*Arthur Moorehead, Down Beat*

☆ **Live** / Stefanotis 239214

Comprehensive four-disc set of his material from 1959-1985 in
every context. —*Ron Wynn*

☆ **Martial Solal** / I Grandi Del Jazz 97

Italian release with fabulous graphics and liner notes. The music
is also first- rate. —*Michael G. Nastos*

Eddie South

b. Nov. 27, 1904, Louisiana, MO, **d.** Apr. 25, 1962, Chicago, IL
Violin / Swing

Classically trained violinist Eddie South studied at the Chicago
Musical College for many years and in 1924 became the music
director of Jimmy Wade's Syncopators. After traveling extensively
in Europe after 1928, he returned to Chicago in 1931 and started
a band with Milt Hinton that recorded with Victor. South subsequently made recordings with Stephane Grappelli and Django
Reinhardt. His incredible technique and dark tone led to his nickname "dark angel." —*Michael Erlewine*

★ **In Paris** / DRG 8405

Rare cuts from the late '30s featuring violinist Eddie South,
whose beautiful, swinging solos were unfortunately seldom
recorded. These songs were cut when South was living in Paris
and playing with such European jazz greats as Django Reinhardt
and Stephane Grappelli. —*Ron Wynn*

○ **Eddie South** / DRG 8405

This is one of the very few Eddie South albums available. The talented violinist made comparatively few recordings during his career for a player of his stature, and he suffered quite a bit of criticism because some jazz critics felt his tone was a bit too
"legitimate." Well, South's talents should be beyond dispute by

now, and in case proof is needed, this date will suffice. —*Scott Yanow, Cadence*

Muggsy Spanier (Francis Joseph Spanier)

b. Nov. 9, 1906, Chicago, IL, **d.** Feb. 12, 1967, Sausalito, CA
Cornet / Dixieland
Muggsy Spanier had personality and charisma and was a good performer in traditional style. He began on drums and switched to cornet at 13. He joined the Ted Lewis orchestra in 1929, staying with him until 1936, when he joined Ben Pollack's band for two years. The Ragtimers, a short-lived band he formed in the late '30s for dates at the Sherman Hotel in Chicago and Nick's in New York, was among the most popular trad bands of its day. Spanier rejoined Lewis for a short time and from 1941-1943 led his own big band that was modeled after the Bob Crosby Orchestra, in which he'd played in 1940-1941. He played with Lewis again in 1944 and then led various small groups in the '50s and '60s, also working for a time with Earl Hines. —*Ron Wynn*

○ **Muggsy Spanier (1924-1928)** / **i.** Feb. 1924-Apr. 1928 / Retrieval 108
The music of the two earliest groups on Muggsy Spanier's LP—the Bucktown Five (1924) and The Stomp Six (1925)—was peculiarly transitional. While the ensemble work owed its structure largely to the approach of the Original Dixieland Jazz Band, Spanier's cornet playing was significantly influenced by King Oliver and Louis Armstrong. From the Bucktown Five to the Stomp Six, however, the ensembles became increasingly loose-limbed, as Spanier mirrored Armstrong's gradual relegation of the ensemble to the stature of a framework for solo performance. —*Chris Sheridan, Cadence*

○ **Great Sixteen, The** / **i.** 1939 / RCA 1295

★ **Columbia, the Gem of the Ocean** / Jun. 13-14, 1962 / Mobile Fidelity 857
Excellent recording of fine '50s date. —*Ron Wynn*

James Spaulding (James Ralph Spaulding, Jr.)

b. Jul. 30, 1937, Indianapolis, IN
Alto sax, flute / Hard bop, progressive big band, modern creative
James Spaulding is a tremendous alto sax and flute player with one of jazz's slimmest profiles. Spaudling came to prominence during the '60s and '70s as a stirring alto soloist with one foot in bop and one in the free, expressive style being pioneered by Ornette Coleman. He was also among the best flute players, able to play lengthy lines and swirling solos, sweetly or with funk and bite. He dropped out of sight for while in the '80s but has been a steady contributor to many sessions for small jazz companies in late '80s and '90s. —*Ron Wynn*

○ **Gotstabe a Better Way** / May 31, 1988 / Muse 5413

★ **Brilliant Corners** / Nov. 25, 1988 / Muse 5369

Spyro Gyra

Group / Early jazz-rock, instrumental pop
Spyro Gyra's perhaps the best-selling and most popular fusion group ever. It was started in the mid '70s by saxophonist Jay Beckenstein and pianist Jeremy Wall and was at first primarily a studio band cutting faceless instrumentals. Then their 1979 album *Morning Dance* went gold, and they became an international success. During the '80s and '90s they've had a string of similar sounding recordings, have been derided repeatedly by many jazz critics, and have become a staple on adult contemporary, new-age, and easy listening stations. —*Ron Wynn*

Morning Dance / Aug. 1979 / MCA 37148

★ **Access All Areas** / Nov. 17+19, 1983 / MCA 6893
An excellent live double album that includes live versions of songs from early albums. —*Paul Kohler*

Alternating Currents / **i.** 1985 / MCA 5606
Great songwriting and playing, and nice work by keyboardist Tom Schuman. —*Paul Kohler*

Breakout / 1986 / MCA 5753
An album with more midtempo jazz-style tunes and nice arrangements, with Julio Fernandez. Synths programmed by Eddie Jobson. —*Paul Kohler*

Stories without Words / **i.** Jan. 1988 / MCA 42046

A nice mix of jazz, with tenor and soprano-sax melodies that really sing. —*Paul Kohler*

○ **Collection** / GRP 9642

Jess Stacy (Alexandria Stacy)

b. Aug. 11, 1904, Bird's Point, MO
Piano / Swing, big band
A superb pianist in vintage swing style, with one of the greatest right-hands ever, Stacy arrived in Chicago from Merge Point, MO, in the mid-'20s and worked for many groups in dance halls, clubs, and speakeasies, showing the skills he'd developed from playing on riverboats with such visitors as Bix Beiderbecke and Tony Catalano. Through the efforts of John Hammond, Stacy joined Benny Goodman in 1935 and stayed with him until 1939, attaining jazz immortality by playing a brillant solo on the 1938 Carnegie Hall performance of "Sing Sing Sing." He spent three years from 1939 to 1942 with Bob Crosby. Stacy went to the West Coast and played in piano bars in the '50s and early '60s. He came back in 1973, doing the soundtrack for the film *The Great Gatsby* and then getting a standing ovation at the 1974 Newport Jazz Festival. He began recording again for Chiaroscuro in the mid- and late '70s, and his classic '40s sessions are being reissued —*Ron Wynn*

○ **Piano Solos** / Nov. 16, 1935-Mar. 3, 1959 / Swaggie 1248
1935-1956. Includes a nice cross-section of influential, fine Stacy cuts. —*Ron Wynn*

★ **Jess Stacy and Friends** / Apr. 30, 1938-Nov. 25, 1944 / Commodore 7008

Jeremy Steig

b. Sep. 23, 1943, New York, NY
Flute / Early jazz-rock
Steig was among the first to find a good midpoint between the emerging electronic breakthroughs of the '70s and traditional acoustic instrumentation and arrangements in jazz and pop. His father was a famous artist, and Steig began playing recorder at 6, taking flute lessons at 11. He worked with Paul Bley and Gary Peacock in 1961, and in 1966, he was part of a jazz-rock band that included Tim Hardin. The next year he began leading his own groups. His band Jeremy and the Satyrs was among the early, innovative groups truly able to do either impressive jazz tunes or authentic rock pieces. Steig was also an early proponent of electronics, incorporating them into his band without gimmickry or faddism. Steig was a star in Europe in the '70s, and his flute solos were among the most accomplished in either jazz or rock. His album output diminished greatly after the '70s. —*Ron Wynn*

★ **Flute Fever** / **i.** 1963 / Columbia

○ **This Is Jeremy Steig** / 1969 / Solid State 18059

○ **Music for Flute & Double Bass** / Dec. 1978 / Creative Music Prod.

☆ **Rain Forest** / Feb. 1980-Mar. 1980 / CMP 12
Virtuoso flute player. An improvisational tradition of various groupings. With Eddie Gomez (b), Jack DeJohnette (d), Mike Nock (k), and Nana Vasconcelos (per). —*Michael G. Nastos*

★ **Jigsaw** / Feb. 1989 / Atlantic 82027
Jigsaw, flutist Jeremy Steig's return to recording action after 10 years away, is also a feather in the cap of former Steely Dan Walter Becker's nascent jazz producer career. The title cut is an enticingly quirky assemblage, with a smirking, restless tonal center. Better yet, Steig's "Sifu's Song" has an almost chamber-jazz quality in its incisive melody that frames a beautifully elliptical drum solo by Joe Chambers. —*Josef Woodard, Down Beat*

Mike Stern (Michael Stern)

b. Jan. 10, 1954, Boston, MA
Guitar / Early jazz-rock, instrumental pop, modern creative
An ex-Miles Davis electric guitarist, Mike Stern looks more toward rock-edged tone. But he's also good in a neo-bop setting. His sound is more steely and psychedelic. —*Michael G. Nastos*

○ **Standards (and Other Songs)** / **i.** Sep. 23, 1992 / Atlantic 82419
Just as the title implies this is an album of mostly jazz standards augmented by several of Stern's own original compositions. Also featured are Jay Anderson (b), Randy Brecker (t), and Bob Berg (ts). This is perhaps Stern's finest recording. —*Paul Kohler*

Rex Stewart (William Stewart, Jr.)

b. Feb. 22, 1907, Philadelphia, PA, **d.** Sep. 7, 1967, Los Angeles, CA

Cornet / Swing, big band

Cornetist Rex Stewart was known for his "half-valve" technique, in which he pushed the cornet or trumpet valves halfway down and created a wealth of quarter tones and fresh sounds. Stewart developed this method in part to create alternative, individual sound and help him deal with the challenging music he faced when he replaced his idol Louis Armstrong in Fletcher Henderson's orchestra in the '20s. Though he also worked with Elmer Snowden prior to joining Henderson, and later played with McKinney's Cotton Pickers and Luis Russell, Stewart attained star status during a 12-year tenure with Duke Ellington from 1934-1945. While with Ellington, Stewart's solos became famous on a pair of masterpieces, "Trumpet in Spades" and "Boy Meets Horn." Later he led his own groups, toured Europe and Australia, lived in New Jersey for a while in the '50s, organized and led a Fletcher Henderson reunion band, played at Eddie Condon's, and recorded there as well. He led various groups under the banner of the Ellingtonians on several labels from 1936 to 1941. —*Ron Wynn*

○ **Rex Stewart and the Ellingtonians** / Jul. 23, 1940-1946 / Riverside 1710

○ **Big Reunion, The** / Nov. 1957-Dec. 2, 1957 / Jazztone 1285

○ **Henderson Homecoming** / Aug. 1, 1958 / United Artists 4009

○ **Rendezvous with Rex** / Jan. 28, 1959+Jan. 31, 1958 / Felsted 7001

Rendezvous with Rex brought together two Rex Stewart dates: 1/28/58 and 1/31/58. Stewart will inevitably be tagged an Ellingtonite, and things will usually be related in some degree relative to that. That is understandable as it was with Ellington where he was most magnificent. That said, note that this was not a recording in the Ellington genre, except for a little of the harmonic ensemble blending that might suggest that association. —*Bob Rusch, Cadence*

★ **With Henri Chase** / Jun. 12, 1966 / Polydor 623234

Slam Stewart (Leroy Elliot Stewart)

b. Sep. 21, 1914, Englewood, NJ, **d.** Dec. 10, 1987, Binghamton, NY

Bass / Swing

As with Clark Terry, Stewart's fondness for mugging on stage and his trademark technique of bowing a bass solo and humming along in unison sometimes led observers to consider him more an entertainer than a first-class musician. Stewart also had a long-running collaboration and act with vocalist Slim Gaillard, and the team of Slim and Slam had several delightful vocal hits, among them "Flat Foot Floogie" and "Buck Dance Rhythm." They also appeared in the film *Stormy Weather*, and they toured and recorded with Art Tatum and Benny Goodman as well as having their own trio. Stewart worked with many great musicians on his own from the '40s until the '80s, including Lester Young, Tatum, Rose Murphy, Goodman, and Beryl Booker. He also headed his own groups in the '70s. The 1981 release, *Shut Your Mouth*, paired him with Major Holley, doing the familiar hum-scat-humor routines Stewart had patented earlier with Gaillard. —*Ron Wynn*

○ **Two Big Mice** / Jul. 14, 1977 / Black & Blue 59124

○ **Dialogue** / 1978 / Stash 201

★ **Shut Yo' Mouth!** / Dec. 6, 1981 / Delos 1024
W/ Major Holley. Two great bassists get together for a good time. Highly recommended. —*Michael G. Nastos*

Sonny Stitt (Edward Stitt)

b. Feb. 2, 1924, Boston, MA, **d.** Jul. 22, 1982, Washington, DC

Sax / Bop, hard bop

Sonny Stitt was one of the premier saxophonists in jazz history. He began recording in 1946 after appearing with Tiny Bradshaw, Billy Eckstine, and Dizzy Gillespie. His early recordings are on Savoy and Galaxy (via Sensation). He switched from alto to tenor sax in 1949 and created a sensation with Prestige/New Jazz recordings featuring Bud Powell, John Lewis, and J. J. Johnson and then joined forces with Gene Ammons in 1950, playing both saxes (and, occasionally, baritone sax as well). His Prestige

recordings of 1950-1952 are all worth hearing as are his sessions for Roost, Argo, and Verve throughout the '50s. Stitt was a free-lance recording artist throughout much of his career, which accounts for the large number of recordings done for different labels during the same period. In the '60s, Stitt got into organ sessions with players such as Jack McDuff and Don Patterson. More often than not the organ sessions lack the spirit of his more bop-oriented recordings. From 1966 to 1971 Stitt made use of electronic attachments for his saxophone, which tended to dull his tone and dampen the fire of the music. Those should be avoided. Stitt made well over a hundred albums in his career but those in his later years that are especially recommended are those on the Muse label. Sessions involving pianist Barry Harris are among the best of all Sonny Stitt recordings. —*Bob Porter*

○ **Sonny Stitt with Bud Powell and J.J. Johnson** / Oct. 17, 1949-Dec. 11, 1949 / Prestige 009

○ **Sonny Stitt Plays Arrangements of Quincy Jones** / Oct. 17, 1955 / Roost 2204

○ **New York Jazz** / Sep. 14, 1956 / Verve 8219
When Sonny Stitt was hot, and had a mind to, he could play most inspired music. *New York Jazz* was recorded in 1957 with Jimmy Jones (piano), Ray Brown (bass), and Jo Jones (drums), and it was a serious, but average (good) session. —*Bob Rusch, Cadence*

○ **Burnin'** / Aug. 1, 1958 / Argo 661

○ **Sonny Stitt and the Top Brass** / Jul. 16-17, 1962 / Atlantic 90139
Some wonderful Sonny Stitt alto solos, both in collaboration with the brass section and as a soloist. This early '60s release matched Stitt with a full brass section playing the customary blues, ballads, and standards. His soaring, exuberant playing never overwhelmed the accompaniment but sometimes transcended it, other times elevated it. —*Ron Wynn*

☆ **Soul Classics / i.** 1962-1972 / Prestige 6003
Fine playing, frequently galvanizing solos. 1988 reissue of cuts from 1962-1972. —*Ron Wynn*

★ **Stitt Plays Bird** / Jan. 29, 1963 / Atlantic 1418
Logging in at 45:08, this CD reissue excels its LP predecessor by some eight minutes because of its first-time presentation of the only previously unreleased titles from Sonny Stitt's January 29, 1963, session, "Now's the Time" and "Yardbird Suite." Of course, Stitt fanciers should be grateful for this long overdue act of completion, if not contrition, by the powers that be. —*Jack Sohmer, Jazz Times*

☆ **My Mother's Eyes** / May 1963 / Pacific Jazz 71

○ **Salt and Pepper** / Sep. 5, 1963 / Impulse 52

★ **Tune-Up!** / Feb. 1972 / Muse 5334
Sonny Stitt was more respected than loved. He epitomized bebop as contest. Stitt's work, even at its hard-driving best like this, appears as a routine reissue. Routine or not, this reissue will be welcomed. Musicians and critics respected him, and with his smoothed out bop horn style, he exerted a strong influence on younger players. —*David Dupont, Cadence*

★ **Constellation** / Jun. 27, 1972 / Muse 5323
On February 8, 1972, Sonny Stitt recorded what I rate as the finest album of his last decade, *Tune Up*. His followup session *Constellation* was a close second and is happily available again. Sonny Stitt's style featured a complete mastery of the bop language, the ability to think and play very fast, and an individual sound on both alto and tenor.... Sonny Stitt led over 150 recording sessions in his career, but few were more consistently exciting than the brilliant *Constellation*. —*Scott Yanow, Cadence*

○ **My Buddy: Stitt Plays for Gene Ammons** / Jul. 2, 1975 / Muse 5091
On this album alto and tenor saxophonist Sonny Stitt started off well on the opening track ("You Can Depend on Me"). Stitt turned to alto only on the Charlie Parker tune ("Confirmation").... The best aspect of this release was pianist Barry Harris. Bassist Sam Jones took a few good solos, but his sound was marred by that dull flatness too many bassists in this day of electric pickups seem to prefer to the full acoustic sound. The recorded sound was good, although there was little stereo separation. —*Jerry De Muth, Cadence*

☆ **Blues for Duke** / Dec. 3-04, 1975 / Muse 5129

☆ **I Remember Bird** / 1977 / Catalyst 7616

I Remember Bird featured the fine trombonist Frank Rosolino, who also appeared on several Catalyst dates, and a rhythm section of Dolo Coker, piano; Allen Jackson, bass; and Clarence Johnston, drums. This was essentially Sonny Stitt playing Sonny Stitt; he worked his patented Stitt licks, turned those familiar phrases, and always made them sound new." —*Herb Nolan, Down Beat*

○ **Sonny Stitt with Strings** / 1977 / Catalyst 7620
Stitt with Strings was dedicated entirely to the music of Duke Ellington and covered some of Ellington's most famous melodies like "Take The 'A' Train," "Cotton Tail," "Sentimental Mood," and so on. Among the more refreshing aspects of this album were Bill Finegan's string arrangements, which were often coarse, subtle, and filled with spaces for Stitt to play around and through. —*Herb Nolan, Down Beat*

○ **Last Stitt Sessions—Vol. 1 & 2** / Jun. 1982 / Muse 6003
Some early '80s dates by saxophonist Sonny Stitt, which were issued in single album form shortly after his death. They've been combined and reissued in one two-disc package, and are also available in single disc fashion. Though Stitt was on his last legs, he summoned enough energy and strength to play some booming blues and intense uptempo originals and standards. —*Ron Wynn*

○ **Last Stitt Sessions—Vol. 1** / Jun. 1982 / Muse 5269
This Muse album was another in the series of good solid Sonny Stitt sessions for that label, with pianist Junior Mance adding an extra filip to the session. The outstanding track here was "Angel Eyes," but the session as a whole was successful—not the equal of his most outstanding Prestige and Verve sessions of earlier years, but certainly well worth having. —*Shirley Klett, Cadence*

Billy Strayhorn (William [Swee' Pea] Strayhorn)

b. Nov. 29, 1915, Dayton, OH, **d.** May 31, 1967, New York, NY
Piano, arranger, composer / Swing, big band
Billy Strayhorn was among the greatest jazz arrangers and composers in history, and the partner and confidant of Duke Ellington from 1939 to 1967. Strayhorn met Ellington in 1938 after completing high school in Pittsburgh. He began writing lyrics for Ellington a year later, after playing piano briefly in a band led by his son Mercer. In fact, Strayhorn actually composed his most famous song, "Lush Life," before he joined Ellington. The two became so close some observers claimed it was impossible to distinguish between their styles, though some argue that Strayhorn was more conventional in his voicings and arrangements. His list of compositions includes such classics as "Day Dream," "Chelsea Bridge," and the signature song "Take the 'A' Train." Ellington later had some of his extended pieces published with "Ellington-Strayhorn" joint credit. Strayhorn was also a fine instrumentalist, though he seldom appeared in public with the orchestra or any of the small combos. He cut duets with Ellington, made trio and septet recordings with Johnny Hodges, and in 1963 directed the band in a lavish Ellington concept piece "My People." —*Ron Wynn*

○ **Billy Strayhorn Septet** / i. 1958 / Felsted 2008
★ **Cue for Saxophone** / Apr. 14, 1958 / Verve 820604
Billy Strayhorn Sextet. Fine Strayhorn arrangements for session of topflight Ellingtonians. Johnny Hodges (sax) takes honors. Reissue of 1959 date. —*Ron Wynn*

○ **Lush Life** / i. 1967 / Red Baron 52760
A '92 reissue of a rare session issued under the name of noted arranger-composer Billy Strayhorn, providing the inspiration and material for a combo with Duke Ellington, trumpeters Cootie Williams and Cat Anderson, and drummer Sam Woodyard, and featuring his most famous composition. —*Ron Wynn*

String Trio of New York

Group / Modern creative
Billy Bang, James Emery, and John Lindberg were the original members of the String Trio of New York; they were a violinist, guitarist, and bassist. They made complimentary music and worked as a tight-knit yet free-wheeling trio playing music that maximized intragroup harmony but also spotlighted each player's own unusual style. The group began recording in 1979; Bang departed in the late '80s and was replaced by Charles Burnham. Things changed again in '93, when Regina Carter

recorded with holdovers Emery and John Lindberg. They've done sessions for Black Saint, Stash, and Arabesque. The String Trio has some sessions available on CD. —*Ron Wynn*

● **Area Code 212** / i. Nov. 1980 / Black Saint 0048
○ **As Tears Go By** / i. Dec. 1987 / ITM 0029
○ **Ascendant** / Jun. 1990 / Vintage Jazz 532

Frank Strozier (Frank R. Strozier)

b. Jun. 13, 1937, Memphis, TN
Alto sax / Postbop
One of many alto saxophonists in the '50s and '60s who forged ahead after initially being heavily influenced by Charlie Parker. The Memphis-born Strozier moved to New York and recorded with likes of George Coleman, Harold Mabern, and other fellow Memphians who'd moved to the East Coast. Strozier subsequently moved to a looser, freer alto style; in recent years he has switched to piano. His finest recordings from the '50s and '60s are slowly reappearing in print. —*Ron Wynn*

★ **March of the Siamese Children** / Mar. 28, 1962 / Jazzland 70

John Stubblefield (John Stubblefield IV)

b. Feb. 4, 1945, Little Rock, AR
Sax, flute / Post-bop, Neo Bop
John Stubblefirled is a good modern saxophonist who's recorded mostly for foreign labels like Enja, but has also been featured on small domestic independents. A versatile player, his best instrument is soprano, but he also has recorded on flute, alto, and tenor. A hard bop, mainstream type and capable soloist, he has yet to release the definitive or breakout session that would give him widespread visibility and notoriety. —*Ron Wynn*

○ **Prelude** / i. 1976 / Storyville 4011
★ **Bushman Song** / Apr. 22-23, 1986 / Enja 79660

Idrees Sulieman (Idrees Dawud ibn Sulieman)

b. Aug. 7, 1923, St. Petersburg, FL
Trumpet, flugelhorn / Bop
Trumpeter Idrees Sulieman has been a valuable member of several groups, most notably the Kenny Clarke-Francy Boland Big Band. He left America for Switzerland in the '60s and settled in Copenhagen, Denmark, in the '70s. His early career was spent working with the Carolina Cotton Pickers and the Earl Hines Band in the '40s. Sulieman worked with Thelonious Monk and Mary Lou Williams in the mid '40s and was quick to recognize the changes in the jazz world and embrace bop. He worked with Monk, Coleman Hawkins, and others in the late '40s and through the '50s, before departing from America. —*Ron Wynn*

★ **Coolin'** / Apr. 14, 1957 / New Jazz 8216

Charles Sullivan (Charles Henry Sullivan)

b. Nov. 8, 1944, New York, NY
Trumpet, flugelhorn, bandleader / Bop
A most underrated trumpeter, Charles Sullivan has excellent technique; fine tone; and a bright, shimmering sound and is effective in hard bop, free, big band, or bebop contexts. He's simply not gotten the credit he deserves, though he also doesn't have a large legacy of recordings. Sullivan studied at the Manhattan School of Music in the '60s, and worked for off-Broadway productions. He played with Lionel Hampton and Roy Haynes's Hip Ensemble in the late '60s and toured briefly as Count Basie's lead trumpeter in 1970 and with Lonnie Liston Smith in 1971. He played with Sy Oliver in 1972 and with Norman Connors in 1973. Sullivan toured Europe and recorded with Abdullah Ibrahim in 1973 as well and then worked and recorded with Sonny Fortune, Carlos Garnett, Bennie Maupin, Ricky Ford, Eddie Jefferson, and Woody Shaw, as well as cutting his own records, through the remainder of the '70s. Despite all that activity, Sullivan couldn't expand his audience or gain more recognition. He began heading the band Black Legacy in the late '70s, and continued into the '80s. Sullivan currently has no sessions available on CD, but can be heard on reissues by Shaw, Jefferson, Fortune, and others. —*Ron Wynn*

● **Genesis** / Jun. 20, 1974-Jun. 21, 1974 / Inner City 1012
Charles Sullivan deserved full honors for this lyrical debut album. Though his liner notes referred to a Scorpio's need to be re-

born phoenixlike from the ashes of his own existence, the trumpeter's style was so warm and creative it was difficult to believe he had to negate himself to arrive at such celebratory and stimulating music. Each of the compositions was Sullivan's own, as were the simple but effective arrangements that forged a collection of talented sidemen into an inspired ensemble. —*Howie Mandel, Down Beat*

Ira Sullivan (Ira Brevard Sullivan, Jr.)

b. May 1, 1931, Washington, DC
Winds, trumpet, sax / Bop
Ira Sullivan is one of the great multiinstrumentalists of modern jazz. Long associated with the Chicago modern-jazz scene, Sullivan moved to Florida in the mid '60s and has remained there for most of his career. Fluent on trumpet, fluglehorn, flute, and all the saxophones, Sullivan has almost always been involved with small groups. Sullivan has made a dozen or so albums under his own leadership, and all are challenging, inspired modern jazz. His work with Red Rodney in a co-led group delighted fans in the early and mid-'80s and the albums they recorded for Muse and Elektra/Musician are well worth seeking out. —*Bob Porter*

○ **Nicky's Tune** / Dec. 24, 1958 / Delmark 422
Some stirring solos by trumpeter and saxophonist Ira Sullivan makes this late-'50s session delightful. There's also excellent piano from the sadly neglected pianist Jodie Christian. Sullivan was soon to take a long hiatus from the music business but at this juncture was playing with flair and conviction. —*Ron Wynn*

★ **Ira Sullivan** / Dec. 9, 1976-Mar. 9, 1976 / A&M 706

○ **Incredible, The** / Stash 208
Multiinstrumentalist Ira Sullivan puts on an impressive display of technique as he plays several saxes, plus trumpet and flutes. His facility, solos, and spirit are what make this album interesting. The backing band, arrangements, and production are rather routine, but Sullivan's domination keeps it from bogging down. —*Ron Wynn*

Maxine Sullivan (Marietta Williams)

b. May 13, 1911, Homestead, PA, **d.** Apr. 7, 1987, New York, NY
Vocals, trombone, flugelhorn / Swing, ballads & blues
Maxine Sullivan is a popular vocalist who also plays valve trombone and flugelhorn. Among the more subtle and stylized musicians, Sullivan enjoyed major success in several decades as a jazz vocalist. She sang in clubs and on radio in Pittsburgh and enjoyed what became a signature hit with the 1937 song "Loch Lomond," which was arranged by Claude Thornhill. She got national exposure for two years on CBS radio singing with her husband John Kirby's band in the late '30s; the show "Flow Gently Sweet Rhythm" was the only Black show on the radio network at that time. After touring with Benny Carter in 1941, she retired for awhile in 1942 and then made a comeback a few years later. She retired once more in 1954 but returned again in 1958, this time singing and playing valve trombone and flugelhorn. She did several festival dates and recorded in the '60s and '70s with the World's Greatest Jazz Band, Earl Hines, Ike Isaacs, Bob Wilber, and Dick Hyman. In the '80s, her popularity and profile continued to rise, and she made concept albums of Harold Arlen, Ted Koehler, and Jule Styne songs, plus a good date with the Scott Hamilton quartet. —*Ron Wynn*

○ **Biggest Little Band in the Land, The** / i. 1941 / Circle 125

● **Tribute to Andy Razaf** / i. 1956 / Dcc 610
The Maxine Sullivan CD is a release of a 1956 session for Period that has been virtually impossible to find for 30 years or so. The album concept was in honor of Andy Razaf, one of the great lyricists. Inevitably, it also honors Fats Waller, who wrote so much of the music to which Razaf put words. And the collection is a delightful reminder of Sullivan's ability, without strain or pretense, to interpret a song with feeling, sensitivity, and swing. —*Doug Ramsey, Jazz Times*

★ **Sings the Music of Burton Lane** / i. 1991 / Mobile Fidelity 773

☆ **Maxine Sullivan** / Riff 659004

Sun Ra (Herman "Sonny" Blount)

b. May 22, 1914, Birmingham, AL, **d.** May 30, 1993, Birmingham, AL

Piano, bandleader, composer / Big band, postbop, early free, progressive big band, modern creative
Celestial traveller and master of the swing tradition Sun Ra was the most wonderfully confounding figure in the entire spectrum of jazz (make that music in general). Rocketing out of Chicago in the mid '50s, the Arkestra created sounds that defied their time and place, with perhaps a closer kinship to the great Black orchestras of the prewar years than the then-current bop stylings. Already notable were the excellent line of soloists, the long-term members like Marshall Allen, Pat Patrick, and John Gilmore, acknowledged as a substantial influence on John Coltrane. There were also the lesser-known players, such as the brilliant Hobart Dotson and alto player James Spaulding. Even Ra's own keyboard work is fascinating, with electric piano and even primitive synthesizers popping up in the mix. By the time *The Magic City* was released at the turn of the '60s, Ra had cut his earthly ties and begun operations in the free-jazz territories, a pattern for better than the next decade and a half. Strengthing his usage of African lore, the Arkestra can clearly be seen as a forerunner of later groups such as the Art Ensemble of Chicago. When some were shocked to see Ra's eventual return to swing, we could safely say that once again, Sun Ra was way ahead of the "new traditionalists." With the exhaustive Saturn catalog finally being unravelled, the time for the discovery of Sun Ra is here and now. —*Steve Aldrich*

○ **Sun Song** / i. Jul. 12, 1956 / Delmark 411

○ **We Travel the Spaceways / Bad and Beautiful** / i. 1956-1960 / Evidence 22038
The opening numbers range from the humorous and futuristic bent of "Interplanetary Music" and "We Travel the Spaceways" to the more musically expansive "New Horizons" and "Space Loneliness." Trumpeter Phil Cohran and the superb horn section of Marshall Allen, John Gilmore, and Pat Patrick sometimes remain in the maze, other times explode with short but peppery solos. The other songs mix bop and swing tunes with more experimental fare like "Ankh" and "Exotic Two," where Patrick, Gilmore, Ra, and Allen soar while bassist Ronnie Boykins and drummer Tommy Hunter maintain the rhythmic center. —*Ron Wynn*

○ **Sound Sun Pleasure** / 1958-1960 / Evidence 22014
Sun Ra's kalediscope of sounds was just taking shape in the '50s and early '60s when the 13 tracks comprising this CD were recorded. His Astro-Infinity Arkestra included several emerging musicians who would later become major stars, like baritone saxophonist Charles Davis, Bob Northern on flugelhorn, and James Spaulding, who is featured on various reeds. The great jazz violinist Stuff Smith is even along on "Deep Purple," providing a dazzling, bluesy solo that is right at home in the Ra mix. —*Ron Wynn*

★ **Nubians of Plutonia, The** / i. 1959 / Impulse 9242
By the time of *The Nubians of Plutonia* session, the strongly rhythmic undercurrent of Sun Ra's hard bop band had developed into his heavy percussion period. Three events on the LP were of special interest. The brief "Watusa" was two themes that began in 6/4, like Mongo Santamaria, then grew increasingly strong as they ascended, and the tempo speeded. There was alto saxophonist Marshall Allen's 40-measure solo on "Star," a curious collection of phrases marked by original accenting and a raw Jackie McLeanlike sound. —*John Litweiler, Down Beat*

○ **Cosmic Tones for Mental Therapy / Art Forms Of...** / i. 1963 / Evidence 22036
There has always been some controversy revolving around Sun Ra, but few of his albums ever generated more discussion than *Cosmic Tones for Mental Therapy*, which covers half the 12 numbers on this two-LP, single disc outing. Ra played "astro space organ," and the array of swirling tones, funky licks, and smashing rhythms, aided and abetted by John Gilmore on bass clarinet, Marshall Allen flailing in the stratosphere on oboe, and arrangements that sometimes had multiple horns dueling in the upper register and other times pivoting off careening beats, outraged those in the jazz community who thought Eric Dolphy and John Coltrane had already taken things too far. —*Ron Wynn*

★ **Heliocentric Worlds of Sun Ra—Vols. 1 and 2, The** / Apr. 20, 1965 / ESP 1017
The Heliocentric Worlds of Sun Ra, Vol 1 made Sun Ra's cult reputation in 1965; and though it's no longer shocking, it still has the power to unsettle. The tightly plotted compositions rumble with

ominous percussion, creak with haunted-house horns, and shiver with the spooky timbres of Ra's marimba and celeste. —*Larry Birnbaum, Down Beat*

○ **Monorails and Satellites** / 1966 / Evidence 22013
Although he did not record nearly as much solo piano as he should have, whenever Sun Ra did take the keyboard spotlight the results were memorable. That was certainly the case on this 1966 date with Ra showing the complete range of his styles and influences. There are rumbling boogie progressions and angular bop harmonies, bluesy passages, free sections, and even stride and Afro-Latin references. —*Ron Wynn*

Atlantis / 1967-1969 / Saturn
Sun Ra was soaring far and wide on these late '60s sessions, most notably the 20-minute-plus title cut. This was one of his earliest dates on nothing but electric keyboards, and his manipulation of sounds, noise, whirling phrases, and rhythms was creative and innovative. The other shorter pieces move from somber, almost morose arrangements of *Mu* to the teaming beats of *Bimini* and the otherworldliness of both the Saturn and Impulse versions of *Yucatan*. As usual, Ra's band meshes hard bop, bebop, cool, free, and swing elements, with John Gilmore, Marshall Allen, and company alternately wailing, colliding, and complementing the master's dashing clavinet, synthesizer, and organ journeys. An essential and excellent set. —*Ron Wynn*

○ **Holiday for Soul Dance** / 1968-1969 / Evidence 22011
Sun Ra never concerned himself with the issues of innovation vs. preservation that seem to be the rage in current jazz circles. Instead, his music was both futuristic and classic, embracing the past and anticipating the future. A prime example is this fine eight-track collection of prerock standards done in 1968 and 1969, long before the debate about what is and is not "in the tradition" ever began. But of course Ra would not simply cover these numbers in a reverential manner; instead, he and the Astro-Infinity Arkestra stomp, romp, twist, strut, and cut through a collection ranging from "But Not for Me" through "Early Autumn" and "Body and Soul." —*Ron Wynn*

○ **My Brother the Wind—Vol. 2** / 1969-1970 / Evidence 22040
Sun Ra's synthesizer, organ, and electric keyboard playing were probably the most underrated elements of his arsenal. Even those who did not understand them acknowledged that his compositions were special, and few detractors would dismiss the capabilities of his band members. But Ra's piano and electronic keyboard journeys were often viewed as gimmicky, clowning, or musically illiterate ramblings. Sadly, this ignorance was the prevailing view for much of his career. In retrospect Ra's playing is being celebrated. The remarkable phrases, rhythms, progressions, statements, and solos he offers throughout this 11-cut late '60s and early '70s session are a tribute to his understanding of the moog synthesizer's possiblities and options. —*Ron Wynn*

★ **Space Is the Place** / 1972 / BLUE THUMB
Here is a genuine bonus, some previously unissued cuts. *Space Is the Place* is the soundtrack to a film that was made but never released, and the tunes are among his most ambitious, unorthodox, and compelling compositions. Between June Tyson's declarative vocals, chants, and dialogue and Ra's crashing, flailing and emphatic synthesizer and organ fills, and with such songs as "Blackman/Love in Outer Space," "It's After the End of the World," and "I Am the Brother of the Wind" this disc offers aggressive, energized and uncompromising material. —*Ron Wynn*

○ **Live at Montreux** / Jul. 1976 / Inner City 1039
All but one of the cuts were Sun Ra compositions. Each was a series of moments that dissolved into one another. A swinging dance band passage melted into an arkestral free-for-all; a French horn ripped repeatedly up to the same note; suddenly everything stopped except for one horn that soloed alone, unmetered, and unafraid of taking risks. These moments may have been wild, comic, serious, lyrical, hip. Some sections were pure noise, almost unbearable; all involved the most direct kind of musical expression. —*Douglas Clark, Down Beat*

○ **Unity** / i. Oct. 24+29, 1977 / Horo 20
Live at Storyville in New York. The Arkestra's best live album. Loaded with standards. Incredible musicianship. —*Michael G. Nastos*

○ **Solo Piano—Vol. 2** / i. 1978 / Improvising Artists 373858

★ **Strange Celestial Road** / i. 1980 / Rounder 3035

○ **Of Mythic Worlds** / i. Jun. 1981 / Philly Jazz 1007
Taken from a performance in Chicago (I assume this was in 1979) the album largely highlighted Sun Ra's keyboard work, along with the solo skills of saxophonists John Gilmore and Marshall Allen. By and large, the ensemble interplay of the entire Arkestra was ignored. —*Carl Brauer, Cadence*

○ **Sun Ra Visits Planet Earth / Intersteller Low Ways** / Evidence 22039

John Surman (John Douglas Surman)

b. Aug. 30, 1944, Tavistock, England
Baritone sax, soprano sax, clarinet, synth, electronics / Early jazz-rock, modern creative
A striking player of multireeds and synthesizer, whose range, mastery of the lower register, and knowledge of harmonics, as well as his flexibility and arranging and composing skills, have made him a heralded musician on both sides of the Atlantic. His earliest professional collaboration was with Mike Westbrook in 1962, and he also played in some of Alexis Korner's early blues-rock bands. Surman won the best soloist award at the 1968 Montreux festival and in 1969 got his first major international recognition for his playing on John McLaughlin's *Extrapolation*, where he sparkled on both baritone and soprano. He led his own groups throughout the '70s, with the band SOS being particularly popular in the mid-'70s, as Surman gradually worked electronics and synthesizers into his musical mix. Surman was part of Miroslav Vitous's quartet from 1979 to 1982, toured Australia with him in 1983, and returned there with vocalist Karen Krog in 1985. —*Ron Wynn*

★ **Westering Home** / 1972 / Island 10

○ **Morning Glory** / i. 1973 / Island

☆ **S.O.S.** / Jul. 27-28, 1974 / Ogun

☆ **Upon Reflection** / May 1979 / ECM 825472

Steve Swallow (Stephen W. Swallow)

b. Oct. 4, 1940, Fair Lawn, NJ
Bass, composer / Postbop, early jazz-rock, modern creative
Bassist and composer Steve Swallow ranks as one of the innovators on the electric bass, someone who's redefined the instrument and actually approached it as a totally different animal from its acoustic counterpart. Swallow changed the fingering system and played it like a guitar, and also sought out situations and songs where the electric bass was the requisite instrument. He joined Paul Bley's trio in the '60s and then worked with George Russell, Jimmy Giuffre, and Art Farmer before joining Stan Getz's group from 1965 to 1967 and participating in Gary Burton's radical ensemble from 1967 to 1970. This quartet was a forerunner of the true fusion group, playing jazz, rock, and country in seamless mix and emphasizing electric rather than acoustic context. This experience led Swallow to give up the acoustic bass. He's worked extensively with Mike Gibbs and Carla Bley in the '70s and '80s, and has also become a prolific composer, with works recorded by Bley, Burton, Gibbs, and Chick Corea, among others. —*Ron Wynn*

★ **Swallow** / Sep. 1991-Nov. 1991 / ECM 511960
Swallow rarely departs from the recipe used in the bassist's 1987 *Carla* and in recent small-group Carla Bley records (with similar personnel). Cushy arrangements padded with multiple keyboards frame springy stop-and-go rhythms. Bley's three-chord organ vamps set up Swallow's lead bass and solos from former employers vibist Gary Burton and guitarist John Scofield. Grooves (fast and slow) are everything here. —*Jon Andrews, Down Beat*

Harvie Swartz

b. Dec. 6, 1948, Chelsea, MA
Bass / Early jazz-rock, modern creative
Bandleader, composer, and bassist Swartz has worked with the group Urban Earth and recorded with Sheila Jordan, Mike Stern, and others. —*Ron Wynn*

★ **Underneath It All** / Mar. 1-02, 1980 / Gramavision 8202
This bassist's debut album is with Ben Aranov on piano and John D'Earth on trumpet. This is challenging music, approaching fusion. All selections are Swartz's originals. His later albums don't quite match up, but this is virtuoso. His best is on the way. —*Michael G. Nastos*

○ **Full Moon Dancer** / i. 1991 / Blue Moon 79150

Gabor Szabo

b. Mar. 8, 1956, Budapest, Hungary, **d.** Mar. 1, 1982, Budapest, Hunagary

Guitar, composer / Cool, early jazz-rock

Hungarian guitarist and composer Gabor Szabo didn't come to America until he was nearly 20, but he was still a successful contributor to several jazz groups and sessions. He made his first impact as a member of Chico Hamilton's groups and later worked with Gary McFarland and Charles Lloyd. He co-led a group with Cal Tjader and McFarland in 1968-1969 and then did some recording in which Lena Horne was the featured vocalist. Szabo led other West Coast bands in the '70s, among them the fusion and jazz-rock unit Perfect Circle in 1975, and later recorded with Chick Corea. —*Ron Wynn*

○ **Gypsy '66** / 1965 / Impulse 9105

○ **Spellbinder** / May 6, 1966 / Impulse 9123

○ **Sorcerer, The** / Apr. 14-15, 1967 / MCA 33117

★ **Greatest Hits** / MCA
This is a combination of tracks that guitarist Gabor Szabo recorded over a three-year period (1965-1967) plus a pair of tracks from his earlier association with drummer Chico Hamilton's group. The 18 cuts literally ranged from the sublime to the ridiculous. —*Richard B. Kamins, Cadence*

Lew Tabackin (Lewis Barry Tabackin)

b. May 26, 1940, Philadelphia, PA

Tenor sax, flute / Bop, postbop, progressive big band

Tenor saxophonist and flutist Lew Tabackin is well respected as one of jazz's finest flutists, an excellent soloist and strong accompanist on tenor. He moved to New York in 1965 and worked with Maynard Ferguson, Clark Terry, the Thad Jones-Mel Lewis big band, Joe Henderson, and several combos before starting his own trio in 1968-1969. Following a tour of Switzerland, a jazz workshop in Hamburg, and a stint as featured soloist with the Danish Radio Orchestra, Tabackin married pianist Toshiko Akiyoshi and toured Japan with her in the early '70s. They moved to Los Angeles in 1972 and began a series of workshops. Their workshop big band evolved into the Akiyoshi-Tabackin big band, one of the decade's finest. Tabackin alternated big-band and session work in the '70s and early '80s, and he and Akiyoshi moved back to New York in 1982, the same year he won *Down Beat's* critics poll on flute. Later he and Akiyoshi began their own label, Ascent Records. Among his best recent releases was a 1983 session with Freddie Hubbard titled *Sweet Return.* —*Ron Wynn*

★ **Dual Nature** / Aug. 31, 1976+Sep. 3, 1976 / Inner City 1028
Tabackin on flute (he is unbelievable), alto, and tenor sax, with the Don Friedman Trio. Tunes are from Tabackin, Toshiko Akiyoshi, Bill Mays. Also included are three standards. Tabackin is on sax on one side and flute on the other. There is some astounding musicianship from all. —*Michael G. Nastos*

○ **Tenor Gladness** / Oct. 13-14, 1976 / Inner City 6048
Dueling tenors with Warne Marsh. Six originals were written by the principles or Toshiko Akiyoshi. It is a bit progressive and a thoroughly satisfying date from two virtuosos. —*Michael G. Nastos*

☆ **Rites of Pan** / 1977 / Inner City 6052
1977-1978. Tabackin here is on flute alone with the Toshiko Trio. This is deep harmonic music from the participants' pens as well as some from Dizzie Gillespie, Fats Waller, and Kurt Weill. The flute is startling, but for open ears. —*Michael G. Nastos*

○ **I'll Be Seeing You** / **i.** 1992 / Concord Jazz 4528
Lew Tabackin's is an arpeggiated tenor sax approach, chords up and down, with a throaty attack made up of equal parts cataclysmic slurs and staccato runs. His vibrato is a broad swipe: Horse laugh meets a slow, hot wind. He likes to decorate a melody, as Thelonius Monk's "Ruby, My Dear" and Duke Ellington's "Isfahan" make clear. —*Owen Cordle, Down Beat*

Jamaaladeen Tacuma

b. Jun. 11, 1956, Hempstead, NY

Bass / Early jazz-rock, instrumental pop, modern creative

Jamaaladden Tacuma is a premier electric bassist, best known for his stint with Ornette Coleman's Prime Time Band. Extremely influenced by the style and technique of Stanley Clarke and Jaco

Pastorius, Tacuma is one of the fastest and cleanest players, able to execute rapid-fire passages and huge, thick accompanying lines and essentially play like a guitarist. His releases outside of Coleman's band have largely been disappointing. —*Ron Wynn*

○ **Show Stopper** / 1982-1983 / Gramavision 79435
1982-1983. The five-piece electric band for electric bassist shows many positive and eclectic forces rooted in jazz but not stuck in the past. Includes "Bird of Paradise" with the Ebony String Quartet. Title track with Olu Dara and Julius Hemphill is a treat of all-out contempo-bop. Other cameos are by Blood Ulmer on guitar and Cornell Rochester on drums. This is a fun album. —*Michael G. Nastos*

★ **Music World** / 1986 / Gramavision 79437
1990 reissue that again shows Tacuma cannot harness his great talent into an effective showpiece. —*Ron Wynn*

Horace Tapscott

b. Apr. 6, 1934, Houston, TX

Piano / Postbop, early free, progressive big band, neo-bop, modern creative

Horace Tapscott is a Los Angeles cultural hero. He's the leader of the UGMAA (Underground Musicians and Artists Alliance), and a postbop and creative pianist, composer, arranger, and band leader (big and small). His influence on such players as Arthur Blythe and Azar Lawrence was considerable. He's a delicate or dense improviser. —*Michael G. Nastos*

○ **Giant Is Awakened, The** / **i.** May 1970 / Flying Dutchman 107

★ **Dark Tree—Vol. 1, The** / Dec. 14-17, 1989 / Hat Art 6053
Pianist and bandleader Horace Tapscott has defied easy categorization for over 20 years. His compositions are as likely to be hinged on waltz time or melodies tinged with sentiment as they are on propulsive vamps and jagged themes. Stylistically, his playing is all over the map—from Mal Waldronlike distillations to McCoy Tyneresque power. He tenaciously anchors tempo and form, often with elemental left-hand ostinati, and often for far longer than it takes to make the point. —*Bill Shoemaker, Down Beat*

○ **Dark Tree—Vol. 2, The** / **i.** Dec. 1989 / Hat Art 6083
Includes club recordings featuring clarinetist John Carter done by pianist-bandleader Horace Tapscott in 1989. The recordings, which also feature bassist Cecil McBee and drummer Andrew Cyrille, include long stretches of inspired improvisational interplay. —*Bill Shoemaker, Down Beat*

Buddy Tate (George Holmes Tate)

b. Feb. 22, 1913, Sherman, TX

Tenor sax / Swing, big band, blues & jazz

One of the living prototypes of Texas tenor saxophone, Buddy Tate earned his spurs playing in territory bands before joining Count Basie's Orchestra in 1939, replacing the legendary Herschel Evans. He spent nine years with Basie and then worked with Lucky Millinder, Hot Lips Page, and Jimmy Rushing's Savoy band before getting the chance to take up residency at the Celebrity Club in Harlem. While spending 21 years there, Tate did plenty of recording and touring with swing and bop veterans. He continues performing today, playing with the robust, booming tone; quiet swing; and excellent style that has made him a master saxophonist. —*Ron Wynn*

★ **Swinging Like Tate** / Feb. 12, 1958+Feb. 26, 1958 / Verve 820599
Prototypical Kansas City stomping set with Papa Jo Jones on drums. Dynamic, hot solos. —*Ron Wynn*

○ **Tate-A-Tate** / Oct. 18, 1960 / Prestige 184
Bubbly modern mainstream was found on *Tate-A-Tate*, a 10/18/60 date with Buddy Tate leading a group (Clark Terry, trumpet; Tommy Flanagan, piano; Larry Gates, bass; Art Taylor, drums) over six tracks. . . . Clark Terry was right on the money and sounding '60s fresh. —*Bob Rusch, Cadence*

○ **Sherman Shuff** / Jan. 29, 1978 / Sackville 3017
This Canadian Sackville recording stemmed from an ingenious New York mating of mainstreamers Buddy Tate and Bob Wilber with modernists bassist Sam Jones and drummer Leroy Williams. While the tenorman's sustained excellence should surprise no one familiar with his current work, many will note approvingly Bob Wilber's progress on alto sax, an instrument he associates almost exclusively with Johnny Hodges. —*Jack Sohmer, Down Beat*

★ **Hard Blowin'** / Aug. 25-26, 1978 / Muse 5249
This was the sixth Muse LP from the Sandy's Jazz Revival venue, taped during two days when the machine must have been allowed to run around the clock, and it was the second of the six to appear under tenor saxophonist Buddy Tate's name. Unlike the first— in fact, unlike any of the other five—the other horn players involved in these sessions (Arnet Cobb and Eddie Vinson) did not appear on even one track of this latest release. So, what we had here was Tate's puissant tenor in front of a dynamic rhythm section. . . . All in all, one of Tate's tastiest . . . and best. —*Alan Bargebuhr, Cadence*

○ **Live at Sandy's** / Aug. 25-26, 1978 / Muse 5198
It's obvious this was tenor saxophonist Buddy Tate's gig since the other two saxophonists only played on "She's Got It". . . . Since Eddie "Cleanhead" Vinson and Arnett Cobb come from Houston and Tate is from Sherman (more than two hundred miles north), it was no surprise that he and Vinson never played together before. There is a "Texas Tenor Sound" but there is more than what this early generation played. No doubt about it, this is exactly the way dozens of tenor players sounded in the very early '40s. — *Jerry L. Atkins, Cadence*

☆ **Ballad Artistry of Buddy Tate** / Jun. 12-13, 1981 / Sackville 3034
The name of guitarist Ed Bickert could easily be substituted for Buddy Tate's in the title of this album. For while Tate played well, Bickert stole the show. Aside from "B.T. Blues" and a mildly swinging version of "A Foggy Day," this was an album of ballads, something of a switch for Tate. —*Doug Long, Cadence*

Grady Tate

b. Jan. 14, 1932, Durham, NC
Drums, vocals / Bop, ballads & blues
Though he could have been a star as a vocalist, Grady Tate has gained as much fame and recognition as a drummer. He's equally effective pushing and driving the beat or providing shading and subdued rhythms. Tate's recorded bebop, hard bop, swing, big-band, and soul jazz, and his own singing ability makes him the ideal drummer to accompany vocalists. He began playing drums at five, and initially taught himself. Tate later learned more fundamentals and nuances while in the air force during the '50s. He returned to his North Carolina home after his discharge, studying literature, theater, and psychology at North Carolina College while working part-time as a musician. Tate moved to Washington in 1959, where he played with Wild Bill Davis. He moved to New York two years later, where he played in Quincy Jones's big band and with Jerome Richardson. Tate has subsequently worked with Duke Ellington, Count Basie, Jimmy Smith, Wes Montgomery, Rahsaan Roland Kirk, and many others. He's also backed vocalists Peggy Lee, Sarah Vaughan, Ella Fitzgerald, Astrud Gilberto, Chris Connor, Ray Charles, Blossom Dearie, and Lena Horne. Tate's albums for Skye, Impulse, Milestone, and other labels have emphasized his vocals as much, if not more than his drumming. But his drumming is well represented on sessions. Tate currently has a couple of dates available on CD. —*Ron Wynn*

● **By Special Request** / **i.** Apr. 1975 / Buddah 5623
This album represented Grady Tate the vocalist rather than Tate the percussionist. As such it was primarily pop-soul performances wrapped around Tate's sensual voice. —*Herb Nolan, Down Beat*

Art Tatum (Arthur Tatum, Jr.)

b. 1909, Toledo, OH, **d.** Nov. 5, 1956, Los Angeles, CA
Piano / Swing
The most prodigiously gifted pianist to turn his talent to jazz was born with gravely impaired eyesight and received his musical training at an institution for the blind in his native Toledo. Musicians who heard Art Tatum there as early as 1924 claim he was as amazing then as when he became visible on the national jazz scene in the early '30s. He made his first records as accompanist to singer Adelaide Hail, but that was his last job working for someone else: He was a soloist to the manner born. Playing on 52d Street and in nightclubs throughout the United States, he made his first and only trip abroad to England in 1938, but even there he performed not in concert but on the vaudeville circuit. In 1943 he formed a trio with Tiny Grimes on guitar, and Slam Stewart on bass—the format that brought him his greatest popular success. Even so, it wasn't until Norman Granz took him un-

der his wing, just three years before his untimely death, that Tatum was recorded under proper auspices, with the care an artist of his stature deserved. Tatum's technique was staggering and rivaled that of the greatest classical virtuosos, but unlike them, he was able to give free rein to his imagination and fully exercise his phenomenal rhythmic sense. But even when he unleashed a torrent of notes, the melody was kept in focus. Tatum loved to "battle" with other pianists and was as likely as not to smother hornplayers who sat in with him. Yet he could be a marvelous accompanist when he wanted, to singers he liked or to a hornsman (like Ben Webster) who was not a technical whiz but a great melodist. And Tatum was a master of the blues. His audacious harmonic inventions had considerable influence on Charlie Parker, who listened to him with great attention during a New York stay in 1939. Tatum was a phenomenon. —*Dan Morgenstern*

★ **Piano Starts Here** / Mar. 21, 1933-Apr. 2, 1949 / Columbia 9655
Piano also ends here. This LP contains more than its share of stunning performances, consisting of Art Tatum's first recording date (which is highlighted by an incredible version of "Tiger Rag") and a 1949 concert. From the latter, Tatum's reworking of "Yesterdays" and blinding stride on "I Know That You Know" will make many amateur pianists look for day jobs. The studio date has since been reissued on CD but the live performance remains unavailable. —*Scott Yanow*

○ **Art Tatum (1932-1934)** / **i.** Mar. 1933-Oct. 1934 / Classics 507
This comprehensive CD contains Art Tatum's very first recording (a broadcast version of "Tiger Rag"), four selections in which he accompanies singer Adelaide Hall (along with a second pianist!), and then his first 20 solo sides. To call Tatum's virtuosic piano style remarkable would be a major understatement; he has to be heard to be believed. His studio version of "Tiger Rag" may very well be Tatum's most incredible recording; he sounds like three pianists at once! —*Scott Yanow*

★ **Classic Piano Solos (1934-39)** / 1934-1939 / GRP 607
This excellent CD reissues all of Art Tatum's early Decca piano solos cut at three sessions in 1934 and one in 1937. Tatum was decades ahead of his contemporaries not only in technique but also in harmonic ideas. Highlights of this very impressive set include "Emaline," "After You've Gone, "The Shout," two versions of "Liza," and "The Sheik of Araby." —*Scott Yanow*

○ **Standard Transcriptions** / 1935-1943 / Music & Arts 673
In 1935, 1939, and 1943 Art Tatum recorded an extensive series of piano solos 163 in all) for radio airplay; these were not available commercially (and then only piecemeal) until long after the LP era was underway. Music & Arts on this two-CD set gives listeners all of the remarkable music together for the first time. Tatum fans familiar with only his commercial recordings will find much to marvel at during this recommended set. —*Scott Yanow*

○ **Standards** / 1938-1939 / Black Lion 760143
This Black Lion CD features brilliant piano solos from Art Tatum that were originally cut as noncommercial radio transcriptions during 1938-1939. Duplicating part of Tatum's Music & Arts double-CD, *Standards* features a great deal of magic from the remarkable virtuoso. —*Scott Yanow*

○ **Solos (1940)** / 1940 / MCA 42327
MCA's short-lived Decca CD reissue program put out this gem, all of Art Tatum's piano solos from 1940, including two versions of the previously unknown "Sweet Emalina, My Gal." Some of the routines on these standards were a bit familiar by now (this "Tiger Rag" pales next to his 1933 version) but are no less exciting and still sound seemingly impossible to play. Well worth picking up. —*Scott Yanow*

○ **V-Discs, The** / 1944-1946 / Black Lion 760114
This Black Lion CD mostly features the phenomenal Art Tatum playing solo during 1945-1946, really digging into a variety of standards. A rare version of "Sweet Lorraine" (with bassist Oscar Pettiford and drummer Sid Catlett in 1944) and two numbers with his 1945 trio (featuring guitarist Tiny Grimes and bassist Slam Stewart) round out this excellent CD. —*Scott Yanow*

● **Complete Pablo Solo Masterpieces, The** / Dec. 28, 1953-Jan. 19, 1955 / Pablo 4404
During four marathon recording sessions in 1953-1955, Norman Granz recorded Art Tatum playing 119 standards, enough music for a dozen LPs. The results have been recently reissued sepa-

rately on eight CDs and on this very full seven-CD boxed set. Frankly, Tatum did no real advance preparation for this massive project, sticking mosty to concise melodic variations of standards, some of them virtual set pieces formed over the past two decades. Since there are few uptempo performances, the music in this series has a certain sameness after awhile, but heard in small doses it is quite enjoyable. A special bonus on this box (and not on the individual volumes) are four numbers taken from a 1956 Hollywood Bowl concert. —*Scott Yanow*

○ **Tatum Solo Masterpieces—Vol. 1** / 1953-1955 / Pablo 2405-432
The first of eight CDs reissuing the 119 piano solo performances that Art Tatum recorded for Norman Granz during four marathon record sessions has its moments although in general this series lacks the excitement of Tatum's earliest recordings. The pianist interprets such standards on this first volume as "Body and Soul," "It's Only a Paper Moon," and "Willow Weep for Me." —*Scott Yanow*

★ **Complete Pablo Group Masterpieces, The** / Jun. 1954-Aug. 1956 / Pablo 4401
Art Tatum spent most of his career as a solo pianist; in fact it was often said that he was such an unpredictable virtuoso that it would be difficult for other musicians to play with him. Producer Norman Granz sought to prove that the theory was false, so between 1954 and 1956 he extensively recorded Tatum with a variety of other classic jazzmen, resulting originally in nine LPs of material that is now available as eight separate CDs and on this very full six-CD boxed set. In contrast to the massive solo Tatum sessions that Granz also recorded during this period, the group sides have plenty of variety and exciting moments, which is not too surprising when one considers that Tatum was teamed in a trio with altoist Benny Carter and drummer Louie Bellson; with trumpeter Roy Eldridge, clarinetist Buddy DeFranco, and tenor-saxophonist Hen Webster in separate quartets; in an explosive trio with vibraphonist Lionel Hampton and drummer Buddy Rich; with a sextet including Hampton, Rich, and trumpeter Henry "Sweets" Edison; and on a standard trio session. Highly recommended. —*Scott Yanow*

Art Taylor (Arthur S. Taylor, Jr.)

b. Apr. 6, 1929, New York, NY
Drums / Bop, hard bop
A first-rate drummer, able to absorb the classic timekeeping-style of swing and then adjust to the changing roles instituted by coming of bop and hard bop. Taylor's earliest jobs were with Howard McGhee and Coleman Hawkins in the '50s, and his first recording session came with Hawkins. He later toured with Buddy DeFranco and then worked with Bud Powell's trio twice and George Wallington's trio and quintet during the mid- and late '50s. He also had stints in that decade with Miles Davis and the Donald Byrd-Gigi Gryce group, as well as Thelonious Monk. He became a familiar figure in recording sessions at Prestige, Blue Note, and other labels in the '60s, at one point recording with John Coltrane, Jackie McLean, Hank Mobley, and Lee Morgan. He moved to Europe in 1963 and worked with various expatriates and musicians on tour. He conducted numerous interviews with musicians from the late '60s until the early '70s; the results were the acclaimed book *Notes and Tones*. He returned to New York in 1980 and twice during that decade organized tribute concerts to Bud Powell. —*Ron Wynn*

○ **Taylor's Wailers** / Feb. 25, 1956-Mar. 22, 1957 / Prestige 094
This was typical of the recorded jams that regularly flowed from the Prestige-Rudy Van Gelder connection. This LP listed Red Garland on piano, but it was clearly not him and usual credit goes to Mal Waldron, who hadn't yet become the highly identifiable pianist of the '70s (and '80s)or developed the definition found in a stylist like Garland. This was fine Prestige bop of the period. —*Bob Rusch, Cadence*

○ **Taylor's Tenors** / Jun. 3, 1959 / New Jazz 8219

★ **Art Taylor's Delight** / i. Aug. 6, 1960 / Blue Note 84047
Early '60s definitive sides from this drummer and group known as Taylor's Wailers. —*Michael G. Nastos*

○ **Mr. A. T.** / 1991 / Enja 79677
Mr. A. T. reaffirms the jazz values of the '50s and '60s: bebop, hard bop, and the postbop experimentation of John Coltrane (with whom Art Taylor recorded). Taylor is a bop drummer in the Max Roach, Art Blakey, and Philly Joe Jones style. Tenor saxophonist

Willie Williams suggests John Coltrane, Sonny Rollins, and Hank Mobley, and alto saxophonist Abraham Burton has the hard edge and firm note placement of Jackie McLean, his teacher. Pianist Marc Cary is a more mature soloist who gravitates toward energetic lines and Red Garlandlike block chords. —*Owen Cordle, Down Beat*

Billy Taylor (William Taylor, Jr)

b. Jul. 21, 1921, Washington, DC
Piano, educator / Bop
Few people have served jazz more effectively, as a writer, broadcaster, performer, and composer, than Billy Taylor. His many other activities have tended to overshadow his solid playing, which reflects both the influence of being tutored at one time by Art Tatum and his knowledge of and love for the blues and gospel. A fluid two-handed player, Taylor's rhythms in his prime could almost bowl you over, while his sweeping left-hand statements were immaculate and impressive. Taylor met Tatum and other Harlem legends during trips as a teenager from his North Carolina home. He moved to New York in the early '40s and worked with Ben Webster, Dizzy Gillespie, Stuff Smith, and several others. He led the house rhythm section at Birdland in 1951 and had his own trio throughout the remainder of the decade. But when Taylor cofounded the Jazzmobile in 1965, he began a parallel career as jazz advocate that has won him widespread fame, Emmy awards, and recognition. He was the musical director of the David Frost television show, the first Black to hold that position. His book *Jazz Piano* was a critical and educational sensation in 1982, and his interviews and reports on jazz were a monthly staple of Charles Kuralt's "Sunday Morning" broadcast. —*Ron Wynn*

★ **Billy Taylor Touch, The** / Oct. 28, 1957 / Atlantic 1277

☆ **Billy Taylor with Four Flutes** / Jul. 20, 1959 / Riverside 1151
W/ Frank Wess, Herbie Mann, Jerome Richardson, and Phil Bodner. —*Michael G. Nastos*

○ **Wish I Knew How It Would Feel to Be Free** / 196z / Tower 5111
Recorded with a trio and features Taylor's immortal song bearing the title of the album, several pop and jazz standards, Clare Fischer's "Morning" and "Pensativa," Taylor's "CAG." Bandmates featured are Ben Tucker (b) and Grady Tates (d). —*Michael G. Nastos*

★ **Live at Storyville** / Dec. 2-03, 1977 / West 54
Recorded in New York City with drummer Grady Tate and bassist Victor Gaskin, this album includes classic standards and three Taylor originals including "I Wish I Knew . . . ." It ranges from modern to bop to ballads. This is standard virtuosity from Taylor—you expect nothing less. —*Michael G. Nastos*

○ **Jazzmobile Allstars** / Apr. 1989 / Taylor Made 1003

Cecil Taylor (Cecil Percival Taylor)

b. Mar. 15, 1929, New York, NY
Piano, composer / Early free, modern creative
To say that pianist Cecil Taylor is a revolutionary musician is an understatement. Since the late '50s he has changed the method by which jazz improvisation can be approached as much as John Cage has influenced contemporary sound and concept. Taylor has a free-flowing, take-no-prisoners style, a recognizable voice that emphasizes chord clusters, connected phrases, and bluesy, dense ruminations to form an endless string of original ideas. For those perhaps intimidated by the music of a firebrand and maverick, try his early albums on Contemporary, or the *N.Y. City R&B* album. Later albums with his combo, the Unit, or his revelatory solo albums impart much of his knowledge and uncanny sixth sense as a true original. Taylor has another weapon in his arsenal. He is a wonderful poet who uses words in ethnic tongues and dialects in performance, melded with martial arts dance movements that leave a lasting impression of visual imagery along with the very potent music he creates. —*Michael G. Nastos*

○ **New York City R&B** / Jan. 1961 / Candid 79017
This was a Buell Neidlinger (bass) session that was originally intended to be issued on Candid Records in 1961. It wasn't released until 1971 and then was billed as a co-led session with Cecil Taylor (piano). Taylor's presence does initially overshadow the participation of everyone. . . . But clearly the date is Neidlinger's.

His presence should not be underestimated. —*Robert Iannapollo, Cadence*

★ **Unit Structures** / May 19, 1966 / Blue Note 84237

○ **Student Studies** / Nov. 30, 1966 / Affinity 770
The music on this two-record set was recorded in concert in Paris. As usual, the whole was much larger than the sum of the parts, and I found there was enough inspired listening here to easily recommend the music. *Student Studies* tells some good tales and was full of the Taylor dynamics and at the same time quite accessible. —*Bob Rusch, Cadence*

○ **Great Paris Concert** / i. 1966 / Freedom 10
This three-record set contained a 90-minute performance entitled "Second Act of A" and a 20-minute encore. The main work—consisting of quartets, trios, duets, and solo passages—proceeded with almost unrelieved intensity. Even the few lyrical segments, arcane and shimmering, ached under the strain. There was only one dynamic level—loud—occasionally broken by bursts of volume or sudden lulls. —*Douglas Clark, Down Beat*

★ **Great Concert of Cecil Taylor** / i. Jul. 29, 1969 / Prestige 34003
Boxed set with Taylor in searing live concert alongside Sam Rivers (sax) and Jimmy Lyons (as). Three discs of amazing playing. —*Ron Wynn*

○ **Fondation Maeght Nights—Vol. 1, 2 & 3** / i. Jul. 1969 / Jazzview 001
Originally issued in separate volumes, this classic live recording of the Cecil Taylor Unit at Saint-Paul-de-Vence, France, has been made available as a boxed, three-record set. The music was gloriously alive with a depth and richness that grew with each new listening. —*Carl Brauer, Cadence*

○ **Spring of Two Blue Jays** / i. 1973 / Unit Core
It's impossible to be indifferent to Cecil Taylor's music; one either loves it or hates it. Taylor. . . has essentially forged a revolutionary approach to jazz piano. Sections of *Spring of Two Blue Jays* sound as if they were recorded at half speed and then accelerated, such was the velocity and brilliance of Taylor's upper register work. —*Jon Balleras, Down Beat*

☆ **Unit** / Apr. 3-06, 1978 / New World 201
The inclusion here of Ramsey Ameen's violin alongside the familiar trumpet and sax completed the full symphonic tonal palette in miniature, rounding out a rich timbral blend that augured possible larger-scaled projects. On the other hand, the intimacy of the quintet permitted a degree of spontaneous interplay impossible in larger formats, a responsiveness quite remarkably illustrated in this tour de force of empathetic improvisation. This beautifully packaged and annotated album captured pianist Cecil Taylor at the peak of his maturity, employing essentially the same conceptual group framework he has utilized at least since *Unit Structures*. —*Larry Birnbaum, Down Beat*

○ **One Too Many Salty Swift and Not Goodbye** / Jun. 4, 1978 / Hat Hut 3R02
With drummer Ronald Shannon Jackson in peak rhythmic form, the group that made *One Too Many Salty Swift and Not Goodbye* in 1978 was arguably the finest larger Cecil Taylor unit to date. Recorded shortly after the landmark studio sessions for New World Records, this is the sextet's epic final concert, restored to its entirety on two CDs with the addition of three Taylorless stage warmers. —*John Corbett, Down Beat*

★ **Historic Concerts** / i. 1979 / Soul Note

○ **It Is in the Brewing Luminous** / Feb. 8-09, 1980 / Hat Art 6012

○ **Fly, Fly, Fly, Fly, Fly** / Sep. 14, 1980 / MPS 7108
A solo piano album that defines Taylor's individuality and does indeed fly. Diamond Award Winner in 1981. —*Michael G. Nastos*

○ **Eighth, The** / Nov. 1981 / Hat Art 6036
The chemistry of this group combined with pianist Cecil Taylor's structural landmarks and the *drive* were the essence of this music. . . . Some of Taylor's work with just the bass and drums (William Parker, Rashid Bakr) during sections missing from the original release spotlighted an attractive rough, ragged approach where he chopped at the piano in flurried or pounded fragments. —*Milo Fine, Cadence*

★ **Complete Candid Recordings of Cecil Taylor** / i. Jun. 1990 / Mosaic 127
The sessions that comprise the four discs on this first-rate Mosaic boxed set were done in 1960 and 1961 for the short-lived Candid

label. Taylor's concept had not yet evolved into a finished package. If one impression dominates these discs it is that Taylor himself was not always sure where he was going. There are solos that begin in one direction, break in the middle, and conclude in another. Tenor saxophonist Archie Shepp often sounds unsure about what to play, whether to try and interact or establish his own direction. At the same time, there is plenty of exceptional playing from Taylor, Shepp, and the drum-bass combination of Buell Neidlinger and Dennis Charles. You cannot honestly say everything works on these four discs, but there is never a dull moment. It will not please everyone, but listeners ready for a challenge should step right up and take on this set. —*Ron Wynn*

Jack Teagarden (Weldon Leo Teagarden)

b. Jul. 19, 1905, Vernon, TX, d. Jan. 15, 1964, New Orleans, LA
Trombone, vocals / Dixieland
Jack Teagarden was a jazz immortal, superb trombonist, and one of the real class acts and humorists in the music's long history. No one had ever so easily and completely mastered the trombone prior to Teagarden, and precious few since have had his total control over the instrument. He played difficult phrases, tricky lines, incredible solos, and pithy licks with such ease that his excellent, charming vocal abilities were thoroughly overshadowed. Teagarden's reputation began to grow when he played in Peck Kelley's band in 1921. Teagarden then worked with Willard Robison, Doc Ross, and Ben Pollack and then spent five years with Paul Whiteman, becoming his principal soloist despite having little respect for most of what he was playing. Teagarden formed his own band in 1939 and spent the next seven years heading various groups, before joining Louis Armstrong's All-Stars in 1946. He stayed until 1951 and for the rest of his life led different aggregations and made many remarkable records. Many of Teagarden's innovations, among them varying the volume at which he played, using water-glass mutes, and revolutionizing the use of the slide, have become a mandatory part of the trombone vernacular. —*Ron Wynn*

☆ **That's a Serious Thing** / Mar. 1928-Jul. 1957 / Bluebird 9986

★ **King of the Blues Trombone** / i. 1928-1940 / Sony Special Products 6044

○ **I Gotta Right to Sing the Blues** / Feb. 1929-Oct. 1934 / ASV 5059

○ **Indispensable, The** / i. 1929-1933 / RCA 45695
1929-1933. With a wide variety of bands—Eddie Condon, Ben Pollack, Paul Whiteman, Budd Freeman, and others—this is a great overview of the trombonists carreer. There are several vocals on the 31 cuts and four alternate takes. —*Michael G. Nastos*

○ **100 Years from Today** / i. 1931 / Grudge 4523

○ **Jack Teagarden's Big Eight / Pee Wee Russell's Rhythmakers** / Aug. 31, 1938-Dec. 15, 1940 / Riverside 1708
W/ Pee Wee Russell (cl). 1938 & 1940. Two titans of classic New Orleans style make a great match. —*Ron Wynn*

☆ **Meet Me Where They Play the Blues** / Nov. 1954-Nov. 12, 1954 / Bethlehem 6040
The 12 tracks from these 1954 sessions were issued by the Jazztone Society in the '50s, and the serious record buyer would do well to keep searching the bargain bins for the reissue of that five-star LP. This more expensive LP had only 10 titles, and the long "Blue Funk," by far the best performance from the Leonard Feather date, is among the missing. —*John Litweiler, Down Beat*

☆ **Columbia Special Products** / i. Dec. 1979 / XFL 14940
This Jack Teagarden set is three discs containing a total of 48 tracks, covering a period from November 27, 1928 ("Whoopee Stomp"), to July 23, 1940 ("Shi-Me-Sha-Wabble"). The only real gaps are between mid-1936 and mid-1939, a Paul Whiteman period (Decca and RCA), and, considering what usually surrounded his work with that orchestra, its exclusion is of little loss. There are some cornball tracks in the Teagarden set, but not the music from Teagarden's horn. The individuals making up the discography of these sides reads like a Who's Who of Chicago jazz. —*Bob Rusch, Cadence*

● **Accent on Sound** / Fresh Sound

Clark Terry (Clark [Mumbles] Terry)

b. Dec. 14, 1920, St. Louis, MO
Trumpet, flugelhorn, vocals / Big band, bop, progressive big band

Clark Terry is a superior trumpeter and one of the first to introduce the flugelhorn as a legitimate second instrument for jazz brass players. Indeed, Terry's utilization of vocal effects on trumpet, plus his striking rhythmic abilities, have made him highly admired among his peers. He got his early experience playing in St. Louis bands and in Navy bands during World War II, where he met and worked with Willie Smith. He spent a brief period with Lionel Hampton and then worked with Charlie Barnet, Count Basie, Duke Ellington, and Quincy Jones from the late '40s until 1960. He spent 12 years in the "Tonight Show" band, becoming one of the first Black musicians hired for that august group in the '60s. He's also done plenty of studio work, led a periodic big band, participated in many clinics, and co-led a group with Bob Brookmeyer. —*Ron Wynn*

☆ **Clark Terry** / Jan. 3-04, 1955 / Emarcy 36007

○ **Serenade to a Bus Seat** / Apr. 17, 1957 / Original Jazz Classics 66
Why it took so long for Clark Terry to be recognized for his fine stylized trumpet work is hard to understand, as even by the time of this date he had quite well established himself as a capable individual voice. —*Bob Rusch, Cadence*

★ **In Orbit** / May 7+12, 1958 / Riverside 302
Quartet with Thelonious Monk. Terry shows he can fit into any setting, even with Monk's always arresting, unorthodox piano style. Date also has Sam Jones (b) and Philly Joe Jones (d). CD has bonus cut, 1988 reissue. —*Ron Wynn*

★ **New York Sessions** / **i.** Oct. 3-04, 1961 / Fontana

☆ **Gingerbread Men** / 1966 / Mainstream 373
W/ Bob Brookmeyer (tb) Quintet. This is a fine set, reissued recently. —*Ron Wynn*

★ **Clark Terry's Big B-A-D-Band Live at the Wichita Jazz Festival** / Apr. 21, 1974 / Vanguard 79355
That this band didn't work steadily made its performance here even more remarkable. Much credit had to go to the unit's arrangers, especially to Phil Woods and Ernie Wilkins. Note Wilkins's now revised "Take the 'A' Train" chart, a masterpiece of ensemble writing and reed voicings. Even more impressive was Woods's ballad "Randy." It's impossible to imagine this chart played better—perfect articulation, perfect intonation, perfect balance. —*Jon Balleras, Down Beat*

○ **Clark Terry and His Jolly Giants** / 1975 / Vanguard 79365
Clark Terry had his thing down pat; a small group drawn from his active big band recorded a lighthearted selection of tunes, either familiar or blues-based. Up tempos alternated with medium speeds, and there wasn't one sloppy moment. —*Howie Mandel, Down Beat*

○ **Ain't Misbehavin'** / Mar. 15-16, 1976 / Pablo 105
This served as a sprightly showcase for tunes either written or associated with Fats Waller. Outstanding in his role as front-line mate was the underappreciated alto saxophonist Chris Woods. Clark Terry's unforced humor was evident throughout this session, but be advised that the current (1986) pressing is not up to the standard of the original Pablo. —*Bob Rusch, Cadence*

☆ **Big Bad Band Live at Buddy's Place** / 1976 / Vanguard 79373
What we really got for our money on this album was an assortment of fine soloists working out with an alternately conventional and funky rhythm section with a few big-band punctuations dropped in like cameos. Not surprisingly, the best sounds were rooted in a time when giants wrote big-band music. —*John Mcdonough, Down Beat*

○ **Jive at Five** / **i.** Feb. 1986+Jul. 1988 / Enja 6042
This is a wondrous combination. Trumpeter-flugelhornist Clark Terry and bassist-pianist Red Mitchell represent the apogee of the mainstream meld where bebop meets swing. —*Chuck Berg, Jazz Times*

Jean Toots Thielemans (Jean Baptiste Thielemans)

b. Apr. 29, 1922, Brussels, Belgium
Harmonica, guitar / Swing, bop, Latin-jazz
Jean "Toots" Thielemans is a Belgian harmonicist-guitarist. He's influenced by Django Reinhardt and played with Benny Goodman and George Shearing. Thielemans composed the famous "Bluesette." He has incredible boplike facility on chromatic harmonica. Though he has a tendency toward sweet ballads, Thielemans can also can play modally. —*Michael G. Nastos*

★ **Man Bites Harmonica** / Dec. 30, 1957+Jan. 7, 1958 / Riverside 1738
Early period. Definitive harmonicist from Belgium. W/ Pepper Adams, Kenny Drew, Wilbur Ware, and Art Taylor. —*Michael G. Nastos*

☆ **Silver Collection** / Apr. 1974-Apr. 1975 / Verve 825086

○ **Captured Alive** / Sep. 1974 / Choice 1007
There was a decidedly schizophrenic quality to the music—the feeling of split personality ran all through the performances—that resulted from very real conceptual differences at the core of Toots Thielemans's playing and that of the rhythm section. Coming from basically the same place, pianist Joanne Brackeen, bassist Cecil McBee, and drummer Freddie Waits worked well together, playing a hard, tight, sinewy modernized bebop of an absolutely pared-to-the-bone economy. It was Thielemans on harmonica who was the odd man out, his broadly romantic, frequently florid approach to this music very much at variance with the no-nonsense muscularity of the trio. —*Pete Welding, Down Beat*

☆ **Only Trust Your Heart** / Apr. 1988-May 1988 / Concord Jazz 4355
A bit too sentimental, good playing. CD version has two prime cuts. —*Ron Wynn*

Ed Thigpen (Edmund Leonard Thigpen)

b. Dec. 28, 1930, Chicago, IL
Drums / Bop
Ed Thigpen's a highly-respected, seasoned drummer and percussionist with great skills in every phase of his craft. Thigpen plays with sensitivity and swing; he uses brushes as expertly as sticks; he can provide a driving, steady beat, vary the pulse, solo with flair, or remain anchored in the background. He's also written several books on drumming and led international workshops. Thigpen worked with Cootie Williams, Dinah Washington, Johnny Hodges, Lennie Tristano, Bud Powell, Jutta Hipp, and Billy Taylor in the '50s. He played in Oscar Peterson's trio with Ray Brown from 1959 to 1965 and then joined Ella Fitzgerald's backup band. He moved to Los Angeles in 1967 and rejoined Fitzgerald from 1968 to 1972. Thigpen relocated to Copenhagen in 1972 and taught at the Malmo Conservatory in Sweden while forming the group Action-re-action. He's worked with numerous players in the '70s and '80s, among them Monty Alexander, the Berlin Contemporary Jazz Orchestra, Kenny Drew, Art Farmer, Dexter Gordon, Lionel Hampton, Boulou and Elios Ferre, and Johnny Griffin. Thigpen has recorded as a leader for Verve, GNP Crescendo, Reckless, Timeless, and Justin Time. He has a couple of sessions available on CD as a leader. —*Ron Wynn*

● **Mr. Taste** / Apr. 1991-Jul. 1991 / Justin Time 79379

Gary Thomas

b. 1962
Sax / Neo-bop, modern creative
Strong young-lion saxophonist from Baltimore, whose reputation for aggressive, sprawling solos is becoming well known. Thomas is more in the hard-bop mainstream than some contemporaries and has even recorded an album of standards. But his releases also include the use of synthesizers and sometimes veer into rock and funk. —*Ron Wynn*

★ **While the Gate Is Open** / 1986 / Verve 834439
Despite some rough moments in his solos, this is worth checking out. Emblematic of new wave of '90s jazz types with one foot in other camps. —*Ron Wynn*

○ **By Any Means Necessary** / May 1989 / JMT 834432
Aggressive, young-lion-led session with R&B, electronic elements. Thomas is an explosive, constantly growing improviser. —*Ron Wynn*

Joe Thomas

b. Jun. 16, 1933, Newark, NJ, **d.** Feb. 18, 1981
Tenor sax / Swing, big band
A fine swing era player whose sound and style emphasized rhythmic invention rather than melodic or harmonic development. Thomas was a flashy player who doubled as a vocalist and was a star in the Lunceford band of the '30s and '40s. He started as an alto saxophonist playing in the bands of Earl Hood and Horace

Henderson in the early '30s and then switched to tenor sax and played with Stuff Smith and Guy Jackson before joining Lunceford in 1933. He remained in the Lunceford orchestra until 1947. Thomas became coleader with Eddie Wilcox before leaving to form his own band. He led this band until the early '50s and then temporarily retired to join his father's undertaking business. Thomas kept playing on a periodic basis, appearing at the 1970 Newport Jazz Festival and recording with a quartet featuring Jimmie Rowles in 1979. He made only a few sessions as a leader for such labels as Melodisc and Uptown. Thomas can be heard on various Lunceford orchestra reissued CDs. —*Ron Wynn*

● Blowin' in from K.C. / Dec. 9, 1982 / Uptown 2712

Leon Thomas (Amos Leone Thomas, Jr.)

b. Oct. 4, 1937, St. Louis, IL
Vocals / Ballads & blues, early free
Leon Thomas is a well-known, deep-throated vocalist who worked with Count Basie, Pharoah Sanders, and blues bands. He's an expert yodeler whose forays in that area enlivened several of Sanders's '70s releases. He's since recorded for Flying Dutchman, Portrait (Columbia), and Mappleshade among others. Thomas also recorded with Santana.—*Michael G. Nastos*

○ In Berlin / Nov. 6, 1970 / Flying Dutchman 10142

★ Blues and the Soulful Truth / i. Aug. 1973 / Flying Dutchman 10155
This is his best studio album. Contains many of his best numbers. —*Michael G. Nastos*

○ Facets / Flying Dutchman 10164
A compilation of late '60s and early '70s material that is well put together. —*Michael G. Nastos*

Lucky Thompson (Eli Thompson)

b. Jun. 14, 1924, Columbia, SC
Tenor sax, soprano sax / Bop
Tenor and soprano saxphonist Lucky Thompson got his start playing with the Trenier Twins in the early '40s. He then moved from Detroit to New York, where he had brief stints with many bands, among them Lionel Hampton, Don Redman, Billy Eckstine, Lucky Millinder, and Count Basie, before leaving for the West Coast in 1946. He recorded with Dizzy Gillespie and Charlie Parker, as well as Boyd Raeburn and the Stars of Swing band, before returning to Detroit in 1947, moving back to New York in 1948. Thompson got involved in R&B song publishing, recording, and writing and also led a band at the Savoy before going back to full-time jazz playing in the mid-'50s. He appeared on the classic Miles Davis *Walkin'* session in 1954 and later worked with Milt Jackson, Jo Jones, Quincy Jones, Oscar Pettiford, and several others. He was a master at making definitive, searing statements, despite beginning with a softer tone than normal in the bop mode. A fine recording he made for Vanguard in 1954 has recently reappeared, entitled *Quartet*. —*Ron Wynn*

○ Lucky Thompson / Jan. 27, 1956-Feb. 1956 / Paramount 111

★ Lucky Thompson Featuring Oscar Pettiford / Jan. 27, 1956-Feb. 1956 / Jasmine
Very neglected tenor on a super album, backed by great Pettiford (b). —*Ron Wynn*

☆ Paris (1956) / Mar. 12+14, 1956 / Swing 30030
This Lucky Thompson recording is comprised of two sessions with the only change in personnel being the replacement of bassist Pierre Michelot with Benoit Querson. . . . For the most part, his dry and fleet tenor was the centerpiece on these standards, but pianist Martial Solal did have some good moments as well. —*Carl Brauer, Cadence*

★ Lucky Strikes / Sep. 15, 1964 / Prestige 194
Lucky Thompson brought along Hank Jones (piano), Richard Davis (bass), and Connie Kay (drums) to back him on two standards and six originals. The program here was quite strong, and the leader, on both tenor and soprano, brought a soulful and personal approach to his playing. —*Bob Rusch, Cadence*

Malachi Thompson

Trumpet / Modern creative
Malachi Thompson is a Chicago trumpeter and a stylistic extension of Lee Morgan or Freddie Hubbard. He's known as a creative improviser but plays tunefully. He's been a member of Lester

Bowie's Brass Fantasy, AACM, and RA Ensemble. Thompson is not really a screamer; he plays bluesy tunes. —*Michael G. Nastos*

★ Seventh Son, The / May 1972 / RA 102

○ Spirit / Delmark 442

Sir Charles Thompson (Charles Phillip Thompson)

b. Mar. 12, 1918, Springfield, OH
Piano / Bop, soul-jazz
Pianist-organist Sir Charles Thompson came up in the bop school of Bird and Diz and was able to keep up, even push his speed-demon compatriots. —*Michael G. Nastos*

○ Takin' Off / i. 1945-1947 / Delmark 450
This is a reissue of the classic Apollo series. The 1945 and 1947 sessions feature legendary bands with Charlie Parker, Dexter Gordon, Buck Clayton, Danny Barker, J. C. Heard, Joe Newman, Freddie Green, Pete Brown, and Shadow Wilson playing 16 cuts, 7 previously unissued. This is prime bop. —*Michael G. Nastos*

★ And His All Stars / i. 1950 / Apollo 103
W/ Charlie Parker (as), Dexter Gordon (ts), and Leo Parker (bar sax). —*Michael G. Nastos*

○ Sir Charles Thompson Sextet / i. 1953 / Vanguard 8003

○ Sir Charles Thompson Quartet / i. 1954 / Vanguard 8006

○ Sir Charles Thompson Trio / i. 1955 / Vanguard 8018

Claude Thornhill

b. Aug. 10, 1909, Terre Haute, IN, d. Jul. 1, 1965, New York, NY
Piano, arranger / Swing, big band, progressive big band
Pianist Claude Thornhill is among the more gifted and distinctive arrangers in jazz history. Thornhill combined dance-based arrangements and improvisational elements and did some innovative things in utilizing different instrumentation (notably French horns) and space and time within his compositions. Thornhill had conservatory training but got his practical experience in Midwest territory bands before moving to New York in the '30s. He worked briefly for Paul Whiteman, Benny Goodman, and Ray Noble and then did extensive session work as an arranger, including doing songs for Billie Holiday and providing a hit setting for Maxine Sullivan with "Loch Lomond" in 1937. He later toured with Sullivan in 1937-1938 and then took over a West Coast band that had been headed by Gil Evans, coleading it with vocalist Skinny Ennis. Thornhill had his own band from 1940 to 1942, with Evans rejoining him in 1941. He re-formed his band in 1946, this time with a group that included Lee Konitz and Red Rodney. In 1948 Thornhill, Evans, Konitz, Gerry Mulligan, and Miles Davis among others, participated in the landmark "Birth of the Cool" sessions; these dates helped pave the way for whole West Coast school that took its lead from the softer, more subtle Thornhill-Evans approach. Thornhill continued to head dance-oriented bands into the '50s and '60s. —*Ron Wynn*

★ Claude Thornhill and His Orchestra / 1947 / Hindsight 108

○ Real Birth of the Cool / i. 194z / Columbia
A formative date featuring Thornhill's band doing "cool" arrangements back in the early and mid-'40s. Has never been widely available in America, even the import. —*Ron Wynn*

☆ Tapestries / Affinity
A comprehensive, two-disc set of his prime cuts, with 17 arranged by Gil Evans. —*Ron Wynn*

Clifford Thornton (Clifford Edward Thornton III)

b. Sep. 6, 1936, Philadelphia, PA, d. 1989
Trumpet, trombone / Modern creative
Clifford Thornton played trumpet and trombone in addition to being a composer and bandleader. He was a very staunch progressivist and rarely recorded. He was also active in jazz education during the final phase of his career. —*Michael G. Nastos*

○ Freedom and Unity / Jul. 22, 1967 / Third World 9636

★ Ketchaoua / Aug. 18, 1969 / BYG 529.323
Paris studio date with Fire-breathers Archie Shepp (sax), Grachan Moncur III (tb), Dave Burrell (p), and Sonny Murray (d). —*Michael G. Nastos*

○ Gardens of Harlem, The / Apr. 1974 / JCOA 1008

Definitive, brilliant creative statement from the visionary trombonist with the Jazz Composers Orchestra. A must-have for progressive music listeners. —*Michael G. Nastos*

Henry Threadgill (Henry Luther Threadgill)

b. Feb. 15, 1944, Chicago, IL
Alto sax, composer / Modern creative
Whether it's for arranging, writing, or playing, alto-saxophonist Henry Threadgill ranks among the best contemporary musicians operating in the improvisational sphere. He played in gospel and blues bands growing up and then joined Muhal Richard Abrams's experimental band in the early '60s and was a founding member of the AACM. His trio Air was one of the greatest and most versatile bands of the '70s, doing free pieces, blues-tinged originals, and ballads. Since Air's demise, Threadgill has headed a combo and also worked with other musicians, notably Oliver Lake. He's a master at incorporating R&B, blues, gospel, and swing voicings into his pieces and balancing freedom with discipline in his group's performances. —*Ron Wynn*

★ **Just the Facts and Pass the Bucket** / 1983 / About Time 1005
Sextet (actually seven pieces). Dynamite open-ended compositions, especially surly "Black Blues" and the determined "Man Called Trinity Deliverance." Features Olu Dara, Pheeroan Aklaff, John Betsch, and bassist Fred Hopkins. All pungently original material. —*Michael G. Nastos*

☆ **When Was That?** / **i.** 1983 / About Time
Same band as 1983 except for bassist Brian Smith. The title track is a riot on record. Some extraordinary improvising and spontaneous combustion going on here. Landmark recording. —*Michael G. Nastos*

☆ **You Know the Number** / Oct. 1986 / Novus 3013
A wonderful release with quirky, jerky cuts; resolute, superb solos. —*Ron Wynn*

☆ **Rag, Bush and All** / Dec. 1988 / Novus 3052
Ted Daniel (trumpet), Bill Lowe (bass trombone), and Newman Baker (percussion) are in. "Off the Rag," "The Devil Is Loose," and "Dance with a Monkey" are on. —*Michael G. Nastos*

★ **Spirit of Nuff ... Nuff** / Nov. 1990 / Black Saint 120134
The latest Threadgill armada proves every bit as appealing as his past brigades. —*Ron Wynn*

○ **Too Much Sugar for a Dime** / **i.** 1993 / PolyGram 514258
When it comes to compositional cunning, Henry Threadgill is hard to beat. Yet the sheer eccentricity of *Very Very Circus*—which includes two tubas, two electric guitars, trap set, and an alto and French horn front line—might well stump a less ambitious composer. Not this one. Just listen to "Little Pocket Size Demons," for example, in which Threadgill's alto and Mark Taylor's French horn declaim over a bed of guitar noise and tuba riffs. —*James Marcus, Jazz Times*

Bobby Timmons (Robert Henry Timmons)

b. Dec. 19, 1935, Philadelphia, PA, **d.** Mar. 1, 1974, New York, NY
Piano / Hard bop
Perhaps the finest gospel-tinged pianist ever (with exception of Horace Silver) and a major mover in the funk school of jazz. A Philadelphia native, Timmons began to get noticed in the late '50s through his work with Kenny Dorham, Chet Baker, Sonny Stitt, Maynard Ferguson and attained jazz stardom through two stints with Art Blakey's Jazz Messengers in 1958-1959 and 1960-1961, plus one year with Cannonball Adderley in 1959-1960. For the rest of his life, Timmons led either trios or small combos, where his merger of blues feeling, gospel chording, and jazz timing were extremely popular. His two most famous pieces in gospel-funk style "Dis Here" and "Dat Dere," both of which he penned while with Cannonball. Timmons also picked up the vibes in the mid '60s. —*Ron Wynn*

○ **This Here Is Bobby Timmons** / Jan. 13-14, 1960 / Riverside 104
Trio with Sam Jones (b) and Jimmy Cobb (d). This pianist's single best album. —*Michael G. Nastos*

★ **Moanin'** / Aug. 12, 1960-Sep. 10, 1963 / Milestone 47031
Compilation of five different albums 1960-1963. Great collection and collectable. —*Michael G. Nastos*

☆ **Workin' Out** / Oct. 21, 1964 / Prestige 7387

☆ **Live at the Connecticut Jazz Party** / 1981 / Early Bird 104

Pianist Bobby Timmons had the good fortune to get visibility with drummer Art Blakey and later with alto saxophonist Cannonball Adderley, and of course as a composer. . . . These were workmanlike performances that won't waste your time or insult your mind. This was an album of interest. —*Bob Rusch, Cadence*

Cal Tjader (Callen Radcliffe Tjader, Jr.)

b. Jul. 16, 1925, St. Louis, MO, **d.** May 5, 1982, Manila
Vibes / Cool, Latin-jazz
Vibist Cal Tjader may have been the finest non-Latin bandleader and player to ever achieve fame in Latin-jazz circles. His groups, particularly those of the early '60s with Willie Bobo or the late '50s with Mongo Santamaria, never failed to hit the right groove, and Tjader's solos were always solidly in the spirit. His mother was a pianist, and Tjader played in the late '40s and early '50s with Dave Brubeck and joined George Shearing in 1953-1954. After meeting bassist Al McKibbon, who sparked his emerging interest in Latin music, Tjader began to immerse himself in this style. Throughout the '50s, '60s, and '70s, Tjader's groups made numerous excellent Latin-jazz releases, as well as an occasional mainstream outing. He continued that pattern into the '80s and, at the time of his death, had well over 40 albums in print. —*Ron Wynn*

★ **Tjader Plays Mambo** / Aug. 1954-Sep. 1954 / Fantasy 3221
Tjader Plays Mambo and *Mambo with Tjader* feature three fall 1954 sessions with vibist-pianist Tjader playing two dozen Latinized standards. Four of the tracks found Tjader in the company of a small orchestra for added brass accents. The remainder of the tracks were without the horns and with Verlardi added as a third Latin percussionist. —*Bob Rusch, Cadence*

Jazz at the Blackhawk / Jan. 20, 1957 / Fantasy 436
Quartet. Expressive playing, pretty basic Afro-Latin Tjader groove. W/ Vince Guaraldi (p), Gene Wright (b), and Al Torre (d). —*Ron Wynn*

☆ **Monterey Concerts** / Apr. 20, 1959 / Prestige 24026
Outstanding combination of his sessions with Bobo and Santamaria plus *Concerts by the Sea* LP linked in two-record package. —*Ron Wynn*

☆ **Night at the Blackhawk** / 1959 / Fantasy 278
A Night at the Blackhawk stretched out even further and offered up a program that included some of Cal Tjader's stronger jazz material. On board was Vince Guaraldi (piano), who builds some fine solos and should impress the listener with his inspiration, and Joe Silva, whose Getzian-Hawkish tenor added some nice touches, though he seemed reticent to really assert his playing. —*Bob Rusch, Cadence*

★ **Soul Sauce** / Nov. 20, 1964 / PolyGram 27756
One of his most influential '60s releases with Willie Bobo, Donaly Byrd, and Kenny Burrell. —*Ron Wynn*

○ **El Sonid Nuevo (The New Soul Sound)** / **i.** May 24-26, 1966 / Verve

☆ **Primo** / **i.** 1970 / Original Jazz Classics 762

○ **La Onda Va Bien** / Jul. 1979 / Concord Jazz 4113

☆ **Bamboleate** / Tico

○ **Greatest Hits—Vols. 1 and 2** / Fantasy 4527

Tambu / Fantasy 9453
W/ Donald Bryd (tpt). Fine collaboration between two prominent Latin-jazz players. —*Ron Wynn*

Charles Tolliver

b. Mar. 6, 1942, Jacksonville, FL
Trumpet / Hard bop
Charles Tolliver is a high-powered and fleet-fingered trumpeter whose ability is second to none. He specializes in postbop modal forms, and is one of a handful of great composers. Tolliver was also involved along with pianist Stanley Cowell in the creation of Strata-East Records, an African-American owned and operated record label in the '70s. Tolliver was a member of bands led by Gerald Wilson, Max Roach, and Jackie Mclean and also headed Music Inc. with Cowell. —*Michael G. Nastos*

○ **Ringer, The** / Jun. 2, 1969 / Freedom 1017

Music Map

Jazz Trombone

Parade Bands–c. 1900

1920s
Increase of Trombones in Large Bands
Fletcher Henderson & Duke Ellington

Early Trombonists
Ike Rodgers (Rec. 1929-1934)
Jim Robinson (1892-1976) w/Sam Morgan 1927
George Lewis (1900-1968)
Charles Irvis (1899-1939)
Charlie Green (1900-1936)

Major Early Players
George Brunies (1902-1974)
Kid Ory (1890-1973)

Miff Mole (1898-1961)
Influence on trombonists, bandleaders:
Glenn Miller (1904-1944)
Jack Teagarden (1905-1964)
Tommy Dorsey (1905-1956)

Trummy Young (1912-1984)
Jimmy Harrison (1900-1931)

Duke Ellington's Trombonists:
Juan Tizol (1900-1984)
Tricky Sam Nanton (1904-1946) (w/Ellington from 1926)
Lawrence Brown (1907)
Quentin Jackson (1909-1976)
Britt Woodman (1920)
Buster Cooper (1929)

Swing-Era Trombonists
Tommy Dorsey (1905-1956)
Jack Teagarden (1905-1964)
Vic Dickenson (1906-1984)
J.C. Higginbotham (1906-1973)
Benny Morton (1907-1985)
Al Grey (1925)
Fred Beckett (1917-1946)

Humor associated with
Dicky Wells (1907-1985)
Trummy Young (1912-1984)

Traditional Jazz Revival in late 1930s

Bop Trombonists
Bill Harris (1916-1973)
Lou McGarity (1917-1971)
Kai Winding (1922-1983)
Bennie Green (1923-1977)
J.J. Johnson (1924)
Frank Rosolino (1926-1978)
Carl Fontana (1928)
Bill Watrous (1939)
Curtis Fuller (1934)

Bob Brookmeyer (1929) (valve trombone)
George Roberts (bass)

Slide Hampton (1932)–circular breathing
Jimmy Knepper (1927)–w/Charles Mingus

Multiphonics
Dick Griffin
Ray Anderson (1952)
Phil Wilson (1937)
George Lewis (1952)
Albert Mangelsdorff (1928)

European Free Jazz
Eje Thelin (1938)
Paul Rutherford (1940)
Albert Mangelsdorff (1928)

American Free Jazz
Roswell Rudd (1935)
Ray Anderson (1952)
George Lewis (1952)
Craig Harris (1954)
Grachan Moncur III (1937)
Julian Priester (1935)
Steve Turre (1948)

Trombone in Jazz-Rock
Chicago – Tower of Power – Blood, Sweat and Tears

Modern Big-Band Use
Gil Evans (1912-1988)
Thad Jones (1923-1986)
Maynard Ferguson (1928)
Mel Lewis (1929)
Toshiko Akiyoshi (1929)
Lew Tabackin (1940)

R&B Influence
Fred Wesley

Fusion
Wayne Henderson (1939) (Crusaders) – Bill Watrous (1939)

Includes five Tolliver originals with the Stanley Cowell Trio. All the cuts are important, but "Plight" and "On the Nile" are particularly gripping. Cowell solos marvelously. —*Michael G. Nastos*

★ **Live at Slugs—Vols. 1 and 2** / May 1, 1970 / Strata East 1972
These four sides were part of a live session done in the intimate East Village club Slugs on May Day, 1970. While a certain "same-ness" tended to envelop the two volumes, the improvisational strength of the artists kept the session on such a high level that the music consistently sounded fresh and spontaneous. Tolliver's horn style wasn't revolutionary, but it was possessed of a melodic warmth and compactness of expression shared by few other trumpeters. —*Ray Townley, Down Beat*

☆ **Grand Max** / **i.** 1972 / Black Lion 760145
A brilliant showcase for Charles Tolliver . . . superb rhythm section . . . makes one realize how underrated he has consistently been. —*Bob Rusch, Cadence*

○ **Live at Loosdrecht Jazz Festival** / Dec. 1973 / Strata East 19470
This two-record set from Strata-East was recorded in 1972 at the Loosdrecht Jazz Festival in Holland, and was an exquisite Charles Tolliver showcase. On four sides there were just five compositions, giving everybody plenty of room to play. As a matter of fact, it was a great date for everybody; pianist John Hicks, bassist Reggie Workman, and drummer Alvin Queen worked together beautifully. —*Herb Nolan, Down Beat*

☆ **Impact** / Jan. 17, 1975 / Strata East 51-004
Six spectacular performances from trumpeters. 23-piece plus eight-piece string section orchestra. Great solos from Tolliver and pianist Stanley Cowell on "Plight" and throughout by James Spaulding (as), George Coleman (ts), Charles McPherson (sax), and Harold Vick (ts). As powerful a record as you're likely to hear. —*Michael G. Nastos*

☆ **Live in Berlin at the Quasimodo—Vol. 1** / **i.** 1988 / Strata East 9003
A quartet recording from 1988, this features a stunning elongated version of "Ruthie's Heart" among four originals. There is great group interplay. —*Michael G. Nastos*

Mel Tormé (Melvin Howard Tormé)

b. Sep. 13, 1925, Chicago, IL
Vocals / Ballads & blues
At the age of 3, he was singing in public; at 4, he was on the radio; at 9, he was acting professionally, and at 15, he published his first composition—an instrumental. After playing drums and singing in Chico Marx's band (1942-1943), he formed a vocal ensemble, the Mel-Tones, for which he wrote exceptional arrangements; it performed with Artie Shaw's band. From the late '40s on, Tormé has pursued a career as solo singer with consistent success, also acting in films and on television and writing songs ("The Christmas Song" and "Born to Be Blue" have become standards). He has published a novel, a reminiscence of Judy Garland, an autobiography, and a biography of his friend and frequent coworker, Buddy Rich. Tormé is clearly a man of exceptional gifts; his voice has remained an astonishingly consistent and accurate instrument, and his upper range—always a special feature of his style—remains intact in his seventh decade of performing. He has few peers as an interpreter of the great American songbooks. —*Dan Morgenstern*

○ **Gone with the Wind** / **i.** 1946 / Musicraft
Momentous 1946 and 1947 cuts that indicate Tormé's something special. —*Ron Wynn*

☆ **Mel Torme Swings Schubert Alley** / Jan. 21, 1960-Feb. 11, 1960 / Verve 821581
This Mel Tormé set comes from around 1959 and presented the carefully controlled and complimentary West Coast backing of Marty Paich's Orchestra, which when called upon offered a solo or two of substance. This was prime "fog" as Tormé hiply handled 12 pieces of American stage music and he never sounded in better voice. —*Bob Rusch, Cadence*

★ **Duke Ellington and Count Basie Songbooks** / Dec. 12, 1960+Feb. 2, 1961 / Concord Jazz 4382
Recorded with the Johnny Mandel Orchestra at sessions in Los Angeles, it includes one half Duke Ellington and one half Count Basie, plus Leroy Carr's "In the Evening (When the Sun Goes Down)." With all these things going for it, how can Tormé do wrong? —*Michael G. Nastos*

○ **A New Album** / Jun. 1977 / Gryphon 916
If vocalist Mel Tormé's fine 1975 album *Live at the Masionette* got a Grammy Award nomination, then *A New Album* should have been in line for a Nobel Prize. It was a winner, with few serious weaknesses and at least one track that was a masterpiece of lyric, arrangement, and performance. Here he took on Billy Joel ("NY State of Mind"), Janis Ian, Stevie Wonder ("All in Love Is Fair") and Paul Williams ("Ordinary Fool"), bringing out the qualities in their work that are likely to survive the zeitgeist of their own ear. And because he did, they were all that much closer to comparison with the ranks of Jerome Kern, George Gershwin, Irvin Berlin, and other masters. —*John McDonough, Down Beat*

☆ **Live at Marty's** / **i.** 1981 / Finesse 37484
Trio sessions with guests Cy Coleman (p), Gerry Mulligan (sax), and Jonathan Schwartz (p); these are Tormé's finest live dates, a twofer loaded with standards and fun. Everyone really enjoyed this one, and Tormé's voice is unfettered. —*Michael G. Nastos*

○ **Evening at Charlie's** / Oct. 1983 / Concord Jazz 4248

○ **Elegant Evening** / May 1985 / Concord Jazz 294
By the choice of material and tempos, this LP is ideal for romantic evenings. The music to be heard is redolent of the late at night and to the warm of heart. Engineer Edwards, no doubt in consultation with Tormé, has even added a whiff of mist to the traditional English song "Brigg Fair." In all fairness, this album should have been billed as a Mel Tormé LP with Shearing in accompaniment as that is essentially what it is. —*Shirley Klett, Cadence*

○ **And Rob McConnell's Boss Brass** / May 20, 1986 / Concord Jazz 306
With Rob McConnell's Canadian big band. Pop to swing, including a monster Ellington medley and the spirited "Cow Cow Boogie." —*Michael G. Nastos*

○ **Mel and Geo. Do WWII** / 1990 / Concord Jazz 4471

Ralph Towner (Ralph N. Towner)

b. Mar. 1, 1940, Chehalis, WA
Guitar, piano / World fusion, modern creative
This unique acoustic guitarist brought the craft and discipline of classical guitar into modern improvisational settings. Towner is very active as composer and member of the well-known group Oregon. Raised in a musical family, he studied trumpet and piano and earned a degree in composition. Though he worked as a jazz pianist, his real love is the acoustic guitar: he studied classical guitar intensively with Karl Scheit in Vienna. After playing with the Paul Winter Ensemble, he cofounded the eclectic ensemble Oregon in 1971; his many compositions are mainstays of that popular and artistically successful group. Also an innovator on 12-string guitar, his fine solo on the Weather Report album *I Sing the Body Electric* contributed to his early recognition. An early solo album *Diary* and his duets with John Abercrombie on *Sargasso Sea* show the clarity and energy of his style. Towner's unusually meticulous approach to artistic and technical issues on the guitar, combined with his fine ability as a composer, make all periods of his recorded work well worth investigating. —*David Nelson McCarthy*

☆ **Diary** / Apr. 4-05, 1973 / ECM 829157
Solo guitar and piano. Quintessential melodic content is like no other. —*Michael G. Nastos*

★ **Matchbook** / Jul. 26-27, 1974 / ECM 835014
Definitive duets with vibist Gary Burton and Ralph Towner (g). Buy it on CD. —*Michael G. Nastos*

○ **Solstice** / Dec. 1974 / PolyGram 825458
Those who waited to hear guitarist Ralph Towner in a rhythmic environment more highly-charged than the gossamer wings giving flight to the group Oregon were no doubt pleased with polyrhythmist drummer Jon Christensen. His restless, clean attack underscored Towner's tendency to peculiar turns of rhythm, fleshing out in bold relief a cragginess often smoothed by the rolling tablas of Oregon's Collin Walcott. —*Charles Mitchell, Down Beat*

○ **Old Friends, New Friends** / Jul. 1979 / ECM 829196

○ **Solo Concert** / Oct. 1979 / ECM 827268
Comprising excerpts from live recorded dates in Zurich and Munich during the fall of '79, Ralph Towner's *Solo Concert* was most impressive and again demonstrated that one needn't be electric to be electrifying. —*Stephen Mamula, Down Beat*

Lennie Tristano (Leonard Joseph Tristano)

b. Mar. 19, 1919, Chicago, IL, **d.** Nov. 18, 1978, New York, NY
Piano / Postbop, cool, early free
Blind from age 9, the Chicago-born musician played clarinet and tenor sax professionally early in his career and had a working knowledge of almost every instrument in jazz; at 19 he led his first band. After graduating from the American Conservatory he concentrated on piano and became seriously involved in teaching; among his first students were Lee Konitz and trombonist, composer, and arranger Bill Russo. He moved to New York in 1946 and formed a trio (with Billy Bauer on guitar and Arnold

Music Map

Jazz Trumpet

Early Jazz (New Orleans)
Buddy Bolden (1877-1931) – Manuel Perez (1871-1946)
Freddie Keppard (1890-1933) – Buddy Petit (1897-1931)

Chicago
Joe "King" Oliver (1885-1938)

Bob Shiffner – Louis Metcalf (1905-1981)
Dave Nelson (1905-1946) – Mutt Carey (1891-1948)

Major Player
Louis Armstrong (1901-1971)

Hot Lips Page (1908-1954) – Wingy Manone (1900-1982)
Mugsy Spanier (1906-1967)

Bix Beiderbecke (1903-1931) – Jimmy McPartland (1907)
Max Kaminsky (1908) – Wild Bill Davison (1906)
Bobby Hackett (1915-1976) – Tommy Ladnier (1900-1939)

Ellingtonians
Bubber Miley (1903-1932) – Cootie Williams (1911-1985)
Rex Stewart (1914-1987) – Ray Nance (1913-1976
Clark Terry (1920) – Freddie Jenkins (1906-1978)

Bunny Berigan (1908-1942)

Swing Era
Jabbo Smith (1908) – Henry Allen (1908-1967)
Roy Eldridge (1911) – Buck Clayton (1911-1992)
Charlie Shavers (1917-1971) – Cat Anderson (1916-1981)
Tommy Ladnier – Doc Cheatham (1905)
Bill Coleman (1904-1981)

Maynard Ferguson (1928)

Bop
Dizzy Gillespie (1917-1993) – Fats Navarro (1923-1950)
Clifford Brown (1930-1956) – Howard McGhee (1918-1987)

Johnny Coles (1926)
Red Rodney (1927)
Ira Sullivan (1931)

Cool Jazz
Miles Davis (1926-1991)

Chet Baker (1929-1988)
Shorty Rogers (1924)
Jack Sheldon (1931)

Hard Bop
Donald Byrd (1932)
Lee Morgan (1938-1972)
Freddie Hubbard (1938)
Woody Shaw (1944-1989)
Booker Little (1938-1961)
Kenny Dorham (1924-1972)
Hugh Masekela (1939
Marvin Peterson (1948)
Bill Hardman (1933-1990)
Wilbur Harden (1925)

Free Jazz
Don Cherry (1936)
Bill Dixon (1925)
Michael Ray
Lester Bowie (1941)
Mike Mantler (1943)
Leo Smith (1941)
Ted Curson (1935)
Joe McPhee (1939)
Barbara Donald (1942)
Mike Lawrence
Allen Shorter
Donald Ayler (1942)

Jazz-Rock
Miles Davis (1926-1991)
Maynard Ferguson (1928)
Chuck Mangione (1940)
Don Ellis (1934-1978)
Bill Chase
Randy Brecker (1945)

Wynton Marsalis (1961)
Phillip Harper
Bill Mobley – Melton Mustafa
Ryan Kisor – Marlon Jordan
Roy Hargrove – Brad Goode

Charles Tolliver (1942)
Olu Dara
Eddie Henderson
Butch Morris (1940)
Baikida Carroll (1947)

Fishkind on bass) with which he made his first commercially released records. Championed by critic Barry Ulanov, Tristano enjoyed his greatest fame in the years 1948-1950, leading a sextet with Konitz and tenorist Warne Marsh, recording with and arranging for the Metronome All Stars, and broadcasting with Charlie Parker and Dizzy Gillespie. But Tristano, while a modernist (he pioneered what later became known as "free jazz," to an extent), was not a bebopper. He had his own ideas about how jazz should be played. As the years went by, Tristano played less

and less in public. Though his prowess as a pianist didn't decline—he was exceptionally agile and had a profound knowledge of harmony and structure—he concentrated on teaching. His best students almost always became disciples as well and were expected to follow the master's way. Less directly, however, he had an influence on pianists as disparate as Martial Solal, Bill Evans, and Cecil Taylor. His best records—both as pianist and leader—stand as a very special contribution to jazz. *—Dan Morgenstern*

○ **Continuity** / i. 1952 / PolyGram 830921

This album consists of two live sessions recorded six years apart at the Half Note in New York and featured the pianist with his best-known disciples, alto saxophonist Lee Konitz and tenor saxophonist Warne Marsh. —*Peter Leitch, Cadence*

● **Descent into the Maelstrom** / 1953-1956 / Inner City 6002
Scarcity alone made *Descent into the Maelstrom* valuable, but it was also a magnificent potpourri of bits and pieces recorded from 1952 through 1966. Side one was solo Tristano. . . . Side Two found Tristano in the company of two pairings of drummers and bassists, not surprisingly a generally unhappy marriage in light of Tristano's avowed disdain for the way these instruments were played. . . . And yet, with the subtle accompaniment of Roy Haynes' brushes, a track like the allegedly overdubbed "Pastime" shimmered with layer upon layer of dense, successful, multiline improvisations. —*Jon Balleras, Down Beat*

○ **Lennie Tristano Quartet** / Jun. 11, 1955 / Atlantic 1224
These are previously unreleased performances from the Sing Song Room date. . . . Here pianist Tristano presented his music in more refined terms with alto saxophonist Lee Konitz' interplay both in the Tristano tradition and on his own personal terms. This was a set of excellent vintage, which remains remarkably stimulating. —*Bob Rusch, Cadence*

○ **Requiem** / Jul. 1962-Aug. 1962 / Atlantic 7003
This two-record set represented pianist and composer Lennie Tristano's last outings for Atlantic, two sessions spanning 1955 to 1962. They came at a time when his reputation was at its highest in decades. Were it rereleased while he was alive, it might have precipitated a return to public activity. Tristano was a bit of a visionary and as such he seemed to accept ultimate posthumous acceptance. —*Kirk Silsbee, Down Beat*

● **Complete Lennie Tristano on Keynote** / Mercury 830921

Steve Turre (Steve Turré)

b. Sep. 12, 1948, Omaha, NB
Trombone / Neo-bop, modern creative
Steve Turre is a dynamic trombonist equally versed in hard-bop, mainstream, and Latin-jazz, and currently a member of the "Saturday Night Live" pit band. Turre got his start playing with Woody Shaw, and in recent years he has been an active bandleader and one of the premier trombone soloists among the contemporary generation. He's gaining recognition as a composer as well; he can play brisk uptempo pieces, slow ballads, or funk and R&B-flavored tunes. His latest release includes a song where he displays facility with mutes and knowledge of plunger and wah-wah techniques reminiscent of jazz greats like Tricky Sam Nanton and Al Grey. —*Ron Wynn*

○ **Viewpoint** / Feb. 7-08, 1987 / Stash 270
Viewpoint afforded trombonist Steve Turre and his guest sidemen a chance to bring great texture to the jazz tradition and the many swinging styles he had played, from hard swing to bebop, from New Orleans to the avant-garde, from the blues to Salsa. One of the most imaginative offerings was his version of the Miles Davis classic "All Blues (Flamenco Sketches)." . . . *Viewpoint* was a dandy debut and one long overdue. —*Ken Franckling, Jazz Times*

★ **Fire and Ice** / i. Feb. 5-06, 1988 / Stash 7
Steve Turre has been steadily gathering all the major strands of the jazz trombone tradition, weaving in the process a musical fabric that bears his imprint. On *Fire and Ice* Turre was in the cooking company of pianist Cedar Walton, bassist Buster Williams, and drummer Billy Higgins, and on half the selections, the string Quartette Indigo, with John Blake and Gayle Dixon on violins. —*W. Royal Stokes, Jazz Times*

☆ **Right There** / Mar. 1991 / Antilles 510040

Stanley Turrentine (Stanley William Turrentine)

b. Apr. 5, 1934, Pittsburgh, PA
Tenor sax / Blues & jazz, soul-jazz
Stanley Turrentine is one of the greatest tenor saxophonists of the past 30 years. He made his first records with Max Roach after apprenticeship with Lowell Fulson, Earl Bostic, and others. His own recordings began on Blue Note 1960, and he is also a part of key Jimmy Smith albums (*Midnight Special, Back at the Chicken Shack*, and *Prayer Meeting*). He had a long association with Shirley Scott, with frequent recordings under his and her names

throughout the '60s. He was one of the first key artists to join CTI in 1970 and established himself as a top-selling artist with that label (*Sugar, Salt Song*), Fantasy (*Pieces of Dreams*) from 1974-1978, and later Elektra and Blue Note (again). He is equally at home in a commercial setting or with straightahead jazz accompaniment. Turrentine's work for Blue Note ('60s) is exemplary, as is his CTI work in the '70s. His work for other labels can be very good or rather dull, depending on the concept and its execution. Still one of the true saxophone stars of today, Turrentine is almost always worth a listen. —*Bob Porter*

○ **Blue Hour** / Dec. 16, 1960 / Blue Note 84057
Recorded at Englewood Cliffs, NJ. W/ the Three Sounds. Small group. A beautiful album of relaxed, bluesy sound. —*Michael Erlewine*

★ **Comin' Your Way** / Jan. 20, 1961 / Blue Note 84065
Recorded at Englewood Cliffs, NJ. Small group. 1988 reissue of sumptuous '60s soul-jazz date. Horace Parlan (p) at his bluesy best. —*Ron Wynn*

○ **Up at Minton's—Vol. 1** / Feb. 23, 1961 / Blue Note 4069
○ **Up at Minton's—Vol. 2** / Feb. 23, 1961 / Blue Note 84070
○ **Jubilee Shout** / Oct. 18, 1962 / Blue Note 84122
This long-awaited twofer was as much brother Tommy Turrentine's as it was its leader's and raises the question of why he never made it big like Donald Byrd or Freddie Hubbard, who were hardly fit to even mooch Turrentine's valve oil. A dramatic style and ever-dependable sense of melody instead of vacuous technical displays characterized Turrentine's art: a simplification of Clifford Brown, it was incapable of any falsehood; though generally light-hearted, there was never a frivolous moment. On song after song, on 9 of these 11 tracks, Turrentine's long, singing tones added grace and creativity in a rewardingly creative way. —*John Litweiler, Down Beat*

○ **Let It Go** / Apr. 15, 1966 / GRP 104
Recorded at Englewood Cliffs, NJ. Small group. Some recorded on September 21, 1964. Husband and wife team Turrentine and Shirley Scott (organ) produce one lovely album—blues-jazz, funky. —*Michael Erlewine*

★ **Sugar** / Nov. 1970 / Columbia 40811
Recorded at Englewood Cliffs, NJ. Larger group. By far the best thing he ever made on CTI. Among the handful of genuine jazz albums that were cut on that label. —*Ron Wynn*

○ **Cherry** / May 17, 1972 / Columbia 40936
Recorded at Englewood Cliffs, NJ. Small Group. Lush, wonderful playing by Turrentine, Jackson, despite very uneven material. —*Ron Wynn*

○ **Don't Mess with Mister T.** / Jun. 7, 1973 / Columbia 44173
○ **Wonderland** / 1987 / Blue Note 46762
The music of Stevie Wonder. Recorded at Yamaha Studios, Glendale, CA. —*AMG*

○ **La Place** / 1989 / Blue Note 90261
○ **More Than a Mood** / i. 1992 / Music Masters 65079
After a three-year gap in recording, tenor saxophonist Stanley Turrentine came back with a winner. His playing on *More Than a Mood* swings with the kind of sophistication it takes years to develop and with none of the mannerisms that sometimes occur along the way. Turrentine gets an unusually sweet, honed sound for a tenor player. The crisp, economical pianism of Cedar Walton, the discreet but always firmly guiding bass of Ron Carter, the time press rolls and delicate brushwork of Billy Higgins highlight Turrentine's considerable talents. —*Elaine Guregian, Down Beat*

Tommy Turrentine (Thomas Walter Turrentine, Jr.)

b. 1928
Trumpet / Bop
Tommy Turrentine is the brother of saxophonist Stanley Turrentine and a good trumpeter who played on a few Blue Note albums and cut his own date on Bainbridge in 1960. —*Ron Wynn*

★ **Tommy Turrentine** / i. Jun. 1960 / Bainbridge 1047
A good bop date led by trumpeter Turrentine . . . joined by brother Stanley on tenor, trombonist Julian Priester, pianist Horace Parlan, bassist Bob Boswell, and drummer Max Roach. —*Carl Brauer, Cadence*

Charles Tyler (Charles Lacy Tyler)

b. Jul. 20, 1941, Cadiz, KY, **d.** Jun. 27, 1992
Baritone and alto sax, teacher / Early free, progressive big band, modern creative

One of the freer, more flamboyant baritone saxophonists, as well as a capable alto stylist, Charles Tyler unfortunately never attained widespread recognition. He had complete command of the baritone, was expressive in every register and played with speed, lyricism, or energy. Tyler studied clarinet and alto sax as a child before playing baritone in an army band. He moved to Cleveland in 1960, where he played with Albert Ayler. Tyler later moved to New York, where he became involved in the city's free jazz scene, recording and working extensively with Ayler. He was featured on the albums *Bells* and *Spirits Rejoice*, and also played C-melody sax on a bootleg album with Ayler and Ornette Coleman on trumpet. He made his recording debut as a leader on ESP in the late '60s. Tyler also played with Sunny Murray and others. He moved to California, teaching music for four years at Merritt College and working with Arthur Blythe, David Murray, and Bobby Bradford. Tyler was featured on a Stanley Crouch album in 1973. When he returned to New York in 1976, Tyler began leading his own groups. He recorded for Ak-Ba, Nessa, and Adelphi in the '70s and Sonet, Storyville, Silkheart, Mustevic, and Nessa in the '80s. He worked with Dave Baker, Dewey Redman, Frank Lowe, Steve Reid, and Cecil Taylor and recorded and played with the Billy Bang Ensemble in 1981 and 1982. Only a couple of Tyler sessions are available on CD. —*Ron Wynn*

● **Definite / i.** Oct. 1981 / Storyville 4099
This session took the sax into the Ornette Coleman and post-Coleman era with Charles Tyler's alto and baritone joined by trumpeter Earl Cross, bassist Kevin Ross, and drummer Steve Reid. Side one featured Tyler's alto sax, which, combined with Cross's Don Cherrylike bit and the floating rhythm of Ross and Reid, gave the music a strong Coleman sense.... The passion and involvement continued on side two, though at a slower pace as here Tyler played the baritone sax. —*Kevin Whitehead, Cadence*

○ **Autumn in Paris / i.** Jun. 1988 / Silkheart 118

McCoy Tyner (Alfred McCoy [Sulaimon Saud] Tyner)

b. Dec. 11, 1938, Philadelphia, PA
Piano / Postbop, neo-bop

It's hard to imagine what John Coltrane's classic '60s quartet would have sounded like without the presence of pianist McCoy Tyner. He was just a youngster, not yet 21, when he joined the acclaimed hard-bop Jazztet of Art Farmer and Benny Golson. His prodigous technique soon landed him a job with Coltrane, and from 1960 to 1966 Tyner occupied the piano bench in one of jazzdom's most spectacular and hard-working groups. His was an inventive, expansive sound that breathed excitement into Trane's lengthy modal improvisations, employing thunderous right-hand chords that anchored and propelled the music at the same time. In many ways McCoy was the glue that held this explosive group together, providing a flexible foundation for the saxophonist's free flights while complementing drummer Elvin Jones and bassist Jimmy Garrison with his percussive dynamism. Subsequent solo recordings for Blue Note, Milestone, Impulse, and others have not been so fiery as the early '60s were, but Tyner has shared Coltrane's penchant for African themes and has also gone to the music of Asia for thematic material and instrumentation. As a leader he has had a consistent and well-rounded career, often applying his distinctive touch to straight jazz standards in piano-trio formats when he's not pursuing modal or avant-garde settings. McCoy is still a busy club and festival performer, collaborating with the biggest names in jazz and leading a variety of groups as he continues to hone his bold piano style. —*Myles Boisen*

★ **Inception / Nights of Ballads and Blues /** Jan. 10, 1962-Apr. 4, 1963 / MCA 42000

○ **McCoy Tyner Live at Newport /** Jul. 5, 1963 / Impulse 48

○ **McCoy Tyner: The Early Trios—Vol. 6 / i.** 1966-1968 / ABC/Impulse 9338
Adherents of McCoy Tyner's current emotive pedal style may be surprised at the dry sophistication he brought to his early '60s trio work with members of various Coltrane rhythm sections. Although the composer he favored most often was Duke

Ellington, his pianistic inspiration was clearly derived from Bud Powell, with the decorative proclivites of Art Tatum much in evidence. —*Larry Birnbaum, Down Beat*

★ **Real McCoy, The /** Apr. 21, 1967 / Blue Note 46512

○ **Tender Moments /** Dec. 1, 1967 / Blue Note 84275

○ **Reflections: A Retrospective (1972-1975) /** Jan. 1972-Apr. 9, 1973 / Milestone 47062
When pianist McCoy Tyner moved to CBS in the early '80s, Milestone released *Reflections*, a two-record retrospective of Tyner's recordings from 1972 to 1975. The selections were taken from *Sahara, Song for My Lady, Echoes of a Friend, Song of the New World, Enlightenment, Sama Layuca, Atlantis,* and *Trident,* and involved groupings from solo piano to large band. What they all had in common was an uncompromising commitment to good music. —*Bob Rusch, Cadence*

★ **Sahara /** Jan. 1972 / Milestone 311

★ **Echoes of a Friend /** Nov. 11, 1972 / Milestone 650

○ **Song of the New World /** Apr. 6-09, 1973 / Milestone 618
Pianist McCoy Tyner took a number of his most attractive themes, as well as Mongo Santamaria's "Afro Blue," and provided them large orchestral settings using two groups, one a bank of strings and woodwinds, the other brass and reeds. —*Pete Welding, Down Beat*

○ **Enlightenment /** Jul. 7, 1973 / Milestone 55001
McCoy Tyner's work adds support to the idea that, since around the death of Coltrane, it's been the pianists who've been on the cutting edge of the music's development, and who will be remembered as the seminal artists of the '70s. Unlike most of his fellow keyboard trendsetters, however, Tyner eschewed the electric instruments and devoted himself to an exploration of the frontiers of acoustic piano sound. *Enlightenment* testified to the brillant sound of his endeavors. —*Steve Metaliz, Down Beat*

○ **Sama Layuca /** Mar. 26-28, 1974 / Milestone 9056
Sama Layuca had much of the feeling and direction of *Song of the New World,* recorded with a large orchestra. The album also represented the sum total of where McCoy Tyner's musical mind was heading at that point—his blending of instruments and his concept of rhythm and melody. The group assembled for *Layuca* was Tyner's then current band (soprano and tenor saxophonist Azar Lawrence, bassist Buster Williams, drummer Billy Hart, percussionist Guillermi Franco) augmented by John Stubblefield on oboe and flute, Mtume on percussion and congas, alto saxophonist Gary Bartz and Bobby Hutcherson on vibes and marimba. —*Herb Nolan, Down Beat*

○ **Asante / i.** Jun. 1974 / Blue Note 223
Recorded in 1970, pianist McCoy Tyner's music here, as we've come to expect, was vibrant and cohesive, and it was the kind of music that resisted conventional terminology and categories. This was almost entirely an excursion in group improvisation. Tyner himself stayed mostly in the background, emerging to solo only occasionally. When he did, it was usually in an uptempo section. And as we would have expected, his playing was marked by long, deft lines, rhythmic excitement, and harmonic density. —*Jon Balleras, Down Beat*

☆ **Trident /** Feb. 18-19, 1975 / Original Jazz Classics 720
McCoy Tyner's rolls of exploratory thunder, always virtuosic, but occasionally overgymnastic, were controlled here through the presence of some sobering influences. Yet these elements did not restrain creativity. As all constructive input should and does, they enhanced, they broadened, and they perfected. —*Arnold Shaw, DownBeat*

○ **Fly with the Wind /** Jan. 19-21, 1976 / Milestone 699

○ **Supertrio /** Apr. 9-10, 1977 / Milestone 55003
In formulating *Supertrios,* producer Orrin Keepnews decided to pair McCoy Tyner with two diverse and potentially heady rhythm sections, the teams of bassist Ron Carter and drummer Tony Williams and bassist Eddie Gomez and drummer Jack DeJohnette. In particular, the Tyner-Williams-Carter sessions were effusively expressive without being thoughtfully reactive. Tyner was typically romantic and dramatic, his percussive left hand ostinatos melding effectively with his lucid right hand exercises, an always interesting blend of bluster and blues. Still, tracks like "Waves" and "The Greeting" were undeniably visceral, fully real-

ized fusions of muscular passion with form. —*Mikal Gilmore, Down Beat*

★ **4 X 4** / Mar. 3, 1980-May 29, 1980 / Milestone 550072
4 X 4 may not have appeased all of McCoy Tyner's recent critics. It certainly didn't open any untamed territory for this seminal pianist. But it did offer some of the variety everyone had been screaming for at that time, and was yet another solid addition to Tyner's impressively consistent discography. —*Cliff Tinder, Down Beat*

☆ **La Leyenda De La Hora** / i. 1981 / Columbia 37375
For *La Leyenda*, his Columbia debut date, McCoy Tyner chose to use a nonet plus a string section and to play five originals, four of which were in an Afro-Cuban vein. . . . While Tyner produced more memorable musical moments, *La Leyenda* was still a rewarding listening experience. —*Zan Stewart, Down Beat*

○ **Uptown-Downtown** / Nov. 1988 / Milestone 9167
Live date at the Blue Note in New York. Quintessential Tyner big band. You can't live without this one. —*Michael G. Nastos*

Things Ain't What They Used to Be / 1989 / Blue Note 93598
Upbeat attitude, with struttin' solos from John Scofield (g), George Drams. —*Ron Wynn*

Remembering John / i. 1991 / Enja 79668
A trio session that's mainly Tyner extrapolations on Coltrane compositions, matches his peerless keyboard improvisation with the equally adventurous bass work of Avery Sharpe, and good, though not exceptional, drum support from Aaron Scott. —*Ron Wynn, Rock & Roll Disc.*

○ **Turning Point, The** / i. 1992 / Verve 513573
The 15-piece ensemble, heavier on brass than reeds, is a modal juggernaut that possess the uncommon ability to inspire us in both musical and emotional terms. McCoy Tyner's revival of "Passion Dance," immortalized by his ace quartet in the Blue Note late '60s, is intelligent excitement typified. Avery Sharpe's fleet bass serves as the mooring for sinewy solos and onslaughts of reactive sectional work. —*Frank-John Hadley, Down Beat*

James Blood Ulmer

b. Feb. 1942, St. Matthews, SC
Guitar, vocals / Early free, early jazz-rock, contemporary funk
James Blood Ulmer is a guitarist and vocalist, among the most influential to emerge in the '70s. He sang gospel and learned guitar as a child, moved to Philadelphia as a professional in 1960, and worked with organ funk bands. He went to New York in 1971 and worked at Minton's for several months. Ulmer played with Paul Bley, Art Blakey, and others in the early '70s before studying with Ornette Coleman. Ulmer was in Coleman's band in the late '70s, appearing at the Ann Arbor Jazz and Blues Festival. He recorded with Joe Henderson and Arthur Blythe and cut his own session on Artists House. During the '80s, he recorded for Rough Trade, Columbia, the Caravan of Dreams, and Blue Note. He was in the group Phalanax with George Adams and has recorded on DIW with David Murray. —*Ron Wynn*

★ **Tales of Captain Black** / Dec. 5, 1978 / Artists House
Tales of Captain Black was the first release by guitarist James Blood (Ulmer) and represented a greenhouse for his artistic intuition. Here Blood was joined by alto saxophonist Ornette and drummer Denardo Coleman and the highly gifted bassist Jaamaladeen Tacuma. Each player comfortably coexisted with the others, though a generation separated the soloists from the rhythm section. The band operated within three improvisational systems—ensemble, reed soloist with trio accompaniment, and guitar soloist with rhythm accompaniment—with a freedom that beguiles each song's formal construction. There was dissonance, as you might expect, explored in each musician's individual sound and in the harmonic overtones of the guitar-saxophone pairings that were delightful in their fragile opulence. —*Jim Brinsfield, Down Beat*

○ **Are You Glad to Be in America** / i. 1980 / Rough Trade 16
America isn't really a jazz record, but James "Blood" Ulmer's no one-chord guitar player. . . . On these jams he allowed himself freer rein. Here, too, the horns were used more prominently and to greater advantage. . . . *America* was no jazz player's get-rich-quick record like Oliver Lake's lame reggae LP *Jump Up;* this was the real stuff. —*Kevin Whitehead, Cadence*

☆ **Freelancing** / 1981 / Columbia 37493

Freelancing, Blood Ulmer's first major label release, was also his most eclectic. Columbia appeared to be hedging a bit, eager to display its Great Black Hope as both spacey conceptualist and post-Hendrix funkster, e la the *No Wave* and *America* albums respectively. Accordingly, Ulmer's basic power trio—featuring drummer G. Calvin Weston and bassist Amin Ali (drummer Rashied's son)—was displayed in three setting: alone, with a rock-oriented chorus, and with the neo-jazz horns of David Murray, Oliver Lake, and Olu Dara. —*Larry Birnbaum, Down Beat*

Michael Urbaniak (Michal Urbaniak)

b. Jan. 22, 1943, Warsaw, Poland
Violin, tenor sax, bandleader / Early jazz-rock, world fusion, instrumental pop
Polish violinist, tenor saxophonist, and bandleader Michael Urbaniak was a breath of fresh air when he first appeared on the American music scene in the mid-'70s. His violin playing had warmth, wit, and flair, and his electric violin, and violectra (an electronic bowed string instrument with an octave lower sound than the violin) were both a curiosity and a different sound and voice. His sawing, bluesy phrases and interesting, if at times raw, sax playing, coupled with his wife Urzula Dudziak's scatting and vocal gymnastics, added welcome unpredictability and edge to what was already becoming a dreary landscape as jazz-rock's promise was fading into fusion's profitability. But Urbaniak never fulfilled that initial potential, and he has enjoyed a very successful but aesthetically uneven career. He studied violin as a child, as well as soprano sax and later played tenor. He experimented with traditional jazz and swing and then concentrated on bebop. He played with Zbigniew Namyslowski, Andrzej Trzaskowski, and Krzysztof Komeda in the early and mid-'60s, while working as a classical violinist. Urbaniak led a group in Scandinavia with Dudziak in 1965 and returned to Poland in 1969. He formed Constellation with Dudziak, Adam Makowicz, Czeslaw Bartkowski, and Pawel Jarzebski (later Roman Dylag). Urbaniak and Dudziak came to America in 1974, and he formed Fusion. They performed and recorded until 1977 and made some compelling albums blending Dudziak's vocals and vocal effects, Polish folk melodies, and irregular meters, plus Urbaniak's scintillating violin solos. Urbaniak worked and recorded with Larry Coryell and Dudziak in the '80s and also led his own bands. His albums became less free-wheeling and more restrained and overproduced. Urbaniak also did sessions with Archie Shepp. He has recorded as a leader for Columbia, Muza, Jazz America Marketing, Milan, Rykodisc, and Steeplechase. Urbaniak has a couple of sessions available on CD. —*Ron Wynn*

● **Fusion** / i. 1975 / Columbia 32852

Dave Valentin

Flute / Latin-jazz, instrumental pop
An Afro-Latin and Latin-jazz flutist who's recorded mainly for GRP. His albums have been nice, middle-of-the-road affairs, and one with Herbie Mann is quite substantial. —*Ron Wynn*

★ **Live at the Blue Note** / i. 1988 / GRP 9568

Nana Vasconcelos

b. 1945, Recife, Brazil
Percussion / World fusion
Nana Vasconcelos is a renowned Brazilian percussionist who has maintained a broad world music focus in his jazz-based recordings with Don Cherry, Ron Carter, Pat Metheny, Egberto Gismonti, and others. —*Myles Boisen*

○ **Saudades** / Mar. 1979 / ECM 829380
If percussionist Nana Vasconcelos solo is provocative, on *Saudades,* Vasconcelos plus guitarist Egberto Gismonti plus strings plus voices is awesome and utterly disarming. The berimbau, on whose one string slides a pitch-altering resonating gourd, is wonderfully suited as a solo improvising instrument, and with Vasconcelos in control, its music is remarkably rich in texture and tone. . . . This was a very special record, with sounds and shapes you'd probably never experienced before. —*Michael Zipkin, Down Beat*

★ **Bush Dance** / 1986 / Antilles 842897
The singer and master of the musical-bow berimbau played percussion, synthesizer, and other keyboards and was occasionally joined by Arto Lindsay, Mario Toledo (electric guitar), or Peter

Scherer (keyboards). Mr. Rhythm Machine played drums on most tracks, and as on any album where he appears, the beat was as stiff as a clergyman's collar; where Vasconcelos' chants and vocal colorations were recognizably Brazilian, the results supported an incongruous rain forest dance party. —*Kevin Whitehead, Cadence*

Sarah Vaughan (Sarah Lois Vaughan)

b. Mar. 27, 1924, Newark, NJ, **d.** Apr. 3, 1990
Vocals / Bop, ballads & blues
Sarah Vaughan sang and played piano in church in her native Newark, but on a dare entered the famous Apollo Theater Amateur Hour contest and won, singing "Body and Soul." Billy Eckstine heard her, recognized her very special talent, and recommended her to his boss, Earl Hines. This was in 1943, when Charlie Parker and Dizzy Gillespie were in the Hines band; she followed them into Eckstine's new and revolutionary big band in late 1944. By 1946 she was out on her own and pursued a successful solo career until the end of her life. Sarah (or "Sassy," as her fans called her; she was also known as "The Divine One") had a voice that would have served for an operatic career (or that of a gospel singer), but to our good fortune she chose jazz, though she often "crossed over" into pop. Her ear was as good as any improvising horn player's, her range spanned three full octaves. At her best, Sarah Vaughan had not only the finest voice ever applied to jazz singing but also the creative ideas to match it. —*Dan Morgenstern*

○ **It's You or No One** / May 1946-Apr. 1948 / Musicraft 55
● **Columbia Years (1949-1953)** / 1949-1953 / CBS 44165
★ **With Clifford Brown** / Dec. 1954 / Emarcy 814641
★ **Gershwin Songbook** / i. 1954-1957 / Mercury 814187
There were occasional lapses into operatic excess and vibrato abuse, but in general she put the melody and Ira Gershwin's wonderfully urbane lyrics first, letting the songs sell themselves. . . . This is a great refresher course for people who are cynical about the Gershwin brothers' achievements—and Vaughan's. —*Kevin Whitehead, Cadence*

○ **Sassy** / Apr. 1, 1956-Apr. 8, 1956 / Emarcy 36089
★ **Irving Berlin Songbook** / 1957 / Emarcy 822526
After Hours / Jun. 1961 / Sony Special Products 660
Excellent early '50s cuts that haven't always been available domestically. —*Ron Wynn*
Sarah Slightly Classical / May 1963-Jul. 1963 / Roulette 95977
Again, its value is in relation to appreciation of the concept. She sings wonderfully. CD 1991 reissue, six bonus cuts. —*Ron Wynn*
★ **Sassy Swings the Tivoli** / Jul. 18, 1963 / Mercury 832788
Sassy Swings the Tivoli was an even, swinging live jazz set with backing by Kirk Stuart (piano), Charles Williams (bass), and George Hughes (drums). Stuart joined Vaughan briefly on vocals, but besides that this was not all that usual a date for the singer. It was, however, one of her *jazz* dates. Part of this was reissued on the Mercury twofer *Record Live*. —*Bob Rusch, Cadence*
Sassy Swings Again / Jan. 1967 / Mercury 814587
○ **Jazz Fest Masters** / i. 1969 / Jazz Masters 75244
★ **Complete—Live in Japan** / i. 1974 / Mobile Fidelity 844
She gave the string section time off and worked with a cooking rhythm trio. Especially interesting was the piano of Carl Schroeder. . . . Jimmy Cobb played the drums well, and John Gianelli would have been a fine bassist if he hadn't been so far up on the mix. Vaughan's good taste in tunes, which brought us such fine oldies as "Mean to Me" and "My Kinda Love," was shown in her selection of such fine current material as "Singing Off" and "If You Could See Me Now." Such gems as "Foggy Day," "Funny Valentine" and "Over the Rainbow" spoke well for her ability to size up tunes that wore well but hadn't been done to death. —*Joe Klee, Down Beat*
Duke Ellington Songbook—Vol. 1 / Aug. 15, 1979-Sep. 12, 1979 / Pablo 2312-111
Nice '70s update on Songbook concept. Some of her last truly great singing. —*Ron Wynn*
Duke Ellington Songbook—Vol. 2 / Aug. 15, 1979-Sep. 12, 1979 / Pablo 2312-116
○ **Send in the Clowns** / Feb. 1981-May 1981 / Pablo 2312-130

Jazz Violin

Music Map

Solo Instrument in Ragtime Orchestras (c.1915)

Territory Bands
Andy Kirk (1898-??) Band
Alphonso Trent (1905-1959) Band

Soloist Claude Williams (1908)

Matty Malneck (1903-1981) w/Paul Whitman's band
Erskine Tate (1895-1978)

Great Soloists
Joe Venuti (1903-1978) (w/Eddie Lang)
Stephane Grappelli (1908) (w/Django Reinhardt)
Stuff Smith (1909-1967)

Swing-Era Violinists
Svend Asmussen (1916)
Eddie South (1904-1962)–recorded with Grappelli/Reinhardt
Ray Nance (w/Duke Ellington)

Experimental, Free Jazz Players
Zbigniew Seifert (1946-1979)
Jean-Luc Ponty (1942)
John Blake
Didier Lockwood (1956)

Fusion
John Blake
Michael White (1933)
Sugarcane Harris
Papa John Creach

Avant-Garde
Ornette Coleman (1930)
Leroy Jenkins (1932)
Billy Bang (1947)
Charles Burnham
Michael White (1933)

Violectra
Jean-Luc Ponty (1942)
Micha Urbaniak (1943)

Viola
Maxine Roach

Vaughan's in a less distinguished phase of her career, but she maintains her dignity. This collaboration with the Basie orchestra isn't what it would have been in the '50s or '60s, but it's still nice. —*Ron Wynn*

☆ **Sarah Vaughan on Mercury** / Mercury
Complete on Mercury. Monumental six-disc set that covers her extensive and exhaustive Mercury career. Of course, the company has also hacked this up into multiple packages to get separate profits off each. You can get it either way; I prefer the boxed set. —*Ron Wynn*

Charlie Ventura (Charles Venturo)

b. Dec. 2, 1916, Philadelphia, PA, **d.** Jan. 17, 1992
Sax / Swing, bop
Charlie Ventura was a swing to bop saxophone all-star. He had a deep understanding of the instrument and gained extensive ex-

perience with Gene Krupa in the '40s and '50s. —*Michael G. Nastos*

○ **Euphoria** / Aug. 28, 1945 / Savoy 2243

★ **Charlie Ventura and His Sextet** / May 1946 / Imperial 3002

Joe Venuti (Giuseppi Venuti)

b. Sep. 16, 1903, Philadelphia, PA, **d.** Aug. 14, 1978
Violin / Dixieland, swing

One of the greatest practical jokers in jazz history, the man who put jazz violin on the map was cagey about his date and place of birth. Was it Italy or Philadelphia? 1894 or 1903? We may never know for sure, but it is certain that Venuti went to school in Philly with the great guitarist Eddie Lang and that the two friends formed a team that made the first chamber-jazz records (in 1926) and was in great demand in the recording and radio studios and on the musical stage. Joe and Eddie appeared as special attractions with Paul Whiteman, and Eddie became Bing Crosby's favorite accompanist. When Lang died suddenly in 1933, Venuti was at first inconsolable, but he soon found his form again. He toured Europe in 1934, had his own big band at the height of the swing era, and in 1944 settled in Hollywood to do film work. Almost forgotten, he resurfaced in the '60s, making lots of records, touring worldwide, and surprising fellow musicians and audiences with his undiminished vitality and joy in making music. As a violinist, Venuti did not have a big tone but he did have exceptional facility and a sense of swing that was superior to that of most players on the '20s scene. His style hardly changed (though he amplified his instrument from the '50s on), but he sounded as hip in the '70s as he he had 50 years before. —*Dan Morgenstern*

★ **Joe Venuti with Eddie Lang—Vols. 1 & 2** / **i.** 1926-1927 / JSP 10
In at least one respect, the Joe Venuti-Eddie Lang set sounds very up to date; there are a lot of funny instruments—bass sax, comb, kazoo, hot fountain pen, bassoon, and, of course, Frankie Trumbauer's C-melody sax. For good measure, Tommy Dorsey plays exciting trumpet on "Hot Heels," Jimmy Dorsey not-so-good trumpet (according to Robert Parker), and Venuti bass on "Vibraphonia." There was much talent and playful inventiveness among these New Yorkers, but they lacked swinging rhythm sections 'til the Chicagoans came to their rescue. —*Stanley Dance, Jazz Times*

☆ **Violin Jazz 1927-1934** / 1927-1934 / Yazoo 1062
The 14 selections on this disc include several marvelous examples of the close communication Venuti had with guitarist Eddie Lang. Anyone seeking a clue to the roots of the swing era will hear it clearly on these songs; this is danceable, joyful jazz from an era when rhythm, rather than harmony, was king. —*Ron Wynn, Rock & Roll Disc.*

○ **Venupelli Blues** / **i.** 1969 / BYG 529122

○ **Joe and Zoot** / 1973-1974 / Chiaroscuro 128
In 1964, Dick Gibson got violinist Joe Venuti and tenor-soprano saxophonist Zoot Sims together on stage, and the music that culminated in this recording began. It could have been argued that Sims was not familiar with some of the older numbers like Venuti's "Wild Cat," or "It's the Girl," which hadn't been heard since the Boswell Sisters recorded it. It could also have been argued that the more recent material, like "My One and Only Love," wasn't the best vehicle for Venuti. But if anybody was uncomfortable with the repertoire, they sure didn't let on. Whether they were stompin' through "Lady Be Good" or essaying a pretty ballad like "Small Hotel," everybody was right on target. —*Joe Klee, Down Beat*

○ **Blue Four** / **i.** Jun. 1974 / Chiaroscuro 134
There was nothing but warmth and happiness here, with wily old master violinist Joe Venuti conducting a magical history tour of some classic music. "Blue Too," "Lady Be Good," and "String the Blues," for example, were duo tracks using just violin and acoustic guitar (Bucky Pizzarelli), while "Diga Diga Doo" and "Blue Room" found Venuti with Spencer Clark's bass sax, pianist Dill Jones, and Pizzarelli. Besides the overall good feeling this album conveyed, there was a joyous bounce that never faded. —*Herb Nolan, Down Beat*

Harold Vick (Harold Edward Vick)

b. Apr. 3, 1936, Rocky Mount, NC, **d.** 1987

Sax / Postbop, soul-jazz, progressive big band
Harold Vick was a saxophonist who could hit the note on many levels of jazz: soulful, funky, straightahead, or fusion. —*Michael G. Nastos*

★ **Steppin' Out** / May 21, 1963 / Blue Note 84138

Leroy Vinnegar

b. Jul. 13, 1928, Indianapolis, IN
Bass / Postbop, cool

One of the popularizers of the "walking" bass technique, where the normal four-to-the-bar bass lines are embellished through big, thick tones and nimble playing. Vinnegar would pluck open strings with the left hand, providing a much heavier accent and impact on the composition. Vinnegar and pianist Carl Perkins went to school together in Indianapolis and later became colleagues in Los Angeles after working in Chicago backing Charlie Parker and Sonny Stitt. He later worked with Stan Getz, Barney Kessel, Herb Geller, and Shelly Manne. Vinnegar led some sessions on his own and also worked with the Teddy Edwards, Joe Castro, and Gerald Wilson bands and did some classic recordings with Sonny Rollins, Phineas Newborn, the Jazz Crusaders, and Kenny Dorham, plus a heralded appearance at the 1969 Montreux Festival with Les McCann. His finest releases from the late '50s and early '60s have been reissued. —*Ron Wynn*

★ **Leroy Walks!** / Jul. 15, 1957-Sep. 16, 1957 / Contemporary 160

○ **Leroy Walks Again** / Aug. 1, 1962-Mar. 5, 1963 / Contemporary 454
This bop session was for the most part, music of the moment.... It's notable for being Freddy Hill's recorded debut (at 28 years old) and for Roy Ayers's solid solos —*Bob Rusch, Cadence*

☆ **Jazz's Great Walker** / 1964 / Vee Jay 2502

Eddie "Cleanhead" Vinson

b. Dec. 18, 1917, Houston, TX, **d.** Jul. 2, 1988, Los Angeles, CA
Alto sax, vocals / Bop, blues & jazz, soul-jazz

Eddie "Cleanhead" Vinson combined bop and blues vocals in a completely unique manner. Influenced by Johnny Hodges, Vinson's alto sax work with its spiraling lines, intense tone, and forceful sound were delivered with a searing intensity. His blues singing had a jagged, animated edge but also a tender underpinning, and he performed with a mix of earthy humor and resigned irony. The actual composer of both "Tune Up" and "Four" (Miles Davis was wrongly credited), Vinson performed his bop-blues hybrid from the '30s to the '80s. He joined Arnett Cobb and Illinois Jacquet in Chester Boone's big band one year after he'd begun playing alto sax. He stayed in the band from 1935 until 1941, while it changed leaders to Milt Larkin in 1936 and Floyd Ray in 1940. Vinson toured the South with blues vocalists Big Bill Broonzy and Lil Green and then went to New York, joining Cootie Williams's band. He had a huge hit in 1944 with "Cherry Red Blues." He recorded with Williams's band on Okeh, Hit, and Capitol. Vinson led a big band in 1946 and 1947 and a septet with John Coltrane, Red Garland, and Johnny Coles in 1948. There were sessions with Mercury and King in the late '40s and early '50s and later for such labels as Bethlehem, Riverside, Delmark, and Blues Way. He kept working and recording but didn't enjoy renewed popularity until 1969, when a European tour with Jay McShann and a recording of "Wee Baby Blues" alerted old and new generations about Vinson. This band also recorded for Black and Blue. Vinson played and recorded frequently in the '70s and '80s, working with Count Basie, Johnny Otis, Arnett Cobb, and Buddy Tate, even Roomful of Blues. He did sessions in the '70s and '80s for Muse, Fantasy, Circle, and Pablo. Vinson's playing strongly influenced Cannonball Adderley; a healthy number of Vinson dates are available on CD, much of the Muse and Pablo, as well as material on Black & Blue, Delmark, Fantasy, Bluebird, and Landmark. His King sessions are currently unavailable on a domestic label. —*Ron Wynn*

○ **Eddie Cleanhead Vinson Sings** / **i.** 195? / Bethlehem 5005

○ **Cherry Red** / Mar. 1967 / Bluesway 6007

● **Kidney Stew** / Mar. 26+28, 1969 / Black & Blue 233021

○ **Hold It Right There!** / Aug. 25, 1978-Aug. 26, 1978 / Muse 5243
Eddie Vinson, Arnett Cobb, and Buddy Tate (tenor saxes), together with a top-drawer rhythm section, made a fine group for an engagement in August of 1978 at Sandy's Jazz Revival in

Beverly, MA, and Bob Porter was on hand to record the event. Porter sorted out the performances according to the featured musician, and several LPs on the Muse label were issued. This was the second volume of the Vinson specialties. . . . Cobb and Tate were present only on the title number and "Take the 'A' Train," while the rhythm section (pianist Ray Bryant, bassist George Duvivier, drummer Alan Dawson) purred along in firm support and added solo work of its own. —*Shirley Klett, Cadence*

○ **Live at Sandy's** / Aug. 25, 1978-Aug. 26, 1978 / Muse 5208
Here, in just one of several LPs to have resulted from a historic confrontation of three top-ranking Texas saxmen in a popular Massachusetts Jazz club, Eddie "Cleanhead" Vinson had the stage almost entirely to himself. And, because of the heady atmosphere that was most certainly engendered by the uniqueness of the situation, he succeeded in registering what was arguably his best work on record to date. —*Jack Sohmer, Cadence*

● **And Roomful of Blues** / Jan. 27, 1982 / Muse 5282
Pairing Eddie "Cleanhead" Vinson with Roomful of Blues was one of those ideas that seemed so natural one wonders why it wasn't done sooner. Listeners shouldn't expect any great revelations, but they'll hear hard, swinging jazz and blues that would make Count Basie proud. —*Carl Brauer, Cadence*

○ **Cleanhead & Cannonball** / 1988 / Landmark 1309

○ **Bosses of the Blues—Vol. 2** / Bluebird 8312

Miroslav Vitous (Miroslav Ladislav Vitous)

b. Dec. 6, 1947, Prague
Bass, guitar, composer, educator / Early jazz-rock, world fusion, modern creative
A virtuoso bassist and among the finest players ever to come to America from Europe, Vitous (whose father was a saxophonist) studied violin at 6 and then piano before starting on bass at 14. He played with Jan Hammer and his brother Alan in a junior trio at the Prague Conservatory. Vitous studied at Berklee from 1966 to 1967 and then went to New York and worked with Art Farmer, Freddie Hubbard, and the Bob Brookmeyer-Clark Terry quintet. He worked for a brief time with Miles Davis and had an extended stint with Herbie Mann from the late '60s until the end of 1970. Later, he was a founding member of Weather Report and remained with them from 1971 to 1973. Vitous headed his own groups in 1976 and continued to do that, plus extensive session work, throughout the '80s. —*Ron Wynn*

★ **Mountain in the Clouds** / i. 1973 / Atlantic
A groundbreaking LP for fusioneers—pre-Weather Report—with John McLaughlin, Joe Henderson, Herbie Hancock, Jack DeJonette, and Joe Chambers. All Vitous originals except "Freedom Jazz Dance," clocking in at 11 minutes. Originally "Infinite Search." —*Michael G. Nastos*

○ **Miroslav** / Dec. 1976-Jul. 1977 / Freedom 741040
1976-1977 sessions with Don Alias and Armen Halburian on percussion. Vitous overdubs bass and keyboards. A stunning musical trip through Afro-jazz texture music. "Tiger in the Rain" is absolutely captivating. —*Michael G. Nastos*

☆ **First Meeting** / May 1979 / ECM 1145
Seven pieces written by Vitous. With John Surman (sax, b, cl), a very young Kenny Kirkland (p), and stellar Jon Christenson (d). This is very listenable music, rooted in freedom of expression. —*Michael G. Nastos*

Abdul Wadud (Abdul Khabir Wadud)

b. Apr. 30, 1947, Cleveland, OH
Cello / Modern creative
An outstanding cellist, Abdul Wadud has concentrated solely on the instrument since the age of nine and never decided to double on bass. His plucking and bowed solos have been featured in jazz and symphonic-classical settings, and he's easily the finest cellist to emerge from the '60s and '70s generation. He studied at Youngstown State and Oberlin in the late '60s and early '70s. He played in the Black Unity Trio at Oberlin and met Julius Hemphill; the two subsequently worked together well through the '80s. Wadud played in the New Jersey Symphony Orchestra in the '70s, and earned his master's degree in 1972. He played with Arthur Blythe for the first time in '76, and has since maintained a working relationship with him. He also worked and recorded with Frank Lowe, George Lewis, Oliver Lake, Sam Rivers, Cecil

Taylor, David Murray, Chico Freeman, Anthony Davis, and James Newton in the '70s and '80s. Wadud, Newton, and Davis were in both the octet Episteme and a trio from 1982 to 1984. Wadud recorded as a leader for Bishara and Gramavision in the '70s and '80s and in a duo with Jenkins for Red in the '70s. He has one session currently available on CD. —*Ron Wynn*

By Myself / **i.** 1977 / Bishara 101

Collin Walcott

b. Apr. 24, 1945, New York, NY, **d.** Nov. 8, 1984, Magdeburg, Germany
Percussion, sitar / World fusion
Trained in classical percussion, Walcott's interest in Indian music led him to be one of the first and only Westerners to master both sitar and tabla (Indian hand drums). He studied sitar with Ravi Shankar and tabla with Alla Rakha. Walcott had early recordings with Tony Scott and Miles Davis and became a member of the Paul Winter Consort in 1970. He is probably best known for his work with the chamber jazz ensemble Oregon, which he co-founded with Ralph Towner, Paul McCandless, and Glen Moore. Oregon was unusually successful in creating artistically valuable music from eclectic influences, and Walcott's contribution on tabla and sitar was an important component of the group's tone and ambience. He also had an association with Don Cherry and Nana Vasconcelos in the group Codona. Collin died in an accident in East Germany while touring with Oregon. —*David Nelson McCarthy*

○ **Cloud Dance** / Mar. 1975 / ECM 825469
Collin Walcott's effective *Cloud Dance* produced a series of life-giving musical showers. Taking the form of intimate conversations among musical friends, these protean exploratory dialogues radiated warmth, trust, and adventure. As a trio, Walcott's sitar and John Abercrombie's guitar mingled above Dave Holland's bass in an open terrain of infinite dimensions. —*Chuck Berg, Down Beat*

★ **Works** / 1975-1984 / ECM 837276

☆ **Grazing Dreams** / Feb. 1977 / ECM 827866
W/ Don Cherry, John Abercrombie. His glory. Group music based around Walcott's sitar and tabla work. —*Michael G. Nastos*

Mal Waldron (Malcolm Earl Waldron)

b. Aug. 16, 1926, New York, NY
Piano, composer / Hard bop
Among the more quirky, unpredictable pianists, with a style equally suited to avant-garde or more conventional settings, Mal Waldron earned a degree in music from Queens College in the '50s and then worked with Big Nick Nicholas, Ike Quebec, Della Reese, and various R&B groups. He became a regular member of various Charles Mingus bands from 1954 to 1956 and also was Billie Holiday's accompanist from 1957 to 1959. He led his own bands in the '60s, including backing both John Coltrane and Eric Dolphy, appearing on the immortal "Live at the Five Spot" sessions in the early '60s. During the '70s and '80s, he worked often with soprano saxophonist Steve Lacy, also did hard-bop with Clifford Jordan and Philly Joe Jones. A wonderful soloist, adept accompanist, and fine songwriter. —*Ron Wynn*

● **Mal—Vol. 1 and 2** / Nov. 9, 1956-Apr. 19, 1957 / Prestige 611
On these early dates, the first under pianist Mal Waldron's leadership, he had not developed the strength that characterized his later work on Prestige—both as a sideman with Eric Dolphy and Steve Lacy and as a trio leader on his *Impressions*. His best contributions to this reissue were the haunting, stark arrangements of "Don't Explain" and "Yesterdays". . . Not bad music by any means, but not very remarkable either—suitable for hard bop combers. —*Martin Davidson, Down Beat*

○ **Wheelin'** / **i.** Apr. 1957+Sep. 1957 / Prestige 24069

○ **Up Popped the Devil** / Dec. 28, 1973 / Enja 2034
Pianist Mal Waldron's music is characterized by a heavily brooding rhythmic quality, with the left hand usually carrying the theme at one repetitious tempo while the right hammers away in juxtaposition with a countertempo (usually faster). Such was the case with "Up Popped the Devil," "Snake Out," and "Changachangachang," three very Waldronian pieces in both structure and execution, the latter deriving its melody from the whole-tone scale. Aside from Waldron, the record's strongest

points were bassist Reggie Workman and drummer Billy Higgins, their work being sensitive and supportive throughout. —*Bob Rusch, Down Beat*

★ **Hard Talk** / May 4, 1974 / Enja 2050
Mal Waldron accompanied Lady Day (Billie Holiday) during her last years and worked with Charles Mingus and others. During his lengthy stay in Europe he came to grips with free jazz. He didn't try to emulate players like Cecil Taylor, but rather fused his somewhat stiff but recognizable and immensely enjoyable style with players of the modern school. —*Milo Fine, Cadence*

○ **Crowd Scene** / **i.** 1989 / Soul Note 121218
Mal Waldron can sound miraculous in the right environment, but he is just a little off this time around.... There are moments of glory. Waldron helps himself out with an insistent blues solo on "Scene," and Workman plays with outstanding virtuosity in his solos. —*Jerome Wilson, Cadence*

Fats Waller (Thomas Wright Waller)

b. May 21, 1904, New York, NY, **d.** Dec. 15, 1943, Kansas City, MO
Piano, organ, vocals, bandleader, composer / Stride, boogie-woogie
Huge in girth and filled with mirth, Fats Waller was not only one of jazz's greatest pianists but also one of the century's greatest entertainers. On records (he made hundreds), radio (he had his own programs at a time when Black artists were not often recognized), and in film (he appeared in only three feature films and a handful of shorts but stole every scene), his marvelous sense of humor (he was a champion ad libber), his tremendous time (he was swing incarnate), and his sheer physical force impressed audiences of every stripe. A prodigious creator of melodies, he wrote (with his chief partner, lyricist Andy Razaf) such evergreens as "Ain't Misbehavin'," "Honeysuckle Rose," "Black and Blue," "The Jitterbug Waltz," and dozens of others. At the time of his death, he had a hit show running on Broadway and could be seen on screens throughout the land in *Stormy Weather*, his best movie. Too much food and drink—Fats consumed liquor by the gallon—and not enough rest did him in at 39. But Waller records haven't been out of print since and he still makes new fans—not least among piano players. —*Dan Morgenstern*

● **Giants of Jazz** / **i.** Oct. 21, 1922-Jan. 23, 1943 / Time Life 15
Although now difficult to find, this three-LP boxed set gives listeners a perfect summation of Fats Waller's career and hits most of the highpoints. —*Scott Yanow*

Rare Piano Roll Solos—Vol. 1 / **i.** 1923-1924 / Biograph 1002
Rare Piano Roll Solos—Vol. 2 / **i.** 1924-1931 / Biograph 1005

★ **Turn on the Heat: The Fats Waller Piano Solos** / Feb. 16, 1927-May 13, 1941 / Bluebird 2482
With the exception of a third take of "I've Got a Feeling I'm Falling" and his two earliest records from 1922, all of Fats Waller's recorded piano solos are on this superior double-CD set. Over half of these recordings are from 1929, but fortunately Fats also cut three sessions of piano solos after he became much more famous as a comedy personality with his Rhythm sides. Highlights include the virtuosic "Handful of Keys," the earliest version of "Ain't Misbehavin'," "Clothes LIne Ballet," "I Ain't Got Nobody," and "Honeysuckle Rose." A special bonus are a pair of piano duets with Bennie Payne ("St. Louis Blues" and "After You've Gone"). Classic music. —*Scott Yanow*

○ **Fats Waller—1927-1929** / **i.** May 20, 1927-Dec. 18, 1929 / Swaggie 850
This Swaggie CD has many of Fats Waller's hotter band sides from the 1920s. Waller is heard playing piano and pipe organ with cornetist Thomas Morris's Hot Babies (making the other musicians sound old-fashioned in comparison), there are a couple of his solo pipe organ recordings from 1927, and Fats takes his first recorded vocal, scatting on "Red Hot Dan." The second side of this LP has the classic Fats Waller and His Buddies recordings of 1929; best are "The Minor Drag" and "Harlem Fuss." Classic early jazz (much of which has since been reissued on CD) from the masterful stride pianist before he became famous. —*Scott Yanow*

★ **Fats Waller and His Buddies** / May 20, 1927-Dec. 18, 1929 / Bluebird 61005
This CD has most of Fats Waller's best band recordings of the 1920s, including eight selections by his "Buddies" (highlighted by "The Minor Drag" and "Harlem Fuss"), six (counting two alternate takes) from the Louisiana Sugar Babes (an odd quartet featuring Fats's organ and James P. Johnson's piano), and seven selections on which Waller sits in with cornetist Thomas Morris's Hot Babies in 1927. Surprisingly, other than his scat vocal on "Red Hot Dan," Fats Waller is heard strictly as a pianist, but his talents were so giant as an instrumentalist that one never minds. With trombonists Charlie irvis and Jack Teagarden and trumpeters Red Allen and Jabbo Smith among the strong supporting cast, the one word for this superior CD is hot! —*Scott Yanow*

★ **Complete Fats Waller—Vol. 1** / **i.** May 16, 1934-Mar. 6, 1935 / RCA 5511
This double-LP was the first in a planned series of reissues that would document all of Fats Waller's popular Rhythm recordings. Lack of corporate interest and the rise of CDs led to this particular series stopping after the fourth volume but these are all worth acquiring. Starting in 1934 Fats Waller, then best known as a pianist and composer, began recording with a two-horn sextet called his "Rhythm." Fats from the start of this series emerged as a superior jazz vocalist and an often hilarious personality, generally satirizing the lyrics of the inferior material his band was often given to record. One can fully understand his great popularity from hearing the recordings on this initial volume, particularly such tunes as "A Porter's Love Song to a Chambermaid," "How Can You Face Me," "You're Not the Only Oyster in the Stew" and "Honeysuckle Rose." Recommended. —*Scott Yanow*

○ **Complete Fats Waller—Vol. 2 (1935)** / Mar. 6, 1935-Aug. 20, 1935 / RCA 5575
Although this double-LP series was originally planned to reissue all of Fats Waller's Rhythm recordings, it only made it to the fourth volume. Vol. 2 has 32 exciting examples of his band's music, featuring solos from trumpeter Herman Autrey, Rudy Powell's clarinet and alto, and the leader's powerful stride piano. However it was Waller's humorous and often satirical vocals that really sold these hot recordings. Among the classics on this set are "What's the Reason I'm Not Pleasin' You," "Oh Suzanna Dust Off That Old Pianna," "You've Been Taking Lessons in Love from Somebody New," "My Very Good Friend the Milkman" and the touching (and relatively straightforward) hit version of "I'm Gonna Sit Right Down and Write Myself a Letter." —*Scott Yanow*

○ **Definitive Fats Waller—Vol. 1: His Piano His Rhythm, The** / Mar. 11, 1935-Aug. 7, 1939 / Stash 528
In addition to his many studio recordings for Victor, the popular pianist-singer-composer Fats Waller recorded two extensive sessions of radio transcriptions that could be used to fill in time between radio shows. These have now been reissued in full on two CDs. The first volume finds Waller performing seven songs in 1935 (two duets with the reeds of Rudy Powell and five solos with some vocals) in addition to 23 performances from 1939 (17 with his Rhythm, an excerpt from an organ solo and five unaccompanied piano solos). Throughout Fats Waller, who never really needed an audience, is in exuberant form, playing material that was generally superior to the dog tunes he was often handed at recording sessions. A fun set. —*Scott Yanow*

○ **Definitive Fats Waller—Vol. 2: Hallelujah, The** / **i.** Mar. 11, 1935-Apr. 3, 1939 / Stash 539
This second volume of rare Fats Waller items includes 24 selections performed at a marathon radio transcription session in 1935 (there were actually 31 pieces played, 7 of which are on Volume I!). Waller is heard solo, singing and playing piano without the assistance of his sidemen, and he is in top form on a wide variety of material. This CD concludes with previously unreleased items from three different occasions: a 1936 solo broadcast from Bluefield, West Virginia, two selections privately recorded in London in 1939, and Waller's appearance on the George Jessel Show during the same year. A superior release from the great stride pianist, vocalist, composer, and personality. —*Scott Yanow*

○ **Complete Fats Waller—Vol. 3 (1935-1936)** / Aug. 20, 1935-Jun. 5, 1936 / RCA 5583
Although this "complete" reissue of Fats Waller's Rhythm sides was never finished (it only made it to four volumes), each of the four twofers that did get released are perfectly done. Volume 3 features many fine solos by trumpeter Herman Autrey and Gene Sedric on tenor and clarinet, has three examples of Fats Waller's exciting big band (which on "I Got Rhythm" finds Waller "battling" fellow pianist Henry Duncan), and contains quite a few memorable recordings including "Got a Bran' New Suit," "I've

Got My Fingers Crossed" and "All My Life." Throughout even the weakest selection, Fats Waller's powerful stride piano and verbal interjections really drive the ensembles. —*Scott Yanow*

○ **Complete Fats Waller—Vol. 4** / **i.** Jun. 5, 1936-Nov. 29, 1936 / Bluebird 5905
The fourth and unfortunately final twofer from this "complete" series of Fats Waller Rhythm recordings brings the program up to near the end of 1936. With a sextet that also features solos from trumpeter Herman Autrey, Gene Sedric on clarinet and tenor, and guitarist Al Casey, Fats Waller romps through most of these 28 performances. Highlights include "Black Raspberry Jam," "I'm Crazy 'Bout My Baby," "The Curse of an Aching Heart," the somewhat hilarious "Floatin' Down to Cotton Town," and two versions of "Swingin' Them Jingle Bells." All four volumes of this series are highly recommended, at least until the music eventually resurfaces on CD. —*Scott Yanow*

○ **Fats Waller and His Rhythm: The Middle Years, Pt. 1** (1936-1938) / **i.** Dec. 24, 1936-Apr. 12, 1938 / Bluebird 66083
Since virtually all other Fats Waller and his Rhythm reissue programs have started out with his first Victor recordings from 1934 and then have petered out before reaching the end of the huge quantity, it was decided to start the new Bluebird CD series with Waller's final studio recordings and work one's way backwards! This particular three-CD set (which follows "The Last Years") picks up around where Vol. 4 of the "Complete" LP series ended and includes no less than 70 recordings from Fats Waller's "middle years." Highly recommended. —*Scott Yanow*

○ **Jugglin' Jive of Fats Waller and his orchestra** / **i.** Jul. 16, 1938-Oct. 18, 1938 / Sandy Hook 2097
This very enjoyable CD contains three radio broadcasts featuring Fats Waller and his Rhythm in 1938. Despite some dated chatter (and not-so-subtle racism) from a radio announcer, the music on these live performances is quite spirited with Waller singing and playing heated stride piano with his sextet. While trumpeter Herman Autrey and Gene Sedric's reeds are major assets, Fats is virtually the whole show, really driving his sidemen and stimulating both a memorable party atmosphere and creative swinging jazz. —*Scott Yanow*

George Wallington (Giacinto Figlia)

b. Oct. 27, 1924, Palermo, Sicily, d. Feb. 15, 1993
Piano, composer / Bop
George Wallington was a swing-to-bop piano giant with phenomenal technique. He worked mostly in trios and occasionally in small groups. He was also a prolific composer. —*Michael G. Nastos*

★ **Jazz for the Carriage Trade** / Jan. 20, 1956 / Prestige 1704
This was a 1/20/56 date with Donald Byrd (trumpet), Phil Woods (alto sax), Teddy Kotick (bass), and Art Taylor (drums), and it was also reissued as part of a twofer. The session had a lasting hard bop edge and closely parallels what the Messengers were sounding like at the time. It was an exemplary sample of New York bop. —*Bob Rusch, Cadence*

○ **Dance of the Infidels** / Nov. 14, 1957 / Savoy 1122
Pianist George Wallington had his critics, but I jump to everything he did, and his groups (on this session trumpeter Donald Byrd, alto saxophonist Phil Woods, bassist Knobby Totah, drummer Nick Stabulas) produced some of Phil Woods's greatest playing. —*Jerry L. Atkins, Cadence*

Cedar Walton (Cedar Anthony Walton, Jr.)

b. Jan. 17, 1934, Dallas, TX
Piano / Postbop
This keyboard great was better known as a superb accompanist than as a soloist, although he's delivered many masterly statements over the years. Walton moved to New York from Dallas in the late '50s and was part of J. J. Johnson's sextet from 1958 to 1960. Later he replaced McCoy Tyner in the Jazztet in 1960-1961 and then spent three pivotal years with Art Blakey's Jazz Messengers, whom he rejoined briefly in 1973. During his Messengers tenure, Walton's long lines, keen harmonic sense, and ability to interact with Blakey and the horn front line put him in the upper echelon of jazz pianists. He began to get plenty of work on Blue Note and Prestige sessions and also started to release his own albums. Walton went to Europe in 1970 and has since spent lots of time there. During the '70s he made several memorable releases with

Clifford Jordan, George Coleman, Hank Mobley, and others, was part of two excellent small combos, and also did an excellent series on Timeless under the banner of Eastern Rebellion. —*Ron Wynn*

○ **Plays Cedar Walton** / Jul. 10, 1967-Jan. 14, 1969 / Prestige 6002
1967-1969. 1988 reissue of Walton giving his own work a showcase. Host of great players, among them Kenny Dorham (tpt) and Clifford Jordan (ts). CD has bonus cut. —*Ron Wynn*

★ **Breakthrough** / Feb. 22, 1972 / Muse 5132
This was a reissue of an album originally minted in 1972. It was in fact a classic all-star session with all personnel playing at or near the peak of their prowess. Tenor saxophonist Hank Mobley particularly sounded better than he had since his brilliant salad days in the 1950s. "Breakthrough" by Mobley featured a sax battle between Hank and Charles Davis on baritone in vintage hard bop fashion with pianist Cedar Walton comping up a storm. —*Larry Birnbaum, Down Beat*

★ **Night at Boomer's—Vol. 2, A** / Jan. 4, 1973 / Muse 5022
January 4, 1973, was a doubly fortuitous night at Boomer's for it produced not one but two excellent recordings. To my ears, Cedar Walton's piano style blended Bud Powell's forceful, percussive touch with Bill Evans's linear melodic invention, sprinkled with the slightest bit of current McCoy Tyner; this eclectic mixture produced an entirely transparent style, never obscuring the music itself. Tenor saxophonist Clifford Jordan was equally fascinating. Primarily a lyrical player whose tenor sounded almost like a Paul Desmond alto at times, he, like Walton, was mainly a linear improviser. Yet his playing had a subtle sense of form: In a typical solo he'd start in his ax's lower register and gradually ascend to its heights, roughening his tone as he went along and ending with a minor flurry of light cries, an approach with its own kind of organic logic. —*Jon Balleras, Down Beat*

★ **Night at Boomer's—Vol. 1, A** / Jan. 4, 1973 / Muse 5010
The late tenor saxophonist Clifford Jordan met the mainstream requirements of this occasion with aplomb and, obviously, pleasure. The way pianist Cedar Walton, bassist Sam Jones, and drummer Louis Hayes emphasized on "This Guy's in Love with You" was something approaching a working definition of jazz. —*Doug Ramsey, Down Beat*

○ **Eastern Rebellion—Vol. 2** / **i.** 1975 / Timeless

☆ **Eastern Rebellion—Vol. 1** / **i.** 1975 / Timeless
Recorded slightly more than a year apart, these quartet dates were welcome additions to the discography of one of the consistently fine jazz composer-performers active over the last several decades. . . . Thanks largely to Walton's forceful shaping of the group's music, the longstanding participation of bassist Sam Jones and drummer Billy Higgins, no less than the quite similar approaches of the saxophonists, the two sets possessed a strong cohesiveness of conception and execution that came as no surprise to those familiar with Walton's music. These albums maintained his standards of creativity and musicianship within the bebop rubric to which he held steadfast. —*Pete Welding, Down Beat*

Carlos Ward (Carlos Nathaneil Ward)

b. May 1, 1940, Ancon, Panama Canal Zone
Sax / Postbop, world fusion, neo-bop, modern creative
Carlos Ward is a Jamaican-born saxophonist and flutist. He's done steady work w/ Carla Bley and Abdullah Ibrahim and is as reliable, consistent, and rich with ideas as any. Ward also has substantial funk and R&B credentials, including a stint with B.T. Express. —*Michael G. Nastos*

★ **Lito** / Jul. 1988 / Leo 166
Live date at the North Sea Jazz Festival for saxophonist-flutist with quartet featuring trumpeter Woody Shaw. Extended work. Excellent. —*Michael G. Nastos*

David S. Ware (David Spencer Ware)

b. Nov. 7, 1949, Plainfield, NJ
Tenor sax / Modern creative
A powerhouse tenor saxophonist, David S. Ware's swirling solos with their overblowing, energized screams and intensity make him one of the few current players willing to display ties to the '60s free style. Ware also smartly employs multiphonics and false fingerings. He played baritone, alto, and tenor sax as a teen and attended Berklee from 1967 to 1969. Ware formed the group

Apogee in 1970 and played in Boston until they relocated to New York. Ware played in Cecil Taylor's orchestra during his 1974 Carnegie Hall concert. He spent two years with Andrew Cyrille in the mid-'70s, while also working in a trio with trumpeter Ralphe Malik and touring Europe with Taylor. Ware and Barry Harris made a duet album in 1977, and Ware and Cyrille rejoined forces, recording in 1978 and 1980. Ware has recorded as a leader in the '80s and '90s. He's done sessions for DIW/Columbia and Silkheart. Ware has a couple of dates available. —*Ron Wynn*

○ **Great Bliss, Vol. 1** / **i.** Jan. 1990 / Silkheart 127
Great Bliss, Vol. 1 is David S. Ware's statement of purpose, a bold, sometimes chaotic, always gripping excursion. The young pianist Matthew Shipp is especially inspiring in his grasp of the free tradition. The tunes are long, the structure expendable, dictated by the spirit of the moment. But lyricism is not lost: "Bliss Theme" has a different sort of gospel luster. —*Josef Woodard, Down Beat*

● **Flight of I** / Dec. 1991 / Columbia 52956
Flight of I, recorded a year after David S. Ware's *Great Bliss, Vol. I*, combines fiercely original pieces with two standards. The blend is beguiling. Ware finds a wholly new way to say "There Will Never Be Another You," checking in with the chord changes and the melodic chassis only peripherally. Ware plays the head to "Yesterdays" with a fluttering, beehivelike quality. —*Josef Woodard, Down Beat*

Wilbur Ware (Wilbur Bernard Ware)

b. Sep. 8, 1923, Chicago, IL, **d.** Sep. 9, 1979, Philadelphia, PA
Bass / Bop, hard bop, postbop
A wonderful, exciting bassist, Wilbur Ware managed to overcome some stylistic limitations by his ability to break up the beats He could sometimes befuddle others on the bandstand by this method, but he always managed to link his statements thematically and resolve things to the success of the composition. He had great touch and articulation but didn't approach or roam over the instrument like some other players, preferring to emphasize the lower end in his playing. Ware was a self-taught banjo player, and his foster father made him a bass. He played in string bands around Chicago and then worked in groups led by Stuff Smith, Roy Eldridge, and Sonny Stitt in the late '40s. During the '50s he periodically had his own bands, while working with Eddie "Cleanhead" Vinson, Art Blakey, Buddy DeFranco, Thelonious Monk, and J. R. Monterose. He returned to Chicago in 1959 but went back to New York in the late '60s and reunited with Monk in 1970. The last part of his life he played with Clifford Jordan and Paul Jeffrey. He led a group that included Johnny Griffin, John Jenkins, and Junior Mance and recorded on Fantasy in the late '50s. —*Ron Wynn*

★ **Chicago Sound** / Oct. 1957+Nov. 1957 / Riverside 1737
Quintet. Legendary bassist. With Johnny Griffin (ts) and John Jenkins (as). A classic. —*Michael G. Nastos*

Earle Warren (Earl Ronalde Warren)

b. Jul. 1, 1914, Springfield, OH, **d.** 1994
Alto sax / Swing, big band
Earle Warren was the first outstanding alto saxophonist ever in Count Basie's band and one of the few who took some attention away from the perennially popular tenors like Herschel Evans and Lester Young. Warren joined Basie in 1937. He spent nearly 13 years with Basie, playing and doing some vocals. He left in 1950, later was a manager for such performers as Johnny Otis, and had three stints with Buck Clayton. He continued to tour in the '70s and '80s and worked into the '90s with The Countsmen. He died in 1994.—*Ron Wynn*

★ **Count's Men, The** / Jul. 9, 1985 / Muse 5512
The leader of the Countsmen was alto saxophonist Earle Warren, who after replacing Caughey Roberts, was the leader of the Count Basie band's saxophone section and sometimes vocalist with the band. . . . This was a nice set of swinging jazz, though there was nothing spectacular here, just some Basie standards and some ballads performed with feeling and panache. —*Ronald B. Weinstock, Cadence*

Grover Washington, Jr.

b. Dec. 12, 1943, Buffalo, NY
Sax / Soul-jazz, instrumental pop, contemporary funk

One of the most commercially successful saxophonists in jazz history and a versatile reed specialist, Washington is equally at home on soprano, alto, or tenor sax and has recorded on flute and baritone sax. A much more creative improviser than his hit-making saxophone competitors, Washington has had hits with almost everything he has done since his first album (*Inner City Blues*) for Kudu in 1971. His biggest albums, *Mr. Magic* (Kudu) and *Winelight* (Elektra), have also spawned hit singles. His recordings for Kudu, Motown, Elektra, and Columbia are mostly commercial in content but, given that, Washington's saxophone work is always first rate and a good distance in front of his closest fusion rivals. —*Bob Porter*

● **Inner City Blues** / **i.** 1972 / Motown 5189
Definitive early '70s soul-jazz date. Washington has seldom been more convincing. Ron Carter is stalwart on bass. W/ Bob James (p), Eric Gale (g), Airto (per), and Thad Jones (tpt). —*Ron Wynn*

● **Mister Magic** / Nov. 1974 / Motown 5027

☆ **Winelight** / **i.** Jun. 1980 / Elektra 305
Winelight combined total commerciality with unfailing good taste. Saxophonist Grover Washington Jr. hit on a sure-fire funk success formula, and en route to the bank he blew some very pleasant stuff. Washington extended the soul-jazz set tradition of Arnett Cobb, Gene Ammons, Stanley Turrentine, and others. Within that middle-of-the-road entertainment contest—always responsive to popular trends—he did indeed get down. Essentially *Winelight* was top-of-the-line mood music, soothing, relaxing, and eminently danceable. —*Ben Sandmel, Down Beat*

☆ **Then and Now** / **i.** 1988 / Columbia 44256
We are pleased to observe that Grover Washington, Jr. has—at least for the moment—returned to the fold, eschewing gimmickry and the trappings of pop, with the no-nonsense straightahead *Then and Now*, a nice balance of ballads and uptempos, standards and originals, and the leader's tenor, alto, and soprano. —*W. Royal Stokes, Jazz Times*

Dinah Washington (Ruth Lee Jones)

b. Aug. 29, 1924, Tuscaloosa, AL, **d.** Dec. 14, 1963, Detroit, MI
Vocals / Ballads & blues
They called her "the Queen of the Blues," but as Dinah herself said, she could "sing anything—anything at all." At first, she sang gospel with the Sallie Martin Singers. In 1943, having been discovered by manager Joe Glaser, she was with Lionel Hampton's band, getting a new name but little exposure on records. By 1946 , she was on her own with a Mercury Records contract. Her earliest hits were in the rhythm & blues field, but before long she "crossed over," with such material as "Harbor Lights" and, especially, "What a Difference a Day Makes." With a great gift for projecting lyrics, a sardonic sense of humor, and a voice that was made for blues and jazz, Dinah Washington was also a terrific performer. Her records in a jazz setting (her horn accompanists included trumpeters Clifford Brown, Clark Terry, and Maynard Ferguson; her pianists Wynton Kelly and a young Joe Zawinul) rate with the best of the period, and had she lived, there's no telling what she might have accomplished. Her many emulators include the late Esther Phillips and Nancy Wilson. —*Dan Morgenstern*

★ **Mellow Mama** / Dec. 1945 / Delmark 451
Recorded in Los Angeles in 1945, shortly after she had left Lionel Hampton's band, Dinah Washington's 12 classic blues performances, which include "Rich Man's Blues," "My Voot Is Really Vout," "No Voot No Boot," and "My Lovin' Papa," are now available for the first time in one package. For pure jazz fans, the best news is that the young, salty mama's accompaniment is provided by tenor great Lucky Thompson and a carefully assembled combo of then-L.A. residents, including Milt Jackson and Charlie Mingus. —*Jack Sohmer, Down Beat*

★ **Complete Dinah Washington on Mercury—Vols. 1—7, The** / **i.** 1946-1963 / Mercury 832444
If you buy one, you'll want them all. Important musical documents. —*Michael G. Nastos*

○ **Wise Woman Blues** / **i.** 1949-1963 / Rosetta 1313

○ **Dinah Jams** / Aug. 1954 / Emarcy 814639

★ **Jazz Sides** / **i.** 1954-1958 / Emarcy 824883

1954-1958. Great two-record set that accents her mid-'50s jazz cuts. Until recently that was about all the jazz of Dinah's that was in print. —*Ron Wynn*

★ **Bessie Smith Songbook** / 1957-1958 / Emarcy 826663
Recorded in three sessions, this had Dinah Washington in fine, full voice handling the material in her own fashion and style. The weakness was in the setting, not the singer. Washington was both a great soul singer and a great jazz singer, as her more open jam session for EmArcy will attest. Here she was dealing with material very well suited to her strengths, but instead of being an instrument among other instruments, reflecting and improvising on a theme, she was placed above the pack. —*Bob Rusch, Cadence*

What a Diff'rence a Day Makes! / 1959 / Mercury 818815
Title cut is one of her biggest hits ever. Everything else is a bit overarranged, but she sounds great. Billboard #34. —*Ron Wynn*

○ **Unforgettable** / **i.** 1963 / Mercury 510602
Here we get the incredible voice and spirit of Dinah Washington with the pop confectionary sweetings of a sumptuous studio orchestra in a reissue of material from 1959. In addition to the heartfelt title track, there is a vibrant duo with the great pop baritone Brook Benton and a host of other melodramatically presented ballads, such as "This Love of Mine." Still, Washington's incredible musicianship and three-hankie dramaturgy command attention. —*Chuck Berg, Jazz Times*

☆ **Back to the Blues** / Roulette 25189
Washington, known as the "Queen of the Blues," showed how she'd earned the nickname with this marvelous set of basic 12-bar compositions. She'd moved away from this style by the early '60s but proved immediately and often that she hadn't lost the ability to sing these kinds of songs better than anyone else. —*Ron Wynn, AMG*

Sadao Watanabe

b. Feb. 1, 1933, Utsunomiya, Japan
Alto sax, soprano sax, flute / Bop, world fusion, instrumental pop, contemporary funk
Sadao Watanabe is a Japanese alto and soprano saxophonist with three main strengths: commercially oriented jazz-funk, avant-garde leanings, and the bop roots of his main influence, Charlie Parker. —*Michael G. Nastos*

Nabasada and Charlie / Jun. 27, 1967 / Catalyst 7911
An excellent date with fellow saxophonist Charlie Mariano. Standards played with verve. —*Michael G. Nastos*

★ **Dedicated to Charlie Parker** / Mar. 15, 1969 / Denon 7689

☆ **Bird of Paradise** / May 4, 1977 / Elektra 60748
Just looking at the cover photos of alto saxophonist Sadao Watanabe and Bird and reading Watanabe with the Great Jazz Trio (pianist Hank Jones, bassist Ron Carter, drummer Tony Williams) immediately evoked the question: How well did Japan's best saxophonist play Charlie Parker's best material? To these ears, as well as anybody could no matter where they came from. —*Jerry L. Atkins, Cadence*

○ **I'm Old Fashioned** / May 22, 1986 / Inner City 6015
This session predates much of alto saxophonist and flutist Sadao Watanabe's available recordings. This was a brillant recording, opening with Bird's (Charlie Parker) "Confirmation" and the altoist very much in Bird's groove. This rhythm section was something to hear, and pianist Hank Jones placed a magnificent lingering chord on the end.... This was superb alto and a rhythm section that was rarely equalled in this vein of jazz. —*Jerry L. Atkins, Cadence*

Parker's Mood / Jul. 13, 1986 / Elektra 60475
Close to his best, both on his merit and thanks to aid from James Williams (p) and Jeff Watts (d). 1986 date. —*Ron Wynn*

Benny Waters (Benjamin Waters)

b. Jan. 23, 1902, Brighton, MD
Alto sax, clarinet, arranger / New Orleans traditional, swing, big band
Benny Waters is one of the great jazz veterans, whose experience and grounding extends back to the '20s. An alto saxophonist, clarinetist, and arranger, Waters managed to retain the energy and drive of a youngster while continuing his career well into his '80s. But he's an exceptional alto saxophonist, capable of executing dif-

ficult passages at top speeds easily and demonstrating extensive harmonic knowledge and creativity as a soloist. Waters studied at the Boston Conservatory before playing with Charlie Johnson's band from 1925 to 1932 and also recording with Clarence Williams and King Oliver. He spent time with Hot Lips Page and Fletcher Henderson in the '30s and then worked with Claude Hopkins and the Jimmie Lunceford orchestra in the years before World War II. He led his own groups in the '50s and then left America for Europe, joining Jacques Butler's band in 1955. He became a star in Europe for 15 years, making tours, recordings, and periodically coming back to America for a visit. —*Ron Wynn*

★ **From Paradise (Small's) to Shangrila** / **i.** Jun. 26, 1987 / Muse 5340

○ **Memories of the Twenties, Stomp Off** / **i.** 1988 / Southern Studios 1210

Doug Watkins (Douglas Watkins)

b. Mar. 2, 1934, Detroit, MI, **d.** Feb. 5, 1962, Holbrook, Az
Bass / Hard bop, postbop
Doug Watkins is a popular Detroit bassist whose list of credits dwarfs all except his better-half, Paul Chambers. He was a bastion of the '50s, and a post-to hard-bop giant. —*Michael G. Nastos*

★ **Watkins at Large** / Dec. 8, 1956 / Transition 20

○ **Soulnik** / May 17, 1960 / New Jazz 8238

Julius Watkins

b. Oct. 10, 1921, Detroit, MI, **d.** Apr. 4, 1977, Short Hills, NJ
French horn / Hard bop, postbop, progressive big band
Julius Watkins is the preeminent postbop French horn player in jazz. He's been a prolific arranger and composer and is another of the Detroit jazz legends of the '50s. —*Michael G. Nastos*

★ **Julius Watkins Sextet—Vol. 2** / Mar. 19, 1954 / Blue Note 5064

○ **New Faces-New Sounds: Julius Watkins Sextet** / 1954 / Blue Note 5053

Bill Watrous (William Russell Watrous II)

b. Jun. 8, 1939, Middletown, CT
Trombone / Hard bop, early jazz-rock
Though he's possibly the most skilled and facile trombone technician and stylist in the modern era, Watrous has become increasingly irrelevant from a recording standpoint; his late '80s sessions were routine mood music, and he's had only one recent release, a '92 GRP outing. But his beautiful tone, command, and fluidity with the slide show and remain impressive. His father was also a trombonist, and introduced his son to music. Watrous is largely self-taught, though he took a few lessons and played in traditional jazz bands as a youngster. He studied with Herbie Nichols during his military stint and then made his professional debut with Billy Butterfield. Watrous worked with Kai Winding's various groups from 1962 to 1967. He also did many studio sessions, working and recording with Quincy Jones, Maynard Ferguson, Johnny Richards, and Woody Herman. Watrous was in Merv Griffin's studio band from 1965 to 1968 and on the CBS staff from 1967 to 1969. He joined the jazz-rock band Ten Wheel Drive in the early '70s and led his own group Manhattan Wildlife Refuge in the mid- and late '70s, gaining critical praises for his playing and arrangements. Joe Beck, Dick Hyman, Ed Soph, Danny Stiles, and Ed Xiques were among his musicians. Watrous moved to Los Angeles in the late '70s, where he continued recording and heading bands. He played throughout Germany in 1980 with Albert Mangelsdorff and Winding in the group Trombone Summit, and in London in 1982. Watrous has recorded as a leader for Famous Door, Columbia, Soundwings, and GRP. He has some sessions available on CD. —*Ron Wynn*

● **Tiger of San Pedro** / 1975 / Columbia 33701
Second albums, like second novels, are harder to bring off than firsts, but the Manhattan Wildlife Refuge managed to improve on their excellent debut LP with this superior effort. The music here was more varied, the ensemble playing more secure and relaxed, and the soloists in as good or better form. —*Dan Morgenstern, Down Beat*

Bobby Watson (Robert Michael Watson, Jr.)

b. Aug. 23, 1953, Lawrence, KS
Alto sax / Hard bop, postbop, neo-bop

Alto saxophonist Bobby Watson has steadily emerged as a top player and now must be considered among the premier alto saxophonists on the jazz scene. He has a bright, full tone and a vibrant sound and is versatile enough to have recorded bop and contemporary R&B yet has not turned to fusion or instrumental pop. He moved to New York in the mid '70s and was a member of Art Blakey's Jazz Messengers from 1977 to 1981, attaining at one point the position of musical director for the group. During the '80s Watson played with several groups, among them George Coleman's octet, Charlie Persip's Superband, the Louis Hayes quartet, and the 29th Street Saxophone Band, as well as Sam Riuck's Winds of Manhattan, Philly Joe Jones, Dameronia, Panama Francis, and the Savoy Sultans. His current band is Horizon, and Watson recently released his first album for the Columbia label to unanimous praise. —*Ron Wynn*

○ **E.T.A** / 1977 / Roulette 5009

★ **Advance** / i. Aug. 8, 1984 / Enja 79653
This 1991 reissue heralded the arrival of former Jazz Messenger Bobby Watson as a major figure in 1984. —*Ron Wynn*

☆ **Post-Motown Bop** / i. Sep. 17-18, 1990 / Blue Note 95148
Despite the title, this is an excellent and traditional set. Watson is sparkling. —*Ron Wynn*

Ernie Watts (Ernest James Watts)

b. Oct. 23, 1945, Norfolk, VA
Tenor sax, soprano sax / Hard bop, progressive big band, early jazz-rock
Ernie Watts is a good tenor and soprano saxophonist best known for his extensive work in the studios. He's played on Quincy Jones, Cannonball Adderley, Joe Sample, and other jazz and pop albums and has issued some recordings under his own name. Watts has also made several appearances with the "Tonight Show starring Johnny Carson" band, worked on television shows, and done arrangements for pop and rock groups. Though he's a fine blues and ballad stylist and a technically impressive saxophonist, he's moved away in recent years from challenging jazz dates and concentrated on lucrative pop and rock sessions and studio work. —*Ron Wynn*

● **Ernie Watts Quartet** / Dec. 1987 / JVC 3309
This is a delightful disc; crisp and sophisticated, rich with emotion and craftmanship. Ernie Watts, an alumnus of dozens of groups ranging from Buddy Rich's band to the Tonight Show Orchestra to Wayne Henderson's group, is a highly listenable saxophonist. . . . Watts's style is one that bespeaks years of honing and polish, and he has chosen an absolutely flawless rhythm section here to grace his playing. —*Denny Townsend, Jazz Times*

Jeff Watts

Drums / Neo Bop
A marvelous drummer, Jeff Watts was the rhythm anchor for Wynton Marsalis' group from its beginnings until he departed along with Kenny Kirkland and Branford Marsalis. Watts found a suitable replacement gig; he's now in the Tonight Show orchestra alongside Marsalis and Kirkland. Watts can also be heard on all the early Marsalis sessions on CD. —*Ron Wynn*

Megawatts / i. Jul. 1991 / Sunnyside 1055D

Weather Report

b. 1971
Group / Early jazz-rock, world fusion
Weather Report fired some of the first shots in the fusion revolution, and for the majority of the decade and a half of its existence were its premier exponents. Founded by Joe Zawinul and Wayne Shorter, two key participants in Miles Davis's initial fusion breakthrough, the duo was joined by a host of rhythm section members throughout the band's duration. At the outset, Weather Report remained firmly within jazz structures while working with voicings borrowed from rock. Miroslav Vitous's upright bass quickly gave way to Alphonso Johnson's electric work. Zawinul's Rhodes piano would ultimately be replaced by polyphonic synthesizers, further altering the texture of the group's sound. The arrival of bassist Jaco Pastorius not only gave Weather Report a dazzling new voice, but also gave the group another excellent composer. It was during this period that the group enjoyed its greatest popularity, breaking from the often-impressionistic style

of its earlier work to a more open, pop-influenced direction. Still, Weather Report always avoided the pitfalls of many of their contemporaries, never resorting to mundane funk workouts. The considerable skills and musicianship of Zawinul and Shorter kept Weather Report well above the rest. —*Steve Aldrich*

★ **I Sing the Body Electric** / Nov. 1971 / Columbia 46107
A great record from the days when they were still a serious jazz band. —*Ron Wynn*

Weather Report / i. 1971 / Columbia 37616
Jaco Pastorius (b) ruled the day. The 1971 release that heralded their coming. At the time, they were a breath of fresh air, with sterling compositions and great solos from Wayne Shorter (sax), Joe Zawinul (k), and Miroslav Vitous (b). —*Ron Wynn*

★ **Mysterious Traveller** / 1973-1974 / Columbia 32494
Soprano and tenor saxophonist Wayne Shorter was less in the spotlight on the fourth Weather Report outing, primarily because *Mysterious Traveller* showed a preponderance of Joe Zawinul influence. Rousing synthesizer and crowd yells ushered in Zawinul's "Nubian Sundance," a frisky African celebration possessing automated eeriness as well as jungle playfulness. Shorter appeared sparingly on the 10-minute cut, as the percussionists reigned over the latter half. —*Marv Hohman, Down Beat*

○ **Live in Tokyo** / i. 1977 / Columbia 1213

○ **8:30** / i. Dec. 1979 / Columbia 83670
Weather Report live at last! Famous for their meticulously produced albums—one a year since 1971 (throughout their tenure)—the once and future fusion band came out of the studio with three sides that struck the color and power of an electrical storm (side four contained four new studio cuts). —*Douglas Clark, Down Beat*

Chick Webb (William Henry Webb)

b. Feb. 10, 1909, Baltimore, MD, **d.** Jun. 16, 1939, Baltimore, MD
Bandleader, drums / Swing, big band
His career was short, and Chick Webb seemed cursed with only bad luck. He was a hunchback and died at 30 from TB of the spine. But during his short lifetime, Webb was a propulsive, dominating figure behind the drums. He was a dynamo, whose speed, power, and rhythmic skills were never fully captured on record according to many who saw him repeatedly triumph in head-to-head battles with swing era royalty. Gene Krupa reportedly was in awe of Webb and spoke in shell-shocked tones after being blown away at the Savoy in a legendary combat that occurred only a few months before Webb died. Webb overcame being unable to read music by memorizing the arrangements. He led the band from a raised platform in the center, cuing sections via his drumming. He ranged over a huge kit with specially constructed pedals and cymbal holders and was an imaginative stylist who shoved drum technique ahead through dashing fills and crashing cymbals. He moved to New York in 1924 and formed a band two years later. Webb cut his first record in 1927. By the early '30s he'd recruited Hilton Jefferson, Jimmy Harrison, John Trueheart, and Benny Carter. Later came Mario Bauza, Taft Jordan, John Kirby, and Edgar Sampson. Louis Jordan was another luminary in the band. They recorded for Decca and later ARC. Sampson's "Stompin' at the Savoy" became a hit for Webb's orchestra in 1934. The next year he discovered Ella Fizgerald, and she helped them score 11 hits between 1934 and 1939. "A-Tisket, A-Tasket" topped the charts in 1938. Goodman also had a hit with his version of "Stomping at the Savoy" in 1936. Webb's illness worsened in 1938, and he was gone by the summer of 1939. Fitzgerald sang "My Buddy" at his funeral and kept the band together two more years. Webb had adopted her when her mother died. —*Ron Wynn*

★ **Chick Webb (1929-1934)** / i. Jun. 1929-Nov. 1934 / Classics 502

○ **Jazz Heritage: A Legend (1929-1936)** / 1929-1936 / MCA 1303

☆ **Jazz Heritage: Princess of the Savoy (1934-1939)** / 1934-1939 / MCA 1348

○ **Ella Swings the Band (1936-1939)** / 1936-1939 / MCA 1327

○ **Immortal Chick Webb, The** / i. 1967 / Columbia 9439

○ **Immortal Chick Webb: Stompin' at the Savoy** / i. Jun. 1967 / Columbia 2639

Eberhard Weber

b. Jan. 22, 1940, Stuttgart, Germany
Bass, cello, composer / World fusion, new age, modern creative

Eberhard Weber is among Europe's greatest jazz bassists. He worked with Wolfgang Dauner from 1962 to 1972, became a full-time musician in 1972, and worked with Dave Pike in 1972-1973 and Volker Kriegel's Spectrum in 1973-1974. These extensive experiences enabled Weber to become skilled in every phase of bass playing, both jazz and rock, and led him in the early '70s to create a new instrument he called an "electrobass," an upright with electric properties. Weber began recording prolifically for ECM, both as a leader and with Gary Burton and Ralph Towner, before forming his group Colours in 1975 and heading it until 1982. He joined Jan Garbarek's band in 1982 and began to do solo concerts in 1985, while remaining part of the United Jazz and Rock Ensemble. —*Ron Wynn*

● **Colours of Chloe, The** / Dec. 1973 / ECM 833331

The abilities bassist Eberhard Weber brought to this date were formidable. He was a more than capable player, a gifted lyricist (catch the line of the title cut, before it etches itself indelibly in your mind's ear), an effective if monochromatic orchestrator. All that was missing was a sense of freedom. —*Steve Metaliz, Down Beat*

☆ **Works** / ECM 825429

Ben Webster (Benjamin Francis Webster)

b. Mar. 27, 1909, Kansas City, MO, **d.** Sep. 20, 1973, Amsterdam
Tenor sax / Swing, big band
Tenor sax legend Ben Webster was originally a pianist. After working with a series of great midwestern bands, among them Bennie Moten's and Andy Kirk's, he joined Fletcher Henderson in 1934, in the chair of his idol, Coleman Hawkins. Later he worked with Cab Calloway and Teddy Wilson's fine, short-lived band. But it was when he joined Duke Ellington in 1939 that Webster truly came into his own with such famous solos as "Cottontail," "All Too Soon," and "Sepia Panorama." The warmth of his tone, the drive of his beat, and the majestic simplicity of his melodic conception all came together in the settings the Duke devised for him. All of this was a big influence on his younger contemporaries. After leaving Ellington in 1943, he mostly worked with his own small groups, recording prolifically. He also toured with Jazz at the Philharmonic but didn't visit Europe until 1965; once there, however, he stayed for good, living mostly in Copenhagen and Amsterdam and becoming a beloved elder statesman of jazz. His ballad playing of the later years is among the true glories of jazz. —*Dan Morgenstern*

● **Complete Ben Webster on Emarcy (1951-1953), The** / 1951-1953 / Emarcy 824836

This is two records, with fine program notes by Dan Morgenstern, full discographical information, nicely packaged, wonderful music, and all at a special twofer price.... My only gripe was noisy pressings. —*Bob Rusch, Cadence*

○ **King of the Tenors** / Dec. 8, 1953 / Norgran 1089

○ **Ben Webster** / i. Jul. 14, 1954 / Norgran 1001

○ **Ben Webster and Associates** / i. 1959 / Verve 835254

You can't go wrong with Webster, Coleman Hawkins (sax), Budd Jones (b), and many other masters of ballads, blues, and standards. —*Ron Wynn*

Ben and Sweets / Jun. 1962 / Columbia 40853

1987 release of super date. Harry Edison (tpt) is dynamic, Webster his usual impressive self. —*Ron Wynn*

○ **Trav'lin Light** / Sep. 20, 1963+Oct. 14, 1963 / Milestone 47056

In 1956, a year after tenor saxophonist Ben Webster's sessions with Art Tatum, one of these four sides was recorded; the others were from 1963 sessions by the former roomates Webster and pianist Joe Zawinul—long before the latter became known for the various electronica he made famous with Weather Report.... This twofer provided more documentation of the stylist who not only absorbed the prime elements of Hawkins, but those of Lester Young and Johnny Hodges as well. —*Brent Staples, Down Beat*

○ **Stormy Weather** / Jan. 1965 / Black Lion 760108

The first seven selections on *Stormy Weather* were originally issued on Black Lion in 1974 under the title *Saturday Night at the Montmarte*, that particular occasion being January 30, 1965, in the city of Copenhagen. However, added to the CD release are the three final tracks, which bring the total time up to an almost respectable 55:47. —*Jack Sohmer, Jazz Times*

○ **Meets Bill Coleman** / Apr. 27, 1967 / Black Lion 760141

★ **Ben Meets Don Byas** / Feb. 1-02, 1968 / Verve 827920

Both Ben Webster and Don Byas stemmed from Coleman Hawkins, and Byas was Webster's junior by a mere four years. Nevertheless, by the time of this recording (1968) Byas had begun to move into his final, somewhat unfortunate stylistic phase. Hitherto, his melodic sense had never betrayed him, but now he was beginning, in a desire to remain "modern," to adopt some surface aspects of Sonny Rollins and John Coltrane. Webster, on the other hand, remained wholly himself to the end, and his simpler, more direct style and brilliant use of space wore better. —*Dan Morgenstern, Down Beat*

○ **For the Guv'nor (Tribute to Duke Ellington)** / May 26, 1969 / Charly 15

○ **At Work in Europe** / May 26, 1969 / Prestige 24031

Ben Webster was, and almost always has been, considered one of the leading tenor saxophonists, and while the Black Lion 1965 dates were probably by far the finest results of his last years in Europe, there remains precious little in today's record racks by which to judge this master's value. The soul LP (on this Prestige twofer package) was *Blow Ben Blow*, from a Scandinavian label; the Ellington tribute was from a Dutch label; both LPs were from '69. Like his stylistic mentor, Johnny Hodges, Webster toward the end of his career was highly variable, and on these 10 songs he tended to rely on his big, lovely sound (guaranteed to melt a cold heart at 50 paces).... If the soul LP had shorter ideas, the second was more mellowed out ("I Got It Bad (and That Ain't Good)" and the jaunty relaxation of "Rockin' in Rhythm"). On the whole, however, the soul set was a mite better. —*John Litweiler, Down Beat*

○ **Live at the Haarlemse Jazzclub** / May 9, 1972 / Cat 11

The unmistakable tenor "whoose" that announces the first tune of *Live at the Haarlemse Jazz Club* tips the listener off to the identity of the saxophonist. Captured on the bandstand of a nitery in Haarlem, Holland, it is yet another late period sampling of Ben Webster doing his wonderful thing with a pickup trio (Tete Montoliu, piano; Bob Langeris, bass; Tony Inzalaco, drums) over a set of standards, the last of which, "Perdido," did not appear on the original issue. —*Larry Hollis, Cadence*

○ **My Man** / Jan. 11-19, 1973 / Steeple Chase 1008

This session was taken from a series of recorded nights live at the Montmarte, and tenor saxophonist Ben Webster, whether relaxed or jumping, was on the money. —*Bob Rusch, Cadence*

○ **Ben and the Boys** / i. Apr. 1977 / Jazz Archives 35

This covered tenor saxophonist Ben Webster betwixt and between. On "Tea for Two" we had the rough Webster, on the next track the mellow warmth more closely associated with his later work and, I think, really his forte. For the most part it was the mellow Webster on the 1944 radio transcriptions (excellent sound). —*Geoff Millerman, Cadence*

○ **Saturday Night at the Montmartre** / i. 1987 / Jzm 5029

○ **Plays Duke Ellington** / Storyville 4133

Kid and the Brute, The / Verve

Here is another excellent pairing, this time with Illinois Jacquet (ts). —*Ron Wynn*

Dicky Wells (William Wells)

b. Jun. 10, 1907, Centerville, TN, **d.** Nov. 12, 1985, New York, NY
Trombone / Swing, big band
Dicky Wells numbers among swing's most admired, influential trombonists. His playing balanced comedy with sophistication, could be bluesy or harsh, and was often dazzling and fluid. He had a rich, expressive, and flashy approach and cleverly utilized growls and smears. Wells's solos were characterized by superb melodic skills and expert pacing and note selection. He played in local bands as a teen in Louisville, where he first encountered the music of a player who was a lifelong influence, Jimmy Harrison. Wells moved to New York in 1926. During the early '30s he worked in the bands of Fletcher Henderson, Benny Carter, Spike Hughes, and Teddy Hill and earned national acclaim during his first stint with Count Basie. He played with Basie from 1938 to 1945, and penned "After Theatre Jump" during this tenure. He played with Sy Oliver in 1946 and 1947 and returned to Basie from 1947 to 1950. Wells played with Jimmy Rushing in the early '50s and toured Europe with Buck Clayton in 1959 and 1961. He spent 1961-1963 in the Ray Charles Orchestra and also worked in

the '60s for B.B. King. Wells did freelance recording and touring the remainder of his career, occasionally cutting sessions with various Basie sidemen and alumni under the banner the Countsmen. He made a fine album in 1981 with Buddy Tate. Wells's autobiography "Night People" was both hilarious and informative. —*Ron Wynn*

● **Dickie Wells in Paris** / Jul. 7, 1937-Jul. 12, 1937 / Prestige 7593
○ **Bones for the King** / Feb. 3-04, 1958 / Felsted 2006
This LP was comprised of two different dates, 2/3/58 and 2/4/58. The 2/3 date found Wells in a trombone choir with Vic Dickenson, Benny Morton, and George Matthews, backed by Skip Hall (organ), Major Holley (bass), and Jo Jones (drums). It was a very nicely arranged session, though still relaxed and open with some nice jive bantering on "Sweet Daddy." The next day's session had a more jamming ambience with Skip Hall, now on piano; Jones; and Holly now joined by Buck Clayton (trumpet), Rudy Rutherford (clarinet-baritone sax), and Buddy Tate (tenor sax), and an effective Everett Barksdale on guitar. —*Bob Rusch, Cadence*

○ **Trombone Four in Hand** / Apr. 21, 1959 / Felsted 2009
○ **Lonesome Road** / i. Oct. 1982 / Uptown 2707
This was Dicky Wells's first LP in over 20 years and a remarkable achievement in view of the fact that he suffered a savage beating during the course of a robbery in 1975 and spent most of that year and 1976 in and out of the hospital. A layoff of this length of time when you are in your mid-60s would be difficult for any musician, but particularly so for a trombonist. Indeed, Wells started off the very first track out of tune, which gave a poor initial impression. . . . However, on "Dicky's Famous Break," he concentrated all his resources and produced a fine example of trombone playing. —*Shirley Klett, Cadence*

Dick Wellstood (Richard McQueen Wellstood)

b. Nov. 25, 1927, Greenwich, CT, **d.** Jul. 24, 1987, Palo Alto, CA
Piano
A gifted, aggressive pianist who choose to play mostly traditional styles rather than contemporary material, Dick Wellstood excelled at boogie-woogie, stride, and ragtime, as well as traditional jazz and swing since the mid-'40s. One of the most knowledgeable harmonic technicians, Wellstood also mastered bebop and included in his concerts such songs as "Giant Steps," along with Fats Waller and Scott Joplin. His playing wasn't simply repertory; it blossomed and featured his own distinctive sound and flair, no matter what style. Wellstood played with Bob Wilber in the mid-'40s and then worked with Sidney Bechet in Chicago. He later played with Rex Stewart and Charlie Shavers at Nick's in New York. Wellstood toured with the World's Greatest Jazz Band and played with the Blue Three featuring Kenny Davern and Bobby Rosengarden in the '80s. He did numerous dates for Chiaroscuro, as well as sessions for Jazzology, Swingtime, and Statiris, among others. Wellstood's list of musical associates included Roy Eldridge, Conrad Janis, Henry "Red" Allen, Coleman Hawkins, Wild Bill Davison, Vic Dickenson, Buster Bailey, Gene Krupa, and society orchestra bandleader Paul Hoffman. He's well represented on CD. —*Ron Wynn*

○ **Dick Wellstood Alone** / Nov. 1970-Mar. 1971 / Jazzology 73
● **Dick Wellstood and His Famous Orchestra Featuring Kenny** / Jul. 1973-Dec. 1973 / Chiaroscuro 129
The album's title was a put-on; Dick Wellstood and Kenny Davern were the only two members of this "orchestra," and their mood was equally lighthearted. The feeling was unabashedly retrospective as these men nostalgically glanced at the Chicago jazz scene of the '20s. —*Jon Balleras, Down Beat*

○ **Live at Hanratty's** / 1981 / Chaz Jazz 108
The choice of tunes here—and there were nearly two dozen of them—was excellent. It was a canny mixture of less-often heard standards (though it required "Ain't MisBehavin'" was included) and jazz and blues tidbits. Basically this was an album of one of our finest solo pianists, playing on a piano of his own choosing in a relaxed club atmosphere that inspired him to various heights without causing him to reach for flashy effects. —*Lee Jeske, Down Beat*

○ **I Wish I Were Twins** / i. Mar. 1983 / Swingtime 8204
○ **Plus the Blue Three** / i. 1992 / Chi-Sound 129

Frank Wess (Frank Wellington Wess)

b. Jan. 4, 1922, Kansas City, MO
Flute, tenor sax, alto sax / Bop, postbop, progressive big band
Kansas City born, Frank Wess is a flutist and saxophonist with few peers. He played with Count Basie in the '50s and '60s, and with Sir Roland Hanna in the New York Jazz Quartet in the '70s. A premier soloist with the Toshiko Akiyoshi Big Band in the '80s, he has recently been leading his own big band, with roots in the music he has always played—thoroughly swinging. —*Michael G. Nastos*

○ **Flutes and Reeds** / Aug. 2, 1955 / Savoy 12022
○ **Jazz for Playboys** / Jan. 5, 1957 / Savoy 412
★ **I Hear Ya' Talkin'** / i. Dec. 8, 1959 / Savoy 1136
This was the initial release of the '59 Savoy recording by tenor saxophonist-flutist Frank Wess. It came as a surprise, mainly for Thad Jones's three arrangements (in light of his later big band charts and success). He composed and arranged "Liz," "Opus," and "Struttin." Two of these employed Wess's flute in ensemble and solo; the third, "Struttin'," was a fast vehicle for Wess's early Sonny Rollinslike tenor. The session was oriented toward Basie and the blues. —*Owen Cordle, Down Beat*

☆ **Flute Juice** / Apr. 8, 1981 / Progressive
○ **Flute Talk** / i. 1981 / Progressive
With Tommy Flanagan Trio and guitarist Chuck Wayne, Wess is unbelievable. Includes four standards and two Wess originals. This might be tricky to locate, but dig for it. It is a great album. —*Michael G. Nastos*

Randy Weston (Randolphe E. Weston)

b. Apr. 6, 1926, Brooklyn, NY
Piano, composer, bandleader / Postbop, progressive big band, world fusion, neo-bop, modern creative
Randy Weston has been among the most visionary artists in jazz, incorporating elements of African and Indian music into his work long before it was either fashionable or commonplace to do so. He's especially innovative as a composer in the area of rhythm, and his arrangements are equally compelling, whether for small combos or large orchestras. Weston worked with Art Blakey in the '40s and began heading his own groups in the mid-'50s. He's lived and studied in Africa for many years and at one time ran a club in Tangiers. He's also been a label owner for a short time, while recording for United Artists, Jubilee, Dawn, Roulette, CTI, Verve, Atlantic, and recently Antilles. —*Ron Wynn*

★ **Uhuru Africa / Highlife** / i. 1961 / Roulette 94510
Futuristic exploration of link between Africa and jazz, done in 1961 and 1964. Great players and both traditional jazz and African, and Latin. Reissue with many of this pianist's best compositions. —*Michael G. Nastos*

○ **Blue Moses** / Mar. 1972-Apr. 1972 / CTI
Very rare date on CTI, one of the few that wasn't geared to pop-R&B public but was ambitious and aggressive. —*Ron Wynn*

● **African Cookbook** / i. 1972 / Atlantic
○ **Little Niles** / i. Aug. 1977 / United Artists 4011
Little Niles gathered three long unavailable late '50s Randy Weston sessions under the same title. The first, the entire reissue of the 1958 *Little Niles*, was probably the most opulent and fulfilling Weston work readily available, an intricate fabric of charging percussive layers and tight performances, underscored with a sprawling sensuality. Like Duke Ellington and Charles Mingus's boldest music, *Little Niles* was elegant, patient, and mystically urbanized in spite of its pastoral influences. The remaining sessions, an interpretative sampling of *Destry Rides Again* and a *Live at the Five Spot* album, are similarly magnetic and progressively looser. —*Mikal Gilmore, Down Beat*

☆ **Spirits of Our Ancestors** / i. 1991 / Antilles 511896
Weston with 11-piece band and guests Pharoah Sanders and Dizzy Gillespie. The stellar arrangements are by Melba Liston. Familiar themes are "The Healers," "Blue Moses," "African Cookbook," and "African Village/Bedford Stuyvesant." Most of the ten tracks are extended on this two-CD set. —*Michael G. Nastos*

☆ **African Sunrise—Selections from "The Spirits...** / i. 1992 / Antilles 517177
○ **Perspective** / Denon 8554

Kirk Whalum

Sax / Instrumental pop, contemporary funk
A Memphis-born saxophonist who worked at one time with
Arnett Cobb, Kirk Whalum ranks alongside George Howard and
Najee as the current rage of the urban-Quiet Storm set. He's had
several popular albums and occasionally displays the kind of
bombastic attack and sense of swing one would associate with a
straightahead player. But most of the time Whalum has made
rather standard fusion-instrumental pop recordings. —*Ron Wynn*

And You Know That! / i. 1988 / Columbia 40812
Light pop-fusion though Whalum's a very good player. —*Ron
Wynn*

Cache / i. 1993 / CBS 46931

Give Me Your Love / Columbia 38-07688

Kenny Wheeler (Kenneth Vincent John Wheeler)

b. Jan. 14, 1930, Toronto
Trumpet, flugelhorn / World fusion, modern creative
Canadian-born, British resident Kenny Wheeler plays trumpet
and flugelhorn. He's worked in traditional and progressive big
bands and free-music ensembles. His own group has an atmospheric, introspective quality, accounting for his personal sound.
Wheeler is hard to categorize; he's an improviser and melodicist
first. —*Michael G. Nastos*

○ **Gnu High** / Jun. 1975 / ECM 825591
This is longwinded and worthwhile, w/ the Keith Jarrett (p) Trio.
—*Michael G. Nastos*

★ **Deer Wan** / Jul. 1977 / ECM 829385
For *Deer Wan*, Kenny Wheeler emerged a romanticist in the
grand heroic mode. His compositions and trumpeting suggested
an Olympic majesty. There was grace and eloquence, as well as a
purity of sound and purpose. The players shared Wheeler's point
of view. —*Chuck Berg, Down Beat*

Andrew White (Andrew Nathaniel White III)

b. Sep. 6, 1942, Washington, DC
Sax, educator, transcriber / Postbop, early free, modern creative
Andrew White is a meticulous transcriber of John Coltrane,
Charlie Parker, and Ornette Coleman. He's also a progressive and
entertaining performer, who doubles on several instruments, in-
cluding oboe. He's truly a one-of-a-kind player. —*Michael G.
Nastos*

★ **Maxine Spotts and Brown / i.** Nov. 9, 1975 / Andrew's Music 24
Live recording at Top O' the Foolery with quartet. Includes the
lengthy "Dizzy Atmosphere." Very good. —*Michael G. Nastos*

○ **I Love Japan** / Oct. 12-14, 1979 / Andrew's Music 38
Live recording at the One Step Down with quartet and this DC
historian-transcriber-progressive saxophonist. —*Michael G.
Nastos*

Paul Whiteman

b. Mar. 28, 1890, Denver, CO, d. Dec. 29, 1967, Doylestown, PA
Bandleader / Big band, instrumental pop
Born in Denver, where his father was supervisor of school music,
Paul Whiteman played in the local symphony but became interested in the new dance rhythms and formed a band in San
Francisco. A 1919 Atlantic City engagement brought a Victor
Records contract, and the band scored a tremendous 1920 hit
with "Whispering." Pianist and composer Ferde Grofé was mainly
responsible for Whiteman's early style; instead of playing stock
arrangements, the band had its own original scores, and it soon
became the pacesetter for modern dance music. Always ambitious, Whiteman branched out into popular concert music and in
1924 presented his famous concert of "symphonic jazz" in New
York. For that occasion he commissioned young George
Gershwin to write "Rhapsody in Blue." Dubbed "The King of
Jazz," Whiteman by now was the world's most famous and best-
paid band leader; he toured Europe in 1926 and in the following
year, aware that his ever-growing band was not strong in real jazz
players, hired the stars of the bankrupt Jean Goldkette band.
Among these were Bix Beiderbecke, Frank Trumbauer, and
arranger Bill Challis. Eddie Lang, Joe Venuti, Red Nichols, and the
Dorsey Brothers had already worked with Whiteman, and a
young singer named Bing Crosby was creating a new style (he

was also a member of the hip Whiteman Rhythm Boys trio).
Later, Whiteman featured such jazz stars as Jack Teagarden and
Bunny Berigan, but it was from 1927 to 1930, when Challis, Tom
Satterfield, Lennie Hayton, and William Grant Still were among
his arrangers, that Whiteman came even close to justifying his title. (It must be kept in mind that "jazz" in the '20s did not con-
note what it does today—it simply meant snappy dance music of
the day, not the music of Louis Armstrong and Duke Ellington.)
Whiteman's unfortunate royal title cost him much of the respect
he well deserves as a force for higher standards in popular music
and as a great talent spotter who paid generous wages and
treated his musicians very well. Whiteman retired from bandleading by 1943 (one of his last record dates featured Billie
Holiday) but was frequently heard and seen on radio and TV as a
host of popular-music programs. He left his enormous library of
arrangements to Williams College. —*Dan Morgenstern*

☆ **Paul Whiteman and His Orchestra with Bing Crosby** /
Columbia 2830
This set, along with the two-record albums produced by Epic and
Columbia and the early '30s set (*Ace of Hearts*), provide a bounty
for the Crosbian, old or new; the new collector will find a great
deal of jazz on these tracks, perhaps much that they were heretofore unaware of. —*Wayne Jones, Coda*

★ **Victor Masters** / RCA 9678
Some fine sessions. Regardless of anyone's feeling about whether
he was overrated due to racial politics, Whiteman's music was
very influential on a certain level. Some fine sessions. —*Ron
Wynn*

Gerald Wiggins (Gerald Foster Wiggins, Sr.)

b. May 12, 1922, New York, NY
Piano, arranger, organ / Bop, postbop
Gerald Wiggins is a veteran pianist who plays bop and postbop.
He's been well-traveled as a sideman for singers such as Lena
Horne, Eartha Kitt, Helen Humes, and even The Supremes. —
Michael G. Nastos

○ **Relax and Enjoy It / i.** May 1962 / Contemporary 3595
Pianist Gerald Wiggins led this trio date (1961) with Joe Comfort
(bass) and Jackie Mills (drums). While most people have probably
heard Wiggins in support, here is a record that spotlights him
(he's made numerous recordings under his name but most for
very obscure labels). —*Bob Rusch, Cadence*

★ **Live at Maybeck Recital Hall—Vol. 8** / Aug. 1990 / Concord Jazz
4450
Outstanding solo set, shows Wiggins in more straight jazz setting.
CD version has three bonus cuts. —*Ron Wynn*

Bob Wilber (Robert Sage Wilber)

b. Mar. 15, 1928, New York, NY
Soprano sax / Dixieland, swing
Along with Kenny Davern, Bob Wilber's a tremendous soprano
saxophonist, steeped in traditional and swing jazz history and
technique. Bob Wilber began playing clarinet at Scarsdale High
School and later studied under both Sidney Bechet and Lennie
Tristano while a teen. He formed a band known as The Six that
mixed old and new conceptsin the '50s and then joined Eddie
Condon before playing clarinet and vibes for a year with Bobby
Hackett. During the '60s he was both a frequent contributor to
sessions and a founding member of the World's Greatest Jazz
Band, a group that elevated the notion of trad and vintage New
Orleans music by drawing on contemporary as well as classic
sources. He founded Soprano Summit in 1973 with Kenny
Davern, a player with a very similar background. The Summit
played together about three years, broke up, and recently got
back together for some recording sessions on Concord. —*Ron
Wynn*

○ **New Clarinet in Town** / 1960 / Classic Editions 8

○ **Music of Hoagy Carmichael, The** / Jun. 1969 / Monmouth 6917

○ **Soprano Summit / i.** 1973 / World Jazz 5
This was a pleasant collection of songs quite well done, and how
good it was to hear the soprano played in an old-fashioned, big,
"pretty" manner! —*John Litweiler, Down Beat*

○ **Chalumeau Blue / i.** Apr. 1977 / Chiaroscuro 148
Soprano saxophonist Bob Wilber has good taste, swings, is rewarding and exciting. This was another fine Hank O'Neal pro-

duction with good tunes ("Black and Tan" would make Duke Ellington smile), good performances, an interesting cover, and necessary liner notes. —*Dennis R. Hendley, Cadence*

★ **Soprano Summit—In Concert** / i. 1990 / Concord Jazz 4029
Soprano Summit in Concert took a moment or two to get off the ground, with Kenny Davern providing the lift in "Stompy Jones"—but once they were up they didn't come down until the teasing final bars of "Swing That Music." —*Joel Ray, Cadence*

Lee Wiley

b. Oct. 9, 1915, Fort Gibson, OK, **d.** Dec. 11, 1975, New York, NY
Vocals / Ballads & blues
Lee Wiley numbers among the best jazz singers for articulation, phrasing, and charm. She was a brilliant interpretative artist, never failing to fully present or exploit a lyric or convey a song's sentiment or theme. Wiley sang in many bands from the '30s through the '50s, and made a comeback in the early '70s. She also wrote lyrics, adding words to Victor Young's music for the songs "Got the South in My Soul" and "Anytime, Anyday, Anywhere." She worked with Johnny Green, Leo Reisman, Young, and Eddie Condon in the '30s, was married for a time to pianist Jess Stacy, and toured with his band in the '40s. She also made a series of excellent recordings doing definitive versions of classic pop songs during the late '30s and throughout the '40s. Many have been reissued on Halcyon or Chiaroscuro, as has her 1971 return release on Monmouth-Evergreen, which was rereleased on Audiophile. —*Ron Wynn*

○ **Complete Young Lee Wiley (1931-37)** / 1931-1937 / Vintage Jazz Classics 1023

★ **Sings the Songs of Rodgers and Hart & Harold Arlen** / Audiophile 10

☆ **Sings the Songs of Ira and George Gershwin...** / Audiophile 1

☆ **As Time Goes By** / Bluebird 3138

Buster Williams (Charles Anthony Williams)

b. Apr. 17, 1942, Camden, NJ
Bass / Postbop, neo-bop
Buster Williams is an outstanding bassist who's played with many major jazz stars since the '60s. He's appeared on numerous albums but is probably best known for working in Ron Carter's two-bass group during the '70s. Carter played piccolo bass while Williams played conventional acoustic, and their duets were often spectacular. He's a favorite session contributor due to his tendency not to overwhelm or dominate. Though a capable player, he prefers accompaniment to soloing. —*Ron Wynn*

○ **Crystal Reflections** / Aug. 1976 / Muse 5430
Excellent set. No reed or brass soloist, but Kenny Barron (p) and Jimmy Rowles (p) are super. One of the last times Roy Ayers plays vibes in jazz context on record. —*Ron Wynn*

★ **Heartbeat** / Mar. 28, 1978-Apr. 3, 1978 / Muse 5171
A diverse session of jazz touches by pop guests on the four originals by bassist Williams, one standard, and one by Jimmie Rowles. Includes Rowles (p), Kenny Barron (p), Ben Riley (d), vocalist Suzanne Klewan, and strings from Pat and Gayle Dixon. —*Michael G. Nastos*

Clarence Williams

b. 1896, Plaquemine, LA, **d.** Nov. 6, 1965, New York, NY
Piano, vocals / New Orleans traditional
Organization and consistency were what made Clarence Williams a key figure among early jazz musicians. He rivaled Fletcher Henderson for being the most recorded black performer during the '20s, and published and promoted the work of such seminal stars as Fats Waller, James P. Johnson, Willie "The Lion" Smith, and Spencer Williams, while cowriting major songs like "Royal Garden Blues," "Squeeze Me," "Baby, Won't You Please Come Home," and "T'ain't Nobody's Business If I Do." In addition, his groups, especially The Blue Five, were an important repertory ensemble and backing band for several vocalists. Williams's piano playing and vocals were merely effective at best, but the 300 Williams songs issued between 1921 and 1938 included many extraordinary performances. Williams was part Creole and part Choctaw; at one time due to both his widow and his death certificate Williams's birth date was given as 1898, but further research now shows it was 1893. His childhood included periods

where he worked in a hotel and sang in a street band. He came to New Orleans in 1906 and traveled with a ministrel show as an emcee, singer, and dancer until 1911. Williams began managing a cabaret in 1913 and then started a music-publishing venture with A.J. Piron. Williams moved to Chicago later in the decade, before relocating permanently in New York City in 1920. Prior to going to Chicago, he toured with Piron. Williams cut his first records in 1921, singing with a white band. By 1923 he'd become Okeh's "race music" A&R director, and in that capacity, as well as being a bandleader, he became a conduit for the jazz community. The careers of Louis Armstrong, Sidney Bechet, Buster Bailey, King Oliver, Don Redman, Coleman Hawkins, Lonnie Johnson, Bubber Miley, Tommy Ladnier, and Jimmy Harrison were aided either by him employing them or getting them recording sessions. Williams played on Bessie Smith sessions, and she cut several of his songs; he also backed vocalists Butterbeans & Susie, Sara Martin, Sippie Wallace, and Eva Taylor (whom he married in 1921). The original Blue Five included Thomas Morris, Charlie Irvis or John Mayfield, Sticky Elliott or Bechet, and Buddy Christian. Armstrong was a member in 1924 and 1925, and later came Bailey, Aaron Thompson, Hawkins, Redman, and Miley. They continued recording through 1927. Williams later made nearly 100 recordings for Okeh, Vocalion, and Victor from 1927 to 1939 with "washboard" bands that included Ed Allen, Bailey or Cecil Scott, and Floyd Casey. Williams concentrated on writing after the late '30s but led a final Blue Five session in 1941 with James P. Johnson, Wellman Braud, and Taylor doing vocals and then sold his catalog to Decca in 1943. He was a shop owner in Harlem, but went blind after being hit by a taxi in 1956. Nearly 11 years after his death, a comprehensive biodiscography *Clarence Williams* by Tom Lord put his accomplishments into perspective. —*Ron Wynn*

○ **Complete Sessions—Vol. 1 (1923-1926), The** / Jul. 30, 1923-Nov. 14, 1923 / EPM 5107

○ **Complete Sessions—Vol. 2 (1923-1931), The** / Nov. 1923-Mar. 1925 / EPM 5109

● **Clarence Williams (1927-1934)** / 1927-1934 / DRG 36829

○ **Jazz Heritage: Music Man (1929-1934)** / 1929-1934 / MCA 1349

Cootie Williams (Charles Melvin Williams)

b. Jul. 10, 1911, Mobile, AL, **d.** Sep. 15, 1985, New York, NY
Trumpet, bandleader / Swing, big band
A majestic soloist, Cootie Williams turned the trumpet into a sonic weapon. Whether playing open or muted, Williams performed ringing anthems that could sear paint off the walls or reduce listeners to tears with their shimmering beauty. He was just as masterful accompanying singers and rivaled any Delta or gutbucket vocalist in his blues interpretations. Duke Ellington's "Concerto for Cootie" and "New Concerto for Cootie," done 23 years apart, are clinical workouts reflecting trumpet greatness, then experience. Williams played in his school band on Long Island. At 14, he played one summer with the Young Family band, in the process meeting Lester Young. Williams toured Florida with Edd Hall and worked in Eagle Eye Shields's band before going to New York with Alonzo Ross's Dixie Syncopators. He worked briefly with Chick Webb and Fletcher Henderson before replacing Bubber Miley in the Ellington Orchestra in 1929. Besides being featured on several combo sessions with Ellingtonians outside the orchestra, Williams amazed the jazz world with marvelous solos on "Echoes of Harlem" in 1936 and "Concerto for Cootie" in 1940. Williams made his own outside sessions from 1937 to 1940, heading a combo billed as the Gotham Stompers. It blended Ellington and Webb band personnel plus vocalist Ivie Anderson. Williams also recorded with Lionel Hampton, Teddy Wilson, and Billie Holiday during this period. He left Ellington to join the Benny Goodman orchestra in 1940 and was featured on some impressive recordings. These included "Breakfast Feud," "Wholly Cats," and "Royal Garden Blues." After a year, Williams left to form his own band, which he led during most of the '40s. The group at various times included Charlie Parker, Eddie Davis, Ben Thigpen, Kenny Clarke, and Bud Powell, though they never achieved much success. They recorded an early version of Thelonious Monk's "Epistrophy" under the name "Fly Right." The band scored its biggest hits in the mid-'40s with "Tess Torch Song" featuring vocalist Pearl Bailey, and

"Cherry Red Blues" with lead singer Eddie Vinson. After more tours, Williams served as a session musician on various R&B dates in the early '50s. He continued leading groups and teamed with Rex Stewart on some studio dates in 1957 and 1958. He rejoined Ellington in 1962. Illness began to affect his playing, and Ellington featuring him primarily as a soloist in the '70s rather than with the trumpet section. He remained in the band after Duke died and played with it into the late '70s. —*Ron Wynn*

● **Sextet And Orchestra: 1944 Recordings** / Jan. 6, 1944-Aug. 22, 1944 / Phoenix 1

○ **Big Challenge, The** / **i.** Apr. 1957+May 1957 / Jazztone 77

○ **Cootie and Rex** / **i.** Dec. 12, 1957 / Jazztone 1268

James Williams

b. Mar. 8, 1951, Memphis, TN
Piano / Neo-bop
Another in the long line of Memphis piano players, Williams attended Memphis State in the '70s and then moved to New York and worked for a time in Art Blakey's Jazz Messengers. During the '80s and '90s he has recorded some exceptional trio and small-combo sessions and done extensive sessions. His style and technique include healthy doses of gospel and blues influence, as he was once a church organist and worked in several blues and R&B groups in Memphis. A first-rate soloist and fine composer, he is one of the few modern players who don't trace their approach directly to McCoy Tyner. Phineas Newborn is Williams's mentor, especially in his phrasing and voicings. —*Ron Wynn*

Arioso Touch / Feb. 1982 / Concord Jazz 192
Wonderful 1982 date; great solos, blues influences. Buster Williams (b) and Billy Higgins (d) are great. —*Ron Wynn*

○ **Alter Ego** / Jul. 19+20, 1984 / Sunnyside 1007
This reissue, recorded in 1984, was notable for Williams's writing and engaging piano solos. With a front line of Bill Easley (saxophones, flutes, and clarinet), Billy Pierce (tenor and soprano), and Kevin Eubanks (whose guitar often functions like a third horn), Williams fashioned several attractive ensemble combinations. —*Owen Cordle, Jazz Times*

★ **Progress Report** / 1985 / Sunnyside 1012
Progress Report featured three Art Blakey alumni: James Williams (keyboards), Billy Pierce (reeds), and guitarist Kevin Eubanks (a member of Blakey's short-lived 1980 big band). None of the six originals (half by the leader, one from Eubanks and a pair by Donald Brown) had memorable melodies, but all contained plenty of room for explorative chord-based improvisations. —*Scott Yanow, Cadence*

☆ **Magical Trio 1** / **i.** 1987 / PolyGram 832859

Magical Trio 2 / **i.** 1989 / Emarcy 834368
Date that's just as great as predecessor. Elvin Jones (d) in the driver's chair this time. —*Ron Wynn*

Joe Williams (Joseph Goreed)

b. Dec. 12, 1928, Cordele, GA
Vocals / Big band, blues & jazz, ballads & blues
An all-time giant among male jazz singers, Joe Williams was gifted with one of the deepest, strongest voices ever, plus a charisma and ability to sound sophisticated without sacrificing urgency or empathy in his delivery. Williams sang in Chicago clubs with Jimmie Noone in the '30s and worked with Coleman Hawkins and Lionel Hampton in the early '40s. He later toured with Andy Kirk in 1946-1947 and cut his first record with him in New York before joining Hot Lips Page in the '50s. He spent a few months with Count Basie and then scored an epic hit with King Kolax's R&B band in 1951, cutting the signature version of Memphis Slim's "Every Day I Have the Blues." Williams became a superstar the second time around with Basie, working with him from 1954 to 1960. He gradually began to do sentimental ballads and all types of pop material, as well as blues and jazz, though never opting for rock. He worked with Harry Edison for a time in 1960 and has led his own groups ever since. Williams has never gone out of style and has always been in demand. Though not a huge album seller, he's periodically made some superb releases, and nothing he's ever done is without value. The last few years he's made impact on the television scene playing Bill Cosby's father-in-law on "The Cosby Show." —*Ron Wynn*

★ **Count Basie Swings / Joe Williams Sings** / **i.** Jul. 17, 1955-Jul. 26, 1955 / Verve 825770
This is the definitive Joe Williams record, cut shortly after he joined Count Basie's orchestra. Included are his classic versions of "Every Day I Have the Blues," "The Comeback," "Alright, Okay, You Win," "In the Evening," and "Teach Me Tonight." Williams' popularity was a major asset to Basie, and getting to sing with that swinging big band on a nightly basis certainly did not harm the singer! This gem belongs in everyone's jazz collection. —*Scott Yanow*

☆ **A Swingin' Night At Birdland** / Jun. 1962 / Roulette 52085
In 1961, after six years as one of the main attractions of Count Basie's orchestra, Williams (with Count's blessing) went out on his own. One of his first sessions was this live recording cut at Birdland with a strong quintet that featured trumpeter Harry "Sweets" Edison and Jimmy Forrest on tenor. Williams mostly sings standards and ballads but also tosses in a few of his popular blues (including "Well Alright, OK, You Win" and "Goin' to Chicago") during a well-rounded and thoroughly enjoyable set. —*Scott Yanow*

☆ **Overwhelmin', The** / **i.** 1963-1965 / Bluebird 6464
A CD sampler taken from five former LPs, this fine CD features Joe Williams doing three songs from Duke Ellington's play *Jump for Joy*, five numbers at the 1963 Newport Jazz Festival (during which he is joined by trumpeters Clark Terry and Howard McGhee and tenor greats Coleman Hawkins, Zoot Sims, and Ben Webster), four blues backed by an all-star jazz group, and five ballads in front of an orchestra. Although it would be preferable to have each of the five original albums intact, this superb collection features Joe Williams on a wide variety of material, and he is heard close to his peak throughout. —*Scott Yanow*

★ **Joe Williams Live** / **i.** 1978 / Fantasy 438
Williams meets the Cannonball Adderley septet on this rather interesting session. The expanded rhythm section (which includes keyboardist George Duke and both acoustic bassist Walter Booker and the electric bass of Carol Kaye) gives funky accompaniment to Williams, while altoist Cannonball and cornetist Nat have some solo space. Actualy the singer easily steals the show on a rather searing version of "Goin' to Chicago Blues," his own "Who She Do," and a few unusual songs, including Duke Ellington's "Heritage." —*Scott Yanow*

○ **Prez Conference** / **i.** 1979 / GNP 2124
Dave Pell's Prez Conference was to Lester Young what Supersax is to Charlie Parker. Pell's short-lived group featured harmonized Lester Young solos recreated by three tenors and a baritone; their matchup with singer Joe Williams is quite enjoyable. Since Young was in Count Basie's orchestra when Jimmy Rushing was the vocalist, Joe Williams has a rare opportunity to give his own interpretation to Rushing and Billie Holiday classics like "I May Be Wrong," "You Can Depend on Me," "If Dreams Come True," and "Easy Living." A delightful and swinging date. —*Scott Yanow*

○ **Nothin' But the Blues** / **i.** Mar. 1983 / Delos 4001
Sticking to blues, Joe Williams is in prime form on this special session. His backup crew includes such all-stars as tenor-saxophonist Red Holloway, organist Brother Jack McDuff, and (on alto and one lone vocal) the great Eddie "Cleanhead" Vinson. The many blues standards are familiar, but these versions are lively and fresh. —*Scott Yanow*

○ **Everyday I Have the Blues** / **i.** Mar. 1985 / Roulette 52033

○ **Ballad and Blues Master** / **i.** May 7, 1987-May 8, 1987 / Verve 511354
Taken from the same sessions that had previously resulted in *Every Night*, the identical adjectives apply. Joe Williams was in superior form for this live date, putting a lot of feeling into such songs as "You Can Depend on Me," "When Sunny Gets Blue," and "Dinner for One Please, James." A closing blues medley is particularly enjoyable, and the backup by a quartet that includes pianist Morman Simmons and guitarist Henry Johnson is tasteful and swinging. —*Scott Yanow*

○ **Jump for Joy** / RCA 2713

Mary Lou Williams (Née Mary Elfrieda Scruggs)

b. May 8, 1910, Atlanta, GA, **d.** May 28, 1981, Durham, NC
Piano, composer, arranger / Swing, big band

Married to saxophonist John Williams in her teens, pianist Mary Lou Williams went on the road with his little band; when he joined Andy Kirk, she filled in for the band's regular pianist at their first recording session (he overslept) and soon had replaced him. She'd already showed great promise as an arranger and composer ("Mess-a-Stomp," 1929), and her first solo record, from 1930, is impressive proof that she heard Earl Hines and James P. Johnson very well indeed. When the Kirk band hit its stride in 1936, Mary Lou was *The Lady Who Swings the Band*, setting the tasteful, swinging style for this relatively small (12-piece) big band. She also freelanced as a writer, contributing such hits as "Roll 'Em" to Benny Goodman's library. Leaving Kirk in 1942, she wrote for Duke Ellington, did radio and nightclub work in New York (she debuted an all-female group in 1945), and wrote a major work for jazz group and strings, "The Zodiac Suite" (1946). Hospitable to the new ideas in jazz, she befriended Budd Powell, Thelonious Monk, and other young musicians and shared her knowledge with them.

She worked with Goodman during his bop flirtation (1949) and spent time in Europe. By 1954, a convert to Roman Catholicism, she retired from playing and did charitable work, but a Jesuit priest convinced her that playing music was not sinful and that she should not neglect her gift. She wrote religious music (*Mary Lou's Mass*, 1970; performed at St. Patrick's Cathedral in New York) but also resumed playing in night clubs and at jazz festivals. In 1977 she accepted a faculty appointment at Duke University, where she taught until her death. As a pianist, arranger, and composer, Mary Lou Williams never needed to be tagged "female"; she simply was up there with the best, respected and admired by her colleagues. She was, as Duke Ellington put it, "never out of style." —*Dan Morgenstern*

★ **Roll 'Em / i.** 1944 / Audiophile
Good 1988 reissue of Williams doing boogie, swing, and blues from the '40s. —*Ron Wynn*

First Lady of the Piano, The / Jan. 23, 1953 / Inner City 7006
Exceptional pieces, with Coleman Hawkins (sax), Don Byas (ts), and other swing lords. —*Ron Wynn*

★ **Live at the Cookery** / Oct. 1975 / Chiaroscuro 146
Mary Lou Williams could, without a doubt, handle solo piano. Here she was playing with rhythm (bass) and left space to be filled by rhythm. Only at times was it filled fully by the bass, the result being that on some of the uptempos ("Praise the Lord," "Grand Night," and "Surrey with the Fringe on Top" in particular) there was an imbalance, openings alluded to, but not fully filled by Brian Torff. —*Carol Boer, Cadence*

☆ **Embraced** / Apr. 17, 1977 / Pablo 108
This record documented one of 1977's "big events," the meeting of pianist Mary Lou Williams and Cecil Taylor, at Carnegie Hall, on April 17, 1988, a get-together mounted with much pomp and circumstance. Most of the music consisted of superimpositions of Williams' traditional blues-based approach and Taylor's volcanic eruptions of multinoted flurries. —*Chuck Berg, Down Beat*

○ **Mary Lou Williams Solo Recital** / Jul. 16, 1978 / Pablo 2308218
On this live recording from the Montreux Jazz Festival of 1978, pianist Mary Lou Williams' musical pictures included forms that go back as far as ragtime, boogie, and early swing. The mastery of so many diverse styles became the foundation of her recent compositions and the heart of her multisided improvisation. —*Bradley Parker-Sparrow, Down Beat*

Richard Williams (Richard Gene Williams)

b. May 4, 1931, Galveston, TX, **d.** 1985
Trumpet / Hard bop
Richard Williams was a trumpeter who played with Eric Dolphy, Sun Ra, and Booker Ervin. Tart tone and tremendous ideas flowed from this fine artist's horn. —*Michael G. Nastos*

★ **New Horn in Town** / Nov. 1960 / Candid 79003
Richard Williams' *New Horn in Town* joined trumpeter Williams with the later expatriate altoist-flutist Leo Wright, along with a typical hard bop rhythm section including pianist Richard Wyands and bassist Reggie Workman. Much of the music contained on this record reflected the genre of music that was being exemplified by the Horace Silver Quintet and the Jazz Messengers. —*Spencer R. Weston, Cadence*

Tony Williams (Anthony Williams)

b. Dec. 12, 1945, Chicago, IL
Drums, bandleader / Postbop, early jazz-rock, neo-bop, modern creative
The arrival of Tony Williams into the Miles Davis group altered the trumpeter's course in a way no one had since the brief stay of Bill Evans. Where Miles's early '60s work fell off the pace of the previous decade, Williams kicked the old book into overdrive. The mid-'60s brought him recognition as the decade's most important jazz drummer, rivaled only by Elvin Jones. The original Lifetime lineup was one of the most volatile ensembles anywhere, and a later version of the group with guitarist Alan Holdsworth remains sadly underrated. With the '80s came a return to acoustic jazz, with a fine, long-running group, furthering Williams's reputation as a composer and bandleader. Through all of his various phases, Tony Williams remains one of the most astonishing and musical drummers ever. —*Steve Aldrich*

★ **Life Time** / Aug. 21, 1964 / Blue Note 84180

○ **Spring** / Aug. 12, 1965 / Blue Note 46135
Early-period Blue Note recording with Sam Rivers (sax). Powerful music. —*Michael G. Nastos*

★ **Emergency** / May 26+28, 1969 / Polydor 849068

☆ **Tony Williams Lifetime, The** / Jan. 17, 1970 / Polydor 244021
Groundbreaking early fusion in the late '60s with Jack Bruce (b), Larry Young (organ), and John McLaughlin (g). —*Michael G. Nastos*

○ **Ego** / 1970 / Polydor 2425070

★ **Joy of Flying** / 1979 / CBS 35705
There were three quartet alignments at work here, plus or minus a few studio extras, and two more potent duets. Jan Hammer, then (1979) leading a Jimi Hendrix-influenced rock group and wearing a portable keyboard strapped across his shoulders, supplied the strongest fusion clout on the album. —*Bob Henschen, Down Beat*

○ **Foreign Intrigue** / Jun. 18-19, 1985 / Blue Note 46289
Williams had never led a straightahead recording session before and is a little higher in the mix than drummers usually rate. But despite the fact that he almost drowns out Bobby Hutcherson's vibes at times, Williams playing is consistently colorful and would hold one's interest even if he were underrecorded. —*Scott Yanow, Cadence*

○ **Angel Street** / Nov. 1988-Apr. 1988 / Blue Note 48494
1988 date, first class lineup of young lions fueled by red-hot Williams drumming. —*Ron Wynn*

○ **Story of Neptune** / i. 1992 / Blue Note 98169
The Tony Williams quintet has two obvious assets that put it ahead of most acoustic jazz bands: Williams's powerful and consistently creative drumming and his compositional talents. On this group's fifth Blue Note recording, the drummer contributed the three-part "Neptune," essentially a feature for his drums, a more memorable original, "Crime Scene," and arrangements of three standards. —*Scott Yanow, Cadence*

○ **His Greatest Hits** / Reprise 6006

Larry Willis (Lawrence Elliott Willis)

b. Dec. 20, 1940, NYC
Piano / Postbop, soul-jazz, progressive big band, Latin-jazz, early jazzrock, neo-bop
A veteran sideman and one of the best jazz pianists of all time, Willis plays straight, modal, Latin, and funk. He's been a veteran pianist over four decades and has been in groups ranging from Cannonball Adderley to the Gonzalez Brothers, while working in every context from mainstream to Afro-Latin. He's a truly brilliant player. —*Michael G. Nastos*

★ **Inner Crisis** / 1973 / Groove Merchant 514
Willis plays acoustic and electric. Two different ensembles. Good compositional jazz. —*Michael G. Nastos*

○ **Just in Time** / i. 1989 / Steeple Chase 1251
Here is trio jazz from a veteran pianist, one of the best in America. —*Michael G. Nastos*

☆ **New Kind of Soul, A** / Brunswick 754181

More funky. With viable jazz horn sound for support. Easy to like. Three flugelhorns (Joe Newman, Jimmy Owens, Marvin Stamm). —*Michael G. Nastos*

Cassandra Wilson

b. 1955
Vocals / Ballads & blues, neo-bop, M-Base
Somewhat-controversial vocalist who splits her time between conventional jazz, free-form, R&B, rock, and soul. She's affiliated with Steve Coleman and his Brooklyn-based M-Base group and has a wondrous voice, with a sultry, appealing quality, and excellent timing and articulation. Some question her material, and others consider her the best modern singer working in jazz or related styles. —*Ron Wynn*

○ **Blue Skies** / Feb. 1988 / JMT 834419
Vocalist Cassandra Wilson does not accomplish the integration of her voice into the fabric of the music by assuming the improvisational role of a horn; there is only one, most judicious, instance of scatting in the entire 51 minutes of the CD. She did it, rather, by singing these 10 superb examples of American popular song with understanding of their nature and with respect for their integrity, and yet by transforming them through masterful phrasing, intonation, and command of time. —*Doug Ramsey, Jazz Times*

★ **She Who Weeps** / Nov. 1990-Dec. 1990 / JMT 834443
Very good album, with Rod Williams on piano and Tani Tabbal on drums. —*Michael G. Nastos*

Gerald Wilson (Gerald Stanley Wilson)

b. Sep. 4, 1918, Shelby, MS
Trumpet, arranger / Hard bop, progressive big band
A master arranger and solid trumpeter, Wilson began on piano and learned trumpet while attending college in Detroit. He played with the Jimmie Lunceford band from 1939 to 1942 and then moved to Los Angeles. He worked with Benny Carter and other groups before joining the Navy. He formed his own big band upon his discharge in 1944 and has since been a popular leader, arranger, and musical director. His finest records from a jazz standpoint were done for Pacific Jazz in the '60s, and they are beginning to resurface on reissues. —*Ron Wynn*

★ **Golden Sword, The** / i. 1966 / Discovery 901
○ **Eternal Equinox** / 1969 / Pacific Jazz 10160
○ **Jessica** / Nov. 29, 1982+Dec. 6, 1982 / Trend 531
○ **Orchestra of the '80s** / i. 1983 / Trend 537
○ **Jenna** / i. Jul. 22, 1992 / Discovery 964

Joe Lee Wilson (Joseph Lee Wilson)

b. Dec. 22, 1935, Bristow, OK
Vocals, leader / Ballads & blues
One of the '70s most striking jazz vocalists, Joe Lee Wilson blended a strong, stirring baritone voice and good delivery with a swinging style and savvy selection of material. The results made him quite popular for a few years, especially on college campuses in the Northeast. Wilson studied classical singing and attended Los Angeles City College in the '50s, where he studied jazz. He toured the West Coast and Mexico as a jazz vocalist in the late '50s and moved to New York in 1962. Wilson worked with Sonny Rollins, Lee Morgan, Miles Davis, Pharoah Sanders, and Jackie McLean in the '60s and in 1971 and 1972 sang with Archie Shepp. His dynamic lead vocals on such Shepp albums as *Things Have Got to Change*, and *Attica Blues* won Wilson recognition, as did his recordings as a leader and performances with Sunny Murray, Mtume, and Billy Gault. Wilson operated a loft in New York, the Ladies Fort, from 1973 to 1978, and appeared at the 1973 Newport in New York and 1975 Live Loft festivals. He recorded with Clifford Jordan in 1977 and moved to London in 1978. Wilson toured Europe, performed in London clubs, and did periodic New York dates, but never regained his earlier momentum. Currently none of Wilson's albums are available on CD, though Shepp's *Attica Blues* was reissued in 1993. —*Ron Wynn*

● **Livin' High off Nickels and Dimes** / Jul. 16, 1972 / Oblivion 5
Joe Lee Wilson used his dramatic voice and range with strength and flexibility on his first recording in front of his working group, making personal though careful readings of ballads like "It's You or No One" and "God Bless the Child." Wilson has been heard with large ensembles led by the likes of Archie Shepp, and he

seems one of the few young singers who can give a convincing and meaningful reading to slower, serious works. But the vibrant energy he released on the other four numbers! Through these live broadcast tapes it was easy to imagine Wilson singing "Strollin" atop a Central Park statue or running through Manhattan streets with "You Make Me Want to Dance" on his lips. —*Howie Mandel, Down Beat*

○ **Secrets from the Sun** / Inner City 1042

Nancy Wilson

b. Feb. 20, 1937, Chillicothe, OH
Vocals / Blues & jazz, ballads & blues
Nancy Wilson made her national debut in 1959, fronting the Billy May Orchestra. She has greatly influenced a variety of singers, including Anita Baker and Regina Belle. Wilson's crisp, articulate, intricate jazz phrasing distinguishes her numerous albums (well over 50), which encompass standards, Broadway, blues, jazz, pop, and contemporary soul. —*Bil Carpenter*

○ **Greatest Hits** / i. 1959-1977 / CEMA 9449
● **Nancy Wilson and Cannonball Adderley** / 1961-Mar. 1962 / Capitol 48455
○ **Forbidden Lover** / 1987 / Columbia 40787
○ **With My Lover Beside** / i. 1991 / Columbia 48665
A superbly arranged, produced and mastered session from a wonderful vocalist. Wilson's singing, delivery, and tone are enticing and sensual throughout, even when the songs threaten to get overly sentimental or just sappy. Though the album was aimed at the adult contemporary audience, Wilson never coasted through any number, and this was about as polished and effective as this kind of session could get. —*Ron Wynn*

Teddy Wilson (Theodore Shaw Wilson)

b. Nov. 24, 1912, Austin, TX, d. Jul. 31, 1986, New Britain, CT
Piano / Swing
Teddy Wilson is a swing and big-band era piano giant. The Texas-born artist worked with the big bands of Louis Armstrong, Jimmie Noone, Erskine Tate, and Benny Carter. He frequently accompanied Billie Holiday, and later joined Benny Goodman's famous integrated quartet. Wilson spent his later period in trios and solos, displaying his voice as one based in swing, blues, and elegance. He's a jazz immortal. —*Michael G. Nastos*

★ **Statements and Improvisations (1934-1932)** / 1932-1934 / Smithsonian 13708
When these recordings were made, pianist Teddy Wilson was still in his 20s and somewhat of a sensation. Listening, it was no wonder. Here the cadenzas, harmonics, technics, and sensitivities are all jazz; Wilson had yet to contend with the cocktail element. — *Bob Rusch, Cadence*

○ **Teddy Wilson (1935-1936)** / i. Dec. 1935-Aug. 1936 / Classics 511
○ **Teddy Wilson (1936-1937)** / i. Aug. 1936-Feb. 1937 / Classics 521
○ **Teddy Wilson (1937)** / i. Mar. 1937-Aug. 1937 / Classics 531
○ **Teddy Wilson (1937-1938)** / i. Sep. 1937-Apr. 1938 / Classics 548
○ **Teddy Wilson (1938)** / i. Apr. 1938-Nov. 1938 / Classics 556
○ **Teddy Wilson (1939)** / i. Jan. 1939-Sep. 1939 / Classics 571
★ **And His All-Stars** / i. 193z-1940 / Columbia
This was a blowing ensemble. There was a collective intimacy achieved here that was both soothing and stimulating. Trumpeter Harry Edison, trombonist Vic Dickenson, and soprano saxophonist and clarinetist Bob Wilber made a marvelously liquid blend, to which pianist Teddy Wilson added the carbonation ("June Night," "I'll Get By," "Lonesome and Sorry"). —*John Mcdonough, Down Beat*

○ **Central Avenue Blues** / 1948 / Vintage Jazz Classics 1013
○ **Teddy Wilson Featuring Billie Holiday** / i. 1949 / Columbia 6040
★ **I Got Rhythm** / i. 195z / Verve
○ **With Billie in Mind** / May 1972 / Chiaroscuro 111
Elegant, superior swing and mainstream material, fine tribute to Lady Day. 1990 reissue of 1972 set. —*Ron Wynn*
○ **Piano Solos** / i. 1973 / Affinity 1016

Lem Winchester

b. 1928
Tenor sax, vibes / Postbop
A solid '50s and '60s vibist whose best work was done for the Fantasy label. His finest release, *Winchester Special,* was recently reissued on the OJC label. —*Ron Wynn*

★ **Winchester Special** / Sep. 25, 1959 / New Jazz 1719

Kai Winding (Kai Chresten Winding)

b. May 18, 1922, Aarhus, Denmark, **d.** May 6, 1983, Yonkers, NY
Trombone / Bop
Kai Winding was both a top-flight trombone soloist and a pliable musician who was able to work in many contexts effectively. He was among the ranks of '50s trombonists whose skill and technique helped rescue the instrument from obscurity. Winding came to America at 12 and began to make his mark in the late '40s, playing with Stan Kenton, Charlie Ventura, and Tadd Dameron, among others. He participated in the landmark Birth of the Cool session in 1948; and, from 1954 to 1956, he co-led with J. J. Johnson the influential two-trombone quintet that showed the instrument could do much more than reproduce vocal effects or be plugged into a nostalgic traditional jazz format. Winding expanded the trombone's role even more with a novel four-trombone sextet he led from 1956 to 1961. After working with a supergroup called the Giants of Jazz in the early '70s, Winding essentially retired for a few years, before resurfacing with another two-trombone group with Curtis Fuller in the '80s . He also toured in 1979 with Lionel Hampton. —*Ron Wynn*

★ **Kai Winding, Jay Jay Johnson and Bennie Green with Strings** / Dec. 3, 1954 / Original Jazz Classics 1727
This is an outstanding three-trombone lineup, with understated arrangements. —*Ron Wynn*

○ **Incredible Kai Winding Trombones, The** / Nov. 17, 1960-Dec. 13, 1960 / Impulse 3

Booty Wood (Mitchell W. Bootie)

b. Dec. 27, 1919, Dayton, OH, **d.** Jun. 10, 1987, Dayton, OH
Trombone / Swing, big band
Another of the musicians who excelled on mutes in the Ellington band, Booty Wood provided humorous, effective, and exuberant trombone solos with the plunger and several solid unmuted ones. He began his professional career in the late '30s and worked with Tiny Bradshaw and Lionel Hampton in the early '40s. Wood played in a navy band with Clark Terry, Willie Smith, and Gerald Wilson and reteamed with Hampton after his discharge. He joined Arnett Cobb's small band in 1947 and 1948, played with Erskine Hawkins from 1948 to 1950, and with Count Basie in 1951. Wood left music for a while before joining Ellington in 1959 and working with him until 1960. He rejoined in 1963, but stayed only briefly. Wood returned a third time in the early '70s. He also worked with Earl Hines in 1968 and with Mercer Ellington in the '70s. Wood recorded with the Count Basie orchestra from 1979 to the mid-'80s. He can be heard on Ellington and Basie reissued CDs, as well as some Hampton discs. —*Ron Wynn*

Hang in There / **i.** Nov. 1968 / Master Jazz 8102

Chris Woods (Christopher Columbus Woods)

b. Dec. 25, 1925, Memphis, TN, **d.** Jul. 4, 1985, New York, NY
Alto sax / Bop, blues & jazz
A hard-blowing, evocative alto saxophonist with a great flair for the blues, Chris Woods was great either in a combo, behind a singer, or featured in a large orchestra. He didn't have an overwhelming number of recordings, but anything he did was memorable. Woods worked in Memphis before moving to St. Louis, where he played with the Jeter-Pillars orchestra and with George Hudson. He also recorded as a leader in the '50s and '60s. Woods moved to New York in 1962, where he played, worked and recorded with Dizzy Gillespie and Clark Terry in the '60s. He played with Sy Oliver from 1970 to 1972 and did various sessions. Among those was a tremendous album with Ted Curson. Woods played in the Count Basie orchestra in 1983. He recorded as a leader for Delmark and Futura. Woods currently has no sessions available on CD. —*Ron Wynn*

● **Somebody Done Stole My Blues** / **i.** Dec. 23, 1991 / Delmark 434

Jimmy Woods

b. 1934
Alto sax / Cool, progressive big band
An often fiery, animated alto saxophonist, Jimmy Woods made some fine recordings in the '60s on the West Coast. He studied clarinet at 13, and did his first recording in the early '60s with Joe Gordon. Woods later recorded two albums for Contemporary heading his own group. He played in Gerald Wilson's orchestra in the '60s and with Chico Hamilton. He has not made any records as a leader since the Contemporary dates, which are not available on CD. —*Ron Wynn*

Awakening / **i.** Aug. 1962 / Contemporary 3605

Conflict / **i.** Nov. 1963 / Contemporary 3612

Phil Woods (Philip Wells Woods)

b. Nov. 2, 1931, Springfield, MA
Alto sax, bandleader, clarinet / Bop
Charlie Parker truly lives in the work of Phil Woods and a handful of others who've taken his legacy of alto greatness and both extended it and found their own voice through it without being consumed by it. Woods has a dynamic, soaring tone, unlimited harmonic knowledge, and the wit and technique to execute anything he desires in a solo or on the bandstand. Woods's career began in earnest when he joined the small combo of Jimmy Raney in 1955. He then spent two years with George Wallington, dividing his time there with stints in Dizzy Gillespie's big band and a two-alto unit with Gene Quill in 1957. He was a member of Buddy Rich's big band, staying with him until 1961, and became a prolific studio and session musician in the '60s, working on film soundtracks, cutting his own records, and working on dates by Benny Carter and others. Woods formed the European Rhythm Machine in 1968, which was among the world's best small groups until its demise in 1972. He formed another quartet in the mid-'80s, expanding it to a quintet for a time with trumpeter Tom Harrell. His many recordings from the '50s until the present are almost uniformly excellent; he's resisted the lure of fusion, has also been among the fiercest critics of free music. —*Ron Wynn*

★ **Pairing Off** / Jun. 1956 / Prestige 092
Septet. First-rate '80s reissue of an excellent 1956 date with lots of heavy hitters—Kenny Dorham (tpt), Donald Byrd (tpt), Tommy Flanagan (p), and Woods. —*Ron Wynn*

○ **Four Altos** / Feb. 9, 1957 / Prestige 1734
Familiarity with Phil Woods's later work was all that distinguished his solos on this Prestige session from the solos of lesser lights like Gene Quill, Sahib Shihab, and Hal Stein. Each of the *Four Altos* played well enough, but each sounded so much like the others—sounded, that is, so much but not *quite* like Charlie Parker, even to the deftly interpolated nursery rhymes—that you needed a scorecard to tell them apart (and the sleeve of this no-frills, budget-priced LP didn't give you one). .... There was plenty of good music here—needling piano solos and accompaniment by Mal Waldron, surprisingly detailed arrangements (probably by Waldron or Teddy Charles) on which the altoists blended well as a section, and a remarkable consistency in the alto solos. —*Francis Davis, Down Beat*

☆ **Phil and Quill with Prestige** / Mar. 29, 1957 / Original Jazz Classics 215

★ **Rights of Swing** / Jan. 26, 1960 / Candid 79016
Rights of Swing, composed and arranged by Grammy-winning altoist Phil Woods, was his first major compositional work. Though the work had five parts, each part worked just as well separately as together. .... The album brought together a good sampling of musicians and contained a major contribution from Woods's alto, as the principal soloist. —*Spencer R. Weston, Cadence*

○ **At the Frankfurt Jazz Festival** / 1970 / Embryo 530

★ **Musique du Bois** / Jan. 14, 1974 / Muse 5037
Don Schiltten first assembled the trio of pianist Jaki Byard, bassist Richard Davis, and drummer Richard Dawson for some Booker Ervin dates in the '60s that remain minor masterpieces (they're on Prestige); and the passing years have scarcely tarnished the ensemble's sheen. *Musique du Bois* also demonstrated, for the umpteenth time, that each was a more than worthy soloist. —*Steve Metaliz, Down Beat*

☆ **Phil Talks with Quill** / **i.** Oct. 1981 / Columbia 36808

Alto saxophonists Phil Woods and Gene Quill were given more of the stretch-out room young players seem to need here, and they struck a good balance between competition and cooperation. This was a working band brought into the studio exactly at the point at which night after night on the bandstand had tightened its loose head arrangements just enough. —*Francis Davis, Down Beat*

Reggie Workman (Reginald Workman)

b. Jun. 26, 1937, Philadelphia, PA
Bass / Hard bop, early free
Reggie Workman became a star during the '60s, when his ability to thrive in either free or hard bop settings and work with such musicians as John Coltrane established his reputation. Since then, he's faithfully survived in the jazz jungle, seldom out front, but always making his presence felt with steady, masterfully played bass lines; a solid tone; and brilliantly articulated, impressive solos. Workman's repeatedly proven himself a strong melodic and rhythmic improviser. He played piano, tuba, and euphonium in his youth, settling on bass in the mid-'50s when he was working in R&B bands. Workman began playing with Gigi Gryce in the late '50s and with Red Garland and Roy Haynes. He started with Coltrane in the early '60s, and later in that decade played with James Moody, Art Blakey's Jazz Messengers, Tootie Heath, Yusef Lateef, Herbie Mann, and Thelonius Monk. His recording sessions were no less impressive; they included albums with Coltrane, Freddie Hubbard, Archie Shepp, Lee Morgan, and Cedar Walton. Workman also taught at the New Muse Community Museum of Brooklyn, eventually being appointed director of the music workshop in 1975. He's also taught at several colleges and universities. He remained busy in the '70s, playing with Max Roach, and recording with Charles Tolliver, Billy Harper, Shepp, Art Farmer, and many others. His '80s associations have been with Jubani Aaltonen, Mal Waldron, and David Murray. He presently has only one session as a leader available on CD, an '89 date for the Music and Arts label with Jeanne Lee, Marilyn Crispell, Michelle Navazio, Don Byron, and Gerry Hemingway. —*Ron Wynn*

● Synthesis / Jun. 1986 / Leo 131

World Saxophone Quartet

Group / Modern creative
One of the finest small combos to emerge in jazz during the '80s. A foursome of sax players who, until their last release, recorded and performed all their music without any other accompanists. The original quartet consisted of David Murray, Julius Hemphill, Oliver Lake, and Hamiett Bluiett. Hemphill left last year and was replaced by Arthur Blythe. They began splitting the material between driving originals, avant-garde blowing, and more hard-bop and mainstream pieces. In recent years, they've expanded the repetoire to include an Ellington tribute, an album of classic R&B, and their latest effort, a date with African percussionists. —*Ron Wynn*

○ Steppin' With / Dec. 1978 / Black Saint 0027
Steppin' was the long-awaited first LP by the sort of group that succeds so well in theory but only sometimes in practice: four of the very best modernists, with shared principles of harmony and free melodic motion. The players' differences were distinctive, too, as previous LPs by each showed dissimilar attitudes to line, space, and expression. They played elaborate scores and the four Julius Hemphill pieces each achieved distinction—*Steppin'* through no more than a bass clarinet vamp. —*John Litweiler, Down Beat*

★ Plays Duke Ellington / Apr. 1986 / Nonesuch 79137

Dances and Ballads / Apr. 1987 / Nonesuch 79164
The Quartet extends its reach and scope to include danceable material. —*Ron Wynn*

Rhythm & Blues / 1989 / Elektra 60864
Smashing update of traditional R&B. . . . the masterful ensemble turning R&B and soul classics into dynamic portraits of sax brilliance. The WSB's inspired playing transcends idiomatic considerations; they're an institution and the greatest small combo inside or outside jazz. —*Ron Wynn, Rock & Roll Disc.*

Metamorphosis / i. 1991 / Nonesuch 79258
Amazing mix of African rhythms, African-American harmonies, and solos. Spectacular solos augmented by thrilling African percussion. —*Ron Wynn, Rock & Roll Disc*

World's Greatest Jazz Band

Group / Dixieland
The finest trad-swing group of modern times. This unit grew out of jazz fan and millionaire Dick Gibson's annual jazz parties. After his sixth celebration in 1968, a group featuring Yank Lawson, Bob Haggart, Bob Wilber, Ralph Sutton, and Billy Butterfield were tagged by Gibson as "The World's Greatest Jazz Band." They played together ten years, stressed the collective style of vintage New Orleans music, but were distinguished both by the caliber of players and their willingness not to stagnate and become a camp Dixieland outfit. Their albums surpassed anything else remotely associated with "trad" or Dixieland material. —*Ron Wynn*

○ World's Greatest Jazz Band of Yank Lawson and Bob Haggart / Dec. 10, 1968 / Project 3 3PR5033

★ At Massey Hall / Dec. 4, 1972 / World Jazz 3
Anything from this delightful traditional jazz group is worth hearing. —*Ron Wynn*

Frank Wright

b. Jul. 9, 1935, Grenada, MS, d. 1990
Tenor sax / Early free
An ordained minister, Frank Wright played fiery tenor e la Shepp or Ayler. He was among the more controversial figures of his time. Whether modal or free, Rev. Wright got down. —*Michael G. Nastos*

★ Stove Man, Love Is the Word / May 22, 1979 / Sandra 2106
Live at The Loft in Munich, Germany, with sextet. Rev. Wright is on the edge. This is an extension of Dolphy. Must have open ears. —*Michael G. Nastos*

Richard Wyands

b. Jul. 2, 1928, Oakland, CA
Piano / Bop
A fine ballad and standards player, Richard Wyands is such a strong accompanist that his abilities as a soloist are overlooked. But he plays with taste, delicacy, and sophistication while never ignoring the blues or lacking intensity in his solos. Wyands began playing professionally in the '40s, working with Oakland groups. He backed Ella Fitzgerald and Carmen McRae in the mid-'50s and then moved to New York. Wyands played with Roy Haynes, Charles Mingus, Jerome Richardson, and Gigi Gryce in the late '50s and was extremely active in the early '60s. He was featured on recordings by Oliver Nelson, Etta Jones, Eddie "Lockjaw" Davis, Lem Winchester, Gene Ammons, Willis Jackson, Taft Jordan, and Gryce. Wyands toured and recorded with Kenny Burrell from 1965 to 1974, visiting England in 1969 and Japan in 1971. He also recorded with Freddie Hubbard in 1971. Wyands joined Budd Johnson's JPJ quartet in 1974 and recorded with Benny Bailey in 1978 and Zoot Sims in 1982. He has continued recording and touring through the '80s and '90s, but has done few recordings as a leader. Wyands currently has no sessions available on CD but can be heard on reissued discs by Burrell, Ammons, Hubbard, and many others. —*Ron Wynn*

● Then, Here and Now / i. Oct. 1978 / Storyville 4083

Jimmy Yancey (James Edward Yancey)

b. Feb. 20, 1898, Chicago, IL, d. Sep. 17, 1951, Chicago, IL
Vocals, piano, harmonium / Boogie-woogie
Jimmy Yancey was a truly great stride and boogie-woogie piano man who influenced numerous players during his heyday in the '30s and '40s. —*Cub Koda*

○ In the Beginning / i. 1939 / Solo Art 1
○ Blues and Boogie / Oct. 25, 1939-Sep. 6, 1940 / X 3000
○ Yancey-Lofton Sessions—Vol. 1, The / i. 1943 / Storyville 238
○ Yancey-Lofton Sessions—Vol. 2, The / i. 1943 / Storyville 239
● Yancey Special / i. 1950 / Atlantic 103
○ Lost Recording Date / i. Apr. 7, 1954 / Riverside 1028
○ Yancey's Getaway / i. 1956 / Riverside 12-124
○ Chicago Piano Vol 1 / i. 1972 / Atlantic 82368
   This reissue of a 1951 Yancey session that briefly surfaced in 1959 and 1972 is fine hard-yet-delicate piano soul. Jimmy cut this after his stints with Bluebird, Victor, and Vocalion, but these duets

(Israel Crosby played bass) are prime boogie-woogie, a spirited middle ground between Meade Lux Lewis and Jerry Lee Lewis. —*Jimmy Guterman, Roundup Newsletter*

★ **Volume 1 (1939-1940)** / Document 5041
Yancey's earliest and best sides for the Solo Art label. Beautiful and sensitive performances. (Import) —*Cub Koda*

○ **Volume 2 (1939-1950)** / Document 5042

○ **Volume 3 (1943-1950)** / Document 5043

Yellowjackets

R&B, fusion
Though now known for increasingly sophisticated and polished studio albums with diverse influences, including jazz, world music, and pop, the Yellowjackets started in 1981 as an R&B-oriented band with guitarist Robben Ford. Russel Ferrante (keyboards) and Jimmy Haslip (bass) are the remaining original members, joined by drummer William Kennedy in the most recent lineup. The original idea was that they were studio musicians who wanted to play "real music," and they have crafted a string of very listenable and successful releases. Despite some harping by critics who can't quite find the right label to stick on them, and at least one rather forgettable album (*Shades*), the band has enjoyed well-deserved success behind fine compositions (notably by Ferrante), excellent musicality in its members, and very professional production work in the studio. Their most recent album, *Greenhouse*, received 4 stars from *Down Beat*, no small feat for a band in their genre. —*David Nelson McCarthy*

○ **Shades** / 1986 / MCA 5752
1986 set, prototype fusion. —*Ron Wynn*

○ **Four Corners** / i. 1987 / MCA 5994
Highly popular album, short on jazz feel. —*Ron Wynn*

Politics / i. 1988 / MCA 6236
Features appealing sax of Marc Russo, compositions of Russel Ferrante. Unpretentious, melodic, memorable. Fine studio sound. —*David Nelson McCarthy*

★ **Spin** / i. 1989 / MCA 6304
Clearly their best album. It swings! —*Michael G. Nastos*

Green House / i. 1991 / GRP 9630
Guest sax by Bob Mintzer, with fine orchestration for a real live string ensemble by Vince Mendoza. High level of musicianship all around. Very accessible. —*David Nelson McCarthy*

Larry Young (Khalid Yasin Abdul Aziz)

b. Oct. 7, 1940, Newark, NJ, d. Mar. 30, 1978, New York, NY
Organ / Postbop, soul-jazz, early jazz-rock
An excellent, but greatly overlooked organist, whose approach to the organ was many years ahead of its time. Young offered an alternative to the soul-jazz, bass-pedal-heavy style dominant in the '60s and played in a swirling, loose, and rock-influenced fashion that was most favorably showcased in Tony Williams's Lifetime trio of the late '60s and early '70s and also in his work with Miles Davis. Young made some more conventional jazz dates for Blue Note, but even these displayed a technique that was quite different from that of any other organist of the period. A recent Mosaic boxed set showcases Young's Blue Note material in a comprehensive manner; the Lifetime material has also been reissued. —*Ron Wynn*

☆ **Testifying** / Aug. 2, 1960 / New Jazz 1793
W/ Joe Holiday (ts), Thornel Schwartz (g), and Jimmie Smith (d). —*Michael G. Nastos*

Groove Street / Feb. 27, 1962 / Prestige 7237

★ **Complete Blue Note Recordings** / Sep. 11, 1964-Feb. 7, 1969 / Mosaic
Definitive boxed-set of visionary organist's work. A must-buy. Set includes the first three Grant Green (g) albums. —*Michael G. Nastos*

☆ **Into Somethin'** / Oct. 12, 1964 / Blue Note 4187

● **Unity** / Nov. 10, 1965 / Blue Note 84221
Recorded at Englewood Cliffs, NJ. Innovative, far-reaching organist. —*Ron Wynn*

○ **Contrasts** / 1968 / Blue Note 84266

○ **Heaven on Earth** / Feb. 9, 1968 / Blue Note 84304

Of all the organists around, Larry Young was probably the one with the most ambitious musical outlook. . . . Only occasionally did Young's talent emerge above the surface on this release, for funk was the order of the day —*John Norris, Coda*

Lester Young (Lester Willis Young)

b. Aug. 27, 1909, Woodville, MS, d. Mar. 15, 1959, New York, NY
Tenor sax / Swing
The man who brought a new sound to his chosen instrument and a new sensibility to jazz began as a drummer in the family band led by his father and then also learned violin and saxophone. He left the family band in 1928, worked with various leaders, including King Oliver (1933), and was picked by Fletcher Henderson to replace Coleman Hawkins. But Henderson's musicians couldn't accept Lester's lighter, airier sound and innovative phrasing, so after three months, Lester asked to leave and joined Andy Kirk. It was in 1936, after he invited himself into Count Basie's little band in Kansas City, that doors began to open for Lester. His first record (*Shoe Shine Swing, Lady Be Good*) caused quite a stir, and when he came East with Basie and started to record with Billie Holiday, the stage was set for the return from Europe of Coleman Hawkins and the great tenor divide. Lester's approach became the inspiration for cool jazz—he was also a profound influence on young Charlie Parker. Pres, as he was now known (short for "President," the nickname was given him by Holiday), left Basie in 1940 and led his own little bands for a while with his drummer brother, Lee. Back with Basie in 1943, he was drafted in 1944; his army experience was grim, for he was incarcerated for pot and barbiturate use. Released in 1945, he made some wonderful records (*D. B. Blues, These Foolish Things*), toured with Jazz at the Philharmonic, visited Europe, and maintained his place in jazz despite the rise of bop. But his health got progressively worse, mainly due to alcoholism. He died at the age of 49 in his New York hotel room just hours after returning from a Paris engagement. Lester (who also invented a spoken language of his own) was the creator of a musical vocabulary that was wholly original and profoundly influential. His was a horizontal approach to melody—not the vertical, chord-based one favored by Hawkins, for example—and his long, sinuous lines were filled with unexpected twists and turns, swinging to the hilt. He was one of jazz's great poets and storytellers and a master of the blues. —*Dan Morgenstern*

★ **Complete Lester Young on Keynote** / i. 1944 / Mercury 830920

○ **Master Takes** / i. May 1, 1944 / Savoy 4419
A careful reading of the liner notes reveals that the notion behind this release was to introduce Young to the generally uninformed listener who wanted to hear him without digging through alternate takes of the previous release. —*Milo Fine, Cadence*

● **Pres: The Complete Savoy Recordings** / i. 1944-1949 / Savoy 70819
The method of including master and alternates—thus allowing the listener to hear a piece develop through several recorded attempts—is tried-and-true scholarship, and it helped make the Lester Young collection a wholly excellent experience. There were 25 tracks, but only 15 titles were covered, and there is joy and wonder in hearing Pres treat each of three or four takes as a new piece, creating totally different solos at each opportunity. In some cases, each succeeding take provided a solo extended from the one taken before in overall concept. —*Neil Tesser, Down Beat*

○ **Prez Conferences (1946-1958)** / Mar. 1946-1958 / Jass 18

☆ **Carnegie Blues** / i. 1946 1957 / Verve 825101
All the material here, with the exception of three tracks from 9/19/53 with Lester Young (tenor sax) backed by the Oscar Peterson trio (Herb Ellis, guitar; Ray Brown, bass; Peterson, piano) plus J.C. Heard (drums), was previously unissued. —*Bob Rusch, Cadence*

☆ **Lester Young Quartet and Count Basie Seven** / i. 1950 / Mercury 25015

○ **Lester Swings** / i. 1951 / Verve 22516
Lester Swings consists of five dates with four rhythm sections. Far and away the best of these was the 1945 material with tenor saxophonist Lester Young playing with a sense of adventure sympathetically backed by pianist Nat Cole and drummer Buddy Rich. —*Carl Brauer, Cadence*

☆ **Kansas City Style** / i. Jun. 4, 1952 / Commodore 20021

○ **Pres and Sweets** / i. 1955 / Verve 849391

W/ Harry Edison. Brilliant duo work with Lester Young and Sweets Edison. —*Ron Wynn*

○ **Nat King Cole-Buddy Rich Trio** / **i**. 1956 /

○ **Lester Young in Washington, D.C., 1956—Vol. 2** / Dec. 1956 / Pablo 225

The second of four volumes documenting a particularly strong musical night in the life of the great tenor saxophonist Lester Young features Pres with a very competent trio (led by pianist Bill Potts) performing five standards and Young's two most famous compositions: "Lester Leaps In" and "Jumpin' with Symphony Sid." The recording quality is excellent on this fine showcase for the swinging and emotionally deep style that Young developed in his later years. —*Scott Yanow*

○ **Lester Young in Washington, D.C., 1956—Vol. 3** / Dec. 1956 / Pablo 228

Though much younger than he, Lester Young's accompanists (pianist Bill Potts, bassist Norman Williams, drummer Jim Lucht) on this date at Olivia's Patio Lounge did not seem to share their peers' disdain of earlier styles and stylists. Indeed, they were actually in awe of his very presence, but not so much they could not give him the type of support he wanted. Instead, they treated him with all the loving care and respect a master of his venerable stature deserved. As a consequence, Young played the best he had in years. —*Jack Sohmer, Down Beat*

○ **Lester Young in Washington, D.C., 1956—Vol. 4** / Dec. 1956 / Pablo 230

The fourth of four volumes, all presumably recorded the same night (the liners are a little vague on that matter, although this quartet definitely only played together that week), documents tenor saxophonist Lester Young (only a little more than two years before his death) in excellent form with a complementary trio led by pianist Bill Potts. All four sets are recommended, for Pres sounds quite happy, consistently swings, and comes up with creative ideas on standards and fairly basic originals. Superior postwar Lester Young. —*Scott Yanow*

○ **Lester Young in Washington, D.C., 1956—Vol. 1** / Dec. 1956 / Pablo 2308-219

Collectors who were amazed at "These Foolish Things," "Jumpin' with Symphony Sid," and "Three Little Words" on a mysterious Lester Young Queen-Disc LP will be delighted to hear this entire Pablo album from the same 1956 nightclub sessions. This rhythm section (pianist Bill Potts, bassist Norman "Willie" Williams, drummer Jim Lucht) was highly active, capturing Young's high spirits without intruding, thereby fulfilling one of his own ideals—indeed, there was a special atmosphere of relaxed intensity, confident mastery and straightforward creation about the entire date, and bassist Williams deserved particular credit for inspiring the band's high level of swing. The result was the kind of inner excitement, so different from bombast or high volume, that distinguishes the best jazz combo records. —*John Litweiler, Down Beat*

● **Lester Young-Buddy Rich Trio** / **i**. 1957 / Verve 8164

○ **Lester Young-Nat King Cole Trio** / **i**. 1958 / Score 4019

☆ **Pres at His Very Best** / **i**. Jan. 1966 / Emarcy 26010

These were among the greatest performances Lester Young ever cut. If I had to pick one record with which to spend the rest of my days, it would be this. —*Don DeMicheal, Down Beat*

○ **Coleman Hawkins & Lester Young** / **i**. Nov. 1975 / Zim 1000

This was extraordinary music beautifully reproduced. Every airy puff from Lester Young's tenor came over with sumptuous depth and presence. His work on "I Got Rhythm," "Lady Be Good," and "Sweet Georgia Brown" soared from its first unearthly notes in a tone so sheer you could almost see through it. Buck Clayton was in fabulous form, and Coleman Hawkins performed at his typical high level. But Young's unique tone and his instinct for the surprising turn of phrase stole the ear away from Bean's rolling aggressiveness. —*John Mcdonough, Down Beat*

○ **Pres and Teddy and Oscar** / **i**. Oct. 1976 / Verve 22502

It has been said so often that Lester Young's playing declined after his terrible experience in the Army during World War II that it has almost become unanimously accepted as fact. Only trouble is that many of his recordings dispute that theory. In reality, although Young's health declined gradually throughout the 1950s (until his death in 1959), his solos were often at a high level. This two-LP set contains two of the great tenor's finest recordings, a set with the Oscar Peterson quartet in 1952 and a reunion with

Teddy Wilson in a trio in 1956. Young's performances of "All of Me," "Prisoner of Love," "Just You, Just Me," and melodic renditions of seven straight ballads (the latter from the date with Oscar Peterson) rank with some of the finest work of his career. Essential music for all jazz collections. —*Scott Yanow*

○ **Lester Young Story—Vol. 3, The** / **i**. Jan. 1978 / Columbia 34840

Although it was the same Count Basie orchestra, the sound and character of the Columbia Basies was oddly different from his Deccas. Lester Young was more heavily featured, and the entire band came to sound more and more like a small group, so perfect in its balance and cohesiveness. This was readily apparent on "Taxie War Dance #1," the exquisite "Miss Thing," and "Pound Cake." As for Young, his statements on these tracks were profoundly iconoclastic, particularly the dark, brooding drive of "Pound Cake." —*John Mcdonough, Down Beat*

○ **Giants of Jazz** / **i**. Apr. 1981 / Time Life 13

The pleasant surprise of this Time-Life *Giants of Jazz* offering was the 52-page booklet included with the three-record set, half Lester Young biography and half commentary on the album's recordings. Particularly interesting were the efforts of biographer John McDonough to document the foggy years before and after Young's first stay with the Count Basie band. The strength of the recordings chosen here was that they presented Pres in several different dimensions. To better illustrate his ability as an improviser, the set offered alternate takes of "When You're Smiling" (with Billie Holiday) and "I Want a Little Girl" (Kansas City 6). Young's talents as a soloist tended to overshadow the fact that he provided the finest backing for vocalists in the '30s and '40s of any tenor saxophonist. —*Doug Long, Down Beat*

★ **Lester Young Story—Vols. 1-3, The** / Columbia

Tremendous set that compiles Young's top work for Columbia. —*Ron Wynn*

Snooky Young

b. Feb. 3, 1919, Dayton, OH
Trumpet / Swing, big band, progressive big band
Another prolific studio and session player, and a fine high-note trumpeter, Snooky Young has been playing trumpet since he was five years old and managed to be a member of the Wilberforce College Band in his teens without ever attending the university. He joined the Lunceford orchestra in 1939 after playing in territory bands and stayed there until 1942, becoming famous for his solo on "Uptown Blues." He worked briefly with Count Basie in 1942 and had stints with Lee Young, Les Hite, Benny Carter, and Gerald Wilson, plus another short stay with Basie before he joined him again for two years, from 1945 to 1947. He had his own band for nearly a decade before he hooked up with Basie for a fourth stay, this time from 1957 to 1962. Since then he's been a steady studio player, has appeared with "The Tonight Show" band, and has occasionally issued an album under his own name. —*Ron Wynn*

★ **Horn of Plenty** / Mar. 1979 / Concord Jazz 91

Snooky Young's horn was showcased here against a quartet. The style was middle-of-the-road mainstream. Perhaps the very laidback atmosphere of the date was meant to be, or perhaps it was just a tribute to the professional quality of the musicians. Young has an excellent tone and exercised discipline and control over the music. —*Spencer R. Weston, Cadence*

Joe Zawinul

b. Jul. 7, 1932, Vienna
Piano, keyboards, synth, composer / Hard bop, early jazz-rock, world fusion
No one has ever been able to get a more human, funky sound out of electric keyboards and synthesizers than Joe Zawinul, Vienna's gift to the improvisational world. Zawinul began playing the accordion at six and started studying classical music a year later at the Vienna Conservatory. He worked with Austrian jazz saxophonist Hans Koller in 1952 and with various Austrian groups in the mid- and late '50s, while also playing in France and Germany with his own trio. Zawinul won a scholarship to Berklee in 1959, but spent only a week at Berklee before joining Maynard Ferguson and touring with him for eight months. He became Dinah Washington's pianist after a brief stint with Slide Hampton in 1959 and stayed with her until 1961. After a month in Harry Edison's group, he joined Cannonball Adderley and remained

with his band until 1970. There, Zawinul's skills flourished, and he become a sturdy blues player, good soloist, and excellent accompanist. In 1969 and 1970 he worked in Miles Davis's electric units, gradually moving away from acoustic and concentrating on electric instruments. He cofounded Weather Report in 1971 with Wayne Shorter, and through the '70s and '80s made many influential recordings. Weather Report, especially in its early years, was a true jazz-rock band, able to make appealing, seminal work that had loose, adventurous foundations and energetic solos. Zawinul's synthesizer solos were never dry or dependent on gimmicks but showed it was possible to play with individuality and distinction on what many regarded as simply a technological tool. He and Shorter finally went their separate ways in 1986; since then Zawinul has worked with his own bands. —*Ron Wynn*

○ **Zawinul** / **i.** 1971 / Atlantic 1579

★ **Immigrants** / **i.** 1984 / Columbia 40969
Again, a wildly eclectic menu. Interest depends on how much you enjoy improvisatory music filtered through lots of styles rather than the straight-jazz approach. —*Ron Wynn*

John Zorn

b. 1953, New York
Alto sax, duck calls, composer / Modern creative
The term *avant-garde* truly fits John Zorn; he falls into no easily definable category or school of playing or composition. His splaying, screaming alto sax solos; use of duck calls; and fondness for film soundtracks and mixing of rock, free, pop, and bop settings confound foes and friends alike. He's been identified with the New York "downtown" crowd, a tag he disdains. Zorn's work began to get wide attention in the mid-'80s, especially the *Cobra '86* album on Hat Art, with its molecular system for 13 players, plus Zorn's live act, which has included him blowing a mouthpiece under water. He's also worked with the Kronos Quartet and rockers the Golden Palaminos; been featured on tribute albums to Thelonious Monk and Sonny Clark; done solo, trio, duo, and combo recordings; and utilized studio technology like multitrack dubbing quite creatively —*Ron Wynn*

Pool / Mar. 1+04, 1980 / Parachute
An album that is anarchic, chaotic at times. Gripping and emphatic always. —*Ron Wynn*

Big Gundown / Sep. 1984-Sep. 1985 / Elektra 79139
Music of Ennio Morricone. 1984-1985. Ambitious, rambling, and reflective of Zorn's flirtations with rock and the New York downtown scene. —*Ron Wynn*

Yankees / **i.** 1984 / Celluloid
Far, far afield with ear-splitting exchanges between Zorn, George Lewis (tb), and string-breaker Derek Bailey (g). —*Ron Wynn*

Cobra / Oct. 21, 1985 / Hat Art 26040
Not sure if this is "jazz" in strictest sense. Zorn leads 13-piece group through songs based on a "molecular" system and doesn't play himself. Still, it's as interesting as it sounds. —*Ron Wynn*

Spillane / Aug. 1986-Sep. 1987 / Elektra 79172
An album of nice, dense, and foreboding concept work, with everything from shuffle guitar by Albert Collins to the Kronos Quartet. —*Ron Wynn*

★ **Voodoo: The Music of Sonny Clark** / **i.** 1987 / Black Saint 0109
This is not an album by Sonny Clark, but a tribute to him by John Zorn. Essential Clark repertoire played by progressivists, with John Zorn on alto sax and Wayne Horvits on piano. —*Michael G. Nastos*

○ **News for Lulu** / **i.** Aug. 1987 / Hat Art 6005
This is a great power trio with George Lewis (tb), and Bill Frisell (g). —*Ron Wynn*

★ **Spy vs. Spy: The Music of Ornette Coleman** / **i.** Aug. 1989 / Elektra 60844
On *Spy vs. Spy*, John Zorn and his quintet play 17 Ornette Coleman tunes ranging chronologically from 1958's "Disguise" to four selections from 1987's *In All Languages*. The performances are concise, with all but four songs being under three minutes and seven under two, but there is absolutely no variety in moods or routines. —*Scott Yanow, Cadence*

★ **Naked City** / **i.** 1990 / Nonesuch 79238

His most intriguing, nicely conceived and executed date, with sparkling solos by Bill Frisell (g), Wayne Horovitz (k), and Joey Baron (d). CD has three bonus cuts. —*Ron Wynn*

☆ **Heretic: Jeux Des Dames Cruelles** / Avant Garde 01

Jazz Collections

○ **1930's: Singers—Columbia Jazz Masterpieces, The** / 193? / Columbia 40847

○ **1930's: Small Combos, The** / 193? / Columbia 40833

○ **1940's Big Bands, The** / 194? / Columbia 38574

● **1940's the Singers—Columbia Jazz Masterpieces** / 194? / Columbia 40652

○ **1940's: Bebop —Columbia Jazz Masterpieces, The** / 194? / Columbia 38575

○ **1950's the Singers—Columbia Jazz Masterpiece, The** / 1950 / Columbia 40799

○ **1960's: Singers—Columbia Jazz Masterpieces, The** / 196? / Columbia 38579

○ **40 Years of Women in Jazz: Feminist Retrospective** / Jass 9/10

○ **50 Years of Jazz Guitar** / Apr. 1977 / Sony Special Products 33566

● **Ahmet Ertegun's Cabaret Music** / Atlantic 81817

○ **Americans in Europe—Vol. 1** / Aug. 1963 / Impulse 36

○ **Americans in Europe—Vol. 2** / Aug. 1963 / Impulse 37

Atlantic Jazz: Boxed Set / 1947 / Atlantic 81712
This entire series is worth having and can be purchased in one 12-volume disc set or one 15-LP or cassette set. In compiling the discs, Atlantic for some reason omitted some cuts, making the vinyl a better buy. Of course, the vinyl is now deleted. —*Ron Wynn*

○ **Be Bop Era, The** / Sep. 1965 / RCA 519

○ **Bebop Revolution, The** / Bluebird 2177
A 1990 reissue. Nice formative cuts from the '40s with Dizzy Gillespie, Kenny Clarke, Coleman Hawkins, Lucky Thompson, and Allen Eager. —*Ron Wynn*

Best of the Swing Bands / Vanguard 311
A good cross-section, heavy on big names. —*Ron Wynn*

● **Best of Blue Note—Vol. 1 & 2** / Blue Note B2-96110
Japanese import. An incredible (just the best!) collection of the very best cuts from the Blue Note label. A perfect introduction to hard-bop and soul jazz, if you can find it. —*Michael Erlewine*

● **Best of Chess Jazz** / MCA 6025
This is actually a nice package of cuts pulled from various Argo sessions. —*Ron Wynn*

Best of the Big Bands / Madacy 2308
This offers a nice cross-section of Decca sets, especially Woody Herman. —*Ron Wynn*

Best of the Jazz Saxophones / Lester Recording Catalog 9025

Bethlehem's Best (3 Albums) / Mar. 7, 1956 / Bethlehem EXLP 6

Jazz 'round Midnight / 1992 / PolyGram 513462
Anthology presenting various ballads by jazz greats such as Billie Holiday, Ella Fitzgerald, Sarah Vaughan, Shirley Horn, Mel Tormé, Dinah Washington, and others. Strictly for newcomers; the tracks are great but can all be found elsewhere on recently or newly issued discs, for the most part. —*Ron Wynn*

Big Band Jazz: Various / Delmark 439

Big Band Sampler: Best of the Big Bands / Columbia 45476
A nice overview of the big-band era. —*Ron Wynn*

Big Band's Greatest Hits: Vol. 1 / Columbia 30009
Well-known, easily obtainable, swing era material. —*Ron Wynn*

Swing (4 CD Box Set) / MCA 80724

● **Big Bands of the Swinging Year—Vol. 1** / Collectables 5096

○ **Big Bands of the Swinging Year: Vol. 2** / Collectables 5097

○ **Birdology** / Oct. 1990 / Verve 841 132
Sampler with various alto saxophonists doing Charlie Parker tunes or otherwise showing their stylistic debt to his approach. Another concept album aimed at what major labels see as increasingly profitable new, young audience interested in learning

about jazz and purchasing these grab-bag anthologies. —*Ron Wynn*

○ **Birth of Bop—Vol. 1, The** / 1953 / Savoy 9022

○ **Birth of Bop—Vol. 2, The** / 1953 / Savoy 9023

○ **Birth of Bop—Vol. 3, The** / 1953 / Savoy 9024

○ **Birth of Bop—Vol. 4, The** / 1953 / Savoy 9025

○ **Birth of Bop—Vol. 5, The** / 1953 / Savoy 9026

○ **Black Jazz & Blues: First Sound Films** / Sandy Hook 2068

○ **Black Jazz in Europe 1926-1930** / Dec. 1926-Dec. 1930 / EMI Pathe/Jazztime 252714-2

○ **Black Lion at Montreux** / Mar. 1975 / Black Lion 213

○ **Blue Montreux: 1978 Montreux Jzz Festil** / Bluebird 6573

Blue Note 50th Anniversary Collection—Vol. 1—1939-1956—from Boogie to Bop / Dec. 9, 1991 / Blue Note 92465
1939-1956. Boogie to bop. Parts of the 50th Anniversary boxed set. Formative label sessions with boogie-woogie piano up to hard bop. —*Ron Wynn*

Blue Note 50th Anniversary Collection—Vol. 2—1956-1965—the Jazz Message / Aug. 5, 1991 / Blue Note 92468
1956-1965. Jazz Message. Dynamic cuts, hard bop and avant-garde. —*Ron Wynn*

Blue Note 50th Anniversary Collection—Vol. 3—1956-1967—Funk & Blues / Dec. 9, 1991 / Blue Note 92471
1956-1965. Funk and blues. The birth of soul-jazz. —*Ron Wynn*

Vol 4: Outside in 1964-89 / 1964-1989 / Blue Note 92474
1964-1989. Outside in. Avant-garde, explosive cuts. —*Ron Wynn*

Vol 5: Lighting the Fuse 1970-89 / 1970-1989 / Blue Note 92477

Bluebird Sampler / RCA 6389

Bluebird Sampler 1990 / 1990 / Bluebird 2192-2-RB11

○ **Boogie Woogie Masters** / Black & Blue 590632

○ **Bop Session, The** / Apr. 1978 / Sonet 692

● **Candid Jazz** / 1988 / Candid 79000

50th Anniversary Box / 1942 / Blue Note 98931
Comprehensive boxed set showcasing the complete range of Capitol as a jazz label. The set includes intimate piano trio work, big bands, cool jazz, torch and nightclub singers, even some hard bop and a little free music, plus fusion. —*Ron Wynn*

○ **Charlie Parker 10th Memorial Concert 3/27/65** / Mar. 27, 1965 / PolyGram 826985

● **Chicago Boogie** / May 1977 / Barrelhouse 04

● **Chicago Jazz (1923-1929)** / 1923-1929 / Biograph 12005

● **Chicago Jazz (1925-1929)—Vol. 2** / 1925-1929 / Biograph 12043

Chicago Jazz Summit / Atlantic 81844-2
A 1988 release of some nice cuts done by Chicago jazz veterans at the 1986 JUC festival. —*Ron Wynn*

○ **Chicago South Side Vol.2** / Jun. 1969 / Historical 30

Chicago: At the Jazz Band Ball / RCA 6752

Chicago: The Living Legends—Vol. 1 / Sep. 1-08, 1961 / Riverside 12-389

Chicago: The Living Legends—Vol. 2 / 1960 / Riverside 12-390

● **Clarinet Summit—Volumes 1 & 2** / 1984 / India Navigation 1062

○ **Southern Bells** / Mar. 29, 1987 / Black Saint 0107

In Concert at the Public Theater / Innovative 1062
Wondrous performances by the outstanding Clarinet Summit at Public Theater. Includes the late John Carter (cl). —*Ron Wynn*

Classic Female Jazz Artists / RCA 6755
1939-1952. Despite a dubious title, this is a worthwhile anthology of both blues and jazz artists. —*Ron Wynn*

● **Classic Jazz: Vol. 1—5** / Smithsonian 331
The Smithsonian Collection of Classic Jazz is itself somewhat of a classic, referred to in many books and used as the main learning source in at least one. If you don't know what you like in jazz and are looking for a well-put-together introduction, this set is a good bet. It starts with ragtime's Scott Joplin and proceeds through Bessie Smith, Louis Armstrong, Art Tatum, Duke Ellington . . . all the way up to and including the free jazz of Ornette Coleman, and even the World Saxophone Quartet. Of

course John Coltrane, Thelonious Monk, Miles Davis, and all the other big guns are there—even Horace Silver and Lennie Tristano. This five-CD set (94 tracks) contains classic cuts in most cases. This set is a great place to begin. —*Michael Erlewine*

● **Classic Jazz Piano** / Jun. 1927-Feb. 1966 / RCA 6754
1927-1957. An excellent compilation of some seminal players and styles. CD has three bonus cuts. —*Ron Wynn*

● **Classic Jazz Piano Styles** / Oct. 1967 / RCA 543

☆ **Cole Porter: A Centennial Celebration** / RCA 3090
This master of the urban lyric and chic tune is himself heard here singing demos of three of his standards. Includes 20 performances from the '30s to '80s, featuring Fred Astaire, Artie Shaw, Lena Horne, and others. This is the cornerstone of 20th-century music. —*Mark A. Humphrey*

Columbia Jazz Masterpiece Series / CBS 40799
A good starter collection spotlighting jazz in the period when it still had some pop influence. This is a recent cross-section of jazz-based, scat, and popular song stylists. —*Ron Wynn*

Columbia Jazz Masterpiece Series: 1930s Big Band / 193? / CBS 40651
An excellent single-disc overview of '30s bands, both big names and obscure groups. —*Ron Wynn*

Columbia Jazz Masterpieces: 1940s—the Singers / 194? / CBS 40652

Columbia Jazz Masterpieces: Sampler—Vol. 1 / Columbia 40474

Columbia Jazz Masterpieces: Sampler—Vol. 2 / Dec. 20, 1991 / CBS 40798

Columbia Jazz Masterpieces: Sampler—Vol. 6 / Columbia 45146

○ **Commodore Jazz Sampler—Classics in Swing, The** / 1988 / Commodore 7000

● **Complete Blue Note Recordings of Hall/Johnson/Deparis/Dick** / Apr. 1986 / Mosaic 6 109

● **Complete Commodore Jazz Recordings Vol. 1** / Dec. 1988 / Mosaic 123

● **Complete Commodore Jazz Recordings Vol. 2** / Feb. 1990 / Mosaic 128

● **Complete Commodore Jazz Recordings Vol. 3** / Feb. 1990 / Mosaic 134

● **Complete Master Jazz Piano Series, The** / Mosaic 140

● **Dancing Twenties** / Smithsonian/Folkways RF-27

○ **Dixieland Jazz Gems** / 1950 / Commodore 20010

☆ **Dixieland's Greatest Hits** / Pro Arte 8018

○ **Early and Rare: Classic Jazz Collectors Items** / Oct. 1960 / Riverside 12 134

● **Early Black Swing—the Birth of Big Band Jazz: 1927-1934** / 1927-1934 / Bluebird 9583-2-RB11
1927-1934. Valuable, classic tunes from jazz pioneers, swing, and classic New Orleans. First-rate examples of vintage swing from the '20s and '30s. Plenty of examples from the cream of the crop, including Armstrong, Ellington, Fletcher Henderson. Great introductory item. —*Ron Wynn*

○ **Exciting Battle: Jatp Stockholm '55** / 1955 / Pablo 2310713

○ **Fabulous Ellingtonians on Keynote, The** / 1987 / Mercury 830 926

○ **Bass Is** / May 18, 1992 / Enja 2018

○ **First Esquire Concert, The** / 1944 / Laserlight 15723
January 18, 1944, was definitely the night to be at the Metropolitan Opera House. It was the night Louis Armstrong, Art Tatum, Coleman Hawkins, and some equally famous colleagues—all winners in Esquire magazine's first annual jazz poll—made their Met debut. Recordings of that evening were originally issued by the U.S. Government on V-Discs for distribution to GIs overseas, but the concert was also broadcast live. A handful of small labels have made this astonishing event available to collectors over the years, but this CD release offers the best technical quality I have heard so far.
. —*Chris Albertson, Stereo Review*

○ **First Sessions 1949-1950** / 1949-1950 / Prestige 24081

● **Footnotes to Jazz—Vol. 2:** / Smithsonian/Folkways 31

- **Footnotes to Jazz—Vol. 3:** / Smithsonian/Folkways 32
- **Four Giants of Swing: S'wonderful** / Flying Fish 900035
○ **Free Music One and Two** / Jun. 1971 / ESP 1083
- **From Spirituals to Swing—Carnegie Hall Concerts, 1938-1939** / May 1974 / Vanguard 2-47/48
- **Fun on the Frets: Early Jazz Guitar** / Yazoo 1061
  A companion volume to Yazoo Record's *Pioneers of the Jazz Guitar.* This compilation (1939-1949) features George Van Eps, Carl Kress, and Tony Mottola. —*Richard Lieberson*

  Grp Super Live in Concert / GRP 1650
  A live two-CD set of Ritenour, Gruisin, Scott, and 60 minutes of the Chick Corea Elektric Band. An excellent performance and a fantastic digital recording. —*Paul Kohler*
- **Giants of Funk Tenor Sax** / Prestige 2302
  A great two-disc introduction to both honking-blues and funk (soul-jazz) tenor saxophone. Great for beginners, but should be in any collection. Over three hours of blues-funk greats like Arnett Cob, Eddie "Lockjaw" Davis, Sonny Stitt, Willis Jackson, Houston Person, Stanley Turrentine, Rusty Bryant, and Gene Ammons. A classic collection. —*Michael Erlewine*
- **In Berlin 1971** / 1971 / PolyGram 834567
  Fine supergroup pairing with Dizzy Gillespie, Monk, Sonny Stitt, Kai Winding, Art Blakey, and Al McKibbon. The all-star lineup unites and makes quality music. —*Ron Wynn*
- **Giants of Small Band Swing—Vol. 1** / 1946 / Riverside 1723
  Fine combo dates, mostly bop, plus occasional classic New Orleans style.
  A tremendous 1990 reissue of 1946 recordings featuring various small combos in vintage swing style. —*Ron Wynn*
- **Giants of Small Band Swing—Vol. 2** / 1945-1946 / Riverside 1724
○ **Giants of Traditional Jazz** / Savoy 2251

  Great Trumpets (Classic Jazz to Swing) / Feb. 1927-May 1954 / Bluebird 6753
- **Greatest Jazz Concert in the World, The** / Nov. 1975 / Pablo 2625 704

  Guitar Workshop in L.A. / 1988 / JVC 3314
  Nice jazz-fusion guitar work featuring Jeff Baxter and Buzzy Feiten. —*Paul Kohler*

  Happy over Hoagy/We Dig Cole / Jass 5
- **Honkers & Bar Walkers—Vol.1** / Delmark 438
  1952. A blasting R&B sax anthology consisting of early '50s tracks from the Regal and United labels. —*Michael G. Nastos*
○ **Horizons—Cross Cultural Jazz Sampler** / Music of the World 308
  Includes tracks from *Asian Journal, Malaga to Cairo, Piano Crossroads, Basic Tendencies,* and *Ramama* and features new recordings with Jim Bowie (banjo) and Anders Rosen (saxophone quartet). Great sounds in a modern world music sampler. —*Music of the World*

  Hot Jazz for Cool Nights / 1992 / Music Masters 65089
  Anthology featuring vintage performers doing classic traditional jazz cuts. Earl Hines, Charlie Johnson, Tiny Parham, The Missourians, The Jungletown Stompers, and Musical Stevedores are the acts presented. —*Ron Wynn*

  Illuminations / 1989 / Axiom 422-848958
  Compilation featuring cuts from Axiom artists on the stylistic cutting edge. The list includes Sonny Sharrock, Bill Laswell, Ronald Shannon Jackson and Shankar. It covered jazz, African and Caribbean, fusion, and dance-rock. —*Ron Wynn*

  Impulse Collection: Best of—Vol. 1 / MCA 8026
  Cross-section of good performances from the larger set. —*Ron Wynn*

  Impulse! Jazz—a 30 Year Celebration / 1991 / GRP 101
  A two-record set that has many fine cuts celebrating this distinguished label's three decades. —*Ron Wynn*
- **Jatp: Historic Recordings** / 1944 1946 / Verve 2-2504
☆ **Bird & Pres: The '46 Concerts** / 1946 / Verve 833565-1
  Jazz at the Philharmonic (JATP). Great session with Charlie Parker (as), Dizzy Gillespie (tpt), and Lester Young (ts). Ultimate melding of swing era and bop musicians. —*Michael G. Nastos*

- **Jatp: Tokyo—Live** / Nov. 18, 1953 / Pablo
○ **Exciting Battle** / Pablo
  Frenetic jam session date done in 1955 in Stockholm with an all-out tenor battle between Illinois Jacquet, Flip Phillips, and many others. This has been reissued on CD. —*Ron Wynn*
- **Jazz at Santa Monica Civic '72** / 1972 / Pablo 2625701
  JATP-styled blowing date with well-known Pablo acts. A three-record set from 1972. —*Ron Wynn*
○ **Jazz at the Hollywood Bowl (2 Lps)** / 1958 / Verve 8231
○ **Jazz Band Ball** / Fantasy 12005
  Jazz Club: Alto Sax / PolyGram 40036
  Jazz Club: Alto Sax Clarinet & Flute / PolyGram 45145
  Jazz Club: Bass / PolyGram 40037
  A fine addition in a rare worthwhile compilation series. CD has one bonus cut. —*Ron Wynn*
  Jazz Club: Big Band / PolyGram 40030
  Jazz Club: Drums / PolyGram 40033
  Jazz Club: Guitar / PolyGram 40035
  Jazz Club: Guitar & Bass / PolyGram 45150
  Jazz Club: Piano / PolyGram 40032
  Jazz Club: Tenor & Baritone Sax / PolyGram 45146
  Jazz Club: Tenor Sax / PolyGram 40031
  Jazz Club: Trombone, Mainstream / 1991 / Polydor 845 144
  Jazz Club: Trumpet / PolyGram 40038
  Jazz Club: Vibraphone / PolyGram 40034
○ **Jazz Guitar Classics (1953-1974)** / Dec. 1953-Feb. 1974 / Original Jazz Classics 6012
○ **Jazz Heritage—Big Bands Uptown** / MCA 1323
○ **Jazz Heritage—Blues & All That Jazz** / MCA 1353
○ **Jazz in a Vertical Groove** / May 31, 1991 / Biograph 12057
  Jazz Loves Paris / Speed Record 5002
  A Buddy Collette session with wonderful arrangements and nice solos. It's available once more after a long absence. —*Ron Wynn*
  Vocalists / Jul. 31, 1992 / RCA 66072
  A '92 anthology that spotlights vocal numbers done by both instrumentalists and singers. The list included Lionel Hampton, Fats Waller, Mildred Bailey, Jack Teagarden, Lee Wiley, Dave Lambert, Jon Hendricks, Joe Williams, and Nina Simone among others. —*Ron Wynn*
- **Jazz Men Detroit** / 1955 / Savoy 12083
  Jazz Piano / Smithsonian
  Four discs—68 cuts and over 40 artists—all the way from Jelly Roll Morton through Teddy Wilson, Art Tatum, Erroll Garner, Bud Powell, Thelonious Monk, Tommy Flanagan, Bill Evans . . . up to Chick Corea, Keith Jarrett, and Herbie Hancock—a great survey of piano styles. This collection focuses on piano solos, and most are unaccompanied. Overall, a very nice collection. —*Michael Erlewine*
- **Jazz Sampler: Classics in Swing 1938-1944** / 1938-1944 / Commodore 7000
- **Jazz Singers** / Prestige 24113
  Good range of featured artists aimed at novices and new fans. Very fine two-record set with an extensive cross-section from early Armstrong to Flora Purim. This is worth having, regardless of your jazz knowledge. —*Ron Wynn*
- **Jazz Singers: Vocals by Great Instrumentalists , The** / Oct. 23, 1992 / Bluebird 3137
- **Jazz Tribe, The** / 1990 / Red 123254
  Jazz Trumpet: Classic Jazz to Swing / Prestige 2301
  Vol. 1. An excellent anthology covering a range of trumpet styles in the first phase of jazz. —*Ron Wynn*
- **Jazz at the Philharmonic: Hartford, 1953** / 1953 / Pablo 2308-240
  Includes a 15-minute jam on "Cottontail," an Oscar Peterson Quartet set with Lester Young (ts). J. C. Heard and Gene Krupa are on drums with Ben Webster (ts), Flip Phillips (ts), Benny Carter (as/tpt), and Roy Eldridge (tpt) as jammers. —*Michael G. Nastos*
  Jazz at the Philharmonic: London (1969) / 1969 / Pablo 2620-119

London 1969. This is a nice two-record set. More intensity than usual. —*Ron Wynn*

● **Jazz at the Philharmonic: Stockholm (1955), The** / Feb. 2, 1955 / Pablo 2310-713

● **Jazz in the Thirties** / Disques Swing 8457
A very nice anthology with lots of cuts from underrated performers. —*Ron Wynn*

○ **Jazz in the Ussr** / Mobile Fidelity 21-00890
Wonderfully-recorded collection spotlights Soviet artists. —*Ron Wynn*

● **Jazz—Vol. 10** / 1951 / Smithsonian/Folkways 73/4
● **Jazz—Vol. 11** / 1951 / Smithsonian/Folkways 75/6
● **Jazz—Vol. 1: The South** / 1951 / Smithsonian/Folkways 53/4
● **Jazz—Vol. 2: The Blues** / 1951 / Smithsonian/Folkways 55/6
● **Jazz—Vol. 3: New Orleans** / 1951 / Smithsonian/Folkways 57/8
● **Jazz—Vol. 4: Jazz Singers** / 1951 / Smithsonian/Folkways 59/60
● **Jazz—Vol. 5: Chicago** / 1951 / Smithsonian/Folkways 63/4
● **Jazz—Vol. 6: Chicago #2** / 1951 / Smithsonian/Folkways 65/6
● **Jazz—Vol. 7** / 1951 / Smithsonian/Folkways 66/8
● **Jazz—Vol. 8** / 1951 / Smithsonian/Folkways 69/70
● **Jazz—Vol. 9** / 1951 / Smithsonian/Folkways 71/2

○ **Jazzin' Baby Blues: Hot Piano Roll Solos** / Biograph 117
● **Jazzmen: Detroit** / 1956 / Savoy 12083
○ **Jazzology Poll Winners** / Aug. 1965 / Jazz Crusade 2004

Tribute to Emily Remler—Vol. 2 / 1992 / Justice 503
This was the second of two albums done by an all-star lineup assembled to record two tribute albums following guitarist Emily Remler's death in 1989, with all proceeds going to her Jazz for Kids fund in Pittsburgh. The roster included Herb Ellis, Bill O'Connell, Eddie Gomez, Marvin "Smitty" Smith, and David Benoit. They made a reverential, yet loving and energetically played tribute. —*Ron Wynn*

Just Friends— Gathering in Tribute to Emily Remler, Vol. 1 / 1992 / Justice 0502-2
The first album of two all-star tributes to guitarist Emily Remler by her distinguished friends. They got together in 1989 and cut these sessions for the Austin, Texas Justic label, with all proceeds going to Remler's Jazz for Kids fund in Pittsburgh. There are no stars or supporting musicians here, just several great musicians saying goodbye to their friend. —*Ron Wynn*

● **Kings of Ragtime Banjo** / Yazoo 1044

Legends of Guitar: Jazz—Vol 1 / Rhino 70717

Legends of Guitar: Jazz—Vol 2 / Rhino 70722

● **Manhattan Project, The** / 1990 / Blue Note 94204
... much of this sounds wonderful, especially by comparison with recent releases, but it still lacks some of the crispness, flair, and fire that they achieved in days past. — *Ron Wynn, Rock & Roll Disc.*

● **Mercury 40th Anniversary** / 1985 / PolyGram 24116
○ **Metronome All Stars, The** / 1949 / Columbia 2528
○ **Metronome All-star Bands** / Apr. 24, 1991 / Bluebird 7636-2-RB11

● **Modern Art of Jazz: Modern Art of Jazz** / Biograph 120
A 1991 sampler with collected nice performances showing the growth of bop and hard bop. —*Ron Wynn*

Modern New Orleans Masters / Rounder 11514
Excellent current music by well-known New Orleans performers. —*Ron Wynn*

More Best Dixie: Compact Jazz / PolyGram 38347
Another decent compilation drawing from various traditional performances. —*Ron Wynn*

Music of the Brazilian Masters / 1989 / Concord Jazz 4389

Musicmasters Jazz Sampler / Music Masters 5022

Down Yonder / 1989 / Rounder 11562
An '89 anthology featuring current New Orleans brass bands. The roster includes Dejan's Olympic Brass Band, the Chosen Few, the Rebirth Marching Jazz Band, and the Dirty Dozen Band. —*Ron Wynn*

New Orleans Brass Bands: Down Yonder / Rounder 11562

An eclectic sampler of some of New Orleans's best: the Dirty Dozen, Dejan's Olympia, the Rebirth, and the Chosen Few. — *Bruce Boyd Raeburn*

○ **New Orleans, Chicago, New York** / Jul. 1918-Sep. 1934 / BBC 3CD 821

○ **New Orleans Jazz—Vol. 1 (1942-1955)** / 1942-1955 / Wolf 1001
○ **New Orleans Jazz—Vol. 2 (1926-1951)** / 1926-1951 / Wolf 1002
● **New Orleans Jazz/Heritage Fest: 10th Anniversary** / Flying Fish 99

Vol. 3—Various / DRG 6182
The third in the Robert Parker import series featuring vintage early jazz performers. This set includes selections by Bessie Smith, Fletcher Henderson, Duke Ellington, Louis Armstrong, and Benny Goodman. —*Ron Wynn*

○ **Newport Festival All Stars** / Oct. 1960 / Atlantic 1331

Newport Jazz Festival All Stars / Jul. 1985 / Concord Jazz 4260
Nice, loose date with specially assembled group of mostly veterans, plus one or two younger players performing in vintage jam session style. This is modeled after old Jazz at the Philharmonic dates, and the atmosphere and musical performances come close to equaling that fervor. —*Ron Wynn*

○ **Newport Rebels** / Dec. 1978 / Candid 79022
○ **Nipper's Greatest Hits: 30s-Volume 1** / 1930 / RCA 9971
○ **40s-Volume 2** / 1940 / RCA 9864
Another in an extensive series covering historical recordings from the RCA family of labels. This second volume continued on the identical trail of its predecessors, covering material from a varied lineup including Glenn Miller, Frank Sinatra, and Artie Shaw. It was mostly swing era, prerock, novelty, and jazzy pop material. —*Ron Wynn*

○ **On the Edge—Progressive Music Pushing The...** / 1991 / Antilles 848 210

○ **On-The-Road Jazz** / 1957 / Riverside 12-127
○ **Opus De Bop** / 1957 / Savoy 12114
○ **Opus in Swing** / 1956 / Savoy Jazz 144
● **Parlor Piano** / Apr. 1971 / Biograph 1001Q

Piano Giants / Prestige 24052
A two-record anthology featuring vintage performances by various piano greats taken from Prestige sessions. The styles range from updated stride to hard bop, mainstream, and soul-jazz. Some featured artists include Duke Ellington, Chick Corea, Keith Jarrett, McCoy Tyner, Red Garland, Earl Hines, and Art Tatum. —*Ron Wynn*

○ **Pioneers of Boogie Woogie** / 1953 / Riverside 1009
● **Pioneers of the Jazz Guitar** / Yazoo 1057
Terrific compilation of '20s and '30s acoustic jazz guitar music featuring Eddie Lang, Carl Kress, Lonnie Johnson, Dick McDonough, and others. Yes, Virginia, there was jazz guitar before Charlie Christian. This volume is preferable to Yazoo's companion—*Fun on the Frets*. —*Richard Lieberson*

Prestige 1st Sessions—Vol. 1—Various / 1949 / Prestige 24224
Early material from artists who were cutting dates that were among the first issued by the Prestige label. Performers include Roy Haynes, Don Lanphere, Fats Navarro, Duke Jordan, Al Haig, and Oscar Pettiford. —*Ron Wynn*

Prestige 1st Sessions—Vol. 2—Various / 1949 / Prestige 24115
The second volume in the series devoted to the early recordings issued on the Prestige label in 1949 and 1950. More from Don Lanphere, Leo Parker, Tubby Phillips, Al Haig, and Max Roach, among others. —*Ron Wynn*

Prestige 1st Sessions—Vol. 3—Various / 1950 / Paris 24116
The third volume in the series covering early sessions issued on the Prestige label, this one moving into the '50s. Eddie "Lockjaw" Davis, Dizzy Gillespie, Red Rodney, and Bennie Green are among the artists presented on this release. —*Ron Wynn*

☆ **Prestige Soul Masterpieces** / Original Jazz Classics 1201
Fine intro to funk or soul jazz on the Hammond organ. 15 cuts from classic funk albums by Charles Earland, Billy Butler, Jack McDuff, Gene Ammons, Charles Kynard, Oliver Nelson, King Curtis, Jimmy Forrest, Rusty Bryant, Shirley Scott, Stanley Turrentine, Willis Jackson, Houston Person, Harold Mabern, Eddie

Davis, Red Holloway, Arnett Cobb, Richard Holmes, and many featured soloists. This is the real stuff. —*Michael Erlewine*

● **Earthy** / Jan. 25, 1957 / Prestige 1707-2
Dazzling stints by Kenny Burrell (g), Art Farmer (tpt), and Mal Waldron (p) on otherwise standard cuts. Limited edition release. —*Ron Wynn*

Roots / Oct. 25, 1957 Dec. 6, 1957 / Prestige 062
More big-band bop with a stellar cast that includes Cecil Payne, Pepper Adams, and Idrees Sulieman on saxes and Bill Evans on piano. —*David Szatmary*

○ **RCA Victor Jazz Workshop: the Arrangers** / Bluebird 6471

● **Ragtime Piano Originals** / Oct. 1974 / Smithsonian/Folkways 23

○ **Real Sound of Jazz, The** / Dec. 1985 / Pumpkin 116

● **Rhythm & Blues Sax Anthology** / Atlantic 81666

Riverside Presents...: History of Classic Jazz / Riverside 1575

● **Smithsonian Collection—Jazz Piano Vol. 1** / Smithsonian 0391

● **Smithsonian Collection—Jazz Piano Vol. 2** / Smithsonian 0392

● **Smithsonian Collection—Jazz Piano Vol. 3** / Smithsonian 0393

● **Smithsonian Collection—Jazz Piano Vol. 4** / Smithsonian 0394

☆ **Sound of Chicago: Jazz Odyssey—Vol.2** / Nov. 1964 / Columbia 32

☆ **Sound of Chicago: Jazz Odyssey—Vol.3** / Nov. 1964 / Columbia 33

○ **Memorable 1957 Telecast** / 1957 / CBS 45234

○ **Sound of Jazz, The** / May 1958 / Columbia 1098

● **Picante** / Concord Jazz 295
An anthology featuring cuts from various Afro-Latin and Latin-jazz artists. The roster includes Cal Tjader, Poncho Sanchez, Tania Maria, Tito Puente, Laurindo Almeida, Charlie Byrd, and Monty Alexander. —*Ron Wynn*

● **Spirituals to Swing** / Feb. 1973 / Columbia 30776

● **St. Louis Barrelhouse Piano (1929-1934)** / 1929-1934 / Document 5104

○ **Stride Piano Summit: a Celebration of Harlem...** / 1990 / Milestone 9189

Sullivan Years: Louie Armstrong, The / Tee Vee Toons 9427

An anthology from the recent collection featuring various material recorded on the long-running Ed Sullivan television show. This time it contains selections from the many times Louis Armstrong appeared on the program. Some marvelous playing and singing, juxtaposed with the usual large amounts of show business. —*Ron Wynn*

Swing Time! (1925-1955) / 1925 / Columbia 52862
Extensive multidisc set that presents overview of swing and big-band era with performances from numerous bands in hot, sweet, and pop contexts. The anthology hasn't been weighted toward any one period or style, and it doesn't necessarily offer all the genre's finest works. But it does give a thorough presentation of what defined the period and its appeal. —*Ron Wynn*

○ **This Is Acid Jazz** / Jan. 1991 / Instinct 2250

○ **Timeless All Stars: Time for the Timeless All Star** / Early Bird 101

○ **Town Hall Concert 1945** / 1945 / Commodore 7006

○ **Township Swing Jazz Vol. 1** / Harlequin 8

Tribute to John Coltrane—Live under the Sky / Dec. 20, 1991 / Columbia 45136

● **Tribute to Duke, A** / Concord Jazz 4050

Vocal Jazz / Adventures in Music 53

● **Hal Willner Presents Weird Nightmare: Meditations on Mingus** / Nov. 12, 1992 / Columbia 52739
Another installment in Hal Willner's series of tribute albums. This time, Willner assembled a house band for his guests (including Keith Richards, Chuck D, Elvis Costello, Bill Frisell, Vernon Reid, Charlie Watts, Gary Lucas, Leonard Cohen, and Henry Rollins) to sit in with. *Weird Nightmare—Meditations on Mingus* is predictably uneven and wildly entertaining; it is a fitting tribute to the genius of Charles Mingus —*AMG*

● **Women (Classic Female Jazz Artists: 1939-1952), The** / 1939-1952 / RCA 6755

Yazoo's History of Jazz / Yazoo 1070
Interesting approach, focuses on some of the label's quirkier, expressive artists from the '20s and '30s. —*Ron Wynn*

Young Lions, The / May 25, 1960 / Vee Jay 3013

GOSPEL

Religion has existed for thousands of years, but gospel music is just a few decades old. The term was coined by blues pianist Thomas A. Dorsey in 1920 soon after he wrote "If You See My Savior," his first religious song. After Dorsey established a firm that published his "Gospel" songs and those of others (the first such company), the name stuck.

Gospel music was born out of the blood, sweat, and tears of African slaves working on Southern plantations and in cotton fields. They attended segregated Protestant churches, where White ministers led them in worship. Over time, Blacks combined the Southern folk music, Protestant hymns, and European elements of the worship service with their African traditions and Negro spirituals (which were not religious songs but songs of vexation, e.g., "Nobody Knows the Trouble I've Seen"), and the distinct Black gospel sound was born.

In those early years, Gospel was segregated along racial lines: Southern gospel became a catchword for White gospel when Black gospel was equally Southern in its styling. Mahalia Jackson was the primary influence of her era, although the Swan Silvertones, the Clara Ward Singers, the Five Blind Boys, and others made significant contributions to early gospel. In Southern gospel, the Speers reigned "king of the charts," winning contracts on major labels such as Columbia and RCA, where they recorded such standards as "I'm Building a Bridge" and "I'll Meet You in the Morning."

As the 50s approached, there was a greater amalgamation of gospel, folk, and blues styles, which together were the foundation of rock & roll. Elvis Presley, Jerry Lee Lewis, and Little Richard were just a few of the singers with strong gospel backgrounds to make the leap into the secular arena. Groups like the Soul Stirrers and the Pilgrim Travelers supplied secular music with Sam Cooke, Johnnie Taylor, Lou Rawls, and others.

In the 70s, social movements began to influence what the White gospel young adults were recording. Artists such as Larry Norman pioneered "Jesus Rock." When a contemporary Christian music (CCM) magazine writer asked him if his 1969 *Upon This Rock* album was the first Christian rock album, Norman was cautious. "I can't really tell you if it was the first Christian rock album or not," he said. "I had never heard any. I was a Baptist, and the only Christian songs I had ever heard were the hymns and Negro spirituals .... So when Elvis Presley came along in 1956, and all those other boys, I thought, 'That's nothing new.' They were just stealing Black church music ... so I decided to steal it back."

A similar revolution was taking place among young Black musicians who had tired of the same old "church" beat. Edwin Hawkins has taken a lot of credit for sparking the contemporary Black gospel movement. Actually, Rance Allen was doing it better, and long before Hawkins.

Toward the very late 70s, Andrae Crouch did the unmentionable: he began making music that not only pleased his Black constituency and a progressive White audience but also touched mainstream pop. Amy Grant would later pick up on Crouch's theme and run with it.

During the 80s, gospel had its most lucrative decade to date. Many of the biggest hits were by women. Shirley Caesar and Tramaine Hawkins crisscrossed the traditional and contemporary Black audiences. Sandi Patti held down the inspirational arena as Amy Grant held the pop/rock youth market. Grant's success and subsequent influence in pop led to a lot of copycatting.

An area women did not get into was heavy metal, or heaven's metal as it's called in CCM. Bands that grew up on Aerosmith, Led Zeppelin, Black Sabbath, and other premier hard rock outfits, began to merge Christian lyrics with this type of music. Petra and Stryper are examples.

As the 90s kick in, the direction of the future is uncertain. Amy Grant has moved into the secular field, though she still commands a large gospel audience. Sandi Patti's records do well but don't strike gold as often. Now that the push for crossover success in the 80s has proven fruitless in most cases, gospel artists are returning to their music's roots and explicit message. After all, unadulterated gospel is the most intimate and emotional of all music forms. No matter what your usual music proclivity (be it country or rap), you'll find something in the following review that fits your musical tastes.

– Bil Carpenter

Jimmy A.

Co-founder of '80s alternative pop band Vector who has also worked extensively with Charlie Peacock, strikes out on his own with creative solo efforts that feature his exceptional guitar work and low-key vocal approach. — *Thom Granger*

○ **Entertaining Angels** / i. 1991 / Sparrow 1279
Appealing guitar-pop record in the Charlie Peacock tradition. Peacock appears here, as does vocalist Vince Ebo, most notably on "Thin but Strong Cord," where the two share lead vocals with Abegg. But it's Abegg's show down the line, as he writes and produces the bulk of the material, showing real promise. — *Brian Mansfield*

Abyssinian Baptist Gospel Choir

Group / Gospel
Prof. Alex Bradford directed this choir, some of whose members recorded with the famous Back Home Choir of Newark. — *Opal Louis Nations*

○ **Shakin' the Rafters** / i. 1960 / CBS 47335
An energetic choral release spotlighting one of the most popular, large (100-plus) vocal aggregations of the '60s. — *Ron Wynn*

Acappella

Group / Inspirational
Founded by Keith Lancaster, whose Church of Christ background did not permit instrumental music in worship, this male vocal en-

semble established itself making clever recordings using a variety of sounds, all created by the human voice. —*Thom Granger*

○ **Better Than Life** / **i.** 1987 / Word 9335-608
Soft, synchronized a cappella on original songs. —*Bil Carpenter*

Adam Again

CCM, Alternative pop/rock
Alternative rock act from Southern California whose early albums anticipated synthesis of rock and funk to be later expressed by groups like Red Hot Chili Peppers, Spin Doctors, etc. Group leader Gene Eugene is also a talented producer in Christian alternative music. —*Thom Granger*

In a New World of Time / **i.** 1987 / Blue Collar
Original Howard Finster cover let hipsters know something was worth checking out on this first effort. —*Thom Granger*

Ten Songs / **i.** 1988 / Broken
Band's style begins to solidify here. Includes a killer cover of Bill Withers' "Ain't No Sunshine." —*Thom Granger*

● **Homeboys** / **i.** 1990 / Broken
Urban rock music was met with urban concerns on this excellent collection, including a cover of Marvin Gaye's "Inner City Blues." —*Thom Granger*

Dig / Brainstorm
Emotionally powerful set was less than easy to listen to, due to clues that leader Eugene's marriage to vocalist Riki Michele was coming apart at the seams. —*Thom Granger*

Ric Alba

Vocals, guitar / Gospel
As a former singer/guitarist, Alba worked with the Christian alternative bands The Choir and the Altar Boys. —*Bil Carpenter*

○ **Holes in the Floor of Heaven** / **i.** 1991 / Glasshouse 7014700022
An album with abstract lyrics and a rock guitar focus, with a British sound. —*Bil Carpenter*

Rance Allen Group

Group / Soul, Rock, Black gospel
This Detroit-based, traditionally trained Black gospel group formed in the '60s and were the first traditional gospel group to incorporate rock, jazz, and soul into their music. They were harbingers for the contemporary Christian music movement popularized in the late '70s by Andrae Crouch, Amy Grant, and the Winans.
    Rance Allen scored a Top 30 R&B hit in 1979 with "I Belong To You," one of two Stax singles that year to make the charts. His recordings for Gospel Truth, Capitol, and Stax proved quite popular among gospel audiences, and had some success attracting soul fans as well. —*Bil Carpenter and Ron Wynn*

○ **Ain't No Need of Crying** / **i.** 1958 / Stax 8507
Rance Allen's brand of soul-tinged gospel was at its best on this '75 release. The title track cracked the R&B charts, and Allen's soaring voice, coupled with the fine harmonies provided by his brothers Tom, Steve, and Esau, as well as assistance from cousins Judy, Linda, and Annie Mendez, resulted in some arresting songs. —*Ron Wynn*

Straight from the Heart / **i.** 1972 / Stax 4109
Gospel singer Rance Allen enjoyed some crossover soul success in the early '70s, recording on Stax's Gospel Truth label. His explosive, soaring voice was especially effective on upper register notes and inspirational ballads. This was one of his biggest albums, especially the single "I Belong To You." —*Ron Wynn*

★ **Soulful Experience** / **i.** 1975 / Truth 4207
Another in a string of well-produced gospel albums that incorporated soul influences and relied on Rance Allen's booming, yet also anguished and soulful delivery. This LP contained examples of Allen's ability to explode in the upper register and generate a high-pitched cry that was dazzling and effective. —*Ron Wynn*

I Feel Like Goin' On / **i.** 1980 / Stax 4136
Although not as smartly produced or containing compositions as memorable as some earlier releases, Rance Allen still generated some mild R&B attention with this LP, as well as the usual good response in gospel circles. But the Allen style was becoming more predictable, and would soon lose favor as huge choirs and

slick, Urban Contemporary-style groups and artists began to dominate the modern gospel scene. —*Ron Wynn*

○ **Best of the Rance Allen Group** / **i.** 1988 / Stax 8540
Creative, influential hits with a Memphis flavor. —*Bil Carpenter*

Phenomenon / **i.** 1991 / Bellmark 71806
Consistent with earlier recordings. —*Bil Carpenter*

The Allies

Group / Gospel, CCM
This California-based melodic pop-style rock group, formed in the '80s by Jesus music vetrans Bob Carlisle and Randy Thomas, was influenced by blues/rockers and R&B groups. —*Bil Carpenter*

● **Shoulder to Shoulder** / **i.** 1988 / Dayspring 4164-627
Band's most commercial offering features mid '80s pop and power ballads, best exemplified by bands like Hall & Oates. —*Thom Granger*

Long Way to Paradise / **i.** 1989 / Dayspring 4174-622
A hard, bluesy rock sound. —*Bil Carpenter*

Margaret Allison

Vocals / Spiritual
Margaret Allison and the Angelic Gospel Singers formed in 1944. Their "Touch Me Lord Jesus" (Gotham) hit was #13 on R&B charts in August 1949. Traditional-style quartet music. Current lineup: Allison; Darryl and John Richmond; Frances Leggett; and Theresa McDowell. —*Bil Carpenter*

● **Out of the Depths** / **i.** 1987 / Malaco 4424
An album of traditional cuts featuring "It Could've Been the Other Way" and "Up above My Head." —*Bil Carpenter*

He's My Ever Present Help / **i.** 1992 / Malaco 4447
An album of new traditional favorites, most notably the title song and "I'll Go." —*Bil Carpenter*

My Sweet Home / Nashboro 7003
"Jesus Is All the World to Me" and "Goin' Over Yonder" are outstanding. —*Bil Carpenter*

Altar Boys

Group / CCM, Rock
Punk trio formed by guitarist Mike Stand in 1981. They opened for the Jesus and Mary Chain in the late '80s. —*Bil Carpenter*

● **Collection: Best of 1986-1991** / Frontline
Hard-edged rock music with introspective lyrics. —*Bil Carpenter*

Michael Anderson

CCM
Former A&M pop artist and successful songwriter ("Maybe It Was Memphis") now records for gospel label. —*Thom Granger*

Saints & Sinners / **i.** 1993 / ForeFront
An interesting mixture of pop, country, and southern rock styles. —*Thom Granger*

Inez Andrews

b. Oct. 19, 1935
Vocals, Soul, Spiritual
Inez Andrews' powerful contralto voice has been among gospel's greatest since her days with the Caravans in the late '50s. Andrews' nickname, "Songbird," was taken by Don Robey when he formed a gospel subsidiary label of his Backbeat/Peacock operation. Andrews was among the first gospel artists he signed. She later recorded for Savoy and Spirit Feel. Her most recent release was *Raise Up a Nation* with the Thompson Community Singers in 1991 for Word/Epic. —*Ron Wynn*

○ **Lord Don't Move the Mountain** / **i.** 1972 / MCA 20651
This crossover pop album has a traditional mood. —*Bil Carpenter*

The Two Sides of Inez Andrews / **i.** 1987 / Spirit Feel 1006
It is perhaps ironic that gospel music has the capacity to move secular audiences, the same listeners that dismiss most Christian music, and indeed most religious music, with distaste. Thus is the power of the great voice of Andrews. The gospel veteran is backed by a band that is grounded in the classic elements of the style: incisive piano, effusive electric organ. Surprisingly, the somewhat slick "New Name" (written by Andrews) is one of the highlights, though there are fine standards like "Lord, Lord, Lord." Though there is a balance between the explosive and reflective,

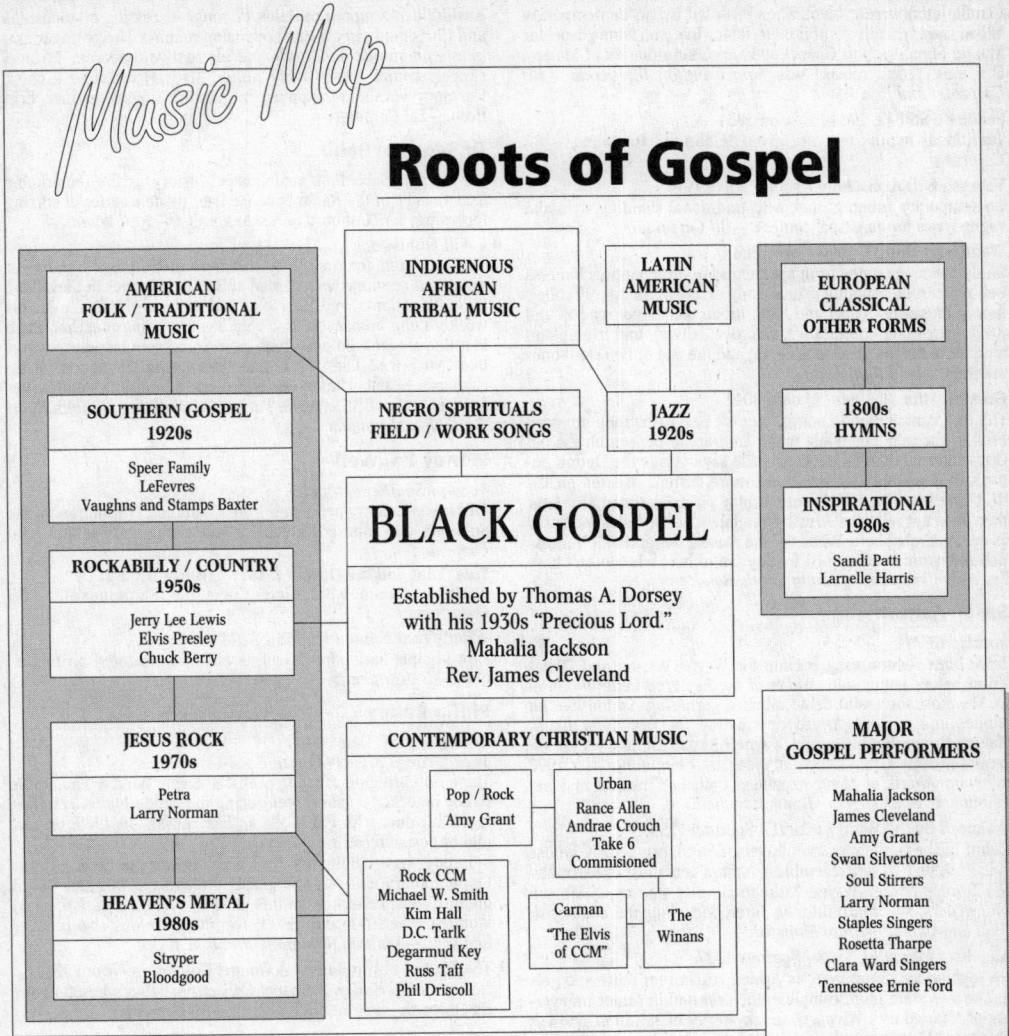

Music Map

Roots of Gospel

AMERICAN FOLK / TRADITIONAL MUSIC

INDIGENOUS AFRICAN TRIBAL MUSIC

LATIN AMERICAN MUSIC

EUROPEAN CLASSICAL OTHER FORMS

SOUTHERN GOSPEL 1920s
Speer Family
LeFevres
Vaughns and Stamps Baxter

NEGRO SPIRITUALS FIELD / WORK SONGS

JAZZ 1920s

1800s HYMNS

INSPIRATIONAL 1980s
Sandi Patti
Larnelle Harris

BLACK GOSPEL

Established by Thomas A. Dorsey with his 1930s "Precious Lord."
Mahalia Jackson
Rev. James Cleveland

ROCKABILLY / COUNTRY 1950s
Jerry Lee Lewis
Elvis Presley
Chuck Berry

JESUS ROCK 1970s
Petra
Larry Norman

CONTEMPORARY CHRISTIAN MUSIC

Pop / Rock
Amy Grant

Urban
Rance Allen
Andrae Crouch
Take 6
Commisioned

MAJOR GOSPEL PERFORMERS
Mahalia Jackson
James Cleveland
Amy Grant
Swan Silvertones
Soul Stirrers
Larry Norman
Staples Singers
Rosetta Tharpe
Clara Ward Singers
Tennessee Ernie Ford

HEAVEN'S METAL 1980s
Stryper
Bloodgood

Rock CCM
Michael W. Smith
Kim Hall
D.C. Tarlk
Degarmud Key
Russ Taff
Phil Driscoll

Carman
"The Elvis of CCM"

The Winans

Andrews is probably most effective singing those numbers that demand unbridled passion. Andrews proves that Christian music needn't be toothless and middle-of-the-road fare. —*Dorian Cohen, Option*

If Jesus Came to Your Town Today / i. 1988 / Miracle

This album features Inez Andrews' famous parched, wearied leads and earnest, at times serene tone. She includes one pop tune, Curtis Mayfield's "People Get Ready," although her version restores the spiritual/church element often missing from other renditions. "Praise the Lord" and "We've Got Work To Do" are the tribute pieces, while "If Jesus Came to Your Town Today" mixes a sociopolitical undercurrent with a plea for the believers to get their act together, and "We've Got Work To Do" reminds us of the tasks left undone. Andrews can still wail and shout, and it's great that she's getting the opportunity to do so without having to compete with a funk backbeat or multi-tracked synthesizers and cloying background vocalists. —*Ron Wynn, Rejoice*

Raise Up a Nation / i. 1991 / Word 48594

Traditional Black arrangements with choir backing. —*Bil Carpenter*

Angelo & Veronica

Italian macho heritage meets Puerto Rican feminine pluck in this husband and wife duo that occasionally out-Winans BeBe, CeCe, and the boys. —*Thom Granger*

○ **Higher Place** / i. Sep. 8, 1992 / A&M 540011
This soulful husband and wife team make a smashing debut with an 11-song set of powerful vocals and jamming instrumentation. Whether belting out ballads or growling out the dance grooves, the Petrucellis sing with a passion rarely heard in gospel or secular music these days. Co-producers Joe Hogue (Billy and Sarah Gaines, Larnelle Harris) and Fred Hammond (Commissioned) are to be applauded for putting together a fine first effort for a couple who are definitely headed for a higher place on the contemporary Christian music scene. —*Edwin Smith, Rejoice*

Vanessa Bell Armstrong

b. Oct. 2, 1953, Detroit, MI
Vocals / Dance, Soul, Gospel
Born in Detroit, MI, Armstrong is a belting R&B singer toeing the line between traditional and contemporary Black gospel.

Armstrong has juggled spiritual and secular music through the '80s and '90s. She did the theme song for the television series "Amen," where her links to Rev. Al Green (and ultimately to Rev.

Claude Jeter) were evident. She's recorded Urban Contemporary ballads and lyrically neutral material for Jive, and done gospel for Muscle Shoals Sound Gospel and Onyx, subsidiaries of Malaco. Her most recent release was *Something on the Inside*. —*Bil Carpenter and Ron Wynn*

○ **Peace Be Still** / **i.** 1984 / Benson 3831
Traditional hymns that are given "Holiness" treatment. —*Bil Carpenter*

Vanessa Bell Armstrong / **i.** 1987 / Jive 1074
Contemporary urban gospel, with traditional shouting style and vague lyrics for its gospel content. —*Bil Carpenter*

Wonderful One / **i.** 1990 / Jive 1200
While the songs range from spectacular to disappointing, Vanessa Bell Armstrong's singing is uniformly excellent on this '90 collection of crossover gospel and light, urban contemporary pop and R&B. Armstrong's declarative, assertive delivery and triumphant manner make the good songs great and the one or two great ones unforgettable. —*Ron Wynn*

● **Greatest Hits** / **i.** 1990 / Malaco 8012
This is a compilation of songs Vanessa Bell Armstrong recorded back in the mid '80s while under contract to Benson on the old Onyx International label. As the title says, this is the Detroit native's best product, for while her more current releases on the RCA/Jive label have had more airplay on mainstream airwaves, they have not reflected Armstrong's talent at her fullest potential as demonstrated here. Whatever the reason, this is classic Vanessa Bell Armstrong and a must for any fan of hers who doesn't have her earlier material. —*Edwin Smith, Rejoice*

Susan Ashton

Vocals / CCM
Texas-born Ashton sang backup for Wayne Watson and Dallas Holm before going solo. *Wakened by the Wind* became one of CCM's most successful debut albums, garnering Ashton five hit singles and a Dove Award nomination for Best New Artist. Having Brown Bannister and Wayne Kirkpatrick, two people essential in Amy Grant's success, didn't hurt her, either. Her 1992 followup *Angels of Mercy* expanded both her musical and her emotional vocabularies. —*Brian Mansfield*

Wakened by the Wind / **i.** 1991 / Sparrow 1259
Debut in the contemporary-folk vein, á la Shawn Colvin (whose voice Ashton's closely resembles). Ashton gets most of her material from producer Wayne Kirkpatrick, also one of CCM's top songwriters; she contributes to three, including the countryish "Ball and Chain." —*Brian Mansfield*

○ **Angels of Mercy** / **i.** 1992 / Sparrow 1327
No sophomore slump here, as Ashton reaches for more and gets it. The topics are more complex—the devastating rumor mongering of "Started as a Whisper," the mysteries of salvation, and fallibility in "Alice in Wonderland"—and the music is more dramatic. —*Brian Mansfield*

Audio Adrenaline

A '90s pop hybrid band, incorporating rock, rap and funk influences. —*Thom Granger*

Audio Adrenaline / ForeFront 2936
A decent debut, highlighted by the EMF-like single, "PDA (Public Display of Affection)." —*Thom Granger*

Don't Censor Me / **i.** 1993 / ForeFront
More pop-savvy and less edgy than its first, the band began to blow up big with singles like "Big House." —*Thom Granger*

John Austin

b. 1969
Vocals, guitar, harmonica / CCM
Born in Chicago, Austin began his career just after high school. He plays acoustic guitar and harmonica and writes most of his own material. He is one of the few rising voices in alternative Christian music. Based on his first effort alone, he's made a contribution to linking authentic gospel messages with uncommercial light-rock music/folk styles. His firm but mellow vocal style is reminiscent of '60s folk heroes such as the Byrds. —*Bil Carpenter*

○ **The Embarrassing Young** / **i.** 1992 / Glasshouse

Austin's debut album contains 12 songs discussing relationships and Christianity in a nonproselytizing manner. Heavy guitar emphasis on mostly light-rock and alternative-style cuts. Musical support comes from Buddy Miller, Mark Heard, and a choir. Harmony vocals are supplied by Austin's singing partner, Erin Echo. —*Bil Carpenter*

Dr. Morgan Babb

Dr. Morgan Babb first made gospel history as the remarkable lead vocalist of the Radio Four. He later made a series of stirring recordings for Nashboro as a solo vocalist. —*Ron Wynn*

● **I Will Not Bow**
This collection, first issued by Nashboro in 1975, is a grab-bag of songs and sermonettes recorded at Baptist churches in Cleveland, St. Louis, Atlanta, and Babb's own ministry in Nashville for his weekly radio broadcasts. Not only a soul-stirring preacher, Babb is a fine singer who adds both power and compassion to songs like "No Friend Like Jesus" and the rousing "Invitation." It includes an hilarious interview with Renate Johnstone, staff writer for the London BBC's "Radio Times." —*Opal Louis Nations, Roots & Rhythm Newsletter*

Wendy Bagwell

Vocals / Southern gospel
This folksy country performer from Chamblee, GA, sings with the Sunliters duo. She is known for humorous story-songs. —*Bil Carpenter*

○ **This, That and the Other** / **i.** 1971 / Heartwarming
A classic album with "Here Come the Rattlesnakes." —*Bil Carpenter*

What's That Name / **i.** 1988 / A&M 8404
Down-home, back-porch, Georgia pickin' is featured on this album. —*Bil Carpenter*

Philip Bailey

b. May 8, 1951, Denver, CO
Vocals, conga drums / Dance, Soul
The falsetto-singing co-lead vocalist in Earth, Wind & Fire, Philip Bailey launched a solo career during the band's hiatus, resulting in his hit duet with Phil Collins, "Easy Lover," in 1985. He also makes gospel records.
Bailey has continued the juggling act between Urban Contemporary material and gospel through the '80s and '90s. A greatest hits collection of his gospel singles was issued by Word/Epic in 1991, and his LP *Family Affair* was also reissued that year. —*William Ruhlmann and Ron Wynn*

● **The Best of Philip Bailey: A Gospel Collection** / Word 77004
Best of Philip Bailey: A Gospel Collection. Bailey's falsetto voice rips through inspiring R&B gospel. —*Bil Carpenter*

Bishop Jeff Banks

Vocals / Black gospel
The Banks Brothers were pupils of Mary Johnson Davis. They enjoyed some success teaming with the Greater Harvest Choir in the '60s for Savoy. —*Ron Wynn*

○ **Caught Up in the Rapture** / **i.** 1987 / Savoy 14787
A traditional spiritual choir sound. Donald Malloy sings. —*Bil Carpenter*

Love Lifted Me / Savoy 14749
Traditional Black gospel. —*Bil Carpenter*

Willie Banks & the Messengers

Group / Black gospel
Willie Banks is the ex-leader of the Jackson Southernaires. —*Opal Louis Nations*

Look at the Blessings / **i.** 1986 / Malaco 4428
Willie Banks sang with the Flying Clouds in the '40s, and has maintained with his own group, The Messengers, an awareness of the old gospel style despite often incorporating lyrics with a more modern tinge. On *Look at the Blessings*, for example, such songs as "Can't Keep From Crying Sometimes" use an image very familiar in soul music, although Banks and company don't even suggest a pop tilt. Other songs, such as "He's Bringing Love to the Nation" and "A Prayer for the Children," could fit into a broadminded urban or Black station's playlist, due to their dual inspi-

rational themes of religious salvation and social emancipation. Banks is a strong, distinctive vocalist, and the engineering and production keep the voices at the top, spread-out keyboards on the bottom, and ensure that the guitar and bass parts are adequately heard. Thus, while it's clear that this was done recently, it doesn't compare unfavorably to many of Banks' past gospel releases. —*Ron Wynn*

● **Heaven Must Be a Beautiful Place** / MCA 20611
Very soulful early '70s sides. —*Hank Davis*

○ **Masterpiece** / Malaco 4437
Engaging modern gospel with some deep harmony. —*Hank Davis*

Barnes & Brown

Group / Black gospel
Rev. F.C. Barnes and Janice Brown of North Carolina, where they are pastors at Red Budd Holy Church in Rocky Mountain, came together to record many traditional albums in the '80s. —*Bil Carpenter*

○ **Rough Side of the Mountain** / i. 1980 / Atlanta 10059
Mellow, bluesy, traditional Black gospel. —*Bil Carpenter*

Luther Barnes

Black gospel
The brother of F.C. Barnes (of Barnes & Brown), Luther Barnes combines traditional excitement with contemporary backbeats. He leads the Red Budd Choir. —*Bil Carpenter*

○ **See What the Lord Has Done** / i. 1987 / Atlanta 10116
Upbeat, testimonial-style traditional cuts. —*Bil Carpenter*

The Barrett Sisters

b. Dec. 3, 1926, Chicago, IL (Delois)
Vocals / Black gospel
Delois, Billie, and Rodessa Barrett began singing in the Chicago-based Morning Star Baptist Church in the '40s as children. Under the direction of their aunt, Mattie Dacus, they were originally known as the Barrett and Hudson Singers before becoming the Barrett Sisters. Delois was recruited for the Roberta Martin Singers while a high school senior at Englewood High. After graduation, she joined Martin's group full time and remained a member for 18 years. Rodessa Barrett became a choral director of Galileo Baptist church and Billie Barrett became a church soloist after taking voice lessons at the American Music Conservatory. They formed the Barrett Sisters in 1962 and have remained together ever since. Their first LP was recorded for Savoy in 1963. They currently record for I Am Records in Chicago. —*Ron Wynn*

○ **Nobody Does It Better** / Word 3815-87
Here's one of the hottest gospel albums ever from this great trio. Their shimmering voices and precise yet spontaneous-sounding interaction on every tune expertly conveys gospel's hypnotic charm. They're particularly inspiring on "Christ Is All," "Rapture," "All My Help," and "Nobody But Jesus." They haven't de-emphasized the overt religious base of the songs or tried to hedge the themes and lyrics. But anyone who doubted whether a trio could sustain the same clout and drive as a quartet or large group should hear "Walk and Talk" or "Fly Away": the Barretts can sing up a storm. —*Ron Wynn, Rejoice*

What a Wonderful World / I Am 4006
A more contemporary production, geared toward fans of a modern approach. —*Ron Wynn*

● **What Will You Do with Your Life** / Savoy 14683
Classic "golden age" gospel, shouting vocals, and tight harmonies. —*Ron Wynn*

Live! Nobody Does It Better / A&M 8428
This classic female gospel group, who through lead singer Delores Barrett Campbell trace their roots to the Roberta Martin Singers, scored a winner with this record. This album finally lived up to their electrifying live appearances and was a great improvement over some prior releases. The sound was sharp, the vocals weren't drowned by the instrumental accompaniment, and the "live" in the title referred to a digital recording session in a Chicago studio rather than in front of an audience. This might have been the best album they'd done up to that time (1989). —*Russell Schoenwetter, Roots & Rhythm Newsletter*

Southern White Gospel

Gospel songs from the beginning formed a large part of the country music repertoire. Two subgroups quickly formed. First came the traditional British ecclesiastical songs, reflecting a fundamental Protestant view of life as a vale of tears and suffering. But another form of gospel songs, one that tolerated joy in both worlds, became increasingly popular because of the upbeat, optimistic message of its lyrics and its fast-tempo melody. Whatever the mood of the musicians and audience, there was an appropriate gospel song: If you are feeling unreasonably good, "This World Is Not My Home" will bring you crashing back to earth; but if your daily life has so much real woe and suffering that a gospel dirge would be the last nail in your coffin, then request the band to play "I'll Fly Away" or "God Put a Rainbow in the Cloud." Southerners, Black and White alike, found gospel music a contrast to country music's standard fare of songs about family and home, good love and broken love, working men and failures, rambling and jail.

Most of country's great performers learned gospel music first, and a large number have returned to it after the pressures of the business drove them to self-destruction – in the old days with alcohol, but more recently with drugs. Thus, gospel songs often have saved not only the audience but the singers, who in the very act of singing "Amazing Grace" have found what the lyrics promise.

Because the church often offered the only opportunity for singing and musicmaking (fiddle and banjo music especially were thought to be the devil's music in the old days), country performers since the 50s have made it standard fare to record a gospel album after "making it" with mass-audience material. The Carter Family, Uncle Dave Macon, Roy Acuff, Bill Monroe, Hank Williams, Red Foley, Tennessee Ernie Ford, Elvis Presley, George Jones, Ricky Skaggs – these are only a few of the legions of country stars who have showcased gospel music in their careers. Bluegrass music, with its base of tradition, emphasizes gospel songs, often sung a cappella. The Lewis Family is the best example of a bluegrass/country group that has created a high reputation over many years by performing gospel and pretty much only gospel. Meanwhile, the Oak Ridge Boys, the epitome of country/rock in the 80s, began as a gospel group. So did the Statler Brothers, who toured as the Kingsmen with Johnny Cash in 1963. Southern gospel is now a subgenre of country music, with its own charts and awards and many groups who perform nothing but gospel. From the earliest country recordings through the most recent, gospel has permeated country music.

– David Vinopal

Sweet Emma Barrett

b. Mar. 25, 1897, New Orleans, LA, **d.** Jan. 28, 1983, New Orleans, LA
Piano, Vocals / Blues, Ballads, Gospel
Stalwart performer with powerhouse vocal technique and bluesy, driving pianist as well. Barrett's career began in the early '20s, and she became known as the "bell gal" for her habit of wearing red garters with bells that jingled while she sang and played. Barrett was part of the Original Tuxedo Orchestra in the '20s and '30s. The group was initially co-led by Papa Celestin and William Ridgley, then Ridgley took over from 1925-1936. Barrett also sang and played with Sidney Desvigne, John Robichaux and A.J. Piron. She appeared at Happy Landing in the '50s, and became a Preservation Hall regular after 1961. Barrett toured with their traveling band overseas, and also did dates outside New Orleans. She overcame a 1967 stroke that caused paralysis on her left side,

and kept performing playing only with her right hand until her death. —*Ron Wynn*

● **Sweet Emma Barrett and Her New Orleans Music** / Sep. 1963 / Southland 241

This is both classic blues, done in the requisite sassy, double-entendre fashion, and traditional jazz that also touches on gospel, brass band and other pop styles. Though not the finest pure singer, Sweet Emma could belt out numbers and make suggestive remarks with abandon. —*Ron Wynn*

Martha and Fontella Bass

b. Jul. 3, 1940, St. Louis, Missouri
Vocals / R&B, Gospel
They are progressive gospel singers, although Fontella is better known for her R&B hit "Rescue Me." —*Michael G. Nastos*

○ **From the Root to The Source** / i. 1980 / Soul Note 1006
Traditional and gospel music updated. Quintessential music, with Amina Myers on piano. —*Michael G. Nastos*

○ **Martha Sings Mahalia** / Chess 91534
Martha Bass paid homage to the great Mahalia Jackson with poignant, exuberantly performed versions of her best songs. Although neither as gifted as Jackson (who is?) nor coming exactly from her more formalized gospel tradition, Bass nonetheless offered creditable tributes to gospel's all-time queen, while also demonstrating her own considerable powers. —*Ron Wynn*

Helen Baylor

Vocals / Soul, Gospel, CCM
Toured with *Hair*. Former backup for Aretha Franklin, Chaka Khan, B.B. King, and others. —*Bil Carpenter*

● **Highly Recommended** / i. 1990 / Word 47763
Modern pop/soul with class. The title says it all. —*Bil Carpenter*

Look a Little Closer / i. 1991 / Word 48781
More Southern R&B-infused than her debut. Highly Recommended. —*Bil Carpenter*

Margaret Becker

Vocals, guitar / CCM
The hardest female rocker/guitarist in CCM, she was influenced by a variety of styles that she incorporates into a unique sound, most built on guitar arrangements. Her hardy vocals cut through any style. —*Bil Carpenter*

Never for Nothing / i. 1987 / Sparrow 1134
A debut with strident proselytizing. —*Bil Carpenter*

The Reckoning / i. 1988 / Sparrow 1161
Spiritual renewal and thickly textured rock music. —*Bil Carpenter*

○ **Immigrant's Daughter** / i. 1990 / Sparrow 1202
She sings about degrees of holiness. Minimalist rock. —*Bil Carpenter*

Simple House / i. 1991 / Sparrow 1261
British influences on the usual power rock. —*Bil Carpenter*

★ **Steps of Faith 1985-1992** / i. 1992 / Sparrow 1354
Becker's best, with a heavy emphasis on *Immigrant's Daughter* and *Simple House*, shows just what a talented pop stylist she is. The one new cut, "This Love," is essential Becker. —*Brian Mansfield*

Soul / i. May 18, 1993 / Sparrow 51343
Shows movement toward European pop/R&B, influenced by artist Annie Lennox and producer Charlie Peacock. —*Thom Grainger*

Margaret Bell

Vocals / Soul, R&B, Gospel, CCM
Younger sister of Vanessa Bell Armstrong. A former commercial jingle singer, she is married to Keith Byars of the Philadelphia Eagles. —*Bil Carpenter*

○ **Over & Over** / i. 1991 / Reprise 26345
A strong voice on refined crossover pop/R&B. —*Bil Carpenter*

Bob Bennett

One of CCM's more thoughtful singer-songwriters, featuring acoustic pop á la James Taylor and introspective lyrics. —*Thom Granger*

Songs from Bright Ave. / i. Sep. 1991 / Urgent! 2837
A painfully honest account of Bennett's impending divorce, not easily received by CCM fans. —*Thom Granger*

● **Lord of the Past** / Urgent! 2789
A fine anthology of Bennett's best songs, with a few new ones thrown in for good measure. —*Thom Granger*

Lisa Bevill

Vocals / CCM
Dance-pop diva who focuses on the teen audience with pumped-up tracks about chastity and clean living. Formerly sang backup for David Meece. —*Brian Mansfield*

○ **My Freedom** / i. 1992 / Sparrow 2201
A Christian record with an emphasis on dance. Heavily textured tracks like "My Freedom" and "Place in the Sun" dominated pop-oriented Christian radio during much of the spring and summer of 1992. —*Brian Mansfield*

Scott Blackwell

Former secular club DJ/mixmaster who brought his skills to the church, causing youth group leaders worldwide to decide whether or not dancing is a sin. —*Thom Granger*

Walk on the Wild Side / i. 1992 / Myx
Producer Blackwell introduces original tunes and his stable of vocalist proteges intended to move feet. —*Thom Granger*

Myx'd Trip to a Gospel House, A / i. 1992 / Myx
Several classic contemporary gospel tunes are fairly radically remixed with a house attack, with fun results. —*Thom Granger*

Robert Blair & the Fantastic Violinaires

Group / Black gospel
Blair began his contemporary quartet group in the '60s and became known for his Julius-Cheeks-like falsetto shouting and raving. The group has recorded up to the present. While their recent Air Records albums have been good, their best music was recorded in the '60s on the Chess and Checker labels. —*Bil Carpenter*

○ **The Pink Tornado** / i. 1988 / Air
Smooth, old-style traditional gospel, with Blair's renowned panting on the title track. A younger member does falsetto on "People Get Ready." —*Bil Carpenter*

Sing with the Angels / Malaco 4415
Strong material with passionate vocals. —*Hank Davis*

○ **Today Is the Day** / Malaco 4399
Excellent modern gospel from an eight-man "quintet." —*Hank Davis*

● **Their Greatest Sides, Vol. 1** / MCA 91526
A collection of some of their best Chess album sides from the '50s and '60s, featuring Robert Blair. Includes "Mother Used to Hold Me," a song known to reduce entire audiences to tears. —*Billy C. Wirtz*

Bloodgood

b. Washington, D.C.
Group / Heaven's Metal, Hard rock
Straightahead power metal band. —*Bil Carpenter*

Alive in America
Bassist Michael Bloodgood and the trio of born-again metalheads, with which he has recorded four studio albums, can definitely rock. They also have a knack of isolating Christianity's more intense and violent imagery so that the message fits the medium—lots of invoking of the Apocalypse and the crucifixion. Still, in music whose very existence is a result of, and response to, the ugliness of Western decay, this live album finds Christian metal in finer form than Christian punk ever was. —*Arsenio Orteza, Rejoice*

Shakin' The World (Bloodgood Live)
Bloodgood vocalist Les Carlsen's phlegmy pipes, while resilient, are ultimately typical of why metal doesn't cross over. It's too ugly

too much of the time. But *Shakin' The World* contains "Crucify," in which Carlsen plays Pilate and the backup singers scream for blood, and "Eat The Flesh," a peculiarly meaty Eucharistic celebration for brethren as Protestant as these. —*Arsenio Orteza, Rejoice*

Detonation / i. 1987 / Frontline 9019
Metal by rote. It's not innovative, but a good sound. —*Bil Carpenter*

● **Rock in a Hard Place / i.** 1988 / Frontline 09036
Mainstream metal sound with strong melodies and lyrics. —*Bil Carpenter*

Debby Boone

b. Sep. 22, 1956, Hackensack, NJ
Vocals / Gospel, Inspirational
This light-voiced singer was born in Hackensack, NJ, and is especially known for the #1 pop hit, "You Light up My Life" (1979). She has done easy-listening albums followed by a string of CCM and inspirational albums. —*Bil Carpenter*

○ **Friends for Life / i.** 1987 / Benson 3034
This is an inspirational/pop offering, featuring "Every Generation." —*Bil Carpenter*

● **Reflections / i.** 1988 / Benson 3014
Her biggest gospel hits. —*Bil Carpenter*

Kim Boyce

b. 1961, FL
CCM
Born in Florida, Boyce rejected a network news position to go into the music ministry. —*Bil Carpenter*

○ **Time and Again / i.** 1988 / Myrrh 6861-619
Christian dance music that would make Madonna jealous. —*Bil Carpenter*

This I Know / i. 1991 / Myrrh 6905-616
There's an urban and rhythm focus on this Tim Miner production. —*Bil Carpenter*

Prof. Alex Bradford

b. 1926, Bessemer, AL, **d.** Feb. 15, 1978, Newark, NJ
Vocals / Black gospel
Born in Bessemer, AL, and influenced by the Blue Jays and Swan Silvertones, Bradford sang with groups such as the Protective Harmoneers, the Birdettes, and the Banks Family. He formed the Bradford Specials in 1954, an eight-man chorale, and appeared in "Black Nativity" and other musicals. Nicknamed "The Professor," he is known for the cuts "Let God Abide" and "Walking with the King." —*Bil Carpenter*

○ **Too Close / i.** 1953-1958 / Specialty 7042
This 29-song package includes his biggest hits, particularly the incredible "Too Close to Heaven," a remarkable three-minute piece that merges theatrics, lyrical metaphors and fire-breathing vocals into a transcendent tour de force. There's also seven newly released numbers, including "Move Upstairs," a 1958 duet between Bradford and Bessie Griffin that turns the song inside out and back around again. —*Ron Wynn*

● **The Best of Alex Bradford / Specialty 2133**
A comprehensive selection of his fiery, stomping cuts with the Bradford Specials all-male quintet on Specialty Records. —*Ron Wynn*

He Lifted Me / Specialty 2143
A good "hard gospel" outing, spiced with animated leads from Bradford. —*Ron Wynn*

○ **Rainbow in the Sky / Specialty 7015**
A broad range of formats and self-penned songs by one of gospel's greatest writers, producers, and soloists. Some issued for the first time here (ca. 1954-58). —*Opal Louis Nations*

Walking with the King / Savgos 5007
Prof. Alex Bradford delivered a series of smashing, aggressive, animated hard gospel anthems here, singing with the fire and fury normally associated with Golden Age material, yet also incorporating some elements of modern production. While not quite as majestic as Brother Joe May, Bradford could moan, shout, and holler with almost any singing evangelist, and he demonstrated that on these numbers. —*Ron Wynn*

Gospel Terms

BLACK GOSPEL – An art form that is essentially Black in tone. The term was coined around the popularity of Thomas Dorsey's "Precious Lord." Black gospel is usually traditional music, often choir-oriented. Mahalia Jackson, Clara Ward Singers, James Cleveland, etc.

CONTEMPORARY CHRISTIAN MUSIC – Picked up where Jesus rock left off, incorporating more funky and harder music elements, often soft-rock. Amy Grant, Michael W. Smith, and BeBe & CeCe Winans are such performers.

HEAVEN'S METAL – "Heavy metal meets gospel lyrics" is how this style is best defined. Strong bass lines, electric/amplified guitar riffs, and steel drumming. Stryper, Bloodgood, and the latter-day Petra coterie exemplify this form.

INSPIRATIONAL – Not unlike middle-of-the-road (MOR) music in the pop sphere, easy-listening, or adult contemporary. Heavy on strings and grandiose orchestrations. Sandi Patti, Dallas Holm, and Dino fall into this category.

JESUS ROCK – A contemporary "White" music style popularized in the late 60s and early 70s, coinciding with the Jesus movement. Pioneers of the form brought rhythm & blues, rock & roll, and folk elements into standard praise tunes. Larry Norman and Randy Stonehill were among the purveyors of the form.

QUARTET SINGING – Based on the old barbershop quartet styles, with gospel lyrics. Usually four-part harmony performed by traditional Black gospel or Southern gospel musicians. Usually performed by males.

SOUTHERN GOSPEL – A country music gospel art form with emphasis on steel and rhythm guitars as its foundation. Draws on bluegrass, blues, and hillbilly elements. Southern gospel groups tend to use four-part harmony with a high tenor and baritone. The Happy Goodmans, the Speers, and Gold City are examples.

SPIRITUAL – A Black gospel art form rising from the Negro spirituals and blues tradition. Characterized by wailing and guttural sounds. Inez Andrews and Shirley Caesar are examples.

STREET POETRY – Whether the term developed in Christian circles is uncertain; however, Christian rap musicians prefer this term to "rap." An urban, funk style of rap with, in this case, Christian lyrics.

– Bil Carpenter

Bride

One of CCM's hardest rocking outfits, lead singer Dale Thompson resembles Guns N' Roses' Axl Rose at times. —*Thom Granger*

Live to Die / Pure Metal 7900602933
This album by Bride contains no ballads and is chock full of straight-ahead metal. Lyrically the album is more graphic than most. "Hell No" is a far too clever and precious attempt to appear they are swearing. No doubt it's an attempt to relate to secular kids. This album is much like Stryper and their "To Hell With The Devil" campaign, only less original. —*Devlin Donaldson, Rejoice*

Willmer Broadnax

b. 1916
Vocals / Black gospel
This bespectacled, dynamic lead tenor worked with various groups in Southern California before gaining a wider audience when he joined the Spirit of Memphis in 1950. Listed variously during his career as Willmer, Wilmer, Wilbur, and Willie "Little Ax" Broadnax, the "ringing tenor" led the Southern Gospel Singers, the Golden Echoes, and later the Spirit of Memphis Quartet during the '50s. —*Bil Carpenter & Kip Lornell*

○ **So Many Years** / Gospel Jubilee 1403
Broadnax's unique and influential voice in a variety of settings following World War II. —*Kip Lornell*

Brooklyn All-Stars

Group / Gospel
A late '50s male quartet featuring Hardie Clifton on leads. They recorded several cuts for Peacock in 1959, including "Rest Awhile" and "Meet Me in Galilee." —*Bil Carpenter*

○ **Our Greatest Hits** / Nashboro 27183
Powerful material drawn from a variety of '60s and '70s Nashboro albums, led principally by the soaring tenor of the underrated Hardie Clifton. —*Opal Louis Nations*

Rev. Milton Brunson

Vocals / Black gospel
He founded the Chicago-based Thompson Community Singers in 1948 and is pastor of Christ Tabernacle Baptist Church in that city. —*Bil Carpenter*

● **Available to You** / **i.** 1988 / Word 5027-658
Traditional, Black mass choir music. —*Bil Carpenter*

Open Our Eyes / **i.** 1990 / Word 47826
More of the same as *Available to You.* —*Bil Carpenter*

My Mind Is Made Up / **i.** Feb. 25, 1992 / Word 48784
Rev. Milton Brunson and The Thompson Community Singers follow up their immensely popular *Open Our Eyes* project of two years ago with yet another collection of strong songs and intricate choral arrangements. The standouts are the title cut and "He Will Deliver," but there's not a weak number in the set. —*Edwin Smith, Rejoice*

Shirley Caesar

b. Oct. 13, 1938, Durham, NC
Vocals / Spiritual
Born in Durham, NC, Caeser sang with the Caravans in the early '60s before going solo in 1966. A strict traditionalist known for her shouting style and evangelizing messages. —*Bil Carpenter*

First Lady / **i.** 1977 / Hob 3515
Secular songs and Christian themes are mixed here. —*Bil Carpenter*

Live in Chicago with Rev. Milton Brunson & The Thompson Community Singers / **i.** 1988 / Word 5021-65
Traditional Black gospel testifying, singing, and storytelling, recorded with the Thompson Community Singers and Albertina Walker. —*Bil Carpenter*

Celebration / **i.** 1990 / Myrrh 8299
Like all the great gospel singers, Shirley Caesar is a survivor; she began with the Caravans, and she's still a star. Sheer vocal talent aside, and as this fine pop-gospel hit album from a couple of years ago confirms, she has always managed to steer a course between conservatism and selling out, in the enduring gospel tradition of drawing on the secular music of its time. —*John Storm Roberts, Original Music*

● **Her Very Best** / **i.** 1991 / Word 47806
This collection is taken from four of her '80s Word albums, plus two unreleased cuts (10 in all). Moments of glory include the choir-backed "Jesus, I Love Calling Your Name," and "Sailing on the Sea of Your Love" with Al Green sharing lead vocals (both are album title cuts). The set also features an extremely interesting rendition, in good Nashville style, of the country gospel classic "No Charge." —*Opal Louis Nations, Roots & Rhythm Newsletter*

○ **I Remember Mama** / **i.** Feb. 25, 1992 / Word 9108-601
Shirley Caesar's poignant remembrances of her mother set the stage for this album that mixed sentimental fare with rockin' evangelism and surging performances. No Golden Age gospel artists have been more successful at retaining their zeal while adapting to contemporary production and arranging tendencies than Caesar. She doesn't compromise her lyrical message, but will hold still for electronics, strings, and even an occasional funk backbeat. This resulted in another hit LP for a gospel legend. —*Ron Wynn*

Jesus, I Love Calling Your Name / **i.** Apr. 28, 1992 / Word 47811
More fervent lyrical material from Shirley Caesar, backed by both choral and contemporary production and arrangements. The

results weren't always successful, but when they clicked, they were masterful. The title track was a sizable hit on gospel radio, and Caesar continued her string of successful LPs that blended traditional vocals and modern/mainstream voicings and backing. —*Ron Wynn*

○ **Sailin'** / **i.** Apr. 28, 1992 / Word 48800
Shirley Caesar and Rev. Al Green made a magnificent team on the title track, which helped win each a Grammy. Caesar's evocative leads and Green's shimmering harmonies and equally spectacular leads were a session highlight, although there were some other fine numbers spotlighting Caesar as well. —*Ron Wynn*

○ **Rejoice** / Myrrh 8106
The title track featured Shirley Caesar in peak form, soaring, shouting, and declaring her love for God. The LP overall wasn't quite as strong as some other Caesar releases, lacking consistent material or top performances. Still, Caesar often managed to salvage things solely with her vocal power and personality. —*Ron Wynn*

● **The Best of Shirley Caesar with the Caravans** / Savoy 14202
This anthology covers Caesar's Savoy material during the period when she initally left the Caravans. It's mostly traditional gospel, often superbly performed, though not as well produced or engineered as her later releases for Word. —*Ron Wynn*

Steve Camp

Vocals / CCM, Inspirational
A well-read and opinionated singer/songwriter, Camp infuses his scholarly knowledge and themes into his music. —*Bil Carpenter*

○ **Consider the Cost** / **i.** 1991 / Sparrow 1272
Bible-based songs with pop and inspirational sounds. —*Bil Carpenter*

Caravans

Arguably the greatest women's gospel group ever, the Caravans at one time included Albertina Walker, Inez Andrews, and "Little" Shirley Caesar, with Rev. James Cleveland on piano. Later, the group also included Cassietta George. They recorded for Savoy through the '50s and '60s. —*Ron Wynn*

★ **Till I Meet The Lord**
The collection here is taken from the two Vee-Jay albums recorded in the early '60s between two lengthy contracts with Herman Lubinsky's Savoy label. Featured singers include founder, manager, and lead Albertina ("Tina") Walker, ably supported by Cassietta George, the great Shirley Caesar, and Josephine Howard, supported by James Herndon and Kenneth Woods on organ and piano. There's some fine high-spirited moments with Walker's raspy wails and Caesar's amazing glissandos. —*Opal Louis Nations, Roots & Rhythm Newsletter*

○ **The Best of the Caravans** / Savoy 7012
This doesn't necessarily contain their best material, only those songs that garnered either chart success or radio airplay during the '50s and early '60s. Like all Savoy releases, there's almost no discographical information, although Walker, Andrews, and Caesar are the artists featured most prominently. —*Ron Wynn*

Michael Card

b. Apr. 11, 1957
Banjo, piano, dulcimer, guitar, violin / Inspirational
Called the "Christian Dan Fogelberg" for his folk guitar style and Bible-based songs, Card learned the banjo from country legend Earl Scruggs and later picked up piano, dulcimer, guitar, and violin. He dropped out of a Ph.D. program to go into the music business. —*Bil Carpenter*

○ **The Final Word** / **i.** 1987 / Sparrow 1126
Pensive, acoustic, and spiritually correct. —*Bil Carpenter*

The Way of Wisdom / **i.** 1991 / Sparrow 1223
Superb, with mellow instrumentation and potent lyrics. —*Bil Carpenter*

● **Joy in the Journey** / **i.** 1994 / Sparrow
Card's best known songs are collected here, with the earliest ones newly re-recorded for this album. —*Thom Granger*

Carman

b. Jan. 19, 1956

Vocals / CCM
Born Dominic Licciardello. He was "saved" at an Andrae Crouch concert. After he was discovered by Bill Gaither, he started his own ministry with a recording arm. He sings in CCM and R&B formats, with a heavy evangelistic message. —*Bil Carpenter*

○ **Live . . . Radically Saved** / i. 1988 / Benson 2463
A breakthrough album with Christian rap, R&B, and a little rock. —*Bil Carpenter*

Shakin' the House / i. 1991 / Benson 2681
A live Black gospel revival set with Commissioned and the Christ Church Choir. —*Bil Carpenter*

● **The Absolute Best** / i. 1993 / Sparrow 51339
A collection of what this unconventional artist does best, spotlighting his story-songs and hits and featuring one new song produced by David Foster. —*Thom Granger*

The Standard / i. Sep. 27, 1993 / Sparrow Records 51387
Carman tries his hand at some new musical directions, with less extended stories and more song-oriented material, alienating some old fans but winning some new ones in the process. —*Thom Granger*

Sister Wynona Carr

b. Aug. 23, 1924, Cleveland, OH, **d.** 1976
Vocals / R&B, Gospel
One of the top gospel artists on the Specialty label during the early '50s, Carr later made some fine R&B. Born in Cleveland, Carr moved to Detroit and joined Rev. C.L. Franklin's New Bethel Baptist Church Choir. She began cutting gospel as Sister Wynona Carr for Los Angeles-based Specialty in 1949, enjoying success with "The Ball Game." Carr went secular in 1955, rocking out on "Boppity Bop (Boogity Boop)" and "Nursery Rhyme Rock." Her lone R&B chart item in 1957, the bluesy "Should I Ever Love Again," was covered by rockabilly great Gene Vincent.
    Wynona Carr's secular and gospel material has recently been reissued by Fantasy, the holders of the Specialty catalog. —*Bill Dahl*

○ **Jump Jack Jump!** / i. 1985 / Specialty 2157
This 24-track set covers her R&B tunes, with many unissued but fine tunes such as "If These Walls Could Speak," "Finders Keepers," and "Weather Man" finally getting out of the vault. The CD also includes her trademark upbeat, sassy songs "Jump Jack Jump," "Boppity Bop (Boogity Boop)," "Ding Dong Daddy," and "Nursery Rhyme Rock." Thematic variety wasn't a label strong suit when it came to Carr's material, and they might have done better with more numbers like "Please Mr. Jailer" and "It's Raining Outside" and fewer boogies and jump pieces. Carr eventually left Specialty, recorded some nicely performed but commercially limp material for Reprise, then faded into obscurity. This CD, as well as her Specialty gospel cuts, show she deserved a better fate. —*Ron Wynn*

★ **Dragnet for Jesus** / i. 1992 / Specialty 7016
This first-ever retrospective of Wynona Carr's gospel period with Specialty (1949-54) showcases a truly dazzling singer and innovative lyricist. Included in the 26 tracks (17 of them previously unreleased) are her biggest hit, "The Ball Game," "15 Rounds for Jesus," and the wonderful (but never released) title track. Throughout, Carr's work swings with a sure-footed sense of joy, devotion, and an underlying sexiness that is as delightful as it is unexpected. There are two fine duets with Brother Joe May, including the great "I See Jesus." Worth the price of the CD alone is the final cut, a hypnotic 1954 performance of "Our Father" with the Rev. C.L. Franklin and his New Bethel Baptist Church Choir; Carr's house-wrecking, completely uninhibited vocal shakes the rafters. Perhaps a young Aretha Franklin was listening. Essential. —*Christine Ohlman, Roundup Newsletter*

Bruce Carroll

Mellow acoustic-based country pop singer-songwriter, closer to James Taylor than Ricky Skaggs. —*Thom Granger*

★ **Sometimes Miracles Hide** / i. Nov. 12, 1991 / Word 48782
Bruce Carroll has few peers in the country/adult contemporary Christian market and they (Paul Overstreet and Wayne Kirkpatrick) appear on this CD. Also lending a hand are Ricky Skaggs, Vince Gill, Mark O'Connor, Twila Paris, Tom Hemby, and Brown Bannister. Enclosed in this package are 10 songs encour-

aging, celebrating, and examining the Christian life. This is Carroll's fourth Christian album and he consistently raises the standards of the industry and broadens his new country genre. —*Pepper Smith, Rejoice*

The Cathedrals

Group / Southern gospel
Formed in 1965, this traditional Southern gospel group appeared regularly on Rex Humbard's "Cathedral of Tomorrow" broadcast in the '60s. The Cathedrals are led by George Younce and Glen Payne, who are known for their on-stage humorous exchanges. —*Bil Carpenter*

○ **Cathedrals Collection, Vol. 1** / i. 1988 / Benson 2471
A fine collection of recent hits, styled in the manner of their old hits. —*Bil Carpenter*

Eric Champion

Young wunderkind writes, sings, plays a variety of instruments, and has released a handful of albums, but Prince influences still loom large as he looks for his own approach. —*Thom Granger*

● **Vertical Reality** / Myrrh Records 6975-614
Tommy Sims production helped focus this concept album based on computer hackers, virtual reality and eternity. —*Thom Granger*

Revolution Time / i. 1991 / Word 47997
Several of the tunes on *Revolution Time* in particular are quite danceable. The two ballads ("Always Here" and "Feeling of Your Love") are both smooth and soothing. All the songs carry good, positive messages, to be sure, yet none plainly point listeners to repentance and faith in Jesus. As such, they are too ambiguous to bring about the spiritual revolution Champion seeks to promote. —*Edwin Smith, Rejoice*

Save the World
As always, Eric Champion's lyrics reflect his fervent desire to see the youth of his generation on fire for God and his kingdom. His vocals are excellent (when are they not excellent?) and are highlighted by live musicians and backup singers as opposed to overdubs and synthesizer programming. —*Edwin Smith, Rejoice*

Gary Chapman

Texas-born songwriter came to early fame with "My Father's Eyes," made popular by Amy Grant, whom he later married. Has also had songs recorded by T.G. Sheppard, Kenny Rogers and other country artists. —*Thom Granger*

Light Inside / i. 1994 / Reunion
Grammy-winning producer Michael Omartian teams with Chapman for a comfortably satisfying album, including remakes of two songs from his earlier (and out of print) Lamb & Lion albums. —*Thom Granger*

● **Everyday Man** / RCA 6375
Chapman's first album in years was prescient in its marriage of pop and country styles on this set, having the unfortunate effect of missing the moment with both audiences. —*Thom Granger*

Steven Curtis Chapman

b. Nov. 21, 1962, Paducah, KY
Vocals, guitar / CCM
Born in Paducah, KY, this singer, songwriter, and guitarist is one of the best CCM songwriters. As a singer, his music is a cross between '70s-style light rock and orchestrated pop. —*Bil Carpenter*

First Hand / i. 1987 / Sparrow 1139
Chapman's freshman debut is infused with country, soft rock, and pop. —*Bil Carpenter*

○ **Real Life Conversations** / i. 1988 / Sparrow 1160
Harder-edged, elaborate, guitar-focused light rock. —*Bil Carpenter*

★ **For the Sake of The Call** / i. 1990 / Sparrow 1258
Chapman's songwriting voice continues to mature, and the stirring title anthem helped make this his most successful album. —*Brian Mansfield*

The Great Adventure / i. 1992 / Sparrow 1328
Chapman flirts with country, rap, and Springsteenian rock on his most ambitious project, both musically and lyrically. Includes

guest appearances from Ricky Skaggs, DC Talk, and BeBe Winans. —*Brian Mansfield*

Heaven in the Real World / **i.** 1994 / Sparrow
Chapman moves into rockier, more electrified territory with his down-home story songs and values. —*Thom Granger*

The Charioteers

Group / Black gospel
The group was led by the great high tenor Billy Williams, who later fronted the Billy Williams Quartet. —*Opal Louis Nations*

○ **Jesus Is a Rock in the Weary Land** / Gospel Jubilee 1407
Some fine jubilee harmony singing from the early '40s. —*Kip Lornell*

Rev. Julius Cheeks

Vocals / Black gospel
Cheeks was the hardest-singing gospel lead in postwar quartet singing. —*Opal Louis Nations*

Family / Savoy 14504
Nice vocals and more midtempo song sermons. —*Ron Wynn*

● **Somebody Left on That Morning Train** / Savoy 14554
Marvelous leads and a good production. This is the best album Cheeks has made as a solo singer. —*Ron Wynn*

We'll Lay Down Our Lives / Savoy 7040
Representative, but a cut below his best single sessions. —*Ron Wynn*

The Choir

Group / CCM, Alternative pop/rock
Alternative rock band influenced by noise pop bands like Cocteau Twins and My Bloody Valentine. More melodic than most, with strong enough songs to cross into pop. —*Thom Granger*

Wide-Eyed Wonder / **i.** 1990 / Word 6885-615
More accessable than *Chase the Kangaroo*, this album helped the band build a larger following through Christian rock radio. —*Thom Granger*

★ **Circle Slide** / **i.** 1991 / Word 47734
Its best set to date, marked by the band's usual high standards of songwriting, extended soloing and better production. —*Thom Granger*

Speckled Bird / **i.** 1994 / R.E.X.
National release of songs from its indie album Kissers and Killers, which, along with the few new tunes, showed increasing love for noise pop genre. —*Thom Granger*

Chase the Kangaroo / Word 6869-61
First movement into Euro alternative guitar pop, sets direction for later albums. —*Thom Granger*

Chosen Gospel Singers

Group / Gospel
Among the original members were Lou Rawls, Joe Hinton, and Joe Medwick, all of whom went on to successful secular careers. Largely an a cappella group, they later became the Gospel Keynotes with the shearing lead vocals of Paul Beasley. —*Bil Carpenter*

Meet The Selah Jubilees
The Chosen Gospel Singers were a spiritual group in the sanctified style fronting such vocalists as the sing-and-preach Bob Crutcher, Joe Johnson from The Trumpeteers, jazz-soul singer Lou Rawls and the hard working Tommy Ellison who later went on to form the Five Singing Stars. These are exciting selections from various labels recorded between 1952 and 1963. Side B features the great Thermon Ruth and the Selah Singers who sang both R&B and gospel under various aliases during the '40s and '50s. The material here from their postwar Arista, Continental, Gotham & Mercury period is entirely gospel—close jubilee harmonies with sparse accompaniment. The songs are taken from rare 45s and 78s. There's good overall sound quality (cassette only). —*Opal Louis Nations, Roots & Rhythm Newsletter*

○ **The Lifeboat** / **i.** 1954 / Specialty 7014
Some of the most powerful gospel vocalizing likely to be heard this or any other year on CD reissue comes from the men of this "mystery group," so called because the personnel seemed to change with almost every session. Variety breeds dazzlement in this case as a revolving door of singers—including a young Lou Rawls—turns out one heart-fixing a cappella performance after another. The accompanying sound of slowly stomping feet on plywood lends a dark, brooding air to songs like "One-Two-Three" and "Prayer for the Doomed," and E.T. Ratley's tenor is particularly impressive on the heart-rending "I Tried." It's hard to pick a favorite cut or vocalist. The overall quality of the artistry and depth of feeling on this disc make it a *total* treasure. It's the current favorite on my CD player and gets my highest recommendation. —*Christine Ohlman, Roundup Newsletter*

Chuck Wagon Gang

Group / Gospel, Southern gospel
A traditional-style country gospel quartet that's been singing with varying personnel since the early '40s. —*Bil Carpenter*

Greatest Hits / **i.** 1920 / Arrival 753
Featuring sixteen tracks, *Greatest Hits* is a solid compilation of some of the Chuck Wagon Gang's best tracks and offers a good introduction to this contemporary country-gospel vocal group. —*Stephen Thomas Erlewine*

Old Time Hymns, Vol. 2 / **i.** 1921 / Arrival 30012
The Chuck Wagon Gang's heart-felt renditions of some well-known traditional hymns are somewhat hampered by the sterile production of the disc, but their strong performances carry the disc. —*Stephen Thomas Erlewine*

Family Tradition / **i.** 1973 / K-Tel 1116
Contains "Standing on the Premises" and other performances that show that throughout the many lineup changes this group has experienced, their sound remains a constant. —*AMG*

Looking Away to Heaven / **i.** 1976 / CBS 36035
One of the best of the more recent Columbia sets. —*Charles S. Wolfe*

★ **Columbia Historic Edition** / **i.** 1990 / CBS 40152
The best set of the group's vintage '30s and '40s sides, well-mastered, with excellent annotations. —*Charles S. Wolfe*

In Harmony / Copperfield 1114
Features "We Are Climbing" and other gospel favorites. —*AMG*

○ **Old Time Hymns, Vol. 1** / Copperfield 1126

The Clark Sisters

Group / Gospel, CCM
Formed in early '80s by the four daughters of Mattie Moss Clark. The contemporary Black style of this quartet is influenced by the Detroit gospel style of the Winans. "You Brought the Sunshine" hit the R&B charts in 1987, and the sisters later appeared in the Melba Moore video, "Lift Every Voice and Sing." Members: Dorinda, Twinkie, Karen, and Jackie Clark. —*Bil Carpenter*

○ **Heart and Soul** / **i.** 1985 / Word 5010-658
A caterwauling urban-funk set. —*Bil Carpenter*

Ashley Cleveland

Vocals / Rock
Earthy acoustic rocker writes worldly-wise songs from a decidedly Christian point of view, and sings them like her life depended on it. —*Thom Granger*

● **Big Town** / **i.** 1991 / Atlantic 82185

Rev. James Cleveland

b. Dec. 5, 1932, Chicago, IL, **d.** Feb. 9, 1991
Vocals, piano / Black gospel
Born in Chicago, Cleveland was one of the pioneers of the trend toward mass choirs that developed in the '50s. He led this movement in Southern California but maintained his national reputation as a teacher, performer, and recording artist until his death in 1991. He played the piano behind the Roberta Martin Singers in the '50s and moonlighted with the Caravans during the same period. By the early '60s he had branched out on his own and gained a Savoy Records contract. He started the "traditional Black choir sound" with the 1962 *Peace Be Still* album and continued to promote the sound through the founding of the Gospel Music Workshop of America in 1968 to train mass choirs in the Cleveland sound. —*Bil Carpenter*

★ **Peace Be Still** / **i.** 1962 / Savoy 14076

A set of original Cleveland tunes and traditional hymns done in the choir format he pioneered with the Angelic Choir of New Jersey. This live recording, done with crude technology, is helped somewhat by the high-fidelity pressing. It includes "I Had a Talk with God" and "I'll Wear a Crown." Cleveland's gruff vocals appear on most cuts. —*Bil Carpenter*

○ **Having Church** / **i.** 1991 / Savoy Gospel 7099
There are those who claim Cleveland's later recordings with the Southern California Community Choir don't quite match those with the group from Nutley, NJ. Perhaps—even probably. He's also lost some power as he's gotten older. But whether led by Cleveland or by other singers (notably the magisterial Lavora Wilson) the material on this CD is powerful and joyous enough to make that kind of distinction irrelevant. —*John Storm Roberts, Original Music*

Victory Shall Be Mine / **i.** 1991 / Savoy 14541
This is among Cleveland's best later works. —*Kip Lornell*

○ **Gospel Music Workshop of America** / Savoy Gospel 7100
A typically strong Cleveland performance with an all-star choir. —*Kip Lornell*

Dorothy Love Coates

b. 1930, Birmingham, AL
Vocals / Black gospel
Born in Birmingham, AL, Coates started singing in the '40s with the Original Gospel Harmonettes, who had the hits "I'm Sealed" and "Get Away." —*Bil Carpenter*

☆ **Get on Board** / **i.** 1956 / Specialty 7017
Dorothy Love Coates is one of only three gospel vocalists (Marion Williams and Mahalia Jackson being the others) included in the list of "greatest jazz singers" compiled by New Yorker jazz critic Whitney Balliett. Coates is, truly, an explosive, knock-'em-dead performer and the composer of some of gospel's most enduring classics. This 24-track set includes alternate takes of some of her biggest hits, including "99½," "Get Away Jordan," and "That's Enough" as well as classics like "Wade in the Water" and "Waiting for Me." Taken together with *The Best of Dorothy Love Coates, Volumes 1 and 2*, it provides a complete retrospective of her 1951-56 tenure at Specialty. —*Christine Ohlman, Roundup Newsletter*

★ **The Best of Dorothy Love Coates, Vols. 1 & 2** / **i.** 1957 / Specialty 7205
A great overview that spotlights the ragged Coates voice and collects many of her best compositions. —*Ron Wynn*

The Best of Dorothy Love Coates/Orig. Gospel Harmonettes, Vol. 2 / **i.** 1991 / Specialty 2141
The group sang hard and sanctified to the point of almost total exhaustion. They're one of the truly great postwar female gospel quintets. This has great improved sound. —*Opal Louis Nations, Roots & Rhythm Newsletter*

The Original Gospel—Vols. 1 & 2 / Specialty 2134
Dynamic lead vocals from Coates, plus superb harmonizing and rollicking instrumental accompaniment. —*Ron Wynn*

Code of Ethics

Techno-pop band delivers catchy tunes influenced by European acts like Depeche Mode but with a decidedly more positive outlook. —*Thom Granger*

Visual Paradox / **i.** 1991 / R.E.X.

Code of Ethics / **i.** 1993 / ForeFront

Daryl Coley

b. 1955, San Francisco
Clarinet, piano, keyboard / Soul, R&B, Jazz, Black gospel
Born in San Francisco, Coley grew up on jazz music and learned to play clarinet and piano. He played keyboards for the Hawkins Family from 1977 until he left to collaborate with James Cleveland in 1983. Later he did work with jazz artists Nancy Wilson and Rodney Franklin and pop singer Philip Bailey. —*Bil Carpenter*

I'll Be with You / **i.** 1988 / Light
Coley shows his jazz technique on the heavily improvisational title cut, with breaks and gaps throughout. Further, the vocal

arrangements are not in standard choir style. Otherwise, mostly upbeat Black gospel. —*Bil Carpenter*

● **He's Right On Time—Live from L.A.** / **i.** 1990 / Sparrow 1234
A live fusion of jazz, classical, and traditional gospel, wrapped up in Coley's zestful, upbeat arrangements. —*Bil Carpenter*

When the Music Stops / **i.** 1992 / Sparrow 1324
Daryl Coley's last album (*He's Right On Time—Live from L.A.*) was a smash hit, and this followup is more of the same. Using a variety of contemporary styles, Coley pulls out all the stops, giving outstanding vocal performances on each cut. Choice Sides are "Real" (a mellow jazz groove), "It Shall Be Done," and the title cut. —*Edwin Smith, Rejoice*

Commissioned

Group / Soul, Funk, R&B, CCM
An urban Black gospel band with crossover appeal. In concert they are an extremely evangelistic group who put on such a dramatic show that the altars are routinely packed with repenters following their performances. Members Fred Hammond and Keith Staten have done solo projects. —*Bil Carpenter*

Will You Be Ready? / **i.** 1989 / Light 019
A mix of contemporary and traditional spirituals. —*Bil Carpenter*

Number 7 / **i.** 1991 / Benson 8527
The group's trademark brassy harmonies and horn-like lead vocals are still there, but the songs and instrumentation have a harder edge with heavy emphasis on the rhythm line. In a word, this is dance music suitable for play at house parties and in clubs. Commissioned seems to be aggressively seeking a substantial share of the R&B secular market. The lyrics are solidly scriptural and the beat is prominent here. —*Edwin Smith, Rejoice*

● **State of Mind** / **i.** 1991 / Benson 2653
An R&B/urban CCM spectacle with tight harmonies. —*Bil Carpenter*

Lee & Cindy Condran

Group / Inspirational, Southern gospel
Commercial jingle writers creating a gospel music community in Annville, PA. In an articulate style, they cover many idioms, principally Southern gospel and MOR. —*Bil Carpenter*

○ **Styles** / **i.** 1991 / Condran 005
Crystal-clear production, from MOR to reggae to Southern gospel. —*Bil Carpenter*

Consolers

This Florida husband and wife duo became extremely popular during the '50s and '60s with their song sermons and downhome stories of spiritual triumph. "Brother" Sullivan Pugh played a blues-tinged guitar and was lead vocalist, while his wife Iola provided harmony. At one point, only Rev. James Cleveland topped their sales figures on the gospel circuit. —*Ron Wynn*

○ **Give Me My Flowers** / **i.** 1993 / ACE 425
This disc reissues material from the Nashboro label recorded between 1955-1963. Included are the foundation shaking "My Soul's Salvation" and large helpings of originals with traditional Christian messages, such as "I Shall Not Want" and "Peace Will Prevail." The pair is backed primarily by the reverberating Pops Staples-ish guitar of Sullivan, though as often as not some drums and a piano also sound in the background. —*Jeff Colburn, Roots & Rhythm Newsletter*

Billy Crockett

Singer-songwriter adept at clever wordplay and catchy acoustic guitar stylings. —*Thom Granger*

● **Any Starlight Night** / Urgent 2782
Any Starlight Night moves beyond the clever into deeper territory. —*Thom Granger*

Andrae Crouch

b. Jun. 1, 1950, San Francisco, CA
Piano / CCM, Christian rock
A groundbreaking pioneer in contemporary gospel music, Crouch combined the classic motif of call-and-response, solo with choir approach with pop songwriting techniques and production, resulting in albums accepted by both Black and White audiences.

Many of Crouch's early songs are now considered 'Jesus Music' standards. After a ten-year hiatus from recording, during which he dabbled in music for film and TV scores, Crouch signed with Quincy Jones' Qwest label for a triumphant return to form with *Mercy.* —*Thom Granger*

Mercy / Qwest 45432
A potpourri of musical styles from Caribbean to African, laid down with impeccable taste in arrangment and production, and exceeding the expectations that come from ten years away from the studio. —*Thom Granger*

☆ **Andrae Crouch & The Disciples** / **i.** 1978 / Light 5717
Andrae Crouch & The Disciples—Live in London has all the groundbreaking rock riffs, motifs, and crossover elements that had him labeled a "devil" by conservatives. —*Bil Carpenter*

Let's Worship Him / **i.** May 1993 / Arrival 3089
Featuring driving beats and funky guitars as well as more contemplative slower numbers, *Let's Worship Him* is a good compilation of Crouch's late '70s and early '80s work, which was considerably more in touch with modern trends than his earlier records. —*Stephen Thomas Erlewine*

● **His Best** / Arrival 620
As the title suggests, *His Best* features some of Crouch's finest moments from the early '70s, including "Jesus is the Answer" and "My Tribute." A good introduction to this popular gospel singer. —*Stephen Thomas Erlewine*

Sandra Crouch

b. Jun. 1, 1950, San Francisco, CA
Drum / Black gospel
Born in San Francisco, CA, with twin Andrae, she's an accomplished drummer and a Black gospel performer and songwriter of high esteem. —*Bil Carpenter*

With All of My Heart / **i.** Aug. 10, 1992 / Sparrow 1325
After a seven-year hiatus from recording, Sandra Crouch is back with her biggest (14 songs) and best recording. Recorded at her father's church in Pacoima, California, and with the best musicians and singers available assisting her, Crouch and friends deliver an excellent balance of traditional and contemporary gospel. Crouch's contralto is in fine form, but she doesn't monopolize the recording. Instead, she shares the stage with members of her choir. —*Edwin Smith, Rejoice*

● **We Sing Praises** / Light 5825
More traditional than her brother Andrae on this fine set of worship pieces, including "Completely Yes." —*Bil Carpenter*

Rick Cua

Vocals, piano / CCM
This singer/pianist with the Outlaws turned down a Spyro Gyra post and turned to gospel in the '80s. —*Bil Carpenter*

You're My Road / **i.** 1985 / Sparrow 170
Moderate rock; includes "Don't Say Suicide." —*Bil Carpenter*

○ **Can't Stand Too Tall** / **i.** 1988 / Reunion 0030-723
Hard-rock message music, with a couple of ballads. —*Bil Carpenter*

Dakoda Motor Co.

Alternative pop band from Southern California features aggressive guitar attack and sunny vocals of lead singer Davia Vallesillo, reminiscent of former Go-Go Belinda Carlisle. —*Thom Granger*

● **Into the Son** / Myrrh
Thrashing guitars meet pop vocals and lyrics straight out of the early Jesus Music songbook, for this most enjoyable debut. —*Thom Granger*

Daniel Amos (Dä)

Group / CCM, Alternative rock/pop
Chameleonic Christian-rock band started out as a Gram Parsons-influenced country band. By the late '70s, the group had become a rock band before the collapse of its record label delayed the release of the landmark *Horrendous Disc.* During that time, frontman Terry Taylor discovered Elvis Costello and the Talking Heads. The few fans who stuck around during the band's three-year recording absence were shocked to hear the new-wave *Alarma!!* released hot on the heels of the mainstream *Horrendous*

Disc. The band, also known as Dä, now follows its own music, with little concern for audiences and marketing. Taylor has become one of the most influential figures in Christian rock, as both a performer and a producer (Randy Stonehill, Jacob's Trouble, Scattered Few). —*Brian Mansfield*

○ **Daniel Amos** / **i.** 1976 / Maranatha Music 08749
Christian country-rock, along the lines of the Flying Burrito Brothers, but hardly *Gilded Palace of Sin.* However, Gram Parsons sideman Al Perkins does contribute pedal steel. —*Brian Mansfield*

○ **Shotgun Angel** / **i.** 1977 / Maranatha Music 8727
Country-rock album, tighter than *Daniel Amos*, with pop harmonies, which made them Christian music's answer to the Eagles. It also made *Shotgun Angel* one of the most popular albums of its time. —*Brian Mansfield*

★ **Kalhoun** / **i.** 1991 / Brainstorm 7100522846
"It's the magic word they claim came down from ancient Babylon," Taylor sings by way of explaining the title word. "Don't know exactly what it means, it's just a sacred kind of thing." Satirical, often scathing, rock that brooks no compromise. —*Brian Mansfield*

○ **Doppelganger** / **i.** Jan. 1992 / Stunt
The Alarma!! Chronicles—Vol. 2. After making (but before releasing) *Horrendous Disc*, Terry Taylor discovered new-wave, and Daniel Amos was never the same. *Alarma!!* stripped the band down to bare bones, but *Doppelganger* returned the production values that typified Daniel Amos records. *Doppelganger* is the second of the four-part *Alarma!!* saga, but it works just fine on its own. Stunt's 1992 reissue of the album includes three live bonus tracks. —*Brian Mansfield*

○ **Horrendous Disc** / **i.** Feb. 1992 / Solid Rock
The country influences of *Daniel Amos* and *Shotgun Angel* almost gone, *Horrendous Disc* established Daniel Amos as a rock band with huge melodies and huge guitars, sweetened by Beatles-influenced harmonies. —*Brian Mansfield*

Bibleland / **i.** 1994 / WAL
A return to a harder-edged alternative rock sound, less melodic but very much alive. —*Thom Granger*

● **Motor Cycle** / Brainstorm
A swirling, sonic song cycle, more accessable than most of Dä's catalog to a larger audience, with great production and tons of Beatle-esque fun. —*Thom Granger*

Davis Sisters

Group / Spiritual
The group was founded by Ruth "Baby Sis" Davis in Philadelphia. Other members included Alfreda, Audrey, and Thelma Davis; Imogene Greene; Curtis Dublin on piano; Jackie Verdell, lead vocalist. They recorded for the Savoy label until 1962. Verdell recorded secular sides for Peacock 1961-1964. Though a quintet, they sounded like a small choir with their full sound. Four members died in separate but tragic fashions. One was burned to death. Ruth died in 1970, while still a young woman after fighting diabetes, liver disease, and kidney disease. —*Bil Carpenter*

★ **The Best of the Davis Sisters** / Savoy 7017
Best of the Davis Sisters of Philidelphia. A remarkable family gospel unit, plagued by personal tragedies. A nice anthology of their Savoy songs. —*Ron Wynn*

DC Talk

Street Poetry
Inter-racial trio whose blend of pop, hip-hop and rap have brought them to gold-record selling status over the course of three albums distributed primarily in the Christian market. —*Thom Granger*

Nu Thang / **i.** 1991 / Heartwarming 2682
Crossover, pop-style Christian rap. —*Bil Carpenter*

★ **Free at Last** / **i.** 1992 / ForeFront
Its breakthrough album, expanding the group's musical boundaries and appeal, with impressive covers of "Jesus is Just Alright" and "Lean on Me," and the trio's best original compositions to date. —*Thom Granger*

De Garmo & Key

Group / CCM
Eddie De Garmo & Dana Key are Memphis-reared guitar rockers who started with the Globe band in early 1972. Later they gave it up to create the Christian rock group called the Christian Band, changing the name to De Garmo & Key later in the decade. They were influenced by ZZ Top, Jimi Hendrix, ELP, and others. —*Bil Carpenter*

Straight on / **i.** 1979 / Lamb & Lion 1043
Bluesy Southern rock that was ahead of its time. —*Bil Carpenter*

● **Destined to Win** / **i.** 1992 / Benson
A greatest hits collection featring most of its radio favorites and an acoustic medley of earlier material. —*Thom Granger*

Heat It Up / **i.** 1993 / Benson
Duo celebrates its 15th year together by producing a well-rounded example of everything it does; pop songs, rockers, ballads are all here. —*Thom Granger*

○ **To Extremes** / **i.** 1994 / Benson
Mid-age crises causes D&K to churn out its hardest rocking effort in years, highlighted by some stellar guitar soloing by Key. —*Thom Granger*

○ **No Turning Back/Live** / Lamb & Lion 1063
A good sampler of the band's early sound, typified by Kansas/Emerson, Lake & Palmer-type guitar/keyboard interplay; before the band ventured into poppier waters. —*Thom Granger*

Feels Good to Be Forgiven / Heartwarming 2510
A solo effort by Eddie De Garmo of bluesy Southern rock. —*Bil Carpenter*

Go to the Top / Benson 2771
A good example of D&K's pop side, with compact, catchy (if somewhat clichéd) tunes with enough hooks to land the band a larger following. —*Thom Granger*

The Journey / Heartwarming 2638
A light, soft-rock solo effort by Dana Key. —*Bil Carpenter*

The Pledge / Power Discs 01096
Competent, keyboard-dominated arena-rock. Upside: "Aliens and Strangers," an insightful (and amusing) U2 knock-off. Downside: the labor-dispute metaphors of "Boycott Hell." —*Brian Mansfield*

Dino

b. 1942, New York, NY
Vocals / Dance, Dance-pop, Gospel, Inspirational
Born in New York, NY. Studied at Julliard and later with Arthur Rubenstein. Flashy instrumentalist known as Christian Liberace. —*Bil Carpenter*

○ **Peace in the Midst of The Storm** / **i.** 1987 / Heartwarming 2571
Inspirational piano music, on the fringes of classical. —*Bil Carpenter*

The Dixie Hummingbirds

Group / Black gospel
Formed by James Davis in Greenville, SC, ca. 1928. Personnel: Davis (baritone), Ira Tucker (lead), Beachey Thompson (tenor), and William Bobo (bass). Early on, they sang hymns and jubilees with spare accompaniment and tight harmonies. In the late '60s, they began to infuse jazz, blues, and rock elements into their material. Notable cuts include "Somebody is Lying" and "You Don't Have Nothin' If You Don't Have Jesus." They backed Paul Simon on "Loves Me Like a Rock" in 1973, recorded at Muscle Shoals Studios.

Changes loomed as the Dixie Hummingbirds moved into the '80s. James Davis retired after 56 years in 1984. Willie Bobo, the great bass vocalist who joined them in 1939, died in 1976. But they continued performing into the '90s, with Ira Tucker and James Walker still featured. —*Bil Carpenter and Ron Wynn*

Christian Testimonial / **i.** 1959 / MCA 28000
Includes "The Devil Can't Harm a Praying Man." —*Bil Carpenter*

○ **The Best of the Dixie Hummingbirds** / **i.** 1973 / MCA 28021
A short (12 cuts) selection that is hardly their best, but still a worthwhile collection of sides from the early '60s. —*Kip Lornell*

★ **Live** / **i.** 1976 / Mobile Fidelity 771
With these 75 minutes of fine performances, good sound quality and a varied repertoire make this the one to buy. —*Kip Lornell*

○ **In the Storm Too Long** / Gospel Jubilee 1405
Their classic early recordings from 1939-1949. This is their pre-Peacock Records material, from before lead singer James Walker joined the quartet. —*Kip Lornell*

O'landa Draper & the Associates

Group / Black gospel
Draper attended Memphis State University, where he formed a mass choir (the Associates) that later performed with Shirley Caesar (on "Hold My Mule"), the Winans, Nicholas, Timothy Wright, Myrna Summers, and others. They currently record for Word/Epic. —*Bil Carpenter*

● **Above & Beyond** / **i.** 1990 / Word 48687
Contemporary Memphis-based choir; good singing, heavily arranged. —*Ron Wynn*

Do It Again / **i.** 1990 / Word 48560
This is the most recent release from this modern gospel orchestra. —*Ron Wynn*

Phil Driscoll

Vocals, trumpet / Church, Inspirational
This White trumpeter, with raspy vocals similar to Ray Charles, performs soulful pop arrangements. —*Bil Carpenter*

● **I Exalt Thee** / **i.** 1983 / Sparrow 1074
Spiritual wailing and trumpet playing on old hymns. —*Bil Carpenter*

Classical Hymns, Vol. 1 / **i.** 1988 / Triloka 1406
An orchestral, symphonic session featuring Driscoll's trumpet solos. —*Bil Carpenter*

The Picture Changes / Word
Driscoll trades in his blustery, Joe Cocker-ish vocal style for a more subdued approach that suits his range better. Vocals are featured more than trumpet here, though understated approach is employed instrumentally as well, to good effect. —*Thom Granger*

Bryan Duncan

Vocals / Rap, Gospel, CCM, Reggae
Former lead singer for Sweet Comfort Band has cut a bushel of albums as a solo artist, but has really honed both his singing craft and lyrical perspective in the early '90s. —*Thom Granger*

Strong Medicine / **i.** 1989 / Word 4602-608
Reggae, rap, and the strong title-track ballad. —*Bil Carpenter*

Now and Then / **i.** 1989 / Light
Collection of biggest hits from Duncan's early solo albums for Light. —*Thom Granger*

Anonymous Confessions of a Lunatic Friend / **i.** 1991 / Word 48555
Duncan's extroverted comic side, periodically rearing its head on a number of songs over the years, is balanced here with a few tunes featuring a new, more confessional tone that would mark the artist's direction to come. —*Thom Granger*

● **Mercy** / **i.** Jan. 19, 1993 / Word 53320
Arguably his best album, Duncan digs deep to deal with the things he's been avoiding . . . and turns in the best songs and vocal performances of his career. —*Thom Granger*

Slow Revival / **i.** 1994 / Myrrh
Continuing with the themes spotlighted on Mercy, this album delivered even better lyrical expressions of the ideas, but is ballad-heavy musically and lacks the variety of earlier work. —*Thom Granger*

Jeff and Sheri Easter

Group / Southern gospel
Both members of this husband/wife duo were born into professional Southern gospel singing families. —*Bil Carpenter*

Picture-Perfect Love / **i.** 1989 / Heartwarming 2542
Homey, folksy country music with bluegrass elements. —*Bil Carpenter*

○ **Brand New Love** / **i.** 1990 / Heartwarming 2668
Peppy, guitar-driven country with story lyrics. —*Bil Carpenter*

● **Shining Through** / Benson 2779
If you like your gospel music with a country sound, you will love this album from Jeff and Sheri Easter. The album contains several

songs that would fit a country format radio station just as well as gospel. While not for everyone, this album is for anyone who enjoys their gospel with a country flavor. —*Phil Wammack, Rejoice*

Vince Ebo

Former session singer and member of Charlie Peacock's acoustic trio, cut one solo album for Warners, but cut his career short when he took his own life in early '94. —*Thom Granger*

○ **Love Is the Better Way** / **i.** May 26, 1992 / Warner Brothers 26895
Though this is Vince Ebo's debut solo release, the Charlie Peacock band member and jingle singer is no stranger to performing or recording. His professionalism (seven producers worked on this project) and non-church musical influences (modern jazz, rhythm and blues, rock, and heavy metal) make for a stunning collection of 10 songs—all of which he co-wrote. Musically, this album alternates well between uptempo grooves and mellow ballads. Regardless of the individual song style, Ebo's vocal abilities are always showcased. The lyrics reflect the joys and struggles of his newfound faith. This is a classic debut from an artist with a great future. —*Edwin Smith, Rejoice*

Michael English

Vocals / Gospel, CCM
Michael English's roots are in Southern Gospel; he performed with the Singing Americans, the Goodmans, the Gaither Trio, and the Gaither Vocal Band before going solo in 1991. English began drawing attention to his powerful tenor when he recorded "I Bowed on My Knees and Cried Holy," first with the Singing Americans, then with the Brooklyn Tabernacle Choir. English is established as one of the top young names in the CCM field as he has won Dove Awards for Best New Artist and Best Male Vocalist. —*Brian Mansfield*

● **Michael English** / **i.** 1991 / Warner Brothers 4104
Wildly successful debut that rides the line between adult contemporary and dance-pop. But the real draw is English's eloquent voice, which is showcased to great effect on the likes of "Heaven" and "Solid As the Rock." —*Brian Mansfield*

Hope / **i.** 1993 / Warner Brothers 45207
English traded the sophomore slump for a scandal, as his second solo album made him even more popular, taking home the Dove Award for Artist of the Year in '94, only to leave gospel music a week later as a result of an extra-marital affair, after which his label dropped him from its roster. —*Thom Granger*

Evie (Tornquist)

Vocals / Inspirational
This Norwegian singer made emphatic pop/inspirational albums in the '70s and '80s. She was the most popular woman in contemporary White gospel before the advent of Amy Grant and Sandi Patti. —*Bil Carpenter*

○ **When All Is Said and Done** / **i.** 1986 / Word 9028-608
Tornquist's light voice really rocks on these midtempo songs of joy. —*Bil Carpenter*

The Fairfield Four

Group / Gospel
This group was created in the early '20s by the pastor of Fairfield Baptist Church in Nashville to occupy his sons, Harry and Rufus Carrethers. With John Battle, they became a gospel trio. The group was transformed into a quartet by the '30s and began the first of numerous personnel changes. They recorded for RCA Victor and Columbia during the decade and were known for their reinterpretation of standard hymns, employing staccato basslines and the ebbing soundwaves of their voices dropping from tenor to baritone. They continue to perform, though the original members are either deceased or retired. —*Bil Carpenter*

○ **Fairfield Four**
Here's 33 cuts by this exciting Jubilee quartet, still performing (after more than 68 years) in a cappella. This contains long out of print Dot (Bullet purchases) and Old Town material from out of print Nashboro and Athens album collections, plus two by Joe Henderson, the group's basso in 1960. It's close-harmony '50s singing at its best with the legendary Sam McCrary "hard tenor" lead and the unbeatable Isaac "Dickie" Freeman occasional bass

lead. This is one of today's best traditional quartets. It's very good sound quality (cassette only). —*Opal Louis Nations, Roots & Rhythm Newsletter*

○ **One Religion**
This is a prize collection of some of Nashville's Fairfield Four Dot recordings spanning the years 1951 through 1953. The group on these sides is composed of Rev. Sam McCrary—lead, Willie Love—second tenor, James Hill—baritone, and Willie Frank Lewis—bass. Some of these cuts are thought to be alternate takes of earlier Bullet recordings made during the late '40s. It's classic a cappella singing reminiscent of early Spirit of Memphis material. There's excellent notes by gospel researcher Tony Heilbut. It's highly recommended. —*Opal Louis Nations, Roots & Rhythm Newsletter*

★ **Angels Watching Over Me** / **i.** 1991 / P-Vine 2327
Their recent Warner Bros. album shows them to still be contenders. These 26 tracks feature the group in their prime in the early '50s. The songs are all a cappella and are a perfect blending of the older Jubilee styles and the harder gospel stylings of groups like The Five Blind Boys. Like the best groups, this quartet knows when to be discreet and when to pull out the stops, and the way the lead singer ornaments the notes and the interplay of the voices will raise the hair on the back of your neck. —*Frank Scott, Roots & Rhythm Newsletter*

○ **Standing in the Safety Zone** / **i.** 1992 / Warner Brothers 4137
This wonderful '92 release features often awesome harmonies, a guest appearance from the Nashville Bluegrass Band on "Roll, Jordan Roll" and soaring, magnificent lead vocals from Walter Settles, Isaac Freeman, and W.L. Richardson. Here's old-time gospel at its best, vividly presented via contemporary technology. —*Ron Wynn*

Fernando

b. Ecuador
Vocals / CCM
Born in Ecuador, raised in California, Fernando began his career in the late '80s. With a rather smooth singing voice, he tends to record pop-ish urban dance music and an occasional message rap tune. He's one of the first Hispanics to make a strong presence in gospel music; However, because of his outspoken pride in his Latin heritage, he's also become a visible role model to young Hispanics (mostly of a nontraditional Protestant bent) who are increasingly beginning to listen to gospel music. —*Bil Carpenter*

● **True Love** / **i.** 1990 / Movin' Up
This is all-English, Top 40 pop-style gospel with catchy hooks, heavy use of background vocals, with sequenced instrumentation. —*Bil Carpenter*

Latin Perspective / **i.** 1992 / Movin' Up
His second album has a definite mix of urban Black music and traditional South American music styles, with a few English/Spanish cuts. —*Bil Carpenter*

First Call

Group / Inspirational
Bonnie Keen, Marty McCall, and Melody Tunney (replaced by Marybeth Jordon). First Call is similar to Manhattan Transfer, with a Christian message. —*Bil Carpenter*

Human Song / **i.** 1992 / Epic 52462
Michael Omartian-produced move for the secular adult-contemporary market. Breezy dance-pop includes a remake of Stevie Wonder's "Don't You Worry 'Bout a Thing." —*Brian Mansfield*

● **Something Takes Over** / Dayspring 4161-628
A range of styles, including Swahili, jazz, and a cappella. —*Bil Carpenter*

Five Blind Boys of Alabama, The

Group / Black gospel
Evolving out of the Happyland Jubilee Singers, this traditional Black gospel quartet was formed in 1937 at the Talladega Institute for the Deaf and Blind in Alabama. By the '40s they became "The Blind Boys" and recorded for Specialty, Vee-Jay, Savoy, Elektra, and other labels. Their first hit was "I Can See Everybody's Mother but Mine" in 1949. Current lineup: Joe Watson, Jimmy Carter, Sam & Bobby Butler, Curtis Foster, Johnny

Fields, and Clarence Fountain. They appeared on Broadway in *Gospel at Colonus.* —*Bil Carpenter*

☆ **The Sermon** / i. 1953-1956 / Specialty/Fantasy 7041
This is a 27-track compilation featuring cuts done during the mid '50s for Specialty. Besides Fountain's smashing voice (among gospel's finest and most charismatic artists) the set's further distinguished by the contributions of four singing preachers: Paul Excano, Samuel K. Lewis, George W. Warren and Percell Perkins, and the insertion of jazz, Latin and comedic elements into the musical mix. —*Ron Wynn*

○ **The Five Blind Boys of Alabama** / Gospel Heritage 315
An excellent 16-track anthology that predates their Specialty recordings by four years, with leads shared by Clarence Fountain and the legendary Paul Excano. With scholarly notes and photos, a must for collectors. —*Hank Davis*

● **Oh Lord Stand By Me/Marching up to Zion** / Specialty 7203
Superb '50s Specialty sides. Hair-raising leads from Clarence Fountain, Rev. Samuel K. Lewis, and Rev. Percell Perkins. —*Hank Davis*

Five Blind Boys of Mississippi, The

Group / Black gospel
The Five Blind Boys of Mississippi are among the greatest singing groups in popular music history. Their smashing harmonies and the amazing leads of Archie Brownlee not only influenced numerous gospel ensembles, but such secular artists as Ray Charles. Their origins date back to the '30s, when Archie Brownlee (Brownley in some accounts), Joseph Ford, Lawrence Abrams, and Lloyd Woodard formed a quartet. They were students at the Piney Woods School near Jackson, Mississippi. They began as the Cotton Blossom Singers, and did both spiritual and secular material. The quartet sang on the school grounds in 1936, then were recorded in 1937 by Alan Lomax for the Library of Congress. After graduation, they decided to become professional singers and for a time performed under dual identities; they were the Cotton Blossom Singers for popular songs and the Jackson Harmoneers for gospel. They became a quintet when Melvin Henderson joined. When Percell Perkins replaced Henderson in the mid '40s, they became the Five Blind Boys. Oddly, Perkins, who doubled as their manager, was not blind. They made their recording debut for Excelsior in 1946, after meeting label owner Leon Rene in Cleveland. They recorded for Coleman in 1948, the same year Joseph Ford was replaced by J.T. Clinkscales. But when they joined Don Robey's Peacock label in 1950, the Five Blind Boys became superstars. The single "Our Father" was a Top 10 R&B hit, and they became a prolific ensemble, recording 27 singles and five albums for Peacock through the '60s. Brownlee died in New Orleans in 1960. His riveting, chilling screams and yells were among gospel's most amazing. Perkins left the group soon after becoming a minister. The list of replacements included Revs. Samy Lewis and George Warren, as well as Tiny Powell. Roscoe Robinson took over for Brownlee, and was assisted by second lead Wilmer Broadnax, who was also a masterful singer. The Five Blind Boys continued through the '70s and '80s and into the '90s. Woodard died in the mid '70s, and Lawrence Abrams in 1982. But the group was still going as of 1993. *Counting On Jesus,* their most recent release, was issued on Soul-Potion Records. —*Ron Wynn*

★ **Best of the Five Blind Boys of Mississippi, Vol. 1** / i. 1973 / MCA 28022
These Specialty recordings truly represent some of the best by this popular group. Arguably the greatest "quartet" ever. Featuring the wondrous Archie Brownlee. —*Kip Lornell & Ron Wynn*

My Desire/There's a God Somewhere / i. 1974 / Mobile Fidelity 769
My Desire/There's a God Somewhere combines two fine albums from the Peacock vaults. Also known as the Original Five Blind Boys and the Jackson Harmoneers. The lead vocals by Archie Brownlee have been known to slay souls and reduce grown men to tears. Powerful material! —*Hank Davis*

○ **Best of Five Blind Boys** / Chameleon 74785
Here are 11 great sides recorded for Vee-Jay in the late '50s featuring the soaring lead vocals of the magnificent Archie Brownlee. —*Roots & Rhythm Newsletter*

Best of the Five Blind Boys of Mississippi, Vol. 2 / MCA 28044
More gems from this seminal ensemble. —*Ron Wynn*

Soon I'll Be Done / Chess 91524
The Chess edition, with the first sighted member, Roscoe Robinson, who shares lead work with Willmer "Little Ax" Broadnax. It doesn't quite equal its predecessors. —*Ron Wynn*

● **You Done What the Doctor Couldn't Do** / Gospel Jubilee 1402
Eighteen stunning hard gospel performances (recorded between 1948-59) by arguably the greatest practitioners of the art. Brownlee was master of controlled vocal pandemonium, his deft leaps from the decorous to the delirious prompting the faithful to "fall out" in ecstatic fits. His "Amazing Grace" becomes an extraordinary plea for deliverance, while the Blind Boys' vamp on the Lord's Prayer ("World Prayer") is a beautifully-tiered tour de force of prayer and song. Anyone wanting to experience the fervor of hard gospel at its intense yet artful best should hear this profoundly heartfelt and masterfully performed music. —*Mark Humphrey, Roundup Newsletter*

☆ **Great Lost Blind Boys Album** / Vee-Jay 601
This Vee-Jay reissue from the late '50s is a testimony to the genius of their lead, Archie Brownlee. Originally issued as two separate albums, this CD contains false starts and studio chatter. After hearing "No Need To Cry," previously unissued, there is no question where doo-wop was born. All in all, the quality of the singing on this CD greatly overshadows any of the rough spots. You'll find definitive versions of almost all of the Blind Boys' repertoire, including the closing cut, "Leave You in the Hands of the Lord." For anyone interested in hearing spirited quartet singing at its best, this is an esssential recording. —*Mark E. Earley, Rejoice*

Florida Boys

Group / Southern gospel
This Southern gospel quintet was first formed in 1947 as the Gospel Melody Quartet. —*Bil Carpenter*

● **Together** / i. 1986 / Canaan 9955-533
Foot-tapping Southern gospel quartet singing. —*Bil Carpenter*

○ **Home Once Again**
This album is pure Florida Boys, containing the type of songs that have pleased their audiences for the past 45 years. [It] may not gain any new fans for the Florida Boys, but for anyone who has been a fan for years, this is a must buy. —*Phil Wammack, Rejoice*

Four Him

CCM
Contemporary inspirational male vocal quartet formed originally as a spin-off from larger choral group Truth, and spearheaded by Kirk Sullivan, whose distinctive phrasing has influenced a generation of young inspirational singers. —*Thom Granger*

Ride / i. 1994 / Benson
Though the foursome teamed up with super-producer Michael Omartian and others for its fifth album, the results showed nothing particularly new. —*Thom Granger*

● **The Basics of Life** / Benson 2960
The group's breakthrough recording, with a title song that said it all about returning to traditional values to its growing number of fans. —*Thom Granger*

The Season of Love / Benson 2187
Christmas album, showed more musical diversity than its normal fare. —*Thom Granger*

Rev. C. L. Franklin

Vocals / Black gospel
The pastor of Detroit's Bethel Baptist Church, confidant of Martin Luther King Jr., and father of Aretha Franklin, this charismatic preacher is known for "hair-raising" sermons. —*Bil Carpenter*

○ **23rd Psalm, The** / Chess 91528
This is both a performance and a lesson, this improvised and yet tightly structured sermon weaves its message around and between the words of possibly the best-known passage in the Bible. Tremendously moving—if you're into qawwali or kriti, you ought to listen to this, even if you don't care that it's an example of the US' leading form of oral literature. —*Carl Hoyt, Original Music*

● **Give Me This Mountain**

The African-American sermon has been little written about, and then usually ponderously. Jeff Todd Titon breaks the mold with a collection of annotated sermons and biographical notes about one of the greatest of preachers. Note: Most of Franklin's recorded sermons are out of print and all are very rare. —*John Storm Roberts, Original Music*

○ **The Eagle Stirreth in Her Nest** / MCA 91529
One wrenching, sweaty, hellfire sermon recorded for Joe Von Battle in the mid '50s. —*Bil Carpenter*

Rodney Friend

Vocals / Gospel, CCM
Friend sang with the group Nicholas and did session work at the Command stable. —*Bil Carpenter*

○ **Don't Lose Sight** / Word 5506-033
Urban contemporary inspirational ballads. —*Bil Carpenter*

Billy and Sarah Gaines

Group / CCM
A husband/wife duo who met while students on the Virginia Commonwealth University campus, they sang with the CCM group Living Sacrifice until 1980. Together they sing in CCM/inspirational style. Billy's is a mellow voice, while Sarah's is high-pitched. —*Bil Carpenter*

Billy & Sarah Gaines / **i.** 1986 / Heartwarming 2301
Pop praise music, with stirring ballads. —*Bil Carpenter*

● **He'll Find a Way** / **i.** 1988 / Heartwarming 2468
An R&B, urban CCM collection of slow and uptempo cuts. —*Bil Carpenter*

Bill and Gloria Gaither

b. Mar. 28, 1936, Alexandria, IN (Bill)
Group / Gospel, Inspirational
Aside from recording as a duo, they have recorded with other artists as the Gaither Vocal Band and the Bill Gaither Trio. The Gaithers are the most successful songwriters in Christian music. Their songs tend to be praise- and worship-oriented but often cross various music barriers stylistically; however, their most significant material is contemporary pop. —*Bil Carpenter*

○ **Live Across America** / **i.** 1980 / Word 8847-656
A fine live double album of their '70s pop-gospel hits. —*Bil Carpenter*

M. C. Ge Gee

Vocals / Street poetry
The first female rapper in Christian music. Born in the Bronx and raised in Dallas, where her parents run an inner-city youth outreach program that was the subject of the film "The Cross and the Switchblade." In the middle of the rap fray, she's not a hard one, nor a pop one. She's picked up the serious issue-oriented street-poetry legacy of her late brother, D-Boy Rodriguez. —*Bil Carpenter*

○ **And Now the Mission Continues** / **i.** 1991 / Frontline
A Tim Miner production of midrange rap that is not too hard and not too pop. The style is urban funk with spare sampling. Most of the album is message-oriented, such as "I Caught the Mike," a pickup of D-Boy's "I Dropped the Mike," which speaks to the continuance of his ministry to youth by Ge Gee. —*Bil Carpenter*

Jon Gibson (Gospel)

Blue-eyed soulster whose instincts and songwriting made his too-close-for-comfort Stevie Wonder-like vocals worth tolerating. Later albums are better, as Gibson evolved into a vocal style more his own. Songs and production are improved as well. —*Thom Granger*

Body & Soul / **i.** 1989 / Frontline
Includes remake of mentor Wonder's "Have a Talk With God," featuring Stevie's own harmonica on the solo. —*Thom Granger*

Jesus Loves Ya / **i.** 1990 / Frontline
A solid outing, featuring hits like "Love Come Down" and the title cut. —*Thom Granger*

● **Hits** / **i.** 1991 / Frontline

A good place to start with Gibson featuring most of his hits, a Scott Blackwell remix of "Jesus Loves Ya" and a new Christmas song. —*Thom Granger*

Forever Friends / **i.** 1992 / Frontline
More slammin' blue-eyed soul from the still less-than-well-known stylist. —*Thom Granger*

Change of Heart / Frontline 9032
Features remake of James Ingram's "Yah Mo B There" and a duet with MC Hammer on "The Wall" before he blew up big. —*Thom Granger*

Glad

Group / Inspirational
They began in 1972 as the Fellowship, drawing upon jazz and pop-rock influences for their unique sound, which centers on tight, meticulous vocal harmonies. —*Bil Carpenter*

○ **The Acapella Project** / **i.** 1988 / Heartwarming 2445
Old church hymns sans instrumentation. —*Bil Carpenter*

Floodgates / Benson 2959
Glad has to be one of the best vocal groups in contemporary Christian music today. This project demonstrates why. From the remake of the 2nd Chapter of Acts' "Which Way the Wind Blows" to the madrigal style of "We are Receiving a Kingdom," these four men blend their voices into a smooth aural tapestry that blankets your living space with lovely inspirational music. You can comfortably listen to this and never be overwhelmed by technological tricks. It's just good, easy-listening gospel music. —*Edwin Smith, Rejoice*

Gold City

Group / Southern gospel
Formed in the '70s, Gold City is a gospel quartet rife with excellent baritone and high tenor vocals. This is kick-back Southern gospel. —*Bil Carpenter*

● **Answer The Call**
Answer The Call is a near perfect album for anyone who loves modern Southern gospel music. In short, this release receives the highest recommendation. There is not a bad song on the entire set and that is rare. Gold City has once again proved itself worthy of being called the number one group in gospel music today. —*Phil Wammack, Rejoice*

○ **Portrait** / **i.** 1989 / Heartwarming 2446
Superb harmonies on this camp-meeting-style country music. —*Bil Carpenter*

Golden Eagle Gospel Singers

Group / Black gospel
An Alabamian a cappella outfit that later developed roots in Chicago, the Golden Eagles were formed in the '30s by Thelma Byrd. On a level with the Golden Gate Quartet, their popularity was strongest in the Midwest. Unlike other groups of the time, who were usually male and Baptist, this one was coed and Sanctified. Much of their music had a fast-paced blues feel, most notably on 1937's "Tone the Bell" and 1940's "He's My Rock," which showcased Hammie Nixon on blues harmonica. They recorded for the Decca label. —*Bil Carpenter*

● **Complete Recordings 1937-1940**
This is a fine collection of 16 songs by this mixed male/female group. The first six sides from 1937 are old time gospel singing, mostly featuring the female voices with accompaniments with guitar & piano. The rest of the tracks are more interesting with more of a quartet feel with both male and female voices evident with some wonderful vocal bass singing on some tracks. These are basically a cappella except for the presence of harmonica player Hammie Nixon on some cuts. Nixon's brittle playing weaves beautifully in and around the vocals. It's lovely music. —*Frank Scott, Roots & Rhythm Newsletter*

○ **The Golden Eagle Gospel Singers** / Eden 4200
Gems from the three Chicago sessions (ca. 1937-1940) of this important mixed 10-member aggregation led by Thelma Byrd and supported at times by Hammie Nixon. —*Opal Louis Nations*

Golden Gate Quartet

Group / Black gospel

Pioneer Virginia gospel/pop quartet of the '30s and '40s. Calling their innovative approach to sacred hymns "jubilee" singing, the Golden Gate Quartet, propelled by Willie Johnson and William Langford, enjoyed massive acceptance far outside the church. Their smooth Mills Brothers-influenced harmonies made the Gates naturals for pop crossover success, and they began recording for Victor in 1937. National radio broadcasts and an appearance on John Hammond's 1938 "Spirituals to Swing" concert at Carnegie Hall made them coast-to-coast favorites. By 1941 the Gates were recording for Columbia minus Langford, and movie appearances were frequent: *Star Spangled Rhythm*, *Hollywood Canteen*, and *Hit Parade of 1943*, to name a few. Some experiments with R&B material didn't pan out during the late '40s, and Johnson defected to the Jubilaires in 1948. The group emigrated to France in 1959; led by veteran bass singer Orlando Wilson, the Golden Gate Quartet's vocal blend is as powerful as ever. —*Bill Dahl*

○ **Travelin' Shoes** / i. Sep. 1992 / Bluebird 66063
This CD features 25 Golden Gate Quartet songs recorded between 1937 and 1939, including many of their most popular items. The group was very popular and influential with their beautiful unaccompanied vocal harmonies. Although much of their repertoire was gospel, they also delved into pop and jazz sometimes doing instrumental imitations with their voices. — *Frank Scott, Roots & Rhythm Newsletter*

★ **35 Historic Recordings** / RCA 42111
Breathtaking sides from 1937-1939—largely a cappella, with both gospel and pop music. The album also includes a landmark version of "Stormy Weather" that is at the root of doo-wop. —*Hank Davis*

○ **Spirituals to Swing** / Jazz Time 791469
An inspired effort, recorded between 1955 and 1969. —*Kip Lornell*

☆ **Swing Down, Chariot** / CBS 47131
The most influential "jubilee" quartet of the late '30s and '40s in inspired and deftly syncopated performances. An archetype. —*Mark A. Humphrey*

The Golden Gate Quartet / Carrere 96702
Recent recordings of familiar spirituals ("Shadrack," "Joshua Fit the Battle of Jericho," "Amen," "Glory Glory Hallelujah") mixed in with a predominantly pop repertoire ("Blue Suede Shoes," "The Great Pretender," "Only You," "Frankie & Johnny"). 18 tunes by this latter-day incarnation of the influential gospel group. —*Roots & Rhythm Newsletter*

The Happy Goodman Family

Group / Southern gospel
Founded in 1963, this Kentucky-based group dominated Southern gospel charts for years, picking up Dove and Grammy awards. They were associated with the PTL Club in the '80s. Members include Vestal, Howard, Rusty, and Sam Goodman, all legends in their own right. —*Bil Carpenter*

○ **Greatest Hits** / i. 1985 / Canaan 9889-530
A live recording of the Goodman Family's country gospel. —*Bil Carpenter*

Tanya Goodman

Rusty Goodman's daughter is a fine songstress, capable of building bridges between her Southern Gospel roots and crossing over them to adult pop pastures, with good results. —*Thom Granger*

Innocent Eyes / i. 1993 / Benson

The Gospel Harmonettes

Group / Black gospel
○ **Camp Meeting** / i. 1993 / Vee-Jay 607
The link between gospel music and the Civil Rights era has never been clearer than on the two albums that comprise this CD reissue. Both issued in the mid '60s, the rough-hewn, earthy and bluesy voice of Dorothy "Love" Coates and her inspirational songs were tailor-made to elevate the spirits of those fighting for social justice. Numbers like "Camp Meeting," "I Won't Let Go," "The Righteous on the March" and "Step By Step" don't have overt political lyrics, but certainly speak to the ultimate victories anticipated by civil rights workers. There's also plenty of more

traditional spiritual material, sung with spirited, passionate belief. —*Ron Wynn, AMG*

The Gospel Harmonettes (Demopolis)

Group / Black gospel
Not to be confused with the famous Dorothy Love Coates group, this convincing a cappella female quartet from Central Alabama recorded in 1991 and have strong roots in the Baptist church and Jefferson County singing tradition. —*Kip Lornell*

○ **Gospel Harmonettes** / Vee-Jay 607

Amy Grant

b. Nov. 25, 1960, Augusta, GA
Vocals / CCM, Pop
The most influential (and certainly most successful) artist to emerge from contemporary Christian music. Grant's natural, unassuming style has won her many fans and made her a star in both the gospel and pop markets; her talents as a singer and songwriter have won her respect worldwide. —*Thom Granger*

Age to Age / i. 1982 / Reunion 6697-274
Grant's first breakthrough in gospel, featuring a solid group of songs and players, and a best-seller for years to come. —*Thom Granger*

☆ **A Christmas Album** / i. 1983 / Word 6768-279
Amy's first seasonal offering is still a perennially strong seller, and one of the best contemporary Christmas albums ever recorded. —*Thom Granger*

Unguarded / i. 1985 / Reunion 6806-278
The artist's first foray into crossover, featuring dance-pop music, and yielding a Top 20 hit, "Find a Way." —*Thom Granger*

● **The Collection** / i. 1986 / Reunion 6843-270
An early gospel hits package, including "El Shaddai." —*Bil Carpenter*

☆ **Lead Me On** / i. 1989 / A&M 5199
Grant's best album, all things considered; a mature statement of faith that digs deeper than most of the genre, with songs that remain relevant. —*Thom Granger*

○ **Heart in Motion** / i. 1991 / A&M 5321
Her mainstream multi-platinum breakthrough, a pure pop treat that yielded a handful of hits and established her as a pop star in the general market. Not a gospel album, but the album's closer, "Hope Set High," left the cards face up on the table. —*Thom Granger*

Home for Christmas / i. Oct. 6, 1992 / A&M 540001
A year (1993) after her mainstream success, contemporary Christian's most popular (and controversial) female vocalist is back with a very nice Christmas album—her second such project in her almost 17-year career. There's no rollicking "Baby, Baby" or "Good For Me" in this set, and Grant and her long-time producer Brown Bannister go for a softer, easy-listening, middle of the road sound. —*Edwin Smith, Rejoice*

House of Love / i. 1994 / A&M
After a duo of detours (a youth worship record and a second Christmas offering), Grant returns with an album that doesn't even pretend to be gospel, but still reflects her ideologies. Mellower than *Heart in Motion*, the album sounds more like *Lead Me On*, but doesn't plumb its depths. —*Thom Granger*

Keith Green

d. Jun. 1982
Vocals / Inspirational
Green founded Last Days Ministries with his wife Melody in the late '70s. A reformer trying to purge the church of unbiblical habits, Keith's music was lyrically a mix of Jesus Movement protest and 19th-century evangelical writings. He died in a plane crash in July 1982. —*Bil Carpenter*

○ **The Ministry Years, Vol. 1** / i. 1987 / Sparrow 1146
1977-1979. Green makes the piano keys sing. —*Bil Carpenter*

The Ministry Years, Vol. 2 / i. 1988 / Sparrow 1170
1980-1982. Theological questioning and stirring MOR. —*Bil Carpenter*

○ **No Compromise** / i. 1990 / Sparrow 1024
Green tackles controversial doctrinal issues, and still makes you want to listen. —*Thom Grainger*

● **For Him Who Has Ears to Hear** / **i.** 1991 / Sparrow 1015
The debut of a major songwriter in Christian music. —*Thom Grainger*

Steve Green

Vocals / Inspirational
Green sang with White Heart and the Gaither Vocal Band before his solo outings. —*Bil Carpenter*

● **For God and God Alone** / **i.** 1986 / Sparrow 1120
A big symphonic sound and righteous lyrics. —*Bil Carpenter*

Tienen Que Saber / **i.** 1987 / Sparrow 1137
A Spanish-language MOR set. —*Bil Carpenter*

Guardian

Hard Rock, Heavy Metal
Bluesy rock outfit has become the Aerosmith of CCM, cranking out a series of albums that have improved consistently. —*Thom Granger*

● **Miracle Mile** / Epic 57112
The band's tour de force, showcasing its hookiest songwriting (on both ballads and rockers) and most powerful playing to date. —*Thom Granger*

The Harmonizing Four

Group / Black gospel
Quartet based in Richmond, VA, comprising Tommy "Goat" Johnson (tenor), Lonnie Smith (baritone), "Gospel Joe" Williams, and Jimmy Jones. Recorded for Vee-Jay and Nashboro labels in the '50s. —*Bil Carpenter*

The Best of the Harmonizing Four / Capitol 74801
Featuring the bass voice of Ellis Johnson or the legendary Jimmy Jones. —*Opal Louis Nations*

★ **Gospel in My Soul** / Chameleon 74801
This truly fine collection of 11 close-quartet gospel songs is from Vee-Jay sessions conducted during the late '50s and issued on a Vee-Jay LP in the early '60s. This is one of the few worthwhile Vee-Jay quartet albums that has never been reissued over the ensuing years. The Richmond group is led here by Thomas Johnson (first tenor) and his son Ellis Johnson (bass). Other members of long standing include Lonnie Smith and Joe Williams. This is an excellent collection. —*Opal Louis Nations, Roots & Rhythm Newsletter*

Child of a King / Peacock 182
"Nobody Knows" and the original gospel cut of "Stand by Me," later popularized by Ben E. King. —*Bil Carpenter*

Larnelle Harris

Vocals, Sax, percussion / Inspirational
This singer, saxophonist, and percussionist was at one time a member of the Spurrlows, First Gear, and the Gaither Vocal Band gospel groups. —*Bil Carpenter*

From a Servant's Heart / **i.** 1987 / Heartwarming 3956
MOR, inspirational best. —*Bil Carpenter*

○ **The Father Hath Provided** / **i.** 1988 / Heartwarming 2370
Signs of pop progression with a little soul. —*Bil Carpenter*

● **The Best of 10 Years, Vol. 1** / **i.** 1991 / Benson 2840
Few performers have powerful enough voices to overwhelm the psuedo-orchestral arrangements of modern inspirational music; Harris does. With *Volume 2*, this provides an excellent overview of the singer's work. —*Brian Mansfield*

○ **The Best of 10 Years, Vol. 2** / **i.** 1991 / Benson 02846
Gets the edge over *Volume 1* because it has the soulful "Friends in High Places" and "I Can Begin Again" from 1989's *I Can Begin Again* album. —*Brian Mansfield*

Larnelle Live—Psalms, Hymns & Spiritual Songs / Benson 2696
Backed by the equally spectacular Brooklyn Tabernacle Choir and accompanied by the lush orchestrations of a full symphony, Larnelle Harris' gorgeous tenor voice never sounded in better form than it does here. His emotional, passionate delivery and impeccable enunciation make it possible to visualize his face aglow with the glory of the Lord as he joyously celebrates all aspects of Christian living. For music, message, and memorable moments, *Larnelle Live!* is m-m-m-good! —*Edwin Smith, Rejoice*

The Edwin Hawkins Singers

b. Aug. 1943
Group / Gospel
Through his mass choir worship seminars, Edwin Hawkins has kept traditional Black gospel styles in vogue, particularly among youth. —*Bil Carpenter*

○ **Oh Happy Day** / **i.** 1969 / Pair 3301
A classic traditional Black gospel recording from 1969. —*Bil Carpenter*

● **The Best of the Edwin Hawkins Singers** / **i.** 1985 / Savoy 7077
They began as the Northern State Youth Choir in 1967 and were co-founded by Edwin Hawkins and soprano Betty Watson. They later became the Edwin Hawkins Singers and became crossover sensations when their single "Oh Happy Day" cracked the Top 10 on both the pop and R&B charts in 1969, peaking at number two R&B (four pop). It was their biggest hit and one of the seminal tunes in contemporary gospel history. Here's a collection featuring other successful Hawkins family numbers. Dorothy Morrison later went on to a solo career. —*Ron Wynn*

Face to Face / **i.** 1989 / Lection 841811
Contemporary, with a spiritual mass choir sound. —*Bil Carpenter*

Tramaine Hawkins

Vocals / Soul, R&B, Black gospel
Briefly singing with the R&B group Honey Cones in the early '70s, she married Walter Hawkins and became a featured singer with the Hawkins Family. She is known for a hard, Black gospel singing style. —*Bil Carpenter*

The Search Is Over / **i.** 1989 / Word 5110
Urban-funk/R&B, crossover gospel. —*Bil Carpenter*

○ **Tramaine Hawkins Live** / **i.** 1990 / Sparrow 1246
Traditional Black gospel belting. —*Bil Carpenter*

● **The Joy That Floods My Soul** / Sparrow 1173
Tramaine Hawkins has sometimes drawn fire from conservative types for being too risky and experimental in her work. There shouldn't be any such worries with *The Joy That Floods My Soul.* The mood is more restrained, the arrangements less linked to prominent, driving backbeats, and Hawkins' rising, glorious soprano is assisted by swirling voices and a soulful choir rather than a barrage of synthesizers and blaring guitars . . . [This] should quiet those who have questioned Tramaine Hawkins' faith or direction; she shows she can sing straight gospel with as much energy and conviction as her crossover tunes. —*Ron Wynn, Rejoice*

Walter Hawkins

b. May 18, 1949, Oakland, CA
Vocals / Black gospel
Born in Oakland, CA, Hawkins earned a Master of Divinity degree from UC at Berkeley. He is pastor of the Love Center Church. —*Bil Carpenter*

○ **Love Alive 1** / **i.** 1975 / Light 5686
Walter and Tramaine Hawkins outsinging one another on this contemporary Black gospel recording. —*Bil Carpenter*

Mark Heard

Vocals / Rock, Folk
Brilliant, poetic singer-songwriter whose work displayed a deep spirituality and an honesty to the human condition uncommon in CCM. Heard died in 1992 of heart failure, and *High Noon* recaps the best material of his last three albums. —*Thom Granger*

Stop the Dominoes / **i.** 1981 / Home Sweet Home Records 2101
More straight rock and roll than his later efforts and more obviously Christian oriented songs. —*Richard Meyer*

Dry Bones Dance / **i.** 1990 / Fingerprint 9001
Includes the great "House of Broken Dreams," the rockin' "Rise From the Ruins" and "Lonely Road." This acoustic album is very forceful but never forced. Each song has a real drive and committed vocals. A great record. —*Richard Meyer*

○ **Second Hand** / **i.** 1991 / Fingerprint 9102
On this album Heard has adopted a more contemporary electric sound. His songs keep getting stronger. Some key tracks are "Nod Over Coffee," "Love Is Not the Only Thing," and "Look Over Your Shoulder." Highly recommended. —*Richard Meyer*

Satellite Sky / i. 1992 / Fingerprint 9751
Mark Heard has gone into overdrive on this, his third Fingerprint CD. Most songs are arranged around his electrified metal bodied mandolin. The personal spiritual message is still here in full force but the songs stand up well. The desparate "Tip of My Tongue," "Love is So Blind" and "Satellite Sky" are key tracks. —*Richard Meyer*

Reflections of a Former Life / i. 1994 / Home Sweet Home
The only way to get even a smattering of Heard's early recordings for Home Sweet Home is on this CD collection, unmercifully brief and hardly a substitute for the real things. —*Thom Granger*

★ **High Noon** / Myrrh 6978-613
Excellent collection of tracks selected from Heard's last three recordings, all of which were exemplary. —*Thom Granger*

Highway QCs

Group / Black gospel
This quartet was started in the '40s. Over the years, the lead singers have included Sam Cooke, Johnnie Taylor, Willie Rogers, and Spencer Taylor. —*Bil Carpenter*

● **Jesus Is Waiting** / Vee-Jay 603
The Highway QCs were considered gospel's greatest farm team, the place where aspiring quartet lead singers would hone their skills before joining an "A-list" group. But that didn't mean the group made inferior music; indeed, the songs on *Jesus Is Waiting*, a single-disc collection combining two albums they cut in the mid '50s and early '60s can stand with any issued by the better name ensembles. A youthful Johnnie Taylor soars, whoops and moans through songs done from 1955-1957, while Spencer Taylor comes on with equal might and ferocity on the later material. They may not have had the reputations, nor kept their members as long, but at times the Highway QCs made music that resounded with as much fury as anyone on the gospel trail. —*Ron Wynn*

○ **The Best of the Highway [QCs]** / Chameleon 74800
A respectable collection for the group that acted as a feeder for the Soul Stirrers and other first-echelon groups. Prior editions included Johnnie Taylor and the unrecorded Sam Cooke and O.V. Wright. —*Ron Wynn*

The Lord Is Sweet / Peacock
Includes "Changes at the End" and "Rock Me." —*Bil Carpenter*

Kim Hill

Vocals, guitar / CCM, Folk-rock
This Mississippi guitarist with a folk-rock style akin to James Taylor and Suzanne Vega has a sturdy, low-alto vocal style. —*Bil Carpenter*

○ **Kim Hill** / i. 1982 / Reunion 0029-725
Semi-philosophical midtempo worship songs. —*Bil Carpenter*

Brave Heart / i. 1991 / Reunion 24346
A vocal Christian statement in a secular folk package. —*Bil Carpenter*

Talk About Life / i. Jun. 1993 / Reunion 0049-726
Honest looks at life crises in an acoustic setting. —*Bil Carpenter*

● **So Far So Good** / i. May 24, 1994 / Bna Entertainment 66332
Hill's first foray into country is of the more current pop/folk- flavored approach, featuring many contemporary Christian musicans on the project. —*Thom Granger*

Dallas Holm

Vocals / Inspirational
Holm is a singer and songwriter. In spite of a restrained, undistinctive, flat vocal style, Holm convincingly brings life to MOR ballads such as his signature song, "Rise Again," without attempting to. —*Bil Carpenter*

○ **Beyond the Curtain** / i. 1988 / Dayspring 4171-623
Inspirational MOR and a reworking of "Rise Again." —*Bil Carpenter*

● **The Early Works: Best of Dallas Holm** / Benson 2767
Adult contemporary pop. —*Bil Carpenter*

The Imperials

Group / Disco, Inspirational
Formed in 1964, the Imperials have shifted back and forth between Southern gospel, MOR, and CCM styles and have launched the careers of other gospel artists, most notably, Russ Taff. —*Bil Carpenter*

Big God / i. 1991 / Star Song
Synthesizers and electric guitars—their hippest date yet. —*Bil Carpenter*

● **The Very Best of the Imperials** / Word 4025-570
Contemporary pop from the '70s and '80s. —*Bil Carpenter*

Iona

British band captures Celtic stylings mixed with folk, rock and jazz for unique approach. —*Thom Granger*

Iona / i. 1991 / ForeFront 2700

Beyond These Shores / i. 1993 / ForeFront

Mahalia Jackson

b. Oct. 1911, New Orleans, LA, d. Jan. 27, 1972
Vocals / Blues, Black gospel
Born in New Orleans, Mahalia Jackson grew up in the Baptist Church, though she also admired blues singers such as Bessie Smith and Ma Rainey. Jackson made Chicago her home beginning in 1927, where she also began a lifelong association with gospel writer and performer Thomas A. Dorsey. She earned the title "Gospel Queen" with her 1947 version of "Move On Up a Little Higher." Tours of Europe and television appearances in the United States followed on the heels of this success. She remained one of gospel's most visible figures until her death. —*Kip Lornell*

Les Plus Grands Themes
It's a joy to hear Mahalia Jackson's early '50s Apollo sides in good, clean digitalized stereo. The quality here is better than all previous reissue material. Soaring and sometimes graceful vocal dynamics by this great diva of gospel and spirituals, but there's a shameful lack of pictures and book notes. This is 18 of the best. —*Opal Louis Nations, Roots & Rhythm Newsletter*

○ **In the Upper Room** / i. 1965 / Vogue 600061
Backed by her longtime pianist Mildred Falls and with vocal support from both the Southern Harmonaires (aka the Larks) and the Melody Echoes, Mahalia Jackson powers her way through the majestic two-part title track, plus "Walk in Jerusalem," "I'm a Child of the City," "His Eye is on the Sparrow," "I Walked in the Garden," "It Is No Secret," and 11 other sacred numbers. The source here is clearly disc rather than tape, and the sound quality reflects that weakness. Part one of the title track is also cut off a bit. Otherwise, this disc features original notes, session details, and lyrics. —*Dave Howell, Roots & Rhythm Newsletter*

The World's Greatest Gospel Singer / i. May 4, 1975 / CBS 644
Contains many songs not included in other anthologies, such as "Keep Your Hand On the Plow," "Out of the Depths," "Jesus Met the Woman At the Well," "I'm Going to Live the Life I Sing About in My Song," and more expressions of her greatness. —*Ladyslipper*

The Mahalia Jackson Collection / i. 1985 / Deja Vu 2006
Probably the greatest gospel singer ever recorded, every rich nuance of this woman's voice embodies spiritual devotion; you don't have to subscribe to Christianity to appreciate her lovely countenance! Contains 20 well-known and loved traditional hymns, including "In the Upper Room" (parts 1 and 2), "Nobody Knows the Trouble I've Seen," "Walkin' to Jerusalem," "My Story," "Bless This House." —*Ladyslipper*

★ **Gospels, Spirituals & Hymns** / i. 1991 / CBS 47083
Her motto was: "Don't let the devil steal the beat from the Lord!" She had pipes that could blow the faithful out of the back pews, but understood restraint far better than some of her disciples. These 36 performances (waxed between 1954-69) present an American archetype in full cry. —*Roundup Newsletter*

☆ **Mahalia Jackson, Vol. 2** / i. Jul. 28, 1992 / CBS 48924
With its excellent sound and liner notes, the second box set of Mahalia Jackson's Columbia recordings is just as essential as the first. —*AMG*

★ **Live at Newport** / Sony 8071

○ **Amazing Grace** / Sony 14358
A nice sampling of Jackson's later recordings. —*Kip Lornell*

Jacob's Trouble

CCM, Pop/rock

Georgia-based band influenced by '60s pop (Beatles, Byrds, Monkees) and Christian alternative mentor Terry Taylor (Daniel Amos, Swirling Eddies), who also produced the band's first two records. —*Thom Granger*

● **Let the Truth Run Wild** / i. 1992 / Alarma
The band's third release was produced by the late Mark Heard. —*Thom Granger*

Jacob's Trouble / i. 1993 / Alarma
Its first self-produced effort, an attempt to forge a more original style. —*Thom Granger*

Diggin' Up Bones / i. 1994 / Alarma
A collection of outtakes, demos, and covers. —*Thom Granger*

Blind Willie Johnson

Vocals, guitar / Blues gospel
A guitar-playing evangelist with a scary, emotion-charged voice, Blind Willie Johnson played the most exquisite slide ever heard. Void of frivolity or uncertainty, his 78s were clearly the work of a pained believer seeking street-corner redemption with a guitar and a tin cup. He was gifted with an incomparable sense of timing and tone, using his pocket-knife slide to duplicate his vocal inflections or to produce an unforgettable phrase from a single strike of a string. With its wide, rough vibrato, his voice was as fierce as Charles Patton's or Son House's, but much easier to understand.
In 1927, Blind Willie Johnson became one of the first gospel guitarists on 78. Among his 30 recorded songs is the landmark instrumental "Dark Was the Night, Cold Was the Ground," described by Ry Cooder as "the most transcendent piece in all American music." Blind Willie spent most of his life singing for the Baptist Church or playing for tips on the streets of Beaumont, TX. Decades later, his music echoed in the styles of Mississippi Fred McDowell and Mance Lipscomb. Still, he remains a slide guitarist without parallel, a player so perfect he's impossible to adequately imitate. —*Jas Obrecht*

☆ **Praise God I'm Satisfied** / i. 1989 / Yazoo 1058
Pre-war gospel blues at its most harrowing and transcendental. Unsurpassed slide guitar! —*Jas Obrecht*

○ **Sweeter As the Years Go By** / i. 1990 / Yazoo 1078
A complement to Yazoo 1058 (*Praise God I'm Satisfied*), this brings us the remainder of Blind Willie Johnson's recorded legacy. The most influential of the "guitar evangelists" to record in the 1920s, Johnson's best work resonates with a timeless urgency. His bottleneck playing, passionate and precise, has never been equalled. In perspective, he may have been the first recorded soul singer. — *Mark A. Humphrey, Rock & Roll Disc*

★ **Complete Recordings of Blind Willie Johnson** / i. 1993 / Columbia/Legacy 52835
If you've never heard Blind Willie Johnson, you are in for one of the great, bone-chilling treats in music. Johnson played slide guitar, and sang in a rasping, false bass that could freeze the blood. But no bluesman was he; this was gospel music of the highest order, full of emotion and heartfelt commitment. Of all the guitar playing evangelists, Blind Willie Johnson may have been the very best. Though not related by bloodlines to Robert Johnson, comparisons in emotional commitment from both men cannot be helped. This two-CD anthology collects everything known to exist, and that's a lot of stark, harrowing emotional commitment no matter how you slice it. Not for the faint of heart, but hey, the good stuff never is. —*Cub Koda*

★ **Complete Blind Willie** / i. 1993 / Columbia/Legacy 52835
All 30 of this amazing Texas gospel artists' master collected up in one place, with the added bonus of improved remastering from the original 78 rpm metal parts and exhaustive liner notes from Sam Charters. With a powerful rasping voice and amazing slide guitar playing, Johnson's music touches on powerful imagery with an equally potent delivery to match it in intensity. No blues or secular music here, but certainly this anthology stands as one of the cornerstones of any American music collection. —*Cub Koda*

Brother Vernard Johnson

Sax / Gospel, Jazz, Inspirational
This saxophonist earned a doctorate in musicology from Southwestern Baptist Theological Seminary in 1982. Influenced by R&B sax man King Curtis, he played in a Kansas City jazz group. Now he plays only gospel-oriented music, touring with a 13-member combo. —*Bil Carpenter*

I'm Alive! / i. 1991 / Nonesuch 61150
Contains some good sax solos, derivative arrangements, timid percussion. —*Ron Wynn*

● **Rocking the Gospel** / ROIR 157
Sanctified, hard-charging sax from gospel's best instrumental improviser since Ben Branch. —*Ron Wynn*

Willie Neal Johnson

Vocals / Black gospel
Johnson has a hard country-blues approach to traditional Black gospel. He currently sings with the Gospel Keynotes. —*Bil Carpenter*

● **Going Back with the Lord** / Malaco 4423
Updated material featuring one-time quartet star Johnson with the Gospel Keynotes. —*Ron Wynn*

I'm Yours Lord / Malaco 4439
These are some fine songs and ordinary performances with the Gospel Keynotes. —*Ron Wynn*

Phil Keaggy

Guitar / Folk, Pop/rock
This premier guitarist played with Glass Harp (which recorded for Decca) before going gospel in the '70s. He was influenced by the Beatles but has won respect for his authoritative style. —*Bil Carpenter*

Love Broke Thru / i. 1976 / Myrrh 6915
These are extended, McCartneyesque guitar solos. Stirring pop/rock. —*Bil Carpenter*

The Wind and The Wheat / i. 1987 / A&M 0758
Several pieces of solo acoustic guitar, and the rest with a small group ensemble. Brilliant acoustic playing. —*Paul Kohler*

○ **Phil Keaggy and Sunday's Child** / i. 1988 / Word 6876-616
Fans of Anglo-rock/pop should love this outing, which has all the tuneful appeal of Crowded House or Jellyfish. Produced by Lynn Nichols (who later helped form Chagall Guevara), *Phil Keaggy and Sunday's Child* sparkles with a fine mix of chiming Rickenbacker guitars and soaring harmonies. Occasionally the Brit-pop focus gives way to a sturdy hard-rock sound, but it's still very well executed. Among the many highlights included are "Sunday's Child," "Tell Me How You Feel," and "I'm Gonna Get You Now." —*Rick Clark*

Town to Town/Ph'lip Side/Play Thru Me / i. 1990 / Myrrh 6945-618
Keaggy's early music has dated rather badly, so while there's some impressive guitar work and some good songs on the two-CD reissue (material 1980-1982), there's a lot to wade through. —*Brian Mansfield*

○ **What a Day/Love Broke Thru** / i. 1990 / Myrrh 6915-611
Keaggy's first two solo albums (from 1973 and 1976 reissued here on one CD) remain among his best. Keaggy was one of the first contemporary Christian musicians to bring an original melodic sense to his songs (indebted as it was to Paul McCartney), and his lyrical naivete comes across as refreshing rather than insipid. —*Brian Mansfield*

○ **Find Me in These Fields** / i. 1990 / Word 48568
His hooks are still firmly rooted in the '60s, but they're big ol' hooks, and a crack backing band makes this a power-pop classic interspersed with guitar instrumentals. —*Brian Mansfield*

Beyond Nature / i. 1991 / Word 47748
An album of solo acoustic guitar and small-group music. An excellent recording. —*Paul Kohler*

★ **Crimson & Blue** / i. 1992 / Word 7016954617
A tour de force of '60s and '70s power trios and extended jams, with songwriting a few cuts above most of the material that inspired it. Mainstream version titled *Blue* features a cover of Badfinger's "Baby Blue," and both feature the Van Morrison tune, "When Will I Learn (To Live in God)." —*Thom Granger*

The Kingsmen (Gospel)

Group / Southern gospel

An old-time quartet, founded by Big Jim Hamill in 1955 and based in Ashland, NC. —*Bil Carpenter*

○ **Mississippi Live / i.** 1987 / Riversong 2387
Booming tenors and resounding baritones. Check out "Inside the Gates." —*Bil Carpenter*

Michael Knott

An important voice in Christian music, Knott delves into dark lyrical territory on many recordings, but still manages a way to communicate the hope of the gospel. —*Thom Granger*

Screaming Brittle Siren / i. 1992 / Bvr 343

Rocket and a Bomb / i. 1994 / Brainstorm

Jan Krist

Critically acclaimed acoustic singer-songwriter shows a way with words and influence from Joni Mitchell. —*Thom Granger*

Decapitated Society / i. 1992 / Storyville

Wing and a Prayer / i. 1994 / Storyville

Andy Landis

New country artist mixes same blend of acoustic folk, pop, and bluegrass stylings that has worked so effectively for artists like Trisha Yearwood. —*Thom Granger*

Stranger / i. 1993 / Star Song
Landis' husband is country producer Steve Buckingham, who does the honors here as well, with guest performances from Dolly Parton, Sweethearts of the Rodeo, and Sonny Landreth. —*Thom Granger*

Cristy Lane (ELEANOR JOHNSTON)

b. Jan. 8, 1940, Peoria, IL
Vocals / Inspirational
Born Eleanor Johnston, this singer of country and pop standards was guided by husband Lee Stoller into a gospel career. She recorded her first record, "Janie Took My Place," on the K-Ark label in 1968. Though the majority of her records are of a secular nature, her biggest hit was "One Day at a Time" from 1979, which is one of the biggest-selling gospel songs of all time and sold several million copies. —*Bil Carpenter*

○ **One Day at a Time / i.** 1978 / Arrival 2073
A simplistic, soft-pop style of gospel from her gentle voice. —*Bil Carpenter*

● **Footprints in the Sand / i.** 1983 / Liberty 48392
Because of the strong selection of songs and consistent performances, this compilation is the one to get out of the several Lane discs available from Arrival. —*Stephen Thomas Erlewine*

All In His Hands / i. 1989 / Heartwarming 2469
Lane's pristine sounds come through best on the '50s-style "He Loves Me Still." —*Bil Carpenter*

My Best to You / i. 1992 / Arrival 3076
A good compilation of some of Lane's most popular gospel material that is somewhat undermined by the number of tracks that are duplicated from *Footprints in the Sand.* —*Stephen Thomas Erlewine*

Mylon LeFevre & Broken Heart

b. Oct. 6, 1945
Group / CCM
Mylon LeFevre sang with his family's Southern gospel group, the LeFevres, at the age of 12. Later he became a songwriter, with his songs recorded by Elvis and others. LeFevre formed the CCM band Broken Heart in 1981. —*Bil Carpenter*

● **Mylon / i.** 1970 / Cotillion 9026
Southern rock, with strong rhythm sections and Joe South guesting. —*Bil Carpenter*

Greatest Hits / i. 1988 / Word 6879-380
Southern boogie/gospel rock and secular music from the early '70s. —*Bil Carpenter*

Crystal Lewis

Lewis began in the cast of *Hi-Tops*, a youth musical, later fronting a rockabilly gospel band (Wild Blue Yonder) and moving on to a solo recording career and a stint with the TV series *Roundhouse.*

A tremendous vocal talent that is surely one of CCM's best-kept secrets. —*Thom Granger*

Simply the Best / i. 1991 / Frontline
A compilation of her better Frontline recordings, including one from a reworking of the melodic idea behind "Be My Baby," by Wild Blue Yonder, "Only One." —*Thom Granger*

★ **Bride / i.** 1993 / Metro One
Though still an uneven record (an ongoing problem), her best vocal work is represented here, including an impressive live take on "Amazing Grace." —*Thom Granger*

Remix Album / i. 1994 / Metro One
Alternate versions stress Lewis' urban and hip-hop instincts, which are formidable (including rap!). Lewis has also released versions of her two Metro One albums in Spanish. —*Thom Granger*

Joe Ligon

Alabama-born vocalist Joe Ligon was the original lead vocalist of the Mighty Clouds of Joy. His sound and approach reflected the influence of both the Rev. Julius Cheeks and Curtis Mayfield. He has remained his lead singer since the '60s, when they signed with Peacock Records. —*Ron Wynn*

○ **Old Revival Back Home** / Word 8279

Kerry Livgren

G/P/COM / Hard Rock, Heavy Metal
Former member and founder of '70s band Kansas, first made Christian statements on solo album *Seeds of Change*, then formed AD and has since retired, making only the occasional 'home made' album. —*Thom Granger*

● **Decade / i.** Feb. 20, 1992 / Sparrow 1320
A two-disc retrospective of Livgren's first 10 years of artistic output as a Christian, nicely packaged and annotated. —*Thom Granger*

Lost Dogs

A 'supergroup' of sorts from the Christian alterntive scene, consisting of Terry Taylor (Daniel Amos, etc.), Mike Roe (77's), Derri Daugherty (The Choir), and Gene Eugene (Adam Again). —*Thom Granger*

Scenic Routes / Brainstorm
A mostly acoustic set, recorded semi-spontaneously in the studio, carrying a surprisingly country flavor on many of the tracks. —*Thom Granger*

● **Little Red Riding Hood** / Word 0536-677
More finely crafted than its first, the foursome reunited for a set of songs that challenged all expectations. —*Thom Granger*

L.S.U.

Alternative rock band fronted by Michael Knott makes music that varies from album to album, but connected by Knott's distinct vision. —*Thom Granger*

● **Shaded Pain / i.** 1987 / Frontline

Claire Lynch

Former lead singer of the Front Porch Bluegrass Band makes an impressive gospel debut with the voice of a mountain-raised angel. —*Thom Granger*

Friends For a Lifetime / i. 1993 / Brentwood Bluegrass

Sallie Martin Singers

Spiritual
A Canadian four-piece band combining heavy guitar-rock riffs with primitive synthesizers, oscillators, and tone generators. The band was capable of recording concise single-length songs as well as breaking loose into long jazz-like improvisations without sounding ponderous as many of their art-rock contemporaries did. —*Jim Powers, Jr.*

○ **Throw Out the Lifeline / i.** 1950-1952 / Fantasy/Specialty 7043
The Sallie Martin Singers were among the finest touring and recording gospel outfits during the '50s, and have had almost none of their output made available until now. The 28 selections (plus a 29th that spotlights her adopted daughter Cora) aren't quite as freewheeling and rampaging as the quartets, but it's no

less powerful and expressive, whether it's Sallie Martin, Cora Martin, or Cora Weston on leads, or the group teaming with special guest Brother Joe May. This is vintage, joyous material from a group that's previously been sorely overlooked. —*Ron Wynn*

○ **Precious Lord** / i. 1993 / Vee-Jay 606
Sallie Martin, a gospel music mainstay as a performer, leader, and publishing maven, had disbanded her famous singing group in the '50s when her daughter told her she didn't want to do any more tours. She briefly resurrected two new editions in the early '60s and cut two albums for Vee-Jay before disbanding them again. Though the 23 songs on this single disc reissue aren't as glorious or memorable as the group's Specialty dates, they are still valuable, both to hear Martin's rough but effective leads and harmonizing with new vocalists, and also because the resignation and mournful quality in Martin's singing during the 1963 sessions were an indication she'd had enough of the performance/recording/touring grind. —*Ron Wynn*

★ **Throw Out the Lifeline** / i. 1993
The most instrumentation these tracks ever had was an organ, a piano, and an occasional drum. originally issued on Specialty Records in the 1950-53 period, these 29 tracks are Black congregational styled numbers, 23 of them previously unissued. These sides also include six selections where Brother Joe May joined the singers. Most of the rest finds Sallie and Cora trading leads. A fine example of Sallie's powers shows up on "Ain't That Good News." —*Bil Carpenter*

The Roberta Martin Singers

b. 1907, d. 1969
Group / Spiritual
This talented pianist started a quartet with Theodore Frye in the '30s. This aggregation gradually evolved into the Roberta Martin Singers by the '50s. It is now known that she copied the piano style of blind pianist Arizona Dranes, who also influenced the Ward Singers. Martin's singers sang loudly and dramatically. She also wasn't concerned about a harmonious sound; when one member of the group was leading a song, whether male or female, you could easily identify the backing voices. This lack of synchronicity made the group's urgent sound a unique and welcome change amid the repetitive quartets of the time. Robert Anderson was one of Martin's principal singers. She herself was referred to as the Helen Hayes of the Gospel World. She died in 1969. —*Bil Carpenter*

○ **The Roberta Martin Singers** / Savoy 7018
Most of Martin's best early work from the late '40s through the '50s is out of print, but this is a nice introduction to this dynamic singer and group leader. —*Kip Lornell*

Brother Joe May

Vocals / Black gospel
A bluesy tenor, May was a protege of Willie Mae Ford Smith. When he began to record in the '50s, he copied her cuts "Search Me Lord" and "Old Ship of Zion" note by note. In the '60s he appeared in the play *Black Nativity*. He was once called the "Thunderbolt of the Midwest." —*Bil Carpenter*

○ **Brother Joe May Live, 1952-1955** / Specialty 7054
Brother Joe May earned his "Thunderbolt of the Midwest" nickname with incandescent, riveting vocals that could blow off a roof or reduce listeners to tears, often at the same time. The 16 tracks on this CD were done live, usually at services or during church performances, and they frequently paired him with the Sallie Martin Singers. While they and Prof. Earle Hines are fine, May is in another dimension. His full, flamboyant and dynamic voice shudders, roars, rises, moans and flails, and he fortifies the songs with commentary that's nearly as inspiring. Even devout atheists will be impressed by the power of Brother Joe May. —*Ron Wynn*

Brother Joe May Story
Here's a 1972 two-record set of 24 gospel songs made popular by Brother Joe May between 1958, when he joined Nashboro after nine years on Specialty, and the time of his demise in 1974. Macon-born May, also known as "The Thunderbolt of the Middle West," was a Pentacostal practitioner of The Willie Mae Ford Smith of gospel singing. May's powerful tenor impressed and inspired many. It includes some live church recordings and sides made with The Joe May Singers. Notable cuts include the rousing

"I've Been Dipped in the Water." This is a fine collection. —*Opal Louis Nations, Roots & Rhythm Newsletter*

☆ **Thank You Lord for One More Day** / i. 1967 / Specialty 2142
Excellent hard gospel, with occasional support from Sister Wynona Carr and the Pilgrim Travelers. —*Ron Wynn*

★ **In Loving Memory . . .** / i. 1974 / Specialty 2151
In Loving Memory of Brother Joe May is a collection of May's finest shouts and duets on Specialty, supported on some cuts by the Pilgrim Travelers, The Sallie Martin Singers, or a live audience. —*Ron Wynn*

○ **Search Me, Lord** / i. 1974 / Specialty 2132
Authoritative gospel and energized vocals with support from the Pilgrim Travelers and The Sallie Martin Singers. —*Ron Wynn*

○ **Thunderbolt of the Middle West** / i. 1974 / Specialty 7033
Brother Joe May, the baritone belter from Macon, Mississippi, could, without much effort, move a church through the power of his voice. On these recordings culled from 1952-1955 sessions, May is ably supported by the vocalizing of The Sallie Martin Singers, Sister Wynona Carr, Annette May, and The Pilgrim Travelers. There are 17 lung-splitting solo outings, 10 previously unissued. It includes such hits as "Search Me Lord" and "I'm Gonna Live the Life I Sing About in My Song." He was the Caruso of postwar gospel. —*Opal Louis Nations, Roots & Rhythm Newsletter*

David Meece

b. 1952
Vocals, piano / CCM
Light pop singer-songwriter whose chameleon-like tendencies has made for an uneven catalog; nevertheless, many of his songs have been smash hits on Christian radio. —*Thom Granger*

● **Chronology** / i. 1940 / Word 6844-277
The best songs from his years with the Myrrh label, making for a good introduction to the artist. —*Thom Granger*

Candle in the Rain / i. 1987 / Myrrh 6864-618
Meece teamed with Gino and Joe Vanelli for this set, resulting in a different musical approach, with good results. —*Thom Granger*

Learning to Trust / i. 1989 / Two-One-Four 5312
A pivotal recording for Meece, as the artist deals with his troubled family history, and crafts some of his best songs in the process. —*Thom Granger*

Rikki Michele

Adam Again chanteuse, one of the few females in the Christian alternative music scene, has also recorded two eclectic solo records. —*Thom Granger*

One Moment Please / Word 1507-027

Big, Big Town / Word 0508-673

The Mighty Clouds of Joy

Group / Soul, R&B, Black gospel
Formed in Los Angeles ca. 1959, the original members were Ermant and Elmer Franklin, Joe Ligon, Johnny Martin, Leon Polk, and Richard Wallace. They had some R&B hits in the 1974-1977 period with "Mighty High" and "Time." They have consistently adjusted their repertoire according to the current trends, having played everything from traditional Black gospel to light rock. —*Bil Carpenter*

● **The Best of the Mighty Clouds of Joy** / i. 1973 / MCA 28019
The title is a bit misleading, but it's still a fair sample of the group's most popular performances. —*Kip Lornell*

The Best of the Mighty Clouds of Joy, Vol. 2 / i. 1973 / MCA 28040
A hodgepodge of lesser material from their Peacock albums and singles. Volume 2 includes some nice sides, but it's weaker than the first volume. —*Kip Lornell*

Mighty Clouds of Joy Live / MCA 22022
At the start of their decline in 1971, the Clouds performed and were recorded live at the Apollo Theater in Harlem. Led by the raspy pipes of Little Willie Joe Ligon, the quintet stirred and quelled the audience through a program of gospel standards and personal hits. Boiling points include a devastating version of "Amazing Grace" and testimonial preaching between selections. Not quite as powerful as the group's 1966 *Live at the Music Hall*

album, but chock full of excitement nevertheless. There's a neglectful lack of pictures and sleeve notes on the otherwise good analog tape transfer. —*Opal Louis Nations, Roots & Rhythm Newsletter*

○ **The Mighty Clouds Live at the Music Hall** / Peacock

Julie Miller

Quirky singer-songwriter has played with mainstream artists Victoria Williams and Shawn Colvin, and an early inspirational pop act, but has bloomed considerably over the course of three solo recordings, produced with taste and care. —*Thom Granger*

● **Orphans & Angels** / Myrrh

Meet Julie Miller / Myrrh

He Walks Through Walls / Myrrh

Tim Miner

Soulful, R&B-based pop from talented singer who also writes and produces for a number of other gospel and R&B artists. —*Thom Granger*

○ **True Story** / **i.** 1990 / Frontline
● **Tim Miner** / **i.** 1992 / Motown 6350
A reworking of the *True Story* album for mainstream R&B market, with significant amount of new material. —*Thom Granger*

Geoff Moore

CCM
Second generation CCM artist influenced by Russ Taff and others, creates dependable heartland pop/rock. —*Thom Granger*

All the Good Music / **i.** 1987 / Benson
Anthology of early music created for the Benson label. —*Thom Granger*

○ **Foundations** / Sparrow 1191
This album places Geoff Moore in the ranks of Petra, Mylon LeFevre, and DeGarmo & Key in the creation of excellent and melodic popular rock music. Like those mentioned, Moore primarily aims his messages at those who are already believers in an attempt to strength their existing faith, to encourage commitment, and to share his understanding of what it means to be a follower of Christ. Moore continues to grow as a songwriter and a leader, one who has cut a niche in the ranks of Christian music stores. His music grows and expands as one listens. It is enjoyable to discover a musician who continues to speak to you and who never fails to expand musically. —*Dan Kennedy, Rejoice*

● **Pure & Simple** / ForeFront 2717
Set represents band at its peak as a rock act; later albums would feature more pop-oriented material. —*Thom Granger*

Cindy Morgan

Songstress shows influences from pop/R&B divas like Mariah Carey and Anita Baker, but manages to craft a sensual style still surprisingly acceptable to White gospel audiences. —*Thom Granger*

Real Life / **i.** Jun. 30, 1992 / Word 52896
Her debut release, *Real Life*, shows much promise as she delivers believable lyrics and urban dance/pop stylings. Morgan's voice falls somewhere between Mariah Carey and Gloria Estefan, but she avoids being a sound-alike. On top of her unique singing abilities, Morgan is a prolific songwriter, addressing spiritual themes without speaking in the usual clichés. Add the hip-hop sound of the streets and she could be the next voice to reach the youth with the message of the gospel. —*Edwin Smith, Rejoice*

Reason to Live / Word

Morning Stars of Savannah

Group
A notable quartet led by Mitchell Williams. —*Opal Louis Nations*

○ **Mama's Old Dress** / Nashboro 47231
Impressive singing and sermonizing from the late '70s. —*Opal Louis Nations*

Rich Mullins

b. 1955
Vocals / CCM

A songwriter whose distinctive point of view makes for some of the more thoughtful lyrics in the genre. Mullins also allows his Celtic/American heritage to influence the instrumental side of his music; the combination has produced a few of the essential albums in contemporary Christian music. —*Thom Granger*

Winds of Heaven, Stuff of Earth / **i.** May 1989 / Reunion 0036-721
Mullins' vision begins to take shape, with help from producer Reed Arvin, on the album that featured the now-classic, "Awesome God." —*Thom Granger*

★ **The World As Best As I Remember It, Vol. 2** / **i.** 1992 / Reunion 24483
A near-perfect song cycle, with moments worthy of the best in pop music history. —*Thom Granger*

○ **A Liturgy, A Legacy & A Ragamuffin Band** / **i.** Oct. 26, 1993 / Reunion 66340
Brilliant concept, where Mullins originals reflecting on the concept of legacy are used as liturgical motifs, making for a thoroughly contemporary and powerful worship experience and artistic statement. —*Thom Granger*

Newsboys

CCM
Band whose principals hail from Australia, has changed musical styles as often as band members. Recent association with Steve Taylor has marked its most artistically fruitful and successful period. —*Thom Granger*

● **Going Public** / **i.** 1994 / Star Song

Nicholas

b. Feb. 18, 1954, (Philip)
Group / CCM
Now a husband/wife duo, Nicholas began as a quartet in the early '80s. As a duo they've been in the forefront of contemporary urban-style Black gospel. —*Bil Carpenter*

○ **Dedicated** / **i.** 1985 / Word 5503-034
The title cut and "Go Tell Somebody" are what modern Black gospel is all about. Their finest work. —*Bil Carpenter*

Nicholas Live in Memphis / **i.** 1989 / Word 5501-031
A spontaneous high-energy set. —*Bil Carpenter*

Larry Norman

Vocals, guitar / Christian rock
One of the founding fathers of 'Jesus Music' in the late '60s, Norman left L.A. band People! to record *Upon This Rock* in late 1969, which, along with Mylon LeFevre's solo debut, marked the beginnings of the genre. His *Only Visiting This Planet* was, and still is for many, a high-water mark for Christian rock. Recent years have found him recording and touring less and less, paritally due to health problems. —*Thom Granger*

○ **Upon This Rock** / **i.** 1969 / Kingsway 6
Counterculture, psychedelic pop. —*Bil Carpenter*

○ **Only Visiting This Planet** / **i.** 1972 / Verve 5092
Contains sociopolitical statements with hard-edged, Jesus rock zeal. —*Bil Carpenter*

Dorothy Norwood

Vocals / Black gospel
A belter with a harsh, gravelly voice, she's probably recorded more songs about wayward children than Shirley Caesar. Before going solo in the '60s, Norwood was a member of the Chimes and the Caravans. —*Bil Carpenter*

A Mother's Son / **i.** 1972 / Word 3813-877
The eight songs on Dorothy Norwood's *A Mother's Son* are ideal to showcase her skill as a master of the song sermon. She uses the war symbolism to marvelous effect on "Battle Field," sounds purposely animated on "Mt. Zion," and turns "I See God Making A Way For You" and "Leave It In The Hand of the Lord" into stirring testaments of belief. Her voice, emphatic pace, and dramatic embellishments are the LP's core; there's sparse background and almost no defined instrumental sound. But Norwood is certainly up to the task; her glorious voice and triumphant spirit make *A Mother's Son* another outstanding classic. —*Ron Wynn, Rejoice*

Live / **i.** 1992 / Malaco 4450

An enthusiastic performance, but the energy level dips whenever Norwood stops singing. —*Ron Wynn*

● **Denied Mother** / Savoy 14140
Norwood's spectacular vocals are supported by the Combined Choir of Atlanta, GA. One of Norwood's greatest song sermons is the title track. —*Ron Wynn*

Faithful Daughter / Savoy 14515
This has another classic single in the title track. —*Ron Wynn*

Look What They've Done to My Child / Savoy 14630
Wonderful anthemic vocals and a textbook selection that's a blueprint of gospel storytelling and lyric imagery. —*Ron Wynn*

Nu Vision

Group / CCM
This Hispanic urban-contemporary vocal band was formed in 1990. Members: David, Pete, and Isaac Hernandez; Rick Olvera. —*Bil Carpenter*

○ **Forever Mine** / i. 1991 / Word 48666
Well-done urban rap/CCM with an obvious R&B influence. —*Bil Carpenter*

Michael Omartian

Vocals, keyboards / CCM
Michael Omartian has enjoyed considerable success in the CCM and secular music fields, as a session sideman, songwriter, solo artist, and producer. During the '70s, Omartian's distinctive keyboard work graced projects by Loggins & Messina and Steely Dan. As a producer, Omartian worked with Christopher Cross (cleaning up at the 1981 Grammys with Cross's self-titled debut), as well as Donna Summer and Amy Grant (notably her platinum *Heart in Motion* album). During the mid '70s, Omartian's solo work helped set the standard for high-caliber pop statements that rivaled the best the secular world had to offer. Omartian continues to release solo efforts, the most recent being *The Race*. —*Rick Clark*

The Race / i. 1991 / Epic 48002
On *The Race*, Omartian collaborates with singer/songwriter Michael Anderson and Bruce Sudano (formerly with Brooklyn Dreams). The style is contemporary keyboard-heavy pop, with several songs sporting strong melodic hooks (particularly "Faithful Forever" and "Heartbreak City"). —*Rick Clark*

★ **White Horse/Adam Again** / i. 1991 / Myrrh 6894-614
This CD combines Omartian's first two solo albums, *White Horse* (1974) and *Adam Again* (1975), both very important to CCM because they heralded the advent of advanced production techniques and sophisticated, multilayered lyrical imagery that went beyond standard gospel metaphors. Musically, these two albums are probably Omartian's most adventurous statements. Highlights include the reflective "Right from the Start" and "The Orphan," as well as the celebratory "Ain't You Glad" and the sweeping ballad "Annie the Poet." "White Horse," "Take Me Down," and "Silver Fish" showcase Omartian's fine arranging and keyboard chops. Nevertheless, certain tracks haven't aged very gracefully, particularly "Alive and Well," which instrumentally sounds like a clichéd '70s "Rockford Files"-style TV soundtrack. Both of these albums utilize the cream of Los Angeles's "A-list" session sidemen, including Lee Ritenour, Leland Sklar, David Hungate, Larry Carlton, and Victor Feldman. —*Rick Clark*

One Bad Pig

Group / Christian rock
A punk quartet that started as a lark for a youth rally in the band's Austin, TX, hometown. The positive reception led to a relatively long career, but the members of the band seemed to understand neither punk's culture nor its philosophy and ended up, depending on where you stood in the audience, as either a generic thrash band or a punk parody. —*Brian Mansfield*

○ **I Scream Sunday** / i. Sep. 17, 1991 / Word 48595
These uninspired punk thrashings, produced by White Heart's Billy Smiley, quickly get tedious. But "Man in Black," a duet with (believe it or not) Johnny Cash, shows the exact spot where punk and Christianity intersect. And Cash comes off as a more committed punk than anybody in the band. —*Brian Mansfield*

Out of the Grey

Husband and wife duo (Scott and Christine Dente) met at Berklee College, and went on to make beautiful music together, distinguished by solid songwriting, catchy guitar figures, and Christine's dreamily lovely vocals. —*Thom Granger*

● **The Shape of Grace** / i. 1993 / Sparrow 51344
Like its debut, the duo works with artist/producer Charlie Peacock to craft a killer collection of songs and hone its sound. —*Thom Granger*

Diamond Days / i. 1994 / Sparrow
More band-oriented that its predecessors, and just as hooky. —*Thom Granger*

Shun Pace-Rhodes

Vocals / Black gospel
Pace-Rhodes hails from a family of singers active in the Church of God in Christ (COGIC) music movement. She and her siblings formed the Anointed Pace Sisters of Atlanta in the mid '70s and were known for their contemporary R&B gospel sound. She sang "That Name" on one of Edwin Hawkins's Music and Arts seminal albums in 1987. It was he who personally went to the head of Savoy-Malaco Records and suggested they sign the belting singer as a solo artist, and they did. Rather than cutting her chops on modern styles, Pace-Rhodes sang music that recalls the days of Mahalia Jackson and the Ward Singers. —*Bil Carpenter*

○ **He Lives** / i. 1992 / Savoy Gospel 14807
The most astonishing traditional female gospel soloist in the church today. Her powerhouse pipes are supported by the Showers of Blessing Choir and the Voices of Power out of Atlanta, GA. —*Opal Louis Nations*

Twila Paris

b. 1958
Vocals / Easy listening, Inspirational
One of modern inspirational music's most prolific singer- songwriters, Paris has already made a formidable contribution to the church worldwide, as a number of her songs have been incorporated into hymnals. —*Thom Granger*

Cry for the Desert / i. 1991 / JCI 5300
Intimate light praise/pop music, with Brown Bannister producing. —*Bil Carpenter*

Sanctuary / i. 1991 / Star Song 8207
Produced by contemporary instrumentalist Richard Souther, this album set new musical standards in the inspirational field for arrangement and production ideas. —*Thom Granger*

● **Heart That Knows You** / i. 1993 / Star Song
Best-of collection of radio hits and re-recordings of early classics that serves to introduce the uninitiated. —*Thom Granger*

Beyond a Dream / i. 1994 / Star Song
Paris spun a few heads with this one, featuring her most contemporary material to date, and a bit of a new and more confident vocal approach to match it. —*Thom Granger*

The Early Works / Benson 2766
A good anthology of Paris' first few albums, featuring songs like "The Warrior is a Child" and "We Will Glorify." —*Thom Granger*

Squire Parsons

b. Newton, WV
Vocals / Southern gospel
Born in Newton, WV, Parsons began his gospel career singing with the Calvary Men. In 1975 he joined the Kingsmen as a baritone, but left in 1979 to pursue a solo career and has since recorded 25 Southern-gospel/MOR albums. Parsons won six *Singing News Magazine* awards, including the prestigious Marvin Norcross Award in 1990. "Sweet Beulah Land" was a #1 song on Southern gospel charts in 1981. —*Bil Carpenter*

○ **His Very Best** / Heartwarming 3872
Includes "Hello Mama," "Jesus Is the Door," and "Sweet Beulah Land." —*Bil Carpenter*

Sandi Patti

b. Jul. 14, 1957, Oklahoma City, OK
Vocals, piano / Inspirational

Born in Oklahoma City, OK, Patti set the standards for light-pop or big-orchestra-style praise songs, which enhance her potent, high soprano delivery. Whereas Amy Grant dominated the '80s youth market, Patti sang for their parents. Her distinctive high notes defined '80s inspirational, string-orchestrated praise balladry and, like Grant, spurred a number of clones. —*Bil Carpenter*

Another Time, Another Place / i. 1973 / Word 48545
A pop crossover setting. —*Bil Carpenter*

○ **A Morning like This** / i. 1986 / Word 9003-273
An inspirational tour de force featuring sweet string arrangements. —*Bil Carpenter*

● **Finest Moments** / i. 1990 / Word 9144-608
Her greatest hits. —*Bil Carpenter*

Make His Praise Glorious / i. Apr. 28, 1992 / Word 9064-604
Make His Praise Glorious is Sandi Patti's eighth, latest, and greatest release. Although there was talk of a new Patti style, most listeners will find no surprises here. Instead it's more of the relatively same songs, arrangements, and phenomenal vocals that have made Patti a household favorite and one of gospel music's best-known artists. —*Steve Rabey, Rejoice*

Le Voyage / i. May 25, 1993 / CBS 53939
Patti stretches out a bit, musically and lyrically, with a sort of "Pilgrim's Progress" set to adult contemporary music and more use of lyrical metaphors than before. —*Thom Granger*

Hymns Just for You / Word 48574
Traditional hymns given Patti's heartfelt imprint. —*Bil Carpenter*

Songs from the Heart / Word 48573
A mix of light CCM and pop-gospel. —*Bil Carpenter*

Michael Peace

Vocals / Street poetry
Michael Peace is the reigning Christian rapper on the scene. He made his debut in 1987 with "Rrrock it Right." —*Bil Carpenter*

Vigilante of Hope / i. 1991 / Reunion 0050-724
Direct, humorless rhymes and a slow groove style. —*Bil Carpenter*

○ **Loud N' Clear** / Reunion 24360
Live, salvation-maniacal, produced by Dez Dickerson (ex-guitarist with Prince). —*Bil Carpenter*

Rrrock It Right / Reunion 24357
Easy rap lingo. Urban-styled, with fresh hooks. —*Bil Carpenter*

Charlie Peacock

Vocals / Christian rock
White-soul singer whose combination of Smokey Robinson-influenced falsetto vocals and cerebral lyrics have helped him develop one of CCM's most individual sounds. He cowrote Amy Grant's 1991 hit "Every Heartbeat." A sought-after producer, he was worked with Margaret Becker, The Choir, the 77's, and Jimmy A. —*Brian Mansfield*

The Secret of Time / i. 1990 / Sparrow 1217
Because of their low-budget production, early Peacock projects classified him as "alternative." "Put the Love Back into Love," "Almost Threw It Away," and "Heaven Is a Real Place" suggested that he had more of an affinity for soul, but "Experience" showed that he still needed to learn that the best grooves are created by instinct, not academia. —*Brian Mansfield*

★ **Love Life** / i. 1991 / Sparrow 1303
Peacock's concept album about the correlation between a man's spiritual relationship with God and his physical relationship with his wife was the masterpiece that *The Secret of Time* pointed to. "After Loving You" made no bones about the object of its affections; it was an unabashed love song for Peacock's wife. But what really shook up the Christian audiences was the sensuous funk of "Kiss Me Like a Woman," nothing less than the first Christian song about foreplay (and a scathing indictment of pop radio). —*Brian Mansfield*

West Coast Diaries—Vols. 1-3 / i. 1991 / Sparrow
Demos and live recordings Peacock released as individual albums between 1986 and 1988; Sparrow reissued them individually and as a boxed set. Peacock's the kind of artist who inspires a desire for completism, so even though these recordings show his tendency to overintellectualize his music, they're still worth

having (especially *Volume 2*, which captures an acoustic concert with guitarist Jimmy A and vocalist Vince Ebo). —*Brian Mansfield*

Coram Deo: In the Presence of God / i. 1992 / Sparrow 1330
This worship-oriented project featuring Michael Card, Michael English, and Susan Ashton reflects writer/producer Charlie Peacock's ongoing preoccupation with the relationship of the Christian life and the omnipresence of God. —*Brian Mansfield*

Maggie Staton Peebles

Vocals / Gospel, Spiritual
Peebles first sang with the Jewell Gospel Trio in the '50s with nine gold records on Nashboro label. Then she became a schoolteacher until returning to gospel in 1988. She has a melodious and sweetly powerful voice. —*Bil Carpenter*

Born Again / Winston-Derek 4891
Black gospel standards of the '50s redone in the '90s. —*Bil Carpenter*

○ **First Fruits** / Winston-Derek 17194
Recorded with a simple rhythm section and traditional arrangements. —*Bil Carpenter*

This Soul of Mine / Winston-Derek 21238
Piano-activated Black gospel. —*Bil Carpenter*

Petra

Group / Gospel, Christian rock
Founded by guitarist Bob Hartman, Petra is Christian rock's biggest and longest-running band, whose first album appeared in 1974 and is still pleasing arena rock fans with its catchy anthems and ballads. —*Thom Granger*

Petra / i. 1974 / Word 48802
A musician's album in a blues/country-rock guitar style. —*Bil Carpenter*

Beyond Belief / i. 1990 / Word 48546
It's no secret that Petra's aiming their music their days at the average teenage male. Sure, their tours of high school gyms attract girls too, but it's mainly "band dad" and longtime Campus Crusade for Christ-affiliate Josh McDowell who gets through to them. The boys wanna rock. So Petra keeps the message simple and the hooks anthemic. —*Arsenio Orteza, Rejoice*

Unseen Power: Backstage Pass / i. 1992
Contemporary Christian music's oldest and most-liked rock band follows up their award-winning album/concept video *Beyond Belief* with a collection of 10 bright, shimmering songs of faith. While Petra has always appealed to the teenage crowd, this release seems to be targeted at possible crossover, too. But Petra fans don't need to worry—the band is not selling out its clear gospel message. With the exception of "Who's On the Lord's Side?" (which was a Black gospel hit for Rev. Timothy Wright), all the compositions were penned by Petra members. Producers John and Dino Elefante do a masterly job of capturing the essence of Petra's charisma on compact disc. —*Edwin Smith, Rejoice*

● **Unseen Power** / i. 1992 / Word 48859
This is a warm, crisp production, aside from its metal and bluesy-pop. —*Bil Carpenter*

PFR

Hailing from Minneapolis, this inventive pop/rock trio shows The Beatles and The Police among its influences. —*Thom Granger*

Pray for Rain / i. Jul. 27, 1992 / Vireo 2202
Originally called Inside Out, the band changed its name to Pray for Rain when signing to Sparrow. Unfortunately, someone else had this name too. —*Thom Granger*

Goldie's Last Day / i. 1994 / Sparrow
Renamed PFR, the band displays a wider range of material and arrangements on its second outing. —*Thom Granger*

Leslie Phillips

Vocals / CCM
Gospel music's she-rebel, Phillips left the gospel industry in the late '80s because of its confining nature. She now records secular material on Virgin Records with producer and husband T-Bone Burnett, under the name of Sam Phillips. —*Bil Carpenter*

● **Recollection** / i. 1987 / Myrrh 6874-613

A greatest-hits package. —*Bil Carpenter*

The Turning / Word 6851-613
Emotionally truthful CCM with eccentric instrumentation. —*Bil Carpenter*

Pilgrim Jubilees

Group / Black gospel
This Jackson, MS, quartet led by Clay and Cleve Graham used great guitar work and unique timing to make their mark in the '50s. —*Bil Carpenter*

Back to Basics / i. 1990 / Malaco 4431
Another solid effort recorded by this label, which helped to bring good Southern gospel music into the '90s. —*Kip Lornell*

● **Gospel Roots** / i. 1990 / Malaco 4419
This dynamic album shows why the Pilgrim Jubilees have remained one of the most respected "hard" gospel groups for so many years. —*Kip Lornell*

The Old Ship of Zion / Peacock
This one includes "Pearly Gates" and "If You Don't Mind." —*Bil Carpenter*

Pilgrim Travelers

Group / Black gospel
This "walking rhythm" gospel quartet was extremely popular around 1950-1954. —*Opal Louis Nations*

Better Than That / Specialty 7053
This is the third Travelers disc to be issued by the folks at Fantasy Records, the current owners of the Specialty catalog, and a fitting companion to the earlier two, *The Best of the Pilgrim Travelers* and *Walking Rhythm*. This time the emphasis is on performances from the early to the mid '50s, when the Travelers were one of the top draws on the gospel circuit. Among the many highlights are "I Could Do Better Than That," "Gonna Walk Right Out," "Go Ahead," "The Life You Save May Be Your Own," and "Hold On," with alternating leads. The numbers here are as fine as those on the earlier releases. The sound quality is good, as is the cover booklet design, and the notes are by the gospel authority Ray Funk. —*Rejoice*

○ **The Best of The Pilgrim Travelers, Vols. 1 & 2** / i. 1990 / Specialty 7204
An aptly named sampler of early sides from the huge Specialty vaults, with the legendary Kylo Turner and Keith Barber on leads. —*Kip Lornell*

● **Walking Rhythm** / i. 1992 / Specialty 7030
The first of two CD collections of prime a cappella close harmony gospel in walking rhythm by The Pilgrim Travelers. Contained are unissued, alternate, and previously issued-on-wax sides from the stunning lead chops of Kylo Turner and Keith Barber, who fronted L.A.'s Travelers during the 1947-1956 Specialty sojourn. The quintet cut over 100 sides during this time. The selection here is drawn from the 1947 through 1951 time frame. They're taken from original 16-inch metal masters and filtered through a non-noise system to produce fine presence and sound clarity. —*Opal Louis Nations, Roots & Rhythm Newsletter*

Sister Lucille Pope with the Pearly Gates

Vocals / Black gospel
○ **The Very Best of Sister Lucille Pope** / Nashboro 48567
Soulful and original '60s/'70s gospel sung in the traditional way by this important Atlanta soloist, supported ably by the male members of her family—the Pearly Gates. —*Opal Louis Nations*

Dottie Rambo

b. Mar. 2, 1934, Madison, KY
Vocals, guitar / Southern gospel
Dottie was born in Madison, KY. (She is the wife of Buck Rambo, mother to Reba Rambo, and mother-in-law to Dony McGuire.) She is more influential for the 700 or more worshipful songs she's written over the years, which have inspired facsimiles and numerous covers, than for her own career as a Southern gospel singer or as one of the first female lead guitarists in gospel. —*Bil Carpenter*

● **The Best of the Rambos, Vols. 1 & 2** / NK 1008
Dottie and Buck's country gospel. —*Bil Carpenter*

Soul of Me / Heartwarming
Late '60s soulful Southern gospel. —*Bil Carpenter*

Sunshine Shine on Me / Heartwarming
Mainstream Southern gospel from the '60s. —*Bil Carpenter*

This Is My Valley / Heartwarming
Rambo's warm voice on moody Southern gospel ballads. —*Bil Carpenter*

Troy Ramey & The Sensational Soul Searchers

Group / Black gospel
○ **Troy Ramey** / Nashboro 7253
Pew-scorching, sanctifying gospel from the '70s by this important Atlanta quartet. —*Opal Louis Nations*

Rev. D.C. Rice

Vocals / Spiritual
Born in Alabama, Rev. Rice relocated to Chicago during WW I to join a Pentacostal church. A moving preacher, he was moved to record after witnessing the success of Bishop Fort Washington McGee on his sermonizing/singing records. Rice mimicked McGee's raucous singing and preaching style. He was a prolific recorder, but 1929's "I'm on the Battlefield for the Lord" on the Vocalion label stands out. —*Bil Carpenter*

○ **Rev. D.C. Rice** / Document 5071
Over twenty exemplary performances of jazz-accompanied, sanctified singing and preaching. —*Kip Lornell*

● **Complete Recorded Works (1928-1930)** / Document 5071

Lulu Roman

Vocals / Southern gospel
One of the "Hee-Haw" regulars, she's full of warmth and humor, with an incredible testimony of healing from drug addiction. —*Bil Carpenter*

○ **Take Me There** / i. 1985 / Word 0001-340
Smooth vocals on this pop-ish Southern gospel. —*Bil Carpenter*

Seawind

CCM
Influential late '70s pop jazz outfit boasted in-the-pocket grooves, clever horn charts, and Pauline Wilson's signature vocals set to lyrics that (more often than not) clearly communicated a Christian worldview. Band's career produce only three albums, but Pauline and husband/drummer Bob released an album in the early '80s, and various other members have made their mark in the L.A. studios, playing on a myriad of projects. —*Thom Granger*

Seawind / i. 1976 / CTI 5002
First outing featured more instrumental than vocal music, but band still made its point with songs like "He Loves You" and "Devil is a Liar." —*Thom Granger*

● **Window of a Child** / i. 1977 / CTI 5007
Though Seawind's second recording came only a year after its debut, this album represents its finest artistic statement, with lyrics that spoke plainly yet poetically, and funky jazz-pop music. —*Thom Granger*

Light the Light / i. 1979 / Horizon 734
Third album with A&M-owned Horizon label exposes band to new audience, but some Christians felt the message was watered down in the process. —*Thom Granger*

2nd Chapter of Acts

Group / Church, CCM
A major Christian-rock act, which began in the early '70s, defined by the sibling harmonies of Annie Herring, Matthew Ward, and Nelly Greisen. Their music brought complex song structures to inspirational music. Their best-known song was 1974's "Easter Song," which achieved moderate mainstream radio airplay (and featured Michael Been, later founder of The Call, on bass). The group's self-deprecating attitudes may have kept them from achieving the renown of some contemporaries. Herring and Ward continued to record solo projects after the group disbanded in 1988. —*Brian Mansfield*

● **20** / i. 1992 / Sparrow 1332

Twentieth-anniversary retrospective is a 41-track overview of the music of this influential group. Includes three early singles for MGM and two previously unreleased cuts.—*Brian Mansfield*

Sensational Nightingales

Group / Black gospel
The Sensational Nightingales were assembled in the '40s. In 1957 they appeared on the Gospel Train tour with the Clara Ward Singers and five other big-name gospel acts. Members: Julius Cheeks (lead), Carl Coates (bass), JoJo Wallace (tenor), Howard Carroll (baritone), and Paul Gwens (tenor). Noted hit: "See How They Done My Lord." One of the earliest gospel quintets, they still record and tour today. Many of their '50s and '60s sides (found on MCA reissues) feature the stunning vocals of Rev. Julius Cheeks. As with Archie Brownlee, Cheeks reaches an intensity that distorts the actual recordings, and his style has been heavily "borrowed" by Bobby Bland, Wilson Pickett, and others. The later recordings by Charles Johnson are smoother and slicker, but still top-notch. —*Bil Carpenter & Billy C. Wirtz*

○ **The Best of the Sensational Nightingales** / i. 1978 / MCA 28020
Twelve selections featuring Cheeks, Johnson, and Herbert Robertson. This album is first-rate, five-star, indispensable, and available as a budget reissue! —*Billy C. Wirtz*

Victory Is Mine / i. 1980 / Malaco 4427
This release has soaring unison vocals on such songs as "He'll Answer Prayer," "He May Not Knock No More," and "Occupy Till He Comes." They also put a nice contemporary touch on "Power in the Blood," and "Open Up My Eyes" has a moving, personalized approach. This isn't earthshaking Sensational Nightingales material, but it's well done, and faithful to the genre in mood and approach. —*Ron Wynn, Rejoice*

○ **Heart and Soul/You Know Not the Hour** / Mobile Fidelity 00767
The CD remastering of these two early '70s albums by this fine harmony quintet is well worth owning. *Heart and Soul* is taken from the better pre-Paramount days (1970-1971), and *You Know Not the Hour* presents the group in a later, more hymnal song setting, both with Charles Johnson on lead. —*Kip Lornell*

The 77's

Group / Christian rock
Quintessential Christian rock band. Fronted by vocalist and guitarist Mike Roe, the band's always-anticipated but infrequent albums make few concessions for CCM compatibility. (Their live album, *88*, for instance, includes a rave-up of the Yardbird's "Over Under Sideways Down.") Drummer Aaron Smith previously played with Ray Charles and the Temptations, including the hit "Papa Was a Rollin' Stone." New band members—bassist Mark Harmon and keyboardist David Leonhardt—made their full-album debut with the band in late 1992, even though they've played live for four years, and promise a new direction for the group. —*Brian Mansfield*

The 77's / i. 1987 / Exit 90565
Promising debut shows a band equally influenced by Bob Dylan and blues/rock. Includes their concert favorite, "The Lust, the Flesh, the Eyes & the Pride of Life," and a killer anthem—"Do It for Love." —*Brian Mansfield*

★ **Sticks and Stones** / i. 1990 / Brainstorm 7100518849
After the departure of keyboardist Mark Tootle, Mike Roe emerged as the dominant figure in the 77's. *Sticks and Stones* points the way to the 77's of the future: biting, guitar-dominated rock with provocative lyrics epitomized by "Perfect Blues." Also includes new recordings of the four best songs from *The 77's.* —*Brian Mansfield*

Seventy Sevens / i. 1992 / Brainstorm
Originally titled *Pray Naked*, the record company went with a self-titled approach instead for this mostly pop collection, with the exception of the Zeppelin-like "Woody" and the unlisted 'title' cut, an eight minute Middle Eastern rave-up. —*Thom Granger*

Drowning With Land In Sight / i. 1994 / Myrrh
Again, an uneven but important album, beginning with a dead-on cover of the Led Zep arrangement on "Nobody's Fault But Mine," and evolving into a hard look at some of life's most challenging realities such as a relationship's dissolution, and its effects on the human spirit. —*Thom Granger*

The Richard Smallwood Singers

b. Nov. 30, 1948, Atlanta, GA
Group / Black gospel
Richard Smallwood was born in Atlanta, GA. He formed the Richard Smallwood Singers in Washington, DC, around 1977. —*Bil Carpenter*

● **Textures** / i. 1987 / Sparrow 51283
Contemporary Black gospel styles, with "Center of My Joy." —*Bil Carpenter*

Portrait / i. 1989 / Word 48559
Piano-backed urban pop-gospel. —*Bil Carpenter*

Michael W. Smith

b. Kenova, VA
Vocals, keyboard / CCM
A singer and songwriter who began as Amy Grant's keyboardist and has grown to be one of CCM's most popular artists, with respectable success in mainstream pop as well. —*Thom Granger*

○ **The Big Picture** / i. Feb. 1986 / Reunion 0010-277
Smith's most rock-oriented project, which garnered him more critical acclaim and less airplay and sales. —*Thom Granger*

The Live Set / i. Mar. 1987 / Reunion 0026-726
A jammin' rock-concert aura. —*Bil Carpenter*

The Michael W. Smith Project / i. Dec. 1987 / Reunion 0002-72
Worshipful, inspirational pop. —*Bil Carpenter*

I 2 Eye / i. 1989 / Reunion 0037-728
A mix of mature pop and soft rock. —*Bil Carpenter*

Go West Young Man / i. 1990 / Reunion 0063-729
The artist's first foray into crossover territory, with "Place in This World" landing on the pop charts and raising the stakes for a new level of acceptance. —*Thom Granger*

○ **Change Your World** / i. 1992 / Reunion 0071-721
Smith's biggest pop production changed his own world, bringing a bevy of hits in both gospel and pop markets, as well as a new level of touring activity. —*Thom Granger*

★ **Wonder Years** / i. 1993 / Reunion
A deluxe two-disc boxed set with Smith's best 35 songs, as well as elaborate packaging and commentary from the artist. —*Thom Granger*

The First Decade: 1983-1993 / i. Oct. 12, 1993 / Reunion 66314
A one-disc greatest hits collection featuring two new songs with a decidedly more mainstream approach. —*Thom Granger*

Rev. Dan Smith

b. 1911, Alabama
Vocals, harmonica / Blues gospel
Smith sang in church and played harmonica as a child. He didn't begin his professional career until the early '60s when he played behind folk legends Rev. Gary Davis and Pete Seeger. However, his musical style is overwhelmingly oriented to Chicago blues. —*Bil Carpenter*

○ **Just Keep Goin' On** / i. 1992 / Glasshouse 52989
All original gospel material set to a 12-bar blues backbeat. Harmonica is the instrumental focus, and the songs are separated by short testimonies by Smith in his folksy gravel of a voice. —*Bil Carpenter*

Mother Smith

b. 1906, Rolling Fort, MS
Vocals / Black gospel
Born in Rolling Fort, MS, she was involved with Thomas Dorsey's National Convention of Gospel Choirs and Choruses and had a 1937 hit with "If You Just Keep Still." Smith had a blues-like contralto and was known for her dramatic vocal fits and improvisational skills on cuts like "Take Your Burdens to the Lord." She performed and recorded sparingly, but was influential by starting a tradition of opening a song with a sermonette. Currently living in Chicago, she was one of the most important gospel singers to emerge in the '30s. —*Bil Carpenter & Kip Lornell*

● **Mother Willie Mae Ford Smith** / Spirit Feel 1010
Mother Willie Mae Ford Smith & Her Children is a compilation that highlights some of the best performances by Ms. Smith and her musical progeny. —*Kip Lornell*

○ **Willie Mae Ford Smith** / Savoy 14739
Includes "I Must Tell Jesus" and "He Never Left Me Alone." —*Bil Carpenter*

Going On with the Spirit / Nashboro 7148
Of special note: "Give Me Wings" and "I've Got a Secret." —*Bil Carpenter*

Steven Soles

Former Dylan sideman (on the Rolling Thunder Revue) and Alpha Band member (with T-Bone Burnett), Soles made two CCM albums in the early '80s that were critically acclaimed, if little heard. —*Thom Granger*

The Promise / i. 1980 / Maranatha! Music
A statement of faith by Soles, with third Alpha Band member David Mansfield contributing. —*Thom Granger*

Walk by Love / i. 1982 / Good News
More commercial than *The Promise*, second solo album features catchier songs and fuller pop arrangements. —*Thom Granger*

The Soul Stirrers

Group / Soul, Black gospel
A legendary gospel group known best for introducing Sam Cooke's mellifluous voice to the world, the Soul Stirrers were tremendously influential on the Black gospel scene from the mid '30s on. Formed in Texas in 1927, the group soon moved their base of operations to Chicago and recorded for the Library of Congress in 1936. A year later, they added lead tenor R.H. Harris, whose advanced concept of modern gospel harmony included alternating leads between two singers, and they became one of the nation's top gospel acts from the '40s on. Harris was replaced by Cooke in 1950, and the charismatic young singer led the group to new heights on Specialty Records through 1956. When Cooke left to go pop, he was succeeded by Johnnie Taylor, later to experience soul hitdom himself. Jimmy Outler and James Phelps also handled front work for a time, and by the mid '60s, when they were signed to Chess, Willie Rogers and Martin Jacox traded leads. A quarter-century later, Rogers and Jacox still lead the active group. —*Bill Dahl*

○ **Heaven Is My Home** / i. 1953-1959 / Specialty/Original 7040
The selections on this reissue cover a significant and too-often ignored aspect of the ensemble's history; the music of its other premier lead singers besides Harris and Sam Cooke. Paul Foster and Johnnie Taylor, the set's feature vocalists, weren't virtuosos like Harris or Cooke; they relied on timing, delivery, and fervor, particularly Foster, whose rousing treatments on "Christ Is All" and "He's My Rock" are disc high points. Taylor, who'd go on to soul and R&B success, has superb solos on "Until Then" and "The Love of God," while teaming with Foster on several other tunes for soaring duets that compare favorably with anything done by their predecessors or successors. —*Ron Wynn*

○ **In the Beginning** / i. 1991 / ACE 280
Here's a great collection of Specialty recordings done by Sam Cooke, solo and with The Soul Stirrers in the early/mid '50s. There's fine gospel singing on "He's My Friend," "Til The End," "Jesus, I'll Never Forget," "I Don't Want To Cry," "Lovable," "Forever," etc. The CD issue has several extra tracks. —*Roots & Rhythm Newsletter*

Sam Cooke with the Soul Stirrers / i. 1992 / Specialty
This 1992 reissue features previously unreleased material. Sam Cooke incorporated the styles of Archie Brownlee, R.H. Harris, and Julius Cheeks (along with his own natural abilities) to become, as many say, the best all-around gospel and R&B singer ever. This recording gives 25 reasons why people might say that. —*Billy C. Wirtz*

○ **Jesus Gave Me Water** / i. 1992 / Specialty 7031
Sam Cooke was one of the most original and influential vocal stylists of all time. You can hear him in all his glory (1951-1955) without edits or overdubs; his peerless soaring melismas are a joy. Catch also the anguished spiritual tones of the great Paul Foster Sr. as he alternates sparingly with Cooke. The first eight cuts are pure unadulterated a cappella. It includes the "long" version (one of three different unissued renderings) of "All Right Now," sung blazingly by gospel's hardest lead, Rev. "June" Julius Cheeks. This is a once in a lifetime treat. —*Opal Louis Nations, Roots & Rhythm Newsletter*

Gospel In My Soul / Vee-Jay 18013
Sam Cooke's smiling face on the cover of *Gospel In My Soul* is momentarily misleading, for the notes point out that the 12 songs included feature four lead vocals each by Cooke, the nimble Johnnie Taylor (Cooke's replacement as the Soul Stirrers' lead vocalist), and Cooke's idol R.H. Harris, whose place in the Soul Stirrers the young, unknown Cooke took in 1951. The confusion doesn't matter, for this is a fine record throughout. Cooke's approach to gospel singing reveals a side of Cooke which his popular hits, with the notable exception of "A Change Is Gonna Come," seldom touched. The carefree good humor is replaced by a forthright beauty and seriousness, but the signature is unmistakable. —*Tom Smith, Roundup Newsletter*

● **The Soul Stirrers** / Specialty 2106
Here's a compilation of the group that is synonymous with intense, inspirational, highly perfected gospel singing. The material—which includes "Wonderful" and "Touch the Hem of His Garment"—spans a decade and features the lead voices of Johnnie Taylor, R.H. Harris, and Paul Foster in addition to Sam Cooke. —*Roundup Newsletter*

● **The Gospel Soul of Sam Cooke, Vol. 2** / Specialty 2128
The Gospel Soul of Sam Cooke & the Soul Stirrers—Vol. 2 is being promoted under Sam Cooke's name, but it's really the Stirrers' show with first-class titles like "Farther Along" and "I'm So Glad." Some of Cooke's greatest moments, ca. 1951-1955, with great second-lead support from Paul Foster Sr. Includes three previously unreleased cuts. —*Kip Lornell*

○ **Shine on Me** / Specialty 7013
Contains 26 previously released tracks, alternate takes, and unissued tracks (ca. 1950) by this legendary quintet and features postwar gospel's finest and most influential soloist, R.H. Harris. —*Opal Louis Nations*

Sounds of Blackness

Group / Dance, Soul, CCM, Reggae
This 30-piece choir and orchestra, formed in 1971 by Gary Hines at Macalester College in Minnesota, combine traditional African elements with contemporary R&B. —*Bil Carpenter*

○ **The Evolution of Gospel** / i. 1991 / Perspective 1000
Primitive, funky, secularized gospel. —*Bil Carpenter*

Greg and Rebecca Sparks

Group / CCM
Husband-and-wife duo who left dance-rockers Bash-n-the-Code to concentrate on acoustic-based rock. They released two albums as Sparks (not to be confused with secular new-wave duo) before adding their first names for 1992's *Field of Your Soul*. —*Brian Mansfield*

○ **Through Flood and Fire** / i. 1990 / Reunion 24403
Using the Memphis Horns and Russ Taff guitarist James Hollihan Jr, this duo (under the moniker Sparks) made a record that matches the power of its convictions. —*Brian Mansfield*

Field of Your Soul / i. 1994
Recorded in 1992, the Sparks got even deeper into roots acoustic rock for this all-but-overlooked recording. —*Thom Granger*

The Speer Family

b. 1921
Group / Southern gospel
The Speers emerged when there were countless Southern gospel quartets and are noteworthy because of their longevity. Though personnel has changed over the years, their music in the '90s is true to the music they were making when the group was formed by patriarch G.T. in 1921. This group is an important reference point in the appreciation of traditional Southern gospel quartet singing. Current lineup: Brock, Ben, and Faye Speer; Robin Mew; Jane Green; Bill Itzel; and Martin Johnson. —*Bil Carpenter*

Hallelujah Time / i. 1990 / HB 9029

● **He's Still in the Fire** / i. 1990 / HB 8911

Spirit of Memphis

Group / Black gospel
This quartet includes: Silas Steele (baritone), Jet Bledsoe, James Darling, and Wilmer Broadnax. —*Bil Carpenter*

○ **When Mother's Gone** / Gospel Jubilee 1404
First-class material from 1948-1958, this includes an enlightening 15-minute radio show. Great lead vocals by "Little Ax" Broadnax, Jet Bledsoe, and Silas Steele. —*Kip Lornell*

The Staple Singers

Group / Soul, Gospel
The Staple's story goes all the way back to Winona, MS, in 1915. It was then and there that patriarch Roebuck Staples entered the world. A contemporary and familiar of Charley Patton, Roebuck quickly became adept as a solo blues guitarist, entertaining at local dances and picnics. Gradually drawn to the church, by 1937 he was singing and playing guitar with a spiritual group based out of Drew, MS, the Golden Trumpets. Moving to Chicago four years later, he continued playing gospel music with the Windy City's Trumpet Jubilees. A decade later Pops Staples (as he had become known) presented two of his daughters, Cleotha and Mavis, and his one son, Pervis, in front of a church audience, and the Staple Singers were born.

The Staples recorded in an older, slightly archaic, deeply Southern spiritual style first for United and then for Vee-Jay. Pops and Mavis Staples shared lead vocal chores, with most records underpinned by Pops's heavily reverbed Mississippi cottonpatch guitar. In 1960 the Staples signed with Riverside, a label that specialized in jazz and folk. With Riverside and later Epic, the Staples attempted to move into the then-burgeoning White folk boom. Two Epic releases, "Why (Am I Treated So Bad)" and a cover of Stephen Stills's "For What It's Worth," briefly graced the pop charts in 1967.

In 1968 the Staples signed with Memphis-based Stax. The first two albums, *Soul Folk in Action* and *We'll Get Over*, were produced by Steve Cropper and backed by Booker T and the MG's. The Staples were now singing entirely contemporary "message" songs such as "Long Walk to D.C." and "When Will We Be Paid." In 1970 Pervis Staples left, and was replaced by sister Yvonne Staples. Even more significantly, Al Bell took over production chores. Bell took them down the road to Muscle Shoals, and things got decidedly funky.

Starting with "Heavy Makes You Happy (Sha-Na-Boom Boom)" and "I'll Take You There," the Staples counted 12 chart hits at Stax. When Stax encountered financial problems, Curtis Mayfield signed the Staples to his Curtom label and produced a #1 hit in "Let's Do It Again." The Staples went on to continued chart success, albeit less spectacularly, with Warner, through 1979. One more album followed on 20th Century Fox in 1981. After a three-year hiatus, they signed a two-album deal with Private I and hit the R&B charts five more times, once with an unlikely cover of Talking Heads' "Slippery People."

The Staple Singers found a new audience in 1994 when they teamed with Marty Stuart to perform "The Weight" on the *Rhythm, Country and Blues* LP for MCA. —*Rob Bowman*

○ **Uncloudy Day & Will the Circle Be Unbroken** / i. 1955-1960 / Vee-Jay 600
The Staple Singers brilliantly fused gospel, folk, blues and soul into a cohesive, commercially potent sound in the '50s and '60s, becoming hit artists when their Stax singles crossed over to the pop charts. They perfected this approach during their tenure at Vee-Jay; the first label that allowed the twangy, expert guitar licks of Roebuck "Pop" Staples to be heard in the group's mix, and fully presented their harmonies. This single disc contains two pivotal Staples albums. *Uncloudy Day* includes such gospel favorites as "I Know I Got Religion" and "Let Me Ride," while *Will the Circle Be Unbroken* offers the splendid title track, plus masterpieces like "Pray On" and "Come Up In Glory." —*Ron Wynn*

Great Day / i. 1963 / Milestone 47028
This two-album Fantasy reissue is an anthology of the material the Staples recorded for Riverside between 1960 and 1963. For Riverside, the Staples recorded mostly gospel but the shouting was toned down a bit. A few modern-day "message" songs make their way into their repertoire as well, including Bob Dylan's "Masters of War." Not quite as cataclysmic as their Vee-Jay material but still essential. —*Rob Bowman*

Freedom Highway / i. 1965 / CBS 47334
A reissue of their first great Riverside collection, with "Daddy" Roebuck and the legendary Mavis Staples as leads. The Staples

once again mix a positive political message with a dash of religion. —*Kip Lornell*

☆ **Pray on** / i. 1968 / Hob 3513
The Staple Singers recorded ten 78s over a four-year period for Chicago's Vee-Jay. These have been reissued countless times in various forms. The Charly CD is simply the most recent. For Vee-Jay the Staples recorded a number of Pops Staples originals as well as radical rearrangements of standards. Pops Staples and Mavis Staples shared the lead singing chores, with Pervis and Cleotha Staples moaning in the background. Superb gospel shouting. —*Rob Bowman*

★ **Best of** / Stax 7
This is a double Vee-Jay set of prime Staples sides, 27 songs picked from the 33 cuts on three Vee-Jay albums that constitute the group's best gospel period (1955-1961) between the earlier States and later Riverside material. The group's close country (Mississippi) harmony, sharpened by the riveting "delta blues" guitar stylings of Pops Staples, is topped off by the impassioned virtuosity of lead singer Mavis Staples, who could reach low into bass notes, then scream and moan her heart out. It includes "Uncloudy Day," "Swing Low," "Pray On," "Stand By Me," "If I Could Hear My Mother Pray Again," "I Know I Got Religion," and "Sit Down Servant." There are about a dozen tracks that are duplicated on a New Cross LP. This is Staples gold. —*Opal Louis Nations, Roots & Rhythm Newsletter*

○ **Greatest Hits** / Fantasy 53308
A reissue of some of the fine Riverside sides (ca. 1962-1964) produced by Orrin Keepnews. This package actually does contain many of their best-known selections (like "Hammer and Nails") and is a good value for the money. —*Kip Lornell*

Candi Staton (CANDI STATON-SUSSEWELL)

b. Mar. 13, 1940, Hanceville, AL
Vocals / Dance, Soul, R&B, Gospel
Born in Hanceville, AL, Staton recorded at Fame Studios. She had disco hits on the Warner label in the late '70s and has done gospel work since 1982. Her weekly music show on the Trinity Broadcasting Network is "New Direction." Staton is one of the overlooked interpreters of Southern soul ballads in the Muscle Shoals sound. Serious listeners will appreciate her hoarsely coarse vocals on such sensual, sassy cuts as "That's How Strong My Love Is" and "I'd Rather Be an Old Man's Sweetheart (Than a Young One's Fool)." She brings equal passion to gospel recordings now that she's exited the secular industry. —*Bil Carpenter*

★ **I'm Just a Prisoner** / i. 1969 / ST 4201
Rick Hall's horns, creeping piano, and Staton's grit. —*Bil Carpenter*

Young Hearts Run Free / i. 1976 / Warner Brothers 56360
Soul meets disco on this classy dance record with tender downbeats. —*Bil Carpenter*

○ **Love Lifted Me** / i. 1988 / Beracah 2010
Traditional gospel reflecting her deep-South roots. —*Bil Carpenter*

Stand Up and Be a Witness / i. 1990 / Beracah 2020
Urban, upbeat psalms and exhortations. —*Bil Carpenter*

Randy Stonehill

Vocals, guitar / CCM
Veteran singer-songwriter who works primarily in acoustic-based settings, but also loves to rock, and displays the occasional penchant for satire. —*Thom Granger*

○ **Welcome to Paradise** / i. 1976 / Solid Rock 2002
Stonehill's first album to receive widespread distribution, an early 'Jesus Rock' masterpiece that still stands the test of time, mostly due to top-notch songwriting. A classic, most unfortunately out of print. —*Thom Granger*

Between the Glory and the Flame / i. 1981 / Myrhh 6679
First pairing with Daniel Amos leader Terry Taylor producing (and band members playing here), on this stripped down pop/rocker reflecting the new wave trends of the time. —*Thom Granger*

Equator / i. 1982 / Myrrh 6742-385
The artist's most successful record, veering from radio-ready ballads to quirky pop peculiarities. —*Thom Granger*

Wild Frontier / i. 1986 / Word 6837-610
After two unsatisfying forays into the more commercial trappings of pop, Stonehill forms new association with producer/player Dave Perkins with larger-than-life rock arrangements and vocals. —*Thom Granger*

★ **Return to Paradise** / i. 1989 / Word 6881-61
Stonehill's work on this collection with Mark Heard (who produced) resulted in the most consistent group of thoughtful, introspective songs in years. Essential. —*Thom Granger*

Wonderama / i. 1991 / Myrrh 6946-38
Randy reunites with Terry Taylor for a psychedelic, Beatlesque song cycle which may have set the stage for Taylor's own version of the same with Daniel Amos, Motor Cycle. —*Thom Granger*

Stories / i. 1993 / Myrrh
A collection of Stonehill's story-songs, mostly ballads, culled from his Myrrh releases. —*Thom Granger*

Stryper

Group / Heaven's metal, Hard Rock
A hard-rock/heavy metal CCM quartet founded in Orange County, CA, in 1983. At the time they signed to Enigma Records in 1984, the group consisted of lead singer Michael Sweet, guitarist Oz Fox, bassist Timothy Gaines, and drummer Robert Sweet. Their first recording was the mini-album *The Yellow and Black Attack*, followed by 1985's full-length album, *Soldiers Under Command*, which reached #84 on the charts. Enigma remixed *The Yellow and Black Attack* and added two songs in 1986, and the new version hit #103. Stryper's second (or third) album *To Hell with the Devil* (1986) went gold and earned the band a Grammy nomination. *In God We Trust* (1988) repeated this success. *Against the Law* (1990) was somewhat less of a hit. —*William Ruhlmann*

In God We Trust / i. 1988 / Hollywood 61186
Balanced soft-rock/metal guitar licks. —*Bil Carpenter*

● **Can't Stop the Rock** / i. 1991 / Hollywood 61106
Can't Stop the Rock: The Stryper Collection 1984-1991 features thundering drums, wailing guitars, keening choruses, pseudo-castrati singing—all the accoutrements of metal, and here in the service of the Lord. This best-of selects from the group's five previous recordings. —*William Ruhlmann*

Swan Silvertones (FOUR HARMONY KINGS)

Group / Black gospel
The Swan Silvertones began their career in the late '30s as the Four Harmony Kings, a community quartet based in Charleston, WV. They were initially influenced by the Golden Gate Quartet and other jubilee-style a cappella groups. Their big break came around 1940 when the Swan Bread Company agreed to sponsor their daily 15-minute program on Knoxville's powerful WNOX. Part of the group's continued appeal has been a willingness to update their sound to meet changing trends; they were among the first quartets, for example, to add a rhythm section in the early '50s. —*Kip Lornell*

○ **Heavenly Light** / i. 1952 / Specialty 7044
The Swan Silvertones only recorded for Specialty Records from 1952 until 1955, and it's generally not considered a prime period in their tenure. But this set of newly released performances from the early '50s, most of which even the label lacks information about, show they did turn in some topflight outings during that period. Ten of the tracks were done live, before hollering, celebrating audiences that weren't attending a concert, but participating in a spiritual renewal. The other eight are studio numbers, but they contain the same intensity and flash that make this a memorable Swan Silvertones document. —*Ron Wynn*

Get Right with the Swan Silvertones / i. 1982 / Rhino 70081
A reissue of various '50s and '60s singles and album sides plus two unissued cuts. Lead vocal dynamics from Rev. Claude Jeter, Paul Owens, and Louis Johnson. This well-rounded and amply annotated cross-section deserves serious consideration. —*Kip Lornell*

☆ **Pray For Me/Let's Go To Church Together** / Vee-Jay 602
The Swan Silvertones perfected their shimmering, explosive vocals while on Vee-Jay Records from 1956-1964. The elastic, dazzling falsetto of Claude Jeter, which was later adapted and reworked by Al Green, was contrasted by any number of powerful second lead singers within the group: Paul Owens, Louis Johnson,

or Azell Monk. The songs on this disc, with one exception, cover the Silvertones last great period and offer resounding harmonies, soaring leads and remarkable music. The lead selection, "Sinners Crossroad," is actually the Silver Quintette, an Indiana group probably most famous for having on its roster two future soul stars in Roscoe Robinson and Joe Henderson. Their song has historical value; everything else has that and musical excellence as well. —*Ron Wynn*

○ **Best of** / Chameleon 74783
This is a reissue of a Vee-Jay LP principally drawn from other Vee-Jay albums issued in 1960 and 1963. Rev. Claude Jeter's swooping falsetto is heard in all its magnificence. So is the preaching style of Louis Johnson and the soft, soulful tones of the great Paul Owens. It contains definitive quintet versions of "The Lord's Prayer," "Blessed Quietness," "Jesus Remembers," and "Great Day In December." These cuts are postwar gospel milestones and memories of how dramatic and spiritually uplifting gospel music had become. It's a must for all serious collectors of postwar gospel music if you don't already have the reissue of these tracks on Rhino or New Cross. —*Opal Louis Nations, Roots & Rhythm Newsletter*

★ **My Rock/Love Lifted Me** / Specialty 7202
Some of the best hard-gospel harmonizing from the middle '50s, most notably "How I Got Over" and "My Rock." The group's toughest sides, with firm conviction from lead soloists Solomon Womack, Rev. Bob Crenshaw, Dewey Young, and Paul Owens.— *Kip Lornell*

Swirling Eddies

Alternative pop/rock, CCM
Another Terry Taylor spin-off, consisting of Adam Again's Gene Eugene and various members of Daniel Amos and related bands listed under pseudonyms, mixing rock and satire with humorous (and occasionally profound) results. —*Thom Granger*

● **Let's Spin** / i. 1988 / Alarma

Outdoor Elvis / i. 1989 / Alarma

Zoom Daddy / i. 1994 / Alarma

T-Bone

Street Poetry
Christian rapper whose highly accomplished skills have won him respect on the street, and whose bold testimony has won him respect in the church. —*Thom Granger*

Redeemed Hoodlum / i. 1993 / Metro One
More authentic than most gospel rap, with in-your-face lyrics. — *Thom Granger*

Russ Taff

b. 1953
Vocals / CCM
Taff first gained recognition as lead vocalist for the Imperials, 1977-1981, but quickly gained a reputation as one of Christian music's most powerful and versatile artists, one whose music could hold its own against the best mainstream acts. His dynamic vocals reflect both the joys and the struggles of the Christian faith. —*Brian Mansfield*

Medals / i. 1985 / Horizon 0751
Second solo set showcases '80s pop styles and hooky songs, resulting in a CCM classic. —*Thom Granger*

Russ Taff / i. 1987 / Word 47765
This self-titled effort finds Taff trying to find himself, a cathartic album, less accessible but deeply felt. —*Thom Granger*

★ **The Way Home** / i. 1990 / Word 6880-613
Taff serves up his best effort here, a blend of well-crafted acoustic pop and roots rock that deserved to be heard beyond the walls of CCM. —*Thom Granger*

★ **Under Their Influence, Vol. 1** / i. 1991 / Word 47733
The musical roots of most CCM artists lie pretty close to the surface, but that's not the case with Taff, the son of a Pentecostal evangelist who preached in California migrant territory. Here Taff pays tribute to Blind Willie Johnson, Brother Joe May, and Mahalia Jackson, among others, with an album that provides the link between gut-level gospel and Southern rock. —*Brian Mansfield*

Take 6

Group / Gospel, Jazz, A cappella
An innovative vocal sextet with an uncanny sense of history and taste, combining classic gospel quartet singing with jazzier approach of groups like Gene Puerling's Hi-Lo's and Singers Unlimited for unparalled arrangements and musicianship. — *Thom Granger*

● **Take 6** / **i.** 1988 / Reprise 25670
Six Nashville gospel vocalists whose collective exchanges and massed harmonies make [it] an unusual, often spectacular release. Their approach more closely echoes classic jubilee than the more common quartet gospel. *Take 6* may yet put some Golden Age fervor back into '80s gospel. — *Ron Wynn, Rock & Roll Disc.*

So Much 2 Say / **i.** 1990 / Reprise 25892
Slightly more contemporary than their debut. — *Bil Carpenter*

Join the Band / **i.** 1994 / Reprise
Its first collection of new material in four years, the group branches out with instrumental backing throughout for the first time, with appearances by Ray Charles, Stevie Wonder, Queen Latifah and a host of stellar sidemen. — *Thom Granger*

Steve Taylor

Vocals / CCM
Sometimes referred to as the "clown prince of Christian music," Steve Taylor brought sarcasm and satire to Christian music. His acerbic lyrics engendered enough controversy to place him among the most visible Christian rockers of the mid '80s. Ultimately he felt stifled by the industry and quit recording for the Christian market, but resurfaced as the lead singer of Chagall Guevara in 1991. He resumed his solo career in 1994. — *Brian Mansfield*

○ **I Predict 1990** / **i.** 1987 / Myrrh 6873-617
It's small surprise the Christian community all but disowned Taylor after songs like "I Blew Up the Clinic Real Good" and "Since I Gave Up Hope I Feel a Lot Better." The songs on *I Predict 1990* don't look for easy answers—they rarely look for answers at all—and they're often unsettling. But half of Taylor's point is that life rarely gives easy answers. The other half is in the final song: "Harder to Believe Than Not To." — *Brian Mansfield*

★ **The Best We Could Find** / **i.** 1988 / Sparrow 1180
This compilation makes an excellent introduction to Taylor's iconoclastic songwriting, with music that frequently sounds like a new-wave Christian sideshow. Taylor gets his licks in on modern culture with "Meltdown (At Madame Tussaud's)," but he more often turns his gaze on the church with songs like "I Want to Be a Clone" and "This Disco (Used to Be a Cute Cathedral)." — *Brian Mansfield*

Squint / **i.** 1993 / Warner Brothers 45479
Taylor returns as a solo act with a renewed sense of satiric mission, and great music to surround his incisive lyrics. — *Thom Granger*

Terry Scott Taylor

Alternative pop/rock, CCM
Though the man behind Daniel Amos and the Swirling Eddies is certainly the father of Christian alternative music, his solo albums often show another side of the artist, with more personal lyrics set in music influenced by the sounds he grew up with, namely Beatles/Beach Boys, etc. — *Thom Granger*

● **Knowledge and Innocence** / **i.** 1987 / Pulse

Briefing for the Ascent / **i.** 1989 / Frontline
Moodier than *Knowledge and Innocence*, due to the lyrics, which deal with the death of Taylor's grandfather. — *Thom Granger*

Miracle Faith Telethon / **i.** 1991 / Frontline
A hodgepodge of outtakes, alternate versions, and humorous segues from Taylor and his various personas. — *Thom Granger*

Pat Terry

Georgia-based artist was one of the few in early Jesus Music worth his salt as a songwriter. Pat Terry Group produced a handful of interesting pop CCM albums in the mid-to-late '70s, but couldn't prepare fans for the trio of artful, introspective solo records made in the early '80s with Mark Heard that were to be

his last in the gospel market. Terry still writes, now for the country market. — *Thom Granger*

Songs of the South / **i.** 1976 / Myrrh
Simple acoustic pop featured "Home Where I Belong" and "Happy Man," later to be hits for B.J. Thomas. — *Thom Granger*

Humanity Gangsters / **i.** 1982 / Myrrh
First solo album finds Terry restless, coming up with more questions than answers, and making arguably better music (with the help of producer Mark Heard who also contributes guitars) than any of his albums with the Group. — *Thom Granger*

★ **Film at Eleven** / **i.** 1983 / Myrrh
The second of three albums produced with Heard found the artist speaking eloquently to the issues of life from a distinctly Christian, though less dogmatic, point of view than his earlier songs, making for an album that, like many of Heard's, stands the test of time. — *Thom Granger*

Silence / **i.** 1984 / Myrrh
Terry completed his trilogy of albums in as many years with another strong collection that featured Leslie (now Sam) Phillips on "Man of Sorrows." — *Thom Granger*

Sister Rosetta Tharpe

b. Mar. 20, 1921, Cotton Plant, AK, **d.** Oct. 9, 1973, Philadelphia, PA

Vocals, guitar / Blues, Black gospel
Born in Cotton Plant, AK, Sister Tharpe toured with P.W. McGhee's tent revivals as a child, singing and strumming guitar. She signed a record deal with Decca in 1938. In addition to her work with gospel artists, she performed folk/blues with Muddy Waters and Lucky Millinder and had R&B Top 10 hits with "Strange Things," "Up Above My Head," and "Silent Night." In a duo with Marie Knight in 1947-1954, their most-noted songs were "Didn't It Rain," "This Train," and "I Looked Down the Line." — *Bil Carpenter*

○ **Sacred & Secular**
This is a beautiful collection of 16 recordings by this fine and important artist covering the period 1941 through 1969. The recordings here feature her with various groups including Lucky Millinder's band (whom she worked with for many years), Leroy Kirkland's Orchestra and smaller groups featuring Sam Price and others. Unfortunately there are none of her tremendous solo recordings made between 1939 and 1941 and the only track that features her along with her guitar is a 1969 live performance which is fine, but not Tharpe at her best. Still many of the tracks here do feature her excellent and distinctive single string guitar playing. There's excellent sound, full discographical details, and extensive notes in a beautiful fold out jacket with great photos. — *Roots & Rhythm Newsletter*

Gospel Train, Vol. 2 / **i.** 1960 / Lection 841391
Recorded later than the material on Volume 1, some of Sister Rosetta's worst, most-overproduced recordings. — *Opal Louis Nations*

Live in Paris—1964 / **i.** 1964 / French Concerts 118
A nice, rather folk-like concert performance in front of an enthusiastic audience. — *Kip Lornell*

Live at the Hot Club De France / **i.** 1966 / Milan 35624
This recording, done in front of French audiences in 1966, starts out as a polite, folky affair. Sister Rosetta Tharpe, perhaps a bit shy in the overseas concert setting, plays it safe with "This Train," "Jesus Met The Woman at the Well," and "He's Got The Whole World In His Hands." Then comes the rip-roaring intro to "Walk All Over God's Heaven," and Tharpe hits her testifyin' stride, and that husky voice can do no wrong (except overloading the mike once in awhile). Her electric guitar is way down in the mix, but thankfully the engineer was paying attention to her show-stopping solo on "Joshua Fit The Battle." Twelve selections, mostly standard spirituals. — *Myles Boisen, Roots & Rhythm Newsletter*

● **Gospel Train** / PolyGram 841134
These are great late '50s Mercury sides with Ernest Hayes on piano and Doc Bagby on organ, among others. The album contains good performances of some of Tharpe's most popular selections. — *Kip Lornell*

○ **Gospel Train** / MCA 1317
Here's a collection of 12 gospel standards recorded in 1956 and originally issued on Mercury. Sister Rosetta Tharpe is accompanied by top R&B and jazz musicians like "Doc" Bagby, Lloyd

Troutman, Panama Francis, and, on a few tracks, the fine gospel quartet The Harmonizing Four. Sister Tharpe turns in stirring renditions of "Jericho," "Two Little Fishes, Five Loaves of Bread," "Can't No Grave Hold My Body Down," "I Shall Know Him," "How About You," "99½ Won't Do," and others. It's essentially a vocal outing for Tharpe, although a few tracks feature her distinctive guitar playing. —*Frank Scott, Roots & Rhythm Newsletter*

Tonio K.

CCM, Rock/pop
Eighties rock misogynist finds salvation and changes his mind without changing his tune. —*Thom Granger*

Notes from the Lost Civilization / Word 6868-389
Further development of themes on *Romeo Unchained*, A&M version included the hilarious "What Women Want." —*Thom Granger*

★ **Romeo Unchained** / What 8340
A brilliant treatise on love in a fallen world, delivered with characteristic wit and heretofore uncharacteristic compassion. —*Thom Granger*

Tramaine

Vocals / Soul, R&B, Gospel
Spent about two weeks with the Honey Cones in the late '60s before joining the Edwin Hawkins Singers. Married Walter Hawkins and was a featured singer with the Hawkins Family in the '70s. Went solo in the '80s with albums on Light, A&M, and Sparrow labels. Strident, shrill belting style on usually traditional-styled Black gospel numbers or ballads such as "Highway" and "The Potter's House." —*Bil Carpenter*

○ **The Search Is Over** / i. 1983 / A&M 5110
Though Tramaine insisted she never deserted the church, it was hard to tell the difference between most of this album's songs and standard urban contemporary, secular material. They were sung with the same vigor and fire that Tramaine Hawkins brought to her gospel tunes, but only someone with a truly generous definition of gospel would equate *The Search Is Over* with religious or spiritual material. —*Ron Wynn*

Kathy Troccoli

Vocals / CCM
Next to Amy Grant and Sandi Patti, New Yorker Kathy Troccoli was probably CCM's most popular female singer before leaving the business in 1986 when her record label, Reunion, couldn't produce the mainstream stardom she sought. Troccoli returned to Reunion when the label had mainstream possibilities (after signing a distribution pact with Geffen) to release hit *Pure Attraction* in 1991. —*Brian Mansfield*

○ **Pure Attraction** / i. 1991 / Reunion 24453
Troccoli's first recording after a five-year absence was her most commercial, with the Diane Warren-penned "Everything Changes" hitting Top Five on CHR radio. Troccoli had developed her songwriting during her time away; she wrote seven of *Pure Attraction's* cuts, emphasizing the torch-song style she loves. —*Brian Mansfield*

The Trumpeteers

Group / Black gospel
Influenced by the Golden Gate Quartet and led by the spectacular singing of Joe Johnson, this quartet hit the public's consciousness in the late '40s with "Milky White Way," which they recorded for Score Records. Other members included Raleigh Tunrage (tenor), Joseph Armstrong (baritone), and James Keels (bass). There were numerous personnel changes, and they disbanded upon Johnson's death in 1948. —*Bil Carpenter & Kip Lornell*

★ **Milky White Way** / i. 1956 / Score 4021
A wonderful sampling of the recordings made by this first-rate a cappella vocal group during the late '40s and early '50s. The title cut became one of this postwar quartet's heaviest-selling gospel 78s. Fine, smooth lead choruses from Joseph Johnson. —*Kip Lornell*

Truthettes

Group / Black gospel
The Oklahoma City-based Morgan Sisters began recording in the late '80s. Personnel: Tiffanie and Tammy Morgan, Jennifer and Angela Tooley. —*Bil Carpenter*

● **Every Step of the Way** / i. 1987 / Malaco 4421
Contemporary-style traditional gospel. —*Kip Lornell*

Flowing / Malaco 4434
Strong harmonies on this album of organ-dominated modern Black music. —*Kip Lornell*

The Twelfth Tribe

Group / Street poetry
The California duo of Dave Portillo and Eddie Sierra began rapping in 1985 under the name of Deity. Influenced by soul and heavy metal, they like the rap of Kool Mo Dee, Houdini, and the Fat Boys. They take their name from the twelfth tribe of Israel: the Benjamites, mighty warriors. They portray a tougher image than most Christian rap artists and have a hard street rap sound. —*Bil Carpenter*

○ **Knowledge Is the Tribe of Life** / i. 1991 / Frontline 9261
Produced, engineered, and mixed by master urban dance musician Scott Blackwell who easily moves into the hard, funky side of Christian rap here. There are 15 rhymes on war, peace, and knowing God. The sound is very Black, very hard, with a few metal elements; a good set though not overly original outside of the gospel music industry. —*Bil Carpenter*

Undercover

Alternative pop/rock, CCM
Seminal Christian punk band led by Joe Taylor, its music has evolved radically since its inception but still delivers a straightahead lyrical approach. —*Thom Granger*

Branded / i. 1987 / Broken

Balance of Power / i. 1990 / Brainstorm

Devotion / i. 1992 / Brainstorm

3/28/87 / Benson 0500-672

Vector

Early '80s alternative pop band boasted Charlie Peacock in its first album lineup, while Jimmy Abegg and Steve Griffith have continued to the present, recording the occasional album project under the moniker. —*Thom Granger*

Simple Experience / i. 1989 / Gaga

Please Stand By / Exit 0012-385

Albertina Walker

b. Aug. 1930, Chicago, IL
Vocals / Black gospel
Born in Chicago, Walker sang with the Pete Williams Singers and the Robert Anderson Singers before forming the Caravans in 1951. Among the Caravans' classics were "Mary Don't You Weep," "Soldiers in the Army," "The Solid Rock," and "The Blood Will Never Lose Its Power." Since 1960 Walker has been a solo singer, maintaining her ties to traditional gospel. —*Bil Carpenter*

Tell the Angels / i. 1960 / Savoy 3051
Her 1960 debut, after the Caravans. —*Bil Carpenter*

○ **God Is Love** / i. 1975 / Lection 839259
A fine collection by this influential performer. —*Kip Lornell*

You Believed in Me / i. 1991 / Benson 2673
This recent album includes "Working on a Building." —*Bil Carpenter*

Clara Ward & the Ward Singers

b. Aug. 1924, d. Jan. 16, 1973
Group / Gospel, Spiritual
The Clara Ward Singers scored in the '50s with swinging traditional Black gospel songs like "Packing Up, Getting Ready to Go." In the '60s they became a mainstay, performing at Las Vegas hotels and drawing the wrath of the gospel music industry for "selling out." Ward died after suffering a stroke in 1972. The remaining members and new personnel continue to perform under the same name. —*Bil Carpenter*

○ **Gospel Soul of Clara Ward**
Here's a surprising set of joyful-sounding gospel songs recorded some time in the early '70s that gives us an idea of how magnificent the Ward Singers sounded in their heyday during the '50s. All the songs are carefully arranged to evoke the feel of a live

church performance, with high-spirited renditions of "What Jesus is to Me" and "It May Be The Best For Me." There's lots of jubilant singing and tambourine banging. —*Opal Louis Nations, Roots & Rhythm Newsletter*

★ **Clara Ward Singers**
Here's 22 sides recorded for the Roulette label in 1963—these are solid gospel winners featuring the unbeatable voice of Clara Ward. An added feature in these jubilant surroundings is a fantastic unnamed slide guitarist, who really goes to town on a few numbers. This is excellent. —*Myles Boisen, Roots & Rhythm Newsletter*

Ernestine Washington

Vocals / Black gospel
Born in Arkansas, Madame Ernestine B. Washington grew up on the sanctified gospel of the '20s, singing primarily for her husband's church and denomination, Washington Temple COGIC. Though inspired by the controlled Baptist style of the Roberta Martin Singers, she had a strident voice and was known to be a singing shouter in the mode of Mahalia Jackson. Her rare and most important recordings were executed from the late '40s through the '50s. —*Bil Carpenter*

○ **In Washington Temple** / Collectors Issue 5529
Gospel Singing in Washington Temple. Sensational solos supported rousingly by Brooklyn's Congregation of the Washington Temple COGIC. Reissue of material recorded in 1958. —*Opal Louis Nations*

Wayne Watson

b. Wisner, LA
Vocals / Gospel, Inspirational
Born in Wisner, LA, he was known for ballads early on, but is now making serious commentary on Christian living. —*Bil Carpenter*

Watercolour Ponies / **i.** 1987 / Word 4155-628
Children-inspired rock/pop ballads. —*Bil Carpenter*

○ **The Fine Line** / **i.** 1988 / Word 4175-572
Sober, down-tempo reflections on life and faith. —*Bil Carpenter*

White Heart

Group / Christian rock
Band of "musician's musicians" with a revolving-door membership; their sound borders on hard-rock/prog-rock. Original vocalist Steve Green became a major inspirational act as a solo artist. Founder and guitarist Dann Huff became Los Angeles' premier studio guitarist in the late '80s before forming the arena rock group, Giant; bassist Tommy Sims joined Bruce Springsteen's road band in 1992. —*Brian Mansfield*

Freedom / **i.** 1989 / Sparrow 1194
White Heart took the album's name to heart, allowing themselves more creative leeway on this than on any previous album. Most Christian arena-rock sounds derivative of its secular counterparts—not *Freedom*; even its weak spots are undeniably original. —*Brian Mansfield*

○ **Souvenirs** / **i.** 1990 / Sparrow 1250
White Heart found its voice in 1986 with *Don't Wait for the Movie*, the first album with lead singer Rick Florian. *Souvenirs* collects the productive years that followed, including five tracks from *Freedom* and an unusual hard-rock remake of "The Little Drummer Boy." —*Brian Mansfield*

Tales of Wonder / **i.** 1992 / Star Song
Band turns in its most popular album in years, showing continued growth and depth in its songwriting, better than the simplistic anthems that typify the arena-rock genre. —*Thom Granger*

● **Highlands** / **i.** 1994 / Star Song
Another artistic high-water mark for the band, which now inlcudes Adam Again member Jon Knox on drums. Influence of '70s prog-rockers like Yes and Kansas is interwoven with Celtic themes for a Christian rock classic. —*Thom Granger*

Whites

Gospel, Folk, Country
Originally a traditional country/bluegrass group known as the Down Home Folks, this family band consists of father Buck and daughters Cheryl and Sharon. Close harmony and exceptional instrumentation (Buck is an extraordinary mandolin player) are their trademark. In recent years, gospel has dominated their material. Sharon and her husband Ricky Skaggs won a Country Music Association Award for the duet "Love Can't Ever Get Better Than This." The Whites were the Gospel Group of the Year in 1989. —*David Vinopal*

○ **Greatest Hits** / **i.** 1987 / Curb 77498
Early '80s sweet harmony from dad and his daughters. —*Mark A. Humphrey*

Steve Wiggins

Vocals / CCM
Outspoken young singer/songwriter (and sometimes street evangelist) from Memphis by way of Arkansas. —*Brian Mansfield*

○ **Steve Wiggins** / **i.** 1991 / Sparrow 1280
The bare-bones production of Wiggins's debut captures the direct, almost confrontational religious nature of his songwriting. He's got the soul of a street preacher and the heart of a Memphis rocker. —*Brian Mansfield*

Stephen Wiley

Vocals / Street poetry
Wiley was the original gospel rapper, but his lightweight talents have been superseded by more skilled practitioners. —*Bil Carpenter*

○ **Rhythm and Poetry** / **i.** 1990 / Star Song 0157
Hip-hop music. Sharper MC skills and a pop sound. —*Bil Carpenter*

The Williams Brothers

Group / Black gospel
The group was organized in 1960 by Leon "Pop" Williams, who is the founder and father of the Williams Brothers. They were then known as the Little Williams Brothers, but as the group grew in talent, experience, and performance, the name changed to the Sensational Williams Brothers. Today the group is simply called the Williams Brothers. All of the group members were born and reared in Mississippi in a little community called "Smithdale," about 100 miles south of Jackson, MS, where a road has been named in their honor. They have been writing and arranging most of their music since 1970 and producing since 1979.

The group recorded its first album in 1973 on the Songbird label, which included the instant hit, "Jesus Will Fix It." Since then they have recorded 16 albums listed as Top 10 in *Billboard* and *Cashbox* magazines, out of which came three #1 records and a Grammy nomination. Their repertoire of hits includes songs such as "Jesus Will Never Say No," "I Won't Let Go My Faith," "He'll Understand," "Sweep Around Your Own Front Door," and "A Ship Like Mine," to name a few. They also performed on the Winans's grammy-winning song, "Ain't No Need to Worry," featuring Anita Baker. In April 1991 the group formed their own record label, Blackberry Records, which is the first Black owned-and-operated label in the state of Mississippi that has major distribution. Their first release on the label, "This Is Your Night," reached #4 on the *Billboard* gospel chart. —*Billy C. Wirtz*

● **Blessed** / Malaco 4400
Slick, well-crafted modern gospel, complete with synthesizer, strings, and percussion overdubs. —*Hank Davis*

Hand in Hand / Malaco 4409
For proof that in quartet change is not decay, look no further. The sermonette "The Goat" might have come off an early Clouds single, and time and again the accompaniment returns to the great, simple, classic piano/organ combination. But the four Williams Brothers are up for most anything, including Walter Hawkins on one track and rappers on another. —*John Storm Roberts, Original Music*

Dewey Williams

Vocals / Black gospel
Born at the turn of the century, Williams has been the leader of the African-American shape-note movement in Southern Alabama for over 50 years. In the late '80s, he was honored with a Heritage Award from the National Endowment for the Arts/Folk Arts. —*Kip Lornell*

☆ **Wiregrass Notes: Black Sacred Harp Singing from the South** / Wiregrass Music
This is a self-produced cassette of a rare Black religious tradition that is downhome and unique. —*Kip Lornell*

Marion Williams

b. Aug. 29, 1927, Miami, FL
Vocals / Black gospel, Spiritual
Born in Miami, Williams sang with a Florida gospel group before joining the Famous Ward Singers (later the Clara Ward Singers) in 1947. Upon leaving the group in 1959, she formed the Stars of Faith, which she left in 1965. She starred on Broadway and in a global tour of *Black Nativity* in the early '60s. She has been singing since the late '60s and is known for her sweet but muscular style of traditional Black gospel. —*Bil Carpenter*

O Holy Night / i. 1959 / Savoy 14032
A Christmas album with the Stars of Faith. —*Bil Carpenter*

○ **Surely God Is Able** / i. 1989 / Spirit Feel 1011
A very strong soloist who reworked classic gospel material from the '30s and '40s into a wonderful 1989 album. —*Kip Lornell*

★ **Strong Again** / i. 1991 / Spirit Feel 1013
Eclectic though satisfying 20-cut album by this major singer, her most impressive solo set in recent years. Sparse accompaniment; mainly traditional material. Excellent. —*Kip Lornell*

○ **Can't Keep It to Myself** / i. 1993 / Shanachie/Spirtfeel 6007
This new disc features 22 awesome performances recorded with minimal, sympathetic accompaniment and little production support. It is mostly Williams with smashing, note-bending and soaring vocals. She flies on slow, bluesy numbers, testifies and shouts on her originals like "Ride in the Clouds" and "I'll Never Return No More," and turns old standards such as Roberta Martin's "God's Amazing Grace" and Rev. Thomas A. Dorsey's "Live the Life I Sing About in My Song" into gripping, fresh reaffirmations of her own faith. Nothing tops gospel for immediate, unforgettable impact, and no one is providing more of it than Marion Williams. —*Ron Wynn*

Somebody Bigger Than You and I / Relic 7004
Her first album after leaving the Ward Singers. Recorded in 1958, it includes "I Can't Forget." —*Bil Carpenter*

The Winans

Group / CCM, Black gospel
These four brothers hail from Detroit, MI. Their contemporary Black gospel style reflects traditional Black gospel roots. They sang gospel all their lives and began their professional careers in the '80s. Members: Marvin, Carvin, Ronald, and Michael Winans. They have performed several times with the likes of Michael McDonald, Anita Baker, and Vanessa Bell Armstrong. —*Bil Carpenter*

Let My People Go / i. 1985 / Qwest 25344
Their distinctive, muddy, percussive, and jazzy sound. —*Bil Carpenter*

Decision / i. 1987 / Qwest 25510
Fine R&B with Anita Baker and Michael McDonald. —*Bil Carpenter*

Return / i. 1990 / Qwest 26161
New jack swing and urban soul. —*Bil Carpenter*

● **Tomorrow** / Light 5853
The title track, a sparkling MOR-style ballad, is the hymn of the '80s. —*Bil Carpenter*

Live at Carnegie Hall / Qwest
A dynamic concert, with all the hits drawn out, on this double album. —*Bil Carpenter*

BeBe and CeCe Winans

Group / Soul, Gospel, Urban
Detroit-born brother and sister BeBe (Benjamin) and CeCe (Priscilla) Winans are part of the gospel-singing Winans family that also includes the Winans, their four brothers. As a duo, BeBe and CeCe maintain the gospel message, although their records have the production values and style of contemporary R&B. They released their debut album, *BeBe & CeCe Winans*, in 1987 and scored a moderate hit (#49) in the R&B charts with the single "I.O.U. Me" scoring on the R&B and adult-contemporary charts.

This earned them three Grammy nominations and one award (gospel). Their second album, *Heaven*, came in 1988 and found them scoring three R&B hits with the title track, "Lost Without You," and "Celebrate Life." The album reached the R&B Top 10 (#95 in the pop chart) and went gold. 1991's platinum selling *Different Lifestyles* was their biggest hit yet, topping the R&B album chart and featuring the R&B #1s "Addictive Love" and "I'll Take You There." —*William Ruhlmann*

○ **Lord Lift Us Up** / i. 1985 / PTL
Pop/MOR-oriented praise tunes. —*Bil Carpenter*

BeBe & CeCe Winans / i. 1987 / Capitol 46883
R&B, urban-crossover CCM ballads. —*Bil Carpenter*

○ **Heaven** / i. Sep. 1988 / Capitol 90959
If you listen carefully, the songs *are* about Jesus rather than love sweet love, but even a casual hearing lets you know this is one of the most soulful duos to come along since Marvin Gaye and Tammi Terrell. Keith Thomas gives the production a contemporary R&B sheen. —*William Ruhlmann*

Addictive Love / i. 1991 / Capitol 15732
More of the same, with Mavis Staples and MC Hammer. —*Bil Carpenter*

Different Lifestyles / i. Jun. 24, 1991 / Capitol 92078
Different Lifestyles, the third outing by BeBe and CeCe Winans, is more of the music their fans have come to expect. Contained herein are 11 songs (10 of them original) combining rap, hip-hop, rhythm and blues, jazz, and soul music with messages of hope, worship, and faith. All in all, *Different Lifestyles* is good, but one wonders if BeBe and CeCe Winans can maintain their originality and uniqueness while producing music that caters to commercial success. —*Edwin Smith, Rejoice*

Relationships / i. 1994 / Capitol
The duo's first outing without the involvement of producer Keith Thomas finds them heading toward more downtempo, ballad-heavy R&B, with Cedric Caldwell and BeBe himself at the producer helm, along with mainstream heavyweights Arif Mardin and David Foster. —*Thom Granger*

Gospel Collections

○ **16 Golden Gospel Greats** / Tripindicular 37
Late '50s sides from the Vee-Jay label. Prime work from the Harmonizing Four and others. —*Hank Davis*

☆ **Ain't That Good News** / Specialty 2115
Super '50s gospel from the Specialty vaults, compiled by Barrett Hanson (aka Dr. Demento). Each cut is a true gem. Of special interest to audiophiles: the tracks carefully segue into each other, with no space between (which could be annoying to some). A spellbinding effect and a great album. —*Barry Lee Pearson*

○ **All of My Appointed Time** / Stash 114
Some of the finest a cappella gospel performances from the fabulous Famous Blue Jay Singers and other greats can be found on this collection. —*Kip Lornell*

Assassination / 1991 / Zu-Zazz 2019
Fine '60s quartet music. Primary features include Ollie Nightingale & the Dixie Nightingales, and the famous Memphis Gospel Writers. —*Opal Louis Nations*

At the Foot of the Cross / 1991 / Glasshouse
A unique worship-oriented album, spearheaded by alternative rock artists Steve Hindalong and Derri Daugherty (from The Choir), and a variety of guests. Album mixes traditional liturgical ideas, some with Latin texts, with less than traditional church music for another part of the congregation. —*Thom Granger*

○ **Atlanta Gospel** / Gospel Heritage 312
A regionally focused compilation by very fine (but virtually unknown) groups like the Five Trumpets and the National Independent Gospel Singers. Drawn from rare 78 rpm sides ca. 1946-1951. —*Kip Lornell*

○ **The Best of Gotham Gospel** / Gospel Heritage 04
This welcome CD covers the extensive Philadelphia-based Gotham label. Drawn from previously unreleased and rare sides from the '40s and '50s. —*Kip Lornell*

○ **Black Religious Singers (1927-42)** / Hans Klement 4008

Extremely rare gospel soloist material by nine performers, notably Rev. D.C. Rice, Sister Clara Hudmon, Elder Curry, and Bozie Sturdivant. —*Opal Louis Nations*

○ **Bless My Bones** / Rounder 2063
Bless My Bones: Memphis Gospel Radio—1950s highlights eight stellar ensembles in a stunning set of radio transcriptions from Memphis's WDIA. Includes "99½ Won't Do" by the Song Birds of the South and "Milky White Way" by the Spirit of Memphis, as well as tracks by the Dixie Nightingales, Southern Wonders, and Sunset Travelers. —*John Floyd*

Brow Beat / 1993 / Alarma
Recognizing the popularity of going 'unplugged' in the early '90s, a number of Christian alternative rock's best bands contributed stripped-down, acoustic performances of mostly new songs to this collection. —*Thom Granger*

○ **Chicago Gospel Pioneers** / 1991 / Spirit Feel 1004
Fine contemporary recordings by Delois Barrett Campbell, Robert Anderson, and Little Lucy Smith. —*Kip Lornell*

Coram Deo / 1991 / Sparrow
Charlie Peacock gathered a flock of popular CCM artists for this group of worship tunes written by Peacock, which are more conventional in song structure than most praise choruses. —*Thom Granger*

○ **Country Gospel Guitar Classics (1927-51)** / Wolf 115
Quintessential guitar rarities from A.C. and Blind Mamie Forehand, Dennis Crumpton, Robert Summers, Sister Mathews, Willie Mae Williams, and Sister O.M. Terrell. —*Opal Louis Nations*

☆ **Early Negro Vocal Quartets (1894-1928)** / Document 5061
A strong collection of mostly religious sides by some pioneering a cappella groups, beginning with an 1894 cylinder by the Standard Quartet. —*Kip Lornell*

○ **Get Right with God** / Gospel Heritage 01
An eclectic, exceptionally entertaining overview of African-American gospel solo and quartet material popular in the early, post-WW II era. —*Kip Lornell*

○ **Go Devil Go—Modern/Kent Gospel Masters** / P-Vine 3017
Distinguished postwar female aggregations plus the notable veteran Prof. James Earle Hines and Rev. G.W. Killens, from rare 78 rpm material. —*Opal Louis Nations*

○ **God's Mighty Hand—Gospel Evangelists** / Gospel Heritage 09
If you like your gospel on the wild side, then these preacher-singers will shake you to your soul. Included are 25 tracks by the likes of the spectacular Sister O.M. Terrell, Rev. Utah Smith, Brother Willie Eason, and the stupendous Elder A. Johnson, coming on like an evangelizing Hasil Adkins with "God Don't Like It." Accompaniment is sparse—mostly just guitar; the mood is raw and intense. This is charismatic stuff, not for the faint of heart. I can't recommend it highly enough. —*Christine Ohlman, Roundup Newsletter*

○ **Going on Home to Glory** / P-Vine 2187
Going on Home to Glory—Trumpet Gospel Anthology. Priceless quartet music from the early '50s. Featuring the Blue Jay Gospel Singers, Carolina Kings of Harmony, Argo Gospel Singers, and others. —*Opal Louis Nations*

○ **The Golden Age of Gospel Singing** / Folk Lyric 9046
The Five Blind Boys, Zion Travelers, and others provide an invaluable overview of gospel quartet singing from the late '40s and early '50s. —*Kip Lornell*

○ **Gospel Rarities (1926-1930)** / Eden 5200
Prime rare 78 rpm material focusing on five soloists, the most impressive being Rev. P.W. Williams and Homer Quincy Smith. —*Opal Louis Nations*

○ **Gospel Stars in Concert** / 197? / Specialty 2153
Historically and spiritually important early '50s live performances by the Gospel Harmonettes with Dorothy Love Coates, Brother Joe May, and the Pilgrim Travelers. Side 2 features three riveting cuts by Sam Cooke and the Soul Stirrers. —*John Floyd*

○ **The Gospel Tradition: The Roots and the Branches, Vol. 1** / 1991 / CBS 47333
The *Gospel Tradition: The Roots and the Branches—Vol. 1* is one of the few gospel collections that ignores the barriers between White and Black gospel music, *The Gospel Tradition* contrasts the blues of Bessie Smith and the Western swing of Bob Wills, the

rough edge of Mitchell's Christian Singers and the smooth polish of the Sons of the Pioneers. Lots of obscure sides dating back to 1927, and a wide range of styles from sanctified women to choral spirituals. —*Brian Mansfield*

☆ **Gospel Warriors** / Spirit Feel 1003
Gospel Warriors: 50 Years of Great Solo Performances is not misnamed and does include some of gospel's most moving soloists from the '40s to the present, most notably Bessie Griffin. —*Kip Lornell*

○ **Gotham Gospel—Vols. 1 & 2** / Collectables 5312
A noteworthy two-volume anthology of obscure Black quartets from the "golden era" of a cappella gospel singing. Late '40s to early '50s recordings emphasize unissued and alternative takes. Very intense and emotional. —*Hank Davis*

☆ **Great Golden Gospel Hits, Vol. 4** / Savoy 14262
A tremendous and far-reaching assortment of vintage gospel by such masters as the Ward Singers, the Davis Sisters, the Staples Singers, and the Gospel Harmonettes. —*John Floyd*

☆ **The Great Gospel Men** / Shanachie 6005
A wide range of magnificent, awesome vocals are displayed on *The Great Gospel Men*, a 27-song anthology. Some names such as Brother Joe May, Rev. James Cleveland and Professor Alex Bradford are familiar even to non-gospel fans; others like the intense Robert Anderson, Professor J. Earle Hines, Norsalus McKissick, Robert Bradley and R.L. Knowles are known only to the hardcore, and even they probably haven't heard many songs by any one artist. This collection alternates nicely between slow and fast pieces, giving all artists a chance to demonstrate their skills. It's hard to say anyone emerges as greater than the others, although Robert Anderson may squeak out on the strength of his amazing "If Jesus Had to Pray." —*Ron Wynn*

☆ **The Great Gospel Women** / Shanachie 6004
Like its male counterpart, this anthology spotlights contributions from both famous stars (Mahalia Jackson, Marion Williams, Dorothy Love Coates, Sister Rosetta Tharpe) and obscure figures (Mary Johnson Davis, Jessie Mae Renfro, Lucy Smith, and Goldia Haynes among others). Here's one disc that really takes advantage of the CD medium with a hefty 31 selections. While some might quibble that celebated stars Jackson and Williams get six tracks apiece, it's hard to argue with the greatness of what's presented by them. Others who turn in head-turning performances include Frances Steadman, Roberta Martin, and Clara Ward. —*Ron Wynn*

○ **Greatest Gospel Gems** / 1991 / Specialty 7206
An excellent 24-song sampling of '50s and '60s sacred testifying from the vaults of Specialty Records. Includes essential cuts from Dorothy Love Coates, the Swan Silvertones, and Sam Cooke and the Soul Stirrers. —*John Floyd*

○ **I Hear the Music in the Air: A Treasury of Gospel Music** / 1990 / RCA 2099
I Hear the Music in the Air: A Treasury of Gospel Music offers great quartet-style singing (and three mini-sermons too!) for RCA Victor between 1926 and 1942. Features the likes of the Golden Gate Jubilee Quartet, the Morris Brown Quartet, and the Southern Sons. Also includes the first recording of Thomas Dorsey's "Precious Lord, Take My Hand," performed in 1937 by the Heavenly Gospel Singers. —*Brian Mansfield*

I Predict a Clone / 1994 / R.E.X.
Tribute to Steve Taylor, whose edgy, satiric rock influenced many of the artists who cover his music here in sometimes faithful, sometimes radically rearranged renditions. —*Thom Granger*

○ **In the Spirit, Vol. 1** / Apr. 1967 / OJL 12
The first of two albums that bring together 32 of the most striking prewar sacred commercial recordings by rural Black singers, including Charley Patton and Bukka White. —*Kip Lornell*

Infinite Flight / 1991 / Sparrow
Fifteen of the label's favorite songs celebrating its 15th anniversary, and collecting some CCM history in the process. —*Thom Granger*

○ **Jesus Is Listening** / P-Vine 3016
Jesus is Listening—Modern/Kent Gospel Masters. Treasure trove of postwar male quartets (late '40s/early '50s). The Echoes of Zion of Atlanta, Swanee River Quartet, and others. —*Opal Louis Nations*

★ **Jubilation, Vol. 1 (Black Gospel)** / Jan. 1992 / Rhino 70288
The Rhino *Jubilation: Great Gospel Performances* series is a terrific overview of Black gospel and country gospel. If you don't buy any other gospel CDs, or if you're looking for a good place to start, try this set. The first volume includes Mahalia Jackson, the Swan Silvertones, the Soul Stirrers, Aretha Franklin with James Cleveland, Shirley Caesar, the Trumpeteers, and many others. — *Billy C. Wirtz*

★ **Jubilation, Vol. 2 (More Black Gospel)** / Feb. 1992 / Rhino 70289
The amazing singing on this volume qualifies it as my favorite. Things heat up right away with the Soul Stirrers, featuring a young Sam Cooke (hear his trademark vocal glissandos years before pop music claimed them), and there's great "hard" gospel vocalizing from the Davis Sisters, the Sensational Nightingales (the wonderful "Burying Ground"), the speaker-splintering Archie Brownlee and the Five Blind Boys ("Our Father"), Staple Singers, Swan Silvertones, Alex Bradford, Dorothy Love Coates, and more. — *Christine Ohlman, Roundup Newsletter*

○ **Jubilation, Vol. 3 (Country Gospel)** / Mar. 1992 / Rhino 70290
The superstars of country music continually pay homage to their gospel roots, as witnessed by classic recordings from the Carter Family, Kitty Wells, the Louvin Brothers, Roy Acuff, George Jones and Tammy Wynette, Bill Monroe, Johnny Cash, Ricky Skaggs, and more. Tunes like Hank Williams' "I Saw the Light," which kicks off the set, and A.P. Carter's "Will the Circle Be Unbroken" from the Nitty Gritty Dirt Band's LP of the same name, have a haunting purity that lingers in the collective American consciousness. — *Christine Ohlman, Roundup Newsletter*

○ **Memphis Gospel Quartets** / High Water 1002
Many of the interesting community-based groups on *Memphis Gospel Quartets—Happy in the Service of the Lord* make their recording debut here. — *Kip Lornell*

○ **New York Grassroots Gospel** / Global Village 206
New York Grassroots Gospel—The Sacred Black Quartet contains strong recordings from the late '80s of contemporary but older-style quartets. — *Kip Lornell*

○ **No Compromise: Remembering the Music of Keith Green** / 1992 / Sparrow 1329
Petra, Steven Curtis Chapman, Russ Taff, and others cover songs by the late Keith Green, probably CCM's most influential early songwriter and performer. Most of the chosen material has worn fairly well over the years. — *Brian Mansfield*

Our Family / 1993 / Everland
Inventive arrangements and good performances earmark this collection of songs for parents and their children, in contrast to the typical children's album made with strictly tots in mind. — *Thom Granger*

Our Hymns / 1989 / Word 9107-605
The first of Word's *Our . . .* series, gathering many popular artists from its labels for new renditions of favorite hymns. — *Thom Granger*

○ **Preachin' the Gospel: Holy Blues** / Apr. 9, 1991 / CBS 46779
Serious inspiration from Blind Willie Johnson, Arizona Dranes, Josh White, Washington Phillips, and others on a digitally cleaned-up recording. — *Jas Obrecht*

○ **Raisin' the Roof** / Mobile Fidelity 760
Indispensable early '60s Sunsets material with O.V. Wright, Rev. Julius Cheeks and the Four Knights, plus great Swan Silvertones material led by Claude Jeter and Louis Johnson, from '60s Vee-Jay sources. — *Opal Louis Nations*

○ **Religious Recordings (1924-1931)** / Five-O-Four 20
Religious Recordings from Black New Orleans 1924-1931. A first-rate booklet and first-rate recordings make this a model for presenting historical recordings. — *Kip Lornell*

○ **Rural Gospel Styles (1944-1951)** / Eden 11200
The two Gospel Keys plus gems by Rev. Utah Smith, Rev. Chas White, Sister Littlejohn, Prophet B. West, and Brother Willie Easton. Essential. — *Opal Louis Nations*

○ **Sanctified Country Girls** / Wolf 119
A fascinating collection of pentecostal-style gospel performances by wonderful (though obscure) artists: Jessie Mae Hill, Cally Fancy, and Rev. Sister Mary Nelson. — *Kip Lornell*

○ **Say Amen Somebody** / DRG 12584

The soundtrack from the wonderful documentary film of the same name. — *Kip Lornell*

○ **Something Got a Hold of Me** / 1983 / RCA 2100
Country music has always had strong ties to Christianity, and this collection of RCA Victor country-gospel music from 1927-1941 demonstrates that heritage, starting with the Carter Family and continuing through the Monroe Brothers, Bill Monroe, the Blue Sky Boys, Uncle Dave Macon, and others. The standouts are A.P. Carter's title track and Dorsey Dixon's "I Didn't Hear Nobody Pray," but there is an outpouring of fervor for "the old-time religion" through every one of these performances. — *William Ruhlmann*

Songs from the Loft / Reunion
Simple but effective songwriting marks this worship project from Amy Grant and husband Gary Chapman, who wrote these choruses for teens that gathered in their barn for youth group-style meetings. — *Thom Granger*

○ **Stained Glass Hour** / 1992 / Rounder 11563
Ricky Skaggs dominates this collection, both as a bandleader and as a member of Boone Creek and the New South. Beyond that, *Stained Glass Hour: Bluegrass and Old-Timey Gospel Music* is an excellent sampler of religious-based bluegrass, past (the Blue Sky Boys, the Johnson Mountain Boys) and present (the Nashville Bluegrass Band, Dry Branch Fire Squad). — *Brian Mansfield*

Strong Hand of Love / 1994 / Myrrh
Tribute to the late Mark Heard, featuring mainstream and CCM artists' renditions of this excellent material. — *Thom Granger*

○ **Ten Years of Black Country Religion** / Yazoo 1019
A first-class overview of Southern rural religious music, including striking performances by Jaybird Coleman and Crumpton & Summers. — *Kip Lornell*

○ **The Truth in the Gospel (1937-50)** / Eden 10200
Essential collection of gospel divas: the first sides of Mahalia Jackson (1937), Sister Goldia Hayes with the Joe Liggins Trio, plus Sister Ernestine Washington with and without the Dixie Hummingbirds and Heavenly Gospel Singers. — *Opal Louis Nations*

☆ **White Gospel** / Collectables 5315
An interesting presentation of jubilee-inspired White-gospel quartets. — *Mark A. Humphrey*

○ **White Spirituals from the Sacred Harp** / New World 80205
The *Sacred Harp* is a collection of four-part hymns compiled in 1840 and widely used through various revisions across the south. In 1959, Alan Lomax made a stereo recording in Fyffe, Alabama of the 24 selections that comprise this stirring release. Quite unlike conventional white gospel, sacred harp singing employs 18th century harmony and "fuguing tunes" that, when sung by a hundred country voices as in this recording, is extraordinarily powerful. Admirers of Balkan vocal music would do well to give this homegrown tradition a listen, as would anyone interested in the variety of American sacred folk song. A 24-page booklet includes a history of the tradition and the music (in shape notes) and texts of the songs. — *Mark Humphrey, Roundup Newsletter*

☆ **The Young Lions** / 1960 / Vee-Jay 902
The '80s and '90s aren't the first time record companies have generated a publicity blitz about youthful jazz musicians. During the '60s, there was another wave of hype about talented prodigies, only then the names were Morgan and Shorter and Timmons rather than Hargrove, Connick, and Marsalis. *The Young Lions* was an album designed to showcase these developing stars, and it included not only Lee Morgan, Wayne Shorter and Bobby Timmons, but Frank Strozier on alto sax, Bob Cranshaw on bass and Louis Hayes alternating drum duties with Albert Heath. Each of these musicians developed their own signature sound, even though some (Morgan) didn't enjoy overly long careers, and others (Cranshaw, Hayes) became better known for their contributions to groups than their prowess as leaders. But they all blossomed from their beginnings as "young lions," and their potential is fully displayed throughout this eight-track anthology, which includes three bonus cuts. — *Ron Wynn*

SOUNDTRACKS

The motion picture soundtrack as we know it today dates from the early 40s, although film music itself goes back much farther than synchronized sound. Piano and organ accompaniments were played live in theaters from the beginning of the century, and it was during 1916 that Victor Schertzinger wrote the first full orchestral and choral score for a motion picture.

During the 30s, it became customary for record companies to release official recorded versions of songs heard in musical films. Hence, much of the musical history of Fred Astaire's RKO work, in films such as *Top Hat* and *Swing Time*, was captured simultaneously on the Brunswick label (now reissued by Columbia Records). And certain orchestral scores by recognized composers, such as Arthur Bliss's music for Alexander Korda's 1936 science-fiction epic *Things to Come*, found a separate life in the concert hall.

But it wasn't until 1942 that a record company fixed on the notion of recording and releasing the major parts of a full orchestra score. The film was *The Jungle Book*, produced by Alexander Korda and scored by Miklos Rozsa. One piece of Rozsa's, the waltz from his score for the 1942 film *Lydia*, had previously been recorded on a single 78 RPM disc by RCA Records with some success. Shortly after *The Jungle Book*'s release, RCA brought Rozsa to New York to record a suite of the key movements from his new score with the NBC Symphony Orchestra, with a narration of the story provided by Sabu, the star of the film. This set of 78 RPM records, which has since been issued many times, marked the start of the movie soundtrack as a record genre.

The next major development took place in 1945, when MGM established its record label, MGM Records. The studio had originally planned to start the label in 1941, with Tommy Dorsey heading it, but the war intervened with a five-year delay. The first "musical biography" was *Till the Clouds Roll By*, inspired by the life and songs of Jerome Kern. It seemed logical to release eight of the musical highlights from the film in a set of four 78 RPM records, which was precisely what was done, with some modifications to make the songs suitable for release on record. These included the removal of lengthy instrumental breaks and sound effects that were germane to the screen presentation but not to the record.

Till the Clouds Roll By was a success, if not a raging best-seller, but it established the pattern for musical soundtracks. Its release ahead of the film secured radio play for the songs, thus promoting the film, and also made the record-buying public aware of the release of the movie in a way that print advertising alone would not have. Subsequently, with the advent of the long-playing record two years later, studios would release their musicals in reasonably complete form, either on their own labels or under contract to other record companies.

Looking at this history more than 40 years later, one must bear in mind just how important the soundtrack album was to the public. In the days before home video (and the boom in movie memorabilia shops), the soundtrack album was the only piece of a movie a fan could actually own, take home, and enjoy at will, without having to depend on the movie studio or the local theater or, in later years, the television station. Additionally, the early soundtrack albums appeared in the era of radio, before the visual medium completely overwhelmed popular culture, and their impact and importance were that much greater at the time.

For the film studios, the soundtrack album (whether devoted to dramatic film scores or musicals) became a major marketing tool, promoting the film by its release weeks ahead of the opening date, securing radio play for the major songs, and promoting the studio's own music-publishing interests. This often led to peculiarities in song and musical lineups. Most movie musical albums, for example, failed to include dance numbers, incidental music, and choral pieces, since these were not hooked to specific singing personalities. Additionally, the running-time restrictions on 78s and early long-playing records required the cutting of extended instrumental breaks, however pleasant.

Finally, there were the peculiarities of the music and movie businesses themselves: Frank Sinatra, who was under contract to MGM Studios for a period of five years and turned in at least one major musical performance on screen during that time (*On the Town*), never appeared on an MGM soundtrack album because he was under exclusive contract to Columbia Records in the 40s. However, the soundtrack album to MGM's 1956 *High Society*, featuring Sinatra, Bing Crosby, and Louis Armstrong, did appear on Capitol Records, where Sinatra was recording in the 50s.

The soundtrack business went along as an adjunct to the movie business until the 60s, when changes began occurring, most notably a splintering of the market. Swept up by the boom in pop and rock music and a decline in traditional entertainment and subjects, studios stopped making musicals (except for major, multi-million-dollar blockbusters) and began demanding a lighter touch in the scoring of their dramatic films. At the same time, two generations of listeners and fans – one that had grown up when the older films were originally in the theaters, and one that had grown up with them on television – began expressing an interest in the music that had filled their lives.

The business of reissuing soundtracks had existed, particularly where musicals were concerned, since the switch from 78s to long-playing records. But in the early 60s, various labels (most notably Capitol, Decca/London, and Warner Bros.) began commissioning new recordings that made use of the dramatic improvements that had been made in record fidelity and stereo sound. *Gone with the Wind* by Max Steiner, *Ben Hur, El Cid,* and *King of Kings* by Miklos Rozsa, and the *Adventures of Robin Hood* by Erich Wolfgang Korngold were just a few of the scores represented in new recordings, often done under the supervision of their original composers.

By the beginning of the 70s, with the recognition of film's cultural importance (it even became a field of academic study), re-recordings had become common. Producers

Peter Munves and George Korngold and conductor Charles Gerhardt brought the first successful extended series of such efforts to RCA Records in the form of the *Classic Film Scores* series, with each volume devoted to a specific composer (e.g., *The Classic Film Scores of Alfred Newman*). The Gerhardt series was ideal for the serious listener and the novice just getting started. Careful attention was paid to the details and nuances of the music itself, and the material was assembled in suites of easily absorbed length.

Meanwhile, on a more intensive level, Elmer Bernstein (himself a major movie composer) had begun a concerted effort to preserve scores and secure rights for the original composers and their estates. As an adjunct to this effort, he made a monumental series of re-recordings in England of vintage film scores in their entirety, through his Film Music Society label.

The 70s and 80s saw a veritable explosion in the field of film music, as a second generation of major screen composers – Elmer Bernstein, Jerry Goldsmith, Leonard Rosenman, Ennio Morricone (whose music for the Clint Eastwood/Sergio Leone "man with no name" Westerns virtually revolutionized that genre) – achieved wide recognition and major composer status. Along with new soundtrack albums, which now seem to accompany virtually every film release, even of the lowest-budgeted picture, re-recordings became still more common using various European orchestras, which work under far less restrictive union rules and for far less money than their American counterparts.

The 80s also saw the establishment of a new kind of soundtrack album, which actually had its roots in the 70s: the rock & roll soundtrack. Films built around rock groups and personalities had been common from the 50s onward (most notably the relatively well-made early films showing the young, lean Elvis Presley; the early British films of Cliff Richard and the Shadows; and the one great work in the genre, the Beatles in *A Hard Day's Night*), but the 70s saw the emergence of the rock soundtrack as a separate screen entity. It began with George Lucas's *American Graffiti*, the soundtrack which, filled with a superbly selected body of rock oldies, was nearly as prominent in the film as any of the actors. The accompanying double album also became a massive seller.

Francis Ford Coppola's *Apocalypse Now*, with its use of 60s hits, moved the formula up a decade and a notch in dramatic intensity, even if its most famous scene involved Wagner's "Ride of the Valkyries" and a helicopter attack. But it was *Fast Times at Ridgemont High*, another film about adolescent life, that brought the formula first used in *American Graffiti* into a contemporary time frame, with an enviable assembly of catchy singles and FM-style hits by contemporary rock artists. From there on, the die was cast: producers saw the path to success with otherwise flawed and conceptually weak movies was simply to license the right rock tracks, and many movies of the 80s and 90s acquired the feel of a jukebox in operation. With varying degrees of success, the specific music involved everything from post-new-wave (*I Was a Teenage Zombie*) to such vintage music-and-myth-mixing efforts as Oliver Stone's *The Doors*, where the songs structured the film and occasionally the soundtracks outperformed and outlasted the movies themselves.

– Bruce Eder

○ **Above the Rim** / Interscope Records 92359
An excellent set of some fine rap and urban R&B featured in the basketball film, *Above the Rim*. Although it's simply a collection of songs, the tracks hold together as an album; it is also a good snapshot of hip-hop circa 1994. —*AMG*

Adventures of Robin Hood / 1988 / Varese Sarabande 47202
A surprisingly dull score (from the 1938 movie) by Erich Wolfgang Korngold—one that he reportedly had a lot of trouble finishing. The music is well and rousingly re-recorded and elevated by its moments of inspiration, which are fewer in number than typical for this composer. —*Bruce Eder*

Against All Odds / 1984 / Atlantic 80152
The soundtrack to this remake of *Out of the Past* is highlighted by the title song, "Against All Odds (Take a Look at Me Now)," a dramatic ballad sung by Phil Collins that topped the charts for three weeks. It also contains songs by Stevie Nicks, Peter Gabriel, Big Country, and Kid Creole & the Coconuts, plus selections from the score by Michel Colombier and Larry Carlton. —*William Ruhlmann*

☆ **Aladdin** / 1992 / Disney 60846
Disney's restored winning streak with animated musicals stretched to three with this film, scored (as were its predecessors, *The Little Mermaid* and *Beauty and the Beast*) by Alan Menken, who collaborated both with his usual partner, Howard Ashman (Ashman died before production was completed) and with Tim Rice, known as the lyricist on Andrew Lloyd Webber's early musicals. The standout performances, as in the film, are by Robin Williams, playing the Genie, on such songs as "Friend Like Me" and "Prince Ali." The score also contains Peabo Bryson and Regina Bell's hit single, "A Whole New World." Note that, while early copies of this album contain what some Arabs considered objectional lyrics in the lead-off song, "Arabian Nights," the lyrics have been redone on later copies. —*William Ruhlmann*

○ **The Alamo** / 1960 / Varese Sarabande 5224
A famous Dimitri Tiomkin score, which suffers from a lack of melodic invention and extended flat passages broken by a few memorable moments. It has its fans, however. —*Bruce Eder*

○ **Alamo Bay** / 1985 / Warner Brothers 25311
One of Ry Cooder's more impressive scores ties in with the Texas location of the film with some Tex-Mex mood music. Most of Cooder's usual session friends are present, including Van Dyke Parks, David Lindley, Jim Keltner, and John Hiatt. Lee Ving of Fear makes a guest appearance, and Cesar Rosas and David Hidalgo of Los Lobos sing on one track. —*William Ruhlmann*

☆ **Alien** / 1980 / Virgin 90975
Jerry Goldsmith's music, recorded under the baton of Lionel Newman, holds up nearly as well as Ridley Scott's 1979 movie, with long, lyrical passages broken up by genuinely unsettling timbral effects. —*Bruce Eder*

○ **American Gigolo** / 1980 / Polydor 813632
Danceable electronic score by Eurodisc master Giorgio Moroder, including "Call Me" by Blondie, which was Number 1 for six weeks. —*William Ruhlmann*

☆ **American Graffiti Soundtrack, Vol. 1** / 1973 / MCA 8001
A stunner of an oldies soundtrack that revolutionized the licensing and use of classic rock songs in movies. One of the great rock oldies collections. It's enjoyable on every level. —*Bruce Eder*

☆ **An American in Paris, An** / CBS 45391
An expanded edition of the George Gershwin showcase soundtrack from the 1951 movie, with good sound (especially on the title ballet, re-scored by Saul Chaplin). —*Bruce Eder*

○ **Anatomy of a Murder** / May 29, 1959-Jun. 2, 1959 / Rykodisc 10039
Duke Ellington's music was used surprisingly little in movies. *Anatomy of a Murder* was a landmark film and Duke's writing fit in perfectly. As in all good soundtracks, the music's role was to accompany and enhance the story, so hearing the soundtrack on CD does leave one with a somewhat incomplete feeling. However Ellington's writing was colorful enough to largely stand on its own even in this setting. This set, although not essential, does not disappoint. —*Scott Yanow*

Ascenseur Pour L'echafaud / Dec. 4, 1957 / Phonogram 8225662
In 1957 Miles Davis went to France for a short tour, and while there he recorded the soundtrack for the film "Ascenseur Pour L'Echafaud." This CD contains the original LP of material plus 19 minutes of unreleased alternate versions. Better than many soundtracks, this music (which also features the tenor of Barney

Wilen and pianist Rene Urtreger) does not really stand on its own without the film. Of mostly historical interest. —*Scott Yanow*

Back to the Future—Original Soundtrack / 1985 / MCA 6144
Huey Lewis and the News scored a Number 1 hit with the typically bouncy "The Power of Love" from this album. Completists will also want to note the appearance of otherwise unavailable tracks by Lindsey Buckingham and Eric Clapton. —*William Ruhlmann*

○ **Back to the Future—Part 2** / 1989 / MCA 6361
This is mostly "effect" or "mood" music, without much that would draw your attention during the movie. Of course, there is a healthy sprinkling of variations on the theme that Alan Silvestri uses in all the *Back to the Future* movies. —*Tavia Hobart*

○ **Back to the Future—Part 3** / 1990 / Varese Sarabande 5272
More of the same from Silvestri, with perhaps a bit more thematic material. It also includes ZZ Top's "Doubleback," arranged (by Silvestri) for banjo, fiddle, and bass. —*Tavia Hobart*

○ **Backbeat** / Mar. 8, 1994 / Virgin Records America, Inc. 39386
Boasting a band filled with alternative rock superstars—Don Fleming and Thurston Moore on guitar, Mike Mills on bass, Dave Grohl on drums, and Greg Dulli on vocals, as well as vocals from Dave Pirner on two cuts—this collection of early rock & roll standards performed in the Beatles movie *Backbeat* is energetic and inspired, if not transcendent. —*Stephen Thomas Erlewine*

○ **Balkan—Mysterious Voices of Bulgaria** / Virgin 91368
Film soundtrack recordings, mostly original music, offering a departure from the *Mystere des Voix Bulgares* repertoire. —*Myles Boisen*

☆ **Batman (Original Motion Picture Score)** / May 1989 / Warner Brothers 25977
The best of all the Danny Elfman soundtracks. The "Batman Theme" is familiar to all who've seen the film, but anyone who hasn't listened to the "Finale" is in for a real treat. Without a doubt Elfman has a flair for writing for brass. —*Tavia Hobart*

Batman TV Soundtrack / PolyGram 834908
Nelson Riddle's TV soundtrack. —*AMG*

Batman Returns / 1992 / Warner Brothers 26972
As anyone would expect, this is more of the same thematic material as in the first movie. However, Elfman does use more of the choral effects of which he seems to have become so fond. Includes "Face to Face," performed by Siouxsie and the Banshees and cowritten by the group and Elfman. —*Tavia Hobart*

Beaches / 1989 / Atlantic 81933
The soundtrack to Midler's musical comeback film, featuring her version of "Wind beneath My Wings." —*William Ruhlmann*

○ **Beauty & the Beast** / 1991 / Disney 60618
This music by Alan Menken and lyrics by Howard Ashman are positively delightful. While not as good as the *Little Mermaid* score, this album has its moments, such as "Be Our Guest" (in an *A Chorus Line* style). Includes both orchestral and vocal selections, featuring the talents of Robby Benson, Paige O'Hara, and Angela Lansbury, among others. Album also includes "Beauty and the Beast" as a duet between Celine Dion and Peabo Bryson. —*Tavia Hobart*

○ **Beetlejuice** / 1989 / David Geffen Co. 24202
Danny Elfman's score for this 1988 Tim Burton film is dark, rollicking fun. It includes Harry Belafonte's hits "Day-O (The Banana Boat Song)," and "Jump in Line (Shake, Shake Senora)." —*Tavia Hobart*

○ **Belle of New York** / 1991 / CBS 47701
A deliberate period-music collection from the 1952 movie, lacking in topflight songs but a good showcase for Fred Astaire's voice. —*Bruce Eder*

Ben-Hur / 1990 / Silva Screen 43
Miklos Rozsa conducting the Royal Philharmonic Orchestra. This '70s re-recording by the composer of the 1959 movie has a very bright sound and most of the highlights, but lacks the weight of the original recordings. —*Bruce Eder*

☆ **Ben-Hur** / Sony 47020
A monumental double CD of Miklos Rozsa's music, assembled from the complete two original albums plus the original film tracks, all cleaned up and properly re-sequenced. —*Bruce Eder*

Benny & Joon / 1993 / Varese Sarabande 5419

Irving Berlin

Irving Berlin (1888-1989) was the most successful songwriter of the 20th century. Though, like his contemporaries, he spent the better part of his career writing songs (usually both words and music) to be used in Broadway musicals, he is better remembered for the songs themselves than for the shows (and sometimes films) in which they were introduced. This is because Berlin was a master at the kind of music that flourished from the turn of the century until World War II, shows that were really just collections of production numbers, scenes, and novelty acts (organized vaudeville presentations, really) rather than the story musicals that became prevalent starting with Rodgers and Hammerstein's *Oklahoma!* in 1943. It is also because Berlin, who did not read music and could play the piano in only one key and only on the black notes (he used a special piano with a lever that changed keys for him and employed a musical secretary to notate his compositions), wrote songs, not scores.

But what songs! Out of more than a thousand, a short list would include "Alexander's Ragtime Band" (his first major hit, in 1911), "God Bless America," "A Pretty Girl is Like a Melody," "Always," "Blue Skies," "Puttin' on the Ritz," "How Deep is the Ocean?," "Cheek to Cheek," "Let's Face the Music and Dance," "White Christmas," "There's no Business Like Show Business," "I Love a Piano," "What'll I Do?," "Easter Parade," and "Oh, How I Hate to Get Up in the Morning." The last came from one of the two shows Berlin organized and performed in during the two world wars (he can be seen in the film version of the second one, *This is the Army*).

Berlin became his own song publisher and built and owned a Broadway theater, the Music Box, to house his shows. Perhaps his greatest and his last hit came with the musical *Annie Get Your Gun* in 1946, though he did write three more before retiring in 1962.

– William Ruhlmann

Scotland's Proclaimers got a belated Number 3 hit with their four-year-old "I'm Gonna Be (500 Miles)" when it was taken up as the theme song of this offbeat romantic comedy. The rest of the soundtrack album features Rachel Portman's score, which emphasizes the movie's whimsical nature. —*William Ruhlmann*

☆ **Bernard Herrmann—Classic Fastasy Film Scores** / 7014
Four of Bernard Herrmann's fantasy film scores written for the movies of Ray Harryhausen (*Seventh Voyage of Sinbad*, etc.) and taken from the original film recordings. The sound is a little soft and compressed, which is understandable given its origins, and the representation of *Jason and the Argonauts* here is a bit of a cheat, but the rest of the material has never been excerpted as fully. —*Bruce Eder*

☆ **Bernard Herrmann—Film Fantasy: Cinema Gala** / London 421266
Bernard Herrmann—Film Fantasy: Cinema Gala is an extraordinarily fine collection of some of Herrmann's most famous film music, originally well-recorded by the composer during the '60s, and remixed for a bright sound today. Worth owning just for the suite from *The Day the Earth Stood Still*, but it's all first-rate. —*Bruce Eder*

Best Of James Bond—30th Anniversary Collection / Capitol 98413
For those who don't want all the extra rarities included in the limited-edition two-disc set, yet still would like to own the most popular theme songs from the James Bond films, this single-disc collection will satisfy their needs quite nicely. —*AMG*

Best Of James Bond—30th Anniversary Collection Ltd. Edition / Capitol 98560

A fine two-disc collection featuring all of the theme songs to the James Bond movies, as well as excerpts from the scores and some unreleased material. *—AMG*

The Beverly Hillbillies [TV Soundtrack] / 1993 / CBS 9202
"The Beverly Hillbillies" television series, which ran from 1962 to 1971, was a situation comedy, not a musical show, other than its famous Flatt & Scruggs theme song. Nevertheless, after three years on the air, the show spun off this album, in which members of the cast, prominently featuring Buddy Ebsen and Irene Ryan, sang songs based on their characters. The result is a novelty, with a vengence. Ebsen, a former musical comedy star, comes off fine, but even fans of the show may not be ready to hear Max Baer sing out about the foibles of life in Beverly Hills. Long out of print, the album was released on CD in 1993 in anticipation of the movie version of the show. *—William Ruhlmann*

The Beverly Hillbillies / 1993 / Fox 66313
Just as the movie version of "The Beverly Hillbillies" television show features an all-new cast playing the parts of the original stars, the soundtrack album features a bunch of current Nashville stars covering roadhouse oldies associated with others, from Joe Diffie's take on George Jones' "White Lightnin'" to Jerry Scoggins' version of Flatt & Scruggs's "The Ballad of Jed Clampett." And as in the film, the newcomers mostly have nothing on their progenitors. Joe Walsh and Steve Earle are the chief exception, their version of "Honey Don't" showing no respect for Carl Perkins and being all the better for it. (The Texas Tornados' version of "Wasted Days and Wasted Nights" is something of a ringer, since lead singer Freddy Fender wrote and recorded the original.) *—William Ruhlmann*

○ **Beverly Hills Cop** / 1984 / MCA 5553
Two million copies of this album were sold within a year of release, which is no surprise, given that it contained such hits as Patti LaBelle's "New Attitude," Glenn Frey's "The Heat Is On," and Harold Faltermeyer's "Axel F." Another notable aspect of the recording is the small-print admission "Contains additional songs that are not in the film." In other words, this is more of a compilation than a soundtrack album *per se*. That didn't bother anybody, though. *—William Ruhlmann*

☆ **The Big Chill** / 1983 / Motown 6062
Motown scored big with this album, which contains ten 60s hits, from Marvin Gaye's "I Heard It through the Grapevine" to Procol Harum's "A Whiter Shade of Pale," just the sort of thing the yuppie thirtysomethings in the movie loved, and just what the audience that saw the film was longing to rediscover. *—William Ruhlmann*

The Big Country / Silva Screen 030
A good idea not brought off well. Jerome Moross' sweeping score for the 1958 movie *The Big Country* (re-recorded digitally) has been performed much too flaccidly, with none of the verve the music demands, despite some fine attention to detail by Tony Bremer and the Philharmonic Orchestra. *—Bruce Eder*

Black Nativity—Broadway Cast / 1990 / Vee Jay 2501
The 1961 release of "Black Nativity," a gospel production performed on Broadway, alerted the theatrical set to the power and transcendence of religious music. The performance featured stirring vocals from gospel stars and text provided by noted playwright Langston Hughes. Though this disc is woefully short at 30 minutes, the vocals by Marion Williams, Prof. Alex Bradford and others are spectacular. Hughes knew that the brilliance of these stars would make the biblical story even more meaningful; something underscored from the opening moments of "My Way's Cloudy," throughout the disc. *—Ron Wynn*

○ **The Blade Runner** / 1982 / Full Moon 23748
A somewhat unsatisfying orchestral re-recording of Vangelis's original electronic score, but acceptable in the absence of the Vangelis music on record. *—Bruce Eder*

Blankman / 1994 / Epic Soundtrax 64328
"Anyone Can Be a Hero," a song here sung by Lalah Hathaway, seems to be the theme of this Damon Wayans comedy, and to accompany it, music supervisor Pila McCurry has assembled a sampler of contemporary African American music by a variety of acts, including the New Power Generation, until recently the backup group for the Artist Formerly Known As Prince, who produced, arranged and composed their selection, "Super Hero." Rap is represented by Tag Team, among others; Silk has an a cappella

gospel tune in "Cry On"; and there's a cover of "Could It Be I'm Falling In Love," by II D Extreme with Patra toasting over it. The rest is big beat mediocrity, but you can dance to it. *—William Ruhlmann*

Blown Away / 1994 / 550 Music/Epic Sound 66145
If the downside of soundtracks containing orchestral scores is that the writing is at the service of the story rather than musical sense, waxing lyrical or tensing up to match the plot points, the concomittant with song-based soundtracks is that, while the songs may match the film's scenes, on record they can sound like an arbitrary jumble of tunes. This album is a good example—what do two songs from Aretha Franklin's pop-jazz era on Columbia Records in the early '60s, U2's hit "With or Without You," and a love ballad called "Take Me Home," sung by Joe Cocker and Bekka Bramlett in the style of "(I've Had) The Time of My Life" (Bill Medley and Jennifer Warnes' hit from *Dirty Dancing*), have to do with each other? Nothing, except that they're all featured in this summer thriller. There's a certain Irish tone here (U2, a song by the Pogues), but no real thematic unity. *—William Ruhlmann*

○ **Blue Velvet** / Varese Sarabande 47277
Angelo Badalamenti's score for David Lynch's psycho-sexual thriller *Blue Velvet* is one of his best. *—AMG*

Bodies, Rest & Motion / 1993 / Big Screen 24506
Michael Convertino's score for Michael Steinberg's "little relationship story" Consists of 20 short pieces (15 are under two minutes each) running about half an hour and based on Indian chants: voices vocalize various nonsense syllables, drums pound individually, single reed instruments play little melodies. It's a miniaturist approach that is individual, if a little odd. *—William Ruhlmann*

○ **The Bodyguard** / 1992 / Arista 18699
The main draw of the *Bodyguard* soundtrack is the biggest single of all time, "I Will Always Love You" (14 weeks at Number 1!) which is surrounded by other adult-contemporary/urban-pop songs from Whitney Houston that are equally appealing to fans of her mega-hit. *—AMG*

Border Radio / 1987 / Capitol 73221
Former Blasters and X songwriter/guitarist Dave Alvin scored this film and brought in his friends—the cream of the early '80s Los Angeles rock scene—to help. Various tracks feature Alvin, fellow X member John Doe, Green on Red, Steve Berlin of the Blasters, and Los Lobos, among others. *—William Ruhlmann*

○ **Born on the Fourth of July** / 1989 / MCA 6340
The first eight tracks on this disc are rock and pop, including songs from Edie Brickell & the New Bohemians, Don McLean, and the Temptations. The last six are from the pen of John Williams. *—Tavia Hobart*

Brazen / 1994 / Epic Dance 66192
The word may be out of date, but this is a disco album. The big beat dominates every track of what is in essence a dance sampler. If you are looking for something to enliven your next party, you've just been hired to act as DJ at your local club, or you like to keep up a steady rhythm in your exercising, this may be the record for you. Certainly, the nomial artists seem interchangeable, the lyrics are romantic but rudimentary, and all is at the service of the relentless beat. But it's a hard record to listen to while sitting still. *—William Ruhlmann*

The Breakfast Club / 1985 / A&M 3294
Anchored by the Simple Minds hit "Don't You (Forget About Me)," this also features tracks by Wang Chung and Jesse Johnson and several good instrumentals by producer Keith Forsey (producer of Billy Idol, and the Psychedelic Furs). *—Scott Bultman*

☆ **Brigadoon** / 1988 / Sony 45440
This pleasant Lerner and Loewe soundtrack is sung with sincerity, if not great power, by Gene Kelly, and features a couple of near-hits. *—Bruce Eder*

○ **Bright Lights, Big City** / 1988 / Warner Brothers 25688
Excellent contemporary dance music on this album, including M/A/R/R/S, Prince, New Order, Bryan Ferry, and Depeche Mode, plus a rare song by Steely Dan's Donald Fagen. *—William Ruhlmann*

Brimstone and Treacle / 1982 / A&M 3245

The better part of this album is given over to songs by the Police and by Sting (who starred in the film), though IRS labelmates the Go-Go's and Squeeze also turn up. — *William Ruhlmann*

Broadway Classics, Vol. 1 / 1991 / MCA 10051
The choice seems nearly random but this sampler of Broadway songs from Broadway shows originally released on Decca includes everything from "The Impossible Dream" to "Don't Cry for Me, Argentina." Listen, and then seek out the complete show. — *William Ruhlmann*

A Bronx Tale / 1993 / Epic 57560
The music from this motion picture consists of period tunes heard in the Bronx and elsewhere in the 1950s and '60s, starting, naturally, with homeboys Dion and the Belmonts and running through the Jimi Hendrix Experience. That's quite a stretch, of course, but it is bridged by interludes given over to recreations of the period sound by Cool Change. And from the Cleftones' "Little Girl of Mine" to the Rascals' "A Beautiful Morning," the selections are such classics it's hard to argue with them. Still, without the movie's images to hold them together, the collection seems virtually random. — *William Ruhlmann*

☆ **Buccaneer** / 1958 / Varese Sarabande 5214
A rousing Elmer Bernstein score, written for a larger-than-life swashbuckler. — *Bruce Eder*

The Buddy Holly Story / 1978 / CBS 35412
In the movie, these performances hold up well, but on record Gary Busey's performances of Holly's originals are pale and flawed and have been supplanted by MCA's definitive Holly collection. — *Bruce Eder*

Buffy the Vampire Slayer / Jul. 28, 1992 / CBS 52854
An average collection of the out-takes of a bunch of medium-level rockers assembled for an amusing but forgettable teen horror comedy. For completists who must have everything by Matthew Sweet, Susanna Hoffs, Toad the Wet Sprocket, Divinyls (a reasonable cover of "I Ain't Gonna Eat Out My Heart Anymore"), Ozzy Osbourne, or the Cult. Post-Judas Priest singer Rob Halford has a solo selection, "Light Comes Out of Black." — *William Ruhlmann*

○ **Cabaret—Soundtrack** / 1972 / MCA 37125
Liza Minnelli hit a career peak in this film musical, and she dominates the soundtrack, lending personal meaning to such songs as the title track (in which she almost seems to be singing about her mother, Judy Garland). Joel Grey is equally impressive. — *William Ruhlmann*

☆ **Camelot** / Sep. 22, 1987 / Warner Brothers 3102
The Lerner and Loewe music in this film version is sung with passion, if not great control, by Richard Harris and Vanessa Redgrave, and is livelier than the movie. — *Bruce Eder*

☆ **The Carl Stalling Project: Music from Warner Bros. Cartoons 1936-58** / 1990 / Warner Brothers 26027
The Carl Stalling Project: Music from Warner Brothers Cartoons is music almost everyone will recognize. Generations of children and adults know Carl Stalling's music, whether consciously or not. This CD collects nearly 80 minutes of Stalling's music from 1936 to 1958. He was a master of making the music fit the animation, using every style of music from the time, including jazz, classical (Wagner, Mendelssohn, and Mozart), big band, children's songs, and Christmas music. An excellent collection of highly innovative soundtrack music. Guaranteed to spark all of your cartoon memories. — *Tavia Hobart*

○ **Casualties of War** / 1989 / CBS 45359
A dark, brooding, and surprisingly restrained work by Ennio Morricone, also more sentimental than his usual standard, and very operatic—parts of it sound like music for a Broadway extravaganza waiting to happen. — *Bruce Eder*

Cat People / 1986 / MCA 1498
David Bowie's featured "Putting Out Fire (With Gasoline)" is the best part of this otherwise predictable electronic score from the 1982 movie. — *Bruce Eder*

○ **Chariots of Fire** / 1982 / Polydor 800020
Vangelis' Academy Award-winning score to the movie continues to be his most famous album, probably because the theme is immediately recognizabl, yet quickly lures listeners into a musical world that stands on its own. — *Linda Kohanov*

○ **Chess** / 1984 / RCA 5340

This is a studio recording made prior to any staged version of the musical, with music by former ABBA members Benny Andersson and Bjorn Ulvaeus and lyrics by Tim Rice about an international chess tournament. A UK Top10 hit, it includes Murray Head's hit version of "One Night in Bangkok." — *William Ruhlmann*

○ **Christine** / 1983 / Varese Sarabande 5240
An exuberant collection of late '50s pop and rock songs, plus George Thorogood's "Bad to the Bone." Put it on and have a sock hop. — *William Ruhlmann*

Cincinnati Kid / MCA 25012
The acclaimed soundtrack for the Steve McQueen film was supplied by Lalo Schifrin. It mixed in snatches of traditional jazz with light mood music, and was among Schifrin's most successful film scores—both sales wise and artistically. — *Ron Wynn*

Cinderella / 1957 / CBS 2005
Perhaps Rodgers and Hammerstein's most seen but least performed musical, *Cinderella* was written for and played on television, for only one, non-taped time. The typically lovely music and affecting lyrics softened some of the harder aspects of the fairy tale, and Julie Andrews gave a wonderful performance in the title role. This recording features the TV cast, and was made a couple of weeks before the broadcast. The score features memorable songs such as "Do I Love You Because You're Beautiful?" — *William Ruhlmann*

○ **Cinema Gala: Citizen Kane** / Decca 417852
Performed by the London Philharmonic Orchestra and National Philharmonic Orchestra. The *Citizen Kane* material isn't as interesting as that on Charles Gerhardt's RCA collection, but the material from *The Devil and Daniel Webster* and *Jason and the Argonauts* is a necessary part of any collection. (Unicorn Records has a still-better rendition of the former that simply has never turned up on CD.) — *Bruce Eder*

☆ **Citizen Kane—Herrmann Film Scores** / Jun. 1974 / RCA 0707
Citizen Kane: The Classic Film Scores of Bernard Herrmann is probably the best of the entire series by conductor Charles Gerhardt and the National Philharmonic Orchestra. Every track is worthwhile and memorably played, especially *Beneath the 12-Mile Reef* and the suite from *Citizen Kane*, the latter highlighted by Kiri Te Kanawa's performance of the Strauss-like aria from *Salammbo*. — *Bruce Eder*

☆ **Classic British Film Music** / Silva Screen 072
An essential import recording of several long-neglected English film scores, most notably Ralph Vaughan Williams' "Coastal Command"; the playing is competent if not always inspired. Kenneth Alwyn and the Philharmonic Orchestra. — *Bruce Eder*

○ **A Clockwork Orange** / Mar. 14, 1989 / Warner Brothers 2573
Although it sounds slightly dated now, the electronic score for Stanley Kubrick's *A Clockwork Orange* still sounds very eerie, especially in conjunction with the classical pieces used in the rest of the film. — *AMG*

○ **Close Encounters of the Third Kind** / 1977 / Varese Sarabande 5275
John Williams's score draws too much from Ravel for its own good, but the sound is impressive and the effects are entertaining. — *Bruce Eder*

Club Paradise / 1986 / CBS 40404
For all intents and purposes, this is a Jimmy Cliff album, which means some high-quality, pop-oriented reggae. On one track, "Seven-Day Weekend," Cliff duets with Elvis Costello (they also wrote the song together), along with The Attractions. — *William Ruhlmann*

Cocktail / 1988 / Elektra 60806
The four-million-selling summer party album of 1988, featuring the Number 1 hits "Don't Worry, Be Happy" by Bobby McFerrin and "Kokomo" by the Beach Boys, plus radio hits by Starship, the Fabulous Thunderbirds, the Georgia Satellites, and John Cougar Mellencamp. — *William Ruhlmann*

○ **Cocoon** / 1985 / Polydor 827041
This James Horner score includes music ranging from ethereal to big band. One can't help but be touched by the plaintive oboe theme found throughout the album. It also includes "Gravity" by Michael Sembello. — *Tavia Hobart*

○ **A Collector's Sondheim** / 1985 / RCA 5480

A four-LP boxed-set compilation that gathers material from a variety of Stephen Sondheim scores over 30 years 1954-1984 (those for which he provided only lyrics are excluded). This is an outstanding, if pricey, sampler that features many rarities is a must for Sondheim fans. — *William Ruhlmann*

The Color of Money / 1986 / MCA 6189
Ex-Band songwriter/guitarist Robbie Robertson put together this soundtrack, which allowed him to collaborate with blues master Willie Dixon and jazz master Gil Evans, though it was his collaboration with Eric Clapton that produced the album's hit song, "It's in the Way that You Use It." Also featured: Don Henley, Robert Palmer (three tracks), and B.B. King. — *William Ruhlmann*

○ **Coma** / Bay Cities 3027
A pure thriller score from the 1978 by Jerry Goldsmith, filled with eerie musical effects that anticipated his soundtrack for *Alien*. It transferred well to CD. — *Bruce Eder*

The Commitments / Aug. 13, 1991 / MCA 10286
Alan Parker's film about a Dublin, Ireland, cover band sparked this wildly popular soundtrack of R&B remakes. Male vocalist Andrew Strong shouts like a working-class Michael Bolton, and all three female singers have knelt at the altar of Queen Aretha. The band's competent, as bar bands go, and the songs are good—any album that includes "The Dark End of the Street" and "Slip Away" has to have something going for it. — *Brian Mansfield*

The Commitments, Vol. 2 / 1992 / MCA 10506
More R&B retreads from Ireland's favorite fictional white-soul band. Seven of the eleven tracks are billed as new recordings, so this is really film leftovers plus some filler. It shows, too—it's a long way down from volume one's "I Can't Stand the Rain" to "Too Many Fish in the Seas." — *Brian Mansfield*

Coneheads / Warner Brothers 45345
A by-the-books pop soundtrack hodge-podge, with a mediocre R.E.M. out-take and "Soul to Squeeze," the Red Hot Chili Peppers' rewrite of "Under the Bridge," being the sole highlights. — *AMG*

Consenting Adults / Oct. 27, 1992 / Milan 35630
Thirteen run-of-the-mill instrumental pieces by Michael Small made to accompany a contemporary romantic thriller, plus a couple of moody songs sung by Q. Rose, one of which is Charlie Rich's "No Headstone On My Grave." — *William Ruhlmann*

Cool Runnings / 1993 / Chaos 57553
It was inevitable that a comedy about a Jamaican bobsled team would have a reggae soundtrack. What is surprising is that it is so enjoyable in a light, unforced way. Worl-A-Girl note the unlikeliness of Jamaica having a bobsled team; Diana King covers Bob Marley's "Stir It Up"; and Wailing Souls cover Talking Heads' "Wild Wild Life." Best of all (if somewhat redundant), Jimmy Cliff got his first chart hit in 23 years with a cover of the 21-year-old "I Can See Clearly Now," by Johnny Nash. — *William Ruhlmann*

○ **Country—Original Soundtrack** / 1984 / Windham Hill 1039
Charles Gross composed and conducted this score, but it's played by several of the new-age artists from Windham Hill Records, notably pianist George Winston, whose distinctive piano playing actually dominates the proceedings. — *William Ruhlmann*

Crossover Dreams / 1986 / Elektra 60470
An album of salsa music prominently featuring the work of Ruben Blades, who also starred in the 1985 film. — *William Ruhlmann*

Crossroads / 1986 / Warner Brothers 25399
The ersatz blues story of the film gives Ry Cooder leeway to turn in an impressive blues-derived soundtrack featuring Sonny Terry along with his usual collaborators Van Dyke Parks, Jim Keltner, Nathan East, and others. But it's Cooder's guitar playing that highlights the album. — *William Ruhlmann*

○ **The Crow** / Atlantic Records 82519
Featuring some of the biggest names in hard-rock, heavy metal, and alternative rock (Stone Temple Pilots, Nine Inch Nails, Rollins Band), the soundtrack to *The Crow* holds together as an album, since most of the bands have a dark, unifying sound. — *AMG*

The Crying Game / 1993 / SBK 89024
The movie that gave new meaning to the line "I know all there is to know about the crying game" has a soundtrack that features both Dave Berry's 1964 UK hit version of the title track and Boy George's remake, which was a U.S. hit. That track, and a few others, were produced by those gender-benders, Pet Shop Boys;

while Lyle Lovett sings his version of Tammy Wynette's "Stand By Your Man," and there is some orchestral scoring by Anne Dudley. As a souvenir of the movie, the soundtrack is a success, but otherwise it's miscellaneous. — *William Ruhlmann*

○ **Dances with Wolves** / Aug. 1990 / Epic 46982
This majestic John Barry score is slightly under-recorded but very rewarding, despite its occasional overreliance on material all too familiar from the James Bond movies. — *Bruce Eder*

Darkman / 1990 / MCA 10094
The music is dark, as the title suggests. Danny Elfman definitely achieves a sinister quality. — *Tavia Hobart*

○ **David Shire—at the Movies** / 1991 / Bay Cities 3021
A too-often overlooked composer gets to play some of his best movie music at the piano, with help from Maureen McGovern. The album includes material from *Norma Rae*, *Farewell My Lovely*, *The Conversation*, and *Return to Oz*. — *Bruce Eder*

☆ **Deep Blues** / 1992 / Atlantic 82450
One thinks of delta blues as a music largely played in the 1930s or so, but journalist Robert Palmer has captured a group of contemporary bluesmen, such as Big Jack Johnson and Roosevelt "Booba" Barnes in his documentary film and on this soundtrack album. Some of the cuts come from the film, and some do not, either way, this is an impressive album and true to its title. — *William Ruhlmann*

○ **Deep in My Heart** / CBS 47703
The Sigmund Romberg material is generally extremely well performed, even by Jose Ferrer, and this collection, from the 1954 movie, is unique in terms of content. — *Bruce Eder*

○ **Diamonds Are Forever—Original Soundtrack** / 1972 / EMI America 96209
John Barry wrote a big, impressive-sounding score for this 1971 film, which on record comes off as a good follow-up to "You Only Live Twice." — *Bruce Eder*

Dirty Dancing / 1987 / RCA 6408
This album includes songs from the hit movie—both old favorites (Bruce Channel's "Hey Baby," "In the Still of the Night," from the Five Satins, and Mickey & Sylvia's "Love Is Strange") and recent ones (Eric Carmen's "Hungry Eyes" and "(I've Had) The Time of My Life," performed by Bill Medley and Jennifer Warnes). "She's Like the Wind" is performed by Patrick Swayze, who played the male lead in the movie. While this may not be "the time of your life," as the album cover advertises, it is a fun collection. — *Tavia Hobart*

○ **Diva—Soundtrack** / 1982 / Rykodisc 10010
A spellbinding mix of opera and new-age music—haunting and memorable. — *Bruce Eder*

Dr. No / 1963 / EMI America 96210
John Barry's "James Bond Theme" from the 1962 movie is the best part of this weakest of the James Bond soundtracks, which otherwise boasts pseudo-Jamaican melodies and a couple of guitar instrumentals. — *Bruce Eder*

☆ **Doctor Zhivago** / 1990 / CBS 45437
A lush, beautiful score for an epic film. "Lara's Theme" was the biggest hit from the 1965 movie, but there were enough secondary tunes to turn it into one of the biggest-selling soundtrack albums in history. Glittering and gorgeous. — *Bruce Eder*

☆ **Easter Parade** / 1989 / Sony 45392
The sound of these 1947 recordings is old, but the assembly of Irving Berlin tunes sung by Fred Astaire, Judy Garland, and Ann Miller is one of the best—especially "Drum Crazy." — *Bruce Eder*

○ **Eddie & The Cruisers—Soundtrack** / 1983 / RCA 5202
There was a year's delay before this film, which concerns the mysterious death of a fictional '60s rock star, took off via video and cable TV; but when it did, the soundtrack album, featuring such songs as "On the Dark Side" and "Tender Years," by John Cafferty and the Beaver Brown Band, took off with it. To most, the music sounded like Bruce Springsteen clones, but it was appealing nonetheless. — *William Ruhlmann*

Edward Scissorhands / 1990 / MCA 10133
This Danny Elfman soundtrack uses a considerable amount of choral effects, including both an adult chorus and a boys choir. The result is a pleasant (albeit occasionally dark) and ethereal score. Includes "With These Hands" as performed by Tom Jones. — *Tavia Hobart*

○ **El Cid** / 1977 / CBS 47704
Rozsa and most listeners agree that *El Cid*, from the 1961 movie, was his last great score. Overall, it is a surprisingly lyrical and sensitive body of music for what was essentially an epic-scale action film. Much of the material has been most inventively derived from medieval Spanish and Arab sources, and while the recording has an unfortunate softness to modern ears, the playing is exceptionally polished and the 1962-vintage stereo separation still holds some surprises. — *Bruce Eder*

☆ **The Empire Strikes Back** / 1980 / Varese Sarabande 5353
Here is an album that includes what are probably some of the most overplayed, overused themes in the history of film scores. However, if you can get past the familiarity and actually *listen* to what's there, you'll find another well-written score from John Williams. — *Tavia Hobart*

Endless Summer II / 1994 / Reprise 45615
Power trio instrumental electric guitar rock to accompany footage of surfers, ranging from raging metal to wailing ballads. Jimi Hendrix lives again, and this time his name is Gary Hoey. — *William Ruhlmann*

○ **Evening with Alan Jay Lerner** / 1987 / DRG 5175
Star-studded two-disc live album taken from a benefit concert. The best of Lerner's songs and stories, sung, spoken, and played by a Broadway/West End who's-who, including Sally Ann Howes, Burton Lane, Marti Webb, Len Cariou, Tim Rice, Douglas Fairbanks, and others. — *William Ruhlmann*

☆ **Exodus** / 1986 / RCA 1058
A grand-scale orchestral soundtrack. Contains the hit title theme from the 1960 movie and a brace of accompanying material done in the best grand style of the era. — *Bruce Eder*

○ **The Falcon and the Snowman** / 1985 / EMI America 48411
Pat Metheny and Lyle Mays lent their trademark sound to the sweeping (occasionally orchestral) score of this original soundtrack. Featuring vocals by David Bowie on "This Is Not America." — *Scott Bultman*

Fallen Angels / 1993 / Verve 519 903
This is the soundtrack to a six-part cable television series based on detective stories set in Los Angeles in the 1940s and '50s. It contains mostly small-band jazz from the Verve Records catalog, and features people like Charlie Parker, Stan Getz, Nat "King" Cole, and Billie Holiday. As such, it functions as a neat jazz sampler separate from the series. — *William Ruhlmann*

○ **Falling from Grace** / 1991 / Mercury 512004
For the soundtrack to his motion picture directing debut, John Mellencamp brought together such artists as Dwight Yoakam, John Prine, and Nanci Griffith. For a record of country, folk, and rock, it is nearly as expansive and rich as his best albums: *Scarecrow*, *The Lonesome Jubilee*, and *Big Daddy*. — *AMG*

☆ **Fame** / 1980 / Polydor 800034
The film's setting in the New York High School of the Performing Arts provided a frame for one of the most inspiring soundtracks of a film in the '80s. Film star Irene Cara scored with the chart-topping title track and the Top 20 "Out Here on My Own." This soundtrack, most of it by Michael Gore, is a knockout. — *William Ruhlmann*

☆ **Fantasia** / 1991 / Disneyland 60007
One of the best and earliest full orchestral scores available (it was recorded for the 1940 film), featuring Leopold Stokowski and the Philadelphia Orchestra in top form. Avoid the digital re-recording from the '80s at all costs. — *Bruce Eder*

○ **Far and Away** / 1992 / MCA 10628
A fine score (as is to be expected from John Williams), although parts of it are reminiscent of his scores from *Hook* and *JFK*. The Chieftains are featured on three tracks, and the album includes Enya's "Book of Days." One thing is puzzling, however. Why, when "Book of Days" is in Gaelic on Enya's *Shepherd Moons* album, is it translated into English for a movie about people from Ireland? — *Tavia Hobart*

☆ **Far from the Madding Crowd** / 1985 / Sony 47023
Possibly the best score written for any English picture since the '40s heyday of Vaughan Williams and William Walton's film work—Richard Rodney Bennett has composed a haunting, melodic yet atonal score for this 1967 movie, built on English folk melodies, that lingers long in the listener's memory. James Galway's flute playing is a bonus. — *Bruce Eder*

Danny Elfman

Since 1980 Danny Elfman has enjoyed modest success as frontman for the eccentric alternative band Oingo Boingo, but an opportunity to score Tim Burton's 1985 film *Pee Wee's Big Adventure* opened up a lucrative career as a composer of TV and film soundtracks. Since then, his credits have included *Batman, Dick Tracy, The Simpsons, Edward Scissorhands, Scrooged, Beetlejuice, Big Top Pee Wee*, and too many more to mention.

– Rick Clark

Faraway, So Close! / Jan. 25, 1994 / Sbk Records 27216
Director Wim Wenders assembled a modern rock who's-who for this soundtrack, which includes tracks by U2 (both of which also turn up on their *Zooropa* album), Lou Reed, Nick Cave, Jane Siberry, and Laurie Anderson. The result is a moody, evocative set that works with the film and as a consistent collection of contemporary songs. (Almost half of the album is given over to selections from Laurent Pettitgand's low-key score.) — *William Ruhlmann*

☆ **Fast Times at Ridgemont High** / 1982 / Asylum 60158
The first great rock & roll compilation soundtrack of the '80s, which sold in the millions (justifiably) and gave Jackson Browne a Top10 hit with "Somebody's Baby." — *Bruce Eder*

○ **Fastest Guitar Alive** / 1985 / CBS 45405
The soundtrack to this 1968 Roy Orbison movie is better than the film (based on a leftover Elvis Presley script), with two good tunes and the rest quite enjoyable. — *Bruce Eder*

Fathers and Sons / 1992 / Chaos 48972
This is an 11-song various artists sampler of some up-and-coming performers, in the guise of a soundtrack album. James McMurtry and Chris Whitley are singer/songwriters in the Bob Dylan tradition. Julianna Hatfield and John Gorka are somewhat more distinctive (in fact, Gorka's "I'm From New Jersey" is the stand-out track here). And ex-Bangle Susanna Hoffs, not so much a developing artist as a near-has-been, does a cover of the old Seekers bit "You Were on My Mind." — *William Ruhlmann*

● **55 Days at Peking** / 1963 / Varese Sarabande 5233
One of Dimitri Tiomkin's better '60s scores, with more interesting material than usual and fewer sluggish spots—the one to get. — *Bruce Eder*

○ **The Film Music of John Barry** / 1988 / CBS 44376
An interesting if predictable compilation, touching most of the key parts of the composer's 1960 output. — *Bruce Eder*

○ **Finian's Rainbow** / 1948 / CBS 4062
Ella Logan, Donald Richards, and David Wayne starred in this mixture of Southern politics and Irish blarney, which was the most successful of Burton Lane's musicals. — *William Ruhlmann*

○ **Firm** / 1993 / MCA/GRP 2007
Dave Grusin's score for this Sydney Pollack treatment of the John Grisham legal thriller starring Tom Cruise consists of jazzy acoustic piano pieces, a surprisingly low-key, yet effective approach. It is augmented with some pop and fusion songs, notably tunes by Jimmy Buffett, Lyle Lovett, and Nanci Griffith, to give a feel of the contemporary southern locale. — *William Ruhlmann*

○ **Flashdance** / 1983 / Casablanca 811492
Giorgio Moroder's score for this dance fantasy album turned into a blockbuster (five million copies and counting) due to the title track, sung by Irene Cara, Michael Sembello's "Maniac," and a bunch of other modern dance tracks. — *William Ruhlmann*

○ **Footloose** / 1984 / CBS 39242
Featuring several hits—including the title tracks, "Let's Hear it for the Boy," "Almost Paradise," "Holding Out for A Hero," and "Dancing in the Sheets"—*Footloose* became one of the biggest soundtracks of the '80s, selling over seven million copies. Today, it sounds a bit dated, yet there's still plenty of fine pop singles on the album. — *AMG*

☆ **Forbidden Planet—Original Soundtrack** / 1978 / Small Planet 1

This startling and overpowering score from the 1956 movie is based on electronic tonalities rather than orchestral performance. A real wonder, and years ahead of its time. — *Bruce Eder*

○ **Forrest Gump** / 1994 / Epic Soundtrax 66329
The surprise hit of the 1994 summer movie season traces the life of a half-wit through the major historical events of the 1950s, '60s, and '70s, and this soundtrack album is a travelog of the same period, from Elvis Presley's 1956 hit "Hound Dog" to Bob Seger's 1980 hit "Against the Wind." Like the movie, the soundtrack to Forrest Gump succeeds at repackaging the familiar—in the film, we revisit everything from desegregation and the Vietnam War to the self-centered trends of the '70s, and on the soundtrack, we hear the concurrrent hits for the umpteenth time—though, unlike the movie, the soundtrack doesn't trivialize what it recycles. Playing it is basically like listening to an oldies radio station, minus the commercials and annoying DJ patter, but, just like many other song-oriented soundtracks, this is still a miscellaneous collection. That, however, didn't keep it from shooting into the Top 10 as the movie became a blockbuster. The double-CD version contains eight more tracks than the cassette. — *William Ruhlmann*

Forrest Gump—Original Score / 1994 / Epic Soundtrax 66430
Forrest Gump was a sugar lump of a movie, a fact driven home by this album containing Alan Silvestri's saccharine score, all cute little piano high notes and swatches of melody rolling out of the string section. There is also a two-disc soundtrack album containing pop songs heard in the picture. It's music to watch feathers waft in the breeze by, and is therefore appropriate to the film, though it has little value on its own. — *William Ruhlmann*

Four Weddings & a Funeral / Apr. 5, 1994 / London Records 828509
Not surprisingly, we have a cornucopia of love songs here, the best of them perhaps being Elton John doing Gershwin on "But Not for Me." (The older rockers get, the more they want to do pop standards.) John also is heard on his own "Crocodile Rock" and on

George Gershwin

In a career tragically cut short in mid-stride by a brain tumor, George Gershwin (1898-1937) proved himself to be not only one of the great songwriters of his extremely rich era, but also a gifted "serious" composer who might bridge the worlds of classical and popular music. The latter is all the more striking, given that, of his contemporaries, Gershwin was the most influenced by such styles as jazz and blues.

Gershwin's first major hit, interpolated into the show *Sinbad* in 1919, was "Swanee," sung by Al Jolson. Gershwin wrote both complete scores and songs for such variety shows as George White's *Scandals* (whose annual editions thus were able to introduce such songs s "I'll Build a Stairway to Paradise" and "Somebody Loves Me").

After 1924, Gershwin worked primarily with his brother Ira as his lyricist. The two scored a series of Broadway hits in the 20s and early 30s, starting with *Lady be Good* (1924), which included the song "Fascinatin' Rhythm." 1924 was also the year Gershwin composed his first classical piece, "Rhapsody in Blue," and he would continue to work in the classical field until his death.

By the 30s, the Gershwins had turned to political topics and satire in response to the onset of the Depression, and their *Of Thee I Sing* became the first musical to win a Pulitzer Prize. In the mid 30s, Gershwin ambitiously worked to meld his show music and classical leanings in the creation of the folk opera *Porgy and Bess*, with lyrics by Ira and by Dubose Heyward. The Gershwins had moved to Hollywood and were engaged in several movie projects at the time of George Gershwin's death.

– William Ruhlmann

Jerry Goldsmith

Jerry Goldsmith (born in Los Angeles in 1929) is the leading figure in film music of his generation. After starting out in radio, he moved to television and into motion pictures in the early 60s, where his instrumental inventiveness and superb melodic sense quickly moved him to the top of his profession. His scores are seldom less than inspired and are always absorbing, whether they are written for thrillers (*The Prize*, "The Twilight Zone" TV series), science fiction (*Logan's Run*), military subjects (*Patton*, *The Blue Max*), or serious drama (*A Patch of Blue*).

– William Ruhlmann

"Chapel Of Love," and when he's not singing, we are getting remakes of "La La La (Means I Love You)" and "Smoke Gets In Your Eyes." Well, what did you expect from a movie that has four weddings in it? And speaking of the funeral, the album concludes with John Hannah's reading of W.H. Auden at the movie's most solemn moment. Thankfully, the film itself ends on a more up note, and you can always program your CD player to play only the wedding material. — *William Ruhlmann*

☆ **From Russia with Love** / 1975 / EMI America 95344
Probably the best of the James Bond scores, with radiant music for strings and startling percussion passages punctuating this recording from the 1963 film. — *Bruce Eder*

Funny Girl / Aug. 1968 / CBS 3220
As a movie, *Funny Girl* is even more of a Barbra Streisand star vehicle than it was as a Broadway show. The main differences between the cast album and this, the film soundtrack, are that there are fewer songs from the Bob Merrill-Jule Styne score, there is less singing for the leading man, in this case non-singer Omar Sharif, and Streisand gets to sing two songs actually associated with Fanny Brice, who she portrays, "I'd Rather Be Blue over You (Than Happy With Somebody Else)" and "My Man." — *William Ruhlmann*

Funny Lady / 1975 / Bay Cities 3006
Barbra Streisand is not known for singing standards, so the chief virtue of this soundtrack to the disappointing sequel to *Funny Girl* is hearing her singing songs like "Am I Blue." This is not a great virtue, however, especially when you also have to endure the singing of James Caan. — *William Ruhlmann*

G.B.H. / Feb. 22, 1994 / Rykodisc Usa Records 20284
This is Elvis Costello and Richard Harvey's music for a British TV series. (The letters stand for "Grievous Bodily Harm.") Scored for a small orchestra, it is typical accompanying music to a dramatic thriller, but unremarkable on its own. Despite the presence of Costello, none of it is vocal music or related to rock & roll. — *William Ruhlmann*

Geronimo—American Legend / 1993 /
Director Walter Hill hired Ry Cooder to do the score for a movie he describes on the back cover as "a drama about two cultures," and Cooder (with such cronies as David Lindley and R. Carlos Nakai) has delivered an appropriate mixture of sounds identifiably based in Native American music and in nineteenth century American folk music—music for the campfires of both camps, as it were. Cooder is steeped in such styles, and the result is effective, if not one of his more independent scores. — *William Ruhlmann*

○ **Get Yourself a College Girl** / 1964 / CBS 52420
A pretty cool soundtrack for a pretty lousy movie. Featured here are the Dave Clark Five, the Standells, the Animals, and Stan Getz. — *Bruce Eder*

☆ **The Ghost and Mrs. Muir** / 1975 / Varese Sarabande 47254
Elmer Bernstein conducting the Royal Philharmonic Orchestra. An excellent re-recording from the 1947 movie, and one of Bernard Herrmann's finest scores—a dark, brooding, romantic work that is lovely and haunting. — *Bruce Eder*

☆ **Giant** / Apr. 12, 1989 / Capitol 92056
The best of Dimitri Tiomkin's original soundtrack albums, in a crisp, dense mono that is extremely impressive on CD. This al-

bum, from the 1956 movie, is a treat for the ears, and well worth owning. —*Bruce Eder*

☆ **Gigi** / 1958 / Sony 45395
One of the finest musical scores ever recorded. A warm, witty, romantic confection highlighted by Andre Previn's spirited conducting, Betty Wand's delectable singing, and Lerner and Loewe's greatest film score. —*Bruce Eder*

○ **Godspell—Soundtrack** / 1973 / Arista 8337
A stirring rock/pop score by Stephen Schwartz and a strong lead performance by Victor Garber make a success of this film version of the stage hit emphasizing the religious nature of Christ (as opposed to the secular *Jesus Christ Superstar*). Robin Lamont's rendition of "Day by Day" was a Top 15 hit. —*William Ruhlmann*

○ **Goldfinger** / 1964 / EMI America 95345
The first of the hit James Bond albums, driven by Shirley Bassey's inimitable performance of the title track. —*Bruce Eder*

☆ **Gone with the Wind** / Sony 45438
An expanded and remastered edition of the original 1939 track, with much of the echo and distortion removed. —*Bruce Eder*

○ **Gone with the Wind** / Polydor 817116
A satisfying CD transcription of the original 1939 Max Steiner tracks, but marred by many imperfections in the original sources and too much echo. —*Bruce Eder*

☆ **The Good, the Bad & The Ugly** / 1988 / EMI America 48408
Probably Ennio Morricone's most appealing and enduring Western score—funny, intense, dramatic, and filled with haunting melodies. The CD's stereo separation adds to the fun of this 1967 soundtrack. —*Bruce Eder*

The Gospel at Colonus / 1984 / Warner Brothers 25182
The original cast recording of the Bob Telson/Lee Breuer musical based on Sophocles's *Oedipus at Colonus* has music written in gospel style and sung by the Five Blind Boys of Alabama and other gospel groups. It is beautifully produced by Telson, Daniel Lazerus, and the Steely Dan team of Donald Fagen and Gary Katz. —*William Ruhlmann*

○ **The Graduate** / Jan. 1968 / Columbia 3180
An okay release from the 1967 movie, featuring some of Simon & Garfunkel's tunes alternating with instrumentals by Dave Grusin. —*Bruce Eder*

Grand Canyon—Soundtrack / 1992 / RCA 61115
A very diverse score by James Newton Howard. It uses everything from rock styles and jazz to delicate orchestral tracks and a huge brass fanfare. It also includes "Searching for a Heart," by Warren Zevon. —*Tavia Hobart*

○ **The Great Escape** / 1963 / Intrada 7025
An impressively remastered recording, with a very rich sound, despite a little more hiss than one might like. —*Bruce Eder*

○ **Great Western Themes (W/Geoff Love & Orch.)** / EMI 52031
Twenty-four tracks done with verve but not much insight, highlighted by "The Big Country," "The Big Valley," "Wagon Train," and a creditable version of "The Virginian." —*Bruce Eder*

☆ **Hang 'em High/Guns for San Sebastian** / CBS 47705
Dominic Frontiere's *Hang 'Em High*, from the 1968 film, is a spare, clever score, but Ennio Morricone's *Guns for San Sebastian* (1968) is practically an opera without words—intense, draining, and magnificent. —*Bruce Eder*

☆ **A Hard Day's Night** / Capitol 11921
The first great rock & roll soundtrack album from the 1964 movie, equal in quality to the best non-film-related albums by the Beatles. Filled with jewels. —*Bruce Eder*

☆ **The Harder They Come** / 1972 / Mango 9202
Jimmy Cliff starred in this gritty film about street life in Kingston, Jamaica. The album is a brilliant compilation of early reggae music, and Cliff's own songs. "You Can Get It If You Really Want It," "Many Rivers to Cross," "The Harder They Come," and "Sitting in Limbo," are among the best of a very good lot. —*William Ruhlmann*

Hello Dolly / 1969 / 20th Century-Fox 5103
The movie version of *Hello Dolly!* was considered to be something of a disappointment, which may help explain why the soundtrack album is one of the few records Barbra Streisand is associated with that hasn't even gone gold. Streisand's wild miscasting is less apparent on record than on film, however, and she sings effectively. The album also features Louis Armstrong, who

Bernard Herrmann

The dean of film composers, Bernard Herrmann was probably the most gifted musician ever to work in films, with barely a note of music to his credit that is not worthwhile. A classically trained composer, Herrmann worked for Orson Welles's Mercury Theatre and the CBS radio network before he went to Hollywood with Welles in 1940. His first two film scores, *Citizen Kane* and *The Devil and Daniel Webster*, were both nominated for Oscars in the same year (*Webster* won), and he was established from then on. Herrmann worked principally for 20th Century-Fox from the mid 40s until the end of the 50s, and did brilliant work on such films as *The Ghost and Mrs. Muir*, *The Day the Earth Stood Still*, *Beneath the 12-Mile Reef*, and *Journey to the Center of the Earth*. In the 50s and 60s, Herrmann also contributed notably to the success of Alfred Hitchcock's films and wrote inspired scores for early films by Brian De Palma and Martin Scorsese. He died the night he finished work on *Taxi Driver*.

– William Ruhlmann

bad a hit with the title song (not this version) and, in a small part, Michael Crawford, later the award-winning *Phantom of the Opera*. On the other hand, Walter Matthau can't sing. —*William Ruhlmann*

Holiday Inn / 1950 / MCA 25205
Bing Crosby and Fred Astaire perform on this soundtrack featuring "White Christmas." —*AMG*

○ **Hollywood Screen Classics** / Chesky 71
Charles Gerhardt conducting the National Philharmonic Orchestra. Chesky has done unexpectedly well with these mostly 1968-vintage recordings. Although the sound is a little compressed compared with Gerhardt's later work, the detail is all there, and the work does have a youthful freshness. Highlights include perhaps the best of all *Gone with the Wind* suites, plus oddities such as the music from *Rashomon*. —*Bruce Eder*

Home Alone / 1990 / CBS 46595
In this score, John Williams manages to cleverly interweave traditional Christmas music with his own Christmas themes. It also includes "O Holy Night" and "Carol of the Bells," both performed by a children's chorus, and Mel Torme's rendition of "Have Yourself a Merry Little Christmas." —*Tavia Hobart*

○ **Honeymoon in Vegas** / Aug. 11, 1992 / Epic 52845
Country singers rule this soundtrack of Elvis Presley covers, which is every bit as flawed, frivolous and fun as the film from whence it came. While Billy Joel parodies "All Shook Up" and "Heartbreak Hotel," John Mellencamp labors to avoid parodying "Jailhouse Rock," and U2's Bono transforms "Can't Help Falling in Love" into an obsessive parable about hero worship, folks like Ricky Van Shelton and Trisha Yearwood just sit back and sing the things, which at least makes them pleasant after more than one playing. Dwight Yoakam's power-chord-country version of "Suspicious Minds" and Travis Tritt's "Burning Love" rank with their best remakes. Breaking the trend are pop crooner Bryan Ferry, who sings a seductive British soul version of "Are You Lonesome Tonight?" and the usually trustworthy Vince Gill, whose Pat Boone-style rendition of Arthur Crudup's classic blues "That's All Right" cleans up the grammar. —*Brian Mansfield*

○ **Hook—Original Soundtrack** / 1991 / Epic 48888
A John Williams masterpiece. The emotion that he evokes through this music is incredible: it can make you experience what the characters in the movie are feeling—see the menace of Captain Hook, or find your happy thought and fly. It includes the vocal selections "We Don't Wanna Grow Up" and "When You're Alone." —*Tavia Hobart*

The Hot Spot—Soundtrack / 1990 / Antilles 846813
This score is credited to "The Ultimate Blues Band," and you can't argue with the name when the personnel includes John Lee

Hooker and Miles Davis. A moody, slinky, bluesy, jazzy, improvised score that's full of treats. —*William Ruhlmann*

House Party 2—Original Motion Picture Soundtrack / 1991 / MCA 10397
Starts off right with a cut by Tony! Toni! Tone! that features Maceo Parker on sax, then keeps the party going all the way to the end with "It's So Hard to Say Goodbye to Yesterday" (even though it's not Boyz II Men's hit version). Includes tracks by Bell Biv DeVoe, Eric B & Rakim, Ralph Tresvant and, of course, Kid 'N Play. —*Brian Mansfield*

☆ **How the West Was Won** / 1985 / Sony 47024
This soundtrack, from the 1962 movie, was the most successful Western film album ever issued, and justifiably so—spacious, poignant, and inspired. —*Bruce Eder*

○ **I Was a Teenage Zombie** / 1987 / Enigma 73296
An excellent compilation album featuring a who's-who of the premier roots-rock bands of the '80s: the Fleshtones, the Del Fuegos, the dB's, Dream Syndicate, the Violent Femmes, the Smithereens, Los Lobos, Alex Chilton, the Ben Vaughn Group, and Bob Pfeifer. Want to know what '80s alternative rock sounded like? Just put this album on. —*William Ruhlmann*

○ **In the Blood** / 1990 / Rykodisc 20174
Director George Butler's 1990 film *In The Blood* was quite controversial in its depiction of the glories of hunting and President Theodore Roosevelt's exploits in Africa. What wasn't questioned, however, was the film's marvelous African music. The soundtrack contained both vintage sounds and newly composed gems, thanks to Olatunji, who was responsible for both old and fresh material. The selections range from contemporary tracks featuring guitarist David Torn and Olatunji to classics by various groups and individual performers, some of which were adapted. Things never slow down or become predictable through 25 selections. —*Ron Wynn*

In the Name of the Father / 1994 / Island Records 518841
U2 alert: The opening and closing songs here were co-written by Bono, and he co-sings the first one, the title song. At the end, there's "You Made Me the Thief of Your Heart," sung with her usual abandon by Sinead O'Connor. In between, the usual mixture of suspenseful instrumental music, composed by Trevor Jones, plus a couple of miscellaneous oldies—"Voodoo Chile," by the Jimi Hendrix Experience and "Dedicated Follower of Fashion," by the Kinks. None of this makes much sense outside the context of the movie, and the Bonofied songs aren't all that good, but completists will want to know. —*William Ruhlmann*

○ **It's Always Fair Weather** / 1955 / Sony 47026
This curious Comden/Green/Previn score is generally downbeat, but highlighted by two killer numbers featuring Dolores Grey and released in stereo for the first time. —*Bruce Eder*

JFK / 1992 / Elektra 61293
This is a very diverse soundtrack album. It includes tracks by John Williams, a performance of the Royal Scots Dragoon Guards (drummers), jazz from Tony Bennett, the first movement of a Mozart horn concerto, and more. —*Tavia Hobart*

○ **Jacques Brel Is Alive and Well . . .** / 1974 / Atlantic 1000
This film version of the musical revue of the songs of Belgian singer/songwriter Jacques Brel retains the pleasure of the stage version of *Jacques Brel Is Alive and Well and Living in Paris* and adds to it by including the author himself on the moving "Ne Me Quitte Pas" (known in English as "If You Go Away"). But the standout performer is Mort Shuman, who, with Eric Blau, also provides the English translations. —*William Ruhlmann*

☆ **James Bond 13 Original Themes** / 1977 / Capitol 46079
A greatest-hits album of sorts, overall very impressive, especially for its diversity of styles. —*Bruce Eder*

○ **Jaws** / 1975 / MCA 1660
This is an outstanding John Williams score. Almost everyone is familiar with the driving and repetitive main theme, but few would recognize anything else from this score. There's some really good stuff here, and it's worth investigating. —*Tavia Hobart*

○ **The Jazz Singer** / 1980 / Capitol 46026
Diamond's only notable screen appearance was his starring role in this remake of the 1927 movie that was Hollywood's first real talkie and originally featured Al Jolson. Diamond wrote a new score, featuring his biggest latter day hits, "Love on the Rocks," "Hello Again," and "America," and as a result this soundtrack al

bum became his biggest seller ever—five million copies and counting. —*William Ruhlmann*

Jennifer 8 / Nov. 1992 / Milan 66120
Christopher Young's score for this detective thriller is based on slow, contemplative piano figures augmented with strings in the wistful, ominous, and threatening tones consistent with the movie's theme. Bits of "Madame Butterfly" and "Silent Night" fill out the score. —*William Ruhlmann*

☆ **Jerome Robbins' Broadway** / 1989 / RCA 60150
A two-disc cast album from Robbins' anthology show, which includes his re-creations of production numbers excerpted from such shows as *On the Town, West Side Story, The King and I, Gypsy,* and *Fiddler on the Roof.* Onstage it was breathtaking; on record it makes for a sort of Broadway's-greatest-hits album, albeit with re-recorded versions. —*William Ruhlmann*

○ **Jerry Fielding—Film Music** / Bay Cities 4002
A very imposing and worthwhile volume of amazingly good music from surprisingly lackluster movies. Each one stands on its own. The music is a worthy memorial to an underrated composer. —*Bruce Eder*

○ **Jerry Fielding—Film Music 2** / Bay Cities 4003

Jimmy Hollywood / 1994 / Atlas Records 523070
This Barry Levinson-directed film came and went so quickly that it would have been easy to miss its soundtrack, which is the work of ex-Band guitarist/songwriter Robbie Robertson. Robertson has constructed several excellent soundtracks in the past (*Carney, The Colour of Money*). and this is another good one. He himself performs several tunes, and he selects others, including tracks by the Iguanas, Sand Rubies, and Concrete Blonde. A smokey, and smokin' set, whatever happened to the movie. —*William Ruhlmann*

☆ **John Williams—Tribute to Spielberg** / CBS 45997
This is a must-have for any John Williams fan who hasn't started a collection yet, as some of the scores from which these tracks were taken may be difficult to find. Includes music from the Indiana Jones movies, *Empire of the Sun, E.T., Always, Jaws, 1941, Sugarland Express,* and *Close Encounters of the Third Kind.* A great representation of some of his finest scores. —*Tavia Hobart*

Judgment Night soundtrack / 1993 / Immortal/Epic Soundtr 57144
Well, it looked like a good idea on paper. Matching (mostly) hardcore rap groups with (mainly) cuttin-edge alternative hard-rock seemed like a good idea, but the results are considerably weaker than its potential. None of the tracks sound like the artists recorded in the same studio together, making the album sound static and weak. Only Mudhoney and Sir Mix-A-Lot's wonderfully mindless "Freak Momma" approaches a real rock and roll moment; the rest is stunningly predictable and frightfully boring. —*Stephen Thomas Erlewine*

Jurassic Park / 1993 / MCA 10859
John Williams's score for what has become the most successful movie of all time is similar to his scores for other popular Steven Spielberg films. He remains firmly in the tradition of the lush, heavily orchestrated score. This is the first horror movie he and Spielberg have collaborated on since *Jaws,* but there is nothing like the threatening theme that helped define that monster movie here. Instead, there is a lot of quiet music, a much more subtle touch, and a wistful theme that runs throughout—though things do come to a boil now and then. —*William Ruhlmann*

Kalifornia / Aug. 3, 1993 /
An undistinguished rock sampler, the highlights of which are X's "Lettuce and Vodka" and David Baerwald's "Born for Love." Score composer Carter Burfell is restricted to one moody track. —*William Ruhlmann*

King and I / Jun. 11, 1956 / Angel 64693
The film soundtrack to Walter Lang's *The King and I* is distinguished from the Broadway cast album chiefly by Alfred Newman's expanded orchestrations and by the presence of Marni Nixon in the role of Anna Leonowens. On film, the part was played by Deborah Kerr, but Nixon, one of the best invisible voices in Hollywood (she also ghosted Audrey Hepburn in *My Fair Lady*) is the wonderful singer of songs like "I Whistle a Happy Tune" and "Getting to Know You," sung onstage by Gertrude Lawrence, who died before the film was made. Yul Brynner repeats his performance as the king, and Rita Moreno

gets to play Tuptim and sing "We Kiss In a Shadow." This is a Hollywood adaptation done right—bigger and more dramatic than Broadway can be, with a show that benefits from the frills—and makes you wonder why they didn't always do as well. — *William Ruhlmann*

○ **Kings Row** / 1979 / Varese Sarabande 47203
Charles Gerhardt conducting the National Philharmonic Orchestra. A well-produced, early digital recording of Erich Wolfgang Korngold's 1942 score for the classic melodrama, capturing the original's majesty. —*Bruce Eder*

Kismet / 1961 / Sony 45393
The Wright/Forrest movie score, released for the first time in stereo, and chock-full of fine singing and those Borodin melodies. —*Bruce Eder*

☆ **Kiss Me Kate** / 1990 / Angel 54033
A two-disc, non-stage, orchestral version of the score of the Cole Porter show, conducted by John McGlinn and featuring the London Sinfonietta. It contains large, instrumental parts of the score not previously recorded. — *William Ruhlmann*

Knight Moves / 1993 / RCA 35632
Composer Anne Dudley thanks director Carl Schenkel for inspiration on her score to his thriller about a chess champion and says that in her notes with him she took down the words "very dark ... threatening ... abstract ... classic film noir ... slightly weird." In her score, she tried to match the description by using what she calls a "dark string orchestra with violas outnumbering violins and a disproportionate number of double basses." She also relied heavily on sound effects, clocks ticking, doors slamming, etc. The result is a functional score guaranteed to set your teeth on edge even if the movie doesn't. — *William Ruhlmann*

○ **Last Action Hero** / 1993 / Columbia 57127
Fueled by power-house tracks by AC/DC and Alice in Chains, the soundtrack to Arnold Schwarzenager's box-office bomb is absolute dynamite, a perfect showcase for the best that heavy metal and hard-rock has to offer in the '90s. —*AMG*

Last Action Hero (Original Score) / 1993 / Columbia 57393
This second soundtrack album from the Arnold Schwarzenegger flop features Michael Kamen's instrumental score for the picture. There's one rock track, played by studio musicians who include members of Cheap Trick and are dubbed "the Los Angeles Rock & Roll Ensemble Featuring Buckethead," but the rest is standard-fare orchestral music, with many classical borrowings. — *William Ruhlmann*

☆ **The Last Emperor—Soundtrack** / 1987 / Virgin 90690
Ex-Talking Head David Byrne and actor/composer Ryuichi Sakamoto (who co-starred in the film) each get a side of this beautiful score to Bernardo Bertolucci's Academy Award-winning film, and each took home Oscars and Grammys for their efforts. — *William Ruhlmann*

A League of Their Own / May 1992 / CBS 52919
Various Columbia Records-affiliated pop singers contribute covers of period songs to the soundtrack of this film, which is a tribute to the all-girls baseball league that existed during World War II. James Taylor performs "It's Only a Paper Moon" and "I Didn't Know what Time It Was," making them his own as he frequently does with material he didn't write. Billy Joel recreates Duke Ellington's "In a Sentimental Mood," Art Garfunkel does nicely with "Two Sleepy People," and the Manhattan Transfer apply their jazz vocal abilities to "Choo Choo Ch'Boogie" and "On the Sunny Side of the Street." The song that got the most attention, however, was Carole King's original tune, "Now and Forever," which hit the Adult Contemporary chart. The album is filled out with music from Hans Zimmer's score, which is appropriate to the film's nostalgic and inspirational themes. (Note that Madonna's Number 1 hit "This Used to Be My Playground," heard in the film, does not appear on this album for contractual reasons.) — *William Ruhlmann*

☆ **Legendary Italian Westerns** / RCA 9974
This rousing and entertaining collection contains highlights from Morricone's most famous scores and provides quite a few surprises. —*Bruce Eder*

Less Than Zero / 1987 / Def Jam 44042
Rap/metal producer Rick Rubin put together this hard-edged soundtrack, which features rockers Aerosmith, Poison, and Slayer, plus rappers L.L. Cool J and Public Enemy, though the hit from

Erich Wolfgang Korngold

A composer and performer prodigy from an early age, Erich Wolfgang Korngold (born in 1897) was already an established and respected author of operatic and orchestral works by his twenties. He bid fair to be a successor to Richard Strauss when a chance offer to go to Hollywood to supervise the scoring of *A Midsummer Night's Dream* brought him to America. He stayed for over a decade, bringing his skills to bear on some of the most celebrated movies of that period. Beginning with *Captain Blood* in 1935, he was inextricably associated with the intense and rousing music for Errol Flynn's swashbucklers, but he also wrote the landmark dramatic scores to such serious films as *Kings Row* and *Between Two Worlds*. He returned to Europe during the period after WWII and attempted to resume his career in serious music, but he found that tastes and styles had altered too radically and that his work was regarded as archaic. He died in 1957.

— William Ruhlmann

the album was a remake of Simon & Garfunkel's "Hazy Shade of Winter," performed by the Bangles. —*William Ruhlmann*

Light of Day / 1987 / Blackheart 40654
Ian Hunter and the Fabulous Thunderbirds turn up on this mainstream rock soundtrack, though it's dominated by the film band, the Barbusters, led by Joan Jett and Michael J. Fox, notably on the Bruce Springsteen title tune. —*William Ruhlmann*

Like Water for Chocolate / Jun. 22, 1993 /
Leo Brower's score for the highest grossing foreign film in American history is by turns lushly romantic (and played by an orchestra) and contemporary to the pre-World War II setting of the story in Mexico, with elements of ragtime and norteno styles. In all modes, it helps recall the moods of Alfonso Arau's evocative movie, with its magical realist approach to cooking and romance. —*William Ruhlmann*

The Lion King / 1994 / Disney Records 60858
Walt Disney Pictures had its fourth straight massive hit with an animated movie musical in the summer of 1994 with its tale of the coming of age of a young lion. The movie studio changed composers, replacing Alan Menken, who wrote *The Little Mermaid*, *Beauty and the Beast*, and *Aladdin*, with Hans Zimmer (instrumental score) and Elton John (songs); lyricist Tim Rice, who took over on *Aladdin* after the death of Howard Ashman, remained in place. John took a leaf from the Paul Simon *Graceland* songbook and filled his music with references to South African mbaqanga. But there wasn't that much of it: We're only talking about five songs here, three of which are repeated at the end in versions by John (one of those, "Can You Feel the Love Tonight," became a hit single). And an already padded soundtrack was further padded with four excerpts from Zimmer's score. Pretty skimpy, all things considered, but that didn't keep this album from topping the charts as the movie harvested hundreds of millions of dollars all summer. — *William Ruhlmann*

○ **The Lion in Winter** / 1968 / Varese Sarabande 5217
An unusually stark and serious John Barry score, nicely remastered. —*Bruce Eder*

☆ **The Little Mermaid—Original Soundtrack** / 1991 / Disney 018
A delightful soundtrack by Howard Ashman and Alan Menken, creators of *Little Shop of Horrors*. The first half is vocal numbers, the last ten are instrumental, with styles that range from English to French, Caribbean to Broadway. This may be the best music from a Disney movie yet. —*Tavia Hobart*

○ **Logan's Run—Original Soundtrack** / Bay Cities 3024
Jerry Goldsmith's brilliant, witty, often very touching score for this 1976 big-budget science-fiction thriller was easily the best part of the movie, and it has been cleaned up and polished up considerably for this CD reissue. It's the first time this music—a

Lerner and Loewe

Alan Jay Lerner (1918-1986) and Frederick Loewe (1901-1988) wrote some of the most stylish, sophisticated theater music of the 20th century. The collaboration didn't come until relatively late in the career of each. New York-born, Harvard-educated Lerner wrote material for radio and for individual performers in the 30s. Loewe, born in Berlin, came to the US in 1924 and gradually worked his way into theater music. The two were introduced in 1942. They scored their first hit, the fantasy *Brigadoon*, in 1947.

The Lerner-Loewe formula was to combine Loewe's lush, melodic music, redolent of Viennese waltz, with Lerner's witty, literate lyrics. This they did in some of the most popular and best-remembered musicals of the 40s, 50s, and 60s, notably *Paint Your Wagon*, *My Fair Lady*, and *Camelot* (plus the film musical *Gigi*). After Loewe's retirement, Lerner wrote with other composers, most successfully with Burton Lane (*On a Clear Day You Can See Forever*).

– William Ruhlmann

mix of hauntingly lyrical orchestral passages and electronic tonalities—has been properly treated. —*Bruce Eder*

○ **Lost Horizon: the Classic Film Scores of Dimitri Tiomkin** / RCA 1669
Tiomkin was arguably the least talented of the major composers associated with Hollywood, and a surprising amount of the material here simply doesn't hold up. On the other hand, the 23-minute suite from *Lost Horizon* does, and then some—a radiant pastiche of largely Russian influences that surges and soars brilliantly. Charles Gerhardt conducts the National Philharmonic Orchestra. —*Bruce Eder*

○ **Lovely to Look at** / 1988 / Sony 47027
This film version of Jerome Kern's *Roberta* is updated, with some humorous bits added on and some pleasing new arrangements. —*Bruce Eder*

Malcolm X / 1992 / 40 Acres & A Mule 53190
Composer/conductor Terence Blanchard, better known as one of the Wynton Marsalis-era young jazz traditionalists and an outstanding trumpet player, turns in a score worthy of the scope of Spike Lee's biographical drama. He mixes jazz segments with effective orchestral mood pieces for a series of musical settings in keeping with the heroic sweep of the film. —*William Ruhlmann*

○ **The Man Who Would Be King** / Bay Cities 3007
This soundtrack, from the 1975 film, was probably Maurice Jarre's best movie music of the '70s, lyrical and powerful. —*Bruce Eder*

☆ **Manhattan** / 1978 / CBS 36020
A brisk rescoring of George Gershwin's music for the 1979 Woody Allen film—very pleasant. —*Bruce Eder*

○ **Married to the Mob** / 1988 / Reprise 25763
Director Jonathan Demme has a talent for compiling terrific soundtrack albums, and this is a good example, featuring Sinead O'Connor, New Order, Chris Isaak, Debbie Harry, Ziggy Marley and the Melody Makers, Tom Tom Club, the Feelies, and Brian Eno. Quite a mixture, but it all works. —*William Ruhlmann*

☆ **Mary Poppins** / Disney 60842
A wonderful, classic story with timeless songs. For children ages three through ten. —*Bob Hinkle*

Medicine Man / 1992 / Varese Sarabande 5350
This Jerry Goldsmith score uses a great many ethnic styles and drums, as well as some emotional themes. At times it's reminiscent of Cusco's new-age compositions. —*Tavia Hobart*

Metropolis / 1984 / CBS 39526
As an album, *Metropolis* is an interesting if unexceptional rock collection. It was notable on screen for its dubious taste, although it made a bundle. —*Bruce Eder*

○ **The Most Happy Fella** / 1992 / RCA 61294

A new Broadway cast recording led by opera singer Spiro Malas. The two-piano arrangement lacks the sweep of the classic original orchestrations but brings out the material in a relatively unadorned fashion that probably works better onstage in the more naturalistic '90s than the original score might. —*William Ruhlmann*

Moviola / 1992 / Epic 52985
John Barry specializes in lush, romantic, symphonic themes for big-budget motion pictures. Here, he conducts the Royal Philharmonic Orchestra, playing a series of them, from *Born Free* to *Dances with Wolves*. —*William Ruhlmann*

Mr. Lucky—TV Soundtrack / RCA 2198
Henry Mancini tried for something similar to Peter Gunn in his music for this Blake Edwards-produced series, but didn't quite succeed. This music is moody and occasionally interesting, but nowhere near as driving as the other. —*Bruce Eder*

Music by Erich Wolfgang Korngold / 1991 / Dcc 117
The granddaddy of all film score re-recordings, this 1962 vintage collection is also one of the best, presenting Korngold's most popular film work in well-chosen excerpts performed by the Warner Brothers Orchestra, conducted by Lionel Newman. Steve Hoffman has done an exceptionally fine job remixing the CD, and even the original insert booklet is re-created. Probably the best recorded version of Korngold's *Adventures of Robin Hood* music too. —*Bruce Eder*

☆ **Music for a Darkened Theater** / 1990 / MCA 10065
A very representative collection of some of Elfman's best work for films and television. It includes music from *Batman*, *Dick Tracy*, *Midnight Run*, among others—even the theme from "The Simpsons." —*Tavia Hobart*

Music from "Mission Impossible" / 1967 / Dot 25831

Music from the Films of Audrey Hepburn / 1993 / Big Screen/Giant 24503
In his liner notes to this collection, Henry Mancini, who wrote 5 of the 11 selections, makes the case that Audrey Hepburn was the inspiration for his writing for the pictures she starred in, and who is to disagree with him? Certainly, some of Mancini's most memorable work came with his Hepburn movies of the early '60s—*Charade*, *Two for the Road*, and of course, *Breakfast at Tiffany's*. Other pieces here cannot be tied so closely to Hepburn; Frederick Loewe's music for *My Fair Lady* predated her. Still, it is Hepburn's image that comes to mind when one hears Fred Astaire singing "He Loves, She Loves" from *Funny Face*, even if composer George Gershwin died when she was nine. In any case, this compilation makes for a charming listening experience, especially at its end, when Hepburn is heard singing "Moon River." —*William Ruhlmann*

☆ **Music from the Great Hitchcock Movie Thrillers** / London 820277
Bernard Herrmann—Music from the Great Hitchcock Movie Thrillers is a well-programmed and well-performed overview of Herrmann's work in association with Hitchcock. None of the scores is anywhere near complete, but all of the famous movie selections from *Psycho*, *North by Northwest*, *Vertigo*, and *The Trouble with Harry* are represented. —*Bruce Eder*

☆ **The Music of Disney: A Legacy in Song** / Disney 60957
A beautifully packaged terrific three-CD boxed set of Disney music throughout the years. Disney buffs will love this set, although there are some popular songs missing. Overall, *The Music of Disney: A Legacy in Song* proves how significant the music from Disney's films and television shows were to pop music and pop culture in general. —*AMG*

Naked Lunch / 1992 / RCA 35614
Ornette Coleman's score for David Cronenberg's film adaptation of William Burroughs's *Naked Lunch* perfectly fits the warped 1950s ambience of the movie. In fact, its stronger than the movie itself. —*AMG*

Nashville Rebel (Soundtrack) / 1973 / RCA 3736
Not only did Waylon provide the music for the film (the whole first side of the album and one track on the second side), but he starred in the title role of the film. While the songs are better than those found on many soundtrack albums, it's not one of Waylon's best. From a distance, the title seems prophetic. —*Jim Worbois*

○ **The Natural** / 1984 / Warner Brothers 25116

This Randy Newman score is spectacular! The main theme is such that one feels that something wonderful has happened, even without knowing anything about the film. It includes some big-band-style tracks and a fragment of "Take Me Out to the Ball Game," which should come as no surprise in a baseball movie score. — *Tavia Hobart*

○ **New Jack City** / 1991 / Giant 24409
A fine collection of New Jack, urban R&B, and hip-hop, *New Jack City* features Ice-T's "New Jack Hustler" and Color Me Badd's "I Wanna Sex You Up." — *AMG*

New York, New York—Orig. Soundtrack / 1977 / EMI America 46090
A movie musical with songs by John Kander and Fred Ebb. They tell the story of the evolution of popular music from the swing era to the singer era and bebop, with reference to the lavish movie musicals of the late '40s. Liza Minnelli sings brilliantly, especially on the title song and on "But the World Goes 'Round," while big-band sax player Georgie Auld handles the music for Robert De Niro. — *William Ruhlmann*

○ **The Nightmare Before Christmas, The Soundtrack** / 1993 / Walt Disney Records 7
Danny Elfman, who has scored many of Tim Burton's imaginative films (*Edward Scissorhands*, his two *Batman* films, etc.) is a perfect musical partner for the somewhat macabre director, and never more so than here, where, in fact, Elfman gets not only to write the music but to play the part of the main character. *The Nightmare Before Christmas* is an animated movie musical about the abduction of Christmas by the denizens of Halloween land, and Elfman sings the part of Jack, the pumpkin king. The score is in his usual lush, but threatening style (Kurt Weill is his biggest influence), but the highlight is Elfman's singing. Even in his rock band, Oingo Boingo (now merely Boingo), Elfman doesn't get to sing like this. Granted, the soundtrack album inevitably lacks the film's outlandish visuals, but it tells the story on its own, and one is better able to appreciate Elfman's excellent performance. — *William Ruhlmann*

○ **North by Northwest** / 1980 / Varese Sarabande 47205
Laurie Johnson conducting the London Studio Symphony Orchestra. A fair account of the classic Bernard Herrmann 1959 score, suffering only from poor dynamics as one of the earlier digital recordings. — *Bruce Eder*

○ **Odds Against Tomorrow—Soundtrack** / 1959 / CBS 47487
This superb jazz score by John Lewis was later turned into a hit by the Modern Jazz Quartet. It's dark and dynamic, and a classic. — *Bruce Eder*

☆ **Of Thee I Sing/Let 'em Eat Cake** / 1987 / Columbia 42522
The Brooklyn Academy of Music staged concert versions of these two Gershwin political musicals of the '30s, one a sequel of the other, with Michael Tilson Thomas as music director and conductor and a cast including Maureen McGovern, Larry Kert, and Jack Gilford. The result is an exquisite recording that restores valuable Gershwin material to the record racks. — *William Ruhlmann*

☆ **On Her Majesty's Secret Service** / 1969 / EMI America 90618
A complex, lyrical John Barry score from the 1969 movie, featuring his greatest song ("We Have All the Time in the World") amid its brilliant instrumentals. — *Bruce Eder*

○ **On the Town—Studio Recording** / 1960 / CBS 2038
This is a studio re-creation of the 1944 show about three sailors on leave for a day in New York City, featuring original cast members Nancy Walker, Betty Comden, and Adolph Green, plus John Reardon. Comden and Green provided lyrics to this delightful work, and the music is by Leonard Bernstein, who conducts here. In addition to such standards as "New York, New York" and "I Can Cook Too," this version includes a great deal of instrumental dance music. — *William Ruhlmann*

○ **110 in the Shade** / RCA 1085
Based on an N. Richard Nash play that also became the Katharine Hepburn/Burt Lancaster film *The Rainmaker*, this film was a moderate success in 1963. The Harvey Schmidt/Tom Jones score is not their best but shouldn't be overlooked. Stephen Douglass singing the opening number "Gonna Be Another Hot Day" evokes *Oklahoma!*, clearly an inspiration to this production. — *Marjorie Ellen Ruhlmann*

One Trick Pony—Soundtrack / 1980 / Warner Brothers 3472

Ennio Morricone

Morricone (an Italian composer born in 1928) came out of a mixed jazz and classical background and first started scoring low-budget action/adventure films in the early 60s. His music for Sergio Leone's three Clint Eastwood "man with no name" Westerns brought him to the attention of moviegoers around the world, who appreciated his mix of refined, elaborate scoring (often with chorus as well as full orchestra) and witty, clever humor – all rather like serious comic opera, and eminently listenable. In addition to his work with Leone, Morricone is famous for his music for such films as *The Mission* and has, by his own estimate, scored 600 or more films.

‾ William Ruhlmann

This is usually categorized as a regular Paul Simon album, although its songs were featured in the Simon-written-and-starring film of the same name. Featuring New York session aces like Steve Gadd, Richard Tee, Tony Levin, and Eric Gale, the music has a contemporary jazz feel, and typical of a Simon album there are some extraordinary lyrics. "Late in the Evening" was the hit, but that's only the beginning. — *William Ruhlmann*

○ **One from the Heart** / 1982 / CBS 37703
A series of romantic duets by the seemingly unlikely couple of Tom Waits and Crystal Gayle in fact works surprisingly well, bringing out the ballad side of each. The score is heavily integrated into the film and tells its story of love and loss in Las Vegas. — *William Ruhlmann*

Original Music From The Films Of Francois Truffaut / 1993 / Milan 35658
Specifically, these soundtrack excerpts are taken from Francois Truffaut's series of biographical films, starting with *The Four Hundred Blows*, tracing the life of the character Antoine Doinel, played over a period of 20 years by Jean-Pierre Leaud. As such, the music is wistful and nostalgic at first and then, in such later films as *Bed and Board*, more jarring. As the liner notes indicate, Truffaut tended to use music sparingly and in short interludes in his films, while these pieces are longer. Also, the music has been assembled from various sources, not all of them directly from the soundtracks. Nevertheless, the album suggests the moods of the films. — *William Ruhlmann*

○ **Pal Joey—Studio Recording** / 1951 / CBS 4364
Rodgers and Hart's *Pal Joey*, with a book by John O'Hara, was a sophisticated, downbeat tale about a gigolo. It may have been a bit too dark for audiences in 1940, when it had a moderate run on Broadway. More than a decade later, Columbia Records' Goddard Lieberson decided to make a studio recording of the show, which included such classic songs as "I Could Write a Book" and "Bewitched, Bothered and Bewildered," with Harold Lang and Vivienne Segal in the main roles. It is *not*, as the album jacket suggests, a "Broadway cast," although, just to confuse matters, the success of this album led to a Broadway revival starring Lang and Segal. — *William Ruhlmann*

The Paper / 1994 / Reprise 45616
Usually, these days, when a soundtrack album is subtitled, "Music from the Motion Picture," that's a signal that it contains songs featured in the movie, but not the instrumental score, which is signalled by the subtitle, "Original Motion Picture Soundtrack." But just to be confusing, this album of Randy Newman's score to *The Paper* says it contains "Music from the Motion Picture." The music will be familiar to anyone who knows Newman's work, with its sweet strings, ragtime feel, and strong melodies. And it does conclude with a song, "Make Up Your Mind," on which Newman duets with Alex Brown. — *William Ruhlmann*

Paris, Texas / Mar. 14, 1989 / Warner Brothers 25270
This Ry Cooder score has a spare, evocative sound created by the guitarist, with partners Jim Dickinson and David Lindley. Star Harry Dean Stanton is also heard, providing some of the dialog from the 1984 film. — *William Ruhlmann*

Passenger 57 / 1992 / Slamm Dunk 53232

Cole Porter

Cole Porter (1891-1964) has been described as the greatest songwriter of the century; he was unquestionably the wittiest. A child of enormous wealth, Porter did not turn his complete attention to songwriting until the 1920s, but from then until the end of the 40s, he turned out nearly a show a year, and he even managed three more in the 50s, not to mention a fair amount of work for motion pictures. Porter, who wrote both words and music, had a flair for melody, but his gift for lyrics was unparalleled. Like Irving Berlin, his work of the 30s is better remembered for individual song hits than complete scores, and those songs included "Let's Do It," "You do Something to Me," "What Is This Thing Called Love?," "Night and Day," "Begin the Beguine," and "Just One of Those Things." An exception to this rule was *Anything Goes* (1934), which, in addition to the title song, included "You're the Top" and "I Get a Kick out of You." The entire score is brilliant, and the show has been revived on stage and in films frequently.

Porter was severely injured in a riding accident in 1937 and lived in pain for the rest of his life. His work, however, continued largely without interruption. His greatest success came with an adaptation of Shakespeare's Taming of the Shrew called Kiss Me, Kate in 1948, after which he worked less frequently, though Can-Can (1953) and Silk Stockings (1955) were notable later hits.

– William Ruhlmann

The score to this *Die Hard* clone picture starring Wesley Snipes is by fusion jazz bassist Stanley Clarke, who contributes both some characteristic bass-dominated electric jazz instrumentals and some typical suspense music for the film's many tense moments. *—William Ruhlmann*

☆ **Patton** / 1970 / PolyGram 810366
A stunning, haunting martial score by Jerry Goldsmith. This is possibly the finest military film score ever written. *—Bruce Eder*

The Pelican Brief / 1994 / Big Screen Records 24544
Most of James Horner's score for the second John Grisham adaptation is quiet, contemplative, and a little tense—music for people to study worrisome briefs by. None of it rises above standard-fare mediocre movie music. *—William Ruhlmann*

○ **Pennies from Heaven—Orig. Soundtrack** / 1981 / Warner Brothers 3639
Original recordings from the '20s and '30s by Bing Crosby, Helen Kane, Fred Astaire, Rudy Vallee, and others formed the soundtrack to this Steve Martin/Bernadette Peters film. A collection of timeless show tunes, this album is sadly out of print. *—Scott Bultman*

Perfect World / 1993 / Reprise 45516
The scene-setting songs featured in this chase picture are Western swing and country & Western favorites, starting with a live version of "Ida Red" by Bob Wills and His Texas Playboys and including music by Don Gibson, Johnny Cash, Marty Robbins, and others. There are also a couple new recordings in a traditional vein by Chris Isaak and some instrumental music by the film's director/star, Clint Eastwood. *—William Ruhlmann*

○ **Performance** / 1970 / Warner Brothers 26400
Future soundtrack composers Randy Newman and Ry Cooder contributed heavily to this film, which was written by veteran Jack Nitzsche. Singers include Merry Clayton, Newman, and Buffy Sainte-Marie, though the most memorable song is "Memo from Turner," the film's star Mick Jagger's only recorded solo performance until his first album in 1985. *—William Ruhlmann*

☆ **Peter Gunn—TV Soundtrack** / 1989 / RCA 1956
This was televison's first big hit music track. The title theme from this series produced by Blake Edwards is one of the finest things

Henry Mancini ever wrote. Here is driving, popular jazz, with a beat and style. *—Bruce Eder*

○ **Peter Pan—Original Cast** / 1950 / CBS 4312
This 1950 version of J.M. Barrie's children's classic predates the more familiar Mary Martin production by four years. Words as well as music are by Leonard Bernstein in one of his earliest Broadway efforts. It stars Jean Arthur and Boris Karloff. — *Marjorie Ellen Ruhlmann*

○ **Peter Pan** / 1954 / RCA 3762
A minor success in 1954, this show owes its persistence in the American consciousness to two television broadcasts. The second (in 1960) was taped for posterity and re-run religiously in the '60s, so the whole baby-boom generation can sing "Tender Shepherd," "I've Gotta Crow," "Never Never Land," "I'm Flying," and "I Won't Grow Up" in a giant chorus. Mary Martin stars as the little boy traditionally played by adult actresses. Betty Comden, Adolph Green, and Jule Styne are among those who contributed to the score. *—Marjorie Ellen Ruhlmann*

○ **Philadelphia** / 1993 / Epic Records 57624
Director Jonathan Demme has developed a reputation for assembling especially interesting soundtracks to such previous movies as *Something Wild* and *Married to the Mob*, but he's never gotten quite such high-powered talent to work for him as be has on this collection of songs from *Philadelphia*. Topping the list, of course, is Bruce Springsteen's Golden Globe and Academy Award winning gold Top 10 hit, "Streets of Philadelphia" (even if it seems to be as much about homelessness as about AIDS, the movie's subject). But also included is Neil Young's "Philadelphia," arguably a better song, and a new number by Peter Gabriel, "Lovetown." Those are the major contributions, though Spin Doctors do a nice version of Creedence Clearwater Revival's "Have You Ever Seen the Rain?" and Indigo Girls' take on Danny Whitten's "I Don't Want to Talk About It" is equally enjoyable. And there's the excerpt from the opera Andrea Chenier by Maria Callas that makes such a striking scene in the movie (minus Tom Hanks's commentary), and a piece of Howard Shore's score. *—William Ruhlmann*

Pirate / 1990 / CBS 48608
An interesting fantasy score by Cole Porter, not quite successful but featuring one classic ("Be a Clown"). *—Bruce Eder*

○ **Plan 9 from Outer Space** / 1958 / Performance 391
A silly and sublime sound recording from one of the most enjoyably silly sci-fi films ever made. The music cues from this 1959 movie are fine familiar fun; the dialog is a hoot. *—Bruce Eder*

Poetic Justice / 1993 / Epic 57131
"Music from the motion picture" means a rap/R&B sampler, highlighted by the singles "Get It Up," by TLC (written by Prince), "Indo Smoke," by Mista Grimm, and "I Wanna Be Your Man," by Chaka Demus & Pliers. Most of this material is average, however, and the most notable song from the movie, Academy Award nominee "Again," sung by female lead Janet Jackson, does not appear for contractual reasons. *—William Ruhlmann*

Point of No Return / 1993 / Milan 66225
Hans Zimmer contributes four selections from a synthesized score to John Badham's thriller, punctuating it with lots of ululations by Sam Ellis. Alternately uplifting and tense (but usually melodic), the music follows the plot, but has little life outside the film. But the other half of the album gives us five performances by Nina Simone, including "Here Comes the Sun" and "Black Is the Color of My True Love's Hair." Her sultry, forceful performances may not have much to do with the film, but they're terrific. *—William Ruhlmann*

☆ **Porky's Revenge!—Soundtrack** / Mobile Fidelity 797
Dave Edmunds produced this album of rockin' tunes featuring a couple of his own, though it's really an album of high-profile ringers: George Harrison, Jeff Beck, Willie Nelson, Robert Plant, and Phil Collins all make appearances, and the result is a rollicking set of songs from the 1985 film that are far above the usual soundtrack effort. *—William Ruhlmann*

○ **Pretty in Pink** / 1986 / A&M 3293
The Psychedelic Furs achieved stardom with their re-recorded version of the title track, an old song of theirs, but the soundtrack album also makes a good modern rock sampler, featuring tracks by Orchestral Manoeuvres in the Dark, New Order, Echo and the Bunnymen, and the Smiths, plus the Suzanne Vega/Joe Jackson collaboration "Left of Center." *—William Ruhlmann*

○ **The Princess Bride—Soundtrack** / 1987 / Warner Brothers 25610
A charming, low-key instrumental score, appropriate to the funny, wistful tone of the film, by Dire Straits leader Mark Knopfler. — *William Ruhlmann*

The Prisoner—TV Soundtrack / 42
An interesting score with a great title theme by Ron Grainer, but there's too much mood and effect music stuck in for all but hard-core fans. — *Bruce Eder*

○ **Providence** / 1980 / DRG 9502
A lyrical, subtle score by Miklos Rozsa from the 1977 movie—one of his most accomplished and most enjoyable pieces of music. — *Bruce Eder*

Pure Country / 1992 / MCA 10651
Soundtrack to the movie of the same name, in which notoriously unflashy Strait plays a country superstar who doesn't believe in arena theatrics. Wonder who he was thinking about. — *Dan Cooper*

☆ **Quo Vadis** / London 820200
A well-produced re-recording of the classic 1951 score by Miklos Rozsa and the Royal Philharmonic Orchestra, with a bright but not too brittle sound and excellent stereo balances. The music itself sounds hokey, but only for having been imitated so many times since 1951. — *Bruce Eder*

Ragtime / 1981 / Elektra 565
It's probably not necessary to describe the style of music on this album, though it is worth noting that the music was written and largely performed by Randy Newman, and that the record contains more music than is heard in the film. — *William Ruhlmann*

○ **Reality Bites** / 1994 / RCA
A fine slice of twenty-something alternative-pop from the '90s, the soundtrack to *Reality Bites* presents the finest of the decade's mainstream alternative pop artists. Crowded House, the Juliana Hatfield 3, and U2 all shine with previously released tracks, Lenny Kravitz turns in a solid new number, Dinosaur Jr. hands in a strong B-side, and World Party offers the sublime musical in-joke "When You Come Back to Me," where they rearrange David Bowie's "Young Americans" for the '90s. On the lesser side, the rerecording of Squeeze's "Tempted" is unnecessary and the remix of "My Sharona" removes any trace of its kitschy charm. — *Stephen Thomas Erlewine*

○ **Repo Man** / 1984 / MCA 39019
A classic compilation of early '80s punk and hardcore; Black Flag might be a highlight, but the majority of the record features LA punk bands. — *AMG*

○ **Reservoir Dogs** / 1992 / MCA 10541
Only five songs here were featured prominently in Quinten Tarantino's rousing crime film ("Little Green Bag," "Hooked on a Feeling," "I Gotcha," "Stuck in the Middle with You," and "Coconut"), but they all include Steven Wright's introductions from the film (separately indexed, thankfully); Tarantino's infamous, profane interpretation of the meaning of Madonna's "Like a Virgin" and Harvey Keitel's monologue on how to rob a jewelry store are included as well. In total, that's about fifteen to twenty minutes of material. Padding out the rest of the disc are three new songs that are barely discernable in the film—"Fool for Love" is very good, "Harvest Moon" passable, and "Magic Carpet Ride" is abominable. After those three songs, the disc has passed the half hour mark by two minutes. Even if *Reservoir Dogs* is very short, it faithfully recreates the spirit of the movie and is compulsively listenable. — *Stephen Thomas Erlewine*

A River Runs through It /
Mark Isham's score for this family saga has much the same warm, nostalgic tone as Robert Redford's film. It's a period piece, and there are touches of the '20s here and there, but for the most part, Isham mixes slow, string-filled passages with stately small group pieces. It makes for good Sunday afternoon background music. — *William Ruhlmann*

Robin Hood—Prince of Thieves / 1991 / Morgan Creek 20004
Eight fantastic tracks of instrumentals plus the Bryan Adams hit "(Everything I Do) I Do It for You" and Jeff Lynne's "Wild Times." — *Tavia Hobart*

The Rocky Horror Picture Show / 1974 / Rhino 70090
The first American production of this sci-fi/rock & roll pastiche from Britain, presented at the Roxy in Los Angeles and featuring

Miklos Rozsa

Born in Hungary in 1907, Miklos Rozsa is the last surviving veteran of moviemaking's "golden age," having scored his first film in 1936 and his latest in 1984. His early success as a serious composer, working in an idiom inspired by the work of Bartók and Kodaly, gave Rozsa the foundation for his dual career in motion pictures. A post-romantic who never accepted atonalism, his best work – and there is much of it – is derived from the texture of native Hungarian folk songs. He began collecting these as a child, giving him a unique command of orchestral timbre and the most distinctive approach of any composer of his generation.

After working for Alexander Korda's London Films, where he provided the memorable and brilliant scores for *The Four Feathers*, *The Thief of Baghdad*, and *The Jungle Book*, Rozsa took up residence in Hollywood in the early 40s, and by mid-decade had made his mark in the area of film noir. The rhythmic nature of his music and his facility with dark melodic lines gave a brooding savagery to films like *The Killers* and *The Naked City*. In the 50s he became the master of the religious epic. His sweeping scores for *Quo Vadis*, *Ben Hur*, *King of Kings*, and *El Cid* found favor among serious choral groups as well as the public, who devoured his albums (originally on the MGM Records label) including two complete albums of music from *Ben-Hur*.

The end of the studio system, the increasing demand for pop tunes in movie soundtracks, and the general coarsening of film subjects in the 60s didn't serve Rozsa well, and his activity in films declined steeply after 1963. Fortunately, he had his career as a serious classical composer to keep him occupied, and by the 70s, filmmakers such as Alain Resnais (*Providence*), Nicholas Meyer (*Time after Time*), and Carl Reiner (*Dead Men Don't Wear Plaid*) gave him a chance for a satisfying "Indian summer" prior to his retirement in the mid 80s.

– William Ruhlmann

Tim Curry, who originated the starring role of Dr. Frank N. Furter in London. Richard O'Brien's score has passed into legend, but it's still fresh here. — *William Ruhlmann*

☆ **The Rocky Horror Picture Show** / 1975 / Rhino 70712
It took almost six years for this soundtrack of the all-time midnight movie favorite to go gold, but it is one of the most memorable film scores (and show scores, for that matter) of the '70s, combining old-time rock & roll with campy horror movie cliches. Tim Curry and Meat Loaf star. — *William Ruhlmann*

The Rocky Horror Picture Show / 1990 / Rhino 71011
This 15th Anniversary four-CD boxed set contains the film soundtrack, the Roxy cast album, a disc of international performances, and a disc of rare tracks by such film principals as Tim Curry and Little Nell. There's also a booklet of photos and such. Pricey, but essential for Rocky fans. — *William Ruhlmann*

Romeo Is Bleeding / 1993 / Verve 521 231
Mark Isham's score for this thriller features low-key traditional jazz (which gets more intense and electronic as it goes along) led by his trumpet and flugelhorn, mostly muted. Echoes of Miles Davis are everywhere, and the album works as a mood piece separate from the film. Abbey Lincoln and A.J. Croce each contribute one vocal track. — *William Ruhlmann*

○ **The Rose** / 1979 / Atlantic 16010
The soundtrack to Midler's successful film, with the title track written by Amanda McBroom. — *William Ruhlmann*

Round Midnight Soundtrack / 1963 / CBS 40464
Soundtrack from late '80s film that won Dexter Gordon an Oscar nomination. Gordon and Herbie Hancock, who did the soundtrack, are among the featured musicians. — *Ron Wynn*

○ **Royal Wedding** / Sony 47028
This witty Alan Jay Lerner and Burton Lane score from the 1951 film is sparked by one great novelty number and the personalities of Fred Astaire and Jane Powell. —*Bruce Eder*

○ **Classic Rozsa** / DRG 13101
Some of Miklos Rozsa's most endearing folk-based classical material. Not in a league with his most heavyweight pieces, but enjoyable and very direct expressions of his love of native Hungarian music. —*Bruce Eder*

Rush / Aug. 1991 / Reprise 26794
Eric Clapton's sublime bluesy score to *Rush* is highlighted by two new original songs including the moving tribute to his son, "Tears in Heaven." —*AMG*

☆ **Saturday Night Fever** / 1977 / PolyGram 800068
One of the biggest-selling albums of all time, this double-disc soundtrack features the Bee Gees hits "Stayin' Alive," "Night Fever," and "How Deep Is Your Love"; Yvonne Elliman's "If I Can't Have You"; and a selection of popular disco hits by Tavares, K.C. & the Sunshine Band, and others. This wasn't only the soundtrack to a film, it was the soundtrack to an era; that era is over, but it's evoked by the music. —*William Ruhlmann*

Scream for Help / 1985 / Atlantic 7 80190
The score for this otherwise forgotten Michael Winner film was written by former Led Zeppelin member John Paul Jones and performed by Jones with Zeppelin guitarist Jimmy Page, Madeline Bell, and Yes singer Jon Anderson. It is unremarkable, but since it represents Jones' only recorded work since Led Zeppelin's demise in 1980, completists may wish to seek it out. —*William Ruhlmann*

○ **Screenplaying (Music from the Films "Local Hero," "Cal," "Princess Bride," "Last Exit")** / 1993 / Warner Bros. 45457
This album presents excerpts from four movie scores written and performed by Dire Straits leader Mark Knopfler: *Cal*, *Last Exit to Brooklyn*, *The Princess Bride*, and *Local Hero*. The music is reminiscent of the calmer parts of Dire Straits songs, melodic, lyrical, and touching. —*William Ruhlmann*

○ **The Sea Hawk** / 1987 / Varese Sarabande 47304
With the Utah Symphony Orchestra. A lush, spirited re-recording (from the 1940 movie) of Erich Wolfgang Korngold's best action score, including all of the choruses. A great achievement. —*Bruce Eder*

○ **The Secret Policeman's Third Ball** / Atlantic 90643
Above-average rock-performance soundtrack, sparked by a superb duet between Kate Bush and David Gilmour. —*Bruce Eder*

○ **Seven Brides for Seven Brothers** / 1954 / CBS 52422
An engaging folk-like musical, this soundtrack was remastered into stereo for the first time and sounds quite crisp. —*Bruce Eder*

○ **She's Having a Baby** / 1988 / IRS 6211
A charming collection of modern rock songs based on the themes of marriage and family, including Dave Wakeling's title song (the best thing that came from his brief solo career), XTC's "Happy Families," Kate Bush's "This Woman's Work," and especially the infectious "Apron Strings" by Everything but the Girl. —*William Ruhlmann*

○ **Short Cuts** / 1993 / Imago 21014
In the movie *Short Cuts*, Annie Ross (formerly of Lambert, Hendricks & Ross), plays a jazz singer, and Lori Singer, who can play cello, plays her cello-playing daughter. This soundtrack album of "music from and inspired by the film" alternates songs by Ross, many of which appear in the film, with classical music performances by Singer, alone and with a quartet. Though they sound like old jazz standards, most of the Ross songs are newly written pieces, with her singing, playing, and songwriting collaborators including a who's-who of rockers—Bono and The Edge of U2, Terry Adams of NRBQ, Doc Pomus and Dr. John (who contribute four compositions), Elvis Costello, Iggy Pop, and Michael Stipe of R.E.M. All of them subsume their usual tendencies to fit into the smokey, late-night ambience of the approach. And Ross, her voice full of knowledge beyond even the sophisticated lyrics, dominates the proceedings. The result is a brilliant album that works well with or without the movie it was constructed to accompany. —*William Ruhlmann*

★ **Show Boat—Broadway Score** / 1928 / Sony 55
This album, originally issued on 78s, presents eight selections recorded by members of the original 1927 Broadway production

of the landmark musical, plus Paul Robeson's rendition of "Ol' Man River." (Robeson was in the original London production and the first Broadway revival.) *Show Boat* is the crowning achievement of Jerome Kern's career. It is the prototype for the unified story musicals that followed it, especially after World War II. It begins lyricist Oscar Hammerstein II's series of socially conscious musicals. And its songs, especially in these versions, are unforgettable. Here you also get Helen Morgan singing "Bill" and "Can't Help Lovin' Dat Man." —*William Ruhlmann*

Show Boat—A Collector's Show Boat / 1976 / RCA 1741
Performances culled from various recordings of *Show Boat*. It leans heavily on a 1956 version featuring Robert Merrill and Patrice Munsel, but also includes 1928 recordings by Paul Robeson and Helen Morgan. —*William Ruhlmann*

☆ **Show Boat** / 1988 / Capitol 49108
This lavish three-CD studio reconstruction of the original score is more than complete: it includes outtake material cut from the show before the opening and also restores controversial lyrics. This was lovingly and thoroughly put together by John McGlinn, who brought in such opera singers as Frederica von Stade and Jerry Hadley, backed by the London Sinfonietta, and is the most exhaustive rendering of perhaps the most important American musical of the 20th century. —*William Ruhlmann*

☆ **Showstoppers** / 1989 / RCA 9590
A collection of 20 songs from Broadway show recordings made between 1909 and 1941. This features such stars as Fanny Brice, Al Jolson, George M. Cohan, Beatrice Lillie, Helen Morgan, Paul Robeson, Eddie Cantor, Ethel Merman, Fred Astaire, Noel Coward, Cole Porter, and Gertrude Lawrence. —*William Ruhlmann*

★ **Sinatra** / 1992 / Reprise 9 45091
This is the two-disc soundtrack to a 1992 television mini-series about the life of Frank Sinatra. There is no musical scoring, and there are no rerecordings. Rather, this is a collection of 30 songs recorded between 1931 and 1979, most by Sinatra, though Bing Crosby, Benny Goodman, and Billie Holiday also make appearances. What is notable about the set is that it is the only album to combine tracks from Sinatra's recordings on Columbia, RCA Victor, Capitol, and Reprise, and thus the only one offering the breadth of his work over a period of 40 years. Of course, it remains a sampler, and there's far more great Sinatra material, but the unique circumstances make this an excellent compilation for the beginner. —*William Ruhlmann*

☆ **Singin' in the Rain** / Sony 45394
A towering film score from the 1952 movie made up of some grand tunes of the '30s, climaxing with the extended "Broadway Ballet." —*Bruce Eder*

☆ **Singles** / Jun. 30, 1992 / Epic 52476
This is what Seattle sounds like. Although Nirvana is not included, there is no better introduction to modern rock of the early '90s than the *Singles Soundtrack*. Most of the significant Seattle bands—Pearl Jam, Mudhoney, Alice In Chains, Screaming Trees, Soundgarden, and Mother Love Bone—are featured on the album as well as Chicago's Smashing Pumpkins and ex-Replacements leader Paul Westerberg. "State of Love and Trust" is arguably Pearl Jam's finest moment, and Mother Love Bone's track proves Eddie Vedder truly is a better, more original vocalist than the late Andrew Wood. Westerberg's first songs since the breakup of the Replacements are here; "Dyslexic Heart" and "Waiting for Somebody" are excellent acoustic-based rockers in the vein of the last Replacements album "All Shook Down," perfect for the twenty-something angst of the film. Smashing Pumpkins deliver the churning, hypnotic "Drown." Mudhoney's "Overblown," an attack on the marketing of the Seattle scene, is the only true slice of grunge, complete with pummeling fuzz guitars and whiny vocals; Alice In Chains's grinding "Would?" and Screaming Trees' pop/psychedelic guitar rave-up, "Nearly Lost You" are equally impressive. —*Stephen Thomas Erlewine*

○ **Sleeping with the Enemy** / CBS 47380
A lyrical, moving Jerry Goldsmith score, which soars to elegant heights of wistfulness and menace. —*Bruce Eder*

Sleepless in Seattle / 1993 / Epic 53764
A collection of romantic pop standards sung by everyone from Jimmy Durante to Carly Simon, the soundtrack to *Sleepless in*

Seattle will delight fans of the movie seeking to recapture the magical romance of the film. —*AMG*

[Sleepless in Seattle]—More Songs for Sleepless Nights / 1993 / Epic 57682

None of the songs on *More Songs for Sleepless Nights* were featured in the film *Sleepless in Seattle*, but for those who enjoyed the movie's actual soundtrack, this collection offers several songs in the same vein. —*AMG*

Sneakers—O.S.T. / Sep. 29, 1992 / CBS 53146

Sneakers was a light, high-tech suspense yarn, and James Horner presents a score long on drawn-out, uncertain passages and sudden bursts of sound, combining the standard orchestra with sound effects and synthesizer blips. Featured player Branford Marsalis is mostly invisible, though he takes a nicely melodic lead on the concluding track, "... And the Blind Shall See." —*William Ruhlmann*

☆ **Snow White And the Seven Dwarfs** / 1993 / Walt Disney 60850

The re-release of Walt Disney's first full-length animated feature in theaters in 1993 prompted the record division of Disney to put together the first full-length soundtrack CD, timing out at more than 73 minutes and containing most of the film's music. The bulk of it was written by Frank Churchill, with lyrics on such songs as "Whistle While You Work," "Heigh-Ho," and "Some Day My Prince Will Come" by Larry Morey. By now, this music has charmed generations of children, and there's no reason why it won't charm even more. —*William Ruhlmann*

So I Married an Axe Murderer / 1993 / Chaos/Columbia 57303

A modern rock sampler, this soundtrack to a forgettable Mike Myers comedy features both new songs by the likes of Soul Asylum, the Boo Radleys, and Chris Whitley and more familiar numbers by Spin Doctors ("Two Princes"), Big Audio Dynamite II, and others. Listened to together, the experience of bearing these strummed electric guitars and adenoidal vocals is like living through 1966 all over again in an alternate universe—not unpleasant, but odd. Oh, and there's also a parody of Beat poetry by Myers called, "This Poem Sucks." Speaking for critics everywhere, we always appreciate it when the artist provides his own review. —*William Ruhlmann*

○ **Something Wild** / 1986 / MCA 6194

Another brilliant compilation of unusual music handled by director Jonathan Demme. The hit was "Ever Fallen in Love," by Fine Young Cannibals, but the album also includes tracks by David Byrne (one of his earliest Latin American outings), Oingo Boingo, Jimmy Cliff, Jerry Harrison, and New Order, among others. —*William Ruhlmann*

Sondheim / 1985 / Book of the Month Club 7515

A three-LP boxed set of newly recorded Sondheim songs, featuring such singers as Cris Groenendaal, Bob Gunton, and Debbie Shapiro, and conducted by frequent Sondheim orchestrator Paul Gemignani. The album presents Sondheim's songs outside a theatrical context, in renditions by great singers. A welcome addendum to the Sondheim library. —*William Ruhlmann*

Spellbound Soundtrack by Charles Gerhardt/National PO / RCA 0911

A surprisingly lackluster collection, except for the music from *The Red House* and *The Lost Weekend*, and featuring unusually flaccid playing by the NPO. —*Bruce Eder*

☆ **A Star Is Born (Judy Garland)** / CBS 44389

This album, from the 1954 movie, was Judy Garland's last musical soundtrack of any note, sounding a little compressed but not severely marred by age. Garland is in fine voice and spirits on the songs themselves, and the notes are about as full and informative as they get. —*Bruce Eder*

○ **Star Trek** / 1979 / CBS 36334

Jerry Goldsmith's music, alternately eerie and savage, was the best part of the movie. It still holds up. —*Bruce Eder*

○ **Star Trek TV Soundtrack, Vol. 1** / 1990 / GNP 8006

The first "Star Trek" TV soundtrack includes some of the finest music written for television during the '60s—moody, atmospheric, and very striking, all broken into relatively short cues. Unfortunately, the source tapes haven't held up well, and the quality leaves a lot to be desired. —*Bruce Eder*

○ **Star Trek, Vol. 2** / GNP 8025

Far more impressive sonically than the first volume, this consists of cues from two second-season episodes, "Amok Time" and "The Doomsday Machine." It is unexpectedly rewarding. —*Bruce Eder*

☆ **Star Wars** / 1977 / Polydor 800096

John Williams at his most ostentatious, a grand Wagnerian-scale soundtrack that deserves credit at least for reviving interest in the classic Hollywood film score. —*Bruce Eder*

Staying Alive—Soundtrack / 1983 / Polydor 813269

This sequel to *Saturday Night Fever* lacked the box office clout of the original, and the soundtrack album was likewise a disappointing seller, but it actually contains some of the better Bee Gees work of the '80s, notably the sad ballad "Someone Belonging to Someone." —*William Ruhlmann*

Straight Talk / 1992 / Hollywood 61303

Dolly Parton makes her periodic West Coast pop move. The results vary, depending on how far Parton strays from her Appalachian roots. "Light of a Clear Blue Morning," which originally appeared on her first solo album, polishes up nicely—all the L.A. glitz in the world can't hide the pure gospel beauty of that chorus. "Straight Talk" isn't nearly as strong as Parton's other big movie hit, but the way she sings it makes it nearly irresistible. Even one of Tennessee's most distinctive voices, however, can't save "Fish Out of Water" and "Thought I Couldn't Dance." —*Brian Mansfield*

○ **Straight to Hell** / 1987 / Enigma 73308

This soundtrack to Alex Cox's bizarre Western features British new-wave graduates the Pogues, Joe Strummer, and the MacManus Band (i.e., Elvis Costello). They also appeared in the film. —*William Ruhlmann*

Streets of Fire—Soundtrack / 1984 / MCA 5492

Jim Steinman (the melodramatic writer behind Meat Loaf's *Bat out of Hell*) is the author of many of the tracks here, and they have his typical rock & roll *Sturm und Drang*, especially when the backup group consists of members of Bruce Springsteen's E Street Band. Also on hand are the Blasters, Maria McKee, and Ry Cooder. The album's hit single turned out to be Dan Hartman's "I Can Dream about You." —*William Ruhlmann*

Strictly Ballroom / 1992 / CBS 53079

The Australian film is off-beat, and the soundtrack dances to its own drummer too, with tango and samba rhythms (and heavy drum tracks) added to songs like "Tequila" and other music borrowed from all over, everything from Cyndi Lauper's "Time After Time" to "The Blue Danube," as played the Bogo Pogo Orchestra. This is a party album. —*William Ruhlmann*

○ **Subterraneans** / 1960 / CBS 47486

A very effective, moody jazz score by Andre Previn, featuring Gerry Mulligan and Carmen McRae, which holds up better than the movie for which it was written. —*Bruce Eder*

☆ **The Sullivan Years: Best of Broadway—Original Cast** / 1992 / Tee Vee Toons 9436

This two-disc set collects TV performances of some of Broadway's biggest hits as they were done with original cast members on Broadway. Among the priceless material from shows like *Camelot*, *West Side Story*, and *My Fair Lady* is a bonus interview with Richard Rodgers and Oscar Hammerstein II (not on the cassette version). —*William Ruhlmann*

Sweet Charity / 1986 / EMI America 46562

This revival stars Debbie Allen in the title role and features Michael Rupert. The score is somewhat modified from the original, so it conforms more to the movie version. —*Marjorie Ellen Ruhlmann*

○ **Television's Greatest Hits, Vol. 1** / Tee Vee Toons 1100

An uneven but enjoyable compilation of the good, the bad, and the forgettable among TV music themes from the '50s and '60s, with variable sound quality to boot. But it's unique. —*Bruce Eder*

Tex Avery Cartoons / 1993 / Milan 35635

Tex Avery was an animator at MGM during World War II and just after, and his work was characterized by a nonstop, hellzapoppin approach, full of manic energy and wild characters. The scores to his cartoons, by Scott Bradley, had to match Avery's madness, and on these six they do so—helped along by the cartoon dialogue. With the 'toons turning up frequently on Ted Turner's Cartoon Network, the music is newly timely, and Droopy remains a deadpan favorite. —*William Ruhlmann*

☆ **That's Entertainment, Part 2** / 1974 / CBS 46872
The 43 tracks on both volumes represent complete versions of pieces either abridged or left off entirely from the original album. Covering song and dance numbers by everyone from Cole Porter to Arthur Freed, this is a magnificent panorama of musical gems from Hollywood. —*Bruce Eder*

Thelma & Louise / 1991 / MCA 10239
The soundtrack for Ridley Scott's feminist road parable contains just what you'd expect—plenty of driving music. You can get the gist of Scott's message from Toni Child's "House of Hope" and Marianne Faithfull's electro-pop cover rendition of the hit "Ballad of Lucy Jordan." But you can find music to help you down those long stretches of road also in Chris Whitley's "Kick the Stones," as well as in covers by Martha Reeves (Van Morrison's "Wild Night"), Charlie Sexton (John Hiatt's "Tennessee Plates"), and Kelly Willis (X's "Little Honey"). —*Brian Mansfield*

The Three Musketeers / 1974 / Bay Cities 3013
This is Michel Legrand's lush soundtrack to Richard Lester's comic version of the Alexandre Dumas novel. It's some of the most romantic and stirring instrumental music to turn up in a film in years. —*William Ruhlmann*

Threepenny Opera / 1976 / CBS 34326
A marvelous staging of the Brecht/Weill musical by the New York Shakespeare Festival and a cast headed by Raul Julia. The new translation by Ralph Manheim and John Willett is fresh and highly singable. —*William Ruhlmann*

Threesome / 1994 / Epic Records 57881
There are some curious covers on this modern rock compilation. A reformed General Public does the Staple Singers' "I'll Take You There" (and earns a hit single for its trouble), U2 tries Patti Smith's "Dancing Barefoot," Teenage Fanclub appropriates Madonna's "Like A Virgin," and, perhaps most imaginatively, Duran Duran resurrects Steve Harley & Cockney Rebel's "Make Me Smile (Come Up and See Me)." Also featured: originals by Tears for Fears and Bryan Ferry. As usual with such "music from the motion picture" collections, there's a sense of randomness here, but there are enough interesting tracks to keep you listening. —*William Ruhlmann*

○ **Thunderball** / 1978 / Capitol 90628
John Barry's fourth James Bond score from the 1965 movie shows a little weariness, as some material is repeated and the new stuff isn't always memorable. —*Bruce Eder*

☆ **Till the Clouds Roll By** / CBS 47029
This soundtrack is an all-star tribute to Jerome Kern, without the climactic Frank Sinatra "Ol' Man River" but filled with worthwhile performances. —*Bruce Eder*

Tommy / 1972 / Rhino 71113
This lush, orchestrated version of the rock opera, done with Pete Townshend's participation and blessing, featuring Roger Daltrey, Rod Stewart, Ringo Starr, and Merry Clayton. Pretentious in its proportions and bombast, but often moving if this sound is your cup of tea. —*Bruce Eder*

Tonight Let's All Make Love in London / 1968 / CBS 47893
Peter Whitehead's 1967 film *Tonight Let's All Make Love In London* was an attempt to document the mid '60s swinging London pop scene at its peak. The soundtrack was an instant collector's item, divided between interview snippets with such scene-makers as Michael Caine, David Hockney, Julie Christie, and Mick Jagger; and marginal incidental music by ummemorable pop acts produced by Rolling Stones manager Andrew Loog Oldham (Vashti and Twice as Much). The Small Faces' contribution, "Here Comes the Nice," is easily available elsewhere. Allen Ginsberg (misspelled "Alan" on the original sleeve) reads the poem that gave the film its name. The chief attraction of this CD reissue is the addition of two lengthy, otherwise unavailable cuts by the original Pink Floyd lineup in 1967 (mere snippets had appeared on the original LP). Their 16-minute version of "Interstellar Overdrive" (re-recorded for their first LP) starts off scintillatingly, then degenerates into a rather aimless jam. The 12-minute "Nick's Boogie," not available in any other version, is a considerably more aimless, free-form instrumental piece dominated by scraping guitars. Even in its expanded CD reissue, this album will only appeal to hardcore collectors. —*Richie Unterberger*

Trespass / 1992 / Sire 26978

This first soundtrack album from Trespass (there is also an album of Ry Cooder's score) contains "music from the motion picture" "plus bonus tracks." It is a gangsta rap sampler featuring Ice-T and Ice Cube, who star in the film, along with Public Enemy and others. In other words, there's a lot of rage, many threats of violence, and a generous helping of obscenities, all set to some busy rhythms. —*William Ruhlmann*

○ **Trespass: Original Score** / 1993 / Sire 45220
In the music for *Trespass*, which starred Ice-T and Ice Cube, the disembodied groans of Cooder's guitars combine with Jim Keltner's percussion and Jon Hassel's otherworldly trumpet playing to create a dark, frightening mood. Outside of "King of the Streets," which features film dialogue, and Austin singer Junior Brown's boozy country song "Party Lights," the music here possesses the ambience of an urban street Western. One of Cooder's scariest scores. —*Brian Mansfield*

Trouble in Mind / 1986 / Island 842891
Mark Isham provides the brooding instrumental texture and Marianne Faithfull adds her gravelly chanteuse vocals to the score of this Alan Rudolph film. —*Scott Bultman*

True Lies / 1994 / Lightstorm Music/Epic 64437
The most notable song on this soundtrack album is Living Colour's remake of Cream's late 1960s hard rock classic "Sunshine of Your Love," which is heard in two different mixes. But primarily, the album consists of Brad Fiedel's orchestral score to the Arnold Schwarzenegger action picture, which is characteristically bombastic and portentous. —*William Ruhlmann*

☆ **Twilight Zone, Vol. 1** / 1983 / Varese Sarabande 47233
Ignore the slightly compressed sound and take in the eerie, beautifully wrought compositions, every one of them memorable not only from the series but from lots of subsequent use. —*Bruce Eder*

○ **Twin Peaks** / Sep. 11, 1990 / Warner Brothers 26316
Composer Angelo Badalamenti (*Cousins*) set the tone for David Lynch's bizarre television soap with a haunting theme created from electric piano, synthetic strings and the twangiest guitar this side of Duane Eddy. The love theme, appropriately enough, sounds like a funeral march. (The series' central character was found dead at the beginning of the first episode.) The rest of the music, instantly recognizable to anyone who saw even one episode of the series, borders on fever-dream jazz. Lynch favorite Julee Cruise sings the only three vocal songs. The music from Twin Peaks is dark, cloying and obsessive—and one of the best scores ever written for television. —*Brian Mansfield*

Twin Peaks—Fire Walk with Me / Aug. 11, 1992 / Warner Brothers 45019
Composer Angelo Badalamenti, who wrote the music for the television series for which this movie served as a "prequel," presents another low-key score mixing after-midnight jazz with ambient sounds, never taken at more than a medium tempo. The mood is dark and languid, appropriate to the unusual tone of the TV show and movie. Jimmy Scott and Julee Cruise contribute eerie vocals to songs with lyrics by director David Lynch. —*William Ruhlmann*

○ **The Unsinkable Molly Brown** / 1981 / CBS 45442
Debbie Reynolds sparks this homespun early '60s movie musical version that has proved a favorite over the years. She can be a bit overbearing, but it works, and Harve Presnell sings well. —*Bruce Eder*

○ **Until the End of the World** / Warner Brothers 26707
One of the rare collections of song-oriented soundtracks that sounds like a cohesive album, the dark, atmopheric *Until the End of the World* features rare tracks from R.E.M. ("Fretless"), Elvis Costello (a cover of the Kinks' "Days"), U2 (a different mix of the title track), and Lou Reed (an alternate version of "What's Good"), as well as a host of other artists. —*AMG*

○ **Valley Girl (Music from the Soundtrack)** / Rhino Records, Inc. 71590
A compulsively listenable collection of early '80s New Wave tracks that range from the familiar ("Who Can It Be Now?") to the obscure ("Johnny Are You Queer?"), without any lapse in quality. —*AMG*

Warsaw Concerto: Cinema Gala / London 421261
A handy if unexceptional collection of mostly '60s-vintage recordings from the Decca Records vaults by various conductors and or-

chestras. It is notable for Bernard Herrmann's slow but powerful renditions of Arthur Bliss's "Things to Come" and the prelude from Ralph Vaughan Williams's "49th Parallel." —*Bruce Eder*

☆ **The Way West, Scalphunters ...** / 1967 / EMI 4946
The Way West/Scalphunters/Hang 'Em High. Bronislav Kaper's moody, lyrical music from *The Way West* gets its deserved first-class treatment with surprisingly good sound. *The Scalphunters* is adequately represented, as is *Hang 'Em High. —Bruce Eder*

○ **Wayne's World** / Feb. 18, 1992 / Reprise 26805
With Queen's "Bohemian Rhapsody" and Jimi Hendrix's "Foxy Lady" among other hard-rock tracks, the soundtrack to the smash hit *Wayne's World* perfectly conjures up the small-town teen culture portrayed in the movie. —*AMG*

○ **Wayne's World 2 soundtrack** / 1993 /
Yes, it tries to replicate the gleeful AOR festival of the first film but it *succeeds*. With Joan Jett's "I Love Rock & Roll," Norman Greenbaum's "Spirit in the Sky," and "Superstar" by Urge Overkill and Chrissie Hynde recording as Superfan leading the way, *Wayne's World 2* is every bit as enjoyable as the first film's soundtrack. —*AMG*

☆ **West Side Story** / 1962 / CBS 20004
This film version of the Leonard Bernstein/Stephen Sondheim score of a modern, urban *Romeo and Juliet* spent more weeks at Number 1 in the charts (54) than any other album in history. It is an effective rendition of the score, featuring Natalie Wood, Richard Beymer, Russ Tamblyn, Rita Moreno, and George Chakiris, and features all of the show's important songs, among them "Something's Coming," "Maria," "Tonight," and "Somewhere." —*William Ruhlmann*

○ **The Western Film World of Dimitri Tiomkin** / Unicorn 2011
Laurie Johnson conducting the London Studio Symphony Orchestra and the John McCarthy Singers. A brace of long-overdue modern recordings of Tiomkin's best Western music, including a good (but not complete) accounting of his score for *Red River. —Bruce Eder*

What's Love Got to Do with It / Jun. 15, 1993 /
This is the soundtrack for the Tina Turner film that got Oscar nominations for Angela Bassett and Lawrence Fishburne. There's little here that you couldn't get elsewhere in better versions, but if you only want a hint of the music Tina Turner's made in various contexts with and without Ike, this would be a serviceable purchase. Otherwise, get the film and hear the music in the correct setting. —*Ron Wynn*

○ **When Harry Met Sally...** / Jun. 1989 / CBS 45319
The soundtrack that made Connick an MOR star. —*Ron Wynn*

Who's the Man? / MCA 10794
Mary J. Blige took "You Don't Have to Worry" to Number 11 on the R&B chart, and other chart entries were Jodeci's "Let's Go Through The Motions" and House of Pain's title track. But this is mediocre, formula rap, in the typically boastful, lustful, mock-angry style, and none of it is memorable. —*William Ruhlmann*

Wild Palms / 1993 / Capitol 89098
Ryuichi Sakamoto's score for this futuristic televsion mini-series "presented" by Oliver Stone is rhythmic and spooky. There are also five pop oldies (one of them a remake) that are always nice to hear. —*William Ruhlmann*

Willow—Soundtrack / 1988 / Virgin 90939
This James Horner score goes along with the landscape in the movie—lush, sweeping, and absolutely breathtaking. Of course, it has its share of bad-guy themes too. As a whole, you could hardly ask for a more beautiful score. —*Tavia Hobart*

With Honors / 1994 / Maverick/Sire/Warner 45549
Starting with a Duran Duran cover of Led Zeppelin's "Thank You" (!) and paced by Madonna's "I'll Remember" (Maverick is her vanity label, by the way), this rock sampler is a mixed bag. The highlights are the Pretenders' cover of Bob Dylan's "Forever Young," Lyle Lovett's cover of Irving Berlin's "Blue Skies," and Lindsey Buckingham's "On the Wrong Side." —*William Ruhlmann*

☆ **The Wizard of Oz** / Sony 45356
What else can one say about this bright, tuneful 1939 score—it's a treasure! —*Bruce Eder*

○ **Wonderful Town—Television Soundtrack** / 1958 / Sony
This is a studio recording employing the cast (most of it from the original Broadway production) of a TV telecast made five years

after the stage version. Since there is no film version of *Wonderful Town*, this expensively mounted album, which is a match for the cast album above, stands as the only other recording. Rosalind Russell is again the leading figure. —*William Ruhlmann*

○ **Woodstock Two** / 1971 / Atlantic 400
This is actually more interesting than *Woodstock*, in terms of repertoire and artists. —*Bruce Eder*

You Gotta Walk It Like You Talk It ... Or You'll ... / 1992 / See For Miles 357
This is the reissue to a soundtrack for a low-budget 1970 film, notable because the composers and performers are Walter Becker and Donald Fagen, who went on to form Steely Dan. It has some of the Dan's humor and musical twists, but is really only of interest to show how much the duo had developed two years later when they put Steely Dan together. —*William Ruhlmann*

○ **Zabriskie Point** / 1970 / CBS 52417
Classic psychedelic rock soundtrack, with three otherwise hard-to-find Pink Floyd songs and a Jerry Garcia solo piece. —*Bruce Eder*

Cast Recordings

Allegro / 1947 / RCA Victor 52758
Rodgers & Hammerstein were coming off the twin successes of *Oklahoma!* (1943) and *Carousel* (1945) when they produced this, their third Broadway musical. Not surprisingly, the pre-opening box office was record-breaking, but that was all that kept the show going for 315 performances that disappointed audiences. Today, it is remembered for experimental effects that eventually made their way into later musicals, but this cast album (10 songs originally issued as a five-disc 78 r.p.m. set, now a short CD) indicates that it wasn't one of R&H's better scores. Only Lisa Kirk's showstopper "The Gentleman Is A Dope" is really worthwile. —*William Ruhlmann*

☆ **Annie** / 1977 / CBS 34712
One of the biggest Broadway hits of the '70s, this Charles Strouse and Martin Charnin musical based on the *Little Orphan Annie* comic strip charmed audiences with its Depression-era nostalgia and a score that is highlighted by the standard "Tomorrow." —*William Ruhlmann*

☆ **Annie Get Your Gun—Original Cast** / 1955 / MCA 10047
Although this recording does not quite represent the "original Broadway cast" of the 1946 Irving Berlin musical, it's the next best thing, starring Ethel Merman, Ray Middleton, "and members of the original cast, chorus, and orchestra, under the direction of Jay Blackton." Merman is in fine voice, and the score remains one of Broadway's best collections of songs, from "Doin' What Comes Naturally" to "They Say It's Wonderful" and "Anything You Can Do," not to mention "I Got Lost in His Arms," "The Girl that I Marry," and the showstopping standard "There's No Business like Show Business." —*William Ruhlmann*

☆ **Annie Get Your Gun** / 1966 / RCA 1124
This revival of the Irving Berlin show once again stars Ethel Merman and also features Jerry Orbach. It includes the newly written "An Old-Fashioned Wedding." —*William Ruhlmann*

☆ **Anyone Can Whistle** / 1964 / CBS 2480
Stephen Sondheim's second complete Broadway score, with a book by Arthur Laurents, was not a success onstage, running only nine performances. But the cast album has kept the show alive, due to such outstanding songs as "There Won't Be Trumpets," "With So Little to Be Sure Of," and the title tune, plus a cast led by Lee Remick and Angela Lansbury. —*William Ruhlmann*

☆ **Anything Goes** / 1987 / RCA 7769
This classy 1987 revival features Patti LuPone's spirited interpretations of Cole Porter classics, including the title song, "I Get a Kick out of You," "You're the Top," and "Blow, Gabriel, Blow." —*Marjorie Ellen Ruhlmann*

Anything Goes / 1989 / Angel 49848
This is a re-creation of the original 1934 score, not a cast album, put together by John McGlinn and featuring such opera singers as Kim Criswell, Cris Goenendaal, and Frederica Von Stade, along with the London Symphony Orchestra. It is most notable for con-

Cast Recordings

The truth is that the Broadway musical does not travel well. Conceived as a combination of comedy, drama, song, and dance for one of those thousand-seat theaters that sit on a handful of streets in midtown Manhattan, the Broadway musical, if it is successful, immediately gets translated into a variety of forms into which it doesn't really fit. A road version may travel the country, playing before abbreviated sets in much larger theaters. A film version may appear that, even if it doesn't alter the work in other ways, somehow looks less impressive on film than it does when you're in the theater. Why is it easy to accept that a person onstage may just burst into song, when it looks silly on celluloid? Maybe the stages are the real dream factories – in movies, things are just too realistic. And then, of course, there are the cast albums, which, in a sense, are the farthest-removed translations of Broadway musicals. Here are a few songs, but no story, no dance. The volatile chemistry of opposing art forms that gives birth to the musical simply isn't present. A cast album is a souvenir, but no more to be confused with the real thing than a three-inch model of the Statue of Liberty you can buy at Battery Park.

And yet Broadway musicals have been the spawning ground for some of the most important popular music of the 20th century. In the first few decades of this century, when most people heard new songs by obtaining the sheet music and playing them themselves, Broadway introduced America to most of its new music. Musicals then were often what we would now call revues, developed out of vaudeville and really just collections of individual scenes and songs. But the country's best songwriters – George M. Cohan, Irving Berlin, George Gershwin – were devoting their efforts to the Broadway stage. Despite this dominance, only occasionally was anything resembling an "original Broadway cast" recording made. Recordings had limited popularity, especially after the start of the Depression when record sales fell precipitously, and while Broadway served as a source for pop songs, usually they were recorded by other singers. One reason for this, of course, was that the record industry's main format – the 78 RPM single – allowed for two songs, each no more than about 3 minutes in length. "Albums" (bound collections of several 78s) were rarities, though *Show Boat*, for example, appeared in this form a year after it hit Broadway in 1927. But *Show Boat* was different in many ways. For one thing, it told a single, unified story, and the songs were mostly integrated into the plot.

By the 40s, the style set by *Show Boat* became the norm for most shows, especially after *Oklahoma*. At the same time, CBS developed the 33 1/3 RPM, long-playing record, and CBS president Goddard Lieberson recognized the Broadway cast album to be ideal for the new medium. As a result, cast albums frequently became big hits. From 1945 to 1965, *Song of Norway* (1945), *Carousel* (1945), *Kiss Me, Kate* (1949), *South Pacific* (1949), *Three Little Words* (1950), *Guys and Dolls* (1951), *The Music Man* (1958), *My Fair Lady* (1958), *Flower Drum Song* (1959), *The Sound of Music* (1959), *Camelot* (1961), *Carnival* (1961), and *Hello Dolly!* (1964) all hit #1 on the *Billboard* album charts. The peak of popularity came in the late 50s and early 60s. Then came the rock & roll era, and Broadway show music (like many other pre-rock styles) was swept into a marginalized pop category. Only *Hair* (1968), a rock pastiche, got to the top of the charts, and most cast albums sold modestly.

Stephen Sondheim, the acknowledged master of the Broadway musical in the 70s and 80s, has enjoyed no genuinely successful cast albums, though his song "Send In the Clowns (from *A Little Night Music*) has become a standard. Andrew Lloyd Webber, on the other hand, has largely bucked the trend, starting with his *Jesus Christ Superstar*, of which the pre-stage studio version went to #1 in 1970. Webber has gone on to enjoy million-selling hit cast albums for *Evita*, *Cats*, and *Phantom of the Opera*. Alain Boublil and Claude-Michel Shonberg have also sold a respectable number of copies of *Les Miserables*. These are the exceptions, however. For the most part, not only is the Broadway cast album no longer a commercial sure shot, it may not even get made. Used to be, the week after a show opened and good reviews indicated a hit, the cast would be in a recording studio to get the album out fast. Today, it may be six months before a cast album appears. Recent cases in point include *The Will Rogers Follies* and *The Secret Garden*, both of which opened in the spring of 1991, with their cast albums not available until December. And *Grand Hotel* was at the conclusion of its two-year run before a cast album appeared, by which time it was impossible to append the word "original," since one of the principal actors had died. If this is what happens with big hits, you can imagine how things are for less successful shows.

In spite of all this, there is probably more recording of show music going on now than at any time in the past. Archivists such as John McGlinn, John Mauceri, and Thomas Z. Shepard are hard at work restoring full scores of vintage shows and presenting them in new studio recordings with classically trained singers, further blurring a line between musical and opera already grown fuzzy enough as opera companies have incorporated musicals like *Sweeney Todd* and *South Pacific* into their repertoires. In addition, a plethora of small labels – First Night, Bay Cities, DRG – have taken up the task of recording shows with limited popular appeal, while the majors are digging into their vaults and reissuing long-out-of-print cast albums on compact disc. And then, of course, people keep writing musicals, and audiences keep going to them. How much worry can we have for the musical when we look to the 1992-1993 Broadway season and see on the horizon a version of *Jekyll and Hyde* that already has a cast album out, as well as a new Lloyd Webber musical, *Sunset Boulevard*? Even if the original Broadway cast album is the souvenir of a great evening (as it's always been) and no longer the blockbuster seller it was 30 years ago, it's still the repository of some of the best music of yesterday and today.

– William Ruhlmann

---

taining the show's incidental music as well as its famous songs. —*William Ruhlmann*

Assassins—Original Cast Recording / 1991 / RCA 60737

Stephen Sondheim's show about presidential assassins is unusual to say the least—which may be why it never got beyond an off-Broadway showcase—but it's filled with brilliant songs. —*William Ruhlmann*

☆ **Barnum—Original Cast** / 1980 / CBS 36576

This musical about the life of the great promoter, with music by Cy Coleman and lyrics by Michael Stewart, is dominated by Jim Dale's bravura performance in the title role, although Glenn Close, in one of her few musical-comedy appearances, is also featured. —*William Ruhlmann*

☆ **Bells Are Ringing** / 1956 / CBS 2006

Book and lyrics by Betty Comden and Adolph Green, music by Jule Style. The recording documents Judy Holliday's genius for musical comedy. "The Party's Over" and "Just in Time" are the most memorable numbers in a clever score. —*Marjorie Ellen Ruhlmann*

☆ **The Best Little Whorehouse in Texas** / 1978 / MCA 31007
Tommy Tune staged this rip-roaring, country-style musical, and while you can't see the dance steps on record, Carol Hall's songs accurately express the show's down-home vitality. —*William Ruhlmann*

Beyond the Fringe / Nov. 5, 1962 / Angel 64771
This British comedy revue, featuring Peter Cook, Dudley Moore, and Jonathan Miller, was a precursor to Monty Python's Flying Circus, with its zany humor, though its satire is somewhat more political and brutal. While some of it is no longer topical, most of it remains hilarious. —*William Ruhlmann*

Blood Brothers / 1988 / RCA 61689
This is the London revival cast recording of Willy Russell's weepy melodrama, originally released in England in 1988 at the time of the revival, and released in the U.S. in 1993 to commemorate the opening of the show on Broadway. Russell is steeped in '60s British pop music, and the show is full of catchy songs, though the contrived and dreary subject matter, and the repetitiousness may drive some to distraction. *Blood Brothers* is more than a tearjerker; it suctions tears out of its audience with a vacuum cleaner. To be fair, there are many who love it for that, and even those who don't will have trouble not humming its score on the way out of the theater. —*William Ruhlmann*

☆ **Boyfriend** / 1955 / RCA 60056
A tribute to the frivolous musicals of the '20s, this tongue-in-cheek entertainment was one of the few successful musicals of its time to originate in Great Britain. It's notable for introducing the 19-year-old Julie Andrews to Broadway. —*William Ruhlmann*

☆ **Brigadoon** / 1947 / RCA 1001
The tale of an 18th-century Scottish village that travels through time and its romantic encounter with two 20th-century visitors became the first major hit written by the team of Alan Jay Lerner and Frederick Loewe. It features "Almost like Being in Love." —*William Ruhlmann*

Brigadoon / 1992 / Angel 54481
This is a studio recreation of the Lerner and Loewe musical, performed by the Ambrosion Chorus and the London Sinfonietta, conducted by John McGlinn and featuring soloists Brent Barrett, Judy Kaye, Rebecca Luker, John Mark Ainsley, and Frank Middlemass. It is notable for containing instrumental music from the score not heard on previous albums (it runs a CD-busting 79 minutes), but is otherwise not a striking version of the show. —*William Ruhlmann*

○ **Bubbling Brown Sugar** / 1976 / Amherst 93310
A musical revue featuring some of the most memorable jazz-age tunes of African-American '30s composers such as Duke Ellington, Eubie Blake, and Fats Waller: "Sophisticated Lady," "Honeysuckle Rose," and more. On record, the show becomes essentially a sampler of that music, and it's effective for that, though the listener should also check out the original versions. —*William Ruhlmann*

○ **Buddy—the Buddy Holly Story (London Cast)** / 1989 / Combat 1046
Buddy—The Buddy Holly Story is the London cast recording of a biographical musical about the rock & roll legend. It contains Holly's greatest hits enthusiastically performed by Paul Hipp, who also performed the role on Broadway. —*William Ruhlmann*

☆ **Bye Bye Birdie** / 1960 / CBS 2025
The original Broadway cast album of the Charles Strouse/Lee Adams musical that fictionalizes the impact Elvis Presley's departure for the army had on American teenagers. The authors deftly satirize teen life and early rock & roll and provide a typical Broadway musical love story involving Dick Van Dyke and Chita Rivera. Paul Lynde is also a standout, singing "Kids." The other hit of the show is "Put On a Happy Face." —*William Ruhlmann*

☆ **Cabaret—Original Cast** / 1966 / CBS 3040
With a malevolent grin and the words "Willkommen, bienvenue, welcome," actor Joel Grey established his future as well as the dark tone of this 1966 Tony Award-winning musical. This recording includes a number of songs not in the film version, several performed by the remarkable Lotte Lenya (widow of composer Kurt Weill, whose work clearly influenced the Kander and Ebb score). —*Marjorie Ellen Ruhlmann*

☆ **Camelot** / 1960 / CBS 32602
One of the great Lerner & Loewe musicals, based on the King Arthur legend, starring Richard Burton and Julie Andrews. The music is both a Broadway landmark and a delight. Highlights include the title song, "How to Handle a Woman," and "If Ever I Would Leave You" (sung by Robert Goulet). —*William Ruhlmann*

○ **Camelot—London Cast** / 1982 / Varese Sarabande 47206
Richard Harris took over the stage role of King Arthur (he played the part in the film) and played it on the road and in revivals. Here he appears in a London revival and brings great presence to the part. The album is well recorded and includes some music not found on other recordings. —*William Ruhlmann*

☆ **Can Can** / 1974 / Capitol 92064
A Cole Porter dalliance set in Paris and featuring a young Gwen Verdon, plus such memorable songs as "I Love Paris" and "It's All Right with Me." —*William Ruhlmann*

☆ **Candide** / 1974 / CBS 32923
A complete recording of the revised version of the Bernstein musical (containing some additions to the lyrics by Stephen Sondheim), taken from its most successful theatrical run. Some of Leonard Bernstein's best show music. —*William Ruhlmann*

Candide / 1986 / New World 340/341
A recording by the New York City Opera, based on its 1982 revival of the show, once again with revised music. —*William Ruhlmann*

○ **Carnival—Original Cast Recording** / 1961 / Polydor 837195
Bob Merrill produced his best-loved score for this delicate musical based on the 1953 French film *Lili* about an orphan taken in by a traveling carnival. Michael Stewart was the lyricist, and the stars included Anna Maria Alberghetti and Jerry Orbach. The title song, "Theme from Carnival (Love Makes the World Go 'Round)," became a standard. —*William Ruhlmann*

○ **Carousel** / 1965 / RCA Victor 1114
The Twentieth Anniversary Lincoln Center revival of the Rodgers and Hammerstein classic, with John Raitt re-creating his original portrayal of Billy Bigelow. He's still in good voice, and the stereo recording is superb. —*William Ruhlmann*

○ **Carousel** / 1994 / RCA 62506
This is the original London cast album of the 1993 Royal National Theatre revival starring Michael Hayden and directed by Nicholas Hytner. Hytner takes a far more down-to-earth approach to Rodgers and Hammerstein's second show, bringing out its more tragic aspects. The effect is to bear it anew. (Hayden only was carried over to the 1994 New York production, which is set to have its own cast album.) —*William Ruhlmann*

☆ **Carousel—Original Cast** / MCA 10048
This was Rodgers and Hammerstein's 1945 followup to their landmark hit *Oklahoma*. It includes such chestnuts as "If I Loved You" and "You'll Never Walk Alone," as well as John Raitt's soaring vocals. —*Marjorie Ellen Ruhlmann*

☆ **Cats** / 1981 / David Geffen Co. 2017
The original London cast album of Andrew Lloyd Webber's musical revue celebrating T.S. Eliot's *Old Possum's Book of Practical Cats*. It contains Elaine Paige's UK Top 10 recording of "Memory." —*William Ruhlmann*

☆ **Cats—Original Cast** / 1983 / David Geffen Co. 2031
This is the original Broadway cast album, containing slight musical alterations from the earlier London version and, of course, different singers, though it is not very different. Geffen 2031 is a two-disc complete version of the show. There is also an abridged, single-disc version, Geffen 2026. —*William Ruhlmann*

● **Celebrate Broadway, Vol. 1—Sing Happy** / 1994 / RCA 61987
The first in a series of compilations of songs from Broadway shows recorded by RCA Victor, this album puts together an hour's worth of what used to be called "eleven o'clock numbers." These were the show-stoppers that woke you up shortly before the end of the show and got you ready to hit the street with a smile on your face. (Though, to tell the truth, some of these are first act finales meant to send you into the lobby anticipating the rest of the evening.) "Blow, Gabriel, Blow," from Anything Goes, "I've Gotta Crow," from Peter Pan, "Oklahoma!" from *Oklahoma*, these are the big, bright Broadway songs audiences have hummed to themselves for generations. The RCA catalog is mixed—not all of these performances are taken from the original casts, and the notes

don't make that clear—but this is a good sampler for the casual fan who likes Broadway's stirring songs. —*William Ruhlmann*

Celebrate Broadway, Vol. 2—You Gotta Have a Gimmick / 1994 / RCA 61988

For this collection, RCA has scoured its vaults for Broadway novelty songs, comic numbers frequently performed by the supporting players in shows that provide a change of pace and some laughs. Songs like "I Cain't Say No," from *Oklahoma!* and "Arthur In the Afternoon" from *The Act* show that being risque is not a problem, but just as often these songs are just odd: What else to say about the celebratory "Lizzie Borden," from *New Faces of 1952?* That song, from a revue, had no real context in a show, and some of these songs are actually ringers, such as Fats Waller's "Your Feet's too Big" from *Ain't Misbehavin'* and the "Caribbean Plaid" medley from *Forever Plaid,* material not actually written for Broadway. This is an episodic album, to be sure, but you won't get through it without laughing a few times. —*William Ruhlmann*

○ Celebrate Broadway, Vol. 3—Lullaby of Broadway / 1994 / RCA 61989

Broadway has always had a great ability to celebrate itself, actually, and that ability is showcased on the third volume of RCA's anthology series in songs about show business, starting with the title track (actually written for the movie musical *Forty-Second Street,* which then became a Broadway musical) and ending, inevitably, with "There's No Business Like Show Business." In between are songs by Sondheim, Coleman, Styne, Herman, Kern, Yeston, and Kander, all exploring aspects of the biz. As with the other volumes in this series, the caveat is that these songs come from various sources including but not limited to original Broadway cast albums—concert versions, revivals, revues, etc.— but there isn't a performance here that isn't good, and the selection makes a powerful case for Broadway. —*William Ruhlmann*

Celebrate Broadway, Vol. 4—Overtures! / 1994 / RCA 61990

Overtures introduce Broadway audiences to the music they're going to hear during the course of the evening. Played one after another, they can take on the quality of Muzak, not unpleasant but not compelling. This collection of 12 overtures taken from shows that played on Broadway between the 1940s and 1980s displays the consistency of style in Broadway music. Much of it is appealing, but then, that's the problem—it's like trying to make a dinner out of appetizers. —*William Ruhlmann*

Celebrate Broadway, Vol. 5—Hello Young Lovers / Jul. 19, 1994 / RCA Victor 09026-61991

On its fifth Celebrate Broadway compilation, RCA explores the variety of love, with the emphasis on variety. Indeed, only somewhat complicated love songs have been chosen here, starting with the title song, from *The King and I,* which is sung by an older woman who is not involved in romance, and including "The Human Heart," from *Once On This Island,* which is about universal love; "My Cup Runneth Over," from *I Do! I Do!,* and "I Still Get Jealous," from *High Button Shoes* by way of Jerome Robbins' Broadway, which concern mature relationships; and "Who Can I Turn To?" from *The Roar of the Greasepaint, the Smell of the Crowd* and "In Buddy's Eyes," from *Follies,* which have a real sense of emotional dependency that comes across as desperate. But then, Broadway has treated love in many ways, from *Show Boat's* fanciful 1927 flirtation, "Make Believe," to *Hair's* knowing 1968 revelation that it's "Easy To Be Hard." So, don't expect to put this album on in preparation for a romantic evening with your companion—it's liable to convince the two of you that you should give it up instead. Though the *Celebrate Broadway* series has made extensive use of performances other than original cast recordings, this compilation goes a little farther, with a full two-thirds of the selections drawn from Off-Broadway, revivals, and concert versions. —*William Ruhlmann*

Celebrate Broadway, Vol. 6—Beautiful Girls / Jul. 19, 1994 / RCA

This is a case of going with what you've got. Many of Broadway's greatest divas are represented here, including Ethel Merman, Mary Martin, Julie Andrews, Liza Minnelli, and Barbara Cook. But they are not necessarily heard in their most memorable performances because, for example, RCA Victor has rights only to Julie Andrews' appearance in the recent *Putting It Together* rather than her earlier triumphs. And a few great ones, such as Carol Channing, are missing entirely. There's nothing wrong with

what's here, of course, but as an anthology of Broadway's leading ladies, *Beautiful Girls* doesn't show its women to their best advantage. —*William Ruhlmann*

☆ A Chorus Line—Original Cast / 1975 / CBS 33581

Michael Bennett's 1975 valentine to "gypsies," the dancers who are often treated as so much mobile scenery in Broadway musicals, is sometimes considered to have broken new ground with its frank portraits of talented but frustrated performers. The score by Marvin Hamlisch and Edward Kleban is a favorite of "theater people" everywhere, but was designed to showcase the abilities of dancers rather than singers. Consequently, only the ballad "What I Did for Love" has had a life outside of the show's context. — *Marjorie Ellen Ruhlmann*

○ City of Angels—Original Broadway Cast / 1990 / CBS 46067

The original Broadway cast version of a musical set in Hollywood in the '40s, exploring the interaction between a writer of hard-boiled detective novels and his gumshoe hero. Cy Coleman has turned in some low-key, jazzy period music, and David Zippel's witty lyrics are a match for the book, which was written by Larry Gelbart, the man who brought you the TV series "M*A*S*H." — *William Ruhlmann*

City of Angels / Oct. 12, 1993 / RCA 61973

The London cast recording of Cy Coleman and David Zippel's City of Angels is a virtual carbon copy of the Broadway cast album, though, since that one has a slightly more distinctive cast, it gets the edge. —*William Ruhlmann*

○ Closer Than Ever—Original Cast / 1990 / RCA 60399

A follow-up to Richard Maltby, Jr. and David Shire's previous off-Broadway revue, *Starting Here, Starting Now,* featuring two discs' worth of smart songs about the ups and downs of modern life—especially romance. —*William Ruhlmann*

☆ Company—Original Cast / 1970 / CBS 3550

Winner of both the Drama Critics Circle and Tony awards in 1970, this show established composer Stephen Sondheim as a demigod of the contemporary musical theater. The story of a bachelor afloat in a sea of the very married was certainly of its time, but it has proven to have enduring appeal, as has Sondheim's deliciously tongue-twisting libretto. —*Marjorie Ellen Ruhlmann*

○ Crazy for You / 1992 / Capitol 54618

Broadway's 1992 Tony winner for Best Musical is a newly written show that borrows Gershwin songs primarily from *Girl Crazy,* but also from some of the Hollywood musicals of the '30s. You've heard the songs before, but they're freshly, enthusiastically presented here, and there's enough of the show's book in the lengthy CD to get a sense of the new context. Harry Groener and—especially—Jodi Benson shine in the starring roles. —*William Ruhlmann*

Crazy for You / Nov. 9, 1993 / RCA 61993

This is the London cast recording of "the new Gershwin musical comedy" *Crazy for You,* which repeated its New York success by winning the Olivier Award for Best Musical. The album is similar to the American recording, though the American West accents affected by the British actors are a bit less certain and the cast is slightly less distinctive. —*William Ruhlmann*

○ Curtain Up! Overtures of the American Musical Theater / 1993 / Met 80

It is traditional in the theater that musicals begin with instrumental medleys of the show's songs, probably because that allows everyone time to get in their seats. But some of these orchestral pieces are quite accomplished. In fact, in some cases (Cy Coleman's *On The Twentieth Century,* included here, is an example) they provide as much as you really need of a show. So, here are 16 Broadway musical overtures in 64 minutes, gathered by the Metropolitan Opera Guild to lead off its series of Broadway compilations. First up, appropriately, is John McGlinn's 1988 restoration of *Show Boat,* and we also have music by most of the greats of the American theater, including George Gershwin, Richard Rodgers (note how differently he writes for Lorenz Hart and for Oscar Hammerstein II), Irving Berlin, Leonard Bernstein, Jule Stein, and Stephen Sondheim. One might quibble and note that the likes of Cole Porter, Jerry Herman, Jerry Bock, John Kander, and Andrew Lloyd Webber are missing, but what's here is terrific. —*William Ruhlmann*

☆ Damn Yankees—Original Cast / 1955 / RCA 3948

The Faust legend is retold, in sports terms, as a baseball fan sells his soul so his team can win the pennant. Stars Gwen Verdon and Ray Walston. The score is by Richard Adle and Jerry Ross. Highlights are: "Whatever Lola Wants," and "Heart." — *William Ruhlmann*

○ **Do I Hear a Waltz?** / 1965 / Sony Classical 48206
With music by Richard Rodgers and lyrics by Stephen Sondheim, based on the Arthur Laurents play *The Time of the Cuckoo* (which also served as the basis for the Katharine Hepburn movie *Summertime*). It was not a big success, though some of the songs do reflect the talent that created them, especially the humorous "What Do We Do? We Fly!" — *William Ruhlmann*

Do Re Mi / Jan. 1961 / RCA 61994
Jule Styne's followup to *Gypsy*, was this sendup of the music business, starring Phil Silvers, fresh from his years on TV's "Sgt. Bilko," and Nancy Walker. Other principals were lyricists Betty Comden and Adolph Green, and writer/director Garson Kanin. With all that proven talent, the show should have been better, and as it was, it wasn't a total flop—it got good reviews and ran for about a year, though it closed at a loss. The score proves to have been one of Styne and Comden/Green's less successful ones, with the one memorable song being "Make Someone Happy," though the irrepressible Silvers, one of the great clowns of the era, makes a strong impression. (Originally released in 1961, this cast album was reissued on CD in 1994 with extensive liner notes by theater historian Steven Suskin.) — *William Ruhlmann*

○ **Dreamgirls—Original Cast** / 1981 / David Geffen Co. 2007
This rags-to-riches story of an African-American '60s girl group was a 1981 success for director/choreographer Michael Bennett, in part due to speculation about its possible similarity to the real-life rise of the Supremes. The score by Henry Krieger and Tom Eyen deliberately evokes the pop and R&B sounds that are the play's subject matter. Jennifer Holliday's rendition of "And I Am Telling You I'm Not Going" stopped the show and began her musical career. — *Marjorie Ellen Ruhlmann*

○ **Evening with Frank Loesser** / 1992 / DRG 5169
This disc contains performances associated with three Frank Loesser shows—*Guys and Dolls, The Most Happy Fella*, and *How to Succeed in Business Without Really Trying*. Loesser has a good, sometimes gruff voice and puts the material across well while accompanying himself on piano. These are early versions—lyrics changed and songs were replaced before these scores got to Broadway—so this is in a sense an album for Broadway scholars, though mere fans will have a good time, too. The material from *The Most Happy Fella*, dating from three years before the actual production, features Maxene Andrews of the Andrews Sisters and is previously unreleased. — *William Ruhlmann*

Evita—London Cast / 1978 / MCA 11003
The two-disc pre-stage studio recording by Andrew Lloyd Webber and Tim Rice, billed as "an opera" about Argentine political figure Eva Peron, was a massive UK hit, reaching Number 4, with Julie Covington's "Don't Cry for Me, Argentina" hitting Number 1 and Barbara Dickson's "Another Suitcase in Another Hall" reaching the Top 20. — *William Ruhlmann*

☆ **Falsettoland** / 1990 / DRG 12601
Original off-Broadway cast album from William Finn's sequel to his previous off-Broadway show, *March of the Falsettos*, and one of the most impressive musical scores in years, a fact confirmed when the combined shows came to Broadway under the title *Falsettos* and won a Tony for best score. — *William Ruhlmann*

☆ **The Fantasticks—Original Cast** / 1960 / Polydor 821943
Overwhelmingly the world's longest-running musical, it debuted May 3, 1960, at the Sullivan Street Playhouse in Greenwich Village, where it remains ensconced at this writing. Boy meets girl, boy loses girl, boy gets girl in the end. The simple and utterly charming score by Tom Jones and Harvey Schmidt includes "Try to Remember," "Soon It's Gonna Rain," and "They Were You." — *Marjorie Ellen Ruhlmann*

☆ **Fiddler on the Roof** / 1964 / RCA 7060
Original Broadway cast recording of Sheldon Harnick and Jerry Bock's massively successful musical based on Sholem Aleichem's stories about poor Russian Jews at the turn of the century, starring Zero Mostel, who gets to sing such songs as "Tradition," "If I Were a Rich Man," and "To Life." One of the great musicals of all time, this album was a Top 10, gold-selling hit. (Note: This edition

is a 1986 CD reissue containing two previously unreleased tracks. The still-in-print cassette version, RCA 1005, does not contain these new songs.) — *William Ruhlmann*

○ **Fiddler on the Roof—Original London Cast** / 1984 / CBS 30742
This is the original London cast recording and features Israeli actor/singer Topol in the starring role of Tevye. Topol has since gone on to play the part on film and in a Broadway revival, which means his version is by now more familiar than that of the role's originator, Zero Mostel. Topol's Tevye is notably less comic than Mostel's, but he brings great warmth to his performance, and this, not the film soundtrack, is his definitive rendition. — *William Ruhlmann*

Finian's Rainbow—Original Cast / 1960 / RCA 1057
Revival of the 1947 musical by E.Y. Harburg and Burton Lane. The story is too complicated by half, but that doesn't matter on record, and the music is some of Lane's best. The songs include "How Are Things in Glocca Morra?," "Look to the Rainbow," "Old Devil Moon," and "If this Isn't Love." — *William Ruhlmann*

○ **Fiorello!—Original Broadway Cast** / 1989 / Capitol 92052
Based on the life and times of New York City's most beloved mayor, Fiorello La Guardia. This show won the 1959 Pulitzer Prize for drama, a rare feat for a musical. It was the first success for the composer/lyricist team of Jerry Bock and Sheldon Harnick, and was Tom Bosley's Broadway debut in the title role. — *Marjorie Ellen Ruhlmann*

Five Guys Named Moe / Jul. 1992 / Columbia 52999
This Original Broadway Cast Recording is a good example of the kind of music that can be vital and exciting in a theater and redundant on disc. *Five Guys Named Moe* is a musical revue with the thinnest of story lines, the music for which is taken from the repertoire of jump blues star Louis Jordan, who filled the R&B charts with songs like "Is You Is Or Is You Ain't My Baby" and "Choo Choo Ch'Boogie" in the 1940s and '50s. It makes for a delightful theater going experience, but on record it has to compete with Jordan's originals, and it doesn't. Also, this show originated in the West End, and there is a London Cast album that is virtually identical. — *William Ruhlmann*

○ **Flower Drum Song—Original Cast** / 1961 / CBS 2009
Rodgers and Hammerstein return to a theme that had served them well in both *The King and I* and *South Pacific*: misunderstanding and reconciliation between individuals of differing cultural backgrounds. This 1958 musical revolved around the meeting of old and new worlds in San Francisco's Chinatown. *Flower Drum Song* has a serviceable score but is not the team's most exciting. The novelty "I Enjoy Being a Girl" is more often excerpted than the lovely and overlooked "Love Look Away." — *Marjorie Ellen Ruhlmann*

Follies / 1971 / Capitol 92094
Stephen Sondheim's show about aging follies girls remains one of his greatest scores. This Broadway cast recording is somewhat abbreviated, even though the 1989 CD reissue includes previously unreleased material. — *William Ruhlmann*

★ **Follies—In Concert—Studio Cast** / 1985 / RCA 7128
This performance, recorded live at New York's Avery Fisher Hall, features a dream cast singing Stephen Sondheim's ambitious and fascinating score. With Barbara Cook, George Hearn, Mandy Patinkin, Lee Remick, Betty Comden, Adolph Green, Liliane Montevecchi, Elaine Stritch, Phyllis Newman, and Carol Burnett, among others. — *Marjorie Ellen Ruhlmann*

Follies / 1987 / Encore 3
A two-disc London cast recording of the complete score as revised by Sondheim for a West End production. This includes newly written songs. — *William Ruhlmann*

○ **42nd Street—Original Cast** / 1977 / RCA 3891
In a reversal of usual practice, producer David Merrick turned to the 1933 movie musical for this stage musical, which uses Harry Warren and Al Dubin's venerable songs—such as "You're Getting to Be a Habit with Me," "We're in the Money," "Lullaby of Broadway"—and the chorus-girl-becomes-a-star storyline. The result was new and exciting, almost 50 years later. Stars Tammy Grimes and Jerry Orbach. — *William Ruhlmann*

☆ **Funny Face** / 1980 / Smithsonian 019
A reconstruction of the 1927 George and Ira Gershwin musical, using period recordings by Fred and Adele Astaire, various or-

Jerome Kern

Jerome Kern (1885-1945) is arguably the father of the modern American musical theater. Born in New York of German heritage, he attended the New York College of Music and began to break into Broadway theater during the first decade of the century by having songs of his interpolated into shows. An Anglophile and friend of P. G. Wodehouse, Kern scored his first success with songs inserted into *The Girl From Utah*, a British import, in 1914, including the ballad "They Didn't Believe Me." Breaking away from the European model of waltz music, Kern proved adept at adapting contemporary dance music into his songs as well as producing subtle, inventive ballads. He collaborated with Guy Bolton and, later, Wodehouse on a series of shows presented at the Princess Theater in the middle of the decade, notably *Very Good Eddie*, and continued to score successes into the 20s.

But Kern really entered the history books with *Show Boat* (1927), the first truly modern American musical, with an integrated story and such memorable songs as "Ol' Man River" and "Can't Help Lovin' Dat Man." Like many of his contemporaries, Kern divided his time between Broadway and Hollywood in the 30s, after sound came to the movies, and his movie hits included the Fred Astaire-Ginger Rogers film *Swing Time*, which such songs as "A Fine Romance" and "The Way You Look Tonight" (with lyrics by Dorothy Fields). Kern worked steadily – he wrote or contributed to 37 shows during his career – and was beginning work on *Annie Get Your Gun* when he died suddenly in 1945. He left behind one of the richest catalogs of show music in history.

– William Ruhlmann

chestras, and even a couple of piano recordings by George Gershwin himself. — *William Ruhlmann*

Funny Girl / 1964 / Capitol 2059
The Jule Styne/Bob Merrill musical about Ziegfeld Follies comedienne Fanny Brice became a star vehicle for Barbra Streisand— her first and last starring role on Broadway. It also provided her with some of the best material of her early repertoire: "I'm the Greatest Star," "People," and "Don't Rain on My Parade." This album went gold and reached Number 2. — *William Ruhlmann*

Funny Thing Happened on the Way—Original Cast / 1962 / Bay Cities 3002
A Funny Thing Happened on the Way to the Forum, Stephen Sondheim's first musical as both composer and lyricist, was a delightful comedy hit set in ancient Rome and starring Zero Mostel. It included "Comedy Tonight," one of the great opening numbers in Broadway history. This is a reissue of the original Broadway cast recording. — *William Ruhlmann*

George M!—Original Cast / 1968 / CBS 03200
Joel Grey's second triumph on Broadway (after *Cabaret*) was this musical biography of George M. Cohan, who ruled the Great White Way at the turn of the century. Unlike the Jimmy Cagney movie, the show pulled no punches, but what really mattered were the Cohan songs, including his biggest hits, "Over There" and "Give My Regards to Broadway." A young Bernadette Peters played Cohan's sister. — *William Ruhlmann*

☆ **Gigi—Original Cast** / 1974 / RCA 0404
A Broadway version of the film musical by Alan Jay Lerner and Frederick Loewe, this recording is notable for a cast that includes Alfred Drake and Agnes Moorehead and introduces four new songs, including the cynical and witty "The Contract." — *William Ruhlmann*

Girl Crazy / 1990 / Asylum 79250
A non-stage restoration of the original 1930 show by George and Ira Gershwin, conducted by John Mauceri and featuring Lorna Luft, Judy Blazer, and Frank Gorshin. — *William Ruhlmann*

Godspell—Original Cast / 1974 / Arista 8304
Stephen Schwartz's reverent musical based on the St. Matthew gospel actually opened off-Broadway (which is where it stayed) before the Broadway version of *Jesus Christ Superstar*, to which it was a kind of response. As a piece of theater, *Godspell* was much more successful, running more than five years. This cast album appeared several years into the run, but it effectively captures the show's rock/pop score and Schwartz's re-reading of the Bible into the American vernacular (he had done much the same with Leonard Bernstein on *Mass*). — *William Ruhlmann*

The Gospel at Colonus—Original Cast / 1988 / Nonesuch 79191
This is a little complicated. Bob Telson and Lee Breuer's musical, which mixes gospel music sung by gospel singers with Sophocles's *Oedipus at Colonus*, was originally performed off-Broadway, and a cast album was released. A year later, it was videotaped for the PBS series "Great Performances," and that is the version heard on the album reviewed here. Then three years later, it opened on Broadway. But there's no Broadway cast album. Got that? Okay. This version is similar to the one above (in fact, one track is taken from that recording), but it is a little looser, and in gospel music that's all to the good. — *William Ruhlmann*

Grand Hotel / 1992 / RCA 61327
It took until 1992 for this Tommy Tune musical to reach disc, during which time one of the leads, David Carroll, died (he is remembered in a club performance of one of the songs, included as a bonus track). But most of the rest of the principals—Liliane Montevecchi, Karen Akers, Michael Jeter—are here, making the most of this musical adaptation of the famous movie about a hotel in Berlin in the '20s. The score, by Robert Wright and George Forrest, with significant additions by Maury Yeston, is not the show's strong point (the staging and choreography were what made it a hit), but it gives a good sense of the story and is true to the original source. — *William Ruhlmann*

The Grass Harp / 1971 / Painted Smiles 1354
This Kenward Elmslie/Claire Richardson musical, based on a novel by Truman Capote, was a flop, but it is notable for Barbara Cook's outstanding starring role performance. — *William Ruhlmann*

Grease / 1994 / RCA Victor 09026-62703
For this Broadway revival of the 1972 show, Jim Jacobs and Warren Casey's score has been reorchestrated and a genuine oldie has been added, the Skyliners' "Since I Don't Have You." But *Grease!* is still the same shallow pastiche of 1950s high school references, still unsure whether it wants to celebrate or satirize. The new cast sings with gusto (including star Rosie O'Donnell, who is more comedienne than vocalist), but this still isn't much of a show. — *William Ruhlmann*

○ **Greenwillow** / 1960 / CBS 13974
The original Broadway cast recording of the Frank Loesser musical (perhaps his least well known, but still imbued with his musical talent), starring Anthony Hopkins. — *William Ruhlmann*

☆ **Guys & Dolls—Original Cast** / 1951 / MCA 10301
Frank Loesser's brilliant musical version of the stories of Damon Runyon was a massive hit, running 1200 performances, and this original Broadway cast album shows why, with songs like "The Oldest Established," "A Bushel and a Peck," "Luck Be a Lady," and "Sit Down You're Rockin' the Boat," sung by a cast including Stubby Kaye, Sam Levene, Robert Alda, and Vivian Blaine. — *William Ruhlmann*

○ **Gypsy—Original Cast** / May 1959 / CBS 32607
This tribute to burlesque was a star vehicle for Ethel Merman. The score by Jule Styne and Stephen Sondheim includes the Merman standard "Everything's Coming Up Roses," and the song that is invariably used to introduce anything having to do with the strip tease, "Let Me Entertain You." — *Marjorie Ellen Ruhlmann*

☆ **Hair—Original Cast** / 1968 / RCA 1150
The appearance of "The American Tribal Love Rock Musical" on Broadway in April of 1968 had an effect not unlike the arrival of the motion picture *Woodstock* two years later. *Hair* helped to popularize and, ultimately, to trivialize the "counterculture" it sought to celebrate. But the Gerome Ragni/James Rado/Galt MacDermot score remains one of the most appealing artifacts of the "Age of Aquarius." — *Marjorie Ellen Ruhlmann*

Hello Again / Jun. 28, 1994 / RCA Victor 09026-62680
Michael John La Chiusa's off-Broadway 1994 musical *Hello Again*, based on Arthur Schnitzler's play La Ronde, contains 10 two-character scenes chronicling sexual encounters in different decades of the 20th century—"The Soldier and the Nurse" in scene two, "The Nurse and the College Boy" in scene three, "The College Boy and the Young Wife" in scene four, etc. As such, it is an ambitious undertaking and necessarily episodic. Onstage, there may have been many unifying visual elements, but on record, the sung-through scenes pass by quickly and sketchily, simultaneously full of deep feeling and passion, yet not presented in enough detail to convey those emotions fully to the listener. Though there are nods to musical styles across the century, much of the music is in a post-Sondheim musical recitative style: It's a musical because the dialogue is sung, not because there are real songs, which means it loses more in mere audio form than a standard musical might. A talented effort, then, but relatively inaccessible. — *William Ruhlmann*

Hello, Dolly!—Original Cast / 1964 / RCA 3814
Jerry Herman's musical (with book by Michael Stewart) based on Thornton Wilder's *The Matchmaker* was one of the last great old-style musicals and a massive hit. Even today, its songs (including the title track, "Before the Parade Passes By," and "So Long Dearie") are so memorable most people can hum them. Herman used a turn-of-the-century, major-chord, big-melody approach, effectively kidded and overcome by Carol Channing in the title role. It's precisely because Channing doesn't quite have the range for these melodies that she's able to express the character so well (an effect lost in the Barbra Streisand movie version, though Streisand has no trouble expressing character in other ways). And the supporting cast, including Charles Nelson Reilly, Eileen Brennan, and David Burns, is ideal. — *William Ruhlmann*

Hello, Dolly! / 1967 / RCA 1147
This is the recording of the cast that took over the show more than three years into its run, with Pearl Bailey and Cab Calloway in the lead roles. Though less accomplished than the original, it is notable for Bailey's individual interpretation of Dolly. Bailey was sadly underrecorded during her career, and this is a highlight of what little there is. — *William Ruhlmann*

☆ **House of Flowers—Cast Recording** / 1955 / Sony 2320
With a score by Truman Capote and Harold Arlen and a cast that included Pearl Bailey and Diahann Carroll (in her stage debut), this had the elements of a great show. They're best heard on this cast album in such songs as "A Sleepin' Bee" and "Two Ladies in de Shade of de Banana Tree," which bring out the show's Caribbean flavor. It was a flop onstage for reasons too complicated to explain here, but the soundtrack is very much a hit. — *William Ruhlmann*

○ **How to Succeed in Business ...** / 1961 / RCA 60352
Frank Loesser's satire on the business world, *How to Succeed in Business without Really Trying*, is as meaningful today as ever. Starring Robert Morse and Rudy Vallee, it features such highlights as "The Company Way" and "I Believe in You." It's overdue for a revival, but this original cast album is probably unbeatable. — *William Ruhlmann*

I Can Get It for You Wholesale / 1962 / Sony 2180
Harold Rome's musical about the garment trade, *I Can Get It For You Wholesale*, has long been remembered for the Broadway debut of 19-year-old Barbra Streisand, who played the part of a secretary and sang a song about it, "Miss Marmelstein." This is due not only to her obvious talent, but also to the mediocre nature of the rest of the show, a charmless tale of an unscrupulous businessman played by Elliott Gould. — *William Ruhlmann*

○ **I Do! I Do!** / 1966 / RCA 1128
The main draws to this two-character musical are the two stars: Mary Martin and Robert Preston. *I Do! I Do!* traces 50 years of a marriage, and the show's relative banality is overcome by the strong performances of the principals, as well as the quality of the Tom Jones score which includes the standard, "My Cup Runneth Over." — *William Ruhlmann*

☆ **Into the Woods—Original Cast** / 1987 / RCA 6796
Stephen Sondheim and James Lapine's re-telling of children's stories is an intricate, moving show that works on many levels. The music and lyrics are among Sondheim's best (which is to say, the best there are), and the performances, especially those of

Bernadette Peters and Chip Zien, are outstanding in this original Broadway cast recording. — *William Ruhlmann*

Into the Woods—London Cast / 1991 / RCA 60752
An excellent recording of the Sondheim classic. — *William Ruhlmann*

☆ **Jacques Brel Is Alive and Well—Original Cast** / 1987 / CBS 40817
This 1968 off-Broadway revue of *Jacques Brel Is Alive and Well and Living in Paris* established an "in concert" style of presentation for dramatic music that has often been used since. The poetic lyrics of Jacques Brel, expertly translated by Mort Shuman and Eric Blau, lend themselves to this bookless format. Its best-remembered numbers include "Marathon (Les Flamandes)," "Amsterdam," "Carousel (La Valse a Mille Temps)," and "If We Only Have Love (Quand On A Que L'Amour)." — *Marjorie Ellen Ruhlmann*

Jelly's Last Jam / 1992 / Mercury 314-510846
The good news is that Gregory Hines, playing the part of Jelly Roll Morton in this successful Broadway musical, creates a full-bodied character and performs it with conviction and gusto. His Jelly is proud, impressive, and ultimately tragic. The bad news is that he is also fictional: Writer-director George C. Wolfe has distorted Jelly Roll Morton's true story to tell a fable about African-American assimilation and the evolution of jazz. Unfortunately, Luther Henderson's musical adaptation does to Morton's music what Wolfe does to his life, and the result will be frowned upon by jazz fans, even though it conforms to Broadway conventions. — *William Ruhlmann*

☆ **Jesus Christ Superstar—Original Cast** / 1970 / MCA 10000
Writers Andrew Lloyd Webber and Tim Rice set several precedents with this album. First, it is a pre-stage studio version, and it topped the US charts upon release. Second, it is the first show to successfully put rock music in a theatrical context (*Hair* is really a pop/show-music pastiche, not rock). Third, it is a "sung-through" musical without spoken dialog, technically an operetta. Fourth, though musicals had turned more serious at this point, writing a show about Jesus Christ from the point of view of Judas was about as daring as you could get. It succeeds in all ways. In addition to the title song (a Number 14 hit sung by Murray Head), it includes "I Don't Know How to Love Him" by Yvonne Elliman. — *William Ruhlmann*

Joseph & The Amazing Technicolor Dreamcoat / 1993 / Polydor 314-511130
Andrew Lloyd Webber's first musical to be based on Biblical sources, written in 1967 when he was still a teenager, has taken on greater importance in the wake of his subsequent success. It finally hit Broadway in 1982, and there was a London revival in 1992. This cast album (which is at least the fifth recording) chronicles an American revival production that opened in Los Angeles in February 1993, starring Michael Damian. By now, the short musical has expanded to full length (the CD runs 73 minutes, including the nine-minute discoish "Joseph Megamix" medley), but it remains a rock pastiche with an uncertain tone. Lloyd Webber and lyricist Tim Rice would find their feet with this kind of approach in 1970 when they recorded *Jesus Christ Superstar*, and *Joseph* is still best understood as a dry run for that success. — *William Ruhlmann*

☆ **The King & I** / 1955 / CBS 53328
This 1951 Rodgers and Hammerstein triumph is one of those few musical comedies that gives definition to the art form. This original cast recording stars Gertrude Lawrence, for whom the show was written, as well as Yul Brynner. "I Whistle a Happy Tune," "Getting to Know You," and "Shall We Dance?" are among the classics that grace the score. — *Marjorie Ellen Ruhlmann*

○ **The King and I** / 1992 / Philips 438 007
This is a studio recreation of the Rodgers and Hammerstein musical by the Hollywood Bowl Orchestra, conducted by John Mauceri, with soloists Julie Andrews and Ben Kingsley. Andrews is perfect casting; she restores to the show its true nature as a star vehicle (it was written for Gertrude Lawrence), she embodies the role of the English tutor, and she sings brilliantly. Kingsley brings a contemporary distanced cool to the role of the King of Siam, and the cast is effectively filled out by Lea Salonga and Peabo Bryson (as the lovers who sing "We Kiss In a Shadow"), and by Marilyn Horne (who sings "Something Wonderful"). Mauceri has opted to use the orchestrations developed for the movie version,

which gives the score an added sweep and depth. This is the exception to the many oper-singers-doing-a-musical recreations we've been seeing over the last few years. It makes you wish Andrews and company would take it to New York. —*William Ruhlmann*

☆ **Kismet** / 1953 / CBS 32605

This adaptation of Edward Knoblock's play about a Baghdad beggar who rises to the rank of Emir in one magical day is notable for its score, adapted by Robert Wright and George Forrest from the music of classical composer Alexander Borodin (Borodin even won a Tony!) and for the lead performance by Alfred Drake. This cast album was a big hit, reaching Number 4 in the charts, and "Stranger in Paradise" got to Number 2 in a contemporary recording by Tony Bennett. Onstage, the song was a duet between Doretta Morrow and a young Richard Kiley. —*William Ruhlmann*

☆ **Kiss Me Kate—Original Cast** / 1961 / CBS 4140

Cole Porter's most successful show and his most popular score came with this adaptation of Shakespeare's *The Taming of the Shrew*, updated by the addition of a contemporary backstage subplot. Songs such as "I Hate Men," "Too Darn Hot," "Where Is the Life that Late I Led?," and "Always True to You (In My Fashion)" shows that Porter had lost none of his lyrical wit or compositional skill, especially when heard in the voices of a cast led by Alfred Drake and including Lisa Kirk. This cast album spent 10 weeks at the top of the album charts in 1949 and stayed in the best-seller lists over a year. The show ran more than a thousand performances. —*William Ruhlmann*

Kiss Me Kate / 1987 / Relativity 88561-8258

It's scandalous that there hasn't been a Broadway revival of this Porter masterpiece, but at least the Royal Shakespeare Company in England tried it, and here's the result: a cast led by Paul Jones and Nicola McAuliffe enthusiastically enunciating every delicious bit of wordplay, while a full orchestra plays the music beautifully. —*William Ruhlmann*

Kiss of The Spider Woman: The... / 1993 / RCA Victor 61579

John Kander and Fred Ebb's music for *Kiss of the Spider Woman* tied for the 1993 Tony Award for Best Score with The Who's *Tommy*. The material seems ideal for the longstanding team, who have specialized in writing star vehicles (notably for Liza Minnelli) and have an interest in political themes (Cabaret). *Kiss*, which is set in a South American prison and features a prisoner who dreams of a gaudy movie star, would seem to offer them opportunities for both elements. In practice, though Chita Rivera does her best as the title character, this is not on a par with *Cabaret*, which is to say, good but not great Kander/Ebb. (Though it features the major performers from the Broadway cast, this recording is not technically an original Broadway cast recording, but in fact an original London cast recording, since it was made in London at the time of the West End run, prior to the show's coming to Broadway.) —*William Ruhlmann*

☆ **La Cage aux Folles—Orig. Cast** / 1983 / RCA 4824

Composer Jerry Herman finds much greater depth in this French farce about a club for transvestites in St. Tropez than did the original play or the film, turning it into a virtual proclamation of gay pride ("I Am What I Am"). The score has his typically catchy tunes and slangy lyrics, and it remains touching, perhaps even more so in the age of AIDS. George Hearn is outstanding in the lead role. —*William Ruhlmann*

○ **Lady Be Good!** / 1977 / Elektra 79308

A reconstruction of the 1924 George and Ira Gershwin musical featuring period recordings by Fred and Adele Astaire, George Gershwin himself, and others. The songs include "Fascinating Rhythm" and "The Man I Love." —*William Ruhlmann*

○ **Lenny** / Blue Thumb 9001

A two-disc version of the Broadway play based on the comedy routines of Lenny Bruce, starring Cliff Gorman. Funny and heartbreaking, the play served as the basis for a film directed by Bob Fosse and starring Dustin Hoffman. —*William Ruhlmann*

☆ **Les Miserables—Original Cast** / 1985 / David Geffen Co. 24151

This is the original London cast recording of the musical by Alain Boublil and Claude-Michel Shonberg and starring Colm Wilkinson. A riveting theatrical experience, the show is somewhat less impressive in a merely aural version, but it remains an excellent souvenir for the millions who have seen this show all over the world. —*William Ruhlmann*

○ **Les Miserables—Complete Sym.** / 1990 / Combat 1027

This is quite easily the most impressive complete symphonic recording of *Les Miserables* on the market. The three-disc set is the entire production, not just the major numbers. The company is an all-star cast taken from productions around the world; and the singers hail from New York, Los Angeles, London, Sydney, and Tokyo. Perhaps the most remarkable performance is from Kaho Shimada of Tokyo in the role of Eponine. Shimada herself speaks virtually no English, but you wouldn't be able to tell by listening to this recording. A simply outstanding set. —*Tavia Hobart*

○ **Let's Face It** / 1979 / Smithsonian 016

A reconstruction of the 1941 Cole Porter musical featuring performances by Danny Kaye and Hildegard. Also included on the album are five selections from *Red, Hot, and Blue!*, a 1936 Porter show with Ethel Merman, and three from *Leave It to Me!*, the 1938 show that introduced Mary Martin. —*William Ruhlmann*

○ **Li'l Abner—Original Musical Comedy** / 1956 / Sony 5150

The Johnny Mercer/Gene de Paul musical captures the arch, sometimes cynical tone of *Les Miserables* comic strip and contains all those hayseed characters. Songs like "Jubilation T. Cornpone" and "The Country's in the Very Best of Hands" are much more satiric than anything one normally associates with the '50s, but they certainly don't sound dated today. The cast includes Edith Adams, Stubby Kaye, Tina Louise, and Julie Newmar. —*William Ruhlmann*

○ **A Little Night Music—Orig. Broadway Cast** / 1973 / CBS 32265

This recording of Stephen Sondheim's musical based on the Ingmar Bergman film *Smiles of a Summer Night* is at least as charming as its source material. Sondheim sets the romantic roundelay of the story to a series of waltzes with lyrics that bring out the ups and downs of "Liaisons," to borrow one song title. "Send In the Clowns" was the show's hit, but it is no more impressive than "The Glamorous Life," "You Must Meet My Wife," or "The Miller's Son." The score is effectively handled by a cast led by Len Cariou, Glynis Johns, Hermione Gingold, and Beth Fowler. —*William Ruhlmann*

○ **A Little Night Music—Original London Cast** / 1975 / RCA 5090

Original London cast album of the Sondheim hit, featuring Jean Simmons (a better singer than Broadway's Glynnis Johns), Hermione Gingold (reprising her Broadway performance), and Joss Ackland. —*William Ruhlmann*

○ **Loesser by Loesser** / 1992 / DRG 5170

Composer Frank Loesser (who wrote *Guys and Dolls, The Most Happy Fella*, and other Broadway shows as well as many movie songs) was married to actress/singer Jo Sullivan, who starred in *The Most Happy Fella*. In the years since Loesser's death, Sullivan has toured with a concert revue called *The Songs of Frank Loesser*, and this, with Don Stephenson and the Loessers' daughter Emily, is something of a recreation of that show. It features a selection of some of Loesser's best, well sung and played by a small band. As such, it contains such songs as "Heart and Soul" and "Two Sleepy People," along with medleys from Loesser's shows. —*William Ruhlmann*

○ **Lost in the Stars—Original Cast** / Nov. 1949 / MCA 10302

A 1949 musical with an African-American cast, dealing with racial unrest in South Africa. Music by Kurt Weill, words by Pulitzer Prize-winning playwright Maxwell Anderson. Based on Alan Paton's condescending novel *Cry, the Beloved Country*. The score is lovely but not very African. —*Marjorie Ellen Ruhlmann*

☆ **Mame—Original Cast** / 1966 / CBS 3000

Jerry Herman's score hasn't a weak song, and it has some very strong ones, starting with the title tune and including "We Need a Little Christmas" and "If He Walked into My Life." Add a cast headed by Angela Lansbury and a book by Jerome Lawrence and Robert E. Lee (based on the Patrick Dennis novel about a boy and his zany aunt), and you have a big Broadway hit. —*William Ruhlmann*

☆ **Man of La Mancha—Original Cast** / 1965 / MCA 31065

The musical version of Cervantes's *Don Quixote, Man of La Mancha* opened inauspiciously in an off-Broadway house in the fall of 1965, moved to Broadway, and became the hit of the 1965-1966 season. The original cast recording, with Richard Kiley in the title role, was a gold-selling hit that stayed on the best-seller charts more than three years, and no wonder, with a Mitch Leigh/Joe Darion score that included the stirring title song and the anthemic "The Impossible Dream." — *William Ruhlmann*

○ **Me & My Girl** / 1986 / MCA 6196
A revival/revision of Noel Gay's '30s musical comedy about a Cockney who is heir to an earldom, this Broadway cast album has plenty going for it: Robert Lindsay, who gives a delightful star turn in the main role, and a score including such favorites as "The Lambeth Walk" and "Leaning on a Lamppost." — *William Ruhlmann*

Me and Juliet / 1953 / RCA Victor 61480
Of Rodgers & Hammerstein's three relative flops, *Allegro*, *Me and Juliet*, and *Pipe Dream*, *Me and Juliet* was the most successful. In fact, it broke even. But after 40 years, the only memorable thing about it remains the song that was already a bit on opening night, "No Other Love," based on a theme Rodgers had previously used in *Victory At Sea*. Rodgers & Hammerstein were trying for a light romantic comedy in the style of Rodger & Hart, but Hammerstein was not Hart, and this wasn't *Pal Joey*. — *William Ruhlmann*

Merrily We Roll Along—Original Cast / 1982 / RCA 5840
Stephen Sondheim wrote one of his typically outstanding scores for this show, tracing the lives of a composer and lyricist—backwards. It was a complete flop onstage, but the album proves its quality. RCA 5840 is a 1986 CD reissue of the LP version (RCA 4197), containing one song that previously didn't fit. The cassette version lacks the added song. — *William Ruhlmann*

○ **Miss Saigon—Original London Cast** / 1990 / David Geffen Co. 24271
Alain Boublil and Claude-Michel Schonberg's follow-up to *Les Miserables* is another sung-through operetta with a serious theme and a classic source: They have placed *Madame Butterfly* in the waning days of the Vietnam War. Jonathan Pryce stands out as a pimp named the Engineer in this London cast recording, and the score has the same rock feel as Schonberg's *Les Miserables* music. — *William Ruhlmann*

Mr. Wonderful—Original Cast / 1956 / MCA 10303
This Jerry Bock/Larry Holofcener/George Weiss show is remembered today for boosting Sammy Davis, Jr. to stardom. It also featured a young Chita Rivera. — *William Ruhlmann*

Moby Dick / May 11, 1993 / RCA 61707
Now, here's an oddity. Robert Longden and Hereward Kaye wrote a musical version of *Moby Dick* as it might have been performed by an English girls school and got it on—briefly—in the West End. This cast album was recorded live onstage and, on two discs, is the complete show. Given the apparently satiric setting, you'd expect the result to be funnier than it is: the authors can't seem to decide what their take on the material should be. — *William Ruhlmann*

☆ **The Music Man—Original Broadway Cast** / 1958 / Capitol 46633
The original Broadway cast of Meredith Willson's most successful musical was headed by Robert Preston, who played the part of Harold Hill, a conman who breezes into an Iowa town and tries to sell the inhabitants on non-existent boys band equipment. Willson concentrates on percussive effects and rapid-fire spiels for Preston, though the musical standout is Barbara Cook as Marian the Librarian. Highlights of this perennial hit show include "Seventy-Six Trombones" and "Till There Was You." — *William Ruhlmann*

The Music Man—Studio Recording / 1991 / Telarc 80276
Erich Kunzel leads the Cincinnati Pops Orchestra in this concert version of the score, which features more incidental music than previous albums. Timothy Noble is only adequate in the lead role, but Doc Severinsen proves a surprisingly effective Marcellus Washburn on his featured number, "Shipoopi." — *William Ruhlmann*

☆ **My Fair Lady—Original Broadway Cast** / 1956 / Sony 5090
The original Broadway cast recording of Alan Jay Lerner and Frederick Loewe's musical, based on George Bernard Shaw's *Pygmalion*, about the relationship between an elocutionist and a flower girl. This is one of the great musical scores, including "Wouldn't It Be Lovely," "I Could Have Danced All Night," and "On the Street Where You Live," sung by a cast that includes Rex Harrison, Julie Andrews, and Stanley Holloway. The album spent 15 weeks at Number 1 in the charts. — *William Ruhlmann*

Rodgers and Hammerstein

Composer Richard Rodgers (1902-1979) and lyricist Oscar Hammerstein II (1895-1960) had both had extensive careers in Broadway theater music before they scored their first hit together with Oklahoma! in 1943. Rodgers first teamed with Lorenz Hart (1895-1943), with whom he scored a series of Broadway successes that began when the team's song "Manhattan" was interpolated into *The Garrick Gaieties of 1925*. Rodgers and Hart's shows included *Present Arms* (1928), *On Your Toes* (1936), *Babes in Arms* (1937), and *Pal Joey* (1940), among others, and they are responsible for a slew of song standards including "You Took Advantage of Me," "Dancing on the Ceiling," "There's a Small Hotel," "Where or When," "The Lady Is a Tramp," "My Funny Valentine," "I Wish I Were in Love Again," "Isn't It Romantic," and "Bewitched, Bothered and Bewildered." But Hart's health declined, and Rodgers had sought out Hammerstein prior to his partner's death from pneumonia.

Hammerstein, scion of a theatrical family (his grandfather owned several theaters and wrote shows and his father and brother were also involved in the theater), attended Columbia University, where he wrote college shows with Rodgers. He was a considerable success in the 1920s, collaborating with Jerome Kern on *Show Boat* (1927) and also working with Sigmund Romberg, but he went for a long stretch in the 30s without having a hit.

The Rodgers and Hammerstein team returned to the plot-oriented, socially conscious style of *Show Boat* for a series of landmark musicals in the 40s and 50s, notably *Carousel* (1945), *South Pacific* (1949), *The King and I* (1951), and *The Sound of Music* (1959), among others.

Rodgers, who had the luck to work with two of the most gifted lyricists of the century, continued after Hammerstein's death, though without lucking into a third major partner. He wrote music and lyrics to *No Strings* in 1962, and tried working with Stephen Sondheim on *Do I Hear a Waltz?* (1965), but his later work was less successful.

– William Ruhlmann

○ **My Fair Lady—Original London Cast** / 1975 / CBS 2015
This mega-hit moved into the Drury Lane Theatre in London in April of 1958 with the British stars of the Broadway version intact; hence the original London cast recording is very similar to its more familiar American counterpart. At present this album in CD form is often rather less expensive than the original-Broadway-cast CD, and it is far better to have this *My Fair Lady* than none at all. — *Marjorie Ellen Ruhlmann*

○ **My One and Only—Original Broadway Cast** / 1983 / Atlantic 80110
"The New Gershwin Musical" was the subtitle given this musical, but most people knew it as the new Tommy Tune musical, since he starred in it (with Twiggy) and staged and choreographed it (with Thommie Walsh). On record, Tune's personality comes across even if his long legs aren't visible, and the mostly understated arrangements of Gershwin favorites sound newly minted. — *William Ruhlmann*

○ **No, No, Nanette—Broadway Cast** / 1971 / CBS 30563
A revival of a 1925 musical by Vincent Youmans, Irving Caesar, and Otto Harbach, mounted in an essentially faithful style 41 years later with a cast featuring Ruby Keeler and a production supervised by Busby Berkeley. A romantic roundelay with a flapper at its center, it proved a success all over again in the '70s, probably because it still had a score featuring such songs as "I Want to Be Happy" and "Tea for Two." — *William Ruhlmann*

Stephen Sondheim

According to most critics and theater historians, Stephen Sondheim (b. 1930) stands among Broadway show composers and lyricists not only as the greatest of his generation but as the *only* great one of his generation. There may be many reasons why Broadway has failed to produce consistently great writers to follow the Rodgers and Hammersteins and Lerner and Loewes of the 40s and 50s, but the fact remains that, though he operates without serious competition, Sondheim clearly ranks with such masters, as well as with the Jerome Kerns and Irving Berlins of an even earlier generation.

Sondheim became a mentor of Hammerstein's after befriending the lyricist's son in school, but he got his first big break when he was hired to write lyrics to Leonard Bernstein's score for *West Side Story* (1957), which turned out to be one of the biggest hits and most memorable works of its time. This led to a lot of lyric-writing work, though Sondheim always wanted to write music as well. Nevertheless, he worked with Jule Styne on *Gypsy* (1959), another enormous hit, and would later agree to do the same with Richard Rodgers for the unsuccessful *Do I Hear a Waltz?* (1965).

Before that, however, Sondheim scored his first success as composer and lyricist with *A Funny Thing Happened on the Way to the Forum* (1962). It was his last hit until *Company* (1970), a show about contemporary life and mores that did much to revolutionize the Broadway musical and, as Hammerstein's 50s shows had, move it more toward serious and exotic subjects. Since that time, Sondheim's shows have been amazingly daring in terms of subject matter, with unusual musical ideas and stunningly original lyrics. But they have not always been big hits and have marked a time in the theater when Broadway show music became a marginalized art form in terms of popular culture.

Nevertheless, Sondheim's shows of the 70s and 80s are benchmarks of the genre: *Follies* (1971) brought together aging follies girls for a look at middle-aged American life; *A Little Night Music* (1973) is based on Ingmar Bergman's film *Smiles of a Summer Night* and contains Sondheim's sole hit song, "Send in the Clowns"; *Pacific Overtures* (1976) ambitiously took on the subject of Japanese-American relations; *Sweeney Todd* (1979) was an operetta based on the British grand guignol tale of a murderous barber; *Sunday in the Park with George* (1984) was a biography of impressionist painter Georges Seurat; and *Into the Woods* (1987) wove together children's fairy tales with the theories of psychologist Bruno Bettelheim. At this writing, Sondheim's latest show is *Assassins* (1991), a short piece about presidential killers. In recent years, he has turned more to films (he wrote a score for Stavinsky in the 70s), writing songs for Madonna in *Dick Tracy* in 1990 and reportedly currently working on an original movie musical.

– William Ruhlmann

○ **Oh, Kay!** / 1978 / Smithsonian 011

A reconstruction of the 1926 George and Ira Gershwin musical, featuring recordings by Gertrude Lawrence, with George Gershwin playing many of the piano parts. Songs include "Clap Yo' Hands," "Do, Do, Do," and "Someone to Watch over Me." — *William Ruhlmann*

☆ **Oklahoma!—Original Cast** / 1955 / MCA 10046

Rodgers and Hammerstein's first collaboration in 1943 created the mold from which most musicals were made for the next twenty-five years. The combination of a serious book, with score and ballet truly subservient to the plot, proved a successful formula, particularly in the hands of this team. Alfred Drake's dreamy "Oh, What a Beautiful Mornin'" and Celeste Holm's "I Cain't Say No" are irresistible. — *Marjorie Ellen Ruhlmann*

○ **Oklahoma!—Broadway Revival** / 1980 / RCA 3572
An excellent Broadway revival of the 1943 Rodgers and Hammerstein show that still ranks among their greatest works, and which gets a hi-fidelity workout here. — *William Ruhlmann*

☆ **Oliver!—Original Broadway Cast** / 1962 / RCA 4113
Lionel Bart's musical version of *Oliver Twist*, Charles Dickens' novel of Industrial Revolution London in the late 19th century, was far more entertaining than the subject matter would suggest. The show has Dickens' sad story of poverty and crime, but also one of the strongest scores heard on Broadway in the '60s—"I'd Do Anything," "Be Back Soon," "Oom-Pah-Pah," "As Long As He Needs Me"—in fact, it's one hit after another (no wonder this album reached Number 4 in the charts and went gold). And it has the incomparable Georgia Brown too. — *William Ruhlmann*

○ **Once on This Island** / 1990 / RCA 60595
A wonderful Caribbean-influenced musical by Lynn Ahrens and Stephen Flaherty. You can't see the fluid staging of Graciela Daniele on this disc, but the music almost makes up for it. — *William Ruhlmann*

Over Here! / Mar. 1974 / Sony Classical 32961
The Andrews Sisters returned to active duty as a duo in this musical, which bears a certain similarity to the movies they made during World War II, with a score by Richard M. and Robert B. Sherman (who spent most of their career writing for Walt Disney Movies) that apes the polka and boogie-woogie styles of the Andrews' pop hits of the '40s. Unfortunately, it's all a bit too broad and knowing—"The Good-Time Girl" is a warning against venereal disease, and "Wait For Me, Marlena" is a parody of Marlene Dietrich—and doesn't match the era or the material it simultaneously salutes and satirizes. (Originally released in 1974, *Over Here!* was reissued on CD in 1992.) — *William Ruhlmann*

Pacific Overtures—Original Cast / Jan. 1976 / RCA 4407
One of Stephen Sondheim's most ambitious works, treating the relations between Japan and the West and, in retrospect, containing some of Sondheim's best songs, among them "Pretty Lady" and "Someone in a Tree." Mako leads a distinguished Asian-American cast. — *William Ruhlmann*

☆ **Paint Your Wagon** / 1951 / RCA 60243
Alan Jay Lerner and Frederick Loewe turn their attention to the American West and come up with a story that anticipates the romantic triangle of *Camelot*. On the way, they present one of their best scores, featuring such songs as "They Call the Wind Maria" and "Wand'rin' Star." James Barton stars. — *William Ruhlmann*

○ **The Pajama Game—Original Cast** / 1954 / CBS 32606
This 1954 comedy about organized labor launched Bob Fosse's Broadway career. The jazzy score by Richard Adler and Jerry Ross includes "Steam Heat," "Hernando's Hideaway," and "Hey There." This recording features John Raitt, one of the era's most popular actor/singers. — *Marjorie Ellen Ruhlmann*

○ **Pal Joey—Froman, Beavers & the Broadway Cast** / 1952 / Capitol 91249
One of the biggest hits of the 1951-1952 Broadway season was the revival of *Pal Joey*. Capitol got the rights to the cast album, but couldn't use the stars, who had already recorded the score for Columbia, so they substituted with Jane Froman and Dick Beavers, plus the revival cast. They sing wonderfully, however, and with a score this good, how could they miss? — *William Ruhlmann*

Phantom / 1993 / RCA 61660
Composer/lyricist Maury Yeston (Nine) actually began work on this musical version of Gaston Leroux's novel *The Phantom of the Opera* before it attracted the attention of Andrew Lloyd Webber (and before it fell out of copyright). But Lloyd Webber got to the stage first and had a spectacular success with his show, so the Yeston version is doomed always to be known as "the other Phantom." Nevertheless, it has gotten some productions (though not in New York or London), and this "premiere cast recording" reveals it to be a respectable effort, free of the bombast of Lloyd

Webber, if not quite the superior treatment claimed in the liner notes. —*William Ruhlmann*

○ **The Phantom of the Opera—Orig. Cast** / 1987 / Polydor 831273
This is one of Andrew Lloyd Webber's most highly acclaimed productions. The two-disc set comes with a booklet that has not only the lyrics, but also the dialog and stage directions. Sarah Brightman stars as Christine Daae (the heroine) and Michael Crawford as the Phantom. Also available in a one-disc "highlights" version. —*Tavia Hobart*

○ **Pippin—Original Broadway Cast** / 1972 / Motown 37463-5243
The biggest hit of the 1972-1973 season on Broadway, *Pippin* is perhaps better remembered for Ben Vereen's performance and for the choreography by Bob Fosse than for the songs by Stephen Schwartz. The score is not as good as Schwartz's masterpiece, *Godspell*, but nevertheless has an appealing pop style, especially on such songs as "Corner of the Sky" and "Spread a Little Sunshine." —*William Ruhlmann*

Porgy and Bess / 1977 / RCA Victor 54680
The Houston Grand Opera mounted a revival of George Gershin's 1935 musical/opera *Porgy and Bess* in July 1976, and brought it Broadway in September. In November, RCA Victor recorded a full-length cast album of the show, released as a multi-record set in 1977. In 1983, a one-disc abridgement of highlights was released, and this is the CD version of that album, which was reissued in 1993. Unlike recordings that have taken a pop, jazz, or Broadway approach, this one positions *Porgy and Bess* squarely as an opera, with singing that emphasizes musical embellishment over lyrical expressiveness. As such, it is likely to appeal more to opera fans than to show music fans, but the quality of the Gershwin score, from "Summertime" to "I Loves You, Porgy," is unmistakeable. —*William Ruhlmann*

☆ **Porgy and Bess—Original Cast** / 1989 / MCA 1631
According to Alan Jay Lerner, "It was the first of its kind and remains to this day the greatest triumph of the modern musical theater." According to noted African-American theater historian Loften Mitchell, it was "a work generally hailed by Whites and disliked by many Negroes." George Gershwin's 1935 "folk opera," with lyrics by Ira Gershwin and Du Bose Heyward, based on Heyward's novel, introduced "Summertime," "I Got Plenty o' Nuttin'," and "It Ain't Necessarily So." Even if, as Mitchell says, the characters are stereotypical and the story "not as moving as its source," the musical importance of *Porgy and Bess* is undeniable. —*Marjorie Ellen Ruhlmann*

Premiere Collection I / 1993 / MCA 10053
This 16-track various artists album, a sequel to the 1988 *Premiere Collection* compilation, features everyone—from Placido Domingo to Barbra Streisand—singing some of the more minor entries in Lloyd Webber's catalog. Streisand gets to do "Memory" from Cats, probably the closest thing to a hit here, but the album is more interested in resurrecting material from such duds as *Starlight Express* and *Aspects of Love*. The composer told annotator Baz Bamighoye that the latter show's score "will last longer than *Cats* and *[The] Phantom [Of The Opera]*. Don't bet on it. —*William Ruhlmann*

○ **Pump Boys & Dinettes—Original Cast** / CBS 37790
An ensemble piece written and performed by John Foley, Mark Hardwick, Debra Monk, Cass Morgan, John Schimmel, and Jim Wann. This was quickly promoted from supper club to off-Broadway, and then to Broadway in 1982. It's a warm, small-scale, country-style celebration of life among the denizens of the Double Cupp Diner and the filling station across the highway, somewhere in the contemporary American South. —*Marjorie Ellen Ruhlmann*

○ **Purlie** / 1970 / RCA 60229
This musical comedy adaptation of Ossie Davis's play about a Black preacher who returns to his Southern hometown has a boisterous gospel score written by Gary Geld and Peter Udell and also boasts a cast including Cleavon Little, Melba Moore, Linda Hopkins, and Sherman Hemsley. —*William Ruhlmann*

○ **Return to the Forbidden Planet** / 1991 / Rhino 70480
What a jumble of sources! This is the original London cast recording of a musical based on the sci-fi movie *Forbidden Planet* and Shakespeare's *The Tempest*, employing pop songs of the '50s and

Andrew Lloyd Webber

Andrew Lloyd Webber (b. 1948) is the most successful composer of musicals of his generation and also a breaker of molds for the type. His predecessors were for the most part American: New York-based songwriters steeped in Broadway tradition. Lloyd Webber saw his share of shows as a child, too, but he was born in London, the son of William Lloyd Webber, director of the London College of Music, and was trained at the Royal Academy of Music, hardly the sort of place where you'd be likely to hear *Oklahoma!*

Nevertheless, Lloyd Webber hooked up with lyricist Tim Rice, and the two began work on what would be a typical project for them, a musical based on the Biblical story of Joseph and his coat of many colors. Titled *Joseph and the Amazing Technicolor Dreamcoat*, it brought in a strong rock & roll influence. After writing a second unproduced musical, the two hit on the idea of writing a musical based on the life of Jesus Christ from the point of view of Judas (not the sort of idea likely to occur to a Broadway composer) and, again, imbued with rock. Unable to finance a stage version, Lloyd Webber and Rice did manage to record their show, and *Jesus Christ Superstar* went on to sales in the millions all over the world. The hit musical version followed.

Lloyd Webber and Rice then split, with the composer writing film scores and working on an abortive musical with playwright Alan Ayckbourne (*Jeeves*), after which Rice returned with another audacious idea: a musical based on the life of Argentine dictator (or dictator's wife, depending on how you look at it) Eva Peron. *Evita* (1976) repeated the pattern of *Jesus Christ Superstar*, with its hit record album followed by a successful theatrical run in the West End and then on Broadway.

The Lloyd Webber-Rice partnership having proved itself again, it was severed (Rice went on to write *Chess*), and Lloyd Webber next wrote a musical revue based on T. S. Eliot's whimsical poems about *Cats* (1981). This time the show came before the album, and it's still running. By this time, Lloyd Webber had largely abandoned the rock elements of his work in favor of what critics found a pastiche style largely borrowed from classical and opera sources. He had also become a brand name (and a corporation, the Really Useful Company) that assured at least a modest success for subsequent shows, though critics were often unimpressed with his efforts.

Downgrading the status of his lyricists, Lloyd Webber went on to a series of successful shows (*Song and Dance, Starlight Express*) before scoring another long- (and still-) running hit in 1987 (1988 in New York) with a musical adaptation of *The Phantom of the Opera*. *Aspects of Love* (1989-1990) was less successful, however. Lloyd Webber is presently working on a musical based on the Billy Wilder film *Sunset Boulevard*.

— *William Ruhlmann*

'60s—On record, it's just a bunch of rock oldies—but it's still fun. —*William Ruhlmann*

○ **The Roar of the Greasepaint—Orig. Broadway Cast** / 1965 / RCA 60351

Roar of the Greasepaint, the Smell of the Crowd. A sequel to Anthony Newly and Leslie Bricusse's previous show, *Stop the World—I Want to Get Off*, and almost as winning a score, largely sung by Newly and Cyril Ritchard. Featuring "Who Can I Turn To (When Nobody Needs Me)." —*William Ruhlmann*

○ **Runaways** / 1978 / CBS 35410

Elizabeth Swados conducted this show about teenage runaways, which features a child cast who turn in outstanding performances on some terrific pop-rock material. It's the kind of thing Broadway needs more of. — *William Ruhlmann*

Sarafina! / 1987 / Shanachie 43052

An abbreviated version of the Mbongeni Ngema musical about South African school children. It was recorded in South Africa prior to the show's arrival in New York. Cheaply made, but stirring. — *William Ruhlmann*

○ **Sarafina!** / 1988 / RCA 9307

This is the more complete Broadway cast version of this show, which by November 1988 had turned into the most moving evening in a Broadway theater. Ngema's music captures the newly popular mbaqanga sound of the homelands, and the story paints apartheid in its most glaring colors. — *William Ruhlmann*

She Loves Me—Orig. Broadway Cast / 1976 / Polydor 831968

Sheldon Harnick and Jerry Bock's musical version of *The Shop Around the Corner* was not a stage success (unlike their *Fiddler on the Roof* the following year), but the score has been well remembered in this near-complete recording (originally on two LPs), especially for Barbara Cook's performance. — *William Ruhlmann*

Show Boat—Original Cast / 1962 / CBS 2220

Non-stage studio recording featuring John Raitt, Barbara Cook, William Warfield, Anita Darian, Fay De Witt, Louise Parker, and the Merrill Staton Choir, conducted by Franz Allers. Cook is especially impressive (she went on to a stage revival of the show four years later). — *William Ruhlmann*

Show Boat—London Cast / 1972 / Stanyon 107

This is a well-recorded 1971 London revival, starring Cleo Laine. — *William Ruhlmann*

☆ **Side by Side by Sondheim—Orig. London Cast** / 1976 / RCA 1851

A two-disc London cast recording of a revue culled from songs written by Stephen Sondheim for such musicals as *A Funny Thing Happened on the Way to the Forum*, *Company*, *A Little Night Music*, *Follies*, *Anyone Can Whistle*, *Pacific Overtures*, *Do I Hear a Waltz?*, *West Side Story*, and *Gypsy*, and more obscure works such as "Evening Primrose" (a TV show), *The 7% Solution*, and *The Mad Show*. In anthology and presented starkly, the songs are (if possible) even more impressive than when heard in the shows for which they were written. If there was any doubt that Stephen Sondheim is the greatest talent writing contemporary musicals, this show erased it. — *William Ruhlmann*

Silk Stockings—Original Broadway Cast / 1955 / RCA 1102

Cole Porter based this charming musical on the movie *Ninotchka*, about a Russian official tempted by the romantic and capitalistic elements of Paris. Hildegarde Neff inhabits the Greta Garbo role, while Don Ameche plays Melvyn Douglas' film part. It isn't one of the great Porter scores, but with lyrics like the ones in "Siberia" and "It's a Chemical Reaction, That's All," it is full of Porter's typical wit. — *William Ruhlmann*

Sondheim—Putting It Together / 1993 / RCA 61729

Nominally, this is a sequel to the anthology show *Side By Side By Sondheim*, which selected some of the composer's songs for individual performance by a small cast in a revue format. In practice, it's closer to *Marry Me A Little*, which attempted to build a new book show out of existing Sondheim songs. The five characters in *Putting It Together* are upper-class types having a dinner party, with songs from such Sondheim shows as *Company*, *Follies*, and *Merrily We Roll Along*, which treated such people prominently, interpolated into the proceedings. The songs are terrific, of course, and the cast is talented; this off-Broadway production marked Julie Andrews' return to the theater for the first time in decades. But the story doesn't really work, and the treatment of the material is sometimes odd, as when Christopher Durang finds himself singing "I [YOU] Can Drive a Person Crazy," originally written for a female trio in Company. Nevertheless, when Andrews takes on "Getting Married Today," it's easy to forgive all. — *William Ruhlmann*

Sondheim: A Celebration at Carnegie Hall / 1993 / RCA Victor 61516

This two-CD set is the recording of a benefit concert for Carnegie Hall performed at the hall on June 10, 1992 and featuring the American Theatre Orchestra, conducted by Paul Gemignani, supporting a variety of soloists doing songs written by Stephen Sondheim for Broadway musicals and films. As several anthologies of Sondheim's work and tributes to him have been recorded in the past, the organizers weren't able to find much new in the composer's catalog, and they have settled for sometimes gimmicky arrangements of his familiar songs. Nevertheless, many of the performances are strong, and the stars are many: Glenn Close ("Send In the Clowns"), Madeline Kahn ("I'm Not Getting Married Today"), Patti Lupone ("Being Alive"), Liza Minnelli (the sole new song, "Water Under the Bridge"), and Bernadette Peters ("Not a Day Goes By") are stand-outs, but the cream of Broadway is represented. Also, it's worth noting that, while the album may be a disappointment to diehard Sondheim fans, newcomers not familiar with this material may well be bowled over by its quality. Sondheim is Broadway's top contemporary composer, and this album demonstrates that as well as any. (Also available as a video, which actually works better, given that some of the numbers have strong visual elements.) — *William Ruhlmann*

Sondheim: a Musical Tribute / 1973 / RCA 60515

A two-disc recording of a special benefit show held March 11, 1973, featuring many of the original performers from Stephen Sondheim musicals, reprising their performances of his songs. Thus, the album is a kind of "Sondheim's Greatest Hits," with the added excitement of being a one-time event. Originally isssued as a two-LP set by Warner in 1973, it was reissued by RCA on CD/cassette with previously unreleased tracks. — *William Ruhlmann*

○ **The Sound of Music—Original Cast** / Nov. 1959 / CBS 32601

The Sound of Music was a huge hit in 1959 for Rodgers and Hammerstein, and a highlight in the remarkable career of Mary Martin. The book by Howard Lindsay and Russel Crouse was based on Maria von Trapp's autobiography. It's a rather cloying story that involves nuns, Nazis, and seven cute kids, but it has pleased audiences for years. The title song, "Climb Every Mountain," "My Favorite Things," "Do-Re-Mi," "Sixteen Going on Seventeen," and "Edelweiss" all entered the culture through this score. The cast album features Theodore Bikel in the romantic lead, which unfortunately became a non-singing role in the subsequent film. — *Marjorie Ellen Ruhlmann*

South Pacific / 1986 / CBS 42205

A studio recording featuring a combination of opera singers (Kiri Te Kanawa, Jose Carreras), jazz singers (Sarah Vaughan), and Broadway singers (Mandy Patinkin), with the London Symphony Orchestra, directed by Jonathan Tunick. — *William Ruhlmann*

☆ **South Pacific—Original Cast** / CBS 32604

Adapted from James A. Michener's *Tales of the South Pacific*. Starring Mary Martin and opera star Ezio Pinza, with music and lyrics by Rodgers and Hammerstein, it enjoyed the largest advance ticket sale ever recorded on Broadway when it opened in 1949. The book intertwines two wartime love stories complicated by American prejudices against Asians. The brilliant score includes "A Cockeyed Optimist," "Some Enchanted Evening," "There Is Nothin' Like a Dame," "I'm Gonna Wash That Man Right Outa My Hair," and "Younger Than Springtime." — *Marjorie Ellen Ruhlmann*

○ **Starting Here, Starting Now** / 1977 / RCA 2360

This celebrated off-Broadway revue serves as a retrospective of the work of Richard Maltby, Jr. and David Shire, a songwriting team that has done just about everything *except* write a successful Broadway musical. Contemporary mores are examined in a series of songs including the title tune and "What About Today," both previously recorded by Barbra Streisand. — *William Ruhlmann*

○ **A Stephen Sondheim Evening** / 1983 / RCA Victor 09026-61774

Stephen Sondheim must be one of the most anthologized Broadway composers, his shows having been cannibalized into several revues, reconceived musicals, and concert performances. This is a particularly good one. It is a concert featuring a cast of eight, among them Cris Groenendaal, Bob Gunton, George Hearn, and Angela Lansbury, recorded in 1983 and featuring songs written for shows ranging from Sondheim's unproduced first effort, *Saturday Night*, to what was then his latest, *Merrily We Roll Along*. Particularly notable are the songs cut from shows, such as "There's Something About A War" from *A Funny Thing Happened on the Way to the Forum*. The composer himself turns up toward the end to play piano for Lansbury on "Send In the Clowns" and help sing "Old Friends." (The original two-LP set, released in 1983 [CBL2-4745]) contained 21 selections. When the album was released on CD in 1994 [09026-61174-2], two songs, "Fear No More" and "You're Gonna Love Tomorrow" were cut to keep the time down to the limits of one CD.) — *William Ruhlmann*

○ **Stop the World, I Want to Get Off!**—Orig. Cast / 1962 / Polydor 820261
Stop the World, I Want to Get Off!, Anthony Newley and Leslie Bricusse's innovative show, holds up very well after 30 years, due as much to the score as to Newley's singing on such standards as "Gonna Build a Mountain" and "What Kind of Fool Am I?" — *William Ruhlmann*

○ **Sunday in the Park with George**—Orig. Cast / 1984 / RCA 5042
Stephen Sondheim's musical, imaginatively based on the life of French painter Georges Seurat, is a meditation on life and the creative process, brilliantly realized by Mandy Patinkin and Bernadette Peters. — *William Ruhlmann*

☆ **Sweeney Todd**—Original Cast / 1979 / RCA 3379
A complete, two-disc recording of Stephen Sondheim's *grand guignol* operetta about a barber who cuts things close. This show is a masterpiece full of stirring music and witty, intricate lyrics, lustily delivered by a cast led by Angela Lansbury and Len Cariou. Don't confuse this complete score with a single-disc "highlights" album also in print. — *William Ruhlmann*

○ **Sweet Charity**—Broadway Cast / 1966 / CBS 2900
Gwen Verdon is the standout performer in this recording of the Cy Coleman/Dorothy Fields score, but consider that the songs she has to sing include "Big Spender," "If My Friends Could See Me Now," and "Where Am I Going?" — *William Ruhlmann*

Take Me Along / Oct. 1959 / RCA 51050
Based on playwright Eugene O'Neill's sole comedy, *Ah, Wilderness*, the musical *Take Me Along* was mounted on Broadway in 1959 as a vehicle for TV star Jackie Gleason. It ran for a little over a year and lost money, though it has gone into the black since. Robert Merrill's score is only functional, though it does provide showcases for Gleason on such songs as "Single Kid" and "I Get Embarrassed" (a duet with Eileen Herlie). Walter Pidgeon also makes a strong impression and Robert Morse took a big step to stardom playing the juvenile and singing "I Would Die" with Susan Luckey. Nevertheless, *Take Me Along* never competes with the great musicals of the era. — *William Ruhlmann*

○ **They're Playing Our Song**—Original Cast / 1979 / Casablanca 826240
A successful musical with a book by Neil Simon and songs by Marvin Hamlisch and Carole Bayer Sager. It concerns the on-again, off-again relationship between a composer and lyricist. *They're Playing Our Song* has a pop music score characteristic of its time, even to the point of the disco style of some of its songs. Robert Klein and Lucie Arnaz are the principals. — *William Ruhlmann*

☆ **The Threepenny Opera**—Original Cast / 1954 / Polydor 820260
Marc Blitzstein's translation of the Kurt Weill/Bertolt Brecht musical ran for six years off-Broadway and established the work as a major theater piece in the U.S. This excellent recording not only presents Blitzstein's terrific versions of the songs but also a cast led by Jo Sullivan, Beatrice Arthur, and Lotte Lenya. — *William Ruhlmann*

Unsinkable Molly Brown—Broadway Cast / 1960 / Capitol
Meredith Willson's followup to *The Music Man*, about a *nouveau riche* Colorado mine owner's wife who survives the sinking of the Titanic, is not quite as impressive as its predecessor, but the irrepressible Tammy Grimes does much to make it a success on record. — *William Ruhlmann*

Weird Romance: Two One-Act Musicals . . . / 1993 / Columbia 53318
Weird Romance: Two On-Act Musicals of Speculative Fiction is the cast album for an off-Broadway production of a couple of mini-shows with music by Alan Menken (who has composed the Disney film musicals *The Little Mermaid*, *Beauty and the Beast*, and *Aladdin*) and new lyrical collaborator David Spencer, plus

book writer Alan Brennert. Both shows are love stories set in science fiction scenarios (one was filmed as a "Twilight Zone" episode). The first, "The Girl Who Was Plugged In" attempts social criticism in a tale of mechanical transubstantiatio, and largely fails; but the second, "Her Pilgrim Soul," which concerns holograms and past lives and is played sincerely, works well and contains two first-rate songs: "Need to Know," a science nerd's explanation of his life; and "A Man," a timely dissection of the male gender by a couple of knowing women. — *William Ruhlmann*

West Side Story / 1985 / Deutsche Grammophon 415253
Leonard Bernstein conducts his own score on this studio recording, which features opera singers Kiri Te Kanawa and Jose Carreras. The singers somewhat overwhelm the material (and it's more than a little odd that the only person with a Spanish accent is Carreras, who plays Tony, the American Romeo), but the music is magnificent. — *William Ruhlmann*

☆ **West Side Story**—Original Cast / CBS 32603
A fabulous collaboration of Jerome Robbins (concept, direction, choreography), Arthur Laurents (book), Leonard Bernstein (music), and Stephen Sondheim (lyrics). This modern retelling of the *Romeo and Juliet* story debuted on Broadway in 1957. Larry Kert and Carol Lawrence sing the leads magnificently. Bernstein's instrumental ballet music for this show is probably as familiar as its many standout songs: "Maria," "Tonight," "I Feel Pretty," and "Somewhere," among others. — *Marjorie Ellen Ruhlmann*

The Who's Tommy / 1993 / RCA Victor 68174
The Broadway cast album of *Tommy* (called *The Who's Tommy* presumably to alert Who fans that this really is the stage version of the group's 1969 "rock opera" and not some unrelated Tommy) is the best recording of Peter Townshend's song cycle since the Who did the original. Beatles producer George Martin was in the recording booth, and a stellar cast led by Michael Cerveris sings fervently. That's the good news. The bad news is that Townshend has radically re-thought his ideas in 24 years, and rewritten nine songs to reflect his many changes of heart. Artists rarely improve their work by changing it years later, though they frequently succumb to the temptation, and anyone familiar with the original who tries to sing along to this album is in for a rude surprise. The Broadway *Tommy* has been secularized and domesticated; no longer a messiah, he now longs for normality. It's too bad that Townshend didn't have the wisdom to bring Tommy to the stage intact. (*The Who's Tommy* tied for the 1993 Tony Award for Best Score.) — *William Ruhlmann*

○ **The Will Rogers Follies**—Original Cast / 1991 / CBS 48606
This original Broadway cast recording of the musical by Cy Coleman, Betty Comden, and Adolph Green, (book by Peter Stone), tells the story of the humorist and Ziegfeld Follies star—"a life in revue." Directed and choreographed by Tommy Tune, it won the 1991 Tony Award for Best Musical. On disc, the show's charm comes across, especially when star Keith Carradine is before a microphone. — *William Ruhlmann*

○ **Wonderful Town**—Original Broadway Cast / 1953 / MCA 10050
Leonard Bernstein brings a typical sense of invention and musical ambition to this score, and Betty Comden and Adolph Green their usual street-smart New York lyrics, for a show based on the play *My Sister Eileen* about two siblings struggling in Greenwich Village in the '30s. Rosalind Russell leads a strong cast. — *William Ruhlmann*

☆ **Words & Music** / CBS 47711
An all-star (or nearly so) tribute to Rodgers and Hart, and worthwhile for the Judy Garland and Mel Torme numbers. — *Bruce Eder*

○ **Zorba**—Original Broadway Cast / 1968 / Capitol 92053
John Kander and Fred Ebb's score to this musical adaptation of *Zorba the Greek* was less accomplished than their last show, *Cabaret*, and clearly under the influence of *Fiddler on the Roof*, but it is performed in a spirited manner by a cast led by Herschel Bernardi and Maria Karnilova. — *William Ruhlmann*

CHILDREN'S

If children's music can be defined as musically amplifying thoughts, ideas, and concepts in young minds (minds that are themselves expanding at a great rate) then the first children's music may have been the initial fetal sounds heard by the first well-developed human womb-dweller. Perhaps a mother's sonorous voice. Certainly a mother's heartbeat.

Since then, music for children (and indeed families) has developed right along with the rest of the human condition. But what, you may rightly ask, makes some of this music more worthy than the rest? How does one decide what to expose a child to (and yourself – over and over again) and what to leave alone?

There seem to be many answers to that question – almost as many as there are people to answer. Here, however, are some general thoughts that seem to recur as criteria to use in selecting music and related products for children:

1. Try to find age-appropriate music for your child. The 2-year-old and the 4-year-old are ships passing in the night, so different are they in the cumulative milestones of child development.

2. As a general rule, steer clear of the grossly exploitive. Though children's music has come a long, long way, there are still marketers whose sole thought is to get in quick, exploit at all costs, and get out. This product will almost always be evident to the individual caregiver if he/she simply looks and listens. Sometimes, purely exploitive music is the kids' market "flavor of the month" and will be asked for in plain terms by a child. If for no other reason, it seems worth resisting because of the aural torture you, the caregiver, can save yourself.

3. Under no circumstances purchase a recording that "looks down its nose" at children. Kids know it instantly and they'll turn off. There is no subject too sophisticated for a child to grasp on some level. Challenge the children a little. They'll love it.

4. The great children's music, that which will last and grow, is almost always that which has some appeal to big people as well as little people. "Clever" is a good key word here. So is "melody." So is "non-cutesy."

5. If you can help it, don't buy purely by price. The budget stuff may be good, but it also may be garbage.

6. If you're not sure about an artist or a recording, don't assume the record store clerk knows any more than you do. He or she may know (especially if it's a small, owner-operated retailer) about the world of children's music, but odds aren't good. If possible, listen to some of the music yourself. Make your own judgments. Awards won by particular recordings (*Parent's* Choice, American Library Association, Notable Recording, etc.) will pretty much guarantee the recording isn't junk, but unfortunately it is no guarantee beyond that.

7. Go with your children to concerts and other events that expose them and you to children's music. You'll find out fast what they really like.

8. Make a commitment to use music to expand your children, not simply to placate; to teach, not just babysit; to be proactive, not to create mini-couch potatoes. This requires some forethought and the use of suggestions 1-7, but if you're truly into parenting, the rewards outweigh the effort a thousandfold.

9. Don't get discouraged. You'll find the right recording.

10. It's OK to admit you really like this music too.

That brings us to the listings. We've tried to be as inclusive as possible, but the children's audio field is growing so rapidly right now that I apologize in advance for any omissions. We'll get you next time. Many of the artists putting out the best audio are not nationally known or released. To that end, we've done the best we could to provide a list of sources at the chapter's end to allow access by the reader to all the music we've run into. A few artists have not been reachable, but we've given all the information we had.

The video section is incomplete. Some video releasing companies didn't respond to our questionnaire, some did so partially. Further, much children's video is not essentially musical. We used our best judgment. Again, the second edition will exhibit a higher percentage of the total.

Finally, childhood and parenthood will be made richer, more texturally varied, and – last but not least – more fun if a dose of children's and family music is added. The big people and little people will know each other better, and both will benefit from the knowing.

Our overall goal is to make "totally adult" an obsolete concept.

– Bob Hinkle

● **A-Z Alphabet Animal** / Perfect Score Song Music 01
There are many animal alphabet recordings. This is one of the very best. Ages 4-7. —*Bob Hinkle*

☆ **Abel's Island** / Random House 394-89870
Great story. The art is wonderful and the narration is quirky and appealing. Children's Circle is the originating company of this tape. Their stuff is generally very high quality—you can't easily go wrong. —*Bob Hinkle*

Abracadabra / Educational Graphics 621
For ages 3-8. —*Bob Hinkle*

Addition Facts from 1—12 / Uncle Wilton 002

Singing and Rapping the Addition Facts from 1-12 is for ages 5-10. —*Bob Hinkle*

○ **Adoption Adventure** / Adoptive Parents Educ. 1

This unique collection of songs about adoption explores the feelings and perspectives of all members of the adoption triad: birthparents, adoptive parents, and adoptee. Several of the participants in this project are adoptees, others adoptive parents; the material deals with subjects like self-esteem, searches and reunions with birthparents, adopting a child from another land, loss and separation as well as love and happiness. Very well done, enlightening, entertaining. Recommended for educators, caseworkers, all triad members, relatives, and general listenership, young and adult both. —*Ladyslipper*

○ **Aesop's Fables: Book One; Book Two** / Audio Image
A pleasure to listen to, these stories, each approximately ten minutes in length, are presented by capable actors. —*Janet Schnol*

○ **African American Folk Rhythms** / Smithsonian/Folkways 45003
Ella Jenkins and the Goodwill Spiritual Choir of Chicago celebrate the musical heritage of African Americans. These simple work songs, rhythmic chants, and inspiring spirituals express suffering, warm humor, and aspirations for freedom and equality. Percussion instruments and hand clapping accompany the songs. "A fine contribution" —*Roundup newsletter*

☆ **African Songs & Rhythms for Children** / 1988 / Smithsonian/Folkways 45011
Properly set up by parent or caregiver, these can be exciting as well as eye-opening. It's music every child, regardless of culture, should know something about. Ages 4-10. —*Bob Hinkle*

☆ **Alerta Sings** / 1992 / Smithsonian/Folkways 45012
With this collection of songs in Spanish and English, Suni Paz and her friends from Alerta provide a fun way to teach children about Latin America, the Caribbean and Hispanic culture. —*Roundup Newsletter*

☆ **Alice in Wonderland—Story/Songs** / Disney 60214
This classic belongs in your collection. Boys and girls 3-6. —*Bob Hinkle*

☆ **All for Freedom** / 1989 / Music For Little People 42505
This is technically a children's album, but will inspire and be enjoyed by adults and children alike. Drawing on their rich heritage of African musical traditions, Sweet Honey has put together this dynamic and empowering collection of African songs, African stories, and gospel songs, including "Calypso Freedom," "Kumbaya," "Juba," "The Little Shekere," and title. —*Ladyslipper*

All of Us Will Shine / 1987 / Music For Little People 201
For ages 3-7. —*Bob Hinkle*

○ **Alphabet Album** / Golden Music 4107
There are better alphabet recordings, but this one has those lovable characters. Ages 3-6. —*Bob Hinkle*

○ **American Children** / Alcazar 1002
Alcazar's album features Richie Havens, Taj Mahal, Rick Danko and Dave Van Ronk. —*Janet Schnol*

American Folk For Children / 1954 / Smithsonian/Folkways 7601
American Folk Songs for Children is for ages 3-7. —*Bob Hinkle*

○ **American Folk Songs for Children** / Smithsonian/Folkways 11543-44
For ages 3-7. —*Bob Hinkle*

○ **American Industrial Ballads** / 1957 / Smithsonian/Folkways 40058
This colection demonstrates Pete Seeger's interest in and respect for workers of all stripes. A wonderful record. —*Richard Meyer*

○ **Anansi** / Rhino 70417
Adapted by Brian Gleeson, illustrated by Steven Guarnaccia, read by Denzel Washington. An addition to the *We All Have Tales* series. As on all Rabbit Ears audio cassettes, side two carries the score without narration—this one is a gem. Music by UB40. —*Janet Schnol*

And Tigger Too /
For ages 2-6. —*Bob Hinkle*

☆ **And the Honey Tree** / Disney 60229
Here is Pooh at his best. Recommended. I think these stories should live on and on. Ages 2-6. —*Bob Hinkle*

☆ **Animal Express TV Series** / 1991 / MCA 10290
Shelly Duvall is a staple in a good collection of children's recordings. Ages 3-5. —*Bob Hinkle*

○ **Animal Tales** / 1993 / Lightyear 75191
Cheers to Shontz's first solo effort. (He is half of the duo Rosenshontz.) Sure to have great audience appeal, there are no simplistic kiddie songs in this top notch production. —*Janet Schnol*

● **Anthology of African American Poetry for Young People, Read by Arna Bontemps** / Smithsonian/Folkways 45044

A major part of the African American contribution to American Literature has been lyrical verse. Selected and read by Arna Bontemps, the poems in this recording deal with washing dishes, rainy days, an incident on the streets of Baltimore—in short, the details of everyday life. This anthology includes works by some of the outstanding poets of the twentieth century, including Sterling Brown, Countee Cullen, Langston Hughes, Georgia Douglas Johnson and the Reflections, Johnson and Claude McKay. —*Roundup Newsletter*

○ **Are You Afraid of the Dark II** /
Book and cassette by Ned Kandel and D.J. McHale. —*Janet Schnol*

Ariel & the Secret Grotto / Disney 60234
For ages 3-5. —*Bob Hinkle*

☆ **The Aristocats—Story/Songs (Read-Along Book & Tape)** / Disney 60219
One of the better story soundtracks in Disney's catalog for ages 3-6. —*Bob Hinkle*

☆ **Arlo Guthrie: Baby's Storytime** / Lightyear 022448
Arlo's understated narration and music make these classic stories easy to listen to. —*Bob Hinkle*

Around the Campfire / Price Stern Sloan 0742
For ages 2-4. —*Bob Hinkle*

Australia / Price Stern Sloan
For ages 2-4. —*Bob Hinkle*

Australian Animal Songs / ABC 836054
For ages 4-8. —*Bob Hinkle*

○ **Baby Beluga** / 1980 / Shoreline 10036
This is probably the world's most popular whale. This record is a delight. Ages 3-8. —*Bob Hinkle*

☆ **Baby Songs (W/ Hap Palmer)** / Media Home Entertainment 0015
Hap Palmer's famous series. Much positive interaction between the children and parents means a real "feel good" series. —*Bob Hinkle*

☆ **Baby's Bedtime** / Lightyear 5102
Judy Collins sings 17 best-loved lullabies, to animation by Sesame Street animator Dan Ivanick; based on the book by Kay Chorao. Includes "Hush Little Baby," "The Land of Nod," "Lullaby and Good Night," and other childhood classics. Ages infant to 5. —*Ladyslipper*

○ **Baby's Morningtime** / Lightyear 5104
Judy's voice is the main good point with both of these—but that's a very good point. Ages 2-3. —*Bob Hinkle*

○ **Baby's Nursery Rhymes** / Lightyear 5107
Cosby's TV wife does synth-backed nursery rhymes—a lot of them. I love Ms. Rashad's voice, but that is where this album stops. Ages 1-3. —*Bob Hinkle*

Babysongs / High Top 0015
For ages 1-3. —*Bob Hinkle*

Babysongs Presents Baby Rock / M 022733
For ages 2-5. —*Bob Hinkle*

Balloon-Alloon-Aloon / 1987 / Sony Kids' Music 52881
Fish, crows, monkeys, and less familiar folk, such as "The Woolly Booger" and "The Thing That Isn't There," populate Tom Paxton's second delightful collection of children's music, part of a series called "the kid stuff tapes." (78 Park Place, East Hampton, New York 11937.) —*William Ruhlmann*

☆ **Bambi—Story/Songs (Read-Along Book & Tape)** / 1990 / Disney 60205
Bambi is virtually a metaphor for some of the fears and joys of childhood. A must, for 4- to 6-year-olds especially. A classic. Should be seen and heard by every child. Ages 3-10. —*Bob Hinkle*

○ **Songs for the Earth** / Music For Little People
Environmentally correct silliness plus great bluegrass music, especially for 5- to 6-year-olds. —*Bob Hinkle*

Adventures ... / Music For Little People 2159
Adventures on the Air Cycle. For ages 5-7. —*Bob Hinkle*

Slugs at Sea / Music For Little People 2141
As one of the finest musical groups in the ecology category, The Banana Slug String Band's nature songs are not pedantic or

preachy. This latest album uses classic rock, pop, funk, and blues. The group's other albums, *Adventure on the Air Cycle* and *Dirt Made My Lunch*, are also fun, well informed and performed with flair. —*Janet Schnol*

○ **Bananas in His Eyebrows** / Banana 4822
For ages 3-6. —*Bob Hinkle*

☆ **Beauty & the Beast: Story and Songs** / Disney 60970
The Disney classic. Ages 3-6. —*Bob Hinkle*

○ **Beethoven Lives Upstairs** / 1990 / Children's Group 4200
This is the best of the series by far. A classic. Ages 3-10+. —*Bob Hinkle*

Belly Button / 1982 / Children's Group 023
Rated the top children's album in 1983 by the CBC\Canada's National Radio Network, this is assuredly one of the more delightful kids' LP's around. Some great rock, country, and good-time instrumentation. Heather produced and mixed. —*Ladyslipper*

Bert & Ernie: Side by Side / Golden 4104
Sesame Street products are generally kid-friendly (this one too) and educationally worthy. The production is a bit behind the times but the voices are familiar. This is particularly good. Ages 3-6. —*Bob Hinkle*

☆ **The Best of Burl's for Boys and Girls** / 1982 / MCA 98
The voice has been singing folksy songs to all ages for three generations. It's not modern and not well produced or flashy, but it still works after all this time. Ages 2-6. —*Bob Hinkle*

The Best of Ernie / Golden 4102
If you like Ernie, you'll like this. Ages 3-5. —*Bob Hinkle*

★ **The Best of Sesame Street** / Golden Entertainment 4105
Exactly what it implies, a compilation. It's quite good. For ages 3-6. —*Bob Hinkle*

☆ **Best of the Baby Sitters** / 1959 / Vanguard 6001
Lee Hays (a former Weaver) and then-future acting star Alan Arkin led this folk quartet, whose music is a kind of children's version of the Weavers. They play originals, Woody Guthrie songs, and traditional material for an audience ideally aged from 1-5. —*William Ruhlmann*

○ **Bethie's Really Silly Songs About Animals** / Discovery/BMG
Another high caliber production from Discovery. —*Janet Schnol*

Bible Songs / Price Stern Sloan 1780
For ages 2-4. —*Bob Hinkle*

○ **Big Big World** / A&M 73
Harley is an award-winning performer and NPR commentator. —*Janet Schnol*

○ **Big Ideas** / Fragile Glass 0010
As one of the few Asian-American singers and writers for children and families, Patricia Shih has made a very strong recording. One flaw—the production isn't up to the songs or vocals. Otherwise, this is a "voice" that should be heard. "Color Song" and "Eating Is Fun ..." are worth the cost all by themselves. Ages 4-7. —*Bob Hinkle*

Birds, Beasts, & Bigger Fishes & Foolish Frog / 1955 / Smithsonian/Folkways 7611
For ages 3-7. —*Bob Hinkle*

○ **Birds, Beasts, Bugs & Little Fishes** / 1955 / Smithsonian/Folkways 7610
These two recordings, *Birds Beasts Bugs & Little Fish* and *Birds Beasts Bugs & Bigger Fish* are the heart of what Pete Seeger has to say to children. They still work—especially for younger ones. For ages 3-7. —*Bob Hinkle*

A Blustery Day / Disney 60230
For ages 2-6. —*Bob Hinkle*

○ **Bob McGrath's Favorite Street Songs** / A&M 414
Bob from Sesame Street sings well-arranged, well-orchestrated, and well-produced songs. His positive approach, gentle manner, and "rose-colored glasses" style make one tend to forget his vocal weaknesses. Ages 3-6. —*Bob Hinkle*

● **Boomer Esiason—Story and Songs** / Disney 60535
One of three "audio all-stars". The voice is surprisingly good. The stories are OK. This is for older children, ages 6-10. —*Bob Hinkle*

○ **The Boy Who Drew Cats** / Rabbit Ears 10262
Narrated by William Hurt, music by Mark Isham. —*AMG*

○ **Bremen Town Musicians** / AMME 109
For ages 3-7. —*Bob Hinkle*

○ **Brer Rabbit & the Wonderful** / 1989 / Windham Hill 0716
Truly wonderful. I recommend it. Ages 3-8. —*Bob Hinkle*

○ **Can You Sound Just Like Me?** / 1987 / Children's Group 4203
For very young children. Gets them participating. This one's a good addition to a collection. Ages 2-5. —*Bob Hinkle*

Canciones Para El Recreo / 1973 / Smithsonian/Folkways 45013
For ages 4-8. —*Bob Hinkle*

Captured Live ... / 1978 / Rainbow Morning 7
Captured Live and in the Act is for ages 4-5. —*Bob Hinkle*

○ **Car Songs** / Kimbo 9119
For ages 2-4. —*Bob Hinkle*

Care Bears Sing-A-Long / Care Bear 004
For ages 2-4. —*Bob Hinkle*

Carmen Sandiego: Out of This World / 1994 / Zoom Express
This is the soundtrack to a computer game that, in turn, is based on the children's television series "Where In The World Is Carmen Sandiego?" Be that as it may, it consists largely of songs by Greg Lee, plus selections by Rockapella, XTC, and They Might Be Giants (who explain the sun), and much of its is appealing pop-rock music. —*William Ruhlmann*

☆ **Chanukah at Home** / Rounder 8017
A joyful celebration in song, featuring some of the West Coast's top children's performers. The combination of traditional Jewish and Yiddish material with many new songs yields an album that is fun and instructional for kids of all ages. —*Roundup newsletter*

○ **Charles the Clown** / 1990 / A&M 1500
For ages 2-4. —*Bob Hinkle*

○ **1-2-3 for Kids** / 1990 / Red House 33
This is a really good and musical album. Recommended. For ages 3-7. —*Bob Hinkle*

○ **Child to Child (Lullabies/New Age)** / Projazz 730
Don't just buy this for kids! Yes, you can make a great gift for a child with this... but these gorgeous classical guitar renditions of such sweet tender melodies deserves to be heard and savored by us oldsters too (insomniacs and all)! —*Ladyslipper*

○ **A Child's Christmas** / 1992 / Sony Kids' Music 52774
Tom Paxton proves that clever lyrics deftly sung are not ever lost on children. Ages 3-8. —*Bob Hinkle*

☆ **A Child's Gift of Lullabyes** / JAB
A beautiful record for very young children, including lullabies with vocals on side one and singalongs without vocals on the second side. A Grammy Award winner. Ages 2-4. —*Bob Hinkle*

○ **A Child's Happy Birthday** / Big 001
Longtime folkie Bob Gibson gives us a gentle record for younger kids (3-5) to celebrate with. A nice birthday present. —*Bob Hinkle*

○ **Children of the Morning** / 1922 / Children's Group 1024
One of Canada's new contributions to children, providing gentle music with a positive outlook. Ages 3-8. —*Bob Hinkle*

○ **Children of the World: Rhythmic Activities** / Kimbo 9123
For ages 2-4. —*Bob Hinkle*

○ **Children's All-Time Favorite Dances** / Kimbo 9126
For ages 2-4. —*Bob Hinkle*

○ **Children's Favorite Silly Songs** / Disney 2528
For ages 2-5. —*Bob Hinkle*

Children's Favorites 3 / Disney 60606
For ages 3-5. —*Bob Hinkle*

Children's Favorites 4 / Disney 60608
For ages 3-5. —*Bob Hinkle*

Children's Favorites 2 / Disney 60605
For ages 3-5. —*Bob Hinkle*

○ **Children's Games** / Kimbo 9068
For ages 2-4. —*Bob Hinkle*

The Children's Musical Companion / SAN 1012
For ages 3-7. —*Bob Hinkle*

○ **Children's Record** / Red Rover 222

Chicago's teacher extraordinaire gives us two diverse and wonderful recordings, especially "Daddy Plays Drums." For ages 4-8. —*Bob Hinkle*

Chipmunk Punk / 1980 / Excelsior 6008
Alvin, Simon, and Theodore enter the current pop mainstream. Covers of Billy Joel, Tom Petty, Blondie, and more. Ages 2-5. —*Larry Lapka*

The Chipmunk Songbook / 1973 / Pair 1124
For ages 2-4. —*Bob Hinkle*

The Chipmunks Sing the Beatles Hits / 1964 / Liberty 48379
The best Fab Four parody of all. Ages 2-5. —*Larry Lapka*

★ **Chopsticks** / Zoom Express 416
The best Combe, especially the title track. Ages 2-10. —*Bob Hinkle*

Circle Around / 1983 / Music For Little People 214
For ages 3-5. —*Bob Hinkle*

○ **Circle Time** / Music For Little People 215
Thirty-four favorites presented by Lisa Monet with her sweet voice and lush harmonies leading the way, all aimed at ages 1-5. These are songs that we all know, ready to be introduced to a new generation of music lovers. Family sing-alongs are a sure thing with songs like "Itsy, Bitsy Spider," "Little Teapot," and the immortal "Fuzzy Wuzzy!" —*Backroads Music/Heartbeats*

○ **Citizens of the World** / Seatofourpants Prod. 2
A good recording with uneven production. Seona McDowell has a good touch for kids and teaches some big ideas well. Ages 3-6. —*Bob Hinkle*

Classic Children's Tales / 1989 / Rounder 8015
Jackie Torrence's stories bring her characters absolutely to life. Her delivery usually gets the attention of even the most rambunctious kid. Some of her tales capture the African-American oral tradition as well as any. Ages 4-10. —*Bob Hinkle*

Classic Nursery Rhymes / 1989 / North Star
If you enjoy traditional music, this is for you. Among the instruments played by the Hubbards on *Olde Mother Goose* are recorders, hurdy-gurdies, bagpipes, washboards, flutes, viol, harp bassoon, and cornet. My 4-year-old and 6-year-old boys give it two thumbs up. They could not stop dancing. —*Chip Renner*

★ **The Collection** / Children's Group 84207
Without question, the best way to introduce young children to the major classical composers and their music. Adults learn a lot too. Ages 3-10+. —*Bob Hinkle*

○ **Collections** / Oak Street/Dino Music 19180
This one's better. —*Bob Hinkle*

○ **Color Me Wild—Inside Your Own Mind You Are Perfectly Free** / 1990 / Alcazar 1003
Rory Block has a wonderful sense of communication with children, particularly mid-childhood. Ages 4-5. —*Bob Hinkle*

Come Dance by the Ocean / 1991 / Smithsonian/Folkways 45014
This 1991 summer release is a wonderful collection of songs about caring for the environment and enjoying other cultures, languages and places, from one of the foremost child educators. Ella Jenkins remarks that the ocean symbolizes life, that its characteristics are vitality, energy, contrast and change, and that it resembles children at play. Includes "A Solution to Pollution," "A Humpback Whale," "Environment Game," and "You Can't Sink a Rainbow." —*Ladyslipper*

Come on Out & Play / Red Rover 107
Ages 3-8. —*Bob Hinkle*

Comin' to Your Town / 1992 / Zoom Express 35015
These recordings sound like the Mamas and the Papas of children's music. Rich harmonies, well-produced and well-written songs, and expressive voice. Ages 3-9. —*Bob Hinkle*

Cool in School / 1987 / Round River 104
Cool in School—Tales from the Sixth Grade is for ages 6-10. —*Bob Hinkle*

○ **Corner Grocery Store ...** / 1979 / Shoreline 10041
Raffi is something of an heir to the children's music of such folkies as Pete Seeger and the Babysitters. In *Corner Grocery Store and Other Singable Songs*, he is especially interested in adapting some familiar folksongs—"Pick a Bale o' Cotton," "Goodnight Irene"—as children's songs, along with such tradi-

tional material as "Frere Jacques." He has a light, bouncy singing style that is irresistible to children and parents alike. Ages 3-7. —*William Ruhlmann*

○ **Cowboy Album** / Kid Rhino
Cassette in hangable plastic case; 65-3 norelco; 79-3 CD. —*Janet Schnol*

○ **Cowboy Animals Dance Time Jubilee** / Newport Kids Audio
Perfect for car trips and at home ho-downs. High quality production and first rate musicians combined with silly, yet clever lyrics make this tape a sure fire favorite for young cowpokes and their caregivers. —*Janet Schnol*

○ **Cowboy Critter Campfire Tales** / Newport Kids
This is an original collection of songs and stories based on the old West. —*Janet Schnol*

Creatures of Summer / Zoom Express 35003
While Creatures of Summer Sleep includes stories and songs that are also for very young children. Ages 2-4. —*Bob Hinkle*

○ **Crocodile Smile: 10 Songs of the Earth as the Animals See It** / HarperCollins/Geringer
Sarah Weeks, illustrated by Lois Ehlert, produced and arranged by Michael Abbott. HarperCollins/Geringer. —*Janet Schnol*

○ **Curious George** / Houghton Mifflin
H.A. Rey's fifty year old favorite is now available as a kid-friendly book and cassette. —*Janet Schnol*

☆ **Dancin' Magic** / 1991 / Discovery 4408
Rock 'n' roll from the'50s and '60s is interspersed with more topical songs, as well as old "chestnuts," as sung by Joanie Bartels, sound just right alongside tunes like "Happy Feet," "The Polkadot Polka" and "Hokey Pokey." Delightful versions of "La Bamba," "The Peppermint Twist," "Rockin' Robin" and "Loco-Motion" not only make for great listening but introduce today's youth to a truly great era of music. Closing out the tape is the soon-to-be classic "Dinosaur Rock 'n' Roll," bound for heavy airplay on kid's charts. —*Backroads Music/Heartbeats*

○ **Daring Dewey** / 1992 / Song Wizard 102
Consistent songs, same great voice. Ages 3-6. —*Bob Hinkle*

A Day for Eeyore / Disney 60232
For ages 2-6. —*Bob Hinkle*

○ **Dear Mr. Johnstone** / Dandelion 7248
For ages 3-7. —*Bob Hinkle*

Deep in the Jungle / Educational Graphics 913
For ages 3-8. —*Bob Hinkle*

○ **Dennis Sings Again** / 1921 / Berner
Hard recordings to find, but quite good for ages 3-6. —*Bob Hinkle*

○ **The Dinosaur & More** / Beanstalk 111
Excellent writing in various musical styles. Very good voices and good blend. Recommended. Ages 3-6. —*Bob Hinkle*

Dinosaur Ride / 1981 / Rainbow Planet 3104
Jim Valley cowrites most of his songs with children, giving the songs a particular kind of energy and thrust. Each title is remarkably consistent as well as imaginative. *Dinosaur Ride* is a good place to start. For ages 3-7. —*Bob Hinkle*

○ **Dinosaur Rock** / 1983 / Caedmon 1739
For ages 3-8. —*Bob Hinkle*

Dinosaurs / Price Stern Sloan
"The Monsters Emerge," "Flesh on the Bones," "The Nature of the Beast," "The Death of the Dinosaur" PBS's excellent, high-quality documentary is as engrossing as it is informative. —*Janet Schnol*

Dinosaurs Never Say Please / 1987 / Round River 103
For ages 4-9. —*Bob Hinkle*

Dinosaurs, Dragons & Other Children's Songs / 1992 / Sony Kids' Music 52811
For ages 3-5. —*Bob Hinkle*

Dirt Made My Lunch / Music For Little People 2171
For ages 4-7. —*Bob Hinkle*

Disney Children's Favorites 2 / Disney 60601
For ages 2-5. —*Bob Hinkle*

Disney Children's Favorites 3 / Disneyland 60607
For ages 2-5. —*Bob Hinkle*

Disney Collection—Best Loved Songs #2 / Disney 60817
For ages 2-5. —*Bob Hinkle*

Disney Collection—Best Loved Songs #3 / Disney 60818
For ages 2-5. —*Bob Hinkle*

Disney Collection—Best Loved Songs #1 / Disney 60816
Of these three collections, I like #1 best, just for the integrity of the sequencing, song selection, and such. Chestnuts abound. Ages 3-7. —*Bob Hinkle*

○ **Disney Songs the Satchmo Way** / Mar. 1968 / Disney 6
Only Louis Armstrong could turn songs like "Heigh Ho," "Bibbidi-Bobbidi-Boo" and "The Bare Necessities" into worthwhile jazz. The matchup of Armstrong with Walt Disney tunes is quite logical and an unexpected success. This CD will appeal to tolerant jazz fans and children alike. —*Scott Yanow*

Division Facts from 1-12 / Uncle Wilton 004
Singing and Rapping the Division Facts from 1-12 is for ages 5-10. —*Bob Hinkle*

○ **Dr. Seuss—the Shape of Me & Others** / Random House 679-81031-5
The books are better but these are fun. —*Bob Hinkle*

○ **Doug & Garry** / Surf Productions VO 1
This live concert for families, *Doug & Garry—Adventures of the Happy Pirates*, has much to recommend it. It's silly, musical, very interactive, but most of all, it's fun. If big people can get past Gary's role as an oversized eight-year-old, they'll like it too. —*Bob Hinkle*

○ **Doughey, the Pancake Man** / Mole End 001
One terrific pancake. He takes kids away to fight pirates, with butter and syrup dripping from his rounded self. Ages 3-7. —*Bob Hinkle*

○ **Down by Bendy's Lane: Irish Songs & Stories For...** / Green Linnet 1085
A delightful children's album featuring songs and stories Sands has picked up since childhood. "The Boy with No Story" will have you on the edge of your seat. "Moya Is My Darling," about his daughter, is priceless. Even an adult can enjoy this one. —*Chip Renner*

○ **Dream Catcher** / Music For Little People/Earth
Locke offers evocative flute music, sound effects, for instance rain, crickets, and birds, and a few vocals. —*Janet Schnol*

○ **Dreams and Illusions** / Rounder 8019
Dreams and Illusions—Tales of the Pacific Rim has good artistic potential, largely unrealized. Ages 2-5. —*Bob Hinkle*

○ **Drumming up Business** / Disney 60235
For ages 3-5. —*Bob Hinkle*

○ **A Duck in New York City** / Children's Group 027
Winner of the Gold Parents' Choice Award, and following in the tradition of "Bellybutton" and "Purple People Eater," Heather Bishop's third children's album is much more than a collection of songs—it's the story of the adventures of a country duck in the big city. From a chance meeting with a robot on the street to playing a guitar solo with the Slug Opera, Heather's whimsical fantasy abounds—funny and touching in turns. —*Ladyslipper*

○ **Dulcimer Lullabies** / Dargason 111
Featuring Joemy Wilson on hammered dulcimer with her usual ensemble of Celtic harp, guitar, violin and flute, this all-instrumental 1991 collection of lullaby favorites ("Brahms' Lullaby," "All Through the Night," "Hushabye") as well as some less familiar quiet-time gems from several countries is bound to be a favorite of adults as well as kids! —*Ladyslipper*

○ **Dumbo—Story and Songs (Read-Along Book & Tape)** / Disney 60201
Much-loved music—especially "When I See an Elephant Fly," which is one of the great 3- to 7-year-old mind-stretcher word-game songs. —*Bob Hinkle*

○ **Early Ears Zero** / 1921 / Zoom Express 35005
This series is a way to put music for a particular age (0-6) in the hands of children of that age. The titles are self-explanatory. This is a personal favorite—especially since I created it! *Zero* is for pregnant moms and dads and for infants under 12 months. *One* is still somewhat for parents and for infants 12-23 months and so on, up to *Six* for first graders. The series is based loosely on the milestones in child development occurring during each year of childhood up to six. *Zero* is very soft and a bit ethereal; beautiful music and sentiments. It contains one of the most beautiful pieces ever written for kids: "Mother and Child Suite for Horn

and Harp," by composer Paul Riggio. Also toe-counting, first steps, and loving. —*Bob Hinkle*

○ **Early Ears One** / 1922 / Zoom Express 35006
Low-key, this has some activity. Age 1. —*Bob Hinkle*

○ **Early Ears Two** / 1923 / Zoom Express 35007
Two-year-olds are active, establishing their separate identities. The recording is more upbeat, with more songs directed at the child: toddling, puddle-jumping, learning colors in Spanish, feeling happy. Age 2. —*Bob Hinkle*

○ **Early Ears Three** / 1924 / Zoom Express 35008
More active than earlier ones, speaking more directly to the children. More cleverness: giving up "blankie," skating on the moon, playing double kazoo, going on safari, and hugging. Age 3. —*Bob Hinkle*

○ **Early Ears Four** / 1925 / Zoom Express 35009
Extremely active. Participation abounds. Very clever; funny and silly too. Singing dog duets, dancing, getting the best of the bogeyman, learning space words, making friends, fooling parents. Age 4. —*Bob Hinkle*

○ **Early Ears Five** / 1926 / Zoom Express 35010
A bit more sophisticated than some in this series. It includes a fair amount about friends and socialization, with songs that include a still-active school bus as monster, wishing to fly, a grandpa song, best friends, and a rock & roll dog. Age 5. —*Bob Hinkle*

○ **Early Ears Six** / 1927 / Zoom Express 35011
The most sophisticated. Becoming aware of the opposite sex, food song ("Fish is Delish"), brotherhood (in the larger sense), one-person-can-make-a-difference song, reggae song. Upbeat, happy, and thoughtful. Age 6. —*Bob Hinkle*

○ **East of the Sun, West of the Moon** / Rhino 70419
For ages 4-8. —*Bob Hinkle*

○ **Easter Egg Mornin'** / Rincon Children's Entertainment70427
This series is positive for younger children 3 to 6. It's a little cutesy, though. —*Bob Hinkle*

☆ **Eight Days of Hanukah** / High Top 362
Wonderful songs written by George David Weiss. He is a masterful writer. All kids' voices, and a fun way to learn about the Maccabees, etc. Recommended. Ages 4-10. —*Bob Hinkle*

Elephant Show / Elephant 308
For ages 2-5. —*Bob Hinkle*

Even More Babysongs / Media Home Entertainment 22535
For ages 2-4. —*Bob Hinkle*

Even Trolls Have Moms / Educational Graphics 730
A personal favorite. Ages 3-8. —*Bob Hinkle*

Evergreen Everblue / 1975 / Shoreline 10060
Raffi's first environmental statement. This is not really a children's recording, and apparently Raffi didn't intend it to be. However, since some of the most ferocious recyclers I know are children, and since these kids will inherit our mess, I think older children would benefit from it. Ages 10+. —*Bob Hinkle*

○ **Every Cowboy Needs a Horse** / 2 M 9001
Texas swing for kids by a singer from Western Canada. A great band. Mostly very familiar songs. This is a good door for kids into "Western" music. Ages 4-8. —*Bob Hinkle*

○ **Everybody's Invited** / 1960 / Lovable Creatures 108
This second recording shows development and further promise. A group to watch. Ages 3-8. —*Bob Hinkle*

○ **Everything Grows** / Shoreline 10039
For ages 3-7. —*Bob Hinkle*

○ **Eyes Of The Amaryllis, The** / Live/Family Home Entertainment
The video is based on Babbitt's haunting mystery set in 1880 Nantucket. —*Janet Schnol*

○ **Family Folk Festival** / Music For Little People
With Taj Mahal, Pete Seeger, Doc Watson and Sweet Honey in the Rock. This excellent compilation offers a version of "Puff the Magic Dragon" with a particularly upbeat ending. —*Janet Schnol*

○ **Family Folk Festival** / Music For Little People 2105
Subtitled *A Multi-Cultural Sing-Along*, this anthology includes great old favorites and new tunes by Lillian Allen, Maria Muldaur, Pete Seeger, Claudia Gomez, Taj Mahal, Doc Watson, and John McCutcheon in addition to those listed above, all with

acoustic accompaniment. Includes "The Garden Song," "Little Red Caboose," "Puff the Magic Dragon," and more. —*Ladyslipper*

○ **Family Hug** / Hootentoot 1989
This regionally popular (upper Midwest) group makes recordings with at least two or three wonderful original tunes and some chestnuts. Well produced and well conceived, this is a worthy addition for 3- to 8-year-olds. —*Bob Hinkle*

● **Family Pie** / 1986 / Children's Group 1021
My personal favorite from the Brodeys. Ages 3-7. —*Bob Hinkle*

☆ **Family Tree** / 1988 / Sony Kids' Music 48990
Tom Chapin is one of the most professional and literate children's performers. His recordings, which include "Family Tree" and "Shovlin'," are among the wittiest and most appropriate for children (and big people love them too). Tom's recordings are among the best produced for children. This one is my favorite. Ages 3-10. —*Bob Hinkle & Chip Renner*

★ **Family Vacation** / 1988 / Lightyear 75186
This personifies Rosenshontz. It's well produced, with good songs, and is more adventurous than their other records. If you can only have one Rosenshontz, this is it. Ages 2-8. —*Bob Hinkle*

○ **Favorite Songs for Little People** / Kimbo 10
For ages 2-4. —*Bob Hinkle*

○ **Feathers, Fur or Fins** / ABC 836053
If you want children to know about Australia, this is your guy. Folksy, down under fun, particularly *Australia for Kids* and *Australian Animal Songs*. Ages 4-8. —*Bob Hinkle*

○ **Feel Better Friends** / Golden Music
Bill and Gary are better on audio. —*Bob Hinkle*

○ **Ferngully: The Last Rainforest** / MCA
Available on home video and as a soundtrack album. —*Janet Schnol*

○ **Festival of Light** / Music For Little People 435
For ages 3-6. —*Bob Hinkle*

○ **Fifty Ways to Fool Your Mother** / 1986 / Round River 102
For ages 3-9. —*Bob Hinkle*

A Fish That's a Song / Smithsonian/Folkways 45037
For ages 3-7. —*Bob Hinkle*

○ **Fisher-Price—Little Red Riding Hood** / Media Home Entertainment 22190
Good—but only for very young children. —*Bob Hinkle*

● **Flashbeagle** / Disney 2518
Snoopy music. How can a dog that doesn't talk, bark, or sing get away with making music? The imagination is a wonderful thing. Ages 3-10. —*Bob Hinkle*

○ **Folk Dance Fun** / Kimbo 7037
For ages 2-5. —*Bob Hinkle*

Folk Songs for Young People / 1959 / Smithsonian/Folkways 7532
This cassette-only reissue contains a number of children's favorites such as "Skip to My Lou," "On Top of Old Smokey," "John Henry," "Goodnight Irene," and many others. With complete lyrics, *Folk Songs for Young People* is a children's classic. Originally issued in 1959. — *Roundup Newsletter*

For Our Children / Disney 60616
To benefit the Pediatric AIDS Foundation, several diverse and top-selling talents have created this 1991 compilation. It features songs by: Bette Midler, Carole King, Paula Abdul, Meryl Streep, Ann and Nancy Wilson of Heart, Bob Dylan, Ziggy Marley, Sting, Bruce Springsteen, Elton John, Jackson Browne and Jennifer Warnes, James Taylor, Paul McCartney, Little Richard, and many more. Over an hour of songs we loved as kids ("The Ballad of Davy Crockett," "Itsy Bitsy Spider") as well as new ones, to be enjoyed by folks big and small. —*Ladyslipper*

● **Fred Penner's Place** / Oak Street/Dino Music 0401
This artist is much better than "Fred Penner's Place" would indicate. The TV show would suffocate a lesser artist. Fred is a good singer and player who knows how to communicate with children. I like Fred better than the recording. Ages 3-6. —*Bob Hinkle*

★ **Free to Be You & Me** / 1972 / Arista 8325
A real groundbreaker, this recording caught the fancy of hundreds of thousands well before modern children's music. The values it imparts are still important, particularly in the area of equality of males and females. Ages 3-10. —*Bob Hinkle*

Free to Be a Family / 1988 / A&M 5196
Just a list of the artists who appear on this follow-up to the original *Free To Be* is enough reason to present this to every child you know. Whoopi Goldberg, Lily Tomlin's brilliant Edith Ann, Bea Arthur playing fairy godmother to Gilda Radner's comic Cinderella, Bonnie Raitt singing on "I'm Never Afraid (To Say What's On My Mind)," there's Ladysmith Black Mambazo, Carly Simon, Kermit the Frog and the Muppets, Robin Williams, Mel Brooks, Jane Curtin, Pat Benatar, and the list goes on. A companion piece to the best-selling book by the same name, or all by itself, the songs, stories and poems on this album encourage kids to feel part of the universal family. —*Ladyslipper*

Friendship Train / 1982 / Rainbow Planet 3102
For ages 3-7. —*Bob Hinkle*

Fun-A-Rooey / 1991 / Song Wizard 101
Wonderful voice. The songs are uneven, but the production is good. Worth a second look. Ages 3-6. —*Bob Hinkle*

Fun-n-Folk / Price Stern Sloan
For ages 2-4. —*Bob Hinkle*

G'night Wolfgang / Music For Little People 2108
For ages 4-8. —*Bob Hinkle*

Gift of Story / Three Feathers 101
Good stories for very young children. It's liable to lose anyone above age 6. —*Bob Hinkle*

○ **Girls & Boys Come Out to Play** / 1991 / Music For Little People 2275
This has a wonderful interactive music. Ages 3-7. —*Bob Hinkle*

Goes on Vacation / A&M 408
For ages 3-7. —*Bob Hinkle*

Gold Dog / American Melody 110
For ages 3-6. —*Bob Hinkle*

The Golden Glow / Golden Glow 103
For ages 2-5. —*Bob Hinkle*

Good / 1989 / A&M 409
For ages 3-6. —*Bob Hinkle*

Good Morning / 1987 / Music For Little People 232
Good Morning, Good Night is for ages 2-6. —*Bob Hinkle*

Good Morning Sunshine / Golden Glow 102
For ages 2-5. —*Bob Hinkle*

○ **Good Morning to You** / Virginia Arts 8305
This is one of the finest children's albums this reviewer has heard. Adele Abrahamse's voice is crystal clear and a delight to listen to. The music is a combo of jazz, folk, broadway, and lots more. All songs are original and a few such as "The Dinosaur Song" and "Shoes" make this album a treasure. Includes a 36-page resource book that outlines possible dances and body movements, variations on words, and on one song—seven language translations of a little ditty (the resource book doubles as a coloring book!) There's easily a full afternoon of entertainment here, for even the fussiest child. —*Ladyslipper*

○ **The Good, the Bad and the Two Cookie Kid** / A Better Place
A Better Place's Celebrity Series is a very welcome addition to a genre that is too often the outpost of mediocre product. The other entry in the series uses B.B. King's talents. —*Janet Schnol*

● **Grandma Slid Down the Mountain** / 1984 / Rounder 8010
Cathy Finksings, plays, and produces up a storm. Imaginative songs imparting good general positive values. Ages 4-7. —*Bob Hinkle*

○ **Granny, Will Your Dog Bite?** / Random House 85363-6
For ages 3-5. —*Bob Hinkle*

○ **Great Mouse Detective—Story/Songs (Read-Along Book & Tape)** / Disney 60218
For ages 4-7. —*Bob Hinkle*

○ **Green Album** / 1990 / Disney 17
Various rock bands. Very cute. Listenable for parents as well, at least those into pop music. Ages 3-10. —*Bob Hinkle*

☆ **Growing up Together!** / 1989 / Gemini 1004
Aside from their children-and-family music, identical twins Sandor and Laszlo Slomovitz have recorded twelve albums of international folk dance music for the High/Scope Educational Research Foundation, to teach movement and dance to young children. These well-known singer/songwriters are superb vocal-

ists, and both play a variety of instruments very well. For ages 4-10 and family listening. *Growing Up Together!* received a *Parents Choice Award* and was cited by the American Library Association as a notable children's recording. —*Michael Erlewine*

Grownups Are Strange / Round River 106
Ages 3-8. —*Bob Hinkle*

○ **Gumby Celebration** / Family Home Enter. 22448
I love Gumby, and this stretches the imagination. —*Bob Hinkle*

○ **Halloween Fun** / Kimbo 9113
For ages 2-4. —*Bob Hinkle*

○ **Hans Christian Andersen/Tubby the Tuba** / 1952 / MCA 148
For pre-MTV kids, this is a must. If Hans Christian Andersen had been around in the '50s, he'd have been Danny Kaye. For ages 2-6. —*Bob Hinkle*

☆ **Happy Anniversary, Charlie Brown** / United Media 1
The understated humor, character interaction, and great jazz music make these classics. Adults love them too. Ages 4-9. —*Bob Hinkle*

Happy Birthday / Elephant 0309
For ages 2-5. —*Bob Hinkle*

Harmony Ranch / 1991 / CBS 48589
For ages 3-6. —*Bob Hinkle*

Help Yourself / 1990 / Rounder 8021
A how-to-take-care-of-yourself recording, with Marcy Marxer. I usually find such albums a bit preachy, but this one is much less so. Ages 4-7. —*Bob Hinkle*

○ **Homemade Band** / Random House 58022-5
Hap Palmer is considered by many to be a big figure in children's music. He communicates very well with children and sings directly to them. These recordings have integrity. Ages 3-7. —*Bob Hinkle*

○ **Homemade Games and Activities** / Kimbo 9106
For ages 2-4. —*Bob Hinkle*

○ **Horse Sense for Kids and Other People** / Music For Little People
This offers great roundup and campfire music. —*Janet Schnol*

○ **How the Leopard Got His Spots** / 1989 / Windham Hill 0715
I like this one. With a wonderful story, narration by Danny Glover, and perfect music backing from Ladysmith Black Mambazo, it is one of the few times when the "celebrity" formula actually works well for kids. Ages 3-8. —*Bob Hinkle*

○ **Howjadoo** / 1983 / Rounder 8009
John McCutcheon's first album for kids. Quite good. Ages 3-7. —*Bob Hinkle*

Hug the Earth / 1985 / Music For Little People 236
For ages 3-7. —*Bob Hinkle*

Huggables / Rincon Children's Entertainment 70464
For ages 3-5. —*Bob Hinkle*

○ **Humpty Dumpty** / Bumblebeez 803
For ages 2-4. —*Bob Hinkle*

○ **I Am Who I Am** / 1985 / Zoom Express 35004
Lois LaFonol and her band the Rockadiles (from Colorado) stretch children's imaginations with great music and outstanding vocals. For moms and the very young. Ages 2-5. —*Bob Hinkle*

○ **I Eat Kids (& Other Songs for Rebellious Children)** / 1975 / Rainbow Morning 4347
Barry Louis Polisar is an acquired taste. Parents are generally left out, and Barry sings extremely silly songs to younger children. Parents, on the other hand, do get to watch their children laugh wildly at songs about full diapers, nose picking, and other not-quite-so-graphic subjects. There's no great attempt to educate or stretch a young mind. It's lowest-common-denominator fun. You can tell by the titles that these recordings bear a strong relationship to each other. —*Bob Hinkle*

○ **I Got Shoes** / Music For Little People
Brilliant harmonies abound on the a cappella group's second album for children. —*Janet Schnol*

○ **I Like Dessert** / 1987 / Perfect Score Song Music 02
I Like Dessert is hard to find but well worth the search. David Polansky is a wonderful writer, especially of songs depicting the daily drama of child-parent relationships. Ages 3-8. —*Bob Hinkle*

★ **I Like My Music with a Beat** / 1992 / Zoom Express 35001

Glenn Bennett's latest. The second side has a wonderful piece about an orchestra, which educates kids about orchestras and about life. Excellent. Ages 3-10. —*Bob Hinkle*

○ **I Must Be Growing** / 1992 / Zoom Express 35002
More clever Glenn Bennett songs with good, clever pop arrangements and great vocals. Ages 3-10. —*Bob Hinkle*

I'm Going to Let It Shine / Round River 401
Ages 3-8. —*Bob Hinkle*

I'm Just a Kid / May 19, 1992 / Sony Kids' Music 48696
Adults trying to turn into kids on record make my caution-light come on. This is a very good-sounding production, with a few really good songs ("Bubble Bath Is Even Better"). This would be more believable if the artist would do almost the same thing as more of an adult. There is a spark about this recording that I like. Ages 3-5. —*Bob Hinkle*

I'm a Happy Pirate / Playtime 01
For ages 3-7. —*Bob Hinkle*

● **Imaginary Window** / 1921 / Children's Group 1009
Jack Grunsky's first record. Both listed here are current products, consistently good for ages 3-8. —*Bob Hinkle*

Imagine That / 1982 / Rainbow Planet 3103
For ages 3-7. —*Bob Hinkle*

○ **Imagine That!** / 1992 / Rhino 70474
For ages 3-7. —*Bob Hinkle*

○ **Improvise with Eric Nagler** / 1989 / Rounder 8018
Eric Nagler is a mainstay on Sharon, Lois, and Bram's "Elephant Show." A good singer, good player. Creative and interactive. Ages 3-7. —*Bob Hinkle*

In Harmony / 1980 / Warner Brothers 3481
For ages 3-7. —*Bob Hinkle*

○ **In a Child's Heart** / Golden 4063
For ages 2-6. —*Bob Hinkle*

In the Schoolyard / 1981 / Elephant 302
For ages 3-5. —*Bob Hinkle*

Inch by Inch / Children's Group 1017
For ages 3-6. —*Bob Hinkle*

○ **Isiah Thomas—Story and Songs** / Disney 60534
For ages 6-10. —*Bob Hinkle*

It's the Truth / 1984 / Lightyear 75184
The guys start to go rock & roll. Very good. Ages 3-7. —*Bob Hinkle*

○ **Jack & the Beanstalk** / 1991 / Rhino 70415
For ages 3-7. —*Bob Hinkle*

☆ **Jack & the Beanstalk** / Score 20094
A credible version of the classic. Ages 3-5. —*Bob Hinkle*

○ **Jambo & Other Call & Response Songs & Chants** / 1970 / Smithsonian/Folkways 45017
This beautiful recording of singing and chants is a wonderful means of involving young children in group participation. Ella Jenkins skillfully uses songs and chants in many languages (African, Arabic, and others) to stimulate and entertain children, and in this collection her genius at blending songs, rhythms and chants results in a superb set. Originally issued in 1957; lyrics enclosed. —*Ladyslipper*

Jazz Impressions of a Boy Named Charlie Brown / 1964 / United Media 6
Still the original Charlie Brown good light jazz sound. —*Bob Hinkle*

○ **Joe Montana—Story and Songs** / Disney 60536
For ages 6-10. —*Bob Hinkle*

○ **John Lithgow's Kid-Size Concert** / Media Home Entertainment 22602
Lithgow's warmth of personality and sincere love of children shine through on this minimal production. Ages 3-5. —*Bob Hinkle*

○ **Johnny Appleseed** /
Read by Garrison Keillor, music by Mark O'Connor. —*Janet Schnol*

○ **Joseph the Tailor ...** / Syd Lieberman 103
Joseph the Tailor & Other Jewish Tales. Anyone (young or old) who appreciates the subtleties, twists, turns, and universal humor and pathos in stories will like this one. Ages 5-10. —*Bob Hinkle*

○ **Jubilee!** / 1991 / Boston Skyline 113
To my knowledge, this is the only band for children and families that sounds like the Grateful Dead. Even though the lead vocalist, is clearly a woman, it somehow still reads as Dead-like. Good playing, good songs. Worth having. For ages 3-8. —*Bob Hinkle*

○ **Jump Children** / 1986 / Rounder 8012
Marcy Marxer has a gentle, smart approach to children's music. She's best when concentrating on fun and mind-stretching—like here. For ages 3-6. —*Bob Hinkle*

Jump Tales / Rounder 8020
A jump tale is a tale that makes you jump—it has to have a surprise at the end! On this 1991 release, Jackie presents 5 of her favorite jump tales, about pirates, ghosts and plain everyday people. Two tales are drawn from her family repertoire, complementing a pair of traditional stories and one original. —*Ladyslipper*

○ **Jumpin' in a Puddle** /
For ages 2-5. —*Bob Hinkle*

☆ **The Jungle Book** / 1967 / Disney 60612
A surprisingly crisp 1942 recording of the Miklos Rozsa score, with Sabu narrating. A rich, expressive score. —*Bruce Eder*

Keep the Spirit / Music For Little People 428
For ages 3-6. —*Bob Hinkle*

○ **Keepers of the Earth & Keepers of the Animals** / Fulcrum
Native American storytelling at its finest. Book and cassette. The book offers background information and many activities. —*Janet Schnol*

○ **Kermit Unpigged** / Jim Henson Records
Kermit and the Muppets are joined by Don Henley, Linda Ronstadt, Vince Gill, Jimmy Buffett and others. —*Janet Schnol*

Kiddin' Around / Music For Little People 247
For ages 3-8. —*Bob Hinkle*

○ **Kidding Around** / Youngheart 74772
For ages 4-6. —*Bob Hinkle*

○ **Kids in Motion** / Youngheart 74775
From the same-name video. Good songs. For ages 3-7. —*Bob Hinkle*

○ **Kids of Widney High** / 1989 / Rounder 8014
Kids of Widney High—Special Music from Special Kids is for ages 3-7. —*Bob Hinkle*

☆ **Lady & the Tramp—Story/Songs** / Disney 60213
The story spans generations. Children love it. Ages 3-6. —*Bob Hinkle*

○ **Lamb Chop in the Land of No Manners** / 1991 / A&M 0422
Excellent. Shari Lewis is one of the very few whose act has been universally well presented, consistent, and truly funny. And not just to kids. Lamb Chop frequently says and does things kids see themselves doing or wish they could. Ages 4-10. —*Bob Hinkle*

Late Last Night / Educational Graphics 421
For ages 3-8. —*Bob Hinkle*

○ **Laugh-Along Songs** / Kimbo 8035
Most Kimbo recordings are essentially educational. Not that they're flat or dull—just that their first priority seems to be education, not entertainment. Ages 2-5. —*Bob Hinkle*

Le Hoogie Boogie: Louisiana French Music for Children / 1992 / Rounder 8022
This is a concept whose time has come: Cajun music for children. Both Louisiana French music and children's music have grown in popularity during the past few years, so the merger was inevitable. Vocalist and multi-instrumentalist Michael Doucet, along with some of his friends, family members, and musical allies in the group, Beausoleil, got together to record something special for children. — *Roundup Newsletter*

☆ **The Legend of Sleepy Hollow** / Windham Hill 0711
Though the "celebrity descends from heaven, reads for the kiddies, and leaves" formula is generally not my cup of tea, this is quite good. Ages 5-8. —*Bob Hinkle*

○ **Let Your Inside Out** / Uncle Fred/Pinwheel 602
These songs are terrific. The recordings sound very fresh and clever. Uncle Fred is the Randy Newman of the genre. Ages 3-7. — *Bob Hinkle*

○ **Let's All Sing with the Chipmunks** / 1959 / Liberty 3132

May be out of print, but the TV/music tie-in presented on this album was later used for the Monkees and the Partridge Family. Ages 2-4. —*Larry Lapka*

○ **Let's Go on Safari** / Zoom Express
Glenn Bennett is one of the great treasures of children's entertainment. Clever, funny rock & roll for early and middle childhood. Glenn refuses not to be loved. Ages 3-10. —*Bob Hinkle*

Let's Have Fun / ABC 846596
For ages 3-6. —*Bob Hinkle*

○ **The Lion King: Far from the Pride Lands** / Walt Disney Records
Book and cassette. —*Janet Schnol*

○ **The Lion King: the Brightest Star** / Walt Disney Records
Book and cassette. —*Janet Schnol*

○ **Little Broadway** / 1992 / Sony Kids' Music 48697
Broadway for children is a great idea. The songs here are well and cleverly chosen. The delivery is a little obvious and should be cleverer. Nevertheless, children can learn a bit about theatrical music here. Ages 4-6. —*Bob Hinkle*

☆ **The Little Mermaid—Orig. Soundtrack** / 1991 / Disney 018
A delightful soundtrack by Howard Ashman and Alan Menken, creators of *Little Shop of Horrors*. The first half is vocal numbers, the last ten are instrumental, with styles that range from English to French, Caribbean to Broadway. This may be the best music from a Disney movie yet. —*Tavia Hobart*

★ **The Little Mermaid—Story/Songs** / Disney 60222
The original soundtrack is a wonderful recording. One of the best of the '90s. This recording has the story too. —*Bob Hinkle*

The Little Mermaid Collection / Disney 60956
Little Mermaid Collection—Read-Along Special Edition is for ages 3-10. —*Bob Hinkle*

○ **Live in Concert** / Youngheart 011
These two are personalities many young kids have been aware of through school for quite a while. Positive values, helping kids feel good about themselves, and fun music make this a worthwhile record. —*Bob Hinkle*

Live in Concert / Elephant 307
For ages 3-5. —*Bob Hinkle*

A Long Time to Freedom / Smithsonian/Folkways 45034
This album of Ella Jenkins's favorite songs on the theme of freedom is dedicated to the Reverend Martin Luther King, Jr. For grade school, high school and adult audiences, they are adaptations of traditional African American songs which have been sung on the long road to freedom. —*Ladyslipper*

○ **Look Both Ways** / 1989 / A&M 406
Here is some clever material that seems to be aimed at mid-childhood. Production could be better. Good vocals. His albums have a sameness. Ages 4-7. —*Bob Hinkle*

Love & Warm Fuzzies / Dandelion 2
For ages 3-7. —*Bob Hinkle*

○ **Lullaby Berceuse** / Music For Little People 2206
This French-English bilingual collection won the 1989 Juno Award in Canada...Includes her own lullabies and traditionals like "All Through the Night," Connie Kaldor sings the lullabies, Carmen Campagne the berceuses—can you guess the translation? Sure to calm and soothe. —*Ladyslipper*

● **Lullaby Magic 1** / Discovery 4400
Joanie Bartels's recordings are called the *Magic Series*. They are consistently good for young children. Joanie is a gentle person but also has enthusiasm. *Lullaby Magic 1* and *2* are both excellent. —*Bob Hinkle*

Lullaby Magic 2 / Discovery 4402
A fine concept, appealing to kids of all ages, and enjoyable for any parents listening in! On each tape, side one has pleasing renditions of modern and traditional songs or lullabies, while side two has the music without the vocals. —*Backroads Music/Heartbeats*

Lumpkin, the Pumpkin / 1992 / Rincon Children's Entertainment 70477
For ages 3-6. —*Bob Hinkle*

○ **Lyric Language Japanese** / Penton Overseas/Penton Kids
The latest addition to Penton's musical language-learning series. —*Janet Schnol*

Magical Zoo / 1981 / Disney 60225
For ages 3-5. —*Bob Hinkle*

● **Mail Myself to You** / 1988 / Rounder 8016
Clever songs, great playing, good vocals. Just plain enjoyable for big and little people alike. Ages 3-8. —*Bob Hinkle*

○ **Mainly Mother Goose** / 1984 / Elephant 301
For ages 2-4. —*Bob Hinkle*

○ **Make Believe** / 1986 / A&M 404
A top-notch performer for younger children. Her recordings are consistently good. Ages 3-5. —*Bob Hinkle*

Make Believe Day / 1992 / Sony Kids' Music 48695
A more adult-like record makes the vocals more believable. The songs, though, are not as good as those on the first recording. Ages 3-6. —*Bob Hinkle*

○ **Make the Right Choice** / Kimbo 9114
Make the Right Choice (Issues Kids Are Confronted With) is for ages 4-9. —*Bob Hinkle*

★ **The Marvelous Toy & Other Gallimaufry** / 1984 / Flying Fish 408
Tom Paxton's humor and winning performing style (plus such songs as the title track, a long-time concert favorite) make him a natural children's performer, but it was only 25 years into his career that he made an album for kids. The result is a charming collection, full of rabbits and elephants and, of course, that famous toy that makes all the funny noises. For ages 3-8. —*William Ruhlmann*

○ **Mary Poppins** / Disney 60842
A wonderful, classic story with timeless songs. Ages 3-10. —*Bob Hinkle*

○ **Me and My Bean Bag (Bean Bag Games)** / Kimbo 9111
For ages 2-4. —*Bob Hinkle*

● **Micky Dolenz Puts You to Sleep** / Oct. 22, 1991 / Rhino 70413
Monkee Dolenz makes his solo debut with this children's album. His covers of '60s standards by the Beatles, Hollies, Paul Simon, and Neil Young won't erase the originals from anyone's mind, but they're pleasant enough. —*Jeff Tamarkin*

○ **Mirandy and Brother Wind** /
Illustrated by Jerry Pinkney, read by Cicely Tyson, music by Guy Davis. Knopf book and cassette. Southern dialect, blues riffs and Pinkney's festive illustrations, make this one of the best book and cassette packages on the market. —*Janet Schnol*

○ **Mischief City** / Children's Group 1014
Originally a play mounted in Toronto, this one's really fun. Good songs, well done. The title says it. Ages 4-7. —*Bob Hinkle*

○ **Monsters in My Room** / Round River 101
Clever and assertive, Bill Harley takes the child's point of view bravely and unswervingly. Parents also recognize their own foibles in Bill's songs. Ages 3-8. —*Bob Hinkle*

○ **Moonboat** / 1989 / A&M 0403
More clever songs and arrangements. Tom Chapin's voice seems particularly accessible on this one. "Don't Play with Bruno" is spectacular. Ages 4-10. —*Bob Hinkle*

More Babysongs / High Top 0028
For ages 2-4. —*Bob Hinkle*

○ **More Singable Songs** / 1977 / Shoreline 10038
Not much letdown here. Still excellent. Ages 3-7. —*Bob Hinkle*

○ **Morning 'n' Night** / 1992 / Disney 60834
A little cute, but good for very young children. It nearly underestimates its audience. Ages 3-5. —*Bob Hinkle*

Morning Magic / 1987 / Discovery 4401
For ages 2-5. —*Bob Hinkle*

Mother Earth / 1979 / A&M 0413
Tom Chapin brings a lot of his folk music into his albums for children, and this album is no exception. Ages 4-10. —*Chip Renner*

○ **Mother Goose—(Deluxe) Red** / 1991 / Smarty Pants 70001
These recordings are generally OK, but just OK. You can do better. They're meant for very young kids. For ages 2-4. —*Bob Hinkle*

○ **Mousercise Songs** / Disney 6516
A workout for children, conducted by that omnipresent mouse and friends. Mickey Mouse, can you see your toes? My limited experiments showed kids will get moving around with this one, but

it also fades, and doesn't stand many workouts. For ages 3-6. —*Bob Hinkle*

○ **Mozart's "Magic Flute"** / Children's Group 1023
This one's a bit frenetic but has some wonderful moments. A young girl gets mysteriously caught as an extra character in the opera. Ages 3-10+. —*Bob Hinkle*

○ **Mr. Bach Comes to Call** / 1990 / Children's Group 4201
The ghost of Johann Sebastian visits a young pianist. Ages 3-10+. —*Bob Hinkle*

☆ **Multiplication Facts from 1-12** / Uncle Wilton 001
Singing and Rapping the Multiplication Facts from 1-12. Anyone listening to this "Rap the Facts" series will be hard-pressed not to know their basic math when they're finished. The Professor's (Uncle Wilton) love and concern for kids is plain throughout the series. I wish someone had released it when I was learning the multiplication tables. Ages 5-10. —*Bob Hinkle*

○ **Mushroom Man; Rosebud and Red Flannel, The** / Audio Bookshelf
Another wonderful spoken-word production from Audio Bookshelf. —*Janet Schnol*

Music for Children by Dennis / 1920 / Berner 6320
A little-known artist. These hard-to-find recordings are quite good for ages 3-6. —*Bob Hinkle*

★ **The Music of Disney: A Legacy in Song** / Disney 60957
A beautifully packaged three-CD box set of Disney music throughout the years. Disney buffs will love this set, although there are some popular songs missing. Overall, *The Music of Disney: A Legacy in Song* proves how significant the music from Disney's films and television shows were to popular music and popular culture in general. —*AMG*

The Music of Disneyland, Walt Disney World, & Epcot / 1988 / Disney 007
For ages 3-5. —*Bob Hinkle*

○ **A Musical Adventure with Fivel** / MCA 10458
A good story and OK music. Kids seem to like these characters. Ages 3-6. —*Bob Hinkle*

○ **Musical Playtime Fun** / Kimbo 9120
For ages 2-4. —*Bob Hinkle*

○ **Musical Treasure Chest, Vol. 2** / Disney 119
For ages 3-5. —*Bob Hinkle*

Musical Treasure Chest, Vol. 3 / Disney 120
For ages 3-5. —*Bob Hinkle*

My Best Friend / Music For Little People 2300
For ages 3-7. —*Bob Hinkle*

My Brother Thinks He's a Banana / 1977 / Rainbow Morning 4762
My Brother Thinks He's a Banana is for ages 3-5. —*Bob Hinkle*

○ **My Family Tree: A Recorded History** / Caedmon
In this unusual interactive book and cassette, with guided imagery and flowing celtic harp strains, children are encouraged to visualize and then write their own family stories. —*Janet Schnol*

○ **My First Green Video: A Kids' Guide to Ecology And Environment** / Sony
Based on Dorling Kindersley's "My First" books, this addition to Sony's informative video series offers 13 projects and experiments plus information on environmental problems. —*Janet Schnol*

Naughty Songs... / Rainbow Morning 3
Naughty Songs for Boys and Girls is for ages 4-5. —*Bob Hinkle*

○ **Newspaper Mama** / Zoom Express 038
For ages 3-8. —*Bob Hinkle*

○ **Nitey-Nite** / Golden Glow 101
The *Golden Glow* series is an instrumentally rich, well-conceived series for very young children. Ages 2-5. —*Bob Hinkle*

○ **Noah's Ark** / Lightyear 5101
James Earl Jones's voice carries the day on this well-told tale. Ages 5-8. —*Bob Hinkle*

Nursery Days / 1958 / Smithsonian/Folkways 45036
In *Songs to Grow On—Vol. 1 (Nursery Days)*, Guthrie once again effectively evokes the child's point of view with such simple, yet exciting songs as "Car Song" (with its chorus "Goin' for a ride in

the car car") and "Put Your Finger in the Air." Ages 3-5. — *William Ruhlmann*

Nursery Rhymes and Lullabies / Price Stern Sloan 1925
For ages 2-4. —*Bob Hinkle*

○ **Nursery Rhymes for Little People** / Kimbo 0820
For ages 1-3. —*Bob Hinkle*

Off-Color Songs for Kids / 1983 / Rainbow Morning 5141
For age 5. —*Bob Hinkle*

Oh! Good Grief / 1941 / Warner Brothers 1747
More Charlie Brown sound. Wonderful. Ages 4-9. —*Bob Hinkle*

○ **Old MacDonald Had a Farm** / Score 20064
For ages 1-3. —*Bob Hinkle*

☆ **Old World Lullabies** / Rincon Children's Entertainment70312
Wonderful old lullabies recorded in their original environs with old instruments. A great idea that's well executed. For ages 1-4. — *Bob Hinkle*

Oliver & Company—Story/Songs / Disney 60221
Not what Dickens had in mind, but it's a typical Disney shaggy-dog story that works, if a bit fluffy. Ages 3-5. —*Bob Hinkle*

○ **On the Sunny Side** / 1992 / Music For Little People 42503
Maria Muldaur's voice works surprisingly well for kids. Great arrangements, wonderful song choices. A well-thought-out, very successful recording. Recommended. Ages 4-8. —*Bob Hinkle*

○ **One Hundred One Dalmations—Story/Songs** / Disney 60217
The famous Disney dog story. A good one, worth having. For ages 3-6. —*Bob Hinkle*

○ **One Light One Sun** / 1985 / Shoreline 10040
Raffi turns more to his own originals on this, his best collection, but also turns in excellent versions of traditional songs such as "Apples and Bananas" and claims some nominally adult songs such as "Octopus's Garden" for the children's market. For ages 4-9. — *William Ruhlmann*

One Wide River: Songs & Stories / 1988 / American Melody
A nice collection of folk ballads, folk songs, and stories that can be enjoyed by adults and children alike. Jonathan Edwards and Dave Mallett offer up their usual strong performances. Tom Callinan, Phil Rosenthal, and Phil Bloch do a great version of "The Ragglin' Bog." This is not the kind of music that will wind up your children at bedtime. —*Chip Renner*

★ **One World** / 1989 / Zoom Express 35003
Fantastic world-beat music for kids, by Lois with the Rockadiles and Orchestra King Mama—styles include Soukous, Soca, Highlife, Mbaqanga, plus jazz and blues! These are rhythms that acknowledge the child's musical sophistication, lyrics that build self-esteem and respect for humanity, ideas that honor the child's intelligence, sounds that foster a world consciousness... — *Ladyslipper*

○ **One World, Songs from America & Other Places** / Big Bear 01
These songs are all a bit too synthesized (and same-sounding) for big people to get the multicultural effect, but it's perhaps a good start for kids. Ages 4-7. —*Bob Hinkle*

○ **Oops!** / 1988 / Rounder 8007
Dan Crow's sweet heart and genuine love for children shine through. It's fun but thin (musically and in production). Ages 2-4. —*Bob Hinkle*

○ **Out of This World** / Children's Group 1007
Kim and Jerry Brodey communicate well. Musically they've kept up with the times, doing an exceptional job of teaching positive values, self-esteem, and the wonders of common and uncommon occurrences in childhood. They sing and blend beautifully. Ages 3-7. —*Bob Hinkle*

○ **Outer Space** / Astro 995
A lovable, wonderful eccentric. One of the best visual performers for children. She's *just* crazy enough. Ages 3-8. —*Bob Hinkle*

○ **Over in the Meadow** / Music For Little People 285
For ages 3-8. —*Bob Hinkle*

Over in the Meadow / Price Stern Sloan
For ages 2-4. —*Bob Hinkle*

○ **Over the Moon** / Over The Moon 001
This duo has made a wonderful tape that sounds sometimes like The Byrds, sometimes like early rock & roll, but always like two mommies singing and playing their hearts out. A rough-sounding

recording, but the energy and honesty are unmistakable. Ages 3-10. —*Bob Hinkle*

○ **Party Gras!** / Disney 60827
For ages 2-6. —*Bob Hinkle*

Pass the Coconut / 1991 / A&M 421
For ages 3-6. —*Bob Hinkle*

○ **Patrick's Dinosaurs/What Happened to Patrick's Dinosaurs?** / MCA Universal
Based on the book by Carol Carrick, illustrated by Donald Carrick, animation by Arthur Leonardi, narrated by Martin Short. An addition to "Shelley Duvall's Bedtime Stories" video series, the two tales presented here are beautifully adapted to the format. —*Janet Schnol*

○ **Paul Bunyan** /
Read by Jonathan Winters, music by Leo Kottke. —*Janet Schnol*

○ **Peace by Peace** / 1988 / Golden Entertainment 41042
A more peace- and issue-oriented recording. Sally Rogers still sounds wonderful. The songs are even better; the production is better too. Ages 3-7. —*Bob Hinkle*

Peachboy / Rhino 70416
For ages 4-8. —*Bob Hinkle*

Peanut Butter Pie / 1992 / Sony Kids' Music 52438
The newest one. Very clever. Tom Paxton's voice clicks with kids. Mom and Dad probably already know it. Ages 3-6. —*Bob Hinkle*

○ **Peanuts—Snoopy Come Home** / Golden Entertainment 191242
Our favorite beagle on the lam. It's good. Ages 3-10. —*Bob Hinkle*

Pegasus / 1985 / Lightyear 5105
This story is a bit confusing, perhaps, for younger children, but well read. The music is not very meaningful. Ages 5-7. —*Bob Hinkle*

○ **Pegasus (Stories to Remember)** / Lightyear
Mia Farrow's narration is quite good. The animation is very basic, and the characters look a bit like Saturday morning cartoons. —*Bob Hinkle*

☆ **Peter & the Wolf** / Alcazar 1004
I confess to being a bit jaded and overexposed to this piece. As Snoopy said in the comics upon being exposed to it for the umpteenth time, "I hope the wolf eats him." However, new ears tend to like our friend Peter. Never has there been a wolfier voice than Van Ronk's. Ages 3-8. —*Bob Hinkle*

○ **Peter Pan—Story** / Bumblebeez 812
Take the Disney version if you're needing a Peter Pan of this sort. The original or *Hook* might be better. Ages 2-6. —*Bob Hinkle*

Peter Rabbit, Book and Cassette / Smarty Pants 8001
For ages 2-5. —*Bob Hinkle*

○ **Peter Rabbit, Story** / Bumblebeez 401
For ages 2-5. —*Bob Hinkle*

○ **Peter, Paul & Mommy** / Warner Bros
Audio and video. —*Janet Schnol*

○ **Piggies** / Harcourt Brace
This fantasy, read by Carl and Jennifer Shaylen, includes seven original songs. —*Janet Schnol*

Piggyback Planet / 1989 / Round River 301
Sally Rogers has a truly beautiful and expressive soprano voice that is capable of a whole range of emotions, including love, mischief, mystery, and constructive silliness. Very good songs, but the production doesn't live up to the voice. Ages 3-6. —*Bob Hinkle*

☆ **Pinocchio—Story** / Bumblebeez 812
Disney wins again. Ages 3-5. —*Bob Hinkle*

○ **Play Me a Story** / Knopf
Introduces the music of 17 classical composers. Book and CD. —*Janet Schnol*

Playtime Parade / Golden Glow 104
For ages 2-5. —*Bob Hinkle*

☆ **The Point** / Vestron 4415
Harry Nilsson's classic about finding one's own place and overcoming ostracism. Wonderful music and narration. Though the animation is a bit basic, it is quite clever. This one's a must—if you can find it. —*Bob Hinkle*

○ **Prelearning Skills** / Kimbo 7059
For ages 1-2. —*Bob Hinkle*

○ **Preschool Action Time** / Kimbo 9110
For ages 1-3. —*Bob Hinkle*

○ **Prince Ivan & the Frog Princess** / Delos 6003
For ages 4-8. —*Bob Hinkle*

○ **The Prince & the Pauper—Story/Songs** / Disney 60227
For ages 2-5. —*Bob Hinkle*

○ **Princess Scargo & the Birthday Pumpkin** /
Read by Geena Davis, music by Michael Hedges. —*Janet Schnol*

Pulling Together / 1987 / Gemini 1003
Received a *Parents* Choice Honors Award. Combination of traditional and original materials. —*Michael Erlewine*

Purple People Eater / Children's Group 026
Heather Bishop decided to focus her considerable talent, wit, and warmth on another kids' album. Opening with a moving rendition of "Ghost Riders in the Sky" complete with female pronouns, she then swings into "The Fairy Song" and the rollicking "The Name Game"...Connie Kaldor, Tracy Riley and Ilena Zaremba contribute inspired back-up vocals and again, production and instrumentation is highly sophisticated. Recommended for pre-school, middle young. —*Ladyslipper*

○ **Puss in Boots** / 1993 / Rhino 70456
Narrated by Tracey Ullman, music by Jean-Luc Ponty. —*AMG*

○ **Put Down the Duckie: New Hits from Sesame Street** / 1971 /
Golden Music 4108
Sesame Street, hipper than usual. *Put Down the Duckie—New Hits from Sesame Street* is one of the most musical of the CTW records. Recommended. Ages 3-6. —*Bob Hinkle*

○ **Put on a Happy Face & Sing with Dr. Mike** / Amee Lu 1990
Dr. Mike is a real dentist. The recording is good for a first effort. Here's an artist to watch. Ages 3-5. —*Bob Hinkle*

Quiet Time / Random House 80801
A simple, quiet, mostly acoustic recording. Good for young children. Ages 2-5. —*Bob Hinkle*

○ **Radio Woof Presents Forbidden Folklore!** / Alcazar/Well-In-Tune
This high-spirited melange of traditional tales and music has the added spark of grade school humor. Bill Wellington has several other Radio Woof recordings. —*Janet Schnol*

○ **Radum Scadum** / ABC 838980
This mostly instrumental Australian music is interesting, fun, and electric. Ages 7-9. —*Bob Hinkle*

☆ **Raffi in Concert with the Rise & Shine Band** / 1989 / Shoreline 10035
Here is the first really major figure in modern children's music. He blazed the trail for many to follow. Every recording is recommended. Raffi is Canada's gift to children everywhere. Ages 2-6. —*Bob Hinkle*

○ **Rainbow Earth** / Local Folkel 6682
This shows promise. Wait until the next one. Anita Silvert is good, but new to the market as a writer and producer. Ages 3-6. —*Bob Hinkle*

○ **Rainbow Planet** / 1984 / Rainbow Planet 3101
For ages 3-7. —*Bob Hinkle*

○ **Rainbow Sign** / 1992 / Rounder 8025
This is a well crafted compilation. —*Janet Schnol*

Rainy Day/Sunny Day / Bumblebeez 22
Good young children's material. Ages 2-4. —*Bob Hinkle*

○ **Recycled Songs** / Random House 82643
This is the best recording from Don Cooper. Good teaching songs, such as what kids can do about recycling. —*Bob Hinkle*

○ **Red Riding Hood & Goldilocks** / Windham Hill 0718
For ages 3-7. —*Bob Hinkle*

○ **Red Riding Hood; Goldilocks and the Three Bears** /
Read by Meg Ryan, music by Art Lande. —*Janet Schnol*

The Rescuers—Story/Songs / 1989 / Disney 60210
Rescuers and *Rescuers Down Under* both originate with the animated feature films of the same name. They are exciting stories for younger children. —*Bob Hinkle*

○ **The Rescuers Down Under—Story/Songs** / Disney 60228
For ages 3-6. —*Bob Hinkle*

○ **Rhythms for Basic Motor Skills** / Kimbo 9074
For ages 1-2. —*Bob Hinkle*

○ **The Riddle King's Riddle Songs** / Steve Charney 590-60842-8
Steve and his friend Harry the dummy are corny and silly, but this works for me somehow. I think it's the way Steve and Harry fence with each other. Ages 3-6. —*Bob Hinkle*

○ **Rise & Shine** / 1982 / Shoreline 10042
Apparently this is to be Raffi's last recording mostly for children. He's since turned his attention to the environment and somewhat away from children's recordings. This is a fine album. Ages 3-8. —*Bob Hinkle*

○ **Robin Hood Story/Songs (Read-Along Book & Tape)** / Disney 60203
For ages 3-7. —*Bob Hinkle*

Rock 'n Roll Teddy Bear / 1986 / Lightyear 75183
More rock. The fun continues. Ages 2-6. —*Bob Hinkle*

○ **The Rock-A-Bye Collection** / JAB
This is the second recording from the people who brought you *A Child's Gift of Lullabies*. Ages 1-2. —*Bob Hinkle*

Romp in the Swamp / Do Dreams 18027
For ages 4-7. —*Bob Hinkle*

○ **Rootin' Tootin' Rangers** / Disney 60237
For ages 3-5. —*Bob Hinkle*

○ **Rounder Kids** / Rounder 6
For ages 3-7. —*Bob Hinkle*

○ **Rumpelstiltskin** / 1993 / Rincon Children's Entertainment70458
For ages 3-7. —*Bob Hinkle*

○ **Saddle Pals** / Rounder 8011
The Riders introduce children to Western music in a really fun way. If one becomes enthralled with the music, these are a real find. Ages 3-6. —*Bob Hinkle*

○ **Sam the Snake and Dance with the Bears; Little Miss Mousie** / Discovery/BMG
Both book and cassette packages feature songs from the "Really Silly" series in addition to stories and activities. —*Janet Schnol*

● **The Sandman ...** / Marlboro 04
The Sandman, Lullabies & Other Night Time Songs is a truly lovely lullaby-type album. Recommended. Ages 1-3. —*Bob Hinkle*

○ **Save the Animals, Save the Earth** / Kimbo 9124
For ages 4-7. —*Bob Hinkle*

○ **Seasons of Change** / 1983 / Flying Fish 309
Priscilla Herdman presents a compelling rural landscape, singing in a clear, reassuring voice of struggling farmers, family ties, and feminist consciousness. She continues the interpretive folksinging tradition of Joan Baez and Judy Collins, updating it for the '80s and '90s. —*William Ruhlmann*

○ **Sebastian—Songs** / Disney 60811
The crab from Disney's the *Little Mermaid*, Sebastian is the children's answer to the party band. It is almost impossible to sit still for a whole side. Caribbean rhythms abound. —*Bob Hinkle*

Seeds of Victory / 1990 / Disney 60236
For ages 3-6. —*Bob Hinkle*

Shake It to the One ... / Music For Little People 2211
Shake It to the One You Love the Best. The only blues hero doing real children's music. Parents will like this music almost as much as their children will. Ages 3-8. —*Bob Hinkle*

○ **Shake It to the One That You Love the Best** / 1989 / Music For Little People 2211
Shake It To The One That You Love: The Best Play Songs and Lullabies from Black Musical Traditions is another excellent compilation from Music for Little People. —*Janet Schnol*

Shake Sugaree / 1988 / Music For Little People 42502
Renowned blues singer Taj Mahal plays and sings for children on this award-winning tape. From "Fishin' Blues" to "Little Brown Dog," this is a fun-filled listening experience that everyone will enjoy, and even the little ones (2-5 years) will delight in the humorous and soulful delivery by this true master. Taj's roots in Afro-American culture shine through, and his own children's chorus (he's the father of six) help to portray island life, West Africa and the deep South in a most folksy and funky way. —*Backroads Music/Heartbeats*

Sidewalk Shuffle / Children's Group 1018
For ages 3-6. —*Bob Hinkle*

Silly Songs / Price Stern Sloan 3
For ages 2-4. —*Bob Hinkle*

○ **Sillytime Magic** / 1980 / Discovery 4404
One of Joanie Bartel's most popular. Recommended for ages 2-6.
—*Bob Hinkle*

○ **Simple Folk Dances** / Kimbo 07042
For ages 3-5. —*Bob Hinkle*

Simple Magic / 1984 / Children's Group 1020
For ages 3-7. —*Bob Hinkle*

Sing a Happy Song / Random House 80805
For eight recordings and a number of years, Bill and Gary have
helped to define fun for children across the U.S. Ages 3-6. —*Bob
Hinkle*

Sing with Me ... & Counting Songs / Random House 88810
For ages 2-3. —*Bob Hinkle*

Sing with Me Animal Songs / Random House 88809
For ages 3-5. —*Bob Hinkle*

Sing with Me Christmas Songs / Random House 89355
For ages 3-5. —*Bob Hinkle*

Sing with Me Lullabies / Random House 88811
For ages 1-3. —*Bob Hinkle*

Sing with Me Mother Goose / Random House 88812
For ages 2-3. —*Bob Hinkle*

Sing-Along Take Along Library / Random House 899660
For ages 2-3. —*Bob Hinkle*

○ **Sing-a-Long** / Bumblebeez 400
For ages 2-4. —*Bob Hinkle*

○ **Singable Nursery Rhymes** / Kimbo 8035
For ages 2-4. —*Bob Hinkle*

★ **Singable Songs for the Very Young** / 1976 / Shoreline 10037
This is the one that started it all. Still one of the most popular
recordings for children. Ages 4-10. —*Bob Hinkle*

Singing 'n Swinging / 1980 / Elephant 303
For ages 3-5. —*Bob Hinkle*

○ **Singing Games for Little People** / Kimbo 0880
For ages 3-4. —*Bob Hinkle*

☆ **Sleeping Beauty—Story** / Bumblebeez 817
The classic. Ages 3-5. —*Bob Hinkle*

Sleeping Beauty—Story/Songs (Read-Along Book & tape) /
Disney 60207
For ages 3-6. —*Bob Hinkle*

Sleepytime on Sesame Street / Golden Music 4103
The inclusion of the characters makes it desirable. Otherwise, it's
just OK. Ages 2-5. —*Bob Hinkle*

Smorgasbord / 1979 / Elephant 304
For ages 2-5. —*Bob Hinkle*

○ **Sneakers—Music for Sophisticated Kids** / Smithsonian 210
Enthusiasm and good basic values taught with songs that range
from OK to very good. The vocals are uneven. Production will get
better as they go along. Ages 4-8. —*Bob Hinkle*

The Snow Queen / Delos 6004
For ages 3-8. —*Bob Hinkle*

○ **The Snow Queen** / Lightyear 75108
For ages 4-8. —*Bob Hinkle*

☆ **Snow White & the Seven Dwarfs—Story/Songs** / Disney 60199
Disney wins this one. This one has life, the other one kind of sits
there. Ages 3-6. —*Bob Hinkle*

Snow White & the Seven Dwarfs—Story / Bumblebeez 809
For ages 3-6. —*Bob Hinkle*

○ **Snow White; The Night Before Christmas** /
Book and cassette by Diane Eskenazi. —*Janet Schnol*

Snuffy, the Elf Who Saved Christmas / 1992 / Rincon Children's
Entertainment 70476
For ages 3-6. —*Bob Hinkle*

Something New / 1987 / Boulder's Children's Prod. 03
A very good, eclectic collection of songs from several cultures for
infants, parents, and very young children. Ages 4-10. —*Bob
Hinkle*

Song & Play Time / Smithsonian/Folkways 7526
For ages 2-4. —*Bob Hinkle*

○ **Songs Rhythms and Chants for the Dance** / Smithsonian/Folk-
ways 45004
This recording teaches children about the different activities and
professions involved in dance performances. With the help of Pat
Johnson and the Reflections, Burma West, and the Larry Novack
Trio, Ella Jenkins sings, presents dance-rhythm concepts, and interviews dance professionals. — *Roundup newsletter*

Songs and Rhythms from Near and Far / Smithsonian/Folk-
ways 7655
Ella Jenkins focuses on the theme of travelling on this delightful
recording. Through the world of music, she and her friends take
listeners with them on a journey to countries such as Greece,
Switzerland, Poland, Israel, Holland, Italy, and Canada. Songs
from these regions are represented through a variety of musical
sounds and textures. The expedition then winds up back in the
United States, where some American musical traditions are explored. — *Roundup Newsletter*

○ **Songs for Children of All Ages** / Flying Fish 438
For ages 3-7. —*Bob Hinkle*

Songs for Little Kids / Zoom Express 040
Great Aussie-flavored songs for young children. Ages 2-5. —*Bob
Hinkle*

Songs of America / Random House 80613
For ages 3-6. —*Bob Hinkle*

☆ **Songs to Grow on for Mother and Child** / 1956 /
Smithsonian/Folkways 45035
Some of the last songs written and recorded by Woody Guthrie
were his children's songs. Their strength, shown in *Songs to Grow
on for Mother and Child*, is an unusually strong identification
with actually being a child, in all its simplicity and charm, along
with the ability to win over listeners. Good examples on here are
"Rattle My Rattle" and "I Want My Milk." Guthrie is an acquired
sonic taste worth acquiring. Ages 3-5. —*William Ruhlmann &
Bob Hinkle*

○ **Songs to Sing** / Children's Group 1011
Clever, understated, and mostly just plain fun. Ages 4-8. —*Bob
Hinkle*

○ **Spaghetti Bolognaise** / Zoom Express 039
Australia's version of the Pied Piper, this is very clever material,
with Peter Combe's own unique delivery. Ages 3-9. —*Bob Hinkle*

Stanley Stole My Shoelace... / Rainbow Morning 5
Stanley Stole My Shoelace and Rubbed It in His Armpit is for
ages 3-6. —*Bob Hinkle*

○ **Stay Cool in School** / Do Dreams 19017
Billy B. is a folky pop artist. Clever lyrics and pretty good recordings. Especially good on environment. —*Bob Hinkle*

Stay Tuned / 1976 / Elephant 0306
Children's music's "arena" act. SL & B are more than
Nickelodeon's "Elephant Show." They are so well loved, by virtue
of their wit, perceptiveness, and ability, that children want to be
like them. These recordings could be purchased according to desired subject matter. They do tend to be a bit alike. Pick up the
package and have a look. Ages 2-4. —*Bob Hinkle*

Stayin' Up / Kamotion 1988
For ages 2-5. —*Bob Hinkle*

○ **Step It Down** / 1981 / Rounder 8004
For ages 3-7. —*Bob Hinkle*

○ **Steppin' to the Music** / Linda Saxon Brown
For ages 3-6. —*Bob Hinkle*

Stinger, King of the Bees / 1992 / Rincon Children's
Entertainment 70478
For ages 3-6. —*Bob Hinkle*

Story Cassette / Bumblebeez 407
For ages 3-6. —*Bob Hinkle*

○ **Story and Songs** / Disney 60243
For ages 3-6. —*Bob Hinkle*

☆ **Story/Songs** / Disney 60204
The Disney version is the best of them. Ages 2-5. —*Bob Hinkle*

○ **Storymaker, Tunes and Tales** / CL 3385
A good storyteller for very young kids. Not for repeated listening
by big people. Ages 3-5. —*Bob Hinkle*

Subtraction Facts from 1-12 / Uncle Wilton 003

Singing and Rapping the Subtraction Facts from 1-12 is for ages 5-10. —*Bob Hinkle*

○ **Sunshine Cake** / Alacazam!
The Mike and Carleen McCornack offer timeless songs that are perfect for quiet activities. —*Janet Schnol*

○ **Surfin'** / Playtime
This duo, Doug and Gary, from Rochester, NY, is consistently good. Particularly good vocals for ages 3-7. Humor and cleverness without condescension. —*Bob Hinkle*

Sweet Dreams / CBS 44998
For ages 2-4. —*Bob Hinkle*

○ **The Tailor Of Gloucester** /
Read by Meryl Streep, music by the Chieftains. —*Janet Schnol*

○ **The Tailor of Gloucester** / 1988 / Windham Hill 0710
What a great combination—Meryl Streep and the Chieftains make the recording fly by. Ages 4-7. —*Bob Hinkle*

○ **Tailybone & Other Strange Stories** / High Windy 1203
For ages 5-10. —*Bob Hinkle*

○ **Tale of Peter Rabbit** / 1988 / Rincon Children's Entertainment 708
For ages 3-6. —*Bob Hinkle*

○ **Tales From The Cryptkeeper** /
Book and cassette by Richard Donner, Joel Silver, Robert Zemeckis, Ed Naha. —*Janet Schnol*

★ **Teaching Peace** / 1986 / Children's Group 4202
Teaching Peace is one of the top five children's recordings of all time. Red Grammar's fantastic tenor voice would be successful in any musical genre. A man with a very big heart. Ages 3-10. —*Bob Hinkle*

○ **The Teddy Bears' Jamboree** / Lightyear
The child favorite duo of Gary Rosen and Bill Shontz present their fourth annual free concert at Boston Common for an audience of 10,000 on this live performance video. —*Janet Schnol*

☆ **The Story (Read-Along Book & Tape)** / 1980 / Disney 60216
For ages 3-5. —*Bob Hinkle*

○ **There's a Hippo in My Tub and Dinosaur Rock 'n' Roll; Sillie** / Discovery/BMG
Both book and cassette packages include songs from the "Magic" series in addition to stories and activities. —*Janet Schnol*

○ **There's a Dinosaur ...** / Music For Little People 2123
There's a Dinosaur in My Bed. For ages 3-5. —*Bob Hinkle*

This Lil' Cow / Red Rover 111
For ages 4-8. —*Bob Hinkle*

☆ **This-A-Way That-A-Way** / Smithsonian/Folkways 45002
The great lady of music for young children. Having a serious children's music collection without Ella Jenkins is like collecting rock & roll without Chuck Berry. Different people like different titles. Shop around, look at titles, and listen if you can. —*Bob Hinkle*

○ **The 3 Billy Goats Gruff/3 Little Pigs** / Windham Hill 0713
Surprisingly good Holly, especially the goats. Ages 3-7. —*Bob Hinkle*

○ **Three Hairs from the Devil's Chin** / BAMME 108
For ages 4-8. —*Bob Hinkle*

Three Litttle Pigs—Story and Songs (Read-Along Book & tape) / 1983 / Disney 60212
The Disney version is the better of the choices. Ages 3-5. —*Bob Hinkle*

○ **The Three Little Pigs** / Score 20104
For ages 3-5. —*Bob Hinkle*

○ **Three Little Pigs; The Three Billy Goats Gruff, The** /
Read by Holly Hunter, music by Art Lande. —*Janet Schnol*

○ **Thumbelina** / Random House
Judy Collins, *Thumbelina,* a book and cassette package, Random House. —*Janet Schnol*

Tickles You! / 1980 / Lightyear 75180
A little more rambunctious. Ages 2-5. —*Bob Hinkle*

○ **Time Can Be So Magic** / 1988 / North Star
Produced by Bill Thomas. A collection of songs from "The Captain Kangaroo Show" featuring Noel Paul Stookey, Dave Mallett, Cheryl Wheeler, Paul Geremia, and Peter, Paul & Mary. A thoroughly enjoyable and classy recording. —*Chip Renner*

○ **Time's Running Out** / Three Feathers 1
Pleasing vocals in unevenly produced recordings. A good live artist who communicates well with children. Ages 3-6. —*Bob Hinkle*

○ **Toes Up, Toes Down** / Kimbo 7041
For ages 2-4. —*Bob Hinkle*

Toffee Apple / Zoom Express 037
For ages 3-8. —*Bob Hinkle*

○ **Totally Minnie** / Disney 6521
Disney finally emphasizes a female character, and it only took 50+ years. Children should know that female mice can be popular too. Ages 2-5. —*Bob Hinkle*

○ **Traffic Jams** / Educational Graphics 604
Great writing, a sense of humor, and consistency characterize Joe Scruggs work. As a vocalist and communicator in general, he is eminently likable. Ages 3-8. —*Bob Hinkle*

Travelin' Magic / Discovery 4403
For ages 2-6. —*Bob Hinkle*

○ **A Treasury of Earth Mother Lullabies** / Earth Mother 05
Fourteen of the best selections (68 minutes) from Pamela's 3 volumes of *Earth Mother Lullabies,* from all over the world, proven effective for sleeplessness in both children and adults. —*Ladyslipper*

○ **True Blue** / 1990 / Golden Entertainment 4101
For ages 2-5. —*Bob Hinkle*

Turn on the Music / Media Home Entertainment 22121
For ages 2-4. —*Bob Hinkle*

Two of a Kind / 1991 / Gemini 1005
Uptempo, exuberant songs of family celebration. Also storytelling. Recommended. —*Michael Erlewine*

Uh Oh / Lightyear 75181
Also very good. Ages 3-5. —*Bob Hinkle*

○ **Un Voix Pour Les Enfants** / Children's Group 029
For ages 5-7. —*Bob Hinkle*

○ **Unbearable Bears** / 1986 / Marlboro 01
Kevin Roth's accessible voice and super playing make his recordings a positive for any collection. This one's really all bears all the time. Ages 2-6. —*Bob Hinkle*

☆ **Velveteen Rabbit** / Dancing Cat 3007
This classic story by Margery Williams has re-captured the imaginations of children of all ages. Narration by Meryl Streep, original music by George Winston. 30 minutes. —*Ladyslipper*

Very Best of Peter Combe ... / Zoom Express 993
The Absolutely Very Best of Peter Combe (So Far). Recorded in concert. Ages 3-9. —*Bob Hinkle*

○ **Vivaldi's Ring of Mystery** / 1991 / Children's Group 84206
A fanciful stay in old Vienna. Ages 3-10+. —*Bob Hinkle*

○ **Voyage for Dreamers** / Earth Mother 03
Pamela Ballingham's enchanting voice captures the essence of soothing music, rich and gracefully woven. An embracing empathy for the Earth touches all who listen, and her gentle music, on piano, strings and guitar, is heartening and reassuring for children of all ages to enjoy. This tape reminds us "dreams are never too far". —*Backroads Music/Heartbeats*

Walk a Mile / 1959 / Lovable Creatures 101
One of the most animated, contemporary, professional, hippest kids' recordings; it should have strong appeal to kids from a wide range of cultural and socio-economic backgrounds, as it cures the problem of boring children's music...Great messages, about independent thinking, justice, truthfulness, conflict resolution, and more. Winner, 1989 Parents' Choice Award. —*Ladyslipper*

○ **Warm Fuzzies** / Medicine Show 004
"Story of the Star Spangled Banner" and "One Hand, One Heart" are sentiments every child should be exposed to. Other songs are also excellent. Highly recommended. Ages 3-9. —*Bob Hinkle*

● **We All Live Together** / Youngheart 74768
Chances are, more young children than adults know about this duo because they've crisscrossed the country playing in schools for years. Positive values, self-esteem, and fun characterize these recordings. The *We Live Together* recordings are a good bet. Ages 3-6. —*Bob Hinkle*

○ **We Are Singamajig** / S 1991

For ages 3-4. —*Bob Hinkle*

○ **We Like Kids: Letters & Numbers** / Goodyear
Selections on this large compilation include the electric rock of Craig & Co.'s Craig Taubman and Bethie. —*Janet Schnol*

○ **We Like Kids: Songs for the Earth** / Good Year Books
A thoughtfully assembled compilation album that comes with a sturdy, well designed songbook. —*Janet Schnol*

○ **Wee Sing** / Price Stern Sloan
At the risk of going counter to a substantial-selling, long-standing, and extensive catalog for very young children, I find many of these albums underestimate their listeners, under-think their stories, and manage to do all of this at a very reasonable price. Many people obviously disagree with this assessment. Low price should not by definition rule out quality products. Ages 2-4. —*Bob Hinkle*

Wee Sing and Play / Price Stern Sloan
For ages 2-4. —*Bob Hinkle*

Wee Sing King Cole's Party / Price Stern Sloan
For ages 2-4. —*Bob Hinkle*

Wee Sing America / Price Stern Sloan
For ages 2-4. —*Bob Hinkle*

Wee Sing for Christmas / Price Stern Sloan
For ages 2-4. —*Bob Hinkle*

○ **Wee Sing Around the World** / Price Stern Sloan/Putnam
This book and cassette package is a praiseworthy extension of Pamela Conn Beall and Susan Hagen Nipp's proven formula for presenting well-researched, traditional music. —*Janet Schnol*

○ **Wee Sing Under the Sea** / Price Stern Sloan/Putnam
The duo's ninth video takes children into the briny depths. —*Janet Schnol*

Well-Behaved Children / Rainbow Morning 4
Songs for Well-Behaved Children is for ages 4-5. —*Bob Hinkle*

○ **What Do You Dream About?** / Kaleidoscope 5001
Kathy Kallick is well-known in bluegrass circles as lead singer of The Good Ol' Persons. Her first kid's tape is a delight for young and old, with some strong bluegrass influences on "The Doggy Medley," "Sweet Betsy From Pike," "Buffalo Gals," the title cut and others. Delightful! —*Backroads Music/Heartbeats*

○ **What's in the Sea? Songs about Marine Life** / Kimbo 9116
For ages 3-5. —*Bob Hinkle*

○ **When We Grow Up** / 1921 / Disney 60223
Seems like the Minnie Mouse emphasis a while back just might have been a bit of a Disney nod toward women: progress. Minnie's recordings, however, tend to be sugarcoated and without substance. Not that everything has to be fraught with message, but this stuff just disappears as it plays. For ages 3-5. —*Bob Hinkle*

○ **When the Rain Comes Down** / 1987 / Rounder 8013
A definitively outstanding children's production by a woman who has been a leader in providing excellent material for kids...First-rate youngsters deserve first-rate music like this—recommended! —*Ladyslipper*

○ **Who Will Speak for the Children** / 1988 / Rounder 8008

These kids speak for themselves clearly. The production allows them to. This wonderful record is from mostly older Black kids from Alabama. It is fun and very musical, but the message communicated by the very existence of the recording is important in and of itself. Ages 4-10. —*Bob Hinkle*

○ **Wizard of Oz—The Story/Songs (Read-Along Book & Tape)** / Disney 60209

For ages 3-8. —*Bob Hinkle*

○ **Wonderful Planet** / Malibu/BMG

Opens and closes with the sounds of Aaron Copland's "Appalachian Spring" and includes scenes of moose, otter, penguin and wild horses in their natural habitats in addition to footage of bulldozers razing the land. —*Janet Schnol*

○ **The Wooleycat's Favorite Nursery Rhymes** / 1992 / Discovery 94409

T-Shirt and tape gift set. —*Janet Schnol*

○ **The World Is a Rainbow** / Rainbow Music 9C827

A little-known and hard-to-find record, but very good. For ages 4-8. —*Bob Hinkle*

○ **Yes, I Can** / Children's Group 1010

Sandra Beech specializes in positive childhood values, with an emphasis on self-esteem. Productionwise and vocally, not up to current standards, but there's much charm for younger children. Ages 3-6. —*Bob Hinkle*

○ **Yes, Yes, Yes** / Coco 1991

Dan Conley is extremely tuned to the young child's point of view. His songs stretch children's imaginations. Big things can be expected from Dan. Ages 3-9. —*Bob Hinkle*

You Wanna Be a Duck / 1987 / A&M 407

For ages 3-5. —*Bob Hinkle*

★ **You'll Sing a Song ...** / 1966 / Smithsonian/Folkways 45010

You'll Sing a Song and I'll Sing a Song. Born in St. Louis, raised in Chicago, Ella Jenkins has been a folksinger since 1956. Concentrating on educating music teachers through her now-famous "Adventures in Rhythm" workshops, she demonstrated new group-singing and rhythm-building techniques. Author of two books and any number of albums, Jenkins is possibly *the* major talent in children's music. Her talent is so great that, once heard, she is never forgotten. This is how kids' songs should sound. No family should be without at least one album, and this classic is the place to start. —*Michael Erlewine*

★ **You're in Trouble** / 1989 / A&M 0424

My favorite. Wonderful songs. Ages 3-9. —*Bob Hinkle*

Children's Music Sources

2 M Records, Box 364, Stn G, Calgary, Alberta, Canada T3A 2G3

A Gentle Wind Productions, Box 3103, Albany, NY 12203

Alkazar, PO Box 429, Waterbury, VT 05676

Amee Lu Records

Astro Records, 8033 Sunset Blvd. Ste 685, Los Angeles, CA 90046

Australian Broadcasting Corporation, Polygram

Banana Records, Station A Box 405, White Rock, B.C. V4B 5G3

Beanstalk Productions, 160 Madison Avenue, 6th Fl., New York, NY 10016

Berner Publishing Co., 6320 Cartwright Drive, New Orleans, LA 70122

Big Bear Music, PO Box 532, N. Egremont, MA 01252

Big Records, 1812 W. Hood, Chicago, IL 60660

Boston Skyline, Paul, Peggo (603) 623-1458, (603) 225-8986

Bumblebeez, 21535 Claretta Ave., Lakewood, CA 90715

Caedmon Records, 1995 Broadway, New York, NY 10023

Care Bears, Score Productions, 3414 Peachtree Rd., Atlanta, GA 30326

Castle of Dreams Music, PO Box 147,
    Bedford Hills, NY 10507-0147
Children's Circle, Weston, CT 06883
The Children's Group, 561 Bloor St. W, #300
    Toronto, Ontario, Canada M5S 1Y6
Coco Records, Dan Conley, 10 Weavers Hill,
    Greenwich, CT 06831
Dandelion Music, 275 King St. E., Ste 22,
    Toronto Ontario, Canada M5A 1K2
DBV Walt Disney Records, 500 S. Buena Vista St.,
    Burbank, CA 91521
Discovery Music, 4130 Greenbush Avenue,
    Sherman Oaks, CA 91423
Do Dreams Music, 2770 S.171 St., PO Box 248,
    New Berlin, WI 53151-0248
Easy Street Records, 2 Easy Street, Woodbury CT 06798
Educational Activities, Box 392, Freeport, NY 11520
Elephant Records, PO Box 101 Station Z, Toronto, Ontario,
    Canada M5N 2Z3
Ellen Feldman, BMI, PO Box 17561,
    West Hartford, CT 06117
Family Home Entertainment, 15400 Sherman Way,
    Box 10124, Van Nuys, CA 91410
Fragile Glass Music Publishing, PO Box 1554,
    Huntington, NY 11743
Gemini, 2000 Penncraft Court, Ann Arbor, MI, 48103
Golden Glow, 800 Livermore St., Yellow Springs, OH
    45387
Golden/Western Publishing, 1220 Mound Ave.,
    Racine, Wisconsin 53404
High Top/Media Home Entertainment, 5959 Triumph
    Street, Commerce, CA 90040-1688
High WindyRecords, Fairview, NC 28730
Imagine If Productions, 41 Brookside Ave.,
    Valley Cottage, NY 10989
J. Aaron Brown, 1508 16th Avenue South,
    Nashville, TN 37212
Kamotion Music, PO Box 844, Bala Cynwyd, PA 19004
Kimbo Educational, Box 477, Long Branch, NJ 07740
Launch Pad Records, 16 Stacey St., Randolf, MA 02368
Laura Simms/Gentle Wind Productions, Box 3103,
    Albany, NY 12203
Light Year/Media Home Entertainment, 5959 Triumph
    Street, Commerce, CA 90040-1688
Local Folkel, Box 17196, Rochester, NY 14617
Lois LaFond, Boulder Children's Productions, PO Box 4712,
    Boulder, CO 80306
Lovable Creatures Music, 105 King Street, Ithaca, NY
    14850
Magic Dragon, PO Box 1952, London, Ontario N6A 5J4
Marlboro Records, 845 Marlboro Spring Road,
    Kennett Square, PA 19348
Media Home Entertainment, 5959 Triumph Street,
    Commerce, CA 90040-1688
Medicine Show Music, PO Box 389, Hughsonville, NY
    12537

Moles End Music, RD #3, Box 118, Hampton, NJ 08827
Music For Little People, PO Box 1460, Redway, CA 95560
Musical Munchkins, PO Box 356, Pound Ridge, NY 10576
Over the Moon, (201) 659-8369
Pax Records, 78 Park Place, East Hampton, NY 11937
Perfect Score Music, PO Box 5061, Cochituate, MA 01778
Peter Pan Records, 88 St. Francis Street, Newark, NJ 07105
Playtime Music, 282 Wimbledon Rd., Rochester, NY 14617
Price Stern Sloan, 410 N. Cienega Blvd.,
    Los Angeles, CA 90048
Rabbit Ears, 2225 Colorado Avenue,
    Santa Monica, CA 90404-3555
Rabbit Shadow Records, PO Box 180476, Austin, TX 78718
Rainbow Enterprises, PO Box 733, Clinton, IA 52732
Rainbow Morning Music, 2121 Fairland Road,
    Silver Spring, MD 20904
Rainbow Planet, PO Box 735, Edmonds, WA 98020
Random House, 400 Hahn Rd., Westminster, MD 21157
Red Rover Records, PO Box 6490, Evanston, IL 60202
Rhino/Rincon Recordings, 2225 Colorado, Ave.,
    Santa Monica, CA 90404-3555
Roar Records, 2 Wisconsin Circle, Ste #800,
    Chevy Chase, MD 20815
Rosenshontz, RS Records, Box 651, Brattleboro, VT 05302
Round River Records, c/o Debbie Block, 301 Jacob St,
    Seekonk, MA 02771
Score Productions, Atlanta, GA
Seatofourpants Productions, 1250 Riverbed,
    Cleveland, OH 44113
Sid Leiberman, 2522 Ashland, Evanston, IL 60201
Singamajig, PO Box 147, Madison, NJ 07940
Smarty Pants, 15104 Detroit Ave., Ste 2,
    Lakewood, OH 44107
Song Trek, 2600 Hillegass, Berkley, CA 94704
Song Wizard, PO Box 93242, Los Angeles, CA 90093
Spring Board Records, 2140 Shattuck Ave., Box 2317,
    Berkeley, CA 94704
Steve Charney, 2199-8 Stoll Rd., Saugerties, NY 12477
Storymaker Records, 18 Village Green,
    Port Chester, NY 10573
Surf Productions, 282 Wimbleton Rd., Rochester, NY 14617
Three Feathers Music, 311 Sixth Avenue,
    Brooklyn, NY 11215
Timeless Tunes, PO Box 240, Roslyn, NY 11576
Uncle Fred Records/Pinwheel Productions, 211 W. 56th St,
    Ste 8J, New York, NY 10019
Uncle Wilton Productions, Wilton Banks, PO Box 490,
    Desoto, TX 75115
United Media, 200 Park Avenue, New York, NY 10166
Well in Tune Productions, 301 Thompson St.,
    Staunton, VA 24401
Youngheart Music, 2413 1/2 Hyperion Avenue,
    Los Angeles, CA 90027
Zoom Express, 568 Broadway, Suite 1104,
    New York, NY 100120

EASY LISTENING

Listening to music can have either a primary or a secondary focus. The musical genre we call easy listening clearly falls into the latter category. Its main function is usually as background music; for example, it can provide a pleasant backdrop for dinner, a romantic evening, or just relaxing. While one can't deny the musical contributions of artists such as Miles Davis, Jimi Hendrix, or Bob Dylan, they are not most people's idea of dinner music. In short, there is a time and place for everything. Not all music is meant to challenge or stimulate.

Easy listening is comprised of two elements: 1) soft string-laden arrangements of old familiar standards with some newer pop tunes and 2) the vocal stylings of such perennial favorites as Perry Como or Andy Williams and the lighter fare of artists such as Frank Sinatra, Tony Bennett, or Elvis Presley. Ironically, according to Joel Whitburn's *Top Easy-Listening Records 1961-1974* – which was compiled from *Billboard*'s Easy Listening Charts – the #1 artist on the chart during this period was Elvis Presley; however, you will not find Elvis listed in the Easy Listening section of this book, as his main musical contributions lie elsewhere. Also, for the sake of conformity, vocalists will be found in the Vocal section. Basically, this section consists of albums that are primarily instrumental, with some including an occasional vocal. Some of the most famous artists here are Liberace, Percy Faith, Lawrence Welk, and Mantovani, whose name is almost synonymous with the term easy listening. If there is one common denominator for most of the artists in this section, it is that they have not created a body of work readily identified with them but have relied mostly on interpreting songs that were proven hits. Two notable exceptions to this are Henry Mancini and Leroy Anderson.

Newer artists in this field, such as Zamfir and Richard Clayderman, have relied heavily on TV advertising and mail-orders to sell their records and establish an identity. The two most likely reasons for this are: 1) most easy listening stations do not announce what they play, and 2) many fans of this music feel uncomfortable walking into the average record store, which clearly caters to the youth market.

The audience for easy listening can perhaps best be described as the parents of the baby-boomers, for they were the main buyers of the music when it was a much more dominant force in the marketplace, and they continue to support it today. But the times are changing. In 1979, *Billboard* changed the name of its Easy Listening Chart to Adult-Contemporary, acknowledging the shift in musical tastes of the baby-boomers themselves. Adult-contemporary, or soft-rock as it is sometimes called, features the familiar soft-rock hits of the last 30 years, and some stations sprinkle new-age instrumentals into the mix. It's a different name but the same concept for a younger generation. The more things change, the more they stay the same.

– Ken Cassidy

Ronnie Aldrich

b. Feb. 15, 1916, Erith, Kent, England
Piano
An English pianist, Aldrich studied at the Guildhall School of Music in London. During World War II he joined the RAF Dance Orchestra (later renamed the Squadronaires). He remained with them until 1964, when he embarked on a successful solo career. —*Kenneth M. Cassidy*

Melody and Percussion for Two Pianos / London 444007

Aldrich Feeling / London 820282

● **Ronnie Aldrich & His Two Pianos** / London 44018

Leroy Anderson

b. Jun. 29, 1908, Cambridge, MA, **d.** May 18, 1975
Composer
Leroy Anderson was a light-classical pop composer, most popular in the '40s and '50s. He began his career in 1935, writing and arranging for Arthur Fiedler and the Boston Pops Orchestra. The sound effects he incorporated into many of his compositions became his musical signature. Among his most popular songs are the Christmas classic "Sleigh Ride," "The Syncopated Clock" (the old "Late Show" theme), "Blue Tango," and "Forgotten Dreams." Anderson's witty, melodic compositions gained wide acceptance in both pop and classical circles. —*Kenneth M. Cassidy*

○ **Fiddle Faddle** / 1967 / Vanguard 6008

Blue Tango—Leroy Anderson's Greatest Hits / 1982 / Pro Arte 8011

★ **Leroy Anderson Collection** / MCA 9815

His best, including "Sleigh Ride," "Blue Tango," "Syncopated Clock," and "Forgotten Dreams." —*Kenneth M. Cassidy*

Burt Bacharach

b. May 12, 1928, Kansas City, Missouri
Composer
Along with lyricist Hal David, Burt Bacharach formed one of the most successful songwriting teams of the 1960's. Their songs displayed a reverence for classic American pop songwriting while keeping abreast of current pop trends. They were responsible for some of the most sophisticated pop songs of the 1960's.

Beginning with a string of hits written for Dionne Warwick, the duo achieved chart success rivaled by few. Hits written for other artists include: "This Guy's In Love With You," What the World Needs Now is Love," "Close to You," and the Oscar winning "Raindrops Keep Falling on My Head."

The songwriting partnership ended in the early 1970's Bacharach's muse seemed to desert him until the 1980's when he returned with a vengeance, scoring major hits with "Arthur's Theme," "On My Own," and "That's What Friends Are For."

Throughout his career, Bacharach recorded a series of solo albums with limited success. While it is always interesting to hear a writer's interpetation of his own work, Bacharach's reputation will always rest firmly on his exceptionally fine songwriting. — *Kenneth M. Cassidy*

● **Greatest Hits** / 1974 / A&M 3321
Greatest Hits collects all of the hits Bacharach had as a recording artist, making it a good introduction to his style. —*AMG*

○ **Classics, Vol. 23** / A&M 2521

While it doesn't feature any songs recorded by Bacharach himself, *Classics* is a good collection of hits other artists had with his songs. —*AMG*

Les Baxter

b. Mar. 14, 1922, Detroit
Composer, Sax
Composer, arranger, and tenor saxophonist who composed and arranged for the top swing bands of the '40s and '50s. Baxter's exotic mambos with strings and flugelhorns were for listening and making love. Baxter came to national attention in 1948 via his three 78rpm album "Music Out of the Moon" which introduced the "Theremin" that is played by the motions of the hands in the air over an electronic field. —*Max Salazar*

Ritual of the Savage / 1952 / Capitol

Tamboo / 1954 / Capitol 655

For Dancers Only: Favorite Tangos / 1992 / CEMA 57010

African Blue: Brazil Now / 1992 / GNP 2036

Skins! / Capitol 774

● **Les Baxter's Best** / Capitol 91218

Richard Clayderman

b. 1954, Paris, France
Piano
Pianist Richard Clayderman is France's most internationally successful recording star. His grand style has earned him more than 114 gold albums. He offers a mix of classical standards and originals played in soft piano stylings and bathed in soothing strings. —*Michael Erlewine*

● **Plays Love Songs of the World** / 1987 / CBS 40472

Classic Collection / Quality 15167

Ray Conniff

b. Jun. 11, 1916, Attleboro, MA
Trombone, arranger
Conniff came up through the big-band ranks of the late '30s, eventually landing staff work on network TV by the early '50s. Arranging slick pop studio hits for singers Johnnie Ray, Don Cherry, Johnny Mathis, and others, he became most successful with a long series of chorus-laden easy-listening albums for the non-rock & roll market. —*Cub Koda*

Somewhere My Love / 1966 / Columbia 9319
The lushest of all Conniff albums, this one features the theme from *Dr. Zhivago*. —*Cub Koda*

's Awful Nice / 1977 / Columbia 8001

○ **Conniff Meets Butterfield** / 1978 / Columbia 8155
Showing off a jazzier side to Conniff that recalls his big-band work, this is a nice album with great trumpet work from Billy Butterfield. In and out of print. —*Cub Koda*

S' Marvelous / 1978 / Columbia 8037

★ **Essence of Ray Conniff** / Jun. 1, 1993 / CBS
A brief collection of Conniff's biggest hits. —*AMG*

B'way Rhythm / CBS 8064

Floyd Cramer

b. Oct. 27, 1933, Shreveport, LA
Piano
A Nashville session man extraordinaire, Cramer's style of "slip-note" playing probably makes him the most widely imitated piano player in Country music history. Chet Atkins suggested that Floyd become a session player, which he did in 1955; for the next ten years he must have recorded on one-quarter of all releases during the peak of the "Nashville Sound" (middle-of-the-road country-flavored music). Floyd's highly distinctive "slip-note" style (one note forward, one note back) made him an immediate hit with the fans. He wrote his famous "Last Date," an instrumental hit, in 1960. —*Cub Koda & David Vinopal*

Last Date / 1961 / RCA Victor 2350

On the Rebound / 1961 / RCA Victor 2359

Floyd Cramer Gets Organ-Ized / 1962 / RCA Victor 2428

I Remember Hank Williams / 1962 / RCA Victor 2544

★ **Best of Floyd Cramer** / 1970 / RCA 56322

Almost Persuaded & Other Hits / Camden 2508
This album includes such hits as "King of the Road," "Born Free," "I'm a Believer," and "Strangers in the Night." —*AMG*

Jesse Crawford

b. Dec. 2, 1895, Woodland, CA, **d.** May 28, 1962, Sherman Oaks, CA
Organ, piano
This popular organist began his professional career in 1911. He went on to play at Grauman's Theatre in Los Angeles and at the Paramount Theatre in New York. Crawford scored four Top 20 hits in the 1920's. He later went on to performing background music on radio. His album *Wedding Music* remains one of the most popular of the genre. —*Kenneth M. Cassidy*

○ **Organ Favorites** / MCA 243

★ **Wedding Music** / MCA 27080

Lenny Dee

Dee was a versatile organist who enjoyed a Top Twenty hit with "Plantation Boogie" in 1955 and recorded a series of albums. He is best known for being able to make his organ sound like a wide variety of other musical instruments. —*Kenneth M. Cassidy*

● **Golden Organ Favorites** / 1971 / MCA 182

Percy Faith

b. 1908, **d.** 1976
Piano, composer
He started as a child piano prodigy, giving his first recital at Massey Hall at age 15, until an accident injuring his hands cut short his concert career. He broke into early radio, arranging for orchestras, developing a lush pop-instrumental style. Faith joined the Columbia staff in the early '50s after tenures at RCA Victor and Decca. He pioneered the "songs from Broadway shows" album format in the early '50s to great effect. He also wrote several film scores including hit songs like "Theme from *A Summer Place*," his first Grammy win. As rock & roll took over and his work became more schlocky in format (easy-listening arrangements of Beatle songs, etc.), the musical quotient remained high, thanks in large part to Faith's arranging skills and penchant for picking good material. —*Cub Koda*

★ **16 Most Requested Songs** / 1978 / Columbia 44398
A basic collection of Faith's biggest hits. —*AMG*

○ **All-Time Greatest Hits** / 1978 / CBS 31588
Here it makes sense to stick with the tried and true. Much of the best of Faith's filmscore work (including "Theme from *A Summer Place*") is included here. —*Cub Koda*

Soft Lights and Sweet Music / RCA
Early-50s compilation of pre-Columbia work; lush and romantic. —*Cub Koda*

Ferrante & Teicher

Group
A piano duo, Arthur Ferrante and Louis Teicher met while both were studying at Juilliard in the late '40s. After years of being guests in front of large orchestras and cutting several cleverly arranged duo albums, they hit their stride in the early '60s with a string of lush orchestrated hit singles and albums based around their interlocking piano style. —*Cub Koda*

★ **Greatest Hits** / 1965 / Curb 77338

○ **West Side Story & Other Motion Picture & Broadway Hits** / United Artists
Despite the unwieldy title (*West Side Story & Other Broadway & Motion Picture Hits*), some of their best work. —*Cub Koda*

○ **Theme from "The Apartment"** / United Artists
Their breakthrough album, both in chart success and the establishment of the orchestrated formula that would carry them through the '60s. —*Cub Koda*

Arthur Fiedler

b. Dec. 17, 1894, Boston, MA, **d.** Jul. 10, 1979, Brookline, MA
Conductor
Arthur Fiedler, the conductor of the internationally known Boston Pops Orchestra, has introduced much of America to classical music, if only on the lighter side. He has recorded dozens of

albums over the years; most of them make excellent easy-listening music. —*Michael Erlewine*

● **Fiedler's Greatest Hits** / RCA Victor 3383

Greatest U.S. Marches / RCA 1334

○ **Popular Favorites** / Pair 1022

Myron Floren

Accordion

There is no doubt that Myron Floren is one of the finest accordion players in the world today. He first gained national attention on *The Lawrence Welk Show* and has recorded many albums, most of them polkas. —*Michael Erlewine*

● **World's Greatest Polkas** / Ranwood 8230

○ **Polka King** / Ranwood 8147

Rudolf Friml

b. Dec. 7, 1879, **d.** Nov. 12, 1972
Piano, composer
An American/Czech pianist/composer of operatic and film music. —*AMG*

○ **Romantic World of Rudolf Friml** / Silva America 9764

James Galway

Internationally renowned Irish flautist James Galway first tasted success at the tender age of ten by winning the Irish Flute Championship. Since then he has forged successful careers in both classical and pop music. In the classical world, Galway has won awards for his recording of John Denver's "Annie's Song," and with his album collaborations with Cleo Laine ("Sometimes When We Touch") and Henry Mancini ("In the Pink"). Currently, Galway continues to tour and record extensively. —*Kenneth M. Cassidy*

○ **Greatest Hits, Vol. 2** / May 1992 / RCA 61178

Enchanted Forest: Melodies of Japan / RCA 7893

● **Greatest Hits** / RCA 7778

Jackie Gleason (HERBERT JOHN GLEASON)

b. Feb. 26, 1916, **d.** Jun. 24, 1987
Vocals
Not only was he one of the finest comedians America has ever produced, Gleason applied his prodigious talents to music as well. With a strong jazz roots background (leaning to mesmerized idolatry when dealing with good trumpet players), Gleason developed a chart-topping series of mood albums, citing his reason for their existence: "Every time I ever watched Clark Gable do a love scene in the movies, I'd hear this really pretty music, real romantic, come up behind him and help set the mood. So I'm figuring that if Clark Gable needs that kinda help, then a guy in Canarsie has gotta be dyin' for somethin' like this!" —*Cub Koda*

○ **Night Winds/Music to Make You** / 1953 / Capitol 92088
Gleason's late-night-and-lonely album, lush and emotional, all the right feelings in place. —*Cub Koda*

Lush Moods / 1984 / Pair 1069

● **Best of Jackie Gleason** / 1993 / Capitol

Champagne, Candlelight and Kisses / Capitol
Not enough Os in smooth to describe this one; everything the title implies and more. —*Cub Koda*

Movie Themes-for Lovers Only / Capitol
Gleason conducting double string orchestra with jazz soloists Charlie Ventura and Pee Wee Irwin, interpreting a dozen film-score melodies with typically lush Gleason results. Uniformly excellent. —*Cub Koda*

Earl Grant

d. Jun. 11, 1970
Singer/pianist/organist Earl Grant achieved his greatest success in the late 1950's, early '60's. His single "The End" was a Top 10 hit in 1958. His career was cut short by his death in a car accident in 1970. —*Kenneth M. Cassidy*

● **Ebb Tide/Spanish Eyes** / MCA 38023

Earl Grant at Basin Street / Decca 74299

End / MCA 20270

Bert Kaempfert

d. Jun. 21, 1980
Bandleader
A band whose sound and selections put them much more in the arena of middle-of-the-road music than in jazz, though they're loved by many of the same people who enjoy Lawrence Welk and Glenn Miller. —*Ron Wynn*

○ **Bert Kaempfert's Greatest Hits** / Decca 74810

● **Best of Bert Kaempfert** / Mobile Fidelity 795

Jerome Kern

b. 1885, **d.** 1945
Composer
An American composer/songwriter for Broadway musicals like *Show Boat* (1927). His songs include *The Way You Look Tonight* (1936). —*AMG*

Jerome Kern Showcase / Pearl Flapper 9767

● **Columbia Album** / CBS 47861

Andre Kostelanetz

b. 1901, St. Petersburg, Russia, **d.** 1980, USA
Composer
This music successfully straddles the borders between light classical and "highbrow" pop music. Kostelanetz was particularly effective at doing spectacular arrangements on Gershwin and Cole Porter material. —*Cub Koda*

● **16 Most Requested Songs** / 1972 / Columbia 40218

○ **Stereo Wonderland of Golden Hits** / Columbia 8839

Erich Kunzel

Classically trained conductor who has also worked extensively in the jazz and pop fields. He has collaborated with Dave Brubeck, Duke Ellington, Ella Fitzgerald, and many others. In 1977, he founded the Cincinnati Pops Orchestra and has since made many pop recordings with them. —*Kenneth M. Cassidy*

● **Mancini's Greatest Hits** / 1989 / Telarc 80183

Classics of the Silver Screen / 1990 / Telarc 80221

Night at the Pops / Pro Arte 359

○ **Kunzel Plays Gershwin** / Pro Arte 408

○ **Kunzel on Broadway** / Fanfare 9017

James Last

James Last is a German bandleader with a large following in Europe, who has made occasional inroads in the States. He is best known for his series of "party albums," and his recordings of "The Seduction," a top 30 US hit in 1980, and "Music From Across The Way." —*Kenneth M. Cassidy*

Non Stop Dancing / PolyGram 825115

● **Romantic Dreams** / Polydor 800033

Alan Jay Lerner

b. Aug. 31, 1918, **d.** Jun. 14, 1986
This Broadway musical lyricist, librettist, screenwriter, and author, usually paired with composer Frederick Loewe, is best known for the shows *Brigadoon, Paint Your Wagon, My Fair Lady,* and *Camelot.* Lerner also wrote the score for the film *Gigi* and an Oscar-winning screenplay for *An American in Paris.* —*William Ruhlmann*

○ **Evening with Alan Jay Lerner** / 1987 / DRG 5175
Star-studded two-disc live album taken from a benefit concert. The best of Lerner's songs and stories, sung, spoken, and played by a Broadway/West End Who's Who including Sally Ann Howes, Burton Lane, Marti Webb, Len Cariou, Tim Rice, Douglas Fairbanks, and others. —*William Ruhlmann*

Liberace (WLADZIU VALENTINO LIBERACE)

b. 1919, **d.** Feb. 4, 1987
Piano
Born Wladziu Valentino Liberace on the outskirts of Milwaukee, Liberace learned piano from his father and received encouragement for a classical career from Paderewski. He opted for work in nightclubs and in 1940 moved to New York, where he became

well known for his semi-classical repertoire. During the '50s he became famous through his involvement in television, known for the candelabrum on his piano (modeled after Chopin) and his flashy clothes. He published his autobiography in 1973. —*David Szatmary*

● **Best of Liberace** / 1972 / MCA 4060
This is an excellent sampler that showcases the flamboyant, semi-classical style of the pianist, including "Shubert's Serenade." —*David Szatmary*

Guy Lombardo

b. Jun. 19, 1902, d. Nov. 5, 1977
Vocals

"The Sweetest Music This Side of Heaven" was the logo of Guy Lombardo & His Royal Canadians, who by 1930 had established themselves as America's top dance band. Unfairly lumped in with unswinging "mickey mouse" bands of the era, the music of Lombardo's outfit was actually top-notch, and they were constantly cited by Louis Armstrong as his favorite band for their purity of intonation. A cache of early sides for Gennett reveals that the band was capable of playing "hot" any time they wanted to, but sweet music and singing novelties featuring brother Carmen is what the public wanted, and Lombardo failed to disappoint. He became a national institution hosting televised New Year's Eve broadcasts from New York, making his rendition of "Auld Lang Syne" part of our national memory chest and his lasting legacy. —*Cub Koda*

Legendary Performer / RCA 2047
A nice selection of middle-period material in straightahead mono. —*Cub Koda*

Guy Lombardo Medleys / Capitol
The first volume in a continuing series, featuring nice bandstand medleys done in the typical Lombardo fashion with nice fidelity. —*Cub Koda*

★ **Best of Guy Lombardo** / MCA 4041
All the hits, including the legendary "Boo Hoo." —*Cub Koda*

Magic Organ

Group
No easy-listening collection would be complete without at least one Magic Organ album. And there are dozens of theater-organ album masterpieces to choose from: old-standards, carousel music, waltzes, and, most of all, polkas. —*Michael Erlewine*

○ **Magic Organ** / 1983 / Ranwood 8108

★ **22 All Time Organ Favorites** / 1984 / Vanguard 7019

Henry Mancini

b. 1924
Composer

If the recognition of one's peers is the true measure of success, then few men are as successful as composer, arranger, and conductor Henry Mancini. In a career that has spanned 40 years, writing for film and television, Mancini has won four Oscars and twenty Grammys, the all-time record for a pop artist. For 1961's *Breakfast at Tiffany's* alone, Mancini won five Grammys and two Oscars. *Breakfast at Tiffany's* includes the classic "Moon River" (lyrics by Johnny Mercer), arguably one of the finest pop songs of the last 50 years. At last count, there were over 1000 recordings of it. His other notable songs include "Dear Heart", "Days of Wine and Roses" (one Oscar, two Grammys), and "Charade," the last two with lyrics by Mercer. He also had a #1 record and won a Grammy for Nino Rota's "Love Theme from *Romeo and Juliet*."

Among his other notable film scores are *The Pink Panther* (three Grammys), *Hatari!* (one Grammy), *Victor/Victoria* (an Oscar), *Two for the Road, Wait Until Dark,* and *10.* His television themes include "Peter Gunn" (two Grammys, recorded by many rock artists), "Mr. Lucky" (two Grammys), "Newhart," "Remington Steele," and the *Thorn Birds* television mini-series.

What has kept Mancini's work fresh is his ability to write in almost any style imaginable and his successful experimentations with unusual sounds and instruments. In his 1989 memoir *Did They Mention the Music,* Mancini's coauthor Gene Lees wrote that "More than any other person, he Americanized film scoring, and in time even European film composers followed in his path," and that Mancini wrote scores that "contained almost as many

fully developed song melodies as a Broadway musical." Had he not remained true to his first love, film scoring, Mancini would have more than likely made as large an impact on the Broadway stage as he made on the silver screen. At the time of his death, Mancini was working on a stage adaptation of *Victor/Victoria.* —*Kenneth M. Cassidy*

Music from "Peter Gunn" / 1959 / RCA 1956
Soundtrack and incidental music from Mancini's early "Hollywood jazz" period. Great listening. —*Cub Koda*

★ **Best of Mancini** / 1987 / RCA 53822
Mancini's most memorable scores, including "The Pink Panther," "Moon River," and others. The best overview of his voluminous work. —*Cub Koda*

Mr. Lucky—TV Soundtrack / RCA 2198
Henry Mancini tried for something similar to Peter Gunn in his music for this Blake Edwards-produced series, but didn't quite succeed. This music is moody and occasionally interesting, but nowhere near as driving as the other. —*Bruce Eder*

Mantovani

b. Nov. 15, 1905, Venice, d. Mar. 30, 1980, England
Violin, composer

Violinist, composer, and conductor Annunzio Paolo Mantovani was born in Venice, Italy. He started working in London at 16 and was conducting the Hotel Metropol Orchestra by 1925. Mantovani was a major pioneer in the heavy use of strings and one of the first to be almost exclusively interested in recorded rather than live music. He also was one of the first popular artists to concentrate on producing albums rather than singles. He had seven million-selling albums, including *Immortal Classics* (1954) and *Exodus and Other Great Themes* (1960). In 1935-1936 Mantovani had hits in the US with "Red Sails in the Sunset" and "Serenade to the Night." He was soon recognised as the undisputed king of easy listening, or mood music, as it was called then. He had 51 hit albums in the US alone. —*Michael Erlewine*

Incomparable Mantovani (London) / 1964 / Bainbridge 6269

● **Golden Hits** / 1982 / Bainbridge 6288

Paul Mauriat

French composer/conductor Paul Mauriat is a classically trained musician who decided to pursue a career in popular music. His first major sucess came in 1962, as a co-writer of the European hit, "Chariot." In 1963, the song was given English lyrics, renamed "I Will Follow Him," and became a number one American hit for Little Peggy March. Mauriat is best remembered for his 1968 world-wide smash, "Love is Blue." —*Kenneth M. Cassidy*

Best of France / 1967 / Philips 834370

● **Love Is Blue** / 1967 / Mercury 830769

Sergio Mendes

b. 1941
Piano

An early proponent of his native Brazil's bossa-nova style, he formed the group, Brasil '65 (which later became Brasil '66 and was updated in semi-yearly increments) and scored hits with soothing, Latin-tinged pop throughout the '60s. —*Cub Koda*

● **Greatest Hits of Brasil '66** / A&M 3258
Smooth-as-silk arrangements. His best sides and major hits such as "Fool on the Hill" and "The Look of Love." —*Cub Koda*

'66 Four Sider / A&M 6012

Frank Mills

Canadian born composer/pianist Frank Mills scored a minor US hit in 1972 with, "Love Me, Love Me Love." It wasn't until the release of "Music Box Dancer" and its subsequent success in 1979, that Mills became more of a household name. Success was to be short lived however, and it wasn't long before Mills was back to performing in his native Canada. —*Kenneth M. Cassidy*

● **Music Box Dancer** / Polydor 6192

Jerry Murad & His Harmonicats

Group
Murad & His Harmonicats perform easygoing '50s pop, all built around a harmonica orchestra. —*Dan Heilman*

○ **Jerry Murad's Harmonicats' Greatest Hits** / 1990 / CBS 9511
Contains "Peg o' My Heart" and other hits. —*Dan Heilman*

Peter Nero

b. May 22, 1934, Brooklyn, NY
Piano
Nero is a pianist and New York native who started with Paul
Whiteman, then moved up to symphony until the late '50s, when
RCA Victor signed him and successfully promoted him into a pop
music interpreter. He won the 1961 Grammy for Best New Artist.
His lush orchestrated albums continued through the early '70s,
when he returned to a harder jazz format, recording with a trio.
—*Cub Koda*

Nero Goes =Pops= / RCA
An interesting, largely successful album with Arthur Fiedler and
the Boston Pops Orchestra. —*Cub Koda*

● **Peter Nero's Greatest Hits** / CBS 33136

Now / Concord Jazz 48
This is a smartly played set of standards interpreted in a trio setting. —*Cub Koda*

○ **Hail the Conquering Nero** / RCA
The biggest of his early-60s successes. —*Cub Koda*

101 Strings Orchestra

Group
Published by Alshire International Inc., there are over 200 albums
in this series of lush string-laden instrumentals designed for easy
listening. —*Michael Erlewine*

● **Best of the 101 Strings** / Alshire

Nelson Riddle

b. Jun. 1, 1921, Oradell, NJ, **d.** Oct. 6, 1985, Los Angeles, CA
Composer
While Nelson Riddle had experience as a trombonist and
arranger for Charlie Spivak, Jerry Wald, and Tommy Dorsey in
the '40s and was a staff arranger for NBC radio later in that era,
he achieved his greatest success and notoriety during the '50s.
Riddle was the arranger and conductor for Judy Garland, Jimmy
Wakely, Betty Hutton, Ella Mae Morse, and many others in the
early '50s, including Nat King Cole, but became the top arranger
in Hollywood through his collaborations with Frank Sinatra during 1953. Riddle's orchestrations and careful, intelligent use of
first-class jazz musicians accented Sinatra's voice perfectly, without obscuring, challenging, or threatening. No one was better at
knowing when to increase the brass section's volume, how to support a singer, and what soloist to spotlight and for how long.
Riddle enjoyed some success on his own during the '50s, including a Grammy award in 1958 and a #1 pop hit in 1955. He later
expanded his activities to work with Ella Fitzgerald, Oscar
Peterson, Rosemary Clooney, and Johnny Mathis; and became a
busy film soundtrack arranger, composer, and conductor as well.
He contributed to hit movies such as *The St. Louis Blues* and
Pajama Game, and did the theme music for the TV shows "Route
66" and "The Untouchables." He was musical director for the Julie
Andrews variety show in the '70s and came back from health
problems to arrange and conduct Grammy-winning albums for
Linda Ronstadt in the '80s. His last work was a 1985 arrangement
for opera singer Kiri Te Kanawa. —*Ron Wynn*

Route 66 and Other Great TV Themes / 1980 / CEMA 9452

★ **Best of Nelson Riddle** / Capitol 1990

Doc Severinsen

b. Jul. 7, 1927, Arlington, OR
Trumpet, bandleader
Longtime "Tonight Show" bandleader and Johnny Carson foil,
trumpeter Doc Severinsen spent several years playing in bop
groups and jazz clubs before attaining his high visibility, big paying television gig. During the '40s, he worked with Charlie
Barnet, Sam Donahue, and Tommy Dorsey, and did several sessions in studios. His studio reputation got him a chance to work
at NBC, and he played in the bands for Steve Allen shows and
other programs. He became a member of the Tonight Show orchestra, and assembled a first-class aggregation that often included many top players from major swing and big bands.
Severinsen in the '80s has led his own big band and small combo

when away from the Tonight Show, and won a Grammy in 1986.
He's often been a guest soloist and conductor with various symphony orchestras, and he can hit high notes and play ballads and
standards with ease. —*Ron Wynn*

Tonight Show Band with Doc Severinsen / Aug. 5, 1986+Aug.
7, 1986 / Amherst 93311

Big Band Hit Parade / Feb. 1989 / Telarc 8077
The former Tonight Show bandleader (he was still in that position at the time of this recording) heads his big band through old
warhorses and pre-rock standards. Lots of brass and bombast,
plus some decent solos. Severinsen is a much better trumpet
soloist than his image conveys. —*Ron Wynn*

● **Best of Doc Severinsen** / MCA 4168

○ **Once More, with Feeling!** / Amherst 94405

Billy Vaughn

b. Apr. 12, 1919, Glasgow, KY, **d.** Sep. 14, 1991
Vocals
Kentucky-born Vaughn began his career with the vocal group the
Hilltoppers in 1952. He worked as music director for Dot Records,
and as an arranger and conductor for Pat Boone, the Fontaine
Sisters, Gale Storm, and other Dot artists. His '50s hits include
"Melody of Love" and "The Shifting Whispering Sands." —*AMG*

● **Billy Vaughn & His Orchestra Play 22 of His Greatest Hits** /
Ranwood 7025

Lawrence Welk

b. 1903, **d.** May 17, 1992
Accordion
Long the butt of many a comedian and music fan's jokes,
Lawrence Welk survived into the '90s as America's most successful bandleader. From dirt-poor beginnings in rural North Dakota,
the relatively uneducated and heavily accented Welk seemed an
unlikely candidate to carve out a successful, 60-plus-year career
in the music business, but through sheer dogged persistence and
belief in himself, that's exactly what transpired. His "Champagne
music" style (lighter and less rhythmic than Guy Lombardo's) remained remarkably unchanged over the years. Changes in music
have been constant—the end of the big band era, rock & roll,
country & western, the Beatles, disco—with Welk seemingly impervious to it all, and a built-in audience that felt the same way.
While jazz legends like Coleman Hawkins were lucky to land a
Timex jazz special once a year, Welk was on ABC-TV twice a
week! After being dropped by that network, he was one of the
first to successfully move into television syndication, ending up
more visible than he had been on ABC at his "peak." Expanding
his musical family to include tap dancers, jazz musicians (notably
Pete Fountain), and multitudes of singers (The Lennon Sisters,
etc.), Welk made no pretense of being remotely "hip," merely delivering simple, well-played music and solid, family-oriented entertainment year after year. —*Cub Koda*

★ **16 Most Requested Songs** / Columbia 45030
A brief compilation that captures Welk's style nicely. —*AMG*

Calcutta! / Dot 8024
Welk's early-60s stab at pop/rock & roll instrumentals. —*Cub
Koda*

○ **In Concert** / Ranwood 6001

Pick-a-Polka! / Coral 57067

Favorites / Coral
A nice 12-song overview of Lawrence's '50s television band. No
big hits, just nicely played and sequenced. —*Cub Koda*

Paul Weston & Jo Stafford

Group
Hilarious sendups of cocktail piano/chanteuse duos by bandleader Paul Weston and pop singer Jo Stafford (husband and wife)
as Jonathan and Darlene Edward. Jonathan can't play, Darlene
can't sing, and the whole melange is hilarious from start to finish.
—*Cub Koda*

Crescent City / 1991 / Corinthian 116

● **Music for Memories/Music For Dreaming** / Jan. 20, 1992 /
Capitol 92091

Mason Williams

b. Aug. 24, 1938, Abilene, TX
Guitar
A talented guitarist and comedy writer who came into prominence on the late-60s TV show "The Smothers Brothers." Williams scored a major pop hit with the instrumental "Classical Gas," and he continues to write and perform interesting folk-based acoustic guitar pieces. —*David Szatmary*

Phonograph Record / 1968 / Warner Brothers 1729

● **Music 1968-1971** / 1969 / Vanguard 137
A humorous collection from this underrated guitarist. —*David Szatmary*

○ **Hand Made** / 1970 / Warner Brothers 1838
The best from this folk picker, who is sometimes moving, somewimes humorous. Includes the hit "Classical Gas." —*David Szatmary*

Roger Williams (LOUIS WEERTZ)

b. 1925
Piano
Juilliard-trained, Williams attained chart popularity with overwrought but cleanly played instrumentals like "Autumn Leaves" and the film theme "Born Free." He placed 38 albums in the Top 200 between 1956 and 1972. —*Cub Koda*

● **Best of Roger Williams** / 1989 / MCA 4106
All the hits, with nice fidelity, in one neat package. The perfect place to start. —*Cub Koda*

Zamfir

Romanian panpipe player Gheorghe Zamfir first reached #4 on the UK charts in 1976 with an ethereal hit called "Doina De Jale"—a traditional Eastern funeral piece. He has gone on to make dozens of albums and entrance millions of buyers with the other-worldly sound of the pan pipes. His repertoire includes Romanian folk music and classical melodies, but most of all popular film themes. —*Michael Erlewine*

● **Lonely Shepherd** / 1984 / Mercury 822787

Easy Listening Collections

22 Great Guitar Favorites / 1986 / Ranwood 7014

○ **Hooked on Themes** / 1977 / K-Tel 1663

Hooked on Big Bands / K-Tel 6082

○ **Hooked on Classics—Best of Hooked on Classics** / 1986 / K-Tel 247

○ **Hooked on Classics, Vol. 1** / K-Tel 6113

Hooked on Swing—Best of Hooked on Swing / 1986 / K-Tel 507

○ **Hooked on Swing, Vol. 1** / 1986 / K-Tel 7853

Songs from MGM Musicals / Chandos 8781

○ **Orchestral Space** / Varese Sarabande 47253

Romantic Sax for Lovers / PolyGram 816185

Sax for Lovers / PolyGram 816185

☆ **Secret Agent File** / GNP 2166

Slow Dancing the Night Away / Madacy 5465

Songs & Waltzes from Vienna / CBS 47682

VOCAL

If the human voice is the oldest musical instrument of all, then it's also the most recorded one in the history of the medium itself. In essence, this section reflects how that instrument has been part and parcel of the development of American pop music since recorded performances were being etched into cylinders in Thomas Edison's laboratories.

What we now know as popular or "pop" music started right around the turn of the century. Song publishers were flourishing in a section of New York City known as "Tin Pan Alley," selling sheet music like crazy, while the recording industry was just getting off the ground. Once the sheet music publishers found they needed someone to sing or "plug" that song and make it popular, and the record companies realized that the singer in question could sell a lot of records for them by singing that song, we saw the birth of popular music and the pop singer.

As pop music, even before the advent of rock & roll, took many stylistic twists and turns, so it is with the artists profiled in this section. If one rule of thumb may be applied:

the pop music we're talking about predates rock & roll and is of the Tin Pan Alley variety, the artists profiled belonging to all the various offshoots that genre entails. We're covering nearly a century's worth of recordings from early vaudeville performers like Al Jolson to modern-day artists singing material that clearly falls outside of rock music's several subgenres, and pretty much everything in between. Vocal pop music embraces everything from Rudy Vallee to Barbara Streisand, the Andrews Sisters to Frank Sinatra, and Bette Midler to Tony Bennett. That's a lot of stylistic ground to cover, but the genre itself maps out the same territory, adding decided left-hand turns to include song-and-dance men like Fred Astaire and "international" favorites like Marlene Dietrich and Yma Sumac. Given the current climate of music, one can only wonder what will constitute an entry into this section by the 21st century. As long as people keep singing, the boundaries of vocal/pop music will keep expanding.

– Cub Koda

Ames Brothers

Group
Brothers Ed, Vic, Joe, and Gene Ames formed a group in their native Malden, MA, going on to score 23 Top-40 hits between 1949 and 1960. When rock & roll made chart success more and more difficult to attain, they split up, Ed going on to a solo career of his own. —*Cub Koda*

★ **Best of the Ames Brothers** / 1958 / RCA Victor 1859
Though their early hits recorded for Coral (now MCA) will probably be anthologized at some point, this one features all their biggest and best: "You, You, You," "The Man with the Banjo," "Melodie d'Amour," "Tammy," and "The Naughty Lady of Shady Lane." Smooth as silk. —*Cub Koda*

The Andrews Sisters

Vocals
This American vocal trio consisted of sisters Patty (b. 1920), Maxine (b. 1918), and LaVerne Andrews (1915-1967). Their tight-knit harmonies were a direct descendant of the groundbreaking work done in the early '30s by the Boswell Sisters, but they soon developed their own successful strain. They went on to sell over 60 million records, cashing in on the boogie-woogie fad of the '40s and becoming wartime favorites with film appearances in *Buck Privates* and *Stage Door Canteen*, among others. They are still the biggest-selling girl group ever. —*Cub Koda*

● **50th Anniversary, Vols. 1 & 2** / 1990 / MCA 42044
A two-volume definitive overview, with their best and most interesting sides from a long and successful career. —*Cub Koda*

○ **Capitol Collectors Series** / 1991 / Capitol 94078
A terrific overview of their mid-'50s output for Capitol, including such songs as "Rum and Coca-Cola," "Boogie Woogie Bugle Boy," "Don't Sit under the Apple Tree (with Anyone Else but Me)," "Begin the Beguine," and "Beat Me Daddy, Eight to the Bar." — *Stephen Thomas Erlewine*

Harold Arlen

b. Feb. 15, 1905, Buffalo, NY, **d.** Apr. 23, 1986
Vocals, composer

An American songwriting legend and son of a cantor, Harold Arlen was fascinated early in his life with the sound of ragtime. While singing in his father's synagogue he also played ragtime piano in local Buffalo bands and accompanied silent films.

After arranging for the Buffalodians, Arlen moved to New York. His jobs included arranging for Fletcher Henderson and serving as a rehearsal pianist for radio and theatre. A vamp he devised while practicing was later turned into the song "Get Happy," with lyrics from Ted Koehler. Arlen and Koehler wrote eight revues for the Cotton Club, one of which included the anthem "Stormy Weather," first performed by Ethel Waters.

Though he moved to Hollywood in the '30s, Arlen kept penning songs for Broadway, working with lyricists such as Dorothy Fields, Les Robin, Johnny Mercer, Yip Harburg, and Ira Gershwin as well as Koehler. His list of hits and accomplishments is amazing; They include songs for the films *Take a Chance, Star-Spangled Rhythm, The Sky's the Limit* and his most famous, *The Wizard of Oz*. Arlen also composed tunes for the plays *Earl Carroll Vanities, Rhythm Mania* and *St. Louis Woman*. His incredible array of unforgettable compositions includes "I've Got the World on a String," "I Gotta Right to Sing the Blues," "The Devil and the Deep Blue Sea," "Come Rain or Come Shine," "It's Only a Paper Moon" and "Over the Rainbow."

Numerous jazz artists have recorded his songs, as well as pop performers across the spectrum. Arlen made a few albums as a performer, among them sessions with Duke Ellington and Barbra Streisand. —*Ron Wynn*

● **Harold Sings Arlen (with Friends)** / 1966 / Vox Cum Laude 2920
Harold Arlen and others, including Barbra Streisand. —*AMG*

Fred Astaire (Franz Austerlitz)

b. May 10, 1899, Omaha, NE, **d.** Jun. 22, 1987, Los Angeles, CA
Vocals, dancer, actor
Although best known for his dancing and acting, Astaire was a limited but extremely popular singer whose recordings of numerous pop standards have become the best-known versions. — *Bruce Eder*

Irving Berlin Songbook / Dec. 1952 / Verve 829172

An unusual reconsideration of Astaire's best repertoire, with the singer fronting a jazz combo. Uneven but interesting. —*Bruce Eder*

● **Starring Fred Astaire** / Columbia 44233
The best of Astaire, featuring songs by Berlin, Gershwin, Kern, and others that were written specifically for him. —*Bruce Eder*

Pearl Bailey

b. Mar. 29, 1918, Newport News, Virginia, US, d. Aug. 17, 1990, Philadelphia, Pennsylvania
Vocals
Bailey started in show business by winning an amateur contest at age 13. Her eventual move from Washington, D.C., to New York City established her as the darling of the cabaret/night club circuit. Bailey's languid, bluesy style, with assorted humorous asides and dialogs, only improved with time as movies and Las Vegas beckoned. In the '40s and '50s, Bailey was one of the first women to bring salacious lyrics into the mainstream (witness her seduction of Hot Lips Page, "Baby, It's Cold Outside"). She was also the first female rapper (check "Tired"). In her rich, expressive alto, Bailey didn't just sing a song, she lived it as few artists had done before or have done since. —*Cub Koda and Bil Carpenter*

Intoxicating Pearl Bailey / 1956 / Mercury 20277
Spicy, sing-song storytelling. —*Bil Carpenter*

☆ **Pearl Bailey Sings for Adults Only** / 1959 / Roulette 25016
Delightfully wicked set of standards done up in the inimitable Pearl Bailey manner, with immaculately swinging support from husband/drummer/bandleader Louis Bellson. —*Cub Koda*

Porgy and Bess / Apr. 30, 1959 / Forum 9024
Backed by the Buddy Baker orchestra. —*Bil Carpenter*

★ **Best of Pearl Bailey** / 1961 / Roulette 25144
Sassy and outlandish, this anthologizes most (but not all) of Bailey's best sides, including "It Takes Two to Tango." —*Cub Koda*

○ **16 Most Requested Songs** / 1991 / Columbia 47082
Her most memorable '40s and '50s pop cuts. —*Bil Carpenter*

Definitive Pearl Bailey / CBS 985
Her earliest "rapping" from 1946. —*Bil Carpenter*

Josephine Baker

b. 1906, St. Louis, Missouri, US, d. Apr. 12, 1975, Paris, France
Vocals
After drawing attention to herself with comic dancing in the all-Black chorus line of *Shuffle Along*, Baker became the sensation of Paris during the Jazz Age. Her silvery voice (said to be strong enough in her prime to be able to fill a theater without the use of a microphone), exotic good looks, and energetic manner made her a legend for over a half century in France, with movies, musicals, revues, and hit records to her credit. However, success eluded her in the United States. She was still active in a one-woman show (with a dozen costume changes) in 1975 when she died in her sleep after giving 14 well-received performances. —*Cub Koda*

★ **Josephine Baker** / 1951 / Dcc 614
One of a few examples of great Josephine Baker songs available. Brassy, classy, and vital cuts. Great sound. —*Ron Wynn*

Mae Barnes

Vocals
An entertaining, bombastic singer who handled blues, ballads, bawdy tunes, and standards with zest. She enjoyed some success in '50s and '60s, recording for Atlantic and Vanguard. —*Ron Wynn*

Fun with Mae Barnes / 1953 / Atlantic 404
● **Meet Mae Barnes** / 1958 / Vanguard 9036

Shirley Bassey

b. Jan. 8, 1937, Tiger Bay, Cardiff, Wales
Vocals
The Welsh belter supplied the strident theme song for one of Sean Connery's action-packed James Bond films, *Goldfinger*, in 1965. Bassey had scored a bundle of hits in Great Britain prior to landing the movie theme. Among her later U.S. chart items for United Artists was the title song to another Bond flick, 1972's *Diamonds Are Forever*. —*Bill Dahl*

Live at Carnegie Hall / 1973 / United Artists 111
● **Best of Shirley Bassey** / EMI America 92879
CD release spotlights dynamic international showbiz star. —*Ron Wynn*

Harry Belafonte

b. Mar. 1, 1927, New York, NY
Vocals
The Harlem-born vocalist spearheaded the mid-'50s calypso movement in America, although he started out as a more conventional pop artist. Belafonte's clear diction, pure voice, and strikingly handsome features made him a national sensation when RCA released "Jamaica Farewell" in 1956 and "Banana Boat (Day-O)" the next year. Although much of his subsequent RCA output was calypso-oriented, Belafonte dabbled in everything from blues to Gershwin over the next few years. In addition to his music, Belafonte has starred in several movies, including *Buck and the Preacher*, in 1972, and *Uptown Saturday Night*, in 1974. His daughter Shari is a successful actress. —*Bill Dahl*

○ **Calypso** / 1956 / RCA 53801
His third album, which made him a star. —*Ron Wynn*

☆ **Belafonte at Carnegie Hall** / 1959 / RCA 6006
Landmark late-'50s live set. —*Ron Wynn*

○ **Legendary Performer** / 1978 / RCA 52469
Good retrospective. —*Ron Wynn*

★ **All-Time Greatest Hits, Vols. 1-3** / 1987 / RCA 9771

Day-O & Other Hits / 1990 / RCA 52082
A recent collection of past hits. —*Ron Wynn*

Tony Bennett (Benedetto, Anthony Dominick)

b. Aug. 3, 1926, New York, NY
Vocals
One of the great pop singers of his generation, Tony Bennett reached stardom with a series of hits starting with "Because of You," a 10-week number one in 1951. Other chart-toppers were "Cold, Cold Heart" (1951) and "Rags to Riches" (1953). Bennett scored fewer hits in the second half of the '50s as popular music turned toward the rock & roll style of Elvis Presley, but he became more interested in jazz, recording albums with Count Basie and other jazz musicians. He scored a major popular comeback with "I Left My Heart in San Francisco" in 1962, a tune that won him a Grammy and became his signature song. Through the rest of the '60s, Bennett's albums were top-sellers, and he put his mark on a series of excellent songs from old standards to new movie themes.

In the '70s, Bennett made a couple of outstanding albums with jazz pianist Bill Evans, but he then stayed out of the recording studio for many years, preferring to avoid commercial pressures while performing for fans all over the world. He made a triumphant return to recording in 1986 with *The Art of Excellence* and was the subject of a four-CD boxed-set retrospective of his career, *Forty Years: The Artistry of Tony Bennett* in 1991.

With his ease of manner and warm vocal tone, Bennett has always been a singer's singer, garnering high praise from such peers as Frank Sinatra as well as from critics and fans, and he shows every sign of continuing to please them for many more years. —*William Ruhlmann*

☆ **Count Basie Swings, Tony Bennett Sings** / Nov. 19, 1958 / Roulette 25072

○ **Bennett and Basie Strike Up the Band** / 1961 / Roulette 25231

☆ **I Left My Heart in San Francisco** / 1962 / CBS 8669

○ **Tony Bennett at Carnegie Hall** / 1962 / Sony Special Products 823

○ **Bill Evans Album** / Jun. 10, 1975-Jun. 13, 1975 / Fantasy 439

Bennett/Berlin / 1987 / CBS 44029
A fine Bennett release from the late '80s. —*John Floyd*

☆ **Jazz** / 1987 / Columbia 40424
A splendid collection of material recorded between 1954 and 1967, highlighting Bennett's skills as a jazz vocalist. —*AMG*

Astoria: Portrait of the Artist / 1990 / CBS 45348
This represents some of Bennett's finest late-'80s output. —*John Floyd*

☆ **Forty Years: The Artistry of Tony Bennett** / Oct. 7, 1991 / Columbia 46843

If there were one greatest-hits package that did the job correctly, novices wouldn't have to spring for this four-disc boxed set. However, this is where Bennett's genius and, as the title says, his artistry, proves itself most effectively. Buy this and you'll never need another Bennett disc. —*John Floyd*

○ **Perfectly Frank** / 1992 / Columbia 52965

Think no one can touch the Chairman on his own turf? Think again. Bennett's tribute is such an obvious move, it's odd that it's taken this long to materialize. Sinatra has made no secret of his admiration of Bennett, who puts his spin on this collection of Francis Albert classics. In the process, we wind up with Bennett's best in years. —*Steve Aldrich*

○ **Art of Excellence** / Mar. 4, 1992 / Columbia 40344

Steppin' Out / 1993 /

Bennett's tribute to songs that Fred Astaire made famous (including standards by Gershwin, Cole Porter, Irving Berlin, and Jerome Kern) is as strong a record as anything he has made recently, including the acclaimed *Perfectly Frank.* —*AMG*

● **Essence of Tony Bennett** / Jun. 1, 1993 / CBS

A good but brief introduction to Bennett. —*AMG*

★ **All-Time Greatest Hits** / CBS 31494

The best single-disc introduction to Bennett's music. —*AMG*

Irving Berlin

b. May 11, 1888, Temun, Siberia, Russia, **d.** Sep. 22, 1989

Songwriter

Irving Berlin was one of the greatest songwriters of the 20th century, his first success coming in 1911 with the song "Alexander's Ragtime Band," his last major hit being the Broadway musical "Call Me Madam" in 1950. In between, he wrote everything from "God Bless America" to "White Christmas." As a performer, Berlin was seen on Broadway, around the country, and on film in his wartime shows "Yip Yip Yaphank" and "This Is the Army." —*William Ruhlmann*

★ **Irving Berlin: A Hundred Years** / 1988 / Columbia 40035

● **Girl on Magazine Cover** / RCA 3704

William Bolcom

b. May 26, 1938

Composer, piano

An American composer and pianist whose music makes use of many traditional and contemporary styles (like ragtime and jazz) and focuses on spiritual and religious themes. —*AMG*

Euphonic Sounds: The Scott Joplin Album / 1988 / Omega 3001

The Boswell Sisters

b. USA

Group

Vocal trio hailing from New Orleans with lead singer Connee (1907-1976) and sisters Helvetia and Martha Boswell. Their purity of intonation and bluesy, infectious swing of harmonies became the role model for the Andrews Sisters, Ella Fitzgerald, the McGuire Sisters, and Bette Midler. Connee went solo in the mid '30s, appearing in movies and radio. She entertained the troops during World War II and remained active through the mid '50s. The Boswell Sisters' jazz-like phrasing and strong New Orleans roots made a transitional move away from the stiff pop singing of the '20s. Their trailblazing style lives on today in their numerous progeny. —*Cub Koda*

★ **Everybody Loves My Baby** / Dec. 7, 1992 / Pro Arte 550

It's sad that so far there's only one CD of this extraordinarily gifted trio's work. The dexterous harmony singing and unusual repertoire, anticipating the Andrews Sisters, shines through. —*Bruce Eder*

● **Early Sides: 1931-1935** / Take Two 209

☆ **Boswell Sisters** / CBS

A truly comprehensive multi-record boxed set from Columbia. Inspired programming and notes by Michael Brooks. —*Bruce Eder*

Teresa Brewer

b. May 7, 1931, Toledo, OH

Vocals

Specializing in bright, chirpy melodies, spunky Teresa Brewer was one of the top pop thrushes of the '50s. Raised in Toledo, OH, she was a regular on "The Major Bowes Amateur Hour" as a child. Brewer scored her first huge hit in 1950 at the tender age of 18 with "Music! Music! Music!" and followed it up with an impressive string of smashes for Coral Records that spanned the entire decade. Several of Brewer's mid-'50s hits—Fats Domino's "Bo Weevil," Ivory Hunter's "Empty Arms"—were sanitized R&B covers. Brewer has pursued jazzier directions in recent years, still retaining her youthful vocal delivery. —*Bill Dahl*

● **Best of Teresa Brewer** / 1989 / MCA 1545

This 1989 anthology is comprised of cuts from her Coral albums. —*Ron Wynn*

Memories of Louis / May 11, 1992 / Red Baron 48629

Nice tribute. Excellent production and arrangements. —*Ron Wynn*

○ **American Music Box, Vol. 1 (Songs of Irving Berlin)** / Doctor Jazz 40231

This contains some wonderful selections. —*Ron Wynn*

Hoagy Carmichael (Howard Hoagland Carmichael)

b. 1899, Bloomington, IN, **d.** Dec. 27, 1981, Palm Springs, CA

Vocals, piano, songwriter

One of America's greatest songwriters, Carmichael started in on the ground floor of jazz, working with Louis Armstrong, Jack Teagarden, and his closest friend, trumpet legend Bix Beiderbecke. His lazy, in-the-pocket style of piano playing and singing gave his best performances a wistfulness that appealed to everybody, non-jazz fans included. But it's his songs that have endured best: "Stardust" (one of the most recorded and performed songs of the 20th century), "Up a Lazy River," "Rocking Chair," "Two Sleepy People," "Lazybones," "In the Cool, Cool, Cool of the Evening" and the venerable chestnut "Georgia on My Mind" all have ensured his place as one of the greats of American popular music. —*Cub Koda*

Stardust (1927-1932) / 1927-1932 / Historical 37

This session presents a dozen early Hoagy Carmichael sides that make a nice complement to other recently (1982) reissued Decca sides. These tracks are earlier (1927-1932) and have greater jazz interest in both solos and arrangements. There is also a good helping of Carmichael vocals mixed in with Cliff Williams and Scrappy Lambert. There are two previously unissued tracks, and the overall sound is fair to good. —*Bob Rusch, Cadence*

Stardust Road / 1958 / MCA 1507

Hoagy Carmichael, The Stardust Road is a set of Decca recordings from the '40s chock full of the Carmichael vocal charm and ambiance, but only of peripheral jazz interest. —*Bob Rusch, Cadence*

○ **Hoagy Carmichael Collection** / Smithsonian

A definitive, triple-volume set, mostly devoted to others' interpretations of his work, including recordings by Louis Armstrong and the Boswell Sisters. —*Bruce Eder*

● **Stardust & Much More** / RCA/Bluebird 8333

A wide-ranging collection of recordings of his work by Carmichael and others, covering 1927 to 1960. A good starter on his work. —*Bruce Eder*

Vikki Carr (Florencia Martinez Cardona)

b. Jul. 19, 1941, El Paso, TX

Vocals

After singing at various school functions and in local groups and Pepe Callahan's Mexican-Irish band, Carr began her solo career in earnest in the early '60s. Her solo debut was in Reno, NV, supported by the Chuck Leonard Quartet, which led to a record contract with Liberty. While not gathering much attention in the United States, her first single, "He's a Rebel," was a hit in Australia and led to numerous television appearances and a spell as a regular on the "Ray Anthony Show." In the late '60s, Carr scored three Top-40 hits, including the number three "It Must Be Him." Her American sales dwindled at the beginning of the '70s. With the release of her 1980 album, *Vikki Carr y el Amor,* Carr gained enormous success in the Latin music world. In 1991 Carr won a Best Latin Pop Album Grammy for her *Cosas del Amor.* — *Stephen Thomas Erlewine*

● **It Must Be Him: The Best of Vikki Carr** / 1992 / EMI America 93450
A 23-track compilation of Carr's '60s singles, containing her three Top-40 hits, "It Must Be Him," "The Lesson," and "With Pen in Hand," as well as her version of "He's a Rebel," which was cut before the Crystals version. — *Stephen Thomas Erlewine*

June Christy

b. Nov. 20, 1925, Springfield, IL, **d.** Jun. 21, 1990
Vocals
After a mid-'40s stint as Stan Kenton's vocalist, "The Misty Miss Christy" recorded a series of '50s albums that both jazz and pop fans could dig. The smoky-voiced singer managed to project sexiness and sophistication without sacrificing a wholesome, girl-next-door quality. What a gorgeous voice! — *Richard Lieberson*

○ **Uncollected June Christy with the Kentones (1946)** / 1946 / Hindsight 219
Previously unissued June Christy material from late 4'0s and '50s with knockoff unit from Stan Kenton orchestra. It's designed for completists, as its alternate takes and unreleased cuts that were judged inferior or left over. There's nothing wrong with some of them, but these are not the songs that made Christy famous. — *Ron Wynn*

Interlude / 195 / Discovery 911
Trademark late-'50s recording, full of delicately performed lush and "torch" numbers that displayed both her jazz roots and pop sophistication. — *Ron Wynn*

★ **Something Cool** / Dec. 27, 1954-May 9, 1955 / Capitol 96329
Christy's classic first album, plus ten other '50s sides. The best introduction to Christy. — *Richard Lieberson*

Road Show / 1959 / Capitol 96328
Fine live recording of June Christy with Stan Kenton & the Four Freshmen from 1959. Christy is a bit below par due to a cold on the day of the recording. — *Kenneth M. Cassidy*

Rosemary Clooney

b. May 23, 1928, Maysville, KY
Vocals
Her imaginative choice of material made Rosemary Clooney a household word during the '50s. Clooney and her sister Betty sang over a Cincinnati radio station before joining Tony Pastor's orchestra. Signing with Columbia in 1949, Clooney hit with the inviting number-one smash "Come on-a My House," cowritten by Ross Bagdasarian (who was soon to unleash a trio of electronically created chipmunks on the world as David Seville). Subsequent chart-toppers included "Half as Much" in 1952 and "Hey There" and the country-based "This Ole House" in 1954 (the same year she married actor Jose Ferrer). Clooney also starred in several movies, most notably Bing Crosby's *White Christmas* in 1954. Today Clooney sings in a jazzier vein, as alluring as ever. — *Bill Dahl*

Blue Rose / 1956 / Columbia 872
A moody 1956 collaboration with Duke Ellington. Well worth seeking out. — *Charles S. Wolfe*

● **16 Most Requested Songs** / 1964 / Columbia 44403
Vintage hits from the '50s, including a number of the novelty songs done with Mitch Miller. — *Charles S. Wolfe*

Sings the Lyrics of Ira Gershwin / Oct. 1979 / Concord Jazz 4112
First of a series of '80s albums in which Rosie, backed by a jazz combo, pays tribute to the great pop composers. The whole series is worth having. — *Charles S. Wolfe*

Sings the Music of Cole Porter / 1982 / Concord Jazz 4185
The second in a series of repertory albums that featured Clooney's interpretations of songs by America's principal pre-rock pop composers, this is arguably the best. Clooney brings to Porter songs the sophistication, touches, lyric shadings, and performances that only vocal veterans who truly understood them could provide. — *Ron Wynn*

Sings the Music of Harold Arlen / 1983 / Concord Jazz 4210
A singer whose profile and critical evaluations have soared in the '80s and '90s covers vintage songs from Harold Arlen, most of them done elsewhere by other performers. Clooney is an excellent technical vocalist; these are certainly outstanding interpretations. — *Ron Wynn*

Sings Ballads / Apr. 1985 / Concord Jazz 4282
With jazzman Scott Hamilton and his sextet. — *Charles S. Wolfe*

Sings the Music of Jimmy Van Heusen / 1987 / Concord Jazz 4308
Another sparkling repertory work from this top-flight standards and pre-rock pop vocalist. Clooney does the same delightful job with Jimmy Van Heusen's music that she did with Harold Arlen's, and everything else—production, arrangements, song sequencing, engineering—is equally satisfying. — *Ron Wynn*

Sings Lyrics of Johnny Mercer / Aug. 1987 / Concord Jazz 4333

Sings Rodgers, Hart & Hammerstein / Oct. 1989 / Concord Jazz 4405

Girl Singer / Nov. 1991-Dec. 1991 / Concord Jazz 4496
Contemporary set that reveals that Clooney's voice hasn't lost its luster or effectiveness. This set featured her singing with a big band composed of West Coast session pros. Date reflects traditional Concord conservatism in terms of selections and production, but it's certainly well done. The CD contains a bonus track. — *Ron Wynn*

● **Come on a My House** / Sony 14382
An anthology that contains the classic title song plus other tunes Clooney made popular during '50s. It's a good introductory package, also perfect for those who only want a little Clooney or just the best known items. — *Ron Wynn*

Perry Como (Pierino Como)

b. 1912, Cannonsburg, Pennsylvania
Vocals
Starting out as a barber in his hometown of Cannonsburg, PA, Como gained national attention with the Ted Weems Orchestra in the mid '30s. After World War II, he signed with RCA Victor as a solo artist and started amassing hits, 42 of them in the Top 10 between 1944 and 1958. His laidback, laconic delivery and persona served him well when he became the most successful "band singer" in TV's early days, hosting his variety show for over eight years. Changing over to whimsical novelty material, he still had hits when rock & roll first started dominating the charts. After a 25-year layoff, Como started performing live again in 1970, to devoted audiences, and has maintained a modest touring schedule to this day. — *Cub Koda*

Legendary Performer / 1976 / RCA 51752

★ **Pure Gold** / 1984 / RCA 0972

Today / 1987 / RCA 6368

Harry Connick, Jr.

b. Sep. 11, 1967, New Orleans, LA
Vocals, piano
Much of Connick's music is rooted in the '40s and early-'50s world of big-band swing. Like Mose Allison, another Southern jazz musician, Connick has given an increasingly prominent role to vocals in his repertoire. People come to his concerts expecting to hear him sing, and they are not disappointed. Connick's revival is working. His audiences are youthful and enthusiastic. He's got them laughing at his corny patter, watching his softshoe routines, and listening to sophisticated band arrangements instead of Mötley Crüe or Bon Jovi.

Connick has not paid dues on his multifaceted talent or broad interests. "You haven't heard me do my New Orleans funk stuff yet," he told columnist Stephen Holden. "Maybe a recording of Chopin etudes. There are a million things." Just how much breadth Connick's audience will tolerate remains to be seen. Evidence of his stylistic wanderlust already exists. His 1990 all-instrumental piano trio album *Lofty's Roach Souffle* surprised many people and sounded for all the world like the reincarnation of Thelonious Monk.

Connick's immense popularity is refreshing, even encouraging, despite the fact that he champions decidedly nonmainstream music. Connick had more albums on the *Billboard* best-seller list in November 1991 than any other artist. Moreover, his success will allow him the creative freedom to ensure his far-reaching musical goals. Connick's big-band swing, vocals, and trio work are antidotes to the corporate Top-40 product that has become the background noise in our daily lives. — *Hank Davis*

Harry Connick Jr / 1987 / Columbia 40702
A versatile, nervy pianist whose gift for rhythmic variation and countermelody is well displayed on this debut album, especially when he tackles such standards as "Love Is Here to Stay" and "Sunny Side of the Street." — *William Ruhlmann*

20 / 1989 / Columbia 44369
Even more confident and exuberant than his debut, Connick's second album (the title refers to his age) finds him pulling out the stops on Irving Berlin's "Blue Skies" and trying out his limited but earnest vocal style on a few tunes, notably "Do You Know What It Means to Miss New Orleans?" — *William Ruhlmann*

● **When Harry Met Sally . . .** / Jun. 1989 / CBS 45319
The soundtrack that made Connick an MOR star. — *Ron Wynn*

○ **We Are in Love** / 1990 / Columbia 46146
Sentimental, pre-rock pop-oriented music. Nicely done, though quite mannered. — *Ron Wynn*

Lofty's Roach Souffle / 1991 / Columbia 46223
Still in a pronounced jazz phase, this shows his debt to James Booker and New Orleans barrelhouse blues influences. — *Ron Wynn*

Blue Light, Red Light / Dec. 10, 1991 / CBS 48685

Barbara Cook

b. Oct. 25, 1927, Atlanta, GA
Vocals
A singer with a warm, light soprano, Barbara Cook became a successful Broadway musical performer in the '50s and '60s. By the '70s, she had moved largely into cabaret singing, at which she was equally successful. Born in Atlanta, she made her professional debut at the Blue Angel nightclub in New York in 1950 and her Broadway debut in *Flahooley* (1951), one of several flops in which she got good notices. Another of these was the original version of *Candide* (1956). Cook finally found a Broadway show with legs when she created the role of Marian the librarian in *The Music Man* (1957). The most successful of several shows in which she appeared in the '60s was *She Loves Me* (1963). By the mid '70s, she was popular enough to move up to concert halls, and this is reflected in her album *Barbara Cook and Carnegie Hall* (1975). Her more recent accomplishments include her appearance in the special recording *Follies in Concert* (1985), her inclusion in a new studio recording of *Carousel* (1987), and her delightful album of songs associated with Walt Disney children's films, *The Disney Album* (1988). — *William Ruhlmann*

It's Better with a Band / 1986 / Moss Music 104
A live recording from Carnegie Hall. Includes a wonderful Leonard Bernstein medley, as well as "The Ingenue," a song written for Cook by Wally Harper and David Zippel. — *William Ruhlmann*

● **Disney Album** / 1988 / MCA 6244
A dream match: Barbara Cook's warm, optimistic voice singing songs taken from Disney films—"Some Day My Prince Will Come," "A Dream Is a Wish Your Heart Makes," and more. — *William Ruhlmann*

Bing Crosby (Harry Lillis Crosby)

b. May 2, 1904, Tacoma, WA, d. Oct. 14, 1977, Madrid, Spain
Vocals
An American institution, Crosby started as part of the Rhythm Boys trio with bandleader Paul Whiteman, but he soon went on to major solo success. The first singer to truly understand the microphone (then a relatively new invention), he single-handedly revolutionized pop-music vocalizing by using it as if he were performing to an audience of one. Great success in both records and movies followed, with Crosby's laidback, easy-going style serving him well in both fields. With his roots in Louis Armstrong and Al Jolson, Crosby's laconic phrasing and uncanny ability to sing "in the pocket" have been matched by few singers before or since. — *Cub Koda*

When Irish Eyes Are Smiling / 1952 / MCA 519
One of the most popular of all Crosby collections, from his '40s Decca years. — *Charles Wolfe*

Bing & Basie / 1972 / Emarcy 824705
An excellent date with the Basie big band. — *Ron Wynn*

★ **Best of Bing Crosby** / 1980 / Decca 184

No single package can hold all of Crosby's hits, but this is a start: original cuts from '30s and '40s, with many favorites. — *Charles Wolfe*

Bing Crosby Story, Vol. 1: Early Jazz Years / 1984 / Sony 201

○ **Bing Crosby (1927-1934)** / 1987 / BBC
The best sounding presentation of his formative '20s and '30s cuts. — *Ron Wynn*

○ **And Jazz Friends** / GRP 603
Bing at his best; vintage '40s Decca sides with everyone from Louis Armstrong to Lionel Hampton. — *Charles Wolfe*

Crooner / Columbia 44229
Classic Columbia sides 1928-1934, with fine remastering and good notes. — *Charles Wolfe*

Radio Years, Vol. 1 / GNP 9051
Radio air checks that contain some unusual songs and interesting duet partners. — *Charles Wolfe*

Sammy Davis, Jr.

b. Dec. 8, 1925, d. May 16, 1990
Vocals
When Sammy Davis, Jr. died in 1990, the entertainment world lost one of its reigning superstars. The versatile Davis hailed from a showbiz family and started young, tap dancing up a storm in the 1933 featurette "Rufus Jones for President." His uncle headed the Will Mastin Trio along with Sammy and his dad, and they were a popular lounge act during the '40s. Davis signed with Decca as a singer in 1954, charting with "Hey There," but an auto accident that year cost him an eye. "Something's Gotta Give" was a major hit for Davis in 1955, but his recording career took a back seat for a time to cavorting with the Rat Pack, an all-star crew of Las Vegas swingers headed by Frank Sinatra and Dean Martin. They starred en masse in the films *Ocean's Eleven* (1960) and *Robin and the Seven Hoods* (1964). Moving to the Reprise label, Davis scored with the dramatic ballads "What Kind of Fool Am I?" (1962), "The Shelter of Your Arms" (1963), and "I've Gotta Be Me" (1968), but his only number-one hit came on a very untypical 1972 effort, the saccharine "Candy Man," a million-seller on MGM. A superstar of Broadway, film, and recordings, Sammy Davis, Jr. earned his ranking as one of America's leading entertainers. — *Bill Dahl*

○ **Sammy Davis Jr. Sings, Laurindo Almeida Plays** / 1966 / Dcc 55
Surprising but effective team-up. — *Ron Wynn*

★ **Greatest Hits 1 & 2** / 1978 / Dcc 1848
His best, most complete hits package. — *Ron Wynn*

Decca Years / 1990 / MCA 10101

○ **Capitol Collectors Series** / Jun. 18, 1990 / Capitol 94071
Fine retrospective of pop- and jazz-flavored cuts. — *Ron Wynn*

Doris Day

b. Apr. 3, 1922
Vocals
Though better known for her film roles and "all-American girl" image, Doris Day was a professional vocalist from her teens and enjoyed pop stardom as a lead singer with the Les Brown Orchestra. Critics still dispute whether she was truly a jazz singer. She was certainly no improviser, but she was effective on light novelty fare and innocent tunes of the '40s and '50s, like her Oscar-winning hit "Que Sera, Sera (Whatever Will Be, Will Be)". — *Ron Wynn*

● **Greatest Hits** / 1958 / Columbia 8635

Hooray for Hollywood, Vol. 1 / Jan. 1959 / Columbia 8066

Hooray for Hollywood, Vol. 2 / Feb. 1959 / Columbia 8067

Best of the Big Bands / Columbia 46224

Marlene Dietrich (Von Losch, Maria Magdalena)

b. 1901, d. May 6, 1992
Vocals
Probably Europe's most valued export of the late '20s, Dietrich rocketed to fame in the movie *The Blue Angel*. Her vamp blonde hair and corset-and-black-stockings look is still in use today (Madonna, Madeline Kahn's spoof of her in Mel Brooks's *Blazing Saddles*). Dietrich's deep, almost foghorn-like voice served her

well into grandmotherhood, delighting audiences all around the world. —*Cub Koda*

● **Essential Marlene Dietrich** / Sep. 14, 1992 / Capitol 96450
The best Marlene Dietrich collection available. —*AMG*

○ **Her Complete Decca Recordings** / MCA 1501
Though Dietrich recorded (and re-recorded) many of her best-known tunes for a variety of labels, this compilation catches her in fine form and features an excellent reading of her biggest hit, "Falling in Love Again." —*Cub Koda*

Michael Feinstein

b. 1956
Piano, vocals
Michael Feinstein was born in Columbus, OH, and developed an interest in the piano and in show music at an early age. After moving with his family to Los Angeles in 1976, he met Oscar Levant's widow, who in turn introduced him to Ira Gershwin. He was hired by Gershwin in 1977 to help organize the Gershwin archives, and continued to work with the lyricist until Gershwin's death in 1983.

In 1984 Feinstein launched a career as a pianist and singer devoted to the music of the '30s and '40s, playing at private parties in the Los Angeles area. He had a seven-month residence at the Mondrian Hotel, during which Liza Minnelli threw a party in his honor (February 1985) that got his name around. In January 1986, he opened at the Algonquin Hotel in New York, where a 6-week engagement stretched to 16 weeks.

Feinstein's debut album, *Live at the Algonquin*, mixed the songs of Irving Berlin and Oscar Levant with more current material by Stephen Sondheim and Gretchen Cryer. By 1988 he had been signed to Elektra Records, for whom he has recorded a series of albums spotlighting the work of specific composers, as well as a recent children's album. —*William Ruhlmann*

Live at the Algonquin / 1986 / Elektra 60743
Feinstein in his element. The limitations in his vocal range are made up for by an evident understanding of and enthusiasm for the material, starting with Ray Jessel's "Wanna Sing a Show Tune." —*William Ruhlmann*

● **Pure Gershwin** / 1987 / Elektra 60742
Pure delight. Feinstein's reading of other composers is very, very good, but his feeling for Gershwin (as might be expected from a man who worked with Ira Gershwin for years) is nearly perfect. Feinstein's piano playing is excellent here, and he relishes every syllable of the words. 'S wonderful. —*William Ruhlmann*

Remember: Michael Feinstein Sings Irving Berlin / 1987 / Elektra 60744
The first of Feinstein's theme albums, and one of the best. He captures the simple (and at times deceptively clever) sentiment of Berlin with an unadorned approach that brings out the sturdiness of the melodies as well. —*William Ruhlmann*

Jose Feliciano

b. Sep. 8, 1945
Vocals, guitar
Jose Feliciano's virtuoso guitar work and impassioned vocals have been spotlighted in numerous contexts, notably on his hit adaptation of the Doors hit "Light My Fire." Born in Puerto Rico and blind since birth, Feliciano was raised in New York City. He began his lengthy string of successes on RCA in 1968 with his intimate reworking of "Light My Fire," winning a Grammy for Best New Artist that year. He wrote the theme song for Freddie Prinze's acclaimed TV sitcom "Chico and the Man" and acted in numerous programs. Feliciano continues to perform frequently today. —*Bill Dahl*

● **All-Time Greatest Hits** / 1965 / RCA 6903
Includes his versions of "Light My Fire," "California Dreamin'," "Suzy Q," and "Walk Right In." —*AMG*

Jose Feliciano / 1980 / Bmgi 2490
Nice set of pop/soul. Disco remakes of "I Second That Emotion" and "Ain't That Peculiar," plus a minor hit, "Everybody Loves Me," written by the late Doc Pomus. —*Bil Carpenter*

Eddie Fisher

b. Aug. 10, 1928, Philadelphia, PA
Vocals

A major pop star during the pre-rock '50s, Eddie Fisher's roller-coaster career includes seven million-sellers and two famous ex-wives (actresses Debbie Reynolds and Elizabeth Taylor). The Philadelphia-born Fisher sang with Buddy Morrow's orchestra before getting his big break on Eddie Cantor's radio show in 1949. He started his amazing string of hits for RCA Victor with "Thinking of You" in 1950, quickly developing into a teen heart-throb and peaking in 1953 with the chart-topping "I'm Walking behind You" and "Oh! My Pa-Pa." Fisher attempted to go with the rock & roll flow in 1955 with "Dungaree Doll," another big hit, but his style was unabashedly pop-oriented, and the rock revolt all but pushed him off the charts. Fisher continues to sing, and his daughter, Carrie Fisher, is a well-known actress and writer. —*Bill Dahl*

● **All-Time Greatest Hits #1** / 1991 / RCA 9592

George Formby

Vocals, banjolele
Formby was one of the greatest stars of that most English urban genre, the music hall. He was famous for his banjolele, but also for comic songs like "When I'm Cleaning Windows" (for a Nosy Parker It's an Interesting Job)," "The Lancashire Hot Pot Swingers" (not that—we're talking the 1930s here!), "Grand-dad's Flannelette Nightshirt," and the charming "Leaning on a Lamp-Post," which was featured in the recent revival of "Me and My Girl," though it wasn't part of the original show. —*John Storm Roberts*

○ **When I'm Cleaning Windows** / ASV 5079

Four Freshmen

Group
With their highly advanced concepts of group harmony, the Four Freshmen scored a few hits during the '50s, deeply influencing the vocal blend of the Beach Boys. Formed at an Indianapolis music conservatory, the Four Freshmen were brought to Capitol Records by jazz bandleader Stan Kenton, and the quartet (Bob Flanigan, brothers Ross and Don Barbour, and Ken Arrair) hit with "It's a Blue World" in 1952. Their top seller was "Graduation Day" in 1956, but six chart items in all by the Four Freshmen don't begin to indicate the influence of their breathtakingly close harmonies on subsequent vocal groups. —*Bill Dahl*

○ **Capitol Collectors Series** / Jan. 21, 1991 / Capitol 93197

Four Lads

Group
Soaring four-part harmonies were this Toronto group's stock in trade, and they parlayed their robust sound into a string of pop hits during the pre-rock era. Signed to Columbia Records as background vocalists in 1950, they harmonized behind Johnnie Ray on his 1951 smash "Cry" before making the most of their own shot in the spotlight with "The Mocking Bird" the next year for Okeh. Led by tenor Bernie Toorish, the Four Lads tallied numerous hits for Columbia, including "Skokiaan" in 1954, the powerful "Moments to Remember" in 1955, and "No, Not Much!" and "Standing on the Corner" in 1956. The Four Lads continued to chart frequently through 1959. —*Bill Dahl*

Moments to Remember / 1955 / Columbia 11369
More of their melodic early-'50s pop hits and harmonies. —*Hank Davis*

● **16 Most Requested Songs** / 1991 / Columbia 46158
Features melodic early '50s pop hits by this Canadian quartet. Big-selling, extremely appealing harmonies. —*Hank Davis*

The Four Preps

Group
While performing at a Hollywood High School talent show in 1956, the Four Preps impressed a Capitol Records producer enough to sign them to a long-term contract. By the end of the year, the wholesome, clean-cut group had their first chart single, "Dreamy Eyes." From 1956 to 1964 the Four Preps (Bruce Belland, Ed Cobb, Marv Ingraham, and Glen Larson) charted 13 times on the Hot 100. As the British Invasion stormed U.S. shores, their popularity withered away, although they continued to record until 1967. —*Stephen Thomas Erlewine*

○ **Capitol Collectors Series** / 1989 / Capitol 91626

All the Four Preps songs you'll ever need are included on this 20-track compilation. Every one of their Top-40 hits is here, as are many smaller hits and unfamiliar songs, including their last chart hit, "A Letter to the Beatles." —*Stephen Thomas Erlewine*

Judy Garland

b. Jun. 10, 1922, **d.** Jun. 22, 1969
Vocals
Immortalized while a teenager in the 1939 film musical *The Wizard of Oz*, Judy Garland also recorded often. Of course, her classic rendition of "Over the Rainbow" from *Oz* was a smash that same year on Decca, and she scored numerous hits during the '40s. By 1954, Garland was recording for Columbia, and her rendition of "The Man That Got Away," from her hit movie *A Star Is Born*, helped to define the Garland mystique. She hosted her own TV variety show in the early '60s and continued to belt out her classic material until her premature death. Daughters Liza Minnelli and Lorna Luft are very talented chips off Garland's brilliant block. —*Bill Dahl*

Judy / 1956 / Capitol 92345
Wonderful 1956 studio album recorded with Nelson Riddle's orchestra. —*Charles S. Wolfe*

○ **Judy at Carnegie Hall** / 1961 / Capitol 90013
The best of the later Garland live at a 1961 concert. —*Charles S. Wolfe*

● **Best of the Decca Years, Vol. 1** / 1990 / Decca 31345
Prime early Garland, including the original "Over the Rainbow," as well as pieces from the '40s, like "The Trolley Song." —*Charles S. Wolfe*

One & Only / Nov. 25, 1991 / Capitol 96600
A comprehensive four-disc boxed-set designed with hardcore fans in mind. —*AMG*

Eydie Gorme

b. Aug. 16, 1931
Vocals
Usually paired vocally with her husband, Steve Lawrence, Eydie Gorme cashed in on a Latin-flavored dance craze in 1963 with her bubbly "Blame It on the Bossa Nova" for Columbia Records. The Bronx, NY, product signed on as a regular on Steve Allen's "Tonight Show" in 1953, and the next year had her first chart hit with "Fini" on Coral. Moving to ABC-Paramount, Gorme's perky pipes rode the charts with the likes of "Love Me Forever" in 1957 and "You Need Hands" the next year. She married Lawrence, another "Tonight Show" regular, in 1957, and they're a popular TV and concert attraction to this day. —*Bill Dahl*

Eydie Swings the Blues / 1957 / Paramount 192
Gorme spreading her jazz wings and digging into a nice selection of pop/jazz/blues-style material. —*Cub Koda*

● **Eydie Gorme's Greatest Hits** / 1967 / Columbia 9564
Just what the title says, including "Blame It on the Bossa Nova" and her best pop material. —*Cub Koda*

Softly, as I Leave You / 1967 / Columbia 9394
One of Gorme's best ballad albums. Nicely done. —*Cub Koda*

Robert Goulet

b. Nov. 26, 1933, Lawrence, MA
Vocals
A robust vocalist whose handsome profile has turned up on countless TV variety programs, Goulet first made an impression while starring on Broadway in *Camelot*. He hit in 1962 on Columbia with "What Kind of Fool Am I?" and in 1964 with "My Love Forgive Me (Amore, Scusami)." Goulet still thrives as an actor and easy-listening crooner. —*Bill Dahl*

● **Greatest Hits** / 1969 / Columbia 9815
"If Ever I Should Leave You" and all the rest. —*Bil Carpenter*

Annette Hanshaw

b. 1910, **d.** 1985
Vocals
If there's a female pop/jazz vocalist from the '20s whose record work deserves a much wider hearing, it's undoubtedly Annette Hanshaw. Dubbed "the personality girl," her voice could jump from cute and bubbly on uptempo material to break-your-heart-

in-two emotional on torch ballads, effortlessly. Though she was part of the early brigade of radio stars from the late '20s and early '30s, few could match her rhythmic bounce, instinctive reading of the lyric,or her ability to adapt her voice to exactly what each song needed. Certainly few could sing "in the pocket" as well as she.

In her brief professional career she sang everything. Her remarkable versatility allowed her to tackle romantic ballads, comedy nonsense, uptempo pop material of the day, Hawaiian novelties, and dead-on Betty Boop impressions—all with consummate ease. The backing on all her records is equally superb, most featuring jazz legends like Benny Goodman, Eddie Lang, Red Nichols, Tommy Dorsey, Joe Venuti, and Jack Teagarden, to name a few.

Although she was quite popular on radio and records through the early '30s (even making a few short films for Paramount), she found show business not to her liking and retired in 1934 at the ripe old age of 23. Her unique, original voice and stylings only improved in the all-too-brief eight years she recorded. Her recordings became a lasting legacy not only to her superb work but to a genre of pop music we most assuredly will never see the likes of again. —*Cub Koda*

○ **Sweetheart of the Twenties** / Oct. 1926-Sep. 8, 1927 / Halcyon 5
A solid collection of Hanshaw's earliest sides, 1926-1928, with superb jazz backing. —*Cub Koda*

Rare BG 1927-29 / 1927-1929 / Sunbeam 112
Features Benny Goodman backing Hanshaw on two Betty Boop-style sides originally issued in the '20s under the pseudonym "Dot Dare." —*Cub Koda*

★ **It Was So Beautiful** / 1932-1934 / Halcyon 119
Superlative collection of Hanshaw's last recordings, with "Say It Isn't So," "Give Me Liberty or Give Me Love," and "I'm Sure of Everything but You" being particular standouts. —*Cub Koda*

Benny Goodman Accompanies "The Girls" / Sunbeam 111
Annette shares this compilation album with tracks by Ethel Waters and the Boswell Sisters, but her five tracks here (especially "I Hate Myself" and "Would You Like to Take a Walk") are major treasures and showcase her at her best. —*Cub Koda*

Phil Harris

b. Jan. 16, 1904, Linton, Indiana
Bandleader, vocals
Better known as a longtime actor who made his first film appearance in 1933, Phil Harris was also a successful drummer and singer. Harris played drums with Francis Craig and led his own groups during the '30s, using the song "Rose Room" as a theme. Harris was a regular on Jack Benny's radio show for the decade from 1936-46 and had his own show with Alice Faye from 1947-54. He had a number of novelty hits in the '40s and early '50s. —*Ron Wynn*

Uncollected Phil Harris & His Orchestra (1933) / 1933 / Hindsight 215

● **Phil Harris** / 194z / SWG 1006
Some nice recordings from '40s, before Harris more or less deserted music for an acting career. —*Ron Wynn*

Richard Harris

b. Oct. 1, 1932
Vocals
A veteran actor of the stage and screen, Richard Harris made his pop debut in 1968 with the Jimmy Webb composition "MacArthur Park," one of the most talked-about records of that year. Webb wrote most of Harris's early material, and his songs were perfect for Harris's dramatic delivery. Harris never achieved the success with other writers that he did with Webb and by the mid-'70s was back to acting full time. Harris can also be heard in the role of King Arthur on the movie soundtrack of *Camelot*. —*Kenneth M. Cassidy*

● **His Greatest Performances** / 1979 / MCA 27091

Al Hibbler

b. Aug. 16, 1915
Vocals
This blind pop/jazz singer worked with Duke Ellington's orchestra for eight years before waxing a series of stately pop ballads in the mid '50s. Hibbler debuted in 1942 with Kansas City pianist

Jay McShann's combo for Decca before joining Ellington the next year. Hibbler was on the R&B charts four times in 1948-51 for major independent labels like Chess and Atlantic, but he signed with Decca and crossed over to the pop lists in 1955, battling Roy Hamilton for top honors on "Unchained Melody." The deep-voiced Hibbler encored with the inspirational "He" and the blues-tinged "After the Lights Go Down Low," retaining his reputation as one of the jazz world's leading vocalists until his death. —*Bill Dahl*

After the Lights Go Down Low / 1956 / Atlantic 1251
Post-Decca period. The title track is a remake of the 1956 hit. The backing has a heavier backbeat than earlier efforts. —*Hank Davis*

● **Best of Al Hibbler** / MCA 4098
This contains all his mid-'50s pop, such as like "Unchained Melody" and "After the Lights Go Down Low," done in his compelling and at times bizarre vocal style with a big-band backing. —*Hank Davis*

Lena Horne

b. Jun. 30, 1917
Vocals, actress
A pop/jazz singer and a glamorous star of stage, screen, and TV, Lena Horne will forever be associated with the beautiful theme song of her 1943 hit movie *Stormy Weather*. Horne's immortal rendition was her first hit, although the pop charts don't do justice to her magnificent career. She appeared on Victor, MGM, RCA, and many other labels, but her striking presence in movies such as *Cabin in the Sky, Ziegfeld Follies*, and, more recently, *The Wiz*, remains her chief legacy. —*Bill Dahl*

● **Stormy Weather: The Legendary Lena (1941-1958)** / 1941-1958 / Bluebird 9985
A wonderful anthology covering her '40s and '50s show tunes, blues, and ballads. —*Ron Wynn*

Lena Horne Sings Your Requests / 1963 / Charter 101
A double CD of two fine Horne albums from the '60s. —*Ron Wynn*

Lena Goes Latin / 1963 / DRG 510
Vintage Lena Horne set from early '60s, with backing from the Lennie Layton Orchestra. Horne made a nice adjustment to Latin tempos and rhythms, though there's lots of show biz touches and flourishes as well. She wasn't really doing traditional Latin material, it's more like Latinized pop, but she did it with distinction. —*Ron Wynn*

Men in My Life / 1967 / Three Cherries 64411
A great session with Joe Williams and Sammy Davis, Jr. —*Ron Wynn*

Lena & Gabor / Oct. 11, 1969 / Gryphon 908
Collaboration between Horne and guitarist Gabor Szabo, who proved one of her most sympathetic accompanists. They made expert duo recordings, with Szabo's delicate, sometimes emphatic playing smoothly accompanying the distinctive Horne vocals. —*Ron Wynn*

○ **Live on Broadway (Lena Horne: The Lady & Her Music)** / 1981 / Qwest 3597
A triumphant cast album that effectively captured Lena Horne's acclaimed one-woman Broadway show on a two-record set. The album served both as a vinyl autobiography and also as a centerpiece to document her rise to symbolic importance for Black performers. —*Ron Wynn*

At Long Last Lena / Jul. 1, 1992 / RCA 66021
A package of standards and ballads that showcase her less jazz-oriented side. —*Ron Wynn*

The Ink Spots

Group
The Ink Spots played a large role in pioneering the Black vocal group-harmony genre, helping to pave the way for the doo-wop explosion of the '50s. The quavering high tenor of Bill Kenny presaged hundreds of street-corner leads to come, and the sweet harmonies of Carlie Fuqua, Deek Watson, and bass Hoppy Jones (who died in 1944) backed him flawlessly.

Kenny's impeccable diction and Jones's deep drawl were both prominent on the Ink Spots' first smash on Decca in 1939, the sentimental "If I Didn't Care." From then through 1951 the group was seldom absent from the pop charts, topping the lists with "We Three (My Echo, My Shadow, and Me)" (in 1940), "I'm Making

Believe" and "Into Each Life Some Rain Must Fall" (both in 1944), and "The Gypsy" and "To Each His Own" (both in 1946).

Watson eventually split to form his own group, the Brown Dots, and appeared in numerous low-budget film musicals, while Kenny attempted a solo career, notching a solo hit in 1951 with the uplifting "It Is No Secret." Countless groups masquerading as the Ink Spots have thrived across the nation since the '50s. —*Bill Dahl*

★ **Greatest Hits 1939-46** / 196z / MCA 31347
The authentic Decca recordings showcase this seminal doo-wop vocal unit. —*Ron Wynn*

Al Jarreau

b. Apr. 12, 1940, Milwaukee, WI
Vocals
Jarreau, a onetime rehabilitation counselor with a Master's degree in psychology, used to sing at parties. He landed a deal with Reprise in the '70s and made an impact in 1975 with the album "We Got By." For a while, his passion, his ability to imitate instruments in the best Mills Brothers tradition, and his sense of swing overcame his showbiz tendencies. Later, as he became the darling of an upper-class/professional Black and urban audience, his albums grew more and more self-indulgent. At his best, he is reminiscent of early Johnny Mathis. —*Ron Wynn*

● **We Got By** / 1975 / Reprise 2224
Jarreau's best release, which shows him still improvising and interpreting. —*Ron Wynn*

○ **Look to the Rainbow** / Jan. 1977-Feb. 1977 / Warner Brothers 3052
Fine live sets, with Jarreau at his best. —*Ron Wynn*

All Fly Home / 1978 / Warner Brothers 3229

○ **This Time** / 1980 / Warner Brothers 3434
A big hit on the urban, R&B, and fusion landscape. —*Ron Wynn*

○ **Breakin' Away** / 1981 / Warner Brothers 3576
Some nice R&B/pop cuts on this platinum album. —*Ron Wynn*

All Fly Home/This Time / 1983 / Warner Brothers 23948
A single-disc combination of two hit albums. —*Ron Wynn*

Jarreau / 1983 / Warner Brothers 23801
Pretty pop, R&B, and fusion on this gold album. —*Ron Wynn*

Al Jolson (Asa Yoelson)

b. 1888, **d.** Oct. 23, 1950
Vocals, dancer, comedian
An entertainment dynamo who quickly established himself as Broadway's leading star by the dawn of the 20th century, Jolson was America's first superstar, years before the word was coined. A truly competitive and high-energy performer, Jolson left most of the competition in the dust with his impassioned singing, dancing, and jokes (borrowing much from Black ragtime music and early jazz, and performing in the then-popular, now-taboo minstrel blackface style). His place in popular history was assured when he starred in the first successful talking picture, *The Jazz Singer*, in 1927. His tireless efforts performing for American troops during World War II (he almost single-handedly started the USO) won him a whole new audience who had never seen him perform in his halcyon days. When the film biography of his life became a major hit 20 years later, Jolson's popularity leapt to legendary status, making no one doubt his title of "The World's Greatest Entertainer." —*Cub Koda*

● **Early Years** / Pearl Flapper 9748
Great single-disc compilation of the earliest Jolson material, which made him a sensation on Broadway. Essential sides and a fascinating glimpse into vaudeville's heyday. —*Cub Koda*

Legendary Al Jolson / CBS
A three-disc set of Jolson's early Columbia recordings (1914-1923), with a sixth side devoted to early-'30s Brunswick recordings from his movie days. Some duplication with the above-mentioned *Early Years* compilation, but worth having nonetheless. —*Cub Koda*

Etta Jones

b. Nov. 25, 1928, Aiken, SC
Vocals
Often confused with Etta James, Jones is a nice jazz and popular-standards vocalist who was frequently a partner of tenor saxist

Houston Person in the '70s and '80s. She is an understated, dynamic singer who can express emotions without gimmicks or excessive animation. —*Ron Wynn*

Don't Go to Strangers / Jun. 21, 1960 / Prestige 298
An overlooked excellent set. Some of Jones's blues and strong leads. Recorded June 21, 1960. —*Ron Wynn*

○ **Something Nice** / Sep. 16, 1961-Mar. 30, 1961 / Prestige 221
An excellent reissue of some prime cuts with Oliver Nelson (reeds) and Roy Haynes (drums) from 1960 and 1961. Recorded on September 9, 1960 and March 30, 1961. —*Ron Wynn*

Lonely and Blue / Apr. 6, 1962-May 4, 1962 / Prestige 702

● **Etta Jones' Greatest Hits** / 1967 / Prestige 7443

○ **Fine & Mellow/Save Your Love for Me** / 1987 / Muse 6002
A worthwhile combination of two good records (from 1987 and 1980) into one disc. —*Ron Wynn*

I'll Be Seeing You / Sep. 1987 / Muse 5351
With good Houston Person tenor sax cuts. Originally recorded on September 23, 1987. —*Ron Wynn*

Danny Kaye (David Daniel Kominsky)

b. 1913, d. Mar. 3, 1987
Vocals
Kaye began his career in vaudeville and gained notice on Broadway in such shows as *Straw Hat Review* (1939). He became prominent in musical comedies on the stage and in film and, though never learning to read music, conducted several major orchestras. —*David Szatmary*

● **Best of Danny Kaye** / 1982 / MCA 31058
The best available overview of Kaye's work. —*Stephen Thomas Erlewine*

Sammy Kaye

b. Mar. 31, 1910, d. Jun. 2, 1987
Reeds, bandleader
Kaye's band was a textbook example of "sweet" dance bands: large groups whose arrangements seldom swung in the true sense, but were very popular among those who enjoyed overly sentimental light pop and novelty tunes. Kaye began building his reputation in college, then became a hit on radio in Cincinnati. He moved to Pittsburgh and eventually became a national staple. His radio show "Sunday Serenade" was a huge hit in the '40s and '50s. Kaye had many pop hits, some of them adapted for Broadway shows. His gimmick of having fans volunteer to lead his band was highly popular and was transferred to television in the '50s. Perry Como and Nat King Cole had hits with Kay material. His was far from being a jazz band in the real sense, but made enjoyable material of its kind and is a big favorite to this day. —*Ron Wynn*

● **Best of Sammy Kaye** / 1974 / MCA 4027
Decent collection of his Decca dates. —*Ron Wynn*

○ **Best of the Big Bands** / Columbia 45342
Decent overview. —*Ron Wynn*

Gene Kelly

b. 1912, Pittsburgh, PA
Vocals
Showing an early aptitude in both gymnastics and dance, Eugene Curran Kelly had devoured, by his early teens, everything he could about dance in general and ballet in particular. He was already a successful dance teacher in his hometown when he began his ascent in the original Broadway production of Rodgers and Hart's *Pal Joey*. This led to a film contract with David O. Selznick, which was sold to MGM before Kelly even reported to Hollywood.

The allegiance with MGM proved a godsend for both the studio and Kelly, who (with the help of producer Arthur Freed) came to energize the film company's musical output for the next 15 years. Kelly quickly revealed himself to be a quintuple threat: dancer, actor, singer, choreographer, and director. Beginning with his first film, *For Me and My Gal*, he showed an engaging personality on screen, and his voice, while never strong, was equally pleasing. As his influence at the studio grew, Kelly began proposing more ambitious projects as a director as well as a choreographer and performer.

Kelly was never a popular singer, despite the fact that he acquitted himself onscreen alongside even the likes of Frank Sinatra in several films, but his on-screen geniality and overall popularity—as a younger, more masculine, and more conventionally handsome rival to Fred Astaire (who was at MGM at exactly the same time)—allowed him to effectively repopularize many songs by George Gershwin, Arthur Freed, Nacio Herb Brown, and others through his performances of them in films such as *An American in Paris* and *Singin' in the Rain*. His most popular and influential work as a singer can be found on the soundtracks for those films, plus *Brigadoon, It's Always Fair Weather, Summer Stock,* and the compilation soundtrack *That's Entertainment Part 2.*

As the '50s wore on and the public's taste for musicals waned, Kelly turned increasingly toward directing (*Gigot, Hello Dolly!*) and producing, allowing his acting—which he had never entirely forsaken but had never built into great prominence before the public either—to become the focus of his film work in movies such as *Marjorie Morningstar* and *Inherit the Wind*. He proved to be as adept at drama as he had been at dance. And in the '70s, spurred on by the growing interest in America's cinematic past that coalesced around MGM's compilation feature *That's Entertainment*, Kelly directed the equally fine follow-up, *That's Entertainment Part 2*. —*Bruce Eder*

● **Song & Dance Man** / DRG 15010
Kelly's best output from feature film recordings early in his career. This collection pales next to the work on the soundtracks of *That's Entertainment Part 2* and *Singin' in the Rain*. —*Bruce Eder*

Morgana King (Morgana Messina)

b. Jun. 4, 1930, Pleasantville, NY
Vocals, actress
An accomplished actress, King has also made some albums in the jazz vein. She worked in several New York clubs during the late '50s and early '60s. Her 1964 album, *A Taste of Honey*, made some impact, although King didn't display strong jazz technique. Her late-'70s albums for Muse had better material and more convincing performances, but didn't match her appearances in the films *The Godfather* and *The Godfather Part II* for wide-ranging impact. King makes nice, occasionally arresting albums, and is a very good vocalist. —*Ron Wynn*

○ **Taste of Honey** / 1964 / Mainstream 707
Nice cuts, clean vocals. —*Ron Wynn*

Everything Must Change / Aug. 8, 1978 / Muse 5190
Good interpretations and arrangements from King. —*Ron Wynn*

Portraits / Oct. 19, 1983+Oct. 21, 1983 / Muse 5301
Competent set presenting actress/vocalist Morgana King doing jazz-oriented pop, standards, and ballads backed by a tight combo. She has good technique, delivery and style. There was nothing innovative or particularly original about either the material or the performances, but they were thoroughly professional, often enjoyable. —*Ron Wynn*

Simply Eloquent / 1986 / Muse 5326
Smooth and tasteful. Recorded on February 24, 1986. —*Ron Wynn*

This Is Always / 1992 / Muse
Though King doesn't have the range or power she used to have, she's got the experience and subtlety to find fresh ways of approaching shopworn standards. She wisely doesn't over-sing or extend such numbers as "Let's Get Away from It All" and "I Can't Believe That You're In Love with Me," making the points quickly and singing with precision and concise clarity. Even on longer tunes her pacing is expert and she doesn't linger in uncomfortable registers. Her backing group includes steady musicians who don't rush or impede her vocals, and the absence of horns and brass ensures that she stays in the spotlight. This is restrained and entertaining vocal fare, neither background material nor spectacular or fiery performances. —*Ron Wynn*

Eartha Kitt

Vocals
This alluring vocalist enjoyed a series of pop hits in 1953 and 1954, including the seductive Yuletide perennial "Santa Baby." Kitt's exotic style was first showcased in the Broadway production of *New Faces of 1952* (a film version was made in 1954), and she

waxed the enticing "C'est Si Bon" in 1953 for RCA Victor. "Santa Baby" arrived in time for the 1953 holidays, and her 1954 output included "Somebody Bad Stole de Wedding Bell (Who's Got de Ding Dong)." Kitt has remained active as an actress and singer; she was a convincing Catwoman on the campy mid-'60s TV series "Batman," and she costarred in the recent movies *Pink Chiquitas* and *Erik the Viking. —Bill Dahl*

○ **Best of Eartha Kitt** / 1975 / MCA 1554
Decent overview that concentrates on her pop-oriented material. —*Ron Wynn*

Frankie Laine (Lo Vecchio, Frank Paul)

b. Mar. 30, 1913, Chicago, IL
Vocals
Laine, one of the biggest recording stars of the late '40s and early '50s, is famous for his robust baritone. After working radio shows, dance marathons, and a brief stint replacing Perry Como in Freddy Carlone's band, Laine broke into the national spotlight in 1947 with his million-selling "That's My Desire." Nearly 70 Top 100 hits followed, with "Jezebel" and "I Believe" among the finest. (Note: Frankie Laine has re-recorded his Columbia hits numerous times; thus most Laine compilations contain later material with little warning. Check the label and select CBS if possible.) — *Stephen Thomas Erlewine, Bil Carpenter, and Hank Davis*

Mercury Years / PolyGram 510435
This starts with studio chatter and runs through 22 tracks, dated 1946-1950. Far more bluesy/jazzy than his later Columbia material. —*Hank Davis*

★ **Greatest Hits** / Columbia 8636
The essential collection—wild and energetic—with "Jezebel" and others. —*Hank Davis*

Peggy Lee

b. May 26, 1920
Vocals
Although she was one of the top pop singers of the '40s and '50s, Peggy Lee's love for jazz usually surfaced in her hip phrasing, and her cool cover of Little Willie John's "Fever" gave her a smash in the midst of rockmania in 1958. Lee was singing professionally by 1936, and she joined Benny Goodman's orchestra in 1941. Her tasty rendition of Lil Green's "Why Don't You Do Right?" gave Goodman a major hit in 1943, and by the end of the war, Lee was recording solo for Capitol. She and her husband Dave Barbour wrote "Mañana (Is Good Enough for Me)," a million-selling chart-topper in 1948, while "Lover" was one of her first big items for Decca in 1952. Lee had returned to Capitol by the time "Fever" emerged, and her anthemic "I'm a Woman," penned by Jerry Leiber and Mike Stoller, has proven an enduring favorite. The offbeat "Is That All There Is?" was Lee's final pop-chart bow in 1969. —*Bill Dahl*

Close Enough for Love / 1979 / DRG 5190
Vintage pop and swing material. —*Ron Wynn*

○ **Sings with Benny Goodman** / 1984 / Columbia 7005
Her best songs that featured Benny Goodman. —*Ron Wynn*

Sings the Blues / 1988 / Music Masters 5005
A late-'70s date, with Lee updating her blues tracks. —*Ron Wynn*

All-Time Greatest Hits / 1990 / Curb 77379
A decent collection of past triumphs. —*Ron Wynn*

★ **Capitol Collectors Series, Vol. 1: The Early Years** / May 21, 1990 / Capitol 93195
Capitol Collectors Series, Vol. 1: The Early Years is the best collection of Lee's jazz and blues hits. —*Ron Wynn*

P's & Q's / Aug. 31, 1992 / Capitol 99921
Contemporary meeting between Peggy Lee and Quincy Jones that's part of Jones's recent return to some jazz playing and producing in addition to his highly profitable R&B and pop work. Lee still has her idiosyncratic tone, delivery,and enunciations, along with her timing. —*Ron Wynn*

The Lettermen

Group
Though styles changed drastically and frequently throughout the '60s, the Lettermen held still (for the most part), producing light pop songs full of easy harmonies. Tony Butala (b. 1940), Jim Pike

(b. 1938), and Bob Engemann (b. 1936) formed the trio in Los Angeles in 1960, cutting their first record a year later. The Lettermen charted 20 times on the Hot 100 from 1961 to 1971, a surprising rate of success considering the times. —*Stephen Thomas Erlewine*

● **Capitol Collectors Series** / 1992 / Capitol 98537
All six of the Lettermen's Top-40 hits are here, along with a generous selection of lesser-known singles and album tracks. Informative liner notes and excellent sound help make this the definitive Lettermen collection. —*Stephen Thomas Erlewine*

Limeliters

Group
A folk group formed in 1959 by Louis Gottlieb (bass), Alex Hassilev (baritone, guitar, banjo), and Glenn Yarbrough (tenor, guitar). They played in concert and at folk houses like San Francisco's Hungry I. After their 1965, the Rain Must Fall" in 1965, they appeared on TV and radio nationwide. They disbanded in the mid '60s. —*Michael Erlewine*

Slightly Fabulous Limeliters / 1961 / RCA 2393
This album reached number eight on the charts in 1961. —*Michael Erlewine*

● **Tonight in Person** / 1961 / RCA 2272
Live concert at the Ash Grove. One of their best sellers. —*Michael Erlewine*

Julie London

b. Sep. 26, 1926, Santa Rose, CA
Vocals
Not only was Julie London absolutely gorgeous, she possessed one of the sultriest vocal deliveries around (perhaps best spotlighted on her smoky 1955 pop smash "Cry Me a River"). Born in Santa Rosa, CA, London landed roles in several films during the '40s and married tight-jawed "Dragnet" cop Jack Webb. London's singing ability was encouraged by her next hubby, Bobby Troup (the composer of "Route 66"). She signed with Liberty and hit big with "Cry Me a River," performing it in a memorable scene in the 1956 rock flick *The Girl Can't Help It*. Although that was her only pop hit, London's many Liberty albums were perfect mood music for late-night makeout sessions, and her acting résumé includes a long stint during the '70s as a nurse of the Webb-produced TV hospital drama "Emergency." —*Bill Dahl*

● **Time for Love: Best of Julie London** / 1991 / Capitol 99804
Often over-orchestrated but still effective, these are her best-known songs. —*Dan Heilman*

○ **Julie Is Her Name, Vols. 1 & 2** / Liberty 91675
A '50s album with Julie accompanied by bass and by Barney Kessel's guitar with hip chord voicings. This made a big splash in its day, with many guitarists working to decipher Kessel's work. —*Richard Lieberson*

Trini Lopez

b. May 15, 1937
Vocals
Trini Lopez recorded a series of upbeat tunes for Reprise during the mid '60s, including a smash rendering of the folk standard "If I Had a Hammer" in 1963. The Dallas native cut some Ritchie Valens-influenced rockers for the King label prior to his discovery by producer Don Costa. Lopez's hits capture the excitement of his live performances, and his driving renditions of "Kansas City" (1963), "Lemon Tree" (1965), and "I'm Comin' Home, Cindy" (1966) were substantial sellers. Reportedly one of Dean Martin's favorite performers, Lopez hosted his own network TV variety program and co-starred as one of *The Dirty Dozen* in the popular 1967 movie. —*Bill Dahl*

25th Anniversary Album / Warner Brothers 72868
Remakes of hits plus new recordings, with a contemporary production that suits Lopez's style well. —*Jeff Tamarkin*

Trini Lopez / Bella Musica 89909
Original Reprise records hits and some remakes fill this hard-to-find import. —*Jeff Tamarkin*

● **From the Original Master Tapes** / Reprise 3538
This Japanese import is an exquisite-sounding 20-song collection of the Mexican-American folk-rocker's '60s hits. It serves as evi-

dence that the nearly forgotten Lopez deserves more credit as an interpretive artist. —*Jeff Tamarkin*

Jon Lucien

b. 1942
Vocals
During the '70s, Jon Lucien became a popular figure as a jazz-tinged romantic-song specialist. Lucien's deep, prominent baritone, his penchant for sentimental fare, and his suave, commanding personality and presence made him enormously popular on the cabaret/supper-club circuit as well as among fans of love ballads and similar material. After a long absence, Lucien returned in 1991 with a release that was very much what he'd done in his peak '70s years. Unfortunately, the response wasn't anywhere near what it had been before. —*Ron Wynn*

Listen Love / Apr. 24, 1991 / Mercury 848532
The comeback/return project for '70s romantic sensation Jon Lucien. Lucien, who'd once been among the top vocalists making orchestrated, jazz-tinged R&B, tried to equal his past success by doing essentially the same material with updated production touches (more synthesized support). Despite heavy promotional backup from the record label, he was unable to recapture his position at the top of the heap, though the release was just as solid as his past efforts. —*Ron Wynn*

● **Best of Jon Lucien** / RCA 6851
A good anthology of a vocalist who was a phenomenon for a while in the '70s. He had a deep, very arresting, and sensual voice, not unlike a latter-day Billy Eckstine or Arthur Prysock, and the quasi-jazz backgrounds and romantic lyrics for his songs gave him a matinee idol appeal. Lucien didn't sustain this popularity very long, but for a short time he was the equivalent of what Luther Vandross represents in the '90s: soul for those who like it sweet and polished rather than dirty and funky. —*Ron Wynn*

Dean Martin

b. Jun. 17, 1917
Vocals
Martin's boozy, easygoing vocal style doesn't feature Sinatra's dazzle or Bennett's kitsch, but it remains one of the friendliest in pop. He made his debut in 1948 with "That Certain Party," a duet with then-partner Jerry Lewis, but Martin's best work came in the early '50s, when he had scores of singles in the pop Top 40. His nonchalant way of twisting syllables and slurring notes played a major role in the development of Elvis Presley's ballad style; compare Martin's "I'd Cry Like a Baby" with Presley's "Love Me." He recorded a slew of albums, but his chart run was exhausted by the '60s. He's now a fixture in Las Vegas, where he rubs stage elbows with the likes of Frank Sinatra and Liza Minnelli. —*John Floyd*

★ **Capitol Collectors Series** / Oct. 25, 1989 / Capitol 91633
Terrific 20-song overview of the Capitol years includes everything you need, from "That's Amore" and "Volare" to "Ain't That a Kick in the Head." —*John Floyd*

Al Martino (Alfred Cini)

b. Oct. 7, 1927, Philadelphia, PA
Vocals
Italian singer Al Martino had four hits from 1952 to 1953 and then vanished until the end of the decade—the result of being too young to handle his success and having various disreputable elements vying for control of his career. Martino tried to continue recording in England, to no avail, and returned to America in 1958. After re-signing to Capitol Records the following year, he launched a string of 34 Hot 100 singles that would last until 1977. During the '60s Martino blended country elements with pop songs, blurring the lines between the two genres. In 1972 he appeared in Francis Ford Coppola's masterpiece, *The Godfather*, as singer Johnny Fontaine, a role that strongly resembled Frank Sinatra's life. —*Stephen Thomas Erlewine*

Spanish Eyes / 1966 / Capitol 91231

● **Capitol Collectors Series** / 1992 / Capitol 96430
All of Martino's major hits—"Here in My Heart," "Take My Heart," "I Love You Because," "I Love You More and More Every Day," and "Speak Softly Love" (the love theme from *The Godfather*)—are included on this comprehensive 25-track compilation, along

with informative, lively liner notes and sparkling fidelity. The best Martino collection available. —Stephen Thomas Erlewine

Johnny Mathis

b. 1935
Vocals
Mathis (born James Royce Mathis) made the smoothest makeout music ever recorded, and his rise to stardom in the mid '50s flew in the face of rock & roll's early domination. Staying almost exclusively with lushly orchestrated ballad material, Mathis racked up hit after hit and now has had albums in the charts for 30 years, an achievement few will better. —*Cub Koda*

○ **Music of Johnny Mathis: A Personal Collection** / Columbia Records

○ **Open Fire, Two Guitars** / 1959 / Columbia 8056
A warm and intimate setting, with stellar guitar work from Al Caiola and Tony Mottola. —*Cub Koda*

★ **Johnny's Greatest Hits** / 1962 / Columbia 34667
The original greatest-hits package, which stayed on the charts for ten years. Includes "Chances Are," "It's Not for Me to Say," "Wonderful! Wonderful!" and "The Twelfth of Never." It seldom gets more romantic than this. —*Cub Koda*

Better Together: Duet / Oct. 8, 1991 / Columbia 47982
Mathis's romantic duets with Regina Belle, Patti Austin, Deniece Williams, Take 6, Angela Bofill, Jane Olivor, Dionne Warwick. Aside from the million-selling duet, "Too Much Too Little Too Late" with Williams, includes their stellar reunion on Major Harris's "Love Won't Let Me Wait." Also features the unheralded masterpiece, "You Brought Me Love," with Austin. —*Bil Carpenter*

How Do You Keep the Music Play / May 4, 1993 / CBS 53204
Eleven heavily string-orchestrated renditions of Alan & Marilyn Bergman and Michel LeGrand tunes, such as "Something New in My Life," "Summer Me, Winter Me" and "Something in the Way She Makes Me Feel." LeGrand plays the ivories as a backdrop to Mathis's unctuous vocal delivery. —*Bil Carpenter*

In the Still of the Night / Columbia 44336
One of Mathis's best recordings to date. Contemporary updates of '50s classics, such as "You Belong to Me" and "It's All in the Game." Take 6 supplies guest vocals on the title track. Clean, uncomplicated orchestration. —*Bil Carpenter*

Amanda McBroom

Vocals
This Los Angeles-based songwriter and cabaret singer is probably best known for her song "The Rose," a hit in 1979 for Bette Midler. McBroom has also appeared on stage in "Jacques Brel Is Alive and Well" and "See Saw," and she also tours regularly. Her debut album, *Growing Up in Hollywood* with Lincoln Mayorga, was a best-seller for the prestigious Sheffield Labs label, as was her follow-up, *West of Oz*. —*AMG*

Growing Up in Hollywood Town / 1980 / Sheffield Lab 13
With the help of master pianist Lincoln Mayorga, McBroom sings her own world-weary songs of love and experience and well-chosen oldies like "You've Lost That Lovin' Feelin'." —*William Ruhlmann*

● **Dreaming** / 1986 / Gecko 001
Amanda McBroom remains best known for her composition "The Rose," the hit that served as the title song for the Bette Midler movie. McBroom's version of the song is included here, along with a collection of equally moving love songs. —*William Ruhlmann*

Maureen McGovern

b. 1949
Vocals
Maureen McGovern was a secretary when she was hired by Russ Regan to sing the theme from the movie *The Poseidon Adventure* in 1973. It was a number-one hit. The following year, McGovern sang the theme from *The Towering Inferno*, "We May Never Love like This Again," which was not a hit, though it did win an Academy Award. McGovern went on to other movie themes, then distanced herself from such work, appearing on Broadway in *The Pirates of Penzance*. She built a reputation as a sophisticated pop singer to the point that she was able to headline at Carnegie Hall

by the '90s, singing show music and standards by George Gershwin and other songwriters. — *William Ruhlmann*

Morning After / 1973 / 20th Century 419
Contains that big ballad, of course, though there is no album compiling all of McGovern's movie themes. — *William Ruhlmann*

○ **Naughty Baby** / 1989 / CBS 44995
McGovern as sophisticated pop singer, effectively handling an album of Gershwin material. Includes "Of Thee I Sing," the theme from a show in which she starred in 1987. — *William Ruhlmann*

● **Greatest Hits** / Curb 77337
The best of her movie work and other hits, including "Different Worlds." — *Cub Koda*

Johnny Mercer

b. Nov. 18, 1909, Savannah, GA, **d.** Jun. 25, 1976, Los Angeles, CA
lyricist, Vocals
In the course of a remarkable career, Johnny Mercer wore many hats. He was one of the best and most prolific lyricists of his time ("One for My Baby," "Blues in the Night," "Ac-Cent-Tchu-Ate the Positive," "Moon River") and a fine composer ("Dream," "Something's Gotta Give"). He was also cofounder and president of Capitol Records, where he signed Nat King Cole and Peggy Lee, among others, and a cofounder and president of the Songwriters' Hall of Fame.

He was a recording star in his own right in the '40s. Mercer did not rely strictly on his own material, nor did he possess a technically great voice, but he sang in an appealing, easygoing, swinging style, backed mainly by the Paul Weston Orchestra and the Pied Pipers on background vocals. Mercer's recordings are a bit reminiscent of the Sinatra swing albums of the '50s. His recording of "Ac-Cent-Tchu-Ate the Positive," one of his most popular, enjoyed renewed interest in recent years with its appearance in the movie *Bugsy* and its use as the theme of the TV show "Homefront." Mercer was one of those rare individuals who seemed able to achieve anything he put his mind to and do it well. — *Kenneth M. Cassidy*

Uncollected Johnny Mercer (1944) / 1940 / Hindsight 152
A collection of radio transcripts, recorded in 1944 with the Paul Weston Orchestra. — *Kenneth M. Cassidy*

Two of a Kind / 1963 / Atco 90484
An album of duets with Bobby Darin. — *Kenneth M. Cassidy*

● **Capitol Collectors Series** / Jul. 26, 1989 / Capitol 92125
A collection of his best recordings from the '40s. — *Kenneth M. Cassidy*

Too Marvelous for Words / 1991 / Capitol 96791
Too Marvelous for Words: Johnny Mercer has Capitol recording artists, including Mercer himself, singing his songs. — *Kenneth M. Cassidy*

Johnny Mercer Songbook / RCA 9788
A collection of RCA recording artists singing the songs of Johnny Mercer. — *Kenneth M. Cassidy*

Mabel Mercer

b. 1900, **d.** 1984
Vocals
Popular in cabaret work, both in France and the United States, for years. Mercer's strong interpretive skills as a chanteuse and her penchant for popularizing obscure tunes such as "Fly Me to the Moon" brought her a loyal cult following. Admirers of her work included Lena Horne, Nat King Cole, and Frank Sinatra. — *Cub Koda*

○ **Art of Mabel Mercer** / May 21, 1952 / Atlantic 602
Good two-record anthology that features outstanding cabaret vocalist Mabel Mercer. Her approach was brilliant, but not for everyone. It was stiff by jazz-phrasing standards and put far more emphasis on technique than feeling. Yet few have been better at doing highly stylized material. This has not yet been reissued on CD. — *Ron Wynn*

● **Sings Cole Porter** / Atlantic 81264
A great song stylist working in a perfect lyric setting. — *Ron Wynn*

Ethel Merman (Ethel Agnes Zimmerman)

b. 1908, New York, **d.** 1984
Vocals
Merman developed her booming vocal style on her own. She attracted attention in Gershwin's *Girl Crazy* (1930), capping the show with her rendition of "I Got Rhythm." Dubbed the "Queen of Broadway," Merman starred in Cole Porter's *Anything Goes* (1934) and Irving Berlin's *Annie Get Your Gun* (1946) and *Call Me Madam* (1950). She also appeared in 14 movie musicals, including *There's No Business like Show Business.* — *David Szatmary*

● **Musical Autobiography** / 1963 / Decca 153
Two-album set that provides a solid introduction to Merman's distinctive style. — *David Szatmary*

Bette Midler

b. Dec. 1, 1945, Paterson, NJ
Vocals
Bette Midler counts singing as only one of her talents; at times since 1972, when she first came to national recognition, it has seemed to be the least of her talents. Still, she has managed to score a number of major hits in a roller-coaster career as a recording artist. Born in Paterson, NJ, and raised in Hawaii, Midler early on showed an interest in singing and acting, and by the '60s she had moved to New York and gotten a role in the long-running Broadway hit *Fiddler on the Roof.* Midler developed a nightclub act that included comedy and singing of a variety of kinds of material, including show tunes, pop hits, and even a takeoff on the Andrews Sisters, and appeared with increasing frequency in New York with her accompanist, Barry Manilow. She was signed to Atlantic Records and released *The Divine Miss M* (1972), which went gold and included a Top-Ten single cover of the Andrews Sisters' "Boogie Woogie Bugle Boy." *Bette Midler* (1973) was similarly successful.

Midler's album sales fell off during the rest of the '70s, though her records always reached the Top 100 in the album chart. But in 1979 she starred in the film *The Rose,* a fictional account of the life of Janis Joplin, and the title track became a Top-Ten hit. The year 1980 saw the release of Midler's concert film, *Divine Madness,* and her best-selling book, *A View from a Broad.* Her next film, *Jinxed* (1982), however, was a major flop, and subsequent records didn't fare well. Midler made a cinematic comeback with *Down and Out in Beverly Hills* (1986), but it wasn't until 1989 that she had another pop hit, when her version of "Wind beneath My Wings" from her film *Beaches* became a number-one hit. This rejuvenated her singing career, and 1990's *Some People's Lives* became a Top Ten, million-selling album, with the song "From a Distance" hitting number two. Midler's soundtrack album to her 1991 film *For the Boys* was also a gold-selling hit. — *William Ruhlmann*

○ **Divine Miss M** / 1972 / Atlantic 7238
Midler's early camp style is captured in this debut album, which features her torchy version of "Do You Want to Dance?," the bubbly remake of "Boogie Woogie Bugle Boy," and Buzzy Linhart's "Friends," all Top-40 hits. — *William Ruhlmann*

Bette Midler / 1973 / Atlantic 7270
An earthy mix of blues, R&B, and '40s boogie-woogie. — *Bil Carpenter*

○ **Songs for the New Depression** / 1976 / Atlantic 18155
Notable for a duet with Bob Dylan on "Buckets of Rain" and an excellent version of Tom Waits's "Shiver Me Timbers." — *William Ruhlmann*

Thighs & Whispers / 1979 / Atlantic 16004
A disco set. — *Bil Carpenter*

○ **Rose** / 1979 / Atlantic 16010
The soundtrack to Midler's successful film, with the title track written by Amanda McBroom. — *William Ruhlmann*

○ **Divine Madness** / 1980 / Atlantic 16022
This record showcases Midler at her liveliest, during a concert at Pasadena Civic Auditorium. — *Larry Lapka*

No Frills / 1983 / Atlantic 80070
Top-40 pop and light rock. — *Bil Carpenter*

Beaches / 1989 / Atlantic 81933
The soundtrack to Midler's musical comeback film, featuring her version of "Wind beneath My Wings." — *William Ruhlmann*

Some People's Lives / 1990 / Atlantic 82129
Midler's most successful regular album release in some time, featuring "From a Distance." — *William Ruhlmann*

For the Boys / 1991 / Atlantic 82329
A film placing Midler in the Andrews Sisters' milieu of World War II was an inspired choice, and the soundtrack shows her abilities on period material as well as giving her a chance to sing a touching version of the Beatles' "In My Life." — *William Ruhlmann*

★ **Divine Collection** / Jun. 22, 1993 / Atlantic
Bette Midler's first compilation features most of her hits, including "Wind beneath My Wings," "The Rose," "Boogie Woogie Bugle Boy," "From a Distance," and her version of "One More for My Baby (and One More for the Road)," recorded on one of the final episodes of "The Tonight Show" starring Johnny Carson. *Divine Collection* is the greatest-hits collection that Midler has needed for quite some time. — *AMG*

Mills Brothers

Group
Few Black vocal groups had the impact of the Mills Brothers, either commercially or musically, and their long-lasting reign as hitmakers stretched from the early '30s to the late '60s. John, Herbert, Harry, and Donald Mills were born in Piqua, OH. After polishing their harmonies around Cincinnati, they scored their first number-one hit in 1931 with the rousing "Tiger Rag." The group's enduring gimmick involved imitating various instruments vocally, with John providing guitar backing until his death in 1935 (his father, John Sr, replaced him).

Major stars of records, radio, and film, the Mills Brothers were tremendously popular. "Paper Doll" and "You Always Hurt the One You Love" were wartime favorites on Decca. The group gently swung to the top of the charts with "Glow Worm" in 1952, and even took a tentative stab at rock & roll in 1958 with a cover of the Silhouettes' "Get a Job." As late as 1968, the group, by then a trio after their dad's retirement, registered a solid seller with "Cab Driver," and they remained a popular TV and nightclub attraction through 1982 (when Harry died). — *Bill Dahl*

Four Boys and a Guitar / 1954 / GNP 9016

☆ **Greatest Hits** / 1958 / MCA 31035

Close Harmony / 1969 / Ranwood 3008

★ **Best of Decca Years** / Decca 31348
Most of the Mills Brothers' best-known hits, remastered well, with good notes. — *Charles S. Wolfe*

Our Golden Favorites / MCA 188

Liza Minnelli

b. 1946
Vocals
The daughter of Judy Garland and movie director Vincente Minnelli, Liza started in show business early on, guest-dueting as a youngster with her mother, from whom she inherited much of her energetic singing and performing abilities. She scored on Broadway at age 20 with the original cast of *Cabaret*, later winning an Oscar for the movie version. Hollywood beckoned, as Minnelli is a fine actress, but her musical show and cabaret roots hold fast to this day. — *Cub Koda*

○ **Liza with a "Z"** / 1972 / Columbia 31762
An Emmy-winning TV concert performance. — *Larry Lapka*

Singer / 1973 / Columbia 32149
Early-'70s contemporary music. A change of pace for her. — *Larry Lapka*

Liza Minnelli at Carnegie Hall / 1981 / Telarc 85502
Concert performances from 1979. — *Larry Lapka*

Results / 1989 / Epic 45098
Produced by the Pet Shop Boys, this album has a more contemporary sound. — *Larry Lapka*

Marilyn Monroe (Norma Jean Baker)

b. 1926, **d.** Aug. 5, 1962
Vocals
Hollywood's most enduring legend was also a fine jazz-influenced singer, with a larger discography than one might expect. — *Cub Koda*

☆ **Some Like It Hot** / 1956 / United Artists 4030

The soundtrack of Billy Wilder's comedy features Monroe's breathy versions of several '20s jazz/pop classics, including a steamy "Running Wild." Out of print, but worth the search. — *Cub Koda*

Remember Marilyn / 1959 / 20th Century 901

● **Marilyn Monroe Collection** / Deja Vu 2001

○ **Gentlemen Prefer Blondes** / Disques Swing 101
Another soundtrack album, her first, featuring "Diamonds Are a Girl's Best Friend" and duets with Jane Russell. In and out of print. — *Cub Koda*

Vaughn Monroe

b. 1911, **d.** May 21, 1973
Vocals, trombone, bandleader
Big-voiced baritone who caught on at the tail end of the big band era with theme "Racing with the Moon" and followed with over 20 Top-Ten hits through the early '50s, among them "There! I've Said It Again," "The Trolley Song," "Cool Water," "Ghost Riders in the Sky," and "Red Roses for a Blue Lady." Pleasing delivery and deep voice worked well for him when he became a pitchman for RCA in 1955, doing commercials to introduce America to the latest thing, color TV. — *Cub Koda*

● **Best of Vaughn Monroe** / 1987 / MCA 1559
This big-band leader's original hits, including "Ghost Riders in the Sky," "Racing with the Moon," and "Ballerina." Until RCA reissues its collection, these versions will suffice. — *Hank Davis*

There I Sing, Swing It Again / 1989 / RCA Victor 1799

Yves Montand

b. 1921, **d.** 1991
Vocals
Perhaps he's best known as a political revolutionary or as Marilyn Monroe's co-star in *Let's Make Love*, but he was also a dynamic showman known for his almost somnambulistic style of crooning. — *Bil Carpenter*

● **By Request** / CBS
C'est excellent. Montand crooning en Français on such standards as "Les Feuilles Mortes" and "Planter Cafe." — *Bil Carpenter*

Ella Mae Morse

b. Sep. 12, 1924, Mansfield, TX
Vocals
One of the most talented and overlooked vocalists of the '40s, Ella Mae Morse blended jazz, country, pop, and R&B; at times she came remarkably close to what would be known as rock & roll. At not yet 14, Morse had her first taste of the big time when Jimmy Dorsey's band came to Dallas for a stay at the Adolphus Hotel and she called for an audition. Unbeknownst to her, the band needed a new female vocalist. Believing that Morse was indeed 19, as she and her mother claimed, Dorsey hired her. When he received a letter from the school board declaring that he was responsible for the Morse's care, he fired her. Morse joined former Dorsey pianist Freddie Slack's band in 1942. She was only 17 when they cut "Cow Cow Boogie," which became Capitol Records' first gold single. The following year, Morse began recording solo. Although her recordings were consistently solid and sold fairly well (frequently charting better on the Black charts than on the pop charts), Morse never obtained a huge following. She retired from recording in 1957. — *Stephen Thomas Erlewine*

Morse Code / 1957 / Capitol 898

Hits of Ella Mae Morse and Freddie Slack / 1962 / Capitol 1802

★ **Capitol Collectors Series** / 1992 / Capitol 95288
After being out of print for many years, a well-chosen sampling of Morse's groundbreaking recordings is now available on this splendid compilation. Her ten charting solo singles are here, along with sides recorded with Freddie Slack and some obscure tracks. Morse blazes through every song, particularly "House of Blue Lights," "Milkman, Keep Those Bottles Quiet," "Pig Foot Pete," "The Blacksmith Blues," and her first recording, "Cow Cow Boogie." This is an album with terrific liners and superlative sound. Snatch it up and pray Capitol reissues more Morse material. — *Stephen Thomas Erlewine*

Nana Mouskouri

b. Oct. 13, 1936, Athen, Greece
Vocals
Born in Athens, Greece, Mouskouri grew up listening to American jazz and Black gospel music. She attended a classical music conservatory but was thrown out for playing jazz. Later she worked with Harry Belafonte and Quincy Jones. Mouskouri possesses an articulate, resonant soprano.—*Bil Carpenter*

Tu M'Oublies / 1986 / Polydor 830563
French pop songs. "Parle-t-il de Moi?" and "L'amour, Qu'est-ce Que C'est?" are the best cuts. —*Bil Carpenter*

○ **Magic of Nana Mouskouri** / Jan. 21, 1988 / Philips 836497

Oh Happy Day / 1990 / Philips 848108
This tribute to Black gospel has 14 soulful cuts done with an earthiness never shown on previous records. "In the Upper Room" and "Slow Train" stand out. —*Bil Carpenter*

● **Only Love: The Best of Nana** / 1991 / Philips 510229
Nana's English covers of '80s hits like Cyndi Lauper's "Time After Time." —*Bil Carpenter*

Wayne Newton

b. 1942
Vocals, guitar
Though best known for his long-standing love affair with Las Vegas-style entertainment, Newton actually started in a country & western/rockabilly act with his brother Jerry, recording as the Newton Rascals. Wayne came to national prominence early in the '60s with regular appearances on the "Jackie Gleason Show." Though most effective with ballad material and a Vegas-glitz style of performing, Newton is actually a fine guitarist whose voice packs more wallop than critics generally give him credit for. —*Cub Koda*

Danke Schon / 1963 / Capitol 1973

Best of Wayne Newton / 1967 / Capitol 16083

★ **Capitol Collectors Series** / 1989 / Capitol 91634

Wayne Newton in Person / Capitol 2029

Ray Noble (Raymond Stanley Noble)

b. Dec. 17, 1903, Brighton, England, **d.** Apr. 2, 1978, London, England
Bandleader, arranger, composer
An arranging and compositional mainstay as well as a good pianist and top bandleader, England's Ray Noble enjoyed great popularity both in America and Europe. He cleverly infused his songs with jazz, swing, and pop influences, creating numbers that were popular and artistic successes. Noble was HMV's music director in the late '20s and early '30s, and wrote such early '30s hits as "Love Is the Sweetest Thing," "The Very Thought of You," "The Touch of Your Lips" and the instrumental anthem "Cherokee." Charlie Barnet had a hit with the latter in 1938, and Charlie Parker was quoted as saying it was improvising on the song that let him play the music he'd been hearing in his mind.
Noble scored four number one hits in 1933 and 1934, among them "Isle of Capri" and "The Old Spinning Wheel." He came to America in 1934 with Al Bowlly and drummer/manager Bill Harty. Glenn Miller assembled a band for him that included Bud Freeman, Claude Thornhill, and Will Bradley. The results were such songs as "Paris in the Spring" and "Let's Swing It" in 1935. Noble backed Fred Astaire on the hit songs "Nice Work If You Can Get It," "A Foggy Day," and "Change Partners" in the late '30s on Brunswick. He signed to the label as an artist, then moved to Columbia in 1940. The song "By the Light of the Silvery Moon" was on the charts in 1941 and 1944. Noble's last number-one hit was "Linda" in 1947. He recorded on Victor in America, and also for Sunbeam, Aircheck, and Monmouth Evergreen, among others. Import and jazz specialty stores are the place to consult for Noble CDs. —*Ron Wynn*

● **1935-1936** / 1976 / Jazz Band 2112

Jane Olivor

b. 1947, New York
Vocals
A tender-voiced singer who made her mark in pre-World War II European cabaret-style music. Though influenced by Johnny

Mathis and Simon & Garfunkel, Olivor is often compared to Edith Piaf. —*Bil Carpenter*

○ **Chasing Rainbows** / 1977 / Columbia 34917
Melancholy '40s Parisian cafe-style music. —*Bil Carpenter*

Stay the Night / 1978 / Columbia 35437
A subtle, sensitive try at the Top 40. —*Bil Carpenter*

Best Side of Goodbye / 1980 / Columbia 36335
Forlorn and moody—easy listening. —*Bil Carpenter*

In Concert / 1982 / Columbia 37938
Near-riotous crowds feed this heartful cabaret act. —*Bil Carpenter*

Patti Page (Clara Ann Fowler)

b. Nov. 8, 1927, Claremore, OK
Vocals
Patti Page was one of pop music's leading singers during the early '50s. Her double-tracked vocals, highly innovative at the time, translated into gigantic commercial success. By the age of 19, Page was working as a singer at a Tulsa radio station, and she signed with Mercury in 1948. Page's use of multi-tracked vocals gave her a unique, full sound, and in 1950 her renditions of "All My Love" and "Tennessee Waltz" were both pop chart toppers, the latter for a good three months. "Mockin' Bird Hill" (1951), "I Went to Your Wedding" (1952), and "Doggie in the Window" (1953) were only a few of her gold records for Mercury, and she persevered through the early rock era with "Allegheny Moon" in 1956 and "Old Cape Cod" the next year. Her last major pop smash in 1965, "Hush, Hush, Sweet Charlotte," was the theme song to a popular movie. —*Bill Dahl*

★ **Mercury Years, Vol. 1** / Jan. 1991 / Mercury 510433
Original hits from 1948-1952. Includes "Tennessee Waltz." Excellent package. —*Hank Davis*

○ **Mercury Years, Vol. 2** / Feb. 1991 / Mercury 510434
Original hits from 1948 to 1952. Includes "Tennessee Waltz." Excellent package. —*Hank Davis*

Mandy Patinkin

b. Nov. 20, 1947
Vocals
Versatile stage and screen actor and singer, Patinkin first gained notice in the Broadway musical *Evita*. He has since made his mark in films (*Ragtime*, *The Princess Bride*) and most especially on Broadway in *Sunday in the Park with George*, *The Secret Garden*, and his own one-man show, *Dress Casual*. He began his recording career in 1989. —*William Ruhlmann*

● **Mandy Patinkin** / 1989 / Columbia 44943
Patinkin has reserves of emotion that seem boundless on this tour de force collection mainly given over to show songs. Employing a vocal range that begins in a clear high tenor and plunges to a gruff baritone, Patinkin is able to act and sing duets with himself or sing beautifully alone. But feeling—sometimes overflowing feeling—is the core of his sense of interpretation. As a result, some very old songs sound newly written in his hands. —*William Ruhlmann*

○ **Dress Casual** / 1990 / Columbia 45998
An enormously ambitious collection of show and film music dominated by suites and medleys taken from Stephen Sondheim's obscure *Evening Primrose* (with guest Bernadette Peters) and *Pal Joey*. —*William Ruhlmann*

The Pied Pipers

Group
Originally consisting of eight members, the Pied Pipers had their greatest success after nearly half of the members left the group. The remaining Pipers (Billy Wilson, Chuck Lowry, Jo Stafford, and Stafford's then-husband John Huddleston) joined the Tommy Dorsey Band in 1939, backing Sinatra on many classic recordings. In 1942 the Pied Pipers broke away from Dorsey, and Huddleston joined the army, to be replaced by Hal Hopper, one of the original eight members. The group backed Johnny Mercer on several tracks during the early '40s, including "Candy" and "Blues in the Night." Their first single ("Deacon Jones"/"Pistol Packin' Mama") was released in 1943. Stafford had by then become quite busy with her solo career, and she left the group in 1944, to be replaced by June Hutton. Throughout the rest of the decade the

Pied Pipers charted frequently, yet their popularity waned in the '50s. A group bearing the Pied Pipers' name still tours today. —*Stephen Thomas Erlewine*

★ **Capitol Collectors Series** / 1992 / Capitol 95289
A terrific 20-track overview of this early vocal group. Features all of their best known songs, including "The Trolley Song," "Dream," "Open the Door, Richard," "Mam'selle," and "My Happiness." The remastering is top-notch, and the liner notes contain many anecdotes and much information. —*Stephen Thomas Erlewine*

Louis Prima

b. Dec. 1911, New Orleans, LA, d. Aug. 24, 1978, New Orleans, LA
Vocals, trumpet
Though he started in his native New Orleans—heavily influenced by Louis Armstrong's playing and singing and composing the jazz anthem "Sing, Sing, Sing" —Prima really hit his stride in the mid '40s. Combining Armstrong's scat singing style with Neapolitan gibberish and an irresistible rhythm, Prima created a string of hits that presaged the coming of rock & roll by a good dozen years. He moved to Las Vegas by the early '50s, hooked up with his wife Keely Smith and saxophonist Sam Butera, and ruled the late-night scene there for almost 20 years. A manic performer with an unbelievable sense of rhythm and humor, Louis Prima remains a true American music original. —*Cub Koda*

Wildest Show at Tahoe / 1955 / Capitol 908

Las Vegas Prima Style / 1958 / Capitol 1010

Hits of Louis & Keely / 1961 / Capitol 91208

Play Pretty for the People / 1964 / Savoy 4420

★ **Capitol Collectors Series** / 1991 / Capitol 94072
An excellent, rocking, and very funny overview of his Capitol years. —*Dan Heilman*

● **Zooma Zooma: The Best of Louis Prima** / Rhino 70225
Eighteen Capitol recordings from 1956 to 1958, including the title track, "Just a Gigolo/I Ain't Got Nobody," "That Old Black Magic," and "I've Got You under My Skin." Great sound on tracks that rock like crazy. —*Cub Koda*

Johnnie Ray

b. Jan. 10, 1927, d. Feb. 25, 1990
Vocals
Although he was practically deaf, Johnnie Ray's tear-inflected delivery tabbed him as an early-'50s sensation. Leaving Oregon for Detroit, Ray found a gig at the Flame Club, an R&B and jazz institution. In 1951 Ray signed with Columbia's R&B subsidiary Okeh Records, although "Cry," his histrionic million-seller that year, was a pop entry all the way, with background vocals by the Four Lads. Produced by Mitch Miller, "Cry" remained perched atop the pop charts for nearly three months. Ray encored with "The Little White Cloud That Cried" before moving to the parent Columbia logo and enjoying a steady stream of pop hits, including "Walkin' My Baby Back Home" in 1952 and a cover of the Prisonaires' "Just Walking in the Rain" in 1956. Ray's frenzied antics set off riots among female admirers during his heyday, but the advent of rock soon dulled his hit-making powers. By 1959, the hits were through. Guidelines: Stick with original Columbia recordings and select the most generous sample, such as *16 Most Requested Songs*. —*Bill Dahl*

★ **16 Most Requested Songs** / 1991 / Columbia 46095
The original '50s recordings of Ray's best, including "Cry" and "Just Walking in the Rain." —*Hank Davis*

Helen Reddy

b. Oct. 25, 1942, Melbourne, Australia
Vocals
Reddy began performing at the age of four in her native Australia; by the early '60s she had her own television series. Between 1971 and 1978, Reddy hit the Top 40 fourteen times with her smooth, airy light-pop singles, including number ones "Delta Dawn," "Angie Baby," and "I Am Woman." As her hits petered out toward the end of the '70s, her acting work increased, including roles in *Pete's Dragon*, *Sgt. Pepper's Lonely Hearts Club Band*, and *Airport 1975*. —*Stephen Thomas Erlewine*

I Am Woman / 1972 / Capitol 11068

Greatest Hits / 1975 / Capitol 46490
Reddy's biggest light-pop hits. —*Bil Carpenter*

No Way to Treat a Lady / 1975 / Capitol 11418
Smooth, pristine pop. —*Bil Carpenter*

Music, Music / 1976 / Capitol
A diverse mix of light rock, chilling jazz. Includes "Get off Me." —*Bil Carpenter*

Imagination / 1983 / MCA 5376
Funky R&B pop. —*Bil Carpenter*

Debbie Reynolds

b. Apr. 1, 1932, El Paso, TX
Vocals
Reynolds grew up in Burbank, CA, where she won a celebrity-impressions contest that led to a movie contract. Her biggest hit, "Tammy," a million-seller from 1957, pushed Buddy Holly's "That'll Be the Day" out of the number-one slot on the pop charts. Reynolds also starred in numerous films. —*Bil Carpenter*

● **Best of Debbie Reynolds** / 1972 / Curb 77435
Reynold's sweet voice against soft string arrangements. Includes the hit "Tammy." —*Bil Carpenter*

Paul Robeson

b. Apr. 9, 1898, d. Jan. 23, 1976
Vocals
Paul Robeson's commanding voice was capable of many wonders—he powerfully sang spirituals and acted in Shakespearean plays and numerous movies (including "The Emperor Jones" in 1933 and "King Solomon's Mines" in 1937). Robeson recorded for Victor in 1925, the same year he began collaborating with pianist Lawrence Brown, and his immortal "Ol' Man River" was immensely popular in 1928. As the decades passed, Robeson proved an eloquent spokesman for equality and freedom. —*Bill Dahl*

Paul Robeson Sings 'Ol' Man River' & Other Favorites / 1972 / Angel 47839

Golden Classics, Vol. 3 / 1977 / Collectables 6504
This erratic collection ranges from decent to marvelous. —*Ron Wynn*

○ **Power & the Glory** / 1991 / CBS 47337
This is a retrospective of Robeson's best known spirituals and folk music. —*Bil Carpenter*

Golden Classics, Vol. 1: American Balladeer / Collectables 6502
A great singer tries hard on established standards. —*Ron Wynn*

☆ **Ballad for Americans** / Vanguard 117
Superb songs, Americana, and more. —*Ron Wynn*

★ **Essential** / Vanguard 57
Some of his strongest and most defiant vocals. —*Ron Wynn*

Man & His Beliefs: A Golden Classics, Vol. 2 / Collectables 6503
Political/topical material. —*Ron Wynn*

Dinah Shore

b. Mar. 1, 1917, Winchester, TN
Vocals
Shore's public debut came at the age of four in Nashville. She sang at WSM there before moving in 1937 to New York, where she did radio shows with Eddie Cantor. Later she starred in Hollywood musicals and her own TV talk show. During the '50s, Shore was one of the top singers in the country. —*Bil Carpenter*

Bouquet of Blues / 1942 / RCA 1214
This is a superb album of blues cuts in pop style. It includes "St. Louis Blues" among others. —*Bil Carpenter*

● **16 Most Requested Songs** / Columbia 45315
Her best hits, including the peppy "Buttons & Bows." —*Bil Carpenter*

Frank Sinatra (Francis Albert Sinatra)

b. Dec. 12, 1915, Hoboken, NJ
Vocals
Frank Sinatra's public image as a boorish, Mafia-hobnobbing, wife-abusing, obnoxious right-wing lout is in direct conflict with the personality that dominates his finest music. From his ascent

to pop stardom in the '40s up to his last moment of brilliance in the '60s, Sinatra was pop music's quintessential romantic, someone who could tell you how much love hurts and then jump and wail about how good it feels, with overwhelming amounts of conviction and sincerity. A character emerges from his best music who is searching unflaggingly for the perfect love; when he doesn't find it, he explores the bowels of abandon and heartbreak with equal diligence.

This isn't the place to discuss the innovations Sinatra brought to pop vocalizing and album-making in the 20th century (buy the highlighted discs to discover that). Nor is this the place to discuss the vulgarity that has characterized his public life (check out Kitty Kelly's bio). The CDs highlighted below offer a biography of Frank Sinatra that is unarguably the most important. On record the guy was a sucker for love, and if you have a hard time relating to that, put this book back on the shelf and go browsing in the automotive section.

After cutting his teeth with the orchestras of Harry James and Tommy Dorsey in 1942, Sinatra pursued a career as a soloist. The rest, you could say, is history. Under the tutelage of producer Axel Stordahl, Sinatra developed a vocal style that stretched syllables with perfect amounts of subtlety and showmanship and gave millions of bobby-soxed girls their first sex symbol.

Sinatra left Columbia in 1953, disgusted by the shoddy material his label was tossing him. He hooked up with Capitol that same year and, with Nelson Riddle and producer Voyle Gilmore, took full advantage of the then-new long-play record by recording thematically linked albums. He also worked with arranger/conductors Billy May and Gordon Jenkins, who, along with Riddle, would embellish Sinatra's conceptual endeavors with perfectly suited accompaniment, adding new facets to his musical personality. For those keeping score, Riddle specialized in jazzy, sprightly arrangements, while May favored splashy, pounding thumpers, and Jenkins piled on thick gobs of orchestration, heavy on the strings.

Sinatra left Capitol in 1961 to form his own label, Reprise. Unfortunately, the magic that was so abundant during the first 20 years of his career had withered. His voice had lost most of its charms, becoming rougher and less dazzling in both emotion and technique. There's good stuff from this period but, sadly, not much. —*John Floyd*

○ **Voice: The Columbia Years (1943-1952)** / 1943-1952 / Columbia 40343
An exhaustive six-disc presentation of his formative years, divided into six themes: saloon songs, standards, screen, love songs, swing, and stage. It might be too much for skeptical novices, but this is a marvelous set. —*John Floyd*

☆ **Songs for Young Lovers/Swing Easy** / 1955 / Capitol 48470
This brings together Sinatra's first two 10-inch releases for Capitol, with zesty arrangements by Nelson Riddle and a new-found bounce and confidence in Sinatra's vocals. —*John Floyd*

☆ **In the Wee Small Hours** / 1955 / Capitol 96826
His first full-blown concept album (from 1955) is a gut-wrenching collection of maudlin ballads, including definitive readings of "I'll Be Around," "Ill Wind," and "Dancing on the Ceiling," with Nelson Riddle's most beautiful soundscapes. —*John Floyd*

★ **Songs for Swingin' Lovers!** / 1956 / Capitol 46570
The title says it all. Soaring big-band arrangements and the best set of songs Sinatra's ever sung make this release the best introduction to his swinging world. —*John Floyd*

☆ **Where Are You** / 1957 / Capitol 91209
The first of Sinatra's three collaborations with Gordon Jenkins, who wraps his vocals in a lush, warm blanket of compassion and sympathy. The CD contains four Nelson Riddle-conducted bonus cuts. —*John Floyd*

Swingin' Affair! / 1957 / Capitol 94518
Features some fine Nelson Riddle swingers and a decent song selection but lacks the thematic wallop of *Swingin' Lovers.* Fanatics will enjoy it, though. —*John Floyd*

Close to You (& More) / 1957 / Capitol 46572
Another fine set of Nelson Riddle-arranged weepers, highlighted by the tear-jerking title cut and "I Couldn't Sleep a Wink Last Night." —*John Floyd*

○ **Frank Sinatra Story in Music** / 1958 / Sony 20709

A stunning two-disc collection of Sinatra's early years. His nickname at the time was "The Voice," and you can hear why: If you could hear velvet, it would sound like Sinatra's vocals on "I Concentrate on You" and "I've Got a Crush on You." —*John Floyd*

☆ **Sings for Only the Lonely** / 1958 / Capitol 48471
Gone is Nelson Riddle's trademarked light-swing jazz. Gone is the bounce in Sinatra's voice. This morose, almost gothic set of torch songs captures "The Voice" in the furthest regions of commiserative torment. —*John Floyd*

☆ **Come Fly with Me** / 1958 / Capitol 48469
Once you've exhausted the other swingin' sets, check out this Billy May-powered set of dance-floor wailers, which was Sinatra's last album on Capitol. —*John Floyd*

No One Cares / 1959 / Capitol 94519
Another Jenkins-conducted set of weepers. Essential cut: "I Can't Get Started." —*John Floyd*

☆ **Come Dance with Me!** / 1959 / Capitol 48468
A bright, splashy set of hard-thumping dance-floor invitations. Sinatra's voice is showing signs of wear, but Billy May's arrangements make them easy to ignore. —*John Floyd*

○ **Sinatra's Swingin' Session!!! (& More)** / 1961 / Capitol 46573
This decent collection of upbeat bouncers features the gorgeous "September in the Rain," one of Frankie's best moments. —*John Floyd*

Come Swing with Me / 1961 / Capitol 94520
Once you've exhausted the other swingin' sets, check out this Billy May-powered set of dance-floor wailers, which was Sinatra's last album on Capitol. —*John Floyd*

○ **It Might as Well Be Swing** / Dec. 1964 / Reprise 1012

☆ **September of My Years** / 1965 / Reprise 1014
After four years of duds on his own label, Sinatra and Gordon Jenkins bounced back with a set that examines the meaning of life, confronting both the ghosts of the past and the specter of old age. —*John Floyd*

Sinatra at the Sands / 1966 / Reprise 1019

Francis A. Sinatra & Edward K. Ellington / 1968 / Reprise 1024

Hello Young Lovers / 1986 / Columbia 40897
A 26-song grab bag that rounds up some choice leftovers from the Columbia years. —*John Floyd*

Sinatra Rarities: The Columbia Years / 1988 / Columbia 44236
Don't let the title fool you—this batch of overlooked material (which includes a breathtaking version of "Why Shouldn't I?") is all grade-A Sinatra. —*John Floyd*

★ **Capitol Years** / 1990 / Capitol 94777
A well-selected three-disc set that contains the high marks of his Capitol era, but you really should hear them in their original contexts. —*John Floyd*

○ **Reprise Collection** / 1990 / Reprise 26340
A lavishly packaged four-disc hodgepodge of later years. For fanatics it's essential, but it unintentionally documents the demise of Sinatra's talents. —*John Floyd*

● **Capitol Collectors Series** / 1990 / Capitol 92160
Rounding up the best material from otherwise mediocre albums like *This Is Sinatra, Nice and Easy,* and *All the Way.* —*John Floyd*

★ **Sinatra Reprise: The Very Good Years** / Mar. 26, 1991 / Warner Brothers 26501
This contains the worthwhile material from *The Reprise Collection* in a less cumbersome single-disc package. A necessary addition to your Sinatra collection. —*John Floyd*

Sings the Select Cole Porter / Jun. 24, 1991 / Capitol 96611
Here's a vibrant, joyous and vocally rich Sinatra backed by superb arrangements from an orchestra conducted by Nelson Riddle. The 16 numbers include such triumphs as "Night And Day," "I Get a Kick out of You" and "What Is This Thing Called Love." —*Ron Wynn*

Duets / Oct. 25, 1993 / Capitol
Although it was a gigantic hit, *Duets* doesn't present Sinatra at his best—his voice is worn and he shows no interaction with his partners, probably because their parts weren't recorded at the same time. It's more of a marketing success than a artistic accomplishment. —*Stephen Thomas Erlewine*

○ **Sinatra & Sextet: Live in Paris** / 1994 / Reprise Records

A rare recording of Sinatra with a small combo, *Live in Paris* captures him at a the top of his form, even if his stage patter is embarrassing and, at one point, borderline racist ("Ol Man River"). Nevertheless, this album is a fascinating historical document and it has some splendid music. — *Stephen Thomas Erlewine*

☆ **Columbia Years (1943-1952): The Complete Recordings** / Columbia
For serious students of popular singing, this 12-disc boxed set is indispensable. During his early years at Columbia, Sinatra defined what popular singing was, and these 285 songs show why he was so revolutionary. For many, 12 discs is too much music, but for collectors, the set is essential. — *Stephen Thomas Erlewine*

Barbra Streisand

b. Apr. 24, 1942
Vocals
Despite having to compete with rock singers during what is known as the "rock era," Barbra Streisand has turned out to be one of the most successful recording artists since World War II. As of the end of 1989, she had collected more platinum records than any other person, and her gold albums were exceeded only by Elvis Presley's. Streisand is also a successful actress and film director.

She got her start in New York City nightclubs and in musical comedy, appearing in *I Can Get It for You Wholesale* on Broadway when she was signed to CBS Records (now Sony Music). She went on to a starring role in *Funny Girl* (she would also star in the film version), by which time she had released her first album, *The Barbra Streisand Album*. During the mid-'60s, Streisand's albums were consistent sellers, though only her first single, "People," made the Top Ten. That meant she appealed primarily to adults and, as the '60s wore on, the music business became increasingly youth oriented. In addition, Streisand turned more of her attention to Hollywood, resulting in a slight fall-off in her popularity as a singer.

She began to address this in the early '70s by singing more rock-oriented material, notably a Top-Ten version of Laura Nyro's "Stoney End," but by the mid '70s she had found a niche as a singer of contemporary ballad material (for example, the theme song from her hit film *The Way We Were*). Streisand helped her own cause by cowriting the number-one hit "Evergreen" from her next film, *A Star Is Born*, and thereafter displayed a remarkable versatility that even found her at home in duets with disco diva Donna Summer and Bee Gee Barry Gibb. She was less active as a recording artist in the '80s, though in 1985 she scored an amazing success with *The Broadway Album*, probably her best-selling album ever. In 1991 she released a boxed-set retrospective, *Just for the Record . . .*, and in 1992 was thought to be close to re-signing a lucrative deal with Sony, covering both her musical and film activities. — *William Ruhlmann*

☆ **Barbra Streisand Album** / 1962 / Columbia 8807
The birth of a legend, best exemplified by Streisand's slow ballad treatment of "Happy Days Are Here Again," which transforms it from a frothy celebration song into a far more complicated mixture of remorse and warmth. — *William Ruhlmann*

Happening in Central Park / 1968 / Columbia 9710
Streisand's personality is on full display here, and her singing is mesmerizing. — *William Ruhlmann*

What about Today? / 1969 / Columbia 9816
Streisand's first tentative attempt to try out the work of contemporary songwriters. — *William Ruhlmann*

★ **Greatest Hits** / 1970 / Columbia 9968
Barbra's best of the '60s. — *William Ruhlmann*

○ **Barbra Joan Streisand** / 1971 / Columbia 30792
A confident Streisand takes on the songs of John Lennon and Carole King and even throws in an otherwise-unheard tune by Steely Dan's Walter Becker and Donald Fagen. — *William Ruhlmann*

☆ **Barbra Streisand's Greatest Hits, Vol. 2** / 1978 / Columbia 35679
The best of Barbra in the '70s. — *William Ruhlmann*

Guilty / 1980 / Columbia 36750
A chart-topping collaboration with Barry Gibb, featuring three Top-Ten hits. — *William Ruhlmann*

★ **Broadway Album** / 1985 / Columbia 40092

Streisand's abandonment of Broadway was the worst thing that happened to the theater in the '60s. This album, including masterful versions of the work of Stephen Sondheim along with some older classics, is some small recompense. It is also the best work of a very great career. — *William Ruhlmann*

○ **Greatest Hits . . . and More** / 1989 / Columbia 45369
This is really the third volume of Barbra's greatest hits. Her best from the '80s. — *William Ruhlmann*

Yma Sumac (Sumac del Castillo, Zoila Imperatriz Charrari)

b. 1928
Vocals
A singer with an amazing four-octave range, Sumac was said to have been a descendant of Inca kings. Her offbeat stylings became a phenomenon of early '50s pop music. While her album covers took advantage of her strange costumes and voluptuous figure, rumors abounded that she was, in actuality, a housewife named Amy Camus. It mattered little, since there has been no one like her before or since in the annals of popular music. — *Cub Koda*

● **Enchantress** / Pair 1172
Early-'50s recordings by a self-proclaimed Incan princess. Exotic music and a multi-octave vocal range. — *Hank Davis*

Spell of Yma Sumac / Pair 1172

Toni Tennille

b. May 8, 1943
Vocals
Throaty Alabama singer made a career as a '40s-style standard singer after her Captain & Tennille phase. — *Bil Carpenter*

● **Do It Again** / USA Music Group 596
A collection of previously released pop-style standards. — *Bil Carpenter*

More Than You Know / Mirage 90162
Husky, full-throttle vocals on '50s standards. — *Bil Carpenter*

Rudy Vallee

b. Jul. 28, 1901, d. Jul. 3, 1986
Vocals
Rudy Vallee was an immensely popular vocalist in the late '20s and '30s. Singing into a megaphone became his vocal trademark. At the height of his popularity, he had his own national radio show. As his singing career faded with the arrival of Bing Crosby, he switched to a career on the stage and screen. The 1966 novelty hit "Winchester Cathedral" was inspired by Vallee. He attempted a brief, unsuccessful comeback, recording an album that included his own version of "Winchester Cathedral." — *Kenneth M. Cassidy*

○ **Young Rudy Vallee** / 1961 / RCA Victor 2507

★ **Vagabond Lover** / Pro Arte 459
The best of Vallee's recordings from the '20s and '30s. — *Kenneth M. Cassidy*

Bobby Vinton

b. Apr. 16, 1941, Canonsburg, PA
Vocals, clarinet
As a child, Vinton played clarinet and was influenced by the big-band sound of Les Brown and Stan Kenton. He signed with Epic in 1960. He was renowned as the "King of Polka" for his Polish roots, but during the upbeat musical '60s he distinguished himself as an ultra-smooth, sentimental balladeer of the first order. — *Bil Carpenter*

● **Greatest Hits** / 1964 / Curb 77253
Some of the most beautiful ballads recorded, including "I Love How You Love Me" and "Blue Velvet." — *Bil Carpenter*

○ **All-Time Greatest Hits** / 1972 / Columbia 31487
A classy set of hits and other soft string ballads. — *Bil Carpenter*

Melodies of Love / 1974 / ABC 851

Roger Whittaker

b. 1936, Kenya, Africa
Vocals
British singer and whistler Roger Whittaker was born in Kenya. His first break came in 1970 with "Durham Town", a number-12 hit on the U.K. charts. This was soon followed by a string of hits

that became in time an avalanche of hit albums. *The Very Best of Roger Whittaker* reached number five on the U.K. charts and logged an incredible 42 weeks on the British charts. With almost 100 albums in print, Whittaker has become one of the most popular of the easy-listening singers. —*Michael Erlewine*

All Time Heart Touching Favorites, Vol. 1 / Apr. 23, 1990 / Liberty 90601

All Time Heart Touching Favorites, Vol. 2 / May 21, 1990 / Liberty 94151

● **Best of Roger Whittaker** / 1991 / RCA

Andy Williams

b. Dec. 3, 1928

Vocals

Andy Williams parlayed his relaxed vocal delivery into massive pop success and TV stardom during the '60s. After starting out singing with his brothers over various midwestern radio stations as a youth, the Wall Lake, IA, native went solo in 1952 and became a regular on Steve Allen's "Tonight Show" through 1955. He signed with Archie Bleyer's Cadence Records the next year and hit with "Canadian Sunset," topping the charts with a cover of Charlie Gracie's rock-tinged "Butterfly" in 1957. "Are You Sincere" (1958) and "Lonely Street" (1959) preceded a move to Columbia in 1961 and the huge seller "Can't Get Used to Losing You" in 1963. Williams has long been one of America's top middle-of-the-road entertainers, hosting his own TV variety series throughout the '60s, and he remains a highly popular attraction. —*Bill Dahl*

★ **Andy Williams' Best** / 1962 / Cadence 25054

A nice retrospective of Williams's early sides. —*Cub Koda*

Moon River & Other Great Movie Themes / 1962 / Columbia 8609

The hit title song and lush interpretations of movie-theme classics. —*Cub Koda*

Million Seller Songs / 1978 / Cadence 25061

Greatest Hits, Vol. 2 / 1981 / CBS 32384

Picks up where the Cadence compilation left off, including "Can't Get Used to Losing You," "Days of Wine and Roses," "Dear Heart," and others. —*Cub Koda*

Pia Zadora

b. 1955

Vocals

The daughter of violinist Skip Schipani is known as a low-budget movie star, but she also recorded several albums in the '80s. (Jermaine Jackson appeared on a couple of songs.) Zadora also toured with Frank Sinatra during the decade. —*Bil Carpenter*

● **Pia & Phil** / 1985 / Epic 40259

Her robust voice belts out great standards. —*Bil Carpenter*

I Am What I Am / 1986 / CBS 40533

A second set of well-executed standards. —*Bil Carpenter*

Pia Z. / 1989 / Epic 45273

A good stab at the pop charts. Youth oriented. —*Bil Carpenter*

Vocal Collections

Capitol's Great Ladies / 1992 / Capitol 98014

○ **Hits of 1940** / Living Era 5087

○ **Modern a Cappella** / 1992 / Rhino 71083

○ **Nipper's Greatest Hits: 1902-1920** / 1991 / RCA 3031

Al Jolson, George M. Cohan, Enrico Caruso: RCA Victor was there at the beginning, and this 20-song volume captures the times nicely. —*Jeff Tamarkin*

○ **Nipper's Greatest Hits: The 30s, Vol. 2** / Apr. 19, 1991 / RCA 9972

As strong as the first volume. Louis Armstrong, Artie Shaw, Gene Krupa—the big-band era begins here. —*Jeff Tamarkin*

○ **Nipper's Greatest Hits: The 40s, Vol. 1** / 1940-1949 / RCA 9855

With the likes of Frank Sinatra, Tommy Dorsey, Glenn Miller, and Spike Jones, this is a solid set. —*Jeff Tamarkin*

☆ **Rodgers & Hart Songbook** / RCA 8590

A 20-track compilation album of show songs by Richard Rodgers and Lorenz Hart, recorded by a variety of pop singers in the '50s and '60s, among them Perry Como, Jack Jones, and Ann-Margret. —*William Ruhlmann*

☆ **Sentimental Journey, Vol. 1** / Jun. 15, 1993 / Rhino 71249

The first volume of Rhino's pop vocal collection, *Sentimental Journey*, covers the years 1942-1946 and includes such vocalists as Bing Crosby, Doris Day, Judy Garland, Jo Stafford, Vaughn Monroe, and Frank Sinatra (with "Swinging on a Star," "Sentimental Journey," "The Trolly Song," "Candy," "There! I've Said it Again," and "Night and Day," respectively). Not only does the music sound great, but the liner notes are extensive, with complete musician credits. —*AMG*

☆ **Sentimental Journey, Vol. 2** / Jun. 15, 1993 / Rhino 71250

Sentimental Journey: Pop Vocal Classics, Vol. 2 (1947-1950) includes Dinah Shore's "Buttons and Bows," Patti Page's "The Tennessee Waltz," "Again" by Mel Torme, "Eileen Barton's "If I Knew You Were Comin' I'd've Baked a Cake," and (on CD) "Goodnight Irene" by the Weavers and "Music! Music! Music!" by Teresa Brewer among its 18 tracks. —*AMG*

☆ **Sentimental Journey, Vol. 3** / Jun. 15, 1993 / Rhino 71251

Sentimental Journey: Pop Vocal Classics, Vol. 3 (1950-1954) includes Johnny Ray's "Cry," Tony Bennett's "Because of You," "Come on-a My House" by Rosemary Clooney, Jo Stafford's "You Belong to Me," Kay Starr's "Wheel of Fortune," Dean Martin's "That's Amore" and "How High the Moon" by Les Paul & Mary Ford. Another good installment in the Rhino pop vocal series. —*AMG*

☆ **Sentimental Journey, Vol. 4** / Jun. 15, 1993 / Rhino 71252

Arguably the best, most consistent entry in Rhino's pop vocal series, *Sentimental Journey, Vol. 4 (1954-1959)* includes "Mack the Knife" by Bobby Darin, Peggy Lee's "Fever," Dinah Washington's "What a Diff'rence a Day Makes," Guy Mitchell's "Singing the Blues," Doris Day's "Que Sera, Sera (Whatever Will Be, Will Be)," Dean Martin's "Memories Are Made of This," and "Chances Are" by Johnny Mathis. —*AMG*

○ **Sentimental Journey: Capitol's Great Ladies of Song, Vol. 2** / Mar. 2, 1992 / Capitol 98014

☆ **Sweet and Lovely: Capitol's Great Ladies of Song, Vol. 1** / Jan. 20, 1992 / Capitol 97802

GAY

With the major labels reporting $10 billion in cassette and CD sales, 1993 was a record-breaking year for the international music industry. It was also the biggest year ever for gay music. More new artists emerged, more albums with openly gay themes were recorded and released (most on independent labels), and more gay albums were purchased than ever before in the history of the community. In fact, according to Overlooked Opinions, a national market-research firm, gay and lesbian people buy eight times as many tapes and CDs as the average consumer.

Although gay literature is enjoying popularity and shows like *Angels in America* and *Kiss of the Spider Woman* have had big commercial breakthroughs, gay music has been the poor stepchild of the gay cultural arts. Barbara Streisand, Bette Midler, the Village People, and Taylor Dayne were staples in the musical diets of gay people for years, and mainstream record companies focused on mega-selling album artists, in the process overlooking the needs of the gay community to hear its stories represented in pop music. This critical oversight has pushed an incredible array of diverse artists into the independent record scene. Ten years ago, Romanovsky & Phillips were just emerging to join Tom Wilson Weinberg in what for years would be the only representation of gay male recording artists in the community. Today, dozens of gay artists and groups are making great albums in the fields of pop, rock, alternative, folk, dance, and country & western. Pop music is slowly emerging from the closet!

At the same time, the gay movement is at a crossroads, continuing to define itself and working to represent a widely diverse, constantly evolving population of human beings. There has never been more need—or opportunity— to support music with a specifically gay perspective—music that speaks to the lives of gay people everywhere. And more than ever before, there is good reason to believe that gay people will discover and enthusiastically embrace their own new music and help bring it into the mainstream.

Every movement has its music, and now we are creating our own. With the recent passing of Stonewall 25, we still don't know how far ahead equal rights for gay people may lie, but we can be sure that through all our struggles, the music will be there—for gay men and lesbians, for our families, for straights, and for anyone who will listen to this bold new music.
—Will Grega

Adult Children of Heterosexuals

Rock, cabaret
Part of Boston's Theatre Offensive and founded by members of the legendary United Fruit Company, this hard-edged, cogender cabaret band entertains in an exciting and provocative way with a blend of high camp and low humor. — *Will Grega*

Adult Children of Heterosexuals / 1993 / Mcmillan Records
"I'm So Hard so I'm So Easy" and "I Never Liked You Anyway" (read up, down, and in every direction) are two of the screamingly hilarious gender-bending romps on this raucous blend of avant-garde jazz, cheesy synths, sax, and vocal ensemble. — *Will Grega*

Tina Benez

Rock, pop
Benez is a self-styled drag queen goddess, with solid pop smarts, unlimited ambition, chart savvy, and a fervent following all too willing to propel him/her to superstardom. — *Will Grega*

☆ **Glamour Overdose** / 1994 / Benez Popaganda Muzik
Benez delivers one of the most wildly original albums of the '90s. "Hitler's Daughter (High Fascist Model)" is a chilling peep into the fascistic (but highly fashionable) future of the world politic. "Glamour Overdose (G.O.D.)," a scream from start to finish, is delivered over a highly polished Eurodance/rock track. The vocal samples and overall production are brilliantly tasty. "Ghost in You" is a phenomenal ballad with an arrangement reminiscent of Ennio Morricone's spaghetti-Western film scores. — *Will Grega*

Richard Bone

Alternative dance, pop
A founding member of New York City's electronic music scene, Richard Bone started his career by writing music for off-Broadway theater productions (using homemade processors) and has worked with neo-legendaries Lenny Kaye and Reeves Gabrels. In 1980 he joined Shox Lumania but soon went solo and released a string of singles on Chrysalis Records. He has produced singles for Rubber Rodeo, composed original music for award-winning cable and broadcast television, and has been involved in the music video production of his own work released on the experimental Sony "Video 45's" in the early '80s. — *Will Grega*

● **Quirkwork** / 1992 / Quirkworks Laboratory
Tricky arpeggiated passages, layered vocals, and deft production combine to make these dance-floor friendly tracks a real treat. Tracks include "Last Days of Heaven," "Calling All Cars," and "Eveready Strut." — *Will Grega*

○ **Ambiento** / 1994 / Quirkworks Laboratory
Bone's delightful foray into ambient music. Stylized, peppered with fantastic samples and a sense of humor about itself, *Ambiento* serves to humanize the genre. — *Will Grega*

Michael Bonti

Folk, pop
Long Island native with a masterful voice and a gift for writing melodic folk music. — *Will Grega*

Michael Bonti / 1993 /
Gorgeous melodic acoustic pop that weaves social insight ("Quilted City") and downright horny playfulness. — *Will Grega*

Joe Bracco

Pop
Joe Bracco represented one of gay music's best hopes when he died of AIDS in March 1991 at age 30. But thanks to Paul Phillips of Romanovsky & Phillips, Bracco's buoyant performances live on. Phillips took a collection of the late Bracco's rough home recordings and demos and layered them with lush instrumental arrangements to create a wonderful posthumous tribute to a true pop talent. — *Will Grega*

○ **True to Myself** / 1992 / Fresh Fruit
The collection sparkles with Bracco's warm personality, melodic pop/New Wave influence, and true gift for lyric writing. "Friend

in My Pocket" is a goofy tribute to condom use. These recordings are proof that Joe Bracco was a rare and compelling talent—a New Wave Bruce Springsteen—and Paul Phillips is to be commended for bringing Bracco's superlative gift to light. —*Will Grega*

Butt Boy

Techno, ambient, leather

Thrust Recordings specializes in music written expressly as sensuous sounds for those serious about leather. This sensual music has the mellowness of New Age, the orchestral influence of classical music, the sharp edge of rock, and the futuristic sounds of techno pop, with a heavy leaning toward early Pink Floyd and the synthesized electronic pop of Jean Michel Jarre. —*Will Grega*

Feel the Music / 1993 / Thrust Recordings

Already an accomplished composer in video, radio, and theater, Butt Boy brings his sexual music into the private places of the leather community and sets the mood required for a mind trip into the erotic. "Dance of the Whip" builds its swirling sound around the rhythmic pattern of a cracking whip. This is an album that should come with protection! —*Will Grega*

Michael Callen

Rock, pop, vocal

After he learned he had the disease in 1982, leading AIDS activist Michael Callen singlehandedly redefined the public's concept of a person with the disease by giving speeches, writing articles, appearing on national television, giving interviews, organizing within the community, campaigning, and singing at a tempo that would exhaust most healthy people. His political efforts have been chronicled in Randy Shilts's classic book, *And the Band Played On.* His musical output is nothing less than amazing, including two albums recorded as a member of the Flirtations (see listing). His debut solo release was recorded six years after he was diagnosed with HIV, had established the PWA Coalition, and testified at congressional hearings on AIDS. —*Will Grega*

☆ **Purple Heart** / 1988 / Significant Other

Purple Heart is nothing less than the most stunning gay album recorded to date. The album has a pop/rocking set that segues into a more intimate set of six songs with Michael at the piano and includes the classics "Living in Wartime," "Love Don't Need a Reason," and Callen's ultra-campy reading of "Where the Boys Are." It is a must-have by an outstanding human being, a hero of our community, and one of the most wondrous voices ever recorded. Elizabeth Taylor said about him, "His life is a shining symbol of hope, strength, and courage." —*Will Grega*

Keith Christopher

Pop, rock, soul

An exceptionally talented vocalist with a wide range and a personable, embraceable quality, Keith Christopher produces music that is melodic, endearing, and just plain thrilling to hear. His songs reflect the emotions and issues of today in a style that is strong and vulnerable, passionate, and clear. He has composed special material for the United Nations Environmental Program as well as the Names Project. —*Will Grega*

○ **Keith Christopher** / 1993 / Kct Productions

Sublime and gratifying songs reinforce his belief in the power of love as a force for personal growth and physical health. The tracks on this debut are muscular and lush, with hip '90s rhythms that surround his made-for-radio, big White soul voice. —*Will Grega*

David & Jane

Gospel, pop

David & Jane are a unique combination of a gay man and lesbian woman singing gospel music. They are vanguards in the use of inclusive language, a testimony to their belief in God's love for everyone. Both are ministers based in the greater New York City area, and they have been featured at New York City Gay Pride festivals since 1991. —*Will Grega*

David & Jane. . . Not Ashamed / 1993 / Heifer Records

This is fun—the kind where you jump up on your chair and wave your hands and say hallelujah—with first-rate originals ("Standing on the Promises," "Bless It Back," "Rejoice") and stirring covers ("My God Is Real" and "Farther Along"). A collection of glorious songs that only goes to prove that God is on our side! —*Will Grega*

Diamond Rose

Folk

With rare honesty and haunting melodies, this diverse acoustic duo writes from the heart. JayDee is bluesy and playful; Steven Gellman is woeful and bummed—and together they create an entertaining, compelling blend of styles. Gellman plays a handmade stringed instrument that has become a trademark of the Diamond Rose sound. The "strumstick," a cross between a banjo, mandolin, and dulcimer, is unique in sound and appearance. —*Will Grega*

○ **This Road Called Life** / 1992 / Blue Guitar

A promising premiere by future killers, Diamond Rose are seriously committed performers who will challenge your perceptions of acoustic music. Steve Gellman's voice, like his lyrics, is powerful and sensitive. The duo's lyrics consistently achieve a delicate balance between humor and poignancy, while the hypnotic chord changes evoke a REM-like dreaminess. JayDee's lyrics are laugh-out-loud hysterical, and her voice brings to mind Natalie Merchant; at times fragile, at times sardonic and playful, it is a voice that captures both the depth and whimsy of her lyrics. —*Will Grega*

David Diamond

New country

A legend while still in his teens—he was a founding member of Berlin ("The Metro," "Sex I'm A . . . ")—and racking up numerous gold records, David Diamond discovered that country music was what really saddled his horse. He's a fine producer and writer, gifted with a voice that sounds remarkably like that of the Eagles' Don Henley and evokes the whole Southern California country sound of the late '70s. —*Will Grega*

Qowboy / 1993 / 2 Butch 4 U

Delivered with intelligence and solid pop smarts, with slide geetar and California country/rock thrown into the stew, Qowboy's music is pure country/pop cooked up by a superb stylist. Diamond balances the release with good-time songs of the Highway 101 honky-tonk variety and cryin'-in-your-beer numbers. He explores the pain of a shattered soul loving too well, losing, and bruising—hard stuff that goes down smooth. —*Will Grega*

The Fabulous Pop Tarts

Dance, club, house

Two of the busiest men in show business, the Pop Tarts have produced three hit television series (including "The Best of Manhattan Cable" for England's Channel 4), written a book (about Michael Milken!), masterminded the career of supermodel/singer RuPaul, and composed and recorded this 17-song CD—all in the past 12 months! Superachievers of the world! —*Will Grega*

○ **Gagging on the Lovely Extravaganza** / 1992 / World of Wonder

Running through smooth dance grooves in Erasure's and Pet Shop Boys' territory without sounding nearly as alienating as the mass of house music being churned out today, this album speeds you along the freeway of love with no exit ramps. Guest luminaries include Dan Hartman, RuPaul, and Dee-Lite's Lady Kier Kirby. —*Will Grega*

Flirtations, The

A cappella

If there is one group that embodies the state of gay culture today, it's the Flirtations. The Flirtations gained national prominence in the late '80s as the only openly gay, positive a cappella group. Oh, it helped that they had tremendous voices and chose outstanding material. In a few short years, these media darlings became everybody's group-of-choice as ambassadors of homosexuality the world over. Little could they have known at their first Greenwich Village street performance in 1988 that within five short years they would appear on "Donahue," "Good Morning America," "Nightwatch," "MTV News," and National Public Radio; that they would gather rave reviews across the country; and that they would actually be making a living doing what they love most: being gay and singing about it. —*Will Grega*

○ **Flirtations** / 1990 / Significant Other
Their eponymous, fully digital premiere contains some of their best-loved material: "To Know Him Is to Love Him," "Something Inside So Strong," "Everything Possible," and "Surfin' U.S.A." camped to perfection. A group like this comes along only once in a lifetime. Among the brilliant harmonies, general silliness, and giddy repertoire a splendid time is guaranteed for all. — *Will Grega*

☆ **Live: Out on the Road** / 1992 / Flirts Records
Stunning, exciting, moving, engrossing, and hysterically funny, this album gives you a front-row seat for the best gay act in America. Recorded in Vancouver in December 1992, *Out on the Road* captures all the excitement of the Flirts' live performances. The album contains Flirts faves "Boy from New York City," "Johnny Angel," "Lesbian Love," "The Homecoming Queen's Got a Gun," and "Living in Wartime." There is a wonderful excitement in hearing the group live and experiencing the audience interplay and reaction. — *Will Grega*

Ted Fox

Folk, pop
Uplifting, political, and stridently queer! The spirit is reborn in Ted Fox, and it is mighty! He is an out and proud gay man singing songs of defiance and positive self-affirmation. — *Will Grega*

○ **One of Us** / 1992 / Heymanee Records
Fox's debut features folkie melodies sung with self-assurance and the social commitment that Peter, Paul & Mary mined in the '60s heyday of the folk form. The beautifully executed lyrics and the coffeehouse energy make this album well worth a listen, and the sentiment comes through loud and queer. "Sink or Swim," an anthem for our struggle, is the real winner here. — *Will Grega*

Jesse Hultberg

Pop, folk, rock
Former mastermind behind cult band 3 Teens Kill 4 steps out (way out) to begin an auspicious solo career. "I Was Raised a Straight Boy (But I'm Not Today)" is used as the theme for cable's "Party Talk" program. — *Will Grega*

☆ **Jesse Hultberg** / 1994 / Wild Monk
Whether delivering an acoustic rendering of "If I Can't Have You," or lightly hip-hopping along a Joni Mitchell buried gem ("The Priest Song"), Hultberg proves himself the master of blending acoustic and high-tech genres. Best song title in a long time: "Am I Raquel Welch Starring in *Fantastic Voyage*?" — *Will Grega*

Grant King

Folk, pop
Grant King's recordings capture surprisingly well the warmth and sensuousness of his incredible live performances. He writes from the heart and never fails to win over audiences. He is and always has been an unflinching and proud gay singer-songwriter. — *Will Grega*

Where to Now / 1992 / Open Secrets Musicwor
King's easy, James Taylor–like charm oozes out of the tracks on his debut. Some of his more popular performance pieces—"To Hold and Be Held" and "Your Roses Came Today"— are here. His amazing rhythm guitar work drives "Loving Cup" in a manner reminiscent of Lindsey Buckingham's guitar work with Fleetwood Mac. — *Will Grega*

● **Entitled to Bloom** / 1993 / Open Secrets Musicwor
Entitled to Bloom includes more heartfelt, deeply personal lyrics that bring one much closer to the artist. King uses the crystal clarion of his voice to communicate straight to your heart. Also featured on this tape is King's collaboration with Rob Costin, "James and Me," a sweet song sung from the perspective of an adoring child about the tall, strong, older brother he looks up to. It could well be the most innocently subversive song ever penned by a gay songwriter. — *Will Grega*

Ben & Ellie Kreader

Synth, pop, soul
Writer-producer Ben Kreader began singing in college after placing an ad in the *Chicago Reader* for a woman who "smokes at least a pack a day." When nobody responded, he ended up dis-

covering his own voice without the aid of Marlboros. — *Will Grega*

Sink or Swim B/w Blizzard-cassingle / 1993 / Eat Your Wheat
Kreader's sister, Ellie, takes vocal lead on the first track, "Sink or Swim." Ellie Kreader has a dream voice, a voice with the elasticity and how-dee-do of K. T. Oslin, able to convey every little quirk of emotion. The tracks are dark, rhythmic masterpieces that call to mind early work by the Eurythmics. Ben Kreader's voice (he sings "Blizzard") is big, bluesy, and R&B tinged. These two tracks are from an elaborate multimedia performance of Ben's that involves rear screen projection, handheld lights, glowsticks, road flares, flashlights, and pinwheels and that pulls 17 of his songs into a narrative story line. — *Will Grega*

Rob Krikorian

Folk, pop
Rob Krikorian writes about time and love: how time passes and how love heals. Krikorian's voice is perfectly suited to this mellow style of music popularized by Dan Fogelberg and others—contemporary folk for those with a taste for quiet music, with an interest in lyrics/imagery, and with a sense of humor. — *Will Grega*

○ **Quicksand in the Hourglass** / 1990 / Common Time
"Aren't We Born to Dance," alluding to the Stonewall riots, is the most direct of this set. The title song works in a particularly moving manner, and "Send in $9.95" takes a jab at televangelists peddling Jesus. *Quicksand* is a lovely, polished work, a gentle disc on which Krikorian conveys a Michael Franks style, easiness, and charm. — *Will Grega*

Dan Martin & Michael Biello

Pop, vocal
Dan Martin and Michael Biello are the fathers of the newly born gay music scene and are responsible for many new artists coming to light in our community. Martin has written scores for films and videos including "Clones in Love," winner of the San Francisco Gay & Lesbian Film Festival's top prize for best short. His score for Lauren Malkasian's video "The Last Run" is currently being aired on PBS. Martin has also written the score for Jim Hubbard's "The Dance," which chronicles Martin's and life-partner Michael Biello's relationship and has screened at the Berlin Film Festival, MOMA, and festivals around the world. Martin has also written instrumental music for Hazelden Publishing's Sound Recovery series of subliminal healing cassettes, and for Erospirit's sexual environments series. Martin is the founder of OutMusic, the organization of lesbian and gay composers, lyricists, and musicians that produces the only annual festival of gay and lesbian music. He has brought to the stage numerous queer music-theater pieces with Biello, a performing visual artist and Martin's lyricist. — *Will Grega*

Homo Love Song / 1990 /
The material is riveting on their debut release, so you don't mind the spare piano/vocal production, though these artists deserve the full treatment. Martin's delivery runs the gamut from downright bratty (when called for) to heartbreakingly tender. This release introduced two gay standards: "Forgive Me," and the much-covered "Hold Me in Your Arms." Compassionate, raunchy, romantic, and beautiful, the songwriting talents of Martin and Biello seem unending. — *Will Grega*

★ **Human Being** / 1992 /
From anthems like "You Do Not Know Me" and "Lay Your Burden Down" to the butt-shaking beat of "Drag Dance" and the mechanical dance rhythms of "Strange Now," *Human Being* delivers consistent entertainment pleasure. The spiritually uplifting pieces are emotionally ardent songs that resonate in the heart and soul. — *Will Grega*

Tom McCormack

Pop, rock, vocal
McCormack represents the best our community has to offer. His outstanding voice, superb writing and production skills, and inspiring artistry embody the future of gay music. — *Will Grega*

○ **Running with Light** / 1991 / Spotted Dog
McCormack's debut showcases his more subdued, spiritual side and contains some devastating songwriting, most notably on "Everything," which *Billboard* called "a warm and affecting bal-

lad of earnest delivery complemented by a stark, piano-dominated arrangement." *Running with Light* speaks with the language of the heart to a contemporary audience that yearns to mine more deeply the power of each person's passionate journey. — *Will Grega*

○ **Rose Colored Glasses** / 1993 / Spotted Dog
McCormack uses a rock sound that is an intentional throwback to the '70s sound; at times recalling Billy Joel, Elton John, and Crosby, Stills, Nash & Young. This kick-ass set of astonishing songs includes "I Am Alive," "Here I Am," and current crowd-pleaser "Falling Down Kind of Love." On this second album he journeys still deeper into the gray areas of life with stories of money, desire, and identity. — *Will Grega*

☆ **Missing** / 1994 / Spotted Dog
One gets the feeling that this is the definitive gay album that artists in our community have been trying to write for years. "In Secret," "Don't Tell," and "Love Is Love Is Love," eloquently speak for the collective gay subconscious. — *Will Grega*

Rus McCoy

Alternative rock, pop
An artist whose ultimate goal is to be an openly gay rock artist who achieves regular airplay on mainstream radio, McCoy was born to write and sing affecting alternative rock. The arrangements soar thanks to Ace, his producer-collaborator, and set him squarely in Simple Minds/New Order/Depeche Mode territory. — *Will Grega*

☆ **Ace Sessions** / 1991 / Stonewall Records
"Never Tell a Soul" is a synth-pop standout that deals with alienation, self-induced silence, and internalized homophobia. With guitar work that demands striking comparison to U2's Edge, songs like "Happy Birthday, Baby Butch" grab your ears immediately. From ambitious Springsteen-like suites to a sound reminiscent of early LA New Wave, McCoy hits the mark every time. — *Will Grega*

Bill McKinley

Pop, vocal
It is the rare performer who emerges and is granted instant and universal legendary status, but the sheer power of Bill McKinley's musical gifts has propelled him to mythic stature in a few short years. He is a showman and artist who possesses that winning combination of show-biz savvy and utter naturalness that is the unmistakable mark of The Genuine Article. — *Will Grega*

☆ **Everything Possible** / 1992 / Everything Possible
An openly gay performer on the cabaret circuit, McKinley has a talent and a passion that he deserves his own 76-piece orchestra on call 24 hours a day. Fresh, subtle, a showcase for astonishing technique, *Everything Possible* is a beautiful gift to the community and so stunningly brilliant it leaves you gasping. A command performance, this is not just an album; it's an arrival. — *Will Grega*

Will McMillan

Vocal / cabaret
This Sondheim tribute is actually a soundtrack, taken from McMillan's one-man show that opens with him as a tuxedoed man who gradually transforms himself into a woman and then back into a man. — *Will Grega*

○ **Will Sings Sondheim** / 1992 / Mcmillan
This is a remarkable album of intelligent and sensitive interpretations of Sondheim classics that span the songwriter's career, up to and including "More," written for the *Dick Tracy* soundtrack. The songs are performed with the reverential emotion and loving restraint of an adoring fan. Entertaining, and a welcome relief from those over-the-top ultratheatrical Sondheim tributes of late, this is a collection praised by the master himself.—Will Grega

Gustavo Motta

Piano / vocal
Motta's songs were performed in concerts and cabarets in New York, San Francisco, and Philadelphia during years when he was staging productions for the Houston Grand Opera, the Washington Opera, and Cincinnati Conservatory of Music; they have also been performed at the Metropolitan Opera. Only after

testing positive for HIV in 1987 did he devote himself full-time to recording and performing his music in solo concerts and at AIDS benefits and begin an effort to ensure that his songs would be preserved and performed. — *Will Grega*

○ **Songs 1963-1993** / 1993 / Motta Music
This abundant tribute to Gustavo Motta, who died in 1993, is a collection of 30 years' worth of intelligent songwriting in traditions that borrow from cabaret, theater, pop/rock, and world influences. Readings by male and female voices lend nuance to the song interpretations, and they all feature Motta himself on piano. Motta's 30-year output reveals a super tunesmith whose songs deserve good homes. — *Will Grega*

Pansy Division

Punk, rock
San Francisco band that celebrates deep subculture fringes of gay life. — *Will Grega*

Undressed / 1993 / Lookout Records
Sex punks tunefully and loudly wagging their penises and preferences about. The most successful track here is a departure for the band, the Byrds-influenced "Boyfriend Wanted." — *Will Grega*

Andrew Paralic

Jazz
Composer-pianist Andrew Paralic has an extraordinary facility for jazz composition and utilizes an ensemble's supple execution of his Coltrane-like pieces to re-create a mood and an era. Paralic is a graduate of Baruch College and has attended the Berklee College of Music and the Jazz Mobile. — *Will Grega*

○ **Three Tunes** / 1993 / Paralic
The pieces on this release are reflections of his own gayness with titles like "Too Little, Too Late" (about AIDS funding), "Out Tune," and "Finally" (about the total acceptance of his lifestyle by his family). — *Will Grega*

Phideaux

Progressive art rock, Celtic pop
Phideaux Xavier has performed in the New York area since the '80s, when he fronted the punk/pop combo Sally Dick & Jane. Early 1990 saw the birth of The SunMachine, a sextet consisting of guitar, bass, percussion, flute, violin, and cello with three strong singers besides Xavier, whose boyish exuberance and soulful intensity create one irresistible package. — *Will Grega*

○ **Friction** / 1993 / Bloodfish
The Celtic pop poetry and art rock pieces cast a beautiful, dreamlike spell that charms and disorients at the same time. The surrealistic imagery and elaborate introductions create a strangely unified whole, though the pieces career stylistically from psychedelic pop to urban dance to dance/pop and sensitive ballads. — *Will Grega*

Elliot Pilshaw

Singer, songwriter
Elliot Pilshaw has been recording as an out gay musician since his debut release in 1982. He is cofounder of the Flirtations, an original cast member of Tom Wilson Weinberg's "Ten Percent Review," and founder of Sons & Lovers, a new gay a cappella quintet. Alongside his work in the larger gay community, Pilshaw has been especially active in the Jewish gay and lesbian community. He has performed at the International Conferences of Gay and Lesbian Jews, traveled and performed extensively throughout Israel, and is currently a cantor at Congregation Beth Simchat Torah, New York's gay and lesbian synagogue. — *Will Grega*

Bending the Rules / 1982 /
His debut release has a fresh sound for a work that was recorded 12 years ago. That just goes to prove that there's something timeless about Pilshaw. On *Bending the Rules*, Lorin Sklamberg and Pilshaw combine musical excellence with social awareness to give us all yet another means to celebrate and affirm the beauty and validity of our lifestyle. Covers include "Millwork" (James Taylor), "Something about the Women" (Holly Near), and a remarkably moving interpretation of Kristin Lem's "How Nice." — *Will Grega*

Native Tongue / 1984 /

This release is a collection of 12 hauntingly beautiful songs by some of Israel's most well-known contemporary songwriters, including Shalom Hanoch, Yehudit Ravitz, and David Broza. With its elegant simplicity, beautiful harmonies, and warm acoustic sound, *Native Tongue* will delight the ears of both Hebrew- and non-Hebrew-speaking listeners. Titles include "Etz Ha-alon," "Ein-Gedi," and "Shir Ha-Emek." — *Will Grega*

○ **Feels Like Home** / 1986 /
Teamed with John Bucchino and engaging material, Pilshaw delivers an album that finds its way home into the heart. Weaving together pop, jazz, folk, and Broadway musical styles, Pilshaw has delivered an album of songs that glow with the goodness of gay love, life, and friendship. Provocative lyrics, dazzling piano arrangements, and Pilshaw's breathtaking vocals combine to make this album a landmark of gay men's cultural expression. He sings of liberation without blaming or apologizing, informed by pride and a spirited political intelligence; John Bucchino provides lush and elegant piano accompaniment. — *Will Grega*

Queer Conscience

Pop
A community activist along with his husband, Rick Cresswell is compelled to get at the greater truths of our struggle for human rights. The couple received a lot of press in 1991 when they participated in a "visibility action" at Boston's Stocks and Bonds bar. In that action, the two were attacked by a uniformed Boston police officer because the couple refused to stop kissing each other. — *Will Grega*

It's a Queer Nation / 1992 / Scream Sync
QueerCon's debut features militantly queer pop songs from Rick Cresswell and gang that bounce along happily in bubble-gum-groovy '60s melodies and arrangements. Cresswell has a muscular tenor that calls to mind Harry Chapin, and he uses it to put over songs of defiance that deal with shame, rejection, societal indifference, and self-acceptance. — *Will Grega*

● **Back to the Other World?** / 1993 / Scream Sync
Rick Cresswell's supple tenor complements the forthright, unflinching lyrics with determination that is gentler than on the group's debut. Queer Conscience is committed to pushing a blatantly direct queer agenda with such songs as "Telling Someone" and "The Ballad of Harvey Milk." In "OUTside Information," Cresswell sings about the need to be obviously and visibly queer. With blunt and bruisingly political songs, and a particularly striking album cover collage, this collection will make you want to march. — *Will Grega*

Curtis A. Robertson

Rock, pop, parody
Fusing wide-ranging influences from Herman's Hermits to Ray Stevens to Randy Newman, Robertson's parodies turn our reverential and taken-for-granted concepts of pop music inside out. — *Will Grega*

○ **Stinkwater & the Page Boys** / 1994 /
Deranged set in which Curtis Robertson imagines himself as two groups, one a white-trash country unit, the other a New Wave Herman's Hermits. "This Isn't Love in My Eyes (I'm Just Tired)," "Kiss Me like You Mean It," and "I'm Gonna Hurt to Have to Hate You" are the countrified standouts. — *Will Grega*

Rick Robertson

Alternative rock, pop
Robertson is blessed with a voice that was made to be recorded, and a gift for writing terrific lyrics that lock into the mood of the musical settings. — *Will Grega*

Six / 1993 /
These songs are the result of two unique musical collaborations, and both succeed brilliantly at exploring the farther fringes of alternative pop driven by synthesizer technology, detached alienation, and the longings of a man in limbo. The sound of this release calls to mind the Cure, New Order, and Depeche Mode. The moody "For Saturday" is a standout smash, but also check out the Rob Costin collaborations "Magnificent Man," "The Lover's Tent," and "Carry Me." (Costin himself is an exciting writer and performer of stunning power now at work on his own debut album.) The ease, power, and poetic language of this release are pure ge-

nius, and Robertson may just be our own little psychedelic-era Bob Dylan, a poet and prophet of queerdom. — *Will Grega*

Romanovsky & Phillips

Pop, rock
Romanovsky & Phillips (R&P) are easily the most popular out-of-the-closet singing duo in history. Having toured extensively in the US, Canada, and Australia, R&P have earned the title "Ambassadors of Homosexuality." Prolific and long-standing members of the gay music community, R&P have a hysterically comic bent on contemporary gay life. Each of their albums is also peppered with beautifully romantic ballads and sensitive and politically impassioned numbers that give their releases exhilarating balance. Fifties doo-wop parodies with silly kazoo solos don't seem out of place beside poignant ballads in the musical world of R&P. As the most successful gay group in the history of our community, R&P have been on the forefront of gay entertainment for more than a decade. Since gay people love to hear about nothing more than themselves, these two brilliant young men write about what we couldn't possibly hear enough about, our favorite subject: ourselves. And why not? Gay people have been invisible in the media and American society, so it's about time we Hear Queer. — *Will Grega*

I Thought You'd Be Taller / 1984 / Fresh Fruit
This album, the folkie beginning of the dynastic duo, reflects the sound they honed in their humble, hummable beginnings as a San Francisco folk duo in the early '80s. As such it showcases the wonderful harmonic vocal arrangements of their two distinctive voices and contains their most naive, but always charming, material. — *Will Grega*

● **Trouble in Paradise** / 1986 / Fresh Fruit
Expertly tuned into gay fascinations and foibles, R&P nail the issues in love and politics right on the head. More classics: "What Kind of Self-Respecting Faggot Am I?," "Wimp," "Homophobia," "Must've Been Drunk," "The Answering Machine Song," and "Don't Use Your Penis for a Brain." This "sounds" like a hit album should sound and is probably their best-known work. With *Trouble in Paradise* they grew leaps and bounds above their auspicious debut and became international gay pop stars. — *Will Grega*

Emotional Rollercoaster / 1988 / Fresh Fruit
On the third album they changed the formula a little bit and captured the crazy cabaret ambiance of their live performances, leaning toward vaudeville. But it's the vaudeville treatment given this album that nearly covers up the most incisive and brilliantly observed lyrics of R&P's career. Classics: "The Sodomy Song," "Give Me a Homosexual," "My Mother's Clothes," and "I've Created a Monster." — *Will Grega*

★ **Be Political, Not Polite** / 1991 / Fresh Fruit
It was three years before R&P managed a follow-up to their record three releases of blatant gay pop music. In the meantime they had become the most successful, beloved, and prolific group in the history of gay music. Packed with 15 songs of love, anger, politics, and hope, this album is a feast of R&P at the top of their form and covers a wide range of subjects, from lesbian/gay parents to lesbian/gay teachers, from surviving AIDS to surviving dating. As always, the harmonies are terrific. Classics include "Tango Indigesto," "Queers in the Closet," "When Heterosexism Strikes" and "OH NO I'm in Love (with My Therapist)." — *Will Grega*

Ron Romanovsky

Pop, rock
One of the duo Romanovsky & Phillips, he recorded his first solo album in 1992. — *Will Grega*

☆ **Hopeful Romantic** / 1992 / Fresh Fruit
The music is mostly upbeat and covers a wide variety of musical styles woven together with some of Romanovsky's best vocals ever. At his tenderest he evokes Don McLean, but in the mould of Ron Romanovsky, a polka party never seems out of place. As a solo artist, Romanovsky ventures into new territory with the Gershwinesque "A Measure of Sadness," the rock & roll riffs of "The Perfect Crime," and the seductive cabaret blues of "Baby Take Advantage of Me." — *Will Grega*

Tommie Saeli

Alternative rock, glam rock

Saeli is a retro rocker, best known as the host of cable's "Gay Dating Game." The rock cello-wielding Saeli (a former go-go dancer at New York City's Pyramid Club) is a hot, muscled Italian boy in a pink glitter metallic suit and feather boa who offsets the sexy Billy Idol growl of his voice with a Yoko Ono-like falsetto accompanying him in unison on many of his songs. With dazzlingly mind-bending lyrics that blend myth, fantasy, and magic, Saeli weaves a psychedelic spell once he gets that Marc Bolan groove going. — *Will Grega*

○ **Hello** / 1993 / Howling Wolf

The crunchy sound of this disc is a throwback to the early '70s glam rock of gender-benders David Bowie and T. Rex: heavy drumming, handclaps, and football cheer choruses. It's a hard sound with no guitars, just layers of rock cello and cathedral organ. With the exception of the drumming, the album is a one-man tour de force. "Rock & Roll Queen" evokes Elton John's ripping "Saturday Night's Alright for Fighting." "Michaelangelo Irreducible" is a Motown (Supremes. . . surprised?) take-off. "Lady of the Well" sports a Moody Blues harpsichord. Take the savage sweetness of John Lennon, add the guts of David Bowie, the flash fame of Nirvana, the magic of Sigfried and Roy, and shake . . . don't stir. Say hello! — *Will Grega*

Joseph Victor Sieger

Synth, pop, alternative

Pyscho semipornographic music for the groin, San Francisco's Sieger composes poetic electronic music that disc reeks of RUSH, leather, and mansweat. His voice ranges from pleasing to deranged; his lyrics are an incredibly hot journey into the supersexual psyche of Master Sieger. — *Will Grega*

☆ **Self-portrait** / 1993 / Siegerwerke

Absolutely uncompromising, without-a-net performance of over the edge, self-ghettoized, gay-sex-obsessed material. This release combines an '80s retro synth-pop sound with touches of '90s techno and freely mixes rap with balladry, consistently exhibiting an experimental electronic edge. The album also contains a brave a cappella reading of Village People's "San Francisco (You Got Me)." — *Will Grega*

Doug Stevens & the Outband

Contemporary country, rock

Doug Stevens and the Outband are consistently winning fans in the gay and straight country-music communities. In the short time they have been together, they've played Gracie Mansion, Town Hall in New York City with Joan Rivers, the Rainbow Room at Rockefeller Center, and the 1993 March on Washington. At the march they were seen by three million people around the world on C-SPAN and millions more on the "NBC Evening News" affiliates. They have appeared three times on "In The Life" and have played at many two-step dances and concerts on the east coast and in the Midwest. This thoroughly entertaining and consistent album is produced with sparkling clarity and punch. The pansexual lineup includes the wicked fiddle work of John Cordes and the electrifying lead guitar work of Desiree, who has a strong guest spot as lead vocalist on the self-penned "Cactus Country." — *Will Grega*

★ **Out in the Country** / 1993 / Longhorn

The runaway favorite of the year, this pop biography could have been called "Meet Doug Stevens," because Stevens not only writes and sings good songs, but he also has lived them. The Tupelo, MS, native begins with his tale of kissing boy cousins ("Out in the Country") and southern intolerance ("Born in Mississippi"). He then leaves for the big city ("Git While the Gittin's Good"), falls in love ("Sweet Breath of Love"), looks back in anger ("White Trash"), loses his lover when he's diagnosed with HIV ("HIV Blues"), and emerges stronger and renewed of spirit ("Act Up"). The Outband owes much to country/rock crossover traditions like Linda Ronstadt, the Eagles, and Neil Young. On this debut that is nothing less than a gay-music cultural milestone, Doug Stevens & the Outband embody what the best "country music" should be: rock with an accent. — *Will Grega*

Pussy Tourette

Rock, pop, blues

Beginning as a go-go dancer in San Francisco's teeming underground scene, Tourette was acclaimed as the hottest and sauciest act on the city's cabaret scene when she started singing her original compositions live. Touring nationally has helped her develop nothing less than a fanatical following. Five Tourette songs are featured in *Sex Is*, which won the Best Gay Film Award at Berlin's International Film Festival. — *Will Grega*

☆ **Pussy Tourette in Hi-fi** / 1993 / Feather Boa

With a gift for self-invention, this fiercest of drag divas constructs the myth and legend of Pussy Tourette while simultaneously deconstructing queer misconceptions. From the New Orleans' Dr. John camp of "If I Can't Sell It . . . " to the gritty Led Zeppelin-influenced heavy blues of "Free Pussy," it's clear that Ms. Tourette is not the girl next door. Tourette has a streetwise, gritty gift for rock/blues. "French Bitch" is an instant queer classic (the video has more slaps per minute than any other music video in history!). Warning: This pussy is no kitten! — *Will Grega*

Turtle Creek Chorale

Choral

The Turtle Creek Chorale (TCC) is a Dallas-based male chorus under the direction of Dr. Timothy Seelig. Membership in the TCC currently stands at 200 singing members. The repertoire of TCC can best be described as eclectic, drawing on everything from Bach to Broadway and both sacred and secular works. In 1993 the chorale debuted at Carnegie Hall. They have also been the focus of the PBS special "After Goodbye: An AIDS Story," chronicling the stages of loss and grief recovery from AIDS by looking at the impact of the disease on the members, families, and friends of the TCC. (The choir has lost 60 members during the past ten years.) Among other luminaries, the TCC has performed for Texas Governor Ann Richards and the Queen of England. This chorale, with four albums, presents very intelligent song-cycle selections. — *Will Grega*

● **From the Heart: Live** / 1990 /

For choral music lovers, Turtle Creek is heaven. Each disc is stuffed with more than an hour's worth of song. *From the Heart* was voted "Best Choral Recording of 1990" by the readers of the national publication *CHORUS*. Like they say, the turtle only makes progress when he sticks his neck out. Standouts on this gorgeous disc include "Not While I'm Around" (Sondheim), "Pie Jesu" (Webber), and "Bring Him Home" (Boublil). — *Will Grega*

Peace / 1991 /

A gorgeous feast of choral music, which includes holiday favorites "The First Noel," "White Christmas," "O Holy Night," "What Child Is This?" and "Ave Maria." — *Will Grega*

Testament / 1992 / Reference Recordings

TCC rises to new heights of accomplished, dramatic, downright thrilling sound with punchy orchestral brilliance—all derived from a new sound process called "high definition." Joined by the Dallas Wind Symphony, the chorale jumps off the disc, and it truly feels as if the performance is taking place in your living room. Focusing on the music of five 20th-century American composers—Ron Nelson, Howard Hanson, Randall Thompson, Aaron Copland, and Leonard Bernstein—*Testament* is a lesson in American history that will revive old-fashioned patriotism. — *Will Grega*

○ **When We No Longer Touch** / 1993 /

A transformative work of raw beauty, and a breakthrough in choral recordings, this original piece addresses the stages of grief recovery (denial, isolation, anger, bargaining, depression, acceptance, and hope) and benefits AmFAR. Based on Peter McWilliams's poems from the book *How to Survive the Loss of Love*, this incredibly moving work is a testament to the strength and resilience of the human heart and soul. Its blending of wit and sorrow makes it a poignant, near-flawless tribute to lost love. — *Will Grega*

Tom Wilson Weinberg

Show music

Before reclaiming the name Weinberg in 1983, Tom Wilson released two albums of original songs, *Gay Name Game* and *All-American Boy*. Wilson Weinberg has traveled and performed extensively and continues to do so, but in recent years his writing has been focused on musical theater. His new show *Get Used to It* played off Broadway in 1992, and he is now at work on a musical. He was awarded the honor of writing and producing the official CD of Stonewall 25 in 1994. —*Will Grega*

Ten Percent Revue / Aboveground
This album is a studio-cast recording of the musical revue that had a long run off Broadway in 1988 and played in more than two dozen cities. Two men and two women sing such songs as "Flaunting It," "Turkey Baster Baby," and "The Supremes" (a spoof on our highest court). —*Will Grega*

★ **Get Used to It** / Aboveground
Joyous, romantic, uplifting, and satirical, Weinberg's cast recording of his latest revue is an incisive, humorous look at the serious gay issues of our time. From the wacky opening number "No Opening Number" to the heartwarming "I'll Call You Lover" through the defiant (but bouncy) "Breaking the Penal Code with You," this is superb musical theater and a great gift from one of the most talented members of the gay community. —*Will Grega*

● **Don't Mess with Mary** / Aboveground
This benefit album (the official CD of Stonewall 25) is a disc no gay person should be without. Featuring hard-edged new mater-

ial with a scorching rock vocal by Jan Tilley and a fierce reading of the title track performed by drag diva Tina Benez, these tracks (which even include a dance re-mis) represent a departure in style for Weinberg, although Weinberg favorites "Safe Sex Slut" and "Before Stonewall" (from Ten Percent Revue) have been specially rerecorded for this project. —*Will Grega*

Windy City Gay Chorus

Choral
This chorus is a stunning example of the revival of male choral singing in North America. Windy City Gay Chorus's precision, flexibility of style, warmth of color, well-balanced tone, firm diction, and meticulous attention to detail add up to what some have termed the finest male chorus in the country. WCGC is now into its second decade of music making. They have won first place in the Great American Choral Festival and have received grants based on musical excellence from the National Endowment for the Arts, the Illinois Arts Council, and ChorusAmerica. —*Will Grega*

● **Mostly Love** / 1991 / Wcpa
Accessible and well paced, this tape could convert even the most resolute disparagers of choral music. The work charms, lulls, and ultimately seduces. What really works here is the blending of ob-

Record Company Addresses

Y'All
235 East 10th Street, Studio G, New York, NY 10003-7666

Benez Popaganda Muzik
c/o William Spring, 353 6th Avenue, 3rd fl., New York, NY 10014

McMillan Records
8 Westwood Road, Somerville, MA 02143-1518

Longhorn Records
31-65 29th Street #A-6, Astoria, NY 11106

Feather Boa Records
584 Castro Street, Suite 260, San Francisco, CA 94114

Siegerwerke, Inc.
PO Box 14348, San Francisco, CA 94114-0348

Windy City Performing Arts
3023 North Clark #329, Chicago, IL 60657

Worm
2103 Harrison NW, Suite 2414, Olympia, WA 98502

Aboveground Records
PO Box 2233, Philadelphia, PA 19103

Fresh Fruit Records
369 Montezuma #209, Santa Fe, NM 87501

Elliot Pilshaw
PO Box 021616, Brooklyn, NY 11201

Phideaux Xavier
c/o Bloodfish Music, 172 East 4th Street #7E, New York, NY 10009

Scream Sync Production
137 Hollett Street, Scituate, MA 02066-2036

Motta Music
PO Box 1245 Cathedral Station, New York, NY 10025

Paralic
PO Box 20231, New York, NY 10011

Everything Possible
PO Box 1483, Indianapolis, IN 46206-1483

Tommie Saeli
Howling Wolf Records, 75 2nd Avenue #2, New York, NY 10003

Spotted Dog
PO Box 40-0041, Brooklyn, NY 11240-0041

Rob Krikorian
c/o CommonTime Productions, PO Box 1076, Brookline, MA 02146

Dan Martin
PO Box 1575 Canal Street Station, New York, NY 10013

Open Secrets Musicworks
PO Box 132 Old Chelsea Station, New York, NY 10113-0132

Heymanee
1415 Steele Street #3, Denver, CO 80206

Flirt Records
PO Box 421 Prince Street Station, New York, NY 10012-0008

World of Wonder
80 Varick Street #7B, New York, NY 10013

David Diamond
2 Butch 4 U Productions, 1427 Sanborn Avenue, Silverlake, CA 90027

Heifer Records
304 East 38th Street #2C, New York, NY 10016

Diamond Rose
PO Box 0077, Rockville, MD 20848

KCT Productions
230 Riverside Drive #14F, New York, NY 10025

Significant Other, Inc.
PO Box 1545 Canal Street Station, New York, NY 10013

Thrust Recordings
PO Box 29212, Dallas, TX 75229

Quirkworks
PO Box 229, Greenville, RI 02828

Wild Monk Records
147 2nd Avenue #477, New York, NY 10003

scure and familiar material. "The Great Peace March" (Holly Near), "What'll I Do?" (Irving Berlin), and "Where Is Love?" (Lionel Bart) are among the familiar. — *Will Grega*

Don We Now... / 1992 / Wcpa

Tasty selections of Christmas favorites, including "Deck the Halls," "Silent Night," and "White Christmas." — *Will Grega*

Worm

Synth, pop, folk

Worm is a one-of-a-kind vocal/songwriting duo of twins: a gay brother and a lesbian sister. On their debut release, they tap an analog synth production sound that hearkens back to Yaz and early Eurythmics. The duo blends beautifully balanced harmonies as well as vocal solos that brother and sister trade off. — *Will Grega*

Worm / 1992 / Worm

With honesty, clarity, and pop melodic hooks, the Seattle siblings grapple with issues of acceptance, same-sex relationships, justice, coming out, freedom, equal rights, and world peace. Best tracks here are "Woman of the Third Wave" and "Gay Nineties." The wonderful acoustic guitar work of sister Janie is showcased on her contributions while keyboardist Jamie explores synth-pop grooves on his compositions, and that's what works best about this release: it is the ultimate in inclusion. Gay male and lesbian/feminist viewpoints exist side by side as well as merge. This

formula is what it's all about, coming together as brothers and sisters. — *Will Grega*

Y'all

White-trash country gospel

As a lowbrow, southern-fried, trailer-park Simon & Garfunkel, Y'all astonishes in the amazing way they illumine the gay experience. It is really surprising that they have gotten overwhelming positive and downright affectionate coverage for their stage act (performed by the six-foot, three-inch Jay Byrd in his lucky green dress and shirtless Steven Cheslik-DeMeyer in beat-up overalls) in both the gay and straight media. Their sound is a mix of rural Americana: gospel, country-western, and bluegrass music performed "Hee-Haw" style with superb harmonizing. James Dean Jay Byrd is the son of a tent revivalist from Okey-Dokey, TX, and the nephew of a trailer-home salesman and crossdresser. His pardner Steven is a former corn farmer from Corn Flake, IN, and the 17th child of former Catholics. — *Will Grega*

○ **Evening of Stories & Songs, An** / 1993 / Y'all Records

"I Am the Queen of the Rodeo" and "Man Who's Not in My Family Tree" (about Grandpa's boyfriend) are knee-slappin' standouts in these homespun tales of rural gay life. All of Y'all's songs are heartfelt originals, from lonely trail-riding tunes to everybody-join-in hillbilly ditties to classic-styled gospel numbers. — *Will Grega*

WOMEN'S

"Women's Music" is about women more than it is about music. Formally, "Women's Music" is the name applied to the songs which were one of the earliest expressions of the feminist cultural network. The folk and protest music traditions—themselves responses to the oppressiveness of the 1950s—lingered from the 1960s. Feminist and gay liberation movements were gathering speed; and the possibilities of a diverse and visible Lesbian community exploded into reality. Women's bookstores, art by and for women, woman-only space, even new spellings of the words "woman"/"women," minus references to "man"/"men" (womon, womoon, wimmin, womyn), were explored.

Women's Music got its start with Lesbians. It all began in 1971, with the first two Lesbian-oriented records produced in the U.S.: Maxine Feldman's *Angry Atthis* and Madeline Davis's *Stonewall Nation* (both 45 rpm). The idea of music written, arranged, and played by and for women; the concept of taking a women-only show on the road (as happened with Women on Wheels); the thought of producing, manufacturing, distributing, and promoting music made by women—all caught on like wildfire.

Among the most popular artists of that era was Alix Dobkin, who brought her years of experience as a folksinger to homegrown songs about her new Lesbian identity (*Lavender Jane Loves Women*, Women's Wax Works, 1974); Dobkin has recently released a retrospective commemorating her career as a Lesbian troubadour (*Love and Politics: A 30-Year Saga* (Women's Wax Works (1992)). Meg Christian's *I Know You Know* (Olivia Records, 1974) was soft and gently Euro-classical, in contrast to her strong butch look; Cris Williamson, fresh from gigging as an interpreter of modern folk, lent her breathtakingly resonant voice to her metaphorical ballads. Williamson's seminal *The Changer and the Changed* (Olivia Records, 1975) remains the best-selling independent album of all time. All three mid-1970s albums, plus the myriad of other music from artists like Deidre McCalla, Ginni Clemmens, Kristin Lems, and Margie Adam, were collected eagerly and played endlessly. These records' very existence, as much as their lyrics, opened up a world of exciting, challenging, and radical contingencies to their mostly Lesbian audience.

Other women, whose music was based on more complicated or less mobile modalities (electric, band, multi-instrumental, or chorus, for example) were less well-known but every bit as important in setting precedents. Collective experience was gained from—and great sounds played by—BeBe K'Roche, Gwen Avery, Heather Bishop, Linda Tillery, Mary Watkins, Nancy Vogl (Berkeley Women's Music Collective), Robin Flower, Sue Fink, Vicki Randle (now on Jay Leno's Tonight Show), and Woody Simmons.

There were also women in the mainstream who, like their Women's Music counterparts, were learning the business of music. Some of these women subsequently entered the Women's Music arena, able to teach the essentials to other women—minus the unwanted hierarchal industry politics. June Millington, a rock guitarist, teamed with her bass-playing sister, Jean, and several other women musicians to form Fanny, the first all-women's band to be signed by a major label. Through four successful albums with Warner Brothers, Fanny served notice that women could do more than simply sing. Helen Hooke, of Deadly Nightshade fame, has also been making music for over twenty years, first on the RCA label and currently self-produced. The all-women quintet, Alive!, tore up the jazz world; their two recent Northern California reunion concerts sold out, a testament to the recalled power of their collaboration. Two other mainstream women artists—Bertha, and Goldie and the Gingerbreads—also made significant recordings. There was also a handful of notable women musicians who made music with men, including April Lawton (guitarist with Ramatam) and Tret Fure (lead guitarist with Spencer Davis).

Even before there was Women's Music, there were women who were determined to be heard, and to have other women's (including Lesbians') voices heard. In 1973, ten of these women—some associated with the radical Lesbian feminist newspaper *The Furies*—got together in Washington, D.C. Through hard work, strong wills, self-denial, and a benevolent Goddess, they were able to record a 45 rpm single of Meg Christian's rendition of "Lady" (Carole King/Gerry Goffin), backed with Cris Williamson's "If It Weren't for the Music." The spirit spread, money was raised, and the newly-born Olivia Records was able to release the aforementioned early discs by Meg Christian and Cris Williamson—along with the tide-turning, innovative, and witty *Lesbian Concentrate*, designed as a response to Anita Bryant's vicious campaign against homosexuals.

For 20 years now, Olivia has produced Lesbian and feminist Women's Music featuring such artists as Cris Williamson, Deidre McCalla, Lucie Blue Tremblay, Teresa Trull, Nancy Vogl, Mary Watkins, June Millington, Linda Tillery, Dianne Davidson, and Tret Fure (the latter two on the Second Wave label, a division of Olivia). Another record company that has figured vitally in Women's Music is Redwood Records, founded in 1972 when Holly Near recorded *Hang in There*, and now known as Redwood Cultural Work. Redwood has produced and distributed records, and presented concerts, by dozens of artists—male and female, from many cultures—who sing for peace, justice, feminism, and human rights.

Other individuals and organizations have played roles in the development of the feminist cultural network. The groundbreaking book *Lesbian/Woman*, by Del Martin and Phyllis Lyon, was initially printed amid the tidal wave of post-Stonewall gay activism; following 1991's National Lesbian Conference, Volcano Press reprinted it in a special 20th-anniversary edition (1992). The Naiad Press, founded in 1973 by Donna McBride and Barbara Grier, remains the largest publisher/supplier of Lesbian titles in the world.

The National Women's Music Festival (the oldest festival of its kind) and the Michigan Womyn's Music Festival (the largest of its kind) celebrate their 20th anniversaries in 1994 and 1995, respectively. As of 1994, there are at least 15 major festivals of Women's Music in the South, Alaska, Hawaii, the West Coast, and the East Coast (including Northampton, MA, or "Lesbianville," according to the *National Enquirer*). The Ladyslipper Catalog, the largest listing of Lesbian and other women's music products in the world, was founded by Laurie Fuchs nearly 20 years ago, and still functions as an important resource in a rapidly changing industry. *Hot Wire: The Journal of Women's Music and Culture*, widely acknowledged as the most thorough current chronicler of Women's Music, unfortunately ended production after ten years.

At one time, it was possible to own all the "Women's Music" that had been recorded. As *The Changer and the Changed* has gracefully aged, women musicians have hit the scene playing all styles including soul, rock, rap, Latin American, jazz, funk, Bebop, house music, Caribbean/island, African, reggae, country/western, gospel/hymnal, punk/thrash, folk, R&B, Australia aboriginal, swing, chanty, klezmer, Native American/Canadian, big-band, taiko, and Euro-classical. There are singers, instrumentalists, songwriters, solo acts, backup musicians, duos, trios, dance ensembles, and larger groupings. The Ladyslipper Catalog mentions 68 pages worth of women's music, and one would need hundreds of CDs and cassettes to boast of an up-to-date collection.

Many people think of Women's Music as an exclusively "white-woman-with-guitar" genre, because some of the movement's pioneers were visible in the established and accepted tradition of folky-with-guitar. In fact, not all of those pioneers were white, and not all were guitar players; nonetheless, the label "white-women-with-guitar" has stuck to Women's Music. Simplification and prejudice aside, Women's Music currently transcends this label, and goes far beyond any specific performer or performance.

Where once only a handful of labels released Women's Music—Olivia, Redwood, Icebergg, Flying Fish, Ladyslipper—many sisters are are doing it for themselves: self-production. Multitudes of local producers, promoters, distributors, managers, booking agents, engineers, and other technicians facilitate the process. Along with the expansion in roles and realities for women making music, new resources have developed.

In 1986, a group of visionary women agreed that the time had come for a national organization of Women's Music and culture. In 1987, the Association of Women's Music and Culture (AWMAC) was founded by a steering committee that included performers Deidre McCalla and Sue Fink, festival producer Lisa Vogel (of the Michigan Womyn's Music Festival), record producer/engineer Leslie

Ann Jones, and Olivia Records founder and president Judy Dlugacz. AWMAC currently sponsors an annual National Conference in conjunction with the National Women's Music Festival, plus more intimate regional meetings. The organization strives to encourage Women's Music and culture by assisting its members' networking and education, and by offering members other support services.

Also in 1987, June Millington realized her dream of creating new possibilities for women pursuing careers in music—a dream born of her own frustrating experiences in the male-dominated music industry. Millington founded the Institute for the Musical Arts (IMA), a nonprofit, multicultural teaching and performing-arts organization that trains women in skills that are useful in the music business.

Finally, *Women's Music Plus* (edited by Toni Armstrong, Jr., one of the founders of *Hot Wire*) is a comprehensive resource that suggests the levels of competence, complexity, and diversity in Women's Music and culture. This directory lists performers, live-event and record producers, record labels, record distributors, recording technicians, stage workers, women's choirs and choruses, comedians, dance artists, storytellers, theatre artists, cartoonists, festivals, American Sign Language interpreters, artists' representatives, photographers, film/video/television professionals, feminist writers and broadcasters, feminist publishers, periodicals, libraries and archives, bookstores, and other catalogs and directories. Where Northern California was once the exclusive "capital" of Women's Music—Olivia and Redwood both make their homes in the San Francisco Bay Area, as do AWMAC and the IMA—the Women's Music Plus list spans North America, and in fact the globe.

In summary, Women's Music is a broad cultural phenomenon—and more than music. Not all Women's Music is about Lesbians, or stridently feminist, or even about women. But Women's Music does convey words, ideas, and role models that are supportive of, and culturally relevant to, Lesbians. Its broader themes embrace a range of ecofeminist, anti-patriarchal, pro-peace, and humanitarian philosophies.

Women's Music and Women's Culture represents an international movement whose boundaries are constantly being stretched—whose definition is known to many listeners, but can't be adequately written down. One definition of Women's Music would include all performers who appear at Women's Music festivals; another definition might simply include all those who define themselves as participants in Women's Music. Whatever the definition, it is certain that the existence of Women's Music and her products nourishes Lesbian feminists, heterofeminists, and other open-hearted listeners.

—Laura Post

Margie Adam

Margie Adam is a singer-songwriter known to the feminist and progressive communities for her blend of passionate love songs, goofball humor, and thoughtful political observation. In the decade spanning the mid 70s and early 80s, Adam helped to define and expand notions about Women's Music as an art form, a political force, and an industry.

While performing on university campuses, at festivals, in theaters and clubs, and at the conventions of many major women's organizations (NOW, Women in the Law), Adam created a recorded body of work on her own label, Pleiades Records. Her albums include *Margie Adam, Songwriter* (1976), a solo piano album; *Naked Keys* (1980), recorded live; *We Shall Go Forth!* (1982); and *Here Is A Love Song* (1983).

Adam's performance history includes the thrilling experience of leading 10,000 women at the National Women's Conference in Houston in singing a three-part harmony version of "We Shall Go

Forth!" The song was later placed in the archives of the Political History division of the Smithsonian Institution. In 1980, the National Women's Political Caucus sponsored Adam on the first national concert tour designed specifically to raise funds for feminist candidates. Adam had the honor of headlining a concert at Constitution Hall that coincided with the July 1, 1982, Equal Rights Amendment ratification deadline, and was attended by members of 80 national women's organizations.

In 1984, Adam came off the road for a "Radical's Sabbatical." In the following years she studied piano and voice, and returned to college, where she obtained credentials for working in the field of chemical dependency.

To the surprise of many—particularly of Margie Adam herself—she began to write music again in 1990. As she developed a new repertoire, Adam made the decision to perform the music in public. Constant requests for a new recording led her to gather together a group of women musicians to record her latest album, *Another Place*, which exemplifies the balance of humor, politics, and passion which is the hallmark of Margie Adam's work. —*Laura Post*

○ **Here Is a Love Song** / 1983 / Pleiades
An elegant, beautifully instrumented LP of beautiful swoons and fun songs, with an extra-hot group of musicians: Jean Fineberg and Ellen Seeling on horns, Vivian Stoll on vibes, Barbara Cobb on bass, Barbara Borden, Susanne Vincenza, Carolyn Brandy, Diane Lindsay, and Michele Sell—who used to play with Frank Sinatra—on harp. —*Ladyslipper*

★ **Best of Margie Adam** / 1990 / Olivia 961
This late 1990, double-length edition is one of Olivia's *Women's Music Classics* collections, with songs chosen from all of Margie's albums to commemorate one of Women's Music's best-selling pianists and songwriters—and the first time Margie's work is available on CD! Includes "Best Friend (The Unicorn Song)," "Tender Lady," "Naked Keys," and 14 more. —*Ladyslipper*

○ **Another Place** / 1993 / Pleiades 2751
...A lovely collection of songs, chock-full of her trademark wry and gentle observations on the ways of the heart. Her voice has matured and deepened, and by bringing together some of today's best Women's Music artists (old and new), she breathes a new, steady life into the scene. —*Ladyslipper*

Alive!

Group / Ballads, Latin jazz, post-bop
All-female quintet from San Francisco area. Hard-swinging, with Latin leanings. As they said in a song, "for lack of a better word, call it jazz." —*Michael G. Nastos*

★ **Alive!** / Sep. 5, 1979-Sep. 7, 1979 / Urana 84
All-female group swung like mad and held no punches. All-original contents include three by lead singer Rhiannon and one from Michelle Rosewoman. "City Life" is an absolute knockout. Features Barbara Borden on drums, Carolyn Brandy (per), Janet Small on piano, Suzanne Vincenza on bass. Where are they now when we need them? —*Michael G. Nastos*

Call It Jazz / May 17, 1981-May 19, 1981 / Alive 8484
If you love Rhiannon as a vocalist, but weren't around when she fronted this ensemble, take our word for it: you'll love this!! Recorded at the Great American Music Hall in San Francisco in May, 1981. It's dynamite...this recording actually preserves that elusive, most magical spirit that Alive! embodied in performance. Produced by Helen Keane. —*Ladyslipper*

○ **City Life** / Nov. 1982 / 543
"A triumph of human and musical spirit—that is *City Life* at its best. Their individual and collective mastery of idioms—from Bebop and ballads to Afro-Cuban and pop—is abundantly evident on this album." This quote from their jacket sums it up. The reasons Alive! is gaining recognition and respect in the greater jazz world will be no mystery to listeners. —*Ladyslipper*

Altazor

Group / Women's
Formed in 1987, this groundbreaking Latin American ensemble combines the multinational talents of Chilean Lichi Fuentes, Venezuelan Jackeline Rago, Cuban Dulce Arguelles, and Asian-American Vanessa Whang. The group's name comes from the Spanish "alta" (high) and "azor" (hawk), words that suggest the soaring vocal harmonies of the singers, as well as the high-flying spirit with which the group's haunting, passsionate music is created. Its repertoire includes traditional Latin American vocal and instrumental arrangements, along with the more socially-conscious lyrics of New Song. Altazor employs an impressive range of instruments that includes the quena, tiple, tres, and charango, as well as the more familiar flute, mandolin, guitar, and piano. —*AMG*

● **Altazor** / 1989 / Redwood 8904
...All-acoustic instrumentation including guitar, mandolin, charango, flutes, congas and percussion. The songs range from poignant ballads to lively dances, with the group really cutting loose on two instrumental tracks—one of which features a wild guitar and charango duet. —*Backroads Music/Heartbeats*

Jamie Anderson

Known for her warm voice and her unique, sometimes outrageous songs, Jamie Anderson has reached many people with her music. In 1990 and 1991, she was voted Favorite New Performer by readers of *Hot Wire*, an international journal of women's music and culture.

Anderson is a versatile performer who has been touring nationally since 1987, playing everywhere from coffeehouses to concert halls all over the U.S. In 1990 alone, Anderson performed for audiences in 22 states, and she has been featured at several Women's Music festivals including Campfest, East Coast Lesbians' Festival, National Women's Music Festival, New England Women's Musical Retreat, Southern Women's Music and Comedy Festival, and West Coast Women's Music and Comedy Festival.

Anderson introduces new listeners to the subtleties of lesbian culture while promoting self-pride and affirmation for other lesbians. —*Laura Post*

★ **Center of Balance** / 1992 / Tsunami 1002
Jamie's second release continues with the humorous, pointed material she's become quite known for, and contains many of the songs she's performed on tour...plus her usual array of contemplative and/or weird songs. Vocal assistance given by Sue Fink, Mimi Baczewska, Leah Zicari. —*Ladyslipper*

Closer to Home / Tsunami
This is a wonderfully lesbian-identified album filled with warmth, humor and honesty...Jamie explores topics near and dear to many of us! Her voice is sweet, the delivery straightforward, and the lyrics direct, thoughtful, and refreshing. —*Ladyslipper*

Ruth Barrett

Parthenogenesis / 1990 / Aradia 110
...An award-winning collection of original songs with powerful woman-identified mythic imagery, celebrating the Goddess with a unique blend of contemporary and traditional instrumentation. Kay Gardner calls Ruth a musician/priestess to lead us into the next century, and this album a *must* for anyone who believes in the political power of women's spirituality. —*Ladyslipper*

Laura Berkson

○ **Laura Berkson** / 1989 / Brave Ann 101
Debut album by a talented singer-songwriter with solid roots in folk, Jewish, and women's traditions—and for whom music is a medium for personal growth, community empowerment, and world change. Included here are many originals of note, including "Marie," the story of two high school girls who won the right to attend their prom together. (It's a famous story now, mostly because of Laura's song!) —*Ladyslipper*

BETTY

○ **Hello Betty!** / 1991 / Betty Rules DDD
The debut release from this favored harmonizing Diva Rock trio—it features the hit singles "Wolfwoman," "Betticoat Junction," "Ms. Snake," "Picnic Love Affair," "Go Ahead and Spit, Mr. Amoeba Man." 21 songs in all, 48 minutes of fun. —*Ladyslipper*

Heather Bishop

Vocals, guitar / Folk
Heather Bishop possesses one of those resonant, endlessly expressive voices that make audiences want to sing along and weep at the sheer beauty. What sets Bishop apart is the grounded spiritual energy that infuses all her work, live and recorded. Her career has spanned two decades of spreading her messages—sometimes joyous, sometimes painful, always passionate—in U.S. and Canadian urban centers (Bishop hails from Manitoba), fly-in Yukon villages, festivals, and conferences.

In her teens, Bishop began to study the acoustic guitar; by the late 1970s, she was touring across the North American continent, building bridges between communities and generations. Although she is an artist who moves easily among genres, Bishop considers herself to be a folk musician who belts out the blues, croons ballads, and delivers stirring political songs.

Her current release, *Old*New*Borrowed*Blue* (Mother of Pearl Records, 1992), is her ninth. It features remixed/digitally mastered versions of "old" tunes from her five albums for adults, "new" tunes (five of them, by Canadian women), cuts "borrowed" from artists whom Bishop has admired, and several blues numbers. —*Laura Post*

Grandmother's Song / 1979 / Mother Of Pearl 001

Heather's very first release. The title song gives the perspective of a pioneer woman growing old on the prairies. Heather is also a painter, and used a beautiful original of her grandmother for the cover art. —*Ladyslipper*

I Love Women ... Who Laugh / 1982 / Mother Of Pearl
This album is the embodiment of a successful transition in style, from a solid blues background to a more rock-oriented, funkier sound. Utilizing an incredible array of synthesizers, plus congas and saxophone, Heather produces strong moods and currents of emotion. Mostly original and clearly woman-identified material. —*Ladyslipper*

☆ **A Taste of the Blues** / 1987 / Mother Of Pearl 006
This 1987 release is another serving of Heather's tasty blues, which is the style her voice was obviously created for...that's power, eh?...Sumptuous jacket, fine production, excellent artistry, wonderful woman. —*Ladyslipper*

★ **Old New Borrowed Blue** / 1992 / Mother Of Pearl 009
This 1992 compilation has two or three selections from each of Heather's albums for adults: *Walk That Edge, A Taste of the Blues, I Love Women Who Laugh, Celebration*, and *Grandmother's Song*...[and] five newly recorded songs, including "Ancient Cry" and "Yes To Life." Lots of her best work here. —*Ladyslipper*

Blazing Redheads

Group / Latin jazz
All-female septet from California who play upbeat Latin jazz on the funky side. S.F. Bay Area darlings. (P.S. None are actually redheads.) —*Michael G. Nastos*

★ **Blazing Redheads** / Aug. 11, 1987-Aug. 12, 1987 / Reference 26
Worth getting. Latin-jazz, funky, get-down music. —*Michael G. Nastos*

Crazed Women / Dec. 10, 1990-Dec. 12, 1990 / Reference 41
...Jazzy and percussion-rich, with elements of Latin, R&B, and even rock...fun and exciting! Joy Julks plays bass on this one. —*Ladyslipper*

Barbara Borden

Lady of the Serpent Skirt / 1988 / Cloud 9 1
Barbara Borden and Sheilah Glover are veterans of the Bay Area women's music scene who, in their first collaboration, explore together the interface between spacious electronic music and world-beat drum stylings.... *Lady of the Serpent Skirt*'s primal, sensual music makes for an intriguing release—full of interesting textures and colorful sounds, alive with the magic of the Earth and the mystery of the soul. —*Backroads Music/Heartbeats*

○ **All Hearts Beating** / 1990 / Cloud 9 2
Drummer Barbara Borden's first solo album develops many of the musical themes originally introduced on *Lady of the Serpent Skirt*, her earlier collaboration with Sheilah Glover ... Combining rich earthiness with delicate space impressionism, *All Hearts Beating* is an exhilarating meeting of heaven and earth, where the rhythms of nature are given expression in the organic voice of the drums. —*Backroads Music/Heartbeats*

★ **Portraits of Passion** / 1992 / Cloud 9 333
In keeping with the spirit of their first collaboration, *Lady of the Serpent Skirt*, *Portraits of Passion* continues to explore the interface between electronic music, acoustic timbres, and world-beat drum stylings—with an intriguing theme to wrap it up. *Portraits of Passion* draws on the life and times of six historical visionaries, portraying the individual spirit of each one in imaginative and sometimes wildly experimental ways that reflect their extremely personal vision...The results are creative spaces well-grounded in earthy rhythms.... —*Backroads Music/Heartbeats*

Meg Christian

Vocals / Folk-pop, Women's
Meg Christian recorded Olivia's first album and, along with Cris Williamson, brought the whole field of Women's Music into its golden age. A singer/songwriter with a folk and classical bent, her music tends to be impassioned and filled with intense feelings, and her sound very elegant and restrained. Although she retired from performing during the '80s, her work still looms large among older listeners, and she is revered within the field. —*Bruce Eder*

Face the Music / 1982 / Olivia 913
The poignant and reflective lyrics are balanced against an opulent sound. Featuring the supporting talents of Holly Near and Sweet Honey in The Rock. —*Bruce Eder*

○ **Turning It Over** / Olivia 925
...her first release since 1977, with love ballads, lovely instrumentals, reflective and humorous tunes. As always, Meg infuses her music with her "personalness." Yet there is also something new here...a sense of self-recognition which will hit home for many...perhaps another season in the cycle. —*Ladyslipper*

★ **The Best of Meg Christian** / Olivia 957
Here are all of the landmark songs from this remarkable singer/songwriter and her decade-long career. Probably the best introduction to her work. —*Bruce Eder*

I Know You Know / Olivia 902
The first "produced" Women's Music record, this has held up with its humor and poignancy, although it may seem dated to some modern ears and sensibilities. —*Bruce Eder*

Kate Clinton

Comedy
Kate Clinton began performing her political comedy in 1981, the same year as Ronald Reagan. Like Reagan, Kate Clinton has built her success upon breaking the rules. Her fast-paced, cutting-edge performance style skewers political egos and shreds taboos.

She focuses on topical world concerns and an affirmative feminist agenda, while drawing on her "recovering-Catholic" roots and years of experience as a high-school English teacher.

Kate Clinton has emerged as a national force outside those traditionally male-dominated bastions, the comedy clubs. With four self-produced albums on her own WhysCrack label to her credit— *Making Light* (1982), *Making Waves* (1983), *Live at the Great American Music Hall* (1985), and her current disc, *Babes in Joyland* (1991)—Kate has built a wide following in her 10 years of performing professionally. —*Laura Post*

Live at Great American Music Hall / 1985 / Whyscrack 103
In her inimitable style, where every breath packs a punch, Kate relates experiences as a recovering Catholic (coveting her neighbor's wife), sensitively and deeply describes Californians Discussing Relationships, satirizes personals in papers, sings her song for parthenogenesis, and tells how she answered the question "What Do YOU Do?" at an S/M workshop. Though Kate's audiences continue to expand at a rapid rate, and the types of people for whom she performs has broadened significantly, she never omits her lesbian material; get your TV sets tuned up! —*Ladyslipper*

★ **Babes in Joyland** / 1991 / Whyscrack 104
Recorded live in Boston, Kate draws on her recovering-Catholic roots, years of high-school English teaching, and her authority on Bush and bawdy politic to build laughter of fears fading and connections made. It's hard to be a dominatrix in a kinder, gentler nation, so her comedy is more stand-with than stand-up! —*Ladyslipper*

Catie Curtis

Vocals / Urban-folk
A Boston-area singer/songwriter whose politics are at once humanist, feminist, and gentle. —*Richard Meyer*

○ **Dandelion** / 1989 / Mongoose
Curtis's debut cassette, featuring 12 songs, is not as polished as her *From Years to Hours* CD. Her acoustic guitar work is good, and she uses just enough backup to add to her music without overpowering it. Good effort. —*Chip Renner*

● **From Years to Hours** / 1991 / Mongoose 102
Curtis shines on her second release, really maturing as a songwriter. Her music is well produced (Darleen Wilson), and her songwriting is intelligent and thought-provoking. "Hole in the Bucket" is the key song on this collection. —*Chip Renner & Richard Meyer*

Dianne Davidson

Vocals, guitar / Soul, blues-rock, Women's
Some of this singer/songwriter's musical talents may have been inherited: her grandmother was an opera singer, and her mother claims Davidson came out of the womb singing. As a child,

Davidson even toyed for a while with the piano and saxophone, before settling on being a singer and developing her personal vocal style.

Davidson's recording career began at age 19 when she produced and recorded her own LP for Janus Records, following a period of belting out soul standards with an eight-piece band. Two more LPs for Janus followed, before the label went out of business in 1974. More recently, Davidson has been recording for Oakland's Olivia Records. The robust, passionate voice featured on her own albums has also provided backup vocals for Linda Ronstadt and Tracy Nelson. Although Davidson handles the blues, R&B, and pop ballads with skill, her strongest songs are the rousing rockers that allow her to belt out the lyrics loud and clear. —*Laura Post*

☆ **Breaking All the Rules!** / 1988 / Second Wave 22011
An excellent showcase for Davidson's powerful voice and guitar, highlighted by her loud, raunchy version of Willie Dixon's "Built For Comfort." —*Bruce Eder*

Hunter Davis

Harmony / 1986 / Hunter Davis Music 8601
● **Torn** / Redwood 8803

Caryl De Groot

○ **Womoon to Womoon** / Rolling Easy 1
Lovely lesbian music by a folkie Phoenix performer, who has written unabashed love songs in a strong woman-identified tradition. Guitar and harmony vocals accompany "Gentle Womoon," "Womoon Rise Up Rising," "Come and Dance," and "Lay Me Down." Tired of vague references? This is for you. —*Ladyslipper*

Melanie DeMore

Come Follow Me / 1986 / Melanie Demore 1
Recipient of standing ovations, Melanie is one of the most exciting new recording/performing artists in women's music of the '90s. "Hard as obsidian," "sweet as chocolate," "strong as knots," and "round as a waterdrop" are some of the attempts that have been made to describe her voice in words. Others have compared her to Patti (of Tuck and), or Joan Armatrading. She's the director of Voices, the Bay Area Lesbian Choral Ensemble, and her expertise in vocal possibilities is evident here—as is her incredible range. —*Ladyslipper*

● **Share My Song** / 1992 / Redwood 9203
Melanie's buoyant vocals and rich lyrics, rooted in the African-American folk tradition, are captured in this 1992 release. —*Ladyslipper*

Deuce

● **Deuce** / 1986 / Redwood 8602
A very jazzy and funky album, primarily instrumental, by a New York ensemble led by Jean Fineberg (flute, sax) and Ellen Seeling (horns). Lots of Latin rhythms courtesy of Nydia Mata, vocal contributions by Teresa Trull and Carol MacDonald, and an urban energy await you; don't be late to this date! —*Ladyslipper*

Ani DiFranco

Vocals, Guitar
What does androgynous, twentysomething, New Wave folk-punksinger Ani (Ah-nee) DiFranco have in common with feminist author/speaker/activist Gloria Steinem? They have both developed ardent followings through preaching a contemporary commonperson's gospel. They are both charismatic onstage. And they both believe in the power of the Revolution Within.

Ani DiFranco is an inadvertent messiah to the "Nose-ring Generation," identified by body piercings, undaunted attitude, and haircuts that would get you fired from the bank: tufted, dyed, and shaven to the scalp. They are spunky, dramatic, brimming with awareness, and bursting with a social consciousness unimagined by their forebears at the same age.

DiFranco's understated voice powers her unflinching lyrics. She delivers the intensity of Janis Joplin, but will never drown in the discontent that she stirs. Her songwriting melds the down-home sensibility of Dolly Parton with the biting energy of metal, and the jittery beat of thrash. The beat used to come from her guitar alone. Now drummer Andy Stochansky joins her gigs.

DiFranco's genuine warmth takes some of the edge off her righteous rage. The unarguable rightness of her vision, and the tunefulness of her compositions, temper the harsh details of her vignettes.

She briefly attended art school in her native Buffalo, then moved to New York City and enrolled at the New School for Social Research. Playing gigs in bars at the same time, she quickly built a strong local following. A West Coast live-events producer, Tracye Lawson, had brought a relatively unknown DiFranco to Santa Cruz, CA, early in 1993; by the time of DiFranco's return engagement in the fall of the same year, her audience had multiplied incredibly.

Following the startling popularity of her sparely self-produced debut recording, *Ani DiFranco* (Righteous Records, 1990), she generated enough revenue to finance a second album, *Not So Soft*, in 1991. In 1993, she released *Puddle Dive* (Righteous Babe Records), which spent 10 weeks on the college charts, providing another quantum leap in the direction of recognition.

Having employed a small posse of session players on *Puddle Dive*, Ani gave the same treatment to some of her older solo material on 1993's *Like I Said/Songs 1990-1991. Out of Range* (Righteous Babe Records, 1994) is DiFranco's latest. —*Laura Post*

Ani Difranco / 1989 / Righteous 001
A fine debut from this young songwriter, singer, and guitarist, whose songs and poems are literate, melodic, feminist, well-arranged, and full of meaningful imagery. Plus she's got a lovely, versatile voice. —*Ladyslipper*

Not So Soft / 1991 / Righteous 002
The delivery is sweet and urgent here, giving blood to her poetry and making the listener get active in the listening...She employs a very rich acoustic guitar on most songs, does some beautiful self-harmonizing, and also adds some conga drum and dust broom! —*Ladyslipper*

○ **Imperfectly** / 1992 / Righteous 003
With her third (1992) album, Ani achieves a level of intensity that folk-rock rarely reaches. Unflinching in her pursuit of honesty, she strikes sparks incessantly as she challenges sexual politics, social conventions, and the meaning of existence, including her own...For the first time, other musicians appear as accompanists, adding shadings of viola, trumpet, mandolin. —*Ladyslipper*

● **Puddle Dive** / 1993 / Righteous 004
On this 1993 release, her most complex effort to date, Ani goes boldly where no one has gone before...joined at various moments by pianist Ann Rabson from Saffire, the Uppity Blueswomen, virtuoso violinist Mary Ramsey from the folk-rock duo John & Mary, and English harmonica sensation Rory McLeod. An in-your-face lyricist who exposes our hidden thoughts and feelings, she confronts the status quo in sex, psychology, and society by reaching unflinchingly into her experience and personal politics. —*Ladyslipper*

Alice Di Micele

Make a Change / 1988 / Alice Otter
...Her strong, deep, textured vocal quality will pull you right in and mesmerize you, as it effectively communicates her ideas: love for the Earth and all creatures; and a strong commitment to peace, political and social change, and personal and political growth. ...Primary accompaniment is cello, guitar. —*Ladyslipper*

It's a Miracle / 1989 / Alice Di Micele 102
Alice's second recording features a fuller sound—acoustic guitars and cello are joined by some sizzlin' sax and drums—and [offers] a lyrical exploration of the Earth's wonders, spiritual connections, love and loss. —*Ladyslipper*

● **Too Controversial** / 1990 / Alice Di Micele 103
This 1990 release features more of Alice's trademark heartfelt lyrics and soulful voice, plus tightly arranged accompaniment (acoustic guitar, bass, keyboards, percussion, soprano sax and cello). Many songs focus on detailing the oppressive aspects of American culture, but what saves this from being a ranting political manifesto is Alice's gorgeous vocal treatment—alternately sweet and growly, whispery and full-throated—and the integral acoustic instrumentation. ..."Personally political" music. —*Ladyslipper*

disappear fear

Group

Echo My Call / 1988 / Refined 1002

Sonia and Cindy Rutstein are blood-sisters with captivating sister-harmonies, and their duo album is characterized by haunting melodies, by content that reaches from the personal to U.S. intervention in Central America, and by a soulful folkbeat delivery. All the material is by husky-voiced lead singer and guitarist Sonia. Nice debut. —*Ladyslipper*

● **Live at the Bottom Line** / 1989 / Disappear Fear 1006

Fifty minutes, 13 songs...primarily live performance, acoustic and vocals from a November, 1991, concert at this special NYC club. Plus four tracks from *Box of Heaven,* and an extra new studio track. —*Ladyslipper*

Deep Soul Diver / 1990 / Disappear Fear 1004

With not much more than two voices, a guitar, and a tambourine, this duo has created a surprisingly sophisticated sound. Sisters Sonia and Cindy combine engaging melodies with catchy and thoughtful lyrics. This 1990 album balances emotional sincerity with irreverence in songs like "For Hollywood I Will" and "Sexual Telepathy." —*Ladyslipper*

Alix Dobkin

Vocals / Women's, topical, political folk

When Alix Dobkin graduated from college with a Bachelor of Fine Arts degree in 1962, she headed right for New York City's Greenwich Village, where she initiated a career for herself as a folksinger.

In 1973, having discovered women in her life, she released *Lavender Jane Loves Women.* A model in its clear feminist lyrics and its unwavering pro-Lesbian stance, it set an early standard with its independence of production (her own Women's Wax Works label) as well as for its collective spirit.

Since that time, Alix Dobkin has been the most visible and vocal Lesbian feminist in the community. Unlike some other performers, Dobkin has shared the process of her life with her audience. Unlike most other performers, she has been personally available to non-performers after gigs—and on-site at festivals, doing workshops on topics like the sexism and misogyny of commercial album art. Like few other performers, she publicly claimed her own identity—as a Jewish Lesbian—and brought music from her culture into her shows.

Twenty years and five albums later, she has released a 30-song cassette and CD, *Love & Politics,* highlighting many of the songs—from *Living With Lesbians, Xx Alix, These Women/Never Been Better,* and *Yahoo Australia!*—that have established her as a foremother of contemporary Lesbian culture.

The FBI named Dobkin a "troublemaker." To her peers, she is "Head Lesbian." —*Laura Post*

Xx Alix / 1980 / Women's Wax Works 003

Alix's material just gets better and better. This collection of songs is, as usual, highly personal, concrete, articulate, thoughtful, and thought-provoking. Her originality, observations, and experiences emerge as...simultaneously aesthetic and contentful; vulnerable and solid-as-a-rock. —*Ladyslipper*

These Women / Never Been Better / 1986 / Women's Wax Works 0050

Ever in a ground-breaking, controversial mode, Alix will shock her folkie fans with some of these selections! Mixing high-tech sound with unadulterated feminist and lesbian messages, Alix joins with Carol MacDonald and Witch to create the honest, scathing "Boy-Girl Rap," "Some Boys," and a country remake of her classic "The Woman in Your Life Is You." Then, switching to her more familiar and still-dear folk style, she delivers "Big Girls," "Crazy Dance," "100 Easy Ways to Lose a Man," and the lovely "These Women." —*Ladyslipper*

Yahoo Australia! Live from Sydney / 1990 / Women's Wax Works 006

A live concert featuring Dobkin at her best and having fun with her subjects, even as she stridently sings out on any number of political issues. —*Bruce Eder*

★ **Love & Politics: A 30 Year Saga** / 1992 / Women's Wax Works 007

Basically a *Best of Alix* collection, this album documents Dobkin's life in songwriting—and the landmarks of her life that

inspired those songs. It's well-balanced, with 20 songs spanning 1962-1992: six generic love songs, six specific love songs, six political-analysis songs, and two "inspirational" songs—one generic and one specific. In addition to some of everyone's favorites, she includes a brand-new recording of the previously unreleased, very controversial "My Lesbian Wars"...plus a 1970 pre-lesbian recording of "Shinin' Through." The CD has the complete liner notes and lyrics. —*Ladyslipper*

☆ **Lavender Jane Loves Women** / Women's Wax Works 001

A pioneering Lesbian-oriented record, with a clever collection of material—such as an interpretation of Dusty Springfield's "I Only Want To Be With You" that holds up well today. —*Bruce Eder*

○ **Living with Lesbians** / Women's Wax Works 002

A surprisingly lively follow-up, with earthy, powerful material featuring basic guitar and all-woman backup singing. —*Bruce Eder*

Tracy Drach

● **Another Door** / 1990 / Drach 'n Droll 001

Long a local favorite, this singer/songwriter/guitarist exemplifies both versatility and consistency in crowd-pleasing—whether performing solo, or opening for such acts as k.d. lang or the Washington Sisters. This late 1990 release demonstrates how her intensity and honesty reach out to the listener. With a little piano help from Nancy Day, and a style that is uniquely Tracy. —*Ladyslipper*

Dyketones

Group

● **Live in P-Town (Double)** / 1988 / Rock n' Role 1001

A full hour-and-a-half by everyone's favorite "rock n' role" five-woman band, performing their trademark slightly-reworked hits from the 50s and early 60s, at a dance party at Dyke High! From "To Know Her Is To Love Her" to "My Girlfriend's Back" to 24 others, hear them croon and rock out to the max....With help from the Dykeangelle Choir and Dyke High Chorus! —*Ladyslipper*

Carole Etzler & Bren Chambers

● **Rainbows in My Mind** / Sisters Unlimited 4

This 1989 album reaches out and lifts the spirit. From the delicate chimes of "Cup of the Moon" to the drumbeats of "Chant for Mother Earth," the music touches the threads of our relationships with each other and with the planet. Carole and Bren interweave cello, guitar, voices, piano, chimes, Aztec drum, gong, Celtic harp, and Tibetan singing bowls into a joyful celebration of life. —*Ladyslipper*

Ferron

Vocals / Women's

In listening to Ferron's music, audiences are allowed to acknowledge the passage of time, people, memories, and hopes through her poetic metaphors. Her familiar vernacular, direct statements, enlightened associations, warm and husky voice, and engaging stage presence have permitted identification with her experiences and her process, her struggles and her wisdom—and with universal anguish and strength. Beginning in 1986, however, many of her followers began to wonder at, and mourn, her absence from recording and touring.

Born on June 2, 1952, Ferron grew up in a semi-rural suburb of Vancouver, British Columbia, the eldest of seven children in a working-class family. After leaving home at 15, she scrambled financially, supporting herself by driving a cab, waitressing, shoveling gravel, and packing five-pound bags of coffee in a factory. From her basement, she recorded and distributed *Ferron* (1977) and *Ferron Backed Up* (1978). Since both albums are now out-of-print collector's items, Ferron has decided to re-release much of their material on subsequent albums.

In 1978, Ferron was "discovered" by Gayle Scott, an American working in film production in Vancouver, who became Ferron's first and only manager and business partner. Ferron and Gayle collaborated on Ferron's next two studio albums—*Testimony* (Lucy Records, 1980) and *Shadows on a Dime* (Lucy Records, 1984)—on which Ferron continued to convey her polished messages of raw truths through sharply lyrical, soothingly melodic music. The songs dealt with the cyclicality of relationships, with questions of survival and identity, and with maintaining optimism amid fear. Despite a small budget assembled through loans and contributions—and in the absence of any organized promotion—*Shadows on a Dime* received a four-star rating from *Rolling Stone* Magazine.

In October, 1985, Ferron received a Canada Council arts grant, enabling her to take a much-needed year off—ostensibly to write and take voice lessons, but also to recover a long-neglected personal life. Recognizing that she would need more time than a year to fully heal from the hardships of the road and the vagaries of the business, Ferron remained withdrawn from the spotlight. After the grant money ran out, she earned a living by laboring as a carpenter's assistant and a bartender, and by working in daycare. Ferron has since returned to the studio and the stage, having reconnected with her physical and spiritual roots, having reaffirmed and redefined her own needs, and having come to a remarkable new peace and with a fresh body of work: *Phantom Center* (1990), *Resting With The Question* (1992), and *Not A Still Life* (1992). —*Laura Post*

★ **Testimony** / 1982 / Redwood 3
Considered her best record, this is a collection of song-poems that run the gamut of deep and intense emotions. —*William Ruhlmann*

☆ **Shadows on a Dime** / 1989 / Redwood 4
Literate songs by one of the best singer/songwriters, on an elaborate follow-up album with a special instrumental luster, courtesy of producer Terry Garthwaite. —*Bruce Eder & William Ruhlmann*

☆ **Phantom Center** / 1990 / Chameleon 74830
Connecting rich, poetic, archetypal imagery with vibrant musical textures, it is guaranteed to create an immediate emotional impact. Instrumentalists include Barbara Higbie and Novi. —*Ladyslipper*

○ **Not a Still Life** / 1992 / Cherrywood Station 007
This 1992 in-concert album, subtitled *Live at the Great American Music Hall*, contains selections from all her previous releases of vocal music, including her 1970s releases *Ferron* ("I Am Hungry") and *Ferron Backed Up* ("Light of My Light," "Call Me Friend," and "Dear Marly"). Also includes a couple of selections not included on any previous albums: the concert favorite "I Know A Game," and "Shady Gate." ... A great retrospective of her songwriting career, and a chance to enjoy her in a more personal way than the studio recordings afford. —*Ladyslipper*

● **Resting with the Question** / Cherrywood Station 006
Who'd have guessed that Ferron's musical gift could express its poetry through instrumental music as well as through songs with lyrics?...Eloquent compositions performed on synthesizer are saturated with emotion: lush, wistful, yearning, haunting, rich, and circular...elegant and probing dreamscapes. And you'll probably lapse into thinking you're hearing flutes, classical guitars, strings, piano, and human voices. A highly recommended opportunity to experience another dimension of this woman's artistry. —*Ladyslipper*

Cathy Fink

Vocals, guitar, banjo, dulcimer / Folk, childrens'

Cathy is a singer/songwriter who has performed with Blue Rose, and has produced several children's tapes. She is an excellent guitar, banjo, and dulcimer player. Her music spans folk, bluegrass, and country, and she has released several high-quality childrens' albums of her own. —*Chip Renner*

○ **Banjo Haiku** / Community Music 202
This 1992 release is a terrific collection of 26 clawhammer banjo tunes, played by an award-winning, expert instrumentalist. Diverse enough for the banjo connoisseur, and tasteful enough for all acoustic instrumental fans to enjoy, she covers a wide variety of tunings, tempos, and timbres demonstrating the versatility of the old-time banjo... . —*Ladyslipper*

Cathy Fink & Duck Donald / Flying Fish 053
This album features skillful performances of old-timey and hillbilly music, some of it comic, all of it sprightly. —*AMG*

Sue Fink

Vocals / Rock

Sue Fink is a multitalented, multifaceted artist. As a voice teacher, she has been sought out by the likes of Brian Wilson (of the Beach Boys), and by backup singers for Aretha Franklin and Marvin Gaye. Other artists have hired her to produce and arrange their recordings, and to write songs for them. The National Association of Independent Record Distributors (NAIRD) gave *Big Promise* (1985), Fink's first solo album, an award of excellence; and the Washington Post loved it. While critics acclaim Fink's serious talent, festivals and conferences have also recognized her acute sense of humor by inviting her to emcee their events.

Sue Fink grew up in Beverly, Hills practicing piano four hours daily. She graduated *magna cum laude* from UCLA's music department, and continued there in graduate school. Fink has sung on television, on albums, and at Nixon's presidential inauguration. Prior to becoming involved with women's music, she amassed professional credits including a State Department-sponsored, 13-nation tour of Asia with the California Chamber Singers, and a singing tour of Europe, Israel, Canada, Hawaii, and the continental U.S. with the Roger Wagner Chorale.

Fink toured with Meg Christian during the spring of 1984, playing synthesizer. The following year brought the release of Fink's critically acclaimed, techno-synthesizer *Big Promise*, and an album tour in collaboration with Diane Lindsay. Fink then started to tour solo; as such, she has performed or emceed at all of the major women's festivals in the U.S. She also founded the Los Angeles Women's Community Chorus, and was featured on KCBS Television's "Two on the Town" as the group's energetic conductor. With her humor, heart, and concern, Sue Fink reached new depth as an artist with her 1989 album *True Life Adventure*, featuring R&B ballads and released on her own Frostfire label.

Most recently, Sue Fink was voted favorite songwriter, emcee, and MIDI programmer by *Hot Wire*, the international journal of women's music and culture; her song "Leaping Lesbians" was, as usual, included as an all-time favorite song. Fink played and/or sang on several new recordings by Pam Hall, Jamie Anderson, and Margie Adam. More recently, she coproduced (with Jamie Anderson) a compilation entitled *A Family Of Friends*—a modern "Lesbian Concentrate," released as a fundraiser to fight the "family values" crusade while demonstrating our own sense of family. Fink, Anderson, Millington, and others co-wrote the title song, which was recorded with a "We Are the World" cast of women's music. —*Laura Post*

True Life Adventure / 1989 / Frostfire 101
A strong and long-awaited follow-up with a jazzy torch style. Sophisticated and polished. —*AMG*

★ **Big Promise** / Ladyslipper 201
From New Wave dance tunes to ballads to rock, Sue's polished debut contains strong political statements delivered in a fun and enjoyable manner. —*AMG*

Judy Fjell

Judy Fjell's performing career began as a teenager, when she picked up a guitar at a garage sale, learned a few chords, and began entertaining folks in her small Montana home town with favorites from the "Hootenanny" radio program.

In the mid-1970s, inspired by the Women's Music movement and encouraged by a close poet friend, Fjell began to write her own songs, featuring messages of social change right alongside her deeply personal lyrics. With her six albums on her own Honey Pie Music label, through her private lessons and Music Empowerment Workshops, Fjell travels and inspires in the minstrel tradition. —*Laura Post*

○ **Dance in the Moment** / 1988 / Honey Pie 105
Her famous "Middle-Aged Body (with Teenage Emotions)," the song that speaks for a generation, is preserved on this 1988 album...Judy's humor helps us keep things in perspective. —*Ladyslipper*

Livin' on Dreams / 1990 / Honey Pie 106
Some 73 minutes of live music, humor, and stories from this Norwegian lesbian singer/songwriter. Her political wit is still finely tuned... . —*Ladyslipper*

★ **Love and Justice** / 1991 / Honey Pie 107
This 1991 release is a collection of Judy's political songs (plus a few by Malvina Reynolds). It started out to be a small, simple, available-only-at-concerts project, until folks started clamoring

for it to be more widely available. Here it is, in its simple and straightforward essence. She deals with lesbian/gay, peace, environmental, feminist, and labor issues, just to name a quick few. — *Ladyslipper*

Robin Flower & Libby McLaren

Vocals / Women's

Robin Flower and Libby McLaren have been breaking ground with their novel fusion of Irish, Cajun, bluegrass, and western swing—progressive bluegrass, they call it. In their songs, they yearn for connection with kindred spirits in diverse forms: she-wolves, faraway women, grandmothers, conscientious interveners in cycles of abuse, courageous interveners in larger political dramas, and romantic lovers.

Flower's career began with auspicious laudatory reviews from the *Village Voice, Frets,* and *Billboard.* Teaming with flatpicker Nancy Vogl, Flower released her first album, *More Than Friends* (Spaniel, 1979). In 1982 came *Green Sneakers* (Flying Fish), then 1984's *First Dibs* (Flying Fish—awarded Best String Band Jazz by N.A.I.R.D.) and 1987's *Babies with Glasses* (Flying Fish—awarded Best Women's Music Album by N.A.I.R.D.).

In the the late 1980s, Flower teamed with equally committed and competent musician, Libby McLaren, whose pop view has softened Flower's sophisticated, technical approach. In previous outings, McLaren had applied her rich keyboards, clear voice, and ear for instrumental interplay to recording, arrangement, and accompaniment for such peers as The Roches, Ronnie Gilbert, and Holly Near.

Flower and McLaren found that they were both very focused, intent upon hard practice, and unquestioning about the need to collectively arrange and assign instrumental and vocal parts. They were so focused and intent that they split from Nancy Vogl, with whom they had initially believed they would play as a trio. In the present scenario, several talented Bay Area women musicians have accompanied them: fiddler-vocalist Crystal Reeves, harpist Michelle Sell, and guitarist-singer Teresa Chandler.

During their first few years together, in the late '80s, Flower and McLaren played for diverse audiences: folk (though they were often labeled "too progressive" or "too electric" for folk purists), mainstream pop, and Women's Music.

Their debut recording as a duo, *Angel of Change,* was released on Little Cat Records (2468 Hearst Avenue, Oakland, CA 94602). Future plans include doing a wholly instrumental album, and a more purely folk-styled album—perhaps one recorded live-in-studio, rather than overdubbed. — *Laura Post*

Robin Flower & Libby Mclaren! / 1989 / Robin Flower & Libby CS

This self-produced 1989 cassette features the talents of two of the industry's finest instrumentalist/singer/songwriters. Their lyrics are catchy and relevant, the arrangements tight, and their voices light and sweet. — *Ladyslipper*

● **Babies with Glasses** / Flying Fish 428
This 1987 release chronicles the development of this instrumentalist/singer/songwriter's new acoustic sound: a mixture of bluegrass with jazz influences and bits of rock and classical strains. — *Ladyslipper*

Tret Fure

Vocals, guitar / Rock

Pop-rocker Fure's personal background is as diverse as her many musical talents. Born in Iowa, she grew up in Illinois and on Michigan's Upper Peninsula, then moved to the West Coast to attend the University of California at Berkeley. She began her music-writing career when she was 19, and worked for a time as a vocalist and guitarist for Spencer Davis, before putting her music-making skills to work as a successful engineer and producer for Olivia Records. There, she engineered, co-produced, and performed on albums for Cris Williamson and June Millington, as well as Olivia's landmark double album, *Meg/Cris at Carnegie Hall.* Her own first (self-titled) solo album was released in 1973 on RCA Records, and shortly thereafter she toured extensively, opening for such groups as the J. Geils Band, Yes, and Poco. Following the release of her second album, *Terminal Hold* (Olivia), Fure focused on her solo career, and with the appearance of her third album, *Edges of the Heart,* she became firmly established as a leading pop-rock performer with unusual depth and

diversity. In her most recent album, *Time Turns the Moon* (Olivia), Fure has continued to pay homage to her roots in folk and rock & roll. Look for her albums on Second Wave Records, a division of Olivia. — *AMG*

★ **Time Turns the Moon** / 1991 / Olivia 22015
One of the best women's music records ever, and one of the finer rock albums of 1990. Assertive and sensitive, tough and reflective, with a sense of humor nearly as prominent as its beat. — *Bruce Eder*

Edges of the Heart / Second Wave 22009
Not as strong as *Terminal Hold,* but with one seriously sexy number ("Tight Black Jeans"); well worth owning. — *Bruce Eder*

○ **Terminal Hold** / Second Wave 22003
Half of this record (most of one side) rocks beautifully hard and breaks a lot of new ground, with help from Dave Davies of the Kinks and Lou Reed alumnus Steve Hunter. — *Bruce Eder*

Kay Gardner

Flute / New Age

An internationally-known composer of healing music, and a pioneer in the women's spirituality movement, Kay Gardner takes the listener on an inspirational journey through the curative and transformative ingredients of music and sound—offering insights into their origins and mysteries, and into how they may be used in the healing process.

Kay Gardner's many albums, on the Ladyslipper label, have featured acoustic instrumentation using the principles of droning, toning, mantra, and chant. She uses harmonics as a stairway to the spiritual, rhythm as the pulse of her music, and melody as its heart and soul.

Gardner has written for several professional music journals, for women's music and culture publications, and for spirituality pages. She regularly teaches workshops on the healing properties of music and sound at the Omega Institute of Holistic Studies, and has been invited to medical schools (including Yale) to present her views. Years of research on this subject went into Kay's book, *Sounding the Inner Landscape: Music as Medicine.* Her most recent project is the oratorio, *Ourbourosa,* a broad work featuring soloists, a 40-piece orchestra, and a 100-voice chorus. She lives on the coast of Maine. — *Laura Post*

○ **Ocean Moon** / 1991 / Urana 85
Combining all the best from *Mooncircles* (all the instrumental tracks) and from *Emerging* (the entire album minus one track), this extra-long-playing compact disc brings Kay's early classic discography into the technological age... This collection features some of Kay's most important work. — *Ladyslipper*

Amazon / 1992 / Ladyslipper 111
Another masterpiece of improvisation from Kay...brings the full sound and ambiance of the Peruvian Rainforest right into your head(set) and heart. Alto flute meditations are blended with Kay's own onsite recordings of birds, tree frogs, rainfall, waterfalls, and pan pipes, which she made when she visited the Amazon River with a women's tour in February of 1992. — *Ladyslipper*

Fishersdaughter / Even Keel 44
Some of Gardner's most fascinating work outside of classical/new age. She recreates folk music in a distinctly woman-centered mode. Not to all tastes, but resounding with a lot of heart. — *Bruce Eder*

Garden of Ecstasy / Ladyslipper 107
Her follow-up to *A Rainbow Path* is just as lush and surprising with its medieval and mystical flavors. — *Bruce Eder*

Mooncircles / Vrana 80
Her earliest instrumental album is a mellow, luscious collection of compositions for her own instrument, the flute, with piano and guitar accompaniment. — *Bruce Eder*

★ **A Rainbow Path** / Ladyslipper 103
A multi-year project that embraces medieval and Eastern influences, yet is almost new age in its ambience. This is the closest that any record has gotten to the feel of Van Dyke Parks's classic *Song Cycle.* — *Bruce Eder*

○ **Moods & Rituals** / Even Keel 39
Subtitled *Meditations for Solo Flutes,* and intended for meditation and relaxation, this sequence of 4 compositions truly has the effect of evoking tranquility, a feeling of well-being and wide-

open space. ...This represents another stage in Kay's research into the use of music in healing. —*Ladyslipper*

Avalon / Ladyslipper 106
This tape of solo flute meditations was created when Kay co-led a "women's mysteries" tour in Glastonbury, England, where Brigid, the Goddess of wells, flames, oaks, creative arts, music, and healing once dwelled, and was once worshipped. ... Remarkably good quality, quieting, and very suitable for meditation. —*Ladyslipper*

Sounding the Inner Landscape (Tape) / Ladyslipper 109
This extended-play tape (68 minutes long) is Kay Gardner's first foray into the arena of guided/self-help tapes, and is intended as a companion piece for her new book, *Sounding the Inner Landscape: Music as Medicine*. Her approach is relaxed, unhurried, and extremely comprehensive. ... If clarity of purpose and pure intent are the basis of all healing, as Kay suggests, then she has succeeded nobly with a most ambitious project. —*Backroads Music/Heartbeats*

Terry Garthwaite

Guitar, vocals, composer

● **Moving Day** / 1985 / Foojoonjoy 007
This 1985 release contains mostly original material in a contemporary vein, softer than previous releases, and one she considers to be more truly representative of her sound, with her sultry expressive voice right up front. —*Ladyslipper*

Ronnie Gilbert

Vocals / Folk

Ronnie Gilbert is no stranger to success or to controversy. Born to working-class Jewish parents in New York City, she refused to participate in her 1940s high-school senior play because she was convinced of the racial injustice of its minstrel-show theme. In the 1950s, singer Gilbert melded her joyous contralto with the radical voices of Pete Seeger, Lee Hays, and Fred Hellerman in their celebrated group the Weavers. They brought folk rhythms and social activism to the mainstream—even while being branded subversives, and blacklisted, amid the hysteria of the McCarthy era.

In 1963, divorced both from her husband and from the cultural expectations of a wife, Gilbert was beginning to build a solo singing career when she met Joseph Chaikin, who was then a young actor/director with the fledgling experimental troupe The Open Theater. In the 1970s, Gilbert's career took yet another surprising turn, when she earned an M.A. in clinical psychology and worked as a therapist for several years.

The 1980s saw Gilbert make her debut appearance at the Michigan Womyn's Music Festival, reading a Lesbian-themed poem. Gilbert met, was inspired by, and sang with Holly Near; the two recorded *Lifeline* (live, 1983) and *Singing With You* (1986), and Gilbert recorded *Harp* (1985) with Near, Arlo Guthrie, and Pete Seeger.

Gilbert's debut solo album, *The Spirit Is Free* (1985) was released on the feminist Redwood label. Her live album *Love Will Find A Way* (1989) was released on the Abbe Alice label—the collaborative product of a new alliance with manager/partner Donna Korones. In 1990, Gilbert gave the keynote speech at the annual conference of the Association of Women's Music and Culture (AWMAC). More recently, Gilbert opened another new direction by performing her one-woman theater piece on the life of the legendary American labor agitator, Mother Jones. —*Laura Post*

★ **The Spirit Is Free** / 1985 / Redwood 408
Gilbert retains a strong vocal presence on standards and feminist-oriented originals. A rousing mix of old standards, such as "The Midnight Special," with new material such as "Mothers, Daughters, Wives." A good startup album. —*Bruce Eder*

Love Will Find a Way / 1989 / Abbe Alice 915
A very honest and representative live album, consisting of a dozen numbers drawn from her current repertoire. —*Bruce Eder*

Lifeline / Redwood 404
A fresh and vibrant concert album with Holly Near, and with a repertoire ranging from current topical songs like "Biko" to romantic classics like "Stormy Weather." Followed up by the album *Singing With You.* —*Bruce Eder*

Girls in the Nose

Group

● **Girls in the Nose** / 1990 / Girls In The Nose 1
Wild, raunchy, sexy, thrilling, and hysterically funny lesbian-feminist—yet politically incorrect—rock n' roll. Loosely translating their philosophy as Viva la Vulva, this 6-woman band includes Gretchen Phillips from Two Nice Girls, here in her wilder persona. —*Ladyslipper*

Origin of the World / 1992 / Girls In The Nose 2
Nine great songs from one of our all-time favorite bands, "kick-ass lesbian rockers from the Lone Star State." ... This 1992 release contains "Breast Exam," "More Madonna, Less Jesus," "Pink Guitar," "Medusa," "Sodomy," "Incongruity," and more, sung to and with sexuality, passion and humor. —*Ladyslipper*

Monica Grant

Harbor Girl / 1989 / Gans 1
Produced by Melanie Monsur and featuring the supporting talents of Gayle Marie, Nina Gerber and other women, this 1989 debut tape contains such humorous originals as "PMS," "Best Girl," and "Coming Out Story," plus the more serious "Lover's Lullaby" and title song. —*Ladyslipper*

● **The Heart of It** / 1991 / Gans 102
Backed by a full band for her 1991 release, this Bay Area singer/songwriter/guitarist/humorist serves up a righteous helping of her original witty, heart-ful, and honest songs. —*Ladyslipper*

Gypsy Heart

Gypsy Heart / Lodestar 003
Known for doing bluegrass from a woman's perspective, this Georgia ensemble consists of Louisa Branscomb (harmony vocals, banjo, mandolin, lead and rhythm guitar) and Kathleen Hatfield (lead and harmony vocals, rhythm guitar), with Dede Vogt, Sally Brooks, and Al Pieper. Featured here are 9 originals by Louisa, including "Steel Rails" (later covered on Alison Krauss' 1991 Grammy winner *I've Got That Old Time Feelin*'). —*Ladyslipper*

Pam Hall

● **Honey on My Lips** / 1992 / Fabulous 303
This sultry-voiced album from Mississippi's own features songs filled with love, feminist insight, and woman-power. Whether it be blues, rock or ballads, taste a little *Honey on My Lips*—nothing could be sweeter. ... (Her voice has been compared to Joan Armatrading's.) Brilliantly produced by June Millington. —*Ladyslipper*

Bonnie Hayes

● **Good Clean Fun** / 1982 / Slash 112
Bonnie's an S.F. Bay Area rock icon—writing for the likes of Huey Newton, and performing regularly with her band, Wild Combo. She's got light, saucy vocals, and rollicking good-time rock & roll, San Francisco style—plus a habit of writing infectious pop melodies infused with fun lyrics. —*Ladyslipper*

Susan Herrick

Her 2-1/2-octave range voice is equally comfortable with haunting whispers and resonant power. Her melodies innovatively blend folk, jazz, and pop styles, and the words that she writes offer the revolutionary gifts of personal revelation and precious insight. She is Susan Herrick, singer-songwriter, guitarist, pianist, drummer, and sacred healer.

In 1985, Susan received a B.Sc. degree in music therapy, with emphasis on classical voice and composition. While establishing a private practice as a music therapist, she toured her first independent album, *Loving Me*, an acoustic collection that reached thousands of listeners. On the heels of that success came multiple challenges: the breakup of a seven-year relationship, and the recalling of sexual abuse. Fortified by self-healing, Susan released her second recording, *Truth & the Lie*, in 1991. It was issued on the Watchfire label, which Susan cofounded with her partner Jessie Cocks. —*Laura Post*

★ **Truth & The Lie** / 1991 / Watchfire 1

A remarkable recording from a remarkable artist and performer. On this album, she sings original songs about the childhood sexual abuse she suffered, and about the discovery and healing process she has undergone as an adult. ... Her lyrics are full of depth and grace; her voice is tender yet strong, her harmonies are sweet; and the production is excellent. —*Ladyslipper*

Loving Me / 1991 / Susan Herrick 1
Her debut folk recording. While not specifically dealing with recovery issues, there is a strong healing theme—not surprising from a music therapist. —*Ladyslipper*

Helen Hooke

Helen Hooke was first known in her 1970s incarnation, as the inspired fiddler for the country/feminist/rock touring band Deadly Nightshade. While Olivia and Redwood were just beginning, Deadly Nightshade released two albums (*The Deadly Nightshade* and *F&W*) on the RCA label. The group received press in *Rolling Stone, The New York Times,* and *Ms.* Magazine as harbingers of feminism. Deadly Nightshade played alongside such feminist luminaries as Bella Abzug and Gloria Steinem, at gatherings of groups like NOW.

In the mid 1980s, after several more bands and managers oriented towards national distribution, Hooke decided to put her next album independently: *Verse-Ability* (Montana Blake Productions, 1988). She was pleased with her involvement in the music from beginning to end, and was drawn to the women's music and culture circuit in which such independent production is possible. She appeared at the 1991 Michigan Womyn's Music Festival, and at the 1991 Association of Women's Music and Culture (AWMAC) annual conference. Hooke recently released her new album, *Your Body's a Rocket* (Montana Blake Productions, 1992). —*Laura Post*

● **Verse-Ability** / 1988 / Montana Blake 1001
The spirit and sound of the groundbreaking '70s feminist rock group *Deadly Nightshade* is alive and well, and dwelling in the music of this former member. Helen puts forth some of her multi-instrumental best on this self-produced 1988 release, blending electric violin, guitar, synthesizer, accordian, drums and percussion. The songs take on a personal, heartfelt nature, and are testimony to her "Live in the moment" attitude. —*Ladyslipper*

Pat Humphries

○ **Same Rain** / Moving Forward 360
Pat's the kind of songwriter you stumble upon very infrequently—one with the ability to anthemize common struggles and triumphs. This album represents seven years of work, "most of it internal." She sings, in a clear, steady voice—and often in lovely self-harmonies—songs that name us, for all our differences, as beings all washed by the same rain. —*Ladyslipper*

Jasmine

○ **Wild Strings** / Icebergg 217
...It is magnificent, intelligent, absolutely a pleasure. The duo is now a trio (Carol and Michelle have been joined by Lydia Ruffin), and their awesome harmonies are even fuller. They have sustained their incredible powerhouse energy, plus strength in lyrica, rhythm, melody. Mostly original material; produced by ace Terry Garthwaite, and recorded with a full band. —*Ladyslipper*

Justina & Joyce

● **So Strong** / 1991 / HSP 101
Rich, dark timbres and sweet harmonies characterize the magic that this duo works; each song rings with an uncommon emotional depth and vocal beauty—not to mention gorgeous acoustic instrumentation and exquisitely clear recording quality. —*Ladyslipper*

Connie Kaldor

Vocals / Women's
Kaldor is from Alberta, and is one of the main figures of the contemporary Canadian singer/songwriter community. —*Richard Meyer*

One of These Days / 1980 / Coyote 1317
The voice of this Canadian singer/songwriter is exceptionally fine and strong on this release. —*Ladyslipper*

○ **Gentle of Heart** / Oak Street/Dino 019
A 1989 release of original songs, infused with this Canadian artist's prairie-derived independence and sense of spaciousness. Performed in her magnificently deep, emotive, resonant voice. —*Ladyslipper*

○ **Moonlight Grocery** / Redwood 8504
A late '84 release by one of our favorite singer/songwriters. Includes "Maria's Place," the very feminist "Get Back the Night," "Talk Without Speaking," "Caught in the Crossfire," and more. —*Ladyslipper*

○ **Wood River** / Coyote 9101
Subtitled *Home Is Where the Heart Is,* this beautiful, haunting collection of Connie's songs from the Canadian prairies has finally captured the warmth and emotion of the artist's live show. It contains new material as well as her classics. —*Ladyslipper*

Kitka

○ **Kitka** / Kitka 1
Kitka (pronounced Keet-kuh) is a nine-woman choral group from the San Francisco Bay Area that specializes in the vocal music of Eastern Europe. While three of the tunes have instrumental accompaniment (cello, cimbalom, flute and recorder), the other seventeen are sung a capella—as solos, duets, or quartets, or by the full choir. ... Kitka has delivered a spiritual album of masterful renditions of traditional and contemporary Eastern European vocal music. —*Backroads Music/Heartbeats*

Lisa Koch

● **Colorblind Blues** / Tongueinchic 1
A.k.a one-fourth of the fabulous *Venus Envy* band, or half of the comedy duo Dos Fallopia, former *Fabulous Dyketone* Ms. Koch ("Coke") has put together a smashing first solo release. Great production, vocals, lyrics—shades of June Millington meets Kate Clinton! —*Ladyslipper*

Lynn Lavner

I'd Rather Be Cute / 1986 / Bent 81369
This Jewish lesbian from Brooklyn performs humorous material in a cabaret style, from "A Mother's Lament" ("Please, Lynnie, don't wear leather pants to the seder/and please cover your tattoo at the seder") to "First Dyke On *Dynasty.*" —*Ladyslipper*

● **You Are What You Wear** / 1988 / Bent 33176
Yet another funny album from the dyke queen of cabaret camp. —*Ladyslipper*

Zoe Lewis

● **Soup Kitchen ""Swing"** / 1991 / Zoe Lewis 1
With a pleasantly high-range voice, given to leaping into jazz inflections at the drop of a hat; a lighthearted sense of humor, crossed with a social consciousness; and a great band (guitar, sax, bass, percussion, fiddle)—Zoe throws quite the bash! —*Ladyslipper*

Libana

Group
Libana is a unique feminist performing group, interpreting ethnic and spiritual woman-themed music from around the globe. They have performed at educational institutions, folk/ethnic events, and women's music and culture festivals across North America for 15 years.

Libana was formed in 1979 when 25 women came together to explore women's music from different genres. At the time, the Women's Music scene, proper, was flourishing, but these 25 women believed that their approach would be different. They wanted to look cross-culturally at the music of, by, and about women.

Over the years, the group of 25 has been reduced to eight—although five of the current eight have been performing together since Libana's founding. The group has recorded and released seven albums, including one on the feminist Ladyslipper label (*Fire Within*), and their latest two (*Sojourns* and *Borderland*) on the world-music Shanachie label. Despite these changes, Libana's music has been steadily defined by its cross-cultural focus. —*Laura Post*

Handed Down / 1985 / Spinning 001
On this 1985 tape, they sing songs from Eastern Europe and the Middle East, with some accompaniment from instruments such as oud, violin, and dumbek. The sound is at times reminiscent of the Bulgarian Women's Choir. —*Backroads Music/Heartbeats*

A Circle Is Cast / 1986 / Spinning 002
This 1986 release is a departure from the feminist ensemble's previous recordings. It highlights Libana's spiritual basis of celebrating community and reverence—reverence for the Earth, for the nuances of seasons, for the solitude of meditation, and for the Divine within. —*Ladyslipper*

Sojourns / 1991 / Shanachie 67001
Sojourns features tunes mainly from the Balkans and the Middle East, sung choral-style with joy and conviction, to the accompaniment of guitars, violins, dumbeks and other instruments...a lively and captivating work, full of all kinds of pleasures for fans of choral and/or world music. —*Backroads Music/Heartbeats*

● **Fire Within** / 1993 / Ladyslipper 108
The latest release from this eleven-woman vocal group again offers a bouquet of traditional tunes from around the world. Notably absent are any songs from the Balkans and the Middle East, which have been heavily featured on previous albums. Instead, there are 18 pieces from countries as geographically and culturally diverse as Spain and Hawaii, Sweden and Japan, Kenya and the United States—as well as a couple of original tunes. —*Backroads Music/Heartbeats*

○ **Libana, A Women's Chorus, Vol. 1** / Libana 1
Formed in 1979, this ensemble researches and performs vocal, instrumental, and folk-dance music that celebrates women's traditions from a variety of cultures through the ages. Their first tape, recorded live in concert, celebrates women and nature with primarily Eastern European/Balkan music, plus a little early medieval music and contemporary folk. —*Ladyslipper*

Libana, A Women's Chorus, Vol. 2 / Libana 2
Fourteen women's voices celebrate women's work and women's spirit, with songs and dances of Celtic, Jewish, and Slavic origins. Recorded partly in concert, partly in studio. —*Ladyslipper*

Laura Love

Over the past several years, Laura Love has become quite acclaimed in the Northwest music scene as an unparalleled vocalist, bassist, and songwriter.

Love's style is a synthesis of inner-city funk with a folkish sensibility. One of a musician's most difficult tasks is to find an apt label for her music; in Love's case, the descriptions "folk/funk," "African/Appalachian," and "House/Celtic" have been bandied about. Whatever you choose to call it, Love's original music is at once fresh, def, and rooted in tradition.

Although a popular headliner in her own right, she has opened for John Lee Hooker, Lyle Lovett, Bo Diddley, Karla Bonoff, and Elayne Boosler. She has also been invited to join the lineup at a number of folk and eclectic music festivals.

Born in Lincoln, Nebraska, Laura Love began her career at the age of 16, singing jazz and pop standards at the Nebraska State Penitentiary. Since then, Love has played in a blues/grunge outfit, and in a duo, a trio, and the funny feminist foursome, Venus Envy. Love has released three albums: *Menstrual Hut* (1989), *Z Therapy* (1990), and *Pangaea* (1993), all on her own label, Octoroon Biography. —*Laura Post*

● **Menstrual Hut** / 1989 / Octoroon Biography 1
Laura identifies strongly as a lesbian/feminist woman of color, and her material reflects this consciousness—both her original songs and some carefully selected traditional folksongs. To her own guitar accompaniment, she presents—with a voice laden with depth and texture—her songs "I'm Your Daughter's Lover," "Listen To Me" (a tribute to Native American women), and "W-I-M-M-I-N." Other highlights are a spectacular rendition of the traditional "Wayfaring Stranger," plus the title song and more. —*Ladyslipper*

○ **Z Therapy** / 1990 / Octoroon Biography 2
Laura's second release is a beautifully produced follow-up to her debut, on which she is accompanied by—among others—the Therapy Sisters and Z-Helene Christopher from the Z-Band. Except for her marvelous rendition of "Swing Low, Sweet Chariot," all the songs are originals. Several songs impart a world beat, with instrumentation such as cymbals, dumbek, congas, and bongos; plus Laura on acoustic and bass guitars. —*Ladyslipper*

○ **Pangaea** / 1992 / Octoroon Biography 3
Fabulous, kickin', polished, vibrant—all these words exemplify this self-produced 1992 release. ... With more than a passing resemblance to Nanci Griffith's emotional warmth, this is an artist with clear vision, lots of ideas, a great band, and a marvelous set of pipes. —*Ladyslipper*

Deidre McCalla

Vocals, Guitar
This urban singer/songwriter has been said to combine the delivery of Nina Simone with the lyrical insightfulness and social commentary of Phil Ochs. McCalla came of age in New York City during the McDougal Street pop/folk heyday, when artists sought to give musical expression to the nation's anger and unrest.

Transplanted now to a new home base in Northern California, McCalla continues to tour across the country, her travels having made her an articulate, contemporary troubadour. She plainly admits what every rocker knows: that life begins with an acoustic guitar.

McCalla's first two albums, *Don't Doubt It* and *With A Little Luck*, have received numerous New York Music Award nominations. Her most recent LP, *Everyday Heroes & Heroines*, was produced by Teresa Trull, and featured contributions from Mike Marshall, Linda Tillery, Bonnie Hayes, and others. —*Laura Post*

★ **Everyday Heroes & Heroines** / 1992 / Olivia 965
This 1992 release—beautifully produced by Teresa Trull, and Deidre's best to date!—again demonstrates this singer/songwriter's exceptional talent with bright, energetic material. —*Ladyslipper*

○ **Don't Doubt It** / Olivia 965
Very hip, very contemporary, very danceable. Deidre's unique sound is clearly brought out by the superb production skills of Teresa Trull. If you like Cris Williamson or Teresa Trull, you're sure to like Deidre. —*Ladyslipper*

○ **With a Little Luck** / Olivia 953
Her second album is even better than her first—from the irrepressible celebratory exuberance of "All Day Always" (bound to become a classic), to her pursuit of a woman in "Would You Like to Dance," to a vocal duet with Teresa Trull that's just too hot for words. —*Ladyslipper*

Carol McComb

Vocals / Folk
McComb is a California singer/songwriter whose music ranges from country to folk. —*Chip Renner*

○ **Tears into Laughter** / 1989 / Kaleidoscope 41
McComb's album is very compelling. The sad "Faded Dresden Blues," about the effects of Alzheimer's disease on her grandmother, touches the soul. She is backed by Nina Gerber (Kate Wolf's guitar player) on acoustic guitar, Sally Van Meter (Good Ol' Persons) on dobro, Laurie Lewis on vocals, and Barbra Higbie on piano. —*Chip Renner*

June Millington

V/G/COM
Back in 1969, when June Millington began her career as lead guitarist for Fanny—a mainstream all-women band—she recognized that mainstream music was largely inaccessible to women. During the five years that Fanny was active in the 1970s, few women made significant establishment recordings.

Through four successful albums with Warner Brothers (*Fanny*, *Charity Ball*, *Fanny Hill*, and *Mother's Pride*), June Millington and Fanny served notice to the rock world that women could do more than simply sing—they could also write and play rock & roll passionately. Yet there were hardly any women technicians supporting either live tours or the studio recording process; and women booking agents, managers, and promoters were few and far between.

Then, in 1975, Millington was asked to play on Cris Williamson's seminal album, *The Changer and the Changed*. For Millington, it had been a leap from fooling on the ukulele as a child in her native Manila, to rock fluency in California; it was a greater leap from mainstream fame to "Women's Music."

Resonating with the politics of women making music, Millington established her own label, Fabulous Records, and released several albums: *Heartsong* (1981), *Running* (1983), and *One World, One Heart* (1988). Then Millington began to conceive of mentorship for women pursuing music and allied professions.

The Institute for the Musical Arts (IMA) was born out of Millington's desire to empower women, especially women of color, in their pursuit of careers in the field of music. It aims to bridge the gap between women in mainstream music and those in "Wwomen's Nusic," and attempts to promote social justice and equality within the music industry and in other social and cultural spheres.

Millington's idea immediately drew some of the most experienced women in the music industry to IMA's advisory boards: Bonnie Raitt, Linda Tillery, Teresa Trull, and Cris Williamson. Today, IMA is a nonprofit, multicultural national teaching and performing-arts organization based in the San Francisco Bay Area. Through classes, apprenticeships, and work experience in live performance and studio recording, IMA students learn essential skills in such areas as artist management, concert lighting/sound, entertainment law, instrument/voice development, marketing, music composition, promotion, sound technology, stage management, video production, and recording/engineering. IMA has nurtured several new albums by up-and-coming artists, released on the Fabulous Label. —*Laura Post*

Heartsong / 1981 / Fabulous 929

Running / 1983 / Fabulous 101

★ **One World, One Heart** / 1988 / Fabulous 202

Melanie Monsur

Melanie Monsur wants to be known as a composer. Perhaps best recognized for her supple piano accompaniments for The Washington Sisters, June Millington, Ronnie Gilbert, Cheryl Wheeler, Gayle Marie, and Sylvia Kohan, Melanie has also released two albums of original music, *Dragonfly* and *Opus K4*.

Melanie learned piano in the lessons that she and her siblings all took. In adolescence, Melanie rebelled against rigorous piano practice, and took up the guitar. After earning a B.A. in music theory and composition from the University of Massachusetts at Amherst, Melanie got to know folksinger Cheryl Wheeler, an association that helped her decide to pursue a performing career.

Although Melanie had played her first live gig while she was in the 8th grade, and had played coffeehouses while in high school, she says that her professional performing career really started when she joined forces with two men, and scrambled between gigs for several years. In 1983, the lure of working with other women musicians drew Melanie to the San Francisco Bay Area.

Melanie recorded her first album, *Dragonfly*, in 1987—teaming with a woman engineer, and working with a low budget and no producer. Melanie's second album, *Opus K4* (the name of a synthesizer), was recorded live at June Millington's Institute for the Musical Arts (IMA), in Bodega, California.

In 1991, Melanie moved from the San Francisco Bay Area to New Mexico, seeking time and space to write. Since then, Melanie has amassed a body of new Mexican-influenced, instrumental piano tunes. In addition, she currently travels monthly to New York to perform Persian-influenced music for students of the philospher Gurdjieff. —*Laura Post*

● **Opus K-4** / Melanie Monsur Music 2

Her second recording features her all-instrumental compositions, performed on her Kawai K-4 digital synthesizer. The result is a captivating blend of styles and moods—both contemplative and rhythmic, melodic and just plain lovely. —*Ladyslipper*

Musica Femina

Group

● **Returning the Muse to Music** / 1989 / Lilac 3

Janna and Kristan blend lovely classical and new age sounds by historical and contemporary women composers on this 1989 release. Featured are a commissioned piece by Therese Edell, and compositions by: Theresa Clark; Isabella Leonarda, the early Baroque Italian nun composer; and Maria Theresia von Paradis, of 18th century Vienna. There are also a few by Janna, including "Tremolo for Kristan," a gorgeous guitar solo. Demonstrates the

strength, beauty, and diversity of acoustic instrumental music by women. —*Ladyslipper*

More Flute & Guitar Music by Women / Musica Femina 2

Upholding their commitment to insure that women's contributions to music not be lost or ignored, Kristan Aspen (once flutist of Izquierda Ensemble) and Janna MacAuslan (once Meg Christian's guitar teacher) record and perform works by classical and contemporary women composers. —*Ladyslipper*

Holly Near

Vocals / Women's

Holly Near is one of the most respected singers of our time. To her legion of fans, she is a consummate entertainer who retains her integrity amidst the rise and fall of fads in the music industry. She has recorded 15 albums, selling well over 1.5 million copies. More concerned with peacemaking than with hitmaking, Near's uncompromising vision has led her to defend originally unpopular causes. For her achievements, she was named Woman of the Year by *Ms.* Magazine.

Near has relentlessly pushed forward, exploring new genres. Recently she appeared in the critically acclaimed feature film, *Dog Fight*, with Lili Taylor and River Phoenix, and on the popular television show, *L.A. Law*. She also appeared as herself in the independent film, *Emma and Elvis*.

Near recently added author and playwright to her list of accomplishments. Her autobiography, *Fire in the Rain...Singer in the Storm* (William Morrow), details her life as an artist and activist, and was recently published in paperback after selling 30,000 hardback copies. Her first children's book, based on her inspiring song, "The Great Peace March," was published by Henry Holt.

Near has also written a musical "docudrama," which she staged in Los Angeles with her sister Timothy. It ran through the fall of 1992 as part of the prestigious Mark Taper Forum's season. Her video releases include a 30-minute mix of live concert footage and candid background banter, and a two-hour video autobiography that includes over 20 cuts of her music.

Near got her start in a local talent show at the age of seven. After high school, Near attended UCLA, where she was "discovered" and immediately put to work in film and television. She appeared in George Roy Hill's film *Slaughterhouse 5*, in the film *Minnie and Moscowitz*, and in the Broadway production of "Hair." She was also seen on such popular television shows as *All in the Family, Room 222*, and *Mod Squad*.

Throughout the '70s and '80s, Near worked for peace and feminism. She has a passion for Central and Latin America, and was one of only a handful of North American performers who performed in war-torn El Salvador. In the last 20 years, she has toured the world as an ambassador of peace and hope.

One of Near's greatest accomplishments is the founding of Redwood Cultural Work. Started 20 years ago as a record label that supported artists who were otherwise marginalized from the music industry, it has since become a leading multicultural, nonprofit arts organization. —*Laura Post*

○ **A Live Album** / 1974 / Redwood 3700

Her 1974 classic second album, which captures the dynamic quality of her performances, is now back in print. Contains many of the best-loved songs about women. —*Ladyslipper*

○ **You Can Know All I Am** / 1976 / Redwood 3600

Powerful, sometimes playful, and sometimes painful look at the conditions of many kinds of women: in prison, organizing in factories, initiating relationships. More produced than her previous albums, but Holly's voice still sparkles through. —*Ladyslipper*

Imagine My Surprise! / 1979 / Redwood 401

A playful, quirky feminist record with elements of jazz, country, and even a little bit of Broadway. —*Bruce Eder*

Speed of Light / 1982 / Redwood 403

A lively, snappy followup to *Imagine My Surprise!*, with extra pop wrinkles. —*Bruce Eder*

Journeys / 1984 / Redwood 405

A handy retrospective, covering Near's first six albums. —*Bruce Eder*

☆ **Don't Hold Back** / 1987 / Redwood 413

Near's party album, a thoroughly pleasing collection of love songs, with guest appearances by Bonnie Raitt and Kenny Loggins. —*Bruce Eder*

Watch Out! / 1989 / Redwood 406
Here she collaborates with the West Virginia folk and traditional quartet Trapezoid—well-known for their Appalachian instruments and styles—and so enters yet another musical genre, acoustic folk music. —*Ladyslipper*

Singer in the Storm—Life/Music of.. / 1990 / Chameleon 74832
This live recording defines what Near is about. Divided between love songs and political statements, it is spirited and well-executed. —*Bruce Eder*

★ **Fire in the Rain** / 1993 / Redwood 402
Offering musical highlights from Near's autobiographical play of the same title,this is in effect a compilation of some of Near's best work. This ranges from standards like "I Can't Give You Anthing But Love" and "If I Loved You," to feminist and lesbian anthems like "Started Out Fine" and "Simply Love"—dating back 20 years and re-recorded. She is in wonderful voice, and accompanied by pianist John Bucchino and occasional strings. This is a good way to sample Near's warm, political, triumphant style. —*William Ruhlmann*

Sky Dances / Redwood 8902
A folky, intimate, and emotion-filled 1989 release that features Holly at her absolute best—singing songs by such contemporary writers as Ferron, Bernice Johnson Reagon, Ruben Blades, Phil Ochs, and Malvina Reynolds. —*Ladyslipper*

○ **Lifeline [with Ronnie Gilbert]** / Redwood 404
A majestic collaboration of generations and spirits. In the '40s and '50s, Ronnie was one of the Weavers: a folk group that loudly voiced the progressive and humanist concerns of the American people, until the blacklist virtually silenced them; and that won the hearts and devotion of a huge following... . This is a live recording from the Great American Music Hall in San Francisco. Styles encompass Broadway, folk, jazz, and Gospel. —*Ladyslipper*

○ **Singing with You [with Ronnie Gilbert]** / Redwood 410
Both studio and live recordings from this inimitable duo. Includes a medley of old favorites ("Imagine My Surprise," "Something About the Women," and more); Ruth Pelham's sweet, touching song from the perspective of a child whose parents have divorced, "I Cried"; Ferron's "Kid's Song" (from her out-of-print record *Ferron Backed Up*); and a variety of others that relate to social issues, friendship and love. —*Ladyslipper*

Faith Nolan

Vocals, bass, guitar, harmonica, tambourine / Women's
Faith Nolan was born in Nova Scotia, a fifth-generation Canadian in a predominantly Black community whose cultural roots resemble those in the Southern United States. As a Black activist from a musical family, Nolan sings about topics like Canadian Black history and heritage, feminism, and workers' and children's rights. Her musical abilities are enhanced by her educational background in theatre, opera, and writing, and by her commitment to community work.

Faith Nolan is a singer and composer who plays folk guitar sprinkled with funk and reggae; who plays slide guitar, tambourine, and harmonica in the earliest blues traditions; and who speaks the cultural language of African-North American music: spirituals, gospel, jazz. Nolan's concern for common people is articulated in her three albums: *Africville, Sistership,* and *Freedom To Love* (Redwood Records, 1989). Faith Nolan finds her strength in music, and her music finds its strength in her acutely sensitive awareness of issues that are made invisible and rarely addressed in mainstream music. —*Laura Post*

● **Freedom to Love** / 1989 / Redwood 8903
One of Faith's best releases! Includes an original rock anthem, "I Black Woman"; an incredible rendition of Billie Holiday's "Strange Fruit"; the title song, which equates homophobic laws with slavery; Ma Rainey's lesbian song "Prove It On Me"; and more, each with a clear and inspiring message of liberation. Backed by some of Vancouver's finest musicians. —*Ladyslipper*

○ **Africville** / Multi-cultural Women 11161
Focusing on Black women, historically and presently, Faith's original songs give voice to issues while instilling a sense of strength, through a variety of styles—blues, jazz, reggae, funk, African

drumming... . The title song is about the relocation of the largest Black community in Canada. All accompanying musicians are Black Canadians. —*Ladyslipper*

○ **Sistership** / Multi-cultural Women 11162
This album focuses on the struggles and contributions of Black women. Some songs relate to sexuality and lesbianism ("She's Sixteen": "...she is young, Black, and gifted and gay..."). Others relate to various political struggles. ... Faith plays almost every instrument on the album: electric bass, 12-string and 6-string guitars, slide guitar, harmonica, and tambourine. —*Ladyslipper*

Rashida Oji

● **Big Big Woman** / 1991 / Fabulous 404
This 1992 release has been described as honest, playful, innovative, intense, powerful...and as "bleeding, crying, and laughing all at the same time." Oji combines the honesty of women's stories with contemporary music, drawing from spiritual, folk, and rap. Her deliveries range from the a cappella "Vyry's Song" (about an enslaved black woman), to acoustic ballads, to dance tunes recorded with a full band, such as title cut. Also includes the notable "No Way," about the pain of incest and battery. —*Ladyslipper*

Ova

● **Possibilities** / 1981 / Stroppy Cow 444
This 1985 release is strong and tender—full of love for women, our possibilities and sexualities; and full of love for the earth, as well as despair over its abuse... . Strong on harmonies and rhythms, using a variety of African and South American instruments, plus drum machine. ... This collective (4 women at this release) produces another very worthwhile album. —*Ladyslipper*

Who Gave Birth to the Universe / 1988 / Stroppy Cow 888
From "Healing Touch" to "Rainforest" to "Political Beings," Jana and Rosemary bring their wide perspective and accomplished musicianship to a variety of concerns and musical styles on this 1988 release. Import. —*Ladyslipper*

Out of Bounds / Stroppy Cow 666
Calm strength is the word that comes to mind when listening to this album. Jana and Rosemary (joined by the Amazon Voices) weave a musically colorful quilt of songs that celebrate and reflect our lives as a whole. Musically diverse, it is simultaneously moving and humorous, and highly recommended. —*Ladyslipper*

Parachute Club

Group
○ **At the Feet of the Moon** / RCA
The overall production and instrumentation is tighter, and highly synthesized, while the lyrics remain political and inspiring. —*Ladyslipper*

● **Wild Zone: Essential Parachute Club** / RCA 17284
This 15-track retrospective contains some of the most incredible, political material this band has ever recorded. —*Ladyslipper*

Phranc

Vocals / Folk-pop
Born in 1959 in Southern California, a Jewish girl attends 13 years of Hebrew School and loves to swim. Who knew that little pigtailed Suzy Gottlieb, who fooled around with the guitar at age nine, was to come out as a lesbian separatist, then a punk rocker, then a radical folksinger named Phranc—effective at dissolving prejudice and barriers, and the only lesbian solo artist to perform to mainstream audiences?

Tracing her lyrical roots to Allan Sherman (she has listened to "My Son The Folksinger" since age five), Phranc has toured with The Smiths and The Pogues; has appeared in the film *The Fall of Western Civilization* with her band, Nervous Gender; has been interviewed for *People* Magazine; and has released three albums: *Folksinger* (1985, Rhino Records), the campy *I Enjoy Being A Girl* (1989, Island Records), and, most recently, *Positively Phranc* (1991, Island Records).

Phranc says the strong foundation of her lesbian youth allowed her to make the transition between radical separatist and affirmative lesbian missionary. Experiencing consistent, positive, role models; living and working within a disciplined, politically thoughtful collective; and being shown personal tolerance—all cultivated the inner reserve and confidence necessary for confronting, and thriving within, the straight world. Though Phranc's early path often was unproductive—sometimes wild and occasionally self-destructive—she nonetheless retained a firm commitment to coming out and staying out, with her own opinions as well as with her lesbian identity. —*Laura Post*

Folksinger / 1985 / Island 846358
Her debut album of modern acoustic folk with a rock edge. Voice, guitar, and harmonica. —*AMG*

★ **I Enjoy Being a Girl** / 1989 / Island 842579
Her pop breakthrough, with songs like "Take Off Your Swastiska." She doesn't mince words, and as with the great folksingers of the past, her music is just as good as the message. Politics infused with humor and irony. A great album cover! —*AMG*

Positively Phranc / 1991 / Island 848282
This is harder and more electric, with a song about Billy Tipton and a wonderful a cappella cover of the Beach Boys classic "Surfer Girl." —*AMG*

Ranch Romance

Group / Country

● **Western Dream** / 1990 / Sugar Hill 3799
From several opening dates for k.d. lang to their 1990 debut women's-festival performances, this four-woman trad-but-rad band has brought their flawless harmonies, driving rhythm, hot instrumental work, and wild yodeling to thousands of new fans around the country! Perfect for two-stepping, or any other partner dancing you'd care to do, as well as feet-stomping and finger-snapping. —*Ladyslipper*

○ **Blue Blazes** / 1991 / Sugar Hill 3794
This 1991 release is a hot mix of "regressive country" originals, incorporating acoustic honky-tonk, rockabilly and swing. Characterized by thoughtful original lyrics, entertaining music and great arrangements for guitar, fiddle, accordian, and bass, it has been described as "k.d. lang and Patsy Cline meet Bob Wills." —*Ladyslipper*

Bernice Johnson Reagon

Contemporary

● **River of Life / Harmony: One** / 1972 / Flying Fish 70411
Reagon studied her concept of harmony and "what voices are supposed to do" in the Gospel listening lab of the Black congregation; she developed it with Sweet Honey in the Rock; and she now offers its mature incarnation in this one-woman, multi-tracked choral masterpiece. *River of Life* presents Reagon's interpretations of nine traditional gospel spirituals and Civil Rights songs (including "Since I Laid My Burden Down"), and three originals. The album includes Reagon's notes about the personal significance of each piece. — *Erin Ryan, Roundup newsletter*

○ **The Songs Are Free** /
This is the soundtrack from the video of the same title, in which Bernice traces the history of communal singing and the repertoire rooted in the Black church. She follows this repertoire from songs of resistance, courage, and pride to songs of determination and faith. She also explores the songs' roles in Black life, from the Underground Railroad period through the Civil Rights movement and into the present. Includes dialogue, instruction, and performance—solo and with both the SNCC Freedom Singers and Sweet Honey in the Rock. —*Ladyslipper*

Toshi Reagon

Vocals, guitar / Folk

Toshi is the daughter of Bernice Johnson Reagon (from Sweet Honey in the Rock). She plays guitar and delivers beautiful soul-laden vocals. —*Chip Renner*

Demonstrations / 1985 / T&R 582
Not only a "strong voice in a new generation of Black women's music"—a really *fine* voice, fine song writing, and stylistically distinctive musicianship from this woman of diverse and growing talents. Toshi plays electric lead and rhythm guitars, acoustic guitar, drums, and bass, and does lead and background vocals. Co-producer with Toshi is her mom, Bernice Reagon of Sweet Honey in the Rock. The folky and rock & roll-ish numbers here are equally strong. —*Ladyslipper*

Justice / 1992 / Flying Fish 526
The material here is mostly original, though she does include a Georgia Sea Island song, and Sting's "Walking in Your Footsteps." With her famous mother, Bernice Johnson Reagon of Sweet Honey in the Rock, as well as Casselberry-Dupree and Annette Aguilar. —*Ladyslipper*

Ann Reed

By Request / 1992 / Aml 11006
This 1992 release is just what it says: material that Ann has issued by request of her fans. Ann, with her glorious voice and 12-string, is accompanied by Joan Griffith on bass and 6-string. Includes "Lisa's Song," "Every Long Journey," "Styrofoam," and more. —*Ladyslipper*

Hole in the Day / 1993 / A Major Label 11008
This 12-song, 1993 release features her thrilling brown-sugar-and-molasses voice, that damn-fine guitar playing, and, of course, her wry love songs. —*Ladyslipper*

● **Just Can't Stop** / Red House 11
Ann is a fine 12-string guitarist, with a fluid Fahey/Kottke style. Here she plays with a rhythm section, including several women—sax, keyboards, bass, drums, and percussion fill out her original tunes. Includes one instrumental, "For Jane"; some jazzy tunes; and a song written for Ann Bancroft, the first woman to reach the North Pole by dog sled (in May 1986). —*Ladyslipper*

○ **Talk to Me** / Red House 24
Ann's back, with some great songwriting and guitar-playing. With the same ensemble and producer as *Just Can't Stop,* she turns out originals that are melodically strong, exciting, and romantic yet solid...intelligently dealing with interpersonal relationships. —*Ladyslipper*

○ **Back & Forth** / Aml 11005
This contains the best from her first releases *Carpedium* and *Room and Board,* such as "The Woman You'd Love," "Jessie," and "Jaynie"; plus three new songs: "Push the River," "What Made You Love Her," and "Where the Hell Is Boston?" —*Ladyslipper*

Road of the Heart / Aml 291
...Compelling, introspective, and all-acoustic, in a folky/jazzy/bluesy vein. —*Ladyslipper*

Reel World String Band

Group

● **Appalachian Wind** / 1990 / Flying Fish 517
This all-woman band celebrates their tenth anniversary of making music together with this 1990 album, featuring several additional female musicians as guest performers. They alternate lead vocals on this great selection of songs—several original, and several about women. —*Ladyslipper*

Rhiannon

Vocals / Jazz

Best known through her ten years as vocalist with the jazz group Alive!, Rhiannon blends classical drama with multicultural street theater and scat phrasings, in her innovative genre of jazz storytelling. Born into the homogeneity of the Dakotas, Rhiannon was lured to California by burgeoning lesbian passions. She received support from a mostly-dyke audience that came to hear her double-bill with Helen Hooke's group Deadly Nightshade, and was subsequently introduced to the world of women's music and culture in 1975, at the First National Women's Music Festival in Champaign, Illinois. Alive! formed soon after, going on to wow jazz clubs across the U.S. for 10 years.

Most recently, Rhiannon has taught voice; has released two cassettes for voice training; has toured with her moving and intensely personal one-woman show, *Toward Home* (a version of which was recently released on cassette); and has joined Voicestra, a multicultural, mixed-gender, gay-and-straight, all-vocal ensemble orchestrated by longtime friend and collaborator, Bobby McFerrin. —*Laura Post*

☆ **Toward Home** / 1991 / Ladyslipper 202
With material by Betsy Rose, Janet Small, and Carolyn Brady, Rhiannon shows her stuff. Accompanied by Nina Gerber and Barbara Borden, she displays her range and diversity. —*AMG*

Libby Roderick

○ **If You See a Dream** / 1990 / Turtle Island 1001
For fans of music that delivers a message, the voice of this Alaska feminist is not to be missed. Her acoustic sound accents vital and beautiful lyrics in songs inspired by the many struggles of women. Perhaps most notable is "Rosa"—a tribute to women of color in general, and to Audre Lorde, Winnie Mandela, Alice Walker, Fannie Lou Hamer, and Rosa Parks in particular... . An excellent debut album. —*Ladyslipper*

● **Thinking Like a Mountain** / 1991 / Turtle Island 1002
This exquisitely produced 1991 release from Alaska's feminist phenomenon contains 11 original songs that Libby often performs in concert. —*Ladyslipper*

Rude Girls

Group

Rude Awakening / Flying Fish 424
Dedicated to rude girls everywhere, and to their awakening, this lively women's acoustic quartet presents a fine debut folk album. High on heart-breaking harmonies, stringed instruments, and original tunes... . Excellent production by Cathy Fink; back-up by Abby Newton, Marcy Marxer and other women. —*Ladyslipper*

Carla Sciaky

● **The Undertow** / 1991 / Green Linnet 2103

Anne Seale

● **Sex for Breakfast** / 1991 / Anne Seale 1
What an odd, *different* sort of tape! Frankly lesbian lyrics, with a 1930s lounge sound and Allan Sherman-type humor and rhyming... her original songs include "Body Hair," "I Get a Rash from Relationships," "Your Women's Bookstore," "Provincetown," and "A Lesbian Cemetery." —*Ladyslipper*

Michelle Sell

New Age, adult alternative, chamber jazz

● **Circle 'Round the Moon: Harp Music** / Moon Circle 1102
Michelle Sell's debut solo release offers something a bit different for lovers of harp music. Rooted in the gracefulness of the classical tradition, Michelle's music offers rich melodies and a wide variety of rhythmic colorings. Five tracks are collaborations with master cellist David Darling, and several other fine musicians also contribute their talents—including Radhika Miller on flute and recorder, Jannine Del Arte on saxophone, and percussionists Tony D'Anna and Kim Atkinson from the group Tokenki. There are a couple of harp solos, but *Circle 'Round the Moon* mostly features tasteful and elegant ensemble playing with crossover appeal. —*Backroads Music/Heartbeats*

She Is

● **Kissing In the Deep End** / 1992 / Lickety-Split 495
Rippling dream of consuming passion...sweet, soft longing...young love...hot funky leather and lace...bubbling cool fun. This is a five-song collection of original women's music by this D.C.-area four-woman band; includes the *Billboard* Magazine award-winning song, "In My Dreams." —*Ladyslipper*

Judith Sloan

● **The Whole K'CUFIN' WORLD** / 1992 / Earsay 002
This 1992 release captures Judith in a selection of live performances replete with her assortment of characters. "Muriel" runs for president, "Belinda" attacks US Foreign Policy, "Jennifer" talks about Japan, "Ethel" gives advice, and the compassion of "Sophie" shines through. With her sharp and insightful social and political commentary, this artist is guaranteed to keep you laughing and thinking, as she explores war, media, sexuality and plastics! —*Ladyslipper,*

Judy Small

○ **Home Front** / 1988 / Redwood 8808
This wonderful folk artist presents a late '88 album of political songs covering a wide range of concerns...Thoughtful and

thought-provoking, Judy is one of the most important songwriters of our time. —*Ladyslipper*

○ **Snapshot** / 1990 / Redwood 9003
This 1990 release, coinciding with a repeat U.S. tour, is a welcome addition to her collection of political and humorous protest songs. If you liked her previous albums, you'll love this one! —*Ladyslipper*

○ **Mothers, Daughters, Wives** / Redwood 3100
The second release from this Australian feminist songster contains stories of everyday life...including the title cut, which charted on Australian radio. (This is the U.S. release of the album released in Australia under the title *Ladies and Gems*.) —*Ladyslipper*

○ **One Voice in the Crowd** / Redwood 8503
Australian feminist and social-protest themes are conveyed through her serious portraits ("A Heroine of Mine") and wry parodies ("The I.P.D."—a male equivalent of the I.U.D.). Includes "The Family Maiden Aunt" from her first Australian release, *A Natural Selection*, and a few songs that decry the power of the U.S. presence—military and otherwise—on the international scene. —*Ladyslipper*

Starhawk

The Way to the Well / Starhawk 1
Utilizing drumming, song, chanting, and visualization, this contemporary guided meditation is subtitled *A Trance Journey for Empowerment*. The title itself refers to accessing the well of power within us all, rather than always searching outside of ourselves for fulfillment. The listener is encouraged to become the protagonist of the story, thus facing an opportunity for transformation. —*Ladyslipper*

Carol Steinel

I'm Dangerous! / Carol L. Steinal 0191
In this 1991 debut album, the songster/comic from Portland tells her own story troubadour-style: that of a self-described "raging, bad-assed dyke." Lots of great queer material, including "Dangerous," and "Old Friends Ain't," a lesbian C&W tune. There is also Steinel's "hate trilogy"—"God Is Love," "Leviticus," and "Dying For Love"— which exposes the hypocrisy of the bible-thumpers (or the "biblical schizophrenia" phenomenon, as she calls it). Recorded live, so it includes her concert commentary and humor as well as audience enthusiam. Steinel accompanies her songs on guitar. —*Ladyslipper*

Suede

Easily Suede / 1988 / Easily Suede 1001
Suede's debut solo album features an intriguing blend of jazz and light rock styles; she communicates everything from a dream for world peace, as in "From a Distance," to the strictly fun and seductive "Doncha Wanna Know (You Got Me Where You Want Me)." Self-produced, with Suede on all vocals, piano, guitar, and trumpet. —*Ladyslipper*

● **Barely Blue** / 1992 / Easily Suede 1002
This long-awaited follow-up to Suede's debut is more jazzy/bluesy in style, and includes several concert favorites ("Sister," "My Foolish Heart"), as well as previously unrecorded works. She interprets two John Bucchino songs—"If I Ever Say I'm Over You" and "Puddle of Love"—as well as "Measure of Sadness," co-written by John Bucchino and Ron Romanovsky. —*Ladyslipper*

Sunny McHale SkyeDancer

Lesbian Nation / Sunny Mchale Skyedancer 9110
You'll appreciate the wry and affirming humor shining through Sunny's lyrics in these 13 songs...her voice is strong and versatile, and her acoustic guitar accompaniment clear and melodic. In songs such as "Got No Need For Scared," "Keep Comin' Out," and "Hummingbird Sweet," she takes the essence of her life as a lesbian and distills it into songs that contain insight and celebration, weave webs of cultural power, shatter shackles of homophobia, and offer unexpected resolutions to daily problems. —*Ladyslipper*

Sweet Honey in the Rock

Group / Women's

These days, the voice as a dominant instrument is finding new favor among music lovers. The group that has been central to this development within the contemporary music scene is a quintet of electrifying vocalists based in Washington, D.C., Sweet Honey in the Rock.

Singing unaccompanied, except for body and hand percussion instruments, this ensemble of African-American women singers has, in 17 years, built a solid international reputation and following. The strength of Sweet Honey lies within its repertoire, rooted in the tradition of African congregational choral style and its many extensions. One hears the moan of blues, the power of early 20th-century Gospel, echoes of the community quartet, and jazz choral vocalizations freshly tinged with church melodic and harmonic runs. A Sweet Honey in the Rock concert is a transforming experience, drenching audiences with harmonies. The rhythms change, leads change, and women dance: it's breathtaking music.

The women of Sweet Honey sing fiercely of being fighters, tenderly of being in love, and knowingly of being women. They take their ever-growing audiences through a complex journey of celebration and struggle, rooted in African-American history.

The concept and leadership of the group rest primarily with Bernice Johnson Reagon, who, as vocal director of the D.C. Black Repertory Theater, founded Sweet Honey in 1973. Reagon began her work as a socially conscious artist in 1961, during Albany, Georgia's Civil Rights Movement campaign. The musical and political groundwork that Reagon sets is constantly expanded by the other singers who join her on Sweet Honey's stages. Twenty African-American women singers have lent their voices over the past 17 years, so that there could be Sweet Honey in the Rock. — *Laura Post*

Sweet Honey in the Rock / 1976 / Flying Fish 70022
This album features original compositions and traditional Gospel music. — *AMG*

B'lieve I'll Run on (See What the End's Gonna Be) / 1978 / Redwood 3500
Second album of a cappella vocals, with a clear Gospel influence and an emphasis on harmonies. Original songs about: women who have loved other women, as mothers, daughters, sisters, lovers; Black women's experiences; and specific Black women of uncommon strength—Sojourner Truth and Fannie Lou Hamer. — *Ladyslipper*

Good News / 1982 / Flying Fish 245
Recorded live in Washington, D.C., in 1981. Includes "Breaths," probably their finest and most breathtaking track ever—a topnotch "circular sharing of historic wisdom, boundless energy and love." — *Ladyslipper*

The Other Side / 1986 / Flying Fish 70366
Sweet Honey addresses a spectrum of issues, with a blend of contemporary, protest, topical, personal and love songs. Includes "Venceremos (We Will Win)," "Mandiacappella" (a vocal improvisation based on West African drum rhythms), Woody Guthrie's "Deportees," and Bernice Reagon's original "Mae Frances." — *Ladyslipper*

★ **Live at Carnegie Hall (Double)** / 1988 / Flying Fish 70106
Probably the group's best showcase, playing to their audience in high spirits and with excellent sound. — *Bruce Eder*

☆ **Breaths** / 1989 / Flying Fish 70105
A CD-only compilation of their best tracks from the Flying Fish label. Over an hour of music. — *AMG*

We All... Everyone of Us / 1989 / Flying Fish 317
These five Black women need and use nothing more than their voices to create music more complete and moving than a full orchestra. This 1983 release includes the favorites "More Than a Paycheck" and "Battle for My Life." Powerful lyrics join intertwining harmonies, to deliver a message that haunts you long after the record stops spinning. — *Ladyslipper*

○ **Feel Something Drawing Me on** / 1989 / Flying Fish 70375
A different album concept from their previous discs, and a unique release. This is an album of sacred music: from Christian Gospel songs sung by congregations in the Deep South and in Liberia, to traditional lullabies, to the West African funeral song "Meyango." Here, Sweet Honey gives voice to many of the root traditions underlying their more contemporary music, and beautifully document the diverse cultural, spiritual, and artistic powers of sacred song. — *Ladyslipper*

○ **In This Land** / Sep. 15, 1992 / Earthbeat! 42522
In the inspired congregational tradition of African American culture, this 1992 album goes straight to the hearts and souls of our lives, sharing truth, tragedy, comfort, outrage, hope, love, healing, solidarity, and wisdom—doing so always at the highest levels of beauty and art. — *Ladyslipper*

Lynn Thomas

● **Courage** / 1992 / Lynn Thomas 1
Using a variety of upbeat styles, and singing with a vocal strength reminiscent of Bette Midler, Lynn pens and performs songs like "Lavender Love," "Best Friend," "Gone Fishing," and the lovely "Conditions." — *Ladyslipper*

Linda Tillery

Vocals / Blues-rock

She shared the stage with John Mayall and Tiny Tim in the early 1970s, before it was fashionable for women to play music alongside of men. Her rock band, The Loading Zone, had released a self-titled album on RCA (1969), and Tillery's debut solo disc, *Sweet Linda Divine* (CBS), came out a year later to enthusiatic reviews and high praise.

Around the time that the Women's Music and Culture movement was getting started, Linda Tillery—Tui to her friends—lent her percussive and vocal skills to albums by Mary Watkins and Teresa Trull. Tillery's own second solo effort, *Linda Tillery,* was released on the Olivia label in 1978. She has since played and/or sang on some 40 albums, collaborating with such female musical powerhouses as June Millington, Deidre McCalla, Barbara Higbie, Margie Adam. Tillery can also be heard on the Olivia Tenth Anniversary Album, *Meg/Cris Live At Carnegie* (1983).

In 1985, Tillery released *Secrets,* on her own 411 label; distributed by Redwood Records, it returned her to center stage. In recent years, she has assembled a large band that plays jazzy, funky blues—and receives repeated standing ovations at Women's Music festivals. Tillery and Skin Tight played at Olivia's 20th anniversary dance, in Oakland, California, in 1993. — *Laura Post*

☆ **Secrets** / Redwood 736
A powerful collection of sultry, potent rock and R&B, driven by Tillery's forceful voice and personality. — *Bruce Eder*

Tofa'ah

● **The Sound of Joyous Song** / Tofa'ah 7
An absolutely gorgeous album by a group of seven women who now live in Jerusalem, Israel, but originally hail from the U.S. and Australia. They combine a variety of musical heritages to create new and original Jewish music, which speaks of individual and collective Jewish struggles and joys. Their instruments are their voices, acoustic and electric guitar, bass, percussion, banjo, flute, and violin. Songs are in Hebrew, with translations enclosed. — *Ladyslipper*

Lights / Tofa'ah 3
A collection of songs exclusively by and for women, beautifully performed by this ensemble from Israel on their third release. Dedicated to awakening and inspiring the Jewish spirit through music, with some of their work focusing on the joys and struggles of Jewish women. Tofa'ah artfully blends voices and instruments: flutes, guitar, harp, clarinet, sax, and more. — *Ladyslipper*

Topp Twins

Group

Lynda and Jools Topp—identical twins, with that eerie twin kinship and an irresistible propensity for finishing each other's sentences—are as different from each other as they are from the stereotypical Kiwi. Together, the Topp Twins are lesbian country & western political-theatrical humorists. Lynda, the more physically solid of the two, has the magnificent yodel. Jools, sparer in size and in conversation, sports a dry sense of humor and comes alive onstage, pacing their musical sets with her guitar.

Raised on a dairy farm on the North Island of New Zealand, Lynda and Jools milked cows from ages five to 15, and obtained the "educational certificates that we needed in order to leave school." Taking inspiration from their mother, who used to sing, and using a guitar given to them by their brother when they were 11, the Topp Twins got their chance to play and sing at a yearly local shindig. Lynda and Jools later moved to Christchurch, the biggest city on the South Island, supporting themselves with blue-collar jobs. They played their first real gig to 300 people there. A women's fundraiser followed, as did skits and theater bits, before their debut tour in 1979. Touring with Helen Caldecott in New Zealand, and with Billy Bragg in England, brought them an eclectic and loyal following. They were voted New Zealand's Entertainers of the Year in 1987. Their commissioned theater show was voted the country's Best T.V. Performance in the same year.

The Topp Twins' un-self-conscious charm, and their sense of fun, have caused audiences to swell around them—across tiny New Zealand, but also across the broader expanses of Australia, Canada, the United States, and the U.K. At the recent National Women's Music Festival in Illinois, the audience liked the Topp Twins' yodeling so much that, following a mainstage appearance, the twins drew a standing-room-only crowd for an after-hours coffeehouse set. —*Laura Post*

○ **No War in My Heart** / 1987 / Topp Twins 29029
Their 1987 album juxtaposes biting political satire with beautiful love songs. Includes "President's Men," "Throw Down Your Guns," "Dolly Parton," "The Queen," "Untouchable Girls," and more. —*Ladyslipper*

● **Hightime** / 1992 / Topp Twins 3
Jools and Lynda Topp, our favorite New Zealand sibling duo, bring their offbeat humor, genetic harmonies, and a unique acoustic guitar sound to this 1992 release. —*Ladyslipper*

Adrienne Tori

● **Find a Way** / 1990 / ABT 226
○ **Brooklyn From the Roof** / A Bongo 519
A fairly spectacular instrumental album for piano and synthesizers, by a virtuosa composer and keyboardist who gained initial exposure as Holly Near's accompanist. ... Each piece has a varied sound and rhythm, keeping the listener's interest active: ...from avant garde to upbeat, to emotional and intense, to mellow and lyrical. —*Ladyslipper*

Lucie Blue Tremblay

Vocals / Folk
Tremblay's music has an intensity that also soothes. This Canadian-born singer/songwriter's bilingual background has proved a valuable asset, and her keyboard and guitar-playing skills have provided fine accompaniment to her poignant, spellbinding ballads, ever since she first arrived on the Canadian music scene in 1984.

Her self-titled debut album was voted one of the Top 10 Albums of the Year by the *Boston Globe* in 1986. In subsequent albums, she has continued to turn personal experience into compelling song, interspersing studio recordings with concert cuts, and alternating English lyrics with songs in French.

Tremblay serenades us with a rich, warm voice that can soar from a throaty purr to strong, crystal tones. Her songs combine a soft melodic essence with a depth of feeling that is riveting—particularly in her love songs. Her performing credits include appearances at New York's Carnegie Hall, and at the Canadian Pavilion at 1992's World's Fair in Seville, Spain. She has recently been heard with James Taylor and Randy Newman on National Public Radio's weekly broadcast, *E-Town*. —*Laura Post*

☆ **Lucie Blue Tremblay** / 1986 / Olivia 947
Her debut features sweetly sung material in both French and English, although the listener should have no trouble following the emotional content of either. One live side and one studio-recorded side, featuring backing vocals by Cris Williamson, Teresa Trull, Tret Fure, and Deirdre McCalla. —*AMG*

Tendresse/ Tenderness / 1989 / Olivia 955
Beautiful love songs, political statements, and traditional folk music show her diversity. Poignant stories in both French and English. —*AMG*

I Want You To Know Who I Really Am / 1991 / Demi-soeurs 001

Also known as Lucie's "Coming-Out Kit," this cassingle (1-song tape) is perfect to send to parents, family, and old friends: "...And if you love me as much as I love you/then you'll love me/even if I'm not like you..." The insert even gives contact addresses for organizations like PFLAG (Parents and Friends of Lesbians and Gays). —*Ladyslipper*

★ **Transformations** / 1992 / Olivia 967
Another charmed release from this charming performer; songs, in both English and French, include "Chez Nous," "All Out of Love Tonight," "Homeless," "Sail Away," and "The Guilty One." —*Ladyslipper*

Teresa Trull

Vocals, keyboard / Country-Pop
Brought up in Durham, North Carolina, where she was steeped at an early age in blues, Gospel, and R&B, Trull began her musical career singing Gospel in churches, then served as the lead singer in a rock & roll band for several years before joining the East Coast nightclub circuit. Since the release of her first album, *The Ways a Woman Can Be* (1977), Trull's gutsy rock & roll vocal style, along with her songwriting and record production talents, has won the fiery-haired singer ever-widening recognition.

In particular, Trull's album *Acclaimed*, a collaboration with Barbara Higbie, received high critical praise. Other musicians with whom Trull has performed and recorded include Bonnie Hayes, Dave Sanborn, Andy Narell, Darol Anger, Mike Marshall, Alex DeGrassi, Joan Baez, Linda Tillery, Cris Williamson, Holly Near, and Tracy Nelson.

A songwriter of considerable renown, Trull co-wrote two songs on the Whispers' gold album *Love for Love*, including the title track (which she wrote with Roy Obiedo). Her production talents were recognized in 1985 when she was nominated for a New York Music Award as Best Producer of an Independent Album. Blessed with an endless supply of energy, Trull's live performances have been described as combining the high power of Nona Hendryx with the irreverant wit of Bette Midler. Her albums bear witness to the daring new steps she's been willing to take to broaden her musical career. —*AMG*

★ **A Step Away** / Redwood 412
Trull's best. A high-quality work of hope and joy from this vocalist/keyboardist. —*AMG*

Unexpected [with Barbara Higbie] / Second Wave 22001
The women of this dynamic duo show their stuff on this LP, as they have been doing on tour around the country. An eclectic bunch of styles—country, Gospel, ballads—with some simple songs, and some fairly produced. Barbara is a pianist extraordinaire; don't miss her LPs on Windham Hill. —*Ladyslipper*

Two Nice Girls

Group
● **2 Nice Girls** / 1989 / Rough Trade 59
They're not two, they're not nice, and they're not girls; they *are* three talented women who make great music together. If you can imagine a mixture of the Roches' layered harmonies and humor, a true women-identified sensibility, and vibrant, kaleidoscopic imagery, you'll have an inkling of the Girls' style. They spoof hetero love in "I Spent My Last $10.00 (On Birth Control and Beer)"; they sing of their women lovers un-self-consciously. —*Ladyslipper*

○ **Like a Version** / 1990 / Rough Trade 78
This 1990 EP release primarily contains covers...of material by artists from Donna Summer to Sonic Youth, the Carpenters to Janis Martin! Also included is "I Spent My Last $10.00," from their debut album. Six songs in all. —*Ladyslipper*

Chloe Liked Olivia / 1991 / Rough Trade 262
Funny, kitschy, feisty, smart, brave, sexy, political, warm, or just plain wonderful...all of these qualities are in abundance on their 1991 release—a musical hybrid that transcends the boundaries of most genres. From the faux-disco of "Let's Go Bonding," to the smooth-as-Smokey "Swimming in Circles," to "The Queer Song" and "Princess of Power," the Girls have outdone themselves with ten brilliant songs that run their usual range from tender to tongue-in-cheek. —*Ladyslipper*

Edwina Lee Tyler

● **Drum Drama!** / Percussion Piquant 1
One of the most dramatic percussionists around, Edwina Lee Tyler is a master of djimbe drum, marimba, tambourine, and cymbals. Recorded live at the People's Voice Cafe in Greenwich Village, this album begins with "the cool side," then progressively heats up: Edwina performs original percussion instrumentals ("Out of Bondage"), and new arrangements—with vocals—of a traditional spiritual ("Wade in the Water") and a West African song ("Ki Yak Ki Yak"). As you listen, the movement and dance will absolutely come alive—in your mind and your body. —*Ladyslipper*

Venus Envy

Group

● **I'll Be a Homo for Christmas** / 1988 / De Milo
A highly recommended seasonal release, containing the following: "Rhonda the Lesbo Reindeer," "It Came Upon a Midnight Queer," "O Little Town in Michigan," "The 12 Gays of Christmas," "Here Comes the Fairy Queen," "I Hate the Holidays," "I'll Be a Homo for Christmas," and more! Nothing will bring as much holiday cheer as this terrific collection of songs. With Laura Love, Linda Schierman, Lisa Koch, and Linda Severt. —*Ladyslipper*

Unarmed and Dangerous / 1990 / Venus Envy 1
Outstanding tri-vocals by Laura Love, Lisa Koch, and Linda Schierman, with bass, guitar, and harmonica—plus Linda Severt on percussion. This six-song tape features great covers (and improvisations) of "Venus," "She's Not There," "Thank You for Letting Me Be Myself," and "Under the Boardwalk," plus "Nelson" and the hilarious "Beaver Cleaver Fever." —*Ladyslipper*

Nancy Vogl

Vocals, Guitar
Vogl began picking out tunes on a beat-up, nylon-string guitar when she was 13, then graduated to steel strings when she was 20. From there, she went on to become a founding member (in Berkeley, CA) of one of the first feminist bands, and ended up touring nearly every major folk club and university in the United States.
 She released her first solo album, *Something to Go On* (Redwood Records), in 1984. A trip to Nashville two years later produced her album *Fight Like the Dancer* (Olivia Records), a contemporary mix of country, blues, and swing. Vogl's reflective, challenging, and visionary lyrics combine the grace and humor of 1940s musical show tunes with the solid power of 1970s acoustic rock. They wed the heartbreak of country ballads to the clean-picking fun of folk. —*Laura Post*

● **Something to Go on** / Redwood 3000
Nancy's mastery of acoustic steel-string guitar-picking is something to contend with! Certainly, not many could match her skill. She is a veteran—now into her second decade—of women's music tours and recordings. On her first solo effort, she has structured one side instrumental, featuring original duets with musical partner Suzanne Shanbaum; and the other side vocal. Her song "Crime of the Century" is an outstanding indictment of homophobia and other oppressions. Her insight into economic, social, and political history infuses the work with an extra intelligence. —*Ladyslipper*

Peggy Ward

● **We Are the Dance** / 1990 / Laughing Out Loud 1
Anyone who recognizes the vast talent that's emanating from Canada these days will want to check out this Alberta woman! Her voice is deep and strong and sure and beautiful; her lyrics are woman-affirming, anti-racist, anti-patriarchal, pro-gay, pro-environmental—all those good things. Includes "Sophie's Song," "Bring 'er Around Lass," and "People Belong to the Land." —*Ladyslipper*

Washington Sisters

Group
Once upon a time, two little girls stayed up through the night, singing every song they knew. Years later, identical twins Sandra and Sharon Washington have taken their late-night ramblings and laughter on the road.

Bold. Joyful. The Washington Sisters bring an uplifting spirit of hope to their two albums, *Understated* (Iceberg Records, 1987) and *Take Two* (Shsawa Music, 1991). The Washingtons have performed hundreds of concerts, including over two dozen appearances at music and cultural festivals in the U.S. and Canada. Their blend of a capella jazz, swing, blues, Gospel, and island rhythms provides a unique basis for their message of peace, women's rights, pride, and cultural diversity. —*Laura Post*

Understated / 1987 / Icebergg 221
This debut album of hot sounds by identical twins Sandra and Sharon is full of unique harmonies and special songs: "Breaths," "Sweet Inspiration," "Brown Like Me," "Find the Spirit," and more. A cappella funk is combined with contemporary pop/folk/jazz, and a touch of calypso. Back-up vocals by Linda Tillery and Vicki Randle; expertly produced by Teresa Trull. —*Ladyslipper*

● **Take Two** / 1991 / Shsawa 222
Even better and more stylistically diverse than the harmonizing twins' first album, this 1991 follow-up includes blues, jazz, swing, country, and love songs. ... Produced by Teresa Trull, with such backup artists Linda Tillery, Melanie Monsur, Nina Gerber, Paul McCandless, John Bucchino, and even Teresa herself. —*Ladyslipper*

Mary Watkins

Piano, composer / Folk, Progressive big band
An eclectic composer who works comfortably in both the classical and jazz traditions, Watkins draws no firm boundaries around any one style. Elements of blues, Gospel, country/folk, and pop slip easily into her work, and her versatility as a composer, arranger, pianist, and producer is reflected in the pieces she has composed for symphony orchestras, chamber ensembles, films, and the theater.
 Born in Denver, Watkins began her formal musical training when she was four, and by the age of eight was already starting to improvise and compose short piano pieces. After receiving a degree in music composition from Howard University in 1972, she performed with jazz combos in the Washington, D.C., area, then moved out to the West Coast and established her own jazz quartet. Several albums soon followed, as did numerous commissions and awards. Notable among Watkins' many compositions is her jazz score for the musical play *Lady Lester Sings the Blues*, based on the life of Lester Young, and her score for *The Revolutionary Nutcracker Sweetie*, a jazz adaptation of Tchaikovsky's *Nutcracker* ballet. —*AMG*

Winds of Change / Oct. 16, 1981-Oct. 17, 1981 / Palo Alto 8030
Large ensemble/orchestral recording, made at Herbst Theatre in San Francisco. Watkins plays piano in the spirit of artists like Duke Pearson and Melba Liston. A fine album to find. —*Michael G. Nastos*

★ **Spirit Song** / 1985 / Redwood 8506
Different, perhaps arty. Imaginative. Worth looking for. —*Michael G. Nastos*

○ **The Soul Kings** / 1992 / Wenefil 1001
Mary treats familiar Gospel hymns softly and tenderly here, in a generous attempt to share their healing and soothing qualities with a frenzied and wounded world. Performing solely on her synthesizers and electric pianos, she presents such gems as "Amazing Grace," "Blessed Assurance," "Pass Me Not," "By and By," and "I'll Fly Away." They are arranged and interpreted with care and great affection. —*Ladyslipper*

Sam Weis

● **So True!** / Silver Road Music 101
With a deep, earthy voice, and celestial 12-string guitar, Sam Weis is a delightful songwriter focusing on love...Also includes an incandescent instrumental, "Nasty Habits." Nicely produced. —*Ladyslipper*

Ilene Weiss

b. 1953
Songwriter / Folk
Weiss is a very perceptive writer of songs about romantic irony. Her compositions have been covered by Anne Hills, Deidre

Resources in Women's Music

Women's music is closely associated with two record companies, Olivia and Redwood Records, both of which have figured prominently in the advancement of Women's Music. For 20 years, Olivia (and its sister label, Second Wave Records) has produced the music of such artists as Cris Williamson, Deidre McCalla, Lucie Blue Tremblay, Teresa Trull, Dianne Davidson, and Tret Fure. Redwood Records (now Redwood Cultural Work) was started in 1972 when Holly Near recorded *Hang In There*. Since then, Redwood has produced and distributed records and presented concerts by dozens of artists, male and female, from many different cultures, all of whom sing for peace, justice, feminism, and human rights.

Where once only a handful of labels (Olivia, Redwood, Icebergg, Flying Fish) released Women's Music, many sisters are now doing it themselves, via self-production. Multitudes of local producers, promoters, distributors, managers, booking agents, engineers, and other technicians facilitate the process. Along with the expanded roles and realities for women interested in making music, new resources have clearly developed as well.

Other individuals and organizations have also played leading roles in the development of the feminist cultural network. The ground-breaking book *Lesbian/Woman* by Del Martin and Phyllis Lyon, initially printed following the tidal wave of post-Stonewall gay activism, was reprinted after the 1991 National Lesbian Conference for a special twentieth anniversary edition by Volcano Press (1992). And the Naiad Press, founded in 1973 by Donna McBride and Barbara Grier, remains the largest publisher/supplier of Lesbian titles in the world.

The Ladyslipper Catalogue, founded by Laurie Fuchs nearly 20 years ago and now containing the largest listing of Lesbian and other women's music products in the world, continues to function as an important resource in a rapidly changing industry. *Hot Wire: The Journal of Women's Music and Culture*, widely acknowledged as the most thorough current chronicler of Women's Music, unfortunately ended production after ten years.

At one time, it was possible to own all the "Women's Music" that had ever been recorded. However, as *The Changer and the Changed* has gracefully aged, more and more women musicians playing all styles (including soul, rock, rap, Latin American, soul, jazz, funk, bebop, house music, Caribbean/island, African, reggae, country/western, gospel/hymnal, punk/thrash, folk, R&B, Australian aborig-

inal, swing, chanty, klezmer, Native American and Canadian, big band, karaoke, taiko, and euro-classical) have hit the scene. There are singing musicians, instrumentalists, songwriters, solo acts, back-up musicians, duos, trios, dance ensembles, and larger groupings. *The Ladyslipper Catalogue* devotes 25 pages to Women's Music listings, and one would have to own hundreds of CDs and cassettes today to boast of having an up-to-date collection.

The National Women's Music Festival (the oldest Women's Music festival) and the Michigan Womyn's Music Festival (the largest Women's Music festival) will be celebrating their 20th anniversaries in 1994 and 1995, respectively. As of 1993, there are at least fifteen major festivals of Women's Music being held throughout the United States: in the south, on the east and west coasts, in Northampton MA ("Lesbianville," according to the National Enquirer), and in Alaska and Hawaii.

In 1986, a group of visionary women agreed that it was time to form a national organization of Women's Music and Culture. In 1987 the founding Steering Committee—including performers Deidre McCalla and Sue Fink, festival producer Lisa Vogel (Michigan Womyn's Music Festival), record producer/engineer Leslie Ann Jones, and Judy Dlugacz, founder and president of Olivia Records—appointed a bylaws committee to draft governing principles for the nascent Association of Women's Music and Culture (AWMAC). AWMAC, which currently sponsors an annual National Conference in conjunction with the National Women's Music Festival (as well as a number of more intimate regional meetings), strives to encourage and empower Women's Music and Culture through networking, education, and support services for its members.

Finally, the comprehensive resource *Women's Music Plus* (edited by Toni Armstrong, Jr., one of the founders of *Hot Wire*) reflects the competence, complexity, and diversity of Women's Music and Culture. Listed are performers, artists in film, video, and television, women's choirs and choruses, record and live event producers, artists' representatives, American Sign Language interpreters, record distributors, stage workers, technicians, feminist press and other writers, feminist broadcasters, photographers, publishers, festivals, periodicals, bookstores, libraries and archives, record labels, catalogs and directories, cartooning, crafts, comedy, dance, storytelling, and theatre. Where northern California was once the exclusive "capital" of Women's Music (Olivia and Redwood both make their homes in the San Francisco Bay Area, as do AWMAC and the IMA), the *Women's Music Plus* list, although emphasizing North America, virtually spans the globe.

—*Laura Post*

McCalla, Robin Flowers, Marcy Marxer, Cathy Fink, among others.

Originally from Philadelphia, Weiss now resides in New York City. She has been nominated for a BMI Songwriters Award and two New York Music Awards. She is a contributor to *The Fast Folk Musical Magazine*. —*Chip Renner & Richard Meyer*

○ **Outside and Curious** / 1992 / Gadfly 111591
This CD is just Weiss singing and playing guitar—and doing both very well. What stands out, though, is her songwriting: her songs are often filled with humor, yet they can make you think. A very good release. —*Chip Renner*

Erica Wheeler

Strong Heart / 1989 / Blue Pie 010
No stranger to attendees of several women's music festivals, we hope Erica will soon be no stranger to a wider group of listeners,

thanks to this 1989 debut tape. Her voice is resonant, yet with a certain vulnerable quality—the type that mesmerizes and holds the listener. Her lyrics are thoughtful and poetic, with the heart being her main theme. —*Ladyslipper*

● **From That Far** / 1992 / Blue Pie 200
This Massachusetts singer/songwriter embodies the finest qualities of folk music: the vocal warmth, the clear acoustic tones, the simple recounting of the stories of our lives. Erica's voice is silky and sweet on this 1992 release, her songwriting direct and poetic. —*Ladyslipper*

Cris Williamson (Chris Williamson)

Vocals, songwriter / Rock
For the fans who who have bought her 14 albums, and who flock to her sold-out concerts, Williamson's music and its messages are restorative balms that soothe, enlighten, and inspire. Her timeless

classic, *The Changer and the Changed*, remains one of the best-selling independent albums of all time—and *the* top-selling women's music album.

An avid environmentalist and humanitarian, Williamson frequently lends her name, talent, and support to causes that others might consider lost—such as those involving terminally ill children. She brings her special brand of energy and hope to these efforts.

Williamson's "Don't Lose Heart" serves as the theme song for Henry Jaglom's acclaimed motion picture *New Year's Day*, and she has contributed compositions to a variety of other feature films and TV documentaries, including the PBS documentary "Is Anyone Home on the Range?" Williamson also wrote, produced, and narrated the Parents' Choice Award-winning sci-fi fable for children, *Lumiere*, which is now part of the curriculum of several Montessori schools. A blend of toughness, honesty, and intimacy marks her strongly personal, pop-styled ballads. As a musician, poet, and teacher of "the art of the possible," Williamson creates music that feeds the spirit and calms the soul. —*Laura Post*

○ **Cris Williamson** / 1971 / Olivia 927
A remastered reissue of her first album. Very basic and raw, with veiled hints of things to come. —*Bruce Eder*

○ **The Changer and the Changed** / 1975 / Olivia 904
The record that set a new standard in the field. Soulful, passionate, and poignant. —*Bruce Eder*

Strange Paradise / 1980 / Olivia 921
Musically on par with *The Changer and the Changed*, but with more of a rock & roll influence and some phenomenal synthesizer. Joined by Jackie Robbins, June Millington, and (on one cut) Bonnie Raitt. —*Ladyslipper*

○ **Blue Rider** / 1982 / Olivia 931
Bonnie Raitt guests on this, Williamson's most highly regarded rock album. A successful mix of electric guitars and topical concerns, with some very personal lyrics. —*Bruce Eder*

Meg/Cris at Carnegie Hall (2-Set) / 1983 / Second Wave 933
A deluxe double volume of the entire herstory-making Carnegie Hall performance of Nov., 1982, that celebrated Olivia's tenth anniversary. ... The CD version is a single disc, and contains all but two of the selections. —*Ladyslipper*

Portrait / 1983 / Olivia 935
This retrospective, compiled in 1983, is a collection of favorites drawn from her previous albums. —*Ladyslipper*

Snow Angel / 1985 / Olivia 943
This is a winter holiday album, with songs for the variety of seasonal holidays...you *could* think of it sort of as a "Cris-Ms." album. —*Ladyslipper*

Wolf Moon / 1987 / Olivia 951
This varied selection of songs has one common thread: a wolf theme running throughout, from "The Run of the Wolf" (a poignant dedication to Kate Wolf), to the love song "Home Free" ("...No longer the lone wolf"...), to the title song (about listening to Wolfman Jack's radio show). —*Ladyslipper*

Country Blessed / 1989 / Second Wave 22013
Recorded as a duo with Olivia Records' ace producer Teresa Trull, in a somewhat countrified vein. An especially unusual record, it showcases Williamson performing songs by other writers. —*Bruce Eder*

☆ **Prairie Fire** / 1989 / Olivia 941
Her hardest rocker ever—and her cleverest, most pointed collection of songs, with their concerns ranging from Native Americans to new age vacuousness. —*Bruce Eder*

★ **Circle of Friends: Cris Live...** / 1991 / Olivia 963
This live recording of the *15th Anniversary of The Changer and the Changed* show, as performed in Berkeley in 1990, brings back the special magic of that remarkable album, which influenced so many of us in the early years. Includes selected highlights from *The Changer...*—"Waterfall," "Sweet Woman," "Shooting Star," "Dreamchild," "Sister," and "Song of the Soul"—as well as previously unrecorded songs from Cris' early repertoire: "If It Weren't For the Music," "Circle of Friends," "Sisters of Mercy," "Olivia," "Millworker," "Hey Good Lookin'," and more. In all, 72 minutes of music. A wonderful way to remember and honor the album and the era. —*Ladyslipper*

The Best of Cris Williamson / Olivia 959

It's not quite what the title says. The folk material dominates, leaving out some cool and hot rock numbers. —*Bruce Eder*

Women's Alliance

● **Drumming -1991 Her Voice, Our Voices** /
Women's Alliance offers summer camps for women that incorporate spirituality, Earth wisdom, psychology, and the arts...and their music sounds amazing. This is an exciting compilation of live drumming, along with other musical and narrational tidbits from their 1991 summer camp. Recorded by Maya Novelli. A wonderful way to bring the incredible energy of camp into your home! —*Ladyslipper*

Yasmeen

● **Yasmeen of Sweet Honey in the Rock** / Summer 1
This four-song cassette represents the solo debut of Yasmeen, a 13-year member of the acclaimed a cappella group Sweet Honey in the Rock. Loosening up with a jazzy, contemporary R&B band behind her, she shows off her songwriting skills and her gorgeous sultry voice—and just generally throws her hat into the Anita Baker ring. —*Ladyslipper*

○ **Still Walking In the Way of Love** / Summer 2
Features an array of R&B, jazz, songs with spiritual content, and topical songs, in the tradition of Sweet Honey in the Rock. Included are: the title song, about homelessness; "Colors," a pro-choice song; "Monrovia, Liberia"; and covers of "Knocking on Heaven's Door" and James Brown's "I Feel Good!" Absolutely recommended for all Sweet Honey fans. —*Ladyslipper*

Yer Girlfriend

We Won't Be Silent / 1989 / Esther 101
Yer Girlfriend is five Kentucky women who are committed to maintaining a strong political voice through the medium of popular music. They aim to break down walls of homophobic prejudice and traditional stereotypes about women, while their audiences are tapping their toes to music that's fun. They do just that on this debut tape of original, wonderfully-out lesbian and feminist songs, employing beautiful vocal harmonies. —*Ladyslipper*

● **L-Word Spoken Here** / 1992 / Esther 102
Their 1992 release is a rededication to the out and proud lyrics, and the toe-tapping sounds, that audiences can't get enough of. Blues, rock, or folk, they deliver each song with style, energy, and heart. From the ballad "Still Waters," a song about taking risks, to "Take Back Our Lives," suggesting that women have more to conquer than just the night, their messages are as clear as their sound is hot. —*Ladyslipper*

Leah Zicari

● **Wouldn't That Be Fun?** / 1990 / Gender Bender 62233
A pretty super-duper lesbian-affirming tape, by a femme dyke-with-bike-with-guitar. A must for every woman who's ever had a crush on "Martina"...and several other lovely lesbian songs. Add to that a good voice, accompaniment, and arrangements. —*Ladyslipper*

Women's Collections

☆ **Family of Friends** / Tsunami 1003
This 1993 release may be the best sampler of women's music ever created. The title song, an anthem-to-be and a must-have for every women's music lover, is one of the sweetest and most memorable tunes ever composed... . As a collaboration, it expresses some of the highest spirit of our lesbian culture. It was co-written by Sue Fink, Jamie Anderson, June Millington, Jane Emmer, and Dakota, and is performed by the songwriters along with Margie Adam, Deidre McCalla, Cris Williamson, Tret Fure, Sharon Washington, Jean Millington, Susan Herrick, Robin Flower, Monica Grant, Helen Hooke, Mary Watkins, Barbara Borden, and others.

There are also tracks (many previously released) by the following individual artists and groups: Alix Dobkin (including her previously unreleased "My Kind of Girl"), Pam Hall, Venus Envy, Yer

Girlfriend, OneSpirit (Kay Gardner and Nurudafina Pili Abena), Sue Fink, June Millington, Mimi Baczewska, Laura Berkson, Diane Lindsay, Leah Zicari, and Jamie Anderson. Some profits will be donated to a lesbian organization. A great introduction for friends and "family" new to women's music, and a classic for the confirmed. —*Ladyslipper*

○ **For Therese** / 1990 / Sea Friends 312
On March 10, 1990, a group of artists and friends gathered to celebrate Therese Edell's 40th birthday in a unique way: they put on a one-of-a-kind concert as a loving tribute to Therese and her musical contributions. Sixty minutes of this event have been preserved on this album, produced by Therese. It features musicians like Sue Fink, Betsy Lippitt, Kay Gardner, Deidre McCalla, Nydia Mata, the Atlanta Feminist Women's Choir, and the MUSE choir,...instrumentation such as flute, oboe, bassoon, cello, harp, and glockenspeil,...and songs that include Betsy's "For Therese," Therese's own "Emma" (performed by Sue Fink), "Sister Heathenspinster's Calendar Days," "Katie's Song," "Good Friends Are the Best," "Holly's Waltz," and "O My Friends," co-written by Therese. Some songs even feature *combined* choirs! —*Ladyslipper*

★ **Michigan Live 85—Womyn's Music Fest** / 1986 / August Night 10
This double album is the definitive sampler of women's music, joyfully reflecting all the richness and diversity of the women's cultural movement at its best. Live performances by Holly Near, Kay Gardner, Alix Dobkin, Ferron, Lucie Blue Tremblay, and oth-ers have been superbly engineered into a body of work that flows as beautifully as the landmark festival it commemorates. A must for every lover of women's music, and a perfect gift for anyone! —*Ladyslipper*

○ **Peace Camp Sings** / Tallapoosa 2

This album contains 38 songs collected by Sorrel Hays, primarily at the Greenham Common and Seneca Women's Peace Camps between 1983 and 1985. Several were recorded later by Marilyn Ries in her living-room studio. Some of the songs were composed by individuals, some are collective efforts, and others set new lyrics to well-known melodies; they are sung by a variety of artists. The album includes Naomi Littlebear's "You Can't Kill the Spirit," recorded at the Barbara Deming Memorial Service; "We're Shameless Hussies," "My Old Mom's a Lesbo," "Fuck Off Sexist Pigs," "I'm a Dyke," "Ron with the Neutron Bomb," "Rocka My Soul in the Bosom of Sisterhood," "We Are the Weavers," and many more priceless expressions of the strength of womankind. Proceeds go to women's peace camps. —*Ladyslipper*

○ **Redwood Collection** /

This sampler album includes selections by Holly Near, Ronnie Gilbert, Inti-Illimani, "H.A.R.P.," Ferron, Linda Tillery, Mary Watkins, Guardabarranco, Judy Small, and Nancy Vogl—all of whom have released records on the Redwood label. Great for introducing new audiences to the Redwood roster. —*Ladyslipper*

CHRISTMAS

In 1942, Irving Berlin wrote "White Christmas" for the movie *Holiday Inn*, and while not an overnight success, once the GIs overseas besieged the Armed Forces Radio with requests for this song (sung by Bing Crosby), the top-selling Christmas single of all time was also on its way to becoming the most recorded song of all time. Berlin collected an Academy Award for "Best Song" and the market for Christmas music was now well-established.

One of the great things about Christmas records: there's something for everyone, be it blues, jazz, country, pop, R&B, rock & roll, novelty, or even reggae! While there are probably more sacred Christmas recordings, the emphasis in this chapter is on the secular releases. There may have been more artists recording holiday tunes in the '50s and '60s than in the present, but now we see artists getting together to record Yule classics for worthwhile causes, such as the two A&M CDs, *A Very Special Christmas*, for the Special Olympics. Record labels also continue to release seasonal compilations of artists from their rosters, with mixed results. This idea was first generated (and best executed) by Phil Spector with his 1963 paragon, A Christmas Gift for You from Phil Spector. Even though the 45 has gone the way of the 8-track; searching the used record stores, the flea markets, the yard sales, and whatever way one hunts down the elusive Christmas 45, 78 or LP from the past can bring lots of pleasure (I'm especially proud of my 78 of Art Carney doing a beatnik version of "'Twas the Night Before Christmas"). Rhino Records has done the most commendable job of reissuing classic "Cool Yule" 45s on various compilations, and more labels seem ready to enter the Christmas reissue marketplace. Another great way to find buried treasures

(there's probably a longer list of artists who haven't recorded a Yule tune than of those who have) is to trade tapes with people who have made it an annual tradition to make a new holiday tape to send to friends and fellow collectors as a combination Christmas card/gift; over the years, I have acquired rarities from all over the world on tape.

With so many holiday treats to choose from, keep in mind that compilations of various artists are often the best way to go, as many artists could not maintain a full album's worth of high-quality material. Here, then, in alphabetical order, are my recommended "Twelve CDs of Christmas."

— *Decibel Dennis MacDonald*

Charles Brown: Please Come Home for Christmas / KING CD 5019 (1961)
James Brown: Santa's Got a Brand New Bag / RHINO CD 70194 (1966-70)
Elvis Presley: Elvis' Christmas Album / RCA CD 5486 (1957)
Ventures: The Ventures' Christmas Album / EMI CD 94994 (1965)
Various: A Christmas Gift for You from Phil Spector / ABKCO CD 4005 (1963)
Various: The Best of Cool Yule / RHINO CD 75767 (1988)
Various: Christmas Kisses: Christmas Classics from Capitol's Early Years (1990)
Various: Christmas Party with Eddie G. / SONY CD 46919 (1990)
Various: Hipster's Holiday: Vocal Jazz and R&B Classics / RHINO CD 70910 (1989)
Various: Merry Christmas Baby / HOLLYWOOD CD 900
Various: Santa Claus Blues / JASS CD 3 (1988)
Various: Soul Christmas / ATLANTIC CD 82316 (1991)

Johnny Adams

Christmas in New Orleans / 1988 / ACE 2046

A disappointing effort from "The Tan Canary" who is in fine voice but weighed down with poor arrangements. Adams also stays in control too much, rarely letting that tenor voice take flight. — *Decibel Dennis MacDonald*

Air Supply

☆ **The Christmas Album** / 1987 / Arista 8528

The adult-contemporary sounds of the season, from light-rock radio's favorite Australian group. — *David A. Milberg*

Alabama

☆ **Alabama Christmas** / RCA 7014

A must for your C&W Christmas, it contains the classic "Christmas in Dixie." — *David A. Milberg*

Herb Alpert & The Tijuana Brass

○ **Christmas Album** / 1968 / A&M 3113

A million-seller from 1968. This is an essential part of any Christmas collection, especially their hit version of "The Christmas Song." — *David A. Milberg*

Julie Andrews w/ Andre Previn

☆ **Christmas Treasure** / 1968 / RCA 3829

Orchestra with Andre Previn arrangements that feature Andrews. — *AMG*

Eddy Arnold

Christmas with Eddy Arnold / 1961 / RCA 52554

This is the immortal "Tennessee Plowboy's" classic Christmas album. First released in 1962, it still sounds great today. — *David A. Milberg*

Joan Baez

☆ **Noel** / 1966 / Vanguard 79230

An album of stately beauty as Baez's pure, soaring soprano is accompanied by a consort of recorders and viols, lute, harpsichord, baroque organ, winds, strings, and percussion. Her rendition of the "Coventry Carol" is as stirring as any recorded version I've heard, and Baez pours her heart into "The Carol of the Birds." Considering Baez's politics, one would never know she recorded this album in the Vietnam War era. It's timeless. — *Decibel Dennis MacDonald*

The Beach Boys

The Beach Boys' Christmas Album / Oct. 1964 / Capitol 95084

What more can you say about this all-time classic? A million-seller from 1964, featuring "Little Saint Nick" and "Man with All the Toys." —*David A. Milberg*

Harry Belafonte

☆ **To Wish You a Merry Christmas** / 1962 / RCA 2626
A mostly subdued setting for Belafonte as he is backed by an orchestra and chorus throughout. Traditional fare, including sacred and secular, with two medleys, along with the calypso feel of "Mary's Boy Child" and "A Star in the East." Includes a sung version of Henry Wadsworth Longfellow's "I Heard the Bells on Christmas Day." —*Decibel Dennis MacDonald*

Tony Bennett

☆ **Snowfall: The Tony Bennett Christmas Album** / 1968 / CBS 09739
Tony Bennett at his peak in 1968, adding an uncommon style to the common standards of the day. —*David A. Milberg*

David Benoit

☆ **Christmastime** / Oct. 31, 1991 / Blue Moon 79161
Pleasant piano stylings. Perfect for meetings under the mistletoe. —*David A. Milberg*

Booker T. & the Mgs

In the Christmas Spirit / Oct. 1966 / Atlantic 82338
Booker T. and the MG's find the groove to come up with funky instrumentals of Yule classics "Jingle Bells," "Silver Bells," and the percolatin' "We Wish You a Merry Christmas." Steve Cropper makes his guitar sing on the down 'n' bluesy "Merry Christmas Baby." —*Decibel Dennis MacDonald*

Boston Camerata w/ the Boston Shawm & Sackbut Ensemble

☆ **Noel, Noel! (Noels Francais/French Christmas Music (1200-1600)** / Erato 45420
Joel Cohen conducts medieval/renaissance French Christmas music with the Boston Shawn and Sackbut Ensemble. Very fine traditional music. —*Michael Erlewine*

Liona Boyd

☆ **A Guitar for Christmas** / 1989 / CBS 37248
Classical guitarist extraordinaire manages to shine once in a while, even when the Muzak production is smothering her in a morass of holiday Velveeta cheese—Richard Clayderman for classical guitar music. —*Rick Clark, Rock & Roll Disc*

Brave Combo

★ **It's Christmas, Man!** / 1991 / Rounder 9033
Originally recorded for the Japanese market (!), this Denton, Texas "polka band" (they play many styles beyond polka) have recorded one of the funnest, albeit goofiest, seasonal delights you'll ever hear. "O, Christmas Tree" is done as a samba, "The Christmas Song" is performed in the ska style, while "Feliz Navidad" makes your feet want to dance to the cumbia. The traditional "Hanukkah, Oh Hannukah" is turned into a hora and "The Little Drummer Boy" into a wild guaguanco, whatever that is. Brave Combo also add several original songs to the Christmas canon, including the cha cha "It's Christmas," but the CD's high point is the frenzied polka, "Must Be Santa." Highly recommended fun, and danceable too ! —*Decibel Dennis MacDonald*

Jack Brokensha w/ Lenore Paxton

☆ **Holiday Inventions** / 1968 / US Steel 836
One side has vibist Brokensha with Bess Bonnier on piano; the other has pianist Paxton and vocalist Robert Chambers. Crystalline chamber Christmas jazz. The album was subsidized by US Steel. —*Michael G. Nastos*

Garth Brooks

○ **Beyond the Season** / Aug. 17, 1992 / Liberty 98742
One of the most succesful Christmas albums ever, Beyond the Season is a varied collection for a country star, even one as

"progressive" as Brooks. The tunes range from a gospel version of "Go Tell It on the Mountain" to a song-play where Brooks' songwriters take the roles of animals in the manger. It's about half traditional and half original, with Brooks cowriting the hardest rocking tune, "The Old Man's Back in Town." —*Brian Mansfield*

Charles Brown

★ **Please Come Home for Christmas** / Deluxe 5019
These dozen tracks from rhythm & blues singer/pianist Charles Brown are among the most essential Yule tunes ever recorded, including his original, oft-covered "Please Come Home for Christmas" and "Merry Christmas, Baby." Brown's smoother-than-aged-brandy voice is perfectly suited to an intimate evening at home with that special someone beneath the mistletoe. —*Decibel Dennis MacDonald*

James Brown

★ **Santa's Got a Brand New Bag** / 1988 / Rhino 70194
Compiled from three Christmas LPs and various singles released by the "Santa of Soul" between 1966-1970, this 16-track collection includes one of JB's most over-the-top screamfests on "Let's Make Christmas Mean Something this Year," while he gets loose and funky with "Soulful Christmas." Others have tried, but nobody can beat the Godfather on his ballad "Sweet Little Baby Boy," and nobody but the "man who put the 'wet' in sweat" can pull off "Santa Claus Go Straight to the Ghetto." This is as essential as it gets. —*Decibel Dennis MacDonald*

Kenny Burrell

☆ **Have Yourself a Soulful Little Christmas** / Oct. 1966 / Cadet 91567
Have Yourself a Soulful Little Christmas is recently back in print after its original release on Cadet Records in 1966. Pensive, meditative, precise playing. A must-have, with a definitive jazz version of "Little Drummer Boy." —*David A. Milberg & Michael G. Nastos*

The California Raisins

☆ **Christmas with the California Raisins** / Priority 7923
From their 1988 claymation CBS-TV special. The cut "Hark" is especially worth hearing. —*David A. Milberg*

The Cambridge Singers

☆ **Christmas Night—Carols of the Nativity** / Collegium 106
The lovely Cambridge Singers as conducted by John Rutter—one of the most brilliant living composers. If you yearn for an elegant Christmas album in the traditional style, this is it. Includes 22 carols. —*Michael Erlewine*

Glen Campbell

☆ **Merry Christmas** / Aug. 19, 1991 / Liberty 96383
A great combination of easy-listening and C&W treatments of Christmas standards. —*David A. Milberg*

Larry Carlton

☆ **Christmas at My House** / MCA 6322
One of the greatest jazz/rock guitarists of the '80s & '90s provides this classic Christmas guitar album. —*David A. Milberg*

The Carpenters

○ **Christmas Portrait** / 1978 / A&M 5173
An essential album for your fireside Christmas. It sold a million in 1978 and contains the classics "Merry Christmas, Darling" and "Have Yourself a Merry Little Christmas." —*David A. Milberg*
○ **An Old Fashioned Christmas** / 1978 / A&M 4726
Their second Christmas album. More of the soft sounds of the season, made for mistletoe and someone you love. —*David A. Milberg*

Ray Charles

○ **Spirit of Christmas** / 1987 / Columbia 40125

Ray's capable of better than this, but it ain't half bad, either. Freddie Hubbard knocks off a fine solo during the hard-swinging break on "What Child Is This" and Ray almost gets down on "Santa Claus Is Coming to Town." "All I Want for Christmas" is another highlight. The drawback is that for every good cut, there's a throwaway track. But some Ray is a lot better than no Ray at all. —*Rick Clark, Rock & Roll Disc*

The Chipmunks

Christmas with the Chipmunks / 1962 / EMI America 48378
Their first Christmas album, with the classic "Chipmunk Song." Great for kids of all ages. —*David A. Milberg*

Christmas Jug Band

Mistletoe Jam / Relix 2036
Led by multi-instrumentalist/vocalist Dan Hicks, the CJB are best heard in small doses (unless, of course, you truly enjoy the novelty of jug bands). "Somebody Stole My Santa Claus Suit" is the highlight (and can also be found on Rhino's *Bummed Out Christmas* collection). —*Decibel Dennis MacDonald*

Cincinnati Pops Orchestra/Erich Kunzel

☆ **Christmas with the Pops** / Telarc 80226
Trim your tree with the full orchestral delights of holiday standards with a true maestro. —*David A. Milberg*

Nat King Cole

☆ **The Christmas Song** / Oct. 27, 1986 / Capitol 46318
Cole recorded the definitive version of "The Christmas Song" in 1946, and while this 1960 re-recording is sublime, it is worth seeking out the original. Although there is a heavy-handed use of orchestras and choruses on this record, Cole rises above the dreck with stellar versions of "Adeste Fidelis," "O Holy Night," and more. —*Decibel Dennis MacDonald*

☆ **Cole, Christmas, & Kids** / Sep. 10, 1990 / Capitol 94685
More Christmas magic with touching tunes like "The Little Boy that Santa Forgot." —*David A. Milberg*

Mitzie Collins w/ Roxanne Ziegler & Glennda Dove

☆ **Nowell** / Sampler 8606
Hammer dulcimer, with harp and flute accompaniment. Lesser-known but lovely works done in a creative and bright way. —*Michael Erlewine*

Perry Como

★ **Christmas Album** / 1968 / RCA 1929
A million-seller with an updated version of his 1950 classic "There's No Christmas Like a Home Christmas." —*David A. Milberg*

☆ **I Wish It Could Be Christmas Forever** / 1982 / RCA 4526
His fans will delight in this Christmas present. His most recent recording of the sounds of the season. —*David A. Milberg*

Ray Conniff

☆ **Christmas Album** / 1962 / CBS 38300
This album, also known as *Merry Christmas to All*, was a million-seller in 1962 and a top-seller for ten years. A good '60s sound-of-the-season timepiece. —*David A. Milberg*

★ **We Wish You a Merry Christmas** / 1962 / Columbia 8692
This is a million-selling album, and includes their hit version of "Silver Bells." —*David A. Milberg*

☆ **Here We Come A-Caroling** / Columbia 40499
More classics with the Conniff touch, from 1965. His second-most-popular Christmas album collection. —*David A. Milberg*

Floyd Cramer

☆ **We Wish You a Merry Christmas** / RCA 53828
Nashville's most famous pianist recorded and released this in 1967. Great C&W easy-listening. —*David A. Milberg*

Bing Crosby

☆ **Bing Crosby's Christmas Classics** / 1962 / Capitol 91009
This is a reissue of Crosby's 1962 album *I Wish You a Merry Christmas*. Above-standard renditions of famous Christmas standards. —*David A. Milberg*

Christmas Songs / 1990 / Vintage Jazz 1017
This 75-minute CD is in four parts, including the complete Kraft Music Hall broadcast of December 21, 1944, in which Crosby performs "Adeste Fidelis" and "Jingle Bells"; other performers are included. There are selections from various broadcasts, 1942-46, and a Christmas Eve 1944 Philco Radio Hall of Fame broadcast with the Paul Whiteman Orchestra, including a performance of "White Christmas." The CD concludes with excerpts from a Christmas 1946 broadcast, including a duet with Skitch Henderson on "The Christmas Song." —*Decibel Dennis MacDonald*

○ **Merry Christmas** / MCA 31143
"Der Bingle" in two distinctly different moods: from the solemnity of "Silent Night" and "Adeste Fidelis" (sung in English and Latin) to the playfulness ("gonna have a lotta fun") on "Jingle Bells," with the Andrews Sisters providing some smiles with their "Ji-ji-jingle" vocals. They duet on two more, including "Mele Kalikimaka." Also includes a remake of "White Christmas." —*Decibel Dennis MacDonald*

★ **Bing Crosby Sings Christmas Songs** / MCA 5765
Includes his definitive "White Christmas." —*Michael Erlewine*

Original White Christmas / Unreleased Studio Masters from Holiday Inn and Blue / Vintage Jazz Classics 1012
The musical *Holiday Inn* garnered Irving Berlin an Academy Award for Best Song, "White Christmas." The film version is on this CD, transferrred from a radio transcription disc, as "Der Bingle" duets with Marjorie Reynolds on this and a medley of "Happy Holiday/Let's Start the New Year Right." —*Decibel Dennis MacDonald*

Bobby Darin

25th Day of December / 1961 / Atco 91772
Give Darin credit for choosing mostly American spirituals for this release, but he would have fallen flat had he not been backed by the Bobby Scott Chorale on "Go Tell it on the Mountain," "Jehovah Hallelujah," and other rousing numbers. On the hymns, however, Darin is lost in syrupy arrangements. —*Decibel Dennis MacDonald*

Danny Davis & The Nashville Brass

Christmas with Danny Davis & the Nashville Brass / RCA 4377
This album was a Christmas hit in 1970, and the smooth C&W stylings of Christmas standards still sound great after 20 years. —*David A. Milberg*

Doris Day

☆ **Christmas Album** / 1964 / CBS 30016
The Doris Day sound of the '60s. Includes a notable new (at that time) Christmas number, "Christmas Present." —*David A. Milberg*

John Denver

○ **Rocky Mountain Christmas** / 1975 / RCA 1201
This million-seller is a must! It contains the classics "Aspen Glow" and "Christmas for Cowboys." —*David A. Milberg*

A Christmas Together with the Muppets / 1979 / RCA 3451
John Denver and the Muppets. The most fun since David Seville & the Chipmunks. Moving renditions of "Have Yourself a Merry Little Christmas" and "We Wish You a Merry Christmas." —*David A. Milberg*

Placido Domingo

☆ **Christmas with Placido Domingo** / 1984 / CBS 37245
A perennial favorite. Christmas standards in the great tradition of legendary operatic tenors. —*David A. Milberg*

Fats Domino

Christmas Is a Special Day / Nov. 16, 1993 / The Right Stuff

Music Map

Christmas

MEDIEVAL FOLK MUSIC
YULETIDE SONGS

20s BLUES

30s JAZZ/BIG BAND

40s CROONERS & BIG BANDS

Bing Crosby's
"White Christmas"

COUNTRY & WESTERN			JAZZ
Louvin Brothers	Les Brown	Glenn Miller	Louis Armstrong
Eddy Arnold	Harry James	Guy Lombardo	Miles Davis
Ernest Tubb	Frank Sinatra	Andrews Sisters	Jimmy Smith Collections
Gene Autry			

50s POP/NOVELTY

ROCK/POP/NOVELTY	Perry Como	EASY LISTENING
Elvis Presley	Tony Bennett	Andy Williams
James Brown	Nat King Cole	Johnny Mathis
New Kids On The Block	Spike Jones	John Denver
California Raisins		

It's amazing that 40-plus years after recording "The Fat Man," Fats Domino's voice is virtually unchanged. Hearing that lazy N'awlins drawl on his original "I Told Santa Claus" and "Christmas is a Special Day" is a delight *despite* the electronic keyboards and rhythm machine used on the latter. Fats romps through other seasonal favorites, "Jingle Bells," "Silver Bells," and "Blue Christmas" among them. Once you get past the rhythm machine (three drummers are credited ?!?), you can enjoy the return of the "Fat Man." —*Decibel Dennis MacDonald*

Michael Doucet w/ Beausoleil

Christmas Bayou / 1986 / Swallow 6064
Cajun fiddler extraordinaire and leader of Beausoleil, Michael Doucet is backed by swamp guitar whiz Sonny Landreth, accordionist Pat Breaux, and others on this unique assortment of French fare and rollicking instrumental versions of "Deck the Halls" and "Auld Lang Zyne" (sic)—be prepared to do some two-steppin' and waltzing under the mistletoe when you throw this one on. —*Decibel Dennis MacDonald*

Elmo & Patsy

☆ **Grandma Got Run over by a Reindeer** / CBS 39931
Worth buying, if only for the classic title tune. —*David A. Milberg*

John Fahey

Christmas Album / 1975 / Burnside 0004
Fahey's latest Christmas project includes accompaniment from a small acoustic band. — *Roundup Newsletter*

○ **Christmas Guitar** / 1989 / Varrick 11503
Fahey's studious acoustic guitar explorations of traditional music won him a lot of notoriety in folk circles during the '50s and '60s.

Christmas Guitar features cuts previously available on other Fahey Christmas albums. Fahey's style is a distinctive blend of blues, folk, and ragtime. Even though his playing sometimes sounds a little too stiff and academic, all of the songs on this collection are wonderfully rendered. —*Rick Clark*

Percy Faith

☆ **Music of Christmas** / 1966 / CBS 38302
Hit album with a notable rendition of "Silver Bells." —*David A. Milberg*

● **Christmas Is** / 1989 / CBS 9377
This had its debut at Christmastime 1954. It's a great "time peace" of the decade's sounds of the season. —*David A. Milberg*

Arthur Fiedler

● **Pops Christmas Party** / 1959 / RCA 3436
This album is most famous for the classic version of "Sleigh Ride." —*David A. Milberg*

☆ **A Christmas Festival** / RCA 6428
Fiedler and the Boston Pops are in good form on this holiday album. —*David A. Milberg*

Ella Fitzgerald

● **Ella Fitzgerald's Christmas** / 1967 / Capitol 94452
1968 hit album representing a change in Ella's style after her switch to Capitol. Re-released in 1978 as *Ella Fitzgerald Sings Christmas.* —*David A. Milberg*

☆ **Wishes You a Swinging Christmas** / Polydor 27150
Originally released in 1960 as *A Swinging Christmas*, this album is representative of Fitzgerald's Verve label career. —*David A. Milberg*

Scott Fitzgerald

○ **A Child's Music Box Christmas** /
A recording of Christmas music especially for children, played on music boxes, and woven together with other sounds of the season. —*Backroads Music/Heartbeats*

○ **Old Fashioned Country Christmas** /
Stir up memories of the perfect Christmas, with the sounds of a jingle-bell sleigh ride, chestnuts roasting on the open fire, and Christmas melodies played on music boxes and the old family organ. —*Backroads Music/Heartbeats*

Rita Ford

☆ **Joyous Music Box Christmas** / Music Masters 60116
Christmas music played on old music boxes. —*Michael Erlewine*

● **Music Box Christmas** / CBS 8498
This one has been part of the Christmas record scene continuously since 1961. Warm and pleasant sounds for a fireside Christmas. —*David A. Milberg*

Tennessee Ernie Ford

☆ **The Star Carol (Reissue 2)** / Capitol 91010
A best-seller for ten years; the sacred sounds of the season never sounded better! —*David A. Milberg*

Frankie Valli & The Four Seasons

○ **Christmas Album** / 1967 / Rhino 70234
A reissue of their 1966 best-selling Christmas classic on the Philips label. "Santa Claus Is Coming to Town" is a great rocker. "Joy to the World Medley" is a surprise treat. —*David A. Milberg*

Connie Francis

○ **Christmas in My Heart** / 1959 / Polydor 823561
Originally released in 1959. Vintage Connie Francis. —*David A. Milberg*

James Galway

☆ **Christmas Carol** / RCA 5888
Galway's magic flute is perfect for a fireside Christmas Eve with the entire family. —*David A. Milberg*

Art Garfunkel w/ Amy Grant

○ **Animal's Christmas** / 1986 / Columbia 40212
One of the best Christmas albums of the '80s, featuring "Carol of the Birds." —*David A. Milberg*

Edward Gerhard

Christmas / Oct. 1991 / Virtue 1920
A sterling collection of seasonal standards from Gerhard, an acoustic guitar fingerpicking virtuoso from New Hampshire. (He produced and played on Bill Morrissey's *North* album on Philo, and has a solo album of his own, *Night Birds*, also on Virtue.) —*Roundup newsletter*

Jackie Gleason

☆ **Merry Christmas** / 1956 / Capitol 94686
Originally released in 1956, this is the album for Christmas cuddling, in the great tradition of Jackie Gleason instrumental arrangements. —*David A. Milberg*

Merry Christmas / Sep. 10, 1990 / Capitol 94686
"The Great One" tended to be overly sentimental in the orchestrations he used on his many "mood" LPs, but on this seasonal release, the arrangements, while somewhat cloying, somehow work, making this a fine choice for the over-sixty set. His original "Christmas in Paris" is a bitter-sweet standout. —*Decibel Dennis MacDonald*

Amy Grant

☆ **A Christmas Album** / 1983 / Word 6768-279
Amy's first seasonal offering is still a perennially strong seller, and one of the best contemporary Christmas albums ever recorded. —*Thom Granger*

Home for Christmas / Oct. 6, 1992 / A&M 540001
A year (1993) after her mainstream success, contemporary Christian's most popular (and controversial) female vocalist is back with a very nice Christmas album—her second such project in her almost 17-year career. There's no rollicking "Baby, Baby" or "Good For Me" in this set, and Grant and her long-time producer Brown Bannister go for a softer, easy-listening, middle of the road sound. —*Edwin Smith, Rejoice*

Al Green

○ **White Christmas** / 1986 / Word 48597
Although seasonal albums can be ponderous affairs, Rev. Al Green made sure that wasn't the case on this mid '80s work. He attacked traditional carols, hymns and holiday material with the same devotion as he did soul anthems and gospel classics. Even if you're not a fan of holiday albums (and I for one am not) this deserves high praises. —*Ron Wynn*

David Grisman

☆ **Acoustic Christmas** / 1983 / Rounder 0190
The Dawg's new tricks include wayward wanderings amid medieval settings (Respighi airs), swing ("Santa Claus Is Coming to Town"), the light fantastic (a wonderful "Winter Wonderland" like a hail of radiant snowflakes) and an odd, slummy, delightful "Silent Night." Except for the bad duck joke on the mercifully brief "We Wish You a Merry Christmas" and the sax-soggy "White Christmas," the level of music is consistently out of this world. The mood ranges all over the place, but what virtuosity! —*Bob Coltman, Roundup newsletter*

Vince Guaraldi

☆ **A Charlie Brown Christmas** / Jan. 16, 1992 / Fantasy 8431
The original soundtrack to this annual CBS TV special is one that both children and the child in all of us can enjoy. Aside from the association with the Charles Schulz cartoon characters, Guaraldi's light piano touch makes this a nice CD to throw on when the Christmas party is over. —*Decibel Dennis MacDonald*

Merle Haggard

☆ **A Christmas Present** / 1973 / Curb 77352
While Hag keeps the mood light with selections such as "Santa Claus and Popcorn" and more traditional fare, he also has some bite with the high and lonesome "Daddy Won't Be Home for Christmas." His matter-of-fact tale about layoffs at the factory, "If We Make It through December," has become timeless in tough times. —*Dennis MacDonald*

John Wesley Harding

God Made Me Do It—the Christmas EP / 1989 / Warner Brothers 26093
On this four-song EP (plus "A Cosy Promotional Chat" with ex-Bonzo Dog Band Viv Stanshall), Harding, apparently at the behest of his label, wrote one seasonal song, the Bob Dylan-inspired "Talking Christmas Goodwill Blues," a free-association acoustic folk ditty. Amusing. —*Decibel Dennis MacDonald*

Emmylou Harris

☆ **Christmas Album (Light in the Stable)** / Jul. 1979 / Warner Brothers 3484
An album of soaring beauty, as if from angels on high. Neil Young, Dolly Parton, and Linda Ronstadt add harmony vocals to the moving title track, aided by James Burton's electric guitar and Hank DeVito's pedal steel. Beauty beyond belief. Recently reissued on CD. —*Dennis MacDonald*

Michael Hedges w/ Kelly McGillis

☆ **Santabear's First Christmas** / Windham Hill 0700
A story disc. Kelly McGillis narrates a Christmas tale over the lovely acoustic guitar of Hedges. —*AMG*

Tish Hinojosa

○ **Memorabilia Navidenia** / 1991 / Watermelon 1006
One does not have to understand Spanish to be moved by the beauty of Hinojosa's voice on "A La Nanita Nana," a traditional

Spanish lullabye from "Las Posadas" ("The Inns," a Christmas re-enactment). The remaining tunes are Hinojosa originals, including Spanish and English versions of "Arbolito" (Little Christmas Tree") and "Milagro," recalling the message of peace, hope and love from the Nativity. A release of rare beauty. —*Decibel Dennis MacDonald*

Paul Horn

☆ **The Peace Album** / 1988 / Kuckuck 11083
This holiday release from 1988 is by one of the greatest flutists of our time. The exquisite elegance of the music comes partly from the uniquely conceived "multi-flute orchestra," in which Horn is the only musician, adding unusual depth and dimension to the performances of these pieces, ranging from "Silent Night" to "We Three Kings" to "Ave Maria." This Celestial Harmonies release is dedicated to the peace inside each one of us and offers sterling performances throughout. —*Backroads Music/Heartbeats*

Engelbert Humperdinck

☆ **Merry Christmas** / Epic 36765
This was a hit album in 1980. All the romance of a typical Humperdinck album. —*David A. Milberg*

Inner Voices

Christmas Harmony / 1990 / Rhino
Four women whose a cappella voices will mesmerize you as they take flight on mostly sacred material, although they do a finger-snappin', sultry version of "Merry Christmas Baby" and "Boogie Woogie Santa Claus" accompanied by sleigh bells. Inner Voices have a fan in Johnny Mathis who said "I am a fan forever." —*Decibel Dennis MacDonald*

Burl Ives

○ **Have a Holly Jolly Christmas** / MCA 25992
An all-time holiday favorite. Includes the classic "Santa Claus is Coming to Town." —*AMG*

The Jackson 5

○ **The Jackson 5 Christmas Album** / 1970 / Motown 5250
One of the greatest holiday albums ever, and that's coming from someone who doesn't care for Christmas LPs. But Michael and company carry off the seasonal bit well, and their versions of these dusty hymns and carols could even charm Scrooge. —*Ron Wynn*

Alan Jackson

☆ **Honky Tonk Christmas** / Oct. 12, 1993 / Arista
One of the best country Christmas albums, with a smart blend of old and new songs and not a traditional carol in the bunch. Jackson starts off strong with the rocking "Honky Tonk Christmas," then sings a gorgeous duet with Alison Krauss. He adds his voice to a previously taped track by the late Keith Whitley on "There's a New Kid in Town," and does a credible job with Merle Haggard's "If We Make it Through December." Fabulous, save for a silly duet with the cartoon Chipmunks. —*Brian Mansfield*

Mahalia Jackson

☆ **Silent Night (Songs for Christmas)** / 1962 / CBS 38304
Whether or not you like sacred music, one cannot help but be moved by the power and passion with which Mahalia Jackson sings "Sweet Little Jesus Boy" and the spiritual "Go Tell it on the Mountain." Her rendition of "Silent Night, Holy Night" is simply inspirational. —*Decibel Dennis MacDonald*

☆ **Christmas with Mahalia Jackson** / Special Music 4608
This was the second of her two legendary gospel Christmas albums for Columbia. A worthy companion to her earlier *Silent Night* album. —*David A. Milberg*

Jambalaya Cajun Band

Joyeux Noel / Swallow 6100
This Cajun band sings six of the fourteen songs included here in French and another five more bi-lingually. Lyrics are provided for all songs in both French and English, as Jambalaya add some spice to seasonal favorites and include original compositions alongside old traditional Cajun fare, e.g. "Il Est Ne" ("He Is Born," which used to be sung in French Catholic masses). With twin fiddles and pumping accordion, this includes the most rollickin' instrumental of "Joy to the World" you may ever hear. —*Decibel Dennis MacDonald*

The Jets

Christmas with the Jets / 1986 / MCA 5856
A somewhat charming holiday album by the Minneapolis family group the Jets. But they'd lost their commercial clout some time back, and by now were beginning to sound like one more faded teen troupe. As with most Christmas releases, if you enjoy the genre, you'll find room for one more. —*Ron Wynn*

Evan Johns & His H-Bombs

○ **Please, Mr. Santa Claus** / Aug. 23, 1991 / Rykodisc 30169
Put this nine-song mini-album CD in the Christmas stocking of any rock & roll fan. The "crash and burn" guitar style of Johns recalls Santo and Johnny ("Snowed In") and Jimmy Bryant ("Santa's Little Helper"), while his snarly vocals on the title track bring new meaning to "cool yule." Spiced with original instrumentals and a cover of "Telstar," this is a must for Evan Johns fans and those who want a little bite in their yuletide listening. —*Dennis MacDonald*

Etta Jones

Christmas with Etta Jones / Jan. 1991 / Muse 5411
Well done holiday album featuring the underrated singer Etta Jones putting her spin on traditional Christmas favorites. It's strictly for Christmas music fans, but maintains integrity and jazz connection through fine vocal and instrumental performances, production and song selection. —*Ron Wynn*

Spike Jones

☆ **It's a Spike Jones Christmas** / 1970 / Rhino 70196
A real oddity, this features Spike Jones's usual sense of musical humor, with spoofs of holiday standards intermingled with reverently-sung Christmas carols by his 25-voice choir. Includes his novelty hit, "All I Want for Christmas Is My Two Front Teeth," and "Jingle Bells" sung in Pig Latin. How curious are you? —*Roundup newsletter*

The Judds

☆ **Christmas Time with the Judds** / RCA 6422
Country Christmas with Wynonna and Naomi Judd. Strong performances. —*AMG*

Peter Kater

☆ **For Christmas** / 1987 / Silver Wave 503
Supper-club piano stylings of familiar holiday songs. Very fine pianist. It works. —*Michael Erlewine*

○ **The Season** / Nov. 26, 1991 / Silver Wave 702
Expanding the scope and repertoire of his previous holiday recording, Kater is joined here by a violin, sax and flute on six traditional and four original Kater compositions, making for another classic recording. —*Backroads Music/Heartbeats*

Stan Kenton & His Orchestra

☆ **Merry Christmas!** / 1961 / Capitol 94451
A hit album from 1961. A definite Kenton collectible. —*David A. Milberg*

○ **Kenton's Christmas** / Feb. 21, 1961-Mar. 14, 1961 / Creative World 1001
Traditional carols arranged for the Kenton brass and rhythm—no saxes. "O Holy Night," "Angels We Have Heard On High," "O Tannenbaum," "The Holly and the Ivy," and more. Recorded in 1961. — *Roundup newsletter*

King's College Choir

☆ **O Come All Ye Faithful** / Argo 414042

Sixteen traditional carols done by this classic Christmas choir. This is what carols were meant to sound like. —*Michael Erlewine*

The Kingston Trio

☆ **The Last Month of the Year** / 1960 / Capitol 93116
An essential part of any Christmas album collection. True Christmas folk songs, from spirituals to Old English rounds. A must! —*David A. Milberg*

Gladys Knight & The Pips

That Special Time of Year / 1971 / Columbia 38114
A good Christmas album from Gladys Knight and the Pips, a great one if you're a fan of holiday releases. They don't have to fake intimacy since they're a family group, and Knight's voice sounds both sincere and moving on the hymns, carols and seasonal items. Unfortunately, at present it's out of print. —*Ron Wynn*

Lyn Larsen

The Pipes of Christmas / Pro Arte 282
A large theater organ (Paramount Theater) and Christmas songs add up to a trip to the 1930s. —*Michael Erlewine*

Peggy Lee

☆ **Christmas Carousel** / 1960 / Capitol 94450
This is the classic Christmas sound of Peggy Lee during her peak recording years. —*David A. Milberg*

The Lettermen

☆ **For Christmas this Year** / Sep. 10, 1990 / Capitol 94687
Here is the early Lettermen sound of 1966. Put a log on the fire, sit back, and enjoy. —*David A. Milberg*

Ramsey Lewis Trio

The Sound of Christmas / 1960-1961 / Chess 91566
The good half of this classic jazz yule release features just the trio having a swingin' time with "Here Comes Santa Claus" and "Winter Wonderland," and cookin' on the funky original, "Christmas Blues." The bad half kicks in when Riley Hampton adds a ten-man string section to the last five tunes. —*Decibel Dennis MacDonald*

☆ **More Sounds of Christmas** / MCA 91569
Again hampered by strings on too many cuts, on the plus side, this does contain the ultra-cool original, "Eggnog," featuring Lewis on celeste. —*Decibel Dennis MacDonald*

Norman Luboff Choir

☆ **Christmas with the Norman Luboff Choir** / RCA 2941
This one debuted in 1964 and made the *Billboard* charts. If you like the choral group sound of the early '60s, you'll love this one. —*AMG*

Madeline MacNeil

☆ **Christmas Comes Anew: Christmas Music with Dulcimers and Singing** / Kicking Mule 247
European and American Christmas songs with the bright voice of MacNeil backed by acoustic guitar, dulcimer, and strings. —*Michael Erlewine*

Henry Mancini

☆ **Merry Mancini Christmas** / RCA 3612
Mancini magic at its best, for the holidays. Perfect background music for holiday family get-togethers. —*David A. Milberg*

Barry Manilow

○ **Because It's Christmas** / Arista 8644
Christmas classics in the Manilow style. Nestle under the mistletoe with this one. —*David A. Milberg*

Mannheim Steamroller

☆ **Fresh Aire Christmas 1988** / American Gramaphone 1988

A worthy successor to their first *Christmas Album.* —*David A. Milberg*

Mantovani Orchestra

☆ **All-Time Xmas Favorites, Vol. 1 & 2** / Deram 820341
Great music to wake up to on Christmas morning. Many cuts taken from his 1953 million-selling album. —*David A. Milberg*

Christmas Carols / London 913
This album made the Billboard Top 40 charts for five consecutive years, 1957-1961, with the peak of Number 3 in 1958. —*AMG*

Manzanera & Mac

Christmas the Player / 1989 / Rykodisc 10125
Christmas carols played on traditional instruments by British street musicians, led by Roxy Music's Andy MacKay. — *Roundup newsletter*

Wynton Marsalis

☆ **Crescent City Christmas Card** / 1989 / Columbia 45287
This elegant Christmas album swings with heart and soul and is certain to be a standard. — *Rick Clark, Rock & Roll Disc.*

The Martin Best Medieval Ensemble

☆ **Thys Yool—a Medieval Christmas** / May 1988 / Nimbus 5137
Elegant music. Early Christmas celebrations on original instruments. —*Michael Erlewine*

Johnny Mathis

☆ **Merry Christmas** / 1958 / Columbia 8021
Of the several Christmas LPs Mathis has recorded, this one gets the nod. With empathetic arrangements by Percy Faith, it's impossible to say how many babies were born the following September after parents heard Johnny Mathis crooning "The Christmas Song." Smo-o-o-oth! —*Decibel Dennis MacDonald*

Give Me Your Love for Christmas / 1969 / Columbia 09923
A million-seller featuring the Mathis sound after he returned to Columbia Records from the Mercury label. —*David A. Milberg*

Christmas Eve with Johnny Mathis / 1986 / Columbia 40447
More romantic sounds of the season, '70s-style, featuring "Christmas Is." —*David A. Milberg*

John McCutcheon

Winter Solstice / 1984 / Rounder 0192
A collection of hammer dulcimer music for Christmas, Chanukah, and the New Year's season. With help from members of the Washington Bach Consort and the group Trapezoid, McCutcheon leads a musical journey through many lands and cultures, all in the holiday spirit. —*Roundup newsletter*

Maureen McGovern

☆ **Christmas with Maureen McGovern** / CBS 45869
Velvety smooth. Great for Christmas cuddling. —*David A. Milberg*

Jacob Miller

Natty Christmas / 1978 / RAS 3103
Along with DJ Ray I, Jacob sends up Xmas; "Deck the Halls with Boughs of Collie" sets the pace. —*Roger Steffens*

Mitch Miller

● **Christmas Sing-Along with Mitch Miller** / 1958 / CBS 38298
The first *Sing Along with Mitch* Christmas album. The MOR sound of the '50s. —*David A. Milberg*

☆ **Holiday Sing-Along with Mitch Miller** / 1961 / CBS 38297
This album made the Billboard Top 40 in both 1961 and 1962. —*AMG*

The Miracles

Christmas with the Miracles / 1963 / Motown 5254
Recorded in October, 1963, when the Miracles still included Claudette Robinson, Smokey's wife, in the lineup; she sings lead on "Let It Snow." Smokey contributes one original, the mid-tempo "Christmas Everyday," that stands as one of the finest Motown

seasonal favorites and one of Smokey's most memorable performances of his long career. —*Decibel Dennis MacDonald*

Jim Nabors

☆ **Christmas Album** / 1990 / CBS 9531
An easy-listening treat that includes one of the best versions of "White Christmas" ever. —*David A. Milberg*

Willie Nelson

☆ **Pretty Paper** / 1979 / CBS 36189
Worth the price just for the title song. —*David A. Milberg*

New Edition

○ **Christmas all over the World** / MCA 39040
A musical Christmas party, featuring the title tune. —*David A. Milberg*

Mojo Nixon & The Toadliquors

Horny Holidays! / Triple X 51117
Irreverent and raunchy, would you expect anything less from Mojo Nixon? Not for the kiddies or Tipper Gores of the world, this CD is hilarious if you listen to it in the spirit it was recorded (a few trips to the spiked eggnog punchbowl might help). "Mr. Grinch" is a perfect vehicle for Nixon's from-the-gutter vocals, while his original "It's Christmas Time" recalls the Memphis soul-struttin' of Rufus Thomas crossed with Clarence Carter's down 'n' dirty style. "We Three Kings" is turned into a tale of debauchery as Nixon growls "We were drunk for three days straight, feeling like we were Tom Waits." Play this not to be sanctified but to be amused. —*Decibel Dennis MacDonald*

NRBQ

○ **Christmas Wish** / Rounder 2501
NRBQ bring a sense of goofy fun to this eight-song mini-album, covering standards in their wacky style and contributing a few originals—Terry Adams's "Electric Train" and Joey Spampinato's "Christmas Wish." The cover photo of NRBQ decked out in their winter pajamas is a real hoot. —*Dennis MacDonald*

Laura Nyro

Christmas and the Beads of Sweat / 1970 / Columbia 30259
One of her most wonderful early albums; includes "Brown Earth," "When I Was a Freeport and You Were the Main Drag," "Up on the Roof," and more. —*Ladyslipper*

Odetta

☆ **Christmas Spirituals** / 1960 / Alcazar 104
Odetta's husky voice is often stunning, both in her a cappella performances and her songs with accompaniment. Odetta says these songs are traditional spirituals; neither purely African nor purely American, but songs that emerged from the sufferings of slavery. Powerful stuff. —*Dennis MacDonald*

Alexander O'Neal

○ **My Gift to You** / 1988 / Tabu 45016
So good I want to play it year 'round. Decent contemporary holiday discs are hard to come by, but Minneapolis's finest soul singer and producers Jimmy Jam and Terry Lewis created a disc that nearly rivals Spector's in concept (all the originals are brilliant) and Elvis Presley's in performance. "Sleigh Ride" is the hardest piece of Xmas funk James Brown never cut, and the brassy treatment given to "Winter Wonderland" would make Sinatra proud. —*John Floyd, Rock & Roll Disc*

Eugene Ormandy

☆ **Glorious Sound of Christmas** / CBS 6369
Although they're not credited in the title, this album also features the Mormon Tabernacle Choir. It was a million-seller when it was first released in 1962. —*David A. Milberg*

Greatest Christmas Hits / CBS 7161
This album also includes the Temple University Choir, combined with the Philadelphia Orchestra for a truly classical Christmas. —*David A. Milberg*

Osmond Family Christmas

○ **Osmond Family Christmas** / Curb 77513
Donny and his brothers singing smooth harmonies for the holidays. —*David A. Milberg*

Buck Owens

☆ **Christmas with Buck Owens** / Curb 77349
Buck adds fun to the season's festivities when dishing out country corn such as "Santa Looked a Lot like Daddy." The Buckaroos turn in a romping instrumental of "Jingle Bells," and Buck contributes a honky-tonk Christmas classic with "Blue Christmas Lights." —*Dennis MacDonald*

Patti Page

☆ **Christmas with Patti Page** / 1956 / Mercury 20093
Holiday standards and sacred sounds, as with the hit "Happy Birthday, Jesus." —*David A. Milberg*

Stevan Pasero

☆ **Christmas Classics for Guitar** / Sugo 8602
Guitar transcriptions and arrangements of a variety of traditional Christmas fare, folk tunes, and classical compositions. —*Michael Erlewine*

Kim Pensyl

A Kim Pensyl Christmas / 1991 /
This 1989 Christmas release comes from the composer of the popular *Pensyl Sketches*. Kim blends his inimitable piano style with extensive synthesizer orchestrations to produce an album that varies from dynamic uptempo renditions to gentle, introspective colorings. A couple of original pieces complement the selection of traditional Christmas tunes, making this an exciting year-end release. —*Backroads Music/Heartbeats*

Peter Paul & Mary

☆ **A Holiday Celebration** / 1988 / Gold Castle 71316
This 1988 release contains songs they made famous such as "Blowin' In the Wind" plus "A Soalin'," "Children Go Where I Send Thee," "O Come O Come Emmanuel," "Light One Candle," "The Cherry Tree Carol," and more; joyfully and elegantly performed live-in-concert, many with full choir and orchestra. —*Ladyslipper*

Michael Petri

☆ **Noel! Noel! Noel!** / RCA 60060
Christmas music from one of the world's finest recorder players. Backed by the Westminster Abbey Choir and the National Philharmonic with Martin Neary. —*Michael Erlewine*

The Platters

○ **Christmas with the Platters** / PolyGram 822742
Christmas standards with the Platters touch, plus a couple of Buck Ram originals: "Come Home for Christmas" and "Merry Christmas, Baby." —*David A. Milberg*

Elvis Presley

○ **Christmas Album** / Nov. 1957 / RCA 5486
From playful takes on "White Christmas" to bluesy, low down readings of "Blue Christmas" and "Santa Claus Is Back in Town," to the straight interpretations of yuletide standards that close it out, there's simply no other Christmas album that sounds quite like this. —*Cub Koda & Rick Clark*

Memories of Christmas / RCA 4395
Compiled in 1982, this collects some of the King's most-loved Christmas material—"Blue Christmas," "Santa Claus is Back in Town"—and adds four unreleased versions of seasonal songs, the standout being a sizzling eight minutes of "Merry Christmas, Baby" showing that this boy from Memphis could grind out the blues with the best of 'em. —*Decibel Dennis MacDonald*

Sings the Wonderful World of Xmas / RCA 4579
The least of the Elvis seasonal releases, notable only for his version of "Merry Christmas Baby." —*Decibel Dennis MacDonald*

Charley Pride

☆ **Christmas in My Home Town** / 1970 / RCA 4406
The title tune was a great Christmas hit. Mellow C&W for the holidays. —*David A. Milberg*

Raffi

☆ **Raffi's Christmas Album** / Shoreline 10043
This is an essential collection that's perfect for kids and still enjoyable for adults. —*David A. Milberg*

Lou Rawls

Merry Christmas Ho! Ho! Ho! / Sep. 10, 1965 / Capitol 94703
Early Lou Rawls at his best, including his hit version of "Little Drummer Boy." —*David A. Milberg*

Leon Redbone

Christmas Island / 1989 / Private Music 2061
The enigmatic Leon Redbone gives his time-warp treatment to a predictable bunch of Christmas standards. Fans of Redbone's low-key camp style will enjoy this, particularly the duet with Dr. John on "Frosty the Snowman." —*Rick Clark*

Ren & Stimpy

Crock O' Christmas / Sony Wonder
What hath Nickelodeon begat? Celebrate that shabbiest holiday of the year, Yaksmas Eve, with the hairballing Stimpy and high-strung Chihuahua, Ren, as they trash Christmas classics : "Fleck the Walls," "Cobb to the World," "The Twelve Days of Yaksmas"— you get the idea. Stupidity knows no limits unless, of course, Beavis and Butthead get to release *Huh Huh Holidays*. —*Decibel Dennis MacDonald*

Paul Revere & The Raiders

Christmas Present & Past / 1967 / CBS 45310
A rocking-great trip back to the 60s with Mark Lindsay and Paul Revere. An essential oldie-but-goodie. —*David A. Milberg*

Bob Rivers Comedy Corp

☆ **Twisted Christmas** / Critique 90671
This is one of the funniest Christmas albums of all time! Essential! Includes the classic "Message from the King." —*David A. Milberg*

Marcus Roberts

○ **Prayer for Peace** / 1991 / Jive/Novus 63124
Outstanding piano solos, so good that even those who loathe holiday music might find it hard to ignore if they give it a listen. Roberts' solo dates have moved more and more back to early styles like stride, ragtime and boogie-woogie, but here he's more contemporary and introspective than reflective. —*Ron Wynn*

Kenny Rogers

☆ **Christmas** / Sep. 1981 / EMI America 46558
Kenny Rogers does his thing with old and new Christmas tunes. Just what you would expect. —*AMG*

Rotary Connection

○ **Peace** / 1968 / Chess 91568
A great Christmas present from the '60s, featuring the late Minnie Riperton. —*David A. Milberg*

Royal College of Music Choir/Brass Ensemble

☆ **Carols for Christmas** / 1989 / Rykodisc 10004-5
These 41 carols and hymns are done, for the most part, a cappella. Spacious. Lovely. —*Michael Erlewine*

Royal Philharmonic w/ David Newman

☆ **It's a Wonderful Life; a Christmas Carol ...** / Telarc 88801
Royal Philharmonic with David Newman. Original scores for three of the greatest Christmas films of all time, *It's a Wonderful Life*, *A Christmas Carol*, and *Miracle on 34th Street*. Restored and recorded in pristine digital sound. —*Michael Erlewine*

Sackville All Stars

☆ **Christmas Record** / Mar. 29, 1986-Mar. 30, 1986 / Sackville 3038
Jazz improvisations on standard Christmas tunes. With Milt Hinton on bass, Gus Johnson on drums, Ralph Sutton on piano, and Jim Galloway on soprano saxophone. —*Michael Erlewine*

Mike, Peggy, and Penny Seeger

☆ **American Folk Songs for Christmas** / 1989 / Rounder 0268-0269
Lovers of traditional serious folk music will enjoy this double CD set, which features everything from earnestly untrained a cappella performances to a whole array of acoustic instrumentation, including mandolin, dulcimer, guitar, psaltery, autoharp, banjo, and so forth. —*Rick Clark*

Doc Severinsen

☆ **Merry Christmas** /
"Tonight Show" band treatment of Christmas classics. —*David A. Milberg*

Robert Shaw Chorale

☆ **Many Moods of Christmas** / 1962 / Telarc 80087
This is one of the later, and better, Christmas offerings from these performers. —*David A. Milberg*

Harry Simeone Chorale

☆ **The Little Drummer Boy** / 1984 / PolyGram 822744
Contains the definitive version of the title song and similar performances of other sounds of the season. Essential. —*David A. Milberg*

Frank Sinatra

☆ **The Sinatra Christmas Album** / Nov. 11, 1987 / Capitol 48329
Essential Sinatra Christmas sounds of his Capitol era, with "Christmas Waltz" and "Have Yourself a Merry Little Christmas." —*David A. Milberg*

Christmas Dreaming / 1989 / CBS 40707
A collection of Sinatra sides cut between 1944 and 1950 to commemorate the season. The refinement of his phrasing and vocal timbre during those years is stunning. Even though his best work was yet to come, this is a worthwhile CD for Sinatra lovers. —*Rick Clark, Rock & Roll Disc*

Chris Stamey Group

○ **Christmas Time** / 1986 / Coyote 8564
An expanded reissue of the 1986 Coyote LP, this is a popmeister's heaven as ex-dB's Stamey reunites with the dB's on the title track and duets with Wes Lachot on the Badfinger soundalike, "Christmas is the Only Time (I Think of You)." Cult figure Alex Chilton turns in a fairly straight version of "The Christmas Song" and his "Jesus Christ" (from his last Big Star LP) is here as well. Syd Straw turns in a Phil Spector "Wall of Sound" version of Blondie's "(I'm Always Touched by Your) Presence, Dear"(with the title changed to "Presents"). More ear candy from the dB's, Peter Holsapple and others, and look for that hidden track eighteen ! —*Decibel Dennis MacDonald*

The Statler Brothers

☆ **Statler Brothers Christmas Card** / 1979 / Mercury 822743
Wonderful stuff, with "I Believe in Santa Claus." —*David A. Milberg*

Doug Stone

The First Christmas / Apr. 1992 / Epic 52844
Given the number of songwriters in Nashville, it's surprising the town hasn't produced more Christmas songs. The First Christmas gets a bunch of them, though. Song like "An Angel Like You" play off Stone's romantic-balladeer image, and "When December Comes Around" wound sound great any time of year. "Sailing Home for Christmas" depicts the irony of soldiers celebrating the

coming of "peace on earth" while stationed on a battleship. — *Brian Mansfield*

Barbra Streisand

☆ **Barbra's Christmas Album** / 1967 / CBS 9557
An essential collection including "Sleep in Heavenly Peace (Silent Night)" and "Jingle Bells." —*David A. Milberg*

Supremes w/ Stevie Wonder

○ **Merry Christmas/Someday at Christmas** / Motown 8141
Contains the classics "Twinkle, Twinkle Little Me" and "Someday at Christmas." Truly supreme wonders. —*David A. Milberg*

Russ Taff

The Christmas Song / Oct. 5, 1992 / Sparrow 1338
Jazzy, '50s pop vocal and instrumental approach reminds of classic Cole/Sinatra seasonal sets. —*Thom Granger*

Take 6

☆ **He Is Christmas** / Feb. 1992 / Reprise 26665
Take 6 makes the sacred Christmas repertoire their own with their unique blend of gospel, jazz and vocal magic. *He is Christmas* features the original title track along with nine traditional Christmas carols transformed in arrangements by the soul-stirring rhythms and ear-shaking dissonances of the Take 6 fundamental style. Joey Kibble, brother of chief arranger Mark Kibble, joins the sextet for the first tune on the album; and the Yellowjackets provide instrumental accompaniment on "God Rest Ye Merry Gentlemen." — *Erin Ryan, Roundup newsletter*

The Temptations

○ **Christmas Card/Give Love at Christmas** / 1900 / Motown 8117
This two-album CD contains all of their Christmas hits, including "Rudolph the Red-Nosed Reindeer," "Give Love at Christmas," and "Silent Night." —*David A. Milberg*

The Christmas Card / Oct. 1970 / Motown 5251
The Christmas sound for the "Big Chill Generation," including a great rendition of "Rudolph the Red-Nosed Reindeer." —*David A. Milberg*

Give Love at Christmas / Aug. 1980 / Motown 5279
A nice holiday package, and arguably the company's best, along with the Jackson Five christmas album. The group didn't just coast through the carols and hymns, but really injected some energy into them, particularly Eddie Kendricks. —*Ron Wynn*

Dylan Thomas

☆ **A Child's Christmas in Wales** / Caedmon 1002
Everyone should hear Dylan Thomas read this lovely prose piece. Enchanting, in the true sense of the word. Also included are Thomas poems such as "Do Not Go Gentle into that Good Night." —*Michael Erlewine*

Eric Tingstad & Nancy Rumbel

☆ **The Gift** / 1989 / Sona Gaia 62751
Tingstad and Rumbel, who have a couple of the best cuts on the *Narada Christmas Collection*, blend a spatial new-age sensibility with straight melodic readings of traditional Christmas music, performed on acoustic string and wind instruments. Sometimes the exquisite technique is a little bloodless, but all in all, very well done. —*Rick Clark, Rock & Roll Disc*

Randy Travis

☆ **Old-Time Christmas** / Aug. 29, 1989 / Warner Brothers 25972
Ten Christmas songs, some old, some new, one by Travis ("How Do I Wrap My Heart for Christmas," written with Paul Overstreet). "God Rest Ye Merry Gentlemen" is outstanding. —*Brian Mansfield & AMG*

Trinity College Choir

☆ **Carols from Trinity** / Conifer 501
Twenty-seven carols (old and new) from renowned Trinity College Choir, with Richard Marlow. Classic and elegant. —*Michael Erlewine*

Travis Tritt

Loving Time of the Year / May 1992 / Warner Brothers 45029
The harder Tritt rocks on *Loving Time of the Year*, the better he sounds. His Southern-boogie versions of "Winter Wonderland" and "Silver Bells" make a perfect antidote to sleigh-bell burnout. When he tries to be an "interpretive singer" on "Have Yourself a Merry Little Christmas," he falls flat on his face. Elsewhere, Tritt writes the title track while covering two by Buck Owens and one by Sonny James. —*Brian Mansfield*

Bobby Vee

Merry Christmas / 1962 / EMI America 94993
Not just the standards, but some tasty originals like "A Not So Merry Christmas" in this '60s Christmas time capsule. —*David A. Milberg*

The Ventures

★ **Ventures' Christmas Album** / Oct. 22, 1990 / EMI America 94994
This is easily one of my Top 10 favorite Yuletide albums of all time. Recorded in 1965, at the height of the Ventures popularity, the group takes seasonal classics and with their trademark Mosrite guitars in hand, they adapt the tunes to incorporate hits of the day : "Santa Claus is Comin' to Town" crossed with "Wooly Bully"; "Frosty the Snowman" with a little "Tequila" thrown in; even the original "Sleigh Ride" reprises the group's smash hit "Walk—Don't Run." Highest recommendation. —*Decibel Dennis MacDonald*

The Whispers

○ **Happy Holidays to You** / 1979 / CBS 75305
A hit when it was first released, the title tune is especially good. —*David A. Milberg*

Slim Whitman

☆ **Christmas Album** / 1969 / EMI America 94995
This is a reissue of an album originally released in 1969. Vintage Slim Whitman for the holidays. —*David A. Milberg*

Roger Whittaker

☆ **Christmas Album** / 1978 / RCA 2933
This is the sound of Roger Whittaker at the peak of his career. A worthwhile stocking-stuffer. —*David A. Milberg*

Andy Williams

☆ **Christmas Album** / 1963 / CBS 8887
An essential Christmas classic! A million-seller in 1963, and a perennial hit ever since. —*David A. Milberg*

Christmas Present / 1965 / CBS 33191
This was Andy Williams's second million-selling Christmas album, and with good reason. Here is Andy's sound at its peak. —*David A. Milberg*

Merry Christmas / CBS 40169
Andy's voice is custom-made for Christmas. Here are 17 tunes crooned by an expert. —*AMG*

Joe Williams

That Holiday Feeling / 1990 / PolyGram 843956
Dave Pell's Prez Conference was to Lester Young what Supersax is to Charlie Parker. Pell's short-lived group featured harmonized Lester Young solos recreated by three tenors and a baritone; their matchup with singer Joe Williams is quite enjoyable. Since Young was in Count Basie's orchestra when Jimmy Rushing was the vocalist, Joe Williams has a rare opportunity to give his own interpretation to Rushing and Billie Holiday classics like "I May Be Wrong," "You Can Depend On Me," "If Dreams Come True" and "Easy Living." A delightful and swinging date. —*Scott Yanow*

Jackie Wilson

○ **Merry Christmas from Jackie Wilson** / 1963 / Rhino 70574

After being out of print for years, this 1963 gem from one of the most exciting R&B entertainers of all time is finally available. Essential. —*David A. Milberg*

George Winston

☆ **December** / 1982 / Windham Hill 1025
The mother of all solo instrumental albums, and with good reason. Mixing traditional carols with Pachelbel's Canon and a few originals, Winston produces a solo piano album of unparalleled—and undeniable—beauty. How can music be simultaneously stirring and soothing, relaxed yet exalted? Millions have found the answer here, and an industry has spent more than a decade trying to duplicate it. — *William Ruhlmann*

Frank Yankovic

☆ **Christmas Memories** / Smash 830396
This one won a Christmas-music Grammy, and with good reason. You'll love this version of "Blue Christmas." —*David A. Milberg*

Christmas Collections

Acoustic Christmas / 1990 / CBS 46880
All but two of the dozen tracks were recorded specifically for this compilation; Harry Connick, Jr.'s solo piano rendition of "Winter Wonderland" was cut for the movie When Harry Met Sally. . . . Tops on this CD is Rosanne Cash's tender version of "It Came Upon a Midnight Clear," accompanied by guitar, violin and mandola. T Bone Burnett turns in a sparse "God Rest Ye Merry Gentlemen," with sonorous dobro and violin from Jerry Douglas and Mark O'Connor. Shawn Colvin steams things up a bit with a jazzy "Have Yourself a Merry Christmas" but the most unusual track belongs to the unlikely pairing of Poi Dog Pondering with the Dirty Dozen Brass Band : prepare to second-line for their festive version of "Mele Kalikimaka." —*Decibel Dennis MacDonald*

★ **All Star Christmas Jubilee** / Vintage Jazz Classics 1016
This 77-minute disc includes two Armed Forces Radio Service Christmas Jubilee shows (1945 and 1947) and other '40's holiday tracks. The Delta Rhythm Boys harmonize on a snippet of "Jingle Bells" before the master of patter and jive, Ernie "Bubbles" Whitman takes over as MC. Count Basie and His Orchestra are the house band for the '45 show, with guests including Lena Horne on "Silent Night" and a hilarious Christmas jive routine with Whitman and Eddie Green. Duke Ellington and His Orchestra are the backing band for the '47 show, jumping into the festivities with "Ring Dem Blues." The Nat King Cole Trio deliver a smooth take of "The Christmas Song," Perry Como wanders through a "Winter Wonderland" and there are non-Yule selections from other jazz artists. The non-Jubilee selections include four from Frank Sinatra, Kay Starr's "December" and a novelty version of "Jingle Bells" from Mel Blanc & the Sportsmen. Although approaching half a century old, these performances are every bit as entertaining today. Highly recommended. —*Decibel Dennis MacDonald*

The Alligator Records Christmas Collection / 1992 / Alligator 9201
To really get that Christmas party smoking, throw *The Alligator Records Christmas Collection* (Alligator/Warner Music) on the disc player and another log on the fire. The legendary blues label dishes up the goods and turns up the heat with a set of mostly original compositions. Koko Taylor peels wallpaper with "Merry, Merry Christmas"; William Clarke's wailing harp drives "Please Let Me Be Your Santa Claus"; Charles Brown sets the tone with "Boogie Woogie Santa Claus"; and Lonnie Brooks serves the seasonal gumbo with "Christmas on the Bayou." For an updated traditional, just try sitting still for Katie Webster's "Deck the Halls with Boogie Woogie." —*Roch Parisien*

Alligator Stomp, Vol. 4—Cajun Christmas / 1992 / Rhino 71058
If you're throwin' a Yule dance party, I don't know of a better seasonal collection that features two-steps and waltzes. Of the 17 tracks, 15 were licensed from THE Cajun label, Swallow Records. Beausoleil recorded two songs especially for this compilation, the original "Christmas Bayou" and "It Came Upon a Midnight Clear," performed as an instrumental Cajun waltz. Four tracks are

drawn from Beausoleil's fiddler/singer/leader Michael Doucet's Swallow *Christmas Bayou* CD, including this CD's closer, "Auld Lang Syne," which starts out traditionally slow before finishing off as a spirited two-step. Other highlights include Belton Richard's versions of "Blue Christmas" and "Please Come Home for Christmas," both sung in Cajun French: Richard's mournful vocals and the accompanying steel guitar give both songs added depth. Caveat emptor: if you hate accordions, fiddles, or just having a good time, do not buy this CD. —*Decibel Dennis MacDonald, Roundup newsletter*

Austin Rhythm and Blues Christmas / 1989 / Epic 40576
Originally issued on the Austin label in 1983, this rockin' release was reissued with a new cover on Epic in 1986. Standouts include the Fabulous Thunderbird's spirited instrumental "Rockin' Winter Wonderland," and vocalist Kim Wilson pouring his harp and soul into Hop Wilson's "Merry Christmas, Darling." Two of Austin's finest blues divas, Angela Strehli and Lou Ann Barton, turn in smokey and sultry covers of yule classics, but it is bassist/vocalist Sarah Brown who sizzles with her original "My Christmas Is Hung with Tears." —*Dennis MacDonald*

Big Band Christmas / CBS 40948
Big bands, often with pop vocalists, including Les Brown with Doris Day singing "The Christmas Song," Red Norvo with vocalist Mildred Bailey on "I've Got My Love to Keep Me Warm" and Benny Goodman with Peggy Lee and Art Lund duetting on "Winter Weather." Laster Lanin's arrangement of "Christmas Night in Harlem" is one that'll have you flip, flop and flying, but most of this CD is on the slower, sentimental side. —*Decibel Dennis MacDonald*

☆ **Billboard Greatest Christmas Hits: 1955-1989** / 1989 / Rhino 70636
Billboard Greatest Christmas Hits: 1955—Present / Vol. 2 features Elvis on "Blue Christmas," Bobby Helms ("Jingle Bell Rock"), and Brenda Lee ("Rockin' around the Christmas Tree"). On the novelty side, this disc has "Grandma Got Run Over by a Reindeer," "The Chipmunk Song," and others. —*Rick Clark*

☆ **Billboard Greatest Christmas Hits: Country** / Rhino 70639
Primarily late '40s and late '50s hits, many more novelty than C&W. The Texas Troubadour, Ernest Tubb, hit the charts twice with his 1949 A-side, "Blue Christmas," and then the B-side, "White Christmas" (both are here). Country corn from Tex Ritter, Buck Owens, Eddy Arnold, and others, alongside Johnny Cash's solemn "The Little Drummer Boy." —*Dennis MacDonald*

☆ **Billboard Greatest Christmas Hits: 1935-1954** / Rhino 70637
Some of the biggest seasonal classics are represented on these two discs. *Vol. 1* opens with Bing singing (guess what?) "White Christmas" and runs through Gene Autry's "Rudolph the Red-Nosed Reindeer," "The Christmas Song" (Nat King Cole), "Let It Snow, Let It Snow, Let It Snow" (Vaughn Monroe), the annoying "All I Want for Christmas (Is My Two Front Teeth)" by Spike Jones, and more. —*Rick Clark*

○ **Billboard Greatest R&B Christmas Hits** / Rhino 70638
Includes the original version (1947) of "Merry Christmas, Baby" by Johnny Moore's Three Blazers, featuring Charles Brown's smoother-than-brandy vocals; jump-blues from Mabel Scott on "Boogie-Woogie Santa Claus"; vocal group contributions from the Orioles and the Cadillacs; Chuck Berry's "Run Rudolph, Run"; and five more. —*Dennis MacDonald*

☆ **Blue Yule—Christmas Blues and R&B Classics** / Rhino 70568
A stellar 18-song compilation with many tracks that are not duplicated on other in-print collections. Treasures abound here: rare tracks from John Lee Hooker and Lightnin' Hopkins, Hop Wilson's original "Merry Christmas, Darling" (covered by the Fabulous Thunderbirds on *An Austin Rhythm & Blues Christmas*), Louis Jordan's last recording (1968, "Santa Claus, Santa Claus"), and more. —*Dennis MacDonald*

Bob Hope's Christmas Party / 1945 / Vintage Jazz Classics 1031
"Command Performances" were half-hour radio programs recorded for the Armed Forces Radio Service shipped to the WWII troops on 16-inch platters. On this collection there is a humorous sketch from Mel Blanc as "P-P-Private Sad Sack, "using the Porky Pig voice; banter with Hope, Bing Crosby, Judy Garland and other celebrities; and musical performances from Dinah Shore, Harry James, Johnny Mercer, and others. Carols performed

by Garland, Shore, Crosby and more conclude the CD. —*Decibel Dennis MacDonald*

☆ **Bummed-Out Christmas!** / Rhino 70912
Not just for the Scrooge on your holiday list. This album has a rare gem from the Everly Brothers, "Christmas Eve Can Kill You." George Jones is equally mournful on "Lonely Christmas Call" from 1963, but the most powerful track comes from the duo of Johnny & Jon with the deep soul ballad, 1966's "Christmas In Vietnam"—their call-and-response style is textbook Sam and Dave. On the lighter side, there's the Christmas Jug Band (featuring Dan Hicks). This compilation ranges from the humorous (Sherwin Linton, "Santa Got a D.W.I.") to the mournful (George Jones, "Lonely Christmas Call"). —*Dennis MacDonald*

☆ **Christmas Album** / CBS 39466
A wonderful holiday sampler. Includes Tony Bennett, Frank Sinatra, Andy Williams, Johnny Mathis, and others. —*David A. Milberg*

☆ **Christmas Cheers from Motown** / Motown 6292
A hit album from 1973 with great Christmas presents from the Temptations, Diana Ross & the Supremes, Stevie Wonder, and Smokey Robinson & the Miracles. —*David A. Milberg*

☆ **Christmas Classics** / 1989 / Rhino 70192
A well-rounded compilation of R&B, rock & roll, pop, and rocking instrumentals (the Ventures and Santo & Johnny). Aretha Franklin is elegant on "Winter Wonderland," while Stevie Wonder and the Supremes represent "The Motown Sound." Roy Orbison is in top form on "Pretty Paper," and Bobby "Boris" Pickett would make the Grinch smile with "Monsters' Holiday." —*Dennis MacDonald*

☆ **The Christmas Collection** / Dec. 12, 1991 / Prestige 6011
Devotees of acoustic combo jazz will love *The Christmas Collection.* Every song is a highlight on this who's-who of jazz giants, featuring Dexter Gordon, Paul Bley, Art Blakey, Charles Mingus, Gene Ammons, Bobby Timmons, Eddie "Lockjaw" Davis, Bill Smith, Don Patterson, and more. There is a continuity from beginning to end that makes this a very playable collection. Its a must! —*Rick Clark, Rock & Roll Disc*

☆ **Christmas Comedy Classics** / Priority 9306
Collectibles by Dancer, Prancer & Nervous—the Singing Reindeer (Stan Freberg, Mel Blanc, and Yogi Yogesson). —*David A. Milberg*

☆ **Christmas Gift Set** / Sep. 16, 1991 / Capitol 97990
With tracks from Bing Crosby, Nat King Cole, and Frank Sinatra, it is essential stuff for a nostalgic Noel. Cuddle under the mistletoe or by a warm fireplace with this one. —*David A. Milberg*

★ **Christmas Gift for You from Phil Spector** / 1963 / Phillies 4005
Featuring Phil Spector's "Wall of Sound" in its prime and his early stable of artists, the Ronettes, Crystals, Darlene Love, and Bob B. Soxx & the Blue Jeans, this stands as inarguably the greatest Christmas record of all time. Spector believed he could produce a record for the holidays that would capture not only the essence of the Christmas Spirit but also be a pop masterpiece, standing against any work these artists had already done. He succeeded on every level, with all four groups/singers recording some of their most memorable performances, from Ronnie sounding sexy as ever on the Ronettes' "I Saw Mommy Kissing Santa Claus" to the playfulness of the Crystals on "Santa Claus is Coming to Town." The star on top of this Christmas tree, however, is Darlene Love, with her impassioned "Christmas (Baby Please Come Home)." This is the Christmas album by which all later holiday releases have to be judged and it has inspired a host of imitators. It's absolutely essential. (Note: This CD is available separately and as part of the highly recommended four-CD boxed set, *Phil Spector: Back to Mono (1958-1969)* Abkco CD 7118 1991) —*Decibel Dennis MacDonald*

☆ **Christmas Kisses** / Oct. 1, 1990 / Capitol 94701
An outstanding 22-track compilation from Capitol's vaults, 1944-1963, covering many styles, from the folk blues of Leadbelly to the entrancing pop vocals of Nancy Wilson. Doo-wop, honky-tonk, piano boogie, and the playful girl group Pop of the Bookends on "Christmas Kisses" all fit in with Les Paul's dazzling display of guitar virtuosity on "Jingle Bells" and the irresistible "Rudolph the Red-Nosed Reindeer Mambo" from Billy May and his orchestra. —*Dennis MacDonald*

☆ **Christmas Memories** / RCA 8563

Relive the Christmas sounds of pop singers and artists of the '40s and '50s. —*David A. Milberg*

☆ **Christmas Party with Eddie G.** / 1990 / CBS 46919
If there is a more entertaining Christmas compilation than this CD, I have not heard it. This is a party platter that includes international Christmas greetings and amusing comedy bits from old radio in between 17 tracks of R&B, blues, country, exotica, rock, novelty, and more. Most tracks are unavailable elsewhere on CD. From the surf sounds of Untamed Youth to the strains of Monty & Marsha Brown's "Cajun Christmas," this is a nonstop Christmas party. —*Dennis MacDonald*

☆ **A Christmas Present for You from Phil Spector** / Rhino 70235
There is no doubt that Phil Spector's production vision was brilliant. This Christmas album is one of his greatest achievements (which is saying a lot). Features Darlene Love, the Ronettes, Bob B. Soxx & the Blue Jeans, and the Crystals. Spector focuses Christmas through the attitude of early '60s pop magic the way Crosby did for music of the '40s. —*Rick Clark*

☆ **Christmas Rap** / Profile 1247
Early rap-masters from the early '80s, including Run D.M.C., Sweet Tee, Surf MCs, Derek B, Dana Dane, Spyder-D, and others! —*David A. Milberg*

☆ **Christmas Rock Album** / Priority 9465
Great Christmas hits from Elton John, Foghat, Queen, Beach Boys, Elvin Bishop, Waitresses, and others. Super stuff! —*David A. Milberg*

Christmas Soul Special / Varrick 15
This 1982 session brings together many great soul singers of the '60s—Mary Wells, Martha Reeves, Shirley Alston (of the Shirelles), Sam Moore (of Sam & Dave), Ben E. King—but only Wilson Pickett rises to the occasion with incendiary versions of "Jingle Bells" and "Silver Bells." —*Decibel Dennis MacDonald*

☆ **Christmas with the Canadian Brass** / RCA 4132
Christmas favorites performed by this popular brass choir, plus the great organ of St. Patrick's Cathedral. The combination works. Fine traditional arrangements with some modern flavor. —*Michael Erlewine*

○ **Cool Yule** / Rhino 75767
Eighteen tracks culled from two out-of-print "Cool Yule" albums, this includes "Santa Claus" by the '60s garage band the Sonics (set to the tune of "Farmer John"); the hilarious R&B novelty "Christmas in the Congo" from the Mar-Keys; Tina Turner's wailing on "Merry Christmas, Baby"; and more essential offerings from James Brown, Solomon Burke, and others. —*Dennis MacDonald*

○ **Cool Yule, Vol. 2** / Rhino 70193
Subtitled "A Collection of Rockin' Stocking Stuffers," this platter delivers with Johnny Preston's humorous rockabilly number "(I Want a) Rock and Roll Guitar" and the girl-group delights of Honey and the Bees "Jing Jing a Ling." The Pacific Northwest's kings of garage rock, the Sonics, turn in an original, "Santa Claus" that cops the "Farmer John" riff and gets their wish list straight: "I want a brand new car / a twangy guitar / a cute little honey / and lots of money." More R&B and R&R from Huey "Piano" Smith, Jack Scott, the Uniques, Gary "U.S." Bonds, and more. Pass the eggnog. —*Decibel Dennis MacDonald, Roundup Newsletter*

☆ **Country Christmas, Vol. 1** / RCA 4812
Great stuff from the '70s and '80s by Alabama, Charley Pride, Willie Nelson, Razzy Bailey, and others. —*David A. Milberg*

Country Christmas Collection / 1991 / PolyGram 848999
An uneven collection with a few standouts: Bob Wills & His Texas Playboys turn in a playful "Santa's on His Way" and the more sentimental strains of "When It's Christmas on the Range." Jerry Lee Lewis, an underrated Country singer, can break your heart with "I Can't Have a Merry Christmas, Mary, Without You" and George Jones is high and lonesome on "Maybe Next Christmas." Dave Dudley turns his "Six Days on the Road" into a seasonal treat with "Six Tons of Toys." —*Decibel Dennis MacDonald*

☆ **Creole Christmas** / 1990 / Epic 47045
Featuring some of the finest singers of New Orleans, including Aaron Neville, Johnny Adams, Irma Thomas, and more. —*Dennis MacDonald*

○ **December's Eve** / RCA 8374

Fireside Christmas sounds from RCA's popular (not rock & roll) artists of the '50s. —*David A. Milberg*

Dr. Demento Presents: Greatest Xmas Novelty CD / 1989 / Rhino 75755

Dr. Demento's novelty collections are usually in sync with those folks who think *Mad Magazine* is essential reading. Nothing wrong with that, even though this collection is at times overbearingly cute and the humor often too dated to be meaningful or funny for those who didn't remember the songs the first time around. Nevertheless, where else can you find "Grandma Got Run over by a Reindeer," Bob & Doug McKenzie's (of SCTV) "Twelve Days of Christmas," the Barking Dogs, Wild Man Fischer, Weird Al Yankovic, Cheech & Chong, and Stan Freberg on one disc? If Handel's *Messiah* represents the loftier aspects of Christmas, then *Dr. Demento Presents* is the season's whoopee cushion. —*Rick Clark, Rock & Roll Disc*

☆ A Grp Christmas Collection / 1989 / GRP 9574

Chick Corea's Elektric Band, Special EFX, Lee Ritenour, David Benoit, Tom Scott, Gary Burton, Mark Egan, and a host of others run through a batch of standards with an inhumanly high level of virtuosity. As with many GRP releases, the state-of-the-art sound tends to take precedence over sparks. Gary Burton's mathematically precise "God Rest Ye Merry Gentlemen" does for jazz what Gentle Giant did for rock. Dave Grusin, Szakcsi, and Lee Ritenour turn in emotive solo performances, and the unique Kevin Eubanks arrangement of "Silver Bells" work well. —*Rick Clark*

☆ A Grp Christmas Collection, Vol. 2 / GRP 9650

If you loved the first one, you'll love this too. —*David A. Milberg*

☆ God Rest Ye Merry Jazzmen / 1981 / CBS 37551

A compilation of tracks not on any other albums. With Dexter Gordon Quartet, McCoy Tyner (solo), Arthur Blythe Quartet, Heath Brothers, Paquito D'Rivera Duo, Wynton Marsalis Quintet in modern and modal settings. —*Michael G. Nastos*

○ Handel's Messiah—a Soulful Celebration / 1992 / Warner Brothers 4141

Contemporary soul/pop artists, including Patti Austin, Tevin Campbell, Stevie Wonder, Quincy Jone, Take 6, Howard Hewett, and Dianne Reeves, take a pop-song approach to Handel's classic Christmas oratorio. Handel's wonderful melodies are updated with synthesizers, drum machines, and slick pop production that Quincy Jones and Take 6's Mervyn Warren. —*AMG*

☆ Have Yourself a Jazzy Little Christmas / Verve 840501

This 15-track CD has something for everyone : the smooth vocal styling of Billy Eckstine on "Christmas Eve," the purring Dinah Washington on the seductive "Ole Santa," and Ella Fitzgerald showing her soft and sentimental side on the single, "The Secret of Christmas." Billie Holiday, with help from Benny Carter and Sweets Edison, warms up the punchbowl with "I've Got My Love to Keep Me Warm," while Sister Rosetta Tharpe raises the rafters on her powerful rendition of "O Little Town of Bethlehem." Jimmy Smith and his funky Hammond B3 invigorate "Jingle Bells," but by adding tympani and horns, he totally re-invents "God Rest Ye Merry Gentlemen." —*Decibel Dennis MacDonald*

Have Yourself a Merry Little Christmas / 1989 / Rhino 70911

... a well-intentioned effort with a portion of the proceeds going to some unspecified charity. Eclectic, but ultimately too uneven to make this ecumenical effort a satisfying listen. — *Rick Clark, Rock & Roll Disc.*

☆ Have a Merry Chess Christmas / 1989 / Chess 25210

A fine cross-section of R&B and blues plus three tracks from the out-of-print 1968 Chess Gospel Christmas album, "A Christmas Dedication." It includes the Meditation Singers doing a plaintive "Blue Christmas" (not the Elvis classic), '60s soul from the O'Jays and Rotary Connection (featuring the late Minnie Ripperton), Chuck Berry singing "Run Rudolph, Run," a smokey take on "Merry Christmas, Baby," and more. —*Dennis MacDonald*

☆ Hillbilly Holiday / 1989 / Rhino 70195

To date, the best compilation of Christmas Country ranging from the Louvin Brothers wrapping their harmonies around "It Came Upon a Midnight Clear" to unabashed fun from Hank Snow ("Reindeer Boogie"), Buck Owens, Loretta Lynn, and the downright amusing "Daddy's Drinking up Our Christmas" from Commander Cody. —*Dennis MacDonald*

☆ Hipsters' Holiday: Vocal Jazz & R&B Classics / Rhino 70910

Typical of Rhino releases, *Hipster's Holiday* has very well laid-out annotation and pictures. This collection covers tracks from 1946 to 1988. Eartha Kitt's "material girl" ode, "Santa Baby," as well as its antithesis in the Miles Davis "Blue Xmas (To Whom It May Concern)," are here, as well as the hyper-scat singing of Leo Watson and Lambert, Hendricks & Ross. Both of the former are also on the CBS *Jingle Bell Jazz* collection, but they sound better here. As with the Jass and Savoy discs, Rhino has drawn from some performances of off-vinyl sources. All in all, this disc sounds cleaner and more detailed than those two releases, primarily due to the more recent vintage of recordings. —*Rick Clark*

Home Alone 2: Lost in New York / 1992 / Fox 11000

Bruce Springsteen had always sought to re-create Phil Spector's "Wall of Sound" with his E-Street Band (one listen to "Born to Run" is all the proof you need), so when Steven Van Zandt wrote "All Alone on Christmas" for ex-Phil Spector singer par excellance Darlene Love, he also used four other former E-Streeters to back her up on this full-scale production, adding six horns, bells, tambourines and extra percussion to outdo the "Boss" in apeing the "Wall of Sound." The remainder of the CD, unfortunately, is filled with dreck from Bette Midler, Atlantic Starr, even a later (read: subpar) Johnny Mathis track. Will someone please give Darlene Love her own record? —*Decibel Dennis MacDonald*

Home for the Holidays / RCA 2276

This nine-song CD is mediocre at best with one gem: Foster and Lloyd's original "Christmas List," a power-popper that recalls Marshall Crenshaw. Other tracks by Clint Black, K.T. Oslin, Keith Whitley, and more. —*Decibel Dennis MacDonald*

Hot Jazz for Cool Nights / 1992 / Music Masters 65089

Anthology featuring vintage performers doing classic traditional jazz cuts. Earl Hines, Charlie Johnson, Tiny Parham, The Missourians, The Jungletown Stompers and Musical Stevedores are the acts presented. —*Ron Wynn*

☆ It's Christmas Time Again / Stax 8519

Only the *Soul Christmas* collection of Atlantic beats this compilation of Christmas soul and blues. Rufus Thomas, Mack Rice, and Albert King sound downright salacious, while the Rance Allen Group sanctify "White Christmas" in a way Bing Crosby never could. The Emotions joyously set the record straight with "Black Christmas," and the Staples Singers sermonize in their special fashion with "Who Took the Merry out of Christmas?" Isaac Hayes, the Temprees, and Little Johnny Taylor are also in great form here. —*Dennis MacDonald & Rick Clark*

☆ Jingle Bell Jazz / 1989 / CBS 40166

Jingle Bell Jazz is a single-CD compilation of two previously released CBS holiday jazz albums, *Jingle Bell Jazz* (1974) and *God Rest Ye Merry Jazzmen* (1985). This disc is loaded with strong performances by Herbie Hancock, McCoy Tyner, Dexter Gordon, Wynton Marsalis, Duke Ellington, Lionel Hampton, Miles Davis, and more. —*Rick Clark, Rock & Roll Disc*

Just in Time for Christmas / 1990 / IRS 13052

When Phil Spector assembled his stable of artists in 1963 to create the masterpiece, *A Christmas Gift for You from Phil Spector*, he probably did not suspect that other labels would try to imitate his success: this collection shows how bringing together bands from a label's stable can fail miserably. Except for contributions from Squeeze (the quirky "Christmas Day") and the dB's (the powerpop "Home for the Holidays"), this is fairly unnecessary fare. —*Decibel Dennis MacDonald*

★ Legends of Christmas Past, a Rock N' R&B Holiday Collection / EMI America 99987

A "must" for any cool yule fan, this 20-track CD will delight collectors with nine rare or previously unreleased cuts, including two rockin' tracks from Bill Haley. Lon Chaney, Jr. escapes from the vaults to unleash the playful "Monster Holiday," while Canned Heat boogie down with their original "Christmas Blues" and attempt to make Alvin & the Chipmunks hip on a remake of "The Chipmunk Song." Gorgeous Doo-Wop from the Five Keys and Marvin & Johnny; blues from Amos Milburn and Charles Brown; rock 'n' roll from Jan & Dean and the Belmonts; and more from Eddie Cochran with the Holly Twins, Manfred Mann, others. —*Decibel Dennis MacDonald*

☆ Lump of Coal / Oct. 8, 1991 / First Warning 75702

These are old holiday standards performed in a punk/new-wave style. Fun and nicely done. —*David A. Milberg*

Mas! a Caribbean Christmas Party / 1992 / Rykodisc 10150
Christmas releases tend to sound the same, mainly because there's only so many ways to sing shopworn carols and holiday tunes. But here's actually a Christmas alternative; a nine-track CD with Caribbean artists putting their spin on the season. El Gran Combo, Joseph Spence, Lord Nelson and Machel don't distort the traditional meaning of the lyrics, but they certainly bring a fresh quality to their holiday numbers, while performing much more upbeat versions than you'll hear on many rote Christmas discs. —*Ron Wynn*

☆ **Merry Christmas Baby (King)** / King 5018
The original issue of this classic was subtitled *Intimate Christmas Music for Lovers*, and with five of the dozen tracks featuring the smoothest of the smooth vocalists, Charles Brown, that subtitle is appropriate. Other King artists represented here are bluesmen Lowell Fulson and Jimmy Witherspoon and Lloyd Glenn on "Sleighride" doing a swinging piano workout. Mabel Scott's original jumping "Boogie-Woogie Santa Claus" can be found here. —*Dennis MacDonald*

☆ **Merry Christmas Baby (Paula)** / Paula 12
R&B and blues from 15 artists on 23 songs including some re-recordings by Charles Brown and Lowell Fulson. Includes the riveting "Christmas in Vietnam" by deep-soul duo Johnny and Jon. —*Dennis MacDonald*

☆ **Merry Christmas Baby—Romance & Reindeer** / Sep. 30, 1991 / Capitol 97459
For that beneath-the-mistletoe mood-setter, this compilation of crooners and pop singers is hard to beat. You'll be put under the spell of sultry sounds from Julie London and Nancy Wilson or the silky soul of Nat "King" Cole. Dean Martin's dreamy "Winter Romance" is here, along with the seductive pairing of Johnny Mercer and Margaret Whiting on "Baby, It's Cold Outside." 25 tracks from 1946-1968. —*Dennis MacDonald*

The Mother of All Flagpole Christmas Albums / Fla 6001
Culled from three Christmas tapes released by Flagpole Magazine, this includes performances recorded 1990-92 from 21 Atlanta and Athens, GA bands. Most of the songs are diverse "alternative" originals but there's also a bizarre guitar/sax duet of "Jingle Bells" from the Flat Duo Jets, a cover of Spinal Tap's "Christmas with the Devil" by Allgood, an okay version of the Sonics' "Santa Claus" by the Woggles, "You're a Mean One, Mr. Grinch" from the Labrea Stompers, and more spotty fun. —*Decibel Dennis MacDonald*

The Narada Christmas Collection / 1989 / Narada 63902
Even though Narada is known as a new-age label, this collection maintains the musical attitude of that genre, while embracing the classier pieces of the Christmas holiday, such as, "What Child Is This," "It Came Upon a Midnight Clear," "O Holy Night," and so forth. Nice, unobtrusive, polite—ultimately the kind of stuff that may teeter a little too close to easy listening for some listeners. —*Rick Clark*

New England Christmastide / North Star 0002
These 14 Rhode Island performers on folk instruments come from separate musical traditions—sea, Irish, singer-songwriter, classical—with a determination not to leave Christmas to the choirs, orchestras and trumpeters. They have fashioned an unassuming gem: an album full of warm colors and quiet delights... a bounty of beautiful (and unimpeachably traditional) Christmas music, done in ways that are fresh, sprightly, reverent and deeply Christmasy. Recommended. — *Bob Coltman, Roundup newsletter*

Nipper's Greatest Christmas Hits / RCA 9859
Nipper's Greatest Christmas Hits is a time-warp escape into the '50s world of the Ames Brothers, Roger Whittaker, Dinah Shore, Perry Como, and Arthur Fiedler. —*Rick Clark*

○ **Reggae Christmas** / RAS 3101
Here are all your favorite carols with a Rastafarian twist from Eek-A-Mouse, Mighigan & Smiley, Freddie McGregor, and others. —*AMG*

○ **Rhythm & Blues Christmas: 20 Songs** / Hollywood 369
Among the 20 tracks included here are two from Hank Ballard and the Midnighters alone would be worth the price of admission: "Christmas Time for Everybody but Me" rivals the most testifyin' pleas of King labelmate James Brown, and Ballard turns in another outstanding performance with "Santa Claus Is

Coming." While there is some duplication with other in-print collections (especially *Merry Christmas Baby*, on Starday/King), this marks the only CD appearance of many holiday classics from the King vaults. Recommended highly. —*Decibel Dennis MacDonald, Roundup newsletter*

○ **Rock & Roll Christmas** / ACE 2040
Reissue of Huey "Piano" Smith and the Clowns' *Twas the Night before Christmas* album on Ace, with six added tracks from other New Orleans artists. Oddly, the tracks are not identified by artist, but that won't spoil your yule dance party. You can mambo to Smith's "Almost Time for Santa" and do the Popeye to "All I Want for Christmas (Is a Little Bit of Music)." A nutty but danceable party platter. —*Dennis MacDonald*

☆ **Rockin' Little Christmas** / MCA 25084
A dozen sides of rock & roll, R&B, girl group (the 1964 "Love for Christmas" by the Gems), and more. "Mambo Santa Mambo" by the Enchanters and "Hey, Santa Claus" by the Moonglows are unbeatable fun. —*Dennis MacDonald*

Santa Claus Blues / Jass 3
There isn't a seasonal CD that'll keep the hepcats swingin' more than Santa Claus Blues. Spanning 1925-1971 with a generous 23 tracks, this includes the gutbucket blues of Lionel Hampton and His Orchestra on "Merry Christmas, Baby," Fats Wallers' humorous arrangement of "Swingin' Them Jingle Bells," Jimmy Rushing as the vocalist in Count Basie's Orchestra on "Good Morning Blues (I Want to See Santa Claus)" and a mournful-sounding Victoria Spivey on "Christmas Morning Blues." From the Crescent City there's the title cut from the Clarence Williams Five (with Louis Armstrong and Sidney Bechet), Louis Prima's playful "What Will Santa Claus say (When He Finds Everybody Swingin')," and Louis Armstrong finishes with five selections, including "Cool Yule" and "Zat You, Santa Claus?" This album is highly recommended. —*Decibel Dennis MacDonald*

☆ **Santa Claus Blues** / Jass 3
Santa Claus Blues, covering almost 50 years of jazz, blues, and swing, will appeal to archivists of those forms. Victoria Spivey wails on the "Christmas Morning Blues," and Duke Ellington's Hot Five (with Ozie Ware) get down with "Santa Claus, Bring My Man Back." Some of the other artists that shine on *Santa Claus Blues* are Fats Waller, Count Basie, Woody Herman, Ella Fitzgerald, and Lionel Hampton. Many of these tracks have been taken from vinyl sources, but the transfers are generally very good. Nevertheless, the Louis Armstrong tracks can be found in much better shape on Rhino's *Hipster's Holiday* and MCA's *Traditional Classics*. Unfortunately, this compilation lacks decent liner notes, a feature that should be standard on releases like this. —*Rick Clark*

Scrooged / Arista 10Y3058
While only a portion of this soundtrack has a Yule theme, the duet of blue-eyed soul diva Annie Lennox and the ever-in-style Al Green on "Put a Little Love in Your Heart" sends a message that should be broadcast year-round. Also includes Robbie Robertson's "Christmas Must Be Tonight" and Natalie Cole reprising her father's "The Christmas Song"; surprisingly, she didn't think to turn this into a duet and video with her father. —*Decibel Dennis MacDonald*

○ **Soul Christmas** / 1968 / Atlantic 82316
This 1991 reissue includes eight of the original 11 tracks included on the Atco 1968 release (a rare album still worth seeking) with 11 more tracks added from the Atlantic vaults. Few, if any, Christmas compilations are more essential than this one. Otis Redding's performances of "White Christmas" and "Merry Christmas, Baby" are alone worth the price of admission. Clarence Carter's funky "Back Door Santa" and Joe Tex's ballad "I'll Make Every Day Christmas (For My Woman)" are only two more tracks that make this an absolute must-have CD. —*Dennis MacDonald*

In a Christmas Mood—A Swing Era Big Band Celebration / Mobile Fidelity 796
Christmas big-band-style, performed by the Starlight Orchestra. The playing is very tight, professional, and true to style, but like Glenn Miller (to whom this collection tips its hat), *In a Christmas Mood* might be too much white bread for certain lovers of jazz. As with all Mobile Fidelity discs, the sound is impeccable. —*Rick Clark*

★ **Street Carols** / Sep. 1991 / Street Gold 4131

Recorded in 1991, this a capella recording has a timeless quality as hand-in-velvet-glove harmonies work their magic on songs new and old, with blasts from the past in Jerry Butler, the Spaniels, the Chi-Lites, but credit must go to the group, Stormy Weather, who not only organized this Doo-Wop project but also sang five of the fifteen selections, including the original "Street Carols" that sounds like a lost gem from 1954. David Somerville, ex-lead singer of the Diamonds, does all four vocal parts on "The Last Month of the Year" but the CD peaks with Ronnie Spector's version of Frankie Lymon's "Creation of Love" (with re-worked lyrics to fit the Yule theme). —*Decibel Dennis MacDonald*

Sugar Plums: Holiday Treats from Sugar Hill / Sugar Hill 3796

Most of this CD is imbued with soft, sublime sounds of the season, including Jerry Douglas's double-tracked dobro/guitar rendering of "Away in a Manger," Dan Crary's guitar and sleigh bells version of "What Child is This?" and the stately bluegrass harmonies of John Starling, Larry Stephenson and Rickie Simpkins on "Beautiful Star of Bethlehem." Robin and Linda Williams sing Steve Earle's "Nothing But a Child" as if it were a Yule folk standard. The all-female Ranch Romance vamp up Elvis's "Santa Bring My Baby Back (To Me)" with sizzling accordion and fiddle, and Red Knuckles & the Trailblazers end the proceedings with a medley that'll make you "n'yuk n'yuk n'yuk." —*Decibel Dennis MacDonald*

Swinging Big Band Christmas / Laserlight 15464

Of the ten selections included here, only a few really swing: the Gene Krupa Trio's (drums/sax/piano) live version of "Jingle Bells" is tops, and both the Larry Clinton Orchestra and the Les Brown Orchestra work wonders with Tchaikovsky ("Dance of the Sugar Plum Fairies" and "The Nutcracker Suite", respectively). Otherwise, much of this CD is "sweet music" of Guy Lombardo, Jack Teagarden and others. —*Decibel Dennis MacDonald*

The Texas Christmas Collection / Amazing 1026

Sixteen Texas artists, but only a handful offer a worthwhile performance here. Willie Nelson turns in a delicate version of "Silent Night" while guitarists Eric Johnson and Van Wilks pair up for an acoustic rendering of "What Child is This?" Jerry Jeff Walker calls his friend up to say he's coming home in "Mason Dixon's on the Line" and Beto & the Fairlanes liven the party up with a salsa instrumental take of "We Three Kings." The real gem in this Lone Star compilation belongs to Long Tall Marcia Ball with her impassioned version of Charles Brown's seasonal chestnut, "Please Come Home for Christmas." —*Decibel Dennis MacDonald*

☆ **Traditional Christmas Classics** / 1989 / Adventures in Music 024

Why the artists performing on this disc aren't listed on the outside of the package is a mystery. Mel Torme does "The Christmas Song," and there's Bing Crosby's "White Christmas." "Christmas in New Orleans" by Louis Armstrong is easily the highlight on this outing. Easy-listening kingpins Billy Vaughn, LeRoy Anderson, and Roger Williams are here doing their most famous Christmas music contributions. —*Rick Clark*

A Very Special Christmas / A&M 3911

Recorded to benefit the Special Olympics, this has some of the biggest names in contemporary music, most covering seasonal favorites with mixed success. Outstanding tracks include the Pretenders "Have Yourself a Merry Little Christmas" with Chrissie Hynde giving a touching performance. Run-D.M.C.'s topical "Christmas in Hollis" relies heavily on sampling "Back Door Santa" and may head you toward the dance floor. Alison Moyet's stately version of "The Coventry Carol" is beautifully haunting. Only the "Material Girl," Madonna, embarrasses herself with an overly campy "Santa Baby." —*Decibel Dennis MacDonald*

A Very Special Christmas 2 / Oct. 20, 1992 / A&M 540003

Although not even half of this CD is outstanding, it was recorded for a worthwhile cause (Special Olympics) and contains some songs I certainly wouldn't want to be without, most notably Tom Petty and the Heartbreakers' "Christmas All Over Again"—this is jingle/jangle pop at its best. Boyz II Men wrap their a capella voices around "The Birth of Christ" and the two "Wall of Sound" standouts, Darlene Love and Ronnie Spector, bring their powerful voices together for the first time on "Rockin' Around the Christmas Tree." Bonnie Raitt duets with Charles Brown on his sexy "Merry Christmas, Baby" while Aretha Franklin shows why she's called the "Queen of Soul" on "O Christmas Tree." —*Decibel Dennis MacDonald*

Warner Bros. Records Presents a Christmas Tradition, Vol. 3 / Warner Brothers

This CD is worth the price of admission for the Texas Tornados' Farfisa-fueled, accordion-pumped "Rudolph the Red-Nosed Reindeer," one of the best Tex-Mex Christmas party records you'll ever hear. The gospel quartet, the Fairfield Four, sing "The Last Month of the Year" a capella—another standout. Holly Dunn contributes a spirited rendition of "Feliz Navidad" with a lively percussion break and empathetic accordion and Brenda Lee re-does her classic "Rockin' Around the Christmas Tree." —*Decibel Dennis MacDonald*

☆ **A Winter's Solstice—Vols. 1 & 2** / Windham Hill 1201

This is a superb sampler with 15 artists from the label performing original pieces as well as their own renderings of traditional works. The artists include Hedges, Aaberg, Nightnoise, Dalglish, Ackerman, Stein and Walder, McCandless, Metamora, and Therese Schroeder-Sheker, plus others. In the finest Windham Hill tradition, this is a truly stirring collection. —*Backroads Music/Heartbeats*

☆ **Yuletunes** / Black Vinyl 12591

Inspired by the Beatles Fan Club Christmas EPs and Phil Spector's Christmas LP, popmeisters, the Shoes, put together this compilation of 16 bands, most relatively obscure, and came up with some pure pop delights. This Yule punchbowl is filled with jingley/jangley guitars, Beatlesque melodies and harmonies, Spector "Wall of Sound" sleigh bells, and more to brighten your holiday listening. Standouts are many, including the Shoes' "This Christmas," Bill Lloyd's Marshall Crenshaw-ish "Underneath the Christmas Tree," the Idea's Byrdsy "It's About that Time," Matthew Sweet's "Baby Jesus" and the Cavedogs' "Three Wise Men and a Baby" sounds like an outtake from The Beatles (a.k.a. *The White Album*). —*Decibel Dennis MacDonald*

CELTIC & BRITISH ISLES

There is in me (faint memory of a smile)
The soul of a shivery old cat –
Let the wood-grey body be wounded, beaten,
Whatever be at it, it will live.

These words, written in the 14th century by the Welsh bard Dafydd ap Gwylim, express the unquashable endurance of the Celtic cultures of Europe. Through centuries of oppression, of systematic attempts by foreign occupiers to destroy Celtic cultural identity, their expressive arts have continued to develop and to spawn new and emergent forms. It is a supreme and fitting irony that we consider English folk music under the rubric of "Celtic and British Isles" music.

The term "Celtic" in its most rigid sense refers to languages: to Irish, Manx, and Scots Gaelic, and to Welsh, Cornish, and Breton Brythonic. However, what we think of as Celtic music is performed by both Celtic speakers and speakers of English and French, in the Celtic homelands in the British Isles, Ireland, Brittany and a diaspora that spans the globe from Australia to America. It is defined here as music that has sprung from the ancient, ever-developing musical tradition of the Celtic homelands.

There are various levels of "professionalism" and "traditionality" among performers of this music. The tradition continues of amateur musicians and singers who watch and listen to their elders, gradually learning to express themselves within the medium of traditional musical performance. On the other hand, a revival of interest in traditional music since the 60s has created an international demand for newer groups influenced by classical, folk, jazz, and pop music. The result is a musical system with many genres and styles, ranging from unaccompanied singing or solo playing to highly structured arrangements of folk ensembles and to rock & roll bands belting out jigs and reels with a vicious backbeat.

The standard of musicianship in this music is extraordinarily high. This is due partly to the important role of music in the cultural and national identities of the countries and ethnic groups in question, partly to vigorous systems of musical competition leading to national championships for each instrument. The high standard of performance, combined with the multifarious genres and styles considered in this section, lead to a problem of sorts: there are a huge number of good records to buy and limited space for us to guide you to them. This section concentrates somewhat on the newer, revival acts, which have a broader appeal than strictly traditional approaches. Many of these groups list their traditional sources in the notes to their albums, giving the interested listener leads for further listening.

This, then, is but a tip of the old cat's tail, a vantage point from which to begin your own explorations of the rich realms of Celtic and English folk music.

– Stephen Winick

Albion Band, The

Group / English

The musicians hired to accompany Shirley Collins in 1971 were called the Albion Band and later became a group in their own right. Bass player Ashley Hutchings, who had previously founded and left both Fairport Convention and Steeleye Span, is the driving force behind this group. The members use acoustic and electric instruments to create a folk-rock sound that is something like Fairport Convention's but usually more typically English in character. They have existed as the Albion Band, the Albion Country Band, and the Albion Dance Band. —*Stephen Winick*

Rise Up Like the Sun / 1978 / Carthage 4431
Traditional and modern songs with a less folky sound. —*Stephen Winick*

A Christmas Present from the Albion Band / 1988 / Tracer 003
Carols, songs, and recitations pertaining to the holiday, featuring the lovely singing of Cathy LeSurf. —*Stephen Winick*

Give Me a Saddle, I'll Trade You a Car / 1989 / Topic 454
A refreshingly original and challenging project. Familiar themes associated with the American West(ern) are explored. —*Dirty Linen*

● **Battle of the Field** / 1989 / Carthage 4420
Recorded in 1973, released in 1976, this lovely album was the band's debut as a separate entity. —*Stephen Winick*

Songs from the Shows / 1990 / Road Goes on Forever 0006
A pastiche of concert and studio recordings from the Albion's words-and-music presentations from 1977 to 1989. It's a nicely crafted program, pleasantly strung together. —*Danny Carnahan*

Songs from the Shows 2 / 1991 / Albino 005

Again, material from *Here We Come A-Wassailing* (1977), *Albion Hymn* (1981), *An Easter Garland* (1985), *Wild Side of Town* (1987), and *Key to the North* (a 1989 film) has been unearthed, most of it new to the Albion fan who merely knows the band's numerous albums. Well chosen and thoughtfully sequenced. —*Dirty Linen*

○ **Live in Concert** / 1993 / Windsong 041
Combines material from two BBC radio concerts, one in 1977 and the other in 1982. This is classic Albion Band material from two of its most exciting periods, blending traditional music with pop and loving it. —*Stephen Winick*

1990 / Topic 457
Smart catchy songs that have traditional roots and simple but innovative arrangements. —*Dirty Linen*

Martin Allcock

A former member of the Bully Wee Band, Martin Allcock took his multi-instrumental talents into Fairport Convention in the mid '80s. —*Stephen Winick*

○ **Maart** / 1990 / Woodworm 012
Features traditional and original tunes and songs. Maart sings and plays everything under the sun, cooking up a well-balanced folk-rock stew. —*Stephen Winick*

Altan

Group / Celtic

Ireland's most electrifying current group features fiddles, flute, bouzouki, and guitar in driving and precise arrangements of dance tunes, along with airs and songs by the stunning Mairead Ni Mhaonaigh. The band began as a duo, Ni Mhaonaigh on vocals and fiddle, and her husband, Frankie Kennedy, on flute. They have added accompanists and lead players to the group over the last decade and now exist as a five-piece band. Altan explores the music of their Ulster and Donegal heritage—as well as some from further afield—with uncompromising sensitivity and innovative flair. Each of their recorded projects has surpassed its predecessors, a truly amazing accomplishment. —*Stephen Winick*

Ceol Aduaidh / 1983 / Green Linnet 3090
Like *Altan*, this album is by Mairead Ni Mhaonaigh (fiddle and vocals) and Frankie Kennedy (flute). It also includes Ciaran Curran, still an Altan member, on cittern. Synthesizers are added by Eithne Ni Bhraonain, who would later become a pop sensation as Enya. Like all recordings by these spectacular musicians, this one is an excellent piece of work. —*Stephen Winick*

Altan / 1987 / Green Linnet 1078
This album is technically credited to Mairead Ni Mhaonaigh and Frankie Kennedy, but it's clearly the first step in Altan's development into a tight band. It's full of beautiful, fiery music, a little less dense and powerful than the later recordings. —*Stephen Winick*

Horse with a Heart / 1989 / Green Linnet 1095
This album was evidence that Altan would become the best Irish traditional band in the world. —*Stephen Winick*

The Red Crow / 1990 / Green Linnet 1109
Superb. The band really nails down its sound on this one. —*Stephen Winick*

● **Harvest Storm** / 1992 / Green Linnet 1117
Their latest and best. A true necessity. —*Stephen Winick*

Alistair Anderson

b. Mar. 18, 1948, Wallsend, Tyne and Wear, England
Northumbrian pipes, concertina
A pioneering force in Northumbrian folk music, Anderson plays Northumbrian pipes and concertina. —*Stephen Winick*

Plays English Concertina / 1972 / Trailer 2074
And he plays it well, on his first solo album. Features several of the Boys of the Lough as guests. —*Stephen Winick*

The Concertina Workshop/Topic / 1974 / Free Reed 501
The title says it all. —*Stephen Winick*

○ **Steel Skies** / Flying Fish 288
Anderson and band perform recently composed tunes. —*Stephen Winick*

William Andrews & Liam Walsh

Group
Both Andrews and Walsh, two very different pipers, were born in the 19th century. Andrews was winning contests before World War I, and both men had direct contact with the giants of the older tradition. —*John Storm Roberts*

○ **Classics of Irish Piping** / Topic 262
Virtually all of the album's recordings date from the late '20s. These reels, airs, hornpipes, and jigs represent a highly important link with the past. —*John Storm Roberts*

Dan Ar Bras

Vocals, guitar
A truly great acoustic and electric guitarist, and a good singer as well, Ar Bras was the guitar wizard in many of Alan Stivell's arrangements. He has also had a long and productive solo career. —*Stephen Winick*

Douar Nevez / 1977 / Hexagone 883009
A Breton rock concept album relating the story of Ys, the Breton equivalent of Atlantis. —*Stephen Winick*

○ **Allez Dire a La Ville** / 1978 / Hexagone 883021
A well-crafted pop album with Celtic leanings, this foregrounds Ar Bras' electric guitar and voice, as well as several songs written by poet Xavier Grall. —*Stephen Winick*

○ **Acoustic** / 1985 / Green Linnet 3035
Highly personal compositions with a Celtic feel. —*Stephen Winick*

Les Iles de la Memoire / 1992 / Keltia Musique 32

Classic Ar Bras. Impeccably textured acoustic guitars, electric work alternately delicate and searing, and tunes that stir the heart and live on in the memory. —*Dirty Linen*

Xavier Grall Chante par Dan Ar Bras / 1992 / Keltia Musique 33
Musical realizations of words by Xavier Grall. The singing is forceful, and the arrangements are varied and stimulating. —*Dirty Linen*

Arcady

Group / Celtic
A Galway band featuring several former members of De Danann, as well as fine singing by Frances Black. —*Stephen Winick*

○ **After the Ball** / 1991 / Shanachie 79077
Features traditional Irish tunes, sentimental ditties, and one French song from Brittany. —*Stephen Winick*

Ar Log

Group / Celtic
ArLog is Wales's premier folk group. Their style has evolved from an early folky period to a more refined, almost classically orchestrated approach. —*Stephen Winick*

Ar Log / 1978 / Dingles 305
This debut is full of great singing and playing even though it is still a little rough. —*Stephen Winick*

● **Ar Log II** / 1981 / Dingles 310
Smooth vocal harmonies and powerful virtuoso playing. Their best. —*Stephen Winick*

Ar Log III / 1982 / Dingles 315
Very similar in style, presentation, and quality to *Ar Log II*, with gentle electric bass accompaniment. —*Stephen Winick*

Meillionen / 1982 / Dingles 715
This all-instrumental release of tunes for dancing features Ar Log's classically tinged arrangements as well as new sounds like accordion and keyboards. Ar Log did not consider *Meillionen* a regular Ar Log album, but rather a special project. —*Stephen Winick*

Pedawar / 1985 / Ar Log 001
Pedwar is Welsh for "four"; this fourth Ar Log release (not counting the *Meillionen* project) is very much like its predecessors, highly orchestrated but still sprightly. —*Stephen Winick*

ArLog V / 1988 / Sain 1468
As strong as ever. —*Dirty Linen*

Frankie Armstrong

b. Jan. 13, 1941, Workington, Cumbria, England
Vocals / English
One of the most powerful voices in English folk song, Armstrong has been part of Ewan MacColl's Critic's Group. Her solo albums are all worth listening to. —*Stephen Winick*

Out of Love, Hope and Suffering / 1974 / Bay 206
Serious, humorous, and bawdy songs and ballads. —*Stephen Winick*

Frankie Armstrong—Songs & Ballads / 1975 / Antilles 7021
Classic old ballads. —*Stephen Winick*

★ **And the Music Plays So Grand** / 1981 / Briar 4211
A live performance of traditional and contemporary songs, held in Sweden in 1978, is captured on this wonderful album. —*Stephen Winick*

I Heard a Woman Singing / 1984 / Flying Fish 332
The traditional and original songs on this album address women's issues. —*Stephen Winick*

Anne Auffret & Yann-Fanch Kemener

Anne Auffret is a singer and harp player with an angelic voice who specializes in religious music and hymns. Yann-Fanch Kemener is one of the most important Breton singers of the current generation. It was largely through his influence that many younger people became interested in Breton songs. He is also known as Jean-Francois Quemener. —*Stephen Winick*

● **Roue Gralon Ni Ho Salud** / 1994 / Keltia Musique 42
The two unearthly voices and the gentle ring of the harp make this an album of rare beauty. —*Stephen Winick*

Barely Works

This English dance band draws on eclectic instrumentation and influences to create stimulating and original music. —*Stephen Winick*

Don't Mind Walking / Green Linnet 3071
Punchy and upbeat album featuring accordion, brass, drums, guitar, and vocals. —*Stephen Winick*

Barley Bree

An Irish Canadian act, Barley Bree sounds a lot like the Clancy Brothers and Tommy Makem. —*Stephen Winick*

○ **No Man's Land** / Shanachie 52012
Consistently well played and sung, overbrimming with nostalgia, this is the group's best album. —*Stephen Winick*

Margaret Barry & Michael Gorman

An Irish tinker lady of high renown, Barry possessed a remarkable, strong voice and a unique, untutored banjo style. —*Stephen Winick*

○ **Folk Songs (Ireland)** / Smithsonian/Folkways 8729
Barry sang some of her best material on this album. —*Stephen Winick*

Barzaz

Barzaz is one of Brittany's most innovative bands, producing unmistakably Breton music on instruments that are recent imports to the Breton scene. Jean-Michel Veillon's wooden flute, Gilles Le Bigot's guitar, Alain Genty's fretless bass, and David Hopkins's bamboo flutes and percussion are a perfect foil for Yann-Fanch Kemener's vocals, the one truly traditional aspect of Barzaz's sound. —*Stephen Winick*

Ec'honder / 1989 / Escalibur 828
Both slow, meditative songs and quicker dance songs fill this debut disc. —*Stephen Winick*

● **Den Kozh Dall** / 1992 / Keltia Musique 29
A fuller, more confident sound is achieved, and some dark and moody arrangements are created. —*Stephen Winick*

Battlefield Band

Group / Scottish
The Glasgow-based Battlefield Band is one of Scotland's foremost folk-revival bands. Their older albums are quite traditional in style and content, but their later ones are tinged with pop. Along the way, they were among the first bands to incorporate the sounds of electric keyboards and the great Highland bagpipe into a folk-pop setting. —*Stephen Winick*

Battlefield Band: Scottish Folk / 1976 / Arfolk 349
Battlefield Band's first recording features Alan Reid, Brian McNeill, and Ricky Starr. They sing and play pretty arrangements of tunes and songs from the Scottish tradition. —*Stephen Winick*

Battlefield Band 2 / 1977 / Arfolk 358
This third album had the same year and lineup as their second, and a very similar title. It features different material and was released on a different label, however. It also features three guests who add three different types of bagpipes to Battlefield's sound. Buy it if you can find it. —*Stephen Winick*

○ **At the Front** / 1978 / Topic 381
A brilliant older album, featuring the singing of Jamie McMenamy (later of Kornog) and Pat Kilbride. —*Stephen Winick*

Stand Easy / 1979 / Topic 404
This fine release was their first to feature a Highland piper (Duncan MacGillivray) as a band member. —*Stephen Winick*

○ **Home Is Where the Van Is** / 1980 / Temple Music 2006
Their first U.S. release, this excellent album introduces Ged Foley, later of the House Band. It is also the first to feature Brian McNeill's excellent songwriting, and it achieves a very nice balance between their traditional roots and their modern sensibilities. —*Stephen Winick*

The Story So Far / 1982 / Flying Fish 274
A compilation of some of their older material, including rare tracks. —*Stephen Winick*

Anthem for the Common Man / 1984 / Temple Music 2008

Musical Instruments of England and the Celtic Countries

Bagpipes – Bagpipes are found all over the world. In its simplest form, a bagpipe consists of an air reservoir (or bag), a chanter (a pipe fitted with a double reed), and a means of inflating the bag. It may also be fitted with one or more drones (pipes that sound a single continuous note). Scottish Highland pipes, called "warpipes" in Ireland, have a mouth pipe to inflate the bag, three drones, and a nine-note fingered chanter. In the lowlands of Scotland and the north of England, mellow-toned, bellows-blown smallpipes are the norm. In Ireland, the Uillean pipe, the world's most complex bagpipe, reigns supreme. It consists of bellows, a bag, a two-octave chanter, three drones, and three regulators (keyed drones controlled by the player's wrist) that can play short rhythmic bursts of any of a number of chords as accompaniment to the chanter.

Free Reeds – Named after their metal reeds, which are free to vibrate on three sides, these instruments include the harmonica and various squeezeboxes. The harmonica (or "moothie" in Scotland) is popular all over Britain and Ireland, owing to its affordability and small size. The melodeon (or diatonic accordion) is a squeezebox with one, two, or three rows of buttons tuned to different diatonic scales. The accordion can be the familiar piano-keyed instrument or a melodeon whose rows are tuned a half-step apart, creating a chromatic instrument. In general, chromatic-button accordions are the most popular in Ireland, melodeons are the most popular in England, and piano accordions are the most popular in Scotland, but all forms are played in all countries. The concertina is a squeezebox of hexagonal cross-section, whose buttons are spread over both ends.

Woodwinds – The whistle is a metal tube with either a wooden fipple or a plastic mouthpiece, with fingerholes like a recorder. The flute, either wooden or metal, was popular originally in Ireland but is beginning to find popularity elsewhere as well. The bombarde, a high, piercing oboe, is one of the national instruments of Brittany.

Strings – The fiddle, or violin, is popular everywhere in Europe. The harp is a very important instrument, historically speaking, to the Celtic countries; it is still the national symbol of Ireland. Celtic harps are smaller and have fewer strings than the familiar concert harp, and have no pedals. Fretted, plucked, and strummed strings like guitars, banjos, and mandolins have become important to the folk revival, both as accompaniment to singing and as solo instruments. The bouzouki, a Greek instrument imported to Irish music, and the cittern, a revived Renaissance instrument, as well as mandolas and mandocellos, also grace the music frequently.

Percussion – Anything handy may be knocked together as percussion, but the most common are spoons and bones, which can become amazingly precise, rhythmically speaking, in the right person's hands. In Ireland, the bodhran, a goatskin on a wooden frame, is the drum of choice, and this has spread all over the Celtic lands. In Scotland, side drums and snare drums are used, mostly in military music.

– Stephen Winick

Alistair Russell replaces Foley; Dougie Pincock replaces MacGillivray. They begin to experiment with electronics and with new sounds and rhythms. —*Stephen Winick*

Celtic Hotel / 1987 / Temple Music 2002
The band's longest-lived lineup made their last and best trip to the studio when they recorded this album. *Celtic Hotel* is one of Battlefield's best. It features almost exclusively original material based on Scottish traditions. —*Stephen Winick*

★ **After Hours** / 1987 / Temple Music 2001
This compilation of material from Battlefield's Temple Records releases is probably the place to start listening. —*Stephen Winick*

Home Ground / 1989 / Temple Music 2034
The lineup's curtain call was this live album on which they perform old and new favorites. —*Stephen Winick*

Home Ground Live / 1989 / Temple Music 34
The band captured live in the Highlands, performing old and new favorites. —*Stephen Winick*

The Battlefield Band's Hi-Light / 1991 / Tonn Mor
A good set from the new lineup, caught live in the Scottish Highlands. —*Stephen Winick*

New Spring / 1991 / Temple Music 2045
This new lineup finds Pincock replaced by veteran piper Iain MacDonald and McNeill, one of the band's founders, replaced by seventeen-year-old whiz kid John McCusker. They still make equally fine music. —*Stephen Winick*

★ **Opening Moves** / 1993 / Topic 468
This CD combines most of the material from *At the Front* with extra tracks taken from *Battlefield Band* and *Stand Easy*. It's the essential compilation of Battlefield's Topic period. —*Stephen Winick*

Sarah Bauhan

Bauhan is an excellent whistle and flute player from New England. —*Stephen Winick*

● **Chasing the New Moon** / 1991 / Whistler's Music 9859
Bauhan and her guests perform traditional and original tunes full of variety and beauty. A brilliant debut! —*Stephen Winick*

Untamed Grasses / 1993 / Alcazar 116
More magnificent music from Bauhan and friends. —*Stephen Winick*

Derek Bell

Harp, timpani, oboe, piano / Irish
Best known as the harpist with the Chieftains, Derek Bell periodically records solo albums that allow his instrumentals to take center stage, backed by his fellow Chieftains on whistle, bodhran, and fiddle. —*Bruce Eder*

Carolan's Receipt / 1992 / Shanachie 79013
Bell's tribute to 17th-century harpist Turlough Carolan, backed by the New Irish Chamber Orchestra. —*Bruce Eder*

● **Carolan's Favorite** / Shanachie 79020
Probably Bell's best and most mystical album, a subdued and varied account of Turlough Carolan's music. —*Bruce Eder*

Derek Bell's Musical Ireland / Shanachie 79042
A more general look at Irish music spanning numerous periods in various styles. —*Bruce Eder*

Peter Bellamy

b. Sep. 8, 1944, Bournemouth, Dorset, England, **d.** Sep. 24, 1991
Vocals / English
Bellamy was one of the English folk revival's greatest voices. He was born in Norfolk in 1944. In early 1965 he moved to London, where he met up with Royston Wood and Heather Wood, and the three got a regular gig at a club whose name they would eventually adopt—The Young Tradition. Their performances featured flamboyant costumes, witty presentation, and the startling power of Bellamy's voice. The group entertained a lot of audiences, recorded a pair of albums, gained a reputation for excellence, and were still unable to make a living as performers. In 1969, they broke up. As Bellamy would later point out, they became important and influential, even legendary, after they had ceased to exist.

Bellamy first thought of setting the poems of Rudyard Kipling to music in 1970. This fascination with Kipling continued until Bellamy's death, resulting in no fewer than five albums of Kipling songs. Also in the '70s, Bellamy composed *The Transports*, a bal-

lad opera in the mold of Ewan MacColl's work, and recruited such people as Martin Carthy, Nic Jones, A.L. Lloyd, and Cyril Tawney to record it. It was released as an album in 1977 and also had several stage runs in England. During the '70s and '80s, Bellamy was trying to find an audience wider than the traditional folk crowd, so he cut back on the traditional songs in his shows, turning them into multimedia historical presentations. But traditional singing was in Bellamy's blood, and the beginning of the '90s found him performing a mostly traditional repertoire once again, with the exuberant enthusiasm he has always been known for. Bellamy felt there was a lack of appreciation for the music to which he had devoted his life, observing more than once that countless performers had abandoned traditional music for other forms of "folk" music. Some, he felt, did it for money, something he no doubt understood but regretted. More often, though, he expressed regret that interest in traditional song was simply on the wane, not only with audiences, but also with performers. He always acknowledged that his own unwillingness or perhaps his inability to compromise had led to the demise of the Young Tradition. Perhaps, some 22 years later, it also helped lead to his own demise; in September 1991, Peter Bellamy took his life. All Peter Bellamy recordings are recommended. —*Stephen Winick*

Peter Bellamy Sings the Barrack-Room Ballads of Rudyard Kipling / 1974 / Green Linnet 1002
Bellamy performs songs of Rudyard Kipling. —*Stephen Winick*

Tell It Like It Was / 1975 / Trailer 2089
Over the ten years prior to this release, Bellamy had been writing tunes to traditional words and words to traditional tunes. This release showcased some of the results. —*Stephen Winick*

☆ **The Transports** / 1977 / Free Reed 022
Bellamy's masterpiece ballad opera, starring himself and other influential folk singers. —*Stephen Winick*

○ **Songs an' Rummy Conjurin' Tricks** / 1991 / Fellside 5
Recorded live a scant nine months before his death, this album is an excellent example of Bellamy's charm as a live performer. —*Stephen Winick*

● **Both Sides Then** / 1992 / Fledg'ling
Traditional songs of England, Ireland, and America, sung in Bellamy's amazing voice and accompanied by guests such as Louis Killen and Dave Swarbrick. Simply beautiful.
This CD rerelease contains one extra track as well as copious extra liner notes. A brief and moving biographical essay by Martin Carthy completes the package. —*Stephen Winick*

Mary Bergin

Mary Bergin is a member of a musical family from Dublin. She learned to play the tin whistle as a child and was all-Ireland champion in her teens. Not primarily a performer, she teaches whistle and makes uilleann pipes and flutes. —*Stephen Winick*

★ **Feadoga Stain** / Shanachie 79083
Bergin is joined by members of De Danann, who accompany her through an outstanding display of tunes and talent. —*Stephen Winick*

○ **Feadoga Stain 2** /
We waited 14 years for another solo album, and it's worth it! —*Stephen Winick*

Black Family, The

This talented singing family features Mary Black, who gained recognition with the group De Danann and then broke through to great fame on her own, as well as Frances Black, whose work with Arcady seems sure to catapult her to similar success. Their brothers Martin, Michael, and Shay round out the group. —*Stephen Winick*

★ **Black Family, The** / Dara 023
One of the best albums of Irish singing you'll find, this features old ballads, sea shanties, and contemporary numbers. —*Stephen Winick*

Time for Touching Home / 1990 / Dara 035
A combination of traditional selections and some contemporary pieces in the "folk" mold, written by the likes of Nanci Griffith, Jez Lowe, and Dougie MacLean. —*Dirty Linen*

Mary Black

b. May 22, 1955, Ireland
Vocals
A premier Irish vocalist, Mary Black has produced albums with the Black Family and as a solo artist. —*Chip Renner*

● **Collected** / 1984 / Gifthorse 10006
This 1986 album contains both previously released and unreleased material; many traditional songs with Irish instrumentation (uilleannn pipes, bouzouki, fiddle, sitar, etc.), including a beautiful Gaelic ballad and "She Moves Through the Fair." —*Ladyslipper*

No Frontiers / 1989 / Gifthorse 77308
Mary Black's strong vocals take hold of you on this CD, along with the strong producing and guitar work of Declan Sinnott. Features Noel Bridgeman, Garvan Gallagher, Pat Crowley, and Carl Garaghty. Black shines on past the point of rescue on the lighthearted "Carolina Rua" and the "Moving Hearts Sounding Another Day." —*Chip Renner*

○ **Babes in the Woods** / 1991 / Gifthorse 77528
Mary Black's crystalline voice is highly regarded in her native Ireland, where this disc entered the charts at number one. Thoughtful songs colored by dobro, mandolin, accordion, fiddle, sax, and other instruments. —*Roundup newsletter*

Bleizi Ruz

Group / Celtic
One of Brittany's top bands, blending traditional accordion and bombarde playing with the newer sounds of electric guitars, bass, and drums. —*Stephen Winick*

En Concert / 1991 / Escalibur 836
A live album featuring innovative instrumentals and traditional and original songs. —*Stephen Winick*

Hent Sant Jakez / 1993 / Shamrock 1018
With guests like Spain's La Musgaua and Leilia, Ireland's Desi Wilkinson, and Brittany's Laurent Jouin, Bleizi Ruz perform music relating to the pilgrimage from France to Santiago, Spain. Eclectic and enjoyable. —*Stephen Winick*

○ **Coz Lizoriou-Klask Ar Plac'h** / Pluriel 65
Two albums on one CD. A lot of good, solid, instrumental music, and one song. —*Stephen Winick*

Blowzabella

Group / Irish
Blozabella was formed in the early '80s by a group of musicians studying instrument making. The idea was to make traditional dance music based on the use of melody-accompanied drones. Original members included Sam Palmer and Cliff Stapleton (hurdy-gurdies) and Dave Roberts (melodeons, piano). Over the years they evolved into a highly electric band featuring Andy Cutting (melodeons, percussion), Nigel Eaton (hurdy-gurdies, cello, percussion), Jo Freya (vocals, tenor saxophone, clarinet), Paul James (saxophone, bagpipes, rauschfeife, percussion), and Jon Swayne (saxophone, bagpipes). Their music has been influenced by Middle Eastern, Irish, and Bulgarian music. —*Stephen Winick & Chip Renner*

Blowzabella / 1982 / Plant Life 038
Subtitled *Traditional Dance Music,* this album is intended for dancing, and the notes include dance instructions as well as detailed descriptions of their instruments. The music is mostly French, with English music taking second place. —*Stephen Winick*

In Colour / 1983 / Plant Life 051
Like their first album, this live follow-up includes mostly French music played on bagpipes, hurdy-gurdy, melodeon, and woodwinds. It's got great energy and verve, and also has dancing instructions included. —*Stephen Winick*

○ **Bobittyshooty** / 1984 / Plant Life 064
The Blowzabella boys began to foreground their own compositions on this LP. Spirited and enjoyable, this is one of their best. —*Stephen Winick*

○ **Vanilla** / 1990 / Green Linnet 3050
You'll hear all types of European influences on this CD. Not for the faint of heart; only fans of the eclectic need apply. —*Chip Renner*

Bothy Band, The

Group / Celtic
This groundbreaking Irish band of the '70s folk revival includes pipes, flute, fiddle, guitar, and more, plus the unbelievable singing voice of Triona Ni Dhomhnaill. —*Stephen Winick*

○ **1975—The First Album** / 1975 / Green Linnet 3011
Brilliant 1975 debut, featuring fiddler Tommy Peoples. —*Stephen Winick*

★ **Old Hag You Have Killed Me** / 1976 / Green Linnet 3005
An electrifying set, *Old Hag* features some of the Bothy Band's strongest material and best performances. It marks the debut of Kevin Burke as a member. —*Stephen Winick*

Out of the Wind into the Sun / 1977 / Green Linnet 3013
Perhaps their weakest album, this is still very much worth hearing. It features more synthesizer and electric piano than before and marked an era when the band was uncertain of its future. —*Stephen Winick*

● **After Hours (Live in Paris)** / 1979 / Green Linnet 3016
The Bothy Band are back at their peak on this live farewell album. Some of their greatest hits are reprised, and some new material is introduced in a concert context. —*Stephen Winick*

★ **Best of the Bothy Band** / 1988 / Green Linnet 3043
Intricate arrangements, lovely singing, powerful rhythms. An absolute must. —*Stephen Winick*

La Bottine Souriante

Quebec's traditional music is a blend of French and Irish styles. This is Quebec's top folk ensemble, incorporating fiddle, accordion, guitar, and more. —*Stephen Winick*

Les Epousailles / 1981 / Gamma 256
Their second album, with a lot of good material. —*Stephen Winick*

Y a Ben du Changement / 1982 / Gamma 265
This sounds much like *Les Epousailles.* —*Stephen Winick*

Je Voudrais Changer D'chapeau / 1989 / Rounder 6041
This '90 CD won a Juno award in Canada, and it brilliantly mixes diverse styles ranging from folk to Cajun to French to country, featuring Michel Bordeleau's mandolin and violin, Yves Lambert's accordion, Andre Marchand's guitar, Denis Frechette's piano, and Martin Racine's violin and mandola, plus a string quartet and special guest Robert Ellis's bass trombone. The members of the group share vocal duties, and their exuberant harmonies, spirited arrangements, and rousing uptempo themes are uniformly appealing throughout. Despite structural and linguistic differences, La Bottine Souriante's music has elements that fans of many American idioms should recognize and admire. —*Ron Wynn*

● **Jusqu'aux P'tites Heures** / 1991 / Mille Pattes 2037
La Bottine Souriante have melded with a brass quartet to becoming a driving Quebec folk orchestra. Astoundingly entertaining. —*Stephen Winick*

Chic N' Swell / Green Linnet 3042
Their first U.S. release is a strong follow-up to their first two albums. —*Stephen Winick*

○ **La Traversee De L'atlantique** / Green Linnet 3043
Their most Irish-sounding album, with a bodhran player adding to the distinctly Canadian percussion of heavy boot tapping. —*Stephen Winick*

Robin Huw Bowen

Bowen is the greatest exponent of the Welsh triple harp. He has been a member of the group Mabsant as well as a solo musician. —*Stephen Winick*

Cyfarch Y Delyn (Greet the Harp) / 1988 / Sain 1460
A collection of beautiful airs and dances played by Bowen on solo harp. —*Stephen Winick*

○ **Telyn Berseiniol Fy Ngwlad (The Sweet Harp of My Land)** / Flying Fish 70610
More of the same. This CD features two tracks from Cyfarch Y Delyn as bonus tracks. —*Stephen Winick*

Boys of the Lough, The

Group / Celtic

A folk-revival group featuring members from England, Ireland, and Scotland and led by the great Shetland fiddler Aly Bain. — *Stephen Winick*

○ **The Boys of the Lough** / 1973 / Shanachie 79002
This debut album is particularly brilliant because of Robin Morton's and Dick Gaughan's contributions. —*Stephen Winick*

Second Album / 1973 / Rounder 3006
Live album. Good sound quality. —*Chip Renner*

Lochaber No More / 1975 / Philo 1031
Another excellent album of dances, airs, and songs. —*Stephen Winick*

Live at Passim's / 1975 / Philo 1026
A great early album, still with Morton. —*Stephen Winick*

Wish You Were Here / 1978 / Flying Fish 070
Live-performance recordings of this traditional Irish group's Shetland Islands tour. —*AMG*

Regrouped / 1980 / Flying Fish 225
This album features traditional Celtic folk music in a variety of styles, from airs and hornpipes to reels, a cappella ballads, and jigs. —*AMG*

To Welcome Paddy Home / 1986 / Shanachie 79061
The tragic death of guitarist Tich Richardson left the band short and shocked for a while, but they bounced back beautifully on this album. —*Stephen Winick*

Far from Home / 1986 / Shanachie 79065
Highly recommended. —*Chip Renner*

Farewell and Remember Me / 1987 / Shanachie 79067
One of their finest records. —*Chip Renner*

Sweet Rural Shade / 1988 / Shanachie 79068
Includes their top three releases. —*Chip Renner*

Fair Hills of Ireland, The / 1993 / Sage Arts 3022
The boys celebrate their 25th anniversary with this excellent studio album. —*Stephen Winick*

Live at Carnegie Hall / Sage Arts 301
A good live album. The crowd is into the show. —*Chip Renner*

Brass Monkey

Brass Monkey were a most unusual and appealing English folk group. Composed of Martin Carthy (guitar, mandolin, vocals), John Kirkpatrick (squeezeboxes, vocals), Howard Evans (trumpet, flugelhorn, vocals), Martin Brinsford (saxophone, mouth organ, percussion), and, depending on the date, either Roger Williams or Richard Cheetham (trombone), they were a powerful and commanding group. Unfortunately, these very busy musicians were unable to find enough time for the band to continue. —*Stephen Winick*

○ **Brass Monkey** / 1971 / Rare Earth 523
This was the band's majestic debut album, featuring Carthy and Kirkpatrick's singing backed by the innovative combination of instruments. —*Stephen Winick*

See How It Runs / 1986 / Topic
A worthy successor, this features more bold and brassy arrangements of traditional songs. —*Stephen Winick*

★ **Complete Brass Monkey** / 1993 / Topic 467
CD rerelease of all the Brass Monkey material. Thoroughly indispensable, this is the one to buy. —*Stephen Winick*

Anne Briggs

b. Sep. 29, 1944, Toton, Nottinghamshire, England
Vocals / English
Both a singer of traditional songs and a songwriter, Briggs was an influence on many important revival singers—June Tabor, Maddy Prior, Sandy Denny, Jacqui McShee, Christy Moore, and others—before she gave up performing for a quieter life. Her lovely voice and accompaniments on guitar and bouzouki still sound fresh and vital. —*Stephen Winick*

The Time Has Come / 1971 / CBS 64612
Quiet, introspective original songs. —*Stephen Winick*

★ **Classic Anne Briggs** / 1990 / Fellside 78
This CD rerelease captures all of her recordings for Topic between 1964 and 1971. Almost every folk song she recorded is here. An absolute must! —*Stephen Winick*

Robin Bullock

Multi-instrumentalist Robin Bullock is a bluegrass-turned-Celtic string wizard. He is currently a member of the group Helicon. —*Stephen Winick*

● **Green Fields** / 1993 / Dorian Discovery 80112
Bullock plays Celtic instrumentals on cittern, guitar, and other instruments, and uses the studio to its fullest effect. Wonderful energy and imagination. —*Stephen Winick*

Joe Burke

b. Mar. 16, 1884, Philadelphia, PA, d. Jun. 9, 1950, Upper Darby, PA
Accordion / Celtic
One of Ireland's best-known accordion players, Burke comes out of the great Galway squeezebox tradition. —*Stephen Winick*

The Tailor's Choice / 1983 / Green Linnet 1045
Burke mostly plays a boxwood flute. Maire Ni Chathasaigh joins him on harp. —*Stephen Winick*

Happy to Meet & Sorry to Part / 1986 / Green Linnet 1069
Trio album with Michael Cooney and Terry Corcoran featuring pipes, accordion, guitar, and singing. —*Stephen Winick*

○ **Traditional Music of Ireland** / Green Linnet 1048
Recorded in 1972 and 1973, this album was released in this country in 1983. A truly classic accordion album with impressive lift and verve. —*Stephen Winick*

Kevin Burke

Fiddle / Celtic
The most fluid and mesmeric fiddler playing Irish music, Burke has been a member of Patrick Street and the Bothy Band. — *Stephen Winick*

If the Cap Fits / 1978 / Green Linnet 3009
A showcase of Burke's amazing talents. —*Stephen Winick*

Promenade / 1979 / Green Linnet 3010
With Michael O Dhomhnaill. Not to be missed. —*Stephen Winick*

● **Eavesdropper** / 1981 / Green Linnet 3002
Kevin and Jackie Daly show amazing empathy for each other's playing—a true musical union. —*Stephen Winick*

○ **Portland** / 1982 / Green Linnet 1041
Another fine display, with Michael O Domhnaill. —*Stephen Winick*

○ **Up Close** / 1984 / Green Linnet 1052
A gem, featuring guests like Matt Molloy, Joe Burke, and the Murphy family of harmonica players. —*Stephen Winick*

○ **Open House** / 1992 / Green Linnet 1122
An astounding disc from Burke and his band. —*Stephen Winick*

○ **Celtic Fiddle Festival** / 1993 / Green Linnet 1133
Magnificent fiddle album also stars Johnny Cunningham and Christian LeMaitre of Kornog. —*Stephen Winick*

Buttons & Bows

Group / Celtic
This group is made up of Jackie Daly, along with brothers Seamus and Manus McGuire on fiddles. —*Stephen Winick*

The First Month of Summer / 1987 / Green Linnet 1079
More of a good thing. —*Stephen Winick*

Ian Campbell

Vocals / Scottish
Ian Campbell and the Ian Campbell Folk Group were Britain's favorite folk performers, bar none, during the '60s. Based in Birmingham, they featured singers Ian and Lorna Campbell of Aberdeen as well as Dave Swarbrick and Dave Pegg, later of Fairport Convention. Their arrangements are somewhat dated today, but with their rousing guitar, banjo, and fiddle accompaniments, some songs still sound fresh, and Swarbrick in particular was ahead of his time. —*Stephen Winick*

Across the Hills / 1964 / Transatlantic 118
A good general Campbell album. —*Stephen Winick*

● **Coaldust Ballads** / 1965 / Transatlantic 123
Mining songs, mostly from the Northeast. —*Stephen Winick*

The Singing Campbells / 1965 / Topic 12T120

Ian and Lorna, plus their sister Winnie; their parents, Dave and Betty; and their friend Bob Cooney. All unaccompanied traditional songs, including old ballads and modern street songs. Wonderful! —*Stephen Winick*

Tam o' Shanter / 1968 / Xtra 1074
Ian Campbell alone, performing songs by Robert Burns. — *Stephen Winick*

Capercaillie

Group / Scottish
Featuring accordion, fiddle, whistles, and guitar along with an array of electronics, Capercaillie makes new Scottish folk music. — *Stephen Winick*

Crosswinds / 1984 / Green Linnet 1077
Still a bit tentative, but a good album. —*Stephen Winick*

● **Sidewaulk** / 1989 / Green Linnet 1094
Donal Lunny's production and the band's skill make this collection of driving, syncopated tunes and songs very exciting indeed. —*Stephen Winick*

Danny Carnahan

Danny Carnahan and Robin Petrie come from San Francisco. Carnahan is a singer and songwriter who plays fiddle, guitar, and mandolins, while Petrie concentrates on hammered dulcimer. They have recorded both Celtic traditional and original folk music. —*Stephen Winick*

● **Journeys of the Heart** / 1984 / Celtoid 70102
One of the best recordings of traditional and original Irish and Scottish material from an American act, this features Carnahan's voice and instruments backed by Petrie on a few tracks. — *Stephen Winick*

Two for the Road / Flying Fish 364
Another great set of tunes and songs, this features more participation by Petrie. —*Stephen Winick*

○ **No Regrets** /
Mostly contemporary folk-style material with a Celtic flavor, this is a new direction for the duo. It works well. —*Stephen Winick*

Liz Carroll

Fiddle / Celtic
A fantastic Irish fiddler from Chicago, Liz Carroll has been a member of Cherish the Ladies and of the Green Fields of America. She's also part of one of the greatest Irish trios performing today, along with Billy McComiskey and Daithi Sproule. Her solo work also deserves attention. —*Stephen Winick*

Friend Indeed—Irish Fiddle and Piano / 1978 / Shanachie 29013
Carroll's light and quick but firmly accented fiddling is backed by Marty Fahey's better-than-average piano on this, her first solo album. —*Stephen Winick*

Kiss Me Kate—Irish Fiddle and Accordion / 1978 / Shanachie 29010
Carroll is joined by button accordion player Tommy Maguire for some tight duo playing that predicts her later work with Billy McComiskey. —*Stephen Winick*

○ **Liz Carroll** / 1988 / Green Linnet 1092
Powerhouse tunes, some of which she wrote herself. Accompanied by guitarist Daithi Sproule. —*Stephen Winick*

★ **Trian** / 1992 / Flying Fish 70586
Utterly brilliant. Carroll and Billy McComiskey play as one, and Daithi Sproule's accompaniment and singing are as good as it gets. The best Irish trio there is.—*Stephen Winick*

Martin Carthy

b. May 21, 1940, Hatfield, Hertfordshire, England
Vocals, guitar / English
Martin Carthy is one of the pioneers of the folk revival that swept Britain in the early '60s. As a singer, he has introduced many beautiful and moving traditional songs to audiences worldwide. As a guitarist, he's credited with helping invent a style of accompaniment prevalent in British folk music. He has created many songs from shreds and patches of traditional material, fragments that were too beautiful to be discarded. Others he has created out of whole cloth. For all his accomplishments he has been called

"the best-known urban revival singer in England," and, more succinctly, "a living legend."

Martin recorded his first album in 1965, and on it he was accompanied by fiddler Dave Swarbrick, who played with the Ian Campbell Folk Group, at the time one of Britain's most successful folk acts. Carthy and Swarbrick became fast friends and musical accomplices, touring and recording together from 1966 to 1969. Together they were one of the most important folk-revival acts in Britain. Since that time, Martin has been a member of many groups, including one of the first and one of the last lineups of the enormously successful folk-rock outfit Steeleye Span, the first lineup of the less-successful Albion Country Band, the excellent and innovative group Brass Monkey, and the a cappella singing family the Watersons (of which he remains a member). Recently, he and Dave Swarbrick recemented their musical partnership. —*Stephen Winick*

Martin Carthy / 1965 / Fontana 5269
Carthy's debut album, while a bit rudimentary by his later standards, sounds remarkably good 30 years later. —*Stephen Winick*

Second Album / 1966 / Fontana 5362
Carthy and Swarbrick start sounding more comfortable together on this fine album. —*Stephen Winick*

○ **Byker Hill** / 1967 / Fontana 5434
Carthy and Swarbrick become a fully integrated musical personality. The title track is simply astounding. —*Stephen Winick*

But Two Came By / 1968 / Fontana 5477
Carthy and Swarbrick first received equal billing on this album. A fine collection. —*Stephen Winick*

Prince Heathen / 1969 / Fontana 5529
Another astounding title track put together from traditional fragments by Carthy. —*Stephen Winick*

Because It's There / 1971 / Rounder 3031
Carthy and his pal John Kirkpatrick left a two-year stint in the folk-rock group Steeleye Span in 1978, then teamed up again for this album. Wonderful, brassy arrangements feature trumpeter Howard Evans and predict Carthy's work with Brass Monkey. —*Stephen Winick*

Crown of Horn / 1971 / Rounder 3019
Carthy's guitar gets a real workout on songs like "The Bonny Lass of Anglesey" and "Old Tom of Oxford." Really impeccable playing and singing. —*Stephen Winick*

○ **Out of the Cut** / 1971 / Rounder 3075
Trio of Carthy, Kirkpatrick, and Evans are back for this album, one of Carthy's very best. —*Stephen Winick*

Sweet Wivelsfield / 1971 / Rounder 3020
Carthy goes it alone, on his first album without Swarbrick. The result is quite good. —*Stephen Winick*

Right of Passage / 1988 / Topic 452
This set is good but not as stunning as we might expect after a six-year hiatus in which to work up material. —*Stephen Winick*

○ **Life & Limb** / 1991 / Green Linnet 1143
Singer/guitarist Martin Carthy and fiddler Dave Swarbrick, stars of the '60s British folk circuit, are reunited on a fine '90s set. Fleet and passionate playing. —*Mark A. Humphrey*

○ **Skin & Bone** / May 1992 / Green Linnet 3075
A new studio album from the re-formed (though not reformed) Carthy/Swarbrick team is finally here. It's full of class and grace. —*Stephen Winick*

★ **Collection** / 1993 / Green Linnet 1136
The tracks on this compilation were picked by Martin himself from his solo recordings. A must! —*Stephen Winick*

Mike Casey

A native of North Carolina, Casey has adapted Irish banjo and mandolin techniques to the Appalachian dulcimer. Along the way, he's learned to play flute in the East Galway style. —*Stephen Winick*

○ **Hourglass** / 1992 / Celtic Trader 7730
This lovely disc features Casey's delicate dulcimer and wooden flute backed by several guests. Very tastefully done. —*Stephen Winick*

Celtic Thunder

This Baltimore-area group has been around for 15 years, playing souped-up Irish and Irish American music. —*Stephen Winick*

Celtic Thunder / 1988 / Green Linnet 1029
The first Celtic Thunder album is full of sprightly energy. Mick Moloney guests. —*Stephen Winick*

The Light of Other Days / 1988 / Green Linnet 1086
More polished, slick, and commercial than their first album. —*Stephen Winick*

Ceolbeg

Ceolbeg is an impressive Scottish band for the '90s, featuring Highland bagpipes, harp, flute, and other traditional instruments next to drums, bass, and keyboards. It's all held together by the voice and guitar of singer-songwriter Davy Steele. —*Stephen Winick*

Seeds to the Wind /
More polished and confident than their first album, this established Ceolbeg as one of Scotland's most important recording folk groups. Traditional and original songs alternate with excellent instrumentals. —*Stephen Winick*

● **Unfair Dance** / 1993 / Greentrax 058
This one features some breathtaking modern arrangements of traditional songs and new material. —*Stephen Winick*

Ceoltoiri

Maryland band Ceoltoiri perform traditional music on Celtic harp, hammered dulcimer, and guitar. —*Stephen Winick*

Celtic Lace / 1989 / Maggie's Music 203
Beautiful duo arrangements, with accompanists here and there. Harpist Sue Richards's greatest strength is her command of Scottish traditional music. Karen Ashbrook's sprightly hammered dulcimer playing is an excellent complement to Richards's harp. Even the cover art is cool! —*Stephen Winick*

Silver Apples of the Moon / 1992 / Maggie's Music 202
Connie McKenna's guitar and singing add the right amount of gentle Irish charm. An excellent album for the fan of Irish and Scottish music. (Rating: Best of Artist+.) —*Stephen Winick*

Cherish the Ladies

Group / Irish
This group started with a concert series produced by the Ethnic Folk Arts Center in New York City. The theme was young women in traditional Irish music. Out of that series grew an ensemble of women musicians, fronted by flute player Joanie Madden, that is one of America's great Irish music groups. —*Stephen Winick*

★ **The Back Door** / 1992 / Green Linnet 1119
Their first album as an ensemble is also one of the finest American Irish records ever. Features dance music, airs, and songs sung by Cathy Ryan. —*Stephen Winick*

Out & About / May 1993 / Green Linnet 1134
This follow-up to *The Back Door* is another marvelous display of tight group playing and soloing. Johnny Cunningham produced it. —*Stephen Winick*

Chieftains, The

Group
The original traditional Irish folk band, as far as anyone who came of age in the '70s is concerned, is the Chieftains. Their sound, built principally around Paddy Moloney's pipes, is otherworldly, entirely instrumental. Over the 20 years since they first emerged (several years after the recording of their debut album, *Chieftains I*), the Chieftains have done more to reintroduce the sound of pipes, bodhran, and whistle to the world outside of Ireland than any other group of musicians. Their breakthrough to an audience beyond the ranks of Irish-music enthusiasts came with the group's appearance on the sound track of Stanley Kubrick's movie *Barry Lyndon* (their "Women of Ireland" became a radio hit and led to extensive further film work). Since the late '70s, their albums have settled into an effective but less than fully inspired mode of creativity as the group has sought to add new wrinkles to an old repertory without repeating themselves. —*Bruce Eder*

The Chieftains 1 / 1964 / Shanachie 79021

A rather tame debut album, exploring what was truly unknown territory during the mid '60s. Better things would follow. —*Bruce Eder*

The Chieftains 2 / 1969 / Shanachie 79022
More fully developed and secure sound, with Moloney stepping out in front and the rest of the group forming up nicely. —*Bruce Eder*

The Chieftains 3 / 1971 / Shanachie 79023
The group's first great record, a haunting trip through an Ireland of song, story, and legend. —*Bruce Eder*

○ **The Chieftains 4** / 1973 / Shanachie 79024
The record that broke the group with college audiences in the mid '70s—this is elegant, wistful, and ethereal in equal measures. —*Bruce Eder*

Bonaparte's Retreat / 1976 / Shanachie 79026
The group's attempt to merge their traditional sound with a progressive form. It was only partly successful—it was overdone and overambitious but still worth hearing. —*Bruce Eder*

● **Chieftains Live!** / 1977 / Shanachie 79027
An older lineup performs a rousing live set. —*Stephen Winick*

The Chieftains 7 / 1977 / CBS 35612
A boisterous and exuberant traditional album. —*Stephen Winick*

☆ **The Chieftains 10: Cotton-Eyed Joe** / 1981 / Shanachie 79019
More great traditional sounds. —*Stephen Winick*

Ballad of the Irish Horse / 1985 / Shanachie 79051
Quite a concept album—songs devoted to the Irish horse and its importance and role in legend and history. —*Bruce Eder*

Chieftains in China: Video / 1985 / Shanachie 204
The Chieftains have dedicated themselves to keeping Irish traditional music—jigs, reels, and the like—alive and kicking. During their two decades of recording and performing, they have become musical ambassadors, spreading their lively sound throughout the world. This video documents the Chieftains' memorable trip to China and the resulting musical/cultural bond that was forged. The *Irish Times* called it "the most satisfying and extraordinary episode in their 20-year career." — *Roundup newsletter*

Irish Heartbeat / 1988 / Polydor 834496
Van Morrison sings traditional Irish songs with the Chieftains. —*Stephen Winick*

Reel Music: The Film Scores / 1991 / RCA 60412
The group's collected film tracks, which constitute their best-known work to the public at large. A generous collection. —*Bruce Eder*

☆ **The Bells of Dublin** / Oct. 1991 / RCA 60824
Joined by Nanci Griffith, the Irish group presents a superb concert blending folk and country music. Well recorded and well photographed. —*Bruce Eder*

Irish Evening / 1992 / RCA 60916
Guests are Nanci Griffith and Roger Daltrey. —*Stephen Winick*

● **The Best of the Chieftains** / Jan. 14, 1992 / CBS 48693
Twelve favorites from Ireland's foremost cultural ambassadors. — *Roundup newsletter*

Clancy Brothers, The

Group / Celtic
This singing family from Carrick-on-Suir, County Tipperary, are the most famous Irish folksingers in the world. They usually have a lead singer from outside the family. (They have sung with Tommy Makem, who comes from a singing family in Keady, County Armagh.) —*Stephen Winick*

By the Rising of the Moon / 1959 / Tradition 1006
Their first album, recorded in Kenneth S. Goldstein's kitchen with Tommy Makem. Free from some of the hokeyness of later efforts. —*Stephen Winick*

Greatest Hits / 1973 / Vanguard 53
A set with Lou Killen, a famous singer of Northumberland folk songs and sea shanties. Killen and the Clancys make an interesting combination and a record worth getting. More Scottish material than is usual for the Clancys. —*Stephen Winick*

○ **Live!** / 1982 / Vanguard 79445
With nephew Robbie O'Connell, from Waterford City. Another indication of their skill at handling the audience. —*Stephen Winick*

Reunion Concert / 1991 / Shanachie 202

Recorded at the Royal Ulster Hall in Belfast, this is an example of what the lads can do for an audience. —*Stephen Winick*

Aiofe Clancy

The daughter of Bobby Clancy, one of the Clancy Brothers, Aiofe is a fine singer in her own right. She has sung in folk clubs and concert halls from Ireland to Australia, and now lives in the United States. —*Stephen Winick*

It's About Time / 1994 / Rego 3017
An impressive debut that features Clancy singing songs old and new, accompanied by some great Irish musicians. —*Stephen Winick*

Liam Clancy

One of the original three singing Clancy Brothers, Liam later went off with Tommy Makem to form a duo, and then on his own as a solo act. —*Stephen Winick*

The Dutchman / Shanachie 52005
Mostly sad, slow songs fill this solo album. —*Stephen Winick*

● **Liam Clancy** / Vanguard 79169
A classic old album of Irish songs in Clancy's gentle style. An excellent introduction to this artist. —*Stephen Winick*

Clannad

Group / Celtic
Made up of three siblings and their twin uncles, this Irish family band went on to great fame as a pop group. However, their pre-pop days produced albums far more exciting to Celtic music fans, with Celtic harp, flutes, and other instruments backing up lovely Gaelic singing. —*Stephen Winick*

○ **Clannad 2** / 1974 / Shanachie 79007
Crisp and subtle arrangements. —*Stephen Winick*

Dulaman / 1976 / Shanachie 79008
The exquisite voice of Maire Ni Bhraonain centers the vocal harmonies, and her harp playing provides the focal point for the instrumental arrangements. Their repertoire consists of traditional Gaelic songs that they infuse with an uptempo, improvisational, yet precise and delicate, musicianship. —*Ladyslipper*

Crann Ull / 1980 / Tara 3007
This 1980 recording from Dublin's Tara Records contains pure traditional Gaelic and Irish material, impeccably performed, naturally revolving around Maire's heavenly voice. It's one of the last straightforward, all-acoustic albums Clannad recorded before they embarked on their experimentation with more contemporary sounds. —*Ladyslipper*

● **Fuaim** / 1982 / Atlantic 82481
This 1982 release (the only one with Enya) contains the beginnings of their ingenious blending of contemporary modes with the traditional: you will hear intermittent touches of synthesizer, clarinet, sax, electric guitar, and percussion. That, coupled with these six-part genetic harmonies, makes this a must for every Enya and Clannad fan. —*Ladyslipper*

○ **Macalla** / 1985 / RCA 8063
1985's *Macalla* is one of Clannad's strongest albums. The songs are mainly midtempo or slower and combine the poignant beauty of Irish balladry with the immediacy of a rock-band lineup. Traditional Irish instruments come and go, along with touches of sax, and on "In a Lifetime," soulful guest vocals by fellow Irishman Bono, of U2. *Macalla* is a well-rounded album of melodic folk-pop, infused with that beautiful warm sadness that seems to pervade Irish music and culture. —*Backroads Music/Heartbeats*

● **Pastpresent** / 1989 / RCA 9912
This 16-track anthology concentrates on this premier Celtic pop group's five major label releases (and adds two new tracks). Clannad weds acoustic, ethnic instruments to modern studio technology and ethereal, hook-filled melodies. All the tracks are well chosen. Too bad some of their earlier material couldn't be included. —*Brad Bradberry, Rock & Roll Disc*

○ **Anam** / 1990 / Atlantic 82409
Anam has primarily an acoustic sound, with the ongoing variety of 12 tracks covering vast musical terrain. Fans of Loreena McKennitt and Enya (onetime Clannad member) will also appreciate the subtle harmonies and vocal clarity of Maire Brennan.

The domestic version has two extra tracks: "In a Lifetime," a duet with Bono of U2 that was previously heard on *Macalla,* and "Harry's Game," a longtime favorite from the classic *Magical Ring.* —*Backroads Music/Heartbeats*

Banba / 1994 / Atlantic 825503
Clannad continues the trend of their last few albums with their latest release, *Banba.* Though it is certainly a pop effort, the Celtic influences are still present, this time in a more subdued, low-key production. —*David Jehnzen*

Clishmaclaver

Maryland-based duo Jennifer Culley and Brooke Parkhurst specialize in Irish, American, and Scottish songs sung in bright harmonies. Both have studied singing with Irish ballad singer Frank Harte. —*Stephen Winick*

Hearing Double / Bright Phoebus 001
Two beautiful voices treat a number of Irish ballads, English laments, and American hymns. A backing band that includes Billy McComiskey (accordion) and Myron Bretholz (bodhran) adds punch. This is an impressive debut! —*Stephen Winick*

○ **Roots Entwined** / Bright Phoebus 002
Parkhurst and Culley display talent, feminist sensibilities, and good humor on their second album. There's a lot of Scottish and American material here, sung with skill. On this album, the backing band is all-female and equally excellent. —*Stephen Winick*

Jack & Charlie Coen

Vocals, whistle, flute / Celtic
These two musicians, formerly of Woodford, County Galway, emigrated to New York in the '50s. Both have played whistle and flute, though Jack now concentrates on flute and Charlie on concertina. Charlie, also a fine singer, is known in Irish music circles simply as "Father Charlie," since his day job is serving the Church as a priest. —*Stephen Winick*

○ **The Branch Line** / 1977 / Green Linnet 3067
A 1992 rerelease of a classic 1977 Topic album. Reels, jigs, hornpipes, flings, and polkas, performed solo by each musician and as a duo. Real traditional Irish music at its best. —*Stephen Winick*

Michael Coleman

b. 1891, d. 1945
Michael Coleman of Killavil, County Sligo, is one of the seminal figures in Irish and Irish American traditional music. He came to the United States in 1914 and became a successful performer of Irish music in vaudeville and variety theaters across America. He settled in New York City, where Irish music was in great demand by the large Irish population. Between 1921 and 1944 he recorded many 78 rpm recordings of fiddle music that even today exert a great influence on players both here and in Ireland. Coleman's recorded material is one of the reasons that the Sligo fiddle style and tune repertoire predominate in much of Irish and Irish American fiddling. Many of Coleman's classic recordings have been rereleased on albums. —*Stephen Winick*

★ **Michael Coleman 1891-1945** / 1992 / Gael-Linn/Viva Voce 161
This stunning double CD release features 48 of Coleman's hugely influential sides, as well as a booklet over 100 pages long with fascinating accounts of Coleman's life and music. It's the best Coleman compilation available. —*Stephen Winick*

Shirley Collins

b. Jul. 5, 1935, Hastings, Sussex, England
Vocals / English
One of the most important singers and collectors of the early revival, Collins was a source from whom groups like Pentangle got many of their songs. Her sweet, sweet voice and Sussex accent made her quite popular for a time, but she gave up recording years ago. —*Stephen Winick*

● **Folk Roots, New Routes** / 1964 / Decca 4652
Collins with Davy Graham, a fantastic guitarist. —*Stephen Winick*

The Sweet Primeroses / 1967 / Topic 170
Her sister, Dolly Collins, adds portative pipe organ to Shirley's voice and banjo. —*Stephen Winick*

No Roses / 1971 / Antilles 7017

Features a truly impressive folk-rock backing band, later to become the Albion Band. —*Stephen Winick*

Seamus Connolly

Seamus Connolly has won all-Ireland fiddle titles a whopping ten times. He has also been a judge at the same competition, a solo musician, and a teacher. Currently, he teaches traditional Irish music at Boston College and tours and records when he can. —*Stephen Winick*

Notes from My Mind / Green Linnet 1087
This brilliant debut established his reputation among listeners as a master performer. It is slightly marred by weak sound in places, but the musicianship is impeccable. Guests include Liam O'Flynn (uilleann pipes) and Tommy Hayes (percussion). —*Stephen Winick*

● **Here and There** / Green Linnet 1098
Connolly's second album surpasses his first. Robust sound is a big improvement, and the tunes are unusual and exciting. Accompanists include Mick Moloney and Tommy Hayes. —*Stephen Winick*

Copper Family

Group / English
Farmers, shepherds, carters, and innkeepers, the Coppers have sung for at least 200 years in the same Sussex village, Rottingdean, Sussex, England, in a style reflecting the tradition of pub bard on Saturday, church choir on Sunday. —*John Storm Roberts*

○ **Coppersongs** / 1988 / EFDSS 004
Four generations of this most important of English singing families continue, delightfully, as an unusually pure example of living tradition. —*John Storm Roberts*

Arthur Cormack

Arthur Cormack won the 1983 gold medal in Gaelic singing at the national Mod, or music competition, the highest accolade for a Scottish Gaelic singer. He was only 18 years old at the time. Since then, Cormack has continued to sing Gaelic songs and has released two albums. —*Stephen Winick*

Nuair Bha Mi Og: Gaelic Songs by the Mod Gold / 1984 / Temple Music 2016
Accompanied by members of the Battlefield Band and by Alison Kinnaird, Cormack uses his naturally strong voice to great effect. —*Stephen Winick*

● **Ruith Na Gaoith** / Temple Music 2032
Many of the same accompanists, plus some new ones, join Cormack for his second album. Like his first, this one is restrained and tasteful. The arrangements are a bit more contemporary in sound, making it just a bit more accessible. —*Stephen Winick*

Craobh Rua

Craobh Rua is a relatively new band from Northern Ireland, who perform stirring music on uilleann pipes, fiddle, banjo, guitar, and vocals. Their greatest success has been in Scotland, where their albums and live shows have been accepted warmly and heartily by both fans and influential musicians. They could be one of the groups to watch in the future. —*Stephen Winick*

Not a Word About It / 1990 / BTB 0010
Craobh Rua's debut album has real verve in the instrumental passages, but the vocal selections are less forceful. —*Stephen Winick*

● **More That's Said, the Less the Better, The** / 1992 / BTB 0020
Both the playing and the singing convey the group's passion. —*Stephen Winick*

Critic's Group, The

Group / English, Scottish
This folk-song discussion group led by Ewan MacColl eventually began recording albums as singers. They included Frankie Armstrong, John Faulkner, and some other people who later became well known. All are well worth hearing. —*Stephen Winick*

The Female Frolic / 1968 / Argo 82
Songs addressing women's issues. —*Stephen Winick*

○ **Waterloo-Peterloo** / 1968 / Argo 86

Songs of laborers and soldiers. —*Stephen Winick*

As We Were A-Sailin' / 1970 / Argo 137
Sea songs, featuring MacColl himself. —*Stephen Winick*

Tony Cuffe

Vocals, whistle, guitar / Scottish
Tony's voice, whistle, and guitar are as wonderfully expressive alone as they were when he sang with Ossian. —*Stephen Winick*

○ **When First I Went to Caledonia** / 1988 / Iona 011
Beautiful selections, beautifully done. —*Stephen Winick*

John & Phil Cunningham

Group / Celtic
John, an outstanding Scottish fiddler, was a founding member of Silly Wizard. Phil, an equally impressive accordionist, joined after the group lost its original accordion player. Though known best for their work with the Wizard, John and Phil have a few other records available. —*Stephen Winick*

● **Against the Storm** / 1980 / Shanachie 79017
Scottish pipe tunes, Irish reels, and haunting slow airs fill this lovely album. —*Stephen Winick*

Thoughts from Another World / 1981 / Shanachie 79029
John's first solo album, an impressive debut including Celtic and American tunes. —*Stephen Winick*

○ **Fair Warning** / 1983 / Green Linnet 1047
Great fun from John Cunningham. Quicksteps and reels rub shoulders with slower, more haunting pieces. —*Stephen Winick*

○ **Airs & Graces** / 1984 / Green Linnet 3032
A Phil Cunningham solo outing. Not only accordion but also great whistle playing and moody synthesizer sounds make this an outstanding recording. —*Stephen Winick*

★ **Palomino Waltz** / 1988 / Green Linnet 1102
The Palomino Waltz / 1989 / Green Linnet 1102
Another Phil Cunningham solo album, and a nice follow-up to his other work. —*Stephen Winick*

Tom Dahill

Tom Dahill grew up in Irish neighborhoods in St. Paul, Minnesota, where he met many old-time Irish musicians. He learned to play the fiddle and to sing from such figures as Terence "Cuz" Teahan and Pat Hill. He has been a member of several bands and has toured extensively in the United States and Ireland. —*Stephen Winick*

Ragged Hank of Yarn / Flying Fish 490
Glenn Walker Johnson adds Irish harp and whistle. Dahill's singing is still less than thrilling, but this record is saved by its unusual selection of songs. —*Stephen Winick*

Jackie Daly

Accordion / Celtic
Daly is one of Ireland's top accordion players and has been a member of De Danann, Buttons & Bows, Arcady, and Patrick Street. —*Stephen Winick*

● **Buttons & Bows** / 1984 / Green Linnet 1051
Dance tunes from the Celtic lands as well as Scandinavia, in impressive arrangements. —*Stephen Winick*

Shaun Davey

Shaun Davey is a classical composer from Belfast whose work frequently features traditional motifs and instrumentation. He is best known for several compositions that feature the uilleann bagpipe, perhaps the only bagpipe refined enough to sit in with a symphony orchestra. —*Stephen Winick*

★ **The Brendan Voyage** / 1991 / Tara 3005
The Brendan Suite was Davey's first work for orchestra. It is based on the journey of a sixth-century monk who may have been the first European in America. The uilleann pipes, played by Liam O'Flynn, represent the boat. This innovative work, combining classical and traditional folk music, made Davey's reputation. —*Stephen Winick*

Pilgrim / Tara 3011
Features selections from the Lorient Festival Suite, composed for 1983's Interceltic Festival in Lorient, Brittany. This one features

orchestra, Welsh choirs, Scottish pipe bands, Galician bagpipes, Breton bombardes, and, of course, Liam O'Flynn. — *Stephen Winick*

○ **Granuaile** / Tara 3017
This one features orchestra, Liam O'Flynn's pipes, and Rita Connolly's singing. The songs and music, all written by Davey, tell the story of a 16th-century outlaw noblewoman. — *Stephen Winick*

Meg Davis

American-born singer Meg Davis now spends a lot of time in Ireland, where she sings with Joe Burke's trio. — *Stephen Winick*

Claddagh Walk / 1990 / Lismor 9030
Davis's voice treats some lovely songs, and the arrangements are classy and clean. — *Stephen Winick*

Deanta

Deanta is a young band with lots of talent and energy from the north of Ireland who play spirited arrangements of songs and tunes from their native tradition. — *Stephen Winick*

Deanta / Green Linnet 3081
A very energetic album full of great playing and singing. A bit marred by overproduction in places. — *Stephen Winick*

De Danann

De Danann began by producing the traditional music of Galway and Kerry, two of Ireland's musically rich counties, in vibrant arrangements. Influenced by both the instrumental sound of the Chieftains and the more vocally dominated sound of Planxty, this band built up a name for itself in the wake of the Chieftains' rise to international fame. Its members, especially the support singer, have come and gone with dizzying regularity, so that many of the greatest musicians in Ireland, including Frankie Gavin, Johnny Moynihan, Johnny McDonagh, Jackie Daly, Martin O'Connor, Dolores Keane, Mary Black, and Maura O'Connell have passed through its ranks. They've also changed the spelling of their name over the years; they go by either De Danann or De Dannan.— Stephen Winick & Bruce Eder. — *Stephen Winick*

○ **De Danann** / 1976 / Decca 5287
Their debut, featuring singer Dolores Keane. — *Stephen Winick*

Star-Spangled Molly / 1978 / Shanachie 79018
This time, the singer du jour is Maura O'Connell, and the theme is Irish American music of the '20s. — *Stephen Winick*

○ **The Mist Covered Mountain** / 1980 / Shanachie 79005
One of their strongest albums instrumentally, this release also features the singing of Tom Phaidin and Sean O Conaire. — *Stephen Winick and Bruce Eder*

A Jacket of Batteries / 1983 / Green Linnet 3053
This album features many new members but achieves sound of remarkable continuity with De Dannan's previous albums. — *Stephen Winick*

○ **Song for Ireland** / 1983 / Sugar Hill 1130
Mary Black contributes the stunning vocals that have made her famous, and the instrumentals have even more energy than usual. — *Stephen Winick*

Anthem / 1985 / Dara 013
On this album, the band has lots of former members back on board, including Dolores Keane. Both Jackie Daly and Martin O'Connor play accordion, and Mary Black sings a few songs. The band's name changed spelling between the two covers of this LP. — *Stephen Winick*

Selected Jigs Reels & Songs / 1988 / Shanachie 79001
This one features Johnny Moynihan's singing and bouzouki. — *Stephen Winick*

☆ **The Best of De Danann** / 1991 / Shanachie 79047
Probably as good a way to start off as any, with the most popular cuts from the group's albums. — *Bruce Eder*

1/2 Set in Harlem / 1991 / Green Linnet 1113
They blend their traditional music with gospel, klezmer, and other styles. — *Stephen Winick*

Ballroom / Green Linnet 3040
Features music-hall songs sung by Dolores Keane, along with more great instrumentals. — *Stephen Winick*

Johnny Doherty

A Donegal Traveler, John Doherty was one of the great masters of his own region's traditional fiddle style. — *Stephen Winick*

○ **Bundle & Go** / Green Linnet 3077
A collection of excellent field recordings made by Allen Feldman and Eamonn Doherty. — *Stephen Winick*

Mickey Doherty

Fiddle / Irish
For some perspective on all the revivalist "Celtic" music around, here is an undisputed grand master of Irish tradition. Mickey Doherty was one of the great names of Donegal fiddling and storytelling. — *John Storm Roberts*

○ **Gravel Walks** / 1949 / Irish Folklore Commission 002
These superb recordings, his first, were made pretty much by happenstance during a 1949 field trip. — *John Storm Roberts*

Tom Doherty

Born in Donegal, Ireland, Tom Doherty learned to play the melodeon in the early '20s. He traveled to find work, first to Scotland and England, and then to the United States, settling in Brooklyn. All the while, he kept alive the now-rare tradition of Irish melodeon, playing at dances, parties, and sessions. — *Stephen Winick*

○ **Take the Bull by the Horns** / Green Linnet 1131
Doherty recorded his first solo album when he was well into his 70s. Backed by many great younger musicians, including his daughter, he achieves a refreshingly light and experimental approach. — *Stephen Winick*

Johnny Doran

Uilleann pipes / Irish
An undisputed grand master of Irish tradition. Doran, a traveler from Clare, was heir to a major family tradition of pipers and a true original (he was a major influence on Willy Clancy, among others). — *John Storm Roberts*

○ **The Bunch of Keys** / Irish Folklore Commission 001
This tape includes the handful of recordings he made for the Irish Folklore Commission in the mid '40s. — *John Storm Roberts*

Dubliners

Irish musician and folklorist Mick Moloney calls the Dubliners "the bearded Bohemians of the Irish folk scene." They had a gritty, urban image that contrasted with some of the prettier origins of other bands. Although they're still around today, their great recordings were made years ago, with singer Luke Kelly and banjo player Barney McKenna. — *Stephen Winick*

Live at the Albert Hall / 1969 / Starline 5194
An early live set shows what all the fuss was about. — *Stephen Winick*

● **20 Original Greatest Hits** / 1978 / Chyme 1028
You can't go wrong with this compilation, which spans about ten years of the Dubliners. — *Stephen Winick*

○ **A Pacel of Rogues** / Arc 1061
Out of all the Dubliners' original albums, this one shines the brightest. — *Stephen Winick*

Seamus Egan

Banjo, flute, whistle, uilleann pipes / Celtic
A young virtuoso from Philadelphia, Egan has won the all-Ireland championship on four different instruments. — *Stephen Winick*

Traditional Music of Ireland / 1985 / Shanachie 29020
Seamus and his sisters, Siobhan and Rory Ann, rip through some fine tunes. — *Stephen Winick*

★ **Week in January** / 1990 / Shanachie 65005
Seamus Egan's fine flute and banjo playing make for an exciting album. — *Stephen Winick*

Seamus Ennis

Vocals, pipes, whistle / Celtic
A folklorist, singer, storyteller, and performer on uilleann pipes and tin whistle, Ennis was one of the pioneering figures in Irish folklore. His fluency in English and every dialect of Irish and

Scottish Gaelic made him an excellent cultural ambassador, telling translated Gaelic tales and playing venerable tunes to English audiences with a flair that revealed the genius hidden in folklore. —*Stephen Winick*

Forty Years of Irish Piping / 1974 / Green Linnet 1000
A musical biography of Ennis, plotting the development of his playing. Compiled by Pat Sky. —*Stephen Winick*

● **Feidlim Tonn Ri's Castle** / 1977 / Claddagh 19
On *Feidlim Tonn Ri's Castle*, "The King of Ireland's Son," Ennis tells a long Gaelic heroic folktale in English, with music on his pipes and whistle. Literally wonderful. —*Stephen Winick*

The Wandering Minstrel / 1977 / Green Linnet 3078
Solo piping by Ennis. —*Stephen Winick*

Meredydd Evans

A tutor at the University of Bangor, Wales, Meredydd Evans studied Welsh folk songs. He became quite influential, and his singing and teaching can be heard today in the repertoire of many Welsh folk groups. —*Stephen Winick*

● **Welsh Folksongs** / Smithsonian/Folkways 6835
Unaccompanied performances of many songs. Evans's beautiful voice floats. —*Stephen Winick*

John Faulkner

Better known as the former husband and singing partner of Dolores Keane, John Faulkner is also a formidable talent in his own right. He was a member of Ewan MacColl's Critic's Group in the '60s and continues to perform today. He sings and plays several instruments.—*Stephen Winick*

Nomads / 1992 / Clo-Iar Connachta 071
Features a seven-track "concept side" concerning the Highland clearances in Scotland. Faulkner is joined by many friends, including Dolores Keane. —*Stephen Winick*

● **Kind Providence** / Green Linnet 1064
Faulkner plays every instrument, including guitar, bouzouki, fiddle, and hurdy-gurdy. He also sings many lovely songs. An excellent album. —*Stephen Winick*

Figgy Duff

Group / Canadian
In Newfoundland, the proximity of traditional performance to American rock & roll produced naturally what Fairport Convention and Steeleye Span produced consciously in England: a hybrid of traditional English and Celtic music with rock. Figgy Duff is the most important exponent of this Newfoundland music, featuring the haunting voice of Pamela Morgan combined with a strident rock & roll approach. —*Stephen Winick*

● **Figgy Duff** / 1980 / Hagdown
Their debut, and their folkiest outing. —*Stephen Winick*

After the Tempest / 1984 / Celtic Music 023
Their second album, featuring a lot of great music, traditional and new. —*Stephen Winick*

Weather Out the Storm / 1989 / Hypnotic 1000
Powerful pop music with Celtic roots. —*Stephen Winick*

○ **Downstream** / 1993 / Hypnotic/A&M
Downstream completes a four-album evolution for Newfoundland's Figgy Duff. This latest consists entirely of songs written by core members Noel Dinn and Pamela Morgan. You can slice through *Downstream*'s atmosphere like a heavy maritime fog, and the whole project turns on Morgan's smoky, evocative vocals. You still find fiddle, mandolin, pennywhistle, and the occasional bout of bodhran, but the ten tracks stir up an inviting contemporary fusion—from the sultry swing of "Sweet Temptation" and world-beat feel of "Allanadh" to former Tom Cochrane guitarist Ken Greer's weeping pedal steel on "Pirates of Pleasure." —*Roch Parisien*

Fisher Family, The

Group / Scottish
Children of an occasional singer who was a Gaelic speaker from the isle of Barra and a Glasgow police inspector who sang choral music, opera, and music-hall songs, the Fishers have become respected traditional and contemporary folksingers. Archie Fisher sings the old songs in addition to writing his own; Ray sings the old ballads in a magnificent voice; and Cilla, with her husband, Artie Tresize, performs both traditional and contemporary music as well as a large repertoire of children's music. The siblings occasionally unite for tours or special appearances, but most of their recorded material is separate. —*Stephen Winick*

○ **The Fisher Family** / 1965 / Topic 12T137
In 1965, when this was recorded, Cilla was barely a teenager. Still, she makes valuable contributions along with Archie, Ray, and her sisters Joyce, Audrey, and Cindy. Archie's guitar accompaniments are little more than simple strumming, but all the singing is wonderful. This is a real collector's item. —*Stephen Winick*

Archie Fisher

Guitar, vocals / Scottish
See the biography for the Fisher Family. —*AMG*

Archie Fisher / 1968 / Celtic Music 007
Released in 1968, this first album shows off Fisher's gentle voice and guitar accompaniments. —*Stephen Winick*

● **The Man with a Rhyme** / 1976 / Folk Legacy 61
More gentle singing and guitar. His best. —*Stephen Winick*

Off the Map / 1986 / Snow Goose 1112
Archie Fisher's singing and guitar wedded to Garnet Rogers's fiddle and flute. —*Stephen Winick*

○ **Will Ye Gang, Love** / Green Linnet 3076
Fisher was one of the first good Scottish folk guitarists, and this shows off both his guitar playing and his singing. —*Stephen Winick*

Cilla Fisher

Vocals, guitar / Scottish
See the biography for the Fisher Family. —*AMG*

For Foul Day and Fair / 1978 / Folk Legacy 69
The album is the first and only U.S. release for Cilla Fisher and Artie Tresize. —*Stephen Winick*

○ **Cilla and Artie** / 1979 / Topic 12TS405
Riveting arrangements of excellent traditional and contemporary songs, with Artie Tresize. —*Stephen Winick*

Ray Fisher

Scottish
See the biography for the Fisher Family. —*AMG*

Bonny Birdy / 1972 / Trailer 2038
Superbly passionate renderings of ballads, backed by an all-star cast of folk-revival musicians including members of Steeleye Span and the High Level Ranters. —*Stephen Winick*

Willie's Lady / 1982 / Folk Legacy 91
This one's more sparsely arranged than *Bonnie Birdy* but no less gorgeous. —*Stephen Winick*

☆ **Traditional Songs of Scotland** / 1991 / Saydisc 391
This proves that a voice can get even better over time. A brilliant 18-track achievement. —*Stephen Winick*

Winston Fitzgerald

Winston "Scotty" FitzGerald was a pioneer recording artist of Scottish fiddle music in Cape Breton Island, Nova Scotia. His influence in Canada's Maritime Provinces is similar to that of Michael Coleman on Irish American music. —*Stephen Winick*

● **Classic Cuts** / 1992 / Breton 001
This CD compilation brings together 22 medleys of breathtaking Scottish fiddle music. —*Stephen Winick*

Five Hand Reel

Group / Scottish
A great '70s folk-rock group from Scotland, featuring Dick Gaughan. —*Stephen Winick*

Five Hand Reel / 1976 / Rubber 019
Magnificent electrified traditional songs. —*Stephen Winick*

● **For A' That** / 1977 / Black Crow 212
Five Hand Reel's best recording, featuring a rare occurrence: Gaughan singing in Gaelic. —*Stephen Winick*

Earl O'moray / 1978 / RCA 25150
Their third album, recorded in 1978. A fine effort, though not as good as the first two. —*Stephen Winick*

Four Men & a Dog

This five-piece band from Ireland is one of the most promising acts of the '90s. —*Stephen Winick*

● **Shifting Gravel** / Green Linnet 3084
The playing still outshines the singing, but songwriter Kevin Doherty at least gives us some new and interesting songs. —*Stephen Winick*

Barking Mad / 1991 / Topic 461
A debut album with fire. The instrumental work is really superb, but the singing and songs are pretty dispensable. —*Stephen Winick*

Finbar & Eddie Furey

The sons of fiddler Ted Furey from Ireland, Finbar and Eddie rose to fame in the '60s. Finbar is a flamboyant and forceful uilleann piper who won his first all-Ireland championship at the age of 15, while Eddie is a singer and guitarist. They have been members of the Furey Brothers and Davey Arthur, but their most charming recordings are the ones they did as a duo. —*Stephen Winick*

Finbar & Eddie Furey / 1968 / Transatlantic 168
A good set of tunes and songs, including Irish and Scottish songs and dance tunes. —*Stephen Winick*

● **Best of Finbar & Eddie Furey** / 1991 / Harp 1006
One of the few currently available collections of early Finbar and Eddie. —*Stephen Winick*

The Irish Pipes of Finbar Furey / Nonesuch 72048
A modern piper, sometimes with guitar or flute. —*David L. Mayers*

Dick Gaughan

Vocals, guitar / Scottish
Gaughan is one of the finest singers and guitarists on the Scottish scene and has applied his talents to both traditional music and contemporary political material. —*Stephen Winick*

☆ **No More Forever** / 1972 / Leader 2072
His first album, all traditional and wonderful. —*Stephen Winick*

Coppers and Brass / 1977 / Green Linnet 3064
Originally released in 1977, this is a brilliant all-instrumental set of guitar tunes. —*Stephen Winick*

○ **Gaughan** / 1978 / Topic 384
This CD rerelease features all of the excellent 1978 album *Gaughan* plus four sets from *Coppers and Brass* and two from his guest spots on the High Level Ranters album *Bonnie Pit Laddie*. —*Stephen Winick*

● **A Handful of Earth** / 1981 / Green Linnet 3062
Another fine album. "Song for Ireland" is a classic. Features Brian McNeill, Phil Cunningham, and Stewart Isbister. Voted Album of the Decade of the '80s by *Folk Roots* magazine, *A Handful of Earth* is Gaughan's best blend of traditional and contemporary songs. —*Chip Renner & Stephen Winick*

A Different Kind of Love Song / 1983 / Folk Freak 404013
The sound of this import CD is stellar. There is a chilling song, "Prisoner 562," to make you "think again." I can't fault a thing on this one. Buy it. —*Chip Renner*

Frankie Gavin

Frankie Gavin comes from Connemara, one of the Irish-speaking areas of Ireland. He is best known as De Danann's fiddle player, but he also plays the flute and records solo records. —*Stephen Winick*

○ **Up and Away** / 1983 / Gael Linn 103
Gavin plays mostly flute on this album but also fiddle and even accordion! He is backed by Ringo McDonagh's bodhran and Charlie Lennon's piano, and gives a great performance. —*Stephen Winick*

○ **Frankie Goes to Town** / 1991 / Green Linnet 3051
A superb album of fiddling, backed by Alec Finn's bouzouki and Charlie Lennon's piano. —*Stephen Winick*

Irish Fiddle & Bouzouki / 1991 / Shanachie 29008
A live-in-the-studio, one-session album, recorded with Alec Finn (bouzouki) in Greenwich Village during a De Danann tour. The players are relaxed, and the tunes flow nicely. —*Stephen Winick*

Hugh Gillespie

Hugh Gillespie was a Donegal man who immigrated to New York, where he joined a community of Irish musicians. A fantastic fiddler, he was soon well known and began recording 78s in the late '30s. —*Stephen Winick*

Classic Recordings of Irish Traditional Fiddle Music / Green Linnet 3066
The tracks on this fine disc have been collected from Gillespie's 78 rpm recordings. Listen for echoes of Michael Coleman. —*Stephen Winick*

Goadec Sisters, The

Three sisters from rural Brittany, the Goadecs are acclaimed as the greatest of Brittany's traditional singers to make it onto recordings. —*Stephen Winick*

○ **Moueziou Bruded a Vreiz** / 1975 / Keltia Musique 11
The CD rerelease of a classic 1975 LP, this record contains both sad ballads and songs for dancing. —*Stephen Winick*

Great Big Sea

A rollicking young band from Newfoundland, Canada. Great Big Sea plays music derived from Irish and English traditions. —*Stephen Winick*

Great Big Sea / 1993 / NRA 1002
Debut album of upbeat, fun music. —*Stephen Winick*

Green Fields of America, The

Group / Celtic
Mostly a touring ensemble, Green Fields has included many of the very finest musicians on the Irish American scene. —*Stephen Winick*

○ **Live in Concert** / 1989 / Green Linnet 1096
A fine showcase of a lot of talent, including Mick Moloney, Seamus Egan, Eileen Ivers, Robbie O'Connell, and Jimmy Keane. —*Stephen Winick*

Gwerz

Group / Celtic
Erik Marchand's startling voice and Soig Siberil's guitar work helped Gwerz become one of Brittany's best-known bands, and deservedly so. —*Stephen Winick*

Musiques Bretonnes De Toujours / 1985 / Dastum
Interesting arrangements, but not as masterful as the second album. —*Stephen Winick*

● **Au Dele** / 1987 / Escalibur 821
Their best album. —*Stephen Winick*

○ **Gwerz Live!** / 1992 / Gwerz Pladenn 001
This one was recorded live during a reunion concert in 1992. It features live versions of their most popular songs. —*Stephen Winick*

Tim Hart & Maddy Prior

Group / Celtic
A young duo from St. Albans who founded Steeleye Span with Ashley Hutchings and Gay and Terry Woods. Most of their influence on the music scene has been with that band, but their solo albums are also classics. —*Stephen Winick*

Folk Songs of Olde England / 1968 / AdRhythm 3
Simple accompaniments with guitar, banjo, and dulcimer grace two volumes of top-flight renditions of traditional songs. —*Stephen Winick*

Folk Songs of Olde England 1 / 1968 / B&C 105
Simple accompaniments with guitar, banjo, and dulcimer grace this volume of top-flight renditions of traditional songs. —*Stephen Winick*

● **Summer Solstice** / 1971 / Shanachie 79046
An album that features fuller, more mature arrangements. —*Stephen Winick*

Folk Songs of Olde England 2 / 1976 / Mooncrest 26
More of what made volume one a classic. —*Stephen Winick*

Frank Harte

Vocals / Celtic

A source of traditional songs among folk-revival singers, Harte has collected thousands of songs and has published a book and several albums of Dublin street songs. —*Stephen Winick*

Dublin Street Songs / 1967 / Topic 12T172
Includes classic ballads as well as humorous pieces. With Alf Edwards on concertina. —*Stephen Winick*

● **And Listen to My Song** / Ram 1013
Broadside ballads of old Dublin, with Donal Lunny on bouzouki and Bertram Levy on concertina. —*Stephen Winick*

Through Dublin City / Topic 12T218
Just Harte, unaccompanied. —*Stephen Winick*

Martin Hayes

A native of East Clare, Ireland, Hayes played with his father in the great Tulla Ceili Band before immigrating to America. —*Stephen Winick*

○ **Martin Hayes** / Nov. 1992 / Green Linnet 1127
Hayes's lingering, lyrical fiddle style is refreshingly different. —*Stephen Winick*

Joe Heaney (O HEANAA, SEOSAIMH)

Vocals / Celtic
A magnificent singer in both Gaelic and English, Heaney sings in *sean-nos*, the highly ornamented style of traditional Irish song. —*Stephen Winick*

● **Joe and the Gabe** / 1979 / Green Linnet 1018
Heaney's remarkable voice is joined by the flute, whistle, and fiddle playing of Gabe O'Sullivan, for a fine cross-section of Galway music and song. —*Stephen Winick*

O Mo Dhuchas / Gael Linn 051
All unaccompanied, all Gaelic. For really hard-core fans. —*Stephen Winick*

Heather Heywood

○ **By Yon Castle Wa'** / Greentrax 054
Heywood's second recording and her first CD, this features her warm and remarkable voice on 14 songs, traditional and contemporary. She joins Ray Fisher as one of the quintessential ballad singers of the Scottish revival. —*Stephen Winick*

High Level Ranters, The

Group / Celtic
A Northumbrian group, formed in the late '60s and featuring Alistair Anderson, Tom Gilfellon, Johnny Handle, and Colin Ross. The High Level Ranters were very regionally oriented, with lovely songs in broad Geordie dialect and tunes identified with the region. —*Stephen Winick*

High Level / 1971 / Trailer 2030
They first perfected their arrangements on this album. —*Stephen Winick*

○ **A Mile to Ride** / 1973 / Trailer 2037
Beautiful singing from Handle and Gilfellon, subtle but rousing work on the tunes. Highly recommended. —*Stephen Winick*

● **Bonny Pit Laddie** / 1975 / Topic 12TS271
A double album of songs about the lives of coal miners. Very well done, with guest appearances by Dick Gaughan and Harry Boardman. —*Stephen Winick*

Noel Hill

The concertina in Irish music is associated with County Clare. Noel Hill is certainly one of Clare's best-known concertina players, and one of the best in Ireland. —*Stephen Winick*

The Irish Concertina / 1982 / Shanachie 79073
Backed by Charlie Lennon's piano, Hill plays jigs, reels, hornpipes, and airs. The dry little squeezebox never sounded better. —*Stephen Winick*

● **Noel Hill & Tony MacMahon** / Shanachie 34003
Along with ace accordionist Tony MacMahon, Hill played three evenings in a pub in County Cork in October 1985. The sessions were taped and a live album produced. It's the kind of album that makes you wish you'd been there. —*Stephen Winick*

Horslips

Group / Celtic
The first group in Ireland to mix electric rock with traditional music. Their early albums are the most interesting for Celtic music fans. —*Stephen Winick*

○ **Happy to Meet, Sorry to Part** / 1973 / Atco 7030
Raw and raunchy folk-rock with fiddle, banjo, and flute along with electric guitars, bass, and drums. Traditional songs and Tull-like rockers. —*Stephen Winick*

● **The Tain** / 1974 / Atco 7039
A concept album relating the story of Tain Bo Cuailgne, Ireland's great medieval epic. —*Stephen Winick*

House Band

This excellent British group features Ged Foley (voice, guitar, Northumbrian pipes), Chris Parkinson (vocals, melodeon), and John Skelton (flutes, whistles, bombardes). They specialize in blending traditional English, Scottish, and Breton music with other sounds both traditional and contemporary. —*Stephen Winick*

Word of Mouth / 1988 / Green Linnet 3045
Ged Foley's vocals are a bit dreary on this record, but the fresh and inspired instrumentals make it more than worth having. —*Stephen Winick*

● **Stonetown** / 1991 / Green Linnet 3060
Same story, but the vocals pick up just a bit. The instrumentals are still the group's strength. —*Stephen Winick*

Paul Huellou

Vocals / Breton
Paul Huellou is well known in his native Brittany, where he has become one of the foremost singers of the Breton music tradition. —*Music of the World*

Songs from Brittany / Music of the World 209
This recording features Paul Huellou (vocals), J. Pol Huellou (flutes), Paddy Keenan (pipes), Brendan Fahy (guitar), and Pascal Segart (violin). —*Music of the World*

Irish Rovers, The

Group / Irish
This quintet started out in the late '50s (curiously, by way of Canada) and by the mid '60s were a popular folk ensemble on television on two continents. Although their work, exuberant and boisterous, has relatively little scholarship, lacks a traditional sound, and became less fashionable with the ascent of groups like the Chieftains, the Irish Rovers continue to have a devoted core following. —*Bruce Eder*

The Unicorn / 1971 / MCA 15
The single most popular record that the Irish Rovers ever made. Their cover of Shel Silverstein's slyly written "The Unicorn" stands apart from the more straightforward material on this album, which is devoted to good times, family, religious differences, and other significant elements of Irish song. —*Bruce Eder*

● **Irish Rovers' Greatest Hits** / 1981 / MCA 4066
The record to start with to get to know the Irish Rovers. It isn't representative of their full range of material. —*Bruce Eder*

Irish Tradition, The

Group / Celtic
Baltimore-area trio featuring Billy McComiskey's accordion and Brendan Mulvihill's fiddle, as well as the sweet singing and skillful guitar of Andy O'Brien. —*Stephen Winick*

The Corner House / 1978 / Green Linnet 1016
Impressive second album. —*Stephen Winick*

● **The Times We've Had** / 1985 / Green Linnet 1063
A thoughtfully performed album, varied in material but consistent in quality. —*Stephen Winick*

Andy Irvine

Vocals / Irish, traditional folk
A principal songwriter with the Irish folk groups Planxty and Patrick Street. —*Richard Meyer*

○ **Andy Irvine and Paul Brady** / 1976 / Green Linnet 3006

Irvine and Brady (former Planxty members) team up for one of the greatest albums of traditional Irish songs ever produced. Their unique sound will stay with you long after you've heard it. —*Stephen Winick & Chip Renner*

Andy Irvine and Dick Gaughan: Parallel Lines / 1983 / Green Linnet 3201

Irvine and Gaughan make a formidable duo, performing both traditional and contemporary material. Nicely balanced. —*Stephen Winick & Chip Renner*

○ **Rude Awakening** / 1991 / Green Linnet 1114

This is a celebratory bunch of songs about a very interesting crew. It's quite a cast: Woody Guthrie; Antarctic explorers; novelist-wildman Sinclair Lewis; Irish patriots James Connolly and Michael Dwyer; Mexican revolutionary Emiliano Zapata; and Raoul Wallenberg, a Christian Swede who saved thousands of Hungarian Jews from the SS. Like most story songs, even the most evocative of these tales do more to whet one's appetite to learn more about the personalities involved than actually define them in song, but that's okay, particularly when the introductions are made by someone as blessed with a fine voice and melodic sense as Andy Irvine. Now we know what the man's been reading in his spare time! —*Tom Smith, Roundup newsletter*

Eileen Ivers

A fiddle virtuoso, Eileen Ivers was born in New York City to parents who had emigrated from Ireland. At the age of eight she began to learn fiddle from Martin Mulvihill, the great fiddler and teacher from County Limerick. Between the ages of 11 and 19, she won eight all-Ireland championships, culminating in the senior championship in 1984. She has been a member of Cherish the Ladies, the Green Fields of America, Chanting House, and even Hall and Oates's band. —*Stephen Winick*

○ **Eileen Ivers** / 1994 / Green Linnet 1139

Tradition and innovation go hand in hand on Ivers's surprising, fresh, and impeccably played solo recording. —*Stephen Winick*

Dafydd Iwan

Dafydd Iwan has been a tireless activist in attempting to revitalize Welsh language and culture. He is also a marvelous singer and songwriter with many recordings to his credit. —*Stephen Winick*

Yma O Hyd / 1993 / Sain 2063

This CD features tracks from two albums Iwan recorded with the band Ar Log. It contains almost the entirety of *Rhwng Hwyl A Thaith* (1982) and *Yma O Hyd* (1983). It's stirring stuff, but it's mostly lost on non-Welsh speakers. —*Stephen Winick*

○ **Canueuon Gwerin** / 1993 / Sain 2063

Iwan's renditions of traditional songs, with punchy, pop-tinged arrangements. —*Stephen Winick*

Johnstons

The Johnstons rose to prominence in Dublin in the late '60s. Formed by Luci, Adrienne, and Michael Johnston, the group featured harmony singing with guitar accompaniment. Eventually, Michael left the group and was replaced by Mick Moloney (vocals, mandolin, banjo) and Paul Brady (vocals, guitar). This four-piece band became extremely popular in Ireland and toured the world, starting off the careers of both Moloney and Brady. Unfortunately, their albums are equally split between innovative treatments of traditional material and fairly derivative covers of American folk-pop. Look for the traditional stuff! —*Stephen Winick*

○ **The Johnstons** / 1968 / Mercury 640

An excellent debut full of the good stuff. —*Stephen Winick*

○ **The Barleycorn** / 1969 /

More great ballads and songs. —*Stephen Winick*

● **Transatlantic Years** / 1992 / Transatlantic/Demon 13

This anthology is about equally split between their traditional material and their arrangements of Joni Mitchell, Gordon Lightfoot, Leonard Cohen, and so forth. It's a great way to get a feel for the group. —*Stephen Winick*

Nic Jones

Vocals, guitar / English

Jones, one of the best English singers and guitarists in folk music, had a relatively short career before being paralyzed in an auto accident. All of his albums are worth buying. —*Stephen Winick*

● **Ballads and Songs** / 1970 / Trailer 2014

Debut album that established him as one of the best. —*Stephen Winick*

Nic Jones / 1971 / Trailer 2027

Beautiful follow-up to *Ballads and Songs*. —*Stephen Winick*

The Noah's Ark Trap / 1977 / Shanachie 79003

A few guests join him to fill out the arrangements. —*Stephen Winick*

○ **Penguin Eggs** / 1980 / Shanachie 79058

Even better than *The Noah's Ark Trap*. Many critics consider this his best. —*Stephen Winick*

Ron Kavana

Vocals / Celtic

A singer, songwriter, and guitarist, Kavana took the Irish music world by storm a few years ago with the group Alias Ron Kavana. His solo recording is the place for folk-music lovers to start. —*Stephen Winick*

● **Home Fire** / 1991 / Green Linnet 3070

Angry, impassioned, gritty singing. Wild, boisterous, irreverent playing. Excellent musicianship, songwriting, and production. It adds up to one heck of an album. —*Stephen Winick*

Dolores Keane & John Faulkner

Group / Celtic

An English husband and Irish wife in a harmonious (though temporary) partnership. She sings with an angel's voice; he also sings and plays guitar, bouzouki, and fiddle. —*Stephen Winick*

○ **There Was a Maid** / 1978 / Claddagh 23

After she left De Danann, Keane recorded this lovely solo album, accompanied by another band, Reel Union. —*Stephen Winick*

● **Brokenhearted I'll Wander** / 1979 / Green Linnet 3004

Features Reel Union, a band including pipes and fiddle, as backup. A truly gorgeous album, this is Keane and Faulkner's best work. —*Stephen Winick*

Farewell to Eireann / 1980 / Green Linnet 3003

Poignant emigration ballads, including the lovely "Galway Bay." —*Stephen Winick*

Sail Og Rua / 1983 / Green Linnet 3034

Mostly Gaelic songs, with guests including Keane's Aunt Sarah, a well-known traditional singer. —*Stephen Winick*

★ **Dolores Keane** / 1988 / Round Tower 1

James Keane

James Keane was well known as an accordion player in his native Dublin before he immigrated to New York. He is the brother of Sean Keane, fiddler with the Chieftains. —*Stephen Winick*

That's the Spirit / 1994 / Green Linnet

A magnificent follow-up, 14 years later. This features some of New York's best musicians backing Keane's robust button box. —*Stephen Winick*

Sean Keane

Sean Keane is a singer and flute player from County Galway, Ireland. He is the brother of well-known singer Dolores Keane. —*Stephen Winick*

All Heart No Roses / Shanachie 79085

A lovely album of unusual songs and great singing. —*Stephen Winick*

Kelly/O'Brien/Sproule

James Kelly is a Dubliner by birth and currently one of the best Irish fiddlers anywhere. Paddy O'Brien is a fine accordionist from County Offaly. Daithi Sproule of Derry city is one of the best guitarists in Irish traditional music and a great singer. All three are based in the United States, although this trio, which called itself Bowhand, no longer performs together. —*Stephen Winick*

○ **Spring in the Air** / Shanachie 29018

Tight trio playing from this extremely talented group makes this a fine listen if traditional tunes are your bag. Sproule's two songs are also beautiful. —*Stephen Winick*

Pat Kilbride

Vocals, guitar, cittern / Celtic

A virtuoso cittern and guitar player and an excellent singer and songwriter, Pat Kilbride is one of the most dynamic solo performers in Irish music. He was a member of the Battlefield Band for a brief time in the '70s, then moved to Belgium and eventually Brittany, where he performed in a more pop-oriented group. In the '90s, Kilbride's a New Yorker and plays music both solo and with the Kips Bay Ceili Band. —*Stephen Winick*

● **Rock & More Roses** / 1989 / Flying Fish 2011
This extra-length CD and cassette includes the entirety of Kilbride's 1980 *Rock and Roses* album, along with six tracks of instrumental music recorded in 1986 and 1987. Brilliant and a bargain to boot. —*Stephen Winick*

○ **Undocumented Dancing** / 1992 / Green Linnet 1120
This album has everything that made *Rock & More Roses* great, plus Kilbride's original songs. It's great! —*Stephen Winick*

Kips Bay Ceili Band

This New York-based quartet features Pat Kilbride (vocals, guitar, cittern), John Whelan (button accordion, keyboards), Steve Missal (drums, percussion, vocals), and Richard Lindsey (bass). They perform original and traditional folk, rock & roll, and Irish music. —*Stephen Winick*

Digging In / Green Linnet 1130
Some powerful tracks, some lightweight ones. See them live instead. —*Stephen Winick*

John Kirkpatrick

Melodeon / English

A fine melodeon player, Kirkpatrick has been a member of Steeleye Span. He is a champion of English music and dance and also heads a Morris dance team. —*Stephen Winick*

The Rose of Britain's Isle / 1974 / Topic 247
Lovely material, lovely performances with Sue Harris. Harris, Kirkpatrick's wife, sings and plays the oboe, and also heads a dance team. —*Stephen Winick*

☆ **Plain Capers: Morris Dance Tunes** / 1976 / Free Reed 010
A pioneering effort at producing an acoustic yet modern setting for Morris dance music, *Plain Capers* features such guests as Sue Harris (oboe, hammered dulcimer) and Martin Carthy (guitar). Impeccably researched and performed, this album is a delight! —*Stephen Winick*

Shreds and Patches / 1977 / Topic 355
Excellent follow-up with Sue Harris. —*Stephen Winick*

● **Going Spare** / 1978 / Free Reed 030
All original songs and tunes, some of them weird and hilarious. —*Stephen Winick*

Kornog

Group / Scottish, Breton

Brittany's greatest instrumentalists team up with Scottish singer and instrumentalist Jamie McMenamy (previously of Battlefield Band) for an unbeatable combination. —*Stephen Winick*

Kornog / 1983 / Escalibur 811
Debut album. Overlaps in material with *Premiere* but is still worth having. —*Stephen Winick*

● **Premiere** / 1984 / Green Linnet 1055
Live in Michigan. The ambiance of a live album and some great Scottish ballads make this Kornog's best album. —*Stephen Winick*

Ar Seizh Avel / 1985 / Green Linnet 1062
This is a pretty album of traditional and original tunes and songs. —*Stephen Winick*

Christine Kydd

Christine Kydd is a singer and guitarist based in Edinburgh. She performs traditional and contemporary songs, both solo and as a duo with Janet Russell. —*Stephen Winick*

● **Heading Home** / 1993 / Fellside 93
An excellent album, mostly of slow, pensive folk songs. Kydd's rich, full voice is worth seeking out. —*Stephen Winick*

Sam Larner

b. 1878, **d.** 1965
Vocals / English

The fens, farms, and fishing ports of East Anglia were among the richest lodes of southern English traditional songs, and Larner was one of the finest East Anglian source singers. He was a fisherman from the age of 12, but his repertoire went far beyond sea songs and the standard broadside ballad fare. —*John Storm Roberts*

○ **A Garland for Sam** / Topic 244
Splendid notes amplify splendid music. —*John Storm Roberts*

Grey Larsen & Andre Marchand

Grey Larsen is a well-known American flute and concertina player. He has played with Malcolm Dalgliesh and with the group Metamora. Andre Marchand is one of Quebec's most important folk-revival figures. His vocals, guitar, and tapping feet were among the ingredients in La Bottine Souriante. —*Stephen Winick*

○ **The Orange Tree** / 1993 / Sugar Hill 1136
Larsen and Marchand explore their Irish and French Canadian roots on this album. The material is marvelously played and sung, and mostly upbeat and fun. —*Stephen Winick*

Tomas Lynch

Tomas Lynch is an Irish uilleann piper, singer, and guitarist living in Britain. —*Stephen Winick*

Crux of the Catalogue / 1993 / Linecheck 002
This bold, hardboiled debut album features gritty singing and fast piping. Guests include June Tabor. —*Stephen Winick*

Mac-talla

In 1993, producer Robin Morton asked a group of extraordinary talents in the field of Scottish Gaelic music to get together and record. This led to their creation of a working, touring group. The members are singers Arthur Cormack, Eilidh MacKenzie, and Christine Primrose and instrumentalists Blair Douglas (keyboards, accordion) and Alison Kinnaird (Scottish harp, cello). —*Stephen Winick*

Mairidh Gaol Is Ceol / 1994 / Temple 2054
Brilliant performers sing and play some fine Gaelic material on this disc. Sad songs of parting rub shoulders with upbeat *Puirt-a-beul*, mouth music intended for dancing. —*Stephen Winick*

Ewan MacColl

b. 1915, **d.** 1989
Vocals / Scottish

Ewan MacColl may well have been the most influential person in the current British folk-song revival. From his early manhood until his death in 1989, he remained passionately committed to folk song, though not exclusively; he was also a poet, a playwright, an organizer, an activist, a songwriter, a husband, and a father. MacColl was born in Scotland in 1915. His father was a Lowland man who spoke Scots English, his mother a Highlander who spoke Gaelic. Both of his parents were singers. MacColl left school at 14 to busk and act in the streets and was quickly discovered by the BBC. Soon he was not only singing, but also writing programs for the radio. He founded the first folk club in England, the Ballads and Blues Club, as well as the Critic's Group, an influential early singing group that included such singers as Frankie Armstrong, Anne Briggs, and John Faulkner. He himself was one of the foremost interpreters of traditional songs ever recorded. The most ambitious project he undertook was to record a representative sampling of Professor Francis James Child's English and Scottish popular ballads.

While his early repertoire consisted mainly of street songs and traditional material, he has always been an important songwriter. Most impressive was his competence in producing expressions that had appeal to all levels of society; his songs have been covered by performers as diverse as Dick Gaughan, the Pogues, Roberta Flack, and Elvis Presley, and many have been collected in several versions from the oral tradition. They range from savage political satire to tender love songs and are supremely effective at producing the desired emotions.

Beyond his activities as a singer and songwriter, MacColl was an actor and a playwright. In 1947, George Bernard Shaw commented, "Apart from myself, MacColl is the only man of genius writing for the theatre in England today." His playwrighting and songwriting joined seamlessly in his "radio ballads," radio plays that bordered on ballad operas. Many of his most lovely and best-remembered songs were written for these plays, some of which have been released in album form.

MacColl was married to Peggy Seeger, herself a singer of folk songs (and half-sister of American folk icon Pete Seeger). Together MacColl and Seeger, sometimes accompanied by their children, who are also skilled musicians and singers, recorded numerous albums.

Many of MacColl's albums are out-of-print products of long-defunct record companies. Some, however, are readily available. All, like MacColl himself, are important factors in the history of the folk revival, to be cherished by all who encounter them. This great singer made many, many albums over many years. All of them are recommended for fans of great singing, though some may be a bit specialized (e.g., unaccompanied singing in broad Scots dialect) for some listeners. —*Stephen Winick*

○ **English/Scottish Popular Ballads (The Child Ballads)** / 1956 / Riverside 629
English and Scottish Popular Ballads, a nine-album set, edited by Kenneth S. Goldstein and performed by MacColl and A.L. Lloyd, is the first systematic attempt to record a representative sampling of the Child canon of ballads in a traditional British singing style. It is important for academic reasons, but more so for those who simply love the English-language ballad. Exquisite performances by MacColl and Lloyd. —*Stephen Winick*

The Wanton Muse / 1968 / Argo 85
Bawdy and sexually suggestive songs. —*Stephen Winick*

The Angry Muse / 1968 / Argo 83
Protest songs. —*Stephen Winick*

★ **Black and White** / 1990 / Green Linnet 3058
A compilation of 20 important tracks that will lead you to further listening. —*Stephen Winick*

○ **Real MacColl** / 1993 / Topic 463
CD reissue of tracks recorded during the '50s and '60s. The arrangements are somewhat dated, but the singing is marvelous. —*Stephen Winick*

Scots Street Songs / Riverside 612
Urban folk song at its best. —*Stephen Winick*

Eilidh MacKenzie

Eilidh MacKenzie is a Gaelic singer who has won the Ladies' gold medal at the national Mod, or music competitions. —*Stephen Winick*

Eideadh Na Sgeulachd (The Raiment of the Tale) / Temple 2048
This CD features traditional and original songs in Gaelic. Some are sung unaccompanied; some feature excellent backup musicians. —*Stephen Winick*

Talitha MacKenzie & Martin Swan

The former lead singer of Mouth Music, this American-born doyenne of Scottish Gaelic singing has performed sea shanties, waulking songs, and *peurit-a-beul,* the Gaelic term for nonsense songs intended as accompaniment for dancing. —*Stephen Winick*

Solas / Shanachie 79084
Solas combines traditional Gaelic singing with African percussion and funky electronics. It's not for traditionalists, but it's very accessible to folks who don't have much knowledge of traditional music. —*Stephen Winick*

Mouth Music / Rykodisc 196
Truly a remarkable, innovative, mesmerizing synthesis of the traditional Gaelic singing style called *puirt a beul,* "mouth music," with African rhythms and modern keyboard technology! MacKenzie is the vocalist on this intense material, which she discovered when she traveled to Edinburgh to study Scottish and ancient Gaelic culture in depth; Swan is the instrumentalist and arranger (except on one that Talitha arranged). They say it's a matter of finding a strong rhythm that complements the tradi-

tional song structures and then creating some kind of tension or powerful or surprising harmonic context in which they happen, and they've certainly accomplished just that. Highly recommended! —*Ladyslipper*

Dougie MacLean

Vocals, guitar, fiddle
This singer, guitarist, songwriter, and fiddler has been a member of the Tannahill Weavers and Silly Wizard. He now owns his own studio and record label in his hometown of Dunkeld. —*Stephen Winick*

Singing Land / 1985 / Dunkeld 004
Mostly original songs. —*Stephen Winick*

Real Estate / 1988 / Dunkeld 008
Same story. His songs revolve around ideas of home, land, and love. —*Stephen Winick*

○ **Indigenous** / 1991 / Dunkeld 15
His latest and best album. Also mostly originals, with two by Robert Burns. —*Stephen Winick*

Tony MacMahon

Tony MacMahon is an excellent button accordion player from Miltown Malbay, County Clare, a noted center of traditional music. Among his influences were accordionists Joe Cooley and Sonny Brogan, as well as piper Willie Clancy, fiddler Bobby Casey, and singer and piper Seamus Ennis. —*Stephen Winick*

○ **Traditional Irish Accordion** / Shanachie 34006
MacMahon's solo album is a great listen and is a frequently consulted reference work for other accordionists. —*Stephen Winick*

Catherine-ann MacPhee

MacPhee, an extremely talented Gaelic singer from Barra, rose to fame with Edinburgh's well-known 7:84 theatre, with whom she sang and acted in various shows. Her activities with the theater brought her exposure and many requests for a recording. She has since become a recording artist to meet that demand. —*Stephen Winick*

● **Canan Nan Gaidheal (The Language of the Gael)** / 1987 / Greentrax 009
A fascinating collection of work, play, and protest songs in Scottish Gaelic, this album features MacPhee's beautiful voice accompanied by members of the group Ossian. —*Stephen Winick*

Chi Mi'n Geamhradh (I See Winter) / 1991 / Greentrax 038
MacPhee's voice treats more wonderful songs in Gaelic. —*Stephen Winick*

Malicorne

Group / Celtic
Malicorne founder Gabriel Yacoub, taking his inspiration from the French and Celtic explorations of Alan Stivell and Dan Ar Braz as well as the British folk-rock of Steeleye Span, led his crew in producing rich, haunting arrangements of the folk music of France, Brittany, and francophone Canada. The band's later recordings feature original compositions and more contemporary instrumentation yet retain a traditional flavor. —*Michael P. Dawson*

Malicorne (Hexagone) / 1974 / Hexagone 883002
Their debut. More acoustic and folky than their later works, and just as terrific. —*Stephen Winick*

Malicorne Two / 1975 / Hexagone 883004
Malicorne's second album is much like their first: solid and well-played arrangements of traditional material, folkier than their later outings. —*Stephen Winick*

○ **Almanach** / 1976 / Hexagone 883007
Beautifully packaged album consisting of seasonal songs and music from around France. Malicorne's most consistently excellent album. —*Stephen Winick*

Malicorne IV / 1976 / Hexagone 883015
This excellent album features some stirring songs with orchestral arrangements. —*Stephen Winick*

Quintessence / 1977 / Antigon 3224
A compilation of tracks from Malicorne's early albums. —*Stephen Winick*

L'Extraordinaire Tour de France d'Adelard Rousseau / 1978 / Elektra 52272
Concept album following a *compagne*, the French equivalent of a Freemason, through his rite of passage, a tour of France. Dan Ar Bras guests. —*Stephen Winick*

○ **En Public a Montreal** / 1979 / Ballon 13010
Malicorne's live album features material from their albums as well as five new tracks. A set of French Canadian reels drives the Montreal audience wild! —*Stephen Winick*

Bestiare / 1979 / Ballon 13012
Concept album of animal songs, some dealing with lycanthropy. Somewhat more pop-oriented and more uneven. —*Stephen Winick*

● **Legende: Deuxieme Epoque** / 1991 / Hannibal 1360
Legende is an anthology gleaned from five albums by a group touted for all the best reasons as "France's answer to Fairport Convention." From 1973 on, Malicorne mined and expanded France's folk-ballad tradition with good songs, alluring singing, both arcane and ultramodern instruments, and oddball studio tricks that worked in their favor. Their music is so melodically rich that it won't matter if your command of French doesn't even get you through a Folger's commercial. — *Roundup newsletter*

Trio Erik Marchand

Erik Marchand, formerly of the group Gwerz, is a powerful singer of Breton songs. His trio came into being when accompanist Thierry Robin discovered that the oud, or Middle Eastern lute, could reproduce the unusual intervals of traditional Breton vocal music. Soon the duo had recruited Hameed Khan, a tabla player, to round out their Breton-Arabic fusion. —*Stephen Winick*

Chants du Centre-Bretagne "An Henchou Treuz" / 1990 / Ocora 559084
The first outing by this innovative trio blends Middle Eastern rhythms and melodic improvisation with old Breton ballads. —*Stephen Winick*

Tri Breur / 1991 / Silex 4225008
More of the same. Marchand's startling voice is joined by Yann-Fanch Kemener on one track. —*Stephen Winick*

Cormac McCarthy

Vocals, guitar, harmonica / Irish
McCarthy is a Boston-based singer-songwriter who plays guitar and harmonica. —*Chip Renner*

○ **Troubled Sleep** / 1990 / Green Linnet 2102
McCarthy delivers rich, strong vocals and is backed by Patty Larkin, Peter Gallway, Devonsquare, Rich Watson, Bob Thompson, Teg Glendon. His songs are well written in a folk-pop style. If you like the classic folksinger with rich production, you will enjoy what this CD has to offer. —*Chip Renner*

Billy McComiskey

Accordion / Celtic
Simply the best Irish accordion player in America, and one of the best in the world. —*Stephen Winick*

○ **Makin' the Rounds** / 1981 / Green Linnet 1034
Billy is joined by a few friends, including the late great accordionist Sean McGlynn, for a rousing and expertly arranged album of dance music. —*Stephen Winick*

Cathal McConnell & Len Graham

Cathal McConnell, a singer and flute player from the north of Ireland, has been a member of the Boys of the Lough for many years. Len Graham is a folk-revival singer of great renown. He fronts the group Skylark. Both are all-Ireland champions. — *Stephen Winick*

On Lough Erne's Shore / 1989 / Flying Fish 058
The Boys of the Lough's whistle and flute player performs traditional Irish music solo and in duets. —*AMG*

For the Sake of Old Decency / 1992 / Sage Arts 22012
This was recorded live in concert in Pittsburgh. It's a nice cross-section of the repertoires of two of Ireland's important singers and musicians. —*Stephen Winick*

Andy McGann

Andy McGann is a legendary name in New York and Irish music circles and has influenced some of this generation's best musicians. In his younger days he played with Michael Coleman, probably the most important fiddler who ever recorded. Since then he's remained at the top of the field for traditionalists. —*Stephen Winick*

○ **It's a Hard Road to Travel** / Shanachie 29009
When you hear this album, the reason McGann was revered as the Bronx's top fiddler will be obvious: a robust, almost classical tone combines with an easy grace and fluttering ornaments for a distinctive and masterful sound. Paul Brady's guitar accompaniments bring out the best. —*Stephen Winick*

Andy McGann & Paddy Reynolds

See Andy McGann for notes on this fine fiddler. Paddy Reynolds is from County Longford, Ireland, and immigrated to the United States in the late '40s. He and McGann lived close to each other and played together throughout the '50s. Although their individual styles are quite different, they accommodate each other so well that they become an extremely tight duo. —*Stephen Winick*

Traditional Music of Ireland / Shanachie 29004
Simple major-key jigs, reels, and hornpipes fill this tight duet album. Paul Brady accompanies on guitar. —*Stephen Winick*

Seamus & Manus McGuire

Group / Celtic
The McGuire brothers are two of Ireland's great fiddle players who rarely tour internationally. They can be heard on several grand recordings, though, including those by Buttons & Bows. Daithi Sproule is a distinguished Gaelic singer and guitarist now living in the United States. He, too, has played with several great bands, including Skara Brae and Altan. —*Stephen Winick*

○ **Carousel (with Daithi Sproule)** / 1984 / Gael Linn 105
They breeze through reels, waltzes, and jigs, and Sproule sings three lovely songs in Gaelic. —*Stephen Winick*

Joe & Antoinette McKenna

Joe McKenna is a piper, and his wife, Antoinette (née Bergin), is a singer and harp player. Both hail from Dublin, where Joe learned to play pipes from Leo Rowsome and other members of the famed Pipers' Club. —*Stephen Winick*

Magenta Music / 1975 / Shanachie 79076
Strange and almost psychedelic songs invade the serene musical world of the McKennas. The result is interesting but uneven. —*Stephen Winick*

At Home / Shanachie 29016
The McKennas and accompanists Mick Moloney and Irene Herrmann explore some sensitive slow airs as well as songs and dance music. —*Stephen Winick*

Farewell to Fine Weather / Shanachie 79043
More songs and tunes in fairly conservative folk-revival style. —*Stephen Winick*

Irish Pipes & Harp / Shanachie 29011
Their recording debut, this one features two songs by Antoinette and lots of dance music from Joe. It's all impeccably played. —*Stephen Winick*

Brian McNeill

Brian McNeill was involved in the Edinburgh folk scene in the '70s, when he formed the Battlefield Band with Alan Reid. Although he originally specialized in the fiddle and is still a superb fiddle player, he is also a multi-instrumentalist of amazing breadth and a songwriter of the first order. His solo works, both before and after leaving Battlefield at the end of 1990, are varied in content but consistent in quality. —*Stephen Winick*

Monksgate / 1978 / Greentrax 062
McNeill's friends, including members of the Battlefield Band, perform a rousing set of instrumental selections. —*Stephen Winick*

Busker & the Devil's Only Daug / 1979 / Temple Music 2042
This one includes both traditional and original numbers, and is populated by guests like Cilla Fisher and Battlefield personnel. More excellent original songs and tunes, plus a few staples of the busker's repertoire. —*Stephen Winick*

○ **Unstrung Hero** / 1985 / Temple 017
McNeill gives us an album of completely original tunes and songs, on which he sings and plays violin, viola, guitar, mandolin, mandocello, bouzouki, cittern, tenor banjo, concertina, xylophone, hurdy-gurdy, synthesizers, acoustic and electric bass, and drums. Astoundingly well done. —*Stephen Winick*

Horses for Courses / 1993 / Greentrax 071
This album is by the duo McNeill and Tom McDonagh. McDonagh's Irish songs and string picking back up McNeill's usual slew of instruments. Dick Gaughan guests on voice, guitar, and synthesizer. It's entertaining and solid but not as amazing as some of McNeill's solo work. —*Stephen Winick*

● **The Back o' the North Wind** / Greentrax 047
A brilliant historical labor of love, this solo outing is the musical half of his daring and exquisite stage show tying together Scots and American history through the stories of five very different emigrants, both willing and reluctant. McNeill is a truly great songwriter, and this album includes some of his best work. —*Danny Carnahan.*

Ed Miller

An Edinburgh native living in Texas, Miller has earned a reputation as one of North America's best Scottish singers. He has also earned a Ph.D. in folklore from the University of Texas. —*Stephen Winick*

● **Scottish Voice** / 1993 / Wellfield 030
Miller's commanding vocal presence and impeccable taste in songs make this his most enjoyable album. —*Stephen Winick*

Home & Away / Folk Legacy
Miller sings excellent and moving renditions of songs associated with Scotland's folk revival. Songwriters include Robert Burns, Adam MacNaughton, Matt Armour, Mary Brooksbank, Nancy Nicholson, Hamish Henderson, Ian Sinclair, and Miller. —*Stephen Winick*

Border Background / Folk Legacy 115
A tribute to his dual nationality. —*Dirty Linen*

Jacky & Patrick Molard & Jacques Pellen

This trio is made up of Jacky and Patrick Molard, who have been members of Gwerz and Pennou Skoulm, and Jacques Pellen, an innovative guitarist. —*Stephen Winick*

Triptyque / 1993 / Gwerz Pladenn 002
Jacky Molard plays fiddle, mandolin, and guitar; his brother Patrick plays bagpipes; and Pellen holds it all together on guitar. This is an impressive album of experimental Breton music. —*Stephen Winick*

Matt Molloy

Flute / Celtic
Matt Molloy of Ballaghadereen, County Roscommon, Ireland, is one of the standards against whom Irish flute players are measured. His characteristically strong blow and robust tone make him a powerful addition to any session. He was an original member of the Bothy Band in the '70s; then, when the band broke up, he joined Donal Lunny in the reformed Planxty. After his stint in Planxty, he replaced Mick Turbidy in the Chieftains, Irish music's most famous instrumental group. With them he's toured the world, from China to the United States. Along the way he has recorded several solo, duo, and trio projects and settled down as a pub owner in County Mayo, Ireland. —*Stephen Winick*

Matt Molloy with Donal Lunny / 1984 / Green Linnet 3008
Molloy plays reels and airs as no one else can. —*Stephen Winick*

Contentment Is Wealth / 1985 / Green Linnet 1058
This album pairs Molloy with fellow Chieftains member Sean Keane for some amazing flute and fiddle duets. Arty McGlynn accompanies on guitar. —*Stephen Winick*

○ **Matt Molloy with Tommy Peoples & Paul Brady** / 1985 / Green Linnet 3018
A 1985 release of 1977 studio sessions, with fiddler Peoples and guitarist and singer Brady joining Molloy for unbelievably fiery trio playing. —*Stephen Winick*

Stony Steps / 1987 / Green Linnet 3041
Molloy again demonstrates his amazing virtuosity. —*Stephen Winick*

● **Heathery Breeze** / 1988 / Shanachie 79064
Molloy's flute is once again backed only by Donal Lunny's guitar, bouzouki, and synthesizer. Brilliant, again! —*Stephen Winick*

● **Music at Matt Molloy's** / Jan. 22, 1993 / Real World 2324
Live music from the locals at Matt Molloy's pub in County Mayo. Molloy himself plays flute. One of the better recordings of "live-in-the-pub" style Irish music anywhere. —*Stephen Winick*

Moloney, O'Donnell & Keane

Group / Celtic
Mick Moloney came to the United States in 1973 and soon met fiddler Eugene O'Donnell. Seamus Egan was only four years old at the time, but he grew up to become one of the country's finest young musicians. —*Stephen Winick*

There Were Roses / 1986 / Green Linnet 1057
A brilliant title track. Fiddler Liz Carroll guests. —*Stephen Winick*

● **Kilkelly** / 1988 / Green Linnet 1072
The title track is an absolute classic. —*Stephen Winick*

Mick Moloney

Vocals / Celtic
Moloney is one of the most active members of the Irish American musical community. In the '60s he played with the Johnstons, one of the most important early revival bands. A singer, instrumentalist, and folklorist, Moloney hails from Limerick but now lives in Philadelphia, where he recently earned his Ph.D. in folklore with a brilliant dissertation on Irish music in America. —*Stephen Winick*

We Have Met Together / 1973 / Green Linnet 1010
Interesting first solo album, including traditional and modern songs and tunes. —*Stephen Winick*

● **With Eugene O'Donnell** / 1978 / Green Linnet 1010
A beautiful album, with lovely songs and tune arrangements. Derry-born O'Donnell is the king of slow airs and set dances on the fiddle. —*Stephen Winick*

○ **Strings Attached** / 1980 / Green Linnet 1027
Mick's only all-instrumental recording, featuring his mastery of tenor banjo and mandolin as well as guitar and bouzouki accompaniments. —*Stephen Winick*

Uncommon Bonds / 1984 / Green Linnet 1053
Classic Irish and Irish American material with Eugene O'Donnell. —*Stephen Winick*

Christy Moore

Vocals / Celtic
Founder of Planxty and Moving Hearts, Moore has also had an important solo career and has played both traditional music and folk-tinged pop music. —*Stephen Winick*

Prosperous / 1971 / Tara 2008
Guests include Andy Irvine, Liam O'Flynn, Donal Lunny, and Kevin Conneff. A collector's item, mainly because it was the album that spawned Planxty. —*Stephen Winick*

Live in Dublin / 1978 / Tara 2005
Christy at his best on this better-than-average live album. —*Chip Renner*

The Iron Behind the Velvet / 1978 / Tara 2002
His band on this one includes Moore's brother Barry, aka Luka Bloom. —*Stephen Winick*

The Time Has Come / 1983 / Green Linnet 3033
Great solo effort featuring traditional and political songs. —*Stephen Winick*

○ **Ride On** / 1984 / Green Linnet 3302
A powerful CD featuring "Ride On," "City of Chicago," "Lisdoonvarna," and "Among the Wicklow Hills." This one is so good it can make his other good ones seem weak. —*Chip Renner*

Ordinary Man / 1985 / Green Linnet 3301
A notch below *Ride On.* Featuring "Delirium Tremens," "Reel in the Flickering Light," and "Quiet Desperation." —*Chip Renner*

Nice 'n Easy / 1986 / PolyGram 823099
This import contains "Sacco & Vanzetti," "Nancy Spain," and "Lanigan's Ball." —*Chip Renner*

Unfinished Revolution / 1987 / Warner Brothers 242134

Very good. Contains "Biko Drum," "A Pair of Brown Eyes," and the title track. Produced by Donal Lunny. —*Chip Renner*

Voyage / 1989 / Atlantic 82034

What makes it so compelling a disc is Moore's brilliant use of the philosophy of the whisper. You're compelled to by the aural spaces he leaves wide open. His brogue, recorded purely, is the sound of a man who's chosen not to adopt the transatlantic dialect favored by the younger generation. —*Danny McCue, Rock & Roll Disc*

The Christy Moore Folk Collection / Tara 1972

A hard-to-find collection of Moore's early works. Buy it if you see it. —*Chip Renner*

● **Christy Moore (Polydor)** / Polydor 2383426

Terrific album of traditional songs and ballads. —*Stephen Winick*

Moving Hearts

Group / Folk, Irish

This Irish folk-rock group of the first half of the '80s had a lineup including Brian Calnan, Keith Donald, Donal Lunny, Christy Moore, Eoghan O'Neill, and Davy Spillane. It was the forerunner of such followers as the Pogues, the Mekons, and the Oyster Band and mixed a traditional approach (they played acoustic instruments, such as bodhran and uilleannn pipes, as well as electric ones) with a contemporary repertoire, some of it socially conscious material. For example, *Moving Hearts* in 1981 included "Hiroshima Nagasaki Russian Roulette." The second album, *Dark End of the Street*, was internationally hailed.

The band's talented lineup had trouble staying together, and *Live Hearts* in 1983 was their last real album, though *The Storm* in 1985 was an interesting instrumental collection. The band's influence has been extensive, and Christy Moore has gone on to a successful solo career. —*William Ruhlmann*

○ **Moving Hearts** / 1981 / Green Linnet 3305

This compilation album features *Hearts* standards such as "Hiroshima," "Nagasaki, Russian Roulette" and "McBrides," as well as a version of Jackson Browne's "Before the Deluge" that turns it into an Irish folk song. —*William Ruhlmann*

Martin Mulhaire, Seamus Connolly & Jack Coen

Accordionist Mulhaire, fiddler Connolly, and flute player Coen come from the East Galway/East Clare region of Ireland. All now live in America. —*Stephen Winick*

☆ **Warming Up** / 1993 / Green Linnet 1135

Masterful performances by all three musicians and their accompanist, Felix Dolan, make for a fine album of straight-out Irish instrumental music. —*Stephen Winick*

Brendan Mulvihill

Brendan Mulvihill is the son of influential fiddler and music teacher Martin Mulvihill. His unique style and fine technique have contributed to the success of the group the Irish Tradition, as well as to his own work. —*Stephen Winick*

● **Morning Dew** / 1993 / Green Linnet 1128

Mulvihill shares the billing on this release with Donna Long, a gifted pianist and harpsichord player. Together they extend the boundaries of Irish music. —*Stephen Winick*

Flax in Bloom / Green Linnet 1020

Mulvihill is backed by Mick Moloney's guitar and banjo on this album of traditional fiddle tunes. His tone and flamboyant style are undeniable, but his innovative ornaments may distract fans of traditional fiddling. —*Stephen Winick*

Martin Mulvihill

Martin Mulvihill, a fiddler who came from Limerick, Ireland, to the Bronx, had a major impact on Irish music in the eastern United States. It was not so much his playing as his teaching that influenced others; Mulvihill ran a highly successful Irish music school and even went on the road to other cities to teach Irish music to interested youth. Many of the good and great young players studied with Mulvihill. —*Stephen Winick*

● **Traditional Irish Fiddling from County Limerick** / Green Linnet 1012

There's nothing flashy or fancy here, just solid and spirited playing from Mulvihill and his accompanist, Mick Moloney. —*Stephen Winick*

Denis Murphy

Siblings Denis Murphy and Julia Clifford were from the area of County Kerry, Ireland, known as Sliabh Luachra. Both were students of the fiddle master Padraig O'Keeffe. —*Stephen Winick*

☆ **The Star Above the Garter** / 1992 / Shanachie 34002

This rerelease of an early '60s album shows the richness and variety of Kerry's musical tradition through the repertoire of these talented siblings. —*Stephen Winick*

Phil, John & Pip Murphy

The late Phil Murphy and his sons John and Pip hail from County Wexford, Ireland. They are among the best-known harmonica players in the Irish tradition. —*Stephen Winick*

● **Trip to Cullenstown** / 1991 / Claddagh 55

Sprightly tunes are played on various harmonicas. —*Stephen Winick*

Na Fili

Group / Celtic

This important trio set an early high standard for group playing on pipes, fiddle, and whistle. —*Stephen Winick*

● **An Ghaoth Aniar: The West Wind** / 1969 / Mercier 9

Playing is augmented by explanations of the tunes and songs right on the record. —*Stephen Winick*

Farewell to Connacht / 1971 / Outlet 1010

Another fine Na Fili album. —*Stephen Winick*

Na Fili 3 / 1972 / Outlet 1017

Features several religious songs sung in Gaelic. —*Stephen Winick*

Maire Ni Chathasaigh

Vocals, harp / Celtic

Considered one of Ireland's finest clarsach (harp) players, Ni Chathasaigh is also a fine singer in Gaelic and English. —*Stephen Winick*

● **The New-Strung Harp** / 1985 / Temple Music 019

Ni Chathasaigh shows off all her talents, particularly that of arranging dance tunes on the harp. —*Stephen Winick*

Out of Court / 1991 / Old Bridge Music 03

With Ni Chathasaigh's husband, Chris Newman, an eclectic talent on the guitar. Together they make lovely and lively instrumental music. —*Stephen Winick*

Mairead Ni Dhomhnaill

Vocals / Celtic

Maighread Ni Dhomhnaill of Donegal is one of Ireland's finest traditional singers. She was a member of Skara Brae with her siblings Triona Ni Dhomhnaill and Micheal O Dhomhnaill. She takes most of her songs from the Donegal tradition, many of them from her own family. —*Stephen Winick*

Mairead Ni Dhomhnaill / 1976 / Gael Linn 055

As fine as her sister's solo album, this features some excellent musicians backing Mairead (as she then spelled her name) on fiddle, concertina, guitar, whistle, and keyboards. —*Stephen Winick*

● **Gan Dha Phingin Spre (No Dowry)** / 1991 / Gael Linn 152

Fifteen years later, Maighread is back with a new way to spell her name and a new way to arrange her songs: '90s style. Smooth production and arrangements by Donal Lunny make this a winner. —*Stephen Winick*

Triona Ni Dhomhnaill

Vocals, harpsichord / Celtic

A member of Skara Brae and the Bothy Band, Ni Dhomhnaill always seems to be part of an interesting musical outing. Her clear singing voice and harpsichord playing are an asset to any lineup. —*Stephen Winick*

○ **Triona** / 1975 / Green Linnet 3034

Solo album that features some of her loveliest recorded songs, some in English and some in Gaelic, with accompaniment by some of Ireland's greatest players. —*Stephen Winick*

Chris Norman

Chris Norman is a classically trained flute player from Canada now living in the Baltimore area. He plays with the world-music group Helicon and the early-music ensemble The Baltimore Consort. —*Stephen Winick*

● **Man with the Wooden Flute** / 1992 / Dorian 90166
Norman's sweet-toned flute leads a rousing set of tunes from Britain, Ireland, the United States, and Canada. —*Stephen Winick*

Beauty of the North / 1994 / Dorian 90190
This time, Norman and friends concentrate on tunes from Quebec and Maritime Canada. It's beautiful playing, somewhat classical in sound. —*Stephen Winick*

Nowell Sing We Clear

This four-man group features John Roberts, Tony Barrand, Fred Breunig, and Steve Woodruff. They perform traditional English songs of the Christmas season. —*Stephen Winick*

● **Nowell Sing We Clear** / 1977 / Front Hall 013
Midwinter carols sung by Roberts and Barrand and accompanied by Breunig (fiddle) and Woodruff (accordion). Tasty vocal harmonies and a spirit of joy fill this one. —*Stephen Winick*

Second Nowell / 1981 / Front Hall 026
More carols in Roberts and Barrand's trademark style. —*Stephen Winick*

Nowell Sing We Clear, Vol 3. / 1985 / Front Hall 036
Mostly new material, with a few new versions of previously recorded songs. —*Stephen Winick*

Nowell Sing We Clear, Vol. 4 / 1988 / Front Hall 039
This CD introduces Andy Davis (who replaces Steve Woodruff). It features mostly fresh versions of songs that the group has recorded before. —*Stephen Winick*

● **Best of Nowell Sing We Clear, The** / 1989 / Front Hall 301
This picks the best tracks from the first three albums. It's a great introduction to the group. —*Stephen Winick*

Sean Nua

This group features Joe McKenna (uilleann pipes, accordion, whistles) Antoinette McKenna (harp, voice), Gerry O'Donnell (flute, whistle), Joe McHugh (uilleann pipes, bouzouki, keyboard), Jo Partridge (guitar), and Mario N'Gomo (percussion). —*Stephen Winick*

The Open Door / Shanachie 79082
A very nice, contemporary take on traditional music, this features both spirited dance music and contemplative pieces. —*Stephen Winick*

Paddy O'Brien

Paddy O'Brien was a giant in the world of traditional Irish music. In 1954, he recorded three 78 rpm records that highlighted his own style of buttonbox playing, a style that allowed him to graft the full range of keys and of ornaments from traditional fiddle playing onto his accordion. Few accordionists in Irish music today have not been influenced by this innovative and inspired style of playing. Seamus Connolly, O'Brien's partner, is one of the top Irish fiddlers in the world. He teaches Irish music at Boston College. —*Stephen Winick*

Stranger at the Gate / 1988 / Green Linnet 1091
O'Brien's button accordion is backed by Daithi Sproule's sensitive guitar. —*Stephen Winick*

Robbie O'Connell

Vocals / Celtic
This nephew of the world-famous Clancy Brothers is also a fine folksinger and a respected songwriter. —*Stephen Winick*

● **Close to the Bone** / 1982 / Green Linnet 1038
O'Connell's gentle voice and guitar perform traditional songs. Quite a treat. —*Stephen Winick*

Love of the Land / 1989 / Green Linnet 1097
Mostly original songs that prove he's a fine songwriter. —*Stephen Winick*

Never Learned to Dance / Green Linnet 1124

Features O'Connell's voice and guitar on new original songs. Some of the tracks are serious and some funny, but all are fine work. —*Stephen Winick*

Martin O'Connor

Button accordion player Mairtin O'Connor has been a member of the ensemble De Danann as well as an influential solo musician. —*Stephen Winick*

Perpetual Motion / 1990 / Claddagh 26
O'Connor explores many styles of music, from Basque fandangos to rock & roll. But he maintains a characteristically Irish lift in his playing —*Stephen Winick*

Eugene O'Donnell

This native of Derry city now lives in the Philadelphia area. He is a master of slow airs and set dances on the fiddle. —*Stephen Winick*

● **Slow Airs & Set Dances** / Green Linnet 1015
An excellent showcase for O'Donnell's talents. His fiddle weeps and sings. —*Stephen Winick*

3 Way Street / Green Linnet 1129
Egan's flute and banjo fit in perfectly with O'Donnell's fiddle and Moloney's voice, guitar, and strings. Tracks go from delightful to devastating. —*Stephen Winick*

Liam O'Flynn

An uilleann piper from County Kildare, O'Flynn was a founding member of Planxty. This innovative performer has recorded with pop, folk, and classical musicians and on film sound tracks in a variety of styles. —*Stephen Winick*

Liam O'Flynn / 1988 / WEA
O'Flynn's piping is backed by former members of Planxty, among others. —*Stephen Winick*

Fine Art of Piping / 1991 / Celtic Music
Solo album shows off O'Flynn's amazing talents. —*Stephen Winick*

● **Out to an Other Side** / 1993 / Tara 3031
O'Flynn's most eclectic album, this one features solo tracks as well as folk-revival and orchestral arrangements. —*Stephen Winick*

Ossian

Group / Scottish
Formed in the mid '70s, Ossian went on to become one of Scotland's best-loved folk-revival bands. Members have included fiddler John Martin, Highland bagpipe virtuoso Iain MacDonald, composer and multi-instrumentalist Billy Jackson, and singer and guitarist Tony Cuffe. The group broke up after Cuffe and Jackson moved to the United States. The other members have remained prominent on the Scottish folk scene. —*Stephen Winick*

St. Kilda Wedding / 1978 / Iona 001
Features Billy Ross singing in English and Gaelic. —*Stephen Winick*

Seal's Song / 1981 / Iona 002
Another lovely, lovely album. Singer Tony Cuffe shines. —*Stephen Winick*

Dove Across the Water / 1982 / Iona 004
Another beautiful album, this one features compositions by Billy Jackson and Tony Cuffe as well as traditional material. —*Stephen Winick*

● **Borders** / 1984 / Iona 007
A masterpiece; every tune and song is gorgeous. —*Stephen Winick*

Light on a Distant Shore / 1986 / Iona 009
Lots of compositions by Billy Jackson presage his later compositional work. Wonderful playing and singing make this another fine effort. —*Stephen Winick*

Jerry O'Sullivan

Jerry O'Sullivan is one of the United States' finest uilleann pipers. He won the all-Ireland piping championship in 1979; since then he has played at major Irish events up and down the east coast and has spent several years in County Clare continuing to hone his piping skills. He has appeared on several film sound tracks, including *Far and Away*. —*Stephen Winick*

The Invasion / Green Linnet 1074
For Jerry, music is a social force, a thing to be shared with friends. This is reflected in his solo album, which features several of his musical pals, including Joanie Madden (flute), Eileen Ivers (guitar), and Seamus Egan (flute, banjo, whistle). —*Stephen Winick*

Niamh Parsons

Niamh Parsons is a fine singer from Ireland. Her roots are traditional, but she sings in a variety of styles. —*Stephen Winick*

● **Loosely Connected** / Greentrax 052
A lovely showcase for Parsons's voice, this album features some traditional and folk material from Ireland, along with some contemporary material with pop and country leanings. Her singing is very much worth hearing. —*Stephen Winick*

Patrick Street

Group / Celtic
Veterans of a lot of old, great bands like Planxty, the Bothy Band, and De Danann got together in the mid '80s to form Patrick Street. The most consistent members are Kevin Burke, Jackie Daly, Andy Irvine, and Arty McGlynn. —*Stephen Winick*

Patrick Street / 1986 / Green Linnet 1071
Much lighter, airier, and less intense than a lot of Irish music. It's a style that fits the artists well. —*Stephen Winick*

○ **All in Good Time A** / 1986 /
The four original recording members are back as a cohesive band for another excellent outing. —*Stephen Winick*

No. 2 Patrick Street / 1988 / Green Linnet 1088
Another thoroughly enjoyable album. —*Stephen Winick*

● **Irish Times** / 1990 / Green Linnet 1105
The addition of pipes and another fiddle makes for a fuller sound. Their best work. —*Stephen Winick*

Tommy Peoples

An electrifying fiddler from Donegal, Tommy Peoples has converted more than one person to the religion of Irish traditional music. A member of the Bothy Band in 1975, he was the propulsive fiddler who powered that group's landmark first album. He also has some magnificent solo work. —*Stephen Winick*

High Part of the Road / Shanachie 29003
Shortly after his stint with the Bothy Band, Peoples recorded this masterful solo album. Even on his slower tunes, his rolls are lightning flurries of notes. He's backed by Paul Brady, who was then Ireland's premier guitar accompanist. —*Stephen Winick*

● **The Iron Man** / Shanachie 79044
This features extremely strong fiddling backed by Daithi Sproule's guitar. A set of Donegal strathspeys steals the show. —*Stephen Winick*

Plankerdown Band, The

This fine folk-rock band from the Canadian province of Newfoundland features former members of Figgy Duff. —*Stephen Winick*

Jig Is Up / 1993 / Pigeon Inlet 7331
An all-instrumental debut album, this features fresh and vibrant arrangements of tunes from the Newfoundland tradition, which includes English and Irish heritage. —*Stephen Winick*

Planxty

Group / Celtic
This band grew out of the sessions that produced Christy Moore's album *Prosperous*. Originally, it featured Moore, Donal Lunny, Andy Irvine, and Liam O'Flynn, a lineup that made two albums in 1973, before Lunny went off to join the Bothy Band. His replacement was Johnny Moynihan, a former member, along with Irvine, of Sweeny's Men. This lineup recorded the next Planxty LP in 1974, after which Moore left the group. Planxty recorded no more albums before they broke up in 1975. The group was back together in 1979 and recorded albums with new members until 1983, when they evolved into Moving Hearts. —*Stephen Winick*

★ **Planxty** / 1973 / Shanachie 79009

Stunning 1973 debut featuring arrangements of traditional songs and tunes with both punch and subtlety. —*Stephen Winick*

○ **The Well Below the Valley** / 1973 / Shanachie 79010
Not quite as compelling, perhaps, as the debut album, but still a treasure. —*Stephen Winick*

○ **Cold Blow and the Rainy Night** / 1974 / Shanachie 79011
Lunny is replaced by Johnny Moynihan of Sweeny's Men and De Danann fame. —*Stephen Winick*

The Planxty Collection / 1976 / Shanachie 79012
Just a notch below *Well Below the Valley*. Well produced. —*Chip Renner*

● **After the Break** / 1979 / Tara 3001
Brilliant tunes and songs featuring Matt Molloy. —*Stephen Winick*

The Woman I Loved So Well / 1980 / Tara 3005
Some of the fire is gone from their arrangements, but a few of the songs are their best ever. —*Stephen Winick*

Plethyn

A group from Wales that bases its harmony singing style on the Plygain carol tradition, Plethyn features the lovely voice of Linda Healy. —*Stephen Winick*

Drws Agored / 1991 / Sain 4033
Bright harmonies and simple accompaniment make this a pleasant listen. The words are in Welsh, but there are some English translations in the booklet. —*Stephen Winick*

Maddy Prior

Group / Folk
Singer Maddy Prior gained a following in England's folk clubs as a member of a duo with Tim Hart. In the late '60s she recorded several albums with Hart (*see* Tim Hart and Maddy Prior). After meeting Ashley Hutchings at a folk festival, Prior and Hart joined Steeleye Span, the highly acclaimed electric folk group that Prior still fronts today. Along the way she has been part of another duo with June Tabor, called "Silly Sisters." She has also recorded several albums solo and with her husband, Rick Kemp. —*Stephen Winick*

Carols & Capers / Park 9
Prior is joined on this release by the Carnival Band, an early-music instrumental group, for Renaissance arrangements of Christmas carols. —*Stephen Winick*

○ **Year** / 1993 / Park 20
Year features a few traditional songs, plus a suite of songs written by Prior about the passing of the year. Intriguing stuff! —*Stephen Winick*

● **Summer Solstice** / Shanachie 79046
This heralded British folk release by Prior and Hart led to the creation of Steeleye Span. It includes "Three Drunken Maidens," "Fly Up My Cock," "Bring Us in Good Ale," "Sorry the Day I Was Married," and nine others. —*Roundup newsletter*

Jean Redpath

b. Apr. 28, 1937, Edinburgh, Scotland
Vocals / Scottish
A singer of Scottish traditional songs and ballads, Jean Redpath immigrated to the United States from Scotland in 1961. She sings unaccompanied in a clear and gentle voice, and has been well known on the folk circuit since the '60s and '70s for her renderings of ballads and children's songs. —*Michael Erlewine*

The Jean Redpath Scottish Ballad Book / 1964 / Elektra 7214
Scottish ballads, beautifully done. —*Stephen Winick*

Laddie Lie Near Me / 1967 / Elektra 7274
More of the same. —*Stephen Winick*

★ **Frae My Ain Countrie** / 1973 / Folk Legacy 49

● **First Flight** / 1989 / Rounder 11556
This 60-minute-plus collection brings together the best of her long out-of-print first recordings made for Elektra in the '60s. Recently over from Scotland, she sings traditional songs from varied sources, accompanying herself on guitar. —*Ladyslipper*

The Songs of Robert Burns / Philo
Ambitious multivolume set aims at recording all of Burns's songs, with authentic accompaniment. —*Stephen Winick*

Sue Richards

Sue Richards specializes in Scottish and Irish material on the Celtic harp. She is well known to audiences in the DC area and beyond as a three-time American Scottish harp champion and as a member of the groups Ceoltoiri (Celtic music) and Ensemble Galilei (early music). —*Stephen Winick*

Grey Eyed Morn / 1991 / Maggie's Music 201
Richards plays mostly Scottish tunes, along with a few Irish and Welsh pieces. Guests include Bonnie Rideout (Scottish fiddle) and members of Ceoltoiri. —*Stephen Winick*

● **Morning Aire** / Maggie's Music 204
This one's split equally between Irish and Scottish material. Billy McComiskey (accordion, concertina) and Myron Bretholz (bodhran) add an Irish touch to arrangements. Wonderfully played all round. —*Stephen Winick*

Bob Roberts

Accordion
The accordion was an important British folk and popular instrument from the mid 19th century on and was also very much a sailors' instrument. Roberts, who worked on sailing cargo wherries much of his life, was a fine melodeon player and singer with a very wide repertory: a hilarious epic about a North Sea oil rig; "The Grey Hawk," of Renaissance origin; "The Foggy Dew" in an eastern English version; shanties; and more. —*John Storm Roberts*

○ **Songs from the Sailing Barges** / Topic 361
The accordion, particularly the button melodeon, was an important British folk and popular instrument from the mid 19th century on. Accordions were also sailors' instruments. Roberts, who worked on sailing cargo wherries much of his life, was a fine melodeon player and a singer with a very varied repertory: a hilarious epic about a North Sea oil rig; "The Grey Hawk," of Renaissance origin; "The Foggy Dew" in an eastern English version; shanties; and more. —*John Storm Roberts, Original Music*

John Roberts & Tony Barrand

Group
Roberts and Barrand are a pair of singers from England who used to live in Vermont. In the '70s they started singing English traditional songs in harmony, which is unusual (though not unheard of) in the English tradition. Over the years they've recorded many albums as a duo and as part of the group Nowell Sing We Clear. —*Stephen Winick*

Spencer the Rover Is Alive & Well / 1971 / Swallowtail 0001
English traditional songs, ranging from drinking songs to ancient ballads to cockney music-hall ditties, performed in pretty two-part harmonies. —*Stephen Winick*

Mellow with Ale from the Horn / 1975 / Front Hall 04
A mixed bag of songs is performed by Roberts and Barrand, this time accompanying themselves on a few instruments. Material ranges from the tragic to the wacky. —*Stephen Winick*

● **Dark Ships in the Forest** / 1977 / Folk-Legacy 65
Fascinating ballads of supernatural encounters are made even more compelling by the presence of Fred Breunig and Steve Woodruff (fiddle and button accordion) as accompanists. This is among Roberts and Barrand's best albums. —*Stephen Winick*

To Welcome in the Spring / 1980 / Front Hall 022
This album of seasonal songs also features Steve Woodruff and Fred Breunig. It predates the quartet's recordings as Nowell Sing We Clear and features a similar theme. —*Stephen Winick*

Eat Bertha's Mussels / 1983 / Front Hall 031
Captures Roberts and Barrand live at Holstein's in Chicago. They sing mostly drinking songs and other lighthearted material. Good choruses get the audience singing along. —*Stephen Winick*

★ **A Present from the Gentlemen** / 1992 / Golden Hind 101
A mixed bag of songs, with Roberts and Barrand's trademark harmonies. Great material lovingly arranged makes this their best work to date. —*Stephen Winick*

Across the Western Ocean / Swallowtail 4
Roberts and Barrand sing sea shanties and forebitters. There are fewer songs in harmony and more with choruses than on their first release. This is a fine selection of material performed beautifully. —*Stephen Winick*

Loeiz Ropars

Loeiz Ropars is one of the fathers of the Breton music revival. In the early '40s he became interested in revitalizing the *kan ha diskan*, a special kind of call-and-response singing used to accompany dances, and later made himself a part of the postwar reawakening of Breton cultural identity. His background of peasant life and his involvement in the the the *Cercle Celtique* of Poullaouen, a Celtic cultural association, led him to the idea of creating a new type of event for Breton music and dancing. It would be like the community based *fest-noz*, "night party," except that it would bring people together from different parts of Brittany. His idea, the "new-style" *fest-noz*, is the most important type of folk-music event in Brittany today. —*Stephen Winick*

○ **Kan Ha Diskan** / 1992 / Keltia Musique 28
This is an album of pure, unaccompanied vocals. It's melodically and rhythmically catchy, and sung with enthusiasm by Ropars and his partners. Still, the inaccessibility of the language makes this a release for diehard fans of Breton music. For those diehard fans, it's a treasure. —*Stephen Winick*

Leo Rowsome

Leo Rowsome was one of the most influential pipers of his generation—*indeed, of all time. He came from a long line of Wexford pipers but lived in Dublin, where he taught many of the current generation of pipers. He died in 1970.* —Stephen Winick

☆ **The King of the Pipers** / Shanachie 34001
Originally released on Dublin's Claddagh label in the '60s, this classic is now available again on CD. Rowsome's open piping style flows beautifully. —*Stephen Winick*

Russell & Kydd

The duo of Janet Russell and Christine Kydd perform traditional and contemporary songs in harmony. —*Stephen Winick*

● **Janet Russell & Christine Kydd** / 1987 / Greentrax 011
This CD features delightful songs and sublime harmonies. —*Stephen Winick*

Russell Family, The

Micho, Pakie, and Gussie Russell, three brothers from the town of Doolin, County Clare, were among the smoldering coals that fed the Irish folk revival. Micho in particular, through extensive touring and sharing of his music and songs, was an important link between the essentially urban folk revival and the roots of Irish rural music. His tragic death in 1994 in an auto accident saddened all lovers of Irish music. —*Stephen Winick*

☆ **The Russell Family** / Mar. 1993 / Green Linnet 3079
A classic album of traditional tunes and songs in rural style, this is a wonderful CD for lovers of the older Irish traditional music. —*Stephen Winick*

Janet Russell

From Buckhaven in Fife, Scotland, Janet Russell is one of the finest voices in contemporary Scottish folk. Steeped in traditional song but also fond of songwriting, Russell stresses the unity of old and new songs. —*Stephen Winick*

Gathering the Fragments / 1988 / Harbourtown 003
The emphasis in Russell's debut is on powerful arrangements of contemporary Scottish songs, with a few older gems thrown in. —*Stephen Winick*

Ben Sands

Ben Sands is a member of the Sands Family of County Down. He specializes in singing gentle love songs, both traditional and contemporary ones. He also plays guitar and mandolin. —*Stephen Winick*

○ **Take Your Time** / 1993 / Spring 1029
Unlike his brothers Tommy and Colum, Ben Sands is not a prolific songwriter, so this album is full of songs written by others, including traditional ones. Most are gentle love songs with an easy, uplifting feeling. —*Stephen Winick*

Colum Sands

A member of the Sands Family of County Down, Colum Sands is a fine singer and an inspired songwriter, much like his brother Tommy. —*Stephen Winick*

● **March Ditch** / 1991 / Spring 1014
Colum's songs are full of hope, irony, humor, and political consciousness. His singing is accompanied by members of the Sands Family, among others. —*Stephen Winick*

Tommy Sands

○ **Beyond the Shadows** / 1992 / Green Linnet 3068
Tommy's "We Will Rise Again" and "1999" are songs of hope. "Red Wine" and "Make Me Want to Stay" are finely written love songs. "When the Boys Come Rolling Home" is an infectious, good-time song. This CD is my pick for Top Ten of 1992. Keep up the good work, Tommy! —*Chip Renner*

☆ **Singing of the Times** / Green Linnet 3044
Jam-packed with great songs and emotions, "There Were Roses" is a classic, dealing with the senseless killing in Northern Ireland. "I'm Going Back on the Bicycle" and "Don't Wake Me Early in the Morning" are fun songs. "Humpty Dumpty Was Pushed" questions us, and "Your Daughters & Your Sons" has been used as an anthem throughout the world. Highly, highly recommended! —*Chip Renner*

Scartaglen

Group / Irish
Scartaglen is a four-piece Kansas City band that plays traditional Irish music. The members of the band include Connie Dover (vocals, keyboards), Michael Dugger (vocals, fiddle, guitar, banjo), Roger Landes (bouzouki, mandolin, guitar, bodhran), Kirk Lynch (uilleann pipes, tin whistle, guitar, bouzouki), and Rebecca Pringle (fiddle). —*Chip Renner*

The Middle Path / 1986 / Castle Island
A very good album featuring great vocals—a totally satisfying sound. —*Chip Renner*

● **Last Night's Fun** / 1992 / City Spark 3342
Their finest release to date. Everything about their music has matured to the point that I feel Scartaglen is one of the finest Celtic bands on the scene to date. Highly, highly recommended. —*Chip Renner*

Shanachie

A quintet from Germany, Shanachie have spent a lot of time in Miltown Malbay, County Clare. There, in a pub called the Ocean View, they've learned to play Irish music better than many Irish bands do it. —*Stephen Winick*

Ocean View / 1990 / Errigal 008
A debut album full of verve. They do sound a bit stilted in the vocal department, but the playing is quite good. —*Stephen Winick*

○ **Second Home** / 1993 / Airborne 02
The playing's more polished, and—even better—they've imported singer Olga Vaughan from Ireland. A truly impressive album. —*Stephen Winick*

Sharon Shannon

Sharon Shannon is a young, gifted accordion player from Galway. Her pared-down, speeded up, and rocked-out approach to traditional music appeals to other artists as much as it does to her fans. It earned her a place in the Waterboys and in Christy Moore's band before she toured Europe and the United States with her own successful band. —*Stephen Winick*

○ **Sharon Shannon** / Jul. 1, 1993 / Philo 1153
Shannon and band breeze through some great material with amazing virtuosity. This one'll keep your toes tapping for weeks. —*Stephen Winick*

Soig Siberil

An innovative guitarist, Soig Siberil has been a member of many great Breton bands, including Kornog, Gwerz, Den, Pennou Skoulm, and Kemia. —*Stephen Winick*

○ **Digor!** / 1993 / Gwerz Pladenn 005
Siberil's rhythm guitar skills are matched by his beautiful lyrical lead abilities, and his compositions are equally captivating. Many

styles and moods are explored. The band includes flute, percussion, banjo, bagpipes, mandolin, fiddle, and bass along with the guitars, which keeps everything interesting and fresh. —*Stephen Winick*

Sileas

Group / Scottish
Patsy Seddon and Mary McMaster are Sileas (pronounced SHE-LISS). Both sing and play the Celtic harp. Their music features both the standard nylon-strung acoustic harp and the bright-sounding camac electro-harp. —*Stephen Winick*

Delighted with Harps / 1987 / Green Linnet 3039
This is a pretty collection of traditional melodies and songs. Material includes dance music, airs, and songs in both Scots and Gaelic. —*Stephen Winick*

Beating Harps / 1987 / Green Linnet 1089
More fine tracks. One original composition by Seddon. —*Stephen Winick*

● **Harpbreakers** / 1990 / Lap Wing 127
Sileas continue their trend of playing top-quality Scottish and Irish music on harps. They also keep up the lovely singing. —*Stephen Winick*

Silly Sisters

Group / English
Steeleye Span's Maddy Prior and folk diva June Tabor teamed up in 1976 for the first Silly Sisters album. It was more than a decade before they followed it up with a second, but both recordings feature a gorgeous melding of Prior's clear, brassy soprano with Tabor's darker tones. —*Michael P. Dawson*

★ **Silly Sisters** / 1976 / Shanachie 79040
Maddy Prior and the then little known June Tabor team to keen a delightful lark of an album. An enduring minor piece with many, many of the English folk revival's best players. Whimsical and spirited. —*Mark A. Humphrey*

○ **No More to the Dance** / 1980 / Shanachie 79069
A long-awaited second collaboration between June Tabor and Steeleye Span's Maddy Prior. —*Michael P. Dawson*

Silly Wizard

Group / Scottish
Generally considered the world's finest performers of traditional and contemporary Scottish music—and with good reason. Silly Wizard's music is at once driving and sensitive, powerful and poignant—at times hypnotic, often humorous—with sensitive group interplay and virtuoso-level musicianship, particularly from brothers Phil (accordion, keyboards, whistles, guitar, vocals) and Johnny Cunningham (fiddle). Their repertoire includes centuries-old instrumental dance music along with traditional and contemporary narrative ballads: tales of joy and woe, of men and women, of time and travel, of love and loss. Silly Wizard is not just another folk-music group; they rank with the greatest creators and performers from any country from any time.

Several members of the group, particularly the Cunningham brothers and vocalist Andy Stewart, have made solo and duo recordings and have performed and recorded with other artists, primarily Scottish traditionalists. These recordings are also well worth investigating, but get the Silly Wizard stuff first. —*Niles J. Frantz*

Caledonia's Hardy Sons / 1978 / Shanachie 79015
A wonderful early album; Stewart's voice is sweeter and more innocent than on later works. —*Stephen Winick*

So Many Partings / 1980 / Shanachie 79016
Another great early set. —*Stephen Winick*

● **Wild & Beautiful** / 1981 / Shanachie 79028
A brilliant set, featuring some great original songs by Andy and some breathtaking tunes from the Cunninghams. —*Stephen Winick*

The Best of Silly Wizard / 1985 / Shanachie 79048
Really only the best of their Shanachie releases; still, it's a great compilation. —*Stephen Winick*

☆ **Live Wizardry** / 1988 / Green Linnet 3036
This two-for-one bargain captures the group live in 1988, at the culmination of their career. A brilliant set. —*Stephen Winick*

Skara Brae

Group / Celtic

A vocal quartet featuring Michael O Dhomhnaill and his sisters Triona and Mairead Ni Dhomhnaill of Rann na Feirste in Donegal and Daithi Sproule from Derry city. —*Stephen Winick*

○ **Skara Brae** / Shanachie 79034

Michael and Triona went on to form the Bothy Band, and Daithi became a fine solo artist and a member of groups like Altan, but this was their first recorded effort, made in the early '70s, of beautifully performed Gaelic songs. The four vocalists are skillfully backed by Micheal and Daithi on guitar and by Triona on harpsichord. —*Stephen Winick*

J. Scott Skinner

b. 1843

Fiddle / Scottish

James Scott Skinner, born in 1843, was already playing by 1855. Skinner was no folk artist, but a virtuoso of a drawing-room style that drew from both the folk and classical traditions. —*John Storm Roberts*

○ **The Strathspey King** / Topic 280

These extraordinary recordings link us with a style first formed about 150 years ago, and a musical idiom not just dead but unjustly forgotten. —*John Storm Roberts*

Skolvan

One of the top bands on the Breton dance-music scene, Skolvan use fiddle, bombarde, guitar, and more to create rousing and intricate arrangements of Breton music. —*Stephen Winick*

★ **Come to the Dance** / 1991 / Keltia Musique 16

Guest vocalists Yann-Fanch Kemener and Marcel Guilloux add another dimension to this excellent album of dance music. —*Stephen Winick*

Skylark

Group / Celtic

An excellent group featuring Len Graham of Antrim, one of Ireland's great singers, along with Gerry O'Connor's fiddle and Garry O'Briain's mandocello and guitar. —*Stephen Winick*

● **All of It** / 1979 / Green Linnet 3046

Several guests add fullness to the arrangements; otherwise, it's more of the same good thing. —*Stephen Winick*

Skylark / 1979 / Shanachie 29021

Skylark's first album, featuring Andrew McNamara's accordion. This is dance music, along with singing in Graham's rich voice. —*Stephen Winick*

Daithi Sproule

A former member of the group Skara Brae, Daithi Sproule of Derry city now lives in Minneapolis. He is one of Irish music's greatest guitar accompanists and also a fine singer in English and Gaelic. He currently performs part-time in the groups Trian and Altan. Although his guitar accompaniment and vocals have been featured on many albums, he has not recorded much as a solo artist. —*Stephen Winick*

★ **Heart Made of Glass** / Green Linnet 1123

Simply a stunning debut, this is the kind of album that will never be last year's model. Liz Carroll and Peter Ostroushko help create simple, beautiful arrangements for ten songs and two instrumentals featuring Sproule's unparalleled voice and guitar. —*Stephen Winick*

Andy M. Stewart

Vocals, guitar, bouzouki / Scottish

The lead singer of Silly Wizard, Stewart has also had an impressive career on his own and with Manus Lunny, who backs his vocals with expert playing of bouzouki and guitar. —*Stephen Winick*

○ **By the Hush** / 1982 / Green Linnet 3030

Excellent solo album, winner of *Melody Maker*'s Folk Album of the Year award in 1983. —*Stephen Winick*

Fire in the Glen / 1986 / Shanachie 79062

This album features Stewart along with Phil Cunningham and Manus Lunny. It's a fine piece of work. —*Stephen Winick*

● **Dublin Lady** / 1987 / Green Linnet 1083

A masterpiece, and a must for Celtic music fans. With Manus Lunny. —*Stephen Winick*

Songs of Robert Burns / 1990 / Green Linnet 3059

Anybody with a fondness for Burns's poetry should hear this album. Andy's renditions are stirring and beautiful, even if the arrangements are a little weaker than Lunny's usual. —*Stephen Winick*

At It Again / 1990 / Green Linnet 1107

With Manus Lunny. Not as fantastic as *Dublin Lady*, but still a fine record. —*Stephen Winick*

Man in the Moon / 1994 / Green Linnet

Credited to Stewart as a solo artist, this one features Gerry O'Beirne handling much of the accompaniment and production work. Some great songs, plus a few sappy ones. On balance a beautiful album. —*Stephen Winick*

Alan Stivell

Vocals, bagpipes, harp / Breton

Probably the best-known artist from Brittany, and the most influential. He began by performing traditional Celtic music on the Breton harp, an instrument his father reinvented. Later, he delved into folk-rock music with a band that included Brittany's best musicians and original compositions, playing bagpipes and singing as well as playing the harp. —*Stephen Winick*

Renaissance of the Celtic Harp / 1972 / Rounder 3067

With its release this little gem started the current renaissance in Celtic harp. Alan Stivell is a master of his art, and this album is a true delight. Performed entirely on acoustic instruments (harp, cello, flute, and hand drums), his beautifully simple treatments speak directly to the heart. Stivell performs with skill, grace, and love. —*Backroads Music/Heartbeats*

From Celtic Roots / 1974 / Fontana 6325304

Features Irish, Scottish, and Welsh music as well as Breton, with an electric folk-rock band. —*Stephen Winick*

In Dublin / 1975 / Fontana 9299547

This nice little live album features folky and electric arrangements of traditional music. —*Stephen Winick*

● **E Langonned** / 1976 / Fontana 332

Stivell's finest acoustic band performing traditional and original material. —*Stephen Winick*

Journee a La Maison / 1978 / Rounder 3062

Stivell's arrangements here are tinged with jazz and pop, but it's still very Breton. —*Stephen Winick*

Legend / 1984 / Celtic Music 022

Based on the ancient Irish invasion legends, this album is atmospheric and new-agey in feeling. —*Stephen Winick*

Alan Stivell in Concert / Shanachie 806

Stivell is backed by acoustic guitarist Bernard Coutelan and performs a beautiful program of tunes and songs. —*Stephen Winick*

Strobinell

An excellent folk-revival group from Brittany, Strobinell feature mostly wind instruments and guitar. —*Stephen Winick*

Aoutrou Liskildri / 1991 / Keltia Musique 26

Several ballads and many instrumentals fill this album. —*Stephen Winick*

David Surette

David Surette is a well-known performer on the New England contra-dance and Celtic music scene. He has played and recorded with many of the area's finest acoustic musicians. —*Stephen Winick*

● **Back Roads** / 1993 / Madrina Music 201

Surette's guitar, mandolin, and bouzouki playing is quite impressive on this disc. The range of tunes he plays includes traditional music from New England, Ireland, Scotland, Sweden, France, Canada, Brittany, and Appalachia as well as original Surette compositions. All in all, it's impeccable and full of surprises. —*Stephen Winick*

Dave Swarbrick

Fiddle / English, Celtic

This fiddler is best known for his partnership with Martin Carthy and his participation in groups like the Ian Campbell Folk Group and Fairport Convention. He also has many excellent solo albums to his credit. —*Stephen Winick*

● **Rags, Reels & Airs** / 1967 / Polydor 236514

○ **Swarbrick** / 1976 / Transatlantic 337
Swarb's first solo album, featuring old buddies from his Ceilidh band days as well as Martin Carthy and Fairport Convention. A lot of good dance music, plus a few slower tunes. —*Stephen Winick*

Swarbrick 2 / 1977 / Transatlantic 341
Really a continuation of *Swarbrick*, with the same personnel and producer. Swarbrick even wears the same shirt for the cover photo! —*Stephen Winick*

Lift the Lid & Listen / 1978 / Sonet 763
Continues the trend started on his first two albums. —*Stephen Winick*

Sweeny's Men

Group / Celtic
An early and important Irish group that influenced both the acoustic and the electric folk revival. It featured Andy Irvine, later of Planxty and Patrick Street; Johnny Moynihan, later of Planxty and De Danann; and Terry Woods, later of Steeleye Span and the Pogues. —*Stephen Winick*

● **1968** / 1968 / Transatlantic 37
Mostly traditional songs. A great collector's item. —*Stephen Winick*

The Legend of Sweeny's Men / 1988 / Demon 004
The best of Sweeny's Men. —*Stephen Winick*

June Tabor

b. Dec. 31, 1947, Warwick, England
Vocals / Folk, traditional jazz, English
One of the folk revival's greatest voices, Tabor has sung with the duo Silly Sisters as well as with the Oyster Band. She also has several solo recordings. —*Stephen Winick*

○ **Airs & Graces** A / 1976 / Shanachie 79055
This album features mostly traditional songs, as well as Eric Bogle's now-classic ". . . and the Band Played 'Waltzing Matilda,'" in its first recorded version. —*Stephen Winick*

Ashes and Diamonds / 1977 / Green Linnet 3063
American CD rerelease of this 1977 album. The overall sound is a bit dated, but lovely singing from Tabor and Nic Jones's guitar make this a treat. —*Stephen Winick*

● **A Cut Above** / 1980 / Topic
This one features Martin Simpson on guitar. More brilliant renditions of traditional songs. —*Stephen Winick*

Abyssinians / 1983 / Shanachie 79038
Few people can wrap vocals around a folk melody the way June Tabor does. Here she breathes life into "The Month of January," "A Smiling Shore," "I Never Thought My Love Would Leave Me," and seven more. — *Roundup newsletter*

○ **Some Other Time** / 1989 / Hannibal 1347
English folksinger sings American popular ballads. A lovely album from a lovely vocalist. —*Michael G. Nastos*

Taillevent

Taillevent is a group of amateur singers who came together during a 1990 workshop on sailors' songs in Sarzeau, Brittany, France. Since then, they have ventured forth to entertain bars and pubs with traditional maritime shows. —*Stephen Winick*

En Revenant du Large / Taillevent 001
Ernest and energetic, if unpolished, this album is loads of fun and a great collection of maritime material from Brittany. —*Stephen Winick*

Tannahill Weavers

Group / Folk
The Tannahill Weavers, who started as a band 20 years ago, occupy a unique position among the groups on the Scottish folk scene. Stalwarts Roy Gullane and Phil Smillie have surrounded themselves with a rotating cast of great musicians. Their music,

which uses the Highland bagpipe, flute, and fiddle as its melodic core, is tighter, more intense, and harder driven than that of the Battlefield Band, Silly Wizard, or other contemporaries. Despite their mostly acoustic sound, they're the closest thing to a rock & roll band in intensity and attitude than the Scottish traditional music scene has to offer. —*Stephen Winick*

Are Ye Sleeping Maggie / 1976 / Plant Life 001
A tentative debut, this features some nice tunes and songs, but none of what the Weavers became famous for—bagpipes. —*Stephen Winick*

Old Woman's Dance / 1978 / Plant Life 010
An excellent early effort featuring Alan Macleod's Highland pipes. —*Stephen Winick*

○ **Tannahill Weavers** / 1979 / Green Linnet 3101
A classic album of Scottish folk music featuring fiddle, bagpipe, flute, and more. —*Stephen Winick*

Tannahill Weavers IV / 1982 / Green Linnet 3102
Another classic, this one features some favorites of their concert repertoire. —*Stephen Winick*

Passage / 1984 / Green Linnet 3031
The Weavers add electric guitarist Bill Bourne for an excursion into electric folk. —*Stephen Winick*

Land of Light / 1986 / Green Linnet 1067
Back to a mostly acoustic sound, this is a solid Tannahill album. —*Stephen Winick*

○ **Dancing Feet** / 1987 / Green Linnet 1081
This album finds the Weavers as energetic as in the days of their classic early albums. —*Stephen Winick*

● **Best of 1979-1989** / 1989 / Green Linnet 1100
A great compilation, this is the place to start. —*Stephen Winick*

Cullen Bay / 1990 / Green Linnet 1108
Fiery and ferocious, they're up to their old ways once again. —*Stephen Winick*

Mermaid Song / 1992 / Green Linnet 1121
Their arrangements are beginning to sound a little formulaic, but there are great material and fine performances here. —*Stephen Winick*

Cyril Tawney

Cyril Tawney has been a mainstay of the English folk scene for many years. He is well known both as an interpreter of traditional material and as an excellent songwriter. His songs have been sung by many other folk-revival performers, further enhancing his reputation. He is strongly associated with his native region of Devon and Cornwall, and has recorded much material from that part of southern England. The years he spent in the Royal Navy also make him a natural interpreter and writer of sea songs. —*Stephen Winick*

Outlandish Knight / 1965 / Polydor 236 577
Tawney performs versions of some of the "big ballads," the narrative songs that are an important part of England's folk poetry. —*Stephen Winick*

Children's Songs from Devon and Cornwall / 1969 / Argo 4
Some cute and silly material offered in Tawney's warm voice. —*Stephen Winick*

Mayflower Garland / 1970 / Argo 9
This contains both traditional and original songs, and was recorded in honor of the 350th anniversary of the sailing of the Mayflower. —*Stephen Winick*

○ **In Port** / 1972 / Argo 28
Original Tawney songs focusing on the sea fill up this album. Many of his best-known songs appear on this album, including "Sally Free and Easy," "The Grey Funnel Line," and "The Ballad of Sammy's Bar." —*Stephen Winick*

I Will Give My Love / 1973 / Argo 87
Tawney returns on this album to the traditional songs of southwestern England. —*Stephen Winick*

● **Sally Free & Easy** / 1990 / Neptune 002
Fresh interpretations of some of the material from *In Port*, plus new songs. —*Stephen Winick*

Seamen Bold / 1993 / Neptune 005
Traditional and original songs of the sea. —*Stephen Winick*

Little Boy Billee / 1993 / Neptune 006

Tawney lends his voice and guitar to more children's songs. —*Stephen Winick*

Scan Tester

b. 1887, d. 1972
Accordion / English
Accordionist Scan Tester was that great rarity, a southern English traditional instrumentalist who was repeatedly recorded. —*John Storm Roberts*

○ **I Never Played to Many Posh Dances** / 1990 / Topic 6
The music here, all from the late '50s to mid '60s, includes solos (including some traditional Sussex fiddle), duets, and group numbers. Wonderful music, a very thorough job, and a unique record of the range and style of a pub-cum-village-hop musician. Not to be missed by any lover of English traditional music. —*John Storm Roberts*

Carol Thompson

Carol Thompson is an American harpist of Anglo-Welsh background. She performs traditional music on the neo-Celtic harp, the classical pedal harp, and the fascinating Welsh triple harp. —*Stephen Winick*

● **Carolan's Welcome** / 1993 / Dorian 90176
Thompson is back, this time with friends Billy McComiskey (accordion, concertina), Jack Coen (wooden flute), and Darcy Fair (neo-Celtic harp). Her repertoire includes more dance music on this one, making it both uplifting and gentle. —*Stephen Winick*

The Enchanted Isles / 1993 / Dorian 90120
Thompson's first CD recording finds her playing a variety of airs on a variety of harps. It's one of the finest solo harp discs available, for quiet times and moods. —*Stephen Winick*

Kathryn Tickell

Bagpipes, fiddle / Folk, traditional bluegrass, English
A young virtuoso on the Northumbrian bagpipes and fiddle, Tickell was named official piper to the lord mayor of Newcastle-upon-Tyne in 1984. She is the first person to hold that title in more than 150 years. —*Stephen Winick*

○ **On Kielder Side** / 1984 / Saydisc 343
An excellent collection of English and Celtic tunes from Tickell and her small band. —*Stephen Winick*

★ **Kathryn Tickell Band** / 1991 / Black Crow 227
Sizzling contemporary arrangements of traditional material fill this album. —*Stephen Winick*

Steve Tilston

This married couple from England (Tilston) and Ireland (Boyle) are one of the most compelling acts in this genre of music. His songwriting, singing, and guitar work are all excellent, and her singing of traditional songs and her instrumental work are likewise impressive. —*Stephen Winick*

Life by Misadventure / 1988 / Run River 001
Steve Tilston has a voice not unlike Nick Drake's, a unique guitar style that relies heavily on the nylon-string guitar, and song-writing skills that run the gamut from wild pitch to strikeout. —*Dirty Linen*

☆ **Swans at Coole** / 1989 / Capitol 71366
An absolutely beautiful album of guitar music, this features traditional tunes played in a classical vein. —*Stephen Winick*

★ **Of Moor & Mesa** / 1992 / Green Linnet 3087
An extremely well-balanced album, this features beautiful traditional songs sung by Boyle and equally lovely original songs written and sung by Tilston. Accompaniments on guitar, flute, and other instruments help make this a joy to hear. —*Stephen Winick*

Triskell

Identical twins Pol and Herve Queffeleant both play the harp. Together, they are Triskell. —*Stephen Winick*

○ **La Harpe Celtique** / 1990 / Le Chant du Monde 274916
A rerelease CD featuring materials from two LPs of 1976 and 1977, this finds the brothers playing traditional dance music and original compositions backed by an interesting band. —*Stephen Winick*

Paddy Tunney

A magnificent singer and lilter from County Fermanagh in Ulster, Paddy Tunney has a huge repertoire of songs and is a singer of consummate skill. He has many recordings, but most are hard to find and out of print. —*Stephen Winick*

○ **Stone Fiddle** / Green Linnet 1037
This cassette contains 11 songs from the Fermanagh region where Tunney was reared. If you like unaccompanied singing, this is perfect. —*Stephen Winick*

Jean-Michel Veillon

Jean-Michel Veillon was a child prodigy on the bombarde, that piercing woodwind characteristic of Breton music. Later in life, he became interested in Irish music, and particularly the wooden flute, which was not played in Brittany. Through his exemplary work with groups like Galorn, Kornog, Barzaz, Den, and Pennou Skoulm, Veillon has made the wooden flute an acceptable instrument in the Breton tradition. —*Stephen Winick*

★ **E Koad Nizan** / 1993 / Gwerz Pladenn 004
Accompanied by the best musicians Brittany has to offer, Veillon plays the flute in a lovely, lilting style. This is the first album ever to focus on Breton music played on the wooden transverse flute, and it's a landmark for that reason. But buy it just because it's wonderful. —*Stephen Winick*

Voice Squad, The

Fran McPhail, Phil Gallery, and Gerry Cullen are the Voice Squad, a three-part harmony singing group from Ireland. —*Stephen Winick*

Good People All / Shanachie 79081
Lovely ballads in an easy, flowing a cappella style fill this recording. —*Stephen Winick*

John Whelan & Eileen Ivers

Group / Celtic
A great button accordion player, Whelan has won the all-Ireland championship on the instrument six times and the all-Britain seven times. His playing is exciting and fresh, if not strictly traditional. Ivers is his match, a seven-time winner of the all-Ireland fiddle titles. —*Stephen Winick*

○ **Fresh Takes** / Green Linnet 1075
Accompanied by Mark Simos and Triona Ni Dhomhnaill, Whelan and Ivers tear into some wonderful tunes, using consistently fresh and newfangled arrangements to keep the album interesting. —*Stephen Winick*

Chris Wood & Andy Cutting

An English duo who play fiddle and melodeon. Cutting has been a member of Blowzabella. —*Stephen Winick*

Lisa / 1992 / RUF 002
A debut album of quirky charm. —*Stephen Winick*

Tri Yann

Group / Celtic
This band is the most important exponent of urban folk-rock from Brittany. Over the years their music has ranged from punchy acoustic arrangements of traditional songs to rock & roll that is based on the Breton and Gallo traditions. —*Stephen Winick*

Suite Gallaise / 1974 / Marzelle 6325700
Their best acoustic album, full of bouncy energy. —*Stephen Winick*

○ **La Decouverte Ou L'Ignorance** / 1976 / Marzelle 836 414
An excellent album, this was their first to use electric guitars, drums, and other rock instruments in a mostly folk setting. —*Stephen Winick*

Les Filles des Forges / 1977 / Marzelle 6641896
Early double-album compilation. —*Stephen Winick*

Urba / 1978 / Marzelle 510 770
Tri Yann continued their exploration of folk-rock on this album about urbanization in Brittany. —*Stephen Winick*

Heol A Zo Glaz, An / 1981 / Marzelle 836 413

Another good collection of folk-rock tunes and songs, this one features a suite about Breton resistance to a French nuclear power plant. —*Stephen Winick*

● **Si Mort a Mors** / 1982 / Philips 814613
Excellent double-album compilation that covers the first ten years or so, without overlapping *Les Filles des Forges*. —*Stephen Winick*

Cafe du Bon Coin / 1983 / Marzelle 814 276
More of an electric feel is brought to this album. The band is still excellent. —*Stephen Winick*

Belle Et Rebelle / 1990 / Marzelle 848 229
Breton folk-rock for the '90s. —*Stephen Winick*

Le Vaisseau De Pierre / Marzelle 834724
A sort of rock opera on CD, this features a new lineup and a really rock & roll sound. —*Stephen Winick*

Celtic & British Isles Collections

○ **The Best of the Irish Folk Festivals—The Seventies** / Green Linnet 7478
This collection features more than 60 minutes of live music from De Danann, Clannad, Liam O'Flynn, Mick Hanly, Dolores Keane, John Faulkner, Jackie Daly, and Eddie and Finbar Furey. The recordings are from the Irish folk festivals held in West Germany. —*Chip Renner*

○ **The Big Squeeze: Masters of Celtic Accordion** / 1988 / Green Linnet 1093
Nine of the finest accordion players are presented on this collaboration featuring Joe Burke, Phil Cunningham, Jackie Daly, James Keane, Jimmy Keane, Billy McComiskey, Sean McGlynn, Paddy O'Brien, and John Whelan. —*Chip Renner*

Bothy Ballads / Tangent 109
Recording from the School of Scottish Studies of Edinburgh University, with solid documentation. The bothies of northeastern Scotland were basically dormitories for unmarried farm labor that became music incubators. Here are instrumental jigs, diddling (mouth-music), ballads old and new on themes heroic and pretty, all in the anglophone Lowland tradition. —*John Storm Roberts*

☆ **Celebration of Scottish Music** / 1988 / Temple Music 028
A compilation featuring the Battlefield Band, Cilla Fisher, and other great players and singers. —*Stephen Winick*

○ **Celtic Folk Festival** / 1982 / Calig 50588
Live in concert. Features the Welsh music of Ar Log as well as the Breton band Bleizi Ruz. —*Stephen Winick*

○ **Celts Rise Again** / 1990 / Green Linnet 104
Green Linnet shows off its stable of Celtic artists, and it's our gain. Featuring 18 tracks by Altan, Capercaillie, John and Phil Cunningham, Andy Irvine, Matt Molloy, and Robbie O'Connell. Great sampler. —*Chip Renner*

○ **Feed the Folk** / Temple Music 01
Featuring tracks from the Chieftains, the Battlefield Band, Fairport Convention, Steeleye Span, Martin Carthy, Paul Brady, and others. All proceeds go to charity. —*Stephen Winick*

Fiddler and His Art / Tangent 141
This presents examples of five regional styles played by seven of Scotland's finest musicians in recordings ranging from the '30s on. An enormously valuable recording enhanced by admirable notes and delightful packaging. —*John Storm Roberts*

☆ **Flight of the Green Linnet—The Next Generation** / Rykodisc 20075
Flight of the Green Linnet is a first-class collection of Scottish, Irish, and British music featuring Relativity, Silly Wizard, Capercaillie, the Chieftains, Patrick Street, the Tannahill Weavers, and many more. Seventy minutes of excellent music and song. A favorite. —*Chip Renner & Stephen Winick*

○ **Folk Songs of Britain: Songs of Courtship** / 1970 / Topic 157
How to sum up this stunning set? Ten volumes, organized by themes, of a huge body of field recordings by Peter Kennedy, Alan Lomax, Hamish Henderson, and several other collectors over a period of some 15 years (and originally issued, though long deleted, on the Caedmon label). Some performers (the Copper Brothers of Sussex, Jeannie Robertson, and Sean Ennis) are familiar source singers; others are totally unknown. All are outstanding and authentic artists. Together they present an unprecedentedly full picture of a rich but cohesive tradition. —*John Storm Roberts*

Gaelic Psalms from Lewis / Tangent 120
Lewis's superb psalm style is a truly Celtic flowering. —*John Storm Roberts*

○ **Gathering** / 1981 / Greenhays 705
Features the likes of Donal Lunny, Matt Molloy, Paul Brady, and Andy Irvine. —*Stephen Winick*

☆ **Heart of the Gaels** / 1992 / Green Linnet 105
A follow-up to *The Celts Will Rise Again*, this 18-track sampler of Celtic music features over 70 minutes of Altan, Patrick Street, the Tannahill Weavers, Dick Gaughan, Matt Malloy, Sean Keane, Andy Irvine, and others. —*Scott Bultman*

○ **High Kings of Tara** / 1980 / Tara 3003
Features Planxty, Christy Moore, Andy Irvine, and more. —*Stephen Winick*

Irish-American Dance Music & Songs / Folk Lyric 4010
Historic recordings from the late '20s. —*David L. Mayers*

Melodeon Greats / Topic 376
Features pre-1920 recordings of Scots polkas, reels, jigs, marches, and the like in early 20th-century urban popular style, mostly with piano accompaniment. —*John Storm Roberts*

☆ **Music and Song of Scotland** / Greentrax 030
A CD sampler from a great company in Scotland, featuring music that should point you in new, exciting directions. —*Stephen Winick*

Music from the Western Isles / Tangent
The Western Isles are among the few areas in which Scots Gaelic is not extinct. —*John Storm Roberts*

○ **Boston College Irish Fiddle Festival: My Love Is in America** / 1991 / Green Linnet 1110
A toe-tappin' collection guaranteed to get you on your feet, featuring some of the finest Irish fiddlers. This CD was recorded at a concert at Boston College on Mar. 25, 1990, featuring Kevin Burke, Seamus Connolly, Eileen Ivers, and many more. A good way to get into Irish fiddle music. —*Chip Renner*

○ **Celtic Fiddle Collection—Playing with Fire** / 1989 / Green Linnet 1101
With 16 Celtic fiddlers, this well-thought-out album is long overdue. Don't fiddle around—pick it up! —*Chip Renner*

○ **The Rights of Man: The Concert for Joe Doherty** / 1991 / Green Linnet 1111
This is a great collection of music from the Feb. 24, 1990, benefit in New York City for political prisoner Joseph Doherty. Celtic Thunder, Cherish the Ladies, Seamus Connolly, Seamus Egan, Eileen Ivers, Jimmy Keane, Pat Kilbride, Donal Lunny, Robbie O'Connell, and John Whelan are featured. Highly recommended. —*Chip Renner*

Scottish Tradition 2—*Music from the Western Isles* / Tangent
Some "waulking" (cloth-fulling) songs by women, with bagpipes and flutes. Good notes. —*David L. Mayers*

Shetland Fiddle Music / Tangent 117
Shetlanders are also great fiddlers, virtuosi in a tradition still richly individual. —*John Storm Roberts*

Waulking Songs / Tangent 111
Besides the Gaelic "waulking" songs, there are pipe reels, mouth music, laments, pibroch, a hymn, and even a Fenian song. —*John Storm Roberts*

WORLD MUSIC

Any book with a single chapter on "world music" runs straight into a very basic problem. You can tell it like it really is, from the perspective of the proverbial "musical Martian," giving a balanced picture of styles (99% of which are totally unknown to Americans,) or you can wildly distort reality and produce something your public can relate to. The latter course is the only reasonable one in a book like this, but the result is a little like a supermarket with three shelves: "soup," "pretzels," and "everything else."

Even if you simply divide the world into *The West* and *The Rest*, ignoring the fact that a good deal of Western music ends up in the World category, we're looking at one chapter devoted to at least 85% of the world's music. Obscure stuff, of course – like Chinese music, which is relevant to a mere one-fifth of the world's population (a bit more than that, if you count the millions of overseas Chinese). Or Indian music, with not one but two major classical traditions, three "universal" religions, and many more regional ones. Latin America: 33 nations, two major languages, and styles that have transformed the whole rhythmic basis of popular music in the United States. And if international influence rather than numbers is the issue, there's Cuba: an island of 10.5 million people whose sounds beat the US out for enduring influence on other cultures.

Just as no chapter (and no book and no ten-volume series) can really offer more than a drop in the ocean of world music, there's no way I can pretend to sum things up in a few hundred words. Instead I've decided to point out a few hidden confusions and traps in the American (and therefore this chapter's) concept of the subject.

Much the most important of these is the very major difference between what I like to call "other people's music" and the intercultural experiments of Western musicians, whether it's Yehudi Menuhin playing with Ravi Shankar, Art Blakey playing with Solomon Ilori, or Annababoula mixing various Middle Eastern styles with various Western idioms. Though these mixes have recently come to be called "world beat," they're really Western styles with non-Western elements, just as willow-pattern Delft china was Dutch plates with Chinese motifs.

This would be a lot more obvious if almost every music in the world didn't stem from a mix of other music, very frequently from different cultures. There may be a couple of Amazonian nose-flute players and a didjeridu virtuoso in central Australia who was never influenced from outside, but that really isn't the way most music works, and the richest cultures are usually the most mixed (United States, Balkans, Latin America, India). On this level, pretty much all music is crossover music.

"Other people's music" is in fact most of the music that exists. This would be more obvious if the US weren't so large, so geographically isolated, and so musically deprived. I know somebody who did a survey of recordings on sale in an open-air market in Abidjan, the capital of Ivory Coast. There were local recordings. There were recordings from other African countries. There was soul. There was jazz. There was French pop. There were the Beatles. There was US country music (lots of it, though stressing Jim Reeves). There was New York salsa. There were several sorts of Cuban music. There was more, which I've forgotten. All of this in a stall next to a woman selling yams. I defy anybody to find an equivalent range of music in your average US mall.

We also tend to overestimate our influence on the rest of the world. So it comes as a bit of a surprise to learn that, while the rest of the world has consumed US music quite freely for the last half century, Cuba and Argentina have been overwhelmingly more influential internationally over the last 75 years or so. Over the long term, the powerhouse has been the Middle East, which gave both Asia and the West most of their musical instruments.

One reason for listening to "world music" is because it's most of the music there is. The second reason – and most important – is because it's enriching beyond belief. World beat can be nifty, but the real thing can strike like lightning – it can raise the hair on the nape of your neck. It wasn't some worldbeat recording (or Xavier Cugat) that really launched the Latin takeover in the US in 1930; it was a recording of "The Peanut Vendor" by a genuine Cuban band. And the same is true for individuals. I've known people whose entire lives have been changed by the revelation of Cuban or Indian music (or, in my case, calypso-and-blues-and-flamenco-and-Arabic music all at once).

So, welcome to "other people's music" in all its many-splendored glory.

– John Storm Roberts

WORLDBEAT

Annabouboula
Group / Worldbeat
Lead singer Anna Paidoussi sounds like the Cowboy Junkies' Margo Timmins on speed. Their hit "I'd Rather Set Myself on Fire" illustrates their hybrid sound—traditional Greek harmonies and instrumental work, set against a modern rock production. Challenging and unusual music. —*Hank Davis*
○ **Greek Fire** / 1990 / Shanachie 64027

The rough edges of the Greek/house-music merger have been sanded off. Good news if you like your dance music seamless, bad if you crave the unexpected dash of grit and spice. —*Bob Tarte*

Bahia Black
Worldbeat
○ **Ritual Beating System** / 1991 / Axiom 314-510856
Collision between Brazilian drum troupe Olodum, American jazz artists (Herbie Hancock, Wayne Shorter, Henry Threadgill), bucket drummers (Larry Wright, David Chapman), rap, samba, funk, rock, and more—produced by Bill Laswell. Whatever kind of music this is, I want to hear more of it. —*Bob Tarte*

Boiled in Lead

Group / Worldbeat, Rock

Boiled in Lead is a midwestern Celtic-rock band. The band was originally Drew Miller, Jane Dauphin, Brian Fox, Mitch Griffin, and Dave Stenshoel. Later on Robin "Adnan" Anders and Todd Menton replaced Jane, Brian, and Mitch. The current band is Robin, Drew, and Todd. —*Chip Renner*

From the Ladle to the Grave / 1989 / Atomic Theory 1104

This CD has a great sound combining the Irish influences with good old rock. "Madman Mora Blues" and "Step It Out, Mary" are very strong. This record was in the Top 20 of the Folk Roots critics poll. —*Chip Renner*

○ **Orb** / 1990 / Atomic Theory 1108

Worldbeat with a twist the 3 Mustapha 3 way—and with an undercurrent of punk aggressiveness. Nothing intimidates these Minnesotans, neither Serbian kolos, Romanian klezmer, Scottish ballads, nor traditional Armenian fare. Produced by Hijaz Mustapha himself. —*Bob Tarte*

Old Lead / 1991 / Omnium 2001

This CD contains the band's first two releases, "Boiled in Lead" and "Hotheads." 24 songs. The BIL section of the CD is raw compared to the Hotheads section. By the time Hotheads came out the band had added Todd Menton who gave the band a more polished sound. —*Chip Renner*

Bratsch

○ **Transports En Commun** / 1991 / Griffe 1902

French troupe of purported Gypsy musicians display astonishing virtuosity throughout a wide range of styles: Bulgarian, klezmer, flamenco, jazz, classical touches. —*Bob Tarte*

Dan Del Santo

Vocals / Worldbeat

Del Santo lives in Austin, TX, where he has assembled a mighty group of players who can leap from reggae to juju to rock and back again without breaking into a sweat. He coined the term "worldbeat" to describe his music, a mix of Western and African pop that draws from many influences without ever sounding watered down or "commercial." —*J. Poet*

○ **Off Your Nyash** / 1990 / Flying Fish 551

Del Santo's politically aware lyrics give you plenty to think about while the band's rhythms motivate your feet. —*J. Poet*

Diga Rhythm Band

Worldbeat

○ **Diga Rhythm Band** / 1976 / Grateful Dead 41062

Grateful Dead drummer Mickey Hart has long been a proponent and student of world music. He produced this 1976 all-percussion outing, which is a compelling and powerful recording that draws in the listener with its spellbinding rhythms. —*Jeff Tamarkin*

Earth Island Orchestra

○ **Earth Island Orchestra** / 1992 / I Wanna 1

Detroit's Arab and Indian community contribute pieces to this wild jigsaw puzzle of international influences. —*Bob Tarte*

Mickey Hart

b. Sep. 11, 1943
Drums / Worldbeat

Mickey Hart is a drummer, an ethnomusicologist, and an author. He joined the Grateful Dead as its second percussionist in 1967. In 1970 Hart left the Dead and cut the solo album *Rolling Thunder* in 1972, featuring various members of the Dead. Hart returned to the band in 1974.

Hart's musical activities outside the Dead have been extensive. In 1976, the Dead's Round Records label released *Diga* by the Diga Rhythm Band, an early experiment in worldbeat fusion put together by Hart. His interaction with drummers from around the world sparked an abiding interest in the role of the drum in other cultures—and a steadily expanding curiosity about non-Western musics. 1979 and 1980 saw the release of two albums of music from the film *Apocalypse Now*, much of it contributed by Hart. In 1983 Hart released albums under the heading *The World.* These began with a reissue of *Diga Rhythm Band*

(an album by Babatunde Olatunji produced by Hart). Then came a series of albums of music Hart had recorded around the world. In 1989 Hart released *Music to Be Born By*, an album based on the heartbeat of his son in the womb, and 1990 saw the simultaneous release of Hart's first book, *Drumming at the Edge of Magic*, and an album, *At the Edge*. In 1991 another book and disc, both called *Planet Drum*, appeared. Both albums made the upper reaches of new-age and world-music charts. —*William Ruhlmann & Bob Tarte*

Rolling Thunder / 1972 / Grateful Dead 40112

This is the nearest thing to a conventional pop-rock album Mickey Hart ever made. It features Grateful Dead members Bob Weir, Jerry Garcia, and Phil Lesh, as well as other San Francisco rock musicians, and contains early versions of the Dead songs "Playing in the Band" and "Greatest Story Ever Told." —*William Ruhlmann*

The Apocalypse Now Sessions / 1980 / Rounder 10109

Hart's soundtrack work for *Apocalypse Now* expanded into these free-ranging, rather abstract tracks with fellow Grateful Dead drummer Billy Kreutzmann. —*Bob Tarte*

○ **Dafos** / 1983 / Rykodisc 10108

An established audiophile classic for its thrilling, nearly overpowering sonics, this percussion-based journey to a mythical country features Brazilian percussionist Airto Moreira and vocalist Flora Purim. —*Bob Tarte*

Music to Be Born By / 1989 / Rykodisc 20112

This hypnotic 70-minute album features Mickey's son Taro's heartbeats—recorded in utero!—with subtle drums, bass guitar harmonics, and wooden flute. This is music designed to have a calming effect on women in labor, through the use of a single musical pattern repeated with slight variation throughout. —*Backroads Music / Heartbeats*

At the Edge / 1990 / Rykodisc 40124

Sounds like we're at the edge of the rainforest on this atmospheric recording that uses a variety of unusual instruments and employs such musicians as Jerry Garcia, Babatunde Olatunji, Airto Moreira, and Zakir Hussain. —*William Ruhlmann & Bob Tarte*

○ **Planet Drum** / Dec. 1991 / Rykodisc 10206

A dazzling all-percussion workout with plenty of muscle and deep grooves featuring many of the world musicians from *At the Edge*. Loosely tied to Hart's book of the same name. —*Bob Tarte*

○ **Yamantaka** / Celestial Harmonies 13003

A collaboration recorded in 1982 at the Grateful Dead Studios which combine Hart with the composers and performers of the *Tibetan Bells* series. Since *Yamantaka* is the Tibetan god of the dead and lord of the underworld, you might guess that the tone of this release is dark and other-worldly, with music played on unusual and invented percussive instruments that seem to build and appear almost from out of nowhere. —*Backroads Music / Heartbeats*

Ofra Haza

Vocals / Disco, Ethnic, Israeli

By the early '80s, Ofra Haza was already a popular teen singer/songwriter in Israel, before she exploded onto the international scene with a glossy album of ancient Yemenite songs updated for the nightclub set. Since then, pop sensibilities have overshadowed the Jewish traditions in her music, and she has even applied her gorgeous, sensual singing to English-language chart attempts. —*Myles Boisen*

50 Gates of Wisdom / 1984 / Shanachie 64002

Like the Berber songs of Algeria's Markunda Aures, Haza's contemporary versions of Yemeni Jewish songs feature tradition-based singing with pop backings. Her gorgeous voice carries all before it, but the arrangements are over-slick at times. Still, this was Haza as kibbutz pop-star, unlike her later worldbeat wanderings. —*John Storm Roberts*

Shaday / 1988 / Sire 25816

This CD made Haza a household name throughout Europe because it was her first to sell literally millions of copies there, earning her the nickname the "Israeli Madonna." She combines Hebrew, Yemenite, and English in prayers and original compositions with a driving European dance beat. Includes the international hits "Im Nin Alu" and "Galbi" (later made famous after rap stars Eric B. & Rakeem sampled it for one of their hits). Also available domestically on Sire with bonus remixes of the above tracks. —*Phil Fink*

Desert Wind / 1989 / Sire 25976
Most of the songs on Ofra's 1990 release, which fittingly coincides with her first US concert tour, are sung partially in English; but the content is still about the Yemenite Jewish community, Yemenite tradition, and peace in the Middle East, with the imagery and rhythm of the desert an integral part of this music. "Fantamorgana," a tribute to her mother and other Yemenite Jews who were persecuted and banished to Yemen's desert, includes the voice of her mother chanting in Arabic. The time's ripe for this sort of world music to gain a foothold in the arena of commercial recognition and success. —*Ladyslipper*

Kirya / 1992 / Shanachie 64043
Whether she's singing in Hebrew, Aramaic, or English, Ofra Haza entrances with the exotic allure of her golden voice. Her latest disc mixes traditional Yemenite sounds and stories with new lyrics and occasional hip-hop beats. But even on songs like "Daw Da Hiya," with punk godfather Iggy Pop narrating over an industrial rhythm, the focal point is the mesmerizing swirl of Haza's vocals. "Barefoot" finds her voice dancing with a saxophone as an acoustic guitar caresses a sensual groove, while the mysterious pulse of the title track is boosted by her soaring, quivering outbursts. Haza's music is a call for peace, love, and equality, delivered with soulful sonic beauty. —*Mark J. Cadigan, Roundup Newsletter*

Zakir Hussain

Percussion, tabla, concerta / World Fusion
The son of table drumming master Alla Rakha learned at his father's knee from an early age. Today, he is the most widely-recorded North Indian tabla performer, almost always giving dynamic support in a sideman role. His few efforts as a session leader are usually in world music fusion groups; to discover the true substance and breadth of his classical raga playing seek out a store with a good Indian music selection and you are bound to find his contributions with a variey of top-ranked traditional instrumentalists. —*Myles Boisen*

Venu / Apr. 1990 / Rykodisc 20128
Classical flute master Chaurasia and one of India's leading young tabla players, Zakir Hussain, in a 1974 live recording, which was remixed a couple of years ago. The entire CD is devoted to one raga, "Rag Ahir Bhairav," a light-classical, early-morning raga that mixes a well-known classical piece, "Bhairav," with a folk melody called "Ahir." Superb music, finely recorded with good notes. —*John Storm Roberts*

Magical Moments of Rhythm /
Magical Moments of Rhythm is a series of excerpts, recorded live in concert in both India and the USA, that focuses on Zakir's astonishing mastery of the complex rhythms of the tabla, arguably the most sophisticated hand drums in existence. All the main melody instruments of Indian classical music—sarod, sitar, santoor, sarangi, and bansuri—are heard here, albeit primarily in supporting roles, played by such prominent musicians as Ustad Sultan Khan and Hariprasad Chaurasia. Particularly outstanding are the extended tabla solos that close out each side, played with tremendous passion and focus, often at dazzling speeds, by this extraordinary virtuoso. —*Backroads Music / Heartbeats*

Zakir Hussain & The Rhythm Experience /
Zakir Hussain & The Rhythm Experience is World Music at its very best, weaving the rhythms of India, Cuba, Africa, the Middle East and Indonesia into combinations of skillfully improvised exchanges with precise unison drumming. Guest artists include Bay Area notables such as Mickey Hart, Narada Michael Walden, Mel Martin and Jim Loveless, as well as Zakir's father Ustad Alla Rakha. —*Heartbeats*

Nusrat Fateh Ali Khan

Vocals / Qawwali
Like the Sabri Brothers, Khan has captured the attention of the world music community with the vocal intensity of his qawwali music. But his performances have more of an individual focus, with emphasis on dramatic improvisational cascades and other flashy singing techniques. He has been recorded on a number of import labels, and has even done a pop-fusion album for Peter Gabriel's Real World label. —*Myles Boisen*

○ **En Concert a Paris** / Ocora 559072/73/74
A five-volume concert recording released in three component parts, in a word this set is magnificent. For those who wish to dive headlong it captures best the man's magic. —*Ken Hunt*

Magic Touch / Oriental Star 030
Bally Sago's anthology of sometimes good, mostly too blatantly commercial, mixes of material by Nusrat Fateh Ali Khan, polarises taste. Love it or leave it. But there are far worse pains that can be inflicted in the name of qawwalli. Bally Sagoo is actually very good at his job. —*Ken Hunt*

Last Prophet, The / Real World 2341
For a while there I'd somewhat lost interest in Nusrat, whose recent Western releases seemed to me only okay. Well, pass the crow pie. This is the finest qawwali recording I've heard in years, by one of the greatest qawwali singers, and certainly the most impassioned. This is just simply perfection—musically speaking—and the notes aren't bad in their non-technical way. —*John Storm Roberts, Original Music*

Mustt Mustt / 1990 / Atlantic 91630
This one tries to bring him to the World Beat party with a band that includes producer/guitarist Michael Brooks and former Neville Brothers bassist Darryl Johnson. The songs (some of which are merely vocal exercises) haunt and enchant, particularly the delightfully loping title track. Most fascinating artistic experiment of the year. —*Roundup Newsletter*

Day, Night, Dawn, Dusk / 1991 / Shanachie 64032
Not the best collection of the great qawwal's output but a convenient taster of his style because of its widespread availability. —*Ken Hunt*

☆ **Shahbaaz** / 1991 / Real World 91735
This shows Kahn taking chances with tradition, pushing his dynamic voice and ensemble to new expressive heights. —*Myles Boisen*

Shahen-Shah / Apr. 1991 / Atlantic 91300
Four lengthy selections of Sufi devotional music with impassioned chorus and accompaniment. —*Myles Boisen*

★ **Devotional Songs** / 1992 / Real World 2
A well deserved favorite. Its opener named "Allah Hoo Allah Hoo" (although the piece is neither fixed in shape nor lyric) became a rallying cry for early qawwali converts. —*Ken Hunt*

○ **Love Songs** / 1992 / Real World 32
The complementary piece to Devotional Songs and therefore one of the spearheads of Real World's assault on the West's qawwali taste buds. —*Ken Hunt*

○ **Traditional Sufi Qawwalis Vols. 1 and 2** / 1993 / Navras 0016 & 0017
Recorded live in London in December 1989, these two single volumes are exemplary illustrations of the sort of repertoire the listener might expect if they attend a qawwali concert where the audience is made up largely of Muslims of Asian descent. (He tends to adjust his repertoire and performance style to take account of the style of venue, the devotional situation—for example, his presence at Sufi shrine—or the composition of his audience.) —*Ken Hunt*

Ilham / 1993 / Audiorec 2075
The title translates a Revelation. Released in 1993 but consisting of material recorded some fifteen years before, Ilham is exclusively in his mother tongue, Punjabi. —*Ken Hunt*

Live in Paris—Vols. 1 & 2 / Ocora C558658/59
There is no single greatest singer of qawwalis, the ancient Sufi songs that have become central to popular religion and popular music in Pakistan. But if there were, his name would be Nusrat. Khan inherits a family tradition of qawwali singing going back several centuries, and in live performances like this concert he can be emotionally devastating. —*David L. Mayers*

Angelique Kidjo

○ **Logozo** / 1991 / Mango 162-539918
State-of-the-art production and mainstreamed African dance beats are poised to propel this talented singer from Benin to international pop stardom. Branford Marsalis, Ray Lema, and Manu Dibango contribute. —*Bob Tarte*

Ray Lema

Nangadeef / 1990 / Mango 9829
If Herbie Hancock's "Rock-It" had been recorded by the Zairian diaspora in Paris, it might have sounded something like this. Though the low spots are pretty generic, the frequent thunderclaps on this forward-looking disc are worthy of Youssou N'Dour at his best. —*Bob Tarte*

Gaia / 1991 / Mango 9895
Kraftwerk meets the rain forest as Lema refines his vision of Africa as reference point for the rest of the world. May be the source of the most mind-boggling computer-rhythms ever commited to disc. An organic approach to synthesis laden with insight and wit. —*Bob Tarte*

Benjamin Lew & Steven Brown

Group
Brown was a founder of the West Coast group, Tuxedomoon; Lew is a Belgian composer/filmmaker. —*John Storm Roberts*

Twelfth Day / 1984 / Original Music 301
Their first recording's acoustic/electronic mix had African overtones with echoes witty or wistful of idioms ranging from the Orient to baroque Germany and '30s French cabaret. The result is both original and all of a piece—one of those recordings that doesn't really fit into any neat definitional box, and thus has remained the preserve of a too-small number of passionate devotees. —*John Storm Roberts*

Carlos Lomas

From Malaga to Cairo / 1986 / Music of the World 304
Carlos Lomas is a masterly interpreter of the flamenco guitar and an exciting composer. Together with his friends who play Indian sitar, Middle Eastern drums, flutes, banjo, and violin, he creates a very special type of world music with a flamenco flavor. —*Music of the World*

Mandingo Griot Society

Group
Foday Musa Suso is a Mandingo (West African tribe) griot (hereditary musician and cultural curator) who can trace his hereditary lineage back to the first performer on the 21-string kora lute. After a traditional apprenticeship in Africa, he came to the US in 1977 and formed the Mandingo Griot Society to bring his native sounds to a new, receptive audience. The group included Adam Rudolph (who recently appeared on Hassan Hakmoun's *Gift of the Gnawa* CD) and had featured jazz trumpeter Don Cherry as a guest, anticipating world music fusion many years before the worldbeat era. —*Myles Boisen*

○ **Watta Sitta** / 1971 / Celluloid 6103
This is another great kora electrification project. Watta Sitta bravely attempts to mold an international dance music sound around Muso's African harp, while Herbie Hancock provides moral support. —*Bob Tarte*

Mouth Music

○ **Mouth Music** / Jan. 18, 1991 / Rykodisc 10196
Intriguing blend of puirt a beul (traditional Gaelic vocal music intended for dancing) with African and other drumming styles plus the requisite drum machine and synths, resulting in the world's first Irish-roots house music. —*Bob Tarte*

Osibisa

Group
The brainchild of Teddy Osei, a Ghanaian sax player, composer, and drummer who came to London to study music, Osibisa was one of the first African bands to win worldwide popularity. Their mix of African (especially highlife) and Caribbean forms made them a sensation in the mid '70s and their popularity continues today, even though recording dates have fallen off. —*J. Poet*

○ **Woyaya** / 1971 / Decca 5327
One side of this album has three jazzier, more improvisatonal cuts, the other a good sampling of the band's Afro-funk groove. —*J. Poet*

Heads / 1972 / Decca 75368

Funk, Latin, and reggae accents add spice to the band's highlife groove. —*J. Poet*

Ojah Awake / 1976 / Antilles 7058
The band's commercial high water mark with two hits, "Coffee Song" and "Dance the Body Music." —*J. Poet*

Outback

Group / Worldbeat
Outback's ebullient, accessible, yet highly irregular style could be described as "tribal new-acoustic." The group is anchored by two multi-instrumentalists, Graham Wiggins and Martin Craddick, who in 1988 met by chance in Oxford and began playing as a duo all over England. A former jazz pianist, Wiggins taught himself to play the didgeridoo (sometimes spelled *didjeridu*), an Australian aboriginal wind instrument made of a hollowed-out wooden tube. Through the use of various techniques (including circular breathing), the instrument produces an earthy, gritty, and at times almost electronic sound. Curiously enough, Wiggins's didgeridoo takes on a folksy quality similar to the resonant twang of a mouth harp when combined with Craddick's acoustic guitar and mandolin strummings. After the success of their first international release *Baka*, the two refined and expanded upon this unusual sound by adding the talents of Sagar N'Gom on West African percussion and Ian Campbell on drums. Outback's latest release also features French fiddle player Paddy LeMercier. —*Linda Kohanov*

○ **Baka** / 1990 / Hannibal 1357
Acoustic guitarist Martin Craddick makes a strong team with Graham Wiggins, whose axe of choice is the Australian aboriginal instrument, the didjeridu. Wiggins's unorthodox techniques on this instrument—which generate percussive patterns as well as animal barks—finds their equal in Craddick's narrative instrumental style. —*Bob Tarte*

Dance the Devil Away / 1991 / Hannibal 1369
An expanded Outback adds violin, synthesizer, and all sorts of drums to the mix, giving this album a more complete sound. The percussion and acoustic guitar form a nice wall of sound with Wiggins's didgerido slicing out and hypnotizing the listener. —*Bob Tarte & Chip Renner*

Lakshiminarayan Shankar

b. 1950
Violin / World Fusion, Jazz-fusion
This violinist has found a comfortable style that melds and combines classical Indian influences and jazz devices. He moved to America in 1969, eventually earned a doctorate in ethnomusicology at Wesleyan, where he began meeting jazz musicians like Ornette Coleman, Jimmy Garrison, and John McLaughlin while working as a teaching assistant and concert master of the university chamber orchestra. He studied with McLaughlin in 1973, and two years later, they cofounded the group Shakti, which was active until 1978. During the '80s and beyond, Shankar has recorded periodically as a leader, doing both jazz-based material and Indian classical music. He's also worked with rockers Peter Gabriel, Phil Collins, and Frank Zappa. —*Ron Wynn*

● **Who's to Know** / Nov. 1980 / ECM 827269
This is more like it. Genuine Indian classical ragas, though the somber quality robs session of vitality. —*Ron Wynn*

Song for Everyone / Sep. 1984 / ECM 823795
One of Shankar's best. —*Ron Wynn*

Nobody Told Me / 1990 / PolyGram 839623
Exquisite recording, moments of beauty. —*Ron Wynn*

Soul Searcher / 1991 / Axiom 422-846755
1991 date with special guest Peter Gabriel. Decent, occasionally surprising. —*Ron Wynn*

3 Mustaphas 3

Group / Worldbeat
The 3 Mustaphas 3 pratfell onto the burgeoning worldbeat scene from out of nowhere in 1986—or from Szegerely, somewhere in the Balkans, if you believe their press releases. According to Mustapha mythology, the Balkan Beat Boys first sharpened their musical teeth at the Crazy Loquat Club under the guidance of Uncle Patrel Mustapha Bin Mustapha. Then, seeking broader horizons, they stole away one night, accompanied by their fa-

vorite refrigeration equipment, to seek world success from a UK base.

The Mustapha's humor has been a double-edged scimitar, however. In the beginning it allowed them to introduce difficult music to unsuspecting audiences new to the worldbeat sound. But the burlesque that initially forwarded their agenda also worked against them by threatening to consign the group to the purgatory of novelty act. An increasing emphasis on solid musicianship, plus their collaboration with revered African performers like Stella Chiweshe, have begun to win the band the critical respect they deserve. And no one else makes a crash course in world music so much fun. —*Bob Tarte*

Shopping / 1987 / Shanachie 64006
Egyptian film music is a major influence here in the fezsters's first full-length release. But don't miss the hilarious Mustapha rap tune "Fiz'n" or the terrific cover of Morrocan artist Najat Atabou's searing "Shouffi Rhirou." —*Bob Tarte*

○ **Heart of Uncle** / 1989 / Rykodisc 20156
Convincing tour of world capital backstreets, featuring crisp arrangements of an Indian film music classic ("Awara Hoon") plus forays into taarab, benga, klezmer, merengue, Bulgarian vocal music, and more. Stunningly creative. —*Bob Tarte*

☆ **Soup of the Century** / 1990 / Rykodisc 10195
Stung by allegations that they're nothing but a "joke band," the Mustaphas cook up their hardest set yet, recorded live in the studio with minimal overdubbing. Look for mindboggling genre fusions plus molten clarinet and electric bazouki breakouts. —*Bob Tarte*

○ **Friends, Fiends & Fronds** / 1991 / Omnium 2003
A portrait of the artists as an evolving concept is presented in this collection of singles, B-sides, and remixes. Worth its weight in premium goat's cheese for the two versions of their masterpiece "Linda Linda" and a pair of brand new songs. —*Bob Tarte*

Glen Velez
....

Percussion / Modern Creative, World Fusion

Handdance: Fame Drum Music / 1984 / Music of the World 301
Glen Velez is an internationally recognized authority on tambourine history and playing techniques from around the world. On this recording [with Layne Redmond] he plays tambourines and mbira (African thumb piano), and utilizes harmonic singing. "A multi-fingered rain forest of percussion." *Washington Post.* —*Music of the World*

Ramana / 1990 / Music of the World 307
A remarkable hand percussionist, Glen Velez specializes in frame drums from all over the world. Glen plays frame drums, unbira, and steel drums, and is joined by Layne Redmond (percussion) and Howard Levy (harmonica). "Magic happens when he begins to play." *The Village Voice.* —*Music of the World*

AFRICA

Africa Collection

☆ **Africa Dances** / 1972 / Original Music 002
This groundbreaking pan-African anthology was the first and is still the only continent-wide survey, also the only one to compare and contrast pan-African developments during the crucial '50s-'70s period. The CD has music from 13 countries, two more than the LP/cassette versions. —*John Storm Roberts*

○ **Sound d'Afrique** / Oct. 1982 / Mango 9697
The first compilation of African dance music to be issued in North America by a major label and still one of the best. —*J. Poet*

○ **Compact d'Afrique** / 1986 / Globestyle 907
New-wave soukous from Congo and Zaire: faster and hotter than the old style pioneered by Franco and Rochereau. Great cuts by Kanda Bongo Man, Papa Wemba, Choc Stars, and Les Quatres Etoiles. —*J. Poet*

○ **African Moves, Vol. 1** / Jan. 1987 / Rounder 11513
This CD has soukous from Tabu Ley Rochereau, juju from Ebenezer Obey, and highlife from African Brothers as well as other artists. —*J. Poet*

○ **African Moves, Vol. 2** / Feb. 1987 / Rounder 1029

African Music

There's no way to write coherently about the music of a continent covering 52 independent nations, between 800 and 1600 languages (depending on your definition), and at least five major cultural groupings. The confusions inherent in this kind of diversity are many, but a few stand out. Some of the confusion stems from the fact that African music has been both influential and influenced. The direct or indirect influence on new-world popular music has been varying, but all of it, "White," "Black," or "Latin," has at least a touch of Africa. And the compliment has been returned. African music has always been (and remains) essentially local, but African musicians have always drawn from elsewhere: over a thousand years from Islam, over a couple of hundred from Europe, over half a century from the Americas, somewhat (and increasingly) from US African-American styles and reggae, greatly in the past from US country music, and enormously from Cuba and Latin New York.

More confusion results from the Western stereotype that associates drums with African traditional music. In reality, western Nigeria (for example) has a dozen or so 20th-century urban styles for voices and percussion alone, and at least one of these outshines in popularity all the Nigerian musicians known to the West.

There's another confusion of much greater immediate importance to this listing of African recordings. Different circumstances have led to noticeably different levels of "Africanness" in contemporary pop styles. At the most "African" level, there's what happens when a whole culture falls in love with an overseas influence, as the Congolese did with Cuban music. Sophisticated individual bands sometimes develop styles with an abnormally high proportion of overseas influence (Fela Kuti, Manu Dibango). When expatriate musicians form bands to play the music of their homeland, as did Osibisa in London, they come under different influences and produce a different mix. Different yet again are groups combining expatriate African musicians with Europeans, like the Germano-Ghanaian "Burger-Highlife" bands in Germany. Lastly, famous musicians with a local or expatriate African audience (N'Dour, Ade, many others) have recently been trying to "cross over" internationally, with still different results.

All this tends to mislead newcomers to African music. At first, naturally enough, people tend to like music that's not too foreign, which means very American-influenced. So we latch onto individual musicians with a strong American element and assume, usually incorrectly, that Africans think as much of them as we do. The result is that Fela and Manu Dibango get described as "African superstar" when they are not by any means the superstars of their own countries and are pretty much unknown elsewhere in Africa. (In fact, the only musicians with a real pan-African appeal are the big names of soukous, and even they don't have any noticeable following in South Africa.)

All of which means that if you want to explore African music, albums by Fela or the recent big-label recordings of Youssou N'Dour make handy vehicles for starting the journey. But if that's as far as you go, you haven't even landed yet.

– John Storm Roberts

A sampler featuring crossover artists, musicians that mix African and Western styles, especially funk and reggae, for a sound pleasing to Europeans as well as the folks back home. Solid work by Salif Keita, Papa Wemba, and Aster Aweke, among others. —*J. Poet*

○ **Africa on Mango** / 1988 / Mango 9816
Pleasant collection of very accessible contemporary pop-oriented music from Africa. Some sung in English and some in native tongues. Rhythmic, "happy," generally uptempo, easy on the ears. Features the Bhondu Boys, Salif Keita, Mbougeni Ngema, and others. —*Niles J. Frantz*

○ **African Acoustic: Sounds Eastern and Southern** / 1988 / Original Music 108
More of Africa's enchanting acoustic guitar styles: 1981 recordings by both adults and kids. The only name known even to megabuffs is the late Losta Abelo, once a friendly rival of Mwenda Jean Bosco. The most bewitching cuts of all, in my view, are by a Tanzanian who plays only for friends; one song is briefly and unintentionally accompanied by the clattering of crockery. The kids include a group of blind school children making very adept music with homemade instruments, and a hell-for-leather cut for high-pitched voices and tomato-can banjo. —*John Storm Roberts*

○ **Out of Africa** / 1988 / Rykodisc 20059
A good continental selection that includes Senegal's Youssou N'Dour, South Africa's Mahotella Queens, Nigeria's juju master Ebenezer Obey, and Rochereau. —*J. Poet*

★ **Rhythms of Resistance: Music of Black Africa** / 1988 / Earthworks 86058

○ **Izibani Zomgqashiyo** / 1989 / Shanachie
One of the lively, hip, funky Mgqashiyo rhythm's hottest exponents is this group of five women from Southern Africa, mostly around Soweto, who have been together since 1964. They were voted the 1975 Radio Bantu Best Group of the Year. At times, they are also accompanied by their male "groaners" (Robert Mbazo Mkhize, Potatoes Mazambane, and Joseph Mthimkhulu) and a super band. Highly recommended. — *"Blue" Gene Tyrrany*

Forgotten Music/Kamtole / Ocora 559055
Both ends of the musical continuum of the islands: the Afro-Malagasy, with part-French melodies accompanied by various instruments including percussion, in lullabies, canoe songs, topical songs, drummed dance music, and even a dance-drama; and the Afro-French Indian Ocean music, with fiddles and percussion playing waltzes, schottisches, and the like in a style that kept much of the 19th-century delicacy of the originals while beefing them up with percussion. —*John Storm Roberts*

Music of Africa / Kaleidophone 1
The most outstanding contribution to documenting African music is the *Sound of Africa* series by Hugh Tracey. That entire collection can be found only in particular college libraries and homes of collectors, but the ten-volume *Music of Africa* is available on the Kaleidophone label: *Musical Instruments 1, Strings*; *Musical Instruments 2, Reeds (Mbira)*; *Musical Instruments 3, Drums*; *Musical Instruments 4, Flutes & Horns*; *Musical Instruments 5, Xylophones*; *Musical Instruments 6, Guitars 1*; *Musical Instruments 7, Guitars 2*; *Rhodesia 1*; *Tanzania 1*; and *Uganda 1*. —*David L. Mayers*

Sacred & Secular Music of The Middle Atlas / Ocora 559057
The French have a special gift for making recordings both totally authentic and immediately attractive, as is this collection of vocal and instrumental pieces, mostly for flute and drum but including some lute-playing. Not only truly beautiful, it is also fairly unusual, since double-reed pipes are more common in the Maghreb region (and in Sufi music) than flutes. —*John Storm Roberts*

Sahara: Music of Gourara / Auvidis 8037
Gourara, an area of oases, was once prosperous and wealthy, and though some of its music is common to the whole Sahara, some of the most ancient reflects a strong cultural individuality. There's a wide range of music here, some religious, some secular, but mostly reflecting a classic sacred/secular unity-in-duality. The singing is mostly choral with a strong solo lead, and much of it is underpinned with percussion, but there's also some fine reed flute and spike fiddle. —*John Storm Roberts*

○ **Fulani** / Auvidis 8006
The six million or so Fulani are scattered through several Sahelian countries, but these recordings are all from two groups, one living in North Dahomey and the other in Niger. This re-release from the old UNESCO World Atlas series is simply splendid: varied, superbly played, well recorded, and well documented. A lot of fine flute playing, praise songs to lute and other instru-

ments, and various ritual and work songs—as well as an unduly substantial example of jaw harp, the recording's only longueur. — *John Storm Roberts*

Algeria

Houria Aichi
....

Chants de l'Aures / Auvidis 6749
Music of the Aures mountains south of Constantine, recorded in a vein now regarded as old-fashioned (for which read traditional or even classic), with flute and percussion backing. Wonderful. — *John Storm Roberts*

Aissaoua
....

Aissaoua / Club du Disque Arabe 647
An extremely rare recording—in that the only one I know—of a powerful percussion-heavy music for ghaita oboe, frequently played at women's get-togethers in traditional Algerian society. It was originally linked with the trance-inducing ceremonies of North African Sufi mysticism, and still serves a somewhat secularized psycho-spiritual role. —*John Storm Roberts, Original Music*

Chaba Fadela
....

Vocals / Ethnic, World-Arab, Rai
One of the Rai Rebels from Algeria. —*Michael G. Nastos*

Fi 'Nselfik / Mango 9915
Here's a wonderful recording by the queen of rai. Her gorgeous singing is backed by synth work ideally suited to translate the long, mellifluously gutsy lines of North African tradition into the post-Moogian cosmos. It's a truly strange and inevitable album despite the familiarity that has since bred taking-for-granted (Note: though Mango doesn't bother to tell you, this is a reissue of the *Attitude* album). —*John Storm Roberts, Original Music*

○ **Hana Hana** / 1978 / Mango 9856
On this album, backed by a more modern sythesizer sound and pristine French production, the queen and king (her husband Cheb Sahraoui is here also) of rai unite for a series of solid duets. —*Bob Tarte*

○ **You Are Mine** / 1988 / Mango 9827
"N'sel Fik" by Fadela and her husband Cheb Sahraoui is the biggest Algerian hit in the country's history. The rest of the tracks here aren't bad either. See the *Rai Rebels* listing. —*J. Poet*

A. Igman
....

Rray lw / Aladin 2218
Subtitled "Berber Folklore of Kabylie," this is a treasure. Sharing some elements with rai (though much closer to their common ancestor), this music is earthier, less studio-controlled and ultimately more personal and less bombastic. The line-up is a simple one of drums, bass, flute, a very unobtrusive synth, and Igman's mandol. If rai is the U2 of Algeria, Igman is its Pogues. —*Carl Hoyt, Original Music*

Cheb Kader
....

Vocals / World-Arab, Rai
The Elvis of rai music. Potent hybrid—emotional Arabic vocals and melodies set against contemporary rock percussion and production. —*Hank Davis*

El Awama / Michel Levy Prod. 303
Kader is a young France-based whiz kid whom producer Levy found when Mami got drafted. He's an attractive singer, though a little lightweight, and his style (backings in any event) is heavily but effectively influenced by rock, reggae, and so on. —*John Storm Roberts, Original Music*

○ **From Oran to Paris** / Shanachie 64029
An odd hybrid of emotional Arabic vocals and melodies set against contemporary rock production. —*Hank Davis*

Cheb Khaled
....

Vocals / Rai
Many got their first exposure to Algerian rai music through Cheb Khaled, who set the pace for most of the young Chebs with his

youthful good looks and rebellious, streetwise stance. With noted producer Rachid Baba behind him, Khaled brought the sensuous rhythms and high-tech gloss of pop-rai to the English-speaking world, leaving an indelible mark with his soaring vocals and tales of debauchery. —*Myles Boisen*

○ **Kutche** / 1989 / Intuition 7909342
Though its heart-of-hearts is in the right place, even the best Algerian rai usually suffers from a less than state-of-the-art synthesizer sound. Not so here. Collaboration between Paris-based keyboard whiz Safy Boutella and one of rai's most powerful voices sets tough standards for other discs. —*Bob Tarte*

Mohamed Khaznadji

○ **Nouba du Mode Maya** / Esperance 2691
Half of what was once a double-LP set by one of the best contemporary classical vocalists in the andalus style that goes back to the idiom brought by refugees from the collapse of Muslim Spain. Here he sings a nouba (vocal suite) in Maya mode, whose title in English is "Wedding Morning," backed by string and percussion orchestra. Thorough French notes accompany the release. —*John Storm Roberts*

Cheb Mami

Vocals / Rai
Mami was one of the first "Chebs" to be heard in the West when rai music came out into the open in 1985-86. Known as the prince of rai, he presented a clean-cut, fashionable image consistent with the Paris scene, but maintained a rootsy stance on his first few recordings. —*Myles Boisen*

Prince of Rai / 1989 / Shanachie 64013
Unlike most rai, this disc features live musicians, including a wailing Arabic fiddle guaranteed to raise goose bumps. —*J. Poet*

Let Me Rai / 1990 / Priority 57142
Recorded in Los Angeles using session musicians, this album is more Western, but retains enough Algerian influence to keep things interesting. Includes a couple of interesting reggae/rai fusions. —*J. Poet*

Bellemou Messaoud

○ **Le Pere du Rai** / World Circuit 011
Messaoud was not only an early pop-rai luminary but a man with the bizarre but ultimately successful notion of using a trumpet in Maghrebi music. This release, with new vocalist Cheb Ourrad Houarri, features a basically acoustic band consisting of accordion, guitar, keyboards, and rhythm. —*John Storm Roberts*

Cheikha Remitti

○ **Ghir el Baroud** / Michel Levy 306
A stunning new recording by the Bessie Smith of rai. Aside from the sheer splendor of the performance, its flute-and-percussion backing is the "missing link" between urban styles like chaabi and the electronic rai of the new generation. The controlled emotional charge of this antiestablishment music comes with a subdued humor, but the overriding effect is of power. —*John Storm Roberts*

Algeria Collection

Rai Planete / Cooking Vinyl 004
A wonderful example of the creative chaos that is pop-rai, from a faintly daft reggae-rai opener by Cheb Mami to Raina Rai's rock guitar licks and Gypsy-ish fiddle behind Cheb Kader to "classic" electronic rai, plus Khaled, Moumen, Tati. The one huge flaw is the absence of Fadela, Zahaounia, or any of the great women singers! Ridiculous!! —*John Storm Roberts, Original Music*

☆ **Rai Rebels** / 1988 / Earthworks 91000
Virgin's collection goes beyond the obvious rai heavies, though it includes Fadela's "N'sel Fik" yet again. Here are the great Chaba Zahouania and a particularly fine newcomer, Houari Benchenet, who gets a great deal of mileage out of mixing the older harmonium sound with his electronics—plus, natch, Sahraoui, Khaled, and Hamid. Adequate sound, rather ragged editing, wonderful music. —*John Storm Roberts*

African Musical Terms

Afrobeat – West African dance music with strong Afro-American influences, symbolized by Fela Anikulapo-Kuti of Nigeria.

Apala – 20th century Islamic-influenced street music with vocals and percussion.

Batá – Nigerian lap drums (three double-headed drums played together) used for religious purposes in Cuba.

Benga – Guitar music originating with the Luo people of Western Kenya but now widely popular throughout the country.

Fuji – Post World War II Western Nigerian percussion and vocal music.

Griot – A traditional bard of the Mandingo people, revered and respected as an essential member of their community, performing at all ritual functions.

Highlife – A complex of dance styles from English-speaking West Africa, developed around the turn of the century. Guitar band music heard with jazz-like horn sections or in rural areas with just multiple guitars.

Jit – Music from Zimbabwe that features percussion and vocals. The Bhundu Boys and James Chimombe were among those who adopted more modern styles.

Juju – Talking drums, multiple guitar lines, and call and response vocals are prime lements of this music, with links to the traditional drumming of theYoruba tribe of western Nigeria. Ebenezer Obey, I. K. Dairo, and King Sunny Ade are the grand masters of juju music.

Kora – A 21-string harp-lute linked to Mandingo culture, and frequently played in Mali, the Gambia, Guinea, and Senegal.

Kwassa kwassa – Zairean dance fad popular in the late 80s.

Kwela – South African pennywhistle street music developed in the 50s.

Makossa – Cameroon's major contemporary dance rhythm, combining soukous with traditionally local elements.

Mbalax – A Senegalese percussion music. Also the modern dance style of Youssou N'Dour and others.

Mbaqanga – South African township music first popular in the mid 60s.

Mbira – The Zimbabwean name for the finger piano widespread throughout sub-Saharian Africa.

Mbube – A choral music style from South Africa with roots in the glorious local traditions and Afro-American gospel.

Milo jazz – The namesake of Milo malt drink, this is a Sierra Leone street dance.

Palm wine guitar – An older West African acoustic guitar music named after the drink.

Rai – Although an older form, contemporary rai is a teenage rebel music, mixing electronics with Algerian street idioms.

Soukous – A popular teenage dance music from 70s Zaire. From the French word for "shake," it is the generic name for an influential music of Zaire and the Congo that has spread across Africa. Combining local musical ingredients with Cuban/Caribbean rhythms and elements of 30s and 40s American country music (the guitar sound of Jimmie Rodgers, for example).

Taarab – Afro-Arab urban music of the East African coast in the Swahili language. This is listening, not dance music, typically heard at wedding parties.

☆ **Rai Rebels, Vol. 2: Pop Rai & Rachid Style** / 1989 / Atlantic 91407
The anthology includes selections from Cheb Zahouzni, Cheb Khaled, Chaba Zahouania, etc. An excellent intro to the East African pop sound of rai. —*Ron Wynn*

○ **Folklore Kabyle** / Club du Disque Arabe 033
The Kabylie mountain dwellers of Algeria maintain a fierce cultural independence. The backbone of the resistance against the French, they have since proven a thorn in the side of the independent government. Musically, they have contrived both to preserve their tradition and to refresh it. These recordings include several by the great Kabylie women singers, Hanifa, Djamila, as well as the superb younger Daughters of Djudjura, plus examples of traditional double reeds and drumming. Much of the music is not so much traditional as popular-infused-by-traditional. Adequate English notes. —*John Storm Roberts*

Angola

Teto Lando

Esperances Idosas / Sonodisc 68585
This has the generalized Afro-Caribbean backings of bland massmarket world-beat, but it's also very charming—especially Lando's irresistible Portuguese crooning. —*Carl Hoyt, Original Music*

Burundi Collection

Burundi: Traditional Music / Ocora 559003

Congo (Brazzaville)

Ali & Tam's with Orchestre Malo

/ Zone 5
More of the Kinshasan Alternative, this one is also distinguished by highly percussive bass and an extremely effective integration of local marimba with the mostly Western instruments. Again, there's lots of horn work (including some charming solo sax influenced by older Caribbean styles) and percussion, delicate acoustic guitar, together with melodies that hark back less to traditional music than to the very early days of the urban style. Here's another real treat. —*John Storm Roberts, Original Music*

Bantous de la Capitale

Les Bantous De La Capitale 1963/1969 / Sonodisc 36527
Les Bantous were a splinter group of the Orch. Rock A Mambo, a very influential early band that could not really survive the defection of the musicians who went on to become Les Bantous. The founder of Les Bantous was Nino Malapet the clarinetist. Joining him were Essous the saxophonist, the singers Kosmos, Tchico, and Pamelo Mounk'a, and guitarists Papa Noel and Master Mwana Congo—quite the all-star band! Ronnie Graham in his excellent book says about these early recordings: "Buy on sight!," and I can see why—the clarinet is just perfect for the early rumba sound and these guys have a more funky groove than any other early bands—even Franco, Kalle, or Nico. Not that they are necessarily better, just groove harder (they even do a guaguanco number—"Maria Linda"!). —*John Storm Roberts, Original Music*

Monument / Sonodisc 5506
This recent offering by one of the long-lived greats of the style provides hope for soukous fans amid the potboiling. Others may hit-hunt, but Les Bantous still hew gloriously to the classic two-part song, with all-real musicians and an understated groove that kicks much harder than the new funko-soukouzouk. —*John Storm Roberts, Original Music*

Diblo Dibala

Guitar / Soukous
Dibala began playing guitar when he was 12. By the time he was 15 he almost beat Franco, Zaire's top guitarist and band leader, in a guitar duel, and Franco offered Diblo a job in his band. Dibala became Zaire's top session player and arranger, playing and composing material on over 60 albums by other artists. In 1979 Kanda Bongo Man lured Dibala away from Franco; the band re-located to Paris where their success can be traced in large part to the fiery solo work he has contributed to Bongo Man's albums. In 1986 Dibala left Kanda to form Loketo with singer Aurlus Mabele. —*J. Poet*

Loketo

Guitar / Soukous
Loketo's Diblo Dibala may be Zaire's finest guitarist. Since forming the band with singer Aurlus Mabele in 1986, Diblo's amazingly sharp fretwork and melodic phrasing has made Loketo one of the top attractions on the Parisian and African music scene. Loketo is one of the best purveyors of "new-wave" soukous. —*J. Poet*

Congo (Brazzaville) Collection

○ **Anthologie De La Musique Des Pygmaes Aka (Anthology of Aka Pygmy Music)** / Ocora 559012-3
Poly-rhythmic, soft voiced, continuously inventive jungle pattern music accompanying almost all aspects of pygmy life. Sample songs/rites include "Rituel précédant le départure a la chasse" (Ritual preceding leaving for the hunt), "Berceuse" (Lullaby), "Deux chantfables: L'oiseau, taillefine" (Two story songs: The bird, slender waist). Highly recommended. — *"Blue" Gene Tyrrany*

○ **Mbuti Pygmies of Ituri Rainforest** / 1992 / Smithsonian/Folkways 40401
This CD reissue combines two long-out-of-print recordings that were among Folkways' most popular African releases of the '50s. Anthropologist Colin Turnbull's field recordings may not match the sonics of today's digital productions, but their scope still impresses. Spotlights the gorgeous, free-flowing vocal style called hocketing, where singers pass short melodic lines from person to person in sort of a round that forms shimmering harmonic patterns. —*Bob Tarte*

○ **Music of the Rainforest Pygmies** / 1992 / Lyrichord
Another reissue of Colin Turnbull's field recordings, this one from 1961. Song types are more varied than his Folkways collection because selections include the Mbuti influence on music of neighboring peoples. Contains a delightfully baffling Twa pygmoid rendition of "(Oh, My Darling) Clementine," presented to Turnbull as a very old and sacred song. —*Bob Tarte*

Music of the Baka Pygmies / Auvidis 8029
My favorite music from the Cameroons. There is one particular track that features young girls singing and slapping the water. —*David L. Mayers*

Cameroon

Francis Bebey

b. 1929, Douala, Cameroon
Vocals, guitar / Neo-traditional
A composer, guitarist, and novelist from Cameroon, Bebey has combined Latin American, Western (pop and classical), and African elements into his compositions. —*J. Poet*

○ **Akwaaba: Francis Bebey** / 1984 / Original Music 005
These compositions for sanza (thumb piano), drums, and claves are accompanied by singing, including a technique called double voice, a method of singing two notes at the same time. The music is peaceful, eerie, and spiritual. —*J. Poet*

Moni Bile

b. Aug. 1957, Douala, Cameroon
Bass

10 Anniversaire / Mad Production 52711
Bile goes (almost) all the way into Afro-zouk, though there are still Cameroonian elements, mostly the guitar and choruses. Which said, Bile is a very intelligent musician, and this recording is full of original touches, subtle and less subtle. —*John Storm Roberts, Original Music*

Moni Bile Story, Vol. 1 / Moni Bile Productions 6818
After several "greatest hits" packages that were actually dopey re-recordings of old tunes, here is new evidence of why Bile got so big. From the opening chords of "Osi Tapa Lambo Lam" to the last notes of "New Look Makossa" he reveals his mastery of this

polished, elegant, almost too sweet dance music. —*Carl Hoyt, Original Music*

○ **Moni Bile** / MB 115
Cameroonian makossa has more drive that Zairian zoukous, and a larger dollop of local traditional rhythms. Bile is an absolute top makossa artist, and this excellent album shows why, with drive, fine solos, and variety in arrangements. —*John Storm Roberts*

Charlotte Mbango

○ **Maloko** / Energy 54681
Mbango is a very nifty singer in a vein reminiscent of Mbilia Bel, whose backings mix zouk influences and Cameroonian instrumental sound. Mix and match maybe, but a mix that does indeed match. Nothing blindingly innovative, just warmth, charm, bounce. Toto Guillaume, Joe Mboule, Naimro zouk it to 'em on keyboards. Outrageously short, but that's all too standard in makossa/soukous/zouk. —*John Storm Roberts*

Bella N'Joh

Belle Mère / Sim's Productions 49909
Here's high-energy Paris Afro-zouk, as opposed to Paris Antillo-zouk (as if life weren't too complicated already!), and it's much more entertaining. This is the way zouk should have gone when popularity side-tracked it. The arrangements are happening, the rhythms hot and experimentation is more than a mere sampling of funny noises. Cast a vote for freshness . . . —*Carl Hoyt, Original Music*

Les Tetes Brulées

Group
Africa's first "punk" band appears on stage in tribal paint, wearing shades and outrageous costumes, and plays a blistering guitar pop that's almost heavy metal in its attack. The first African guitar band to radiate "attitude" with a capital A, with the musicianship to back up their aggressive stance. Their style has been dubbed "Bikutsi" and expands on many of the current melodic and rhythmic formulas of West African pop. —*J. Poet & Myles Boisen*

☆ **Hot Heads** / Apr. 1991 / Shanachie 64030
Exciting, electric "new wave" band from Cameroon. Funky and punky. —*Myles Boisen*

Bikutsi Rock / 1992 / Shanachie 64042
Cameroon's "hotheads" sweeten their sound with the Mory Kante Group's horn section and multilayered vocals by Charlotte Mbango. This comes across less like African punk than like a Gold Coast funk and soukous experiment. —*Bob Tarte*

Cape Verde

Cesaria Evora

Mar Azul / Melodie 79533
Ravishing is the word that springs to the lips: one of those tiresome British understatements, but it'll have to do. Evora has the most glorious voice, the melodies are heartrendingly Portuguese, the guitar-runs have escaped from a fado recording, the harmonica and clarinet and muted trumpet simply add to the soul-saturating aura, and the very un-Portuguese (but quite Brazilian in spots) zip of the rhythms just top the whole thing off. I keep reaching for synonyms for perfection, and ecstasy, and pardon-me-while-I-melt. —*John Storm Roberts, Original Music*

Cape Verde Collection

○ **Cape Verde Islands: The Roots** / Playasound 65061
A 1990 recording of the Afro-Lusitanian tradition of Cape Verde, which leans heavily toward the Portuguese end of the Verdean spectrum; mornas and coladeiras for cavaquinho and viola (guitar family), and funanas for accordion and metal scraper—all radiating the nostalgic melancholy the Portuguese call saudade. Of special interest, on the more Afro end, is a song for the rare cimboa spike fiddle. —*John Storm Roberts*

African Pop

The roots of popular US music can be traced to Africa. The guitar, the world's favorite folk instrument, is a North African lute that was modified by the Spanish during the Moorish conquest. The origins of the blues, which led to rhythm & blues, rock & roll, soul, heavy metal, disco, new-wave, rap, and every other youth music of the past several hundred years, can be traced back to the rhythms of West Africa brought to the new world by slaves. Jazz was born in New Orleans, a city where Africans mixed their music with that of their English, French, and Spanish neighbors. Salsa is a combination of African drumming and Spanish folk music with the rhythms of the native peoples of Cuba and the Dominican Republic; soca is African with a dose of English and Latin folk music; zouk is what happened when Africans, native Islanders, and French people mixed in Guadeloupe – the permutations are endless. Despite the racism and economic exploitation of European incursions, African rhythms have emerged triumphant whenever outsiders came in contact with Africans.

Attempting to compile a basic library of African music is a difficult task. Imagine for a moment that someone had never heard any (North) American music. Where would you send that person to begin an investigation? Mississippi blues? Miami or New York salsa? Tex-Mex accordion music? Zydeco? Rock? Disco? Polka? And the US is only one country. Africa is a continent that includes several Arabic nations as well as thousands of Black ethnic groups, each with their own music, language, and culture. There are some obvious starting points. The impact of artists like Franco, Fela, Kuti, Mahlathini, Ladysmith Black Mambazo, Salif Keita, and Youssou N'Dour on our planet's growing international consciousness has been increasing and will continue to do so, but they don't begin to tell the story. While the listings here merely scratch the surface, they should provide you with a starting place. With a few exceptions, these are confined to current recordings that should be easy to track down in any large record store.

– J. Poet

Central African Republic Collection

Musique Centrafricaine / Auvidis 8020
This is the best overview of various tribal musics throughout the Central African Republic. It includes music from the following peoples: Azande, Babinga, Bagandou, Bianda, Bofi, Broto, Dakpa, Isongo, Linda, and Ndokpa. —*David L. Mayers*

Ethiopia

Mahmoud Ahmed

Vocals
Mahmoud Ahmed is a well-dressed elder statesman of Ethiopian popular music, leading the field for over 20 years at home, and even making concert appearances in the US. He is a master vocalist in the highly ornamented East African style and is known for inducing the uninhibited shaking of "eskeukta" on the dance floor. —*Myles Boisen*

☆ **Ere Mela Mela** / 1986 / Hannibal 1354
Ere Mela Mela: Modern Music from Ethiopia is a dark and brooding mix of '60s San Francisco rock ambience with Ethiopian modality. Driven by bluesy sax riffs and Ahmed's passionate vocals. —*Bob Tarte*

Aster Aweke

Vocals

Washington, DC, singer who combines Ethiopian melismatic singing with contemporary dance beats. —*AMG*

○ **Aster** / 1989 / CBS 46848
If Aretha Franklin had been born in Ethiopia, she might have grown up to be Aster Aweke. The singer mixes jazz, soul, funk, and Ethiopian strains to produce a form that's made her a superstar back home and a fast-rising talent in the US. American soul music has been a force in Ethiopia since the '60s, so Aweke's fervent vocalizing should ring a bell with most listeners. —*J. Poet*

Kabu / 1990 / CBS 47846
The second effort of this amazing Ethiopian songwriter and vocalist has more of an Afro-pop musical sound, with the exception of the haunting love ballad, "Kabu," which means "sacred rock" and employs a slow marimba for both rhythm and melody . . . simply lovely! Backed up on other cuts by a variety of percussion instruments, horns, keyboards and acoustic bass, Aster's voice is again rich and enchanting. Lyrics are translated in the liner notes. Also includes several traditional Ethiopian songs with contemporary arrangements. Recommended! —*Ladyslipper*

Aster Aweke / Triple Earth 107
Aside from a couple of voice-and-krar-lute duets as relief, here one of Ethiopia's leading singers mostly fronts an Anglo-Amharic Afrosoul ensemble—no new concept, as owners of *Africa Dances*, let alone *Mahmoud Ahmed*, are aware. It's exhilarating stuff from a very fine vocalist. —*John Storm Roberts, Original Music*

Seleshe Damessae

Tesfaye: Vocal & String Music of Ethiopia / 1986 / Music of the World 107
Seleshe Damessae, an accomplished singer and musician from Ethiopia, offers a wonderful selection of compositions rendered in complex vocal stylings and sung in Amharic, his native language. He accompanies himself on the krar, a six-string lyre, which dates back to the ancient civilizations of the Nile. —*Music of the World*

Ethio Stars & Tukul Band

Ethio Stars/Tukul Band / Piranha 44
Far too little of the great soul-based modern Ethiopian sound is available in the West, and much of what's available is often crossover. So double yippee for a CD that would have won the JSR Seal of Excellence anyway on quality alone. There's two bands, one hardcore Cushitic soul, the other using a more adventurous version of the same sound with added traditional instruments. It's an absolute Must Buy! —*John Storm Roberts, Original Music*

Mindanoo Mistiru

○ **Mindanoo Mistiru, Vol. 1** / Lyrichord 7243
A good introduction. Avoids restrictive definitions and offers contemporary barroom music for accordion and percussion as well as some of Africa's most ancient idioms. —*John Storm Roberts*

Ethiopia Collection

Golden Seventies, The / Blue Silver 002
Transfixed by US soul music, the Ethiopians transformed it into a vividly African sound. James Brown is a presence, but Ethiopia's mystical, minor-key edge accentuates the rawness of the groove. Aweke, Ashete, and the Wallias Band are hot here and their musical mixing as it should be! —*Carl Hoyt, Original Music*

○ **Jewish Liturgies of Ethiopia** / Inedit 260013
Though their own legends make the Falasha, or Ethiopian Jews, descendants of the Queen of Sheba, the oldest solid records go back to the 14th century AD, and the oldest scholarly guesstimate I've seen goes to the 4th. Whatever, their liturgical music is very different from both local secular forms and Ethiopian Orthodox Christian liturgy. Here are parts of Sabbath offices, wedding prayers, and circumcision songs. —*John Storm Roberts*

○ **Music of Ethiopia, Vol. 3** / Barenreiter Musicaphon 2314
The baganna, the magnificent "harp of David," here on *Music of Ethiopia—Three Chordophone Traditions*, plays its essential role as accompaniment to songs of meditation. The krar, known as the devil's instrument, is used to accompany love and topical songs. The masinqo, a spike fiddle of a type common in Africa, as well as the Middle East and the Balkans, is heard in music for wed-

dings and other social gatherings. All are played on this album by exceptional musicians. —*John Storm Roberts*

Gambia

Alhaji Bai Konte

b. 1920, West Gambia, **d.** 1983
Kora / Kora
Traditional kora player from the Gambia, an elder of the West African pop generation, and father of Dembo Konte. —*Myles Boisen*

○ **Kora Melodies—Music from Gambia, West Africa** / 1979 / Rounder 5001
This 14-cut disc features everything from a 58-second fragment "Tuning Kora" to a spectacular six-minute plus triumph "Cedo." During the disc, he demonstrates the properties, appeal and charm of the kora, playing with power, passion, charm, strength and integrity, sometimes going through uptempo pieces that accent his speed, other times probing and exploring an ancient number in a manner that showcases his knowledge of and reverence for vintage African music, a reverence that makes listening to this a stunning experience. —*Ron Wynn*

Dembo Konte

Baa Toto / World Records 005
Konte and Jobarteh, a younger generation of the family of the great Alhaji Bai Konte, have appeared on several similar British recordings. The performances here are as good as any I have heard by this duo, and certainly the price is right. The notes, on the other hand, are not particularly impressive. —*John Storm Roberts, Original Music*

○ **Jali Roll** / 1990 / World Circuit 5020
In their own right, these masters of the West African kora harp captivate. Backed by bass, drum, guitars, and accordion, courtesy of the 3 Mustaphas 3, they achieve a new dimension without sacrificing subtleties. Many brilliant, beautiful moments with Kausa Kuyateh. —*Bob Tarte*

Foday Musa Suso

Vocals
Foday Musa Suso is a master musician with one foot on the dance floor and one foot in the villages of Africa. Suso was born in Gambia to a distinguished family of griots (musician storytellers) that can trace his line back almost a thousand years. He has been tireless in his efforts to spread African music and culture to all corners of the globe. On his solo recordings, and as a member of his Mandingo Griot Society, he plays traditional African folk music. On his Mandingo records he leads an electro funk fusion band that can rock the house with the best rap, funk, and house groups. He's played extensively with Herbie Hancock (that's his voice on "Rockit") and frequently collaborates with Bill Laswell on various Afro-fusion experiments. —*J. Poet*

○ **Hand Power** / 1969 / Flying Fish 70318
A solo album of traditional Gambian acoustic music. —*J. Poet*

The Dreamtime / 1969 / Creative Music Prod. 3001
On *The Dreamtime* he presents us with a selection of traditional vocal and instrumental tunes, characterized by lively dancing kora patterns played over solid bass lines, with much use of repetition, creating an almost hypnotic effect. On some pieces he multitracks himself, adding, in places, the raspy voice of the nyanyery (a one-string violin), talking drums, kalimba (thumb piano) and karinyan (metal scraper). The kora provides a delightful alternative to more familiar stringed instruments. —*Backroads Music / Heartbeats*

New World Power / 1981 / Axiom 422-846853
On this album Suso continues his Afro-funk experiments with Bill Laswell and other members of New York's Downtown Art/Rock Mafia. —*J. Poet*

Ghana

Alhaji Ibrahim Abdulai

Master Drummers of Dagbon, Vol. 1 (Northern Ghana) / 1987 / Rounder 5016
Led by Alhaji Ibrahim Abdulai, the Master Drummers of Dagbon's playing over 20 selections and 75-plus minutes never wavers in intensity, appeal, or depth. You hear unison rhythms and spectacular individual playing as well as amazing drum progressions and movements; the songs are designed to support traditional dances, and the mood ranges from teeming to lush, aggressive to enticing. —*Ron Wynn*

Master Drummers of Dagbon, Vol. 2 / 1988 / Rounder 5046
Here's another 16 performances by the incendiary troupe from Northern Ghana, the Master Drummers of Dagbon. Once more, the ensemble turns their drumming into a hypnotic, enchanting rhythm ceremony, creating waves of shimmering, exploding beats, accents and patterns. What's so impressive about the Master Drummers, besides their obvious abilities, is the way melodic and harmonic developments emerge from what seems like an obsession with rhythm. Their seamless lines, rippling phrases and non-stop propulsive energy key these songs, which, like the previous CD's numbers, are tied to traditional dances, celebrations and expressions of worship and joy. It's hard to imagine even the most ardent non-world music fan not being attracted to the Master Drummers' material; it's simply irresistible. —*Ron Wynn*

Mustapha Tettey Addy

Drums, dance. Part of a drumming family, Ghana's Mustapha Tettey Addy eventually became its most famous member. He was initiated into ritual drumming and dancing by his father, a fetish priest. Addy became 'dadefoiakye,' the head of the ritual drummers, after his father's death. He was a full-time member of the Ghana Dance Ensemble during the '60s, and also loosely associated with the Institute of African Studies at the University of Ghana. Widespread travels throughout West Africa in the early '70s alerted Addy to other styles and techniques, which he utilized when he formed his group Ehimono in '74. Addy toured Europe several times in the '70s, then returned there in the '80s, this time mainly as a teacher. A master of complex, intricate and intense rhythms, Addy's superb '70s and '80s recordings *Master Drummer Vol. 1* and *Master Drummer Vol. 2* are essential, while his 1990 release *Come and Drum* with his son Abdul Rahman Kpany Addy and two German musicians, aims at simplifying and breaking down tricky rhythms without destroying the music's essence. —*Ron Wynn*

○ **Master Drummer from Ghana** / Lyrichord 7250
Addy, a Ga from Accra, spent many years learning the major traditions of other groups as well as such recent developments as kpanlogo, a style developed by Accra teenagers in the '60s. Good technical quality; adequate notes. —*John Storm Roberts*

Obo Addy

Drummer, composer / Worldbeat
Obo Addy may be the most widely traveled member of this celebrated Ghanian family. He began his professional career in Joe Kelly's band in 1954, learning to play Western music for highlife audiences in hotels and nightclubs. Addy switched groups in 1959, becoming a member of the Builder's Brigade Band, one of Kwame Nkrumah's state ensembles. He toured the country extensively, and two years later was invited to join the Farmer's Council of Ghana. Addy became the Farmers' Band's deputy leader by 1962. After working briefly with the Ghana Broadcasting Band, Addy decided he wanted to save and publicize vintage drum and dance traditions. He took a job at the Arts Council, honed his compositional skills and continued exploring fusions of the old and the new. Addy helped form Anansi Krumian Soundz, a band that exclusively used traditional instruments. In 1972 Addy joined with his brothers to form Obuade (Ancient), which received worldwide acclaim and popularity. Obo Addy spun off his own band in 1981, Kukrundu, cutting two albums in '83 and '84 on the Avocet label. He issued two albums in '86, one spotlighting traditional Ghanian music on cassette, the other a contemporary effort titled *African-American*. With inter-est growing in traditional African material, Obo Addy gained more stature and fame as the '80s ended. He formed a smaller band in '88 Okropong. —*Ron Wynn*

Okropong / Earthbeat! 2500
On *Okropong* he presents several traditional songs sung in a vigorous call and response style to the accompaniment of many African hand drums and gongo bells. Also included are two original instrumentals featuring lively melodies played on a soft-toned wooden xylophone. Obo Addy multi-tracks himself to create his complex drum orchestra and chorus, playing all the instruments on all but one cut on this dynamic and highly rhythmic album. —*Backroads Music / Heartbeats*

○ **Let Me Play My Drums** / Burnside 10
When it comes to spectacular drumming and dance rhythms—and the horn arrangements—Obo Addy and Kukrudu are definitely open for business. If you're into drumming and haven't yet discovered Addy, check this out. —*John Baxter, Option*

The African Brothers Band

Ghana's African Brothers Band has thrived and survived through three decades of social and political transition and turmoil throughout their homeland. They have reigned supreme atop the highlife hierarchy almost since their inception. They're currently led by Nana Kwame Ampadu the Third, and record at Ambassador studios in Kumasi. A couple of years ago, they did their first shows in England since 1984. The African Brothers emerged as superstars in 1967, with their first hit "Ebi Tie Ye." They were part of the new highlife sound that fused rock and reggae bits into a tight, multiple guitar front line, accenting lyricist and leader Nana Ampadu's exhaustive, metaphor-driven sermons drawn from stories of the animal kingdom. They have several other releases available on the international market, plus many other cassette-only items not sold outside Ghana. —*Ron Wynn*

○ **Me Poma** / 1984 / Rounder 5018
The African Brothers band has been around a while now—its leader, Nana Ampadu, was a pioneer in developing a local Afrobeat which he calls Afrohili. Soul-funk touches in the rhythm section, classic sweet-sour highlife vocals, guitars and horns, some tasty though unobtrusive organ—a good example of what's happening in a style that's been strangely ignored lately. —*John Storm Roberts*

Eric Agyeman

Highlife Safari / Stern's 3002
Ghanaian pop music has always been on the softer end of the spectrum—the harmonies are sweet, the horns fat, and the synth, I'm sorry to say, saccharine. However, this 1979 recording is a real gap-filler of a CD. Agyeman began to inject Zairian influences into his guitar playing with these songs, though without the attack of soukous and its cousins. Still, it's about time we get to hear classics from this era. —*Carl Hoyt, Original Music*

A.B. Crentsil

Moses / 1982 / African Music 11
Aided by a denunciation from the Christian Council of Ghana, *Moses* brought Crentsil new stardom after his career slumped somewhat when the Sweet Talks collapsed. —*John Storm Roberts*

Kafo Mpo Dzidzi / 1983 / Dymtex 8801
Crentsil's 1982 *Moses* with the Ahenfo Band brought him new stardom after something of a slump and established him as one of highlife's more imaginative talents. Despite a couple of cuts in English, the recent *Kafo Mpo Dzidzi*, recorded in the US, is typical of contemporary highlife in its keyboards, horn lines, and general mix of sophistication and strong local sound. —*John Storm Roberts*

○ **Reminiscin' in Tempo** / 1991 / African Music 301
A.B. Crentsil & the Sweet Talks were major figures in the highlife renaissance of the '70s. This 1978 "Hollywood Highlife Party" recording, the band's last, is one of the best '70s highlife offerings I know. —*John Storm Roberts*

Kakraba Lobi

Xylophone / Neo-traditional
Kakraba Lobi, who comes from a family of xylophonic virtuosi, is one of a large and growing number of African musicians who ex-

pand traditional music from within besides teaching it at university level. —*David L. Mayers*

Xylophone Player from Ghana / Tangent 130
On this deeply satisfying recording, Lobi plays mostly his own compositions and arrangements of traditional material, supported by percussionist Mustapha Tettey Addy. —*David L. Mayers*

E. T. Mensah & Tempos Dance Band (Emmanuel Tetteh Mensah)

b. 1919, Ussher Town, Accra, Ghana
Group
Mensah has had the longest reign of any of African music's self-crowned kings. The King of Highlife made his first records in 1952 and was an instant success with his Latin and Caribbean-inspired danceband style. He played in England in 1953 and toured West Africa steadily in the '50s and '60s. In the '70s, the sweet and swinging sounds of highlife were drowned out by a profusion of new styles, but Mensah's influence was still strongly felt. —*Myles Boisen*

○ **All for You** / 1986 / Retro 01
This highlife pioneer from Ghana merged the rhythms of calypso, Latin, and local tradition to establish the first African supergroup. —*J. Poet*

Day by Day / 1987 / Retro 02
Here is another stunning collection from Mensah and the Tempos. —*J. Poet*

Oboade

○ **Kpanlogo Party** / Lyrichord 7251
Contrary to the notions of many Westerners, African percussion musics are by no means all traditional. Kpanlogo, which surfaced in Accra during the '60s, was a new music created by teenagers hanging out, and it met the usual disapproving reaction from the older generation. Oboade, a family group led by master drummer Mustapha Tettey Addy, played it superbly. —*John Storm Roberts*

Ghana Collection

Shambros/Melody Aces/Black Santiagos / Original 026
Benin-born trumpeter De Souza's hot and soloist-heavy·groups were on the leading edge of Accra's 1960s highlife golden age. With the Black Santiagos, he introduced Congolese music in the mid 1960s, launched Afro-beat in Ghana around 1968, and took in twist, shake, and anything else passingly hip, along with a steady flow of your standard great highlife numbers. —*John Storm Roberts, Original Music*

○ **Giants of Danceband Highlife** / 1990 / Original Music 11
In their palmy days, E.T. Mensah's '50s Tempos were the most influential band in West Africa. Here are four of their most charming early hits. The Ramblers—one of the hottest bands of the '60s—and the Uhurus were both jazz-oriented. The Ramblers stuck to straightahead dance music; Uhuru experimented, with phenomenal results, in the early '70s. This was the cutting edge of highlife in its time, and its extinction was a real loss. —*John Storm Roberts*

Ancient Ceremonies: Songs & Dance Music / Nonesuch 72082
A Nonesuch re-release of music recorded in the '70s and the best general introduction to Ghanian traditional music that I've met, in that there's variety in singing styles, types of music, and instrumentation, along with excellent playing and very fine recording quality. —*John Storm Roberts*

○ **Music of the Northern Tribes** / Lyrichord 7321
Reissue of an admirable mid '70s set of recordings by ethnic groups from Ghana's northern savannah. Much of this music shows the influence of Islam in its tight tone and vocal shake. There's a lot of variety here in styles and instrumentation (the Dagarti, for example, are noted xylophonists), and a sharp contrast with the better-known sounds of the southern forests. —*John Storm Roberts*

Guinea

Balla Et Ses Balladins

Balla Et Ses Balladins / Popular African Music 302
I had never heard of this incredible band before this CD arrived—in tone I would have to say they're an interesting mix of Bembeya Jazz and Orch. Baobab. The Balladins are yet another one of the amazing Guinean National Bands that were sadly broken up in the '80s as the economy went south. As if all this background wasn't enough, included here are Kante Manfila, Famoro Kouyate, the slinkiest guitar work in the world and even some solo trombone! Even though I say it quietly, they're better than Baobab—don't pass this up! —*Carl Hoyt, Original Music*

Bembeya Jazz National

Regard Sur le Passé / Syliphone 42064
A CD from 1982, a time when Guinean nationalism was in full swing and the restrictions of the hard-line government had been slightly relaxed. The music was not so much a product as an expression of cultural identity, mixing the ever-present Cubanisms with a very strong traditional element. It makes the band at this period less smooth and more emotive, with an undisguised fervor for the re-emerging Africanism of the time. Balafon and guitar, horns and percussion—by now a familiar blend, but never less than fresh and new (including some nasty funk and a mind-blowing neo-Robert Fripp guitar solo!). —*Carl Hoyt, Original Music*

○ **Wa Kele** / Sonodisc 8460
Bembeya Jazz National, one of the oldest and greatest of all Sahelian bands, was the inspiration for more famous groups (Les Ambassadeurs among them). Alas, none of their superb music from the '70s is currently available, but the '80s material is almost as good. Like any working band, they keep up with the trends (at times too much so). But they're still one of the freshest of all Sahelian bands despite the commercial pressures that have so damaged Youssou N'Dour and other big names. Instead of hunting transitory international glory, they've stuck to their glorious mix of swooping Afro-funk and hot Afro-Cuban, sparked by the other-worldly guitar of Sekou "Diamond Fingers" Diabate. —*John Storm Roberts*

Sekouba Diabate

Le Destin / Popular African Music 202
Not Sekou "Diamond Fingers" Diabate, but very close. Sekouba was a young singer with Bembeya Jazz when the collapse of Guinea's Marxist government brought the dissolution of that fabulous state-sponsored band. As the money dried up the instruments disappeared, and the musicians went back to kora, balafon and n'goni. The result is the same languid groove and sleepy funk without a horn section (though a very tasteful synth drum is used). —*Carl Hoyt, Original Music*

Sona Diabate

Vocals, guitar / Sahelian pop
Sona Diabate comes from an extensive family of hereditary griot musicians from Guinea that includes many of the biggest names in traditional West African music. She is a particularly gifted singer who, as part of her occupation, must memorize vast amounts of oral history and compose "praise songs" to important figures and benefactors. She has also performed as a singer and guitarist with the band Les Amazones de Guinea. —*Myles Boisen*

○ **Girls of Guinea** / 1988 / Shanachie 65007
Two female vocalists and a pair of intertwining acoustic guitars weave in and out of the deep recesses of the heart in an urgent appeal to traditional values. Recorded live to two-track tape with acoustic guitar backing by guitar master Sekou Diabate and background singing from Les Amazones, this stirring set of vaguely Western-sounding songs bristles with passion and immediacy. —*Bob Tarte & Myles Boisen*

Fatala

Gongoma Times / Real World 2331
This is a reissue of a 1988 WOMAD recording of this neo-traditional ensemble that included balafon but laid particular emphasis on percussion. The performance is admirable, the singing slightly under-recorded. A splendid plus is leader Yacouba Camara's harmonica. It's a rarely recorded instrument in African rural music, and Camara's playing makes that a major mystery. —*John Storm Roberts, Original Music*

Jali Musa Jawara (Diawara)

b. Northern Guinea

Vocals, harp, guitar / Sahelian pop

Jali Musa Jawara, the half-brother of African pop star Mory Kante, performs traditional Manding songs of West Africa, praising important citizens and delivering well-intentioned advice. His glittering kora (multi-stringed gourd harp) is the centerpiece of gentle folk groups that include the marimba-like balafon, guitar, and a characteristic West African vocal chorus. —*Myles Boisen*

Soubindoor / 1988 / Mango 9832

Guinean pop musician Jawara returns to his roots with a folk ensemble built around kora (Mandikan harp), balafon (marimba), guitar, and soaring high-energy vocals. —*Bob Tarte*

☆ **Yasimika** / May 1991 / Hannibal 1355

This new US release was first issued in France in 1983. Two koras, a balafon, and a splendid female chorus backing Jawara's lead make for a deserved bestseller among Africans in France. This is contemporary-traditional Mandingo music, purely and wonderfully performed and admirably recorded. A treasure, in fact. —*John Storm Roberts*

Kouyate Sory Kandia

Kandia, Kouyate Sory / Sonodisc 6814

Singer/kora-player Kandia was a major artist in the neo-traditional vein who died far too young. As this rare 1977 recording shows, he was a superlative singer with a power and subtlety well set off by a large chorus and fine flute, fiddle, and balafon, as well as his own kora. Technically only adequate, musically a glory. Notes in French only. —*John Storm Roberts, Original Music*

Guinea Collection

Musics of Fouta-Djalon / Playasound 65028

Fouta-Djalon, in North Guinea, is home to groups with a strong griot tradition. This collection includes string and flute ensembles, a rare type of transverse flute, balafon, and of course various forms of song. —*David L. Mayers*

Nyamakalas from Futa Jalon, The / Buda 925302

The Nyamakalas are representatives of the most recent incarnations of ancient forms of expression. This recording was made in November of 1991 as part of the National Direction of Culture project. In conjunction with this project, there is an ethnological study and a documentary film being made. The sound quality is extra special, as are the notes and photographs. In between the cuts are sounds of roosters, children, the ocean, and other outdoor sounds. There are mostly traditional instruments, but also occasional electric guitar and accordion. I find the singing particularly intimate, locally rooted, but Muslim influenced. —*Raissa St. Pierre, Original Music*

Ivory Coast

Aicha Kone

Poro Dance / Tamaris 92008

Kone, a local star since the 1970s, has a warm voice à la Zaire's Mpongo Love and Togo's Bella Bellow, but she's emphatically her own woman. Unlike most Ivorians, she sings in Bambara—not French—to backings that span charming acoustic guitar, punchy soukous and quirky kwela. She was virtually ignored in the West for decades but produced two CDs in a year—about time, too! —*John Storm Roberts, Original Music*

Kenya

Maulidi and Musical Party

○ **Mombasa Wedding Special** / 1990 / Globestyle 058

Charming urban-Kenyan version of Swahili taarab, so freewheeling and laidback it's a wonder the music doesn't whirl apart. Recorded live at a women-only wedding celebration. —*Bob Tarte*

Daniel Owino Misiani

Guitar / Bengal

D.O. Misiani, the king of Kenya's "Benga" pop music, is an energetic and varied guitarist. His band Shirati Jazz is also featured on *The Nairobi Beat* (Rounder 5030) with other important Benga groups, and it's good to see him getting his due in the world music explosion of the '80s. —*Myles Boisen*

☆ **Benga Blast** / 1990 / Atlantic 91314

This features classic dance music from this Kenyan pioneer. Wild guitar! —*Myles Boisen*

○ **Shirati Jazz** / Globestyle 046

The Shirati Jazz release is a really outstanding collection of the benga heavies' early recordings, with founder Misiani. There's no date given here, but we'd guess mid '70s from the sound. The album consists of yet more recordings from a fine and influential band, these recently made. —*John Storm Roberts*

Orchestra Virunga

Group / Soukous

Samba Mapangala left Zaire and settled in Kenya in the late '70s. He first led a soukous band of Zairian musicians called Les Kinois (Kinshasa Boys). When they broke up, he looked for local talent and formed Virunga, a group that takes soukous and adds Kenya's benga beat, as well as Western rock and blues influences. —*J. Poet*

○ **Virunga Volcano** / 1990 / Earthworks 91408

This disc, with Samba Mapangala, compiles the band's early hits including "Malako," the tune that made them famous. —*J. Poet*

Feet on Fire / 1991 / Stern's Africa 1036

At the end of Virunga's sold out European tour the band went into a London studio to document their sound, ca. 1991. The band now carries a hard hitting horn section, but their sound remains true to their African roots. —*J. Poet*

Kenya Collection

☆ **Guitar Paradise of East Africa** / 1990 / Earthworks 2420

The "other" guitar sound of Africa. Rootsier than soukous—with an emphasis on melody to match the propulsive rhythms—benga dance music from Kenya explodes in a sweet, energy-laden combination of fraternal vocal harmonies and chiming electric guitars. —*Bob Tarte*

○ **Kenya Dance Mania** / 1991 / Earthworks 2423

A retrospective of rhumba and benga-influenced mega-hits recorded during Nairobi's heyday as a trendsetting recording center in the late '70s and early '80s. Astonishing guitar breakouts, bottomless bass lines, and homespun homilies vie for center stage. —*Bob Tarte*

○ **Nairobi Sound** / 1993 / Original Music 023

This is still the only release covering the '60s pre-benga electric guitar, and the acoustic material fills the gap between Kenya Dry and the more recent British releases. Both the acoustic and electric sounds back then—before soukous took over the world—were strongly local and idiosyncratic, and this set offers a side of each (including the original version of "Malaika," which Miriam Makeba once turned into an international hit). —*John Storm Roberts*

○ **Songs the Swahili Sing** / 1994 / Original Music 024

The first compilation of the Muslim music of East Africa's coast. With Indian film music and occasional rock and salsa influences grafted onto its basic Afro-Arab stock, this is a totally unexpected monument to the diversity of the Black experience. This, incidentally, was the release that brought taarab to the attention of the outside world, and it's still the most varied introduction, with fine singers male and female in idioms that range from near-Arab to one of the world's most improbable cha cha chas. —*John Storm Roberts*

Madagascar

Rakotofrah

○ **Flute Master of Madagascar** / Globestyle 027

Among the European styles reworked in Africa and the Caribbean was military fife-and-drum music and its civilian pipe-and-tabor equivalent, both of which fit nicely with various African equivalents. This is an enchanting (though awfully short) example of the sort of thing that resulted: a new music with clear European as well as local roots. The results sound very Caribbean—unless you know the older sega of Mauritius, Reunion, and the Seychelles. —*John Storm Roberts*

Rakotozafy

○ **Valiha Malaza** / Globestyle 028
The tube-zither valiha is one of the pinnacles of Malagasy music, typical in its mix of Southeast Asian and African ingredients. This re-release of the '60s recordings of the instrument's best-known master is much the best of Globestyle's Malagasy issues, and a worthy substitute for the vanished Ocora valiha album (which also, incidentally, included cuts by Rakotozafy). —*John Storm Roberts*

Rossy

○ **Island of Ghosts** / 1991 / Real World 91782
Seventeen tracks by Madagascar's most popular musician, originally commissioned for the PBS documentary, "Madagascar: Island of Ghosts." — *Roundup Newsletter*

Madagascar Collection

○ **Madagasikara One** / 1986 / Globestyle
Madagasikara One: Current Traditional Music of Madagascar features the rapid, tumbling accordion styles and the sound of the valiha box-harp that typify the airy music of the Malgasy Republic. Also contains selections by master flutist Rakotofrah and the out-of-place military-band troupe Tsimialona Volambita. —*Bob Tarte*

☆ **Madagasikara Two** / 1986 / Globestyle
Madagasikara Two: Current Popular Music of Madagascar. Island-accented township jive, Trio FA's irresistible accordion jam, and a pair of African outreach cuts by rising star Rossy testify to the richness of island culture. The diversity of material here (and its uniqueness) is impressive. —*Bob Tarte*

Mali

Ambassadeurs Internationaux

☆ **Ambassadeurs Internationaux** / 1984 / Rounder 5013
The Ambassadeurs go back a long way, but the period just after Salif Keita and Kante Manfila had moved the group to Ivory Coast and before they split up was certainly one of their great periods. This fine anthology presents the group at its best, playing for Africans and with none of the hit-hunting encumbrances that made the much-hyped Soro so disappointing. —*John Storm Roberts*

Fanta Damba

○ **Mamadou Magadji** / Esperance 7518
Fanta Damba is a peerless singer in the classical Malian vein, a vocalist of power, restraint, and subtlety with centuries of Afro-Islamic tradition behind her. —*John Storm Roberts*

Maravillas De Mali

Maravillas De Mali / Disco Stock 8060
Here is a very revealing oddity. In 1964 an entire Malian band led by flutist Boncana Manga (a different-drummer who later started a Euro-classical orchestra in Ivory Coast before making a couple of successful popular recordings) went to Cuba to study. This is their graduation recording so to speak, and it certainly suggests where the '70s Malian groups got their Cuban tinge. It is, in fact, largely straight charanga though with enough Africanisms to keep you interested. It's Rarisimo stuff. —*John Storm Roberts*

Zani Diabate

○ **Zani Diabate and the Super Djata Band** / 1988 / Mango 9814
Malian beats roil and boil beneath Diabate's sheets of electric guitar à la Jimi Hendrix, Freddie King, and a touch of the Doors. Psychedelic solo fever resembling nothing else in African music. —*Bob Tarte*

Mory Kante

b. 1950, Kissidougou, Guinea
Vocals / Dance, Sahelian pop
Along with Salif Keita, Mory Kante was an early member of the seminal Rail Band of Bamako, joining as a singer when he was in his teens. After a stint as lead vocalist, he left the band to form his own theatrical troupe, which included dozens of performers and his brother Jali Musa Jawara. In the '80s he became an international pop star, exploring neo-traditional Manding music on the kora, as well as club-ready dance mixes. His "Yeke Yeke" became the biggest-selling African release to hit the European pop charts. —*Myles Boisen*

10 Cola Nuts / 1986 / Barclay 829087
After early success in his native Guinea, Kante moved to Paris where he began making waves with his blend of funk, rock and traditional African sounds. This disc is short (25 minutes), but compelling. —*J. Poet*

○ **Akwaba Beach** / 1987 / Barclay 833119
The first single from *Akwaba Beach*, "Yeke Yeke," was a major European dance hit for Kante in 1987. Dismissed by some for his heavy dance beat, Kante's crossover sound is a perfect way to ease your ears into the joys of African pop. —*J. Poet*

○ **Touma** / 1990 / Mango 9903
A breakthrough release featuring an international band with guest stars Carlos Santana and Ray Phiri, but the unsung heroine is backing vocalist Djanka Diabate, who showers spice on Mory's cool. —*Bob Tarte*

Salif Keita

b. Djoliba
Vocals / Afro-pop
Salif Keita was born in Mali into a family that can trace their roots back to Soundjata Keita, the warrior king who founded the Malian Empire in 1240. Keita was born an albino (a bad omen), and his family frowned upon his choice of a musical career. When he refused to follow a traditional path of study, Salif's father disowned him and he was left to wander the streets of Bamako, Mali's capitol. After years of singing on street corners and in small clubs, Keita landed a job as vocalist for the Super Rail Band, a government-sponsored group that was gaining national fame with their mixture of traditional and Western (especially Cuban) music. Mali is one of the northernmost states in Black Africa, and has always been a cultural melting pot, with Arabic, French, Spanish, and regional ethnic groups contributing to a unique musical and cultural mixture. In the Rail Band, Keita met guitarist Kante Manfila, another musician with an international pop vision, and together they pursued their vision of a Cuban/Zairean/Malian fusion. In 1973, the duo left the Rail Band and joined Les Ambassadeurs Internationaux, where their stylistic hybrid began to earn them an international reputation. As Les Ambassadeurs became more successful, they also became more aware of their roots and, as the Arabic influences of their culture crept back into the music, they developed one of Africa's most unique and hypnotic sounds. In 1987 Keita left the Ambassadeurs to pursue a solo career in Paris. With the cream of that city's African session players, he recorded *Soro*, the international hit that brought him to the attention of Island Records, who now record his music for international distribution. —*J. Poet*

● **The Mansa of Mali . . . A Retrospective** / Mango 162-539937
The 10 cuts on this anthology range from the late '70s "Mandjou," with its stinging guitar riffs, throbbing organ, and gorgeous sax backing to the spectacular "Souareba," in which Keita's vibrant vocals are backed by electric drums, synthesized backing and capably arranged by Francois Breant and Jean Phillippe Rykie, plus "Tenin," from the LP *Ko-yan*. This was produced by Joe Zawinul and included his contributions on keyboards, assistance from the great Antillean bassist Etienne M'Bappe, and appearances by many other African music superstars. The anthology covers Keita's three Mango releases, plus the LP *L'Enfant Lion*. While it's not a substitute for the complete LPs, those unaware of Keita's vocal prowess and mastery will hopefully be persuaded to get the complete package by this fine sampler. —*Ron Wynn*

○ **Soro** / 1987 / Mango 162-539808
The album that propelled Keita into the front ranks of the international scene. —*J. Poet*

Ko-yan / 1989 / Mango 162-539836
A cabaret touch invades this Parisian production, which blends straightahead Afro-pop and punk with lacy electronic ornamentation. —*Bob Tarte*

○ **Amen** / 1991 / Mango 162-539910
Produced by Joe Zawinul (Weather Report), this set is more international in scope, with guest shots by Carlos Santana and Wayne Shorter adding to its commercial appeal. —*J. Poet*

Kante Manfila

○ **Kankan Blues** / 1991 / African Music 201
A stunning record. Ace Afro-Frankfurter Gunter Gretz went to Manfila's hometown of Kankan and recorded him and various relatives, including balafonist Balla Balla. As you'd expect of a family of griots, there's magnificent traditional singing here, along with acoustic and electric guitar and superb balafon. Gretz's notes are both eccentric and very revealing, with a long account of the sundry hazards of field recording. —*John Storm Roberts*

○ **Diniya** / Esperance 8467
I'm ambivalent about Diniya, as about Soro and many other Afro-Parisian productions since the "world music" boom. Not a patch on Manfila's older recordings: far too much hit-hunting paraphernalia, from Synclavier to synth to the usual Afro-zouk horns. Manfila sings beautifully, as do the backup singers, and there are certainly splendid moments. —*John Storm Roberts*

Oumou Sangare

Moussolou / "Women" / 1989 / World Circuit 021
This traditional recording (produced by Ibrahim Sylla, who turned the knobs for Salif Keita's international breakthrough *Soro*) was West Africa's biggest-seller in 1989. Sparkling kora (African harp), driving percussion, and a stunning multi-tracked voice that often recalls an African version of the Shirelles makes this one a winner. —*J. Poet*

Sali Sidibe

Wassoulou Foli / Stems 1047
A 25-year-old star of the youngest Wassoulou generation, Sidibe backs gorgeously classic Malian vocals with instrumentals combining mellow flute and funk keyboards with strongly neo-traditional elements (the notes claim nobody uses as many traditional instruments). It works stunningly—even the heavily soul-funk final cut. —*John Storm Roberts, Original Music*

Ali Farka Toure

African
Often hyped as "the African John Lee Hooker," Ali Farka Toure has a relationship to blues music much deeper than this derivative label would suggest. The blues came to America with the slave trade, on ships loaded in West Africa. Farka Toure's music reclaims these forms by bringing the country blues back to its ancestral home. —*Myles Boisen*

☆ **Ali Farka Toure** / 1988 / Mango 9826
At first blush you think you're hearing American Delta blues— then the Malian-language vocals kick in. Starkly beautiful acoustic guitar with tasty calabash and bongo percussion. —*Bob Tarte*

○ **The River** / Jan. 1990 / Mango 9897
Toure's second release expands his adventuresome blues-based approach, with a harmonica, sax, and native violin beefing up the sound on several cuts. —*Bob Tarte*

African Blues / Feb. 1990 / Shanachie 65002
A compilation of formative import recordings from this West African bluesman. —*Myles Boisen*

○ **Source** / 1991 / Hannibal 1375
African guitarist Ali Farka Toure's previous releases were wonderful mixes of traditional language and rhythms being supported by contemporary concerns, instrumentalists and producers. His most recent session features his working band backing Toure in a series of impassioned, animated tunes that are done in both his native tongue and English. The similarity between Toure's sparse playing and percussive writing and early blues songs has been noted. What also deserves mention is the cohe-

sive qualities his band have and the way his electric and acoustic playing, with its light, frilly air, fills in the spaces underneath his vocals easily. —*Ron Wynn*

Talking Timbuktu / 1993 / World Circuit 1381
The seamless, haunting melodies, enchanting rhythms, and wonderful vocals make this 10-track CD a memorable and exciting project. —*Ron Wynn*

Mauritania

Khalifa Ould Eide with Dimi Mint Abba

○ **Moorish Music from Mauritania** / World Circuit 019
Mauritanian music has been unavailable for so long, this would be an important release even if it were not also an absolutely gorgeous example of the enormously rich brew of Afro-Islamic nexus. The two women singers featured (the country's most famous) sing in a contemporary-traditional idiom like those of Fanta Sacko and other Malians. A total must-have. —*John Storm Roberts*

Mauritius

Jean Claude

Sega
Pat Patoua / Piros Disques 5147
Attractive mainline sega—a pop sound, but a strictly local one. Most of Jean-Claude's numbers have the familiar backwards 6/8 rhythm, but others are underpinned by a more traditional-sounding beat. The backings are basic small-group, with insistent but not aggressive rhythm, and the lead instrument is a feisty electric guitar. Nice stuff! —*John Storm Roberts*

Morocco

Abdelhadi Belkhyat

El-Kamar El-Ahmar / Tichkaphone 05
Belkhyat built high-octane vocals, Egyptian-derived strings setting off 'ud or khanoun interspersions, rubato to the max, an occasional cut with an unnamed woman singer, into a Moroccan sound. No discoid or Euro-pop trimmings, but a sound of great self-assurance and integrity with an odd grandeur and sweep to it. Dazzling, in a word. —*John Storm Roberts, Original Music*

Hassan Erraji

○ **Traditional Arabic Music** / 1991 / Saydisc
Erraji excels on 'ud, darbouka, bandir, ney, and vocals in performances with his trio. —*Linda Kohanov*

Hassan Hakmoun

○ **Gift of the Gnawa** / 1991 / Flying Fish 571
Moroccan musician Hakmoun's compelling vocals and sintar (lute) playing rides the tide of Adam Rudolph's fierce tabla foundation. Joined by Don Cherry's trumpet and Richard Horwitz on ney (flute), they produce an intensely evocative fusion. —*Bob Tarte*

Cheikh Salah

☆ **Arabo-Andalusian Music** / Buda Musique 925092
The late Cheikh Salah led one of the finest modern orchestras, playing North African classical music based on forms brought by refugees from the great music school of Cordoba at the collapse of Muslim Spain. This is pure and authentic style, superbly sung and backed by a small ensemble of local instruments. Dismal notes, short measure for a steep price, but the superb music more than compensates. —*John Storm Roberts*

Morocco Collection

Hadra of the Gnawa of Essaouira / Ocora 560006
The first Western field recording of ritual music from the Afro-Moroccan Gnawa's syncretic religious cults. The performances, backed by the remarkable three-stringed bass guembri and per-

cussion, are less virtuosic than earlier recordings of individual performers, and the recording quality less perfect—but fans of Hassan Makmoun note: these are his roots. —*John Storm Roberts, Original Music*

☆ **Master Musicians of Jajouka (Morocco)** / 1972 / Adelphi 3000
A field recording of hypnotic Moroccan oboe, string, and drum ensembles made famous by Brian Jones (Rolling Stones guitarist). —*Myles Boisen*

○ **Gnawa Music of Marrakesh: Night Spirit Masters** / 1991 / Axiom 9881
Gnawa Music of Marrakesh: Night Spirit Masters—the great lost Led Zeppelin all-acoustic tapes? Naw! Primal rock from Morocco's Gnawa people—used in trance rituals and therapeutic practices—throbs with layered percussion and ecstatic vocals. Could be the authentic roots of a sound heard round the world. Excellent contemporary recording of one of the many traditional Moroccan, drum-based styles. Heavily atmospheric moods. —*Bob Tarte & Myles Boisen*

Rwayes Anthology—Berber Songs and Instrumental Music ... / Inedit 260023 (4)
Rwayes Anthology—Berber Songs and Instrumental Music from the Sous Region is included in a large and highly recommended series from Morocco on the Inedit series of recordings put out in France by the Maison des Cultures du Monde. —*David L. Mayers*

Mozambique

Orchestra Marrabenta Star

○ **Independance** / Piranha 15
Almost the hardest of all African music to find is the Portuguese-influenced idiom of Angola and Mozambique. This is no street music but the country's top band, using local rhythms and elements ranging from South Africa to the US via Youssou N'Dour (with a good dollop of Portuguese here and there). The results are quite varied, and fresh as well as polished. —*John Storm Roberts*

Nigeria

Admiral Dele Abiodun

b. Bendel State, Nigeria
Vocals, guitar / Juju
"Admiral" Dele Abiodun has had a steady music career of approximately 20 years. As a singer, composer, and guitarist, Abiodun is considered to be one of the best juju musicians. He started his music career at a young age dropping out of school and moving to Ghana to study music and to find a job. In Ghana he played the bass for several different highlife bands, but in 1969 he decided to go out on his own and he formed his own band called Sweet Abby and the Tophitters. The year following the formation of the band, Abiodun created a new style and used that in many of his performances. The new style of music that was created is known as Adawa, which in translation means Independent Being. After the introduction of the Adawa style, Abiodun and his band released several LPs and singles. In 1981 Abiodun released the hit album *Beginning of a New Era* and in 1983 he released another hit album titled *Ma Se'Ke*. In more recent times, Abiodun and his band have released two albums almost back to back. In 1985 they released *Confrontation*, which is a mini-LP, and in 1986 they released the record *Oro Ayo* in Nigeria. —*AMG*

Prince of Juju / Shanachie 43032
Abiodun himself says his style is a mix of juju and highlife. That isn't too obvious, except at times in the guitar work, and perhaps in a more driving approach than is the juju norm. But he's the latest big name in Lagos, and it's easy enough to see why from this collection of several of his latest big sellers. —*John Storm Roberts, Original Music*

King Sunny Ade (Sunday Adeniyi)

b. 1946, Oshogbo, Nigeria
Group / Juju
King Sunny Ade was the first modern African musician to "benefit" from the music industry's star-making machinery. In 1982, Ade was signed to Island Records who tried to promote him as

"Africa's Bob Marley." The problem was that Ade's music, a Nigerian style called juju, really requires intensive listening and the uneducated ears of Europe and America just weren't ready for the kind of polyrhythmic percussion that is juju's stock-in-trade. A typical Ade gig presented six guitars each playing different lead lines, seven or more drummer/percussionists in full flight, various horn and keyboard players and several singers and dancers filling the stage. A magnificent spectacle, but one that boggled the minds of people used to a basic four-piece rock band. After pumping millions into Ade's organization, Island Records admitted defeat and dropped Ade in 1984. —*J. Poet*

Master Guitarist Vol.2 / African Songs 8010
Here's early Ade, from his Green Spot days—strongly guitar-oriented and more solidly rooted in the classic juju sound than many of his later work. But already, especially with the second, late-Green Spots-era album, Ade was beginning to stand out, the cool, crystal-clear style starting to move toward his later individuality. At the same time, it was still firmly within what was already becoming a guitar-oriented juju tradition. —*John Storm Roberts, Original Music*

Juju Music / 1982 / Mango 162-539712
The first of Ade's international releases on Mango, the record that made North American and British fans aware of the richness of African music. A classic. —*J. Poet*

○ **Synchro System** / 1983 / Mango 162-539737
High-tech sound and some electronic instruments give this an international appeal. —*Myles Boisen*

Aura / 1984 / Mango 162-539824
This mid '80s recording has studio gloss, but still delivers. Includes harmonica work by Stevie Wonder. —*Myles Boisen*

Live Juju Live / 1988 / Rykodisc 80047
An entire set (70+ minutes) that captures some of the live power of Ade and his band; recorded in 1988. —*J. Poet*

The Return of the Juju King / Mercury 832522
More contemporary grooves from Ade's own label. —*Myles Boisen*

Segun Adewale & His Superstars

b. 1955, Oshogbo, Nigeria
Group / Juju
Adewale was a willing participant in the juju boom of the early '80s, with an eclectic mix of Nigerian and Western styles he dubbed "yo-pop." He never quite made the splash that Obey or King Sunny did, but he produced a couple of exciting, distinctive albums in his heydey. —*Myles Boisen*

Ojo Je / 1988 / Rounder 5019
Adewale's second US release amplifies the juju tradition with heavy rock touches in the guitar work and a heavy, rolling bass-guitar that coexists with the percussion on pretty much even terms. Which, of course, is how the style moves onward—feeding on influences from all over. —*John Storm Roberts, Original Music*

○ **Play for Me** / 1988 / Rounder 5015
Adewale's juju style is less guitar-centered than that of other, more popular Nigerian groups. The vocal harmonies are a major attraction here, as are the tracks in apala style, with just vocals and throbbing drums. Some English lyrics. —*Myles Boisen*

Akanni Animashaun & Apala Group

Group / Apala
Traditional Nigerian drum ensemble. —*Myles Boisen*

☆ **Akanni De Alawiye Orin** / 1984 / Shanachie 43022
A very important introduction to Yoruba percussion. —*Myles Boisen*

Barrister (Sikiru Ayinde)

b. 1948, Lagos, Nigeria
Vocals / Fuji
Sikiru Ayinde, also known as Barrister, started his music career at the age of 10 singing in traditional musical competitions. In 1963 he joined the military, but continued to study music. After his release from the Army, he released three singles, two EPs and several albums. Barrister and his band the Supreme Fuji Commanders played fuji music, which Barrister himself introduced to the music world. —*AMG*

Fuji Garbage / Globestyle 067
Barrister is perhaps the greatest name in fuji, a splendid Yoruba percussion style that surfaced in the mid 1960s. This new recording has the expected wonderful drumming and singing, along with splendidly idiosyncratic pedal steel and synth—an irony, since fuji was in part a reaction against juju's adoption of Western instruments. —*John Storm Roberts, Original Music*

○ **More Fuji Garbage** / 1991 / Globestyle 067
Take Nigerian juju, strip it down to its rhythmic essentials, discarding everything else but atmospheric bursts of Hawaiian guitar and Barrister's incantory voice, and you've got the meanest, leanest sound this side of rap. —*Bob Tarte*

I.K. Dairo (Isaiah Kehinde Dairo)

b. 1930, Offa, Nigeria
Group / Juju
Considered by many to be the "father of juju" for his many innovations, Isaiah Kehinde Dairo was born in Kwara State, Nigeria, in 1931. One story has it that his lifelong love of music stemmed from a drum that his father, a carpenter, made for him in his youth and that accompanied him wherever he went. In early adulthood, Dairo tried earning a living as a barber, a construction worker, a cloth merchant, and with other jobs. Dairo sat in with early juju bands at night, led by musical pioneers Ojoge Daniel and Oladele Oro. In the mid '50s he formed his own group, the ten-member Morning Star Orchestra, which gained fame later as the Blue Spots. Though highlife was the most popular form of band music in West Africa at the time, Dairo and his band released a long succession of influential singles that, by the end of the Nigerian Civil War in 1970, helped establish juju as the premier Nigerian sound. Dairo changed the tenor of juju by introducing the accordion and talking drums to the orchestra and singing in a variety of regional dialects, which widened the rural appeal of the music. When his appeal began to wane at the end of the '70s, he gave up performing, turning first to managing clubs and a hotel in Lagos, then to a ministry in the Cherubim and Seraphim church movement. In 1990 he recorded his first album in 15 years with a re-formed Blue Spots band. —*Bob Tarte*

☆ **Juju Master I.K. Dairo, MBE** / 1990 / Original Music 009

○ **I Remember** / 1991 / Music of the World 212
One of the founding fathers of Nigerian juju returns after a 15-year retirement from the music business. The accordion anchor to his sound is a charming antidote to over-produced, technology-heavy pop. —*Bob Tarte*

○ **The Glory Years** / 1991 / Original Music 009
I.K. Dairo, the most influential juju master ever, created its gorgeous vocal sound by borrowing the harmonies of the local Church of the Cherubim and Seraphim, besides widening its appeal beyond the Yoruba core audience. These are the early '60s recordings that made him the king overnight (and won him the MBE the Beatles also got). Splendid guitar, soaring vocals, great percussion, plus the jaunty accordion playing he also introduced. The major Dutch music magazine called it the "re-release van het jaar" (re-release of the year). Savvy chaps! —*John Storm Roberts*

Fela Anikulapo Kuti

b. 1938
Vocals / Afro-beat
Fela Kuti was born the son of a strict minister father and a mother named Funmilayo, who went on to become one of Nigeria's leading feminists. Fela was a problem child in grammar school, and by the age of 16 he was singing in a highlife band, much to the chagrin of his parents. Upon the death of his father, Fela convinced his mother to send him abroad to study music. He landed in London in 1957 where he studied trumpet, got married, and formed his first band, Koola Lobitos. In 1963, Fela and the band moved back to Nigeria and began experimenting with various stylistic innovations ranging from highlife to jazz to soul. In 1968, after hearing the music of James Brown (through cover versions played by the band of Geraldo Pino from Sierra Leone), Fela added funk to his mixture and called it "Afrobeat." In 1969 he took his band on an extended US tour, where a month's residence in Los Angeles brought him in contact with the Black Panthers and other American Black Nationalist groups. He attended con-

sciousness-raising groups, read widely in Black and African history, and returned to Nigeria with a militant gleam in his eye. Between 1970 and 1977 Fela released over 30 albums of incendiary African agit-pop that took the Nigerian Military government to task for corruption, brutality, and mismanagement. In 1977 the soldiers responded by burning Fela's living quarters and nightclub to the ground; Fela was jailed and tortured. On his release, he continued to make records that made the government squirm as much as they made the common folk dance. As his reputation grew, Fela added more and more musicians and dancers, until his troupe grew to a revue of some 80 people. Although most of his recent music has been rather perfunctory in nature, his '70s classics stood out in the African pop landscape. —*J. Poet*

Volumes 1 & 2 / 1977 / EMI 15983/84
A two-album anthology on EMI (France) of Kuti's Nigerian hits from the early to mid '70s, when he was at the height of his lyrical and musical powers. —*J. Poet*

Army Arrangement (Original version) / 1985 / Celluloid 6109
One of the tunes that got Fela in trouble with Nigeria's military government, a hard-hitting bit of rhythmic agit-pop. This (Celluloid 6615) was also released in an inferior remixed and overdubbed version aimed at the dance club market under the same title on Celluloid 6109. Be sure to read the small print. —*J. Poet*

The Best of Volumes 1 & 2 / Oceana 4104
A nice overview of Kuti's incendiary recordings for the Celluloid label. —*Myles Boisen*

○ **Fela's London Scene** / Makossa
A superb early '70s album of funky Afro-pop, one of his most successful efforts at blending Nigerian music with James Brown-style soul grooves. —*Myles Boisen*

Los Angeles 1969 / Stern's 3005
I have never liked Fela's music, but his African lounge jazz funk throbs with purpose in comparison to the contemporary African lounge jazz funk heard lately. These songs were recorded in 1969, just before he and the band were kicked out of the US, and include a sweet highlife/rumba, somewhat marred by dopey spoken lyrics. If you like Fela, you'll love this. —*John Storm Roberts, Original Music*

The Lijadu Sisters

Group
Kehinde and Taiwo Lijadu are a rarity in the African music scene—liberated twin sisters, who share the spotlight on smooth close harmonies and command a sharp, inventive backing band. —*Myles Boisen*

☆ **Double Trouble** / 1984 / Shanachie 43020
Apala is just one of many Yoruba street-popular styles for voices and percussion. Among the others is a women's equivalent called waka. And waka is the strong local root that makes the Lijadu Sisters' pop style blossom. Not only is their singing rich with its glorious choral sound, but the electric bass line and guitars are equally balanced by Yoruba percussion. All of which makes this a very fine recording, outclassing many of those with more famous names. —*John Storm Roberts*

Prince Nico Mbarga (Nicholas Mbarga)

b. 1950, Abakaliki, Nigeria
Vocals, guitar / Panco
With his band, Rocafil Jazz, Prince Nico scored the biggest African hit ever. His 1976 triumph was a song called "Sweet Mother" and its appeal (13 million copies sold) was largely due to Mbarga's pan-African mix of Cameroonian, Nigerian, and Zairian styles. Despite his multi-instrumental talents and ownership of his own record label, Prince Nico has not been able to sustain his success, and seems fated to go down in history as a one-hit wonder. —*Myles Boisen*

○ **Aki Special** / 1987 / Rounder 11545
Mbarga plays panco, a style from East Nigeria that borrows from reggae, funk, soukous, highlife, and more. This CD collects most of the tracks from Mbarga's two Rounder albums *Sweet Mother* and *Free Education*. —*J. Poet*

○ **Sweet Mother** / Rounder 5007
More Nigerian highlife, this one with touches of music from neighboring Cameroon—not too surprising, since Mbarga himself

and his band of the period were both half-Cameroonian. The title track, a smash in its time, remains a song of great charm. —*John Storm Roberts, Original Music*

Ebenezer Obey

b. 1942, Idogo, Western Region, Nigeria
Vocals, guitar

Chief Commander Ebenezer Obey has been a Nigerian superstar since the '60s, producing dozens of classic juju recordings. His "miliki" style differs from King Sunny Ade's (his only competition as a star bandleader) in its Christian messages and traditional orientation (except for the occasional Euro-disco-tainted release). —*Myles Boisen*

○ **Je Ka Jo** / 1983 / Virgin 2283
His first international release on Virgin UK, a shimmering masterpiece of hypnotic polyrhythmic madness. —*J. Poet*

☆ **Juju Jubilee** / 1985 / Shanachie 43031
Obey and Sunny Ade are the kings of juju, and for 20 years each has tried to top the other by adding more guitars, more singers, pedal steel licks, and so forth. This compilation, Obey's first US release, collects Obey's best-selling singles and album tracks from the early '80s. —*J. Poet*

Get Yer Jujus Out / 1989 / Rykodisc 20111
This is how juju music should be—live and full of "juice." Drum heaven. More than 75 minutes of juju's polyrhythmic madness by one of the genre's inventors. —*Myles Boisen & J. Poet*

Babatunde Olatunji

Percussion / World Fusion, Traditional drumming

Olatunji came to the US in the early '60s to study medicine, but when a group of African expatriates he put together to combat homesickness took off, he became one of the first African musicians to make a major impact on the American market. —*J. Poet*

★ **Drums of Passion** / 1959 / CBS 8210
This set came out on vinyl in 1959 and stayed on the charts for several years, an amazing feat for a record of traditional chanting and drumming. Olatunji's success allegedly sparked John Coltrane's interest in African culture, and the music has lost none of its power over the years. —*J. Poet*

Drums of Passion: The Beat / 1989 / Rykodisc 10107
The Beat, recorded in 1986, is a collection of songs that celebrates the evocative power of the drum, with Olatunji's massive bass drums leading a fiery percussion assault of djembe, agogo, talking drums, and other West African instruments. Impassioned call and response vocals give melodic shape to the intense rhythms, while bass, guitars, guitar synthesizer and some wailing electric lead from guest musician Carlos Santana, add spice to the brew . . Produced by Micky Hart, as part of his World series on the Ryko label, *The Beat* more than delivers on the promise of its title. —*Backroads Music / Heartbeats*

Drums of Passion—Invocation / Rykodisc 10102
The first in a pair of releases that featured percussionist Olatunji showcasing his celebrated multi-rhythmic style in a fresh context. Olatunji was adding African beats to jazz and R&B dates back in the '60s, and does roughly the same thing on this date, fueling careening, expansive tracks that are long enough to incorporate everything from singers to numerous drummers playing traps, congas, shekeres and all other matter of drum. It's teeming, infectious, and among the best blends of traditional and contemporary African and American elements. —*Ron Wynn*

Oriental Brothers

Highlife

○ **Heavy on the Highlife!** / 1991 / Original Music 012
Two of the top bands playing the kicking, East Nigerian brand of highlife. This has developed into a tough style, with ferocious guitar and hoarse, urgent vocals. This album includes both Sir Doctor Warrior and Dan Satch's versions of the band in 70 minutes of music covering 1973-1988. One reviewer called this "the dance groove of the year." If all you have heard is the Ghanian version, you ain't heard nothing. This one would sear steak. —*John Storm Roberts*

Nigeria Collection

○ **Juju Artists: 1930s to '50s** / 1930-1950 / Rounder 5017
The earliest juju music evolved from the West African palmwine guitar style and went through many changes before emerging as a potent world music phenomenon in the hands of Sunny Ade. This is a superb "roots" collection, as well as one of a very few non-import compilations of African 78 rpm recordings. Scholarly notes are a plus. —*Myles Boisen*

○ **Igede of Nigeria** / 1989 / Music of the World 117
To the polytheistic Igede of rural Nigeria, adding Christianity to local cults means that hymns about the crucifixion coexist happily with songs about ancestor worship. Their music suggests that the Igede are a solid community with a rich spiritual life. Similar to New Orleans social clubs which ensure that their fellows get a proper send-off, Igede music ensembles joyfully honor deceased members and their earthly achievements. The music itself is dominated by drumming and small-group choral singing about community duties and Biblical tales. Igede speech influences the rhythm and melody lines, with musicians reproducing its tonal patterns on talking slit-drums, antelope horns, clay pots, and a variety of rattles and bells. The 16 tracks included here add up to about 50 minutes of the cultural life of one African community. Well recorded, good notes. —*Tom Smith, Roundup Newsletter*

○ **Yoruba Street Percussion** / 1992 / Original Music 16
The true stars of West Nigerian pop music are the percussionists, who mix Islamic singing, local drumming, and Afro-Cuban feedback in endless permutations of voices and drums. Here are five different styles, all 20th century, all true street music, all different, all recorded for the local market in the '60s. Percussive offshoots of juju are joined by very early fuji, apala, sakara, the Latin-tinged agidigbo, and waka, the women's music. —*John Storm Roberts*

Benues—Rise up Africa / World 007
The Tiv of Benue State are a highly musical people whose culture is unknown outside Nigeria (despite Charles Keil's excellent book *Tiv Song*). The music here is for voices, percussion, and the swange shawm, and is essentially traditional material performed by a largely young group. The notes give some background and track detail, but not where it was recorded. —*David L. Mayers*

Senegal

Pascal Diatta

○ **Simnade** / Rogue 2017
An outstanding recording by a fine woman singer and a man who developed his own acoustic guitar style, avoiding any conscious influence from outside. (Unconscious influences, of course, are a different issue.) This is the real thing, by a local hero of the southern Casamance recorded (extremely well) on location. Altogether exceptional acoustic guitar, and more evidence that African acoustic guitar is alive and highly creative, even if the local record industries have blinders. —*John Storm Roberts*

Etoile de Dakar

Etoile De Dakar Vol. 2: Thiapatholy / Sterns 3006
Youssou N'Dour and friends, vintage 1980, show just how to update African music with non-African elements for modern audiences without stripping it of any of its essential Africanness. The rhythm is a beefy Cuban-derived slink, with juicy dynamic changes and gorgeous solos which provide a perfect accompaniment to N'Dour's voice. —*Carl Hoyt, Original Music*

Nahawa Doumbia

○ **Didadi** / Shanachie 64015
Fine album from a young female vocalist. Her first album has a somewhat over-hip backing in places, but mostly it works well, and Doumbia herself is gorgeous. —*John Storm Roberts*

Djimo Kouyate

West African Kora Music / 1983 / Music of the World 101
The kora is a 21-string harp from West Africa played by oral historians, who pass on their traditions from generation to genera-

tion. Djimo Kouyate from Senegal sings and plays kora and drums on this recording. "His playing is gentle, the sounds haunting, and the final effect vital and original" *New York Times.* — *Music of the World*

Ismael Lo

Sahelian

○ **Ismael Lo** / 1992 / Mango 162-539919
Moody guitar finger-picking and Dylanesque harmonica playing kick off this attractive pop amalgam of American and Manding folk styles, which untimately shifts into straightahead mbalax. — *Bob Tarte*

Baaba Maal

Vocals / Sahelian
One of the most accomplished performers in the high-pitched vocal tradition of West Africa, Senegal's Baaba Maal is also one of his country's biggest international stars, right up there with Youssou N'Dour. —*Myles Boisen*

☆ **Baaba Maal, Mansour Seck & Djam Leelii** / 1989 / Mango 9840
Baaba Maal and Mansour (Thione) Seck, two of Senegal's biggest pop stars, return to their roots (and the roots of the blues, from the sound of it) on this beautifully hypnotic picking session, which also features Djam Leelii. Two guitars, accented by a bit of African percussion and some tasty electric fills by Aziz Dieng, produce pure magic. —*J. Poet*

Baayo / 1991 / Mango 9907
Baayo is a superlative effort. It shouldn't be missed by anyone interested in new African talent. Translations are provided. — *Roundup Newsletter*

○ **Wango** / Syllart 8348
Senegal's Maal borrows from reggae, funk, and Tuculeur traditions for his take on international pop. *Wango* is one of his strongest efforts. —*J. Poet*

Djam Leelii / Mango 9840
This splendid recording combines some cuts from a semi-legendary two-acoustic-guitar cassette with some rediscovered tracks by an early version of his electric band. Both are magnificent, and the contrast of this often stark sound is a fine contrast with the Sona Diabate album listed under Guinea. —*John Storm Roberts, Original Music*

Youssou N'Dour

b. 1959, Dakar, Senegal
Vocals, drums / Sengalese
N'Dour was born in Senegal to musician parents, and was performing ceremonial music at circumcisions and baptisms before he was a teen. His first single, "M'Ba," was released before his 14th birthday, and by 16 he was the featured vocalist with the Star Band. In 1977 he left the Star Band with six other musicians to form Etoile de Dakar. Their first record, *Xalis Money*, was a major hit, earning them enough money to move to Paris, where N'Dour reorganized them as Super Etoile de Dakar in 1979. After seeing a concert by Toure Kunda in 1981, N'Dour decided to combine more international rhythms—reggae, funk, soca—into his traditional mbalax style. His early '80s albums for Virgin International (*Set*, *Immiges*, *The Lion*) and high-profile collaborations with Peter Gabriel cemented N'Dour's place as *the* African singer to watch in the '90s. —*J. Poet*

Djamil / Celluloid 4625
Djamil is a collection of previously unreleased cuts from 1984 and 1985. On one level, you know what to expect. But most of the numbers here are less synthesized, more straightforward—and at the same time quite rich, with excellent horns as well as the usual very individual singing. —*John Storm Roberts, Original Music*

Immigres / 1988 / Earthworks 91020
Senegalese hard rock. This is the album that got Peter Gabriel hooked on African Music. —*J. Poet*

The Lion / 1989 / Virgin 91253
N'Dour's evocative tenor shows an amazing range. He'll moan, shriek, hum, chant, speak, or run a sax-link scat improvisation up and down the scale to make his point, and while the effect is always stunning, his vocal improvisations owe much to Arabic mu-

sic and it can sound slightly alien to most ears weaned on rock. — *J. Poet, Rock & Roll Disc.*

☆ **Set** / 1990 / Virgin 91426
The title tune became the anthem of Senegalese youth in 1990. This is the first album N'Dour hasn't re-recorded for the international market. It's very African, and his best recorded work to date. —*J. Poet*

Eyes Open / 1992 / 40 Acres & A Mule 48714
N'Dour's ongoing quest for a truly global African pop spurs his smoothest—you might say most homogenized—disc yet, one that basks in assimilation and transformation. He is becoming to mbalax what Milton Nascimento is to Brazilian, which means a gain in sophistication but a certain loss of directness. —*Bob Tarte*

Orchestre Baobab

○ **Pirate's Choice** / 1982 / World Circuit 014
Too many current releases are hit-hunting hybrids truly deserving of the vile "Afro-pop" label, which overshadow the superb music made in Africa by Africans for Africans. This charming recording from 1982 is the real thing, driving, delicate, and wholly African. It is to much of the Afro-Parisian stuff on the market as fresh-squeezed orange juice is to lukewarm Kool-aid. — *John Storm Roberts*

Omar Pene / Super Diamono

Fari / Sterns 1051
Diamono was mixing Sahelian vocals and rhythms with electronics and jazz-funk out of conviction long before hit-hunting or zouk horns became a vogue. Once again the result is music with passion and integrity and quirkiness, hugely enhanced by Pene's compelling vocals, all low-key Angst. This has always been an under-rated band. —*John Storm Roberts, Original Music*

Toure Kunda

Group / Sengalese, Djabdong
Toure Kunda was formed in Senegal by Amadou Tilo Toure to provide singing and drumming accompaniment to the djabadong ceremonies of their native region. To some, djabadong sounds much like reggae, so when Amadou Tilo and his three brothers moved to Paris in the '70s, it seemed natural for them to experiment with a djabadong/reggae fusion. As their popularity increased, the brothers Toure added electric guitars, keys, and more percussion, finally hiring on more musicians from Africa and the French Caribbean. After the death of Amadou Tilo the band reorganized and went on to become one of the top commercial attractions in France with their winning mix of reggae, rock, funk, and traditional Senegalese rhythms. —*J. Poet*

Casamance au Clair de Lune / 1984 / Celluloid 6102
An acoustic set of traditional tunes from Senegal. —*J. Poet*

○ **Live** / 1984 / Celluloid 6710/11
One of the few live albums that lives up to its name, worth its hefty import (French) price. All their early hits in extended versions recorded before an adoring crowd that pushes the musicians to their limits. Also available as a single CD. —*J. Poet*

○ **1983-1884** / 1985 / Celluloid 6781
A CD compilation that contains most of *Amado Tilo* and *Casamance au Clair de Lune*. —*J. Poet*

○ **E'mma Africa** / 1985 / Celluloid 6129
The first hit album from the brothers Toure includes "E'mma," one of the most irresistible of African pop tunes. —*J. Poet*

Karadindi / 1989 / Celluloid 6137
Good African pop, with growing rock and funk influences. Lots of catchy, danceable hits. —*J. Poet*

○ **Salam** / 1990 / Trama 710321
The brothers Toure still use traditional material, but there's more funk and a more commercial edge to the production in evidence; very user-friendly to non-African ears. An import recording on the French label Trama. —*J. Poet*

Senegal Collection

Musique Des Peul Et Des Tenda / Ocora 560043
Presenting the music of five groups in one region of southern Senegal near the Guinean border, the aim is to show the range of

musical idioms indigenous to one relatively cohesive region. The most featured instrument is spike-fiddle, but above all there's track after wonderful track of singing. Superb music, excellent notes—Ocora at its best. —*John Storm Roberts, Original Music*

Djabote / Real World 2340
Unlike most drummers in the West African traditions, Rose has always tended to work with large ensembles. Yet their enormous power has mostly come with little loss of subtlety, as these recent recordings attest. This open-air set involving no less than 50 drummers and as many singers has a sweep and strength that take your breath away. —*John Storm Roberts, Original Music*

Sierra Leone Collection

Sierra Leone Music / Zensor 41
Here's a delicious brass band, some church music and an example of Salia Koroma along with a slew of other delights. Gorgeous packaging, thanks to the German government and radio money. —*John Storm Roberts, Original Music*

○ **African Elegant** / 1992 / Original Music 15
Freetown, Sierra Leone's capital, early developed a charming, calypso-like Creole-language palm-wine guitar music. The style's undisputed king was Ebenezer Calendar, whose Maringar band (acoustic guitar, tuba, percussion) ruled the roost for 30 years. His gentle, extraordinarily catchy hits, on the order of "Jollof Rice" and "Arriah Baby," dominate this unique collection. Also present are several recordings by the Kru seamen who first developed the guitar style that was to travel via Ghana to the world, as well as some Mandingo and Mende groups with wonderfully eccentric brass playing. —*John Storm Roberts*

Somalia Collection

○ **Jamiila: Songs from a Somali City** / 1987 / Original Music 007
Jamiila: Songs from a Somali City. Somali popular music has almost never been recorded, yet it has a rich musical culture whose Afro-Islamic ingredients have Swahili, Italian, and Indian garnishes. These delightful performances from 1984 include songs for the 'ud; 'ud and flute; acoustic guitar; and guitar with slightly batty electronic organ (replacing the old portable harmonium). An authentic grassroots sound, with its unselfconcious mix of tradition and gadgetry, and the street-corner hipness of a music that's strictly a neighborhood affair. —*John Storm Roberts*

South Africa

African Jazz Pioneers

Live at the Montreux Jazz Festival / Celluloid 6009042
There's jazz, and there's "township jazz," meaning jazz-influenced dance music, and then there's a township jazz, pretty much a fifty-fifty blend, that is the world's only really solidly based non-US jazz idiom. The Pioneers play this third wonderful style, and last year they blew their audience away in two appearances in Switzerland. This recording lets you hear them do it. —*John Storm Roberts, Original Music*

Boyoyo Boys

○ **Back in Town** / 1987 / Rounder 5026
The Boyoyo Boys, among South Africa's premier township ensembles, had to regroup following the 1984 slaying of drummer Archie Mohlala. They took a break following 15 years of hit records and acclaimed tours, before regrouping for this smashing comeback set in 1987. The 10 tracks on this CD were prototype Boyoyo Boys material; all were three-minute, steaming workouts with punchy guitar lines, torrid sax and funky bass/drum interplay, everything linked by rousing group vocals and harmonies. Despite being only a 30-minute disc, it doesn't qualify as a ripoff item. There's no way any Boyoyo Boys date, no matter how short, doesn't give world music fans their money's worth. —*Ron Wynn*

○ **Tj Today** / Aug. 1989 / Rounder 5036
The Boyoyo Boys, a four-member South African ensemble, offered boiling hot examples of '80s township music on this 10-cut disc Rounder issued in 1988. As saxophonists Lukas Pelo and Thomas Phale provided a mix of outside riffs and funky, bluesy licks, bassist Vusi Xhosa laid down booming, yet solidly in-the-

groove lines with guitarist Vusi Nkosi skittering, flickering, and riding the waves atop the beat. The songs were short, catchy and hook-laden workouts, done at fever pitch. A bonus was violinist Noise Khanyile, whose sawing, spiraling solos turned several selections into bubbling, explosive triumphs. —*Ron Wynn*

Johnny Clegg (Juluka/Savuka)

b. Jul. 13, 1953, Rochdale, Lancashire, England
Group
Johnny Clegg was the founder and chief songwriter of Juluka, South Africa's first interracial and intercultural rock & roll band. For the first year and a half, Juluka played mostly in Black areas where Whites didn't see them, but as they became more popular they often risked their lives (literally) to play the kind of music they loved. Clegg met Sipho (See-poe) Mchunu, a "formidable guitarist," when they were both 17. They formed a strong musical and personal bond and in 1976 cut an album of Zulu ethnic songs under the name of Juluka ("sweat"). The next albums added elements of South African folk, rock, funk, and Zulu street guitar. By 1979 they had a Zulu/rock, South African folk/fusion band with six members (three White and three Black) and a platinum album. Juluka's success helped break down the racial barriers that separated musical styles, and before they disbanded in 1985 they even had a Top 40 hit in Europe with "Scatterlings of Africa," a poignant tribute to the African diaspora. As the political situation heated up in the late '80s, Clegg returned with another interracial band called Savuka ("we have arisen"), this time writing and singing highly political material. After a tumultuous tour of South Africa and western Europe, Savuka inked a worldwide deal with EMI International (Capitol in the US). —*J. Poet*

African Litany / 1982 / Priority 57145
Juluka's second release with Johnny Clegg, the first album by an integrated rock band in South Africa, went gold in three months. This first single "Impi" was based on a Zulu war chant and was considered a call to revolution by people in the know. —*J. Poet*

Ubuhle Bemvelo / Jan. 1982 / Priority 57146
Juluka's follow-up to *African Litany*, a selection of traditional Zulu folk songs done in a rock & roll style. —*J. Poet*

Scatterlings / Oct. 1982 / Warner Brothers 23898
A good Juluka set featuring "Scatterlings of Africa" and "Simple Things." —*Scott Bultman*

○ **Third World Child** / 1987 / Capitol 46778
"Asimbonanga (Mandela)" is an anthem already adopted by Joan Baez and others, while the title tune devastatingly discusses what it's like to be asked to "walk in the dreams of the foreigner." —*William Ruhlmann*

Cruel, Crazy, Beautiful World / 1989 / Capitol 93446
By his third album with Savuka, Clegg had adopted some Los Angeles production techniques, such as those booming drums, perhaps in an attempt to meet the marketplace. But the message is still there: "Woman Be My Country" brilliantly examines Clegg's conflicting feelings about his homeland, while the title song expresses his alternating realism and optimism: "It's your world, so live in it!" —*William Ruhlmann*

☆ **The Best of Juluka** / 1991 / Rhythm Safari 57138
A good summary of Clegg's work with Juluka. —*Scott Bultman*

Adama Drame

Rhythms of the Manding / Philips/UNESCO 6586042
The Mande peoples, who live in parts of several Sahelian countries, have a particularly rich griot-based musical culture. Westerners are particularly aware of Manding kora and balafon playing, but the music of the djemb or jembe drum has also achieved some status (Paris is said to have at least several hundred non-African players, serious or dilettante). Drame's shows and recordings have had a good deal to do with that. This excellent late 1970s album was the first to introduce him to Westerners. —*John Storm Roberts, Original Music*

Noise Khanyile

Art of Noise, The / Globestyle 045
This is dynamite Zulu fiddling, with township bands and more rural groups, by a man who played with most of the big names of the time. This has to rank as one of the best reissues of downhome 1970s sounds so far—one not to be missed. The notes are

better than most, too, despite the misuse of the word traditional—an irritating inaccuracy that seems to be spreading. —*John Storm Roberts, Original Music*

Ladysmith Black Mambazo

Group

Ladysmith Black Mambazo was founded by Joseph Shabalala in 1974. They've cut 29 albums over the past 14 years, but the group did not become well known outside of South Africa until Paul Simon asked them to perform on *Graceland.* Shabalala was born into a poor family that lived on a White man's farm near the town of Ladysmith. There were eight children in the Shabalala family, and, as the oldest boy, it was Joseph's duty to take care of the family after his father died. Shabalala's first musical experience, save for a bit of fooling around on the guitar, came with a choral group called the Blacks. Shabalala eventually took over leadership of the group and became its main composer. The Blacks won most of the local vocal competitions and became the most popular Zulu vocal group, but Shabalala felt that something was missing. "I had been hearing a voice inside me," Shabalala said. "I didn't know it, but it was the voice of God." When the voice told him to fast, Shabalala obeyed, and on his fast, he had a vision of a new kind of vocal music. Shortly thereafter he became a Christian. Taking the choral music he heard in the Christian church, he combined it with the Zulu tradition to create his own style. When the Blacks refused to take part in Shabalala's experiments, he formed Ladysmith Black Mambazo. The group consists of seven bass voices, an alto, a tenor, and Shabalala singing lead. Even if you don't speak Zulu, when they hit a low rumbling note, you can literally feel the power of their voices in your body. "In Zulu singing there are three major sounds," Shabalala explains. "A high keening ululation; a grunting, puffing sound that we make when we stomp our feet; and a certain way of singing melody. Before Black Mambazo you didn't hear these three sounds in the same songs. So it is new to combine them, although it is still done in a traditional style. We are just asking God to allow us to polish it, to help keep our voices in order so we can praise Him and uplift the people." —*J. Poet*

Induku Kethu / 1984 / Shanachie 43021
This group can be heard at its most direct and unadorned on this collection, with Joseph Shabalala leading the ensemble through some swooping vocal harmonies and the group's unique stop-and-start call-and-response sequences. (In Zulu.) (Also recommended: The religious collection *Ulwandle Oluncgwele.*) —*William Ruhlmann*

○ **Shaka Zulu** / 1987 / Warner Brothers 25582
In the wake of their participation on his *Graceland* album, Paul Simon produced this Ladysmith album, their most accessible work for Western ears, which is pristinely recorded and sung partially in English. —*William Ruhlmann*

Two Worlds One Heart / 1990 / Warner Brothers 26125
A great album that joins the vocal traditions of North America and South Africa. Includes collaborations with George Clinton, Ray Phiri (*Stimela* and *Graceland*), and Gospel star Marvin Winnans. —*J. Poet*

Classic Tracks / 1991 / Shanachie 43074
A selection of tunes from Ladysmith's many South African albums. —*J. Poet*

○ **Best of** / 1992 / Shanachie 43098
For over 20 years, the members of South African vocal group Ladysmith Black Mambazo have been considered the foremost singers of the style known as Mbube. Directed by lead vocalist Joseph Shabalala, the group displays tight harmonies and glorious arrangements on this 16-song collection. Around 10 years ago, more people outside of South Africa started to become aware of the beautiful stylings of these nine voices and the powerful, jubilant energy they generate. This CD effectively captures the group's rich, exhilarating sound. —*J.J. Rassler, Roundup Newsletter*

Inala / Shanachie 43040
Here's releases from one of the top modern groups in the style usually called mbube or iscathamiya, the soul-shaking vocal sound that stems about equally from traditional Azanian choral music, US gospel and the Inkspots—a group whose importance goes far beyond its contribution to Paul Simon's recent *Graceland*

album. These, of course, are straight, no Simon . . . —*John Storm Roberts, Original Music*

Sipho Mabuse

○ **Harari** / 1981 / A&M 4887
A solid but unhappily out-of-print album by the pop band Mabuse and Harari led in the mid '70s. —*J. Poet*

Burn Out / 1985 / CBS 440524
The EP that introduced Europe and America to Mabuse. The title track is an African dance/pop classic and worldwide hit. CBS sold several thousand copies of this one to American dance clubs in 1985, but they were unable to get it to cross over to the pop market. —*J. Poet*

○ **Sipho Mabuse** / 1987 / Virgin 90676
One of the first African pop records to get wide US distribution. Contains "Burn Out" and several other tracks from the South African album of the same name, but again the market wasn't ready. —*J. Poet*

Chant of the Marching / 1989 / Earthworks 91271
Another South African take on funk, rock, and Zulu pop, with many tracks in English. —*J. Poet*

Mahlathini

b. 1937
Vocals / Mbaqanga
Simon Nkabinde Mahlathini (nicknamed "the Lion of Soweto") came to international attention via the 1985 sampler *The Indestructible Beat of Soweto.* He began to tour internationally with female singers the Mahotella Queens, although he has been playing and singing his brand of mbaqanga (Zulu pop music, heavily influenced by traditional singing styles) since the early '60s. Mahlathini started singing on street corners, graduated to men's choral music, and went on to form his own smaller group in the mid '60s. When he "went electric" in the mid '70s, his new sound caused a sensation, and much controversy. With the Mahotella Queens supplying their dynamic backing vocals and fancy dance routines (think of a South African version of the Supremes) and Mahlathini's primal groaning filling the air, you don't have to understand the language to get the message, although the group has occasionally recorded in English. Another part of Mahlathini's success is the backing supplied by West Nkosi and the Makgona Tsohle Band. "Makgona Tsohle means 'Jack-of-all-trades,'" says Nkosi. "Our mbaqanga is a blend of traditional styles with modern instruments, a music anyone can relate to." —*J. Poet & William Ruhlmann*

○ **The Lion of Soweto** / 1987 / Earthworks 90867
The compilation that introduced Mahlathini to the rest of the world. Primal, growling mbaqanga (with backing vocals by the Mahotella Queens) that prompted many critics to call Mahlathini the "Howlin' Wolf of South Africa." —*J. Poet*

Thokozile / 1988 / Earthworks 90920
Another exemplary outing from Mahlathini and the Mahotella Queens, with a kwela-like swing to the arrangements. —*J. Poet*

Paris—Soweto / 1989 / Polydor 839676
More of Mahlathini and the Mahotella Queens. Recorded in Paris at the end of their first post-*Graceland* tour. More produced and glossier than their Shanachie recordings, with a slight concession to the international dance market in the rhythms, but not lacking in musical and vocal fire power. —*J. Poet*

○ **Rhythm & Art** / 1990 / Shanachie 43068
More Zulu and accordion jive from Mahlathini and the Queens, with several songs in English. —*J. Poet*

The Lion Roars / 1991 / Shanachie 43081
Mbaqanga was in disfavor when Paul Simon's *Graceland* rekindled interest in the form. This is a late '80s reunion album that shows Mahlathini and the Queens have lost none of their fire. —*J. Poet*

Mahotella Queens

Group / Mbaqanga
The Queens, often heard in concert and on record with deep-voiced "groaner" Simon Mahlathini, represent the South African township style with absolute perfection. Established in 1964 as a session harmony group, they came to prominence in the '70s with their tough vocal style and rock-solid mbaqanga backing band.

Some of the original Queens have toured the States with Mahlathini recently, displaying their sprightly dancing and gusty harmonies to appreciative Western audiences. They are also heard to great effect on the collection album *Soweto Never Sleeps—Classic Female Zulu Jive* (Shanachie 43041) with other sister groups. —*Myles Boisen*

☆ **Izibani Zomgqashiyo** / 1986 / Shanachie 43036
One of the lively, hip, funky Mgqashiyo rhythm's hottest exponents is this group of five women from Southern Africa, mostly around Soweto, who have been together since 1964. They were voted the 1975 Radio Bantu Best Group of the Year. At times, they are also accompanied by their male "groaners" (Robert Mbazo Mkhize, Potatoes Mazambane and Joseph Mthimkhulu) and a super band. Highly recommended. —*"Blue" Gene Tyrrany*

Marriage Is a Problem / Jun. 1991 / Shanachie 43080
Very danceable, upbeat, certain to lift any dragging spirits! Highly recommended. —*Ladyslipper*

Women of the World / 1993 / Shanachie 6407
Though usually heard backing the groans and surging vocals of Malathini, the Mahotella Queens can certainly perform on their own. A working unit since 1964, they show on this new release that their harmonies and leads deserve attention on their own. There are celebratory praise songs such as "Africa" and the title track, numbers done in both their traditional language and English, a wonderful remake of Bob Dylan's "I Shall Be Released," and potent message tracks "Homeless" and "I'm Not Your Good Time Girl." —*Ron Wynn*

Miriam Makeba

b. Mar. 4, 1934, Johannesburg, South Africa
Vocals / Protest
Born in Johannesburg, South Africa, she played with the Black Mountain Brothers from 1954 to 1957. In 1959 she met Harry Belafonte, who brought her to the States and groomed her career. Makeba's Black Nationalist position in the late '60s led to public backlash, which she did not overcome until the '80s. —*Bil Carpenter*

☆ **Evening with Belafonte/Makeba** / 1965 / RCA
A '60s album of folk music. —*Bil Carpenter*

The World of Miriam Makeba / 1986 / RCA 2750
Includes material in Spanish, English, and African languages; songs include "Forbidden Games," "Dubula," "Pole Mze," "Tonados de Media Noche." —*Ladyslipper*

○ **Sangoma** / 1988 / Warner Brothers 25673
Makeba's comeback album, her first US release in almost a decade. A beautiful collection of traditional South African songs with spare production values that highlight the power of Makeba's vocals. An excellent set of Xhosa folk songs Miriam learned as a child. —*J. Poet & Bil Carpenter*

Miriam Makeba / 1989 / RCA 2267
The first American album from Makeba, this is a long-out-of-print classic. —*J. Poet*

○ **Africa** / Oct. 1991 / Novus 3155
This 1991 compilation encompasses several recordings from Miriam's early US career, from 1960-1965, yet the content and arrangements sound fresh and timely! Includes works from her collaborations with Harry Belafonte, and former husband Hugh Masekela, with spare instrumental backup—guitar, percussion—and a lovely backup chorus . . . 23 songs in all. —*Ladyslipper*

Welela / Mercury 838208
This dynamic 1989 release contains songs in both English and African dialects, including a re-interpretation of her classic "Pata Pata," which means "Touch, Touch," as well as "African Sunset, Soweto Blues." —*Ladyslipper*

○ **The Click Song** / Esperance 155564
This is a classic: Miriam's first long-playing album, recorded with the Belafonte Folk Singers! It includes her well-known songs, "The Click Song," "Mbube," another version also known as "Wimoweh," "House of the Rising Sun," "Iya Guduza," which triple-tracks Miriam's voice and was probably the first multiple recording in Zulu, the humorous "One More Dance," and others, performed in Xhosa, Swazi, Zulu, and English. —*Ladyslipper*

The Best Of . . . /

Recorded in 1958-59, this amazing compilation gives us a glimpse of Miriam's earliest years, and in a sort of "girl group" situation paralleling the movement here in the West; she and several women were "adopted" by a studio that put them together with veteran studio musicians and engineers, and turned them loose! Enhancing their popularity was the fact that they combined traditional elements with contemporary ones, interjecting political references as well. —*Ladyslipper*

Dorothy Masuka

○ **Pata Pata** / 1991 / Mango 162-539911
This Zimbabwean woman has a beautiful, flowing voice and is backed up by other female vocalists and a "typical" Afro-pop band—twangy finger-picked electric guitar, steady percussion with lots of hand claps, keyboards and horns, yielding a tribal, hypnotic effect, some of it great for dancing . . . this is her first worldwide album release. —*Ladyslipper*

Busi Mhlongo

Babhemu / Sterns 1053
At last a release that isn't copycat mbaqanga or mbube! Among the specialties of South African music have been: a uniquely glorious female lead vocal style; a long-term openness to the US; and the world's only truly naturalized jazz and soul styles. Mhlongo has all of that going for her, along with a super voice and a fine band that is somewhat in the polished Soul Brothers' vein. —*John Storm Roberts, Original Music*

Mthembu Queens

Mthembu Queens / Rounder 5034
Here's fine 1970s-style mbaqanga, with both kick and subtlety—plus the variety that comes from having both female and male lead singing. An additional pleasure is the interplay between an outstanding guitarist and some sensational somersaulting bass-playing (also some unusual soukous influence). *Graceland* led to many so-so Azanian releases; this is one of the good ones. —*John Storm Roberts, Original Music*

Emjindini / 1985 / Rounder 5034
Though the Mthembu Queens aren't as celebrated as Malathini and the Mahotella Queens, they showed on this 1989 CD that they don't have to take a back seat to anyone. With Mthembu's deep-throated gurgles, moans, wails, and vocals superbly contrasted by the Queens spirited singing, it doesn't matter that the lyrics aren't in English. The jutting rhythms, flickering guitar and harmonizing have universal appeal to anyone who loves great music. —*Ron Wynn*

Mbongeni Ngema

Ngema wrote and performed *Woza Albert*, an anti-apartheid comedy/drama that got rave reviews when it toured the US in 1984. Along with Hugh Masakela, Ngema wrote *Sarafina*, a musical drama that told the story of a day in the life of a South African township as seen through the eyes of a group of high school children. —*J. Poet*

☆ **Sarafina—Original Cast Album** / 1988 / RCA 93072
The songs express the conflicting feelings of hope, terror, love, and struggle of life under the gun. —*J. Poet*

Time to Unite / 1988 / Mango 9811
More songs of struggle and liberation; featuring the cast of *Sarafina*. —*J. Poet*

Philip Tabane

○ **Man Phily** / African Music 04
This rich anthology ranges over 17 years and a stylistic range with room for hand piano as well as electric guitar, for kwela and marabi and blues. —*John Storm Roberts*

○ **Unh!** / Nonesuch 79225
Tabane in extremely laidback mood. One of those jams—a little like some roots dub—that will either bliss you out or blah you out. Not the best Malombo by a long chalk, in our book, though Malombo's music is always intelligent even when it isn't quite working. What it's doing on the Explorer series of all things is another and more mysterious question! —*John Storm Roberts*

South Africa Collection

★ **Indestructible Beat of Soweto** / 1986 / Shanachie 43033
This anthology of South African artists surprised everyone by becoming a best-seller. It introduced worldbeatniks to Ladysmith Black Mambazo, Mahlathini, and Moses Mchunu and paved the way for Paul Simon's *Graceland*. Winner of *The Village Voice*'s Jazz and Pop Poll for Best Record of 1987. An essential sampler of modern African stylings. A revelation and a joy. —*J. Poet & Hank Davis*

○ **Siya Hamba** / 1989 / Original Music 003
Two faces of '50s Azanian music, from recordings by Hugh Tracey of the International Library of African Music. The first side covers a wide range of rural sounds, including some amazing harmonica (dances with vocals and strange hyperventilations, bluesy solos); concertina; an entirely unexpected piece backed by autoharp; and various wonderful country guitar styles. Side two is a session of smalltown dance music from the jazz- and jump-blues-influenced kwela period, with some terrific women singers. — *John Storm Roberts*

☆ **Freedom Fire** / 1990 / Earthworks 91409
The third of the Earthworks *Indestructible Beat* series (distributed by Virgin) is as good as, if not better than Vol. 1. —*J. Poet*

○ **Singing in an Open Space** / 1990 / Rounder 5027
This set of Zulu semi-rural music from 1962 to 1982 is emphatically the best South African release I've heard in the current glut. None of it is traditional (as the above-average notes rightly point out, the word is routinely misused). All of it—voices, guitars, fiddles, harmonicas—is far more intense than the usual city sounds. —*John Storm Roberts*

★ **Indestructible Beat of Soweto, Vol. 2** / Earthworks 90866

Mbube Roots: Zulu Choral Music from South Africa / Rounder 5025
South African a cappella vocals are spotlighted on this 16-track anthology that begins with the Baritu Glee Singers and concludes with well-known contemporary artists Ladysmith Black Mambazo. The similiarity between early Mbube and pre-quartet African-American gospel (jubilee) is astonishing, as are the vocalists' range, soaring harmonies, smashing leads, and swirling accompaniment. Unfortunately, there's erratic sound quality here, as many of these were done long before the era of sonic superiority. But the majesty of the voices overcomes any technical difficulties. —*Ron Wynn*

Zulu Beats from South Africa / Hannibal 4410
Fine dance music from various electric guitar bands. —*Barry Lee Pearson*

Sudan

Hamza El Din

Lute, 'ud / Neo-traditional
Hamza El Din is recognized worldwide as the musical ambassador from Sudan, and he is one of the greatest masters of the 'ud, a fretless lute popular throughout the Arab world. He is a celebrated concert performer and an evocative singer, keeping the musical traditions of the Nubian region alive. —*Myles Boisen*

Music of Nubia / 1964 / Vanguard 79164
A luminous expression of the sensuous and nurturing aspects of Arabic culture. Good explanations of the songs in the notes. Recommended. —*Tom Smith, Roundup Newsletter*

☆ **Escalay: The Water Wheel** / 1968 / Nonesuch 72041
Extensive selections of a unique style of music personally developed by the soloist-vocalist on 'ud and tar. *Escalay: The Water Wheel—Oud Music of Nubia* is the recording that brought El Din's Nubian traditions to the attention of many in the West—an ethnomusicological classic. —*Myles Boisen & David L. Mayers*

○ **Eclipse** / 1978 / Rykodisc 10103
Meditatively paced traditional songs by a master of Sudanese music. Hamza's deep, smoky voice is accompanied by the 'ud—a precursor to the lute—and by compelling use of a simple Nubian frame drum called the tar. A beautiful, even lush recording of El Din's latest 'ud mastery. —*Bob Tarte & Myles Boisen*

A Song of the Nile / JVC

A beautiful introduction to Nubian culture of Sudan. For many of us Hamza is a true hero of world music. He introduced this deep tradition to people all over Europe, the US, and Asia. I must admit that music from the Horn of Africa has a very powerful pull on me. The most beautiful recordings I've found are on the Museum Collection of West Berlin. These recordings by Robert Gotlieb feature stunning performances from the Blue Nile region. —*David L. Mayers*

Abdel Aziz el Mubarak

○ **Abdel Aziz el Mubarak** / 1987 / Globestyle 023
Mubarak is one of Sudan's most popular bandleaders, a man who combines Western influences (including reggae) with his country's age-old Muslim traditions. —*J. Poet*

○ **Straight from the Heart** / World Circuit 010
Mubarak was featured on an earlier World Circuit release with a small group, but this is a much better release: Mubarak as the Sudanese hear him, backed by a ten-piece group including accordion and saxophones. A fine live recording (made at a London concert) that shows off one of the most exciting and least known of the Afro-Arab pop idioms. —*John Storm Roberts*

Abdel Gadir Salim

○ **Nujum Al-Lail/Stars of the Night** / 1989 / Shanachie 64039
Silky-voiced Sudanese bandleader delivers a strong set of swaying music highlighted by the gentle alto saxophone of Abdel Hadi. Contains "A'Abir Sikkah," a successful attempt to meld reggae with a local village rhythm. —*Bob Tarte*

○ **The Merdoum Kings Play Songs of Love** / 1991 / World Circuit 024
Backed by the All Stars, a seven-piece band with an understated but compelling orchestral sound, Abdel Gadir returns with more lush music from the Sudan. The complex layering of instruments and medium-boil tempos suggests the effortless flow of a juju all-nighter. —*Bob Tarte*

Sudan Collection

○ **Sounds of Sudan** / 1990 / World Circuit 018
Arabic pop music by Abdel Aziz el Mubarak, Abdel Gadir Salim, and Mohamed Gubara. —*J. Poet*

Tunisia

Hassan Elgharbi

○ **Enchanted Kanun** / CDDA 046
Elgharbi, Tunisia's leading player of the kanun zither, is a major virtuoso. In 1976 he won the grand prize at Iran's prestigious Shiraz Music Festival. Here he plays the piece that gained him the prize, along with various other improvisations on traditional modes and personal compositions (one backed by a bassist!). The CD winds up with a couple of recordings by an Egyptian virtuoso of the early 20th century. —*John Storm Roberts*

Tanzania

Mlimani Park Orchestra

○ **Sikinde** / Africassette
A great compilation of '80s recordings. A big group and, thanks to the flexibility of cassette (Tanzania has no record industry), it lays out at length in fine style. Recently released in the US on Africassette—a unique release with great horns, real-thing strength, and total absence of worldbeat slickness. —*John Storm Roberts*

Nyota

○ **Nyota** / Globestyle 044
Fine taarab (wedding music of the Swahili) by Black Star and Lucky Star, two groups that helped keep the coastal style alive by stylistic changes and the development of orchestras featuring accordion and the like. A thrilling retrospective on an all-but-forgotten genre. —*David L. Mayers & Bob Tarte*

Remmy Ongala

Songs for the Poor Man / 1990 / Real World 91315
This Tanzanian take on soukous is as restrained as the Zairian form is hedonistic. Ongala's songs on social themes are delivered with winning conviction. —*Bob Tarte*

○ **Mambo** / 1991 / Real World 92129
Backed by Orchestre Super Matimila, Ongala trades the laidback soukous of his first US release for political songs—in English and Swahili—whose directness recalls Nigeria's Fela Anikulapo Kuti and includes touches of contemporary Latin music and a shot of rhythm and blues. —*Bob Tarte*

○ **Nalilia Mwana** / WOMAD 010
Life gets very confusing in East Africa! Ongala is Congolese by origin, and his group consists mostly of expatriate Zairians. Not that the sound is soukous: it's a mix of truly Tanzanian elements with early '70s boucher. The results are highly individual—and, given that contemporary Tanzanian bands just don't get recorded, not to be passed up. —*John Storm Roberts*

Orchestra Super Mazembe

○ **Kaivaska** / 1982 / Virgin 2263
This Tanzanian band with a heavy Congolese influence can really tear it up. Check out "Malamba d'Amour" ("Words of Love") to see what Buddy Holly would have sounded like if he'd been born in Africa. —*J. Poet*

Hukwe Ubi Zawose

Hukwe Ubi Zawose / JVC 25011
Ilimba (66-key finger-piano) virtuoso Zawose is quite well known to WOMAD audiences and featured largely on Triple Earth releases. Zawose is essentially on the more traditional end of a large and varied spectrum of African musicians working to transmute traditional forms to keep them relevant in changing times. —*David L. Mayers*

Mateso / Triple Earth 104
Perhaps the world is at last waking up to the fact that musicians all over Africa are exploring various ways of renewing traditional idioms without betraying or ossifying them. —*David L. Mayers*

Tanzania Collection

○ **Sound d'Afrique, Vol. 2** / 1982 / Mango 9754
Soukous and soukous-influenced sounds from other West African countries. Highly recommended. —*J. Poet*

○ **Tanzania Sound** / 1987 / Original Music 106C
In the '50s, Tanzania built its own blend of local Afro-Cuban and Congolese ingredients into a new dance style. Here are its '50s and '60s classics—both the early bands, like the legendary Kiko Kids with their strong Afro-Arab tinge, and the groups of the classic era. The Tanzanian bands, more driving than their Congolese models and more dance-oriented than their Kenyan neighbors, used local rhythms earlier than the proto-soukous bands themselves and contained some splendid hornmen with very individual sounds. They also had a melancholy vocal sound entirely different from their Congolese models. —*John Storm Roberts*

○ **Music of Zanzibar—Taarab 2** / 1988 / Globestyle 033
The vocal approach is borrowed from Indian film music, the instrumentation from Arabic orchestras, and the rhythms from Latin America—but the music's heart is as large as its influences. Deliciously cornball in the best pop-music sense. From Zanizibar (now part of Tanzania). —*Bob Tarte*

○ **Music of Zanzibar—Taarab 3** / 1990 / Globestyle 040
This is a collection of hits by some of Zanzibar's best taarab bands, including supergroups Ikhwani Safaa Musical Club and Culture Musical Club. —*J. Poet*

Uganda

Geoffrey Oryema

Exile / 1958 / Atlantic 91629
Oryema plays the nanga, a zither described as having seven strings, though mine has one string that runs seven times across the instrument making it hell to tune. This is half of a terrific

CD—wonderful except when Brian Eno and Co get in on the act and undercut it. —*John Storm Roberts, Original Music*

Samite

Vocals, piano, flute / Neo-traditional
Singer and multi-instrumentalist Samite is a little like Francis Bebey in that he over-dubs both his own voice and various African and Western instruments (including the big East African litungu lyre, finger piano, and flutes). While he has a slight, slight folky edge in places and is not a strong solo singer, his over-dubbed polyphonic vocals and most of his instrumental work is gorgeous. —*John Storm Roberts*

○ **Abaana Bakesa** / 1992 / Shanachie 65003
Abaana Bakesa—Dance, My Children, Dance offers joyful, endearing, traditional-based songs performed on marimba, kalimba (finger piano), and litungu (Ugandan harp). Samite's mellifluous vocals exert a powerful charm. Recommended for listeners with children. —*Bob Tarte*

Pearl of Africa Reborn / 1992 / Shanachie 65008
Fuller instrumentation and punchier production than his first release help embed firmly in memory these bright pop songs derived from Ugandan stories. Musicians from Senegal, the United States, and Barbados join the avuncular Samite in a loving tribute to his mother that's perfect for families everywhere. —*Bob Tarte*

Zambia Collection

○ **From the Copperbelt: Zambian Miners Songs** / 1989 / Original Music 004
If you're into country blues, Mwenda Jean Bosco, or roots in general, this is for you. The remarkable guitarists of the '50s Zambian copper mines were mostly wandering minstrels who roamed from mine to mine, crisscrossing the border between Zambia and Katanga and forming part of a guitar movement that has always been incorrectly credited to East Zaire alone. There's an enormous variety here, from rugged, rootsy stuff to the beginnings of an urban-influenced sound with US and South African as well as Congolese elements. —*John Storm Roberts*

Zaire

Empire Bakuba

○ **Massassi Calcule** / ACMPI 1001
Inventors of the recent kouassa-kouassa dance craze, and arguably the greatest contemporary hard-soukous band bar none, Bakuba is heavy on the guitars and with no time for horns or pop frills. Leader and lead vocalist Pepe Kalle has a voice a little similar to the late Franco, set off beautifully by the backup singers. Guitarist Boeing 737 (really!) is more adventuresome than the recently hyped Diblo Dibala, with a bare-feet-on-a-hot-road guitar style and very well integrated echoes of funk and rockabilly. Typical of soukous bands, though Bakuba is one of the monsters of the '80s and '90s, it has been recording since the late '60s. —*John Storm Roberts*

M'bilia Bel

b. Jan. 10, 1959, Kinshasa, Zaire
Soukous

○ **Bameli Soy** / 1987 / Shanachie 43025
One of our top pix for the year! By one of Africa's top female vocalists . . . the album is replete with Congolese rhythms, harmonies, percussion, and energetic joyousness. —*Ladyslipper*

○ **Phenomene** / Melodie Makers 35004
Bel sang for years with Rochereau and went out on her own in 1988. Bameli Soy presents her in the Rochereau days. The marvelous *Phenomene* was the first fruit of her artistic freedom and it's wonderful, with ace arranger Rigo Star's work framing her sensuous style without making it soupy. And given how well Bel's style and voice blended with the benign drive of Afrisa International, as Bameli Soy attests, her solo success was against considerable self-competition. —*John Storm Roberts*

Franco (L'Okanga La Ndju Pene Luambo Makiadi)

b. 1938, Sona-Bata, Zaire, **d.** 1990
Guitar / Soukous
After World War II, Kinshasa (the capital of what is now Zaire) became a bustling city where the popular music of Ghana (highlife),
Cuba (rumba), and various local groups simmered down into the
folkloric form of pop known as soukous. Franco, "the Sorcerer of
the Guitar," was the leader of the TPOK Jazz Band, the most influential and popular band in Africa's modern history. A natural
guitar talent, Franco joined Ebengo Dewayon's Watam band
while in his early teens, cutting his first guitar solo record,
"Bolingo Na Ngai Beatrice," at the tender age of 13. He formed
the first edition of TPOK at the age of 15, and the group dominated the charts from that moment until Franco's death in 1990.
—J. Poet

20eme Anniversaire / 1976 / African Music 360.082/832
A two-record (French import) set released to celebrate Franco's
20th year in the music business; a good buy if you can find it. —
J. Poet

○ **Franco & His All Powerful TPOK Jazz** / 1984 / Makossa 2814
One of the master's last big hits, "Tres Impolie," has a catchy chorus, great guitar fireworks, and a relentless groove. *—J. Poet*

Originalite / 1987 / Retro
Remastered from original 78-inch singles cut between 1956 and
1959, these are the hits that established Franco (and TPOK Jazz
Band) as Africa's reigning guitar god. *—J. Poet*

Kanda Bongo Man

b. 1955, Inongo, Zaire
Guitar, Vocals / Soukous
One of the biggest stars of the fashion-conscious Parisian soukous
scene, Kanda Bongo Man issued his own records in Paris and
Zaire before hitting it big internationally. His long-time lead gui-
tarist Diblo Dibala is now a star bandleader in his own right. —
Myles Boisen

☆ **Amour Fou/ Crazy Love** / 1988 / Hannibal 1337
Sharp soukous from two Paris albums. Diblo Dibala's agile guitar
is a real plus on this American debut. *—Myles Boisen*

Kwassa Kwassa / 1989 / Hannibal 1343
More dance-floor fun. Very uptempo and infectious Zairian pop.
—Myles Boisen

○ **Kanda Bongo Man** / 1990 / Globestyle 005
Early hits by one of the hottest new-wave soukous bands; features lead guitarist Diblo Dibala (see Loketo). *—J. Poet*

○ **Sai-Liza** / Hannibal
The recording that introduced the kouassa-kouassa dance has
been a runaway smash in Paris and Africa. Unsure why this has
been one of the biggest hits in quite a while? Try Dibala on lead
guitar, Lokassa ya Mbongo backing him up, and Pablo Lubadika
on bass guitar, all of them in top form. Add KBM's admirable liking for a small tight group—aside from those mentioned, there's
only synth, drum, and a two-voice backup vocal group. Kanda
Bongo Man is one musician who almost always deserves the
semi-adulation Western buffs have given him. *—John Storm
Roberts*

Extra Ball / 1991 / Shanachie 64028
Loketo's swansong as a group is their most highly charged, hook-
filled release yet, with dazzling guitar pyrotechnics from Diblo
Dibala and friends. *—Bob Tarte & J. Poet*

Pablo Lubadika

Okominiokolo / Sterns 1052
A new one from Pablo, session man extraordinaire. He plays with
all the current biggies but his heart is in the music, not the trends.
A fact that he proves joyously here, crafting outrageously catchy
melodies that coil around the soaring guitars and his own excellent bass playing. *—Carl Hoyt, Original Music*

Aurlus Mabele

Soukous

○ **King of Soukous** / 1991 / Warner Brothers 89005
Brief as an aerobics workout and just as stimulating, this 30-
minute disc presents the voice of Loketo after the breakup of that
massively popular band. Filled with can't-miss spiraling soukous

rhythms, saucy backup vocalists, and great guitar by Dally
Kimoko. *—Bob Tarte*

Madilu

Sans Commentaire / Sterns 1055
Hired by Franco in 1984, Madilu-Bialu blossomed into a vocalist
of particular expressiveness. Franco's ghost is here in spots, but
there's also some dynamite input from Lokassa, Syran M'Benza,
Pablo, and—above all—the less-known guitarist Popolipo Zero
Faute. This kind of talent could get slick, but this is all swing and
charm, tightness and ease. *—John Storm Roberts, Original Music*

Sam Mangwana

Vocals / Zouk / Soukous
This former singer with Rochereau and Kanda Bongo Man has
added elements of soca and zouk into his high-octane soukous
style. *—J. Poet*

○ **Aladji** / 1978 / Shanachie 64017
This album contains hits from several African albums; one of the
hottest African dance compilations of the late '80s. *—J. Poet*

Antoine Moundanda

Mosseka / Celluloid 668882
Once upon a time there was a new music in what is now Zaire,
in which almost anything could happen and probably did, so creative was the ferment. Among the mighty men who bestrode the
musical landscape was one Antoine Moundanda, who mixed the
sanza finger-piano with guitars and percussion, and lo there was
a sound of great joy, the like of which is rarely to be heard. So, of
course, he waxed rich and famous har har har. The good news is
that that quirky genius Zao recently resurrected Moundanda and
paired him with sax, flute, guitars and other soukousian elements
of great quality, on equal terms. *—John Storm Roberts, Original
Music*

Tshala Muana

○ **Soukous Siren** / 1985 / Shanachie 64031
Forget soukous. Muana hits hardest when she throws herself into
mutuash, a dizzying rural polyrhythm the Zairian singer/song-
writer backs up with strong melodies and molten arrangements.
—Bob Tarte

☆ **Nasi Nabali** / Es Paranza 9689
One of the best recordings by a singer whose reputation just
keeps growing—and rightly so. The ingredients are familiar
enough—what's done with them is what counts. Muana and her
chorus work almost as one unit, and the backings balance fluid
guitars, tough disco elements, and jaunty traps; punchy horns
that blend R&B licks with older Afro/Carib references; and local
traditional elements to subtle and splendid effect. She has the
best voice of all the Zairian women singers. *—John Storm Roberts*

Docteur Nico

○ **Docteur Nico & the Orchestra African Fiesta** / 1966-1968 /
African Music 36516
Whatever any Zairian guitarist does (and therefore almost any
African guitarist from anywhere), he is in some way echoing
something created 20 years ago by the late Docteur Nico. A constant experimenter, Nico did for the guitar what Rochereau (his
colleague in both African jazz and African fiesta) did for Congo
music vocals, blending and reworking the idiom's Cuban and local strains into something brilliantly new. All these recordings,
therefore, are basic to any soukous collection. *—John Storm
Roberts*

Tabu Ley Rochereau (Tabu Pascal)

b. 1940, Bundundu, Zaire
Vocals
Tabu Ley (Rochereau), with Franco, is the father of modern
African pop. His band, Africa International, was a leading inno-
vator and changed the way Congolese (and later Zairian music)
music was played. In an interview with Ronnie Graham, later
reprinted in Graham's *Guide to Contemporary African Music* (Da
Capo, 1988), Tabu Ley spoke at length about his life and music.
"Tabu is my father's name; Ley is my father's father's name.
Rochereau is a name I got in grammar school. During a French

history lesson I was the only one who knew the names of Napoleon's generals; the rest of the class was punished because of it. They teased me and called me Rochereau, but I liked the sound of it and kept it as my artistic name." Rochereau learned sacred and secular music at the Catholic grammar school he attended, although he'd been singing at home since he was a child. At the age of 14, he wrote his first hit, "Besama Muchacha," which was recorded by L'African Jazz, the band of Le Grande Kalle, the greatest bandleader of the '40s, '50s, and '60s. Because Rochereau was underage, the songwriting credit was taken by Kalle. When Rochereau finished high school, Kalle gave him a job as a singer with L'African Jazz, and the first tune he wrote for them, "Kelia," made Rochereau an instant success. In 1965 Rochereau left Kalle to form African Fiesta with Docteur Nico, another Kalle alumnus. Since then, Rochereau has led the pack in musical innovations and creative drive. He's written more than 2000 songs for himself and other artists, and recorded more than a hundred albums, with almost every new release bringing a new facet of his creativity to the fore. He's added Latin, jazz, soul, and disco elements to his music. His organization is a fertile training ground for other musicians, who have gone on to fame and fortune (including Sam Mangwana and Mbilia Bel). —*J. Poet*

○ **Omana Wapi** / 1976 / Shanachie 43024
Picked by *The Village Voice's* Robert Christgau as one of the greatest albums of the '80s, this historic collaboration teams Rochereau, Zaire's greatest singer and guitarist, for one of the few "supersessions" worthy of the title. —*J. Poet*

Man from Kinshasa / 1991 / Shanachie 43089
In a nod to contemporary logic, the Zairian master gets behind a drum machine. With another nod to roots, he dares accordion-driven soukous on one of the many highlights here, including "Tour Eiffel." —*Bob Tarte*

Papa Wemba (Shungu Wembadia)

b. Kasai, Zaire
Vocals, guitar / Soukous
Besides being a sartorial role-model who launches fashion after fashion, Wemba has come to symbolize the younger generation of soukous. He started with Zaiko Langa Langa and sticks to an updated version of the driving ZLL style. No heavy funk/R&B overlays, no horns: at most some bluesy flashes in the scintillating guitar work. Just a sparkling, glittering interplay of guitars and drums and voices that doesn't let up. —*John Storm Roberts*

○ **La Voyageur** / 1992 / Earthbeat! 42516
American debut by one of the continent's most arresting vocalists, who is loathe to let a syllable escape his throat without first gift-wrapping it in brightly colored knots. Compositions hurl themselves from soukous to mbube, dashing against the rocks only during flirtations with mellow rock and jazz—but his amazing cockcrow of a voice continually triumphs. —*Bob Tarte*

☆ **L'Esclave** / Gitta 1024
This recording, a massive hit for a full six months when it first came out, testifies to a driving Zairian style that other big names have neglected in favor of more laidback sounds. —*John Storm Roberts*

○ **Amour Kilawu** / Esperance 8438
This collaboration with Viva La Musica (a band of ZLL alumni) is among his very best from the mid '80s. The collaboration with Modogo (full title: *Papa Wemba, Modogo Gian Franco Ferre and Viva la Musica: Nouvelle Generation a Paris.* Phew!) is an outstanding example of how they moved the basic sound forward a notch for the '90s. —*John Storm Roberts*

○ **Papa Wemba with Modogo** / Esperance 8459
Full title: *Papa Wemba, Modogo Gian Franco Ferre and Viva la Musica: Nouvelle Generation a Paris.* I've not been a big Wemba fan; what I've heard seemed to exemplify the blustery, over-produced Afro-Parisian sound that so overvalues the trendy. But, and this is a big BUT, this is a great LP. No horns, no synth, no kwassa kwassa, just the laid-back hipness I've come to expect from Zaiko Langa Langa and its satellites. (Yes, this is yet another one!) — *John Storm Roberts*

Zaiko Langa Langa

Group / Soukous
In the early '70s, the Zaikos hoisted the banner of change in Zairian music by stripping soukous down to its rhythm, guitar, and vocal essentials. The absence of horn players and their rebellious attitude established ZLL as the new wave of youth music, and a host of new bands came from their ranks. Offspring of the "Clan Langa Langa" include Papa Wemba, Bozi Boziana, and the groups Zaiko WaWa, Langa Langa Stars, Choc Stars, Anti-Choc, and many more. —*Myles Boisen*

Langa Langa F.D. / 1990 / Celluloid 6155
One of the few non-import CDs available. —*J. Poet*

La Zai komania

L'Amour du Travail Bien Fait / Bono Music 5005
The grandson of ZLL . . . That's what the notes seem to be claiming in any event, though J.P. Buse, who sings lead, is no new-hatched chickie. However, this 1989 album is super stuff with all the cunning simplicity that is a trademark of ZLL and its spinoffs at their best. There are no goddam drum machines, but the jaunty traps-playing that the 1970s groups pioneered, joyous guitar, kicky keyboards and general niftiness. —*John Storm Roberts, Original Music*

Zaire Collection

☆ **Merveilles du Passe** / African Music 36501
From the late '50s onward, the music of Zaire that came to be called soukous has been an overwhelmingly huge influence on all other Black African styles, with the exception of South Africa. This wonderful collection documents some of the gems of the early days, from the adolescence of the '50s through the '70s new-wave of Zaiko Langa Langa and such. Here—though not always at their super-peak—are most of the influential names in African music: Le Grand Kalle, Franco, Verckys, Bavon Marie-Marie, Rochereau, and on and on. If you want to know African music at any level, you have to know this stuff. —*John Storm Roberts*

Zimbabwe

Bhundu Boys

b. Zimbabwe
Group / Jit
The Bhundus built up a national following in Zimbabwe by taking the more traditional guitar styles of chimurenga (made popular by Thomas Mapfumo), adding some English/American-style finger-picking and a heavy disco-like bass drum beat, and playing with a lilting, rhythmic swing that's part highlife and part soukous. They call their hybrid "jit." In 1986 the Bhundu Boys put out their first record; when Scottish booker Gordon Muir heard it, he called Zimbabwe and flew the Bhundu Boys to England for a tour that became a year-long residence. With music industry heavies like Elvis Costello and Madonna touting them to the press, the Bhundus were soon under contract to Warner Brothers International (Island in the US). Influenced by the Rolling Stones and soukous as well as the traditional music of their native Zimbabwe, the Bhundu Boys are one of Africa's most ass-kicking guitar bands. —*J. Poet*

☆ **Shabini** / 1986 / Disque Afrique 02
An earlier album with a relatively under-produced sound. Guitars, bass, keyboard, and percussion. Exciting music from Zimbabwe. —*Hank Davis*

Tsvimbodzemoto / 1987 / Disque Afrique 03
Their second album, another great recording that mines the roots of Zimbabwe and serves them up with plenty of dazzling rock guitar. —*J. Poet*

○ **True Jit** / 1988 / Mango 162-539812
Their international debut is considered "watered down" by some purists, but it'll still knock your socks off. With a fuller sound and some English lyrics. —*J. Poet & Hank Davis*

Pamberi / 1990 / Mango 162-539858
Highly melodic and rhythmic music from Zimbabwe. —*Hank Davis*

Stella Chiweshe

Vocals, mbira / Neo-traditional, Mbira
As a woman in a male-dominated field, Stella Chiweshe has faced many struggles to survive as a musician and keep her na-

tive traditions alive. But her persistence has paid off and, along with her own small mbira (also known as sanza or thumb-piano) groups, she has recorded numerous traditionally oriented import albums of Zimbabwean folk music. —*Myles Boisen*

○ **Ambuya/Ndizyozvo** / 1988 / Globestyle 029
As you can hear on the last four tracks of this CD, Chiweshe experiments with a fusion of rock and traditional Zimbabwean styles. (This import version includes material from the *Ndizyozvo* EP that the Shanachie version does not.) —*J. Poet*

○ **Ambuya** / Shanachie 65006
An earthy, deeply satisfying document of traditional and original Zimbabwean thumb-piano (mbira) music by this talented performer. —*Myles Boisen*

Thomas Mapfumo

b. 1945, Marondera, Zimbabwe
Vocals, guitar / Chimurenga
Thomas Mapfumo made revolutionary changes in Zimbabwe's pop-music scene by recording a song for which he'd written his own music. Before Mapfumo, songs in the traditional style were always based on tunes that had been handed down for generations. Mapfumo's music, chimurenga ("music of struggle"), became popular during the civil war against White minority rule, but his popularity made the government unhappy. In 1977 he was sent to a prison camp for subversion. To obtain his release, Mapfumo agreed to perform for the ruling party, but at the concert he sang only his most revolutionary songs. "I told them that since I'd been in detention, I didn't have time to write new ones." Mapfumo grew up in the country, went to a British colonial school, and worked as a herd boy, watching over the cattle. After hearing the Beatles and Wilson Pickett in the early '60s, Mapfumo taught himself guitar and started a band that played pop music from African countries as well as Beatles, Rolling Stones, funk, and soul. Mapfumo left Western music behind to form the Acid Band. Their first album, *Hokoyo* ("Beware"), contained the songs that led to Mapfumo's detention. After Zimbabwe's liberation in 1978, Mapfumo formed Blacks Unlimited and released *Gwindingwe Rine Shumba* (Lion in the Bush), a joyous celebration of his country's independence. Jumbo Van Renen, the president of Earthworks Records, arranged to put out Mapfumo's music in England; when Van Renen later became CEO of Island Records in the UK, he signed Mapfumo again, this time to an international recording contract. —*J. Poet*

Indangariro / 1984 / Shanachie 44012
These were done shortly after the Zimbabwean independence and still have that youthful fire. —*Myles Boisen*

☆ **Chimurenga Singles** / 1984 / Shanachie 43066
The early hit singles by Mapfumo and Blacks Unlimited. These sides were recorded during the long civil war; their musical and lyrical content completely revamped the face of pop music in Zimbabwe. A classic. —*J. Poet*

Corruption / 1989 / Mango 162-539848
Mapfumo's first international release. This has more stunning guitar, and the title tune is sung in English to a calypso-like beat. A joyful mix of innovation and traditional roots. Great dance music. —*J. Poet & Myles Boisen*

Chamunorwa / 1991 / Mango 162-539900
Sidestepping his characteristic flinty sound, Mapfumo digs in deep with extended trance-inducing grooves propelled by thundering bass-drum heartbeats. —*Bob Tarte*

Shumba: Vital Hits of Zimbabwe / 1991 / Earthworks 1022
An anthology of Mapfumo's biggest hits from the late '70s and early '80s. Includes most of *Gwindingwe Rine Shumba*, an album released by Mapfumo to celebrate Zimbabwe's independence. —*J. Poet*

Dumisani Maraire

Chaminuka: Music from Zimbabwe / 1988 / Music of the World 208
This is an unparalleled recording that features the rhythms and melodies of Zimbabwe from the master musician Dumisani Maraire. Maraire sings and plays mbira and is joined on several selections by Minanzi III, a powerful marimba-and-percussion ensemble. Together, these two elements provide a fascinating glimpse into the music of Zimbabwe. —*Music of the World*

Zimbabwe Collection

○ **Viva! Zimbabwe** / 1983 / Hannibal 4411
Post-liberation pop with generous samplings of jit, soukous, chimurenga, and other styles. —*J. Poet*

○ **Take Cover** / 1986 / Disque Afrique 01
Guitar pop from Zimbabwe by various artists, in the chimurenga style pioneered by Thomas Mapfumo. Pick hit: "Tarira Nguva," the African take on country & western, by the Family Singers. —*J. Poet*

ASIA

Asia Collection

Asia / Pan 2020
The revenge of the colonized! Unbelievably varied marching bands from Nepal, India, Indonesia, the Moluccas and the Philippines: some large, some small; some shahnais, some with flutes; some with walls of sound such as Spector never dreamed of; some inhabited by the ghosts of King Oliver. To be icily objective about it, it's sheer, unadulterated rapture. —*John Storm Roberts, Original Music*

☆ **Islamic Music of Asia** / Inedit 260022
Muslim music from Pakistan, India, Malaysia, and Indonesia. Here are a call to prayer from Pakistan, a qawwal from India and one from Pakistan (Sabri Brothers); a Pakistani ghazal; a Malaysian maulidd, and a salawat dulang, a two-singer vocal contest special to Indonesia. Admirable idea, fine music. —*John Storm Roberts*

☆ **Tuva: Voices Center of Asia** / Smithsonian/Folkways 40017
Not only have we here 33 examples of some of the most impressive vocal techniques in the world (including chordal throat-singing, with some almost equally remarkable instrumental work, but the notes, though cheaply produced, are extremely thorough. —*John Storm Roberts & Myles Boisen*

Bangladesh Collection

Songs of the Madmen / Arion 274715
The "madmen" are the Bauls, the wandering mystics of Bengal, who "proceed against the tide of habit, received ideas, and generalization." Not surprisingly, therefore, they set great store by singing, dancing, and ornamentation of the body, making this a very lively recording. The thorough notes include English translations of the songs. —*Carl Hoyt, Original Music*

Cambodia

Sam-Ang Sam Ensemble

○ **Music of Cambodia** / World Music Institute 007
Sam-Ang Sam is affiliated with Seattle's Cambodian Studies Center. He here leads various groupings of traditional musicians in wedding music and other songs traditional and contemporary. Good notes. This is part of the World Music Institute's New Americans series. —*John Storm Roberts*

Cambodia Collection

Royal Music of Cambodia / Philips 6586 002
A long piece by pinpeat orchestra, wooden-keyed xylophones predominating with gongs. Various smaller ensembles and mohori orchestra. —*David L. Mayers*

China

Guo Brothers & Shung Tian

Group
The Guo Brothers (Guo Yue and Guo Yi) come from a musical family, and distinguished themselves as young woodwind players in offical Chinese orchestras. After leaving China, their musical

horizons have broadened, but still reflect the austerity and poise of their native traditions. —*Myles Boisen*

○ **Yuan** / 1990 / Virgin 86154
These young brothers put some new twists into traditional Chinese music. Gorgeous recordings of an accessible small group. —*Myles Boisen*

Lu-Seng Ensemble

○ **Shantung . . .** / Nonesuch 72051
Shantung Folk & Traditional Instruments. Peaceful melodies from the Lu-Sheng Ensemble and excellent examples of folk and classical music played on sona (oboe), drum and cymbals, sheng, cheng, t'unti, nan'hu, and ti-tzu. Truly the people's music, not fussy or Westernized. —*Myles Boisen & David L. Mayers*

Li Xiantang

○ **Art of the Qin** / Ocora 560001
Li's performance of compositions from 223 to 1937 highlights the transcendence of styles and eras typical of the seven-stringed qin zither (and indeed Chinese music as a whole). Bizarre, maybe, but as a bassist, I'm fascinated by the qin. Not only are some new basses like a vertical version of it, but Li's techniques provide a wonderful model, from the delicate, breathy slides of the rare "Fisherman's Song" to the vigor of "Flowing Waters." —*Carl Hoyt, Original Music*

China Collection

China / Barenreiter Musicaphon 2032
A varied and very beautiful set, recorded in mainland China, of classical compositions for stringed instruments—pipa, qin, and zheng—plus one for xiao bamboo flute and qin. The pieces are all several hundred years old (dates are often disputed). The musicians are of different generations and reflect several approaches to their tradition. The notes and illustrations are, as always, admirable. —*John Storm Roberts*

China—Music of the Pipa / Nonesuch 72085
Folk and classical instrumentals on the four-string Chinese lute by master Lui Pui-Yuen. —*Myles Boisen*

Chinese Turkestan/Xinjian Uighur Music / Ocora 559092/3
Music from the Mideast/Asia interface. Though ruled by China, Uighur and Dolan are Muslim, and their music (despite Asian influences more obvious in the look of its instruments than in its sound or structure) is a highly individual descendant of the Arabo-Persian nexus. A superb recording of instrumental and vocal pieces, with very full notes. (144 minutes) —*John Storm Roberts*

Hong Kong: Instrumental Music / Auvidis 8031
A re-release of an old *Musical Atlas* album mostly devoted to solo music, notably (though not solely) to stringed instruments: pipa lute, butterfly harp, and ch'in zither are all represented along with various wind instruments, all in particularly fine performances. The term "classical" may be unsuited to the Chinese tradition, but this is art music, old and new, of high order. —*John Storm Roberts*

☆ **Spring Night on a Moonlit River** / Nonesuch 72089
Spring Night on a Moonlit River—Music of the Chinese offers beautiful Chinese classical music, featuring the soulful sounds of the seven-string ch'in. —*Myles Boisen*

India

Jitendra Abhisheki

○ **Hymns From The Vedas And Upanishads, Vedic Chants** / Ravi Shankar Music Circle
Music from the depths of the soul. Born into a family of priests in Goa, India, Abhisheki's father was the "pujari" (chief priest) at the Mangeshi temple, a position now held by Abhisheki's brother. The contrast of the devotional songs and the traditional Vedic rhythmic punctuations with the Upanishad poetry and romantic emotion in more fluid raga-style singing, show Abhisheki to be a singer of great gifts and psychological understanding. The combined rhythmic delivery with high emotion in the mixed ragas of the "Hymn on the Greatness of Shiva" is direct and masterful. The combination of beauty and philosophy in the "Peace Chants"

is also remarkable ("Om. That is full, this is full, From the full the full has been taken, Having taken the full from the full, the full alone remains. Om. Peace, peace, peace"). —*"Blue" Gene Tyrrany*

Ali, Salamat and Nazakat

Salamat and Nazakat Ali / 1988 / Hannibal 1332
A 1970 recording by two leading khayal singers—rarer in that Nazakat has since died. They perform two ragas that are musically close but emotionally very different. Rag Megh is associated with love, anticipation and the rainy season. Rag Bairagi is associated with sadness and devotion. The performance is superb: Richard Henderson, who studied under Pandit Pran Nath as did the Alis, finds this the finest Indian vocal recording he's ever heard. —*John Storm Roberts, Original Music*

Vijaya Anand

Dance Raja Dance / Luaka Bop 268742
Anand is a kingpin of new-wave southern Indian filmi music, though more uptempo, brassier, and hipper than his elders, with lots of electric guitar and synth as well as the usual tablas, dholak, violins, harmonium, sitar. This stuff will stimulate all your acupuncture points—guaranteed. Truly outstanding notes are a major bonus. —*Raissa St. Pierre, Original Music*

Apache Indian

Bhangra
"Move Over India," a crossover dance hall hit mixing elements of bhangra, rap, reggae, and ragga, brought the British-based Apache Indian to a wide mixed race audience in Britain. (Compound nouns describing his Afro-Caribbean-Asian musical hybrid proliferated: bhangramuffin was a favorite). *No Reservations* also scored considerable success in India. —*Ken Hunt*

No Reservations / 1993 / Mango 1625399322
While his music is not bhangra in any accepted sense, he grew out of the bhangra scene. His is a remarkable bhangra-related dance music often carrying a social message in a mix of Punjabi, English, and West Indian patois. Tracks such as "Chok There" (meaning 'Tear the House Down'), "Move Over India," "Don Raja," and "Arranged Marriage" made it a remarkable debut. (With one qualification: several tracks had previously appeared on an independent mini-album for Jet Star.) —*Ken Hunt*

Nikhil Banerjee

The Hundred-Minute Raga / 1982 / Raga 207
Two CDs. The Raga label specializes in concert recordings of classical Indian music, on the eminently logical ground that concert music is at its best in concert. This splendid performance by the late Nikhil Banerjee, one of the greatest of sitar players, was given in Berkeley in 1982. As the name suggests, it consists of the whole of one lengthy raga (except the start of the introductory alap, which was missed for reasons explained). The notes are adulatory but informative, and an interview with Banerjee is included. —*John Storm Roberts*

Live: Berkeley 1982 / 1982 / Raga 104
This extensive raga—"Misra Kafi"—shows Banerjee at his best (especially since it was recorded in the second part of the concert). Very fine digital recording. —*John Storm Roberts*

○ **Immortal Sitar of Pandit Nikhil Banerjee, Ragas: Purabi Kalyan, Zila-kafi, Kirwa** / 1986 / Chhanda Dhara
One of the best and unfortunately last recordings of Banerjee, an incomparable sitarist. His beautiful rendering of "Purabi Kalyan," a combined raga, expresses with restraint the peaceful and devout mood of this twilight raga through an original melody. Another combined raga "Zila-Kafi" is next, played with liberal development of the romantic mood. The concluding South Indian raga "Kirwani" begins in a mood of devotion and develops into a fast Jhala. —*"Blue" Gene Tyrrany*

Raga Patdeep / Sonodisc 8414
Both his sense of musical architecture and the influence of Ali Akbar Khan can be heard clearly in the extended development of this evening raga. (48+ minutes) —*John Storm Roberts*

Jagdeep Singh Bedi

Soft & True / 1989 / Music of the World 108
Features the surbahar (bass sitar) and sitar of Jagdeep Singh Bedi, a virtuoso who creates a kaleidoscope of sound and melody with his instruments. Side 1 features solo surbahar with tanpura; Side 2, sitar and flute duets with tabla accompaniment. —*Music of the World*

Jotin Bhattacharya

Raga Lalita Gouri/Raga Bhagawati / Ark 85601
Little-known in the West but a major musician, sarod-player Bhattacharya is the pupil of the great Ustad Allaudin Khan who is regarded as closest to the master's spirit and style, which reconciled the freedom of khyal and the intensity of drupad. —*John Storm Roberts*

Balbir Bobby

Giddha
Giddha like bhangra is quintessentially a folk dance. Far more graceful than its male counterpart it traditionally was performed to dholki accompaniment. Boliyans (traditional folk songs) formed its core repertoire and like other Punjabi folk music its content could be scurrilous verging on the crude. Balbir Bobby's subtitle "Non-Stop Boliyan" says it all. —*Ken Hunt*

Jullunduro Paar / 1990 / Audiorec
Music by Varinder Bachan. Lyrics traditional. —*Ken Hunt*

Ajo Chakrabarty

○ **Raga Malkauns (Bara Khayal In Ektal / Chota Khayal In Tintal) / Raga Mishra Bhai** / 1991 / IAM (India Archive Music)
Chakrabarty is an amazing inventive vocalist with a unique style. He continuously produces fresh, brief, well-defined phrases, never lapsing into sequences of repeated gestures in order to "push" the music along. In the two khayals in Raga Malkauns, he therefore achieves considerable depth of feeling as if the experience was absolutely spontaneous. There is a sonic lavishness of coincident harmonies between the two tamburas, harmonium, and voice at times in this raga that will sweep the listener away. Excellent understated tabla playing by Samar Saha. —*"Blue" Gene Tyrany*

Hariprasad Chaurasia

Flying Beyond—Improvisations on Bamboo Flute / Earthbeat! 89004
Hariprasad is an acknowledged virtuoso on the bansuri, or bamboo flute. Backed only by tambura, Hariprasad improvises around a traditional raga to produce this album of deep meditative music. The pure tones of his flute rise and fall over the drone of the tambura creating a timeless mood of peacefulness and profundity. —*Backroads Music / Heartbeats*

○ **Rag Kaunsi Kanhra** / Nimbus 5182
Sensuous evening raga for the bamboo bansuri flute, with tabla by Sabir Khan. Lovely. —*Myles Boisen*

Dagar Brothers

Rag Kambhoji / 1989 / Music of the World 114
Dhrupad is one of the oldest and most respected forms of classical Indian music, and the Dagar Brothers are its internationally acclaimed master vocalists. This outstanding release features Ustads N. Zahiruddin and N. Faiyazuddin Dagar singing "Rag Kambhoji." They are accompanied by Mohan Shyam Shara (pakhawaji drum) and Mussarat and Wasif Dagar (tamburas). —*Music of the World*

Kadri Gopalnath

Jugalbandi / Magnasound 15036
Of all Western instruments recently introduced to Indian classical music, I find Gopalnath's Carnatic saxophone the most interesting, because the sax is flexible enough to adapt well to non-European intervals and tonally distinctive enough to give the effort real point. Wadvati's Hindustani clarinet is almost equally successful. A really superb recording both conceptually and in its results. —*John Storm Roberts, Original Music*

The Music of India

The music of India has enjoyed a worldwide explosion since coming into vogue in the psychedelic 60s. Most Indian musicians come from musical families and begin study from an early age at the knee of a father or uncle. In the classical tradition (the majority of recordings available in the US are by North Indian classical musicians), music is a prestigious, life-long pursuit where sustained solo expression figures prominently. Centuries-old scales called ragas serve as the basis for extended improvisation in small groups, typically involving a tabla drummer and tambura player, whose ethereal drone reinforces the mood of the raga for the lead instrumentalist.

Popular lead instruments in the North Indian school are the multi-stringed sitar, sarod, sarangi, and santour, and woodwinds – bamboo flute and shehnai – a double-reed oboe sometimes heard in larger ensembles. The voice is also featured in both North and South Indian classical forms – in the South the dominant art music is the Carnatic style, which emphasizes highly ornamented improvisation based on long melodies of folk, sacred, and classical origin. Common instruments in the South are the stringed vina and violin, often used in larger groups with singers and a variety of percussion – the double-headed mridangam, clay-pot drum, and tambourine. In recent years, Western instruments – mandolin, guitar, clarinet, piano, and even the saxophone – have been embraced by younger innovators and incorporated into the classical tradition (though not without protest).

India also has a rich legacy of regional folk music; religious songs of various sects; theatrical epics involving mythology, dance, and music; pop forms; and of course an extremely prolific film-music industry, just beginning to be appreciated abroad. Recordings offered by American companies are just the tip of the iceberg – go to an Indian market in a major city and you will find a bewildering array of national styles, most on inexpensive cassettes.

– Myles Boisen

Gulabi Sapera

Music of Rajasthan / Silex 225213
The northwestern state of Rajasthan is a treasure house of traditional music of almost unparalleled variety, depth, and vibrancy, much of it performed by professional or semi-professional castes of musicians. The Silex release, which is confined to one group, is musically just as fine (take special note of the highly unusual final cut). It also has lyrics in Rajasthani and English, but zero background on music or musicians! —*John Storm Roberts, Original Music*

Gangubai Hangal

The Voice of Tradition / Wergo 15012
At 75 years, Hangal may be the last representative of a generation that valued tradition and simplicity over show. She has been singing publicly since the late '20s and still performs with a group that includes her daughter and granddaughter. These performances of ragas from the "Kirana Gharana" are an important rarity amid the multiple recordings of familiar virtuosos. —*John Storm Roberts*

Medhi Hassan

Best of Mehdi Hassan, The / EMI India 012
Mehdi Hassan is arguably the premier male ghazal singer, taking both talent and popularity into consideration. This "best of . . ." shows him in classic vocal form, though with backings that will strike Westerners as highly pop-oriented—an issue that appears

Indian Film Music

Filmi, as Indian film music is known wherever Indian film is shown, doubles as India's foremost popular music form. It is a music which profoundly appeals to the Indian psyche throughout the subcontinent. It also commands a loyal following elsewhere. Indian film, for example, is a popular form of entertainment in places as far apart as Indonesia and Israel, the Gulf States and Ghana, England and Egypt but not necessarily just among Indian diaspora communities. Among Indians film is the most popular form of entertainment, sometimes the only form of entertainment on a daily basis available in urban communities. For decades Bombay, Calcutta, Madras and a scattering of regional centers have dominated India's musical outpourings. Towering over them all is Bombay or Bollywood as it came to be nicknamed.

General film song is known as filmi gana, as opposed, for example, to filmi qawwali, an immensely popular, secularly debased form of the Islamic devotional music called qawwali. Filmi music in essence is the lingua franca of India and Indians. For Indians of all classes and creeds filmi's finest are as instantly recognisable as hits like Barbra Streisand's "Memories," Frank Sinatra's "Chicago," Bing Crosby's "White Christmas" and Paul McCartney's "Mull of Kintyre" are to Westerners. At best filmi has aspirations towards immortality, is timeless, at worst it is irritatingly disposable and ephemeral–to flirt with mixed metaphor, the opposing poles of popular music's balancing act the world over. Yet as a popular music genre, statistically, commercially and aesthetically, filmi has few serious rivals or peers in the whole world of popular music.

The arrival of India's first talkie in 1931 ushered in a new era. Ardeshir M. Irani's Alam Ara (Beauty of the World) had started life as a theatrical piece in the Parsee Theater. Transferring it to the celluloid screen, Irani retained the original drama's use of song. The decision was significant on four counts. Alam Ara reeled out a link with its folk the-

ater origins, it played out what would become the institution of film song, it gave Indian cinema its first vocalist, and it proved a hit in India and further afield in Ceylon (Sri Lanka), Burma (Myanmar) and what one film commentator rather open-endedly called "West Asia." The talkies brought major headaches for the Indian film industry.

The silent cinema had revealed itself to be an unimaginable motherlode of spectacle, wonderment and lucre. Language threatened to undermine all that since talkies accentuated the nation's linguistic divide. With films being made in around 15 major languages, music was able to woo the largely illiterate audience to the cinema. Indian film moguls found their Hollywood grail in the film song. Because of their familiarity even to illiterate audiences, their respectability as subject matter and their wide-ranging appeal, the early pioneers of the silent cinema had used mythic and religious stories to entice the public. Music provided–and proved–to be that necessary new ingredient in the recipe. Thanks to Ardeshir M. Irani, filmi had its first singer in Wazir Mohd. Khan. Shellac would shortly turn to film song. (As early as January 1933 HMV (India) was predicting that "the key to prosperity...in the immediate future" would lie in "Indian Talkie records and Radio-Gramophones".) The introduction of film song played tunes on box office tills.

Westerners often find the appeal of Indian films and filmi baffling, banishing it to a Cahiers du Cinema critic's wilderness. Plagiarised or hackneyed plots are the norm. Head-splitting sound enhancements concuss. Eyeball-blitzing jarringly juxtaposing jarringly incongruous images is commonplace. It can all combine to prompt the question: How much money would the drugs cost to get as weird as the cutting room and sound effects team? Film song has contributed to Indian film's unique narrative style, developing the convention of interleaving song and, frequently, lavish dance routines. For westerners such interjections disconcertingly break up and suspend the narrative flow. Indians, long attuned to such conventions, do not so much as blink. Musical arrangements may have the kitchen-sink

not to bother Indian listeners overmuch. —*John Storm Roberts, Original Music*

Anup Jalota

Farmaish / Music India 033
Devoted to the traditional Persian-derived love songs called "ghazals" that have recently re-entered Indian pop music with a vengeance. Jalota is mostly known for religious bhajans, but this is a really splendid set in a semi-classical vein, wonderfully sung to violin, harmonium, and percussion accompaniment. (61+ minutes) —*John Storm Roberts*

Brij Bhushan Kabra

○ **Raga Puriya Alap** / Celluloid Records
In this reissue of a 1983 recording, this amazing slide guitarist not only makes astonishing and spontaneous melodic inventions but also evokes surprising new sounds from his instrument. A tremolo-inflected cry, a stream of fire rising into space will suddenly turn into a heartfelt, personal sigh. Confident statements underlined by strong rhythms soon follow. Raga Puriya, played at sunset, is a meditation on renunciation, subtle and complex to play. Serious listening will be highly rewarded. —*"Blue" Gene Tyrrany*

Salamat Ali Khan

Two brothers from Pakistan (Nazakat is now dead) who challenged and inspired each other to great vocal heights in a stirring duet form usually heard in Indian music. Salamat has gone on to record as a soloist. —*Myles Boisen*

○ **Salamat & Nazakat Ali Khan** / 1988 / Hannibal 1332
Classical vocal duets in the uplifting Khayal tradition. —*Myles Boisen*

○ **Raga Gunkali/Saraswati/Durga** / Nimbus 5307
Vocal ragas. —*Myles Boisen*

Sultan Khan

○ **Rag Bhupali, Rajasthani Folk Song In Rag Bhup Mand** / 1991 / Moment
A slow lyrical performance on the sarangi expressing love and sadness begins "Rag Bhupali," one of the oldest and simplest of ragas, and the exposition develops into exciting virtuosic exchanges between Khan and the famous Zakir Hussain on tabla. Perhaps the nicest surprise this album offers is the warm, sweet Rajasthani folk song, which is alternately sung and then played on the sarangi, beautifully varied but never overdone by Khan and Hussain, who actually provide a decrescendo section at the end instead of simply stopping. —*"Blue" Gene Tyrrany*

Ustad Ali Akbar Khan

Sarod / Classical
One of the greatest Indian musicians of the 20th century (many would argue *the* greatest), although his fame has always been eclipsed by that of his cousin Ravi Shankar. The reigning master of the fretless sarod, Ali Akbar Khan has done hundreds of recordings in India and runs an influential Indian music school in California. An important innovative force outside of India. —*Myles Boisen & John Storm Roberts*
Journey / Aug. 1990 / Triloka 184

approach to a degree touching on the parodic. Musical effects may be crassly applied. Even Kumar Sanu's blockbuster hit of 1994, the superbly melodic "Ek Ladki Ko Dekha," added clumsy reverb. Music directors–as songwriting teams tend to be called Ö~ may be contracted for years ahead. Many burn out or shamelessly recycle, often apparently without anybody noticing for several soundtracks, the weight of their names carrying the film forward in the cinematic equivalent of the Emperor's New Clothes. Caveats aside, scattered throughout its illustrious history are many, many examples of people of rare vision.

Traditionally the filmi industry was renowned for its well-known cabal of playback singers, the voices behind the screen image, the name singers who could tip the balance and make a potential flop a hit. Historically the position had been very different. As the singer and Gramophone Company of India producer G.N. Joshi wrote in Down Melody Lane, "Even unmusical heroes and heroines like Devika Rani, Motilal, Savita Banerji, Leela Chitnis and Ashok Kumar came before our microphones a number of times." Gradually a coterie of uncredited, unnamed singers arose. For over a decade it was industry policy not to credit playback singers. This was because it was believed that so doing would detract from the celluloid heroes' popularity. For example, the early post-war film Mahal gave the playback singer–Lata Mangeshkar–as Kamini, the name of the role played by the actress Madhubala. Only in the 1940s did this position change. The existence of these professional vocalists became an open secret and the public demanded to know whose voice as behind the moving lips. Once their names began rolling on the credits, the names of the playback singers became as celebrated as the film stars themselves. Yet Indian producers' extreme conservatism created the situation whereby a small, highly select band of playback vocalists came to monopolize most sessions. This is because such vocalists came to be seen as a major factor in the box office success of any film and nobody wanted to meddle with the alchemy of success. A coda is needed.

While the playback singer may seem an alien concept to many, Hollywood too had its version. Audrey Hepburn in the 1957 version of Funny Face sang with the voice of Marni Nixon when she sang "How Long Has This Been Going On?" India merely raised the convention to the status of an art form.

Over the years a carousel of names has spun by. In Bollywood the old hierarchy came to revolve around singers such as Noor Jehan (especially popular in Pakistan from Partition in 1947 onwards and a major influence on the Queen of the playback singers, Lata Mangeshkar), Lata Mangeshkar (reckoned to be the most recorded artiste anywhere in the world), her sister Asha Bhosle, Kishore Kumar, Mukesh and Mohd. Rafi (as the spelling was finally standardized). Others overshadowed to some degree but estimable vocalists nevertheless included female playback artists such as Geeta Dutt, Suman Kalyanpur and Suraiya, and male counterparts such as C.H. Atma, Manna Dey, Hemant Kumar and Talat Mahmood. During the 1990s a core of new singers including Abhijeet, Sudesh Bhosale, Kavita Krishnamurty, Udit Narayan, Anuradha Podwal and Kumar Sanu arose.

All the regional film industries have their quota of homegrown playback heroes and heroines. While some singers have broken through to the Hindi-speaking nation–S.P. Balasubramanyam is a notable example, having worked with Naushad and scored several major Hindi hits–most, like Yesudas, T.M. Soundarajan and Ghantasala, are content to exploit the considerable Southern market. S.P. Balasubramanyam remains a reigning champion, commanding large fees. Even so a new generation of singers such as Mano, S. Janaki, P. Sushila and Chitra Shankar have emerged, for there are crowns to be wrested and won. Southern singers as a whole remain local heroes. Many Tamil and Telugu soundtracks (even on EMI India), for example, use packaging which is incomprehensible outside their linguistic community and such albums carry no English translation.

On *Journey,* Khan displays both his instrumental prowess and his inventiveness in fusing Western musical idioms with Indian sensibilities. The album consists entirely of original material, with clearly discernable chord changes and strong melodies . . . *Journey* is a daring statement by a brilliant artist. —*Backroads Music / Heartbeats*

☆ **Duet** / RSM 103
A near-perfect example of the classical duet. This superb live concert features star violinist L. Subramaniam and tabla drummer Zakir Hussein. —*Myles Boisen*

○ **Signature Series–Vols. 1 & 2** / Alam Madina 9001
His long-unavailable 1967 recordings for the Connoisseur Society were the gateway to raga for many Americans. More than that, they are examples of one of the great schools of Hindustani classical music. Among the first of the Connoisseur series to be reissued, these and all his recordings are essential. Volume 1 has ragas "Chandranandan," "Gauri Manjari," "Jogiya Kalingra"; Volume 2, ragas "Medhavi," "Khammaj," "Bhairavi Bhatiyar with Ragmala." —*John Storm Roberts*

Ustad Sabri Khan

Raga Darbari/Raga Multani / Auvidis 6754
Ustad Sabri Khan is one of the greatest living masters of the Indian violin. His most important contribution to the advance of the tradition (like many 20th-century masters) has been to give his instrument an important solo role, after a period in which it had fallen into disrepute. Here he plays two ragas associated with khayal, which express more tension than most chosen by contemporary musicians. —*John Storm Roberts*

Ustad Sabri Khan with Ghulam Sawar Sabri / ARCD 1172
The sarangi is strongly associated with accompaniment, but even in solo–a recent development pioneered by Sabri Khan–the sarangi normally follows khayal and thumri forms. —*John Storm Roberts*

Ustad Sultan Khan

Sarangi / Classical
Along with his contemporary Ram Narayan, Ustad Sultan Khan is one of a handful of Indian classical musicians keeping the sound of the sarangi alive. This archaic instrument is bowed, with the performer sliding his fingernails along the melody strings; the many sympathetic strings vibrating in harmony produce a haunting drone accompaniment. —*Myles Boisen*

☆ **Sarangi: The Music of India** / 1975 / Rykodisc 10104
This shows many emotional sides of the living master of the sarangi, an ancient bowed string instrument. —*Myles Boisen*

Ramnad Krishnan

Vocals / Carnatic
The Carnatic style is primarily a showcase for vocalists, who must present long composed pieces in addition to intense and demanding improvisations. Ramnad Krishnan began studying at the age of six and, after achieving celebrity status in both South and North India, went on to teach at Wesleyan University in Connecticut. —*Myles Boisen*

☆ **Vidwan–Music of South India–Songs of the Carnatic Tradition** / Nonesuch 72023
Ramnad Krishnan: Vidwan—Songs of the Carnatic Tradition features vocals with violin and mridangam. Extended perfor-

mances, lengthy alap. An essential record of the South Indian vocal art in all its complexity. —*David L. Mayers & Myles Boisen*

S. and R. Maharajapuram

Carnatic Music / Auvidis 6746
Sathanam and Ramachandran Maharajapuram, the father-and-son team, among the major singers of their respective age groups, are also the sixth and seventh generation of a major vocal dynasty. Their duet style is as beguiling as it is authentic. —*John Storm Roberts*

Mala

Giddha
While bhangra, folk, and filmi dominate the Punjabi market, giddha (or gidha) is still a vital force. Mala performs in the giddha style. A prevalent and deeply entrenched Punjabi male view has it that giddha's cultural association with womankind makes it unfitting for men to dance to its rhythms. —*Ken Hunt*

Gidha Pao Gidha / Multitone 1125
One of the main popularizers of giddha. —*Ken Hunt*

Ram Chatur Mallik

○ **King Of Dhrupad: Ram Chatur Mallik In Concert** / 1988 / Wergo
Three unusual ragas, recorded in Vrindaban, the religious center of Krishna worship and the home town of Dhrupad, sung by the last great court singer of Darbhanga in the Northeast of India. "Raga Vinod," being a creation of Mallik's father Rajit Ram, will not be found in any textbook. The alap is sung here in a majestic style, as a pure composition without embellishment or distortion, followed by a dhrupad with a poem about separation from a beloved. "Raga Sindura" is sung with striking rhythmic improvisations in a "dhamar" style of uneven 14-beat cycle, a tradition of the Bihar province. The text concerns a young girl being reprimanded for not joining in the festivities of the spring rites of Holi, the festival of colors. "Raga Paraj" is sung again as a dhamar with a text about the red Gulal powder and colored water thrown during Holi, concluding traditionally with a fast Sulphakta in ten beats with a text about Krishna, who is called the dark, beautiful one. This CD is intense listening, more for the edge of your seat than reclining with your eyes closed. —*"Blue" Gene Tyrrany*

Mitalee

Best of / EMI India 5006
Ghazals are love poems traceable back to medieval Persia via the Moghul dynasty. These days, they are performed in a huge range of styles. This duo specializes in pop ghazals, with arrangements that use a full range of backings from traditional to full-string-section pop. There's even a charming and entirely successful French influence in Bhupinder's "Dhundlaye Huye Waade," for example. —*John Storm Roberts, Original Music*

Budhaditya Mukherjee

Rag Bagesri/Rag Des / May 1989 / Nimbus 5268
Sitar ragas. —*Myles Boisen*

○ **Rag Ramkali/Rag Jhinjoti** / May 1989 / Nimbus 5221
Sensitive sitar from one of the instrument's leading younger exponents, specializing in the vocal-derived gayaki style. —*Myles Boisen*

Ram Narayan

☆ **Rag Lalit** / 1989 / Nimbus 5183
Dark and dissonant—the most intense Indian music I've heard. Mostly solo sarangi (an ancient bowed instrument), with some tablas to break up the 73-minute length. —*Myles Boisen*

Rag Bhupal Tori/Rad Patdip / Nimbus 5119
Ragas on sarangi by the best-known contemporary practitioner. —*Myles Boisen*

Premi

Bhangra Ten Years On / Multitone 1212
This band was a pioneer of pop bhangra, the wild teenage Indo-Brit spin-off of a Punjabi folk form that over the past decade created a whole new music by combining Punjabi vocals and traditional rhythms and instruments (harmonium, various drums including the obligatory Punjabi dholak) with Western ingredients including funk, occasional reggae, electric piano and assorted synthesized sounds. —*Raissa St. Pierre, Original Music*

Satyajit Ray

Indian Art Film Music
★ **Jalsaghar** / Ocora 559022
For 1959's Jalsaghar (The Music Room) Ray brought in Vilayat Khan, vocalists Salamat Ali Khan and Akhatari Bai (Begum Akhtar), and shehnai player Bismillah Khan to create a momumental piece of work. Exemplary choice of musicians. Taste personified. —*Ken Hunt*

○ **Music of Satyajit Ray** / EMI India 5448
From 1961 Ray branched out, composing, scoring, and arranging the soundtracks for his own films. This selection presents tracks from *Teen Kanya* (*Three Daughters*) (1961) and *Shakespearewallah* (1966) to *Ganashatru* (*An Enemy of the People*) (1989) and his last completed film *Aguntuk* (*The Visitor*) (1991). Music was indissoluble from film in his overall vision. The booklet notes also reproduce a piece of staff notated score with delightful parading elephants—Ray was also a graphic artist and typographer. —*Ken Hunt*

Apna Sangreet

Bhangra
Like Alaap, one of the old guard and one of bhangra's legends. Gurcharan Mali's percussion work is a trademark. —*Ken Hunt*

Bhangre Da Raja / Multitone 1110
Dressed up to kill on the cover, Apna Sangeet's image presented bhangra's traditional face. The music straddled the divide between the traditional and contemporary. The title is not misspelled. —*Ken Hunt*

Ronak Mela / Multitone 1145
Drum-driven music from one of bhangra's finest bands. —*Ken Hunt*

Trichy Sankaran

Laya Vinyas / 1989 / Music of the World 120
Laya Vinyas (*Rhythmic Elaborations*) is a lively tape of Indian drumming showcasing the skills of an acknowledged virtuoso, who plays the mridangam, a double headed barrel drum that is the main percussion instrument of South India. On a couple of tracks Sankaryan is joined by the resonant vina, South India's answer to the sitar, while tambura and occasional finger cymbals and kanjira (frame drum) add their rhythmic voices. Center stage is Trichy's nimble fingered playing, amply displaying the subtle sophistication of the mridangam. —*Backroads Music / Heartbeats*

Shri Emani Shankara Sastry

Art of the Vina / Playasound 65015
The vina, an ancestor of the sitar, is the most important instrument of the South Indian Carnatic tradition. Shri Sastry is an heir to several generations of vina virtuosity. This 1974 recording (48+ minutes) contains lengthy ragas and shorter pieces. An outstanding performance, with superb notes and photos. —*John Storm Roberts*

Aruna Sayeeram

Carnatic Song / Auvidis 6747
Sayeeram sings a program with many kritis (religious songs somewhat like bhajans), accompanied by violin and the usual supporting instruments. (65:05) —*John Storm Roberts*

Lakshmi Shankar

Season & Time / Ocora 558615
Lakshmi Shankar is one of the greatest contemporary vocalists in the northern Indian classical tradition, a brilliantly expressive interpreter of khayal and bhajan forms. —*John Storm Roberts, Original Music*

Evening Concert / Ravi Shankar Music Circle 102

Lakshmi Shankar has a heavenly voice, sweet and clear. The "Khyal in Raga Dhaani" in a blues-like pentatonic scale and the romantic Thumri are delivered in an innocent, direct, lyrical melodiousness. The bhajan "Gopala" by the 16th century poet Nidhiram is totally engaging in its pleading yet devotional quality, with Shankar beginning at a high point right from the onset. "Janama Marana" by the saint-poetess of the 16th century, Mirabai, who gave up her life as a Queen for devotion to Lord Krishna, has a loving, serious quality. A throughly enjoyable album. —*"Blue" Gene Tyrrany*

Songs of Devotion / Auvidis 6745
Shankar sings mostly religious bhajans and semi-classical thumri in the khayal style, accompanying herself on the swaramandal zither—a relation to the santur. —*John Storm Roberts*

Ravi Shankar

b. 1920
Sitar / Classical
Known worldwide as the ambassador of Indian classical music, thanks largely to Beatle George Harrison and fiery performances at important '60s rock festivals, Ravi Shankar is also one of the most proficient North Indian musicians. He is a particularly nimble and exciting performer on the many-stringed sitar, especially in duet situations. Albums and tapes of his many '60s and '70s recordings are almost always available at used-record stores and/or Indian grocery stores in metropolitan areas, and his recent works, often in the world music/fusion vein, are easy to find. —*Myles Boisen*

Music of . . . / Ocora 558674
Ravi Shankar, of course, is not just a major proponent of cultural interchange, but (as sometimes seems to be overlooked these days) a musician equalled only by Ustad Ali Akbar Khan in his generation, a major influence on younger Indian players, and a profound and far-ranging exponent of the Hindustani sitar tradition. —*John Storm Roberts, Original Music*

☆ **Ragas** / 1973 / Fantasy 24714
A less-than-perfect recording, but this double-album is an impeccable document of inspired raga duets by the masters Ravi Shankar and Ali Akbar Khan. —*Myles Boisen*

Raga Parameshwari / 1976 / Capitol 10561
A full raga cycle, with his best tabla drum accompanist, Alla Rakha. —*Myles Boisen*

Shankar Project: Tana Mana / 1987 / Private Music 2016
A new-age-oriented project, not traditional classical sitar music. —*Myles Boisen*

Inside the Kremlin / 1988 / Private Music 2044
A collaboration with the Russian Folk Ensemble, Chorus, and Orchestra. —*Myles Boisen*

The Genius of Ravi Shankar / CBS 9560
Another worthy effort from Shankar's period of worldwide fame. —*Myles Boisen*

○ **The Sounds of India** / CBS 9296
Good notes and a spoken prolog by Shankar make this a fine introduction to North Indian classical music. —*Myles Boisen*

Shivkumar Sharma

☆ **Rag Madhuvanti/Rag Mishra Tila** / Nimbus 5110
Glittering classical rags on the rarely heard santur, an Asian version of the hammer dulcimer. —*Myles Boisen*

Colours of 100 Strings / EMI 5076
Until Sharma brought it into the classical canon quite recently, India knew the santur largely as a Kashmiri folk instrument. On this recording he plays an extended "Rag Vachaspati" and a shorter piece, based on a Rajasthani folk form, that creeps into the classical canon. —*John Storm Roberts*

○ **Shringar** / Real World 91317
Ragas for sarod and violin in the southern Carnatic tradition, recorded in concert by two brothers (Shivakumar and Sridhar) from the younger generation of musicians. "Raga Bageshri" is a late-night raga, while the extremely popular "Bhairavi" is played at any time of the day. Here they are both given somewhat contemplative renderings that focus on spiritual depth rather than technique. —*John Storm Roberts*

K. Sridhar

Nadanjali / Auvidis 6736
A 74-minute raga malkauns in dhrupad tradition, out of which Sridhar has apparently made a personal composition he has named "Nadanjali," the divine sound. —*John Storm Roberts, Original Music*

Parween Sultana

○ **Raga Rageswari, Raga Hamsadwani, Bhajans** / Oriental Records
This is a married musical duo, a "jugabanddi" par excellence. The clarity of line of perfectly complementary soprano and tenor voices, the emotional depth, and the sheer rollercoaster-ride thrill of their musical development is exceptional even in the richness of Indian music. Parween Sultana has the distinction of singing in musical festivals of both the North and South to sold-out audiences. —*"Blue" Gene Tyrrany*

Khayal / Esperance 8412
Khayal developed (like the European romantic movement) to reassert the primacy of expressiveness over rules that are too rigid; lyricism, freedom, improvisation, and virtuosity are its hallmarks. Sultana and Khan, perhaps the most highly regarded of India's younger singers, perform both solos and duets in a recording that is, at times, breathtaking. —*John Storm Roberts*

From Dawn to Dusk / Auvidis 6748
Sultana and Khan perform in the expressive khayal style. —*John Storm Roberts*

Pankaj Udhas

Paimanes / Music India 003
Devoted to the traditional Persian-derived lovesongs called "ghazals" that have recently re-entered Indian pop music with a vengeance, the Udhas set is quite as good as their *Farmaish* but in a more pop vein, with backings that draw from an intriguing mix of Indian and overseas (including Greek and Spanish) influences. —*John Storm Roberts*

India Collection

★ **Golden Voices From the Silver Screen Volume 1** / GlobeStyle 054

★ **Golden Voices From the Silver Screen Volume 2** / GlobeStyle 056

★ **Golden Voices From the Silver Screen Volume 3** / GlobeStyle 059
Western compilations have tended to focus on filmi songs with quirky and gimmicky arrangments. GlobeStyle's three volumes have their share of them but theirs are a balanced selection revealing the genre's grandeur. Matchless compilations with extensive notes that explain the context of this music. —*Ken Hunt*

Asia Classics 1 / Luaka Bop 2684
Madras has been under-represented when it has come to Western filmi anthologies, most of which have zoomed in on Hollywood's clique of playback vocalists. Largely, a peek at the world of the Madras-based playback singer S.P. Balasubramanyam (alternatively spelled S.P. Balasubramaniam), this is a first rate introduction to the Anand's magpie-eyed blending and borrowing tendencies. Any musical sound or genre is fair game. —*Ken Hunt*

Kismat & Shaheed & Bandhan / EMI India 20229
Featuring three films from the 1940s, this album captures a selection of earlier playback singers. Kismat (1943) features Arun Kumar and Ameerbai as its two main vocalists. Shaheed (1948) is noteworthy for the singing of the remarkable Punjabi folk singer Surinder Kaur in a playback role and Geeta Roy. Bandhan (1940) features Arun Kumar and the previously mentioned actress Leela Chitnis. One of the filmi reissues of 1994. —*Ken Hunt*

○ **Anarkali & Mughal-E-Azam** / EMI India 5112
A mighty combination. Anarkali featuring music by C. Ramchandra (the nom de plume of Ramchandra Chitalkar) is largely a vehicle for peak period Lata Mangeshkar. The excellent Hemant Kumar provides the male voice. *Muhal-E-Azam* is one of Naushad's masterworks. Lata Mangeshkar features prominently. It also contains a cameo performance by the venerable Bade Ghulam Ali Khan singing "Shubh Din Aayo" and anything by

this truly special Hindustani classical vocalist is worth listening to. A highly recommended coupling. —*Ken Hunt*

○ **Pakeezah & Razia Sultan** / EMI India 5129
Two further classics of Indian cinema paired together. *Pakeezah* (*Pure of Heart*) even carries the lonesome whistle blowing motif of the film into its music. Lata Mangeshkar, Rajkumari, Mohd. Rafi, and even the light classical vocalist Parween Sultana contribute to this magnificent movie. Razia Sultan also strongly feature the omnipresent Lata Mangeshkar. Asha Bhosle and Jagjit Kaur and Mahendra Kapoor and Bhupinder duet. Highly recommended too. —*Ken Hunt*

Baiju Bawra & Shabab / EMI India 5176
For the first of these films Maushad coaxed one of the finest classical male vocalists, Ustad Amir Khan, into the studio to sing with a jugalbandi (duet) with the marvellous Pandit D.V. Paluskar (in a scene reenacting a legendary jugalbandi between Tansen and Baiju). The usual suspects such as Mohd. Rafi, Shamshad Begum, Manna Dey, Hemant Kumar and, naturally Lata Mangeshkar were roped in for these soundtracks. —*Ken Hunt*

Mississippi Masala / JRS 35809
The soundtrack to Mira Nair's 1992 social drama set against the aftermath of the Ugandan-Asian exodus is noteworthy for its original score by the Southern Indian classical violinist Dr. L. Subramaniam and its non-Indian tracks. Untypically for an Indian soundtrack Subramaniam mixes Smiley Lewis, Otis Redding, a token Mukesh (his hit "Mera Joota Hai Japani"), and others. An Indian rather than a filmi soundtrack. —*Ken Hunt*

○ **1942—A Love Story** / EMI India 110048
1994's premiere film soundtrack outshone all others—even before its cinema permiere—due to one song. Kumar Sanu's interpretation of "Ek Ladki Ko Dekha" (roughly I Saw a Girl) proved that melody was in and that the spate of crudity and double-entendres that had haunted the early 1990s had had their day. Lata Mangeshkar's contribution lacks the power of her peak years but her presence acts as official validation. Completing the picture are six older tracks by Rahul Dev Burman (hence the *& Memorable Hits of R.D. Burman* of the full CD title). —*Ken Hunt*

★ **Thiruda Thiruda & Pidhiya Mugam** / Magnasound/OMI 0705
With music by A.R. Rehman and performances by Mano, Ahahul Hamid, Anupama, Chitra, Unni Menon, Sujatha, and S.P. Batasubramaniam, these two Tamil soundtracks are more accessible to World Music audiences than many from the Northern film industry. Their clever arrangements can evoke Okinawan music and Queen or can sound like renegades from Sally Potter's *Orlando* (Varese Sarabande VSD 5413). —*Ken Hunt*

Qawwalis From Films Volume 1 / EMI India 5333
A collection of filmi qawwalis drawm from movies such as *Mera Naam Joker, Zanjeer, Painter Babu*, and *Karma*. Asha Bhosie, Mukesh, Kishore Kumar, Manhar and Mahendra Kapoor are among the playback singers featured. A tastefree zone. —*Ken Hunt*

Jai Jai Ram Shreeram / Music India 100
The Hindu devotional songs called bhajans are a life-work for some singers, and powerful attraction for others better known in other genres. There are classical versions of bhajans, and mass-pop versions, and there is a core style that might be called traditionally-rooted popular. This album brings together three singers: Lata, who is best known for her filmi recordings, Pandit Bhimsen Joshi, and the most popular of all bhajan singers, Anup Jalota. Squarely in the traditional-popular vein, without pop trimmings or non-Indian instruments, this is wonderful. —*John Storm Roberts, Original Music*

Shyam Brass Band Street Music / TIPS 5221
The Shyam band's hallucinatory versions of Indian film tunes are a truly magnificent example of the extraordinary co-optation of brass band by Asian musicians. De Souza is having kittens where he is, but this combination of faintly maniacal horns and Indianized percussion (executed with a lot of technical chops, so you know they mean every assonance) is plainly and simply irresistible. —*John Storm Roberts, Original Music*

Professional Popular Musicians / Ocora 580044
The northwestern state of Rajasthan is a treasure house of traditional music of almost unparalleled variety, depth, and vibrancy—much of it performed by professional or semi-professional castes

of musicians. This release is the widest-ranging, both musically and chronologically. —*John Storm Roberts, Original Music*

Langas & Manganiyars / King 5117
The northwestern state of Rajasthan is a treasure house of traditional music of almost unparalleled variety, depth and vibrancy—much of it performed by professional or semi-professional castes of musicians. King's superlative World Music Library recording focuses on two major castes. —*John Storm Roberts, Original Music*

○ **Festival of India: A Hindustani Sampler** / 1990 / Music of the World 121
The great masters of North India perform classical and folk music on this landmark production, *Festival of India: A Hindustani Sampler*. Featured artists include V.G. Jog (violin), Sultan Khan (sarangi), G.S. Sachdev (bamboo flute), Purna Das Baul (Bengali folk ensemble), and the Dagar Brothers (Dhrupad vocal music). An excellent introduction to North Indian music. —*Music of the World*

○ **Inde Centrale/traditions Musicales Des Gond (central India/Musical Traditions of)** / 1990 / VDE-Gallo
India is the homeland for more than 40 million "tribals," aboriginals or indigenous peoples, whose ancestors lived there before the Aryans arrived in approximately 1500 BC. Many of these people live in the more inhospitable forests and mountain regions, are hunters, farmers, and some have become "outcast" Hindus. There are about four or five million Gond who speak an unwritten Dravidian language, and this recording is primarily of the Gond who live in Bastar, the southernmost district of Madhya Pradesh. Many of their villages show characteristics of megalithic civilization with menhir grave monuments and enormous stone slabs that serve as roofs and fences. There is a wide variety of songs presented here from a drumming "Rain Dance" to the fascinating "L'Escorte de la Mariée" (Bridal Escort) for antiphonal chorus of friends and family wishing her farewell as she makes a strange noise like weeping, to the joyous "Pani mali gala jai" (The Rainshowers Pour Down) and a heartfelt "Ode to Bastar" sung in elegant Halbi by a famous poet met on a deserted mountain road on the hottest day of the year. Rough and real and intriguing. —*"Blue" Gene Tyrrany*

Carnatic Music / Barenreiter Musicaphon 2021
A very fine recording involving vocals by Semmangudi Srinavasa Aiyar, the vina player K.S. Narayanaswami, and mridangam player Palghat Ragu. They perform two kritis by Muttuswami Dikshitar, one of the three founders of Carnatic music, along with two raga medleys. Major musicians (this series is bizarre in its reluctance to treat performers as individual artists rather than carriers of a style), excellent notes, and recording by John Levy. —*John Storm Roberts*

Folk Music of Uttar Pradesh / Barenreiter Musicaphon 55802
Any collection from India's most populous state is clearly only going to scratch the surface, but this one is unusually impressive. It's basically an overview—a range of instrumental cuts (lots of percussion) followed by vocal music of all sorts. But this is an overview quite out of the ordinary because of the incredibly detailed notes—84 pages of English (a few credits aside). Moreover, the recording quality is superb. A fine start for Musicaphon's CD series. —*John Storm Roberts*

☆ **Indian Classical Music** / Caprice 2022
This standout set of two LPs covers several different approaches to both of the major classical traditions. Young sitarist Debu Chaudhuri takes a strongly traditional approach. So does S. Balachander, the greatest Carnatic vina player of the older generation. Bhimsen Joshi, too, sings khayal and thumri with more austerity than vocalists like Parveen Sultana. Lastly, flutist Hariprasad Chaurasia and santurist Shivkumar Sharma play Vivaldi and Bach in performances that are airy and playful, while in no way less serious. —*John Storm Roberts*

○ **North Indian Folk Music** / Auvidis 8033
A really fine glimpse into an enormously rich musical culture. Aside from their very great instrinsic merits, many of these recordings—among them a bhajan by a wandering monk, a shahnai solo, an episode from the *Ramayana*—give a feeling for the popular equivalents of music more familiar in their classical aspect in the West. (50:30) —*John Storm Roberts*

Bhangra

Traditional bhangra is a secular folk dance and music form of Punjabi origin. It is closely associated with the Sikh Baisakhi festival celebrating harvest home although Baisakhi itself is celebrated throughout Northern India. Bhangra later took on other shadings and became a sophisticated popular music form albeit one that has largely failed to become popular outside its primary, Indian audience. Baisakhi, unlike most Punjabi melas (literally fairs or festivals but now used as a catchall for bhangra shows) which are based on a lunar calendar, falls on April 13 (although every 36 years, as happened in 1975, it falls on April 14) and is the start of the Punjabi New Year. Traditionally performed by Punjabi menfolk, bhangra has a female counterpart called giddha (or gidha). This too is performed at harvest time and to celebrate the birth of a son. During the 1990s female singers such as Kamaljit Neeru encroached on bhangra's male preserve. Sung in Punjabi in its original folk form, bhangra's popular version was later adopted and adapted by Gujaratis and other ethnic groups. 'Bhangra' is said to derive from 'bhang', a word meaning herbal cannabis, since bhang fuelled the festivities. Culturally Sikhism permits dance as the spontaneous expression of joy and happiness; its holy book, however, frowns upon 'ritualistic dancing,' as typified by Hindu dance forms.

During the early 1960s when the Indian community in Britain was still predominantly male, a folk-styled bhangra reminded them of home. Amongst early acts performing bhangra were Deedar Singh Pardesi, Mohinder Kaur Bhamra, and Bhujangy. Gradually a more commercial form developed. Amplification came in and Western instruments like electric guitar and bass became commonplace additions. Nevertheless traditional institutions have stood their ground. Foremost are dholak (a double-headed wooden drum with sheephide membranes) and dholaki (a smaller version) played with curved wooden sticks called khunti or the hands respectively. These drums power the music and provide bhangra's heartbeat. Even the relatively quiet chimta, a tong-shaped instrument with five pairs of metal discs, tambourine- fashion, along each arm, has retained its place with the aid of amplification.

Pop-bhangra—an alternative label concocted to differentiate it from the music's traditional roots—had emerged by the late 1970s. Its stomping ground was the Punjabi community in Britain, especially localities to the West of London (around Southall in Middlesex) and in the Midlands. Initially bhangra was largely performed by amateur or semi-professional bands at weddings and other functions. Increasingly nowadays it is the domain of professional groups, ones capable of filling major venues.

Even so these bands continue to perform at parties and wedding receptions and continue to live in their old neighborhoods. Gradually bhangra joined the repertoire of Indian cover bands whose main repertoire hitherto largely consisted of filmi hits. Canada and Australia have also developed thriving bhangra scenes.

The Southall-based Alaap group was one of the earliest groups to make its mark. In turn the excitement of their music communicated itself to a new audience in the Indian sub-continent. Coverage in the white press at the time trumpeted bhangra as the voice of disaffected Asian youth. There was something in this even if it overplayed the sociological. Bhangra remained first and foremost a dance music. In Britain it was important in furnishing Asian youth with a voice. It grew into the main form of cultural expression for second and third generation Asians and helped them to define themselves culturally and socially. Several dynasties of musicians arose, bridging the gap between bhangra's folky roots and the contemporary bhangra form. Bhangra's foremost acts are Alaap, Malkit Singh's Golden Star (UK) and Heera.

Increased audience expectations led to increased sophistication and showmanship. Premi and Apna Sangeet epitomised these developments; gold and silver lamÇ became very chic. A cabaret style, as newer bhangra bands dubbed it, became popular. By the mid 1990s the most popular British-based bhangra acts playing either Alaap-style or modern bhangra included Achanak, Azaad, Malkit Singh's Golden Star (UK), Holle Holle, Pardesi, Premi, The Sahotas and Johnny Zee.

Towards the end of the 1980s a new era of experimentation dawned. Labelled by some New Wave or Fusion Bhangra, these experiments drew on American and Afro-Caribbean forms such as funk, rap, reggae and ragga and in some cases bhangra became but one ingredient in the music. Head and shoulders above the competition was the singer Apache Indian who signed with Island Records in 1992 after a series of independent label crossover dance hall hits. The 1990s also saw bhangra reflect other trends in Western popular music. Fusion forms—with various cod names like BhangRagga and Bhangramuffin—appeared. Ragga For The Masses (Multitone DMUT 1236) in 1992 featuring Sasha, D.C.S. and Bindusri was the first major attempt to distribute and sell the music—BhangraRagga—outside the immediate Indian market. Despite a partnership with the multinational BMG, it stalled. Remix compilations like Street Dance (Audiorec ARCD 2065) in 1994 featured DJ-style revisitings of material by acts such as Apna Sangeet and Premi have become a feature. Such experimentation spread the word. Bhangra of whatever hue is one of the true success stories of Asian music.

–Ken Hunt

Indian diaspora

Alaap

Bhangra

Alaap provides a practical demonstration of bhangra's progress. Founded in 1977 in Southall, their debut album was on their own label, focused on traditional Punjabi folk music. Under the influence of producer Deepak Khazanchi and the high energy of disco and rock, Alaap's music went electric and employed drum machines. Later albums took religious themes (Shabe Ghat Ram Bole) or paired them with guests such as Asha Bhosle (Chham Chham Machdi Phiran) and Anuradha Paudwal (Na Dil Mang Ve). —Ken Hunt

Remixx Extra Hot 4 / Multitone 1162

This band was a pioneer of pop bhangra, the wild teenage Indo-Brit spin-off of a Punjabi folk form that over the past decade created a whole new music by combining Punjabi vocals and traditional rhythms and instruments with Western ingredients including funk, occasional reggae, electric piano, and assorted synthesized sounds. A studio remix of some of their bigger hits boosts the bass and drum sounds with echoed techniques and other various dramatics. —Raissa St. Pierre, Original Music

Dance With Alaap / 1981 / Multitone 1009

Alaap's second album blessed with a strong sense of identity. — Ken Hunt

○ **Chham Chham Nachdi Phiran** / 1990 / Multitone 1125

Billed as Alaap with Asha Bhosle. The validation of the presence of Asha Bhosie, one of India's most illustrious and more innovative playback singers, brought Alaap a new respectability and broke new ground. Leader Channi Singh's interest in filmi was showing. —*Ken Hunt*

Na Dil Mang Ve / 1991 / Multitone 1195
Alaap's second collaboration, this time found them in the good company of Anuradha Paudwal. —*Ken Hunt*

The Best of Alaap / Multitone 001
Alaap, one of the top groups, is relatively laidback and rather traditional, but overall quite eclectic. —*John Storm Roberts*

Ashwin Batish

Guitar / Fusion
Ashwin is a dynamic younger member of the Batish family, who brought their rich musical heritage from India to Santa Cruz, California, where they run a cassette-only label and tape-duplicating service. He is a nimble and energetic performer on the sitar, recording with his father Pandit Shiv Dayal Batish as well as with various fusion musicians and renowned tabla-master Zakir Hussain. —*Myles Boisen*

○ **Sitar Power** / 1987 / Shanachie 64004
The logical extension of Indian-music flirtations of the Beatles and the Rolling Stones. High-energy raga rock! —*Myles Boisen*

Sheila Chandra

Vocals / Vocal, Indo-British, Indi-pop
Like Najma, Sheila Chandra has brought her Indian ancestry to the open ears of the British pop market, scoring with a series of dance records throughout the '80s. Her music relies mainly on Western harmonies and rhythms, typically in a beat-heavy dance mold, with her supple voice supplying a sheen of Eastern exoticism. —*Myles Boisen*

○ **The Struggle** / 1984 /
Released in the spring of 1985 *The Struggle* is the most heavily rhythmic of all of Sheila's albums. Electronic drums are right up front and, along with some furious tabla, they propel the East-West instrumentation through the 11 tunes . . . Funky and tough, *The Struggle* is a high-energy dance-oriented workout, the perfect counterpart to the serenity of *Quiet.* —*Backroads Music / Heartbeats*

Out on My Own / 1984 /
As the title implies, this is Sheila Chandra's first solo album, released in January 1984, a statement of her independence both as an artist and as a young woman. Continuing in the musical vein of Monsoon's *Third Eye,* this album overflows with catchy pop songs, with piano and sitar providing the main melody lines, and a full-tilt percussion section consisting of tabla, mridangam (a double-headed barrel drum), ghatam (a large round clay pot), cabassa (shaker), and electronic drums . . . This CD release also includes four tracks from the 1985 LP-only *Nada Brahma.* —*Backroads Music / Heartbeats*

Nada Brahma / 1985 / Indipop 4
Released in July 1985, only three months after *The Struggle,* this LP-only release combines the meditative colorings of *Quiet* with the rhythmic emphasis of *The Struggle.* The 27-minute title track (which translates as "Sound is God") is a multi-part and multi-tracked atmospheric collage emphasizing the expressiveness of Sheila's voice. Using simple instrumental backing—mainly piano, dulcimer and tambura—Sheila explores many Indian as well as Western vocal styles. —*Backroads Music / Heartbeats*

☆ **Silk 1983-1990** / 1991 / Shanachie 64035
A career retrospective of one of the innovators of the British Indi-pop style, this album contains moody and danceable hits collected from various '80s releases. *Silk* combines classical Indian music and Western pop. Exotic club dance music. —*Bob Tarte & Myles Boisen*

Najma

b. England
Vocals / Indo-British
Najma Ashtar, a beautiful and talented young woman born in England of Indian parentage, seems bound for stardom in our world-music-conscious age. She sings traditional lyrics of the Urdu-language poets primarily, backing the complex poetry with a very contemporary musical palette that includes pop, jazz, and popular Indian music. Recently she has branched out to include qawwali, Indian ragas, and Western songs in her repertoire, always keeping her sensuous music close to its roots. —*Myles Boisen*

☆ **Qareeb** / 1989 / Shanachie 64009
This beguiling album showcases the ethereal, haunting music of this stunning Indian vocalist based in Great Britain. With power and grace, she mixes ancient Indian ghazals (short romantic poems) with original melodies in an "Indipop" style, combining traditional and Western instrumentation. An album of great immediacy and impact, offering an arresting new musical experience. —*Ladyslipper*

● **Atish** / 1990 / Shanachie 64026
Atish is Urdu for "fire," and this extension of ideas first explored on *Qareeb* burns with the flame of inspiration. This follow-up album (which contains English vocals) is a liquid, sensual blend of jazz, pop, rock, and various Indian vocal styles exploring the complexity and pitfalls of love. —*Bob Tarte & Myles Boisen*

Indonesia Collection

Gamelan Semar Pegulingan Saih Pitu / CMP 3008
Semar Pegulingan gamelans were originally royal ensembles and used a seven-tone scale. Later, various different ensembles with the same name developed, all of them pitched higher and with a brighter, more delicate sound than gong gede. This group is one of the few remaining seven-tone Semar Pegulingan gamelans. Its music seems almost weightless, slower, and less insistently virtuosic than modern styles. —*John Storm Roberts, Original Music*

Jegog of Negara / King 5157
Jegog are West Balinese ensembles of bamboo xylophones, some of them gigantic, to which drums and small metal percussion may be added. Performances often involve competitions (mebarung) between two groups playing different pieces at the same time. The winner is the group that throws the other off. There are two performances in mebarung style here, plus one uncontested piece with added drums and metal percussion. —*John Storm Roberts, Original Music*

☆ **Music from the Morning of the World** / Jun. 17, 1988 / Nonesuch 79196
This combines two classic Nonesuch albums to offer a good survey of gamelan music from Bali, along with the famous monkey chant ritual. —*Myles Boisen*

Indonesia (Bali) Collection

○ **Gamelan Semar Pegulingan Saih Pitu—the Heavenly Orchestra of Bali** / Sep. 1991 / Creative Music Prod. 3008
This recording features one of Bali's rarest and most beautiful orchestras, the Gamelan Semar Pegulingan Saih Pitu owned by the village of Kamasan. The 29-piece orchestra performs traditional holy music. Recorded in Kamasan, September 1991. —*Roundup Newsletter*

Balinese Contemporary Music / Barenreiter Musicaphon 2575
These early-to-mid '80s recordings give examples of the gamelan gong kebyar in the villages of Pinda and Sawan—both centers of the most widespread contemporary Balinese gamelan sound. Kebyar is one of those few forms that develop out of tradition with little or no outside influences (a much more common procedure than is sometimes realized). The music is splendid and the documentation and photos, as usual, outstanding. —*John Storm Roberts*

☆ **Golden Rain—Balinese Gamelan Music** / Nonesuch 72028
An introduction to the exciting Balinese kebjar style, plus a long excerpt from the gripping ritual drama known as ketjak (monkey chant). —*Myles Boisen*

Indonesia (Java)

Gamelan Sekar Tunjung

The Music of K.R.T. Wasitodiningrat / 1992 / Creative Music Prod. 3007
This landmark LP recording presents gorgeous compositions in classical Javanese forms by the great artist and teacher known as "Pak Cokro." The gamelan is heard throughout, with solo instru-

ments coming to the fore, and several works have Wasitodiningrat's characteristic multi-part vocals. Performed by Gamelan Sekar Tunjung in Yogyakarta, directed by Djoko Waluyo. Available from the American Gamelan Institute, Box 5036, Hanover, NH 03755-5036, USA. — *"Blue" Gene Tyrrany*

Idjah Hadidjah

Vocals / Jaipongan
Idjah Hadidjah is the gorgeous voice of Gugum's' Jugala group, an outstanding female singer from a whole generation who avoided Western and Indian influences in favor of a distinctive regional sound. —*Myles Boisen*

☆ **Tonggeret** / 1987 / Nonesuch 79173
An Indonesian delight. An exotic document from one of Sunda's most popular jaipongan singers. —*Myles Boisen*

Euis Komariah

Jugala Orchestra / Globestyle 057
On the island of Sunda in the 1970s, a new popular style emerged that was entirely based on older local forms and instruments, yet appealed to the young and eventually to Indonesians on the other islands as well. Komariah, produced by a (perhaps the) creator of jaipongan, is a fine, slightly pop-oriented singer. Here she sings covers of the Jugala cassette label's major hits over the years. Here's wonderful music and admirable notes. —*John Storm Roberts, Original Music*

Jaipongan Java / 1990 / Globestyle
Euis's frail and plaintive vocals adrift in a landscape of jagged gamelan percussion and rhythms. Capricious, moody, inspired, and dosed with shots of wit. —*Bob Tarte*

○ **The Sound of Sunda** / 1990 / Globestyle
Western vocal harmonies combine with music-box-style gamelan-derived instrumentation in a recording of torch songs in the popular degung genre. Playing the part of heart-wrenched lovers, the entwining yearnings of Euis and Yus Wiradiredja recall the best and most soulful American male-female pop duets. Highly recommended. —*Bob Tarte*

Nasidaria Group Semarang

☆ **Keadilan** / Piranha 26
This is a truly wonderful recording. The all-woman Nasidaria is a supergroup by Javanese standards, with 32 cassette releases under their belts. This is yet another of the great Muslim crossover sounds, with Indian and Arabic (including contempo-Cairo) influences, but also a sound totally its own. Traditional Qasidah was epic poetry accompanied by percussion and response singing. Indonesian Muslims use the form as a kind of Islamic calypso of social and topical comment, and Nasidaria added synth, guitars, and so on, along with Indian drumming, *filmi* touches, and all the usual wonderful stuff. —*John Storm Roberts*

Indonesia (Java) Collection

☆ **Street Music of Java** / 1989 / Original Music 006
Three major street-popular idioms. Kroncong, a seductive music for fiddle, ukulele, and guitar, is thought to have originated under Portuguese influence as far back as the 17th century. Dangdut is a newer style, with strong Muslim influences (including Egyptian film music). The street versions here are based on the percussion that gives it its name. Langgan Jawa is a regional form of kroncong with stronger musical links to other local styles. Also included is some village ronggeng and a guitar-backed style called melayu that crosses local, Latin, and Indian influences. —*John Storm Roberts*

○ **Java—Vocal Art** / 1990 / Auvidis 8014
This is Javanese macapat poetry, which clearly shows the introspective and subtle character of much of Java's vocal music. — *Gino Robair, Roots & Rhythm*

Flute & Gamelan of West Java / Tangent 137
Recordings by the National University group of Jakarta, featuring Indonesia's best-known flute player, Sulaeman. The first side is devoted to music for bamboo flute accompanied by kacapi zither. The gamelan pieces are played by a group half-a-dozen strong, in the coastal style. —*John Storm Roberts*

○ **Javanese Court Gamelan . . .** / Nonesuch 72044

The Music of Indonesia

One of the most populous regions of the world, Indonesia is also extremely culturally diverse, spread out across nearly 3000 islands. Although only the three larger islands of Java, Sumatra, and Bali are represented by current recordings, they comprise elements of many ethnic influences, including Hindu, Buddhist, Tao, Islamic, Christian, and animist religions. This diversity reflects the influences from their Indian and Asian neighbors as well as the European presence of the Dutch.

Perhaps the best known of Javanese and Balinese music is gamelan (orchestra) music. Gamelan is an ensemble of instruments consisting of gongs (kempul), hand drums (kendhang, ketipung), wooden and bronze xylophone-like instruments (gembang, saron), and bronze kettles, gongs, and bowls (bonang, kenong, kethuk) as well as bowed lutes, plucked zithers, and flutes. Derived from centuries of Indonesian bronzesmithing, the gamelan accompanies ceremonial rituals, dance-dramas, and the wayang (leather shadow puppet theater tracing its origins to the Indian epics *Mahabharata* and *Ramayana*). Some of these performances can last the better part of one day and well into the next morning. The percussive and metric melodies of gamelan music are beautifully ornate, embellished by various instruments in the ensemble. The effect is hypnotic; in fact, the music is used for trance-induction in certain rituals.

The musical tradition in Indonesia is so rich and varied, we don't have room here to describe all the many styles. Here are just a few. *Ketjak* (or monkey chant) is a ritual drama and trance-inducing dance in which a choir of singers chants the sound "Chak". *Kroncong* is a style of solo vocal accompanied by small groups of European-style instruments, including ukelele (the word kroncong refers to a similar Indonesian instrument), violin, guitar, plucked three-string cello, or (on the Muslim northern coast) accordion. This urban folk-music style, popular from the 20s to the 60s, is now primarily nostalgic "oldies" music for middle-aged Indonesians. *Langgam jawa* (Javanese song) is a regional form of kroncong from Central Java, especially Surakarta, that is sung in Javanese.

Dangdut, another folk music, is the "country music of Indonesia," with songs about the misfortunes of ordinary people. Rhoma Irama is the principle figure in dangdut music and can be heard on the Smithsonian/Folkways recording *The Music of Indonesia - Vol. 2*.

Jaipongan is a contemporary dance and musical form created by producer and musical *auteur* Gugum Gumbira Tirasondjaja in the Sundanese section of West Java during the cultural revolution of the 60s.

Another contemporary style, called *pop Indonesia*, or simply pop, is cross-cultural mass-market music intended to appeal to a wide diversity and unite the various ethnic groups.

– Scott Bultman

Javanese Court Gamelan from the Pura Paku Aleman, Jogjakarta offers some extended stately and beautiful pieces by a very traditional Central Javanese gamelan. —*David L. Mayers & Myles Boisen*

○ **Java, Vol. 1 (Opera of Danuredjo 7)** / Ocora 559014
World premiere recording of Langen Mandra Wanara, a once-popular form of Javanese opera. —*Peter Garellick, Roots & Rhythm*

Iran Collection

☆ **Classical Music of Iran . . .** / 1991 / Smithsonian/Folkways 40039

The *Classical Music of Iran: The Dastgah Systems* collection of classical Iranian music performances was recorded before the 1979 Iranian revolution drove many accomplished players into exile. Extensive liner notes add to the appeal of this historic document. —*Linda Kohanov*

Japan

Japanese Koto Consort

○ **Japanese Koto Consort** / Lyrichord 7205
Very fine recordings of sokyoku, instrumental music for koto, shamisen, and shakuhachi, two of them accompanying vocals. Though the instruments are a lot older, these ensembles took hold during the Edo period when a new mercantile class was having a profound effect on what had until then been mostly a courtly and religious tradition. The notes are sparse but fairly informative, the duration chintzy even for an LP reissue, but the music delightfully combines authenticity and accessibility. —*John Storm Roberts*

Shoukichi Kina

○ **The Music Power from Okinawa** / 1991 / Globestyle
Delirious, high-spirited ditties shelter a tough sense of nationalism, cultural identity, and opposition to colonialism—hence Bob Marley's admiration for Kina, captured here in a 1972 live recording, which is deliciously ragged. A pair of bonus studio tracks demonstrate the power of Okinawan pop at full high-tech tilt. —*Bob Tarte*

Kodo

Heartbeat Drummers of Japan / 1985 / Sheffield Lab 2222
Authentic Japanese Taiko-drum ensemble, who sometimes add modern and/or Western touches to their thunderous drumming repertoire. —*Myles Boisen*

Kohachiro Miyata

Shakuhachi—the Japanese Flute / 1976 / Nonesuch 720762
Five solo pieces recorded in 1976 by one of Japan's leading shakuhachi players. All are parts of the standard repertoire, and most are meditative in nature. The music is magnificent, the recording excellent, and the notes exemplary in their combination of clarity and information. Short measure at 34+ minutes. —*John Storm Roberts*

Tadashi Tajima

Shungetsu / Music of the World 124
Traditional Chamber Music / Auvidis/SAGA 6784
Tajima plays the shakuhachi flute, the ideal instrument for these honkyoku, pieces handed down through the centuries as "blowing meditation." By contrast, the voice is pre-eminent in the chamber music of the Nihon No Oto Ensemble (though there is one honkyoku played in, as far as can be told, quite a different style than Tajima). The singer slides, jumps and stretches around the texts while the instruments (koto Zither, shakuhachi, and biwa and shamisen lutes) accent, comment, and agree in glorious slow-motion synchronization. —*Carl Hoyt, Original Music*

Shingetsu / 1991 / Music of the World 124
The shakuhachi, a notched bamboo flute, is the most important wind instrument of Japan. This recording features eight pieces for solo shakuhachi played in a distinctive style by Tadashi Tajima, one of Japan's finest traditional shakuhachi masters. Tajima's breath, phrasings, and use of long flutes combine in making this an exceptional recording. —*Music of the World*

Kinshi Tsuruta

Satsuma-biwa / Ocora 559067
The satsuma-biwa, a type of lute, has its own traditions and repertoire. The energetic and percussive style featured in the music composed for this instrument appeared in 16th-century South Kyusu, whose then-ruler wrote its first lyrics. Tsuruta, one of the major living interpreters of satsuma-biwa, sings three contrasting songs here. Exemplary music; brief but adequate notes. —*John Storm Roberts*

Japan Collection

○ **Gagaku: The Imperial Court Music of Japan** / Lyrichord
An long overdue reissue of this magnificient recording and performance of this majestic, other-worldly music played by the Kyoto Imperial Court Music Orchestra. The "gagaku" (refined, elegant or correct music) style is an amalgam of various court musics from India, China, and Korea from as long as 1500 years ago. Because of the continued support, gagaku music may be heard today much as it sounded millenia ago. Included are classics such as "Etenraku" (music of divinity), the masterpiece "Manzairaku" for the majestic dance of four persons in bird costumes, the sword dance "Embu," and "Hassen" the music of the crane dances. Also the dragon dance "Nasori," "Goshoraku" with tones based on the five Confucian principles, music to the Indian bird "Karyobin," and the opening prelude "Irite." —*"Blue" Gene Tyrrany*

Shomyo Buddhist Ritual: Shingon School / Chant du Monde 274976
Shomyo liturgical chant, introduced to Japan in the 9th century, is characterized by pure vocal monody and free, unmeasured rhythm. In general effect it is like a graver Gregorian chant (which makes it particularly accessible to Western ears). A singularly beautiful recording, though the notes aren't quite up to Ocora's Shomyo release. —*John Storm Roberts, Original Music*

Okinawa / King 2025
Though there's quite a range of music here, from folk to classical, this charming set reveals the more mainstream styles as frequently jaunty and even boisterous, very different from the mainstream Japanese idioms to which we have been accustomed. The performers are well-known professional classical and folk performers. An ear-opening pleasure. —*John Storm Roberts, Original Music*

Jam Session of Tsugaru-Shamisen / King 2024
Three leading experimental musicians in what might be called new-traditional vein play a series of improvisations for shamisen lute, shakuhachi, and percussion (including djembe and darbukka). Carl's comment: "When the percussion and flute kick in, it sounds like Japanese jazz by way of NYC-style improv and Indian film music." Whatever . . . —*John Storm Roberts, Original Music*

☆ **Flower Dance—Japanese Folk Melodies** / Nonesuch 72020
Ten ancient folk tunes—lullabies, drinking songs, dances, and so forth—featuring the Noday family performing on shamisen and koto (both stringed instruments), plus percussion and bamboo flute. —*Myles Boisen*

○ **Kabuki & Traditional of Japan** / Nonesuch 72084
A nice recording of Japan's dramatic but austere theater music. —*Myles Boisen*

○ **Koto Music of Japan** / Bescol 374
Stately art music for the resonant Japanese zither, played in solo or ensemble settings. —*Myles Boisen*

Noh Play/Recitation to Biwa / Barenreiter Musicaphon 2017
Lyrical Noh choral drama, developed in the late 14th century and largely unchanged since, consists largely of recitative and song. Includes *Hagoromo*, one of a class of plays concerning romantic and nature spirits. Also includes an example of a pre-Noh-play narrative tradition. —*John Storm Roberts*

○ **O-Suwa-Daiko Drums** / Auvidis 8030
Originally used in Shinto rituals, later also as military music, complex percussion ensembles of the Suwa valley use other instruments only as garnishes. As privileged audiences in the US have recently discovered, this is one of the great percussion traditions of the world, overwhelming even on record. (41:51) —*John Storm Roberts*

Shinto Music / Barenreiter Musicaphon 2016
Traditional Music of Japan—Shinto Music. Shinto music goes back to the 4th century, but it was much reworked in the mid 19th century. Here are religious dance-songs and other music, including both wind and stringed instruments. —*John Storm Roberts*

Traditional Vocal & Instrumentals / Nonesuch 72072
A nice variety of Japanese singing and instrumental styles from the traditional Ensemble Nipponia. —*Myles Boisen*

Korea

Park Sang Won

○ **The Kayagum—Korea, Vol. 1** / Disques Esperance 165.528
Park's technique on the 12-string kayagum is formidable. —*Myles Boisen, Roots & Rhythm*

Samulnori

Record of Changes / Feb. 1988 / Creative Music Prod. 3002
Contemporary-traditional ritual song and percussion. Salumnori is a young group that composes (or re-creates) compositions stemming from ancient Korean ceremonial music, arranged and played by 20th-century Koreans. As such, it is part of a quite widespread attempt to adapt tradition to modern life and beliefs. —*John Storm Roberts*

Korea Collection

Lam Saravane/Khen Music / Ocora 559058
In the lam, performed at various important village occasions, male and female vocalists sing a kind of competitive love song in which he charms and she exposes the shallowness of his charming. A performance of delicate strength, backed by flute and khen (bamboo) mouth-organ. To this performance by one of the great women lam singers is added a number of solo pieces for khen. Fine performances, excellent recording, good notes. —*John Storm Roberts*

☆ **P'Ansori: Korea's Epic Vocal Art & Instrumental** / Nonesuch 72049
Although difficult for Westerners, the p'ansori vocal style featured on *P'Ansori—Korea's Epic Vocal & Instrumental* is highly regarded in Korea, and singer Kim So-Hee is a national treasure. —*Myles Boisen*

Laos Collection

Laos / Barenreiter Musicaphon 2001
An admirable introduction to the varied classical and village idioms of this musically rich nation, with its ancient Indian as well as Chinese and Southeast Asian elements. Included are several varied pieces for the khene, a bamboo mouth organ that is the precursor to the Chinese cheng, and various classical orchestras, some dominated by strings, some by xylophones, one (in a *Ramayana* epic) by oboe and percussion. Fine photos, slighter notes than usual in this series. —*John Storm Roberts*

Mongolia

Shu-de

Voices from the Distant Steppe / Real World 2339
Tuva's various remarkable forms of often-shamanic "throat singing" are almost unique: other cultures' versions tend to be far less diverse. Shu-de is a young group that has made a considerable splash on tour in Europe. The performances are almost startlingly fine. —*John Storm Roberts, Original Music*

Mongolia Collection

Mongolian Folk Music / Hungaraton 18013
In a world with ever more fine recordings of once-unobtainable music, this two-CD collection of 1967 recordings by a Hungarian ethnomusicologist remains almost hors concours (even from Jean Jenkins's Tangent set). Superb recording quality does justice to a very wide selection of vocal and instrumental pieces that are remarkable in their beauty and variety (three different musical subcultures). One song is also remarkable in its almost spookily Scots-Irish sound. English notes. —*John Storm Roberts*

Philippines

Kulintang Arts

Ancient Rhythms/Urban Sounds / Kulintang Arts

Qawwali

Put simply, qawwali is a form of religious observance, of worship. Qawwali is the premier Islamic devotional music form. Its singers are called qawwals. Only the light classical ghazal form of Persian descent is a contender for the hearts of Muslims. Closely associated with the mystical Sufi brotherhood, the word 'qawwali' derives from the Persian qaul meaning 'to tell'; qawwali itself means 'utterance'. Its popularity transcends religious and geographical boundaries. Hindus, Sikhs and Muslims alike sing its praises.

Related Islamic musical forms do not seem to feature in commercially available forms. For example, nothing comparable to the Sufi recitations on Turquie Ceremonie des derviches Kadiri (VDE CD-587) seems to be generally available although tarannum–chanted Urdu poetry–is an art form widely appreciated where Urdu is the main literary language. A secular form, tarannum, being chanted is not classed by Islam as sung and therefore avoids the theological debate that has dogged qawwali.

Islamic theologians have long debated whether music is prohibited or permissable. Nevertheless the faithful have long been great lovers of music. Qawwali is not the recipient of universal acceptance among Muslims or even Sufis. Of the four silsilahs (literally 'chains' or 'lines') or Sufi orders, found in any numbers in the subcontinent, namely the Chishti, Suhrawardi, Naqshbandi and Qadiri, only the Chishtis traditionally sought ecstatic inspiration in music. The Suhrawardis were indifferent to music's charms. The Naqshbandis rejected it outright. The jury is still out.

Like most other Hindustani musical forms, its artistic–as opposed to its spiritual–potency lies in the qawwal's skill to extemporize. As far as Western audiences are concerned two performers dominate but there are scores of first-class qawwals–singers of qawwali: Nusrat Fateh Ali Khan and the Sabri Brothers. Among other noted qawwali acts whose work is worth keeping a mental note of are Aziz Mian, the Warsi Brothers and Jafar Husain Khan Badauni & Party

–Ken Hunt

Kulintang is South Philippine music for string, gongs, and percussion. This multimedia group of young Bay Area Philippinos plays a contemporary version of kulintang and also various offshoots, fusions, and parallels. The cassette has one side of kulintang, and one of a mixed bag of compositions ranging from jazz-oriented to a folky sound also common in the Philippines. —*John Storm Roberts*

In Concert / Kulintang Arts
Kulintang is a southern Philippine music for string, gongs, and percussion. The cassette mixes driving gongs and even more driving percussion with jazz trumpet and bass clarinet in a genuinely fresh jazz fusion that swings amazingly. True innovators and a real discovery, as exhilarating as early Cubop. —*John Storm Roberts*

Pakistan

Iqbal Bano

Ghazals / Music Today 1035
Iqbal Bano has for a quarter of a century been one of the greatest of semi-classical singers specializing in thumri, ghazals, and geets, and her backing artists here include the great sarangi player Sabri Khan, along with Azhid Khan on harmonium. This particular CD is part of a series called Gulistan, which translates roughly as a garden in full flower. —*John Storm Roberts, Original Music*

Sabri Brothers

Group / Qawwali
The Sabri Brothers are not brothers by birth but members of a mystical Islamic Sufi brotherhood. They were the first group to bring their devotional qawwali songs to the West from Pakistan, recording and giving concerts of this boisterous and highly rhythmic music outside of its religious setting. Their sound is full of interplay and group singing, in contrast to the style of soloist Nusrat Fateh Ali Khan. —*Myles Boisen*

Qawwali / 1978 / Nonesuch 72080
The first Pakistani Sufi record issued in the US, and a fine example of full-throated qawwali. —*Myles Boisen*

○ **Ya Habib** / 1990 / Plan 9 2311
Excellent performances by the Sabri Brothers—heirs like Nusrat Fateh Ali Khan to generations of virtuosity—in which they hew closer to Sufi tradition than in more recent recordings aimed at the Pakistani market. Superb. —*John Storm Roberts*

Pakistan: The Music of the Qawal / 1990 / Auvidis/Unesco 8028
Uncredited anywhere but in the booklet, this volume consists of four performances by the Sabri Brothers. The opening piece is an allegory in ghazal form (a light classical poetic form) on, as Alain Danielou's notes put it, "the emotions of love and transitory aspects of the world." Amen apart from pointing out that qawal is an alternative spelling. —*Ken Hunt*

Pyar Ke Morr—Live in U.K. Vol. 1 / 1993 / Oriental Star Agencies 058
A word to the wise. Such releases are everywhere and, while they fuel theories about the (predominately male) drive to collect, they add little of spiritual or aesthetic value to the debate. —*Ken Hunt*

Sri Lanka Collection

Singhalese Music . . . / Barenreiter Musicaphon 2566
Singhalese Music—Singing & Drumming is the music of Sri Lanka's majority ethnic group. The first recording is mostly religious folk, with a side devoted to unaccompanied vocals, including various agricultural songs. The second consists of drumming with and without vocals: notable are part of the "heavenly elephant" dance and the fine drum duet. —*John Storm Roberts*

Kolam—the Masked Play / Barenreiter Musicaphon 2569
Music of Sri Lanka's majority ethnic group. Kolam, more like a masquerade than a drama in the European sense (involving dance, mime, and highly elaborate costumes), belongs mainly to three villages in southern Sri Lanka, and even there it is dying out. This recording includes songs and music for the dance sections, and comes with outstanding notes and photos of the intricately beautiful masks and costumes. —*John Storm Roberts*

Tibet

Ache Lhamo

Tibetan Musical Theatre / Esperance 8433
Ache Lhamo is a form of traditional theater that has been very popular at all Tibetan social levels since it developed in the 15th century, but pretty much unknown to the world at large. Members of the India-based Tibetan Institute of Performing Arts here perform scenes from an early libretto, accompanied by the traditional drums and cymbals. —*John Storm Roberts*

Karma Kagyu Institute

○ **Chenresik** / Karma Kagyu Institute 1
An authentic version of the Tibetan Buddhist ritual to Chenresik, the Bodhisattva of Compassion. This complete version of the classic ritual chant practice also includes the remarkable "Calling the Guru from Afar" written by the First Jamgon Kongtrul Lodro Thaye. Produced at the Karme Thegsum Choyang Studio with authentic personnel, this is the actual ritual as it has been practiced for hundreds of years in Tibet. —*Michael Erlewine*

Tibet Collection

Tibetan Buddhist Chant / King 5164

Parts of the Kalacakra Offering chants, performed by monks of the Nyamgyal Monastery, headquarters of the Dalai Lama's Gelugpa sect. As so often with King's World Music Library, the details given in the English notes are a little confusing, but these recordings were definitely made in a Tokyo recording studio—as the technical quality attests. —*John Storm Roberts, Original Music*

○ **Shartse College of Ganden Monastery** / 1978 / Bridge 9015
Three extended pieces by monks of the Gelugpa (Dalai Lama) sect of Tibetan Buddhism, two a cappella, and one with a full ritual orchestra—cymbals, handbells, conch shells, long and short trumpets, drums, etc. One of these pieces is the song of the great Tibetan saint Tsongkhapa to the Buddha, and the other two involve the dharma protectors Setab and the fierce Yamantaka. —*Michael Erlewine*

○ **Tantras of Gyuto** / 1978 / Nonesuch 79198
Two extended pieces by monks of the Gelugpa (Dalai Lama) sect of Tibetan Buddhism. These monks from the Gyuto Tantric college (some 40 monks) chant from two of the most profound Tibetan texts, the one dedicated to the deity Guhyasamaja (*Sangway Dupa*), which concerned with the self-existing sacredness of the universe; and the other dedicated to the fierce dharma protector Mahakala—Tibetan Buddhism's chief protector. —*Michael Erlewine*

○ **Gyoto Monks: Tibetan Tantric Choir** / 1987 / Windham Hill
Astonishingly recorded—as if you are sitting right next to or among the singers. The profound liturgical chanting is also astonishing . . . at times the monks are co-ordinating not only rhythm and extraordinary overtone singing, but the very micropulses of the vocal waveforms are exactly in sync, precisely as if they were one voice guided by a universal computer. The first chant is from the Guhyasamaja Tantra—Chapter II and the second, Melody for Mahakala, is interrupted with dramatic instrumental sections played by an ensemble of skull drum, small bell, several pairs of cymbals, a pair of conch shells, two long copper horns, a pair of short bone trumpets, and several large drums struck with sticks. Highly recommended. —*"Blue" Gene Tyrrany*

Ladakh Monastic/Village Music / Chant du Monde 274662
Ladakh is a large plateau, bordered by the Himalayas and the Karakorams, where China, India, and Pakistan meet. The monastic music here consists of an extract from a single ritual, performed by a choir, shawms, oboes, and percussion. The village music is more varied, including music for archery for oboe and kettle-drums, a song in honor of a lama with the same instrumentation, and solo songs. —*John Storm Roberts*

○ **Tibet: Musiques Sacrees** / Ocora 559011
This album was recorded in Nepal at Tibetan Buddhist monasteries of the Gelugpa and Nyingmapa sects. Most of the cuts are Gelugpa, including part of the Chod—a cleansing ritual. Other sections include the assembly call (with conch horns), prayer wheel, prostration rites, and more. A second group of tracks includes a ritual to Vajrayogini—a major female deity in Tibetan Buddhist practice. Various ritual instruments (thigh-bone trumpets, hand drums, cymbals, oboes, etc.) are heard. —*Michael Erlewine*

○ **Tibetan Ritual Music** / Auvidis 8034
A rare recording of an entire Tibetan ritual from the Nyingmapa monastery of Dehra Dun. Divided into three parts, each of which has both chanting and music for metal horns and trumpets as well as oboes and drums. Nominally an invocation to the goddess Yeshiki Mamo, though the notes overstate the shamanistic elements involved. (44:51) —*Carl Hoyt, Original Music*

Thailand

Saman Hongsa & Group

○ **Isan Slete** / Globestyle 051
Modern songs and music from northeast Thailand, sung by a husband-and-wife team with traditional ties and instruments but a modern attitude (and an electronics shop). The instrumentals, including kaen, xylophone, panpipe, and lute, are played by traditionalists rather than village musicians. Exhilarating music; fine notes. —*John Storm Roberts*

Thailand Collection

La Hu Nyi of Thailand / Barenreiter Musicaphon 2572
Music of a minority group living in North Thailand, Burma, Laos, and part of China's Yunnan province. Unlike in Thailand as a whole, the bamboo mouth organ is a major instrument here and heavily represented. The examples on this recording include music for a New Year's dance and for a lunar festival, mostly for mouth organ. Also here are love songs, some accompanied by lute. —*John Storm Roberts*

Mongolia

Shu-de

Voices from the Distant Steppe / Real World 2339
Tuva's various remarkable forms of often-shamanic "throat singing" are almost unique: other cultures' versions tend to be far less diverse. Shu-de is a young group that has made a considerable splash on tour in Europe. The performances are almost startlingly fine. —*John Storm Roberts, Original Music*

Vietnam

Tran Quang Hai

Landscape of the Highlands / 1985 / Music of the World 203
Original compositions for the dan tranh, a sixteen-string zither from Vietnam. The mesmerizing sound of this instrument combined with the virtuosity of Tran Quang Hai make this a unique and very special recording. "Deliriously beautiful and highly rhythmic." *New Age Journal.* —*Music of the World*

Dreams & Reality / Playasound 65020 S19.98
Tran Quang Hai, a virtuoso of the dan tran zither as well as many other instruments, is also a well-known author and researcher. Singer Bach Yen started professional life as a Saigon pop singer before she went to Paris to study voice. Both have been working for years outside Vietnam: Bach Yen sings in Hebrew and several European languages as well as Vietnamese, and Tran Quang Hai's playing shows clear, though intermittent signs of influence by European harp playing. As you'd expect, their performances are colored by these experiences in a personal way that is rather different from the customary intercultural cross-fertilizations. —*John Storm Roberts*

Phong Nguyen Ensemble

○ **Music of Vietnam** / World Music Institute 008
As musician and ethnomusicologist, Phong Nguyen is one of the major international figures of Vietnamese music. Here he joins other expatriate musicians (including the 77-year-old master of the dan nguyet lute, Nguyen Cia Cam) to perform a wide range of traditional and contemporary music. (These recordings were made at two WMI concerts in New York City.) Excellent recording, notes, and production as always with the World Music Institute. —*John Storm Roberts*

Vietnam Collection

Eternal Voices / New Alliance 053
Superb recordings by an ensemble of major US-resident Vietnamese musicians. Directed by Phong Nguyen, five singers and ten musicians present gorgeous performances of just about all the major traditional forms. The notes are wonderful, the packaging exceptional. —*John Storm Roberts, Original Music*

Ca Tru & Quan Ho / Auvidis 8035
Two traditional forms from North Vietnam. Ca Tru is a rather delicate women's art-music form based on codified modes, rhythms, and ornamentations and accompanied by various combinations of lute, zither, flute, and percussion. The equally beguiling but notably more robust quan ho songs, a form for young men and women, also has a traditional repertory but is often improvised. In this recording, made in Hanoi in 1976, they are backed by wind and stringed instruments but without percussion. (46:47) —*John Storm Roberts*

Tradition of Hue / Barenreiter Musicaphon 2022

Covers musicial idioms from central Vietnam. The *Hue* album devotes a side to several forms of court music, and another to ritual and entertainment music. Includes pieces for a wide range of wind, string, and percussion groups. Fine notes and photos. —*John Storm Roberts*

CARIBBEAN

Caribbean Collection

Zoop Zoop Zoop / New World 80427
Admirably recorded music from US Virgin Islands, well annotated. Most of the cuts on this smashing recording are by scratch bands, funji groups, and there's a lot of interesting sax work as well as more traditional sounding material. Varied, exhilarating and authentic: What more can one expect? —*John Storm Roberts, Original Music*

☆ **Under the Coconut Tree** / 1984 / Original Music 201
Music of Grand Cayman, off Jamaica, and Tortola in the British Virgin Islands. Cayman has a remarkable fiddle tradition, with US country as well as Scot-Irish roots, with Creole polka drumming under all! Tortola's funji groups mix guitar and mandolin with percussion and washtub bass. Add homegrown calypso plus roots music of all sorts—none ever recorded before—and you have some very special stuff. —*John Storm Roberts*

☆ **Caribbean Island Music** / Nonesuch 72047
I recorded this material on my first field trip in 1971. Many of these recordings are still unique: Jamaican country mento, digging songs, and nine-night songs; a Haitian acoustic merengue group; Dominican merengues, salves, tonadas, drum groups, and the English-language Mummies later featured in the British "Repercussions" TV/video series. Enjoy! —*John Storm Roberts*

○ **Caribbean Revels** / Smithsonian 10102
Caribbean Revels: Haitian Rara & Dominican Gaga. Rara and Gaga are basically the same thing—vaudou-related Easter parade music using (traditionally) African-derived single-note shawms, and—quite often these days—trumpets and saxes as well as percussion. Gaga is distinct from rara to the extent that the Haitian minority in the Dominican Republic has developed its own traditions. Both branches are exuberantly documented here through street recordings of both traditional and trumpet-led examples. Joyous stuff from a beleaguered people. —*John Storm Roberts*

☆ **Salt & Tabasco** / Mango 9852
A good anthology that blends soca, reggae, Afro-Cuban, and Latin selections. Includes the Cuban group Los Van Van, plus Arrow and others. —*Ron Wynn*

Dutch Antilles Collection

Tumna Cuarta & Ka'i—Music from Aruba & Curacao / Original Music 202

French Antilles

Les Aiglons

Group / Zouk
A classic Guadeloupian band of the '70s cadence era who, like nearly all bands of the period, were heavily influenced by the Haitian music that literally overwhelmed the Antilles from the late '50s to the early '80s. Les Aiglons held the record for the most sales of a record (*Cuisse-La*) of any Antilles band until the overwhelming success of Kassav' with *Zouk-La Se Sel Medikamen Nou Ni* in 1985. The band broke up quietly after their 1987 release, *Bon'm La*, but two members resurfaced in the summer of 1988 as a more commercial project called Love Stars. —*Gene Scaramuzzo*

Le Cerveau / 1983 / Henri DEBS 725

Bidimbo/Ay Lopital / 1985 / Henri DEBS 2427

○ **Bon'm La** / 1987 / Henri DEBS 2435

Alphonso et son Orchestre Antillais

Group / Zouk

A biguine artist who represents the classic form of the biguine as it evolved through the war years. —*Gene Scaramuzzo*

○ **Vive La Biguine** / Disques Festival 273

Anzala

Group / Gwo ka

One of the preeminent stars of the Guadeloupian music called "gwo ka," featuring two-hand drums of the same name. In an effort to compete with the zouk market, Anzala has released a couple of successful records that add electric instruments to the basic drum and vocal gwo ka sound. —*Gene Scaramuzzo*

○ **Se Roule Moin Ka Roule** / 1983 / Henri DEBS 730

An early '80s effort featuring the rawer gwo ka for which he is most famous. —*Gene Scaramuzzo*

Batako (Patrick Parole)

Group / Zouk

Band led by Guadeloupian guitarist Patrick Parole, who plays strongly in the Haitian mini-jazz-band guitar style. Because of this, Batako records continue to be among the more Haitian-sounding and thus stand apart from formula zouk efforts. —*Gene Scaramuzzo*

○ **Chiraj** / 1988 / Henri DEBS 2459

Parole's release was one of the best of what has, admittedly, not been a particularly inspiring period for zouk. It's mellow but not soupy, with a nice Creole tinge to some of the melodies, a lot of Haitian influence (what goes round comes round), and such passing felicities as a neat trumpet solo. Evidence that zouk's recent pop orientation doesn't necessarily mean triviality. —*John Storm Roberts*

Belenou

Group / Belair

A decade-old Martiniquan band that uses bele (belair) rhythms as a foundation for experimentation that ranges in sound from jazz to Afro-beat. Uneven, but when it works it's very unusual and exciting. —*Gene Scaramuzzo*

Emosyon Tambou-A / 1990 / APAL 04

Jocelyne Béroard

Vocals / Zouk

Martiniquan lead singer for Kassav' whose popularity soared in 1986 because of her endearing stage personality and her convincing vocals on Kassav' classics like "Pa Bisouin Pale" and "Move Jou." —*Gene Scaramuzzo*

☆ **Siwo** / 1987 / Georges DEBS 036

This lead female vocalist from Kassav' sings zouk love ballads better than anyone. Backed by the group Kassav'. Excellent. A zouk classic. Import. —*Robert Leaver & Gene Scaramuzzo*

Milans / 1991 / CBS 14-468723-10

Her second solo effort. A formula success pleasing all but those who wished to hear her break new ground. —*Gene Scaramuzzo*

Black Jack (Pipo et Ronald)

Vocals / Zouk

A studio zouk project by Ronald Rubinel and Kassav's Jean-Philippe Marthely, that includes contributions by every major star imaginable. Featured is a kind of techno-zouk, heavy on programmed drums, that is the trend of zouk in the '90s. —*Gene Scaramuzzo*

○ **Black Jack (Pipo et Ronald)** / 1991 / Sonodisc 7233

Nods to rap and raggamuffin reggae are accomplished with moderate success. The raggamuffin-style "Machand Poisson" was one of the huge hits of 1991. —*Gene Scaramuzzo*

Eric Brouta

Vocals / Zouk

A Guadeloupian singer/songwriter who is among an elite clique of studio musicians including Luc Leandry. Always with a crisp, highly percussive sound, but his quality of songwriting varies. —*Gene Scaramuzzo*

○ **Telephone** / 1988 / Henri DEBS 2453

A particularly strong release. —*Gene Scaramuzzo*

Pa Ka Tenn / Debs

This drummer and vocalist from Henri Debs's studio became a star with this record. —*Robert Leaver*

Bwa Can'non

Group / Cadence

An extremely interesting Martiniquan band in that their records present the complete range of music to be found in the Antilles repertoire: cadence, biguine, quadrille, Creole mazurka, calypso, merengue . . . everything but zouk. —*Gene Scaramuzzo*

○ **Amour Passion** / 1986 / Solo Gammes 1001

Champagn'

Group / Zouk

A zouk studio project by Zouk Allstar Frederic Caracas, always enlisting a star-studded cast of singers and musicians. Their consistently above-average songwriting leans toward "zouk love" but features the kind of strong instrumental accompaniment that would be expected of a member of the Zouk Allstars. —*Gene Scaramuzzo*

○ **Hit ("Tire Baton La")** / 1988 / Moradisc 4038

Chiktay

Group / Zouk

One of the best of the Guadeloupian zouk vocal groups. They're consistently good, always employing a strong stable of studio musicians. —*Gene Scaramuzzo*

○ **Balanse Le Dam** / 1987 / Bamboo 022

Max Cilla

Hand drums, flute / Folklore

A Martiniquan bamboo flutist who is a favorite guest for live performances of traditional music. These two wonderful records have a strong foundation of hand drums and flute, with rhythms ranging from chouval bwa to bele to ti kannot. —*Gene Scaramuzzo*

La Flute Des Mornes—Vols. 1 & 2 / 1988 / Hibiscus 88004

Henri Debs

Clarinet, Sax, Whistle

A Guadeloupian entrepreneur who began his career as a biguine artist and gained renown as the creator of a style dubbed 'biguine kombas.' Currently he is best known for his studio in Point a Pitre, Guadeloupe, known sometimes as Studio Zouk La Terreur. As a former musician, he is more involved in the production of the Debs stable of stars than most record producers, especially his brother Georges who owns the now-defunct Georges Debs label out of Martinique. With his background and resources, he occasionally indulges himself by performing and releasing compilations of classic Antilles music, usually a bit on the overly sentimental side. (Also see 'Max et Henri') —*Gene Scaramuzzo*

30th Anniversary / Debs 2437

Henri Debs is an old-hand singer/guitarist as well as record executive. This album with Severin, another veteran vocalist, has an odd mix of Antillean and salsa musicians (Hector Zarzuela and Mauricio Smith, e.g.). But the results are fresh beyond expectation. Frisky horn arrangements and a strong creole feel make this more interesting to us than Kassav' and its clones. —*John Storm Roberts, Original Music*

Georges Decimus

Vocals / Zouk

Two early solo efforts by one of the founders of Kassav'. After more than a decade with Kassav', Georges went off in 1990 to form his own band, called Volt-Face. —*Gene Scaramuzzo*

☆ **La Vie** / 1982 / Moradisc 4001

Recorded during the highly experimental phase of Kassav' and featuring the prototype formula soon adopted by the group and by zouk artists in general. —*Gene Scaramuzzo*

★ **Nwel** / 1983 / Liso Musique 6011

Another example of the experimental phase of Kassav'. A classic. —*Gene Scaramuzzo*

Pierre-Edouard Decimus

Zouk

Caribbean Music Styles

Biguine – Throughout the long history of the biguine, the dominant sound has been that of the clarinet and trombone, both solo and as a duet, and, while the phrasing often recalls New Orleans jazz, the overall sound is unmistakably Caribbean. The signature sound of the biguine is the interplay between the clarinet and trombone, which can still be heard today throughout the Antilles musical milieu, from the most traditional music to the music of the cadence era or the pop sounds of today's zouk. Any contemporary music that uses biguine as its base, even that which ventures as far off as contemporary jazz, is considered "biguine moderne." The classic music of carnival in the Antilles is an uptempo version of the biguine rhythm, called "biguine vide."

Cadence –A constantly changing style that evolved primarily among the islands of Guadeloupe, Martinique, Dominica, and Haiti. The cadence era was exciting and extremely fertile, requiring musicians of only the highest calibre, who could master not only Antilles pop styles like biguine and Creole mazurka but also those of Haiti and the other neighboring islands. The cadence years saw the evolution of the pop influences that embellish the rootsier foundation of today's Antilles musicians, allowing for expression in an internationally familiar musical language: electric instruments, riffing horn sections, trapset drums, topical lyrics, and specific stylings of rock music, reggae, soca, American Black music, and more. In addition to Les Aiglons, this was the heyday of big bands like La Perfecta, Typical Combo, La Selecta, Les Maxels, Les Léopards, Les Vikings de la Guadeloupe (whose co-leader, Pierre-Edouard Decimus, went on to create Kassav' at the end of the decade), and Gordon Henderson's Exile One of Dominique. Recordings from this era, while fascinating and enjoyable, often suffer from out-of-tune instruments and sub-par recording quality. Cadence led directly into the early 80s and the rise of zouk, and it was the musicians schooled in cadence who were the first zouk stars. The major catalyst behind the emergence of zouk was the desire to produce a new Caribbean music that treated the multifaceted music of the Antilles to the state-of-the-art recording technology of the Paris studios.

Chouval bwa – A rural Martiniquan style of music that evolved as accompaniment to the "manege" (or carousel). Originally featuring a large drum like a bass drum, hand drums, and ti bwa, chouv' was led by melodic instruments like accordion, bamboo flute, and wax-paper/comb-type kazoos. One young artist, Claude Germany, is attempting to carry on the traditional form of chouval bwa, while others have updated it minimally (by the addition of electric bass) or dramatically (as in the case of zouk chouv', which features an array of electric instruments, including synthesizer). Chouval bwa is Creole for the French term "cheval bois," meaning "wooden horse."

Compas – Haitian dance music, started by Nemours Jean-Baptiste in the 50s, known first as compas-direct.

Gwo ka – The various indigenous rhythms of Guadeloupe are played on a two-drum family of hand drums called gwo ka. Gwo ka music is rhythm-driven by the two drums and is often accompanied by a mounted stick or bamboo log hit with sticks called a ti bwa. The drummers lead the way for dancers, and usually there is singing accompaniment. Gwo ka has been an underlying element of zouk from day one, and, in fact, Kassav's first album was entitled *Love and Ka Dance*. Anzala and Ti Celeste (or Ti Seles) are two gwo ka artists still recording today, the latter sticking to the roots while the former has electrified his sounds.

Road March – Chosen at the carnival in Trinidad, this is the most popular song of the year.

– Gene Scaramuzzo

The founder of Kassav' and the father of zouk. Look under Kassav' and Soukoue Ko Ou for further information on Decimus. *—Gene Scaramuzzo*

Waya Se Sa Ki Peyi La / 1983 / Liso Musique 6019
Waya Se Sa Ki Peyi La/Carnaval Ave Le Roi et La Reine is a typical early carnival effort. *—Gene Scaramuzzo*

Jacob Desvarieux

Zouk

One of the three founding members of Kassav', Desvarieux credits the title cut from *Banzawa* as being the spark that touched off the zouk explosion. *—Gene Scaramuzzo*

☆ **Banzawa** / 1983 / Georges DEBS 016
After listening to the title cut (and the entire album), there will be no question in one's mind as to why this set off the zouk craze. *— Gene Scaramuzzo*

☆ **Yelele** / 1984 / Georges DEBS 22
As with all solo Kassav' efforts, these albums include participation by all members of the band. Among the more than two dozen Kassav'-related records released since 1979, *Yelele* and *Goree*, duo efforts by Desvarieux and Georges Decimus, are among the absolute cream of the crop. *—Gene Scaramuzzo*

Djo Dezormo

Vocals / Biguine vide

One of the most unusual of all the contemporary artists of Martinique, Dezormo is best known for being one of the few singers of "angaje" (political/social-commentary) lyrics, always releasing his records at carnival time in order to add some spice to the festivities. From the separatist community of Riviere-Pilote, Dezormo is a political activist in a country not known for activism. His commentaries have included everything from local politics to French presidential candidate Jean-Marie Le Pen. His Carnival 1990 "Voici les Loups" (Here Come the Wolves), a huge success, pictured Europe as a wolf devouring Martinique, alluding to a European Community agreement that will soon allow citizens of any member country to buy land in any other member country, which includes by default Martinique and Guadeloupe. Brother of biguine moderne artist Michel Godzom, Dezormo also loves biguine, Creole mazurka, and waltz, always incorporating these styles into his music. *—Gene Scaramuzzo*

Sa Pe Change / 1988 / Solo Gammes 40110
The Creole lyrics are a barrier to understanding his clever messages, but fortunately the fine music carries the day. *—Gene Scaramuzzo*

Ethnikolor

Group / Traditional

One of the surprise hits of the 1991 carnival and indicative of the growing revival of interest in classic Antilles pop music. The brainstorm of Martiniquan "living legend" Ronald Rubinel, the Ethnikolor discs feature a Who's Who of Antilles artists ranging from Kassav' members to biguine moderne clarinetist Michel Godzom to chouval bwa stars Marce Pago and Dede St. Prix. *— Gene Scaramuzzo*

Bel Biguine / 1991 / New Deal 50 073
The Carnival 1991 release featured two long medleys, one a biguine, the other a Creole mazurka, much in the spirit of the early '80s Soukoue Ko Ou Carnival releases but with more of a live feeling. *—Gene Scaramuzzo*

☆ **Vol. 2: La Fete Antillais Continue . . .** / 1992 / New Deal 40239
The Carnival 1992 release was even better, covering an even wider range of Antilles sounds and including a rootsy, percussive tribute to the late Eugene Mona. *—Gene Scaramuzzo*

Experience 7

Group / Zouk

A Guadeloupian band from the '70s cadence era, led by Guy Houllier and Yves Honore (who have the further distinction of directing the studio band at the Henri Debs studio in Point a Pitre, Guadeloupe). While the band can be heard lending their particular sound to countless successful projects involving the Debs studio, their own records as Experience 7 are usually uneven, due to an admirable willingness to experiment far beyond the zouk formula. —*Gene Scaramuzzo*

Mwen Ke Devire / 1985 / Henri DEBS
An early zouk record that features Eric Brouta and Tanya Stival. —*Robert Leaver*

○ **Sundama** / 1989 / Henri DEBS 2470

Fal Frett

Group / Biguine moderne

One of the best of the contemporary jazz bands from the French Antilles, a small list that also includes artists like Lucien Joly, Caraibes Jazz Ensemble, and the West Indies Jazz Band. —*Gene Scaramuzzo*

Cha Pastiche / 1985 / Celluloid 6774

Flamme Abymienne

Group / Quadrille

Members of a Guadeloupian society for the preservation of the Creole form of the European dance called the quadrille. The band still plays occasional dances on the island and were coaxed into traveling to Louisiana in 1991 to perform at the Festival International de Louisiane alongside old-time Cajun accordion and fiddle bands. —*Gene Scaramuzzo*

○ **Festival De Quadrille** / 1975 / Henri DEBS 512

William Flessel

Message Ka / VideoTop 70809
Unusual: Guadeloupian gwo-ka percussion music without a singer. Although strangely vacant without the bittersweet vocal melodies, the drumming is just as entrancing by itself, and in fact, it is revealed more clearly as a discrete branch of Afro-American drumming, quite different from Brazilian or Cuban forms. This is a six-man band and the guys are good. —*Carl Hoyt, Original Music*

Gilles Floro

Zouk

One of the star crooners of the "zouk love" style, Floro produces hit after hit. Every album contains chartbusters, not only the ones listed below. —*Gene Scaramuzzo*

Pa Pawol Anle, A / Liso Musique 6050B
This recording is enriched by strong biguine and compas touches in among the zouk, and by Floro's own jazz-influenced playing. —*John Storm Roberts, Original Music*

○ **Reve Bleu** / 1986 / Liso Musique 9708

Michel Godzom

Clarinet / Biguine moderne

One of the great biguine moderne artists of Martinique (an all-encompassing term that includes any contemporary styles using biguine as the basis). Clarinetist Godzom is a great experimenter, exploring the limits of biguine, mazurka, quadrille, and waltz, usually hitting solidly on the mark as he did on the album listed below. —*Gene Scaramuzzo*

☆ **Hotel Diamant Des Bains** / 1984 / Georges DEBS 021

Bod Guibert

Zouk

Unlike most Antilles artists of the zouk era that have basically copied Zairian soukous, producing a not overly interesting sound I've dubbed "zoukous," Guibert has managed to produce quality zouk combining equal amounts of both African and Antillais. The unique sound captured on his albums has made them collector's items. —*Gene Scaramuzzo*

Normalement (Bibiche) / 1989 / BG 001

Features a melange of elements African and Antillais. Hard to find. —*Gene Scaramuzzo*

○ **Ma Mail La** / DEG SA 300067
Totally unique Afro-zouk of unsurpassed quality. A collector's item. —*Gene Scaramuzzo*

Simon Jurad

Vocals / Zouk

Simon Jurad is one of the few Martiniquan musicians who can be found playing live somewhere on the island almost every night of the week, his gigs including everything from tourist bar/lounge performances to hip zouk shows. His career began in the cadence era, so as both singer and musician he has a wealth of experience under his belt. Jurad's biggest strength is his consistent ability to write catchy, musically interesting songs, although contractual complications have prevented him in recent years from being able to credit himself as songwriter on his albums. —*Gene Scaramuzzo*

Faut Pas Faire / 1986 / Melodie Makers 8210

☆ **Mama** / 1989 / Georges DEBS 046

Glorye La Te A / 1991 / Akatoto 020.1

Kali

Banjo / Folklore

Kali began his professional music career in what many consider to have been Martinique's finest reggae band, Sixieme Continent, which hit big with a 12-inch single called "Reggae Dom-Tom." In the late '80s Kali picked up a century-old family heirloom, a banjo, and began exploring roots music of a different nature . . . music of the Martiniquan capital St. Pierre that was destroyed at the beginning of the century by the eruption of Mount Pele. He can often be heard contributing his banjo to zouk and traditional projects alike, from recordings by Pier Rosier and Ze Top to Max Ransay and the latest by Malavoi. —*Gene Scaramuzzo*

○ **Racines—Vols. 1 & 2** / 1989 / Hibiscus 88020
A re-exploration of the classic forms of Antilles music. This vocalist and banjo player performs neo-traditional biguine moderne. Charming. —*Gene Scaramuzzo & RVR*

Live Au New Morning / 1991 / Hibiscus 88047
A live recording of classic Antilles music, which helped put Kali on top of the list of Martiniquan roots music artists. —*Gene Scaramuzzo*

☆ **Roots** / 1991 / Philips
The best cuts from Kali's first three albums. —*Gene Scaramuzzo*

Kali / Affirmations 2
A simple recording yet harmonically stunning, especially on the a cappella numbers, as well as quite woman-identified . . . or, as their press release says, "a rich vocal texture and lyrics that express concern for the quality of relationships on our planet—humans and the earth, women and men, life and death; celebrating those that are mutually enhancing and questioning those that are not." —*Ladyslipper*

Kassav'

Group / Zouk

○ **Eva** / 1982 / 3A 210
This, their fourth album, was the first with the touch of total greatness. —*Gene Scaramuzzo*

Passeport / 1983 / Sonodisc 7240
This is precisely the sound that made zouk so influential—a modified Haitian beat, Stevie-Wonder-style keyboards, and heaps of traditional gwo ka percussion—surprising when you consider the techno-monster the style has become. Includes two songs from *Oh Madiana*. —*Carl Hoyt, Original Music*

Aye / 1984 / Georges DEBS 018
One of the earlier LPs by the now almost late, great zouk powerhouse, *Aye*, from 1984, has all the US influence wrapped around the swinging (loping would be a good word) Antillean beat. —*Carl Hoyt, Original Music*

○ **An-Ba-Chen'n La** / 1985 / Georges DEBS 027
Kassav's output has always intriguingly tended to veer before the roots and funk sides of their mix. *An-Ba*, the one that cemented the band's position as the biggest deal pretty much anywhere on the Afro-French circuit, returned to the individual approach and

Zouk

When zouk music from the French Antilles islands of Guadeloupe and Martinique exploded onto the international music scene in the mid 80s, attention was again focused on a part of the Caribbean that hadn't been heard from musically since the popularity of the biguine in the early 20th century. Created in the late 70s by a small clique of Guadeloupian musicians residing in Paris, zouk presented a mélange of global influences that touched millions in the French-speaking African diaspora, subsequently acting as a catalyst for an exciting mid-80s period of musical experimentation.

With the Paris recording studios as a common meeting ground, francophone musicians from Africa and the Caribbean gathered to exchange ideas and "zoukify" their respective pop music forms, placing an indelible mark on the soukous of Zaire/Congo, the makossa of Cameroon, and a host of others. Haitian musicians, themselves a major influence on the French Antilles music scene, were in turn deeply affected by zouk, as were eventually (to a much lesser degree) English-speaking Caribbean artists from the Virgin Islands to Montserrat to Antigua.

Zouk truly draws its power from the rich musical heritage of Africa and the Caribbean. In its bubbly, light, loping beat can be heard elements from Guadeloupe, Martinique, Dominica, and Haiti, with dashes thrown in from Paris, Zaire, Antigua, Trinidad, Cuba, Puerto Rico, the Dominican Republic, and more. With so many influences, it's not surprising that popular zouk can range from highly percussive, driving dance music to slow ballads that hover dangerously close to French disco and cabaret singing.

Since the late 80s, zouk has become somewhat locked into a restrictive formula not unlike soca, and from an international viewpoint, its popularity has waned. Ironically, this has obscured from view the fact that today the French Antilles are bubbling with exciting musical experimentations involving many classic types of Antilles music like the biguine, chouval bwa, bele (belair), and ti kannot (kalenda). Inspired by a renewed sense of identity (and a dramatically increased knowledge of recording technology) afforded by the success of zouk, older Antilles musicians are returning to the musical riches of their islands. As we move into the 90s, the overall musical output of the Antilles is bursting with rhythmically propulsive, melodic sounds like zouk, zouk chouv', biguine moderne, biguine vide, and more.

With zouk (and to a lesser extent the modernized forms of classic music), the Antilles music scene revolves around the studio rather than live performance. Only a dozen or so self-contained bands exist that actually tour outside of Paris and the islands. Like many forms of Caribbean music, the majority of Antilles recordings reflect studio projects involving certain cliques of musicians, and it's not unfair to say that looking at the musicians' names on the record jacket will give a fair idea of the music within, before the shrink wrap is ever peeled off. As for the lyrics, aside from a few rare exceptions, all projects are in Creole and avoid anything "angaje" (political or social commentary).

Records come out twice a year in the Antilles, timed either for summer vacation or for the Christmas holidays leading into carnival. Most recordings are done in Paris, with Henri Debs's studio in Guadeloupe running second, and J-P Mauriello's Hibiscus Studio in Martinique running a far-distant third. Excluding sure sellers like Kassav' and occasional huge successes, most releases are treated to only one pressing by Antilles record producers. This means records quickly become hard to find after their initial appearance. Fortunately, compilations featuring collections of hits are becoming increasingly available and often represent the only means of hearing the music. Of even more interest is the recent appearance of a few anthologies of artists, like the superb Hibiscus Records releases of early music by Eugene Mona and other classic music from the defunct 3A label.

– Gene Scaramuzzo

general hang-loose joviality of the earlier salsa-based style at its best. It was also a very highly worked album: "thanks also to" brass, string, and synthesizer types outnumbered the basic band. —*John Storm Roberts, Original Music*

Vini Pou / 1987 / CBS 44420

Kassav's first US disc is one of the strongest yet. [It] is full of tricky beats, catchy choruses that'll have you singing along in two seconds flat. — *J. Poet, Rock & Roll Disc.*

Kassav' Aux Zenith / 1987 / Georges DEBS 38/39

I've always found Kassav' to be a variable band, capable of great music but too prone to lapse into an overslick funk typical of any pickup group of session-men (which is how they began life). These tending to be studio-oriented faults, it's perhaps not surprising that this live concert recording was one of the most genuinely exciting Kassav' sessions ever recorded. —*John Storm Roberts*

● **Zouk Is the Only Medicine We Need** / 1989 / Greensleeves

A superb greatest-hits collection from the top band. —*Robert Leaver*

Edith Lefel

Vocals / Zouk

A Martiniquan zouk singer whose sparkling strong voice graced many records by Lazair, Simon Jurad, Kassav', and others before she attempted her own record. —*Gene Scaramuzzo*

○ **La Kle** / 1988 / Georges DEBS 043

A huge success even though (or because) Lefel opted to sing in the weak, rather wimpy vocal style that was the rage of late '80s zouk-love. —*Gene Scaramuzzo*

Love Stars

Group / Zouk

A Guadeloupian "zouk love" studio project involving three singers, two of whom were original members of Les Aiglons. As with many Henri Debs productions, it includes a star-studded cast. —*Gene Scaramuzzo*

Ipokrit / 1988 / Henri DEBS 2449

This album is, in fact, excellent, and particularly notable for fine solo sax rather than the usual ensemble riffs, as well as for a pleasingly batty edge and plenty of verve. —*John Storm Roberts*

○ **Yo Malade/Jane** / 1989 / Henri DEBS 2469

La Maafia

Group / Compas

A Martiniquan band led by drummer, singer, and songwriter Jean-Michel Cabrimol, and one of a handful, including Diapason, Filpak, and Nouvelle Galaxie, that specializes in playing a Martiniquan version of classic Haitian mini-jazz. La Maafia's albums are typically a balance of uptempo dance numbers and slow ballads graced by flute. It's certainly not formula zouk but very popular, nonetheless, because of the long-time Antillean love of Haitian music. —*Gene Scaramuzzo*

☆ **Mama Afrika** / 1988 / JMC 007

Exquisite Antilles funk jazz (a Martinquan version of Haitian compas) featuring flute, sax, trumpet, and conga. —*Robert Leaver*

Malavoi

Group / Folklore

Led by Martiniquan pianist Paulo Rosine, Malavoi has been recording since the late '60s. The original band featured a horn section and consisted mainly of Latin music enthusiasts. The band added a string section in the late '70s and recorded a superb album of charanga-style music that included percussion by Dede St. Prix. Only this one album captured the brief period when Malavoi had both a horn section and a string section; the horns left soon afterward. An anthology of hits from this era is now available on the Hibiscus label release *L'Autre Style*. The albums listed below are among the best of the band as it exists today, presenting a varied repertoire of "Creolized" European dance forms like the quadrille, mazurka, and waltz along with strong elements of biguine and charanga. Pipo Gertrude, who replaced long-time Malavoi vocalist Ralph Thamar in late 1987, appears on *Jou Ouve* and *Souche* (which is not listed because it's not among their best), as well as the group's latest. The *Live au Zenith* album features Thamar. —*Gene Scaramuzzo*

Zouel / 1983 / Georges DEBS 014-15
Wow! Phoosh! When it comes to string-band arranging, this one has the kitchen with faucets. I mean, lush!! And lush is the word— the calorie count has to be enormous, but the cream is real and rich, the chocolate dark and gorgeous. Ralph Thamar sings. Vocalist Marijose Alie, who has been listening to the Brazilians with good results, is featured on one cut. Seriously, the uptempo numbers swing mightily, the traditional ones update perfectly (great quadrille!), and the slow ones, by the very splendor of their richness, simply obliterate the usual sub-bolero plod. Oh, yes, demon bass and dynamite piano too. —*John Storm Roberts*

La Case a Lucie / 1987 / Blue Silver 8221
After some ill-received forages into zouk on their previous album, Malavoi have decided to stick with the mellow, delicate sound that crosses Cuban charanga with earlier Martiniquan stras. Not that they're in any time warp—there's some quite effective synthesizers in spots, and a lot of kick in the rhythm section. A couple of cuts don't make it, including the title track. But five elegant successes out of seven ain't bad, and it's always nice to hear from the French Antilles' more neglected idioms. —*John Storm Roberts, Original Music*

○ **Live au Zenith** / 1989 / Blue Silver
A classic 1987 concert from this large orchestra. "String Creole music" featuring Edith Lefel on vocals. —*Robert Leaver*

○ **Malavoi—L'Autre Style** / 1992 / Hibiscus 88052
This is for everyone tired of zouk, but who wished he wasn't. —*Carl Hoyt, Original Music*

Marce et Toumpak

Group / Chouval bwa
Drummer Marce Pago, along with Dede St. Prix, took the torch first lit by Eugene Mona in the '70s and ran with it to bridge the gap between the growing early '80s zouk scene and a rural percussive form of Martiniquan music called chouval bwa. Dispensing with chouval bwa's large bass-drum-like tambour, but adding electric instrumentation to the basic lineup of rhythmic vocals, hand drums, bamboo flute, and occasional accordion, both Marce and St. Prix took chouval bwa to a level of popularity right alongside zouk. Marce coined the term for this new form, "zouk chouv'," with his 1987 album of the same name. His early albums, prior to *Zouk Chouv'*, are not strong on electric instruments and are, in fact, in many ways more in keeping with the return-to-roots trend of the '90s. —*Gene Scaramuzzo*

☆ **He Binzot** / 1985 / Georges DEBS 030

Zouk Chouv' / 1987 / Globestyle
Neo-traditional with heavy roots percussion and great horn riffs. —*Robert Leaver*

Mirage (Myraj)

Group / Zouk
This studio zouk project under the direction of Rodrigue Nouel usually produces some fine music. All the records in their catalog are worth hearing although *Pou Zot* is of special value because of its unique variation on traditional zouk. —*Gene Scaramuzzo*

○ **Pou Zot** / 1989 / EMI 7920411
This album stands out from Mirage's others due to its successful deviation from formula zouk. —*Gene Scaramuzzo*

Eugene Mona

d. Aug. 1991

Flute / Zouk
This legendary bamboo flutist, songwriter, and performer was an extremely creative musician who, on the one hand, was a keeper of the flame of rural music traditions and who, on the other hand, was not afraid to experiment with the addition of contemporary sounds. He set the stage onto which later came Dede St. Prix, Marce Pago, Pakatak, and others. Mona died in August of 1991. —*Gene Scaramuzzo*

Témoignage / 1989 / Hibiscus 88024/25
This live album features raw roots music. —*Gene Scaramuzzo*

○ **Blan Manje** / 1991 / Hibiscus 88037
Recorded nearly five years after *Temoignage*, *Blan Manje* is a percussive/electric treat. —*Gene Scaramuzzo*

● **Mona—Vols. 1 & 2** / 1992 / Hibiscus 88050/51
This anthology of Mona's '70s music is a must for any fans of Dede and Marce. —*Gene Scaramuzzo*

Pakatak

Group / Chouval bwa
This Martiniquan tambour group under the leadership of Krisyan Jesophe has been around for a long time, though members change. —*Gene Scaramuzzo*

Chouval Bwa / PKT 003
A fine example of of this band's work. —*Gene Scaramuzzo*

Dominique Panol

Zouk

○ **Bolotte** / 1987 / Georges DEBS 1503
Panol, a perennial sideman himself, features Decimus, Maimro (on acoustic piano!), St. Eloi, and Alibo, and still comes up original. His fortes are tough beat propelled by his own bass, and a total lack of moderation: more machine-like drum machines, more synthetic synth, larger and richer backup vocals, even a Malavoi-like string quartet. As campy as hell. Also terrific. —*John Storm Roberts*

Plastic System Band

Group / Biguine vide
An approximately 80-piece carnival street band that consists of horns, stiltwalkers, and dozens of percussionists playing on plastic drums and ti bwa. In the Martiniquan carnival tradition, their recordings are medleys of everything from French nursery songs to popular zouk songs to the myriad of Antilles carnival songs. These recordings give a superb introduction to Martiniquan carnival music. *Bel Je* includes both songs found on the "Kalot Kannaval" 12-inch single. —*Gene Scaramuzzo*

Kalot Kannaval / 1988 / Solo Gammes 40109

☆ **Bel Je** / 1991 / Plastic System Band 02

Max Ransay

Vocals / Zouk, Biguine moderne
This original member of the '70s Martiniquan cadence band Les Leopards made a stunning reappearance in 1988 with the first biguine to make Radio Caraibe DJ Balthazar's Creole Hit Parade in nearly a decade. The follow-up album is a fine collection of biguine, zouk, and ti kannot (kelenda). Earlier '80s efforts by Ransay are also worth hearing. —*Gene Scaramuzzo*

☆ **Au Secours en Mwe!** / 1989 / Hibiscus 88018

Folklore Martiniquais Traditionnel / RN 1148
Ransay and Michel Thimon; two original Les Leopards members team up. —*Gene Scaramuzzo*

Pier' Rosier

Vocals / Zouk
A Martiniquan singer of traditional music who went the zouk route in 1985 with a first-rate group of Paris-based musicians calling themselves Gazoline. Artistic differences between Rosier and the band led to their breakup in late 1987, so Rosier went on to form his own handpicked band of underlings, which he named Gazolinn'. His entire catalog, with both bands, is worth hearing, strong on chouval-bwa-influenced rhythms and providing some of the most serious hard-edged "zouk chire" this side of Kassav' (in terms of technical and songwriting excellence). The Shanachie Records anthology is a fine introduction and includes many of

the best of Rosier's collaborations with the original Gazoline. — *Gene Scaramuzzo*

○ **Le Bidongaz** / 1989 / Cyclonn' 001
A friend of ours describes Bidongaz as "Gazolin's Kraftwerk album"—a good line with a good deal of truth. But Rosier's idiosyncracy still flashes plentifully from the technology like lightning from a storm cloud. —*John Storm Roberts, Original Music*

☆ **Zouk Obsession** / 1990 / Shanachie 64021
Among the top Zouk groups on the worldbeat circuit. This 1990 release of their greatest hits spotlights the great Pier' Rosier. — *Ron Wynn*

Ronald Rubinel

Keyboard / Zouk
Aside from Michel Alibo, there is no Antilles musician with a longer list of musical credentials, both live and on record, than Ronald Rubinel. He was a staple of touring Haitian bands in the '70s, who was heard adding rare keyboard parts to soukous recordings by Loketo and the other superstar Zairian bands. In the Antilles, he was a cadence star in the '70s and a zouk star in the '80s through to today. He is also the catalyst behind Martinique's most exciting carnival creation of the past two years, Ethnikolor. Besides playing on nearly as many zouk releases as the members of the Zouk Allstars, he has released a handful of his own recordings, always featuring a Who's Who of Antilles stars. *Bal Boutche* may be the best introduction. —*Gene Scaramuzzo*

○ **Bal Boutche** / 1989 / Georges DEBS

Dede St. Prix

Drums, flute / Chouval bwa
A hand drummer, bamboo flutist, and songwriter, St. Prix is one of the rootsmen of Martinique. After stints as percussionist in many local bands (including E+, Malavoi, and Pakatak), he formed his own band, Avan Van, in the early '80s and has never looked back. His pioneer efforts were in the melding of zouk sounds with a rural musical tradition called chouval bwa. As a songwriter he has lent his efforts to a variety of projects, reaching a pinnacle with an extremely funky cut called "Amazon" that appeared on Joelle Ursull's *Black French* album. *Mi Se Sa*, reissued on Mango Records, is the most electric and not the most indicative of the total recorded output of St. Prix, even though it's likely to be the easiest to find. —*Gene Scaramuzzo*

Mi Se Sa / 1988 / Mango 9813
Altogether successful at putting over a classical chouval bwa, freshened but not threatened by the contemporary touches. (33:39). —*John Storm Roberts*

☆ **Leve/Arrete Ton Delire** / 1991 / Karac 44402

Tanya St. Val

Vocals / Zouk
The darling of the French Antilles music scene, St. Val's records benefit from strong support by the best the islands have to offer. Her voice is hefty, much in the way of Grace Slick, and her interpretations are always convincing. She is definitely deserving of her star status. —*Gene Scaramuzzo*

○ **Tamboo** / 1987 / Henri DEBS 2436
This 1986 album was the rocket that propelled St. Val from the semi-obscurity of backup singing to stardom, incidentally putting Béroard on notice and confirming pop or lovers' zouk as the wave of the then future. Though this last has to be chalked up as a negative, Tamboo—like St. Val herself—is full of charm and bounce. —*John Storm Roberts, Original Music*

Sartana

Vocals / Zouk
This prolific Guadeloupian zouk star uses gwo ka as the basis of his sound. Some may find Sartana's very unusual voice unpleasing, although in some ways it adds a sense of authority and demands attention much like Peter Tosh. Early albums include collaboration by most members of Kassav', although ironically his later releases are more zoukish. —*Gene Scaramuzzo*

Ostilite / Polidisc 64101
Zouk may be dead, but—thanks to Sartana and his ilk—it just won't lie down. The gloriously kicking opener signals that the joy

The French Antilles (Martinique & Guadeloupe)

These two Caribbean islands are technically part of France, with Martinique being more developed and Guadeloupe the poorer sister island. The creole culture has seen a wide mix of peoples and, therefore, music. The beguine was the first Antilles popular music to reach international audiences and was influential in jazz, Brazilian, and African music. As it faded in the late 50s, cadence became popular, being similar to the popularity of Haitian compas in the 60s and 70s.

As people were listening to other Caribbean music, traditional African-derived "gwo ka" drumming and chanting survived. Ti Celeste and Marce' et Tumpak have become popular, playing such traditional music. Exile One merged music from Haiti, Trinidad, and the Antilles into a new popular music called "cadence-lypso." They helped revive the local music scene and influenced other Caribbean musicians as they toured extensively.

As many Antilleans moved to France (especially Paris) in search of work, a collective of musicians named Kassav' began blending cadence, compas, and other Caribbean styles into a new dance music called zouk. They quickly became an international phenomenon in the 80s as they took their high-energy dance music to the world.

Recorded and live music experienced an unprecedented boom for Antilles music. Countless zouk artists emerged, and *le zouk* could be heard all over Paris, the French Caribbean, Francophone Africa, and dance floors the world round. At the same time, other traditional or neo-traditional music thrived, including the creole string music of Malavoi, the chouval bwa of Dede Saint Prix, and the Haitian compas of J. M. Cabrimol et La Maafia. Musically, these little islands have become massive.

– Robert Leaver

is back, with its early-Kassav' oomph and sparkling salsa-style keyboards for zest. And so it goes: dance heaven with the variety, the constant little fresheners and above all the pazazz that says "We aren't just doing this—we mean it!" —*John Storm Roberts, Original Music*

○ **Bom'me Lacrimogene** / 1988 / Tropic 1118

Soukoue Ko Ou

Group / Biguine vide
This is the best of four carnival/Christmas medleys put out in the early '80s by Kassav' founder and Guadeloupian Pierre-Edouard Decimus, utilizing the same core of musicians used on the early Kassav' records. The unsophisticated use of programmed drum machine kills the joy of most of these discs, but the superb songs on *Vacances* cannot be beaten down. See the listings for Pierre-Edouard Decimus for an earlier such effort. —*Gene Scaramuzzo*

○ **Vacances** / NR 1153

Souskay

/ Moradisc 4025B
This the first recording by a young Martiniquan group—two men, one woman. On some levels they're a bit like Maurinier, but they score on the blend of sharp strings and fat brass, as well as an excellent bassist (crucial in this kind of zouk, if it isn't to bland out). —*John Storm Roberts, Original Music*

○ **Mr. Sho** / 1988 / Moradisc
A big hit—ultra fast. —*Robert Leaver*

Libertine / 1992 / JE Productions 69812
Souskay have let 'er rip electronically this time. They always were ones for the Godzilla drum machines, but this time it's let joy be

unconfined. I like the woman singer, Patsy Geremy, who's all over Side 2. Play that first and you'll feel benign about Side 1. —*John Storm Roberts*

Stellio

☆ **Et Son Orchestre Antillais** / Music Memoria 30838
Classic biguine was a manically charming dance style with a front line consisting of clarinet and trombone. Clarinetist and bandleader Stellio was the great name of between-the-wars biguine, a major composer and leader of the most popular and influential band of the era, both in Paris and back in the islands. These biguines, mazurkas, and so forth cover his prime, from the late '20s to late '30s. A bedrock-indispensable part of any Caribbean—hell, just plain any—collection. —*John Storm Roberts*

Au Bal Antillais / Folk Lyric 9050
We love the old Martiniquan biguine, with its manically jaunty clarinet/trombone age, like early New Orleans jazz the night the trumpeter overslept. This album is devoted to the greatest name the style produced, and these are his original recordings—the earliest in pure island vein, some of the later ones (typically) in collaboration with Cuban musicians. —*John Storm Roberts*

Tatiana
Zouk
○ **Tatiana & Zouti** / 1988 / Debs 2452
Tatiana and Zouti came on the scene a year or so ago, with this sleeper second album. The sound is familiar enough, but zouk (especially lovers' zouk) is in the ascendant. Lead singer Tatiana and her equally young group have an oomph that several bigger names are beginning to lose. —*John Storm Roberts*

Ralph Thamar
Vocals / Zouk
A longtime lead singer for Malavoi, who went his separate way in 1987. Thamar is known for very hard-edged, techno-zouk, creative songwriting, and rather classical-style singing. —*Gene Scaramuzzo*
○ **Caraibes** / 1991 / Declic100% 05

Michel Thimon
Vocals / Zouk
A singer with the legendary Martiniquan cadence band Les Leopards, Thimon is now a music writer for the France-Antilles of Martinique, occasionally still dabbling in music projects. —*Gene Scaramuzzo*
La Maafia Presente . . . ("Le Ou Se on Neg") / 1989 /

Ti Emile
Group / Belair
One of the best opportunities to hear traditional Martiniquan bele (belair) drumming and singing. —*Gene Scaramuzzo*
○ **25 Ans de Bel-air** / 1977 / 3A 016

Ti Raoul (Grivalliers)
Group / Zouk
A very raw, exciting example of Martiniquan belair singing and drumming. —*Gene Scaramuzzo*
○ **La Rivye Leza** / 1988 / APAL 03

Ti Seles (Celeste)
Group / Gwo ka
Basic gwo ka drums and singing but a real standout because of Seles's authoritative voice, beautiful singing, and occasional use of very melodic sax. —*Gene Scaramuzzo*
Ti Celeste / 1984 / Henri DEBS
An excellent recording of traditional gwo ka percussion and vocals. —*Robert Leaver*
○ **Ou Pa Kare** / 1985 / Henri DEBS 2423
● **Ses Plus Grands Succes** / 1991 / Henri DEBS
○ **Virus La** / Wirem 4579
Singer Ti Seles has the reputation variously of a gwo ka traditionalist and a modernizer of the form, both of which theories are true. His "Hommage a Robert" (a gwo ka legend) is rootsy drum-

ming, and his voice is always deep and rural. But for several tracks he adds synth and piano, very successfully, in a quite effective adaptation of zouk to the far more local Guadeloupian sound of gwo ka. —*John Storm Roberts*

Turbo II
Group / Zouk
They do Kassav'-related carnival medleys relying heavily on past Kassav' hits. (See 'Soukoue Ko Ou') —*Gene Scaramuzzo*
Tu Di k'Tu N'm Pa Sa / 1989 / Georges DEBS 045
Vol. 2 / 1992 /

Joelle Ursull
Vocals / Zouk
An original member of the Guadeloupian female vocal trio Zouk Machine until she was manipulated out of the band, Ursull went on to become a solo star with the help of an incredible musical cast on *Miyel* and later with a crossover masterpiece, *Black French*. —*Gene Scaramuzzo*
☆ **Miyel** / 1988 / CBS 462433
Black French / 1990 / CBS 466854
Includes a collaboration with none other than French bad boy Serge Gainsbourg. The Gainsbourg/Ursull duet "White and Black Blues" took Europe by storm in summer of 1990, but it's the Dede St. Prix composition, "Amazon," that makes the album worth buying. —*Gene Scaramuzzo*

Guy Vadeleux
Bass / Zouk
This hardworking Martiniquan artist, recording since the cadence days, got his start as a bassist for Pierre Rassin's authentic biguine band, where he was properly schooled in all the musical traditions of the Antilles. It's for this reason that Vadeleux's albums of the zouk era are unusual and popular, containing familiar references to biguine, cadence, and Creole mazurka, while never failing to hit the zouk bull's-eye. Vadeleux can be seen most nights of the week playing solo and group gigs in tourist spots, although those hoping to hear a sound similar to his records will be disappointed. —*Gene Scaramuzzo*
Ambiance Bo Kaille / 1984 / 3A 235
○ **Mazouk' Potpourri** / 1991 / Solo Gammes

Francky Vincent
Composer / Zouk
Probably the best way to get acquainted with this master of suggestive lyrics is through the recent anthology on Declic Records, although the other one listed may still be in print. Vincent's album jackets and music are often downright hilarious, although the clever wordplay will be lost on non-Creole-speaking listeners. The reason his records are listed as of high interest is the irony that instrumentally his music is superb, featuring sparkling production, ringing instruments, and creative songwriting. One of the true talents of the Antilles. —*Gene Scaramuzzo*
15 Ans Deja . . . (Braguette d'Or) / 1989 / Bleu Caraibes 82444
○ **Coquinement Zouk** / 1991 / Declic100% 50236

Zaza
Vocals / Zouk
One of Martinique's carnival stars, who often releases her work only on 45 rpm records. —*Gene Scaramuzzo*
○ **The Best of Zaza** / 1989 / Hibiscus 88022
This recent anthology provides a rare opportunity to experience her music. —*Gene Scaramuzzo*

Ze Top
Group / Zouk
This first-class gathering of musicians casts a witty, irreverent look at zouk and Antilles music in general. —*Gene Scaramuzzo*
○ **Ka Dance** / 1991 / Hibiscus 88040
This record came out at carnival time 1991 and is already one of the classics. It will probably remain available for years to come. —*Gene Scaramuzzo*

Zouk Allstars

Group / Zouk

The Zouk Allstars are Dominique Gengoul, Jean-Luc Alger, Frederic Caracas, and Charles Maurinier, four young musicians who have made an indelible mark on Antilles music of the '80s and early '90s. To call them prolific is a gross understatement; pick up any ten zouk albums, and it's likely that one or more of their names will appear on at least seven as producers and/or instrumentalists. Solo projects include studio groups like Karata, Mazout', Champagn', and Lazair. The crystal clarity of their production, the funkiness of their playing, and their ceaseless creativity are the reasons behind their popularity. —*Gene Scaramuzzo*

○ **An Nou Swe** / 1987 / Moradisc 4029

● **Vol. 2** / 1988 / Moradisc 4037

Top Niveau / 1989 / Moradisc 4050

Zouk Machine

Group / Zouk

A Guadeloupian female vocal trio who incorporate many American Black music elements into their music, a trait that has made them extremely popular in Paris and the Antilles but has left most Americans cold. It was erroneously thought by many Antilleans that Zouk Machine, along with backup provided by Experience 7, would be the zouk band to break the American market. The 1986 release includes Joelle Ursull, who was replaced shortly afterward by Jane Fostin. —*Gene Scaramuzzo*

Zouk Machine / 1986 / Henri DEBS

Includes the hit "Pisime Zouk." —*Robert Leaver*

○ **Min Ne Nwen** / 1987 / Liso Musique 6057

○ **Maldon** / 1988 / Henri DEBS 2451

French Antilles Collection

Antilles D'aujourd'hui / 1978 / Festival 402984

Undoubtedly the best, and probably only, collection of Antilles music circa mid to late '70s. Includes cuts from many of the biggest names of the era, usually their most popular songs. This collection confirms what was said earlier about the diverse talents of Antilles musicians, presenting everything from cadence and Haitian compas to biguine, Creole mazurka, and calypso. Still occasionally surfaces in Paris record stores. —*Gene Scaramuzzo*

☆ **Dance! Cadence!** / 1985 / Globestyle 002

A wonderful look at cadence, biguine moderne, ti kannot, (kalenda), and early zouk by the likes of Eugene Mona, Georges Decimus, and Michel Godzom. A classic. —*Gene Scaramuzzo*

○ **Zoukollection—Vols. 1-3** / 1988 / Hibiscus

Although much the same argument can be made for these compilations (released 1988-1990) as for the *Planete Zouk* discs, the difference is that these are mostly all artists from the Hibiscus label, a stable of unusual artists who are much more involved in experimentation and a return to classic forms like biguine, ti kannot, etc. —*Gene Scaramuzzo*

☆ **Hurricane Zouk** / 1989 / Atlantic 90882

Classic high energy mid '80s zouk. It includes some collaboration with African musicians in Paris. —*Robert Leaver*

Le Grand Merchant Zouk / 1990 / Sonodisc

A live concert featuring all the top zouk musicians (Kassav', F. Caracas) playing together. —*Robert Leaver*

Generation Zouk, Vol. 3 / 1991 / New Deal 334

○ **Planete Zouk—Vols. 1 & 2** / 1991 / Declic100% 50230

An abridged version of Vol. 1 was reissued as *Planet Zouk: The World of Antilles Music (Rhythm Safari)*, and there are plans to do the same soon with Vol. 2. These are compilations of radio hits from a variety of record labels circa 1988-1991 from Paris and the French Antilles. The cuts feature samples from a Who's Who of Antilles greats, from Kassav', Dede St. Prix, Malavoi, and Ronald Rubinel to lesser known but also accomplished artists like Edith Lefel, Ralph Thamar, Eric Virgal, and Experience 7. Many good songs can be found here, from the biguine tinges of Thamar's "Polisson" to the underlying soukous feeling of Experience 7's "Goudjoua." Eric Virgal's "Pa Fe Mwen la Pen" is a fine example of zouk-love, while Edith Lefel's lead vocal on her

Compas

Haitian bandleader Nemours Jean-Baptiste coined the phrase "compas direct" in the 50s to refer to his style of music. "Compas" means musical measure in Spanish, and "direct" refers to the absence of a third chord. Although similar to merengue, compas has a more driving rhythm; its moderate tempo is paced by a steady bass, which anchors the drum and cowbell percussion.

The instrumentation changed from a big band with a full horn section to the smaller "mini-jazz" combos of the later 60s and 70s, who introduced electric guitars and trap drums while retaining the solo saxophone (most typically, the alto sax) and sometimes the accordion. Compas now had a less direct meaning and became a generic term to refer to the Haitian style or, more specifically, rhythm. New York City became home to the top compas bands as the immigrant community grew. Compas spread to Miami, Montreal, Paris, and throughout the Caribbean, especially Guadeloupe and Martinique. In exile, compas has been influenced by soul and funk and more recently by zouk, a popular dance music inspired by Haitian compas.

– Robert Leaver

cocomposition with Ronald Rubinel ("Sensation") shows the best melding of zouk with American soul sounds, an oft-made attempt that is rarely successful. The fact that these are all radio hits implies a common thread that runs throughout the set of music: strong on formula, weak on experimentation. This is a "safe" set of music, which features good songs but few surprises and few moments of pure zouk ecstasy. —*Gene Scaramuzzo*

☆ **Zouk Attack** / 1992 / Rounder 5037

This anthology featured such appealing zouk groups as Pier' Rosier and Gazoline, Love Stars, Typical and Tatiana and Zouti, but sounds just a bit smooth in many places. It's a reminder that zouk was and is a roots-oriented pop sound, and as such has a soft center as well as frenetic edges. —*Ron Wynn*

Generation Zouk, Vol. 2 / New Deal

○ **Generation Zouk, Vols. 1-3** / New Deal

Arguably the best of the collections of radio hits, but please refer to the *Planete Zouk* record entry to read more on this. The New Deal/Carrere label features some of the best music made in the Antilles, and whoever was responsible for compiling these collections (which feature artists from all labels) showed typical good taste. —*Gene Scaramuzzo*

Les Rois du Zouk / Riahi 7242

Desvarieux, Grammacks, Jeff Joseph, Panol, and a couple of others, plus instrumentals. It could have been a disaster, but zouk is in the details, and the details here are mostly real tasty. This is no groundbreaker, but it's a real cute listen. The major cuts are "An Nou Alle" (Desvarieux); "Creole Mix" (K. Rodney); "Sensations" (Panol); "Hot Music" (Jeff Joseph); "Laisse Moin Vive" (Sylvie Drai); "Reggae Boulevard" (Grammacks); "Debar Debar" (Jeff Joseph); "Reminiscence" (Kassav'). —*John Storm Roberts*

Bahamas

Joseph Spence

b. Aug. 1910, Andros, Bahama, **d.** Mar. 18, 1984

Vocals, guitar / Bahaman

Born on the island of Andrus in the Bahamas, Spence created an idiosyncratic (and inimitable) guitar style rife with percussive and improvisatory vamps around staid hymns and such "square" standards as "Coming in on a Wing and a Prayer." He was a folk guitarist's Thelonious Monk, and his growling vocal counterpoint and surprising inventions are one of folk music's great delights. —*Mark A. Humphrey*

○ **The Complete Folkways Recordings (1958)** / 1958 / Smithsonian/Folkways 40066

When I first heard Spence's singing and guitar I couldn't stop laughing from joy and amazement. Both this and his recording with the Pinder family are absolute musts! *1958* is Spence alone in his first recordings and I defy anyone to speak of his guitar playing without a six-volume thesaurus—his feet thumping out the beat, he picks in a such a crazily syncopated style that you have to play every song twice just to believe it! He plays mostly hymns that he has adapted himself. —*Carl Hoyt, Original Music*

Happy All the Time / 1964 / Carthage 4419
Waxed for Elektra in 1964, this has better sound than the Folkways recordings and offers some of Spence's most percussive playing. —*Mark A. Humphrey*

The Real Bahamas, Vol. 1 / 1965 / Nonesuch 2013
The recordings on *The Real Bahamas in Music and Song—Vol. 1* date from 1965 and feature Spence accompanying members of the family of his sister, Jenny Pinder. They may be available on CD. In any event, the Folkways, Elektra, and Arhoolie albums are pretty much "the essential" Spence. —*Mark A. Humphrey*

The Real Bahamas, Vol. 2 / 1965 / Nonesuch 72078
The second volume of a two-volume set. It may be available on CD. —*Mark A. Humphrey*

Living on the Hallelujah Side / 1987 / Rounder 2021
This set of '70s performances, reissued on CD, included evocative renditions of "A Closer Walk With Thee," "More and More With Jesus," and "When the Saints Go Marching In," plus equally arresting versions of "Irene Goodnight" and the holiday ditty "Santa Claus is Comin' to Town." Spence was incapable of self-indulgence or fakery; his lines, phrasing, riffs and solos are enchanting, while his vocal effects and accompaniment often come close to surpassing his playing. This was simply magical material, the kind that comes only from the genuine originals. —*Ron Wynn*

○ **Good Morning Mr. Walker** / 1990 / Arhoolie 1061

Bahamian Guitarist / 1990 / Arhoolie 349
His Boston concert, 1971, plus informal recordings. Spence chortles at his twists on tradition. Carter Family purists should lend an ear to "Will the Serpent Be Unbroken!" —*Mark A. Humphrey*

○ **Music of the Bahamas, Vol. 1** / Smithsonian/Folkways 3844
○ **Music of the Bahamas, Vol. 2** / Smithsonian/Folkways 3846
○ **Music of the Bahamas, Vol. 3** / Smithsonian/Folkways 3847

Haiti

Bossa Combo

Accolade / Mini 1069
Bossa Combo has always been one of my favorite bands for its original arranging style. Here, after the rather subdued first cut, they'd sear steak. —*John Storm Roberts*

Boukman Eksperyans

○ **Vodou Adjae** / 1991 / Mango 539 899
○ **Kalfou Dangare** / 1992 / Mango 9927
○ **Vodou Adjae** / Mango 9899
Boukman Eksperyans blend the rhythms of rural *rara* drumming and its cautionary vocal tradition with subdued modern keyboard and electric guitar lines, making music with extraordinary melodic and rhythmic undertow. The Creole patois and lilting harmonies may sometimes disguise the hard-edged lyrical content—these folks are from Haiti, after all—but there's no missing the fact that this is a burning debut. Translations provided. —*Roundup Newsletter*

Caribbean Sextet

En Gala / Mini 1002
The Caribbean Sextet, one of my favorite Haitian bands, opens here a bit heavily into the synth. But after a dreamy opening, the second cut kicks into a righteous Creole number, and joy reigns. Fine sax here, too, with a slight R&B edge, flute (rare in Haitian music), and a fine trumpeter. —*John Storm Roberts*

Frantz Casseus & Marc Ribot

Haitian Suite / 1989 / Music of the World 202

Frantz Casseus, the genius of contemporary Haitian guitar music, was the first classical guitar composer to draw inspiration from the African-derived music of his homeland. Marc Ribot, a highly accomplished guitarist, interprets these timeless and haunting beautiful melodies. —*Music of the World*

Coupé Cloué

Vocals / Haitian

An enigmatic guitarist and singer, Coupe Cloue acquired this nickname (translated as "kickout") from his prowess on the soccer field. He is famous, or rather notorious, for his lyrics containing sexual double-entendre, long "raps" ranging from risque to romantic, and social satire. His "compas mamba" (peanut compas) seems very African, with a guitar style resembling West African highlife and the use of Cuban bongo drums and bamboo tubes played with sticks in addition to the standard conga and drum kit. Appearing on many album covers wearing African clothing, Coupe Cloue with his shaved head cuts a striking figure. This may explain why he was given the title "Le Roi" (the king) when he played in the Ivory Coast, West Africa, in 1975. Of all the electric Caribbean bands, Coupe Cloue has the strongest African sound, which shows the strength of his roots, for he claims he never heard African music before his 1975 trip. —*Richard Lieberson*

○ **The World of** / 1979 / Mini
Coupe Cloue's always had the capacity to beguile me all over again, however many of his recordings I hear. But this 1979 release, which I'd never heard before, has to be one of the man's very finest. Every track is catchy to the max, egg-full of the jaunty charm that defines Haitian mini-jazz, and rich in simply wonderful guitar. —*John Storm Roberts*

L'essentiel Coupe Cloue / Mini 1067
Gesner Henry (Coupe Cloue) runs one of the prettiest guitar bands on either side of the Atlantic, though Tabou Combo's hit-hunting has kept C.C. out of the international spotlight. Here are the interlocking guitars, rootsy percussion, and chatty vocals that make Coupe in general, and this mid '70s collection in particular, one of our undisputed faves. —*Carl Hoyt, Original Music*

○ **Sociss (With Terio Select)** / Marc's Records 281
When *Sociss* was recorded, I'm not sure: late '70s? It's decently recorded, and among the favorites around here musically speaking. This is unpretentiously but outstandingly catchy three-guitar band stuff, gentle and rippling but still with a kick, and there are very few Haitian recordings that really overshadow these guys, particularly in their good-humored creole genre. A definite classic. —*John Storm Roberts*

Full Tank / AP Records 104
This is an irresistibly jaunty example of hardcore string-band by Haiti's finest guitar-band. *Full Tank* (the group's latest) has a fair amount of keyboards, but the guitars and the singing are the albums' heart. —*John Storm Roberts, Original Music*

The Preacher / Mini 1062
Eight classic '70s cuts and "Myan Myan." —*Robert Leaver*

Djet-X

Egal Ego / Mini 1211
Djet-X leader Gerard Daniel was Shleu Shleu's last saxist before it transmogrified into Ska-Shah #1. Great band. This 1990 recording combines contempo keyboards and oddments like a smattering of rap with your basic mini-jazz guitar band bounce and (not surprisingly) neat horns. —*John Storm Roberts*

Ensemble Nemours Jean-Baptiste

☆ **A Musical Tour of Haiti** / Ansonia 1280
One of Haiti's most popular artists is Nemours Jean-Baptiste. His experience in orchestral work has been long and varied, including a prosperous tour in the United States. On this album, the orchestra performs the beautiful rhythmic dance, the Haitian merengue. —*Roundup Newsletter*

GM Connection

You and I / Mini 1105
GM is salsa-oriented, with longer horn lines, a more stretched-out swing, more fine sax solos, and some strings on the order of Martinique's great Malavoi. —*John Storm Roberts*

Les Gypsies de Petion-Ville

Courage / Macaya 116
'70s style from Haiti, not New York City. —*Robert Leaver*

Magnum Band

Adoration / Mini Records 1140
Here's another gorgeous recording from a consistently fine band, this one made in 1982. Magnum was an example of having it all: good solos, good singers, all buoyed up by a killer rhythm section and horns that cook consistently. And along with the tightness and joy was the humor the new young bands are missing: a humor that allowed the lead guitarist to build a fine solo from a mix of "Alone Again, Naturally" and some great Nashville fills! —*John Storm Roberts, Original Music*

Rara Machine

Break the Chain / 1991 / Shanachie 64038
Undoubted winner of the 1991 award for the most startlingly rapid improvement. Rara Machine's first album was amiable enough but exceedingly bland—and on the whole, Haitian recordings for non-Haitian companies have a poor track record. So imagine my surprise when I let this one loose and discovered an altogether outstanding set with a really good mix of Creole singing, percussion roots, mini-jazz arrangements, and just enough zouk in the trimmings. Such surprises bless the day. —*John Storm Roberts*

Les Shleu Shleu

Group / Mini jazz
Shleu Shleu, the Haitian forerunner of what in NYC became Ska-Shah #1, was one of the great bands. Their combination of swing and delicacy was one reason, but from this distance what stands out from that pre-funk era is their strong Creole flavor, not just in the melodies but in the wonderful solo sax, a style no longer heard. Here's a question: given the Congo touch in the guitars, who was influencing whom? —*John Storm Roberts*

○ **Les Shleu Shleu** / 1978 / Dada's 04
Unmistakably creole, yet still quite cosmopolitan with its jaunty sax and Congolese-style guitar, Haitian music of this period (1978) had an influence only more remarkable for the fact that Haiti is only half of a small island. It's my impression that bands like Shleu Shleu played more for love than money. It certainly sounds that way. —*John Storm Roberts*

Ce La ou Ye / 1990 / Mini 1004
Early '70s classic mini-jazz. —*Robert Leaver*

6eme Anniversaire / Feb. 1990 / Mini 1005
This reissue bears a 1990 copyright date, but I'd guestimate it as '60s or very early '70s. —*John Storm Roberts*

Pionniers / 1991 / Melodie Makers 1014
A new, different band. Modern sound with soukous-like guitar and full horn section. —*Robert Leaver*

☆ **Ace Frape** / Mini 1011
Early/mid '70s. —*Robert Leaver*

Tete Chauve / Mini 1003
Includes a mambo instrumental. —*Robert Leaver*

Ska-Shah #1

Group / Mini jazz
See Les Shleu Shleu. —*AMG*

For Ever / Mini 1111
Ska-Shah has great swing, kicking alto and tenor sax solos, flashes of soukous-like guitar, and a general hell-for-leather exuberance that makes me want to laugh aloud. —*John Storm Roberts*

Ska-Shah #1 / Ska-Shah 201
Mid '70s album with one of Ska-Shah's biggest songs. —*Robert Leaver*

Tabou Combo

Group / Haitian
Formed in the Port-au-Prince suburb of Petion-Ville by the Chancy brothers, Albert on bass and Adolphe on guitar, this young band won the Radio Haiti mini-jazz competition in 1968.

They relocated to Brooklyn in 1971, and their song "New York City," which spoke of the difficulty of life in exile, reached #1 on the Paris pop charts in August 1975. They competed with Ska-Shah for top band honors in the '70s and '80s and fought "musical duels" similar to the Weber Sicot/Jean-Baptiste Nemours battles of the '50s and '60s. An irresistible live band, Tabou Combo takes Haitian compas to the widest of audiences. From their regular appearances in the '80s at the famous Zenith Theatre in Paris, to an audience of 20,000 in New York's Central Park, to the Jazz and Heritage Festival in New Orleans, in football stadiums throughout the Caribbean, and on the turntables of the top DJs, this band makes people dance. Influenced by funk and soul in their adopted home, Tabou took on the likeness of the Commodores on the covers of their late '70s releases. They even made a demo tape with hopes of a Motown contract. Their desire to reach the Black US market remains unsatisfied, but they should be proud that popular musicians such as Kassav' from the Antilles/Paris and Wilfrido Vargas from the Dominican Republic have absorbed their music. —*Richard Lieberson*

8eme Sacrement / 1974 / Mini 1044
The CD is from 1974, which some regard as the band's golden age. Back then it was essentially a guitar band (with accordion to link back to Nemours!), with a perfect blend of drive and simplicity. "New York City," the biggest Haitian hit of all time, is featured on this live album. —*John Storm Roberts*

Live au Zenith / 1989 / Esperance 8057
The band's relative recent success outside its core community led to hit-hunting that marred its 1989 release. Happily, however, there's little of it in this Zenith set, recorded at a gig in Paris. This double album (also available on video) has plenty of zouk influence, but on the whole it's a return to the band's '80s sound at its best. —*John Storm Roberts*

Any Antilles / 1989 / TC 8056
New sound. Ultimate Haitian dance music. —*Robert Leaver*

Toto Bissainthe

○ **Chante Haiti** / Arion 64086
With Marie-Claude Benoit and Mariann Matheus. Slave songs from the Vodoun cult. Powerful, beautiful, and haunting. —*Robert Leaver*

Haiti Collection

☆ **Konbit Burning Rhythms of Haiti** / A&M 75021-5281
Filmmaker Jonathan Demme compiled this sharp package of classic (and rarely heard) Haitian music from 1957 to the present, with most tracks coming from the last half of the '80s and containing potent political sentiments, not to mention potent dance rhythms. —*Myles Boisen*

Trinidad

Allrounder

○ **Whey Going On!** / 1989 / Crosbys
One of the more hilarious tunes of 1989 was Allrounder's tongue-in-cheek defense of Jimmy Swaggart in "Innocent Jimmy" from this EP. —*Gene Scaramuzzo*

Arrow

Vocals / Soca, Party soca, Calypso
From Montserrat, Arrow got his start as a first-class calypsonian in the traditional Trinidadian style but soon began exploring ways to bring the music to an international level. Always an innovator, he played around with mixing elements of cadence, salsa, and American R&B guitar into his music. In 1983 he experienced his first pan-Caribbean success, "Hot Hot Hot" (a song that later became an international hit). Since then he has branched out to include a wider array of world-music elements, from hip-hop to the sounds of various African nations, while concentrating on lyrics that act predominantly as a vehicle to drive the music to a higher frenzy. A late '80s contract with Island/Mango Records has made him the soca artist most widely distributed and most easily available in the States. His 1992 release, *Zombie Soca*, was notable for including three songs with social commentary lyrics. Unlike those of most calypsonians,

Arrow's early releases, including those preceding the Island/Mango albums, are still easily available. —*Gene Scaramuzzo*

Outrageous / Arrow
Continuing with a bit of social commentary but jamming hard with tunes like "Pressure" and "Physical." —*Gene Scaramuzzo*

○ **Instant Knockout** / 1980 / Charlie's
From his heavily cadence-flavored period, featuring the original version of the social commentary "Bills." —*Gene Scaramuzzo*

○ **Hot Hot Hot** / 1983 / Arrow
An exciting album not only for the title cut; every song is great. Still featuring social commentary. —*Gene Scaramuzzo*

Soca Savage / 1984 / Arrow 023
Early Arrow album with two major dance hits, "Party Mix" and "Columbia Rock," one of soca's best Latin fusion tunes. —*J. Poet*

Knock Dem Dead / 1988 / Mango 162-539809
Arrow's strongest musical statement to date. The disc kicks off with "Groove Master," the first track to mix rap and rock guitar with a supersonic soca beat. Another major innovation is the addition of South African township jive on "Tell Mama" . . . The rest of the disc is typical non-stop Arrow party music. — *J. Poet, Rock & Roll Disc.*

○ **Massive** / 1989 /
Re-mixed as *O'la Soca* on Mango. —*Gene Scaramuzzo*

O'la Soca / 1989 / Mango 162-539835
Hot tracks and exuberant, though sometimes irritating vocals. A remix of his 1989 *Massive* album. —*Ron Wynn*

Soca Dance Party / 1990 / Mango 162-539878
Arrow's latest exploration of Caribbean rhythms includes an excursion to Guadaloupe entitled "Zouk Me." —*J. Poet*

☆ **Hot Soca Hot** / 1990 / Arrow
Outstanding anthology of hits. Unlike other Arrow anthologies, this one was put together by the man himself, and therefore features what he knows is the best. —*Gene Scaramuzzo*

Zombie Soca / 1992 / Arrow
This is an outstanding album by Arrow, including the superb dance hall soca "Wine Yuh Body." Complete with several re-mixes, social commentaries, and a total of 70 minutes of music, this is the best Arrow album to come along in a while. —*Gene Scaramuzzo*

Bally

Vocals / Soca
An extremely consistent young calypsonian who has already won the Jr. Calypso Monarchy Crown and usually places in the finals for the National Calypso Monarchy competition. More often than not, his hits have meaningful lyrics. —*Gene Scaramuzzo*

Honey / JW Prod.
"Jam & Wine" from this LP was one of the year's best commentaries on the jam and wine controversy. The best LP from what otherwise has been a rather lackluster 1990s for Bally. —*Gene Scaramuzzo*

○ **Bally with Love** / 1988 / Love People
Features "Shaka Shaka" and "Bacchanal Start." —*Gene Scaramuzzo*

Pleasure / 1989 / Love People
Contains "Maxi Dub," the first commentary on the invasion of Jamaican dancehall into T&T. —*Gene Scaramuzzo*

Baron

Vocals / Soca
Known for his sweet voice, dark skin, and multitudes of gold jewelry, Baron is one of the favorites among the ladies. His topics are rarely political, sticking more to love songs, tales of risque encounters, and global messages about peace. Every album is good. —*Gene Scaramuzzo*

○ **Full of Fire** / 1987 / B's
One of his biggest years, including the suggestive "Say Say." —*Gene Scaramuzzo*

Party Fusion / 1989 / JW Productions
"Somebody" was possibly his biggest hit ever. —*Gene Scaramuzzo*

Becket

○ **Gal Ah Rush Me** / 1990 / Cocoa
From the island of St. Vincent, Becket often hits hard with party soca, but "Gal Ah Rush Me" and "Teaser" from this album were huge hits. —*Gene Scaramuzzo*

Black Stalin

Group / Soca, Party soca, Social commentary
Stalin is the master of socially conscious lyrics combined with infectious soca dance music, and is a revered legend in T&T (the Trinidad & Tobago style). Song topics range from local concerns like support for the steel drums and calypsonians to concerns of African and Caribbean unification, with occasional global topics like the litany against world leaders in "Burn Dem." Between 1967 and 1992 Stalin has been a finalist contender for the coveted National Calypso Monarchy crown 16 times, winning it four times. —*Gene Scaramuzzo*

Help / Straker's
The title cut is rather whiney, but is left in the dust by superb cuts like "Black Man Killing Black Man," "Kaiso Music," and "Wey de Wok." —*Gene Scaramuzzo*

Rebellion / Ice
More cuts than necessary on this first Ice Records release for Stalin, but there is a core of songs here that would have made an excellent normal length LP. —*Gene Scaramuzzo*

○ **Caribbean Man** / 1979 / Makossa
The album that brought him his first Calypso Monarchy crown with "Caribbean Unity" and "Play One." —*Gene Scaramuzzo*

Wait Dorothy Wait / 1985 / Charlie's
Twelve-inch single backed with "Ism Schism;" these two songs brought him his second crown. —*Gene Scaramuzzo*

I Time / 1987 / B's
Includes "Burn Dem," the most internationally known of any Stalin composition. Brought him his third crown. —*Gene Scaramuzzo*

☆ **Roots Rock Soca** / 1991 / Rounder 5038
Rounder collected 11 Stalin gems on this '91 anthology, which has been recently been released on CD. Such numbers as "Caribbean Unity," "Black Man Music," and "Burn Dem" have a pronounced Afro-Latin bent, showing soca's ties with Latin jazz and Afro-Cuban rhythms. Material done later in the '80s has a faster pace, and Stalin begins including more synthesized backbeats and contemporary arrangements. Anyone unfamiliar with either soca's delights or Stalin's music will get a fine introduction via this CD. —*Ron Wynn*

The Bright Side / 1991 / Straker's
A great album that will go down in history for including his first hit with party lyrics, "Ah Feel to Party." The song brought him his fourth crown. Excellent from beginning to end. —*Gene Scaramuzzo*

○ **Cry of the Caribbean** / 1992 /

Blueboy (Superblue)

Vocals / Soca, Party soca, Social commentary
Blueboy may very well be the most loved of T&T's calypsonians. After dominating the Road March competition in the early '80s, a difficult bout with personal problems removed him for a while from the big leagues. His triumphant return in 1991 (as "Superblue") was met with overwhelmingly positive response by a public that had been truly empathetic during his "lost years." In both 1991 and 1992 Superblue was so far ahead in the Road March competition that his ultimate victories were pronounced long before Carnival Tuesday, but in '93 he even exceeded this feat by writing the most popular Road March ever (in terms of votes tallied), "Bacchanal Time." Look under Blueboy for the best of his earlier efforts, but consider both albums as Superblue to be essential listening. —*Gene Scaramuzzo*

○ **Soca in the Shaolin Temple** / 1980 / Charlie's 1001
Classic early '80s album. —*J. Poet*

Thundering Soca / 1984 / CCP 007
Soca with a hard rock edge. —*J. Poet*

Caribbean Magic / 1988 / B's

The still-embattled Blueboy managed to come through with hints of his past grandeur with this album, which includes "Ding Ding" and "Look the Devil Deh." —*Gene Scaramuzzo*

○ **Poom Poom** / 1990 /
After 1990, Blueboy began going by the name Superblue. —*Gene Scaramuzzo*

10th Anniversary / 1991 / Charlie's
A soca masterpiece. Contains the 1991 Road March, "Get Something and Wave." —*Gene Scaramuzzo*

☆ **Jab Jab** / 1992 /

Brother Resistance

Vocals / Soca, Rapso
Main artist in a dub-poetry style of soca called rapso. Eloquent in interviews and in lyrics, he is an artist who would be of great interest outside of T&T if only better known. In his homeland, he often must struggle to find a spot in a calypso tent and only infrequently releases a record. —*Gene Scaramuzzo*

Tonight Is De Nite / 1988 /

○ **Heart of the Rapso Nation** / 1992 /

Burning Flames

Group / Soca
From Antigua, this band represents the epitome of the high-energy, multiple-influenced, synthesizer-driven soca bands of some of the other soca islands. Years of tourist gigs and a stint as backup band to Montserrat calypsonian Arrow laid the groundwork for their solo debut . . . total domination of the Antigua carnival in 1986 with *Stiley Tight*. Elements of rock, funk, reggae, cadence, zouk, and more, put to frenetic tempos of amphetamine-like proportion, were the trademark of this band until 1989's "Workey Workey," a funky, zoukish second-line that was an international sensation. They zouked it out further in 1990 with "Chook and Dig" and shortly afterward were anthologized on a Mango release, *Dig*, although the re-mixing done for the record worked to the detriment of each cut. They have taken Antigua Road March almost every year since 1985. —*Gene Scaramuzzo*

Hard Fu Ded / Dr. G Prod
"De Donkey" took '92 Road March honors, initiating a donkey craze that exploded a few months later at the '93 T&T Carnival. —*Gene Scaramuzzo*

Brigiding Biff / BF
Every kind of liquid imaginable was being tossed around at Antigua Carnival '93 because of "Wet Down," the Road March winner from this LP. —*Gene Scaramuzzo*

○ **Me Na Freard** / 1989 / BF
Many songs from this album, including "Workey Workey," were selected and re-mixed for Mango's *Dig* anthology. —*Gene Scaramuzzo*

Dig / 1991 / Mango 162-539914
Re-mixes of some of the band's best late '80s output, surprisingly de-emphasizing the frenzied tempos that first made them famous. —*Gene Scaramuzzo*

Calypso Rose

Vocals / Soca, Party soca, Calypso, Social commentary
Rose has won more national and international awards than any other calypsonian save for Sparrow and Kitch. The National Calypso King Competition had to be changed in name to the National Calypso Monarchy Competition as a result of her being the first female to ever take the crown (in 1978). Her material is often feminist in nature, and the music is much in the style of Antigua's Swallow . . . heavy on the cowbell and horn section. It is no exaggeration to say that every album by Rose is worth hearing. —*Gene Scaramuzzo*

Soca Diva / Ice
Her first album away from the Straker label in more than a decade, a perfect collection of social comentary, always from an amused but experienced perspective. —*Gene Scaramuzzo*

○ **Trouble** / 1984 / Straker's 2252
One of calypso's small number of women performers and the only female Carnival "King," Rose has a strong message of Black pride and feminist consciousness, often turning in scathing criticisms of the way men treat women. This album is one of her best. —*J. Poet*

● **Pan in Town** / 1985 / Straker's 2261
This one is among her best; includes "Huttam Pullam," "Put It on the Table," and "Turn On the Pressure." —*Gene Scaramuzzo*

Soca Explosion / 1988 / Straker's 2299
This above-average album from one of soca's top singers is especially notable for a really fine Indo-calypso (an old calypso tradition that has produced many fine songs) in "Indian Baccanal," and a rare and welcome bonus: lots of solo horn to freshen the backings. —*John Storm Roberts*

Carl & Carol

Vocals / Soca, Party soca
Longtime leaders of the T&T brass band Savage and now residents of Miami, Carl & Carol appear as backup singers on countless calypso records. They release a 12-inch single or album nearly every year, their 1988 release being particularly noteworthy. —*Gene Scaramuzzo*

We Wanna Live / 1988 / Ice
"Savage" and "Scandal" were Road March contenders. —*Gene Scaramuzzo*

Chalkdust

Vocals / Soca, Social commentary
An extremely dedicated social commentator, schoolteacher Chalkdust predominantly limits his lyrics to local concerns, with a point of view that often forces Trinidadians to look within themselves for the causes and answers to the country's problems. He has won the Monarchy crown five times since 1976, most recently in 1993 for "Kaiso in Hospital" and his remarkably timely surprise song at the Monarchy Finals, "Misconceptions." A kaiso legend, but probably not very accessible to those with a passing interest in calypso. —*Gene Scaramuzzo*

Visions / Straker's
The '93 T&T Carnival raged in controversy over new styles of music entering the calypso/soca scene. Chalkdust's finger-pointing "Kaiso in Hospital" was the widely accepted as the "official" viewpoint on the matter, even if a bit extreme in its accusations. One of Chalkie's best LPs ever, including other great commentaries like "The Acid Test" and "Stickman's Lament." —*Gene Scaramuzzo*

○ **Chaffeur Wanted** / 1989 /

○ **Total Kaiso** / 1989 / Straker's
"Chauffeur Wanted" is a scathing indictment against the prime minister of the time, a song that brought Chalkdust the National Calypso Monarchy Crown in 1989. —*Gene Scaramuzzo*

Charlie's Roots

Group / Party soca
A T&T brass band that had been popular for many years prior to the emergence of one of their lead singers, David Rudder, as a solo calypsonian in 1986. In that year Rudder won both the Road March and the National Calypso Monarchy crown. In 1988 another Charlie's Roots lead singer, Chris "Tambu" Herbert, began a three-year domination of the Road March as a solo artist. Despite the solo careers of the two, they remain to this day as singers for Charlie's Roots, although as of 1988 they began to release albums under their own names, with the band listed as backup artists. Albums are still released occasionally under the group's name. Sire Records reissues Rudder's music with Charlie's Roots in nice packages that are more easily available than the original Charlie's releases. Their tendency to mix songs from different years may confuse those who really wish to familiarize themselves with Rudder as a developing artist. —*Gene Scaramuzzo*

☆ **The Hammer** / 1986 / Charlie's 3451
The album that made Rudder a legend, released under the Charlie's Roots name. It won him the title of Road March King, King of Carnival, and Best New Artist, a feat unprecedented in the history of calypso. —*J. Poet*

10th Anniversary / 1987 / Charlie's
Featuring Rudder again, this time with "Dedication" and "Calypso Music." This album, along with the previous year's "Bahia Gyal," was reissued on Sire Records as *This Is Soca—Vol. 1*. —*Gene Scaramuzzo*

☆ **Total Party** / 1992 / Charlie's
This album, which features Rudder on "Savannah Party," was one of the finest releases from Carnival 1992. —*Gene Scaramuzzo*

Crazy

Reggae, Soca
As #2 he certainly tries harder. There is perhaps no artist in T&T who more consistently composes a party masterpiece aimed at the Road March and yet loses time and again, usually placing second. Best known internationally for his Indian soca success, "Nani Wine," he has actually been responsible for many huge hits, including "Ain't Bong for You" (from 1984), "Drive It" (1988), "Gimme More" (from 1990), and "Penelope/Party Now Start" (from 1992). Only once, in 1985, did he win the Road March, with "(Suck Me) Soucouyant." For all-out party soca, any record by Crazy will do. —*Gene Scaramuzzo*

Let's Go Crazy / JW Prod
"Paul" from this LP got banned from Children's Carnival but it only opened the door for another great tune, "Jump Up and Wail," to jump into the battle for the Road March race. —*Gene Scaramuzzo*

Craziah Than Ever . . . / JW Prod
On first listen maybe a lesser LP than others by Crazy, but nonetheless contains three hits during Carnival '94 . . . "Dis Is How," "OPP In the Party," and "La La Lay La La La Lo." —*Gene Scaramuzzo*

New Directions / 1984 /
Contains two great songs for the road, "Ain't Bong for You" and "Soca Tarzan." —*Gene Scaramuzzo*

Soucouyant / 1985 / Trinity 001
Another three-song "LP" from Crazy. A soucouyant is a Trinidadian spirit that can suck the life out of you, but Crazy is so pumped up on soca energy that he taunts the apparition with one of the great double entendre lines of the '80s, "Suck Me, Soucouyant." —*J. Poet*

☆ **Nani Wine** / 1989 / Trinity 001
The title song, written by Superblue, is an infectious Indian soca response to Drupatee's "Mr. Bissessar" from the year before. Crazy's most well-known song. —*Gene Scaramuzzo*

○ **Crazymania** / 1992 / JW Productions
Most music lovers of T&T agree that "Penelope" from this LP could have been the Road March if it hadn't advised "if you can't find a woman, take a man." —*Gene Scaramuzzo*

Cro-Cro

Vocals / Soca, Social commentary
Little known outside T&T, Cro-Cro is responsible for some of the most scathing calypso diatribes against corruption and political chicanery. Because his topics are of local interest, he rarely tours internationally, even in the years when he has won the National Calypso Monarchy crown. Another legend, like Chalkdust, whose records will probably be fairly inaccessible to those with only a general interest in calypso. —*Gene Scaramuzzo*

○ **Still De Best** / 1991 / Straker's
Probably the most accessible of his albums. —*Gene Scaramuzzo*

Dealberto

Vocals / Party soca, Social commentary
He has never been a major figure in carnival but he consistently produces a humorous, topical calypso. —*Gene Scaramuzzo*

Pan Woman/Rambo the Avenger / 1987 / B's
A fine pan tune backed by a silly but amusing fantasy of Rambo coming to rescue us all from the problems of the world. A minor hit in 1987. —*Gene Scaramuzzo*

Designer

My Burning Desire / 1983 / Charlie's 335
An up-and-coming singer drops rock and funk rhythms into the mix for a style that appeals to Islanders living in the USA as well as Trinidad. "Rockin' Fever" is a perfect example of rock done calypso style. —*J. Poet*

○ **Ra-Ti-Ray** / 1992 / JW Productions
Infectious melody and chorus with throwaway lyrics; one of the biggest party hits of 1992. —*Gene Scaramuzzo*

Drupatee (Ramgoonai)

Vocals / Soca, Party soca
East Indian singer who nearly took the Road March in 1988 with "(Roll Up the Tassa) Mr. Bissessar," an Indian soca that was the motivation behind the following year's "Nani Wine" response by Crazy. —*Gene Scaramuzzo*

Down In Sando / Spice Island
Contains the instant classic "Lick Down Me Nani (Careless Driver)," whose lyrics can be taken innocently or so lewdly that the song was banned for '93 Kiddie Carnival. —*Gene Scaramuzzo*

☆ **Mr. Bissessar** / 1988 / KPS
A classic 12-inch single. —*Gene Scaramuzzo*

○ **Hotter Than Ah Chullah** / 1989 / Akash

Pepper Pepper/Hotter Than Ah Chullah / 1989 / Akash
This 1989 effort was almost as popular as the previous year's hit, and was the last offering by Drupatee that played a major part in carnival. —*Gene Scaramuzzo*

Duke (Mighty)

Vocals / Soca, Social commentary
A legendary calypsonian for his unduplicated feat of winning the calypso Monarchy four years in a row. Considered one of the major figures in calypso, Duke releases albums that are always of interest. He never fails to deliver a party soca for the Road March competition but has only once captured it (in 1987 with "Is Thunder"). His topics range from party lyrics to global concerns, addressing only on rare occasions something of local concern. —*Gene Scaramuzzo*

○ **Calypso Forever** / 1983 / Straker's 2235
Duke (aka Mighty Duke) is one of calypso's founding fathers; this is one of his best efforts from the early '80s. —*J. Poet*

● **Yesterday, Today and Tomorrow** / 1987 / LEM's
Containing the 1987 Road March, "Is Thunder." —*Gene Scaramuzzo*

○ **Poison** / 1988 /

Party for Yuh Life! / 1989 / JW Productions
"Yahhhhhhh" was among the hottest songs of 1989. —*Gene Scaramuzzo*

○ **Total Disorder** / 1990 /

The Phung-Uh-Nung Sweet / 1992 / Straker's
Title cut and "Rocket in Yuh Pocket" are worth hearing. —*Gene Scaramuzzo*

Explainer

Vocals / Soca, Social commentary
A severely underrated calypsonian who rarely makes it to the Monarchy finals but who nearly always releases an album of interest. His albums are always a talented mix of social commentary and (often risque) party tunes. —*Gene Scaramuzzo*

○ **Nature** / 1982 / Charlie's 317
Mostly songs about sex and romance, told with much humor and compassion. —*J. Poet*

○ **The Awakening** / 1984 / B's
"Caribbean Change" was one of the best commentaries on the unrest being caused by foreign intervention in the Caribbean (Grenada, Cuba, etc.). A gem. —*Gene Scaramuzzo*

Dedicated to You / 1985 / B's 020
Explainer is very political, and one of the few soca singers who can tell a tale from the women's perspective. Features "Lunch Time," an amusing celebration of oral sex. —*J. Poet*

☆ **Positive Vibrations** / 1989 / Vista 4003
One of the few calypsonians to date to have his past work anthologized, this disc provides a taste of all the styles of lyrical commentary that make Explainer great. —*Gene Scaramuzzo*

Tongue / 1991 / Charlie's
Especially good; includes the party hit "Curfew Jam" as well as one of the first soca tunes ever written about a love affair between a calypsonian and his hand. —*Gene Scaramuzzo*

Francine (Singing)

Vocals / Party soca, Social commentary
A calypsonian who rarely plays a major role in carnival but who often makes a good commentary on some local issue. 1988's

"Carnival Controversy" and 1989's "Sing for the Judges" show her to be unafraid to speak out against the T&T government, and these in fact represent two albums that would provide a good introduction to her music. —*Gene Scaramuzzo*

She/Chinaman / 1984 /
A 12-inch single with funky soca featuring steel drum lead that livened up Carnival '84. —*Gene Scaramuzzo*

○ **Reaching Out** / 1988 / Straker's
"Cultural Controversy" was a major commentary of 1988. —*Gene Scaramuzzo*

Dedication / 1989 / Straker's
"Sing for the Judges" was mentioned above, but "Soca Do That" is also a fine tune from 1989, although admittedly it was not among the biggest hits. —*Gene Scaramuzzo*

Gabby (Mighty)

Gabby is undoubtedly Barbados' finest calypsonian as he has proved again and again in the past dozen years. —*Gene Scaramuzzo*

○ **Boots** / 1984 / Ice 1283 003
By Gabby of Barbados, a hard-hitting anti-war commentary deploring the use of tax money for a costly acquisition of boots for the military. It had a particularly strong impact coming as it did in the same year as the invasion of nearby Caribbean island Grenada. —*Gene Scaramuzzo*

Soca Trinity / 1993 / Ice/Ras 930602
Six songs by Gabby on this collection also including '93 tunes by Bajan calypsonians Grynner and Bert "Panta" Brown. "Pow Pow (Arm the Police)" was his forceful solution to addressing the growing crime problem in Barbados. —*Gene Scaramuzzo*

Iwer George

Vocals / Soca, Party soca
An artist who often releases a 12-inch single of a very hot Road March contender. His lyrics range from suggestive to irritatingly obscene, the high-water mark being "Boom Boom Time" in 1987, with the depths being reached in 1992 with *X-Rated*. —*Gene Scaramuzzo*

Nuff Respect / 1991 / Wrecker
Includes Road March contenders "The Party Hot" and "Wine & Jump Up." —*Gene Scaramuzzo*

Gypsy

Gypsy is one of the outstanding calypsonians of T&T who annually since 1988 has won the National Extempo Calypso crown, a competition in which contestants must compose lyrics on the spot. He has had a roller-coaster career that has reached the extremes of peaks and valleys. His "Sinking Ship: SS Trinidad" from his classic 1986 release was considered by most to be the crowning blow that brought on the downfall of the PNM government, which had been in power for nearly 30 years. Despite this triumph, he lost out that year to David Rudder's "Bahia Gyal/The Hammer." Somewhat bitter (a 1987 calypso, "Sing Ram Bam," sarcastically refers to the "inane" lyrics of Rudder's "Bahia Gyal"), and further embattled by other career setbacks, he has nonetheless gone on to compose outstanding calypsos each year. Any album by Gypsy is recommended. —*Gene Scaramuzzo*

☆ **The Action Too High** / 1986 / MRS
A classic featuring the aforementioned "The Sinking Ship." The title cut is also one of the most danceable commentaries ever written in soca style concerning the drug problem. —*Gene Scaramuzzo*

We Need More Love / 1987 / J&M 34887
One of the best albums from the sometimes uninspired second half of the '80s. Gypsy, who is consistently good and consistently underrated, devotes one side to party and topical lyrics. The title track is a tearaway, but my own favorite cut is "Sing Ram Bam," which has a classic calypso melody and nice acid guitar punctuations. —*John Storm Roberts*

I Believe in You / 1990 / MRS
A true calypsonian who comments on the issues of the times, Gypsy sings on the previous year's incident, in which toilet paper was thrown at him during a live performance, and on the terrible

new Value Added Tax, in "No VAT." He boogies down in "Gimme the Thing." Another great album. —*Gene Scaramuzzo*

Bad Behavior / 1992 / MRS
Another first-rate offering. —*Gene Scaramuzzo*

Humanoids

○ **Humanoids** / 1990 / Etienne
The band hails from St. Thomas, V.I. With Georges "Soul" Thomas of the legendary group Gramacks, and Herrie Etienne of Swinging Stars, both of Dominique, this album is a wonderful blend of soca sounds with '70s-era cadence music. Worth hunting down. —*Gene Scaramuzzo*

Jam Band

○ **We Run Things** / 1988 / Parrot Fish
Another high-energy band à la Burning Flames, this time from St. Thomas, V.I. This band has dominated the St. Thomas Road March competition in recent years. —*Gene Scaramuzzo*

Kaiso Genius

○ **Going Back to Africa** / 1980 / Makossa 2346
Older, pre-soca-style calypsos, which deal with the usual topics: sex, romance, politics, and Black pride. —*J. Poet*

Johnny King

Vocals / Soca, Party soca, Social commentary
A policeman who annually releases a 12-inch single or EP with meaningful lyrics backed by an uptempo dance tune. Some years, such as 1985, it was the meaningful melody that caught on, although he has hit very big in other years with serious Road March contenders. 1988 was probably his highest party moment with "Wet Me Down." —*Gene Scaramuzzo*

Appreciation/Ah Want It / 1985 / King

Illusions / 1987 /

○ **Wet Me Down/War Mongers** / 1988 / Hibiscus

Don't Rub Me/Pan Victory / 1989 / M Chanka Prod.

Kitch (Lord Kitchener)

Vocals / Soca, Party soca, Social commentary
Kitch is, along with the Mighty Sparrow, the most well-known of any calypsonian of T&T. With a career spanning over four decades, he has an extremely large catalog of annual releases, complicated further by an unknown number of anthologies and reissues. Amazingly, none are bad. Several anthologies of pre-soca-era material are listed below as starters, along with a handful of the best annual releases from the soca era, beginning with the early '80s release, *Kitchener Goes Soca*, in which he dramatically demonstrated that he was more than capable of keeping abreast of any latest musical fashion. —*Gene Scaramuzzo*

Longevity / JW Prod
Unbelievably, "Mystery Band" from this LP was an even bigger success than "Bee's Melody" from '92. —*Gene Scaramuzzo*

Still Escalating / JW Prod
This LP came out early in a short carnival season during which there were very few early releases. It may explain why two otherwise average songs, "Earthquake" and "No Wuk for Carnival," were such big hits. —*Gene Scaramuzzo*

Klassic Kitchener / Ice
A several volume set that includes high quality versions of the original hit songs by Kitchener from the beginning of his career to the onset of the soca era in the late '70s. —*Gene Scaramuzzo*

Classic Carnival Hits / Ice
Between them, Lord Kitchener and the Mighty Sparrow have written 18 Road Marches between 1956 and 1994. Nine of the 10 written by Kitch are included on this wonderful collection. —*Gene Scaramuzzo*

Goes Soca / 1980 / Charlie's 262
One of the first hit soca albums. —*J. Poet*

Kitchener Goes Soca / 1981 / Charlie's
There is no denying that Kitch is the master here as he picks up the tempos and delivers some of the best soca tunes of the day. Includes "Soca Jean" and "Kitchener It Bon Down." —*Gene Scaramuzzo*

☆ **Roots of Soca** / 1984 / Charlie's
This album doesn't have a single second-rate song on it. One of the high points of Carnival 1984. —*Gene Scaramuzzo*

○ **Master at Work** / 1985 / Kalico
"Soca Misinterpretation" may very well be the best party song Kitch has written in the '80s, aided by a fantastic echoed mix courtesy of arranger Leston Paul. —*Gene Scaramuzzo*

The Grand Master / 1987 / B's
Includes "Pan in A Minor," a huge hit among the steelbands in 1987 and more than enough reason to search out this album. —*Gene Scaramuzzo*

The Honey in Kitch / 1992 / MCA
The popularity of "Bee's Melody" among the steelbands in 1992 may have even surpassed their enthusiasm in 1987 for Kitch's "Pan in A Minor." —*Gene Scaramuzzo*

○ **King of Calypso** / Melodisc 12-200
One of the pioneers of calypso. This collection reaches back to the hits of the '40s and early '50s for classics like "Black & White," "Life Begins at 40," and "Short Skirts." —*J. Poet*

Spicy Delight / Melodisc 12-129
More early Kitch, leaning toward the bawdy tunes that first made him popular. —*J. Poet*

Lloyd Lovindeer

Soca Babylon Boops / 1986 / TSOJ
Simultaneous to hitting big in Jamaica with a reggae version of "Babylon Boops," Jamaican Lovindeer released this soca version famous for the slack B-side in which he goes into great detail as to how he's going to defend the lady in trouble. —*Gene Scaramuzzo*

○ **Soca Nights** / 1987 / TSOJ
Hot on the heels of "Soca Babylon Boops" came this album famous for "Big Panty Lady" with its request to "show me your panty size." Plenty slack and a big hit. —*Gene Scaramuzzo*

Maestro

Vocals / Soca
One of the founding fathers of soca music, Maestro was tragically killed in the late '70s. —*Gene Scaramuzzo*

○ **Anatomy of Soca** / 1978 / Charlie's
This one and *Soca Explosion* by Lord Shorty are the two albums that most dramatically re-defined T&T music. —*Gene Scaramuzzo*

Melody (Lord)

Vocals / Calypso
Another of the legends of calypso who died just at the end of the '80s. Responsible for many classic songs. —*Gene Scaramuzzo*

○ **Through the Looking Glass** / 1960 / Cook 927
Melody gained fortune, if not fame, by writing hits for Harry Belafonte, including "Momma Look at Boo Boo." This early '60s album contains some of his biggest hits, including "Si Senior," an early Latin-influenced calypso, which Belafonte recast as "Sweetheart from Venezuela." —*J. Poet*

I Man / 1979 / Charlie's
This was Melody's first crack at soca, just a year after Maestro and Shorty started the ball rolling. A classic that still sounds great. —*Gene Scaramuzzo*

Lola / 1982 / B's 1022
A strong soca effort from 1982, which shows Mel rocking just as hard as the young turks. —*J. Poet*

Merchant

Rock It / 1984 / Benmac 0051
Merchant won King of Carnival with the title tune from this EP. —*J. Poet*

Ah Coming Too / 1987 / Straker's
A strong album from Merchant's large catalog of releases. "Ah Coming Too," a feminist tale, was the hit, but "Tumble Down" was another great tune done in a funk fashion. —*Gene Scaramuzzo*

Sparrow (Mighty)

Vocals / Calypso
In the late '80s he released two volumes of his early, calypso-era hits redone in a soca style that are very popular, and was anthologized in a three-volume set by Ice Records in '93. —*Gene Scaramuzzo*

○ **25th Anniversary** / 1980 / Charlie's 001
A double-record set released to celebrate 25 years of calypso classics. Features "Wanted: Dead or Alive" a worldwide pop hit later covered by the Manhattan Transfer. —*J. Poet*

The Greatest / 1983 / Charlie's 1006
There are no bad Sparrow records, but some are better than others, including this masterpiece from 1983. Includes a critique of inflation, "Capitalism Gone Mad," as well as "Phillip My Dear," a nasty account of what "really" happened when that stranger crept into Queen Elizabeth's bedroom. —*J. Poet*

Vanessa / 1984 / B's 024
The title track is an ode to the "nasty" Miss America Vanessa Williams. —*J. Poet*

☆ **King of the World** / 1984 / B's
Includes the classic "Doh Back Back," a hopelessly infectious soca that brought Sparrow the Road March title. —*Gene Scaramuzzo*

Party Classics 1 & 2 / 1985 / Charlie's 7194
The aforementioned two volumes of '50s through '70s hits by Sparrow, redone in a soca style. Titles like "Jean & Dinah" and "Mr. Walker," which appear on Volume I, are surely known by most of the world. The biggest hit, though, "Congo Man," was on Volume 2. —*Gene Scaramuzzo*

○ **A Touch of Class** / 1986 / B's
Another classic with "Coke Is Not It," "Ah Fraid De AIDS," and "Invade South Africa," all performed to killer soca beats. One of the most topical of Sparrow's '80s releases. —*Gene Scaramuzzo*

Hot Like Fire / 1992 / Rohit 7755
In a move that brought on enough controversy to enliven conversations for the next year, Sparrow re-entered the Monarchy competition in 1992 with "Both of Them" from this album. He won, but that's another story. —*Gene Scaramuzzo*

Dancing Shoes / Ice 930102
An all around good LP but it shines for "More the Merrier," which takes a jab at calypsonian Shorty for his "holier than thou" criticism of Sparrow's '92 tale of debauchery, "Both of Them." —*Gene Scaramuzzo*

Marcia Miranda

○ **Come Fly with Me** / 1991 / Straker's
In her first year on the scene as a solo artist, Miranda hit very hard with this album, which is good from start to finish. One of the great albums of Carnival '91. —*Gene Scaramuzzo*

Machel Montano

Vocals / Party soca, Social commentary
The youngest calypsonian to ever reach the National Monarchy finals (in 1986 at the age of 11), Montano has consistently put out above-average material. It wasn't until 1991 that he repeated the level of success of 1986, though, with "1st in De Party" and the repatriation sentiment of "Take Me Back." —*Gene Scaramuzzo*

Too Young to Soca? / 1986 / Macho 24-11-74
Montano was only 11 years old when he burst on the scene with this fine EP. —*J. Poet*

One Step Ahead / 1991 / Straker's
Probably his best since "Too Young . . ." —*Gene Scaramuzzo*

Obstinate (King)

Vocals / Party soca, Social commentary
One of Antigua's best calypsonians, a frequent winner of the Monarchy competition. —*Gene Scaramuzzo*

Murder With An Attitude / Charlo's
The melodic, bubbling "Jumbie" from this LP proved to be a big hit for Obstinate. —*Gene Scaramuzzo*

○ **Obstinate** / 1987 / Greenbay
Includes two uptempo party tunes, "Voyier y Montez" (in a zouk style) and "Jam Band Beat" (a Road March contender). —*Gene Scaramuzzo*

Organizer

○ **That's Ah Bandit** / 1989 / Wrecker
This social commentary was one of the runaway hits of Carnival
'89, describing the many different ways that the people of T&T
had been ripped off. The melody is really pretty on this, also. —
Gene Scaramuzzo

Our Boys Steel Orchestra

Pan Progress / 1991 / Mango 162-539916
The second Mango album from one of Trinidad & Tobago's oldest
and best pan ensembles. *Pan Progress* celebrates the work of Len
"Boogsi" Sharpe—the instrument's most prolific composer—and
includes compositions by Ray Homan and producer Andy Narell.
In short, a musical celebration of some of the sweetest sounds
around. —*Mango*

○ **Our Boys Steel Orchestra** / Mango

Leston Paul

Vocals / Party soca
One of just a handful of arrangers who are responsible for nearly
the entire yearly crop of records coming out of T&T. Most years
he releases an album that includes his versions of the songs from
that year that he enjoyed the most. —*Gene Scaramuzzo*

○ **Soca Invasion** / 1985 / B's 030
Check the back of any soca album from the early '80s on and
you're likely to find Paul credited with keyboards, drum programs, and arrangements. On this instrumental recording Paul
introduces his version of several standards, which include
Arrow's "Tiny Winey," Merchant's "Rock It," and Crazy's
"Socouyant." —*J. Poet*

Penguin

Vocals / Party soca, Social commentary
Penguin has consistently produced first-rate records during his
career but has never repeated the level of popularity he enjoyed
in the early '80s. —*Gene Scaramuzzo*

○ **Touch It** / 1984 / B's 004
In 1984, with this album, he dominated the Road March competition with "Sorf Man" (although he lost out to Sparrow) and took
the Monarchy crown with "We Livin' in Jail" and "Sorf Man." —
Gene Scaramuzzo

Ken "Professor" Philmore

Vocals / Soca, Party soca
Longtime arranger for Fonclaire Steel Band who has moved over
temporarily (?) to Phase II Pan Groove, Philmore has written a
song each year driven by pan and sung by a calypsonian on
record. He has hit especially big on two occasions, in '88 and
again in '93. —*Gene Scaramuzzo*

☆ **Pan by Storm** / 1990 / Straker's
One of the true gems of Carnival '90, sung by Designer. If you like
pan, you must find this one. —*Gene Scaramuzzo*

Plain Clothes

Vocals / Soca, Social commentary
An often humorous, always witty, calypsonian who each year has
something interesting to offer. —*Gene Scaramuzzo*

Chambers Done See / 1985 /
One of the great double-entendre calypsos of the '80s, this one
can be found on Rounder's *Say What? Double Entendre Soca
From Trinidad.* —*Gene Scaramuzzo*

Denyse Plummer

Vocals / Caribbean
Enlisted by Phase II Pan Groove steelband arranger Len
"Boogsie" Sharpe in 1986 to sing his band's Panorama entry,
Plummer began making a name for herself as a calypsonian. In
1988, with yet another Len "Boogsie" Sharpe pan tune, "Woman
Is Boss," she arrived at the National Calypso Monarchy finals and
also won the Calypso Queen crown. Since then she has taken the
Calypso Queen crown a total of four times and has won the World
Calypso Crown three times. Blessed with a strong voice and al-
ways an outstanding composition, Plummer makes records that
are fresh and exciting. —*Gene Scaramuzzo*

☆ **The Boss** / 1988 / Weldon's
Includes "A Nation Forges On" and "Woman Is Boss." —*Gene
Scaramuzzo*

Still the Boss / 1989 / Boss
With "Together Right Here" and "The Champ." —*Gene
Scaramuzzo*

Victory / 1990 / Oscar's
A 12-inch EP with "DJ Fever" and "The Message," which brought
Plummer her third Calypso Queen crown. "DJ Fever" was a
much-welcomed tribute to the DJs worldwide who push soca. —
Gene Scaramuzzo

Carnival Killer / 1991 / Dynamic Sounds 3466
The title track brought her yet another Calypso Queen Crown, her
fourth. —*Gene Scaramuzzo*

Poser

Soca

Heavy Action / 1987 / Straker's
A particularly good year for Poser, with "Tonight" and the social
commentary "Ah Never Thought." —*Gene Scaramuzzo*

○ **The Bus Conductor** / 1990 / Wrecker
"Bus Conductor" was a surprise party hit that took off early in the
season and continued strong in popularity right through carnival.
A classic from 1990. —*Gene Scaramuzzo*

Protector

Vocals / Soca, Party soca, Social commentary
Among the top of the list of underrated calypsonians, Protector
has yet to release a bad record. He delivers plenty of good party
soca but is also very skilled at social commentary (local and
global) and has several times made it to the Monarchy finals. Any
Protector album is recommended. —*Gene Scaramuzzo*

Simply Beautiful / 1985 / Charlie's
An EP that lives up to its name, featuring the killer "Spanish
Party" and the slow, funky tale of unrequited love, "Charmaine."
—*Gene Scaramuzzo*

Going Places / 1989 / Straker's
Includes the excellent commentary on today's youth, "Young-
Restless." —*Gene Scaramuzzo*

○ **Total Protection** / 1990 / Straker's
The superb "Crossover Sweet" is enough reason to look for this
album, but the whole package is another fine offering from this
talented calypsonian who is not that well known outside T&T. —
Gene Scaramuzzo

Rootsman

Vocals / Soca, Party soca, Social commentary
A calypsonian who usually aims for the Road March although
he's not unfamiliar with social commentary. It's undoubtedly his
party music that brings him to the forefront, with the records below being of particular interest. —*Gene Scaramuzzo*

Rack Me Rack Me / 1985 / Charlie's

○ **Jam on de Parkway (Parkway Rock)** / 1986 / B's

Miami Vibes / 1987 / Love People

David Rudder

b. 1953
Vocals / World Fusion, Soca, Calypso
Rudder has become perhaps soca's most visible performer, and
one of the few on a major American label. Rudder began singing
in 1965 as a member of a group called the Solutions. He began
heading his own group in 1970, doing pop and soul songs, then
turned to soca in the late '70s, working with the great Kitchener
before joining Charlie's Roots in 1980 as a replacement for lead
vocalist Chris "Tambu" Herbert. Rudder finished third in the
Road March competition for Carnival '85, then in 1986 became
one of the few performers to win the Young King and Calypso
Monarch titles. Rudder has gotten heavy criticism from calypso
traditionalists for his incorporation of R&B, blues, funk, and rock
elements into his soca compositions, but his popularity has increased to the point that he's appeared at international jazz and
blues festivals as well as carnival and soca events. —*Ron Wynn*

Ministry of Rhythm / Lypsoland

A fine ip throughout but featuring one of his biggest hits ever, a commentary on the state of affairs in T&T presented through the image of the steel band controversy of '92, "Dus' In Deh Face." The CD version includes a bonus rhythm track. —*Gene Scaramuzzo*

☆ **Haiti** / 1988 / Sire 25723
In terms of Road March power, 1988 was Rudder's finest moment, with "Bacchanal Woman" and the superb social commentary, "Panama." The title cut was a remarkable ode to Caribbean unity. Sire reissued this album with cuts from the previous two years under the same title, *Haiti*. —*Gene Scaramuzzo*

☆ **1990** / 1990 / Sire 26250
A concept album from the king of contemporary soca, which details the international struggle against racism with particular emphasis on South Africa. —*J. Poet*

Frenzy / 1992 / Lypsoland
"Knock Them Down" and "Stiff Waist Man" were popular, but "De Long Time Band," with its unusual percussion and old-time sound, is a song that will long be remembered. —*Gene Scaramuzzo*

Scorcher

○ **The Hoper** / Straker's 2240
Excellent album that mixes a nonstop party vibe with militant Afrocentric lyrics. —*J. Poet*

Scrunter

Vocals / Soca, Party soca, Social commentary
Another calypsonian who presents a problem in deciding which of his records to list. He's so consistently good that all are recommended. He often presents social commentary, but his party music is what really stands out. —*Gene Scaramuzzo*

Doh Jam Dis / 1985 / 2 Guys
A killer 12-inch single from 1985. —*Gene Scaramuzzo*

○ **Every Shadow** / 1986 / Charlie's
Every song on this record is great, and plenty are risque. "Ah See You" was a party hit, "Every Shadow" a commentary on crime, "Nanny" and "John Dick" not very subtle odes to sex, and "Me No Want No Man" a great story from a woman's perspective. —*Gene Scaramuzzo*

Soca Bacchanal / 1987 / Hibiscus
"She Want Me to Sing in She Party" was the big hit on this 12-inch single, but "Lost Tenor" is a fantastic pan tune. —*Gene Scaramuzzo*

Shadow

Bass / Soca, Party soca, Social commentary
There are many calypso lovers who await Shadow's annual release more than that of any other calypsonian. Like Stalin and just a handful of others, Shadow is a totally unique calypsonian; there is no other like Shadow. Since 1974 and his landmark composition "De Bassman," he has never failed to deliver some of the toughest basslines, most infectious grooves, and most original compositions of anyone in the Caribbean. On top of all this, he has a low, authoritative voice that lends an air of truth and finality to all he sings. His social and political commentaries are delivered in such a clever way (and propelled as they are by his unique soca beat) that the messages often sink in subliminally, a testimony to his unique lyrical skills. With this in mind, how does one narrow down his nearly 20 records to a handful of recommendations? —*Gene Scaramuzzo*

Moods of the Shadow / Kisskiddee
It's hard to single out any one song as the best on this LP that delivers outstanding soca, reggae, and funk. —*Gene Scaramuzzo*

Dingolay / Kisskiddee
"(Pak Pak) Pay de Devil" and the rapso "Poverty Is Hell" were the two most popular songs of Carnival '94. Shadow's exclusion from the Calypso Monarchy Finals was the scandal of the year. —*Gene Scaramuzzo*

○ **De Bassman** / 1974 /
The legendary album that brought Shadow to fame. —*Gene Scaramuzzo*

If I Coulda I Woulda I Shoulda / 1979 / Charlie's

A particularly outstanding album from this era of Shadow's career, featuring a raw sound worth hearing. Quite different from the Shadow of today. —*Gene Scaramuzzo*

Return of De Bassman / 1984 / Straker's 2251
The end of an era for a particular raw sound to Shadow's music. As always, a killer mix of hits like "More Music," "Snakes," and the title cut. —*Gene Scaramuzzo*

○ **High Tension** / 1988 / Straker's 2279
This represents the epitome of Shadow's late '80s recorded output. "Tension" was a killer in the Road March arena, yet was in serious competition with two other songs from this same album, "Bad Boy Peter" and "Garden Want Water" (with sexual tension in all three). "Crazy Computer" was a favorite in the tents, giving Shadow four hit songs in one year. —*Gene Scaramuzzo*

☆ **Columbus Lied** / 1991 / Shanachie 64033
Shadow is one of the few calypsonians who has been anthologized on an American label. This recent release presents eight of the best of his songs from 1988 through 1990, a landmark period in his career. —*Gene Scaramuzzo*

Winston Bailey Is the Shadow / 1992 / Kisskidee
A decidedly different approach on this album. Only one song on this album, "Hard Head," was Road March bound. Neither "Soucouyant," the superb commentary on AIDS, nor the late-bloomer "Music" (aka "Dingolay") were typical uptempo grooves, showing that Shadow can hit no matter how far he strays from formula. —*Gene Scaramuzzo*

Shandileer (Brass Band)

Group / Party soca
A T&T brass band that consistently produces party hits, although some years the songs tend to sound alike. You can't go wrong with the ones listed below, but any others are worth hearing. —*Gene Scaramuzzo*

De Pong/The Donkey Dance / Sorrel
Although the lesser of the two donkey songs for '93, this one certainly added fever to "doin' the donkey." —*Gene Scaramuzzo*

○ **Happy** / 1988 /
A serious Road March contender in 1988. —*Gene Scaramuzzo*

Do What You Want / 1991 / Sorrell
Another highlight in their bid for Road March; includes "Do What You Want" and "We Pushin'." —*Gene Scaramuzzo*

Shorty (Lord)

Vocals / Soca, Social commentary
The founding father of soca music who, along with Maestro, brought a new image to calypso at the end of the '70s, and he still occasionally releases records as Ras Shorty I. He became involved in the jam and wine controversy of '92 that made him the butt of Sparrow's '93 calypso, "The More the Merrier." —*Gene Scaramuzzo*

○ **Soca Explosion** / 1978 / Charlie's
The ultimate classic. —*Gene Scaramuzzo*

Collection / 1985 / Carotte
A wonderful anthology covering Shorty's scandalous early career of extremely suggestive calypsos, including a handful of cuts from *Soca Explosion*. Sound quality is rather poor, unfortunately. —*Gene Scaramuzzo*

Squibby

Pan Running Wild / 1984 / B's
An absolutely thrilling, breathtaking soca featuring double tenor pans on lead. —*Gene Scaramuzzo*

Sugar Aloes

Vocals / Soca, Party soca, Social commentary
Sugar Aloes sounds like . . . wears lots of gold like . . . moves on-stage like . . . Baron. Nonetheless an entity unto himself who, since his entry in 1990, has consistently reached the Calypso Monarchy semi-finals (and usually the finals) with a biting political commentary while at the same time aiming at the Road March with great party tunes. All his LPs are worth hearing. —*Gene Scaramuzzo*

○ **Solid As a Rock** / 1990 / Wrecker

Calypso and Steelband Music of the Caribbean

The musical output of Trinidad & Tobago – calypso, steelband music, and now, soca – is centered around the carnival season that begins shortly after Christmas and culminates with "Carnival Tuesday," the day before the Catholic feast of Ash Wednesday. The island calypsonians compose (or buy) at least two new songs annually, which they then perform nightly throughout carnival season at the "calypso tents." Of course, all those who can arrange it will also produce recordings of their songs that will be released sometime between Thanksgiving and a few weeks before Carnival Tuesday.

The annual music crop is highly affected by two major music contests in which the vast majority of calypsonians compete during carnival season, the National Calypso Monarchy (best calypsonian of the year) and the Road March (best party song of the year), as well as by a host of other smaller competitions like Junior Monarch, Calypso Queen, and Extempo Monarch. Most compositions are a reflection of attempts of calypsonians to win these competitions. Consequently, they fall into two camps: party songs vying for Road March and lyrically strong calypsos vying for the Monarchy by addressing a wide range of social and political topics.

Recordings of calypso (whose more uptempo contemporary form is called "soca," from the words Soul and Calypso) feature a fairly standard formula of programmed drums and rhythm section, calypso guitar, occasional lead or tenor pans (steel drums), horns, and a syncopated bass guitar that gives the music its true soul. While the lyrical content and cleverness will differ dramatically from song to song, a calypso album will typically include some songs strong on lyrics and some that put lyrics secondary to a strong dance beat. The best of the lot are undoubtedly those that combine infectious dance beats with thoughtful or timely messages.

Although on a much smaller scale, similar competitions exist on most of the other soca islands (Antigua, Barbados, Virgin Islands, Aruba, etc.), influencing their calypsonians to produce records in much the same way as in Trinidad and Tobago.

The strongest trend both in Trinbago and the other soca islands is the greater visibility of brass bands (the name given to self-contained bands with horns). In days past, the main function of the brass bands was to play covers of the hits of the day, but since 1986 and the emergence of David Rudder from the Charlie's Roots brass band, these bands are beginning to be responsible for many of the original hits of carnival. In T&T, the lead singers of these bands are beginning to be looked upon as bonafide calypsonians (not without controversy), but this facet of brass-band emergence is not happening on the other islands. Instead, the strong trend in non-Trinidadian brass bands is a group effort to produce a supercharged soca with frenetic tempos and touches of outside influences like rock, funk, rap, dancehall reggae, and more. These wild forms of soca are coming from the Burning Flames of Antigua, Jam Band of St. Thomas, WCK of Dominique, the Humanoids of St. Thomas, Arrow of Montserrat, and many others.

A discussion of Trinidad & Tobago calypso/soca wouldn't be complete without mention of the steel drum (simply called a "pan" in the islands). For decades, the steel bands, large and small, waited to hear the annual crop of new music and then selected their favorite to arrange and perform during carnival. Since the mid 80s, however, there has been a growing trend for steelband arrangers to write an original song and record it as soca, with a calypsonian singing. This has added exciting new music to carnival that very often features virtuoso lead or tenor panplaying. In Carnival '92 there were a remarkable dozen popular tunes written by steelband arrangers.

In searching for interesting calypso records, a good rule of thumb is to select those that enjoyed a high measure of success during a given carnival season, be it Trinidad & Tobago or any of the other calypso/soca islands like Antigua, Barbados, the Virgin Islands, and St. Vincent. This practice will provide the opportunity to experience a wider range of artists than just those found internationally, like the Mighty Sparrow, Lord Kitchener, Shadow, David Rudder, and Calypso Rose. At the same time it will introduce the listener to the cream of the crop as seen through the eyes of the islanders, an important lesson considering that past success does not guarantee popularity at every carnival: the biggest sensations of one year's carnival could be the kiss of boredom the next.

Likewise, the age of CDs is bringing to us for the first time a host of easily available compilations and anthologies, another excellent way of getting a broader taste. Aside from the CDs, don't expect to find many liner notes on albums, but do look for the names of the three major arrangers, Frankie McIntosh, Leston Paul, and Pelham Goddard, in order to experience their somewhat differing approaches to the calypso/soca art form. The major labels as we move into the 90s are Charlie's, Lypsoland, Charlo's, Straker's, and JW's.

– Gene Scaramuzzo

This year's joint Young King crown-winner is an unabashed soca-romantico, and his tendency toward soupiness is just barely overcome by the novelty of the sound. His big number here, "The Judge," is remarkably slow and gentle for soca, and his voice adds an appropriate tone of reproach to what could easily have become standard anti-government whining. —Carl Hoyt, Original Music

○ **Pure Sugar** / 1991 / Wrecker

○ **Special Assignment** / 1992 / Wrecker

Superblue

Named after the Freddie Hubbard tune. All-star band led by trumpeted arranger Don Sickler. Plays mainstream, post-bop blue-note-type material. —Michael G. Nastos

Flag Party / Ice
The very late arrival of this disc for Carnival '94 prevented Superblue from achieving his fourth consecutive Road March victory. In fact, in T&T this album was rush released in a plain white sleeve under the subtitle "The Late But Great '94 Album." —Gene Scaramuzzo

★ **Superblue** / Apr. 1988 / Blue Note 91731

Top-flight octet includes Bobby Watson (as), Roy Hargrove (tpt), Mulgrew Miller (p). This group should have gotten more mileage out of its fine 1989 release. —Ron Wynn

Superblue 2 / Apr. 24-25, 1989 / Blue Note 92997

Nice follow-up with revamped personnel features Wallace Roney (tpt), Ralph Moore (ts), Rene Rosnes (p), and holdovers Bobby Watson (as), Don Sickler (tpt, conductor)—impressive. —Ron Wynn

Bacchanal Time / Ice 930302

Although the rest of the cuts are less exciting, the title cut ranks as the ultimate pastiche of commands, countdowns, and song hooks. —Gene Scaramuzzo

Swallow

Vocals / Party soca

Antigua's undisputed party master who pleases everyone from the Caribbean to NYC to Toronto with cowbell- and horn-driven soca. Talented beyond compare, able year after year to compose infectious hooks with catchy lyrics. There's not a bad release by Swallow throughout his long career. *—Gene Scaramuzzo*

Subway Jam, Pace Yourself / 1981 / Charlie's 477
Swallow specializes in party jams, usually without any social or sexual message beyond "Have a good time." "Subway Jam," the title tune, is an all-time soca anthem. *—J. Poet*

Party in Space / 1983 / Charlie's 342
The title track has Sally Ride jammin' to the soca beat with her fellow astronauts and a saucerful of aliens. A great party album. *—J. Poet*

○ **First Take** / 1984 / Charlie's
This one will leave you breathless. Includes "Flagwoman," "Town Mash Down," and "Satan Comin' Down." *—Gene Scaramuzzo*

Flagwoman / 1985 /
Flagwoman/Satan Comin' Down Town Town Mash Down.

Hit Man / 1987 / Charlie's 6857
Here is one of the best albums from the second half of the '80s. Swallow's 1987 "Hit Man" is notable for a very fine kick-em-up about the Brooklyn carnival. *—John Storm Roberts*

☆ **Swallow on the Streets of Brooklyn** / 1988 / Charlie's
"Fire in the Backseat" had everyone moving in 1988. *—Gene Scaramuzzo*

Steam / 1990 / Charlie's
The title cut was another gem. *—Gene Scaramuzzo*

Tambu (Chris Herbert)

Vocals / Party soca, Social commentary

This Charlie's Roots singer began his solo career after fellow Charlie's Roots singer David Rudder's successful attempt in 1986. Tambu succeeded in capturing the Road March title three years in a row with basically the same song recycled, as well as making it to the Monarchy finals each of those years. Tambu is a good singer and, despite the fact that he recycles song ideas, capable of writing very catchy choruses. His pursuit of a music degree at Berkeley has kept him out of the '92 through '94 T&T Carnivals. *—Gene Scaramuzzo*

○ **Culture** / 1988 / Sire 25741
The title cut was somewhat of an anthem during Carnival '88, calling for the preservation of T&T's unique cultural achievements like steelband, limbo, calypso, and East Indian tassa drumming, although it was "This Party Is It" that captured the Road March. A great album from 1988. *—Gene Scaramuzzo*

The Journey / 1989 / Lypsoland
Road March #2 was "Free Up" from this album. *—Gene Scaramuzzo*

The Cry / 1990 / Lypsoland
"No No We Eh Going Home" and "Let's Do It" brought Tambu his third Road March victory and again brought him to the Monarchy finals. *—Gene Scaramuzzo*

Reach Out / 1991 / Lypsoland O14
Ironically, "Rant and Rave" and "Not Me Is the Music" from this album were two of Tambu's better songs, but they were crushed in the Road March competition by Superblue's "Get Something & Wave." *—Gene Scaramuzzo*

Taxi (Brass Band)

Johnny / 1987 / Rohit
An uptempo, catchy soca 12-inch single from 1987. *—Gene Scaramuzzo*

○ **Made in Trinidad** / 1991 / Rainbow Music
This features the legendary sex-on-the-dance-floor romp, "Dollah," a Caribbean anthem on a par in popularity with Arrow's "Hot Hot Hot" and "Workey Workey" by Burning Flames. *—Gene Scaramuzzo*

Trini (Mighty)

Vocals / Party soca

Rarely a major force in carnival celebrations, Trini nonetheless comes through on occasion with a big hit. "Sailing," from 1988, was fairly strong in the parties, but 1987's "Curry Tabanca" was probably his pinnacle to date. *—Gene Scaramuzzo*

Curry Tabanca / 1987 / Rohit
A 12-inch single about a man going through severe "curry" withdrawal. A great double entendre soca from 1987. *—Gene Scaramuzzo*

Wck

○ **Culture Shock** / 1991 / Charlo
This Dominiquan band was a surprise hit during T&T's 1991 Carnival with the title cut. A splendid mix of zouk, cadence, and soca, in a genre similar to Burning Flames but leaning much more heavily toward the French Antilles. *—Gene Scaramuzzo*

Trinidad Collection

☆ **This Is Soca** / 1987 / Sire 25650
This two-record set makes for a fine introduction to soca/calypso. Record #1 is David Rudder's strong 1987 effort, while record #2 is a compilation of hits, including Stalin's "Burn Dem." *—J. Poet*

○ **Calypso Pioneers—1912-1937** / 1989 / Rounder 1039
This companion CD to a prior Rounder anthology devoted to classic calypso from the '30s to the '40s, these 16 cuts present formative songs from 1912-1937. The music is still emerging from a confluence of American dance band sounds, African and Afro-Latin rhythms, plus Caribbean social situations and influences. As carnival became an entrenched celebration within the Caribbean community, the songs composed to be performed during that time came to be known as calypso. The anthology includes early performances by such calypso heroes as Atilla the Hun, Wilmouth Houdini, Phil Madison, Julian Whiterose and Sam Manning. Vocal styles, instrumental backing, lyrics, arrangements and production are quite unsophisticated and uneven on the early cuts, but then a sound and unified approach began to appear in the middle section and is quite evident by the final numbers. This was the foundation music for Caribbean people outside of Jamaica, but it never enjoyed the widespread international exposure until the '50s, when Harry Belafonte briefly triggered a calypso explosion. The mastering and annotation work, as always, is thorough and instructive. *—Ron Wynn*

○ **Calypso Season** / 1989 / Mango 539861
A fine collection full of unintended ironies. Most of it is in fact soca, balanced between names (Baron, Tambu, Sparrow) and unknowns (All Rounder). But there are two old-calypso cuts with acoustic guitar by Roaring Lion, and one by classic steelband the Desperados—and all three strike like a cool breeze in a crowded dancehall. Still and all, the soca cuts are just fine in their own affably shallow way. Whoever selected this lot had fine ears (pity Mango couldn't have spared the time or the bucks for at least some kind of notes, fer crine out loud). *—John Storm Roberts*

○ **Trinidad Carnival** / 1989 / Delos 4012
Various steelbands recorded live at the 1989 Trinidad Carnival, issued on Delos's Caribbean subsidiary label. Fine sound. *—Ron Wynn*

○ **Carnival Jump-Up** / Feb. 1989 / Delos 4014
Anthology featuring various steel-bands from Trinidad and Tobago. All recordings were made on location, and it includes songs by Amoco Renegades, Carib Tokyo, Neal and Massy Trinidad All-Stars, etc. Sterling sound. *—Ron Wynn*

☆ **Calypso Breakaway** / 1990 / Rounder 1054
This new set of classics from 1927 to 1941 brings more gems from Atilla the Hun, Tiger, Executor, Caresser, Beginner, and other great names. I've never bought the anti-soca line of many old-hand calypso buffs: there were plenty of feeble calypsos back then too. But the vocal and instrumental verve of the best calypsos have never been equalled. *—John Storm Roberts*

☆ **Heat in De Place: Soca from Trinidad** / 1990 / Rounder 5041
A wonderful collection of modern soca tunes, with a good mix of topical and socio-political selections. *—Ron Wynn*

☆ **Say What? Double Entendre Soca** / 1990 / Rounder 5042
Anthology featuring contemporary soca and calypso musicians from Trinidad who specialize in songs containing sexual innuen-

dos and explicit/implicit messages. The roster includes Shadow, Bally, Monarch, Poser, etc. —*Ron Wynn*

○ **Wind Your Waist** / 1991 / Shanachie 64034

Fine selection of soca dance hits by Arrow, Shadow, and Kitch; includes Tambu's 1987 anthem, "This Party Is It." —*J. Poet*

○ **Calypsos from Trinidad** / Arhoolie 7004

The subhead of this CD is a lot more to the point than the title: *Politics, Intrigue and Violence in the 1930s, Including the Butler Calypsos.* This is a dynamite collection of political comment—not just about Butler's union activities and their aftermath, but Mussolini in Abyssinia and depression at home. The lyrics make current soca sound tame, and the melodies, singing, and backup playing make a delicate fire that would make you want to ban electric sockets from the market. This, all in all, is probably the best of the several superb classic calypso sets now available. A terrific 24-page booklet adds to it all. —*John Storm Roberts*

○ **Calypsos: Afro-Limonese Music of Costa Rica** / Lyrichord 7412

Like Panama, Costa Rica has a substantial minority of English-speaking inhabitants. These pieces—mostly calypsos, after a terrific percussion comparsa—were recorded in the Costa Rican port city of Puerto Limon. They have a spread from wonderful to tentative, but this is street-music pure, presenting a range of singers and styles mostly old and unaffected by commercial recordings. Very unspecific notes, disgracefully short measure even for an LP, let alone CD, but very rare music that is never less than charming. —*John Storm Roberts*

○ **Heart of Steel: Steelbands of T&T** / Flying Fish 522

Modern steelbands from Trinidad and Tobago. Little duplication with other anthologies, and it's also better produced. More instructive than inspirational. —*Ron Wynn*

○ **Jazz N' Steel from Trinidad & Tobago** / Delos 4013

Another anthology, this one featuring the Rudy Smith Trio and Annise Hadeed Quartet. It features steelbands that combine improvisational flair and eclectic approach. —*Ron Wynn*

☆ **Pan Classics** / Blue Rhythm 1114

For decades now, steelbands have been playing arrangements of popular European classical and semi-classical pieces, and that—augumented by piano from time to time—is what is featured here. Four of Trinidad's most popular steelbands play Handel, Johann Strauss, Vivaldi, and even Wagner! I frankly hate this stuff and deeply regret the much less grandiose steelband of the early days. Still, it's an authentic local phenomenon, and the groups here—Samaroo Jets, Solo Harmonites, Tropical Angel Harps, and Trinidad Cement Ltd Skiffle Bunch Steel Orchestra (!)—are no flash-in-the-pan (sorry . . .). —*John Storm Roberts*

☆ **Rebel Soca: When the Time Comes** / Shanachie 64010

Unlike reggae, soca plays not a Messianic-rebellious role in Trinbago society, but a pragmatic reformist one. The three weakest tracks here seem attempts to justify a basically inappropriate concept. The rest, ranging from good to terrific, are from mainstream soca commentators from Stalin and Nelson to Ras Iley and Red Plastic Bag. —*John Storm Roberts*

US Virgin Islands

Blinky and the Roadmasters

○ **Crucian Scratch Band Music** / 1990 / Rounder 5047

Blinky & the Roadmasters offer a '90s variation on the classic "Crucian" (St. Croix) style. They feature a frontline with two alto saxophonists interacting with an electric guitarist and banjo or ukelele player. The rhythm section blends electric bass with congas and other percussion devices. The feel and sensibility, as well as the vocal arrangements and style combine the floating flavor of classic calypso with the modern intensity and improvisational flavor of rock, plus Afro-Latin rhythmic elements. Such songs as "Ay Ay Ay" and "Labega's Carousel" have a folk wit and irony. Blinky and the Roadmasters are also an excellent musical unit, cohesive, funky, and entertaining. If you're unfamiliar with Crucian music, here's a great introduction. —*Ron Wynn*

NATIVE AMERICAN

Native American Collection

○ **Songs of Earth, Water, Fire & Sky** / 1991 / New World 80246

Nine ceremonial dances from various tribes of the American Southwest, plus East and West Coast tribes. Clear and vibrant field recordings from 1975. —*Myles Boisen*

○ **Arctic Circle** / Ocora 559021

This is very important recording, done by the scholar Jean Malaurie. Includes Inuit chants and drums from Thule to the Bering Strait. —*David L. Mayers*

○ **Inuit Games and Songs** / Auvidis 8032

A recording like this was my introduction to ethnic music, and the sonic complexity and communal nature of the breath games has had a tremendous impact on my musical thinking. In addition to the games, this CD contains goose imitations, a shamanic song, and a very rare piece for Inuit violin. Good, if not too extensive, notes. (45:01) —*Carl Hoyt, Original Music*

Navajo Songs from Canyon De Chelly / New World 80406

Powwow Songs: Music of the Plains Indians / New World 80343

The Copper Eskimo Tradition / Auvidis/UNESCO 8053

Though they never sang outdoors (in case the spirits stole the words and thus the life of the singer), song accompanied every ritual, social, or even commercial transaction of the Copper Eskimo. Though the traditional songs have largely been forgotten now, this fine reissue of the old UNESCO musical Atlas compensates somewhat. —*John Storm Roberts, Original Music*

○ **Canada: Jeux Vocaux des Inuit (Inuit du Caribou, Netsilik Et Igloolik) (Inuit Vo)** / 1989 / Ocora

Ninety types of gestures and games, mostly sung by two people facing each other, sometimes alternating arm movements, sometimes holding shoulders, crouching, drop to heels and then standing up; they make throat sounds, pant, quack like ducks, and make other noises, with half of the games telling a story; some songs are made by two women with there heads side by side singing into a basin, or alternately by one woman singing into metal bowls which act as a resonator (in older times, they used water bags made from caribou hide); some games are based on single words repeated in a sequencing pattern drawn from a story without the whole story ever being told; stories of fish, dogs, a woman who counts the stars to find out how many children she will have, but the stars are covered by cloud and fog; games to make your friend laugh, and to imitate the sound of zero degree weather. Enjoyable for the sound of the songs and fascinating for the sheer variety, and the depth of their poetry and philosophy of experience. —*"Blue" Gene Tyrrany*

EUROPE

Albania Collection

Folk Music of Albania / Topic 154

Sandwiched between Yugoslavia and Greece, part Christian, part Muslim, Albania is a tiny land with a rich and ancient musical culture. Fine recordings by A.L. Lloyd of songs, dances, and instrumentals, among them bagpipe, flutes, and lutes. Given the country's beleaguered history, the vocals include many epic ballads old and new. —*John Storm Roberts*

Marcel Cellier Presents Albanian Folklore / Cellier 010

Another great project by the man who brought us the *Mystere des Voix Bulgares.* Twelve traditional selections for solo and group voices, flute, clarinet, and folk orchestras, with many interesting similarities to the music of Greece and neighboring Baltic countries. Recommended. —*Roots & Rhythm*

Armenia

Djivan Gasparyan

☆ **I Will Not Be Sad in This World** / 1989 / Opal 25885

These singularly beautiful pieces backed by a second duduk acting as a drone are, so to speak, meditations on folk themes rather than traditional performances. *—John Storm Roberts*

Armenia Collection

Armenia 1 . . . / Ocora 559001
Armenia 1—Liturgical Songs and Instrumental Music. Reissue of two Ocora albums of Armenian music. The first half is devoted to stark Christian hymns from the medieval period. The initial eight selections feature early male choir works with haunting two-part melodies that are profoundly affective, but the following six solo voice pieces are less pleasing. After the final contemporary mixed chorus piece we move on to the instrumental portion of the disc, which showcases ten solo, duo, and small-group settings of modern social music on traditional instruments. As is the case with the music of neighboring Iran and Turkey, a rich confluence of Arabic, Oriental, and eastern European influences is extant here, and the variety of styles is astounding. My particular favorites are the introspective duets for fiddle and recorder, but all tracks are worthwhile, making the second half a satisfying conclusion to this eclectic 72-minute program. *—Myles Boisen, Roots & Rhythm*

Austria

Slavko Avsenik

○ **Freude and Musik Mit . . .** / Koch International Corp. 501
Avsenik's music—all of which is self-composed—is quite polished (though not too fancy), but I find the mix of accordion, clarinet, and oompah irresistible. A tuba does weird and wonderful things to a waltz. *—John Storm Roberts*

Austria Collection

Austrian Folk Music—Vols. 1 & 2 / Arhoolie 3003
Austrian Zither / Playasound 65067
Twenty-two zither zingers with a distinctive alpine flavor, including Anton Karas's "Harry Lime Theme" played by J.C. Ollier-Urfer. *—Myles Boisen, Roots & Rhythm*
○ **Lieder u. Jodler aus den Bergen** / Koch International Corp. 399205
Alpine yodeling is one of humanity's most remarkable vocal techniques, and commercial "Jodlerlieder" are worthy of much more attention than they get. Some of the best stuff is on ill-documented collections like this one, which mixes some outstanding "Jodler" with pretty zither playing. *—John Storm Roberts*
Mountain Songs and Yodeling of the Alps / Smithsonian/Folkways 8807

Bulgaria

Mystere Des Voix Bulgares

Group
The Mysterious Voices of Bulgaria belong to the National Radio and Television Chorus, the premier women's choir popularized worldwide through the efforts of ethnomusicologist Marcel Cellier. His recordings, issued on various import labels before appearing on Nonesuch, made a big splash in western Europe and the US, cultivating vast new audiences for the group's dramatic adaptations of folk singing styles. Their spine-chilling harmonies, punctuated by whoops and quavers, are presented in full choral arrangements and smaller groups—duos and trios—with and without instrumental backing. *—Myles Boisen*
Les Mystere Des Voix Bulgares, Vol. 3 / 1991 / PolyGram 846626
When the first volume in this series was released in 1975 it created a sensation, as Western European and North American audiences fell in love with the dazzling dissonant harmonies of the all-female Bulgarian State Radio and Television Choir. *Volume 2*, released in 1987, included pieces by other choirs, while *Volume 3* divides itself among four groups, including the original State Choir and the mesmerizing Trakia Choir. Bulgarian folk music, with its roots in Central Asia, heavily features diaphonic singing,

Bulgarian Music

Although the Bulgarian Mysterious Voices get all the publicity, there is a profusion of highly developed vocal and instrumental groups within the borders of Bulgaria. A number of ethnically and geographically distinct regions – Piron/Macedonia, Thrace, Rhodope, Shope, and others – boast their own village groups, heard on various compilations. And with heightened interest in the usual national folklore ensembles, plus the opening of borders in Eastern Europe, a new wave of recordings can be expected. Already many female and male choirs have entered the market, and classic recordings of the Philip Koutev folklore ensemble are being reissued. Wedding Band clarinetist Ivo Papasov (an ethnic Turk) has toured the US twice with his red-hot Wedding Band and his wife, a stunning vocalist in the traditional Thracian style. Complex rhythms and exotic instruments like the gaida (bagpipe), the gadulka (a primitive violin with droning strings), breathy kaval and ravalcheta flutes, the clarinet, accordion, and more, add to the appeal of the richly varied Bulgarian expression.

– Myles Boisen

a technique in which two voices (solo or choral) track each other in intervals that are both startling and enchanting to Western ears. Along with yodels, yelps, and harmonies that shift back and forth between sweet consonance and bracing dissonance, the choirs produce an earthy style of vocal music full of power, passion and a strange beauty. While it may puzzle and challenge the mind, the body wakes up and the heart rejoices. *—Backroads Music / Heartbeats*
○ **Le Mystere des Voix Bulgares** / Nonesuch 79165
This is the record that started the boom. An excellent introduction to this thrilling Bulgarian women's choir. *—Myles Boisen*

Ivo Papasov & His Orchestra

Group
This very popular Bulgarian bandleader is a fierce clarinetist known for brilliant improvisations and blazing interpretations of all manner of Balkan melodies. His Bulgarian Wedding Band has caused a sensation, particularly among younger Bulgarians, with its blending of traditional music and high-octane Western rock, delivered at the upper limits of speed and volume. *—Myles Boisen*
Orpheus Ascending / 1989 / Hannibal 1346
An energetic debut of this thrilling Bulgarian clarinetist and wedding band leader. *—Myles Boisen*
☆ **Balkanology** / 1991 / Hannibal 1363
Faster than the Ramones, more frantic than Mahavishnu, and as precise as Bach, this disc kicks me into overdrive every time. Dance music for the blessed. *— Roundup Newsletter*

Pirin Folk Ensemble

State Ensemble for Folk Dances / 1990 / Balkanton 060060
Excellent one-hour CD of authentic Bulgarian music by the leading traditional folk music ensemble, led by long-time director and scholar Kiril Stefanov. Most of the 19 selections are vocal settings with instrumental accompaniment by kaval (flute), zurna (oboe), stringed instruments, etc. A must-have for pure folk enthusiasts. *—Myles Boisen, Roots & Rhythm*

Bulgaria Collection

Folk Music of Bulgaria / 1966 / Topic 107
This release nicely complements the *Village Music of Bulgaria* album on Nonesuch Records and includes some other far-flung regions. *—Myles Boisen*
Village Music of Bulgaria . . . / 1968 / Nonesuch 72034
Recordings from four major Bulgarian regions, each with its own captivating style of singing and accompaniment, are featured on

this album, *Village Music of Bulgaria—A Harvest, a Shepherd, a Bride*. This is the real thing. —*Myles Boisen*

○ **Music of Bulgaria—Balkana** / 1987 / Hannibal 1335
Ten of Bulgaria's leading professional musicians illustrate the breadth of Bulgarian traditional music. Includes the unmistakable vocal sound of Trio Bulgarka and the exhilarating flute-and-bagpipe romps of Trakiiskata Troika (the Thracian Trio). —*Bob Tarte*

○ **Bulgarian Village Singing . . .** / 1990 / Rounder 1055
In *Bulgarian Village Singing—Two Girls Started to Sing*, the roots of the commercially acclaimed Bulgarian "mystery" vocals are explored in this field recording of harvest, wedding, and ritual songs of remote villages. A vibrant document of a vanishing musical form. Features extensive helpful liner notes. —*Bob Tarte*

○ **Balkan—Mysterious Voices of Bulgaria** / Virgin 91368
Film soundtrack recordings, mostly original music, offering a departure from the *Mystere des Voix Bulgares* repertoire. —*Myles Boisen*

Byelorussia / Auvidis 8805
This wonderful recording covers a relatively small area, but a particularly rich one. The extraordinary Slavic contrapuntal choral music is there in pure form, along with other songs, plus fiddle, pipe, and other instrumentals. —*John Storm Roberts*

○ **Macedonian Songs & Dances** / Nonesuch 72038
A nice variety of singing, from solo to choirs, from the Turkish-influenced region of Pirin-Macedonia. —*Myles Boisen*

☆ **Village & Folk Music of Bulgaria** / Nonesuch 79195
Combining two of the best Nonesuch collections into one unbeatable folk music document. —*Myles Boisen*

Byelorussia Collection

Byelorussia

Byelorussia / Auvidis 8805
This wonderful recording covers a new (or more properly renewed) country with particularly rich traditions. The extraordinary Slavic contrapuntal choral music is here in pure form, along with other songs, and fiddle, pipe, and other instrumentals. —*John Storm Roberts*

Czechoslovakia Collection

Czechoslovakia / Planett 242003
Kind of a generic release, as you'll gather from the fact that it really has no discernible title. But the music is nice enough. What you get is a series of regional groups and singers that smack overmuch of your standard over-arranged National Folk Ensemble but which contain some signs of local roots. Among them are some more-than-just-agreeable performances. It badly needs a few rude boors to give it more zip and vulgarity, but it's very amiable. —*John Storm Roberts*

Cyprus Collection

○ **Folk Music of Cyprus** / Lyrichord 7329
Music of the Greek, Turkish, and Maronite communities. The major traditions, Greek and Turkish, exist separately in Cyprus, each with links to its metropole. But each has distinctly Cypriot elements and a considerable amount of common ground (as indeed is true of Greece and Turkey). Fine recordings by Wolf Dietrich, with scruffily reproduced but adequate notes. —*John Storm Roberts*

Finland

Konsta Jylha

Master Fiddler / Finnish Folkmusic Institute 23
Jylha became an icon of the Finnish folk revival. A fiddler whose groups also played popular music for village hops, he was both authentic and versatile. Side 1 is devoted to superlative traditional playing backed by accordion. Side 2, a 1971 concert, has fine but more familiar playing. —*John Storm Roberts*

European Music

As the small list here suggests (even allowing for the fact that Great Britain and Ireland are taken care of in the Celtic and British Isles section), the reaction against Euro-centrism can go too far. True, Eastern Europe has recently been "discovered," with much harrumphing from the marketing departments, but even here the proportion of derivative to authentic is notably out of whack. But the traditional music of western Europe is not only extraordinarily varied (perhaps most startlingly so in the case of Italy), but much of it formed the other major root of New World styles of all kinds. Spain isn't so badly off, though the focus is exclusively on flamenco. Portugal is beginning to surface. Greece is beginning to take an interest in its roots. But the rest is – almost everywhere – silence. While there are plenty of revivalists, less than a dozen recordings of true traditional French singers ever existed and all but two are now deleted. Germany is not so badly off, thanks only to an active regional commercial industry: German ethnomusicologists no sooner hatch than they fly south to Africa and beyond, like so many geese in winter.

– John Storm Roberts

Piirpauke

○ **Algazara** / Rockadillo 2009
An excellent group performing imaginative arrangements of a wide variety of tunes stemming from different ethnic sources. —*Roots & Rhythm*

Eino Tulikari

Kantele / Finnish Folk Music Institute 1
Like the Alpine zither or the African finger-piano, the kantele zither—the "national instrument" of Finland—is a reminder that genuine rural traditions aren't all raunch and fireworks. Eino Tulikari was the greatest 20th century kantele player, and this brilliant recording deserves a place in the world-music Top 100 rather than the obscurity in which it languishes. —*John Storm Roberts, Original Music*

France Collection

○ **Corsica: Chants Polyphoniques (Polyphonic Chants)** / 1987 / Harmonia Mundi
Highly ornamented religious and secular poetical chants by a local group of singers (E Voce Di U Cumune—The Voice of the Community), most of whom do not read music yet sing remarkably complex traditional styles with a raw, warm energy. Harmonies are often in ancient parallel fifths, in natural non-"trained" modal tuning, at times sliding into place with emotion. Sometimes several voices ornament together and a glorious chord emerges from the midst. Truly moving and honest music. —*"Blue" Gene Tyrrany*

○ **Corsica—Religious Music . . .** / 1989 / Auvidis 8012
Among the most neglected of idioms are the oral religious traditions of Europe, and particularly western Europe. *Corsica—Religious Music of the Oral Tradition* offers recordings of an ancient polyphonic church style from the remote village of Rusiu that are probably unique: certainly I know nothing quite like them (some Sardinian singing is loosely similar). The outstanding a cappella music is backed by outstanding notes. —*John Storm Roberts*

☆ **Chansons de la Belle Epoque** / Music Memoria 30188
France's Cafe Concert style under its various names was as rooted in the urban working class as in English music hall, but it reached further into cafe society and produced international stars as the London music hall never did. Here are some great early moments—major stars like Yvette Guilbert and Mistinguett and huge hits like Bruant's original "Aupres de Ma Blonde," but mostly earlier and more obscure names like Paul Lack, who in-

fluenced Chevalier and Felix Mayol (a song about the *maxixe*, a Brazilian dance introduced at the same time as the tango but without the staying power). Rotten notes. (57:39) —*John Storm Roberts*

Grand Bal Folk / Hexagone 193782

A wonderful collection of traditional French dance music performed by four of France's best folk groups in the '70s—La Bamboche, Malicorne, Le Grand Rouge, and La Chiffonie. A delightful collection of bourrees, branles, marches, waltzes, among others, played on guitars, accordions, hurdy gurdies, bagpipes, dulcimer, fiddle, etc. —*Frank Scott, Roots & Rhythm*

Songs & Dances of Correze / Arion 33492

Correze lies in the isolated Massif Central, and its dances are typical of heartland French tradition. The dance-oriented notes (French only) include an illustration of the basic steps of the bourree as well as descriptions of the polka piquee, the demi-valse, various bourrees, and many other dances played by a local bagpipe and fiddle band that has the real sound. —*John Storm Roberts*

Georgia

Rustavi Choir

Group / Georgian choir
The Rustavi Choir is an all-male vocal group, the best known of the many ensembles now active in the Georgian Republic (formerly USSR). Their traditional repertoire encompasses many Georgian regions and is largely polyphonic, with rich intertwining melodic lines and dramatic vocal effects. —*Myles Boisen*

○ **Georgian Voices** / 1989 / Nonesuch 79224
A soulful representation of the distinctive Georgian vocal chorus sound. Similar to Bulgarian music, with a different sense of drama. —*Myles Boisen*

Georgia Collection

Polyphony of Svaneti / Chant du Monde 274990
For obvious political reasons, the rich and ancient Georgian polyphonic singing tradition has gone relatively unnoticed until recently. This is the first recording to have been made in the singers' usual social setting, from choirs ranging from village and even regional level to groups of friends at home. Much, though not all, is a cappella. Stunning singing, splendid notes. —*John Storm Roberts, Original Music*

Germany Collection

German Drinking Songs / Bescol
Octoberfest / Pro Arte 4003

Greece

Sotiria Bellou

40 Sotiria Bellou / 1988 / Lyra 0001
Nineteen selections by this rembetika star, commemorating her 40 years as a renowned singer. The sound is very good, which leads me to believe that these must be recent, instead of "vintage," recordings. Compared to her more impassioned early songs the material is a little on the light and delicate side, but even if this CD doesn't persuade you to make a marathon run to the bottom of a bottle of ouzo it's still a great rembetika without the scratches and grit. An important contribution to the small world of authentic Greek music on CD. —*Myles Boisen, Roots & Rhythm*

☆ **Sotiria Bellou** / Margo 8323
Fourteen vintage recordings by one of the most highly regarded female rembetiko singers. A+ rating. —*Roots & Rhythm*

George Dalaras

Fifty Years of Rembetika Songs / Minos 248/9
Recent recordings of 19 rembetika songs, totaling 68 minutes. Although the title implies that Mr. Dalaras is a venerable rembete, his clear and supple voice leads one to believe that he is a

newcomer, providing us with updated versions of a half century of classic pieces by Tsitsanis, Tountas, and others. As a "revivalist" work it is quite good (although I'm sure that purists hate this sort of thing), conveying much of the feeling and form of the old songs by way of the clean and simple studio recording. The arrangements are played expertly in the lilting, yet mournful Greek manner, and Dalaras's voice is plaintive and technically precise. His only shortcoming is that he fails to deliver the soulful passion that the "golden age" singers possessed, in this praiseworthy effort to keep their music alive. —*Myles Boisen, Roots & Rhythm*

Iota Lidia

○ **Mega Souxe** / EMI 1703372
Lidia was at her considerable peak in the urban music called laika and the country-based dimotika, which varied as much as anything in their instrumentation (bouzouki + accordion equals laika, clarinet + fiddle equals dimotika, in a justified oversimplification). The songs here, of whatever idiom, are gems of the point where Europe and the Middle East intersected. I have a passion for the more Eastern rhythms of Lidia. A superb CD. —*John Storm Roberts*

Iorgos Mangas

New Urban Greek Folk Music for Dancing & Listening / 1987 / Globestyle
Uptempo instrumental music from master clarinetist Mangas. —*John McCord, Roots & Rhythm*

○ **Iorgos Mangas** / Globestyle
Mangas is a fine clarinetist in the dimotiki tradition, which long since left the villages to play a role more like US "country" music. His first solo album is fusion music with accordion from the urban laika style, various traditional instruments, electric guitar from the pop idiom, and rembetika touches. It's not a new mix, but this band does it well. —*John Storm Roberts*

Poly Panou

○ **Mega Souxe** / EMI 1703292
By Panou's time, the earlier styles of laika and dimotiki had coalesced into something mainstream but still very Greek. Panou arguably out-sings Lidia by a hair on this superb CD. —*John Storm Roberts*

Bassiles Perpiniades

○ **Bassiles Perpiniades** / Margo 8331
Fourteen selections by a bouzouki performer, on the acclaimed Margo rembetiko series. —*Roots & Rhythm*

Mikis Theodorakis

b. Jul. 29, 1925
COM

Canto General / Minos 15010
Large-scale work by Theodorakis, which sets the poems of Pablo Neruda to an orchestral score. Complete version, recorded live in Germany with the Stockholm Orchestra, St. Jakob's Chorus, and featured vocalists Maria Farandouri and Petros Pandis. —*Myles Boisen, Roots & Rhythm*

Vasillis Tsitsanis

Concert at Herakleio Crete / Minos 486/7
Thirty-two songs recorded live (no date given) by a legendary and popular singer. —*Myles Boisen, Roots & Rhythm*

Iordanis Tsomidis

Bouzoukee: The Music of Greece / Nonesuch 72004
Flashy fretwork with an old-fashioned group. —*Myles Boisen*

S. & N. Gatsos Xarchakos

Rembetiko / CBS 450637
CD contains 13 of the songs issued on the Greek import two-LP set. Excellent contemporary Greek music. —*Roots & Rhythm*

Greek Music

The folk music of Greece is some of the most varied and so-phisticated of any in the world, enriched by a multitude of modern and Hellenic cultures. Musical notation was used in Greece centuries before the birth of Christ, and these pieces have been dramatically revived on a French album entitled *Musique de la Grece Antique* (Hamonia Mundi 1015). From the dawn of the recording era, Greek folklore was docu-mented on 78 RPM records. The most sought-after record-ings from the period between the wars are in the *rembetiko* style. Rembetiko was the music of the rembetes, a poverty-stricken subculture who carried knives, ran afoul of the law, and took solace in drink, hashish, and soulful songs about their origins in western Turkey, across the Aegean Sea. This was the blues of Greece, sung in passionate, melancholy scales by men and women alike, accompanied by the 8-string bouqouki and sometimes a violin or other stringed instrument.

Like the blues music of the US, the character of rembetiko changed after WWII (outstanding early rembetiko collec-tions have just come out on the Rounder and Arhoolie la-bels). It had become popular, even respectable, and was pre-sented in the tavernas instead of the hash dens. This mass acceptance was followed inevitably by lighter renditions of the music at faster tempos; gradually the music of the un-derworld became slick, glitzy folk-pop, known as "laiki." In tavernas today (even in the US, where tight-knit communi-ties abound), you can still hear echoes of rembetiko in the slow "zembekiko" dance, done usually by a lone man from the audience who turns slowly, lost in introspection, arms outstretched.

In this country, tavernas and the rare Greek gift-shop/gro-cery provide your best chances to learn about the music first-hand. The best folk-music recordings (or pop, for that matter) are not produced for English language consumers and are rarely found in mainstream stores. Used-record stores might yield the occasional gem, but beware of generic-looking albums with pictures of the Parthenon or polyester-clad bouzouki players on the cover. The American labels Nonesuch, Folkways, Peters/PI, and Olympic have is-sued good folk collections; recommended Greek labels in-clude Intersound, AF, EMI, Columbia, Margo, Lyra, and Venus. If there is English writing, look for the words "Demotika" or "Ahmotika." Bouzouki collections often fea-ture a mixture of rembetika, pop, and folk, with flashy fret-work guaranteed on at least a few cuts.

Genuine folk recordings often focus on a particular region, instrument, or dance style. Some of my favorite instruments are bagpipes, the bouzouki and other members of the string family, the accordion, and especially the clarinet (clarino), which takes on a fluid, vocal quality with dramatic leaps added for effect. Of course the vocalist's art is highly devel-oped here; Greek singers have been breaking hearts for thousands of years! The proximity of Greece to Arabic and Balkan cultures endows even the roughest village music with the best of many worlds. Intense emotion, virtuosity, improvisation, swirling melodies, and unusual rhythms are plentiful.

Another musical resource is folk-dancing clubs, which can still be found scattered around college towns and major cities. Go there on Greek-dance nights to hear and learn the hassapiko (butcher's dance), zembekiko, tsifteteli (rela-tive of the belly dance), syrtaki (from *Zorba the Greek*), the athletic tsamiko, and tricky odd-meter dances from the north, also common in Albania, Yugoslavia, and Bulgaria. And if all else fails, ask a Greek friend, or meet one – I have always found Greek people to be very friendly and more than willing to talk music with genuinely interested Americans.

Vitality, pride, and love of music seem to be part of the na-tional character and can be found in abundance in even the most average Greek recordings, so don't be afraid to go shopping or take a chance – you'll be glad you did.

– Myles Boisen

Y. & Y. Sarris Xintaris

Songs from the "Dawn Song in the Minor" / Minos 471/2
Contemporary rembetika from this Greek TV series—23 selec-tions by Tsisanis, Vamvakaris, and others, performed by modern ensemble. —*Myles Boisen, Roots & Rhythm*

Greece Collection

Clarinet Virtuosi of Greece / 1980 / Disques Cellier 67.469
Traditional clarinet field recordings. —*Myles Boisen*

This Is the Best of Bouzouki / 1981 / EMI 026-71180
Popular masters of the eight-string bouzouki. —*Myles Boisen*

Greece Is . . . Magic / 1989 / Falireas Brothers 1016
Ok, so this looks like a tacky "tourist" item, there's hardly any English info on the thing, and it's expensive. But in spite of being a merchandising failure, this CD contains 13 examples of *the* most soulful modern Greek music I've ever heard—the kind of passionate tunes that make you want to soak up ouzo like a sponge and smash glasses 'til dawn. The heartfelt sounds of vio-lin, accordion, 'ud, bouzouki, and an abundance of mournful clar-inet dominate the instrumental landscape, with just one powerful vocal number starting off the program. I believe these recordings (all done in the studio) come from the Greek AF label; clarinet legend Yiorgos Mangas is included, as well as samples from a gorgeous AF record of Byzantine music. I'm not sure about the origin of the rest, but every one is a gem, the variety of styles is captivating, and I'll bet my last drachma that you'll be yelling for more when this hour-long disc is done. —*Myles Bosien, Roots & Rhythm*

Greece: Chansons et Danses Populaires / 1991 / VDE 552
A lovely collection of traditional music from various parts of Greece, recorded between 1930 and 1959 by ethnomusicologist Samuel Baud-Bovy. There are six performances recorded in 1930 in the Dodecanese Islands including lyra and lauto instrumental duets, a couple of gorgeous duet vocals, and a couple of solo vo-cals. There are 16 performances recorded in Crete in 1954, fea-turing a wide range of vocal and instrumental music. Finally there are seven tracks recorded in continental Greece between 1930 and 1959, including solo vocals and instrumental perfor-mances on flute, clarinet, and lute. Sound is excellent, even on the earliest recordings. The booklet, with notes in English and French, has extensive information on the source of the record-ings, background to the music, and a discussion of every track, and there are a handful of wonderful photos. —*Roots & Rhythm*

☆ **Folk Music of Greece** / Topic 231

Rural Greek music is commonly divided into the Mountains and the Islands. This collection opens with a variety of mainland mu-sic, including some splendid clarinet as well as the usual impas-sioned and highly decorated vocals. The second side focuses on the very different styles of the Aegean Isles, stressing fiddle and lute as well as the ancient Balkan bagpipe. Good notes; great mu-sic. —*John Storm Roberts*

☆ **Kalamatiana/Syrta** / EMI 707532

EMI's huge Demotic Anthology was a treasury and it's wonderful to see a CD version starting. These were not village recordings but very fine performances by professionals close to the roots, with traditional backings. Among those splendidly present are singers Iota Lidia, Rosa Abatsi, Yoryos Nakos (superb, underrated), Papasideres, and clarinetists Karakostas and Malliaras. — *John Storm Roberts*

Kassatina / EMI 170751/841
Greece has spawned a huge variety of rich musical expression, making the term "Greek music" (like African, Asian, or American music) an almost useless generalization. This Greek import disc graciously leads the listener into a rewarding in-depth examination of many traditional musics heard in Greece, still presenting only a fraction of the multitude of regional and historical styles. The respected scholar Alain Danielou has assembled 14 top-quality selections recorded in seven isolated areas where the native traditions have been preserved more-or-less intact. Follow him to Epirus, Macedonia, the Peloponnese, Thrace, the island of Crete, and farther east into present-day Turkey, in search of some of the most distinctive instrumental work and plaintive singing heard anywhere in the Mediterranean. Good recordings, and the notes, though not long-winded, are extremely informative. Essential. — *Roots & Rhythm*

☆ Rembetica / Rounder 1079
A welcome collection, especially since the Folklyric LP is now history. I do have some musical and conceptual cavils, but each is more than balanced by a strength. Some of the cuts are far from their singers' best, and the Papaioannis piece is plain unworthy. But there's a great deal of fine music from unfamiliar as well as familiar artists (including the first recorded bouzouki solo—check out the "Moonlight Sonata" piano!). Anyway, how many CDs are 100% flawless? Buy it, enjoy. —*John Storm Roberts*

○ Rembetiko 1930-60 / Margo 8302
Fourteen various rembetiko performers on an excellent reissue label. —*Roots & Rhythm*

Rembetiko 1950-60 / Margo 8307
Fourteen more rembetiko songs. —*Roots & Rhythm*

Soul Dances of the Greeks / Peters 33
A sampler of favorite folk dance styles by a solid group. —*Myles Boisen*

Hungary

Karikas Egyuttes
Group
This six-person band combines strong throaty female vocals, often in unison duet, over a background of tamburas, citterns, and string bass, with lots of fiddle and some clarinet and Hungarian end-blown flute. The result is a powerful yet poignant sound, with a rhythmic drive that characterizes folk dance music. —*Roots & Rhythm*

Ez a Vilag Olyan Vilag / Radioton 18148
Highly recommended traditional album. —*Roots & Rhythm*

Kalyi Jag

Gypsy Folk Songs from Hungary / Hungaraton 18132
Interesting and very listenable record of Hungarian Gypsy songs adapted for performance by the four young members of Kalyi Jag. Their approach to the Gypsy legacy is analogous to the treatment of folk material during the American folk music boom of the early '60s ... The end result is an album of 19 lovely vocal pieces, including energetic renditions of uniquely Gypsy singing techniques, with understated strings and percussion accompaniment ... This fine studio recording is sure to delight many of you, especially fans of European folk song. —*Roots & Rhythm*

Kolinda

○ Kolinda / 1978 / Hexagone 193672
A CD reissue of a 1978 album by a fine progressive Hungarian group. —*Roots & Rhythm*

Kolinda / 1987 / Pandisc 128
A new album by this progressive Hungarian group. —*Roots & Rhythm*

Muzsikas (Marta Sebestyen)
Vocals / World Fusion
The diminutive Marta Sebestyen is a giant of Hungarian music leading the folk revival field, and also experimenting with pop forms. Her strong and expressive voice is often backed by the Muzsikas, a young group who have revived interest in a number of Hungarian ethnic styles with their energetic, traditional performances. Marta also records with other folkloric ensembles such as Vujicsics. —*Myles Boisen*

☆ Prisoner's Song / 1988 / Hannibal 1341
Dark and powerful statement of life in a Cold War climate, explored through traditional Hungarian songs and instruments. Marta Sebestyen's amazingly evocative voice connects with the medieval sound of the hurdy gurdy and the sting of Mihaly Sipos's Gypsy violin. —*Bob Tarte*

Blues for Transylvania / 1990 / Hannibal 1350
Their second domestic release, also with Sebestyen, is part celebration and part commemoration of a troubled history. This recording explores the traditional music of the Romanian region of Transylvania (taken from Hungary after WW I). Even the fast and furious songs have a meditative quality. Another outstanding release from one of Europe's premier folk ensembles. —*Bob Tarte & Myles Boisen*

○ Marta Sebestyen with Muzsikas / Hannibal 1330
A lovely solo effort by the premier Hungarian singer, once again with her performing group Muzsikas. —*Myles Boisen*

Vujicsics
Group
Named after a popular Hungarian musicologist, Vujicsics is a group of schooled and professional musicial folklorists who concentrate on preserving the traditions of Serbia and Croatia (southern Hungary and Yugoslavia). They are highly regarded for their broad repertoire of collected songs and spirited performances with a variety of singers, including Marta Sebestyen. —*Myles Boisen*

☆ Vujicsics / 1988 / Hannibal 1310
Stunning instrumental wizardry and undiluted Slavic songs from southern Hungary. *Vujicsics* features Marta Sebestyen and others. —*Myles Boisen*

Serbian Music from Southern Hungary / 1989 / Hannibal
Serbian Music from Southern Hungary is another landmark recording of vibrant Hungarian music from the Hannibal label . . . this collection of songs and dance tunes will have you whirling so fast you just might lose your borscht if you're not careful. —*Roots & Rhythm*

Hungary Collection

Sixth Hungarian Dance-House Festival / 1989 / Hungaraton 8144
Sixth Hungarian Dance-House Festival is a beautiful collection of Hungarian music recorded in 1987, featuring mostly young folk revivalists along with some traditional performers. Lots of that distinctive fiddle and bowed bass sound that is so appealing in Hungarian music plus some fine bagpipe playing, flute, and some wonderful singing, including a powerful performance by Balazs Nagy with the Taltos Ensemble and an unaccompanied lullaby by the incomparable Marta Sebestyen. —*Roots & Rhythm*

Bukovinai Szekelyek Magyarorszagon / 1989 / Hungaraton 18131
Bukovinai Szekelyek Magyarorszagon is a collection of Hungarian folk songs of the much-displaced Bukovinian Szekelys. These are not professional performances but field recordings of seven different women, most of them housewives, singing unaccompanied songs of lamentation, regret, disappointment, and displacement that date back almost two centuries. The performances are stark (solo voice) but conscientious, broken up only by occasional interludes by fiddler Laszlo Laszlo. The melodies and especially the lyrics are quite beautiful. A booklet is included containing background info, lyrics with translations, and written music of each song. —*Russ Schoenwetter, Roots & Rhythm*

Eastern Carpathian Traditional Music / Quintana 1903029
These recordings made in Ukrainian areas that were once part of Hungary have the strengths and weaknesses of a seriously imperiled tradition. The music (including Gypsy and Jewish material) is enormously rare and precious. The performances are sometimes limited, though some of the instrumentals are charming. —*John Storm Roberts*

Gypsy Folk Songs / Quintana 903028

Despite its importance in Hungarian tradition, the music Gypsies play and sing for each other is much rarer on record than, say, Australian Aboriginal. Here are solo voices, and also some songs backed by remarkable guitar. None of it is professional, and much is less than polished, but it has all the emotional reality the tea-room czardas lack. By contrast, the notes are an outrage: titles in three languages and names of performers but zero other information. P.S.: From memory I'd say this isn't the material on the Hungaroton Gypsy release, but I haven't heard that for several years, so no guarantees. (74:46). —*John Storm Roberts*

☆ **Szatmari Bandak** / Hungaraton 18192

Four local Gypsy string bands from Hungary's northeastern Szatmar region, an area with a particularly rich but rapidly disappearing musical tradition. Perhaps the most fascinating cuts are old Hungarian Jewish tunes preserved by the Gypsies, but all of this is outstanding in the semi-professional vein of many Gypsy musicians—musically skilled but down-to-earth and locally rooted. Very thorough notes in English. (53+ minutes) — *John Storm Roberts*

○ **Transylvanian Folk Music** / Fonti Musicali 581115

Like many relatively isolated out-groups, the Hungarian minority of Romania preserved forms often lost in Hungary itself. This is a rich, varied, admirably recorded collection of music ranging from solo voice to small dance band. The standard of playing is remarkable. What isn't clear is the provenance of the performers, though (given that one of the singers is Marta Sebestyen) it's pretty clear these weren't recordings made in situ. —*John Storm Roberts*

Italy Collection

Festival Music of Calabria / Inedit 260051

This CD was recorded over a decade at all sorts of religious and secular festivals. A great deal of it is instrumental, from solo bagpipe through accordion groups to diverse marching bands, as well as equally varied processional and party-time singing. Another reminder of just how rich Italian traditional music really is. Fine notes, with photos, round things off. —*John Storm Roberts, Original Music*

Bagpipe in Italy / Lyrichord 7343

Bagpipes, of course, are extraordinarily widespread throughout the world. But Italy, it's fair to say, is not one of the areas most buffs would identify as pipes heaven. Wrong, as this album licensed from the superb Italian Albatros collection reveals. Here are pipes small and pipes huge, mostly from the Mezzogiorno, but including two examples from the north and one from Sardinia. Also included are low-tech but thorough photocopied notes, a big plus. —*John Storm Roberts*

☆ **Folk Music of Calabria** / Barenreiter Musicaphon 55803

The new Musicaphon CDs are all remarkable for the quality of their documentation (here, a 70-page English booklet filled with photos as well as admirable text). This one is also the most remarkable so far for the quality of its material. Italian traditional music, with its range of influences from French to Berber, is staggeringly rich and varied. That Calabria—the toe of the Italian boot—is as rich as any, the music here amply proves. Extraordinary bagpipe music, ancient and magnificent polyphonic singing, accordion, shepherd's pipe, on and stunningly on. —*John Storm Roberts*

○ **Polyphonies of Sardinia** / Chant du Monde 274760

If Italian traditional music is the richest in western Europe, Sardinian is some of the most extraordinary, with Arabic and ancient Berber as well as mainland influences. Except for one track, the music here is an amazing four-voice a cappella polyphonic idiom with an improvising lead on a two-voice bass of extraordinary deep vocalizations unlike anything I have heard from Europe or the Mediterranean. The last track is a more orthodox song to guitar and jaw-harp. The effect of this interpolation is a little odd: I could have used either more variety or a total concentration on the one form. —*John Storm Roberts*

Sicily / Argo 71

Short selections but great variety of folk music, some surprising and raucous, some plaintive and charming. —*David L. Mayers*

Kurdistan

Nawaal

/ Buzaidphon 57

Nawaal is a major name in what amounts to a Kuwaiti New Sound. This 1987 tape is splendid. Not only is Nawaal a very beguiling singer, but her backing is amazing. The elements are familiar enough—string section, kanoun, synthesizer, percussion. But the arrangements are really fresh, there's some superb acoustic piano and even better rai-ish solo fiddle. —*John Storm Roberts, Original Music*

Norway

Mari Boine Persen

Vocals

Persen began her musical career singing about the trials of the Lappish people, who have been rapidly assimilated into other Scandinavian cultures. She still gives voice to protest, keeping homeland issues and music alive with a fusion of traditional and contemporary folk music popular throughout the region. —*Myles Boisen*

☆ **Gula Gula** / 1989 / Real World 91631

Gula Gula means "Hear the Voices of the Foremothers," and many of the songs here are reflective of an oppressed woman's rage and determination to succeed. Titles include "Vilges Suola" ("White Thief"), "Balu Badjel Go Vuoittan" ("When I Win Against Fear"), "Eadnan Ba'kti" ("To Woman"), and "Oppskrift for Herrefolk" ("Recipe for a Master Race"). Sung in Sa'mi, with English translations; the label is Peter Gabriel's, designed to promote world music. —*Ladyslipper*

Norway Collection

Nordic Folk Instruments / Caprice 1233

The Nordic countries are—by northern European standards—remarkably rich in instrumental music. No fewer than 24 instruments, indigenous and naturalized, are presented in this admirable album, from the simple birchbark through flutes, fiddles, zithers, to accordions and guitar. A lavish illustrated booklet has an English translation. —*John Storm Roberts*

Poland

Kurpianka

Kurpianka / Polskie Nagrania 0683

Polish folk songs for weddings and dances. —*Roots & Rhythm*

Poland Collection

Evening at a Polish Tavern / Apon 2821

Polkas, waltzes, songs. —*AMG*

Portugal

Francisco Fialho

Best of Fado / Arc 1165

It isn't that, of course, but Fialho is a really fine singer in the somewhat starker Coimbra vein, and the duo backing (Alfredo Marceneiro and Fernando Farinha) are also right on the money. Lots of saudade and all the fixings, in fact. —*John Storm Roberts*

Fernanda Maria

Fado . . . Fados! / Arion 64072

One of the younger artists in the pure Lisbon fado vein, Fernanda Maria adds to the traditional saudade a predilection for more uptempo numbers, sometimes accompanied by accordion and/or triangle as well as the classic guitars of fado itself. Ever less Lisbon fado being available, this is one to celebrate. —*John Storm Roberts*

Carlos Paredes

Guitar

The Portuguese guitar is a 12-string instrument with double courses (string pairs) and a small body, similar in tone to the mandolin or Greek bouzouki. Its penetrating sound is championed by Carlos Paredes, a sensitive, even shy performer who balances tradition and spontaneous invention. His original approach was likened to the freshness of Ornette Coleman by bassist Charlie Haden, who is himself a minor cultural hero in Portugal. *—Myles Boisen*

○ **Dialogues** / 1990 / Antilles 422 849 309
A collaboration with jazz bassist Charlie Haden. A marvel of sensitive string playing. *—Myles Boisen*

Guitarra Portuguesa / Mar. 1990 / Nonesuch 79203
The old-fashioned crystalline beauty of this instrument has made Paredes an overnight sensation. *—Myles Boisen*

Amalia Rodrigues

Lisboa a Noite / Planet 6002
This is a too-rare gift: a CD of the queen of fado, and one of the ultra-voices of the 20th century. From internal evidence (the overall sound plus the presence of what sounds like the original version of the bilingual "Coimbra"), I'd say these recordings came from the mid 1950s, by me her last great period. I melt, as always—especially, interestingly, at the ranchera "Gorioncilla," one of a handful of fine Spanish-language songs. *—John Storm Roberts*

Raizes / Planet 6005
More evidence that fado is one of the great urban sounds, and Amalia herself, at her best, one of the finest singers this century has produced. No frills here, just enchantment backed by the equally classic duo of guitars, Portuguese (Jaime Santos) and six-stringed (Domingos Camarinha or Santos Moreira). Three cuts are in Spanish. The rest are pure Lisbon saudade. *—John Storm Roberts, Original Music*

☆ **Fados e Guitarradas** / Festival 401132 S21.98
Almost all of Amalia Rodrigues's greatest recordings were made during the 78 rpm era when she was a purely national treasure. Many have disappeared, but some of the best are available on a French release with gorgeous packaging but no notes beyond the titles, lengths, and composers. The CD version consists of only one of the LPs in the vinyl set. Still, here are some of the great moments in 20th-century urban popular music. *—John Storm Roberts*

Fernando Machado Soares

Coimbra Fado / Ocora 559041
Coimbra fado, for centuries the heritage of that city's university students, has a pure and impassioned classicism unique in my experience. Vocals and guitar backings are both ravishing beyond my power to describe or even suggest. The fact that this is the only example available is, to my mind, proof positive of the doctrine of the Cosmic Fall. *—John Storm Roberts*

Portugal Collection

Portuguese String Music / Heritage 5
Lovely instrumental music from various string bands emerging from the Portuguese traditions of choros, fados, and Cape Verde Creole music. The earliest selections are four splendid choros from the Bahia region of Brazil, from 1908, with two featuring charming flute, guitar, and cavaquinho (or ukelele), and two lively "tangos" on mandolin and guitar. The eight Portuguese tunes are instrumental variations on popular fados from 1926 to 1929, played on guitar and lute, with those of Joao de Mates, Eduardo Alves, and Ricardo Borges de Sousa especially lilting and sensuous. Finally, four fiery fiddle, guitar, and cavaquinho pieces from Cape Verde Creoles recorded in the US in the '30s round out this eye-opening and very welcome release. Now for some Portuguese vocal music. *—John McCord, Roots & Rhythm*

Portuguese Traditional Music / Auvidis 8008
Seventeen selections from four different areas of Portugal—the provinces of Beira Baixa, Alentejo, and Douro Littoral, and fados from Lisbon. *—Roots & Rhythm*

Romania

Sandor Fodor

○ **Hungarian Folk from Transylvania** / Hungaraton 18122
The toughest thing to find is music falling between the pure field-recording and the neo-folk music of Muszikas and their ilk. Fodor is a superb example of a regional semi-professional, a man of regional fame with far more technical skill than village musicians. He and his string band play wonderful dance music, with Romanian, Hungarian, and Gypsy influences. *—John Storm Roberts*

Romania Collection

Romania: Village Music—Oltenia / 1991 / VDE 537
Rough but potent folkloric recordings from the Constantin Brailoiu collection, recorded by Braliloiu and his assistants between 1933 and 1943. Featured are 23 selections of authentic peasant music from the province of Oltenia, where Gypsy traditions enrich the performance of ancient long songs, dance music, and ceremonial music. Many vocal selections, and some remarkable work on flute and string instruments. *—Myles Boisen, Roots & Rhythm*

○ **Reflections of Romania . . .** / Nonesuch 72092
Reflections of Romania—Village & Urban Folk Traditions combines the best this musically rich country has to offer—rough Gypsy peasant songs contrasted with polished ensemble work. *—Myles Boisen*

Romania: Transylvania / Ocora 559070
A wide-ranging survey of musical folklore from the Transylvanian region of Romania, collected during the '70s. Every one of these selections is a genuine, and often surprisingly primitive, example of peasant music. The emphasis here is on solo vocals, vocal ensembles, flute music, and tarafs—small ensembles, primarily of Gypsy origin, that feature violin as the lead instrument. Although the recording quality is inconsistent and somewhat distracting from one cut to the next, the variety and potency of the pieces are more than sufficient to hold one's attention throughout the 20-track, 50-minute program. A must for those who lust after the pure untainted folk sound from Drac's backyard. *—Myles Boisen, Roots & Rhythm*

○ **Roumanian Songs and Dances** / Playasound 65031
This album is a well-rounded and truly inspired compilation of traditional music. *—Myles Boisen, Roots & Rhythm*

Russia

Valia & Aliocha Dimitrievitch

○ **The Russian Gypsies** / Disc AZ 102222
Russian Gypsy music—12 by Valia and Aliocha, and eight from the Matrioschka Ensemble. *—Roots & Rhythm*

Russia Collection

Journey to the USSR / Chant du Monde 274920/5
Unparalleled in their scope, the six CDs in this collection cover both instrumental and vocal music in, respectively (and at times illogically), Russia, Ukraine, and Bielorussia; Uzbekistan (!); Kirghizistan, Azerbaijan, and Turmenistan; North Caucasus; the Volga/Urals region; and Siberia. The musical range is just as wide: from wonderful, authentic music to the kind of pseudo-folk ensemble ruined by unsuitable arrangements from some party hack of a third-rate composer. Worth it, though, for the good stuff. *—John Storm Roberts*

Marvels of Polyphony in Sakartvelo / JVC 1296
I picked up this CD upon a friend's insistence that the finest vocal music in the world comes from Soviet Georgia (in the Caucasus mountain range, bordering on Turkey and the Black Sea). Inside the vague Japanese packaging, I was most pleased to find 15 live recordings of truly unforgettable choral music. The first half presents nicely varied female ensemble pieces, some in Western hymn style, others in a more East European "mysterious voices" mode. More remarkable are the male choir works which follow—a potent combination of modern and ancient harmonies,

uniquely layered rhythms, and some very robust singing. Incorporated in many of these pieces is an unparalleled yodeling style; also heard is a small amount of applause and noise from the audience, who are unable to control their enthusiasm at a few points. Get this one and you may have a few uncontrolled outbursts of your own! CD only; 48 minutes long. —*Myles Boisen, Roots & Rhythm*

Spain

Jacinto Almaden

Cante Flamenco / 1989 / Fandango 3
Excellent singer (1899-1968), born Jacinto Antolin Gallego in Almaden, in the Cuidad Real mining province north of Cordoba. An admirer of Antonio Chacon, his strong suit was the Andalusian (non-Gypsy) cantes, especially malaguenas, tientos, marinetes, and mining cantes. With fine accompaniment from Pepe Badajoz and Melchor De Marchena, these '30s recordings have a haunting intensity that makes them extremely attractive. —*John McCord, Roots & Rhythm*

Manolo Caracol

Manolo Caracol / 1989 / Fandango 5
Fine '30s and '40s recordings from this flamboyant Gypsy singer, whose passionate voice led him to great popularity . . . Backed by Paco Aguilera, his treatment of seguriyas, alegrias, and bulerias is stunning. —*John McCord, Roots & Rhythm*

Paco DeLucia

World Fusion, Contemporary flamenco
Guitar. A premier acoustic and flamenco player who has recently attracted interest from American audiences through his duets with Al Dimeola. —*Ron Wynn*

Fabulosa Guitarra De Paco DeLucia / 1984 / PolyGram 818145
Amazing solos and playing throughout. —*Ron Wynn*

Entre Dos Aguas / 1986 / Polydor 814106
Any and all of his albums have a great blend of traditional elements and virtuoso playing. —*Ron Wynn*

★ **Sirocco** / 1987 / Polydor 830913
At times, flamenco phenomenon DeLucia has branched out into jazz, bossa nova, and Cuban mixes. Here, however, he plays essentially solo compositions based on pure flamenco, though with a virtuosity and reach that belong in a concert hall rather than in the traditional settings. —*John Storm Roberts*

★ **Live . . . One Summer Night** / Polydor 822540
Ranges from sentimental to animated. —*Ron Wynn*

Fernanda and Bernarda de Utrera

Cante Flamenco / Ocora C58642 S3996
Fernanda de Utrera emerged from the Andalucian heartland in 1959, acclaimed by many sound critics as the finest pure flamenco singer of her generation. Her younger sister, Bernarda, is regarded at least as highly. —*David L. Mayers*

Jacinto Antulin Gallego

El Nino De Almaden / Mandala 4832
A miner from the town of Almaden, Jacinto Antulin Gallego was perhaps the greatest non-Gypsy vocalist of the great 1920s and 1930s era, a singer of power and always controlled passion. Pedro Soler, his guitarist for many years, contributes a perfectly matched backing. —*John Storm Roberts, Original Music*

Gipsy Kings

Group / World Fusion, Flamenco
The very popular Gipsy Kings developed out of the family group Los Reyes, led by patriarch Jose Reyes in the '70s and '80s. In 1983, they brought the sound of Spanish gypsy guitarists to the world as the Gipsy Kings, keeping their traditions intact on the first few releases. —*Myles Boisen*

☆ **Gipsy Kings** / Feb. 1988 / Elektra 60845
Originally released in 1987 in Europe, *Gispy Kings* is an ebullient disc brimming with thoroughly refreshing music. . . . What makes the Kings so enjoyable is their freshness. On their US debut disc, the Kings swing. —*Jim Fusilli, Rock & Roll Disc.*

Allegria / Jul. 1989 / Elektra 61019
This album features raw, early recordings from this Gypsy family. Very authentic. —*Myles Boisen*

Luna De Fuego / Aug. 1989 / Philips 834064
Both sides of this album run continuously as though in a live performance, but there is no audience apparent. What background noise there is sounds like group interaction and is not intrusive, rather it adds to the feeling of excitement and fiery authenticity. Recommended for all those who like to dig a little deeper into "overnight successes," and for those who have any interest in flamenco and/or gypsy music. —*Roots & Rhythm*

Mosaique / Nov. 1989 / Elektra 60892
Latest release—a little slicker than last year's model, with drums, synthesizer, electric guitar, among others thrown in. Twelve cuts. —*Myles Boisen, Roots & Rhythm*

Pepe Habichuela

Flamenco
○ **A Mandeli** / 1983 / Hannibal 1315
Guitarist Habichuela, born into a well-known flamenco clan in 1944, wears two hats. Under one, he is an eminent traditionally oriented guitarist. Under the other, he has recorded with Don Cherry and with North African musicians. Several tracks on this album are traditional: on others he works with electric bass, percussion, and even lute. Either way, he's dazzling. —*John Storm Roberts*

Ketama

Group
This Spanish group consists of the brothers Carmona, their cousin Jose Miguel (son of the great flamenco artist, Pepe Habichuela) and Jose Soto, a leader of the "new flamenco" movement. —*Scott Bultman*

○ **Ketama** / 1987 / Hannibal 1336
The funk-fusion-flamenco of Ketama is by now a very well-established style. To the Andalucian root, this young trio adds Cuban and vaguely disco touches, but also what sounds remarkably like Indian passages (presumably from lute, since there's no Indian instrument in the credits). I find the results interesting but less than 100% successful—mostly because the flamenco underpinnings are hardly virtuosic. —*John Storm Roberts*

La Niña de Puebla

b. 1909
Vocals / Flamenco
Born in La Puebla De Cazalla, near Seville and named Dolores Jimenez Alcantara, Nina was blinded as a youth, turned to singing and made her debut in 1931. —*John McCord, Roots & Rhythm*

Cante Flamenco / 1989 / Fandango 1
She specialized in cante chico styles like fandangos and zambras, some with popular influences, but all, like "Y No Llores como un Nino" and "Hiciste Sangre en Mis Labios," are quite intense, featuring her strong voice and intricate ululations, and fine backing by Manolo de Badajoz, Antonio Delgado, and Luis Yance. —*John McCord, Roots & Rhythm*

Pastora Pavon

b. 1890
Vocals / Flamenco
Doubtless the greatest female flamenco singer to have recorded, Pastora Pavon, or La Nina de los Peines (the Girl of the Combs) was born to a gypsy family in Seville in 1890. Successful from her youth, she performed in Madrid, Seville, and Bilbao with such as Manuel Valle, Antonio Chacon, brother Tomas, and husband Pepe Pinto. —*John McCord, Roots & Rhythm*

○ **Nina de los Peines, La** / 1989 / Chant du Monde 274859
Able to chant the most intense siguriyas or bulerias or a frivolous cante chico with equal beauty and sublime originality, she casts a spell on these '30s recordings, aided by the guitars of Manalo de Badajoz and Melchor de Marchena, that is unforgettable. With no duplication of the *Chant du Monde* set and excellent sound, this is essential. —*John McCord, Roots & Rhythm*

Paco Peña

Flamenco

Flamenco / 1978 / PolyGram 826904
This 1971 recording shows instrumental flamenco in full and wonderful flower. —*John Storm Roberts*

Pepe Pinto

Pepe Pinto / 1989 / Fandango 8
Pepe Pinto, born in 1903 in Seville, had a mellow singing voice which, along with his extensive repertoire and sense of theater, made him quite popular, though a bit commercial in the '40s and '50s. Married to the great La Nina de los Peines, he performs here in a pure style, accompanied mostly by guitarist Melchor de Marchena, on these fine recordings from 1930-1946. —*John McCord, Roots & Rhythm*

Niño de Ricardo

Nino de Ricardo / Chant du Monde 274927
The superb guitarist I knew as Nino Ricardo without the "de" backed La Nina de los Peines (who sings on the last cut here) and other great singers of the '30s. This set was almost all recorded in the mid '50s when he took up solo playing late in life, when guitarists began to move out from under the vocals. (59:25) —*John Storm Roberts*

Juanito Varea

Juanito Varea / 1989 / Fandango 4
These '30s recordings are mostly excellent examples of pure, breathtaking cante flamenco, as the alegria "Mariquita Mia" or the solea "A una Gitarilla una Tarde." With Nino Ricardo, Paco Aguilera, and occasional orchestra. —*John McCord, Roots & Rhythm*

Antonia Gilibert Vargas

○ **La Perla de Cadiz** / Chant du Monde 274934
Cadiz singer Antonia Gilibert Vargas, "La Perla de Cadiz," was the daughter of a major singer, married to another, and is regarded as the finest singer of *bulerias* of her generation. This is outstanding classic flamenco—*cante hondo* enough to please all but the most picky, by a singer of power and unusual joy: one of the greatest of singers from a city with a major flamenco tradition of its own. —*John Storm Roberts*

Spain Collection

Best of Sevillanas: Vols. 1-4 / 1990 / Oro 704
These four volumes, culled from a mid '70s LP series, showcase the popular flamenco-based Sevillanas, the joyful carnival music that fills the springtime air in Seville and surrounding Andalusia. It's a catchy sound, undeniably Spanish, with energetic brass and group vocals driven by clattering castanets, guitars, and a variety of innovative drums, pianos, and strings. Artists interspersed among the discs include Los Hermanos Reyes (early Gipsy Kings), El Pali, Los Marismenos, Amigos de Gines, Los Romeros de la Puebla, and more. Recommended for those of us who like to keep up on world music currents, as well as fans of Spanish flamenco and the Gypsy music of the Andalusian region. —*Myles Boisen, Roots & Rhythm*

Riches Heures du Flamenco / 1990 / Chant du Monde 274262
Flamenco recital with singers Pepe de la Matrona and El Nino de Almaden, dancer La Joselito, and Pedro Soler on guitar. Ten selections. —*Roots & Rhythm*

☆ **Young Flamencos** / Nov. 22, 1991 / Hannibal 1370
Devoted to various of the young fusion flamenco types: Pata Negra, Ketama, and some less-known groups. Purist buffs become hypertensive over this stuff. Personally, I find it interesting, not necessarily good (most of the singing is plain weak), but then some really lousy performances form part of important stylistic change. —*John Storm Roberts*

Early Cante Flamenco (1934-1939) / Folk Lyric 9001
Includes the classic "La Niña de los Peines." These are historic recordings. —*David L. Mayers*

Former Soviet Republics Collection

☆ **Musics of the Soviet Union** / 1989 / Smithsonian/Folkways 40002
A superb sampler of traditional regional styles covering many of the significant republics. The uniformly genuine quality makes this highly commendable. A fine overview with good non-academic notes. —*Myles Boisen & David L. Mayers*

Music of the Tundra & Taiga / Inedit 260019
A rare collection of the music of Russian Asian groups, bordering on Mongolia: notably the Burait, but also Tungus, Yakuts, Nenets, and Nganasans. Some of the vocal styles are extremely impressive, but the most extraordinary cuts are of jaw-harp playing, almost a parody of electronic music. —*John Storm Roberts*

Women's Songs from Old Russia / Inedit 260018
Songs, in fact, from the women's choirs of three villages, one in the far north, a second a little south of Moscow, and the third (settled by exiles) near Lake Baikal. As obvious as the common roots of this ancient idiom are the differences between the three groups. But, whatever the level of complexity, all are grassroots versions of the great Slavic choral sound. —*John Storm Roberts*

Sweden

Filarfolket

Smuggel / Amalthea 71
Filarfolket continue to use Swedish folk music as a starting point for their own blend of music. "Tuffepolskan," "Karnevalspolska," "Polska Lucumi," "Tartan," "Rockan," and others. —*Roots & Rhythm*

1980-1990 / Amalthea 76
A 19-cut retrospective taken from this eclectic unit's recordings on the Amalthea label. —*Roots & Rhythm*

Norrlatat

Korpens Tecken (1974-1987) / Manifest
An entertaining selection of 17 songs and tunes drawn from six albums recorded by this popular Swedish group between 1974 and 1987. The music is consistently varied and imaginative and ranges from the lovely traditional twin fiddle sound to a more electric group sound. Instrumentation includes fiddles, soprano sax, trombone, accordion, bass, piano, guitar, and synthesizer, among others, and there are several fine vocals by Hans Alatalo. Well worth a listen. —*Frank Scott, Roots & Rhythm*

Sweden Collection

Accordion Music from Angermanland / Caprice 1231
The northeast Swedish province of Angermanland is an accordion stronghold, where old melodeons as well as contemporary instruments can be heard. The music here is played on a large number of different types (plus one harmonica), with an extraordinary range of sound quality. The results are equally varied, and highly beguiling. English notes included. —*John Storm Roberts*

America Swedish Spelmans Trio / Rounder 6004

Folk Fiddling from Sweden / Nonesuch 72033

○ **Harmonica & Accordion** / Caprice 1
Accordion and harmonica playing from all over Sweden: polskas, polkas, waltzes, and other dances on a wide variety of instruments, finely recorded in the homes of local musicians. Excellent illustrated notes in English as well as Swedish. An extraordinarily varied recording of a tradition virtually unknown outside its homeland. —*John Storm Roberts*

○ **Have You Heard the Terrible News?** / Caprice 1222
From "Sir Patrick Spens" to "Frankie and Johnny," the recounting of crime and tragedy has been central to traditional music; and in Sweden as well as Britain, street-singers hawking the printed versions that have come to be called broadside ballads spread their material through the land with remakrble speed. Here, typically, are Lincoln's assassination and an accidental shooting of purely local fame, the tragedy of Elvira Madigan, and the murder of a pregnant maidservant. The notes' tracing of roots and procedures is outstandingly good, as are the illustrations. —*John Storm Roberts*

○ **Master Fiddlers from Narke & Vastmanland** / Caprice 1146
A wonderful collection of cylinder recordings, including music for fiddle, nyckelharpa (keyed fiddle), clarinet, and jaw harp. The inherent value of recordings made before the international folk movement (which influenced as well as preserved traditional styles) is obvious. But these performances are also beautiful—and the sound quality, despite underlying crackle, amazing. *—John Storm Roberts*

○ **Singing Tornedalen** / Caprice 1162
The Tornedalen region of northeastern Sweden borders on Finland. It is Finnish- and Lappish- as well as Swedish-speaking, and very different from the rest of Sweden in its singing style (instrumental music was, for religious reasons, unknown until recently). Most of the examples here are in Finnish, the rest in Swedish and Lappish. Wonderful notes and photos. *—John Storm Roberts*

○ **So Makaroni . . .** / Caprice 1224
So Makaroni: Living Children's Tradition in Sweden. Children's songs and games are extraordinary in the way they preserve ancient elements while changing constantly. One rhyme here seems to come from the pre-Reformation Latin missal; another uses Hitler as material. Crucial even though, alas, only the general parts of the notes are translated. *—John Storm Roberts*

○ **Visor I Skillingtryck** / Caprice 1097
Skillingtryck were cheap booklets of songs. Like the British broadside ballad, the great era of the skillingtryck was the 18th and 19th centuries, but both have remained fresh in traditional singers' memories. Both often told of drama and murder and moralistic mayhem. Some derived from very ancient themes. One sung here is well known in English and Appalachian balladry. *—John Storm Roberts*

Switzerland Collection

Juuzli: Muotatal Jodel / Chant du Monde 274716
One of the very few available recordings of the true mountain jodel (as opposed to commercial recordings of jodler, which are regional popular songs). As such, it is essential to a European collection. *—John Storm Roberts*

Ukraine Collection

Music of the Tatar People / Tangent 129
Music of both the Muslim majority and Orthodox minority of Tatars, mostly unaccompanied vocals (including remarkable duets and trios), but with examples of a local copper pipe, jaw harp, and violin. A remarkable documentation of one of the obscure frontiers between Europe and Asia that are home to so much superlative music. *—John Storm Roberts*

Ukraine / Auvidis 8206
Like just about all of the series, this reissue of the old *UNESCO Musical Atlas* (which was designed specifically for non-academic listeners) has an unusually fine balance of authenticity and variety. The multifarious splendors of Slavic choral singing are very well represented, but there's also plenty of splendid instrumental work. *—John Storm Roberts*

Yugoslavia

Jova "Besir" Stojilkovic'

○ **Blow "Besir" Blow** / 1988 / Globestyle 038
True "heavy metal" music delivered by Stojilkovic' and his raucous brass band, Brass Orkestar. Incredibly dynamic performances of festival and wedding standards that seem constantly on the verge of dissolving into chaos. Cheery and invigorating. *—Bob Tarte*

Yugoslavia Collection

Folk Music of Yugoslavia / Topic 224
Given Yugoslavia's ethnic diversity and geographical position, the variety of its music is hardly surprising. Here are open-throated singing in the magnificent Slavonic choral style, decorated vocals of Balkan-Turkish ilk, ancient diaphonic duets, Gypsy songs, clarinet/violin duos, and solos for bagpipes, one-string fiddle, flute,

and other ancient instruments—all of it superb. *—John Storm Roberts*

Islamic Ritual Music from Yugoslavia . . . / Philips 6586 015
Islamic Ritual Music from Yugoslavia—Zikr of the Rufai Brotherhood offers strange, ecstatic, trance-like music. *—David L. Mayers*

○ **Serbia: Pastoral Dances and Melodies** / Auvidis 6759
A splendid recording of non-vocal music recorded in the '70s, divided by instrument: violin trio, bagpipes small and large, ditto flutes, and one of those irresistible local brass bands—a very fine one, both lyrical and marginally comic. The notes are very thorough (sometimes to the point of irrelevance), the recording quality is remarkable by any standard, but the music is simply superlative. *All* of it, which is far from always the case. (75 minutes) *—John Storm Roberts*

Songs & Dances of Yugoslavia / Playasound 65044
Serbian, Macedonian, and Bosnian folk songs, mostly played by the Rakija ensemble. Not particularly inspired performances, but they do present a wealth of traditional melodies in a sort of polished folk style. *—Roots & Rhythm*

LATIN CONTINUUM

Latin Collection

Musica de la Tierra, Vol. 1 / 1988 / Music of the World 206
Talented musicians from all over Latin America present a wonderful selection of instrumental music from South America, Mexico, and the Caribbean. Featured artists: Pepe Santana, Atahualpa Poalasin, Gonzalo Mata, Sukay, Marc Ribot/Frantz Casseus, Los Troveros Cuyanos, Aires Comombianos, and El Sexteto Criollo. An excellent instrumental sampler. *—Music of the World*

Musica de la Tierra, Vol. 2 / 1988 / Music of the World 207
Presents a sampling of instrumental and vocal melodies from Brazil, Ecuador, Colombia, Argentina, Peru, Mexico, and Haiti. Artists include Tico Da Costa, Tahuantinsuyo, Los Troveros Cuyanos, Atahualpa Poalasin, Los Pregoneros del Puerto, and Aires Colombianos. A dynamic cross-section of Latin American music. *—Music of the World*

Argentina

Raul Barboza

Villa Nueva / La Lichere 167
It's not all tango . . . bandoneon-player Barboza leads a quintet including harp in an "evocation" of Guarani Indian music, mostly devoted to the complex Guarani chamame rhythm, along with a couple of waltzes, polkas and such. *—John Storm Roberts, Original Music*

Carlos Gardel

Vocals / Latin pop, Tango
Carlos Gardel was one of the biggest stars of the Argentine tango in its classic period between the wars. He was a handsome, passionate singer backed by the leading "orquestras tipicas," and also enjoyed considerable fame in Paris when tango and other Latin American music was all the rage. His most popular songs are issued on RCA International, and a comprehensive reissue series has come out on the import El Bandoneon label. *—Myles Boisen*

○ **Classic Gardel** / 1985 / Original Music 402
Carlos Gardel was the greatest of the classic tango singers, and according to many, the man who moved the style from the Buenos Aires deminode to the international scene. At his purest, he was backed only by two guitars, and this Custom Cassette presents him that way, at his best and simplest. In both lyrics and singing style, tracks like "Milonga Sentimental" evoke with remarkable richness the tango worldview of machismo and sentiment. *—John Storm Roberts*

○ **16 Hits, Vol. 1** / Capitol 42196
An appearance in 1917 at the Teatro Colon in Buenos Aires made Gardel a star the like of which has rarely been seen, and launched the tango as a vocal form. This collection is often grotty

(some cuts must have come from 78s and/or soundtracks), but technical issues pale before the wonderful mix of early guitar- and orchestra-backed material. —*John Storm Roberts*

Astor Piazzolla

b. 1921, d. Jul. 5, 1992
Accordion / Opera, Tango
Often referred to as the originator of the "nuevo tango," Piazzolla was an Argentine visionary who endured the wrath of many of his countrymen for adapting their national dance to his own modern ends. A soulful and accomplished performer on the ac- cordion-like bandoneon, Piazzolla's many recordings have placed him as a leading international composer. Besides his own hand- picked groups, he recorded with a mix of jazz and classical play- ers in the US. —*Myles Boisen*

Maria de Buenos Aires / 1991 / Milan 73138-35602
Recent "opera tango." —*Myles Boisen*

★ **Tango: Zero Hour** / Apr. 23, 1992 / Pangaea 42138
Astor says it's his best—I agree. The perfect haunting, passionate recording from the master of the new tango, with his best group. —*Myles Boisen*

○ **The Late Masterpieces** / 1993 / American Clave 1022
American Clave's three-disc retrospective covering Piazzolla's en- tire label work merits its title; the opening volume alone reaf- firms it. Piazzolla considered *Tango: Zero Hour* his finest effort and with good reason. Its sweeping bandoneon solos, sensual arrangements and dramatic presence are astonishing. But the other two releases do not drop the ball; if you think three discs of tango are too much, pay close attention to Astor Piazzolla. In his case, three are not nearly enough. —*Ron Wynn*

Concierto para Bandoneon / Nonesuch 79174
This recording with a classical orchestra is Piazzolla's apotheosis. For years he has been turning a dance form into an art music. Here he essentially crosses into the regional conservatory style called national music. —*John Storm Roberts*

Love Tanguedia / Tropical Storm 74919
Highlights from Piazzolla's work on two films, *South* and *Enrico IV*. Interesting fusion of tango, classical, jazz, and pop. Includes "Tanguedia III." —*Roundup Newsletter*

New Tango / Atlantic 81823
A beautiful, although not representative recording of Astor paired with jazz vibraphonist Gary Burton. —*Myles Boisen*

Rough Dancer & the Cyclical Night / American Clave/Pangaea 1019
Along with *Tango: Zero Hour*, one of his crowning achievements, nostalgic yet uncompromisingly modern. —*Myles Boisen*

Five Tango Sensations / Elektra 79254
More soul-stirring contemporary tangos with the Kronos Quartet, surprisingly well-suited to Kronos's modern string quartet format. —*Myles Boisen*

Horacio Salgan

Tango Vol. 1 / Mandala 4830
From the mid 1940s on, Salgan has been one of the great tango pianists, influenced by jazz without straying into crossover. In 1959 he began playing in duet with guitarist del Lio, and this live 1988 recording is something of a tango pinnacle, with more ele- gance and freedom than the dance-oriented groups but more drive and snap than the nuevo version. —*John Storm Roberts, Original Music*

Tierra Del Fuego

Tierra del Fuego / Adda 581125
Well! Roll over Piazzolla! If Astor's tango is nuevo, these guys play avant nuevo! But it's tough to place them at all, what with tango/danza references, a tendency to carry the classical elements already inherent in the style to extremes, and jazz touches. They work with various combinations of flute (and bass flute), cello, guitar, piano, double-bass (plucked and bowed), and percussion. After an initial boggle or two I decided I really like this one. — *John Storm Roberts*

Brazil

Alcione

b. 1947, São Luis, Maranhão
Samba, bossa nova
A former schoolteacher from the northern state of Maranhaó, Alcione Nazar is strongly identified with samba but excels at re- gional styles and ballads as well. —*Terri Hinte*

● **Personalidade** /
An exciting sampling of her work, including "Etelvina Minha Nega" (composed by her father João Carlos), the dreamy ballad "Amantes da Noite," and the anthemic "Não Deixe o Samba Morrer." —*Terri Hinte*

Alemão (Olmir Stocker)

Instrumental
○ **Bem Brasileiro** /
Samba, choro, and rhythms from Brazil's Northeast are inter- preted by this guitarist/composer's quartet. Cascading arpeggios and a wide array of exotic percussion sounds create a quietly cap- tivating mood. —*David Rumpler*

Brasil Geral /
This instrumental guitar duo has strong Northern Brazilian influ- ences. —*David Rumpler*

Leny Andrade

b. 1943
Brazilian jazz, bossa nova
A carioca (native of Rio de Janeiro), Andrade has been called Brazil's First Lady of Jazz, but she is a masterful interpreter of the great Brazilian composers, classic and contemporary. —*Terri Hinte*

○ **Cartola 80 Anos** / 1987 /
In this 1987 recording, Andrade's husky contralto and the beauti- ful songs of the samba composer Cartola make an inspired pair- ing. The arrangment on this album was done by keyboardist Gilson Peranzzetta. —*Terri Hinte*

Banda Mel

Axé music
○ **Mãe Preta** /
This samba-reggae pop band from Bahia is a welcome relief from the overly synthesizer-driven bands that dominate the current Bahian pop music scene. Banda Mel has won acclaim for its strong vocals, subtle use of electronics, and taut, no-nonsense arrangements. This energetic, danceable release is their best ef- fort to date. —*David Rumpler*

Jacó do Bandolim

b. 1918, d. 1969
Choro
● **Mandolin Master of Brazil** /
Mandolin, no: he plays an instrument that is its big brother. But the "master" bit is right. This is choro, a rough parallel to ragtime, and a particularly fine string-band sound. The recordings here date mostly from the '50s and include some mellow accordion on three cuts. This is true but polished music from the magic (and very rare) moment when a virtuoso develops an idiom out of a street sound without doing it in. (67:08) —*John Storm Roberts*

Jorge Ben

b. 1940
MPB, World Pop
Born in 1940, this carioca singer and guitarist devised an inge- nious synthesis of samba and pop rhythms that helped earn him many worldwide hits, notably the oft-covered "Mais Que Nada." — *Terri Hinte*

Sacudim Ben Samba (1964) /
Ben's third album, one of the best from this early period, already shows his signature blending of North and South American pop. The music reflects his preference for constructing melodies over simple, often modal, harmonies. His low-key bossa-nova vocals

Brazilian Music

For many Americans, Brazilian music means bossa nova and "The Girl from Ipanema" or perhaps summons up a vague image of Carmen Miranda in an extravagant tropical headdress. The truth is that Brazil's popular music has more diversity, more vitality, and more impact in the world arena than that of any other country except the United States.

The last decade has seen Brazilian music enjoying a resurgence of popularity beyond its home borders: many artists have been able to record for US labels and tour in North America, Europe, and Japan. But in fact an ongoing Brazilian-American cultural exchange of significant proportions has been in progress at least since the bossa nova explosion of the early '60s.

There are many parallels between the two countries' histories and many affinities between the two melting-pot cultures. Brazil was colonized by a European power (Portugal) that decimated native Indian populations and instituted African slavery. Regional styles of music—such as baião, frevo, chorinho, forró, afoxé, carimbó—arose as European, Indian, and African elements collided, converged, and blended.

Samba, which originated in a Black urban setting in Rio de Janeiro, is at the root of it all. It is fundamental in Brazilian music, just as the blues—born in the Black rural American South—informs most American popular music.

Out of samba came the cool, captivating syncopation of bossa-nova, whose creators and popularizers—João Gilberto, Antonio Carlos Jobim, Luiz Bonfá, Vinícius de Moraes, Nara Leão, Baden Powell—found themselves part of a giant wave that would break on distant shores. Bossa nova proved irresistible to the rest of the world, and so too has much of the music that has followed in its wake.

In the late '60s, the rock-influenced tropicália movement was spearheaded in Salvador, Bahia, by Gilberto Gil, Caetano Veloso, Gal Costa, and Maria Bethania, all of whom are still active and successful recording artists. MPB, or Musica Popular Brasileira, was a loose confederation of post-bossa-nova singer/songwriters who emerged in the '70s and whose ranks included Milton Nascimento, Chico Buarque, João Bosco, Djavan, and Ivan Lins. It was an exciting, unusually fertile period that represented an apogee of artistic development for these individuals and for Brazilian music overall.

The music of Brazil is generally distinguished by an unrivaled integration of melodic and harmonic sophistication with rhythmic invention and richly poetic lyrics. Whatever the style, it is invariably imbued with saudade, a yearning for a person or place or thing that conveys itself as a sadness or melancholy. (Music, of course, is the celebration that helps to matar, or alleviate, saudades.)

Since I wrote the introduction to the first edition of this chapter, a good deal has happened in "world music." A slew of new recordings has still been released in the US and Europe, though the old imbalance has to some extent been preserved. (There's still far more northern than southern Indian classical music. There still isn't a single field-recording of the Portuguese-derived music of Brazil's majority tradition. There's still lots of Indonesian, not much Thai, essentially no Philippines and on and on.) Still, there have been changes. One is the rise of a world-music-as-ecology tendency. Another, related, is sudden fashion for small, preferably aboriginal and if possible nomadic traditions: in particular the joik of Lapland and the Australian didjeridu. The Worldbeat phenomenon has proliferated like kudzu. And last but far from least, along with all this has come the birth of all sorts of small labels with outreach agendas – most notably Holland's Pan Records, whose releases have ranged from Tuvan throat music to some wonderful Asian, African and Latin-American brass-band CDs.

The inscription "Disco é cultura" (Records are culture) that appears on many Brazilian albums demonstrates an awareness on the part of Brazilians that their music is an authentic expression of who they are, that it is an uplifting, unifying force. It is at the same time a universal language understood everywhere, enriching all who listen.

— Terri Hinte

---

are spiked with bluesy twists and idiosyncratic slides into the upper register. —*David Rumpler*

☆ **Personalidade (Best of Brazil)** / 1991 /

Truly a best-of collection, including "Mais Que Nada," "País Tropical," "Oba, Lá Vem Ela," and "Taj Mahal," which years later was transmogrified into Rod Stewart's megahit "Do Ya Think I'm Sexy?" —*Terri Hinte*

Maria Bethania

b. 1946, Santo Amaro da Purificacão

Tropicália, MPB

Possessed of a magisterial yet sensuous contralto, Bethania has been at the forefront of Brazilian music for 25 years and is one of Brazil's biggest international stars. —*Terri Hinte*

★ **Alibi** / 1978 /

On this breakthrough million-selling 1978 album, Bethania sang romantic ballads by some of Brazil's best young composers: Chico Buarque, Gilberto Gil, and her brother Caetano Veloso. —*Terri Hinte*

Memoria da Pele/Memory of Skin / 1990 /

Bethania, of course, is one of the great names. Above all, she is a fine, smoky ballad singer with a gorgeous voice, as this 1989 release of songs by composers from João Bosco to Djavan amply testifies. The best cut, among many great ones, is a simply gorgeous song to fado-style guitars. —*John Storm Roberts*

Luiz Bonfá

b. 1922

Bossa nova

From Rio de Janiero, Bonfá was already well-established as a composer and guitarist when he was invited to contribute to *Black Orpheus*. He was both progenitor and popularizer of the bossa-nova style. Famous for writing "Manhá de Carnaval" and "Samba de Orfeu," he worked with Stan Getz on bossa-nova recordings of the '60s. —*Terri Hinte & Michael G. Nastos*

Non-Stop to Brazil / 1989 /

Recent but classic jazz-bossa by one of its defining spirits. The elusive Bonfá, an important influence on US jazz-bossa who has pretty much vanished, is superbly evanescent in style. The recording expresses the close links of bossa nova and jazz. Bonfá is joined for a trio of tracks by NY guitarist Gene Bertoncini. (46:55) —*John Storm Roberts*

○ **Bonfá Magic** / 1991 /

A sublime 1991 recording, his first in Brazil in 30 years, of Bonfá compositions old and new. Guaranteed to transport the listener to a Rio cafe, complete with tropical breeze and caipirinha. —*Terri Hinte*

João Bosco

b. 1946, Minas Gerais

MPB

A virtuosic guitarist and galvanic performer, João Bosco was born in the state of Minas Gerais. He emerged in the '70s as a leading

MPB (Música Popular Brasileira) composer, whose urban sambas have been recorded by many top artists. —*Terri Hinte*

○ **Galos de Briga** /
This classic early Bosco with mysterious ballads and boleros and strong samba contributions features surrealistic and irreverent lyrics by long-time partner Aldir Blanc. Includes complete Portuguese lyrics. —*David Rumpler*

○ **Caça à Raposa** /
Stylistically, this is a more upbeat companion to *Galos de Briga*. Includes complete Portuguese lyrics. —*David Rumpler*

Ao Vivo 100ª Apresentação /
This live solo concert demonstrates the tremendous energy and momentum Bosco can generate with just his guitar and voice. Includes complete Portuguese lyrics. —*David Rumpler*

★ **O Bebado e o Equilibrista** /
An excellent greatest hits collection drawn from his early LPs. —*David Rumpler*

○ **Gagabiró** / 1984 /
Bosco's lengthy and productive partnership with lyricist Aldir Blanc reached a creative peak on this 1984 recording, a dazzling, highly sophisticated fusion of African and Brazilian rhythms and styles. —*Terri Hinte*

Chico Buarque
b. 1944
Bossa nova, MPB
Chico Buarque de Hollanda is widely considered to be the most gifted poet in the Portuguese language. He is also a superb composer, and many of his songs are popular standards. —*Terri Hinte*

○ **Construção** / 1971 /
With *Construção* Buarque makes the transition from gifted songwriter to an impassioned critic of modern Brazilian life, though his criticism was encoded to avoid censorship. This recording ranks among Buarque's best and features many treasures including the haunting "Olha Maria," composed with Antonio Carlos Jobim and Vinícius de Moraes. —*David Rumpler*

Quando o Carnaval Chegar / 1972 /
Although it falls short of his best efforts, there's quite a bit to recommend this film soundtrack, which includes Maria Bethania (in particularly fine form) and the intimate voice of Nara Leão. Skip the ponderous orchestral interludes and go directly to Buarque's "Quando o Carnaval Chegar," "Caçada," and "Mambembe," Bethania's performance on Buarque's "Bom Conselho," and the charming renditions of songs by 1920s and '30s composers Assis Valente and Lamartine Babo. —*David Rumpler*

Chico Canta / 1973 /
Dated synthesizer sounds and mediocre arrangements throw a wet blanket on this one. Only the songs "Tatuagem," "Barbara," and "Fado Tropical" keep it from sinking entirely. —*David Rumpler*

Francisco / 1978 /
This is one of Buarque's least adventurous efforts. Only in spots (on "Cantando no Toró," for example) does he supply the unexpected twists that elevate his music to the level of his literate and thought-provoking lyrics. —*David Rumpler*

★ **Vida** / 1980 /
A mid-career tour-de-force featuring some of Buarque's greatest songs and the work of three of Brazil's outstanding arrangers: Francis Hime, Antonio Carlos Jobim, and Roberto Menescal. The Buarque/Jobim collaboration "Eu Te Amo," and the film theme "Bye Bye Brasil" are enough to make it worth acquiring. —*David Rumpler*

○ **Chico Buarque** / 1978 (Polygram 518220) /
Another strong and consistent Buarque LP, this selection of uptempo sambas and ballads features guest appearances by Elba Ramalho, Zizi Possi, and a duet with Milton Nascimento on "Cálice," the classic protest song. —*David Rumpler*

Beth Carvalho
Samba

● **Canta o Samba de São Paulo** /
Carvalho's latest is a relaxed, enjoyable live recording focusing on composers from the metropolis of São Paulo. Unlike "Ao Vivo na Olympia", the sound here is much closer to studio quality, with just enough audience mixed in to keep things exciting. —*David Rumpler*

○ **Pérolas** /
This 1992 recording marks a return to the rootsy, acoustic smallgroup style that brought Carvalho acclaim in the '70s. As always, Carvalho's backup is the best that samba has to offer. The young musicians on this recording capture the style of the old-time players, even if some of the idiosyncratic, rough-edged charm has been smoothed out. —*David Rumpler*

★ **Mundo Melhor** /
This Japanese CD (originally recorded in Brazil in '74) is the only currently available example of a series of exceptional LPs Carvalho recorded in the '70s. From a particularly fruitful period in her career, it has the hallmarks of her greatest recordings: strong, tuneful singing, unobtrusive arrangements, superb samba accompaniment, and an unequalled attention to detail in recording multiple percussion instruments. I highly recommend any of her recordings from this period, including De Pé no Chão, Sentimento Brasileiro, Suor no Rosto, Coração Feliz and Traço de União, should they be reprinted. —*David Rumpler*

Dori Caymmi
b. 1943
MPB
Dori, son of Dorival Caymmi, has worked extensively as a producer and arranger in both Brazil and the US. He is a major artist in his own right, a singer, guitarist, and composer whose songs have been widely covered. —*Terri Hinte*

● **Brasilian Serenata** / 1988 /
His second American release is a lush, impressionistic work of great beauty. He sings his own material (in English and Portuguese) and two of his father's classics ("Voce já Foi à Bahia," "Pescaria"). —*Terri Hinte*

★ **Dori Caymmi** / 1988 /
If you like *Brasilian Serenata*, you'll want this one too. —*Michael G. Nastos*

Dorival Caymmi
b. 1914
Northeast, Sambas
Called Brazil's greatest living composer by no less than Tom Jobim, Caymmi has vividly and lovingly depicted his native Bahia in songs, much as Jorge Amando has done in his novels. —*Terri Hinte*

○ **Caymmi's Grandes Amigos** / 1986 /
The master and his remarkable offspring (Dori, Nana, and Danilo Caymmi) sing each other's compositions together and separately. Their sonorous vocal blends and obvious affinities make this album uncommonly satisfying. —*Terri Hinte*

Nana Caymmi
b. 1941
Samba canção, ballad styles
A singer of exceptional sophistication and emotional power, specializing in ballads and boleros (some by her father and brothers) and with a fine ear for new composers. —*Terri Hinte*

○ **Nana Caymmi** / 1979 /
Caymmi is backed on this 1979 date by top musicians such as João Donato, Robertinho Silva, and Toninho Horta. With her brothers also on hand as writers and sidemen, she invites listeners into her magic inner circle. —*Terri Hinte*

Roberto Correa
Viola Caipira /
This is not strictly traditional music (though played on a traditional Brazilian guitar) but compositions by a young player with classical training as well as traditional roots. As such, they lack the fire of their source but retain an elegance reminiscent of classic Coimbra fado guitar. The notes are so all-encompassing as to be confusing. (68:20) —*John Storm Roberts*

Gal Costa
b. 1946
Bossa nova, MPB, tropicalia, samba-reggae

Maria da Graça Costa Penna Burgos, an artist of extrordinary range, went on from early associations with fellow baianos Veloso, Gil, and Bethania to sustain a career as Brazil's top female singer. — *Terri Hinte*

○ **Trilha Sonora do Filme Gabriela** / 1957 /

○ **Personalidade (Best of Brazil)** / 1974 /

☆ **Gal Canta Caymmi** / 1975 /
In this 1975 release, Costa sings ten of Dorival Caymmi's musical vignettes of life in Salvador, Bahia, about which she knows a great deal (it's her hometown). — *Terri Hinte*

Fantasia / 1981 /
A huge record for Costa in 1981, containing songs by Ivan Lins ("Roda Baiana"), Caetano Veloso ("Meu Bem, Meu Mal"), and Djavan ("Faltando um Pedaço"). — *Terri Hinte*

Bem Bom /
Bem Bom was tropicalista Costa's bid for superstardom in the mid '80s, with the involvement of everybody who is anybody (well, almost). The jazz and R&B touches are more mainstream than before—but the Brazilian pop avant-garde has long drawn heavily on US sources, besides being more sympathetic to lushness than its US counterparts. — *John Storm Roberts*

Maria D'Apparecida

Maria D'Apparecida/Baden Powell /
Apparecida started out as a classical singer and switched to popular music after a car accident in France, where she lives permanently. Despite her background, she's not just technically good, but amazingly authentic. And of course any recording with Baden Powell is basically a must. — *John Storm Roberts*

Martinho da Vila

b. 1939

○ **Samba Enredo** /
Martinho's somewhat languorous vocal delivery contrasts intriguingly with the busy rhythms percolating behind him on these dozen sambas-enredo (the "theme song" performed by each samba school during Carnival.) — *Terri Hinte*

Vinícius de Moraes (De Moraes, Vinícius)

b. 1913, **d.** 1980
MPB, bossa nova
Songwriter. A carioca who once described himself as "the blackest white man in Brazil," Vinicuis was a poet, diplomat, and frequent collaborator of Jobim's, among many other bossa-nova figures. — *Terri Hinte*

★ **Toquinho e Vinícius/Personalidade** /
Guitarist and composer Toquinho (b. 1946) and Vinícius recorded as a duo during the '70s (until Vinícius's death). Together they created exuberant, joyful music that was also very popular—in Brazil and abroad. — *Terri Hinte*

Djavan

b. 1950
Bossa nova, MPB, world pop
A Brazilian singer/vocalist hailing from the northeastern state of Alagoas, he has fashioned an appealing and influential blend of Brazilian, African, and rock rhythms that have been called "South American global pop." — *Terri Hinte*

★ **Seduzir** / 1981 /
Djavan's third album (1981) has all the hallmarks of his unique style, which includes asymmetrical melodies and captivating rhythms, and some of his most memorable tunes ("Pedro Brasil," "Luanda," "Seduzir"). — *Terri Hinte*

Gilberto Gil

b. 1942, Salvador, Bahia
Bossa nova, MPB, tropicália, reggae, world pop
An important Brazilian vocalist, composer, and political activist who has been on the cutting edge of Afro-Latin music over at least three decades. Gil was a pioneer in utilizing everything from reggae to rock in his music. He is idolized by many American rockers and was one of a wave of musicians signed by US labels in an attempt to reap the worldbeat harvest. Gil is an outstanding and charismatic vocalist. — *Ron Wynn*

☆ **Realce** / 1978 /
A good example of how Gil mixes it all up: recorded in Los Angeles with a Brazilian/American cast, this 1978 session combines Gil's unique samba-rock-funk fare with a Portuguese version of Bob Marley's "No Woman, No Cry." — *Terri Hinte*

João Gilberto

b. 1932, Bahia
Bossa nova
One of the greatest Brazilian singers of all time. It would be difficult to overestimate the influence of João Gilberto on Brazilian music. "Everything he did, and does," Caetano Veloso has remarked, "illuminates the past and the future of the music in Brazil."

Born in Bahia in 1932, Gilberto electrified the country with his 1958 recording of Jobim's "Chega de Saudade." Just a few years later the colossal hit "The Girl from Ipanema," which he recorded with then-wife Astrud and saxophonist Stan Getz, precipitated the worldwide bossa-nova phenomenon.

Gilberto is generally recognized as the architect of bossa nova: he condenses samba polyrhythms into his syncopated, thoroughly original guitar style, while his cool, caressing, utterly free vocals define intimacy and swing. — *Terri Hinte*

Amoroso / 1977 /
This 1977 classic is to swoon over: Gilberto singing in Portuguese, Spanish ("Besame Mucho!"), Italian, and English, with strings arranged and conducted by Claus Ogerman. Que beleza . . . — *Terri Hinte*

★ **Legendary João Gilberto** / 1990 /
A 1990 compilation of Gilberto's alluring bossa-nova recordings (1958-1961), containing a generous 75 minutes of music. At the time of its original release, it changed the musical landscape of Brazil and beyond. — *Terri Hinte*

João / 1992 /
Recent but classic jazz-bossa by one of its defining spirits. Vocally, Gilberto is in fine muttering form, communicating intensely with somebody in his breast pocket, and his guitar is as delicate as ever. This recording expresses the close links of bossa nova and jazz. *João* has Clare Fisher arranging and on some cuts playing keyboards, along with one of those saccharin string-sections even the most avant-garde Brazilians love. — *John Storm Roberts*

Egberto Gismonti

b. 1947, Carmo, Brazil
Brazilian jazz, instrumental, MPB
This brilliant, prolific composer, guitarist, and multi-instrumentalist has in effect created his own genre of music, with elements from the entire spectrum of Brazilian styles as well as classical and jazz influences. — *Terri Hinte*

○ **Dança das Cabeças** / 1976 /
The initial American release features extended pieces for guitarist and percussionist Naná Vasconcelos. Side 1 is a tour de force, with the pieces segueing together beautifully. —*Michael G. Nastos*

★ **Sol do Meio Dia** / 1977 /
Guitarist Egberto Gismonti's *Sol do Meio Dia* was very colorful, involved music. . . .The music on this recording was dedicated to the Xingú Indians of the Amazon. Each song was a dedication to the various deities that are a part of the Xingú cosmology. The music was folkloric and Gismont's talents gave the music a deep spiritual quality. —*Spencer R. Weston, Cadence*

Sanfona / 1980, 1981 /
These are virtuoso solo performances and group sessions including a suite and Gismonti's famous "Frevo." This is a double-record set full of prominent Brazilian jazz. —*Michael G. Nastos*

Works / 1983 /
Excellent compilation. —*Michael G. Nastos*

Infância / Jul. 15, 1991 /
A stunning effort by Egberto and his current (1991) working group: guitarist/synthesist Nando Carneiro, bassist Zeca Assumpção, and cellist Jacques Morlenbaum. —*Terri Hinte*

Açademia De Dancas /
An ensemble with strings enhances the beauty of Gismonti's improvisations. —*Michael G. Nastos*

A Incrível Bateria

Samba de Enredo-

○ **O melhor dos Sambas-Enredos /**
This outstanding studio recording of carnaval samba was produced by the legendary Marçal Sr., father of percussionist Marçal Jr. (renowned for his work with the Pat Metheny group), and features splendid versions of some of the greatest sambas-enredo ever written. Strong, tuneful singing complemented by breathtaking samba school drumming. Includes complete English/Portuguese lyrics. —*David Rumpler*

Antonio Carlos Jobim

b. 1927

Bossa nova

One of the greatest 20th-century composers of popular music. The extraordinary body of work created by Antonio Carlos Brasileiro de Almeida Jobim has had an incalculable influence on Brazilian and American music.

His music, he has said, comes from nature. It is romantic, urbane, lyrical, rhythmically and harmonically sophisticated, and very, very beautiful. Jobim himself, as singer, pianist, and arranger, is one of the finest interpreters of his own songs, but they've held strong appeal for an incredible array of international artists over the last 35 years.

"Wave," "Corcovado," "Águas de Março," "Felicidade," "Once I Loved," "Dindi," "The Girl from Ipanema," "One Note Samba," "Desafinado," "Triste"—these are just a few of the carioca composer's classics. —*Terri Hinte*

★ **Elis and Tom** / 1974 /
A perfect record: Brazil's beloved cantora Elis Regina singing an all-Jobim program, accompanied by the composer, who also joins her for several duets, notably his masterpiece "Águas de Março." —*Terri Hinte*

Urubu / 1976 /
This beautiful 1976 session features Claus Ogerman's incomparable string arrangements. In fact, half the album is orchestral-only; on the other half, Jobim sings such gems as "Correnteza," cowritten by Bonfá. —*Terri Hinte*

Terra Brasilis / 1980 /
Once again teaming with arranger Claus Ogerman on this 1980 double album, Jobim reworks many of his classic compositions, including "Dindi," "One Note Samba," and of course "The Girl from Ipanema." —*Terri Hinte*

Passarim / 1987 /
Jobim's "Banda Nova" is a family affair (including wife Ana, daughter Elizabeth, and son Paulo Jobim), which has been touring the world since the mid '80s. Danilo Caymmi is a featured band member. —*Terri Hinte*

Nara Leão

b. 1942, d. 1989

Vocals / Bossa nova, MPB

Nara Leão was known as "the muse of bossa nova," but she also recorded samba de morro ("from the hills," i.e., the real thing) and was later an integral part of Tropicália (with Gil, Gal, Bethnia, Caetano). —*Terri Hinte*

○ **Personalidade (Best of Brazil) /**
Practically a bossa sampler: Leão's gentle voice caresses some of the classics of the genre, such as "Sabe Voce" (by Carlos Lyra and Vinícius), "Telefone" (Roberto Menescal), and several by Jobim and Buarque. —*Terri Hinte*

Ivan Lins

b. 1945

MPB

The carioca singer, composer, and pianist got his first break with Elis Regina's 1970 hit of his "Madalena." Since then he's had a distinguished solo career; American jazz musicians are especially enamored of Lins. —*Terri Hinte*

★ **A Noite** / 1979 / EMI (import)
A Noite contains impassioned performances of some of Lins's best-known songs—"Antes Que Seja Tarde," "Comecar de Novo" ("The Island"), and "Velas" (a Grammy winner as recorded by

Quincy Jones). Now reissued on CD with 1977's *Somos Todos Iguais Nesta Noite.* (2 in EMI series, import) —*Terri Hinte*

Edu Lobo

b. 1943

Bossa nova, MPB

Although only sporadically active in recent years, this singer, composer, and guitarist had enduring contributions in the post-bossa era. His "Arrastão" (written with Vinícius) helped launch the career of Elis Regina. —*Terri Hinte and David Rumpler*

● **Personalidade** / 1987 /
Lobo's warm vocal style and intricate northeastern-flavored guitar work make this compilation a must. "Upa Neguinho" and "Borandá" are among the highlights; the Tamba Trio backs him on several tracks. —*Terri Hinte*

Marisa Monte

MPB, Rock Brasileiro

Mais /
Despite a few NYC credits (notably John Zorn and a couple of recording studios), this is Brazilian with extensions rather than worldbeat. There's muito rock in this, which gives it an attack harder than the familiar bossa-nova mega-mellowness, but there aren't enough Americanisms to swamp the basic Brasileirismo. Fresh and interesting. (64:34) —*John Storm Roberts*

Milton Nascimento

b. 1942

Vocals / MPB

Milton Nascimento grew up in the small town of Três Pontas in Minas Gerais, and retains a strong indentity as a mineiro (i.e., resident of Minas). Since making his recording debut in 1967, Nascimento has enjoyed broad international acclaim as a singer and composer; he's also been a favored collaborator of many American artists, notably Wayne Shorter, Pat Metheny, and Paul Simon. Nascimento's songs incorporate influences as diverse as the Beatles, Gregorian chants, American jazz, African rhythms, bossa nova, and mineiro folk music, and address both the personal and political. A singer of uncommon emotional power whose plaintive tenor can soar to an otherworldly falsetto, he is "the Voice of Brazil" for audiences around the world. —*Terri Hinte*

○ **Minas** / 1975 /
Milton's debut American release. Includes famous tunes "Cravo e Canela" and "Nada será como Antes," with Herbie Hancock, Wayne Shorter and Raul Souza, Toninho, Airto Moreira, Roberto Silva. An important document. —*Michael G. Nastos*

○ **Geraes** / 1976 /
Stylistically and emotionally a counterpart to *Minas*, *Geraes* (an obsolete spelling of "Gerais") includes some of Nascimento's most haunting melodies, as well as a powerful duet with Chico Buarque, "O Que Ser (A Flor da Pele)." —*Terri Hinte*

Missa dos Quilombos / 1982 /
Quilombos were settlements established by runaway slaves during the Portuguese colonial period. Nascimento's mass (recorded in 1982) "celebrates the death and resurrection of the Negro people in the death and resurrection of Christ." It was banned by the Vatican. —*Terri Hinte*

★ **Sentinela** / Nov. 7, 1990 /
Folk themes with sacred overtones: this 1980 session is one of the most spectacular examples of how Nascimento weaves many threads into his music. The title track is an unforgettable duet with Nana Caymmi. —*Terri Hinte*

Clara Nunes

Samba

★ **The Best of Clara Nunes /**
Another excellent compilation, drawn mostly from "Brasil Mestiço" and "Nação" plus a handful of other songs. —*David Rumpler*

● **2 in 1 Series /**
This CD import re-releases two of Nunes's best LPs, "Brasil Mestiço" and "Nação". The first providing an excellent overview of Brazilian folkloric music including several styles of samba and forro. "Nacao" features the captivating rhythm called afoxé, plus

a number of other rhythms native to the state of Bahia in Brazil's Northeast. —*David Rumpler*

★ **O Canto da Gueirreira Vols 1 and 2** /
These two excellent "best of " CDs contain a total of 30 songs spanning Nunes career. Inevitably there is some overlap with "The Best of Clara" (World Pacific), but also a substantial amount of material (about half of each CD) that is not included on the U.S. "best of" collection. —*David Rumpler*

Hermeto Pascoal

b. 1936, Lagoa da Canoa, Alagoas
Instrumental, Brazilian jazz

Brasil, Universo / 1988 /
This brilliant, unconventional, uncompromising music draws on jazz, choro, Northeast rhythms and Hermeto's gift for inventing new instruments and combining existing instruments in fascinating new ways. Don't expect the easy sway of bossa nova. This is music that challenges and inspires. Also recommended: *Lagoa da Canoa Município de Arapiraca* (Happy Hour HH5005-2) and *Hermeto Pascoal E Grupo* (Happy Hour HH5009-2) —*David Rumpler*

Hermeto / 1972 /
Brazilian multi-instrumentalist with a 35-piece orchestra (string heavy) approaches Gil Evans-like sonorities. All compositions are by Pascoal. The album, produced by Airto Moreira and Flora Purim, has some marvelous sounds and joyous music. —*Michael G. Nastos*

Elis Regina

b. 1945, d. 1982
Bossa nova, MPB
Arguably the greatest female singer Brazil has ever produced, Elis Regina was born in the southernmost state of Rio Grande do Sul. A drug overdose in 1982 took her life at the height of her popularity and artistic powers. —*Terri Hinte*

● **Saudade do Brasil** /
This well-recorded 2-CD set catches Elis in extremely outgoing and expressive form. Highlights include inventive reworkings of classics such as Nascimento's "Cançao da America," (complete with Andean flutes and percussion). The most daring piece is Ary Barroso's "Aquarela do Brasil." Here the '50s standard is superimposed on Native Indian tribal chanting, giving new meaning to the song's lyric, "Brazil, my Brazilian Brazil." This is one of Elis' greatest recordings, and those best acquanted with her music will most enjoy it. Complete Portuguese lyrics included. (Note: disc 1 was released in the US in 1992 on Tropical Storm as Elis Regina *That Woman—Vol. 2*. A 1991 Tropical Storm release entitled *Elis Por Ela* includes three cuts from disc 2, but omits the remaining seven.) —*David Rumpler*

○ **Elis Especial** /
This recording features classic early Elis accompanied by an un-credited, relentlessly swinging piano trio. The sound quality could be better (it was recorded in 1968), but by the end of the first song you won't care anymore — you'll be blissfully tapping your foot! —*David Rumpler*

13th Montreux Jazz Festival /
Not as well-recorded as *Saudade do Brasil* or *Transversal do Tempo*, this 1979 CD shows Elis in good form, but not taking many chances. Five songs from this CD have been re-released on *Elis Por Ela* (Tropical Storm), including the Milton Nascimento medley, the Montreux CD's most emotional segment. —*David Rumpler*

● **Transversal do Tempo** /
Transversal is one of Elis's most passionate recordings — an excellent example of her artistry. Her voice conveys deep anger and sadness, even as the music inspires. Includes complete Portuguese lyrics. —*David Rumpler*

★ **Essa Mulher** / 1979 /
A beautifully produced and conceived collection of songs (by João Bosco, Danilo Caymmi, Cartola, Baden Powell, Joyce) on which Regina arrasou (outdid herself, that is to say). —*Terri Hinte*

Elis / Feb. 5, 1991 /
It's not her very best, but a solid 1974 studio session with great songs by Nascimento, João Bosco, and Gilberto Gil, plus a rare recording of "Na Batucada da Vida" by Ary Barroso. Includes complete Portuguese lyrics. —*David Rumpler*

★ **Art of Elis Regina** / 1992 /

★ **Elis Por Ela** / 1993 /
This "best of" collection features live and studio recordings from her middle and late albums. Contains five tracks from the live "Saudade do Brasil," four tracks from "Live at Montreux," and five studio tracks, notably a resuscitated (finally!) version of "Beguine Dodoi," whose mastering was completely botched on the U.S. release of "Essa Mulher." Includes complete Portuguese lyrics. —*David Rumpler*

Bola Sete

b. 1923, Rio de Janeiro, Brazil, d. 1987 , Greenbrae, CA
Guitar / Instrumental
Sete ranks among the better Brazilian and Latin-jazz acoustic guitarists. He came to America in 1960 and has worked with Dizzy Gillespie, Paul Horn, and Vince Guaraldi among others. Sete has made solo releases, straight jazz dates, and bossa-nova records, and is equally accomplished playing in flamenco or Latin settings. —*Ron Wynn*

☆ **Bossa Nova** / 1962-1963 /
Tremendous guitar solos, authentic Brazilian fare done in a main-stream jazz context. —*Ron Wynn*

○ **Incomparable Bola Sete** / May 1965 /
His finest instrumental playing. —*Ron Wynn*

☆ **Bola Sete at the Monterey Jazz Festival** / Sep. 17, 1966 /

☆ **Autentico** / 1966 /
Brilliant recordings with his New Brazilian Trio. —*Ron Wynn*

Simone

b. 1949
MPB, Samba Canção

○ **Amar** / 1982 /
One of Simone's most satisfying albums, with masterful versions of tunes by Buarque, Jobim, Nascimento (including the title track), and the baiano Moraes Moreira ("Pão e Poesia"). —*Terri Hinte*

Tamba Trio

○ **Tamba Trio** / 1975 /
Though recorded past the group's heyday, this 1975 album captures them in their finest bossa form. They're joined by guests Toninho Horta, Danilo Caymmi, João Bosco, and Ivan Lins, who each contributed songs. —*Terri Hinte*

Alceu Valença

b. 1946

Alceu Valença /
Valenca is less well known than many MPB stalwarts, but quite as good. Musically, in fact, he is more individual than many big wheels in this rather text-oriented genre. He has a liking for harder rock influences than most of his compatriots, but also at times turns to a very pretty classic Luso-Brazilian acoustic guitar sound. —*John Storm Roberts*

Velha Guarda da Portela

Samba

Grandes Sambistas /
Fine examples of one of the most traditional small group samba styles, from the musicians of one of the major competitors in the Rio carnival. This compilation includes two seriously important composers, Wilson Moreira and Nelson Sargento and members of the Portela samba school playing a Saturday-night string-band style with the cavaquinho and guitars very audible. There's also some nice jazz trombone in places. —*John Storm Roberts and David Rumpler*

Caetano Veloso

b. 1942
MPB, Bossa nova, Tropicália
From his emergence as one of the aesthetic revolutionaries in the tropicalia movement, Caetano has been a risk-taker-ground-

breaker who has contributed immeasurably as singer, composer, and social conscience. — *Terri Hinte*

● **Cores Nomes** / 1982 /
The compositions on this 1982 recording by Djavan, João Donato, Dorival Caymmi, and of course, Veloso, are exquisitely matched to Caetano's refined vocal style (which owes much to fellow Bahian João Gilberto). — *Terri Hinte*

Tom Zé

b. 1936
MPB, Tropicália, Experimental

○ **Brazil Classics 4—Best of Tom Ze: Massive Hits** / 1984 /
A cofounder of the tropicalista movement with Veloso, Gil, Bethania, et al., Zé has faded into obscurity as his music becomes more and more experimental and eccentric. This is by far the best Brazilian recording I've ever heard (caveat emptor!), partly because of the gentleness of Zé's weirdness and partly because he sounds so Brazilian even as the other tropicalistas come to associate "avant-garde" with increasingly Pan American pop-soup. (42:42) — *Carl Hoyt, Original Music*

○ **Brazil 5: The Hips of Tradition** / 1992 /

Brazil Collection

Amazônia: Cult Music of Northern Brazil / Lyrichord
This features the Afro-Brazilian religious music of Amazônia, which is very different from that of the Bahian version mostly because it mixes Amerindian ingredients with its Yoruba elements. Though most of the music on the album is religious, there are also a couple of splendid examples of *carimbó* by a local band. — *John Storm Roberts*

☆ **Black Orpheus ...**
Black Orpheus—Original Soundtrack Recording. The prodigious talents of Antonio Carlos Jobim and Vinícius de Moraes ("Felicidade") and Luiz Bonfá ("Manhã de Carnaval") were introduced to the world on this unforgettable soundtrack. — *Terri Hinte*

Bossa Nova—Trinta Anos Depois (Thirty Years Later) / PolyGram 826870
A collection of early Brazilian recordings that is not just a great listen, but a salutary reminder about a music that has attracted a lot of nonsense talk. Bossa nova—the authentic, real, genuine stuff—was from the start strongly jazz-oriented and heavily pop in musical aesthetic. Here to prove it are Velosa, Regina, Gilberto, Toquinho, and all sorts of other legends semi- and total. — *John Storm Roberts*

★ **Brazil—Roots—Samba** / 1989 /
Examples of classic and vintage samba, with cuts from Wilson Moreira, Nelson Sargento, Velha Guarda da Portela, etc. — *Ron Wynn*

★ **Brazil Classics 3: Forró, Etc.** / 1985 /
The third volume in the *Brazil Classics* series. — *AMG*

★ **Brazil Classics: Beleza Tropical** / Oct. 1989 /
The first of a three-volume set, compiled by David Byrne, that gives gringos a chance to pick up on the salacious sounds that've been going on in Brazil. Fans of Talking Heads' later work or Paul Simon's African excavations will enjoy these well-done sets. — *John Floyd*

★ **Brazil Classics 2: O Samba** / Jan. 1990 /
The tracks on this disc, recorded over the last 20 years or so, are entertaining ... a good starting point for those who may wish to explore further, or a fair sampler for those who only want to dabble. — *Richard Riis, Rock & Roll Disc.*

★ **Brazil Forró** / 1989 /
Brazil Forró: Music for Maids and Taxi Drivers is a textbook anthology, capturing the sound of Brazil's newest music form forro, a style that's more rhythmically aggressive and stimulating than any of their recent genres. Well-packaged and well-produced, and with excellent sound and a nice cross-section, *Brazil Forró* features José Orlando and Toinho de Alagoas, among others. — *Ron Wynn*

Brazil: The Sound World of The Bororo Indians /
This recording may be an indicator of the future of world music. Collected here are field recordings from a small tribal group,

> If Brazilian CDs are hard to come by in your area, a good mail-order source is Brazil CDs. They carry a wide variety of styles including bossa nova, samba, Axé music from Bahia and Brazilian jazz. The staff is friendly and knowledgeable and they can special order any Brazilian title in print. For a ree catalog, call 617-524-5030 or write to them at Brazil CDs P.O. Box 382282, Cambridge, MA, USA 02238-2282

which up until recently may have been regarded as "primitive." They have a remarkably rich mythology and cosmology, with which their music is intimately connected. This digital recording covers both specifically religious and more secular songs and dances. What grabs me is the attention to music and nature being intertwined. — *David L. Mayers*

Bresil—Musiques Du Haut Xingu /
Interesting long horns, animal songs, and flutes. Fascinating people fast disappearing. — *David L. Mayers*

Bresil 88 /
An attractive anthology with a largely samba-based feel. Some cuts are by artists known in the US—Jorge Ben, Milton Nascimento, Elis Regina, Gilberto Gil—but more who are at least as good though less famous here: Jovelina Pérola Negra, Maria Creuza, Marcos Valle, Wando, Filo, and more. — *John Storm Roberts*

Creadores de Lambada / TH-Rodven 2678
In its origins, the lambada (like bossa nova, though on a much smaller scale) was something authentic. The first version of the enormous Brazilian hit "Chorando se Foi," which is included here in its Spanish-language version, was stupendous in its drive and its echoes of Bolivian flutes. The other cuts on this satisfying CD are samba with a lot of fine jazz-tinged soloing. — *John Storm Roberts*

In Praise of Oxalá & Other Gods ... / Nonesuch 72036
In Praise of Oxalá & Other Gods—Black Music of South America is festive music from Colombia, Ecuador, and Brazil. — *David L. Mayers*

Music of Mato Grosso—Brazil /
Especially interesting for animal calls and eight-foot long flutes. From the Xingú area. — *David L. Mayers*

● **Sambas Enredo de Sempre** /
This "all-time greatest carnival sambas" collection features some of the most memorable "theme sambas" written during the past thirty-five years, and offers a tremendous variety of singing styles and band arrangements. Overall production and recording quality is excellent. Highlights include rare samba de enredo performances by Clara Nunes, Martinho da Vila, and Roberto Ribeiro, the highly regarded puxador (lead singer) of the Império Serrano school. — *David Rumpler*

○ **Sounds of Bahia, Vol. 1** /
○ **Sounds of Bahia, Vol. 2** / 1991 /
Bahia stands alone as a distinctive contributor to Brazilian popular music, producing the country's most outstanding composers, musicians and singers. The region has a strong historical link to Africa, due to the great numbers of African slaves brought there from Angola and the Guinea coast. This thirteen-track compilation presents a sampling of some of the best contemporary music of the region in which the African influence is quite evident. — *Roundup Newsletter*

● **Quatro Grandes do Samba** /
With Nelson Cavaquinho, Candeia, Guiherme de Brito, Elton Medeiros. Four of the greatest traditional samba composers from Rio's *morro,* or hillsides were re-united for this outstanding small-group session. Among the best recordings of this rarely heard samba style, this Japanese import is worth searching for. — *David Rumpler*

● **Encontro com a Velha Guarda** /
This top-notch reunion session features old-time samba greats from the *morro,* including Mano Décio da Viola, Noel Rosa de Oliveira and Ismael Silva. A companion volume to "Quatro Grandes do Samba", this Japanese import is also excellent. — *David Rumpler*

Chile Collection

☆ **Hispano-Chilean Metisse Traditional Music** / Auvidis 8001
From the re-released *UNESCO World Atlas* series, this is almost the only recording of Hispano-Chilean traditional music. Included are religious music, including parade-dances influenced by the Andean Indians, various types of guitar-accompanied ballads, harp-backed cuecas, and more. Thorough notes, though the English translation is eccentric and in a couple of places positively cryptic. —*John Storm Roberts*

Colombia

Joe Arroyo

b. Nov. 1, 1955, Cartagena, Columbia
Salsa

16 Exitos / Fuentes 5648
While Niche has a tight but pretty standard salsa sound, Arroyo uses all sorts of Colombian rhythms (including cumbia), thus giving his universality strong local roots. —*John Storm Roberts, Original Music*

○ **Fuego** / Fuentes 5674
Arroyo had become a major favorite among European salsa buffs, and a considerable success on the Latin concert circuit. Novelty aside, I think the reason is that while he hews to a tight but pretty standard salsa sound, he uses all sorts of Colombian rhythms (including cumbia), thus giving his universality strong local roots. —*John Storm Roberts*

Cesar Castro

Cesar Castro Y Sus Cumbiamberos / Fuentes 201341
Castro is a major big deal in hardcore cumbia, and here he cuts loose with one of those jovially batty sonoras. There's no baritone horn, alas, but lots of singularly fine clarinet. Castro himself plays a mean accordion, too heavy to bother with flash most of the time. The mix of killer playing and cut-up atmosphere, along with the cumbia's ponderous grace—elephants dancing—is indescribable. On no account deprive yourself. —*John Storm Roberts*

Lisandro Meza

De Fiesta por el Mundo / Fuego 041
This particular CD is most all quartet, but with such added trimmings as nifty old-Carib sax and gorgeous acoustic guitar in a cut or two. —*John Storm Roberts, Original Music*

Estas Pillao / Faisan 501
Meza is not your average rural accordionist, but he manages to be both sophisticated and true to what is, at its best, very much a roots music. In fact it's amazing how many changes he can ring on what is, theoretically, a fairly simple idiom. His own playing is both sharp and bluesy, and there's some acoustic guitar on this album that's sheer bliss. —*John Storm Roberts, Original Music*

Mandamas, El / 1986 / RCA 9916
The great accordionist/bandleader and all-round maestro of vallenato. —*John Storm Roberts*

Cancion para Una Muerte Anunciada / Toboga 600
This riff on a famous novel is just part of what makes Meza the finest vallenato musician extant. He takes the Marques story and re-works it back into a small-town drama with brilliance, setting it to a melody that is amazingly sophisticated without ever going beyond tradition. —*John Storm Roberts*

Toto la Momposina

Music of the Atlantic Coast / ASPIC 55509
Tota la Momposina sings the music of the Atlantic coast backed by a percussion group that includes a marimbula or bass finger-piano and sometimes a cane flute. These days, she is an international performer very popular in France, but this is the nearest thing available to Afro-Colombian roots music, and a pleasure. This and the collection album *La Ceiba* are non-vallenato releases for a change. —*David L. Mayers*

Sonora Dinamita

De Nuevo 16 Exitos / Sonotone Latino 1632

Fine batty dance-band cumbia with a mess of singers male and female, all good. This is jovial double-entendre country music by and large, from the opening "No Provoques me Pichiche" (giggle giggle) on down. Everything is real crisp, real easy, and real good. —*John Storm Roberts*

Linda Conjunto with Carmen Rivero Vera

A Bailar la Cumbia / CBS 80227
Re-release of a very fine band from the '50s. Vera is a fine singer in the semi-plaintive, semi-humorous cumbia vein, and the mambo-inflected band (two trumpets, two saxes) is with her all the way. Fine though some of the new Colombian salsa groups are, the cumbia bands have much more regional flavor, and this one is a classic. —*John Storm Roberts*

Colombia Collection

☆ **Cumbia Cumbia** / World Circuit 016
Running from the '50s to the '80s, these cuts perfectly showcase the most charming of Latin American music—a kind of musical equivalent to the poetry of Edward Lear. —*Carl Hoyt, Original Music*

Mejores Duetos / Sonolux 9
One of a slew of compilations devoted to the old duet style of Colombian popular music, mostly accompanied by guitars but occasionally running to a piano (or even an organ) or other small-scale instrumentation. Most of this stuff must go back a long way, before the salsa influences became unavoidable. It's simple, often sentimental, sometimes courtly, and most enchanting. —*John Storm Roberts*

○ **Sacred & Profane Music of the Ika** / Smithsonian/Folkways 4055
Music of the mountain Indians of North Colombia. Dance music played on accordion with rasp. Recordings of Puerto Rican mountain music include the great Ramito, Jibarito, and La Callandria, all major discoveries. —*David L. Mayers*

Cuba

Armenteros, Chocolate & Chappottin

Prefiero el Son / SAR 1009
Chocolate is one of the greatest of Cuban trumpeters, playing in a jazz-tinged style straight from the 1940s conjunto Golden Age (he had the trumpet chair in Arsenio Rodriguez' greatest band when Chapotin left it). This 1980 recording is pure, classic, wonderful conjunto, with ravishing trumpet, lots of tres and all the fixings. —*John Storm Roberts*

○ **Estrellas De Cuba** / Antilla 1995
Chappottin and Chocolate were perhaps the two greatest names of the generation that developed Cuba's jazz-oriented conjunto trumpet sound. Chocolate still records in New York. Chappottin, his equal, was nicknamed the Louis Armstrong of Cuba; he's now forgotten by all but the buffs. The music here is from one of 20th-century popular music's greatest Golden Ages. —*John Storm Roberts*

Don Azpiazu & His Havana Casino Orchestra

Group

Don Azpiazu was until recently a forgotten giant. This was the band whose 1930 "Peanut Vendor" not only became a huge national hit, launching a decade of rumbamania, it was also the first US recording of an authentic national Latin style (in other words, Latin music, not US music to a Latin rhythm, like the '20s tangos). Equally important, Azpiazu's "Peanut Vendor" introduced to the US all those Cuban percussion instruments we now take for granted. His second recording, "Green Eyes," was the first example of true crossover with a North American vocalist. More important yet, this was simply a very fine band indeed, by the standards of its own or any other day. —*John Storm Roberts*

○ **Don Azpiazu & His Havana Casino Orchestra** / Harlequin 10

Don Barreto

Don Barreto 1932-1935 / Harlequin 06

Singer and guitarist Emilio "Don" Barreto was one of many expatriate Cuban musicians who kept the rumba going in Europe, and indeed his group was an important missionary of the genre. His band already shows influences from Martinique, and in fact a lot of the cuts here are biguines. The whole thing is very mellow and charming, with admirable clarinet (a Martiniquan element that was pretty much dying out in Cuba), as well as fine Cuban flute, guitar, and singing. —*John Storm Roberts*

Cachao (Israel "Cachao" Lopez)

b. Sep. 14, 1918, Havana, Cuba
Composer / Salsa
Without question, Cuba's greatest loss since 1959. Cuban music historian Helio Orovio wrote in Cuba's music dictionary that it was Cachao's bass lines that inspired his brother to create the Danzon mambo. The word "Cachao" is a selling factor in album sales; it represents top quality, libido stimulus, arousing, exciting, all of the adjectives that describe a best seller. He left Cuba in 1962 for New York. His reputation preceded him and was responsible for employment in every top-quality music orchestra in the USA. —*Max Salazar*

Cachao Y Su Descarga '77, Vol. 1 / May 1978 / Salsoul 4111
One of the greatest Cuban bassists (and the bass is what pegs all that superb rhythmic interplay), Cachao has played with all the greatest names in his time. Alas, I don't know the personnel of this superlative 1960s recording, but greatness is everywhere present. And not just greatness in the splendid tres playing, the brilliant trumpet and singing and on and on, but richness and variety. The numbers range from extremely Afro-centric pieces to classic son ("Tres Lindas Cubanas," and the delights along the way include a rare-as-hen's-teeth clarinet solo of enormous charm. Quintessential about sums it up . . .). —*John Storm Roberts*

Caridad Cuervo

Sonaron 12 Companas / Areito 3904
One of the great Afro-Cuban guaracheras. The voice is still redolent of power and grace. The backing is one of those splendid everything-bands that Cuba has gone in for recently, with mule-kick trombones, rock-ish keyboards and guitar, strings, you name it. This is the sort of group that can even more or less carry off the boleros that reduce most salsa groups to banality. —*John Storm Roberts*

Conjunto Casino

15 Exitos Originales / Kubaney 0269
The Conjunto Casino was one of the greatest bands of Cuba's '40s and '50s golden age. This CD has zilch notes—who plays the super piano on some cuts, I don't know—and the sound is a bit muffled. But the music is so good and so rare as to turn the flaws into minor irritants. —*John Storm Roberts*

Celia Cruz

Homenaje a Los Santos / Mar. 8, 1994 / Polydor 314-521757
Here's a wonderful early recording! *Homenaje . . .* consists of songs to and around the spirits of lucumi/santeria backed by dance-type bands, a slightly odd Cuban sub-genre. It's an interesting genre, with wonderful singing, variable but sometimes superb backings. (LP-length) —*John Storm Roberts, Original Music*

○ **The Best** / Sony Discos 80587
One of the reigning queens of salsa, Celia's music is celebratory and relentlessly energetic, with lots of percussion, horns and harmonies. This album, originally issued on Fania Records, includes "Yo Soy laVoz," "Isadora," and "Latinos en Estados Unidos." —*Ladyslipper*

Nostalgia Tropical / Orfeon 000808
This is a wonderful early recording! It's not just Celia with Matancera, but includes other Sonora Matancera hits from the 1950s. —*John Storm Roberts*

Celina Gonzalez

Salsa

A Santa Barbara / Suaritos 103
You may have come across the British issue of an '80s Celina Gonzalez album. But her great days were much earlier, when she

was singing with her late husband, Reutilio. They specialized in what may seem to an outsider a slightly odd form: Afro-Cuban religious pop songs backed by a group of guitar (Reutilio), rhythm, and (excellent and distinctive) piano. Celina was a more restrained singer than Celia Cruz, but this is magnificent music from a magnificent period. —*John Storm Roberts*

○ **Que Viva Chango!** / Qbadisc
The queen of campesino, or Cuban country music, in a one-hour anthology of her Cuban albums. The music is rootsy, light, and moves forward with tremendous momentum. —*Ned Sublette*

Beny More

Vocals / Sonero
Venerated by buffs of the '50s Cuban sound, Beny More was, like New York's Tito Rodriguez, not only a dynamic sonero but a fine, fine bolero singer. He was also a big deal as a bandleader fronting full-throated mambo bands. The first Cuban artist to have his own TV show, he was, as far as I know, the only Cuban singer to have an entire book written about him. —*John Storm Roberts*

Homenaje Postumo a Joseito Fernandez / Mediterraneo 10072
This 1950s set dedicated to the composer of the international hit "Guajira Guantanamera" (no, not Pete Seeger!!) is mostly sones and totally superb (in every respect except recording quality which is ho-hum-minus). It even has a couple of superb charanga cuts—rare as hen's teeth, I'd say. Certainly I've never heard More with charanga before. Cuban-music-wise, if you don't know More you're faking it, so why not come in out of the cold? —*John Storm Roberts, Original Music*

☆ **The Most from Beny More** / 1976 / Bmgi 2445
Even though this reissue lacks documentation except for titles, his biggest '50s hits are a basic item for your collection. Worth every cent and more. —*Ned Sublette & John Storm Roberts*

Y Hoy Como Ayer / Bmgi 3203
Beny More, "El Barbaro del Ritmo," was one of the greatest singers of Cuba's 1950s golden age. Like New York's Tito Rodriguez, he was not only a dynamic sonero, but a fine bolero singer. He also ran a dynamite big-band in the Cuban version of high-energy mambo style, as this fine collection amply proves: everybody who was anybody blew their socks off in it at one time or another, and somewhere the palm trees are still swaying from the impact. —*John Storm Roberts, Original Music*

Inigualable, El / Discuba
More, "El Barbaro del Ritmo," is venerated by buffs of the 1950s Cuban sound. Even though this reissue lacks all documentation except titles, it's worth every cent and more. —*John Storm Roberts, Original Music*

Los Munequitos de Mantanzas

Rumba Caliente / 1992 / QBadisc 9005
Much harder to find than the religious drumming of Cuba is the secular street rumba generally known as guaguance—a rowdy, dance-party music with all the complexity and precision of its religious cousins and added touches not generally approved of by the pious, including a good dose of humor. This is absolutely terrific and a great excuse to party! —*Carl Hoyt, Original Music*

○ **Cantar Maravilloso** / Globestyle 053
Recorded in a good studio in London on their first trip ever outside of Cuba (in 1989!), Cuba's most famous rumba group. (The classic sides, recorded for Puchito in 1952, are out of print now.) —*Ned Sublette*

Rumba Caliente / Qbadisc
A coupling of cuts from two albums recorded 12 years apart—one in 1989, the other produced by musicologist Maria Teresa Linares in 1977. Real street rumba—nothing on Munequitos's records but voices and percussion. —*Ned Sublette*

Orquesta Aragon

○ **Aragon** / Monitor 820

○ **Grandes Exitos De Orquesta Aragon** / RCA 8361

○ **That Cuban Cha-Cha-Cha** / Bmgi 2446
This group—which still exists—was world famous in the '50s. This is as good an introduction to them as you'll find. —*Ned Sublette*

Orquesta Casino De La Playa

Sus Grandes Exitos / RCA 9739
This is a total gem. In the late '30s and early '40s, Casino de la Playa was the most important band in Cuba. Perez Prado was their pianist before he split for Mexico, fame and fortune. Miguelito Valdez recorded with them (including the first "Babalu") before adding lustre to the last decent version of the Xaver Cugat band. And here it all is—the seminal "Bruca Manigua," a great "Peanut Vendor," on and on. Depite its length, it's not just a must, but a must must! —*John Storm Roberts*

○ **Memories of Cuba** / Tumbao
It doesn't get any better than this. The great Miguelito Valdes— the man who made "Babalu" famous—sang with this orchestra. You hear a little of him in virtually every important Cuban singer who came after. —*Ned Sublette*

Orquesta Reve

Group / Latin pop
Led by Elio Reve (timbales player), they play an original style of Afro-Cuban music called son, an eastern Cuban dance music. The 60-year-old Reve has led the Orquestra since the mid '80s and has led many other bands since the '50s. —*Michael G. Nastos*

○ **La Explosion Del Momento!** / 1989 / Real World 91301
Hot Latin jazz with good horn chants and choral vocals. Led by Elio Reve Matos. Twelve tracks, four pieces written by Reve Matos and Juan Carlos Alfonso. —*Michael G. Nastos*

○ **Suave Suave + 3** / Discos Habanos 002
One of Cuba's three or four finest modern bands in a fine example of the hot mix of flute-and-fiddle charanga with trombones— in this case heavier on the trombones than shared by several contemporary Cuban bands. Reve is hot enough to sear steak, and a super mix of classic and new (the singing style re-creates the high nasality of the golden age). The band's also notable for a brilliant pianist. Fire-and-filigree, in an idiom that's one of the most amazing survivals-by-adaptation in New World dance music. —*John Storm Roberts*

Isaac Oviedo

○ **Routes of Rhythm, Vol. 3** / 1992 / Rounder 5055
Isaac Oviedo, Cuba's greatest living guitar maestro, got a most deserved place in the spotlight on the final release in Rounder's 1990 CD series spotlighting classic and contemporary Afro-Cuban music. Oviedo's mix of Spanish and African influences could be heard in his lines, riffs, colorations and phrasing while his voice and manner conveyed everything from teasing suggestions to overt invitations and sentimental asides. Though he wasn't singing in English, Oviedo's voice on such tunes as "Ta Jose," "Ccoballende," and "Yuya" registered with anyone possessing open ears. Both Rounder and the Public Broadcasting System, which broadcast a companion television series for the music, deserves kudos for a job well done. —*Ron Wynn*

Los Papines

Homenaje a Mis Colegas / Vitral 4105
There are only three great voices-and-percussion guaguanco or rumba callejera groups left, and their recordings come and go confusingly. Here one of them, Los Papines, has added musicians, including ex-Irakere trumpeter Arturo Sandoval. The effect varies between rumbon with horns, and conjunto with amplified percussion. —*John Storm Roberts*

Guaguanco / Bravo 105
The vocals of this set are not their best, but the drumming is well up to speed. A year or two ago it was well nigh impossible to find secular Afro-Cuban music like this, but paradoxically enough the CD-driven decline of the LP has also led to the cassette reissue of all sorts of very rare recordings. —*John Storm Roberts*

Pello El Afrokan

Un Sabor Que Canta / Vitral 4122
The mozambique was the first and perhaps only Afro-Cuban creation of the Castro era (when Eddie Palmieri recorded one in New York, he got death threats!) Its creator was Pello el Afrokan. This is deep Afro—a contemporary trombone-led sound but very heavy on the percussion, and with vocals far more African than

Cuban Music

You can't imagine American music in the 20th century without the influence of Cuban music. Period. In the 19th century, the port cities of New Orleans and Havana traded licks across the shipping route between them. Later, the synocopated basslines of Cuban son helped the rhythm of jazz move from a foursquare chunk to something hipper. Many rock standards use typically Cuban beats, transplanted and disguised. And then there's salsa, which is Cuban music mixed with Puerto Rican and other influences.

Cuban music has seen many styles in this century: the 20s son; the danzon-playing charangas of the 30s; the blazing-trumpet conjuntos of the 40s; the cha cha cha of the 50s; the ever-present rumba; and, of course, in back of it all, African religious music. Cuban musicologists – and common people as well – know not only what the Afro-Cuban religious music is, but where in Africa it comes from. They know what is Yoruba, what is Dahomeyan, what is Kongo, what is Abacua. I know a salsa musician in New York who says, "If you want to know about Africa, go to Cuba."

Cuban music is alive and kicking. The rhythms are still rooted in the land and the people, and the popular beats continue to evolve.

– Ned Sublette

standard salsa singing. It's arguably the most original happening in Cuban tipico since the 1950s. And it's stunning stuff. —*John Storm Roberts*

Arsenio Rodriguez

b. Aug. 30, 1911, Guira de Macurijes, Matanzas, Cuba, **d.** Dec. 31, 1971, Los Angeles, CA
Guitar / Conjunto
Rodriguez was blinded at age three when kicked in the face by a horse. The Marvelous Blind One, as he was fondly referred to, changed the course of Afro-Cuban dance music when he became the first to utilize the conga drum in a dance band in 1937. His son montuno sound was first heard in 1944, four years after he formed his trumpet conjunto. Considered one of Cuba's best composers and tres guitarist, he left Cuba in 1952 for New York City. —*Max Salazar*

○ **Cuban Counterpoint: History of the Son Montuno** / 1992 / Rounder 1078
The son montuno is perhaps the best example of the mixed genre of Cuban popular music, the result of a long and complex process of interpenetration of African and Spanish elements. This anthology sketches its development, from its folk beginnings to its entry into the Cuban popular music mainstream. Strummed guitars backed by gently insistent percussion give way to later songs, such as the horn-driven numbers sung by Celia Cruz. A rich musical odyssey that spans 40 years. —*Roundup Newsletter*

○ **A Todos Los Barrios** / Jun. 1992 / RCA 3336
Oh, glory—music from the greatest period of one of the greatest names in classic Cuban conjunto. This is the long overdue re-release of Rene Lopez's great 1974 compilation. The original recordings date from 1946-1950. The length is shabby, even for a former LP, and the CD is totally without information beyond titles. But music of any sort—certainly Cuban music—simply does not come more classic than this. —*John Storm Roberts, Original Music*

○ **Afro Cuban Classic** / Ansonia 1337
From Cuba, we present the extremely talented artist and composer, Arsenio Rodriguez. This album was also reviewed by Peter Watrous of the New York *Times*: "Afro Cuban Classic," it says simply on the back cover, and this isn't hype. Mr. Rodriguez, a blind Cuban who played the tres, led a terrific band in the '50s and '60s and was an excellent songwriter as well, having written, among other tunes, the standard, "Bruca Manigua." Mr. Rodriguez was known as a master of Afro-Cuban music and the disk is loaded

with different types of rhythms, ostinatos, and riffs that are kicked off by his insistent yet graceful figures." *—Roundup Newsletter*

○ **Arsenio Rodriguez y Su Conjunto** / Ansonia 1337
This CD version of two albums from his New York period brings together just about all of his material currently available. *—John Storm Roberts*

Silvio Rodriquez

Nueva trova
Modern Cuban pop music. Utterly beautiful, passionate, hip, and melodic. Even without subtitles, this is compelling music. *—Hank Davis*

Dias y Flores / 1988 / Hannibal 1322
Silvio Rodriquez, one of Cuba's finest guitarists, tried to link the music in his homeland with newer styles from Latin America on 1975's *Dias y Flores*, issued on compact disc in 1988 by Hannibal. The results were both intriguing and uneven; the playing was always impressive, but sometimes the vocals seemed unfocused or rambled, with Rodriquez and company trying to fit their work into styles they weren't thoroughly familiar with. But most of this is gripping, magical material, particularly the sections where Rodriquez's guitar and the rhythms laid down by Leoginaldo Pimentel, Ignacio Berroa, Norberto Carrillo, and Daniel Aldama converge seamlessy. *—Ron Wynn, AMG*

Ñico Saquito

Good-bye Mr. Cat / World Circuit 035
Saquito was the driving force of the great son trio Los Guaracheros de Oriente. He last recorded in 1982, backed by some truly wonderful string-picking. His voice had faded slightly—after all, he was in his '80s. But both he and his backup have a rarely surpassed charm and flair. Downhome without raunch, masterly without flash, this is some kind of perfection. *—John Storm Roberts, Original Music*

Sexteto Habanero

Son Cubano / Tumbao T001
These 1924-1927 recordings caught them in their early prime. This is what they play in Heaven when the Andeans and the Burmese put down their harps . . . *—John Storm Roberts, Original Music*

○ **Sexteto Habanero** / Tumbao
Tumbao is a Swiss label that's turned up this year with some previously unavailable classic sides. This is one of the greatest of the great son groups of the '20s. *—Ned Sublette*

Sintesis

○ **Ancestros** / Qba 9001
The most important progressive rock album in Cuba, ever. Authentic Afro-Cuban religious ritual melodies, sung passionately and with great fidelity to the originals, arranged for contemporary instrumentation with electric guitar and synthesizer. People fall in love with this album. *—Ned Sublette*

Sonora Matancera

50 Anos / Seeco 4001
The recordings here were all from the 1950s, and even then the list of vocalists is amazing: Miguelito and Valdez, Bienvenido Granda, Myrta Silva (superb), Daniel Santos, on and on and superbly on . . . Oh, yes, not to forget Celia Cruz. *—John Storm Roberts, Original Music*

65 Aniversario / Orfeon 000822
Sonora Matancera, founded in 1924, is one of the great conjuntos and the way to stardom for a zillion singers. This splendid compilation includes a track each by 15 vocalists. Celia is here with Yerbero Moderno, but it's the other cuts that are the most interesting—including one by the brilliant Miguelito Valdez, the original Mr. Babalu but also a Havana heavy in his time. *—John Storm Roberts, Original Music*

Trio Matamoros

○ **Ecos de Cuba** / 1975 / Kubaney

About the only thing you're likely to find by this extremely influential group. Matamoros was the composer of some of the biggest standards in the popular Cuban repertoire—"Lagrimas Negras" and "Son de la Loma," to name two. *—Ned Sublette*

Lagrimas Negras / 1980 / Kubaney 115
The Trio Matamoros was one of the greatest of the incomparable Cuban guitar-and-percussion sones groups, (and a seminal influence on early African guitar). The title cut here is one of the most beautiful of Cuban melodies. Also here is a track with an oboe-like reed instrument descended (really!) from the Chinese shona and only heard during carnival in Oriente. *—John Storm Roberts*

☆ **20 Exitos Inolvidables** / 1985 / Kubaney 150
If I had to live with only one popular recording for all eternity, this might well be it. "Son de la Loma," "Lagrimas Negras," "El Que Siembra Su Maiz," "Santiaguera," the great Matamoros wrote them all, and here they all are. True, the luscious "Olvido" is missing, but there's probably such a thing as too much bliss. *—John Storm Roberts*

Trio Matamoros / Ansonia 1251
Ciro Rodriguez, Rafael Cueto, and Miguel Matamoros comprise the Trio Matamoros, the pride of Cuba. The trio is an authentic example of an institution of Cuban art. All three were pioneers of popular Cuban music and their songs have been heard in all four corners of the world. For over 35 years, they have been inseparable, acting and singing the popular music of Cuba. *—Roundup Newsletter*

Bebo Valdes

b. Oct. 9, 1918, Quivican, Havana, Cuba
Piano
A brilliant composer, pianist, and arranger, he began his pro career in 1938 with the orchestra of Happy Happy D'Ulasia. Valdes has performed with Havana's best orchestras, which included Julio Cuevas and Amadeo Romeu's Tropicana Orquesta. In 1952, when Valdes recorded a fill-in tune "Con Poco Coco" for Norman Grantz's Mercury label, he became the first Cuban to record a Cuban jam session. Valdes has lived in Sweden since 1963, and still performs and records there. He is the proud father of Chucho Valdes of Cuba's "Irakere." *—Max Salazar*

Con Poco Coco / 1952 / Mercury

Los Van Van

Bailando Mojao / World Pacific 806002
This set is a compilation covering 1984-1990, plus a cut recorded live in Havana by QBADisc's Ned Sublette. All the numbers stretch out, and the live one is a monumentally cooking 12-plus minutes. Background notes on the band and the style would have been a vast improvement on the translations of fairly undistinguished lyrics, but the music is superb—and blessedly plentiful. *—John Storm Roberts*

Songo / 1988 / Mango 9825
Van Van is the unchallenged #1 dance band in Cuba, formed in 1969 and going full blast today. I sometimes say I don't like this album—the mix is a little cold, I think—but I play it a lot. A high-tech re-recording, in Paris, of some of their '80s tunes—including their biggest hit, "Muevete," and an irresistible "Que Palo Es Ese." It's a great record, really, but the band has an even greater one in them. *—Ned Sublette*

Dancing Wet (Bailando Mojao) / World Pacific
An anthology of killer tracks from the '80s through 1990, including a very hot live cut. *—Ned Sublette*

Los Van Van / Vitral 4118
A heavy CD from one of Havana's heaviest contemporary groups. Van Van, a cross between a charanga and a trombone conjunto, is perhaps less adventurous than Irakere, but it doesn't recycle familiar material nearly as much and is more consistently terrific. It also has one of the finest pianists in the whole Latin field. *—John Storm Roberts*

Carlos Varela

○ **Jalisco Park** / Eligeme
Good luck trying to find this one; it's on a tiny Spanish label, but it's worth the trouble. At 28 years of age, Varela is an independent voice; his lyrics register as daring in the political context of Cuba. He's the poet of young Havana in the early '90s. This album,

Salsa

In 1974 Salsa became a household word in the Hispanic communities. It was first heard when Cuba's Ignacio Pineiro's Sexteto Nacional introduced his tune "Echale Salsita" at the 1932 Chicago World's Fair. Salsa, the Spanish word for spicy sauce, was uttered when dancers urged bandleaders to swing the music. The word lay dormant until 1962 when Seeco Records released Joe Cuba's *Stepping Out* album, in which vocalist Jimmy Sabater's tune "Salsa y Bembe" appeared for the first time after 30 years. Salsa's thrust to national recognition occurred after Cal Tjader's 1964 recording of "Soul Sauce" (Salsa del Alma), which received airplay on jazz, R&B, and Latin-music programs across the United States. It achieved international acceptance after the fiery music of the Fania All-Stars and the bands of Larry Harlow, Johnny Pacheco, Ray Barretto, Eddie Palmieri, Orchestra Broadway, La Sonora Poncena, Willie Rosario, El Gran Combo, the Willie Colon/Ruben Blades combination, and Tito Puente modernized the Afro-Cuban sound in the 70s.

The roots of salsa sprouted with the Cuban *son*, a rhythm created in Santiago De Cuba by Theodora Ginez. El son began its rhythmic change in 1791 after hundreds of White Frenchmen and Haitians fled the revolution and relocated in Cuba. During the 18th century, the Cuban government forbade the playing of el son, in that its lyrics protested the inhuman slavery conditions, causing riots. Soldiers from as far away as Havana were sent to Oriente. Those who were musicians returned home with the new rhythm, and it soon found its way throughout Cuba.

In 1920, during a carnival in Havana Guillermo Castillo's Grupo Tipica, Oriental played el son. After the carnival, the group became El Sexteto Habañero, and the era of the trumpet conjunto and the popular el son rhythm began.

In April 1930, the Cuban orchestra of Don Aspiazu started the New York salsa era when it overwhelmed its audiences with its version of "The Peanut Vendor." From the RKO Palace in midtown Manhattan, the tune's infectious melodies filtered to all of New York. RCA Victor recorded it on May 13, 1930, and released it five months later. "El Manisero" was the background music for the 1931 movie *Cuban Love Song.* By the mid 30s, every Latin music aggregation included el son in its repertoire. The most popular groups were those of Vicente Sigler, Nilo Melendez, Alberto Socarras, Rafael Hernandez's Grupo Victoria, Augusto Coen, Xavier Cugat, Montecino's Happy Boys, and Alberto Iznaga's La Siboney. In Cuba during the late 30s, Afro-Cuban rhythms were demonstrating further innovations. Orestes Lopez, a revered musician of Antonio Arcano's charanga (a piano, flute, strings, and rhythm section) invented the danzon mambo rhythm in 1938. The mambo became the standard third part of the danzon, adding an overwhelming excitement that has not yet been improved upon. During the 40s, the Cuban guaracha rhythm joined el son in popularity; the best recordings were by Miguelito Valdes, Machito and the Afro-Cubans, Anselmo Sacassas, Noro Morales, José Curbelo, and Marcelino Guerra.

The next innovation occurred in 1943 at La Conga Club in midtown Manhattan. On Sunday evening, May 28, 1943, the Machito orchestra finished playing a tune. While the next number was being searched for, pianist Luis Varona began to play the introduction to the tune "El Bottellero" (The Bottlemaker). All of a sudden, bassist Julio Andino joined in, plucking the same notes. At a rehearsal the following evening, Mario Bauza (trumpeter and Machito's musical director) told Varona and Andino to play the same introduction while he sang out the broken chords he wanted saxophonists and trumpeters to repeat. Bauza then wrote a melody for the band to play on top of the broken chords. Thus the tune "Tanga" was conceived, and Afro-Cuban jazz (now Latin jazz) was created.

In 1949, Perez Prado's "Mambo #5" became a monstrous hit and officially kicked off the mambo era. Among the then-new bandleaders who revised Prado's sound for New York dancers were Tito Puente and Tito Rodriguez, whose orchestrations were the model for the Palladium mambo. In addition to the two Titos, the most popular bands of the 50s included Machito, Miguelito Valdes, Pupi Campo, Joe Loco Quintet, Alfredito, La Playa Sextet, Cal Tjader, and Noro Morales, along with the Cuban bands of Arsenio Rodriguez, Orquesta Aragon, Enrique Jorrin, Felix Chappotin, Jose Fajardo, Roberto Faz, Bebo Valdes, Cachao y Su Descargo, and Beny More.

The pop dance bands of the 60s were Johnny Pacheco, Charlie Palmieri, Eddie Palmieri, Joe Quijano, Orlando Marin, Joe Cuba Sextet, Ricardo Ray, Pete Rodriguez, and Lou Perez, along with the boogaloo bands of Johnny Colon, King Nando, Joey Pastrana, the Le Bron Brothers, and Joe Bataan. The 70s was an exciting decade because of Gerald Masucci, president of Fania Records. Mr. Masucci spent thousands of dollars in the 60s and 70s promoting unknown musicians who today are superstars earning great sums of money. Masucci bought three hours of air time in every large Hispanic-populated city, including San Juan, Puerto Rico. He flew artists all over the world until they became well known. Eddie Palmieri was the superstar of the 70s. Ray Barretto's tune "Cocinando" was the best of the 70s. The most popular bands were those of Larry Harlow, Johnny Pacheco, Ray Barretto, Bobby Valentine, Willie Colon, Willie Rosario, Tipica Novel, Bobby Rodriguez y La Compania, Angel Canales, La Sonora Poncena, El Gran Combo, Mongo Santamaria, and the sizzling Orchestra Broadway, who never failed to pack ballrooms.

The 80s saw the comeback of Tito Puente among the top bands, with great Concord Jazz label recordings. Joining Puente were Orchestra Broadway, Oscar DeLeon, Louis Ramirez, Willie Rosario, Ray Barretto, Eddie Palmieri, Luis "Perico" Ortiz, Roberto Torres, Papaito Munoz, Charanga America, Conjunto Candela, Grupo Fascinación, Santiago Ceron, Wayne Gorbea, Libre, and the red-hot Conjunto Clásico. So far the 90s have included Poncho Sanchez, Bongologic, Shades of Jade, José Alberto, Tito Nieves, Columbia's Joe Acosta, Santo Domingo's Cuco Valoy, and Japan's Orquesta de la Luz. Salsa would have never achieved its heights of popularity without music arrangers, the music-makers who create hit records – for example, Marty Sheller, Louie Ramirez, Papo Lucca, Oscar Hernandez, Isidro Infante, Alfredito Valdes Jr, Hector Rivera, Rene Hernandez, Lou Perez, Israel "Cachao" Lopez, Arturo "Chico" O'Farrill, Ray Santos, Joe Loco, and Tito Puente.

– Max Salazar

recorded in Spain with Spanish sidemen, is an impressive debut by someone who will likely be a major artist in years to come. — *Ned Sublette*

Cuba Collection

Real Rumba / Corason 110
The real thing in rumba still is fairly rare on record. Even rarer are recordings by groups other than Los Munequitos, Los Papines or Carlos Embales. More than half the cuts on Real Rumba are by virtually unknown groups: Afrocuba de Matanzas, Columbia de Puerto and Cutumba. What's more, it includes the other major rumba styles as well as guaguanco: columbia, yambu, and a new development involving bata drums and called batarrumba. It has decent notes. — *John Storm Roberts, Original Music*

Fiesta De La Rumba / Egrem 0019
The Egrem release is mostly the Big Three, plus a couple more— notably Celeste Mendoza. It is in Spanish only. — *John Storm Roberts, Original Music*

○ **Cuban & Puerto Rican Music** / 1987 / Music of the World 111
Side 1: Orlando Puntilla Rios and Nueva Generacion perform sacred Yoruba santeria music sung and played on Afro-Cuban drums and percussion. Side 2 features Puerto Rican jibaro music by Israel Berrios and El Sexteto Criollo, and bomba and plena by Los Pleneros de la 21. A great introduction to the Afro-Carribbean tradition. — *Music of the World*

○ **Cuba Classics 2: Dancing with the Enemy** / 1988 / Luaka Bop 26580
I'm biased, I admit: I helped compile *Cuba Classics 2—Dancing with the Enemy*. At the burrito joint where I eat lunch, they play it every day, and Peter Watrous at *The New York Times* gave it #2 on his Ten Best of 1991 list. These are obscure recordings mostly, the majority from the '60s and '70s. Damn good, if I do say so. — *Ned Sublette*

Routes of Rhythm—Vols. 1 & 2 / 1988 / Rounder 5049/50
Volume 1 is subtitled *Carnival of Cuban Music* and the second volume is subtitled *Cuban Dance Party*. (See Isaac Oviedo for Volume 3.) — *AMG*

○ **Cuba Classics 1: Canciones Urgentes** / Warner Brothers 26480
An anthology, compiled by David Byrne, of various tracks by Silvio Rodriguez, one of the leaders of Cuba's nueva trova (new song) movement. — *Ned Sublette*

○ **Cuba Classics 3** / 1992 / Warner Brothers 45107
This album is more forward-looking. Buy with confidence. — *Ned Sublette*

☆ **Cuban Counterpoint** / Rounder 1078
A lengthy history of African and Iberian musical interface that results in the various styles and sounds that comprise the Cuban genre son montuno. This 22-track anthology issued by Rounder in 1992 covered this wide ranging idiom and its diverse, yet related forms. It included segments from the '20s to the '70s; there were Spanish vocal arrangements and ensembles, polyrhythmic African percussion, linguistic elements of each, and material that sometimes sounded like the songs heard in saloons and cantinas on the Mexican border and other times like the bustling jam sessions heard in East Coast clubs. The songs were mostly short (none longer than three and a half minutes) and included several contributions from the great bandleader Arsenio Rodriguez as well as cuts by Sexteto Habanero, Benny More and the Cachao All Stars featuring El Nino Rivera. It was an exhaustively annonated and valuable anthology that shed fresh light on the enchanting mix that constitutes modern Afro-Cuban music. — *Ron Wynn*

○ **Dances of the Gods** / Ocora 559051
Here's something crucial for percussion buffs: field recordings covering all the major religious traditions (lucumi, arara, palo monte, tambor yuka, abakwa, transplanted Haitian), along with a couple of street rumbas (guaguanco and columbia). More of the latter would have been nice, and the notes are a bit confused on relationships between denominations. But this is still essential stuff. — *John Storm Roberts*

○ **Joyas Tropicales** / Ansonia 13034
Most of this gem is devoted to cuarteto and septeto music, including many cuts by the Trio Matamoros and Guaracheros de Orients. Others in this vein include the Cuarteto Marcano, the

Puerto Rican Cuarteto Borniquen, and others less well known. Most of the rest is from the Sonora Matancera. Pretty much all of it is gold, a most long-buried treasure trove. — *John Storm Roberts*

○ **Sabroso!: Havana Hits** / Earthworks
Probably the standout in this various-artists compilation is Los Van Van's original recording of "Muevete." — *Ned Sublette*

Dominican Republic

Jossie/Patrulla Esteban

15 Exitasos / TTH 1931
Esteban has had less publicity than Vargas (of whom he was a protege like practically all the younger merengueros), Belkis, or Villalona. But he's chalked up some hefty hits over the last few years on a mix of tearaway vocals, humor, and a tight, tight band. Heard again in this best-of, most of them stand up just fine. — *John Storm Roberts*

Los Grandes Del Merengue

☆ **Grandes del Merengue Tipico, Los** / Jose Luis 093
This album is a selection of the young Turks who have brought the country-style accordion sound roaring back from the trashcan of history, updating it into a splendidly happening sound. Fefita La Grande, Francisco Ulloa, and the older Ciego de Nagua are here, but so are a bunch of younger up-and-comers. Most add a sax in the jovial lunacy called perico ripiao. The whole thing is as much re-creation as revival, and wonderfully so. — *John Storm Roberts*

Tatico Henriquez

20 Exitos / Bachata 6007
I recorded country merengue in the field in the early 1970s, Henriquez peak era. So I can vouch personally for the fact that Henriquez, like the other great names of last-generation accordion-quartet merengue tipico, stood out only on quality, not style, from the guys who came into town on Sunday to play for dimes. The craggy rural voice, the punch of the accordion, the drive of the tambora drum, the slashing guira scraper, are all (marvellously) as close to the roots as you can get. — *John Storm Roberts*

La India Canela

Que Siga la Fiesta / Jose Luis 07
Yet another female accordionist to add to Maria Diaz and the unparalleled Fefita la Grande. This one, known to her buddies as Mery Hernandez, is no Fefita, but she's less shaky than Maria Diaz can sometimes be, in the same effective and mellow style, with the mania being (in traditional fashion) provided by the saxist. — *John Storm Roberts*

Milly & Jocelyn & Los Vecinos

Ahora Es! / Musical Productions 6021
This band is tight and imaginative, melodies and arrangements fresh and punchy, Jocelyn is a fine singer. But they all pale beside Milly. The woman's a total wipe-out: an absolute killer, riffing and jamming like you wouldn't believe, like some kind of merengue Celia Cruz. Stunning, we tell you, stunning! — *John Storm Roberts*

7+1 = Vecinos / Musical Productions 6038
Milly comes out as if she's looking to bite somebody, but she's marginally mellower here than in previous albums, though consistently ebullient (and a lifestyle away from cutesy types like Las Chicas del Can, Belkis, or for that matter her sister Jocelyn). Aside from that, the usual originality in both vocal and instrumental arrangements. — *John Storm Roberts*

○ **14 Grandes Exitos** / Capitol 424862
It doesn't fool with any crossover elements (Debbie Gibson covers for example), just pushes ahead with an oomph higher and mightier than I would have believed possible. I listen to a lot of merengue; now I listen to 56 minutes more. — *Carl Hoyt, Original Music*

Wilfrido Vargas

La Musica / Sonotone 1406

Vargas goes from strength to strength, using success as license to experiment with uniformly musical results. Whether it's flavors of acoustic guitar and marimba or twisting the merengue two-four into a mock-pompous march, a moment of tenderness or a fit of jovial mayhem, he plays *e pluribus unum* in his latest album like only Willie Colon before him, though with very different results. —*John Storm Roberts*

○ **Wilfrido 86** / Karen 95
Vargas was the most creative head of '80s merengue, and in fact pretty much masterminded the entire merengue renaissance of the period. Virtually every Dominican band or singer of the '80s either started out with him or was encouraged by him. He had hit after hit, and used his popularity as license for experiments. A list of the external novelties—harmonica, highly original guitar licks, what sounds like harp (though none's credited), ditto harpsichord—no way does justice to the general air of jovially manic creativity. —*John Storm Roberts*

Johnny Ventura

○ **Y Su Combo** / Kubaney 117
With the rise of the merengue new-wave, Ventura, once the hippest of the salsa-merengueros, has become something of a Grand Old Man—an elder statesman à la Tito Puente. Here are the original versions of some of his greatest hits going back a couple of decades, including "El Pinguino," and "El Problema de Ramon." This stuff holds up. —*John Storm Roberts*

Angel Viloria

○ **Y Su Conjunto Cibaeno** / Ansonia 1206
This was the band that set off the first New York merengue craze, 20 years or more ago. The Cibao is merengue heartland, and this group had it all, including lots of the loopy C-melody sax that is a basic part of the sound (as well, of course, as great accordion and vocals, metal scraper, and tambora). —*John Storm Roberts*

Dominican Republic Collection

Bachatazos, Vol. 1 / Jose Luis 116
Bachata Rosa, though pretty enough, was basically the pop sound you'd expect from a big hit. The music in this first-of-its-kind compilation is the real bachata, the small-town guitar-based music that grew from Dominican backyard barbecues of the same name. It's mostly bolero-based, but its influences (other than local) are enormously varied: from classic trios to Mexican to Puerto Rican. Delicious. —*John Storm Roberts*

Ecuador

Karu Nan

Chimbaloma / Tumi 027
Ecuadorian music of any kind is rare on record, as is Andean music not by New Age-tinged PC middle-class bands with Quechua names. These guys are all peasants and craftsmen living in the village of Chimbaloma, and—polished though they are—they have real roots. —*John Storm Roberts, Original Music*

Mexico

Los Alegres De Teran

El Golpe Traidor / CBS Latino 20477
Here's a hugely popular norteno group. The basic sound here is the older duo/trio style, in which accordion and bajo sexto are underpinned by electric bass, but not traps. Unlike many of the Alegres' many recordings, the core unit is joined here by solo sax rather than mariachi trumpet, which gives this release a more downhome sound than some of the Alegres' recordings. —*John Storm Roberts, Original Music*

Triunfadores del Norte / CBS 20660
A hugely popular norteno group introduced to Anglos by Chris Strachwitz's reissues. As in most of the Alegres's many recordings, however, the core unit is joined on-and-off by mariachi backings. —*John Storm Roberts*

Lola Beltran

La Grande . . . / Peerless 0148
Lola Beltran has claims to be the greatest woman singer in the high-octane pop-ranchera style. The Beltran CD has a wide range of superb songs. Perhaps the finest is one, somewhat out of her main line, called "Pelea de Gallos"; there's also a "Caballo Blanco," which is worth comparing with Jimenez's original. —*John Storm Roberts*

Hermandos Vega

Esto Es Puro Norteno / Dos coronas 9403
Pure Norteno indeed: clean and crisp and classic, with punchy, mellow accordion and all the fixin's. Notably fine bass-player, too. The Brothers Vega recently took top honors at the Arizona Battle of the Norteno Bands. —*John Storm Roberts, Original Music*

Lydia Mendoza

Tex-Mex

La Gloria de Texas / Arhoolie 3012
Accompanied only by her 12-string guitar, "The Lark of the Border" strips down the high-octane Tex-Mex "country" sound into a strictly personal and greatly moving style. One of the most moving guitar-and-voice recording since Hank Williams' solo demo tapes. —*Carl Hoyt, Original Music*

Pregoneros del Puerto

Music of Veracruz / 1985 / Rounder
Here's entrancing, often ethereal songs from Los Pregoneros del Puerto, playing music from Veracruz. The most immediately striking characteristic is the harp playing of Gonzalo Mata. His strumming, swirling lines are punctuated by tremendous singing from Jose Gutierrez and equally effective harmonizing. Likewise, the guitar interplay and percussive support adds depth to the setting. While this isn't as rhythmic or percussive as other Latin music genres, it's got widespread harmonic and melodic appeal. The songs are short (none longer than three and a half minutes) but long enough and performed with enough vigor to get and hold your attention. —*Ron Wynn*

Sones Jarochos / 1990 / Rounder
A lovely record. The sones of the harp-led groups of Vera Cruz are a lot more complex than norteno music both rhythmically and in playing style, and arguably even more impassioned. Los Pregoneros del Puerto are an old-established professional group with a regional base, so they are both authentic and virtuoso, which is by no means always the case. Superb music; very full notes with lyrics and translations. Four stars at least. —*John Storm Roberts*

Lucha Reyes

Exitos / Bmgi 8526
I know nothing about Reyes except what I hear; a powerful ranchera singer with a fresh and natural style nearer to the grass-roots than most later singers. The original copyright of this collection is 1964 but she both sounds and looks earlier. I imagine she was, like most, a singer/filmstar, but both her singing and the instrumental backing date from a simpler time. —*John Storm Roberts*

Mexico Collection

Music from Mexico & Colombia / 1987 / Music of the World 113
Los Pregoneros del Puerto sing and play traditional Veracruz melodies using harp, jarana, and requinto. Side two presents Aires Colombianos who perform music from the mountains and plains of Columbia with vocals, string, and percussion instruments. Also featured are Mexican-American songs by the legendary Lydia Mendoza. —*Music of the World*

Fiestas of Chiapas & Oaxaca / Nonesuch 72070
An excellent selection ranging from church music to brass band, small string ensemble, solo singer, and guitar. David Lewiston must be highly commended for this brilliant recording. Now available on CD. —*David L. Mayers*

Music of the Tarascan Indians / Smithsonian/Folkways 4217

Some fine guitar and violin music, chirimias and flutes from one of the most musically interesting areas of Mexico. —*David L. Mayers*

Peru

Leandro Apaza

Peruvian Harp & Mandolin / 1984 / Music of the World 105
This selection of traditional Peruvian folk songs was recorded in the ancient Incan city of Cuzco. The artists (blind street-musicians) play 33-string harp and 10-string armadillo-shell mandolin, and they sing in Quechua and Spanish. These beautiful love songs and haunting melodies represent the strongest musical tradition in the Americas. —*Music of the World*

Huayno Music of Peru

Group / World fusion
Huayno is the popular music of the Indians from the Andean mountain regions of Peru. Many of these indigenous people have left their homes to find employment in Lima and other cities, bringing back a cross-fertilizing element of urban culture and music to their villages. —*Myles Boisen*

☆ **Huayno Music of Peru, Vol. 1** / Arhoolie 320
The popular huaynos of Peru go back hundreds of years and come in all sorts of forms, from village square to (relatively) bigtime pop. Part Spanish, part Indian, they are almost nothing like the better-known Latin forms in feeling or rhythm. As this superlative collection shows, the truly popular versions are almost hypnotically beguiling. Stunning. —*David L. Mayers*

Inti-Illimani

Group / Peruvian
A six-piece South American folk group with ethnic instrumentation. —*Michael G. Nastos*

○ **Imagination** / 1984 / Redwood 8505
Andean folkloric instrumental music; 14 tracks with the emphasis on joy and light. —*Michael G. Nastos*

Leyenda / Jan. 1990 / CBS 45948
Inti-Illimani's assortment of wind, string, and percussion instruments, in collaboration with the two master guitarists, has now yielded a world music recording that celebrates unity in diversity while managing to communicate the deep-rooted commitment to freedom and human rights at the core of Inti-Illimani's music. —*Backroads Music / Heartbeats*

De Canto Y Baile (Of Song and Dance) / Redwood 8901
The latest album by this venerable group of ambassadors of South American music is essentially a vocal album. Unlike *Imagination*, this is not a collection of lively pan-flute tunes, but of impassioned songs about life, love, and death, very much in the Nueva Cancion (New Song) tradition. —*Backroads Music / Heartbeats*

Palimpsesto / Redwood 3400
Also a good representation of their work. —*Michael G. Nastos*

Sukay

Group
Sukay specializes in Peruvian music of the Andes Mountains. Led by the Badoux's, musicologists from S.F., these are storytellers with romantic presence. —*Michael G. Nastos*

○ **Music of the Andes** / 1978 / Flying Fish 212
Traditional music of Peru, Argentina, Ecuador, and Bolivia. Music of wooden panflutes is most prevalent. Led by Edmond and Quentin Badoux, who play Peruvian traditional music. Beautiful. —*Michael G. Nastos*

Huayrasan / Flying Fish 70501
Huayrasan mixes lively instrumental pieces with impassioned songs sung primarily by a female member of the group. The tunes skate along to the swirling rhythms of charango, guitar, and mandolin, with melodies played on a variety of wooden flutes and panpipes. This is music to lift the spirits and bring joy to the soul, overflowing with the joie-de-vivre that makes this South American music so appealing —*Backroads Music / Heartbeats*

Mama Luna / Flying Fish 433

This one-woman two-man trio presents lovely Ecuadorian, Peruvian, and Bolivian music featuring notched bamboo flutes, pan pipes, and charangos or Andean guitars, with lead vocals by Quentin Howard (a woman). Some contemporary material with Spanish lyrics is included in addition to their trademark traditional instrumentals; so this, their fifth release, should appeal to an even broader audience. —*Ladyslipper*

Peru Collection

Flutes and Strings of the Andes / 1984 / Music of the World 106
An outstanding recording from an area almost entirely represented on record by imitators rather than source musicians. It casts a fairly wide net, with examples for voices, flutes, strings, and percussion from three provinces. Track by track, the music is marvelous, and the cassette is admirably programmed for diversity as well as authenticity. Good notes, too, for a cassette. —*John Storm Roberts*

Mountain Music of Peru, Vol. 1 / 1986 / Smithsonian/Folkways 40020
What makes a satisfactory national compilation is obviously to some extent a question of ideology. For my money, this one is superb as an overview and introduction. It ranges from shepherd pipe, solo voice, and carnival music, to popular huaynos from the towns. Unlike the plethora of middle-class groups with a political agenda that beclutter the field, this one does music that is real and superb, as are John Cohen's notes. Some were released in 1966, but 15 minutes' worth has been added for this re-release. (68:17) —*John Storm Roberts*

Paucartambo: Festival Music from the Central Andes / 1987 / Music of the World 109
The selections on *Paucartambo: Festival Music from the Central Andes* were recorded live at the festival of La Mamacha Carmen in Paucartambo, Peru. This fiesta is one of the most deeply rooted mestizo celebrations in the entire Andean region. Flutes, strings, accordions, brass, and percussion instruments are used, and several selections are sung in Quechua and Spanish. —*Music of the World*

Panama Collection

○ **Street Music of Panama** / 1988 / Original Music 8
Panamanian music is among the most exciting in the whole Afro-Latin area. On the Afro end are the voices-and-drums tamboritos, sung and played superbly here by groups of young women. The fiddle-and-percussion cumbia and guitar-backed mejorana are both real Creole idioms, whose Spanish and African elements are both crucial. Then there's the carnival music of the diablitos, and oddest of all, the howling gritos of the midnight hours. This is the real thing, taped before the tradition began to fade. It is also the only album devoted to this wonderful idiom, and capped by a charming piece of Choco Indian flute playing. —*John Storm Roberts*

Puerto Rico

Canario Y Sus Pleneros

Plenas / Ansonia 1232
The tremendous popularity of the plena (most typical rhythm of Puerto Rico) prompted Ansonia Records to produce this album, featuring 12 great plenas, interpreted by the Master of the Plena, Canario. Such favorites as "Cortaron a Elena," "Cuando Las Mujeres Quieren a Los Hombres," and "Santa Maria" are included in this gem of an album. —*Roundup Newsletter*

☆ **Canario Y Sus Pleneros** / Ansonia 1232
The plena is to Afro-Rican music what the calypso is to Trinidad—dance music, oral history, and Op-Ed page in song. Canario was perhaps the greatest composer of plenas ever, and this brand-new CD version of his only reasonably available recording contains many of his best-known recordings, among them "Cartaron a Elena" and the classic "Santa Maria." —*John Storm Roberts*

El Gran Combo

Piano, composer / Salsa

Led by Puerto Rican pianist-composer-arranger Rafael Ithier, which was the Rafael Cortijo y su Combo in 1959. Since the '70s El Combo has become a top seller and sells out performances. — *Max Salazar*

Boogaloos Con . . . / Gema 3044
This album comes from the band's very early days and is the genuine 1960s Real Thing. It also has a lot of straight salsa in its typical downhome sound, and Andy Montanez sang lead. —*John Storm Roberts*

○ **Nuestra Musica / 1971 / Combo 2045**
El Gran Combo is a perennial sellout on pure tight mainstream salsa alone—mainstream in the contemporary sense, which includes a lot of Puerto Rican tinge. Here they carry the Boricua sound especially far, with an album rich in plena, bomba, and even jibaro riffs and rhythms. They're also pretty funny guys: the jibaro-style "No Hay Cama Pa' Tanta Gente" rings a very cute change on the standard let's-mention-everybody. —*John Storm Roberts*

Latin-Up / 1973 / Combo 2070
The title cut of the band's newest release is a kind of a sort of a boogaloo in spots. As was and is customary, this album has a lot of straight salsa as is typical of the Combo's sound. Arranged by Rafael Ithier. —*John Storm Roberts*

○ **Mejor Que Nunca / 1976 / EGC**

Innovations / Cmo 2043
It's a more mainstream album, this—and therefore a good way to find out what's so special about these fellows. One thing is a tendency to surprising little touches like a sudden soprarno sax solo. But the most important ingredients are bedrock: a fine, flexible, individual singer in Charlie Aponte, intelligent leadership by Rafael Ithier. —*John Storm Roberts, Original Music*

Romantico . . . Sabroso / Cmo 2054
Here's more from one of the island's finest salsa groups. EGC, of course, is a little mellower, as befits an institution. —*John Storm Roberts*

Luis Miranda

Mi Musica Borincana / Ansonia 1626
Miranda's style and material are typical of the older generation. Quintero, a cuatro-player the equal of any, is wonderful on the album: he's at his best working within the constraints of backing a singer. Miranda, incidentally, provides a bonus in the form of a controversia—a theoretically improvised musical bicker using the ancient and complex decima form—with Joaquin Mouliert. — *John Storm Roberts*

Willie Rosario

b. May 6, 1930, Cuomo, Puerto Rico
percussion / Salsa
Arriving in New York City from Puerto Rico in 1948, Rosario was moved by Tito Puente's drumming ability at the Palladium Ballroom. He began his percussion studies and made his pro debut with Johnny Sequi's band in 1953. When Sequi moved to Puerto Rico, Rosario took over the band and today it is among the most popular salsa and Latin jazz aggregations in Latin America. —*Max Salazar*

Roaring Fifties / Sonotone Latino 2511
Percussionist Rosario moved back to Puerto Rico in the '70s, but he came up in NYC. He once told me his influences were the likes of Tito Rodriguez and Herbie Mann, not the Cubans. He also said, "I like clean music, music that has definition." Put those two elements together and you have a dynamite big-band sound: crisp, elegant, and driving. I'd call it timelessly classic, but this band plays as freshly as if they'd only just invented the sound! —*John Storm Roberts*

Eddie Santiago

○ **Atrevido Y Diferente / Thl 2424**
The biggest name in the newish salsa-romantica vein, which combines lushness and swing. This was Santiago's first real smash—something like a year in the Top Three!—and in retrospect it was, I think, his best recording. Part of his effect comes from a tendency to move more readily than traditional salsa singers from a low register to a fine, clear high one—a simple but effective way of gaining emotional clout. Almost as important was a dynamite

Latin American Terms

Berimbau – Originally an African instrument brought to Brazil, this bow-shaped instrument has one steel string and a gourd resonator.

Bossa nova – Syncopated Brazilian dance music that developed out of a mixture of samba and cool jazz from the late 50s and early 60s.

Charanga – A delicately fiery Cuban ensemble featuring violins, solo flute, timbales, piano, and unison singing. The cha cha cha originated from a charanga group.

Conjunto – A small group, itrumpet-led in Cuban music and accordion-led in Mexico. It additionally features vocals, piano, bass, conga, and bongos.

Cuatro – Puerto Rican ten-stringed guitar used in "jibaro" music.

Cumbia – An accordion-led "vallenato" style combining Andean Indian, African, and European elements. Hugely popular in Colombia.

Danzón – An older Cuban ballroom-dance style played by charanga orchestras.

Forró – Down-to-earth, jaunty music of Northeastern Brazil, comprising accordions, triangles, and a shallow drum called a zabumba.

Güiro – A percussion instrument, it is shaped like a gourd, has carved ridges, and is scraped with a stick.

Jíbaro music – Puerto Rican mountain music featuring guitar, cuatro, maracas, guiro, and voice. Its beginnings are found in Spanish-derived traditions of verse.

Lambada – Extremely popular in Europe in 1989, this close dance is done to Afro-Brazilian-Caribbean rhythms.

Mambo – Hugely popular Cuban big-band music that swept the US in the 50s. Also the name of the instrumental section in contemporary salsa.

Merengue – The "national" music of the Dominican Republic. Played with a tambora drum and güiro in both accordion-led and big-band styles.

Méringue – An older Haitian dance rhythm, related to the Dominican rhythm.

MPB – An acronym for Musica Popular Brasileira, it is a common term for a recent, text-oriented Brazilian popular music (of Milton Nascimento and others), which followed the bossa-nova.

Partido alto – A form of the samba featuring a slow tempo.

Plena – Puerto Rican street music lyrically similar to Trinidadian calypso and played on panderetas (hand-held frame drums), güiro, harmonica, and accordion.

Rumba – A US misnomer for the son, which became an international dance craze in the 30s. Afro-Cuban percussion music with various offshoots.

band, crisp and tight, with a particularly fine pianist. —*John Storm Roberts*

Sigo Atrevido / TH-Rodven 2497

Here's the king of salsa romantica, the 1980s blend of salsa-and-sentiment that is giving this Miami-based company such a long lease on the top of the charts. —*John Storm Roberts, Original Music*

La Sonora Ponceña

Group / Salsa

One of Puerto Rico's most popular orchestras, which was founded by Quique Lucca in 1954 in Ponce, Puerto Rico. La Ponceña is directed by Lucca's son, the brilliant composer, arranger, and keyboardist, Papo, born in 1950. Papo Lucca's career started in 1964 when he became the band's pianist. At the moment, La Ponceña is among the top five salsa and Latin jazz bands in Latin music. —*Max Salazar*

○ **Into the '90s** / Inca 1085
Sonora Ponceña, always a tight, fresh avant-mainstream group, has arguably become one of the great bands. With this recent release they're adding things around the edges—an effective touch of soul, an entirely out-of-idiom piano intro, a gravely beautiful bowed-bass break, and all sorts of other unexpected doings. All of which makes the title a little more substantial than such slogans usually are. —*John Storm Roberts*

On the Right Track / Inca 1084
Sonora Ponceña is one of the best bands around—and not just in Puerto Rico, though that's where it's based. With the possible exception of pianist Papo Lucca, these aren't names—just a very tight, fresh group with the ability to make a tradition-based sound brand new. Listen to the sudden trumpet duet in "Odiame" and rejoice! —*John Storm Roberts*

Edwin Colon Zayas

Bien Jibaro / Rounder 5056
We're talking major discovery here. Zayas is a cuatro player the equal of the better-recorded greats—Yomo Toro, Tonito Ferrer and Nieves Quintero—echoes of all of whom occasionally resonate in his playing. He backs Arturo Santiago, Jr., an award-winning trovador, in mountain seises and other forms including the decorously charming old Puerto Rican danza. —*John Storm Roberts, Original Music*

Puerto Rico Collection

Puerto Rico in Polynesia / Original Music 020
Hawaii's Puerto Rican plantation laborers not only preserved their own traditions but also picked up songs from their fellow-workers with wonderful cross-over effect. The usual great Jibaro cuatro-picking, craggy accordion, rootsy aguinaldos, elegant old-style danzas and the like are joined by unique—and splendid—Japanese, Hawaiian, and Filipino, Puerto-Rican blends. —*John Storm Roberts, Original Music*

○ **Music of Puerto Rico 1929-1946** / Harlequin 2075
A very fine set of recordings, mostly string groups, mostly from the mid '30s. Many of them are by New York-Puerto Rican groups in the fashionable Cuban idioms of the time—boleros, sones, and so forth—by major composers like Pedro Berrios and Rafael Hernandez. These have a lot of charm, but the gems are a handful of truly Puerto Rican forms: seises, aguinaldos, and plenas. A major bonus is a two-clarinet-lead danza. The only bummer: the greatest of all early pleneros, Canario, appears just once, playing a commercial bolero! —*John Storm Roberts*

United States

Bad Street Boys

○ **Looking for Trouble** / JAP 708
The most interesting group to come out of Latin New York's English-language salsa substyle for decades—a joyous early '80s update of the boogaloo traditions, trombones, chutzpah, and all. Who could resist a group that moves from urbane rap through "The Lady Is a Tramp" to "When Sunny Gets Blue" done boogaloo? —*John Storm Roberts*

Batacumbele

Group / New York salsa
A hot Afro-Cuban outfit that rivals any today. —*Michael G. Nastos*

Con Un Poco De Songo / 1981 / Disco Hit 008
A recording by one of the most adventurous, interesting, and—more simply—best bands extant. The story is told by the instrumentation, which includes one trumpet, baritone sax, flute, clarinet, bata drums, and cuatro. Which translates into a sound drawing from a very wide range of traditions, mixing charanga and conjunto and the rest in a more varied way than the standard orquesta sound. —*John Storm Roberts*

★ **In Concert Live at the University of Puerto Rico** / 1988 / Montuno 526-527

This is hot and heavy Latin/Afro/Cuban music from this stellar 20-plus-piece band. Mostly includes traditional themes extended with improvisation. This is one you cannot live without. — *Michael G. Nastos*

Ruben Blades

b. Jul. 16, 1948, Panama City, Panama
Vocals / Salsa, New York salsa, Latin soul
The Panamanian-born Blades is one of salsa's leading artists and the first to incorporate rock consistently into his boiling sound. He has remained a prominent voice of leftist Latino politics through his topical songwriting and his active/activist role in Panama's political system. —*John Floyd*

Bohemio Y Poeta / 1979 / Fania 541
This release was a transition between Blades's post-Willie Colon sound and the '80s *Seis del Solar*. The salsa sounds predominate much of the time, and there's a Cuban classic in among his own compositions. But keyboards and vibes (presumably from Louie Ramirez, who did some of the arranging) point to a new dispensation in the offing, with their (here, at least, very successful) fusion edge. —*John Storm Roberts*

○ **Buscando America** / 1984 / Elektra 60352
A masterful concept album (the title means "searching for America") that spins hard-hitting tales of Latino strife and American injustice. This album includes some of his most gorgeous ballads. —*John Floyd*

Escenas / 1985 / Elektra 60432
There's a lot going on here, aside from Blades's agreeable duet with Linda Ronstadt and the Joe Jackson solo, which got the press. Besides, pianist Ricardo Marrero has long been on our "most-underrated" list. —*John Storm Roberts, Original Music*

Crossover Dreams / 1986 / Elektra 60470
An album of salsa music prominently featuring the work of Ruben Blades, who also starred in the 1985 film. —*William Ruhlmann*

○ **Agua De Luna** / 1987 / Elektra 60721

○ **Nothing But the Truth** / 1988 / Elektra 60754
Blades' first album in English. . . . While by no means excising Latin rhythms from his music, Blades has made a point of adding a host of other forms: reggae, pop, power guitar rock, light jazz. "Ollie's Doo-Wop" explains itself. — *Susan Korones, Rock & Roll Disc*

Amor Y Control / 1992 / Discos Cbs International 80839
Ruben Blades, the Panamanian actor/writer/singer, weighs in here with an impressive collection of affecting, humanistic, and black-humored songs in Spanish.—*Alanna Nash, Stereo Review*

Antecedente / Elektra 60795
Although sung in his native tongue, his return to exuberant, dance-oriented salsa breaks through all language barriers. —*John Floyd*

☆ **Ruben Blades Y Son del Solar . . . Live!** / Elektra 60868
A smoldering set, recorded live with his 11-piece band, Son del Solar, who romp and stomp for over an hour. Perfect for parties. —*John Floyd*

Carabali

Salsa

Carabali / 1981 / Mango 9888
A super young band working in the great vibes-led Latin-jazz-inflected quintet sound of the '50s and early '60s! You've heard Cal Tjader and, I hope, stopped sneering at George Shearing. But the great groups in this vein—the TNT Band and the like, even Joe Cuba, were filled with New York Latinos and cut much closer to the salsa bone. Carabali has the whole thing down pat, including the change-of-pace English language songs and terrific vibist Valerie Naranjo working off Oscar Hernandez's piano just like the hippest of mellow old times. Joy cometh in the morning . . . —*John Storm Roberts*

Milton Cardona

○ **Bembe** / 1985 / American Clave/Pangaea 1004
Cardona, one of New York salsa's finest percussionists, is an initiate in the lucumi faith that traveled from West Africa to the New World. This New York recording of the songs for various orisha is

part of a widespread religious practice whose local differences are mostly superficial. (Worth comparing with the Afro-Cuban anthology issued by Areito.) —*John Storm Roberts*

Willy Chirino

Salsa

○ **Acuarela Del Caribe** / Sony Discos 80228
Like his great *Zarabanda* album, Chirino's new one superbly exploits the riches of the Miami sound, which stem from a true verbal and musical bilingualism. The opener is just staggering: a kind of mad medley veering between tipico and rock; between (literally) Sergeant Pepper and "Purple Haze" and "Son de la Loma." —*John Storm Roberts*

14 Exitos / Thl 151
Chirino is a leader of the Miami-Latin sound, which draws from disco and other Anglo forms, Cuban music, and New York salsa. Alas, his best-ever song "San Zarabanda" isn't included. But it's good to see a break in the usual neglect of this creative and individualistic Florida idiom. —*John Storm Roberts*

Willie Colon

b. Apr. 28, 1950, Bronx, NY.
Vocals / Salsa, New York salsa, Latin soul, Latin jazz
Born to Puerto Rican parents, Colon began music studies in 1964 while he directed his group. He signed with Fania Records in 1967 and immediately established his name with the tracks "Jazzy" and "I Wish I Had a Watermelon." Colon is idolized outside the US. He's a cultural hero in Latin America. He improves with every recording. —*Max Salazar*

Guisando / 1969 / Fania 370
Colon's third album with, for trivia buffs, his second-favorite cover. Colon was 20 at the time, and this is still the funky, riotous, sometimes mildly ragged and chaotic sound of his early days. The hallmarks are exuberance, humor, innovation, lots of Colon compositions and, as a bonus, the fine piano of the band's African-American pianist, Mark Diamond. —*John Storm Roberts*

★ **The Good, The Bad, The Ugly** / 1975 / Fania 484
A classic recording by one of the most creative heads in New York salsa. In 1975 *The Good...*, a New Directions release after Colon got fed up with the two-trombone sound, was the evidence that he could reach beyond his youthful sound into an idiom both wider and deeper. It was also the last album with Hector Lavoe, who had decided to stay with being a teen idol. *The Big Break, Asalto Navideno*, and this album in their different ways were pinnacles of early to mid '70s salsa. —*John Storm Roberts*

Canciones Del Solar De Los Aburridos / 1983 / Fania
The Colon/Blades partnership produced the tightest combinations of musical creativity and lyrical intensity in recent salsa. This 1981 album is among their finest: ominous harmonies, meaningful lyrics, tradition shot with experimentation: constant surprise and constant pleasure. —*John Storm Roberts*

Asalto Navideno / Fania 449
A groundbreaking early '70s recording, *Asalto Navideno* was a Christmas album, and Christmas is the time when the old jibaro mountain sound comes briefly into its own. Colon hired cuatro player Yomo Toro and gave him a leading role, launching him on a new career. A major album, which includes one of Colon's finest Panamanian-flavored early hits, "La Murga." —*John Storm Roberts*

Especial No. 5 / Sonotone Latino 100
One half of this album was recorded in Colombia, the other in New York. Neither is Colon at his best, in our view, but for the record (tee-hee) here it is. —*John Storm Roberts*

○ **Metiendo Mano** / Fania 500
Salsa history in the making: the album in which Willie Colon introduced Ruben Blades to the wider world! An obvious classic, given Blades's subsequent history, but also a gorgeous album with Yomo Toro on two tracks (one playing guitar), the great pianist Sonny Bravo on two cuts, and ace percussion with Milton Cardona and Nicky Marrero. —*John Storm Roberts*

☆ **The Big Break/La Gran Fuga** / Fania 394
Colon's third album and clearest early sign of his individuality, with a Ghanaian children's song, the first of his Panamanian-influenced numbers, and a prophetic venture into Brazilian rhythms. —*John Storm Roberts*

Tiempo Pa' Matar / Fania 631
Colon, one of the most creative heads of the '60s, has retained the same restlessness and inquiring mind, and the same ability to come up with music both beguiling and intelligent. (Check out the use of the female *coro* in "Volo" on this album.) Fine vocals, fine musicians, and who would dare claim to spot all the stylistic sideglances under the surface of this subtle and enchanting album? —*John Storm Roberts*

○ **El Malo** / Fania 337
El Malo was Colon and Hector Lavoe's first-ever recording, made in 1967 when Colon was a mere 17 years old. Every number's a killer: "Jazzy," "Juana Pena," "Borinquen," "El Malo." *Plus* boogaloo! —*Carl Hoyt, Original Music*

Joe Cuba (Gilberto Calderon)

b. Apr. 22, 1931, New York, NY
Group / New York salsa
Cuba's music career started with La Alfarona X in 1950. In 1955 the Joe Cuba Sextet came into being and his vibraharp sound caught on. In 1962, when the group recorded "To Be With You" for Seeco Records, the band began to soar to popularity because of Nick Jimenez's arrangements and the vocals of Cheo Feliciano and Jimmy Sabater. When the boogaloo era arrived, the majority of the popular New York bands were put out of work. The Cuba sound changed with its recordings of "El Pito" and "Bang Bang"; it not only sold millions but enabled the Cuba sextet to enjoy the #1 spot in the Latin music world along with the Eddie Palmieri Orchestra. —*Max Salazar*

○ **Joe Cuba Sextet** / Tico 1133
The '50s/'60s cusp saw a last flowering of the bilingual, Cubop-inflected, often vibraphone-led quintet sound. Puente was one of its heavies, but in New York at least, the tradition was maintained into the pachanga and even boogaloo era of the '60s by Joe Cuba. Jaunty mambo, soupy English-lyric boleros, Latin-jazz or neotipico; this was an archetypal Latin New York sound. —*John Storm Roberts*

Henry Fiol

○ **Sonero** / 1983 / Earthworks 1019
In the mid '80s Fiol recorded on his own Corazon label some of the most consistently elegant recordings in Cuban-tipico vein. As this British compilation from Corazon shows, he's a terrific singer, light and throwaway for a sonero. And his band's mix of classic elements with versatile tenor sax punctuations works a treat. Elegant is the word; alas, too short are two more equally valid ones. —*John Storm Roberts*

HMA Salsa

California Salsa II / Dos Coronas 9405
A big band like the classic mambo groups, with three lead singers. Justo Almerio, Alex Acuna, and Poncho Sanchez guest-star, but the other folks are just dynamite musicians. The arrangements are swirling, rich and brassy, and the solos range from blow-you-down to stunning. —*John Storm Roberts, Original Music*

Noro Morales

b. Jan. 4, 1911, Puerto de Tierra, Puerto Rico, d. Jan. 16, 1964
New York salsa
Morales was in New York in 1935, played briefly with the bands of Alberto Socarras and Augusto Coen before establishing the Brothers Morales (Noro-Humberto-Esy) orchestra in 1939. The 1942 Decca 78 "Serenata Ritmica" gave Morales instant recognition. During the decade of the '40s his and Machito's bands were the most popular in NYC. —*Max Salazar*

○ **His Piano and Rhythm** / Ansonia 1272
The fabulous Noro Morales has long been idolized by a faithful multitude of music lovers. His distinctive arrangements and unique style have earned him a reputation to be envied by his fellow musicians. He has appeared in Europe, throughout the United States and Puerto Rico, and for many years conducted his orchestra at the annual Harvest Moon Ball. He is also a gifted composer. "Vitamina" and "Mi Guajira" are hits. —*Roundup Newsletter*

Manny Oquendo (Manyy Oquendo Y Libre)

b. Jan. 1, 1931, New York, NY
Percussion / Salsa

He began percussion studes in 1945 and gained drumming experience with the bands of Carlos Valero, Luis del Campo, Juan "El Boy" Torres, Jose Budet, Juanito Sanabria, Marcelino Guerra, Jose Curbelo, and Pupi Campo before becoming Tito Puente's Bongo player in 1950. Four years later Oquendo was with Tito Rodriquez and with Vicentico Valdes in 1955. For the following six years, Oqundo freelanced and recorded for New York's top bands. In 1962 he settled with the Eddie Palmieri orchestra. Before 1974 ended, Oquendo's Conjunto Libre came into being. Oquendo gained world-wide recognition in 1983 with his recording of "Little Sunflower," considered the best recording of the year. —*Max Salazar*

Con Salsa & Con Ritmo / 1976 / Salsoul

Incredible / 1981 / Salsoul

Ritmo, Sonido, Estillo (Little Sunflower, Montuno) / 1983 /

Johnny Pacheco

b. Mar. 25, 1935, Santiago de los Caballeros, Domincan Republic
Sax, percussion, flute / Salsa

Relocated to New York during the late 1940s. In high school he learned to play sax, percussion and flute. In September, 1959, he left Charlie Palmieri's flute and strings orchestra to organize his own. With his first recording, *Pacheco y su Charanga*, released by Alegre Records in 1961, three tracks, "Oyeme Mulata," "El Guiro de Macorina," and "Que le Pasa a mi Mama," changed the sound of music throughout Latin America and ushered in the "Pachanga" (a strenous dance) era, which faded out in 1964. Pacheco and attorney Gerald Masucci founded the Fania label in 1964 and with its first album, LP #325 (Pacheco's birthdate) kicked off the yet unborn salsa era in New York City. —*Max Salazar*

Que Suene la Flauta / 1962 / Alegre
Pacheco's first avatar was as a flutist, first with Charlie Palmieri's groundbreaking 1959 charanga, then—until he switched to conjunto in 1964—with his own flute-and-fiddles group. Though the band followed Cuban models (far too closely, some Cuban musicians grumbled), his own style was very distinctive, tougher, and less flowing than his Cuban rivals, and his wildly successful band benefited also from a very fine singer in Elliot Romero. "Alto Songo," from this album, was one of his personal classics. —*John Storm Roberts*

Compadres / Fania 00400
The early '70s *Compadres* was one of the finest of all Cuban-derived New York tipico salsa recordings. Even then, Conde was one of the great soneros of the Big Manzana, and Pacheco already knew all there was to know about getting the last snap, crackle, and pop out of a conjunto. This was one of the band's great moments. —*John Storm Roberts*

Early Rhythms / Mpl 3162
This had me floored. I know all Pacheco's groups, and he never ran a mambo-type big band. Yet here he is, fluting away like Johnny-Begone in front of full brass and sax sections. This is Pacheco freelancing, in about 1962, with what was essentially Machito's band. It's an unusual disc, with fine flute, and great Rene Hernandez arrangements. —*John Storm Roberts, Original Music*

Charlie Palmieri

b. 1927, New York, NY, d. 1988
Piano / New York salsa, Latin jazz

Palmieri began piano studies at six, was sitting in with bands at dances at 14, and was a full-time musician at 16. He formed his group, El Conjunto Pin Pin, in 1948. He played piano for Pupi Campo, Tito Puente, Tito Rodriguez, Bicentico Valdes, and Pete Terrace before forming his Charanga Dubonney group in 1958. —*Max Salazar*

● A Giant Step / 1988 / Tropical Budda

Impulsos / Mpl 3118
The late Charlie P. was a greater pianist than his brother, as deeply musical, as universally loved, and with far more sense. He picked musicians by talent not fame, and they blew their hearts out for him. This mid '70s session has the swing, as hot as EPs but more benign; the jazz solos and tipico ensembles. Our loss is heaven's gain. —*John Storm Roberts*

○ Adelante Gigante / Alegre 7013
Eddie Palmieri always said his elder brother was the better player, and by the time of his death, Charlie Palmieri was well enough known outside the barrio to get an obituary in the *New York Times*. This classic mid '70s album has all his usual taste, talent, classic piano (and in a couple of places organ) along with his favorite lead singer, Vitin Aviles, and a tight band. —*John Storm Roberts*

Lou Perez

b. Jun. 21, 1928, New York, NY
Composer / Salsa

Born to Puerto Rican and Cuban parents. Perez is a most underrated musician in that very few people know of his musical genious. He's a composer and cracker-jack arranger who began studying music in 1945. He has recorded 15 albums, all for dancers only. What makes Perez special is his rich imagination, which is evident in three outstanding LPs. Movie star Patrick Swayze became a star after dancing to Perez's De Todo un Poco in the box office hit *Dirty Dancing*. A Lou Perez album is a collector's item. —*Max Salazar*

Para la Fiesta Me Voy / Recomar 3361
When the charanga sound first hit New York in 1959, one of the earliest and finest groups to form was launched by pianist Lou Perez. This album became an instant hit and has remained as an underground classic, little known but highly prized by the aficionados. It's a reminder of just what a fine mix was produced by Cuban delicacy and NYC drive at their best. —*John Storm Roberts*

Rudy Regalado

La Gloria / Dos Coronas 9407
More very successful eclecticism. Venezuelan-born Regalado builds strongly on New-York-style big-band salsa, adding rather more jazz horn, a touch or more of crisped-up salsa romantica, a nicely judged balladry, a cut blending chachacha and bembe, a pleasant rap number. Several singers, including an admirable woman vocalist: Thania Sanchez. —*John Storm Roberts, Original Music*

Mon Rivera

○ Karakatis-ki / Ansonia 1356
Rivera was probably the true originator of the trombone conjunto sound associated with early Eddie Palmieri and Willie Colon. But he was also an important figure in the period when Puerto Rican influences in general and the plena and bomba in particular were at their peak in New York salsa. And most basically he was a fine (and at times comic) singer with a smoking band. —*John Storm Roberts*

Tito Rodriguez

b. Jan. 4, 1923, San Juan, Puerto Rico, d. Feb. 28, 1972, New York, NY
Vocals / New York salsa

Rodriguez came to New York in 1939, where he sang with the orchestras of his brother Johnny Rodriguez, Enric Madriguera, Caney, Xavier Cugat, Noro Morales, and Jose Curbelo. Rodriguez formed a quintet in 1947 and enlarged it in 1948 to a trumpet conjunto. In 1963 his recording of "Inolvidable" in Argentina sold 1,500,000 copies throughout Latin America. —*Max Salazar*

○ Un Retrato de . . . / TR 120
The great TR was, of course, part of the New York mambo troika of which Puente and Machito were the other members. A fine singer of both mambo and romantic material, he ran a band as fiery as any. Here are "Mama Guela" and "Yambu" in the former vein, and the monster hit "Cuando Cuando" in the latter, as well as much more. A major re-release. —*John Storm Roberts*

○ Uptempo / Tico 1427
An interesting cut-out of relatively unfamiliar Rodriguez mambos, cha-cha-chas, and such, including his version of "El Manicero." Rodriguez was a major heart-throb, and his albums always had plenty of schmaltz. Not being into big-band bolero, which seems to me a major waste of a rhythm section, I'm happy to have the hotter stuff unsullied. —*John Storm Roberts*

Candi Sosa

Cuba . . . Mi Corazon Te llama / Dos Coronas 9402
The bicultural Miami sound moves from salsa to Anglo-mellow balladry to funk in one record, one cut or one chorus. Now here's an L.A. version, solidly enough based in Cubanismo to sound like adventurousness and not just rootlessness. Nifty in the details, too: the pop-jazz-ballad "Caribbean Blue" is given a delicate tang by a gentle finger-piano undertone. —*John Storm Roberts, Original Music*

United States Collection

○ **Caliente—Hot** / 1977 / New World 244
Five fine NYC roots groups re-create classic idioms from Afro-Cuban drumming through plena to the pure conjunto and sones sound: the Pleneros de la 110th Street, Julito Collazo, Hector Rivera y Su Conjunto, Sexteto Criollo Puertorriqueno, and the Sepeto Son de la Loma. —*John Storm Roberts*

○ **Sixties Gold** / Musica Latina 53
The Gran Manzana of the '60s, the era of the boogaloo and Latin soul, was an enormously creative and rackety time. This was the era of East Harlem Black-Latin crossover. It brought forth names still famous—Barretto, Pacheco, Colon—and names forgotten—Pagan, Bataan, Colon. (Buy the record! Educate yourself!) Here are Ray's original "El Watusi," Joe Cuba's "Bang Bang," Mongo's "Watermelon Man," and a dozen other pearls of musical mayhem in a purely neoyorquino style the looming tipico revolution was about to kill stone dead, to the great loss of the scene. —*John Storm Roberts*

○ **Salsa Greats, Vol. 2** / Fania 524
This fine compilation dates back to 1978, but most of it not only stands up but is still jumping. Present, and more than correct, are classics like Eddie Palmieri's great "Azucar," Puente's "Para los Rumberos," Barretto's "Mirame de Frente," Larry Harlow's "Aresnio," Willie Colon's "Che Che Cole," and less familiar numbers by Pacheco, Roberto Roena, Ricardo Ray, Bobby Valentin, and the Sonora Poncera. —*John Storm Roberts*

Venezuela

Billo & His Caracas Boys

Viejo Pero Sabroso / Discolando 8468
Despite all the competition from Cuban and US bands, Billo and the lads were popular well beyond the borders of Venezuela in the '60s and '70s. The sound was mainstream mambo-era big band but with the variations you might expect from a South American group, particularly but not only in the group's excursions into cumbia. —*John Storm Roberts*

Julio Jaramillo

Sentimental de America / Fonodisco 10
Jaramillo was a fine singer in the elegant older Venezuelan vein, whose backings included harp, guitar, and occasional fiddles and/or accordion. This was a style that, while definitely pop rather than traditional, owed little or nothing to any outside source (with the notable and obvious exception of the Argentine tango). —*John Storm Roberts*

Coleccion de Pasillos / Discolando 8278
A mid '70s recording. This is elegant, delicate, charming, and very Venezuelan singing with guitar-led backings (bass, a touch of harp) to match. Jaramillo had an international name at times, but this is far more local than the pan-Latin trio music of groups like Los Panchos. It would be nice to see this kind of classic sound rediscovered. —*John Storm Roberts*

Pastor Lopez

En Mexico / Discolando 8537
Lopez became a big-time exponent on the heartthrob end of contemporary cumbia, but he started real rootsy. The band here has horns along with its accordion, but this is still a great small-town sound, and Lopez himself is super. —*John Storm Roberts*

Maria Rodriguez

Tremenda, La / World Circuit 001
Rodriguez came out of the Venezuelan street comparsa, became a Cuban-style pop singer in the '40s, and then went home to teach and sing the traditional comparsas and joropos. On this admirable first album by a new British label she is backed by a classic quartet of mandolin, cuatro, guitar, and maraccas, and a few more beautiful sounds. —*John Storm Roberts*

Venezuela Collection

Folk Music from Venezuela / Reportage 18101
Side 1 of this cassette is devoted to a semi-pro revivalist—or at least preservationist group, which performs fulias and other forms from all over Venezuela in a pretty authentic style. Side 2 is given over to field recordings of all three types of Venezuelan music—Euro-Venezuelan, Afro-Venezuelan, and Indian. Particularly fine is some of the drumming, but the string groups playing for joropos are also a rarity. Outstanding notes, for a cassette. —*John Storm Roberts*

○ **Grandes del Cuatro, Los** / Leon 1131
A tremendous recording of a little-known member of the American guitar family, the four-string Venezuelan cuatro, fronting five small guitar-and-percussion combos in a variety of styles: mainly Venezuelan folkloric, but including the occasional bossa and jazz number. The playing is even more manically virtuosic than flamenco, echoes of which surface here. Andean touches are also prevalent. —*Carl Hoyt, Original Music*

○ **Music of Venezuela** / Zu-Zazz 2018
A very fine set of recent recordings by amateur and semi-professional groups, with a focus on stringed instruments—violin as well as members of the huge family of Latin guitars and mandolins. Many of the styles included are available on commercial recordings, but not on the whole in such grassroots idioms, nor with such excellent notes. This album is also available in the US on the High Water label. —*John Storm Roberts & Myles Boisen*

MIDDLE EAST

Middle East Collection

☆ **Holy Quran: Surat Yusuf** / Oriental 101
Orthodox Islam has always viewed music with ambivalence, if not downright disapproval. Yet the recitation of the Holy Koran and the call to prayer form the aesthetic bedrock of all the music of the Islamic world. The late Sheikh Mahmoud Khalil El Houssary, a former head of the Al Azhar Mosque in Cairo, here recites Surat Yusuf, the Koranic story of Joseph (no coat of many colors, but the pit and the fat and lean king are there). —*John Storm Roberts*

Jewish Music / Philips 6586 00 1
Religious chants from the Mediterranean-Middle Eastern area from Gibraltar and Morocco to Turkey and Yemen. —*David L. Mayers*

Sung Poetry / Auvidis 8025
In most cultures the distinction between recitation and song, poem and lyric, is not nearly as distinct as in the West. Many great poems of the Middle East are still sung, and cantatas or song-cycles with particular structures are the backbone of the Andalus classical tradition, whether in Syria or the Maghreb. The examples here are in Turkish, Farsi, and Arabic. —*David L. Mayers*

Azerbaijan

Haji Baba Huseynov

Maqam of Azerbaijan / Inedit 260026
One cultural benefit of recent events is that the former Soviet Middle East is no longer an inaccessible mystery land. This means, for example, that Azeri classical music can reclaim its position as a major tradition within the Persian-Turkish-Arabic nexus. A fine recording by leading exponents of vocal style, tar

lute, and kemantche fiddle. Splendid music; informative notes. — *John Storm Roberts*

Alem Kassimov

Two Mugam / Inedit 260015
Azeri art music is one of the lesser known of major idioms within the Mideastern/Islamic tradition. Of the two mugam (loosely, modes) for tar lute, spike fiddle, and daf frame drum performed here, the 51-minute "Mugam rast" is overwhelmingly the major work with its 19 vocal and instrumental sections. Excellent performance; fine recording; passable notes. (61:58) —*John Storm Roberts*

Azerbaijan Mugams / Melodiya C30 24023
Although it is a Soviet republic, the music of Azerbaijan has a strong Middle Eastern sound related to neighboring Turkey and Iran. This album presents the trememdously powerful and acrobatic singer Alim Gasymov in front of a traditional three-piece ensemble, doing two side-long "mugam" suites. Highly recommended. —*Myles Boisen, Roots & Rhythm*

Azerbaijan Collection

Land of Flames / Pan 2012
A fine recording of Azerbaijani music, which is nearer to Iranian than anything else. The instrumentation here is tar lute, kamancha fiddle, and def percussion. The performers are all fairly young and apparently at the height of their powers. The music includes a substantial dastagah, a couple of shorter vocal pieces and two fine solo mugam, one for tar and the other for kamancha. Wonderful music, good notes. —*John Storm Roberts, Original Music*

○ **Azerbaijan—Traditional Music** / 1991 / Chant du Monde 274901
A great collection that details the wonders of musical cross-pollination. —*Myles Boisen, Roots & Rhythm*

Egypt

Mohamed Abdel Wahab

Vocals

As singer and as influence on Egyptian music during its renaissance, Abdel Wahab was equaled only by Umm Kulthum. But while she was a traditionalist to the core, Abdel Wahab believed in learning from Western music. Yet he too was a musical nationalist, renewing rather than diluting Egyptian tradition. Starting from a highly traditional sound as a teenager, he gradually moved into a highly varied (and internationally popular) film-based repertoire. But besides contributing to the pop world, he introduced more fundamental elements, such as long instrumental passages, a major element in his work. —*John Storm Roberts*

Vol. 1 (1920-1925) / 1970 / Artistes Arabes 011
This set of Wahab's earliest recordings is an event of supreme importance. It's also superb—and as a double bonus, it has fine notes (translated into English) by a man who knew him most of his artistic life. Major, major stuff. —*John Storm Roberts*

○ **Vol. 10 (1939)** / 1971 / Artistes Arabes 021
The most recent in this ongoing series dedicated to Egypt's greatest 20th-century singer/composer. Consists of music from a film, *Youm Said*. Whether or not it was his first, I have no idea. But both Abdel Wahab's singing and the accompaniments (despite a little accordion and piano here and there) were mostly far more traditional than his later movies. A significant transition period. —*John Storm Roberts*

Cleopatra / 1991 / Soutelphan 501
Abdel Wahab and Umm Kulthum, king and queen of 20th-century Egyptian music, also epitomized opposing approaches. While Kulthum was traditionalist to the core, Abdel Wahab believed in learning from Western music. Yet he too (as this mid-period recording shows) was nothing if not a musical nationalist, using new ideas and practices to refresh rather than to dilute ancient tradition. —*John Storm Roberts*

Mohamed Abdel Wahab A'habib Al-Uaghoul / Cairophon 604

This second of two classic recordings, done a quarter-century after its predecessor, shows Abdel Wahab's consistent development of long instrumental passages, a major element in his work, as well as the splendid singing of his maturity. —*John Storm Roberts, Original Music*

Amina

Dance

○ **Yalil** / 1989 / Mango 162-539892
Egyptian motifs tangle with hot Parisian production styles in the service of pouty-voiced diva Amina, who knows the power of sexy exotica over the feet of continental clubgoers. An intriguing experiment in widening North African pop. —*Bob Tarte*

Asmahan

Early Recordings / Club du Disque Arabe 865
Like Leila Mourad, Asmahan was a star of musical films in the '30s and '40s, and her later recordings were tugged back and forth between nationalism and internationalism. But in her early days (from which these splendid recordings date) she worked brilliantly within the tradition-based mainstream of her time, usually with small ensembles of local wind and string instruments. —*John Storm Roberts, Original Music*

☆ **Asmahan & Farid** / 1970 / Baidaphon 601
Farid al Atrache is one of the great names in 20th-century Egyptian popular music. Asmahan had one of the greatest voices of '30s and '40s pop. Both were stars of Egypt's musical cinema. This set of their '40s hits charmingly recalls an era of experiment and eccentricity. —*John Storm Roberts*

Aleik Salat Allah / 1980 / Artistes Arabes 004
This recording—which atypically has English notes—covers rather the same ground as *Asmahan & Farid*, though with more of Asmahan's early classic or neo-traditional recordings along with the crossover film material. —*John Storm Roberts*

Farid Al Atrache

Awal Hamsa / Cairophon 127
This 1972 release was one of Atrache's very finest, both instrumentally and vocally. Following his usual custom in live performances, he opens with oud, and proceeds by a smooth sequence to the main business of the evening, his singing. —*John Storm Roberts, Original Music*

Takasim Oud / Voice of Lebanon 103
These live recordings catch much of his brilliance, as well as his audience's impassioned response. This is one not only for lovers of Middle Eastern music, but for lovers of fine string playing of all kinds. —*John Storm Roberts, Original Music*

○ **Addi Errabi** / Voice of Lebanon 602
In a career that took him from young traditional singer to major film-star and concert artist, Atrache was at the center of Egyptian music for a very long time. This 1973 live recording is typical of his concerts in its progression from solo 'ud to Atrache's tenderly stark vocals, all punctuated by passionate audience response. — *John Storm Roberts*

Aziza Galal

Wal Tekeina Netkabel Sawa / EMI 101
Behind her spectacles, Moroccan-born, Cairo-based Galal clearly has no truck with pop-star glitz in her appearance or her art, but she is one of the finest living singers in the Egyptian vein. She seeks flexibility rather than flash and purity rather than richness of tone, and her accompaniments impeccably vary the now classic string sound with unobtrusive modern touches. —*John Storm Roberts*

Abdel Halim Hafez

Mawood / Soutelphan 509
A smashing concert recording by a major star of the post-World War II generation, Hafez is in typical mellow, yearning voice here, backed by electric guitar (effective) and sax along with the usual 'ud, quanun, and string section, etc. This is quintessential Egyptian mainstream pop without silly frills, much enhanced by the live audience. —*John Storm Roberts, Original Music*

Kariat Al-Fengan / Soutelphan 502

Middle Eastern Music

Though ethnic sounds from throughout the world have been gaining popularity in recent years, Middle Eastern recordings remain the most challenging to American and European ears. Many people, in fact, initially find it uncomfortable to listen to the intricate, microtonal melodies and passionate rhythms of Arabic music. Once you get used to the exotic intensity of these highly evolved styles, however, there's no turning back. The simplistic melodic structures and heavy-handed beats of Western music can seem naive, reserved, and even downright stodgy by comparison. Still, there are several barriers to appreciating Middle Eastern music, most notably the lack of recordings available in the West. Even when you can obtain a few intriguing releases, chances are the liner notes don't include any information about the artists or the music. This is especially true of companies that import albums directly from Near Eastern countries.

The situation has improved somewhat over the last five years through the efforts of Western labels that have started to license and repackage albums by Middle Eastern pop stars, particularly Algerian rai artists who combine the melismatic fervor of their heritage with the glitz and drive of Western rock. Labels like Lyrichord, CMP, Playasound, and Rykodisc, on the other hand, have released their own high-quality recordings of traditional and classically oriented styles. These albums offer an excellent introduction to the Middle Eastern aesthetic, not only because they provide easy-to-grasp explanations of the music in the liner notes, but because the labels choose to present musicians on the basis of consummate artistry, high production standards, and relative accessibility. Many of the younger artists, in fact, temper their mastery of ancestral styles with their appreciation of and exposure to modern Western techniques. Turkish ney (flute) player Kudsi Erguner, Galilee-born oud virtuoso Simon Shaheen, and Lebanese multi-instrumentalist Ali Jihad Racy are three "rising stars" in the West who walk that fine line between tradition and innovation in some satisfying new ways.

"The idea of incorporating Western elements is something that Middle Eastern musicians have valued in the last 50 years or so," explains Racy, who moved to the US in 1968 and currently serves as Professor of Ethnomusicology at UCLA. "I have tried to experiment with my own Arab instruments and see how I can use them to create effects and new sounds to convey certain feelings and ideas. Electronic instruments have been really taking over in our music, for better or worse, and you find that the traditional resources have shrunk. Many musicians are using a more limited number of rhythmic patters and modes. Short, danceable rhythms are important. They make the music more accessible to people in the West. But there are still people who are developing new techniques and taking traditional instruments in some (admirable) new directions. It's an exciting time."

Though their approaches may be quite different, many of these revolutionary artists have retained the sense of ecstasy that Middle Eastern music treasures. From Turkish Sufi meditations to Arabic classical styles and more modern aproaches, the idea of mixing the sublime with the sensual has long been a powerful element. Religious writings in this part of world, in fact, often include amorous poetry in which feelings of earthly love and yearning are used as metaphors for the ultimate love of God. "In our music, the idea of creating ecstatic effects is very important," says Racy. "Mysticism and passion are not incompatible. Rather they work together to create a total experience. The players are skillful and the music is complex, not for the sake of technique, but rather to perfect the ability to emotionally tranform the listener."

This, indeed, is what Middle Eastern music does best. Ultimately, you don't have to understand the forms, modes, and rhythmic cycles to grasp the appeal. At the hands of an accomplished artist, the emotion behind the music comes through loud and clear.

– Linda Kohanov

Concert recording by a major star of the post-WW II generation. Like Lebanon's Fairuz, Hafez fronts settings that range from the now-traditional chorus and strings-and-percussion orchestra to various groups with heavy overseas influences. But his own style and the melodies he sings are both quintessentially Egyptian. — *John Storm Roberts*

Hanan

Haluwa / Slam 1501
Hanan is one of the finest singers on the younger Egyptian scene. There's less Euro-pop on this than on the earlier Slam releases, more strongly Egyptian material, plus a few splendid oddities, such as an intro that sounds vaguely like Astor Piazzolla. —*John Storm Roberts*

Ali Hassan Kuban

Vocals / Nubian
Ali Hassan Kuban is a master singer and popularizer of Nubian music, a typically vocal expression native to the border region of Egypt and Sudan. In the mid '50s, Kuban added electric guitars, keys, a horn section, and percussion to his music, fusing traditional songs of love with uptempo pop instruments in a Western-influenced mix. His group appeals to old and young alike. — *Myles Boisen & J. Poet*

☆ **From Nubia to Cairo** / 1980 / Shanachie 64036
Traditional wedding and love songs of southern Egypt, with propulsive drumming, clapping, and strings, R&B influenced horn charts, and Farfisa-like electric organ underpinning Kuban's arid vocals. A masterpiece. —*Myles Boisen & J. Poet*

Umm Kulthum

Vocals
Umm Kulthum (also known in the West as Oum Kalsoum) is among the greatest singers of the 20th century. She has been called the Bessie Smith of Egypt, and for stark passion she was all of that. But she was also more. She found a way of moving traditional music into the contemporary mainstream without dilution, and, without compromising, achieved a popularity unparalleled by any singer anywhere. —*John Storm Roberts*

Hajrik / Sono Cairo SC119
Her incredible first recordings recordings are backed by the traditional small groups that later grew into positive orchestras. Notes in English are a rare bonus. *Hajrik* is typical of Kulthum at her prime, shortly after the album form allowed live performances to be recorded at length and in depth, both vocally and instrumentally. —*John Storm Roberts*

☆ **El Atlaal** / Sono Cairo 101
Another from her prime, shortly after the LP form allowed her to record songs the way she sang them live. —*John Storm Roberts*

Rubayaat el-Khayyam / Sono Cairo 116
Kulthum sings Omar—though not, of course, the Fitzgerald version. This is another of the best-known recordings of Kulthum's late-classic period from the '40s to the '50s. —*John Storm Roberts*

Faat el-Mi'ad / Sono Cairo 105
On this concert recording from Kulthum's later years, she didn't change her own style but acknowledged contemporary Egyptian musical developments in accompaniments, with far from classic

but fascinating elements: notably sensational taqassim for saxophone. —*John Storm Roberts*

Musicians of the Nile

Group

The Musicians of the Nile are an international performing troupe of professional musicians from the Luxor area. Using only folk instruments, this group keeps the traditions of Upper Egypt alive. —*Myles Boisen*

☆ **From Luxor to Isna** / 1989 / Real World 7567-91316
A first-class collection of Arabic folk music from Egypt from the country's premier touring group. Strictly traditional drums, strings, reeds, and songs from the desert. —*Myles Boisen & J. Poet*

Musicians of the Nile—Vols. 1 & 2 / Ocora 559006
The music of contemporary Egypt has come a long way from the villages of the Egyptian Nile. But its roots are in the flutes, the oboes, the two-stringed fiddles, and impassioned vocalism and drumming of a peasant culture with strong Gypsy roots, in which popular and classical met. —*David L. Mayers*

Ali Jihad Racy

b. 1943, Lebanon
Flute, clarinet

An accomplished multi-instrumentalist, Racy has done much to promote an appreciation for Middle Eastern music in the West. Born in Lebanon, Racy came to the US in 1968, where he earned his Masters and Doctorate degrees from the University of Illinois before accepting a position as Professor of Ethnimusicology at UCLA. His recordings for various labels provide a showcase for his mastery of the flute-like ney and the clarinet-like mijwiz, as well as the stringed instruments 'ud and buzuq, both important to Middle Eastern styles. Racy is currently working on a book tentatively titled *The Art of Ecstacy in Arab Music.* —*Linda Kohanov*

○ **Jazayer** / 1989 / Earthbeat! 2549
Originally recorded by the Grateful Dead's Mickey Hart in 1979, this collection features traditional and contemporary Middle Eastern dance music performed with great spirit and skill by Racy in collaboration with the members of Jazayer, an American ensemble of Middle Eastern music enthusiasts. —*Linda Kohanov*

○ **Taqasim** / Lyrichord
Taqasim (the plural of taqsim) are extended, non-metrical instrumental improvisations. This collection of three such pieces features Simon Shaheen on 'ud and Racy on buzuq, offering a rare opportunity to hear the sublime, at times feverish, interactions of two virtuoso performers. —*Linda Kohanov*

Simon Shaheen

b. 1955, Tarshiha, Galilee
Violin / Arabic classical

A virtuoso on the 'ud as well as the violin, Shaheen is equally adept at performing traditional Arabic music and Western classical styles. Born in the village of Tarshiha in northern Galilee, he learned his craft initially from his father. At the same time, Shaheen also studied Western classical music, graduating from the Jerusalem Music Academy in 1978. Two years later, he moved to New York where he continued his studies at the Manhattan School of Music. In addition to his performances worldwide, Shaheen teaches 'ud and violin, composes for theatrical productions, and produces recordings. —*Linda Kohanov*

The Music of Mohamed Abdel Wahab / 1990 / Axiom 422-846754
Cairo was once a major movie-making capital, and Wahab invented the soundtrack sound that still influences how we think about Egyptian music. 'Ud dervish Simon Shaheen, backed by an energetic orchestra and chorus, interprets some of the composer's most intoxicating pieces. —*Bob Tarte*

○ **Turath (Heritage): Masterworks of the Middle East** / 1992 / CMP 3006
A rarity and a very welcome one: a really outstanding classical recording by a quartet of young musicians. Shaheen, an excellent oud-player and violinist, is joined by fine ney quanun and percussion in a recital of classic and contemporary works in the linked Arabic and Ottoman-Turkish tradition. —*John Storm Roberts*

Ihab Tawfi

Ikmini / Slam 190
This is the cassette from which Island extracted the cut "Masakeen." Tawfi's a fine singer, with a sound locally enough rooted (along with the hip version of local rhythms) to subdue and turn to good purpose the international-pop garnishes. At its best, the newer Egyptian sounds approach rai in intensity, and surpass it in variety. —*John Storm Roberts*

Egypt Collection

☆ **Yalla—HitList Egypt** / 1990 / Mango 539 873
Hard-hitting overview of a variety of gritty, hardworking Egyptian pop that mixes elements of bazaar culture with Eurodisco technocraft. Disc is divided equally between uptown and street styles. Contains "Elli Shatr Enhaa Tgannen," the naughty newlywed rap that had Cairo's elders blushing. —*Bob Tarte & Myles Boisen*

Cairo Tradition / Auvidis 8038
All the music on *Cairo Tradition: Taqasim & Layali* is played by members of the Takht ensemble under the aegis of the Cairo conservatory. There's a lot of excellent kanun zither playing, both solo and under the layali, vocal improvisations on a maqam. There are also admirable 'ud and ney solos. A core recording, all in all. —*John Storm Roberts*

Music of Egypt—Upper & Lower / Rykodisc 10106
The Grateful Dead's Mickey Hart recorded these pieces in 1978, having happened across the music during a tour. The first four are from the Aswan area, the last two are fine instrumentals, one for a mizmar oboe group, the other for tar with a darabukka backing. —*David L. Mayers*

Iraq

Munir with Mohamed Elkassabgi Bachir

Munir Bachir & Mohamed Elkassabgi / CDDA 003
'Ud virtuosi of two generations and two traditions. Munir Bachir is perhaps the finest living player in the great Iraqi school. In the Geneva concert featured in this record, he plays both traditional modes and looser, more personal improvisations of marked Spanish influence. The great Egyptian player Elkassabgi both composed for and accompanied Umm Kulthum in her early glory days: his solos here, mostly from the '30s, are drawn from 78s originals. —*John Storm Roberts*

Iran

Karimi/Musavi

Masters of Traditional Music Vol. 2 / Ocora 560025
These are reissues of two classic 1979 recordings. All are outstanding, but the ney playing, for my money, is simply breath-taking. The second CD in the set is entirely devoted to an equally fine recording of duets by singer Mohammad Karimi and Musavi on ney. The recording is extremely good technically. —*John Storm Roberts, Original Music*

Masters of Traditional Music, Vol. 2 / Ocora 560025
Reissue of 1979 recording. The CD is entirely devoted to a fine recording of duets by singer Mohammad Karimi and Musavi on ney. Extremely good technically. —*John Storm Roberts*

Faramarz Payvar

Composer

Faramarz Payvar is an important composer and conservator of Persian classical music, leading his touring ensemble on the 72-string santur (hammer dulcimer). Various other string instruments are featured in this group, as well as the zarb drum and soloist Khatereh Parvaneh, a prominent female vocalist. —*Myles Boisen*

○ **Faramarz Payvar Ensemble** / 1974 / Nonesuch 72060
Iran has arguably been the world's most important musical culture. It links us with ancient Greece, and is at the root of both Arabian and Indian (and thence Southeast Asian) classical idioms. Santurist Payvar's ensemble brought together some of

Iran's finest classical musicians in the group and solo performances for santur zither, kamancheh fiddle, tar lute, zarb percussion, with—a rare treat—a fine woman singer, Khatereh Parvaneh. —*John Storm Roberts*

Manoochehr Sadeghi

Sounds of the Santur / IER 7151
The Iranian santur is the progenitor of a great sweep of instrumentals from China to southcentral Europe, and a major classical instrument in its own right. Sadeghi is one of the recognized younger leaders of the renaissance in the instrument, whose tradition was being gradually lost. Here he plays two dastgahs (essentially, suites), one of them also played on the ney by Hossein Omoumi. —*John Storm Roberts*

Dariush Tala'i with Mohammad Musavi & Majid Kian

Masters of Traditional Music, Vol. 1 / 1979 / Ocora 560024
Reissue of classic 1979 recording is devoted to instrumentals for tar (Dariush Tala'i), ney (Mohammad Musavi), and santur (Majid Kiani). All are outstanding, but the ney playing, for my money, is simply breathtaking. Superb music; notes that give plenty of general background but are totally lacking in properly attributed track information. Extremely good technically. —*John Storm Roberts*

Iran Collection

Music of Iran, Vol. 1 / Barenreiter Musicaphon 2004
This recording is of music for solo kamantche, voice with tar, and solo sehtar. —*John Storm Roberts*

○ **Music of Iran, Vol. 2** / Barenreiter Musicaphon 2005
A good range of music from renowned musicians of several generations: dumbek solo; piece for santur; mathnavi mystical poem in a mode like one used in Indian devotional chant; ney flute solo; and tar and kamantche duet. —*John Storm Roberts*

Israel

Theodore Bikel

b. Mar. 2, 1924, Vienna, Austria
Vocals, guitar / Yiddish
Singer, guitarist, song collector, and author Theodore Bikel came to New York in 1955 and was soon an integral part of the folk scene in this country. Speaking some 17 different languages, Bikel was popular in the early and mid '60s performing the songs of many countries, but particularly those of Israel. —*Michael Erlewine*

○ **Sings Yiddish Theatre . . .** / 1991 / Bainbridge 2504
Sings Yiddish Theatre & Folk Songs was originally released in the '60s on Elektra. This 1991 reissue features the original liner notes, complete with Yiddish lyrics and English translations for all 16 tracks by one of the Yiddish theater's best-known actors. This also features the arrangements of master maestro Dov Seltzer. —*Phil Fink*

Gloria Feidman

Clarinet / Jewish
Without a doubt, the leader of Klezmer music and a world famous clarinet virtuoso. —*Phil Fink*

○ **Jewish Soul Music: 20 Jewish Tunes** / 1989 / Hed Arzi 15366
This release features both live and studio recordings from the early '70s, digitally remastered on CD. A virtual greatest-hits by this greatest of Klezmers. —*Phil Fink*

David "Dudu" Fisher

Vocals / Yiddish
One of Israel's leading male vocalists, Fisher has recorded numerous albums in Hebrew, ranging from showtunes (he played Jean Valjean in the Tel Aviv production of *Les Miserables* to Chassidic and Hebrew versions of '60s classic rock tunes. —*Phil Fink*

○ **Mamma Loshen (Mother Tongue)** / 1992 / Helicon 8089

Fisher sings 22 of the greatest Yiddish songs ever written. —*Phil Fink*

Moshe Ganchoff

○ **Cantorial Masterworks—Part 1** / 1991 / Musique Int'l 7340
This cassette release only features recordings originally made in 1942, many of which have not been previously issued. —*Phil Fink*

Gidi Gov

○ **Derech Eretz** / 1987 / Hed Arzi 151178
Among Israel's hottest rock stars, Gov teams on this debut album with one of Israel's most famous songwriters, Ychuda Poliker. One of the hardest-rocking albums ever to come out of Israel. —*Phil Fink*

Kleveland Klezmorim

○ **Casbah** / 1989 / WKSU-FM
This CD by a regional Klezmer band combines authentic European Klezmer with original modern compositions performed in a Klezmer style. —*Phil Fink*

Klezmer Conservatory Band

Oy Chanukah! / 1989 / Rounder 3102
This recording, by a band of 15 women and men, contains celebratory instrumentals, informative narratives, and strong vocals by Judy Bressler. Includes "Jewish Heroines," "Dona, Dona," "The Struggle for Freedom," "Chassidim Dance," "Making Latkes" (with recipe and demonstration!), "Klezzified." —*Ladyslipper*

○ **Old World Beat** / Feb. 21, 1992 / Rounder 3115
One of Klezmer's leading exponents, this band has spent the last decade spreading this old world beat around the planet. With traditional melodies alongside brand new tunes, this 1991 release reflects the eclectic nature of Klezmer—alternately brooding and raucous, always spirited and engaging. —*Ladyslipper*

Touch of Klez! / Vanguard 79455
An album of dance tunes and Yiddish songs, with Eastern touches in melody and harmony, for the rest of the year. The stand-outs are the rich vocals by Judy Bressler (described by a fan as a heaven-sent Russian goddess), including her brand of Klezmer scat, and Ingrid Monson's poignant cornet improvisations. —*Ladyslipper*

The Klezmorim

East Side Wedding / Flying Fish 258
Among the best of US klezmer revivalists—the first album here was the recording that arguably sparked the idiom's entire rediscovery. Included are Rumanian, Greek, Serbian, Russian and US pieces. Wedding has what the notes call the "Turkey in the Straw" of eastern Europe, "Yoshke Yoshke." Streets . . . includes a reminder of just how open Balkan musical frontiers were, since it's called taksim—the Arabic word for a free-rhythm improvisation, which presumably got into Jewish music via Turkey and the Balkans or via some similar route. A minor plus for the visually minded is a charming cover by cartoonist R. Crumb of Cheap Suit Serenaders fame. —*John Storm Roberts, Original Music*

First Recordings (1976-1978) / Arhoolie 309
The best of the new Klezmer bands. An admirable effort by young musicians to capture the sound and feeling of the classic Yiddish music. Recorded in Berkeley, California in 1976 and 1978. —*Cliff Martin*

Aaron Lebedeff

○ **Sings 14 Yiddish Favorites** / 1964 / Greater Recording Co. 56
As the title implies, this features the legendary Yiddish vocalist on 14 of the best-known Yiddish songs, including the all-time favorite, "Roumania, Roumania." —*Phil Fink*

The Mazletones

○ **Meshugge for You** / 1989 / Global Village 137
Updated arrangements of Klezmer favorites on this CD release. —*Phil Fink*

Megama

Group / American Jewish pop

American Shalom Levine and Canadian Moshe Yess moved to Israel and formed this group, releasing the two most definitive English-language/Jewish-content albums of the past 20 years. Unfortunately the group split following the release of their second album. —*Phil Fink*

○ **Megama** / 1980 / CBS 84604

Their debut features folksy lyrics and catchy tunes as well as the moving "My Zadie," one of the most popular English-language Jewish songs ever written. —*Phil Fink*

God Is Alive and Well and in Jerusalem / 1982 / CBS 85660

Just as listenable and entertaining as their first album. —*Phil Fink*

Alberto Mizrahi

○ **The Voice of a People** / 1992 / Anshe Emet Synagogue

This CD captures one of America's finest living cantors in digital excellence. —*Phil Fink*

Piamentas

○ **Piamenta 1990** / 1990 / Holyland 805

The first CD release from Avi and Yossi Piamenta, two brothers who are former New York studio musicians who now compose and perform Jewish music with a grinding guitar and an elegant flute sound combined with a rock & roll backbeat. This features "Asher Boro," a prayer sung at Jewish weddings, set here to the tune of Men At Work's "Down Under." —*Phil Fink*

Molly Picon

○ **At the Yiddish Theatre** / 1971 / Greater Recording Co. 220

At the Yiddish Theatre captures the late Yiddish star's greatest hits from her days in the Yiddish theater, many of which were written and produced by her husband Yonkel Kalich. —*Phil Fink*

Dave Tarras

Jewish

○ **Yiddish-American Klezmer Music** / Yazoo 7001

A stunning collection of great Yiddish music, from early instrumental to big band-style pieces with guest vocalists. Also contains some cuts from radio broadcasts. Great stuff! Essential representation of the genre. —*Cliff Martin*

Christobel Weerasinghe

Israel—Its Music and Its People / Desto 503

Folk songs and dances, religious and cantorial music, with a narrative by Weerasinghe. —*Roots & Rhythm*

Israel Collection

Judeo-Hispanic Songs of the Eastern Mediterranean / Inedit 260054

Sephardic music preserved in the Ottoman Empire by refugees from Spain. This charming Latino-language collection includes Romances and holiday, wedding, love, and comic songs as well as a lament for Jerusalem. Historical importance and musical charm aside, what strikes me forcibly is how Spanish/European these songs have remained over the centuries. —*John Storm Roberts, Original Music*

○ **Treasury of Immortal Performances** / 1966 / RCA 6173

A set of three albums each by a different cantor (Josef Rosenblatt, Samuel Vigoda, and Moshe Koussevitsky). Released in 1966, this boxed set repackaged recordings from as early as 1928 and includes a booklet on the cantors. The Koussevitsky portion has been re-released on CD (Israel Music ICD 5002) with two additional tracks, while the Rosenblatt portion (Israel Music ICD 5001) has three bonus tracks. —*Phil Fink*

○ **Very Best of Israel** / 1990 / CBS 460815

This compilation covers material from CBS Israel's vaults, spanning 40 years of Israeli folk and light popular music. —*Phil Fink*

○ **Folklore Israelien, Le** / Atoll 77045

Not field recordings, but a mix of traditional and traditional-style songs of which the best-known is perhaps "Hava Nagila." Many are performed by the Effi Netzer Singers. Also featured are Ianit, Lahakat Hanachal, Luci Arnon, and Danny Granot. —*John Storm Roberts*

○ **Hassidic Tunes of Dancing and Rejoicing** / Smithsonian/Folkways 4209

A delicious album that includes music for clarinets and percussion; a charming dance for clarinet, trumpet, and accordion; a great deal for voices, including some fine "mouth music." Strong Balkan and eastern European, of course, but also a few reminiscent of the western European ballad tradition. These field recordings are backed by extensive notes and photos. —*John Storm Roberts*

○ **Israel—Forty Years** / Atoll 900

An anthology doubly welcome for its wide view of Israeli popular music. Here are rock/disco-influenced idioms (very interesting); straight rock; the more traditional but equally fine Central European sound of the Effi Netzer Singers; the sonic chicken soup of the Kibbutz Folk Singers; and several other styles to boot. Very varied, very unfamiliar, and mostly very good. —*John Storm Roberts*

○ **Israeli Chassidic Song Festival** / Hed Arzi

These "cast" recordings have been released annually on cassette and vinyl since the first festival in 1968. Many of the tunes first released on these albums have passed into the public's consciousness as though they had been written hundreds of years ago. —*Phil Fink*

Kurdistan Collection

○ **Kurdish Music** / Barenreiter Musicaphon 2028

Ethnically and culturally united though they are, the Kurds of the mountainous region that is split between Iran, Iraq, Turkey, and the Soviet Union are also a part of the great Islamic Middle-Eastern cultural block. The music here—all superbly performed—includes flute solos and duets (the Kurds, a pastoral mountain people, have no stringed instruments) and songs epic and romantic, as well as a Soviet Kurdish dance piece. —*John Storm Roberts*

Kurdistan / Auvidis 8023

Though they are spread across several Middle Eastern countries, the Kurds are very much a cultural entity and their music a recognizable subset of the general regional idiom, with strong links to Persian tradition and a particular liking for the Dorian mode. The Kurds are also traditionally nomadic: they have relied largely on shepherd's pipes and the human voice (though they have adopted stringed instruments from their neighbors over time). —*John Storm Roberts*

Kuwait Collection

○ **Stars of Kuwait, Vol. 1** / Buzaidphone 503

In the late '80s, Kuwait developed a whole new take on mainstream Arabic pop, in which a bunch of fresh new singers fronted groups not only with the standard string sections but also with novelties ranging from Greek bouzouki to the only Arab piano playing to use the bottom half of the keyboard. Most of the important names are here: Rabab, Nawaal, Adul Karim Kader, and seven others. Lots of range stylistically, from at least a couple of mini-generations. The singing aside, the Kuwaitis are into a lot of intriguing instrumental stuff including occasional gorgeous solo fiddle. —*John Storm Roberts*

Lebanon

Majida El Roumi

☆ **Kalimaat** / Music Masters 002

A wonderful example of the everything-goes experimentalism of much Arabic pop. El Roumi sounds a little like Fairuz, though with more honey and less smoke. Gorgeous, in a word. In places she shows very strong Indian *filmi* influences, not just in the arrangements but in her singing. One song has a loopy sub-Dixieland backing. Yet others are somewhat more orthodoxly splendid. I love it! —*John Storm Roberts*

Lebanon Collection

Prayer and Religious Incantation / Barenreiter Musicaphon
2030
A particularly fine recording of prayers, muwashaat (hymns), and
other religious material. Druze, Sunni, and Shiite: music of the
mosque, not of the mystical sects. Despite the ambivalence and
intermittent hostility of Islam to music, this is not only beauty of
a high order but the sound that underlies all other vocal idioms
of the whole Islamic world. —*John Storm Roberts*

Morocco

A. Doukali & A. Belkayat

Group
Abdelhadi Belkayat and Abdelwahab Doukali, leaders of the first
wave of big-time Moroccan pop music, both began singing in the
'60s. Both were inevitably influenced by Egypt, and indeed spent
time there. But neither simply "went Egyptian," and both in fact
ended up international stars. In very broad terms, Belkayat is
reminiscent of Egypt's Abdel Hali Hafez. Doukali is a more dramatic singer with lusher and slightly more adventurous backings.
—*John Storm Roberts*
☆ **A. Belkayat & A. Doukali** / Disque Arabe 012
They make a terrific pairing on a super CD. —*John Storm Roberts*

Pakistan Collection

☆ **Treasures of Pakistan** / Playasound 65082
Excellent examples of music for sarinda and sarangi fiddles as
well as the rabab lute, extremely well recorded on location. As a
nice touch, the producer is Kudzi Erguner, a Turkish musician,
rather than the usual Western ethnomusicologist (not the first—I
remember Deben Bhattacharya's recordings with nostalgia—but
still too rare). Brief but cogent notes. —*John Storm Roberts*

Saudi Arabia

Mohamed Abdu

Evening with . . . / Duniaphon 297
This concert recording presents him in typical form, with a youthful style that still (like pretty much all Gulf music) sticks very
close to tradition. Within the general Middle Eastern ambit, this
is a very different idiom from those of Egypt or Lebanon, having
strong Persian, Indian and even African links. —*John Storm
Roberts, Original Music*
○ **Mohamed Abdu** / Saut el Jazira 501
Currently one of the big names of Saudi popular music, Abdu is
squarely in the mainstream. You get here three long songs from a
concert appearance. Vocally he reminds me a little of Abdel
Halim Hafez, though his voice is more sinewy. Instrumentally
there are touches of updating—occasional keyboards, electric gui-
tar, and the like. But the orchestra, and particularly the strongly
Egyptian string sound, would mostly fit fine behind Umm
Kulthum in her later days. —*John Storm Roberts*

Ettab

○ **The Very Best of Ettab** / Relax-In 513
Afro-Saudi Ettab is, in my book, terrific. Like most Saudi singers
she doesn't get as contemporary as, say, the Egyptians. But she's
a vocalist of power and charm both. Moreover, her backings add
to the mainstream strings all sorts of effective garnishes, from accordion to keyboards, that contrive to be at once goofy and effective. —*John Storm Roberts*

Syria

Souheil Arafeh

Magic Touch / Byblos 908
Arafeh uses a mix of highly traditional instruments and styles
with occasional modernisms (drum rhythm, electric organ), in
what amounts to an instrumental suite evocative of various
provincial towns and other places in Syria. The result is a kind of

program music building on tradition, which is relatively unfash-
ionable in modern Arabic music but really very attractive. —*John
Storm Roberts*

Omaya Orchestra/Chorale

Raska al Samah/Waslat Mouachahat / Byblos 907
Syrian andalus classical music differs from its Maghrebi cousin
not just in that it has ancient Byzantine elements but because
Syrian orchestras have been more willing to borrow ensemble
string voicings from the West. These two vocal suites are typical
and splendid, opening with a fine kanoun solo and sung magnificently throughout. —*John Storm Roberts*
Album: Badakhshan / Pan 2024
The Badakhsan region is home to a large minority of Ismailis, followers of the Aga Khan. Badakhshan presents a richly diverse
range of instrumentals and vocals. Most involve various lutes,
though there's also a lament accompanied by accordion! —*John
Storm Roberts, Original Music*

Tadjik Music of Badakhshan / Auvidis/UNESCO 8212
The Tadjik CD, equally lute-rich and varied, includes cuts from
Chinese Tadjiks. —*John Storm Roberts, Original Music*

United Arab Emirates

Abdallah Belkhair

Abdallah Belkhair / Al-Shab 006
A fine singer from Dubai in a strongly traditional style, backed by
strings and percussion of that mixed Egyptian/Bedouin descent
that has become mainstream. In contrast with the "new sound"
singers of Egypt, and Kuwaitis like Nawaal, it is quite devoid of
interpop or overt Westernisms. —*John Storm Roberts*

Turkey

Kudsi Erguner

b. 1952, Istanbul
Flute, ney flute / Sufi
The haunting sound of the flute-like ney is literally in Erguner's
blood. Born in Istanbul, he is the oldest son of Ulvi Erguner, considered to be Turkey's last great master of the instrument and the
man responsible for preserving traditional Turkish music during
the period of cultural upheaval at the end of the Ottoman Empire.
Kudsi Erguner expanded upon his father's role by spreading
Turkish music through the world. Moving to Paris in 1975, he
opened a school for Turkish music. He has since recorded several
beautifully-produced albums of Sufi music and contributed his
talents to scores for plays and films, including Peter Brook's acclaimed production of the *Mahabharata* epic. —*Linda Kohanov*
○ **Turkey: Art of the Ottoman Tanbur** / 1989 / VDE
Kudsi Erguner recorded this album featuring alternating solo performances by two modern masters of the tanbur, Abdi Coskun
and Fahreddin Cimenli. The tanbur is the most commonly used
lute-like instrument in Turkish art music. The musicians here
fully exploit the rich, sonorous timbre of the instrument, which
can be either plucked or bowed. —*Linda Kohanov*
○ **Sufi Music of Turkey** / 1990 / Creative Music Prod. 3005
A powerful recording of Middle Eastern music. Kudsi plays ney
with Mahmoud Tabrizi Zadeh adding the scintillating sounds of
the santur (a type of hammer dulcimer) and the sensual melodies
of the kemantche (a bowed string instrument). Bruno Caillat also
plays zarb and tabla. —*Linda Kohanov*
Whirling Dervishes from Turkey / 1991 / Arion
Another fine performance of Sufi music from Kudsi, collaborating this time with some traditional singers and instrumentalists
who perform a Mevlevi Whirling Dervish ceremony. —*Linda
Kohanov*
Sufi Flutes / JVC 25005
Despite Islam's ambivalent attitude to music, Koranic recitation
and other are at the heart of the music religious incantations of
the Islamic world. The Sufi mystical brotherhoods use music and
dance to induce religious ecstasy, one of many reasons why they
are suspect in the eyes of orthodox theologians. In this CD you
get the pure religious sound in its pristine form, and instrumen-

tal preludes to Sufi ceremonies are played on the ney flute backed by percussion, in a style near to classical music (the Sufis were in fact guardians of the Middle Eastern classical tradition for a while). As a plus, there are English notes for a change! — *John Storm Roberts*

Erköse Ensemble

○ **Tzigane—Gypsy Music of Turkey** / 1992 / Creative Music Prod. 3010
This dazzling album is the only recording currently available of Turkish gypsy music. The five-man Erköse Ensemble combine the violin-like kaman, clarinet, 'ud (lute), kanun (zither) and darbuka (hand drum) in an intoxicating high-energy swirl that will leave you reeling. —*Backroads Music / Heartbeats*

Talip Ozkan

○ **Mysteries of Turkey** / 1988 / Music of the World 115
The mysterious and exotic sound of the saz, a long-necked lute, is the focus of this recording. Talip Ozkan, a master musician from Turkey, presents traditional songs and dances from his homeland with this unique instrument. Both solo saz and accompanying vocal selections are featured on this recording. —*Music of the World*

The Dark Fire / 1992 / Axiom 314-512003
Buzzing, stinging forays into medieval Turkish music by Ozkan, master of the saz—a member of the lute family played with a cherrywood plectrum—accompanied by stark frame-drum and wooden spoon percussion. Fierce performances brimming with slurred runs, angular melodies, and fractal-shaped riffs. —*Bob Tarte*

Bayram Bilge Toker

Bayram Toker / 1991 / Music of the World 122
On this recording he presents both Sufi devotional music and Turkish folk songs, each one delivered with exuberance and skill. He can be dark and emotive in the Sufi song "Haydar, Haydar" or the funeral lament "Ag it." The instrumental lines are complex, giving rhythm to the long vocal lines. Some of the folk dance pieces here are as frenzied as any raga, and as beautifully and expertly played. —*Dirty Linen*

Turkey Collection

○ **Masters of Turkish Music** / 1990 / Rounder 1051
Scholarly (though very entertaining) collection of Turkish 78s, divided evenly between classical vocal music and various instrumental recordings, all demonstrating sophisticated musicianship. —*Myles Boisen*

○ **Best of Turkey** / 1991 / Atoll 8649
Actually Turkish pop. Seven popular Turkish artists are included, each contributing two pieces. —*Gino Robair, Roots & Rhythm*

Turkey: Ceremony of the Kadiri Dervishes / 1991 / VDE 587
Sufi chanting ceremonies of the Kadiri dervishes. Four selections, over an hour long. —*Roots & Rhythm*

Asik / Inedit 260025
The Asik form an ancient Anatolian popular tradition of songs amatory and philosophical, here wonderfully performed by a young woman singer and middle-aged master of the genre, backed by equally fine saz. Like much of this kind of music, it has the subtlety of the classical tradition while being more forthright in overall manner. —*John Storm Roberts*

Uzbekistan

Shashmaqam

○ **Music of Bukharan Jewish Ensemble** / 1991 / Smithsonian/Folkways 40054
A wide variety of passionate music by expatriate members of the Central Asian city of Bukhara mixes a dramatic Hassidic vocal style with Indian and Islamic instrumentals. An intriguing collection of ancient folksongs, ghazals (allegorical love poems), wedding songs, instrumentals, and more from the Jewish repertoire of this fertile region. —*Myles Boysen & Bob Tarte*

Yemen Collection

North Yemen / 1989 / Auvidis 8004
This is a reissue of a long out-of-print UNESCO album surveying the diversity of ceremonial music in North Yemen. —*Myles Boisen, Roots & Rhythm*

PACIFIC

Pacific Collection

Voices of the Rainforest / Apr. 5, 1991 / Rykodisc 10173
This recording deserves a place of its own. Steve Feld's new recordings from Kaluli territory set it in a sonic context reflecting the reality that the rainforest is a "dense, layered aural tapestry to which the Kaluli lend their voices." The arrangement is that of a day in the life of the Kaluli and the rainforest. Its powerful effect is enhanced by outstanding recording technique and admirable notes. —*David L. Mayers*

Music of the Iatmul / Barenreiter Musicaphon 2701
The set was recorded in the early '70s and covers a good deal of the same musical ground as *Music of Middle Sepik.* —*John Storm Roberts*

Polyphonies of Solomon Islands / Chant du Monde 274663
Polyphony—for both voices and panpipes—is crucial to Solomon Islands music. This recording is from Guadalcanal and Savo. This re-release of classic 1974 recordings by Hug Zemp contains fine examples of both (including one amazingly like a shape-note solfa), with very thorough notes and photos. —*John Storm Roberts*

Songs from the Kimberleys / AIAS 13
One in a series of three sets in the outstanding collection issued by the Australian Institute of Aboriginal Studies. The Kimberleys area of Western Australia offers a quite different tradition. Comes with substantial booklet. —*John Storm Roberts*

Australia

David Blanasi

Bamyili corroboree / Grevillea Records 1030
A fine but frustrating tape. The music more involving than any other Aboriginal recording, but there are zero notes and what is gleanable is confusing. Though the title suggests a range of music, it is apparently all by one singer, backed by a small chorus, percussion and what the UK distributor calls a didjeridu but sounds more like a bull-roarer. —*John Storm Roberts, Original Music*

Australia Collection

○ **Australia—Songs of the Aborigines and Music of Papua, New Guinea** / Lyrichord
Reissue of interesting field recordings of two distinct Aboriginal cultures—particularly, the Malkari "Centipede" and "Snake" songs, the Bunggul dance songs "Seagull" and "Spider" with their rhythmically innovative didjeridu accompaniments, the haunting Gizra People's flute piece announcing the coming of the Southeast winds during the rainy season, the surprising sudden dissonances of the "Two Flutes" piece, and the evocative "Magician Song" sung by magicians and their initiates while preparing potions. —*"Blue" Gene Tyrrany*

○ **Australia—Aboriginal Music** / 1992 / Auvidis—Unesco
A good overview of the many varieties of Aboriginal music, also including many selections of the more rarely heard women's music. Mysterious vocal trillings across distances in the "Rain Dreaming" ceremony, an ancient tale of two drowning girls in "Women's Wu-ungka Songs," melissimatic vocalizations like North Indian music in the "Wongga Dance Songs," and wonderful rhythmic inventions in the "Stingray, Dolphin, Curlew and Shark Songs." Excellent notes by the recordist Alice M. Moyle. —*"Blue" Gene Tyrrany*

Aboriginal Sound Instruments / AIAS 14
More than a mere demonstration, because almost all the tracks are performances, with singing where relevant. All are, of course,

musicologically important. Most involving for non-academics are the eerily beautiful didjeridu tracks. The booklet includes the cultural background, thorough notes on individual tracks, and transcriptions of all examples. —*John Storm Roberts*

☆ **Djambidj: An Aboriginal Song Series** / AIAS 16
Clan-song series like *Djambidj* constitutes an important musicopoetic form with strong spiritual and ritual significance. Two singers are accompanied by didjeridu and percussion. This, along with *Goyulan: The Morning Star*, are the only recordings of complete Aboriginal song series. The accompanying very substantial monographs include transcriptions and translations as well as detailed background notes. Crucially for its quality, it is a real collaboration between the main singer and an ethnomusicologist. —*John Storm Roberts*

Goyulan: The Morning Star / AIAS 18
This and *Djambidj: An Aboriginal Song Series* are the only recordings of complete Aboriginal song series. —*John Storm Roberts*

Music of the Torres Strait / AIAS 11/15
Like Native Americans, Aborigines have developed a range of new music as well as drawing on an expansion of their own resources (including intertribal styles) borrowing from other traditions. The two cassettes covering traditional and modern idioms illustrate the process and its results in changing old styles or evolving new ones. Excellent booklet of notes. —*John Storm Roberts*

Songs from North Queensland / AIAS 12
One in a series of three sets in the outstanding collection issued by the Australian Institute of Aboriginal Studies. Contains examples of both traditional music and more syncretic styles from a town in North Queensland. Comes with substantial booklet. —*John Storm Roberts*

Songs from Yarrabah / AIAS 7
One in a series of three sets in the outstanding collection issued by the Australian Institute of Aboriginal Studies. Contains examples of traditional music and more syncretic styles from a town in North Queensland, offering in greater detail one stylistic area in the region covered more generally by the North Queensland album. Comes with substantial booklet. —*John Storm Roberts*

Songs of the Northern Territory / AIAS 1/5
Camp and corroboree singing recorded in 1962-1963 in a wide range of locations in Australia's vast Northern Territory. Most of the music is ceremonial. These tapes are a remarkably thorough exploration of a series of interlocking cultures. The 60-page accompanying illustrated booklet goes into great detail about the individual tracks and background. —*John Storm Roberts*

Hawaii

Sol Hoopii

Steel guitar / Hawaiian
The most celebrated steel guitarist of the Hawaiian golden age was undoubtedly Sol Hoopii, who first came to the mainland as a stowaway in 1919. I believe he is the only performer to appear on every Hawaiian slide compilation, where liner notes typically describe him with a single word—"hot." Most of his 78s (over 200!!) were recorded in Los Angeles, where he enjoyed great popularity in such clubs as the Hula Hutt and Seven Seas. He appeared in many movies, toured the country advancing his highly rhythmic slide techniques, and left his stamp on an entire generation of lap steel and pedal steel guitarists in the emerging country & western style. —*Myles Boisen*

Master of the Hawaiian Guitar, Vol. 1 / 1987 / Rounder 1024
Rounder recently reissued this first of two fine collections from 1977 on CD. The remastering fully accents the creativity and richness of Hoopii's solos, and the speed and fludity he repeatedly demonstrated. Even if the harmonies and vocals on such cuts as "Alekoki" and "Hilo" doesn't bowl you over, it's impossible not to be impressed by Sol Hoopii's instrumental talents. —*Ron Wynn*

☆ **Master of the Hawaiian Guitar, Vol. 2** / 1988 / Rounder 1025
This second anthology featuring songs from the great Hawaiian guitarist Sol Hoopii moves from the late '20s into the '50s, and shows Hoopii extending his technique and displaying his jazz style. Hoopii's voicings, speed, riffs, accompaniment and solos are

---

Hawaiian Music

In the early days of recording history, Hawaiian music was not like the music we associate with tourist hotels and slow hula dances today. Vintage island sounds, passed on to us by a number of outstanding 78 RPM reissues, were hot and peppy, featuring flashy slide guitarists like Sol Hoopii, King Benny Nawahi, and mainlander Roy Smeck. Island guitarists, inspired by hot jazz and blues, traveled to the states regularly, where they enjoyed great popularity and in turn influenced the emerging bottleneck blues style. Country musicians were also fascinated by the Hawaiian-style slide, and the pedal steel is a direct descendant. With the advent of amplification, the guitar had more sustaining ability, and guitarists tended to slow down to a more leisurely pace. The characteristic soaring vocal harmonies of the male and female groups also became more languid, bringing the golden age to a slow, syrupy halt. After decades of kitschy commercialization, the music of the islands has revitalized and returned to its roots, with slack-key guitarists Gabby Pahinui and Raymond Kane again finding favor on this continent, and slide enthusiast Bob Brozman bringing back not only the classic sounds but the surviving members of the celebrated Tau Moe family.

– Myles Boisen

---

varied and unpredictable over the 16 songs, and often are the saving grace compensating for lightweight lead vocals and sleep-inducing harmonizing. —*Ron Wynn*

Melelani Serenaders

Kaulana 'O Ni'ihau / Hula 579
Music from the island of Niihau, Hawaii. —*Roots & Rhythm*

Na Mele O Na Opio

○ **It's a Small World** / Pumehana 4902
Twenty-nine-member youth group performs a variety of Hawaiian styles. —*Roots & Rhythm*

Ohta San

○ **Contemporary Hawaiian Mood** / Poki 9036
Ukelele master with modern Hawaiian music. —*Roots & Rhythm*

Hawaii Collection

☆ **Hula Blues** / 1971 / Rounder 1012
Another great sampling of top Hawaiian and stateside sliders, some with a country beat. —*Myles Boisen*

Hawaiian Steel Guitar 1920s-'50s / 1976 / Arhoolie 9009
Hawaiian Steel Guitar Classics—1920s-'50s features Hawaiian, cowboy, and vaudeville slide experts. —*Myles Boisen*

Hawaiian Steel Guitar, Vol. 2 / 1981 / Arhoolie 9027
Hawaiian Steel Guitar Classics—Vol. 2 (1927-1934) is a Bob Brozman compilation of all-authentic Hawaiian acts, both popular and obscure. —*Myles Boisen*

Vintage Hawaiian Music, Vol. 1 / 1989 / Rounder 1052
Vintage Hawaiian Music—Steel Guitar Masters (1928-1934) contains the earliest Hawaiian 78 rpm recordings. With its companion volume of singers, they are important historical documents. Both volumes are treasures. —*Myles Boisen*

☆ **Vintage Hawaiian Music, Vol. 2** / 1989 / Rounder 1053
Very early Hawaiian 78 rpm recordings, *Vintage Hawaiian Music—Great Singers 1928-1934* has a companion volume of steel guitar. An important historical document. Both volumes are treasures. —*Myles Boisen*

○ **Vintage Original Hawaiian Classics** / 1990 / Vintage Jazz Classics 1003

A lovely collection of '20s and '30s Hawaiian tunes, put together lovingly by Noel McMillan. —*John McCord, Roots & Rhythm*

Hawaiian Guitar / Yazoo 1055
The most agile dazzlers of the 78 rpm era. A slide guitarist's dream come true. —*Myles Boisen*

New Caledonia Collection

Kanak Songs—Feast & Lullabies / Chant du Monde 274909
The culture of the New Caledonian Kanaks east of Australia varies from island to island and community to community (the 60,000 Kanaks speak at least 20 languages), yet the music has a good deal of underlying cohesion. The examples here, including a remarkable recitative speech and many swirling songs to percussion, were mostly recorded on the main island of Grande Terre. The music comes with the usual thorough notes. (45:34) —*John Storm Roberts*

New Zealand

Inia Te Wiata

Waiata Maori / Waikiki 2002
The Maori people are known for their joyous communal singalongs known as waiata. —*AMG*

Papua New Guinea Collection

Music of Middle Sepik / Barenreiter Musicaphon 2700
Thanks in part to geography, Papula/Nugini is surely the territory with the most musical variety per head of population. The recordings (mostly Iatmul), made from the early '60s to early '70s, include fine flute music for solo and ensembles, as well as other wind music and a little percussion. —*John Storm Roberts*

Music of the Abelam / Barenreiter Musicaphon 2704
The Iatmul recordings, made in the early '70s, include fine flute music for solo and ensembles, as well as other wind music and a little percussion. The Kaluli are a small group living in central Papua. This album provides the recordings of the music discussed in Stephen Feld's award-winning book of the same name. The

Original Music

The music librarian of a university with a major ethnomusicological school once wrote, "In my opinion, the easiest way to acquire a good selection of world-music recordings is to go straight to Original Music…" Original Music in fact is still the only mail-order company to specialize in recordings, books and videos on music of all kinds from all over the world, from Indian classical to merengue-rap. A big part of Original Music's strength comes from the fact that its founder/owner is John Storm Roberts, editor of the *All Music Guide* world music chapter. John, who credited by a NYT article with having "invented" world music 20 years ago with his book *Black Music of Two Worlds*, also wrote *The Latin Tinge* besides producing many African and Caribbean albums. For more information, contact: Original Music, 418 Lasher Road, Tivoli, NY 12583; phone (919) 756-2767.

Abelam album, more vocally oriented, is devoted to music for socio-religious events, such as building and consecrating a ceremonial house, yam festivals, and rites of passage. —*John Storm Roberts*

Samoa Collection

Samoan Songs: Historical Collection / Barenreiter Musicaphon 2705

An outstanding recording bringing together Samoan recordings of great rarity. Three were recorded before WW I, three in 1940, and the rest in the mid and late '60s. They include dance songs, war songs, and topical songs of various sorts, including political ones. Music of enormous importance is underpinned by Musicaphon's thorough notes. —*John Storm Roberts*

NEW AGE

As the Beatles took the United States by storm, jazz artist Tony Scott took a deep breath and uttered the first notes of Music for Zen Meditation. Back then, no one really knew what to do with an exotic set of interactions between clarinet, Japanese koto, and shakuhachi flute. Released on Verve in 1964, Music for Zen Meditation remained an anomaly in the jazz label's bebop and swing catalog until this subtle cross-cultural venture was hailed as the first "new-age" album some 20 years later. If Scott had come up with the same American-Japanese collaboration in the 90s, he might just have easily found himself under the "world music" banner.

Scott's story is not unusual among contemporary instrumental artists. If these musicians have anything in common at all, it's their ability and intention to defy categorization. Of course, this sort of attitude tends to confound everyone else: from record labels, distributors, critics, and retailers to listeners trying to find the music in stores.

After a few frustrating decades trying to force innovative, instrumental releases into jazz and classical markets, some members of the record industry thought they had come across a handy new term. In the mid 80s, new-age music became the catchall designation for recordings that didn't seem to fit anywhere else. This phrase arose from the music's success in alternative outlets like health food stores, bookstores, and occult-oriented stores, as well as massage and meditation centers associated with the new-age movement. However, while a small number of artists openly supported new-age lifestyles and concepts through their music, most instrumentalists resented the association. As the 80s came to a close, cynical members of the media were having a field day allying the new-age music-marketing category with crystal gazers and trance channelers, in the process ignoring the merits of serious artists with highly original ideas. The whole thing left a bad taste in everyone's mouth, and much effort has been made in the early 90s to wipe out the stigma of this unfortunate development.

Back when the phrase "new-age" was being thrown around as a possibility, some people lobbied for the more general designation "contemporary instrumental." It wasn't short or catchy enough for most marketing executives, but increasing numbers of artists, record companies, critics, and radio producers have been using it. Contemporary instrumental (or CI for short, if you wish) is one of the few terms broad enough to encompass the myriad approaches and innovations taking place daily in this field. We've also come up with a list of subgenres to distinguish certain trends that have arisen in recent years; however, most artists regularly cross, combine, and recombine these tendencies as well. It's just the nature of CI musicians to create new fusions based on fusions of fusions.

– Linda Kohanov

Philip Aaberg

Vocals, keyboard / Solo instrumental, Adult alternative, Chamber jazz

This Montana-born keyboardist and composer studied music at Harvard on a Leonard Bernstein scholarship before paying his dues on the San Francisco blues scene. Aaberg's wide range of abilities led to guest appearances on over 80 albums. He also toured with artists as varied as Peter Gabriel, John Hiatt, Kenny Rogers, and the Doobie Brothers. Upon signing with Windham Hill in 1985, Aaberg made his eclectic background pay off through a series of solo albums that show off his rigorous keyboard technique, diverse influences, and colorful compositional style. *—Linda Kohanov*

High Plains / 1969 / Windham Hill 1037

Aaberg's Windham Hill debut. Solo piano pieces with folk and impressionistic elements that evoke the wide-open spaces of the American West. *—Linda Kohanov*

● **Out of the Frame** / 1979 / Windham Hill 1069

Lush yet pensive instrumental pieces masterfully combining acoustic and electronic sounds. *—Linda Kohanov*

Upright / 1980 / Windham Hill 1088

Aaberg calls this the first Windham Hill dance record. Upbeat toe-tappers are complemented by graceful slow numbers. *—Linda Kohanov*

Cinema / 1992 / Windham Hill 11110

Aaberg pays tribute to several contemporary film composers with a collection of piano solos. Movements of scores from *Cinema Paradiso*, *Diva*, *My Brilliant Career*, and *Awakenings*, among other films, are elegantly performed and nicely sequenced. *—Linda Kohanov*

William Ackerman

b. Nov. 1949, Germany

Guitar / New Age, Solo instrumental, Adult alternative, Chamber jazz

William Ackerman has gained prominence both as a musician and a businessman, and at least one of those occupations seems to have been unintentional. Though Ackerman has played guitar since the age of 12, when he dropped out of college it was to become a carpenter, and his first company was called Windham Hill Builders. But Ackerman composed guitar music for Stanford University theater productions, and the encouragement of friends led him to record an album of his tunes, *The Search for the Turtle's Navel*, in 1976. The album was surprisingly successful, and Ackerman found himself in the music business.

Since then, Ackerman has continued to record his own albums, to produce Windham Hill albums for such other artists as George Winston, Alex de Grassi, and Liz Story, and to serve in various capacities in the record company. (He stepped down as CEO in 1986; his function now primarily concerns A&R, the liaison between a record company and its artists.) Though Ackerman has long since sickened of the new-age tag, threatening physical violence against anyone categorizing Windham Hill's music with the term, he has had more to do with the rise of acoustic-based instrumental music as a popular form in the 70s and 80s than anyone else. *—William Ruhlmann*

In Search of the Turtle's Navel / 1976 / Windham Hill 1001

For many people, this is the album that invented new-age music. Ackerman's acoustic guitar improvisations, full of shifting moods and tempos, evocative and stirring, transformed him from a carpenter to a record company executive and charmed a surprisingly large audience. The music retains its power to move listeners to-day. —*William Ruhlmann*

Past Light / 1983 / Windham Hill 1028
For his fifth album, Ackerman added new instrumental colors to his guitar work. Especially notable are Michael Manring's bass playing and the one-track "Garden," featuring the Kronos Quartet. The added instrumentation serves only to accentuate Ackerman's typically inventive playing. —*William Ruhlmann*

Opening of Doors / 1992 / Windham Hill 1028
In his characteristically enigmatic manner, Will Ackerman offers his eighth release with "thanks to all who still listen to what I have to say musically after all these years." As always, there are introspective guitar sketches, small ensemble pieces supported by the expressive bass playing of Michael Manring, and song titles that are far more quirky than the music itself. What sets *The Opening of Doors* apart, however, are the three pieces featuring and co-written by Tim Story, whose keyboard musings add simple melodies that intermingle with Ackerman's guitar lines. In addition, there are two tracks that cut loose with electric guitar runs by someone named Buckethead, and two others featuring the smooth, silvery sax of Sapphron Obois. Ackerman's invitation is a warm one for listeners to enter his familiar musical realm. —*Backroads Music / Heartbeats*

● **Windham Hill Retrospective** / 1993 / Windham Hill 11121

Aeoliah

○ **Light At Mount Fuji** / 1994 /
Subtitled *A Live Transmission,* this new recording finds Aeoliah at his most sublime, with two deep space compositions that signify a stylistic change from his previous celestial creations. Recorded live in June of 1992 on the slopes of Mount Fuji in Japan, this album is ideal for deep meditation and inner attunement. This is healing, transforming & uplifting music of the spheres, with transparent ambiance of overtones that are heard slowly turning and opening on the two pieces, each around 31 minutes in length. They have Japanese titles that translate as "We Are One Light" and "We Are One Love." Aeoliah opens interdimensional doorways to the stargates and beyond. —*Backroads Music / Heartbeats*

★ **Angel Love** /
Two long ambiences that are pure warmth and loveliness float you on billows of slow, sweet chords. Synthesized organ and violin ascend and spread, heightened in places by a tender piano line, faraway voices and chimes. Pastel cloudlike, with shifting images—*Angel Love* is like a slow motion sunrise seen from high places. One of Aeoliah's premier releases. —*Backroads Music / Heartbeats*

Alio Die

● **Under an Holy Ritual** / 1990 / Projekt 39
Using sparse instrumentation and heavily processed sound effects, Alio Die submerges listeners into a world of nocturnal reverberations, dripping catacombs and "things that go bump in the night." Fans of O Yuki Conjugate will find commonality with Alio Die's concepts, though the focus is more on atmospherics & less on percussive dynamics. Both appear to imbibe from the same cup of mind-altering elixir. —*Backroads Music / Heartbeats*

Ancient Future

Group / Adult alternative, Ethnic fusion
Ancient Future was formed in 1978 by guitarist Matthew Montfort, who was interested in combining ancient musical traditions with modern technology. The band's inviting melodies, exotic instruments, and ethnic textures helped popularize of world-music fusion. —*Linda Kohanov*

Quiet Fire / 1986 / Sona Gaia 61012
A more subtle approach to the mix of new-age lyricism and world-music rhythms. —*Linda Kohanov*

● **World without Walls** / 1990 / Sona Gaia 62763
Squeaky clean acoustic romp by San Francisco quartet through African and Asian rhythms, with a dose of jazz and a dollop of Zakir Hussain sitting in on Indian percussion. —*Bob Tarte*

Asian Fusion / 1993 / Narada 63023

Ancient Future shines brightly on their latest cross-cultural release. As usual, they blend exotic traditions of the East with a contemporary fusion/synthesis of the West in their intriguing original material. Instruments from eastern realms such as the Gu Zheng, Kokyu or tabla, mix with piano, synth, bass, violin and the many guitars of group leader Matthew Montfort. This eclectic blend cuts across musical boundaries with the greatest of ease. Like a musical travelogue, it spans the expanses of Asia, from the Silk Road to the Spice Islands, & from the Himalayas to the forbidden city of ancient Peking. —*Backroads Music / Heartbeats*

Joel Andrews

● **Iridescence** /
Joel Andrews is able to bring forth the dreamlike sounds of higher realms. A master of the healing Harp, Joel co-creates with nature to manifest refined & rejuvenating sounds. *Iridescence*, divided into 20-minute halves, was commissioned by Dr. C. Norman Shealy for use in the Shealy Pain & Rehabilitation Institute in Springfield Missouri. This is the perfect album for healing, deep meditation, massage, or unwinding from a day at work. —*Backroads Music / Heartbeats*

Darol Anger

Fiddle, guitar, mandolin / New Age, Adult alternative, Chamber jazz, New-acoustic
Fiddler extraordinaire Anger was one of the early proponents of new-acoustic music, a virtuosic blend of folk, bluegrass, and jazz. —*Linda Kohanov*

Live at Montreux '84 / 1984 / Windham Hill 1036
This recording is a precursor to a series of albums released by the band Montreux on Windham Hill. Barbara Higbie's gift for highly melodic piano improvisation mixes well with Darol Anger and Mike Marshall's new acoustic tirades and Andy Narell's Caribbean-flavored steel drums. —*Linda Kohanov*

● **Chiaroscuro** / 1985 / Windham Hill 1043
This 1985 release is still one of the finest examples of new-acoustic music's appeal. Some fiery ensemble pieces are balanced by a few slower, moodier works and even some down-home versions of melodies by J. S. Bach. —*Linda Kohanov*

Tideline / 1986 / Windham Hill 1021
Anger plays various stringed instruments, accompanied by Barbara Higbie on piano. Mike Marshall joins in on a couple of tunes. —*Linda Kohanov*

Duo / 1988 / Rounder 0168
Anger and Mike Marshall were snatched up by Windham Hill soon after this early Rounder release, which offers a look at the duo's stylistic development. —*Linda Kohanov*

David Arkenstone

Guitar, keyboard / Adult alternative, Progressive electronic
Southern California-based Arkenstone honed his chops as a guitarist and keyboardist in various local bands and touring groups before the music of Kitaro inspired him to create a lavish synthesizer-based sound of his own. Most of his albums have enjoyed lengthy runs on the *Billboard* new-age sales chart due to a combination of accessible melodies, pop sensibilities, and cinematic textures. —*Linda Kohanov*

★ **Valley in the Clouds** / 1987 / Narada 62001
Arkenstone's finest album of electronic soundscapes is also his least commercial effort. Nicely designed atmospheres and warm, flowing melodies characterize Arkenstone's first album for Narada. —*Linda Kohanov*

Citizen of Time / 1990 / Narada 62008
A sonic odyssey telling the story of a traveler who visits earth's past and present civilizations. This album has some nice moments but generally the concept is more ambitious than the music. —*Linda Kohanov*

In the Wake of The Wind / 1991 / Narada 64003
One of the better examples of pop electronic music. —*Linda Kohanov*

Spirit of Olympia / 1992 / Narada 64006
David Arkenstone, David Lanz, and Kostia of the Soviet Union have teamed up to create an album in the spirit of the Olympic games, celebrating the beauty, energy, camaraderie, and ideals of

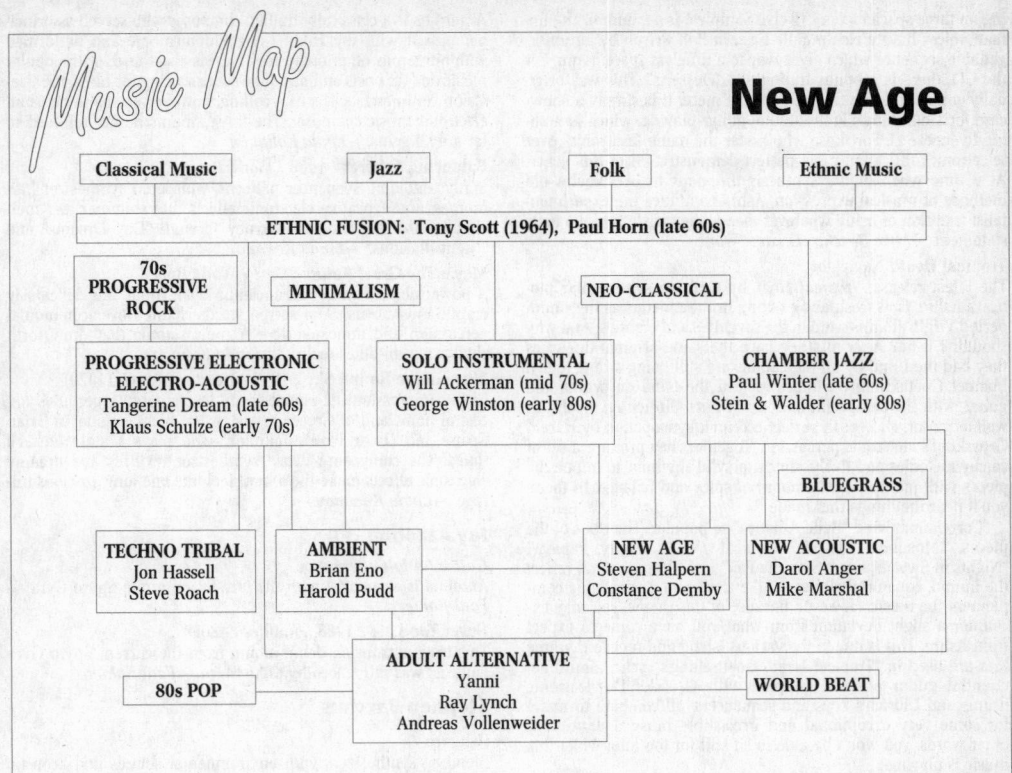

Music Map

New Age

| Classical Music | Jazz | Folk | Ethnic Music |

ETHNIC FUSION: Tony Scott (1964), Paul Horn (late 60s)

70s PROGRESSIVE ROCK

MINIMALISM

NEO-CLASSICAL

PROGRESSIVE ELECTRONIC ELECTRO-ACOUSTIC
Tangerine Dream (late 60s)
Klaus Schulze (early 70s)

SOLO INSTRUMENTAL
Will Ackerman (mid 70s)
George Winston (early 80s)

CHAMBER JAZZ
Paul Winter (late 60s)
Stein & Walder (early 80s)

BLUEGRASS

TECHNO TRIBAL
Jon Hassell
Steve Roach

AMBIENT
Brian Eno
Harold Budd

NEW AGE
Steven Halpern
Constance Demby

NEW ACOUSTIC
Darol Anger
Mike Marshal

80s POP

ADULT ALTERNATIVE
Yanni
Ray Lynch
Andreas Vollenweider

WORLD BEAT

---

athletic competition. They have taken traditional orchestral arrangements and added their own personal style and vision to a modern up tempo rendering via synthesizer, electric guitar, and percussion. Broad in scope and far-reaching in its collective musical vision, Arkenstone and his two comrades provide varied, adventurous listening. —*Backroads Music / Heartbeats*

○ **Chronicles** / 1993 / Narada 64007

With his new collection, simply titled *Chronicles*, it is possible to hear his most influential and successful compositions in one carefully packaged effort. Along with Richard Burmer, Peter Buffet & Patrick O'Hearn, Arkenstone has been one of the most enduring artists of the more active side of the genre. —*Backroads Music / Heartbeats*

James Asher

Group / New Age, Electro acoustic, Synthesiser

First-wave mod punks, led by Paul Weller, began as energetic Who clones but quickly became one of England's most distinct and proudly British combos. Weller's songwriting—alternately political and romantic—and the band's unflagging energy, however, are not just for fawning Anglophiles. —*John Floyd*

● **Great Wheel** / 1989 / Music West 180

Globalarium / Silver Wave 802

Globalarium is a musical portrait of a unified and harmonious world through a multiplicity of ethnic musical styles. Just as Asher's previous *The Great Wheel*, covered a lot of ground, his new *Globalarium* travels far and wide in gathering its musical influences, such as didgeridoo, classical flute, trumpet, shakuhachi, recorder, steel drum and a large selection of sampled and electronic sounds. Adding to the mix are guest performers such as Hossam Ramsy on percussion (has played with Peter Gabriel), Tim Wheater on flute, Joji Hirota (of Trisan trio), and, of course, Asher himself who plays keyboards in addition to being composer, producer and arranger on *Globalarium*. The ingenious combinations and multi-textured pieces command attention and

invite lots of in-depth exploration for rewarding listening all the way. —*Backroads Music / Heartbeats*

Ashra

Group / Adult alternative, Progressive electronic, Ambient, Minimalism

Formed in the late 60s by guitarist and synthesist Manuel Gottsching, this German group was highly influential in the field of contemporary electronic music. Ashra's album *New Age of Earth* (1977) is a classic in that it foreshadows the serene atmospherics used by subsequent "space music" composers. Gottsching continues to record to this day, though the results have been uneven. His rock-based albums are generally uninspiring, while his more recent work, which tends toward a form of trance-inducing electronic minimalism, is interesting though not particularly original. —*Linda Kohanov*

● **New Age of Earth** / 1977 / Blue Plate 1667

The last great Ashra disc—all spacey, floating guitars and synthesizers. —*Michael P. Dawson*

Walkin' the Desert / Navigator

Manuel Gottsching, the mainstay of Ashra (previously, Ash Ra Tempel), has been around the Berliner school of Electronic Rock as long as Tangerine Dream. In fact, Klaus Schulze and C. Schnitzer left T. Dream at different times to join Ashra back in the early '70's. Now paired with Lutz Ulbrich (aka Luul), Gottsching has come out with a beautifully eclectic album of music written for a Cultural festival in Berlin called "E 88". In its original format, there was to be a narrator accompanying the music but it was decided to leave him out for the album recording which doesn't seem to hurt the music a bit. The main idea behind the four movements of this work was to provide "live" interaction between the two performers. Each movement varies accordingly. The first movement is subtitled "Two Keyboards", and is simply one synth playing against a percussive piano. "Six Voices" is an ambient piece featuring six sampled voices with two more added for this album. "Four Guitars" has a chunky rhythm guitar backing up three spacier axes. "Twelve Samples" is a triumph. The human voices have a rich middle Eastern flair driven by an unforgettable sequence which gives way to a timeless space hymn. For the CD, there is a bonus track titled "Desserts". This was originally supposed to be the coda for the piece. It is simply a showcase for Gottsching's Froese-esque guitar playing, which is nothing to sneeze at. For those who prefer the name "esotronic" over "electronic", this album is a perfect demonstration of this genre. At a time when digital synthesis threatens to overwhelm old methods of musical expression, Ashra continues the experimentalist tradition of using whatever means they wish to make their statement. —Mike Birtchet, Dreams Word

○ **Tropical Heat** / Navigator
The latest release, *Tropical Heat*, by German synth/guitar pioneers Ashra, is as fresh and exciting in the nineties as their mid-period Virgin albums were in the seventies and eighties. And why shouldn't it be? After all, they have the same original lineup as they had then, and by all indications are still going strong today! Manuel Goettsching continues to lead the band on synths and guitar, with the competent back-up of Lutz Ulbrich on synths, as well as guitar, all kept in perfect eccentric syncopation by Harald Grosskopf's electronic percussion. Together they produce a set of catchy melodies and lively, almost playful rhythms, to imbue the pieces with just the right amount of spice and balance. In them, you'll hear the things that made
"Correlations" and "Belle Alliance" so popular. The titles of the pieces, "Mosquito Dance", "Tropical Heat", "Pretty Papaya", "Nights in Sweat", "Don't Stop the Fan", and "Monsoon", all reflect the humid, equatorial climate of the tropics, and admirably complement the music. However, because of this theme, you may encounter a slight deviation from what you have come to expect from Ashra. This is due to the various island and reggae rhythms that are used in "Tropical Heat". Goettsching's cyclic, almost sequential guitar phrases, coupled with Grosskopf's electronic drums and Ulbrich's keys and sequencers, all combine to make for some very exceptional and irresistible musical dances. In other words, you won't be able to sit still for too long while this music is playing.
Additionally, it is excellent music to play in the car, but keep your eye on the speedometer while you're driving. Otherwise, you're very likely to experience another type of "tropical heat". Recommended. —Jeff Filbert, Dreams Word

William Aura

Synthesizer / New Age, Adult alternative
Before signing with Higher Octave Records in the late 80s, Aura composed music for the healing arts based on research into psycho-acoustic audio production. He mixed zithers and other acoustic instruments with synthesizers to create a warm, relaxing bath of sounds. Aura has picked up the tempo on his latest albums with pleasant results. —Linda Kohanov

○ **Half Moon Bay** / 1987 / Higher Octave 7002
Aura's first recording for Higher Octave was recorded at a seaside studio in Half Moon Bay, CA. It has lots of ocean ambience and silky synthesizer washes. —Linda Kohanov

● **Timepiece** / 1988 / Higher Octave 7017
Timepiece (A Ten Year Perspective) is a good introduction to Aura's style and appeal. The album is a compilation of selected works from the first 10 years of his career. —Linda Kohanov

Paradise / 1991 / Higher Octave 7008
Some remixes of Aura's early music for healing, complete with 3-D nature sounds. —Linda Kohanov

Every Act of Love / 1992 / Higher Octave 7040
Though the album is billed as "global fusion for the contemporary mainstream," it really has more to do with pop and light jazz than anything ethnic. Aura's characteristic synthesizer timbres are enhanced by saxophone, piano, drums, and flute. —Linda Kohanov

World Keeps Turning / Jan. 15, 1992 / Higher Octave 7022
Aura's first "contemporary dance album" is best used as peppy background music. It withers under closer scrutiny. —Linda Kohanov

Paul Avgerinos

Bass / Progressive electronic, Ethnic fusion, Ambient

Avgerinos is a classically trained composer who served as principal bassist with the Hong Kong Philharmonic and performed with numerous other orchestras. He has also toured with popular music and jazz acts and has done some scoring for films and television commercials. His true calling, however, seems to be as an electronic-music composer. The three albums he has released so far are all gems. —Linda Kohanov

Balancing Spheres / 1988 / World Room
Softly unfolding sequencer patterns, whispered synthesizer harmonies, and evocative electronic effects that shimmer and melt characterize this two-part journey through "Day Dreams" and "Night Illusions". —Linda Kohanov

Maya: The Great Katun / 1988 / World Room
A powerful portrayal of an ancient Mayan ritual, this deliciously cryptic music consists of sacred words chanted over ceremonial percussion and atmospheric electronic sounds that draw forth shadows from other realms. —Linda Kohanov

● **Muse of the Round Sky** / 1992 / Hearts of Space 11029
Richly impressionistic soundscapes inspired by Avgerinos's ancestral homeland of Greece. Guest artists include guitarist Brian Keane and Omar Faruk Tekbilek, who plays Middle Eastern flutes. The composer's dense synthesizer textures and dreamy electronic effects make the album feel like one long, luscious mirage. —Linda Kohanov

Jay Azzolina

Guitar / Adult alternative
Azzolina is a guitarist with the jazz-fusion group Spyro Gyra. —Paul Kohler

○ **Never Too Late** / 1988 / Antilles 842650
This tasty jazz-fusion debut album from the current Spyro Gyra guitarist was influenced by Mike Stern. —Paul Kohler

Stephen Bacchus

★ **Pangaea** /
Blending synthesizers with environmental sounds and acoustic instruments from around the world, Stephen Bacchus takes us on a musical journey through the mists of prehistory to the vast primordial landmass of Pangaea, a mythological continent that gave birth to all the continents as we now know them. The album opens with a neo-classical harp-based track, featuring co-producer/flutist Ron Korb, before slipping into the reflective Eastern modal scales that characterize most of the album. Watery Javanese gamelan gongs, shakuhachi flute, lyrical koto, steel-bright sarod, glistening santur dulcimer & tabla join with lush synths, piano, oboe, flute, running streams, sweet birdsongs, and ocean waves to create exotic landscapes of lingering delicacy. Like a memorable vacation in the tropics, *Pangaea* leaves the listener relaxed, refreshed & inspired by its vision of shimmering beauty. —Backroads Music / Heartbeats

Wally Badarou

b. 1955
Synthesizer / Adult alternative, Ethnic fusion, Ambient, Electro acoustic
Badarou was born in Paris, where his physician parents were educated and his father later served as ambassador from their West African homeland of Cotonon Benin (formerly Dahomey). Although he planned a career as a pilot, he was seduced by synthesizers and rock & roll, eventually becoming a well-known session keyboardist in England and his own Nassau, Bahamas, studio. Badarou's early career included work with M (on the hit "Pop Music"), Joe Cocker, Herbie Hancock, and Island Records artists like Grace Jones, Black Uhuru, and the British funk band Level 42. In addition to his production and keyboard work for Level 42, he has done several film scores, most notably *Kiss of the Spider Woman*. You can hear both the rhythmic sensitivity of his African heritage and the harmonic sensibility of his classical training in his music. His expressive and sophisticated synthesizer textures are full of life, especially on his more dance-oriented *Echoes* album. —Scott Bultman

● **Echoes** / 1984 / Island 842503
You can actually feel Caribbean sunshine with this music. Badarou breathes real life into his synthesizers on this album of happy, upbeat, and danceable instrumentals. —Scott Bultman

New Age Music Types

SOLO INSTRUMENTAL – Solo instrumental recordings launched successful labels like Windham Hill and Narada, ushering in a whole movement oriented toward impressionistic, often folk-inspired originals for piano, guitar, celtic harp, even hammered dulcimer. Though some of these releases offer innovative, emotionally moving performances, enough second-rate opportunists have jumped on the bandwagon to give the genre its "aural wallpaper" reputation. Still, some fine musicians continue to battle this stigma.

ADULT ALTERNATIVE – This genre attracts a wide cross-section of listeners who are looking for something a little different without straying too far from the mainstream. It's actually hard to say whether new adult contemporary radio formats were created to play this music or whether the music was created for radio airplay. Adult alternative styles – whether acoustic, electronic, or electro-acoustic – are heavily influenced by pop, rock, and jazz fusion elements. (Some albums feature a few vocal selections with lyrics, although the main orientation remains instrumental.) The best artists have a flair for melodic invention, colorful instrumentation, and rhythmic vitality while retaining a strong level of accessibility. At worst, adult alternative releases sound like trite pop songs without words.

PROGRESSIVE ELECTRONIC & ELECTRO-ACOUSTIC – This music thrives in more unfamiliar territory. The styles that emerge are often dictated by the technology itself. Rather than sampling or synthesizing acoustic sounds to electronically replicate them, these composers tend to mutate the original timbres, sometimes to an unrecognizable state. True artists in the genre also create their own sounds (as opposed to using the preset sounds that come with modern synthesizers).

In progressive electro-acoustic music, the electronics play an equal if not greater part in the overall concept. Acoustic instruments performed in real time are usually processed through reverb, harmonizing, etc., which adds an entirely new dimension to the player's technique.

At best, this music opens up new worlds of listening, thinking, and feeling. At worst, progressive electronic artists worship technology for its own sake, relinquishing the heart and soul of true artistic expression.

NEW AGE – Born from an aesthetic that aims to induce a sense of inner calm, new-age music emerged from the meditational and holistic fields. Generally these are harmonious and nonthreatening albums that are allied with new-age philosophies encouraging spiritual transcendence and physical healing. Some of these albums are artistically satisfying as well as therapeutic. Lesser musicians, however, often make ridiculous claims in the liner notes as to their ability to catapult listeners into advanced spiritual states through specially designed sonic vibrations and "immaculately conceived" musical ideas.

AMBIENT – A term popularized by Brian Eno but used here in a broader sense. Ambient composers use echo, electronic reverb, and other spatial techniques as important musical elements in creating atmospheric pieces and sonic environments.

The best artists have developed the ability to manipulate the listener's sense of space and time in highly sophisticated ways. Many ambient recordings involve extended compositions that change subtly in content and timbre over a long period of time. Though some musicians use ambient techniques for their meditative benefits (and can thus be allied with the new-age movement), other ambient composers create ethereal, alien environments that are more mysterious and confrontational than comforting.

NEO-CLASSICAL – Many contemporary instrumentalists are conservatory trained, yet don't subscribe to the modern classical world's emphasis on intellectual, atonal forms of composition. As these artists follow their own vision, however, classical music may continue to be an important inspiration. In the context of CI music, the neoclassical distinction refers to any style influenced by classical music, whether the performer is offering updated arrangements of actual works by an established composer (Bach, Pachelbel, and Debussy seem to be popular in this respect) or weaving elements from the baroque, classical, romantic, impressionistic, and/or more challenging 20th-century styles into a more original approach.

NEW-ACOUSTIC – An exhilarating mix of bluegrass and jazz. Folk instruments like the mandolin, fiddle, banjo, and acoustic guitar play lead roles on new-acoustic albums. Virtuosity is the name of the game as the musicians stretch the boundaries of their traditional roles with heated improvisations and complex jazz harmonies.

ETHNIC FUSION – One of the major trends among all contemporary instrumental subgenres is the fusion of ethnic instruments, modes, and rhythms with Western styles. The possibilities are as wide-ranging as the world's vast musical cultures.

TECHNO-TRIBAL – A more specific variation on the ethnic fusion theme, techno-tribal music is becoming more prominent among progressive electro-acoustic artists who are fascinated by the idea of combining man's most primeval musical expressions with his most technologically advanced inventions. Tribal rhythms and instruments from the aboriginal cultures of Africa, Australia, and North and South America are mixed with sophisticated electronics. Though successful efforts are immensely powerful, it takes great skill and sensitivity to keep the music from sounding like cheap parodies of the cultures from which these artists are borrowing.

CHAMBER JAZZ – This style is distinguished by small, acoustic-based ensembles in which improvisation is a major factor. Though some groups are more jazz-based than others, they all tend to employ neo-classical aesthetics, particularly from the Impressionistic period and later 20th-century movements. Ethnic elements are also an important factor. These world-music leanings, however, are usually oriented toward the classical traditions of other cultures (Indian, Middle Eastern, and Oriental), although South American styles also figure prominently in a lot of these recordings.

MINIMALISM – One of the main innovations in the contemporary classical field, minimalism has also influenced many CI composers, particularly in progressive electronic styles where sequencers play an important role. Generally this music is characterized by a strong and relentless pulse, the insistent repetition of short melodic fragments, and harmonies that change over long periods of time.

– Linda Kohanov

Words of a Mountain / 1989 / Island 842446
This album has a more contemplative mood than his last, and a distinctly classical feel, although the atmospheres are no less vivid. —*Scott Bultman*

Matt Balitsaris

New Age, Adult alternative, Ethnic fusion

● **Gypsy Heart** / 1992 / Raven 7922
Matt Balitsaris is a versatile guitarist who is at home in many settings. He weaves dense sonic tapestries that shift in shape and texture right before your ears. Balitsaris plays slide guitar, 12-string, acoustic, electric, MIDI ... virtually anything with strings! The contrasting accompaniment is provided by hand drums, MIDI vibes (Jeff Berman; see p. 13) and fretless bass, with many world music hints, such as chants & other-worldly vocalese. Images of distant lands and wandering souls express the appealing spirit of the *Gypsy Heart.* —*Backroads Music / Heartbeats*

Patrick Ball

Harp / Irish, Solo instrumental
With a vast knowledge of folklore and music from the British Isles, Celtic harp player Patrick Ball calls forth the music of a simpler, more magical time. His scintillating performances on the traditional wire-strung harp are by far the best-selling titles on the Fortuna label. —*Linda Kohanov*

● **Celtic Harp 1—Music of Turlough O'carolan** / Jan. 1983 / Fortuna 17005
Celtic Harp 1—Music of Turlough O'Carolan. All of Ball's recordings that feature traditional tunes from the British Isles are great. —*Linda Kohanov*

Celtic Harp 2—from a Distant Time / Feb. 1983 / Fortuna 17011

Celtic Harp 3—Secret Isles / 1990 / Fortuna 17029

Christmas Rose / 1990 / Fortuna 17077
This is the first Christmas release by this well known Celtic harper. The sixteen carols ring with the crystalline purity of his harp which is strung with brass strings in the manner of the ancient Irish bards. The rich resonance and bright chiming sounds of his harp evoke the joy and magic of the season as he freely mixes old favorites like "The First Noel" and "Silent Night" with more obscure tunes like "Dona Nobis Pacem" and "The Gloucester Wassail." Occasional touches of penny whistle are heard in the background, as well as the stirring strains of the uillean pipes on "The Carol of the Birds." Fittingly, "Auld Lang Syne" is chosen to close out this warm and uplifting album. —*Backroads Music / Heartbeats*

○ **Celtic Harp 4—O'carolan's Dream** / 1991 / Fortuna 17061
A gentle, yet masterful collection of music by the renowned late 17th-century Irish harper Turlough O'Carolan. —*Linda Kohanov*

Tom Barabas

Piano, synthesizer / New Age, Adult alternative, Solo instrumental (piano)
Before developing a taste for rock and jazz, Barabas studied classical music at the Caracas Conservatory in Venezuela. His skills as a pianist are admirable; Barabas's use of synthesizers is not quite so sophisticated but shows some promise. —*Linda Kohanov*

● **Sedona Suite** / Soundings of the Planet 7142
This new-age pop jaunt through Southwestern scenes has some nice moments. —*Linda Kohanov*

Magic in December / Soundings of the Planet 7146
New Age impressionism with a lovely classical feel shines through in the delightful interplay of piano and delicate synthesizer. Includes a nice version of the Pachelbel's "Canon in D," "Ave Maria" and three originals, most notably the "magical" title piece. —*Backroads Music / Heartbeats*

Pete Bardens

Keyboard / Adult alternative, Progressive electronic
Best known for his work with the 70s progressive rock band Camel, Bardens has played with a number of rock legends over the years. His solo instrumental music is catchy and well produced, yet rarely ventures beyond the tenets of pop music and tends to suffer as a result. —*Linda Kohanov*

● **Seen One Earth** / 1987 / Capitol 46868

A concept album based on the space exploration and astronaut book *The Right Stuff.* —*Linda Kohanov*

Speed of Light / 1988 / Atlantic 7489672
A half-instrumental/half-vocal project released as a followup to the popular *Seen One Earth.* —*Linda Kohanov*

○ **Water Colors** / 1991 / Miramar 4001
This soundtrack to a video by the same title is a mixed bag. Some simplistic and superficial selections are balanced by some well-produced, thoughtful keyboard work. —*Linda Kohanov*

Further Than You Know / 1993 / Miramar 2601
Bardens was leader of the group Camel, and has several solo albums since the demise of the group. *Further Than You Know* continues his journey into contemporary vocal compositions, while he remains true to his roots with three exciting instrumentals that showcase his unique, sophisticated and rhythmic blend of jazz and rock styles. —*Backroads Music / Heartbeats*

Barefoot

Percussion, violin / Adult alternative, Ethnic fusion
Percussionist Henry Clay and violinist Steve Kindler came up with the concept of Barefoot, an ensemble inspired by the dance traditions of many different cultures. The band tends to compose collectively, often featuring ethnic dancers on stage to add to the excitement of the music. —*Linda Kohanov*

● **Barefoot** / Nov. 19, 1991 / Global Pacific 79333
Earthy world/fusion/dance music featuring a multicultural ensemble led by violinist Steve Kindler. Kindler is best known for his work with Kitaro and the Mahavishnu Orchestra. —*Linda Kohanov*

Dance of Life / 1992 / Priority 57125
Dance of Life is the second release from this San Francisco Bay Area group headed by Steve Kindler and Clay Henry. With a host of musicians & percussionists playing instruments ranging from violin, panpipes and synthesizers to tuba and talking drum, the focus is fun music that moves the body. "After Hours" provides some primal heat with Peter Apfelbaum's sultry tenor sax, and "Dancing Barefoot" fans the flames with Latin rhythms & vocals by Vicki Randall. The stirring melody "The Heights of Atacama" opens with ethereal pan-pipes, and closes with the deft strokes of Carlos Reyes' Paraguayan harp. We are later led into a flowing fantasy of Old Spain on the cut, "Andalucia," with Spanish guitar, flute, violin & percussion. Barefoot plays music to lift the spirits and inspire unabashed frolicking. —*Heartbeats*

Bearheart

Medicine Songs of the Native American Peyote Lodge / 1994 /
Marcellus "Bearheart" Williams is a respected elder shaman and Road Chief of the Peyote Lodge. He creates an extremely personal I-Thou relationship with each listener on *Medicine Songs.* His voice envelops you in friendship as he sings and shares the meaning of each song comprising the all night medicine ceremony. Uma Silbey's synthesizer and sampler work does a masterful job of conveying the sounds and atmosphere inside the huge ritual teepee where the nature spirits come to bear witness to each individual's prayers. Bob Boyll's heartbeat drumming rides in perfect tandem with Bearheart's hissing rattle throughout. This gift, filled with vitality, offers more than any mere field recording could hope to. —*Backroads Music / Heartbeats*

Robert Bearns

New Age

★ **Golden Voyage, Vol. 1** / Golden Voyage 3001
Produced by Robert Bearns and Ron Dexter, this is some of the earliest and most successful New Age music. Using sounds of nature blended with flutes, bells, piano, guitar and electronic sounds, these timeless explorations through celestial harmonics create a unique and magical experience for the listener. Very visual and indescribably delicious! Now on CD. —*Backroads Music / Heartbeats*

Bruce BecVar

Guitar, synthesizer / Adult alternative
This California guitarist and synthesist writes highly melodic, commercially accessible ensemble music. Though he plays most of the instruments himself, his technique on acoustic guitar is

most admirable. He's also a well-known luthier—one of his hand-crafted guitars is on display at the New York Metropolitan Museum of Art. —*Linda Kohanov*

★ **Forever Blue Sky** / 1989 / Willow 115
A good example of BecVar's style. —*Linda Kohanov*

Arriba / Willow 119
A long-time Heartbeats favorite for his eloquent guitar instrumentals, Bruce BecVar has come up with new inspiration in the flamenco style on his new release *Arriba*. He retains the breezy, evocative feel which made *Rhythm of Life, Forever Blue Sky, The Nature of Things* and *Take it to Heart* so successful as he drifts off to distant lands vibrant with the flamenco spirit...The selections, solo and ensemble, include hints of classical, pop and reggae, as BecVar breathes passion and romance into every note. The trademark fluidity and melodic sense, which give Bruce a "naturally commercial sound," translate perfectly into this new style as he skillfully navigates the line between accessibility and authenticity. —*Backroads Music / Heartbeats*

Rhythms of Life / Higher Octave 7043
On *Rhythms of Life*, Bruce BecVar reaches a new pinnacle of musical heights with the expansive, cascading melodies of his rich guitar music. He is joined on his fourth album by a cast of stellar musicians, and combines elements that travel across and blend many contemporary styles. His music sounds immediately familiar in a number of ways, as innovative musical progressions come to life in his recognizable style, consummately expressed with synthesizer, percussion and melodic vocal tones...Bruce's success is a result of his heartfelt and sensitive acoustic melodies and lead lines combined with dynamic multi-instrumental arrangements. —*Backroads Music / Heartbeats*

○ **Take It to Heart** / Willow 110
Sure, it's a marvel of new age/space music marketing, and yes, it is peaceful, gentle stuff, but the music has a graceful, classical side that leaves behind the cliches. BecVar plays acoustic and synthesizer guitars, with some keyboards. The sound quality is absolutely clear, and the guitar solos are the strongest part of the album; there's depth here, and pleasant listening. —*Dan Maryon, Option*

Nature of Things / Willow 113
The heartfelt sounds of delicately blended instruments takes *The Nature of Things* deep into lyrical heartspace with care and sensitivity. Synthesizer, vocal harmonics, and percussive touches add to the rich acoustic guitar sound, revealing a precious, subtle magic which connects the listener to the uplifting spirit of love, peace and beauty. Bruce's clear-sailing melodic lines are mixed with light, bright folk-picking, and the more spacious pieces on each side glisten and gleam with a depth of beauty that expands and deepens over time. Bruce's second album, *The Nature of Things*, is a musical masterpiece, essential to any collection. —*Backroads Music / Heartbeats*

Stephanie Bennett

New Age

● **Stories Seldom Told** / Harpworld 9001
This lush collection of magical harp-centered pieces is both soothing and challenging, ranging from solo tracks to a 14-piece orchestra. Flutes and recorders, oboes, brass and strings, tablas, timpani and bells help to blend the timeless beauty of *Stories Seldom Told* with passionate, adventure-filled music. On "The Rabbit Who Belonged to the Desert," all the elements mesh perfectly, with a lilting backbeat carrying the fantasy melodies. "A Big Cat Hug," referring to the cougar on the album cover, is a lullaby-like piece that shows Bennett's proficient harp playing, and is the only solo piece. "Dream Dance" is a string-laden dreamy piece with bass flute leading up to the dramatic break in the center, while "Dragonmaker" builds to a full orchestral sound, complete with conductor. —*Backroads Music / Heartbeats*

Pierre Bensusan

Guitar / Solo instrumental, Chamber jazz, Ethnic fusion
This French guitarist was actually born in Algeria and has long been fascinated with his North African roots as well as the Celtic folk traditions of western Europe. After making a name for himself as a folk musician in the late 70s, Bensusan began to incorporate jazz and classical elements into his music, creating a vir-

tuosic, highly original style on the acoustic guitar. —*Linda Kohanov*

○ **Solilai** / 1982 / CBS 44897
Pierre Bensusan did longer, more spirited numbers on this '81 session, which was issued in America in '93 by Dadgad (Rounder distribution). He played both acoustic and electro-acoustic guitar, as well as adding his own (at times) bass and percussive accompaniment. Soprano saxphonist and flutist Didier Malherbe provided fine instrumental support, while special guests fretless bassist Emmanuel Binet ("Doatea") and Yvan Lantos on Hungarian pipes ("Solilai") were excellent in short stints. Bensusan stretched out on "Bamboule," "Suite Flamande Aux Pommes" and the title cut, doing more than slight melodic variations. He demonstrated a craft and ability that indicate he could be a fine improviser if so inclined. Those who've shied away from other Bensusan albums due to the lack of ambitiousness might try this one; it's the closest he's come on any CD to displaying significant jazz skills. —*Ron Wynn*

Spices / 1987 / CBS 42665
Guitarist Pierre Bensusan's fifth album issued on the Dadgad (Rounder distribtion in America) label continued his expansion into brisker, more adventurous music. While there were still laid-back, impressionistic and light songs, Bensusan played with more intensity, stretching out on guitar and going beyond restating the melody and adding teasing, nimble voicings. On "Presqu'ile," "Les Voiles Catalanes" and "Montsegur" his riffs had bite and edge. He was backed by a larger band, and soprano/tenor saxophonist and flutist Didier Malherbe and pianist/keyboardist Franck Sitbon provided some instrumental challenge and encouragement, as did percussionist Denis Benharrosh and bassist Emmanuel Binet. Where most of his other albums were almost totally atmospheric with rhythm either implied or almost missing, this CD had a pronounced Afro-Latin and African tinge at times, due to Benharrosh. This was Pierre Bensusan's most effective and complete album issued among the five available on Rounder. —*Ron Wynn*

Pres De Paris / 1991 / Rounder 3023
Guitarist Pierre Bensusan mixes jazz, folk, New Age, even light fusion elements into his music. These 10 tracks recorded in the mid-'70s include originals from Bensusan, a remake of a '60s folk tune by Bill Keith and Jim Rooney, a reworking of an Irish number, impressionistic cuts and a superb solo mandolin piece, "Lady de Nantes." While Bensusan isn't an energetic or bluesy stylist, he's a lush, sentimental guitarist, whose soothing, delicate touch and lyrical voicings are appealing, as well as his interplay with violinist Phil Fromont, banjo player Bill Keith, bassist Gerard Lavigne, and dulcimer player/guitarist Claude Lefebvre. While occasionally songs become so smooth and relaxed they veer into easy-listening land, Bensusan's music overall has strength and character, as well as beauty. —*Ron Wynn*

● **Musiques** / 1993 / Lost Lake Arts 0092
Pierre Bensusan's a marvelous technical guitarist; he has speed, flair, touch and expressiveness. While he doesn't play with either fire or improvisational elan, he demonstrates tremendous skills throughout the 13 pieces on this anthology of late '70s singles issued in '93 by Dadgad (distributed domestically by Rounder). With the exception of "Perles De Cristal" and "Si Bhig, Si Mnor/The Rakish Paddy," these are short, ethereal atmospheric pieces nicely played with Bensusan. The melodies and voicings are stylish, done in a dreamy, catchy manner. There's bits of flamenco and Spanish guitar, and it's brillantly executed. If you're seeking tough, harsh or gritty material, look elsewhere. Pierre Bensusan's solo playing deliberately avoids those qualities. —*Ron Wynn*

Erik Berglund

New Age, Solo instrumental

● **Angel Beauty** /
Erik Berglund's *Angel Beauty* takes the listener on a peaceful journey through the shimmering tones of his harp. This music is filled with images of beauty, soaring wings, light and healing. Blending his Celtic harp with keyboard synthesizers, Berglund carries one into the realm of angels, of all encompassing love and deep inner trust. The pieces are three to six minutes, and feature a few vocal portions by Erik & Marty Freed, plus synthesizer colorings by Etherium, Anton Mizerak & Berglund. The nurturing

ambience is ideal for massage, meditation, healing, or washing away the cares of the world. —*Backroads Music / Heartbeats*

Harp of the Healing Waters /
Erik Berglund's follow-up to his successful *Angelic Harp Music* takes the listener on a peaceful journey through healing waters. The gentle and lyrical harp melodies are framed by background synthesizer, and the occasional sound of flute, cello, and tinkling chimes, as well as the sounds of water itself on three of the seven tracks. The instruments create a relaxing and nurturing ambience ideal for meditation, massage, healing, or just washing away the cares of the world. —*Backroads Music / Heartbeats*

Steven Berkowitz

Ambient, Minimalism

Dis/Recon / 1994 /
Nature, vision, human, and machine all combine to create a unique synthesis of sound on Steven Berkowitz's second release, *Dis/Recon*. The movement of leaves floating on water is captured by motion camera. A computer converts the photographs into numerical data. Software written by the artists translates images from visual to aural language. The changes in positions of the leaves in physical space determine the changes in positions of notes in harmonic space. The final product, ultimately, is not any single image but the relationships between all when experienced together, a self- referential, lateral arrangement! Simultaneously perceiving the same image through more than one sense creates synaesthesia—a profound state of mind that intimately connects our visions, thoughts and feelings to inspire our very essence. Reminiscent of the pioneering works of Eno and Roach, Berkowitz further pushes the envelope of deep ambient sound sculpting. —*Backroads Music / Heartbeats*

● **Ec(s)tasis /**
Steven Berkowitz calls his work "fluid music," an apt term for these two 30-minute tracks of flowing, shimmering synthesizers. The first track, "Ec(s)tasis," is comprised of watery synth effects, from the essence of a quiet country brook to a waterfall, to a gentle drizzle, to an outright downpour of rain pit-a-pattering against a window. No actual water sounds are heard; the feeling is given only by the way the synthesizers are played. The second track, "(S)tasis," moves into the realm of inner space, with deep bass notes underlining a flowing midrange that shimmers and hangs in the room. This track will take you journeying through the galaxy on a wave of sound and let you hear the distant call of the stars. Reminiscent of Iasos or Brian Eno at their most magical, Berkowitz' music will find fans among those who enjoy the quiet side of Steve Roach, Aeoliah or Kevin Braheny, and serves as an ideal background ambience for relaxing, meditation or massage. —*Backroads Music / Heartbeats*

Jeff Berman

Things She Said / 1994 /
This debut from vibraphonist/percussionist Jeff Berman was produced by Matt Balitsaris, known for his albums on the Raven label. For those wishing to dive into jazzier waters, *Things She Said* will fill the bill, with its breezy rhythms and urban musicality laced with engaging melodic themes. ...*Things She Said* is a mellow release offering companionship for a variety of musical settings. —*Backroads Music / Heartbeats*

Patrick Bernhardt

New Age

★ **Atlantis Angelis** / IMG 2002
An artist of this caliber comes along only once in a great while. The immediate comparisons to the "solid gold" appeal of Enya are obvious, but the music of Patrick Bernhardt stands alone. This superb release combines ethereal appeal with the timelessness of the ancient mystics. Patrick sings Sanskrit mantras taken from Vedic Hindu sources in a rich vibrato voice set to his own inspired music that blends his delicate guitar, piano and synth choir tracks, bringing to mind other artists such as Kitaro, Jon Mark and, above all, Enya herself. Robert LaFond's additional piano and synthesizer, along with the beautifully soaring vocals of Brigitte Pellerin, round out the sound. The spaciousness of the recording is enhanced further by nature sounds and layered production that creates a hypnotic effect, especially in the 30 minute

plus suite, "Song of the Universal Light," which renders a rich panorama of sound images, shimmering colors and hues, and a calling to reconnect with the resounding power of the universe. All in all, *Atlantis Angelis* conveys mystical truths and ancient melodies in an ethereal yet modern western setting where movement dissolves into an eternity and time entertains poised stillness. And if purely soothing, relaxing music is your cup of tea, you can drink deeply from the the magical waters of *Atlantis Angelis*. —*Backroads Music / Heartbeats*

Paul Binkley

● **Closer to Home /**
A beautiful and mostly undiscovered gem of a release. Paul lives in Nashville, and plays guitar in a style not unlike Bruce BecVar. He adds a plaintive, emotional violin to a couple of pieces, and the effect moves between a "front porch" style and studio ensemble interplay. The flow between pieces is especially effective, and works well in many listening environments. Subtle yet deeply expressive, that's the music of Paul Binkley. —*Backroads Music / Heartbeats*

○ **Passages /**
Passages, flows from ensemble pieces, with violin, cello, piano, bass, drums & percussion, to tracks written for acoustic guitar with cradle-like gentleness. Spirited and lively with a warm energy that thoroughly captivates the listener, Binkley's uniqueness translates in a careful development from track to track, tunefully calling on influences from classical, folk and jazz fields. Without any overdubs or electronic orchestration, *Passages* is the result of talented acoustic players gathering to bring to life these well-crafted songs. —*Backroads Music / Heartbeats*

Daniel Blanchet

Guitar / Neo-classical, Progressive electronic, Ambient
A classically trained guitarist, Montreal-based Blanchet is part of a growing electronic music contingent in Canada. He began experimenting with synthesizers in 1985, intrigued by their endless possibilities of sound color and spatial enhancement. Blanchet's early fascination with Bach's oratorios is reflected in his use of electronic reverb to create cathedral-like dimensions for his thoughtful compositions. —*Linda Kohanov*

Le Chemin De L'ermite / 1987 / Rubicon 2302
Blanchet's first album features lyrical pieces that suggest imaginary environments with an innocence reminiscent of Kitaro. —*Linda Kohanov*

● **L'harmonie Des Mondes** / 1991 / Rubicon 2301
An homage to the famous *Harmony of the Spheres* treatise by the 16th-century astronomer Johannes Kepler, this collection explores a variety of musical moods and settings with the same poetic theme of order and beauty that Kepler believed ruled the universe. —*Linda Kohanov*

Les Voilers De L'espace /
Old and new are blended to create a fantasy journey through time and space by Daniel Blanchet on *Les Voilers de L'Espace*, which means "The Voyagers of Space". His previous titles, *Le Chemin* and *Les Harmonies* showed considerable diversity within contemporary spacemusic styles. On his latest venture, Blanchet takes us in several directions. Opening with a five movement suite of gentle synthesizer orchestration supporting acoustic guitar, Blanchet then leads into provocative, modern landscapes with sweeping textures and sensuous harp melodies. Stylistically, the music falls somewhere between Jarre and Lynch with similar planetarium atmospherics to Jonn Serrie. —*Backroads Music / Heartbeats*

Blue Chip Orchestra

Group / New Age, Progressive electronic

★ **Blue Chip Orchestra** / Mercury 426373
Debut release on the German electronic music scene. Presenting the latest techniques in computer music. Synthephonic productions of the highest caliber. —*John Tait, Dreams Word*

Blue Danube

The digital philharmonic sound images of the *Blue Danube* project draw upon the rich orchestral heritage of the Austrian region in this avant garde tribute to some of the most dynamic and brilliant of European classical composters. The Blue Chip Orchestra is the brainchild of Hubert Bognermayr who has fused this inter-play of classically trained instrumentalists and live soloists of the computer age...*Blue Danube* is thoughtful and intelligent music which demands attention, then leaves you wondering "Are these guys serious?" —*Backroads Music / Heartbeats*

Ian Boddy (Ian Biddy)

New Age

Uncertainty Principle / 1994 /
Ian Boddy is a synthesist who specializes in grand scale orches-trations. After three previous albums offered to Heartbeats read-ers, Boddy has produced a magically cohesive work, *The Uncertainty Principle*. Combining his driving style with studio ef-fects of all kinds, Boddy maintains his trademark style while forg-ing into broader territory as far as compositional twists and tech-nical innovation. The music is filled with the multiple sampled sounds of acoustic guitar, strings, horns, choirs and percussion to create a powerful musical experience, using elements from rock and classical romanticism, with a nod in Kitaro's direction, as well as ethnic influences. "Space Cadet" and "Supernova" recall T. Dream at their creative peak, right down to the patterned rhythms. Then the album's highlight, the title track in three parts, before the two closers. At the forefront of UK synthesists, Boddy has delivered his strongest statement to date, majestic music with an epic feel, hinting at the magic of lost times & places. —*Backroads Music / Heartbeats*

○ **Odyssey** /
Odyssey is the latest release on Scotland's Surreal to Real label, the same people who brought us John Dyson's *Evolution*. Boddy is a synthesist who specializes in dramatic large scale orchestra-tions. Most of his pieces revolve around simple four-chord struc-tures, but they are embellished with the sampled sounds of acoustic guitar, strings, horns, choirs and percussion to create grandiose musical experiences. *Odyssey* incorporates rock ele-ments and classical romanticism, with a strong nod in Kitaro's di-rection, plus ethnic influences, such as on the atmospheric "Amazonia". This is majestic music with an epic feel, hinting at the magic of lost times and places. —*Backroads Music / Heartbeats*

Botanica

Group / Progressive electronic
Led by synthesist Sanford Ponder, this group creates music gen-erated by fractal mathematics. The computer programs are con-nected to numerous synthesizers. The musicians then interact with the resulting soundtracks by overdubbing percussion, sax, flute, and piano. For something created by the seemingly impar-tial mathematics of "chaos" theories, this music is surprisingly beautiful and emotionally stimulating. —*Linda Kohanov*

● **Garden of Earthly Delights** / 1989 / Deep Music 001
Though both Botanica releases are well worth owning, the band's first fractal effort is more serene and melodious, thus more ac-cessible. —*Linda Kohanov*

Strange Attractor / 1991 / Deep Music 002
The album's title is probably the best description of this music. Sometimes mysterious and floating, other times aggressively beat-oriented, *Strange Attractor* sounds like something you might encounter in outer space. —*Linda Kohanov*

Liona Boyd

★ **Persona** / 1988 / Columbia 42120
After 20 highly-acclaimed classical guitar records, Liona entered the "New Age" with style in 1988. Starting with the Vangelis piece from *The Year of Living Dangerously* (L'Enfant) and featuring guest appearances from Eric Clapton, David Gilmour (Pink Floyd) and Yo-Yo Ma (#1 cellist in the world), the scope and vari-ety of *Persona* is kind of "beyond belief!" Exciting, beautiful and dazzling, just like the artist herself. —*Backroads Music / Heartbeats*

Kevin Braheny

Composer / New Age, Progressive electronic, Ambient
This Los Angeles-based synthesist builds much of his own equip-ment, including the 3-D binaural recording technology he uses on

his *Secret Rooms* album. His sounds and special effects are so-phisticated and highly evocative, but Braheny's music is not all technique. His graceful improvisations on electronic wind instru-ments bring a lyrical dimension to his music. —*Linda Kohanov*

● **Way Home** / 1978 / Hearts of Space 11001
This lush, romantic space music has an overall feeling of longing. —*Linda Kohanov*

○ **Galaxies** / 1988 / Hearts of Space 11004
Braheny's score for a planetarium soundtrack is filled with slowly evolving, synthesized atmospheres that are appropriately spacey. —*Linda Kohanov*

Secret Rooms / 1991 / Hearts of Space 11015
A varied album, with a few uneven tracks. Overall, the album showcases Braheny's meticulous production standards and virtu-osity on the electronic wind instrument. —*Linda Kohanov*

Spencer Brewer

piano / Adult alternative
This Northern California-based pianist has released a half-dozen records on the Narada label. His pleasant, pop-flavored style and strong melodic sense make for nice easy-listening music that of-ten suffers under the scrutiny of concentrated listening. His col-laborations with other artists on the Narada label are stronger. —*Linda Kohanov*

● **Shadow Dancer** / 1984 / Narada 60144

Emerald / 1986 / Narada 61011
A collaboration with guitarist Eric Tingstad and wind player Nancy Rumble that puts Brewer in a more substantial musical setting than his own albums. —*Linda Kohanov*

○ **Dorian's Legacy** / 1989 / Narada 63008
An optimistic jaunt through contemporary instrumental textures. —*Linda Kohanov*

Piper's Rhythm / 1991 / Narada 63018
More of Brewer's light, yet technically proficient style. —*Linda Kohanov*

Michael Brook

Guitar / Progressive bluegrass, Electronic, Techno-Tribal
This innovative guitarist and producer received early recognition as an engineer and performer on projects with Brian Eno, Daniel Lanois, and Jon Hassell. Brook went on to produce albums on Peter Gabriel's Real World label by African artist Youssou N'Dour and Pakistani singer Nusrat Fateh Ali Khan. Brook also did some fine guitar work on the latter release. His style as a composer is characterized by a unique "infinite guitar" sound (created through heavy signal processing), mixed with Eno-style ambience and Hassell-influenced "fourth world" rhythms. —*Linda Kohanov*

○ **Hybrid** / 1985 / EG 41
An album by which all world-music fusions should be judged. This has incredible musicianship, production, compositional ideas, and voodoo percussion. —*Linda Kohanov*

● **Cobalt Blue** / Jul. 1987 / 4AD 45000
Michael Brook has a decided talent for subtlety. Taking a musical or rhythmic theme, he stretches it, lays out variations, and, when finished, offers us a musical environment that we can climb into. Joining Michael on this album are luminaries Brian Eno, Roger Eno and Daniel Lanois, all of whom Brook has collaborated with in the past. Using such instruments as guitar, infinite guitar, syn-thesizers, and various percussion, Michael and friends lead us into the dreamlike imagery of "Ten", but only after we have ex-perienced the more upbeat "Ultramarine" and "Slipstream". Middle Eastern influences run throughout "Shona Bridge", and "Breakdown" brings us into territory we might call "funky Cajun". "Red Shift" must be that perfect minor-key theme for the good-guy gunfighter all dressed in black. This album is a must for those of us who like to walk a little closer to the edge. —*Backroads Music / Heartbeats*

Harold Budd

b. May 24, 1936, Los Angeles, California
Composer / Neo-classical, Ambient, Avant-garde
Budd is America's sovereign slow-motion composer. You could practically drive a truck through the spaces between each note on

many of his compositions—that is, if you weren't so tempted to ease on the brakes and linger in the expansiveness of the sound. A principal figure in the California avant-garde of the 60s, Budd developed a talent for composing lyrical, liquid music that unfolded at rarefied speeds. His solo albums and collaborations with Brian Eno have since become classics for their depth of expression and masterful execution. With every tone reverberating into a translucent silence, Budd always manages to sustain a keen sense of emotional intensity and anticipation. The effect is that of romantic yearnings and perilous undercurrents turned loose among wide open spaces. —*Linda Kohanov*

Pavillion of Dreams / 1978 / EG 1566
Pavilion of Dreams is a cycle of works composed and recorded by Harold Budd from 1972-1975, each unique in form and inspiration. Strong in electric piano, harp, and voice, this album provides a look at Budd's formative years. —*Backroads Music / Heartbeats*

○ **Ambient 2—The Plateaux of Mirror** A / 1980 / EG 18
A collaboration with Brian Eno on this installment of the *Ambient* series. Meditative solo piano with Eno touch. —*Scott Bultman*

● **Pearl** / 1984 / EG 37
A collaboration with Brian Eno. One of the finest ambient albums of all time. A beautiful, highly emotional work of art. —*Linda Kohanov*

By the Dawn's Early Light / 1991 / Opal 26649
Contemporary chamber music in slow motion, filled with a delicious sense of yearning. —*Linda Kohanov*

Peter Buffett

Piano / Adult alternative, Ethnic fusion
Buffett's full-bodied electronic sound and rock-influenced accessibility make his music a congenial transition between the lighter pop instrumentals that have flooded the market and artists who are pushing the boundaries of modern electronic music with more challenging fare. The Nebraska-born pianist went to Stanford University, where he converted his Bay Area apartment into an efficient recording studio that provides soundtracks for numerous advertising, television, and film companies. Upon hearing of Kevin Costner's plans to create the movie *Dances with Wolves*, Buffett sent the actor a copy of his album *One by One*, which featured several cuts inspired by the plight of Native Americans. Costner was impressed enough to use some of Buffett's music in the film. Buffett's four Narada recordings combine a flair for drama and cinematic-style electronic orchestrations with his interest in Native American cultures. His later albums feature a progressively more prominent use of acoustic timbres, both sampled and authentic. —*Linda Kohanov*

○ **Waiting** / 1987 / Narada 62002
Buffett's first album is characterized by grand sweeps of sound and dramatic themes that are a bit on the trite side at times. —*Linda Kohanov*

One by One / 1989 / Narada 62004
The composer's interest in orchestral grandeur is further refined as he routes various acoustic sources—cellos and guitars to owls and basketball sounds—through his samplers and keyboards to create thick timbral tapestries. His Native American interests emerge on several cuts. —*Linda Kohanov*

● **Lost Frontier** / 1991 / Narada 62012
A collection of sonic essays inspired by the American West and its original inhabitants. Buffett's keyboards are enhanced by an ensemble of strings, woodwinds, and guitar. —*Linda Kohanov*

Yonnondio / 1992 / Narada 62013
Buffett's most recent effort is breezy and lighthearted while maintaining a certain level of instrumental intricacy and imaginative sound construction. —*Linda Kohanov*

Richard Burmer

Sitar, piano / Electronic, Adult alternative, Progressive electronic, Ambient, Synthesiser
Burmer is a gifted melodist and a meticulous electronic craftsman. His style grew out of a love for East Indian and European folk music, as well as an interest in the progressive rock of the 70s a la Moody Blues and Pink Floyd. Adept in sophisticated studio techniques, Burmer honed his craft in the Southern California

electronic scene of the mid 80s before returning to his Michigan homeland at the end of the decade. —*Linda Kohanov*

Mosaic / 1984 / American Gramaphone 690
An early collection of electronic vignettes that showcase an already original style. —*Linda Kohanov*

★ **Bhakti Point** / 1987 / Fortuna 693
A well-balanced collection of Burmer's style. Imaginative, often luxurious electronic textures and themes. —*Linda Kohanov*

○ **On the Third Extreme** / 1990 / American Gramaphone 691
Burmer in a more commercial setting. Well constructed and interesting, yet lacking the soul of his earlier works. —*Linda Kohanov*

○ **Invention** / 1992 / American Gramaphone 692
On the itinerary are explorations like "Curiodance," "Easter Eve," "Walking Summer to Sleep" and "Settle Near the Sunset," which animate the landscape of majestic beauty and whimsical wondering. On "King-fisher's Day," "Promise of Return," "Landing" and "Inventor," Burmer crashes boundaries of musical convention and propels one into the world of high drama and rhythmic, emotional intensity. Incorporating state of the art synthesizers like the Emulator & Proteus with added percussion and guest guitarist Jon Claussen, Richard creates a sweeping orchestral sound which is hard to believe... —*Heartbeats*

Doug Cameron

Violin / Adult alternative, Ethnic fusion
The Ohio-born, classically trained violinist developed an interest in jazz early on. He later toured with Gregg Allman, moved to Southern California, and became a popular session man. His albums as a leader subsist on urban beats and spicy Latin rhythms that provide exhilarating settings for his violin improvisations, yet the compositions themselves often lack the substance to support repeated listenings. —*Linda Kohanov*

● **Mil Amore** / Aug. 1989 / Narada 63010

Journey to You / 1991 / Narada 63020
A few insubstantial compositions grow tiresome after a while, but Cameron's jazz-tinged improvisations show that he has talent. —*Linda Kohanov*

Jim Chappell

Piano / Solo instrumental, Adult alternative, Chamber jazz
While trying to make it as a country/pop star in Nashville, Chappell accidentally hit upon a formula for success. At night, he'd noodle around on the piano to help himself unwind from the frustrations of the music business. A friend suggested he should release some of these piano vignettes instead of struggling in the pop world. Chappell followed the advice, and his first two albums (*Tender Ritual* and *Dusk*) were enthusiastically received by fans of solo piano music. On later albums, he composed and arranged works for various ensemble settings, gaining considerable exposure on the New Adult Contemporary charts. Chappell's strength lies in his ability to create memorable themes with lyrical, impressionistic accompaniments. Though his large-ensemble music leans toward a contemporary easy-listening style, its moodiness saves it from banality. He remains most expressive in the solo piano and small-ensemble realms. —*Linda Kohanov*

● **Tender Ritual** / 1979 / Real Music 0131
Impressionistic solo piano music from a sensitive composer and performer. —*Linda Kohanov*

Dusk / 1987 / Real Music 0132
More piano vignettes. —*Linda Kohanov*

Living the Northern Summer / 1989 / Real Music 0133
Chappell's first ensemble efforts show his promise as an arranger. —*Linda Kohanov*

○ **Nightsongs and Lullabies** / 1991 / Real Music 0135
Although his solo piano efforts are arguably his best, this album (which offers a cross-section of solo piano pieces and works for small ensemble) is a good all-around introduction to Chappell's style. —*Linda Kohanov*

Checkfield

Instrumental Pop, Adult alternative

New age group that uses mostly synthesizers and acoustic guitars. Better than most new age type music due to the arrangements of the songs. —*Paul Kohler*

View from the Edge / 1990 / American Gramaphone 790
Here is the clear maturation of the vision conceived by this duo of musical craftsmen. Their intricate blend of composing and performing skills elevates this release, their fourth, a cut above much of the sound dominating contemporary music radio. The full production also stands out, even during the smoothest, most predictable interludes. And the addition of three vocals to their previously all-instrumental sound completes the "ground-breaking" aspect of *A View From the Edge*. From the Moody Blues-ish vocal album opener, "Hitchhiker" to the final piece, "To Look for America," Checkfield has bestowed upon us a nostalgic, yet new and exciting look into the next decade. This is summer listening at its best. —*Backroads Music / Heartbeats*

Chi

Group / Adult alternative, Ethnic fusion
Taking its name from the Chinese word for energy, this instrumental duo composes the kinds of animated, well-performed, yet sometimes frivolous tunes that new adult-contemporary radio tends to eat up. With its heavy pop/jazz orientation, this is fun music for listeners interested in taking an upbeat aural vacation from the pressures of everyday life. —*Linda Kohanov*

● **Jet Stream** / 1990 / Sonic Atmospheres 80028
Chi core members Tom Chase on guitars and Steve Rucker on keyboards are joined by consummate percussionist Luis Conte and several other guest artists, including the West African Goun ensemble. A colorful, multicultural romp. —*Linda Kohanov*

Pacific Rim / 1990 / Sonic Atmospheres 80029
Chi's debut. —*Linda Kohanov*

Sun Lake / 1991 / Sonic Atmospheres 80038
A little more upbeat and acoustically oriented than the *Jet Stream* album. —*Linda Kohanov*

Colin Chin

Guitar / Adult alternative
This San Francisco native got his start hanging out and eventually touring with the members of Group 87, a late-70s instrumental ensemble that featured Mark Isham and Patrick O'Hearn. With Isham, Chin attended a seminar conducted by Brian Eno on applying advanced technology to music. The event was a revelation for the young guitarist, who was motivated to expand his horizons into the field of electronic music. —*Linda Kohanov*

○ **Intruding on a Silence** / 1988 / Narada 62006
Chin's debut as a leader, though not particularly adventurous, features some well-designed electronic atmospheres with rock influences. Isham and O'Hearn add some characteristic solos as guest artists, giving the entire album a Group 87 reunion feel without the band's original edge. Overall, however, it's a promising beginning for Chin. —*Linda Kohanov*

Suzanne Ciani

Buchla, synthesizer, composer / Adult alternative, Progressive electronic
One of the first and finest woman artists to make a name for herself in the electronic music world, Ciani earned a Masters degree in composition from the University of California at Berkeley, where she studied with electronic pioneers Max Matthews, John Chowning, and Don Buchla. In 1975 she moved to New York, where she got involved in the Soho art scene, and also worked with minimalist Philip Glass. She began to hit the big time with the establishment of Ciani Musica, Inc., one of the foremost commercial production companies in the country. Ciani later expanded into film scoring and gained recognition for her work on Lily Tomlin's *The Incredible Shrinking Woman* as well as the award-winning feature documentary *Mother Teresa*. Ciani's career as a recording artist, however, took a more indirect route. Her 1982 Japanese release *Seven Waves* became an underground hit, prompting its American release in 1984. Then *Velocity of Love* came along, which, with its intriguing synthesizer work balanced by strong melodies and pop sensibilities, helped define various contemporary instrumental radio formats, including the Wave. —*Linda Kohanov*

★ **Velocity of Love** / 198 / Private Music 82085
Her warm electronic journeys make for a "State of the Heart" release which is technically masterful and emotionally warm. The overall feeling is floating in warm, clear water while soaring to the heights of the heart's imagination, with longing, tenderness, and a wonderful touch. "Slowly, slowly, with the velocity of love . . ." —*Backroads Music / Heartbeats*

Hotel Luna / 1986 / Private Music 82090
On her sixth recording, Suzanne Ciani finds a new maturity that does not take away from or dramatically alter her signature style of heartfelt warmth. Her musical flights of fantasy are vividly portrayed through her new compositions, and the depth of sound has expanded due to the increase in supporting players, notably violinist Steve Kindler, Isham/O'Hearn sideman Kurt Wortman on percussion and flautist Peter Gordon. —*Backroads Music / Heartbeats*

○ **Neverland** / 1988 / Private Music 2036
Ciani is a master at constructing complex compositions using electronic keyboard instruments that nevertheless retain the ability to speak to listeners emotionally. On her most accomplished work, Ciani explores a broad musical range, from majestic landscapes to humorous percussive patterns, always retaining a strong sense of melody and overall structure. —*William Ruhlmann*

History of My Heart / 1989 / Private Music 2058
Suzanne Ciani has had great success because of her second and third albums. This new album continues her melodic style with more emphasis on keyboard work. The synthesizers are there but as filler material in the background. Her style appears to be changing to that of Tangerine Dream. Shorter works and more commercially oriented. The album is a pleasure to listen too with its light upbeat music. —*Matt Hargreaves, Dreams Word*

Album of Solo Piano Music / 1990 / Private Music 2073
After 20 years of perfecting her abilities with electronic music, Ciani turned back to the acoustic piano for this live recording of material largely taken from *Neverland* and its excellent followup, *History of My Heart*. Demonstrates that Ciani is not dependent on electricity to produce vital music. —*William Ruhlmann*

○ **Private Music of Suzanne Ciani** / 1992 / Private Music 82103

Tim Clark

Composer, vocals / Progressive electronic, Ethnic fusion, Ambient
You'd expect high-quality electronics from a musician who has clocked in a good 20,000 hours composing soundtracks for Toronto's McLaughlin Planetarium and writing scores for numerous other planetarium programs, award-winning radio dramas, films, and theater productions. Clark's graduate studies in composition also seem to come in handy. Though he only has one solo album out so far, *Tales of the Sun People* is impressive because he refuses to settle for the exciting sounds and few engaging melodies many electronic players work hard to attain. Clark's engaging music is filled with unexpected turns and inventive new twists on old ideas. —*Linda Kohanov*

○ **Tales of the Sun People** / 1990 / Hearts of Space 11017
A clever, richly evocative album of electronic music. It deserved more attention when it was first released. —*Linda Kohanov*

Tim Clement

Composer / Progressive electronic, Ethnic fusion, Ambient
Best known for the electronic environments he created as half of the Canadian duo Danna & Clement, this Toronto-based composer has also written music for theater, dance, and film. His early work with Danna explored ways of translating the serenity of Canada's Ontario wilderness into music through ambient compositions that combine synthesizers with recordings of natural sounds. Clement's first major album as a leader, however, is more tuneful and rhythmic as it successfully incorporates ethnic influences into an engaging electro-acoustic context. —*Linda Kohanov*

★ **Waterstation** / 1990 / Solitudes 23
One of the most creative and eclectic contemporary instrumental albums of 1990. *Waterstation* features everything from an atmospheric take on country music with liquid pedal-steel guitar musings by Kim Deschamps (of Cowboy Junkies fame) to extended pieces fueled by relentless yet almost translucent ethnic

rhythms. Other compositions involve highland bagpipes, Egyptian reed flute, and zither. One selection even features a bizarre union of electronics, glassy trance rhythms, and spoken word tracks. —*Linda Kohanov*

Carolyn Conger

Vision Quest /
On *Vision Quest*, Carolyn Conger guides us through two neo-shamanic visualizations. First she narrates a Native American tale of man's confrontation with his shadow self, in the form of animal spirits, and then we are purified through a dawn healing ritual. Michael Stearns' visionary Spacemusic provides a dramatic score. —*Backroads Music / Heartbeats*

Jessie Allen Cooper

Sax / Adult alternative
This self-taught saxophonist has long had an interest in mixing environmental sounds with his contemporary-jazz-influenced compositions to create relaxing, highly melodic musical vignettes that convey an appreciation for nature. —*Linda Kohanov*

Soft Wave / 1987 / MCA 62753
Cooper's first (and so far only) major release uses the sounds of ocean waves and dolphin cries to accompany his tranquil soprano sax solos. Synthesists Mark Cohen and Rusty Hamilton are also featured. —*Linda Kohanov*

Scott Cossu

Harp, cello, piano / Neo-classical, Adult alternative, Chamber jazz
Scott Cossu's ensemble works have the heart, soul, and skill that come from an artist motivated by personal vision rather than industry trends. His 1980 debut album *Still Moments* featured harp, cello, and vibes as foils for his own pianistic improvisations, at a time when solo instrumentals were the rage. His style has evolved and become more sophisticated over the years. Yet because each stage in his development was carried out with the utmost sincerity and expressive intent, each album he has recorded continues to have a life of its own. —*Linda Kohanov*

Still Moments / 1980 / Lost Lake Arts 0086
His debut, originally released on a small independent label; later remastered and reissued through Windham Hill. —*Linda Kohanov*

Islands / 1984 / Windham Hill 1033
Cossu began to expand his musical vocabulary with larger arrangements featuring horns, bass, and drums. The more impressionistic leanings of his previous releases are also expanded upon through the album's fusion of blues, jazz, Latin, and classical elements. *Islands* features some major contemporary jazz names like flutist Dave Valentin, bassist Mark Egan, drummer Danny Gottlieb, and violinist Michal Urbaniak. —*Linda Kohanov*

● **Wind Dance** / 1984 / Windham Hill 1016
The pianist's first original release for Windham Hill features duets with Alex de Grassi and Dan Reiter. —*Linda Kohanov*

○ **Reunion** / 1986 / Windham Hill 1049
A return to his roots in small ensemble music, this album centers around performances with cellist Eugene Friesen with additional appearances by de Grassi, Shadowfax violinist Charles Bisharat, and English-horn player Bob Hubbard. —*Linda Kohanov*

Switchback / 1989 / Windham Hill 1081
Cossu's forays into rock and blues were coproduced with jazz flutist Dave Valentin. —*Linda Kohanov*

She Describes Infinity / Feb. 14, 1992 / Windham Hill 1063
An artistically satisfying summation of Cossu's previous styles, this album includes lyrical duet and trio performances as well as arrangements for an expanded rhythm section. It's a thoughtful and mature collection of pieces. —*Linda Kohanov*

Coyote Oldman

Group / Ethnic fusion, Ambient
This duo creates highly reverberant soundscapes featuring Native American flutes. Michael Graham Allen began visiting museums to research ancient musical instruments over 20 years ago. He went on to construct and play many kinds of flutes and panpipes, later naming his own flute-building company Coyote Oldman. In

1986 Allen was selling his handcrafted instruments at an Oklahoma arts fair when he met Barry Stramp, an accomplished studio engineer who played flute, keyboards, and guitar. Using synthesizers and other digital processors to manipulate the "physics of echoes," Stramp helped define the Coyote Oldman sound by electronically enhancing and multi-tracking Allen's haunting flute melodies. —*Linda Kohanov*

● **Tear of the Moon** / 1987 / Coyote Oldman 102
Though there is an earlier Coyote Oldman release available on cassette only, *Tear of the Moon* is really the first in which Stramp's special engineering techniques are as important to the music as the flutes themselves. A sophisticated use of reverb augments the effects of primal flute sounds to create an otherworldly, almost aquatic atmosphere. —*Linda Kohanov*

Landscape / 1988 / Coyote Oldman 103
Native American flutes with Incan, Peruvian, and bass panpipes as well as Aztec log drum, bells, and Chapman stick are used in original compositions with plaintive melodies that echo through meditative atmospheres. —*Linda Kohanov, Ladyslipper*

○ **Thunder Chord** / 1990 / Hearts of Space 11022
Allen and Stramp's most masterful execution of the sound that had begun to mature on previous albums. It took 18 months of patient work to record these timeless flute melodies elegantly enveloped in a lush, 3-D digital ambience. —*Linda Kohanov*

Charles Crevier, Francois Kiraly, Jean Francois Crevier

○ **Music From the Sky** / 1994 /
Kiraly and the Creviers belong to the new class of musicians who are no longer musicians in the conventional sense but who act as intermediaries between the physical mundane and the realm of the transcendent and eternal. Aptly titled *Music from the Sky*, this is an album that conveys a profoundly reverent feeling of awe and wonder for the infinite divine. Connecting with the higher firmament by synthesizer and piano, they bring forth rare waves of sound imbued with the qualities of majestic silence and mystical timelessness. This album is the perfect complement for healing work, meditation, or just contemplating the miracle of life. Also recommended is their first album of incredible beauty, *Calypso*. —*Backroads Music / Heartbeats*

Rusty Crutcher

Sax / Progressive electronic, Ambient
A former Los Angeles saxophone studio musician, Crutcher performed with pop stars like Lionel Ritchie and the Commodores before moving to Santa Fe, NM, and developing his own introspective style of music. Crutcher's main body of work falls under his *Sacred Sites* series, a set of concept albums that convey his musical impressions of historic locations. As part of the compositional process, Crutcher visits these ancient areas to record environmental sounds that he weaves into his synthesized soundscapes. Crutcher is producing a new *Sacred Sites* project dealing with the Serpent Mound built by Ohio's prehistoric Hopewell Indian culture. —*Linda Kohanov*

● **Machu Picchu Impressions** / 1988 / Plan 9 8401
One of Crutcher's earliest *Sacred Sites* projects, this album features synthesized atmospheres and subtle melodies with sounds recorded at Machu Picchu. —*Linda Kohanov*

Love Dance / 1989 / Plan 9 8405
A set of spontaneous improvisations pairing Crutcher's alto saxophone with Jim Oliver's subtle, yet highly melodic keyboard work. Tuneful and relaxing, yet not as compelling as Crutcher's *Sacred Sites* releases. —*Linda Kohanov*

○ **Chaco Canyon** / 1990 / Emerald Green 8404
Crutcher went to New Mexico's Chaco Canyon to record environmental sounds primarily during solstices and equinoxes. This prehistoric archeological site is thought to have been the trading and spiritual center for the Anasazi, one of the earliest-known Native American cultures in the Southwest. Crutcher's music, often performed on wind synthesizer, is reminiscent of Native American styles. —*Linda Kohanov*

Ocean Eclipse / Plan 9 8407
Based on Rusty's experience of the total solar eclipse last summer in Baja California, *Ocean Eclipse* lays evocative music over the sounds of the tidal-quieted ocean at Las Cruces near La Paz, Baja,

Mexico. The tracks move chronologically from the morning sunrise to the approaching darkness, the actual total eclipse & the first rays of the sun as it reappears. This living tapestry of life portrayed in sound includes Rusty's flutes, keyboards, & soprano sax, with acoustic guitar by Bruce Dunlap and percussion by Jeff Sussman. —*Backroads Music / Heartbeats*

Crystal Wind

● **Inner Traveler** / Higher Octave 7024
This first release by this group, headed by Kevin Setchko, displays a beautifully lush, jazz-based style featuring flute, sax, guitar and drums all tied together in a fluid manner by synthesizer and keyboards. This colorful ensemble covers a mid-tempo range of original compositions along with "Sacred Journey II" by Kitaro and Paul Winter's classic "Icarus". Crystal Wind combines several divergent influences to create a mainstream sound with a very distinctive style. Recommended. —*Backroads Music / Heartbeats*

Cusco

Group / Adult alternative, Ethnic fusion
Two German keyboardists lead this band: Michael Holm had a long string of Top Ten vocal records in Germany during the 60s and 70s; Kristian Schultze, is one of Europe's busiest studio musicians. They share an interest in South America's prehistoric musical heritage, yet their albums are far from traditional. Cusco combines catchy melodies and steady rock/funk beats with just enough ethnic percussion and electronically generated panpipe sounds to give a South American flavor. —*Linda Kohanov*

● **Apurimac** / 1988 / Higher Octave 7016
Cusco's first US release is the band's celebration of the Amazon River, with plenty of Peruvian rhythms and panpipe sounds to set the mood. Their subsequent albums are variations on this theme. —*Linda Kohanov*

Mystic Island / 1989 / Higher Octave 7021
The German group Cusco exploded on the scene a couple of years ago with *Apurimac*, an album of infectious electronic pop interpretations of the pan flute music of the Andes. On their latest release, the pan flute sound only appears as coloring on a few cuts, dominating only on the outstanding "Catalina," which leaps along to a neo-Andean rhythm, with intoxicating acoustic guitar frills from Sigi Schwab. The remainder of *Mystic Island* is full of catchy melodies, shimmering textures and a bright upbeat charm that makes this instantly likeable music—a quality they share with fellow Germans Tri Atma and the Nightingale artists. —*Backroads Music / Heartbeats*

Water Stories / 1990 / Higher Octave 7031
The third U.S. release by the German keyboard-based group Cusco is a tribute to some of the world's great lakes and seas. The joyful sound of synthesized panpipes and flutes, that first endeared Cusco to American audiences on *Apurimac*, appears on several cuts, notably on the opening track, "Waters of Cesme"...Their catchy melodies and playful spirit of celebration have earned Cusco a place among the best-loved of the more pop-oriented New Age artists. —*Backroads Music / Heartbeats*

Malcolm Dalglish

Vocals, dulcimer / Ethnic fusion, New acoustic
This American hammer dulcimer virtuoso managed to liberate the instrument from its folk roots through his masterful solo recording for Windham Hill. At the same time, he enjoys playing Celtic and northern European traditional music as a member of the group Metamora (see listings under Metamora). —*Linda Kohanov*

● **Jogging the Memory** / Windham Hill 1046
Contempory, highly inventive music for hammer dulcimer. Intriguing and entrancing. —*Linda Kohanov*

Danna & Clement

Group / Electronic, Ambient
Though both artists have released satisfying solo albums (see the separate listings), these Canadian electronic musicians first became widely known as a team. Their music together is an organic synthesis of sounds from nature and softly unfolding electronic ambiences. —*Linda Kohanov*

Gradual Awakening / 1982 / Fortuna 17022

The duo's first release is a haunting collection of tone poems inspired by Canada's untamed landscapes. Synthesizers, guitars, harps, and flutes are enhanced by natural sounds like rushing water and the cries of timber wolves. —*Linda Kohanov*

● **Summerland** / 1984 / Fortuna 17035
This gentle collection of pieces evoking the essence of the summer season combines lush electronics with sounds of surf, gulls, songbirds, and cathedral bells. —*Linda Kohanov*

Mychael Danna

Composer / Neo-classical, Ambient, Progressive alternative
Danna is one of Canada's busiest composers. With a degree in composition from the University of Toronto, he has won numerous prizes for his music, including the prestigious Glenn Gould Award. In addition to his classically oriented work, Danna has long had an interest in electronic music. Since the 80s, he has released several albums of synthesized soundscapes in collaboration with Tim Clement (see Danna & Clement). He also serves as composer-in-residence at Toronto's McLaughlin Planetarium, where his electronic music skills are widely appreciated. —*Linda Kohanov*

★ **Sirens** / 1991 / Hearts of Space 11026
Danna's first widely available album as a leader is sensual and spacey, with episodes of melting pedal-steel guitar solos and sighing female vocals that symbolize his fascination with the mysteriously compelling qualities of feminine archetypes. —*Linda Kohanov*

Skys / 1992 / Hearts of Space 11032
Mychael Danna, known for planetarium & soundtrack compositions, as well as for the Canadian duo Danna & Clement, calls "Skys" "romantic minimalism." These are sound paintings of the mind, inspired by the vast, endless skys of Canada during the cold, grey times of the year. The first parts are moody and portray a deep longing, filled with sweeping orchestral and acoustic keyboard sounds. "Sky #7," is a haunting and beautiful melody, with the sounds of a tinwhistle giving Celtic styling & feel. "Sky #10" has an inner richness; keyboards and sampled voice crescendo into what sounds like a full orchestra, returning back from the land of dreams. —*Backroads Music / Heartbeats*

Chip Davis' Day Parts

● **Impressions** / American Gramophone 993

Romance / American Gramophone 103
Romance is the fourth title in the "Day Parts" series, known as "gourmet music for the four mood groups." New compositions by Richard Burmer highlight the roster of artists, with mastermind Chip Davis, John Archer and Ron Satterfield (aka Checkfield), Liona Boyd, Michael Hoppe and guitarist Doug Smith among others. Classical works by Debussy, Beethoven, Ravel & Rachmaninoff are lovingly interpreted, and several piano pieces fill the over 60 minutes of music. Poetic liner notes are included, designed to be savored and contemplated in life's many opportunities for romance. —*Backroads Music / Heartbeats*

Peter Davison

Synthesizer, Sax, flute / New Age

★ **Winds of Space** / 1987 / Higher Octave 7001
Peter combines synthesizers, flute, sax, Balinese flute and digital drums into a full sound, with some soaring, Kitaro influence in this well-conceived musical work. Sounds great on CD, even with repeated listening over three years. This was a definite breakthrough for this established composer and began a string of "hits" for the Higher Octave label as their debut release. —*Backroads Music / Heartbeats*

Davol

New Age, Progressive electronic

★ **Mystic Waters** / Silver Wave 506
On *Mystic Waters*, Davol uses a host of synthesizers to produce electronic weavings of a first-class nature. These fluid electronic pieces flow from a distinctive spacey style to mid-tempo cruisers, with images of *Mystic Waters* recurring throughout. There are signs of many musical influences, yet Davol's sound remains quite original and very magical. The lush, multi-track arrange-

ments each carry his signature style and sound. —*Backroads Music / Heartbeats*

Alex De Grassi

Guitar / New Age, Solo instrumental, Adult alternative, Chamber jazz, Ethnic fusion
Music has long been a family affair for de Grassi. Though he's primarily self-taught as a guitarist, his grandfather played violin with the San Francisco Symphony and his father was a classical pianist. Even more significant are de Grassi's ties to one of contemporary instrumental music's most influential labels: Windham Hill. In addition to his status as one of the company's finest and most consistently intriguing artists, de Grassi is literally a member of the Windham Hill clan. After earning a degree in urban geography from U. C. Berkeley and performing as a street musician in London, he made ends meet by learning the carpentry trade from his cousin Will Ackerman, who was just starting a small instrumental record label. De Grassi was encouraged to record his first album, *Turning: Turning Back*, for the fledgling Windham Hill company. As it turns out, he had more going for him than good connections. Over the years, de Grassi has proven to be an innovative guitarist and composer whose mastery of acoustic finger-picking styles has grown to include a variety of other techniques and ethnic influences. Though he left briefly to record with RCA Novus, de Grassi has since returned to the Windham Hill fold. In the mid 80s, his travels to Bolivia became a major inspiration. He made numerous field recordings during his visits and first incorporated indigenous influences from the culture on his 1987 RCA Novus release *Altiplano*. His contacts with Bolivia's Contemporary Orchestra of Native Instruments also set in motion the ensemble's first American release *Arawl* on the New Albion label. —*Linda Kohanov*

● **Turning: Turning Back** / 1978 / Windham Hill 1004
An excellent technician, de Grassi is able to vary his effects on the acoustic guitar from textured chording to involved picking, evoking folk and madrigal styles and alternating his approaches at will. He somehow seems to have absorbed all the important guitar styles of the previous 20 years and can mix and recreate them at will. —*William Ruhlmann*

Slow Circle / 1979 / Windham Hill 1009
Celebrated guitarist whose technique and style have made him a hit on contemporary instrumental (New Age) circuit. He's not really either a jazz or fusion player; all albums, this one included, are more suites designed to showcase different moods rather than sessions to present any musical style or message. —*Ron Wynn, AMG*

Deep at Night / 1983 / Windham Hill 1100
Alex de Grassi's reunion with Windham Hill is cause for celebration with this collection of original, lyrical pieces in a wide range of styles and moods. *Deep at Night* is an immediately accessible return-to-form by one of the most important finger-style guitarists recording today. Nine solo guitar compositions are complimented by "Hidden Voices," the album's closing track, which features the debut of the Sympitar, an eastern-influenced guitar variant of intriguing sitar-like character. —*Backroads Music / Heartbeats*

Altiplano / 1987 / Novus 3016
He branched out from his solo guitar albums on Windham Hill to this ambitious effort, which finds him in a variety of band settings that underscore his acoustic flights, bringing out previously unheard aspects of his music. —*William Ruhlmann*

○ **Windham Hill Retrospective** / 1992 / Windham Hill 11113

Constance Demby

Vocals / New Age, Neo-classical, Progressive electronic
Demby is one of the few representatives of the new-age movement (in both her music and her personal philosophies) who consistently creates artistic, highly expressive compositions. She was a member of an East Coast experimental group in the early 70s and began releasing her own music on cassette in 1978, shortly after moving to California. Her early recordings consist primarily of extended pieces for hammer dulcimer, atmospheric compositions featuring instruments of her own design, and (increasingly) original works based on her love of sacred classical music from the Baroque period. She really came into her own, however, when digital sampling synthesizers arrived on the scene. Recording in

her own 16-track studio, Demby integrated electronically sampled sounds of orchestral instruments into her ambitious, two-part masterpiece *Novus Magnificat*, released in 1986. It has since been acknowledged as a classic in the realms of new-age and progressive electronic music. Though subsequent recordings have not matched the scope and emotional power of this work, Demby continues to evolve as an artist in some promising new directions. —*Linda Kohanov*

★ **Novus Magnificat: Thru the Stargate** / 1986 / Hearts of Space 11003
Novus Magnificat (Through the Stargate) is an electronic masterpiece. Demby's extended, classically influenced composition is also a deeply moving work. —*Linda Kohanov*

Sacred Space Music / 1988 / Hearts of Space 11010
An early precursor to *Novus*, this classically influenced, yet meditative album was re-released on CD in 1988. —*Linda Kohanov*

Set Free / 1989 / Hearts of Space 11016
Demby's first release since her landmark recording *Novus Magnificat* features some selections reminiscent of that work, as well as shorter pieces heading in new directions, including some selections influenced by Balinese music and some other tunes more on the pop side. —*Linda Kohanov*

Sunborne / Ladyslipper 2
Subtitled *Fire Series*, part one of *The Elements*, this symphonic poem includes the following movements: "The Dawning," "Darkness of Space," "Lift Thine Eyes," "Sunborne," "One With the Light," and does feel like a journey. Instrumentation includes bowed gamelon, space bass, whale sail. —*Ladyslipper*

Light of This World / Ladyslipper 5
Delightful title cut representing a true departure for the artist: a pop/ rock/gospel song, on which she's joined by back-up vocalists from the Edwin Hawkins Singers!...a rousing New Age Gospel statement of joy and oneness. The remainder is a BEST OF, with selections from her first 5 albums; good for an overview of her work. —*Ladyslipper*

Skies Above Skies / Potentials Unlimited 27
Ethereal, mythical, mystical, celestial, and yes, *beautiful* music for meditation and sheer listening pleasure. This multi-talented woman composed, performed (on hammered dulcimer, cheng, tamboura, synthesizer, cello, piano, organ, and vocal tones), and produced this recording with an East-West spiritual theme: Tibetan chant, St. Francis of Assisi prayer, and more. —*Ladyslipper*

Deuter

Vocals, flute, guitar / New Age, Ethnic fusion, Ambient
Like many artists in the contemporary instrumental realm, Deuter mixes acoustic and electronic instruments, ethnic influences, and sounds from nature—only he's been doing it since the early 70s. Born in the German village of Falkenhagen, Deuter learned flute and taught himself to play guitar but was discouraged from pursuing music as a career. The trauma of a nearly fatal auto accident in 1970, however, motivated him to pursue his dreams. His first recording, *D*, was released on Kuckuck in 1971. (He still records for this label.) Over the years, Deuter's spiritual search has taken him around the world, most notably to India, where he lived on an ashram, studied Indian music, and recorded several albums. In the mid 80s he moved to the US, eventually settling in Santa Fe, NM. Deuter's style is characterized by gentle melodies and joyful rhythms that render his music accessible even as he presents an intriguing blend of Eastern and Western styles. —*Linda Kohanov*

● **Land of Enchantment** / 1978 / Kuckuck 11081
Land of Enchantment is an album of celebration, of jubilant light-hearted tunes that perfectly capture the feeling of springtime. The dominant instruments are bright steel-string acoustic guitar and dancing flutes, supported by and light touches of percussion and tasteful synthesizer that sounds at times like a chiming music-box. —*Backroads Music / Heartbeats*

○ **Silence Is the Answer** / 1981 / Kuckuck 11049
Actually two releases in one, this double set combines the best elements of Deuter's two main styles. "Silence is the Answer," the first half, offers some of the purest meditative music we know, combining bells and gongs with the lightest of synthesizers, recorders and guitar parts. The second half of this recording,

"Buddham Sharnam Gachchami," moves to the other end of the spectrum with the finest of Deuter's "celebration music," strumming guitars and joyous recorders mixed with a bubbly synth sound and rhythmic undertones. *—Backroads Music / Heartbeats*

○ **Call of the Unknown 1972-86** / 1986 / Kuckuck 11076
This compilation features selections from eight releases as well as two works recorded especially for the project. *—Linda Kohanov*

Sands of Time (Dbl Anthology/Live) / 1991 / Kuckuck 12090
Deuter has so much material available that it's best to start with one of several compilations of his work. Although *Call of the Unknown* is also a fine introduction to his music, the double CD *Sands of Time* is really the best choice for several reasons; first because it features some of his most recent compositions (including a selection taken from his video soundtrack to *The Petrified Forest*) that you won't find on any other recording. The first disc also offers a balanced presentation of music from some of his best albums. The second disc, however, is the real treat because it features never-before-released improvisations and extended compositions recorded live in performance. *—Linda Kohanov*

○ **Henon** / 1992 / Kuckuck 11099
Deuter's latest album is consistent with the style he established twenty years ago. The music here, while taking advantage of the latest in recording technology, hasn't evolved much over the last decade, yet it retains its expressive integrity and uplifting, celebratory qualities. *—Linda Kohanov*

Do'ah

Group / Adult alternative, Ethnic fusion
Two New Hampshire residents, Randy Armstrong and Ken LaRoche, are the ringleaders of this long-standing ensemble founded in 1974. The name, which was spelled "Do'a" on the band's first few recordings, comes from an Arabic word signifying a call to prayer and meditation; but the music is often upbeat and festive. The members of Do'ah play somewhere in the neighborhood of 75 instruments from various ethnic persuasions, yet the overall feeling owes much to Western music. Some of their compositions seem a little too good-natured and naive at times; however, you have to admire their virtuosic playing and vision, especially since Do'ah was creating world-music fusions a good 10 or 15 years before the idea hit the mainstream. *—Linda Kohanov*

● **Light upon Light** / 1979 / Philo 1056
Do'ah's first album was recorded back when Armstrong and LaRoche were working as a duo. *—Linda Kohanov*

Ornament of Hope / 1986 / Philo 9000
Do'ah's second album is significant in that Armstrong and LaRoche were beginning to hear larger orchestrations in their compositions. On this release, they brought in other musicians to perform on various pieces. *—Linda Kohanov*

Companions of the Crimson Coloured Ark / 1987 / Philo 9009
Do'ah finally decided on a quintet instrumentation, and that's how the band has operated since. *—Linda Kohanov*

○ **Early Years** / 1988 / Rounder 11539
This is a collection of selected tunes from the band's first two albums and, as such, is a document of Do'ah's early development. *—Linda Kohanov*

John Doan

Guitar, lute, harp guitar / Neo-classical, Chamber jazz
Though Doan is a master of renaissance lute as well as classical and contemporary guitar styles, he's one of the few artists around who has explored the possibilities of the harp guitar. The instrument was popular in America around the turn of the century, yet today has been all but forgotten. The way Doan plays it, you have to wonder how this intriguing medium could ever have slipped into obscurity. In addition to the standard six strings of regular guitars, the harp guitar features five bass strings that add a special warmth and richness, as well as several treble strings that create a translucent sense of delicacy. The Oregon-based artist and guitar professor has so far released only one recording, *Departures*, on the Narada label. *—Linda Kohanov*

● **Departures** / 1988 / Narada 61019
Doan's ensemble settings for harp guitar take full advantage of the instrument's expressive range and rich timbral palette. This is contemporary instrumental music at its finest; however, its thoughtful, often sublime lyricism and subtle classical music in-

fluences didn't add up to commercial success when the album was first released. It's still available, and definitely worth going out of your way to find. *—Linda Kohanov*

Bill Douglas

Bassoon / Neo-classical, Chamber jazz, Ethnic fusion
This Canadian-born artist couldn't have a much more varied musical background. His first band did Elvis covers in the 50s, yet Douglas went on to gain a music degree and spent several years as a classical bassoonist with the Toronto Symphony. Over the years he has also worked as a jazz improviser, an avant-garde composer, and a college professor. He finally settled in Boulder, CO, where he remains music director at the Naropa Institute. For the last seven years, he has toured and recorded with classical clarinetist Richard Stoltzman, as well as writing much of the material for Stoltzman's popular crossover albums *Begin Sweet World* and *New York Counterpoint*. Those who've enjoyed these recordings will find Douglas's own releases for the Hearts of Space label similar in conception. There's no mistaking his sweet, lyrical melodies; his combination of Western, folk, and classical styles; his virtuosity on several instruments; and the poignant sense of innocence in much of his music. *—Linda Kohanov*

★ **Jewel Lake** / 1988 / Hearts of Space 11006
Douglas's debut as a leader was a surprise hit in Spain, of all places. The composer's style on this release, however, may be a little too sweet for some tastes. *—Linda Kohanov*

Cantilena / 1990 / Hearts of Space 11021
This is his most masterly and well-balanced effort so far. Most of the selections are smooth, melodious songs-without-words inspired by everything from spirited-yet-flowing Celtic dances and modal folk songs to some deeply emotional music that conveys a near religious profundity. *—Linda Kohanov*

Mark Dwayne

★ **Angels, Aliens & Archetypes** /
The midi-guitar wizardry that turned everyone's heads with *The Monuments Of Mars* has returned. Mars is no longer the focus, it is now our own planet Earth. The title track has the sound that was so distinctive to his first album. However after that, everything changes...With this second album, Mark has shown his music will not be boxed in and recycled. Mark Dwane's music has its own atmosphere—rarefied and vast. This album is available from—Orbian Music, P.O. Box 45131, Westlake, OH 44145-0131. *—Dreams Word*

○ **Monuments of Mars** /
Mark Dwane's album is based on the photo of potential enigmatic ruins on Mars (ie. the famous photo of the martian surface that looks like there is a face and pyramids on it.) For a first release this is a good effort and worth having in any E-Music collection. There are nine tracks in all with the ninth track being a reprise of the opening track. The opening track, "Eternity" gives the feeling of cold aged desolation, like the ruins are now without the life that built them. All of the other tracks have keyboard based percussion with the other music being created via midi guitar. A good variety of music never becomes repetitive or boring. Simply stated, the music is distinctive, energetic, and a pleasure to listen to over and over. Oh yeah, it has real cool cover artwork like some of the old spacier Roger Dean art. It is not available in stores. Orbian Music, P.O. Box 45131, Westlake, Ohio 44145-0131. *—Matt Hargreaves, Dreams Word*

John Dyson

Guitar, synthesizer, sequencers / New Age, Progressive electronic
● **Aquarelle** /
"Aquarelle" deftly combines some of the better elements of Wavestar (Dyson's former band): the rhythmic sequences, the stratospheric solos, and electronic effects; and the more varied, more experimental melodic approach attempted in *Evolution*. Sprinkled with far better musical ideas and a higher standard of production, the result is one of the more innovative electronic releases to be heard in some time.

The theme of *Aquarelle* is, as the title suggests, water. Some enigmatic hints of the motivations behind this decision are evident in the very amusing liner notes. The tracks range from long, developing, melodic pieces such as "Shadows" and "Colorado

Rainmaker" to the very rhythmic "Analog". The melodic pieces conjure up a metaphor of classic-era TD using the production techniques of their most recent releases. However the tracks are definitely distinguished by Dyson's own flair. The more rhythmic tracks such as "Angel Falls", "Analog", and "Rio Grande" are reminiscent of a refined Wavestar. However, even "Analog" has the interesting twist of being based around a Chopin-ish organ theme. The album closes on a pleasant meditative, but not boring, note with "Tall Ships". The CD totals 60:46 in nine tracks. Every track has a fresh idea which keeps this album from being lost in the recent pile of new E-music releases. The engineering is much more professional sounding than Wavestar or Evolution. Highly recommended. *—Kurt A. Geisel, Dreams Word*

William Eaton

Koto / Chamber jazz, Ethnic fusion, Ambient
Eaton designs and builds many of the stringed instruments he plays, and he's come up with some unique hybrids like the "koto harp guitar," the "o'ele 'n strings" (a double-necked instrument), and even a 26-string guitar. The Phoenix-based artist performs and records most often with Native American flutist R. Carlos Nakai. Together they create haunting, highly resonant, original pieces inspired by places and cultures of the Southwest. (See also albums listed under Nakai.) *—Linda Kohanov*

● **Tracks We Leave** / 1989 / Canyon 7008
An evocative collection of highly impressionistic compositions on which Eaton plays some of his most intriguing instruments (including the lyre and the koto harp guitar) in sparse ensemble settings that feature special guests like Nakai on Native American flutes, Rich Rogers on the Japanese shakuhachi flute and percussion, as well as Udi Arouh on guitar and tablas. *—Linda Kohanov*

Wisdom Tree / Canyon 7009
Having previously worked with R. Carlos Nakai, luthier William Eaton steps out on his own again on *Wisdom Tree*. His handmade wooden string instruments combine melodic structures with improvised musical dialogues to offer a haunting, spontaneous collection. Eaton plays harp guitar, Lyre, Koto harp guitar and his own creation, the O'ele'n Strings (31 strings, 22 pitches). Joining him are the accomplished double bassist Edgar Meyer, violinist Arvel Bird, flutist Ia Tulip and Native American flutist Robert Tree Cody, and Udi Arouh on guitar. Occasional rhythms are played on balafon, shaker, berimbau & water drums. While there are no vocals, the music of William Eaton speaks clearly of an ancient heritage brought to light in modern ways. *— Backroads Music / Heartbeats*

Eko

Ethnic, New Age, Ethnic fusion, Electro acoustic
Logikal / 1992 / Higher Octave 7047
Logikal is the second release from Irish guitarist John O'Connor's eclectic group Eko. The sound centers around O'Connor's guitars as he cooks up an old-world folk music hybrid that extends to Andean, Celtic, Irish and Caribbean influences. Gutsy finger-picking gives way to laid-back Island flavorings and easygoing changes. Several musicians with rock and folk backgrounds are heard, like percussionist Hossam Ramzy, Bob Loveday from Penguin Cafe Orch. and the versatile Danny Thompson on double bass. The sound is ethnically-based and highly charged with large doses of clean, light-hearted fun. *—Backroads Music / Heartbeats*

William Ellwood

Guitar / Neo-classical, Solo instrumental, Chamber jazz
As the story goes, Ellwood cajoled his parents into buying him a cheap, nearly unplayable guitar when he was 12 years old. The instrument was too warped to play chords, so he came up with the right-handed picking style he uses to this day. The Canadian-born artist later developed an interest in renaissance and baroque music, taught himself to play the lute, and eventually designed a 7-string guitar so he could transcribe lute pieces without sacrificing any voicings. Ellwood's classical music leanings are apparent on his Narada recordings, although his music has a gentle, contemporary feel to it as well. *—Linda Kohanov*

Openings / 1986 / Narada 61010
Like many contemporary instrumentalists, Ellwood began his recording career as a solo artist. His debut for Narada is a collection of pieces for guitar. *—Linda Kohanov*

● **Renaissance** / 1987 / Narada 61015
Ellwood expands his scope a bit on this album, with subtle ensemble works that elegantly express his love for renaissance and baroque music in an updated context. Keyboards, percussion, flute, and bassoon are used sparingly and effectively in arrangements that feature several guest artists (including fellow Canadian Bill Douglas). A delicate, well-balanced effort. *—Linda Kohanov*

Vista / 1989 / Narada 61024
Ellwood dives further into ensemble music on his third Narada release. Violinist Billy Oskay of Nightnoise, keyboardist Robert O'Hearn (Patrick O'Hearn's brother), and keyboardist George Mitchell (who performs with Diana Ross) are among the musicians who thicken the sound and provide some nice moments, at the cost of the intimacy of Ellwood's previous albums. *—Linda Kohanov*

Emerald Web

Group / Progressive electronic, Ambient
In addition to releasing a dozen albums on various independent labels, husband-and-wife team Bob Stohl and Kat Epple have scored and produced music for numerous film and TV projects at the state-of-the-art recording studio in their Florida home. These projects have gained them numerous awards, including several Emmy and Addy awards and a 1986 Grammy nomination. In 1990 their close creative partnership ended when Stohl tragically drowned. *Manatee Dreams of Neptune*, one of the finest albums Emerald Web ever made, was recorded shortly before his death. Though many of their releases are difficult to find, the evocative, mood-altering compositions on the releases listed here are exemplary of the Emerald Web sound. *—Linda Kohanov*

Nocturne/Lights of Ivory Plain / 1989 / Fortuna 17012
This CD-only release brings together selections from two albums recorded in 1983 and 1984. Haunting bass flute and Celtic harp melodies flow into the rhythmic permutations of digital synthesizers and the colorful sounds of the Lyricon wind synthesizer. *— Linda Kohanov*

● **Manatee Dreams of Neptune** / 1990 / Scarlet 25707
Emerald Web's last album is arguably the duo's best. The inspiration comes from an unusual juxtaposition of experiences. Several of the selections were inspired by Voyager's photographs of Neptune and its moons (Emerald Web provided music for a network of television programs on the space probe's rendezvous with Neptune). At the time this album was made, the composers were also spending a lot of time watching manatees swim in the waterways near their home, enjoying the graceful movements of these endangered marine mammals. The resulting music is mysterious and otherworldly while conveying a deep appreciation for life on this planet. *—Linda Kohanov*

Roger Eno

Piano / Progressive electronic, Ethnic fusion, Ambient, Avant-garde
Brian Eno's brother plays romantic, heavily processed piano music that sounds like a cross between Harold Budd's poignant minimal phrasing and the classical miniatures of French composer Erik Satie. *—Linda Kohanov*

● **Voices** / 1985 / EG 42
Lilting atmospheric piano music in slow motion. *—Linda Kohanov*

Esteban (Stephen Paul)

Guitar / Neo-classical, Solo instrumental, Ethnic fusion
Guitarist Stephen Paul was affectionately called "Esteban" by his teacher, the legendary classical virtuoso Andres Segovia. Though Esteban has released only one album of original music so far, he shows much promise as both a composer and a performer. *— Linda Kohanov*

○ **Duende** / 1991 / Sound Designs of Arizona 1002
Esteban calls his style "new-world guitar music," an accurate moniker for *Duende*'s combination of classical, flamenco, and ethnic influences from various cultures. Estaban's touch is expressive and his technique impressive—the album was all recorded without editing or overdubbing. *—Linda Kohanov*

Dean Evenson

Flute / New Age, Ambient
In the 70s, Evenson and his wife Dudley traveled across the country with early portable video equipment to document "the awakening consciousness as it was manifesting in people's lives." The couple eventually settled in Tucson, AZ, and built a small empire with their Soundings of the Planet record company. Their stated purpose was to help people "experience the healing energies of music and natural sounds and get in touch with a more peaceful place inside themselves." Soundings of the Planet has had amazing success in creating and distributing recordings that communicate this goal. Evenson produces many of the label's artists. He also has several albums of his own that combine natural sounds with his softly flowing flute melodies and various other acoustic and electronic instruments. —*Linda Kohanov*

○ **Ocean Dreams** / 1989 / Soundings of the Planet 7140
Ocean waves and whale sounds weave in and out of music that is highly atmospheric and melodic. Though the motivation is sincere, it's all been done better before, most notably by Paul Winter. —*Linda Kohanov*

● **Desert Dawn Song** / 1991 / Soundings of the Planet 7144
An environmentally inspired thematic album, more accomplished than *Ocean Dreams.* —*Linda Kohanov*

Wind Dancer / Soundings of the Planet 7149
Wind Dancer takes as its inspiration the grandeur of the Pacific Northwest. With themes built from nature sounds heard intermittently in the background, these seaside soundtracks reflect a watery world of misty isles, as the piano and synth of Tom Barabas blend with the sensuous synthesizers and silver flutes of Dean Evenson. Add saxophone, percussion and guitar, and these majestic, circular melodies allow you to enter a world of mystery and wonder. *Wind Dancer* is less ambient and nature-oriented than prior releases. —*Backroads Music / Heartbeats*

Scott Fitzgerald

Vocals / New Age, Adult alternative, Ethnic fusion, Ambient
● **Thunderdrums** / World Disc 07
This represents Scott Fitzgerald's move into the area of neo-shamanic music. Using appropriate nature sounds to introduce each piece (fire, water, thunder, etc.) Scott uses synthesizers and drums to create a dynamic ambience intended to "explode the mind, move the body and fire the soul." Much of the feeling here, from the catchy title and artwork to the music itself, draws its inspiration from Native American culture, with flute-like sounds and echo-heavy drums dominating. However, African influences are also incorporated, while on "Sampan," Scott's synthesizer creates a lively interpretation of Chinese music. *Thunderdrums* is a strong addition to the growing body of work linking electronics to primal rhythms. —*Backroads Music / Heartbeats*

All One Tribe / World Disc 25
Here's the long awaited sequel to *Thunderdrums,* a new global journey which revs up the previous themes & pushes them into overdrive. Joined by percussionist M. B. Gordy, Scott Fitzgerald has come up with highly melodic and modern interpretations of ancient tribal cultures. He brings influences from North to South America, from the Caribbean to Australia, and from the Middle East to China. —*Backroads Music / Heartbeats*

Robert Fox

★ **Fire and the Rose** /
After the triumphant and critically acclaimed debut *Asfafa,* England's Robert Fox has returned with another stellar album, *The Fire and the Rose.* Robert breathes life into his synthesizer to give rise to emotionally charged and spiritually uplifting sound poems which penetrate to the center of one's soul. Based on the theme of T. S. Elliot's book, *The Four Quartets,* Robert paints with grand symphonic chords, dynamic percussion and tubular bell tones which give one the exalted feeling of ascending in a space cathedral. —*Backroads Music / Heartbeats*

Asfafa /
This release by Robert Fox has all the hallmarks of a classic spacemusic recording. The majesty and grandeur in this music do not overpower the delicate subtleties. It may even invite comparisons to Constance Demby's *"Novus Magnificat,"* as both play as a wholly united piece. Lush symphonic strings, gently weaving patterns, angelic voices and a light rhythmic force through most tracks create a flawless atmospheric production, evoking visions of great peace within beautiful other worlds. As far as spacemusic debuts go, *Asfafa* is right up there with Stephen Bacchus' *Pangaea,* or Daniel Blanchet's *L'Harmonie des Mondes,* although Fox also integrates influences from European synthesists such as Klaus Schulze or Wavestar in his stunning montage of cosmic synths and intricate percussion work. —*Backroads Music / Heartbeats*

Christopher Franke

Keyboard / Adult alternative, Progressive electronic, Minimalism
After nearly two decades as one of the main pillars of the legendary electronic group Tangerine Dream, this German keyboardist struck out on his own in the late 80s. Before he left, his mastery of sequencer-driven synthesizer techniques defined much of the trademark TD sound with its pulsing, multilayered mosaics of precise yet exhilarating note patterns. —*Linda Kohanov*

● **Pacific Coast Highway** / 1991 / Private Music 82094
Franke's first solo album is surprisingly melodic, highly accessible, and immaculately produced. As the title suggests, this music would make the perfect soundtrack for a drive up the California coast. The innovative sequencer work of his Tangerine Dream years has given way on this album to more predictable pop electronic orchestrations that would easily fit into new adult contemporary radio formats. —*Linda Kohanov*

Friedemann

Guitar / Solo instrumental, Adult alternative, Ethnic fusion
West German guitarist Friedemann Witecka is a popular arranger, producer, and studio musician in his homeland. His US releases for Narada prove he's also one of the most imaginative composers of instrumental music influenced by rock and jazz fusion styles. This catchy, spirited music gracefully sidesteps most pop cliches. —*Linda Kohanov*

● **Indian Summer** / 1987 / Narada 63002
The guitarist's North American debut is an engaging mix of styles and instrumental colors. Standard guitars and keyboards are enhanced by Chinese hammer dulcimer, harp, vibes, marimba, and lots of percussion. —*Linda Kohanov*

Aquamarine / 1990 / Narada 63017
Friedemann is working with an even larger palette of colors here (12 guest musicians). —*Linda Kohanov*

Eugene Friesen

Cello / Neo-classical, Chamber jazz
Best known for his work with the Paul Winter Consort, this classically trained cellist was inspired by equal parts sacred orchestral music and mid-60s pop styles. (The innovative use of the cello by the Beatles in some of their arrangements was a strong influence on young Friesen.) His work with a diverse roster of artists over the years has further expanded his scope. He has recorded and performed with everyone from Dave Brubeck and Anthony Davis to Scott Cossu and Steven Halpern. —*Linda Kohanov*

Arms Around You / Living Music 17
Friesen's lyrical cello solos are the highlight of this romantic contemporary instrumental album. —*Linda Kohanov*

Edgar Froese

Guitar, mellotron / Electronic, Adult alternative, Progressive electronic, Ambient
A founding member of the pioneering German synthesizer group Tangerine Dream, Froese proved to be the most ambitious in releasing solo albums alongside the voluminous output of the band. He was also considered a master of the Mellotron, an early keyboard device (made famous by the rock group Moody Blues) that produced its sound through key-activated tape loops of actual recordings of orchestras, choirs, and other acoustic sounds. Froese's individual style has a more direct and personal quality, while still drawing from TD's trademark sequencer sound. These albums also feature his penchant for rock-style guitar work. —*Linda Kohanov*

Aqua / 1974 / Blue Plate 1624

The solo debut from Tangerine Dream's leader. —*Michael P. Dawson*

● **Epsilon in Malaysian Pale** / 1975 / Blue Plate 1625
Lush, entrancing electronic pieces. —*Michael P. Dawson*

Stuntman / 1979 / Blue Plate 1628
A less otherworldly version of Froese's sound. —*Michael P. Dawson*

Gandalf (Hein Strobl)

b. , Austria
Synthesizer / New Age, Adult alternative, Progressive electronic, Ambient
Austrian musician Hein Strobl took his stage name from the goodhearted magician in J. R. Tolkien's trilogy *Lord of the Rings*. As such, the composer's goal is to create music that magically inspires positive thoughts and feelings in his listeners as an antidote to the negative forces of modern life. From his early spatial electronic and guitar soundscapes to his more recent symphonic compositions, Gandalf's work conveys his love of nature and commitment to preserving the environment. —*Linda Kohanov*

More Than Just a Seagull / 1988 / Eurock 2001
Gandalf's USA debut was originally composed as the soundtrack for a multimedia performance of Richard Bach's book *Jonathan Livingston Seagull*. Sounds of the sea mix with bird calls, bells, guitars, synthesizers, Mellotron, and grand piano to create wistful music that floats and soars. —*Linda Kohanov*

○ **Labyrinth** / 1990 / Eurock 2004
This music was composed as the soundtrack to an Austrian experimental film screened at the Berlin and Cannes Film Festivals in 1989. A refreshing departure from Gandalf's eternally optimistic style, *Labyrinth* explores the deeper psychological realms of sound through dense, darkly evocative melodies, minimalist rhythmic patterns and contemplative soundscapes. —*Linda Kohanov*

○ **Gallery of Dreams** / 1993 / Eurock 2009
Gandalf's latest features the talented Steve Hackett, formerly with the popular group Genesis in their heyday. From biting electric leads to serene classical guitars, Hackett adds a new dimension to the Austrian artist Gandalf who has his own multi-faceted approach. Flute and oboe expand the sound even further, and Gandalf's versatility is heard on guitars, keyboards, mandolin, percussion and more. Stately melodies and symphonic flair tie the selections together, while Hackett, who appears on over half the tracks, shows his lyrical side to great advantage without forsaking the power and fluidity of his playing. To top it off, the CD booklet and packaging are perfectly eloquent, adding just the right touch to one of the most powerful & enjoyable releases of 1993. —*Backroads Music / Heartbeats*

● **Reflection** / Eurock 2007
A collection of essential pieces recorded between 1986 and 1990, chosen by Gandalf himself to represent various aspects of his style. Influences range from classical and symphonic music to rock, pop, new age, and oriental. —*Linda Kohanov*

T. K. Gardner

Guitar / Adult alternative
New-age? Light jazz? Adult-contemporary? The 8-string guitar work of T. K. Gardner may be hard to classify, but it makes for great listening. Too much of so-called space music is just that—vacuous. Although Gardner's music has that new spacious sound, it also has definition and real substance—integrity. This is how new-age music should sound. You may have trouble finding his one album, *8 X 10*, in stores, so here is the address: Wildcard Records, P.O. Box 4565, Anaheim, CA 92803. —*Michael Erlewine*

○ **8 X 10** / 1990 / Wildcard

Michael Garrison

Vocals / Progressive electronic, Minimalism
A longstanding American exponent of sequencer-based music, Garrison has released over a half-dozen albums of high-energy electronics. Strongly influenced by European innovators like Klaus Schulze and Tangerine Dream, this Oregon-based artist enjoys propelling listeners into rhythmic travels along the spacetime continuum. —*Linda Kohanov*

○ **Eclipse** / 1983 / Winspell 112882

One of Garrison's finest sequencer scorchers, with some quiet, impressionistic moments to balance things out. —*Linda Kohanov*

Earth-Star Trilogy / 1988 / Windspell
Not quite as frenetic and hard-edged as many of Garrison's previous releases. —*Linda Kohanov*

○ **Rhythm of Life** / 1991 / Windspell
This recent release accelerates into the breathless sequencer work Garrison is known for, though his style is rather predictable at this point. —*Linda Kohanov*

Robert Gass

Vocals / New Age, Neo-classical, Choral, Ambient, Chant
A nationally known lecturer, Gass holds a doctorate in clinical psychology from Harvard and has received classical training in music at the New England Conservatory and Tanglewood. As director of the 30-person performing group On Wings of Song, he has produced a number of recordings under his *Extended Chant* series that feature uplifting, updated versions of sacred choral traditions from around the world. Though many of these works are based on authentic spiritual texts and melodies, Gass's primary goal seems to be oriented toward making the music as comforting and as accessible as possible to modern audiences. However, listeners who enjoy Middle Eastern chanting, American Indian music, and medieval plain-chant singing in their purest, most traditional forms will likely find Gass's interpretations a little too sweet and Westernized. —*Linda Kohanov*

From the Goddess / 1989 / Spring Hill 1010
This celebration of the feminine spirit features a weaving of three well-known goddess chants sung by the 24 women of On Wings of Song, with delicate instrumental accompaniments involving harp, guitar, and percussion. —*Linda Kohanov*

○ **Heart of Perfect Wisdom** / 1990 / Spring Hill 1012
Gass's finest recording to date is his adaptation of the Buddhist heart sutra. Striking a delicate balance between Eastern and Western sensibilities, the album features full chorus, Tibetan bells, Nepalese wooden flutes, and some overtone singing, with a subtle use of acoustic guitar and Celtic harp. This presentation retains a sense of mystery and reverence for Eastern tradition that is lost to various degrees on some of Gass's other recordings, which lean toward the sentimental at the expense of the mystical. —*Linda Kohanov*

Kalama / 1990 / Spring Hill 1011
On *Kalama: A Sufi Song of Love*, the members of On Wings of Song sing ancient Sufi lyrics in Arabic to contemporary melodies and arrangements featuring guitar, violin, tabla, and sarod, among other instruments. —*Linda Kohanov*

Gloria / 1991 / Spring Hill 1014
Gass's arrangement of the *Gloria* from the Catholic mass mixes some elements of Gregorian chant with classical guitar accompaniments. —*Linda Kohanov*

● **Medicine Wheel** / Shm 1015
Medicine Wheel blends the uplifting sounds of On Wings of Song with traditional Native American music. The first half has several meditative chants woven with the sounds of Indian flutes, crickets, cicadas and birds. The second half uses the words of Chief Seattle as a starting point, set to music by Robert Gass in a passionate call to honor and care for the Earth. There are now thirteen titles in the "chants of the world" series, useful for a variety of moods and listening environments. —*Backroads Music / Heartbeats*

Michael Gettel

Composer / Solo instrumental, Adult alternative
This Seattle-based composer and music teacher writes contemporary piano-based ensemble works inspired by family, friends, and the beauty of the Pacific Northwest. Though his uptempo pieces are on the trite side, he is at his best when he creates flowing, impressionistic music involving acoustic piano and melodic instruments like oboe, French horn, and flugelhorn. —*Linda Kohanov*

● **San Juan Suite** / 1988 / Sounding 2701
Michael Gettel has an instantly appealing piano style reminiscent of George Winston. On his first album, Gettel's only accompaniment are the sounds of the ocean, whales and other marine mammals, along with natural ambient sounds. Otherwise, *San Juan Suite* is solo piano only, with each piece a personal portrait. This

music really flows, like the waters of Puget Sound around the San Juan Islands which inspired this album. —*Backroads Music / Heartbeats*

Return / 1990 / Narada 62769
Michael Gettel's covers show a different place in time, more remote and still, yet full of wind and nature, while his music expresses the same feelings, filled with survival and beauty. Besides Gettel's piano, instruments include oboe, classical guitar, fiddle, soprano sax, synthesizer, percussion, accordion and even a chromatic harmonica. The music and each of Gettel's compositions, all between five and seven minutes, stand up well for the most part. While quite different from his popular *San Juan Suite* this release will take Michael Gettel even farther. —*Backroads Music / Heartbeats*

Places in Time / 1992 / Narada 63019
A finely produced album, *Places in Time* features a wide variety of guest artists including violinist Billy Oskay, oboists Nancy Rumbel and Russel Walder, and synthesist David Arkenstone, among others. —*Linda Kohanov*

David Gibney

○ **Shaman Journey** / 1994 /
Composer and keyboard player David Gibney is a musical visionary who takes the listener on an exotic sonic adventure on the *Shaman Journey*. Inspired by his own vision quest experiences, Gibney uses up to 75 tracks at a time on these compositions that are melodically intriguing, rhythmically compelling and dripping with atmosphere. Images of water abound, with influences from such tropic meccas as Bali and Hawaii...Both mystical & accessible, *Shaman's Journey* is a profound work that repeatedly reveals new depth. —*Backroads Music / Heartbeats*

Jerry Goodman

Violin / Adult alternative, Progressive electronic
As a member of John McLaughlin's influential jazz/rock fusion band Mahavishnu Orchestra in the early 70s, Goodman used his violin to create phrasings and sonorities previously associated with the electric guitar. His subsequent albums as a leader for Private Music expand on these experiences to create a dynamic and aggressive style that fuses rock textures with classical dynamics through tightly arranged compositions. —*Linda Kohanov*

Ariel / 1985 / Private Music 2013
Vivid fusion textures and combustible fiddle playing. —*Linda Kohanov*

● **On the Future of Aviation** / 1989 / Private Music 2003
Goodman's debut as a leader features his abilities on guitar, mandolin, synthesizers, and percussion, in addition to violin solos that subsist on his characteristic screaming, electronically distorted sound. —*Linda Kohanov*

Govi

Guitar, mandolin, cello / New Age, Ethnic fusion
This California-based artist was born in Germany. His inspiration and style are similar to that of another German immigrant, Deuter, who co-produced and performed on Govi's debut album *Sky High*. Like Deuter, Govi spent a number of years living and studying in India, where he added sitar to his vocabulary of acoustic and electric guitars, mandola, and cello. His music is a gentle, melodious combination of influences from around the world. —*Linda Kohanov*

● **Heart of a Gypsy** / 1987 / Real Music 0789
On Govi's latest recording, he heads south of the border and lands squarely in the heart of the Andes. But in true gypsy form, he manages to invoke the flavors of other cultures and lands as he travels through the musical spaces on this breezy tour-de-force. The strong South American influence is, however, less in the Inti-Illimani vein than in the style that fellow countryman Deuter has previously explored on a few cuts, and similarities between these two artists are apparent on at least two or three of the tracks on *Heart of a Gypsy*. —*Backroads Music / Heartbeats*

Cuchama / Jun. 1993 /
Govi is a spirited guitarist with a recognizable style that incorporates elements from flamenco, Caribbean and jazz influences to create his musical statements. With no shortage of passion or virtuosity, Govi has a memorable sound that ranges from airy, trop-

ical tempos to slower pieces to lively south-of-the-border rhythms. Other musicians such as Anugama, Karunesh and tabla player Daniel Paul make solid contributions to this fine effort from a superb instrumentalist with an obvious flair for the guitar. —*Backroads Music / Heartbeats*

Wayne Gratz

Piano, keyboard / Solo instrumental, Adult alternative, Chamber jazz
Gratz spent over a decade playing keyboards in a Florida-based pop band before he sent a tape of some of his more reflective solo piano pieces to Narada. The label was immediately intrigued by his songwriting skills and signed him up. Though he's primarily self-taught, Gratz possesses a natural talent for creating lush, impressionistic music that somehow sidesteps the cliches many of his labelmates lapse into. Though he's not as well known as David Lanz or Spencer Brewer, Gratz is in many ways more successful at creating subtle, artistically satisfying compositions. —*Linda Kohanov*

● **Reminiscence** / 1989 / Narada 61023
Gratz's debut for Narada is primarily devoted to solo piano music with a few guest performances by Scottish fiddler Alasdair Fraser and oboist Nancy Rumbel. This is evocative, understated music with an innate sense of elegance. —*Linda Kohanov*

Panorama / 1990 / Narada 61028
Gratz plays keyboards and guitar as well as piano on this collection of ensemble pieces produced by violinist Billy Oskay. Though the composer has managed to keep the subtleties of his own style intact for the most part, the Gratz sound occasionally gets mired in thick arrangements that threaten to obscure his delicate insights. —*Linda Kohanov*

Green Isac

Group / Progressive electronic, Ethnic fusion
Green Isac is a Norwegian-based duo featuring Morten Lund on keyboards, guitar, and flute. His partner Andreas Eriksen is an imaginative percussionist well versed in African and Arabic styles. Their first and only album available so far is astounding in its creative manipulation of a wide range of influences. —*Linda Kohanov*

○ **Strings and Pottery** / 1991 / Eurock 2006
From the intricate minimalist patterns of Steve Reich, the techno-tribal mystery of Jon Hassell, and the tango seductions of Astor Piazzola to the rhythmic vitality of rock and the percussive ecstasy of third-world traditions, Green Isac seems to have summed up the major innovations of the late 20th century in a single well-crafted album. —*Linda Kohanov*

Chuck Greenberg

Flute, Sax, keyboard / Adult alternative, Progressive electronic, Ethnic fusion
One of the founding members of the influential world-music/fusion band Shadowfax, Greenberg plays flutes, saxophones, and keyboards. The California-based artist is also well known for his use of the Lyricon, an electronic wind instrument he helped develop. The Lyricon adds an ethereal dimension to his masterful melodic improvisations. As a composer, Greenberg combines rock, pop, and jazz elements into his music while retaining a progressive edge. —*Linda Kohanov*

○ **From a Blue Planet** / 1991 / Capitol 71362
Greenberg's first album as a leader allows him to shine as a soloist, though he is accompanied by some first-class artists like guitarist Alex de Grassi, as well as fellow Shadowfax bandmates Charles Bisharat on violin and Phil Maggini on bass. An impressive album. —*Linda Kohanov*

Jeff Greinke

● **In Another Place** / 1993 / Linden 2010
This release marks a major step forward in the ongoing evolution of Jeff Greinke's electronic music. Where there was once a predominance of smoky haze there is a delicate luminosity and playfulness, with a new feeling of freshness and vitality that has never surfaced on his previous releases. Even when he applies his characteristic treated piano and synthesizer to the gothic romanticism of the title cut his hands convey a greater level of confident

sensitivity and technical precision. Along with these stylistic changes one can detect more "heart" in Greinke's performance. There is less of the "alien" and more of the "human" for us to connect with this time around. —*Backroads Music / Heartbeats*

Sylvan Grey

Kantele / Neo-classical, Solo instrumental, Ethnic fusion
Grey works wonders with the 36-string Finnish folk zither known as the kantele, which she discovered during a trip to England and studied briefly with Finland's highly regarded teacher Ulla Katajavuori. Back in the United States, Grey devoted herself to composing music for the kantele and honed her chops performing in coffeehouses. She recorded her first album, *Ice Flowers Melting*, for Fortuna Records in 1981. (It was re-released in 1988.) Her finest effort, however, is her rhapsodic followup recording *Recurring Dream.* —*Linda Kohanov*

● **Ice Flowers Melting** / 1981 / Fortuna 17003
Recurring Dream / 1989 / Fortuna 17063
Without the use of electronic processing of any kind, Grey produces a lush, scintillating sound from the kantele through her skillful use of bell-like accents, ringing harmonics, arpeggios, and delicate ostinatos. The music is both stirring and intimate. —*Linda Kohanov*

Paul Halley

Piano, harpsichord, keyboard / Neo-classical, Solo instrumental, Chamber jazz
Though he's best known as a member of the Paul Winter Consort, this English-born pianist has an impressive career of his own. After receiving a Masters degree from Cambridge, with prizes in composition and harpsichord playing, Halley was named Musical Director at New York's Cathedral of St. John the Divine. There he expanded its music program to include a rich combination of contemporary as well as classical styles. He also wrote choral works and Broadway scores. Winter, whom Halley met in 1980, was the first to recognize the keyboardist's talent for improvisation and invited him to join the Paul Winter Consort. Halley has since been a featured performer on many of the Consort's finest albums. —*Linda Kohanov*

New Friend / 1988 / Living Music 7
This is an imaginative collection with Eugene Friesen of improvisations for cello and piano, featuring two of the Paul Winter Consort's long-standing members. —*Linda Kohanov*

● **Pianosong** / 1989 / Living Music 9
Halley's first solo album for Winter's Living Music label consists of rich and varied solo piano improvisations, augmented on three cuts by the sonorous sounds of the Cathedral of St. John the Divine's pipe organ. —*Linda Kohanov*

Steven Halpern

Vocals, piano, Synthesizer / New Age, Neo-classical, Ethnic fusion, Ambient
Halpern is the original new-age artist, in the most accurate sense of the term. In 1975 he released *Spectrum Suite*, his first album of music specifically designed for relaxation and healing. Before that, Halpern had been immersed in the New York City jazz scene as a trumpeter and guitarist. His disgust at the adverse effects of life in the fast lane were accentuated by a move to California, where he perfected his idea of "anti-frantic alternative" music. Based partly on his metaphysical beliefs and partly on more solid scientific research into the effects of sound on the human body, he came to the conclusion that the Western foundation of tension and release in music couldn't by nature provide listeners with relief from stress. He decided the answer was to create music that "didn't go anywhere" in the traditional sense but instead immersed the listener in a positive atmosphere conducive to recuperative and transcendental experiences. Halpern created music that was centered largely around cascades of major-key arpeggios improvised at the electric piano, and he added generous helpings of reverb to create a spacey, other-worldly feeling. He took a certain amount of inspiration from oriental classical music and looked into the ceremonial, magical, and healing aspects of sound used by ancient cultures. While some of his ideas take on the pseudo-science pallor of new-age mysticism, Halpern's importance as one of the true fathers of modern meditational and healing forms of music cannot be overemphasized. He has released

over 50 instrumental and guided-meditation recordings, some of which are better than others. He has also written two books on his theories: *Tuning the Human Instrument* and *Sound Health.* —*Linda Kohanov*

★ **Spectrum Suite** / 1975 / 770
Halpern's first release is a cornerstone of the new-age genre and one of the best examples of the comforting electric-piano reverberations that have continued to dominate his style over the years. —*Linda Kohanov*

○ **Connections** / 1984 / 7838
This collaboration with flutist Paul Horn is appropriately soothing, yet delightful on a purely musical level as well. —*Linda Kohanov*

● **Crystal Suite** / 1988 / 7842
More music for relaxation in the typical Halpern mode, couched in the composer's more eccentric new-age theories involving the healing powers of crystals. —*Linda Kohanov*

○ **Higher Ground** / 1991 / Sound Rx 7848
Arguably Halpern's most artistically accomplished album, *Higher Ground* mixes his trademark sounds of the past with some new directions, particularly a more skillful use of synthesizers. For those interested in Halpern's latest therapeutic developments, there's an added benefit: the composer has included what he calls "binaural beat phrasing" to the music, which he says "sonically entrains your brain to an immediate 8-cycles per second response" that locks you "into phase with the natural harmonics of the Earth." —*Linda Kohanov*

Gaia's Groove / Sound Rx 7845
The two halves of this album feature very different moods and styles. The first half is lyrical and spacious, with Steven's synthesizers and electric piano gracefully opening up ambient vistas along with Tony Selvage's sensitive and atmospheric electric violin. The second half is jazzy and rhythmic with influences both Middle Eastern and Native American, adding David Friesen on bass for "Oceania" and Frank Ekeh on percussion. Included here is a startling version Pachelbel's "Canon," driven along by African drums! —*Backroads Music / Heartbeats*

Soundwave 2000 Series: Recovering from Co-Dependency /
This is the latest release in Halpern's Soundwave 2000 series of Subliminal affirmation tapes. If you are participating in your own process of recovery from patterns of compulsive behaviors, you will find this tape to be a powerful resource that supports you in your recovery. The "harmonic messages", while inaudible, are listed clearly on the insert card, while Halpern's relaxing music is the ideal accompaniment. —*Backroads Music / Heartbeats*

Peter Michael Hamel

b. 1947
Keyboard, piano, organ / Neo-classical, Ethnic fusion, Minimalism
As a young man, Hamel studied music, psychology, and sociology in his native Germany. He then spent three extensive periods in Asia, where his studies of Eastern musical traditions (particularly Tibetan and Indian) had a profound effect not only on his compositional style but on his views concerning Western music as a whole. Hamel shared his unconventional insights on music and its place in society in his influential book *Through Music to the Self.* First published in 1976, the treatise discusses the transformational effects of music through the ages and calls for a more spiritual approach to composition in 20th century Western music. While many of his concepts fueled the American new-age movement, Hamel's music is a far cry from the good-natured doodling often associated with that genre. Though some of his works are more successful than others, they all exhibit the grace and intelligence of classical music, the spontaneity of jazz, the hypnotic qualities of Far Eastern styles, and (quite often) the relentless drive of American minimalist techniques. —*Linda Kohanov*

☆ **Transition** / 1983 / Kuckuck 12063
All of Hamel's albums have their moments, but *Transition* presents some of the composer's most beautiful and most emotionally arresting music. Hamel performs several extended works on piano that combine rhapsodic melodies with rich harmonic flourishes. There's also an ambitious essay for pipe organ, PPG wave computer, and synthesizer that takes listeners out of the realm of everyday experience. The real gem, however, is a 25-minute mas-

terpiece for prepared piano that transforms the standard 88 keys into a sort of mini percussion ensemble. The music on this clever, yet highly expressive work sounds like everything from an Indonesian gamelan to an African bamboo orchestra. —*Linda Kohanov*

● **Let It Play** / 1984 / Kuckuck 11078
Hamel in various moods 1979 to 1983. Samples taken from *Transition, Colours of Time, Bardo*, and a few previously unreleased selections. Fine introduction to his varied style. —*Linda Kohanov*

Organum / 1986 / Kuckuck 11074
Hamel's contemporary interpretation of the medieval musical concept known as "organum," which involved an intricate interplay of modal melodies. Four extended works on pipe organ culminate in acutely intense barrages of sound and sensation. A challenging album. —*Linda Kohanov*

James Hardman

★ **Pleiadian Suite** /
Grand, glorious fanfare in celebration of the eternal spirit. A call forth to all beings both terrestrial and celestial to join in the ecstatic dance of life. This is the music of James Hardman. Hailing from Orcas island in the Pacific Northwest, James stands at the helm of his super sound generator navigating into the heart of dramatic and joyous emotion. With the release of *Pleiadian Suite*, James joins the ranks of classically inspired musicians such as Constance Demby, Raphael and Ray Lynch. His depth of expression and dedication to heartfelt celebration lift this space music to wondrous heights, full of bubbling rhythms, soaring melodic passages and ensuing emotions, Hardman's celestial dances for electronic instruments expand beautifully in these carefully sculptured performances, first released in 1988, now available on CD. Named after the Pleiades star cluster, this is an album that will continue to shine brightly. —*Backroads Music / Heartbeats*

Michael Harrison

Piano / Solo instrumental, Ethnic fusion, Minimalism
A protege of minimalist godfather La Monte Young, this conservatory-trained pianist and composer successfully mixes classical, jazz, and ethnic influences into his music. Harrison also works extensively with alternate tuning systems and invented what he calls the "harmonic piano." This instrument is capable of playing 24 notes per octave (as opposed to the standard 12). The strings are also designed to resonate sympathetically like those of a sitar. —*Linda Kohanov*

● **In Flight** / 1987 / Fortuna 17042
A most unusual album of piano solos that combine lyrical melodies and impressionistic harmonies with some Indian and Oriental influences. A couple of the pieces were also performed in "just intonation." Unfortunately, the passionate and sublime flights of fancy featured on this recording never got the attention they deserved. —*Linda Kohanov*

From Ancient Worlds—for Harmonic Piano / 42
The ancient tuning mode/style called "just intonation" is heard on this release from New Albion. With a harp-like timbre, the instrument allows for playing 24 notes per octave in perfectly tuned intervals. Recorded in the Cathedral of Saint John the Divine in New York. Harrison's studies with the physics of sound and his training in Indian classical music showed him about perfectly tuned intervals, as they apply both to singing and conventionally tuned pianos. As a result, he spent two years modifying a grand piano to create the Harmonic Piano. Due to the tuning and design, his playing produces aural overtones and combinations thereof. This is not easy, but engaging, intense listening. —*Backroads Music / Heartbeats*

Don Harriss

Keyboard / Electronic, Adult alternative
This keyboardist and computer whiz has derived his unique sound from a diverse background that includes classical training, 60s Haight-Ashbury psychedelia, stints of touring and recording with rock idol Pat Travers, and jobs composing corporate film soundtracks. Though he lapses into glitzy pop triteness on occasion, he is light-years ahead of most adult contemporary synthesists in his sophisticated use of texture and sound. He has several albums on the market that did well on new adult contemporary radio, including *Shell Game, Vanishing Point*, and *Elevations*, but his best release by far is *Abacus Moon*. —*Linda Kohanov*

★ **Abacus Moon** / 1989 / Sonic Atmospheres 80026
A brilliant combination of pop sensibilities and playful, imaginative sound designs. —*Linda Kohanov*

Jon Hassell

b. Mar. 22, 1937
Trumpet / Ethnic fusion, Minimalism, Techno-Tribal, Avant-garde
When the album *Earthquake Island* was released in 1978, John Hassell appeared to be a gifted trumpeter working at the edges of jazz with Caribbean and Latin American rhythms. Subsequent releases confounded expectation, however, as it became clear that Hassell's improvisational approach was related less to jazz than it was directly inspired by classical Indian music. Most of his compositions can be thought of as ragas, where fierce African and Asian rhythms lead into coolly detached trumpet soloing influenced by Karnatic vocal techniques. Inseparable from Hassell's flowing, breathy style of playing is the distinctive timbre of his electronically processed horn, which sounds halfway between an African wood trumpet and a digital synthesizer. Hassell's association with Brian Eno brought the Canadian musician into contact with the world of pop. He worked with Talking Heads on *Remain in Light* and contributed to Peter Gabriel's soundtrack for Alan Parker's film *Birdy*.
As if in atonement for his brush with pop, Hassell released a succession of decidedly noncommercial if not abstract releases guided as much by the philosophy as the music of foreign cultures. More recently, his brilliance has shone closer to the mainstream. In 1989, he recorded an album with the west African percussion group Farafina, and his latest release *City: Works of Fiction* chooses hip hop rather than worldbeat as the point of departure. —*Bob Tarte*

Earthquake Island / 1979 / Tomato 269612
"Miles Davis meets the Bermuda Triangle" on Hassell's first album with Miroslav Vitous, Nana, Dom Um Romao, and Badal Roy. Stunning music and cover art. —*Michael G. Nastos*

★ **Fourth World -, Vol. 1: Possible Musics** / 1980 / EG 7
Brian Eno's most satisfying and captivating set of mood music came through this collaboration with Jon Hassell. Evocative, eerie, and druggy. Jungle music on Venus—is an apt description of *Fourth World—Vol. 1: Possible Musics*. With percussionists Nana Vasconcelos and Ayibe Dieng, and bassists Percy Jones and Jerome Harris. Essential. —*John Floyd & Michael G. Nastos*

Fourth World, Vol. 2: Dream Theory in Malaya / 1981 / EG 13
An academic feel proceeds from the subject matter, a meditation on the inspirational seed of artistic composition. It takes its lead from the dream-telling of Malaysian aborigines, the Senoi, whose environment, beliefs, and music shape Hassell's approach. —*Bob Tarte*

Aka Darbari Java / 1983 / EG 31
A wild combination of Pygmy voices, Indian ragas, Senegalese drumming, Javanese gamelan styles, and computer-enhanced trumpet choruses. —*Linda Kohanov*

Power Spot / 1986 / PolyGram 829466
An unexpectedly hot raga approach and rock sensibility contribute to the most accessible of Hassell's solo recordings, which proves he can manipulate Asian and African rhythms in the service of the body as well as the mind. —*Bob Tarte*

City: Works of Fiction / 1990 / Opal 26153
Hassell's "Fourth World" explorations move into a futuristic metropolis. Tribal sensibilities combine with hip-hop rhythms to create a *Blade Runner* atmosphere. —*Linda Kohanov*

Steve Haun

Keyboard / Adult alternative
With his gift for catchy melodies and vibrant keyboard textures, this Colorado-based artist has consistently placed well on both *Billboard* and major NAC/adult-alternative radio charts. Tight musicianship is an important feature of Haun's contemporary jazz- and pop-based ensemble recordings, although his compositional style is not particularly original. —*Linda Kohanov*

Midnight Echoes / 1989 / Silver Wave 507

Inside the Sky was a surprise success, reaching the heart of radio audiences. This sensational follow-up is a work of epic proportion, involving, in parts, a more jazzy sound (swingin' sax from Nelson Rangell), in addition to the full, lush sound provided by a live string section featuring members of the Denver Symphony Orchestra. —*Backroads Music / Heartbeats*

○ **Collage** / 1991 / Silver Wave 607
A nice fusion-flavored mixture of acoustic and electronic sounds. —*Linda Kohanov*

Michael Hedges

Guitar / Guitar-pop, Solo instrumental, New acoustic
A virtuoso acoustic guitarist on the Windham Hill label. On his first two albums, *Breakfast in the Field* and *Aerial Boundaries*, his playing style combined two-handed tapping ostinatos with percussive slides and slaps to produce rhythmic intensity and hypnotic melodies. This is compositional genius, with Hedges coaxing a full ensemble of sounds from his guitar. His acoustic sound is treated with reverb and delays, producing a spacious atmosphere that is warm and inviting. His third album, *Watching My Life Go By*, is a change of pace, on which Hedges adds his voice to the music and interprets Bob Dylan's "All Along the Watchtower." Following a double live album, he returned with the *Taproot* album, on which he again did vocals and, for the first time, included other musicians. —*Scott Bultman*

Breakfast in the Field / 1981 / Windham Hill 1017
Debut album featuring extraordinary guitar work with alternate tunings and his two-handed tapping technique. —*Paul Kohler*

★ **Aerial Boundaries** / 1985 / Windham Hill 1032
Hedges shines on his second album, producing an amazing variety of sounds with just his acoustic guitar and ample reverberation. One track features extensive electronic processing. Very melodic and musical. —*Scott Bultman*

Watching My Life Go By / 1987 / Open Air 0303
Hedges adds his vocals to the mix, with a cover of Dylan's "All Along the Watchtower" and his own well-crafted originals. —*Scott Bultman*

○ **Live on the Double Planet** / 1987 / Windham Hill 1066
This exceptional live release features both vocal and instrumental pieces. Superb recording! —*Paul Kohler*

Taproot / 198z / Windham Hill 1093
Acoustic guitar with a small group, including two tracks of Hedges on electric guitar! —*Paul Kohler*

☆ **Santabear's First Christmas** / Windham Hill 0700
A story disc. Kelly McGillis narrates a Christmas tale over the lovely acoustic guitar of Hedges. —*AMG*

Danny Heines

Guitar / Solo instrumental, Adult alternative, Chamber jazz
The Colorado-based guitarist seems inspired by equal parts jazz, rock, and contemporary acoustic guitar styles exemplified by Windham Hill artists like Alex de Grassi and Michael Hedges. Heines, however, has transcended his influences to create a spirited style of his own. —*Linda Kohanov*

● **Aqua Touch** / 1986 / Silver Wave 501
Debut features solo and ensemble pieces, with guest appearances by woodwind player Paul McCandless and cellist Eugene Friesen. —*Linda Kohanov*

One Heart Wild / 1987 / Silver Wave 604
Another finely crafted collection of Heines's work. —*Linda Kohanov*

★ **Every Island** / 1988 / Silver Wave 505
The richly hued guitar stylings of Heines are enhanced by the lyricism of soprano saxophonist and oboist Paul McCandless and the spicy Latin rhythms of Brazilian percussionist Cafe. —*Linda Kohanov*

Max Highstein

Keyboard / New Age, Adult alternative
With a BA in music, a Masters degree in psychotherapy, and a license to practice massage therapy, this keyboardist began his recording career creating guided relaxation tapes. His later instrumental albums combine gentle pop rhythms with optimistic melodies designed for the new-age-lifestyle market already familiar with his narrated work. —*Linda Kohanov*

★ **Stars** / 1988 / Serenity 008
New-age pop music featuring Highstein on acoustic piano and synthesizers accompanied by some top studio musicians on flute, oboe, violin, cello, trumpet, electric bass, and drums, among other instruments. —*Linda Kohanov*

Touch the Sky / Serenity 010
This is music that soars, for piano, winds, cello, bass, percussion, etc. The 1st cut "Full Circle" was a radio hit and the whole album plays very cohesively with lots of appeal. One piece after another leads the listener through joyous and positive spaces, ranging from "Ferris Wheel" to "Mars in Scorpio" and "Back at the Castle". Make your ears happy with *Touch The Sky*. —*Backroads Music / Heartbeats*

○ **Healing Waterfall** /
This popular guided journey and imagery tape uses the lush synthesizer sound and cascading piano music of Max Highstein. Jill Andre's voice easily facilitates deep relaxation & self-healing to take place. —*Backroads Music / Heartbeats*

○ **Lightbeing** /
Max Highstein in collaboration with Jill Andre. The same team that created the popular *Healing Waterfall* has put together another guided healing journey, this time to another planet (!). This wondrous voyage was written by Max, narrated by Jill, and has music that was composed and performed by Max as well. Side two is music only. —*Backroads Music / Heartbeats*

Himekami

Synthesizer / Adult alternative, Ethnic fusion
This Japanese synthesist creates lush, pop-influenced music that's almost symphonic in conception. A composer of film and television scores in his native country, Himekami is also well known for his multimedia events at historic shrines and temples throughout Japan. His recorded music, however, is inconsistent in quality. Even his "best of" collections released in the United States feature sweet, easy-listening fluff alongside his more masterful musical journeys. —*Linda Kohanov*

● **Moonwater** / 1989 / Higher Octave 7023
Himekami's first release in the US is actually a collection of some of the better selections from his numerous Japanese recordings. Oriental influences are couched in thick synthetic textures and Western harmonies. —*Linda Kohanov*

Snow Goddess / 1991 / Higher Octave 7034
A followup to his successful US debut release, *Moonwater*. —*Linda Kohanov*

Michael Hoenig

Composer / Progressive electronic, Minimalism
Hoenig was one of many German composers to emerge from the innovative, electronic underground scene thriving in that country during the 60s and 70s. He first came to recognition in the progressive rock group Agitation Free in the 70s. After a short stint with Tangerine Dream, Hoenig went on to produce what is considered by many to be one of the most important albums to come out of the German electronic school. He has since moved to Los Angeles, where he currently pursues a career as a film composer. —*Linda Kohanov*

☆ **Departure from the Northern Wasteland** / 1978 / Kuckuck 11079
Departure from the Northern Wasteland, a classic of the progressive electronic genre, contains four pieces that are almost perfect in their realization of the sequencer as a compositional tool. Hoenig took the concept of repetitive music further than most anyone in his homeland and claimed his inspiration was drawn from American minimalist composers Philip Glass, Steve Reich, and Terry Riley. The title track is a sublime 20-minute journey through ever-changing melodic and rhythmic phase relationships, creating the vivid sensation of a train ride through misty Northern European landscapes. —*Linda Kohanov*

Walter Holland

Guitar, synthesizer / Adult alternative, Progressive electronic
This California-based synthesist and guitarist honed his chops in the progressive rock band Amber Route. His solo albums firmly

state his love of powerful, rock-anthem-style electronic pieces inspired in part by Tangerine Dream and Pink Floyd. Holland has also been instrumental in supporting the vital underground electronic scene that continues to develop outside the mainstream music industry. Toward this end, he established his independent Coriolis record label and distribution company, which released the critically acclaimed, multi-artist concept album *Dali: the Endless Enigma* (see entry under the collections and compilations of various artists at the end of this chapter). —*Linda Kohanov*

● **Relativity** / 1986 / Coriolis 0103
Urgent sequencer-driven pieces mixed with searing electric guitar solos and rock-influenced acoustic drums. —*Linda Kohanov*

Transcience of Love / 1989 / Coriolis 0105
Ambitious but inconsistent example of his style. —*Linda Kohanov*

Robert Julian Horky

Flute, keyboard, percussion / New Age, Neo-classical, Ethnic fusion, Ambient, Minimalism
Horky received both classical and modern music training in some of the best music schools in Vienna, Austria. Though he plays keyboards and percussion, his main instrument is the flute. This includes bass, alto, soprano, bamboo, and glass flutes, as well as others of exotic origin. His style is characterized by traces of minimalist, ambient, ethnic, and ritual music. Horky is also closely allied with the new-age movement in his desire to create deeply spiritual, uplifting music. —*Linda Kohanov*

★ **Voyager** / 1986 / Eurock 2003
Horky's first US release ranges from free-flowing meditative pieces to a 30-minute new-age symphony. One of the most intriguing sections, however, is based on ancient Greek scales played on instruments from that period. This is a good cross-section of Horky's varied approaches, with some uneven moments. —*Linda Kohanov*

Ios / 1987 / Eurock 172239
A flute concert recorded live at the Greek island of Ios. —*Linda Kohanov*

Apolys / 1988 / Eurock 150586
An intriguing collection of music for clavichord tuned to an ancient Greek scale. —*Linda Kohanov*

○ **Narayama** /
"Narayama" is a concept album inspired by a Japanese novel and the mountain after which it was named. Austrian artist Robert Julian Horky's main instrument is flute or, more accurately, a whole array of flutes—European alto, soprano and bass, Indian bamboo and even a high-pitched glass flute. To these he adds intriguing instruments such as musical glasses—which produce soft bell-like tones and drones—the hypnotic resonant strings of a polychord, and the mysterious aerophone, along with touches of keyboards, mandolin, cymbals and gongs, to paint a portrait of the quiet power and mystical aura of the great mountain...*Narayama* is a subtle but powerful work that takes the listener on a magic carpet ride where flights of fancy become indistinguishable from deep states of meditation. —*Backroads Music / Heartbeats*

Paul Horn

b. Mar. 17, 1930, New York, NY
flute, clarinet, sax / New Age, World Fusion, Solo instrumental, Chamber jazz, Ambient
This classically trained flutist went on to become a respected jazz artist. After honing his chops in Chico Hamilton's famous band, Horn made numerous recordings with his own jazz groups and received two Grammy Awards in the 60s for his "Jazz Suite on Mass Texts." He also played with the NBC Hollywood Staff Orchestra but soon became dissatisfied with commercial music and the Los Angeles lifestyle. In the mid 60s, Horn flew to India, where he studied Transcendental Meditation with Maharishi Mahesh Yogi (who was to become the Beatles' famous guru). During his stay, Horn recorded *Inside the Taj Mahal*, the album that became one of the cornerstones of the new-age music movement. It was also one of the first albums to explore the creation of a sense of space and ambience in music, years before sophisticated electronic reverb units hit the market. Horn went on to record in such architectural wonders as Egypt's Great Pyramid

and the majestic cathedrals of the former Soviet Union. His cross-cultural collaborations with musicians from China, India, and the Middle East gained critical accolades, as did his highly refined works for more conventional Western ensembles. The British Columbia-based artist continues to record and perform throughout the world. —*Linda Kohanov*

○ **Inside the Great Pyramid** / 1976 / Kuckuck 11060
The flutist continues his travels, arriving in Egypt to record in the Great Pyramid of Giza. The double-CD set features a powerful introspective suite of 40 spontaneously composed "psalms" created by Horn on piccolo, alto, and C flutes. —*Linda Kohanov*

○ **China** / 1983 / Kuckuck 11080
An exquisite collaboration between Horn and Chinese multi-instrumentalist David Mingyue Liang that captures the timeless elegance of oriental music. —*Linda Kohanov*

Traveler / 1985 / Kuckuck 11086
Originally released in 1987, this album is a striking summation of Horn's many talents. Reverberant solo instrumental episodes are complemented by evocative original compositions involving synthesizers, string quartet, even a boys' choir. —*Linda Kohanov*

☆ **Peace Album** / 1988 / Kuckuck 11083
Contemporary instrumental. Fifteen holiday-oriented compositions with the soft, soothing flute of Paul Horn. —*AMG*

● **Nomad** / 1990 / Kuckuck 11087
A collection of pieces from eight of his albums, including *Inside the Cathedral*, *The Peace Album*, *In Concert*, *China*, and *Traveler*, among others. —*Linda Kohanov*

☆ **Inside the Taj Mahal 2** / 1991 / Kuckuck 11085
Horn's most influential album was captured when Horn slipped into the Taj Mahal one night with his flute and a tape recorder. The resulting set of spontaneous solo flute improvisations took full advantage of the magical resonances of India's famous monument. Each tone Horn plays hangs suspended in space for 28 seconds, and the acoustics are so perfect you can't tell when the original sound stops and the echo takes over. —*Linda Kohanov*

○ **Music** / Kuckuck 11101
On this release, flautist Paul Horn steps into the timeless beauty of Baroque music's most quietly appealing composers. Pachelbel, Bach & Palestrina are all represented, with Horn's focus on the extravagant beauty of the flute family, including the low, low sounds of the contrabass flute and combinations of c flute, alto flute and bass flute. Simple purity gives way to massive sonorities created by the three choirs of flutes used in one of Palestrina's motets. After moving through tracks from the 16th through 18th centuries, the album closes with three of the motets written in 1960 by the late Maurice Durufle. Paul Horn's music has been heard in virtually every corner of the globe—a partial list of his recordings takes up no less than thirteen pages in his fine autobiography, *Inside Paul Horn*. —*Backroads Music / Heartbeats*

Lucia Hwong

Vocals, lute / Progressive electronic, Ethnic fusion, Ambient
Hwong has a degree in ethnomusicology, experience in writing for New York dance companies and multimedia artists, and a stamp of approval from minimalist innovator Philip Glass, who has acted as her mentor to a certain extent. Her masterfully produced, electro-acoustic albums on the Private Music label are filled with ethereal yet sensual dreamscapes and breathless, rhythmic journeys through fantastic worlds. Unfortunately, Hwong disappeared from the recording scene after the release of her second album, *Secret Luminescence*. —*Linda Kohanov*

★ **House of Sleeping Beauties** / 1985 / Private Music 2006
Though both of her Private Music releases are excellent, this particular collection of colorful, Oriental-inspired music is stunning. —*Linda Kohanov*

Secret Luminescence / 1987 / Private Music 2021
More ethereal and moody than her first release, this is also downright erotic at times. —*Linda Kohanov*

Soren Hyldgaard

Composer / Neo-classical, Adult alternative, Ambient
An award-winning Scandinavian composer, Hyldgaard has extensive experience composing for theater and films as well as writing concert music in a more traditional classical vein. —*Linda Kohanov*

○ **Flying Dreams** / 1988 / Fonix Musik 0116
Light, breezy melodies set to gentle cinematic orchestrations featuring piano, oboe, guitar, flute, strings, and synthesizers, along with occasional nature sounds. —*Linda Kohanov*

Iasos

Synthesizer / New Age, Electronic, Minimalism
One of the original new-age musicians, this California synthesist creates expansive, uplifting music that floats and shimmers. Iasos has always been sincere in his desire to induce higher states of consciousness through his music. Sometimes his lofty aims get bogged down in an overly sweet presentation, but at other times he succeeds in creating transcendent and artistically satisfying music. —*Linda Kohanov*

★ **Angelic Music** / 1978 / Inter-Dimensional Music
An earlier dose of Iasos's cosmic aspirations. —*Linda Kohanov*

● **Elixir** / 1983 / Sound Rx 7000
The quintessential Iasos recording. Whether the album has the potential to carry people to Nirvana on wings of song is up to the personal experience of each listener. In any case, the music is beautiful and deeply inspired. —*Linda Kohanov*

Bora Bora 2000 / 1991 / 79340
An album of high-energy dance music and musical sketches of the tropics. Dedicated to the "Spirit of Fun," this collection of island rhythms will bring a smile to your face and get you out of your chair. Infectiously happy, the six dance tracks bounce and jump with delight. Performed on synthesizer, like all of Iasos' music, the steel drum sounds, Afro-Cuban percussion and tropical melodies will whisk you off to the shores of Tahiti...With the release of *Bora Bora 2000*, Iasos proves he is equally skilled at creating musical delights for the body as he is at providing celestial journeys for the spirit. —*Backroads Music / Heartbeats*

Essence of Spring / 1993 /
Essence of Spring captures the buoyant enthusiasm and bubbling optimism of Spring. Side one contains five musical selections with nature sounds interspersed, while side two is an environmental tape, with a continuous half-hour of brooks and birds. A great way to start the day! Iasos was this year's recipient of The Crystal Award in the New Age artist category. —*Backroads Music / Heartbeats*

Timeless Sound / 1994 /
This new cassette-only release by Iasos contains two long tracks designed for deep meditation. Side one, "Cloud Prayer," is an extended half-hour version of a track from his release "Wave #1 (Interdimensional Music)," with deep slow drones, soaring highs that advance and recede, and fluttering tones like birds or butterflies occasionally passing through. The second side, "Throne Realms," is a new work in Iasos' trademark flowing celestial style, with shimmering synthesizers floating gently throughout. Each is lovely, and, at thirty uninterrupted minutes per side, offers an extended space for meditation. —*Backroads Music / Heartbeats*

Ralf Illenberger

Guitar / Adult alternative
Inspired by the Beatles and the Rolling Stones, this German guitarist essentially taught himself to play from records, later adding Leo Kottke, J. S. Bach, and Keith Jarrett to his list of influences. Honing his chops in local dance bands, Illenberger graduated to concert dates and eventually released seven albums in Europe before signing with Narada Records in the US. His style is an intelligent mix of pop and jazz, making him one of the better adult-alternative instrumentalists on the market. —*Linda Kohanov*

● **Circle** / 1988 / Narada 63006
Illenberger's American debut mixes colorful instrumentals with some introspective moods. —*Linda Kohanov*

Heart & Beat / 1990 / Narada 63009
This more energetic and lighthearted album features a number of prominent European sidemen. —*Linda Kohanov*

Inkuyo

Group / Ethnic fusion
Inkuyo comprises four musicians who bring the ancient instruments and songs of their South American Incan heritage firmly into the 20th century. Their name and inspiration are taken from a remote mountain village high in the heart of the Andes where the people retain many of the customs their ancestors followed centuries ago. In addition to performing their own arrangements of traditional tunes, the members of Inkuyo present modern compositions inspired by the Chilean "new song" movement, as well as a number of spirited folk-inspired originals. —*Linda Kohanov*

★ **Land of the Incas** / 1988 / Fortuna 17064
Although both of Inkuyo's albums are equal in artistic merit, this is perhaps the best place to start. This festive collage of tradition and innovation features a wide variety of intriguing South American instruments: cane flutes, panpipes of all sizes, and traditional drums and percussion, as well as acoustic guitar, violin, and harp. —*Linda Kohanov*

Temple of the Sun / 1992 / Fortuna 17080
More crisp, evocative performances from these masterful performers. This time the music is inspired by the legends surrounding Coricancha, the famous fallen temple of the sun located in the Incan capital city of Cusco. With its exterior walls covered in gold, the building was mercilessly plundered by the Spanish in the 1500s. Inkuyo succeeds in capturing the mystery, majesty, and tragedy of this historical wonder. —*Linda Kohanov*

Mark Isham

Trumpet, synthesizer / Chamber jazz, Progressive electronic, Ambient
This multi-instrumentalist and composer, born in New York but now based in San Francisco, made his reputation early in the 70s while playing with progressive rock bands and jazz groups like Art Lande's Rubisa Patrol. He has performed or recorded with such artists as Van Morrison, Was (Not Was), and David Sylvian. His trumpet sound is reminiscent of Miles Davis with his use of a mute and his sparse phrasing, but his great talent as a composer lies in his ability to combine synthesizer and acoustic instruments into effective and he is in demand for film scores. Isham's stately and often dreamy music reveals his classical training while inventively exploring the sonic possibilities of electronic instruments. —*Scott Bultman*

★ **Vapor Drawings** / 1983 / Windham Hill 1027
Crystalline synthesizer textures form the perfect atmosphere for Isham's melodic trumpet solos (with percussion from his Group 87 bandmate Peter Van Hooke). His talent for blending electronic and acoustic sounds produces beautiful and organic music, and this first album for Windham Hill cemented his reputation. —*Scott Bultman*

○ **Film Music** / 1987 / Windham Hill 1041
His scores for *Never Cry Wolf*, the Academy Award-winning documentary *The Times of Harvey Milk*, and the Mel Gibson/Diane Keaton film *Mrs. Soffel* showcase his musical depth and dreamy style. On the *Mrs. Soffel* score, Isham's blend of acoustic and synthesizer textures are haunting and deeply moving. —*Scott Bultman*

Castalia / 1988 / Virgin 90900
More jazz-oriented music on this ensemble recording featuring Isham's muted trumpet over a dense and percussive backdrop from longtime Isham sidemen David Torn, Peter Maunu and Patrick O'Hearn, plus Paul McCandless, Terry Bozzio, and Mick Karn. The sweeping strings and classical guitar on "My Wife with Champagne Shoulders" and the evocative "A Dream of Three Acrobats" are highlights. —*Scott Bultman*

Mark Isham / 1991 / Virgin 91293
Isham continues his ensemble-style collaborations with guests Tanita Tikaram, Chick Corea, John Patitucci, and John Novello, and the contributions of sidemen David Torn, Peter Maunu, and Peter Van Hooke. Pleasing group work that provides a nice complement to the two vocal tracks. If you like these, try Isham's soundtrack recording for *Trouble in Mind* with Marianne Faithull. —*Scott Bultman*

Songs My Children Taught Me / 1991 / Windham Hill 1101
Over 70 minutes of Isham's musical accompaniment to the Windham Hill children's story series minus their voice-over. Quite nice as background music. —*Scott Bultman*

Jean Michel Jarre

Vocals, synthesizer / Electronic, Adult alternative, Progressive electronic

Son of film composer Maurice Jarre, Jean Michel became France's most famous electronic musician in the 70s, when two of his finest albums, *Oxygene* and *Equinoxe*, were released. He has since had an interesting, if uneven, career. His later rock-oriented work seems a bit heavy on the testosterone as well as the ego, a development no doubt influenced by the impact of playing for hundreds of thousands of people in settings such as his giant outdoor concert in Houston during the mid 80s. —*Linda Kohanov*

★ **Oxygene** / 1977 / Dreyfus 827885
This album conveys the excitement and freshness you'd expect from a talented young man embarking on a career in what was still a relatively unknown and unjaded electronic music scene. Sometimes innocent and introspective, other times ambitious and even a little spooky, this is a must for anyone interested in electronic music. —*Linda Kohanov*

Equinoxe / 1978 / Dreyfus 800025
Progressive, multilayered electronic music with glistening sequencer patterns, flowing melodies, and futuristic special effects that sound like you're blasting off into outer space. After all these years, most of it holds up. —*Linda Kohanov*

○ **Zoolook** / 1984 / Dreyfus 823763
Jarre went off in an unexpected and intriguing direction on this album. Taped voices in a number of languages are juiced up through electronic processing and then combined with synthesizers and live musicians. Guitarist Adrian Belew and vocal wizard Laurie Anderson add some interesting angles of their own. For adventurous listeners. —*Linda Kohanov*

Rendez-Vous / 1986 / Dreyfus 829125
Jarre explores more conventional rock ground, much of it already hoed by other artists. —*Linda Kohanov*

○ **Waiting for Cousteau** / 1990 / American Gramaphone 8436142
With the release of Jarre's last album "Revolutions", his music took a different direction and some very nice material is starting to emerge. "Revolutions" was Indian influenced rhythm, but repetitive. "Waiting for Cousteau" has four tracks with the title track on the CD running to 46:53. Track 1 "Calypso" is a calypso rhythm based upbeat dance track. "Calypso part 2" is more sequencer rhythm and somewhat spacey in the style of Tangerine Dream. "Calypso part 3" is slower; like a thoughtful blues tune. "Waiting for Cousteau" is similar to the slow space synth music of Steve Roach but with a simple pleasant piano track running throughout. There are occasional sound effects but they do not detract from the drifting feel of the music. Most fans of EM will find this new Jarre release very nice because the material is very diverse. —*Matt Hargreaves, Dreams Word*

○ **Chronologie** / 1993 / Disques Dreyfus
Jarre's latest release comes three years since his last full album and fourteen years since his landmark debut album "Oxygene." Rather than returning to those ambient beginnings, "Chronologie" is an expose of time in many ways. The album begins and ends with a heartbeat, and is alive with the rhythms of life and machines. At the same time, the development of the styles throughout the album in some way parallel the development of Jarre's own music from "Oxygene" through to "Chronologie." Several tracks borrow elements from previous albums in a subtle way which does not detract from this album's originality. We are carried through a progression of early eighties styles to later elements of techno. The sounds of clocks are pervasive, reminding us of the theme of time. Digital watches, sampled analog clocks and the backing rhythm itself, the ringing of alarm bells and the winding of clocks can be heard. Although it combines elements from Jarre's previous works, "Chronologie" stands on its own, and contains enough subtleties to maintain the listener's interest for a long time to come. —*Rob Geraghty, Dreams Word*

Gordon Jeffries

Soothing Classics / 1994 /
Keyboard artist Gordon Jeffries has assembled these classical themes and arranged them to emphasize the melodic beauty. The music is blended with nature sounds, and the tempos have been slowed to a perfect rate, with resonant timbres and softened crescendos for maximum relaxation. Digital sampling technology puts an ensemble of sounds in the hands of one composer, as Jeffries' performances give the feeling of an entire orchestra, set

in the great outdoors. He selects two composers for each of the releases, as shown below. The four-title series is available as a four-pack cassette set or individually on Cassette or CD. Four Volumes: *Chopin/Dvorak, Mozart/Beethoven, Satie /Bach, Vivaldi / Debussy* —*Backroads Music / Heartbeats*

Eddie Jobson

Keyboard, violin / Easy listening, Adult alternative, Progressive electronic
This dynamic rock violinist has played with everyone from UK, Roxy Music, and Frank Zappa to Jethro Tull. Jobson's recordings as a leader showed much promise in their use of keyboards, computer-generated sounds, and wailing electric-violin solos. Too bad he hasn't released more of his own music. —*Linda Kohanov*

Zinc / 1983 / CBS 12275
Jobson's solo debut is mostly instrumental, with a few vocals. —*Paul Kohler*

★ **Theme of Secrets** / 1985 / Private Music 2005
A masterpiece of soundscapes created by using the Synclavier computer. A brilliant album from start to finish. —*Paul Kohler*

Marnie Jones

Vocals, guitar / New Age, Neo-classical
Jones came to a professional recording career late in life—after 15 years of working in the industrial design field. Though she had sung and played guitar as an avocation since childhood, Jones later taught herself to play the harp and began releasing albums of improvised music for that instrument. Her more recent recordings show a steady growth in her abilities as a performer and composer of tender, contemplative music that Jones herself says is great for meditation, relaxation, or massage. —*Linda Kohanov*

● **Journeys** / 1988 / Thrival 035
Jones's harp music is enhanced by guest artists playing flute, clarinet, bells, percussion, synthesizers, and Indian drum. —*Linda Kohanov*

Golden Wave / 1989 / Thrival 036
Another album of tender ensemble settings. —*Linda Kohanov*

○ **Grace** / 1994 / Marnie Jones 38
This gentle and lovely album blends whale and dolphin sounds with Marnie Jones' harp and angelic vocal harmonies. *Grace* flows in the combining of her harp and psaltery with woodwinds and percussion touches. Half of the pieces lead off with the sounds of whales or dolphins, recorded in Hawaii, Florida and the Caribbean. Nearly an hour, *Grace* provides peaceful, inspiring listening as the creatures of the deep move the musicians to create music from their deeper selves. —*Backroads Music / Heartbeats*

Michael Jones

Piano / Neo-classical, Solo instrumental
A native of Ontario, Canada, Jones studied classical piano and kept up his chops throughout his college courses in psychology. During seminars he conducted as part of his own business-management consulting practice, he began including interludes of piano improvisations. Finally, after years of encouragement from friends and clients, he released *Pianoscapes* in 1983. It was the first album ever released on the Narada record label. Over the years, Jones has recorded a number of solo piano and small-ensemble albums. Especially nice is his 1987 duo with cellist David Darling. —*Linda Kohanov*

● **Pianoscapes** / 1985 / Narada 61001
His solo piano debut. —*Linda Kohanov*

Solstice / 1985 / Narada 61008
Seasonal piano pieces from two of Narada's best-selling artists, Michael Jones and David Lanz. —*Linda Kohanov*

★ **Amber** / 1987 / Narada 61014
Jones teams up with cellist David Darling for a delicate set of improvisational pieces. —*Linda Kohanov*

After the Rain / 1988 / Narada 61020
Impressionistic pieces in small ensemble settings. —*Linda Kohanov*

○ **Michael's Music** / Jul. 21, 1990 / Narada 64002
A retrospective of Jones's subtle solo piano and ensemble pieces. —*Linda Kohanov*

Chuck Jonkey

New Age, Ethnic fusion

Peyote Ceremony / 1994 /
Peyote Ceremony was recorded in a teepee within sight of the mysterious "Shiprock" of New Mexico. This sacred ceremony was performed by members of the Ute and Navaho tribes...Nine separate Peyote songs are heard, powerful prayers that petition nature, birds and animals, Jesus and other meaningful subjects. Used for healing & divine assistance, the chants call for, forgiveness, guidance, understanding & cures from all ills. —*Backroads Music / Heartbeats*

Jason Joseph

○ **Steps of the Pilgrim** / 1994 /
This first entry from Jason Joseph skillfully blends the passionate with the contemplative. It is an hypnotic ambiance, drinking at times from the wells of the likes of Eno, Budd, Lanois and Brook. Yet in *Steps of the Pilgrim*, the darker regions explored are more gentle, even angelic. —*Backroads Music / Heartbeats*

Mark Josephson

New Age, Progressive electronic, Electro acoustic

○ **Dreamstate** / 1994 /
Dreamstate is a multifaceted album, full of layered sounds, strong melodies, shifting tempos, key changes, holophonic sound effects, and stereo interplay. Mark Josephson is a synthesist and violinist whose music explores the spaces between electronic rock and symphonic classicism, in a melange of styles often reminiscent of Vangelis. He mixes the straight-ahead dynamism of rock, with thumping bass & forceful drums, as melodies twist and turn, constantly keeping listeners on their toes...This is an intriguing work on a grand scale, dynamic & subtle, rhythmic & spacey, vibrant in its musical paradoxes.—*Backroads Music / Heartbeats*

Peter Kater

Piano / Instrumental bluegrass, Solo instrumental, Ethnic fusion
This German-born pianist and composer currently lives in rural Virginia. Since 1983, he has released over a dozen albums spanning solo piano music to contemporary jazz ensemble projects. Though some of his music comes from more predictable light-jazz molds, his finest work in recent years is featured on two inspired collaborations with Native American flutist R. Carlos Nakai. —*Linda Kohanov*

Spirit / 1983 / Optimism 1001
This is Kater's 1983 debut. —*Linda Kohanov*

★ **Natives** / 1990 / Silver Wave 601
Kater and R. Carlos Nakai's first collaboration got excellent reviews for good reason. —*Linda Kohanov*

● **Collection 1983-1990** / 1991 / Silver Wave 605
A summation of Kater's varied style taken from his numerous albums as a leader. —*Linda Kohanov*

○ **Migration** / 1992 / Silver Wave 704
A quiet, thoughtful album inspired by a desire to "create and experience ritual in one's life." Contemporary melodies coalesce with subtle Native American themes and liturgical-style wordless choral passages. R. Carlos Nakai chants and plays flutes and eagle-bone whistles, trading lines with Kater's piano and synthesizers. Guest artists include cellist David Darling and saxophonists Mark Miller and Bob Read. —*Linda Kohanov*

○ **How the West Was Lost** / Mar. 1993 / Silver Wave 801
This popular pianist records in both solo and ensemble format, and has recently collaborated on two releases with acclaimed Flautist R. Carlos Nakai. Here in full ensemble setting Kater provides the evocative music for the current PBS TV show, *How the West Was Lost*, stories of the frontier days told from Native American perspective. Solos and duets, with and without Nakai, plus a several powerful and complex tracks, combine for a work of depth and poignancy. —*Backroads Music / Heartbeats*

Brian Keane

Guitar / Progressive electronic, Ethnic fusion, Electro acoustic
This virtuoso guitarist and sought-after producer has performed with some of the biggest names in jazz, including Bobby McFerrin, Larry Coryell, and Paco de Lucia. In addition to his own contemporary jazz albums, Keane is an accomplished composer and arranger who has written soundtracks for award-winning films. His score to the documentary *Suleyman the Magnificent* caught the ear of Celestial Harmonies owner Eckart Rahn, who eventually released the soundtrack. The label has since commissioned several other albums of Middle East-inspired instrumentals from Keane, with Turkish multi-instrumentalist Omar Faruk Tekbilek. These exotic recordings are among Keane's finest work. —*Linda Kohanov*

Suleyman ... / 1988 / Flying Fish 452
Suleyman the Magnificent, Keane's imaginative soundtrack to the documentary and traveling art exhibit on the Ottoman Empire, also features Tekbilek and several other Middle Eastern musical experts. —*Linda Kohanov*

Fire Dance / 1990 / Celestial Harmonies 13032
This masterful collection of music mixes traditional Turkish, Egyptian, and North African folk melodies and dances with synthesized atmospheres that sound like hot desert winds blowing over the Sahara. An artful union of Eastern and Western sensibilities, with Omar Faruk Tekbilek. —*Linda Kohanov*

★ **Beyond the Sky** / 1992 / Celestial Harmonies 13047
This latest Middle Eastern venture by Keane and Tekbilek is a continuation of their previous work for Celestial Harmonies. —*Linda Kohanov*

Georgia Kelly

Harp / New Age, Neo-classical, Solo instrumental, Ethnic fusion
Kelly was a major force in popularizing the harp in contemporary instrumental music. Years before American audiences had even heard of Andreas Vollenweider, this West Coast musician was gaining considerable attention for her albums of solo harp performances, which she initially released through her own recording and distribution company. The relaxing and inspirational qualities of her music attracted the attention of hospitals, cancer clinics, and drug-abuse programs, which regularly used her recordings for therapeutic purposes. A sensitive and skillful musician, Kelly has made several noteworthy recordings for Global Pacific, some of which being highly recommended collaborations with other artists. —*Linda Kohanov*

★ **Seapeace** / 1970 / Global Pacific 40724
Originally released in the 70s, Kelly's influential recording of solo harp music is now considered a classic in the CI and new-age realms. —*Linda Kohanov*

Harp and Soul / 1983 / Global Pacific 79311
Kelly mixes her own originals with arrangements of Barbra Streisand's "Evergreen" and the "Trois Gymnopedies" by Satie. Wind player Richard Hardy joins the harpist on several cuts. —*Linda Kohanov*

○ **Fresh Impressions** / 1987 / Global Pacific 79306
This set of classical duos with violinist Steven Kindler offers arrangements of some of the most famous impressionist pieces by Gabriel Faure, Erik Satie, and Claude Debussy, plus two originals in the French style by Kelly and Kindler. —*Linda Kohanov*

○ **Winter Classics** / 1989 / Global Pacific 79337
...*Winter Classics* is a beautiful and sophisticated album that more than lives up to the promise of its title. —*Backroads Music / Heartbeats*

Journey Home / 1989 / Global Pacific 79303
This elegant, heartfelt collaboration with Yugoslavian guitarist Dusan Bogdanovich was inspired by Kelly's quest to connect with her own Yugoslavian roots. Traditional folk songs from the region come to life in contemporary arrangements. Sprinkled between are original compositions inspired by the beauty and spirit of the duo's shared heritage. —*Linda Kohanov*

○ **Gardens of the Sun** / 1994 /
On *Gardens of the Sun*, her latest gift of music, Georgia brings an utter sensitivity to her work, inspired partly by her recent visits to Dubrovnik and Zagreb and her efforts towards bringing about renewed diplomacy and peace in these deeply troubled times. Her music exposes the soulful relationship with the homeland of her relatives, and this poignancy can be heard in the music, along with a hopeful joy and the beauty of nature's creations. Of the eight songs heard, five are harp solos, and show why Georgia Kelly has often been referred to as "the first lady of the harp." The

others are duets—one with former collaborator & guitarist Dusan Bogdanovic on their jointly composed "Requiem," one with flautist Stephen Schultz, and the third adding simply tambourine by recording and mixing engineer Warren Dennis. This uplifting record will bring rays of light into your life. —*Backroads Music / Heartbeats*

Al Gromer Khan

Composer / Electronic, Ethnic fusion, Ambient
German composer Alois Gromer decided to dedicate himself to playing the sitar after he attended a 1969 recital in London given by Indian classical-music master Vilayat Khan. During a 1975 ceremony conducted by respected teacher Imrat Khan, Gromer became the first European to be inducted into the legendary Khan dynasty of sitar players, which dates back to Moghul India. Adding the Khan surname to his professional identity, he created a number of albums that skillfully combined his adopted Eastern heritage with his Western classical birthright. —*Linda Kohanov*

Divan I Khas / 1970 / Beyond 72894
Khan's pop instrumentals with Middle Eastern and Indian influences are interesting, but not entirely successful. —*Linda Kohanov*

★ Mahogany Nights / 1990 / Hearts of Space 11020
This album of "night music" is a collection of exotic, highly atmospheric soundscapes with subdued sitar occasionally wafting out of Khan's lush synthesizer tapestries like a fine incense. Although the composer's sitar talents are better represented on other albums, this is a good, all-around introduction to his style, especially for those who normally shy away from Indian music. —*Linda Kohanov*

Bob Kindler

Cello / Neo-classical, Chamber jazz, Ethnic fusion
This classically trained cellist performed with the Honolulu Symphony for 14 years, played jazz with Dave Brubeck's son Darius, and formed a guild that organized cross-cultural events involving dancers, poets, artists, and musicians from around the world. All of these influences and experiences are apparent in his contemporary instrumental albums, which are eclectic to say the least. —*Linda Kohanov*

Tiger's Paw / 1990 / Global Pacific 79334
An exceptional album of contemporary, ethnic-inspired instrumentals. In addition to cello, autoharp, and flutes, the album features an extended range of tablas (an Indian drum) used in creative settings. —*Linda Kohanov*

● Waters of Life—Music from the Matrix III / Nov. 4, 1991 / Global Pacific 79308
R 83253 Complete title is *Waters of Life—Music from the Matrix III*. —*AMG*

Steve Kindler

Violin / Neo-classical, Chamber jazz, Ethnic fusion
Like his brother Bob, violinist Steve Kindler played in the Honolulu Symphony, but he cut his jazz chops as a member of John McLaughlin's fusion band, Mahavishnu Orchestra. Kindler has also toured and recorded with Jan Hammer, Jeff Beck, and Kitaro. Kindler's smooth yet impassioned violin improvisations are the perfect vehicle for his own highly melodic compositions, combining classical, jazz, rock, and ethnic influences. In addition, Kindler is a member of Barefoot, a co-op world-music dance group. —*Linda Kohanov*

Across a Rainbow Sea / 1970 / Global Pacific 79332
Kindler's melodic gifts are topped off by some sophisticated keyboard work and lively Latin grooves. —*Linda Kohanov*

★ Dolphin Smiles / 1987 / Global Pacific 79301
A series of duets with synthesist Teja Bell, featuring lush, fluid textures and flowing melodies. —*Linda Kohanov*

Ben Tavera King

Guitar / Chamber jazz, Ethnic fusion
A Texas-born master of the nylon-string guitar, King likes to call his music "Southwestern Hispanic jazz." Not only does he combine flamenco with jazz and Native American styles, he throws in influences from Mexico and the Caribbean as well. Acknowledged as a leader in the renaissance of Hispanic music,

King has been the subject of a PBS television special and has performed at Lincoln Center. —*Linda Kohanov*

Desert Dreams / 1984 / Global Pacific 79309
Though not as well produced as *Coyote Moon*, King's debut for Global Pacific is a gem, with lively, more straightforward pieces for guitar, sax, bass, and percussion. —*Linda Kohanov*

● Coyote Moon / Jan. 20, 1992 / Global Pacific 79309
An infectious mix of impassioned flamenco guitar stylings with all kinds of Hispanic references—everything from Tex-Mex grooves to mariachi rhythms with a jazz twist. —*Linda Kohanov*

Turquoise Trail / 1993 /
An intriguing combination of Hispanic guitar, Native American flute and percussion reflect the rich heritage of the Southwest, crossing the boundaries between World Music, New Age and Native American flute styles. —*Backroads Music / Heartbeats*

Gershon Kingsley

★ Anima
The ever-innovative Gershon Kingsley treats us to an eclectic album of his latest electronic compositions. Kingsley, world-renowned as a composer, conductor, and musician, shows his genius on *Anima* in themes that seem to mirror the light, the darkness, the joys and journeys of the spirit in its evolution. Both modern and classical styles are blended seamlessly. Tracks from the out-of-print 1986 classic *Much Silence*, never released on CD, add to the desirability. "Quiet Descent" is a gentle marriage of piano and synthesizers. "Reconciliation" explores rhythms and percussive sounds from around the world. In the more classical "Animus," we experience a majesty that is coupled with a powerful longing. "Spirit Implosions" leads us to a cathedral of digitalized voices celebrating a spiritual homecoming. From the darkly dramatic title cut, "Anima", to the romantic and sometimes whimsical "The Road to the Sun", this pioneer of synthesized music demonstrates a musical maturity and excellence that can only come from years of solid dedication. —*Backroads Music / Heartbeats*

Osamu Kitajima

Guitar, koto, percussion, synthesizer / New Age, Ethnic fusion

Behind the Light / 1991 / Higher Octave 7045
This collection of seven elegant jewels hints at an unusual blend of East-West idioms as Osamu brings his broad musical experience to bear on his first album for Higher Octave. His earlier roots are evident, as is his pop-rock sensibility. While this album is anything but pop, he displays a knack for strong melodies and catchy hooks. Traditional Japanese instruments are used very effectively to create exotic percussive moods that give way to rhythmic "cruisers". The shifting moods are highlighted by the occasional appearance of electric guitar and drums but the music never gets too heavy or too far into hard-driving fusion territory. Through *Behind the Light*, Osamu builds his musical temple, filled with elements that are elusive in nature and filled to the brim with his unique illumination. —*Backroads Music / Heartbeats*

★ Source / CBS 42239
Osamu's first CBS release is the ultimate blend of East and West, electronic and traditional. The themes from *The Source* are memorable, cohesively uniting the three richly-textured pieces. Ever shifting styles, tempos and powerful musical statements are continually heard, and Osamu never loses the flow or continuity of the whole work. From the 25-minute opening piece "Heavensent" (aptly titled!) to the 12 and 13-minute "Through Cosmic Doors" and "Eye to I," we're talking major masterpiece on this one. A group of fine musicians support him, playing lyricon, shakuhachi, synthesizers, acoustic and electric guitar, percussion, harp, and violin. —*Backroads Music / Heartbeats*

Kitaro

Guitar / New Age, Progressive electronic, Ethnic fusion
Kitaro's style is the epitome of the contemplative, highly melodic synthesizer music often associated with the new-age movement. Interestingly enough, this famous Japanese composer taught himself to play electric guitar in high school—inspired by the R&B music of Otis Redding. In the early 70s, Kitaro formed the Far East Family Band, which released two albums of progressive

rock. In 1972, however, he met the innovative German synthesist Klaus Schulze during a trip to Europe. Kitaro was hooked. He built his first synthesizer and began experimenting with all kinds of unusual sounds. His first solo album, *Astral Voyage*, appeared in 1978 and quickly gained a cult following. Two years later, he produced the first of several soundtracks for "Silk Road," a Japanese television documentary series that ran for five years. Several albums of music from "Silk Road" were released to a growing international contingent of fans who admired his combination of lush, majestic textures and gentle, almost naive, melodies. Kitaro, however, was still considered an underground artist in America until he signed with Geffen Records in 1986, which re-released seven of his earlier albums and gave him the support to expand his scope in many ways. For instance, after years of creating albums in the privacy of his home studio near Japan's Mt. Fuji, Kitaro produced his 1987 release, *The Light of the Spirit*, with the help of Mickey Hart. The album featured an array of American musicians and was nominated for a Grammy Award in the Best New-Age Performance category. That same year, Kitaro also made his first live tour of North America and sold two million albums in the US alone. Kitaro's style had changed as well, becoming more theatrical and assertive while retaining a certain level of innocence and purity. His more recent recordings also show a renewed interest in the rock and pop elements that originally attracted him to music in the late 60s. — *Linda Kohanov*

● **My Best** / 1986 / Gramavision 79407
Kitaro's synthesizer-based compositions are extended aural landscapes full of dramatic peaks of intensity and valleys of emotional calm. He is fond of loud, tympani-like drums, sweeps of sound that approximate electronic winds, and majestic melodies played in singing, upper-register tones. And his music is quite consistent. If you like this, you'll probably like every record he's made. — *William Ruhlmann*

☆ **Silk Road I & II** / 1986 / Gramavision 79411
Kitaro's masterwork remains this two-record score for a Japanese TV series. His most ambitious themes and involved playing are found here. — *William Ruhlmann*

● **Light of the Spirit** / 1987 / David Geffen Co. 24163
With the help of Grateful Dead drummer Mickey Hart, Kitaro made this album using American musicians, which gives it slightly more of an ensemble feeling than his usual one-man productions. — *William Ruhlmann*

Kojiki / 1990 / David Geffen Co. 24255
Kojiki is perhaps the most developed and distilled musical statement of Kitaro's illustrious career. His trademark two-finger synthesizer melodies, with their strangely compelling power, and his refined sense of drama remain intact, but the sound is embellished by full blown orchestral arrangements, while many of the pieces undergo sophisticated melodic development reminiscent of symphonic music. The skillful layered arrangements breathe new life into Kitaro's blend of traditional Japanese music, western romantic classicism, rock, and spacemusic, as electronics mix with violin (some played masterfully by Steve Kindler), flute, harp, guitar, drums, and entire string sections to produce an exhilarating work of majestic proportions... *Kojiki* has the grandeur and scope of an epic film score, and may prove to be the definitive work thus far from this major artist. — *Backroads Music / Heartbeats*

Live in America / 1991 / David Geffen Co. 24323
Kitaro's already dramatic music is given even greater force when played before a live audience, as this 1990 show from Atlanta's Fox Theatre demonstrates. — *William Ruhlmann*

○ **Dream** / 1992 / David Geffen Co. 24477
Two giants in contemporary music have joined forces to create one of the most awe-inspiring albums of the nineties. Kitaro has taken his signature style into a new dimension of orchestral drama with three tracks featuring the breath-taking vocals of Jon Anderson, from the group "Yes". Anderson, a long-time Kitaro fan, showed up on Kitaro's Japanese mountain top and hung out for a month. Their ensuing "marriage" of vocals and music is the result. Kitaro composed the music while Jon wrote the lyrics. The songs revolve around the eternal theme of love, as in the transcendental romanticism of "Lady of Dreams" and the ecstasy of spiritual liberation in "Agreement"...This is a special album full of soaring emotion and spiritual upliftment. — *Backroads Music / Heartbeats*

Daniel Kobialka

○ **Rainbows** / Kob 304
On the companion compilation, *Rainbows*, Kobialka gathers six enchanting versions of well-loved classics and folk melodies to soothe & relax children and the adults who love them. Featured is an extended version of "Somewhere Over the Rainbow" plus "Oh What a Beautiful Morning" & "Greensleeves." — *Backroads Music / Heartbeats*

★ **Velvet Dreams** / Kob 305
Pachelbel's "Canon in D" is taken to a new dimension in contemporary music by the principal violinist with the San Francisco Symphony. A gentle, sublime version, nearly 21-minute long, fills the first track of *Velvet Dreams* with floating synthesizers and vibraphone, while two selections each from Bach and Vivaldi make up the remainder. Vivaldi's "Largo from *Winter* of The Four Seasons" and Bach's "Jesu, Joy of Man's Desiring" close with soothing treatments of luxurious relaxation and refined tranquility. — *Backroads Music / Heartbeats*

Bernward Koch

New Age, Chamber jazz

Carole Koenig

After Shadows: Classics for Quiet Moods / Carole Koenig 1007
While most hammer dulcimer players tend to stick to interpretations of Celtic music, Carole Koenig has presented on her previous albums an array of medieval, renaissance and baroque pieces adapted to this venerable folk instrument. On *After Shadows* Carole has turned her attention to the impressionist music of late nineteenth and early twentieth century Europe. With one piece each by George Gershwin and Cyril Scott, the album focuses on the three great composers of this era, Claude Debussy, Maurice Ravel and Erik Satie...The resonant tones of the dulcimer perfectly fit this atmospheric and somewhat mysterious music, resulting in a peaceful yet colorful album of subtlety and elegance. — *Backroads Music / Heartbeats*

Encore!: Renaissance & Baroque Music on the Hammered Dulcimer / Carole Koenig 1006
Renaissance and Baroque music on the hammered dulcimer. Carole is really catching on, with her representations of musical time periods and styles. This time she "goes for baroque", with pieces by Bach, Handel, Praetorius, and others. Additional instrumentation is provided by violin, viola, flute, guitar, and keyboards. — *Backroads Music / Heartbeats*

● **Gala: Classics from a Romantic Era** / Carole Koenig 1008

Gary Lamb

Drums, piano / Solo instrumental, Adult alternative
Lamb's music is exemplary of his early musical interests. The Northern California native grew up listening to R&B and was playing drums in Bay Area rock bands before the age of 20. Along the way, he dabbled in piano and actually took some time off from the club scene to concentrate on building his chops on that instrument. He recorded a couple of solo piano albums in the mid 80s, eventually adding electronic keyboards to the mix on his 1989 release *Watching the Night Fall*, his first album to get national radio airplay. His subsequent recordings mix his love of catchy, generally cheerful, pop melodies with his penchant for rock & roll backbeats. — *Linda Kohanov*

Walk in the Garden / 1987 / Golden Gate 7130
An early album of piano vignettes. — *Linda Kohanov*

Watching the Night Fall / 1989 / Petrale Soul Music 22242
Lamb's first blend of acoustic piano with synthesizers and percussion was inspired by California's Big Sur coastline. — *Linda Kohanov*

● **Distant Fields** / 1990 / Golden Gate 7150
Lamb's all-electronic album retains the sounds of acoustic piano and percussion through the use of sophisticated sampling programs. Though he expands his palette with a few unusual tone colors here and there, the sounds remain fairly conventional.

Generally, these are lively tunes with a subtle use of backbeats. —
Linda Kohanov

Love Themes / 1992 / Golden Gate 7180
With seven releases now available, the prolific Gary Lamb has
shown himself to be a sensitive composer and pianist, sometimes
in a solo setting and sometimes, as on his latest *Love Themes*,
with his own state-of-the-art orchestration. The idea behind this
new album was to describe the many different aspects or themes
of love, and he succeeds in bringing to mind childhood hopes and
dreams, love of nature, and quiet, tender moments. This beautiful,
heartfelt statement provides special listening moments, and is
sure to find a place in your heart. Whether cradling a sleeping
baby, sharing time with friends or enjoying the majestic colors of
the early evening sky, Gary Lamb's intimate music will enhance
your pleasure. —*Backroads Music / Heartbeats*

Imaginations / 1993 / Golden Gate 2224
Those familiar with Gary Lamb's previous releases may be expecting more of the quiet, pretty piano and synthesizer music that
is Gary's signature. *Imaginations* has some of this, but on many
of the cuts the pace has been kicked up a few notches, both in
tempo and by the addition of electronic drums and synthesized
tuned percussion. Gary's musical style continues to develop and
mature, including new elements and depth of passion. Don't be
surprised if the title track and "Modern World," both upbeat and
lively, bring you to your feet dancing. "When You Return to Me"
is full of the hope and joyful expectation that a loved one will
come soon, while "The Boys From Liverpool," Gary's tribute to
the Beatles, includes no Beatles music but has the happy-go-lucky
spirit of their early songs. Three musical portraits of specific locales are included here: Vancouver, Hong Kong, and Claude
Monet's garden at Giverny. Gary Lamb fans and anyone who enjoys pretty, melodic, and lively instrumental music will find much
to delight in on *Imaginations*. —*Backroads Music / Heartbeats*

Pascal Languirand

Vocals, keyboard, guitar, percussion / New Age

● **Gregorian Waves** / 1991 /
Drama, emotion and reverence are intertwining elements which
unite the nine pieces and give *Gregorian Waves* its majesty and
expressive impact. Like *MCMXC A.D.* by the European group
Enigma, another exciting 1991 release, Languirand has found innovative new ways of interpreting Gregorian chanting in a dynamic contemporary context while capturing hordes of listeners.
—*Backroads Music / Heartbeats*

☆ **Ishtar** / 1994 /
Ishtar is new music that delves into the future while calling forth
mystical potency from an ancient past. Pascal combines the energies of outward expression & inward introspection simultaneously. His keyboard playing exposes exotic realms of subtle emotion and jubilant, rhythmic touches that convey the brilliance of
the full moon and richness of ivory. Voices enter twice, on
"Passage" and "The Realm of Enki," sung hauntingly by Daniele
Vince. Additional keyboards and percussion are heard from
Phillippe Attie who co-produced & arranged "Voyager." With a
powerful bottom and solid rhythms, Pascal uses drama, emotion
and a flair for the unusual in his melodic development. Sounding
at times like Mychael Danna, Patrick O'Hearn or Mark Dwane,
Pascal ventures into every facet of today's spacemusic, drawing
on experience and innovation while producing sound that is un-
equivocally modern. —*Backroads Music / Heartbeats*

○ **Minos/De Harmonia Universalis ('78-'80)** / 1994 /
At first, this title seems more progressive, similar to the space-
rock records of that era, but closer listening reveals a sustained
continuum of music not unlike efforts by Steve Roach or Robert
Rich in blending sacred sounds and aural imagery. Majestic yet
gentle, Pascal's pioneering works welcome one into original musical worlds that engage heart & mind. This timely reissue, with
two LPs on one CD, is worth further exploration. —*Backroads
Music / Heartbeats*

David Lanz

Piano / Solo instrumental, Adult alternative
One of the most popular artists in the solo instrumental and
adult-alternative spheres, Lanz played in several rock bands during his teens, then began developing his style as a solo pianist in
a small Seattle nightclub. He introduced some of his originals

into the bar's required mix of standards and pop tunes, receiving
such a positive response from patrons that, before long, he was
playing his own material almost exclusively. His early albums of
solo piano works are still among the Narada label's best-sellers.
His two collaborative efforts with guitarist Paul Speer also hit the
Billboard Top 200 Albums chart; yet as Lanz's national popularity grew, he began to experiment with works for larger and larger
ensembles, culminating in full orchestral accompaniments on
Skyline Firedance (1990). His most recent album is a refreshing
return to his solo piano roots. —*Linda Kohanov*

★ **Cristofori's Dream** / 1988 / Narada 61021
Among the most popular new-age recordings ever made, this is
an album of instrumental piano music (with other instruments,
especially strings and string-like synthesizers, added). Its selections have a calm elegance, as Lanz spends most of his time in
the upper register of the piano, delivering precise, articulated
melodies, culminating in a recreation of Procol Harum's "A
Whiter Shade of Pale" that features original organist Matthew
Fisher. —*William Ruhlmann*

Skyline Firedance / 1990 / Narada 64001
On his popular followup to *Cristofori's Dream*, Lanz turns in two
discs of the same music, one scored for orchestra and the other
played solo on the piano. The alternate approaches to the music
bring out Lanz's talents as a composer. —*William Ruhlmann*

○ **Return to the Heart** / 1991 / Narada 64005
Return to the Heart is a return to Lanz's roots as a solo pianist, yet
his new compositions for this medium show a remarkable sense
of maturity, elegance, and taste. —*Linda Kohanov*

Laraaji

*Zither, guitar, bells, synthesizer / Progressive electronic, Ethnic
fusion, Ambient*
This multi-instrumentalist creates shimmering, meditative tapestries using electronically enhanced zither, autoharp, and other
acoustic instruments. He was first brought to wider audiences
through his association with Brian Eno. —*Linda Kohanov*

★ **Day of Radiance** / 1980 / EG 19
An enchanting recording divided into two moods. The first part is
buoyant with folk-like jigs that move toward a more hazy zither-
in-space sound exemplary of Eno, who produced this album as
part of his *Ambient* series. —*Linda Kohanov*

Max Lasser

Guitar / Adult alternative, Chamber jazz, Ethnic fusion
The Swiss guitarist was best known for his association with boyhood chum Andreas Vollenweider. Lasser's tours and recordings
with the harpist culminated in Vollenweider's Grammy-winning
album *Down to the Moon*. A year later, the guitarist formed Max
Lasser's Ark and made several colorful, versatile albums. —*Linda
Kohanov*

● **Earthwalk** / 1988 / CBS 44520
Max Lasser's Ark combines a wide variety of influences on this
release—everything from classical, jazz, and folk to touches of
ethnic styles. A thoroughly enjoyable romp though a variety of
moods and textures. —*Linda Kohanov*

Timejump / 1990 / Narada 62768
Lasser's release on the Sona Gaia label is slickly produced with
some intriguing approaches to the guitar, from sparkling classical
miniatures and powerful electric solos to Indian raga-style
melodies played on slide guitar, among other things. The album
also features Lasser's abilities on keyboards. —*Linda Kohanov*

Different Kind of Blue / Oct. 1992 / Real Music 5050
Swiss guitarist Max Lasser is an alumnus of Andreas
Vollenweider's band, and his music displays the same fluidity. He
combines catchy melodies with powerful rhythms and rich
arrangements, playing acoustic, electric and slide guitars plus
mandolin, dobro & Chinese cheng. Lasser draws on folk, rock,
jazz & world backgrounds while his band adds keyboards, bass,
drums, woodwinds, marimba & vibes. Included is the aptly titled
"Little China," with delicate cheng & second guitarist Thomas
Fessler, two tracks with Paul McCandless, five cuts with
vibes/marimba ace Emmanuel Sejourne, and the closer, "Ry's
Blues," a tribute to the great slide guitarist Ry Cooder. —
Backroads Music / Heartbeats

Latitude

● **Latitude I & 40 Degrees North** / 1994 /
Here are two classics that have been out-of-print for years. The first Latitude album debuted the synth/vibes/guitar sound that won such a following. Soothing, spontaneous melodies provide an energetic tranquility, as heard on the classic "Wing & A Prayer." Her second effort is more dynamic with colorful, contagious tunes that helped it to reach #1 on the Radio charts. — *Backroads Music / Heartbeats*

Adrian Legg

Guitar / Solo instrumental, Chamber jazz, New acoustic
An acoustic guitarist from England, Adrian has played in many country-based bands. His current work showcases his solo acoustic guitar playing. —*Paul Kohler*

Techno Picker / 1983 / Spindrift 201
Debut from this acoustic guitarist. If you enjoy great guitarists, do yourself a favor and check this album out. —*Paul Kohler*

Fretmelt / 1984 / Spindrift 115
This release features Legg with a small group. Brilliant, with Legg sounding like three guitarists playing at once! —*Paul Kohler*

Lost for Words / 1986 / Making Waves 127
This album from the British acoustic guitar wizard features jaw-dropping playing. —*Paul Kohler*

● **Guitars & Other Cathedrals** / 1990 / Relativity 1045
Using an acoustic guitar modified with banjo tuners, Legg takes his guitar where no one has gone before. Essential listening. — *Paul Kohler*

○ **Mrs. Crowe's Blue Waltz** / 1993 / Combat 1162
This is the third release by eccentric guitar deity Adrian Legg. *Mrs. Crowe's Blue Waltz* strays from Legg's usual all-acoustic format, perhaps in hopes of reaching a wider audience with electric guitar, string and vocal arrangements. In the meantime, you will hear his unique melding of folk, blues, country, jazz and New Age styles, all played with dazzling dexterity and a truly unusual style. —*Backroads Music / Heartbeats*

Andreas Leifeld

Adult alternative, Progressive electronic, Ethnic fusion
This brilliant, yet little-known, German artist has a flair for combining refined ambiences with driving funk bass lines and rock beats. His well-constructed melodies and improvisations are often quite catchy, while his song titles and symbolic sonic imagery are lined with social commentary. Classically trained, Leifeld makes a living as a music teacher in Paderborn, Germany, and his modest apartment is overrun with all manner of electronic gadgetry. He is truly a living, breathing example of the cyberpunk mentality—you get the feeling he would gladly leave earthly concerns behind if he could download the essence of his mind, body, and soul onto a hard disk. —*Linda Kohanov*

Mysterious Messages / 1990 / Musique Intemporelle 907
Though not as polished as *Discoveries*, this album is another fine example of Leifeld's style. Most of the pieces are upbeat with ethereal underpinnings and some disco grooves. On "Tokio" he also hints at the Japanese mentality of technological supremacy by mutating oriental melodies through heavy-handed electronics. —*Linda Kohanov*

○ **Discoveries** / 1991 / Musique Intemporelle 907
Futuristic in conception and execution, this album still harkens back to the sequencer-driven sound of the German electronic school. Yet unlike Tangerine Dream, Leifeld has managed to add rock and pop influences without losing his progressive edge. His two-part suite "African Dreams" delves into the techno-tribal realm. He also adds some amusing political cynicism on the final selection, "Same Old Game," by layering recorded voice fragments of George Bush's most banal catchphrases over combat sounds and a brooding, almost sinister electronic score. —*Linda Kohanov*

Brent Lewis

★ **Earth Tribe Rhythms** /
Of the many drumming titles available, *Earth Tribe Rhythms* is perhaps the most entertaining & fun-filled. Brent Lewis uses the Ikauma Drums, a system of 22 tuned drums mounted on a large stand, allowing him to play tunes as well as a wide variety of percussion styles. Lewis has traveled the world learning his craft, and studied extensively with Kwasi Badu, drummer for the King of Ghana. Lewis plays all the parts on this multi-tracked album, with the melodies most apparent in the strong bass lines that provide the foundation. Most of the tunes are uptempo and range from the almost pop-ish "Bone to Bone" to the tropical undulations of "Caribbean Sea," and from the Middle Eastern "Potent Potion" to the dense jungle impressionism of "Tribal Consciousness." There are no dull moments here, only high-energy dance grooves by this master percussionist. —*Backroads Music / Heartbeats*

Ottmar Liebert

Guitar, percussion / Guitar-pop, Adult alternative, Ethnic fusion
Liebert has said that "flamenco is a music both romantic and dangerous; it is an attitude as much as it is a musical genre." Therein lies the philosophy that catapulted him to fame at the end of the 80s with an engaging mix of subdued flamenco guitar and South American percussion, rock, jazz, and pop influences. Liebert's "attitude" actually suppresses the more challenging and "dangerous" aspects of flamenco in favor of the romantic—and the stylish. He's not a technical wizard on the guitar, but he has a feel for the music's innate sensuality and a gift for creating memorable melodies. Born in Cologne, Germany, to a Chinese-German father and a Hungarian mother, Liebert traveled throughout Russia and Asia before moving to Boston and eventually settling in Santa Fe, NM. After years of trying to hit the big time in various jazz-funk bands, he began playing acoustic guitar in Santa Fe restaurants. His first (self-produced) cassette, *Nouveau Flamenco*, was basically recorded for friends, but the album received heavy radio airplay on WAVE in Los Angeles. Higher Octave Records re-released it nationally in 1990. After his subsequent album *Borrasca* quickly climbed the charts, Liebert was picked up by a major label, Epic. With his exotic good looks and enigmatic stage presence, Liebert has brought flamenco to mainstream America with a certain level of class and accessibility. His prowess as a composer and instrumentalist has steadily improved over the years. —*Linda Kohanov*

★ **Nouveau Flamenco** / 1990 / Higher Octave 7026
Originally released in 1988, this independently produced album went on to top *Billboard*'s new-age chart and sell a half-million copies. The music, however, lacks the craftsmanship of later releases. In fact, almost all of the short selections end in mediocre fadeouts. —*Linda Kohanov*

Poets and Angels / 1991 / Higher Octave 7030
Shirley and company combined novelty numbers ("She Took It Like a Man," "Trashy Women") with outlaw country ("Jesus and Mama," "Queen of Memphis") in a way that connected with the blue-collar country crowd. The album sold 1.5 million copies. — *Brian Mansfield*

Borrasca / 1991 / Higher Octave 7036
This is another nicely produced, flamenco-influenced chart-climber. —*Linda Kohanov*

○ **Solo Para Ti** / 1992 / Epic 47848
Liebert's first recording for Epic is his finest effort to date. Along with his group Luna Negra (bassist Jon Gagan and percussionist Dave Bryant), the album also features a guest appearance by rock guitarist Carlos Santana on a couple of cuts and some subtle vocals by Santa Fe artist Joe Bradley. A few of Liebert's originals also add strings, horns, and piano, although acoustic guitar remains the prominent voice throughout. —*Linda Kohanov*

Lightwave

Group / Progressive electronic, Ambient
A leading French electronic band, Lightwave creates extended works that can best be described as "sonic architecture" in their use of slowly unfolding blocks of synthesized sound and sensation. —*Linda Kohanov*

★ **Nachtmusik** / 1990 / Erdenklang AAAA
After releasing four independently produced cassettes through the European underground, Lightwave has released its first CD on the pioneering German electronic label Erdenklang. The title, translated as "night music," is the perfect description of the dark, delightfully ambiguous compositions. —*Linda Kohanov*

Teo Lima

Batacoto / 1994 /
From the heart of Brazil comes this all-star group led by percussionist Teo Lima. A selection of instrumental and vocal music radiates with the diverse rhythms of the Brazilian people. Appearances by Dionne Warwick, Ivan Lins, Gilberto Gil, Sivuca, Ernie Watts and violinist Jerry Goodman help to showcase the various styles, such as samba, jongo, maracatu, ciranda & two songs of African rhythmic origins. Notes about the various songs and dances are found in the liner notes. Passionate, mellow & pleasantly varied, the 8-member group carries *Batacoto* through 14 tracks, anchored by Lima who is one of the best Brazilian percussionists. —*Backroads Music / Heartbeats*

Lorie Line

● **Storyline** /
Storyline covers various shades of feeling and emotion, presenting semi-autobiographical reflections of the artist's life, glimpsed through a variety of musical windows. From childhood memories and a lullaby for her own new-born daughter, to love songs celebrating freedom, growth and change, to themes inspired by Mozart and old spirituals, Lorie Line's melodious piano and quiet sensitivity evoke a magical tapestry of imaginative musical tales. The artist's fluid piano is delicately augmented by touches of rainstorm ("Whisper in the Wind"), violin ("Alleta Raine") and guitar ("Child of Spring"). If you like the beautiful piano of Danny Wright you will love Lorie Line's graceful debut. —*Backroads Music / Heartbeats*

Joaquin Llevano

Violin / Adult alternative
Llevano gained early recognition for his work with jazz violinist Jean-Luc Ponty before starting his own recording career with Global Pacific. —*Linda Kohanov*

○ **One Mind** / 1987 / Global Pacific 79305
Llevano's debut as a leader is a combination of new-age, jazz, and rock styles. Includes A. West on bass. —*Paul Kohler*

Frank Lorentzen

New Age
● **Hands** / 1993 /
An undiscovered Spacemusic treat is *Hands* by Denmark's Frank Lorentzen. The music is reminiscent of the classic works of Iasos and Aeoliah, as Frank creates gentle synthesizer chords which bathe the listener in a spiritual healing energy of deep, gradual, and ever-lifting tones, encircling the musical body of one's inner presence. This is perfect music for massage or meditation, slowly unfolding to reveal & illuminate. —*Backroads Music / Heartbeats*

Ray Lynch

Lute / New Age, Neo-classical, Adult alternative
Though he's one of the most influential artists in "new-age pop" and adult-alternative circles, Lynch has extensive formal music training. Inspired by Andres Segovia's classical guitar recordings, Lynch studied the instrument in Barcelona, Spain, in the early 60s. He later attended the University of Texas as a composition student. Toward the end of the decade, Lynch moved to New York and became a fixture in the city's "early music" scene as a lutenist with the Renaissance Quartet. A period of personal and spiritual crisis, however, led him to retreat from his career in conventional classical music. He moved to California, spent some time investigating various spiritual traditions and philosophies, and started experimenting with electronic music. His 1983 debut album, *The Sky of Mind*, artfully meshed his early classical music leanings with spatial, synthesized orchestrations and became an underground success with virtually no promotional support. Two years later, he released his most famous album, *Deep Breakfast*. While much of the album continued in a neoclassical vein (with some lyrical duets for viola and keyboards, among other things), Lynch's catchy tune, "Celestial Soda Pop," became a hit in the newly emerging WAVE radio formats. The album was one of the first new-age releases to sell over 500,000 copies. While Lynch's later albums have their moments, his increasingly pop-oriented style seems to have lost the expressive intensity of his earlier work. Still, growing numbers of listeners seem attracted to his vibrant electronic textures and heartrending melodies. —*Linda Kohanov*

○ **Sky of Mind** / 1983 / Music West 101
The Sky of Mind was Ray's debut from 1983. The current version features new arrangement of the six pieces, which are classically-inspired and heartfelt, performed on both acoustic & electronic instruments. The radiant compositions also make for ideal morning listening, with Tibetan bells connecting the pieces, and its emotional nature paving the way for a true musical journey—a classic example of the genius of Ray Lynch. —*Backroads Music / Heartbeats*

★ **Deep Breakfast** / 1986 / Windham Hill 11117
Ray Lynch's synthesizer playing sometimes approximates keyboard instruments and sometimes sounds like individually plucked strings on electrified string instruments, but always has a deeply textured melodic structure and a buoyant rhythmic underpinning. Isolated notes in series and patterns make a pointillistic mosaic of sound that alternately soothes and stimulates. No wonder this is one of the best-selling new-age albums of all time. —*William Ruhlmann*

No Blue Thing / 1989 / Windham Hill 11119
Ray Lynch continues to explore the interface between acoustic and electronic instrumentation, as well as between popular and classical elements, with an obvious debt to the pastoral works of Ralph Vaughan Williams. The synthesizers—with their characteristic plucked, harp-like, and harpsichord tones—are beautifully complemented, on almost every piece, by oboe, flute, English horn, cello, violin, viola or classical guitar, with the acoustic instruments much more prominent than on "Deep Breakfast."...Once again this meticulous artist has produced a sublime album of sensitive and deep compositions and sophisticated yet uncluttered arrangements. —*Backroads Music / Heartbeats*

Music of Ray Lynch / 1990 / 104
A box set. —*Linda Kohanov*

Steve MacDonald

★ **Spinfield** / 1990 / Hearts of Space 11012
Spinfield offers a dramatic and unique vision of dynamic, instrumental "power-pop/space-music," reaching through space into rock styles. There are influences heard from Tangerine Dream and Pink Floyd as well as elements of Tri Atma and Yanni. Through it all, though, this electronic keyboard artist from New Zealand maintains full control of the blistering flight, journeying through zealous cross-rhythms into an array of dazzling space-passages. Power to spare! —*Backroads Music / Heartbeats*

Mannheim Steamroller

Group / Neo-classical, Adult alternative, Progressive electronic
This Omaha-based group has sold a lot of albums over the years with its high production standards and accessible pop orchestral sound. Best known for their extensive *Fresh Aire* series of albums, the members of Mannheim Steamroller mix a certain level of classical inspiration with piano, synthesizers, guitar, bass, drums, and sometimes full symphony orchestra. The resulting music is sometimes fascinating, yet often no better than muzak on amphetamines. In fact, it's extremely difficult to recommend one album over the next: they all offer a few arresting moments next to forgettable music that, at its worst, can be downright embarrassing. (Some of the albums are even accompanied by pretentious liner notes analyzing the music's form and inspiration, yet the compositions inside don't begin to live up to these classical references.) —*Linda Kohanov*

Fresh Aire 1 / 1975 / American Gramaphone 355
The first in composer Chip Davis's ongoing series of instrumental new-age albums is, as the album cover says, "a collection of original music set in a hybrid musical style, combining the long-lived forms of the classics, performed on both old-world and contemporary instruments," to which we might add that Davis also mixes in the sounds of nature, especially rain, on an album meant to evoke spring. —*William Ruhlmann*

Fresh Aire 2 / 1977 / American Gramaphone 359
Davis's "fall" collection is also a recasting of madrigal and Renaissance musical styles—harpsichord and flute sounds in stately cadences. With typical eclecticism he mixes in drums and

rhythms that would not be out of place on a rock stage. —
William Ruhlmann

Fresh Aire 3 / 1979 / American Gramaphone 365
The "summer" album is dominated by a version of a 16th-century
toccata, played rapidly and evoking the energy and life of the season. — *William Ruhlmann*

Fresh Aire 4 / 1981 / American Gramaphone 370
Bach is the touchstone for this 18th-century tribute that constitutes the "winter" selection in the *Fresh Aire* series, appropriately
filled with organ-like sounds. — *William Ruhlmann*

○ **Fresh Aire 7** / 1982 / American Gramaphone 777
...As meticulous in detail as it is epic in scope, *Fresh Aire VII* is a
truly grand statement, fusing the past with the present, creating
music of the future. *Fresh Aire VII* is a powerful album, and was
recently awarded the Grammy in the New Age category. —
Backroads Music / Heartbeats

★ **Fresh Aire 5** / 1983 / American Gramaphone 385
Accompanied by the London Symphony and the Cambridge
Singers, Mannheim Steamroller journeys back in time to 1609,
then takes off for the moon. It's all a dream, but makes for some
of the liveliest music of the series. — *William Ruhlmann*

○ **Saving the Wildlife** / 1986 / American Gramaphone 2086
This 1986 release is the soundtrack from a PBS Special about endangered species. Each cut is devoted to a particular country and
species, such as India, Africa, China, etc. Tributes to seals, pandas,
grizzlies, penguins and whales and others are done in uniquely
playful ways which are cross-cultural and delightfully typical of
the dynamic "Mannheim style". —*Backroads Music / Heartbeats*

Fresh Aire 6 / 1986 / American Gramaphone 386
Siren-like sounds and stately melodies dominate on an album
whose theme is "impressions of Greek mythology." — *William
Ruhlmann*

Classical Gas / 1987 / American Gramaphone 800
Guitarist Mason Williams teams up with the Steamroller for an
orchestrated, synthesized version of his 1968 instrumental hit,
plus more in the same vein. — *William Ruhlmann*

○ **Fresh Aire Motivator** /
Originally designed for runners, this sixty-minute tape is a collection of the most uptempo cuts from the Fresh Aire catalog. A
map and graph are even included to help guide your most opti-
mal run. This is like a "greatest hits", from *Fresh Aire I-V*. —
Backroads Music / Heartbeats

● **Yellowstone: The Music of Nature** / American Gramaphone
3089
Growing out of an attempt to bring positive awareness to the natural cycles and outstanding beauty of Yellowstone National Park,
Chip Davis' inspiration for this album began with his visit there
last Fall. Four classical compositions, by Respighi, Grofe,
Debussy, and Vivaldi, are given full orchestral treatment. Mixed
with several classic Steamroller pieces and assorted nature
sounds, this release has a Fantasia-like dramatic presence of symphonic grandeur. This is also a fund raising effort, the first of its
kind endorsed by the National Park Service. —*Backroads Music /
Heartbeats*

Fresh Aire Interludes / American Gramaphone 373
Interludes consists of the softer, mellow pieces from the "Four
Seasons" series of *Fresh Aire I-IV*. Consistent, resonant keyboard-
centered pieces provide a pleasing backdrop, with environmental
sounds mixed in, showing a more sensitive Steamroller side. —
Backroads Music / Heartbeats

Michael Manring

Bass / Adult alternative, Chamber jazz
Inspired by his teacher Jaco Pastorius, Manring has taken the
electric bass into new territory. A native of the Washington, DC,
area, he played classical bass in high school chamber groups and
orchestra while also working in local Top 40 bands. From 1979 to
1982, he honed his chops in the DC fusion group Natural Bridge
and also started performing with guitarist Michael Hedges.
Manring played on Hedges's Windham Hill debut *Breakfast in
the Fields*. Since then, the bassist has become *the* Windham Hill
session man, recording on albums by Will Ackerman, Ira Stein,
and Russel Walder in addition to his frequent tours with Hedges.
Manring is a also a key member in the label's all-star band,
Montreux. —*Linda Kohanov*

● **Unusual Weather** / 1986 / Windham Hill 1044
Manring's debut as a leader is a striking combination of ethereal
atmospheres and stormy solos. —*Linda Kohanov*

Toward the Center of the Night / 1989 / Windham Hill 1083
Another finely crafted bass exploration. —*Linda Kohanov*

○ **Drastic Measures** / 1991 / Windham Hill 1102
Manring takes drastic measures in his continuing crusade to
push the bass out of the rhythm section and into the spotlight.
Lyrical solos, bass overdubs, some virtuosic arpeggios, and
breathless passage work illuminate ensemble-oriented originals
as well as updated versions of Jimi Hendrix's "Purple Haze" and
Chick Corea's "500 Miles High." —*Linda Kohanov*

Jon Mark

Vocals, guitar / Progressive electronic, Ambient
A top English session musician in the 60s, Mark played with
everyone from the Rolling Stones and Marianne Faithfull to blues
sensation John Mayall. As the decade came to a close, the vocalist, composer, and guitarist began exploring the potential of
jazz/rock fusion as co-leader of the highly influential Mark-
Almond Band. After the group dispersed in the late 70s, Mark
moved to New Zealand, where he has so far produced two albums of impressionistic synthesizer pieces. —*Linda Kohanov*

★ **Standing Stones of Callanish** / 1988 / Kuckuck 11082
Standing Stones of Callanish, Mark's tribute to his Celtic roots, is
a set of elegant synthesizer sketches that capture the mystery and
the simple beauty of the British Isles. —*Linda Kohanov*

○ **Land of Merlin** / 1992 / Kuckuck 11094
Mark's most recent album is almost a seamless continuation of
the softly melodic synthesizer style he established on *Standing
Stones*. *Land of Merlin* was inspired by Mark's childhood experiences traveling through the enchanted landscapes of Cornwall,
the legendary birthplace of King Arthur and home to his fabled
Knights of the Round Table. —*Linda Kohanov*

Alhambra / 1993 / Kuckuck 11100
From the spellbinding majesty of the Alhambra to the thunderous war machine called Conquistadores, Jon Mark has again captured the soul and spirit of a people in his music...As in *The
Standing Stones of Callanish* and *Land of Merlin*, Jon Mark
weaves ancient melodies & rhythms into his electronic tapestry,
this time portraying the elegance and grandeur of Medieval
Spain. With classical guitar accents, sounds of harp, trumpet, and
the hot desert wind adding vivid colorings, *Alhambra* is yet another haunting soundtrack to give wings to our ever-nomadic
imaginations. —*Heartbeats*

Gerald Jay Markoe

Composer / New Age, Electronic, Ambient
Since the early 60s, this composer and astrologer has been fascinated by the relationships among music, meditation, sacred
geometry, and spiritual teachings. Boasting Bachelor and Masters
degrees from Juilliard and the Manhattan School of Music, respectively, Markoe has also received ASCAP awards for his scores
to theatrical productions. Though he's obviously a knowledgeable
musician, his potential as an electronic composer is inhibited by
his blatantly new-age ideas. —*Linda Kohanov*

● **Music from the Pleiades** / 1989 / Astro 01
Eleven synthesizer pieces designed to create the sensation of an
otherworldly voyage to the Pleiades, a star cluster in the constellation of Taurus often cited as the origin of extraterrestrial visitors to Earth. Markoe recorded the album in a studio filled with
crystals, which he says gives the music a very special vibration.
One reviewer called *Music from the Pleiades* "a good tape for out-
of-body projection." However, the spacey, orchestra-inspired compositions themselves don't necessarily stand up to concentrated
listening. —*Linda Kohanov*

Sacred Music from Seven Stars / 1991 / AstroMusic 5
This album is more on the neo-classical side, with thick layers of
synthesized sound suggesting celestial orchestras. —*Linda
Kohanov*

Juan Martin

*Guitar / Easy listening, Guitar-pop, Neo-classical, Orchestral,
    Ethnic fusion, Flamenco*
Classical guitarist. —*AMG*

● **Painter in Sound** / 1986 / Novus 3005
Light and tranquil, this is Spanish-flavored classical guitar with synthesizer and trumpet support from Mark Isham. Each piece is meant as a companion to a famous painting. — *Scott Bultman*

James Owen Matthews

☆ **Liquid Strings** / 1994 /
One of the finest debuts for space music in some time, *Liquid Strings* has already been put to the test with excellent response to airplay on *Music From the Hearts of Space*. Matthews has a sensitive touch in his layering of sound patterns upon stringed textures, warm and inviting to the ear. His solo synthesizer music offers a quiet intimacy and a wonderful journey in sound. *Liquid Strings* is made up of nine "small symphonies," each complete unto itself yet part of the greater whole which blends the expansiveness of the skies above with the voices of the inner soul. The title track and album closer, the nearly 11-minute "Celestial Strings" are just two of the highlights from a soon-to-be Heartbeats favorite, James Owen Matthews. — *Backroads Music / Heartbeats*

Peter Maunu

Guitar / Adult alternative, Progressive electronic
Though he's not publicly well known, this veteran guitarist is highly respected in the inner music circles of Los Angeles for session work ranging from Claus Ogerman, Jean-Luc Ponty, and Mark Isham to Bobby McFerrin, the Commodores, and the Pointer Sisters. Together with Isham and Patrick O'Hearn, Maunu performed in the short-lived but still-talked-about Group 87, an early 80s progressive band. Maunu's single release as a leader is one of the finest albums on the Narada label. — *Linda Kohanov*

★ **Warm Sound in a Gray Field** / 1990 / Narada 62010
An exceptional album of electronically based ensemble music. From atmospheric country-blues numbers to inventive reworkings of Gregorian chants and Sufi whirling-dervish influences, Maunu's music is filled with well-designed synthetic textures, compelling melodies and absorbing solos. Guest appearances by O'Hearn and Isham also give the album a Group 87 reunion feel. — *Linda Kohanov*

Susan Mazer

● **Fire in the Rose** / Rising Sun 306
This classic album of original compositions for electric harp features the lyricon wind synthesizer of Dallas Smith. The music evokes an atmosphere of intimacy and personal celebration, with intricate jazz-based improvisation building throughout the close musical interplay. Mid-tempo tunes with a range of motifs and moods leave plenty of room for Mazer's stellar playing. — *Backroads Music / Heartbeats*

Jim McGrath

Percussive Environments / 1994 /
Not since *Earth Tribe Rhythms* has a drum release generated such enthusiasm. It is no surprise, therefore, to find out that Jim McGrath worked with Brent Lewis on his popular release *The Primitive Truth*. On his own, with capable support, McGrath takes listeners into meditative and hypnotic pieces sculpted around an organic approach to rhythm. This allows the sound to expand and change according to its own whims. He achieves a primal, natural sound, unencumbered by high-tech sound manipulations. The four 15-min. tracks become true percussive environments—essentially a soundtrack to the movie in the listener's mind. Having experienced first hand the hypnotic state that can be created in such a way, McGrath recorded *Percussive Environments* to inspire the listener to experience the same feeling, to tune into the power of the drum. — *Backroads Music / Heartbeats*

Megabyte

● **Powerplay** / Jan. 1987 / Innovative 710062
Recently re-released on CD, the debut album by the mysterious European group Megabyte remains an underground classic for its high-energy psychedelic techno space-rock sound. Operating under aliases for contractual reasons, A. Mega and B. Byte create fantasy electronic soundscapes built on dynamic grooves made up of layered synthesizers, wailing guitar and exciting percussion rhythms. Whether using ultra catchy melody lines, as in the title track, or venturing into highly experimental sound collages, as in "Secret Destination (The Flight of Mathias Rust)," Megabyte's music is stimulating and multi-faceted, full of trippy sound effects and explorations that draw the listener into a world of sonic mind expansion. — *Backroads Music / Heartbeats*

Wim Mertens

Composer / Indie, Neo-classical, Progressive electronic, Minimalism
This Belgian composer is not well known among US audiences, although he has made several highly regarded appearances at the New Music America festivals. In Spain, however, where he was the subject of a major television special, he is a new-music celebrity. Mertens's style employs mesmerizing minimalist techniques with a sense of the romantic that appeals to both serious music aficionados and more mainstream listeners. The keyboardist uses a certain amount of electronics along with some acoustic instruments like violin, flute, and saxophone. — *Linda Kohanov*

● **Close Cover** / 1991 / Windham Hill 1056
Compiled from Mertens's solo and group projects recorded during the early to mid 80s, this Windham Hill collection offers an overview of his textural, multilayered style of minimalist composition. — *Linda Kohanov*

Metamora

Group / Chamber jazz, Ethnic fusion, New acoustic
This trio excels at instrumentals that combine traditional Northern European folksongs, jigs, hornpipes, and reels with modern improvisational techniques. Malcolm Dalglish, Grey Larsen, and Pete Sutherland are all multi-instrumentalists who tackle a virtual bandstand of acoustic and electric sounds. All of their albums provide fresh perspectives on folk music played with grace, humor, and a sense of adventure. — *Linda Kohanov*

● **Morning Walk** / Windham Hill 1068
Though it's difficult to choose among the group's albums based on musical reasons, this Windham Hill release holds the highest production standards. — *Linda Kohanov*

David Michael

These two multi-instrumentalists met in 1973 and founded various ensembles together over the years. Harpist David Michael is also skilled on zithers, guitars, banded psaltery, cello, and bouzouki. Flutist Randy Mead, who has toured and recorded with Ancient Future, is an expert on ancient tunings. He also built the zith-harp played by Michael on the engaging duo project *Petals in the Stream*. — *Linda Kohanov*

★ **Petals in the Stream** / 1987 / Fortuna 17041
A kaleidoscopic jaunt through Renaissance, Baroque, Impressionistic, Oriental, and Irish traditions. — *Linda Kohanov*

○ **Keystone Passage** / 1994 /
This album makes for perfect listening on a warm, breezy afternoon, with its pastoral beauty and acoustic gentleness. Both David Michael and Randy Mead are skilled players, and *Keystone Passage*, third "duo album," is in many ways a culmination of a musical relationship that has spanned twenty years and a variety of creative explorations...Building on the melodic and lyrical character of their earlier works, these soothing and romantic themes sweep the listener through centuries and around the globe, visiting such locales as The Andes, British Isles, Norway and, above all, the beauty of Washington's Olympic Peninsula. — *Backroads Music / Heartbeats*

Stephan Micus

Composer, Bandleader / Neo-classical, Ethnic fusion, Minimalism
This respected German composer and multi-instrumentalist made his first journey to the Orient at the age of 16. He has since traveled around the world. He spent extensive periods of time studying ancient musical techniques in India and Japan and collected a number of ethnic instruments previously unknown in the West. His recordings for the ECM label are essentially solo efforts in which the illusion of an ensemble is created by the composer's extensive overdubs. Micus's intention is not to play these instru-

ments according to tradition, but to combine modes of expression from around the world in exciting new ways. Though he sometimes creates sounds you'd swear were the result of electronic keyboards, Micus is an acoustic purist who often develops unconventional performance techniques on ethnic instruments. — *Linda Kohanov*

East of the Night / Jan. 1985 / ECM 825655
Two long fantasias for guitars and Japanese flutes. —*Michael P. Dawson*

Ocean / 1986 / ECM 829279
A four-part suite, similar to *Implosions* but recorded nine years later. —*Michael P. Dawson*

Twilight Fields / 1987 / ECM 835085
Like all of his albums, this one is haunting and serene. —*Michael P. Dawson*

★ **Music of Stones** / 1989 / ECM 837750

Wings over Water / Aug. 24, 1990 / ECM 831058
He even coaxes beautiful music from ordinary items like tuned flowerpots! —*Michael P. Dawson*

Darkness and Light / Dec. 31, 1990 / ECM 847272
This features his latest find, an elongated wind instrument from Russia. —*Michael P. Dawson*

Dr. Emmett Miller

Letting Go of Stress / 1994 /
With the music of Steven Halpern, Dr. Miller presents his most popular tape, with four different experiences and effective techniques for stress reduction & relaxation. —*Backroads Music / Heartbeats*

Radhika Miller

Flute, harp, piano, cello / Neo-classical, Ethnic fusion
Though she studied classical piano as a child, Miller took up the flute in college after reading some passages about the instrument in a yoga book. It turned out to be more than a whim. By the end of her first year, she was studying in France with famed classical virtuoso Jean-Pierre Rampal. Three years later, Miller graduated from San Francisco State University with a degree in music. Inspired by her love of sacred vocal music, she developed a style she calls "the singing flute." Over the years, Miller has arranged and transcribed sacred classical scores, choral works, and spirituals for her own performances, involving flute, harp, piano, and cello to create prayerful, uplifting works. In 1983 she launched the independent record label Radhika Miller Music (RRM) and has since released over a half-dozen high-quality albums that include soulful interpretations of Gregorian chant, Palestrina, Bach, Debussy, Telemann, Vaughan Williams, American spirituals, and Irish folk music in addition to her own compositions and improvisations. —*Linda Kohanov*

★ **Gems of Grace** / Real Music 1109
Though all of Miller's recordings could be considered gems, this collection of lullaby-like serenades is particularly satisfying in conception and execution. It helps that she has some top-notch musicians with her: cellist David Darling, pianist Allaudin Mathieu, harpist Michelle Sell, and French horn player Alicia Telford. —*Linda Kohanov*

The Modern Mandolin Quartet

Group / New Age, Neo-classical, Chamber jazz, New acoustic
This ensemble was formed in the mid 80s as the brainchild of Mike Marshall, an internationally acclaimed mandolin player best known for his work with David Grisman and Montreux. Marshall was looking for a way to bring respectability to an instrument primarily known for bluegrass and quaint folk tunes. Toward this end, he established a string-quartet-style group featuring the extended family of mandolin instruments. Marshall and Dana Rath play standard mandolins (which take the place of violins), John Imholz plays mandocello (with a range similar to the cello), and Paul Binkley holds up the middle with his mandola (the alto counterpart to the viola). Together they interpret well-known classical works and premiere newly commissioned compositions of "serious mandolin music." —*Linda Kohanov*

Modern Mandolin Quartet / 1988 / Lost Lake Arts 0095

A fine debut for Windham Hill, yet not quite as sophisticated as *Intermezzo.* —*Linda Kohanov*

Montreux

Group / Chamber jazz, New-acoustic
This Windham Hill "all-star" band features Mike Marshall, Darol Anger, Barbara Higbie, and Michael Manring. All of the musicians involved come from eclectic musical backgrounds. Their work in this band mixes folk, bluegrass, and new acoustic elements with more subtle traces of jazz improvisation. —*Linda Kohanov*

○ **Sign Language** / 1987 / Windham Hill 1058
Montreux's debut adds selected percussion and some vocal harmonies to an uplifting, shape-shifting conglomeration of acoustic-oriented styles. —*Linda Kohanov*

Let Them Say / 1989 / Windham Hill 1084
The quartet expands to quintet with drummer Tom Miller. —*Linda Kohanov*

● **Windham Hill Retrospective** / 1993 / Windham Hill 11122

Morthound

Spindrift / 1994 /
Beginning with subsonic rumblings and dancing chimes, Morthound applies the first broad brush strokes from their impressionistic sound palette. With each application, rudimentary shapes emerge and are wedded to a series of metronomic rhythms from a variety of instruments. Whether you're moving to the waltz tempo and waifish vocals of "Herb of Grace" or pondering the sampled dialogue from "Jacob's Ladder" and "Apocalypse Now," there is a consistent post-modern simplicity to this group's style, and fans of O Yuki Conjugate will likely want to get in on this, too.Morthound combines minimalist sensibilities with world music influences and ambient backdrops. Even though this group "paints" in primary colors, the images they convey remain abstract and open to thematic interpretation. — *Backroads Music / Heartbeats*

Lisa Moskow

These Still Waters / 1994 /
Lisa Moskow has been a student and performer of North Indian music since 1969. She studied sarod with maestro Ali Akbar Khan for 15 years and has several previous recordings which have unfortunately never been released on CD. Genji Ito, her collaborator on this new release, is a Japanese-American musician/composer/performer who plays shakuhachi flute & hischiriki oboe. Together they have come up with *These Still Waters*, a satisfying and fully realized merging of their considerable talents. Like a white swan cutting a wake across the glassy surface of a pond, the instruments mingle and dissolve with delicate sensitivity. The bright & plucky sound of the sarod is brilliantly played by Moskow and is far more mature than on her previous recordings. Stir in the sleepy intonations of the shakuhachi and expressive moanings of the hischiriki and the styles of Japanese and Indian music join as one entity, able to relax and refresh like a deep meditation. Go ahead & take a long cool sip from *These Still Waters.* —*Backroads Music / Heartbeats*

R. Carlos Nakai

Trumpet, flute / Neo-classical, Chamber jazz, Ethnic fusion
Tucson-based multi-instrumentalist R. Carlos Nakai is a Native American musician and cultural anthropologist of Navajo-Ute descent. Though he received classical training on the trumpet, his numerous recordings consist primarily of resonant solo performances of Native American flute improvisations with a judicious use of synthesizers, chanting, and nature sounds. Nakai only occasionally features arrangements of traditional melodies from various tribes; instead, he is primarily concerned with creating original compositions that capture the essence of his heritage in highly personalized ways. In addition to his solo recordings, Nakai has had the opportunity to create new avenues of expression for the Native American flute through collaborations with various artists over the years, including the ethnic jazz band Jackalope, keyboardist Peter Kater, contemporary classical composer James DeMars, and multi-instrumentalist William Eaton. — *Linda Kohanov*

★ **Earth Spirit** / 1987 / Canyon 612
At times criticized for modernizing the spirit of Native Americans, Nakai crystallizes these melodies and rhythms into an accessible and enjoyable palette of wonderful meditational music. All his work is very worthwhile, but this is his best. He plays North American flute and is an expert visual artist as well. —*Michael G. Nastos*

○ **Sundance Season** / 1987 / Celestial Harmonies 13024
Native American themes combined with contemporary and classical motifs. Nakai's use of Tibetan bells is intriguing. —*Michael G. Nastos*

Desert Dance / Aug. 1989 / Celestial Harmonies 13033
...*Desert Dance* is a musical meditation on the spirits of the area and forces of nature that shape it. Using flutes, drums, rattles, and voice, Carlos sketches poignant sound pictures of this land rich in history and myth. —*Backroads Music / Heartbeats*

Ancestral Voices / Canyon 7010
In a more cross-cultural vein is *Ancestral Voices*, Nakai's third collaboration with guitarist/luthier William Eaton. In addition to the flute/stringed instrument duets, whistles, rattles and drums, there are two tracks that feature the renowned Black Lodge Singers. —*Backroads Music / Heartbeats*

Emergence / Canyon 609
...*Emergence*, mixes traditional Plains Indian pieces with nature improvisations, as well as occasional rattles, some chanting, digital delay and sparse synthesizers. —*Backroads Music / Heartbeats*

● **Canyon Trilogy** / Canyon 610
Canyon Trilogy represents a return to the simplicity of Carlos Nakai's earlier albums such as *Changes* and *Journeys*. There are no additional instruments here, no rattles, and no chanting, just Carlos' haunting flutes, either solo or multi-tracked. The "Trilogy" in the title refers to the three sections of the tape—"Dawn's Mirage", "Dreamscapes", and "Resonance". —*Backroads Music / Heartbeats*

Nightnoise

Group / Neo-classical, Chamber jazz, Ethnic fusion
The brainchild of American violinist Billy Oskay and Irish guitarist Michael O'Domhnill, Nightnoise has evolved from a studio-oriented duo to a high-energy performing band. The music has been described as "classical Celtic pop" and "Irish-flavored, jazzy chamber music." Whatever you call it, the band's style is infectious, fun, and technically impressive. —*Linda Kohanov*

★ **Parting Tide** / 1990 / Windham Hill 1097
The band's most sophisticated album to date uses computer-triggered synthesizers to expand the palette of colors beyond the already impressive acoustic talents of the quartet. The album also includes originals by O Domhnill's sister, Triona, whose abilities on keyboards, whistle, and accordion are second only to her expressive vocals. —*Linda Kohanov*

Shaina Noll

Songs For the Inner Child / 1994 /
Shaina Noll is from Santa Fe, New Mexico, and she has gathered some of that area's finest musicians to assist her. Jim Oliver produced and plays keyboards, piano and synthesizers, while Rusty Crutcher adds soprano sax, David Ziems guitars and Richard Noll plays alto recorders and sings harmonies. But it is clearly Shaina's crystalline, heavenly voice and tasteful song selection that makes this release stand out. —*Backroads Music / Heartbeats*

Patrick O'Hearn

Cello, violin, bass, flute, synthesizer / Adult alternative, Progressive electronic
In the early 80s, this bassist and synthesist was mired in the glitz and grind of pop music as a member of the group Missing Persons. Then friend Peter Baumann, best known for his work with Tangerine Dream, made O'Hearn an offer he couldn't refuse. Baumann had visions of starting a record label catering to his first love, contemporary electronic music, and he wanted O'Hearn to become a charter member of the new company. Nearly a decade and a half-dozen albums later, O'Hearn is still amazed at the success of *Ancient Dreams*, the richly hued debut release that

established his career as a solo artist and helped launch the Private Music label. Born in Los Angeles and raised in Oregon, O'Hearn was exposed to a wide variety of music by his parents, who were both working musicians. Though he studied cello, violin, and flute, he gained early experience playing bass with his parents' lounge act. As his musicianship began to excel, he found himself accompanying jazz greats like Joe Henderson, Joe Pass, Tony Williams, and Charles Lloyd. While living in San Francisco in the mid 70s, he played with Frank Zappa and co-founded the visionary progressive band Group 87 with Mark Isham and Peter Maunu before joining Missing Persons. O'Hearn's style reflects all of these experiences within the context of a highly personal electronic sound. During the late 80s, however, his innovative vision seemed to blur under the strain of the commercialism infiltrating the new-age and contemporary instrumental realms. Urged on by increasingly conservative, pop-oriented executives at Private Music, O'Hearn conformed to more conventional song forms on albums like *Between Two Worlds* and *Rivers Gonna Rise*. His music suffered from excessive predictability as a result. The record label even released some crass disco mixes of the composer's most tuneful selections on the embarrassing *Mix Up*. Fortunately, O'Hearn's good musical sense prevailed in the long run. His more recent releases *Eldorado* and *Indigo* are both admirable, highly satisfying albums. He is, however, the last remnant of the Private Music label's original roster of innovative, electronic-based instrumentalists. —*Linda Kohanov*

★ **Ancient Dreams** / 1985 / Private Music 2002
Though *Eldorado* and *Indigo* are certainly among O'Hearn's finest albums, his startling debut *Ancient Dreams* remains the purest example of his innovative style. The keyboardist creates a sense of understated drama through a starkly elegant interplay of synthesized melodies and pseudo-pop rhythms. This unpredictable manipulation of the composer's rock and jazz roots suggests the wide open spaces of surreal landscapes. An all-time classic in the contemporary electronic field. —*Linda Kohanov*

Rivers Gonna Rise / 1988 / Private Music 2029
Too watered-down, yet technically proficient, examples of O'Hearn's sound. —*Linda Kohanov*

○ **El Dorado** / 1989 / Private Music 2054
A marvelous experiment in contemporary, Middle-Eastern-flavored electro-acoustic music. O'Hearn seemed to be embarking on a new direction in his musical career with this thoughtful yet sensuous blending of ancient and modern modes of expression. The album features two prominent Iranian artists—singer Shahla Sarshar and violinist Farid Farjad—though the music was obviously ahead of its time in the notoriously conservative world of adult alternative music. Hopefully, O'Hearn will someday be able to return to the exotic world he touched on in *Eldorado* and create more music from the Fertile Crescent. —*Linda Kohanov*

Indigo / 1991 / Private Music 82091
O'Hearn's most recent release is an unabashed return to the style he pioneered on *Ancient Dreams*. His characteristically expansive textures are anchored by booming bass drums that feel simultaneously primeval and futuristic. Lush electronics with a hefty dose of rhythmic testosterone. —*Linda Kohanov*

Hiroshi Okano

Trumpet / New Age, Progressive electronic, Atmospheric
● **1987-1990** / Oct. 1991 / Innovative 720141
Hiroki Okano is a Buddhist monk who also happens to be one of Japan's prominent composers, writing extensively for film, dance and theater productions. *1987-1990* is an anthology of his recent work, a meeting of traditional instrumentation with contemporary electronics in a timeless fusion of austere yet alluring beauty. The nine pieces, most of which overlap each other, build slowly, the sound seemingly arising from and sinking back into a formless space that is both subtle and tremendously potent, like the classic Buddhist meditation on form and emptiness. Almost subliminal synthesizer drones hover like low-lying mist, while rippling bell tones, acoustic and electric guitar, muted drums, woodblocks, chimes, snatches of chants and traditional Japanese string and wind instruments create mysterious soundscapes. The use of echo, minor keys, stereo separation and an equivocating relationship between a relatively simple foreground and a rich background of half-heard sounds creates an intriguing aura, as if something undefined is groping towards definition. Like a leaf-

less tree silhouetted against a strangely bright winter sky, *1987-1990* is an unsentimental expression of the beauty to be found in impermanence and the paradoxical power of stillness. Note: for those who are squeamish about nudity, the cover has front and back photos of a naked Japanese woman tastefully adorned with ink-brush calligraphy. *—Backroads Music / Heartbeats*

Mike Oldfield

b. May 15, 1953, Readings, Berkshire, England
Guitar, bass, keyboard, percussion / Industrial, Progressive electronic, Art-Rock/Progressive-Rock
Had he come along fifteen years later, composer Mike Oldfield might have invented New Age music, which is where he is often lumped today anyway. In 1973, however, he successfully approached youthful entrpeneur Richard Branson with an idea for an experimental album-length instrumental composition, and the result was *Tubular Bells*, whose success—spurred by the music's use as the theme from *The Exorcist*—became the foundation of Virgin Records, Virgin Atlantic Airways, et al (Branson's corporate ventures). Since then, Oldfield—who had previously recorded in a progressive English folk bein with his sister Sally—has never had so massive a hit, but has delved into spacious (some would say aimless) long form instrumentals with an unparalleled degree of success and attention. *—Michael G. Nastos*

★ **Tubular Bells** / 1973 / Reprise 45041
The then-newly-formed Virgin Records allowed Oldfield a year to complete this 49-minute conceptual effort, which required him to record eighty tracks of himself playing 28 different instruments. *Tubular Bells* achieved Top Ten chart success in the US when it was used in the soundtrack for the film *The Exorcist*, selling over 10 million copies. *—Scott Bultman*

Hergest Ridge / 1974 / Virgin 90590
A well-made followup, with a strange, otherworldly quality in evidence. *—Bruce Eder*

Orchestral Tubular Bells / 1975 / Virgin 90894
A nice idea that comes out rather silly—the original record was livelier and fresher, although this version of *Tubular Bells* does offer some distinct timbral differences for those who care enough. *—Bruce Eder*

Ommadawn / 1975 / Blue Plate 1855
New Age meanderings begin to dominate, but the textures change just enough to hold interest. *—Bruce Eder*

● **Essential Mike Oldfield** / 1980 / Audio Visual 011

Tubular Bells II / 1992 / Warner Brothers 45041
...Twenty years later, this reprise risked being over-pretentious; instead, Oldfield incorporates passages that are downright playful and irreverent—take the grunts, groans, and phased vocal sounds of Altered States and the mock bluegrass of closer Moonshine. Well done. *—Roch Parisien*

David Parsons

Drums, Synthesizer / Progressive electronic, Ethnic fusion, Ambient
Since 1975, this New Zealand artist has made numerous trips to India to absorb the culture, study the music, and record performances by indigenous artists. In addition to producing two albums of traditional Tibetan ritual music by the monks of the Dip Tse Chok Ling Monastery (for the Fortuna Records *Sacred Ceremonies* series), Parsons has translated the essence of his oriental journeys through the lush yet profound soundscapes he has created for a number of highly regarded solo albums. Originally a jazz-rock drummer, he became interested in the music of India when he heard a performance by sitar master Ravi Shankar over two decades ago. Parsons bought a sitar and explored the instrument on his own for several years before studying with Krishna Chakravaty, one of Shankar's most accomplished disciples. After several trips to the East, Parsons composed almost exclusively for Indian instruments until 1979 when he purchased his first synthesizer. He now owns one of the largest electronic recording studios in New Zealand, where he composes for radio, TV, and film. His devotion to both Western technology and Eastern music has made for a potent, highly imaginative style of composition. *—Linda Kohanov*

Himalaya / 1989 / Fortuna 17059

An artfully austere sonic ascent of the legendary mountain range. *—Linda Kohanov*

★ **Yatra** / 1990 / Fortuna 18072
Though all of the albums recorded by Parsons are highly recommended, this double CD (which includes 35 minutes of material not featured on the cassette versions) offers a balance of shorter, more uptempo pieces and longer, more contemplative works. *Yatra* (which means "journey" in Sanskrit) is a musical travelog through the Indian countryside, with its busy open-air markets and joyful folk melodies. Gradually, the composer moves into the ethereal realm of Tibet, a landscape imbued with secret ceremonies and hidden knowledge. *—Linda Kohanov*

Tibetan Plateau/sounds of The Mothership / 1991 / Fortuna 17013
Tibetan Plateau/Sounds of the Mothership is a CD collection from the first two Fortuna releases recorded by Parsons in 1980-1982. Deep spatial compositions for synthesizer, enhanced by classical Indian instruments. *—Linda Kohanov*

● **Dorje Ling** / 1992 / Fortuna 17076
Parsons's latest release was inspired by his recent return to Dharamsala, India, the seat of Tibetan Buddhism in exile. Samples of traditional Tibetan music (taken from his recordings for the *Sacred Ceremonies* series) are mixed into these gently evolving electronic compositions. *—Linda Kohanov*

Stevan Pasero

● **Classical Bouquet** / Sugo 9005
Here is a bountiful collection of guitar music, covering many of the world's most beautiful classical pieces of love, memory and sentiment. Pasero brings a tonal clarity to his playing that takes it a notch or two above the level of simple dexterity. The flawless renditions of "Clare de Lune," "Romeo and Juliet," Pachelbel's "Canon," "Sleeping Beauty," and two pieces from Vivaldi's "Four Seasons", plus two originals and many more, range from stirring to sensitive in their performance while remaining faithful to the original in each case. Over an hour in length, this generous portion of music has been gathered from previous Pasero releases to make this fine *Classical Bouquet*, to share or enjoy for a long time. *—Backroads Music / Heartbeats*

Dr. Roger Payne

○ **Songs of The Humpback Whale**
Since 1970 when the first whale recordings were made by Dr. Roger Payne, the haunting beauty & evocative sounds of whale singing have been carefully studied and documented. Something about these initial recordings, recently reissued by Living Music, continues to stand above all other similar efforts. Here are the original whale recordings, complete with digital remastering, preserved in their classic majesty. *—Backroads Music / Heartbeats*

Penguin Cafe Orchestra

Group / New Age, Neo-classical, Ambient
The Penguin Cafe Orchestra creates dreamlike music. It is beautiful, yet illogical, unpredictable, and often bizarre. Lush violins swirl between classical melodies and country hoedowns. Is that Beethoven or "Walk, Don't Run" they're playing? Is that a touchtone telephone playing the melody? Yes to all the above, and much more. And don't forget the repetition. Things go on just a little longer than you think they should. Remember Supersax, the jazz group that fully orchestrated Charlie Parker's sax solos and gave them a fuller and richer sound? Well, it's almost as if the Pengies have taken the two-note picking of Luther Perkins (Johnny Cash's guitarist) and taught his repetitive, minimalist picking to a string quartet. The incredible thing is that these are beautiful, compelling records. You may feel as if you dreamed the whole thing, but it is not a nightmare. Probably because no one knows how to classify their music, Penguin Cafe Orchestra is often described as new-age. Until a better label comes along, don't let that put you off. Instead, find a copy of the album called *Penguin Cafe Orchestra*—great cover!—and see what the subconscious mind sounds like when it's given some stringed instruments to play with. *—Hank Davis*

Music from the Penguin Cafe Orchestra / 1976 / EG 27

In many ways this release is virtually interchangeable with *Broadcasting from Home*. Haunting melodies are played over hypnotically repeated string patterns. —*Hank Davis*

● **Penguin Cafe Orchestra** / 1981 / EG 11
Stunning and inventive string music. —*Hank Davis*

Signs of Life / 1991 / EG 50
"Southern Jukebox Music" is beautiful. This is a superb collection. —*Hank Davis*

Frank Perry

Percussion / New Age, Ethnic fusion, Ambient
Frank Perry is a modern musical mystic who takes his inspiration from ancient ideas concerning the power of sound to transform consciousness. Buddhist traditions, the writings of Plato, and Pythagoras's famous treatise *Music of the Spheres* are all seriously taken into consideration by this percussionist. Perry has rejected the rhythmic qualities of drums, woodblocks, etc., in favor of instruments like Chinese Buddha gongs and Tibetan bells, producing ethereal, elongated resonances. His albums feature extended compositions that are quiet and delicate, yet abstract in nature, and his liner notes are filled with lengthy discussions of the philosophies behind the music. His work is likely to be fascinating to many listeners, especially those who also enjoy the Celestial Harmonies *Tibetan Bells* series of releases by Henry Wolff and Nancy Hennings. However, people with more conventional musical and religious tastes may find Perry's style and ideas disturbing. —*Linda Kohanov*

★ **Deep Peace/New Atlantis** / 1983 / Celestial Harmonies 14007
Deep Peace/New Atlantis, a double-CD collection, features two albums originally recorded in 1980 and 1983. The four extended works featured are exemplary of Perry's mystical, meditative style. They also illustrate his skill in composing for a variety of ancient instruments that are by nature extremely difficult to manipulate artistically. —*Linda Kohanov*

Zodiac / 1986 / Celestial Harmonies 13025
As the title suggests, this album offers a suite of pieces symbolizing the 12 zodiac signs. Due to the appeal of this programmatic element and the shorter selections involved, you would expect this album to be the most accessible introduction to Perry's style. However, with music as abstract and unfamiliar as this, it doesn't really matter. Perry's vision just seems most effective in the long-form mode. —*Linda Kohanov*

Michael Pluznick

Percussion, drums / Adult alternative, Ethnic fusion, Electro acoustic
This New Jersey native has been fascinated with percussion since childhood. Like Mickey Hart, Pluznick has gone beyond Western traditions in his lifelong pursuit of the magic of rhythm. His music weaves electronic drums and synthesized melodies with a vast collection of ethnic instruments and rhythms hailing primarily from Africa, South America, and the Caribbean. —*Linda Kohanov*

Where the Rain Is Born / 1989 / Sona Gaia 62756
Pluznick's debut is a tasteful mix of synthetic imagery and ethnic percussion. —*Linda Kohanov*

Cradle of the Sun / 1990 / Sona Gaia 62762
There are 17 artists and what seems to be nearly a hundred different instruments scattered throughout this album, but the effect is never overpowering. In fact, there's a strong emphasis on Western pop beats and fusion-style synthesizer melodies with some jazzy trumpet solos. The ethnic influences are primarily rhythmic in nature and often quite subtle, making this music accessible to a wide variety of listeners. Some nice keyboard textures add to the appeal of these familiar-sounding yet well-crafted originals. —*Linda Kohanov*

● **Rhythm Harvest** / 1992 / Narada 63022
In his third release, percussionist extraordinaire Michael Pluznick finds all the pieces meshing perfectly in a dynamite brew of Haitian, Caribbean and West African influences. This animated release features male and female vocals, guitar, trumpet, keyboards and, above all, Pluznick on over 20 rhythm instruments. Joel Lindheimer plays guitar and charango, Robert Powell pedal steel guitar, and Kim Atkinson adds extra touches of percussion on several tracks, while lead vocals (often of a call-and-response

nature) are shared between Yagbe "Oba-llu" Onilu, Lygia Ferra and Pedro DeJesus. Highlights are the swaying "Le Bolero Haitien," "Mozambique," based on a Cuban dance craze in the '60's, the catchy "Rumbacito," and "Giant Step," from traditional music that pays homage to the mountain spirit of the Yoruba people of western Nigeria. While the band is undeniably hot, it's Pluznick who holds the reigns, leading his group through complex, dynamic polyrhythms in this fruitful *Rhythm Harvest*. —*Backroads Music / Heartbeats*

Sanford Ponder

Synthesizer / Progressive electronic, Minimalism
This California-based synthesist recorded two albums in the early 80s during the initial years of the Private Music label. He dropped out of sight for a while, then went on to establish the group Botanica, which has so far released two fascinating albums of music created by fractal mathematics programs. (See albums listed under Botanica.) —*Linda Kohanov*

● **Etosha** / 1985 / Private Music 2001
Serene, unpretentious synthesizer music with minimalist underpinnings characterize Ponder's debut album. —*Linda Kohanov*

Tigers Are Brave / 1986 / Private Music 2012
Ponder's second release is more varied in conception and instrumentation with traces of violin and other acoustic instruments. —*Linda Kohanov*

Popol Vuh

Group / Neo-classical, Progressive electronic, Ethnic fusion
One of Germany's premiere progressive electronic bands, Popol Vuh was founded in 1969 by keyboardist Florian Fricke. The band took its name from the Mayan Indian bible, and, in fact, the group's first album *Affenstunde* (*The Time of the Monkey King*) was a strong reflection of Fricke's interest in Mayan lore. Over the course of nearly 20 albums, Popol Vuh combined sacred musical traditions and instruments from around the world with classical, jazz, and rock elements. It also created quite a stir as one of the first bands to use the Moog synthesizer in the early 70s. As such, the band influenced several generations of electronic and contemplative artists. Popol Vuh also gained considerable attention for its scores to films by the celebrated German director Werner Herzog, including *Nosferatu* and *Aguirre, the Wrath of God.* —*Linda Kohanov*

★ **Tantric Songs / Hosianna Mantra** / 1991 / Celestial Harmonies 13006
Tantric Songs/Hosianna Mantra is new-age devotional-rock chamber music that is spacey and spacious on this pairing of two early albums (from 1973 and 1978) on one CD. —*Michael P. Dawson*

● **For You & Me** / Jan. 1991 / Milan 35615
Mixing elements of world music with breathless guitars and inspired vocals, *For You and Me* reestablishes the German group Popol Vuh as a band to be reckoned with. Group founder Florian Fricke holds down the center of creativity, in synch with Daniel Fichelscher on guitar and the stirring vocals of Renate Knaup-Aschauer as they freely mix styles from India, Africa, Tibet, and South America among soaring passages and lilting reggae beats. This surprisingly melodic music tends to linger on and stay right with you in the manner of classic pop innovation. —*Backroads Music / Heartbeats*

Robert Powell

Vocals, horns / New Age, Ethnic fusion, Electro acoustic
★ **Desert Beach** /
Robert Powell is a talented guitarist whose playing has graced several of the past year's more interesting albums by artists as diverse as Opafire, Barry Cleveland, Jim Chappell and Michael Pluznik. On his first solo album Robert travels through many cultures, moods, styles and tempos to offer up a potpourri of globally flavored guitar instrumentals. Though he plays a wide variety of guitars, acoustic and electric, it is his pedal steel work that really stands out and gives *Desert Beach* its distinctive voice. On tunes ranging from the upbeat countrified rock of "Truckstop Mirage" to the languid cruise of "Pony Owens," the pedal steel soars and glides, creating elegant washes of sound that are both lyrical and spacious. World music touches abound, thanks in part

to Michael Pluznik whose atmospheric percussion illuminates three tracks, notably the aptly named "Rhythm Congress" where, using African talking drums and angklung rattles, Michael sets up a densely charged field of rhythm as a foundation for Robert's multi-tracked electric guitars. Drums and bass, both played by co-producer David Burns, complement Robert's guitar orchestra, with occasional background synthesizer and, on one track, Venezuelan harp by Diana Stork from the group Geist. Folk, Hawaiian, country, rock and spacemusic elements are skillfully blended making *Desert Beach* a most auspicious, as well as enjoyable, debut release. — *Backroads Music / Heartbeats*

Giles Reaves

Keyboard, percussion / Progressive electronic, Ambient
Though his music is of the progressive electronic variety, this keyboardist and percussionist got his start through country music channels. While living in Nashville in the 80s, Reaves hooked up with producer Marshall Montgomery and ended up working as his assistant engineer. Eventually Reaves's own music caught the ear of MCA producer Tony Brown, who signed the synthesist up to the company's Master Series label. Reaves recorded two solo albums and one collaboration with Jon Goin before a tightening in the music market forced MCA to let go of artists on its instrumental sub-label. Reaves's latest album for Hearts of Space is a finely produced, technically accomplished evolution of his textural electronic style. — *Linda Kohanov*

★ **Wunjo** / 1986 / MCA 5819
Reaves's debut is arguably his best effort for MCA in its subtle yet refined use of space and electronics. — *Linda Kohanov*

● **Sea of Glass** / 1992 / Hearts of Space 11030
Subdued drums and percussion, liquid soundscapes, and slowly shifting layers of melting electric guitars are among the evocative sounds Reaves uses on this sensitively designed electro-acoustic album. — *Linda Kohanov*

Jorge Reyes

Flute, percussion / Progressive electronic, Ethnic fusion, Techno-Tribal
This enigmatic multi-instrumentalist draws from the diverse culture and history of his Mexican homeland, as well as his early experiences playing in progressive rock bands south of the border. Currently based in Mexico City, Reyes combines flute, pre-Columbian instruments, and percussion with synthesizers and voice to cast a spell of ritualistic intensity. Like shadows from Mexico's sultry and savage past, his music has a dark quality to it that sometimes scares off the unprepared, but adventurous listeners will find plenty to admire in his evocation of jungles, jaguars, and Aztec rites. Though his albums are often difficult to find, most of his imported releases are well worth the extra effort and expense involved. — *Linda Kohanov*

Comala / 1989 / Mundo 8801
If the Aztecs and Mayans had been able to play synthesizers and electric guitars along with their flutes and drums, it might have sounded something like this. — *Linda Kohanov*

● **Bajo El Sol Jaguar** / 1991 / Paraiso
Techno-tribal music to raise the dead, rip the hearts out of your sacrifices, or dance to under the full moon. Reyes's latest album as a leader also features the innovative sounds of Spanish electric guitarist Suso Saiz. Some booming Peter Gabriel-style beats can be found among mysterious atmospheres and virtuosic percussion. — *Linda Kohanov*

○ **Nierika** / Silent 9326
...A must for lovers of powerful trance music, *Nierika* is tribal primal at its core while seeking to discover the transpersonal, the collective unconscious behind the self. — *Backroads Music / Heartbeats*

Robert Rich

Flute, guitar, percussion / Progressive electronic, Ethnic fusion, Ambient, Techno-Tribal
Building his first synthesizers at the age of 13, Rich spent his teen years hiding out in his unique sound environments. While gaining a degree in psychology from Stanford University, he became more adept at translating his interests in dreams and trance states into music. (After graduation, he remained a part of the lu-

cid-dream-research team headed by pioneer Stephen LaBerge.) Rich's all-night Sleep Concerts and all-evening Trance Concerts introduced his style to audiences in the San Francisco Bay Area. At the same time, he was developing his chops by diligently practicing baroque keyboard music, experimenting with ethnic influences, and delving into alternate tuning systems and sacred geometry. Though still in his late 20s, Rich's music has been appreciated throughout the new-music underground in Europe and North America for years, though his three *Hearts of Space* albums have since brought his music to wider audiences. Besides a wide array of synthesizers, Rich plays flutes, steel guitar, and acoustic percussion, which not only add depth to his music, but allow him to explore his obsession with microtonality and tunings based on non-Western scales. Ranging from latticelike polyrhythms and pieces with a strong Indonesian feel, to deep, time-suspended studies of stasis and slow motion, his compositions are meticulous in detail and subtlety. In 1990 Rich also teamed up with longtime friend Steve Roach to create the critically acclaimed *Strata*, which successfully merged their individual sounds into a shared musical vision. Rich and Roach will release their second collaboration, *Soma*, in the fall of 1992. — *Linda Kohanov*

Rainforest / 1989 / Hearts of Space 11014
Robert's debut for Hearts of Space is a finely wrought collection of lush, textural pieces and engaging uptempo works inspired by the intricacies of baroque counterpoint exemplified by Bach and the fluid melodies of Indonesian gamelan music. — *Linda Kohanov*

● **Strata** / 1990 / Hearts of Space 11019
This highly regarded collaboration between Rich and Steve Roach uses layers of the earth as a metaphor for exploring layers of the psyche. With a wide variety of acoustic and electronic instruments, the two create surreal landscapes of throbbing world-music rhythms, broad synthesizer washes, and ethereal sounds. — *Linda Kohanov*

Gaudi / 1991 / Hearts of Space 11028
Like the melting, three-dimensional visions of the album's namesake—early 20th-century Spanish architect Antonin Gaudi—Rich's musical structures are geometrical yet organic. Throughout the recording, his offbeat timbres flow in swirls of mutating patterns, their subtle sense of strangeness resulting from Rich's extensive use of just intonation. — *Linda Kohanov*

Geometry / 1991 / Spalax Music 14279
Originally recorded in 1986-1987, *Geometry* is an early example of the delicate, synthesized latticework Rich creates by mapping various mathematical relationships directly into shimmering, intertwining musical structures. — *Linda Kohanov*

Steve Roach

Vocals / Electronic, Progressive electronic, Ambient, Techno-Tribal
Roach's major longstanding influences are not necessarily musical; rather he draws inspiration from empowered geological places, particularly the Mojave and Sonoran deserts and the aboriginal rock-art sites of the Australian outback. In the early years of his career, however, this former adrenaline addict and motocross racer cited the European electronic scene of the 70s as an important impetus in his fascination with sequencer-based music. Yet by the release of his 1983 album, *Structures from Silence*, it was clear Roach was developing his own style. His thick, breathing waves of sound were initially embraced by listeners, meditators, and therapists in the holistic fields; however, Roach's music was far from angelic or superficially comforting. His inspiration grew from the expansive landscapes of the Southwest, complete with the feelings of danger and mystery he associated with these places. A chance to score music for a PBS documentary on the rock art of the Dreamtime (a system of aboriginal mythology) gave Roach the opportunity to visit a number of sites deep in the Australian outback. He also met up with aboriginal didjeridu master David Hudson, who taught Roach how to play the ancient wind instrument and helped him build his own didjeridu. These experiences fueled his landmark double album *Dreamtime Return*. Now considered a classic in the progressive electronic field, it marked the synthesis of Roach's earlier sequencer-based sound with his expansive, chordal atmospheres and his growing infusion of tribal aesthetics. In the late 80s, Roach moved from

his base in Los Angeles to the Sonoran desert outside of Tucson, Arizona. There he has produced a number of projects that continue to blur the lines between ancient ritual and modern technology. His numerous collaborations include albums with Michael Stearns, Kevin Braheny, Robert Rich, and Michael Shrieve. In addition, he has recently been working with Mexican multi-instrumentalist Jorge Reyes and Spanish guitarist Suso Saiz. Their album *Suspended Memories, Forgotten Gods* is set for release in the spring of 1993. —*Linda Kohanov*

○ **Structures from Silence** / 1984 / Fortuna 17024
This influential album of extended works marked the emergence of his serene, yet haunting synthesizer breaths. —*Linda Kohanov*

★ **Dreamtime Return** / 1988 / Fortuna 18055
Roach's sojourn into the mythological mind of the Australian aborigines demonstrates that electronic music's greatest potential may lie in bringing our most elusive dreams and ancient memories into focus through potent, highly imaginative soundscapes. Altered chords that breathe ever so slowly, floating textures, digitally sampled aboriginal instruments, primitive trance rhythms, and arresting abstract sounds lead you through an unfolding maze of sonic dimensions that depict a sense of mystery and confrontation with the unknown. Double CD has 38 minutes of music not in the cassette version. —*Linda Kohanov*

Quiet Music / 1988 / Fortuna 17044
A subtle collection of ambient pieces with subdued melodies, *Quiet Music* evokes images of shimmering desert mirages. —*Linda Kohanov*

Desert Solitaire / 1989 / Fortuna 17070
The second of two collaborations with Kevin Braheny inspired by the desert, this album pays homage to the Edward Abbey book of the same title. It inadvertently became a memorial to that Southwestern nature writer when Abbey died shortly after the music was recorded. Featuring some powerful work by Michael Stearns, this album taps into the psychological depths of stark Southwestern landscapes through a subtle set of soundscapes depicting the hidden dangers, unseen gifts, and intoxication that the desert promises. —*Linda Kohanov*

Western Spaces / 1990 / Chameleon 74761
This reissue of Roach and Kevin Braheny's first evocation of the American Southwest features several selections not included on the original 1987 version. This album is considered by many to be a classic in the progressive electronic and ambient genres. —*Linda Kohanov*

Australia: Sound of the Earth / 1990 / Fortuna 17071
After the success of *Dreamtime Return*, which was inspired by Australian aboriginal mythology, Roach returned to Australia. He traveled the continent with a tape recorder collecting natural sounds and capturing performances by native musicians, which he then wove into a sonic journey through the outback. The album is significant in that it features high-quality recordings of aboriginal didjeridu master David Hudson, who does some startling things with this ancient wind instrument. There are also some powerful performances by a group of five didjeridu players, as well as some intriguing contemporary compositions by Australian composer Sarah Hopkins. —*Linda Kohanov*

○ **World's Edge** / 1992 / Fortuna 18057
Roach's first solo release since *Dreamtime Return* is another double CD. With shorter pieces on the first disc and a single 67-minute work on the second, *World's Edge* explores the paradoxical relationships between sound and silence, space and rhythm, ancient ritual and modern technology. An accomplished album. —*Linda Kohanov*

Now/Traveler / 1992 / Fortuna 17048
This CD reissue features music from Roach's first two albums, originally recorded in the early 80s. A good example of his early, high-energy, sequencer-based style, with some hints at his developing ambient and tribal leanings. —*Linda Kohanov*

SoMA / 1992 / HOS 11033
Soma, (the first collaboration by Steve Roach and Robert Rich since *Rainforest*) is an atmospheric collection of dark and somber masterpieces. In the studio, these two gifted musicians seem to push beyond reality's frail constraints. This is slowly evolving music with meticulous attention to detail and depth of field. The melodies are soft—like dreamy shadows in an ancient fire-lit cave, and at the same time it is as distant as the stars. This creates a perfect dichotomy of technology and primeval emotion. The title of this CD as explained in the liner notes is from Vedic writings describing SOMA, a drink made from plants with which could one commune with the Gods. The same word also meant "body" to the Greeks. To create this musical Castanada-like vision, Rich and Roach utilized a large assortment of synths, samples, ethnic wind and percussion instruments. The music is so delicately produced that it becomes almost impossible to distinguish what Roach is playing from what Rich is playing. Discreetly adding texture to layers of electronic sound, each instrument is meticulously placed in the compositions at crucial spots. One of the album's longest pieces, "Nightshade," is a great example of how well Rich and Roach work together in this context. They constantly seem to intuitively communicate each other's thoughts through some telepathic zone deep inside their music. *Soma* continues Steve Roach's musical vision of an ever-expanding musical universe incorporating ancient instruments with digital tools to fuse a new direction in electronic/world music. Largely dark and mysterious, this is music whose stretched-out minimal spaces float and shift from moment to moment and from emotion to emotion. It's a remarkable album of primal and ritualistic-feeling music that communicates directly to the inner being of the listener and invites us to the spiritual Dreamtime. Highly recommended. —*Ben Kettlewell, Dreams Word*

Kim Robertson

Meditation

● **Tender Shepherd** / Gourd 112
Celtic harpist Kim Robertson expands the capabilities of this majestic and ancient instrument. On *Tender Shepherd*, Kim focuses on lullabies & airs, providing melodies for quiet times. You'll hear lyrical, heart-touching music played with delicacy, grace and skill in this set of tunes from traditional Irish, Welsh & Scottish lore, plus the classical strains of Bach's "Sheep May Safely Graze." Inspired by a legacy and beauty that is communicated in the music, Kim's unique quality is clearly felt through a sensitive and fluid touch. —*Backroads Music / Heartbeats*

Gabrielle Roth

Vocals / Minimalism, Techno-Tribal
Roth doesn't actually play the ritualistic, heavily percussive music featured on her recordings. Instead, the style emerged from her dance performances and movement workshops in which she strives to unite spiritual and sexual energies into what is often referred to as the "dance of ecstasy." Her book, *Maps to Ecstasy: Teachings of an Urban Shaman*, explains the philosophy behind the music she requisitions for her performances and ultimately her albums. She has her own New York-based label, Raven Recording, which has expanded its scope in recent years to release other artists as well. Listed as "musical director" in the liner notes to her five albums, Roth often "composes" by dancing along with a musician's improvisations to communicate her vision, relying on her husband, percussionist Robert Ansell, to lead their ensemble, the Mirrors. —*Linda Kohanov*

Initiation / 1984 / Raven 5883
The albums *Initiation, Bones, Ritual,* and *Waves* feature techno-tribal trance music of various tempos and moods, designed for everything from meditation and massage to ecstatic dancing. —*Linda Kohanov*

Bones / 1989 / Raven 04
Gabrielle's latest, and her first that is available on CD, is a musical lament for the past and a prayer for the future. With more synth and production emphasis than before, we still find an amazing mix of swirling and engrossing percussion sounds, with some flute and violin added to the basic tracks. *Bones* is a calling to the inner dance, the dance around your bones, one which Gabrielle knows intimately. —*Backroads Music / Heartbeats*

Ritual / 1990 / Raven 06
...with *Ritual*, we are sensing a major release, of true world-music proportions, which traces a sinewy rhythmic progression through several pieces, from the call to spirit of the opening flutes to solid tom-toms and a multitude of drums, with kalimba, violins and other voice and synthesizer effects rounding out the sound. This is deep, all-pervasive music which captures one's attention from the inside out, offering sounds to move with, allowing one the maps with which to search deeply inside one's own

inner movements where the rituals of life are acted out moment by moment as the eternities play on. —*Backroads Music / Heartbeats*

★ **Waves** / 1991 / Raven 07
Roth's most aggressive and accomplished recording features some respected percussionists, including Mino Cinelu. Driving tribal rhythms are the basis for six compositions, several of which also make effective use of wailing female vocals. Some synthesizers and electronic guitars add to the sense of mystery Roth craves in her music. —*Linda Kohanov*

○ **Trance** / 1993 / Raven 5927
Trance is the latest in Gabrielle's cutting edge musical series exploring primeval dance rhythms and ecstatic trance. Since her earlier drum-based efforts, Gabrielle's music has become more world beat in orientation, propelled by a powerful percussion section & various musicians who lend distinctive flavors to the pieces. At times funky and danceable, there are other portions which are airy & melodic, with trilling flutes and smoky sax. Jai Uttal adds to half the cuts, while Daniel Lauter and band leader Robert Ansell join in as well. Rhythmic but restrained, earthy but ethereal, *Trance* is a strong pancultural statement about the hypnotic power of rhythm. —*Backroads Music / Heartbeats*

○ **Totem** / Raven 5862
Totem is urban trance dance music featuring trap drums, assorted percussion and occasional synthesizers, guitar, flute and voice. —*Backroads Music / Heartbeats*

Bernardo Rubaja

Piano / Adult alternative, Ethnic fusion
Raised in Argentina, Rubaja studied piano formally as a child, performed in local pop groups during his teens, and advanced to Argentina's National Academy of Fine Arts. Several years spent studying music in the multicultural climate of Paris added to his skills as a performer and composer. Rubaja, who now lives in Southern California, released his first album as a leader on the Narada label. —*Linda Kohanov*

● **High Plateaux** / 1987 / Windham Hill 1064
High Plateaux, a collaboration with Cesar Hernandez, was Rubaja's recording debut. The album was produced in 1987 by Mark Isham. —*Linda Kohanov*

New Land / 1990 / Narada 63014
Amidst his rich synthesized sounds, pop textures, and spicy Latin rhythms, Rubaja also performs on such exotic South American instruments as the charango (a guitarlike instrument made from an armadillo shell) and the bandoneon (a button accordion made famous by fellow Argentinian Astor Piazzola). Guest artists include trumpeter Mark Isham and percussionist Alex Acuna, among others. —*Linda Kohanov*

Ryuichi Sakamoto

Keyboard / Progressive electronic, Ethnic fusion
Electronic keyboard whiz who received his training at the University of Tokyo. He released his first solo effort in 1978 and shortly thereafter formed the techno-pop band Yellow Magic Orchestra. Sakamoto has successfully combined electronics and world music. He has written the scores for several soundtracks, including half of *The Last Emperor* soundtrack, which won an Oscar. —*David Szatmary*

● **Beauty** / 1989 / Virgin 91294
A world-music tapestry featuring a mixture of Eastern, Western, and African elements and such musicians as Robbie Robertson, Sly Dunbar, and even Brian Wilson. —*David Szatmary*

Neo Geo / Nov. 14, 1991 / Epic 40994
An interesting combination of Japanese and funk rhythms with such notable guests as jazz drummer Tony Williams, reggae star Sly Dunbar, and Iggy Pop. —*David Szatmary*

Somei Satho

b. 1947

● **Mantra / Stabat Mater**
A powerful release from this Japanese composer on New Albion, *Mantra* employs haunting drone vocals to transport the listener deep within. *Stabat Mater* is an all-vocal oratorio composed in honor of the Virgin Mary and all women whose children died. At times startling and dissonant, this is moving neo-religious music. —*Backroads Music / Heartbeats*

Paul Sauvanet

☆ **Eleusis** / 1994 / ?
This is a discreet little gem that resonates with a peaceful tranquility. Quietude and an elusive searching, inspired by the works of Carlos Castaneda, are apparent themes in this work by Canadian synthesist Paul Sauvanet. Bit by bit, the listener is drawn into the subtle magic of these luxuriant incantations, warm and alluring, that call for careful listening to uncover the floating whispers within. Recently featured on *Music From the Hearts of Space*. —*Backroads Music / Heartbeats*

Eberhard Schoener

Composer / Progressive electronic, Ambient
German composer Schoener is a sonic explorer who has not only stepped outside European traditions for inspiration, but has created breathtaking music from the most unlikely sources, both natural and electronic. After an extended journey through the Far East, in which he studied religious as well as musical practices, he came to the conclusion that artists need to come to terms with their own cultural heritages to be truly effective. His 1973 release *Meditation*, for instance, expressed the ideal of spiritual contemplation often associated with the East, through synthesized music rooted in Western experience. —*Linda Kohanov*

○ **Meditation/Sky Music ...** / 1973 / Kuckuck 12059
This double-CD reissue features music originally contained on two albums of extended pieces recorded in 1973 and 1983 respectively. *Meditation* consists of two reflective works for synthesizers. On *Sky Music—Mountain Music*, however, he creates delicate, transparent soundscapes from more natural sources, though it was actually created by attaching tuned whistles to carrier pigeons and allowing the birds to fly through air currents generated by BMW's wind tunnel. —*Linda Kohanov*

● **Trance-formation** / 1977 / Innovative 710131
Recorded in 1977, this classic work is an expression of Schoener's personal and subjective experiences from frequent trips to southeast Asia. Joined by Andy Summers (of The Police) on guitar and the other members of the band, The Secret Society, Schoener's Moog, Mellotron and keyboards lay a unique foundation for Gregorian vocals...It is recordings like this and the worthwhile reissue as first time CDs that show the timelessness of this musical genre. —*Backroads Music / Heartbeats*

Schonherz & Scott

Group / Adult alternative, Progressive electronic, Ambient
This duo features Vienna-born keyboardist Richard Schonherz who has written music for full orchestra as well as soundtracks for Austrian films and television projects. A native of San Francisco, Peter Scott studied guitar privately, then enrolled in the Musicians Institute of Technology where he concentrated on composing and arranging. Both artists have played a wide variety of styles over they years, from classical and jazz to rock and blues. Shortly after the two musicians met, they began producing a series of pop demos as well as a series of instrumental selections. The latter became the basis for the duo's 1987 Windham Hill debut, *One Night in Vienna*. Their pop demos provided the impetus for a second release, *Under a Big Sky*, which includes vocal tunes as well as more pop oriented instrumentals. —*Linda Kohanov*

Under a Big Sky / 1991 / Windham Hill 1105
While the duo has a flair for sensual yet subdued instrumentals, the vocal selections that tend to dominate this album are completely pedestrian. —*Linda Kohanov*

Robert Schroeder

● **Brain Voyager** / Aug. 1985 / Racket 715030
Ever since *Brain Voyager* was released in 1985 it has remained a personal favorite. Its smooth, unfettered electronic keyboard style washes over your mind in pastel waves of aqua and lavender. Sequencer-driven cruisers give way to choral splendor on "Glucksgedanken," sung by Monika Rath. Then the gorgeous theme of "Love Symphony" rises out of the fading stillness. Slipping on headphones, one embarks on a relaxing voyage through the electro-chemical universe of neuro-pathways.

Memories lived or yet to be dissolve into one another like va-porous phantoms. Even as Schroeder builds up tension, layer by layer, a safety valve releases and you drift back on course. Chronologically, *Brain Voyager* is in the middle of Schroeder's many releases, but he has never duplicated this magical style be-fore or since. His melodic themes vary, and never exceed 7 min-utes in length, unlike most of his IC titles, keeping the material as fresh & relevant as when it was released. —*Backroads Music / Heartbeats*

Theresa Schroeder-Sheker

Group / New Age, Neo-classical

★ **Rosa Mystica** / 1987 / Celestial Harmonies 13034
Rosa Mystica is a superb balancing of musical, historical, and spiritual sensibilities. With just her lyric soprano voice, a nylon strung Celtic harp, medieval psaltery & bells on one piece and a sensitive cello performance on another, Ms. Schroeder-Sheker has artfully fashioned a tapestry of piety, beauty, and longing, em-broidered around the mystical symbol of The Rose. Traditional music, gleaned from medieval & 19th century sources, has been lovingly and skillfully augmented with new musical and lyrical additions. Ms. Schroeder-Sheker's exquisitely written notes which accompany the music are the crowning touch. —*Backroads Music / Heartbeats*

Klaus Schulze

Synthesizer / Electronic, Progressive electronic, Minimalism
One of the cornerstone figures in the German electronic scene, this pioneering synthesist has recorded nearly two dozen solo al-bums over the past 20 years. His music has grown and changed with the evolution of technology, but his concept of long-form, highly rhythmic sequencer music pulsing under soaring melodies has remained constant. Though he established his own identity years ago, Schulze was briefly a member of Tangerine Dream, ap-pearing on one album, *Electronic Meditation*, in 1970. He did not, however, cave in to convention or engage in cheap pop-electronic exploits, as did his former TD colleagues in the mid 80s and be-yond. Still, Schulze's collaborations with former Santana drum-mer Michael Shrieve brought a new level of percussive intensity to his music, as well as a wider audience from the progressive rock world. The availability of Schulze's music has always been inconsistent in the US, and many Americans have no idea how strong his influence has been on electronic music worldwide. (He was, for instance, the inspiration behind Kitaro's initial investiga-tions of synthesizer music.) Schulze continues to perform throughout Europe and is tireless in releasing new recordings, some of which are better than others. When Schulze does hit the nail on the head, his music is immensely powerful. —*Linda Kohanov*

○ **Timewind** / 1975 / Blue Plate 1807
Two masterful sequencer essays that make effective use of mini-malistic patterns to suspend and ultimately erase all sense of ob-jective "clock-time" experience. —*Linda Kohanov*

Mirage / 1977 / Audio Visual 033
Mirage gives the listener impressionistic sequencer work depict-ing winter landscapes. —*Linda Kohanov*

X / 1978 / American Gramaphone 8336272
Schulze's 10th solo release marks the peak of his most influential period of work. Presented with a classic sense of German drama, this double-CD artfully combines the composer's synthesizers and sequencer patterns with live drums and full orchestra. Intense, driving, long-form pieces frame surreal, abstract sounds. Each of six pieces is named for a historical figure Schulze ad-mires, beginning with a 24-minute selection titled "Friedrich Nietzsche." —*Linda Kohanov*

Miditerranean Pads / 1990 / Audio Visual 081
One of the old masters of EM returns with a new offering. The al-bum was delayed for a while but was finally released with two other classics. This new recording is not one of his stronger titles. The album has three tracks with a generous running time of 70 minutes. While the three pieces are interesting, none are show grabbers like some of his prior work. Track one is a typical per-cussion and synth piece that runs to 30 minutes. Track 2, the al-bum title piece, is a symphonic choir piece. Track 3, "Percussion Planante" is lots of percussion with piano overlaid. The recording

is of excellent quality but the laid back feel sends me running for older material. —*Matt Hargreaves, Dreams Word*

● **Beyond Recall** / 1991 / Venture 1873
Schulze in a more sedate and reflective mood, with acoustic gui-tar samples creating lyrical melodies. —*Linda Kohanov*

○ **Dresden Performance** / Jul. 12, 1991 / Venture 1865
This double-CD contains a live concert that was performed on August 5, 1989 in Dresden, Germany; at a time when Dresden was still behind the Iron Curtain...The music in the opening se-quence as well as the closing one appears to be influenced by the voice and music style of the Japanese Kabuki theater. The sound quality of both discs is really outstanding. The music style is very percussive and rhythmic. It is nothing like the spacy droning style that was evident in the mid-seventies. Long-time fans of KS will enjoy the music. —*Matt Hargreaves, Dreams Word*

○ **Dome Event** / Apr. 16, 1993 / Venture 1881

☆ **Royal Festival Hall, Vol. 1, and Royal Festival Hall, Vol. 2** /
Klaus Schulze's *Royal Festival Hall* is a challenging two-volume CD set which is sold separately. This album marks a further evo-lution in Klaus Schulze's long and creative career. These two CDs have a combination of live and studio tracks...Whereas Schulze has recently composed large 30-minute tracks with movements based on a single one, these tracks are composed of many sepa-rate movements as one. Schulze uses sampling to effectively con-struct immense surreal, often cubist soundscapes.
    Some people may find Klaus' new direction to be too chaotic and abstract for them and thus may not like this less melodic ap-proach. Others may find this music to be refreshingly more chal-lenging and delightfully more complex. In either case, with nearly 140 minutes of music, there's a lot for everyone. —*Andrew Wedlake, Dreams Word*

● **Dome Event** / Plan 9 1881
The Dome Event, easily achieves a mid-eastern mystical feel, demonstrating that Klaus is more inventive than Gabriel in his orchestration and arranging. This is a fusion of Oriental/Occidental influences uniting the sacred and the pro-fane, as well as the disparate worlds of sensuous dance rhythms and dreamy electronic textures. Schulze's sampling skills are su-perb, both in terms of real instruments and voices and in "found" sounds. It is a magnificent album in every aspect. Recorded di-rectly from Klaus' mixer to digital recording equipment, it's also an audiophile recording...Klaus Schulze remains a distinctive mu-sician, masterful arranger and after over two decades of recording and performing, is still a major force in modern music. —*Ben Kettlewell, Dreams Word*

John Serrie

Composer / Adult alternative, Progressive electronic, Ambient
Leading planetarium composer Serrie has been looking to the heavens for inspiration for over a decade. Coming from a family ensconced in the aviation field, Serrie now soars and glides with his hands on the controls of analog and digital synthesizers. His rhythmic outings often have an understated heroic feel, although he has also done some more pop-oriented instrumentals on his 1990 release *Tingri*. However, he seems most at home in the longer-form space-music journeys for which he initially became known. —*Linda Kohanov*

○ **Flight Path** / 1989 / Miramar 2002
This album offers the best of both worlds in terms of Serrie's style, from sequencer patterns that sail through hyperspace to enigmatic, ambient textures that sparkle like star clusters or float with shrouded density through black holes and other cosmic wonders. —*Linda Kohanov*

Tingri / 1990 / Miramar 2003
The first few cuts have more of a superficial, adult-alternative feel to them. The latter part of the album opens up into beautifully produced spaces that drift and hover. —*Linda Kohanov*

★ **And the Stars Go with You** / Dec. 5, 1990 / Miramar 2001
Serrie's debut release on CD captures the development of 10 years of planetarium work. Lush romantic pieces with episodes of subtle sequencer patterns maintain a consistently peaceful yet wondrous mood, perfect for stargazing. —*Linda Kohanov*

● **Planetary Chronicles, Vol. 1** / 1992 / Miramar 2004

Serrie's most recent effort is a continuation of the liquid stargaz-ing music pioneered on his 1988 debut *And the Stars Go with You.* —*Linda Kohanov*

Nada Shakti

Samadhi /
Samadhi is a magical blend of the ancient chants of India, with the powerful yet subtle vocals of Nada Shakti, accompanied by the exquisite music of Bruce BecVar. For Nada this pure "sound transmission" is the real substance of the heart. The instrumental passages are slight but sensitively added, with words and transla-tions of the sacred Sanskrit chants included. *Samadhi* has the magic and beauty to inspire and uplift, enhanced by Bruce BecVar's Shakti harp & guitar —*Backroads Music / Heartbeats*

Michael Shrieve

Drums, percussion / Adult alternative, Progressive electronic
Shrieve has had a long and interesting career as a rock drummer, percussionist, and progressive electronic composer. Gaining early recognition as the powerhouse drummer for Santana, the teenage Shrieve was launched into the popular culture maelstrom when he performed an extended drum solo during Santana's appear-ance at the legendary Woodstock festival. Over the years, Shrieve has continued to strive for innovative approaches to percussion-based music. His numerous collaborations include work with Stomu Yamash'ta, Klaus Schulze, Steve Roach, David Beal, David Torn, and Andy Summers, to name a few. —*Linda Kohanov*

Leaving Time / 1988 / RCA 3032
Virtuoso percussionist Shrieve teams with synthesist Roach to create some highly atmospheric soundscapes, replete with un-usual sounds and stray melodies. — *William Ruhlmann*

Stiletto / 1989 / Jive/Novus 3050
Always a team player (witness his long stint in Santana), Shrieve puts together an unusual ensemble for his first "solo" album, in-cluding trumpeter Mark Isham and former Police guitarist Andy Summers. The tracks (combining elements of rock, jazz, and in-dustrial noise) are dominated by percussion elements, and even the guitar and trumpet playing are more rhythmically than melodically handled. But this extraordinarily inventive album yields subtle pleasures. — *William Ruhlmann*

● Big Picture / 1989 / Fortuna 17060
This collaboration between Shrieve and the talented young drummer David Beal is an electronic percussion tour-de-force with epic rhythms, powerful melodies, and broad textural brush-strokes. Amazingly enough, this innovative album fell through the cracks when it was first released and didn't get nearly the at-tention or distribution it deserved. —*Linda Kohanov*

Perry Silverbird

● Blessing Way / Celestial Harmonies 13046
The Blessing Way instills a deep sense of power in its crystal clear performances which blend with the sounds of nature.The record-ing begins on location at Canyon de Chelly National Monument in Arizona, as songbirds awaken on a rocky ridge within the canyon. Silverbird's small reed flute begins its melodious poetry, echoing off the massive red walls. The drumming slowly com-mences, as the sun rises higher, opening the way for distant chanting. As the listener is surrounded with the sacred Navajo ceremony of *The Blessing Way,* the sunlight fades and with it the drumming and chanting as well, leaving the lone flute and wind whistling again through the haunting darkness. Produced by his father, J. Reuben Silverbird, this recording is the solo debut of Perry, known as "The Gentle Flute Poet." —*Backroads Music / Heartbeats*

Steve Sisgold

Garden of Wisdom / 1994 /
Accompanied by the soothing music of James Asher's *The Great Wheel,* Steve takes you on a guided journey of your life's purpose, value and vision. This can be used on a daily basis to enhance personal growth and inspire action. Sisgold is an author & pre-senter who also writes music & works with effective communica-tion, money management and relationship issues. —*Backroads Music / Heartbeats*

Mark Sloniker

Keyboard, composer / New Age, Adult alternative
● Paths of Heart / 1994 /
On *Paths of Heart,* his 1986 debut, the music is peaceful and mov-ing; the first half is more jazzy, with a nice ensemble sound sur-rounding Mark's expressive keyboards; the second half is where the real beauty lies, with long flowing pieces that develop with patience and visibility. Tune in to the spaciousness of the Rockies while finding the heart of today's contemporary instrumental sound—that's what Mark Sloniker is all about.
—*Backroads Music / Heartbeats*

Software

Group / Adult alternative, Progressive electronic
Formed in 1983, this German electronic duo owes much to elec-tronic pioneer Klaus Schulze. Software's music usually builds on sequencer patterns and simple melodies, creating a lighter ver-sion of the Schulze style. Their later work is woven into concept albums, yet the music rarely lives up to their poetic aspirations. Software's earlier recordings with Peter Mergener are generally more satisfying. —*Linda Kohanov*

★ Past, Present, Future, Vol. 2 / 1987 / Innovative 710061
An efficient collection of music from five of the group's mid-80s recordings. Vol. 1 (IC 7/10.060) is also nice. —*Linda Kohanov*

Solitaire

Group / Progressive electronic, Ambient, Techno-Tribal
The brainchild of German keyboardist Elmar Schulte, this record-ing entity is based in the small town of Paderborn, yet draws in-spiration from foreign landscapes, particularly the wide open spaces of the American Southwest, Scotland, and Norway. Schulte named the group, in fact, after his admiration for the mu-sic on *Desert Solitaire,* an album by American synthesists Steve Roach, Kevin Braheny, and Michael Stearns (see listing under Roach). Solitaire's dark, textural pieces and occasional ethnic rhythms are a marked contrast to the sequencer-dominated her-itage of the 70s German electronic school popularized by Tangerine Dream and Klaus Schulze. —*Linda Kohanov*

Altered States / 1990 / Musique Intemporelle 597-907
A commendable debut. "Heart of the Desert," a long, hypnotic dirge, is particularly well done. —*Linda Kohanov*

● Plains and Skies / 1992 / Musique Intemporelle 849-907
Schulte's slowly emerging compositional voice is urged along by the obvious influences of his favorite artists, particularly Steve Roach, Jon Hassell, and Michael Brook. —*Linda Kohanov*

Sophia

● Hidden Waters, Sacred Ground /
This exquisite release, Sophia's most popular, is full of lovely in-strumental passages and her beautiful voice. Zither, tambura, bamboo flute & violin combine with Raphael's colorful synthe-sizer, imbued with healing energies & spiritual qualities. For mas-sage, meditation or just filling your space with loving feelings, *Hidden Waters, Sacred Ground* provides a wonderful accompani-ment by combining earth and water elements. —*Backroads Music / Heartbeats*

Richard Souther

Keyboard / Adult alternative, Ethnic fusion
As a promising session keyboardist in Los Angeles, Souther be-gan landing work in recording studios while still in his teens, eventually performing with such artists as Barry McGuire, Debby Boone, the Mothers of Invention, and Phil Keaggy. In 1980, how-ever, a near-fatal bout with food poisoning suspended Souther's career for several years. Following his recovery, he began to focus on developing a solo career that would involve more personal themes, including his Christian perspective on life. Strong, hope-ful melodies are his trademark, yet his albums for the Narada la-bel also reflect his pop background as well as his early classical training, his feeling for contemporary jazz, and his subsequent in-terests in ethnic music. —*Linda Kohanov*

Cross Currents / 1989 / Narada 63007
Optimistic melodies in a pop-jazz ensemble setting. —*Linda Kohanov*

● **Twelve Tribes** / 1990 / Narada 63015
Souther's second release shows a marked evolution in style from his first album, recorded just a year earlier. Not only are his keyboard parts based on more original timbres, Souther also abandons customary drum sounds for a stronger emphasis on live and sampled percussion. Rather than a standard kick drum, for instance, he uses an African log drum. In place of cymbals, he uses samples of someone breathing. The emphasis is still on catchy melodies and contemporary jazz textures, yet Souther's creative use of ethnic rhythms and instruments adds a new level of sophistication to his accessibility. —*Linda Kohanov*

Chris Spheeris

Keyboard / New Age, Adult alternative, Progressive electronic, Ambient

○ **Desires of the Heart** / 1990 / CBS 40478
Desires of the Heart is a balanced collection of 10 instrumentals whose common attribute is beautiful melodic writing and excellent production. The emotional coherence, warmth and "heart" in this music makes for a combination that works great. —*Backroads Music / Heartbeats*

Hilary Stagg

Harp / Adult alternative

Stagg was working as an electrician when he heard Swiss harp sensation Andreas Vollenweider in concert. At that moment, the Northern California native was inspired to learn all he could about the electro-acoustic harp. A few years later, he was releasing his own albums, using his knowledge as an electrician to amplify his instrument to suit the soft, dreamy music he was developing. Stagg also credits the sweet melodic stylings of Loggins & Messina, the Doobie Brothers, and the Moody Blues as influences. Over the course of three recordings, Stagg has grown increasingly accomplished as a performer and composer. —*Linda Kohanov*

Beyond the Horizon / 1987 / Real Music 1795
Stagg's debut release. —*Linda Kohanov*

Feather Light / 1989 / Real Music 1800
Using his customized acoustic-electric harp, Hilary's *Feather Light* style is complemented by judicious use of additional instruments, from the bluesy slide guitar of the opening cut, to violin, dobro, and synthesizer. For the most part these instruments appear separately on different cuts but the final track, "No Pressure", brings several of them together in an upbeat ensemble celebration. As usual, Hilary plays with his trademark light touch to produce this gentle but upbeat album. —*Backroads Music / Heartbeats*

★ **Dream Spiral** / 1991 / Real Music 1805
Though Stagg is backed by an ensemble featuring synthesizer, electric bass, percussion, acoustic guitar, and violin, his custom-electrified Troubadour harp remains the focus of eight originals that take on a silky, dreamlike quality through the composer's resonant techniques. —*Linda Kohanov*

○ **Edge of Forever** / Jul. 1, 1993 / Real Music 1810
With *The Edge of Forever,* Stagg takes his playing to new heights of inspiration. While his instrument has a naturally attractive sound, it is Stagg's sensitive and gently spirited playing that makes this album come together in such a cohesive manner. Additional flute and keyboards add to the sound on the seven tracks, culminating in the 11-minute closer, simply titled "Forever." Cover art by environmental artist George Sumner tops it off perfectly. —*Backroads Music / Heartbeats*

Bruce Stark

Piano / Neo-classical, Solo instrumental

As a physics major in college, Stark found himself spending more time in the dormitory lounge playing piano than doing his homework. Inspired by Keith Jarrett's extended improvisations, the self-taught musician abandoned his scientific studies and just barely managed to get accepted into the music department of California State University at the age of 22. He went on to gain a Masters degree in composition from Juilliard, studying with heavies like Roger Sessions and Vincent Persichetti. Yet along the way, Stark never lost his interest in the tonal, highly improvisational styles that attracted him to music in the first place. Unlike the George Winston clones who gave solo piano music a bad name in the

1980s, this Tokyo-based artist starts out with strong compositional ideas and actually develops them in intelligent and emotionally charged ways. —*Linda Kohanov*

○ **Song of Hope** / 1991 / Hearts of Space 11025
One of the finest solo piano releases in recent years, *Song of Hope* strikes a rare balance between musical literacy and pure emotion. —*Linda Kohanov*

Michael Stearns

The Beam / Progressive electronic, Ambient

An accomplished sound sculptor, Stearns developed an appetite for psychedelic music from listening to Jimi Hendrix and Cream in the 60s while playing in his own rock bands. In 1974, a fortuitous meeting with dance/movement icon Emilie Conrad provided Stearns with the impetus to move to Los Angeles from his hometown of Tucson, AZ, leaving behind plans to become a Sufi mystic in the process. During the next dozen years, Stearns worked in close association with Conrad's Continuum dance collective, creating spontaneous live accompaniment for the group's explorations of movement and sound. In the process, he developed an electronic-based style that mixed environmental recordings with synthesizers and exotic instruments including "the beam," a 12-foot aluminum shaft strung with piano wire that produced extremely low tones. In 1983, Stearns was selected to score the IMAX film, *Chronos*, an opportunity that allowed the composer to further develop his interests in sophisticated multi-channel techniques and mind-expanding soundscapes. Over the last decade, Stearns has scored numerous IMAX and OMNIMAX films and has been able to build and refine a state-of-the-art studio to continue his search for new sounds. —*Linda Kohanov*

★ **Planetary Unfolding** / 1985 / Sonic Atmospheres 307
A masterful electronic symphony based on the idea that the universe is made of sound rather than solid matter (a notion that has its roots in Oriental philosophy as well as in some modern theoretical physics circles). Stearns's performances on the Serge synthesizer actually give the feeling that atoms, cells, planets, and other celestial bodies are creating a complex orchestration that is unfolding on itself and expanding into deep space. —*Linda Kohanov*

Chronos / 1985 / Sonic Atmospheres 312
This soundtrack for the IMAX film by Ron Fricke stands on its own. Stearns's interests in sound design and innovative recording techniques take an equal seat with the music, which captures the drama of large-format film and inspires majestic visuals in the mind of the listener. —*Linda Kohanov*

● **Encounter** / 1988 / Hearts of Space 11008
A musical science-fiction fantasy, *Encounter* is "space music" in the most obvious sense of the word. Stearns's ten-piece suite depicts contact with a UFO, culminating in a journey to the stars. The imagery is so effective that it's probably not advisable to listen to this album alone in the desert. —*Linda Kohanov*

Stein & Walder

Group / Neo-classical, Chamber jazz

Keyboardist Ira Stein and oboist Russel Walder met in 1981 at a series of master classes taught at the Naropa Institute by two of their major influences, Ralph Towner and Paul McCandless. Shortly thereafter, Stein and Walder produced a demo and were signed to Windham Hill. Over the years, their sound has expanded from the acoustic duets of their 1982 debut, *Elements*, to a satisfying blend of electronic keyboards, drums, bass, and intricate studio enhancements. —*Linda Kohanov*

Transit / 1978 / Windham Hill 1042
Produced by Mark Isham, this album added lush electronics and a number of talented sidemen to the mix, including bassist Michael Manring. —*Linda Kohanov*

● **Under the Eye** / 1990 / Narada 62760
An invigorating display of the duo's diversity, maturity, and inventiveness, *Under the Eye* features ensemble settings with guitarist Tom Vatlin, bassist Shido, drummers Robbie Bean and Gene Refkin, and percussionist Marc Anderson. —*Linda Kohanov*

Stillwater, Michael & Maloah

● **Arc in Time** / 1994 /

Arc in Time is a retrospective anthology, spanning 1980-1989 and five separate albums. Heard are heart songs which offer an exquisite musical tapestry for healing, inspiration and living in harmony. Styles range from contemporary folk to soft-jazz, classic choral to mellow rock with continual themes of opening the heart. Since it is the first title by Michael Stillwater on CD, this is ideal either as an archive of favorite Stillwater tunes or as a first title for your collection. Other artists such as Joel Andrews, Buddy Comfort, Dallas Smith, Schawkie Roth and Pamela Polland make various contributions to the songs. Among the 15 songs are "One Light," "Song Universal" and "You Belong to Love." —*Backroads Music / Heartbeats*

Liz Story

Piano / Neo-classical, Solo instrumental, Adult alternative
Story studied classical piano while growing up in Southern California and even thought about becoming a music librarian or theorist for a while. Then she heard jazz pianist Bill Evans at a New York club, and the experience changed her perspective on music overnight. Story, who had studied at Juilliard and was enrolled at Hunter College at the time, abandoned her academic program in favor of jazz lessons with Sanford Gold, a teacher Evans had recommended. Back in Los Angeles, she continued her musical education at UCLA and the Dick Grove Music Workshops, but it was a job playing piano at a French restaurant that sparked her major breakthrough as a composer. Since the front casing of the piano was missing, Story had no place to put her sheet music and was forced to improvise freely. Eventually, she put some of her spontaneous compositions on tape and sent them to Windham Hill. Within four days, Will Ackerman had called her back and the contract was signed for her first release, *Solid Colors*, an album of impressionistic piano miniatures. Over the course of five recordings, including a two-album stint with RCA Novus, Story's style has expanded to include electronic duets with Mark Isham and works for various types of ensembles, yet the piano remains the prominent voice in her finely crafted compositions. —*Linda Kohanov*

● **Solid Colors** / 1983 / Windham Hill 1023
With remarkable technical facility, tremendous feel, and a playful sense of musical progression, Liz Story proves a moving and fascinating pianist on her debut album. Intuitive yet intellectual, Story nevertheless has a strong sense of structure, and her quick, light playing always keeps things moving. —*William Ruhlmann*

Unaccountable Effect / 1985 / Windham Hill 1034
A particularly striking album of rhapsodic piano solos and gorgeous collaborations with synthesist Mark Isham. —*Linda Kohanov*

Part of Fortune / 1988 / Novus 3001
On several tracks of this label debut, Story experiments with added instrumentation—percussion, a cello, strings, a choir—giving her music a more formal cast that does not reduce its attraction. —*William Ruhlmann*

Speechless / 1989 / Novus 3037
Story's second and final recording for RCA Novus is a return to the solo piano realm after her forays into arrangements involving other instruments on her previous two releases. —*Linda Kohanov*

● **Escape of the Circus Ponies** / 1991 / Windham Hill 1099
It's actually difficult to recommend one of Story's albums over all the rest, because they all offer different sides of her musical personality, complete with brilliant moments and less successful ideas. Her 1990 return to Windham Hill, however, shows a level of maturity in her ability to compose for solo piano, especially in her creative use of altered harmonies and her mastery of the thoughtful lyricism associated with her greatest inspiration, Bill Evans. —*Linda Kohanov*

Tim Story

Piano / Neo-classical, Progressive electronic, Ambient
Though he also recorded for Windham Hill at one time, this Ohio-based keyboardist is not related to Liz Story. His intimate style thrives on cavernous spaces, an element that eventually caught the attention of Hearts of Space Records, which released his most recent (and in many ways his best) album, *Beguiled*. Other than some early guitar lessons, Tim Story is self-taught. With experience as a recording engineer and a studio musician under his

belt, he turned his attention to composing and released his first albums on a tiny Norwegian label called Uniton in 1982. His music attracted the attention of Windham Hill's Will Ackerman, who released two of his albums in the late 80s and included several of Story's pieces on some of the label's samplers. Though his melodic voice is often expressed with uncommon delicacy on grand piano, Story sets the contours of his pieces with broad synthesized brushstrokes in hazy, enigmatic veils of color. Like Harold Budd, he also injects a profound sense of ambiguity into his compositions, suggesting emotions for which there are no words. —*Linda Kohanov*

Glass Green / 1987 / Windham Hill 1061
More upbeat selections are included in the midst of Story's characteristically elegant, open-ended lyricism. —*Linda Kohanov*

★ **Beguiled** / 1991 / Hearts of Space 11027
Story's most subtle and masterful work to date can best be described as graceful, visceral chamber music for 21st-century romantics. His miniatures for Steinway grand piano and synthesizers, sometimes enhanced by the velvet richness of Martha Reikow's cello, embody passion at a whisper. —*Linda Kohanov*

Wheat and Rust /
Tim's stately synthesizer and introspective piano evoke images of wintery landscapes; perfect music to listen to while curled up in front of the fire or on a lazy, rainy day. Tim Story has a gift for creating charming little melodic poems full of lightness, grace and whimsy, delicate, unpretentious, skillfully concocted combinations of acoustic piano and synthesizer voicings. —*Backroads Music / Heartbeats*

Strunz & Farah

Guitar / Guitar-pop, Guitar-classical, World music derivative
Combining elements of Latin and middle eastern music (Jorge Strunz is Costa Rican while Ardeshir is Iranian), this acoustic guitar duo's world/jazz fusion style offers an interesting blend of music. Interesting percussion and rhythms from traditional instruments, plus the occasional guest (like India's L. Subramaniam), adds to the blend. —*AMG*

Mosaico / May 1984 / Mesa Blue Moon 79036
The first and still best record for this team of Iranian guitarist Andeshir Farah and guitarist Jorge Strunz. It includes seven originals with a multi-ethnicity that is truly global. Latin, African, and jazz influences most prominent. —*Michael G. Nastos*

● **Americas** / May 12, 1992 / Mesa Blue Moon 79041
The latest from this dazzling and astonishing guitar duo surpasses 1990's award-winning "Primal Magic" with blazing intensity and passion. Their uptempo flamenco sound really vaults way beyond standard fare. Jorge Strunz occupies the left channel, while Ardeshir Farah holds down the right. Visual images abound, conjuring up remote, romantic islands, tropical rainforests and warm, moon-lit waters. "Americas" melds the flair, dexterity and cultural roots of their combined Latin American and Middle Eastern heritages with the surrounding septet of tremendous musicians. This is truly one of the most cohesive and deeply stirring album I have come across in a great while. —*Backroads Music / Heartbeats*

Paul Sutin

● **Serendipity** / Jul. 1985 / Real Music 1853
The magic and beauty of life is expressed through the innocence of nature in this superb spacemusic from Switzerland. Performed on the Kurzweil 250, the spacious sounds are multi-faceted, as Sutin settles in to capture the essence of good fortune with gentle music. This title plays perfectly next to Lynch's *The Sky of Mind*, especially for morning listening. —*Backroads Music / Heartbeats*

Tangerine Dream

Group / Adult alternative, Progressive electronic, Minimalism, Avant-garde
Formed as a rock group in 1967 by Edgar Froese, Tangerine Dream is one of the most important entities to shape contemporary instrumental music over the last 20 years. The turbulent 60s, Froese's association with surrealist painter Salvador Dali, and the arrival of the Moog synthesizer were just a few of the forces that helped to fuel this German electronic group through a barrage of

constant change in style and personnel. Core members over the years have included Froese and Chris Franke as well as Peter Baumann, who went on to start the Private Music label. Curiously enough, the band's most recent addition is Jerome Froese, Edgar's son, whose enigmatic photos as a baby can be found in the artwork to TD's early albums. Over the past 25 years or so, the TD sound has moved from the droning nightmares of *Zeit*, to the mesmerizing sequencer-based masterpieces of *Rubycon* and *Ricochet* in the 70s, to the sparkling high-tech rock of the 80s. A cult phenomenon for decades, Tangerine Dream gained wider recognition when the group's highly evocative music attracted the interest of William Friedkin. This resulted in the score to the film *Sorcerer* and the beginning of a large number of soundtracks. (TD's music for the Tom Cruise scorcher, *Risky Business*, probably attracted the most attention.) In recent years, Tangerine Dream has moved toward shorter, song-based pieces that seem superficial and predictable compared to the group's pioneering work, yet Froese and company must be admired for TD's continuous output and place in electronic music history. — *Linda Kohanov*

Rubycon / 1975 / Virgin 91009
Classic, uncompromising Tangerine Dream. A must for any serious collector of electronic music. — *Linda Kohanov*

● **Logos** / 1982 / Virgin 2257
This live recording captures the Dream at a high point that occurred midway through the band's career. Longer, more intricate pieces are present, yet the action takes place at a brisk pace, moving through many of the trademark TD motifs and soundscapes. The recording's studio quality and engrossing performances are clearly inspired. — *Linda Kohanov*

★ **Le Parc** / 1985 / Combat 8043
A selection of different moods, all of a consistently high quality. Each track takes its name and inspiration from a different park in the world, like Central, or Yellowstone for example. — *Vladimir Bogdanov*

● **Canyon Dreams** / 1987 / Miramar 2801
TD received its first Grammy nomination with this album. The music was originally composed for a scenic video on the Grand Canyon, released under the same title. The style is a rather ingenious combination of the group's progressive style and current commercial leanings, and, as such, is Tangerine Dream's finest album of recent years. — *Linda Kohanov*

Best of / 1989 / Audio Visual 75
This album is a British issue only so far and are not a true BEST OF but what you get is quite good. The problem with the disc is that the material covers only the early years and the eighties material with nothing from the Virgin years. — *Matt Hargreaves, Dreams Word*

Melrose / 1990 / Private Music 2078
Quite a contrast from *Logos Live*, this album is one of the better examples of the band's recent immersion in adult-alternative electronic pop. — *Linda Kohanov*

Rockoon / 1992 / Miramar 2802
Though the music has its moments, TD's most recent album is listed mostly as a reference. — *Linda Kohanov*

220 Volt Live / 1993 / 2804
220 Volt Live is a fine collection of eleven new compositions performed and recorded live during the '92 North American Tour. It's a companion to the full-length video album which is titled *Three Phase* from Miramar ...As a statement of the current TD lineup caught live, it succeeds in every way. — *Ben Kettlewell, Dreams Word*

John Tesh

New Age, Progressive electronic
TV host John Tesh also scores soundtracks and makes light new-age records. — *AMG*

● **Tour de France 1988** / 1988 / Private Music 2040

Garden City / Cypress 0133
Second release from John Tesh, consummate electronic musician and nationally famous host of TV's Entertainment Tonight. His first, on Private Music, gained attention and fairly good sales. With *Garden City*, John is hoping to go all the way, with a bona fide single containing vocals (and lyrics by his wife) and strong critical acclaim. A family affair, you say? Either way, a rewarding

experience for today's contemporary listener desiring more muscle than many New Age releases offer. — *Backroads Music / Heartbeats*

Tingstad & Rumbel

Group / Neo-classical, Chamber jazz
Guitarist Eric Tingstad and oboist Nancy Rumbel create music directly inspired by the chamber-jazz styles of Oregon and the Paul Winter Consort. After studying at Northwestern University, San Antonio-born Rumbel moved to New York. There she met oboist Paul McCandless (who played with the Winter Consort before helping to establish Oregon with guitarist Ralph Towner). McCandless put her in contact with Winter, and before she knew it, Rumbel herself was touring and recording with the Paul Winter Consort. After a five-year stint with the group, Rumbel dropped out to start a family when she met Eric Tingstad at an outdoor festival. The Seattle-based guitarist had been influenced by Oregon's Ralph Towner. Tingstad studied classical guitar in college and spent the better part of the 70s playing lead guitar in a Seattle progressive-rock band. In the 80s, however, he returned to the acoustic guitar and released two solo albums that established his popularity as a regional musician known for creating "Northwest Impressionism." When Rumbel moved to Washington, she and Tingstad agreed to collaborate. They have since recorded a number of contemporary chamber-music-style albums for the Narada label. The musicians, who have a long history of environmental activism, often create albums with outdoor themes and have been known to give away tree seedlings at their live performances. — *Linda Kohanov*

Woodlands / 1987 / Narada 61016
An early collaboration with pianist David Lanz. — *Linda Kohanov*

● **Homeland** / 1990 / Narada 61026
Tingstad and Rumbel's pastoral sound is a bit more aggressive on this album, due to a stronger rhythmic emphasis and the appearance of over a dozen guest artists. The overall effect, however, remains subtle, with snatches of Oriental and South American influences mixed with the duo's usual fusion of classical and North American folk influences. — *Linda Kohanov*

In the Garden / 1991 / Narada 64004
The duo created this album based on their mutual interests in gardening and to promote responsible land stewardship concepts. Some of the proceeds were donated to national gardening organizations. — *Linda Kohanov*

Renewal / 1994 /
Eric Tingstad has made a successful career for himself with his acoustic blends of guitar/oboe compositions, mostly with Nancy Rumbel. Their releases such as *Legends*, *In the Garden* & others have set standards for fine craftsmanship and excellence. Before discovering his current formula, Tingstad released two albums of solo guitar, in 1982 and 1984, which stand up well next to the works of Leo Kottke, though they are closer to the original Windham Hill titles by Ackerman or De Grassi. Seven tracks from *On The Links* and six from *Urban Guitar* comprise this collection. For fans of solo acoustic guitar, *Renewal* will more than satisfy. — *Backroads Music / Heartbeats*

Tri Atma

Group / Adult alternative, Ethnic fusion
Founded in 1977 by German guitarist Jens Fischer and Indian tabla player Asim Saha, Tri Atma specializes in fusing Eastern musical elements with Western electronic pop. In 1982, the duo met Klaus Netzle, a veteran German record and television producer who brought the space-age sounds of the Fairlight and Synclavier computer synthesizers to their music. — *Linda Kohanov*

★ **Yearning & Harmony** / 1982 / Fortuna 016
Buoyant Eastern rhythms and Western grooves support some intricate acoustic guitar work and compelling electronic keyboard solos. — *Linda Kohanov*

○ **Essential Tri Atma** / 1990 / Higher Octave 7028
A collection of digitally remastered pieces from three of Tri Atma's previous recordings with an emphasis on their more pop-oriented fusions. — *Linda Kohanov*

Nik Tyndall

Composer / Progressive electronic, Ambient

As a designer of sound units and amplifiers in the 70s, this German artist made a natural progression into composing for electronic instruments at the end of the decade when he formed the avant-garde duo Tycoon with Rudolf Lager. In the mid 80s, he struck out on his own and released a number of recordings on the German Sky label, in addition to composing soundtracks for film and television. His style combines primarily lush environmental soundscapes with the delicate percussive textures of bamboo, gongs, and windchimes. —*Linda Kohanov*

● **Lagoon** / 1990 / Hearts of Space 11018

Tyndall's first American release concentrates on shorter pieces with each selection exploring a single mood through finely-crafted, primarily computer-generated sounds. —*Linda Kohanov*

Vangelis (Evangelos Papathanassiou)

Keyboard / Neo-classical, Progressive electronic, Ambient

With his lush synthesizer textures, sweeping romantic melodies, and undeniable flair for the dramatic, Vangelis has been called "the electronic Tchaikovsky." This self-taught artist grew up in Athens, Greece, where he shunned piano lessons at an early age in favor of conducting his own musical experiments by playing with radio interference and stuffing the family piano with nails and other foreign objects. After achieving considerable success in Greece with his early-60s rock group, Vangelis moved to Paris at the age of 25 and formed the progressive band Aphrodite's Child. He was even invited to replace Rick Wakeman in Yes, but turned the position down as his interests floated away from rock and into soundtrack work. His early scores to Frederic Roussif's *Apocalypse des Animaux* and *Opera Sauvage* were released as albums. Nearly 20 years later, this music stands on its own as some of Vangelis's finest work. In the mid 70s, the composer moved to London where he set up an extensive electronic music studio. There he recorded some of his most popular solo albums while continuing to create masterful soundtracks for film and television projects, including the theme to Carl Sagan's *Cosmos* and the ethereal, futuristic music for *Blade Runner*. He is best known, however, for his Academy Award-winning score to *Chariots of Fire*. Though many electronic composers have fallen in and out of fashion over the years, Vangelis's music possesses the kind of originality and quality that makes it seem timeless. His sophisticated use of texture and atmosphere is balanced by highly expressive melodies and swells of emotional intensity. It's hard not to be moved by this music. —*Linda Kohanov*

○ **China** / 1979 / Polydor 813653

One of the composer's least-known albums is also one of his best. Exalted invocations of Oriental majesty frame playful, folk-like melodies and mystical rites of passage. —*Linda Kohanov*

○ **Opera Sauvage** / 1981 / Polydor 829663

An early film score with a delicious sense of romanticism. —*Linda Kohanov*

☆ **Chariots of Fire** / 1982 / Polydor 800020

Vangelis's Academy Award-winning score to the movie continues to be his most famous album, probably because the theme is immediately recognizable yet quickly lures listeners into a musical world that stands on its own. —*Linda Kohanov*

Soil Festivities / 1984 / Polydor 823396

A five-movement suite that emerges from a thunderstorm into a celebration of nature's savage beauty. —*Linda Kohanov*

Mask / 1985 / Polydor 825245

Primal rituals in a futuristic setting. —*Linda Kohanov*

Direct / 1988 / Arista 8545

Vangelis released *Direct* in 1988, at the time a major new work that covered all aspects of his previous career. The results were quite exciting, from his familiar dynamic pieces and rhythmic approaches to more reflective passages, and a wonderful "Glorianna" with superb female operatic vocals closing out the first half. —*Backroads Music / Heartbeats*

★ **Antarctica** / 1988 / Polydor 815732

Originally composed for a forgettable Japanese film on the South Pole, this album is a masterpiece of sonic sensations depicting vast plains of ice, sunlight glittering across the snow, and the sting of Antarctic winds. Expansive melodies are punctuated by the lashing sounds of whips urging dog sleds into mysterious and forbidden landscapes. —*Linda Kohanov*

○ **Themes** / 1989 / Polydor 839518

Selections from his most famous soundtracks, including many themes never before available on a recording (such as those from *Blade Runner*, *The Bounty*, and *Missing*). —*Linda Kohanov*

City / 1990 / Atlantic 82248

...Vangelis has created another masterwork of truth, sensitivity, and grace which has received airplay on both Musical Starstreams and Music from the Hearts of Space already. —*Backroads Music / Heartbeats*

○ **1492 Conquest of Paradise** / 1994 /

Suitably grand in scale and far-reaching in its scope, this soundtrack is the first new music from Vangelis since 1990's *The City*. *1492* stands up well next to Vangelis's classic *Chariots of Fire*, due to his inane ability to get right inside the material and provide an integral part of the film itself. Vangelis succeeds in capturing the fifteenth century mood, mixing rich choral portions with modern elements, and portraying the larger than life character of Columbus, complete with full range, dynamic sound. Also: "The City," "Themes," "Chariots of Fire." —*Backroads Music / Heartbeats*

David Van Tieghem

b. Apr. 21, 1955

Drums, percussion / Progressive electronic, Techno-Tribal

New York-based percussionist David Van Tieghem has shown a remarkably broad sense of what constitutes a percussion instrument, "playing" everything from kitchen items to a theater itself. Sometimes coming under the heading "performance art," his work as a soloist with several albums under his own name and as an accompanist to Laurie Anderson and others is wildly imaginative. —*William Ruhlmann*

These Things Happen / 1984 / Warner Brothers 25105

David Van Tieghem is a percussionist, nominally speaking, but as far as he's concerned, everything on earth is a percussion instrument. On this album, which features a variety of found sounds (including radio transmissions) mixed in with more conventional instruments, Van Tieghem plays a wine bottle, a hair comb, metal ashtrays, and balloons, among other things. But this musically arranged junk heap is often amazingly musical. If you like it, try Van Tieghem's three albums on Private Music, especially *Strange Cargo*. —*William Ruhlmann*

● **Strange Cargo** / 1989 / Private Music 2051

This New York artist has built himself a reputation both as an innovative percussionist and sometime performance artist. On his latest album he further explores the quirky fusion of funk, rock, jazz, Asian, and progressive electronic elements that characterize his music. We are taken on a journey through wildly diverse terrains—from tight structured melodies to impressionistic pastiches of weird and wonderful sounds, all multi-layered and full of interesting background effects best captured on headphones. —*Backroads Music / Heartbeats*

Safety in Numbers / Private Music 2015

Not comfortably labeled New Age, or percussion music, or pop, or electronic music, Van Tieghem's music has that "downtown" mix of all these and yet is distinctly his own...from the lush "Crystals" to the droll and rhythm steady "Night of the Cold Noses." This is twisted "easy listening." —Blue *Gene Tyranny*

Viaggio

Voyage /

The Voyage is primarily the work and artistry of Coral Martens-Sims, who plays harp and bass fiddle on this collection of classical, celtic and original compositions. With flute & cello as supporting cast, Coral moves through arrangements as diverse as the traditional Japanese piece, "Sakura," or the soothing "Brahms' Lullaby." Other influences filter in, as heard on 'Loch Lomond' and her own composition, 'Mystic Casbah.' The title cut, also self-penned, display Coral's skills as writer, while others thrive on the trio approach. One vocal, "All Through The Night," nests comfortably in the middle of the program. For peaceful listening with classical appeal, Viaggio's *The Voyage* will take you places that you'll likely enjoy revisiting time and again. —*Backroads Music / Heartbeats*

Andreas Vollenweider

Harp / Adult alternative, Ethnic fusion

Vollenweider was one of the few musicians to gain superstar status as a "new-age artist" back when the term was first used as a marketing category in the mid 80s. The Swiss harpist, however, quickly transcended the need for alternative record sales when his albums simultaneously broached *Billboard*'s pop, jazz, and classical charts in 1986. Born in Zurich in 1953, Vollenweider was ensconced in the city's fine art scene, courtesy of his father, one of Europe's leading organists. After becoming proficient on guitar, flute, and other instruments, the young Vollenweider developed a passion for the harp, which he modified to suit his needs. Not only did he construct a damper to expedite more rhythmic playing, he broadened the harp's tonal range by electrifying it. His buoyant funk beats, exotic pan-cultural influences, and colorful harp improvisations began to sweep Europe in the early 80s as Vollenweider was signing with CBS Records to release *Behind the Gardens ... Behind the Wall*. Three albums later, he won his first Grammy for 1987's *Down to the Moon*. Over the years, Vollenweider has managed to maintain his artistic integrity and vision despite increasing commercial success. The harpist's 1991 album *Book of Roses* is a testament to his ability to expand his scope as a composer while keeping his trademark sound intact. — *Linda Kohanov*

Behind the Gardens (Behind the Wall—under the Tree) / 1982 / CBS 37793
Vollenweider's debut album featured electric harp music. Beautiful sounds. — *Paul Kohler*

★ **Caverna Magica** / 1983 / CBS 37827
A followup album featuring harp in a small group ensemble. Very nice. — *Paul Kohler*

White Winds / 1985 / CBS 39963
A fantastic album of intricate compositions and moods. — *Paul Kohler*

○ **Down to the Moon** / 1986 / CBS 42255
A masterpiece of beautiful melodies and rhythms from Vollenweider's electric harp. — *Paul Kohler*

Dancing with the Lion / 1989 / CBS 45154
A recent release of Vollenweider's new-age/jazz harp music in a large group setting. — *Paul Kohler*

Trilogy / 1991 / CBS 46974
Excellent 2-CD compilation. Contains the first three albums plus *Pace Verde* and half of *Eine Art Suite in 13 Teilen*. — *Paul Kohler*

Book of Roses / 1992 / CBS 48601
A multicultural tapestry combining symphonic, flamenco, African, and Eastern European elements with Vollenweider's characteristic "otherworldly" atmospheres and spirited pop rhythms. — *Linda Kohanov*

Eine Art Suite in 13 Teilen / Audion 88001
A rare import-CD from Switzerland, featuring early material not found on any other release. Worth looking for. — *Paul Kohler*

Vox

Vocals, keyboard / New Age, Choral, Progressive electronic, Ethnic fusion

★ **Diadema** /
Diadema is a powerful album that recasts the inspired music of the twelfth century German mystic Hildegard von Bingen into a contemporary setting...Vox have succeeded beautifully in interpreting this truly spiritual music in such a way that its depth and relevance are more apparent than they would have been through a strictly traditional performance. — *Backroads Music / Heartbeats*

Ware-Patterson

Classical Offering / 1994 /
This soothing release will please both classical aficionados and those who simply wish to enjoy a classical setting of soft, serene ambiance. The music is performed by the accomplished duo of Bettine Clemen Ware on flute & Richard Patterson, who plays classical guitar. They offer sublime versions of beautifully arranged classics by Debussy, Beethoven, Schubert, Bach and others, like "Air on a G String," "Moonlight Sonata," "Fur Elise," & "Simple Gifts," the beloved Appalachian folk song, & more.

Ware's angelic flute playing carries the memorable melodies along on waves of bliss and gentleness. — *Backroads Music / Heartbeats*

Kit Watkins

Keyboard / Adult alternative, Progressive electronic, Ethnic fusion

The Virginia-based keyboardist creates finely crafted music that always seems to straddle a handful of genres with ease. He was a founding member of the short-lived, yet highly original, progressive 70s band, Happy the Man. In the early 80s, Watkins began building his own home studio and produced consistently inviting music that draws on his first-rate keyboard skills and his keen ear for sonic detail. He has recently been exploring a darker, more ambient side with the release of his two *Thought Tones* albums, both of which are highly recommended. — *Linda Kohanov*

Thought Tones, Vol. 1 / 1990 / 2002
Kit Watkins' earlier works strongly reflected his background in progressive rock, but the second half of his last album *SunStruck* marked a distinct shift towards space music. On *Thought Tones* that shift is complete, offering five abstract audioscapes designed to provide an atmosphere conducive to "creative thinking, contemplation, imagination, and other forms of direct and indirect perception." Always the experimenter, Kit Watkins has totally eschewed the use of keyboards of any kind. Instead, three of the pieces respectively feature the sounds of thunder, a dulcimer and saw blades heavily processed by electronic means, while the other two pieces were generated by analog flangers placed in a continuous feedback loop...At times reminiscent of Pauline Oliveros' *Deep Listening* or Brian Eno's *On Land*, *Thought Tones* is a work of great depth and power, an evocative meditation on the paradoxical relationship between formlessness and form, and a masterpiece of ambient space music. — *Backroads Music / Heartbeats*

Azure / 1990 / East Side Digital 80242
A truly eclectic brew of progressive rock, classical, jazz, world, and ambient music. — *Michael P. Dawson*

● **Sunstruck** / 1990 / East Side Digital 80422
Watkins is at his best on the lengthy ambient synthesizer excursions. — *Michael P. Dawson*

○ **Thought Tones, Vol. 2** / 1991 / Linden Music 2005
The second volume in Kit Watkins' *Thought Tones* series continues the exploration of mysterious abstract soundscapes intended to assist "creative thinking, contemplation, imagination, and other forms of direct and indirect perception." While the first volume eschewed the use of synthesizers, *Volume 2* happily employs them, along with interactive software and samplers that draw on the sounds of cars, hummingbirds, cats, sawblades and wine glasses, as well as conventional instruments. — *Backroads Music / Heartbeats*

☆ **Circle** / 1993 / Linden 2009
An hour of continuous environmental sound and quiet music, *Circle* was inspired by the surroundings of his home in Virginia's Blue Ridge mountains. A variety of natural sounds are interlaced with subtle music. — *Backroads Music / Heartbeats*

A Different View / Linden Music
Here, Watkins shows his musical roots as a very competent classical performer in his own right. *A Different View* is a beautiful collection of impressionistic tone poems, lovingly dedicated to the great masters who composed them. — *Jeff Filbert, Dreams Word*

○ **Sampler** / Linden Music
This pleasant mixture contains 70 minutes of diverse material from the former Happy the Man and Camel keyboardist. It is recommended to those not too familiar with Kit's diverse style. It's also for those admire Kit, but don't own much of his stuff. It contains 16 pieces taken from Kit's 6 solo CDs. Nice, professional, independent work. Linden Music, P.O.Box 520, Linden, VA 22642 — *Phil Anderson, Dreams Word*

Tim Wheaton

New Age, Meditation

Green Dream / 1988 /
This 1988 album has a strong emphasis on melodic structure. Tim's flutes & keyboards are complemented by others on keyboards, cello, percussion, guitar and voice, with some sax and

oboe by Andy Mackay from Roxy Music. Tim's flutes are ever present, but the focus is on ensemble playing rather than soloing, with effective interplay between flute, cello, and synthesizers. The mixture of acoustic instruments with synthesizers and classical elements makes *Green Dream* a beautiful and peaceful treasure. —*Backroads Music / Heartbeats*

Calmer Panorama / 1988 /
This release is unlike any other in its ability to create an auditory retreat. *A Calmer Panorama* is a 1988 release with two long tracks, in a meditative vein. Tim's breathy silver flute flows in and out of the nature sounds, creating an effect reminiscent of the serenity and harmonious ebb and flow of a Zen garden. — *Backroads Music / Heartbeats*

○ **Yearning** / 1994 /
One of the most romantic and beautifully conceived releases of this or any year, *The Yearning* joins composer/keyboardist Michael Hoppe with flautist extraordinaire Tim Wheater, whose musical musings are starting to appear on a striking number of releases. Subtitled *Romances for Alto Flute*, this release even has a story behind it. Hoppe's grandfather, the preeminent E. O. Hoppe (1878-1972), photographed many of the most famous and charismatic members of his generation, and his photos have a uniquely tactile and humane quality. Included are Queen Elizabeth, Marlene Dietrich, Mary Pickford, Princess White Deer and eight other celebrated women. The melodically seductive compositions, all written by Michael Hoppe, provide a perfect vehicle for Tim's expressive playing. The romantic ballads combine with the 32-pg. booklet to delight and fill the senses. The exquisite lyricism and healing elements heard in the music are suggestive of the most passionate of love songs, overflowing with the qualities of tenderness, intimacy and, above all, yearning. — *Backroads Music / Heartbeats*

★ **A Calmer Panorama** / Imagemaker Sound & Vision 2001
Tim Wheater is a British flutist. This album, his fifth, is composed of oriental influenced flute playing mixed with synthesizer, sequencer sounds, bird voices, and running water. —*Matt Hargreaves, Dreams Word*

○ **Timeless** /
Timeless presents a veritable kaleidoscope of gentle and passionate states within the body, soul and mind, encompassing elements from classical, spacemusic, world music and beyond. Ultra-dreamy passages with ethereal vocal textures take flight from the start on "The Laughing Sun," giving way to the tribal undertones of "Manna" and the expansive, pastoral beauty of "Hummingbird." Tim's music is bright and airy, a "breathing music" that can fill one's space with images of shafted sunlight, warm and inviting. A sense of humor and a variety of special effects are also present, enhancing the overall sound. The final track, one of several in the 7-8 min. range, is especially lovely, fittingly titled "The Wind of Freedom." —*Backroads Music / Heartbeats*

Whalesong /
Whalesong was inspired by time spent consorting with whales at Platypus Bay in Australia. Haunting notes drift on the ocean swell as flute & whale sing and play together. The first of two 30-min. tracks blends Tim's flutes with the whales; the second adds didgeridoo, hand drums and rhythm stick, while the finale captures the Southern Humpback Whale. Magnificent! —*Backroads Music / Heartbeats*

Awakenings /
This is comforting, pretty music with flute and layered synthesizer. This sensitive and soothing music has a similar feel to *The Fairy Ring*, but more flutey. The blending of electronic sound with the organic sound of the flute creates a celestial synthesis. James Galway calls this "Sensational . . . just too beautiful for words" —*Backroads Music / Heartbeats*

Rob Whiteside-Woo

Keyboard, composer / New Age, Neo-classical

★ **Miracles** / 1988 / Serenity 002
Miracles continues to be a classic six years after release as truly unique music of the spirit for harp, strings and winds. It is simply gorgeous! Rob composed this music to accompany passages from *A Course in Miracles*, and the results are meditative heart music

which is powerful, gentle and loving. —*Backroads Music / Heartbeats*

Ann Williams

● **Summer Rose** / Earthsong 2
Anne plays Irish and Celtic harps, autoharp, bamboo & silver flutes, vocals and bells, with additional flutes, cello & zither making *Summer Rose* a loving journey of unfoldment and emergence. Anne's lyrical voice and serene harp are wonderfully offset by the harmonies and rhythms, resulting in a tape of great sensitivity, at once earthy and reverential. This soothing & uplifting music is pure imagery, sound that is felt rather than heard, celestial seasonings for summer or anytime! —*Backroads Music / Heartbeats*

Wind Machine

Group / Adult alternative, Chamber jazz, New acoustic
Since its inception in 1986, Wind Machine has excelled at creating guitar-based music that dabbles in styles ranging from blues and bluegrass to jazz, rock, and new-age atmospherics. Core members Steve Mesple, Joe Scott, and Blake Eberhard utilize a vast arsenal of instruments ranging from mandolin, dobro, banjo, and some of their own guitar-hybrid inventions to trombone, harmonica, and fretless bass. —*Linda Kohanov*

● **Rain Maiden** / 1985 / Silver Wave 508
Another fine album of contemporary instrumental music. —*Linda Kohanov*

Voices in the Wind / 1991 / Silver Wave 701
Breezy instrumentals with an emphasis on contemporary jazz and folk influences. The production is crystal clear and as smooth as silk, which gives the group's upbeat originals a soothing quality. —*Linda Kohanov*

Road to Freedom / Silver Wave 602
Road to Freedom is the fourth Wind Machine release, following the surprise hit, *Rain Maiden*. The group remains intact, with two dynamite guitarists sharing the leads in bringing Steve Mesple's compositions to their fullest form yet. The twelve tunes range from sweet, serene songs of love to blistering acoustic frenzies. Several tunes are tributes to various freedom fighters, both near and far, and the fervent feelings of the universal struggle for peace and justice are translated well through the music. — *Backroads Music / Heartbeats*

George Winston

Piano / Neo-classical, Solo instrumental
Though George Winston is one of the most popular solo pianists in the history of contemporary instrumental music, he didn't start playing until after high school. Inspired by blues, rock, and R&B styles, he initially gravitated toward the organ and electric piano. Then in 1971 he heard the records of legendary stride pianist Fats Waller, which motivated him to concentrate on the acoustic piano and develop his own style. After recording his first solo album, *Ballads and Blues*, in 1972, he stopped playing for several years. He eventually was encouraged to delve into the instrument again when he discovered the music of New Orleans R&B pianist Professor Longhair. In 1980 he released the first of four solo piano albums for the Windham Hill label. These became amazingly successful and helped create industry support for more pastoral forms of the instrumental music subsequently referred to as "new age." Winston's recording style combines his gift for impressionistic melodies with American folk influences, yet his live performances continue to reflect his longstanding interests in stride and blues piano styles as well. —*Linda Kohanov*

★ **Autumn** / 1980 / Windham Hill 1012
Winston's impressions of the fall season are full of slow chording and sudden melodic runs on his acoustic piano. He captures the mixed feelings of the season, both its final flaring of life and its gradual retreat. —*William Ruhlmann*

★ **December** / 1982 / Windham Hill 1025
The mother of all solo instrumental albums, and with good reason. Mixing traditional carols with Pachelbel's Canon and a few originals, Winston produces a solo piano album of unparalleled—and undeniable—beauty. How can music be simultaneously stirring and soothing, relaxed yet exalted? Millions have found the

answer here, and an industry has spent more than a decade trying to duplicate it. —*William Ruhlmann*

Winter into Spring / 1982 / Windham Hill 1019
In a sense, this second seasonal album follows an opposite direction from *Autumn*, its hard, isolated notes and stop-and-start style gradually giving way from the stasis of winter to the growth and movement of spring. It's a good album for beginning your day. —*William Ruhlmann*

Summer / 1991 / Windham Hill 11107
On *Summer*, his return to the studio after six years, George Winston takes on seven originals plus two traditional tunes and half a dozen contemporary pieces by the likes of Randy Newman ("Living Without You") and Carmine Coppola ("The Black Stallion"), Pete Seeger, Art Lande and label-mate Philip Aaberg. Winston's nine-foot Steinway Grand has a crystal clear sound, and it comes to life in George's hands on *Summer* much in the same way that has delighted his audiences over the past decade. He effortlessly combines both traditional and obscure folk motifs, along with jazz improvisation and New Age introspection into an attractive blend that is uniquely George Winston. —*Backroads Music / Heartbeats*

Paul Winter (Paul Theodore (Jr) Winter)

b. Aug. 31, 1939, Altoona, PA
soprano, alto sax, bandleader / New Age, World Fusion, World music derivative
Environmental causes have been Paul Winter's concern as much, if not more than, music since the '70s. He's joined Greenpeace expeditions, recorded accompanying whales and wolves, and formed an organization linking environmental issues with musical concerns. Winter's music has never been among the more soulful, hard-edged, funky or bluesy; he's utilized improvisation but also incorporated elements from ethnic, European folk, symphonic/classical and other sounds that gradually became known as "New Age," (now contemporary instrumental in some circles.) His alto and soprano sax playing is melodically enticing, but seldom harmonically or rhythmically challenging. Winter founded the Paul Winter sextet while a Northwestern University student. This group was a winner at the 1961 Intercollegiate Jazz Festival held at Notre Dame, where some judges on the panel included John Hammond and Dizzy Gillespie. Hammond got the Consort onto Columbia. They proved quite popular, and the State Department sponsored a Latin American tour for the band in 1962. But five years later, Winter broke from a strict jazz sound with the Winter Consort, a band blending ethnic influences from Africa and Latin America, as well as Europe and America. Ralph Towner, Glen Moore, Collin Walcott, Paul McCandless and David Darling at one time were all members, and the instrumentation included acoustic guitar, sitar, bass, cello, and oboe. But the Consort eventually disbanded, with its core members forming a similiar, even more successful band, Oregon. Winter has blended music and environmental politics throughout the '80s and '90s. He's recorded as a leader for Columbia, A&M, Epic, and Living Music. Winter has several sessions available on CD. —*Ron Wynn and Linda Kohanov*

★ **Icarus** / 1971 / Living Music 4
Saxophonist's definitive statement. W/ members of the group Oregon—Paul McCandless, Ralph Towner (g), Collin Walcott, and Glen Moore. Spiritual and substantive—a rare combination. It works well. —*Michael G. Nastos*

☆ **Icarus** / 1972 / Epic 31643
This, a reissue of saxophonist Paul Winter's finest album, marks a transitional point in his career from jazz to his own brand of contemporary instrumental. But one can simply revel in the lovely melodies, the contemplative sounds, and the tasteful production of George Martin, especially on the justly famous title track by Ralph Towner. —*William Ruhlmann*

★ **Common Ground** / 1977 / A&M 3344
This is a good example of Winter's nature-conscious music, as he has incorporated the sounds of birds, wolves, and humpback whales into his ensemble. It's surprising how close such wild animals come to playing pop music. —*William Ruhlmann*

Wintersong / 1979 / Living Music 12
Dedicated to the spirit of giving and forgiving, this fine musical work from 1986 includes traditional songs from Sweden, Italy, England, France, Germany, the Appalachians as well as Bach's

"Joy," plus "Beautiful Star" by Odetta. Instrumental in its entirety, *Wintersong* is music for dancing, loving, and being alive, full of joy and lyricism. —*Backroads Music / Heartbeats*

○ **Callings** / 1980 / Living Music 1
A musical celebration of the sea and its creatures, with the voices of 15 various sea mammals woven into the fabric of the music. —*Backroads Music / Heartbeats*

○ **Sun Singer** / 1983 / Living Music 3
Striking example of Winter's lyricism. Paul Halley on keyboards and Glen Velez playing frame drum and percussion. —*Linda Kohanov*

○ **Canyon** / 1985 / Living Music 6
Released in 1985, half of the compositions for *Canyon* were actually recorded in the Grand Canyon, while the rest were recorded in St. John's Cathedral in New York. The musicians were Paul McCandless, David Darling, Eugene Friesen, Glen Velez, Paul Halley, John Clark and Oscar Castro-Neves. Powerful and memorable. —*Backroads Music / Heartbeats*

Whales Alive / 1987 / Living Music 0013
For the listener, *Whales Alive!* is a deep, dynamic and dramatic listening experience. Artist royalties from *Whales Alive!* will be donated to the World Wildlife Fund for its efforts to preserve whales. —*Backroads Music / Heartbeats*

● **Wolf Eyes** / 1988 / Living Music 18
This is a retrospective of Paul Winter's work from 1980-1988, featuring cuts from most of his albums of this period (not his two more specialized *Whales Alive* and *Wintersong*). Five of the tracks were recorded in the cathedral of St. John the Divine in New York City, and three were recorded live in the General Assembly of the United Nations on World Environment Day in 1984, including a fine version of "Icarus," the long-time favorite from Paul Winter's repertoire. As usual Paul's soprano sax is supported by his Consort, and augmented by the voices of dolphins, birds, and especially wolves. —*Backroads Music / Heartbeats*

Earthbeat / 1988 / Living Music 15
Billed as the album of original music created by Americans and Russians together, this album features Halley, Velez, guitarist Oscar Castro-Neves, and cellist Eugene Friesen collaborating on some selections with the Dmitri Pokrovsky Singers, a vocal ensemble rooted in the tradition of Russian village music. Traditional music from throughout Russia is mixed with Winter's Brazilian-influenced sound. There are also some beautiful instrumentals and, true to Winter's style, some natural sounds, most notably the calls of the Alaskan tundra wolf and Russian loon. —*Linda Kohanov*

Earth: Voices of a Planet / 1990 / Living Music 19
Winter regulars and some special guest artists have put together a musical journey that starts in North America and travels through Africa, Antarctica, South America, Australia, Asia, and Europe. Selections feature indigenous nature sounds and traditional influences from various regions. —*Linda Kohanov*

○ **Anthems** / Living Music 23
Featuring artists like Paul Halley, Eugene Friesen and Winter himself, this anthology amply displays the tradition of interweaving diverse instruments and voices from different parts of the world. Mid-tempo and jazzy in parts, but consistently melodic, *Anthems* celebrates the people, places, creatures and cultures of the Earth. 17 tracks; 72 minutes in all. —*Backroads Music / Heartbeats*

Wolf

● **Beyond Words** / 1994 /
His second release, *Beyond Words*, interjects several multi-dimensional elements in his attempt to honor the spiritual worlds that Wolf has discovered since his adoption into the Crow tribe by Hollis Little Creek, an Anisnabe elder. Most pieces include nature sounds which add to his self-made Kokopelli flutes. He also performs several duets with Tim Wheater, while violinist Marc Josephson & others are also heard. From thundering drums to sonorous flutes, the selections on *Beyond Words* take you precisely there—to that space of knowledge and awakening, of harmony and balance. —*Backroads Music / Heartbeats*

Wolff & Hennings

Group / Ethnic fusion, Ambient

The mystical sounds of Tibetan bells and singing bowls have been used for centuries in Buddhist meditation and religious rites. Henry Wolff and Nancy Hennings first encountered these instruments during a 1969 trip to India and Nepal where they studied with the Kagyu branch of Tibetan Buddhism. Since 1971, the duo has been releasing a subtle, haunting series of recordings featuring Tibetan bells, including a collaboration with Grateful Dead percussionist Mickey Hart called *Yamantaka*. Wolff and Hennings also contributed their skills to the Philip Glass soundtrack for the film *Koyaanisqatsi*, which brought the transcendent sound of the bells to wider audiences. The uncanny resonances of these acoustic instruments produce music that often sounds electronically generated. —*Linda Kohanov*

● **Tibetan Bells II** / 1978 / Celestial Harmonies 13005
While the duo creates its own compositions, this early album is closer in concept to the way these instruments are traditionally used. —*Linda Kohanov*

Tibetan Bells III: The Empty Mirror / 1988 / Celestial
  Harmonies 13027
Tibetan Bells III: The Empty Mirror is another compelling album of purely acoustic Tibetan bell music. —*Linda Kohanov*

Yamantaka / Celestial Harmonies
Grateful Dead drummer and world musicologist Mickey Hart's most ethereal work is on this collaboration with Wolff & Jennings. —*Linda Kohanov*

Eric Wollo

Guitar / Progressive electronic, Ethnic fusion, Ambient
Norwegian composer Erik Wollo started out as a jazz guitarist and dabbled in jazz-rock fusion on his early recordings. In 1984, however, he came out with *Traces*, an electronic album of startling originality. His most recent release is equally impressive. While there's always a sense of warmth to his atmospheric pieces, his music resounds with the stark beauty of Norway's wintry landscapes. Through his subtle minimalist patterns and nebulous breaths of sound, you can easily imagine the composer staring through windows splayed with ice crystals as Arctic winds whisper across the snow fields and ethereal northern lights pulse steadily in the distance. —*Linda Kohanov*

● **Traces** / 1984 / Badland 003
Expansive synthesizer textures float over the slowly churning, hypnotic drives of sequencer patterns and primal rhythms on this collection of richly hued electronic dreamscapes. —*Linda Kohanov*

Images of Light / 1990 / Eurock 2005
Another sublime set of Northern visions with a few darker, more experimental pieces. On "Urban Space," for instance, some gritty sampled saxophone undulations and long melodic lines successfully romanticize the cold, hard imagery of mechanized life. —*Linda Kohanov*

Danny Wright

Piano
● **Black and White** / 1986 / Moulin D'or 101
○ **Black and White 2** / 1989 / Nichols-Wright 889
This is the sequel to *Black and White*, Danny's very successful solo piano tape of popular show tunes. *Volume 2* continues in the same vein with a couple of modern classical pieces by Debussy and Rachmaninoff mixed in with favorite tunes from Broadway musicals and movie soundtracks. Selections from *Porgy and Bess*, *Out of Africa*, *Phantom of the Opera* and others, plus a fine version of "Moon River", are given Danny's trademark romantic treatment. —*Backroads Music / Heartbeats*

Autumn Dreams / 1991 / Moulin D'or 921
The latest album by the prolific Danny Wright is a meditation on the "dreams of changes... as well as warm memories of times past." Performing on a Steinway concert piano, Danny Wright plays original compositions, all tender ballads glowing with warm introspection. Unlike some of his previous albums there is no synthesizer back-up here, but several of the pieces are graced by wistful violin, gentle oboe and English horn. *Autumn Dreams* once again shows Danny Wright to be a sensitive pianist, a master of sweet sentiment and nostalgic expressiveness. —*Backroads Music / Heartbeats*

○ **Black and White Encore** / 1991 / Nichols-Wright 391

The third release in Danny Wright's extremely popular Black and White series once again offers a selection of tunes from Broadway musicals, movie soundtracks and popular culture. —*Backroads Music / Heartbeats*

○ **Day In The Life** / 1993 / Moulin D'Or 942
Danny Wright's 11th recording is neither a flamboyant improvisational exercise, nor a rigidly structured presentation. Instead, it combines nice piano melodies, elaborate but not pompous or bombastic arrangements and a modicum of synthesizer/electronic backing and orchestration. The results are music that doesn't overwhelm, but holds interest over 11 selections. The songs are short enough and arranged in such a manner that the suite feeling Wright seeks is maintained. The most interesting numbers are "Peace" and "Gabriel's Oboe", longer compositions with more musical variety and thematic contrast than the disc's shorter tunes. It's a well-arranged and produced work, aimed at fans interested in structured material with some degree of individuality. —*Ron Wynn*

David Wright

Ocean Watch / 1994 /
This is a powerful release, advancing considerably the sound of this UK synth wizard who combines warm emotion and rhythmic motion in sublime ways. His atmospheric and melodious themes reach a new height on *Ocean Watch*, balancing tranquil and serene landscapes with his signature sound in unique ways that make it difficult to draw comparisons with other electronic music artists...Electronic embellishments roam above and underscore piano-based arrangements, and state-of-the-art keyboards are employed. —*Backroads Music / Heartbeats*

● **Between Realities** /
David Wright continues his brilliant E-music vision with *Between Realities*. It is part two of a trilogy. *Marilynmba* is part one and the soon to be released *Beyond the Airwaves* is part three. As for this CD, David keeps up his high standards from previous recordings with tracks like "Eastern Innersense". It is largely dominated by a sequenced rhythm, with a flowing, spacey ending to top it off. —*Jeff Misner, Dreams Word*

Yanni

Piano / Adult alternative, Progressive electronic
Yanni's grandiose keyboard style is both accessible and exciting, two elements that have led to his success in the realm of adult-alternative radio. His explosive, pop-influenced instrumentals and romantic pianistic ballads have also made him a popular touring and recording artist for the Private Music label. In addition to his original television, commercial, and film scores, Yanni's music has been used extensively on programs like *Wide World of Sports* and coverage of the Olympic Games. This aspect of his career seems especially appropriate when you consider that he achieved early success not as a musician, but as a member of the Greek National Swimming Team. (He broke the national freestyle record at age 14.) Born in Kalamata, Greece, Yanni arrived in the US after high school and obtained a degree in psychology from the University of Minnesota before diving headfirst into music. It didn't take long for the self-taught keyboardist and composer to establish himself as a studio musician, jingles composer, and producer. After gaining an impressive cult-following for his first independently released album, Yanni was picked up by Private Music and has become one of the label's best-selling artists. One of the most visible artists in the contemporary instrumental realm, Yanni's rise to fame was expedited in the early 90s by his romantic relationship with actress Linda Evans, which gained him coverage on mainstream programs like "Lifestyles of the Rich and Famous" as well as appearances on the daytime talk show circuit. —*Linda Kohanov*

★ **Keys to Imagination** / 1986 / Private Music 2008
Yanni's first Private Music release is a true masterpiece of dramatic synthesizer music. Yanni's music is lusty and brilliant, richly melodious and memorable, full of passion & life as befits his Greek heritage. One of the ultimate car stereo albums, Yanni's flamboyant, superb style of compositions makes *Keys to Imagination* some of the most extravagant, hyperspace music we know. —*Backroads Music / Heartbeats*

Out of Silence / 1987 / Private Music 2024

Yanni's second album, like his first (*Keys to Imagination*) was recorded entirely on synthesizers at his home studio. The composer/performer makes extensive use of the orchestral possibilities of electronics, creating big themes to play across elaborate, echoing rhythm tracks. Unlike much adult alternative music, it's constantly stimulating foreground music with an extremely modern sound. — *William Ruhlmann*

Chameleon Days / 1988 / Private Music 2043

With *Chameleon Days*, Yanni again explores new and fascinating rhythms, while maintaining the same balance between high-energy space-cruisers and gorgeous, evocative ballad-like slower pieces. — *Backroads Music / Heartbeats*

Niki Nana / 1989 / Private Music 2056

Yanni takes a more overtly pop approach here, adding other musicians and vocalists (on the title track) and even playing in dance rhythms, so what was always an engaging style of music becomes more accessible to a wider audience. — *William Ruhlmann*

○ **In Celebration of Life** / 1991 / Private Music 82093

This is a strong collection of pieces from four of Yanni's earlier albums, plus "Song For Antarctica," composed for the *Polar Shift* compilation. The focus is on drama, power and passion, common elements throughout his music. — *Backroads Music / Heartbeats*

Dare to Dream / 1992 / Private Music 82096

Dare to Dream was Yanni's first new music in three years. He seems to have slowed down and become less extravagant in his intricate development and rhythms. Beyond the overall beauty of the new pieces, special attention is likely to go to "Aria," an inspired vocal piece co-conceived by Yanni and Malcolm Mclaren. — *Backroads Music / Heartbeats*

In My Time / 1993 / Private Music 82106

Yanni's latest is another extension of his creative spirit and stirring passion for life. Focusing on piano as his primary instrument, Yanni infuses his "signature" style with timeless, eloquent themes and plenty of romantic energy. No longer are rhythm and dynamic currents as vital to Yanni's sound, since he seems to have stopped fueling his music with "rocket power." His romantic outpourings lend a personal nature to *In My Time*, and this new effort should be received with enthusiasm far and wide. Yanni is uniquely expressive, and this new music is deeply touching on many levels. — *Backroads Music / Heartbeats*

○ **Yanni Live at the Acropolis** / Sep. 1993 / Private Music 82116

● **Reflections of Passion** / Private Music 2067

Here are 15 romantic songs from Yanni's five earlier releases, plus three new songs recorded especially for this album. Much of *Reflections of Passion* is from *Niki Nana* and *Chameleon Days*, while his two earliest are represented by only one cut each, and the tempos vary from the slower, dramatic pieces to his unique "rocket fuel" style, full of dazzling cross-rhythms and intricate development. — *Backroads Music / Heartbeats*

Yas-Kaz

Percussion / Progressive electronic, Ethnic fusion

A university-trained percussionist, Japanese artist Yasukazu Sato gained attention for his international tours as composer for the innovative dance group Sankaijuku. His unusual combination of ancient Oriental forms, spacious musical atmospheres, and ceremonial percussion provided perfect accompaniment to the ritualistic movements and slowly unfolding acrobatic feats of this modern Japanese dance company. He has also scored several award-winning Japanese films, performed with American jazz saxophonist Wayne Shorter and Japanese synthesist Himekami, and recorded a number of imaginative solo albums. — *Linda Kohanov*

★ **Darkness in Dreams** / 1991 / Kuckuck 11092

Compiled from six of his finest recordings, these selections illustrate the composer's gift for translating fantasy into sonic reality. Each cut is a world in itself, in which luminous zither cascades and tribal percussion tracks alternate with joyous folk dances and Oriental melodies for full string orchestra that soar over waves of synthesized sequencer patterns. A good introduction to the varied moods of Yas-Kaz (most of his recordings are rare Japanese imports). — *Linda Kohanov*

Samplers & Collections

The field of contemporary instrumental music has probably inspired more artist collections than any other musical genre. Established CI record companies generally release at least one sampler every year or so, giving listeners a taste of the most engaging and accessible cuts from upcoming albums. As it turns out, these compilations are often the label's best-selling title, a fact that has led several of the companies to produce a number of fine thematic collections as well. The following list distinguishes up to three samplers for each label (though most have released many more), as well as a miscellaneous section for the best collections released through smaller companies.

– Linda Kohanov

New Age Collections

American Gramaphone Sampler #1 / 1987 / American Gramaphone 366

American Gramaphone Samplers #1 & #2 feature a number of selections from Mannheim Steamroller's *Fresh Aire* series as well as pieces by other American Gramaphone mainstays like Eric Hansen, Ron Cooley, and Checkfield. — *Linda Kohanov*

American Gramaphone Sampler #2 / American Gramaphone 3671988

○ **Anthems** / 1992 / Living Music 23

In celebration of the label's tenth anniversary, Living Music has brought together music from 18 of the 22 albums in its catalog, featuring Eugene Friesen, Oscar Castro Neves, Glen Velez, Paul Halley, Russia's Dmitri Pokrovsky Singers, and of course, the label's founder Paul Winter. Though Living Music has two other samplers on the market, *Anthems: Ten Years of Living Music* is by far the most comprehensive. — *Linda Kohanov*

Asia Music / 1994

Asia is a thoughtful blend of the new and old, from musicians representing each major Eastern tradition, with the music of India, Japan, China and Tibet. Indian sitar, Chinese cheng and Japanese koto, as ancient as the cultures themselves, are heard side-by-side with contemporary Asian music and works that combine traditional Oriental sounds with electronic instruments and processing. These selections span the rich catalog of Celestial Harmonies—you'll hear David Parsons, Paul Horn, Stomu Yamashta and Terry Riley as well as Sunazaki, Koga, Yas-Kaz, Asiabeat and the Monks of the Dip Tse Chok Ling Monastery. — *Backroads Music / Heartbeats*

Au-Del Du Rubicon (Beyond Rubicon) / 1994

A host of fine spacemusic artists from Canada plus the prolific Steve Roach make up the 77 minutes of this excellent anthology. Spacey & melodic pieces offer a veritable treasure of sounds, from the acoustic touch of Daniel Blanchet to upbeat cruisers by Serge Laporte and the space drift of Francois Kiraly. The ten-minute track by Steve Roach, "Full Moon Prophesy," is not on any of his releases. Stately, visceral, occasionally solemn and always intelligent, this sampler is a superb intro to this style of music. — *Backroads Music / Heartbeats*

CMP-Ler / 1994

This compilation has selections from the first ten titles on CMP's *3000 Series*, with traditional music from a variety of non-Western cultures. The low price makes *CMP-ler* a great way to taste these high-quality releases. — *Backroads Music / Heartbeats*

● **Dinner Classics**

This is a series of attractively packaged albums put out by CBS Masterworks, sampling classical music of various times and cultures. Each one is thematized around the cuisine of that country and the covers feature overhead shots of tantalizing table spreads of appropriate foods. The inserts also include recipes from Martha

Stewart's best selling book *Entertaining. —Backroads Music / Heartbeats*

● **A Door in the Air** / 1991 / Echodiscs 1001
Like the Hearts of Space record label, Echodiscs is the offshoot of a widely syndicated contemporary instrumental radio program— in this case, *Echoes* (Box 224, Eagle, PA 19480). The company's first release is a collection of noteworthy recordings made especially for broadcast. These "Living Room Concerts" are captured in the homes of the artists by Echoes producer and host John Diliberto. *A Door in the Air* offers a sampling of his favorites by Robert Rich, Stein & Walder, Arco Iris, Michael Brook, David Torn, and Steve Roach. —*Linda Kohanov*

● **Erdenklang Music Sampler, Vol. 2** / 1992
This German label has an extensive roster of European contemporary instrumental artists with an emphasis on electronic music (both pop-oriented and progressive). *Magic Age II* is the second in a series that features evocative pieces of a more ambient nature, including some previously unreleased material from Peeter Vahi, Hector Zazou, Blue Chip Orchestra, and Lightwave, among others. —*Linda Kohanov*

● **Fruits of Our Labor: Global Pacific Sampler** / 1986 / Rhino 79320
The Global Pacific label's first sampler, *Global Pacific—The Fruits of Our Labor*, features the early work of artists like Steve Kindler, Ben Tavera King, Paul Greaver, and Bob Kindler, among others. —*Linda Kohanov*

○ **Global Pacific—Global Voyage** / 1988 / Rhino 79321
Selections from popular Global Pacific recordings by Paul Horn, David Friesen, Georgia Kelly, Bob Kindler, Do'ah, Steve Kindler, and Teje Bell. —*Linda Kohanov*

Harvest Moon / 1994
Harvest Moon features three gifted yet very different proponents of the harp. Kim Robertson, Michelle Sell & Carlos Reyes play, in turn, Celtic harp, Classical and folk harp, & Paraguayan harp. Each has five tracks, all solo; they flow perfectly one into the next, from O'Carolan to Debussy, with Reyes' original compositions providing several highlights. For harp fans of any background this is a winner, right down to the catchy Sugo artwork. — *Backroads Music / Heartbeats*

● **Hearts of Space—Starflight 1** / 1986 / Hearts of Space 100
This album's also originally produced for the popular weekly radio show. Overall feeling is quite different than *Cruisers 1.0*. The ten lush, ambient pieces featured are taken from albums by Michael Amerlan, Tim Clark, and Steve Roach. —*Linda Kohanov*

● **Hearts of Space—Cruisers 1.0** / 1988 / Hearts of Space 11102
Produced in the tradition of the "Music from the Hearts of Space" syndicated radio show, *Cruisers 1.0* is a tightly programmed musical journey in which selections by various artists flow in and out of each other almost seamlessly over the course of an hour— an effect more akin to a "soundtrack for the mind" than a label sampler. Pieces by Don Harriss, Gershon Kingsley, Klaus Schonning, Michael Stearns, and Ken Stover are featured on these gently rhythmic pieces. —*Linda Kohanov*

○ **Hearts of Space—Sampler '90** / 1990 / Hearts of Space 11200
While the previous *Hearts of Space* collections featured music from other labels, the *Universe Sampler '90* is the first compilation of artists signed to the Hearts of Space record company (which grew out of the radio program). Music is by Kevin Braheny, Bill Douglas, Constance Demby, Raphael, and others. —*Linda Kohanov*

Songs of the Great Lakes Indians / 1994
This state-of-the-art recording captures a Native American pow-wow, recorded in northern Wisconsin by Mickey Hart. The wailing and trilling voices create a charged atmosphere celebrating the spiritual dimension of life and humanity's connection to the Earth. —*Backroads Music / Heartbeats*

○ **Inner Landscapes** / 1991 / Clear Productions 9001
The best and most recent Clear Productions venture includes selections by Kit Watkins, John Serrie, Laraaji, and Steve Roach, among others. —*Linda Kohanov*

Living Music Collection 2 / Living Music 16
Paul Winter Consort, Eugene Friesen, Paul Halley, Oscar Castro-Neves, and Susan Osborn provides tracks for this compilation album. —*AMG*

● **Looking East—Poland** / 1990 / Erdenklang 90341

● **Looking East—Hungary** / 1991 / Erdenklang 91348
The unexpected opening of the Iron Curtain has recently given birth to Erdenklang's collections of synthesizer music from Eastern European countries. This album offers an evocative cross-section of pop, cross-cultural, and avant-garde electronic composers who have never before been heard in the West. A noteworthy achievement. —*Linda Kohanov*

Narada Wilderness Collection / 1990 / Narada 63905
Although Narada has released numerous samplers over the years, this Wisconsin-based label has become the leader in producing engaging thematic albums. The *Narada Wilderness Collection* features impressionistic works by company staples like David Arkenstone, Spencer Brewer, Tingstad and Rumbel, Peter Buffett, David Lanz, and others. The extensive CD booklet includes a statement from each artist about the specific landscape that inspired his or her piece, as well as stunning nature photography to go along with it. —*Linda Kohanov*

Narada—a Childhood Remembered / 1991 / Narada 63907
Twelve Narada artists were commissioned to compose pieces inspired by favorite works of children's literature, each colorfully illustrated in storybook fashion in the CD booklet. —*Linda Kohanov*

● **Narada—Alma Del Sur** / 1992 / Narada 63908
One of Narada's classiest packages yet, *Alma Del Sur* is a showcase for contemporary South American music by Argentinian multi-instrumentalist Bernardo Rubaja, Brazilian flutist and percussionist Junior Homrich, Bolivian panpipe virtuoso Gonzalo Vargas (accompanied by the North American band Ancient Future), Paraguayan harpist Roberto Perera, and the Bolivian ensemble Rumillajta, among others. Liner notes include exquisite photos of traditional artwork and overviews of South American history and music, as well as biographies of the artists. Don't be misled into thinking this is a collection of traditional music, however. It is instead a survey of modern styles palatable to a wide variety of listeners. —*Linda Kohanov*

Decade / 1994
Here is a two CD set celebrating the tenth Anniversary of the Narada label. With Lanz, Jones, Buffett, Brewer, Tingstad & Rumbel, Arkenstone and others.
—*Backroads Music / Heartbeats*

Night at the Symphony / 1994
This collection is a "listener's choice" of classical works by Mozart, Bach, Vivaldi and others, culled from thousands of selections of orchestral works. 13 tracks are highlighted by four pieces from Mozart's "Eine Kleine Nachtmusik," Vivaldi's "The Four Seasons" & Bach's "Brandenburg Concerto" are also heard. Pieces range from romantic themes to improvisatory melodies, from introspective movements to lush minuets & waltzes. —*Backroads Music / Heartbeats*

● **Polar Shift** / 1991 / Earth Sea
A benefit for Antarctica including songs from Enya, Yanni, John Tesh, Paul Sutin, Vangelis, Chris Spheeris, Jim Chappeil, Paul Voudouris, Steve Howe, Constance Demby, Kitaro, and Suzanne Ciani. —*AMG*

Private Music Sampler, Vol. 5 / 1990 / Private Music 2077
A more recent sampler with selections by artists like Yanni, Tangerine Dream, Andy Summers, and Patrick O'Hearn. —*Linda Kohanov*

● **Raven: A Sampler** / 1991 / Raven 21
An eclectic sampling of the recordings released on the small New Jersey-based company, Raven Recording, including music by the label's founder and main artist Gabrielle Roth as well as pieces by Matt Balitsaris, Nicholas, and Raphael. —*Linda Kohanov*

○ **Relax with Classics, Vol. 1** / 1994
This popular series offers magnificent Baroque music selected and sequenced for relaxation, work, study and well-being by the LIND Institute. *Vol. 1: Largo* includes the Pachelbel "Canon in D," as well as pieces by Albinoni, Vivaldi, Mozart, Handel and others. Each volume has several outstanding highlights, has 50 minutes plus music, and now comes on Compact Disc. —*Backroads Music / Heartbeats*

The Sun
This 76 minute sampler covers the talented artists of Colorado's Silver Wave label. With upbeat, jazzy overtones on many cuts,

this is like listening to your favorite station playing its best tracks. All the elements of contemporary instrumentals are heard: jazz, acoustic, world, electronic & meditative music. Davol, Heines, Kater & Nakai, Wind Machine, Fowler & Branca are all heard on the energetic and bright *The Sun*. —*Backroads Music / Heartbeats*

Spirit Cries, Vol.1 / 1994
Compiled by Mickey Hart from the Library of Congress Archives, this album features field recordings gathered over a period of four decades from Belize, Peru, Suriname, French Guiana and Jamaica. The stark and emotionally direct sounds of *The Spirit Cries* are subtitled *Endangered Music from the Rainforests of South America and the Caribbean*. —*Backroads Music / Heartbeats*

○ **Visionaries** / 1989 / Clear Productions 8901
Clear Productions (1489 Coddington Rd., Brooktondale, NY 14817) occasionally puts out admirable collections of work by independent artists. Often these pieces are commissioned especially for the project rather than taken from previously released albums. This particular recording features new-age synthesist Iasos, hammered-dulcimer virtuoso Dan Duggan, and pianist Richard Shulman, among others. —*Linda Kohanov*

○ **Windham Hill—Soul of ...** / 1987 / Windham Hill 1062
Windham Hill's *Soul of the Machine* collection of contemporary electronic and electro-acoustic music primarily features little-known artists, many of whom are not signed to the label: Michael Foreman, Fred Simon, Michael Whiteley, Schoenherz and Scott, Colin Chin, Philippe Saisse, Mark Darnell, Tim Story, Roy Finch, Ted Greenwald, Scott Hiltzik. —*Linda Kohanov*

● **Winter's Solstice, Vol. 1** / 1989 / Windham Hill 1045
... quietly emotive meditations on the spirit of the season. Excellent sound and playing make this a disc worth having for those who don't want to be barraged by a predictable menu of Christmas standards. — *Rick Clark, Rock & Roll Disc.*

● **Windham Hill—First Ten Years** / 1990 / Windham Hill 1095

Windham Hill has put out so many samplers that it can be confounding to choose one over another. This double CD, however, features a selection or two from just about everyone who has ever recorded for the *main* label (not the Windham Hill jazz or singer/songwriter divisions). A comprehensive overview of the contemporary instrumental sound for which the company is most famous. —*Linda Kohanov*

Windham Hill Sampler '92 / Sep. 10, 1991 / Windham Hill 11109

A taste of the most recent work from label mainstays like Michael Manring, Alex de Grassi, Nightnoise, Michael Hedges, Mark Isham, Montreux, David Torn, Liz Story, Modern Mandolin Quartet, Phil Aaberg, and Will Ackerman. —*Linda Kohanov*

Mang Zhong Summer / 1994

Bringing the body and mind into a state of equilibrium and harmony is no small feat. Often the use of music can provide an effective aid. For millennia the Chinese have been aware of the healing properties of music, but in recent years research has thrown new light on the relationship between music and the medical and philosophical model. This six volume set is an outcome of this study, a collaboration between medical researchers & leading Chinese composers. Two long tracks offer sweeping melodies performed by the Shanghai Racial Music Troupe, with shimmering strings, soaring flute, piping reeds, massed lutes, tuned bells and assorted percussion. Designed to strengthen the natural defenses within the listener against the conditions of the four seasons, *Mang Zhong: Summer* is an uplifting album that indeed has a calming and healing effect. —*Backroads Music / Heartbeats*

20TH CENTURY AVANT-GARDE

Categories are at best relative, and this is especially true in avant-garde music. In this section you'll find music made with stones and symphony orchestras, home-built computers, and the unadorned human voice. The subjects are diverse—from personal political concerns to meditations on natural phenomena. What these pieces have in common are composers who pursued unique visions intertwined with their lives. These works go beyond any recognized categories and help enhance our sensitivity to the physical and imaginary worlds (both of which are "real" because we do the imagining).

This section covers a wide range of musical invention:

1. Pattern music that gradually evolves over a steady pulse into complex and changing forms in an "eternal present," in the manner of many natural processes, such as the "divine proportion" of the chambered nautilus's shell and the splitting of the amoeba. Examples: Riley, Reich, Tom Johnson, Glass.

2. Music that takes single sounds and other elements out of pop music's usual song forms and styles and formally expands on them to make music of universal vision. Examples: Branca, The Residents, Chatham, Oswald.

3. Music employing chance procedures (sometimes called "aleatory," which is actually a limited special case of chance operations) that produce the unexpected at every moment for performer, listener, and even composer. The compositions are often described as indeterminate of their "realization" (a onetime performance, like sand paintings that are erased after a particular ceremony, with the basic score or tradition remaining until the next realization). This music gives the performer both greater responsibility and greater freedom, while encouraging us to experience the myriad events of every moment outside and inside ourselves—a sort of "ecology of the mind." In a very real sense, this music is not "about" something but is that "something" itself. Examples: Cage, Brown, Wolff, Feldman.

4. Music based on psychoacoustic illusions and other natural phenomena—brainwaves, sonic blasts from sand dunes, chaotic vibrations, radiowave "whistlers" in the ionosphere, a plant's apparent response to fire or emotional stimuli (as in the Backster Effect used in "Plant Music," an unrecorded radio piece by Tom Zahuranec [1972]). Other examples: Lucier, Amacher, Monahan.

5. Compositions for home-built instruments. Examples: Partch, Fullman.

6. Sound installations, often interactive with the public, and other pieces designed to happen in places other than the usual concert halls. Examples: Kuivila, Hunt, Behrman.

7. Music in alternate tunings, creating new sensations of hearing (Johnston, Partch, Wyschnegradsky), and music that explores new ways of playing traditional instruments (Goldstein, Klucevsek, Celli, Goode).

8. Unique approaches to traditionally defined melody, harmony, and rhythm (Hovhaness, Thomson, Garland, Hosokawa), including what could be called "the downtown sound," in which pop, world, techno, folk, and concert musics have all become part of the general vocabulary, not "collaged" in some artificial way but resulting in forms that are an outgrowth of the musicians having grown up hearing and playing all these musics (Pickett, Gordon, Zorn, Sublette, Kroesen).

9. New narrative forms and text/sound pieces. Examples: Ashley, Atcheley, Anderson, Neill, Thorington, Turner.

10. Deeply meditative music of an altered and expanded time sense. Examples: Vierk, Radique, Mostel.

11. Unique "crossover" pieces from jazz, rock, and other genres. Examples: Coleman, Reed, Zappa.

12. Superformalist pieces, by academics who are regarded, even by their peers, as somewhat out of the fold. Examples: Wolpe, Barraque, Babbitt.

13. The vast array of electronic and tape music generated by digital computers or by analog synthersizers: *musique concrète*, made by manipulation of tape speed and editing (also accumulation of sounds created by covering the erase head, delay made by multiple tape loops, and so forth); "live electronic" performance and interactive performance with acoustic instruments and voices; sampling acoustic and electronic sounds and modulating them with a wave-shaping synthesis, etc.; computer-controlled installations; electronically amplified instruments and enviromental sounds; and much more.

14. Collective improvisations and group "process/procedure" work. Examples: Oliveros, Deep Listening Band, Cardew and the Scratch Orchestra, Zorn's groups.

And, of course,

15. Composers/performers and any of their pieces that can be described as employing several of the techniques, aesthetics, and influences mentioned above.

—*"Blue" Gene Tyranny*

John Adams

b. 1947
Composer / Minimalism
An American minimalist composer who is known for *Nixon in China*. —*AMG*

Shaker Loops (1978) / In LCO 8 (London Chamber Orchestra) "Minimalist" / 1990 / New Albion
An exceptionally good performance: rushing, trembling sounds represent the practices of the utopian religious sect the Shakers

and also the musical "shake." The two lovely inner movements, "Hymning Slews" and "Loops and Verses," are Adams's best harmonic writing—a lot of activity for so-called "minimal" music. —*"Blue" Gene Tyranny*

Maryanne Amacher

○ Stain—The Music Rooms/ In "Imaginary Landscapes" / 1989 / Elektra/Nonesuch
Amacher has created some of the finest pieces and sound-installations based on psychoacoustic illusions. Until the advent of CDs,

most of her work was unrecordable partly because of the extreme ranges of pitch and dynamics, the duration of the piece necessary to create some illusions, and the stability of the medium. The "music rooms" are literally that—installed on floors of a house or in adjacent rooms that the audience walks through to create their own mix from enormously amplified environmental and electronic sounds. — *"Blue" Gene Tyranny*

Beth Anderson

b. 1950

Composer / Electronic

Very original composer in a variety of forms and musical styles, including textsound and tape pieces. — *"Blue" Gene Tyranny*

● **Torero Piece (1973) / In "10 + 2 = 12 American Text Sound Pieces"** / 1974 / 1750 Arch Street Records

This unfortunately not-yet-reissued disc contains this duet for the composer and her mother in which the mother describes her relationship to her daughter while the daughter makes unrelated phonemic sounds decoded from a paint-by-number picture she found in a junk antique store. An imaginative and drolly humorous piece by this very original composer who is also known for her opera about Queen Christina. — *"Blue" Gene Tyranny*

Revel (1981/1984) / 1984 / Opus One

Performed by the Richmond Symphony, conducted by Jacques Houtman. New romantic music that combines rock harmony and an interest in world music. — *"Blue" Gene Tyranny*

Jorge Antunes

b. 1942

Musica Electronica / Joias Musicais

This is the first electronic music made in Brazil. Antunes is a wonderful composer who constructed the Center for Chomo-Musical Research in Rio de Janeiro and thereby became the first composer of electronic music in his country. "Valso Sideral" (1962) and "Contrapunctus Contra Contrapunctus" (1965) are early uses of patterning in "rhythmic cells" where the rhythms are gradually distorted. In "Cintra Cita" (1969) the composer has a "bande rendezvous" (tape meeting) with himself over materials and chance rhythms and thoughts used throughout his work. The fascinating "Auto-Retrato sonre Paisaje Porteno" (1969) used a scratch on an old 78 rpm record played on a wind-up phonograph as the basic rhythmic element for the construction of an electronically modified samba where the words are inflected by the composer's voice and lose all actual meaning. "Historia de un Pueblo" (1970) is a dramatic work alternating between sweet persuasion and aggression, a not explicitly narrrative story that can nevertheless be understood by anyone. — *"Blue" Gene Tyranny*

Robert Ashley

b. 1930

Composer / Jazz, minimalism

In the past 15 years, Robert Ashley, influential for several decades as both a composer and writer, has created a series of operas-for-TV that speak on many levels of the lives of the people that constitute present-day America. — *"Blue" Gene Tyranny*

She Was a Visitor / In "Extended Voices" / 1968 / Odyssey

The Brandeis University Chamber Chorus, conducted by Alvin Lucier. Describes musically how "rumor" is spread among people, with leaders of a group selecting phonemes of the chanted line "She was a visitor" and the group sustaining each individual sound. The amassed sound, a "surface" of normalized little disturbances, in which an audience could also participate, begins to resemble airplanes, cars, trains—or perhaps the subatomic world. — *"Blue" Gene Tyranny*

Music Word Fire and I Would Do It Again: The Lessons / 1981 / Lovely Music

Available now in its full videotape form. Robert Ashley, Jill Kroesen, and David Van Tieghem (vocals), with prepared piano solos improvised by "Blue" Gene Tyranny, and instrumental and vocal percussion by Van Tieghem. "This may be the first—dazzling—use of variation form in rock and roll" (Gregory Sandow, *The Village Voice*). — *"Blue" Gene Tyranny*

Yellow Man with Heart with Wings (1978) / 1990 / Lovely Music

An inspired prose-poem in Spanish and English about agriculture and other perspectives and feelings that occur to people in cities and to those who live outside cities. Heart-lifting. — *"Blue" Gene Tyranny*

★ **Perfect Lives** / 1991 / Lovely Music

Available in CD and videotape, *Perfect Lives* is part of a trilogy of operas-for-TV including *Atalanta (Acts of God)* and *Now Eleanor's Idea* (a total of 39 half-hour episodes). *Perfect Lives* was realized for Channel Four of British Television. In this epic work set in the American Midwest, the rhythms of the music, the geometry of the scenes, the relations of the characters all seem to be from the same cloth, as if being described by the martyred first natural scientist Giordano Bruno, who is a "background" character never appearing in this work. For the characters who do appear, this is the basic plot: Raoul de Noget (No-zhay), a singer, and his friend Buddy, "The World's Greatest Piano Player," have come to a small town in the Midwest to entertain at the Perfect Lives Lounge. For some unexplained reason, they have fallen in with two people from the town, Isolde ("nearing 30 and not yet spoken for") and her brother, "D," just out of high school and known as "The Captain of the Football Team" (his parents call him Donnie), to commit the perfect crime (a metaphor for something philosophical): in this case, to remove a sizable amount of money from the bank for one day (one day only) and "let the whole world know it was missing." The seven episodes are "The Park (Privacy Rules)," "The Supermarket (Famous People)," "The Bank (Victimless Crime)," "The Bar (Differences)," "The Living Room (The Solutions)," "The Church (After the Fact)," and "The Backyard (T'Be Continued)." "*Perfect Lives* is nothing less than the first American opera" (Allan Evans, *Fanfare*). — *"Blue" Gene Tyranny*

● **In Sara Mencken Christ and Beethoven There Were Men and Women** / 1991 / Cramps

The text by the legendary John Barton Walgamot traces a hidden story of social progress underneath the gradual repetition, addition, and subtraction of names and organized variation of syntactical parts. The reading voice activates beautiful and humorous electronic sounds designed by composer Paul DeMarinis for this piece. — *"Blue" Gene Tyranny*

☆ **Don Leaves Linda (Improvement)** / 1992 / Elektra/Nonesuch

Don Leaves Linda, in a completely new sound for voices and an electronic orchestra, recalls the Spanish influence in America. By touching and genuinely humorous metaphorical incidents and characters, and a music that is equally intimate and dramatically universal, we are presented with a driving sense of the "eternal present." A masterpiece. — *"Blue" Gene Tyranny*

El / Aficionado / 1994 / Lovely Music

Described in the catalog as "incidences in the life and career of a person who has reason to believe himself to be an 'agent of the department,' featuring Thomas Buckner as The Agent and Jacqueline Humbert, Sam Ashley, and Robert Ashley as his interrogators," this new opera is a grand metaphor of the interior life of most of us who question our actions and thoughts at different times in our lives. Beautiful and mysterious electronic orchestrations by Ashley, working with composer Tom Hamilton. — *"Blue" Gene Tyranny*

Kenneth Atchley

b. 1954

Composer / Modern acoustic blues, electronic

○ **Don Giovanni, Act I, Scenes 1-4 / In "Anthology of Music for the 21st Century"** / 1991 / Leonardo Music Journal, Vol. 1 #1

A musical conversation with the characters of Da Ponte's libretto for Mozart's opera about the cultural myth of Don Juan and the history of our attitudes about sexuality (and "going to hell" for sharing sensual feeling). A subtle, surreal evocation for voices and electronics with a highly poetic and intelligent text by the composer. — *"Blue" Gene Tyranny*

6 House / In the collection "Views from the Imaginary City" / 1995 / Inial

The text is extracted from a much longer libretto about Nikola Tesla. The composer writes, "The inventor believed that human behavior could be described in scientific expressions, explained, and eventually predicted. This excerpt portrays a specific human relationship—a crush—in terms of phase relations. The work also provides a view of the relationship through the filter of

Duchamp's "Nude Descending a Staircase." With K. Atchley (vocal and electronics) and Mark Trayle (electric guitar solo). —*"Blue" Gene Tyranny*

Larry Austin

Hybrid Music: Four Compositions: Quadrants (Event/Complex No. 1/ Second Fantasy on Ives' Universe Symphony—The Heavens/ Catalogo Voce/ Maroon Bells for Voice and Tape / 1980 / Irida
A prolific composer of acoustic and electronic music, Austin's early music combined elements of jazz improvisation with advanced compositional techniques such as in his cantata for soprano and jazz at the University of California at Davis in 1963. Works composed in his "open style" include "Catharsis: Open Style for Two Improvisational Ensembles, Tape and Conductor" (1967) and the theater piece "The Maze" (1966) for percussionists, dancer, tape, and films. He later developed combinatoriale pieces, the "event/complexes" of the '70s, wrote fantasies for voice and the legendary *Source* magazine anthology of new music, and composed many other electro-acoustic works. His recent work with computers on the CDs above continues to combine electronics and acoustical instruments/voices by transforming with a sense of humor recognized historical material into "mini opera-buffas." —*"Blue" Gene Tyranny*

Montage: Themes and Variations for Violin and Computer Music on Tape (1985)/ In "CDCM Computer Music," Vol. 10 / 1985 / Centaur

Sinfonia Concertante: A Mozartean Episode (1988)/ In "CDCM Computer Music," Vol. 1 / 1988 / Centaur

Milton Babbitt

b. 1916
Composer / Classical, electronic, atonal-chromatic
American composer of 12-tone serial music; known for *Partitions* (1957) and *Three Compositions for Piano* (1947). —*AMG*

All Set, for Jazz Ensemble (1957) / 1990 / Elektra/Nonesuch
Formal writing for a jazz group, like experiments for other "progressive jazz" ensembles of the late '40s and '50s—the Sauter-Finegan Orchestra, the Stan Kenton Orchestra, and so forth. This is a piece of its decade, but still interesting. Other works on this CD are by other well-known formalist composers: George Rochberg (1918-), Lalo Schifrin (1932-), Richard Wernick (1934-), and Stefan Wolpe. —*"Blue" Gene Tyranny*

Correspondences for String Orchestra and Synthesizer Tape (1967) / In "Cage/Carter/Babbitt/Schuller" / 1994 / Deutsche Grammaphon
A fascinating classic of electro-acoustic illusions within a formalist style. —*"Blue" Gene Tyranny*

Tadeusz Baird

b. 1928, **d.** 1981
Atonal-chromatic

Psychodrama for Orchestra / Concert for Oboe and Orchestra / Scenes for Cello, Harp, and Orchestra / Canzona for Orchestra / Concer / 1993 / Koch
An interesting blend of dramatic Schunbergian romanticism, serial pointillism, and original orchestral colors written by a composer who went from a rather bland style of what was then imagined to be "people's music" to a radical change in the '60s. —*"Blue" Gene Tyranny*

Llorene Barber

Concierto de Campanas Sacra Lucus (The "sacra Lucus" Concerto for Church Bells) / 1992 / Unio Musics
Written for more than one hundred musicians located in 14 bell towers in Lugo, this astonishing piece, similar to many that Barber has presented in Spanish cities, was presented on June 8, 1991. All traffic ceased during the performance, and suddenly Lugo was transported back in time, as the persistent rhythm of the "Hymn of the Ancient Kingdom of Galicia," with the "Alabado sea el Santisimo" played simultaneously on a cathedral carrillon, began to ring from the outermost bell towers toward the center of the city, the queen tower of the cathedral. The sound is stunning, floating over the area like a sonorous "decibel net" or mystical blanket, or the humming of UFOs. The performers were

given chronometers and a precise time score for their various parts, which required pre-exercising for and strenuous playing during the 40-minute performance. Barber has recently gotten the Spanish navy to cooperate in a piece that uses modern battle cruisers, ancient frigates, cannon, and cathedrals on shore and again the involvement of an entire city for a performance. — *"Blue" Gene Tyranny*

Jean Barraque

b. 1928, **d.** 1973

... au dela du hasard (... beyond Mere Luck) (1959) for Four Instrumental Formations and a Vocal Formation / 1981 / Astree
Barraque was one of the first serialists with a unique style that combined a rich impressionism and extremely formal pointillism. His beautiful "Sonate pour Piano" (1950-1952) (recorded by Claude Helffer on Astre AS 36, out-of-print disc) was praised by jazz critic Andre Hodeir in an early book. This praise and Barraque's use of jazz instrumentalists (playing his serial music) sitting together with classic ensembles led to Barraque being stigmatized socially. This was the late '50s. "... au dela du hasard," like "Chant apres Chant" (1966) for six percussionists, voice, and piano, was inspired by Hermann Broch's poem "The Death of Virgil," not merely setting the text, but reflecting upon it. The titles of the movements will give some idea of this impulse—"The light without rays," "Unable to evolve or regress," "Which ephemeral signs?" "Abusive exaggerations," "In the wandering multitude," "For the unknown edge of chance," "Before the quotation," "Blinded by the dream (quotation)," "Beyond the direct line of sight," "On a thought without night." —*"Blue" Gene Tyranny*

○ **Le Temps Restitu (1968), excerpt from "La Mort de Virgile" (The Death of Virgil) by Hermann Broch** / 1987 / Harmonia Mundi
A work similar in many aspects to "...au dela du hasard," although more in the pointillistic serial style. Beautiful performance by mezzo-soprano Anne Bartelloni. On the same CD is the virtuosic "Concerto" (1962-1968) for alternating trios of instruments (violin-bassoon-trumpet, violoncello-flute-tenor saxophone, and others). —*"Blue" Gene Tyranny*

Louis and Bebe Barron

Group / Electronic
Wrote electronic music for film. The Barrons also assisted John Cage in making "Williams Mix." —*"Blue" Gene Tyranny*

Forbidden Planet (1954) / 1989 / Planet Records
The first Hollywood filmscore to use electronic music (the first all-electronic soundtrack was for Anais Nin's *The Bells of Atlantis* in 1952). The sound results from cybernetic (controlled feedback) circuitry, especially designed by the Barrons, producing Krells and monsters from the Id. — *"Blue" Gene Tyranny*

Martin Bartlett

b. 1939

Pythagoras' Ghost / 1993 / Front
The title piece on this CD is for four electronic wind instruments and contains sections that are lighthearted, even goofy in their sense of humor ("Akousmata—ear whisperings," "Xenomelophilia—love of strange melodies"), one movement of elegant transparency ("Chromopneuma—breath colours"), and a tiny pedantic march ("Gymnosophia—naked philosophies or nude philosophers"). My favorite work is "The Arrival of Sir John Franklin in Paradise" (1988) for a wonderful variety of synthesized sounds surrounding and supporting Bartlett's chanting and sometimes electronically modified voice on texts from Dante. A composer with a definitely original manner. —*"Blue" Gene Tyranny*

David Behrman

b. 1937
Electronic

○ **On the Other Ocean / Figure in a Clearing** / 1977 / Lovely Music
Subtle, sustained, serene. Electronics with flute, bassoon, cello soloists. Innovative interactive performance setup and a beautiful listening experience. —*"Blue" Gene Tyranny*

Leapday Night / 1990 / Lovely Music
Several pieces with computer-aided interactive electronics and improvising musicians on mutatrumpet, trumpets, keyboards, violin. With Takehisa Kosugi, Ben Neill, Rhys Chatham. Warm, beautiful, and gently humorous. — *"Blue" Gene Tyranny*

☆ **Unforeseen Events** / 1992 / Experimental Intermedia
Beautiful interactive computer music with Ben Neill, mutatrumpet. Contains: *Unforeseen Events* with four sections: "View Finder," a canon with gradually more ornate response to what the trumpeter is playing; "Fishing for Complements," a trio for computer, mutatrumpet, and a listener to the interchange who enters changes into the computer on a silent keyboard as the music progresses from simple repeating figures to hundreds of rapidly cascading sounds; "Witch Grass," more complex figures with sustained computer chords gradually slipping away from their tonal centers; and "Canyon," a cerebral canyon with shadowy trains of pitch-shifted chords; "Refractive Light," in which tonal changes occur as "deflections" at the on-and-off edges of overlapping events, has three sections: "Harbinger," "Crisscrossed Eights," and "Ein Glaesele Warems." — *"Blue" Gene Tyranny*

Jacques Bekaert

Summer Music 1970 / 1977 / Lovely Music
12 musical portraits, vignettes in sound with various instrumentalists performing verbal-instruction scores. Varied and charming. At the time of this recording, Bekaert was the voice of the legendary "King Kong" new music radio show for Radio Belgium. — *"Blue" Gene Tyranny*

Luciano Berio

b. 1925
Composer / Classical, electronic, atonal-chromatic
Italian composer of 12-tone and electronic music in most genres, including ballet, vocal, and piano music. —*AMG*

Coro for 40 Voices and 40 Instruments (1976) / 1991 / Deutsche Grammaphon
Performed by the Cologne Symphony Orchestra and Chorus conducted by the composer. Probably Berio's masterpiece in his romantic-pointillism style. — *"Blue" Gene Tyranny*

Johanna Magdelena Beyer

b. 1888, **d.** 1984
Electronic, atonal-chromatic

IV for Percussion (1935) / 1991 / Aerial #3
Performed by Essential Music. Percussion music for nine unspecified (!) instruments, completely unique but appeals to a fundamental feeling. Beyer was involved in much new-music activity but her personal life remains a mystery, her music still largely unperformed. (See *New Music for Electronic and Recorded Media in 20th-Century Collections* in this section.) — *"Blue" Gene Tyranny*

The Bifurcators

Gang of Two / 1995 / Artifact
A new great group with composers Philip Perkins (bowed bass, electronic noisemakers, computers) and Scott Fraser (electric guitar) plus, for this CD, performers Bonnie Barnett (vocals), Tim Perkis (computer), and Doug Carroll (electric cello). Includes: "The Rose Window," inspired by the stained-glass windows of Notre Dame (Paris), for guitar, computers, sampler, and other sound-makers; "White Eagles," a sparse, elegiac work in memory of the Bosnian war dead; "A New Work," a live performance over phone lines to the group improvisation about slowness and inexorability where electronics "shadow" the players like the optical illusion of a steady shadow appearing to move; the performers may or may not "go along with it." — *"Blue" Gene Tyranny*

John Bischoff

b. 1949
Electronic

Next Tone Please / Frog Peak Music
Six subtle and mysterious electronic compositions by this legendary Bay Area composer. See also his "Rendezvous" in *Just for the Record.* — *"Blue" Gene Tyranny*

Rendezvous (1978)/ In "Just for the Record" / 1981 /

Melodic phrases that "sometime go their own separate ways, sometimes drifting apart and at other times coordinating together." Multi-timbral synthesizer sounds suggest an underlying surreal story. — *"Blue" Gene Tyranny*

○ **Artificial Horizon (with Tim Perkis) (1951)** / 1989 / Artifact
Wonderful collaborative and individual compositions for personal computer systems. Includes: "Touch Typing," "Next Tone, Please," "Engagement," "Dovetail," "Artificial Horizon," "Clicks," "Clavitron 6000," "Audio Wave," "Happy Trails." See also *The Hub.* — *"Blue" Gene Tyranny*

The Glass Hand/ In CDCM Computer Music, Vol. 17 / 1994 / Centaur
An eletronically generated live performance piece where "unwanted artifacts," or "low-level synthesizer behaviors" are highlighted, revealing "in a poetic way the often hidden nature of electronic instruments." Mysterious and fascinating. — *"Blue" Gene Tyranny*

Bob and Bob

Across America (1981) / M.I.T.B. Records
A wonderful record as well as a "document" of a performance art piece: poetry and comments and stories from a crosscountry journey. You may also want to follow up with their band record *We Know You're Alone* backed with *We've Been Seeing Things* on Polygram/Polydor Records (New York, 12-inch EP disc, 1983). And one of them, The Dark Bob, has also made *One Bob Job* (includes "Outside of Moab", "The List," "Interstate") (1982, one-sided 12-inch LP) and *Kabbalamobile* (cassette, from soundtrack of theater work), all available from M.I.T.B. Records. — *"Blue" Gene Tyranny*

Lars-Gunnar Bodin

b. 1935
Electronic

For Jon (Fragments of a Time to Come) (1977) / 1978 / Folkways
An out-of-print disc well worth searching for. A "surrealistic science fiction," even cyberpunk (the term wasn't in wide usage at the time) cantata for narrator, chamber choir, and electronics with the text processed through and triggering the electronics. Reflects Bodin's continuing concern with concepts connected with modern science and technology, and the role of art in a post-revolutionary (Marcusean sense) society. — *"Blue" Gene Tyranny*

○ **Anima (1984)/ In "Computer Music Currents 7"** / 1990 / Wergo
A brief work perfectly depicting a profound psychic process—the unification of consciousness with the higher self. The human voice (soprano) hears its counterpart in the computer voice, and gradually the two merge throughout the course of the piece. Beautiful. — *"Blue" Gene Tyranny*

David Borden/Mother Mallard

Continuing Story of Counterpoint, Parts 9-12 (1976-1987), The / 1988 / Cuneiform
Influenced by pattern music, Borden's music nevertheless has its own character made from rich layers of free-wheeling solos over the patterns with some very lovely textures. The structure of the music is built on composer and performer names and birthdates in an elevated soap-opera structure. Performed by Mother Mallard's Portable Masterpiece Co., a well-known 1970's East Coast synthesizer group with Borden, Linda Fisher, and Steve Drews. See also "Double Portrait" in Double Edge's *U.S. Choice.* — *"Blue" Gene Tyranny*

Double Portrait (1987) / In Double Edge "U.S. Choice" / 1992
Influenced by other pattern music composers (Glass, Reich, Riley), Borden's music nevertheless has its own character made from rich layers of free-wheeling solos over the patterns with some very lovely textures. The structure of the music is built on composer and performer names and birthdates in an elevated soap opera structure. Performed by Mother Mallard's Portable Masterpiece Co., a well-known East Coast synthesizer group in the early 1970s (original members: David Borden, Linda Fisher, Steve Drews), which used many modern techniques in its pieces

from chance procedures to pattern music and various forms of improvisation. — *"Blue" Gene Tyranny*

Linda Bouchard

b. 1957

Black Burned Wood / In Dora Ohrenstein's "Urban Diva" / 1993 / CRI

An accomplished composer of more than 50 works in various genres from opera to chamber works, Bouchard has created an intense song concerning a mysterious girl, Sara, running through woods, obsessed, who may have murdered her parents. See also Bouchard's "Lung Ta" for string quartet in *Bang on a Can, Vol. 3.* — *"Blue" Gene Tyranny*

Andre Boucourechliev

Ombres (Shades) (Hommage a Beethoven) / EMI

Performed by the National Chamber Orchestra of Toulouse, directed by Louis Auriacombe. Recordings of Boucourechliev's music are difficult to find but well worth the effort. This is an "hommage" to the Father of Modern Music. Beethoven's Third Symphony *Eroica* and sometimes other works are often credited with being the first modernist compositions, partly because they were built from small "kernels" of ideas rather than as variations on full melodies, and also because the music did not need outside references to justify it. Instead of falling for the rather obvious idea of collaging Beethoven's works, Boucourechliev creates an impression of the "interior" nature of Beethoven's democratic and universal pieces. This is difficult to put in words, but is something like the "feeling" you have left after the music has ended.. This is a transcendental and sustained piece, unique in character. — *"Blue" Gene Tyranny*

Pierre Boulez

b. 1925
Composer / Classical, atonal-chromatic

French composer and conductor whose music includes elements of serialism and the aleatoric. Boulez conducted the New York Symphony Orchestra from 1971 to 1978. — *AMG*

○ **Improvisations Sur Mallarma (Improvisations on Mallarma) I & II (1957) for Soprano and Instrumental Ensemble /** Hungaroton

This composition, together with "Le Marteau sans Maitre (The Hammer without a Master)," established the particular sound of Boulez's approach to serialist composition, a poetic pointillism with a Debussyian sense of timbres that has characterized most of his works and is more interesting than most of the later, rather arid pieces that followed it. This CD also contains two lovely classics of 12-tone music (upon which serialism is based), Arnold Schoenberg's *Pierrot Lunaire, op. 21* (1912) and Anton Webern's *5 Canons on Latin Texts, for Soprano and Instrumental Ensemble, op. 16* (1923-1924), plus two of his songs. — "Blue" Gene Tyranny

Structures Pour Deux Pianos (Livre I, 1952; Livre II, 1961) / 1992 / Wergo

A reissue of the marvelously accurate and colorful performances by the great Alfons and Aloys Kontarsky. — *"Blue" Gene Tyranny*

Paul Bowles

b. 1910
Spoken word, world music derivative

○ **Voices of Paul Bowles, The / Tellus #23**

Audio portrait on cassette of the author/composer with stories, selected works, early compositions (*Music for a Farce, Interlude and Prelude* #2, long unavailable), and environmental recordings made near his Moroccan home. In a library you may still find his wonderful pieces *A Picnic Cantata* (1955) for four women's voices, two pianos, and percussion (including a milk bottle and cigar box) (Columbia LP with pianists Gold and Fizdale); *The Wind Remains* (1943) (an opera based on an abstraction of the third act of Garcia Lorca's "Asi que pasen cinco anos") (MGM Records disc E3549; also contains composer Peggy Glanville-Hick's "Letters from Morocco," which are settings of texts by Bowles). — *"Blue" Gene Tyranny*

Black Star at the Point of Darkness / 1992 / Psalmodia Sub Rosa

A wonderful sound and soul journey featuring the voice of Paul Bowles reading narrations and poems, his recordings of ritual Moroccan music, and the six Preludes for piano. — *"Blue" Gene Tyranny*

Glenn Branca

Composer, guitar

New York classical-punk, composes loud modernist symphonies. — *John Dougan*

○ **Symphony No. 1 (Tonal Plexus) / 1983 / Roir**

Music for Peter Greenaway's Film "The Belly of an Architect" (1987) / 1987 / Les Disques Du Crepescule

A different light-music for string orchestra with the gradually sliding tone-densities of the guitar music transferred to orchestral strings for some of the best moments in the score. — *"Blue" Gene Tyranny*

Symphony No. 6 (Devil Choirs at the Gates of Heaven) for 10 guitars, keyboard, bass, drums / 1989 / Blast First

Studies in gradually denser sonorities ("resultant masses") with a rock-steady pulse, this music digs deep into the mind/feeling to elicit bardo-like sensations often approached by the profoundest Buddhist chant. (Cage and Branca once had a disagreement about Branca's music being "fascist." Cage argued that densities creating a "sustained climax" restrict the mind from opening up. I doubt that fascists would like these symphonies.) — *"Blue" Gene Tyranny*

Henry Brant

b. 1913
Atonal-chromatic, world music derivative

Orbits (1979), A Spatial Symphonic Ritual for 80 Trombones, Organ, and Sopranino Voice / CRI

Played by the Bay Bones Trombone Choir with Brant (organ), Amy Snyder (vocal), and conducted by Gerhard Samuel. One of Brant's most ambitious spatial pieces: sounds accelerate in a circular motion ascending the cupola of St. Mary's Cathedral in San Francisco. His enormous multispatial work *Meteor Farm* (1982), which requires a symphony, two choruses, jazz band, Javanese gamelan, West African drummers and singers, Western percussion groups and two sopranos, has not yet been recorded. — *"Blue" Gene Tyranny*

☆ **Angels and Devils for Flute and Flute Orchestra (1932, revised 1947) / 1991 / Centaur**

Played by the Eastman Wind Ensemble. Brant is the composer who reintroduced spatial distribution as a parameter of musical expression, such as it was in Gabrieli's time. This is Brant's classic work of "spatial music" for 14 flutes with performers standing on ladders or on different levels. — *"Blue" Gene Tyranny*

Ghost Nets (1988) / 1992 / AmCam

Spatial narratives for double bass solo and two separated instrumental groups. Lewis Paar, double bass. This CD also includes Gordin Cyr's "String Quartet #2" (1983). — *"Blue" Gene Tyranny*

Anthony Braxton

b. Jun. 4, 1945, Chicago, IL
Sax, composer / Modern creative, cool
See the Jazz section for his biography.

Four Compositions 1982-1988 / 1990 / Hat Art

☆ **Composition No. 107 (excerpt, 1982) / In CDCM Computer Music Series, Vol. 10 / 1991 / Centaur**

A "dry and glass-like sound universe" punctuated with high-energy improvisation. Excellent performances. Braxton has taken the "graph score" to a new level for his compositions, which involve a combination of spontaneous and charted playing, and has extended his imagination into the future, like Charles Ives in his "Universe Symphony" to be played from mountaintops, to pieces to be played from planet to planet. — *"Blue" Gene Tyranny*

Composition 98 / 1991 / Hat Art

Composition #165 for 18 Instruments / 1992 / Hat Art

Excellent solo and ensemble pieces. — *"Blue" Gene Tyranny*

Two Lines / 1995 / Lovely Music

An excellent CD by two excellent composer/performers. The pre-issue listeners have described it as "very ... very ... fast." See also the CDCM Computer Music Series for other Braxton/Rosenboom performances in each other's compositions. —*"Blue" Gene Tyranny*

Earle Brown

b. 1926
Minimalism

○ **Times Five (1963) / Octet 1 (1953) / December (1952)/ Novara (1962) / CRI**
Elegant kaleidoscopic mobiles for various instrumental combinations and electronics read from various original graphic scores. Brown is one of the composers of The New York School (along with Cage, Feldman, and Wolff) who radically altered our concepts of the freedom possible in music. —*"Blue" Gene Tyranny*

Available Forms II/ In "New Music" / 1968 / RCA Victrola
Ethereally beautiful performance, conducted by Bruno Maderna. The score is constructed in blocks of music ("available forms") that the conductor cues and guides with various signals, like an engineer with tracks of recorded material to mix. A combination of spontaneous music making and precomposed intentions that works well. Enthusiasts may also want to check out his "Four Systems for Four Amplified Cymbals" (1964) in *Electronics and Percussion*, with Max Neuhaus on percussion (Columbia MS 7139 disc, currently out-of-print). —*"Blue" Gene Tyranny*

Folio (1952/1953) / Music for Cello and Piano (1954)/ In "The New York School" / 1993 / Hat Hut
Two classic works by Brown, including four realizations of the famous multidimensional graph score "Folio." —*"Blue" Gene Tyranny*

Leif Brush

Terrain Instruments Are Activated (1990) / 1992 / The Aerial #4
Since 1968, Leif Brush has made sound installations and performances in galleries and public places around the world using his Terrain instruments: Minnesota Permanent Forest Terrain, Signal Disc, Whistler, Wind Ribbons, Rainpattern Tree Filters, Treeharps Networking, Modified Treeways—and an array of transducers (solar-powered sensor amplifiers connected to microprocessors controlled and updated by telephone) and speaker-environments that amplify and articulate natural phenomena. Mysterious and beautiful. —*"Blue" Gene Tyranny*

Gavin Bryars

b. 1943
Percussion / Minimalism
A percussionist and bandleader who's worked with many top European jazz musicians. Byars has had two albums issued on ECM in the late '80s and early '90s. —*Ron Wynn*

First Viennese Dance (M.H.) (1985-1986)/ In "Three Viennese Dancers" / 1986 /
Scored for French horn and percussion, this ethereal, slowly unfolding music is different from Bryar's other "sound" of jauntingly repeating, minimally changing chords that he shares with Michael Nyman. M.H. Mata Hari, the famous World War One spy and one of three famed dancers in Vienna in late 1906. —*"Blue" Gene Tyranny*

Jesus' Blood Never Failed Me Yet / 1993 / Point
Six realizations for orchestra and the gravelly old man's voice of Tim Waits (who sounds very much like the original tape-recorded voice of a street singer used in the earlier Obscure Records recording of this piece). Each realization shows Bryar's gift for invention and variation and simple, appealing emotionality. A very touching and beautiful recording of nearly 75 minutes' duration. Highly recommended. —*"Blue" Gene Tyranny*

Warren Burt

Of Course / Anyway You Can Always Put Language Down to Experience (with Chris Mann) /
This 77-minute piece comes on a cassette accompanied by a plastic glove and a red rock from Australia, but no liner notes. Needless to say, a strange electronic piece with the natural voice as a "trigger." —*"Blue" Gene Tyranny*

Sylvano Bussotti

b. 1931

Rara Requiem / Bergkristall / Lorenzaccio Symphony, The / 1992 / Duetsche Grammaphon
As a talented graphic artist, Bussotti has made some of the most amazing looking graph scores, like the famous "Five Pieces for David Tudor," a score made in 1959 from a drawing made in 1949. Lines run in every direction, there are wild squiggles and vortices, small icons of imaginary characters, laconic word phrases of equal import as the other symbols, formless dark areas. Likewise, the score for "Coeur pour Batteur" in Max Neuhaus's out-of-print Columbia 7139 disc *Electronics and Percussion* is as defined as it is open (synaesthetically) to subjective readings by the performer. In this recording, Neuhaus divides the score into spatial directions for unusual body movements that result in sounds, together with inadvertent body movements, and instruments set up to sympathetically vibrate out of the control of the performer. In Bussotti's later works heard in this two CD reissue of recordings from 1976 and 1978, Bussotti's approach is more traditional in procedure but not in sound: "Bergkristall" is a ballet in one act and seven scenes based on a tale by Adalbert Stifter of a young boy and girl who get lost in a snowstorm on Christmas Day while returning home from the valley where their grandparents live in the dyeworks. Following the spirit of a baker's boy who had once become lost, they wander off toward the "regions of eternal ice." Nature takes on supernatural forms— snow spirits, comets— which dance with the children to keep them awake (together with their mouthfuls of coffee), and in the morning the children are rescued as the sun "burns like fire over the vast expanses of snow and glittering quartz as though a mass of roses were shining." The music is presented often in brief "illustrations," as dense (in a good sense) as multicolored drawings in a children's book. The Christmas tree decorations, the dancing spirits, the icy dissonance. If Charles Ives had decided to write with serialistic gestures and sounds, the result would probably be close to this unusual and exciting score. —*"Blue" Gene Tyranny*

Christopher Butterfield

Music for Klein and Beuys (1987) / Pillar of Snails (1984-1987) / 1993 / Not for Sale (Musicworks)
Highly original chamber music ("Music for Klein and Beuys") by this Canadian composer with snatches of delightful tunelike passages that are somewhat more like melodic gestures, brief responses, bon mots to the accompaniment of percussion that often sounds like amplified crumpled bags. But it's not "joke music". It's something else. "Pillar of Snails" is a piano piece that begins with single unharmonized melodic line statements separated by an appropriate silence, and gradually glorious chords are added but only briefly as a shading. The title refers to a tower or pillar, a massive black basalt cube that once sat on a pedestal but has now fallen and is half-submerged in a marsh in a mausoleum on a hill (The Spindles) in the once ancient Phoenician port of Amrit in what is now Syria. This CD is literally not for sale but came included in a package from the Canadian Musicworks magazine, who may still have some. Butterfield also excellently performs Kurt Schwitter's "Ursonate" (Sonate in Urlauten) on this CD. —*"Blue" Gene Tyranny*

Michael Byron

b. Sep. 7, 1953

○ **Marimbas in the Dorian Mode/ In "Cold Blue Anthology" / 1990 / Cold Blue Records**
Unusual fluttering sounds from four marimbas played in a sustained and very quiet manner—absolutely peaceful. If you run across one, grab a copy of the lovely orchestral pieces on *Tidal* on the defunct Neutral Records. —*"Blue" Gene Tyranny*

George Cacioppo

b. Sep. 24, 1927, d. Apr. 4, 1984

☆ **Time on Time in Miracles/ In "Music from the ONCE Festival" / 1966 / Advance**
Cacioppo produced some remarkably original ensemble music—the graph score based directly on the form of the constellation "Cassiopeia"; "Two Worlds" (1962), which contrasts the worlds of instrumental and vocal sounds; "Advance of the Fungii," based on

ideas in the book by E. C. Large, which describes various plagues that overwhelm plants and animals from time to time; and "Bestiary 1 Eingang. Several works generated pitches and overall form based on Markov chains. — *"Blue" Gene Tyranny*

John Cage

b. 1912, Los Angeles, CA, d. Aug. 12, 1992
Composer / Electronic, minimalism
American composer of avant-garde music based on non-Western philosophy and employing aleatoric, electronic, and prepared instruments. Known for "4'33"" (1952), "HPSCHD" (1969), and "Imaginary Landscape no. 1" (1939). —*AMG*

Etudes Boreales (1978) / Ryoanji (1983) / 1985 / Mode
One of the most beautiful albums of Cage's music: wonderful silences, no sense of pulse, perfectly played gestures on piano, cello with mezzo-soprano vocal, peaceful, eternal. Highly recommended. — *"Blue" Gene Tyranny*

☆ **Empty Words (Part III, Live Teatro Lyrico Di Milano 2 Dec. 1977)** / 1991 / Cramps
Cage reading a gradually fragmenting text based on Thoreau's "Walden Pond," this heartwarming piece shows how Cage's chance procedures serve to enhance, rather than distance, human feeling and attention. The entire *Empty Words* (Parts I-IV) on 8 CDs will be issued in the near future by Lovely Music. — *"Blue" Gene Tyranny*

"John Cage": Music for Marcel Duchamp (1947) / Music for Amplified Toy Pianos (1960) / Radio Music (1956) / 4'33" in Three Parts / 1991 / Cramps
Wonderful performances by composer/performers Hidalgo, Marchetti, Simonetti, and Stratos of these well-known pieces, including the famous "silent piece" (4'33") in three parts. — *"Blue" Gene Tyranny*

☆ **Singing Through/ Vocal Compositions by John Cage** / 1991 / New Albion
Beautifully performed pieces from 1942-1985 by vocalist Joan LaBarbara with piano and percussion. Contains: "A Flower" (1950), "Mirakus" (1984), "Eight Whiskus" (1984), "The Wonderful Widow of 18 Springs" (1942) for voice and closed piano, "Nowth upon Nacht" (1984), "Sonnekus" (1985), "Forever and Sunsmell" (1942), "Solos for Voice (from the Songbooks) #'s 49, 52, 67" (1970), "Music for Two (by One)" (1984). — *"Blue" Gene Tyranny*

Music for Merce Cunningham: Five Stone Wind (Collaboration with David Tudor and Takehisa Kosugi) / Cartridge Music (1960) Realizat / 1991 / Mode
Amplified violin, bamboo flute, nine clay pots, tapes, and live electronics. The spirit of gentle indeterminancy. "Cartridge Music" is a classic of graph music for phonograph cartridges and amplified small objects. — *"Blue" Gene Tyranny*

Cheap Imitation / 1991 / Cramps
With the composer at the piano. A lovely performance of melodies that are fragments and transformations of melodies for Erik Satie's opera *Socrate* on the death of Socrates. Cage had to produce "cheap imitations" of these melodies for a performance when the rights for the Satie score could not be obtained. — *"Blue" Gene Tyranny*

Diary: How to Improve the World (You Will Only Make Matters Worse) / 1992 / Wergo
An 8-CD set of brilliant observations, from the humorous to the speculative to the heart-filling. Cage speaks of lives and notions of the well-known—B. Fuller, Thoreau, the Vietnam War, Meister Eckhart, Schoenberg; being crammed in a subway car and odd confrontations with airplane employees; of unique and everyday events—unemployment, free worldwide communications, dads and moms, electric clothing, workable anarchy. The typography determines the stereo distribution and level of Cage's voice, the effect of someone talking inside your head, disembodied. (The printed texts additionally used color changes to parallel this effect.) Some of the text, pictures of Cage reading and the clean water supply, and chronologies accompany the discs. — *"Blue" Gene Tyranny*

Fontana Mix and Solo for Voice 2 / 1993 / Hat Hut
Three parts of the classic tape music piece "Fontana Mix" are superimposed while the "Solo for Voice 2" is performed simultaneously with them. When certain pieces employed the same chance operations or other similar methods in their composition, Cage would often specify in the score that they could be played at the same time. — *"Blue" Gene Tyranny*

Indeterminancy, New Aspect of Form in Instrumental and Electronic Music / 1993 / Smithsonian/Folkways
A CD reissue of the legendary early '60s discs in which Cage relates enlightening and entertaining stories from his life, from ancient texts, from secondhand sources and spontaneous insight, while pieces composed using indeterminant procedures are performed on piano and live electronics by David Tudor. Essential for an understanding of Cage at the root level. (It's OK that the voice is obscured at times.) — *"Blue" Gene Tyranny*

Concert for Piano and Orchestra / Atlas Eclipticalis / 1993 / Wergo
This has got to be one of the finest recordings of Cage's music ever. The careful consideration given to musical and sonic details by The Orchestra of the S.E.M. Ensemble with conductor Petr Kotik and the wonderful performance of piano soloist Joseph Kubera finally makes understandable in sound Cage's philosophical and poetical insights. In the performance of "Atlas Eclipticalis," for example, we finally hear the ongoing universe of stars, planets, solar winds, and asteroids (etc.) much as Cage may have imagined a performance of his work. These musicians play the music with respect, accuracy, and a more than ordinary sense of what is beautiful. — *"Blue" Gene Tyranny*

Alison Cameron

Alison Cameron / 1995 / Experimental Intermedia
A premiere CD of compositions for chamber ensemble by this innovative Canadian composer. Includes: "Runa" for viola, bassoon, sax, piano, electric piano, and percussion; "Raw Sangudo" for alto sax, C trumpet, and tuba; "Blank Sheet of Metal" for three electric guitars, keyboards, bass, piano, organ, tuba, and percussionists; "Gibbous Moon" for baroque quartet; and "Chamber of Statues" for violin, bass clarinet, French horn, bass, piano, and percussion. — *"Blue" Gene Tyranny*

Cornelius Cardew

b. May 7, 1936, d. Dec. 13, 1981
☆ **Memorial Concert 16th May 1982: First Movement for String Quartet / Octet '71 / Treatise / The Great Learning no. 1 and Other Pieces** / Gelbe Musik
A retrospective of this musically and morally influential British composer's work played by his composer-friends Bryars, Nyman, Dave Smith, John White, John Tilbury, Rzewski, Tom Philips, Christopher Hobbs, Balanescu, Janos Negyesy, and members of the "Scratch Orchestra," a collective performing group for musicians and non-musicians that Cardew cofounded in 1969. In their constitution draft they stated that "the word music is here not understood to refer exclusively to sound (but) is flexible and depends entirely on the members." (See "Scratch Music," edited by C.C., M.I.T. Press, MIT 239, paperback issued 1974.) — *"Blue" Gene Tyranny*

Wendy (Walter) Carlos

b. 1939
Synthesizer / Electronic
Carlos stirred popular interest in synthesizer music with her *Switched-On Bach* recordings, and continues to explore the possibilities of electronic music. —*AMG*

Secrets of Synthesis / CBS
More than just a demonstration disc on electronic music, the examples are original creations from her own works, from the bestselling "Switched-On Bach" to "Digital Moonscapes," and contain extremely interesting theories and a new procedure for harmonic synthesis that results in sounds never heard before. (There's an interesting article on this with a floppy disc demo in *Keyboard*, November,1986.) — *"Blue" Gene Tyranny*

Elliott Carter

b. 1908
Composer / Classical, Atonal-chromatic
American composer influenced by Hindemith, Stravinsky, and Varese. His compositions include ballets, chamber pieces (*First Quartet*, 1951), and symphonic works (*A Symphony of Three Orchestras*, 1976). —*AMG*

○ **String Quartet no. 3 (1971)/ Elegy (1943)/ In "The Music for String Quartet, Vol. II"** / 1988 / Etcetera
Amazing performances by the renown Arditti String Quartet. Pieces that illustrate the best of his early and later styles.. Particularly noteworthy are the dense "abstract expressionist" complexity of the third quartet—instrumental conversations—and the unpredictable but warm, advanced-Coplandesque harmonies of the "Elegy." —*"Blue" Gene Tyranny*

Holiday Overture (1944, Revised 1961) / Suite from Pocahontas / Syringa / 1991 / CRI
Reissues of Carter in his early style. Sweeping energetic performance of the "Holiday Overture." —*"Blue" Gene Tyranny*

Variations for Orchestra (1954-1955)/ In "Cage/Carter/Babbitt/Schuller" / 1994 / Deutsche Grammaphon
The shocking classic that was a signal of Carter's change into a radically new American serialist style. —*"Blue" Gene Tyranny*

Joseph Celli

b. 1944
World music derivative

No World Improvisations / 1992 /
Virtuoso solo and duo improvisations with Jin Hi Kim (b. 1956) (Korean komungo, changgo, and electric komungo) and Celli (Indian Mukha Veena, English horn without reeds, and Yamaha WX-7 MIDI-breath controller). Wonderful. —*"Blue" Gene Tyranny*

No World (Trio) Improvisations / 1992 / O.O. Discs
Imaginative group improvs by Joseph Celli (double reeds), and Jin Hi Kim (komungo and electric komungo), in trio format with different guest soloists, including Alvin Curran (electronics), Shelley Hirsch (voice), and Malcolm Goldstein (violin). —*"Blue" Gene Tyranny*

Sky: S for J (1976) for Five English Horns Without Reeds / In "Organic Oboe" / 1992 / O.O. Discs
New and startling techniques for the English horn. —*"Blue" Gene Tyranny*

Joel Chadabe

b. 1938
Electronic

Modalities/ In CDCM Computer Music Series, Vol. 7 / 1990 / Centaur
Gamelan-like, peaceful. —*"Blue" Gene Tyranny*

Rhys Chatham

b. Sep. 19, 1952

Die Donnergoetter (The Thundergods) (1984-1986) for 6 Electric Guitars, Bass, and Drums / Waterloo, no. 2 (1986) for Solo Percussion / Homestead Records
Rhys merges both pattern rock-influenced riffs (like Peter Gordon) and dense sonorities (like Glenn Branca) to produce music of an extended time sense—with imagery of thundergods, Waterloo complete with the requisite drums and massed trumpets, and the '60s rock trio. —*"Blue" Gene Tyranny*

John Chowning

b. Aug. 22, 1934, Salem, NJ
Composer / Electronic
An American composer of computer music at Stanford University. —*AMG*

☆ **Phone (1980-1981) / Turenas (1972) / Stria (1977)/ Sabelithe (1971)** / 1988 / Wergo
Lyrical and sophisticated FM synthesis computer music with mysterious and surprising psychoacoustic illusions (especially found in "Turenas," the first piece to create the impression of sound sources moving in a 360-degree space). —*"Blue" Gene Tyranny*

Henning Christiansen

b. 1932
Composer / Minimalism
A composer who uses normal instruments and noises and who also makes art objects in the Fluxus tradition: e.g., his "Betrayal, op. 144," a carton filled with various small objects and an EP,

signed and numbered (available from Gelbe Musik). —*"Blue" Gene Tyranny*

Abschiedssymphonie (Farewell Symphony) (1985) / 1985 / Edition Block
The Farewell Symphony was composed for the opening of the Friedensbiennale (Freedom Biennale) in Hamburg, 1985, and is played by artists Joseph Beuys, Nam June Paik, and Christiansen. For further listening try the LPs *Fluxid: Hoehlenmonat* ("A Month in a Hole"); *Concerto for Flute and Noises; Fressmonat* ("A Month of Devouring"); *Concerto for Sax, Cello, and Noises; Fluxyl: Koenig Frost* ("King Frost"); *Concerto for Oboe and Noises; Maskenmonat* ("A Month of Disguises"); *Concerto for Trumpet, Tuba, and Noises* (available from Gelbe Musik). —*"Blue" Gene Tyranny*

Ornette Coleman

b. Mar. 9, 1930, Fort Worth, TX
Alto sax, composer / Early free, jazz-fusion
See the Jazz section for his biography.

☆ **Forms and Sounds** / Bluebird
Legendary as the performer/composer who freed jazz from the harmony and songforms of Tin Pan Alley ballads, these pieces show more of Coleman's path since his densely chromatic orchestral piece "Skies of America" (some movements are entitled "Holiday for Heroes," "Place in Space," "Foreigner in a Free Land," "Sunday in America").This CD includes "Forms and Sounds" (played by The Philadelphia Woodwind Quartet): densities of melodies alternately freely floating or played to an automaton pulse with commentary-like to bluesy to celebratory trumpet interludes played by Coleman—calls to reconsider life; "Saints and Soldiers": repression by the religious and political contrasted with saintly discernment; "Space Flight": flashes of unidentified fluttering things that suddenly disappear (performed by The Chamber Symphony of Philadelphia String Quartet). —*"Blue" Gene Tyranny*

Trinity/ In Malcolm Goldstein's "Sounding the New Violin" / What Next?
Fragments of melodies—joyous to contemplative to spontaneously exploring. —*"Blue" Gene Tyranny*

Nicolas Collins

b. 1954
Electronic

100 of the World's Most Beautiful Melodies / 1989 / Trace Elements
Played by an all-star "downtown" group: Nicolas Collins, Pippin Barnett, Anthony Coleman, Tom Cora, Peter Cusack, Shelley Hirsch, George Lewis, Christian Marclay, Ben Neill, Zeena Parkins, Robert Poss, Ned Rothenberg, Elliott Sharp, Davey Williams, John Zorn, and Peter Zummo. A tongue-in-cheek title, perhaps, depending on your idea of "beautiful melody." Ranges from electronically and physically modified instruments with a definite "edge" to the barely perceptible, and awakes the ear. Collins is also part of the Impossible Music group (with David Weinstein, David Shea, Ted Greenwald, and Tim Spelios) who, performing live, manipulate CD players in the spirit of Plunderphonics and rap-scratch style to create a new style of electronic ensemble with works like the spatial and surreal "Simulcatastrophy"; a performance of Collin's "In CD" (a title pun on Riley's "In C," of course) often humorously re-thinking Beethoven and Mozartian cadences and form (he has made some recent work with Ben Neill along this same line); and the dense work "Salvador Dali's Digital Cinema." —*"Blue" Gene Tyranny*

It Was a Dark and Stormy Night / 1992 / Trace Elements
More ensemble work with a sound like *100 Melodies* but with a more through-composed style. —*"Blue" Gene Tyranny*

Philip Corner

b. Apr. 10, 1933

(Gamelan) The Gold Stone (1985)/ In Malcolm Goldstein's "Sounding the New Violin" / What Next?
Sighing, sliding tones of rough to sweet texture like a "folk" violinist, restrained to pleading. —*"Blue" Gene Tyranny*

Pictures of Pictures, from "Pictures of Pictures" / Frog Peak Music

Ten fascinating movements for piano solo. —*"Blue" Gene Tyranny*

Gong / Ear / 1993 / The Aerial #5
A brief piece for gongs of all nationalities, sizes, and tunings. Slight mysterious gestural sounds (objects tumbling on the rims, rubbings, etc.) to long, sustained resonances. —*"Blue" Gene Tyranny*

Henry Cowell

b. 1897, **d.** 1965
Atonal-chromatic, world music derivative

○ **Quartet Euphometric (1916-1919)** / 1977 / New World
Like the "Quartet Romantic" (1915-1917) and the "Concerto for Rhythmicon and Orchestra," this brief, two-minute work, played here by the Emerson String Quartet, is built on yet another of Cowell's groundbreaking "resources." Converting pitch intervals into rhythms (all tones vibrate in rhythmic cycles but you can hear the separate beats only on very low notes). Although these works were too difficult for players of that decade, they are quite playable now. Cowell was the prime mover of the "ultramodernist" (the term used then) music scene in the early part of the century, who established the vitally important New Music editions (publishing some modern classics) and who produced many concerts of new music (see Rita Mead's *Henry Cowell's New Music 1925-1936*—The Society, the New Music Editions, and the *Recordings*, University Microfilms International, Ann Arbor, Michigan, Research Press, 1981). He invented many technical musical devices (see his 1930 book *New Music Resources*), such as playing inside the piano (in his famous work "Banshee"), producing artificial harmonics on the piano. Like Charles Ives, he was writing "atonally" before the similar technique reached America from Europe (Schoenberg, Berg, Webern, Hauer). His interest in the musical techniques of other cultures led to attempts at synthesizing a "world music" and greatly influenced his later, more conservative works (his writing seemed to change after the sad episode of his undeserved imprisonment—see Michael Hicks' article "The Imprisonment of Henry Cowell" in the *Journal of the American Musicological Society*. Nevertheless, he made the best of the situation, organizing and inspiring prison bands and continuing his editing and correspondence with the help of friends). A recording of his piano works is essential to any new music collection, but at the moment of this writing there are (amazingly) none available. —*"Blue" Gene Tyranny*

Persian Set / 1993 / Koch
This is a collection of Cowell's more conservative but still original later works that reflect a fascination with "world music" and redefining traditional harmony and counterpoint. Performed beautifully by the Manhattan Chamber Orchestra, conducted by Richard Aulden Clark, this CD contains: "Persian Set," "Old American Country Set," "American Melting Pot," "Hymn and Fuguing Tune," "Air," and "Adagio" from "Ensemble." —*"Blue" Gene Tyranny*

Cowell: Piano Music / 1994 / Smithsonian/Folkways
At last, a reissue of the 1963 recording of Cowell playing several of his piano works in his casual style, so that the listener regards the unusual sounds and techniques as completely natural within the context of each piece's imagery. A recording of the complete piano works is definitely needed, but this CD, with Cowell's spoken commentary at the end, is a precious thing to have at the moment. —*"Blue" Gene Tyranny*

Ruth Crawford (Seeger)

b. 1901, **d.** 1954

○ **Quartet 1931 / In "Arditti String Quartet"** / Gramavision
A highly expressive piece and an innovative breakthrough in its use of harmonics and extended tones. Crawford invented structural techniques that have had great influence on avant-garde music. —*"Blue" Gene Tyranny*

Sonata for Violin and Piano / Study in Mixed Accents for Piano (1930) / 9 Preludes for Piano / Diaphonic Suite #1 for Solo Oboe / 1993 / CRI
A CD reissue of mostly earlier pieces by Crawford showing her innovations and originality. —*"Blue" Gene Tyranny*

Alvin Curran

b. 1938
Composer / New age, electronic
American composer and student of Elliott Carter who has written small- and large-scale pieces that make use of environmental sounds. —*AMG*

○ **Electric Rags II** / 1990 / New Albion
Rova Saxophone Quartet with Curran (electronics), Scot Gresham-Lancaster (Oberheim expander). Playing lots of tuneful and rhythmic material ("Z Train," "Corny Island," "Scusami, I Walk Alone," "Continental Shelf-Dance," etc.). The computer spontaneously structures the concert while the sax players control synthesizers, and all is constantly transformed in real time. —*"Blue" Gene Tyranny*

Songs and Views of the Magnetic Ocean / 1994 / Catalyst
Sounding a bit like Terry Riley plus sound effects, this CD is a lovely, almost New Age mix of environmental, vocal, and synthesized sounds. Sections include "At Harmony Ranch" and "Crystal Aires." —*"Blue" Gene Tyranny*

Schtyx (1991) / VSTO (1993) / 1994 / CRI
Schtyx is scored for three dog whistles, piano, prepared piano, harmonica, bass drum, two violins, and percussion. *VSTO* is for string quartet. —*"Blue" Gene Tyranny*

Anthony Davis

b. Feb. 20, 1951, Patterson, NJ
Piano, composer / Modern creative
See the Jazz section for his biography.

Lost Moon Sisters / In Dora Ohrenstein's "Urban Diva" / 1993 / CRI
Best known for his dramatic 12-tone style as in the opera "X, The Life and Times of Malcolm X" (1986) and his incidental music for the award-winning Broadway play "Angels in America," Davis has written here a lovely, modest, blues-influenced (with some echoes of Dave Brubeck) chamber work to a mythically ranging, brilliant text by Diane DiPrima. —*"Blue" Gene Tyranny*

Bob Davis

Piano / Big band
Bop, mainstream pianist who recorded during the late '50s in Minneapolis. —*Ron Wynn*

Ecomania / 1991 / Earwax Productions
Cassette of a wonderful production for radio containing opinions, musical fantasies, natural sound, etc., showing all aspects and attitudes concerning the idea of "ecology." —*"Blue" Gene Tyranny*

Deep Listening Band

○ **Troglodyte's Delight (1989)** / 1990 / What Next?
Exploring the sound properties of the Tarpaper Cave in Rosendale, New York, this group of renown improvisors (Stuart Dempster on trombone and didjeridu, Pauline Oliveros on accordion with voice and whistles, the vocals of Panaiotis and Julie Lyon Balliett, and the percussion of Fritz Hauser). Satisying natural and meditative beauty with two cuts featuring just cave water ("Cave Water"). My favorite cut is "After Dinner with the Trogs." —*"Blue" Gene Tyranny*

Ready Made Boomerang, The / 1991 / New Albion
This time our intrepid new music crew are found enchantingly mucking around underground in the Cistern Chapel, Fort Worden Cistern, Olympic Peninsula, Washington, exploding a balloon ("Balloon Payment") to demonstrate the natural reverberation time of the space, making suspended vocal ("CCCC" or Cistern Chapel Chance Chants) and unusual instrumental sounds, and dropping percussive stuff. Lovely and mysterious. —*"Blue" Gene Tyranny*

Paul DeMarinis

b. 1948
Electronic

I Want You / Kokole / In "Another Coast" / 1988 / Music and Arts
Inventive and charming interactive vocals with electronics. —*"Blue" Gene Tyranny*

☆ **Music as a Second Language** / 1991 / Lovely Language

Interactive electronics outlining voices with computer shadowing melodies, beautiful sustains, gentle humor, and humanity. Contains: "Fonetica Francese," a take-off on language lessons; "Odd Evening," about a Chinese radio play; "An Appeal," "a fit of legal dictation plagued by spurious vocal melodies"; "The Sand Clock"; "Cincinnati 1830-1850"; "The Power of Suggestion," based on the voices of hypnotists, evangelists, and salesmen; and "Beneath the Numbered Sky," based on an Indonesian folksong. Marvelously imaginative. — *"Blue" Gene Tyranny*

Stuart Dempster

b. 1936
Minimalism, world music derivative

○ **In the Great Abbey of Clement VI** / 1987 / New Albion
Mellow solo trombone calls, earth energy drones, and cries of a didjirido invoke the resonate standing waves built into the harmonic geometry of the architecture. — *"Blue" Gene Tyranny*

Robert Dick

b. Jan. 4, 1950

Venturi Shadows / 1992 / O.O. Discs
Music of this flute revolutionary/composer in performances by Neil Rolnick, Steve Gorn, Ned Rothenberg, and Mary Kay Fink. — *"Blue" Gene Tyranny*

Die Toedliche Doris (Deadly Doris)

Naturkatastrophen (Natural Catastrophes) (1985) / Gelbe Musik
7-inch disc with booklet in German and English. Instructions on how to produce do-it-yourself disasters—a way of dealing with "the dread generated by State, society, and nature," as kids do by means of fairy tales, and others do by forms of resistance. TUdliche Doris, "Deadly Doris," is three visual artists, centered in Berlin, who manifest a good sense of humor, a very raw and raucous approach to music, and a lot of well-placed angst, and who refer to their group as "she." This record is one of their milder productions, but be warned: playing this album will definitely not endear you to the neighbors. — *"Blue" Gene Tyranny*

Jaques Diennet

Aubracs: Wuevres pur Batterie, Synclavier et Bande Magnetique (Works for Percussion, Synclavier, and Tape) / 1987 / GMEM
One of the most interesting composers in the lively scene at the Groupe de la Musique Experimentale de Marseilles. This CD contains two atmospheric works: "Aubracs-sur-Maguelonne" (1982) and "Aubracs-les-Canaux" (1984) for percussion sounds and Synclavier synthesizers; many of the percussive type sounds are in fact generated by the eletronics, and the illusion is created in which the listener cannot tell who is playing what. "This is an imaginary place tinkering about the scenery. I may mix limestone (Les Quatre-Maguelonne) with granite (Aubrac) and so hasten the continental drift. The drawing out of sound is also the principle of confrontation: the blunt, almost harsh tone of the percussion instruments and those most sophisticated instruments of digital technology." — *"Blue" Gene Tyranny*

Herbert Distel

Die Reise (The Journey) / 1990 /
A dazzling four-part work designed for radio broadcast. — *"Blue" Gene Tyranny*

Lucia Dlugoszewski

b. 1931
Atonal-chromatic

Tender Theatre Flight Nageire (1971 / 1978) / CRI
A "series of musical rituals involved with the poetic roots of erotic experience, *Nageire* is an oriental aesthetic principle of nondevelopment, of nonlinear, leap. It uses constant and extreme surprise ... leaping into unknown material ... for the flexibility of the mind. One drop of water can unhinge my throat into miracles of swallowing. The sudden shiver of a delicate paper rattle or an unusually sensitive tonguing on a brass instrument becomes transparency utterly alive" (from notes by the composer). For brass ensemble with the composer playing on many of her 100 percus-

sion instruments: lovely silence, surprising sounds. — *"Blue" Gene Tyranny*

○ **Angels of the Inmost Heaven** / 1975 / Folkways
Performed by a brass ensemble, conducted by Gerard Schwarz. Music for a dance by Erick Hawkins, these "Angels" are described by transformations called Nova (bursts of energy), Corona (transparent densities), and Clear Core (tiny distinctions in static walls, a nervous surface of extremely quick pulses). Extraordinary variations of glissandos, fast lip and finger trills, and constant shifting of mutes are the ingredient techniques of a very unique style that flows with high energy and also the eloquence of a Debussy orchestral brass section. — *"Blue" Gene Tyranny*

Fire Fragile Flight / 1979 / Candide
This gorgeous piece, performed by the Orchestra of our Time, is totally unique in sound and conception. A chamber orchestra with an unusual percussion section (four players on slide whistles, hanging bells, playing inside the piano, etc.) recreates the physical phenomena of falling leaves in early March in the Great Lakes country. The music has 65 freely chosen, musically dangerous "leap-points," which trigger whirling "startle-juxtapositions" of varying speed, like the reflected light on turning and falling leaves will sometimes appear to set them on fire. — *"Blue" Gene Tyranny*

Charles Dodge

b. Jun. 5, 1942
Composer / Electronic
An American composer of computer music and the director of the Center for Computer Music at Brooklyn College. — *AMG*

Earth's Magnetic Field (1970) / 1971 / Nonesuch
Realized at the Columbia University Computer Center, this piece is built from directly translating a record of the magnetic changes (Kp indices) for planet Earth in 1961. Eight values a day are read from graphic charts that look so much like music they are popularly known as Julius Bartel's "musical diagrams." An interesting experiment. — *"Blue" Gene Tyranny*

In Celebration / Speech Songs / The Story of Our Lives / 1990 / CRI
Reissue of a 1978 disc in which poetry readings are digitized and restructured in the computer to modify vocal and other sounds. — *"Blue" Gene Tyranny*

Any Resemblance Is Purely Coincidental / 1992 / New Albion
A new collection of Dodge's compositional modifications of pre-existing material. Includes: "Any Resemblance Is Purely Coincidental" for voice (Enrico Caruso) and pianist (Alan Feinberg), "Speech Songs" (see above), "The Waves," and "Viola Elegy." — *"Blue" Gene Tyranny*

Paul Dolden

Threshold of Deafening Silence, The / 1992 / Tronia
Wonderfully uninhibited and compact densities of amassed acoustic sounds, like the 400 tracks of "Below the Walls of Jericho," or the modulated galactic racket of "In the Natural Doorway I Crouch" for alternately tuned balalaikas. Highly recommended. — *"Blue" Gene Tyranny*

Paul Dresher

b. 1951
Electronic, world music derivative
A composer whose work touches on contemporary classical and New Age concepts as much, if not more than, jazz. His compositions were recorded in 1981 by the New Performance Group of the Cornish Institute. — *Ron Wynn*

Other Fire (1984) In "Another Coast" / 1988 / Music and Arts
A rich mix of naturally occurring rhythmic and cycling environmental sounds (birds, temple bells, and more) from tape recordings made during Asian and Southeast Asian travels that nonetheless gives the illusion of electronic synthesis. — *"Blue" Gene Tyranny*

Liquid and Stellar Music / This Same Temple / 1994 / Lovely Music
A CD reissue of these lovely phase music pieces, in which repetitive processes gradually change melodic figures. — *"Blue" Gene Tyranny*

James Drew

The Celestial Cabaret, A Concerto for Pianist and Chamber Orchestra Symphony No. 3 / 1991 / Artistry Production
Called by Nicolas Slonimsky "an authentic American original," Drew has received many awards for composition. Taught at Yale University and UCLA in the '70s, he is also an illusive figure, a legendary underground jazz pianist who has played with Elvin Jones, Clark Terry, Donald Byrd, and Earl Turbinton. He has created a style entirely his own, each piece beautifully conceived. "Symphony No. 3" is one movement of long, slow melodies that create a mysterious yet hopeful feeling with very brief percussion punctuations and chordal brass writing, none of these elements suggesting anything we have heard before yet we somehow understand the meaning. The remarkable "Celestial Cabaret" is built featuring the unaccompanied piano soloist in a lyrical, flowing style that is not romantic but like a commentary, free-flowing thought suddenly surrounded by brief, strange versions of cabaret music of a very refined type, not satirical and not immediately recognizable. You must really hear his music to really get the idea. — *"Blue" Gene Tyranny*

Sonata "Appassionata" for Cello and Piano (1982)/ In "Cello America, Vol. 2" / 1993 / Music and Arts

Marcel Duchamp

○ **Erratum Musical (for Three Voices) (1913)** / "Sculpture Musicale" (Realized as Mesostic by John Cage) and a Version for Music-boxes / 1990 / Edition Block
The S.E.M. Ensemble, directed by Petr Kotik, realizes these early pieces using chance operations for "any instrument in which the virtuoso intermediary is suppressed." Another interesting realization is by percussionist Donald Knaack, who used a large funnel, five open-connected wagons, and numbered balls (Finnadar Records SR-9017, disc, issued 1977, out of print). — *"Blue" Gene Tyranny*

William E. Duckworth

b. 1943
Minimalism

○ **Thirty-One Days (1987) for Alto Saxophone** / 1990 / Lovely Music
Singing and wailing sax, solo and multitracked in ensemble, great playing by Michael Swartz, who uses movement in the stereo space to change presence and "throw" sounds. — *"Blue" Gene Tyranny*

Time Curve Preludes (1982) : Books I and II, Preludes I-XXIV, The / 1990 / Lovely Music
Described quite accurately by a reviewer as a "new-age *Well-Tempered Clavier*," the *Time Curve Preludes* are played elegantly by pianist Neely Bruce. — *"Blue" Gene Tyranny*

☆ **Southern Harmony (1980-1981)** / 1994 / Lovely Music
The Gregg Smith Singers, assisted by the Rooke Chapel Choir of Bucknell University, conducted by Gregg Smith, create the first complete recording of this exceptionally fascinating and moving choral work by concentrating and sampling only certain aspects— such as rhythm and a single gesture—of shaped-note ("sacred harp") singing (a style of the rural South), the interior nature of these hymns is brought to the surface—a very different idea from merely "setting" the hymns with new harmonies. — *"Blue" Gene Tyranny*

David Dunn

b. May 22, 1953

Chaos and the Emergent Mind of the Pond / 1990 /
An assembly of bio-acoustical underwater recordings that lets us listen to a burgeoning level of life we do not normally hear. — *"Blue" Gene Tyranny*

Angels and Insects / 1992 / What Next
"Tabula Angelorum Onorum 49" is based on alchemist John Dee's psychic communications (see also Jerry Hunt's work along these lines). Computer-fractal voices, disembodied informants. Includes an extended re-mix of "Chaos and the Emergent Mind of the Pond," an assembly of micro bio-acoustical underwater events— insect dronings, buzzings, clickings—recorded very (macro-) closely—that lets us listen to a burgeoning level of life we nor-

mally do not hear. Dunn has also edited a splendid book, "Pioneers of Electronic Art," available from Nonsequitur. See also his "...With Zitterings of Flight Released (in Memoriam Kenneth Gaburo)" in the collection "Views from the Perfect City." — *"Blue" Gene Tyranny*

Duke Ellington (Edward Kennedy Ellington)

b. Apr. 29, 1899, Washington, DC, **d.** May 24, 1974, New York, NY
Composer, bandleader, piano / Big band, traditional jazz, swing
See the Jazz section for his biography.

○ **Clothed Woman/ In "Mirage: Avant-Garde and Third Stream Jazz," The** / 1977 / New World
Much is written about the magnificient compositions and career of Duke Ellington in the Jazz and Classical sections of this guide, but this piece, recorded on December 30, 1947 (originally issued on Columbia 38236), deserves special attention as a precursor of the pointillistic style in both advanced Afro-American and Eurocentric music. The opening and closing statements of this short work are in free or open time (no pulse or rhythm) and are made from chordal forms abstracted from Ellington's piano "punctuation" accompaniment style (developed over 20 years at the time of this recording). The resulting sound is several years in advance of a similar sound in serialist music and "free jazz." Avoiding the usual idea of the "bridge" of a song, the midsection of this composition has a steady pulse that he built by placing these gestures over a chromatic boogie-bass figure that serves as a nonmodulating, suspended-in-time nervous drone. — *"Blue" Gene Tyranny*

Suite from "The River" / 1993 / Chandos
A wonderful orchestration by Ron Collier of one of Ellington's many "suites" (Examples: "The Queen's Suite," "The Goutelas Suite," "The Uwis Suite," "Suite Thursday," "Far East Suite") played by the Detroit Symphony Orchestra, conducted by Neeme Jervi. Several of Ellington's own orchestrations can be heard on the MCA Classics CD (1989) of *Ellington: Orchestral Works* with the pieces "New World A'Coming," "Harlem," and "The Golden Broom and the Green Apple." — *"Blue" Gene Tyranny*

Brian Eno

b. May 15, 1948, Woodbridge, England
Synthesizer / Electronic, progressive electronic, ambient, avant-garde, art-rock/progressive-rock
See the Rock section for his biography.

Discreet Music / 1975 / Obscure Records
Taking a cue from Satie's idea of "musique d'ameublement" (furniture music), music that just exists, like furnishings in an apartment, played so as not to draw attention to itself (not really Muzak, a company which seeks to produce a more intentional work-product effect), Eno created several albums of what he termed "ambient music," which combined a softer style of pattern music (influenced by Bryars, Nyman, Harold Budd) with environmental noises. *Discreet Music* is from probably the best of these, using an Oliveros-style tape delay arrangement to slowly change patterns of repeating sounds. — *"Blue" Gene Tyranny*

Robert Erickson

b. 1917
Atonal-chromatic

Robert Erickson: Ricercar e 3 (1967) for Contrabass Solo / Sierra (1984) for Baritone and Ensemble / 1991 / CRI
The "Ricercar" is a bass solo with an improvised quality played sensitively by Bertram Turetzky. "Sierra," with text by Erickson and sung here by Philip Larson with the SONOR Ensemble, is a very peculiar recitative with instrumental colors about the California environs, interspersed with greetings to friends. Erickson's writing is built from "academic" elements but is always personal, unique, and lively. — *"Blue" Gene Tyranny*

John Fahey

b. Feb. 28, 1939, Cecil County, MD
Guitar / Instrumental bluegrass
One of the greatest and certainly among the most influential acoustic guitarists in folk and popular music, Fahey started his own record label, Takoma, in 1959, to release his debut album, *The Transfiguration of Blind Joe Death*. He has since recorded 40 or more albums. A student of rural blues music, Fahey did a Ph.D.

thesis on Charley Patton and incorporated the Delta blues into his increasingly eclectic style. Also important as a record-company executive, Fahey recorded what he liked, resurrecting the career of Bukka White and taking on young protege Leo Kottke, who has never really escaped his influence. Nor have the army of new-age guitarists of the 70s and beyond, many of whom sound like Fahey in isolated moments, though none can keep up with his musical ability and imagination. By now there are elements of almost all genres in his music, yet his playing remains his own. — *William Ruhlmann*

○ **Singing Bridge of Memphis, Tennessee / March! for Martin Luther King in "The Yellow Princess," The** / 1992 / Vanguard
In this CD reissue, we hear how Fahey, like Moondog, has often used environmental sound, not as background, but as integral to his improvised, modern folk-style guitar music, like the mournful train sounds in the distance for his "Raga for Pat" (Takoma Records, out of print). — *"Blue" Gene Tyranny*

Morton Feldman

b. 1926, d. 1987
Composer / New age, minimalism
American composer of quietly textured music, sometimes of extreme length; notable works are *Viola in My Life* (1970-1971) and *Rothko Chapel* (1971). —*AMG*

Pieces for More than Two Pianos / Sub Rosa
Sublime, slowly evolving chordal textures. Contains "Four Pianos," in which the four players all read from the same material but play at their own speed, gradually creating a landscape of indeterminate delays. Sensitively performed by Le Bureau des Pianistes. — *"Blue" Gene Tyranny*

☆ **Rothko Chapel (1971) for Chorus, Viola, and Percussion/ Why Patterns? (1978)** / 1991 / New Albion
After inventing graph notation in the early '50s ("Projection I" for solo cello in 1950), Feldman began to write works that used long tones and wordless singing and were played very quietly (allowing sounds that could not be otherwise heard), creating a changing but unbroken "surface." In the '70s, he began to work with gently pulsing mobile-like rhythmic figures of which "Why Patterns?" is a good example. — *"Blue" Gene Tyranny*

For Samuel Beckett / 1991 / Newport Classic
San Francisco Contemporary Players, directed by Stephen Mosko. Mobiles for chamber orchestra, similar to his last orchestral work, "Coptic Light." Unfortunately, recording was made with instruments at normal volume, which affects the delicate transparency of sound intended by Feldman, and so, even though the producers wish you to "play this CD very quietly," the sound is much fuller and harsher than it would be if they had played quietly from the outset. — *"Blue" Gene Tyranny*

○ **Viola in My Life (1970) / False Relationships and the Extended Ending (1968) / Why Patterns? (1978), The** / 1992 / CRI
Reissues of some wonderful pieces, "False Relationships and the Extended Ending" alternates between exact proportions and "free time" in the vertical style (slowly changing chords, common-tone suspensions) in pieces such as "Atlantis" (1958) and "The Swallows of Salangan"), which came after the counterpoint style of the early '50s graph pieces. "The Viola in My Life" was the next development, adding melody-like gestures. Ethereal, heartfelt. — *"Blue" Gene Tyranny*

String Quartet (1979) / 1994 / Koch
Astonishingly well played by the Group for Contemporary Music, this piece is a masterwork. Continually new inventions of harmonic colors, mobile-like patterns, and crystalline to shockingly rich timbres occur in an unpredictable but ultimately aesthetically satisfying time placement, and the whole performance of 78 minutes and 27 seconds takes the listener through a wide range of transcendental mental spaces. — *"Blue" Gene Tyranny*

Luc Ferrari

b. 1929
Electronic

○ **Brise-glace (et Si Toute Entiere Maintenant...) ("Icebreaker, Supposing Now I Were To ...)** / 1991 / Adda
Winner of the Prix Italia 1987. Surreal, poetic interior monologue of passenger on shipboard near the Arctic Circle. Beautiful and

original blend of orchestral writing, natural and electronic sounds. French text by Colette Fellous. — *"Blue" Gene Tyranny*

Fluxus

☆ **FluxTellus** / Tellus Audio Cassette Magazine #24
Soundworks by the legendary East Coast artists' group who, together with other '60s performers like The ONCE Group in Michigan, radically accepted all activity of art and life in their work. Contributions from George Brecht (organizer of the New Jersey-based Yamday Festivals), Dick Higgins (writer and publisher of the famous *Something Else Press*), Alison Knowles, George Maciunas, Emmet Williams, LaMonte Young, Takaka Saito, Jackson Mac Low, Joe Jones, Tomas Schmit, James Tenney, Robert Watts, Larry Miller. — *"Blue" Gene Tyranny*

Bill Fontana

b. 1947
Electronic

Australian Sound Sculptures / Edition Block
Fascinating sounds by one of the pioneers of sound installation pieces. This work was made while Fontana was a producer for the Australian Broadcasting Commission (1975-1978). Based on eight-channel field recordings he made for a tape archive of Australian environmental sounds, which were presented as an exhibition called "Sound Sculpture" at the National Gallery of Victoria in Melbourne. — *"Blue" Gene Tyranny*

○ **Landscape Sculpture with Fog Horns (Installation Version, 1981; Live Radio Version, 1982)** / 1982 / KQED-FM
The installation version on this unfortunately out-of-print disc, created for the San Francisco New Music America '81 Festival, involved eight loudspeakers each playing a broadcast of ambient sound from distant locations in the Bay Area, as listeners walked along the 600 foot pier (East Wall of Pier 2, Fort Mason Center) on a trajectory towards Angel Island three miles away. A changing and drifting configuration of echo and delay patterns was created by the uncoordinated pulses of the horns and the wide spatial placement of the microphones at Point Blunt, West Garrison, Treasure Island, the Yacht Harbor, Fort Point, China Beach, the Legion of Honor, and the Cliff House. Four locations were used for the live radio version. The sound of a fog horn can travel about 5 miles. Under certain atomspheric conditions, the fog will mask certain pitches (on the radio version, the horns form a mysteriously beckoning major chord with a flat second added, plus seagulls and some brief unintelligible conversation by passersby). Certain horns are louder at a distance than at close proximity. These variations make for a beautiful listening experience. — *"Blue" Gene Tyranny*

Fast Forward

b. 1954
World music derivative

Same Same / Experimental Intermedia
Great new pieces featuring Fast's improvisation group. — *"Blue" Gene Tyranny*

○ **Panhandling** / 1990 / Lovely Music
Not your usual percussion music. Sometimes studies of a single sound: a bullroarer (Africa, Australia) in "Bullroarer"; a metal ball rolled about a waterfilled, tuned oil drum, producing beautiful harmonics, in "Waterball"; ssemblies of metals from life—a bathtub, metal snake, and two temple bells in "Precious Metals." Sometimes there's the bright emotion of steel pan solos in "Red Dance," "The Big Wind," and "Stix," exploring closely placed tones moving on a steady rhythm figure, like some guitar picking, Bach prelude, or African marimba music. — *"Blue" Gene Tyranny*

Fred Frith

Guitar / Rock & roll, 20th century, world music derivative
Brilliant British avant-garde electric guitarist and multi-instrumentalist specializing in improvisation, incorporating trace-elements of free jazz and progressive rock with lots of noise and "treated" guitars a la John Cage's "treated" pianos. Solo, duo, and group (see Henry Cow) recordings range from flat-out noise (*Guitar Solos, With Enemies Like These, Who Needs Friends?*), to lovely, airy, almost lullaby-like compositions (parts of *Gravity*), to

industrial dance music (side two of *Speechless*). Even the prettiest tunes have an edge, and the others (the majority) may make you re-evaluate what you consider music. Challenging and complex. It is hard to be halfway about Frith's music; you either love it or hate it. Definitely not for the weak-hearted, weak-minded, or weak-spirited. — *Niles J. Frantz*

☆ **Technology of Tears (1987) and Other Music for Dance and Theatre, The** / SST Records
"Sadness, Its Bleached Bones Behind Us" and "You Are What You Eat" are unrelenting slices of hard-edged sounds over a pulse. "The Palace of Laughter, The Technology of Tears" is an imaginative, intense, varied suite comparing music that represents the past "frozen tears" of sadness—displayed by the media as images before us—with the "hot tears" of the moment that cannot be absorbed by technology. "Jigsaw" and "Jigsaw Coda" (1986) create patterns with constantly shifting accents and subdivisions—uneven pieces to be fit together. "Propaganda" (1987), music for a theater production, is a series of brilliantly evocative soundpieces with electronics, guitar, and sound effects: feedback and explosions in the distance, tantric harmonizing in the desert: "A Deeper Understanding of Conflict," "The Relentless Landscape," "The Excellent Hyena," "The Wolf Demon." With John Zorn (alto sax), Tenko (voice), Christian Marclay (turntables), Jim Staley (trombone). — *"Blue" Gene Tyranny*

Guitar Solos (1974) / ESD
Made in four days; improvised, some to a roughly preconceived idea. "Glass c/w Steel": "four layers of sound in an eerie haze out of which bounds a rubbery, animal-like line" (Cole Gagne in the book *Sonic Transports*); "Ghosts": distorted chords appearing and disappearing; "Out of Their Heads (on Locoweed)": "like being harangued by an automobile accident" (Gagne); "Hello Music," a cheery welcome; "No Birds": a tour through imaginary landscapes. A remarkable album that predated so much radical guitar playing of the next decades, and still has a lot of originality to offer. — *"Blue" Gene Tyranny*

James Fulkerson

b. 1945
Electronic

James Fulkerson: Co-ordinative Systems No. 10 for Trombone and Tape Delay (1976) / Music for Brass Instruments II (1975) / Antipho / Irida
A talented composer/trombonist who uses alternate mouthpieces to create electronic-like tones, which are fed into delay network in "Co-ordinative Systems No. 10." In "Music for Brass Instruments II," the bass trombone player follows an "aural score" of two other trombones on tape and attempts to follow and blend with them. "We play and think differently when we follow only our ears." — *"Blue" Gene Tyranny*

Ellen Fullman

Staggered Stasis / The Aerial
Rich acoustic waves of sound from Fullman's original invention, the Long String Instrument. Floating harmonics and ancient Pythagorean intervals. — *"Blue" Gene Tyranny*

Body Music / 1993 / Experimantal Intermedia
Five more astonishing compositions on long string sculpture-instruments, including the marvelously flowing "Work for 4," performed on a 145-foot-long string installation, already a modern classic. "Space Between" surprisingly produces some sounds normally associated with electronic music, and "Body Music" suggests a kind of celestial Delta-blues with its bar chording technique. A CD that will appeal to many listeners. — *"Blue" Gene Tyranny*

Diamanda Galas

b. Aug. 29, 1955
Composer
Harsh, assaultive art-punk with quasi-operatic delivery. Not for the fainthearted. — *John Dougan*

☆ **Plague Mass (1984—End of the Epidemic)** / 1991 / Mute
Galas, who has been known for both her own work and as a singer of extremely demanding modern scores, has created this heart-wrenching cry about the physical suffering caused by AIDS, compounded by the shameful arrogance of self-appointed moralists. Maintaining an incredible intensity and depth for over an hour's solo vocal (recorded live at The Cathedral of St. John The Divine, NYC, with suitably minimal band and electronics backup), Gales proceeds through Mahalia Jackson-influenced spiritual singing, breaking at points into high saxophone-like wails, to dramatic dialogs in many dialects and languages ("There are no more tickets to the funeral") to engrossing Portugese "fado" singing to taking on the attributes of Satan (in "Sono L'Antichristo," I Am the Anti-Christ) in order to challenge the concept of a vengeful, instead of compassionate deity (and society), much as Nina Simone did in her controversial song "God is a Killer" in the '60's. The Mass ends with the heartfelt lyrics "I go to sleep each evening now dreaming of the grave and see the friends I used to know calling out my name. O Lord Jesus, do you think I've served my time?" At times, the singing is "self-indulgent", but, well.... — *"Blue" Gene Tyranny*

Masque of the Red Death / 1992 / Mute
Contains: "The Divine Punishment," "Saint of the Pit," and "You Must Be Certain of the Devil (A Plague Mass in 3 Parts)." A two-CD set with pieces similar in intensity to the "Plague Mass." — *"Blue" Gene Tyranny*

Singer / 1992 / Mute
Contains a mix of original, traditional gospel and Chicago blues tunes such as "Balm in Gilead / Swing Low Sweet Chariot" and "I Put a Spell on You" with Galas's personal "twist." — *"Blue" Gene Tyranny*

Ge Gan-Ru

b. 1954
Atonal-chromatic, world music derivative

○ **Yi Feng (Ancient Wind)/ In "New Music China"** / Tellus #19

Gu Yue/ In "Sonic Encounters" / 1990 / Mode
China's first avant-garde composer. After receiving degrees in violin and composition from the Shanghai Conservatory of Music, he was forbidden to play anything but scales during the Cultural Revolution and was later incarcerated and tortured. In 1983 he was awarded a fellowship to Columbia University where he studied with Chou Wen-chung and Mario Davidovsky and received his Doctor of Musical Arts degree. He has composed concert music, as well as music for dance, theater, and several film scores: "Tang Dynasty," "Who Killed Vincent Chin?" (1988 Oscar nominee for Best Documentary Film), and "A Great Wall," the first Chinese-American feature film collaboration. His dramatic and effective music combines "contemporary Western compositional techniques with my Chinese feeling and experience along with Chinese musical characteristics inherited from thousands of years ago, so as to set up a universal music world expressing natural and primitive beauty." Watch for a future recording of his composition "Wu" (Rising to Height) (1986) for piano and chamber orchestra. — *"Blue" Gene Tyranny*

Orlando Jacinto Garcia

○ **La Belleza del Silencio (The Beauty of Silence)** / 1992 / O.O. Discs
Beautiful groups of sounds and soft, sharp, sustained dissonances in constantly varying permutations characterize the music by this Cuban-born, Miami-based composer, who studied with Morton Feldman. Perfect performances by Joan LaBarbara (voice), the Gregg Smith Singers, Jan Williams, percussion, and other musicians. — *"Blue" Gene Tyranny*

Colores Ultraviolados / In "Bang on a Can, Vol. 3" / 1994 / CRI
A lovely rhythmic mobile of sensual sounds from voice, flute, violin, and bass. — *"Blue" Gene Tyranny*

Peter Garland

b. Jan. 27, 1952

Border Music / 1992 / What Next
Early percussion pieces and works for solo harp, as well as a newer piece for harp, violin, and percussion influenced by Yaqui Indian pascola dances. Peter Garland is the publisher of *Soundings Press*, which for years has been an invaluable source for scores and information about new music. — *"Blue" Gene Tyranny*

Walk in Beauty / 1992 / New Albion

Two piano pieces and an ensemble work with Aki Takahashi (piano), and the Abel-Steinberg-Winant trio. The title piece "Walk in Beauty," named after the Beauty Way chant of Navajo curing and peyote ceremonies, is a bit stiff and uninflected in performance and composition, but the final piano work "Jornada del Muerto (in memoriam Lew Welch)" (Journey of the Dead One—name of a place in southern New Mexico in which travelers have perished in its desert and where the first atomic bomb was exploded) has much interesting and beautiful patterning especially in the final section "The View from Vulture Peak"; the eight-section ensemble piece "Sones de Flor" (Flower Songs), based structurally on the Japanese poetic form renga, a chain of linked couplets, played on violin, piano, vibraphone, and tom-tom, is beautiful, clear, and a full realization of Garland's folk music-minimalist-formal aesthetic and also makes for good listening. Listeners may also enjoy checking out Garland's *Nana + Victorio* (1993) on the new AVAN label. — *"Blue" Gene Tyranny*

Peter Gena

b. Apr. 27, 1947

Mother Jones/ In Thomas Buckner's "Full Spectrum Voice" / 1991 / Lovely Music
A new approach to political song, a complex vocalise gradually gains momentum, breaking into a ballad, "The Death of Mother Jones," and then, returning to the vocalise, brings the music into another dimension. — *"Blue" Gene Tyranny*

Jon Gibson

b. Apr. 27, 1940

"Two Solo Pieces": Cycles (1973) / Untitled (1974) / 1977 / Chatham Square
With the composer performing on organ and alto flute. Using seven notes in very slow four-part harmony, Gibson builds an organ texture of exquisite presence; improvising on a simple long melody with dedicated sweetness, Gibson constantly varies with innate musicianship the piece "Untitled," which closes this album of two classics of music truly built on "minimal" means. — *"Blue" Gene Tyranny*

Rainforest/Brazil (He Was Not Disappointed)/ In Thomas Buckner's "Full Spectrum Voice" / 1991 / Lovely Music
From the theater work "The Voyage of the Beagle," with text by Charles Darwin. Rainforest sounds, wood flute, synthesizer mellismatic wanderings, and a gorgeous vocal. — *"Blue" Gene Tyranny*

☆ **Waltz (1981) for Saxophone and Piano / Song Three (1976) Extensions II (1981-1982) for Sound Environment and Sax/ In "Jon Gibson"** / 1992 / Point
The beautiful "Waltz" seems to suddenly become suspended and lead to another dimension of mind. All three pieces are subtle combinations of melody with conceptual patterning. — *"Blue" Gene Tyranny*

Michael William Gilbert

b. Aug. 17, 1954

○ **Moving Pictures (1978)** / 1978 / Gibex
An unfortunately out-of-print disc featuring heavenly electronic music from this Massachusetts composer. Echoes of Far East folk musics combined with synthesizers, flutes, voice, and percussion. — *"Blue" Gene Tyranny*

Janice Giteck

b. Jun. 27, 1946

Home (Revisited) / 1992 / New Albion
An album of pieces dedicated to people living with AIDS, this is music of hope and humanity rather than overt raging. Giteck's music is influenced by the gamelan and cyclic music traditions, especially in the lovely "Om Shanti." "Home (Revisited)" is a heart-filling piece for choir (mostly singing the word "home") and instruments, sung here by the Philandros of the Seattle Men's Choir. There is also the touching "Tapasya" for viola and percussion. See also Giteck's "Breathing Songs from a Turning Sky (excerpt)" in the collection "Music from Mills." — *"Blue" Gene Tyranny*

Philip Glass

b. 1937
Composer / Minimalism, avant-garde, world music derivative
American composer primarily of minimalist music for film, ballet, and opera using an ensemble of electronic and amplified acoustic instruments. Glass also has a body of instrumental works for acoustic instruments. — *AMG*

☆ **Music in 12 Parts** / 1990 / Virgin
Glass is renown for his pattern music style, presented in its most developed form in this early work, and still one of his best. He has developed a method of writing that retains the sense of the timeless "present," while bringing a new possibility to rethink melody and harmony in a nonvirtuosic sense. At times this is very elegant and profound as in this CD, and the opera *Akhnaten* on CBS-2-M2K-42457, and at times verges on the direct appeal of a movie-music sensibility as in *1000 Airplanes on the Roof* on Virgin 91065-2; for having this range he remains a very controversial composer. — *"Blue" Gene Tyranny*

Glass Organ Works: Donald Joyce, Organ / 1993 / Catalyst
With a richer sound and variation of timbres than in the usual Glass keyboard renditions, Donald Joyce plays, with great attention and feeling, various solo works by Glass on a large church organ. Appealing. — *"Blue" Gene Tyranny*

Music with Changing Parts / 1994 / Elektra/Nonesuch
A reissue of the 1971 recording. Glass at his most fundamental and best. — *"Blue" Gene Tyranny*

Vinko Globokar

b. 1934

Les Emigras (The Emigrants) (1982-1986) / 1991 / Hamonia Mundi
Performed by the Ensemble Musique Vivante. A music-theater work by this Yugoslavian composer/jazz trombonist, who lives in Paris and whose works are nearly impossible to classify. "Any model of organisation existing in nature or in culture can become music." Five narrators singing, shouting, and speaking in many languages "give the impression of sitting in a court that is in the process of judging the public," with the listener also placed in a similar situation. We are dealing with people who left their countries in order to survive or improve their way of life. The first part, "Miserere," is an historical allegory: letters from Italians who had emigrated to Brazil and also from Turkish emigrants, interviews with women who follow their husbands, and so on. The second part, "Realities/Augenblicke" (Realities/Flashes), contrasts hope accompanied by dance music against projected images of potential misery. The third part, "Sternbild der Grenze" (Border Constellation), with a text by Peter Handke, is a series of nine tableaux performed by giant puppets contriving to cross "a hermetically sealed border" in a clandestine way. At various points, the singers cross the "border" of the stage and go into the audience. There are also parts for an orchestra, a small choir, two vocal soloists, and a jazz trio. — *"Blue" Gene Tyranny*

Anthony Gnazzo

b. 1936
Electronic, minimalism

Asparagas/ In "Music from Mills" / Music from Mills
A gradual "process piece" using drum-set outtakes from a recording session re-edited to emphasize the rhythmic irregularities into a wild cluster of drum beats. — *"Blue" Gene Tyranny*

Malcolm Goldstein

b. Mar. 27, 1936

Soweto Stomp (1985) / 1991 / Musicworks #46
Performed by the Malcolm Goldstein Workshop Ensemble in Montreal . Freely accessed sax and wind riff patterns with African 6/4 rhythms gradually mutating dense to simple textures suggest some incredible celebration of simultaneous emotions. — *"Blue" Gene Tyranny*

Summoning of Focus (1977)/ In Joseph Celli's "Organic Oboe," A / 1992 / O.O. Discs
A framework for improvisation, a ritual of sorts. A richness of sound textures and depth of intensity and presence sustained to the end. — *"Blue" Gene Tyranny*

Tongues of My Mother's Teaching (1988) / 1992 / Musicworks
A touching piece with Goldstein softly playing violin, picking out strains from collages of old recordings of many types of violin and fiddle folk music. — *"Blue" Gene Tyranny*

Daniel Goode

b. Jan. 24, 1936

Clarinet Songs / 1993 / Experimental Intermedia
A fascinating collection of short pieces for solo clarinet skillfully played by the composer. Each piece features a different playing technique. My personal favorites are "Clarinet Drum," the odd tunings of "Six New Fractal Fingers," the almost-Tibetan "Clarinet Trumpet," and the lovely double stop harmonies of "Long Distance." Daniel Goode is one of the founders of the well-known Downtown Ensemble in New York City and has created many other larger works such as the mixed-media piece "Manaqua-Matagalpa-Music," about the Nicaraguan revolution, and "Three Talking Sculptures for Election Day" (1992), about guns, pornography, and sexual expression. — *"Blue" Gene Tyranny*

Michael Gordon

Big Noise from Nicaragua / 1992 / CRI
Complex works from the '80s by this dynamic composer: "Thou shalt not! Thou shalt not!" (1983), with passages of triple-meter rhythms in strings and winds, countering to quarter notes in the percussion, "The Low Quartet" (1985/1986), for four bass clarinets; "Four Kings Fight Give" (1988), for chamber strings and winds, which has a passage in seven tempi at once, performed by the Michael Gordon Philharmonic, conducted by Linda Bouchard; and "Acid Rain" (1986), played by the Spectrum Ensemble, conducted by Guy Proteroe. — *"Blue" Gene Tyranny*

Peter Gordon

b. Jun. 20, 1951
Horn, composer
Horn/synth player & composer of avant-garde music. —*AMG*

● **Leningrad-Xpress** / 1990 / Newtone Records
Music from dance and theater productions in a musical language equally informed by world music, tough New York City rock, pattern music, Albert Ayler jazz, and electronic music. Gordon makes it all work in these highly original tone poems from the almost Weillian "Leningrad Express" and "Warsaw," to the disco-Italian folk music of "Toscana," to the electronic and dissonant "In the Fields," "Trinity Site," and "Inside the Nuclear Power Plant" (text by Kathy Acker), the sublime atonal chamber music of "Inside Marie," the Chopinesque-Tibetan "Woyzeck's Dream," the 1920's Berlin-style "Der Kindertotentanz," and the unabashedly pretty "Pastis" acoustic guitar solo. — *"Blue" Gene Tyranny*

Geneva / Extended Niceties / 1992 / New Tone
Imaginative polytonal rock songs and instrumentals reissued from post-art-rock times of the early '80s. Bold and beautiful genuine lyricism and humor with various combinations of the Love of Life Orchestra. — *"Blue" Gene Tyranny*

Still Life and the Deadman / 1993 / Newtone
From the lush string orchestra of the first piece, "Awareness," to the excellent performances of the Balanescu and Parsley Club string quartets (respectively in "De Dode (The Dead Man)" music for a Bataille drama and in "Rembrandt Suite"), this melodic, evocative album fulfills the promise of the thorny rose on its cover—romantic harmonies with strange melodic turns, the sweet with the dissonant, the humorous with the plaintive, and the traditional with the "downtown." This CD, with additional winds and percussion, presents a turning point and a maturing of style in Gordon's work. — *"Blue" Gene Tyranny*

Henryk Mikolaj Gorecki

The Essential Gorecki / Olympia
A collection of the earlier more radical and interesting works by this Polish composer whose current tonal style is a kind of syrupy sentimentalism that has a certain popularity. Included are excellent performances of "Epitafium" (Epitaph), for mixed choir and instrumental group (1958); "Zderzenia-Scontri" (Collisions) (1960); "Genesis II: Canti Strumentali per 15 Esecutori" (Genesis II: Instrumental Songs for 15 Performers) (1962); "Refren" (Refrain) (1965); and "Muzyka Staropolska" (Old Polish Music)

(1969). Performances by the Polish National Orchestra and the National Philharmonic Choir. — *"Blue" Gene Tyranny*

Gerard Grisey

b. 1946

Partiels for 16 or 18 Musicians/ Derives for Two Orchestral Groups / Erato
Ensemble Ars Nova, directed by Boris de Vinogradov; Orchestre National de France, directed by Jacques Mercier. Extremely quiet washes of harmonic colors over the orchestral surface with other unusual timbres. — *"Blue" Gene Tyranny*

Tom Hamilton

b. 1946
B / Electronic

Pieces for Kohn / 1976 /
Four electronic pieces that are musical responses to four paintings by artist Bill Kohn, large geometrics of mythical cities. — *"Blue" Gene Tyranny*

○ **Formal and Informal Music** / 1981 / Somnath
Complex and rich live electronic music improvisations. Contains "Formal and Informal Music" (1980) and "Crimson Sterling" (1973), for electronics, winds, and percussion. J. D. Parran (woodwinds and saxes), Rich O'Donnell (percussion). Watch for a 1995 issue of Hamilton's music on the Experimental Intermedia labels. — *"Blue" Gene Tyranny*

Moondog (Louis Hardin)

b. 1916

☆ **Music of Moondog, The** / 1990 / CBS
A reissue of two LPs recorded in 1969 and 1972. Rounds, canons, and other pieces that are the precursor of much pattern music. Incidentally, John Fahey has made a wonderful arrangement of Moondog's "Theme and Variations" (1952) for guitars, percussion and synthesizer on *John Fahey: Rain Forests, Oceans, and Other Themes* (Varrick CD 019). — *"Blue" Gene Tyranny*

More Moondog / The Story of Moondog / 1990 / Prestige
CD reissues of two LPs on the Prestige label from 1956 and 1957. Moondog on the street and everywhere else. The sources in everyday life with music and life blending as a whole. A soundtrack to spur the imagination. Contains: "Softshoe and Hardshoe" (7/4), "A Duet with the Queen Elizabeth Whistle and Bamboo Pipe," "Ostrich Feathers Played on Drums," "All Is Loneliness," "5/8 in Two Shades," "Violetta's Barefoot Dance," "A Portrait of Ninon-A Cocker Spaniel," and others. — *"Blue" Gene Tyranny*

○ **Elpmas** / 1991 / KOPF
Contains: "Wind River Powwow," "Westward Ho!," "Suite Equestria," "Marimba Mondo 1—The Rain Forest," "Fujiyama 1," "Marimba Mondo 2—Seascape of the Whales," "Fujiyama 2," "Bird of Paradise," "The Message," "Introduction and Overtone Continuum," and "Cosmic Meditation"—environmental sounds, gently rocking marimbas, lovely counterpoint for winds, sweetly sung wisdom, "a protest against our treatment of aboriginal people ...and nature, plants, and animals...." — *"Blue" Gene Tyranny*

Lou Harrison

b. 1917
Composer / World music derivative, alternate tunings
American composer whose style has been influenced by Asian music, including the Javanese gamelan. His ensembles rely on Asian folk instruments, especially the percussion. —*AMG*

☆ **Music for Guitar and Percussion** / 1990 / Etcetera
With John Schneider, well-tempered guitar, and the Cal Arts Percussion Ensemble, conducted by John Bergamo. A good overview of Harrison's work, especially the alternately pastoral and crashingly celebratory "Canticle No. 3, for ocarina, guitar and percussion" (1941). The ocarina suggests Native American and Japanese folk melodies; the guitar is used as a percussion instrument along with gamelan-like suspended brake drums and shaker. Also contains the more melodic "Suite no. 1" (1976), (though it's still in unusual Pythagorean, just-tuning, Babylonian/Arabic, and artificial scales); "Plaint and Variations on Song of Palestine"; "Serenado por Gitaro" (1952), with the strange chromatic "Infinite Canon" and Usul movements; "Serenade for Guitar with a Percussion Player" (1978); and "Waltz

for Evelyn Hinrichsen" (1977). Excellent performances. — *"Blue" Gene Tyranny*

Double Music (1941), Collaboration with John Cage, for 4 Percussionists/ In The New Music Consort's "Pulse" / 1990 / New World
A wild and wacky, by-now classic percussion piece, using a small range of pitches, that begins as a modest melody and winds up like a heated and joyous village celebration for many unusual instruments. Excellent example of a successful collaboration in composition. This CD is especially recommended as a good collection of percussion music. — *"Blue" Gene Tyranny*

Gamelan Music / 1992 / Music Masters
Beautiful and meditative pieces that reflect Harrison's abiding affection for the gamelan that has dominated his musical thought in the last few decades. — *"Blue" Gene Tyranny*

Pierre Henry

b. 1927
Composer / Electronic
French composer of electronic musique concrete pieces for ballet and on religious themes. — *AMG*

Variations Pour Une Porte Et Un Soupir ("Variations for a Door and a Sigh") / 1964 /

○ **Le Voyage** / 1964 /

Futuriste / 1980 /
All hauntingly beautiful albums from this composer's over forty years of work in electronic and "musique concrAte" and collaborations with Pierre Schaeffer. Watch for a future reissue of a collection of these currently out-of-print discs. — *"Blue" Gene Tyranny*

Bernard Herrmann

b. 1911, d. 1976
Composer, drums / Vocal, orchestral, chamber music
The dean of film composers, Bernard Herrmann was probably the most gifted musician ever to work in movies, with barely a note of music to his credit that is not worthwhile. A classically trained composer, Herrmann worked for Orson Welles' Mercury Theatre and the CBS radio network before going to Hollywood with Welles in 1940. His first two film scores, *Citizen Kane* and *The Devil and Daniel Webster*, were both nominated for Oscars in the same year (Webster won), and he was established from then on. Herrmann worked principally for 20th Century-Fox from the mid 1940's until the end of the 1950's, and did brilliant work on such movies as *The Ghost And Mrs. Muir*, *The Day The Earth Stood Still*, *Beneath the 12-Mile Reef*, and *Journey to the Center of the Earth*; in the 50's and '60s, Herrmann also contributed notably to the success of Alfred Hitchcock's films, and wrote inspired scores for early films by Brian De Palma and Martin Scorsese. He died the night he finished work on *Taxi Driver*. — *Bruce Eder*

North by Northwest / Unicorn–Kachana
Bernard Herrmann completely changed the idea of the filmscore from heavily operatic and kitschy "incidental music" to the use of bare melody-like gestures or patterns in pure theme-and-variations form, which was to prove an influence on later avantgardists. This procedure is fully demonstrated in the two recordings above, and in his score for Hitchcock's "Vertigo" (1958), with its shocking polytonal harmonies (Mercury, 1986), and in his last score for Martin Scorsese's "Taxi Driver" (1976) (Varese Sarabande, 1986), where the patterns over jazz harmonies are as totally symmetrical as in the work of John Coltrane (especially "Naima" and "Giant Steps"). The orchestrations, with signature extended harp arpeggios, for the two films above recall his music for Nicholas Ray's "On Dangerous Ground" (1951) (videodisc, Image Entertainment, 1989) and Robert Wise's "The Day the Earth Stood Still" (1951) (videodisc, CBS Fox), which sounds remarkably like a Phil Glass score. In interviews, Glass has stated his early interest in Herrmann's music. — *"Blue" Gene Tyranny*

Devil and Daniel Webster Suite / Silent Noon / For the Fallen / Currier and Ives Suite / Koch

Psycho (Complete Music for the Hitchcock Film) (1960) / 1989 / Unicorn–Kachana
Performed by the National Philharmonic Orchestra, conducted by the composer. An early champion of new music, conducting pre-

mieres of several Charles Ives scores in the '30s, Herrmann completely changed the idea of the filmscore from heavily operatic and kitschy "incidental music" to using only the barest of melody-like gestures or patterns in pure theme-and-variations form. This procedure is fully demonstrated in this recording, in his score for Hitchcock's "Vertigo" (1958), with its shocking polytonal harmonies (Mercury 422 106-2, issued 1986), and even in his last score for Martin Scorsese's "Taxi Driver" (1976) (Varese Sarabande VSD-5279, issued 1986), where the patterns over jazz harmonies are as totally symmetrical as in the work of John Coltrane (especially "Naima" and "Giant Steps") and Jon Gibson. The orchestration and extended harp arpeggios recall his music for Nicholas Ray's "On Dangerous Ground" (1951) (issued on videodisc, Image Entertainment, 1989) and Robert Wise's "The Day the Earth Stood Still" (1951) (issued on videodisc, CBS Fox 1011-80), which sounds remarkably like a Phil Glass score. In interviews, Glass has stated his early interest in Herrman's music. Herrmann's concert music is more traditional but still remarkable for its clarity of line (especially recommended is the "Souvenirs de Voyage" for clarinet and string quartet (1967), issued in 1991 on Delos DE 3088). — *"Blue" Gene Tyranny*

Symphony #1 / 1992 / Koch
Herrmann's own concert music is somewhat more traditional—the "Currier and Ives Suite" like Shoshtakovich with "wrong notes" and the lovely "Silent Noon" recalls Delius, whom Herrmann admired—but the music is still remarkable for its clarity of line. Especially recommended are "For the Fallen" in this CD and the "Souvenirs de Voyage" for clarinet and string quartet (1967) in *American Chamber Music from Chamber Music Northwest* issued in 1991 on Delos. The bold, solid brass writing in "The Devil and Daniel Webster Suite", from the 1942 film, is similar to that in his sweeping "Symphony #1" played by the Phoenix Symphony, conducted by James Sedares. — *"Blue" Gene Tyranny*

Juan Hidalgo

☆ **Tamaran—Gocce Di Sperma Per Dodici Pianoforti** / 1990 / Cramps
A brilliant conceptual work for 12 pianos by a leading figure in Spanish avant-garde music. — *"Blue" Gene Tyranny*

Lejaren Hiller

b. 1924
Electronic, atonal-chromatic

Illiac Suite (excerpt)/ In "The Voice of the IBM 7090 Computer" / 1960 / Bell Telephone Labs Records
You'll find this disc only in libraries at the moment. The "Illiac Suite," composed with engineer L. M. Issacson, was the first computer music piece. It demonstrated possibilities for complex rhythms and transpositions of melody, and it suggested a spectrum of controlled to quasi-random systems for composition. The IBM 7090 computer, with the computing ability now possessed by a modest personal computer, occupied two rooms. Included on this disc are brief experiments by Drs. J. R. Pierce, M. V. Mathews, Newman Guttman, David Slepian, David Lewin, M. E. Shannon. — *"Blue" Gene Tyranny*

Algorithms, Versions I and IV (1968) / 1969 / Deutsche Grammmophon
An interesting ensemble piece for acoustic instruments and magnetic tape, composed using the IBM 7094 computer. Titles of the three sections reflect some of the mathematical constructs represented—"The Decay of Information," "Icosahedron," and "The Incorporation of Constraints." Currently out-of-print disc to be reissued on CD. — *"Blue" Gene Tyranny*

Metaphors/ In the Buffalo Guitar Quartet's "New Music for Guitars" / 1990 / New World
Interesting work with new guitar techniques. — *"Blue" Gene Tyranny*

Toshio Hosokawa

b. 1955
World music derivative, alternate tunings

Seeds of Contemplation (Mandara) for Shomyo and Gagaku Ensemble (1986) / Fragmente I for Shakuhachi, Koto, and Sangen (1988) / 1990 / Fontec

Two exquisitely spare compositions combining ancient court-music gestures with matrix-combinatory European compositional techniques. Beautifully paced performances in the "breath" tempo of traditional Gagaku ensembles. Hosokawa studied with Isang Yun and Witold Szaloneck in (West) Berlin and has received commissions and prizes in Japan, Europe, and the United States. His "pure" use of the Gagaku ensemble is different from Takemitsu's somewhat more romantic approach. For comparison with the tradition, listen to the still excellent *Gagaku: The Imperial Court Music of Japan* by the Kyoto Imperial Court Music Orchestra, reissued on CD on Lyrichord. — *"Blue" Gene Tyranny*

Alan Hovhaness (Chakmakjian)

b. 1911
Composer / World music derivative, alternate tunings
Though Hovhaness is primarily known as a classical composer, he is revered as one of the fathers of the new-age and world-music movements. He is without a doubt one of the earliest artists in any genre to make significant use of ethnic music elements, spiritual concepts from other cultures, and sounds from nature in his compositions. In the '30s, he refused to conform to the atonal intellectualism of his colleagues and began combining influences from his Armenian heritage with the great musical traditions of the Far East. A series of fellowships allowed him to travel to India, Japan, and Korea to study and compose during the '50s and '60s. During that time, his eclectic, mystical compositions began to strike a chord with American audiences. Continually ahead of his time, Hovhaness was actually the first to mix the recorded songs of humpback whales in an orchestral context. Carl Sagan even used some of Hovhaness's music in the "Cosmos" television series. Though most of the composer's music is available through classical music outlets, several contemporary instrumental labels have released collections of his piano pieces, bringing his expressive and sophisticated style to wider audiences. — *Linda Kohanov*

Wind Music of Alan Hovhaness: Return and Rebuild the Desolate Places (Concerto for Trumpet) / Symphony no. 7 (Nanga Parvat) (1959) / Mace

An out-of-print disc that can still be found in used record bins. With the North Jersey Wind Symphony and percussion, Keith Brion conducting. Another side of Hovhaness: dissonant clusters, fury and devastation, wild improvised village marches, a mountain frozen forever in treeless snow, the fierceness of volcanic earthquakes, rocks sculptured by tornados. Visions from Armenia. Hovhaness in the church of nature. — *"Blue" Gene Tyranny*

And God Created Great Whales (1970) for Orchestra and Whale Songs / Concerto no. 8 for Orchestra (1953) / Elibris (Dawn God of the Urardu) / 1989 / Crystal

Magnificently beautiful recording of an orchestra in an old abbey and a good overview of the composer's work. — *"Blue" Gene Tyranny*

☆ Lousadek (Dawn of Light), op. 48 (1945) for Piano and Orchestra /Symphony no. 2, op. 132 "Mysterious Mountain" / 1990 / Musicmasters

Performed by the American Composers Orchestra, Dennis Russell Davies conducting, with Keith Jarrett as piano soloist. Informed by the highly mellismatic, floating melodic sense of Armenian song together with simple, refined orchestration, "Lousadek" is a lovely work that nearly caused a riot at its New York premiere as it innocently stepped on the mental toes of the academic chromaticists and the American nationalists in the audience. The symphony "Mysterious Mountain" combines many of the elements of Hovhaness's later style: parallel chordal passages of universal religious feeling (similar to Eastern Orthodox Church chanting), the treatment of canon and fugue in an entirely original manner (more of a variation form), quasi-random pizzicati and strange transparent bells on odd harmonics that suggest landscapes at long distances from civilization. Hovhaness is a prolific composer of nearly 500 compositions to date, but these two pieces wll give the listener a good idea of his general instrumental approach. — *"Blue" Gene Tyranny*

Lady of Light, op. 227 (1968) / 1991 / Crystal

With Patricia Clark (soprano), Leslie Fyson (baritone), The Ambrosian Singers and Royal Philharmonic Orchestra, conducted by Hovhaness,. Simple elegiac chant and solo song with and without text and mixed with sudden random rushings of voices, harmonizations on non-European scales, a protest against war based on the Swiss "Chalabala" legend: "Dancing to the Stars over Bridges of Thread," "I Am Dancing in Heaven," "No More Serve Your Brutal War Lords." — *"Blue" Gene Tyranny*

Mount St. Helen's Symphony (sym. no. 50) / City of Light Symphony (sym. no. 22) / 1993 / Delos

Performances by the Seattle Symphony, conducted by Gerrard Schwartz (sym. no. 50) and the composer Alan Hovhaness (sym. no. 22). Soaring, magnificient works. — *"Blue" Gene Tyranny*

Hub

☆ Hub / Computer Network Music, The / 1989 / Artifact

A totally new idea in live electronic music, the six composers of The Hub play computer music live by interacting with musically sensitive responses to each other's programs, the computers often physically connected through complex networks that make many aspects of their performances spontaneous. Contains: John Bischoff's terrific "Perry Mason in East Germany," Tim Perkis's "Farabi," Chris Brown's "Rol'Em," Phil Stone's "Borrowing and Stealing," Scot Gresham-Lancaster's "Whackers," Perkis/Brown/Stone "Hot Pig," Bischoff/Perkis/Trayle "Dovetail," Perkis's "The Minister of Pitch," and Mark Trayle's "Simple Degradation." — *"Blue" Gene Tyranny*

Jerry Hunt

b. Nov. 30, 1943, d. 1993
One of the most original composers of our time, Hunt, often creating scores of complex physical moves in space, made a concert into an occasion that re-creates music's role in divination of all countries and ages—for example, his "Sur John Dee" (1966) in John Cage's thought-provoking compilation "Notations" (1969, Something Else Press). Hunt was also an innovative computer systems designer and created mysterious alliances of computers and primal energy in his installation pieces (one a voodoo hut with computerized proximity detectors triggering electronic sounds for the New Music America Festival in Houston). — *"Blue" Gene Tyranny*

Transform (Stream) (1977) / Cantegral Segment 18, 17 (1977-1976) / Transphalba (1978) / Volta (Kernel) (1977) / 1979 / IRIDA

An out-of-print disc but well worth searching for. Using various mechanical and electronic instruments and systems, Hunt investigates the relation of nerve bonding in the human body and its descriptive, analogous patterning in electronic systems. IRIDA vinyl discs are still available (see addresses section) and the CRI label will be issuing a new CD soon of 70 minutes of Hunt's music, all of the music that appeared on IRIDA and an early piano work. — *"Blue" Gene Tyranny*

☆ Fluud for Dual Synclaviers/ In CDCM Computer Music Series, vol. 1 / 1988 / Centaur

Ceremonial moves based on Robert Fluud's *monochordum mundi syphiphoniacum* (1622). Otherworldly. — *"Blue" Gene Tyranny*

Babalon (string)/ In "The Aerial #1" / 1990 / Aerial

Mysterious hermetic evocations with shamanic rattles and bells, and an interactive computer system for sound retrieval. — *"Blue" Gene Tyranny*

Ground / Five Mechanic Convention Streams / 1992 / O.O. Discs

In five compositions, Hunt investigates "nonconventional intention" and how it is transformed into gestures, much of this activity based on a system of translation gestures using the angelic tables produced by the mystic John Dee through the skrying of Edward Kelley (1582-1589). Pieces include "Chimanazzi (Olun): Core" for violins, keyed violin, and (electronic) device arrays, "Lattice (Stream): Ordinal" for piano and auxiliary device arrays, and "Bitom (Stream): Link" for cow horns, pianos, and device arrays. Hunt is assisted by composer Rod Stasick and vioinist Jane Henry. — *"Blue" Gene Tyranny*

Haramand Plane / 1994 / What Next?

Jerry Hunt's last recording and it's fabulous! Three "links" of his electronic relays and processes with simultaneous tracks of acoustic percussion in an evocative (literally) ceremonial performance. — *"Blue" Gene Tyranny*

David Hykes

Hearing Solar Winds / 1983 / Ocora
An extended choral work made from Hoomi singing of western Mongolia and the overtone chanting of Tantric Buddhism. Spectacular shimmering surfaces (overtones from clusters of fundamentals beating against each other) and other effects. Some titles are "Multiplying Voices at the Heart of the Body of Sound," "Gravity Waves," and "Rainbow Voice." — *"Blue" Gene Tyranny*

Harmonic Meetings / 1990 / New Albion
A reissue of the two-disc set on CD. Lovely as always. — *"Blue" Gene Tyranny*

Current Circulation / 1992 / Celestial Harmonies
A reissue of the well-known 1984 album. More like single studies of the singing techniques. Includes "Free Ascents," "Subject to Change," "Ascending Mount Summation." — *"Blue" Gene Tyranny*

True to the Times / How to Be? / 1993 / New Albion
Includes: "Worldwind Psalm" and "Prayer Songs for the Sorrow / Pythagoras over Persia." — *"Blue" Gene Tyranny*

Toshi Ichiyanagi

b. 1933
World music derivative

Solo Compositions / 1991 / Camerata
Includes "Cloud Figures for Solo Oboe," "Hoshi-No-Wa" for sho; "Scenes III for Solo Violin," "Time Sequence for Piano." Lovely pieces by the composer who introduced much of new music to Japan by organizing concerts and exhibitions of graph music, and whose early pieces such as "Kaiki" (1960), for sho, organ, koto, harmonica, and saxophone, and early theater music works such as "Sapporo" (1963) are classics. See also his work "Extended Voices" in the collection "Extended Voices." — *"Blue" Gene Tyranny*

Charles Ives

b. Oct. 20, 1874, **d.** May 19, 1954
Composer / Classical
Highly original American composer of orchestral, chamber, and solo vocal and piano music who used and anticipated polytonality, atonality, and polymeter/polytone clusters. A unique quality of his music is the combination of well-known hymns and popular tunes with a complex dissonant accompaniment. Notable works include *Three Places in New England* (1914) and the *Sonata for Piano no. 2, "Concord, Mass"* (1920). — *Mary K. Scanlan*

☆ **Unanswered Question (1908) / Central Park in the Dark (1898-1907) / Holidays Symphony (1904-1913), The** / CBS
This recording by the Chicago Symphony is particularly interesting because both the original and revised versions of *The Unanswered Question* are performed. The dissonant flute-clusters and trumpet theme are played completely free of the consonant, serene chords of the strings in the original version, another innovation by Charles Ives. — *"Blue" Gene Tyranny*

Ives Plays Ives / Record no. 4/ In "Charles Ives, The 100th Anniversary" / Columbia
This out-of-print five-disc set is a treasure of music and memorabilia. Ives playing spontaneously (improvising) on published and unpublished material/ideas. Reveals the creative process in its searching mode (apart from the necessary structural work), with Ives enthusiastically letting his hands discover what cannot be preconceived. Especially remarkable are the so-called "X, Y, Z Improvisations." — *"Blue" Gene Tyranny*

○ **Three Quarter-Tone Pieces/ In "New Music in Quarter-Tones"** / Odyssey
Three beautiful pieces—"Largo," "Allegro," and "Chorale"—for two pianos tuned quarter-tones apart from each other. This is a fine recording and performance, but these pieces should really be heard live. As with much of Ives, additional transparent "ghost" sounds occur in the performance space, caused by the strange combinations of harmonics and tunings, which can be heard by listeners but not recorded. This is especially true for these pieces. As a child, Ives sang tunes, in quarter-tones, along with other children in the family inspired by their bandleader father, George E. Ives, who also staged such experimental spectacles as bands playing different tunes marching from opposite ends of town and

crossing in the middle. That event is re-created in "Three Places in New England." — *"Blue" Gene Tyranny*

Orchestral Music of Charles Ives, The / 1990 / Koch
With the Orchestra New Englan, conducted by J. Sinclair. Includes "Calcium Night Light," "Country Band March," "Largo Cantabile," "Postlude in F," "Set for Theater Orchestra," "Set of Four Ragtime Dances," "Three Places in New England," and "The Yale-Princeton Football Game." Great performances. The collection does not include other orchestral works such as the *Orchestral Set no. 2* (probably the best performance of this was Stokowski conducting the London Symphony Orchestra on the out-of-print disc London Records SPC 21060), or the visionary "Tone Roads," 12-tone piece written many years before that technique found its way from Europe to the States. — *"Blue" Gene Tyranny*

● **Symphony no. 4 (1910-1916) / Robert Browning Overture (1908-1912), Songs: An Election; Lincoln, The Great Commoner** / 1991 / Sony Classical Masterworks
With Leopold Stokowski conducting the American Symphony Orchestra, and the Gregg Smith Singers. A magnificent transcendental vision of life performed with full spirit by Stokowski's orchestra with attention to the polyrhythms, transparent "memory" textures, and harmonic layerings of this completely innovative writing. The songs (especially "Lincoln, the Great Commoner," with its amazing tone-cluster glissandos for voices and strings) are perfect complements to the symphony. — *"Blue" Gene Tyranny*

Leroy Jenkins

b. Mar. 11, 1932, Chicago, IL
Violin, composer, bandleader / Modern creative, avant-garde
See the Jazz section for his biography.

Lifelong Ambitions (featuring Muhal Richard Abrams) / 1981 / Black Saint

Leroy Jenkins Live! (featuring Computer Minds) / 1993 / Black Saint
Two CDs that give an overview of Jenkins's earlier tune-oriented and later free playing. Muhal Richard Abrams is a composer who has served as an important musical, spiritual, and social influence as president of the AACM (Association for the Advancement of Creative Musicians) founded in Chicago in 1965, by members of his earlier group The Experimental Band. His own work may be heard on "Blu Nlu Blu" (Black Saint, 1991) and "Family Talk" (Black Saint, 1993) in excellent performances that reach out to the listener. Abrams's recent and daring work, the masterpiece "Duet for Pianos #1" has yet to be recorded. — *"Blue" Gene Tyranny*

Santa Fe / 1994 / Lovely Music
A magnificent CD of violin and viola solos showing the dynamic "pure music" side of this great composer/performer who worked with the AACM in Chicago in the '60s, then moved to New York City and founded The Revolutionary Ensemble (they recorded five albums). He has composed many large works played by the Brooklyn Philharmonic, the Cleveland Chamber Symphony, the Albany Symphony, and Kronos Quartet and was included in the Kennedy Center's American Composer series; he recently premiered his opera-for-dance "The Mother of Three Sons," commissioned by the Munich Biennale, and his "Off-Duty Dryad" (1990) was played by the Soldier String Quartet with dancers. He is currently at work on a new opera that includes three rappers as characters and a piece about the recently uncovered Negro Graveyard in Manhattan. He is a totally engaging performer who keeps the listener on the seat's edge waiting for the next surprising variation and invention. — *"Blue" Gene Tyranny*

Terry Jennings

b. Jul. 19, 1940, **d.** Dec. 11, 1981

☆ **Terry's G Dorian 12-Bar Blues (9 X 5) + 3 (1962)/ In "Jon Gibson"** / 1992 / Point
Gibson on sax with two synthesizers and percussion. Terry Jennings was one of the first players on any wind instrument to play multi-phonic chords, which are produced by a combination of unusual fingering and overblowing. Classics of extended time-sense music, his ethereally beautiful piano music, and especially the remarkable "String Quartet" (September 1960) (see score in

La Monte Young's *An Anthology*) have yet to be recorded. — *"Blue" Gene Tyranny*

Scott Johnson

b. 1952
Minimalism, rock

○ **John Somebody / No Memory for Electric Guitar, Woodwinds, Percussion, and Electronics (1981-1983)** / 1986 / Elektra/Nonesuch
"Remember that guy ... John Somebody? He was a ... sort of a b..." asks a woman's voice on the repeating master tape loop, as other smaller loops join in, and then pop-jazz instrumental figures imitate the rhythm and add funky melodies and cross-rhythms (built on the smaller samples of the loop) in accumulating levels, which suddenly break and start again with interpretations of the loops. We find ourselves tapping our feet and wanting to dance. An original and appealing album, in which Johnson clearly demonstrates for his listeners the relation between ordinary speech and musical rhythms. Speech in this case also includes the laughter of "Involuntary Songs." *No Memory* is also built on this speech sampling idea but is more complex in its modulation of both the loop sounds and the layering of the more chromatic instrumental phrases. — *"Blue" Gene Tyranny*

Confetti of Flesh/ In Dora Ohrenstein "Urban Diva" / 1993 / CRI
A sensual rhapsody about New York City living with text by Jayne Cortez ("I am new york city of blood police and fried pies"), this chamber piece shows Johnson in a more melodious and somewhat more "uptown" mode than in his previous compositions, the whole texture grown from a three-note motive, but still with an underlying hip beat. Beautifully performed. — *"Blue" Gene Tyranny*

Tom Johnson

b. Nov. 18, 1939

Music for 88 / 1993 / Experimental Intermedia
Just the disc to give to those people who remark inquisitively about the relationship of music and mathematics. Tom actually explains out front before and at times during each piece about the math being used, and at times how musicians and mathematicians differ in their views. Many charming and lovely minimalist pieces for voice and very well-recorded piano with sometimes unintentionally (?) droll humor. A very original piece (as in "Why didn't I think of that?"). (See also his piece "Failing: A Very Difficult Piece for Solo Bass" in *Bang on a Can Live, Vol. 1.* — *"Blue" Gene Tyranny*

Rational Melodies (1982) (21 Pieces for Any Instrument) / 1993 / Hat Art
Lovely conceptual pieces performed by Eberhard Blum on piccolo, flute, alto flute, bass flute. — *"Blue" Gene Tyranny*

Ben Johnston

b. 1926

☆ **Amazing Grace (String Quartet no. 4) (1973)** / 1991 / Elektra/Nonesuch
Heartrendingly beautiful microtonal setting with variations on this traditional melody played by the Kronos Quartet. It is also called the "String Quartet no. 4" on out-of-print vinyl Gasparo GS-205, where it is played in more accurate tuning by the Fine Arts Quartet. — *"Blue" Gene Tyranny*

Calamity Jane to Her Daughter / In Dora Ohrenstein "Urban Diva" / 1993 / CRI
With a text based on a section from a disputed diary (which includes a recipe for a "20-year cake") that may or may not be the authentic account of the historical Calamity Jane's secret marriage to James Butler (Wild Bill) Hickok, Johnston spins a wonderfully melodious vocal line in just intonation with beautiful consonances and dissonances amongst the accompanying instruments. — *"Blue" Gene Tyranny*

Ponder Nothing: Chamber Music of Ben Johnston / 1993 / New World
Compelling works in just intonation played by Music Amici: "Septet," "Three Chinese Lyrics," "Gambit," "Five Fragments," "Trio," and "Ponder Nothing" for clarinet solo. — *"Blue" Gene Tyranny*

Victoria Jordanova

Requiem for Bosnia (An Improvisation for Broken Piano, Harp, and Child's Voice) / Four Preludes for Harp (On a Sunday, A L'Espagnol, By the Seashore, Harp Wind) / Once Upon a Time / Variations / 1994 / CRI
Strong, neo-romantic/modernist works primarily for harp. — *"Blue" Gene Tyranny*

Mauricio Kagel

b. 1931
Classical

Staats Theater (1967-1970) / Deutsche Grammaphon
Kagel takes apart the apparatus of the State Theater of operas, plays, and other spectacles and examines in detail the images and sounds we are presented with apart from plot, libretto, and subject matter. Not a satire but a surreal concentration. Many of Kagel's original instruments and sound-making devices (listen to "Akustica" (1968-1970), a two-disc set on Deutsche Grammaphon, if you can find a copy) are used, both for the sound they make and because of their symbolic value. A steel strip partially strapped to the player's feet (he is part of the circuit) is in the form of a Mobius strip, which is associated with getting from one side, the "real," to the other side, "the figurative," without going over the edge. Likewise, tape music, choral and operatic ensembles, stage sets (Wagnerian to pop-art large soda bottles), stock characters (the Barber, the Imaginary Invalid, Amor, and the Troubadour Knight), and stock themes (Concern, Virginity, Iron Curtain, Investigation, Nighttime), movement (Contradance), the players in the pit, callisthenics done by the performers to keep in shape, and even the resultant waste paper of programs and notices are all presented in their physical and imaginary contexts. — *"Blue" Gene Tyranny*

☆ **String Quartet I (1965-1967) / Pan (1985) for Piccolo and String Quartet / String Quartet II (1965-1967) / String Quartet III (1986-1988)** / 1991 / Disques Montaigne
Played with great sensitivity by the Arditti String Quartet. The marvelous first and second quartets take some late Bartok string techniques to new levels: snap string, tremolos of bow wood (col legno) rebounding off strings, non-vibrato glassy textures, maximum bow "crunch," random pizzicato, playing on the wood of the instrument. The quartet is treated compositionally like electronic music—at turns mysterious, dramatic, and lyrical. With scale-like fragments and operatic "bird" figures, *Pan* seems to reset *The Magic Flute*. The third quartet, like *Pan*, contains elements of past musical gestures treated for their sound value (not as quotes or satire), combined with techniques from the first quartets. All this makes for very original music. — *"Blue" Gene Tyranny*

Les Idees Fixes (Rondo for Orchestra), Musik fur Tasteninstrumente und Orchester (Music for Keyboards and Orchestra), op. 1991 (Concerpiece for Orchestra) / 1993 / Col Legno
Fascinating new pieces played by the Rundfunk Sinfonieorchester (Radio Symphony Orchestra) of Saarbrucken, coducted by the composer, with four pianists. — *"Blue" Gene Tyranny*

Franz Kamin

Rugugmool / 1980 / Station Hill
These two works both have an interesting, unusual combination: linear, poetic texts combined with instrumental music that has structured openness (indeterminacy of well-defined events) and a surface level that suggests narrative atmospheres. "Rugugmool" has an impressionist description of a boatsman piloting a woman to meet lovers and friends, with words and phrases recurring magically, a "one-to-one code language" with everything becoming one, followed by instrumental "dances" based on charts defined in a Book of Animal Models. In "Behavioral Drift II," elements of a constant complex of sounds are traded from instrument to instrument, the whole always being present, and the performers are guided by a light panel controller. The text here is from the composer's book "Ann Margaret Loves You and Other Psychotopological Diversions." Kamin's earlier works include "7 Dog W" for seven supra-audible dog whistles, and "A Concert of Doors," a composition for doors in the woods. — *"Blue" Gene Tyranny*

Jin Hi Kim

b. 1956
World music derivative

Komungo Permutations / 1990 / What Next
Electronic exploration of this ancient Korean instrument, bamboo on silk. — *"Blue" Gene Tyranny*

Guy Klucevsek

b. 1948
Minimalism

○ **Flying Vegetables of the Apocalypse** / 1991 / Experimental Intermedia
Dance music for accordion solo with top-notch combos of winds, strings, saxes, percussion. Unique transitions between the new-music, downtown style, tango, blues, polka, and more—poetic, even hum-a-long. My favorite cuts: "Waltzing Above Ground," "Fez Up." See also *Manhattan Cascade* CD in 20th-Century Collections in this section. — *"Blue" Gene Tyranny*

Alison Knowles

b. Apr. 29, 1933

Frijoles Canyon / 1992 / What Next
An extended work weaving together text and field recordings of the New Mexico landscape by this former member of the Fluxus group. Mixed sounds of rocks, sticks, trees, cacti, and of course beans. — *"Blue" Gene Tyranny*

Gottfried Michael Koenig

b. 1926
Electronic, atonal-chromatic

○ **Klangfiguren II (Soundfigures II) (1955-1956)/ Essay (1957-1958)/ Terminus 1 (1962) / Terminus 2 (1966-1967) / Output (1979) / Funktionen** / 1990 / Bvhaast ("Acousmatrix I/II")
Classic pointillistic electronic music. — *"Blue" Gene Tyranny*

Takehisa Kosugi

b. 1938
World music derivative

Violin Improvisations New York, September 1989 / 1992 / Lovely Music
Warm melodic phrases, sometimes almost romantic, sometimes slipping away like a bird heavenward. Always unpredictable and unanalyzable. — *"Blue" Gene Tyranny*

Petr Kotik

b. Jan. 27, 1942

Petr Kotik's S.E.M. Ensemble / 1991 / Ear-Rational
Petr Kotik's music is a very personal blend of austere and often strange rhythmic feelings and a Gregorian-chant simple melodic sensibility, with sudden startling chromatic and other tonal shifts, hypnotic and compelling music ranging from his now-legendary setting of Gertrude Stein's "Many Many Women" (out-of-print disc set) to the recent magnificent "Explorations in the Geometry of Thinking," a four-hour-long setting of the "Numerology" section of F. Buckminster Fuller's brilliant "Synergetics," scored for three drummers, woodwinds and trombones, and vocal soloists, and partially excerpted from this Ear-Rational CD. Included also is the melodic "Solos and Incidental Harmonies" for flute, brass, and tambourine. — *"Blue" Gene Tyranny*

Jill Kroesen

b. 1949
Rock-derivative

Stop Vicious Cycles / 1982 / Lovely Music
Like the albums of Ned Sublette and Laurie Anderson, this disc presents only the songs that make up part of the material for her extended and inventive performance pieces. Jill Kroesen, a performer as intense as Diamanda Galcs and Lydia Lunch but more flexible, has made stage works, including a ballet *The Lou and Walter Story*, that reduce historical and social icons, like Alexander the Great and even the History of the World (as an icon in itself), to the personal and emotional, thereby stripping away much of the pomposity and abstraction that often accom-

panies the cant of the historical imperative. One European fan said to her, "You try to make everything so simple whereas we try to make everything complex." These songs with a beat also make use of electronic and acoustic noise, free-style brass playing, bizarre percussion and mixing, and a totally new approach to the idea of pitched/non-pitched singing. Some of the pieces are "I'm Sorry I'm Such a Weenie," "I Am Not Seeing That You Are Here," "I'm Just A Human Being" ("I'm just a human being who can hardly keep her own house clean. And I lie in bed and think how the president is just a human being and it scares me to think about the life he leads."), "Alexander The Great" ("...I want to travel all around and get lost conquering everybody's ground. And send plunder to my mother and kill my threatening brother. I'm Alexander and I'm pretty and I ain't in no hurry to get home."), and the legendary "Fay Shism Blues." — *"Blue" Gene Tyranny*

Philip Krumm

b. Apr. 7, 1941

○ **Sound Machine (1966)/ In "Texas Music"** / 1979 / IRIDA
An electronic but somehow also a living being with a gently insistent pulse (or is it a purr?) who sometimes emits quasi-random tiny beeps and sighs. A lovely short piece from the composer of much innovative music: *Music for Clocks* (for multiple clock/metronomes and orchestra, composed several years before Ligeti's *Poeme Symphonique* (1965) for 100 metronomes and before Ichiyanagi's *Music for Electronic Metronome* (1961) was published); the "Piano Variations" (all on one C chord; the "variations" consist of fingering changes affecting the pressure and consequently the timbre of the chord); the outer space *Formations* (*Score of Heavenly Lattices*), and much more. — *"Blue" Gene Tyranny*

Ron Kuivila

b. Dec. 19, 1955

○ **Blurred Genres** / Slowscan #6
Electronic music by a composer renown for his evocative and beautiful sound-installation pieces based on subtle concepts and realized with self-designed and built electronics, his latest work being a high-voltage arcing sound sculpture entitled *Dolci Mura* (Sweet Walls). — *"Blue" Gene Tyranny*

Joan La Barbara

b. Jun. 8, 1947
Avant-garde

○ **Sound Paintings** / 1990 / Lovely Music
Extended vocal techniques (circular breathing, multiphonics like that in Buddhist chant, imitation of environmental sounds, speech just on the edge of comprehensibility) multitracked into some beautiful pieces. I especially like "Erin" on a photograph of an Irish child with his father's coffin, and "Klee Alee," inspired by the imagery of Paul Klee's paintings and the squiggles and brush-strokes when viewed up close. — *"Blue" Gene Tyranny*

73 Poems (Texts by Kenneth Goldsmith) / 1994 / Lovely Music
A beautiful collaboration with both the musical setting and the poems created for the most part at the same time. La Barbara's voice is multitracked and her composition and vocal techniques responsive to both the meaningful content and the physical character of the words; for example, a tone-cluster for a towering wall. — *"Blue" Gene Tyranny*

Mary Jane Leach

Celestial Fires / 1993 / Experimental Intermedia
Beginning from simple means—close harmonies with phasing rhythms, each of the six compositions on this CD gradually blossoms in the intricacy of their exquisite movement and sound. Each uses an ensemble of instruments or voices of a similar family, which emphasizes the textural binding—"Bruchstuck," "Green Mountain Madrigal," "Mountain Echoes," and "Ariel's Song" for eight treble voices; "Feu de Joie" for solo bassoon and six taped bassoons; and the illusionary "Trio for Duo" for live and taped alto flute and voice. Truly beautiful. — *"Blue" Gene Tyranny*

Anne Lebaron

Dish / In Dora Ohrenstein's "Urban Diva" / 1993 / CRI

A sensual and humorous chamber work based on the texts "Seeing You Again Makes Me Wanna Wash the Dishes," "On Being Irresponsible About Lovers and Those Who Swoop on You," and "The Swooper and the Swoopee." LeBaron is an accomplished composer with chamber music recorded on the Mode label. The German Ear-Rational label features her jazz group The Anne LeBaron Quintet with the Phantom Orchestra. The voice in *Dish*, especially at the beginning of the piece, is amplified and echoed to create tactile effects. See also LeBaron's "Blue Harp Study 1" and "Blue Harp Study 2" in the collection *Jewel Box*. Listeners may also enjoy checking out her new album with several ensemble works on MODE records (1993). — *"Blue" Gene Tyranny*

George Lewis

b. 1952

Trombone / Traditional jazz, modern creative, avant-garde, jazz derivative

This self-taught clarinetist made a name for himself in the '20s, working with some of the most popular Black bands in New Orleans. Throughout the decade he also performed on the streets of the city with the Eureka Brass Bands. By the early '30s he was with trumpeter Evan Thomas's Band. Later, during the New Orleans revival, Lewis traveled with Bunk Johnson's band to New York. On returning to New Orleans, he formed the George Lewis Ragtime Band with several of Johnson's former sidemen. By 1950 he was considered by many to be the central figure in the "traditional" jazz revival, and over the course of the next two decades he performed successfully on his own and with the Preservation Hall Jazz Band, touring the nation and making several international trips. Lewis was known for his fluent and highly individual style, which could match emotional intensity with lyrical grace and poignancy. Of the clarinetists identified with the New Orleans revival, Lewis's influence has been the most pervasive, inspiring players like Sammy Rimington, Tommy Sancton, and Woody Allen, among others. — *Bruce Boyd Raeburn*

☆ Homage to Charles Parker / Black Saint

Both of Lewis's compositions on this album are for an ensemble with Anthony Davis (piano), Douglas Ewart (bass clarinet), George Lewis (tenor trombone and electronics), and Richard Teitelbaum (Polymoog, Multimoog, and Micromoog synthesizers). "Blues" (1977) is a "collective orchestration" that builds in a fragmentary style of changing timbres, with a spirit that ranges from happy to that of Tibetan meditation, taken from material arranged in four basically diatonic choruses, using the essential harmonic sequence of the classic blues form as a starting point — but don't expect to hear a traditional "blues" because this music goes to the spirit behind the tune, rather than playing the tune. In the "Homage to Charles Parker" (1978), "the iconography [of the first section] ... represents the life of Charles Parker—what is known, what is thought to be known, what is dreamed, heard, and said—and his 'reality,' i.e., birth and death." The second part is based on the traditional solo with chordal accompaniment form that Charles Parker "brought to a rare level of perfection" and making "loving inferences as to Parker's afterlife," pointing "to a new appraisal of world music after his life—one in which Afro-American creative music decisively affirms its place as a living, growing, vital part of world culture." — *"Blue" Gene Tyranny*

☆ Chicago Slow Dance (1977) / 1981 / Lovely Music

An elegantly slow, evolving introspective portrait of Chicago life. There is a sound of shakers like the clacking of overhead subway rails, solos that range in attitude from resignation to spontaneous joy (Douglas Ewart on musette, bassoon, tenor sax, Ewart flute, bass clarinet, percussion; G. Lewis playing electronics, alto and tenor trombones; J. D. Parran on nagaswaram, baritone sax, piccolo; Richard Teitelbaum on Moog synthesizer). There are gentle surreal dream sounds and melodies evoking many images, perhaps a bird lost in the city, kids playing in vacant lots, night sounds on the edge of town, a passing police car, boats on the lake, your neighbors' noises through the walls of an apartment house—an exquisite and beautifully played work. — *"Blue" Gene Tyranny*

George Lewis / 1990 / Black Saint

A CD reissue of the 1978 disc. Contains: "Monads" for an ensemble with Anthony Davis (piano), Douglas Ewart (bass clarinet), Leroy Jenkins (violin), G. Lewis (alto and tenor trombones),

Roscoe Mitchell (soprano sax), Abdul Wadud (cello) —fleeting melodic fragments amidst pointillistic (but not abstract !) textures, constantly redefined and varied; "Triple Slow Mix," a trio for two pianos and sousaphone—a steady and slowly varied bass passacaglia surrounded by either extremely fast pointillistic playing or banal quote-like figures as if from music "literature," like a blasA music student in the practice room just trying to make it through the day (every once in a while someone shouts "Hey !"), "Cycle" (with Lewis on Moog synthesizer)—humorous and touching solos of mid-range sounds that make you smile without knowing why; "Shadowgraph, 5 (Sextet)" for the large ensemble mentioned above, also with Muhal Richard Abrams on piano and G. Lewis on sound-tube—someone near us is explaining something but we don't quite get it (perhaps it's something "foreign"): a tapestry of gestures, quick shadows of the initial event. — *"Blue" Gene Tyranny*

Changing With The Times / 1993 / New World

Innovative pieces, each with a speaker, poet, or singer reflecting on modern living. Titles include "Chicago Dadagram," "So You Say," "The View From Skates In Berkeley," "Airplane," "Epilogue." Listeners may also enjoy checking out Lewis' new CD "George Lewis" (1993) on the new AVAN label. — *"Blue" Gene Tyranny*

Gyorgy Ligeti

b. 1923

Composer / Classical, electronic, atonal-chromatic

Austrian composer of keyboard, electronic, orchestral, chamber, opera, and choral works. — *AMG*

○ Lux Aeterna, for 16-Voice Mixed Chorus (1966) / Deutsche Grammaphon

Performed by the North German Radio Chorus, conducted by H. Franz. The famed "sound of the monolith" in Stanley Kubrick's film *2001* was lifted from *Lux Aeterna*, in a lovely performance. There's a surface of sustained and overlapping clusters of multitimbral quality that suggests universality without bigness. — *"Blue" Gene Tyranny*

☆ Atmospheres (1961) for Large Orchestra/ Lontano (1967) for Large Orchestra/ In "Wien Modern" / 1990 / Deutsche Grammaphone

Performed by the Vienna Philharmonic, conducted by Claudio Abbado. Transparent washes of neo-impressionistic colors; interdimensional landscapes. Perfect companion pieces; beautiful. — *"Blue" Gene Tyranny*

Annea Lockwood

b. 1939

Electronic, minimalism

Sound Map of the Hudson River, A / 1990 / Lovely Music

This is listening to natural sound in heightened detail, beautiful for the ear and mind. — *"Blue" Gene Tyranny*

Thousand Year Dreaming / 1992 / What Next

An evocation perfectly described by the title. Use of native instruments and percussion sounds from natural objects. Meditative. See also her song "Night and Fog" in Thomas Buckner's vocal CD *Full Spectrum Voice*. — *"Blue" Gene Tyranny*

Alvin Lucier

b. 1931

Electronic, minimalism

○ Music for Solo Performer (1964-1965) for Enormously Amplified Brain Waves and Percussion / 1982 / Lovely Music

The first musical work to use brain waves to generate sound. World instruments, as well as a cardboard box and a trash can, are vibrated by loudspeakers placed near and under them, as bursts and trains of the amplified alpha waves disturb the cones of the speakers. — *"Blue" Gene Tyranny*

☆ I Am Sitting in a Room / 1990 / Lovely Music

A new music classic. 32 repetitions of a simple line of text over 40 minutes, constantly broadcast and re-recorded in a room until the nodal tones of the room and the voices undergo a magical transformation of a sense of person and place into a sense of universal presence. Lucier is the dean of psychoacoustic music. — *"Blue" Gene Tyranny*

Crossings / 1991 / Lovely Music

Pure, profound, and classic. Complex ideas realized simply. This CD includes the pieces "In Memoriam Jon Higgins" (1984), "Septet for Three Winds, Four Strings, and Pure Wave Oscillator" (1985), "Crossings" (1982) for small orchestra with slow-sweep, pure wave oscillator. — *"Blue" Gene Tyranny*

Music on a Long Thin Wire / 1992 / Lovely Music
Recording of an installation made on May 10, 1979, in the rotunda of the US Customs House, Bowling Green, New York City. The wire was extended 80 feet through the oval of the rotunda and was driven by one pure wave oscillator. The wire played itself, registering all changes in volume, timbre, harmonic structure, rhythmic and cyclic patterning, and other sonic phenomena. — *"Blue" Gene Tyranny*

Clocker / 1994 / Lovely Music
For amplified clock, performer with galvanic response sensor, and digital delay system. — *"Blue" Gene Tyranny*

Ralph Lundsten

Fagel Bla (Blue Bird) (1969) / **Tellus (1968)** / 1970 / Telestar
Two wonderful enviromental pieces by these two Swedish composers. *Blue Bird*, commissioned by the Foundations for Nationwide Concerts as inauguration music for the Expo-Norr festival in 1969 at Ostersund, is a two-channel composition performed from giant balloons that floated over the city. The strange effect is that the sounds do not dissipate when over a listener, so that the height of the balloons made no difference; *Tellus*, commissioned by the Swedish Institute, was a sight/sound performance for the 1968 Triennal in Milan. The theme was "global welfare in social, technical, and emotional light." — *"Blue" Gene Tyranny*

Witold Lutoslawski

b. 1913
Piano / Classical, atonal-chromatic
Polish pianist and composer of orchestral, chamber, and piano music. — *AMG*

Preludes and Fugue (1972) for 13 Solo Strings/ Mi-parti for Orchestra (1976) / Novelette (1979) / 1989 / Polskie Nagrania
Performed by the National Chamber Orchestra in Warsaw and the Polish Radio National Symphony Orchestra, conducted by Lutoslawski and Hollinger. Totally redefines "preludes" as mysterious sound-pieces with a "fugue" of brilliant, aleatoric, sliding, perpendicular lines. Both *Mi-Parti* (French for a whole with two parts not the same) and the *Novelette* imply nonspecified narratives. — *"Blue" Gene Tyranny*

Postlude I for Orchestra (1958) / Paroles Tissees (Weaving Songs) (1965) for Tenor, Strings, Harp, Piano, and Percussion / Livre Po / 1990 / Polskie Nagrania
Although his pre-1960 works are almost 19th-century in their gestures and development, the pieces on this CD are strikingly different in their tone-colors and organization, especially the beautiful *Livre pour orchestre* and the highly original *Cello Concerto*. — *"Blue" Gene Tyranny*

Les Espaces du Sommeil (The Spaces of Sleep) / 1990 / Philips
Some lovely timbral effects for a setting of this poem by Robert Desnos about the discovery of one's soul or others' presence ("There is you undoubtedly whom I do not know ...") during the internal wanderings of sleep. The singing of Dietrich Fischer-Dieskau is of course superb. CD also includes the "Symphony No. 3. Both works performed by the Berlin Philharmonic, conducted by the composer. — *"Blue" Gene Tyranny*

Angus Maclise

b. 1938, **d.** 1979

Angus Maclise (Various Works) / 1992 / Mela Foundation
A cassette collection of various works by the marvelous poet, mystic, composer, drummer, and cembalum player who wrote music for independent films (Ron Rice's *Chumlum*, Warhol's *EPI (Exploding Plastic Inevitable)* and combined American forms with music of expanded time sense; for example, "12 I 64 AM NYC the first twelve; Sunday Morning Blues" (1964) for bowed gong, hand drums, sopranino saxophone, bowed guitar, plucked mandola, and viola. — *"Blue" Gene Tyranny*

Jackson Mac Low

b. 1922
Open Secrets / 1994 / Experimental Intermedia
Mac Low began writing music and poetry when he was 15, and later he developed his "simultaneities" after 1953 for speakers, vocalists, instrumentalists, and/or projectionists. His poetry, published to date in 25 volumes, is written following the many indeterminate/nonintentional procedures that he has invented. This CD provides a good overview of Mac Low's creativity: the "1st Milarepa Gatha" (1976), "Thanks" (1960), the "38th and 39th Merzgedichte in Memoriam Kurt Schwitters" (1989), "Phoneme Dance in Memoriam John Cage" (by Mac Low and Anne Tardos) (1993), "Free Gatha 1" (1978), and "Free Gatha 2" (1981) are works for massed, multitracked voices speaking/singing at the same time with complex compositional procedures described in the notes. The "Milarepa Quartet for Four Like Instruments" (1982) employs a letter-to-pitch-class code that translates text into music in the manner of procedures used by Messiaen, Ashley, Cage, and others. "Winds/Instruments" (1980) is for voices and instrumentalists who sometimes speak, and "Lucas 1 to 29: for One or More Instrumentalists (In Memoriam Morton Feldman and for the Musicians of Germany)" (1990) is based on the Lucas sequence. — *"Blue" Gene Tyranny*

Bruno Maderna

b. 1920, **d.** 1973
Atonal-chromatic

☆ **Quadrivium (Crossroads) (1969) for Four Percussionists and Four Orchestral Groups / Aura (1972) for Orchestra / Biogramma (1972) for Lar** / 1990 / Deutsche Grammaphon
A reissue on CD of the 1980 discs. Performances by the North German Radio Symphonie Orchestra, conducted by Giuseppe Sinopoli. The expressive, shimmering neo-impressionism of "Aura" and "Biogramma," and the ever-changing landscape (guided by the conductor's choices, different for each performance) of "Quadrivium," by the poet of the serialist composers. — *"Blue" Gene Tyranny*

Vandalia / 1991 /

Per la Sete Dell-Orecchio (For the Thirst of the Ear) / 1991 /
The legendary, conceptually surreal piano recordings finally reissued. — *"Blue" Gene Tyranny*

Bruno Maderna Dirige Maderna / 1993 / Arkadia
Wonderful performances of Maderna, an accomplished conductor as well as composer, conducting his own music. Contains the "Concerto for Violin and Orchestra" (1970 version), "Grande Aulodia" for flute and oboe soloists and orchestra, and the magnificient "Aura." — *"Blue" Gene Tyranny*

David Mahler

The King of Angels / Frog Peak Music
Two tributes to Elvis Presley: the song "Every Song You Sang" and the tape piece "The King of Angels." Also the word piece "Cup of Coffee." Surprising works by this important Seattle-based composer. — *"Blue" Gene Tyranny*

Chris Mann

La-de-da / Talking About Healesville / 38'37" A Machine for Making Sense / Frog Peak Music
Three cassettes by this influential Australian composer, poet, text sound and visual artist. "La-de-da" is the classic "truly stereo" test piece; "Talking about Healesville" was banned in Healesville; and "38'37" A Machine for Making Sense" is the improvisational group of which Mann is a member. — *"Blue" Gene Tyranny*

The Birth of Peace / NMA
Cassette tape with book of Mann's multimedia piece for goldfish-controlled computers and poets. Includes plastic goldfish. — *"Blue" Gene Tyranny*

Walter Marchetti

☆ **Natura Morta (still Life)** / 1991 /
Vandalia / 1991 / Cramps

Per la Sete Dell-Orecchio (For the Thirst of the Ear) / 1991 /
Cramps
The legendary, conceptually surreal piano recordings finally reissued.
— *"Blue" Gene Tyranny*

Christian Marclay

○ **Black Stucco/ In "Imaginary Landscapes"** / 1989 /
Elektra/Nonesuch
Marclay plays turntables—using the clicks of vinyl discs, by
"scratching," back-and-forward manual rotation, mixing,
varispeed—using recordings as "artifacts" of our society. He has
also created art objects with the same records—"Footsteps" is a
one-sided record containing the sounds of footsteps. 3500 copies
were spread on the floor of the Shedhalle galleries in Z rich and
people were invited to walk on them over the course of six weeks,
and 1000 of the records with dirt and scratches are available from
Gelbe Musik. He has also made a "Record without grooves" with
a gold label housed in a black velour cover with golden writing,
signed and numbered. — *"Blue" Gene Tyranny*

Ingram Marshall

b. 1942
New Age, electronic, minimalism

○ **Fog Tropes/ Gradual Requiem/ Gambuh I** / 1990 / New Albion
Three Penitential Visions / Hidden Voices / 1993 /
Elektra/Nonesuch
Atmospheric, subtle, with almost new-age transparency but more
ideas: one of Marshall's best albums. *Fog Tropes* creates the beautiful landscape suggested by the title, with gently phasing orchestral brass and taped ocean sounds. — *"Blue" Gene Tyranny*

Richard Maxfield

b. 1927, **d.** 1969
Electronic, atonal-chromatic

○ **Night Music in "New Sounds in Electronic Music"** / Odyssey
This exquisite pre-synthesizer electronic music is made like his
pieces *Sine Music* (1959) and *Trinity Piece* (1960), with only the
supersonic bias signal of a tape recorder and a supersonic sawtooth waveform from an oscilloscope producing audio-range difference-tone "ghosts." Identical in feeling to a response to the
sound of birds and insects on a summer night in a city park. —
"Blue" Gene Tyranny

☆ **Richard Maxfield: Electronic Music** / 1992 / Mela Foundation
A cassette reissue of the original out-of-print Advance Recordings
disc (1969), this collection contains some of the most beautiful
and imaginative electronic and "live electronic" music ever made
(I'm serious) using only pre-synthesizer Army-surplus store electronics. *Pastoral Symphony* (1960) for three channels—one behind the audience—is a lovely work, as is *Night Music* on
Odyssey records (see above) and his *A Swarm of Butterflies
Encountered on the Ocean* (unissued). "Bacchanale" (1963) is
made from a noise-improv-collage ensemble with poetry by
Edward Fields, folk music recordings (many from Henry Cowell),
jazz hang-outs, scraping violin noises, underwater clarinet, drum,
typewriter, and parts of Maxfield's *African Symphony* and the poetic *Wind*. The latter is made of events separated from each other
by beautifully timed silences. The sounds are composed of wind
and the sounds of things that wind moves, like squeaking rusty
gates. Maxfield turns it all into an intriguing piece. Other pieces
on this recording include *Piano Concert for David Tudor* (1961),
for piano and tapes made from the performer's improvisations;
Amazing Grace (1960), a mass of tape loops cut to a score (like
Maxfield's *Cough Music* (1959-1961) and *Italian Folk Music*), humorous samples from a religious revival; part of the sketches for
Maxfield's opera *Stacked Deck*. "Composers, Performance, and
Publication," a very interesting essay, appears in *An Anthology* by
La Monte Young.— *"Blue" Gene Tyranny*

Toshiro Mayuzumi

b. 1929
Atonal-chromatic, world music derivative

Mandala Symphony (1960) / Odyssey
Performed by the NHK Symphony Orchestra, conducted by
Hiroyuki Iwaka. Although bordering on a large contemporary romantic work, this symphony attempts to express a Japanese
"Buddhist view of the omnipotent universe," and uses only collections of sounds to achieve this aim. The two parts of the mandala are expressed in the two parts of the symphony: "Kongokai-Mandala symbolizes spiritual awakening through contemplation
and oneness with eternity; Taizokai-Mandala represents the
world of Sokushin Jyobutsu, which is made up of the phases of
life, such as Gakido (a place of hunger and thrist where sinners
go in the afterlife) or Shurado (passage of pandemonium, the
world of the immature until they attain spiritual awakening)."
(See also *String Quartet* by LaSalle in 20th-Century Collections in
this section.) — *"Blue" Gene Tyranny*

Barton McLean

b. Apr. 8, 1938

**A Little Night Music / Demons of the Night/ In CDCM
Computer Music Series, vol. 7, A** / 1990 / Centaur
Nocturnal tone poems, beautifully formed computer sounds expressing different night sensations. — *"Blue" Gene Tyranny*

Olivier Messiaen

b. 1908, **d.** Apr. 28, 1992
*Organ, composer / Classical, electronic, atonal-chromatic, world
music derivative*

French organist and composer of music that is mostly religious in
nature. Messiaen composed in most forms, especially keyboard
(organ, piano) and orchestral. —*AMG*

**L'Ascension (Four Symphonic Meditations for Orchestra)
(1933)** / Koch Schwann
Performed by the Bavarian Radio Orchestra, directed by Karl
Anton Rickenbacher. Compassionate, sacramental, similar to *Les
Offrandes Oubliees* (1930); unlike the severe religious works of
his later style. CD includes *Chronochromie* (1959/1960). — *"Blue"
Gene Tyranny*

**Trois Petites Liturgies (Three Brief Liturgies) (1943-1944) for
Women's Chorus, Chamber Orchestra with Ondes Martenot**
/ Erato
A very curious, Byzantine work with a poetic and controversial
text by the composer, the poetry of gems and colors mixed with
reflections on the presence of the Creator, in us, in others, in
things. — *"Blue" Gene Tyranny*

☆ **Des Canyons Aux Etoiles (From the Canyons to the Stars)
(1971-1974)/ Oiseaux Exotiques (Exotic Birds) (1956)/
Couleurs de la Cite** / 1991 / CBS
London Sinfonetta, directed by Esa-Pekka Salonen. A terrific collection of the best of Messiaen's later style. Pointillistic tone paintings and good performances, but I prefer the out-of-print Erato
discs with Marius Constant conducting. — *"Blue" Gene Tyranny*

O Sacrum Convivium/ In "Of Eternal Light" / 1993 / Catalyst
A warm, hopeful religious work in Messiaen's early style in a
beautifully subtle performance by Musica Sacra, conducted by
Richard Westenburg. This CD also contains the enchanting and
energetic "Return to Earth" by Meredith Monk, and pieces by
Moran and Ligeti. — *"Blue" Gene Tyranny*

Eclairs sur L'Au-Dela (1992) / 1994 / Jade
The generally agreed-upon translation for this title,
"Illuminations from the Beyond," is a little tame compared to the
equally appropriate and somewhat more apt "Lightning-Flashes
from the Beyond." The full-brass unisons with whipcracks and
deep rolls from bass drum and gong in the section "Seven Angels
with Seven Trumpets" elicit the most chilling, majestic feelings
from a pre-modern sense of the eternal mystery. "The Way to the
Invisible" likewise opens gates of the subconscious with beautifully bizarre harmonic sweeps in the strings, full chordal annunciations in the brass, and "total chromatic" backdrops for the song
of the pied butcherbird to wander through. As in several other
Messiaen works, the birds are seen as intermediaries between the
heavenly and the earthly: there is a gorgeous menagerie of 25
bird songs played freely and simultaneously in the section
"Several Birds from the Trees of Life," and birds appear throughout the piece. Lovely, unique melodic strains appear in several
sections: "God Will Wipe Every Tear from Their Eyes"; the very
moving, yet not sensual in the usual manner, "Dwelling in Love";
and the final "Christ, Light of Paradise." This piece is a testament
to faith in the natural revelation of the Great Mystery expressed

in clear, beautiful musical imagers, neither overemotional nor overaustere. Recorded in a live performance by the National Polish Radio Orchestra of Katowice, conducted by Antoni Wit. — *"Blue" Gene Tyranny*

Roscoe Mitchell (Roscoe Edward Mitchell, Jr.)

b. Aug. 3, 1940, Chicago, IL
Reeds, composer / Modern creative, avant-garde, early free
See the Jazz section for his biography.

☆ **Four Compositions** / 1992 / Lovely Music
Fleeting chromatic gestures; bizarre multiphonic acoustics; unusual instruments (triple contrabass, viol, and contrabass sarrusophone); touching, brief melodies; and humor combine to create unique music. Selections include "NONAAH," "Duet for Wind and String," "Cutouts," and "Prelude." Excellent performances. Highly recommended. — *"Blue" Gene Tyranny*

Pilgrimage / 1994 / Lovely Music
Fabulous new pieces featuring the Roscoe Mitchell New Chamber Ensemble: Mitchell, Thomas Buckner (vocal), Joseph Kubera (piano), and Vartan Manoogian (violin). — *"Blue" Gene Tyranny*

Dary John Mizelle

b. Jun. 14, 1940
Polyphonies (1975) for Shakuhachi and Electronic Sounds / Spectra (1975-1979) for Bass and Computer Tape / Primavera-Heterophony, for 24 Celli / 1981 / IRIDA
Polyphonies of earth, air, fire, and water sounds; dualities of musical gesture (such as slow/fast); and varieties of musical organization (drone, pointillistic, gestural, polyphonic, stochastic, and cyclic) in a strange duet. Unique dramatic sounds from massed strings. — *"Blue" Gene Tyranny*

Gordon Monahan

○ **Long Aeolian Piano, The** / 1990 / Musicworks #45
A lovely "aeolian harp," sculpted with Thaddeus Holownia, made from strings attached to an upright piano, stretched down a hill, and set in resonance by the wind. (Incidentally, another lovely "aeolian harp" with metal resonators built by Doug Hollis lives as a permanent installation atop the Exploratorium in San Francisco. See *Soundviews* in 20th-Century Collections in this section.) See also Canadian composer Monahan's piece "Speaker Swinging" (excerpt) in the collections *Imaginary Landscapes* and *Soundviews.* — *"Blue" Gene Tyranny*

This Piano Thing / 1992 / Swerve Editions
Studies in producing unusual sounds from both an unaltered acoustic piano in "Piano Mechanics" and a prepared piano in "This Piano Thing." Monahan has invented several original playing techniques ("Fingers and Arms Becoming Four Hands," "High Trills Becoming Difference Tones," "Voices Emerging along High Tension Wires") that also require an ear sensitive to the momentary buildups of rushing waveforms and overtone changes. Fascinating and original work. — *"Blue" Gene Tyranny*

Meredith Monk

b. Nov. 20, 1942
Keyboards, composer / Avant-garde

Key / 1993 / Lovely Music
Rerelease on CD of the 1973 classic. Monk's modern folk music from her beautiful and noble performance-ceremonies that recall former times and a lineage of human understanding beyond the present state of things. Songs include "Porch," "Under Street," "What Does it Mean?," "Vision," "Fat Stream," "Do You Be?" "Vision" (reprise), "Change," and "Dungeon" with Meredith Monk (voice, organ, jew's harp); and Daniel Ira Sverdlik, Dick Higgins, Colin Walcott, Lanny Harrison, and Mark Monstermaker (voices). See also her beautiful "Phantom Waltz" in the collection *U.S. Choices* by the piano duet Double Edge. — *"Blue" Gene Tyranny*

Atlas / An Opera in Three Parts / 1993 / ECM

Robert Moran

b. 1937
Minimalism
The works listed below have either been unavailable in the U.S. for a long time or have just been newly recorded by this highly original and often lyrical composer. Moran collaborated with

Phillip Glass on the opera *The Juniper Tree.* — *"Blue" Gene Tyranny*

Arias, Interlude, and Inventions from "Desert of Roses" / Ten Miles High over Albania for Eight Harps / Open Veins for Orchestra / 1993 / Argo
A very original composer whose orchestral sound has touches of exotic color, phase music, tuneful invention, Moran collaborated with Philip Glass on the opera *The Juniper Tree.* Highly recommended. — *"Blue" Gene Tyranny*

Charles Morrow

b. 1942
Minimalism, world music derivative

Birth of the War God (1973) / The Cloud Will Break / The Canticle for Brother Sun (1985) for Vocal Ensemble, The / Laurel

BP for bp / Musicworks
Unique works by a composer who has an abiding interest in world music and has produced some fine compositions with minimalist instrumentation. — *"Blue" Gene Tyranny*

David Moss

b. Jan. 21, 1949
Avant-garde

Language Linkage (1988) / 1990 / Aerial #1
Energetic setting of Italo Calvino text for many processed voices, electronic sounds, and percussion. Like a parallel universe. A very different sound. — *"Blue" Gene Tyranny*

Raphael Mostel

Nightsongs / 1991 / Scarlet/Infinity
Not a "new-age" group, this ensemble is described on their first CD cover as creating "new music for old instruments," and that's what they do. Raphael Mostel resonates Tibetan brass meditation bowls, gradually introducing sharp and startling sounds that will awaken the chakras. "Jacob's Ladder" combines didgeridoos, water, and breaking sounds with wailing thighbone trumpets. John Charles Thomas produces a solo on the ancient lyzarden with jazz-line inflections in "Nightsong." The brilliant singer and instrumentalist Mieczyslaw Litwinski is also featured throughout. — *"Blue" Gene Tyranny*

Blood on the Moon / 1992 / Digital Fossils
Original music of a transparent, eternal quality that also suggests many Asian and Middle Eastern traditions, primarily because of the acoustic instruments used to play it: singing bowls, shakuhachi, Tibetan thighbone trumpets, ram's horn, and others. Highly meditative and sustained, with moments of restrained intense emotion. — *"Blue" Gene Tyranny*

Gordon Mumma

b. 1935
Electronic, minimalism
Gordon Mumma is a cofounder, with Robert Ashley, of the Cooperative Studio for Electronic Music in Ann Arbor, MI, which has been in existence since the early '60s. —*AMG*

☆ **Mesa/Pontpoint/Fwyyn** / Lovely Music
Performed by the composer, with Pauline Oliveros and David Tudor (bandoneons). "Fwyyn" is a lament to bring back to life a dancing princess who had been enchanted—beautiful, slowly evolving textures. "Mesa" describes expansive, eroded mesa landscapes, and "Pontpoint" interprets a bridge in a rural French village through an analogous bridging movement in the acoustical space. Pure electronic music, by a cofounder (with Robert Ashley) of the Cooperative Studio for Electronic Music in Ann Arbor, Michigan (1960-1970). — *"Blue" Gene Tyranny*

○ **Dresden Interleaf 13 February 1945/ Music from the Venezia Space Theatre/ Megaton for William Burroughs, The** / Lovely Music
Live electronic music created for multimedia theaters. Performances by the ONCE Group on tour. Fascinating and mysterious. — *"Blue" Gene Tyranny*

Hornpipe (1967)/ In "The Sonic Arts Union" / 1970 / Mainstream

A piece for French horn played with unusual reed mouthpieces, cybersonic circuits, and other devices. We hear the sound of the processing circuits balancing and unbalancing themselves, as the horn player's chosen responses gradually build an "orchestra" of accumulated decisions. A mysterious live performance. —*"Blue" Gene Tyranny*

Conlon Nancarrow

b. Oct. 27, 1912
Composer / Atonal-chromatic, jazz derivative
An American composer residing in Mexico since 1940, Nancarrow's works involve manipulation of the workings of player pianos, producing sounds and gestures not possible for human performers. —*AMG*

☆ **Studies for Player Piano, vol. I-II, vol. III-IV, vol. V** / 1990 / WERGO
Secluded in a quiet suburban district of Mexico City, Conlon Nancarrow spent three decades composing these incomparable pieces, punching the player piano rolls himself. Of unparalleled rhythmic complexity and fascinating energy, with boogie woogie in some studies like you've never heard before. —*"Blue" Gene Tyranny*

Study no.15 (1950s), Transcribed for Piano Four-Hands by Yvar Mikhashoff/ In "Continuum Performs Nancarrow" / 1992 / Musicmasters
The same surprising rhythmic complexities and drive as the piano rolls. Played here by live performers. —*"Blue" Gene Tyranny*

Ben Neill

☆ **Collapse of the Illusory One-Tribe Nation from Itsofomo (In The Shadow of Forward Motion), with Text and Vocals by David Wojna, The** / 1991 / Tellus #25
○ **Mainspring** / 1992 / Ear-Rational
Pieces featuring Neill's invention, the mutatrumpet, a combination of three trumpets plus slide, which makes rapid change between a variety of sonorities possible. An electronic processing system by Robert Moog and a computer program by David Behrman have both been designed to work with the mutatrumpet. This CD exemplifies the idea of "unified multisidedness" in the sounds and the compositional style. For example, "Mainspring" (1985), after a fanfare-type introduction, goes into a riff-steady march tune over a half-stepping accompaniment with steel guitar country music slides and, later, a solo for the bridge— really delightful and peculiar. "Dis-solution 2" (1986) is for mutatrumpet, percussion, and pitch-sensing electronics (David Behrman) providing a lovely treble shadow. "No More People" (1988), with text by Stevie Smith for soprano and band, is a classic aria over constantly intense telegraphic figures. Wow ... — *"Blue" Gene Tyranny*

Itsofomo (In the Shadow of Forward Motion) (Complete Work) / 1993 / New Tone
The raw truth of a personal experience of anti-gay violence: the energetically telegraphing style of the music is excellently imagined and perfectly complements the impassioned text and delivery by the late Wojnarowicz. Extraordinarily moving. —*"Blue" Gene Tyranny*

Phill Niblock

b. 1933
Electronic, minimalism, world music derivative
○ **Four Full Flutes** / 1991 / Experimental Intermedia
Meditative, sustained, divine; slowly changing clusters. —*"Blue" Gene Tyranny*

Music by Phill Niblock / 1993 / Experimental Intermedia
This CD contains two compositions—"Five More String Quartets" and "Early Winter"—both of which are long, sustained sound universes that slowly change in pitch and timbre, redefining the form of the sonic space they simultaneously create and occupy. For example, in "Early Winter" for string quartet, multitracked bass flute, sampled and synthesizer voices, and flute, harmonics slowly appear and vanish like the slow onset of winter weather. "Five More String Quartets" creates ghostly different tones by the detuning/retuning of pitches from multitracked strings. —*"Blue" Gene Tyranny*

Luigi Nono

b. 1924, **d.** 1990
Composer / Classical, electronic, atonal-chromatic
An Italian composer in the 12-tone or atonal style, whose work encompasses many forms, including opera and electronic music. Many fundamental pieces by Nono are out of print: "Y Su Sangre Ya Viene Cantando (And Even Your Blood Comes Singing)," for flute, strings, and percussion, from *Epitaffio per Garcia Lorca* ("Epitaph for Garcia Lorca," RCA Victrola VICS 1313, 1968); the choral settings of texts by Cesare Pavese; and the operas *Intolleranze* ("Intolerance," 1960, which attacks segregation, the bomb, and Nazism); *Al Gran Sole Carico d'Amore* ("To the Great Sun Charged with Love," 1975, about the Paris Commune of 1871). —*"Blue" Gene Tyranny*

Floresta e Jovem e Cheja de Vida (1965-1966) for Soprano, Voices, Clarinet, Copper Plate, and Tape, A / 1979 / Deutsche Grammaphon
A good example of Nono's pieces (like "Non Consumiamo Marx" and "La Fabricca Illuminata," both for voices and tape) that calls for attention to immediate situations, in this case, the escalation of the Vietnam War by American forces. Nono uses tapes that mix multiphonics played on the clarinet with various electronic sounds produced at the national radio RAI studios, as well as texts from pro- and anti-war groups and individuals, a Vietnamese partisan, American workers and students, vocalized by the legendary New York-based group The Living Theater. In live performance with this tape, a soprano and other lives voices sing a lament and deliver other texts, accompanied by five suspended copper metal plates of various thicknesses (ancient sounds of the call to war). —*"Blue" Gene Tyranny*

☆ **Das Atmende Klarsein (fragment) for Bass Flute and Magnetic Tape/ In Roberto Fabbriciani's "Flute XX"** / 1991 / Koch
Breath and the clarity of being—"pneuma moving through metal": mysterious, dramatic, and beautiful. —*"Blue" Gene Tyranny*

Pierre/ Dell' Azzuro Silenzio/ Inquietum for Voices, Winds, and Live Electronics (1985) / Quando Stanno Morendo, Diario Polacco 2 / 1991 / Dischi Ricordi
Excellent set of three works combining acoustical instruments and voices with live electronics (i.e., not on tape). —*"Blue" Gene Tyranny*

○ **La Lontananza Nostalgica Utopica Futura ("Nostalgia for a Far-Away Future Utopia") for Violin and Taped Electronics** / 1992 / Disques Montaigne
With Irvine Arditti (violin). The electronically modulated sound of the violin is distributed among eight loudspeakers according to various structural and dynamical processes. Mysterious and beautiful. —*"Blue" Gene Tyranny*

Fragmente—Stille, An Diotima (1980) ("Fragments—Stillness, to Diotima") / 1992 / Disques Montaigne
Performed by the Arditti String Quartet. Seeking to "externalize as fully as possible that which has been internalized ... that is what matters today." Nono is guided by lines from Holderlin's famous poem (Diotima was Socrate's teacher and is associated with the concept "Time"), which are present only as an unspoken meditation and guidepost written into the score in 52 places, Nono poses the fundamental question "Where am I, and who am I?" by examining old music and memories from the distant past as producers of both pain and hope. Written for the Beethoven Festival in Bonn, Nono uses Beethoven's piano sonata instruction "mit innigster Empfindung " (roughly, "with innermost searching of the heart") to imply a readiness to break out of the habitual "into the open air." This quartet produces a positive sensation that has been used as an instruction in several of John Cage's works—"play until you feel the presence of silence." (There is also a lovely 1986 performance by the LaSalle Quartet on Deutsche Grammaphon 415 513-2.) —*"Blue" Gene Tyranny*

Il Canto Sospeso (1956) / 1994 / Sony Classical
This piece, based on letters of World War II resistance fighters, introduced new choral writing techniques of word fragmentation and suspension. Nono was one of the leading serialist composers who developed the 12-tone techniques of pre-World War II composers, primarily those of Anton Webern. Excellent performance by the Rundfunkchor Berlin (Berlin Radio Choir) and the Berlin Philharmonic, conducted by Claudio Abbado. Mahler's

"Kindertotenieder" (Songs on the Deaths of Children) is also included. — *"Blue" Gene Tyranny*

Michael Nyman

b. 1944
Minimalism, avant-garde

Zed and Two Noughts, A / 1990 / Virgin Records
Score for the film by Peter Greenway. Nyman's filmscores make effective use of baroque harmonies (Pergolesi, Vivaldi, Purcell—often in a traditional "chain of suspensions" technique) and Phil Glass-like harmonies (Wagnerian thirds mixed with modal scales), combined with obsessive patterns in the British "minimalist" style to make a sound of his own. Excellent production by composer David Cunningham. — *"Blue" Gene Tyranny*

Piano Concerto, The / 1994 / Pauline Oliveros
Notwithstanding the rather droll British joke of the title, and barely skirting a style of Romantic period kitsch, this piece still features surprising harmonic changes and lovely melodies a la Nyman, and retains the post-modern "edge" of his earlier film music. The concerto is of course based on Nyman's music for Jane Campion's award-winning movie *The Piano*. — *"Blue" Gene Tyranny*

Pauline Oliveros

b. 1932
Electronic, minimalism

○ **I of IV (1966)/ In "New Sounds in Electronic Music"** / 1968 / Odyssey
This is a good example of Oliveros's earlier electronic music, using a configuration of tape recorders patched into each other with magnetic tape spliced in loops so that a form of "automatic generation" system was created by feedback. Similar to Richard Maxfield, Oliveros used bias frequencies of tape recorders and lower "ghost tones" produced by the interference of very high frequencies. — *"Blue" Gene Tyranny*

Lullaby for Daisy Pauline/ In "Sleepers" / 1985 / Finnadar
A lovely choral work. — *"Blue" Gene Tyranny*

☆ **Roots of the Moment, The** / 1988 / Hat Hut
Oliveros with accordion in just intonation within an interactive electronic environment created by Peter Ward. An amazing hour-long live creation (improvisation). Images of valleys, other universes, whatever comes to mind—an exercise in true "deep listening" as she refers to the concerts her Foundation presents in upstate New York. — *"Blue" Gene Tyranny*

Crone / 1992 / Lovely Music
Oliveros on accordion, with electronics creating various illusionary movements in space. Beautiful. — *"Blue" Gene Tyranny*

Bob Ostertag

○ **Sooner or Later (Tarde o Temprano)** / 1991 / Recrec
Known for his technique of live performance sampling before there were samplers (by recording a performance, cutting the tape, making a loop, and then playing it back on a tape recorder with the tape guards held up by balloons), Ostertag has created a stark and moving work based on the recorded voice of a young Salvadoran boy burying his father, who had been killed by El Salvador's National Guard. "There is the sound of the boy's voice, a fly buzzing nearby, and the shovel digging the grave. In Part Two, there are additional sounds from a 20-second sample of the guitar playing of Fred Frith." Ostertag spent the last 10 years working in or around El Salvador. "I saw a lot of death. In that culture, which is both Catholic and highly politicized, death gets surrounded with all kinds of trappings that are intended to make it heroic and purposeful. God's will, or else it is irrelevant, since the victims "live on in the struggle." It's all glorious and heroic ... but some 70,000 people have died there ... most ... because they were in the wrong place at the wrong time. They didn't want to. There was no plan. There was no glory. Even for the heroes there is a starker, more immediate side to their death ... sooner or later. No angels sang and no one was better. If there is a beauty, we must find it in what is really there ... the boy, the shovel, the fly. If we look closely, despite the unbearable sadness, we will discover it." — *"Blue" Gene Tyranny*

All the Rage (1992) / 1993 / Elektra/Nonesuch

This moving, 17-minute CD performed by the Kronos Quartet concerns responses to the AIDS epidemic. Part of the purchase price is donated to AIDS relief agencies. — *"Blue" Gene Tyranny*

John Oswald

b. May 30, 1953

Rubiyat Plunderphonics / 1991 / Elektra
This promo-CD (PRCD 8247-2) uses copyrighted material lifted from Elektra's own 40th anniversary Rubiyat collection and other issues: imaginative and probing recombinations of musical gestures from the Doors, Carly Simon, Metallica, Tim Buckley, Faster Pussycat, MC5. — *"Blue" Gene Tyranny*

Discosphere / 1991 / ReR Jocd
This is a wonderful compilation of short, effective, single-themed pieces written for dance, or that had dances made to them or with them. From very delicate studies like "Skindling Shades" made from incendiary sounds, the wild rhythmic rock of "Angle" to the thousandfold overdubbing of a tiny bell sound in "Amina" and the hilarious fractured mystery-tale "The Case of Death," Oswald points out the bones and flesh of our illusions with a funny kind of love. — *"Blue" Gene Tyranny*

○ **Nine Examples of Plunderphonic Techniques** / 1992 / Musicworks #47
These are the techniques used to make the legendary, not-for-sale, but nevertheless illegal-to-possess "Plunderphonics" (1989). Copies were destroyed by the Canadian Recording Industry Association, even though the quoted recordings were so distorted by creative sampling that no one would mistake them for the "real" thing. Canadian composer Oswald comments hilariously and surrealistically on sound material that has become the archtypical if not the downright kitsch-geck detritus of civilization. A procedure and attitude reminiscent of presamplers James Tenney ("Collage #1: Blue Suede," 1961), Richard Maxfield ("Amazing Grace" and "Cough Music" from the early '60s), and Gordon Mumma ("Epoxy"). — *"Blue" Gene Tyranny*

Plexure / 1993 / Avan
This nonstop, high-energy mind bender contains brief detailed and formal studies of passion/pleasure textures in pop culture form the musical equivalent of the involuntary entoptic visions ever-present when we close our eyes. Structural numerics guide precise collaging of gestures lifted from many well-known singers, and we as listeners begin to understand as the underlying nature of their emotional expressions/manipulations. Some sections are: "Urge (Marianne Faith No Morrisey)," "Blur (Bolton Chili Overdire: Moment, Wow, Nest)," and "Temperature (Beastie Shop Beach: Tempus Amore/Hyper Love Theme, Tempo Pact)." If this were a painting, it would be Abstract Expressionist Pop/Op Art—for those who can listen with their minds as well as their nerves. — *"Blue" Gene Tyranny*

Harry Partch

b. 1901, **d.** 1974
Composer / World music derivative, alternative tunings
An American composer of music featuring microtonality using self-made instruments, Harry Partch was the most original thinker on tuning theory in centuries (see his *Genesis of a Music*, Da Capo Press), as well as an instrument designer and builder extraordinaire. — *"Blue" Gene Tyranny*

And on the Seventh Day, Petals Fell on Petaluma (1964) / The Bewitched: Final Scene and Epilogue (1952-1955) / **Castor and Pollux** / CRI
The most original thinker on tuning theory in centuries (see "Genesis of a Music," Da Capo Press). Instrument designer/builder extraordinaire of the Chromelodeon (1945-1949), the Blo-Boy (1958), the Cloud-Chamber Bowls (1950-1951), the Boo (1955-1957), the Spoils of War (1950-1955), the Marimba Eroica (1951-1955), the Crychord (1960-1961), the Eucal Blossom (1964-1967), the Xymo-Xyl (1963), the Mazda Marimba (1963), the Quadrangularis Reversum (1965), and the Harmonic Canon III (Blue Rainbow, 1965), just for starters. Partch had a wonderful sense of humor even while he was discussing serious philosophical questions of life and death. "The Letter" is from a fellow hobo traveling the rails in the 1930s: lots of sliding and suggestive sounds of the "if you know what I mean" typem and naturally a kind of world-weariness; there is sophisticated canonic writing in

"Petals ..." and a sublime mystery in the Cloud Chamber Music. — *"Blue" Gene Tyranny*

Delusion of the Fury / Columbia
A ritual of voices, mime, original instruments, dance, lighting, and staging in which instrumentalists sometimes sing and act—complete theatre as ancient as it is new. Titles of some scenes: "A Son in Search of His Father's Face," "The Quiet Hobo Meal," "Pray for Me Again." — *"Blue" Gene Tyranny*

Bewitched, A Dance Satire (1955), The / 1990 / CRI
A total theater experience like "Delusion of the Fury" above. Titles of some sections are: "The Lost Musicians Mix Magic," "Three Undergrads Become Transfigured in a Hong Kong Music Hall," "Exercises in Harmony and Counterpoint Are Tried in a Court of Ancient Ritual," "The Romancing of a Pathological Liar Comes to an Inspired End," and "Two Detectives on the Trail of a Tricky Culprit Turn in Their Badges." — *"Blue" Gene Tyranny*

Maggi Payne

b. Dec. 23, 1945

Airwaves (Realities) (1987)/ In "Another Coast" / 1988 / Centaur
A comparison of consensual reality in desert and urban cultures by slow sound-imaging. One step beyond the idea of the tone poem into a kind of reality-based illusionism. — *"Blue" Gene Tyranny*

Crystal / 1991 / Lovely Music
Some of the most beautiful and well-crafted electronic music ever, suggesting vast interior and exterior dimensions. Some titles are: "Subterranean Network," "White Night" (a French expression for a sleepless night of repeating thoughts), and "Solar Wind" (based on shockwave interactions of Saturn and Venus with the solar wind). — *"Blue" Gene Tyranny*

Krzysztof Penderecki

b. 1933

Composer / Classical, atonal-chromatic
A Polish composer of choral and orchestral music, opera, and chamber music in a modern harmonic setting. — *AMG*

"K. Penderecki, vol. 1": Threnody for the Victims of Hiroshima for 52 Strings (1959) / Polymorphy for 48 Strings (1961) / 1989 / Polskie Nagrania
This collection, performed by the LaSalle Quartet and the Warsaw and Cracow Philharmoni Orechestras and Choirs, is a good overview of the dramatic and original orchestral timbres of Penderecki's early work with, for example, the famous "Threnody" for massed solo strings making sounds never heard before like thousands of objects randomly falling, sirens, searing fire, rushing storms, and wind. The conceptual and emotional spaces of the "Dimensions of Time and Silence" are everything the title promises. Sensitive performances and great pieces. — *"Blue" Gene Tyranny*

Jutrznia/Utrenya (The Entombment and Resurrection of Christ) (1969-1970) for Two Mixed Choirs, Solo Voices, and Symphony Orchestra / 1989 / Polskie Nagrania
Performed by the Warsaw National Philharmonic Orchestra and Choir. Although there are references to sections of the orthodox mass in the program notes, this is rarely heard in this deeply felt music that speaks to the naked soul ... before the churches appeared ... and could be Buddhist just as well as Christian. The elegant choral and orchestral material is made of tone clusters, chants, and percussive punctuation, taking us into intradimensional and at times hair-raising boundless interior and exterior worlds. — *"Blue" Gene Tyranny*

Matrix 5: Penderecki / 1994 / EMI Classics
A splendid collection of Penderecki's orchestral music, performed by the Polish Radio National Symphony Orchestra. Includes: "Anaklasis" (1959), "Threnody for the Victims of Hiroshima" (see comments above), "Fonogrammi" (1961), "De Natura Sonoris no. 1" (1966), "Capriccio" (1967), "De Natura Sonoris no. 2" (1971), "The Dream of Jacob" (1974), and the "Canticum Canticorum Salmonis" (1970). — *"Blue" Gene Tyranny*

Philip Perkins

Neighborhood with a Sky / 1982 / Fun Music

A beautiful album of compositions where the electronic and "natural" sounds are barely distinguishable; significantly, Perkins does not try to simulate the "natural sounds" but lets their dynamic form and movement influence his electronic sounds (somewhat in the way that Cage, using chance methods, tries to imitate nature, not in its appearance but in its manner of working). The "neighborhood" for Perkins is that of the disc itself, where the natural and the artificial coexist successfully. Contains: "Bird Variations," "The Black and White Cat," "Este's Request," "The Fountain," Equinox Weather," "Rico in the Birdhouse" for trombone solo in an environment, and "Retreat." — *"Blue" Gene Tyranny*

Flame of Ambition, The / 1986 / Fun Music
A collection of pieces about people "burning literally with ambition ... the root of both mankind's greatest triumphs and worst self-made calamities," with scenes from a corporate skyscraper, the company fort: "Taking the Stairs," "Worrisome Fanfare/Weekend with the Kids," "At the Bar," "Talk/Exit (for Corazon Aquino)." A good blend of Perkins's electronic, natural sound, and tuneful mixes. — *"Blue" Gene Tyranny*

☆ **Remotes (I) (1990), The** / 1990 / Fun Music
A mix on cassette tape of nine live radio broadcasts of "The Remotes," a live performance work for an interactive electronic system and various guest musicians, where spontaneous playing and processing allows for all sorts of interesting, communal, and intuitive music making. — *"Blue" Gene Tyranny*

Virgo Ramayana and Other Works for Radio / 1992 / Fun Music
An excellent set on cassette tape of four works, each rich in content and original in concept. "Virgo Ramayana" (Perkins was born under the sign of Virgo) is a 23-minute journey of mysterious ambience and soulfulness with sounds recorded in Indonesia—beautifully mixed with aural textures, blending seamlessly as in a dream, and at other times modulating each other with hidden messages. A great performance realization of John Cage's "Radio Music" (1956) follows. The six-minute edit called "Remotitude" comes next, a live electronic work realized at the Berkeley KPFA studios, with sounds difficult to describe in words—like you've tuned in on a broadcast from an alien world. The 45-minute piece "Say Again," a live radio work with a vocalist (Bonnie Barnett), computer synthesist (Tim Perkis), percussionist/guitarist (Scott Fraser), and Perkins mixing radios, signal and MIDI processes, sampler, and tapes and playing electric bass. Beginning with an odd story about a woman from California offering U.S. herbal tea to some Swiss farmers, the piece moves, modulates, and carries you along in the moment-to-moment mental flow of this ensemble. Highly recommended for its healthy avant-gardism. — *"Blue" Gene Tyranny*

Emanuel Dimas De Melo Pimenta

b. 1957

Rings (1989) / Rozart (1989) / Structures II (1988) / Short Waves (1985) / 1990 / Mode
An emerging composer who works in a "pure" style influenced by American and European aesthetics. "Rozart" incorporates the voice of Enrico Caruso. "Short Waves" was written for the dance "Fabrications" by the Merce Cunningham Dance Company. — *"Blue" Gene Tyranny*

Larry Polansky

b. 1954

Movement for Andrea Smith (My Funny Valentine for Just String Quartet)/ In "Just Intonation" / Tellus #14
An extremely slowed-down angularized ballad. How can I possibly describe the pleading feeling? — *"Blue" Gene Tyranny*

○ **Theory of Impossible Melody, The** / 1989 / Artifact
Fascinating formal (transformational) logic programs generating electronic and acoustic pieces, using the HMSL (Hierarchical Music Specification Language, designed by Phil Burk, Polansky, and David Rosenboom). A feeling of the Cabalistic mysteries. Contains: "B'rey'sheet" (In the Beginning)," computer-aided melodic transformations of traditional Hebrew tropes and melodies used for singing the *Torah;* "Cantillation Study no. 1 for Jody Diamond," for voice and electronics; "Four Voice Canons nos. 3-6 (#3 for computer, #4 for marimbas, #5 for percussion,

#6 for computer); "Simple Actions—Rules of Compossibility for Voice and Live Computer"; "Psaltery for Lou Harrison." —*"Blue" Gene Tyranny*

Henri Pousseur

b. 1929
Electronic, atonal-chromatic

○ **Scambi (Exchanges) (1954) / Trois Visages de Liege (Three Faces of Liege) (1961)/ Paraboles-Mix (1972)** / 1990 / BV Haast ("Acousmatrix 4")
The pure evolving electronic masses of "Scambi," a portrait of the city of the composer's youth (and comissioned by the city of Liege), and a semi-improvised live electro-acoustic mixture changed every evening of the performance (containing a "love duet," "Viva Cuba," "Hymn to the Ornithological Zeus," "Aerial View of Haiphong, Massachusetts") by this wonderfully poetic composer. —*"Blue" Gene Tyranny*

Traverser La Foret (1987) / 1993 / Adda
Although it can be a bit coy at times, this odd, mythological Cantata for narrator, two solo voices, choir, and 12 instruments has its charms and probably a hidden meaning that I'm not getting. The vocal writing and harmonies are exquisite and transparent in texture. —*"Blue" Gene Tyranny*

Eliane Radique

b. 1932
Electronic, minimalism

☆ **Kyema, Intermediate States** / 1992 / Experimental Intermedia
Profound and serenely meditative electronic music inspired by the *Bardo Thodol* (*Tibetan Book of the Dead*). Six states: Kyene (Birth), Milam (Dream), Samten (Contemplation), Chikai (Death), Chonye (Clear Light), Sippai (Becoming). This is the real thing. —*"Blue" Gene Tyranny*

Mila's Journey Inspired by a Dream / 1992 / Lovely Music
With Tibetan singing by Lama Kunga Rinpoche, and English singing by Robert Ashley. Wonderful images and stories from the "100,000 Songs of Milarepa," the musical setting of which is Radique's lifelong project. —*"Blue" Gene Tyranny*

Lou Reed (Louis Firbank)

b. Mar. 2, 1942, Freeport, Long Island, NY
Vocals, guitar / Rock
See the Rock section for his biography.

Amine Ring in "Metal Machine Music," The / Great Expectations
On this CD reissue of the original 1975 RCA Records disc, we hear an unrelenting, seeringly beautiful electro-acoustic composition for electric guitar and an array of "consumer-priced" sound-processing devices and amplifiers used by most bands of the mid-'70s. Inspired by La Monte Young's Dream Music installations, this one-time spontaneous production of Reed's predated a great deal of rock-sound inspired new music (Branca, Chatham, and others).Feedback and a lot of the Keith Richards-effect (maximum volume through small speakers) lends a feeling of infinite universal and atomic surface compression permeating everything. "Passion-realism was the key" is the significant line from the otherwise rather posed liner notes. Sudden silences leave the listener floating. —*"Blue" Gene Tyranny*

Steve Reich

b. Oct. 3, 1936
Composer / Avant-garde, 20th century classical
Steve Reich deserves attention as an improviser and percussionist not really fitting into either a traditional jazz or a classical vein. Reich studied both music at Juilliard and philosophy at Cornell and later was a student of Darius Milhaud and Luciano Berio at Mills College in California. He formed his own ensemble in 1966, and immersed himself in African drumming in 1970 by living in Ghana. In 1973, he studied Balinese gamelan music. Recognized as a major figure in the minimalist school, his compositions emphasize repetition, with chords changing one note at a time and arrangements that include ethnic and ancient rhythmic elements. Reich released acclaimed albums in the '70s and '80s featuring multiple drums, marimbas, voices, and unusual instruments. —*Ron Wynn*

○ **Different Trains (1988) for String Quartet and Tape** / 1989 / Elektra/Nonesuch
In an acoustic equivalent to interactive electronics, Reich creates a rhythmic tape of train whistles of the '30s and '40s and of speakers recalling train rides of the past in the U.S.A. and in Nazi-occupied lands. The natural pitch inflections of the voices are then transferred to pitches for the instruments. A rich emotional experience akin to his earlier pieces—"It's Gonna Rain" (1965) and the shocking "Come Out" (1966) (both on Elektra/Nonesuch 79169-2)—a more interesting use of the rather mechanistic edge of his pattern music. —*"Blue" Gene Tyranny*

Brian Reinbolt

b. 1955
Electronic

It's Not That Simple / 1990 / Artifact
Interesting microcomputer music, especially the three-dance set "Simple Dance" ("Simple—dance on the plain of a dream," "IV—the patron saint of lawyers," "Cones—made of ever-increasing and decreasing circles") and "Black Noise." —*"Blue" Gene Tyranny*

The Residents

Group / World music derivative, alternate tunings, 20th century rock derivative, alternative pop/rock
The Residents are one of rock's oddest and most mysterious groups. Their identity has been a closely guarded secret for two decades. In rare public appearances, they are typically disguised as giant eyeballs decked out in tuxes and top hats. But behind all the weirdness is ... more weirdness—primitive mutations of popular songs by the likes of Elvis, James Brown, and Hank Williams; frightening nursery rhymes; elaborate mythological epics that span several albums; and pure sonic explorations. Like the most adventurous modern composers, the Residents understand the emotive power of sound; early pieces like "Eskimo" are unforgettably evocative. Their later projects contain subtle social commentary. Even when the parody verges on self-parody, the music retains shock value and sophistication. —*Myles Boisen*

○ **Commercial Album (1980)** / Ralph Records
40 brief stories, homilies, instrumentals, slices of life, each exactly 60 seconds long: "The Coming of the Crow," "Nice Old Man," "My Work Is So Behind," "Die in Terror," "Floyd," "Act of Being Polite,"—each unique in vocals and instrumentation, and each weirdly humorous and momentarily stunning. —*"Blue" Gene Tyranny*

☆ **God in Three Persons** / 1988 / Ryko
Employing the same stress-scheme as Poe's "The Raven" throughout its 62 minutes, *God in Three Persons* is an extended work in "talking-blues" style for narrator, electronic instruments, and a chorus providing comments not to be found in the libretto—they sing production credits at the beginning, and lines like "something's coming, but not real soon," and "this is a sad part, oh, such a sad part." This surreal and yet directly delivered work is as lovingly human as it is comic, with profound experience simply expressed—in short, an original masterpiece of American music, directly in the tradition of the Thomson-Stein and Robert Ashley operas. As in all Residents pieces, the voices are modified electronically and the musical elements are deceptively minimal—most of its 14 episodes have only two chords which, however, still manage to instantly produce the correct atmosphere (Phil Glass-like Wagnerian thirds for mythic import, tonic-dominant in triplets for '50s teenage love story, and more). There are only passing riffs, more like comments, and the only melody in the whole piece is a wheezy organ quote of the standard doxology hymn "Holy, Holy, Holy (God in Three Persons)." The subject matter is, in part, the derivation of religious and other symbolic images from the naturally erotic, but that's only part of it. Please give this one a listen. —*"Blue" Gene Tyranny*

● **Eskimo (1979)** / 1990 / ESD
A CD re-issue of the 1979 record. A wild vision of what original polar Eskimo life was like before government housing came along in the late '60s. Contains "The Walrus Hunt," "Birth," "Artic Hysteria," "The Angry Angakok," "A Spirit Steals a Child," "The Festival of Death." A totally engaging tone-poem, filled with humor, pathos, shamanism, and all the other great things, with skill-

ful electronic sound-painting and always the right touch. — *"Blue" Gene Tyranny*

Roger Reynolds

b. 1934
Electronic, atonal-chromatic

Whispers out of Time / Transfigured Wind II / 1990 / New World
Lovely and mysterious works for flute and computer-generated tape. — *"Blue" Gene Tyranny*

○ **Voicespace: Still (1975)/ A Merciful Coincidence (1976) / Eclipse (1979) / The Palace (1980)** / 1992 / Lovely Music
A reissue of the two-record set. Four pieces for computer electronics and voices that amplify to an extreme degree the components and expressive qualities of the voice. "Still," with a text from Samuel Coleridge's *The Wanderings of Cain* (1798), moves extremely slowly in a "vocal fry" across the aspirate clicks and wind of the performer; "A Merciful Coincidence," on a text from Samuel Beckett's *Watt* (1953), uses the aggressive-passive inflections of the frog-performers croaking, which seems to have intent, if not syntactical, "meaning"; "Eclipse," with a combined text from Borges, Gabriel Marquez, Issa, James Joyce, Melville, and Wallace Stevens, eclipses strains of modulated texts into one another; "The Palace," on a translated text by Jorge Luis Borges (1976), is a dramatic monodrama about how the Self imagines its confines within the space of the Mind, and a prerecorded, modified voice is added to the singer onstage, yielding an enormous, supra-human quality. — *"Blue" Gene Tyranny*

Electroacoustic Music / 1993 / New World
Dramatic new pieces for instruments and electronics: "Versions/Stages" (1988-1991) and "The Ivanov Suite" (1991) created for Tadashi Suzuki's version of Chekhov's play. — *"Blue" Gene Tyranny*

Terry Riley

b. 1935
Composer / Ambient, minimalism, world music derivative, alternate tunings

An American composer of minimalist electronic keyboard music, whose works are influenced by his studies of East Indian music. —*AMG*

○ **In C** / 1989 / Celestial Harmonies
Performed by the Shanghai Film Orchestra, conducted by Wang Yongji. Truly celestial, with a different feeling from American/European performances of this famous piece. This CDalso contains David Mingyue Lang's gorgeous "Music of a Thousand Springs" and his "Zen (Ch'an) of Water." Highly recommended. — *"Blue" Gene Tyranny*

☆ **Rainbow in Curved Air/Poppy Nogood and the Phantom Band** / 1990 / CBS
A CD reissue of the classic 1969 recording. After several graph compositions and early pattern-pieces with jazz ensembles in the late '50s and early '60s (see "Concert for Two Pianists and Tape Recorders" and "Ear Piece" in La Monte Young's book *An Anthology*), Riley invented a whole new music, which has since gone under many names (minimal music—a category often applied to sustained pieces as well, pattern music, phase music, and others). This music is set forth in its purest form in the famous "In C" (1964) (for saxophone and ensemble, CBS MK 7178). "Rainbow in Curved Air" demonstrates the straightforward pattern technique, but also has Riley improvising with the patterns, making gorgeous timbre changes on the synthesizers and organs, and presenting contrasting sections that have become the basic structuring of his current works ("Cadenza on the Night Plain" and other pieces, Kronos Quartet, Gramavision R22Z-79444, two CDs; "Salome Dances for Peace" (1989), Kronos Quartet, Elektra/Nonesuch 79217-2, two CDs; and the recently premiered and as-yet-unrecorded "The Jade Palace" (1991), commissioned and played by the St. Louis Symphony. Scored for large orchestra with extra percussion and electronics, some of this work's seven movements are: "Star Night," "Blue Lotus," "The Earth Below," and "Island of the Rhumba King.") — *"Blue" Gene Tyranny*

Tread on the Trail (1964-1965) for Sax and Synthesizer/ In "Jon Gibson" / 1992 /
Gibson's exquisite tone shines. — *"Blue" Gene Tyranny*

June Buddhas from "Mexico City Blues" / 1992 / Musicmasters
Another side of Riley. CD also includes Lou Harrison's "Seven Pastorales" and Peggy Granville-Hicks's "Etruscan Concerto." — *"Blue" Gene Tyranny*

Persian Surgery Dervishes / 1993 / Newtone
Reissue of Riley's masterpiece from the '70s. — *"Blue" Gene Tyranny*

Peter Van Riper

Heart (from Acoustic Metal Music) / 1992 / The Aerial #4
Playing on a twirling metal strip about eight feet long, which a sculptor-friend used to make interlocking heart constructions, Van Riper makes a transparently beautiful and almost electronic effect. — *"Blue" Gene Tyranny*

Jean-Claude Risset

b. 1938
Electronic, atonal-chromatic

Songs (Dreams) (1979) / Passages (1982) for Flute and Tape / Computer Suite from Little Boy (1968) / Sud (South) (1985) / 1988 / Wergo
One of the early developers of computer music, with Max Matthews at Bell Laboratories and at IRCAM in Paris. Exquisite textures in an aural space that constantly changes its dimensions—soft velvet to digital glacier edges to the ringing of huge bells after they are struck. "Sud" is filled with electronic tropical sounds and washes like extended raindrops and wind chimes. A delight to the ear. — *"Blue" Gene Tyranny*

Neil B. Rolnick

b. Oct. 22, 1947

Macedonian Air Drumming / 1992 / Bridge
Contains "Sanctus," a computer-generated tape; the complete "Balkanization" (see also *Imaginary Landscapes in 20th-Century Collections in this section*); "ReRebong," for the gamelon Son of Lion; and "Macedonian Air Drumming," for MIDI-controlled instruments. —"Blue" Gene Tyranny

Electricity / 1992 / O.O. Discs
Great performances of Rolnick's music by George Lewis (trombone), the New York Contemporary Music Ensemble, and Robert Dick (flute). — *"Blue" Gene Tyranny*

David Rosenboom

b. 1947
Electronic

Systems of Judgment (1987) / 1990 / Centaur
A many-timbred computer music composition, sweeping in scope: dynamic sonic illusions of natural sound—mythical and philosophical worlds meeting. — *"Blue" Gene Tyranny*

○ **Precipice in Time (1966) / In CDCM Computer Music Series, Vol. 10, A** / 1991 /
A unique blend of "free jazz," live "phantom doubles" (computer re-synthesis of acoustic instruments), and graphed structure. From high energy to quiet anticipations with interior tension. Terrific playing. — *"Blue" Gene Tyranny*

Mikel Rouse

b. 1957

Soul Menu / 1993 / New Tone

Living Inside Design / 1994 / New Tone
In "Soul Menu" there is some excellent, positive, spirited pattern music combined with rock and soul music instrumentation and rhythmic support, material developed for one of Rouse's groups, Broken Consort, which plays his more concert-oriented music; Tirez Tirez is his pop group. Simultaneous Gamelan-like phrases of seven and eight beats occur in "Hope Chest," a tongue-in-cheek jazz riff in the lively "Ranger"; group rhythm studies in "Copperhead" and "Leading the Machine." The CD *Living Inside Design* continues many of these sounds and techniques but applies them to an excellently produced sequence of songs that goes from the almost-pop "Forever Tonight" to the heartfelt "Kiss Him Goodbye" ("Mouth congress: a kiss, a second parade. An orgy of logic, a romance replayed, and up to the minute, a best out of three"), in which multiple voices occur in an overlay and de-con-

struction technique Rouse calls "counterpoetry," backed up with vocal and instrumental drones over a beat. Like Arthur Russell, Rouse at times creates that peculiar cosmically "airy" sound associated in pop music with Julee Cruise, the Cocteau Twins, early Fleetwood Mac, and even the Tuff Records version of "Sally Go Round the Roses." Rouse is currently working on an opera based on Truman Capote's *In Cold Blood.* —*"Blue" Gene Tyranny*

Dane Rudhyar (Daniel Chenneviere)

b. 1895

Piano Music: Paeans (1927), Stars (1927), Granite (1929) / CRI

Syntony / Pentagram III for Piano / Orion
Rudhyar was somewhat like the poet Ezra Pound (who also wrote music), a "Renaissance man"—painter, poet, author of texts on astropsychology and mystic philosophy, a pianist, and a composer. In the 1920s, his discords and polytonal and polyrhythmic writhing made him a young avant-gardist, and he was to be guided by metaphysical and theosophical concepts and "spontaneous exteriorizations of peak experiences" throughout his life. His composition was influenced directly by Debussy (whom he met and wrote a book about, *Debussy and the Cycle of Musical Civilization*), late Liszt and Scriabin, and early Stravinsky in his neoprimitive stage. Rudhyar's sense of large, cyclic phases of life and civilization and individuation led him to write the brilliant classic *The Astrology of Personality* in 1936, but his compositional style remained noncyclic, linear, asymmetrical, and highly emotional. "Five Stanzas" is almost unremittingly tense in sweeping writing reminiscent of Carl Ruggles, but contains an otherworldly Andante expressivo mid-movement pianoworks "Epic Poem" played· by Michael Black. "Syntony," "Penentagram III" played by Michael Sellers, and "Transformation" played brilliantly by Marcia Mikulak alternate dissonant counterpoint melodies with massive chords (reminding one of Ives's "First Sonata"), and the two string quartets "Advent" and "Crisis and Overcoming" move through constant statement-like passages to describe psychic processes —in "Advent" with its movements Visitation, Tumult in the Soul, Tragic Vision, Summons and Response, and Acceptance (referring to Christ's mother Mary), and in "Crisis and Overcoming" from a troubled minor key to a calm major key "realilzation" at the end. A unique voice. —*"Blue" Gene Tyranny*

Five Stanzas for String Orchestra (1927)/ Epic Poem for Piano (1979) / 1983 / CP2

Advent for String Quartet (1976) / Crisis and Overcoming for String Quartet (1978) / Transmutation for Piano (1976) / 1992 / CRI

Carl Spaque Ruggles

b. 1876, East Marion, MA, **d.** 1971, Bennington, VT
Composer / 20th century, atonal-chromatic
Ruggles's eclectic education included private lessons in theory and composition from professors at Harvard. While supporting himself as an engraver, Ruggles honed his compositional craft and gave lectures on modern music. The year 1907 marked the beginning of an active musical period during which Ruggles taught at the Mar d'Mar School of Music in Minnesota, founded the Winona Symphony Orchestra, and began work on the opera *The Sunken Bell.* A move to New York in 1917 brought Ruggles private patronage and acquaintances with Varese and Ives, relationships that opened many professional doors for Ruggles. Ruggles's largest work, *Sun Treader,* for orchestra, was performed in Paris and Berlin in 1932. In addition to a position at the University of Miami as director of composition (1938-1943), Ruggles continued composing and revising his scores. Though he received many honors for his musical work, in later years he began to shift his creative emphasis to painting. Although not a serial composer, Ruggles wrote melodies so that no note was repeated until a set number had been played. His music is atonal with an emphasis on the chromatic. His love for American and English literature is evident in his use of the works of Whitman and Browning as settings for his work. —*Lynn Vought*

○ **Vox Clamans in Deserto (A Voice Crying in the Wilderness) (1923)** / In "The Complete Works of Carl Ruggles" / CBS Masterworks

A magnificent work with texts by Robert Browning, Walt Whitman and C.H. Meltzer, years ahead of its time. Sweeping performance. Performed by Beverly Morgan (mezzo-soprano), with the Speculum Musicae, conducted by M. Tilson Thomas. —*"Blue" Gene Tyranny*

☆ **Sun-Treader (1926-1931)** / 1990 / Deutsche Grammaphon
Dramatic and soaring peformance by the Boston Symphony Orchestra, conducted by Michael Tilson Thomas. Ruggles, like Ives, shared the same Emersonian transcendentalist vision of society and the soul's possibilities, and this work is his most eloquent expression of that insight. Ruggles would work by placing enormous scores on the floor and craft every note and passage in detail. An earlier recording of the orchestral "Lilacs" and "Portals," played by the Juillard String Orchestra, conducted by Frederick Prausnitz, is also recommended. —*"Blue" Gene Tyranny*

Arthur Russell

b. 1951, **d.** 1992
Minimalism

○ **Tower of Meaning** / 1983 / Chatham Square
Julius Eastman conducted an almost medievally pure music in which tone combinations of two or three notes tuned to modal/raga scales are played by various instrumental groups. There is a love of listening to the pure combinations per se, as they are delivered at a regular, moderate pace—then, unpredictibly, rich or dissonant chords will be held that open your mind's ear and take your breath away. The sudden ceasing of the music at certain points also has a similar effect. —*"Blue" Gene Tyranny*

William Russell

b. 1905, **d.** 1992

Made in America / The Complete Works of William Russell / 1993 / Mode
At last! The complete works of composer and ragtime violinist Russell, who during the 1930s composed some of the most cantankerous and original percussion music ever heard. This CD includes such works as his six-minute "Trumpet Concerto"; his lively "Four Dance Movements"; "Three Cuban Pieces"; "March Suite" with the movements School March, Wedding March, Military March, Hunger March, and Funeral March; the "Chicago Sketches," with each movement named after an address (3525 S. Dearborn, 5507 S. Michigan, 4726 S. State); the music for the ballet "Ogou Badagri" (1933), based on the voodoo rites of Haiti; and of course "Made in America" (1936). Another true American original. —*"Blue" Gene Tyranny*

Joel Ryan

b. 1945
Electronic

☆ **Number Readers, The** / OR Ltd (London)
One of our most original writers on the aesthetics of new music, Ryan also has been associated as an original software designer with the S.T.E.I.M. studios in Amsterdam. This elegant work for live computer-driven electronics, video, and spoken text is based on shortwave radio transmissions heard in the evenings, of women's voices reading numbers, with great precision, in German and sometimes Spanish and Czech, sometimes preceded by electronic chime patterns. "No nation or agency has claimed authorship of these broadcasts." Joel observed a middle-aged woman in Amsterdam sitting at the front window of a well-kept old house with pad and pencil in semi-darkness by an old style model radio; he soon began to realize that there was a "synchrony of the number readers' broadcasts with the woman's vigils." Ryan weaves a variety of musical imagery using this central "coding" idea as a stepping-stone: "Codes to protect property," "Julius Caesar's code to confuse the Gauls $c + 3Mod24$," "Code as reason contradicting itself," "The Language of Flowers," "Codes You Can Eat," and many others. Fascinating, innovative work. —*"Blue" Gene Tyranny*

Frederic Rzewski

b. 1938
Conductor, composer / Folk, atonal-chromatic, world music derivative

Coming Together—Attica, for Narrator and Instruments (1972) / 1990 / Hungaroton

☆ **Winnsboro Cotton Mill Blues (1980) / In Double Edge "US Choice"** / 1992 / CRI

The whirring and clanging of the factory mixed with the rhythmic blues of the workers. Thrilling music played with a lot of heart by this astonishingly talented duo. —*"Blue" Gene Tyranny*

People United Will Never Be Defeated, The / 1994 / New Albion

The thrilling, virtuoso, political classic for piano: 36 variations on "El Pueblo Unido Jamas Sera Vencido!" played brilliantly by Stephen Drury, with excerpts from a live performance in Buenos Aires of the tune by Quillapayun. —*"Blue" Gene Tyranny*

De Profoundis (1992) for Speaking Pianist / Sonata (1991) for Piano / 1994 / Hat Hut

Two moving examples of how political concerns can be expressed with rich human emotions. —*"Blue" Gene Tyranny*

Carlos Santos

b. 1940
Text-sound

Voicetracks / P.A. Taylor

A self-described "romantic structuralist." Outrageous humor, vocal virtuosity, sharply contrasting emotions. —*"Blue" Gene Tyranny*

Erik Satie

b. 1866, d. 1925
Classical, atonal-chromatic, minimalism, jazz derivative

Satie's music, in sound and aesthetics, was fundamentally different from the prevailing 19th-century German school that prized ideals of continuity and development. It is music as sound per se (*Musique d'ameublement*, that is "Furniture Music" or "Music for Furnishing," 1920). In *Musiques intimes et secretes* ("Intimate and Secret Music") and the famous "Vexations" from *Pages mystiques*, 1892-1895), Satie describes the conceptual nature of human mental activity and then requires the performers to experience and scrutinize, simultaneously, the exact moments of shifting psychological states. "Vexations" is a short musical passage of neutral feeling (augmented and diminished chords) repeated 840 times very slowly. Satie emphasizes natural and spontaneous mentation apart from "ideas" in *The Dreaming Fish, Heures seculaires et instantanees* ("Ordinary and Snapshot Times") and *Veritables preludes flasquers—pour un chien* ("Authentic Flabby Preludes—for a Dog"). Ironic titles and commentaries poke fun at pomposity, as in *Le duc de Connaught et le President aux manoeuvers* ("The Duke of Connaught and the President on Maneuvers") and *Enfantines* ("Infantile Pieces," 1913, which go by such titles as "The Bean-King's War Chant"; "Importune Peccadillos, I"; "Being Jealous of His Comrade with the Big Head, II"; "Him Eat His Cookie, III"; and "Taking Advantage of His Corns to Steal His Hoop"). Satie's religious feeling was of a mystical, preclerical kind, expressed in works such as *Premiere pensee rosee + croix* ("First Rosey Thought + Cross," 1891, French word play on "Rosicrucians"); the beautiful and compassionate *Messe des Pauvres* ("Mass for the Poor," 1893-1895); and the moving *Socrate* (1918) on the death of Socrates, based on texts by Plato. Satie invented many musical techniques—the use of whole-tone scales, chords built in fourths, pattern melodies, unresolved "dissonances" used for their value as sounds, "open" large forms without contrasting or developing sections, and others. Perhaps more important, he was the first conceptual composer. —*"Blue" Gene Tyranny*

Piano Works, vol. 1 "First and Last Works" / Piano Works, vol. 2 "Mystical Works" / Piano Works, vol. 3 "Etudes" / Piano Works, vol. 4 / 1989 / Angel

Pianist Aldo Ciccolini produced the first complete recordings of all of Satie's piano works, and his playing of them is still the best. He treats them with clarity, lightness, and the appropriate humor but never with the rubato sweetness that some performers slip into. In these piano works, Satie can probably be most clearly seen creating a music that in both its sound and aesthetics is fundamentally different from that produced under the ideals of continuity and development prized by the 19th-century Germanic school (which until about the 1950s still held the most influence in the U.S.). With originality from the root of the soul and some

amazing titles, Satie focuses on music as "sound" per se, especially in "Musique d'ameublement" ("Furniture Music" or "Music for Furnishing") (1920), for piano, three clarinets, and a bassoon. He seems to regard any music as a direct result of the interests of that music's creator regardless of whatever poetic, religious, or other description "out there" has been attributed to the music—he has fun with this in the lovely "Descriptions Automatiques." With Buddhist-like attention and perhaps the first true attempt to describe the "conceptual" nature of human mental activity, he requires the performer(s) to simultaneously experience and examine in detail the exact moments of shifting psychological states, in such works as "Musiques intimes et secrAtes" ("Intimate and Secret Musics": I. Nostalgia, II. Cold Reverie, III. Unfortunate Example), and in his famous "Vexations" from the "Pages mystiques" (1892-1895), a piece that attracted John Cage's attention and was discussed widely by him, making the piece famous: the music is a short musical passage of neutral feeling (or, perhaps, ennui—composed of augmented and diminished chords) to be repeated 840 times very slowly, for a total duration of around 18 hours, 40 minutes, usually requiring 10 pianists. His beautiful "Messe des Pauvres" (Mass for the Poor) (1893-1895 speaks for compassion, in modern harmonies moving in 10th-century parallel monastic singing (organum). Other pieces emphasize natural and spontaneous mentation apart from "ideas": "The Dreaming Fish," "Heures seculaires et instantanAes" ("Ordinary and Snapshot Times"), and "VAritables prAludes flasques—pour un chien" ("Authentic Flabby Preludes—for a Dog": I. Severe Reprimand, II. Alone at Home, III. We Play). He uses ironic titles and written commentaries in his scores to poke fun at pomposity and officialism: "Le duc de Connaught et le PrAsident aux man uvres" (The Duke of Connaught and the Preseident on Maneuvers), "En habit de cheval" (In a Riding Outfit," with movements titled I.Chorale, II. Latin Fugue, III. Another Chorale, IV. A Fugue on Paper); "Sonatine bureaucratique" ("Bureaucratic Sonatina"); and the piano suite "Enfantines" ("Infantile Pieces") (1913), with titles like "The Bean-King's War Chant" and "Importune Peccadillos"—I. Being Jealous of His Comrade with the Big Head, II. Him Eat His Cookie, III. Taking Advantage of His Corns to Steal His Hoop". Satie's religious feeling was of a mystical, precleric kind expressed in works like "PremiAre pensAe rose + croix" (1891) ("First Rose + Cross Thought"), the first and second "PrAlude du NazarAen" ("Prelude of the Nazarene"), and in his moving work "Socrate" (1918) on the death of Socrates based on texts by Plato. Satie invented many musical techniques:use of whole tone scales, chords built in fourths, pattern melodies, unresolved "dissonances" used for their value as sounds, "open" large forms without contrasting or developing sections, and others—but perhaps more importantly, he was the first conceptual composer. —*"Blue" Gene Tyranny*

Complete Ballets, The / 1990 / Vanguard Classics

Wonderful performances by the Utah Symphony Orchestra, conducted by Maurice Abravanel. Contains "Parade" (1917, realist ballet after Jean Cocteau), "Mercure" (Mercury, 1924, plastic poses in 13 scenes, designed by Pablo Picasso), "Relache" (Respite, 1924, instantaneous ballet in two acts, a cinematic intermission, and a dog's tail, designed by Francis Picabia, film by Rene Clair), "Jack in the Box" (1899, pantomime, orchestrated by Milhaud, 1923), "Gymnopedies" 1 and 3 (1888, orchestrated by Debussy—music for ancient Greek gymnastic exercises written in old modal scales), "Trois morceaux en forme de poire" (1903, three pieces in the form of a pear, orchestrated by Desormiere), "Cinq Grimaces pour 'Le Songe d'une nuit d'ete'" ("Five Grimaces for a Planned Cocteau Production of "A Mid-Summer Night's Dream," 1914), "The Grand Ritournelle" from "La belle excentrique" ("The Beautiful Eccentric Lady") (1920). —*"Blue" Gene Tyranny*

Giacinto Scelsi

b. 1905, d. 1988
Classical, atonal-chromatic, minimalism

Pfhat (1974) for Chorus and Orchestra / 1988 / Accord

Unlike the heaviness with which Scelsi at times depicts mythologies of Buddhist, Egyptian, Latin, and other ancient cultures (in a ponderous style sometimes called "the new religiosity"), *Pfhat* employs a concentrated pallette of sounds and compositional ideas—breathing sounds from the chorus, imitation of a single giant ringing bell, and a lovely finale for two flutes holding a dissonance surrounded by (about) a hundred small, tinkling bells.

For comparison, this CDC also contains "Aion" (1961) and "Konxom-pax" (1969). — *"Blue" Gene Tyranny*

Botba / 1992 / Hat Art
Marianne Schroeder (piano). Somewhat more conservative but more concentrated early works beautifully played. Includes "Un Adieu," the "Sonata no. 2," and the interesting "Suite no. 8" (1952), an evocation of Tibet with its monastaries, rituals, prayers, and dances. — *"Blue" Gene Tyranny*

Pierre Schaeffer

b. 1910
Electronic, atonal-chromatic

Erotica "Symphonie Pour un Homme Seul" (Collaboration with Pierre Henry)/ In "Concert Imaginaire" / 1984 / INA.GRM - INA
A short and sweetly humorous feuilleton (or bob-bon, as the case may be) by the composer who led early French work on composing with environmental, extra-musical sounds or "musique concrete"—resulting in his "Concert de Bruits" (Concert of Noises) broadcast in 1948 and the establishment in 1951 of the Groupe de Recherches de Musique Concrete and in 1958 of the Group for Musical Research of the Office of French Radio-Television (O.R.T.F.). "Musique concrete" now also includes electronic and world music. — *"Blue" Gene Tyranny*

Stephen Scott

b. 1944
*New Age, electronic, minimalism, neo bop
See the Jazz section for his biography.*

○ **Minerva's Web (1985) / The Tears of Niobe (1986)** / 1990 / New Albion
Ten musicians of the Colorado College New Music ensemble playing one piano by plucking and bowing the strings. Appealing, slowly developing music with surprising celestial and rhythmic textures. — *"Blue" Gene Tyranny*

Ramon Sender

b. Oct. 29, 1934

Audition (excerpt) / 1986 / Music from Mills
One of my favorite composers ever since I heard, at a ONCE Festival in the mid-'60s, both his electronic tape "Kore" (1962) and "Information": the score was a huge roll of transparent material, for performer(s) giving improvised "information," a few receiving instructions on headphones while performing on accordion with his wonderful electronic tape, "Desert Ambulance." — *"Blue" Gene Tyranny*

Elliott Sharp

b. 1951
Guitar, electronics / Modern creative, avant-garde
Sharp is a reigning member of the electric guitar avant-garde, an unrestrained improviser, and a theory-minded composer who bases much of his work on mathematical models. He is a frequent contributor to the New York new-music scene and has toured with the Knitting Factory crew. He performs solo and leads his own bands. — *Myles Boisen*

○ **Twistmap** / Ear-Rational
Four works performed by the Soldier String Quartet, Carbon, and Sharp. Like the first Kagel quartets, these pieces introduce new playing techniques and sounds, some stimulating the ear and mind with the aural equivalent of painting with gravel. Raw and beautiful, especially the second cut "Shapeshifter." — *"Blue" Gene Tyranny*

● **Hammer, Anvil, Stirrup** / 1989 / SST Records
An excellent rendering by the Soldier String Quartet of some of Sharp's best music. Visceral patterns with seering harmonic content and new string techniques. The unique title piece, present in two takes interesting to contrast, seems to be partly a gritty and humorous take-off on hoedown/cowboy horseback-riding music (as depicted in movies) and partly a wandering into some strange slithery tuning zones traversed by squiggly melodies, using the Fibonacci series to generate tunings, rhythms, and forms. The next selection, "Tessalation Row," delivers an electrifyingly gorgeous image as geometric and scintillating as the Zapotec design from Oaxaca, Mexico, on the CD's cover. "Digital" is a toe-tapping

rhythmic study that uses a strip of spring steel woven into the strings near the bridge as a preparation; the instruments are then all played with a two-handed hammering technique. "Diurnal" and "Ringtoss" study massed and unison melodic gestures using looping and deconstruction techniques. "Re/Iterations" is for string orchestra (made here by over-dubbing the Quartet), with contact microphones attached to the instruments to pick up the subtle difference or "ghost" tones produced by the combinations of high harmonics—dense masses of swirling frequency/rhythm patterns lovely in their rawness. — *"Blue" Gene Tyranny*

Stuart Saunders Smith

Crux / 1992 / O.O. Discs
"The most important part of music … is music's autobiography … the dead other—our made up selves—a mourning of the missed other." This CD is a meeting point of four compositions: "Tunnels" (1982) for musician/actor; "Notebook" (1980) for trumpet, piano, contrabass, flute; "Family Portraits" (1992) (Sylvia, Ivy, Earle) for piano; and "Here and There" (1971) for flute, shortwave radio, and piano interior. A fascinating composer. — *"Blue" Gene Tyranny*

Laetitia Sonami

○ **Pie Jesu—Sounds from Empty Spaces no. 3/ In "Another Coast"** / 1988 / Music and Art
We hear Moslem song, sweet synthesizer tones, CB radio, the beginnings of an anxious explanation, a dog bark, and other environmental sounds that depict an imaginary world built from the drama of "unforeseen change." See also her compositions "What Happened" in the collection *Imaginary Landscapes* (1989), and "Story Road" in the collection *Jewel Box* (1992). — *"Blue" Gene Tyranny*

Laurie Spiegel

b. Sep. 20, 1945

○ **Unseen Worlds** / 1991 / Scarlet Records/Infinity
This album gives a good overview of her approaches to digital synthesis, from folk music-like steady sequences of single sounds to the stately, galactic "Sound Zones," a beautiful and original piece using sweeps of clusters, sounds-within-sounds, images-within-images, tunings never before experienced. A truly moving experience. A similar mix can be heard in her currently out-of-print CD *The Expanding Universe* on Philo PH 9003. — *"Blue" Gene Tyranny*

Cavis Muris (1986) / In CDCM Computer Music Series, vol. 13 / 1993 / Centaur
A charming piece in five parts. Computer-generated using Spiegel's self-designed computer program "Music Mouse—An Intelligent Instrument." The title, meaning "mouse hole" or "the mouse's cave," was a result of her imaging what it would be like for mice to experience our ordinary human spaces: "such a vast and foreign world from their tiny perspectives." — *"Blue" Gene Tyranny*

Jim Staley

b. 1950
Jazz derivative

Don Giovanni / 1992 / Einstein
A reconstructed montage of improvisations: pointillistic pop, primal nonverbal vocals, lyric synchronicity, "A hyper-suite of Mozartean dogfights (by) master virtuosos of the proto-form [who] stir up the red soup." Produced by Fred Frith, this is a terrific "downtown" album with Ikue Mori (drums and electric drums), Zeena Parkins (electric and acoustic harps), Jim Staley (the "kinesthetic trombonist" and on didjeridu), Tenko Ueno (the Tokyo vocalist), and Davy Williams (the Birmingham-based power guitarist). A great "world" mix. — *"Blue" Gene Tyranny*

Mumbo Jumbo / 1994 / Einstein
Reissue of some wonderful improvisational trios with vocalist Shelley Hirsch, Sam Bennett, keyboardist Wayne Horowitz, Elliott Sharp, Bill Grisell, Ikue Mori, John Zorn, and Fred Frith. — *"Blue" Gene Tyranny*

Karlheinz Stockhausen

b. 1928
Composer / Electronic

A German composer in electronic and acoustic media who is concerned with abstract processes in composition, Stockhausen composed for many forms, including opera, orchestral, chamber, and vocal works. —*AMG*

☆ **Konkrete und Elektronische Musik—Etude/ Studie I U. II/ Gesang Der J nglinge (Song of the Youths)/ Kontakte** / Stockhausen Gesamtausgabe CD #3
Classic and well-developed electronic music—some pieces with specific images, like the "Song of the Youths" in the fiery Biblical furnace—and others without extra-musical images. — *"Blue" Gene Tyranny*

Kurzwellen (Shortwaves) / Stockhausen Gesamtausgabe (Complete Edition)
Mysterious transmissions from the ether, the romance of sounds broadcast through and emitting from the universal night. — *"Blue" Gene Tyranny*

Spiral for Solo Performer (1968) / 1993 / Hat Hut
A strange, mysterious composition performed by Eberhard Blum on flute, voice, and shortwave receiver. — *"Blue" Gene Tyranny*

Klavierstucke (Piano Pieces) / David Tudor, Piano / 1994 / Hat Hut
A re-issue of the incredible performances of the Piano Pieces in their first recording made on Sept. 19, 1958, and Sept. 27, 1959, at the WDR Radio in Cologne, Germany. Tudor at that time was the renown pianist of avant-garde music, having played Boulez's monumentally complex "First Piano Sonata" from memory, for instance, and the exponent of the new "indeterminate" music of Cage. At some point after these performances, Tudor swore that he would never play a piece of Stockhausen's again, probably for political reasons. Anyhow, these are astonishing concerts of the Klavierstucke I-VIII, and four versions of Klavierstuck XI. Highly recommended. — *"Blue" Gene Tyranny*

Carl Stone

b. Feb. 10, 1953

○ **Woo Lae Oak (1981)** / 1983 / Wizard Records
Lovely, sustained, and slowly changing music made by classic "musique concrete" means—a rubbed string, blowing in a bottle, and other sounds are made into tape loops and changed by means of precise tape speed change, layering, and other techniques. — *"Blue" Gene Tyranny*

Mom's / 1992 / New Albion
Captivating by their simplicity. Stone has an underlying feeling for modality and rhythm from American folk music without ever imitating it. "Banteay Srey," for example, has a simple two-note pulse to which is gradually added a walking bass line and harmonies, transparent in their textures in a West Coast way, creating an engaging romantic and also otherworldly feeling. "Mom's" has a guitar riff that goes on simply for a while; then suddenly a whole slew of salsa-sampling musicians step in—a sheer delight. Other selections are beautiful character studies. An original and widely listenable composer. — *"Blue" Gene Tyranny*

Ned Sublette

World music derivative, rock derivative

Western Classics with the Southwesterners / 1980 / Lovely Music
Sublette's music is a good example of someone working with known styles whose attitude not toward the music but toward life in general is just a bit "off" from the normative, and somehow this makes the music just slightly different enough to be "avant." This CD, recorded in Albuquerque, New Mexico, is the traditional straight roots music from which Sublette created a unique and eccentric cowboy/downtown music with impossibly great words (the infamous cattle mutilation song, and many others) that appeals equally to both C & W and new-music fans. Recently the music has been evolving through Texas-Mexican Border music and Cuban influences. Sublette recently traveled to Cuba to study the remaining authentic bands and musicians outside the cities. In the late '70s and early '80s, he produced many unusual new-music programs of other composers' music, especially commissioned for National Public Radio in the southwest (single compositions lasting most of the day). He recently produced a score for Chinese instruments, written both in European and in Chinese notations, for an opera, with text by Lawrence Weiner. Sublette

currently runs a distributing company primarily for discs of real Cuban music. — *"Blue" Gene Tyranny*

○ **Cowboys Are Frequently Secretly/ In "Life Is a Killer"** / 1982 / The famous gay cowboy song. — *"Blue" Gene Tyranny*

Ships at Sea, Sailors and Shoes / 1993 / Excellent
To unbelievably great texts by Lawrence Weiner, Ned Sublette sings, in his decidedly cowboy accent, with The Persuasions (yes, those Persuasions! really stretching o.u.t.) in this entertaining CD of fractured doo-wop art songs/pieces with an underlying philosophical earnestness ("There Is No Light at the End of the Tunnel," "Ever Widening Circles of Remorse") with ecological concerns as in "Big Bang/New Flora" ("Row, row, row, your boat as the shit flows gently down the stream ... what we don't flush away we'll blow away another day") and transcendent situations ("Postcards from Heaven," like the title of Cage's piece for harps) with a collage of Spanish dialog, seashore, and choir from somewhere. There are also poetry readings, and the pieces never "develop" in any ordinary song fashion. Deserves both pop and avant-garde bins in the record outlets. Highly recommended. — *"Blue" Gene Tyranny*

Morton Subotnick

b. 1933
Composer / Electronic, atonal-chromatic
American composer of primarily electronic music. —*AMG*

○ **Key to Songs (1985) / Return (1985-1986), The** / 1986 / New Albion
Subotnick's music from the electronic music classics "Silver Apples of the Moon" and "The Wild Bull" has always been descriptive of poetic, lyrical imagery. Similarly, "The Key to Songs" is based on Max Ernst's collage novel *Une Semaine de Bonte* ("A Week of Kindness or the Seven Deadly Elements"). *Return—A Triumph of Reason* refers to the change from dread and foreboding to reason that was accomplished by Edmond Halley upon explaining the circuit of his well-known comet. A good example of modern "tone poem" electronic music. — *"Blue" Gene Tyranny*

Sun Ra (Herman "Sonny" Blount)

b. May 22, 1914, Birmingham, AL, d. May 30, 1993, Birmingham, AL
Piano, bandleader, composer / Big band, modern creative, early free, progressive big band, postbop
See the Jazz section for his biography.

☆ **Heliocentric Worlds of Sun Ra, vol. 1, The** / Base Record
The ESP-Disk 1014, issued 1965, re-pressed. The first of the series by Sun Ra and the Solar Arkestra. — *"Blue" Gene Tyranny*

Voice of The Eternal Tomorrow / The Rose Hue Mansions of the Sun / Saturn 80
This unfortunately out-of-print album has all the spectacular excitement of a live Sun Ra event. "Voice of the Eternal Tomorrow" is a sequence of astonishing solos by members of the Arkestra, and the end solo by Sun Ra is so "out there" that the audience sits in stunned silence before applauding respectfully. "The Rose Hue Mansions of the Sun" begins with a high-energy, loose-chordal hymn by the group and then launches into another incredible 20-minute solo by Sun Ra, punctuated by the band. Sun Ra demonstrates a mastery of electronic modulation. The alternation between solo and the various Arkestra entrances leads unceasingly into the most unpredictable zones. — *"Blue" Gene Tyranny*

Cosmic Explorer (1970)/ In "Nuits de la Fondation Maeght," The / 1981 / Recommended Records
Sun Ra was one of the first instrumentalists to use a Moog synthesizer in live performance. This 20-minute solo improvisation (with minimal extra sounds from the ensemble), ranging between high energy clusters and the lyrical, shows his ability to create an astonishing range of sound and emotion, inspiring a truly "cosmic" conclusion from the Arkestra. — *"Blue" Gene Tyranny*

John Cage Meets Sun Ra (June 8, 1986 at "Sideshows by the Seashore," Coney Island, NY) / 1981 / Meltdown Records
Two on-the-surface apparently different aesthetic approaches on the same stage. It worked as everyone became "attuned to the next moment, the next sound." — *"Blue" Gene Tyranny*

☆ **Cosmic Equation** / 1990 / Magic Music
A retitled reissue of "The Heliocentric Worlds of Sun Ra, vol. 2," ESP-Disk 1017, issued in 1966. The astonishing sessions that

went light years beyond "free jazz" improvisation to create a music of deeply felt explosive and gentle gesture made from sound itself without reference to previous notions of melody or harmony. — *"Blue" Gene Tyranny*

Akio Suzuki

Soundsphere / 1990 / Het Apollohuis Publications
This CD, with a 36-page booket in English and Japanese, features two instruments—an echo instrument created by Suzuki in 1970 called the "Analapos" and his version of a Glass Harmonica used in the installation piece "Space in the Sun." — *"Blue" Gene Tyranny*

Toru Takemitsu

b. 1930
Composer / Atonal-chromatic, world music derivative
Japanese composer in Western media and forms, guided by Oriental aesthetics and occasionally making use of Oriental instruments. —*AMG*

☆ **Works of Toru Takemitsu IV, Includes Music of Tree (1961)/ Coral Island for Soprano and Orchestra (1962) / Kaidan (1966) for Magnetic Tape** / 1988 / JVC
Stunningly beautiful tone poems that ombine pointillistic writing with a Debussyian harmonic sense. The tape composition "Vocalism A-I" ("Ai" means love in Japanese) is already a classic. — *"Blue" Gene Tyranny*

Riverrun for Piano and Orchestra (1984)/ Waterways (1977)/ Rain Coming for Chamber Orchestra (1982)/ Rain Spell (1982)/ Tree Line (1982) / 1991 / Virgin
Pointillistic, colorful tone poems for various instrumental ensembles. with many new orchestral techniques, especially in the elegant "Rain Coming." Played by the London Sinfonetta, conducted by Paul Crossley. — *"Blue" Gene Tyranny*

Visions / 1992 / Denon
The Tokyo Metropolitan Symphony Orchestra, conducted by Hiroshi Horigome, presents Takemitsu classics: the richly harmonic Debussy-like "Requiem for Strings"; "November Steps"; the newer, thinner-in-texture but abundant in orchestral color pieces "Far Calls, Coming, Far" (1980) for violin and orchestra; and the new "Visions" (1989) with its section "Mystere" and an orchestration of his piano work "Les yeux clos" for the second section. — *"Blue" Gene Tyranny*

Cecil Taylor (Cecil Percival Taylor)

b. Mar. 15, 1929, New York, NY
Piano, composer / Modern creative, avant-garde, early free
See the Jazz section for his biography.

Alms/Tiergarten (Spree) (1988)/ In "Cecil Taylor in Berlin '88" / 1989 / Free Music Production
2 CDs from a large set, with an extensive booklet describing the pieces in detail with analyses, and the workshop sessions that led to the final concert, with pictures galore. This set is interesting primarily to hear European musicians interpret Taylor's kinesthetic directing—mostly an intense density of "free playing" (actually following specific internalized instructions and images), with almost everyone going on different gestures at once. Slow unison melodies emerging from the environment. The most interesting series is "Weight—Breath—Sounding Trees." — *"Blue" Gene Tyranny*

Richard Teitelbaum (Richard Lowe Teitelbaum)

b. May 19, 1939, New York, NY
Composer, synthesizer / Electronic, early creative

○ **Blends (1977)** / 1985 / Lumina
As the title promises, one of the most perfect blends of world music, with Katsuya Yokoyama on shakuhachi, Trilok Gurtu on tabla and other percussion, and Teitelbaum on synthesizer.The score is written in different notations based on Japanese, Indian, and American practices. — *"Blue" Gene Tyranny*

James Tenney

b. 1934
Electronic, atonal-chromatic, alternate tunings

★ **Music of James Tenney: Selected Works 1963-1984, The** / Musicworks

Includes: "Three Indigenous Songs no. 3 (Hey, when I sing these songs; Hey, look what happens" (1979) with words based on Iroquois chant coded into instrumental music; "Phases" (1963), a computer-generated tape composition; "Quiet Fan for Erik Satie" (1970-1971), for an ensemble of 13 instruments—lyrical, hypnotically phase-modulated, Satie-like pastoral melodies; "For Ann (Rising)" (1969), a tape composition; "Spectral CANON for CONLON Nancarrow" (1974) for harmonic player piano; "Bridge" (excertp) (1982-1984) for two pianos, eight-hands; "Voice(s)" (1982-1984) for instrumental ensemble, voice(s), tape, and tape delay—like a field of supernatural rainbows. See also his "Septet for Electric Guitars" in *Tellus #4* (collections), "Koan" in Malcolm Goldstein's "Sounding the New Violin," and "Critical Band" played by the Relache ensemble on MODE. — *"Blue" Gene Tyranny*

Selected Works: 1961-1969 / 1992 / Artifact
Some of the earliest and most imaginative electronic and computer-generated music. Tenney was one of the first composers to use Max Mathew's computer music synthesis system at Bell Labs, and this CD includes some works created there: "Ergodos II (for John Cage)" and "Analog #1: Noise Study." Also included are his humorous study of Elvis Presley's voice in "Collage #1 (Blue Suede)," the terrifying "Fabric for Che," and the illusionary "For Ann (Rising)," an audio version of the persistence-of-motion visual illusion (for example, when a stopped train still seems to a passenger to be moving): tones rise but get nowhere—until the final ascension. Also included is a Nancarrow-like player piano piece but with stochastically generated notes. — *"Blue" Gene Tyranny*

Collage no. 2, Viet Flakes (1967) / 1992 / Musicworks
A tape collage with silences utilizing snatches of pop music urging love and sensibility ("think about it") contrasted with ominous classical phrases and folk music. Very subtle way to make political/humanist music. — *"Blue" Gene Tyranny*

Virgil Thomson

b. 1896, **d.** 1989
Composer / 20th century
Highly original American composer who exerted considerable influence as a music critic of the *New York Herald Tribune* and whose compositions reflect a universal approach embracing many idioms and styles. Thomson's score to the film *Louisiana Story* won the Pulitzer Prize in Music in 1948. —*Mary K. Scanlan*

★ **Four Saints in Three Acts (1934)** / Elektra/Nonesuch
A setting of the magnificent text by Gertrude Stein (1874-1946). For this opera, Thomson employed her writing technique of having characters and images just appear on the landscape of the stage—no linear plotline, only a real/historical/imaginary connection to a specified subject. This frees the creative process to attempt great character and language combinations that hopefully will provide insights, making for a completely modern opera where melodies, moods, and other elements follow in surprising sequences but with a sense of the whole being always present, what Stein called "the eternal present." There are humorous choruses about "pigeons on the grass, alas," "Lucy Lily"; subtle lines about perception: "the garden inside and outside of the wall"; St. Ignatius predicting the Last Judgment; St. Teresa painting flowers on very large eggs. An all African-American cast gave the first productions of this opera because Thomson wanted clear American speech. Thomson had set three songs on Stein's texts before attempting this opera. — *"Blue" Gene Tyranny*

○ **Mother of Us All (1947), The** / 1990 / New World
Performed by the Santa Fe Opera. The text for this opera is again by Stein but the organization is somewhat more narrative, with even semblances of a plot. The theme is the life and struggles of suffragette Susan B. Anthony—the weariness of leading a totally public life, and the seemingly endless fight for rights—deep reflections about the meaning of "family" and humanity versus laws. Beautiful atmospheric musical writing. Much of Thomson's other writing is very lyrical, always with a sound of his own, but conventional in structure; however, if you love these operas, try the "Sonata da Chiesa" (Church Sonata) (1926); the award-winning filmscores for "The River" (1937), "The Plow That Broke the Plains" (1936), and the "Louisiana Story" (1948); and "A Portrait Album" (Elektra/Nonesuch D4-79024), which contains selections

from Thomson's 147 musical portraits of friends—a task similar to Stein's many portraits in writing. —*"Blue" Gene Tyranny*

Helen Thorington

Building a Universe: Rifts, Absences, and Omissions (1987) / 1992 / Musicworks
An eerie radiopiece about how medicine has total insensitivity toward women's bodies. See also her piece "In the Dark" in the collection *Aerial #5.* — *"Blue" Gene Tyranny*

Yasunao Tone

Musica Iconologos / 1994 / Lovely Music
In this beautiful CD, Tone continues his refined, elegant work in the transformation of one sense sphere into another (for example, flute tones into computer haiku in "Lyrictron" on Barbara Held's CD in 20th-Century Collections in this section): here, the sound is an encoded description, via a video-to-sound transformation array (bringing to mind David Behrman's '70s installation piece, "Clouds") that scans Chinese character "poems" describing photographic images into an optical music recognition computer program, a very direct process bypassing the electronic-ness of the devices. Intriguing. — *"Blue" Gene Tyranny*

David Tudor

b. Jan. 20, 1926

★ **Microphone (1975)** / 1991 / Cramps
A ressue on CD of this classic. One of the great and wild "live electronic" pieces with sounds that Tudor once described as sounding to him like dinosaur howls echoing in prehistoric caves to timid, sweet calls of unidentifiable creatures.The original circuitry was designed by Tudor and Gordon Mumma. — *"Blue" Gene Tyranny*

Neural Network Plus / 1994 / Lovely Music
Composed incorporating a synthesizer designed around an analog neural network chip by Intel Corporation, this work was a commission from Merce Cunningham and the Paris Opera to accompany the hour-long dance, "Enter." Well known as both a composer and a brilliant pianist, Tudor continues his pioneering electronic work ("Rainforest IV" on BLOCK Records, "Pulsers" and "Untitled" on Lovely Music, and others) with this piece. — *"Blue" Gene Tyranny*

"Blue" Gene Tyranny (Robert Sheff)

b. 1945
Electronic, minimalism, jazz derivative
Robert Sheff, aka "Blue" Gene Tyranny, has composed and performed avant-garde music for 30 years, writing over 60 works for various ensembles of electronic and acoustic instruments and voices. He has produced and recorded many albums of music by other composers, published articles on contemporary music, and composed over 30 soundtracks for film and video productions. He writes for *Music with Roots in the Ether* and *Music Beyond the Boundaries*, and his compositions have been reviewed in *Sonic Transports, Soundpieces 2: Interviews with American Composers*, and *Talking Music: Conversations with Five Generations of American Experimental Composers*. He has received a New York Foundation for the Arts Fellowship in Composition. —*AMG*

Sound to Movement / VRBLU
Beautiful sax music sometimes played while spinning, sometimes mixed with natural sounds. Similar work can be heard in *Room Space* (VRBLU 13) and *Indian Circle* (VRBLU 16). —*AMG*

Real Life and the Movies / 1981 / Fun Music
A cassette retrospective of electro-acoustic pieces from 1958-1980. Includes: some hi- and low-fi soundtracks for independent movies: "Closed Transmission" (1966), realized on a IBM 7090 computer; "The White Night Riot" (1979), based on recordings made while running from police during the riot that followed Dan White's light sentencing for the murders of mayor George Moscone and gay civil rights leader Harvey Milk; and the parapsychological experiment/illusion "Pals/Action at a Distance." —*AMG*

○ **Intermediary, The** / 1982 / Lovely Music
This spontaneously performed piano piece is shadowed interactively by beautiful computer voicings designed by Joel Ryan. An illusion is created—the inspirational "message" seems to occur

sometimes before and sometimes after the performer plays material of similar shape: time both linear and all-at-once. "A genuine delight."—Recordings of Experimental Music. —*AMG*

○ **Free Delivery** / 1990 / Lovely Music
Live keyboard performances from 1983-1989. Includes: "Five Takes on the Nocturne with and without Memory" (1989) for solo piano, "The Country Boy Country Dog Intro" (1984) for piano and tape, "The Intermediary Following Traces of the Song" (1988) for acoustic piano and live sampling keyboard, "The Intermediary with a Rendition of Stardust" (1983) for solo piano and electronics, and "Sunrise or Sunset in Texas" (1983) from a film soundtrack." "Blue" Gene Tyranny: Cecil Taylor's keyboard energy, Morton Feldman's ear—the most original aspect of [his] works is the way they create continuity: they're tonal, yet rigorously asymmetrical. They satisfy the ear without letting it take anything for granted. They evolve, with the labyrinthine irreversibility of deep psychic forces." Kyle Gann (*The Village Voice*). —*AMG*

Blue (Music for the Film by Derek Jarman) / 1994 / Mute/Elektra Nonesuch
To write music to underscore a political message, to protest war, to promote human rights, or, in this case, to respond to the current AIDS plague are difficult enough assignments. To also be sensitive to a brilliant and moving text that contains an artist's deepest feelings in the forms of ironic personal stories ("With yellow infection bubbling at the corner, I said, 'This looks like a planet.' The doctor says, 'Oh, I think it looks like a pizza'. ") and transcendent poetic expression is an even more challenging task. On the screen, and on the CD booklet and disc label, we see only the color blue, no images. And in the soundtrack, with some additional music—Brian Eno, Szymanowski ("Scheherazade" from *The Masques*), "Disco Hospital," Satie, and others—and several excellent surreal environment ambience seques, Turner succeeds in inventing a dramatic score of great variety. It works best when the total sound avoids directly illustrating one-for-one the images in the text; otherwise, at times the effect is like Orson Welles delivering a mythological radio play that overwhelms the humanity and directness of the text. "From the bottom of your heart, pray to be released from image," Jarman exhorts us. "Blue is the universal love in which man bathes—it is the terrestrial paradise." — *"Blue" Gene Tyranny*

Nocturne with and without Memory / In Lois Svard's "With and without Memory" / 1994 / Lovely Music
A lovely and mysterious work, beautifully played by pianist Lois Svard in her premier CD. "With and without memory" refers to sections that resonate (like memories from the day into the evening, contrasted with light, dry, nonresonant sections; and also refers to the second and third movements that sometimes do and sometimes don't recall passages from the first movement. (See comments under Lois Svard in 20th-Century Collections in this section.). —*AMG*

Country Boy Country Dog / How to Discover Music in the Sounds of Your Daily Life / 1994 / Lovely Music
In a small Midwestern town, a natural mystery that's always been there is revealed. Using the procedural score "How to Discover Music in the Sounds of Your Daily Life" (1967), a rich variety of orchestral, electronic, and natural sounds describe the interaction between mental events and the daily environment: the "inside"—intuitive decision, spontaneous mental activity, feeling—and the "outside" that makes up reality. The score sets up an ecological chain in which natural sounds and voices are recorded and analyzed electronically (for hidden rhythmic codes, continuous melodic streams, harmonic attractions), and then electro-acoustical pieces are made from these analyses and played back into the environment. The five parts form an "audio-storyboard" (a movie soundtrack independent of a film): "A Dream without Images" (before dawn, inside); "The CBCD Intro" (sunrise, outside); "Country Boy Country Dog" (midday, inside and out)' "X Marks the Spot (Daydream)" (afternoon, inside); and "The CBCD Variations for Soloist and Orchestra" (twilight, outside). —*AMG*

Vladimir Ussachevsky

b. 1911, d. 1990
Electronic, atonal-chromatic

○ **Suite from "No Exit" (1962)/ Line of Apogee (1967)** / 1990 / New World

Two lyric, eerie, and innovative filmscores for the film of J. P. Sartre's play and Lloyd William's avant-garde film by the master of the Columbia-Princeton electronic music sound. Also employs vocal, animal, and environmental sounds. (See also "Pioneers of Electronic Music" in 20th-Century Collections in this section.) — *"Blue" Gene Tyranny*

David Van Tieghem

b. Apr. 21, 1955
Drums, percussion / Progressive electronic, techno-tribal
New York-based percussionist David Van Tieghem has shown a remarkably broad sense of what constitutes a percussion instrument, "playing" everything from kitchen items to a theater itself. Sometimes coming under the heading "performance art," his work as a soloist with various albums under his own name and as an accompanist to Laurie Anderson and others is wildly imaginative. — *William Ruhlmann*

Safety in Numbers / 1987 / Private Music
Not comfortably labeled new-age, or percussion music, or pop, or electronic music, Van Tieghem's music has that "downtown" mix of all these and yet is distinctly his own: from the lush "Crystals" to the droll and rhythm-steady "Night of the Cold Noses." This is twisted "easy listening." — *"Blue" Gene Tyranny*

Edgard Varese

b. 1883, **d.** 1965
★ **Offrandes (1921) / Integrales (1925) / Octandre (1923)/ Ecuatorial (1934)** / 1990 / Elektra/Nonesuch
The Contemporary Chamber Ensemble, conducted by Arthur Weisberg. Simply the very best performances available of Varese's acoustic and vocal works. "Ancient Forests," "Queen of the Polar Dawns," the sacred Mayan texts—musical and verbal imagery par excellence. — *"Blue" Gene Tyranny*

☆ **Poeme Electronique (1958)/ In "Electroacoustic Music: Classics"** / 1990 / Neuma
A visionary piece: "opacities and rarefactions," the jungle, outer space, the Golden Section, strange ceremonies. The booklet that comes with the CD includes a spectrogram score of the music. — *"Blue" Gene Tyranny*

Integrales for 11 Winds and Percussionists (1924-1925) / Ameriques (1918-1922) / Arcana (1927) for 120 Musicians / Density 21.5 / 1990 / Sony Classical
The wonderful orchestral music conducted by Pierre Boulez—not the best performances but passable, and the only one of "Arcana" currently available. "Ameriques" is played beautifully on Vanguard Classics OVC 4031 by the Utah Orchestra, conducted by Maurice Abravanel. Watch for future recordings of "Deserts" with the original tape interpolations (once available on the out-of-print disc *The Varese Record* on Finnadar SR 9018, issued 1977, with notes by Frank Zappa). — *"Blue" Gene Tyranny*

Lois Vierk

b. 1951
Minimalism, world music derivative
○ **Simoom** / 1992 / Experimental Intermedia
Cuts include "Go Guitars," for five electric guitars; "Cirrus," for six trumpets;. "Simoom," for eight cellos. Sighing, sliding tones, rhythmic pulse, strange harmonics. Reaches an indescribable state, like music from an unknown culture. Influenced by Japanese Buddhist chant. Seriously meditative. — *"Blue" Gene Tyranny*

Manhattan Cascade / In Guy Klucevsek's "Manhattan Cascade" / 1992 / CRI
A beautiful work that gradually develops from repeating single tones to masses of swirling clusters. More of a horizontal "cascade" between harmonic dimensions than a vertical "waterfall." — *"Blue" Gene Tyranny*

Larry Wendt

b. Apr. 5, 1946
Bring Your Mom Too / WEN 04 (Frog Peak Music)
"Sadness Without Brains" is a sound-assembly cassette of small hand tools, amplified auto parts, shortwave radios, stories, junk, and an assortment of other sounds. The tape is packaged in a metal case opened with a Phillips-head screwdriver. Other Wendt

cassettes are available from the same distributor: "Guided Missile Favorites," "Slowscan vol. 3" with Nicolas Collins, "Upper and Lower California," "Live from Bakersfield." — *"Blue" Gene Tyranny*

Kenney Werner (Ken Werner)

b. 1949, **d.** 1992
Piano, synthesizer / Neo-bop, postbop
A fascinating pianist/electronic keyboardist who is bound by few restrictions. An absolutely astounding trio pianist, he can back singers (notably Roseanna Vitro) with perfect empathy and has done some interesting synthesizer programming. —*Michael G. Nastos*

○ **Timing (1978)/ In "Blue" Gene Tyranny's "Just for the Record"** / 1979 / Lovely Music
Improvised, sustained synthesizer chords are changed on a spontaneous verbal cue from the composer. A simple but surprisingly engaging experience for the listener: the externalization of a musical sense that the public normally never hears. Harmonic also created many art installations in the form of walk-in store fronts called "Art While You Wait." (See also *Lovely Little Records* in 20th-Century Collections in this section.) — *"Blue" Gene Tyranny*

Hildegard Westerkamp

Cricket Voice (1987) / 1990 / The Aerial
Score from electronically modified environmental sounds made by "playing" the desert (plucking on cactus spikes, dried roots, and palm leaves; resonance of an old water reservoir). Beautifully assembled. — *"Blue" Gene Tyranny*

Gregory Whitehead

William S. Burroughs Tape Worm Mutation (1991), The / 1992 / Musicworks
A hilarious piece for speaker and audience response, in which the degenerative re-recording of a voice leads one through human aging and the gradual complete breakdown of spoken language. The phrase chosen to be treated to 327 degenerations is aptly, "I am a degenerate." — *"Blue" Gene Tyranny*

Christian Wolff

b. Mar. 8, 1934
Summer (1961) for String Quartet / In "The Avant-Garde String Quartet in the U.S.A." / Vox Box
A sensitive performance of this graph score in the composer's "early" style. — *"Blue" Gene Tyranny*

"For 1, 2, or 3 People" (1964) / In "A Second Wind for Organ" / 1968 / Odyssey
A sensitive, imaginative realization by David Tudor using the baroque organ like a synthesizer. Sounds never to be expected from a baroque organ. Great recording in wide stereo adds to the effect. Tudor has a refined sense of timing. — *"Blue" Gene Tyranny*

☆ **Mayday Materials/ In CDCM Computer Music Series, Vol. 6** / 1990 / Centaur
A "mix of abstraction, lightheartedness, and perhaps political suggestiveness," an interesting combination of Wolff's earlier new-music sensibilities and his later use of folk songs as guiding lines (rather than directly quoted). Nine out of 20 pieces made for a dance by Lucinda Childs. — *"Blue" Gene Tyranny*

Malvina (1989) for Koto / In Kazue Sawai's "Three Pieces" / 1992 / Jasrac
A tribute to Malvina Reynolds, a singer and songwriter who championed the causes of oppressed people. The composer scored variable tuning changes on Reynolds's "On the Rim of the World" and Walter Robinson's song "Harriet Tubman"—six sections of running or sustained sounds, and a certain range of freedom is indicated on how the performer may play. A delicate combination of tune and contemporary procedures. — *"Blue" Gene Tyranny*

For Prepared Piano (1951) / For 1, 2, or 3 People (1964) / In "The New York School" / 1993 / Hat Hut
Two classic turning points in contemporary music. Concerning "For Prepared Piano," Wolff was once asked to close the window while he was playing (I believe it was) this piece. But he declined,

saying that all the sounds happening at that moment constituted the music. Excellent performances and realizations of the score. — *"Blue" Gene Tyranny*

Stefan Wolpe

b. Aug. 25, 1902, **d.** Apr. 4, 1972

○ **String Quartet (1968-1969)** / 1991 / CRI
Performed by the Juilliard String Quartet. Although writing in a strict atonal style, Wolpe wrote clear, angular music that wove gestures directly appealing to the body senses, sometimes with a sense of humor; a nonabstract academic composer (not always recognized as one by contemporary academics). This Quartet is one of his finest works and stands out among the other two works on this CD by Roger Sessions and Milton Babbitt. Also recommended are "Enactments for Three Pianos" (1950-1953) on Elektra/Nonesuch 78024-4 (cassette tape) and the "Passacaglia" from *Four Studies of Basic Rows* (1936) on New World NW-344-2. — *"Blue" Gene Tyranny*

Ivan Wyschnegradsky

b. 1893, **d.** 1979

Compositions for String Quartet and String Trio / 1990 / Edition Block
Performed by the Arditti String Quartet. Includes the three microintervallic string quartets, a Composition (op. 43), and a Trio (op. 53). A pioneer (with Willy Moellendorf, Joerg Mager, Alois Haba, and Fredrich Trautwein) in quarter-tone and "ultrachromatic" music. The "Trio" with its tone leaps that collapse into each other and the first quartet are probably the most unique discoveries. — *"Blue" Gene Tyranny*

Iannis Xenakis

b. 1922
Composer / Classical, electronic, atonal-chromatic
Greek-born French composer whose mathematical compositional techniques and electronic media in orchestral, chamber, choral, vocal, ballet, and acoustic works have considerably influenced the development of composition in Europe and America. — *Mary K. Scanlan*

○ **Medea for Male Choir, Hand-held Stones, and Orchestra** / 1969 / Erato
Perfomed by the Orchestra and Choir of the French Radio-Televisio, directed by Marius Constant. A good combination of Xenakis's more spare abstract music combined with ancient Greek chant: more involving than the often-violent themes or forced humor of his music based on stochastic procedures, transformation groups, Poisson's law of probabilities, etc., where structure is the only content. But some people like that sort of thing. This record also includes "Syrmos," for 18 strings, and "Polytope," for four orchestras disseminated in the audience." — *"Blue" Gene Tyranny*

Mycenae-Alpha (1978)/ In "Electroacoustic Music: Classics" / 1990 / Neuma
Images of natural phenomena digitized directly into dense and intense computer music. — *"Blue" Gene Tyranny*

Gayle Young

Amaranth / Musicworks
A fascinating work by this important Canadian composer, instrument builder, author, and editor of the *Musicworks* magazine. — *"Blue" Gene Tyranny*

La Monte Young

b. 1935
Piano / 20th century
More in avant-garde classical or minimalist mode than jazz, Young is known for the use of repetition, cycles, and modes. Very similar to Steve Reich, though not as creative rhythmically. His keyboard forays have some interest, but no connection to improvisational tradition except in the broadest sense. — *Ron Wynn*

Well-Tuned Piano (1964-81), The / Gramavision
The legendary just intonation work in a set of five CDs. The booklet goes on a bit much, justifying Young's place in history, so just listen to the music, which is pleasant and nonvirtuosic in the usual sense. — *"Blue" Gene Tyranny*

89 VI 8 C. 1:42-1:52 AM Paris Encore from "Poem for Chairs, Tables, Benches, Etc." (1960)/ In "Fluxtellus" / Tellus
A piece with a verbal instruction score (what we used to call "music without notes," "procedural music," or "events," etc.—see the FluxTellus collection) that uses the floor sounds of precisely moved furniture in a resonate space. Young's "early style." — *"Blue" Gene Tyranny*

☆ **90 XII 9C. 9:35-10:52 PM NYC, The Melodic Version (1984) of the Second Dream of the High-Tension Line Stepdown Transformer from the Four** / 1991 / Gramavision
Eight trumpets with Harmon mutes slowly develop, over a 60-plus minute duration, an image, in just intonation tuning, of the gradual accumulation of harmonics one might hear in a high-tension line as voltages change and intermodulate each other. In the liner notes, Young recalls two such listening experiences in his life: one next to a telephone pole in Bern, Idaho, and the other near 20 transformers outside of Montpelier where his grandfather ran a gas station. Mysterious and meditative. Tuning as a function of events compared over time. — *"Blue" Gene Tyranny*

Frank Zappa (Francis Vincent Zappa)

b. Dec. 21, 1940, Baltimore, MD, **d.** Dec. 4, 1993
Guitar / Rock & roll, hard rock, avant-garde, fusion
See the Rock section for his biography.

Freak Out! (1966) / 1966 / Verve
An early "art rock" album with a unified program throughout the whole ("concept album"): characterized by unusual rhythmic meters and a wide use of sound-processing techniques available at that time (speed changes, tape delay, multitracking, echo, and flanging). The final piece, "The Return of the Son of Monster Magnet," is pure musique concrete. The albums *Lumpy Gravy* Verve V6-8741, 1967) and *Uncle Meat* (Bizarre 2Ms-2024, 1969) are also recommended for these techniques, as well as the use of orchestral sections mostly written in a Varese-wannabee style. — *"Blue" Gene Tyranny*

○ **Black Page (1977), The** / 1987 / Keyboard Magazine
A floppy vinyl disc insert of an extremely interesting one-line solo programmed on a Synclavier. The solo is notated in complex polyrhythmic ratios (a la Stockhausen) but has the effect of the "stretch-rhythm" used in the most sensitive jazz solos. A score is included in the text of the magazine. — *"Blue" Gene Tyranny*

John Zorn

b. 1953, New York
Alto sax, duck calls, composer / Modern creative, avant-garde
See the Jazz section for his biography.

Yankees / 1983 / Celluloid Cell
A collective improvisation by Derek Bailey (acoustic and electric guitars), George Lewis (trombone), John Zorn (alto and soprano saxs, clarinets, game calls). Subtle, droll, hilarious takes on the trivia of baseball sounds—Lewis speaks through the trombone, "ball one, ball one"; there are snippets of a slipping and sliding version of "Take Me Out to the Ball Game"; and so on. Sections are titled "City City City"; "The Legend of Enos Slaughter"; "Who's on First"; followed by "On Golden Pond," a tongue-in-cheek tone poem of the flora and fauna, mosquitos, etc.; and "The Warning Track," about a very tiny railroad system. — *"Blue" Gene Tyranny*

Classic Guide to Strategy, The / 1985 / Lumina
Solo woodwind improvisations with gamecalls, parts of saxes and clarinets. Eccentric, pure Zorn. — *"Blue" Gene Tyranny*

Classic Guide to Strategy, Vol, 2, The / 1986 / Lumina
More beautifully intense solo pieces with inflections like ancient Japanese music. Sections are named after various Japanese artists: Aoyama Michi, Enoken, Kazumi Shigeru, Kondo Toshinori, Yano Akiko, Togawa Jun, and Mori Ikue. Cover art is calligraphy of the character for "water." — *"Blue" Gene Tyranny*

Cobra / 1990 / Hat Art
A studio and live performance recording with many of NYC's "downtown" improvisors: Anthony Coleman, Bill Frisell, Wayne Horwitz, Bob James, Guy Klucesvek, Arto Lindsay, Christian Marclay, Zeena Parkins, Bobby Previte, Elliott Sharp, Jim Staley, David Weinstein, J. A. Deane, and Carol Emanuel. — *"Blue" Gene Tyranny*

More News for Lulu / 1992 / Hat Hut

Another CD of wonderful trio improvisations with John Zorn, George Lewis, and, this time, Bill Frisell. Odd, humorous, melodic, dramatic. *—"Blue" Gene Tyranny*

Peter Zummo
b. 1948

○ **Zummo with an X—Contains: Instruments (1980) / Song IV from the Suite Six Songs (Commissioned for Trisha Brown's Dance "Lateral** / 1985 / Loris Bend Foundation
"Instruments" is a pure, spare study of musical intervals with a gently humorous quality, using phase (mobile) techniques to produce variations. The "Six Songs" are all played over the same peacefully persuasive tabla pulse from Bill Ruyle; Arthur Russell's singing and cello playing (harmonics, counter-rhythms) together creating one warm voice; and Peter Zummo's open and muted trombone statements (simple riffs, sweet pleas, and sometimes snores)—all combine to make an irresistible mental dance. Highly recommended. *—"Blue" Gene Tyranny*

Experimenting with Household Chemicals / 1995 / Experimental Intermedia
Another great CD, like a suite but continuous: "Fresh Batteries," "Includes Free Information," "Sung, Played, Heard," "Rocket Scientist," "In Three Movements," and "Peaceful Transportation." With many of the same qualities as the album above, obviously including the gentle humor. Highly recommended. *—"Blue" Gene Tyranny*

Avant-Garde Collections

Aerial #1—A Journal in Sound, The / Aerial AER 1990/1
Contains: David Moss "Language Linkage" / Terry Setter "Aphorism III; Like a Coat or Mask" / Christine Baczewska "Day of the Dead" / Richard Kostelanetz "Murdoch and the Sufi from Invocations" / Rich Jensen "Folly"/ Loren Mazzacane and Suzanne Langille "Haunted House" / Lost Souls "Idumea" / Malcolm Goldstein "Qerneraq; Our Breath As Bones" / Floating Concrete Octopus "Burial Song" / Jerry Hunt "Babalon (String)" / Stuart Sherman "Four Sound Pieces: Doors, Water, Click, Pin-Ball" / Bern Porter "The Last Acts of St. Fuckyou." *—"Blue" Gene Tyranny*

○ **Aerial #2—A Journal in Sound, The** / Aerial AER 1990/2
Contains: Bob Davis and Jon Raskin "Poison Hotel" / David Dunn "Chaos and the Emergent Mind of the Pond" / Jin Hi Kim "Komungo Permutations" / Jeff Greinke "Road to Solo" / Christopher Shultis "Motion/less" / Chris Cochrane "Santiago Penando Estas" / Sue Ann Harkey "In This Year of the Snake" / Annea Lockwood "Nautilus" / LaDonna Smith and Davey Williams "Green Song" / Hildegard Westerkamp "Cricket Voice." *—"Blue" Gene Tyranny*

Aerial# 4, The / Aerial AER 1991/4
Another terrific anthology of the latest. Contains: Brenda Hutchinson "Eeeyah!" / Peter Van Riper "Heart" / Erik Belgum "Dick Tracy All Over His Body" / Leif Brush "Terrain Instruments Are Activated" / Elodie Lauten "Music for the Trine, Part IV" / Elise Kermani "Spiral" / Anna Homler and Steve Mosher "Sirens" / Joseph Weber "Transformation of the Brothers into the Sun and Moon" / Patsy Rahn "Trojan Horse"/ and N. Sean William "Come Window Golds Coming." *—"Blue" Gene Tyranny*

All Guitars / Tellus 10
All the weirdest guitarists on the New York scene. Includes contributions from Lee Ranaldo, Bob Mould, Arto Lindsay, the Butthole Surfers, Blixa Bargeld, Tim Schellenbaum, Elliott Sharp, David Linton, and others. *—"Blue" Gene Tyranny*

☆ **Another Coast (New Works from the West)** / Music and Arts CD-276
Contains: Carl Stone "Wall Me Do" and "Hop Ken" / Paul Dresher "Other Fire and Water Dreams" / Maggi Payne "Airwaves (Realities)" / Paul DeMarinis "I Want You" and "Kokole" / Laetitia Sonami "Pie Jesu—Sounds from Empty Places no. 3." *—"Blue" Gene Tyranny*

Anthology of Music for the 21st Century Leonardo Music Journal vol.1 no.1 /

Contains music by Marc Battier, Sarah Hopkins, Larry Austin, Ed Osborn, Daniel Goode, I. Wayan Sadra (Gamelan), Craig Harris, Amnon Wolman, Graeme Gerrard, Steven Paxton with Paula Claire, David Rothenberg, Simon Running, Erling Wood, and Kenneth Atchley (see review under composers). *—"Blue" Gene Tyranny*

Audio Works by Visual Artists / Tellus 21
Visual artists from the Futurists to the present. Includes pieces by Joseph Beuys, A. Russolo, Kurt Schwitters, Lawrence Weiner, Richard Huelsenbeck, Joan Jonas, Terry Allen, Marcel Duchamp, Y Pants, Magdalena Abakanowicz, and many others. *—"Blue" Gene Tyranny*

Austral Voices / New Albion Records NA028 CD
Avant-garde music by Australian composers. Contains Alan Lamb (b. 1944) "Journeys on the Winds of Time I" (1987-1988), which uses sounds made by three miles of abandoned telegraph wires singing in the wind, a sort of giant Aeolian harp in the Great Southern Hinterland of Western Australia / Alistair Riddell (b. 1955) "Fantasie" for computer-driven piano / Sarah Hopkins (b. 1958) "Cello Chi" (1986), which uses extended vocal and cello techniques such as harmonic singing, bowed harmonics, and circular "didjeridu bowing" / Warren Burt (b. 1949) "Three Inverse Genera" (1989), for four musicians on tuning forks tuned to a 19-tone system recorded in a barn with sounds of the Australian bush country filtering in / Ross Bandt (b. 1951) "Genesis" (1983), for medieval psaltery recorded in a large hollow concrete cylinder five floors underground in Melbourne's Collins Place Car Park / Jeff Pressing (b. 1946) "Butterfly's Dream," for synthesizers / Ross Bolleter (b. 1946) "Nallan Void" (1987), for a ruined piano found at the Nallan sheep station near Cue, 700 km north of Perth (this piano had once graced the bar at the Big Bell Hotel in the '30s and '40s and was now slowly returning to nature). *—"Blue" Gene Tyranny*

Avant-Garde String Quartet in the U.S.A., The / Vox Box SVBX 5306 (3 disks)
Marvelous performances by the Concord String Quartet with quartets by Earle Brown, John Cage, George Crumb, Jacob Druckman, Morton Feldman, Lejaren Hiller, Leon Kirchner, Christian Wolff, Stefan Wolpe. Hopefully it will be reissued . *—"Blue" Gene Tyranny*

○ **Bang on a Can Live, vol. 1** / CRI CD 628
A collection of live performances from the annual new music festival in Manhattan: includes Alison Cameron "Two Bits," Bill Doerfeld "Evening Chant," Michael Gordon "Strange Quiet," Tom Johnson "Failing," Scott Lindroth "Relations to Rigor," Julia Wolfe "The Vermeer Room," and Evan Ziporyn "Luv Time." *—"Blue" Gene Tyranny*

CDCM Computer Music Series vol. 1, CEMI: Center for Experimental Music and Intermedia at the University of North Texas, Denton, The / Centaur CRC 2029
Contains music by Larry Austin "Sinfonia Concertante: A Mozartean Episode" (1988), Thomas Clark "Peninsula" (1988) for piano and computer, Jerry Hunt "Fluud" (1988) (see comments in "composers") for dual synthesizers, and Phil Winsor "Dulcimer Dream" (1988) for amplified piano. *—"Blue" Gene Tyranny*

○ **CDCM Computer Music Series vol. 10, The Virtuoso in the Computer Age—I, The** / Centaur CRC 2110
Music by Paul Lansky "As If" for string trio and computer-synthesized sound / Larry Austin "Montage: Themes and Variations for Violin and Computer Music on Tape" (1985) / John Melby "Concerto no. 1 for Flute and Computer-Synthesized Tape" (1984) / David Rosenboom "A Precipice in Time" (1966) (see comments in "composers") / and Anthony Braxton "Composition no. 107" (excerpt, 1982) (see comments under "composers"). *—"Blue" Gene Tyranny*

CDCM Computer Music Series vol. 2, EAR Studios at Rensselear Polytechnic Institute, The / Centaur CRC 2039
Contains music by Richard Teitelbaum "Golem 1" (1987), Martin Bresnick "Lady Neil's Dumpe" (1987), Neil B. Rolnick "What Is the Use?" (1985), Rick Baitz "Kaleidocycles" (1985), Scott Lindroth "Syntax" (1985). *—"Blue" Gene Tyranny*

CDCM Computer Music Series vol. 3, Experimental Music Studios and Computer Music Project at the University of Illinois at Urbana-Champaign, The / Centaur CRC 2045

Music by Salvatore Martirano "Everything Goes When the Whistle Blows" for Zeta violin and YahaSalmaMAC MIDI Orchestra (1985), John Melby "Chor der Waisen" (Chorus of the Orphans) for computer-generated tape (1985), Sever Tipei "Cunculi" (1986) for five tubas—mostly quietly played clusters with complex beat patterns—pleasant to hear, Scott A. Wyatt "Still Hidden Laughs" (1988) for Synclavier and Yahama systems, Herbert Bruen "Project SAWDUST No. 6: I Told You So!" (1981)—speechlike gestures made from filtered spectrum noise sources for computer-generated tape, and Carla Scaletti "SunSurgeAutomata" (1987)—a mysterious short work built from clicks that are collected to resemble pitch and rhythm. "This is expressive of Lewis Thomas's proposal that the development of life on Earth may have been 'thermodynamically inevitable,' given the steady stream of energy from the sun to the unfillable sink of space by way of the Earth. Thomas suggests that the 'urge to make music' may be a desire to recapitulate this transformation of inanimate, random matter in chaos into the improbable ordered dance of living forms" realized using the Platypus Digital Processor. — "Blue" Gene Tyranny

CDCM Computer Music Series vol. 6, Bregman Electronic Music Studio at Dartmouth College, Hanover, NH, The / Centaur CRC 2052

Music by Jon Appleton "Brush Canyon" (1983)—a wonderful short tone-poem using the Synclavier / Paul Moravec "Devices and Desires" for Synclavier—a "musique concrAte" work about certain social reins / David Evan Jones "Still Life in Wood and Metal" for percussion ensemble and tape / Jon Appleton "Degitaru Ongaku" (1983) for Synclavier / Christian Wolff "Mayday Materials" (see comments in "composers") / and David Evan Jones "Still Life Dancing" for percussion ensemble and tape. — "Blue" Gene Tyranny

CDCM Computer Music Series vol. 7, Ear Studios at Rensselaer Polytechnic Institute, Troy, NY, The / Centaur CRC 2047

Music by Neil B. Rolnick "Vocal Chords" (1988) for voice and digital processors and "A Robert Johnson Sampler" (1987) / Pauline Oliveros "Lion's Tale" (1989) for digital sampler / Julie Kabat "Child and the Moon-Tree" (1989) for vocalist and electronics / Barton McLean "Visions of a Summer Night" (1989) for MIDI-based computer system (see comments in "composers") / and Joel Chadabe "Modalities" (1989) for interactive computer music system. — "Blue" Gene Tyranny

Cassette Mythos Audio Alchemy CD/K7, The / What Next? Records WN000006

So much of the newest music is just in cassettes and computer discs freely exchanged through the mail, contact made by word-of-mouth and small publications soliciting contributions. (I'm reminded of Frankie Mann's remark that some of the best music in the country is made by "12 year olds in their attics with cassettes.") This is a collection with some of the most inspired, sometimes gawd-awful but always unique, samplings of the cassette culture—maybe more in-the-air than underground. 21 selections: Heather Perkins "What You Think Will Happen Will"/ Ric E. Braden "Columbus Ave. 10 PM" / Jim Steele "Splatter Experience of the Green Gods" / Daniel Johnston "Grievances" / John Wiggins "Timbre Melody" / Yximalloo "China-Pong" / Qubais Ghazala "The Delphian Oracle" / Frederick Lonberg-Holm "The Second Minuet" / Costes "Oh Fortuna" / Kitchen Table Ensemble "Exploded Views" / Solomonoff and Von Hoffmanstahl "Banzai Noir" / Vosch "Tunnel at Dawn" / Philip Perkins "Remoting (excerpt from Berkeley Remote)" / Minyy "Sspress" / Triptic of a Pastel Fern "Shiny Things" / Gregory Whitehead "It Makes Me Blush" / Mystery Laboratory "Excerpt from V.T." / Bat Lenny "Delphi ( )" / Collapse/Relapse "Webs" / Hope Organ "Sneaky" / (no composer given) "Tentatively, a convenience drying clothes made entirely from zippers (partial cycle)." — "Blue" Gene Tyranny

Cathy Berberian, Voice / Mainstream MS-5005 (out-of-print)

Astonishing performances by one of new-music's first vocal sound experimenters: Berberian (1925-1983) had many pieces written especially for her. Includes Luciano Berio "Circles" (text by e.e. cummings), Bussotti "Frammento," and an especially noteworthy presentation of the John Cage "Aria with Fontana Mix." You may also wish to hear her "Stripsody for Solo Voice" (1966) on Wergo WER 60054-50. — "Blue" Gene Tyranny

Chicago 82—A Dip in the Lake / Les Disques Du Crepescule TWI 116 (cassette)

Music from New Music America '82. A terrific overview. — "Blue" Gene Tyranny

Cinq Quartuors Espagnols (Five Spanish String Quartets) Arditti Quartet / Disques Montaigne Ref. 789006

Great performances of quartets by Luis de Pablo, Mira Fornes, Ramon Ramos, Tomas Marco, and Cristobal Halffter. — "Blue" Gene Tyranny

○ **Cold Blue Anthology** / Cold Blue Records L10

When you listen to the pieces in their order on the record, an unnameable, evocative narrative seems to underlie the whole. Includes: Chas Smith "Beatrix" / Ingram Marshall "Gradual Siciliano (for Gus)" / Peter Garland "The Three Strange Angels (1972-1973)" for piano, drum, and bullroarer / Daniel Lentz "You Can't See The Forest ... Music, 1971" / Michael Byron "Marimbas in the Dorian Mode" (May Day, 1976) / Jim Fox "Appearance of Red" / Read Miller "Weddings, Funerals, and Children Who Cannot Sleep" / John Kuhlmann "In This Light" / Rick Cox "Necessity" / Michael Jon Fink "Celesta Solo (1981)" / Eugene Bowen and Harold Budd "Wonder's Edge" / James Tenney "Spectral CANON for CONLON Nancarrow" for player piano. — "Blue" Gene Tyranny

Compositoras Madrileuas (Women Composers of Madrid) / RTVE M3/12

Contains: Alicia Santos "Sonata para flauta y piano" (1958) / Marisa Manchado "Obertura" (1956) / Consuelo Diez "Naggareth" for percussion ensemble (1958) / Zulema de la Cruz "Pulsares" for piano and taped electronics (1958) (see comments under "composers") / Maria Escribano "Jondo" for sax ensemble, piano, and percussion (1954) (see comments under "composers"). — "Blue" Gene Tyranny

Computer Music Currents 7 / Wergo WER 2027-2

Contains: Richard Karpen (1957) "Il Nome" (1987) / Jean-Claude Risset "L'autre face" / Lars-Gunnar Bodin "Anima" (1984) / Tracy L. Petersen "Digital Tantra I" (1978) / Frances White (1960) "Ogni Pensiero Vola" (1985) / and Joji Yuasa "A Study in White" (1987). — "Blue" Gene Tyranny

Concert Imaginaire, GRM (Imaginary Concert) / INA C 1000

A good collection of "musique concrAte" pieces by the GRM (Groupe de Recherches Musicales, "Group for Musical Research"): J. Schwarz "And Around" / Bernard Parmegiani "La Roue Ferris" / Pierre Schaeffer-Pierre Henry "Erotica—symphonie pour un homme seul" / Michel Chion "La Ronde" / Jacques Lejeune "L'invitation au dApart" / Ivo Malec "Reflets" / Jean Schwarz "Suite N" / Christian Zanesi "D'un jardin e l'autre" / Denis Dufour "Bocalises" / Philippe Mion "Puzzlasept" / Francois Bayle "ErosphAre." — "Blue" Gene Tyranny

Conducted by Clytus Gottwald / Wergo WER 60111

This volume contains the Brian Ferneyhough (1943) "Time and Motion Study III" (1974-1975) for 16 voices, percussion, and electronics, and also excellent performances of compositions by Mahler, Aribert Reimann (1936), Messiaen, Ligeti, Alban Berg, and Maurice Ravel. Vol. I in this series contains works by Dieter Schnebel (composer of "F r Stimmen ... Missa Est" (For Voices ... Missa Est) (1956-1958, 1964-1968), with movements entitled "dt 31," "AMN," and " ! (Madrasha II)" and "Atemz ge" (Respirations) for voices), Hans Otte, Bussotti, Ligeti, Pousseur, Webern, Nono; and Vol. II has works by Hans Holliger, Schnebel, Penderecki, and Cerha. — "Blue" Gene Tyranny

Confederacy of Dances, vol. 1, A / Einstein Records EIN001

Concert recordings from the Roulette Experimental Music Series. Comes with a 32-page booklet containing essays by Mark Dery, Tim Page, Kevin Whitehead, and David Weinstein on Roulette and the "downtown scene." CD selections are: Bill Frizell "April 16, 1988" / Christian Marclay "Untitled" / Tohban Djan (Ikue Mori and Luli Shioi) "Blue Seed" / Zeena Parkins "Scruples" / Billy Bang "One for Albert" / Anthony Coleman "Acid Jazz Burnout" / David Weinstein "Icetralia" / Chris Cochrane "To Disenfranchise (Repatriation)" / Ron Kuivila "Canon Y" / John Zorn "Sebastopol" / Guy Klusevik "Sylvan Steps" / Davbid Weinstein "Poland" / Hirsch-Mori-Shea-Staley Quartet "Ulula Zone" / and Jeanne Lee and Wadada Leo Smith "Beauty is a Rarity." — "Blue" Gene Tyranny

Contemporary Contrabass; Bertram Turetzky, Contrabass, The / Nonesuch Records 71237 (disc)
Great playing. Contains: John Cage "26' 1.1499" for a String Player" (1955) / Pauline Oliveros "Outline" for flute, percussion, and string bass (an improvisation chart) (1963) / Ben Johnston "Casta Bertram" (1969) for live recording, playback loops, and chance processes. — *"Blue" Gene Tyranny*

Cultures Electroniques / 6: Les Magisteres du 19e Concours International de Musique Electroacoustique (Magisterium of the 19th Electroacoustic Competition) / Harmonia Mundi LDC 278055
An excellent compilation of elegant, subtle, and poetic electronic works including Bernard Parmegiani (1927-) "Exercisme 3" (Exercise/Exorcism 3) (1986) / Barry Truax (1947-) "Riverrun" (1986) / Wilhelm Zobl (1950-) "Andere die Welt, Sie Brauchtes" (Change the World, It Needs Changing) (1973) / and James Dashow (1944-) "Whispers Out of Time" (1976). — *"Blue" Gene Tyranny*

Cultures Electroniques / 6: Prix Quadrivium / Bourges 1991 / Harmonia Mundi LDC 278053/54
Another interesting collection of prize-winning electro-acoustic pieces, although sometimes their "tastefulness" makes them seem somewhat similar. Especially unique are Andrew Lewis (from Great Britain, born 1963) "Time and Fire" / Mike Vaughan (from Great Britain, born 1954) "Ensphered" for soprano sax and tape / Ake Parmerud (from Sweden, born 1953) "Alias" / Justice Olsson (from France, born in Johannesburg in 1949) "Up!" / and Alicyn Warren (USA, 1955) "Longing for the Light." Other compositions are by Cort Lippe (USA, 1953) "Music for Harp and Tape" / David Arzounan (USA, 1955) "Precipitation" / Jon Appleton (USA, 1939) "Stereopticon" / Roderik De Man (Pays Bas, born in Indonesia, 1941) "Chordis Canam" / and Georg Katzer (West Germany, 1935) "Rondo." — *"Blue" Gene Tyranny*

Double Edge / CRI CD 637
Contains: Frederic Rzewski "Winnsboro Cotton Mill Blues" (1980) / David Borden "Double Portrait" (1987) / "Blue" Gene Tyranny "The De-certified Highway of Dreams" (1991) / James Tenney "Chromatic Canon" (1983) / Paul Bowles "Night Waltz" (1949) / "Duke" Ellington and Billy Strayhorn "Tonk" (1940) / Meredith Monk "Phantom Waltz" (1989) and "Ellis Island" (1981) / Mel Powell "A Setting for Two Pianos" (1987) / Morton Feldman "Two Pianos" (1957). — *"Blue" Gene Tyranny*

☆ **Electro-Acoustic Music: Classics** / Neuma Records 450-74
Contains: Varese "Poeme Electronique" / Milton Babbitt "Phenomena" and "Philomel," both with soprano Judith Bettina / Roger Reynolds "Transfigured Wind IV" with Harvey Sollberger (flute) / Iannis Xenakis "Mycenae-Alpha." Some of the best of the European-academic style. — *"Blue" Gene Tyranny*

Electronic Music / Vox Turnabout TV 34046S
Contains: Ilhan Mimaroglu "Agony" (1965), John Cage "Fontana Mix" (1958), and Luciano Berio "Visage" (1961), based on the fabulous vocal sounds of Cathy Berberian. — *"Blue" Gene Tyranny*

Electronic Music / Vox Turnabout TV 34004S
Early compositions utilizing the RCA Mark II synthesizer at Columbia-Princeton. Contains: Andres Lewin-Richter "Study no. 1" / Ilhan Miraroglu "Le Tombeau d'Edgar Poe," "Intermezzo," and "Bowery Bum" / Tzvi Avni "Vocalise" / Walter Carlos "Variations for Flute and Electronic Sound" and "Dialogues for Piano and Two Loudspeakers." — *"Blue" Gene Tyranny*

Electronic Music / Folkways 33436
Early works from independent composers in Canada, the USA, and Australia. Victor Grauer "Inferno" / Jean Ivey "Pinball" / John Robb "Collage" / Hugh Le Caine "Dripsody," one of the first Canadian tape pieces / Walter Olnick-Schaeffer "Summer Idyl Noesis" / Myron Schaeffer "Dance R 43" / Val Stephen "Fireworks" and "Orgasmic Opus." — *"Blue" Gene Tyranny*

Elektroakustische Musik aus Finnland (Electro-Acoustic Music from Finland) / Edition RZ 3004
Music by Patrick Kosk, Petri Hiidenkari, Harri Nouri, Tapio Nevanlinna. — *"Blue" Gene Tyranny*

Experimental Theater / Tellus 18
Sound from "performance art" presentations: Spalding Gray "Sex and Death to the Age 14 (excerpt)"/ Vulcan Death Grip with Ann Magnuson "Get It Up or Get Out" (1986), vocals with band/ Mike Kelley with Sonic Youth "Plato's Cave, Rothko's Chapel, Lincoln's

Profile" (1986) / Jerri Allyn "Queer Revolution" (1984)/ Ann Magnuson "Arachnae X. Pudenda" (1987) / Lydia Lunch "The Cancer Has Finally Become Contagious" (1987). — *"Blue" Gene Tyranny*

Explosions, The Bob James Trio / ESP-Disk 1009 (out-of-print)
Probably the first recording of improvised jazz combined with electronic music, as well as playing inside the piano and other new-music techniques. Contains lively and often humorous compositions by Bob James and Gordon Mumma "Peasant Boy" / Bob Ashley and Bob James "Untitled Mixes" / Bob James "Explosions" / Barre Phillips "An On" / and a version (not the full one for voice and electronics found in *Source* magazine) of "Wolfman" by Bob Ashley and Bob James. With Bob James (piano), Barre Phillips (bass), and Robert Pozar (percussion). — *"Blue" Gene Tyranny*

Exquisite Corpses from P.S. 122 / What Next ? Recordings WN 0002
Not actually a collection, but a collective improvisation by 30 performer/composers, in which each participant was given only a hint of the contributions of other participants, the whole of the improvisations then collected together, unedited and without overdubbing or retakes. A panorama of approaches to the meaning of improvisation. — *"Blue" Gene Tyranny*

☆ **Extended Voices; The Brandeis University Chamber Chorus, Directed by Alvin Lucier** / Odyssey 32 16 0156 (disc)
New pieces for chorus and voices altered electronically. Contains Pauline Oliveros "Sound Patterns" / Alvin Lucier "North American Time Capsule 1967," for voices and Sylvania Electronic Systems Vocoder / John Cage "Solos for Voice 2" electronic realization / Robert Ashley, "She Was a Visitor" / Toshi Ichiyanagi "Extended Voices" / MorTon Feldman "Chorus and Instruments (II)" and "Christian Wolff in Cambridge." Some of the best performances and recording of new-music ever. — *"Blue" Gene Tyranny*

False Phonemes / Tellus 22 (cassette)
A wonderful anthology of works for computer-generated voice. Contains Remko Scha "katadeedo daynatadoh (restored to youth according to beauty I walk)" from Impressions of Africa, and French Recitatif/ Larry Wendt "Galaxy Love" / Brian Reinbolt "Brain Monkey"/ Mark Rudolph "Beautiful but Marred by the Blemish of a Perpetual Dissatisfaction"/ Alice Shields "Mass for the Dead"/ Paul DeMarinis "Mind Power"/ Paul Lansky "Not Just More Idle Chatter"/ Jon English and Jim Pomeroy "The Hartford Address"/ Ron Kuivila "Linear Predictive Zoo"/ John Cage "Writings through the Essay: On the Duty of Civil Disobedience " (excerpt). — *"Blue" Gene Tyranny*

Full Spectrum Voice; Thomas Buckner (vocals) / Lovely Music LCD 3021
An edition of premiere inspirations beautifully sung for voice, instruments, and electronics. Includes Robert Ashley "Odalisque" / Jon Gibson "Rainforest/Brazil (He Was Not Disappointed)" / Nils Vigeland "March, Hymn, and Waltz" / Peter Gena "Mother Jones" / Annea Lockwood "Night and Fog" / and Roscoe Mitchell "because it's," "this," and "dim"—three songs on poems of e.e. cummings. Highly recommended. — *"Blue" Gene Tyranny*

Funnel Zone / Dossier DCD-9017
Music by Vivante Tableaux, Setrakian, Slap, TVD, Marilyn Manson, Quayle, Rivet Ecks, Vociferous Mutes, Happiness Boys, Chameleon Circus, King Felix. Wonderful grass roots new-music and some industrial rock mostly from the Miami, Florida, area. I especially like "Second Nature" and "Haides" by King Felix. — *"Blue" Gene Tyranny*

Futura 1-5 (Soundtext Poetry) / Cramps Records CRSCD 091 - 095
A great series of poetry, utilizing vocal sounds as well as words, called "soundtext" in the U.S. It isn't necessary to know the base language in which the poem-performances are given. Futura 1: "La declamazione futurista (The futurist declamation)" and "Lo Zaum', linguaggio trasmentale (Zaum', the transmental language)"; Futura 2: "Simultaneismo francese (French simultaneism)" and "Precursori e dadaisti in Germania (Forerunners and dadists in Germany)"; Futura 3: "L'urlo: Antonin Artaud (The howl: ultralettristes)" and "La poesia sonora oggi (Sound poetry today)"; Futura 4 and 5: "La poesia sonora oggi (Sound poetry today)". — *"Blue" Gene Tyranny*

Gerd Zacher, Organ / Deutsche Grammophon 139 442

Great realizations of Giuseppe Giorgio Englert "Vagans animula" (1969), Morton Feldman "Intersection 3" (1953), Gerd Zacher "Re" for organ and intoner (1969), and John Cage "Variations III" (1963), realized for three organs, percussion, and winds. — *"Blue" Gene Tyranny*

Images Fantastiques / Mercury Limelight LS 86047
A great collection of musique concrAte pieces. Contains: Luciano Berio "Momenti" and "Omaggio a Joyce" / Bruno Maderna "Continuo" / Luc Ferrari "Visage V" / Iannis Xenakis "Orient-Occident" / Jean Baronnet and Francois Dufrene "U 47." — *"Blue" Gene Tyranny*

☆ **Imaginary Landscapes** / Elektra/Nonesuch 9 79235-2
Contains: Ron Kuivila "Loose Canons" (excerpt) / Shelly Hirsch and David Weinstein "On the Swing" (an excerpt from *Pomp and Circumstances*) / Neil B. Rolnick "Balkanization" (excerpt) / Mark Trayle "Simple Degradation (Border)" / Gordon Monahan "Speaker Swinging" (excerpt) / Laetitia deCompiegne Sonami "What Happened" / Maryanne Amacher "Stain—The Music Rooms" (excerpt) / Alvin Lucier "Music for Alpha Waves, Assorted Percussion, and Automated Code Relays" / David Tudor "Dialects" (excerpt) / Nicolas Collins "Real Electronic Music" / Voice Crack "A Spoonful of Tea in a Barrel Full of Honey" (excerpt) / Christian Marclay "Black Stucco" / "Blue" Gene Tyranny "Somewhere in Arizona 1970" for baritone and electronics. 70 minutes of some of the best and most innovative of new electronic music of varied idiosyncratic approaches. — *"Blue" Gene Tyranny*

○ **Island of Sanity: New-Music from New York City** / Review Records (Dist. No NML 8707CD
Contains: David Linton "Lumbago" / Mofungo "Slimeball Necktie" / Christian Marclay "1930" / Fish and Roses "Checkered Past" / Details at Eleven "Music for Secretaries" / Skeleton Crew "The Sparrow Song" (Frith) / Mark Dery "Banging Khruschev's Shoe"/ Charles K. Noyes "Mouse and Ermine" / Locus Solus "Wrap Backwards and the Usual Snowflakes" and "Beda Fomm" / David Fulton "Border Patrol" / David Garland "The Golden Years" / Bump "Spies in Space / Beer in My Bed" / Chris Vine "Alignment" / Carbon "Cormorant" / Bosho "Boy Yaca" / The Scene Is Now "Lullaby Stomp/Cool Pool" / H/M/D "Runner" / Robert Previte "Requiem for Vincent." Edited by Elliott Sharp, this collection clearly shows the spillover of people and styles from New Music to new-music and art-rock and no-wave bands and other styles, in what may be called the "downtown style." Composer/performers who play gigs at bars and also at new-music festivals in academia. This has been happening with the American avant-garde since Ives played ragtime in East Village bars, or for any composer, familiar with dance and song, who also wants to express the conceptual/meditative flashes that occur in life. — *"Blue" Gene Tyranny*

John Cage Tribute / KOCH
A collection of instrumental and vocal pieces and memories honoring the memory of John Cage: Excerpt from Cage's "Thirty Pieces for String Quartet" played by the Kronos Quartet / "Three Dances for Two Prepared Pianos, Dance #1" played by Patrick Moraz and Jackson MacLow / Anne Tardos "First Four Language Word Event" / Christian Wolff's "Six Melodies Variation" for solo violin (variations on Cage's "Six Melodies") / Ken Nordine's "A Cage Went in Search of a Bird" / composer Earle Brown playing Cage's "Three Solos for Trumpet" from the "Concert for Piano and Orchestra" / Laurie Anderson's "Cunningham Stories: at the age of twelve ..., Merce Cunningham phoned his mother ..., Every morning ..., The Cunningham Company ..."/ Ryuichi Sakamoto's "Haiku FM"/ Larry Austin's "art is self-alternation is Cage is ..."/ David Tudor's "Webwork" music for the Cunningham dance "Shards" / Yoko Ono's "Georgia Stone" / Oregon's "Chance/Choice" / David van Tieghem playing Cage's "Living Room Music" / James Tenney's "Ergodos 1 for John Cage" / Robert Ashley's "Factory Preset" / Frank Zappa performing Cage's "4'33" " / John Cale's "In Memoriam John Cage—Call Waiting" / Meredith Monk singing Cage's "Aria" / and selection marker #82 is simply "New York City." — *"Blue" Gene Tyranny*

Jon Gibson / Point Music CD 434873-2
The essential collection for understanding the variety of expressions possible in pattern or phase music (sometimes rather misleadingly called "minimal" music). Amazingly gorgeous saxophone playing by Jon Gibson. Includes : Terry Riley "Tread the

Trail (1964-1965) / Steve Reich "Reed Phase" (1967) / Philip Glass "Bed from Einstein on the Beach (Act IV/2)" (1976) / John Adams "Pat's Aria from Nixon in China (Act II/I)" (1987) / Philip Glass "Gradus for Jon Gibson" (1968) / Jon Gibson "Waltz" (1981), "Song Three (1976), and "Extensions II" (1981/1982) for sound environment and saxophone / Terry Jennings "Terry's G Dorian 12-Bar Blues (9 X 5) + 3 " (ca. June 1962) / LaMonte Young "Any Integer (to Henry Flynt)" (April 1960). — *"Blue" Gene Tyranny*

○ **Just Intonation** / Tellus 14
"Just intonation" is any tuning system in which all of the intervals can be represented by whole-number ratios, with a strong preference for simple ratios." Contains pieces radically different from each other but all aiming for this "maximum clarity" tuning. — *"Blue" Gene Tyranny*

○ **Just for the Record** / Lovely Music VR 1062 (disc)
"Blue" Gene Tyranny plays multikeyboard works by Robert Ashley "Sonata" with "Trio: Christopher Columbus Crosses to the New World in the Nina, the Pinta, and the Santa Maria Using Only Dead Reckoning and a Crude Astrolabe" / John Bischoff "Percussion" / Phil Harmonic "Timing" / and Paul DeMarinis "Great Masters of Melody." — *"Blue" Gene Tyranny*

LCO 8 (London Chamber Orchestra) "Minimalist" / Virgin VC 7 91168-2
A very well played and good overview of some of the better-known pattern ("minimalist") composers. Contains: John Adams "Shaker Loops" / Philip Glass "Facades" / Steve Reich "Eight Lines" / Philip Glass "Company" / and Dave Heath (1956) "The Frontier." — *"Blue" Gene Tyranny*

Les Ondes Martenots (50th Anniversary of the Ondes Martenot Electronic Keyboard) / Productions Disques Ades 21.007 (two discs)
Classic and newer works for 1 to 6 Ondes Martenots, sometimes with piano. Somewhat patterned after the Russian Theremin, the Ondes Martenot (the "Martenot Waves") was another early electronic music instrument that was first presented publicly in May 1928 at the Parisian Opera House by its inventor Maurice Martenot. This collection contains: "Fete des belles eaux" (1937), "Suite for Ondes Martenot and Piano" (1933) by Darius Milhaud, "3 Poemes" (1935) by Andre Jolivet, and "Hexade" (1973) by Roger Tessier. — *"Blue" Gene Tyranny*

○ **Life Is a Killer** / Giorno Poetry Systems Rec GPS 027 (disc)
A Dial-A-Poem Poets life-centering collection of different ensembles of speakers with and without instrumental music. Works by Amiri Baraka, William S. Burroughs, Jim Carroll, Jayne Cortez, The Four Horsemen (b.p. Nichol, Steve McCaffery, Paul Dutton, Rafael Barreto Rivera), John Giorno, Brion Gysin, Rose Lesniak, Ned Sublette. — *"Blue" Gene Tyranny*

Live Electronic Music Improvised / Mainstream MS -5002
Two influential early European-based "live electronic" bands: M.E.V. (Musica Electronica Viva), centered in Rome with members Alan Bryant, Alvin Curran, Frederic Rzewski, Richard Titelbaum, and Ivan Vandoor, and A.M.M., centered in London with members Cornelius Cardew, Lou Gare, Christopher Hobbs, Eddie Prevost, and Keith Rowe. — *"Blue" Gene Tyranny*

○ **Lovely Little Records** / Lovely Music LP101-06
Box of six 7-inch discs with booklet. Contains: John Bischoff "Silhouette" (1979) and "The League of Automatic Music Composers: Recording, December 17, 1978" / Paul DeMarinis "If God Were Alive (and He Is) You Could Reach Him By Telephone" and "Forest Booties" / Phil Harmonic "Phil Harmonic's Greatest Hits" and "WPA/Composite Mix : John Bischoff and Phil Harmonic" / Frankie Mann "I Was a Hero (from The Mayan Debutante Revue)" and "How To Be Very Very Popular" / Maggi Payne "Lunar Disk" and "Lunar Earthrise"/ "Blue" Gene Tyranny "Harvey Milk (Portrait) Part I: The Action, Part II: The Feeling." — *"Blue" Gene Tyranny*

Mallets, Hands, Sticks, and Drums / O.O. Discs #3
With Brian Johnson, Jan Williams, and drummers from Africa, Cuba, and Brazil. "Channeled violence ... perceptual minimalism full of uncontrollable variations" (*Village Voice*). Features the cut "Snare for Camus." Recorded in Studio B (the Toscanini studio) at Radio City Music Hall. Wild. — *"Blue" Gene Tyranny*

Manhattan Cascade Guy Klucevsek, Accordian / CRI CD 626
A marvelous, uplifting concert of twisted tunes and new uses for the "free bass accordion" containing Mary Ellen Childs' charming

Pygmymusic-like "Oa Poa Polka," Anthony Coleman's plaintive "Below 14th Street, Above 125th Street," Rolf Groesbeck's tone cluster and conjuring "Polka 1," Aaron Kernis's cinematic joke "Phantom Polka" (Kernis is also a composer of some brilliant orchestral music; watch for future recordings), John King's hymn-based "All Together Now," Guy Klucevsek's "Samba D Hiccup," and the lovely "An Air of Gathering Pipers," Christian Marclay's "Ping Pong Polka" with wildly modulated record collage, Lois Vierk's "Manhattan Cascade" (see review under composers), and John Zorn's humorous "Road Runner." — *"Blue" Gene Tyranny*

Music from Mills / Mills College MC 001 (three-disc set)
A centennial anthology produced and compiled at The Center for Contemporary Music at Mills College. Contains: Lou Harrison "Sonata No. 2" for cembalo / Terry Riley "The Ethereal Time Shadow (excerpt)" / Luciano Berio "Chamber Music" / Dave Brubeck "Summer Song" / David Rosenboom "In the Beginning: Etude 1 (Trombones)" / Robert Ashley "Flying Saucer Dialogue from the Opera Atalanta (Acts of God)" / Anthony Braxton "Composition no. 62 (+30 +96)" / David Behrman "Interspecies Smalltalk, Part 2 (Excerpt)" / Elinor Armer "Thaw" / Steve Reich "Melodica" / Maggi Payne "Subterranean Network (excerpt)" / Darius Milhaud "Segoviana" / Pauline Oliveros "Alien Bog (excerpt)" / Anthony Gnazzo "Asparagas" / Katrina Krimsky "Apparitions" / Larry Polansky "Four Voice Cannon #3" / Pandit Pran Nath "Dira Dira Ta Na in Raga Bhairavi (excerpt)" / Janice Giteck "Breathing Songs from a Turning Sky (excerpt)" / "Blue" Gene Tyranny "Remembering" / Ramon Sender "Audition (excerpt)" / and Morton Subotnick "The Key to Songs (excerpt)." — *"Blue" Gene Tyranny*

○ **Music from the ONCE Festival** / Advance FGR-5 (out-of-print)
The only recording of compositions from this legendary festival that presented the newest in avant-garde music, film, and dance from 1961-1968. Contains: Gordon Mumma "Music from the Venezia Space Theatre" / Robert Ashley "Crazy Horse Symphony" / George Cacioppo "Time on Time in Miracles" / Donald Scarvarda "Landscape Journey." — *"Blue" Gene Tyranny*

○ **Music with Memory** / Tellus 9 (cassette)
A collection of works by composers who use microcomputers as their instruments. Includes Nicolas Collins "Devil's Music" (1985) / John Driscoll "Stall" (excerpt) with Phil Edelstein and Peter Labiak's rotating robotic loudspeaker system (1981) / Brenda Hutchison "Interlude from Voices of Reason" (1984) / Ron Kuivila "Parodicals" and "Cannon Y for C.N. " (1985) / Paul DeMarinis "Eenie Meenie Chillie Beenie" (1983) and "Yellow Yankee" (1983). — *"Blue" Gene Tyranny*

Musica Futurista / Cramps CRSCD 046/047 (2 CDs)
A terrific collection of early soundtext, piano, radio, and noise pieces from the Italian futurists 1913-1933 with Italian and English liner notes. Works by Luigi Russolo, Filippo Marinetti, A. Casella, Virgilio Mortari, Franco Casavola, Francesco Pratella, Daniele Napoletano. — *"Blue" Gene Tyranny*

Musik um den Futurismus / Akademie der Kuenste (Aca S-105
More futurist music 1915-1925 including also Russian, French and German composers influenced by this Italian movement. "Formes en l'air—a Pablo Picasso" (1915) by Arthur V. Lourie / "Le temple est mesure—l'espirit est incarne" ("The temple is measured—the spirit is incarnate"), "Je t'attendrai" ("I will wait for you") (1913), "Le Sang !" ("The Blood !") (1918) by Nicholas Obouchov / "Musik fuer Klavier, op. 1" (1916), "Ich hatt' einen Kameraden —Groteske" (I had a comrade—a grotesque) (1919), "Musik fuer Klarinette, Klavier und freihangendes Blechsieb" ("Music for clarinet, piano, and free-hanging perforated sheet metal") (1919) by Hans-Juergen von der Wense / "Streichquartett op. 13 in Vierteltoenen" ("String Quartet op. 13 in Quarter-tones") (1925) by Ivan Wyschnegradsky / "Fragmente aus der Oper 'Laviatore Dro' " ("Fragment from the opera 'Dro the aviator' ") (1914) by Francesco Balilla Pratella / and "La Pioggia" ("The Rain") by Antonio Russolo. — *"Blue" Gene Tyranny*

○ **Musique ExpArimentale Groupe de Recherches Musicales de la R.T.F. (Musical Research Group of French Radio-Television)** / Disques BAM LD 071
An exquisite collection of musique concrAte pieces. "Volumes" (1960) by Francois-Bernard Mache for 12-track tape and a chamber orchestra consisting of seven trombones, two pianos, and two percussionists—cosmic sounds of great import on the distant horizon slowly approaching and suddenly disappearing, great rat-

tlings and small ones like crickets, breaking, impacting percussion; "Crucifixion" (excerpts) by Romuald Vandelle, based on a poem by Poe spoken by a fragmented voice, gloomy and terrifying; the surreal, elegant "Ambiance II (Toast FunAbre)" by Michel Philippot for woman's spoken voice and tape based on a Mallarme text; one of the best musique concrAte compositions, "Tautologos II" by Luc Ferrari—masses of speech-inflected, tape-manipulated sounds like conversations amongst alien beings, bizarre glasslike drones (rotating metal resonators on piano strings), humorous mobiles of sounds combining and recombining: a soundtrack to stimulate the imagination; "Texte II" (1953) by AndrA Boucourechliev, described as "a form in movement" employing "controlled chance," recorded on two tapes to be played simultaneously on two tape recorders so that coincidences of the mono tracks are always variable from performance to performance—an astonishingly rich palette of sounds for such an early piece. — *"Blue" Gene Tyranny*

New American Music, Vol. 4 / Folkways FTS 33904
An interesting collection of new compositions using a variety of compositional techniques and sound sources. Contains: Gordon Mumma "Cybersonic Cantilevers," a live electro-acoustic performance / Joel Chadabe "Echoes," interactive computer music with percussionist / V. Ussachevsky "Conflict," voice plus electronics / Noa Ain "Used to Call Me Sadness," a text-sound piece with violin accompaniment / and Ann McMillan "Whale," modified whale sounds and "Carrefours." — *"Blue" Gene Tyranny*

New Music China / Tellus 19
Contains both new popular and folk music as well as new-music: Fred Houn "I Wor Kuen (The Boxers)" from Bamboo That Snaps Back/ Chen Yi "Xie Zi" / Ge Gan-Ru "Yi Feng (Ancient Wind)" for solo cello / Zhou Long "Kong Gu Liu Shui (Valley Stream)" for traditional ensemble / Wu Wen Guang "Liu Shui (Flowing Water)" for guqin (ancient seven-string zither) / Tan Dun "Plucking Instruments Suite" (excerpt) / R.I.P. Hayman "Nightsongs" score from film about immigrant life in Chinatown / Jing Jing Luo "Monologue Part 1": she also writes for large orchestra and traditional Chinese ensembles. — *"Blue" Gene Tyranny*

☆ **New Sounds in Electronic Music** / Columbia Odyssey 32 16 0160
One of the most beautifully pressed vinyls of electronic music, with three important works: Steve Reich "Come Out" (see comments under "composers") / Richard Maxfield "Night Music" (see comments under "composers") / and Pauline Oliveros "I of IV" (see comments under "composers"). — *"Blue" Gene Tyranny*

New-Music Articles Magazine Cassettes / Frog Peak Music
The NMA is a primary source of new and experimental music in Australia; each issue is accompanied by a tape. NMA Tape 1: computer music, improvised work and computer-controlled piano pieces by Warren Burt, Brian Parish, David Hurst, Graeme Gerrard, John Jenkins, Jon Rose, Alistair Riddell, and Essendon Airport / Tape 2: vocal, electronic, and chamber music by Chris Mann, Ron Nagorcka, Anti Music, Mark Pollard, John Gillies, Ernie Althoff, Les Gilbert, and Rainer Linz / Tape 3: Jon Rose and Martin Wesley-Smith, Richard Vella, Rik Rue, John Oswald, Makers of the Dead, Travel Fast, Japanese Coke Ads, and the Australian Bicentennial Authority / Tape 4: music by women composers, including solo and chamber compositions, electronic and computer music, installations and improvised works by Jennifer Fowler, Ros Bandt, Sarah Hopkins, Annea Lockwood, Caroline Wilkins, Vineta Lagazdina, and others / Tape 5: vocal, instrumental, and electronic work by Chris Mann, Rainer Light, SWSW THRGHT, Syd Clayton, Amanda Stewart, Ernie Althoff, Daniel Kahans, Caroline Wilkins, John Gillies and Greg Hooper, and Densil Cabrera / Tape 6: recent computer and computer-assisted music by Greg Schiemer, David Hurst, Alistair Riddell, Warren Burt, Mark Randolph, Cindy John, Amanda Baker, and Graeme Gerrard / Tape 7: music accompanying the "history" issue: performance and radio pieces, environmental composition, and music theater by Greg Schiemer, Jon Rose, Ron Nagorcka, Helen Gifford, Ernie Gallagher, Percy Grainger. — *"Blue" Gene Tyranny*

New-Music for Electronic and Recorded Media / 1750 Arch Street Records S-1765
A great collection of music by contemporary women composers writing from 1938-1977. Contains a realization of Johanna Beyer's "Music of the Spheres" (1938) / Annea Lockwood "World

Rhythms" / Pauline Oliveros "Bye Bye Butterfly" (1965) / Laurie Spiegel "Appalachian Grove I" / Megan Roberts "I Could Sit Here All Day" / Ruth Anderson "Points" / Laurie Anderson "New York Social Life," "Time to Go," and "For Diego." — *"Blue" Gene Tyranny*

New-Music for Guitars, Buffalo Guitar Quartet / New World Records NW 384-2
Interesting, mostly melodious music with many new techniques of guitar playing, including having the guitars sound like other string instruments: harps, sitars, ancient kithara. Contains Lejaren Hiller "Metaphors" / Stephen Funk Pearson "Mummychogs (Le Monde)" / Walter Hartley "Quartet for Guitars" / James Piorkowski "The Struggle of Jacob" / William Ortiz "Abrazo" / and Loris Chobanian "Sonics." — *"Blue" Gene Tyranny*

New-Music for Piano, Yuji Takahashi (Piano) / Mainstream Records MS-5000
Excellent performances of Xenakis "Herma"/ Reynolds "Fantasy for Pianist" / Takahashi "Metatheses" / and especially Earle Brown's "Corroboree." — *"Blue" Gene Tyranny*

New-Music from Poland 1956-1961 / Philips PHS-900-141
Beautifully recorded orchestral compositions: Penderecki "To The Victims of Hiroshima" (1956) / Grazyna Bacewicz (b. 1913) "Music for Strings, Trumpets, and Percussion" (1958) / Tadeusz Baird "Erotica, Six Lovesongs for Soprano and Orchestra" (1960-1961) / and Kazimierz Serocki (b. 1922) "Sinfonietta for Two String Orchestras" (1956). — *"Blue" Gene Tyranny*

New-Music from South America for Chamber Orchestra / Mainstream Records MS/5017
Music by Oscar Bazan (born 1936, Argentina), Marlos Nobre (born 1939, Brazil), Cesar Bolanos (born in Peru), Gerardo Gandini (born 1936, Argentina), Manuel Enriquez (born 1926, Mexico), Alcides Lanza (born 1929, Argentina). — *"Blue" Gene Tyranny*

Organic Oboe / O.O. Discs 1
Wonderful performances by Joseph Celli in this historic recording rereleased on CD. Contains: the only American release of Stickhausen's "Spiral" (1968) for soloist on shortwave radio and other instruments / Celli "Sky: S for J" (1976) (see comments in "composers") / Elliott Schwartz "Extended Oboe" (1973-1974) for oboe and electronic tape / and Malcolm Goldstein "A Summoning of Focus" (1977) for wind instrument (see comments in "composers"). — *"Blue" Gene Tyranny*

○ **Panorama Alectronique** / Mercury Limelight LS 86048
Classic pure electronic and musique concrAte compositions from studios in Paris and Cologne. Includes: Pierre Henry "Entite" / GyUrgy Ligeti "Artikulation" / Herbert Eimert "Selection I" / Mauricio Kagel "Transition I" / AndrA Boucourechliev "Texte I" / and Henri Pousseur "Scambi." — *"Blue" Gene Tyranny*

Paul Zukofsky, Violin / CP 2 Recordings CP 2/6
Works by three composers beautifully played: Giacinto Scelsi "Anahit," Iannis Xenakis "Mikka" (1972) and "Mikka 'S' "(1975), Philip Glass "Strung Out" (1967). — *"Blue" Gene Tyranny*

Pioneers of Electronic Music / CRI CD - 611
The Columbia-Princeton sound from 1952 to 1971. Compositions by Ussachevsky, Otto Luening (b. 1900), Pril Smiley, Bulent Arel, Mario Davidovsky, Alice Shields. Recommended cuts: "Incantation" by Luening and Ussachevsky, "Stereo Electronic Music" by Arel. — *"Blue" Gene Tyranny*

Portraits / New Albion Records NA 009
A good sampler: excerpts from Ingram Marshall "Fog Tropes," Somei Satoh "Birds in Warped Time," Paul Dresher "Channels Passing," Stephen Scott "Rainbows," Daniel Lentz "O-KE-WA," and John Adams "Light Over Water." — *"Blue" Gene Tyranny*

Pulse, The New Music Consort / New World Records 80405-2
A great collection with some classic percussion music. Contains: John Cage and Lou Harrison "Double Music" (1941), John Cage's rhythmically sophisticated "Second Construction" (1940) and jazzy "Third Construction" (1941), Henry Cowell "Pulse" (1939) for six percussionists, Harvey Sollberger "The Two and the One" (1972), and Lukas Foss "Percussion Quartet" (1983). — *"Blue" Gene Tyranny*

Response: Electronic Music from Norway / Mercury Limelight LS- 86061

A mid-1960s collection. Contains: Arne Nordheim "Epitaffio for Orchestra and Tape" and "Response I" / Alfred Janson "Canon for Chamber Orchestra and Tape" / and the outstanding Bjorn Fongaard "Galaxy for Three Electric Guitars in Quarter-Tones." — *"Blue" Gene Tyranny*

Severino Gazzelloni, Flute with Aloys Kontarsky (Piano) / Time Records 8008 (out-of-print)
Lovely performances of flute solo pieces by Franco Evangelisti "Proporzioni," Luciano Berio "Sequenza," and Yoritsune Matsudaira "Somaksah"; and for flute and piano by Niccolo Castiglioni "Gymel," Olivier Messian "Merles Noir," and Bruno Maderna "Honeyreves." — *"Blue" Gene Tyranny*

○ **Site-Less Sounds** / Tellus 25
Powerful personal and political visions by Shelley Hirsch "#39" / Gregory Whitehead "How to Pronounce 'Prothesis,'" "M is for the Million Things,", and "This Is Not a Test" / David Moss "Conjure" / Jacki Apple, Keith Antar Mason, Linda Albertano, Akilah Nayo Oliver "Redefining Democracy in America: Episodes in Black and White" / David Wojnarowicz and Ben Neill "The Collapse of the Illusory One-Tribe Nation from ITSOFOMO (In the Shadow of Forward Motion)" / Constance DeJong with Brenda Hutchinson "Vanishing Act." Highly recommended. — *"Blue" Gene Tyranny*

Sleepers / Finnadar Records 90266-1 (disc)
Available from Deep Listening Publications. Eight takes on the lullaby. Contains: Doris Hays "Hush"; Annea Lockwood "Malolo"; Ilhan Mimaroglu "Sleepsong for Sleepers"; Daniel Goode "The Red and White Cows"; Tom Johnson "Lullaby"; Pauline Oliveros "Lullaby for Daisy Pauline," a choral piece; Alison Knowles "Mantra for Jessie (Some Help in Sleeping)" for speaker with shaker; Ann Silsbee "Go Gentle" for three flutes. — *"Blue" Gene Tyranny*

○ **Sonic Arts Union, The** / Mainstream MS 5010 (disc)
The famous American new-music group. Contains Alvin Lucier "Vespers" (1968) for echolocation devices / Robert Ashley "Purposeful Lady Slow Afternoon" (see comments under "composers") / David Behrman "Runthrough" / Gordon Mumma "Hornpipe" (1967). — *"Blue" Gene Tyranny*

Sonic Encounters, Margaret Leng Tan, Piano / Mode Records 15
An interesting collection demonstrating the mutual effects of Asian and American aesthetics. Contains: the first recordings of two John Cage pieces, "Primitive" (1942) and "In the Name of the Holocaust" (1942), for prepared piano; Alan Hovhaness "Orbit #2" (1952) and "Jhala" (1952); George Crumb "Five Pieces for Piano" (1962); Somei Satoh "Cosmic Womb" (1975), for two pianos with digital delay; and Ge Gan-Ru "Gu Yue" (1986, premiere recording). — *"Blue" Gene Tyranny*

○ **Soundviews, Vol. One: Sources** / What Next?
An audio magazine with cassette and booklet. Contains excerpts from: Annea Lockwood "A Sound Map of the Hudson River" / Mary and Bill Buchen "Harmonic Compass" / Stephan Von Huene "Totem Tone #2" / Karen McPherson "A Pond at Dusk" / Julius "Music in the Air" / Hildegard Westerkamp "Interview" and "A Walk Through the City" / Andrej Zdravic "Cicadas Head Dance" / Bill Fontana "Landscape Sculpture with Foghorns" / Richard Lerman "Interview" and "Brass Screen and Bronze Screen" / Brigitta Bertoia "Interview" / Harry Bertoia "Energizing" / Jim Pomeroy "Mozart's Moog" / Doug Hollis "Interview" and "A Sound Garden" / Dr. Frederick Scarf "Voyager II; Uranus Fly By" / David Behrman and George Lewis "Installation for Parc de la Villette" / Snapshot "Evening Sounds in Albion, Michigan" / Gordon Monahan "Speaker Swinging"/ Charlamagne Palestine "Carillon Concert" / Bernard Baschet, Michel Deneuve, and Alain Dumont "Extrait d'Resurgence" / Paul Panhuysen and Johan Goedhart "Jan Huygen I" / Liz Phillips "Interview" and "Windspun for Minneapolis"/ Leif Brush "Teleconstructs III" / Ron Konzak "Interview" and "Giant Puget Sound Windharp" / Bart Hopkins "Disorderly Tumbling Forth" / Susan Stone "House With a View" / Jeffrey Bartone "Sky Concert" / Ellen Fullman "Immigration" / Pauline Oliveros, Linda Montano, Tom Jaremba, and children "No More Fear" / Carl Stone "Kuk II Kwan" / John Cage "Interview" / Robert Rutman "Something to Reflect the Misery of Our World Today" / Ellen Zweig "She Traveled the Landscape" / Peter Richards "Wave Organ" / Paul DeMarinis and David Behrman "Sound Fountain" / Annea Lockwood "Interview" / Alvin Curran "Maritime Rites" /

Record Company Addresses

The Aerial (*see* ¿What Next? Recordings)

Het Apollohuis
Tongelresestraat 81, 5613 DB Eindhoven, The Netherlands

Artifact Recording
1374 Francisco Street, Berkeley, CA 94702

BASE Record
Via Collanarini 26, Bologna, Italy

Cold Blue Records (*see* Frog Peak Music)

Cramps Records
Distribuzione Best Sunset srl, Via False, 33, 36050 Monteviale, Vicenza, Italy

Deep Listening Publications
156 Hunter Street, Kingston, NY 12401

Dossier Recordings
Esync Ocular Interchange, PO Box 380621, Miami, FL 33238

Earwax Productions
245 Hyde Street, San Francisco, CA 94102

Edition Block
Gelbe Musik, Schaperstrasse 11, D-10719 Berlin, Germany

Edition RZ
c/o Robert Zanc, Leibnizstrasse 33, D-10625 Berlin, Germany

ESD Records
530 North 3rd Street, Minneapolis, MN 55401

Finnadar (*see* Deep Listening Publications)

Frog Peak Music
PO Box A36, Hanover, NH 03755

Front Records
c/o The Western Front, 303 East 8th Avenue, Vancouver, BC, Canada V5T 1S1

Fun Music
735 Spokane Avenue, Albany, CA 94706

Giorno Poetry Systems Records
Giorno Poetry Systems Institute, Inc., 222 Bowery, New York, NY 10012

Homestead Records
Dutch East India Trading, PO Box 800, Rockville Centre, NY 11571-0800

Inial Group
PO Box 13292, La Jolla, CA 92039-3292

IRIDA Records
Available from Deep Listening Publications, Nonsequitur (*see* ¿What Next? Recordings), or Steven Houseright, Route 1, Box 240, Canton, TX 75103

Leonardo Music Journal
Pergamon Press, 395 Saw Mill River Road, Elmsford, NY 10523

Lovely Music, Ltd.
10 Beach Street, New York, NY 10013

MELA Foundation
275 Church Street, New York, NY

Mills College Records
Mills College, Music Department, 5000 MacArthur Blvd., Oakland, CA 94613

M.I.T.B. Records
PO Box 6461, Beverly Hills, CA 90212

Musicworks
1087 Queen Street W, Toronto, Ontario, Canada M6J 1H3

NMA (*see* Frog Peak Music)

Neuma Records
71 Maple Street, Acton, MA 01720

New Tone Records
Robi Droli, Strada Roncaglia 16, 15040 San Germano (AL), Italy

O. O. Discs, Inc.
376 State Street, Brooklyn, NY 11217-1707

Opus One Records
May 1 through October: PO Box 604, Greenville, ME 04441
November through April: PO Box 795, Napanoch, NY 12458

Orion Master Recordings, Inc.
PO Box 4087, Malibu, CA, 90265-1387

Productions Disques Ades
54, rue Saint-Lazare, 75009 Paris, France

ROIR
Reachout International Records, Inc., 611 Broadway, Suite 411, New York, NY 10012

Slowscan Editions
c/o Jan Van Toorn, PO Box 1548, 5200 BN, 's-Hertogenbosch, Holland; also available from Frog Peak Music

Soundviews (*see* ¿What Next? Recordings)

SST Records
PO Box 1, Lawndale, CA 90260

Stockhausen-Verlag
Kettenberg 15, 5067 Kurten, Germany

Tellus
c/o Harvestworks, Inc., 16 West 22nd Street #902, New York, NY 10010

Tronia Disc
160 Beaconsfield Avenue, Toronto, Ontario, Canada M6J 3J6

Unió Musics
Llorenç Barber, Mesón de Paredes, 14, 28012-Madrid, Spain

VRBLU Records
c/o Peter Van Riper, 73 Calyer Street, Brooklyn, NY 11222

¿What Next? Recordings
Nonsequitur, Inc., PO Box 344, Albuquerque, NM 87103-0344

Widemouth Tapes
PO Box 382, Baltimore, MD 21203

Tony Schwartz "Factory, Whistle Carols." Whew—almost an entire new music festival on one cassette. A very well-organized collection, especially interesting for the many "sound installation" pieces, which are usually never issued on recordings. —*"Blue" Gene Tyranny*

○ **String Quartets; The LaSalle Quartet** / Deutsche Grammaphon 423 245-2

Fundamental statements of new ideas about the string quartet form by composers Cage, Lutoslawski, Penderecki, and Mayuzumi. Sensitive performances. —*"Blue" Gene Tyranny*

○ **Tango** / Tellus 16

Retakes on the idea and spirit of the tango. Includes works by Carlos Gardel, David Garland with Cinnie Cole and Zeena Parkins, Chris DeBlasio, Keith Keeler, B. Hutchinson with Gerry Lindahl, A. Tomlinson, Elodie Lauten, Jo Basile and Orchestra, "Blue" Gene Tyranny, Molly Elder, Mathew Nash, Christopher Berg, Fast Forward, and Mader. —*"Blue" Gene Tyranny*

Upper Air Observation, Barbara Held (Flute) / Lovely Music CD3031

Selections: Nils Vigeland "Vara" (1979) / Alvin Lucier "Self Portrait" (1979/1990) / Yasunao Tone "Trio for Flute Player" and "Lyrictron" / Barbara Held "Upper Air Observation." Remarkable musicality on originally commissioned works producing new possibilities for flute and electronics: Lucier's "Self-Portrait" uses a wind anemometer, activated by streams of air from the flutist's lips, that causes a light beamed through its blades to gradually reveal parts of the player's body; haiku poems are generated by a computer that detects the pitches of the flute in Yasunao Tone's beautiful "Lyrictron"; Held's "Upper Air Observation" uses recordings of a radio sound weather balloon launching and other sounds. — *"Blue" Gene Tyranny*

○ **Utopia Americana** / New Tone Records NT 6707
A wonderful view of what is "American" in contemporary American Music from an Italian producer's perspective. Containing primarily rhythmic-based music and soundtext rhythms from ordinary speech (Ginsberg's works) with some dreamy electronic music by Oliveros and solo jazz by Steve Lacy, this is an interesting collection of new recordings and reissues of tracks from out-of-print or hard-to-get vinyls. Nice cover photo of Joey's Navajo Cafe and Dining Room framed by the grills of several pickup trucks parked outside. Contains: Allen Ginsberg "Hum Bomb" (1992) / Steve Reich "Music for 18 Musicians" (live, 1976) / Michael Galasso "Baroque" (live, 1992) / Ben Neill "Bal" / John Cage "Third Construction" (from a 1983 Italian studio recording) / David Behrman "A Traveller's Dream Journal (EWR-LAX)" (1992) / Pauline Oliveros "A Woman Sees How The World Goes with No Eyes" (from the Lovely Music LCD 1903 "Crone Music") / Steve Lacy "Pannonica" / John Zorn/Andrea Centazzo

"First Environment for Sextet" (recorded in New York WKCR Radio 1978 from "Environment for Sextet" Ictus Records 0017) / Allen Ginsberg "Father Death Blues." — *"Blue" Gene Tyranny*

Voice of the Computer / Decca 710180 (out-of-print)

Bell Labs computer music from the 1960s. Contains James Tenney "Stochastic Quartet" / Max Mathews "Masquerades," "Slider," and "Swan Song" / J. C. Risset "Computer Suite from Little Boy" (see comments under "composers") / J. R. Pierce "Eight-Tone Canon." — *"Blue" Gene Tyranny*

Wai-te-ata Press Music Editions / Frog Peak Music

Independent publisher of new-music by New Zealand composers. — *"Blue" Gene Tyranny*

○ **Wergo Collection: Music of Our Century** / Wergo WER60200-50

An excellent sampler of 15 works giving a quick "taste" of many composers: Herbert Henck, Cage, Ligeti, Penderecki, Henze, Stockhausen, and others. — *"Blue" Gene Tyranny*

Word / Tellus 7

Spoken works with music, processed voices, and many other combinations by novelists and poets. — *"Blue" Gene Tyranny*

CLASSICAL

Though classical music appeals to many people, the diversity, complexity, and even the mystique of "classical music" can be rather intimidating. There is much to know and much to learn about classical music (many people have devoted their lives to studying obscure facets of it), but the encouraging thing about this art form is that you can enjoy what your are hearing without knowing exactly why. While detailed study, investigation, and reading may enhance the enjoyment of the music even further, a scholarly approach is not required. All that is required is a desire to explore and discover new musical territory. The genre of classical music is rich enough to provide a lifetime of wonder and surprises, and a nearly limitless potential for discovery makes the journey well worth the effort.

The basic question is, "Where do I begin?" The important thing to remember is that everyone, from first-time concertgoer to long-time aficionado, has been confronted with this same decision at some point. A certain piece, performer, or composer may have caught his or her attention either at a concert, on a movie soundtrack, or even in a commercial on TV. For example, Pachelbel's *Canon and Gigue in D Major* was hardly noticed in the 20th century until audiences heard it in the soundtrack of the movie *Ordinary People*. Once the listener has become interested, there are a number of different methods by which he or she can go about exploring classical music. The purpose of this guide is to provide some basic information about the appreciation of classical music, and it includes suggestions on possible avenues of investigation that will be useful to the novice and experienced listener alike.

How to Use this Guide

The world of classical music spans nearly ten centuries and encompasses a multitude of styles, forms, and purposes. This section of the guide was compiled to help and encourage diverse people in exploring the abundance of recorded classical music that is now available. This section focuses on composers and compositions that provide a basic repertoire of music representing the various major styles and forms developed over the past millennium in Western Art music.

In this section of the All-Music Guide, we have assembled a list of compositions that we feel form a solid basis for a music collection containing representative works from all periods and styles of the last 900 years. The compositions we have marked with a star (★) are those that provide a basic starting point for getting acquainted with more music by a particular composer or historic period. For each of the compositions listed, we have identified recommended recordings that best present the compositions to the listener through superior performance and recorded sound. This is not to imply that the recordings listed are the only outstanding recordings available for a given work, only that they are representative of the best currently available on CD. We have limited our recommendations to CDs currently available, and at the time this list was prepared every attempt was made to ensure that the recordings listed are currently available. However, availability of recordings is at times a complex and fast-changing issue complicated by distributor and manufacturer offerings in various countries and even regions within countries, as well as changes in label ownership.

This section has been designed to provide a roadmap to classical music in its many forms and styles, and to assist the user in acquiring a collection of recordings that bring this music into the home. We hope this list will help you collect your own library of recordings, become acquainted with the music of different composers, and experience the greatest possible enjoyment of music. A discussion of possible explorative methodologies is presented at the end of this section.

Much more music is offered here than one would expect in a basic library. In this respect you will have more suggestions available in areas where you find the music most congenial and interesting. At times, however, we suggest you sample other composers or periods. (A year or two from now you may find you have been missing some fine music!) As a general rule, the music from the classical and romantic periods is the most accessible and familiar to the modern listener because phrases of these great works are often used in commercials and films. Works from these periods are probably the best place for a novice to start.

Almost anyone will think of pieces of music and performances that "must" be in a basic library but are missing here. Personal taste will influence anyone's choice. Subjective perspectives and interpretations vary widely. We have endeavored to choose recommended recordings that are critically acclaimed and provide a good place to begin exploring specific performances, but readers-listeners should feel free to investigate any alternative that interests them, regardless of what we, or any review publication or classical music guide, specify as the correct course. The information is presented alphabetically by composer, with a short biographical essay followed by recommended compositions and recordings. For major works with many fine recorded performances available we have listed two or more alternative recordings that we feel present the music effectively. When dealing with early music, for which period performance practice may be a factor (see below), we have listed both modern and period instrument performances as applicable. The reader should feel free to choose among the listed recordings when making purchase decisions. It is impossible for this section to list all currently available recordings of excellence. Particularly in certain areas where many wonderful performances are available (Beethoven's or Mozart's symphonies, for example) we have listed only a few of the recordings that provide an overview of the compositions. No attempt has been made to prepare an exhaustive list of all outstanding recordings.

A Word on Authenticity and Period Instruments

For earlier music (i.e., romantic , classical or an earlier period), there has been a great deal of recent exploration of different interpretations in terms of "historically informed" or "period instrument" practices. These don't represent a single movement or school of thought concerning "correct" interpretational choices so much as a philosophy of investigation into long-neglected techniques of playing, instrument construction, ensemble size, choice of tempos, and a variety of other issues. Many "period instrument" performances focus attention on one or more of these aspects. These interpretations have found favor with many CD buyers, and the availability of recordings capturing these performances has increased dramatically. At their best, period performances can illuminate often-heard compositions anew by incorporating smaller instrumental or vocal forces, expose novel sonorities by using instruments similar to those in use at the time the music was first composed, and bring clarity to the inner workings of the music. For example, many of Bach's choral works were scored for four voices alone, not 100-member choruses. However, there are excellent performances of older repertoire using modern instruments and performance practices that bring a fuller more substantial sound to the music. We have tried to recommend CDs that capture outstanding performances whatever the interpretation.

The "authenticity" question is not as straightforward as some would think. The use of instruments similar to or the same as instruments commonly in use at the time the music was written can be important, but so is the performance practice and consideration of what the composer may have intended when she or he wrote the score. These are all intertwined, of course, but early music performers may place emphasis on one or more of these aspects:

1. Period instruments (or copies of ancient instruments from the time the music was written). The hope is that by using such instruments the performer might more accurately convey the tonal qualities in the music that the composer (or the audience of the composer's time) would recognize. Considerations include the actual instrument used, whether the instrument has been modified, and in what way the instrument has been modified. For example, all extant Stradivarius violins have been altered. Because they were made over 300 years ago and have now been altered, they may not be considered authentic for music of the high baroque. Questions of pitch are relevant; today we tend toward a standard pitch of A440 Hz or even slightly higher (as the European A441 Hz), but in Bach's time the standard pitch was probably around A405, almost half a step lower. For stringed instruments the kind of string (gut vs. steel) and how it is wound is of import. For wind instruments the types of pads, keys, valves, mouthpieces, reeds, and bell shapes can drastically affect tonal qualities.

2. Period practice. This is a vigorous discussion in part because so much was accepted in the apprentice system for teaching performers. The oral tradition combined with teaching by example was the primary means of instruction until the time conservatories were established in the late 19th century. Accordingly there are many open questions about bowing, vibrato, makeup and forces in ensembles, and so forth. For instance, many baroque period sonatas were written for one (solo sonata) or two (trio sonata) obbligato instruments and basso continuo. The obbligato parts were written out in full, but it is known that the soloists were given license to embellish the solo parts with ornamentations and improvisations of their own. The extent to which this took place and what forms it took when it was used are very much in question. Was it just the occasional grace note, or were more elaborate additions the norm? We really don't know since few composers were required or concerned—given the conventions of the time—with writing

out specifically how these decorations or improvisations were to be accomplished. The whole question of basso continuo is also problematic. What instruments were used (bass viols, cellos, contrabasses, bassoons, harpsichord, organ, some combination, etc.) and how the parts were delineated and distributed (the composer typically just wrote chord changes—thorough bass or figured bass—intending the performers to provide something more than block chords) all come into question.

3. Musicological research continues on original manuscripts, particularly regarding the intent of the composer. This is also highly problematic. For example, many people think that the composer's written score should be treated as if it were sacrosanct. In matters of dynamics, tempo, phrasing, and dozens of nuances, the performer may interpret what the composer wrote in different ways or ignore what's written altogether. For instance, what tempo is meant by the word *andante?* How about *allegro?* No one from two or more centuries ago bothered to relate this specific information. Metronomes came into existence about the time Beethoven was writing his late works, but they were highly inaccurate. Beethoven often expressed frustration with the way orchestras of his day butchered his works; he saw the metronome as one way of helping musicians play at the tempos he intended, so he went back and added metronome markings to many of his earlier works, including all of his symphonies. However, there is some question whether Beethoven's metronome was accurate. In addition, he may not have marked every change of tempo in precisely the way he wanted the music performed; that is, he may have made mistakes. There is some evidence that during the romantic and modern periods slow movements (movements marked adagio, andante, etc.) have comparatively slowed down and fast movements (movements marked allegro, presto, etc.) have comparatively sped up. Tempo is one of the primary means by which a composer and conductor can convey contrast and add emotion to a work.

Claims made by performers are also relevant. Claims of authenticity and inauthenticity in performance practices are often emotionally loaded. For instance making even a semblance of a claim of authenticity implies that all other interpretations are inauthentic. Likewise any discussion of "historically informed" practice implies that other interpretations are uninformed. Many of the people interested in the "authentic" style of playing and musical exploration avoid problematic terms and public advocacy of these concepts. They have too often been misquoted and misunderstood.

The fact is that the difference in style and interpretation is not clearly defined as many would have us think, particularly those who are opposed to the practice of period performance. For instance, much has been made of recent recordings of the Beethoven symphonies [those most sacred works in modern orchestral concerts]. A specific case in point is the recent complete cycle of the symphonies recorded by the Chamber Orchestra of Europe led by Nicholas Harnoncourt and issued on the Teldec label. Harnoncourt employed "modern" instruments (many of which are actually Stradivarius and Amati instruments used in Beethoven's time and earlier that have since been modified to take higher tunings and produce more volume) with modern bows and strings. He also used period winds to a certain extent (e.g., the valveless hunting horns used during Beethoven's time). He employed an ensemble of approximately the same size as orchestras during Beethoven's time. (Orchestral forces got progressively larger until the early 20th century when we settled on the Mahlerian/Wagnerian/Brucknerian- sized ensembles that have since played Beethoven and Mozart, often with partdoubling. Consider Mahler's *Symphony of a Thousand* compared to a 20- or 30-member orchestra.) Harnoncourt studied the original scores carefully, coming to many of the same conclusions as his colleagues (Roger Norrington et al.) about tempos, phrasing, and dynamics. Note that neither Harnoncourt nor Norrington followed the metronome markings specified in the manuscripts slavishly, but each of them has tried to reflect the original spirit throughout the score.

Is this "authentic?" Harnoncourt and his ensemble devoted more time to questions of musicality than to trying to recreate an authentic historic experience. Music is a personal and highly expressive medium best served by making choices based on musical thoughtfulness and at least a consideration of historicity. Not all period instrument performances are successful, but then neither are all modern instrument performances. It is best to judge each approach individually and decide whether the result is musically satisfying, regardless of the tensions and controversies surrounding the philosophies. Harnoncourt's approach has been judged a success by many, not because it is authentic or somehow historically informed, but because it works as music. Musically informed choices and individual tastes are also relevant to the listener. What are your preferences? Whether you have ideas or know nothing at all about music, the All Music Guide provides you with delineations of the various musical periods that you will find useful in informing your choices.

Musical Periods

Because there has been much interest in historic periods—baroque, Renaissance, and so on—as they apply to music, composers listed here are identified with their period. The terms used for the various historic periods are borrowed loosely from art history and often follow similar developmental trends in painting, sculpture, literature, and architecture. Although any such groupings are at best arbitrary, it may help you to associate composers with the predominant styles flourishing during these periods and thus make it easier to find music that you will like. Please bear in mind that the placement of a composer in a specific period is an arbitrary choice based on flexible definitions. For this reason, dates of certain composers overlap boundaries on the list. The following definitions are provided to assist you in understanding the musical eras:

Medieval

Music developed during the Gothic, or medieval, period, including Gregorian chant, was developed and refined over several centuries. This period covers the period 1000-1450. Music of the medieval period was predominantly sacred and characterized by the slow development of rhythmic independence between voices in polyphonic textures. An advance occurred away from the monophonic style of Gregorian chant and the more straightforward multiple voice textures of organum. Because these composers often did not affix their names to their works, many individuals of this era are unknown to us; even if a name can be associated with a particular work, very little may be known about the specifics of that composer's life. However, a few major composers from this era are known to us, including Abbess Hildegard von Bingen, Perotin Magnus, and Guillaume de Machaut.

Renaissance

As in all forms of art, including music, the Renaissance marked the rebirth of humanism and a revival of achievements for their own sake. Musical innovations were quickly disseminated, primarily because of the advent of music printing. Movable type and various forms of musical print-

ing likewise resulted in the progressive movement of music theory and practice. This period covered the last half of the 15th century and the entire16th century. During the Renaissance broader, more complicated harmonic and contrapuntal structures emerged. Though the musical forms employed were still largely liturgical, the late Renaissance brought a great increase in sophistication for instrumental composition, as well as the continued development and emergence of secular madrigals, dramatic works, and the first operas. Many of these changes were pioneered with the music of Franco-Flemish composers including Johannes Ockeghem, Guillaume Dufay, and Josquin des Prez. The period culminated in the music of Giovanni Palestrina, Claudio Monteverdi, William Byrd, Roland de Lassus, and many others, as the musical styles spread throughout Europe.

Baroque

Music of the baroque era (1600-1750) was characterized by vastness of proportion, rich counterpoint, great splendor, and a highly ornamented melodic line. Its emphasis on the use of great vocal and instrumental color was a departure from the severity of medieval and early Renaissance music. Secular music was now as much in evidence as liturgical music. The harpsichord music of Johann Sebastian Bach, Francois Couperin, and Jean-Philippe Rameau, as well as the instrumental and orchestral music of Georg Frederic Handel, Antonio Vivaldi, Arcangelo Corelli, and Johann Sebastian Bach epitomize the precepts of the baroque.

Classicism

In the music of the classical period there was a revolt against the musical trends of the preceding (baroque) era. To be sure, there is no set date on which one might remark that here the revolution began. But one can see the beginnings of the classical era in the music of the great transitional composer Carl Philipp Emannuel Bach, through the emergence of the galant style, as well as in the productions of the musicians who came to be known as the Mannheim School (Johann Stamitz etc.). Briefly, the characteristics of classicism combined a concern for musical form with more concise melodic expressions and clarity of instrumental color. The compositions of Franz Joseph Haydn and Wolfgang Amadeus Mozart, in particular, exemplified the concepts of classicism. This era culminated with the early music of Ludwig van Beethoven.

Romanticism

Extending the bounds of music beyond the restrictive formality of classicism was the prime function of the romantic period. Formal concern, intellectuality, and concise expression were augmented by sentiment, imagination, and effect. The period of romanticism began with Ludwig van Beethoven's late works (string quartets, symphonies, piano sonatas). It culminated in the form known as "impressionism" (Claude Debussy, Maurice Ravel, etc.), a transitional trend that, with the innovations of Gustav Mahler's symphonies, formed the beginnings of 20th century music.

20th Century

Little attempt has been made to differentiate among the various subgroupings under which music of our century has been placed. There is no compact definition for the contents of this era. The distinctive features include music written since the turn of the century, which does not fit into the category of romanticism for strict chronological reasons, works that attempt to broaden the horizons of music for either orchestral technique or mode of expression, and music that does not categorically belong to the avant garde (see the section on avant garde for further definition). The operative principle for assigning composers to this category was qualitatively one of style. Composers in the classical category are closer in style and outlook to composers of the preceding lists than those in the avant garde section are, though there are, of course, some who could have gone in either list. This category still includes a wide range of styles,

such as neo-classical, neo-romantic, expressionist, and atonal. There is substantial chronological overlap between works listed in this section and those listed in the avant garde section, but on average the compositions in this category fall into the first half of the 20th century and follow the melodic and harmonic patterns and compositional forms of earlier periods.

—*Dave Lampson*

Adolphe-Charles Adam (1803-1856)

Born to the concert pianist Jean Louis Adam, Adolphe-Charles was trained from early childhood to take the piano as his vocation. At the Paris Conservatory he studied organ, counterpoint, and composition. He discovered a talent for composition, especially for opera. At the age of 28 he won acclaim for a comic opera and thereafter produced an average of two operas a year until his death at the age of 52. of his 53 operas, a handful have achieved a permanent place in the repertory. Notable among them are *Le Postillon de Longjumais, Regine,* and his enduringly popular masterpiece, *Si j'etai roi.* His most frequently performed work is the music for the ballet *Giselle,* so full of splendor and memorable melody that it transcends the stage. *Giselle* typifies Adam's gifts of melody, harmony, and dramatic effects.

Near the end of his life, having lost his money in the failure of a business venture, the hapless Opera-National, Adam was rescued by his appointment in 1847 as professor of music at the Paris Conservatory, where he had studied as a young man. Adam was an outgoing, articulate man who traveled frequently in Europe and enjoyed friendships with many of the composers and musicians of his age. Nevertheless, his compositional style was distinctly French, Parisian even, and he stands as one of the seminal influences in the development of the French opera, noted for its lushness (at times, nearly excess) of rich and dramatic melody, music as apt for the dance and spectacle as for the voice. —*Doug Purl*

GISELLE (BALLET)

Giselle (complete ballet) / London 433007-2 or 417505-2
Richard Bonygne/Royal Opera House Orchestra

Alexander Agricola (c.1446-1506)

Agricola was a Franco-Flemish contemporary of Josquin Des Prez who spent most of his working life in Italy. During his lifetime, he was hailed by some writers as the greatest composer in Europe. Agricola's output consists of sacred and secular vocal music, as well as several pieces in chanson style, which survive without text. These last examples serve as evidence of a nascent instrumental genre, to which Agricola must have been a prime contributor, and include such purely instrumental effects as diminution. While Agricola's music uses some of the same structural principles as Josquin's, including a telling ability for working out all voices concurrently, he does not use imitation to the same degree and so looks back somewhat to the previous generation of Ockeghem. Agricola's compositions are all highly polished, with a fine sense of harmony and voice leading. —*Todd McComb*

CHANSONS

Chansons / RCA Deutsche Harmonia Mundi 77038-2-RC
Crawford Young/Ferrara Ensemble, Schola Cantorum Basiliensis

SACRED MUSIC

Magnificat; Motets: "Nobis Sancti Spiritus," "O crux ave," "Regina coeli" (also see Josquin Des Prez) / Chanticleer CR-8808
Chanticleer

Isaac Albeniz (1860-1909)

An important Spanish pianist and composer of solo piano music (*Suite Iberia,* 1906) and opera music (*Pepita Jimenez,* 1896). Albeniz was a precocious, self-taught, and instinctive musician, a stowaway who toured the world in his youth. He wrote with Moorish rhythms, an Andalusian sense of harmony, and ornate decoration. *Iberia* is the poetic height of southern Spanish music and dance forms. —*"Blue" Gene Tyranny*

IBERIA

Iberia/ London 417887-2
Alicia De Larrocha (piano)

SUITE ESPANOLA

Suite espanola #1 & 2, Op. 47 / London 417887-2
Alicia De Larrocha (piano)

RAPSODIA ESPANOLA

Rapsodia espanola, Op. 70 / London 410289-2
Alicia De Larrocha (piano), Rafael Fruhbeck de Burgos /London Philharmonic Orchestra

Tomaso Albinoni (1671-1750)

Albinoni was a famed Italian violinist and prolific composer in all forms, including opera (*Rodrigo in Algeri,* 1702) and secular instrumental works (*Adagio for Organ & Strings*). His output includes more than 50 operas, most of which were produced in his native Venice. The ubiquitous "Adagio in G" was arranged, or rather reconstructed, for organ and strings by Remo Giazotto in the late 1940s from a six-bar fragment of music by Albinoni along principles the composer would have employed. —*"Blue" Gene Tyranny*

ADAGIO (ARRANGED BY REMO GIAZOTTO)

Adagio in G Minor / Nimbus NIM5032
William Boughton/English String Orchestra

CONCERTOS A CINQUE OP. 5

12 Concertos a 5, Op. 5 / Philips 422251-2
Pina Carmirelli (violin), Anna Maria Cotogni (violin), Michael Murray-Robinson (viola), Carol Figeriod (viola)/I Musici

★ **Concertos for Oboe Op. 7 & 9**

8 Concertos, Op. 7 #2, 3, 5, 6, 8, 9, 11 & 12 / Archiv 427111-2
Heinz Holliger (oboe), Hans Elhorst (oboe)/Camerata Bern

12 Concertos, Op. 9 / Philips 426080-2
Heinz Holliger (oboe), Maurice Bourgue (oboe), Felix Ayo (violin)/I Musici

Carl Friedrich Abel (1723-1787)

German-born composer who made his home in London. Best known for his collaborations with Johann Christian Bach that produced a series of popular symphony concerts from 1767 to 1781. —*AMG*

SYMPHONIES

6 Symphonies, Op. 7 / Chandos CHAN8648
Adrian Shepherd/Cantilena

6 Symphonies, Op. 10 / CPO 999207-2
Michael Schneider/La Stagione Frankfurt

Charles-Valentin Alkan (1813-1888)

Alkan, and his four brothers, all musicians, adopted their father's first name as their surname. Alkan Morhange (1780-1855) was the proprietor of a music school in Paris, and he early recognized among the musical talents of his sons the singular ones of young Charles-Valentin. Consequently, at the age of five Alkan was enrolled in the Paris Conservatory of Music, the breeding ground of many outstanding musicians and composers in the 19th century. Alkan studied composition and piano, making his debut at 12 years of age performing his own compositions as well as those of others. He seemed a star ascendant. Before he was 20 he had embarked on the first of two trips abroad (the second came two years later), the only times he was ever to leave Paris in his lifetime.

Music Map **Classical**

Middle Ages 1100 – 1450
Monophonic music (i.e., music in which only one tune, or line, is being played by all the musicians), polyphonic music (many lines being played at once, independent but equal), primarily vocal and sacred.

Forms:
Motet, solo song, mass

Major works:
de Machaut'sMesse de Nostre Dame, Dufay's chansons

Composers:
Perotin (ca. 1155-1250)
Guillaume de Machaut (ca. 1300-1377)
John Dunstable (ca. 1380-1453)
Guillaume Dufay (ca. 1400-1474)
Johannes Okeghem(1410-1497)

Renaissance 1450 – 1600
Polyphonic music, primarily vocal and sacred, although instrumental and secular music start to become important.

Forms:
Madrigal, mass, chanson, dance, anthem, fantasia, variations

Major works:
Palestrina'sMissa Papae Marcelli , Dowland's lute music, Lassus's motets, Morley's madrigals

Composers:
Josquin des Prez (ca. 1440-1521)
Andrea Gabrieli (ca. 1510-1586)
Giovanni Palestrina (ca. 1525-1594)
Orlandus Lassus (1532-1584)
William Byrd (1543-1623)
Tomas Luis de Victoria (ca. 1549-1611)
Giovanni Gabrieli (ca. 1554-1612)
Don Carlo Gesualdo (ca. 1560-1613)
John Dowland (1563-1626)
Orlando Gibbons (1583-1625)

Baroque 1600 – 1750
Strong, rhythmic, highly ornamental instrumental and vocal music, both sacred and secular. Primarily polyphonic, but also the start of music in which one line is more important than the others played at the same time, which accompany it rather than being played independently. First appearance of opera as a form.

Forms:
Opera, cantata, oratorio, concerto grosso, solo concerto, fugue, trio sonata, suite, prelude, chorale

Major works:
Monteverdi'sOrfeo; J. S. Bach'sBrandenburg Concertos, St. Matthew Passion , Well-Tempered Clavier ; Handel'sMessiah and concerti grossi; Vivaldi's concertos

Composers:
Claudio Monteverdi (1567-1643)
Heinrich Schütz (1585-1672)
Dietrich Buxtehude (1637-1707)
Arcangelo Corelli (1653-1713)
Henry Purcell (1659-1695)
Alessandro Scarlatti (1660-1725)
François Couperin ("The Great") (1668-1733)
Antonio Vivaldi (1678-1741)
Jean Phillipe Rameau (1683-1764)
J. S. Bach (1685-1750)
George Frideric Handel (1685-1760)
Domenico Scarlatti (1685-1757)
Johann Pachelbel (1653-1706)
Giovanni Battista Pergolesi (1710-1736)

Classical era 1750 – 1827
Music, primarily instrumental (although opera begins to come into its own), of many types (dominated by the sonata form) and textures, marked by clarity, balance, and restraint. Melody with harmonic accompaniment becomes predominant.

Forms:
Sonata, concerto, symphony, string quartet, opera

Major works:
Mozart's Don Giovanni , "Jupiter" symphony, "Prussian" string quartets; Haydn's symphony no. 88, Creation

Composers:
C. P. E. Bach (1714-1788)
Franz Joseph Haydn (1732-1809)
Wolfgang Amadeus Mozart (1756-1791)
Ludwig van Beethoven (1770-1729)

Romantic era 1827 – 1890
Very expressive music (primarily instrumental, with opera becoming very important) in which melody is the dominant feature, with full-bodied harmonies.

Forms:
Lieder, sonata, symphony, symphonic tone poem, opera, short forms such as nocturne and intermezzo

Major works:
Wagner's Tristan und Isolde, Beethoven's ninth symphony, Schubert's lieder, Tchaikovsky's "Pathétique" symphony, Bizet's Carmen, Verdi's Otello

Composers:
Franz Schubert (1797-1828)
Hector Berlioz (1803-1869)
Fredric Chopin (1810-1849)
Robert Schumann (1810-1856)
Franz Liszt (1811-1886)
Giuseppe Verdi (1813-1901)
Richard Wagner (1813-1883)
Johannes Brahms (1833-1897)
Piotr Ilyich Tchaikovsky (1840-1893)
Antonín Dvořák (1841-1904)
Edvard Grieg (1843-1907)
Giacomo Puccini (1858-1924)
Gustav Mahler (1860-1911)

Contemporary era 1890 – present
Highly eclectic music of various forms and types (melodic and otherwise), such as impressionism, nationalism, neo-classicism. Traditional structures and forms are broken up and recast using influences from non-Western music, technology, and abstract ideas.

Forms:
Symphony, concerto, sonata, opera, many others.

Major works:
Stravinsky'sSacre du Printemps, Bartók's quartets, Berg'sLulu, Webern'sFive Pieces for Orchestra

Composers:
Claude Debussy (1862-1918)
Arnold Schoenberg 1874-1951)
Maurice Ravel (1875-1937)
Béla Bartók (1881-1945)
Igor Stravinsky (1882-1971)
Anton Webern (1883-1945)
Alban Berg (1885-1935)
Sergei Prokofiev (1891-1953)
Aaron Copland (1900-1990)
John Cage (b. 1912-1992)
Benjamin Britten (1913-1976)

In Paris Alkan was a member of an accomplished social circle that included many of the leading names of his times in thought and the arts. In 1838 he appeared in concert with his close friend and neighbor, Frederic Chopin, and was warmly received by critics and public alike. To this day there is no definitive explanation of what ensued from this point, though surmise and conjecture have flourished. For six years Alkan disappeared from the concert stage. He performed again for nearly 2 years and then dematerialized as public pianist for 28 more years; when he appeared again he was past 60.

In his time Alkan was considered the peer of Chopin and Liszt in technique. He is widely thought of as an eccentric par excellence. In his later years he became intrigued with the pedalier, a pedal board that attaches to the piano and enables full performance of organ literature on the piano. He was fond of playing the compositions of Bach on this device and composed copiously for it. His piano works require the utmost of skills, attesting to Alkan's own. Few performers care to attempt the difficulties of the Alkanian oeuvre in public, though some display their uncommon prowess by means of his works. The name of Alkan even now remains one capable of engendering vigorous debate in musical circles. —*Douglas Purl*

PIANO MUSIC

Assorted Pieces including Sonatine Op. 61 / Harmonia Mundi HMA190927
Bernard Ringeissen (piano)

Concerto for Solo Piano, Op. 39 #8-10 / Music & Arts CD-724
Marc-Andre Hamelin (piano)

25 Preludes, Op. 31 / Marco Polo 8.223284
Laurent Martin (piano)

"Grand" Sonata "Les Quatre Ages," Op. 33, Prelude & Etudes / EMI CDM7642802
Ronald Smith (piano)

Etudes, Symphonie & Overture Op. 39 #1, 2, 4-7 & 11 / Marco Polo 8.223285
Bernard Ringeissen (piano)

Georgio Allegri

Allegri's Miserere Mei, Deus is a chant for five-part a cappella choir in nine sections in the falsobordone style, in which four of the voices sing highly embellished and decorative passages, improvised by the original choir and later written down to be preserved. Allegri probably wrote only the basic chant. This work has been sung in the Sistine Chapel during Holy Week every year since it was composed, and the ornamentation was kept secret until historian Charles Burney discovered the original manuscript and reconstructed the complete work. Miserere Mei, Deus is also the work that Mozart transcribed from memory at age 14—a legendary feat of music history. —*"Blue" Gene Tyranny*

MISERERE

Miserere (w/ "Crucifixus" by Lotti, also see Palestrina) / Collins 50092
Harry Christophers/The Sixteen

Arcadelt, Jacob

A French composer of sacred music and many secular madrigals and chansons, known for "Il bianco e dolce cigno" ("The sweet, white swan"). —*AMG*

MADRIGALS

Madrigal Collection / RCA Deutsche Harmonia Mundi 77162-2-RC
Anthony Rooley/Consort of Musicke

Thomas Augustine Arne (1710-1778)

This important British contemporary of Handel composed songs and ballad operas such as *Dido and Aeneas* (1734) and *Alfred* (1740), (which featured the song "Rule, Brittania"). —*Mary K. Scanlan*

SYMPHONIES

4 Symphonies / Chandos CHAN8403
SHEPHERD, Adrian/Cantilena

KEYBOARD CONCERTOS

6 "Favorite" Concertos / Hyperion CDA66509

Paul Nicholson (harpsichord, organ & fortepiano)/Parley of Instruments Baroque Orchestra

Daniel-Francois Auber (1782-1871)

As a young man Auber was sent abroad by his father, a successful Parisian art dealer. In London Auber studied business, but he also established himself in musical circles and began to compose songs. The increasing breakdown of relations between England and France impelled him to return home in 1803. On his return he forsook a business career and dedicated himself to composition, at first for the nascent opera comique. For a long time he was unsuccessful, but his talent was obvious and he received much encouragement, from Cherubini among others. In time he became popular, and eventually he completed about 50 operas, most notable among them being *Fra Diavolo*, which remains in the permanent repertoire.

Auber's career divides between the opera comique and French grand opera; he may be considered a cofounder of both of these media . His style is light, decidedly different from that of his weightier contemporaries. It has often been compared to that of Rossini, though it must be said that Auber's compositions would never be mistaken for those of anyone else. In 1842 he was appointed to the faculty of the Paris Conservatory, a post he retained until his death at the age of 89. —*Douglas Purl*

Overtures

Overture to "Fra Diavolo," "Masaniello" and "The Bronze Horse" / Mercury Living Presence 434309-2
Paul Paray/Detroit Symphony Orchestra

Carl Philipp Emanuel Bach (1714-1788)

The second son of J. S. Bach was a keyboardist, a composer of keyboard sonatas, and author of the *Essay on the True Art of Keyboard Playing*, whose output includes chamber music, songs, and oratorios. His music marks the transition from the baroque to the classical style and features minute attention to the details of expression in the beautiful "empfindsamer Stil" (sensitive style), which led toward a more romantic style of music. —*"Blue" Gene Tyranny*

MAGNIFICAT

Magnificat, Wq. 215 (1749) / London Jubilee 421148-2
Palmer, Watts, Tear, Roberts, Philip Ledger/Choir of King's College, Cambridge, Academy of St. Martin-in-the-Fields

CONCERTO IN A FOR CELLO

3 Concertos, Wq. 170-172 / Virgin VC790800-2
Anner Bylsma (cello), Gustav Leonhardt/Orchestra of the Age of Enlightenment

CONCERTOS FOR FLUTE

5 Concertos, Wq. 165-169; Sonata Wq. 132 / CBS M2K44690
Jean-Pierre Rampal (flute), Janos Rolla/Franz Liszt Chamber Orchestra

3 Concertos Wq. 22, 166 & 168 / Capriccio 10104
Eckart Haupt (flute), Hartmut Haenchen/Carl Philipp Emanuel Bach Chamber Orchestra

2 Concertos Wq. 167 & 169 / Capriccio 10105
Eckart Haupt (flute), Hartmut Haenchen/Carl Philipp Emanuel Bach Chamber Orchestra

CONCERTO FOR 2 HARPSICHORDS

Concerto, Wq. 46 / Archiv 419256-2
Andreas Staier & Robert Hill (harpsichords), Reinhard Goebel/Musica Antiqua Koln

CONCERTOS FOR OBOE

2 Concertos, Wq. 164 & 165 / Capriccio 10069
Burkhardt Glaetzner (oboe), Max Pommer/New Bach Collegium Musicum, Leipzig

SONATAS FOR FLUTE & CONTINUO

4 Sonatas, Wq. 83-86 / Denon 33C37-7807
Andras Adorjan (flute), Huguette Dreyfus (harpsichord)

6 Trio Sonatas, Wq. 124, 127-129, 133 & 134 / Capriccio 10101
Eckart Haupt (flute), Siegfried Pank (viola da gamba), Armin Thalheim (harpsichord)

★ **Sonatas for Keyboard**
6 "Prussian" Sonatas, Wq. 48 / Etcetera KTC1011

Anneke Uittenbosch (harpsichord)

18 Sonatas, 13 Rondos & 6 Fantasias, Wq. 55-60 / CPO
999100-2
Gabor Antalffy (harpsichord & fortepiano)

★ **Symphonies**

"Berlin" Symphonies, Wq. 174, 175, 178, 179 & 181 / Capriccio
10103
Hartmut Haenchen/Carl Philipp Emanuel Bach Chamber
Orchestra

6 Symphonies, Wq. 182 / L'Oiseau-Lyre 417124-2
Christopher Hogwood/Academy of Ancient Music

4 "Hamburg" Symphonies, Wq. 183 / Capriccio 10175
Hartmut Haenchen/Carl Philipp Emanuel Bach Chamber
Orchestra

Johann Christian Bach

The 11th son of J. S. Bach and the youngest to live to maturity,
Johann Christian received his early musical training from his father, than whom music has spawned no greater genius. His father
died when Christian was 14 . Thereupon he studied with his
brother Carl Philipp Emanuel. Four years later he left for Italy,
where he continued his studies and won a patron. Eventually he
became organist at the cathedral of Milan and began to compose
operas, economically the most rewarding of compositional forms
in those days. In 1762 he emigrated to London, his home until his
death 20 years later. The *London* Bach achieved immediate
renown in England, and within two years was appointed music
master to the Queen. Until his health failed, he was the co-orga-
nizer (with Carl Abel) of an acclaimed series of London concerts
that ran from 1764 to 1781. Bach departed from the musical style
of his father and older brothers, anticipating and contributing to
the development of the "classical" era. His tendencies include a
new emphasis on emotional expression, a shift from ecclesiastical
to concert-hall forms and genres, and a conscious featuring of virtuoso instrumental registration. His work embodies the "style
galant" of the last half of the 18th century. Besides his many operas and chamber compositions, Bach wrote around 90 symphonies, productivity akin to that of Haydn. Had Johann
Christian's father J. S. Bach never existed, Johann Christian's place
in musical history would be secure. So profound and excellent
were his talents and knowledge, the child prodigy Mozart was
brought to him in London in 1764 for instruction. Mozart acknowledged his debt to his mentor by using several of Bach's piano sonatas as the bases for his own piano concertos. —*Douglas
Purl*

CONCERTOS FOR HARPSICHORD OR FORTEPIANO

6 Concertos, Op. 1 & 6 Concertos, Op. 7 / Philips 438712-2
Ingrid Haebler (fortepiano), Eduard Melkus/Capella Academica,
Wien

3 Concertos in A Major, F Minor & G Major Op. 7 / 6 / Denon
33C37-7672
Huguette Dreyfus (harpsichord)/Tokyo Solisten

OVERTURES

6 "Favorite" Overtures / L'Oiseau-Lyre 417148-2
Christopher Hogwood/Academy of Ancient Music

QUINTETS FOR FLUTE, OBOE & STRINGS

Quintets, Op. 11 #1 & 6, Op. 22 #1 and Sextet in C Major /
Archiv 423385-2
Various Performers/The English Concert

SYMPHONIES

6 Symphonies, Op. 3 / Philips 422498-2
Neville Marriner/Academy of St. Martin-in-the-Fields

Johann Sebastian Bach (1685-1750)

Bach is considered by many people to have been the greatest
composer in the history of Western music. Bach's main achievement lies in his synthesis and advanced development of the primary contrapuntal idiom of the late baroque, and in the basic
tunefulness of his thematic material. He was able to successfully
integrate and expand upon the harmonic and formal frameworks
of the national schools of the time: German, French, Italian and
English, while retaining a personal identity and spirit in his large
output. Bach is also known for the numerical symbolism and

mathematical exactitude that many people have found in his music—for this, he is often regarded as one of the pinnacle geniuses
of western civilization, even by those who are not normally involved with music.

Bach spent the height of his working life in a Lutheran church
position in Leipzig, as both organist and music director. Much of
his music is overtly religious, while many of his secular works admit religious interpretation on some levels. His large output of organ music is considered to be the greatest legacy of compositions
for the instrument, and it is the measure by which all later efforts
are judged. His other solo keyboard music is held in equally high
esteem, especially for its exploration of the strictly contrapuntal
fugue; his 48 preludes and fugues (*The Well-Tempered Clavier*)
are still the primary means by which these forms are taught. His
other chamber music is similarly lofty, the sets for solo violin and
solo cello being the summits of their respective genres. Bach's
large-scale sacred choral music is also unique in its scope and development. The *St. John* and *St. Matthew* passions and *B Minor
Mass* led to the rediscovery of his music in the 19th century. His
huge output of cantatas for all occasions is equally impressive.
Finally, his large output of concerti includes some of the finest examples of the period, including the ubiquitous *Brandenberg
Concertos*. —*Todd McComb*

★ **Art of the Fugue**

The Art of Fugue, BWV 1080 / Harmonia Mundi HMC901169 /
70
Davitt Moroney (harpsichord)

The Art of Fugue, BWV 1080; Canons, BWV 1086 & 1087 /
Archiv 413642-2
Reinhard Goebel/Musica Antiqua Koln

The Art of the Fugue, BWV 1080 (Early Version) / Archiv 427673-2
Kenneth Gilbert (harpsichord)

★ **Brandenburg Concertos**

6 Brandenburg Concertos, BWV 1046-1051 (w/ Suites) /
Archiv 423492-2
Trevor Pinnock/The English Concert

6 Brandenburg Concertos, BWV 1046-1051 / Archiv 423116-2
Reinhard Goebel/Musica Antiqua Koln

6 Brandenburg Concertos, BWV 1046-1051 (w/ Suites) / RCA
Eurodisc 69219-2-RV
Josef Suk (violin), Max Lesueur (viola), Maurice Bourgue (oboe),
Aurele Nicolet (flute), Manfred Sax (bassoon), Rudolf
Baumgartner/Festival Strings Lucerne

**6 Brandenburg Concertos, BWV 1046a, 1047-1049, 1050a,
1051** / L'Oiseau-Lyre 414187-2
Christopher Hogwood/Academy of Ancient Music
Cantatas (BWV 4, 78, 82, 140, 202)

Cantatas #1-4, BWV 1-4 / Teldec 2292-42497-2
Esswood, Equiluz, Egmond, Nicholas Harnoncourt/Vienna
Concentus Musicus & Boy's Choir

Cantatas #78 & 198, BWV 78 & 198 / Harmonia Mundi
HMC901270
Philippe Herreweghe/La Chapelle Royale Orchestra & Chorus

Cantatas #82, 152 & 202, BWV 82, 152 & 202 / Ricercar
RIC061041
Greta de Reyghere (soprano), Max van Egmond (bass)/Ricercar
Consort

Cantatas #140, 56 & 159, BWV 140, 56 & Anh. 159 / Dorian
DOR-90127
Schellenberg, Gordon, Lichti, Funfgeld/Bach Choir of Bethlehem,
Bach Festival Orchestra

Cantatas #202, 209, 211 & 212, BWV 202, 209, 211 & 212 /
RCA Deutsche Harmonia Mundi Editio Classica 77151-2-RG
Elly Ameling, Gerald English, Siegmund Nimsgern/Collegium
Aureum

CHROMATIC FANTASY & FUGUE FOR HARPSICHORD

Chromatic Fantasy & Fugue, BWV 903 / L'Oiseau-Lyre 433054-
2
Christophe Rousset (harpsichord)

Chromatic Fantasy & Fugue, BWV 903 / Arabesque Z6577
Igor Kipnis (harpsichord)

Chromatic Fantasy & Fugue, BWV 903 / Philips 412252-2
Alfred Brendel (piano)

Chromatic Fantasy & Fugue, BWV 903 / Supraphon 110359-2
Ivan Moravec (piano)

★ **Concertos for Harpsichord(s) (BWV 1052, *1056)**

3 Concertos, BWV 1052-1054 / Archiv 415991-2
Trevor Pinnock (harpsichord)/The English Concert

4 Concertos, BWV 1055-1058 / Archiv 415992-2
Trevor Pinnock (harpsichord)/The English Concert

7 Concertos, BWV 1052-1058 / London 425676-2
Andras Schiff (piano)/Chamber Orchestra of Europe

★ **Concertos for Violin & 2 Violins**

2 Concertos for Violin, BWV 1041 & 1042; Concerto for 2 Violins / L'Oiseau-Lyre 400080-2
Jaap Schroder & Christopher Hirons (violins), Christopher Hogwood/Academy of Ancient Music

2 Concertos for Violin, BWV 1041 & 1042; Concerto for 2 Violins / EMI CDC747005-2
Anne-Sophie Mutter & Salvatore Accardo (violins)/English Chamber Orchestra

2 Concertos for Violin, BWV 1041 & 1042; Concerto for 2 Violins / Archiv 410646-2
Simon Standage & Elisabeth Wilcock (violins), Trevor Pinnock/The English Concert

FANTASIA & FUGUE IN G MINOR FOR ORGAN

Fantasia & Fugue in G Minor, BWV 542 / Telarc CD-80049
Michael Murray (organ)

Fantasia & Fugue in G Minor, BWV 542 / London Weekend Classics 417679-2
Karl Richter (organ)

★ **Goldberg Variations for Harpsichord**

Goldberg Variations, BWV 988 / Harmonia Mundi HMC901240
Kenneth Gilbert (harpsichord)

Goldberg Variations, BWV 988 / London 417116-2
Andras Schiff (piano)

Goldberg Variations, BWV 988 / Kontrapunkt 32023
Lars Ulrik Mortensen (harpsichord)

Goldberg Variations, BWV 988 / Sony SMK52594
Glenn Gould (piano)

Goldberg Variations, BWV 988 / Denon 8175736772
Huguette Dreyfus (harpsichord)

INVENTIONS FOR HARPSICHORD

30 Two- & Three-Part Inventions, BWV 772-801 / Archiv 415112-2
Kenneth Gilbert (harpsichord)

30 Two- & Three-Part Inventions, BWV 772-801 / London 411974-2
Andras Schiff (piano)

ITALIAN CONCERTO FOR HARPSICHORD

Italian Concerto in F Major, BWV 971 / Reference Recordings RR-51CD
Albert Fuller (harpsichord)

Italian Concerto in F Major, BWV 971 / Philips 412252-2
Alfred Brendel (piano)

Italian Concerto in F Major, BWV 971 / Nimbus NIM5080
Vlado Perlemuter (piano)

MAGNIFICAT

Magnificat, BWV 243 / Philips 411458-2
John Eliot Gardiner/Monteverdi Choir, English Baroque Soloists

Magnificat, BWV 243 / Harmonia Mundi HMC901326
Philippe Herreweghe/Collegium Vocale, La Chapelle Royale Orchestra

Magnificat, BWV 243 (w / Vivaldi Gloria)) / Chandos Chaconne CHAN0518
Emma Kirkby & Tessa Bonner (soprano), Michael Chance (countertenor), John Mark Ainsley (tenor), Richard Hickox/Collegium Musicum 90

★ **Mass in B Minor**

Mass in B Minor, BWV 232 / Archiv 415514-2
John Eliot Gardiner/Monteverdi Choir, English Baroque Soloists

Mass in B Minor, BWV 232 / EMI CDS747293-2

Andrew Parrott/Taverner Consort, Choir & Players

MUSICAL OFFERING

Musical Offering, BWV 1079 / Archiv 413642-2
Reinhard Goebel/Musica Antiqua Koln

Musical Offering, BWV 1079 / Harmonia Mundi HMC901260
Davitt Moroney (harpsichord), Janet See (flute), John Holloway (violin), Jaap ter Linden (cello), Martha Cook (harpsichord)

ORGAN MUSIC COLLECTION

Complete Organ Music / Calliope CAL9703 / 17
Andre Isoir (organ)

Toccatas, Fantasias, Fugues, Chorale Preludes, etc. / Harmonia Mundi HMX290772.83
Lionel Rogg (organ)

The Great Organ at Methuen / Telarc CD-80049
Michael Murray (organ)

Preludes & Fugues and Toccatas & Fugues / Erato 2292-45701-2
Marie-Claire Alain (organ)

Choral Preludes / Erato 2292-45702-2
Marie-Claire Alain (organ)

PARTITAS FOR HARPSICHORD

6 Partitas, BWV 825-830 / Archiv 415493-2
Trevor Pinnock (harpsichord)

6 Partitas, BWV 825-830 / RCA Deutsche Harmonia Mundi Editio Classica 77215-2-RG
Gustav Leonhardt (harpsichord)

6 Partitas, BWV 825-830 / London 411732-2
Andras Schiff (piano)

★ **Passacaglia & Fugue in C Minor for Organ**

Passacaille & Fugue in C Minor, BWV 582 / London Jubilee 417711-2
Peter Hurford (organ)

Passacaille & Fugue in C Minor, BWV 582 / Telarc CD-80049
Michael Murray (organ)

Passacaille & Fugue in C Minor, BWV 582 / Philips Concert Classics 422965-2
Daniel Chorzempa (organ)

★ **St. Matthew Passion**

Passion According to St. Matthew, BWV 244 / Harmonia Mundi HMC901155-57
Philippe Herreweghe/Collegium Vocale, La Chapelle Royale Orchestra

★ **Sonatas & Partitas for Solo Violin**

6 Sonatas & Partitas, BWV 1001-1006 / RCA Deutsche Harmonia Mundi Editio Classica 77043-2-RG
Sigiswald Kuijken (violin)

6 Sonatas & Partitas, BWV 1001-1006 / EMI CDS7494832
Itzhak Perlman (violin)

6 Sonatas & Partitas, BWV 1001-1006 / Philips 438736-2
Arthur Grumiaux (violin)

SONATAS & PARTITA FOR FLUTE & CONTINUO

3 Sonatas, BWV 1020, 1031 & 1033; Partita, BWV 1013 / Philips 422061-2
Irena Grafenauer (flute), Maria Graf (harp), David Geringas (cello)

4 Sonatas, BWV 1030, 1032, 1034 & 1035 / Denon 33C37-7331
Aurele Nicolet (flute), Christiane Jaccottet (harpsichord), Mari Fujiwara (cello)

7 Sonatas, BWV 1030-1035 & 1020; Partita, BWV 1013 / Harmonia Mundi HMU907024 / 25
Janet See (flute), Davitt Moroney (harpsichord), Mary Springfels (viola da gamba)

★ **Suites for Solo Cello**

6 Suites, BWV 1007-1012 / Sony Vivarte S2K48047
Anner Bylsma (cello)

6 Suites, BWV 1007-1012 / Deutsche Grammophon 419359-2
Pierre Fournier (cello)

6 Suites, BWV 1007-1012; Sonatas, BWV 1027 & 1028 / Mercury Living Presence 432756-2

Janos Starker (cello)

SUITES FOR HARPSICHORD (ENGLISH & FRENCH)

6 Suites "English," BWV 806-811 / Harmonia Mundi HMC901074.75
Kenneth Gilbert (harpsichord)

6 Suites "English," BWV 806-811 / London 421640-2
Andras Schiff (piano)

6 Suites "French," BWV 812-817 / Virgin Classics VCD759011-2
Davitt Moroney (harpsichord)

6 Suites "French," BWV 812-817 / L'Oiseau-Lyre 411811-2
Christopher Hogwood (Harpsichord)

★ **Suites for Orchestra**
Orchestral Suites, BWV 1066-1069 / Erato 4509-91800-2
John Eliot Gardiner/English Baroque Soloists

Orchestral Suites, BWV 1066-1069 (w/ Brandenburg Concertos) / Archiv 423492-2
Trevor Pinnock/The English Concert

Orchestral Suites, BWV 1066-1069 (w/ Brandenburg Concertos) / RCA Eurodisc 69219-2-RV
Maurice Bourgue (oboe), Aurele Nicolet (flute), Manfred Sax (bassoon), Rudolf Baumgartner/Festival Strings Lucerne

TOCCATAS FOR HARPSICHORD

7 Toccatas, BWV 910-916 / Dorian Recordings DOR-90115
Colin Tilney (Harpsichord)

TRIO SONATAS

6 Trio Sonatas, BWV 525-530 / Philips 422328-2
John Butt (organ)

6 Trio Sonatas, BWV 525-530 / Philips 422328-2
Heinz Holliger (oboe), Tabea Zimmermann (viola), Christiane Jaccottet (harpsichord), Thomas Demenga (cello)

4 Trio Sonatas, BWV 1036-1039 / Harmonia Mundi HMC901173
Stephen Preston (flute), Ingrid Seifert (violin), Charles Medlam /London Baroque

★ **Toccata & Fugue in D Minor for Organ**
Toccata & Fugue in D Minor, BWV 565 / London Jubilee 417711-2
Peter Hurford (organ)

Toccata & Fugue in D Minor, BWV 565 / Philips Concert Classics 422965-2
Daniel Chorzempa (organ)

WELL-TEMPERED CLAVIER

Well-Tempered Clavier Books I & II, 48 Preludes & Fugues BWV 846-893 / Harmonia Mundi HMC901285.88
Davitt Moroney (harpsichord)

Well-Tempered Clavier Book I, 24 Preludes & Fugues BWV 846-893 / London 414388-2
Andras Schiff (piano)

Well-Tempered Clavier Book II, 24 Preludes & Fugues BWV 846-893 / London 417236-2
Andras Schiff (piano)

Well-Tempered Clavier Books I & II, 48 Preludes & Fugues BWV 846-893 / Archiv 413439-2
Kenneth Gilbert (harpsichord)

Well-Tempered Clavier Book I, 24 Preludes & Fugues BWV 846-893 / Sony SM2K52590
Glenn Gould (piano)

Well-Tempered Clavier Book II, 24 Preludes & Fugues BWV 846-893 / Sony SM2K52600
Glenn Gould (piano)

Well-Tempered Clavier Book I, 24 Preludes & Fugues BWV 846-893 / RCA Deutsche Harmonia Mundi Editio Classica 77011-2-RG
Gustav Leonhardt (harpsichord)

Well-Tempered Clavier Book II, 24 Preludes & Fugues BWV 846-893 / RCA Deutsche Harmonia Mundi Editio Classica 77012-2-RG
Gustav Leonhardt (harpsichord)

Wilhelm Friedemann Bach (1710-1784)

The eldest son of J. S. Bach, Wilhelm studied composition, organ, and violin with his father and at Thomasschule in Leipzig. After studying mathematics and humanities at the University of Leipzig, Bach accepted positions as organist, first in Dresden and then in Halle. In his 50s he relocated to Berlin, where he spent the final two decades of his life.

Bach composed for small groups and the orchestra of his day, besides organ and piano. He is closest in temperament and style to J. S. Bach of all the latter's sons. His music lies in the baroque tradition of harmonic elegance. More an able musician than an unusually gifted one, Wilhelm Freidemann is overshadowed by his brothers, Carl Philipp Emanuel, Johann Cristoph Friedrich, and Johann Christian. —*Douglas Purl*

KEYBOARD MUSIC

2 Sonatas, Fantasia, Suite, Fugues, etc. / Harmonia Mundi HMC901305
Christophe Rousset (harpsichord)

3 Sonatas, Polonaises, etc. / Ricercar RIC051043
Guy Penson (fortepiano & harpsichord)

CONCERTOS

2 Concertos in F Minor & F. 43 (w/ Sinfonia F. 65) / Ricercar RIC069049
Guy Penson (harpsichord), Adrian Chamorro/Ricercar Consort

Concerto, F. 46; Sonata F. 10 (also see C.P.E. Bach) / Archiv 419256-2
Andreas Staier & Robert Hill (harpsichords), Reinhard Goebel/Musica Antiqua Koln

SINFONIAS

Sinfonia F. 65 (w/ 2 Concertos) / Ricercar RIC069049
Adrian Chamorro/Ricercar Consort

3 Sinfonias, F. 64, 65 & 67 / Koch Schwann Treasure CD316012F1
Helmut Muller-Bruhl/Cologne Chamber Orchestra

Samuel Barber (1910-1981)

An American singer and composer of modern, accessible, neo-romantic symphonies and chamber music, including *The School for Scandal* (1933), *String Quartet* (1936), and *Adagio for Strings* (1936). Barber's music has integrity, retaining a noble and lyrical sound of its own through changing fashions and never sounding dated. —*"Blue" Gene Tyranny*

★ **Adagio for Strings**
Adagio, Op. 11 / 2 / Nimbus NIM5032
William Boughton/English String Orchestra

Adagio, Op. 11 / 2 / Special Music SCD-8012
Andrew Schenck/New Zealand Symphony Orchestra

Adagio, Op. 11 / 2 / Chandos CHAN9169
Neeme Jarvi/Detroit Symphony Orchestra

CONCERTOS (PIANO, VIOLIN)

Violin Concerto, Op. 14 / EMI CDC7478502
Elmar Oliveira (violin), Leonard Slatkin/Saint Louis Symphony Orchestra

Violin Concerto, Op. 14 / Reference Recordings RR-45CD
Ruggiero Ricci (violin), Keith Clark/Pacific Symphony Orchestra

Piano Concerto, Op. 38 / RCA 60732-2-RC
John Browning (piano), Leonard Slatkin/Saint Louis Symphony Orchestra

KNOXVILLE: SUMMER OF 1915

Knoxville: Summer of 1915 / Nonesuch 979187-2
Dawn Upshaw (soprano), David Zinman/Orchestra of St. Luke's

Knoxville: Summer of 1915 / Virgin 59520
Jill Gomez (soprano), Richard Hickox/City of London Sinfonia

SONATA FOR PIANO

Piano Sonata, Op. 26 / Virgin 59008
Peter Lawson (piano)

Piano Sonata, Op. 26 / RCA 60415-2-RG
Van Cliburn (piano)

SYMPHONIES (1, 2)

Symphony #1, Op. 9 / Chandos CHAN8958
Neeme Jarvi/Detroit Symphony Orchestra

Symphony #1, Op. 9 / RCA 60732-2-RC
Leonard Slatkin/Saint Louis Symphony Orchestra

Symphony #2, Op. 19 / Special Music SCD-8012
Andrew Schenck/New Zealand Symphony Orchestra

Symphony #2, Op. 19 / Chandos CHAN9169
Neeme Jarvi/Detroit Symphony Orchestra

Bela Bartok (1881-1945)

A Hungarian composer and musicologist who transcribed folk melodies and composed ballet, opera, orchestral, and chamber music, including *Dance Suite* (1923), *Sonata for Two Pianos & Percussion* (1937), *Mikrokosmos, 6 Books* (1926-1939), and *Concerto for Orchestra* (1943). Bartok was a 20th-century original who showed how superb intellectual effort (he invented a composition system using Golden Sections, the Fibonnacci series, and quasi-serial techniques) and great passion (as can be seen in his in-depth studies of the Hungarian folk music, the "night music" expressionist social tension between the wars, and his own life as a forced émigré) can combine to make great art. — *"Blue" Gene Tyranny*

★ **Concerto for Orchestra**

Concerto / London 421443-2
Charles Dutoit/Montreal Symphony Orchestra

Concerto / London 425694-2
Christoph von Dohnanyi/Cleveland Orchestra

Concerto / London 400052-2
Sir Georg Solti/Chicago Symphony Orchestra

Concerto / RCA Gold Seal 60175-2-RG or 09026-61504-2
Fritz Reiner/Chicago Symphony Orchestra

★ **Concertos for Piano (*3)**

Piano Concertos #1-3 / Philips 416831-2
Zoltan Kocsis (piano), Ivan Fischer/Budapest Festival Orchestra

Piano Concertos #1-3 / Philips 426660-2
Stephen Bishop Kovacevich (piano), Sir Colin Davis/London Symphony Orchestra & BBC Symphony Orchestra (#2)

Piano Concertos #1 & 2 / Deutsche Grammophon 415371-2
Maurizio Pollini (piano), Claudio Abbado/Chicago Symphony Orchestra

CONCERTOS FOR VIOLIN

Violin Concertos #1 & 2 / London 425015-2
Kyung-Wha Chung (violin), Sir Georg Solti/Chicago Symphony Orchestra & London Philharmonic Orchestra (#2)

Violin Concertos #1 & 2 / Sony SK45941
Midori (violin), Zubin Mehta/Berlin Philharmonic Orchestra (#2)

DANCE SUITE FOR ORCHESTRA

Dance Suite / London 400052-2
Sir Georg Solti/Chicago Symphony Orchestra

Dance Suite / Hungaroton HCD31167
Ivan Fischer/Budapest Festival Orchestra

MIRACULOUS MANDARIN

The Miraculous Mandarin (Suite) / London 430352-2
Sir Georg Solti/Chicago Symphony Orchestra

The Miraculous Mandarin (Complete) / London 411894-2
Antal Dorati/Detroit Symphony Orchestra & Kenneth Jewell Chorale

MUSIC FOR STRINGS PERCUSSION & CELESTE

Music for Strings, Percussion & Celeste / London 421443-2
Charles Dutoit/Montreal Symphony Orchestra

Music for Strings, Percussion & Celeste / London 411894-2
Antal Dorati/Detroit Symphony Orchestra

Music for Strings, Percussion & Celeste / London 430352-2
Sir Georg Solti/Chicago Symphony Orchestra

Music for Strings, Percussion & Celeste / Philips 416831-2
Ivan Fischer/Budapest Festival Orchestra

Music for Strings, Percussion & Celeste / RCA Gold Seal 60175-2-RG or 09026-61504-2

Fritz Reiner/Chicago Symphony Orchestra

PIANO MUSIC

Sonatina, Hungarian Folk Songs, Roumanian Folk Dances, Bagatelles, Op. 6 / Philips 434104-2
Zoltan Kocsis (piano)

Dance Suite, Hungarian Peasant Songs, Roumanian Folk Dances, Rondos / Denon C37-7092
Andras Schiff (piano)

★ **Quartets for Strings**

String Quartets #1-6 / Deutsche Grammophon 423657-2
Emerson Quartet

String Quartets #1-6 / Hungaroton HCD12502 / 4
Takacs Quartet

SONATA FOR SOLO VIOLIN

Violin Sonata / EMI CDC7476212
Nigel Kennedy (violin)

Violin Sonata / Philips 420948-2
Viktoria Mullova (violin)

Sir Arnold Bax (1883-1953)

British composer of modern classical music, characterized by chromatic harmonies, whose works encompass all forms except opera and theatre music; known for tone poems (*Tintagel* (1919)) and *Sonata for Piano no. 2* (1919). — *AMG*

SYMPHONIC POEMS

Symphonic Poems "In the Faery Hills," "Into the Twilight," "Roscatha," "The Tale the Pine Trees Knew" / Chandos CHAN8367
Bryden Thomson/Ulster Orchestra

Symphonic Poems "November Woods," "Summer Music," "The Garden of Fand," "The Happy Forest" / Chandos CHAN8307
Bryden Thomson/Ulster Orchestra

Symphonic Poems "Saga Fragment" and "Winter Legends" / Chandos CHAN8484
Margaret Fingerhut (piano), Bryden Thomson/London Philharmonic Orchestra

SYMPHONIES

Symphonies #1 & 7 / Lyrita SRCD.232
Myer Fredman/ London Philharmonic Orchestra

Symphony #3 / Chandos CHAN8454
Bryden Thomson/London Philharmonic Orchestra

Ludwig van Beethoven (1770-1827)

Beethoven's symphonies, quartets, concertos, and piano sonatas are significant advances in their respective genres, revealing the passion that marked a move from the classical to the romantic period. Naturally democratic, Beethoven strove to express his ideal of a world of freedom and equality. He rose from an adverse childhood in Germany, making his way on charm and self-education (especially shown in his opera *Fidelio* and the famous *Symphony no. 9*), sometimes masking frustration with angry behavior. Beethoven was destined to become the "inventor" of "modern music," composing from a "seed" or "germ" idea rather than a full melody and treating rhythm in new ways (for example, the phase variations in the third symphony). — *"Blue" Gene Tyranny*

★ **Concertos for Piano (1-3, *4, *5)**

Piano Concertos #1-5 / L'Oiseau-Lyre 421408-2
Steven Lubin (fortepiano), Christopher Hogwood/Academy of Ancient Music

Piano Concertos #1-5 and Triple Concerto / Sony Essential Classics SB3K48397
Leon Fleischer (piano), George Szell/Cleveland Orchestra

Piano Concertos #1 & 2 / Sony SK42177
Murray Perahia (piano), Bernard Haitink/Royal Concertgebouw Orchestra

Piano Concertos #3 & 4 / Sony SK39814
Murray Perahia (piano), Bernard Haitink/Royal Concertgebouw Orchestra

Piano Concertos #4 & 5 ("Emperor") / RCA 7943-2-RG

Van Cliburn (piano), Fritz Reiner/Chicago Symphony Orchestra
Piano Concerto #5 ("Emperor") / Philips 416215-2
Claudio Arrau (piano), Sir Colin Davis/Dresden State Orchestra

★ **Concerto for Violin**

Violin Concerto in D Major, Op. 61 / RCA Living Stereo
Jascha Heifetz (violin), Charles Munch/Boston Symphony Orchestra

Violin Concerto in D Major, Op. 61 / EMI CDC7470022
Itzhak Perlman (violin), Carlo Maria Giulini/Philharmonia Orchestra

Violin Concerto in D Major, Op. 61 / Denon 33C37-7508
Jean-Jacques Kantorow (violin), Antoni Ros-Marba/Netherlands Chamber Orchestra

★ **Concerto for Piano, Violin & Cello**

Concerto "Triple," Op. 56 / Denon 33CO-1407
Jean-Jacques Kantorow (violin), Mari Fujiwara (cello), Jacques Rouvier (piano), Emanuel Krivine / Netherlands Chamber Orchestra

Concerto "Triple," Op. 56 / Deutsche Grammophon 415276-2
Anne-Sophie Mutter (violin), Yo-Yo Ma (cello), Mark Zeltser (piano), Herbert von Karajan / Berlin Philharmonic Orchestra

Concerto "Triple," Op. 56 / Teldec 2292-46441-2
Trio Fontenay, Eliahu Inbal / Philharmonia Orchestra

DIABELLI VARIATIONS FOR PIANO

33 Variations ("Diabelli") in C Major, Op. 120 / Philips 416295-2
Claudio Arrau (piano)

33 Variations ("Diabelli") in C Major, Op. 120 and Bagatelles Op. 119 (rec. 1957) / Sony Masterworks MPK44837
Rudolf Serkin (piano)

33 Variations ("Diabelli") in C Major, Op. 120 / Vox Music Group PVT7200
Alfred Brendel (piano)

EROICA VARIATIONS FOR PIANO

17 Variations ("Eroica,") Op. 35 / Philips 412227-2
Alfred Brendel (piano)

17 Variations ("Eroica,") Op. 35 / Teldec 2292-44921-2
Cyrien Katsaris (piano)

17 Variations ("Eroica,") Op. 35 / Deutsche Grammophon 423136-2
Emil Gilels (Piano)

FIDELIO (OPERA)

Fidelio, Op. 72 / Deutsche Grammophon 419436-2
Gundula Janowitz (soprano), Lucia Popp (soprano), Leonard Bernstein/Vienna Philharmonic Orchestra & Vienna Staatsopernchor

Fidelio, Op. 72 / / Philips 426308-2
Jessye Norman, Reiner Goldberg, Kurt Moll, Bernard Haitink/Staatskapelle Dresden & Staatsopernchor Dresden

★ **Missa Solemnis**

Missa Solemnis in D Major, Op. 123 / Deutsche Grammophon 413780-2
Edda Moser (soprano), Hanna Schwarz (alto), Rene Kollo (tenor), Kurt Moll (bass), Leonard Bernstein/Royal Concertgebouw Orchestra & Rundfunkchor Hilversum

Missa Solemnis in D Major, Op. 123 / Teldec 9031-74884-2
Eva Mei (soprano), Marjana Lipovsek (alto), Anthony Rolfe Johnson (tenor), Robert Holl (bass), Nikolaus Harnoncourt/Chamber Orchestra of Europe & Arnold Schoenberg Choir

Missa Solemnis in D Major, Op. 123 / Telarc CD-80150
Sylvia McNair (soprano), Janice Taylor (mezzo-soprano), John Aler (tenor), Tom Krause (baritone), Robert Shaw/Atlanta Symphony Orchestra & Chorus

OVERTURES

Overtures & Incidental Music: Leonore #1-3; Fidelio; Coriolan; Egmont; Creatures of Prometheus; Ruins of Athens; etc. / Vox Music Group CDX 5099
Stanislaw Skrowaczewski/Minnesota Orchestra & Bach Society of Minnesota

★ **Quartets 7-16 (*8, *14)**

5 Quartets #7-11 ("Middle Quartets") / Philips 420797-2
Quartetto Italiano

5 Quartets #12-16 & Grosse Fuge—"Late Quartets" / Philips 426050-2
Quartetto Italiano

5 Quartets #7-11 ("Middle Quartets") / RCA Red Seal 60462-2-RC
Tokyo Quartet

5 Quartets #12-16 & Grosse Fuge—"Late Quartets" / RCA Red Seal 09026-60975-2
Tokyo Quartet

2 Quartets #8 & 13 / Calliope CAL9637
Talich Quartet

2 Quartets #9 & 14 / Calliope CAL9638
Talich Quartet

QUINTET FOR PIANO & STRINGS

Quintet in E Flat Major, Op. 16 (w/ Mozart Quintet) / Sony SK43099
Murray Perahia (piano)/Members of the English Chamber Orchestra

Quintet in E Flat Major, Op. 16 (w/ Mozart Quintet) / Telarc CD-80114
Andre Previn (piano)/Vienna Wind Soloists

SERENADE & TRIOS FOR STRINGS

Trio, Op. 3 and Serenade, Op. 8 / Denon CO-2251-EX
Mozart String Trio

3 Trios, Op. 9 / Denon 8175723032
Mozart String Trio

Trios, Op. 3 & 9 and Serenade Op. 8 / Deutsche Grammophon 427687-2
Anne-Sophie Mutter (violin), Bruno Giuranna (viola), Mstislav Rostropovich (cello)

Trio, Op. 3 and Serenade, Op. 8 / Sony Vivarte SK53961
L'Archibudelli

3 Trios, Op. 9 / Sony Vivarte SK48190
L'Archibudelli

SEXTET FOR WINDS

Sextet, Op. 71 (w/ Octet for Winds)

Amon Ra CD-SAR26
Classical Winds

Sextet in E Flat Major, Op. 71 / Supraphon 111445-2
Vaclav Kyzivat & Zdenek Tesar (clarinets), Zdenek & Bedrich Tylsar (horns), Frantisek Herman & Vilem Horak (bassoons)

★ **Sonatas for Piano #1-32 (*8, *14, 21, *23, *29)**

9 Piano Sonatas #1, 5, 6, 9, 10, 13, 14 ("Moonlight"), 15 ("Pastoral") & 25 / Vox Music Group CDX 5056
Alfred Brendel (piano)

7 Piano Sonatas #2, 3, 7, 8 ("Pathetique"), 11, 12 ("Funeral March") & 24 / Vox Music Group CDX 5060
Alfred Brendel (piano)

8 Piano Sonatas #16, 17 ("Tempest"), 18, 19, 21 ("Waldstein"), 22, 23 ("Appassionata") & 26 ("Les Adieux") / Vox Music Group CDX 5042
Alfred Brendel (piano)

6 Piano Sonatas #27, 28, 29 ("Hammerklavier") & 30-32 / Vox Music Group CDX 5028
Alfred Brendel (piano)

3 Piano Sonatas #8 ("Pathetique"), 13 & 14 ("Moonlight") / Deutsche Grammophon 400036-2
Emil Gilels (piano)

3 Piano Sonatas #21 ("Waldstein"), 23 & 26 / Deutsche Grammophon 419162-2
Emil Gilels (piano)

2 Piano Sonatas #21 ("Waldstein"), 30 & Andante favori / Philips 416145-2
Claudio Arrau (piano)

5 Piano Sonatas #28, 29 ("Hammerklavier") & 30-32 / Nonesuch 979211-2
Richard Goode (piano)

SONATAS FOR CELLO & PIANO #1-5

2 Cello Sonatas #1 & 2, Op. 5 / CBS MK37251
Yo-Yo Ma (cello), Emanuel Ax (piano)

2 Cello Sonatas #3, Op. 69 and #5, Op. 102 / 2 / CBS MK39024
Ma, Yo-Yo (Cello)
Ax, Emanuel (Piano)

Sonata #4, Op. 102 / 1 and Variations / CBS MK42121
Ma, Yo-Yo (Cello)
Ax, Emanuel (Piano)

2 Cello Sonatas #1 & 2, Op. 5 & Variations / Hyperion CDA66281
Anthony Pleeth (cello), Melvyn Tan (fortepiano)

3 Cello Sonatas #3-5, Op. 69 & 102 / Hyperion CDA66282
Anthony Pleeth (cello), Melvyn Tan (fortepiano)

★ **Sonatas for Violin & Piano #1-10 (*5, *9)**

10 Sonatas (complete) including #5 ("Spring") and #9 ("Kreutzer") / Philips 412570-2
David Oistrakh (violin), Lev Oborin (piano)

2 Sonatas, #5 ("Spring") and #9 ("Kreutzer") / Philips 412255-2
David Oistrakh (violin), Lev Oborin (piano)

2 Sonatas, #5 ("Spring") and #9 ("Kreutzer") / London 410554-2
Itzhak Perlman (violin), Vladimir Ashkenasy (piano)

2 Sonatas, #5 ("Spring") and #9 ("Kreutzer") / Philips 8.550283
Takako Nishizaki (violin), Jeno Jando (piano)

★ **Symphonies (1, 2, *3, 4, *5, *6, 7, 8, *9)**

9 Symphonies (complete) / Deutsche Grammophon 429036-2
Herbert von Karajan/Berlin Philharmonic Orchestra

9 Symphonies (complete) / Teldec 2292-46452-2
Nikolaus Harnoncourt/Chamber Orchestra of Europe

9 Symphonies (complete) / EMI CDS7498522
Roger Norrington/London Classical Players

Symphony #3 ("Eroica") / RCA Red Seal 60755-2-RC
Gunter Wand/North German Radio Symphony Orchestra

Symphony #5 / Deutsche Grammophon 415861-2
Carlos Kleiber/Vienna Philharmonic Orchestra

2 Symphonies #5 & 8 / RCA Red Seal 60092-2-RC
Gunter Wand/North German Radio Symphony Orchestra

Symphony #6 ("Pastorale") / RCA Red Seal 60094-2-RC
Gunter Wand/North German Radio Symphony Orchestra

Symphony #6 ("Pastorale") / Telarc CD-80145
Christoph von Dohnanyi/Cleveland Orchestra

Symphony #9 ("Choral") / RCA Red Seal 60095-2-RC
Edith Weins (soprano), Hildegard Hartwig (alto), Keith Lewis (tenor), Roland Hermann (bass), Gunter Wand/North German Radio Symphony Orchestra & Chorus

Symphony #9 ("Choral")/ Telarc CD-80120
Carol Vaness (soprano), Janice Taylor (mezzo-soprano), Siegfried Jerusalem (tenor), Robert Llyod (bass-baritone)/Christoph von Dohnanyi/Cleveland Orchestra & Chorus

★ **Trios for Piano & Strings (*#6 "Archduke")**

11 Piano Trios (complete) / EMI Studio CMS7631242
Pinchas Zukerman (violin), Jacqueline Du Pre (cello), Daniel Barenboim (piano)

2 Piano Trios #4 ("Ghost") and #6 ("Archduke") / Philips 412891-2
Beaux Arts Trio

3 Piano Trios #1, #6 ("Archduke") and #8 / Virgin Classics Veritas VC7590442
Castle Trio

Vincenzo Bellini (1801-1835)

Italian composer noted for his skill in writing long, flowing, graceful, and inventive melodies. Bellini influenced Chopin and many other composers of the early 1800s. He had a pronounced effect on the opera of that time, advocating simplicity over showmanship as a way to touch the heart. —*"Blue" Gene Tyranny*

OPERAS (*LA SONNAMBULA, NORMA, I PURITANI*)

La Sonnambula / EMI CDC7473772 (mono)
Maria Callas, Nicola Monti, Nicola Zaccaria, Eugenia Ratti, Florenza Cossoto, Antonino Votto/Coro e Orchestra del Teatro alla Scalla di Milano

La Sonnambula / London 417424-2
Joan Sutherland, Luciano Pavarotti, Nicolai Ghiaurov, Richard Bonynge/National Philharmonic Orchestra

Norma / EMI CDS7473042
Maria Callas, Mario Filippeschi, Ebe Stignani, Tullio Serafin/Coro e Orchestra del Teatro alla Scalla di Milano

Norma / London 414476-2
Joan Sutherland, Luciano Pavarotti, Montserrat Caballe, Samuel Ramey, Richard Bonynge/Orchestra & Chorus of the Welsh National Opera

I Puritani / London 417588-2
Joan Sutherland, Luciano Pavarotti, Piero Cappuccilli, Nicolai Ghiaurov, Richard Bonynge/London Symphony Orchestra & Chorus of the Royal Opera House, Covent Garden

Alban Berg (1885-1935)

An Austrian composer primarily of atonal music in many genres, including opera; known for *Wozzeck* (1925) and *Three Orchestral Pieces* (1915). Webern, Berg, and Schoenberg (Berg's teacher) made up the Viennese School, Berg being the romantically impassioned point of this composer triangle—highly original and lyrical, with a brilliant sense of orchestral color. Information about his life and love affairs is encoded in many of his works (especially the *Lyric Suite* and the *Violin Concerto*), which are the subjects of controversy. —*"Blue" Gene Tyranny*

CONCERTO FOR VIOLIN

Concerto / London 430349-2
Kyung-Wha Chung (violin), Sir Georg Solti/Chicago Symphony Orchestra

Concerto / Deutsche Grammophon 413725-2
Itzhak Perlman (violin), Seiji Ozawa/Boston Symphony Orchestra

LYRIC SUITE FOR STRING QUARTET

Suite "Lyric" / Deutsche Grammophon 419994-2
LaSalle Quartet

Suite "Lyric" (Orchestral Version of Three Movements) / Deutsche Grammophon 427424-2
Herbert von Karajan/Berlin Philharmonic Orchestra

WOZZECK (OPERA)

Wozzeck (1921) / Deutsche Grammophon 427424-2
Behrens, Langridge, Zednik, Grundheber, Haugland, Claudio Abbado/Vienna Philharmonic Orchestra & State Opera Chorus

Wozzeck (1921) / London 417348-2
Silja, Jahn, Laubenthal, Zednik, Waechter, Christoph von Dohnanyi/Vienna Philharmonic Orchestra & State Opera Chorus

Leonard Bernstein (1918-1990)

An American composer and pianist who conducted the Boston Symphony and New York Philharmonic orchestras and wrote music in many forms, including musicals (*West Side Story*, 1957). —*AMG*

CHICHESTER PSALMS

Chichester Psalms / Deutsche Grammophon 415965-2
Leonard Bernstein/Isreal Philharmonic Orchestra & Vienna Youth Chorus

Chichester Psalms / Telarc CD-80181
Derek Lee Ragin (alto), Donna Carter (soprano), Victoria Blakeney (mezzo-soprano), Rob Lund (tenor), Wayne Baughman (bass), Robert Shaw/Atlanta Symphony Orchestra & Chorus

MASS

Mass (1971) / CBS M2K44593
Leonard Bernstein/Norman Scribner & Berkshire Boys' Choir

WEST SIDE STORY (BALLET MUSIC)

West Side Story—Symphonic Dances / Deutsche Grammophon 410025-2
Leonard Bernstein/Los Angeles Philharmonic Orchestra

West Side Story—Symphonic Dances / Virgin 59619

Edo de Waart/Minnesota Symphony Orchestra

Hector Berlioz (1803-1869)

A renowned French orchestrator and composer of *Symphonie Fantastique* (1830) and opera, vocal, and choral music. Berlioz continued to influence romantics through the late 19th and early 20th centuries with monumental yet graceful orchestrations. He was the embodiment of the romantic sensibility—idealism, a tendency toward pastoral reverie and the macabre, infatuation with the ideal lover (as reflected in the recurrent "theme of the beloved" in the *Symphonie Fantastique*), and a wild, Byronesque lifestyle (the *Symphonie* is built around a program based on DeQuincey's *Confessions of an English Opium Eater*). A great love of nature infuses *Harold in Italy,* and great terror and grandeur is expressed in his *Te Deum.* He revived pure modal tonalities from French folk music, combining them with the turbulence of chromaticism to express the spirit of his revolutionary age. One of the greatest of all melodies, "D'amour l'ardente flamme" ("The ardent flame of love"), occurs within a landscape of dramatic gesture in *La Damnation de Faust. —"Blue" Gene Tyranny*

DAMNATION OF FAUST

La damnation de Faust, Op. 24 / Philips 416395-2
Gedda, Bastin, Veasey, Van Allen, Knight, Sir Colin Davis/London Symphony Orchestra, Wordsworth School Boys' Choir & Ambrosian Singers

L'ENFANCE DU CHRIST

L'enfance du Christ, Op. 25 / Erato 2292-45275-2
Anne-Sofie Van Otter (soprano), Johnson, Jose Van Dam (tenor), Bastin, John Eliot Gardiner/Lyon Opera Orchestra & Monteverdi Choir

L'enfance du Christ, Op. 25 / Denon CO-76863 / 4
M. Zimmermann, J. Aler, E. Wilm Schulte, S. Dean, P Kang, Eliahu Inbal/Frankfurt Radio Symphony Orchestra & Cologne Radio Chorus

HAROLD IN ITALY

Harold in Italy, Op. 16 and Overtures / Deutsche Grammophon 415109-2
Wolfram Christ (viola), Lorin Maazel/Berlin Philharmonic Orchestra

Harold in Italy, Op. 16 / Denon CO-73207
Yuri Bashmet (viola), Eliahu Inbal/Frankfurt Radio Symphony Orchestra

Harold in Italy, Op. 16 and Overtures / London 421193-2
Pinchas Zuckerman (viola), Charles Dutoit/Montreal Symphony Orchestra

OVERTURES

Overtures: "Beatrice et Benedict," "Rob Roy," "Waverly," "King Lear" & "Le Carnaval Romain" / Chandos CHAN8316
Sir Alexander Gibson /Scottish National Orchestra

Overtures: "Les Francs Juges," "La Corsaire," "Waverly," "King Lear" & "Le Carnaval Romain" / Philips 416430-2
Sir Colin Davis/London Symphony Orchestra

REQUIEM

Requiem, Op. 5 ("Grande Messe des Morts") / Philips 416283-2
R., Dowd (tenor), Sir Colin Davis/London Symphony Orchestra & Chorus

Requiem, Op. 5 ("Grande Messe des Morts") / Telarc CD-80109-2
John Aler (tenor), Robert Shaw/Atlanta Symphony Orchestra & Chorus

★ Symphonie Fantastique

Symphonie Fantastique, Op. 14 / London 414203-2
Charles Dutoit/Montreal Symphony Orchestra

Symphonie Fantastique, Op. 14 / EMI CDC549541
Roger Norrington/London Classical Players

Symphonie Fantastique, Op. 14 / Philips 411425-2
Sir Colin Davis/Royal Concertgebouw Orchestra

Symphonie Fantastique, Op. 14 / Telarc CD-80271
David Zinman/Baltimore Symphony Orchestra

LES TROYENS (OPERA)

Les Troyens (1863) / Philips 416432-2
Lindholm, Veasey, Vickers, Glossop, Sawyer, Sir Colin Davis/Royal Opera House Orchestra & Chorus

Franz Berwald (1796-1868)

A Swedish composer of symphonic and chamber works. At various times an orthopedist, manager of a glass works, and part-owner of a sawmill, Berwald is recognized as a great symphonist and the greatest Swedish composer of the 19th century. His four symphonies (Serieuse, Capricieuse, Sinfonie singulire, and the Symphony no. 4 in E-flat) are his best works—fine examples of his audacious sense of modulation combined with a strong classic melodic line. —*"Blue" Gene Tyranny*
Chamber Music

Piano Trios #1-3 / Marco Polo 8.223170
Ilona Prunyi (piano), Andras Kiss (violin), Csaba Onczay (cello)

Quartet for Piano & Winds, Quintet for Piano & Strings and Septet / Koch CD310056H1
Werner Genuit (piano)/Consortium Classicum
Symphonies (1-4)

4 Symphonies #1 "Serieuse," #2 "Capricieuse," #3 "Singuliere" and #4 / Deutsche Grammophon 415502-2
Neeme Jarvi /Gothenburg Symphony Orchestra

Heinrich Ignaz Franz von Biber (1664-1704)

An Austrian violinist and composer who became the most celebrated violin virtuoso of the 17th century. Biber wrote many sonatas for violin that employ both normal tuning and scordatura, where the strings are tuned to a chord instead of in perfect fifths. He also composed many sacred and secular pieces. The Mystery (or "Rosary") Sonatas, for solo violin and various continuo instruments, are musical metaphors, even allegories, of religious mysteries. — *"Blue" Gene Tyranny*
Battalia

"Battalia" a 10; 4 Sonatas, etc. / Archiv 429230-2
GOEBEL, Reinhard/Musica Antiqua Koln

★ **Sonatas "Rosary" for Violin & Continuo**
16 "Rosary" Sonatas / Virgin VCD790838-2
John Holloway (violin), Davitt Moroney (organ), Stephen Stubbs (lute)/Tragicomedia
Sonatas "Fidicinium Sacro-Profanum"

6 Sonatas "Fidicinium Sacro-Profanum" (also see Muffat) / Chandos CHAN8448 / 9
Adrian Shepherd/Cantilena

Georges Bizet (1838-1875)

A French composer of piano, vocal, and dramatic music known for the opera Carmen (1875). Torn between his gift for evocation of narrative imagery with an extraordinary musicality and a respect and love for simple classic form, Bizet achieved a powerful synthesis of the two in the L'Arlsienne Suites and the famous Carmen shortly before he died in his mid 30s. —*"Blue" Gene Tyranny*

★ **Carmen (opera)**
Carmen (1875) / Erato 2292-45207-2
Esham, Migenes-Johnson, Placido Domingo (tenor), Raimondi, Lorin Maazel/Orchestre National de France & Radio France Chorus

Carmen (1875) / London 414489-2
Tatiana Troyanos (soprano), Kiri Te Kanawa (soprano), Placido Domingo (tenor), Jose Van Dam (baritone), Sir Georg Solti/London Philharmonic Orchestra & John Aldis Choir

Carmen (1875) / EMI CDB7543682
Maria Callas (soprano), Pretre, Gedda, Massard, Jose Van Dam, Georges Pretre/Paris Opera Orchestra & Chorus
Carmen Suites and L'Arlesienne Suites

Carmen Suites #1 & 2 and L'Arlesienne Suites #1 & 2 / London 412464-2
Charles Dutoit/Montreal Symphony Orchestra

L'Arlesienne Suites 1 & 2 / Carmen Suites 1 & 2 / Naxos 8.550061
Anthony Bramall/Slovak Philharmonic Orchestra

Ernest Bloch (1880-1959)

A Swiss composer who moved to noise-based composition from neo-classical beginnings. Bloch was a composer of psychologically profound works who was greatly influenced by world music (Hebrew melody, Southeast Asian music, and Tibetan music) in creating a totally original music with a traditional fluidity of inflection. His later works, like the Sinfonia Breve (1952), written when he was 72, developed a bold, energetic dissonance. —*"Blue" Gene Tyranny*
Schelomo

Rhapsody "Schelomo" / Virgin VC790735-2
Steven Isserlis (cello), Richard Hickox/London Symphony Orchestra

Rhapsody "Schelomo" / Deutsche Grammophon 429155-2
Pierre Fournier (cello), Alfred Wallenstein/Berlin Philharmonic Orchestra

Rhapsody "Schelomo" / Vanguard OVC4047
Zara Nelsova (cello), Maurice Abravanel/Utah Symphony Orchestra

Luigi Boccherini (1743-1805)

An Italian composer who specialized almost entirely in chamber music and wrote chamber symphonies, numerous violin and cello sonatas, and guitar music. His profound admiration for Haydn gave rise to the saying "Boccherini is the wife of Haydn." —*Mary K. Scanlan*
Concertos for Cello

12 Cello Concertos (complete) / EBS EBS6058
Julius Berger (cello), Vladislav Czarnecki/Southwest German Chamber Orchestra, Pforzheim

4 Cello Concertos (w / Symphonies) / RCA Deutsche Harmonia Mundi 7768-2-RC
Anner Bylsma (cello), Jean Lamon/Tafelmusik

3 Cello Concertos & 3 Sonatas for Cello / Virgin CDC59015-2
Steven Isselis (cello), Juha Kangas/Ostrobothnian Chamber Orchestra

★ **Quintets for Guitar & Strings (3, *4, 5, 6)**
8 Guitar Quintets (complete) / Philips 426092-2
Pepe Romero (guitar)/Academy Chamber Ensemble

3 Guitar Quintets #1-3 / Harmonia Mundi HMU907039
Richard Savino (guitar)/Artaria Quartet

3 Guitar Quintets #4-6 / Harmonia Mundi HMU907026
Richard Savino (guitar)/Artaria Quartet
Quintets for Strings

3 Quintets Op. 11 #4-6 "dello L'ucceliera" / RCA Deutsche Harmonia Mundi 5472-77159-2
Smithsonian Chamber Players

3 Quintets Op. 39 / Harmonia Mundi HMC901334
Ensemble 415

3 String Quintets, Op. 60 #1& 5 and Op. 61 #1 / Harmonia Mundi HMC901402
Ensemble 415
Symphonies

5 Symphonies Op. 21 #1-5 in B Flat Major, G. 493-497 / CPO 999174-2
Johannes Goritzki/German Chamber Academy of Neuss

4 Symphonies / Harmonia Mundi HMC901291
Chiara Banchini/Ensemble 415

Francois-Adrien Boieldieu (775-1834)

CONCERTO FOR HARP

Concerto in C Major / Vox Music Group CD3X3019
Marie-Claire Jamet (harp), Paul Kuentz/Paul Kuentz Chamber Orchestra

Concerto in C Major / London 425723-2
Marisa Robles (harp), Iona Brown/Academy of St. Martin-in-the-Fields

Arrigo Boito (1842-1918)

Poet, novelist, and composer, Boito is known for the single opera he completed, *Mefistofele*. Like Rossini, who wrote three dozen operas by his mid-thirties, and spent the next forty years of his life unable or unwilling to complete another, Boito underwent some kind of crisis early, and worked 54 years unsuccessfully at completing his second opera.

As a student at the Milan Conservatory, Boito was awarded a stipend after winning composition prizes that enabled him to travel and study abroad for two years. He took advantage of the prize to visit Poland, his mother's birthplace, as well as England, Germany, and France. He was much impressed during these sojourns with the dramatic power of the operas of Beethoven and especially of Wagner. Hence he reshaped the traditional elements of Italian opera to suit the kind of dramatic presentation he had in mind. The result was *Mefistofele*, first performed when the composer was barely 24, for which the highly literary and literate Boito also wrote the libretto. At its premiere performance, a pious contingent, objecting to the thematic modernism of Boito's version of the Faust legend, demonstrated angrily. After the second performance was likewise ill-received, Boito withdrew the opera and undertook to modify it to appease criticism. It has become a staple of the repertoire, one of the most exciting and compelling of operas.

Dry as his font of musical inspiration became, Boito nevertheless retained in full his literary powers. He wrote librettos for Ponchielli's *La Gioconda* and for Verdi's operas *Falstaff* and *Othello*, all regarded as works of the first order. Much of Boito's poetry has never fallen out of favor, and his letters reveal unusual gifts as well. Seldom, if ever, has anyone else secured a seemingly imperishable niche in musical history with so little output. One can only lament the early evaporation of Boito's source of musical inspiration. Had his powers increased, he might have eclipsed all others. —*Douglas Purl*
Mefistofele (opera)

Mefistofele (1868) / Sony S2K44983
Eva Marton, Placido Domingo (tenor), Samuel Ramey, Giuseppe Patane/Hungarian State Orchestra & Hungaroton Opera Chorus

Mefistofele (1868) / London 410175-2
Freni, Caballe, Luciano Pavarotti (tenor), Ghiaurov, Oliviero de Fabritiis/National Philharmonic Orchestra

Alexander Borodin (1833-1887)

A Russian composer in many forms, including opera (Prince Igor, 1887). Borodin was one of "The Mighty Five" Russians who wrote nationalist music. The illegitimate son of a prince and a civil servant, he became an important research chemist and physical scientist. He wrote music of great originality and beauty—bold orchestral tone poems on exotic lands and subjects, as well as Russian nationalist works influenced by folk melodies and featuring astonishing harmonic and rhythmic innovation (chords in fourths, harmonies with nonharmonic "added tones," quasi-jazz syncopation). —*"Blue" Gene Tyranny*
Prince Igor: Polovtsian Dances

Prince Igor: Polovtsian Dances (w / Rimsky Korsakov Scheherazade) / EMI CDC747717
Sir Thomas Beecham/Royal Philharmonic Orchestra

Prince Igor: Polovtsian Dances (w / Rimsky Korsakov Scheherazade) / Deutsche Grammophon 415502-2
Herbert von Karajan/Berlin Philharmonic Orchestra

★ **Quartets (1,*2)**
String Quartets #1 & 2 / EMI CDC7477952
Borodin Quartet

String Quartet #2 (w / Smetana Quartet #1) / Telarc CD-80178
Cleveland Quartet

String Quartet #2 (w / Tchaikovsky Quartet #1) / Collins Classics 12372
Alberni Quartet
Symphony #2

Symphony #2 (w / Polovtsian Dances & Overture) / Musicmasters MMD60100L or ASV Quicksilva CDQS6018
Enrique Batiz/Mexico State Symphony Orchestra

3 Symphonies # 1-3 / Naxos 8.550238
Stephen Gunzenhauser/Czecho-Slovak Radio Symphony Orchestra

William Boyce (1711-1779)

A British composer of instrumental and sacred vocal works and one of the early symphonists. Boyce was the son of a London cabinetmaker. He became hard-of-hearing at an early age but nevertheless attained popular success, writing joyous and lyrical music of classic design, like the collection of overtures and his eight symphonies rediscovered in the 1930s by Constant Lambert. — *"Blue" Gene Tyranny*

Symphonies

8 Symphonies, Op. 2 / Archiv 419631-2
Trevor Pinnock/The English Concert

8 Symphonies, Op. 2 / Nimbus NI5345
William Boughton/English String orchestra

Johannes Brahms (1833-1897)

A German composer of major works in all forms except opera, including symphonies, lieder, and solo piano music. Playing in rough taverns down by the docks as a teenager in order to supplement his family's humble income, Brahms persevered to become a renowned conductor of Bach, Beethoven, Schubert, and Schumann and a great composer, faithful to the traditional architecture and logic of classical forms but a romantic in love with German folksong. He eschewed chromaticism and told a personal and nonprogrammatic story in every composition. — *"Blue" Gene Tyranny*

ALTO RHAPSODY

Rhapsody for Alto, Male Chorus & Orchestra, Op. 53 / Orfeo C025821
Hodgeson (alto), Bernard Haitink/Bavarian Radio Symphony Orchestra & Chorus

M. Lipovsek (alto), Claudio Abbado / Berlin Philharmonic Orchestra & Ernst-Senff Chorus

★ Academic Festival Overture

Academic Festival Overture, Op. 80 / Deutsche Grammophon 423617-2
Claudio Abbado/Berlin Philharmonic Orchestra

Academic Festival Overture, Op. 80 / RCA 7920-2-RC
Leonard Slatkin/Saint Louis Symphony Orchestra

★ Concertos for Piano (1, *2)

Piani Concertos, #1 Op. 15 and #2 Op. 83 / Deutsche Grammophon 419158-2
Emil Gilels (piano), Eugen Jochum /Berlin Philharmonic Orchestra

Concerto #1, Op. 15 / London 425110-2
Andras Schiff (piano), Sir Georg Solti /Vienna Philharmonic Orchestra

Concerto #2, Op. 83 / Deutsche Grammophon 435588-2
Emil Gilels (piano), Eugen Jochum /Berlin Philharmonic Orchestra

Concerto #2, Op. 83 / London 410199-2
Vladimir Ashkenazy (piano), Bernard Haitink/Vienna Philharmonic Orchestra

Concerto #2, Op. 83 / CBS MK42261 or MYK37803
Rudolf Serkin (piano), George Szell/Cleveland Orchestra

★ Concerto for Violin

Concerto in D Major, Op. 77 / RCA Living Stereo 09026-61495-2
Yasha Heifetz (violin), Fritz Reiner /Chicago Symphony Orchestra

Concerto in D Major, Op. 77 / EMI CDM7646322
David Oistrakh (violin), Otto Klemperer /French National Radio Orchestra

Concerto in D Major, Op. 77 / EMI CDC7471662
Itzhak Perlman (violin), Carlo Maria Giulini / Chicago Symphony Orchestra

CONCERTO FOR VIOLIN & CELLO

"Double" Concerto, Op. 102 / CBS MK42024 or MYK37237
Zino Francesatti (violin), Pierre Fournier (cello), Bruno Walter/Columbia Symphony Orchestra

"Double" Concerto, Op. 102 / Deutsche Grammophon 410603-2

Anne-Sophie Mutter (violin), Antonio Meneses (cello), Herbert von Karajan/Berlin Philharmonic Orchestra

★ German Requiem

Ein Deutsches Requiem, Op. 45 / Philips 432140-2
C. Morgiono (soprano), R. Gilfry (baritone), John Eliot Gardiner / Orchestre Revolutionnaire et Romantique & Monteverdi Choir

Ein Deutsches Requiem, Op. 45 / EMI 432140-2
Elizabeth Schwarzkopf (soprano), Dietrich Fischer-Dieskau (baritone), Otto Klemperer /Philharmonia Orchestra & Chorus

Ein Deutsches Requiem, Op. 45 / Telarc CD-80092
Arleen Auger (soprano), Richard Stilwell (baritone), Robert Shaw /Atlanta Symphony Orchestra & Chorus

HUNGARIAN DANCES

21 Hungarian Dances, WoO 1 (original for piano 4-hands) / Philips 416459-2
Katia & Marielle Labeque (piano)

21 Hungarian Dances, WoO 1 (original for piano 4-hands) / Claves CD50-8710
Duo Crommelynck

21 Hungarian Dances (orchestrations) / Philips 411426-2
Kurt Masur/Gewandhaus Orchestra Leipzig

21 Hungarian Dances (orchestrations) / Deutsche Grammophon 410615-2
Claudio Abbado/Vienna Philharmonic Orchestra

21 Hungarian Dances (orchestrations) / Chandos CHAN8885
Neeme Jarvi/London Symphony Orchestra

PIANO MUSIC

Complete Piano Music / RCA 69245-2-RG
Gerhard Oppitz (piano)

7 Fantasias, Op. 116; 3 Intermezzos, Op. 117; and 4 Pieces, Op. 119 / Philips 411137-2
Stephen Bishop Kovacevich (piano)

Scherzo, Op. 4; 4 Ballades, Op. 10; and 8 Pieces, Op. 76 / Philips 411103-2
Stephen Bishop Kovacevich (piano)

16 Waltzes, Op. 39; 2 Rhapsodies, Op. 79; and 4 Pieces, Op. 118 / Philips 420750-2
Stephen Bishop Kovacevich (piano)

QUARTETS FOR STRINGS (1-3)

String Quartets #1, Op. 51 and #1 & 3, Op. 67 / Vox Music Group VU9012
Tokyo String Quartet

String Quartets #1-3 / Deutsche Grammophon 437128-2
LaSalle Quartet

String Quartets #1 & 2, Op 51 / Hyperion CDA66651
New Budapest Quartet

String Quartet #3, Op. 67 (w/ Piano Quintet) / Hyperion CDA66652
New Budapest Quartet

QUARTETS FOR PIANO & STRINGS (1-3)

Piano Quartets #1-3, Op. 25, 26 & 60 / Sony S2K45846
Emmanuel Ax (piano), Isaac Stern (violin), Jaime Laredo (viola), Yo-Yo Ma (cello)

Piano Quartets #1-3, Op. 25, 26 & 60 / Vox Music Group CDX5052
Eastman Quartet

Piano Quartets #1 & 3, Op. 25 & 60 / Virgin Classics VC7592482
Domus

Piano Quartet #2, Op. 26 (w/ Mahler Piano Quartet) / Virgin Classics VC7591442
Domus

Piano Quartets #1-3, Op. 25, 26 & 60 / Arabesque Z6553-2
Cantilena Piano Quartet

★ Quintets for Strings

String Quintets #1 & 2, Op. 88 & 111 / Nonesuch 979068-2
Boston Symphony Chamber Players

String Quintet #2, Op. 111 (w/ Clarinet Quintet) / Delos DE3066

Chamber Music Northwest

String Quintets #1 & 2, Op. 88 & 111 (w/ Quintets & Sextets) / Deutsche Grammophon 419875-2
Cecil Aronowitz (viola)/Amadeus Quartet

String Quintet #2, Op. 111 (w/ Clarinet Quintet) / Harmonia Mundi HMC901349
Gerard Causse (viola)/Melos Quartet

★ **Quintet for Clarinet & Strings**

Quintet in B Minor, Op. 115 / Orfeo C068831A
Karl Leister (clarinet)/Vermeer Quartet

Quintet in B Minor, Op. 115 (w/ Weber Quintet) / Reference Recordings RR-40CD
Eddie Daniels (clarinet)/Composers String Quartet

Quintet in B Minor, Op. 115 (w/ String Quintet #2) / Harmonia Mundi HMC901349
Michel Portal (clarinet)/Melos Quartet

Quintet in B Minor, Op. 115 (w/ String Quintet #2) / Delos DE3066
David Shifrin (clarinet)/Chamber Music Northwest

QUINTET FOR PIANO & STRINGS

Piano Quintet, Op. 34 / RCA 6673-2-RC
Barry Douglas (piano)/Tokyo String Quartet

Piano Quintet, Op. 34 (w/ String Quartet #3) / Hyperion CDA66652
Piers Lane (piano), New Budapest Quartet

Piano Quintet, Op. 34 (w/ Schumann Quintet Op. 44) / Academy Sound & Vision LTD CDDCA728
Peter Frankl (piano)/Lindsay String Quartet

★ **Serenades for Orchestra (*1,2)**

Serenade #1, Op. 11 / RCA 6247-2-RC
Leonard Slatkin /Saint Louis Symphony Orchestra

Serenade #2, Op. 16 (w/ Haydn Variations & Academic Festival Overture) / RCA 7920-2-RC
Leonard Slatkin /Saint Louis Symphony Orchestra

Serenade #1 & 2, Op. 11 & 16 / London Weekend Classics 421628-2
Istvan Kertesz/London Symphony Orchestra

Serenade #1, Op. 11 (w/ Haydn Variations) / Chandos CHAN8612
Vernon Handley/Ulster Orchestra

SEXTETS

String Sextets #1 & 2, Op. 18 & 36 / Naxos 8.550436
Stuttgart Soloists

String Sextets #1 & 2, Op. 18 & 36 / Hyperion CDA66276
Raphael Ensemble

SONATAS FOR CELLO & PIANO

Cello Sonatas #1 & 2, Op. 38 & 99 / EMI Studio CDM7632982
Jacqueline Du Pre (cello), Daniel Barenboim (piano)

Cello Sonatas #1 & 2, Op. 38 & 99 / Hyperion CDA66159
Steven Isserlis (cello), Peter Evans (piano)

SONATAS FOR VIOLA OR CLARINET

2 Clarinet Sonatas, Op. 120 / RCA 60036-2-RC
Karl Leister (clarinet), Gerard Oppitz (piano)

2 Clarinet Sonatas, Op. 120 / RCA 60036-2-RC
Richard Stoltzman (clarinet), Richard Goode (piano)

2 Viola Sonatas, Op. 120 (w/ Joachim Variations) / Conifer CDCF199
Rivka Golani (viola), Konstantin Bogino (piano)

2 Viola Sonatas, Op. 120 / Bridge BCD-9021
Barbara Westphal (viola), Ursala Oppens (piano)

SONATAS FOR VIOLIN & PIANO

Sonatas #1-3, Op. 78, 100 & 108 / EMI CDC7474032
Itzhak Perlman (violin), Vladimir Ashkenazy (piano)

Sonatas #1-3, Op. 78, 100 & 108 (w/ Busoni) / Deutsche Grammophon 423619-2
Gidon Kremer (violin), Valery Afanassiev (piano)

Sonatas #1-3, Op. 78, 100 & 108 / London 421092-2
Josef Suk (violin), Julius Katchen (piano)

★ **Symphonies (*1, 2, *3, *4)**

Symphonies #1-4 / RCA Gold Seal 60085-2-RG
Gunter Wand /North German Radio Symphony Orchestra, Hamburg

Symphonies #1-4, Haydn Variations & Tragic Overture / RCA Eurodisc 69220-2-RV
Sanderling, Kurt/Staatskapelle Dresden

Symphony #1, Op. 68 / Chesky CD19
Jascha Horenstein/Royal Philharmonic Orchestra

Symphony #1, Op. 68 / Deutsche Grammophon 435347-2
Carlo Maria Giulini/Vienna Philharmonic Orchestra

Symphonies #2 & 3, Op. 78 & 90 / Deutsche Grammophon 429153-2
Herbert von Karajan/Berlin Philharmonic Orchestra

Symphony #2, Op. 78, Tragic & Academic Festival Overtures / Deutsche Grammophon 431592-2
Leonard Bernstein/Vienna Philharmonic Orchestra

Symphony #3, Op. 90, and Haydn Variations / CBS MK42022
Bruno Walter/Columbia Symphony Orchestra

Symphony #4, Op. 98, and Tragic Overture / Deutsche Grammophon 410084-2
Leonard Bernstein/Vienna Philharmonic Orchestra

Symphony #4, Op. 98 / Deutsche Grammophon 400037-2
Carlos Kleiber/Vienna Philharmonic Orchestra

TRAGIC OVERTURE

Tragic Overture, Op. 81, and Symphony #4 / EMI CDC7540602
Wolfgang Sawallisch/London Symphony Orchestra

Tragic Overture, Op. 81, and Symphony #3 / Teldec 2292-44972-2
Christoph von Dohnanyi/Cleveland Orchestra

TRIO FOR CLARINET & STRINGS

Clarinet Trio in A Minor, Op. 114, and Piano Trios #2 & 3 / Arabesque Z6608
David Shifrin (clarinet), Colin Carr (cello), David Golub (piano)

Clarinet Trio in A Minor, Op. 114, and Clarinet Quintet / Hyperion CDA66107
Thea King (clarinet), Karine Georgian (cello), Clifford Benson (piano)

Clarinet Trio in A Minor, Op. 114, and Horn Trio / Chandos CHAN8606
James Campbell (clarinet), Yuri Turovsky (cello), Luba Edlina (piano)

★ **Trios for Piano & Strings (*1, 2, 3)**

Piano Trio #1, Op. 8, and Horn Trio / Arabesque Z6607
David Golub (piano), Mark Kaplan (violin), Colin Carr (cello)

Piano Trios #2 & 3, Op. 87 & 101, and Clarinet Trio / Arabesque Z6608
David Golub (piano), Mark Kaplan (violin), Colin Carr (cello)

Piano Trios #1 & 3, Op. 8 & 101 / CRD CD3432
Isreal Piano Trio

Piano Trio #2, Op. 87, and Schumann Trio / CRD CD3433
Isreal Piano Trio

Piano Trios #1-3, Op. 8, 87 & 101 / Chandos CHAN8334
Borodin Trio

Piano Trios #1-3, Op. 8, 87 & 101, and Horn and Clarinet Trios / Philips 416838-2
Beaux Arts Trio

TRIO FOR HORN, VIOLIN & PIANO

Horn Trio in E Flat Major, Op. 40 and Piano Trio #1 / Arabesque Z6607
David Jolley (horn), Colin Carr (cello), David Golub (piano)

Horn Trio in E Flat Major, Op. 40, and Clarinet Trio / Chandos CHAN8606
Michael Thompson (horn), Yuri Turovsky (cello), Luba Edlina (piano)

★ **Variations on a Theme by Haydn (St. Anthony Variations)**

Variations on a Theme by Haydn, Op. 56a, and Symphony #3 / CBS MK42022
Bruno Walter / Columbia Symphony Orchestra

Variations on a Theme by Haydn, Op. 56a, Academic Festival Overture & Serenade #1 / RCA 7920-2-RC
Leonard Slatkin/Saint Louis Symphony Orchestra

Variations on a Theme by Haydn, Op. 56a, and Symphony #1 / Teldec 2292-42429-2
Christoph von Dohnanyi/Cleveland Orchestra

Benjamin Britten (1913-1976)

A popular British composer of operas, such as *Peter Grimes* (1941), and most other musical forms, including choral and orchestral music and solo vocal music. Several of Britten's works, including *A Ceremony of Carols*, are performed on a seasonal schedule. Britten has also achieved renown as an opera composer, using themes from American, Japanese, and British cultures. He is equally famous for his vocal music, whose aesthetics of matching word and music showed the influences of Auden and Isherwood. As a conscientious objector, he spoke eloquently against militarism in his *War Requiem. —"Blue" Gene Tyranny*

PETER GRIMES (OPERA)

Peter Grimes, Op. 33/ London 414577-2
Watson, Pears, Evans, Benjamin Britten/Royal Opera House Orchestra & Chorus, Covent Garden

★ **Serenade for Tenor, Horn & Strings**

Serenade for Tenor, Horn & Strings, Op. 31 / London 417153-2
Pears, Tuckwell, Benjamin Britten/London Symphony Orchestra

Serenade for Tenor, Horn & Strings, Op. 31 / RPO CDRPO7015
M. Hill, J. Bryant, Vladimir Ashkenazy/Royal Philharmonic Orchestra

SINFONIA DA REQUIEM

Sinfonia da Requiem, Op. 20 / EMI CDC7542702
Simon Rattle/City of Birmingham Symphony Orchestra

Sinfonia da Requiem, Op. 20 / Chandos CHAN8983 / 4
Richard Hickox/London Symphony Orchestra

WAR REQUIEM

War Requiem, Op. 66 / London 414383-2
Vishnevskaya, Pears, Fischer-Dieskau, Benjamin Britten/London Symphony Orchestra & Chorus

War Requiem, Op. 66 / EMI CDC7470332
Soderstrom, Tear, Allen, Simon Rattle/City of Birmingham Symphony Orchestra & Chorus

YOUNG PERSON'S GUIDE TO THE ORCHESTRA

Young Person's Guide to the Orchestra, Op. 34 / Telarc CD-80126
Andre Previn/Royal Philharmonic Orchestra

Young Person's Guide to the Orchestra, Op. 34 / London 417509-2
Benjamin Britten/English Chamber Orchestra

Max Bruch (1838-1920)

A German composer of operas, cantatas, and choral works known for his violin concertos and *Kol Nidrei for Cello & Orchestra*. Such works as his *Concerto for Violin & Orchestra no. 1 in g* exhibit a Mendelssohnian melodic warmth in a flowing, beautifully varied texture. —*"Blue" Gene Tyranny*

★ **Concerto #1 for Violin**

Concerto #1, Op. 26 / CBS MK42256 or MYK37811
Isaac Stern (violin), Eugene Ormandy/Philadephia Orchestra

Concerto #1, Op. 26 (w/ Mendelssohn Concerto) / Deutsche Grammophon 400031-2
Anne-Sophie Mutter (violin), Herbert von Karajan/Berlin Philharmonic Orchestra

Concerto #1, Op. 26 (w/ Mendelssohn Concerto) / Deutsche Grammophon 427656-2
Gil Shaham (violin), Giuseppe Sinopoli/Philharmonia Orchestra

KOL NIDREI FOR CELLO & ORCHESTRA

Kol Nidrei, Op. 47 / Mercury Living Presence 432001-2
Janos Starker (cello), Antal Dorati/London Symphony Orchestra

Kol Nidrei, Op. 47 / Deutsche Grammophon 429155-2
Pierre Fournier (cello), Jean Martinon/Lamoureux Orchestra, Paris

SYMPHONIES (1-3)

Symphonies #1-3 / Philips 420932-2
Kurt Mazur/Gewandhausorchester Leipzig

Anton Bruckner (1824-1896)

An Austrian composer of orchestral, chamber, keyboard, and sacred vocal music and several symphonies, who was influenced by Wagner. Bruckner was a deeply religious man. Often misunderstood and underprogrammed in his lifetime, this mysteriously retiring, reticent composer of simple, rustic tastes amazed audiences with his improvisatory skill on the organ. He created nine symphonies of absolutely unique form and expression that speak of an awe of nature. Their flowing sense of development leads into the most unexpected imaginary zones, with thematic material (often drawn from the dances and folk tunes of his homeland) sometimes suddenly reappearing in disguised and metamorphosed visage. — *"Blue" Gene Tyranny*

QUINTET FOR STRINGS

Quintet in F Major / Supraphon 32CO-1744
Lubomir Maly (viola)/Kocian Quartet

Quintet in F Major / Claves CD9006
Vladimir Mendelssohn (viola)/Sonare Quartet

SACRED MUSIC

Motets / Hyperion CDA66052
Matthew Best/Corydon Singers

Mass in E Minor & 6 Motets / Conifer CDCF192
Simon Halsey/CBSO Chorus & Wind Ensemble

Mass in E Minor / Hyperion CDA66177
Matthew Best/Corydon Singers

★ **Symphonies (1-3, *4, 5, 6, 7, 8, *9)**

Symphonies #1-9 / EMI CZS7629352
Eugen Jochum/Staatskapelle Dresden

Symphonies #1-9 / RCA Gold Seal 60075-2-RG
Gunter Wand /Cologne Radio Symphony Orchestra

Symphonies #1 in C Minor & #5 in B Major / Deutsche Grammophon 415985-2
Herbert von Karajan /Berlin Philharmonic Orchestra

Symphony #3 in C Minor / Philips 422411-2
Bernard Haitink/Vienna Philharmonic Orchestra

Symphony #4 ("Romantic") in E Flat Major / London 425613-2
Riccardo Chailly/Royal Concertgebouw Orchestra

Symphony #4 ("Romantic") in E Flat Major / Deutsche Grammophon 431719-2
Herbert von Karajan /Berlin Philharmonic Orchestra

Symphony #6 in A Major / Orfeo C024821
Wolfgang Sawalisch/Bavarian State Orchestra

Symphony #6 in A Major / EMI Studio CDM7633512
Otto Klemperer/New Philharmonic Orchestra
Eliahu Inbal/Frankfurt Radio Symphony Orchestra

Symphony #7 in E Major / London 414290-2
Riccardo Chailly/Berlin Radio Symphony Orchestra

Symphony #8 in C Minor / Deutsche Grammophon 415124-2
Carlo Maria Giulini/Vienna Philharmonic Orchestra

Symphony #9 in D Minor / Deutsche Grammophon 427345-2
Carlo Maria Giulini/Vienna Philharmonic Orchestra

Symphony #9 in D Minor / CBS MBK44825
Alfred Walter /Columbia Symphony Orchestra

Brumel, Antoine (c. 1460-c. 1520)

Brumel was a top composer in the Franco-Flemish tradition during the time of Josquin and Obrecht. Brumel was a pupil of Josquin, and historically significant as the first truly French composer to be associated with the court in Burgundy. Much of his fame rests on the 12-voice *Missa et ecce terrae motus*, which was to be cited until the end of the 16th century and led to the composition of more laments on his death than were received by his contemporaries Obrecht, Mouton, and Agricola combined.

Brumel's style in this mass (and in much of his work) is primarily chordal, largely eschewing contrapuntal intricacy and making sparing use of imitation. As such, his style has more in common with the later Renaissance style as exemplified by Palestrina than the style of Ockeghem or Josquin. The *Missa et ecce terrae motus* ("Earthquake Mass") is hence historically significant for its style, which is somewhat anticipatory of later developments and for its through-composed 12 voices, which produce massive blocked chordal structures.

On the whole, Brumel's music should appeal those who enjoy the later Renaissance style and will, no doubt, find this an interesting example of earlier large chordal music sparse in contrapuntal ideas. —*Todd McComb*

MASSES

Mass et ecce terra motus (Earthquake Mass) / Sony Vivarte SK46348
Paul Van Nevel/Huelgas Ensemble

Antoine Busnoys (d.1492)

Busnoys was perhaps the most highly regarded composer at the court of Burgundy during the final days of the luxurious duchy. His compositions comprise two cantus firmus masses, several motets, and dozens of secular chansons. Busnoys was best known for his secular music; indeed his finest works in these forms compare well with those of the acknowledged master of the age, Johannes Ockeghem. In fact, Busnoys's best-known work, the motet-chanson "In hydraulis," is a tribute to Ockeghem, his teacher. Busnoys' compositions delight in all manner of tricks, from harmonic effects to lyrical acrostics. His secular works represent the apogee of the intricate chanson form (in both poetry and music) of the early Renaissance. —*Todd McComb*

SACRED MUSIC

Mass "O crux lignum triumphale"; "In hydraulis"; 3 Motets & 3 Chansons / Dorian Recordings DOR-90184
Alexander Blachly/Pomerium Musices

Ferruccio Busoni (1866-1924)

An Italian-German pianist and composer of chamber pieces whose later works imply a rethinking of his distinct compositional style. An accomplished concert pianist and visionary musical theorist, Busoni wrote with great subtlety and invention and created a strange tonal world entirely his own. —*"Blue" Gene Tyranny*

CONCERTO FOR PIANO

Piano Concerto, Op. 39 / Telarc CD-80207
Garrick Ohlsson (piano), Christoph von Dohnanyi/Cleveland Orchestra & Male Chorus

Piano Concerto, Op. 39 / EMI CDH7698502
John Ogden (piano), Daniell Revenaugh/Royal Philharmonic Orchestra & Men of John Alldis Choir

PIANO MUSIC

Fantasia "contrappuntistica" on a Theme by Bach; Fantasia on a Theme by Bach / Continuum CCD1006
John Ogdon (piano)

Complete Music for Piano Two Hands / Philips 420740-2
Geoffrey Douglas Madge (piano)

Complete Music for Piano 4-Hands / Jecklin JD579-2
Isabel & Jurg von Vintschger (pianos)

Dietrich Buxtehude (1637-1707)

A Danish (or German) organist and composer of vocal and organ music, sacred cantatas, and chorales. Buxtehude was the famed organist and composer whom J. S. Bach made a 200-mile journey on foot to hear. His organ music (toccatas, preludes and fugues, passacaglias, ciacconas, and chorale preludes) greatly influenced Bach with their clarity of line, nobility, and often daring harmonic invention. His chorale music contains innovations such as the exchange of the normal roles of the orchestra and chorus in *Gott hilf mir* ("God help me"): The orchestra plays the straight chorale tune, while the singers provide elaborate ornamentations. —*"Blue" Gene Tyranny*

ORGAN MUSIC (CHORALES)

Choral Preludes, Fugues, Toccatas, Preludes, etc. / Harmonia Mundi HMX2901484 / 88
Rene Saorgin (organ)

Choral Preludes, Fantasia, Passacaglia, Praeludium, etc. / Chandos Chaconne CHAN0501
Piet Kee (organ)

Choral Preludes, Canzonas Chaconne, etc. / Chandos Chaconne CHAN0514
Piet Kee (organ)

William Byrd (1543-1623)

Byrd was the leading English composer of his generation, and together with his continental colleagues Giovanni Palestrina (c.1525-1594) and Orlando de Lassus (1532-1594), one of the acknowledged great masters of the late Renaissance. Byrd is considered by many the greatest English composer of any age, and indeed his substantial volume of high-quality compositions in every genre of the time makes it easy to consider him the greatest composer of the Renaissance—his versatility and genius outshining those of Palestrina and Lassus in a self-evident way. English music of the period was amazingly rich, dominating the music of the continent in depth and variety, in a way that was not seen before or since. Also, Byrd's preeminent position at the beginning of music publication in England allowed him to leave a substantial printed legacy at the inception of many important musical forms. It would be impossible to overestimate his subsequent influence on the music of England, the Low Countries, and Germany.

Byrd also contributed heavily to the developing genre of the English anthem (including the newer "verse" style with organ accompaniment), composing his widely regarded "Great Service" in this format. However, it was his Latin music that he chose to publish. This was series inaugurated in 1575 with the volume of *Cantiones Sacrae*, a joint collection with Thomas Tallis. Though this publication was not especially successful, Byrd followed it up with two more: the *Cantiones Sacrae* of 1589 & 1591. These "sacred songs" would be called motets on the continent, and represent the most significant English contribution to the motet repertory. Byrd also composed three Latin masses (for three, four, and five voices) during the period 1593-1595. These masses are unusual, not only because they could no longer have a liturgical function, but also because they include settings of the "Kyrie"—something not previously done in English mass composition. Following the three masses, Byrd produced his unparalleled legacy in sacred choral composition: the two huge volumes of *Gradualia* (1605 & 1607). These publications consist of many short pieces of liturgical music set in verse sections, which can be combined in various ways to form liturgically accurate Propers cycles for every significant feast and votive mass of the Roman Catholic rite. Byrd also published numerous smaller scale songs—*Psalmes, Sonets & Songs* (1588), *Songs of Sundrie Natures* (1589), and *Psalmes, Songs & Sonnets* (1611)—a fairly substantial volume of consort music—viol fantasias, variations, and dances of three to six parts and five five-part "In Nomines"—as well as having some of his works arranged by others for the lute. The final, and perhaps most impressive, examples of Byrd's immense legacy of compositions are his keyboard pieces. Taken together, Byrd's huge legacy of music—several hundred individual compositions—makes him one of the most brilliant composers in Western history. —*Todd McComb*

CONSORT MUSIC

Complete Consort Music: Fantasias, In Nomines, etc. / Virgin Classics Veritas CDC5450312
Fretwork

★ Keyboard Music

Nevell Cycle & Second Cycle / Harmonia Mundi HMC901241
Davitt Moroney (harpsichord)

13 Pieces from the Fitzwilliam Virginal Book / Claves CD9001
Ursula Duetschler (harpsichord)

SACRED CHORAL MUSIC

Masses in 3, 4 & 5 Parts; Great Service; Motets; and Anthems / Gimell CDGIM343 / 4
Peter Phillips/Tallis Scholars

Marion Masses from the Gradualia / Hyperion CDA66451
Gavin Turner/William Byrd Choir

Motets / Collegium COLCD110
John Rutter/The Cambridge Singers

Antonio de Cabezon (1510-1566)

Spanish organist and composer. Cabezon's extensive organ music is the earliest attributed music scored specifically for that instrument. His music usually makes use of a strict cantus firmus and is often set in variation form. —*AMG*

ORGAN MUSIC

Historic Spanish Organs—Vol. 1 / Valois 4645
Kimberly Marshall (organ)

Ferdinando Carulli (1770-1841)

Carulli was a noted performer of and advocate of the guitar, for which he wrote numerous pieces, and on which he authored a widely disseminated treatise, *Harmony Applied to the Guitar.* In the middle of his life he relocated to Paris, then perhaps the capital of musical knowledge, where he acquired a large following as a teacher of the guitar. His compositions, numbering above 400, favor the scale that is now called chamber music, though he wrote for full orchestra as well. —*AMG*

WORKS FOR FLUTE & GUITAR

6 Serenades, Op. 109 / Claves CD50-8304
Peter-Lukas Graf (flute), Konrad Ragossnig (guitar)

Concerto in G Major for Flute & Guitar; 2 Duos, Op. 104 #1 & 3; Nocturne, Op. 190; and Fantasy, Op. 337 / CBS MK42130
Jean-Pierre Rampal (flute), Alexandre Lagoya (guitar), Janos Rolla/Franz Liszt Chamber Orchestra

Emmanuel Chabrier (1841-1894)

A French pianist-composer of operas, piano pieces ("Impromptu," 1873), and the orchestral *Espana* (1883). He inspired Ravel. A composer of skillfully written works of bright orchestral imagery and exhilarating energy, Carulli was once called "a musical bridge between our own times and those of Couperin and Rameau" by Csar Franck. —*"Blue" Gene Tyranny*

★ **Espana**

Rhapsody "Espana" & Suite pastorale (w/ Dukas *Sorcerer's Apprentice & La Peri***)** / Chandos CHAN8852
Yan Pascal Tortelier/Ulster Philharmonic Orchestra

Rhapsody "Espana" & Other Works / Mercury Living Presence 434303-2
Paul Paray/Detroit Symphony Orchestra

Gustave Charpentier (1860-1956)

A student at the Paris Conservatory and winner of the Grand Prix de Rome, Charpentier became identified with his advocacy of the working class. His one enduring composition is the opera *Louise*, dedicated to his mistress and named after her, for which he also wrote the libretto. —*AMG*

LOUISE (OPERA)

Louise / Sony S3K46429
Ileana Cotrubas (soprano), Placido Domingo (tenor), Jane Berbie, Gabriel Baquier, Michel Senechal, Georges Petre/New Philharmonia Orchestra & Ambrosian Opera Chorus

Marc-Antoine Charpentier (1645-1704)

A French composer known mainly for church music and motets and as a collaborator with Molière for theater music. —*AMG*

MUSIQUE DE THEATRE

Incidental Music for "Circe" & "Andromede" / Harmonia Mundi HMC901244
Charles Medlam/London Baroque

SACRED MUSIC

Miserere, Motets / Harmonia Mundi HMC901185
Philippe Herreweghe/La Chapelle Royale Orchestra & Chorus

Oratorios: "Caecelia," "Filius Prodigus," and Magnificat / Harmonia Mundi HMC90066
William Christie/Les Arts Florissants

Ernest Chausson (1855-1899)

A French composer of opera, chamber music, and the symphonic poem *Viviane* (1882). The influences of Wagner and Franck are evident in Chausson's music, although he developed an intense individual style. —*Mary K. Scanlan*

CONCERT FOR VIOLIN, PIANO & STRING QUARTET

Concert, Op. 21 / Harmonia Mundi HMC901135
Regis Pasquier (violin), Jean-Claude Pennetier (piano), Roland Daugareil (violin), Genevieve Simonot (violin), Bruno Pasquier (viola), Roland Pidoux (cello)

POEME FOR VIOLIN & ORCHESTRA

Poeme, Op. 25 / EMI CDC7477252
Itzhak Perlman (violin), Jean Martinon/Orchestra of Paris

Poeme, Op. 25 / London 417118-2
Kyung-Wha Chung (violin), Charles Dutoit/Royal Philharmonic Orchestra

SYMPHONY

Symphony in B Flat Major, Op. 20 / Chandos CHAN8369
Jose Serebrier/Belgian Radio Symphony Orchestra

Symphony in B Flat Major, Op. 20 / EMI CDM7646862
Michel Plasson/Toulouse Capitole Orchestra

Frederic Chopin (1810-1849)

Except for some Polish songs and a few works for cello and piano trio, Chopin devoted his life to the creation of a richly melodic and harmonically original literature for the keyboard. From dances of his Polish homeland (such as the polonaise and the mazurka) to original "free" forms (such as the ballade), his music is still loved today and studied by both composition and keyboard students. —*"Blue" Gene Tyranny*

ANDANTE SPIANATO & GRANDE POLONAISE

Andante Spianato & Grande Polonaise Brillante, Op. 22 / Telarc CD-80280
Malcolm Frager (piano)

Andante Spianato & Grande Polonaise Brillante, Op. 22 / Philips 420654-2
Claudio Arrau (piano), Eliahu Inbal/London Philharmonic Orchestra

CONCERTOS FOR PIANO (1, 2)

Piano Concertos #1, Op. 11, and #2, Op. 21 (w / Complete Works for Piano & Orchestra) / Vox Music Group CDX5002
Abbey Simon (piano), Heribert Beissel/Hamburg Symphony Orchestra

Piano Concertos #1, Op. 11, and #2, Op. 21 / Sony SK44922
Murray Perahia (piano), Zubin Mehta/Israel Philharmonic Orchestra

Piano Concerto #1, Op. 11 / EMI CDM7643542
Maurizio Pollini (piano)

Piano Concertos #1, Op. 11, and #2, Op. 21 / Deutsche Grammophon 415970-2
Krystian Zimerman (piano), Carlo Maria Giulini/Los Angeles Philharmonic Orchestra

KRAKOWIAK

Rondo "Krakowiak," Op. 14/Philips 420654-2
Claudio Arrau (piano), Eliahu Inbal/London Philharmonic Orchestra

Rondo "Krakowiak," Op. 14 (w/ Complete Works for Piano & Orchestra) /Vox Music Group CDX5002
Abbey Simon (piano), Heribert Beissel/Hamburg Symphony Orchestra

★ **Piano Music (Ballades, Etudes, Nocturnes, etc.)**

4 Ballades, Op. 23, 38, 47 & 52, and 4 Scherzos, Op. 20, 31, 39 & 54 / Chesky CD44
Earl Wild (piano)

4 Ballades, Op. 23, 38, 47 & 52; Barcarolle, Op. 60; and Fantasie, Op. 49 / Deutsche Grammophon 423090-2
Krystian Zimerman (piano)

4 Ballades, Op. 23, 38, 47 & 52; and 4 Scherzos, Op. 20, 31, 39 & 54 / RCA RCD1-7156
Artur Rubinstein (piano)

12 Etudes, Op. 10, and 12 Etudes, Op. 25 / Deutsche Grammophon 413794-2
Maurizio Pollini (piano)

12 Etudes, Op. 10; 12 Etudes, Op. 25; and 3 Unpublished Etudes / Chandos CHAN8482
Louis Lortie (piano)

4 Impromptus, Op. 29, 36, 51 & 66; Berceuse, Op. 57; Barcarolle, Op. 60; and Fantasie, Op. 49 / CBS MK39708
Murray Perahia (piano)

21 Nocturnes / Hyperion CDA66341 / 2
Livia Rev (piano)

7 Polonaises, Op. 26, 40, 44, 53 & 61 / Deutsche Grammophon 419045-2
Maurizio Pollini (piano)

SONATA FOR CELLO & PIANO

Cello Sonata in G Minor, Op. 65 (w/ Grieg Sonata) / Claves CD50-703
Gerd Starke (cello), Ricardo Requelo (piano)

Cello Sonata in G Minor, Op. 65 (w/ Other Chamber Music) / Le Chant Du Monde LDC278.831 / 832
Stanislas Firlej (cello), Anna Wesolowska (piano)

SONATAS FOR PIANO (2, 3)

Piano Sonatas: #2 ("Funeral"), Op. 35, and #3, Op. 58 / RCA Red Seal 5612-2-RC
Maurizio Pollini (piano)

Piano Sonatas: #2 ("Funeral"), Op. 35, and #3, Op. 58 / Deutsche Grammophon 415346-2
Maurizio Pollini (piano)

LES SYLPHIDES (BALLET ARRANGED BY DOUGLAS FROM CHOPIN'S PIANO MUSIC)

Ballet Suite "Les Sylphides" / Capriccio 10073
Heinz Fricke/Berlin Radio Symphony Orchestra

Ballet Suite "Les Sylphides" / London 430723-2
Richard Bonynge/National Philharmonic Orchestra

VARIATIONS ON "LA CI DAREM LA MANO"

Variations on Mozart's "La ci darem la mano," Op. 2 (w/ Complete Works for Piano & Orchestra) / Vox Music Group CDX5002
Abbey Simon (piano), Heribert Beissel/Hamburg Symphony Orchestra

Variations on Mozart's "La ci darem la mano," Op. 2, and 4 Scherzos, Op. 20, 31, 39 & 54 / Hyperion CDA66514
Nikolai Demidenko (piano)

Johannes Ciconia (1335-1411)

Franco-Flemish composer of vocal music, active mostly in Italy. Ciconia was one of the most important composers of the generation that made the shift from the complex and rhythmically animated lines of the late medieval period to the smoother harmonic contours of the early Renaissance. His works exhibit both of these divergent styles to varying degrees, some making an interesting synthesis. He composed in all genres of the time: mass movements, motets, canons, virelais, madrigals, ballatas, etc. Together with his English contemporary Leonel Power, he represented one of the two stylistic poles that would yield the landmark music of the Franco-Flemish Renaissance, Guillaume Dufay being the most important synthesizer of the two. — *Todd McComb*

COLLECTIONS

Motets, Virelais, Ballate, and Madrigals / Opus 111 30-101
Alla Francesca & Alta

Hommage to Ciconia / New Albion 048
Ensemble Project Ars Nova

Francesco Cilea (1866-1950)

Composer and music professor. Cilea's most famous opera is the durable *Adriana LeCouvreur*. He also composed chamber music and songs. Cilea studied piano and composition at the Naples Conservatory and went on to a distinguished career teaching and finally heading several music conservatories in Italy and Sicily. — *AMG*

ADRIANA LECOUVREUR (OPERA)

Adriana Lecouvreur/ CBS M2K34588

Renata Scotto (soprano), Placido Domingo (tenor), Elena Obraztsova (mezzo-soprano), Sherill Milnes, James Levine/Philharmonia Orchestra ^ Ambrosian Opera Chorus

Adriana Lecouvreur/ Legato LCD111-2
Caballe, Cossotto, Jose Carreras (tenor), DíOrazi, Masini/Tokyo Lirici Italiani

Domenico Cimarosa (1747-1801)

An Italian composer of various concertos, chamber music, and operas, especially in the buffa style, whose vocal writing and orchestration make him an important predecessor to Rossini. — *Mary K. Scanlan*

CONCERTO FOR OBOE

Concerto in C Major / Philips 420189-2
Heinz Holliger (oboe)/I Musici

Aaron Copland (1900-1990)

An American composer of film scores, opera, piano, chamber music, and other forms. Copland is best known for his ballet music (*Appalachian Spring*, 1944; *Rodeo*, 1942) and his orchestral works (*Lincoln Portrait*, 1942; *Fanfare for the Common Man*, 1942). Sincerely concerned about relating to a wide public without compromising his music, Copland succeeded brilliantly both with more complex works like the *Piano Variations* and *Twelve Poems of Emily Dickinson* (1949-1950) and the subtle simplicity of his highly popular ballet music suites. He was the quintessential American nationalist composer. — *"Blue" Gene Tyranny*

★ **Appalachian Spring (Suite or complete ballet)**

Appalachian Spring: Ballet / EMI CDC7497662
Leonard Slatkin/St. Louis Symphony Orchestra

Appalachian Spring: Suite / Telarc CD-80078
Louis Lane/Atlanta Symphony Orchestra

Appalachian Spring: Suite / Sheffield Labs CD-27
Dmitri Kitayenko/Moscow Philharmonic Orchestra

Appalachian Spring: Suite (original chamber version) / Reference Recordings RR-22CD
Keith Clark/Chamber Ensemble

CONCERTO FOR PIANO

Piano Concerto / Chandos CHAN6580
Gillian Lin (piano), John Hopkins/Melbourne Symphony Orchestra

Piano Concerto / Vanguard OVC4029
Earl Wild (piano), Aaron Copland/Symphony of the Air

★ **Fanfare for the Common Man**

Fanfare for the Common Man / Telarc CD-80078
Louis Lane/Atlanta Symphony Orchestra

Fanfare for the Common Man / CBS MK42265 or MYK36257
Leonard Bernstein/New York Philharmonic Orchestra

RODEO (DANCE EPISODES OR COMPLETE BALLET)

Rodeo: Dance Episodes / Telarc CD-80078
Louis Lane/Atlanta Symphony Orchestra

Rodeo: Complete Ballet / EMI CDC7473822
Leonard Slatkin/St. Louis Symphony Orchestra

EL SALON MEXICO

El Salon Mexico / EMI CDC5476062
Eduardo Mata/Dallas Symphony Orchestra

El Salon Mexico / Deutsche Grammophon 419170-2
Leonard Bernstein/New York Philharmonic Orchestra

SYMPHONY #3

Symphony #3 / EMI CDC5476062
Eduardo Mata/Dallas Symphony Orchestra

Symphony #3 / Deutsche Grammophon 419170-2
Leonard Bernstein/New York Philharmonic Orchestra

Symphony #3 / Telarc CD-80201
Yoel Levi/Atlanta Symphony Orchestra

Arcangelo Corelli (1653-1713)

An Italian violinist and composer of trio sonatas and concerti grossi who distinguished himself solely in instrumental music and whose style typified the baroque period. Corelli created some of the most popular compositions of the 18th century<h150>—richly spirited music with a refined and touching melodic sense. —*"Blue" Gene Tyranny*

★ **Concerti Grossi Op. 6**

Opera Omnia (complete works) / Europa Musica 350.202
Carlo Chiarappa/Accademia Bizantina

6 Concerti Grossi, Op. 6 #1-6 / Harmonia Mundi HMU907014
Nicholas McGegan/Philharmonia Baroque Orchestra

6 Concerti Grossi, Op. 6 #7-12 / Harmonia Mundi HMU907015
Nicholas McGegan/Philharmonia Baroque Orchestra

12 Concerti Grossi, Op. 6 / Hungaroton HCD12376 / 77
Janos Rolla/Liszt Ferenc Chamber Orchestra, Budapest

12 Concerti Grossi, Op. 6 / Archiv 423626-2
Trevor Pinnock/The English Concert

12 Concerti Grossi, Op. 6 / Vox Box CDX5023
Paul Angerer/Southwest German Chamber Orchestra, Pforzheim

SONATAS OP. 5

12 Sonatas, Op. 5 #1-12 / Virgin VCD790840-2
Trio Sonnerie

6 Sonatas, Op. 5 #1-6 / Harmonia Mundi HMC901307
Chiara Banchini (violin), Jesper Christensen (harpsichord), Luciano Contini (archlute), Kathy Gohl (cello)

TRIO SONATAS, OP. 1-4

12 Trio Sonatas, Op. 1, and 12 Trio Sonatas, Op. 3 / Harmonia Mundi HMC901344.45
London Baroque

12 Trio Sonatas, Op. 2, and 12 Trio Sonatas, Op. 4 / Harmonia Mundi HMC901342.43
London Baroque

12 Trio Sonatas, Op. 3 / Smithsonian Collection ND035
Smithsonian Chamber Players

Michel Corrette (1709-1795)

ORGAN CONCERTOS

6 Concertos, Op. 26 / Harmonia Mundi HMA1905148
Rene Saorgin (organ), Dr. Gilbert Bezzina/Baroque Ensemble of Nice

François Couperin (1668-1733)

A French harpsichordist and composer known for his boldly harmonized and highly ornamented harpsichord works of dance suites as well as organ, chamber, and sacred music. Possessed of a lively, curious mind and a refined, ironic sense of humor, Couperin (known as "The Great") wrote the *Pièces de Clavecin* as character portraits, both of general types and of specific people of his day, which are studied even today for their deliberate fantasy and innovativeness ("The Player," "The Courteous One," "The Little Nothing," and many others). He was also a master of the Italian and French vocal styles of the period, demonstrated in his profoundly lyrical church motets (*Legions de ténèbres*, for Ash Wednesday; a *Magnificat*). Couperin's music leads from the baroque to the early classical periods. —*"Blue" Gene Tyranny*

D'APOTHEOSE DE CORELLI & D'APOTHEOSE DE LULLY

d'Apotheose de Corelli & d'Apotheose de Lully; Concert #8 / Erato Musifrance 2292-45011-2
John Eliot Gardiner/English Baroque Soloists

d'Apotheose de Corelli & d'Apotheose de Lully / Astree E7709
Hesperion XX

★ **Concerts Royaux**

4 Concerts "Royaux" / Harmonia Mundi HMC901151
Robert Claire (flute), Janet See (flute), Davitt Maroney (harpsichord), Jaap Ter Linden (bass viol)

LES GOUTS-RENUIS OU NOUVEAUX

10 Concerts # 5-14 ("Les Gouts-renuis ou Nouveaux") / Archiv 427167-2
Thomas Brandis (violin), Chiara Banchini (violin), Heinz Holliger (oboe), Marie-Lise Schupbach (oboe), Aurele Nicolet (flute), Christiane Nicolet (flute), Josef Ulsamer (viola da gamba), Laurenzius Strehl (viola da gamba), Manfred Sax (bassoon), Christiane Jaccottet (harpsichord)

LES NATIONS

4 Suites ("Les Nations") / Astree E7700
Jordi Savall /Hesperion XX

4 Suites ("Les Nations") / Archiv 427164-2
Reinhard Goebel/Musica Antiqua Koln

★ **Pièces de Clavecin**

Pièces de Clavecin Book I, Ordre 3 & 8, etc. / RCA Deutsche Harmonia Mundi 77219-2-RC
Skip Sempe (harpsichord)

Pièces de Clavecin Book I, Ordre 1-5 / Harmonia Mundi HMA190351.53
Kenneth Gilbert (harpsichord)

Pièces de Clavecin Book II, Ordre 7 / Newport Classic NCD60051
Mark Kroll (harpsichord)

Pièces de Clavecin Book II, Ordres 6, 11 & 12 / Astree E7754
Blandine Verlet (harpsichord)

Pièces de Clavecin Book II, Ordre 7,8 / Denon 33CO-1719
Huguette Dreyfus (harpsichord)

Pièces de Clavecin Book II, Ordre 11; Book III, Ordre 13 / Denon 38C37-7070
Huguette Dreyfus (harpsichord)

Pièces de Clavecin Book III, Ordre 13-19 / Harmonia Mundi HMA190357.58
Kenneth Gilbert (harpsichord)

Pièces de Clavecin Book IV, Ordre 20-27 / Harmonia Mundi HMA190359.60
Kenneth Gilbert (harpsichord)

Bernhard Henrik Crusell (1775-1838)

The Finn Crusell's compositions concentrate on woodwinds (he was a clarinetist) employed in chamber settings and songs. He studied in Stockholm, Paris, and Berlin, but his music is identified with Nordic traditions. He translated librettos into Swedish and was honored for his services to music by the Swedish Crown. —*AMG*

CONCERTOS FOR CLARINET

3 Clarinet Concertos: #1 Op. 1, #2 Op. 5, and #3 Op. 11 / BIS BIS-CD-345
Karl Leister (clarinet), Osmo Vanska/Lahti Symphony Orchestra

2 Clarinet Concertos: #1 Op. 1 and #3 Op. 11 / Hyperion CDA66055
Thea King (clarinet), Alun Francis/London Symphony Orchestra

Clarinet Concerto #2 Op. 5 (w/ Weber Concerto #2) / Hyperion CDA66088
Thea King (clarinet), Alun Francis/London Symphony Orchestra

QUARTETS FOR CLARINET & STRINGS (3)

3 Clarinet Quartets: #1 Op. 2, #2 Op. 4, and #3 Op. 7 / Hyperion CDA66077
Thea King (clarinet)/Allegri String Quartet

3 Clarinet Quartets: #1 Op. 2, #2 Op. 4, and #3 Op. 7 / Ondine ODE727-2
Kari Kriikku (clarinet)/Avanti Quartet

Jean-Henri D'Anglebert (1635-1691)

French composer of keyboard music. D'Anglebert published four suites for harpsichord, together with a Kyrie and five short fugues for organ. This publication represents some of the most polished French keyboard writing of the time. His style puts an elaborate counterpoint and precise system of embellishments at the service of an elegant melodic line, which is never obscured by these additions—his suites show a facility at working with multiple lines at a time to form a unified counterpoint. Typical of the period, his harpsichord suites include unmeasured preludes and all manner of dances. His celebrated *Tombeau to Chambonnieres* pays homage to the first important French exponent of solo harpsichord performance; his small organ output provides a welcome glimpse into the playing of the period. —*Todd McComb*

PIÈCES DE CLAVECIN

4 Suites ("Pièces de Clavecin") and Pièces d'orgue / Erato 2292-45007-2
Scott Ross (harpsichord and organ)

CLASSICAL

Franz Danzi (1763-1826)

A German composer-cellist with the Mannheim Court Orchestra. He wrote stage music (singspiels, grand opera, etc.) as well as symphonies, sacred music, and numerous chamber pieces for winds. —AMG

QUINTETS FOR WINDS

4 Quintets, Op. 53 & 67 / BIS BIS-CD-532
Berlin Philharmonic Wind Quintet

4 Quintets, Op. 41 & 56 / BIS BIS-CD-552
Berlin Philharmonic Wind Quintet

Claude Debussy (1862-1918)

A French composer of piano music, opera, cantatas, ballets, and orchestral and chamber works. His most notable pieces are *Prélude à l'après-midi d'un faune* ("Prelude to the Afternoon of a Faun") (1894) and *Nocturnes* (1899). Inspired often by pictorial subjects (Monet's water impressions became "Reflections in the Water" for piano) and by the elusive and unnameable in nature (footsteps in the snow; still leaves; and the hypnotic, overwhelming sensations of his rare visits to the French coastline), Debussy's music develops chords, melodies, and orchestration that are connected more by a single surreal observation than by an overriding logic. For example, one note is similar to another in a distantly related, enharmonic chord, but this brief tie is enough to follow, or a single gesture will soon evolve, spreading outward in all directions until a whole orchestral piece is made from a single falling line (*Afternoon of a Faun; Jeux*). Not bad for a kid born over his parents' china shop, who loved Lassus and Palestrina as much as ragtime and Javanese music. — *"Blue" Gene Tyranny*

★ **Clair de lune (Suite Bergamasque)**

Suite Bergamasque / Philips 412118-2
Zoltan Kocsis (piano)

Suite Bergamasque / Denon C37-7734
Jacques Rouvier (piano)

Suite Bergamasque excerpts, including "Clair de lune" / Special Music SCD-6034
Humbert Lucarelli (oboe), Susan Jolles (harp)

Suite Bergamasque #3, "Clair de lune" / Hyperion CDA66340
Susan Drake (harp)

ETUDES FOR PIANO

12 Etudes Books I & II / Nonesuch 79161-2
Paul Jacobs (piano)

12 Etudes Books I & II / Philips 422412-2
Mitsuko Uchida (piano)

IBERIA (SEE IMAGES FOR ORCHESTRA)

★ **Images for Piano (3 sets of 3 each: 1894 ("oubliees")/ 7 (Books I & II))**

3 Images (oubliees) / Philips 412118-2
Zoltan Kocsis (piano)

6 Images Books I & 2 (w/ Chopin piano music) / Vox Music Group CDX5103
Ivan Moravec (piano)

3 Images (oubliees) and 6 Images, Books I & 2 / Denon CO-1411
Jacques Rouvier (piano)

IMAGES FOR ORCHESTRA

3 Images / Philips 420392-2
Pierre Monteux/London Symphony Orchestra

3 Images / London 425502-2
Charles Dutoit/Montreal Symphony Orchestra

Image #2 (Iberia Suite) / RCA Gold Seal 60179-2-RG
Fritz Reiner/Chicago Symphony Orchestra

★ **La Mer**

3 Symphonic Sketches ("La Mer") / London 433711-2 or 421171-2
Ernest Ansermet/Orchestra of the Swiss Romande

3 Symphonic Sketches ("La Mer") / RCA Gold Seal 09026-60975-2
Fritz Reiner/Chicago Symphony Orchestra

3 Symphonic Sketches ("La Mer") / EMI CDC7494722

Michel Plasson/Toulouse Capitole Orchestra

L'ISLE JOYEUSE

L'Isle Joyeuse / Nimbus NIM5080
Vlado Perlemuter (piano)

L'Isle Joyeuse / Stradivari Classics SCD6078
Dubravna Tomsic (piano)

NOCTURNES FOR ORCHESTRA & CHORUS

3 Nocturnes / Philips 433712-2
Ernest Ansermet/Orchestra of the Swiss Romande

3 Nocturnes / London 433712-2
Ernest Ansermet/Orchestra of the Swiss Romande

PELLEAS ET MELISANDE (OPERA)

Pelleas et Melisande / London 430502-2
C. Alliot-Lugaz (soprano), F. Golfier (soprano), C. Carlson (mezzo-soprano), D. Henry (tenor), G. Cachemaille (baritone), P. Thau (bass), Charles Dutoit/Montreal Symphony Orchestra & Chorus

Pelleas et Melisande / Pierre Verany PV.788093 / 4
M. Walker, E. Manchet, Yhar, Le Texier, Meven, J. Carewe/Nice Philharmonic Orchestra & Opera Chorus

★ **Prelude à l'après-midi d'un faune**

Prelude to the Afternoon of a Faun / London 433711-2 or 421171-2
Ernest Ansermet/Orchestra of the Swiss Romande

Prelude to the Afternoon of a Faun / Sheffield Labs CD-24
Erich Leinsdorf/Los Angeles Philharmonic Orchestra

Prelude to the Afternoon of a Faun / EMI CDC7494722
Michel Plasson/Toulouse Capitole Orchestra

Prelude to the Afternoon of a Faun / Unicorn-Kanchana DKP(CD)9103
Boaz Sharon (piano)

★ **Preludes for Piano**

12 Preludes Book I / Denon 38C37-7121
Jacques Rouvier (piano)

12 Preludes Book II / Denon 38C37-7043
Jacques Rouvier (piano)

QUARTET FOR STRINGS

String Quartet, Op. 10 / Telarc CD-80111
Cleveland Quartet

String Quartet, Op. 10 / Hungaroton White Label HRC122
Bartok Quartet

SONATAS FOR CELLO & PIANO; FLUTE, VIOLA & HARP; AND VIOLIN & PIANO

Sonatas for Cello & Piano; Flute, Viola & Harp; and Violin & Piano / Chandos CHAN8385
Athena Ensemble

Sonatas for Cello & Piano; Flute, Viola & Harp; and Violin & Piano / Virgin VC7596042
Nash Ensemble

Cello Sonata / Virgin VC7592562
Steven Isserlis (cello), Pascal Devoyon (piano)

Violin Sonata / Deutsche Grammophon 415683-2
Shlomo Mintz (violin), Yefim Bronfman (piano)

Michel Richard Delalande (1657-1726)

French composer of sacred vocal music and secular instrumental music. He was composer-organist-harpsichordist for the Royal Chapel of Louis XIV and one of the leading composers of motets during the baroque era. His *symphonies* written as table music for the king's feasts have remained popular. —AMG

CAPRICES (SYMPHONIES FOR THE KING)

Symphonies pour les Soupers du Roy—Suites #1-12 and Concert / Harmonia Mundi HMC901337.40
Hugo Reyne/Ensemble "La Simphonie du Marais"

Leo Delibes (1836-1891)

Delibes came, and received his early training, from a musical family. His career as a student at the Paris Conservatory was stellar. There, besides organ, he studied composition with Adolphe Adam, whose influence on Delibes was definitive. Late in his life

Delibes was appointed professor of composition at the Paris Conservatory.

Delibes's mastery of harmony and melody has rarely been equaled. His two most successful ballets, *Coppelia* and *Sylvia*, contain melodies familiar to all lovers of serious music. His operatic masterpiece is *Lakme*, the last opera he completed before his death. He also composed works for chorus, piano, organ, and chamber groups. The loveliness and superior consistency of his greatest works have made them perennially popular.

COPPELIA (BALLET SUITE)

Coppelia: Ballet Suite / Naxos 8.550080
Ondrej Lenard/Slovak Radio Symphony Orchestra, Bratislava

Coppelia: Ballet Suite / Capriccio 10073
Heinz Fricke/Berlin Radio Symphony Orchestra

LAKME (OPERA)

Lakme/ London 425485-2
Joan Sutherland (soprano), Vanzo, Bacquier, Richard Bonynge/Monte Carlo Opera Orchestra

SYLVIA (BALLET SUITE)

Sylvia: Ballet Suite / Naxos 8.550080
Ondrej Lenard/Slovak Radio Symphony Orchestra, Bratislava

Sylvia: Ballet Suite / Laserlight 15616
Frigyes Sandor/Budapest Philharmonic Orchestra

Frederick Delius (1862-1934)

A British composer of opera, vocal, choral, orchestral, and chamber music. The ear of the young Delius was engaged, one summer night in Florida, by the sound of close-harmony Afro-American singing gently wafting over the St. John River (he had been sent to manage an orange plantation). Delius suddenly realized that his vocation was to be a musician. A romantic with the musical vocabulary of the impressionists, he wrote often-imitated but never-matched tone poems of great subtlety and beauty in a very personal style that is not reducible to a formula. — *"Blue" Gene Tyranny*

BRIGG FAIR

Brigg Fair (English Rhapsody) / EMI CDS7475098
Sir Thomas Beecham/Royal Philharmonic Orchestra

Brigg Fair (English Rhapsody) / EMI CDC7499322
Richard Hickox/Northern Sinfonia of England

★ On Hearing the First Cuckoo in Spring

On Hearing the First Cuckoo in Spring / EMI CDS7475098
Sir Thomas Beecham/Royal Philharmonic Orchestra

On Hearing the First Cuckoo in Spring / EMI CDM5650672
Richard Hickox/Northern Sinfonia of England

On Hearing the First Cuckoo in Spring / Chandos Collect CHAN6502
Norman Del Mar/Bournemouth Sinfonietta

TONE POEMS

Tone Poem #1 ("Summer Evening") / EMI CDS7475098
Sir Thomas Beecham/Royal Philharmonic Orchestra

Tone Poem #1 ("Summer Evening") / Nimbus NI5208
William Boughton/English String Orchestra

Tone Poem #2 ("Winter Night") / EMI CDS7475098
Sir Thomas Beecham/Royal Philharmonic Orchestra

Tone Poem #3 ("Spring Morning") / Records International 7012-2
John Hopkins/Slovak Philharmonic Orchestra, Bratislava

Josquin Des Prez (c.1440-1521)

Josquin Des Prez was one of the most influential and widely regarded composers in the history of Western music, so famous that he is known merely by his first name. Josquin was apparently born in the Duchy of Burgundy, in modern Belgium. He spent a large portion of his middle years in various Italian cities in great demand as a master of music and then retired to Conde (in northeast France) late in his life. Josquin's extended sojourns in Italy allowed him not only to spread the northern polyphonic style there but also to pick up some of the southern vitality noticeable in many of his secular works. However, his extended works are always marked by a subtlety and serenity characteristic of the Franco-Flemish school.

Josquin's surviving musical output is very large, comprising masses, motets, and secular songs in both French and Italian. His style is marked by the technique of pervasive imitation, in which different vocal lines share material in a subtle interlocking manner. Most of his compositions are for four voices, though larger textures are not uncommon. Josquin's masses include not only cantus firmus masses, such as the widely reknowned *Missa Pange Lingua*, but also "parody" masses in which entire contrapuntal complexes are borrowed from an earlier source. His secular compositions are highly varied, from light songs called "frottola," to weightier french chansons, such as the widely parodied "Milles Regretz," to the motet-chanson "Deploration on the death of Ockeghem/Nimphes des bois" and its gloomy textures. However, Josquin's motets contain some of his most varied and highly respected output, and it is here that his combination of piety, technical mastery, and individual discretion makes its surest showing.

Today, Josquin's reputation is as high as it has ever been, except perhaps during his lifetime, when he was the most sought after composer in Europe. His command of text and structure makes his music one of the great legacies of Western art. — *Todd McComb*

★ Masses

Mass "Hercules Dux Ferrariae," Miserere mei Deus, etc. / EMI Reflexe CDC7499602
Paul Hillier/Hilliard Ensemble

Mass "Ave Maris Stella," Motets, and Chansons / EMI CDC7546592
Andrew Parrott/Taverner Consort and Choir

Mass "Ave Maris Stella" and Motets / Astree 8507
A Sei Voci

Masses "Pange Lingua" and "la Sol Fa Re Mi" / Gimell CDGIM009
Peter Phillips/Tallis Scholars

Mass "de Beata Virgine," Motets and Chansons / Kontrapunkt 32110
Bo Holten/Ars Nova Ensemble

Mass "Mater Patris," Motets: "Berzerette savoyenne" & "Domine, non secundum peccata nostra" (also see Agricola) / Chanticleer CR-8808
Chanticleer

★ Motets

Motets and Chansons / EMI Reflexe CDC7492092
Paul Hillier/Hilliard Ensemble

Motets and Stabat Mater / Harmonia Mundi HMC901243
Philippe Herreweghe/La Chapelle Royale

Karl Ditters von Dittersdorf (1739-1799)

An Austrian violinist and composer of opera, singspiels, concertos, and instrumental chamber pieces. He was a leader of the Viennese classical school. A close friend to Mozart, Dittersdorf, Michael Haydn, Jan Vanhal, and Mozart met frequently to play each other's string quartets. — *AMG*

CONCERTO FOR DOUBLE BASS

Double Bass Concerto in E Major, Flute Concerto & Symphonies / Olympia Explorer OCD405
Stefan Thomasz (double bass), Nicolae Boboc/Arad Philharmonic Orchestra

SYMPHONIES "METAMORPHOSES"

6 Symphonies "Metamorphoses" / Calig CAL50885 / 86
Kurt Rapf/Vienna Sinfonietta

Gaetano Donizetti (1797-1848)

A leading Italian opera composer of the 1830s and 40s who also wrote sacred and instrumental chamber music; known for *Don Pasquale*, *Maria di Rohan*, *L'elisir d'amore*, and *Lucia di Lammermoor*. As an important exponent of the bel canto style, Donizetti wrote more than 70 operas in his life, which are noted for their fluent melodies, brilliant orchestration, and the individuality and believability of the characters as supported in the music. — *"Blue" Gene Tyranny*

LUCREZIA BORGIA (OPERA)

Lucrezia Borgia / London 421497-2
Joan Sutherland (soprano), Marilyn Horne (mezzo-soprano), Aragall, Wixell, ??????, Richard Bonynge/National Philharmonic Orchestra

LUCIA DI LAMMERMOOR (OPERA)

Lucia di Lammermoor / London 410193-2
Joan Sutherland (soprano), Luciano Pavarotti (tenor), Milnes, Ghaiurov, Richard Bonynge/Royal Opera House Orchestra

Lucia di Lammermoor / EMI Studio CMS7636312
Callas (soprano), Di Stefano, Panerai, Zaccaria, Herbert von Karajan/RIAS Symphony Orchestra & La Scala Chorus

LA FILLE DU REGIMENT (OPERA)

La Fille du Regiment / London 414520-2
Joan Sutherland (soprano), Luciano Pavarotti (tenor), Sinclair, Malas, Richard Bonynge/Royal Opera House Orchestra

La Fille du Regiment / Nuovo Era 6791 / 92
Serra, Tagliasacchi, Matteuzzi, Dara, Campanella/Bologna Teatro Comunale Orchestra & Chorus

DON PASQUALE (OPERA)

La Fille du Regiment / Nuovo Era 6791 / 92
Serra, Bartolo, Corbelli, Dara, Campanella/Teatro Regio di Torino Orchestra & Chorus

John Dowland (1563-1626)

A British composer of melancholy songs, lute music, and sacred and secular vocal music. Dowland was one of the greatest and most insightful songwriters who ever lived. His instrumental works demonstrate a mastery of contrapuntal complexity and a feeling for rhythmic liveliness. His famous *Lachrimae*, or *Seaven Teares*, was also acclaimed in literary circles. — *"Blue" Gene Tyranny*

AYRES

Pilgrim's Solace (selections) and selected Ayres / Virgin Classics VC759521-2
Emma Kirkby (soprano) and Anthony Rooley (lute & orpharion)

Third Book of Ayres / L'Oiseau-Lyre 430284-2
Anthony Rooley/Consort of Musicke

LUTE MUSIC

28 Dances, Fantasias, etc. / Dorian DOR-90148
Ronn McFarlane (lute)

LACHRIMAE

Lachrimae (complete) / Virgin Classics VC545005-2
Fretwork

Lachrimae (complete) / BIS CD-315
Jakob Lindberg/Dowland Consort

Lachrimae (complete) / Hyperion CDA66637
Paul O'Dette (lute), Peter Holman/Parley of Instruments Renaissance Violin Consort

Guillaume Dufay (c.1400-1474)

Dufay was one of the most highly regarded composers of his generation, and one of those principally responsible for inaugurating the Renaissance in music. Dufay was born in Cambrai (now in France, but then in the Duchy of Burgundy)—one of the primary musical centers of the era and a highly significant staging ground for the structural principles of the high Renaissance. He spent a considerable portion of his life in various cities in Italy, and so not only contributed to a refinement in the musical life of bustling Italy but also brought ideas on lively Italian textures to the intellectual centers of northern Europe. Dufay was one of the most cosmopolitan composers of his or any age, and his large musical output contains masterpieces in every genre, from cyclic masses to isorhythmic motets to simply ornamented hymns and dramatic cycles.

Dufay's music flows more smoothly than the characteristically complex rhythmic textures of the late medieval period and is marked by graceful melodies and a compelling sense of direction. As his career progressed and his fame grew, Dufay increasingly took up the four-voice vocal texture that was to be characteristic of the early Renaissance as a whole. His four cantus firmus masses "Se la face ay pale," "L'homme arme," "Ecce ancilla do-

mini," and "Ave regina caelorum" are landmarks in what was to become the dominant style of mass composition. The mass "Se la face ay pale" is probably the earliest surviving mass based on a secular theme, previous cantus-firmus masses having been based on liturgical chant.

Today, we value Dufay's music not only for its grace and invention, but also for its significant historical position in the quickly evolving style of the early Renaissance. The fact that the life of so cosmopolitan a character from this period has been preserved so well in documentation lends invaluable insight on the musical developments of the time. —*Todd McComb*

CHANSONS

Chansons by Guillaume Dufay et Gilles Binchois / Harmonic 8719
Dominique Vellard/Ensemble Gilles Binchois
Masses

Mass "se la face ay pale" / Focus 934
Thomas Binkley/Pro Arte Singers

Mass "l'homme arme," Motets (see below) / EMI Reflexe CDC7476282
Paul Hillier/Hilliard Ensemble

MOTETS

Nuper rosarum flores, Alma redemptoris mater, etc. / EMI Reflexe CDC7476282
Paul Hillier/Hilliard Ensemble

Paul Dukas (1865-1935)

Though he studied at the Paris Conservatory, was possessed of great talent, and was deemed a bright prospect, Dukas composed sparingly. He taught and edited musical scores, but he primarily spent his life as a music critic for various journals. He is known chiefly for his ballet *La Peri* and for his stunning orchestral scherzo *The Sorcerer's Apprentice*, the latter immortalized in the modern age by Leopold Stokowski and Walt Disney in *Fantasia*. Nearing death, he destroyed all his unfinished manuscripts.

SORCERER'S APPRENTICE

Symphonic Poem: The Sorcerer's Apprentice / Deusche Grammophon 419617-2
James Levine/Berlin Philharmonic Orchestra

Symphonic Poem: The Sorcerer's Apprentice / London 421527-2
Charles Dutoit/Montreal Symphony Orchestra

Maurice Durufle (1902-1986)

A French organist and composer in a modal style who is known for his *Requiem* (1947). —*AMG*

★ Requiem

Requiem, Op. 9 / Telarc CD-80135
Robert Shaw /Atlanta Symphony Orchestra & Chorus

Requiem, Op. 9 (third version) / Hyperion CDA66191
Ann Murray (mezzo soprano), Thomas Allen (baritone), Matthew Best/English Chamber Orchestra & Corydon Singers

Antonin Dvorak (1841-1904)

The dean of Czech composers and a violist and composer with a major output of orchestral and chamber music, including *Symphony no. 9, "From the New World"* (1893); *String Sextet in A, op. 48* (1878); and *Trio for Violin, Cello, & Piano no. 3 in f, op. 65* (1883). Dvorak is noted for his symphonies and symphonic poems, which have the emotional energy and scope of conception found in Schubert and Beethoven. —*"Blue" Gene Tyranny*

CARNIVAL OVERTURE

Carnival Overture, Op. 92 / Chandos CHAN8453 or CHAN8767
Vernon Handley/Ulster Orchestra

Carnival Overture, Op. 92 / Virgin VC7591742
Libor Pesek/Royal Liverpool Philharmonic Orchestra

★ Concerto for Cello

Cello Concerto in B Minor, Op. 104 / CBS MK42206
Yo-Yo Ma (cello), Lorin Maazel/Berlin Philharmonic Orchestra

Cello Concerto in B Minor, Op. 104 / Deutsche Grammophon 429155-2

Pierre Fournier (cello), George Szell/Berlin Philharmonic Orchestra

Cello Concerto in B Minor, Op. 104 / Chandos CHAN8662
Raphael Wallfisch (cello), Sir Charles Mackerras/London Symphony Orchestra

Cello Concerto in B Minor, Op. 104 / Vox Music Group CDX5015
Zara Nelsova (cello), Walter Susskind/Saint Louis Symphony Orchestra

CONCERTO FOR PIANO

Concerto in G Minor, Op. 33 / London 417802-2
Andras Schiff (piano), Christoph von Dohnanyi/New York Philharmonic Orchestra

Concerto in G Minor, Op. 33 / Vox Music Group CDX5015 or Mobile Fidelity Sound Labs MFCD814
Rudolf Firkusny (piano), Walter Susskind/Saint Louis Symphony Orchestra

CONCERTO FOR VIOLIN

Concerto in A Minor, Op. 53 / EMI CDC7474212
Nathan Milstein (violin), Rafael Fruhbeck de Burgos/New Philharmonia Orchestra

Concerto in A Minor, Op. 53 / Vox Music Group CDX5015
Ruggiero Ricci (violin), Walter Susskind /Saint Louis Symphony Orchestra

Concerto in A Minor, Op. 53 / CBS MK44923
Midori (violin), Zubin Mehta/New York Philharmonic Orchestra

★ **Quartets** (*10, *12, *14)

String Quartets #10, Op. 51, & #12 ("American"), Op. 96 / Supraphon 110581-2
Panocha String Quartet

String Quartets #10, Op. 51, & #14, Op. 105 / Denon 38C37-7235
Kocian Quartet

★ **Quartets for Piano & Strings**

String Quartets #10, Op. 51, & #14, Op. 105 / Academy Sound & Vision LTD CDDCA788
Lindsey Quartet

String Quartets #12 ("American"), Op. 96, & #13, Op. 106 / Academy Sound & Vision LTD CDDCA787
Lindsey Quartet

★ **Quartets for Piano & Strings**

Piano Quartets #1, Op. 23, & #2, Op. 87 / Dorian Recordings DOR-90125
Ames Piano Quartet

Piano Quartets #1, Op. 23, & #2, Op. 87 / Le Chant du Monde LDC278.1082
Jan Talich (viola)/Prague Trio

Piano Quartets #1, Op. 23, & #2, Op. 87 / Supraphon 111464-2
Josef Hala (piano), Josef Suk (violin), Josef Kodousek (viola), Josef Chuchro (cello)

Piano Quartets #1, Op. 23, & #2, Op. 87 / CBS MB2K45672
Rudolf Firkusny (piano)/Julliard String Quartet

QUINTETS FOR PIANO & STRINGS

Piano Quintets #1, Op. 5, & #2, Op. 81 / Philips 412429-2
Sviatoslav Richter (piano)/Borodin Quartet

Piano Quintets #1, Op. 5, & #2, Op. 81 / Supraphon 104115-2
Jan Panenka (piano)/Smetana Quartet

RUSALKA (OPERA)

Rusalka / Supraphon 103641-2
Gabriela Benackova, Vera Soukupova, Wieslaw Ochman, Richard Novak, Vaclav Neumann/Czech Philharmonic Orchestra & Chorus

SERENADES FOR ORCHESTRA

Serenades #1 for Strings, Op. 22, & #2 for Winds, Op. 44 / Philips 400020-2
Sir Neville Marriner/Academy of St. Martin-in-the-Fields

Serenades #1 for Strings, Op. 22, & #2 for Winds, Op. 44 / London 417452-2
Christopher Hogwood/London Philharmonic Orchestra

Serenade #1 for Strings, Op. 22 / Delos D / CD3011
Gerard Schwarz/Los Angeles Chamber Orchestra

Serenade #2 for Winds, Op. 44 / Orfeo C051831
Brezina/Munich Wind Academy

SLAVONIC DANCES

Slavonic Dances, Op. 46 & 72 / Supraphon 110081-2
Vaclav Neumann/Czech Philharmonic Orchestra

Slavonic Dances, Op. 46 & 72 / London 417749-2
Antal Dorati/Royal Philharmonic Orchestra

★ **Symphonies** (*7, *8, *9 "New World")

9 Symphonies / London 430046-2
Istvan Kertesz/London Symphony Orchestra

9 Symphonies / Chandos CHAN9008 / 13
Neeme Jarvi/Scottish National Orchestra

3 Symphonies: #1 ("The Bells of Zlonice") #2, Op. 4, and #3, Op. 10 / Supraphon 111003-2
Vaclav Neumann/Czech Philharmonic Orchestra

2 Symphonies: #3, Op. 10, and #6, Op. 60 / Naxos 8.550268
Stephen Gunzenhauser/Slovak Philharmonic Orchestra

2 Symphonies: #5, Op. 76, and #7, Op. 70 / Naxos 8.550270
Stephen Gunzenhauser/Slovak Philharmonic Orchestra

3 Symphonies: #7, Op. 70; #8, Op. 88; and #9 ("From the New World"), Op. 95 / London 421082-2
Christoph von Dohnanyi/Cleveland Orchestra

3 Symphonies: #7, Op. 70; #8, Op. 88; and #9 ("From the New World"), Op. 95 / Supraphon 110559-2
Vaclav Neumann/Czech Philharmonic Orchestra

Symphony #9, "From the New World," Op. 95 / Virgin VC759505-2
Libor Pesek/Czech Philharmonic Orchestra

Symphony #9, "From the New World," Op. 95 / Chesky CD31
Jascha Horenstein/Royal Philharmonic Orchestra

★ **Trios for Piano & Strings** (1-3,*4)

Piano Trios #1, Op. 21, and #2, Op. 26 / Denon 33CO-1409
Suk Trio

Piano Trios #3, Op. 65, and #4 ("Dumka"), Op. 90 / Denon 33CO-1410
Suk Trio

Piano Trios #1, Op. 21, and #2 Op. 26 / Newport Classic NCD60074
Raphael Trio

Piano Trio #4 ("Dumka"), Op. 90 / Chandos CHAN8445
Borodin Trio

Piano Trios #3, Op. 65, and #4 ("Dumka"), Op. 90 / Philips 426094-2
Beaux Arts Trio

Edward Elgar (1857-1934)

A British composer of choral, orchestral, chamber, and instrumental music known for the oratorio *The Dream of Gerontius* (1900) and the tone poem *Enigma Variations* (1899). A chronological list of Elgar's works is like an autobiography of his interior life within English society, from the early choral works about the "hero" bringing new vision and even a childlike sense of wonder (*The Black Knight, Op. 25,* 1889), to the mysterious tone poems that, while they lack a specific program, often contain musical portraits of friends and family in the process of self-discovery (*Enigma Variations*), and finally to the stark landscape and lone-survivor solos of the *Concerto for Cello & Orchestra in e* (1919). He is known for developing a unique variation technique for symphonic writing and for the popular *Pomp and Circumstance March no. 1, op. 39. —"Blue" Gene Tyranny*

★ **Concerto for Cello**

Cello Concerto in E Minor, Op. 85 / EMI CDC7473292
Jacqueline Du Pre (cello), Sir John Barbirolli/London Symphony Orchestra

Cello Concerto in E Minor, Op. 85 / CBS MK39541
Yo-Yo Ma (cello), Andre Previn/London Symphony Orchestra

Cello Concerto in E Minor, Op. 85 / Virgin VC75952112
Steven Isserlis (cello), Richard Hickox/London Symphony Orchestra

CONCERTO FOR VIOLIN

Violin Concerto in B Minor, Op. 61 / EMI CDC7472102
Nigel Kennedy (violin), Vernon Handley/London Philharmonic Orchestra

Violin Concerto in B Minor, Op. 61 / Naxos 8.550489
Dong-Suk Kang (violin), Adrian Leaper/Polish National Radio Symphony Orchestra

Violin Concerto in B Minor, Op. 61 / RCA Gold Seal 7966-2-RG (mono)
Jascha Heifetz (violin), Sir Malcolm Sargent/London Symphony Orchestra

ENIGMA VARIATIONS

Enigma Variations, Op. 36 / Telarc CD-80192
David Zinman/Baltimore Symphony Orchestra

Enigma Variations, Op. 36 / Virgin VJ7596432
Andrew Litton/Royal Philharmonic Orchestra

POMP & CIRCUMSTANCE MARCHES

5 Pomp & Circumstance Marches, Op. 39 / Denon CO73534
Sir Charles Groves/Philharmonia Orchestra

5 Pomp & Circumstance Marches, Op. 39 / Chandos Collect CHAN6504
Sir Alexander Gibson/Scottish National Orchestra

★ **Symphonies (*1, 2)**

Symphony #1 in A Flat Major, Op. 55 / Philips 416612-2
Andre Previn/Royal Philharmonic Orchestra

Symphony #1 in A Flat Major, Op. 55 / EMI CDM7640132
Sir Adrian Boult/London Philharmonic Orchestra

Symphony #1 in A Flat Major, Op. 55 / RCA Red Seal 60381-2-RC
Leonard Slatkin/London Philharmonic Orchestra

Symphony #2 in E Flat Major, Op. 63 / EMI CDM7640142
Sir Adrian Boult/London Symphony Orchestra

Symphony #2 in E Flat Major, Op. 63 / Chandos CHAN8452
Bryden Thomson/London Philharmonic Orchestra

Symphony #2 in E Flat Major, Op. 63 / RCA Red Seal 60072-2-RC
Leonard Slatkin/London Philharmonic Orchestra

Georges Enesco (1881-1955)

A Romanian violinist and composer known for rhapsodic, poetic orchestral music (such as *Rhapsodies Roumanains*, 1901) that speaks with an original elegance and a flow of melodic invention, showing a different feeling for this part of Europe than has been expressed by other composers. —*"Blue" Gene Tyranny*

OEDIPE (OPERA)

Oedipe Op. 23 / EMI CDC7540112
Barbara Hendricks, Fassbaender, Lipovsek, Taillon, Gedda, Aler, Lawrence Foster/Monte Carlo Philharmonic Orchestra

★ **Romanian Poem**

Romanian Poem, Op. 1 / Stradivari Classics SCD-6038
Iosif Conta/Romanian Radio & Television Orchestra

★ **Romanian Rhapsodies**

2 Romanian Rhapsodies, Op. 11 / Stradivari Classics SCD-6038
Iosif Conta/Romanian Radio & Television Orchestra

Romanian Rhapsody #1, Op. 11 / Mercury Living Presence 432015-2
Antal Dorati/London Symphony Orchestra

Romanian Rhapsody #2, Op. 11 / Mercury Living Presence 434326-2
Antal Dorati/London Symphony Orchestra

SONATAS FOR VIOLIN & PIANO

Violin Sonatas #1 Op. 2, #2 Op. 6, and #3 Op. 25 / Dynamic CDS41
Mariana Sirbu (violin), Mihail Sarbu (piano)

Violin Sonatas #2 Op. 6, #3 Op. 25, and "Torso" Sonata / Hyperion CDA66484
Adelina Oprean (violin), Justin Oprean (piano)

Ferenc Erkel (1810-1893)

BANK BAN (OPERA)

Bank Ban / Hungaroton HCD11376 / 7
Karola Agay (soprano), Erzebet Komlossy (mezzo-soprano), Jozsef Simandi (tenor), Andras Farago (baritone), Gyorgy Melis (baritone), Janos Ferencsik/Budapest Philharmonic Orchestra & Hungarian State Opera Chorus

Manuel de Falla (1876-1946)

An important Spanish composer of opera, oratorio, piano, and ballet music such as *El amor brujo* ("Love, the Magician") and *El sombrero de tres picos* ("The Three-Cornered Hat"). De Falla wrote bold, passionate, and colorful Andalusian gypsy dance forms with folk-style original melodies (*Fantasia betica*); operas and zarzuelas (a Spanish operetta form) about magic (*El amor brujo* ("Love, the Magician") contains the famous "Ritual Fire Dance" to ward off evil spirits while pots and pans are being forged); and mirthful pieces (*El sombrero de tres picos*, a ballet about a miller's wife and a presuming town official). —*"Blue" Gene Tyranny*

LA VIDE BREVE (OPERA)

La Vide Breve (1904 / 5) / EMI CDH7695902
Victoria de los Angeles (soprano), Rivadeneyra, Cossulta, Rafael Fruhbeck de Burgos/Spanish National Orchestra & Orfeon Donostiarra

EL AMOR BRUJO (BALLET)

El amor brujo / London 403703-2
H. Tourangeau (mezzo-soprano), Charles Dutoit/Montreal Symphony Orchestra

El amor brujo / EMI CDM7647462
Victoria de los Angeles (soprano), Carlo Maria Giulini/Philharmonia Orchestra

NIGHTS IN THE GARDENS OF SPAIN

Nights in the Gardens of Spain / London 410289-2
Alicia De Larrocha (piano), Rafael Fruhbeck de Burgos/London Philharmonic Orchestra

Nights in the Gardens of Spain / Academy Sound & Vision LTD CDDCA775
Joaquin Soriano (piano), Jose Serebrier/English Chamber Orchestra

EL SOMBRERO DE TRES PICOS ("THREE-CORNERED HAT" (BALLET)

El sombrero de tres picos / EMI CDM7647462
Victoria de los Angeles (soprano), Carlo Maria Giulini / Philharmonia Orchestra

El sombrero de tres picos / Delos D / CD3060
Jones (soprano), Gerard Schwarz/London Symphony Orchestra

Johann Friederich Fasch (1688-1758)

A German composer and contemporary of J. S. Bach, he wrote many orchestral pieces, chamber works, and oratorios. His vocal pieces and four operas have been lost. —*AMG*

SONATAS (TRIO & QUADRO)

6 Sonatas a 3 and a 4 / Capriccio 10239
Ingo Goritzki (oboe), Burkhardt Glaetzner (oboe), Thomas Reinhardt (bassoon), Siegfried Pank (viola da gamba), Achim Beyer (violone), Christine Schornsheim (harpsichord)

6 Sonatas a 3 and a 4 / RCA Deutsche Harmonia Mundi Editio Classica 77015-2-RG
Camerata Koln

Gabriel Fauré (1845-1924)

A French organist and composer of orchestral, piano, chamber, vocal, and dramatic music, such as the opera *Penelope* (1913). Fauré wedded the chromatic freedom of the Wagnerian palette with his strong French sensibility for melodic line and transparent timbres, retaining his own compositional voice to create pieces of great beauty. His songs (over 100) establish a new relation of music to words—by never reacting directly to the meaning of the words, Fauré uses the music to change or expand them, making the piano more than a mere accompaniment: It is an integral part of the composition. —*"Blue" Gene Tyranny*

★ **Chamber Music w/ Piano (*Quartets & *Quintets)**

Piano Quartets #1, Op. 15, & #2, Op. 45, and Piano Quintets #1, Op. 89, & #2, Op. 115 / EMI CMS7625482
Jean-Philippe Collard (piano)/Quatuor Parrenin

Piano Quartets #1, Op. 15, & #2, Op. 45, and Piano Quintets #1, Op. 89, & #2, Op. 115 / Vox Music Group CDX5073
Jacqueline Eymar (piano), Gunter Kehr & Werner Heuhaus (violins), Erich Sichermann (viola), Bernard Braunholz (cello)

Piano Quartets #1, Op. 15, & #2, Op. 45 / Hyperion CDA66166
Domus

PAVANE

Pavane, Op. 50 / London 421440-2
Charles Dutoit/Montreal Symphony Orchestra

Pavane, Op. 50 / Telarc CD-80059
Leonard Slatkin/Saint Louis Symphony Orchestra

PELLEAS ET MELISANDE

Pelleas et Melisande Suite, Op. 80 / London 421440-2
Charles Dutoit/Montreal Symphony Orchestra

Pelleas et Melisande Suite, Op. 80 / Telarc CD-80084
Robert Shaw/Atlanta Symphony Orchestra

PIANO MUSIC (BARCAROLLES & NOCTURNES)

Barcarolles (complete) / EMI CDC7473582
Jean-Philippe Collard (piano)

Nocturnes (complete), Preludes (complete), Ballade / EMI CMS7691492
Jean-Philippe Collard (piano)

Preludes (complete), Impromptus (complete), and Theme & Variations / CRD 3423
Paul Crossley (piano)

REQUIEM

Messe de Requiem, Op. 48 / Telarc CD-80135
Judith Blegen (soprano), James Morris (bass), Robert Shaw/Atlanta Symphony Orchestra

Messe de Requiem, Op. 48 / London 421440-2
Kiri Te Kanawa (soprano) Sherill Milnes (bass), Charles Dutoit/Montreal Symphony Orchestra

Messe de Requiem, Op. 48 / Harmonia Mundi HMX2901413.15
Mellon (soprano), Kooy (bass), Philippe Herreweghe/La Chapelle Royale Orchestra, La Chapelle Royale Choir, Les Petits Chanteurs de Saint-Louis & Ensemble Musique Oblique

SONGS

18 Songs / Hyperion CDA66320
Dame Janet Baker (mezzo-soprano), Geoffrey Parsons (piano)

Songs (complete) / EMI CDM7640792
Elly Ameling (soprano), G. Souzay (baritone), D. Baldwin (piano)

John Field (1782-1837)

An Irish pianist and composer of delicate and expressive piano pieces. Field was the inventor of the nocturne, a new concept in romantic music and a precursor to Chopin's work in that form (Chopin taught his pupils Field's work). Field, the proverbially incurable romantic, was on the move all his life—from Ireland to Paris to Vienna to St. Petersburg to Moscow. His lovely piano concertos have the grace and subtle line of his nocturnes. Many of his other piano works remain unplayed. —*"Blue" Gene Tyranny*

CONCERTOS FOR PIANO

Piano Concertos #1-7 / Onyx CD101 / 103
John O'Conor (piano), Janos Furst/New Irish Chamber Orchestra

NOCTURNES

15 Nocturnes, Vol. 1 / Telarc CD-80199
John O'Conor (piano)

3 Nocturnes, Vol. 2, and 4 Piano Sonatas / Telarc CD-80290
John O'Conor (piano)

Johann Caspar Fischer (1665-1746)

PIÈCES DE CLAVECIN

Pièces de Clavecin / Harmonia Mundi HMC901026

William Christie (harpsichord)

Cesar Franck (1822-1890)

A noted French organist and composer of chamber, symphonic, keyboard, and sacred choral music, whose major works include *Six Pièces* (1862) and *Les Béatitudes* (1879). In the late 1800s, when France was still in shock from war and warring factions, Franck and his pupils (d'Indy, Chausson, and others, often called "la bande Franck") steered French composition toward symphonic and chamber music and away from the more conservative opera. Franck incorporated organlike textures, timbres, and immense sonorities of highly chromatic adoration and idealism into his symphonic compositions, with which his graceful chamber works stand in contrast (*Sonata for Violin & Piano in a*, *Variations symphoniques for Piano & Orchestra*—his masterpiece). —*"Blue" Gene Tyranny*

ORGAN MUSIC

Complete Organ Music: Chorales, Cantabile, Fantasie, Priere, etc. / Telarc CD-80234
Michael Murray (organ)

Complete Organ Music: Chorales, Cantabile, Fantasie, Priere, etc. / Dorian DOR90135
Jean Guillou (organ)

Complete Organ Music: Chorales, Cantabile, Fantasie, Priere, etc. / Newport Classic NCD60060 / 1
Anthony Newman (organ)

QUINTET FOR PIANO & STRINGS

Piano Quintet in F Minor / Philips 432142-2
Sviatoslav Richter (piano)/Borodin Quartet

Piano Quintet in F Minor / Nimbus NIM5114
John Bingham (piano)/Medici String Quartet

★ **Sonata for Violin & Piano**

Sonata in A Major / Deutsche Grammophon 415683-2
Shlomo Mintz (violin), Yefim Bronfman (piano)

Sonata in A Major / London 421817-2
Joshua Bell (violin), Jacques-Yves Thibaudet (piano)

Sonata in A Major / Dynamic CDS21 / 1-2
Mariana Sirbu (violin), Sarbu Mihail (piano)

SYMPHONIC POEMS

Symphonic Poems: "Le Chasseur Maudit," "Les Djinns" "Les Eolides," and "Psyche" Parts #1-3 / Ricercar RIC009058 / 059
Paul Strauss/Liege Philharmonic Orchestra

Symphonic Poem "Le Chasseur Maudit" / Telarc CD-80247
Jesus Lopez-Cobos/Cincinnati Symphony Orchestra

Symphonic Poems: "Le Chasseur Maudit" and "Les Eolides" / London 433718-2
Ernest Ansermet/Orchestra of the Swiss Romande

SYMPHONIC VARIATIONS

Symphonic Variations / EMI CDM7638892
Jean-Philippe Collard (piano), Michel Plasson/Toulouse Capitole Orchestra

Symphonic Variations / Ricercar RIC009058 / 059
Aldo Ciccolini (piano), Paul Strauss/Liege Philharmonic Orchestra

★ **Symphony in D**

Symphony in D Minor / RCA 6805-2-RG
Pierre Monteux/Chicago Symphony Orchestra

Symphony in D Minor / Telarc CD-80247
Jesus Lopez-Cobos/Cincinnati Symphony Orchestra

Symphony in D Minor / EMI CDM7690082
Alexis Weissenberg (piano), Herbert von Karajan/Berlin Philharmonic Orchestra

Girolamo Frescobaldi (1583-1643)

An Italian organist and composer primarily of keyboard music and some sacred and secular vocal music, who is said to have had a beautiful singing voice and been an accomplished lute and organ player. Frescobaldi's keyboard pieces transformed the toccata into a much more dramatic form and were used as instrumental breaks during the mass (for instance, when the host was elevated). He introduced the variation technique into the canzone, brilliant chromatic counterpoint in the fugal ricercare, and was one of the few composers whose work J. S. Bach, while learning the craft of music, copied out in full by hand. —*"Blue" Gene Tyranny*

CANZONI FOR RECORDER & CONTINUO

17 Canzonas / Pierre Verany PV.793092
Il Teatro all Moda Ensemble

19 Canzonas / Nuovo Era 7131
Kees Boeke/Tripla Concordia

HARPSICHORD/ORGAN MUSIC (*TOCCATAS, CAPRICCI, ETC.)

Toccatas, Caprices, etc. / Philips 432128-2
Gustav Leonhardt (harpsichord)

Toccatas, Caprices, Partitas, etc. / Dorian Recordings DOR-90124
Colin Tilney (harpsichord)

Complete Toccatas from Book I / Tactus TC580690
Sergio Vartolo (organ)

Complete Toccatas from Book II / Nuovo Era 6799
Lorenzo Ghielmi (organ & harpsichord)

Complete Organ Masses / Tactus TC580690
Sergio Vartolo (organ)

Johann Jakob Froberger (1616-1667)

German harpsichordist and composer, student of Frescobaldi, and resident of Vienna. Froberger's published output is quite small, but manuscripts survive for more than 30 harpsichord suites in a highly personal idiom. He is accorded a prominent place in history for his early writing of established suites of dances and his cosmopolitan unification of the various compositional styles of the time. Besides studying in Italy, Froberger spent time in France where he met many of the prominent composers of the time. His music often exhibits a deep melancholy, expressed in simple counterpoint with a beautiful array of sonorities. —*Todd McComb*

WORKS FOR HARPSICHORD

3 Suites, 3 Toccatas, Capriccio, Fantasia, etc. / RCA Deutsche Harmonia Mundi 7923-2-RC
Gustav Leonhardt (harpsichord)

Suites and Toccatas / Harmonia Mundi HMC901372
Christophe Rousset (harpsichord)

4 Suites, 3 Toccatas, Fantasia, etc. / Astree E8716
Blandine Verlet (harpsichord)

Giovanni Gabrieli (1553-1612)

An Italian composer of sacred and secular vocal music and some instrumental keyboard, string, and wind ensemble pieces. Gabrielli's music is considered the epitome of the High Renaissance Venetian school. He was the perfecter of the impressive and lively ceremonial style of cori spezzati ("broken-up choirs or groups"), in which the musicians are located in widely separated spaces; he also wrote strangely chromatic motets about hell and damnation, promoted the music of Monteverdi, and influenced the young Heinrich Schutz. —*"Blue" Gene Tyranny*

★ **Canzoni for Brass Choirs**

Canzoni, Sonatas, and Motets / EMI Reflexe CDC7542652
Andrew Parrott/Taverner Consort, Players, and Choir

Canzoni, Intonazioni, Mass Movements, and Motets / CBS MK42645
E. Power Biggs (organ), Gregg Smith Singers, Texas Boys Choir, Edward Tarr Brass Ensemble

Niels Gade (1817-1890)

An influential Danish composer, conductor, teacher, and admirer of Mendelssohn and Schumann, who adopted the German romantic style in his own works. —*Mary K. Scanlan*

CHAMBER MUSIC

3 String Quartets / BIS BIS-CD-516
Kontra Quartet

String Octet in F Major, Op. 17 (w/ Schubert Octet) / Sony SK48307

L'Archibudelli & Smithsonian Chamber Players

3 Violin Sonatas / Kontrapunkt 32098
Soren Elbaek (violin), Elisabeth Westenholz (piano)

String Quintet #1, Op. 8, and String Sextet, Op. 44 / Kontrapunkt 32121
Johannes Ensemble

SYMPHONIES

Symphonies #1, Op. 5, and #8, Op. 47 / BIS BIS-CD-339
Neeme Jarvi /Stockholm Sinfonietta

John Gay & John Christopher Pepusch

BEGGAR'S OPERA

The Beggar's Opera (1990 edition by Jeremy Barlow) / Hyperion CDA66591 / 2
Bob Hoskins (The Beggar), Ian Caddy (The Player), Adrian Thompson (Macheath), Charles Daniels (Peachum), Sarah Walker (Mrs Peachum), Bronwen Mills (Polly), Richard Jackson (Lockit), Anne Dawson (Lucy), Roger Bryson (Mab of The Mint), Catherine Wyn-Rogers (Jenny Diver), Jeremy Barlow/The Broadside Band

Francesco Geminiani (1687-1762)

An Italian violinist and composer of instrumental, orchestral, chamber, and some harpsichord music. —*AMG*

CONCERTI GROSSI, OP. 3

6 Concerti Grossi, Op. 3 / L'Oiseau-Lyre 417522-2
Jaap Schroder (violin), Catherine Mackintosh (violin), Trevor Jones (viola), Anthony Pleeth (cello), Christopher Hogwood/Academy of Ancient Music

CONCERTI GROSSI, OP. 7

6 Concerti Grossi, Op. 7 / Academy Sound & Vision LTD CD-DCA724
Iona Brown (violin), Malcolm Latchem (violin), Stephen Shingles (viola), Denis Vigay (cello)/Academy of St. Martin-in-the-Fields

George Gershwin (1898-1937)

An American composer primarily of musicals and songs (with lyricist and brother Ira Gershwin), famous for "Rhapsody in Blue" (1924); other notable works include the folk opera *Porgy and Bess* (1935) and the *Piano Concerto in F* (1925).

Gershwin was probably the first composer of extended musical forms, aside from Scott Joplin in his operas, to embrace fully African-American creative music as a fundamental source of inspiration. Certain works, such as the *I Got Rhythm Variations*, scenes in *Porgy and Bess*, and the *Preludes for Piano*, have a sophistication of variation, technique, and orchestration comparable to the best of modern French melodists, like Poulenc. (Gershwin applied to study with Ravel and then with Nadia Boulanger, but was turned down by each, who did not want to cramp his natural style.) Gershwin's influence on jazz has been enormous (his harmonic sense studied by bebop composers), and his music continues to have freshness and warmth. —*"Blue" Gene Tyranny*

AMERICAN IN PARIS

An American In Paris (Tone Poem) / EMI CDC7471612
Andre Previn/London Symphony Orchestra

An American In Paris (Tone Poem)/ RCA Victrola 7726-2-RV
Eduardo Mata/Dallas Symphony Orchestra

PORGY & BESS (OPERA——SELECTIONS)

Porgy & Bess (Symphonic Picture) / London 430712-2
Antal Dorati/Detroit Symphony Orchestra

Porgy & Bess (Symphonic Picture) / RCA Victrola 7726-2-RV
Eduardo Mata/Dallas Symphony Orchestra

★ **Rhapsody in Blue**

Rhapsody in Blue / CBS MK39699
Michael Tilson Thomas (piano), Michael Tilson Thomas/Los Angeles Philharmonic Orchestra

Rhapsody in Blue / Philips 411123-2
Misha Dichter (piano), Neville Marriner/Philharmonia Orchestra

Rhapsody in Blue (Solo Piano Version) / Special Music SCD-8000
Norman Krieger (piano)

Rhapsody in Blue (Two-Piano Version) / Pro Arte CDD367

James Anagnoson & Leslie Kinton (pianos)

Don Carlo Gesualdo (1561-1613)

An Italian composer of motets (settings for sacred texts) and madrigals (settings for secular texts). As Ernst Krenek once said, "If Gesualdo had been taken as seriously in his time as he is now, music history would have taken an entirely different course." From the amazing works of Gesualdo's contemporary Lassus, back to the strange smoking songs of Johannes Symonis and Solage in the 1300s (*Ars Magis Subtiliter,* Ensemble PAN, New Albion Records NA 021), extreme chromaticism has always been around, and perhaps it's more realistic to view it as a means of expression for some of our more unusual experiences. But the austere, graceful, often slowly developing and surprisingly changing interior feeling of Gesualdo's work exerts the unnameable fascination of an unknown world. Gesualdo's music and bizarre life are still being admired and debated. Even Igor Stravinsky became a Gesualdo fan and wrote a *Monumentum pro Gesualdo. — "Blue" Gene Tyranny*

MADRIGALS

Madrigals (17 selections) / Harmonia Mundi HMC901268
William Christie/les Arts Florissants

Madrigals, Book 5 / L'Oiseau-Lyre 410128-2
Anthony Rooley/Consort of Musicke

TENEBRAE RESPONSORIES

Complete Responsories, Miserere, and Benedictus / ECM New Series 78118-21215-2
Paul Hillier/Hilliard Ensemble

Orlando Gibbons (1583-1625)

Gibbons was the leading English composer of his generation. He was born in Oxford and held positions as Organist of the Royal Chapel, keyboard player in the privy chamber of the all-important court of Prince Charles, and finally organist at Westminster Abbey. He died early at Canterbury Cathedral while awaiting the arrival of the new Queen Henrietta Maria. Gibbons's lifetime corresponded to the highest point in English music—a time when it dominated the music of the continent as it had never done before and would rarely do again—moreover, he was known for "the best finger of that age." His position among the private musicians of Prince Charles (later King Charles I) helped to inaugurate one of the greatest eras in chamber music that Western music has seen. Together with his colleagues—the composers Alfonso Ferrabosco II, John Coprario, and Thomas Lupo—Gibbons pioneered new scorings and approaches in consort music that would lead to a repertory eclipsed in volume and depth only by the works of the Viennese school. It was presumably due largely to his influence that organ accompaniment became standard in consort works for strings.

Gibbons is also well-known for his sacred choral music, of which he left a substantial volume. He was among the first major English choral composers schooled entirely in the Protestant universe, and his highly polished English anthems are among the finest in the repertory. He is still regarded as one of the great masters of the verse anthem, in which sections for full choir alternate with passages for soloists and organ (or viol consort) accompaniment. His magnificent "Second Service" (in the verse style) continues to be one of the most highly regarded masterpieces in the genre. Gibbons also composed numerous consort songs, both as purely vocal madrigals and as solo songs with viol consort accompaniments. His strongly evocative "Cries of London" is one of the most peculiar and strangely effective consort songs of the period. Gibbons's lifetime saw a huge volume of music composed in England, in exactly the genres he employed. However, the quality of his output in both sacred choral and chamber music allows him to stand head and shoulders above the many fine composers of his generation. His music continues to be widely admired today, while his choral music has been a constant part of the English cathedral repertory. In fact, no less a personage than the pianist Glenn Gould has named Gibbons as his favorite composer. — *Todd McComb*

CHURCH MUSIC (ANTHEMS & SERVICES)

Anthems: Almighty & everlasting God; Blessed are all they; Glorious & powerful God; Lord, grant grace; O Lord, how do my woes increase; Sing unto the Lord; This is the record

of John; We praise Thee, O Father (also see Sheppard) / Calliope CAL9621
David Wulstan/Clerkes of Oxenford

★ **Fantasias for Viol Consort**

Fantasias a 2, 3 & 4; In Nomines; "The Cries of London" / Virgin VC790849-2
Fretwork and Red Byrd

Fantasias a 3 & 4 ("Music for Prince Charles") / Hyperion CDA66395
Peter Holman/Parley of Instruments Baroque Orchestra

Gilbert & Sullivan

MIKADO (OPERETTA)

The Mikado / Sony S2K58889
/D'Oyly Carte Opera Company

PIRATES OF PENZANCE (OPERETTA)

The Pirates of Penzance / Sony S2K58889
D'Oyly Carte Opera Company

Alberto Ginastera (1916-1983)

An Argentine composer of energetic and even ecstatic opera (*Don Rodrigo,* 1964), ballet, chamber, vocal, and choral music. Ginastera exhibits a Bartokian sense of harmony, bright orchestral colors, and gripping melodic and rhythmic gestures. — *"Blue" Gene Tyranny*

CONCERTO FOR PIANO

Piano Concerto #1 / Academy Sound & Vision CDDCA654
Oscar Tarrego (piano), Enrique Batiz/Mexico City Symphony Orchestra

Umberto Giordano (1867-1948)

A modest, genial man who once threatened his librettist with a toy pistol (they both burst out laughing), Giordano is now chiefly known for the marvelous opera *Andrea Chenier* (about the French poet who was both a champion and a victim of the French Revolution) and the opera *Fedora* (about a Russian princess in love with a nihilist). — *"Blue" Gene Tyranny*

ANDREA CHENIER (OPERA)

Andrea Chenier / London 410117-2
Montserrat Caballe (soprano), Luciano Pavarotti (tenor), Nucci, Riccardo Chailly/National Philharmonic & Welsh National Opera Chorus

Andrea Chenier / London 410117-2
Tebaldi, Del Monaco, Bastianini, Gavazzeni/Santa Cecilia Orchestra & Chorus

Mauro Giuliani (1781-1829)

An Italian guitarist and composer of duets, quartets, concertos, sonatas, and études for guitar. — *AMG*

CONCERTOS FOR GUITAR & STRINGS

Guitar Concerto #1, Op. 30 / RCA 5914-2-RC
Kazuhito Yamashita (guitar)/Leos Janacek Chamber Orchestra

Guitar Concertos #1, Op. 30, and #3, Op. 70 / Philips 420780-2
Pepe Romero (guitar), Neville Marriner/Academy of St. Martin-in-the-Fields

MUSIC FOR FLUTE & GUITAR

Gran Duetto Concertante, Op. 52; Grande Serenade, Op. 82; Grand Duo Concertant, Op. 85; Serenade, Op. 127 / Centaur CRC2017
Virginia Sindelar (flute), Richard Schilling (guitar)

Grand Potpourri, Op. 53; Pièces faciles et agreables, Op. 74; Potpourri tire de l'Opera Tancredi, Op. 76; Variations, Op. 81, Grand Potpourri, Op. 126 / BIS BIS-CD-413
Mikael Helasvuo (flute), Jukka Savijoki (guitar)

Alexander Glazunov (1865-1936)

A Russian composer of symphonies, ballet (*Raymonda,* 1897), orchestral, and chamber music. The end of *Symphony no. 4* and the beginning of *Symphony no. 5* are genuine emotional experiences, as is the lovely *Concerto for Violin & Orchestra in A* (1904), but despite having tremendous popularity in his day, much of Glazunov's music now sounds formulistic. He is perhaps best seen as a late Russian romantic in the tradition of Glinka and early Tchaikovsky. —*"Blue" Gene Tyranny*

STRING QUARTETS (2, 4, 7)

String Quartets #2, Op. 10, and #4, Op. 64 / Melodiya MCD173
Shostakovich Quartet

String Quartet #7 in C Major, Op. 107 (w/ Quintet) / Mobile Fidelity Sound Labs MFCD875
Shostakovich Quartet

STRING QUINTET

String Quintet, Op. 39 (w/ Quartet #7) / Mobile Fidelity Sound Labs MFCD875
Shostakovich Quartet

RAYMONDA (BALLET)

Raymonda (Ballet Music), Op. 57 / Chandos CHAN8447
Neeme Jarvi/Scottish National Orchestra
The Seasons (ballet)

The Seasons (Ballet Music), Op. 67 / Chandos CHAN8596
Neeme Jarvi/Scottish National Orchestra

The Seasons (Ballet Music), Op. 67 / Marco Polo 8.223136
Ondrej Lenard/Slovak Radio Symphony Orchestra, Bratislava

★ Symphonies (*4, *5, 7)

Symphony #4, Op. 48, and Symphony #5 ("Heroic"), Op. 55 / Olympia OCD101
Gennadi Rozhdestvensky/USSR Ministry of Culture Symphony Orchestra

Symphony #4, Op. 48, and Symphony #7 ("Pastorale"), Op. 77 / Orfeo C148201A
Neeme Jarvi/Bamberg Symphony Orchestra

Symphony #7 ("Pastorale"), Op. 77 / Melodiya SUCD10-00028
Evgeni Svetlanov/USSR Symphony Orchestra

Reinhold Gliere (1875-1956)

A Russian composer in many forms, including orchestral, chamber, and opera; known for "The Russian Sailor's Dance." —*AMG*

SYMPHONIES (1, 2)

Symphony #1, Op. 8 / Chandos CHAN9160
Edward Downes/BBC Philharmonic Orchestra

Symphony #1, Op. 8 / Marco Polo 8.220349
Stephen Gunzenhauser/Slovak Philharmonic Orchestra, Bratislava

Symphony #2, Op. 25 / Marco Polo 8.223106
Keith Clark/Slovak Radio Symphony Orchestra, Bratislava

Symphony #2, Op. 25 / Chandos CHAN9071
Edward Downes/BBC Philharmonic Orchestra

Mikhail Glinka (1804-1857)

A Russian composer of orchestral pieces (*Kamarinskaya*, 1848), instrumental works, and opera (*A Life for the Tsar*, 1836); influenced "The Mighty Five." —*Mary K. Scanlan*

A LIFE FOR THE TSAR (OPERA)

A Life for the Tsar / Sony S3K46487
Boris Martinovich, Alexandrina Pendachanska, Chris Merritt, Stefania Toczyska, Emil Tchakarov/Sofia Festival Orchestra & National Opera Chorus

RUSSLAN & LUDMILLA OVERTURE

Ruslan & Ludmila Overture / Sheffield Labs CD-25
Lawrence Leighton Smith/Moscow Philharmonic Orchestra

Ruslan & Ludmila Overture / Melodiya SUCD10-00166
Evgeni Svetlanov/USSR Symphony Orchestra

Christoph Willibald Gluck (1714-1787)

IPHIGENIE EN TAURIDE (OPERA)

Iphigenie en Tauride / Philips 416148-2
Diana Montague, John Aler, Thomas Allen, Rene Massis, John Eliot Gardiner/Orchestre de l'Opera de Lyon & Monteverdi Choir

ORFEO ED EURIDICE (OPERA)

Orfeo ed Euridice / Accent ACC48223 / 24

Marianna Kweksilber (soprano), Rene Jacobs (countertenor), Magdalena Falewicz (soprano), Sigiswald Kuijken/La Petite Bande & Collegium Vocale

Johann Gottlieb Goldberg (1727-1756)

German composer for whose patron J.S. Bach wrote his famous set of variations, but also a composer of concertos and keyboard works himself.

CONCERTOS FOR HARPSICHORD

2 Concertos / Dabringhaus & Grimm MD&GL3250
Waldemar Doling (harpsichord), Emil Tabakov/Sofia Soloists Chamber Ensemble

Nicholas Gombert (c.1500-1557)

Gombert was one of the leading composers of his generation, and one of the most technically advanced composers of polyphonic vocal music in Western history. Gombert was born in a village in Flanders, in the vicinity of Lille, now part of France. He later became choir master to the most prestigious court in Europe, that of Emperor Charles V in Spain. His position allowed him to travel throughout the continent with the imperial entourage. Contemporaries suggested that Gombert had been a student of Josquin Desprez, but the details of this possible association are unknown.

Gombert's compositions are entirely vocal, some for ensembles of up to 12 distinct voices. Unlike his Italian contemporaries, who had begun work on a more animated and harmonically oriented idiom, Gombert kept entirely within the domain of strict counterpoint—and in fact seemed to hold the new musical developments of the time in low regard. His contrapuntal language is based on that of Josquin, but taken to the next level of complexity. A substantial volume of Gombert's compositions survive, including masses, a large number of motets, secular chansons, a set of eight magnificats (one in each mode), and various isolated movements. Shortly after his death, Gombert was mourned as the last of the great masters of vocal polyphony. Indeed, his style continued to represent the most advanced development of imitative counterpoint, at least until the elaboration of the fugue in the baroque era. —*Todd McComb*

SACRED CHORAL MUSIC

Mass "Tempore paschali" for 6 Voices; Magnificat Secundi Toni; and Five Motets / Sony SK48249
Paul van Nevel/Huelgas Ensemble

Motets & Magnificats / Kontrapunkt 32038
Bo Holten/Vocal Group Ars Nova

Henryk Gorecki (b. 1933)

SYMPHONY #3 ("SYMPHONY OF SORROWFUL SONGS")

Symphony #3 ("Symphony of Sorrowful Songs") / Olympia OCD313
Stefania Woytowicz (soprano), Jerzy Katlewicz/Polish Radio National Symphony Orchestra

Symphony #3 ("Symphony of Sorrowful Songs") / Nonesuch 979282-2
Dawn Upshaw (soprano), David Zinman/London Sinfonietta

Charles Gounod (1818-1893)

A French composer of the opera *Faust* and sacred choral music. —*AMG*

FAUST (OPERA)

Faust / Philips 420164-2
Kiri Te Kanawa (soprano), Francisco Araiza, Evgeny Nestorenko, Sir Colin Davis/Bavarian Radio Symphony Orchestra & Chorus

Faust / EMI CDS7542282
Cheryl Studer (soprano), Richard Leech, Jose Van Dam, Thomas Hampson, Michel Plasson/Toulouse Capitole Orchestra & Chorus

ROMEO ET JULIETTE (OPERA)

Faust / EMI CDS7542282
Alfredo Kraus, Catherine Malfitano, Jose Van Dam, Gino Quilico, Michel Plasson/Toulouse Capitole Orchestra & Chorus

Enrique Granados (1867-1916)

A Spanish composer of opera, orchestral, and piano music who wrote in the romantic style but incorporated Spanish rhythms and melodic instrumental patterns into his music. "Goyescas" was inspired by the paintings and etchings of Goya. —*Mary K. Scanlan*

★ **Goyescas**

Goyescas / RCA 60408-2-RC
Alicia De Larrocha (piano)

SPANISH DANCES

Danzas Espanolas, Op. 37 / London 414557-2
Alicia De Larrocha (piano)

Edvard Grieg (1843-1907)

A Norwegian composer of folk-inspired works, including incidental music for *Peer Gynt* (1875). Grieg wrote for orchestra, solo piano, and string quartet and composed the *Concerto for Piano & Orchestra in A, op. 16.* Norway's most famous composer, actually of Scottish descent on his father's side, Grieg studied the folk tunes of his country in his youth (although he actually quoted them only once in his works) and studied with Robert Schumann in Leipzig, Germany. The clear mountain beauty of a Scandinavian landscape can be felt in the pure modal harmonies of pieces like the famous *Concerto for Piano in A*, with its melodies varied in inflection but not modulated in pitch. Sustained transparent textures combine with the warmth of a Schumannesque melodic sensibility. —*"Blue" Gene Tyranny*

★ **Concerto for Piano**

Piano Concerto, Op. 16 / CBS MK44899
Murray Perahia (piano), Sir Colin Davis/Bavarian Radio Symphony Orchestra

Piano Concerto, Op. 16 / London 417112-2
Jorges Bolet (piano), Riccardo Chailly/Berlin Radio Symphony Orchestra

Piano Concerto, Op. 16 / Philips 412923-2
Stephen Bishop-Kovakovich (piano), Sir Colin Davis/BBC Symphony Orchestra

LYRIC PIECES FOR PIANO

20 Lyric Pieces (selected) / Deutsche Grammophon 419749-2
Emil Gilels (piano)

Lyric Pieces (complete) / Unicorn Kanchana UKCD2033 / 4 / 5
Peter Katins (piano)

★ **Peer Gynt Suites**

Peer Gynt Suites #1, Op. 46, and #2, Op. 55 / Deutsche Grammophon 410026-2
Herbert von Karajan/Berlin Philharmonic Orchestra

Nicolas de Grigny (1672-1703)

French organist and composer. Grigny composed only one work—for organ, a mass and five hymns to be performed in the standard style of alternation between chant and instrument. However, his organ writing is the most universally admired of the French baroque, due to its complex polyphony and superb balance. —*AMG*

ORGAN MUSIC

Les Hymnes / BNL 112813
Bernard Coudurier (organ)/Ensemble Alternatim

George Frideric Handel (1685-1759)

German-born composer second only to J.S. Bach as the leading composer of the high baroque era. His concertos and sonatas show exceptional melodic gifts, and his contribution to the development of modern oratorios and operas is significant.

ACIS AND GALATEA (ORATORIO)

Oratorio "Acis and Galatea"; Cantata "Look down, harmonious saint" / Hyperion CDA66361 / 2
Claron McFadden (soprano), John Mark Ainsley & Rogers Covey-Crump (tenors), Michael George (bass), Robert King/The King's Consort

ARIAS

Arias for Cuzzoni / Harmonia Mundi HMU907036
Lisa Saffer (soprano), Nicholas McGegan/Philharmonia baroque Orchestra

Arias for Montagnana / Harmonia Mundi HMU907016
David Thomas (bass), Nicholas McGegan/Philharmonia baroque Orchestra

Arias for Senesino / Harmonia Mundi HMU905183
Drew Minter (countertenor), Nicholas McGegan/Philharmonia baroque Orchestra

Various Arias / EMI CDC7491792
Kathleen Battle (soprano), Neville Marriner/Academy of St. Martin-in-the-Fields

CONCERTI GROSSI OP. 3

6 Concerti Grossi, Op. 3, HWV 312-317 / Archiv 413727-2
Trevor Pinnock/The English Concert

6 Concerti Grossi, Op. 3, HWV 312-317 / Hungaroton HCD12463
Janos Rolla/Franz Liszt Chamber Orchestra

6 Concerti Grossi, Op. 3, HWV 312-317 / L'Oiseau-Lyre 421729-2
Christopher Hogwood/Handel & Haydn Society

★ **Concerti Grossi, Op. 6**

4 Concerti Grossi, Op. 6 #1-4, HWV 319-322 / Archiv 410897-2
Trevor Pinnock/The English Concert

4 Concerti Grossi, Op. 6 #5-8, HWV 323-326 / Archiv 410898-2
Trevor Pinnock/The English Concert

4 Concerti Grossi, Op. 6 #9-12, HWV 327-330 / Archiv 410899-2
Trevor Pinnock/The English Concert

4 Concerti Grossi, Op. 6 #1-4, HWV 319-322 / RCA Red Seal 7895-2-RC
Guildhall String Ensemble

4 Concerti Grossi, Op. 6 #5-8, HWV 323-326 / RCA Red Seal 7895-2-RC
Guildhall String Ensemble

4 Concerti Grossi, Op. 6 #9-12, HWV 327-330 / RCA Red Seal 7895-2-RC
Guildhall String Ensemble

12 Concerti Grossi, Op. 6, HWV 319-330 / L'Oiseau-Lyre 436845-2
Christopher Hogwood/Handel & Haydn Society

CONCERTOS FOR ORGAN, OP. 4 & 7

6 Concertos, Op. 4, HWV 289-294 / Archiv 413465-2
Simon Preston (organ), Trevor Pinnock/The English Concert

6 Concertos, Op. 7, HWV 306-311 / Archiv 413468-2
Simon Preston (organ), Trevor Pinnock/The English Concert

12 Concertos, Op. 4 & 7 / Teldec Das Alte Werk 4509-91188-2
Herbert Tachezi, Nikolaus Harnoncourt/Concentus Musicus Wien

CONCERTO FOR ORGAN "CUCKOO AND NIGHTINGALE"

4 Concertos: "Cuckoo and Nightingale,"Op. 4 #1 & 4, and Op. 7 #1 / Archiv 419634-2
Simon Preston (organ), Trevor Pinnock/The English Concert

HARMONIOUS BLACKSMITH FOR HARPSICHORD (ALSO SEE SUITES)

Suite #5 "The Harmonious Blacksmith," HWV 430, etc. / Nonesuch 979037-2
Igor Kipnis (harpsichord)

★ **Messiah (oratorio)**

Messiah (oratorio (complete)) / Telarc CD-80093
Kaaren Erickson, Sylvia McNair, Alfreda Hodgson, Jon Humphrey, Richard Stilwell, Robert Shaw/Atlanta Symphony Orchestra & Chorus

Messiah (oratorio (complete))/ Archiv 423630-2
Arleen Auger, Anne Sofie von Otter, Michael Chance, Howard Crook, Trevor Pinnock/The English Concert & Chorus

Messiah (oratorio (complete)) / London 414396-2
Te Kanawa, Gjevan, Lewis, Howell, Sir Georg Solti/Chicago Symphony Orchestra & Chorus

Messiah (oratorio (complete with alternate movements and choruses))/ Harmonia Mundi HMU 907050.52
Lorraine Hunt, Janet Williams, Patricia Spence, Drew Minter, Jeffrey Thomas, William Parker, Nicholas McGegan and the Philharmonia Baroque Orchestra & U.C. Berkeley Chamber Chorus

Messiah (oratorio (selected arias & choruses)) / Telarc CD-80103
Kaaren Erickson, Sylvia McNair, Alfreda Hodgson, Jon Humphrey, Richard Stilwell, Robert Shaw/Atlanta Symphony Orchestra & Chorus

Messiah (oratorio (selected arias & choruses) / Archiv 427664-2
Arleen Auger, Anne Sofie von Otter, Michael Chance, Howard Crook, Trevor Pinnock/The English Concert & Chorus

OPERAS (FLAVIO, TAMERLANO)

Flavio (opera) / Harmonia Mundi HMC901312.13
Jeffrey Gall, Derik Lee Ragin, Lena Lootens, Bernarda Fink, Rene Jacobs/Ensemble 415

Orlando (opera) / L'Oiseau-Lyre 430845-2
Kirkby, Bowman, Thomas, Auger, Robbin, Christopher Hogwood/Academy of Ancient Music

Tamerlano (opera) / Erato 2292-45408-2
Argenta, Findley, Ragin, Chance, Robson, Schirrer, John Eliot Gardiner/English Baroque Soloists

ROYAL FIREWORKS MUSIC

Royal Fireworks Music (w / Water Music) / L'Oiseau-Lyre 400059-2
Christopher Hogwood/Academy of Ancient Music

Royal Fireworks Music (w/ Holst Suites) / Telarc CD-80038
Fredrick Fennell/Cleveland Symphonic Winds

Royal Fireworks Music (w/ Overtures) / Philips 434154-2
John Eliot Gardiner/English Baroque Soloists
S@2:Solomon (oratorio)

Solomon (oratorio) / Philips 412612-2
Watkinson, Argenta, Hendricks, Rolfe Johnson, John Eliot Gardiner/English Baroque Soloists & Monteverdi Choir

SONATAS FOR FLUTE OR RECORDER & HARPSICHORD, OP. 1

3 Sonatas, Op. 1 #1, 5 & 9; "Halle" Sonatas / Accent ACC9180D
, Barthold Kuijken (flute), Wieland Kuijken (viola da gamba), Robert Kohnen (harpsichord)

3 Sonatas, Op. 1 #2, 4 & 7; Recorder Concerto in F Major / Hungaroton HCD12375
Laszlo Czidra (recorder), Jano Rolla/Liszt Ferenc Chamber Orchestra

SUITES FOR HARPSICHORD

8 Suites #1-8 (Book I), HWV 426-433 / Archiv 427170-2
Colin Tilney (harpsichord)

5 Suites #2, 3 & 5-7 (Book I), HWV 427,428,430-432 / Harmonia Mundi HMC90447
Kenneth Gilbert (harpsichord)

SUSANNA (ORATORIO)

Susanna (oratorio) / Harmonia Mundi HMU907030.32
Lorraine Hunt (soprano), Drew Minter (countertenor), Jill Feldman (soprano), William Parker (baritone), Jeffrey Parker (tenor), David Thomas (bass), Nicholas McGegan/Philharmonia Baroque Orchestra

TRIO SONATAS, OP. 2 & 5

6 Trio Sonatas, Op. 2 / / Harmonia Mundi HMC901379
London Baroque

7 Trio Sonatas, Op. 5 / / Harmonia Mundi HMC901389
London Baroque

★ **Water Music**

3 Suites ("Water Music"), HWV 348-350 / Archiv 410525-2
Simon Standage & Elizabeth Wilcock (violins), Trevor Pinnock/The English Concert

3 Suites ("Water Music"), HWV 348-350 / CBC Enterprises SMCD5032
Mario Bernardi/CBC Vancouver Orchestra

Suite ("Water Music") (selections), HWV 348 / Reference Recordings RR-13CD
Tafelmusik

Howard Hanson (1896-1981)

An American composer who wrote in various forms, including choral, solo piano, and symphonic pieces. Hanson's sweeping orchestrations are among the best of the 30s nationalist style. — *"Blue" Gene Tyranny*

SYMPHONIES (1, 2, 3)

Symphonies #1 ("Nordic"), Op. 21, & #2 ("Romantic"), Op. 30 / Mercury 432008-2
Howard Hanson/Eastman-Rochester Orchestra

Symphony #2 ("Romantic"), Op. 30 / EMI CDC7478502
Leonard Slatkin/Saint Louis Symphony Orchestra

Symphonies #3 & 6 / Delos DE3092
Gerard Schwarz/Seattle Symphony Orchestra

Franz Joseph Haydn (1732-1809)

A renowned and prolific Austrian composer, famous for his many symphonies. Not only are Haydn's works vitally important in the evolution of musical form, they are delightful and inspirational. Haydn was directly responsible for establishing the form of the string quartet, and he perfected the classical symphony, synthesizing a range of emotions and anticipating by many years the work of composers from Beethoven through Schumann. His keyboard sonatas are marvels of invention and surprise and the church masses are joyous and full of energy and rhythmic counterpoint. To quote his friend and admirer Mozart, "There is no one who can do it all—to joke and to terrify, to evoke laughter and profound sentiment—and all equally well, except Joseph Haydn." — *"Blue" Gene Tyranny*

CONCERTOS IN C & D FOR CELLO

Cello Concertos, Hob VIIb:1 & 2 / Philips 420923-2
Heinrich Schiff (cello), Neville Marriner/Academy of St. Martin-in-the-Fields

Cello Concertos, Hob VIIb:1 & 2 / Sony SK36674
Yo-Yo Ma (cello), Jose Luis Garcia/English Chamber Orchestra

Cello Concerto, Hob VIIb:1 (w/ Symphonies) / Delos D / CD3062
Janos Starker (cello), Gerard Schwarz/Scottish Chamber Orchestra

CONCERTOS FOR HORN

2 Horn Concertos, Hob VIId:3 & 4 / Nimbus NIM5010
Michael Thompson (horn), Michael Warren-Green/Philharmonia Orchestra

Horn Concerto, Hob VIId:3 (w/ Trumpet Concerto) / L'Oiseau-Lyre 417610-2
Timothy Brown (horn), Christopher Hogwood/Academy of Ancient Music

CONCERTOS FOR KEYBOARD

Piano Concertos #2-4 & 9 (w/ Sonatas) / Vox Music Group CDX 5017
Ilse von Alpenheim (piano), Antal Dorati/Bamberg Symphony Orchestra

★ **Concerto for Trumpet**

Trumpet Concerto, Hob VIIe:1 (w/ Horn Concertos) / Nimbus NIM5010
John Wallace (trumpet), Michael Warren-Green/Philharmonia Orchestra

Trumpet Concerto, Hob VIIe:1 (w/ Horn Concerto) / L'Oiseau-Lyre 417610-2
Timothy Brown (horn), Christopher Hogwood/Academy of Ancient Music

Trumpet Concerto, Hob VIIe:1 / Philips 420203-2
Hakan Hardenberger (trumpet), Neville Marriner/Academy of St. Martin-in-the-Fields

CONCERTOS FOR VIOLIN

Violin Concertos, Hob VIIa:1, 3 & 4 / Archiv 427316-2
Simon Standage (violin), Trevor Pinnock/The English Concert

THE CREATION (ORATORIO)

The Creation ("Die Schopfung") / Philips 416449-2

Edith Mattias, Aldo Baldwin, Dietrich Fischer-Dieskau, Neville Marriner / Academy & Chorus of St. Martin-in-the-Fields

The Creation ("Die Schopfung") / L'Oiseau-Lyre 417610-2

Emma Kirkby, Anthony Rolfe Johnson, Michael George, Christopher Hogwood/Academy of Ancient Music Orchestra & Choir and Oxford New College Choir

The Creation ("Die Schopfung") / Vox Music Group CDX 5025

Wolfgang Gonnenwein / Orchestra of the Ludwigsburger Schlossfestspiele & South German Madrigal Choir

MASS #10 ("PAUKENMESSE")

Mass in Time of War ("Paukenmesse") / Philips 412734-2

Judith Blegen, Brigette Fassbaender, Leonard Bernstein/Bavarian Radio Symphony Orchestra & Chorus

MASS #11 ("NELSON")

"Nelson" Mass (w/ Vivaldi Gloria) / London Jubilee 421146-2

Vaughan (soprano), Janet Baker (mezzo-soprano), Neville Marriner, Academy of St. Martin-in-the-Fields & Choir of King's College, Cambridge

"Nelson" Mass & Te Deum / Archiv 423097-2

Felicity Lott, Carolyn Watkinson, Trevor Pinnock/The English Concert & Choir

★ **String Quartets, Op. 71, 74, *76 & 77 (76 / 3 "Emperor")**

6 Quartets #54-59 ("Apponyi"), Op. 71 & 74 / Hungaroton HCD12246 / 7-2
Tatrai Quartet

6 Quartets #60-65 ("Erdody"), Op. 76 / Deutsche Grammophon 415867-2
Amadeus Quartet

2 Quartets #66 & 67 ("Lobkowitz"), Op. 77 / Hungaroton HCD11776-2
Tatrai Quartet

2 "Apponyi" Quartets #1 & 2, Op. 71/ Hyperion CDA66065
The Salomon String Quartet

2 "Apponyi" Quartets #3 & 4, Op. 71, and Op. 74 #1 / Hyperion CDA66098
The Salomon String Quartet

2 "Apponyi" Quartets #5 & 6, Op. 74 / Hyperion CDA66124
The Salomon String Quartet

3 Quartets #66 & 67 ("Lobkowitz") Op. 77, and Op. 103 / Hyperion CDA66348
The Salomon String Quartet

THE SEASONS (ORATORIO)

The Seasons ("Die Jahreszeiten") / Archiv 431818-2

Barbara Bonney, Anthony Rolfe Johnson, John Eliot Gardiner/English Baroque Soloists & Monteverdi Choir

The Seasons ("Die Jahreszeiten") / Vox Music Group CDX 5045

Wolfgang Gonnenwein / Orchestra of the Ludwigsburger Schlossfestspiele & South German Madrigal Choir

SONATAS (MISCELLANEOUS) FOR PIANO

6 Early Sonatas: #1-3, 5, 6 & 9 / Partridge 1122-2
Anthony Kooiker (piano)

5 Sonatas: #8, 9, 11, 13 & 16 / Koch Schwann CD310094H1
Christine Faron (fortepiano)

4 Sonatas: #20, 29, 31 & 33 / Hungaroton HCD11618-2
Zoltan Kocsis (piano)

6 Sonatas: #34-38 / Albany TROY045
Lola Odiaga (fortepiano)

6 Sonatas: #39-41, 48, 49 & 51 / Albany TROY062
Lola Odiaga (fortepiano)

3 Sonatas: #50, 54 & 62 / Philips 416365-2
Alfred Brendel (piano)

★ **Symphonies (6-8,*45,88,*94,100,*101,103,*104)**

3 Symphonies: #6 ("Le Matin"), 7 ("Le Midi"), & 8 ("Le Soir") / Archiv 423098-2
Trevor Pinnock/The English Concert

6 Symphonies: #42, 45 ("Farewell"), 46, 47, 51 & 65 / CBS M3K39685
Derek Solomons/L'Estro Armonico

6 Symphonies: #35, 38, 39, 49 ("La Passione") 58 & 59 ("Fire") / CBS M2K37861
Derek Solomons/L'Estro Armonico

3 Symphonies: #70-72 / Hyperion CDA66526
Roy Goodman/Hanover Band

3 Symphonies: #73 ("La Chasse") 74 & 75 / Hyperion CDA66520
Roy Goodman/Hanover Band

3 Symphonies: #76-78 / Hyperion CDA66525
Roy Goodman/Hanover Band

3 "Paris" Symphonies: #82 ("The Bear"), 83 ("The Hen") & 84 ("In Nomine Domini") / Virgin Classics Veritas VC790793-2
Sigiswald Kuijken/Orchestra of the Age of Enlightenment

3 "Paris" Symphonies: #85 ("La Reine de France"), 86 & 87 / Virgin Classics Veritas VC790844-2
Sigiswald Kuijken/Orchestra of the Age of Enlightenment

2 Symphonies: #91 & 92 ("Oxford") / Philips 410390-2
Sir Colin Davis/Concertgebouw Orchestra Amsterdam

2 "London" Symphonies: #94 ("Surprise") & 96 ("Miracle") / L'Oiseau-Lyre 414330-2
Christopher Hogwood/Academy of Ancient Music

12 "London" Symphonies: #93-102 / Deutsche Grammophon 437201-2
Eugen Jochum/London Philharmonic Orchestra

TRIOS FOR FLUTE & STRINGS (VARIOUS)

4 "London" Trios & 2 Divertimentos, Op. 100 / 2,6 / CBS MK37786
Jean-Pierre Rampal (flute), Isaac Stern (violin), Mstislav Rostropovich (cello)

6 Trios (transcribed from baryton trios) / Accent ACC68641D
Kuijken Barthold (flute), Sigiswald Kuijken (violin), Wieland Kuijken (cello)

6 Trios, Op. 38 / Accent ACC47807D
Kuijken Barthold (flute), Sigiswald Kuijken (violin), Wieland Kuijken (cello) .

TRIOS FOR PIANO & STRINGS (VARIOUS)

43 Trios, Divertimentos & Partitas (complete piano trios) / Philips 432061-2
Beaux Arts Trio

3 Trios, Hob XV:12-14 / Harmonia Mundi HMC901277
Patrick Cohen (fortepiano), Erich Hobarth (violin), Christophe Coin (cello)

3 Trios: #16-18, Op. 70, Hob XV:18-20 / Harmonia Mundi HMC901314
Patrick Cohen (fortepiano), Erich Hobarth (violin), Christophe Coin (cello)

3 Trios, Hob XV:35-37 / Harmonia Mundi HMC901400
Patrick Cohen (fortepiano), Erich Hobarth (violin), Christophe Coin (cello)

John Hebden (1712-1765)

CONCERTOS

6 Concertos, Op. 2a / Chandos CHAN8339
Adrian Shepherd/Cantilena

Hildegard von Bingen (1098-1179)

German abbess and mystic, one of the earliest known female composers. Hildegard's musical and literary output is immense, including religious treatises, plays, and "abstract" music. The latter is monophonic, in the style of Gregorian chant, making use of the primary forms of the time: sequence, hymn, etc. Her melodic contours are consistently original; being based on mystical visions, they usually have an ecstatic quality. —*Todd McComb*

★ **Symphoniae**

Responsoria, Antiphons and Sequences / RCA Deutsche Harmonia Mundi Editio Classica 77020-2-RG
Sequentia

Antiphons and Sequences / Hyperion CDA66039
Christopher Page/Gothic Voices

Paul Hindemith (1895-1963)

A German composer whose style combined neo-classicism with modern harmonic conventions and jazz elements. Hindemith's works include opera (*Mathis der Maler*, 1935), ballet, orchestral, choral, and chamber music. Although idealizing an aesthetic of use over beauty (*Gebrauchmusik*) as a younger man, Hindemith's best-known works are appreciated for their warm, rich, even opulent orchestral colors and gestures; a unique multirhythmic sense; and flowing, rapid polyphony. —*"Blue" Gene Tyranny*

★ **Mathis de Maler (symphony)**

Mathis der Maler (symphony) / London 421523-2
Herbert Blomstedt/San Francisco Symphony Orchestra

Mathis der Maler (symphony) / Telarc CD-80195
Yoel Levi/Atlanta Symphony Orchestra

Mathis der Maler (symphony) / Chandos Collect CHAN6549
Jascha Horenstein/London Symphony Orchestra

SYMPHONIC METAMORPHOSIS OF THEMES BY WEBER

Symphonic Metamorphoses on Themes of Carl Maria von Weber / London 421523-2
Herbert Blomstedt/San Francisco Symphony Orchestra

Symphonic Metamorphoses on Themes of Carl Maria von Weber /Telarc CD-80195
Yoel Levi/Atlanta Symphony Orchestra

Gustav Holst (1874-1934)

Of Swedish descent, Holst was one of the best of the English "colorists" (Bliss, Vaughan Williams, and others). He was inspired by world religions (*Rig Veda* of 1908-1912, the beautiful opera *Savitri* of 1908, and *Hymn of Jesus* of 1917), English folk melody (*Somerset Rhapsody for Orchestra*), and transcendental poetry (*Ode to Death on Whitman's Words*, the *Choral Symphony* on a text by Keats, and *Egdon Heath*—one of his best pieces—on an excerpt from a Hardy novel). *The Planets* is his best-known work—dramatic and atmospheric. —*"Blue" Gene Tyranny*

★ **The Planets (suite)**

The Planets, Op. 32 / Telarc CD-80133
Andre Previn/Royal Philharmonic Orchestra

The Planets, Op. 32 / London 417553-2
Charles Dutoit/Montreal Symphony Orchestra

The Planets, Op. 32 / EMI CDM7647482
Sir Adrian Boult/London Philharmonic Orchestra

The Planets, Op. 32 / EMI 7471602
Andre Previn/London Symphony Orchestra

Arthur Honegger (1892-1955)

PACIFIC 231

Symphonic Movement #1 ("Pacific 231") / Erato 2292-45242-2
Charles Dutoit/Bavarian Radio Symphony Orchestra
Symphonies #3-5

Symphonies #3 ("Liturgique") and #5 ("Di tre re") / Erato 2292-45208-2
Charles Dutoit/Bavarian Radio Symphony Orchestra

Symphony #4 ("Deliciae Basilienses") / Erato 2292-45689-2
Charles Munch/Orchestre National de líORTF

Alan Hovhaness (b. 1911)

ARMENIAN RHAPSODIES

Armenian Rhapsody #2 / Crystal CD508
David Amos/Israel Philharmonic Orchestra

Armenian Rhapsody #3 / Crystal CD804
Alan Hovhaness/Royal Philharmonic Orchestra

SYMPHONIES

Symphonies #2 ("Mysterious Mountain"), Op. 132, and ("And God Created Great Whales"), Op. 229 / Delos DE3157
Gerard Schwarz/Seattle Symphony Orchestra

Symphonies #22 ("City of Light"), Op. 236, and #50 ("Mount St. Helens"), Op. 360 / Delos DE3137
Gerard Schwarz/Seattle Symphony Orchestra

Johann Nepomuk Hummel (1778-1837)

An Austrian pianist and composer of piano, chamber, and vocal music, as well as opera and ballet music. A student of Mozart and contemporary of Beethoven, he was much respected in his time for his craftsmanship and melodic gift. —*AMG*

CONCERTOS FOR PIANO

Concerto, Op. 89 / Chandos CHAN8507
Stephen Hough (piano), Bryden Thomson/English Chamber Orchestra

SEPTETS FOR PIANO, WINDS & STRINGS

2 Septets: #1, Op. 74, & #2, ("Military"), Op. 114 / Hyperion CDA66396
Capricorn

SONATAS FOR PIANO

2 Sonatas: #1, Op. 2, #3 & #6, Op. 106 / Arabesque Z6564
Ian Hobson (piano)

2 Sonatas: #2, Op. 13, & #5, Op. 81 / Arabesque Z6565
Ian Hobson (piano)

2 Sonatas: #3, Op. 20, & #4, Op. 38 / Arabesque Z6566
Ian Hobson (piano)

Engelbert Humperdinck (1854-1921)

HANSEL AND GRETEL (OPERA)

Hansel and Gretel / EMI CDS7540222
Anne Sofie van Otter, Barbara Bonney, Andreas Schmidt, Hanna Schwartz, Jeffrey Tate/ Bavarian Radio Symphony Orchestra

Hansel and Gretel / London 421111-2
Fassbaender, Popp, Berry, Hamari, Schlemm, Sir Georg Solti/Vienna Philharmonic Orchestra

Jacques Ibert (1890-1962)

A French composer of songs, operas, chamber music, and ballet music, also *Concerto for Flute & Orchestra* (1934). Ibert's music is full of humor and color and exhibits elements of both impressionism and classicism. —*Mary K. Scanlan*

DIVERTISSEMENT

Divertissement / Academy Sound & Vision LTD CDDCA517
Neville Marriner/Academy of St. Martin-in-the-Fields

Divertissement / Telarc CD-80294
Erich Kunzel/Cincinnati Pops Orchestra

Vincent D'Indy (1851-1931)

SYMPHONY ON A FRENCH MOUNTAIN AIR

Symphony #1 ("Symphony on a French Mountain Air"), Op. 25 / RCA 6805-2-RG
Nicole Henriot-Schweitzer (piano), Charles Munch/Boston Symphony Orchestra

Symphony #1 ("Symphony on a French Mountain Air"), Op. 25 / EMI CDM7639522
Aldo Ciccolini (piano), Serge Baudo/Orchestra of Paris

Heinrich Isaac (c.1450-1517)

Dutch Renaissance composer of vocal music, one of the leading contemporaries of Josquin Desprez. Isaac composed in all the forms of the time, preferring a conservative harmonic idiom, usually based on imitation. He was one of the most prolific composers of parody masses, using such unusual themes as "bass dances." Like many of his contemporaries, Isaac spent extensive time in Italy. He was highly influential in the later development of music in Renaissance Germany. —*Todd McComb*

SACRED CHORAL MUSIC

Mass "de Apostolis" for 6 Voices and Five Motets / Gimell CDGIM023
Peter Phillips/The Tallis Scholars

Charles Ives (1874-1954)

PIANO SONATA (#2 "CONCORD")

Piano Sonata #2 ("Concord, Mass., 1840-1860") / Nonesuch 971337-2
Gilbert Kalish (piano)

Sonata #2 ("Concord, Mass., 1840-1860") / Vox Music Group CDX5089
Nina Deutsch (piano)

★ **Three Places in New England**

Three Places in New England(symphony) / Koch International 3-7025-2
James Sinclair/Orchestra New England

Three Places in New England (symphony)/ Mercury 432755-2
Howard Hanson/Eastman-Rochester Orchestra

Three Places in New England (symphony) / Deutsche Grammophon 423243-2
Michael Tilson Thomas/Boston Symphony Orchestra

SYMPHONIES (1-3)

Symphony #1 in F Major / Chandos CHAN9053
Neeme Jarvi/Detroit Symphony Orchestra

Symphony #1 in F Major / Sony SK44939
Michael Tilson Thomas/Chicago Symphony Orchestra

Symphonies #2 & 3 / Sony SK46440
Michael Tilson Thomas/Concertgebouw Orchestra Amsterdam

Symphony #2 / Deutsche Grammophon 420229-2
Leonard Bernstein/New York Philharmonic Orchestra

Symphony #3 ("The Camp Meeting") / Mercury 432755-2
Howard Hanson/Eastman-Rochester Orchestra

Leos Janacek (1854-1928)

A Czech composer of opera (*Jenufa, 1904)* and orchestral, instrumental, and sacred vocal music utilizing folk elements; employed his own "speech melody" concept based on the Czech language. From an early age, Janacek believed that music should follow the natural rhythms of human speech, animals, and birds. He went on to produce works of a completely original sound that are romantic, delight in the natural, and have an "angular" and even ascetic quality and a rhythmic vitality, all at the same time. His best-known piece is probably the *Sinfonietta*, with its wonderfully tuneful brass writing. Among his many popular and masterly operas are the first, *Jenufa; Katya Kabanova* (1919), with its snow scenes sounding amazingly like contemporary pattern or minimalist music; and *The Makropoulos Affair,* about a 300-year-old woman spurning lovers. His string quartets seem to have no precedents in harmonic sense and development and are astonishing. The profound, even terrifying religiosity of the *Slavonic Mass* is almost indescribable. — *"Blue" Gene Tyranny*

CUNNING LITTLE VIXEN (OPERA)

Cunning Little Vixen / London 417129-2
Popp, Jedlicka, Randova, Sir Charles Mackerras/Vienna Philharmonic Orchestra & State Opera Chorus

Cunning Little Vixen / Supraphon 103471-2
Vaclav Neumann/Czech Philharmonic Orchestra & Opera Chorus

GLAGOLITIC MASS (SLAVONIC MASS)

Glagolitic Mass / Supraphon 103575-2
Soderstrom, Drobkova, Livora, Novak, Sir Charles Mackerras/Czech Philharmonic Orchestra & Opera Chorus

Glagolitic Mass / Telarc CD-80287
Brewer, Simpson, Dent, Roloff, Robert Shaw/Atlanta Symphony Orchestra & Chorus

JENUFA (OPERA)

Jenufa / London 414483-2
Soderstrom, Popp, Randova, Dvorsky, Sir Charles Mackerras/Vienna Philharmonic Orchestra & State Opera Chorus

Jenufa / BIS CD-449 / 50
Behackova, Rysanek, Ochman, Kazaras, Eve Queler/Opera Orchestra of New York

PIANO MUSIC

Sonata ("October 1, 1905," "On an Overgrown Path" and "In the Mists") / RCA 60147-2-RC
Rudolf Firkusny (piano)

Sonata ("October 1, 1905," "On an Overgrown Path" and "In the Mists") / Deutsche Grammophon 429857-2
Rudolf Firkusny (piano)

★ **Quartets (1, 2)**

String Quartets #1 ("Kreutzer Sonata") and #2 ("Intimate Letters")/ Calliope CAL9699
Talich Quartet

String Quartets #1 ("Kreutzer Sonata") and #2 ("Intimate Letters") / Denon C37-7545
Smetana Quartet

String Quartets #1 ("Kreutzer Sonata") and #2 ("Intimate Letters") / Deutsche Grammophon 427669-2
Hagen Quartet

★ **Sinfonietta**

Sinfonietta / London 410138-2
Sir Charles Mackerras/Vienna Philharmonic Orchestra

Sinfonietta / Telarc CD-80174
Andre Previn/Los Angeles Philharmonic Orchestra

Sinfonietta / Supraphon 110282-2
Frantisek Jilek/Brno State Philharmonic Orchestra

Sinfonietta / Virgin VC791506-2
Libor Pesek/Philharmonia Orchestra

Sinfonietta / London 410138-2
Sir Charles Mackerras/Vienna Philharmonic Orchestra

TARAS BULBA

Taras Bulba Rhapsody / Supraphon 110282-2
Frantisek Jilek/Brno State Philharmonic Orchestra

Taras Bulba Rhapsody / Virgin VC791506-2
Libor Pesek/Philharmonia Orchestra

Clement Janequin (c.1475-c.1560)

French composer, primarily of secular songs. Janequin was one of the earliest Renaissance masters to concentrate on chansons, taking the genre to a new degree of vitality and inclusiveness by his use of such extramusical elements as bird song & "cries" of Paris. He was highly influential in the subsequent development of the song as a form of personal expression in France. — *Todd McComb*

SECULAR MUSIC

La Chasse and Other Chansons / Harmonia Mundi 901271
Ensemble Clement Janequin

XIX Chansons Nouvelles, Attaignant / Astree E 7785
Charles Ravier/Ensemble Polyphonique de France

John Jenkins (1592-1678)

Jenkins was an English composer of music for viol consort. He was born in Kent, the son of a carpenter, and spent most of his life as a "house musician" traveling between the various estates of influential patrons. His position was possible due to the intense cultivation of music in private circles in England at that time and the great demand for just the sort of chamber music at which Jenkins was most skilled. Jenkins was also a player of lute and viols and a skilled performer on the strange lyra viol. After the postrevolution reestablishment of the monarchy, Jenkins finally obtained a court appointment late in his life. By this time, the musical world had irrevocably changed, and though he tried to adjust—by learning the violin, and composing fantasia suites that incorporated the latest dance forms—Jenkins's most influential music dates from earlier in his life, when the older forms of fantasia, pavan, and "In Nomine" were still widely practiced. Today, Jenkins is seen as a provincial musician without great influence; however, his consort music presents us with a large body of high-quality compositions that are quickly gaining an audience with the resurgence of viol performance. — *Todd McComb*

CONSORT MUSIC

17 Fantasias a 4 / Thorofon CTH2042
Kolner Violen-Consort

Fantasias, Ayres, Pavans, etc. / Naxos 8.550687
Rose Consort of Viols

Late Consort Music / Hyperion CDA66604
Peter Holman/The Parley of Instruments

Aram Khachaturian (1903-1978)

A Russian composer of orchestral, chamber, choral, piano, and ballet music in the tradition of Russian orientalism, featuring folk idioms and colorful orchestrations. — *Mary K. Scanlan*

CONCERTO FOR PIANO

Piano Concerto / Chandos CHAN8542
Constantine Orbelian (piano), Neeme Jarvi/Scottish National
Orchestra

CONCERTO FOR VIOLIN

Violin Concerto in D Minor / Chandos CHAN8918
Lydia Mordkovitch (violin), Neeme Jarvi/Scottish National
Orchestra

Violin Concerto in D Minor / EMI CDC747087
Itzhak Perlman (violin), Zubin Mehta/Isreal Philharmonic
Orchestra

GAYNE BALLET

Gayane (suite) / Vanguard OVC5010
Vladimir Golschmann/Vienna State Opera Orchestra

Gayane (ballet) (4 movements from Suite #1) / Chandos
CHAN8542 or CHAN8945
Neeme Jarvi/Royal Scottish Orchestra

Zoltan Kodaly (1882-1967)

An Hungarian composer and associate of Bartok who incorporated folk music into his operas, chamber, orchestral, and choral
music. Kodaly was a kind of "national hero" of Hungarian
music—a bearded, quiet man who guided musicians through
WWII after years of being famous for his *Psalmus Hungariscus,*
a large-scale religious work. His style was informed by folk music and traditional church music, heard abundantly in the suite
from his opera *Hary Janos. — "Blue" Gene Tyranny*

HARY JANOS: SUITE

Hary Janos (suite), Op. 15 / Chandos CHAN8877
Neeme Jarvi/Chicago Symphony Orchestra

Hary Janos (suite), Op. 15/ Hungaroton HCD12190-2
Janos Ferencsik/Budapest Philharmonic Orchestra

Hary Janos (suite), Op. 15/ Hungaroton HCD12252-2
Gyorgy Lehel/Budapest Symphony Orchestra

PEACOCK VARIATIONS

15 Variations ("Peacock") / Chandos CHAN8877
Neeme Jarvi/Chicago Symphony Orchestra

SONATA FOR SOLO CELLO

Cello Sonata, Op. 8 / Nonesuch 979074-2
Jerry Grossman (Cello)

Cello Sonata, Op. 8 / Delos D / CD1015
Janos Starker (Cello)

Franz Krommer (Frantisek Kramar) (1759-1831)

A Moravian violinist, conductor, and composer, known for his
fine solo concertos for wind instruments. —*Mary K. Scanlan*

WIND SERENADES

4 Octet-Partitas, Op. 57, 71, 76 & 78 / EMI CDC7543832
Sabine Meyer Wind Ensemble

4 Partitas, Op. 45 / Etcetera KTC1141
Jeroen Weierink /Josef Triebensee Ensemble

WIND CONCERTOS

3 Clarinet Concertos: Op. 35, 36 & 86 / Claves CD50-8602
Thomas Friedli & Anthony Pay (clarinets)/English Chamber
Orchestra

2 Oboe Concertos in F major, Op. 37 & 52 / Hyperion
CDA66411
Sarah Francis (oboe), Howard Shelley/London Mozart Players

Edouard Lalo (1823-1892)

A French composer of chamber and orchestral music, opera, and
ballet. Lalo is most famous for his *Symphonie espagnole* (1875),
the brilliant and colorful prototype of French impressionism,
which used Spain as its subject in such pieces as Chabrier's
España and Debussy's *Iberia.* But the real genius of Lalo lies both
in his extraordinary, wholly original orchestration—which anticipated many of the most beautiful scores of the impressionists
(the teenage Debussy was in fact among the audience for the ballet *Namouna* and had to be ejected from the house for defending
it to a partially hostile audience)—and in his synthesis of

Wagnerian harmony and French melodic grace in such works as
his masterpiece, the opera *Le Roi d'Ys* (based on an ancient
Breton story), and in *Namouna. — "Blue" Gene Tyranny*

CONCERTO FOR CELLO

Cello Concerto in D Minor / CBS MK35848
Yo-Yo Ma (cello), Lorin Maazel/National Orchestra of France

Cello Concerto in D Minor / Vox Music Group PVT7203
Laszlo Varga (cello), Siegfried Kohler/Stuttgart Philharmonic
Orchestra

SYMPHONY IN G

Symphony in G Minor / Academy Sound & Vision LTD CD-
DCA709
Yondani Butt/Royal Philharmonic Orchestra

SYMPHONIE ESPAGNOLE

Symphonie Espagnole, Op. 21 / EMI CDC7473182
Anne-Sophie Mutter (violin), Seiji Ozawa/National Orchestra of
France

Pierre de La Rue (c.1460-1518)

La Rue was a Franco-Flemish master of vocal polyphony, and a
highly regarded composer in his native Flanders. La Rue spent
some years in Italy, before returning to Flanders in order to begin
his main compositional output. He served consecutively as singer
in the Imperial Chapel of Maximilian, the Chapel of Philippe le
Beau, and finally as court favorite of Margaret of Austria. La Rue's
output consists entirely of vocal music: masses, motets and chansons. Though he was a younger contemporary of Josquin
Desprez, his style is more properly a continuation of that of
Ockeghem, with its varied technical resources, long finely-spun
melodies, and sonorous lines. La Rue's music also displays an unusual rhythmic vitality. His magnificently dark Requiem and intricate "Missa l'Homme arme" (No. 1) are especially admired today. —*Todd McComb*

★ Requiem

Masses "Pro Defunctis" and "L'homme arme" / Harmonia
Mundi HMC901296
Ensemble Clement Janequin

Mass "Pro Defunctis" (also see Josquin Des Prez) / Amon Ra
CD-SAR24
James Wood/New London Chamber Choir

Orlandus Lassus (1530-1594)

Prolific Franco-Flemish composer of sacred works in most forms
as well as much secular music. His *Prophetiae Sibyllarum,* one of
the most unusual and innovative works of the 15th century, is
one of those trail-blazing compositions that could, potentially,
have changed the course of music, had it been better known in
his lifetime. It was discovered only after his death (by his sons,
who were settling his estate). As the titles of the pieces indicate
("Missa Osculetur Me," "Salve Regina," and "Regina Coeli") these
are choral settings of prophetic statements (often parenthetical, in
abbreviated sentences with definite pronouns). The music captures the tone of the sybil-oracle through devices like the graphic
musical arrangement of the text words, unusual connections accomplished through the musical arrangements of the words, and
extremely strange chromaticism within a predominantly chordal
context, which was a totally new form for that time. By contrast,
his Moresken, or morescas (Moorish dances), were the popular
music of the day—humorous, with word plays and mixtures of
languages, including gibberish. They are still very entertaining
and funny, even today. — *"Blue" Gene Tyranny*

★ Madrigals

**"Lagrime si San Pietro" 20 Sacred Madrigals & Motet for 7
Voices** / Sony SK53373
Paul van Nevel/Huelgas Ensemble

★ Motets

**Magnificat "Ecco ch'io lasso il core" and 15 Motets for 3, 4, 5,
6 & 8 Voices** / Thorofon CTH2103
Detlef Bratschke/Orlando di Lasso Ensemble Hannover

**Te Deum; Magnificat "Praeter rerum seriem"; and 11 Motets
for 3, 4, 5 & 6 Voices** / EMI CDC7491572
The King's Singers

Motet "Infelix ego" and Masses "Entre vous filles" & "Susanne un jour" / Naxos 8.550842
SUMMERLY, Jeremy/Oxford Camerata

REQUIEM

Mass "Pro Defunctis" for 5 Voices; Magnificat "Praeter rerum seriem" for 6 Voices; and Three Motets / RCA Deutsche Harmonia Mundi Editio Classica 77066-2-RG
Bruno Turner/Pro Cantione Antiqua

William Lawes (1602-1645)

William Lawes was, with his brother Henry, a court musician to Charles I. He enjoyed great favor and friendship with the king, and when the king moved the court to Oxford, William followed and was made a commissary in the king's personal life guards. He was shot and killed at Chester while riding with the king, whose troops were attempting to free a garrison there. He was remembered by the king as the "Father of Musick," and his portrait as a cavalier hangs in the Faculty of Music at Oxford. His work consists of instrumental, vocal, and stage works, and he was the most important English composer of stage music prior to Purcell. None of his works was published in his lifetime, but his influence on other composers of his day as well as those who followed was considerable. The rise of Purcell ultimately overshadowed Lawes's work, but he still maintains an important position in the history of mid-17th-century English music. —Lynn Vought

CHAMBER MUSIC

Consort Setts in 5 and 6 Parts "For ye Violls" / Virgin VC759021-2
Fretwork

8 Sonatas for Violin, Bass Viol & Organ / Harmonia Mundi HMC901493
London Baroque

8 Fantasia Suites for Two Violins, Bass Viol & Organ / Harmonia Mundi HMC901423
London Baroque

Jean Marie Leclair (1697-1764)

French composer and violinist, famous for virtuoso string technique that founded the French school of violin playing. Leclair composed numerous chamber works and concertos with violins, adapting the style of Corelli & Vivaldi to the French lyric taste. He also composed in other forms, such as opera. —AMG

CONCERTOS FOR VIOLIN

4 Concertos: Op. 7 #1-3 & 5 / Adda 581040
Daniel Cuiller (violin)/Ensemble Stradivaria

4 Concertos: Op. 7 #4 and Op. 10 #1, 2 & 6 / Adda 581294
Daniel Cuiller (violin)/Ensemble Stradivaria

SONATAS OP. 1, 2, 5 & 9

4 Sonatas, Op. 1 #2 & 5, and Op. 2 #1 & 3 / Accent ACC58435D
Barthold Kuijken (flute), Wieland Kuijken (viola da gamba), Robert Kohnen (harpsichord)

5 Sonatas, Op. 1 #6, Op. 2 #8 & 11, and Op. 9 #2 & 7 / Accent ACC58436D
Barthold Kuijken (flute), Wieland Kuijken (viola da gamba), Robert Kohnen (harpsichord)

6 Sonatas, Op. 3 / Cybella CY875
Dominique D'Arco & Raymond D'Arco (violins)

6 Trio Sonatas, Op. 4 / Chandos Chaconne CHAN0536
Purcell Quartet

3 Sonatas: Op. 5 #6, ("La Tombeau") and Op. 9 #7 & 9 / Academy Sound & Vision LTD CDGAU106R
Monica Huggett (violin), Sarah Cunningham (viola da gamba), Mitzi Meyerson (harpsichord)

6 Overtures & Trio Sonatas, Op. 13 / Chandos Chaconne CHAN0542
Purcell Quartet

Franz Lehar (1870-1948)

Lehar was the leading composer of operetta in the 20th century and played a great role in its revival as a form of international entertainment. He was educated in music at Sternberg and played

horn and violin in various military and civilian organizations. After completing his military service, he began conducting and producing his own operettas at theatres in Vienna. In 1905 he set the libretto for Die lustige Witwe, which enjoyed the greatest success in operetta history. Lehar has been compared to J. Strauss II because of his ability to make melodies that sounded right but were unconventional in their construction. He incorporated social dance rhythms into his work and made special use of a gentle waltz in his pieces. —Lynn Vought

MERRY WIDOW (OPERA)

Die lustige Witwe / EMI CDS7471782
Elisabeth Schwarzkopf, Hanny Steffek, Nicolai Gedda, Josef Knapp, Eberhard Wachter, Lovro von Matacic/Philharmonia Orchestra & Chorus

Die lustige Witwe / Denon DC-8103 / 4
Irosch, Koller, Papouschek, Minich, Prikopa, Huemer, Ruzicka, Rudolf Bibl/Vienna Volksoper Orchestra & Chorus

Ruggero Leoncavallo (1857-1919)

Leoncavallo, an Italian, started as a staunch Wagnerite, his style gradually evolving to the Italian verismo (realism) movement in opera. He wrote many operas, but was never able to duplicate the success of Pagliacci. —Mary K. Scanlan

PAGLIACCI (OPERA)

Pagliacci / EMI CDC7495032
Jussi Bjorling, Victoria de los Angeles, Leonard Warren, Robert Merrill, Renato Cellini/RCA Victor Orchestra, Robert Shaw Chorale & Columbus Boychoir

Pagliacci / EMI CDS7479812
Maria Callas, Giuseppe di Stefano, Rolando Panerai, Tito Gobbi, Tullio Serafin/Teatro alla Scala di Milano Orchestra & Chorus

Franz Liszt (1811-1886)

A Hungarian composer and virtuoso pianist. A major musical sensation of his time, Liszt was influential as a composer of difficult music, primarily for the keyboard, but also of orchestral, chamber, operatic, and vocal music; known for the Hungarian Rhapsodies. Liszt was not only the greatest pianist of his age—revolutionizing piano technique (in such works as the two Concertos for Piano & Orchestra, the Sonata for Piano in B, and the Transcendental Etudes) and giving the first complete "piano recital" in a full evening—but he also created the one-movement symphonic form and an advanced harmonic palette that anticipated by many years the harmonic language of Debussy, Bartok, and Schoenberg. In addition, he invented the compositional technique of the "transformation of themes," in which all the motifs in a work are derived from a single idea—anticipating Wagner's "leitmotiv" and Schoenberg's use of one tone-row for an entire piece (as in Moses und Aron.) —"Blue" Gene Tyranny

ANNEES DE PELERINAGE (1ST, 2ND & 3RD YEARS)

Annees de Pelerinage, First, Second and Third Year (complete) / Vox Music Group CD3X3004
Jerome Rose (piano)

Annees de Pelerinage, First Year: Switzerland, S. 160 / Deutsche Grammophon 415670-2
Daniel Barenboim (piano)

Annees de Pelerinage, Second Year: Italy "Sonetto #47, 104 & 123 del Petrarca," S. 161 / Delos D / CD3022
John Browning (piano)

Annees de Pelerinage, Third Year, S. 163 / Philips 420174-2
Zoltan Kocsis (piano)

Annees de Pelerinage (selections) / London 425689-2
Jorges Bolet (piano)

★ Concertos for Piano (*1, 2)

Piano Concertos #1, S. 124, and #2, S. 125 / Mercury Living Presence 412006-2
Byron Janis (piano), Kirill Kondrashin & Gennady Rozhdestvensky/Moscow Philharmonic Orchestra & Moscow Radio Symphony Orchestra

Piano Concertos #1, S. 124, and #2, S. 125 / Deutsche Grammophon 423571-2
Krystian Zimerman (piano), Seiji Ozawa/Boston Symphony Orchestra

Piano Concertos #1, S. 124, and #2, S. 125 / Philips 412006-2
Sviatoslav Richter (piano), Kirill Kondrashin/London Symphony Orchestra

★ Hungarian Rhapsodies

19 Hungarian Rhapsodies, S. 244 (complete) / Deutsche Grammophon 423925-2
Roberto Szidon (Piano)

19 Hungarian Rhapsodies, S. 244 (complete) / Philips 416463-2
Misha Dichter (Piano)

6 "Hungarian" Rhapsodies (Orchestrations of #2, 5, 6, 9, 12 & 14), S. 359 / Mercury Living Presence 432015-2
Antal Dorati/London Symphony Orchestra

6 "Hungarian" Rhapsodies (Orchestrations of #2, 5, 6, 9, 12 & 14), S. 359 / EMI CDM7690112
Willi Boskovsky/Philharmonia Hungarica

MEPHISTO WALTZ

Mephisto Waltz #1, S. 514 / Reference Recordings RR-25CD
Minoru Nojima (piano)

Mephisto Waltz #1, S. 514 / Denon 32C37-7574
Ranki (piano)

★ Les Preludes

Symphonic Poem #3 ("Les Preludes"), S. 97 / Deutsche Grammophon 427222-2 or 415967-2
Herbert von Karajan/Berlin Philharmonic Orchestra

Symphonic Poem #3 ("Les Preludes"), S. 97 / Chesky CD53
Sir Adrian Boult/New Symphony Orchestra of London

Symphonic Poem #3 ("Les Preludes"), S. 97 / Sony SMK47572
Leonard Bernstein/New York Philharmonic Orchestra

★ Sonata in B for Piano

Sonata in B Minor, S. 178 / Philips 410040-2
Alfred Brendel (piano)

Sonata in B Minor, S. 178 / Delos D / CD3022
John Browning (piano)

Sonata in B Minor, S. 178 / Reference Recordings RR-25CD
Minoru Nojima (piano)

TOTENTANZ

Totentanz, S. 126 / London 414079-2 or 430736-2
Jorges Bolet (piano), Ivan Fischer/London Symphony Orchestra

Totentanz, S. 126 / Deutsche Grammophon 423571-2
Krystian Zimerman (piano), Seiji Ozawa/Boston Symphony Orchestra

★ Transcendental Etudes

12 Transcendental Etudes, S. 139 / MCA MCAD-25890
Janice Weber (piano)

12 Transcendental Etudes, S. 139 / Philips 432305-2 or 416458-2
Claudio Arrau (piano)

12 Transcendental Etudes, S. 139 / London 414601-2
Jorges Bolet (piano)

Pietro Antonio Locatelli (1695-1764

An important Italian composer of violin sonatas and concertos. As a violinist, his feats in double stops and changes in tunings are said to have influenced Paganini. —*Mary K. Scanlan*

CONCERTOS FOR VIOLIN

12 Violin Concertos, Op. 3 ("L'Arte del Violino") / Hyperion CDA66721 / 3
Elizabeth Wallfisch (violin), Nicholas Kraemer/The Raglan Baroque Players

6 Concertos, Op. 7 / Adda 581118
Dr. Gilbert Bezzina (violin)/Baroque Ensemble of Nice

SONATAS FOR FLUTE

12 Sonatas, Op. 2 / L'Oiseau-Lyre 436191-2
Stephen Preston (flute), Anthony Pleeth (cello), Christopher Hogwood (harpsichord)

SONATAS FOR VIOLIN

4 Sonatas, Op. 6 #2, 6, 11 & 12, and Capriccio "Prova del'Intonatione" / Hyperion CDA66363
Elizabeth Wallfisch (violin)/The Locatelli Trio

Matthew Locke (1621-1677)

English composer of chamber music, organ music, and anthems. Locke was the most important English composer of chamber music between William Lawes and Henry Purcell, using both the new violin and the older viol. His various suites and anthems are also highly regarded. —*AMG*

ANTHEMS

Anthems: Descende coelo; How doth the city; O be joyful; Audi Domine; Jesu auctor clementie; Super flumina Babylonis; Be thou exalted Lord; Lord, let me know my end / Hyperion CDA66373
Edward Higginbottom / Choir of New College, Oxford & The Parley of Instruments

CHAMBER MUSIC

CONSORTS OF FOWER PARTS / ASTREE E8519
Jordi Savall/Hesperion XX

Jean Baptiste Loeillet (1680-1730)

SONATAS FOR RECORDER (OR OBOE) & HARPSICHORD

7 Sonatas, Op. 3 #1-7 / Pavane ADW7235
Jacques Vandeville (oboe), Michele Delfosse (harpsichord)

Jean Baptiste Lully (1632-1687)

French composer of operas, sacred vocal music, and harpsichord music. Lully was the most important figure in the French musical establishment during his lifetime, influencing the future course of French music for more than a hundred years. —*AMG*

ATYS (OPERA)

Atys (opera) / Harmonia Mundi HMA1901316.18
Mey, Laurens, Mellon, Gardeil, William Christie/Les Arts Florissants Orchestra & Choir

Witold Lutoslawski (b. 1913)

CHAINS

Chain 2 / Deutsche Grammophon 423696-2
Anne-Sphie Mutter (violin), Philip Moll (piano), Witold Lutoslawski/BBC Symphony Orchestra

Chain 3 / Deutsche Grammophon 431664-2
Krystian Zimerman (piano), Witold Lutoslawski/BBC Symphony Orchestra

CONCERTO FOR CELLO

Cello Concerto / Philips 416817-2
Heinrich Schiff (cello), Witold Lutoslawski/Bavarian Radio Symphony Orchestra

STRING QUARTET

String Quartet / Deutsche Grammophon 413686-2
Hagen Quartet

String Quartet / Disques Montaigne 789007
Arditti Quartet

★ Symphony #3

Symphony #3 / CBS M2K42271
Esa-Pekka Salonen/Los Angeles Philharmonic Orchestra

Symphony #3 / Philips 416387-2
Witold Lutoslawski/Berlin Philharmonic Orchestra

Edward Macdowell (1860-1908)

America's best-known 19th-century composer and pianist and the first to achieve international recognition. Macdowell's compositional style is strongly rooted in the German romantic tradition. —*Mary K. Scanlan*

CONCERTOS FOR PIANO

Piano Concertos #1 in A Minor, Op. 15, and #2 in D Minor, Op. 23 / Olympia OCD353
Donna Amato (piano), Paul Freeman/London Philharmonic Orchestra

Piano Concertos #1 in A Minor, Op. 15, and #2 in D Minor, Op. 23 / Centaur
T. Tirano (piano), V. Kazandjiev/Bulgarian Symphony Orchestra

Guillaume de Machaut (1300-1377)

A French composer and important figure in the French Ars Nova whose works include sacred and secular vocal music, notably *Messe de Notre Dame*. As the great synthesizer and inventor of contrapuntal techniques in the 1300s, Machaut composed works that are wonders of technique and lyricism. Especially notable: the lovely isorhythmic motets ("De bon espoir"; "Puisque la douce rouse"; "Speravi"), where all three texts are sung at the same time; the glorious rhythmic inventions of the *Messe de Notre Dame;* and the rondeau "Ma fin est mon commencement" ("My end is my beginning"). — *"Blue" Gene Tyranny*

★ Notre-Dame Mass

Messe de Notre Dame for 4 Voices; Le Lai de la Fonteinne; and Rondeau "Ma fin est mon commencement" / Hyperion CDA66358
Paul Hillier/Hilliard Ensemble

Messe de Notre Dame for 4 Voices / Harmonic 8931
Dominique Vellard/Ensemble Gilles Binchois

★ Chansons

The Mirror of Narcissus: Ballades, Rondeaux, Motets, etc. / Hyperion CDA66087
Christopher Page/Gothic Voices

Remede de Fortune / New Albion 068
Ensemble Project Ars Nova

Gustav Mahler (1860-1911)

An Austrian conductor and composer of symphonies and lieder cycles whose most notable works include *Das Lied von der Erde* (1909) and *Symphony no. 9* (1909). Mahler was known for the length, depth, and painful emotions of his works. He loved nature and life and, based on early childhood experiences, feared death (family deaths, a suicide, and a brutal rape he witnessed). This duality appears in almost all his compositions, especially in the *Kindertotenlieder* ("Songs on the Deaths of Children"), which are actually about the loss of an innocent view of life. Mahler's orchestral music is clear, complex, and full of musical imagery, from the heavenly to the banal (the family lived near a military barracks, so march tunes sometimes appear; an argument was associated with the sound of a hurdy-gurdy outside the window). The "program" in the incredible symphonies is therefore that of personal tragedy and hope projected onto a universal scale. The traumas of the 20th century are expressed in the *Symphony no. 9* (especially the "Adagio"); the elusiveness of beauty and its loss among harshness and modern tragedies are the subjects of the first and fifth symphonies. Mahler discovered the verbal expression of this auditory imagery in poems translated from the Chinese of the T'ang dynasty; *Das Lied von der Erde* ("The Song of the Earth") was the musical result, expressing the transience of all things in a mixture of warmth and severe beauty. — *"Blue" Gene Tyranny*

KINDERTOTENLIEDER

Kindertotenlieder / Deutsche Grammophon 427697-2
Thomas Hampson (baritone), Leonard Bernstein/Vienna Philharmonic Orchestra

Kindertotenlieder / EMI CDC7477932
Janet Baker (soprano), John Barbarolli/Halle Orchestra

★ Das Lied von der Erde

The Song of The Earth / Deutsche Grammophon 413459-2
Brigitte Fassbaender (mezzo-soprano), Francisco Araiza (tenor), Carlo Maria Giulini/Berlin Philharmonic Orchestra

The Song of The Earth / EMI CDC7472312
Christa Ludwig (mezzo-soprano), Fritz Wunderlich (tenor), otto Klemperer/Philharmonia Orchestra

The Song of The Earth / RCA Gold Seal 60178-2-RG
Maureen Forrester (contralto), Richard Lewis (tenor), Fritz Reiner/Chicago Symphony Orchestra

★ Symphonies

Symphony # 1 ("Titan" (original version)) / Harmonia Mundi HMU907118
James Judd/Florida Philharmonic Orchestra

Symphony # 1 ("Titan") / London 411731-2
Sir George Solti/Chicago Symphony Orchestra

Symphony # 1 ("Titan") / Denon 33C37-7537
Eliahu Inbal/Frankfurt Radio Symphony Orchestra

Symphony # 2 ("Resurrection") / Telarc CD-80081 / 2
Kathleen Battle (soprano), Maureen Forrester (contralto), Leonard Slatkin/St. Louis Symphony Orchestra & Chorus

Symphony # 2 ("Resurrection") / Deutsche Grammophon 423395-2
Barbara Hendricks (soprano), Christa Ludwig (contralto), Leonard Bernstein/New York Philharmonic Orchestra

Symphony # 3 / Unicorn-Kanchana UKCD2006 / 7
Norma Procter (contralto), Jasha Horenstein/London Symphony Orchestra & Ambrosian Singers

Symphony # 3 / Denon C37-7828 / 29
Doris Soffel (mezzo-soprano), Eliahu Inbal/Frankfurt Radio Symphony Orchestra

Symphony # 4 / Philips 412119-2
Roberta Alexander (soprano), Bernard Haitink/Concertgebouw Orchestra Amsterdam

Symphony # 4 / Denon 33C37-7952-EX
Helen Donath (soprano), Eliahu Inbal/Frankfurt Radio Symphony Orchestra

Symphony # 5 / Denon 33CO-1088-EX
Eliahu Inbal/Frankfurt Radio Symphony Orchestra

Symphony # 5 / Deutsche Grammophon 423608-2
Leonard Bernstein/Vienna Philharmonic Orchestra

Symphony # 5 / RCA RCD1-5453
James Levine/Philadephia Orchestra

Symphony # 6 ("Tragic") / London 414674-2
Sir Georg Solti/Chicago Symphony Orchestra

Symphony # 6 ("Tragic") / Deutsche Grammophon 427697-2
Leonard Bernstein/Vienna Philharmonic Orchestra

Symphony # 7 in E Minor / Deutsche Grammophon 413773-2
Claudio Abbado/Chicago Symphony Orchestra

Symphony # 7 in E Minor / Deutsche Grammophon 419211-2
Leonard Bernstein/Vienna Philharmonic Orchestra

Symphony # 8 ("Symphony of a Thousand") / London 414493-2
Soloists, Sir Gerog Solti/Chicago Symphony Orchestra & Vienna State Opera Chorus & Singverein

Symphony # 8 ("Symphony of a Thousand") / EMI CDS7476258
Soloists, Klaus Tennstedt/London Philharmonic Orchestra & Chorus

Symphony # 9 in D Major / Sony SM3K47585
Leonard Bernstein/New York Philharmonic Orchestra

Symphony # 9 in D Major / Deutsche Grammophon 419208-2
Leonard Bernstein/Concertgebouw Orchestra Amsterdam

Symphony # 9 in D Major / Deutsche Grammophon 410726-2
Herbert von Karajan/Berlin Philharmonic Orchestra

Symphony #10 (Adagio) in F Sharp Major / Sony SM3K47585
Leonard Bernstein/New York Philharmonic Orchestra

Symphony #10 (completed by Cooke) in F Sharp Major / EMI CDC7544062
Simon Rattle/Bournemouth Symphony Orchestra

Francesco Manfredini (1684-1762)

CHRISTMAS CONCERTO

Concerto Grosso in C Major, Op. 3 #12 ("Christmas Concerto") / Novalis 150004-2
Thomas Furi/Camerata Bern

Marin Marais (1656-1728)

French composer and bass viol player. Marais composed much of the finest viol music of the era, as well as trio sonatas that are considered the prototype of the form. Marais also wrote four operas and various dance pieces. He has become somewhat better known due to the movie made about his life, *Tous les matins du monde* (*All the Mornings of the World*). — *AMG*

SUITES & PIECES FOR VIOLA DA GAMBA

Pieces de Viole Book I (1686), 2 Suites & Tombeau de Mr. Sainte-Colombe / RCA Deutsche Harmonia Mundi 77146-2-RC

Kenneth Slowik & Jaap ter Linden (viola da gambas), Konrad Junghanel (lute)/Smithsonian Chamber Players

Pieces de Viole Book I (1686) 2 Suites & Chaconne / Astree E7769
Jordi Savall (viola da gamba), Anne Gallet (harpsichord), Hopkinson Smith (lute)

Pieces de Viole Book II (1701), Suite, Les Voix Humaines, and Folies d'Espagne / Astree E7770
Jordi Savall (viola da gamba), Ton Koopman (harpsichord), Hopkinson Smith (lute)

Pieces de Viole Book III (1711) 3 Suites / Astree E8761
Jordi Savall (viola da gamba), Ton Koopman (harpsichord), Hopkinson Smith (lute)

Pieces de Viole Book IV (1717), Suite d'un gout etranger / Astree E7727
Jordi Savall (viola da gamba), Ton Koopman (harpsichord), Hopkinson Smith (lute))

Pieces de Viole Book V (1725), 2 Suites / Astree E7708
Jordi Savall (viola da gamba), Ton Koopman (harpsichord), Hopkinson Smith (lute), Jean-Michel Damian (recitation)

Pieces de Viole Book V (1725) 2 Suites / Accent ACC78744D
Wieland Kuijken & Kaori Uemura (viola da gambas), Robert Kohnen (harpsichord)

14 Pieces en Trio, Suite, and Folies d'Espagne / Hyperion CDA66310
Purcell Quartet

6 Suites / Teldec Das Alte Werk 9031-77617-2
Kees Boeke & Walter van Hauwe (recorders), Wouter Moller (cello), Robert van Asperen (harpsichord)/Quadro Hotteterre

Alessandro Marcello (1669-1747)

CONCERTO FOR OBOE
Concerto in D Minor / Philips 420189-2
Heinz Holliger (oboe)/I Musici

CONCERTOS "LA CETRA"
6 Concertos "La Cetra" / Archiv 427137-2
Heinz Holliger & Louise Pellerin (oboes)/Thomas Furi/Camerata Bern

Pietro Mascagni (1863-1945)

Mascagni's masterpiece, *Cavalleria Rusticana*, must have been a breath of fresh air at the turn of the century to operagoers who for years had heard only impressionism, romanticism, and Wagnerianism. Its realistic portrayal of a Sicilian love tryst and murder is compact, direct, and underscored with music of great warmth and scenic orchestration. — *"Blue" Gene Tyranny*

CAVALLERIA RUSTICANA (OPERA)
Cavalleria Rusticana / Deutsche Grammophon 429568-2
Agnes Baltsa, Placido Domingo, Vera Baniewicz, Juan Pons, Susanne Metzer, Giuseppe Sinopoli/Philharmonia Orchestra & Chorus of the Royal Opera House, Covent Garden

Cavalleria Rusticana / EMI CDS7479812
Maria Callas, Giuseppe di Stefano, Rolando Panerai, Tito Gobbi, Tullio Serafin/Teatro alla Scala di Milano Orchestra & Chorus

Jules Massenet (1842-1912)

A French composer of opera, ballet, and other dramatic music, plus choral, vocal, and instrumental music. Fluid melodies, bright and rich orchestration, and lightly emotional aesthetics characterize much of Massenet's appealing output, such as the highly enjoyable and tuneful ballet *Le Cid* and the portrait of the "amoureuse" in the opera *Manon*. Massenet's harmonic writing influenced the young Debussy. In a way, Massenet is like Mascagni in presenting what is imagined to be basic in the "internal life" of a national character (at least for those times). — *"Blue" Gene Tyranny*

LE CID (BALLET SUITE)
Le Cid (ballet suite) / Naxos 8.550086
Keith Clark/Slovak Radio Symphony Orchestra, Bratislava

OPERAS (ESCLARMONDE, MANON, WERTHER)
Esclarmonde / London 425651-2

Joan Sutherland, Aragall, Tourangeau, Richard Bonynge/National Philharmonic Orchestra & John Alldis Choir

Manon / EMI CMS7635492
Victoria de los Angeles, Henri Legay, Michel Dens, Pierre Monteux/Theatre National de l'Opera-Comique Orchestra & Chorus

Werther / Philips 416654-2
Jose Carreras, Frederica von Stade, Thomas Allen, Sir Colin Davis/Orchestra of the Royal Opera House, Covent Garden

Bohuslav Martinu (1890-1959)

Martinu managed to become not only the greatest Czech composer of his generation but also a major international figure, known especially for his concerti and chamber music. His work tends to command attention from its opening bars. Its rhythmic vitality and pronounced lyricism recall the styles of both Dvorak and Stravinsky.

Martinu began as a follower of Debussy, a rather eccentric choice in the Prague of that time—the major figures having been Dvorak and Richard Strauss. He moved to Paris and became part of the avant-garde there. He experimented with jazz, a Bartokian rhapsodic style, and neoclassic fun-and-games in the manner of Les Six. He comes more and more under the influence of Stravinsky, but unlike many others becomes less like Stravinsky and more Czech. Perhaps he saw the relation of Russian folk music to Stravinsky's highly sophisticated and knowing musical approach and figured out his artistic salvation. Whatever, Czech folk influences become subject to a neoclassic musical view.

During World War II, Martinu fled to the United States. Thereafter, his work opened up emotionally, without losing its considerable craft. He became a major 20th-century symphonist, writing four works in this genre during the war (he ended up with six). The postwar period renewed his interest in vocal music. It includes such pieces as *The Prophecy of Isaiah* and *The Epic of Gilgamesh* and culminates in his opera on Kazantzakis's *The Greek Passion*. The two major orchestral works of this last phase are his sixth symphony and *Three Frescoes of Piero della Francesca*. —*Steven Schwartz*

CONCERTOS
Oboe Concerto / Claves CD50-9018
Ingo Goritzki (oboe), Wojciech Rajski/Polish Chamber Philharmonic

Cello Concertos #1 & 2 / Supraphon 33C37-7868
Angelica May (cello), Vaclav Neumann/Czech Philharmonic Orchestra

Piano Concertos #1-5 & Concertino / Supraphon 111313-2
Emil Leichner (piano)/Jiri Belohlavek/Czech Philharmonic Orchestra

Concerto Grosso / Supraphon 110381-2
Josef Ruzicka & Jaroslav Saroun (pianos), Jiri Belohlavek/Czech Philharmonic Orchestra

Violin Concertos #1 & 2 / Supraphon 110702-2
Josef Suk (violin), Vaclav Neumann /Czech Philharmonic Orchestra

★ **Double Concerto**

Double Concerto for 2 String Orchestras, Piano & Timpani / Supraphon 103393-2
Sir Charles Mackerras/Prague Radio Symphony Orchestra

Double Concerto for 2 String Orchestras, Piano & Timpani / Virgin VC791099-2
Richard Hickox/City of London Sinfonia

FRESCOS OF PIERO DELLA FRANCESCA
Frescos of Piero della Francesca / Supraphon 103393-2
Sir Charles Mackerras/Prague Radio Symphony Orchestra

SYMPHONIES
Symphonies #1-6 / Supraphon 110382-2
Vaclav Neumann/Czech Philharmonic Orchestra

Symphonies #1 & 2 / RCA 60154-2-RC
Claus Peter Flor/Berlin Symphony Orchestra

Symphonies #1 & 2 / BIS CD-362
Neeme Jarvi/Bamburg Symphony Orchestra

Symphonies #3 & 6 / Supraphon 110718-2

Vaclav Neumann/Czech Philharmonic Orchestra

Symphonies #3 & 4 / Chandos CHAN8915
Jiri Belohlavek/Prague Symphony Orchestra

Symphonies #5 & 6 ("Fantasies symphoniques") / BIS CD-402
Neeme Jarvi/Bamburg Symphony Orchestra

Felix Mendelssohn (1809-1847)

Known in his time as a great conductor, Mendelssohn helped promote the works of Bach, which were largely forgotten by that time. Such respect for the beauties of musical form carried over into *Songs without Words*, each an individual gem (often studied by composition students) and lovely to hear for their lyricism and surprising alternatives to the expected melodic and harmonic turns. The works that have endured of this natural talent are primarily his orchestral pieces: the fresh lyricism and invention of the *Midsummer Night's Dream* overture and incidental music; the youthful energy and tone-painting of the "Scottish" and "Italian" symphonies; the brilliant *Concerto for Violin & Orchestra in E*, which has a noteworthy and appealing balance of classical and romantic writing; the thrilling, operatically dramatic oratorio *Elijah, op. 70;* also the skillfully written *Octet for Strings in E-flat*, which is light and floating on the strings. All these survive. I hope more of his solo piano music, which has great depth of feeling (for example, the *Variations serieuses, op. 54*), will someday be equally appreciated. — *"Blue" Gene Tyranny*

★ **Andante & Rondo Capriccioso for Piano**

Andante & Rondo Capriccioso, Op. 14 / Chandos CHAN8326
Lydia Artymiw (piano)

Andante & Rondo Capriccioso, Op. 14 / CBS MK42401
Murray Perahia (piano)

Andante & Rondo Capriccioso, Op. 14 / Nimbus NIM5069
Martin Jones (piano)

CONCERTOS FOR PIANO

Piano Concertos #1, Op. 25, and #2, Op. 40 / CBS MK42401
Murray Perahia (piano), Neville Marriner/Academy of St. Martin-in-the-Fields

Piano Concertos #1, Op. 25, and #2, Op. 40 / Teldec 9031-71104-2 or 9031-75860-2
Cyprian Katsaris (piano), Kurt Masur/Leipzig Gewandhaus Orchestra

Piano Concertos #1, Op. 25, and #2, Op. 40 / Chandos CHAN9215
Howard Shelley (piano)/London Mozart Players

Piano Concertos #1, Op. 25 / Nimbus NI5158
Christopher Kite (fortepiano), Roy Goodman/Hanover Band

★ **Concerto for Violin**

Concerto, Op. 64 / London 410011-2
Kyung-Wha Chung (violin), Charles Dutoit/Montreal Symphony Orchestra

Concerto, Op. 64 / RCA Red Seal 5933-2-RC
Jascha Heifetz (violin), Charles Munch/Boston Symphony Orchestra

Concerto, Op. 64 / Deutsche Grammophon 400031-2
Anne-Sophie Mutter (violin), Herbert von Karajan/Berlin Philharmonic Orchestra

ELIJAH (ORATORIO)

Elijah, Op. 70 / Chandos CHAN8774 / 5
Plowright, Finnie, Davies, White, Richard Hickox/London Symphony Orchestra & Chorus

Elijah, Op. 70 / Philips 432984-2
Yvonne Kenny, Anne Sofie van Otter, Anthony Rolfe Johnson, Thomas Allen, Neville Marriner/Academy of St. Martin-in-the-Fields

★ **Midsummer Night's Dream, Incidental Music**

Midsummer Night's Dream: Overture, Op. 23, & Incidental Music, Op. 61 / CBS MYK37760
George Szell/Cleveland Orchestra

Midsummer Night's Dream: Overture, Op. 23, & Incidental Music, Op. 61 / Philips 420653-2
Sir Colin Davis/Boston Symphony Orchestra

★ **Octet for Strings**

String Octet in E Flat Major, Op. 20 / Philips 420400-2
Academy Chamber Ensemble

String Octet in E Flat Major, Op. 20 / Sony SK48307
L'Archibudelli

String Octet in E Flat Major, Op. 20 / Hyperion CDA66356
Divertimenti

String Octet in E Flat Major, Op. 20 / London 421093-2
Academy Chamber Ensemble

QUARTETS FOR STRINGS

String Quartets (complete) / Deutsche Grammophon 415883-2
Melos Quartet

String Quartets, Op. 12 & 13; Andante, Op. 81 #1; and Scherzo, Op. 81 #2 / Hyperion CDA66397
Coull String Quartet

String Quartets, Op. 44 #2, Op. 80, and in E flat major (1823) / Hyperion CDA66579
Coull String Quartet

String Quartets, Op. 44 #1 & 3, Capriccio, Op. 81 # 3, and Fugue, Op. 81 #4 / Hyperion CDA66615
Coull String Quartet

QUINTET FOR STRINGS #2

String Quintet in B Flat Major, Op. 87 / Philips 420400-2
Academy Chamber Ensemble

String Quintets, #1 Op. 18, and #2 Op. 87 / Musicales Actes Sud M210001
Quintette Mendelssohn

SONATAS FOR ORGAN (1, 6)

Organ Sonatas, Op. 65 #2, 3 & 6 / Argo 414420-2
Peter Hurford (organ)

SONGS WITHOUT WORDS FOR PIANO

Lieder ohne Worte (complete) / Hyperion CDA66221 / 2
Livia Rev (piano)

Lieder ohne Worte (selections) / London 421119-2
Andras Schiff (piano)

★ **Symphonies (3, *4, 5)**

Symphony #3 ("Scottish"), Op. 56 / Telarc CD-80184
Christoph von Dohnanyi/Cleveland Orchestra

Symphonies #3 ("Scottish"), Op. 56 and #4 ("Italian"), Op. 90 / Deutsche Grammophon 415670-2
James Levine/Berlin Philharmonic Orchestra

Symphony #4 ("Italian"), Op. 90 / Deutsche Grammophon 410862-2
Giuseppe Sinopoli/Philharmonia Orchestra

Symphony #4 ("Italian"), Op. 90 / Virgin CDC59135
Sir Charles Mackerras/Orchestra of the Age of Enlightenment

Olivier Messiaen (1908-1992)

French composer and organist, one of the most influential teachers of this century. Messiaen was organist at the Sainte Trinite cathedral, and composed a large body of organ music. His harmonic idiom is always highly colorful and rhythmically ingenius. He was able to unify the rhythmic intensity of Stravinsky with the dodecaphonic technique of Schoenberg, being one of the first instructors to carefully analyze their music and pave the way for such students as Boulez and Stockhausen. Messiaen was also one of the first composers to apply serial principles to rhythmic organization, though serial techniques are used only as one means among many in his arsenal. He had a predilection for cyclic forms, often using juxtaposed blocks of differing sonority in his larger works. His thematic material is drawn primarily from two sources: Catholic religious themes and birdsong. To this is added an advanced feeling for modality, building on the work of Charles Tournemire. Messiaen composed in every form of the time, though his concertos and symphonic works are not entitled as such. His music revels in naturalistic evocations and spiritual meditation. Finally, his *Quartet for the End of Time*, composed in a German prison camp, is one of the signature pieces of the mid-20th century. — *Todd McComb*

ORGAN MUSIC (LA NATIVITE)

La Nativite and Apparition de l'Eglise Eternelle / Calliope CAL9928

Louis Thiry (organ)

Diphyque and Les Corps Glorieaux / Unicorn-Kanchana DKPCD9004
Jennifer Bate (organ)

QUATUOR POUR LA FIN DU TEMPS

Quartet for the End of Time / EMI CDC7474632
Deinzer (violin), Gawrilov (clarinet), Palm (cello), A. Kontarsky (piano)

Quartet for the End of Time / RCA Gold Seal
Kavafian (violin), Stolzman (clarinet), Sherry (cello), Serkin (piano)

TURANGALILA-SYMPHONY

Symphony "Turanglila" / CBS M2K42271
Paul Crossley (piano), Murail (ondes martenot), Esa-Pekka Salonen/BBC Symphony Orchestra

Symphony "Turanglila" / EMI CDS7474632
Peter Donohoe (piano), Murail (ondes martenot), Simon Rattle/City of Birmingham Symphony Orchestra

Symphony "Turanglila" / Deutsche Grammophon 431781-2
Yvonne Loriod (piano), Jeanne Loriod (ondes martenot), Myung-Whun Chung/Bastille Orchestra

VINGT REGARDS (PIANO)

20 Pieces: Regards sur l'Enfant-Jesus / London 430343-2
John Ogdon (piano)

Claudio Monteverdi (1567-1643)

An Italian composer of opera (*Orfeo,* 1607) as well as sacred and secular vocal music. Monteverdi was a significant early composer in the operatic genre. Basing his music on his interpretations of ancient texts by Greek theorists (who were greatly respected by Renaissance intellectuals), Monteverdi produced original music from the material of the prevailing Venetian styles. His music is of almost unsurpassable beauty, especially the *Vespro della Beata Vergine.* Monteverdo's theorizing and experimentation in developing theater-music forms led to the fundamentals of opera in the next century, his most notable work in this genre being *Combattimento di Tancredi et Clorinda* (1624). —*"Blue" Gene Tyranny*

IL COMBATTIMENTO DI TANCREDI E CLORINDA

Il Combattimento di Tancredi e Clorinda (1624) & Madrigals / Hungaroton HCD12952
Maria Zadori (soprano), Guy de Mey & Martin Klietmann (tenors), Jozsef Gregor (bass), Nicholas McGegan/Capella Savaria

Il Combattimento di Tancredi e Clorinda (1624), Altri canti d'amor, Il ballo dell'ingrate & Volgendi il ael (Ballo "Movete") / Hyperion CDA66475
Peter Holman/Red Byrd & The Parley of Instruments

Il Combattimento di Tancredi e Clorinda (1624) / Harmonia Mundi Musique d'Abord HMA190986
Rene Clemencic/Clemencic Consort

LA FAVOLA D' ORFEO (OPERA)

La Favola d' Orfeo / Teldec Das Alte Werk 2292-42494-2
Berberian, Kozma, Hansmann, Equiluz, van Egmond, Nikolaus Harnoncourt/Concentus Musicus Wien & Capella Antiqua

La Favola d' Orfeo / Archiv 419250-2
Rolfe Johnson, Juliette Baird, John Eliot Gardiner/English Baroque Soloists, His Magesty's Sagbutts & Monteverdi Choir

L'INCORONAZIONE DI POPPEA (OPERA)

L'Incoronazione di Poppea / Harmonia Mundi HMC901330 / 32
Danielle Borst, Guillemette Laurens, Axel Kohler, Jennifer Larmore, Michael Schopper, Lena Lootens, Rene Jacobs/Concerto Vocale

L'Incoronazione di Poppea / Teldec Das Alte Werk 2292-42547-2
Donath, Soderstrom, Berberian, Esswood, Langridge, Equiluz, Nikolaus Harnoncourt/Concentus Musicus Wien

★ **Madrigals**

Madrigals Book 2 (complete) / Virgin Classics Veritas VC759282-2
Emma Kirkby / Consort of Music

Madrigals Book 3 (complete) / Virgin Classics Veritas VC759283-2
Emma Kirkby / Consort of Music

Madrigals Book 4 (complete) / Opus111 OPS3081

CONCERTO ITALIANO

14 Madrigals (selections) from Books 6-9 / RCA Deutsche Harmonia Mundi 05472772822
Konrad Junghanel/Cantus Colln

★ **Masses**

Mass "In illo tempore," Mass for 4 Voices, and Motets "Cantate Domine" & "Domine, ne in Furore" / Hyperion CDA66214
Harry Christophers/The Sixteen

★ **Vespro della Beata Vergine**

Vespro della Beata Vergine (1610) / EMI CDC7470782
Andrew Parrott/Taverner Consort, Choir & Players

Vespro della Beata Vergine (1610) / Harmonia Mundi HMC9012472
Philippe Herreweghe/Collegium Vocale, Saqueboutiers de Toulouse and La Chapelle Royale Orchestra

Cristobal de Morales (c. 1500-1553)

Morales is generally regarded as the leading Spanish composer during the so-called Golden Age of Spain; his birth shortly after Columbus's voyage presumably prompted the choice of name he was given, and living in Spain during that time must have been truly an exciting experience. The polyphonic style was brought to Spain by the previous generation of composers led by Penalosa, and the mystical intensity of Iberian music reached its maximum influence in the following generation with Victoria's tenure at Rome. Morales occupies the intermediate historical position between these two, along with the contemporary keyboard music of Antonio de Cabezon; his music shows some influence of earlier polyphony as well as looking forward to functional harmony. Morales's fame is also increased by the fact that his polyphony was performed in Mexico during the early days of the Spanish domination there. —*Todd McComb*

MASSES

Missa Pro Defunctis & Officium Defunctorum / Astree E8765
Jordi Savall /Herpsion XX & La Capella Reial de Catalunya

Missa Queramus cum Pastoribus and 5 Motets / Hyperion CDA66635
James O'Donnell /Choir of Westminster Cathedral

Missa Mille Regretz and 4 Motets / Chanticleer CR-8809
Chanticleer

Moritz Moszkowski (1854-1925)

PIANO MUSIC

Works for Solo Piano including "Etincelles" / Collins 14122
Seta Tanyel (piano)

Piano Concerto in E Major, Op. 59 / Hyperion CDA66452
Piers Lane (piano), Jerzy Maksymiuk/BBC Scottish Symphony Orchestra

Wolfgang Amadeus Mozart (1756-1791)

This Austrian composer and child prodigy was a major figure in the classical period who wrote in most musical forms of the time, especially opera, symphony, concertos, and chamber music; his notable works are too numerous to mention. Mozart had a great and lively mind, which he engaged in such experiments as deciding progressions by playing dice and billiards, placing players in adjacent rooms echoing each other (*Notturno for Four Orchestras,* K. 269), and the encoding of Masonic rituals in *The Magic Flute.* Mozart was capable of the most earthshaking and profound works (*Requiem,* K. 626, written as he lay on his deathbed), the sweetest of arias in his many operas, and the most beautiful of melodic invention and variation (the piano concertos, *Eine Kleine Nachtmusik,* and much more). His feeling for the balance of lines that have separate functions (melody, accompaniment, sostenuto, and melisma) is revealed in the quintets, the *Sinfonia Concertante in E-flat,* and the string quartets. Many structures in his symphonies are copies of innovations by Haydn, in some ways more conservative, but their drive, surprising modulations, and memorable melodies are purely Mozart. — *"Blue" Gene Tyranny*

ARIAS

9 Opera Arias for Tenor / Arabesque Z6598
Rockwell Blake (tenor), Nicholas McGegan/London Symphony Orchestra

7 Opera Arias for Soprano / Philips 426721-2
Cheryl Studer (soprano), Neville Marriner/Academy of St. Martin-in-the-Fields

7 Concert Arias / London 417756-2
Kiri Te Kanawa (soprano), Gyorgy Fischer/Vienna Chamber Orchestra

Opera & Concert Arias / London 430513-2
Cecilia Bartoli (soprano), Andras Schiff (piano), Gyorgy Fischer/Vienna Chamber Orchestra

CONCERTO FOR CLARINET

Clarinet Concerto in A major, K. 622 (w/ Oboe Concerto) / L'Oiseau-Lyre 414339-2
Anthony Pay (basset clarinet), Christopher Hogwood/Academy of Ancient Music

Clarinet Concerto in A major, K. 622 (w/ Clarinet Quintet) / Delos D / CD3020
David Shifrin (clarinet), Gerard Schwarz/Mostly Mozart Orchestra

Clarinet Concerto in A major, K. 622 (w/ Clarinet Quintet) / Hyperion CDA66199
Thea King (basset clarinet), Jeffrey Tate/English Chamber Orchestra

Clarinet Concerto in A major, K. 622 (w/ Clarinet Quintet) / Philips 420710-2
Jack Brymer (clarinet), Sir Colin Davis/London Symphony Orchestra

★ **Concertos for Flute / Oboe**

Flute Concerto #1 in G major, K. 313 / Deutsche Grammophon 426677-2
Susan Palma (Flute)/Orpheus Chamber Orchestra

Flute Concerto #1 in G major, K. 313 / L'Oiseau-Lyre 417622-2
Lisa Beznosiuk (flute), Christopher Hogwood / Academy of Ancient Music

Flute Concerto #1 in G major, K. 313 / Philips 422339-2
Irena Grafenauer (flute), Neville Marriner/Academy of St. Martin-in-the-Fields

Flute Concerto #2 in C major, K. 314 / Philips 426318-2
Irena Grafenauer (flute), Neville Marriner/Academy of St. Martin-in-the-Fields

Oboe Concerto in C major, K. 314 / L'Oiseau-Lyre 414339-2
Michel Piguet (oboe), Christopher Hogwood/Academy of Ancient Music

Oboe Concerto in C major, K. 314 / Hyperion CDA66411
Sarah Francis (oboe), Howard Shelley/London Mozart Players

★ **Concertos for Horn #1-4**

4 Horn Concertos, K. 412, 417, 447 & 495 / Philips 412737-2
Hermann Baumann (horn), Pinchas Zukerman/Saint Paul Chamber Orchestra

4 Horn Concertos, K. 412, 417, 447 & 495; Rondo K. 371 / CBS MDK44906
Dale Clevenger (horn)/Liszt Chamber Orchestra

★ **Concertos for Piano (7-19,*20,*21,*23, 24, 25, 27)**

23 Piano Concertos, #5-27 / Archiv 431211-2
Malcolm Bilson, Robert Levin & Melvyn Tan (fortepianos), John Eliot Gardiner/English Baroque Soloists

25 Piano Concertos, #1-6, 8, 9, 11-27 / Deutsche Grammophon 429001-2
Geza Anda (piano)/Salzburg Mozarteum Camerata

2 Piano Concertos, #9 & 21 / CBS MK34562
Murray Perahia (piano)/English Chamber Orchestra

2 Piano Concertos, #19 & 23 / CBS MK39064
Murray Perahia (piano)/English Chamber Orchestra

2 Concertos #24 & 25 / London 425791-2

Andras Schiff (piano), Sandor Vegh/Camerata Academica des Mozarteums Salzburg

2 Concertos #20 & 21 / Philips 416381-2
Mitsuko Uchida (piano), Jeffrey Tate/English Chamber Orchestra

CONCERTOS FOR VIOLIN (#3-5)

5 Violin Concertos #1-5, Rondos K. 268 & 373, and Adagio K. 261 / L'Oiseau-Lyre 433045-2
Simon Standage (violin), Christopher Hogwood /Academy of Ancient Music

5 Violin Concertos #1-5, Rondos K. 268 & 373, and Adagio K. 261 / Naxos 8.503002
Takako Nishizaki (violin), Stephen Gunzenhauser & Johannes Wildner/Capella Istropolitana /

2 Concertos #1 & 4 / CBS MK44503
Cho-Liang Lin (violin), Raymond Leppard/English Chamber Orchestra

2 Concertos #3 & 5 / Deutsche Grammophon 429814-2
Anne-Sophie Mutter (violin), Herbert von Karajan/Berlin Philharmonic Orchestra

COSI FAN TUTTE (OPERA)

Cosi fan tutte, K. 588 / Deutsche Grammophon 423897-2
Kiri Te Kanawa (soprano), Ann Murray (mezzo-soprano), Marie McLaughlin (soprano), Hans-Peter Blochwitz (tenor), Thomas Hampson (bass-baritone), Feruccio Furlanetto (bass), James Levine/Vienna Philharmonic & State Opera Chorus

Cosi fan tutte, K. 588 / Archiv 437829-2
Amanda Roocroft (soprano), Rosa Mannion (mezzo-soprano), Eirian James (soprano), Rainer Trost (tenor), Rodney Gilfry (baritone), Carlos Feller (bass), John Eliot Gardiner/English Baroque Soloists & Monteverdi Choir

★ **Divertimentos (*#1-3 & *#10)**

3 Divertimentos #1-3, K. 136-138; Serenade #6 ("Serenata Notturna"), K. 239; and Serenade #13 ("Eine Kleine Nachtmusik"), K. 525 / Philips 420712-2
I Musici

3 Divertimentos #1-3, K. 136-138, and Serenade #13 ("Eine Kleine Nachtmusik"), K. 525 / BIS CD-506
Drottningholm Baroque Ensemble

2 Divertimentos #10, K. 247, & #17, K. 334 / Sony Vivarte SK46497
Li'Archibudelli

Divertimentos K. 166, 186, 226 & 227 / Orfeo C163881A
Berlin Philharmonic Winds

Divertimentos #8, 9, 12-14 & 16, K. 213, 240, 252, 253, 270 & 289 / Accent ACC8856D
Octophoros

★ **Don Giovanni (opera)**

Don Giovanni, K.537 / EMI CDS7470372
Thomas Allen (baritone), Carol Vaness (soprano), Maria Ewing (mezzo-soprano), Elizabeth Gale (soprano), Bernard Haitink/London Philharmonic Orchestra & Glynebourne Chorus

Don Giovanni, K.537 / EMI CDS7472602
Eberhard Wachter (baritone), Joan Sutherland (soprano), Elisabeth Schwarzkopf (soprano), Graziella Sciutti (soprano), Carlo Maria Giulini/Philharmonia Orchestra & Chorus

Don Giovanni, K.537 / Teldec 2292-44184-2
Thomas Hampson (bass-baritone), Robert Holl (bass), Edita Gruberova (soprano), Hans-Peter Blochwitz (tenor), Nicholas Harnoncourt/Royal Concertgebouw Orchestra & Netherlands Opera Chorus

★ **Exsultate, Jubilate (motet)**

Exsultate, Jubilate, K. 165 / Li'Oiseau-Lyre 411832-2
Emma Kirkby (soprano), Christopher Hogwood/Academy of Ancient Music & Westminster Cathedral Boy's Choir

Exsultate, Jubilate, K. 165 / Philips 412873-2
Kiri Te Kanawa (soprano), Sir Colin Davis/London Symphony Orchestra & Chorus

IDOMENEO (OPERA)

Idomeneo, re di Creta, K. 366 / Archiv 431674-2

Anthony Rolfe Johnson (tenor), Anne-Sophie van Otter (soprano), Sylvia McNair (mezzo-soprano), H Martinpello (soprano), John Eliot Gardiner/English Baroque Soloists & Monteverdi Choir

Idomeneo, re di Creta K. 366 / Teldec 2292-42600-2
Hollweg (bass-baritone), Schmidt (bass), Rachael Yakar (soprano), Felicity Palmer (soprano), Nicholas Harnoncourt/Mozart Orchestra & Zurich Opera House Chorus

★ **Die Zauberflote "The Magic Flute" (opera)**

Die Zauberflote, K. 620 / London 433210-2
Sumi Jo (soprano), Ruth Ziesack (soprano), Uwe Heilmann (tenor), Kraus, Kurt Moll (bass), Sir Georg Solti/Vienna Philharmonic Orchestra & State Opera Orchestra

Die Zauberflote, K. 620 / Deutsche Grammophon 435395-2
Roberta Peters (soprano), Evelyn Lear (soprano), Lisa Otto (soprano), Fritz Wunderlich (tenor), Dietrich Fischer-Dieskau (baritone), Franz Crass (bass), Karl Bohm/Berlin Philharmonic Orchestra & RIAS Chamber Chorus

Die Zauberflote, K. 620 / Teldec 2292-42716-2
Edita Gruberova (soprano), Hans-Peter Blochwitz (tenor), Barbara Bonney (soprano), Thomas Hampson (bass-baritone), Nicholas Harnoncourt/Zurich Opera House Orchestra & Chorus

MARRIAGE OF FIGARO (OPERA)

Le Nozze di Figaro, K. 492 / LíOiseau-Lyre 421333-2
Barbara Bonney (soprano), Arleen Auger (soprano), Alicia Nafe (mezzo-soprano), Petteri Salomaa (bass), Hakkan Hagegard (baritone), Arnold Ostman/Drottningholm Court Theatre Orchestra & Chorus

Le Nozze di Figaro, K. 492 / Philips 416370-2
Lucia Popp (soprano), Barbara Hendricks (soprano), Agnes Baltsa (mezzo-soprano), Ruggero Raimondi (bass), Jose Van Dam (bass-baritone), Neville Marriner/Academy of St. Martin-in-the-Fields & Ambrosian Singers

Le Nozze di Figaro, K. 492 / London 410150-2
Kiri Te Kanawa (soprano), Samuel Ramey (tenor), Lucia Popp (soprano), Fredericka von Stade (mezzo-soprano), Thomas Allen (tenor), Sir Gerog Solti/London Philharmonic Orchestra & London Opera Chorus

MASS IN C ("THE GREAT")

Mass in C Minor ("The Great"), K. 427 / Philips 420210-2
Anthony Rolfe Johnson (tenor), Diana Montague (mezzo-soprano), Sylvia McNair (mezzo-soprano), Cornelius Hauptmann (bass), John Eliot Gardiner/English Baroque Soloists & Monteverdi Choir

Mass in C Minor ("The Great"), K. 427 / Telarc CD-80150
Edith Wiens (soprano), Delores Ziegler (mezzo-soprano), John Aler (tenor), William Stone (baritone), Robert Shaw/Atlanta Symphony Ochestra & Chorus

★ **Overtures**

Overtures (complete) / Naxos 8.550185
Barry Wordsworth/Capella Istropolitana

Overtures to La Nozze di Figaro, Cosi Fan Tutte, Impressario, & Die Zauberflote / CBS MYK37774
Bruno Walter/Columbia Symphony

12 Overtures / Novalis 150041-2
Leopold Hager/English Chamber Orchestra

QUARTETS FOR FLUTE

4 Quartets for Flute & String Trio, K. 285, 285a, 285b & 298 / Sony SK42320
Jean Pierre Rampal (flute), Isaac Stern (violin), Salvatore Accardo (viola),), Mstislav Rostropovich (cello)

4 Quartets for Flute & String Trio, K. 285, 285a, 285b & 298 (w/ Oboe Quartet) / RCA Deutsche Harmonia Mundi 77158-2
Les Adieux

4 Quartets for Flute & String Trio, K. 285, 285a, 285b & 298 / Denon 38C37-7157
Aurele Nicolet (flute)/Mozart String Trio

QUARTET FOR OBOE & STRINGS

Quartet for Oboe & String Trio, K. 370 (w/ Clarinet Quintet) / L'Oiseau-Lyre 421429-2
Stephen Hammer (oboe)/Academy of Ancient Music Chamber Ensemble

Quartet for Oboe & String Trio, K. 370 (w/ Divertimento K. 251) / Philips 412618-2
Heinz Holliger (oboe)/Orlando Quartet

QUARTETS FOR PIANO

Quartets for Piano & String Trio, K. 478 & 493 / Philips 410391-2
Bruno Giuranna (viola)/Beaux Arts Trio

Quartets for Piano & String Trio, K. 478 & 493 / Archiv 423404-2
Malcolm Bilson (fortepiano), Elisabeth Wilcock (violin), Jan Schlapp (viola), Timothy Mason (cello)

★ **Quartets for Strings (*8-13, 14, 16, *17, 18, 23)**

Complete String Quartets / Philips Complete Mozart Edition Vol. 12 422512-2
Quartetto Italiano

14 "Early" String Quartets / Hungaroton HCD31443 / 45
Festetics Quartet

6 "Haydn" String Quartets / CBS M3YK45826
Julliard String Quartet

6 "Haydn" String Quartets / Hungaroton HCD12983 / 85
Takacs Quartet

2 String Quartets, K. 421 & 465 ("Dissonance") / Hyperion CDA66170
Salomon String Quartet

2 String Quartets, K. 458 ("Hunt") & 464 ("Drum") / Hyperion CDA66234
Salomon String Quartet

★ **Quintet for Clarinet & Strings**

Clarinet Quintet in A Major, K581 (w/ Clarinet Concerto) / L'Oiseau-Lyre 421429-2
Anthony Pay (clarinet)/Academy of Ancient Music Chamber Ensemble

Clarinet Quintet in A major, K581 (w/ Clarinet Concerto) / Hyperion CDA66199
Thea King (clarinet)/The Gabrieli String Quartet

Clarinet Quintet in A major, K581 (w/ Clarinet Concerto) / Delos D / CD3020
David Shifrin (clarinet), Gerard Schwarz/Mostly Mozart Orchestra

Clarinet Quintet in A major, K581 (w/ Clarinet Concerto) / Philips 420710-2
Jack Brymer (clarinet), Sir Colin Davis/London Symphony Orchestra

QUINTET FOR PIANO & STRINGS

Quintet in E Flat Major, Op. 16 (w/ Beethoven Quintet) / Sony SK43099
Murray Perahia (piano)/Members of the English Chamber Orchestra

Quintet in E Flat Major, Op. 16 (w/ Beethoven Quintet) / Telarc CD-80114
Andre Previn (piano)/Vienna Wind Soloists

★ **Quintets for Strings**

6 Quintets for Strings, K. 174, 406, 515, 516, 593 & 614 / Philips Complete Mozart Edition Vol. 11 422511-2
Arpad Gerecz (violin), Max Lesueur (viola)/Grumiaux Trio

2 String Quintets, K515 & 593 / Hyperion CDA66431
Simon Whistler (viola)/Salomon String Quartet

2 String Quintets, K516 & 614 / Hyperion CDA66432
Simon Whistler (viola)/Salomon String Quartet

2 String Quintets, K515 & 516 / Calliope CAL9231
Tallich Quartet

2 String Quintets, K593 & 614 / Hungaroton HCD12881
Takacs Quartet

REQUIEM

Requiem, K. 626 (completed by Sussmayr) / EMI CDC7473422
Kathleen Battle (soprano), Ann Murray (alto), David Randall (tenor), Matti Salminen (bass), Daniel Barenboim/Orchestra & Chorus of Paris

Requiem, K. 626 (completed by Maunder) / LíOiseau-Lyre 411712-2

Emma Kirkby (soprano), Watkinson (alto), Anthony Rolfe Johnson (tenor), David Thomas (bass), Christopher Hogwood/Academy of Ancient Music & Westminster Cathedral Boy's Choir

Requiem, K. 626 (completed by Robbins Landon) / Nimbus NIM5241
Gundula Janowitz (soprano), Julia Bernheimer (mezzo-soprano), Martyn Hill (tenor), David Thomas (bass), Roy Goodman /Hanover Band & Chorus

SERENADE #6 ("SERENATA NOTTURNA")

Serenade #6 ("Serenata notturna"), K. 239; 3 Divertimentos #1-3, K. 136-138; and Serenade #13 ("Eine Kleine Nachtmusik"), K. 525 / Philips 420712-2
I Musici

Serenade #6 ("Serenata notturna"), K. 239; Divertimento #1, K. 136; and Serenade #13 ("Eine Kleine Nachtmusik"), K. 525 / Hungaroton HCD12471
Janos Rolla/Liszt Ferenc Chamber Orchestra

Serenade #6 ("Serenata notturna"), K. 239; 2 Divertimentos #1 & 2, K. 136 & 137; and Serenade #13 ("Eine Kleine Nachtmusik"), K. 525 / Capriccio 10185
Sandor Vegh/Camerata Salzburg

★ Serenade #7 "Haffner"

Serenade #7 ("Haffner"), K. 250 / Hungaroton HCD12944
Janos Rolla/Liszt Ferenc Chamber Orchestra

Serenade #7 ("Haffner"), K. 250 / Erato 2292-45436-2
Ton Koopman/Amsterdam baroque Orchestra

Serenade #7 ("Haffner"), K. 250; and Serenade #6 ("Serenata notturna"), K. 239 / Telarc CD-80161
Sir Charles Mackerras /Prague Chamber Orchestra

SERENADE #9 ("POSTHORN")

Serenade #9 ("Posthorn"), K. 320 and Serenade #13 ("Eine Kleine Nachtmusik"), K. 525 / Telarc CD-80108
Zdenek Tylsar (posthorn), Sir Charles Mackerras /Prague Chamber Orchestra

Serenade #9 ("Posthorn"), K. 320; Marches, K. 335 / Philips 416364-2
Neville Marriner/Academy of St. Martin-in-the-Fields

★ Serenades #10 ("Gran Partita"), 11 & 12 for Winds

Serenade #10 ("Gran Partita"), K. 361 / Deutsche Grammophon 423061-2
Orpheus Chamber Orchestra

Serenade #10 ("Gran Partita"), K. 361 / Philips 412726-2
Neville Marriner/Academy of St. Martin-in-the-Fields

Serenade #10 ("Gran Partita"), K. 361 / LíOiseau-Lyre 421437-2
Christopher Hogwood/Amadeus Winds

2 Serenades #11 & 12, K. 375 & 388 / LíOiseau-Lyre 421437-2
Christopher Hogwood/Amadeus Winds

2 Serenades #11 & 12, K. 375 & 388 / Meridian CDE84107
Albion Ensemble

2 Serenades #11 & 12, K. 375 & 388 / CBC Enterprises SMCD5053
Toronto Chamber Winds

★ Serenade #13 ("Eine Kleine Nachtmusik")

Serenade #13 ("Eine Kleine Nachtmusik"), K. 525, and Serenade #9 ("Posthorn"), K. 320 / Telarc CD-80108
Sir Charles Mackerras /Prague Chamber Orchestra

Serenade #13 ("Eine Kleine Nachtmusik") K. 525, 3 Divertimentos #1-3, K. 136-138, and Serenade #6 "Serenata Notturna," K. 239 / Philips 420712-2
I Musici

Serenade #13 ("Eine Kleine Nachtmusik"), K. 525, and 3 Divertimentos #1-3, K. 136-138 / BIS CD-506

Serenade #13 ("Eine Kleine Nachtmusik"), K. 525 / Deutsche Grammophon 419192-2
Orpheus Chamber Orchestra

★ Sinfonia Concertante for Violin & Viola K. 364

Sinfonia Concertante, K. 364 / Deutsche Grammophon 415486-2
Itzhak Perlman (violin), Pinchas Zukerman (viola), Zubin Mehta/Isreal Philharmonic Orchestra

Sinfonia Concertante, K. 364 / London Serenata 422171-2

Iona Brown (violin), Josef Suk (viola)/Academy of St. Martin-in-the-Fields

Sinfonia Concertante, K. 364 / Naxos 8.550332
Takako Nishizaki (violin), Ladislav Kyselak (viola), Stephen Gunzenhauser/Capella Istropolitana

SONATAS FOR PIANO (8, 11, 13, 15)

17 Piano Sonatas / Philips 422115-2 or 422517-2
Mitsuko Uchida (piano)

3 Piano Sonatas: #4, 8 & 15 / Philips 422583-2
Sviatoslav Richter (piano)

4 Piano Sonatas: #5, 8, 9 & 15 / Hungaroton HCD11835
Deszo Ranki (piano)

4 Piano Sonatas: #4, 10, 11 & 12 / London 417817-2
Alicia de Larrocha (piano)

3 Piano Sonatas: #3, 10 & 13 / Deutsche Grammophon 431274-2
Vladimir Horowitz (piano)

SONATAS FOR VIOLIN (K. 296 & 454)

Violin Sonatas (complete) / Philips Complete Mozart Edition Vol. 15 422515-2
Arthur Grumiaux (violin), Walter Klein (piano), et al.

3 Violin Sonatas, K. 296, 305 & 306 / Deutsche Grammophon 415102-2
Itzhak Perlman (violin), Daniel Barenboim (piano)

4 Violin Sonatas, K. 27, 303, 454 & Variations / RCA Red Seal 60740-2-RC
Pinchas Zukerman (violin), Marc Neikrug (piano)

★ Symphonies (29, 35, 36, *38, 39, *40, *41)

Symphonies / Archiv
Trevor Pinnock/The English Concert

2 Symphonies: #29 & 33 / Philips 412736-2
John Eliot Gardiner/English Baroque Soloists

3 Symphonies: #25, 28 & 29 / Telarc CD-80165
Sir Charles Mackerras /Prague Chamber Orchestra

3 Symphonies: #31 ("Paris"), 36 ("Linz"), & 38 ("Prague") / Academy Sound & Vision LTD CDDCA647
Jane Glover/London Mozart Players

3 Symphonies: #34 ("Paris"), 35 ("Haffner") & 39 / Academy Sound & Vision LTD CDDCA615
Jane Glover/London Mozart Players

2 Symphonies: #35 ("Haffner") & 41 ("Jupiter") / Deutsche Grammophon 415305-2
Leonard Bernstein/Vienna Philharmonic Orchestra

2 Symphonies: #36 ("Linz") & 38 ("Prague") / Telarc CD-80148
Sir Charles Mackerras /Prague Chamber Orchestra

2 Symphonies: #36 ("Linz") & 38 ("Prague") / Deutsche Grammophon 415962-2
Leonard Bernstein/Vienna Philharmonic Orchestra

2 Symphonies: #39 & 41 ("Jupiter") / RCA Red Seal 60714-2-RC
Gunter Wand/North German Radio Symphony Orchestra

2 Symphonies: #40 & 41 ("Jupiter") / Telarc CD-80139
Sir Charles Mackerras /Prague Chamber Orchestra

2 Symphonies: #40 & 41 ("Jupiter") / Philips 434149-2
Franz Bruggen/Orchestra of the 18th Century

★ Trio for Strings

Trio (Divertimento), K. 563 / Meridian CDE84079
Cummings String Trio

Trio (Divertimento), K. 563, and Preludes & Fugues, K. 404 / Sony Vivarte SK46497
LíArchibudelli

Trio (Divertimento), K. 563, and Preludes & Fugues, K. 404 / Philips 416485-2
Grumiaux Trio

TRIOS FOR PIANO & STRINGS

7 Piano Trios (complete) / Philips 422079-2
Beaux Arts Trio

7 Piano Trios (complete) / Dabringhaus & Grimm MD&GL3373 / 74
Trio Parnassus

Piano Trio (Divertimento), K. 254, & Piano Trio, K.548 / Hyperion CDA66093
The London Fortepiano Trio

2 Piano Trios, K. 496 & 542 / Hyperion CDA66148
The London Fortepiano Trio

Georg Muffat (1653-1704)

An organist and court musician in Vienna, Prague, and Salzburg before visiting Italy in the 1680's. Muffat studied in Rome with Pasquini, heard Corelli's concerti grossi and heard his own compositions played at Corelli's home.In 1682 he returned to Salzburg but became disenchanted with the conditions there and took a position as Kapellmeister at the court of the Bishop of Passau. He was a versatile musician and played a role in introducing French and Italian styles to the German music scene. — *Lynn Vought*

CONCERTI GROSSI

3 Concerti Grossi (w/ suites; also see Biber) / Chandos CHAN8448 / 9
Adrian Shepherd/Cantilena

STRING SONATAS ("ARMONICO TRIBUTO")

5 Sonatas ("Armonico Tributo") / Hyperion CDA66032
Roy Goodman/Parley of Instruments Baroque Orchestra

SUITES "FLORILEGIUM"

3 Suites ("Florilegium I"): #3, 4 & 7 (w/ concerti Grossi; also see Biber) / Chandos CHAN8448 / 9
Adrian Shepherd/Cantilena

Suites & Sonatas / RCA Deutsche Hamronia Mundi Editio Classica 77074-2-RG
Sigiswald Kuijken/La Petite Bande

APPARATUS MUSICO-ORGANISTICUS FOR ORGAN

12 Toccatas ("Apparatus Musico-Organisticus") / Panton 811016
Jaroslav Tuma (organ)

Modest Mussorgsky (1839-1881)

A member of the group of Russian nationalist composers known as "The Mighty Five," Mussorgsky wrote opera (*Boris Godounov*, 1868), songs, and incidental music (*Pictures at an Exhibition* for piano (1874)), and *A Night on Bare Mountain*). Leading a very difficult life (nearly impoverished at times, working at the dreary job of a civil clerk, and suffering from alcoholism), Mussorgsky nevertheless produced some of the most original and remarkable songs from Russia, which are now part of the standard repertoire. The beauty, strength, and emotion of Russian folk songs and tales inspired him and fellow composers who were looking for a true Russian sound and voice. This is achieved with great coloristic effect in the famous *Night on Bare Mountain* (usually presented in the reorchestrated version by Rimsky-Korsakov) and with intimately stirring feeling (like that evoked by a good storyteller) in the song cycles *Songs and Dances of Death* and *Bez solntsa* (*Sunless*, or *Without Sun*), not to mention the popular *Pictures at an Exhibition*, with its many moods and memorable melodies. The operas *Boris Godounov*, *Kovanschina*, and *Sorochintsy Fair* should be heard in their original versions whenever possible for an experience of the spirit that was to change Russian music in the next century. — *"Blue" Gene Tyranny*

OPERAS (BORIS GODOUNOV, CHOVANTSJINA)

Boris Godounov / Erato 2292-45418-2
Vishnevskaya, Gedda, Raimondi, Mstislav Rostropovich/National Symphony Orchestra and Choral Arts Society & Oratorio Society of Washington

Chovantsjina (Khovanshchina) (completed by Rimsky-Korsakov and reorchestrated by Shostakovich) / Fidelio 1820 / 22
Petkov, Kostov, Bodourov, Popov, Atanas Margaritov/Sofia National Opera Orchestra & Chorus

NIGHT ON BALD MOUNTAIN

Night on Bald Mountain (symphonic picture) / Telarc CD-80042

Lorin Maazel/Cleveland Orchestra

Night on Bald Mountain (symphonic picture) / Mercury Living Presence 432004-2
Antal Dorati/London Symphony Orchestra

★ **Pictures at an Exhibition**

Pictures at an Exhibition / Delos D / CD1008
John Browning (piano)

Pictures at an Exhibition / Virgin Classics CDC59611
Mikhail Pletnev (piano)

Pictures at an Exhibition (orchestrated by Ravel) / Telarc CD-80042
Lorin Maazel/Cleveland Orchestra

Pictures at an Exhibition (orchestrated by Ravel) / London 417299-2
Charles Dutoit/Montreal Symphony Orchestra

Carl Nielsen (1865-1931)

A Danish composer of many musical forms whose finest achievements are his symphonies. Nielson's music is characterized by its direct expression, clarity like that of a mountain spring, and deep humanity and warmth. In the second movement of his *Third Symphony*, a soprano and baritone sing wordless songs to each other across the expanse of the gently murmuring orchestra—after the listeners have been swept away by a first movement that combines a glorious waltz-like theme and punctuations reminiscent of Beethoven's *Symphony No. 3* (also partly in 3/4 time). There is humor and lyricism in the *Concerto for Clarinet* and a variety of moods and inventive sonorities that is unlike anyone else's in the piano music. — *"Blue" Gene Tyranny*

CLARINET CONCERTO

Clarinet Concerto, Op. 57 / BIS CD-321
Olle Schill (clarinet), Myung-Whun Chung/Gothenburg Symphony Orchestra

Clarinet Concerto, Op. 57 / Chandos CHAN8618
Janet Hilton (clarinet), Matthias Bamert/Scottish National Orchestra

★ **Symphonies (1-5)**

Symphonies #1, Op. 7, and #6 ("Sinfonia Semplice"), Op. 116 / London 425607-2
Herbert Blomstedt/San Francisco Symphony Orchestra

Symphonies #1, Op. 7, and #4 ("The Inextinguishable"), Op. 29 / RCA Red Seal 7701-2-RC
Paavo Berglund/Royal Danish Orchestra

Symphony #2 ("The Four Temperments"), Op. 16 / BIS CD-247
Myung-Whun Chung/Gothenburg Symphony Orchestra

Symphony #3 ("Sinfonia Espansiva"), Op. 27 / BIS CD-321
Myung-Whun Chung/Gothenburg Symphony Orchestra

Symphonies #4 ("The Inextinguishable"), Op. 29, and #5, Op. 50 / London 421524-2
Herbert Blomstedt/San Francisco Symphony Orchestra

Symphony #4 ("The Inextinguishable"), Op. 29 / Deutsche Grammophon 413313-2
Herbert von Karajan/Berlin Philharmonic Orchestra

Symphony #5, Op. 50 / BIS CD-370
Myung-Whun Chung/Gothenburg Symphony Orchestra

Johannes Ockeghem (c.1410-1497)

Ockeghem was one of the most respected composers of the 15th century, and along with Guillaume Dufay & Josquin Des Prez, one of the most influential composers of the early Renaissance. Ockeghem was probably born in the current Belgium, in what was then the Duchy of Burgundy—estimates for the year of his birth vary from 1400 to c.1430, but written sources from the period indicate that he was a very old man by the time of his death in 1497. He was premier chaplain to three kings of France, as well as holding the prestigious position of treasurer at the great cathedral and monastery of St. Martin de Tours. During his lifetime, Ockeghem was known for his personal refinement and fine bass voice. After his death, a famous poem by Guillaume Cretin (set to music by Josquin Des Prez) praised his character, skill, and influence. He was long identified as one of the fathers of Renaissance music, his influence finally fading only years after his death.

Ockeghem's surviving musical output is relatively small, comprising a mere handful of motets, several masses, and a couple of dozen secular chansons. His style is marked by a careful handling of vocal ranges in a primarily four-voice texture and an emphasis on complex and expressive bass lines. This emphasis on lower textures opened up a new world of structural possibilities for Renaissance composers, and Ockeghem's compositions exploit these potentials in a variety of ways. Today he is best known for his masses and his ability to integrate large-scale forms in ways that were as unparalleled then as they are now. By the 16th century, Ockeghem was known primarily as an accomplished technical master, famous for his complex lines and polyphonic structures, which had the appearance of intractable puzzles for all but the most accomplished musicians. This perception of difficulty, as well as the unique texture of his works, is due in part to his emphasis on long lines that gradually unfold with the formal development of a piece—a development accomplished by a carefully executed structural plan that includes the supression of cadential features in one or more voices at otherwise "planned" cadences. Ockeghem's reputation as a purely technical master was also earned by the relatively long survival of his more intricate polyphonic explorations as textbook sources. These include his incomparable *Missa Prolationum*, constructed entirely in canon; his *Missa Cuiusvis Toni*, designed to be performable in any of the available modes (catholicon); and his chanson "Prenez sur moi," which is both a strict canon and a catholicon. However, Ockeghem's music is by no means dominated by these technical features (and even in these works, the result is astonishing); his contrapuntal language is extremely varied and complex, largely abandoning the simpler fauxbourdon style of Dufay, but not resting exclusively on the pervasive imitation characteristic of Josquin and the successive continental masters. Today, Ockeghem is regarded not only as one of the pioneers of Western polyphony, but as one of the supreme masters of both lyrical and contrapuntal invention. —*Todd McComb*

★ **Requiem**

Mass "Pro Defunctis" / Harmonia Mundi HMC901441
Marcel Peres/Ensemble Organum

MASSES

Masses for 3 Voices ("Quinti Toni" & "Sine Nomine") / Lyrichord LEMS8010
Kevin Moll/Schola Discantus

Mass ("Prolationum") and Five Motets / EMI CDC7497982
Paul Hillier/Hilliard Ensemble

CHANSONS

Complete Secular Music / L'oiseau Lyre 436 194
The Medieval Ensemble of London

Jacques Offenbach (1819-1880)

★ **Gaite Parisienne**

Gaite Parisienne / Telarc CD-80294
Erich Kunzel/Cincinnati Pops Orchestra

Gaite Parisienne / London 411708-2
Charles Dutoit/Montreal Symphony Orchestra

Gaite Parisienne / Philips 411039-2
Andre Previn/Pittsburgh Symphony Orchestra

LES CONTES D' HOFFMANN (OPERA)

The Tales of Hoffman / Deutsche Grammophon 427682-2
Placido Domingo, Edita Grubernova, Seiji Ozawa/French National Orchestra & Radio France Chorus

★ **Orpheus in Hades Overture**

Overture "Orpheus in the Underworld" / Sony SMK47532 or CBS MYK37769
Leonard Bernstein/New York Philharmonic Orchestra

Overture "Orpheus in the Underworld" / Chesky CD57
Rene Liebowitz/Paris Symphony Concert Society Orchestra

Carl Orff (1895-1982)

A German composer primarily of dramatic music with primal rhythms and raw emotional effects; known for *Carmina Burana*

(1937). His early works were influenced by Richard Strauss and Schoenberg; around 1930 he began writing *Schulwerk* —teaching methods for schools—which allowed him to delve into his obsession with "primitive" rhythms and turn back to Monteverdi for melodies. The result was the *Catulli Carmina* (1943), seven settings of "gutter Latin" texts from medieval monasteries for a capella choir. His study of Bach and Schutz led to his setting some of their works and inspired *Carmina Burana*, Orff's most popular work. The opera *Antigonae* (which uses *Steinspiel*, or tuned rocks, among its many percussive devices) and *Trionfo di Afrodite* (1950-1951) are particularly interesting for their orchestral effects. —*"Blue" Gene Tyranny*

CARMINA BURANA (SCENIC CANTATA)

Carmina Burana / Philips 422363-2
Edita Grubernova (soprano), John Aler (tenor), Thomas Hampson (baritone), Seiji Ozawa/Berlin Philharmonic Orchestra, Shinyukai Choir & Berlin Cathedral Boys' Choir

Carmina Burana / Telarc CD-80056
Blegen (soprano), Brown (tenor), Hagegard (baritone), Robert Shaw/Altanta Symphony Orchestra & Chorus and Atlanta Boy's Choir

Johann Pachelbel (1653-1706)

Central German organist and composer. Pachelbel composed in all the keyboard forms of the time and is known for his clear counterpoint. His *Canon in D* is one of the most popular pieces in all of classical music. —*AMG*

CANON & GIGUE IN D MAJOR

Canon in D Major / Nimbus NIM5032
William Boughton/English String Orchestra

Canon & Gigue in D Major / Reference Recordings RR-13CD
Tafelmusik

Canon & Gigue in D Major / Archiv 427118-2
Reinhard Goebel/Musica Antiqua Koln

HEXACHORDUM APOLLINIS FOR HARPSICHORD OR ORGAN

9 Pieces ("Hexachordum Apollinis") / FY FYCD074
Huguette Gremy-Chauliac (harpsichord)

9 Pieces ("Hexachordum Apollinis"), 2 Chaconnes / Harmonia Mundi HMU907029
John Butt (organ)

★ **Organ Music**

Choral Preludes, Fantasia, Ciacona, Partita, etc. / Virgin VC791087-2
Werner Jacob (organ)

Nicolo Paganini (1782-1840)

An Italian virtuoso violinist, guitarist, and composer of chamber and orchestral music featuring violin and guitar. Paganini revolutionized the art of violin playing (his *Concerto no. 1 in D* gives some idea of his incredible technique), even as he was surrounded by gossip, often self-promoted, about amorous affairs in Napoleon's court; being supported in his teens by an older mistress (her identity still unknown), who saved him from self-destructive drinking brought on by quick fame; a pact made with the devil that gave him superhuman ability to play his instrument; and so on. —*"Blue" Gene Tyranny*

★ **Caprices**

24 Capricci, Op. 1 / CBS MK44944
Midori (violin)

24 Capricci, Op. 1 / EMI CDC7471712
Itzhak Perlman (violin)

24 Capricci, Op. 1 / EMI CDC7476442
Frank Peter Zimmermann (violin)

CONCERTO #1 FOR VIOLIN

Concerto #1, Op. 6 / Philips 420943-2
Midori (violin), Leonard Slatkin/London Symphony Orchestra

Concerto #1, Op. 6 / EMI CDC7470882
Sir Yehudi Menuhin (violin), Alberto Erede/Royal Philharmonic Orchestra

John Knowles Paine (1839-1906)

After receiving a solid education in organ, piano, harmony, and counterpoint from the German musician Kotschmar in Maine, Paine left to study at the Hochschule fur Musik at Berlin. There he continued his work in organ, composition, and orchestration and began performing on organ for such notables as Clara Schumann. During this time he adopted the German style as his own. Upon his return to Boston in 1861, Paine began an organ recital and lecture series that eventually landed him a position at Harvard as the first professor of music in an American university. He was a leading member of the Boston music scene as a teacher of many distinguished musicians and as advocate for the development of music pedagogy in the university system. His music was greatly respected during his prime and received many favorable reviews. Paine's early works were academic but pleasing. Despite an early renunciation of the corruption of chromaticism, he began to incorporate the technique in later works, without much success. His most important later work is the prelude to *Oedipus Tyrannus*. His music is strongly tonal and sensitively orchestrated with increasing chromaticism and complexity in later years. —*Lynn Vought*

CHAMBER & PIANO MUSIC

Romanza & Humoreske for Cello and Piano, Op. 30; Larghetto & Humoreske for Piano Trio, Op. 32; and Violin Sonata, Op. 24 / Northeastern NR219-CD
Joseph Silverstein (violin), Jules Eskin (cello), Virginia Eskin (piano)

Selected Piano Music / New World Records 80424-2
Denver Oldham (piano)

SYMPHONIES (1, 2)

Symphony #1, Op. 23 / New World Records NW374-2
Zubin Mehta/New York Philharmonic Orchestra

Symphony #2 ("In Springtime"), Op. 34 / New World Records NW350-2
Zubin Mehta/New York Philharmonic Orchestra

Giovanni Pierliugi Palestrina (1526-1594)

An Italian composer of sacred music who was an important musical figure of the Renaissance; known for his "seamless texture" of polyphony. Palestrina composed over 100 settings of the mass (in Richard Wagner's words, with "indescribable depth of expression"), including the *Missa Papae Marcelli*, composed after an edict by Pope Marcellus that the vocal music for the mass "must be sung in a fitting manner, with properly modulated voices, so that everything may be heard and understood." Palestrina succeeded in doing this with remarkable clarity of line, beauty of modal harmony, and a festive rhythmic sense. The *Assumpta est Maria* is probably his best mass, with the voices moving more like orchestra parts than block harmony or contrapuntal choirs. —*"Blue" Gene Tyranny*

MOTETS

29 Motets for 5 Voices from Cantico Canticorum / Collegium COLCD122
John Rutter/The Cambridge Singers

★ **Masses (*Missa Papae Marcelli, Hodie Christus Natus Est (Christmas Mass))**

Masses: "Benedicta es"; "Brevis"; "Nasce la gioja mia"; "Nigra Sum"; "Papae Marcelli"; "Sicut lilium inter spinas" and Two Motets / Gimell CDGIMB400 (4-Disc, 400th Anniversary Commemorative Set)
Peter Phillips/The Tallis Scholars

Mass "Papae Marcelli" and Stabat Mater "Dolorosa" (also see Allegri) / Collins 50092
Harry Christophers/The Sixteen

Mass "Hodie Christus Natus Est" and Six Motets / EMI Eminence CDM7640452
Philip Ledger/Choir of King's College, Cambridge

Francisco de Penalosa (c. 1470-1528)

Penalosa was the most highly regarded composer among the first generation to bring the Franco-Flemish polyphonic style to Spain and the Iberian peninsula. He was associated with the royal court in Aragon, as well as the Cathedral of Seville; he also had an ex-

tended stay in Rome as one of the Pope's most desired musicians. A large number of his works survive in Spanish sources.

Penalosa's style is based primarily on that of Josquin, but one finds much tighter formal structures and highly polished gestures leading to an increased emotional expressivity. In this last sense he represents an important beginning to the Spanish choral style to be exemplified a century later by Victoria. His compositions are entirely sacred in designation, though the wide range of emotionality lends many a character that would later be considered more properly secular in nature. —*Todd McComb*

SACRED MUSIC

Masses "Missa Ave Maria Peregrina" and "Missa Nunca Fue Pena Mayor" / Hyperion CDA66629
James O'Donnell /Choir of Westminster Cathedral

22 Motets / Hyperion CDA66574
Bruno Turner /Pro Cantione Antiqua

Giovanni Battista Pergolesi (1710-1736)

An Italian composer known for comic opera as well as sacred and secular vocal music. In his short life, Pergolesi managed to establish a style of beautiful melodies accompanied by a clear orchestra of harmonic tensions, as in the breathtaking *Stabat Mater*, with its slow build of emotion accomplished apparently by the simplest means (in the centuries following Pergolesi's death, some composers attempted to beef up his lovely music by adding huge, pretentious orchestras). The *Stabat Mater* is essentially a vocal chamber music work inspired by religion, rather than a work for the church. It was composed on Pergolesi's deathbed, and he was paid ten ducats for it—one less than it took to bury him. His lovely and lively concertinos, the *Concerto for Flute, Strings & Cembalo in D*, and his opera *La Serva Padrona* are necessary listening for appreciating the natural talent of this wonderful composer. — *"Blue" Gene Tyranny*

STABAT MATER

Stabat Mater / Hungaroton HCD12201
Magda Kalmar (soprano), Julia Hamari (contralto), Lamberto Gardelli/Ladies of the Hungarian Radio and Television Chorus & Liszt Ferenc Chamber Orchestra, Budapest

Stabat Mater, Salve Regina, and In Coelestibus Regnis / Hyperion CDA66294
Gillian Fisher (soprano), Michael Chance (countertenor), Robert King/The King's Consort

★ **La Serva Padrona (Opera)**

La Serva Padrona / Hungaroton HCD12846
Katalin Farkas (soprano), Jozsef Gregor (bass), Pal Nemeth/Capella Savaria

Perotin (c.1160-1240)

French composer of sacred music, the most highly acclaimed musical figure of the High Gothic period. Perotin worked in Paris, and was the most celebrated exponent of the School of Notre Dame, in which monophonic chant was elaborated into polyphony with a sublime perfection. He composed mostly hymns and sequences, as well as some likely partial attributions of mass cycles (along with his older contemporary, Leonin). His style is typical of the period—a tenor chant in even rhythm, elaborated by long melismas in the upper voices. It was for his supreme mastery of this style that he was dubbed "The Great." — *Todd McComb*

★ **Sequences**

"Beata Viscera," "Sederunt Principes," and Seven Other Works / ECM 837751-2
Paul Hillier/Hilliard Ensemble

Peter Philips (1560-1628)

Philips was an English composer and organist who spent most of his working life in Belgium. He was a Catholic, and as such chose to leave England after a tenure as singer at St. Paul's Cathedral in London. He first went to Brussels and then quickly on to the English College in Rome where he met the English Catholic landowner Lord Thomas Paget. Philips and Paget traveled throughout Europe together, before settling in Antwerp shortly before Paget's death. There Philips obtained a position as organist to the chapel of the Archduke Albrect and met his colleagues

John Bull and Pieter Cornet, as well as probably Jan Pieterszoon Sweelinck. He was also highly regarded as a virginal player, and made a living teaching on this instrument.

Philips was one of the most prolific northern composers of Latin sacred choral music, with a few hundred surviving motets. He also composed music for both instrumental consort and keyboard, many of these pieces surviving in arrangements of both types. These pieces involve the best-known genres of English instrumental music of the time, the fantasia, pavan, and galliard. Philips's motets also contain something of the English style in that they are all written with organ accompaniment; his style of vocal composition, however, is more in keeping with the great continental masters of the period, such as Lassus. His vocal and instrumental writing is extremely smooth, with well-planned harmonies and a general lack of contrapuntal artifice. Philips was one of the outstanding vocal composers of his day, publishing motets in German as well as Latin. —*Todd McComb*

MOTETS

Paradisus Sacris Cantionibus / Accent 8862
Erik Van Nevel/Currende Vocal Ensemble

12 Motets / Hyperion CDA66643
Peter Holman/Winchester Cathedral Choir & The Parley of Instruments

KEYBOARD MUSIC

Harpsichord Music / Etcetera 1022
Anneke Uittenbosch (harpsichord)

Harpsichord Music / Harmonia Mundi HMC901263
Emer Buckley (harpsichord)

Walter Piston (1894-1976)

An American composer with an unique tonalist style and a teacher whose book on music theory, *Harmony*, became an American standard. Piston wrote compositions primarily in an orchestral, tonal style, neo-classical and nationalist in character. We may hear a tune that starts out something like folk music, but soon it stretches off into the eeriest of dark universes, as in *Symphony no. 2*, or into breadth and lyricism and a blaze of major-key glory, as in *Symphony no. 6*.) Piston's sound is fresh, sometimes on a big landscape and sometimes evoking a feeling of being lost in the woods, much like traveling across the United States. —*"Blue" Gene Tyranny*

INCREDIBLE FLAUTIST (BALLET SUITE)

The Incredible Flutist (ballet suite) / Sheffield Labs CD-26
Dmitri Kitayenko/Moscow Philharmonic Orchestra

The Incredible Flutist (ballet suite)/ RCA Red Seal 60798-2-RC
Leonard Slatkin/St. Louis Symphony Orchestra

SYMPHONY #2

Symphony #2 / Delos DE3074
Gerard Schwarz/Seattle Symphony Orchestra

Symphony #2 / Deutsche Grammophon 429860-2
Michael Tilson Thomas/Boston Symphony Orchestra

Amilcare Ponchielli (1834-1886)

An Italian composer whose fame is based upon one work, *La Gioconda*, an opera that contains the famous "Dance of the Hours." Ponchielli also wrote band pieces, vocal chamber pieces, and music for voice and piano. —*Mary K. Scanlan*

GIOCONDA: DANCE OF THE HOURS

La Gioconda, Act 3 "Dance of the Hours" / Sony SMK47600
Leonard Bernstein/New York Philharmonic Orchestra

La Gioconda, Act 3 "Dance of the Hours" / Laserlight 15504
Andras Korodi/Budapest Philharmonic Orchestra

Francis Poulenc (1899-1963)

A French composer of many forms, including choral and vocal music, opera, and piano and orchestral works. Poulenc was described by one of his friends as "moiti moine, moiti voyou" (half monk, half guttersnipe), which seems to fit his distinct type of musical composition. The *Concerto for Organ, Strings & Tympani in g* and the *Gloria for Soprano, Orchestra & Chorus in G* are heroic and often lovely; together with his famous opera, *Dialog of the Carmlites*, they reflect his religious bent with dramatic gestures and clear French melodic lines. The ballet music *Les Biches* is an example of his humor, which verges on triviality but never really falls into it. And there are works that fall somewhere in the middle, like the wonderful *Sonata for Two Pianos* and the *Concert Champtre* (1929), written for harpsichordist Wanda Landowska. —*"Blue" Gene Tyranny*

CHAMBER MUSIC

Complete Chamber Music including Sonatas, Sextet, etc. /
EMI CZS7627362
Various performers including: Alan Civil (horn), Michel Portal (clarinet), Sir Yehudi Menuhin (violin), Jacques Fevrier (piano), Michel Debost (flute), Maurice Bourgue (oboe)

Sextet for Piano & Winds and Wind Sonatas / London 421581-2
Pascal Roge (piano), Michel Portal (clarinet), Maurice Bourgue (oboe), Patrick Gallois (flute), Cazalet (horn), Amaury Wallez (bassoon)

CONCERTO FOR ORGAN, STRINGS & TIMPANI

Organ Concerto in G Minor / Erato 2292-45233-2
Marie-Claire Alain (organ), James Conlon/Rotterdam Philharmonic Orchestra

Organ Concerto in G Minor / Telarc CD-80104
Michael Murray (organ), Louis Lane/Atlanta Symphony Orchestra

PIANO MUSIC

Complete Piano Music / CBS M3K44921
Paul Crossley (piano)

Piano Music, Vol 1 / London 425862-2
Pascal Roge (Piano)

Piano Music, Vol 1 / London 417438-2
Pascal Roge (Piano)

SONGS

Voyage a Paris (20 Songs) / Hyperion CDA66147
Felicity Lott (soprano), The Songmakers' Almanac

Micheal Praetorius (1571-1621)

German composer and theorist, influential as a defining force of German musical practice. Praetorius composed both sacred vocal and secular instrumental music; his dance pieces, *Terpsichore*, are the most popular of the period. —*AMG*

★ Terpsichore

Instrumental Dances from Terpsichore (1612) / L'Oiseau-Lyre 414633-2
Philip Pickett/New London Consort

Terpsichore (selections); Christmas Music / Hyperion CDA66200
David Hill/Parley of Instruments Baroque Orchestra & Westminster Cathedral Choir

Sergei Prokofiev (1891-1953)

A Russian composer whose modernity seems to be inherent in him rather than something artificial or overintellectualized. His natural feeling for melody and rhythm—by turns humorous (*Peter and the Wolf*), lyrical (*Concerto for Piano & Orchestra no. 3*), elegiac (*Visions Fugitives*), aggressive (*Scythian Suite*), or all of the above (*Lieutenant Kije Suite*)—is wedded to a desire for direct communication with the listener and a quality of continually interesting invention. From the piano sonatas, we can see that his style was established at an early age and flowed from his character. It is strange, then, that he should have been criticized on one hand by Soviet authorities for "formalistic deviations and antidemocratic musical tendencies," and on the other by American critics on his 1921 tour for expressing Bolshevism in music. He was guilty of neither, and now we can appreciate his wonderful pieces for what they are. —*"Blue" Gene Tyranny*

★ Classical Symphony

Symphony #1 ("Classical"), Op. 25 / Deutsche Grammophon 423624-2
Orpheus Chamber Orchestra

Symphony #1 ("Classical"), Op. 25 / Delos D / CD3021
Gerard Schwarz/Seattle Symphony Orchestra

Symphony #1 ("Classical"), Op. 25 / Chandos CHAN8400
Neeme Jarvi/Scottish National Orchestra

★ **Concerto #3 for Piano**

Piano Concerto #3 in C Major, Op. 26 / Telarc CD-80124
Jon Kimura Parker (piano), Andre Previn/Royal Philharmonic Orchestra

Piano Concerto #3 in C Major, Op. 26 / Deutsche Grammophon 415062-2
Martha Argerich (piano), Claudio Abbado/Berlin Philharmonic Orchestra

Piano Concerto #3 in C Major, Op. 26 / Vox Music Group CD3X3000
Gabriel Tacchino (piano), Louis de Froment/Orchestra of Radio Luxembourg

CONCERTOS FOR VIOLIN (1, 2)

Violin Concertos #1 in D Major, Op. 19, and #2, Op. 63 / Deutsche Grammophon 410524-2
Shlomo Mintz (violin), Claudio Abbado/Chicago Symphony Orchestra

Violin Concertos #1 in D Major, Op. 19, and #2, Op. 63 / Vox Music Group CD3X3000
Ruggiero Ricci (violin), Louis de Froment/Orchestra of Radio Luxembourg

LIEUTENANT KIJE SUITE

Lieutenant KizhehSuite, Op. 60 / Telarc CD-80143
Andre Previn/Los Angeles Philharmonic Orchestra

Lieutenant KizhehSuite, Op. 60 / Deutsche Grammophon 419603-2
Claudio Abbado/London Symphony Orchestra

★ **Peter and the Wolf**

Peter & the Wolf, Op. 67 / Telarc CD-80126
Andre Previn (narration), Andre Previn/Royal Philharmonic Orchestra

Peter & the Wolf, Op. 67 / Deutsche Grammophon 429396-2
Sting (narration), Claudio Abbado/Chamber Orchestra of Europe

ROMEO & JULIET (EXCERPTS)

Romeo & Juliet (ballet), Op. 64 / Sheffield Labs CD-07 / 08
Erich Leinsdorf/Los Angeles Philharmonic Orchestra

Romeo & Juliet Suites, #1-3, Op. 64a, 64b & 101 / Chandos CHAN8940
Neeme Jarvi/Scottish National Orchestra

★ **Sonatas for Piano (2, *6, *7, *8)**

Sonatas and Piano Music / Harmonia Mundi HMU907086.88
Frederic Chiu (piano)

Sonatas and Piano Music / Newport Classic NCD60092 / 3 / 4
Barbara Nissman (piano)

Piano Sonata #6, Op. 82 / Sony SK45931
Evgeny Kissen (piano)

Sonata #7, Op. 83 / Deutsche Grammophon 419202-2
Maurizio Polini (piano)

Piano Sonatas #7, Op. 83, and #8, Op. 84 / CBS MK44680
Eugene Bronfman (piano)

★ **Symphony #5**

Symphony #5, Op. 100 / Chandos CHAN8450
Neeme Jarvi/Scottish National Orchestra

Symphony #5, Op. 100 / RCA RCD1-5035
Leonard Slatkin/St. Louis Symphony Orchestra

Giacomo Puccini (1858-1924)

An Italian composer of opera in the "verismo" (truth and reality) style, which was a reaction against heavy symbolism. Speaking in a harmonic language that is a mixture of Wagner, Debussy, and early Stravinsky, Puccini adds his gift for the liquescent melodic line that speaks and sighs and builds slowly to a beautiful sostenuto, seeming to evoke rather than be accompanied by the orchestra. Puccini's brave heroines are true, fully developed characters, sometimes straight from the real world, who meet tragic ends (the consumptive in *La Bohme;* the shocking suicide in *Tosca; Madame Butterfly,* based on a magazine story by John Luther Long). — *"Blue" Gene Tyranny*

★ **La Boheme (opera)**

La Boheme / London 421049-2

Freni, Harwood, Luciano Pavoratti, Panerai, Herbert von Karajan/Berlin Philharmonic Orchestra & German Opera Chorus

La Boheme / EMI CDCB747235
Victoria de Los Angeles, Bjoerling, Merrill, Sir Thomas Beecham/RCA Victor Orchestra

LA FANCIULLA DEL WEST (OPERA)

La Fanciulla del West / RCA Red Seal 09026-60597-2
Marton, O'Neill, Plante, Fondary, Leonard Slatkin/Munich Radio Orchestra & Bavarian Radio Chorus

★ **Madama Butterfly (opera)**

Madama Butterfly / Hungaroton HCD12256 / 7
Kincses, Takas, Dvorsky, Miller, Giuseppe Patane/Hungarian State Opera Orchestra & Chorus

Madama Butterfly / London 411634-2
Tebaldi, Bergonzi, Sordello, Tullio Serafin/Orchestra e Choro di Santa Cecilia, Rome

MANON LESCAUT (OPERA)

Manon Lescaut (1893) / Deutsche Grammophon 413893-2
Freni, Placido Domingo, Bruson, Giuseppe Sinopoli/Philharmonia Orchestra & Royal Opera House Chorus

Manon Lescaut / EMI CDS7473922
Maria Callas, Giuseppe di Stefano, Fioravanti, Tullio Serafin/Teatro alla Scala di Milano Orchestra & Chorus

LA RONDINE (OPERA)

La Rondine / CBS M2K37852
Kiri Te Kanawa, Placido Domingo, Rendall, Nucci, Lorin Maazel/London Symphony Orchestra & Ambrosian Opera Chorus

★ **Tosca (opera)**

Tosca / RCA RCD2-0105
Leontyne Price, Placido Domingo, Milnes, Zubin Mehta/New Philharmonia Orchestra & John Alldis Choir

Tosca / Deutsche Grammophon 413815-2
Ricciarelli, Jose Carreras, Raimondi, Herbert von Karajan/Berlin Philharmonic Orchestra & German Opera Chorus

Tosca / EMI CDS7471742
Maria Callas, Giuseppe di Stefano, De Sabata, Tito Gobbi, Tullio Serafin/Teatro alla Scala di Milano Orchestra & Chorus

★ **Turandot (opera)**

Turandot / London 414275-2
Dame Joan Sutherland, Luciano Pavarotti, Caballe, Zubin Mehta/London Philharmonic Orchestra & John Alldis Choir

Turandot / RCA RCD2-5932
Nilsson, Tebaldi, Bjoerling, Tozzi, Erich Leinsdorf/Rome Opera Orchestra & Chorus

Turandot / EMI CDS7479712
Maria Callas, Schwarzkopf, Fernandi, Zaccaria, Tullio Serafin/Teatro alla Scala di Milano Orchestra & Chorus

Henry Purcell (1659-1695)

An English composer in every category and form of music practiced in his time, remembered today for lively trumpet voluntaries and sweet vocal airs. *Dido and Aeneas* has plenty of both. Writing it on commission for the head of a boarding school for "gentlewomen" in Chelsea, Purcell included 17 different dances for the girls amidst the lovely arias of the mythological libretto, a type of "masque"—important in the development of opera and a curiously interesting form of theater today. — *"Blue" Gene Tyranny*

ANTHEMS

Complete Anthems and Services Vol. 1 / Hyperion CDA66585
Nicholas Witcomb, Jerome Finnis, Philip Hallchurch (trebles); James Bowman (countertenor); Charles Daniels (tenor); Michael George, Robert Evans (basses)/Choir of New College, Oxford

Complete Anthems and Services Vol. 2 / Hyperion CDA66609
Nicholas Witcomb, Daniel Lochmann, Philip Hallchurch, Timothy Bowes (trebles), James Bowman (countertenor), Rogers Covey-Crump (tenor), Michael George bass/Choir of New College, Oxford

★ **Dido and Aeneas (opera)**

Dido and Aeneas / Chandos Chaconne CHAN0521

Emma Kirkby, Judith Nelson (sopranos), Jantina Noorman (mezzo-soprano), David Thomas (bass-baritone), Andrew Parrott/Taverner Players & Taverner Choir

FANTASIES

15 Fantasias, Z. 732-747 / EMI CDM7630662
London Baroque

★ **Trio Sonatas for Strings & Continuo**

7 Sonatas a 3 & Pavans / Chandos CHAN8591
Purcell Quartet

5 Sonatas a 3, 2 Sonatas a 4, Pavans & Fantasias / Chandos CHAN8663
Purcell Quartet

8 Sonatas a 4 & Voluntaries / Chandos CHAN8763
Purcell Quartet

12 Sonatas a 3 / Harmonia Mundi HMC901439
London Baroque

10 Sonatas a 4 / Harmonia Mundi HMC901438
London Baroque

Johann Joachim Quantz (1697-1773)

After the death of his father, a blacksmith, Quantz began his musical training under his uncle, a town musician in Merseburg. He studied string and wind instruments and also took lessons on the harpsichord. During this period he came to know the works of the major baroque composers of the preceeding and present generations. Quantz moved to Dresden and became a member of the town band in 1716. After studying counterpoint the following year in Vienna, he next settled in Dresden as oboist for Augustus II in the Polish chapel. He perceived little opportunity for advancement on the oboe and switched to flute during this time. His interest in composition began to grow, especially for works for the flute. Here he had many opportunities to perform for the royalty of Europe. After a distinguished world tour, Quantz was offered a post as a member of the court Kapelle in Dresden. In 1740 he took a special position as composer and flute maker for Frederick, the king of Prussia, where he remained for the rest of his career. Quantz was responsible for many innovations in flute design, including the addition of keys to improve intonation. He was the author of teaching manuals for his own as well as other instruments. His compositions are clearly baroque, although his later works show some development toward the classical style. — *Lynn Vought*

CONCERTOS FOR FLUTE

Concertos in C Major, G Major, G Minor, and D Major ("Potsdam")/ RCA 60247-2-RC
James Galway (flute), Jorg Faerber/Wurttemberg Chamber Orchestra, Heilbronn

Sergei Rachmaninoff (1873-1943)

A Russian virtuoso pianist and composer in the Russian romantic style of piano and orchestral works; known for *Rhapsody on a Theme of Paganini, for Piano & Orchestra, op. 43* (1934). Strange as it may seem, Rachmaninoff's popularity overshadows his contribution to music, which was the continuation of the traditions in sound of two other composers: Tchaikovsky (cf. *Concerto No. 2 in C*) and Grieg (the *Op. 43 Rhapsody*). His symphonies, especially the *Symphony No. 3*, 1936), his tone poem *The Isle of the Dead* (1907); the *Symphonic Dances* (1940); and several choral works, including *The Bells* (1913) and *Vespers* (1915), can still be appreciated as innovations within these traditions—as expansive in imagery and timbre as is the brilliance of his melodic sense for the piano. —*"Blue" Gene Tyranny*

★ **Concertos for Piano (1, *2, *3, 4) and Rhapsody on a Theme of Paganini**

4 Piano Concertos: Op. 1, 18, 30 & 40 and Rhapsody on a Theme of Paganini, Op. 43 / Vox Music Group CDX5008
Abbey Simon (piano), Leonard Slatkin/Saint Louis Symphony Orchestra

2 Piano Concertos: #1 & 4, Op. 1 & 40 and Rhapsody on a Theme of Paganini, Op. 43 / Chesky CD41
Earl Wild (piano), Jasha Horenstein/Royal Philharmonic Orchestra

Piano Concerto #1, Op. 1, and Rhapsody on a Theme of Paganini, Op. 43 / London 417613-2
Vladimir Ashkenazy (piano), Bernard Haitink/Philharmonia Orchestra

2 Piano Concertos: #2 & 4, Op. 18 & 40 / London 414475-2
Vladimir Ashkenazy (piano), Bernard Haitink/Philharmonia Orchestra

★ **Etudes & Preludes for Piano**

Preludes, Op. 23 & 32 / RCA 60568-2-RG
Alexis Weissenberg (piano)

Etudes, Op. 33 & 39, and Preludes, Op. 23 & 32 (selections) / Delos D / CD3044
John Browning (piano)

Etudes, Op. 33 & 39, and Preludes, Op. 23 & 32 (selections) / Olympia OLY337
Sviatoslav Richter (piano)

Etudes, Op. 33 & 39 (complete) / Hyperion CDA66091
Howard Shelley (piano)

Preludes, Op. 23 & 32 / London 414417-2
Vladimir Ashkenazy (piano)

★ **Morceaux de Fantasie**

Morceaux de Fantaisie, Op. 3 / 2 / Hyperion CDA66081
Howard Shelley (piano)

Morceaux de Fantaisie—Prelude, Op. 3 / 2 / RCA 60568-2-RG
Alexis Weissenberg (piano)

SONATAS FOR PIANO

Piano Sonatas #1, Op. 28, and #2, Op. 36 / Hyperion CDA66047
Howard Shelley (piano)

Piano Sonata #1, Op. 28 / London 414417-2
Vladimir Ashkenazy (piano)

Piano Sonata #2, Op. 36 / Delos D / CD3044
John Browning (piano)

SUITES FOR PIANO FOUR HANDS

Suites: #1 ("Fantaisie-Tableaux"), Op. 5, and #2, Op. 17 / Harmonia Mundi HMC901301.02
Brigitte Engerer & Oleg Maisenberg (pianos)

SYMPHONIC DANCES

Symphonic Dances, Op. 45 / London 410124-2
Vladimir Ashkenazy/Concertgebouw Orchestra Amsterdam

Symphonic Dances, Op. 45 / Chandos CAN9081
Neeme Jarvi/Philharmonia Orchestra

Symphonic Dances, Op. 45a (piano version) / Harmonia Mundi HMC901301.02
Brigitte Engerer & Oleg Maisenberg (pianos)

★ **Symphony #2**

Symphony #2, Op. 27 / Telarc CD-80113
Andre Previn/Royal Philharmonic Orchestra

Symphony #2, Op. 27 / Virgin CDC595482 or ZDMC592792
Andrew Litton/Royal Philharmonic Orchestra

Symphony #2, Op. 27 / London 400081-2
Vladimir Ashkenazy/Concertgebouw Orchestra Amsterdam

TRIOS FOR PIANO & STRINGS

"Elegiac" Piano Trios #1 and #2, Op. 9 / Chandos CHAN8341
Beaux Arts Trio

"Elegiac" Piano Trios #1 and #2, Op. 9 / Philips 420175-2
Beaux Arts Trio

Jean-Philippe Rameau (1683-1764)

The great French theoretician who synthesized the current rules of harmonic practice and suggested others in *Trait de l'Harmonie* ("Treatise on Harmony") (1723) and *Nouveau Systme de Musique Thorique* ("New System of Musical Theory") (1726)—works that are studied by composers to this day. Rameau was a bold experimenter in harmony and a master of orchestration who introduced new effects (e.g., storm scenes), especially in the choruses of his "operas" (heroic pastorales, allegoric ballet, fetes—not opera as we think of it now). The finest of these are *Les Indes Galantes* (1739) and *Zoroastre* (1749). His harpsichord pieces are exquisite

miniature studies in harmonic and evocative invention. — *"Blue"*
Gene Tyranny

BALLET MUSIC

Suite from Les Indes Galantes / Harmonia Mundi HMC901130
Philippe Herreweghe/Orchestra de la Chapelle Royale

Suite from Castor & Pollux / Philips 426714-2
Frans Bruggen/Orchestra of the 18th Century

Suites from Dardanus and Les Boreades / Philips 420240-2
Frans Bruggen/Orchestra of the 18th Century

Suite from Hyppolyte et Aricie / RCA Deutsche Harmonia
Mundi Editio Classica 77009-2-RG
Sigiswald Kuijken/La Petite Bande

LES INDES GALANTES FOR HARPSICHORD

Suite from Les Indes Galantes / Harmonia Mundi Musique
d'Abord HMA1901028
Kenneth Gilbert (harpsichord)

★ Pieces de Clavecin

Nouvelles Suites de Pieces de Clavecin & Pieces de Clavecin /
Harmonia Mundi Musique d'Abord HMA1901120 / 1

Nouvelles Suites de Pieces de Clavecin & Pieces de Clavecin /
L'Oiseau-Lyre 425886-2
Christophe Rousset (harpsichord)

Pieces de Clavecin (misc.) / Reference Recordings RR-27CD
Albert Fuller (harpsichord)

PIECES DE CLAVECIN EN CONCERTS

5 Pieces de Clavecin en Concerts / Virgin Classics Veritas
VC7591542
Trio Sonnerie

5 Pieces de Clavecin en Concerts / Pierre Verany PV.785023
Andre Raynaud (harpsichord)/Ensemble Baroque du Festival
d'Aix-en-Provence

ZOROASTRE (LYRIQUE TRAGEDY)

Zoroastre in 5 Acts / RCA / Deutsche Harmonia Mundi Editio
Classica 77144-2-RG
John Elwes, Greta de Reyghere, Mieke van der Sluis, Agnes
Mellon, Sigiswald Kuijken/Collegium Vocale and La Petite Bande

Maurice Ravel (1875-1937)

A French composer known for melodic and tonal invention.
Giving the lie to the idea that turn-of-the-century musical trends
were necessarily elite impressionism or "decadent" (whatever
that may mean), Ravel's music always speaks directly to the heart
in a subtle rhythmic sense through great melody, harmonic richness, and iridescent orchestration. (The art of stacking partials in
Ravel's *Bolero* and in the work of Ives predate harmonic synthesis in electronic music by half a century.) Ravel's ballet *Daphnis
et Chloe*, with its gently sustained, wordless vocal chorus amidst
heaven-on-earth sound-painting, is probably the finest synthesis
of his aesthetic. Ravel's melodic abilities and method of making
subtle timbre changes by harmonic shift (rather than loud/soft articulation) are beautifully amplified in his piano works, including
the famous *Sonatine*, *Gaspard de la Nuit*, and in *Concerto for
Piano* (for the left hand in D), which also contain some of his
most advanced harmonic writing. The expansive *La Valse* shows
a more extroverted Ravel, with much of the same fine orchestral
composition. The *Quartet in F*, with its rich, earthy melodies,
shows perhaps a more intimate side of Ravel. — *"Blue" Gene
Tyranny*

ALBORADA DEL GRACIOSO

Alborada del Gracioso / London 410010-2
Charles Dutoit/Montreal Symphony Orchestra

Alborada del Gracioso / Telarc CD-80171
Jesus Lopez-Cobos/Cincinnati Symphony Orchestra

Alborada del Gracioso / Mercury Living Presence 432003-2
Paul Paray/Detroit Symphony Orchestra

BOLERO

Bolero / Telarc CD-80171
Jesus Lopez-Cobos/Cincinnati Symphony Orchestra

Bolero / London 410010-2
Charles Dutoit/Montreal Symphony Orchestra

CHANSONS MEDACASSES

Chansons Medacasses / CBS MK39023
Jesse Norman, Pierre Boulez/Ensemble Intercontemporain

CONCERTOS IN D (LEFT HAND) AND IN G FOR PIANO

Piano Concertos / Deutsche Grammophon 423665-2
Michel Beroff (in D) and Martha Argerich (in G), Claudio
Abbado/London Symphony Orchestra

Piano Concertos / London 417583-2
Alicia de Larrocha (piano), Rafael Fruhbeck de Burgos/London
Philharmonic Orchestra

Piano Concertos / London 410230-2
Pascal Roge (piano), Charles Dutoit/Montreal Symphony
Orchestra

★ Daphnis et Chloe (ballet)

Daphnis et Chloe / London 400055-2
Charles Dutoit/Montreal Symphony Orchestra

Daphnis et Chloe / Chandos CHAN8893
Yan Pascal Tortelier/Ulster Philharmonic Orchestra

Daphnis et Chloe / Delos DE3110-2
Gerard Schwarz/Seattle Symphony Orchestra

MA MERE L'OYE (BALLET)

Ma Mere L'oye / London 410254-2
Charles Dutoit/Montreal Symphony Orchestra

Ma Mere L'oye / Chandos CHAN8711
Yan Pascal Tortelier/Ulster Philharmonic Orchestra

★ Piano Music (Miroirs, Gaspard de la Nuit, Le Tombeau de Couperin, etc.)

Complete Piano Music / Vox Music Group CDX5012
Abbey Simon (piano)

**A la Maniere de Borodine, A la Maniere de Chabrier, Le
Tombeau de Couperin, Menuet Antique, Menuet sur le Nom
d'Haydn, Valses Nobles et Sentimentales, Sonatine, and
Prelude** / Nimbus NIM5011
Vlado Perlemuter (piano)

**Gaspard de la Nuit, Jeux d'eau, Miroirs, and Pavane pour Une
Infante Defunte"** / Nimbus NIM5005
Vlado Perlemuter (piano)

★ Pavane pour Une Infante Defunte

Pavane pour Une Infante Defunte / London 410254-2
Charles Dutoit/Montreal Symphony Orchestra

Pavane pour Une Infante Defunte / Mercury Living Presence
432003-2
Paul Paray/Detroit Symphony Orchestra

Pavane pour Une Infante Defunte / Nimbus NIM5005
Vlado Perlemuter (piano)

QUARTET

Quartet in F Major / Delos D / CD3004
Sequoia String Quartet

Quartet in F Major / Hungaroton White Label HRC122
Bartok Quartet

★ Rhapsodie Espagnole

Rhapsodie Espagnole / London 410010-2
Charles Dutoit/Montreal Symphony Orchestra

Rhapsodie Espagnole / Telarc CD-80171
Jesus Lopez-Cobos/Cincinnati Symphony Orchestra

Rhapsodie Espagnole / Deutsche Grammophon 423972-2
Claudio Abbado/London Symphony Orchestra

TZIGANE FOR VIOLIN & ORCHESTRA

Tzigane / EMI CDC7477252
Itzhak Perlman (violin), Jean Martinon/Orchestra of Paris

Tzigane / Deutsche Grammophon 437544-2
Anne-Sophie Mutter (violin), James Levine /Vienna Philharmonic
Orchestra

LA VALSE

La Valse / London 410010-2
Charles Dutoit/Montreal Symphony Orchestra

La Valse / Telarc CD-80171
Jesus Lopez-Cobos/Cincinnati Symphony Orchestra

La Valse / Mercury Living Presence 432003-2
Paul Paray/Detroit Symphony Orchestra

VALSES NOBLES ET SENTIMENTALES

"Valses Nobles et Sentimentales" / London 410254-2
Charles Dutoit/Montreal Symphony Orchestra

Valses Nobles et Sentimentales / Telarc CD-80171
Jesus Lopez-Cobos/Cincinnati Symphony Orchestra

Valses Nobles et Sentimentales" / Mercury Living Presence 432003-2
Paul Paray/Detroit Symphony Orchestra

Valses Nobles et Sentimentales / Nimbus NIM5011
Vlado Perlemuter (piano)

Max Reger (1873-1916)

Reger is considered by many to be the most important composer to elaborate on the stylistic traits of Brahms and move German music into the 20th century. He was an extremely prolific composer, surpassing many of the 19th-century masters in volume during his short life. He was also a driven man, consumed by hard living. Reger composed in most every form of the time, except opera and the symphony proper. His style is contrapuntally dense, with extremely fast modulations lending an atonal feel to many of his lines, though the music remains strictly tonal in its harmonic direction. He was one of the main composers to resuscitate the fugue as a living, independent form. His organ music is considered by many to be second only to Bach's in depth and significance. This music, along with much of his output, requires a large degree of virtuosity. His orchestral writing is virtually opaque in color—some would say turgid—having something of the feel of organ registrations, though it lightens with age. Even his concertos often draw on Protestant hymns for thematic material. His large volume of chamber music is perhaps his most significant contribution to the concert repertory. This part of his output contains some of the largest and most emotionally draining music in its genre. —Todd McComb

ORGAN MUSIC

Organ Music, Vol. 1 / MD&G R3350
Rosalinde Haas (organ)

Selected Organ Music / Chandos CHAN9097
Piet Kee (organ)

Choral Preludes and Other Organ Music / Signum SIGX26-00
Heinz Wunderlich (organ)

★ Chamber Music (*Violin Sonatas)

2 Violin Sonatas: #4, Op. 72, and #5, Op. 84 / Accord 200002
Robert Zimansky (violin), Christoph Keller (piano)

2 Violin Sonatas: #6, Op. 122, and 7, Op. 139 / Jecklin JD649-2
Hansheinz Schneeberger (violin), Jean-Jacques Dunki (piano)

2 Piano Trios: Op. 2 and 102 / Etcetera KTC1077
Gobel Trio Berlin

2 String Quartets: #4, Op. 109, and #5, Op. 121 / Koch CD310068H1
Joachim Quartet

Clarinet Quintet in A Major, Op. 146 / Camerata 30CM-95-97
Karl Leister (clarinet), Philharmonia Quartet Berlin

String Sextet, Op. 118 / Jecklin JD543-2
Zurich Chamber Music Ensemble

ORCHESTRAL MUSIC

Concerto, Op. 114 / Koch CD311058H1
Gerhard Oppitz (piano), Horst Stein/Bamberg Symphony Orchestra

Concerto in A Major, Op. 101 / Koch CD311186H1
Walter Forchert (violin), Horst Stein/Bamberg Symphony Orchestra

Variations & Fugue on a Theme by Johann Adam Hiller, Op. 100, and Tone Poems after Arnold Bocklin, Op. 128 / Chandos CHAN8794
Neeme Jarvi/Concertgebouw Orchestra Amsterdam

PIANO MUSIC

12 Pieces ("Traume am Kamin"), Op. 143 / Jecklin JD601-2
John Buttrick (piano)

Variations & Fugue on a Theme by Bach, Op. 81, and on a Theme by Telemann, Op. 134 / Koch CD310008H1
David Levine (piano)

Complete Music for Piano Duo / Jecklin JD609-2
Isabel and Jurg von Vintschger (pianos)

Anton Reicha (1770-1836)

Reicha ran away from his widowed mother to study with his uncle Josef, a virtuoso cellist, composer, and director who taught him violin, piano, and flute. His fellow students included Beethoven and Neefe. In Hamburg in 1794 Reicha taught piano, composition, and harmony and began his personal study of mathmatics, philosophy, and meditation. Reicha's professional career included a position as professor of counterpoint at the Conservatoire in Paris and an appointment as Chevalier of the Legion of Honor. Berlioz and Liszt were among his students. His compositions are difficult to classify as musical, theoretical, or pedogological. They are a blend of the artistic and the didactic and are experimental in mode and meter. He wrote several operas, most of which failed, but Reicha enjoyed considerable popularity in his day. His other compositions include works in counterpoint and choral and chamber works. He is remembered as one of the most important theorists of his time, and his many treatises contained the beginnings of important musical developments for the following generations. —Lynn Vought

WIND QUINTETS

Quintets: #7, Op. 91 #1; #18, Op. 99 #6; and #23, Op. 100 #5 / CPO 999027-2
Albert Schweitzer Quintet

Quintets: #5, Op. 88 #5; and #11, Op. 91 #5 / Hyperion CDA66379
Academia Wind Quintet, Prague

Ottorino Respighi (1879-1936)

An Italian composer of orchestral works, vocal music, and operas who based his music on church modes and plainchant; known for his orchestral arrangements. Respighi's music may perhaps be best described as romantic-impressionist, because the melodies are extended and fully developed and the orchestral sound has the richness of an impressionist landscape. His two best-known (and probably his best) works are The Fountains of Rome and The Pines of Rome. Less known but very rewarding to hear are the works in which he reset older music, such as the fine Ancient Airs and Dances (three sets, 1917, 1924, 1932), or those in which he used a rather poetic interpretation of ancient Greek and Gregorian modality, such as Concerto Gregoriano for Violin & Orchestra (1921) and the interesting Concerto in Modo Misolidio for Piano & Orchestra (1925). A fan of Pines and Fountains may also wish to check out Respighi's Roman Festivals, Brazilian Impressions, and Church Windows. —"Blue" Gene Tyranny

★ Ancient Airs & Dances

Ancient Airs & Dances (3 suites) / Omega OCD1007
Christopher Lyndon Gee/Australian Chamber Orchestra

Ancient Airs & Dances (3 suites)/ Mercury Living Presence 416496-2
Antal Dorati/Philharmonia Hungarica

Ancient Airs & Dances (3 suites)/ EMI CDC7471162
Neville Marriner/Los Angeles Chamber Orchestra

GLI UCELLI (THE BIRDS)

The Birds / Omega OCD1007
Christopher Lyndon Gee/Australian Chamber Orchestra

The Birds / Telarc CD-80085
Louis Lane/Atlanta Symphony Orchestra

BRAZILIAN IMPRESSIONS

Brazilian Impressions / Mercury Living Presence 432007-2
Antal Dorati/London Symphony Orchestra

Brazilian Impressions/ Dorian Recordings DOR-90182
Eduardo Mata/Dallas Symphony Orchestra

FESTE ROMANE

Feste Romane/ London 410145-2
Charles Dutoit/Montreal Symphony Orchestra

Feste Romane / Dorian Recordings DOR-90182

Eduardo Mata/Dallas Symphony Orchestra

★ **Fountains of Rome**

Fountains of Rome / London 410145-2
Charles Dutoit/Montreal Symphony Orchestra

Fountains of Rome / Telarc CD-80085
Louis Lane/Atlanta Symphony Orchestra

Fountains of Rome / Mercury Living Presence 432007-2
Antal Dorati/Minneapolis Symphony Orchestra

Fountains of Rome / Dorian Recordings DOR-90182
Eduardo Mata/Dallas Symphony Orchestra

★ **Pines of Rome**

Pines of Rome / London 410145-2
Charles Dutoit/Montreal Symphony Orchestra

Pines of Rome / Telarc CD-80085
Louis Lane/Atlanta Symphony Orchestra

Pines of Rome / Mercury Living Presence 432007-2
Antal Dorati/Minneapolis Symphony Orchestra

Pines of Rome / Dorian Recordings DOR-90182
Eduardo Mata/Dallas Symphony Orchestra

Nikolai Rimsky-Korsakov (1844-1908)

A renowned Russian theoretician whose book on orchestration (*Principles of Orchestration,* 1913) is still widely studied; part of "The Mighty Five," who revived the Russian musical spirit and sound in the second half of the 19th century. His *Scheherazade,* with its exotic imagery, flowing melodies, and balletic rhythms, is his most famous piece, but Rimsky-Korsakov regarded his operas as his best achievement. In fact, two of the eight operas—*The Invisible City of Kitezh* and *The Golden Cockerel*— are unappreciated masterpieces, and the opera *Mlada* is notable for its Wagnerian influences. The *Russian Easter Overture* is a fine example of his mastery of orchestral timbres. —*"Blue" Gene Tyranny*

★ **Capriccio Espagnole**

Capriccio Espagnole, Op. 34 / Deutsche Grammophon 423604-2
Neeme Jarvi/Gothenburg Symphony Orchestra

Capriccio Espagnole, Op. 34 / Telarc CD-80208
Sir Charles Mackerras/London Symphony Orchestra

Capriccio Espagnole, Op. 34 / Naxos 8.550086
Keith Clark/Slovak Radio Symphony Orchestra, Bratislava

COQ D'OR (BALLET SUITE)

The Golden Cockerel / Philips 411435-2
David Zinman/Rotterdam Philharmonic Orchestra

The Golden Cockerel / Mercury Living Presence 434008-2
Antal Dorati/London Symphony Orchestra

RUSSIAN EASTER OVERTURE

Russian Easter Overture, Op. 36 / Deutsche Grammophon 423604-2
Neeme Jarvi/Gothenburg Symphony Orchestra

Russian Easter Overture, Op. 36 / London 417299-2
Charles Dutoit/Montreal Symphony Orchestra

★ **Scheherazade**

Scheherazade, Op. 35 / Philips 400021-2
Herman Krebbers (violin), Kirill Kondrashin/Concertgebouw Orchestra Amsterdam

Scheherazade, Op. 35 / RCA Gold Seal 09026-60875-2
Fritz Reiner/Chicago Symphony Orchestra

Scheherazade, Op. 35 / Chandos CHAN8479
Edwin Paling (violin), Neeme Jarvi/Scottish National Orchestra

SYMPHONY #2 ("ANTAR")

Symphony #2 ("Antar"), Op. 9 / Deutsche Grammophon 423604-2
Neeme Jarvi/Gothenburg Symphony Orchestra

Symphony #2 ("Antar"), Op. 9 / Hyperion CDA66399
Evgeni Svetlanov/Philharmonia Orchestra

Joaquin Rodrigo (b. 1901)

The Spanish romantic-impressionist composer of *Concierto de Aranjuez,* which is often heard in the setting by Gil Evans for Miles Davis on *Sketches of Spain.* The original has many more

charms and beauty of orchestration; it and its companion piece, *Fantasia para un Gentilhombre for Guitar & Orchestra,* each have elegant, warm, and memorable melodies. —*"Blue" Gene Tyranny*

★ **Concierto de Aranjuez for Guitar and Orchestra**

Concierto de Aranjuez / London 417199-2
Eduardo Fernandez (guitar),Gomez / English Chamber Orchestra

Concierto de Aranjuez / Philips 411440-2 or 432828-2
Pepe Romero (guitar), Neville Marriner/Academy of St. Martin-in-the-Fields

Johan Helmich Roman (1694-1758)

Called the "father of Swedish music" for being the first to write instrumental and choral works that could be favorably compared to German and Italian pieces, Roman wrote at least 400 works in most instrumental and vocal genres. His music shows the influence of Handel. He is known for his orchestral suite *Drottningholmsmusiquen* (1744). —*Mary K. Scanlan*

SINFONIAS

8 Sinfonias / Musica Sveciae MSCD418
Schroder, Jaap/Drottningholm Baroque Ensemble

3 Sinfonias & 3 Violin Concertos / BIS BIS-CD-284
Orpheus Chamber Ensemble of Sweden

THE DROTTNINGHOLM MUSIC

The Little Drottningholm Music (suite) and Concerto Grosso / Capriccio 10624
Ulf Bjorlin/Cappella Coloniensis

The Little Drottningholm Music (suite) / Musica Sveciae MSCD417
Claude Genetay/Chamber Orchestra of the National Museum, Stockholm

THE GOLOVIN MUSIC

The Golovin Music (suite) / Musica Sveciae MSCD404
Drottningholm Baroque Ensemble

Gioacchino Rossini (1792-1868)

A celebrated Italian composer of opera, considered among the greatest masters of the genre. The extroverted style of Rossini's characterization and orchestral writing is still uplifting today. He is known for *The Barber of Seville* (1816), but his operas written for the Paris stage are perhaps his best, especially the very original and powerful *William Tell.* —*"Blue" Gene Tyranny*

BARBER OF SEVILLE (OPERA)

The Barber of Seville / Philips 411058-2
Thomas Allen (tenor), Baltsa, Araiza, Trimarchi, Lloyd, Neville Marriner/Academy of St. Martin-in-the-Fields & Ambrosian Singers

The Barber of Seville / CBS M3K37862
Nucci, Marilyn Horne (soprano), Barbacini, Dara, Ramey (tenor), Ricardo Chailly/La Scala Orchestra & Chorus

L@2:L' Italiana in Algeri (opera)

L' Italiana in Algeri / Erato 2292-45404-2
Marilyn Horne (soprano), Kathleen Battle (soprano), Palacio, Ramey, Zaccaria, Claudio Scimone/I Solisti Veneti & Prague Philharmonic Chorus

★ **Overtures**

8 Overtures / Deutsche Grammophon 415363-2
Orpheus Chamber Orchestra

8 Overtures / Philips 412893-2
Neville Marriner/Academy of St. Martin-in-the-Fields

7 Overtures / EMI CDC7540912
Roger Norrington/London Classical Players

SEMIRAMIDE (OPERA)

Semiramide / London 425481-2
Joan Sutherland (soprano), Marilyn Horne (soprano), Serge, Rouleau, Malas, Richard Bonynge/London Symphony Orchestra & Ambrosian Singers

Albert Roussel (1869-1937)

A French composer of ballet, orchestral, chamber, and piano music. Much of Roussel's work begins with detailed, intimate imagery and experiences, like the humor of an insect ballet in *Le Festin d'Araigne* or ancient dances in the tuneful and rhythmic *Suite in F*; but then he expands the music to vast seascapes or dramatic encounters. Roussel, like his fellow impressionists Debussy and Ravel, is able to build rich orchestrations from seed fragments that seem to grow and occupy intersecting planes of sound, as in the *Symphony No. 3* and the *Rapsodie Flamande*. However, his writing is of a simpler line by choice, with "added note" harmonies and a different, attractive impressionist character. — *"Blue" Gene Tyranny*

BACCHUS ET ARIANE, SUITE 2

Bacchus et Ariane, Op. 43 (complete ballet) / EMI CDM7646902
Georges Pretre/National Orchestra of France

Bacchus et Ariane, Op. 43 (Suite #2 only) / Chandos CHAN8996
Neeme Jarvi/Detroit Symphony Orchestra

SYMPHONY #3

Symphony #3, Op. 42 / Chandos CHAN8996
Neeme Jarvi/Detroit Symphony Orchestra

Symphony #3, Op. 42 / Erato ECD88225
Charles Dutoit/National Orchestra of France

Edmund Rubbra (1901-1986)

English composer and writer, born in a lower-middle-class background, he rose to a position at Oxford. Rubbra is best-known for his ten symphonies, some of the finest examples among the large English output of this century. His music possesses an innate intellectual quality, without being overtly so. His idiom is thoroughly tonal in inspiration, and his orchestral textures are concerned with line over color. He was one of the many English composers of his generation to explore the vast repertory of Elizabethan music as inspiration for original composition. — *Todd McComb*

SYMPHONIES

Symphony #2 / Lyrita SRCD235
Vernon Hadley/New Philharmonia

Symphonies #3 & 4 / Lyrita SRCD202
Norman Del Mar/Philharmonia Orchestra

Symphony #10 / Chandos CHAN6599
Hans-Herbert Schonzeler/Bournemouth Sinfonietta

Camille Saint-Saens (1835-1921)

A French composer and melodist of the Liszt school. Although Saint-Saens is appreciated for the mix of Parisian wit and academic seriousness found in *Carnival of the Animals* and the tone painting in his famous *Danse Macabre*, his work is more beautifully developed in his *Concerto for Piano No. 4, Symphony No. 3 in C*, and *Concerto for Violin No. 3 in B*, which contain harmonically advanced writing (a la Cesar Franck) and some of his most beautiful and fluid melody lines. — *"Blue" Gene Tyranny*

★ **Carnival of the Animals**

Carnival of the Animals / Philips 400016-2
V. & P. Jennings (pianos), Andre Previn/Pittsburgh Symphony Orchestra

Carnival of the Animals / Erato 2292-45772-2
Viktoria Postnikova & Jean-Francois Heisser (pianos), Gennadi Rozhdestvensky/Ensemble Instrumental

Carnival of the Animals / London 414460-2 or 430720-2
Pascal Roge & Christina Ortiz (pianos), Charles Dutoit/London Sinfonietta

CONCERTO #1 FOR CELLO

Cello Concerto #1 in A Minor, Op. 33 / CBS MK35848
Yo-Yo Ma (cello), Lorin Maazel/National Orchestra of France

Cello Concerto #1 in A Minor, Op. 33 / Philips 432084-2
Julian Lloyd-Webber (cello), Yan Pascal Tortelier/English Chamber Orchestra

CONCERTOS #2 & 5 FOR PIANO

Piano Concerto #2 in G Minor, Op. 22 / Philips 410052-2
Bella Davidovich (piano), Neeme Jarvi/Royal Concertgebouw Orchestra, Amsterdam

Piano Concerto #5 ("Egyptian") in F Major, Op. 103 / EMI CDC7478162
Jean-Philippe Collard (piano), Andre Previn/Royal Philharmonic Orchestra

Piano Concertos #1-5 (complete) / Vox Music Group CD3X3028
Gabriel Tacchino (piano), Louis de Froment/Orchestra of Radio Luxembourg

Piano Concertos #1-5 (complete) / EMI CMS7694432
Aldo Ciccolini (piano), Serge Baudo/Orchestra of Paris

DANSE MACABRE

Danse Macabre, Op. 40 / London 414460-2
Charles Dutoit/Philharmonia Orchestra

Danse Macabre, Op. 40 / BIS CD-555
James DePriest/Royal Stockholm Symphony Orchestra

INTRODUCTION & RONDO CAPRICCIOSO

Introduction & Rondo Capriccioso, Op. 28 / EMI CDC7477252
Itzhak Perlman (violin), Jean Martinon/Orchestra of Paris

Introduction & Rondo Capriccioso, Op. 28 / EMI CDC7492762
Nadia Salerno-Sonnonberg (violin), Gerard Schwarz/New York Chamber Symphony

SAMSON ET DALILA (OPERA)

Samson et Dalila / EMI CDS7544702
Placido Domingo, Meier, Ramey, Fondary, Myung-Wha Chung/Bastille Opera Orchestra & Chorus

Samson et Dalila / EMI CDM7478952
Gorr, Vickers, Blanc Georges Pretre/Paris Opera Orchestra & Rene Duclos Chorus

SYMPHONY #3 ("ORGAN")

Symphony #3 ("Organ") in C Minor, Op. 78 / Telarc CD-80051
Michael Murray (organ), Eugene Ormandy/Philadelphia Orchestra

Symphony #3 ("Organ") in C Minor, Op. 78 / London 410201-2
Peter Hurford (organ), Charles Dutoit/Montreal Symphony Orchestra

Symphonies #1-3 ("Organ") (complete) / EMI CZS7626432
Bernard Gavoty (organ), Jean Martinon/Orchestra National de l'ORTF

Pablo de Sarasate (1844-1908)

ZIGEUNERWEISEN

Zigeunerweisen, Op. 20 / Deutsche Grammophon 437544-2
Anne-Sophie Mutter (violin), James Levine/Vienna Philharmonic Orchestra

Zigeunerweisen, Op. 20 / EMI CDM7635332
Itzhak Perlman (violin), Andre Previn/Pittsburgh Symphony Orchestra

Erik Satie (1866-1925)

PIANO MUSIC

Complete Solo Piano Music, Vol 1 / EMI CDC7497022
Aldo Ciccolini (piano)

Piano Music, Vol. 1 / Virgin 59515
Anne Queffelec (piano)

Alessandro Scarlatti (1660-1725)

An Italian composer of opera, sacred and secular vocal music, and some instrumental works. Scarlatti's operas, oratorios, and cantatas made him one of the foremost Neopolitan composers of the day. — *Mary K. Scanlan*

CONCERTI GROSSI

6 Sinfonie di Concerti Grossi: #1-6 / Philips 400017-2
William Bennett & Lenore Smith (flutes), Bernard Soustrot (trumpet), Hans Elhorst (oboe)/I Musici

6 Sinfonie di Concerti Grossi: #7-12 and 3 Flute Concertos / Philips 434160-2
William Bennett & Lenore Smith (flutes), Bernard Soustrot (trumpet), Hans Elhorst (oboe)/I Musici

Domenico Scarlatti (1685-1757)

The sixth son of composer Alessandro Scarlatti. His 555 known harpsichord sonatas, more than half of which were written during the final six years of his life, show him to be the most original innovator of harmony in the 18th century. Some, with their wonderful Italian, Portuguese, and Spanish dance rhythms, combined with lively, surprising harmonic turns, make for very uplifting listening; others are more lyrically sombre and quiet in mood. Scarlatti wrote in many other genres (operas, cantatas, church music). *Salve Regina* (1757), his last work, is beautiful. — *"Blue" Gene Tyranny*

★ **Sonatas for Harpsichord**

19 Sonatas: K. 2, 9, 12, 18, 21, 30, 84, 86–87, 159, 175, 277–278, 302, 314–315, 334, 337 & 418 / Dorian Recordings DOR-90103
Colin Tilney (harpsichord)

23 Sonatas: K. 23, 72, 87, 105, 124, 132–133, 146, 159, 175, 215–216, 377, 380, 397, 421, 430, 443, 450, 461, 519, 531 & 535 / Newport Classic NCD60080
Anthony Newman (harpsichord)

15 Sonatas: K. 24, 30, 46, 118–120, 141, 158–159, 208– 209, 380, 381 & 426 / 427 / Chesky CD75
Igor Kipnis (harpsichord)

15 Sonatas: K. 114–116, 144, 175, 402–403, 449–450, 474–475, 513, 516–517 & 544–545 / London 421422-2
Andras Schiff (piano)

12 Sonatas: K. 27, 141, 263–264, 318–319, 380–381, 417, 446 & 550–551 / Amon Ra CD-SAR27
Maggie Cole (harpsichord)

18 Sonatas: K. 52, 211–212, 248–249, 261–264, 318–319, 347–348, 416–417, 490–493 / Koch 3-7014-2
Elaine Thornburgh (harpsichord)

15 Sonatas: K. 87, 104–105, 124–125, 244–245, 408–409, 420–421, 516–517 & 544–545 / EMI CDC7476542
Virginia Black (harpsichord)

Johann Schobert (1735-1767)

An Austrian composer whose style is highly reminiscent of the Mannheim school, though he never actually worked there. Mozart, who was significantly influenced by Schobert, incorporated movements of this composer's scores into his sonatas and piano concertos. — *Mary K. Scanlan*

CHAMBER MUSIC

2 Piano Quartets, 2 Piano Trios, and 2 Violin Sonatas / Harmonia Mundi HMA1901294
Ensemble 415

Arnold Schoenberg (1874-1951)

Schoenberg, who taught Webern and Berg, is the well-known inventor of the 12-tone system. (Josef Hauer independently invented one on separate principles about the same time.) Schoenberg was, amazingly, a self-taught musician, whose *Harmonienlehre* ("Theory of Harmony") is still studied for the breadth of its understanding of the deepest meaning of structure in music. For all its theoretical underpinning, Schoenberg's music is most often dramatic in a romantic way, at the same time leaping to the horizons of pitch in its melodies and, through fragmentation and "Klangfarbenmelodie" (sound-color-melody), creating an angular, "modern" sound in its rhythm and unique orchestration. Schoenberg's earlier and more romantic scores are *Verklrte Nacht* ("Transfigured Night") for string sextet or orchestra; *Pelleas und Melisande* (no relation to Debussy's work); and *Gurrelieder,* which is Mahleresque in texture; all are conceived on a sweeping scale of interior emotion. The early *Chamber Symphony* combines this style with the angular style that would appear in Schoenberg's violin and piano concertos of the 30s. The first of Schoenberg's works in which tonality is completely absent is the song "Du lehnst wider eine Silberweide" ("You Lean against a White Willow") from *The Book of the Hanging Gardens* (1907). Following this came the brilliant *Five Pieces for Orchestra, Op. 16* (1909), with its entirely new approach to orchestration (the suspended chords and color-melody of "Summer Morning by a Lake"); the *Piano Music, Op. 11 & 19;* and *Pierrot Lunaire;* all of which completely changed the sound of symphonic, chamber, and piano music. The later expressionistic pieces followed— *Variations for Orchestra, Quartets for Strings Nos. 3-4, Von Heute auf Morgen* ("From Today until Tomorrow"), and *Die Gluckliche Hand* ("The Fortunate Hand"). The culmination of these efforts was his masterpiece, the opera *Moses und Aron,* which shares with the early work *Friede auf Erden* ("Peace on Earth") the idea of music being a vehicle for the expression of philosophy. His pleas for humanity during and following the horrors of WWII are contained in *A Survivor from Warsaw* and the *Ode to Napoleon Bonaparte.* — *"Blue" Gene Tyranny*

★ **Chamber Symphony No. 1**

Chamber Symphony #1, Op. 9 / Teldec 2292-46019-2
Heinz Holliger/Chamber Orchestra of Europe

Chamber Symphony #1, Op. 9 / Deutsche Grammophon 429233-2
Orpheus Chamber Orchestra

Chamber Symphony #1, Op. 9 / Sony SMK45894
Marlboro Chamber Musicians

FIVE PIECES FOR ORCHESTRA

Five Pieces for Orchestra, Op. 16 / Mercury Living Presence 432006-2
Antal Dorati/London Symphony Orchestra

Five Pieces for Orchestra, Op. 16 / Deutsche Grammophon 419781-2
James Levine/Berlin Philharmonic Orchestra

PIANO MUSIC

Piano Music / Nonesuch 971309-2
Paul Jacobs (piano)

Piano Music / Deutsche Grammophon 423249-2
Maurizio Pollini (piano)

★ **Pierrot Lunaire**

Pierrot Lunaire / Nonesuch 971309-2
Arthur Weisberg/Contemporary Chamber Ensemble

Pierrot Lunaire / Harmonia Mundi HMC901390
Philippe Herreweghe/Ensemble Musique Oblique

STRING QUARTETS

Complete Music for String Quartet / Deutsche Grammophon 419994-2
La Salle String Quartet

★ **Verklarte Nacht**

Verklarte Nacht, Op. 4 (original string sextet version) / Philips 416306-2
Schoenberg Ensemble

Verklarte Nacht, Op. 4 (string orchestra version) / Deutsche Grammophon 415326-2
Herbert von Karajan/Berlin Philharmonic Orchestra

Franz Schubert (1797-1828)

A short-lived, astonishingly prolific German composer of songs, symphonies, and piano and chamber music who is perhaps the true link in the tradition from Beethoven and Mozart to Liszt and Wagner. Schubert's splendid sense of melody and drama testify to the developing romantic ideals in his music; his harmonic palette is essentially that of Beethoven. *Winterreise,* completed on his deathbed, is regarded as his best song cycle. The quartets, octet, and quintets incorporate many elements of his songwriting styles (and even some of the music, as in his *Quartet in D:* the variations movement on "Der Tod und das Madchen" ("Death and the Maiden"). The piano music (sonatas and impromptus) and especially the symphonies show Beethoven's influence and the melodic line becoming longer, perhaps more graceful, in the romantic style. — *"Blue" Gene Tyranny*

IMPROMPTUS

Impromptus, Op. 90, D. 899, and Impromptus, Op. 142, D. 935 / Deutsche Grammophon 435788-2
Andre Gavrilov (piano)

Impromptus, Op. 90, D. 899, and Impromptus, Op. 142, D. 935 / Philips 422237-2
Alfred Brendel (piano)

★ **Moments Musicaux, D. 780**

Moments musicaux, Op. 94 in C Major, D. 780 / Deutsche Grammophon 427769-2
Maria Joao Pires (piano)

Moments musicaux, Op. 94 in C Major, D. 780 / London 430425-2
Andras Schiff (piano)

Moments musicaux, Op. 94 in C Major, D. 780 / Claves CD50-8011
Jorg Ewald Dahler (fortepiano)

OCTET

Octet, Op. 166 in F Major, D. 803 / Philips 416497-2
Academy Chamber Ensemble

Octet, Op. 166 in F Major, D. 803 / Nonesuch 979046-2
Boston Symphony Chamber Players

★ **Quartets #12, 13 & 14 ("Death & the Maiden")**

String Quartet #12 ("Quartettsatz") in C Minor, D. 703, and #14 ("Death and the Maiden") in D Minor, D. 810 / CBS MBK42602
Juilliard String Quartet

String Quartet #12 ("Quartettsatz") in C Minor, D. 703; #13 ("Rosamunde"), Op. 29 #1 in A Minor, D. 804 / Deutsche Grammophon 419171-2
Hagen Quartett

String Quartet #13 ("Rosamunde"), Op. 29 #1 in A Minor, D. 804 / Telarc CD-80225
Cleveland Quartet

String Quartets #13 ("Rosamunde"), Op. 29 #1 in A Minor, D. 804, and #14 ("Death and the Maiden") in D Minor, D. 810 / Denon DC-8005
Prague String Quartet

String Quartets #13 ("Rosamunde"), Op. 29 #1 in A Minor, D. 804, and #14 ("Death and the Maiden") in D Minor, D. 810 / EMI CDC7473332
Berg Quartet

★ **Quintet for Strings**

String Quintet, Op. 163 in C Major, D. 956 / Denon 33C37-7601
Eberhard Finke (cello), Philharmonia Quartett Berlin

String Quintet, Op. 163 in C Major, D. 956 / Sony SK46669
Smithsonian Chamber Players

String Quintet, Op. 163 in C Major, D. 956 / Academy Sound & Vision LTD CDDCA537
Douglas Cummings (cello), Lindsay String Quartet

★ **Quintet in A ("Trout") for Piano and Strings**

Piano Quintet ("Trout"), Op. 114 in A Major, D. 667 / Telarc CD-80225
John OíConor (piano), Cleveland Quartet

Piano Quintet ("Trout"), Op. 114 in A Major, D. 667 / Philips 400078-2
Alfred Brendel (piano), Cleveland Quartet

Piano Quintet ("Trout"), Op. 114 in A Major, D. 667 / Deutsche Grammophon 413453-2
Emil Gilels (piano), Amadeus Quartet

ROSAMUNDE: INCIDENTAL MUSIC

Overture in C Major, D. 644, and Incidental Music, D. 797 / Deutsche Grammophon 431655-2
Anne Sofie van Otter (soprano), Claudio Abbado/Chamber Orchestra of Europe Europe & Ernst-Senff Chorus

Overture in C Major, D. 644, and Incidental Music, D. 797 / Philips 412432-2
Elly Ameling (soprano), Kurt Masur/Gewandhaus Orchestra & Leipzig Radio Chorus

★ **Sonatas for Piano (D. *664, *959, *960)**

Piano Sonatas: #13 Op. 120 in A Major, D. 664, and #14 Op. 143 in A Minor, D. 784 / Olympia OCD288
Sviatoslav Richter (piano)

Piano Sonatas: #4 Op. 164 in A Minor, D. 537, and #13 Op. 120 in A Major, D. 664 / Philips 410605-2
Alfred Brendel (piano)

Piano Sonata #20 in A Major, D. 959 / Nonesuch 978028-2
Richard Goode (piano)

Piano Sonata #21 in B Flat Major, D. 960 / Nonesuch 979124-2
Richard Goode (Piano)

Piano Sonatas: #19 in C Minor, D. 958; #20 in A Major, D. 959; and #21 in B Flat Major, D. 960 / Philips Duo 438703-2
Alfred Brendel (piano)

Piano Sonatas: #19 in C Minor, D. 958; #20 in A Major, D. 959; and #21 in B Flat Major, D. 960 / Deutsche Grammophon 419229-2 or 427327-2 & 427326-2
Maurizio Pollini (piano)

SONATA "ARPEGGIONE"

Sonata ("Arpeggione") in A Minor, D. 821 / RCA 7845-2-RC
Ofra Harnoy (cello), Michael Dussek (piano)

Sonata ("Arpeggione") in A Minor, D. 821 / Chandos CHAN8664
Nobuko Imai (viola), Roger Vignoles (piano)

★ **Songs**

Die Schone Mullerin, D. 795 / Deutsche Grammophon 415186-2
Dietrich Fischer-Dieskau (baritone), Gerlad Moore (piano)

Schwanengesang, D. 957 / Deutsche Grammophon 415188-2
Dietrich Fischer-Dieskau (baritone), Gerlad Moore (piano)

★ **Symphonies (2, 4, 5, *8, *9)**

Symphonies #1-6, 8 & 9 / Deutsche Grammophon 423651-2
Claudio Abbado/Chamber Orchestra of Europe

Symphonies #1-6, 8 & 9 / RCA Gold Seal 60096-2-RG
Gunter Wand/Cologne Radio Symphony Orchestra

Symphonies: #1 in D Major, D. 82, and #2 in B Flat Major, D. 125 / Denon CM7905
Otmar Suitner/Staatskapelle Berlin

Symphonies: #5 in B Flat Major, D. 485, and #8 ("Unfinished") in B Minor, D. 759 / Deutsche Grammophon 427645-2
Leonard Bernstein/Royal Concertgebouw Orchestra, Amsterdam

Symphony #8 ("Unfinished") in B Minor, D. 759 / Deutsche Grammophon 410862-2
Guiseppe Sinopoli/Philharmonia Orchestra

Symphony #9 ("Great") in C Major, D. 944 / Deutsche Grammophon 427646-2
Leonard Bernstein/Royal Concertgebouw Orchestra, Amsterdam

Symphony #9 ("Great") in C Major, D. 944 / Telarc CD-80110
Christoph von Dohnanyi/Cleveland Orchestra

TRIOS FOR PIANO & STRINGS D. 898 & 929

Piano Trios (complete) / Philips 412620-2
Beaux Arts Trio

Piano Trios, D. 28 & D. 898 / Naxos 8.550131
Stuttgart Piano Trio

Piano Trios, D. 897 & D. 929 / Naxos 8.550132
Stuttgart Piano Trio

★ **Wanderer Fantasie**

Wanderer Fantasie, Op. 15 in C Major, D. 760 / Deutsche Grammophon 419672-2
Maurizio Pollini (piano)

Wanderer Fantasie, Op. 15 in C Major, D. 760 / CBS MK42124
Murray Perahia (piano)

Wanderer Fantasie, Op. 15 in C Major, D. 760 / London 417327-2
Vladimir Ashkenazy (piano)

Robert Schumann (1810-1856)

A German composer of romantic music in many forms, including piano pieces, orchestral music, and lieder. Among his notable works are the *Davisbundlertanze* (1837), *Dichterliebe* (1840), and the *Quintet in E-flat for Piano & Strings*. From his early years, Schumann spoke of the piano as a diary for his thoughts and feelings. Later, while establishing the fundamentals for the journalistic criticism of music in his *Neue Zeitschrift fur Musik* ("New Journal for Music"), he seems to have continued that relationship with all the forms in which he composed. Many of his songs, song cycles, and piano works are collections of musical characterizations, which, like the *Kinderscenen* ("Scenes from Childhood") and *Waldscenen* ("Scenes from the Woods"), are often humorous. In his more dramatic works the meaning is often personal and elusive, with a hidden "program," although often passionately beautiful. Schumann's symphonies, neglected for a long time, are now appreciated for the many innovative qualities of their melody and form. —*"Blue" Gene Tyranny*

★ **Carnaval for Piano**

Carnaval, Op. 9 / Sony SK45742
Cecile Licad (piano)

Carnaval, Op. 9 / Philips 432308-2
Claudio Arrau (piano)

Carnaval, Op. 9 / RCA 5667-2-RC
Artur Rubinstein (piano)

CONCERTO FOR CELLO

Cello Concerto, Op. 129 / CBS MK42663 or M2K44562
Yo-Yo Ma (cello), Sir Colin Davis/Bavarian Radio Symphony Orchestra

Cello Concerto, Op. 129 / Vox Music Group CDX5027
Laszlo Varga (cello), Siegfried Landau/Westphalian Symphony Orchestra, Recklinghausen

★ **Concerto for Piano**

Piano Concerto in A Minor, Op. 54 / London 417112-2
Jorges Bolet (piano), Riccardo Chailly/Berlin Radio Symphony Orchestra

Piano Concerto in A Minor, Op. 54 / Philips 412923-2
Stephen Bishop-Kovakovich (piano), Sir Colin Davis/BBC Symphony Orchestra

Piano Concerto in A Minor, Op. 54 / Vox Music Group CDX5027
Peter Frankl (piano), Janos Furst/Bamberg Symphony Orchestra

Piano Concerto in A Minor, Op. 54 / Dorian Recordings DOR-90172
Ivan Moravec (piano), Eduardo Mata/Dallas Symphony Orchestra

DICHTERLIEBE (SONG CYCLE)

Dichterliebe, 16 Songs, Op. 48 / Denon C37-7720
Hermann Prey (baritone), Leonard Hokanson (piano)

Dichterliebe, 16 Songs, Op. 48 / Philips 416352-2
Dietrich Fischer-Dieskau (baritone), Alfred Brendel (piano)

★ **Kinderscenen**

13 Pieces ("Kinderscenen"), Op. 15 / Deutsche Grammophon 410653-2
Martha Argerich (piano)

13 Pieces ("Kinderscenen"), Op. 15 / CBS MK42409
Vladimir Horowitz (piano)

13 Pieces ("Kinderscenen"), Op. 15 / Philips 432308-2
Claudio Arrau (piano)

KREISLERIANA

8 Fantasies ("Kreisleriana"), Op. 16 / Deutsche Grammophon 410653-2
Martha Argerich (piano)

8 Fantasies ("Kreisleriana"), Op. 16 / CBS MK42409
Vladimir Horowitz (piano)

8 Fantasies ("Kreisleriana"), Op. 16 / Philips 432308-2
Claudio Arrau (piano)

LIEDERKREIS (2 SONG CYCLES, OP. 24 & 39)

Liederkreis, 9 Songs Op. 24 and 12 Songs Op. 39 / Dorian Recordings DOR90132
Victor Conrad Braun (baritone), Antonin Kubalik (piano)

Liederkreis, 12 Songs Op. 39 / Denon C37-7720
Hermann Prey (baritone), Leonard Hokanson (piano)

QUARTET FOR PIANO & STRINGS

Piano Quartet, Op. 47 / Philips 420791-2
Samuel Rhodes (viola), Beaux Arts Trio

Piano Quartet, Op. 47 / Amon Ra CDSAR54
Richard Burnett (fortepiano), Fitzwilliam String Quartet

Piano Quartet, Op. 47 / Sony SMK52684
Glenn Gould (piano), Juilliard String Quartet

★ **Quintet for Piano & Strings**

Piano Quintet, Op. 44 / Philips 420791-2

Dolf Bettelheim (violin), Samuel Rhodes (viola), Beaux Arts Trio

Piano Quintet, Op. 44 / Academy Sound & Vision LTD CD-DCA728
Peter Frankl (piano), Lindsay String Quartet

Piano Quintet, Op. 44 / Amon Ra CDSAR54
Richard Burnett (fortepiano), Fitzwilliam String Quartet

SYMPHONIC ETUDES

18 Symphonic Etudes, Op. 13 / Newport Classic NCD60108
Thomas Lorango (piano)

18 Symphonic Etudes, Op. 13 / CBS MK34539
Murray Perahia (piano)

18 Symphonic Etudes, Op. 13 / Deutsche Grammophon 410926-2
Maurizio Pollini (piano)

★ **Symphonies (*1, 2, *3, 4)**

Symphonies #1-4 / Vox Music Group CDX5019
Jerzy Semkow/Saint Louis Symphony Orchestra

Symphonies: #1 ("Spring"), Op. 38, and #4, Op. 120 / Deutsche Grammophon415274-2
Leonard Bernstein/Vienna Philharmonic Orchestra

Symphonies: #2, Op. 61, and #3 ("Rhenish"), Op. 97 / Telarc CD-80182
David Zinman/Baltimore Symphony Orchestra

Symphonies: #3 ("Rhenish"), Op. 97, and #4, Op. 120 / London 421643-2
Christoph von Dohnanyi/Cleveland Orchestra

Symphonies #1-4 / Philips 416126-2
Bernard Haitink/Concertgebouw Orchestra Amsterdam

TRIOS FOR PIANO & STRINGS

Piano Trio #1 and "Fantasiestucke," Op. 88 / Thorofon CTH2030
Gobel Trio Berlin

Piano Trios #2, Op. 80, and #3, Op. 110 / Thorofon CTH2031
Gobel Trio Berlin

Piano Trios #1, Op. 63; #2, Op. 80; #3, Op. 110; and "Fantasiestucke," Op. 88 / Chandos CHAN8832 / 3
Borodin Trio

Heinrich Schutz (1585-1672)

Schutz synthesized Italian multichordal and rhythmic styles with the German dramatic and melodic sensibility to construct powerfully moving and emotional music with a classical restraint that serves to accent these emotional qualities rather than inhibit them. This is especially evident in the marvelous *Symphoniae Sacrae; Saul, Saul Was verfolgst du mich?* ("Saul, Why Persecutest Thou Me?"); the heartbreaking *Fili Mi, Absalon* ("Absalom, My Son"); the multiple-chorus splendor and tone-painting of the *Psalms of David;* and the funeral mass *Musicalische Exequien.* In his older age, Schutz aimed at a sparer style, as shown in the *Christmas Oratorio* (1664), in which all the characters are accompanied by their own scoring and the evangelist/narrator is accompanied only by the continuo part. —*"Blue" Gene Tyranny*

SACRED MUSIC

12 Symphoniae Sacrae III, Op. 12 / RCA Deutsche Harmonia Mundi 7910-2-RC
Frieder Bernius/Musica Ficta & Kammerchor Stuttgart

Motets & Musicalische Exequien, Op. 7 / Archiv 423405-2
John Eliot Gardiner/English Baroque Soloists & Monteverdi Choir

Psalmen David (26 Psalms), Op. 2 / Sony Vivarte S2K48042
Frieder Bernius/Musica Ficta & Kammerchor Stuttgart

Alexander Scriabin (1872-1915)

A Russian composer known for visionary symphonies and piano music, which grew out of his experience with theosophical mysticism in Switzerland in 1903. Driven to express a vision of the future transformation of the world (in a moment of grand, collective ecstasy, not so different from the rapturists of today, though not apocalyptic), Scriabin began to write wholly original piano music and symphonies (#3, *The Divine Poem,* #4, *The Poem of*

Ecstasy, and #5, Prometheus, the Poem of Fire). Scriabin invented many musical devices (like the octatonic scale and the "mystic" chord) that remained tonal in nature and yet produced a new sound that, while characterized both by the transparency of impressionism and the chromaticism of late romanticism, was a wholly new and strange sensation. —*"Blue" Gene Tyranny*

★ Piano Music (Etudes, Preludes, Sonatas (*5))

Etudes, Poems, and Piano Sonata #5, Op. 53 / Nimbus NIM5176
Marta Deyanova (piano)

Piano Sonatas #3–5 & 10 / Harmonia Mundi HMU907011
Richard Taub (piano)

Complete Etudes / Hyperion CDA66607
Piers Lane (piano)

Jose Antonio Seixas (1704-1742)

Portuguese composer of harpsichord sonatas, contemporary of Domenico Scarlatti. Seixas is known for his highly animated keyboard writing in the basic idiom of the time. —*AMG*

SONATAS FOR HARPSICHORD

11 Sonatas / Amon Ra CD-SAR43
Robert Woolley (harpsichord)

Dmitri Shostakovich (1906-1975)

A Russian composer of orchestral-choral, opera, chamber, symphony, vocal, and piano music. Like Prokofiev, Shostakovich was a highly visible and harshly criticized composer. Often in peril from the Stalinist regime and the advancing German armies in WWII, he nevertheless became the last (for now) great symphonist, producing a style that expressed ironic humor (his ninth symphony), had vast epic qualities (the fifth, seventh, and eleventh symphonies), or had a tragic and desolate visage (the tenth symphony). His melodic sense developed from the warm, rich, and even sweet qualities of the *Preludes (24) for Piano*—which skillfully employ Russian folk song modality and magnificent characterization, updating classical techniques—to the bare, large-interval skips of the later works. At times, Shostakovich was able to reach the public with the most modern of his works (the tragic opera *Lady Macbeth of Mtsensk* (1934), widely popular in the Soviet Union and Europe until the press came down on it.) He was one of the most courageous of composers. —*"Blue" Gene Tyranny*

CONCERTOS

Cello Concertos #1 & 2 / Philips 412526-2
Heinrich Schiff (cello), Maxim Shostakovich/Bavarian Radio Symphony Orchestra

Piano Concerto #1 / Chandos CHAN8357
Dmitri Shostakovich, Jr. (piano), Maxim Shostakovich/I Musici di Montreal

Piano Concerto #2 / Chandos CHAN8443
Dmitri Shostakovich, Jr. (piano), Maxim Shostakovich/I Musici di Montreal

Violin Concertos #1 & 2
Lydia Mordkovich (violin), Neeme Jarvi/Scottish National Orchestra

PRELUDES & FUGUES (PIANO)

24 Preludes & Fugues, Op. 87 / Hyperion CDA66441 / 3
Tatiana Nikolaeva (piano)

24 Preludes & Fugues, Op. 87 / ECM New Series 78118-21469-2
Keith Jarrett (piano)

★ String Quartets (*8)

Complete String Quartets / Teldec 9031-71702-2
Brodsky Quartet

String Quartet #8, Op. 110 / Nonesuch 979242-2
Kronos Quartet

String Quartets: #3, Op. 73; #7, Op. 108; and #8, Op. 108 / Virgin CDC59041
Borodin Quartet

★ Symphonies (1, 4, *5, 6, *10, 14)

Symphony #1, Op. 10 / Sheffield Labs CD-26

Lawrence Leighton Smith/Moscow Philharmonic Orchestra

Symphony #4 in C Minor, Op. 43 / London 425693-2
Vladimir Ashkenazy/Royal Philharmonic Orchestra

Symphony #5, Op. 47 / Chandos CHAN8650
Neeme Jarvi/Scottish National Orchestra

Symphony #6 in B Minor, Op. 54 / Deutsche Grammophon 419771-2
Leonard Bernstein/Vienna Philharmonic Orchestra

Symphony #7 ("Leningrad"), Op. 60 / Chandos CHAN8623
Neeme Jarvi/Scottish National Orchestra

Symphony #8 in C Minor, Op. 65 / London 411616-2
Bernard Haitink/Concertgebouw Orchestra Amsterdam

Symphony #10, Op. 93 / Chandos CHAN8630
Neeme Jarvi/Scottish National Orchestra

Symphony #11 ("The Year 1905"), Op. 103 / Delos D / CD3080
James Depriest/Helsinki Philharmonic Orchestra

Symphony #12 ("The Year 1917"), Op. 112 / Deutsche Grammophon 431688-2
Neeme Jarvi/Gothenburg Symphony Orchestra

Symphony #14, Op. 135 / Chandos CHAN8607
Yuli Turovsky/I Musici di Montreal

Jean Sibelius (1865-1957)

A Finnish composer identified with the Finnish nationalism movement before 1918 who is popularly known for the romantic, nationalist works he produced at that time, including *Finlandia* (written for the Press Celebrations of 1899) and the *Valse Triste*. His last work in this style, written a few years later, was *Symphony No. 2*, with its Scandinavian flavor of open spaces. Sibelius continually sought new techniques and sounds, from the neo-classicism of the third symphony to the almost nontonal-based *Symphony No. 4* (1911). The symphonic poem *Tapiola, op. 112* of 1925 is a good example of his later style. Sibelius also wrote piano music, mostly bagatelle-style pieces but also some that are more serious, like the three *Sonatine, op. 67* and *Kyllikki, Three Lyric Pieces for Piano, op. 41*, based on the Finnish epic *Kalevala*. —*"Blue" Gene Tyranny*

★ Concerto for Violin

Concerto, Op. 47 / CBS MK44548
Cho-Liang Lin (violin), Esa-Pekka Salonen/Swedish Radio Symphony Orchestra

Concerto, Op. 47 / Philips 416821-2
Viktoria Mullova (violin), Seiji Ozawa/Boston Symphony Orchestra

Concerto, Op. 47 / EMI CDC7471672
Itzhak Perlman (violin), Andre Previn/Pittsburgh Symphony Orchestra

Concerto in D Minor, Op. 47 (original and final versions) / BIS CD-500
Leonidas Kavakos (violin), Osmo Vanska /Lahti Symphony

★ Finlandia

Finlandia, Op. 26 / BIS CD-221
Neeme Jarvi/Gothenburg Symphony Orchestra

Finlandia, Op. 26 / Telarc CD-80095
Yoel Levi/Cleveland Orchestra

Finlandia, Op. 26 / BIS CD-366
Erik T. Tawaststjerna (piano)

FOUR LEGENDS FROM THE KALEVALA

Lemminkainen—FourLegends from the Kalevala, Op. 22 (suite)/ BIS CD-294
Neeme Jarvi/Gothenburg Symphony Orchestra

Lemminkainen—FourLegends from the Kalevala, Op. 22 (suite) / RCA 9026-60575-2
Jukka-Pekka Saraste/Finnish Radio Symphony Orchestra

★ Symphonies (1, *2, 3, *4, 5, *6, 7)

Symphony #1, Op. 39 / London 414534-2
Vladimir Ashkenazy/Philharmonia Orchestra

Symphony #2, Op. 43 / Chesky CD-3
Sir John Barbirolli/Royal Philharmonic Orchestra

Symphony #2, Op. 43 / Telarc CD-80095
Yoel Levi/Cleveland Orchestra

Symphony #3, Op. 52 / BIS CD-228
Neeme Jarvi/Gothenburg Symphony Orchestra

Symphony #4, Op. 63 / BIS CD-263
Neeme Jarvi/Gothenburg Symphony Orchestra

Symphonies: #4, Op. 63, and #6, Op. 104 / Deutsche
 Grammophon 415108-2
Herbert von Karajan/Berlin Philharmonic Orchestra

Symphony #6, Op. 104 / BIS CD-237
Neeme Jarvi/Gothenburg Symphony Orchestra

Symphonies: #5, Op. 82, and #7, Op. 105 / Deutsche
 Grammophon 415107-2
Herbert von Karajan/Berlin Philharmonic Orchestra

Robert Simpson (b. 1921)

An important modern British composer. —*AMG*

STRING QUARTETS

String Quartets #3 & 4 / Hyperion CDA66376
Delme Quartet

SYMPHONIES (6, 7, 9)

Symphonies #6 & 7 / Hyperion CDA66280
Vernon Handley / Royal Liverpool Philharmonic Orchestra

Symphony #9 / Hyperion CDA66299
Vernon Handley / Bournemouth Symphony Orchestra

Bedrich Smetana (1824-1884)

The "father of Czech music" suffered through the revolt of June 1848 in Prague, continuing to support Czech nationalism in all of his music. Smetana was strongly influenced by Liszt, who praised him, and his symphonic writing shows a pronounced feeling for scene setting and drama, even containing some of the "leitmotiv" technique of Wagner. Smetana's masterpiece is considered to be the symphonic tone poem cycle *Ma Vlast* ("My Country"), from which "Vltava" (The Moldau) and "From Bohemian Fields and Groves" are the most popular sections. — *"Blue" Gene Tyranny*

★ **Ma Vlast (A cycle of 6 symphonic poems including "The Moldau")**

Ma Vlast / Deutsche Grammophon 429183-2
Rafael Kubelik/Boston Symphony Orchestra

Ma Vlast / Supraphon 110082-2
Vaclav Smetacek/Czech Philharmonic Orchestra

Ma Vlast / Virgin CDC595762
Libor Pesek/Royal Liverpool Philharmonic Orchestra

BARTERED BRIDE: OVERTURE & DANCES

The Bartered Bride Overture & Excerpts / Chandos CHAN8405
Geoffrey Simon/London Symphony Orchestra

The Bartered Bride Overture & Excerpts / Deutsche
 Grammophon 427340-2
James Levine/Vienna Philharmonic Orchestra

★ **Quartets (*1, 2)**

String Quartets #1 ("From My Life") in E Minor and #2 in D Minor / Denon 33C37-7339
Smetana Quartet

String Quartet #1 ("From My Life") / Telarc CD-80178
Cleveland Quartet

String Quartets #1 ("From My Life") / Deutsche Grammophon
 429723-2
Emerson String Quartet

Padre Antonio Soler (1729-1783)

A Catalan monk, organist, and prolific composer of sacred and secular music who studied with Domenico Scarlatti; known today for his keyboard works, which show Scarlatti's influence in their idiomatic keyboard treatment, structure, and affinity for Spanish harmonic and rhythmic inflections. —*Mary Scanlan*

CONCERTOS FOR 2 ORGANS

6 Concertos / Solstice SOCD076
Francois-Henri Houbart & Chasseguet (organs)

FANDANGO

Fandango in D Minor, SR 146, & Sonatas / Philips 432830-2
Rafael Puyana (harpsichord)

Fandango in D Minor, SR 146, & Sonatas / Erato 2292-45435-2
Scott Ross (harpsichord)

Fandango in D Minor, SR 146, & Sonatas / Cedille
 CDR90000004
David Schrader (harpsichord)

SONATAS FOR HARPSICHORD

9 Sonatas, SR 12, 15, 49, 54, 56, 69, 76, 84 & 90 and Fandango
 / Erato 2292-45435-2
Scott Ross (harpsichord)

10 Sonatas, SR 19, 41, 72, 78, 84-88 & 90 and Fandango /
 Virgin Classics Veritas VC791172-2
Maggie Cole (harpsichord & fortepiano)

7 Sonatas, SR 4, 9, 16, 24, 25, 60 & 63 and Fandango / Cedille
 CDR90000004
David Schrader (harpsichord)

**6 Sonatas, SR 19, 21, 84, 88, 90 &117; Concerto; and
 Fandango** / Philips 432830-2
Rafael Puyana (harpsichord)

**11 Sonatas, SR 35, 38, 70, 71, 77-79, 82, 83, 113 & 166 and
 Prelude #8** / Astree E8776
Robert van Asperen (harpsichord)

Fernando Sor (1778-1839)

Spanish composer. Though he wrote for other instruments as well, Sor is best known as one of the premier composers for guitar. Sor also wrote opera, ballet, chamber music, and songs. —*AMG*

MUSIC FOR GUITAR

Etudes, Fantasias & Sonatas / London 425821-2
Eduardo Fernandez (guitar)

Etudes / MCA MCAD-42073
Andres Segovia (guitar)

13 Fantasias (complete) / CPO 999199-2
Luis Orlandini (guitar)

Louis Spohr (1784-1859)

A celebrated German violinist and composer whose compositional style is typical of the transition period between classicism and romanticism. Besides writing extensively for the violin, Spohr composed several operas and symphonies, which were extremely well received in his lifetime and continue to be performed. —*Mary K. Scanlan*

CONCERTOS FOR CLARINET

Clarinet Concertos: #1, Op. 26, and #4, WoO. 20 / Orfeo
 C088101A
Karl Leister (clarinet), Rafael Fruhbeck De Burgos/Stuttgart Radio Symphony Orchestra

Clarinet Concerto #2, Op. 57, and #3, WoO. 19 / Orfeo
 C088201A
Karl Leister (clarinet), Rafael Fruhbeck De Burgos/Stuttgart Radio Symphony Orchestra

CONCERTOS FOR VIOLIN

3 Violin Concertos: #3, 6, and in A Major / CPO 999145-2
Ulf Hoelscher (violin), Christian Frohlich/Berlin Radio Symphony Orchestra

2 Violin Concertos: #7 and 12 / Marco Polo 8.220406
Takako Nishizaki (violin), Libor Pesek/Philharmonic Chamber Orchestra, Bratislava

QUARTETS & "DOUBLE" QUARTETS FOR STRINGS

**3 String Quartets: #3 ("Quatuor brillant"), Op. 11; #4, Op. 15
 #1; and #6, Op. 27** / Marco Polo 8.223254
New Budapest Quartet

2 String Quartets: #13 & 14, Op. 45 #2 & 3 / Marco Polo
 8.223258
New Budapest Quartet

**String Quintet ("Grande Quintetto") in G Major, Op. 33 #2,
 "Double Quartet" #1 in D Minor, Op. 65, and String Sextet
 in C Major, Op. 140** / Sony SK53370
L'Archibudelli & Smithsonian Chamber Players

2 Octets ("Double Quartets"): #3 in E Minor, Op. 87, and #4 in G Minor, Op. 136 / Hyperion CDA66142
Academy Chamber Ensemble

Carl Stamitz (1745-1801)

A German composer, one of the major architects of the classical period. Stamitz wrote many concertos and other instrumental pieces. —*AMG*

OCTETS FOR WINDS

3 Octets and 2 Octet-Partitas / CPO 999081-2
Consortium Classicum

QUARTET IN E FLAT FOR WOODWINDS

Quartet in E Flat Major, Op. 8 #2 / Claves CD50-611
Residenz-Quintett Munich

John Stanley (1712-1786)

An English organist and composer whose cantatas and keyboard works are especially important. Stanley was a friend and associate of Handel. —*Mary K. Scanlan*

ORGAN CONCERTOS OP. 10

6 Concertos, Op. 10 / CRD CRD3409
Gerald Gifford (organ)/Northern Sinfonia Orchestra

STRING CONCERTOS OP. 2

6 Concertos, Op. 2 / Hyperion CDA66338
Roy Goodman/Parley of Instruments Baroque Orchestra

VOLUNTARIES FOR ORGAN

11 Voluntaries: Op. 5 #2, 5, 8; Op. 6 #2, 4-6, 8; Op. 7 #2, 6, 9 / Capriccio 10256
Ton Koopman (organ)

Johann Strauss, Sr. (1804-1849)

RADETZSKY MARCH

Radetzsky March, Op. 228 / Deutsche Grammophon 427217-2
Ferenc Fricsay/Berlin Radio Symphony Orchestra

Radetzsky March, Op. 228 / Telarc CD-80098
Erich Kunzel/Cincinnati Pops Orchestra

1992 New Year's Concert / Sony SK52485
Carlos Kleiber/Vienna Philharmonic Orchestra

Johann Strauss II (1825-1899)

An Austrian composer of Viennese waltzes; known as "the Waltz King." His almost 500 dance pieces are his crowning achievement, while his *Die Fledermaus* is the epitome of operetta. —*Mary K. Scanlan*

DIE FLEDERMAUS (OPERA)

Die Fledermaus / Deutsche Grammophon 415646-2
Varady, Popp, Kollo, Prey, Rebroff, Carlos Kleiber/Bavarian State Opera Orchestra & Chorus

Die Fledermaus / Philips 432157-2
Kiri te Kanawa, Edita Grubernova, Fassbaender, Brendel, Andre Previn/Vienna Philharmonic Orchestra & State Opera Chorus

★ **Waltzes**

Radetzsky March, Op. 228 / Telarc CD-80098
Erich Kunzel/Cincinnati Pops Orchestra

Famous Waltzes, Polkas, Marches, and Overtures, Volume 1-5 / Naxos 8.550336 / 40
Various directors and orchestras from Marco Polo Complete Orchestral Music Edition

1992 New Year's Concert / Sony SK52485
Carlos Kleiber/Vienna Philharmonic Orchestra

Richard Strauss (1864-1949)

A German composer, one of the great "late romantics," known primarily for his great tone poems and innovative operas (*Elektra, Salome,* and *Der Rosenkavalier,* controversial both for their music and their extramusical subject matter). *Don Juan* and *Aus Italien* ("From Italy," 1886; Strauss's first symphonic poem) are good examples of his earlier tone poems, which draw almost operatic pictures and use references to national music. *Also Sprach Zarathustra* (1896) describes the different worlds of con-

sciousness and being (more than Kubrick's *2001* movie would lead you to believe) and thus marks the other trend in Strauss's musical thought. The texts from Oscar Wilde, Stefan Zweig, and Josef Gregor for various operas got Strauss into hot water with the moralists in Boston and with the Nazis. His later, post-WWII works are more refined and energetic. — *"Blue" Gene Tyranny*

ALPINE SYMPHONY

Alpine Symphony, Op. 64 / Philips 416156-2
Bernard Haitink/Concertgebouw Orchestra Amsterdam

Alpine Symphony, Op. 64 / London 421815-2
Herbert Blomstedt/San Francisco Symphony Orchestra

★ **Also Sprach Zarathustra**

Also Sprach Zarathustra, Op. 30 / Denon CO-2259
Herbert Blomstedt/Dresden State Orchestra

Also Sprach Zarathustra, Op. 30 / Deutsche Grammophon 410959-2
Herbert von Karajan/Berlin Philharmonic Orchestra

Also Sprach Zarathustra, Op. 30 / EMI CDC7641062
Eugene Ormandy/Philadelphia Orchestra

CONCERTOS (HORN, OBOE)

Horn Concertos #1 & 2 / London 430370-2
Barry Tuckwell (horn), Vladimir Ashkenazy/Royal Philharmonic Orchestra

Horn Concertos #1 & 2 / EMI CMS7643422
Peter Damm (horn), Rudolf Kempe/Staatskapelle Dresden

Concerto in D Major / Koch 3-7023-2H1
Humbert Lucarelli (oboe), Donald Spieth/Lehigh Valley Chamber Orchestra

Concerto in D Major / EMI CMS7643422
Manfred Clement (oboe), Rudolf Kempe/Staatskapelle Dresden
Don Juan

Don Juan, Op. 20 / Deutsche Grammophon 410959-2
Herbert von Karajan/Berlin Philharmonic Orchestra

Don Juan, Op. 20 / Telarc CD-80262
Andre Previn/Vienna Philharmonic Orchestra
Ein Heldenleben

Ein Heldenleben, Op. 40 / CBS MK44817
Alexander Barantschik (violin), Michael Tilson Thomas/London Symphony Orchestra

Ein Heldenleben, Op. 40 / EMI CMS7643422
Peter Mirring (violin), Rudolf Kempe/Staatskapelle Dresden

★ **Four Last Songs**

The Four Last Songs / Deutsche Grammophon 419188-2
Anna Tomowa-Sintow (soprano), Herbert von Karajan/Berlin Philharmonic Orchestra

The Four Last Songs / EMI CDC7472762
Elisabeth Schwarzkopf (soprano), George Szell/Berlin Radio Symphony Orchestra

METAMORPHOSEN

Metamorphosen / Chandos CHAN8734
Neeme Jarvi/Scottish National Orchestra

Metamorphosen / EMI CMS7643502
Rudolf Kempe/Staatskapelle Dresden

ROSENKAVALIER (OPERA)

Rosenkavalier, Op. 59 / London 417493-2
Crespin, Donath, Minton, Jungwirth, Sir Georg Solti/Vienna Philharmonic Orchestra & Vienna State Opera Chorus

Rosenkavalier, Op. 59 / EMI CDS7542592
Kiri Te Kanawa, Barbara Hendricks, Anne Sofie van Otter, Bernard Haitink/Staatskapelle Dresden & State Opera Chorus

Rosenkavalier, Op. 59 / RCA 6644-2-RG
Caballe, Resnik, Lewis, Milnes, Erich Leinsdorf/London Symphony Orchestra & Chorus

SALOME (OPERA)

Salome, Op. 54 / London 414414-2
Nilsson, Hoffman, Stolze, Kmentt, Wachter, Sir Georg Solti/Vienna Philharmonic Orchestra & Vienna State Opera Chorus

★ **Till Eulenspiegel**

Till Eulenspiegels Lustige Streiche, Op. 28 / London 414043-2
Sir Georg Solti/Chicago Symphony Orchestra

Till Eulenspiegels Lustige Streiche, Op. 28 / Chandos CHAN8572
Neeme Jarvi/Scottish National Orchestra

Igor Stravinsky (1882-1971)

An important Russian composer of totally original and exciting music in many forms. Stravinsky's ballet *The Rite of Spring* (1913), a work of exotic and primal character, marked a shift in modern Western music. In early pieces like *Fireworks* (1908) and the marvelous *King of the Stars* for chorus and orchestra (1911), Stravinsky exhibits a love of orchestral color that seems like a combination of Debussy, Scriabin, and Wagner. The wood-flute song and plainchant intervals form one layer of his music. Other layers are the added harmonic dissonances, either in a rhythmic pattern (like the famous sacrificial dance in *The Rite of Spring*) or in sparkling arpeggios of violin harmonics and woodwinds. Stravinsky wedded the primitive, ancient, and neo-classical to the scale of the present. There seems to be a progression from *Petrouchka* and *The Firebird* for the Ballets-Russes, to the neo-jazz *Ebony Concerto*, to the purity of religious feeling shown in the *Symphony of Psalms* and *Agon*, which begins to use the 12-tone technique in a limited way—but maybe it's more an unfolding of a personality that was there from the start. —*"Blue" Gene Tyranny*

APOLLO

Apollon Musagete (ballet) / EMI CDC7496362
Simon Rattle/City of Birmingham Symphony Orchestra

Apollon Musagete (ballet) / RCA 60156-2-RC
Guildhall String Ensemble

CONCERTO ("DUMBARTON OAKS")

Concerto ("Dumbarton Oaks") (original 2-piano version) / CBC Enterprises SMCD5120
James Anagnoson, Leslie Kinton (pianos)

Concerto ("Dumbarton Oaks") /**Deutsche Grammophon 419628-2**
Orpheus Chamber Orchestra

★ **Firebird: Suite**

The Firebird: Suite / Telarc CD-80039
Robert Shaw/Atlanta Symphony Orchestra

The Firebird (ballet) / London 414409-2
Charles Dutoit/Montreal Symphony Orchestra

The Firebird (ballet) / Mercury Living Presence 432012-2
Antal Dorati/London Symphony Orchestra

★ **Petrouchka (ballet)**

Petrouchka (ballet) / Philips 416498-2
Sir Colin Davis/Concertgebouw Orchestra Amsterdam

Petrouchka (ballet) / Telarc CD-80270
David Zinman/Baltimore Symphony Orchestra

Petrouchka (ballet) / EMI CDC7490532
Simon Rattle/City of Birmingham Symphony Orchestra

★ **Sacre du Printemps**

Le Sacre du Printemps (ballet) / Philips 416498-2
Sir Colin Davis/Royal Concertgebouw Orchestra

Le Sacre du Printemps (ballet) / CBS MYK37764
Pierre Boulez/Cleveland Orchestra

Le Sacre du Printemps (ballet) / EMI CDM7645162
Riccardo Muti/Philadelphia Orchestra

SYMPHONY IN C

Symphony in C Major / London 436416-2
Vladimir Ashkenazy/Berlin Radio Symphony Orchestra

Symphony in C Major / CBS MK42434
Igor Stravinsky/CBC Symphony Orchestra

SYMPHONY OF PSALMS

Symphony of Psalms / CBS MK44710
Leonard Bernstein/New York Philharmonic Orchestra & Chorus

Symphony of Psalms / Telarc CD-80105
Robert Shaw/Atlanta Symphony Orchestra & Chorus

Franz von Suppe (1819-1895)

An Austrian conductor and composer of opera, operetta, and incidental music who is famous for overtures to such works as *Poet and Peasant* and *Morning, Noon, and Night in Vienna*. —*AMG*

OVERTURES

Overtures: "Boccaccio"; "Light Cavalry"; "Morning, Noon & Night in Vienna"; "Pique Dame"; "Poet & Peasant"; and "The Beautiful Galatea" / Mercury 434309-2
Paul Paray/Detroit Symphony Orchestra

Overtures: "Boccaccio"; "Light Cavalry"; "Morning, Noon & Night in Vienna"; "Pique Dame"; "Poet & Peasant"; and "The Beautiful Galatea" / London 414408-2
Charles Dutoit/Montreal Symphony Orchestra

Jan Pieterszoon Sweelinck (1562-1621)

Sweelinck was a Dutch organist, teacher, and composer. He is widely considered to be the greatest of Dutch composers. Sweelinck was born in Deventer and later succeeded his father as organist at the Oude Kerk in Amsterdam, where his family were organists continuously for almost 100 years. His compositions include both keyboard and sacred and secular choral music, though it is for his keyboard music that he is best known today. Sweelinck was extremely influential as a teacher, especially of German students (including Scheidemann, Scheidt, Praetorius, and Hasse) who would propagate his compositional techniques far into eastern Europe. He is one of the major figures in the transition from Renaissance to baroque compositional styles.

Sweelinck was one of the great transitional figures in Western music, known for his formal rigor and theoretical knowledge of the most influential compositional schools of the time. His keyboard compositions continued to be widely and directly influential in Germany until the time of Dietrich Buxtehude. —*Todd McComb*

KEYBOARD MUSIC

13 Toccatas, Fantasias, Pavanas, and Other Pieces / Globe GLO5030
Anneke Uittenbosch (harpsichord, organ & virginal)

9 Fantasias, Toccatas, and Other Pieces / RCA Deutsche Harmonia Mundi Editio Classica 77148-2-RG
Gustav Leonhardt (organ)

Karol Szymanowski (1882-1937)

An eminent Polish composer whose early style was influenced by German romanticism. About 1917, his music began to show an awareness of Scriabin and impressionism and a new style began to emerge. As a director of the Warsaw Conservatory, his compositions and teaching had a strong impact on Polish music. His ballet *Harnasie* (based on a folk legend) and his *Stabat Mater* are among his most important works. —*Mary K. Scanlan*

CONCERTOS FOR VIOLIN (#1)

Violin Concertos #1 & 2 / Marco Polo 8.223291
Konstanty Andrzej Kulka (violin), Karol Stryja/Polish State Philharmonic Orchestra

Violin Concertos #1 & 2 / Marco Polo 8.223291
C. Juliet (violin), Charles Dutoit/Montreal Symphony Orchestra

STRING QUARTETS

String Quartets #1 & 2 / Olympia OCD328
Varsovia Quartet

String Quartets #1 & 2 / Denon CO-79462
Carmina Quartet

Thomas Tallis (1505-1585)

Tallis was the most influential English composer of his generation, as well as one of the most popular Renaissance composers of today. Tallis served as an organist and in other professional capacities for four English monarchs, including in the Royal Chapel. Together with his most famous student William Byrd, he obtained a monopoly right from Queen Elizabeth I for the publication of vocal music. Tallis presided over the most dynamic period in English musical history, during which the continental style of structural imitation was largely adopted by English composers in the wake of the Reformation and suppression of the monasteries.

Though Tallis's music includes a wide range of styles and objectives, the bulk of his output is choral music, both in the older Latin motet style and the newer English anthem style. Lyrical ideas usually dominate his musical impulses, and his polyphony is often primarily chordal or homophonic. He was not especially interested in technical counterpoint as such, and his settings have a consequent air of serenity about them that arises from the straightforward musical means used to develop melodic ideas. His sacred Latin choral music is his most highly regarded achievement; this large output is mostly in the motet genre with a wide range of personally selected texts, set syllabically in the style of the continental Renaissance masters of Italy and the North. His *English Anthems* also played an important role in the early development of this long-lived genre.

Today, Tallis's music continues to be extremely popular. It has been used for motivation by such contemporary composers as Ralph Vaughan Williams and Peter Maxwell Davies, as well as providing much of the impetus for the early music movement in English choral performance. Though Tallis's technical achievements pale by comparison with many of his near contemporaries, his music has a superbly communicative element of human expression which still speaks directly to audiences. —*Todd McComb*

★ **Sacred Choral Music (Spem in alium, Lamentations of Jeremiah, Masses, Motets)**

40-Part Motet "Spem in alium"; Lamentations of Jeremiah; Seven Motets / Chandos CHAN0513
Harry Christophers/The Sixteen

Lamentations of Jeremiah; Nine Motets / Gimell CDGIM025
Peter Phillips/The Tallis Scholars

40-Part Motet "Spem in alium"; Lamentations of Jeremiah; Six Motets / Hyperion CDA66400
David Hill/Winchester Cathedral Choir & Winchester College Quiristers

Mass for 4 Voices; Eight Motets / Naxos 8.550576
Jeremy Summerly/Oxford Camerata

The English Anthems (complete) / Gimell CDGIM007
Peter Phillips/The Tallis Scholars

Giuseppe Tartini (1692-1770)

An Italian violinist, composer, and music theorist who made several important acoustical discoveries (resulting in treatises) and wrote numerous violin pieces, the most famous of which is *The Devil's Trill* sonata. —*Mary K. Scanlan*

CONCERTOS FOR VIOLIN

3 Concertos, D. 56, 96 & 113 / Erato ECD88096
Uto Ughi (violin), Claudio Scimone/I Solisti Veneti

3 Concertos, D. 45, 56 & 86 / Novalis 1500922
Thomas Furi (violin)/Camerata Bern

SONATA FOR VIOLIN "DEVIL'S TRILL"

4 Sonatas, including "Il Trillo del Diavolo" / Hyperion CDA66430
Locatelli Trio

John Taverner (c.1490-1545)

Taverner was the leading English composer of his generation, and one of the most influential of English composers. He was born in Lincolnshire, served in a prestigious post at the short-lived Cardinal College at Oxford, and ended his life back in the Lincolnshire town of Boston. Much of Taverner's music was apparently composed early in his life, before the effects of the Reformation could be fully felt in England and before continental compositional practice would have its full influence. He is best known for his large-scale sacred choral music: several masses, votive antiphons, and magnificats.

Taverner's musical style represents the last major essay in the uniquely English florid repertory, based on elaborate free counterpoint and extended melismatic climaxes for accomplished soloists. However, his technique also incorporates some continental ideas on development, especially in its use of motivic connection within and between movements. Taverner's three large-scale festal masses (*Gloria Tibi Trinitas, Corona Spinea, O Michael*) are particularly admired for their variety of invention and command of form. The beautiful "In Nomine" section of the Benedictus of his *Missa Gloria Tibi Trinitas*—first arranged by

Taverner himself for instrumental ensemble—served as the inspiration for an entirely new English genre of composition, which was to retain its vigor until the time of Purcell. Taverner's music, created during a tumultuous period in English history, is particularly well-thought-of today for its combination of reflective and innovative elements. —*Todd McComb*

FESTAL MASSES

Gloria tibi Trinitas (mass); Dum transisset Sabbatum & Leroy Kyrie (motets) / Gimell CDGIM004
Peter Phillips /The Tallis Scholars

Corona spinea (mass) and O Wilhelme, pastor bone (motet) / Academy Sound & Vision LTD CDGAU115
Francis Grier/Choir of Christ Church Cathedral, Oxford

Sancti Wilhelmi (mass); Dum transisset Sabbatum II, Ex eius tumba and O Wilhelme, pastor bone (motets) / Hyperion CDA66427
Harry Christophers/The Sixteen

(mass) Mater Christi (mass) and Mater Christi sanctissima and O Wilhelme, pastor bone (motets) / Nimbus NIM5218
Stephen Darlington/Choir of Christ Church Cathedral, Oxford

"Western Wind" Masses by Taverner, Tye & Shepperd / Gimell CDGIM027
Peter Phillips/The Tallis Scholars

Peter Ilyitch Tchaikovsky (1840-1893)

Tchaikovsky was the preeminent exponent of the Russian national school in the late romantic period. His concertos and symphonies epitomize the romantic ideal and draw heavily on native Russian influences. Strongly melodic in nature, his music has found enduring appeal among newcomers and experienced music lovers alike. —*AMG*

CAPRICCIO ITALIEN

Capriccio Italien in A Major, Op. 45 / Chandos CHAN8460 or CHAN8672 / 8
Mariss Jansons/Oslo Philharmonic Orchestra

Capriccio Italien in A Major, Op. 45 / London 417300-2
Charles Dutoit/Montreal Symphony Orchestra

★ **Concerto #1 for Piano**

Piano Concerto #1 in B Flat Minor, Op. 23 / Deutsche Grammophon 415062-2
Martha Argerich (piano), Charles Dutoit/Royal Philharmonic Orchestra

Piano Concerto #1 in B Flat Minor, Op. 23 / London 417294-2
Andras Schiff (piano), Sir Georg Solti/Chicago Symphony Orchestra

Piano Concerto #1 in B Flat Minor, Op. 23 / Telarc CD-80124
Jon Kimura Parker (piano), Andre Previn/Royal Philharmonic Orchestra

Piano Concerto #1 in B Flat Minor, Op. 23 / Vox Music Group CDX5024
Michael Ponti (piano), Richard Kapp/Prague Symphony Orchestra

★ **Concerto for Violin**

Concerto in D Major, Op. 35 / London 410011-2 or 430725
Kyung-Wha Chung (violin), Charles Dutoit/Montreal Symphony Orchestra

Concerto in D Major, Op. 35 / London 421716-2
Joshua Bell (violin), Vladimir Ashkenazy/Cleveland Orchestra

Concerto in D Major, Op. 35 / Philips 416821-2
Viktoria Mullova (violin), Seiji Ozawa/Boston Symphony Orchestra

Concerto in D Major, Op. 35 / EMI CDC7471062
Itzhak Perlman (violin), Eugene Ormandy/Philadelphia Orchestra

EUGEN ONEGIN (OPERA)

Eugen Onegin / Deutsche Grammophon 415062-2
Thomas Allen, Mirella Freni, Anne Sofie van Otter, James Levine/Staatskapelle Dresden & Leipzig Radio Chorus

Eugen Onegin / Sony S2K45539
Yuri Mazurok, Anna Tomowa-Sintow, Nicolai Gedda, Emil Tchakarov/Sofia Festival Orchestra & National Opera Chorus
Manfred Symphony

Symphony ("Manfred") in B Minor, Op. 58 / EMI CDC7474122

Riccardo Muti/Philharmonia Orchestra

Symphony ("Manfred") in B Minor, Op. 58 / London 421441-2
Richard Chailly/Concertgebouw Orchestra Amsterdam

Symphony ("Manfred") in B Minor, Op. 58 / Chandos
  CHAN8672 / 8 or CHAN8535
Mariss Jansons/Oslo Philharmonic Orchestra

MARCHE SLAV

Marche Slav in B Flat Major, Op. 31 / Mercury Living Presence
  434305-2
Antal Dorati/Detroit Symphony Orchestra

Marche Slav in B Flat Major, Op. 31 / Deutsche Grammophon
  415379-2
Leonard Bernstein/Isreal Philharmonic Orchestra

★ **Nutcracker (ballet)**

Nutcracker, Op. 71 (complete) / Telarc CD-80137-2
Sir Charles Mackerras/London Symphony Orchestra

Nutcracker, Op. 71a (suite) / London 417300-2
Charles Dutoit/Montreal Symphony Orchestra

1812 Overture

1812 Overture in E Flat Major, Op. 49 / Deutsche
  Grammophon 429984-2
Neeme Jarvi/Gothenburg Symphony Orchestra

1812 Overture in E Flat Major, Op. 49 / Deutsche
  Grammophon 415379-2 or 431047-2
Leonard Bernstein/Isreal Philharmonic Orchestra

QUARTETS

**String Quartets #1 Op. 11, #2 Op. 22, #3 Op. 30, and String
  Sextet ("Souvenir de Florence") Op. 70** / EMI CDS7497752
Yuri Bashmet (viola), Natalia Gutman (cello), Borodin Trio

String Quartet #1 in D Major, Op. 11 / Collins Classics 12372
Alberni Quartet

ROMEO & JULIET FANTASY OVERTURE

Romeo & Juliet (fantasy overture) in B Minor / Chandos
  CHAN8310 / 11
Geoffrey Simon/London Symphony Orchestra

Romeo & Juliet (fantasy overture) in B Minor / EMI
  CDE7677892
Carlo Maria Giulini/Philharmonia Orchestra

Romeo & Juliet (fantasy overture) in B Minor / London 430707-
  2 or 430745-2
Sir Georg Solti/Chicago Symphony Orchestra

SERENADE FOR STRINGS

Serenade in C Major, Op. 48 / Deutsche Grammophon 429488-
  2 or 423060-2
Orpheus Chamber Orchestra

Serenade in C Major, Op. 48 / Omega OCD1010
Australian Chamber Orchestra

SLEEPING BEAUTY (BALLET)

The Sleeping Beauty (suite), Op. 66 / Telarc CD-80151
Sir Charles Mackerras/Royal Philharmonic Orchestra

The Sleeping Beauty (suite), Op. 66 / EMI CDC7470752
Riccardo Muti/Philadelphia Orchestra

★ **Swan Lake (ballet)**

Swan Lake (ballet), Op. 20 (complete) / RCA 7804-2-RC
Leonard Slatkin/St. Louis Symphony Orchestra

Swan Lake (ballet), Op. 20 (complete) / Vanguard OVC5008 / 9
Maurice Abravanel/Utah Symphony Orchestra

Swan Lake (suite), Op. 20a / Telarc CD-80151
Sir Charles Mackerras/Royal Philharmonic Orchestra

Swan Lake (suite), Op. 20a / Chandos CHAN8556
Neeme Jarvi/Scottish National Orchestra

★ **Symphonies (2, 4, *5, *6)**

Symphonies #1-6 (complete) / Chandos CHAN8672 / 8
Mariss Jansons/Oslo Philharmonic Orchestra

Symphony #2 ("Little Russian") in C Minor, Op. 17 / Telarc
  CD-80131
Lorin Maazel/Pittsburgh Symphony Orchestra

**Symphonies: #4 Op. 36, #5 Op. 64; and #6 ("Pathetique") Op.
  74** / Deutsche Grammophon 419745-2

Evgeny Mravinsky/Leningrad Philharmonic Orchestra

Symphony #4 in F Minor, Op. 36 / Telarc CD-80047
Lorin Maazel/Cleveland Orchestra

Symphony #5 in E Minor, Op. 64 / Telarc CD-80107
Andre Previn/Royal Philharmonic Orchestra

Symphony #6 ("Pathetique") in B Minor, Op. 74 / Deutsche
  Grammophon 419604-2
Leonard Bernstein/New York Philharmonic Orchestra

TRIO FOR PIANO & STRINGS

Trio in A Minor, Op. 50 / Dorian Recordings DOR90146
Rembrandt Trio

Trio in A Minor, Op. 50 / Chandos CHAN8348
Borodin Trio

VARIATIONS ON A ROCOCO THEME

10 Variations on a Rococo Theme in A Major, Op. 33 /
  Chandos CHAN8347
Raphael Wallfisch (cello), Geoffrey Simon/English Chamber
Orchestra

10 Variations on a Rococo Theme in A Major, Op. 33 /
  Mercury Living Presence 431001-2
Jano Starker (cello), Antal Dorati/London Symphony Orchestra

Georg Philipp Telemann (1681-1767)

A remarkably prolific, skillful, and forward-thinking German
composer, one of the foremost of his day, who wrote a great many
sacred and secular vocal works as well as orchestral, chamber,
and keyboard music. A contemporary of Bach and Handel,
Telemann shared many of their musical techniques and wrote for
many of the same genres, and though his music is overshadowed
by theirs, it has many charms, perhaps more evident in his modest instrumental works (of which the *Suite for Flute & Strings in
A* is a good choice) than in his 40 operas, 600 overtures, 44 liturgical passions, and other large works. Handel said Telemann
could write an eight-part motet with the ease that someone else
would write a letter. —*"Blue" Gene Tyranny*

CONCERTOS (FOR OBOE, FLUTE, VIOLIN, VIOLA, ETC.)

**Viola Concerto in G Major, 2 Concertos for Flutes & Don Quixote
  Suite**/Musicmasters MMD60210X
Louise Schulman (viola)/Orchestra of St. Luke's

5 Concertos for Violin / Philips 411125-2
Iona Brown (violin)/Academy of St. Martin-in-the-Fields

5 Concerto for Oboe / Philips 412879-2
Heinz Holliger (oboe), Iona Brown/Academy of St. Martin-in-the-
Fields

4 Concertos for Horns / Philips 412226-2
Hermann Baumann, Timothy Brown & Nicholas Hill (horns),
Iona Brown/Academy of St. Martin-in-the-Fields

5 Concertos for Flutes, Bassoons & Lute / Capriccio 10284
Eckart Haupt & Wolfgang Loebner (flutes), Gunter Klier (bassoon), Monika Rost (lute)/Dresden Baroque Soloists

4 Concertos for Violins & Suite / Chandos CHAN0519
Simon Standage, Micaela Comberti, Miles Golding & Andrew
Manze (violins)/Collegium Musicum 90

3 Violin Concertos, Concerto for 2 Flutes & Suite / Chandos
  Chaconne CHAN0512
Simon Standage & Micaela Comberti (violins), Rachel Brown, Siu
Peasgood (flutes), Simon Standage/Collegium Musicum 90

ESSERCIZII MUSICI

Sonata and 4 Trio Sonatas from Essercizii Musici /
  Musicmasters MMD60085W
Aulos Ensemble

6 Sonatas & 4 Trio Sonatas from Essercizii Musici /
  Musicmasters MMD60091F92Z
Aulos Ensemble

FANTASIAS FOR OBOE OR FLUTE

12 Fantasies / Denon 38C37-7089
Heinz Holliger (oboe)

★ **Musique de Table**

18 Overtures, Concertos & Sonatas ("Musique de Table") /
  Archiv 427619-2

Reinhard Goebel/Musica Antiqua Koln

PARIS QUARTETS

5 Quartets ("Paris") Book I (Concertos #1 & 2, Sonatas #1 & 2, and Suite #1) / Ricercar RIC043020
Ricercar Quartet

6 Quartets ("Paris") Book II / Denon 8175796132
European Baroque Soloists

3 Quartets ("Paris") Book III #2, 3 & 6 / Wildboar WLBR8801
Concerto Amabile

6 Quartets (Sonatas) Book IV / Koch 3-7031-2
American Baroque

SONATAS FOR FLUTE, OBOE & CONTINUO

6 Sonatas Op. 5 ("Canonic") / Denon 8175796142
Wolfgang Schulz (flute), Hansjorg Schellenberger (oboe) /European Baroque Soloists

★ **Suite in A for Flute & Strings**

Suite in A Minor, Sinfonia & 2 Concertos / Hyperion CDA66413
Peter Holtslag (recorder), Roy Goodman/Parley of Instruments Baroque Orchestra

SONATAS FOR RECORDER & HARPSICHORD

7 Sonatas from Der Getreue Music-Meister & Essercizii Musici / RCA 77153-2-RG
Camerata Koln

WATER MUSIC SUITE ("HAMBURG TIDES")

Overture ("Hamburg Tides") in C Major & 3 Concertos / Archiv 413788-2
Reinhard Goebel/Musica Antiqua Koln

Ambroise Thomas (1811-1896)

Mignon: Overture

Mignon Overture / Sony SMK47601
Leonard Bernstein/New York Philharmonic Orchestra

Virgil Thomson (1896-1989)

Thomson is one of the few true modernists in America. Thomson's music is almost disconcertingly spare and direct. In the consciously American pieces especially, there is a kind of aural equivalent to cubist collage, as ragtime, waltzes, tangos, two-steps, fiddle tunes, and hymns get pasted onto the texture. Unlike Ives, there's an unsentimental distance and clarity to it all, like someone without illusions able to state exactly what's on his mind. Thomson gets this effect in his prose, too

Although overshadowed by Copland (who, by the way, always ackowledged his debts to Thomson), Thomson achieved far more in the realm of opera and vocal music, in which almost everyone acknowledges him a master. Try the powerful (and, to my ear, deeply American) *5 Songs from William Blake,* the incredibly beautiful *Feast of Love* for baritone and chamber ensemble (a real lesson in how to vary orchestral texture and how to continue a musical line), *4 Southern Hymns* (a choral classic), the sinewy cello concerto, the *Symphony on a Hymn Tune, Acadian Songs and Dances* (which deserve the recognition given to the sister suite Louisiana Story), *Praises and Prayers,* the delicate *4 Songs to Poems of Thomas Campion* for voice and chamber group, and the heartbreaking *Stabat Mater* for mezzo and string quartet. — *Steven Schwartz*

PLOW THAT BROKE THE PLAINS

The Plow That Broke the Plains / ESS.A.Y Recordings CD1005
Richard Kapp/Philharmonia Virtuosi

The Plow That Broke the Plains / Vangaurd OVC8013
Leopold Stokowski/Symphony of the Air

Sir Michael Tippett (b. 1905)

An important English composer in the neo-romantic style who excels in large-scale vocal and instrumental forms and, though incorporating dissonance, operates within a largely tonal framework. Not adverse to unusual effects, Tippett interjects several instances of "heavy glottal aspiration" in his fourth symphony. — *Mary K. Scanlan*

CHILD OF OUR TIME (ORATORIO)

A Child of Our Time / London 425158-2
Haymon (soprano), Clarey (soprano), Evans (tenor), White (baritone), Richard Hickox/London Symphony Orchestra & Chorus

A Child of Our Time / London 425158-2
Elsie Morison (soprano), Pamela Bowden (soprano), Richard Lewis (tenor), Richard Standen (baritone), Sir John Pritchard/Royal Liverpool Philharmonic Orchestra

Giuseppe Torelli (1658-1709)

CONCERTI GROSSI OP. 8

6 Concertos from Op. 8, #2, 3, 6, 8, 9 & 12 / Philips 432118-2
Mariana Sirbu & Antonio Perez (violins)/I Musici

Joaquin Turina (1882-1949)

Spanish composer of songs, opera, symphony, chamber music, and instrumental works (guitar and piano) in the style of Spanish impressionism. —*Mary K. Scanlan*

PIANO MUSIC

Danzas andaluzas—Zapateado, Danzas gitanas— Sacromonte, Sanlucar de Barrameda, 3 Danzas fantasticas, Op. 22 / EMI CDM7645282
Alicia De Larrocha (Piano)

Christopher Tye (c.1505-1573)

Tye was an English organist and composer of choral and instrumental music. Apparently a native of East Anglia, Tye received a doctorate in music from Cambridge in 1537 and was later associated with the priory of Ely. Tye was a contemporary of Thomas Tallis and contributed to the assimilation of continental structural principles into English music during the first half of the 16th century. Little survives of his sacred choral music, but what does remain represents an interesting personal synthesis of the older English florid style and the techniques of structural imitation and syllabic text setting. Tye's sparing use of imitation and the general absence of soloist passages gives his music a tighter cohesiveness than that of the previous generation—his Mass *Euge Bone* is perhaps the most impressive example of the period.

Today Tye is at least as well known as a composer of instrumental ensemble music for viol consort. He left 31 such compositions, apparently composed late in his life. These include 21 settings of the "In Nomine" type—based on Taverner's cantus firmus and incorporating all manner of instrumental ideas within a purely polyphonic context. Tye is credited as the first significant composer of instrumental chamber music, and his examples are of uniformly high quality. They represent a substantial legacy for Western music. —*Todd McComb*

SACRED CHORAL MUSIC

Cathedral Music by Christopher Tye / Hyperion 66424
David Hill/Choir of Winchester Cathedral

CONSORT MUSIC

Consort Musicke Set for Viols / Astree E 8708
Jordi Savall/Hesperion XX

Ralph Vaughan Williams (1872-1958)

Vaughan Williams received his training from Hubert Parry and Charles Villiers Stanford, both composers influenced by Brahms. Early Vaughan Williams works have their Brahmsian (and Wagnerian) moments, but in the early music that has survived we hear something absolutely original and unique. Vaughan Williams became enthralled with the English folk song (he was a major collector).

Vaughan Williams fortunately could absorb from diverse sources—including Stravinsky, Brahms, Parry, Debussy, Ravel, Bach, Byrd, and Hindemith—and yet remain absolutely and recognizably himself. After a brief flirtation with French impressionism (*In the Fen Country,String Quartet No. 1*) and some study with Ravel (who called him "the only pupil who does not write my music"), he hit the ground running with his incidental music to Aristophanes's *The Wasps,* the song cycle *On Wenlock Edge,* and the classic *Fantasia on a Theme by Thomas Tallis.* These are, to my mind, the first works in which we see the "real" Vaughan Williams. From here on, you can't mistake the voice.

Vaughan Williams composed extensively in almost every genre but chamber music. He is one of the great setters of English poetry, and vocal music comprises a large part of his output. Major works include *Five Mystical Songs, Merciless Beauty, Sancta Civitas, Serenade to Music, Hodie, 10 Blake Songs,* and *Dona nobis pacem.* He wrote several operas, not one of which has kept the stage: *Hugh the Drover, The Poisoned Kiss, Riders to the Sea, Sir John in Love,* and *Pilgrim's Progress.* The last three contain magnificent music. *Sir John* in particular is one great tune after another. There's no accounting for taste.

The symphonies, in particular, contain much of Vaughan Williams's range. Not one is like another. Each represents a unique approach to problems of symphonic form. All, however, have great emotional power. He is a major symphonist. — *Steven Schwartz*

★ **Fantasia on a Theme by Tallis**

Fantasy on a Theme by Thomas Tallis / EMI CDC7472132
Sir Adrian Boult/London Philharmonic Orchestra

Fantasy on a Theme by Thomas Tallis / Nimbus NIM5019
William Boughton/English String Orchestra

Fantasy on a Theme by Thomas Tallis / Special Music SCD-8011
Dalia Atlas/Israel Philharmonic Orchestra

FANTASIA ON GREENSLEEVES

Fantasy on "Greensleeves" / Nimbus NIM5019
William Boughton/English String Orchestra

Fantasy on "Greensleeves" / Chandos CHAN8828
Bryden Thomson/London Symphony Orchestra

THE LARK ASCENDING

The Lark Ascending / Special Music SCD-8011
Zina Schiff (violin), Dalia Atlas/Isreal Philharmonic Orchestra

The Lark Ascending / Academy Sound & Vision LTD CDQS6023
Iona Brown (violin), Neville Marriner/Academy of St. Martin-in-the-Fields

The Lark Ascending / EMI CDC7497702
Bradley Creswick (Violin), Richard Hickox/Northern Sinfonia of England

★ **Symphonies (*3, 4, 5, 6)**

Symphonies #1-9 / Chandos CHAN9087-91
Bryden Thomson/London Symphony Orchestra

Symphonies #3 ("Pastoral") and #5 / EMI CDM7640182
Margaret Price (soprano), Sir Adrian Boult/New Philharmonia Orchestra

Symphonies #4 and 6 / EMI CDC7472152
Sir Adrian Boult/New Philharmonia Orchestra

Giuseppe Verdi (1813-1901)

Considered Italy's greatest composer of operas. Verdi's works are remarkable for their melodic beauty, superb dramatic construction, and rich orchestration—evoking worlds that lived more in Verdi's mind than, for instance in *Aida,* in the actual Egypt of ancient times. His ability to balance the subjective, intimate lives of his characters with the objective world in which they are set is another wonder of his operas, as in the contrast in *Aida* between the profound, despairing quality of the love duet in the tomb and the marches and grandeur of the earlier scenes. Verdi's dramatic, operatic sensibilities are carried over directly to the *Requiem Mass,* which in its drive and terror is unlike any liturgical music that came before. — *"Blue" Gene Tyranny*

★ **Aida (opera)**

Aida / London 417416-2
Margaret Price, Gorr, Vickers, Merrill, Tozzi, Sir George Solti/Rome Opera Orchestra & Chorus

Aida / London 417416-2
Millo, Zajick, Placido Domingo, Morris, Ramey, James Levine/Metropolitan Opera Orchestra & Chorus
Falstaff (opera)

Falstaff / Deutsche Grammophon 410503-2
Ricciarelli, Hendricks, Valentini, Gonzalez, Bruson, Nucci, Carlo Maria Guilini/Los Angeles Philharmonic Orchestra & Chorus

Falstaff / EMI CDC7496682
Schwarzkopf, Moffo, Merriman, Barbieri, Alva, Gobbi, Panerai, Zaccaria, Herbert von Karajan/Philharmonia Orchestra & Chorus

Macbeth (opera)

Macbeth / Deutsche Grammophon 415688-2
Cappuccilli, Verrett, Ghiaurov, Domingo, Claudio Abbado/La Scala Orchestra & Chorus

Macbeth / Philips 412133-2
Zampieri, Bruson, Lloyd, Shicoff, Giuseppe Sinopoli/German Opera Orchestra & Chorus

OTELLO (OPERA)

Otello / RCA RCD2-2951
Scotto, Domingo, Milnes, James Levine/National Philharmonic Orchestra & Ambrosian Singers

Otello / RCA RCD2-2951
Ricciarelli, Domingo, Diaz, Lorin Maazel/La Scala Orchestra & Chorus

REQUIEM MASS

Requiem Mass / Telarc CD-80152
Dunn, Curry, Hadley, Plishka, Robert Shaw/Atlanta Symphony Orchestra & Chorus

Requiem Mass / EMI CDC7472572
Schwarzkopf, Ludwig, Gedda, Ghiaurov, Carlo Maria Giulini/Philharmonia Orchestra & Chorus

★ **Rigoletto (opera)**

Rigoletto / London 425864-2
Anderson, Pavarotti, Nucci, Ghiaurov, Verrett, Riccardo Chailly/Orchestra e Coro del Teatro Comunale di Bologna

Rigoletto / Philips 412592-2
Grubernova, Fassbaender, Schicoff, Bruson, Lloyd, Guiseppe Sinopoli/Academia di Santa Cecilia Orchestra & Chorus

★ **La Traviata (opera)**

La Traviata / Deutsche Grammophon 415132-2
Cotrubas, Domingo, Milnes, Carlos Kleiber/Bavarian State Opera Orchestra & Chorus

La Traviata / RCA 4414-2-RG
Moffo, Tucker, Merrill, Fernando Previtali/Rome Opera Orchestra & Chorus

★ **Il Trovatore (opera)**

Il Trovatore / Deutsche Grammophon 413355-2
Plowright, Fassbaender, Domingo, Zancanaro, Carlo Maria Giulini/Accademia di Santa Cecilia Orchestra & Chorus

Il Trovatore / RCA 6194-2-RC
Price, Cossotto, Domingo, Milnes, Zubin Mehta/Philharmonia Orchestra & Chorus

Tomas Luis de Victoria (c.1549-1611)

Victoria is one of the greatest Spanish composers of sacred vocal music. After studying in Spain, he went to Rome in 1565, where he may have studied with Palestrina. In any case, he spent most of his life at the papal chapel in Rome, and eventually became the successor to Palestrina. He subsequently published several sets of masses and motets. Victoria is known for his exaltation of Spanish mysticism and his deep religious beliefs, both of which contribute to the ecstatic quality of his music. — *AMG*

MOTETS (ALSO SEE MASSES BELOW)

"Cantica Beatae Virginia"—11 Marian Motets / Astree E8767
Jordi Savall/La Capella Reial de Catalunya & Hesperion XX

18 Responsories for Tenebrae / Hyperion CDA66304
David Hill/Choir of Westminster Cathedral

MASSES (O MAGNUM MYSTERIUM, ETC)

O magnum mysterium & O quam gloriosum(masses and motets); Ardens est cor meum & Ave Maria (motets) / Naxos 8.550575
Jeremy Summerly/Oxford Camerata

Vidi speciosam (mass & motet) and Ave Maria; Ave Maris Stella; Ne Timeas, Maria; and Sancta Maria, Succurre Miseris (motets) / Hyperion CDA66129
David Hill/Choir of Westminster Cathedral

REQUIEM

Requiem "Officium defunctorum" for 6 Voices (expanded version) / Hyperion CDA66250
David Hill/Choir of Westminster Cathedral

Requiem "Officium defunctorum" (short version); Funeral Motets "Versa est in luctum" by Victoria & Alonso Lobo / Gimell CDGIM012
Peter Phillips/The Tallis Scholars

Heitor Villa-Lobos (1887-1959)

Brazil's best-known composer. Villa-Lobos studied his homeland's Afro-Brazilian music as a young man. After travels in Europe, he returned to form his own symphony orchestra and to play many of the classics in Brazil for the first time. The beautiful *Bachianas brasileiras* for various instrumental and vocal combinations are well known and are of course inspired by Bach's music, which Villa-Lobos very much admired (he gave the first performance in Brazil of Bach's *Mass in B*). Villa-Lobos also ventured into certain experiments, such as the "New York Skyline Melody," written graphically to a photograph of the city. — *"Blue" Gene Tyranny*

★ Bachianas Brasileiras

Bachianas Brasileiras #2, 5, 6 & 9 / EMI CDC7473572
Mady Mesple (soprano), Albert Tetard (cello), Michel Debost (flute), Andre Sennedat (bassoon), Paul Capolongo/Orcestra de Paris

Bachianas Brasileiras #6 / Hyperion CDA66295
William Bennett (flute), Robin O'Neill (bassoon)

CHOROS

Choros #2 / Hyperion CDA66295
William Bennett (flute), Thea King (clarinet)

Choros #8 / Delos DE1017
E. Sawyer & Muniz, S. (pianos), Eleazar de Carvalho/Paraiba Symphony Orchestra

GUITAR CONCERTO

Concerto / Philips 416357-2
Pepe Romero (guitar), Neville Marriner/Academy of St. Martin-in-the-Fields

Concerto / Deutsche Grammophon 429232-2
Goran Sollscher (guitar)/Orpheus Chamber Orchestra

STRING QUARTETS

String Quartets #1, 8 & 13 / Marco Polo 8.223389
Danubius Quartet

Philippe de Vitry (1291-1361)

Vitry was one of the most prominent figures in medieval music. Not only do we know of his existence, but the dates of his birth and death are relatively certain—something which cannot be said for much more recent composers of some renown. Vitry was the author of an important music theory text, *Ars Nova*, which has been taken up as the name of that entire period of music history. In the *Ars Nova*, Vitry was primarily concerned with expanding the rhythmic resources offered to composers; he introduced new rhythmic schemes, along with a new mensural notation that was to play an important role for more than a hundred years after his death. The main result of his innovations was that the different lines of polyphony were given much greater independence than had been done previously—during the so-called Ars Antiqua.

Vitry is credited with a large role in the development of the motet. Vitry's use of rhythm occupies an intermediate place between the older style exemplified by Perotin, in which voices show little rhythmic independence (instead operating as a kind of decorated monody in which chordal progression give a kaleidoscopic effect), and the more modern style of Machaut in which rhythmic devices are integral to a composition. Vitry's music provides much of the new technical means (as well as the specific written means in the *Ars Nova*) which would lead to the increased melodic invention and cosmopolitan subtlety of the following generations of composers, from Machaut to Dufay.

Though we do know something about Philippe de Vitry's life and his positions at the French court, less is known about his actual compositions. The only surviving works (some with greater evidence of authenticity than others) are motets. These motets are primarily secular in nature, though a few use religious texts. However, they are mostly on political rather than romantic subjects. Vitry also uses Latin for his secular works, rather than French as had become standard (and Machaut returns to French in his chansons). One sees him here as an intellectual, expressing the issues of his day in musical form. Vitry was a singular genius

who found new modes of expression that would not be fully refined until many years after his death. Interestingly, the nature of the music suggests that his motivation for the new style may well have been in rhetoric, rather than musical expression per se. — *Todd McComb*

20 Chansons & Motets / RCA Deutsche Harmonia Mundi 77095-2-RC
Sequentia

Antonio Vivaldi (1678-1741)

A prolific Italian composer of over 750 works discovered so far, renowned in his time as a violinist and known for solo violin concertos, including the famous *L'Estro armonico, op. 3*. In tone-painting works such as *I Quattri Stagioni* ("The Four Seasons"), Vivaldi established the essential drama and strong rhythms applied to basic harmonies that would prepare the way for the symphonic sonata-allegro form and the 18th-century "sound." He invented the idea that the soloist and orchestra should be in conflict with each other, holding a dialog that was essentially developmental, with effects like swift scales, arpeggios, and tremoli adding to the drama. — *"Blue" Gene Tyranny*

★ Four Seasons

4 Concertos Op. 8 #1-4 ("The Four Seasons") / Archiv 400045-2
Simon Standage (violin), Trevor Pinnock/The English Concert

4 Concertos Op. 8 #1-4 ("The Four Seasons") / Argo 414486-2
Alan Loveday (violin), Neville Marriner/Academy of St. Martin-in-the-Fields

12 Concertos Op. 8 including ("The Four Seasons") / Virgin Classics Veritas VCD790803-2
Monica Huggett (violin)/Raglan Baroque Players

★ Concertos (for violin, bassoon, cello, oboe, flute, etc.)

5 Oboe Concertos / Capriccio 10116
Burkhardt Glaetzner (oboe), Max Pommer/New Bach Collegium Musicum, Leipzig

6 Flute Concertos Op. 10 / Erato 2292-45401-2
Jean-Pierre Rampal (flute), Claudio Scimone/I Solisti Veneti

12 Concertos for 1, 2 & 4 Violins, Op. 3 / L'Oiseau-Lyre 414554-2
Elizabeth Wilcock, John Holloway, Monica Huggett, Catherine Mackintosh (violins), Christopher Hogwood/Academy of Ancient Music

2 Guitar Concertos, Concerto for 2 Violins & Concerto for 2 Cellos / Deutsche Grammophon 415487-2
Goran Sollscher (guitar), Thomas Furi (violin), Thomas Demenga (cello), Thomas Furi/Camerata Bern

6 Bassoon Concertos / Philips 416355-2
Klaus Thunemann (bassoon)/I Musici

6 Violin Concertos, Op. 6 / Philips 426939-2
Pina Carmirelli (violin)/I Musici

6 Violin Concertos, Op. 11 / Philips 426950-2
Salvatore Accardo (violin)/I Musici

7 Cello Concertos / RCA 60155-2-RC
Ofra Harnoy (cello), Paul Robinson/Toronto Chamber Orchestra

5 Concertos for Diverse Instruments / Unicorn-Kanchana DKP(CD)9050
Richard Studt/Tate Music Group

GLORIA

Gloria, RV 589; "Ostro picta, armata spina," RV 642 (w/ J.S. Bach Magnificat) / Chandos Chaconne CHAN0518
Emma Kirkby & Tessa Bonner (soprano), Michael Chance (countertenor), John mark Ainsley (tenor), Richard Hickox/Collegium Musicum 90

Gloria, RV 589 (w/ Haydn's "Nelson" Mass / London Jubilee 421146-2
Vaughan (soprano), Janet Baker (mezzo-soprano), Neville Marriner, Academy of St. Martin-in-the-Fields & Choir of King's College, Cambridge

SONATAS & TRIO SONATAS FOR VIOLIN & CONTINUO

12 Sonatas ("Manchester") / Harmonia Mundi HMU907089.90
Romanesca

7 Trio Sonatas, RV 2, 6, 64, 68, 75, 77 & 79 / Chandos CHAN0511
Purcell Quartet

7 Trio Sonatas, RV 29, 65, 70-72, 76 & 78 / Chandos CHAN0502
Purcell Quartet

SONATAS FOR FLUTE OR OBOE & CONTINUO, OP. 13 (WRITTEN BY NICHOLAS CHEDEVILLE)

6 Sonatas Op. 13 ("Il Pastor Fido") / Naxos 8.55064
Bela Drahos (oboe), Pal Kelemen (cello), Zsuzsa Pertis (harpsichord)

SONATAS FOR CELLO & CONTINUO OP. 14

6 Sonatas Op. 14 / L'Oiseau-Lyre 421060-2
Christophe Coin (cello), Eugene Ferre (guitar), Tom Finucane (archlute), Christopher Hogwood (harpsichord)

Richard Wagner (1813-1883)

An important German composer of opera and vocal music, with some orchestral and piano works, who used chromatic and dissonant harmonies and conceived all aspects of a performance as a Gesamtkunstwerk or total art work. He composed many notable operas, including *The Flying Dutchman* (1843), *Tristan and Isolde* (1865), and a four-opera cycle *The Ring of the Nibelungen* (1876). The trouble surrounding Wagner's works seems to grow out of the lyrics and his attitudes, and their appeal stems from the hypnotic beauty of music that exists in its own time-suspended world. His anti-Semitic attitudes are widely rumored, though his actual father was the actor Ludwig Geyer, who was Jewish. Wagner makes embarrassingly chauvinistic national appeals at the end of *Die Meistersinger*, but most of the rest is a series of lovely choruses and airs, the whole supposedly conceived as a light comedy. Generations of people have been swept away by the marvelous effects in his works, from the "Ride of the Valkyries" to the "Love Duet" (with the duo floating away into the cosmos). They have also been drawn to the beauty of the gently unfolding revolutionary harmonies, complex transformations, and intertwinings of the "Leitmotivs." Well, art isn't supposed to be easy all the time, and working out one's relation to Wagner's aesthetic is certainly good for the spirit. — *"Blue" Gene Tyranny*

DER FLIEGENDE HOLLANDER (OPERA)

Der fliegende Hollander / Philips 416300-2
Balsev, Schunk, Estes, Salminen, Woldemar Nelsson/Beyreuth Festival Orchestra & Chorus

Der fliegende Hollander / Naxos 8.660025-26
Alfred Muff, Ingrid Haubold, Peter Seiffert, Erich Knodt, Jorg Hering, Marga Schiml, Pinchas Steinberg/Vienna ORF Symphony Orchestra & Budapest Radio Chorus

GOTTERDAMMERUNG: RHINE JOURNEY & FUNERAL MUSIC

Orchestral Highlights from the Ring Cycle / CBS MYK36715
George Szell/Cleveland Orchestra

Orchestral Highlights from the Ring / Telarc CD-80154
Lorin Maazel/Berlin Philharmonic Orchestra

Gotterdammerung: Siegfried's Funeral Music / Sheffield Labs CD-07 / 08
Erich Leinsdorf/Los Angeles Philharmonic Orchestra

LOHENGRIN (OPERA)

Lohengrin / London 421053-2
Norman, Randova, Domingo, Fischer-Dieskau, Sotin, Sir Georg Solti/Vienna Philharmonic Orchestra & State Opera Orchestra

Lohengrin / EMI CDC7490172
Grummer, Ludwig, Thomas, Fischer-Dieskau, Frick, Rudolf Kempe/Vienna Philharmonic Orchestra & State Opera Orchestra

DIE MEISTERSINGER (OPERA)

Die Meistersinger von Nurnberg / London 421053-2
Bode, Hamari, Kollo, Bailey, Weikl, Moll, Sir Georg Solti/Vienna Philharmonic Orchestra & State Opera Orchestra

Die Meistersinger von Nurnberg / London 421053-2
Bode, Cox Ridderbusch, Sotin, Hirte, Silvio Varviso/Beyreuth Festival Orchestra & Chorus

★ **Parsifal: Prelude & Good Friday Music**
Parsifal: Prelude & Good Friday Music / Delos D / CD3053

Gerard Schwarz/Seattle Symphony Orchestra

★ **Der Ring des Nibelungen (4 opera cycle)**
Der Ring des Nibelungen (complete 4 opera cycle) / Philips 420325-2
Nilsson, Rysanek, Dvorakova, Burmeister, Soukupova, Modl, Windgassen, Wohlfart, Adam, Stewart, Neidlinger, Bohme, Nienstedt, Karl Bohm/Beyreuth Festival Orchestra & Chorus

Der Ring des Nibelungen: Das Rheingold / EMI CDC7498532
Lipovsek, Rappe, Zednik, Haage, Schmidt, Morris, Adam, Tschammer, Rydl, Bernard Haitink/Bavarian Radio Symphony Orchestra

Der Ring des Nibelungen: Das Rheingold / London 414101-2
Flagstad, Madeira, Svanholm, London, Neidlinger, Bohme, Sir Georg Solti/Vienna Philharmonic Orchestra

Der Ring des Nibelungen: Die Walkure / Deutsche Grammophon 423389-2
Behrens, Norman, Ludwig, Lakes, Morris, Moll, James Levine/Metropolitan Opera Orchestra

Der Ring des Nibelungen: Siegfried / London 414110-2
Nilsson, Windgassen, Stolze, Hitter Neidlinger, Sir Georg Solti/Vienna Philharmonic Orchestra

Der Ring des Nibelungen: Gotterdammerung / London 414115-2
Nilsson, Watson, Ludwig, Windgassen, Fischer-Dieskau, Frick, Sir Georg Solti/Vienna Philharmonic Orchestra

SIEGFRIED IDYLL

Siegfried Idyll / Chesky CD31
Jascha Horenstein/Royal Philharmonic Orchestra

Siegfried Idyll / Deutsche Grammophon 419169-2
Giuseppe Sinopoli/New York Philharmonic Orchestra

★ **Tannhauser: Overture & Venusberg Music**
Tannhauser: Overture & Venusberg Music / Sony SK45749
Zubin Mehta/New York Philharmonic Orchestra

Orchestral Highlights from the Ring / Telarc CD-80154
Lorin Maazel/Berlin Philharmonic Orchestra

★ **Tristan und Isolde: Prelude & Liebestod**
Tristan und Isolde: Prelude to Act I / Sheffield Labs CD-07 / 08
Erich Leinsdorf/Los Angeles Philharmonic Orchestra

Sir William Walton (1902-1983)

A British composer in most forms, especially orchestral music and including film scores, who has aptly described himself as a lyrical classical composer. His *Symphony No. 1* (1935) and the Vaughan Williams *Symphony No. 4 in F* (1934) are the most important British symphonies of the period between the wars—extroverted, with high symphonic color, magnificence, and a bittersweet lyricism. — *"Blue" Gene Tyranny*

CONCERTOS (VIOLIN, VIOLA, CELLO)

Violin & Viola Concertos / EMI CDC7496282
Nigel Kennedy (violin & viola), Andre Previn/Royal Philharmonic Orchestra

Cello Concerto / CBS MK39541
Yo-Yo Ma (cello), Andre Previn/London Symphony Orchestra

FACADE

Facade / Chandos CHAN8869
Richard Hickox/City of London Sinfonia

Facade / Reference Recordings RR-16CD
Chicago Pro Musica

BELSHAZZAR'S FEAST

Belshazzar's Feast / EMI CDM7647232
John Shirley-Quirk, Andre Previn/London Symphony Orchestra & Chorus

Belshazzar's Feast / Chandos CHAN8760
Gwynne Howell, Sir David Willcocks/Philharmonia Orchestra & Bach Choir

SYMPHONIES

Symphony #1 / Chandos CHAN8313
Sir Alexander Gibson/Scottish National Orchestra

Symphony #2 / Chandos CHAN8772
Bryden Thomson/London Philharmonic Orchestra

Unico Wilhelm van Wassenaer (1692-1766)

Independently wealthy, Wassenaer was an amateur musician and composer. In addition to serving as an ambassador and administrator for his country, he was responsible for many compositions initially attributed to Pergolesi, Birkenstock, and others. His works generally conform to a conservative south Italian style, are richly scored and contain many fugual sections. —*Lynn Vought*

CONCERTOS ARMONICI

6 Concertos Armonici / Hyperion CDA66670
Roy Goodman/Brandenburg Consort

Carl Maria von Weber (1786-1826)

Weber, a German composer, almost single-handedly established the romantic movement in music, or at least paved the way for it. His operas, especially *Der Freischutz*—with its simple human characters surrounded by a wild, mysterious nature imbued with the supernatural in eerie, atmospheric scenes (the casting of the magic bullets, for instance)—paved the way for Wagner, just as his piano music inspired Liszt, Schumann, and Chopin. He was equally an innovator in harmony and orchestral timbre, and his lovely concertos feature the soloist as a character who "speaks" rather than plays an objective, instrumental role. —*"Blue" Gene Tyranny*

CONCERTOS & CONCERTINO FOR CLARINET

2 Clarinet Concertos, Op. 73 & 74, and Concertino, Op. 26 / Orfeo C067831
Eduard Brunner (clarinet), Oleg Caetani/Bamberg Symphony Orchestra

2 Clarinet Concertos, Op. 73 & 74, and Concertino, Op. 26 / Virgin VC7907202
Anthony Pay (clarinet)/Orchestra of the Age of Enlightenment

2 Clarinet Concertos, Op. 73 & 74, and Concertino, Op. 26 / Chandos CHAN8305
Janet Hilton (clarinet), Neeme Jarvi /City of Birmingham Symphony Orchestra

CONCERTOS FOR PIANO

2 Piano Concertos, Op. 11 & 32, and Konzertstucke, Op. 79 / Berlin Classics BER1058
Peter Rosel (piano), Herbert Blomstedt /Staatskapelle Dresden

2 Piano Concertos, Op. 11 & 32, and Konzertstucke, Op. 79 / Vox Music Group CDX5098
Roland Keller (piano), Siegfried Kohler /Berlin Symphony Orchestra

GRAND DUO CONCERTANT FOR CLARINET & PIANO

Grand Duo Concertant, Op. 48 (w/ Clarinet Quintet) / XLNT CD18004
Jon Manasse (clarinet), Samuel Sanders (piano)

Grand Duo Concertant, Op. 48 (w/ Flute Trio & Variations) / Orfeo C067831
Eduard Brunner (clarinet), Gerhard Oppitz (piano)

INVITATION TO THE DANCE

Invitation to the Dance, Op. 65 (Orch. by Berlioz) / London 430201-2
Christoph von Dohnanyi/Cleveland Orchestra

Invitation to the Dance, Op. 65 (Orch. by Berlioz) / Nimbus NIM5154
Roy Goodman/Hanover Band

★ Overtures

10 Overtures / Chandos CHAN9066
Neeme Jarvi/Philharmonia Orchestra

7 Overtures / Capriccio 10052
Gustav Kuhn/Dresden State Orchestra

6 Overtures / Nimbus NIM5154
Roy Goodman/Hanover Band

PIANO MUSIC

4 Piano Sonatas and Complete Piano Music / Arabesque Z6584-2
Garrick Ohlsson (Piano)

QUINTET FOR CLARINET & STRINGS

Quintet, Op. 34 (w/ Brahms Clarinet Quintet) / Reference Recordings RR-40CD

Eddie Daniels (clarinet), Composers String Quartet

Quintet Op. 34 (w/ other Chamber Music for Clarinet) / XLNT CD18004
Jon Manasse (clarinet)/Manhattan String Quartet

Anton von Webern (1883-1945)

An Austrian composer of atonal and 12-tone music in many forms, including songs and orchestral, chamber, and choral music; known for *Six Pieces for Orchestra* (1913). If Berg is the romantic of the Viennese school, and Schoenberg is the dramatic lyricist, then Webern is the pointillistic impressionist. Webern created a completely new sound and way of composing music, and in a sense he is the most "modern" of any composer listed here. From the delicate beauties of *Das Augenlicht* ("The Light of the Eyes") for orchestra and chorus (1936), to the mobilelike stars-in-the-sky symmetries of the famous *Piano Variations* (1936), and the diverse and coloristic mysteries of the *Six Pieces for Orchestra* (1913), Webern sought a simplicity and beauty he viewed as inherent in earlier music (he once refused to show a pianist the structure of a piece, asking him to just "play it like Bach"). Webern is the quintessential pathfinder. —*"Blue" Gene Tyranny*

★ Music for String Quartet

Music for String Quartet / Deutsche Grammophon 419994-2
LaSalle Quartet

Music for String Quartet / Sony SK48059
Artis Quartet

★ Five Orchestral Pieces

Five Pieces for Orchestra, Op. 10 / Mercury Living Presence 432006-2
Antal Dorati/London Symphony Orchestra

Complete Orchestral Works / Sony SM3K45845
Pierre Boulez/ London Symphony Orchestra

Thomas Weelkes (1576-1623)

Weelkes began his career as organist for Winchester College, a position he held for only a few years, during which he wrote his best madrigals. Around 1602 he became organist for Chichester Cathedral. Here he enjoyed initial success, but after the publication of his fourth set of madrigals in 1608, his situation began to deteriorate. After being charged for public drunkeness and neglect of duty, Weelkes was dicharged from his post in 1617. He held one other position as an organist, but again failed to fulfill his duties satisfactorily. When he died in 1623, he left everything to a friend who had supplied him with food, drink, and lodging.

Most of Weelkes compositions are vocal pieces, both sacred and secular. A prolific madrigalist, he has been criticized for his lack of skill in integrating the texts with his melodic lines. However, Weelkes is remembered for his creative musical imagery and his mastery of counterpoint. These attributes make him one of the finest composers of English madrigals in the 17th century. —*Lynn Vought*

CHORAL MUSIC

13 Anthems and Motets for 5, 6 & 7 Voices / Hyperion CDA66477
David Hill/Choir of Westminster Cathedral

Kurt Weill (1900-1950)

A German composer. Searching for music and words that would directly affect and address their contemporaries, Weill and Bertolt Brecht had a big hit with the *Mahagonny-Songspiel* (1927) in Berlin (it was expanded to a full stagework in 1930). Representing the surrounding society on stage and mirroring it back on itself, Brecht and Weill invented what has been called the "educational opera." Others in the genre: *Happy End, Der Jasager* ("The Yes-man"), *Der Lindberghflug* ("The Lindbergh Flight"), and *The Ballad of Magna Carta* (with the famous line "Resistance unto tyrants is obedience to God"). The music was based on the style of the cabaret-theater (an old format for political satire) and developed to a richness never heard before, with modern harmonies, progressions having more to do with the freedom of bebop decades later than the normal song of the Bierhalle, and wonderful melodies ("Alabama Song," "Mackie Messer" ("Mack the Knife"), and many others) connected by scene-developing music of a refined imagination. Weill eventually had to flee Germany when the Nazis burned his music and attacked his publishing house. Amazingly, he managed to become one of the most popular composers on the Broadway stage (*Street Scene; Lady in the Dark; Knickerbocker Holiday; Love Life*), but he always kept up his love for music that fulfilled a responsibility by addressing the real world (*Lost in the Stars,* based on Alon Paton's *Cry the Beloved Country,* about racial conflict in South Africa), paving the way for a kind of American "verismo" in musical theater, such as Bernstein's *West Side Story.* For a full understanding of Weill's musical vision, it is important to hear one of his extended instrumental works. —*"Blue" Gene Tyranny*

THREE PENNY OPERA

Three Penny Opera (1928) / CBS MK42637
Lotte-Lenya, Bruckner-Ruggeberg, Orchestra & Chorus

Silvius Leopold Weiss (1686-1750)

Weiss came from a family of lutenists and learned the lute from his father, starting around the age of ten. As a young man he lived with and played for the Polish Prince Alexander Sobiesky and his mother, Queen Maria Casimira in Rome. The queen employed both Alessandro and Domenico Scarlatti as music directors, and so it is likely that Weiss had contact with these musicians during his stay. After the death of the prince, Weiss returned to Germany and eventually became the highest paid instrumentalist at the Dresden court. His career nearly came to a tragic end when the top joint of his right thumb was nearly bitten off during an attack by a French violinist in 1722. He traveled and played throughout Europe, establishing a reputation as a fine musician wherever he went. Weiss is remembered as one of the finest lutenists ever, and also made a major contribution in the area of compositions for his instrument. He wrote nearly 600 works in the late baroque style, and his compositions are sometimes harmonically inventive. He was known for the 'Weissian method' of lute playing which employed skilled fingerings and a smooth legato style. — *Lynn Vought*

LUTE SUITES & SONATAS

Sonatas, Preludes, etc. / Sony S2K48391
Lutz Kirchhof (lute)

Sonata # 7 in D Minor / Amplitude CLCD-2017
CARDIN, Michael (lute)

Sonata ("Partita Grande") in C Major / Naxos 8.550470
LEI, Franklin (Lute)

Sonata in F Sharp Minor / Astree E8718
SMITH, Hopkinson (Lute)

Hugo Wolf (1860-1903)

One of the finest and most innovative songwriters of the late romantic period, this Austrian composer wrote an astonishing flow of 174 songs in a blast of creative energy over a 33-month period. He was also a gifted lyricist, with a musical and literary talent for bringing characters in a poem to life and expressing psychological depths. Both voice and piano sing in his music, working toward conveying a whole impression. Aside from the songs, his best-known work is the beautiful *Italian Seranade* of 1887 for string quartet, later orchestrated in 1892. His only finished orchestral work was *Penthesilea* (1883-1885). Like many artists who consciously (or subconsciously) sacrifice their well-being for their art, Wolf experienced a breakdown due to mental stress and was institutionalized from 1898 to 1903. —*"Blue" Gene Tyranny*

SONGS (LIED)

Goethe-Lieder / Deutsche Grammophon 415192-2
Dietrich Fischer-Dieskau (baritone), Daniel Barenboim (piano)

Goethe-Lieder & Morike-Lieder (selections) / Hyperion CDA66590
Arleen Auger (soprano), Irwin Gage (piano)

Oswald von Wolkenstein (c.1337-1445)

Widely traveled composer of ballads and settings of poems in two- and three-part counterpoint. Considered the greatest of the German Meistersingers, and the last of the Minnesangers. —*AMG Songs*

Ballads & Songs / RCA Deutsche Harmonia Mundi 77302-2-RC
Sequentia

Jan Dismas Zelenka (1679-1745)

Zelenka was a court musician in Dresden for most of his career. Except for brief periods of travel, during which he studied or participated in music research, he served as a double bass player in the court orcchestra and later aided the ailing Kapellmeister in his duties. Upon the death of the Kapellmeister, the position was awarded to another musician, which led Zelenka to feel disillusioned by the lack of recognition he had received for his achievements. He was a skilled contrapuntalist and a creative harmonic composer. His works are marked by extremely precise dynamic directions, and some contain the unusual notation for crescendo that describes each progression in intensity, for example the words *piano, forte,* and *piu forte* written under one instrumental note. —*Lynn Vought*

TRIO SONATAS

6 Trio Sonatas / Capriccio 10074 / 5 or Berlin Classics BER1070
Burkhardt Glaetzner & Ingo Goritzki (oboes), Knut Sonstevold (bassoon), Walter Heinz Bernstein (harpsichord), Achim Beyer (violone), Siegfried Pank (viola da gamba)

Classical Collections

Historical Recordings

"Greetings to Dr. Edison. I am Dr. Brahms—Johannes Brahms!" Thomas Edison's astounding invention, the phonograph, was a mere 12 years old in 1889 when the greatest composer of the time shouted those words into a large horn and then launched into a vigorous performance of his *First Hungarian Dance.* The crude cylinders used at that time eventually gave way to Emile Berliner's revolutionary flat disc, but the large and cumbersome acoustic horn remained state-of-the-art for several decades to come. While this primitive device was adequate for recording the tenor voice (particularly Caruso and his friend John McCormack), other voice ranges, nonbrass instruments, and orchestras fared considerably less well. Despite its limitations, a steady stream of great composer-performers eventually made acoustic recordings, including Grieg, Saint-Saens, Debussy, and Enesco. And while that precious Brahms cylinder quickly deteriorated to the point where the music became barely audible, we can still enjoy the recordings of some of his closest musical friends, such as pianist Ilona Eibenschutz or the legendary violinist Joseph Joachim. Some considerable patience and imagination is required to appreciate the noisy, attenuated, and tinny sounds of these antique discs. But they can also be extremely rewarding and provide us with a unique insight into the composer's own thoughts on how their music ought to go. The horn was eventually replaced by an electronic recording process in 1924, an innovation that at last made it possible to reproduce the sound of a full orchestra with reasonable fidelity—and to hear the subtle nuances of solo and chamber performances. Still, only 4 1/2 minutes of music could be recorded on each side of a 12-inch 78 rpm disc. Symphonies and other extended works had to be broken up into short sections, and performers had to be extremely careful to match the tempo and dynamics at the end of each portion of the work to the beginning of the next side. A missed note or unbalanced chord could not be easily corrected—the entire side had to be rerecorded. The prevailing philosophy of early recording producers was "get it right the first time or forget it." Despite (or perhaps because of) these highly unfavorable conditions, a great many unforgettable recordings were made. — *Tom Godell*

Conductors

The first half of the 20th century was the golden age of symphony conducting. The great Hungarian Artur Nikisch influenced nearly all of his successors, including Leopold Stokowski, Arturo Toscanini, Vaclav Talich, and Serge Koussevitzky. Unlike the conductors of today, each developed a highly individual and immediately recognizable style. Nikisch himself made a few acoustic recordings, including the first recording of a complete symphony—Beethoven's Fifth. However, the severe limitations of the acoustic process make it quite difficult to appreciate his work today. Like Nikisch, conductor Gustav Mahler was also a powerful influence. His friends and disciples included the wayward but invariably fascinating Oskar Fried, Otto Klemperer, Bruno Walter, and Willem Mengelberg. (Look for Mengelberg's incomparable Mahler Fourth, with its constantly fluctuating tempos, to reappear some day on CD.) Sir Thomas Beecham and Wilhelm Furtwangler were also among the most outstanding interpreters of their era. Sadly, two of Furtwangler's most powerful and moving recordings are not currently available: the apocalyptic 1945 Beethoven Fifth and the 1953 Schubert Ninth, both originally recorded for DG. Beecham, on the other hand, is well represented in the current catalog, and his later stereo recordings of Schubert, Grieg, and Mozart are especially compelling.

Beethoven: Symphonies 1, 3, 6 & 8 / MCA MCAD2-9802
Herman Scherchen/Vienna State Opera Orch & Royal Philharmonic

Beethoven: Symphony 7; Haydn: Symphony 101; Mendelssohn: Midsummer Night's Dream (selections) / RCA 60316-2
Arturo Toscanini/New York Philharmonic

Brahms: Symphony 4; Strauss: Death and Transfiguration / DG 423-715-2
Victor de Sabata/Berlin Philharmonic

Bruckner: Symphony 8 / Music & Arts CD-624
Wilhelm Furtwangler/Berlin Philharmonic

Dvorak: Symphonies 7 & 8 / Koch 3-7007-2
Vaclav Talich/Czech Philharmonic

Mahler: Symphony 2 (1923 / acoustic) / Pearl GEMM CDS 9929
Oskar Fried/Berlin State Opera Orchestra & Cathedral Choir

Mahler: Symphony 9 / EMI CDH 7 63029 2
Bruno Walter/Vienna Philharmonic

Moussorgsky-Ravel: Pictures at an Exhibition; Ravel: Bolero, La Valse, Daphnis and Chloe Suite #2 / RCA 61392-2
Serge Koussevitzky/Boston Symphony

Sibelius: Symphonies 2, 5, 7, Tapiola, Pohjola's Daughter, Maiden with the Roses / Pearl GEMM CDS 9408
Serge Koussevitzky/Boston Symphony

Sibelius: Symphony 4, The Bard, In memoriam, Lemminkainen's Return, En Saga, Valse triste / Koch 3-7061-2
Sir Thomas Beecham/London Philharmonic

Strauss: Ein Heldenleben (Mengelberg / New York Philharmonic), Also Sprach Zarathustra (Koussevitzky / Boston Symphony), Don Quixote (Beecham / New York Philharmonic), Death and Transfiguration (Stokowski / Philadelphia Orchestra) / RCA 60929-2

Vaughan Williams: Serenade to Music / Pearl GEMM CD 9342
Sir Henry Wood/BBC Symphony & the vocal soloists for whom the work was composed

Wagner: Orchestral Works (1943-52) / Music & Arts CD 794
Wilhelm Furtwangler/Various orchestras

Solo & Chamber Music

As with the conductors mentioned above, one finds tremendous amounts of personality, charm, and virtuosity among the finest soloists and chamber musicians of this era. Violinists Fritz Kreisler and Jascha Heifetz are certainly the best-known violinists of the time, but many other performers on this instrument are also worth hearing, particularly Eugene Ysaye, Albert Spalding, Jan Kubelik, Mischa Elman, and Efrem Zimbalist. Among the great pianists of the time, look for issues by Rachmaninov, Josef Hofmann, Percy Grainger, Walter Gieseking, and Arthur Schnabel (who was the first to record all of Beethoven's sonatas). The young Artur Rubinstein and Vladimir Horowitz also made a wide variety of fascinating recordings before the advent of the LP, as did violist William Primrose, cellists Emanuel Feuerman and Pablo Casals, and double-bassist Serge Koussevitzky. Many outstanding recordings are waiting to be reissued. Look especially for two of the greatest string quartets ever to come before the public: the Flonzaley and the Paganini.

Bach: Cello Suites / EMI CDH61028 & CDH61029
Pablo Casals (cello)

Beethoven: Violin Concerto (w/ Concertos by Brahms, Mendelssohn & Mozart) / Music & Arts CD-290
Fritz Kreisler (violin) Leo Blech/Berlin State Opera Orchestra

Elgar: Violin Concerto, Violin Sonata / Pearl GEMM CD 9496
Albert Sammons (violin) Sir Henry Wood/New Queens Hall Orchestra

Prokofiev: Piano Concerto 3; solo piano works / Pearl GEMM CD 9470
Serge Prokofiev (piano)

Prokofiev: Violin Concerto #2; Sibelius: Violin Concerto; Strauss: Violin Sonata / Biddulph LAB 018
Yascha Heifetz (violin)

Collections

Trios by Beethoven, Mendelssohn, Schumann, Haydn, Schubert, with Brahms Double Concerto / EMI CHS7640572
Casals-Thibaud-Cortot Trio

The Complete Solo Columbia Recordings / Biddulph LAB 066
Georges Enesco (violin).

Works by Beethoven, Chopin, Levitzky, Liszt, Mendelssohn, Rubinstein, Scarlatti, Schumann / Pearl GEMM CD 9962
Mischa Levitzky (piano).

The Complete HMV Recordings / Appian CDAPR 7002
Moriz Rosenthal (piano).

Works of Brahms, Chabrier, Dvorak, Faure, Kreisler, Mendelssohn, Schubert, Schumann, Vieuxtemps, Wagner, Wieniawski, & Ysaye / Symposium 1045 (acoustic)
Eugene Ysaye (violin)

Medieval
High Gothic Collections

PARIS

Ecole Notre-Dame / Harmonia Mundi HMA1901148
Marcel Peres/Ensemble Organum

FRANCE

Polyphonie Aquitaine (12th Century) / Harmonia Mundi HMC901134
Marcel Peres/Ensemble Organum

ENGLAND

Sumer Is Icumen In: English Medieval Songs / Harmonia Mundi HMC901154
Paul Hillier/Hilliard Ensemble

SECULAR

Carmina Burana / Harmonia Mundi HMC190336 / 8
Rene Clemencic/Clemencic Consort

Thirteenth Century Collections
Motets

The Marriage of Heaven and Hell: Motets and Songs from the Great Age of the Gothic Cathedrals / Hyperion CDA66423
Christopher Page/Gothic Voices

SPAIN

Cantigas de Santa Maria / Quadrivium 014
Ensemble Micrologus

Codex Las Huelgas / Sony Vivarte SK53341
Paul Van Nevel/Huelgas Ensemble

Secular: Northern France

Trouveres: Courtly Love Songs ca. 1175-1300 / RCA Deutsche Harmonia Mundi 77155-2-RC
Sequentia

Secular: Southern France/Provencal

Le Manuscrit du Roi (vers 1250): Trouveres & Troubadours / Arion ARN68225
Guy Robert/Ensemble Perceval

Lo Gai Saber: Troubadours and Minstrels, 1100-1300 / Erato Musifrance 2292-45647-2

Joel Cohen/Camerata Mediterranea

Ars Nova Collections

FRANCE——SACRED

Messe de Tournai (ca. 1325-1350 Earliest Known Polyphonic Mass) / Harmonia Mundi HMC901353
Marcel Peres/Ensemble Organum

FRANCE——SECULAR

Lancaster and Valois: French and English Music, 1350-1420 / Hyperion CDA66588
Christopher Page/Gothic Voices

ITALY——SECULAR

Francesco Landini and the Italian Ars Nova / Opus 111 OPS60-9206
Alla Francesca

A Song for Francesca: Music in Italy, 1330-1430 / Hyperion CDA66286
Christopher Page/Gothic Voices

Ars Subtilior Collections

FRANCE

Codex Chantilly / Harmonia Mundi HMC901252
Marcel Peres/Ensemble Organum

CYPRUS

The Island of St. Hylarion: Music of Cyprus, 1413-1422 / New Albion NA038
Ensemble Project Ars Nova

Renaissance
Fifteenth Century Collections
Motets

The Brightest Heaven of Invention / Amon Ra CD-SAR56
James Wood/New London Chamber Choir

SECULAR

Le Banquet du Voeu 1454 / Virgin 59043
Dominique Vellard/Ensemble Gilles Binchois

The Castle of Fair Welcome: Courtly Songs of the Later 15th Century / Hyperion CDA66194
Christopher Page/Gothic Voices

ENGLISH SACRED——ETON CHOIRBOOK

The Rose & The Ostrich Feather; Eton, vol. 1 / Collins Classics 1314
Harry Christophers/The Sixteen

The Crown of Thorns; Eton, vol. 2 / Collins Classics 1316
Harry Chistophers/The Sixteen

Sixteenth Century Collections
French Secular Songs

Fricasee Parisienne / Harmonia Mundi HMC1901174
Ensemble Clement Janequin

Chansons sur Poems de Ronsard / Harmonia Mundi HMC901491
Ensemble Clement Janequin

How to Go About Finding Classical Music You Like

The basic methodology I've found to be effective in building a good library of recordings, even though I didn't know much about it when I started, is to use some combination of the following strategies, depending on the resources available at any given time.

1. Listen to as much music as you can.

Many college and community libraries have very large collections of classical CDs that can be checked out. Listening to the radio can also be a good source. Concerts can be very effective as well, though they can be expensive. Many colleges have free recitals and very inexpensive concerts available, and community music groups often have low-cost concerts throughout the year. Experiencing live music will help familiarize you with what music sounds like and make you a better judge of recording and performance quality. Participating in various newsgroups and mailing lists available on the Internet, CompuServe and other online services is also an effective way to become part of ongoing conversations about music, performers, recordings, composers, and other music-related topics.

2. Make note of the piece and composer.

a. Most pieces fall into four basic categories: orchestral (symphonies, concertos, suites, overtures, serenades, etc.); chamber (piano trios, string quartets, wind quintets, etc.); keyboard (piano sonatas, organ works, harpsichord works, etc.); and vocal (opera, lieder/song, oratorios, sacred choral music such as masses and motets, etc.). Many people prefer one category over the other, at least initially.

b. Knowing the composer is important because this provides a somewhat reliable guide to other pieces that you should investigate. If you hear one piece you like by a certain composer, there is a fair chance you'll like other major pieces by the same composer. Learning about times and lives of major composers can be very enlightening. There are many beginner-oriented biographies and dictionaries that provide basic information about a composer's life and works, and about musical terminology in general. Even the notes that come with the recordings can be a good source of basic information.

3. Once you know the piece and its composer, you can check any of several sources for the best recording of that work. Other than the *All Music Guide*, I suggest the *Stevenson Guide* as the best overall source. The *Penguin Guide* is also a good reference, as are the primary review publications: *Fanfare, American Record Guide*, and *Gramophone*. Once you have some experience you can determine which source best fits your personal taste and needs. Above all, remember that in the end it matters little if your tastes coincide with those of the critics. There is no one best performance of a piece, so if you like it, and it brings you pleasure, don't be dissuaded by bad reviews. There are often many excellent recordings and performances of a major work available, so don't get discouraged by the varied selection.

Price is another thing to keep in mind when deciding which CD to buy. There are often many great performances of a certain classical piece, and some of them may cost as little as $5. Don't let the low price fool you. There is often *no* correlation between price and recording or performance quality, and the extremely low cost of some releases can provide great opportunities for experimentation without a lot of risk. Don't be afraid to trust your own instincts. If a recording moves you, you don't need to check other sources to see if it's OK. Music is a personal experience.

4. Finding a good CD store from which to buy the CD you want can be a little frustrating in certain parts of the world. My basic advice is to find a store that has a good selection and wait for sales. Most stores have monthly or quarterly sales that can save you $1 to $4 per CD. This is less critical for bargain ($5-$7) CDs. A good store should also have copies of the Stevenson or Penguin guides for in-store use. It is also nice if the store has a knowledgeable and helpful staff, but this is very rare. Since many less-urban areas don't have a good store, mail order is often the least expensive, or only way to find the music you want. All of the above-mentioned publications list several good mail-order firms.

5. OK, so now you have a good CD of music you really like, what next? This section of the *All Music Guide* is designed in such a way that once you know you like at least one piece by a given composer, you can begin to branch out to other works, composers, and periods. For instance, let's say you've bought a CD of Mozart's symphonies #40 & 41, and like them a great deal. You may try other symphonies by Mozart (e.g., #38), or you might want to try symphonies by another composer. In this case, it might be best to stay within the same period (in this case classical), so the symphonies by Haydn (#45, 94, 101 & 104) or Beethoven (e.g., #3, 5, 6 & 9) would be a good place to start. If you find you particularly like Mozart, you might start exploring his major piano concertos (e.g., #20, 21 & 23) or serenades (e.g., #7, 10-13). You can then start branching out and listen to Mozart's piano sonatas or string quartets, and so on.

Another avenue might be to investigate the roots of the symphony (via the concerto grosso, suites, and sinfonias of the baroque era) or to see how the symphony developed after Mozart, Beethoven, and Haydn by looking into the symphonies of the romantic period. This section of the *All Music Guide* provides a "road map" for any of these explorations. Repeat steps #1-4 each time you identify a new piece you want to know more about, and don't be afraid to customize the process depending on your own likes or dislikes. I've always found that keeping lists of potential pieces or recordings I want to add to my collection (a want list) is very helpful. After a while the whole process will become second nature.

Questions

1. Last time I was at the local music store, I compared several CDs of Tchaikovsky's *1812 Overture,* and noticed that the times differed by as much as 1 minute! Does this mean that it may be slightly cut off in the shorter time performance? This complicates CD buying.

Timing differences are due to differing tempi (as set by the conductor) or to the taking of repeats (mostly applicable to older pieces, i.e., classical period or earlier). This brings up an important point. Once you start listening to more music, you may identify certain musicians and conductors you like better than others. So, what does a conductor do? Here's some information to help answer that very question:

During the actual concert, the conductor's duties are simply to begin the piece and provide tempo reminders and queues of various sorts to the musicians. If an orchestra has been very thoroughly prepared, these might not be necessary. A band director I worked with once said something to the effect that during rehearsals he expected 90 percent of our attention to be on him and 10 percent on the sheet music, but during performances, 90 percent of our attention should be on the music, and perhaps 10 percent on him. This seems to be a valid and pertinent guideline.

The need for a conductor during performance was originally identified prior to the time when ensembles had an established repertoire (or musical canon, as some have called it). In olden times (pretty much any time up until the early 20th century), orchestras were constantly having to learn new music, and rarely played a piece repeatedly over many years. Given the quick turnover in pieces being played, there often was not enough time to practice a piece thoroughly before the concert. Sometimes orchestras were doing very little more than sight-reading a piece in front of an audience. In these cases, conductors (who were often the composers themselves) clearly played a vital role in keeping the ensemble together, leading the tempi, queuing solos, and indicating dynamics.

The director's job these days is really quite different. The director often seeks to create a unique interpretation of a well-known, often-played, composition. This composition may be something like Beethoven's Fifth, which has undoubtedly been performed tens of thousands of times (maybe more!) and is undoubtedly well known to the musicians in the orchestra. A good director (who is also a *musician*), will have studied the score in great detail (all parts), may have studied the history of the piece to establish a historical context or to check the accuracy of a published score vs. the original manuscript and prepare a performing version of the score if necessary, and may even have listened to the interpretations of others (though any director will have heard a piece such as the Fifth many times in concert). Based on this investigation she or he will have come up with a unique vision of the piece, and therefore have a desire to realize this vision.

During the process of rehearsal, the director communicates his or her vision of the piece to the musicians in the ensemble and adjusts that vision to varying degrees based on feedback from them. In essence, the director presents a proposal and then acts as arbiter (though sometimes an autocratic one) for the musical decisions made about the way a piece is performed.

A good director is much more than a baton-waver. This is why you often read or hear references to various recordings as "Klemperer's Haydn," "Horenstein's Mahler," or "Norrington's Beethoven." Good directors have a vision of a piece that brings to light, in a penetrating and often touching way, aspects of the music's artistry for the audience. This is not a trivial task, and this is why directors are sometimes cherished.

Of course, sometimes an orchestra programs a piece because it's expected, popular, or contractually obligated to for a recording company. The vision of the director may not be the driving force; indeed it may be entirely absent. The performance that re-

sults is often mundane or even bad, in any case it is less than effective, and best forgotten. In instances where the director's vision is strong, the director is able to communicate that vision to the musicians, and they possess the necessary musicianship to transmit it to the audience, the effect on the audience is powerful. Such instances are few and far between, but that is the goal.

2. Should one look only for DDD recordings as opposed to ADD or AAD? This further complicates CD purchasing.

No, the SPARS code is pretty much meaningless in and of itself. There are many awful digital recordings (and digital recordings of awful performances) and many more incredibly good analog recordings of great performances. If sound is a main concern (and it is for most people) you will probably want to stick to recordings from the late 50s through the present, though some early stereo and even late mono recordings are excellent (much better than you might guess). High-quality magnetic tape equipment started becoming available about 1954.

The definition of the SPARS (Society of Professional Audio Recording Studios) code included on many CDs is:

DDD: Digital tape recorder used during session recording, mixing and/or editing, and mastering (transcription).

ADD: Analog tape recorder used during session recording; digital tape recorder used during subsequent mixing and/or editing, and mastering (transcription).

AAD: Analog tape recorder used during session recording and subsequent mixing and/or editing; digital tape recorder used during mastering (transcription).

The letters in the code indicate what type of *tape recorder* was used at each step in the process—original recording, editing-mixing, and mastering-transcription respectively. Digital tape recorders are fairly inexpensive these days, however, a 32- or 64-track digital editing-mixing console is still pricy. So what is often done is to make a digital 32-track recording of the original performance, run it through a D/A converter into an analog mixing console, back out through an A/D converter to a 2-track digital edit tape. This same process may occur on the way to a digital master tape. If the SPARS code was meant to represent the totality of the technology used, the code would be something like DADAD, but according to the definition, the CD can carry a code of DDD even though the signal has been processed in its analog form several times in the process.

Some companies are adding "pure digital" or "completely in the digital domain" to their labels to signify that the entire process was digital, with no D/A or A/D conversion. Some companies actually do without the first step entirely (analogous to direct-to-disc LPs) and mix on the fly, then transcribe to the digital master. For instance Digital Music Productions, a jazz label, is known for this. For this type of recording, the SPARS code might be -DD.

Most people think the phrase "digitally remastered from the original analog tape" means that the recording was remixed or edited digitally as well, but it means only that a necessary step was followed in getting the music into the digital domain and ready for encoding on the CD. Since CDs are digital, the master tape from which the CD is made must be digital as well. Therefore, *all* recordings that were originally analog, are remastered to digital for the CD medium.

Taken by itself, the SPARS code is not an indicator of recording quality in any specific sense. Depending on your leanings regarding the acceptability of digital technology in general, using digital technology might be said to result in a higher *potential* for low noise, wider dynamic range, low distortion, and so on. As with any tool, though, the technology is only as good as the application. It's perfectly possible to make a terrible recording using the latest in digital technology. If anything, the more sophisticated and complex the gadgetry, the more potential for error. Early digital recordings often fell victim to engineers that didn't grasp the subtleties of the technology.

For classical recordings, which have a long history of fine engineering and depend greatly on the musicianship and interpretation, the SPARS code should not be a prime determining factor in choosing one recording over another.

3. Should one look for particular conductors or orchestras performing a particular piece? This really complicates CD selection!

Yes, but this can be very subjective, and your preferences can change dramatically over time. Move slowly and form your own opinions based on your listening and reading. This is one of the more interesting and fun aspects of collecting, and it's not really as hard as you might imagine. There is no single best way of interpreting all music, so conductors invariably have better success in some works than in others. A great conductor of Mozart may not have any affinity for Mahler, and vice versa.

4. I was recently listening to *The Planets* by Holst. Strangely enough, much as I liked the movement with the title "Mars," I thought the remainder of the CD was boring.

This could be due to the performance. It could also be due to the fact that *good* classical music has a great many nuances that may not be apparent on first hearing. A musical masterpiece has been said to be a work that is pleasing upon first hearing, and then on repeated listenings reveals even more musical wonders. Most really good music requires a bit of attention and experience, much as a great painting requires more than a quick glance for full appreciation. Listen to the CD again carefully. Put it on as background music while you do something else. Put it away for a while and listen to other classical music. No guarantees, but your impression of a piece after living with it for a while may be quite different.

MUSIC RESOURCES

Aside from the music itself, there are many fine resources available that make your music journey more comfortable and fun. There is no room here for a comprehensive review of all the music books, magazines, mail-order firms, and record companies out there, but here are some that we feel provide a real service.

Record Companies

Mosaic Records

It seems that every generation has a few record labels where there is real magic happening. Jazz is no exception. If Blue Note was the standard-bearer of the 60s, then, in our time, it has to be Mosaic Records. Mosaic is not your average record label. Instead of recording jazz artists, they are expert at picking up on jazz gems neglected by other major labels and obtaining a license to publish them in very limited editions. Mosaic offers complete, chronologically ordered recordings (many previously unavailable) by acknowledged jazz masters at the peak of their careers. The sets include thoroughly researched booklets, including discographies and many photos, which, with the recordings, constitute definitive research documents for the featured musician. The quality of these Mosaic packages sets a standard for our times. Scholarship aside, what makes Mosaic founders Charlie Lourie and Michael Cuscuna great is their ability to search out pockets of recorded jazz that have been overlooked or forgotten and reissuing them. A class act. Best of all, Mosaic has found some of the very best jazz recordings ever made, and made them available. Here is some incredible music, and Mosaic sets never seem to get far from my stereo system. These albums can be obtained only through the mail. A detailed catalog is available by writing to 35 Melrose Place, Stamford, CT 06902; or call 203/327-7111.–Michael Erlewine

Smithsonian Recordings

There are two different companies that share a legitimate tie to the Smithsonian; Smithsonian Recordings is the first. You won't see these recordings in stores (you may get a flyer in the mail if you have used your credit card lately). These are, for the most part, boxed sets (CDs and albums) on different music generes–folk, country, jazz, big band, classical, and others. Many of these sets are well conceived and serve as good introductions to a particular kind of music.–Michael Erlewine

Smithsonian/Folkways Recordings

Folkways Recordings, started by Moses Asch and Marian Distler in 1947, introduced baby boomers to real folk music. Folkways was *the* folk/world label back in the 60s. With 2,100-plus albums in their catalog, Folkways is the way many of us first heard the likes of the New Lost City Ramblers, The Country Gentlemen, Woody Guthrie, Cisco Houston, Leadbelly, and others, not to mention a wealth of indigenous world music. But for a while it looked like Folkways (a real national treasure) would be gone forever. But since 1987, thanks to a special arrangement with Rounder Records, every original Folkways album is once again available under a new company called Smithsonian/Folkways. New and priceless recordings from the archives have been added to the catalog.–Michael Erlewine

The complete Folkways catalog is available by writing to: Smithsonian/Folkways Recordings Center for Folklife Programs Smithsonian Institution 955 L' Enfant Plaza, Suite 2600 Washington DC 20560.

Time-Life Series

The Time-Life Series is available only by mail order. You will find it advertised everywhere–on TV and in many magazines. Time-Life offers sets of recordings on R&B, country, the music of the 70s, hit parade (40s and 50s hits), classic rock & roll, the rock & roll era, and others. Each set consists of many separate albums, each one containing the big hits for a particular year. In the case of rock, there are often second and third albums for a given year featuring additional minor hits.

The bad news is that these CDs are expensive. By the time you pay the shipping and handling, each one costs about $20 a shot, which is just too much. For this reason, I wish I could suggest that you ignore the Time-Life Series, that they were poorly done or there was some other reason not to buy them. But the truth is that these CDs are, for the most part, well conceived and well executed. No other hits collection series is even near as comprehensive. Perhaps some of the early albums in the rock series are a little shabby; still, they are worth having.

Typically, there are from 20 to 24 hits per disc, with good liner notes (and complete discographies!) written by well-known music writers. I am not alone in this opinion. After talking with some of the other editors of the *All Music Guide*, the word is: this series is expensive but a real value. The R&B series is especially nice.–Michael Erlewine

Dunhill Compact Classics (DCC)

Since its inception in 1986, Dunhill Compact Classics has specialized in audiophile-quality reissues. The key player in producing their exceptional sound is Steve Hoffman, who has set standards throughout the industry and whose remastering techniques involve first-generation masters only. DCC entered the Gold Disc Audiophile Field with the "24 Carat Gold" series, featuring classic releases by Bob Dylan, Cream, the Eagles, the Doors, and others.–Rick Clark

Mobile Fidelity

Review:Since the late 70s, Mobile Fidelity has been a leader in audiophile remastering, releasing recordings covering a variety of styles–from classic rock artists such as Pink Floyd, the Who, Moody Blues, Rod Stewart, and the Allman Brothers, to titles by Frank Sinatra and Johnny Mathis. Mobile's remasters of jazz greats such as Miles Davis and classical music have been highly acclaimed.–Rick Clark

Rykodisc

Review:Founded in 1984, Rykodisc was the first CD-only label "ryko" is Japanese for "sound from a flash of light"). Since then, Ryko has expanded into all formats, including DAT. Their catalog is impressively eclectic, ranging from rock to world music, reggae, folk, and jazz. Of particular note is the acclaimed David Bowe "Sound and Vision" series. Rykodisc can be reached at 200 N. 3rd Ave., Minneapolis, MN 55401; or call 612/375-9162.–Rick Clark

Record Labels

There are many record companies besides those just mentioned. Here are addresses for some you may wish to contact.

Alcazar Inc.
P. O. Box 429
Waterbury, VT 05676
802/244-8657

American Gramaphone
9130 Mormon Bridge Rd.
Omaha, NE 68152
402/457-4341

Arhoolie
10341 San Pablo Ave.
El Cerrito, CA 94530
415/525-7471

Canyon Records
4143 N. 16th St.
Phoenix, AZ 85016
602/266-4823
602/266-4659

Chacra Alternative Music
35 Parklane Pl., Dept. 3
Dollard-des-Ormeaux
Québec, Canada H9G 1B8
514/624-0278

Crescendo/GNP-Crescendo
8400 Sunset Blvd.
Los Angeles, CA 90069
213/656-2614

Dancing Cat
P. O. Box 639
Santa Cruz, CA 95061
408/249-5085

Editions EG
c/o J. E. M
3619 Kennedy Rd.
S. Plainfield, NJ 07080
201/753-6100

Eurock
P. O. Box 13718
Portland, OR 97213
503/281-0247

Flying Fish
1304 W. Schubert St.
Chicago, IL 60614
312/528-5455

Fortuna
4549 E. Ft. Lowell
Tucson, AZ 85712
602/326-4400

Gaia
121 W. 27th St.
New York, NY 10001
212/645-5252

Gramavision
260 W. Broadway
New York, NY 10013
212/645-5252

Hannibal
P. O. Box 667
Rocky Hill, NJ 08553
609/466-9320

Hearts of Space
P. O. Box 31321
San Francisco, CA 94131
415/759-1130

Higher Octave Music
8964 Wonderland Park AVe.
Los Angeles, CA 90046
213/856-0039

Innovative Communications
c/o Chameleon Music Group
3355 W. El Segundo
Hawthorne, CA 90250
213/973-8282
800/423-6935 (outside California)

Kuckuck
P. O. Box 30122
Tucson, AZ 85751
602/326-4400

Ladyslipper
P. O. Box 3130
Durham, NC 27705
919/683-1570

Living Music
1047 Amsterdam Ave.
New York, NY 10014

Music of the World
P.O. Box 258
Brooklyn, NY 11209

Music West
2200 Larkspur Landing Circle, #100
Larkspur, CA 94939
415/925-9800
415/459-6000

New World
179 Water St.
Torrington, CT 06790
800/233-1337

Novus
c/o RCA Records
1133 Ave. of the Americas
New York, NY 10036
212/582-0028

Philio
(See Rounder)

Private Music
220 E. 23rd St
New York, NY 10010
212/684-2533

Redwood Records
6400 Hollis St., #8
Emeryville, CA 94608
415/428-9191

Rounder
1 Camp St.
Cambridge, MA 02140
617/354-0700

Shanachie Records
Dalebrook Park
Ho-Ho-Kus, NJ 07423
201/445-5561

Shining Star
200 Tamal Vista Blvd., #417
Corde Madera, CA 94925
800/825-4848

Sona Gaia
1845 N. Farwell Ave., 2nd Fl.
Milwaukee, WI 53202
414/272-6700

Sonic Atmospheres
14755 Ventura Blvd., #1776
Sherman Oaks, CA 91403
818/505-6022

Soundings of the Planet
P .O. Box 43512
Tucson, AZ 85733
602/883-1784

Sound Rx
P.O. Box 2644
San Anselmo, CA 94960
415/491-1930

Spring Hill Music
5216 Sunshine Canyon
Boulder, CO 80302
303/938-1188

Tape Masters
176 Forest Ave.
Pacific Grove, CA 93950

Roundup Records

Review:Roundup Records is a first-class act. They were the first to provide straight talk about recordings, new releases and classic albums alike. Roundup Records can be reached at P. O. Box 154, North Cambridge, MA 02140; or call 617/661-6308 (there is a toll-free order line for credit card purchases: 800/44-DISCS).–Michael Erlewine

Rhino Records

From their inauspicious beginnings in 1973 as a used-records store, Rhino Records has become the foremost reissue label in the industry, known for excellent packaging, sound, and liner notes. Bill Inglot's sparkling remastering work is especially noteworthy. For a catalog, send a dollar to Rhino Records, Inc., Dept. C-10, 2225 Colorado Ave., Santa Monica, CA 90404.–Rick Clark

World Music Resources

Original Music

R.D. 1, P.O. Box 190, Lasher Road
Tivoli, New York 12583
See review in mail order section.

Music of the World

P. O. Box 3667
Chapel Hill, NC 27515-3667
(919) 932-9600
(Free Catalog)

Afropop Worldwide

Listener's Guide National Public Radio
2025 M St. NW
Washington D.C. 20036
(202) 822-2323
A business-size, self-addressed envelope will get you a great overview of African and Caribbean music, complete with lists and maps. A real help.

Center for Cuban Studies

124 W. 23rd St.
New York, NY 10011
Not a record store, but they do sell records and videos imported from–as opposed to licensed from–Cuba; the selection is unpredictable but worth checking out.

Qbadisk

P. O. Box 1256
Old Chelsea Station
New York, NY 10011
This address is for mail-ordering Qbadisk albums.

Round World Music

491 Aguerro Street
San Francisco, CA 94110
415/255-8411

Jacob's Judaic Book & Gift Center

13896 Cedar Road
University Heights, OH 44118
216/321-7200
Contact Jay Steingroot. This and the following two listings are resources for recordings of Jewish music.

Musique Internationale

3012 West Jarvis
Chicago, IL 60645
312/743-3012
This is a resource for Jewish cantorial music.

Dor (Israeli)

21 Edgewood Tenafly, NJ 07670
800/762-4944
Contact Dubi Gerber.

Used CDs

Audio House CD Club

There is a brisk business in used CDs. In the early days, all kinds of things were possible–swap clubs, two-for-one swaps, three-for-two swaps, premiums paid on used CDs, and so on. One major company paid $6 apiece for any used CD! By now, reality has asserted itself and all this has settled down. The oldest and largest of these clubs is the Audio House CD Club. Their newsletter/list, which now contains some 15,000 used CDs, comes out every month or so, at $2 a copy–mention the *All Music Guide*, and then it's free. Write or call Audio House CD Club, 4304 Brayan Drive, Swartz Creek, MI 48473;(313) 655-8639.–Michael Erlewine

Mail Order Sources

Cadence Mail Order

Among its many other functions, each month *Cadence* magazine also conducts monthly sales of CDs, books, and records. It carries numerous labels, including many European imports and American independents. The address is *Cadence*, Cadence Building, Redwood, New York 13679.

Coda Sales

Canada's premier jazz publication also sells records, videos, and books. Specific price information may be obtained by contacting Coda Publications, P.O. Box 1002, Station O, Toronto, Ontario M4A 2N4, Canada.

Record Roundup

Rounder's mail-order service, Roundup, publishes a newsletter periodically that lists current specials, and also prints a catalog each year with more detailed listings. The address is Roundup Records, One Camp Street, Cambridge, Massachusetts 02140.

Roots and Rhythm

For many years known as Down Home Music, Inc., this operation is now Roots and Rhythm. Otherwise, nothing has changed. It remains among the finest and most diverse mail-order services in the world. It has plenty of domestic and foreign label/import jazz, though some of the import prices are a bit to the high side. It also publishes periodic newsletters and has catalogs for many categories. The address: Roots and Rhythm, 10341 San Pablo Avenue, El Cerrito, California 94530.

Stash-Daybreak Express

For pure jazz, the number of labels carried by Stash-Daybreak Express rivals any mail operation. It also carries blues, R&B, soul, and doo-wop, but jazz is its specialty and it is very impressive in the caliber and volume that is available. Stash-Daybreak Express, 140 W. 22nd Street, 12th Floor, New York, New York 10011.

I.M.D.

If you haven't yet disposed of your records, or are looking for recent and/or reissued items that have been deleted and/or cut out, here is a great source. I.M.D. carries both cutout vinyl LPs and records and is particularly good for such treasured items as Smithsonian and Arista/Freedom albums. It also has a free catalog available. I.M.D., 160 Hanford Street, Columbus, Ohio 43206.

Audiophile Imports

Yes, even fusion has its champions, and Audiophile Imports offers an extensive variety of fusion and jazz-rock titles. It is a great source for Miles Davis Japanese imports for one, and Jaco Pastorius titles for another. Audiophile, Dept. JT, P.O. Box 4801, Lutherville, Maryland 21094-4801.

Double-Time Jazz

Double-Time can compete with any mail-order service for volume in old and new titles. It handles domestic independent and major-label products, as well as reissues, cutouts, and imports, while also carrying albums and videos in addition to CDs. Double-Time, P.O. Box 1244, New Albany, Indiana 47151-1244.

Worlds Records

If you're a fan of big band or blues, Worlds may prove your best bet for mail-order service. It also carries a full line of major-label, domestic independent, and foreign import titles. Worlds Records, P.O. Box 1922, Novato, California 94948.

Jaybee Jazz

Another excellent source for cutouts and deleted titles, Jaybee is quite strong with big-band items, records, CDs, and cassettes, as well as other styles. Jaybee Jazz, P.O. Box 411004, Creve Coeur, Missouri 63141.

Rick Ballard Imports

If your tastes run predominantly to styles that are mostly available on imports, here is a good source. Rick Ballard Imports carries an extensive number of titles for such labels as Black Saint/Soul Note, DIW, Philology, Timeless, and many others. Rick Ballard Imports, P.O. Box 5063, Dept DB, Berkeley, California 94705.

Sonic Tiger

Yet another excellent source for cutouts in both domestic and import areas, and at extremely competitive prices. Sonic Tiger, P.O. Box 715, Cambridge, Massachusetts 02140.

Descarga

A great Afro-Latin mail-order service. Here is a major option for Latin jazz and salsa that is on the myriad labels out of the American major-label/independent loop. Descarga carries contemporary and classic titles, publishes a newsletter, and qualifies as a first-class operation. Descarga Records, 328 Flatbush Avenue, Suite 180-L, Brooklyn, New York 11238.

Africassette

World music is its bailiwick, including Latin jazz and salsa. and jazz titles from Africa and the Caribbean. Africassette, P.O. Box 24941, Detroit, Michigan 48224.

Original Music

Original Music is founded and still operated by John Storm Roberts. If there is anyone who knows more about "world" music and its permutations, combinations, hybrids, and multiple genres, I'd sure like to know who it is. Original Music, R.D. 1, P.O. Box 190, Lasher Road, Tivoli, New York 12583–Ron Wynn

Eurock

Archie Patterson, a journalist for more than 20 years, started Eurock Ltd. in 1973 to promote and distribute electronic and progressive music from around the world. He's written about some of today's name artists, before they broke into the mainstream and continues today exploring the far corners of the globe for adventurous new music. Write Eurock at P.O. Box 13718, Portland, OR 97213 or call (503) 281-0247.

Catalogs

The Ladyslipper Catalogue

The Ladyslipper Catalogue, founded by Laurie Fuchs nearly 20 years ago and now containing the largest listing of Lesbian and other women's music products in the world, continues to function as an important resource in a rapidly changing industry. Ladyslipper, Inc., P.O. Box 3124-R, Durham, NC 27715 or call (800) 634-6044.

Record Roundup

This is the grandfather of companies offering music-by-mail-with-reviews. Started in 1979 as an offshoot of Rounder Records, Record Roundup issues a 70-page newsletter free of charge several times a year. Each issue is chock-full of reviews and comments about the quality of the recordings offered. Rounder Records can be reached at P. O. Box 154, North Cambridge, MA

02140; call 617/661-6308 (customer service) or 800/44-DISCS (credit card orders).– Michael Erlewine

Roots & Rhythm (formerly Down Home Music)

If Record Roundup started it all, then the Roots & Rhythm catalog (begun in 1978) has perfected the art of catalog/album reviews. Originally called Down Home Music, and affiliated with the Arhoolie record label, Roots & Rhythm reads more like a magazine of reviews than a catalog. Each issue is filled with expert opinion, comment, and reviews on the latest in domestic and imported releases.

The latest catalog, between 60 and 100 pages, is free. In addition to providing information on domestic labels, Roots & Rhythm stocks and reviews a great number of imported albums that are available nowhere else. Certainly this company deserves some sort of award for the ground-breaking work they have done and the example they have set for catalogs with music reviews. Roots & Rhythm can be reached at 6921 Stockton Ave., El Cerrito, CA 94530; or call 510/525-1494.–Michael Erlewine

Magazines, Periodicals, and Newsletters

Goldmine

Published since 1974, Goldmine is just that–a goldmine of discographical information, extended articles, and great album reviews. Nowhere else will you find in-depth articles on individual artists and groups of this length and breadth. And almost every article is accompanied by a complete discography–almost every album ever made is listed. Goldmine is geared to the record collector. In fact, a good part of each issue is filled with the ads of collectors. Reading through these is an experience in itself. Those of us who don't collect may have little idea of the amount of activity in out-of-print and hard-to-find albums. Thanks to these folks, it is possible to find almost any hard-to-find album.

Goldmine has some of the best writers in the business–almost every major free-lance writer has written for them at one time or another. It is a tabloid-size magazine of about 170 pages published biweekly! There is a lot of information here. If you have never browsed through a copy, you have an experience in store for you. It's an eye-opener. Write to them and mention the All Music Guide and you will receive a free sample issue. Goldmine can be reached at 700 E. State St., Iola, WI 54990; or call 715/445-2214.–Michael Erlewine

Cadence Magazine

If you love jazz and also buy records and CDs, you will love Cadence magazine. Started in 1976 and located in upstate New York, this is the magazine for those who want straight-talk about jazz and lots of reviews! Edited by Bob Rusch, the magazine has reviewed some 26,000 jazz albums over the years (many not reviewed elsewhere), and all back issues are still available. This is also a great place to purchase hard-to-find jazz albums. Not available on many newsstands, this fine magazine is worth checking out. Their record catalog is yours for the asking, and $2.50 will get you a sample issue of Cadence. Write to The Cadence Building, Redwood, NY 13679-9612; or call 315/287-2852.–Michael Erlewine

Down Beat

In publication since 1934 and distributed in 142 countries, Down Beat is the largest (and oldest) jazz publication. You can probably get a copy at your local newstand. If not, write to Down Beat, mention the All Music Guide, and you will receive a free sample issue. Down Beat's address is 180 West Park Ave., Elmhurst, IL 60126.–Michael Erlewine

Jazz Times

Another fine jazz magazine, started in 1970, Jazz Times distinguishes itself via special issues on a variety of topics, including musical instruments, exceptional features on woman in jazz, plus useful directories of jazz festivals, record companies, education programs, and more. Both jazz and blues albums are reviewed. Write to them, mention the *All Music Guide*, and get a free sample issue: *Jazz Times*, 8055 13th St., Suite 312, Silver Spring, MD 20910-4803.–Michael Erlewine

Coda

The international perspective in jazz is well documented by *Coda*, Canada's premier publication for improvising music. It has been published since 1958, with January 1994 marking its 253rd issue and counting. It is now a bimonthly, which requires a bit more generic, nonnews approach to jazz issues, but *Coda* also manages to include plenty of still-topical information about European and/or Canadian events, concerts, news, etc. It also carries a regular column by the ubiquitous Kevin Whitehead (currently also available via *Down Beat, Pulse, CD Review,* and National Public Radio), but his "New York Notes" is quite informative when not used to slay the dragon, Wynton Marsalis. It is also second only to *Cadence* in its inclusion of independent label and underground new and free music acts. Subscriptions are currently $24 per year in the United States and $27 everywhere else. The address is *Coda*, P.O. Box 1002, Station O, Toronto, Ontario M4A 2N4, Canada.

Jazziz

An aggressive, if sometimes puzzling, challenger to *Cadence, Down Beat,* and *Jazz Times* on the domestic front is *Jazziz*. It has also done extensive modification over the years in everything from graphic design and layout to the range of its coverage. *Jazziz* pays considerable attention to international music and also gives more space to fusion and pop-oriented sounds than its competitors. Other coverage areas include video, equipment, and jazz-influenced or related styles such as blues and Cajun. *Jazziz* also carries a radio survey, with a Top 40 chart and station listings. Subscriptions are currently $12.95 for one year or $25 for two. The address: *Jazziz*, 3620 N.W. 43rd Street, Gainesville, Florida 32606.

Latin Beat

No publication covers Afro-Latin music in such a comprehensive manner. From salsa to Latin jazz and all things in between, *Latin Beat* is the best bet. It is even a great inducement to polish up on your high school Spanish, as it is a true bilingual magazine. It comes out 10 times a year. Subscriptions are currently $25 for 10 issues. International orders need an additional $10 for postage. The address: *Latin Beat*, 15900 Crenshaw Blvd., Suite 1-223, Gardena, California 90249.

Rock & Rap Confidential

It has been among the few publications that understands the link between cultural and political struggles and has sought to inform and unite diverse musical audiences behind battles against racism, sexism, censorship, and political hypocrisy. It has also been the rare pop periodical that doesn't view jazz as museumpiece fodder, but also doesn't mistake fraudulent pap for the genuine article. The audience is music lovers with a social conscience anxious to hear something other than the same 30 songs recycled hourly. Subscriptions are currently $27 a year, $44 for two, with the rates being $36 and $60 for foreign subscriptions. The address is *Rock & Rap Confidential*, P.O. Box 341305, Los Angeles, California 90034.

Both sides Now Stereo newsletter

This is the quarterly newsletter from which *Both Sides Now* is assembled. It covers both CDs and vinyl and includes interviews with the people who put together oldies reissue packages, previously unpublished discographies and all kinds of information. Write to *Both Sides Now*, Box 384, Fairfax Station, VA 22039. (*Both Sides Now* is also a book; see under "Books on Music" in this section.)– Michael Erlewine

CCM

CCM is the premiere publication in contemporary Christian music, one of the fastest growing genres in the music business today. The magazine covers a wide range of music, including pop, rock, alternative, R&B, hip-hop, and country; all with a decidedly Christian point of view. Send $19.95 for 12 monthly issues to *CCM*, P.O. Box 55996, Boulder, CO 80321-5996.

Rejoice! The Gospel Music Magazine

With very few publications devoted to gospel music, *Rejoice!* is a welcome find. Lots of articles, pictures, and more on your favorite gospel groups, Black and White. It is published bi-monthly by the Center for the Study of Southern Culture, The University of Mississippi, University, MS 38677. Write to the editors of *Rejoice!*, c/o The University of Mississippi, University, MS 38677.–Michael Erlewine

Living Blues: A Journal of the African-American Blues

This is the principal magazine for the blues in this country. Started by blues expert Jim O'Neal, the magazine is now sponsored and published by the Center for the Study of Southern Culture (as is the gospel magazine *Rejoice!*). *Living Blues* is a high-quality magazine (glossy publication) with many illustrations and up-to-date articles on major blues figures. The Center for the Study of Southern Culture can be reached by writing to The University of Mississippi, University, MS 38677.–Michael Erlewine

Dirty Linen

"The Traditional Magazine of Folk, Electric Folk, Traditional and World Music," *Dirty Linen* extends the range of folk music with "a wild sense of dedication matched only by good humor and intelligence" (*Library Journal*). *Dirty Linen* covers acoustic to electric, traditional to progressive, artists, festivals, new releases, venues, news, reviews, interviews, and more. For more information, write to *Dirty Linen*, P. O. Box 66600, Baltimore, MD 21239-6600.–Michael Erlewine

CD International

This is the most complete catalog of CDs in print we have yet seen. The winter 1991/1992 edition has 73,116 album titles on 120,827 discs (popular music only). If available, the label and number are given for each release in the US, UK, Germany, Japan, and Canada. This is the catalog of choice among the music pros, and the only one that lets you see what is available in other countries at a glance. This 8 1/2 x 11catalog is 650 pages. Write CDI Publishing Corp., P. O. Box 22014, Milwaukie, OR 97222. Michael Erlewine

CD International (American Guide)

CD International offers an additional volume that contains only American CDs–some 21,369 discs. Similar in format to the above and about 300 pages long. For many of these discs, individual track listings and playing times (track by track) are included. CDI Publishing Corporation can be reached at PO Box 22014, Milwaukie, OR 97222.–Michael Erlewine

The Beat

The Beat is a bimonthly publication of reggae, African, Caribbean, and world music, providing information, news, interviews, discographies, reviews, and cultural features to an international market of music fans. It features the work of top writers, artists, and photographers who chronicle this rapidly expanding area of music and the increasing popularity of its associated lifestyle.

Today, *The Beat* is the most widely circulated magazine in the country dedicated exclusively to world music. While feature articles still emphasize Jamaican and African artists, recent issues have been devoted to Brazilian pop and music of the Indian subcontinent. But the magazine's real crackle lies with its host of opinionated reviewers, who leave no corner of the world unexplored in their quest for the latest trends or the most obscure sounds.

While not as slick as *Spin, Rolling Stone,* or *Option, The Beat's* newsprint format (black and white) gives it an immediacy these other publications lack, highlighting it as an excellent source of news today on the inevitable influences on mainstream pop in years to come. *The Beat* can be reached at P.O. Box 65856, Los Angeles, CA 90065.–Bob Tarte

Books on Music

The following are a few of the books that you will find on the shelves of record collectors and that were helpful in checking information listed in the *All Music Guide*.

Record Research

Of particular interest to music lovers is the series of books by Joel Whitburn and his company, Record Research. These books are standard items on the shelves of most music collectors and DJs. Originally basing these books on the various chart and sales data (such as #1 hits) coming out of Billboard magazine (the industry newsletter of the record business), Whitburn has (in recent years) continued to add more and more valuable information. A few of these books may turn up in your local bookstore, but many are known only to DJs and record collectors. These books include (where possible) the complete Billboard chart statistics: the date an album entered the charts, its peak, and the number of weeks on the charts. Most also have the RIAA Platinum/Gold or million-seller album status. Great reference works. Record Research Inc. can be contacted by writing to P. O. Box 200, Menomonee Falls, WI 53052-0200; or call 414/251-5408.–Michael Erlewine

Trouser Press Record Guide

Ira A. Robbins, 1991, 763 pages, Collier Books (formerly the *Trouser Press Guide to New Wave Records*, 1983). A reference guide to alternative music (and some fairly mainstream artists) by the people behind *Trouser Press* magazine. Chock-full of biographies and reviews of obscure, revolutionary, and downright strange musical acts from the late 60s to early 90s. Offshoot bands and solo efforts are combined with the source band to show their evolutionary path. The reviews are fair and informative, and it's obvious that these folks really love the music. This new edition is up-to-date (into 1991), dropping a few of the lesser-knowns from the last volume to make room for the newest groups.–SWB

Rolling Stone Record Guide

1992, 800 pages, Random House. One of the classics.–Michael Erlewine

Blues Who's Who

Sheldon, 1987, 775 pages, Da Capo Press. No blues enthusiast should be without this. It contains in-depth career highlights for known blues singers, plus much useful data.–Michael Erlewine

Both Sides Now

Interested in oldies on CD? Compilations of your favorite artist? Collections of various artists? Hard to wade through a mass of reissues to find the performances you listened to 20 years ago? Here is a book that lists 3,000 CDs, including track listings for almost 2,000 of these; stereo information on some 1,500; ratings on 1,000; also the SPARS code, playing time, and year the CD was released (when available). Of special interest is the section on artist compilations and collections. This alone makes *Both Sides Now* invaluable and virtually unique in pop-music literature. The CDs are listed both by label and title and indexed by artist. Its author is a stickler for indicating which cuts are mono and which are stereo (just what we buyers need to know). This is a great find! (A *Both Sides Now* newsletter is available on a subscription basis by writing to Both Sides Now Stereo Newsletter, Box 384, Fairfax Station, VA 22039.)–Michael Erlewine

Rock On – Vols. 1-3

Norm N. Nite, 1974, 676 pages, Thomas Y. Crowell Co. Standard reference works for the classic rock period.–Michael Erlewine

Rock Record 4

Terry Hounsome, 1991, Record Researcher Publications. Indispensible reference work containing not only a huge number of albums but sidemen and instruments for most of these as well.–Michael Erlewine

Rock Movers and Shakers

Dafydd Rees and Luke Crampton, 1991, 585 pages, Billboard Books, classic rock reference work. Contains details not available elsewhere.–Michael Erlewine

Penguin Encyclopedia of Popular Music

Donald Clarke, 1990, 1378 pages, Penguin Books. A fine reference work providing biographical details plus a list of major albums and their release dates. Worth owning.–Michael Erlewine

Collectible Record Albums 1949-1989

Neal Umphred, 1991, 608 pages, Krause Publications. Many price guides offer prices only for general categories within a particular label. What makes Umphred's books (he has one on 45s and a new one on jazz albums) useful is that they privide prices for each album listed. A useful book even for non-collectors because it provides a thorough list of albums for each artist.–Michael Erlewine

Bring the Noise: A Guide to Rap Music and Hip-Hop Culture

Havelock Nelson and Michael A. Gonzales, 1991, 298 pages, Harmony Books.

The Down Home Guide to the Blues

Frank Scott, 1991, 250 pages, A Cappella Books.A recent release that provides a list of blues albums in-print, along with rating comments. Worth having.–Michael Erlewine

The New Grove Dictionary of Jazz

Barry Kernfeld, 1988, 1360 pages, Macmillan Press Limited. If you can afford it (some $300), this huge two-volume set deserves to be on your bookshelf. It is the best single work on jazz that we have seen.–Michael Erlewine

Encyclopedia of Folk and Country & Western Music

Stambler, Irwin, Landon, Grelun, 1984, 902 pages, St. Martin's Press.

Record Collecting

There have been record collectors as long as there have been records. Special performances of operas and classical vocals were prized and bootlegged before the First World War; Enrico Caruso was a household name in much of middle class and working class America (well, at least in the east coast cities with large immigrant populations). The hobby began to soar when a generation of teenagers were swept up in the swing of the big bands. As these fans grew to maturity, their interest remained and many a successful individual whiled away his or her free hours pursuing elusive V-discs or Benny Goodman or Artie Shaw.

78-rpm singles remained the object of pursuit through the early 50s, especially as another type of collector was searching for Son House, Robert Johnson, and the more obscure pre-War blues and country singers. But the biggest boost came from the new jazz aficionados seeking sides by Bird and Diz and Miles. Many of these fans openly embraced the new LP format. Today, many a collector dreams of the heady feeling that will follow tracking down an elusive Blue Note, although the business of collecting out-of-print albums by pioneering jazz artists of the post-bop era is relatively recent and remains clouded in obscurity.

Until the waning days of the 60s, the 45 obtained the bulk of the hobby's passion and attention (along with the biggest of the bucks), as the "little record with the big hole" defined the listening experience of the mature collectors of that period–those who had come of age in the 50s, digging the wondrous harmonies of Black vocal groups from New York or the crazy rhythms of the Southern rockabillies. While such luminaries as the Five Keys and Elvis all recorded albums during the Eisenhower years, it is their Aladdin and Sun singles that command the hefty prices.

By the early 70s, there was an explosion of interest in collecting albums, sparked in no small part by the new generation of fans coming into some spendable cash: those who had cut their teeth on the Beatles and the Stones. The enormous market enjoyed by rock & roll of the 60s–often referred to as Rock with a capital 'R'– now seems pitifully small compared to the multi-platinum success that even mediocre artists achieved during the excesses of the past 20 years. Still, it was large enough that, along with the worldwide esteem in which much of the music is held, it guarantees that the demand–ever growing as new generations of listeners become enamored of *Pet Sounds* or *Music from Big Pink*–will continue to outweigh the dwindling supply. And that, essentially the true foundation of capitalism (and the much vaunted but disappearing "free market"), is what the business of record collecting is about: simple supply and demand.

While dealers love to tout what is supposed to be a "rarity," the lack of supply of an item is meaningless if there is a corresponding lack of interest (i.e., demand). If there are only a half-dozen known copies of a record on the entire planet and there are only three known collectors, there is a glut of that record on the market! On the other side of the spectrum, an album that sold hundreds of thousands of copies in 1966 can be highly valued if there are hundreds of thousands of interested collectors interested in that record today. Such is the case with the infamous "butcher cover" variation of the Beatles' *Yesterday and Today* album. Arguably the world's most collectable album, by Capitol's own estimation the number of copies initially printed and distributed (with and without the revised, second cover pasted over the offending photo) were as few as 60,000 and as many as 600,000!

Near-mint originals comfortably–and with regularity–sell in the four figures; at least three still-sealed, "first state" stereo copies of *Yesterday and Today* (i.e., a jacket where the second cover had never been pasted over the original; thus the album is in its original or first state) have sold in excess of $10,000. Even relatively trashed copies (referred to as "peel jobs," which range from the expert to the wretched) can bring a hundred dollars. And while virtually every hard-working dealer can turn up a few copies a year, the demand escalates, with the value.

Now, for the novice, wondering where to start .... Easy: Start with the music you like. Joining the collecting community by discovering previously unseen used record shops in your hometown, attending conventions an hour away and scouring through collectors' publications like Goldmine–this puts you in touch with such desirable items as live performances recorded exclusively for syndicated radio programs such as the King Biscuit Flower Hour. Find out what the artist you admire cites as his or her obvious influences and trace down original copies of those artists' work. If Prince is your main man, your shelves will see a steady supply of soul and funk on labels such as Atlantic, Tamla, and Stax. If R.E.M. is your idea of the ultimate contemporary rock/pop ensemble, you'll find yourself with a collection of the original Byrds albums and, most likely, a growing interest in Bob Dylan.

I stress originals for several reasons: the pressings are often superior to those of the reissues (assuring your listening enjoyment); and, of course, we are talking about collecting as a hobby and investment. Originals escalate in value; reissues rarely do. Either way, you're hooked, and another collector has joined the fold!–Neal Umphred

Bootleg Overview

Music bootlegs–illegal reproduction and distribution of recordings–have been with us about as long as sound reproduction itself. Few issues in the music industry inspire as much heated debate. A constant irritant to many record companies and musicians, they are a source of pleasure–albeit a bit of a guilty pleasure–to countless fans.

Despite periodic efforts by the industry to crack down on manufacturers and retailers of unauthorized recordings, bootlegging continues to persist and make an impact upon a large audience, much as independent labels continue to proliferate even as corporate companies seek to consolidate their domination of the music industry.

There are several kind of bootlegs. There are pirates, which reissue official material (usually rare and out-of-print) without official permission. There are counterfeits, which duplicate the content (and often sleeve and label) of a record as it appeared in its original release. The most influential and commonly discussed bootlegs collect totally unreleased performances–live concerts, studio outtakes, demos, and radio broadcasts. Bootlegging was hardly unknown in jazz, classical, and other collector recordings before it began to infiltrate the rock audience. A live recording of the Beatles performing "Some Other Guy," a staple of their early sets that they never officially cut in the studio, made the rounds in Liverpool as early as 1963. That same year, the first unauthorized live recording of the Rolling Stones was pressed, giving hardcore fans a memento of their heroes before their rapid ascent to international fame.

It was a late sixties Bob Dylan bootleg, however, that really got the scene rolling. Titled *The Great White Wonder*, this collection of Basement Tape-era demos and other odds and ends, packaged in a plain white sleeve, was manna from heaven for Dylan acolytes desperate for any word of his continued existence. And here were a clutch of unreleased, more or less realized studio performances, available for just a bit more than the standard price of an LP. Similarly popular bootlegs of the Beatles' early 1969 *Get Back* sessions and a show from the Rolling Stones' 1969 U.S. tour (*Liver Than You'll Ever Be*) quickly followed. Soon there were live and (considerably less frequently) unreleased studio recordings by most of the major bands (and many minor ones) for purchase on the underground market.

Bootleg product ebbs and flows according to periodic crackdowns by the law and the record industry, but basically it's been uninterrupted. At collector conventions, specialty shops, London flea markets, and the streets of New York, illicit recordings spanning several decades continue to swap hands. Search hard enough for those Liz Phair demos, that Patti Smith broadcast, or last week's Elvis Costello show, and you'll find it, though it may involve considerable expense and mileage. Realizing they were unable to stop the massive circulation of live tapes among "Deadheads," the Grateful Dead have more or less condoned the taping and trading of their live performances.

Occasionally, a bootleg album slips through this underground web to make an impact upon the mass audience. Such was the case with Prince's unreleased *Black album* in the late 1980s. Outselling a great deal of its legitimately released competition, it attracted attention and reviews in the mainstream press, and even some airplay on commercial radio stations.

Aesthetically, the most frequent complaint against bootlegs is that they sound terrible. And quite a few of them do, especially the older live ones. But bootleg technology has increased enormously over the last decade. Many boots–perhaps even the majority by now–boast excellent pressings, duplication from first-generation sound board and master tapes, and artwork/packaging that is better than the real thing.

Many labels and performers claim to suffer financial and artistic damage from bootlegs, arguing that they are not being compensated for the sale of their property; that boots are a violation of their sacrosanct artistic wishes; and that unauthorized material damages their artistic reputation. Fans counter that consumers of bootlegs almost invariably own all of the artists' official releases anyway; that many bootlegs expose valuable work to a relatively wide audience and cast new light upon an artist's ouevre; and that any damage, financial or otherwise, suffered by the artist is compensated for by the free publicity illicit material generates.

From corporate boardrooms to on-line bulletin boards, variations of the above debate rage. And the audience for bootlegs continues to grow. Whatever one's position, it is undeniable that bootleggers have been responsible for bringing many great performances to light. No appraisal of Bob Dylan is complete without listening to his legendary 1966 Albert Hall concert with the Band; no picture of the Beatles complete without hearing their BBC tapes, during which they performed 35 covers (and one original!) never released on their official albums; and no assessment of the Beach Boys finished without hearing their legendary unreleased *Smile* album. The list will continue to expand as long as there is a serious interest in musicians and their art.–Richie Unterberger

INDEX

Rosenboom, David, 1282, **1284**, 1293, 1297
Rosewoman, Michele, 844, **864**
Rosier, Pier', 1146, **1148-1149**, 1151
Rosmini, Dick, **522**
Rosnes, Renee, **864**
Rosolino, Frank, 800, 809, **864**, 885
Ross, Diana, 21, 125, 168, 203, **277-278**, 316, 350, 1071, 1218
Ross, Dr. Isiah, **452**
Ross, Sandy, **522**
Rossini, Gioacchino, **1354**
Rossy, **1116**
Rotary Connection, 1068, 1072
Roth, David Lee, 150, **278**, 339-340
Roth, David, 500, 505, **522**
Roth, Gabrielle, **1241-1242**, 1254
Roumi, Majida El, **1198**
Rouse, Charlie, 808, 830, **864-865**
Rouse, Mikel, **1284-1285**
Roussel, Albert, **1354**
Rowan, Peter, 515, 576, 598, 626, **627**
Rowans, The, **627-628**
Rowles, Jimmy, 697, 703, 801, 835, **865**, 912
Rowsome, Leo, 1092, **1097**
Roxette, 8, **278**, 369
Roxy Music, 8, 11, 62, 109, 117, 125, 192, 194, 227, 232, **278-279**, 303, 317-318, 1066, 1227, 1250
Royal College of Music Choir, 1068
Royal Philharmonic Orchestra, 62, 963, 968, 972, 975, 1272, 1314, 1316-1319, 1323, 1325-1326, 1334, 1336, 1347, 1350-1351, 1355, 1359, 1361, 1363-1364, 1368
Royal, Billy Joe, 199, 300, **596**
Rubaja, Bernardo, **1242**, 1254
Rubalcaba, Gonzalo, **865**
Rubbra, Edmund, **1355**
Rubinel, Ronald, 1144-1145, **1149**, 1151
Rudd, Roswell, 674, 685, 728, 805-806, 828, 858, **865**
Rudder, David, 1155, 1157, **1159-1160**, 1161-1162
Rude Girls, **1053**
Rudhyar, Dane, **1285**
Rufus & Chaka Khan, 183, **279**, 326-327, 329, 373, 662, 721, 741, 755, 801, 810, 859, 930, 938
Ruggles, Carl Spaque, **1285**
Ruiz, Hilton, 711, 720, 747, **865**
Rumsey, Howard, 702, 719, 734, 862, **865-866**
Run C & W, 553-555, 559, 563, 576, 578, 587, 592, 596, 603, 606, 610, 613, 615
Run-D.M.C., 368, 377, 631, 633, 646, **652-653**, 654, 659-660, 1074
Runaways, The, 176, **279**
Rundgren, Todd, 25, 35, 39, 72, 112, 144, 212, 227, 240, 260, 274, **279-280**, 288, 339, 361, 376
Rundlett, Gail, **522**
Rush, **280**
Rush, Otis, 139, 370, 405, 415, 418, 430-431, 433, 440, **452**, 454, 467-470, 472
Rush, Tom, **522**
Rushing, Jimmy, 459, 490, 679-680, 758, 781, **866**, 888, 909, 913, 1069, 1073
Russell & Kydd, 1077, 1090, **1097**
Russell Band, Tom, 513, **522**, 535
Russell Family, **1097**
Russell, Arthur, **1285**, 1293
Russell, George, 670, 705-706, 729, 738, 740-741, 750, 770, 778, 787, 804, 819,

866, 867, 887
Russell, Janet, 1090, **1097**
Russell, Leon, 80, 85, 99, 196, **280-281**, 408, 434, 573, 585, 626, 684
Russell, Luis, 668, 671, 676, 775, 779, 840, 843, **866-867**, 879, 884
Russell, Pee Wee, 668, 692, 716, 765, 780, 841, **867**, 872, 891
Russell, William, 907, **1285**
Rustavi Choir, **1166**
Rutles, 47, **281**, 339
Ryan, Joel, **1285**, 1290
Ryder, Mitch, 272, **281**, 348
Rypdal, Terje, 750, **866-867**
Rzewski, Frederic, **1285-1286**, 1295-1296
Sabri Brothers, 1105, 1129, 1141, **1142**
Sackville All Stars, 1068
Sade, 9, **281**, 491
Sadeghi, Manoochehr, **1197**
Saeli, Tommie, **1036**, 1037
Saffire, **452**, 1043
Sahm, Doug, 10, 225, **281**, 282, 292, 324, 467
Saint Etienne, **282**
Saint-Saëns, Camille, **1355**
Sainte-Marie, Buffy, **522**, 537, 974
Sakamoto, Ryuichi, 317, 971, 979, **1242**, 1296
Salah, Cheikh, **1117**
Salgan, Horacio, **1174**
Salim, Abdel Gadir, **1125**
Salt-N-Pepa, 117, **653**
Salvador, Sal, 695, 718, **868**
Sam & Dave, **282**
Sam Brothers, 414, **482**
Sam the Sham & the Pharaohs, **282**, 313
Sam-Ang Sam Ensemble, **1129**
Sample, Joe, 665, 719, 786, 808, **868**, 908
Samples, **282**
Sampson, Edgar, **868**, 908
Samulnori, **1141**
San, Ohta, **1201**
Sanborn, David, 331, 345, 665, 749, 804, **868-869**
Sanchez, Paul Edward, **522**
Sanchez, Poncho, 665, 742, **869-870**, 924, 1185, 1191
Sanders, Pharoah, 665, 667, 677-678, 680, 691, 695, 704, 713-714, 716, 771-772, 795, 818, 834-835, 850, 858, **870**, 874, 881, 893, 910, 915
Sandoval, Arturo, 753, **870**, 1183
Sands, Ben, **1097**
Sands, Colum, 1097, **1098**
Sands, Tommy, 378, **1098**
Sangare, Oumou, **1117**
Sangreet, Apna, **1134**
Sankaran, Trichy, **1134**
Santamaria, Mongo, 665, 677, 691, 702, 746, **870-871**, 886, 894, 899, 1185
Santana, Carlos, 189, **282-283**, 1116-1117, 1120, 1232
Santiago, Eddie, **1189**
Santos, Carlos, **1286**
Sarasate, Pablo de, **1355**
Sartana, **1149**
Sastry, Shri Emani Shankara, **1134**
Satan & Adam, 19, 48, 87-88, 94, 175, 227, **453**, 731, 740, 764, 793, 813-814, 819, 878, 900, 1106, 1117, 1162
Satho, Somei, **1242**
Satie, Erik, 840, 1218, 1228, 1230, 1262, **1286**, 1289, 1355
Satriani, Joe, **283**, 339
Sauvanet, Paul, **1242**

Savoy Brown, 204, **283**
Savoy, Marc, **482**
Savoy-Doucet Cajun Band, 479, **482**
Saxon & Cross, 262, 285-286, 289, 298, 314, 327, 337, 340-341, 350, 374
Sayeeram, Aruna, **1134**
Scaggs, Boz, 216-217, **283-284**, 371, 549, 615
Scarface, 642, 650, **653**
Scarlatti, Alessandro, **1355-1356**
Scarlatti, Domenico, **1356**, 1359-1360, 1370
Scartaglen, 493, **1098**
Scelsi, Giacinto, **1286**, 1298
Schaeffer, Pierre, 1271, **1287**
Schmidt, Claudia, **522-523**
Schnaufer, David, **523**, 534
Schobert, Johann, **1356**
Schoenberg, Arnold, 1260, 1311, **1356**
Schoener, Eberhard, **1242**
Schonherz & Scott, **1242**
Schoolly D, 368, **653**, 659
Schooner Fare, **523**, 536
Schroeder, Robert, **1242**
Schroeder-Sheker, Theresa, **1243**
Schubert, Franz, **1356-1357**
Schuch, Steve, **523**, 532
Schuller, Gunther, 712, 729, 744, 827, **871**
Schulze, Klaus, 1205, 1219-1220, 1230, **1243**, 1244
Schumann, Clara, **1348**
Schumann, Robert, 1331, **1357-1358**
Schütz, Heinrich, **1358**
Schuur, Diane, **871**
Schwarz, Tracy, 515, **523**
Sciacy, Carla, **523**
Sciaky, Carla, **1053**
Scobey, Bob, 664, 676, 781, 793, 836, **871-872**
Scofield, John, 670, 708, 738, 748, 764, 778, 812, 819, **872**, 887, 900
Scorcher, 15, 554, **1160**, 1247
Scorpions, 10, 215, **284**, 337, 349
Scott, Hazel, **872**
Scott, Jack, **596**, 1071
Scott, Shirley, 665, 711, 722, 840, 847, **872**, 898, 923
Scott, Stephen, **872**, 1287, 1298
Scott, Tony, 738, 762, 807, **872-873**, 903, 1203
Scott-Heron, Gil, **284**, 638, 642, 650
Screaming Trees, 191, **284**, 976
Scriabin, Alexander, 839, **1358-1359**
Scruggs, Earl, 521, 548, 586, 604, 617-618, 621-623, 626, **628**, 932
Scruggs, Joe, 1004
Scrunter, **1160**
Seal, **285**
Seale, Anne, **1053**
Seals & Crofts, **285**
Seals, Dan, 532, 544, **596-597**, 614
Seals, Son, 450, **453**
Searchers, The, 79, 100, 157, **285**, 503, 520
Sears, Dawn, **597**
Seawind, **950**
Sebadoh, **285**
Sebastian, John, 201, **285**, 311, 504, 514, 529, 534
Secada, Jon, **285-286**
2nd Chapter of Acts, 940, **950-951**
Second II None, **653**
Sedaka, Neil, 85, 133, **286**
Seeds, The, 74, 98, 137, 210, **286**, 320, 368
Seeger, Mike, 491, 514-515, **523**
Seeger, Peggy, 517, **523-524**, 1091

Also available from Miller Freeman Books

All Music Guide to Jazz
The Best CDs, Albums & Tapes
Edited by Ron Wynn, with Michael Erlewine & Vladimir Bogdanov

This is the most comprehensive, easy-to-use guide to jazz, compiled by some of the best music critics in the nation. These critics have selected 9,000 of the the best recordings, produced by more than 1,150 artists and groups. Special features include music maps, label histories, producers, clubs/venues, and jazz styles and terms. 751 pages, $22.95.

Available at bookstores and music stores everywhere, or directly from the publisher (add $5.00 for shipping and handling in the U.S., plus sales tax in CA, FL, GA, IL, NY, TX, and GST in Canada):

> Miller Freeman Books
> 600 Harrison Street
> San Francisco, CA 94107
> Phone 408-848-5296
> Fax 408-848-5784
> E-mail: mfbooks@mfi.com
> World Wide Web: http://www.mfi.com/mf-books/

Related Products

Miller Freeman publishes many other books for musicians, popular music enthusiasts, fans, and instrument collectors. For a complete list of books, please contact the address above. Coming in Fall 1995: *The All Music Guide to Rock.*

Miller Freeman also publishes *Guitar Player, Bass Player, and Keyboard* magazines, available at newsstands everywhere. For subscription information, please call 415-905-2200.

The *All Music Guide* is also available on CD-ROM (from Selectware Technology, 29200 Vassar, Ste. 200, Livonia, MI 48152; phone 313-477-7340), for hard disk (from Great Bear Technologies, 100 Moraga Way, Moraga, CA 94556; phone 800-795-4325), on CompuServe (GO ALLMUSIC), and on the World Wide Web (http://www.allmusic.com/)